ENCYCLOPÆDIA BRITANNICA

THE UNIVERSITY OF CHICAGO

The Encyclopædia Britannica
is published with the editorial advice of the faculties
of the University of Chicago; a committee composed
of persons holding academic appointments at the
Universities of Oxford, Cambridge, London, and Edinburgh;
a committee at the University of Toronto; and a committee
drawn from members of the faculty of the University of Tokyo

*

"LET KNOWLEDGE GROW FROM MORE TO MORE
AND THUS BE HUMAN LIFE ENRICHED"

ENCYCLOPÆDIA BRITANNICA

VOLUME
10

First Published in 1768

by A Society of Gentlemen in Scotland

ENCYCLOPÆDIA BRITANNICA, INC.

CHICAGO · LONDON · TORONTO · GENEVA · SYDNEY · TOKYO · MANILA · JOHANNESBURG

FOUNDED A.D. 1768

ENCYCLOPÆDIA BRITANNICA

Volume 10

GARRISON TO HALIBUT

GARRISON, WILLIAM LLOYD (1805–1879), U.S. antislavery leader, was born in Newburyport, Mass., on Dec. 12, 1805. His parents were from the British province of New Brunswick. The father, Abijah, a sea captain, drank heavily and deserted his home when William was a child. The mother, whose maiden name was Lloyd, is said to have been a woman of high character, charming in person and eminent for piety. William had little education but made the most of his opportunities. He was set to learn the trade of a shoemaker, first at Newburyport, and then, after 1815, at Baltimore, Md. Then he was apprenticed to a cabinetmaker at Haverhill, Mass., but ran away. In Oct. 1818, when he was 12, he was indentured to Ephraim W. Allen, proprietor of the Newburyport *Herald*, to learn the trade of a printer. He soon became an expert compositor, and after a time began to write anonymously for the *Herald*. His communications won the commendation of the editor, who had not at first the slightest suspicion that Garrison was the author. He also wrote for other papers with equal success. His skill as a printer won for him the position of foreman, while his ability as a writer was so marked that the editor of the *Herald*, when temporarily called away from his post, left the paper in his charge.

The printing office afforded him an opportunity to increase his meagre education. He was enthusiastic about liberty; the struggle of the Greeks to throw off the Turkish yoke enlisted his sympathy; and at one time he seriously thought of entering the West Point academy and fitting himself for a soldier's career. His apprenticeship ended in 1826, when he began the publication of a new paper (actually the old one under a new name), the *Free Press*, in his native place. The paper, whose motto was "Our Country, our Whole Country, and nothing but our Country," was an intellectual force, but was too radical for Newburyport, and the enterprise failed.

Garrison then went to Boston, where, after working for a time as a journeyman printer, he became the editor of the *National Philanthropist*, the first journal established in America to promote the cause of total abstinence from intoxicating liquors; but a change in the proprietorship led to his withdrawal before the end of the year. In 1828 he established the *Journal of the Times* at Bennington, Vt., to support the re-election of John Quincy Adams to the presidency of the United States. This paper also died within a year. In Boston he had met Benjamin Lundy (*q.v.*), who had for years been preaching the abolition of slavery. Garrison had been deeply moved by Lundy's appeals, and after going to Vermont he showed the deepest interest in the slavery question. Lundy was then publishing in Baltimore a small monthly paper, the *Genius of Universal Emancipation*, and he went to Bennington and invited Garrison to join him in the editorship.

Garrison first accepted Lundy's views of gradual emancipation, but soon changed to total and immediate freedom for slaves when he joined Lundy in Baltimore in 1829. Lundy believed that the Negroes, on being emancipated, must be colonized somewhere beyond the limits of the United States; Garrison held that they should be emancipated on the soil of the country, with all the rights of freemen. Garrison saw that it would be idle to expose and denounce the evils of slavery, while responsibility for the system was placed upon former generations, and the duty of abolishing it transferred to an indefinite future. His demand for immediate emancipation fell like a tocsin upon the ears of slaveholders. The *Genius*, when it became a vehicle for this dangerous doctrine, was feared and hated. Baltimore was then one of the centres of the domestic slave trade, and upon this traffic Garrison heaped the strongest denunciations. He was prosecuted for libel by the owner of a slave-carrying vessel, was fined $50, and, in default of payment, committed to jail.

John Greenleaf Whittier, whose first poems Garrison had published in the *Free Press*, interceded with Henry Clay to pay Garrison's fine and thus release him from prison. Clay responded favourably, but before he could act Arthur Tappan, a philanthropic merchant of New York, contributed the necessary sum and set the prisoner free after an incarceration of seven weeks. The partnership between Garrison and Lundy was then dissolved by mutual consent, and Garrison resolved to establish a paper of his own, in which he could advocate the doctrine of immediate emancipation and oppose the scheme of African colonization. He first proposed to establish his paper at Washington, in the midst of slavery, but on returning to New England and observing the state of public opinion there, he came to the conclusion that little could be done in the south while the nonslaveholding north was lending its influence for the sustenance of slavery. He determined, therefore, to publish his paper in Boston, and set himself to the task of awakening an interest in the subject by lectures in some of the principal cities and towns of the north. In Boston, then a great cotton mart, he tried in vain to procure a church or vestry for the delivery of his lectures, until a group under the leadership of Abner Kneeland (1774–1844) proffered him the use of their small hall. He accepted it gratefully, and delivered in Oct. 1830 three lectures, in which he unfolded his principles and plans.

On Jan. 1, 1831, without capital and without a subscriber, he and his partner, Isaac Knapp (1804–43), issued the first number of the *Liberator*, avowing their "determination to print it as long as they could subsist on bread and water, or their hands obtain employment." Its motto "Our Country is the World—our Countrymen are Mankind" shows his changed viewpoint. The paper, in addition to favouring abolition, attacked war, alcoholic liquors and tobacco, and assailed freemasonry, capital punishment and imprisonment for debt. The editor, in his address to the public, uttered the words which have become memorable as embodying the whole purpose and spirit of his life: "I am in earnest—I will not equivocate—I will not excuse—I will not retreat a single inch—and I will be heard." For many months Garrison and his partner made their beds on the floor of the room in which they printed their weekly paper, and where Mayor Harrison Gray Otis of Boston, in compliance with the request of Gov. Robert Y. Hayne of South Carolina, "ferreted them out." Otis decided, however, that the paper could not be suspended. In the same year (1831), $5,000 reward was offered for Garrison's arrest and conviction under the laws of Georgia. The *Liberator*, though in constant financial difficulties, exerted a mighty influence, and lived to record not only President Lincoln's proclamation of emancipation, but the adoption of an amendment to the constitution of the United States forever prohibiting slavery.

Garrison was a pacifist, and sought the abolition of slavery by moral means alone. He knew that the national government had no power over the system in any state, though he thought it should bring its moral influence to bear in favour of abolition. His idea was to combine the moral influence of the north, and pour it through every open channel upon the south. To this end he made his appeal to the northern churches and pulpits, beseeching them to bring the power of Christianity to bear against the slave system, and to advocate the rights of the slaves to immediate and unconditional freedom. When they did not respond, he denounced them, and by 1840 had become very unorthodox. The first society organized under Garrison's auspices, and in accordance with his principles, was the New England Antislavery society in Jan. 1832. The same spring Garrison issued his *Thoughts on African Colonization*, in which he showed from official documents that the American Colonization society was organized in the interest of slavery, and that in offering itself as a practical remedy for that system it was guilty of deception. Garrison was deputed by the New England Antislavery society to visit England for the purpose of counteracting the influence there of agents of the Colonization society. He went in the spring of 1833, and was received with great cordiality by British abolitionists. He took home with him a "protest" against the American Colonization society signed by William Wilberforce and other abolitionists in England.

Garrison's visit to England enraged the proslavery people, and when he returned in September with the "protest" against the Colonization society, and announced that he had engaged the services of George Thompson as a lecturer against American slavery, there were fresh outbursts. The American Antislavery society was organized in December of that year (1833), the declaration of its principles coming from Garrison's pen. The activities of this society and Thompson's lectures aroused such fury that, in the autumn of 1835, Thompson was compelled to return secretly to England. He had announced that he would address the women's antislavery society in Boston, and a mob gathered. Not finding him, it seized Garrison and dragged him through the streets until he was rescued and given protection in the jail until he could leave the city in safety.

The abolitionists of the United States were a united body until 1839–40 when division occurred. Garrison countenanced the ac-

tivity of women in the cause, even appointing them as lecturing agents; moreover, he believed in the political equality of the sexes, to which a strong party was opposed upon social and religious grounds. His attack on the churches caused dissent. Many believed that Garrison injured abolitionism by causing it to be associated in men's minds with these unpopular views on other subjects. These differences led to the organization of a new national antislavery society in 1840, and to the formation of the Liberty party (*q.v.*) in politics (see BIRNEY, JAMES GILLESPIE). The two societies sent their delegates to the world's antislavery convention in London in 1840, and Garrison refused to take his seat in that body, because the women delegates from the United States were excluded. The discussions of the next few years served to make clearer than before that the constitution of the United States supported slavery; and Garrison came to the conclusion that its proslavery clauses were immoral, and that it was therefore wrong to take an oath for its support. Because of this, Garrison burned the constitution, denouncing it as "a covenant with death and an agreement with hell," and thereafter worked for peaceful disunion. When in 1861 the southern states seceded from the union and took up arms against it, he saw clearly that slavery would perish in the struggle and that the constitution would be purged of its proslavery clauses. He therefore ceased to advocate disunion, and devoted himself to hastening the inevitable event. His services at this period were recognized and honoured by President Lincoln and others in authority, and the whole country knew that the agitation which resulted in the abolition of slavery was largely due to his uncompromising spirit and indomitable courage.

In 1865 at the close of the war, he declared that, slavery being abolished, his career as an abolitionist was ended. He counselled a dissolution of the American Antislavery society, insisting that whatever needed to be done for the protection of the freedmen could best be accomplished by new associations formed for that purpose. The *Liberator* was discontinued at the end of the same year, after an existence of 35 years. He visited England for the third time in 1846, and again in 1867, when he was received with distinguished honours, public as well as private. In 1869 he became president of the Free Trade league, advocating the abolition of custom houses throughout the world. In 1877, he again visited England, and declined every form of public recognition. He died in New York on May 24, 1879, at the age of 74, and was buried in Boston, after a most impressive funeral service, four days later. In 1843 a small volume of his *Sonnets and Other Poems* was published, and in 1852 appeared a volume of *Selections* from his writings and speeches.

One of Garrison's sons, WILLIAM LLOYD GARRISON (1838–1909), was a prominent advocate of the single tax, free trade, woman's suffrage and of the repeal of the Chinese Exclusion act, and an opponent of imperialism. Another son, WENDELL PHILLIPS GARRISON (1840–1907), was literary editor of the New York *Nation* from 1865 to 1906.

BIBLIOGRAPHY.—The great authority on the life of Garrison is the thorough and candid work of his sons, W. P. and F. J. Garrison, *William Lloyd Garrison, 1805–1879; the Story of His Life Told by His Children* (4 vol., 1885–89). See also Russel B. Nye, *William Lloyd Garrison and the Humanitarian Reformers* (1955); Ralph Korngold, *Two Friends of Man* (1950).

GARTOK (SGAR-THOG), the capital of Mnga'-ris (pronounced Nga-ri), the western district of Tibet that encompasses the ancient region of Zhang-zhung, is traditionally regarded the birthplace of their pre-Buddhist shamanism called Bon. The renaissance of Buddhism was begun in Mnga'-ris by the 11th-century Tibetan translator, Rin-chen bzang-po (958–1055).

Gartok is the western gateway to Tibet. Caravan routes leading along the Indus River to Leh in Ladakh, via the Shipka Pass to Simla in India, and along the Brahmaputra to Zhikatse in central Tibet have been in use for centuries. Regular fairs were held throughout the summer at Gartok, attracting as many as 2,000 people daily, with hundreds of tents covering the bare plain and hillside during the night. A brisk trade was carried on between nomads from the northern plain, merchants from central Tibet, and traders from India and Nepal. A British, and later Indian, trade agency was established at Gartok in 1904 and continued in operation until 1962, when the Sino-Indian trade agreement of 1954 expired and the agency was closed.

The Tibetan government headquarters for Mnga'-ris were maintained during the summer months at Gartok, also called Garyarsa (*Sgar-dbyar-sa*, "Place of the summer camp"), and then moved in November downstream to Gar Dsong (*Sgar-rdzong*), also called Gargunsa (*Sgar-dgun-sa*, "Place of the winter camp").

Formerly a desolate town in winter, Gartok was enlarged considerably after the Communist Chinese occupation of Tibet in 1951. Postal stations, banks, general stores, and hospitals were built along the Gar River. Chinese-built highways connected Gartok with Nag-chu-kha north of Lhasa, via Zhikatse, and with Khotan in the Sinkiang Province of China. The 157-mi. (253 km.)-long Taklakot Highway linked Gartok with the rich agricultural region around Purang Dsong (Spu-rangs rdzong) on the south. A major airfield was constructed and a large garrison force maintained at Gartok because of the continuing Sino-Indian dispute over the Tibet-Ladakh border.

(T. V. W.)

GARVEY, MARCUS MOZIAH (1887–1940), organizer of the most important nationalistic social movement among Negroes which, reaching its peak of influence in the 1920s, once again gained currency and popularity in the late 1960s among some Negroes disillusioned by the slow progress of integration.

Garvey was born in St. Ann's Bay, Jamaica, on Aug. 17, 1887. His parents were descended from the Maroons, a group of escaped slaves who had fought against the British in 1739 and had been set free. Largely self-taught, he attended school until he was 14, when to help support his family he became apprenticed to a printer. After traveling in Central America and living in London from 1912 to 1914, Garvey returned to Jamaica, where with a group of friends he founded (Aug. 1, 1914) the Universal Negro Improvement and Conservation Association and African Communities League, usually called the Universal Negro Improvement Association (UNIA). Its goals were to promote unity among the Negroes of the world by instilling pride of race, to acquire economic power, and to build in Africa a black-governed Negro nation.

When Garvey failed to attract a following in Jamaica, he went to New York City in 1916. He quickly established a branch of the UNIA in Harlem and in the principal urban ghettos of the North. By 1919 Garvey claimed a membership of 2,000,000, though the exact number of members of the UNIA was never clear. But it is certain that he established what was the largest mass movement among Negroes until his time and beyond. The rapid growth of the UNIA can be traced partly to its fiery leader's powers as a propagandist, and primarily to the discontent of hundreds of thousands of Southern rural Negroes who migrated North during and after World War I in search of equality and higher wages, only to encounter an increasing number of race riots, lynchings, and the then awesome power of the Ku Klux Klan (*q.v.*).

From the platform of Liberty Hall in Harlem, which the UNIA bought in 1919, Garvey spoke of a "New Negro" who was proud of being black. His newspaper, *Negro World*, told of the exploits of the heroes of the race, such as Nat Turner (*q.v.*), and of the splendours of African culture. It taught that Negroes would be respected only when they were economically strong. To accomplish his goals, Garvey founded the Black Star Line to promote trade among Negro peoples. The line consisted of three small steamships which encountered nearly every kind of difficulty. In 1919 he also established the Negro Factories Corporation. He reached the height of his power in 1920, when he presided at a convention in Liberty Hall, with delegates from 25 countries.

Garvey was flamboyant: he announced the Empire of Africa in 1921, appointing himself provisional president while creating the Universal African Legion, Universal Black Cross Nurses, Black Eagle Flying Corps, Knights of the Nile, and other orders. His slipshod business methods, and his doctrine of racial purity and separatism—he approved of the Klan because it sought to separate the races—brought him bitter enemies among Negro leaders, including A. Philip Randolph and W. E. B. Du Bois (*qq.v.*), who deplored his bombast, impracticality, and encouragement of colour

divisions pitting the darker skinned against the lighter skinned. His movement declined rapidly when he and other UNIA members were indicted for mail fraud in 1922 in connection with the sale of stock for the Black Star Line. Garvey had served two years of a five-year prison term, when his sentence was commuted in 1927 by President Coolidge and he was deported as an undesirable alien. Virtually unremembered, he died in London, on June 10, 1940.

See Edmund David Cronon, *Black Moses* (1955); August Meier and Elliott M. Rudwick, *From Plantation to Ghetto* (1966).

GARVIN, JAMES LOUIS (1868–1947), the last polemic editor of an English national newspaper and (1924–29) editor of the *Encyclopædia Britannica*. His lengthy political articles (the "bloody everlastings") in the *Observer* were a feature of British journalism for more than three decades.

Born in Birkenhead, Cheshire, of Irish Catholic parents, on April 12, 1868 (Easter Sunday, a fact that charmed him all his life, though he left the Catholic Church and developed his own brand of Christian mysticism), Garvin early lost his father, a labourer, and his formal education ended at 12½. This meagre ration was supplemented, while a clerk in Hull and Newcastle upon Tyne, by prodigious reading and self-taught languages. Eventually he found a job on the *Newcastle Chronicle* as a proofreader. Six weeks later he was a full-time journalist.

In London, Garvin wrote for the *Fortnightly Review* under pseudonyms, "Calchas" among them. He joined the *Daily Telegraph* as leader and "special" writer in 1898. Acquaintance with Lord Northcliffe led to appointment (Jan. 1, 1908) as editor of the *Observer*, a dying Sunday paper soon to become a profitable "fiery force" under "Garve."

Two main themes occupied his pen before World War I, the German peril and the tariff reform campaign of Joseph Chamberlain, about whom he wrote three biographical volumes (1932–34). The "peril" articles delighted the first sea lord, Sir John Fisher, who fed him information with startling incaution. Proprietorship of the *Observer* changed in 1911, when W. W. (later Viscount) Astor became sole owner, but Garvin remained editor until 1942. He supported Lloyd George throughout the war, but described the Treaty of Versailles as "peace and dragon's teeth." His *The Economic Foundations of Peace* (1919) and his article, "War Guilt," in the *Encyclopædia Britannica* (1929), showed him to be realistic and magnanimous to Germany.

Garvin edited the *Encyclopædia Britannica* without relinquishing his *Observer* post just as earlier he had edited the *Pall Mall Gazette* and the *Observer*. His advocacy of Anglo-American co-operation was a recommendation to the American proprietors. Later he wrote in the *Encyclopædia*: "The English-speaking peoples, and these alone, have in their hands for good or evil the key of the world's destinies." He was responsible for the 1926 Supplement (the 13th edition) and for the 14th edition (1929). He sought in the latter to inform "the general reader."

In 1894 Garvin married Christine Ellen Wilson (d. 1918), by whom he had one son, killed in World War I, and four daughters; and in 1921 he married Mrs. Viola Woods. A rather fearsome person to his family, with an explosive temper, he was yet beloved and admired. His mind was nurtured in the 19th century, and this was reflected in his dramatic writing style, but for long he thundered, and was heard, in the 20th. He died at Beaconsfield, Buckinghamshire, on Jan. 23, 1947.

See Katharine Garvin, *J. L. Garvin* (1948); A. M. Gollin, *The Observer and J. L. Garvin 1908–1914* (1960).

(J. Ae.)

GARY, ELBERT HENRY (1846–1927), U.S. jurist and chief organizer of the United States Steel Corporation, was born on Oct. 8, 1846, near Wheaton, Ill. After graduation from law school in 1867 he entered practice in Chicago. He was elected judge of Du Page County in 1882 and again in 1886. Gary was a leader and an authority in corporation law and insurance matters and became general counsel and a director in a number of large railroads, banks, and industrial corporations. In 1898, on organization of the Federal Steel Company, financially backed by J. P. Morgan, he became its first president. This company merged with the U.S. Steel Corporation in 1901; Gary was elected chairman of the board of directors and was its chief executive officer during 26 years of remarkable development of the steel industry and growth of the corporation.

As chairman of U.S. Steel, Gary advocated and established measures for the welfare of the employees of industrial corporations, including stock ownership by them and participation in profits, high wages, and safe, sanitary, and pleasing surroundings. He was a firm upholder of the open shop and his unwillingness to negotiate this issue led to the strike of 1919. During his chairmanship the 7-day week and the 12-hour day for labour were abolished in the steel mills.

The steel mills and the town of Gary, Ind., were named in his honour. Gary died in New York City, Aug. 15, 1927. (J. A. FA.; X.)

GARY, a city and steel-producing centre of Lake County, Indiana, U.S., is at the southern tip of Lake Michigan. It is the third largest city in the state and claims to be the world's largest city established in the 20th century. It is also the largest city of the northwest Indiana industrial area, which includes the cities of Hammond, East Chicago, Whiting, Portage, and several smaller towns. Gary's 1970 census (175,415) showed a population decrease of nearly 3,000 from the 1960 census. The loss was similar to that sustained by many other U.S. cities, reflecting a movement to the suburbs. (For comparative population figures *see* table in INDIANA: *Population.*) In 1960 Gary was designated a central city of the Gary-Hammond-East Chicago standard metropolitan statistical area, comprising Lake and Porter counties (pop. [1970] 633,367), a part of the Chicago standard consolidated area. (*See* CHICAGO: *Population: Metropolitan Area.*) The city's population comes from numerous ethnic and religious backgrounds. Many are of Slavic origin, and the largest single group are the blacks, constituting more than half the population.

In 1904, when the United States Steel Corporation began looking for a Chicago site for a new plant, Judge Elbert Gary (*q.v.*), the corporation's chairman of the Board of Directors, was considering Waukegan, Ill. A search of the area, however, showed the sand-dune country south and east of Chicago to be almost unoccupied and better for transportation. The mill was begun, and the town, originally a living centre for the company's workers, grew in the sand south of the mill. Gary was incorporated as a town in 1906, as a city in 1909. As Gary expanded, it annexed the community of Tolleston in 1910. Tolleston, now a neighbourhood on Gary's west side, had been started by railroad men in 1857. In 1918 Gary annexed the town of Miller, on the lakefront east of the mills.

Gary's largest industry is the steel complex that bounds most of Gary's northern border along Lake Michigan; it includes U.S. Steel's Gary Steel Works, Gary Sheet and Tin Works, Gary Tube Works, the American Bridge Division, and the Universal Atlas Cement plant. While demand for steel and cement causes fluctuation in employment, these plants normally maintain 30,000 workers. Other important industries include those manufacturing auto parts and accessories, screws and bolts, and lighting equipment.

Gary was one of two cities (Cleveland, O., was the other) to elect the first Negro mayor of a major U.S. city—Richard G. Hatcher took office in January 1968. He was reelected in November 1971. During his first term, more than $100,000,000 in federal moneys went to assist and upgrade Gary's social and educational levels. A major, obvious result of urban-renewal funds was the tearing-out of several blocks of blighted buildings just south of the business district. The downtown shopping area has felt the competition from outlying shopping centres and has suffered economically; there has been a concerted effort to upgrade it.

Being a mill town, Gary has more than its share of air- and water-pollution problems; some progress toward controlling pollution was being made in the early 1970s.

Gary's early school system became a model for study with the establishment of what was known as the work-study-play system, or platoon school. Today, its school system is plagued with the same problems confronting many urban schools. In 1970 an experimental program was set up in one grade school that has been described as both "controversial" in methods and "of national interest" because of the general concern in the need to improve elementary schooling. In 1970 a private firm under a "performance contract" began operating a school on a four-year plan requiring payment only for those underachieving pupils actually raised to grade level in certain basic skills measured in testing. The city has a four-year branch of Indiana University. There are two radio stations and a daily newspaper. Television service comes from nearby Chicago. There are several large parks and its beaches attract persons from the surrounding area.

Gary is well served in the area of transportation. The big mills are served by Gary and Buffington harbours on Lake Michigan, both private. The Gary Municipal Airport was expanded in the late 1960s to accommodate all but the very largest planes. The Indiana Toll Road and interstate highways run through and around the city. Railroads have always been important, since many eastern railroads have to bend south of Lake Michigan to get into and out of Chicago. (W. A. WA.)

GAS, a general term for one of the three states of aggregation of matter; also applied to coal gas. *See* ANESTHESIA AND ANESTHETICS; CHEMISTRY: *Physical Chemistry;* GAS INDUSTRY; CHEMICAL WARFARE. *See also* references under "Gas" in the Index.

GAS CHAMBER: *see* CAPITAL PUNISHMENT; CONCENTRATION CAMPS: *Concentration Camps of Nazi Germany.*

GASCOIGNE, GEORGE (c. 1530-1577), English poet, was one of the most talented of the writers who flourished during the early Elizabethan period, before Edmund Spenser's *Shepheardes Calender* (1579) gave a new direction and impetus to English poetry. The son of Sir John Gascoigne of Cardington, Bedfordshire, he attended Trinity college, Cambridge, began the study of law at Gray's Inn in 1555, and thereafter pursued careers as a politician, country gentleman, courtier, soldier of fortune and man of letters, achieving moderate distinction in each.

Gascoigne was a skilled literary craftsman, and his work is memorable for its versatility and vividness of expression and for his treatment of events based on his own experience; but his chief importance is as a pioneer of the English Renaissance, with a remarkable aptitude for domesticating foreign literary genres. He foreshadowed the English sonnet sequences with groups of linked sonnets in his first published work, *A Hundreth Sundrie Flowres* (1573), a collection of verse and prose. In *The Steel Glass* (1576), one of the earliest formal satires in English, he wrote the first original nondramatic English blank verse. In subject, however, *The Steel Glass* is traditional; it is an attack, in the spirit of *Piers Plowman,* on the worldliness, corruption and Italianate manners of the aristocracy, and a defense of native feudal virtues. In two amatory poems, the autobiographical "Dan Bartholomew of Bath" and *The Complaint of Philomene* (1576), Gascoigne developed Ovidian verse narrative.

"The Adventures of Master F. J." was the first original prose narrative of the English Renaissance. Probably because of embarrassment caused by the factual elements in this tale of love intrigue, Gascoigne revised the work; and it appeared as "The Pleasant Fable of Ferdinando Jeronimi and Leonora de Valasco." Another prose work, *The Spoil of Antwerp* (1576), is an early example of war journalism.

Gascoigne's *Jocasta* (performed in 1566) was the first Greek tragedy to be presented on the English stage. Translated into blank verse, with the collaboration of Francis Kinwelmersh, from Lodovico Dolce's *Giocasta,* it derives ultimately from Euripides' *Phoenissae.* In comedy, Gascoigne's *Supposes* (1566), a prose translation and adaptation of Ariosto's *I Suppositi,* was the first prose comedy to be translated from Italian into English. A dramatically effective work, it provided the subplot for Shakespeare's *The Taming of the Shrew.* A third play, *The Glass of Government* (1575), is a didactic drama on the prodigal son theme. Together with several moralistic works in traditional forms of verse and prose on such commonplace themes as the vanity of human life, the sinfulness of man and the evils of drunkenness, it rounds out the picture of Gascoigne as a typical literary man of the early Renaissance, who never lost contact with native tradition as he made his periodic excursions into foreign literature to bring back new forms and themes.

The standard edition is *The Complete Works of George Gascoigne*, edited by J. W. Cunliffe, published in two volumes (1907–10). The original version of his first published work was reprinted in *George Gascoigne's "A Hundred Sundrie Flowres,"* edited by C. T. Prouty (1942).

See C. T. Prouty, *George Gascoigne, Elizabethan Courtier, Soldier, and Poet* (1942); S. A. Tannenbaum, *George Gascoigne, a Concise Bibliography* (1942). (L. A. Sk.)

GASCONY (Fr. GASCOGNE; Med. Lat. WASCONIA or VASCONIA), a region of southwestern France, which in the last centuries of the *ancien régime* was merged with Guienne (q.v.) in the *gouvernement* of Guienne-et-Gascogne. At its greatest extent, in the early middle ages, Gascony may be regarded as extending from the western Pyrenees northward to the Gironde estuary and from the Bay of Biscay eastward to the lower Garonne valley and even across the upper Garonne; but the northern area, with Bordeaux, was finally regarded as part of Guienne, while in the southwest French Navarre and Béarn were separated from the *gouvernement*. The Gascon areas of the *gouvernement* corresponded approximately to the modern *départements* of Landes, Gers and Hautes-Pyrénées, with parts of Lot-et-Garonne, Tarn-et-Garonne, Haute-Garonne, Ariège and Basses-Pyrénées (qq.v.).

During the period of Roman rule in Gaul, the southernmost areas between the Pyrenees and the Garonne, predominantly Iberian rather than Celtic in ethnic composition, had been detached from Aquitania (see AQUITAINE) to form the separate province of Novempopulana. Taken from the Visigoths by the Franks after the battle of Vouillé (A.D. 507), this country was overrun from A.D. 561 by the Vascones or Basques from beyond the Pyrenees (see BASQUE); and in 602 the Frankish kings recognized Vasconia or Gascony as a duchy under the national leader Genialis. In the latter half of the 7th century the Gascon duke Lupus I extended his power over adjacent areas. In the 8th century, however, the Carolingians, having imposed Frankish authority over Aquitaine, were able to set up the march of Bordeaux as a frontier countship to watch over Gascony. The duke Lupus II recognized Frankish suzerainty in 769, and the title "prince of the Gascons" is recorded in 801 for Lupus Sancho (probably Lupus II's son). Seguin I, a count of Bordeaux whom the Carolingians tried to set up as duke of the Gascons, was displaced in 816, after which Lupus Sancho's son Aznar is found styled "count of Hither Gascony." On Aznar's death (836) his brother Sancho Sanchez or Mitarra made himself duke. Sancho Mitarra's son Garsia Sancho (d. 926) dispossessed his cousin Arnaldus in 887 and is recorded with the style "count and marquis on the borders of the Ocean" in 904. Finally, in the latter half of the 10th century, Garsia Sancho's grandson William Sancho (d. 997), duke of all Gascony, became count of Bordeaux also. Bazadais (the country round Bazas) and Agenais (east of the Garonne) likewise passed into Gascon hands in the same period.

On the death of William Sancho's son Sancho William in 1032 a war of succession broke out. Gascony was eventually won, in 1052, by Guy Geoffrey, stepson of Sancho William's sister Brisca and, from 1058, duke of Aquitaine. Thus in the 12th century Gascony passed with the Aquitanian inheritance to the Plantagenet kings of England. Though Henry III of England in 1259 acknowledged himself as the French king Louis IX's vassal for Gascony as part of the duchy of Guienne, Edward I's jurists were able to claim that Gascony, as distinct from Aquitaine, had previously never been a French fief but was either a fief of the Holy Roman empire or an allodial possession of the dukes. In fact throughout the years of intermittent warfare between England and France up to the definitive French reconquest at the end of the Hundred Years' War (q.v.), Gascony remained the kernel of English power in southwestern France. The dukes' authority, however, had for centuries been only nominal over large areas of the original duchy: Béarn (q.v.) had early shaken off all suzerainty before it was orientated first toward Foix, then toward Navarre; and Armagnac and Albret (qq.v.) pursued practically independent policies.

GAS ENGINE: see INTERNAL-COMBUSTION ENGINE.

GAS INDUSTRY. The gases produced for utilization as sources of heat and energy in private residences and industry include manufactured gas (*e.g.,* coal gas, water gas, producer gas, blast furnace gas), natural gas and liquefied petroleum gas. This article deals chiefly with manufactured gas. For discussions of the other types of gas *see* PETROLEUM. *See also* FUELS: *Gaseous Fuels.*

On a world basis, the use of manufactured gas declined as the use of natural gas and electricity increased. Major producers of manufactured gas in the early 1960s were West Germany, Great Britain, the United States, Japan, Czechoslovakia, East Germany, France, the Netherlands, Belgium and Italy. In about half of these countries, including Britain and the U.S., production had declined slowly in the preceding five years while in the others it was static or had increased slightly. In the U.S. in the early 1960s, the amount of natural gas marketed was almost 50 times greater than the amount of manufactured gas produced. In Britain, however, practically all of the gas consumed was manufactured gas. The principal use for manufactured gas originally was the illuminating of streets and interiors of buildings, but electricity eventually became the chief illuminant. Gas then came to be used chiefly for space heating, cooking and the firing of industrial furnaces.

Most manufactured gas is made from coal, although coke, oil and other starting materials also are used. The process of carbonization, or coking, in which coal is heated in an absence of air, was in the 1960s still the most important method for producing fuels derived from coal, but other gaseous fuels were being manufactured by methods known as gasification; *i.e.,* water gas made by the action of steam upon red-hot coke and producer gas made by blowing air, usually mixed with some steam, through a deep bed of hot coke or coal. Coal gas has the highest heating value, averaging about 500 B.T.U. per cubic foot; water gas averages about 300 B.T.U. but may be enriched with oil vapours (carbureting; Table I) up to or above the value for coal gas. The heating value of producer gases is much lower (120–160 B.T.U. per cubic foot) (X.)

because about one-half or as much as two-thirds of their volume is made up of nitrogen contained in the air used for gasification. In Great Britain, the manufactured gas, or town gas, distributed for public supply after purification is coal gas or coal gas mixed with straight or enriched water gas. In some cases, coke oven gas also may be added; this is essentially similar to coal gas in that it is produced by carbonizing coal, but the process is different because it is directed more to the production of coke than of gas. Producer gas is used mainly for large-scale industrial furnaces, including in particular the retorts used for the manufacture of coal gas. A broad comparison of the properties of these gases is given in Table I. (*See also* CARBONIZATION, LOW-TEMPERATURE; COAL AND COAL MINING: *Preparation and Uses of Coal;* COKE, COKING AND HIGH-TEMPERATURE CARBONIZATION.)

The main divisions of this article are as follows:

I. The Gas Industry in Great Britain
II. The Manufacture of Gas
    1. Retorts
    2. Purification
    3. Water Gas
    4. Producer Gas
    5. Blast Furnace Gas

TABLE I.—*Properties of Coal, Water and Producer Gases*

Properties	Coal gas	Water gas		Producer gas	
		Straight (blue)	Carbureted	From coal	From coke
Composition					
Oxygen	0.4%	—	0.4%	—	—
Carbon dioxide	2%–4%	4.7%	5.6%	4%	5%
Unsaturated hydrocarbons	2%–4%	—	7.0%	0.4%	0.4%
Carbon monoxide	8%–18%	41%	30.5%	29%	29%
Hydrogen	29%–50%	49%	37%	12%	11%
Methane	20%–50%	0.8%	14%	2.6%	0.5%
Nitrogen	4%–9%	4.5%	5.5%	52%	54.5%
Heating value B.T.U. per cubic foot	475–560	295	500	163	132
Density (relative to air=1)	0.4–0.48	0.55	0.63	0.87	0.90

I. THE GAS INDUSTRY IN GREAT BRITAIN

Coal gas, when used as an illuminant, burns with a characteristic yellowish luminous flame. The earliest demonstration of this property has been variously ascribed to Jean Pierre Minckelers of Belgium, to Philippe Lebon of France and to Lord Dundonald and William Murdock of Great Britain; but William Murdock is usually given entire credit for being the first to apply coal gas on any considerable scale. Murdock set up a small experimental plant in 1795, lighted a Soho (Birmingham) factory by gas a few years later and in Feb. 1808 was awarded the Rumford medal of the Royal society of London for his invention as described in a paper read before the society.

In 1813 the foundation was laid for the London and Westminster Gas company, soon to become the famous Gas Light and Coke company. It possessed three manufacturing stations with 15 mi. of mains, and Westminster bridge was lit by its gas. Gas lighting was introduced in Bristol in 1823, by which time the Gas Light and Coke company in London was producing nearly 250,000,000 cu.ft. of gas annually for distribution through 122 mi. of street mains. Rapid expansion followed, so much so that the gas companies that had sprung up in the metropolis and in the provinces are recorded as "innumerable" in 1860. Public supply was governed by many local and general acts of parliament. With the advent of electric lighting in 1882 the industry encountered serious competition, which appeared to threaten its existence. In fact, however, the severe shock that it experienced was a stimulus to the industry to look elsewhere than to lighting for the disposal of its products, and the great potential market available to gas in its capacity of a heating medium was soon recognized. The year 1920 stands out as epoch making in the history of the industry; in that year the Gas Regulation act was introduced, the main provision of which was to make it obligatory to charge for gas on the basis of its declared and attested heating value; furthermore, gas had to be supplied at a minimum pressure of 2 in. water gauge in mains or services of 2 in. or more in diameter. These and earlier regulations, including the requirement that gas should be entirely free from the poisonous and objectionable gas hydrogen sulfide, fully protected the interests of the consumer. At that time the annual production of gas in Great Britain had risen to 250,000,000 cu.ft., and there were 7,000,000 consumers (4,250,000 supplied through prepayment or "slot" meters) receiving gas through approximately 40,000 mi. of mains.

On May 1, 1949, the gas industry passed into national ownership in accordance with the provisions of the Gas act of 1948. Many of the provisions of the acts that previously had nationalized the coal and electricity industries were repeated, but there was one significant difference: the larger measure of decentralization and regional responsibility accorded to the gas industry.

Twelve area boards were constituted to assume the ownership of 1,037 undertakings for the nation. The area boards were separate, corporate bodies, each charged with the prime duty of developing and maintaining an efficient, co-ordinated and economical system for the supply of gas and coke and to develop and maintain efficient methods of recovering the by-products of gas manufacture.

At the same time parliament decided that a central body, the Gas council, was needed to represent the industry as a whole and to be responsible for such matters as capital finance, labour relations, research and others calling for central action. The Gas council was to consist of a chairman, a deputy chairman and the 12 chairmen of the area boards; its duty was to advise the minister of fuel and power on questions affecting the industry and generally to assist the area boards in exercising their statutory functions. Thus, after about 140 years of progressive expansion, the gas industry was unified under its central council but at the same time possessed a regional structure that was acknowledged to be well suited to its particular requirements and conducive of the best service to its consumers. Research was specified to be one of the council's responsibilities, and its obligation in this respect was interpreted as being the search for fundamental knowledge and the development of new ideas up to and including the pilot-plant stage. Large-scale plant development and the normal improvement of appliances were entrusted to the area boards and the plant manufacturers. A permanent committee, including scientists from outside the industry, was set up to advise the council on methods of research. Research stations were established in London and Birmingham; in addition, the council contributed to a number of research associations engaged in work of interest to the industry. It also maintained the industry's close association with the University of Leeds and with the British Ceramic Research association.

As result of research aimed at finding more economical methods for producing gas, an experimental plant that used low-grade coal was built at Westfield, Fife, Scot., in 1961. A similar plant was planned at Coleshill near Birmingham. Oil gasification plants were built at several places, including the Isle of Grain, Kent. A plan for shipping methane from the Sahara was being considered in the early 1960s.

In Great Britain early in the second half of the 20th century the approximately 375 gasworks supplied about 13,000,000 customers with about 600,000,000,000 cu.ft. of gas annually. Half of this amount was used in homes and half in industrial and commercial establishments. About three-fourths of the household gas was used for cooking while the rest was used for space heating, water heating and other purposes. Most British homes were supplied with manufactured gas of the coal gas type except in some remote rural areas where bottled liquefied petroleum gas was used. The industries and businesses that used gas were generally those that required accurately controlled temperatures.

II. THE MANUFACTURE OF GAS

In Murdock's apparatus coal was contained in an inclined iron retort heated by a fire burning on a grate below. Cast-iron retorts were used for a long time in the early days of manufacture. Charged with the coal to be carbonized, the retorts were heated by small coal to temperatures of about 600°–700° C., much lower than those used in modern practice. At this point it is convenient to consider the principles involved in the carbonization process.

Coal is the term applied to those rocks in the earth's crust produced by the decay of plant remains and accumulated many millions of years ago. Coal is thus a complex mixture of organic substances that so far cannot be recognized except in broad terms. The essential elementary constituents are carbon, hydrogen and oxygen, with small quantities of nitrogen and sulfur and some incombustible matter—the ash. When heated out of contact with air, the coal more or less fuses and partially decomposes. Gaseous products of decomposition force their way through the plastic mass and give it a honeycombed structure. As the temperature of the mass increases, the coal becomes less fusible and is transformed into a porous solid known as coke. Further heating drives off more gas and results in shrinking and hardening of the coke. The volatile matter evolved in the lower-temperature stages is rich in easily condensable tarry matter and gaseous hydrocarbons. At temperatures above 800° C. the volatile matter is principally hydrogen, with some carbon monoxide.

The manufacturing process thus consists essentially in driving off the volatile products by heat, leaving the solid residue of coke in the retort for subsequent extraction. The volatile matter, or crude gas, leaves the retorts at a temperature usually between 700°–800° C.; at this temperature the gas is heavily charged with steam (derived from hydrogen and oxygen in the coal as well as from actual moisture) and with condensable tarry vapours, hydrocarbons, some sulfur-containing gases, some hydrogen cyanide and ammonia. These constituents must be removed before the gas is distributed to consumers.

When the gases enter the collecting main they are cooled so that condensation takes place; and this is further assisted by

TABLE II.—*Composition of Coal Gas*

Gases	High temperature			Low temperature
	Horizontal retort	Vertical retorts		
		Without steam	With steam	
Carbon dioxide	2.0%	2.2%	3.4%	4.5%
Unsaturated hydrocarbons	3.1%	2.3%	1.8%	3.8%
Oxygen	0.5%	0.4%	0.7%	0.2%
Carbon monoxide	8.0%	10.3%	15.1%	8.3%
Hydrogen	50.6%	49.5%	49.3%	29.1%
Methane	28.1%	28.5%	21.2%	49.1%
Nitrogen	7.7%	6.8%	8.5%	5.0%

washing with water. Water from condensation or from washing dissolves part of the ammonia and other constituents, forming "ammonia liquor." As a consequence of the condensation process, the volatile matter is divided into three portions; two, the tar and the ammonia liquor, are liquid, but they do not mix; the third is the gas itself, which, after further purification from tar fog, residual ammonia and hydrogen sulfide, is ready for distribution.

The proportions of gas, coke, tar and liquor vary according to the particular method used for carbonization and to the nature of the coals carbonized. In broad terms, however, the yield of these products per ton of coal processed in horizontal retorts is about 14 cwt. of coke, 10 gal. of tar and 30 gal. of liquor, the last representing a recovery of approximately 25 lb. of ammonia as sulfate. Table II shows the composition of coal gas according to the method of carbonization employed. The tar is composed of pitch (61.3%), creosote oil (13%), carbolic oil (12.1%), light oils (9.4%), crude naphtha (2.6%) and water (1.6%). The liquor, when horizontal retorts are used, yields for every 100 ml. of its volume 1.5 g. of fixed ammonia; 0.5 g. of free ammonia; 0.25 g. of sulfide as H_2S; 0.01 g. of cyanide as HCN; 0.1 g. of thiosulfide as S; 0.2 g. of thiocyanate as CNS; and 0.25 g. of phenols as C_6H_5OH.

Of the various circumstances that determine the quantities and compositions of the tar, liquor and gas, the temperature at which the coal is carbonized is particularly important. The low-temperature products are those resulting from the first processes of breaking down in the coal. The high-temperature products contain many of the substances formed by the secondary decomposition of the primary products, brought about by subjecting them to a higher temperature. The difference shows itself very plainly both in the gas yield, which is much higher for high-temperature working, and in the nature of the gas, which contains much more hydrogen and less of the easily decomposable compounds of carbon and hydrogen. The tar is usually smaller in amount for high-temperature working, when it is characterized by the presence of the so-called aromatic hydrocarbons of the benzene type, which are products of secondary decomposition and are absent from low-temperature tars. The increased yield of gas in high-temperature working is partly due to the secondary decomposition of some of the more decomposable tar constituents, although it is mainly accounted for by an extensive formation of hydrogen peculiar to high-temperature working.

1. Retorts.—The volume of gas obtainable by working in iron retorts was limited by the properties of this material. An important advance was made when fire clay was substituted for iron, as a higher temperature was permissible. Further improvements of a radical character followed when, in the heating of these retorts, gas firing and the recuperative principle could be employed.

Recuperative.—The principle of the recuperative retort will be understood from fig. 1, which shows a setting of ⌒-shaped horizontal fire-clay retorts. They are heated by producer gas made by passing air through a deep layer of red-hot coke. This gas, meeting hot air immediately under the retorts, burns around them and carbonizes the coal contained therein. The waste gases, after heating the retorts, do not, however, pass away directly to a chimney, as in older methods of "direct" firing, but are turned downward into the recuperator, where they pass along channels in which they are only separated by a thin fire-clay partition from air traveling upward to meet the gas. In this way some of the heat is abstracted from the waste gases and restored to the air used for combustion. Consequently, less heat leaves the setting and a higher temperature can be attained together with economy in fuel. This system of carbonization in horizontal recuperative fire-clay retorts rapidly became standard practice and remains so to some extent, although horizontal retorts are now obsolescent. It enabled an average gas yield of 10,000 cu.ft. of gas per ton of coal to be obtained; and it lowered the proportion of fuel required for heating the setting from 25%–30% of the weight of coal carbonized to 15%–20%.

Although excellent in many ways, the horizontal retort setting as so far described had the disadvantage of requiring heavy labour for hand charging. This drawback has been to some extent neutralized by the use of mechanical charging machines. Other methods were, however, coming forward by which the aid of gravity could be invoked for the moving of the coal and coke during carbonization and some other advantages secured. In the second half of the 20th century new installations were invariably of the vertical retort type.

In normal horizontal retort practice it may be assumed that for every 100 heat units contained in the coal carbonized 24 will appear in the gas, 42 in the coke available for sale after the heating of the retorts has been provided for and 5.6 in tar, which means that 71.6 of the original 100 heat units have been obtained in the available useful products of carbonization. Otherwise expressed, the thermal efficiency of the carbonization process so conducted is 71.6%, 28.4% having been used and lost in the manufacture. In modern large installations of vertical retorts, higher values would usually be attained.

Vertical.—The simplest form of the vertical retort was one in which the retorts were all set vertically (instead of horizontally, as in the past) and, being filled with coal, were heated until the whole of the charge had been carbonized, after which it was withdrawn. This so-called intermittent vertical system was patented in England by J. Bueb in 1904 after previous trial at the Dessau gasworks. It had the advantage, as compared with the handcharged horizontal retort setting, of reducing labour and requiring less ground space for a given output. Another novel advantage was that the retort could be fully charged, thereby lessening the contact of the volatile matter with red-hot coke and the walls of the retort that gives rise to secondary decomposition. A further advance was made almost at once by the introduction of continuous working into the vertical retort system; instead of completing the carbonization of the whole charge before withdrawing any portion of the coke residue, a continuous feed of coal was made to the top of the retort and coke was continuously withdrawn from the bottom by an extraction mechanism. Fig. 2 illustrates a typical setting of vertical retorts. The heating gas from the producer passes through apertures, which can be regulated, into heating channels surrounding the retorts. The upper sections are heated by waste gases alone.

When the heating quality of gas came to be of paramount importance, the heating value per cubic foot superseded its illuminating power in "standard candles" as the statutory method of defining its quality. The British Gas Regulation act of 1920 introduced the sale of gas by the therm, a therm being 100,000 B.T.U., and allowed gas companies and authorities to specify the standard

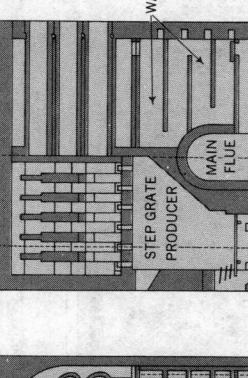

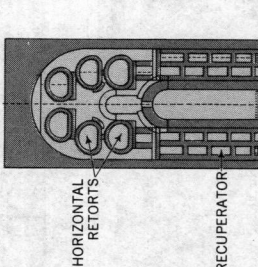

FIG. 1.—CROSS SECTION AND LONGITUDINAL SECTIONS OF A SETTING OF SIX HORIZONTAL RETORTS

quality in B.T.U. per cubic foot of the gas that they would supply (insistence, however, being rightly made upon the maintenance of that standard as all-important). These changes permitted and encouraged such developments in gas manufacture as make for more complete gasification of coal; i.e., for obtaining a larger proportion of its potential heat in the gas made.

Use of High Temperatures.—One method of achieving more complete gasification of coal was to work at a higher temperature. This, in turn, called for special attention to the quality of the refractory materials used in the construction of the retorts and their settings and led to an increase in the use of silica instead of fire clay in vital parts subject to the higher temperatures. In modern practice silica refractories are preferred for the walls of retorts (except for a few feet at the top and the bottom) because of their higher stability, strength and general durability. By such means, higher yields of gas per ton (13,000 cu.ft. per ton) have become common. The gas so made is rich in hydrogen but poorer in illuminating constituents than was the gas usually supplied for lighting purposes; it also is lower in calorific value (say 500 as compared with 600 B.T.U. per cubic foot).

Steaming.—Another widely used method of improving the yield in volume and thermal units is known as the "steaming" of continuous vertical gas retorts; it is carried out by introducing steam at the base where it can react with the red-hot coke. By this means an addition is made to the volume of gas by the interaction of carbon and steam; water gas is thereby generated.

An investigation by the joint research committee of the University of Leeds and the Institution of Gas Engineers, carried out on a Glover-West setting of continuous vertical retorts, showed that a lean coal gave 10,400 cu.ft. of gas per ton with a calorific value of 544 B.T.U. per cubic foot (gross) when steaming was not used. This corresponds to 56.5 therms in the gas per ton of coal carbonized. When steaming was employed, to the extent of 26.4% of steam on the weight of the coal used, the yield increased to 16,900 cu.ft. of gas with a calorific value of 447 B.T.U. per cubic foot, representing 75.7 therms in the gas made per ton of coal.

2. Purification.—As already indicated, the crude gas leaving the retorts contains materials that have to be removed in order to purify the gas before distribution and to recover by-products of commercial value. Many of these constituents are more or less easily condensed or washed out, and the appropriate plant consists of a train of vessels that vary widely in detail from one works to another but are essentially the same in principle. Fig. 3 shows diagrammatically the individual plant units in a typical gasworks

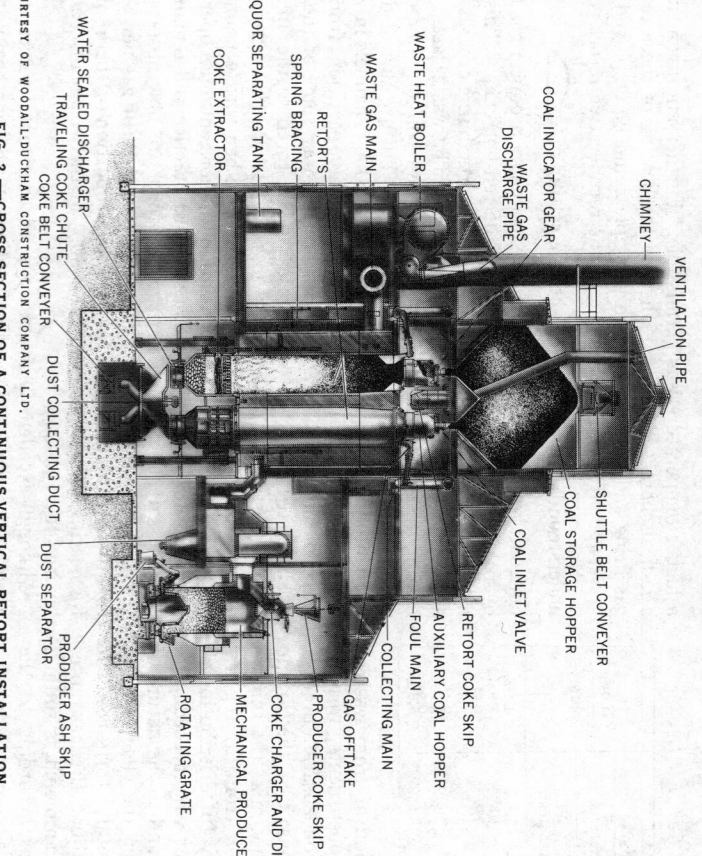

CHIMNEY
VENTILATION PIPE
COAL INDICATOR GEAR
WASTE GAS DISCHARGE PIPE
WASTE GAS MAIN
WASTE HEAT BOILER
RETORTS
SPRING BRACING
LIQUOR SEPARATING TANK
COKE EXTRACTOR
WATER SEALED DISCHARGER
TRAVELING COKE CHUTE
COKE BELT CONVEYER
DUST COLLECTING DUCT
DUST SEPARATOR
PRODUCER ASH SKIP
SHUTTLE BELT CONVEYER
COAL STORAGE HOPPER
COAL INLET VALVE
FOUL MAIN
RETORT COKE SKIP
AUXILIARY COAL HOPPER
GAS OFFTAKE
COLLECTING MAIN
PRODUCER COKE SKIP
MECHANICAL PRODUCER
COKE CHARGER AND DISTRIBUTOR
ROTATING GRATE

BY COURTESY OF WOODALL-DUCKHAM CONSTRUCTION COMPANY LTD.

FIG. 2.—CROSS SECTION OF A CONTINUOUS VERTICAL RETORT INSTALLATION

further cooling and removal of constituents by solution in water are secured. The washers and scrubbers are designed to obtain the greatest possible contact between gas and liquid. In the Livesey washer, for example, the gas stream is repeatedly broken up and forced through water. In modern practice there may follow an electrostatic detarring for the complete removal of tar. Next in sequence are rotary or static washers, in which the gas is brought into intimate contact with water or weak liquor. Ammonia is completely removed from the gas at this stage, although a trace may be allowed to pass forward to preserve alkalinity in the purifiers used later for extracting hydrogen sulphide. Additional scrubbing, using suitable oil solvents, is needed if it is intended to remove volatile tar constituents such as benzene and toluene. The tar and liquor condensed at different points in the system are usually led away to a common well, but there is good reason to suppose that some separation of the various liquors is desirable because some may be more potent than others, with the result that the question of disposal is not equally easy for all liquors.

Hydrogen Sulphide.—It has already been mentioned that law requires the elimination of hydrogen sulphide from gas used for public supply. The final process of purification in ordinary practice is to pass the gas through iron oxide purifiers and thence to gas-holders (storage tanks). The purifiers contain hydrated oxide of iron spread on grids. The oxide absorbs hydrogen sulphide rapidly, becoming converted into iron sulphide. The formation of

and the sequence of steps in the manufacturing process.

Gases travel from the retorts through an "ascension" pipe, which then bends over and dips below the liquid seal in the so-called hydraulic main, the seal being used to prevent access of air to the main when the retort is opened for charging and discharging. Some cooling and consequent condensation of tarry matter occurs in ascension pipes. It is usual for the gas from a number of retorts to be collected in a common hydraulic main. Easily condensable constituents gather there and in the foul main that leads to the condensers.

The condensers consist of nests of pipes cooled externally by air or water; the temperature of the gas within them is thus lowered, resulting in further condensation of both tar and water, which collect at the base of the pipes.

The next stage is the washing or scrubbing of the gas, in which

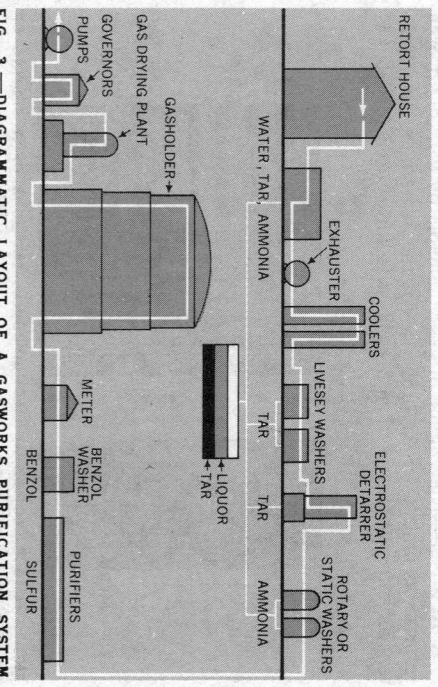

RETORT HOUSE
GASHOLDER
GAS DRYING PLANT
GOVERNORS
PUMPS
EXHAUSTER
COOLERS
WATER, TAR, AMMONIA
TAR
LIVESEY WASHERS
ELECTROSTATIC DETARRER
METER
BENZOL WASHER
LIQUOR
TAR
TAR
ROTARY OR STATIC WASHERS
BENZOL
AMMONIA
PURIFIERS
SULFUR

FIG. 3.—DIAGRAMMATIC LAYOUT OF A GASWORKS PURIFICATION SYSTEM

iron sulfide tends to render the material inactive for absorbing hydrogen sulfide but it can be reactivated by removal and exposure to air, or by admitting a little air into the gas stream so that regeneration takes place *in situ.* In both cases the sulfided material is reoxidized with the formation of free sulfur. When the sulfur content has risen to about 50% the so-called spent oxide is removed and sold for sulfuric acid manufacture. Most of the sulfur in crude coal gas is present as hydrogen sulfide (about 1%) and is completely removed by this process. Smaller quantities of sulfur are present, however, in the form of organic sulfur compounds, which are not extracted to any extent by iron oxide but which may be reduced considerably in amount by special additional processes. In 1942 a special committee set up by the industry recommended that the organic sulfur should be reduced to 10 grains per 100 cu.ft. (about 0.01%) as a first step and that processes should be introduced to obtain lower figures as they became available. The recovery of benzol by oil washing simultaneously removes much of the organic sulfur so that additional processing is more the exception than the rule in general practice. Satisfactory methods for reducing the organic sulfur to, say, 5–6 gr. per 100 cu.ft. are available, however, and are applied when gas of exceptionally low sulfur content is needed. Such processes are frequently used to purify the gas after distribution to the consumer's works.

Ammonia.—Liquor containing the ammonia washed out of the gas is either sold as such or is used at gasworks for the production of ammonium sulfate. Distillation of the liquor with lime drives off ammonia, which may be absorbed in sulfuric acid to form the sulfate, which constitutes a valuable fertilizer. The quantity obtained at gasworks usually lies between 20 and 30 lb. of ammonium sulfate per ton of coal carbonized. The ammonia yield can be increased by steaming the retorts, but the liquor obtained is usually weaker because of the passage of undecomposed steam from the top of the gas retort into the gas. A weaker liquor has a lower commercial value if it has to be sent away for treatment and has the further disadvantage that after distillation for ammonia the residual liquor is greater in amount.

The direct method of recovering ammonia, in which the gas is passed through sulfuric acid for the absorption of ammonia, instead of effecting a separation of the ammonia liquor and distilling it, has found little application in gasworks.

The disposal of the residual liquor after distillation for ammonia, or sometimes of the crude undistilled liquor itself, presents the gas industry with a problem that is serious because of the stringent regulations designed to reduce the pollution of rivers and streams. Although liquor is relatively weak, it is nonetheless a strong trade effluent and its direct disposal into sewers is prohibited. The usual method is to feed it into the local sewer for eventual decomposition in bacteria beds. It has, however, long been known that the constituents of liquor throw an increased load on the sewage purification process, so that the rate at which liquor may be discharged into sewers has to be carefully controlled. Normally the maximum permissible discharge of spent liquor is about 0.5% of the dry weather flow of the sewage. Much attention has been given both to re-examining the amount of liquor that can properly be discharged into sewers and also to developing alternative methods of disposal, the latter being particularly directed to meet the needs of those gas (and coke oven) works whose situation is remote from suitable sewage disposal plant.

Tar.—The tar made at gasworks is subjected to a complicated process of distillation that resolves it into fractions that boil off in different temperature ranges, the fractions being afterward refined. These operations are usually carried out at separate tar distilleries. Among the many products made from tar are toluol, cresol, naphthalene and anthracene, which find application in the production of dyes, medicines, perfumes, disinfectants, solvents, plastics and paints. Tar oil is used for fuel and also for road construction, whereas distilled tar and pitch are used for many purposes; *e.g.,* in connection with building materials, roofing felts, briquettes, etc.

The average yield of tar by the ordinary gasworks process can be taken as 5% of the weight of coal carbonized. At lower temperatures, more tar is produced and the light oil fraction coming over on distillation is usually greater in volume.

3. Water Gas.—Limited gasification of coke in steam can be effected in the continuous vertical retort as already described, but complete gasification of carbon in coke is carried out in an entirely different type of apparatus known as a water gas plant. At high temperatures, carbon decomposes steam into hydrogen and carbon monoxide, but with an absorption of heat according to the equation $C + H_2O \rightarrow CO + H_2 - 56,145$ B.T.U. When the temperature of the carbon has been brought down by this absorption of heat, the reaction is altered with the production of carbon dioxide. An equilibrium tends to be established by the catalytic action of the solid carbon (and inorganic ash constituents) so that a ratio $\dfrac{CO \times H_2O}{CO_2 \times H_2}$ may be set up between the gas constituents, the ratio being constant for any one temperature but falling as the temperature becomes less. The reversible reaction occurring $(CO + H_2O \rightleftharpoons CO_2 + H_2)$ results in a higher carbon dioxide content of the gas as the temperature is lowered; and, moreover, since the velocity of gasification is rapidly lowered with falling temperature, the gas made with the same rate of steam supply comes to contain more undecomposed steam. Carbon dioxide lowers the calorific value of the gas and the steam requires condensation. The high temperature of the carbon can, however, be restored by stopping the steam and blowing with air, thus raising the temperature of the fuel bed and generating a producer gas.

The industrial process based upon this principle of alternately blowing a bed of coke with steam and air was developed by Gaillard (1849), Tessié du Motay and T. S. C. Lowe (1873) and is

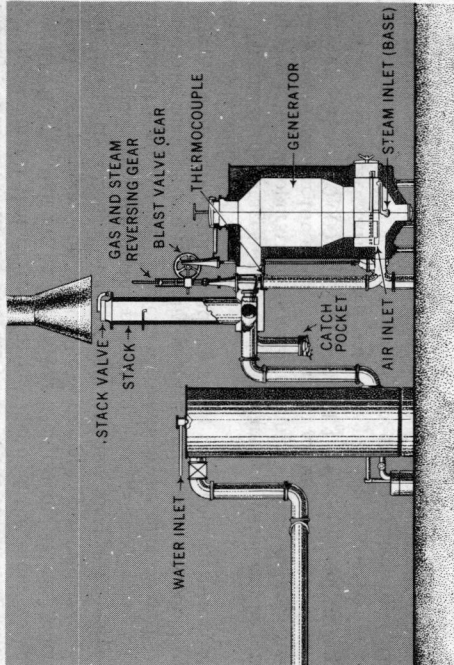

BY COURTESY OF THE INSTITUTION OF GAS ENGINEERS

FIG. 4.—PLANT FOR PRODUCING BLUE WATER GAS

called the water gas process. The plant illustrated in fig. 4 is that of Humphreys and Glasgow. The coke bed, enclosed in a steel casing lined with firebrick, may be blown through the grate below by either air or steam. An arrangement of valves also enables the steam to be introduced above the coke for a "down run." The exact arrangement and time in the up run with steam, down run with steam and blowing with air are varied to suit the fuel and other conditions and constitute a cycle of operations that is carried out systematically and automatically in modern plants. The coke is blown with steam until, as the temperature falls, the carbon dioxide produced in the water gas is reducing its quality too far. During the steam blow, the water gas made is carried forward to a scrubber down which water is running, and then goes forward to join the main gas stream of the works for removal of hydrogen sulfide. This water gas should have a calorific value of 300 B.T.U. per cubic foot. When the steam blast is replaced by air, in order to restore the high temperature in the fuel bed, the producer gas generated, being heavily charged with nitrogen, is not allowed to go forward to the scrubber but is turned up the stack as waste. Use of air continues until a satisfactory high temperature has been re-established in the fuel bed, when steam is again employed. The heaviest thermal loss in the process is that of the potential and thermal heat in the producer gas, but this is lessened in modern plants by the installation of a waste heat boiler.

It has been noted that the water gas made by the process described above has a calorific value approximating to 300 B.T.U. per cubic foot. It is known as "blue" water gas because of the characteristic colour of its flame and is definitely lower in grade than the coal gas made from retorts. The calorific value can be increased, however, by using some of the heat in the gases leaving the generator to crack oil (i.e., to convert it into permanent gas rich in hydrocarbons), so obtaining a "carbureted" water gas of enhanced calorific value. Fig. 5 illustrates a Humphreys and Glasgow plant used for the process. The gas from the generator passes through two chambers, a carburetor and a superheater packed with brickwork, which are raised to redness, some air being admitted for the combustion of the "blow" gas therein. The oil is run in from the top of the carburetor and should be of a grade that can be efficiently cracked under the conditions of the process. (In early stages of the development of the plant the oil was run directly upon the coke in the generator, but this was unsatisfactory for various reasons.) In this plant, blue water gas leaves the generator with a calorific value of 300 B.T.U. per cubic foot but leaves the superheater enriched by the carbureting to an extent determined by the amount of oil used. The extent of carbureting employed is influenced by this factor, by the price of oil and by the quality of the gas desired. In Great Britain, carbureting is usually continued until the calorific value of the carbureted water gas approximates to that of the coal gas made at the same works, say 500 B.T.U.; but in the U.S. it has been usually carried much further. It is plain, too, that blue water gas, enriched by carbureting to the extent desired, can be used as a means of modifying the calorific value of the mixture of coal gas and water gas supplied from a works. The extent to which the coke made in a gasworks may be economically gasified and water gas supplied depends on relative capital and operating costs and the prices of coal, coke and oil.

The main advantages of a water gas plant are that it can be put rapidly into full operation to meet maximum demands and that the yield of gas per ton of fuel is high; for example, modern plants may give about 50,000 cu.ft. of 300-B.T.U. water gas or 70,000 cu.ft. of 500-B.T.U. carbureted water gas per ton of coke.

Modern carbureted water gas plants are entirely automatic with an annular boiler around the generator and self-clinkering grates. A regular quantity of coke is fed to the generator during each gasmaking cycle without interruption to the gasification process. Plants of large capacity are now virtually self-supporting in their requirements of steam.

4. Producer Gas.—Producer gas is simple to manufacture and is the gas usually employed to heat steelmaking and other large industrial furnaces. When air is passed through a deep bed of carbon maintained at a high temperature, i.e., above 1,000° C., in such a way that complete contact with the carbon is attained and equilibrium is maintained, almost the whole of the carbon is obtained as carbon monoxide, according to the equation

$$C + \tfrac{1}{2}\{O_2 + 4N_2\} \rightarrow CO + 2N_2 + 29,000 \text{ cal.}$$

If the temperature is lower, even though the contact is complete and equilibrium is still attained, some carbon will be burned to CO_2 according to the equation

$$C + O_2 + 4N_2 \rightarrow CO_2 + 4N_2 + 97,000 \text{ cal.}$$

If, however, the high temperature has been maintained and the carbon entirely converted to CO, it is plain that the gas will consist of one-third carbon monoxide and two-thirds nitrogen, and the equation representing its formation may be called the ideal producer gas equation. If this producer gas is collected and burned with air, it will generate heat according to the equation

$$CO + 2N_2 + \tfrac{1}{2}\{O_2 + 4N_2\} \rightarrow CO_2 + 4N_2 + 68,000 \text{ cal.}$$

It will be seen that even if the whole of the heat generated in making the producer gas by converting the carbon to CO were lost, some 70% (actually $\frac{68}{97}$) of the total heat of combustion

of carbon to CO_2 would still remain available for use by its combustion of the gas. This large proportion of heat available for the second stage of the combustion of the carbon in burning carbon monoxide to carbon dioxide is the basis of producer gas practice.

Divergence in Composition.—There are various factors that cause divergence in the composition of producer gas from the ideal producer gas equation. In the first place, when coal is used as a fuel and is fed down on the fuel bed, it is at once subjected to a process of distillation or carbonization in the current of producer gas ascending from below, made by the action of the blast upon the carbonized fuel. Producer gas is in this way enriched to some extent with hydrogen, methane, and hydrocarbons, particularly nitrogen is correspondingly diminished. More important, however, is the modification in composition brought about by the steam consequent upon a lower-

TABLE III.—*Producer Gas as Modified by Steam*

Steam saturation, temperature of blast	60° C.	70° C.	80° C.
Percentage composition of gas:			
Carbon dioxide	5.25	9.15	13.25
Carbon monoxide . . .	27.20	21.70	16.05
Hydrogen	16.60	19.65	22.65
Methane	3.35	3.40	3.50
Nitrogen	47.50	46.10	44.55
Total combustibles . .	47.25	44.75	42.20
Cal. value of gas, B.T.U.s per cu.ft. at 0° and 760 mm. {gross	185.6	177.5	169.5
/net	173.0	163.3	154.3
Yield of gas cu.ft. at 0° C. and 760 mm. per ton of coal .	138,250	141,450	147,500
Steam added to blast, lb. per lb. of coal .	0.45	0.80	1.55
Percentage steam decomposed .	87.0	61.0	40.0
*Therms in gas per ton of coal (gross) .	256.6	251.1	250.0
*Weight of steam undecomposed per lb. of coal .	0.09	0.31	0.93
*Therms in gas / Therms in coal × 100	82.4	80.6	80.3

*Not included in the original table.

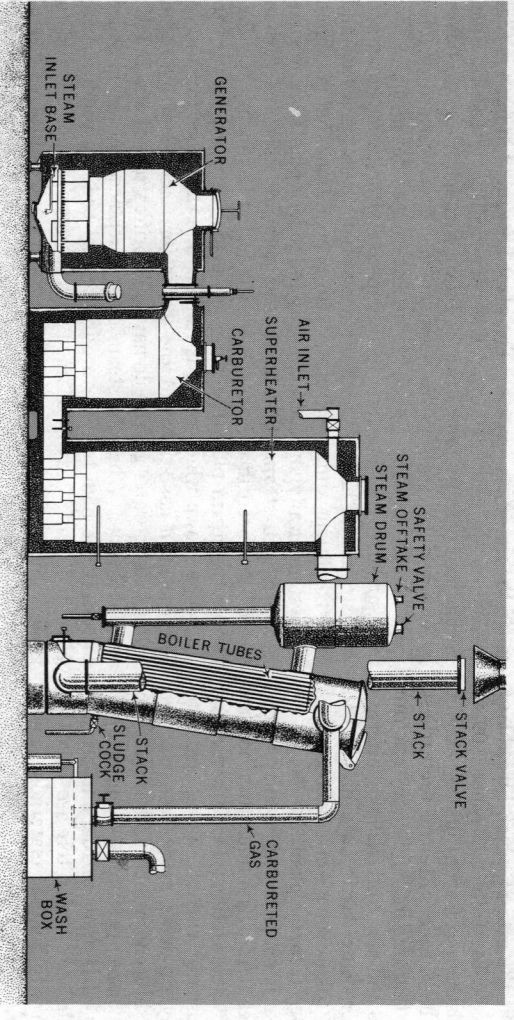

BY COURTESY OF THE INSTITUTION OF GAS ENGINEERS

FIG. 5.—CARBURETED WATER GAS PLANT WITH WASTE HEAT BOILER

ing of the temperature of the fuel bed and the formation of water gas by interaction with carbon. The more steam is used, the lower the temperature and the greater the formation of carbon dioxide and hydrogen at the expense of carbon monoxide. The percentage of nitrogen is further lowered by the admixture with water gas. Moreover, as the quantity of steam is increased and the temperature decreases, the rate of steam decomposition by the carbon lessens and steam passes through the fuel bed undecomposed. The quantity of steam supplied is best controlled by the temperature of the mixed blast at a point well beyond the introduction of the steam, so as to allow a thorough mixing. The temperature of the blast rises with the proportion of steam. It will be understood that undecomposed steam, which begins to occur in quantity as soon as the saturation temperature of 60° C. has been exceeded, is an objectionable constituent in the producer gas, since it is thermally useless and would tend to prevent the attainment of high temperatures on combustion because of its high specific heat. W. A. Bone and R. V. Wheeler followed changes brought about in the composition and yield of producer gas by gradually increasing the proportion of steam, with results shown in Table III. The coal used was washed nut screened over a one-inch mesh.

As the saturation temperature was raised by more steam, the gas composition shows a rise in carbon dioxide from 5% to 13% and a change-over from a carbon monoxide producer gas, in which that constituent is dominant, to a hydrogen producer gas is explained. The nitrogen has fallen and the percentage of total combustibles has also fallen on account of the increase of carbon dioxide resulting from the lower temperature of the fuel bed. The calorific value of the gas has slightly diminished but the volumetric yield has increased, so that the yield in therms contained in the gas per ton of coal gasified shows little change. The weight of steam undecomposed per pound of coal has run up from 0.09 to 0.9 lb. per ton of coal.

Early Producer Construction.—It would appear that the earliest gas producers were deep shafts of brickwork, but the structure most closely identified with the successful establishment of this process of gas manufacture was devised in 1861 by K. W. (Sir William) Siemens; a diagram of his producer is given in fig. 6. It illustrates how the coal falls from the hopper and lies in the producer above the step grate. The producer was connected to a furnace, and the air for gasification was drawn through the fuel bed by natural chimney draft supplemented at times by a siphon effect, induced by the disposition of the main between producer and furnace.

Pressure Producers.—Although producers based essentially on Siemens' simple design were in widespread use, the demands of industry for higher outputs per unit of space and grate area led to the development of producers that work under a positive blast of air and steam. The modern gas producer is essentially of the design shown diagrammatically in fig. 7. The generator is a cylindrical body provided with a grate or tuyère through which the air-steam blast is admitted at the bottom and with an outlet

for gas at the top. The generator is water-jacketed, with the object of preventing adhesion of clinker and at the same time raising the steam needed to saturate the blast. Fuel for a run of about six hours on full load is contained in a feed hopper, from which it falls into the producer through several chutes arranged so as to ensure uniform distribution and to prevent segregation. The Koller grate is a series of superposed cast-iron rings; space between the rings forms horizontal ports through which the blast is distributed evenly. The grate is secured to a revolving ashpan designed to continuously shear the bottom from the column of ash, break up lumps of clinker and discharge both over a plow bolted to the sealing ring. Steam from the annular boiler passes into a vapour box and thence to the air-blast pipe. Blast is supplied by a blower and is measured by a Venturi meter; it is then saturated with steam at any desired temperature and admitted to the producer from beneath the grate. Satisfactory operation of a gas producer depends upon keeping the distribution of blast and ascending gas current as uniform as possible across the section of the fuel bed, so as to give proper contact in all parts with the descending fuel. For this purpose the producer may have holes through which pokers may be inserted to keep the fuel bed level and free from channels that would tend to short-circuit the gas stream. Some designs incorporate mechanical revolving pokers.

In many cases the producer gas can be used hot direct from the generator without further cleaning; the advantage gained is that the sensible heat (*i.e.*, as shown on the wet-bulb thermometer) in the hot gases is retained. When a clean gas is required (as, for example, in a gas engine) the gas must be cleaned and cooled. This is usually effected by means of a washer cooler containing water sprays, in which dust and some tar are removed. Next, a centrifugal washer takes out most of the remaining dust and tar;

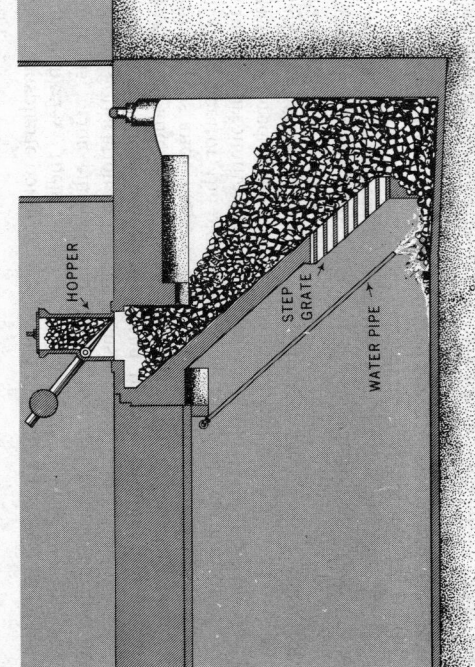

FROM RAMBUSH'S "MODERN GAS PRODUCERS" (BENN BROS.)

FIG. 6.—SIEMENS SYSTEM FOR MANUFACTURE OF PRODUCER GAS

HOPPER

STEP GRATE

WATER PIPE

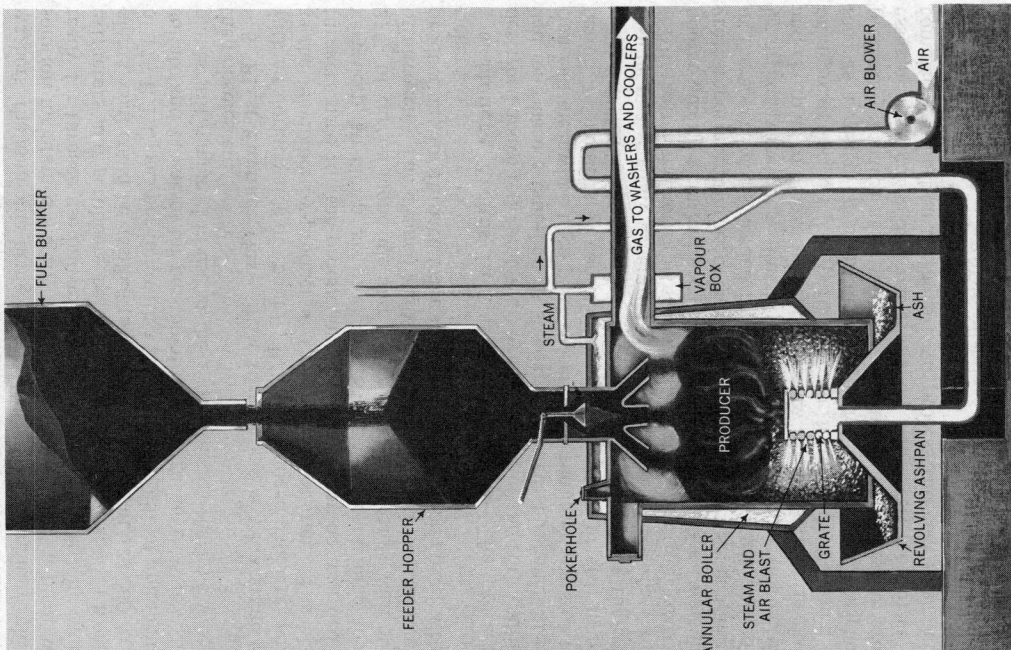

FUEL BUNKER

FEEDER HOPPER

POKERHOLE

STEAM

VAPOUR BOX

GAS TO WASHERS AND COOLERS

AIR BLOWER

AIR

PRODUCER

ANNULAR BOILER

STEAM AND AIR BLAST

GRATE

REVOLVING ASHPAN

ASH

FIG. 7.—MODERN PLANT FOR MAKING PRODUCER GAS

the gas then passes through a moisture eliminator and then to a dry scrubber in which the final removal of dust is accomplished. This scrubber may consist of an oxide box to remove hydrogen sulfide.

In the past, by-product recovery from producer gas was practised on a considerable scale, and modified designs and processes were developed to obtain larger yields of ammonia and tar than were normally obtainable. The essential feature was the use of a very deep fuel bed of coal (12 to 14 ft.) at a lower temperature, which favoured high yields of tar and ammonia. The recovery process called for a rather elaborate plant, the main features of which are indicated in fig. 8. The gas is washed, freed from ammonia and cooled by passing in turn through three Lymn static washers, the ammonia being absorbed in weak ammonium sulfate solution maintained slightly acid. Gas leaving such a plant was ready for furnace use but needed more thorough cleansing by tar extractors and scrubbers before its use in engines. With such plants, coal could be gasified to yield an average of 122,000 cu.ft. of 178-B.T.U. gas per ton, with a recovery of 90 lb. of ammonium sulfate and 21 gal. of tar per ton of dry fuel gasified. A few such plants still remained in use in the 1960s, though the type was by then obsolescent.

5. Blast Furnace Gas.—Blast furnace gas is a low-grade gas with a calorific value of about 95 B.T.U. produced on a large scale as the inevitable by-product of the smelting of iron. The blast furnaces used for the production of pig iron may be regarded as very deep, air-blown gas producers giving a gas containing about 27% of carbon monoxide and 11% of carbon dioxide, with 60% of nitrogen. The cleaned gas is used for steam raising and power production; for furnace firing it usually needs to be mixed with a richer gas.

6. Modern Trends in Gas Manufacture.—The processes described above represent what by the middle of the 20th century had long been established as standard practice; but much attention had meanwhile been paid, especially in the later years of the period, to methods of completing the gasification of coal in one process instead of carbonizing it first and then gasifying the coke residue in a separate generator.

Alternative methods for making gas, particularly from coals of poorer quality than had been used hitherto, then came to assume great importance to the industry because of the increasing scarcity of the special coals needed for the manufacture of gas and coke by orthodox methods. Furthermore, oil fuels became so plentiful and cheap as to demand attention as raw materials for gasmaking on a greater scale. The pattern of the future industry could be seen as a system of interlinked large stations of high efficiency, preferably situated at or near the coal fields and operating processes best suited to the coal available. However, the object of complete gasification methods is to process the coal solely into gas with no solid residue other than ash; the extent to which such processes could be effectively introduced depended upon the balance needed between the supply of gas and of coke (it should be pointed out in this connection that the new emphasis on minimiz-

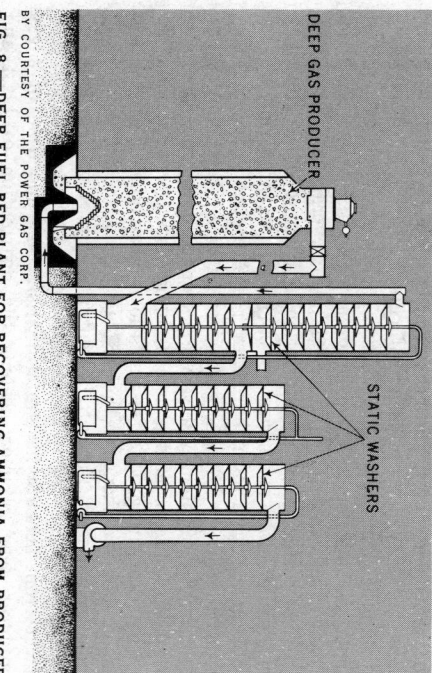

DEEP GAS PRODUCER

STATIC WASHERS

FIG. 8.—DEEP FUEL BED PLANT FOR RECOVERING AMMONIA FROM PRODUCER GAS

ing atmospheric pollution was bound to result in a greater demand for smokeless fuels, such as coke). But complete gasification methods, being efficient and flexible, seemed certain to find extensive application in the gas industry.

Most of these processes depend upon a combination of carbonization and generation of water gas. In the modern plant of Humphreys and Glasgow, the blow gases being led to the carburetor via an annulus surrounding the generator. Available heat in the blow gases is stored in the carburetor and superheater and used to assist carbonization of the coal by transference back to the generator. Part of it may also be used for carbureting. A back-run produced by admitting steam to the top of the superheater and then to the base of the generator gives water gas; the heat in this gas then carbonizes coal in the upper part of the generator. In another part of the run, steam admitted to the generator base, this time without superheat, generates hot water gas, which again passes through the coal in the upper part of the generator. This gas also can be fed to the carburetor if desired. The yield may be from 175 to 190 therms of 345-B.T.U. gas per ton. The plant is designed to gasify coal, coke or any mixture, with subsequent enrichment by oil as may be desirable.

Considerable importance was attached to finding a means of developing these processes and applying them on a large scale. The availability of low-cost oxygen stimulated the development of methods in which the gasification of solid fuels is carried out in oxygen and steam. In Germany and elsewhere, from about 1945, the Lurgi process of gasification in steam and oxygen under pressure was successfully applied on a large scale to lignites (young coals unsuitable for carbonization by orthodox means). This process came to be accepted as having many attractive features for the manufacture of town gas: it can make use of small coal of high ash content and of weakly caking coals unsuitable for carbonization; the plant operates at very high output; and the gas can be readily freed from sulfur and is available at pressure for long-distance transmission. For Great Britain, the search for new gasification processes was given first place in the research program of the Gas council (the former Gas Research board). An important achievement of the British work was the demonstration that the considerable proportion of methane characteristic of Lurgi gas was not due to the synthesis under pressure from carbon monoxide and hydrogen produced on gasification but resulted directly from the hydrogenation of coal, a reaction that proceeds vigorously under pressure. As a consequence, the possibility of manufacturing gas comparable in quality with town gas by gasification methods adapted to favour hydrogenation appeared to be most promising, although many technical problems would have to be solved before large-scale application could follow.

New processes for the direct gasification of oil, without recourse to water gas production, were adopted by certain area boards in Great Britain. The plant developed by the North Thames Gas board and installed at their Southend works produces a rich gas by the partial combustion of oil. Another process, devised by the South Eastern Gas board and installed in its own area and also within the North Eastern board's area, generates gas by the catalytic decomposition of oil. Other methods include the Onia-Gegi, giving an oil gas (from 300 to 1,000 B.T.U.) by the cyclic catalytic cracking of heavy oil, and the Geim process for the continuous production of gas (from 370 to 470 B.T.U.) by the thermal cracking of gas oil. The synthesis of gases rich in methane by hydrogenating coal under pressure was an important objective of the search for new gasmaking processes. (J. W. C.; A. L. Rs.)

III. GAS SUPPLY IN THE UNITED STATES

1. The First Gas Plants.—Following the discovery of gasmaking from coal and the unparalleled success of gaslighting in one or two European cities, gaslighting got its start in the United States in Baltimore, Md. Although there were a few isolated instances of gas being used previously by individuals in other cities, introduction of gaslights in Rembrandt Peale's museum in Baltimore in 1816 proved to be such a success that the city council passed an ordinance on June 17, 1816, permitting Peale and others to manufacture gas, lay pipes in the streets and contract with the city for street lighting. The first recorded demonstration of gas in the United States was in Philadelphia, Pa., in Aug. 1796. The gas was manufactured by M. Ambroise and Co., Italian fireworkers and artists. In 1806, David Melville of Newport, R.I., lighted his home and the street in front with gas that he manufactured. He also lighted a factory at Pawtucket, R.I., and induced the government to use gas at Beaver Tail lighthouse.

2. Growth and Changes in the Industry.—By the second half of the 20th century the gas industry had grown into one of the key industries, showing remarkable ability to adapt itself to meet severe competition, changing raw materials, and drastic economic and labour conditions, while constantly maintaining and expanding its service. When the illumination market was lost after the invention of electric lighting, the gas service emerged as a heat producer; when the severe labour and raw material inflations and dislocations caused by World War II threatened the manufactured gas service and solvency, the industry maintained and expanded its markets by drawing more natural gas from transcontinental pipelines.

The first public utility gas was manufactured by heating a high-volatility coal in a metal retort and subjecting the resulting gas to cooling and purification. A water gas process was introduced later. This injected steam over the coal, which was heated externally. The work of Thaddeus Lowe, a Union balloon officer in the Civil War, made possible the economic manufacture of water gas in internally fired machines. This became the basis of the modern carbureted and blue water gas processes. By-product coke oven gas supplemented and often supplanted coal gas and water gas. Internally fired oil-gas processes were invented and developed. Prior to World War II these were used very little in the United States except on the west coast. Even there prior to World War II the use of oil-gas was declining as natural gas became available.

All these changes were dwarfed by the change from manufactured gas to natural gas. This tremendous exploitation of natural gas followed the discovery and proof of large reserves of natural gas in the midcontinental and southwestern areas in the 1920s. In 1925 seamless electrically welded steel pipe made the transportation of oil and gas for long distances economically feasible. The change was particularly striking after World War II when transcontinental petroleum pipelines became available for gas transmission and the economic inflation and short labour supply made public utility gas manufacture based on solid fuels generally uneconomic.

By the 1960s intrastate and interstate transportation of natural gas by major pipelines had become so far-flung that, except in Maine, Vermont and Hawaii, there was practically no major city in the United States beyond the reach of natural gas supplies.

Long-distance transmission of natural gas changed the engineering and economic problems of the gas industry. It involved heavy investments in long pipelines and, in many cases, the substitution of high thermal value (natural) gas for medium thermal value (manufactured) gas. These changes led to major new developments in gas manufacturing processes, storage and sales. The large investments in long pipelines favour the use of these lines at high load factors; thus natural gas becomes the base gas or the base material for gas manufacture. Off-peak sale of natural gas to industry at attractive rates is favoured with shutoff agreements at times of peak public demands.

A number of oil-gas processes have been designed and developed to utilize the cheaper grades of heavy oils. In many situations component parts of abandoned water gas equipment have been built into the new oil-gas machines. Other studies have developed new equipment as well as new processes for the purpose. In general, such heavy oil-gas making machines use oil and air internally to create the heat they require, then inject oil and steam into the heated zone to make the gas. Partial combustion with air is sometimes simultaneously employed to increase the volume of the gas made. The cycle is then continued by returning to the heating phase, followed by another gasmaking phase. Good heat economy and good heat distribution within the machine are obtained in the same phase by heating alternately in a forward and a reverse direction, followed by making gas in the forward and reverse directions. The incoming oil, air and steam are preheated regeneratively by waste heat from the outgoing products, thereby securing good thermal efficiencies.

Where mixed gases of a total thermal content less than that of natural gas are distributed, or where liquefied petroleum gases are used for enrichment, natural gas, liquefied petroleum gases, gasolines and petroleum oils may be reformed in machines of the water gas or oil-gas type to greater volume, lower thermal content and controlled combustion characteristics and gravity to meet production and mixing needs. The reforming processes may involve partial combustion, pyrolysis or reaction with steam or some combination of these. Reforming, with enrichment of the reformed gas with liquefied petroleum gases or refinery oil gases, may also be used to meet peak loads on natural gas systems.

Unique in post-World War II gasmaking processes was the development of catalytic reforming. The feed stock may be natural gas, propane, butane, refinery oil gases or natural gasoline. The reforming is carried on in chrome-nickel alloy tubes heated externally, usually with light fuel oil. The tubes are filled with a nickel oxide catalyst, and the reforming gas zone is maintained at a temperature of about 982° C. The type of reformed gas depends upon the relative proportions of air and steam in the feed mixture. Pyrolysis of the feed mixture is not attempted. The ultimate capacity depends upon the rate of deposition of carbon, excessive carbon being objectionable. The unit is very flexible. The reformed gas, usually of 180 to 350 B.T.U. per cubic foot (at 15.5° C. and 30 in. mercury barometer saturated with water) with a specific gravity from 0.52 to 0.65 referred to air, is then enriched with undecomposed feed stock. The unit can produce a perfectly matched gas that can be used as 100% replacement of the regular utility sendout. The automatic controls and flexibility of this continuous process permit feeding directly into the distribution system. A minimum of labour is required, capital investment is low, purification of the gas is not necessary and there are no tars and no waste disposal problems. As the plant produces no smoke or dust it can be tolerated in residential locations.

3. Natural Gas.—Although natural gas had been noted in the United States before manufactured gas was introduced, it was not used commercially until long after manufactured gas was distributed.

There is a record of a "Burning Spring," in 1775 near Charleston, W.Va., on land that George Washington dedicated as a public park. In 1821 the first natural gas well in the United States was drilled to a depth of 27 ft. near a "burning spring" at Fredonia, N.Y. In 1854 the first deep gas well, approximately 1,200 ft. deep, was sunk at Erie, Pa. In 1859 Edwin L. Drake began the petroleum industry at Titusville, Pa. Natural gas is frequently associated with petroleum in the earth's crust and its pressure serves to drive the oil to the surface. Oil men in early days ignored natural gas. The gas liberated from the oil at the surface was piped to a flare and burned as a gigantic torch. Wells that gave gas only were flared and allowed to burn themselves out over the years.

The first natural gas corporation in the United States was the Fredonia Gas Light and Water Works Co., organized in 1858. In 1873 Titusville was supplied with natural gas through a two-inch iron pipe five miles long. In 1870 a burning well at Bloomfield, N.Y., was extinguished and connected to a 25-mi. pipeline of white pine logs bored with an eight-inch hole. In 1872 this gas was turned into the mains of the Rochester Gas Co., but the venture soon failed.

By the mid-1960s there were about 100,000 gas wells in the United States; these, with gas producing oil wells, accounted for the annual marketing of about 15,500,000,000,000 cu.ft. of gas.

(See also FUELS: *Gaseous Fuels*.)

4. Liquefied Petroleum Gases.—The liquefied petroleum gases, propane and butane, have been obtained from natural gas condensates at wellheads, in compression operations or at low-temperature points in "wet" gas transmission systems. A very important source has been the crude natural gas gasoline extracted from natural gas by oil absorption. The enriched gasoline-oil mixture is stripped with steam, and the vapours from the crude gasoline are then fractionally distilled. These hydrocarbons are also recovered in petroleum refining and petroleum cracking operations.

Propane alone has sufficiently high vapour pressure at the customary temperatures prevailing over the United States to permit it to be distributed as a gas without admixture. Butane, however, requires a carrier gas. For single consumer installations beyond gas mains a mixture of propane-butane compressed into steel cylinders is sold as bottled gas. Where a number of consumers are to be supplied, propane alone may be distributed by small mains. Communities that are too small to warrant a gas plant may be served with a butane-air mixture in which the content of air must be sufficiently high to avoid condensation of butane from the mixture, but the air content must always be much less than 91.59% and the butane must be more than 8.41% by volume under ordinary atmospheric pressure to prevent explosions. Air content usually does not exceed 67%.

Butane-air gas may be mixed with natural gas under some peak-load conditions to assist in meeting consumer demands. A butane-air plant can be instrumented so that it is operated, controlled and safeguarded completely by automatic devices; consequently its small demands for labour and supervision make it very suitable for service to isolated small communities.

5. Storage of Gas.—The generation and transmission of gas for meeting variable demand loads, e.g., in a public utility, possess an important advantage over electricity in that gas can be stored in large quantities economically, whereas electricity must be generated and transmitted as consumed. This permits gas generating units and long-distance transmission units to be designed for average rather than peak conditions, thereby reducing markedly the capital investment required.

For example, the long-distance transmission of natural gas is maintained at a high load factor in the summer season by moving large gas supplies to storage pools near the customers. Depleted gas fields or natural geological formations of porous rock completely capped by an impervious rock formation can be used for this purpose. They may have storage capacities of billions of cubic feet.

(W. J. HF.)

BIBLIOGRAPHY.—British Gas Federation, *Report on the Planning of the Gas Industry* (1943); J. Mitchell, *British Gas Industry* (1945); G. D. Chandler and A. D. Lacey, *History of the Gas Light and Coke Company* (1949); S. Everard, *History of the Gas Light and Coke Company in Britain* (1949); W. Gumz, *Gas Producers and Blast Furnaces* (1950); Battelle Memorial Institute, *Economics of Fuel Gas from Coal* (1950); Sir Hubert Houldsworth et al., *Efficiency in the Nationalized Industries* (1952); British Gas Industry Productivity Team, *Gas* (1953); American Institute of Mining, Metallurgical and Petroleum Engineers, *Gasification and Liquefaction of Coal* (1953); B. W. Leyson, *Miracle of Light and Power* (1955); A. Key, *Gas Work Effluents and Ammonia*, 2nd ed. (1956); American Society for Testing Materials, *ASTM Standards on Gaseous Fuels* (1958); E. B. Swanson (comp.), *Century of Oil and Gas in Books* (1960); A. Lief, *Metering for America* (1961); J. Lawrie, *Natural Gas and Methane Sources* (1960); American Gas Association, *Historical Statistics of the Gas Industry* (1956), *Gas Facts* (1961), *Proceedings* (annual); *The Register of the Gas Industry* (1962). For current statistics see the UN *Monthly Bulletin of Statistics* and *Britannica Book of the Year*.

GASKELL, ELIZABETH CLEGHORN (née STEVENSON) (1810–1865), English novelist, short-story writer and the first and best biographer of Charlotte Brontë, was a writer of courage and compassion with an instinctive grasp of the story-teller's art. She began her distinguished literary career only in middle life. The daughter of William Stevenson, who was successively Unitarian minister, farmer, editor of the *Scots Magazine* and keeper of the treasury records, she was born in Chelsea on Sept. 29, 1810; her mother died early, and she was brought up from infancy by her maternal aunt, Mrs. Lumb, in Knutsford, Cheshire, spent two years at an efficient boarding school at Stratford-on-Avon, and then lived with her father and an uncongenial stepmother until his death in 1829. When visiting relatives in Edinburgh she met, and married in 1832, the Rev. William Gaskell, Unitarian minister of Cross Street chapel, Manchester, five years her senior. They collaborated in what was intended to be the first of a series of verse "Sketches Among the Poor," published anonymously in *Blackwood's Magazine* (Jan. 1837).

Domestic life claimed Mrs. Gaskell's time but not all her thoughts (the Gaskells had six children of whom four daughters lived to grow up). Her first novel, *Mary Barton: a Tale of Manchester Life*, developed slowly, reflecting the temper and, events of the 1830s, the period of Chartist agitation, and was written mainly in 1845–46, when the death of an infant son had intensified her sense of community with the suffering poor and her desire, as she said, to "give utterance" to their "agony." Delayed by hesitant publishers, the appearance of the novel in 1848 proved well-timed, although it was published anonymously, it won her immediate and widespread fame and an entry to intellectual circles outside Manchester. She had already published short stories in *Howitt's Journal* (under the name "Cotton Mather Mills") and elsewhere, and in the next few years contributed to many other periodicals, Dickens, whom she met in 1849, was eager to have her as a contributor to his *Household Words*; "Lizzie Leigh," another Lancashire tale, appeared in 1850, in the first three numbers, followed by two tragic stories, "The Well of Pen-Morfa" and "The Heart of John Middleton," and in 1851–53 the eight sketches subsequently revised and combined as *Cranford* (1853). There appeared in the related "Mr. Harrison's Confessions," which first appeared in the *Ladies' Companion* in 1851, the isolated country-town society of an earlier generation is presented as a microcosm of life. A vivid chapter of social history, demonstrably faithful to memories of Knutsford (a place which was old-fashioned even then and long remained so), the book is yet more remarkable for its mastery and subtlety of tone, serenely avoiding both the sentimental and the satiric. Writing to John Ruskin, one of its many admirers, in the last year of her life, Mrs. Gaskell said it was the only one of her books she cared to read again.

In her next two novels she again drew attention, though without letting the raised voice of propaganda disturb her art, to neglected claimants upon sympathetic understanding: in *Ruth* (1853) she proposed an alternative to the seduced girl's usual fate in contemporary life and fiction, while dealing perceptively with the moral, domestic and social dilemmas of the dissenting minister who rescues her. In *North and South* (*Household Words*, Sept. 2, 1854–Jan. 27, 1855), she modified the emphasis of *Mary Barton* by making her hero a factory owner and setting Manchester life in a wider context; it is the most balanced and assured of her earlier novels. But publication as a weekly serial proved irksome both to her and to Dickens as editor, and the novel was revised and enlarged by several chapters for publication in two volumes in 1855.

Among the many friends attracted by her writing and her delightful personality was Charlotte Brontë, who died in 1855 and whose biography Mr. Brontë urged her to undertake. *The Life* (1857), written with warmhearted admiration and insight and an unforced narrative skill disposing a mass of firsthand material, is one of the few literary biographies that is at once a work of art and a well-documented interpretation of its subject. But with characteristic impulsiveness she committed some minor indiscretions which brought vexatious controversy, and the work was at first less widely acclaimed than it deserved. For a time she concentrated on the writing of magazine stories of diverse length and subject, including the supernatural; the longest, *My Lady Ludlow* (*Household Words*, June 19–Sept. 25, 1858), included in the collection *Round the Sofa* (1859), is an artfully linked chain of retrospect leading back to life in a noble household 60 years earlier.

All Mrs. Gaskell's 30 or so tales were collected in volumes published between 1854 and 1865. The most outstanding is *Cousin Phillis* (which first appeared in the *Cornhill Magazine*, 1863–64), a sad love story of common life; often, and justly, called "an idyl," it is also a technical triumph of first-person narrative. Like most of her later work, it returns to the past, her share in contemporary problems now taking the form of energetic works of relief in Manchester in the period of unexampled hardship resulting from the American Civil War. This took toll of her health, but her writing remained resilient, exemplifying what a Victorian

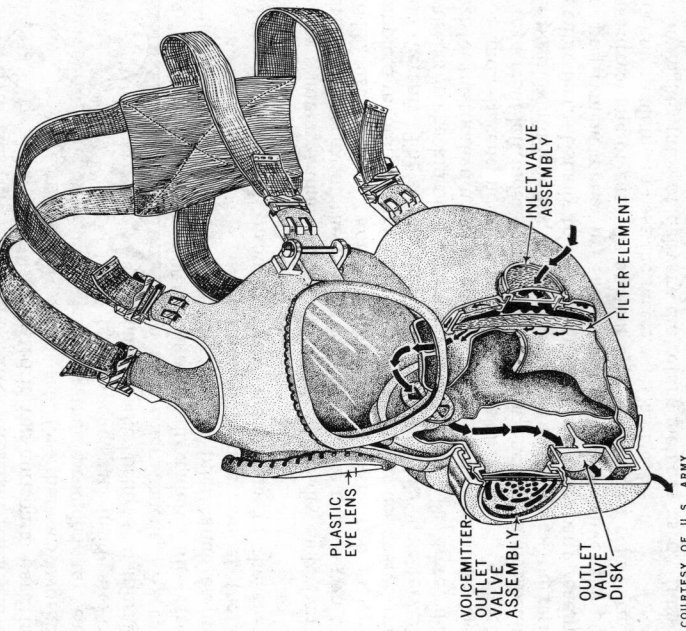

PLASTIC EYE LENS

VOICEMITTER OUTLET VALVE ASSEMBLY

OUTLET VALVE DISK

INLET VALVE ASSEMBLY

FILTER ELEMENT

BY COURTESY OF U.S. ARMY

AIRFLOW PATTERN THROUGH THE M-17 MODEL GAS MASK, CUTAWAY VIEW

critic called her "suppressed gipsiness" (matching her delight in travel), "a restless instinct which impelled her to be constantly making trial in imagination of various modes of life." She was several years at work on *Sylvia's Lovers* (1863), which is set in "Monkshaven" (Whitby) during the Napoleonic Wars and shows the impact of horrifying events upon the quiet life of individual and community in town and homestead. Her powers of moral analysis are at their height in this study of temptation and retribution and remains one of the masterpieces of Victorian fiction.

Wives and Daughters: an Every-day Story, her last and longest novel, which appeared in the *Cornhill Magazine* between Aug. 1864 and Jan. 1866, was nearing its conclusion as a serial at the time of her sudden death at Alton, Hampshire, on Nov. 12, 1865. Set in the period and some of the places of her girlhood, concerned simply with the interlocking fortunes of two or three country families, the novel exhibits some of her distinctive gifts in greater freedom and abundance than any previous work, notably her sense of social nuances and her insight into the relations of parent and child; and her gentle but penetrating portrayal of feminine deceit was compared with George Eliot's. The novel was memorably praised by Henry James. What may be called its summer sadness is not confined to vicissitudes and bereavements; and yet the story tends steadily toward the happy ending of the final, unwritten chapters, which makes it unusual among her novels. In all her work, her sense of the forces that divide individuals and classes is keen, even painful; at the same time, both within each novel and in the reader's response, there is a movement toward reconciliation and understanding, if no more than a mutual understanding of the inevitable differences between the two nations of rich and poor, between north and south, town and country, the old and the young, the good and the clever.

In her lifetime she was regarded pre-eminently as "the authoress of *Mary Barton*," undoubtedly the most influential of her novels in its time, though long since overtaken in popularity by *Cranford*. Her literary affiliations generally are less with novelists of the 19th century (though she owes something to Maria Edgeworth) than with Goldsmith, Crabbe, Lamb and Wordsworth.

Mrs. Gaskell's wish that there should be no biography was respected by the daughters who long survived her, and none that is really definitive yet exists, a prerequisite being the edition of her admirable letters published in 1966.

BIBLIOGRAPHY.—Much primary material may be found in A. W. Ward's introductions to the Knutsford edition of her works, 8 vol. (1906–08); *see also Letters of Mrs. Gaskell and Charles Eliot Norton 1855–1865*, ed. with an introduction by Jane Whitehill (1932); R. D. Waller, *Letters Addressed to Mrs. Gaskell by Celebrated Contemporaries* (1935); *The Letters of Mrs. Gaskell*, ed. by J. A. V. Chapple and Arthur Pollard (1966). The most comprehensive studies are Gerald De Witt Sanders, *Elizabeth Gaskell*, with a bibliography by Clark S. Northup (1929); Annette B. Hopkins, *Elizabeth Gaskell, Her Life and Work* (1952); Edgar Wright, *Mrs. Gaskell, The Basis for Reassessment* (1965); Arthur Pollard, *Mrs. Gaskell: Novelist and Biographer* (1966). The most complete edition of her works is in the World's Classics series, 11 vol. (1901–19), with introductions by C. K. Shorter.
(K. Ti.)

GAS MASK. Casualty gas, as a weapon of war, was first used in World War I by the Germans against the Russians in Poland on Jan. 31, 1915, and against Allied forces north of Ypres in Belgium, on April 22, 1915. (*See* CHEMICAL WARFARE.) The first military gas masks used by the Allies in that war were cumbersome affairs consisting of the mask proper, which fitted around the face, attached by a tube to a canister suspended around the soldier's neck and hung in front of his body. The wearer breathed air through a tube in his mouth from which the poison gases were filtered through charcoal contained in the canister. A nose clip prevented breathing through the nostrils. The use of this type of mask greatly impeded the soldier's movements and efficiency in battle and made it impossible for him to "hug the ground" closely when under attack by machine gun fire.

Considerable improvement in the gas mask was made after World War I and soldiers in World War II were provided with a mask that was lighter in weight, better fitting, ensured clearer and wider-range vision and, by eliminating the nose clamp and mouth inhaler, lowered breathing resistance. Another advantage of the

World War II equipment was that the canister was slung over the shoulder and carried at the soldier's side, thus permitting greater freedom of action in combat.

Although many improvements were made in the mask itself in the decades following World War I, the chemical agencies used to filter impurities from gas-infected air remained fundamentally the same. The canisters were filled with charcoal and soda lime which absorb and neutralize all gases known to be usable for tactical purposes. However, some of the chemicals used to produce poison gases on the battlefield remain suspended in the air as fine, solid particles for long periods. These particles were filtered from the air entering the canisters by pads of felt inserted in the air passage.

For U.S. forces a major improvement came with the M-17 gas mask adopted by the army, navy and marine corps and issued to troops in the early 1960s. The new mask differed radically from earlier versions in that it did not require an external canister or hose. Instead, it filtered air through pads of pliable material enclosed in cavities molded into the facepiece of the mask. It offered protection against gases and aerosols of chemical, bacteriological and radiological agents.

In addition to military uses, gas masks are widely used in industry to protect workmen employed in mining and in chemical and other types of plants where fumes and gases resulting from natural circumstances or manufacturing processes are known to be injurious. Firemen and members of rescue squads also carry gas masks as part of their normal equipment. During World War II masks designed for civilian use in the event of air raid or other form of attack delivering poison gases were also provided, particularly in Europe.
(M. B. H.; X.)

GAS METER, a device for measuring gas volumes. Companies selling gas to the public commonly use a positive displacement meter, a rotary meter, an orifice meter or a heat capacity meter to compute charges for gas usage or purchase.

For small volumes of consumption as in residential premises or most commercial installations, a positive displacement dry meter is used. Its operation involves the alternate expansion and contraction of each side of a double bellows of leather or synthetic material. The meter case, of tin, iron or aluminum, houses two working compartments, each of which encloses a bellows. The compartments are separated by a vertical partition which intersects a horizontal partition above the bellows and below the gear mechanism.

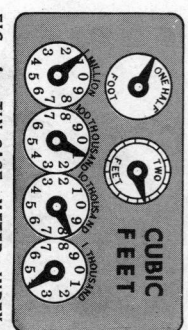

FIG. 1.—TIN-CASE METER INDEX; READING, 1,084,000

Valve parts and seats are located in the horizontal partition, one set for the two working spaces thus provided for each bellows, one space inside and one outside the bellows diaphragm in each compartment. As each bellows alternately fills from the meter inlet and empties through the meter outlet, the gas volume is measured through a gear mechanism to the meter index dial.

The number of index circles in the dial of the dry meter varies with the capacity of the meter. At the top are one or two test circles, usually two. For leak testing, one of the two makes a complete revolution for each cubic foot of gas or designated fraction thereof. The second dial registers two to five cubic feet and is used for checking the accuracy of the meter. The lower dials register the total volume passed. The right-hand index turns clockwise and adjacent indexes turn in opposite directions. The meter is read from left index to right by taking in each the figure behind the position of the index. Three ciphers are added, giving the result in cubic feet. Usually the customer is billed on company readings but prepayment meters are set by an inspector to deliver the purchased volume of gas. In another type, an inserted coin permits a definite volume to pass the meter.

For higher rates of delivery the rotary meter is used. This is a case with semicylindrical ends in which are two or three revolving impellers (rotors). Each rotor moves exactly counter to that adjacent. The entering gas is trapped and must move the rotors to be discharged. The trapped constant gas volume is recorded through gear mechanism to a dial. In some rotary meters the capacity may be large enough to supply gas to a small town.

For measurement of large volumes of gas, an orifice meter is used. Essentially, a steel plate with a centre hole is fitted inside the gas pipe. This obstruction causes the gas to jet downstream, creating there a partial vacuum. A differential pressure can be measured by connecting the upstream space and the downstream space to the two sides of a recording manometer. The differential pressure varies with the flow through the orifice, thus measuring the volume of gas flowing. Orifice meters are relatively simple, sturdy and precise, but they have two disadvantages: there is a large loss of pressure, and the mathematical relations between the differential pressures and the volume of the gas passed are very complex.

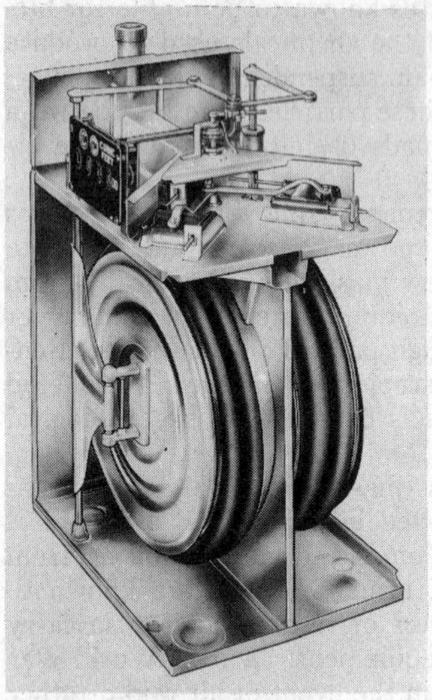

BY COURTESY OF AMERICAN METER CO.

FIG. 2.—CUTAWAY VIEW OF A TIN-CASE METER

Fortunately, natural gas is often available at pressures much higher than is required by consumers, so the loss of pressure may not be objectionable. The mathematical relationships have been carefully analyzed and compiled into tables that simplify the readings.

Where the gas measured has a uniform known heat capacity per unit volume, a device for measuring the passing heat capacity can be employed as a gas meter. Two thermometers of the electrical grid type may be placed some distance apart in a gas pipe. Between these is placed a source of heat, such as an electrical heating coil. The thermometers control the heat input to the coil to maintain a constant rise of temperature between them. The readings of a recording electric wattmeter establish the volumes of gas flowing.

An alternate but similar device measures the varying rise in temperature caused by a fixed rate of heat input. Heat capacity meters cannot be used on gas contaminated with foreign materials such as tar fog, moisture or dust.

See also GAS INDUSTRY. (W. J. HF.)

GASOLINE (PETROL), a volatile, inflammable liquid usually consisting primarily of hydrocarbons derived from petroleum by various processes. By far the most important use is as a fuel for internal-combustion engines (*q.v.*), but it is also used to some extent in special stoves and as a solvent.

In the early days of the oil industry, gasoline (termed "straight run") was simply the portion of petroleum that distilled off at a lower temperature than kerosene, the principal product desired. It was largely wasted until the advent of the automobile. Gasoline became the preferred motor fuel because of two important properties: it had the high energy of combustion typical of hydrocarbons, and it was sufficiently volatile to form a combustible mixture with air in a simple, relatively inexpensive carburetor. It was also cheap and plentiful.

As the demand for gasoline increased during the first two decades of the 20th century, it ceased to be a by-product, and more and more of the kerosene cut began to be included. By 1913 even this became inadequate and a gasoline shortage threatened the further rapid development of the automobile. Fortunately, the first commercial cracking process, the Burton process, was developed about this time to convert heavier oils, particularly the gas oils which boiled just above kerosene, into gasoline by subjecting them to temperatures of around 399° C. and pressures of around 100 lb. As a result of this and many later improvements in cracking processes, gasoline yields have increased to about 50% of the crude oil processed, a figure well over twice the amount of hydrocarbons of suitable boiling point found in average crude oil.

Gasoline is a complex mixture containing hundreds of different hydrocarbons. Most of them are saturated and contain 4 to 12 carbon atoms per molecule, but they differ widely in structure. Motorcar gasoline boils mainly between 32.2° and 210° C., the precise blend being adjusted to the climate and the season. More light, volatile components are needed for quick starting and fast warm up when the weather is cold, but these are likely to cause high evaporation losses and vapour lock at summer temperatures. The heavier portions of the gasoline are valuable for their higher heating value, but in excess they may cause carbon deposits and uneven fuel distribution. Aviation gasoline is a "heart cut" containing less of both the lighter and heavier ends than motorcar gasoline.

As engine designers sought greater efficiency through higher compression ratios, they encountered increasing trouble with engine "knock," a rapid detonation occurring toward the end of the combustion. The shape of the gasoline molecules was found to be very important in determining the knocking tendency of a gasoline. Straight-chain molecules knock much more readily than branched or ring-shaped molecules, especially of the saturated type naturally present in crude oil. It soon became evident that the extent to which the compression ratio, and hence the efficiency, of gasoline engines could be increased depended on changing the kind of molecules present in gasoline.

To establish a definite scale for measuring antiknock characteristics, so-called "iso-octane" (2,2,4-trimethylpentane), a highly branched hydrocarbon, was assigned a value of 100 on the knock-rating scale, and normal heptane a value of 0. The octane number indicates simply that a gasoline has the same knocking tendency (in a standard engine under standard conditions) as a particular blend of heptane and iso-octane, the percentage of the iso-octane in the blend being termed the octane number. However, the actual behaviour in different engines is likely to vary somewhat from the results of the standard test.

The straight-run gasoline found in average crude oil has a low octane number. Needed high-octane components are made by a variety of processes which have been developed over the years. Branched hydrocarbons are plentiful in gasoline made by cracking —particularly if the cracking has been brought about by catalysts instead of by older processes using only heat and pressure. Branched structures are even more abundant in alkylate and polymer gasolines, both of which are made by joining together, with the aid of catalysts, small molecules of gases made as a by-product in most cracking processes. Of the ring-shaped hydro-carbons, among the most valuable are benzene and toluene, which are obtained from coal tar or may be made by passing certain cuts of straight-run gasoline over platinum or other catalysts.

By the end of World War II about 60% of the average motor fuel was composed of synthetic molecules, and aviation gasoline was more than 90% synthetic. By the 1960s most motor gasoline was fully 80% synthetic. This illustrates forcibly the revolution in refining methods brought about by the advent of cracking. The discovery that the cheap hydrocarbons in petroleum could be readily changed in composition and structure led also to a rapidly growing petrochemical industry, which makes from petroleum or natural gas a wide variety of chemicals for solvents, plastics, fibres, synthetic rubber and for many other purposes.

Another important way of increasing antiknock is by the addi-tion of tetraethyl lead, as was discovered by Thomas Midgley in 1922. Though the amount used in motor fuel is less than 0.1% by volume, it may increase the octane number by as much as 15 points. In response to concern about the environment, by the early 1970s lead-free and low-lead gasolines with octane rating of 91 or 92 were marketed, although only the newer automobiles in the U.S. were tuned to use the fuel without knocking.

By the 1960s the average octane number of U.S. gasoline had risen to about 94 for the regular grade and 99 for the premium grade, as compared with a figure of 55 octane or below before the advent of cracking. Military aviation gasoline reached the 100-octane level just before World War II, and still better fuels were later developed. Their antiknock quality is stated in terms of per-formance numbers, which indicate the knock-free power obtainable in an engine of suitable compression ratio as a percentage of the power obtainable from pure iso-octane. The most widely used grade of aviation gasoline had a performance number of 115 under cruising conditions, 145 under take-off conditions. However, fur-ther substantial increases in octane number promised to be quite expensive. As the result of these improvements, the compression ratios of new automobile engines went up from an average of 4.4 to 1 in 1925 to an average of 9.5 to 1 by 1958, with an improvement in the efficiency of gasoline utilization of about 60%.

Additives are also used in gasoline for purposes other than anti-knock improvement. Chlorine and bromine compounds convert tetraethyl lead to relatively volatile salts and thus assist in its removal by the exhaust gases and in reducing the build-up of deposits on exhaust valves, etc. Antioxidants are used to inhibit gum formation. Metal deactivators prevent deterioration caused by contact with the metal of the fuel tank. De-icers prevent engine stalling caused by the icing of carburetor throttle plates. Although petroleum is the principal source of motor fuel, other raw materials are used. Natural gas often contains moderate amounts of liquefiable hydrocarbons, which are recovered as "nat-ural" or "casinghead" gasoline. In Europe alcohol is sometimes in-cluded in motor fuel blends as is motor benzol from coal tar.

Gasoline can be produced by combining carbon monoxide and hydrogen at high pressure in the presence of a suitable catalyst. The needed mixture of gases may be produced by the partial oxi-dation of natural gas (methane) with pure oxygen. To be com-mercial the process requires cheap natural gas as the starting ma-terial, and good prices for the by-product alcohols, acids, ketones and other organic chemicals. In the distant future, coal may be used to provide the hydrogen and carbon monoxide. Direct hydro-genation of coal is also possible, but is expensive. Gasoline can likewise be made from tar sands, of which there are very large de-posits in Canada. The most promising of the long-range sources, however, appeared to be oil shale. The U.S. reserves of shale, are much larger than the country's known reserves of petroleum.

See PETROLEUM; PETROCHEMICALS; *see* also references under "GASOLINE" in the Index.   (R. E. WN.)

GASPARRI, PIETRO (1852–1934), Italian cardinal and canonist, was born at Capovalazza de Ussita on May 5, 1852. He received the degrees of doctor of philosophy, theology and canon law after study at the pontifical seminary at Rome, and from 1880 to 1898 was professor of canon law at the Catholic institute in Paris. In 1904 Pius X, having decided to codify the canon law, confided to Gasparri the direction of the work. The new code was promulgated in 1917 (*see* CANON LAW).

In 1907 Gasparri was made cardinal, and in Oct. 1914 Benedict XV appointed him secretary of state, which office he held through-out the arduous World War I period and the almost equally strenu-ous reconstruction period which followed. He was retained by Pius XI and in 1926 began negotiations which resulted in the Vati-can treaty. He resigned in Jan. 1930 and was succeeded by Eu-genio Cardinal Pacelli (later Pius XII). Cardinal Gasparri died at Rome on Nov. 18, 1934.   (B. Ty.)

GASPÉ, PHILIPPE AUBERT DE (1786–1871), "the grand old man of French-Canadian literature," was the author of the first important novel published in French Canada, *Les Anciens Canadiens* (1863). Born on Oct. 30, 1786, into a distinguished Quebec family whose first Canadian ancestor had been ennobled by Louis XIV of France, De Gaspé was the epitome of gentle-manly dignity as hereditary *seigneur* of his estate on the St. Lawrence river. He received a classical education in Quebec, studied law there and later became sheriff of the city. Bank-ruptcy, for which he spent over three years in debtors' prison, forced him out of public life in his 40s.

After years of reading and meditation, inspired by a rebirth of nationalism in mid-19th century, De Gaspé composed *Les Anciens Canadiens* late in life. It is a romantic historical novel set in Canada at the time of the British conquest (1760), written to preserve the old French traditions for posterity. De Gaspé makes use of known historical material, personal family records, folklore and folksongs. The novel has a nostalgic charm spiced with avuncular humour. It was enthusiastically received and be-came a classic in French Canada, an aristocratic precursor of *Maria Chapdelaine* (1916) by Louis Hémon, and hence of the whole regionalist school that flourished into the 1930s. The com-mon features are idealization of the "good, old days," and of the habitant farmer, loyalty to the soil and distrust of English Canada.

BIBLIOGRAPHY.—Philippe Aubert de Gaspé, *Les Anciens Canadiens* (1863; Eng. trans. *The Canadians of Old* by G. M. Pennée [1864] and C. G. D. Roberts [1890]) and *Mémoires* (1866); Msgr. C. Roy, *Romanciers de chez nous* (1935); J. S. Tassie, "Philippe Aubert de Gaspé," in *Our Living Tradition*, vol. 2 (1959).   (J. S. Te.)

GASPÉ PENINSULA (GASPÉSIA) juts into the Gulf of St. Lawrence and comprises that part of eastern Quebec province which lies between the St. Lawrence river and the province of New Brunswick. It is a hilly to mountainous area with well-forested slopes. The central portion is occupied by the Shickshock range, a continuation of the Appalachians, which rises to over 4,000 ft. (1,219 m.). Settlement is light, occurring only in widely separated coastal villages. The area is known as a tourist centre because of its rugged and picturesque coastal scenery, its striking hills and excellent hunting and fishing. Lumbering and coastal fishing are the principal occupations but there is some mining of copper, zinc and lead and a small production of pulp for papermaking.   (W. F. Ss.)

GAS PLANT (*Dictamnus albus*), a hardy perennial herb of the rue family (Rutaceae), known also as dittany, fraxinella and as burning bush. It has long been a well-known and popular garden ornamental. The stems are stout, woody at the base, bear alternate odd-pinnate leaves, with glossy leathery leaflets dotted with oil glands and surmounted by long, showy, terminal racemes of snowy white or rose-coloured fra-grant flowers with a strong smell of lemon. The gas plant makes a sturdy upright growth, and a clump three feet high and as much in breadth makes a pleasing show when in flower. On a still,

WALTER SINGER
GAS PLANT (DICTAMNUS ALBUS)

sultry summer evening a lighted match held under the flower cluster near the main stem will give a flash, whence the name gas plant.

(J. M. Br.)

GASSER, HERBERT SPENCER (1888–1963), U.S. physiologist and Nobel laureate, was born in Platteville, Wis., on July 5, 1888. After graduating from the University of Wisconsin, and in medicine from the Johns Hopkins school of medicine (1915), he taught at Washington university, St. Louis, Mo., beginning there, with Joseph Erlanger (q.v.), the brilliant series of researches on nerve fibres that led to their joint award in 1944 of the Nobel prize in physiology and medicine. In 1931 Gasser became professor of physiology at Cornell university medical college, and in 1935 director of the Rockefeller Institute for Medical Research, which position he held until his retirement in 1953.

Gasser pioneered in the use of the cathode ray oscilloscope as an instrument for recording the action potentials of nerve impulses. With it he demonstrated the compound nature of the action potential of nerves containing various types of nerve fibres, formulated the rules relating conduction velocity to diameter of the individual nerve fibres, and characterized the several groups of nerve fibres in terms of their electrical properties and conduction velocities. Crucial to this characterization was his study of the after-potentials, which he showed to be different in the several groups of nerve fibres and to be closely correlated with the excitability cycles during recovery of nerve fibres following impulse conduction. An outstanding contribution was his study of the finest of all nerve fibres, the unmyelinated fibres, in which he elucidated their functional properties and, with the aid of the electron microscope, their anatomical structure. He died in New York city on May 11, 1963.

(D. P. C. L.)

GASQUET, FRANCIS NEIL (in religion AIDAN) (1846–1929), Roman Catholic historian and cardinal, was born in London on Oct. 5, 1846. Educated at Downside school, he entered the Benedictine monastery there and was prior from 1878 until 1885. From 1888 onward he published works on monastic history, including the influential *Henry VIII and the English Monasteries* (1888–89), of considerable value but somewhat marred by inaccuracies and bias. He was created cardinal in 1914, and became prefect of the Vatican archives in 1918. Cardinal Gasquet died in Rome on April 5, 1929.

See M. D. Knowles, *Cardinal Gasquet as a Historian* (1957); Shane Leslie, *Cardinal Gasquet* (1953).

GASSENDI (GASSEND), **PIERRE** (1592–1655), French philosopher, scientist and mathematician, famous for his revival of Epicureanism, was born of poor parents at Champtercier in Provence on Jan. 22, 1592. Educated at Digne and Aix, he eventually took holy orders and became professor of philosophy at Aix (1617). After travels in Flanders and Holland (1628–31), he secured an appointment as provost of the cathedral at Digne (1634), which had been disputed for ten years. He then spent some time accompanying the duc d'Angoulême on a tour of his *gouvernement* of Provence. In 1645 Gassendi became professor of mathematics at the Collège Royal in Paris. He died in Paris on Oct. 24, 1655.

Gassendi's writings include: *Exercitationes paradoxicae adversus Aristoteleos* (1624; new ed., 1649); *Epistolica exercitatio in qua principia philosophiae Roberti Fluddi reteguntur* (1630), written at the instance of Marin Mersenne; a letter on the parhelia observed in 1629 (1630); lives of Peiresc and Tycho Brahe (1641 and 1654); a series of objections to the *Meditationes de prima philosophia* of Descartes, which was likewise undertaken at Mersenne's behest and appended to the second edition of the work in question (1642) but republished separately (1644); *Institutio astronomica* (1647); *De vita et moribus Epicuri* (1647); *Animadversiones in decimum librum Diogenis Laërtii, qui est de vita, moribus placitisque Epicuri*, with *Philosophiae Epicuri syntagma* as an appendix (1649); and the *Syntagma philosophicum*, published posthumously among his collected works (1658). The last three works are those on which his lasting reputation depends.

As a philosopher, Gassendi opposed the blind acceptance of Aristotle, revived atomism and advocated an empirical realism. But he was not a consistent empiricist, for while he maintains "that there is nothing in the intellect which has not been in the senses" and that the imaginative faculty is the counterpart of sense, he admits that the intellect, which he affirms to be immaterial and immortal, attains notions and truths of which sensation or imagination can give us not the slightest apprehension. He instances the capacity of forming "general notions" and universals, the notion of God and the power of reflection.

The first part of the *Syntagma philosophicum*, which deals with logic and method, contains a praiseworthy sketch of the history of science and contends that the true method of research is the analytic, rising from lower to higher notions, though it admits that inductive reasoning, as conceived by Francis Bacon, rests on a general proposition not itself proved by induction. In the second part of the *Syntagma*, the physics, Gassendi approves of the Epicurean physics, but rejects the Epicurean negation of God, of particular providence and of an immaterial rational soul, endowed with immortality, capable of free determination and specially created. In the third part, the ethics, there is little beyond a milder statement of the Epicurean moral code and a mass of historical quotations. The final end of life is happiness, and happiness is harmony of soul and body.

GASTEIN, a side valley of the Salzach river in the province of Salzburg, Aus., is situated between 3,000 and 3,500 ft. above sea level and is crossed by the Gasteiner Ache river. The principal settlements in the valley are Badgastein and Bad Hofgastein on the main railway with direct connections to the lines Munich–Venice and Vienna–Zürich.

BADGASTEIN, at an altitude of 3,320 ft., is Austria's most important spa and winter sports resort. Pop. (1961) 5,742. It has radioactive thermal springs with a natural temperature of 43.3° C. (110° F.), an underwater therapy station and, since 1950, a thermal gallery. For skiers there is a gondola cable car leading to the Stubnerkogel (7,365 ft.), and four ski lifts. Badgastein is also known for its magnificent waterfalls.

BAD HOFGASTEIN, the capital of the valley commune, lying at a lower level, is also a spa, the waters being conveyed from Badgastein by a pipeline. Pop. (1961) 4,700. At one time it was, after Salzburg, the richest place in the province because of its gold and silver mines, which were worked from the Roman period until the 20th century.

(H. ZG.)

GASTER, MOSES (1856–1939), Rumanian Jewish scholar, rabbi and Zionist, a noted folklorist and philologist, was born at Bucharest and educated at Bucharest university, where he became lecturer in Rumanian language and literature (1881–85). His championship of the cause of persecuted Jews, which included aiding projects for settling Jews in Palestine, led to his expulsion from Rumania, and he went to England, where he held a lectureship at Oxford in Byzantine and Slavonic languages (1886 and 1891). In 1887 he was appointed chief rabbi of the Sephardic communities of England. Gaster retired in 1919 because of failing eyesight. He died near Abingdon, Eng., on March 5, 1939.

Gaster was author of an enormous body of literature. Among his works were *The Folk Literature of Rumania* (1883); *The Hebrew Version of Secretum Secretorum of Aristotle* (1908); *The Samaritan Book of Joshua* (1908); *Example of the Rabbis* (1924); and many Rumanian translations and contributions to learned journals. His monumental *Crestomatia Romana* was uncompleted at his death.

GASTONIA, an industrial city and seat of Gaston County, is 20 mi. W of Charlotte in south-central North Carolina, U.S. Gaston, a leading cotton-mill county in North Carolina since 1860, in the second half of the 20th century had more cotton mills than any county in the United States. The manufacturing establishments in the county produce principally textiles and textile machinery. Gastonia was incorporated in 1877 and became the county seat in 1909. The county, named in honour of William Gaston, a member of congress and judge of the North Carolina Supreme Court, was formed in 1846. The Technical Division of Gaston College, the Vocational Textile School, and the North Carolina Orthopedic Hospital are located in and near the city. Kings Mountain National Military Park is 20 mi. SW.

In 1929 Gastonia was the scene of a textile strike and severe labour disorders that attracted national attention. Following the death of the Gastonia police chief in a raid on the National Textile Workers Union headquarters, union organizer Fred Beal and six associates were convicted of conspiracy to commit murder.

In 1919 Gastonia adopted the council-manager form of government.

Pop. (1970) 47,142. For comparative population figures see table in NORTH CAROLINA: Population. (R. N. E.)

GASTRIC AND DUODENAL ULCER. Peptic ulcer is an inclusive term referring to a sharply circumscribed, punched-out defect or loss of tissue in the mucosa or lining of the stomach or duodenum. The ulcerative process occurs because of the inability of the mucosal lining of the stomach or duodenum to withstand the corrosive and digestive action of acid gastric juice. It is important to distinguish between gastric (stomach) ulcer and duodenal ulcer because of differences in diagnosis, treatment, and prognosis.

Peptic ulcer is a common cause of recurring or persistent upper abdominal distress, especially in young men. In the United States duodenal ulcer occurs five to ten times more frequently than gastric ulcer. This is not true for other countries. In Japan, for example, the incidence of gastric ulcer is much higher. Duodenal ulcer is more common in men than in women; in gastric ulcer the sex ratio is about equal.

Gastric juice, consisting primarily of hydrochloric acid of a concentration of 0.45% and an enzyme, pepsin, which digests proteins, is secreted by glands in the mucosa of the stomach. It is capable of digesting all living tissue, including the stomach itself. Protective mechanisms, such as secretion of mucus by the stomach glands, dilution of the acid juice by swallowed food and saliva, and intermittency of the secretion, act to prevent digestion of the stomach in the normal person. The secretion of acid gastric juice is controlled primarily by nervous impulses traveling via the vagus nerve. These impulses are stimulated by the sight, taste, or smell of food, by the hormone gastrin, which is liberated from the lower part of the stomach after contact with food, and by other hormones from the duodenum. A person with a duodenal ulcer usually secretes more gastric juice with a higher hydrochloric acid concentration than a normal person does. The fact that this is not true in the case of a person with a gastric ulcer indicates that gastric mucosa may be less resistant than duodenal mucosa to the action of gastric juice.

The causes of peptic ulcers are not completely understood, although many factors have been implicated. Nervous tension, ingestion of certain drugs (such as salicylates and corticoids), and hormonal factors may play roles.

The symptoms of gastric and duodenal ulcer are similar, consisting of gnawing, burning, aching, hungerlike pain or discomfort in the mid-upper abdomen, occurring from one to three hours after meals or when the stomach is empty. Pain frequently occurs at 1 or 2 A.M. This pain is characteristically relieved by ingestion of materials such as food, milk, and baking soda, which dilute and neutralize acid.

Several complicating conditions may occur secondarily to peptic ulcer: obstruction of the stomach outlet, due to inflammation or scar formation, may cause vomiting; hemorrhage may occur, manifested by vomiting of bloody material or material resembling coffee grounds, or by black tarry stools; if the bleeding is excessive, weakness and anemia may occur. The wall of the stomach or duodenum occasionally may perforate, causing severe localized abdominal pain and peritonitis. This catastrophic event requires immediate surgery.

Gastric ulcer is diagnosed by the roentgenographic appearance of a crater or defect in the lining of the stomach. It may also be seen directly through the gastroscope. Gastroscopy, especially when biopsy or microscopic examination of aspirations from the stomach (cytological examination) is also performed, usually enables differentiation of a benign gastric ulcer from an ulcerating carcinoma, symptoms of which are similar. The diagnosis of a duodenal ulcer, invariably benign, is usually based upon the roentgenographic appearance of a characteristic crater or deformity in the duodenum.

Treatment of peptic ulcer is based upon the principle of complete and prolonged neutralization of the gastric hydrochloric acid. This is accomplished by the use of antacids such as combinations of aluminum hydroxide with magnesium hydroxide, or magnesium trisilicate, or magnesium carbonate. Other commonly used antacids are calcium carbonate, dihydroxy aluminum aminoacetate, tribasic calcium phosphate, and milk. Anticholinergic or antisecretory drugs, such as belladonna, atropine, methscopolamine bromide, propantheline bromide, glycopyrrolate, hexocyclium chloride, and oxyphencyclimine hydrochloride, which inhibit the secretion of gastric acid, are also valuable as adjunctive agents. In selected cases, roentgen therapy to the stomach is valuable in producing a decrease in gastric acidity. Sedatives and tranquilizers are used to allay tension and nervousness. In the latter 1960s, the technique of gastric hypothermia was utilized in an attempt to decrease gastric acidity. This technique was of value in controlling gastric hemorrhage. Its long-term effect on the innate tendency toward the ulcer was still to be determined in the late 1960s.

During the first several days of therapy only small feedings of bland foods are allowed. Following this period a full bland diet—meals including two cooked fruits, two cooked vegetables, and lean meat—is tolerated. Prolonged use of a strict diet of pureed foods is rarely necessary. It is, however, best to avoid spices, gas-forming foods, and alcohol or other irritants. Since coffee, chewing gum, and tobacco stimulate gastric secretion, their use should also be discontinued if possible. In addition, a person with an ulcer should understand the nature of the disease so that he may reorient himself to a life of moderation, to relieving nervousness and anxiety, and to obtaining adequate rest and sleep.

Surgical treatment may be necessary in approximately 10% of all cases, either because of complications or because of unwillingness or inability of patients to follow a medical regimen. When it is not possible to differentiate with certainty a benign gastric ulcer from an ulcerating cancer of the stomach, surgery is indicated. In the surgical treatment of a gastric ulcer, the ulcer is removed along with three-fourths of the stomach. In the case of a duodenal ulcer the stomach may be removed in a similar manner, or else the more physiological procedure of vagotomy and gastroenterostomy is employed. In the latter procedure, the vagus nerves to the stomach are severed and an opening is made from the stomach to the small intestine. The purpose of this operation is to eliminate the secretion of gastric juice caused by nervous impulses.

For ulcers in other parts of the gastrointestinal tract, see ULCER.

BIBLIOGRAPHY.—B. W. Sippy, "Gastric and Duodenal Ulcer, Medical Care by an Efficient Removal of Gastric Juice Corrosion," *J.A.M.A.*, 64:1625 (1915); J. B. Kirsner and W. L. Palmer, "The Problem of Peptic Ulcer," *Am. J. Med.*, 13:615 (1952); W. L. Palmer, "Peptic Ulcer," in *A Textbook of Medicine*, ed. by R. L. Cecil and R. F. Loeb, 12th ed. (1967); J. A. Rider et al., "Oral Use of Methscopolamine (Pamine) Bromide in Treatment of Duodenal Ulcer; Effect on Human Gastric Secretion," *J.A.M.A.*, 159:1085 (1955); J. A. Rider et al., "The Effect of X-ray Therapy on Gastric Acidity and on 17-Hydroxycorticoid and Uropepsin Excretion," *Ann. Int. Med.*, 47:651 (1957); J. G. Dragstedt, "Cause of Peptic Ulcer," *J.A.M.A.*, 169:203 (1959); T. L. Cleave, Allen, *Physiology and Treatment of Peptic Ulcer* (1959); T. L. Cleave, *Peptic Ulcer* (1963); David C. H. Sun, *Chemistry and Therapy of Peptic Ulcer* (1966). (J. A. Rr.)

GASTRITIS. The term gastritis signifies inflammation of the stomach, acute or chronic. Acute gastritis is caused usually by dietary indiscretions, excessive intake of alcohol, irritating drugs, food poisoning and infectious diseases. The smooth, glistening, orange-red appearing inner lining (mucosa) of the normal stomach becomes reddened, swollen and dulled; hemorrhages, adherent mucus and occasionally small superficial ulcerations also may develop. The chief symptoms are severe upper abdominal pain, nausea, vomiting, loss of appetite, thirst and diarrhea; the illness develops suddenly and subsides rapidly. The only treatment necessary is temporary avoidance of food, followed by a nonirritating diet, sedatives and antispasmodics; rarely, fluids by intravenous injection may be required. The intentional or accidental ingestion of corrosives (acids, alkalies) causes a severe chemical gastritis, necessitating immediate emptying and thorough washing of the stomach, general supportive care and, if the poison has systemic effects, administration of the specific antidote.

Chronic gastritis is classified into four varieties; mixtures of several types are not unusual. Superficial gastritis is characterized by redness, swelling and hemorrhage of the mucosa, with adherent mucus and erosions. In atrophic gastritis the mucosa is thinned, grayish-green in colour and easily injured; the underlying blood vessels are abnormally visible. In hypertrophic gastritis the stomach wall is thickened, the folds are enlarged and irregular and the mucosa presents a swollen, spongelike appearance. The gastritis following operations upon the stomach combines features of these three types. The incidence of chronic gastritis in the general population is not known; in patients examined because of digestive symptoms the recorded frequency has varied from 15% to 60%. The cause of chronic gastritis and the conditions contributing to its development are not established; excessively hot or cold food, condiments, alcohol, tobacco, irritating medicines, stomach acids, allergy, infection, nutritional deficiencies and emotional disturbances all have been implicated. Since the stomach from early life is exposed continuously to various mechanical, chemical, thermal, bacterial, psychogenic and physiologic influences, chronic gastritis probably results from a combination of factors.

The symptoms in patients with chronic gastritis are indefinite and often resemble the manifestations of functional digestive disorders. They include discomfort, fullness or pain in the upper abdomen, poor appetite, flatulence, belching and variable bowel habits. In erosive gastritis the symptoms may be those of peptic ulcer; bleeding may occur. There are no characteristic laboratory or X-ray findings; these examinations are valuable chiefly to exclude serious organic disease.

There is no specific treatment for chronic gastritis; nor, indeed, is therapy usually necessary. Reassurance as to the absence of serious illness, a bland diet eliminating irritating foods and avoiding large quantities of alcohol, tea and coffee; and sedatives and antispasmodics to relieve nervous tension and quiet the congested, hyperactive stomach are helpful. Vitamins and other nutritional supplements are indicated when the food intake has been poor. Antacids and antisecretory drugs neutralizing and decreasing acid production in the stomach are useful in gastritis with erosions and with bleeding. Surgery is necessary when hypertrophic gastritis cannot be differentiated from tumour, for obstruction at the outlet of the stomach and for uncontrollable hemorrhage; however, such cases are rare. Chronic gastritis tends to be persistent or recurrent, with unpredictable variations in type, severity and distribution. However, it usually does not lead to serious disease. Minor surface alterations, such as congestion, hemorrhage and erosions, usually heal rapidly and completely.

BIBLIOGRAPHY.—J. B. Kirsner and W. L. Palmer, "Gastritis," Cyclopedia of Medicine, 13:157-176A (1955); R. Schindler, Gastritis (1942) and Gastroscopy, 2nd ed. (1950).

GASTROINTESTINAL TRACT

GASTROINTESTINAL TRACT, strictly speaking, is the term applied to that portion of the food canal that includes the stomach and the small and large intestines as an anatomical and a functional unit. The more inclusive term "alimentary canal" (formerly, digestive tube) includes also the esophagus, whereas "digestive tract" denotes the complete food canal, from the mouth through the anal canal. In the adult human being the digestive tract is 25 to 30 ft. long, and the food passes through the following parts one after the other: mouth, pharynx, esophagus, stomach, small intestine, caecum, colon, rectum and anal canal (the caecum, colon, rectum and anal canal constitute the large intestine). Into the digestive tract at various points the salivary glands, liver and pancreas (qq.v.) pour their secretions by special ducts.

This article deals chiefly with the anatomy, comparative anatomy and embryology of the gastrointestinal tract but includes also a discussion of the esophagus. The mouth (q.v.) and the pharynx (see THROAT) are dealt with elsewhere. For the physiology of the digestive tract, see DIGESTION. (See also GASTROINTESTINAL TRACT, DISEASES OF.) The Anatomy section discusses structure in man exclusively; the other two major sections are more general in scope.

ANATOMY

Esophagus.—The esophagus or gullet, a muscular tube lined with mucous membrane, stretches from the lower limit of the pharynx or throat, at the level of the cricoid cartilage, to the cardiac orifice of the stomach. It is about 10 in. long (25 cm.) and ¾ in. to 1 in. in diameter. At first it lies in the lower part of the neck, then in the chest and lastly, for about an inch, in the abdomen. As far as the level of the fourth or fifth thoracic vertebra it lies behind the trachea, but when that tube ends it is in close contact with the pericardium and, at the level of the tenth thoracic vertebra, passes through the esophageal opening of the diaphragm (q.v.), accompanied by the two vagus nerves, the left being in front of it and the right behind. In the abdomen it lies just behind the left lobe of the liver. In both the upper and lower parts of its course it lies a little to the left of the mid-line. Its mucous membrane is thrown into a number of longitudinal pleats to allow stretching.

Stomach.—The stomach is an irregularly pear-shaped bag, situated in the upper and left part of the abdomen. When moderately distended, the thick end of the pear or fundus bulges upward and to the left, while the narrow end is constricted to form the pylorus, by means of which the stomach communicates with the small intestine. The cardiac orifice, where the esophagus enters, is placed about a third of the way along the upper border from the left end of the fundus and between it and the pylorus; the upper border is concave and is known as the lesser curvature. From the cardiac to the pyloric orifice, round the lower border, is the greater curvature.

In front of the stomach are the liver (in part), the diaphragm and the anterior abdominal wall, while behind it are the pancreas, left kidney, left adrenal, spleen, colon and mesocolon. When the stomach is empty it contracts into a tubular organ and the transverse colon ascends to occupy the vacant space.

The pylorus is an oval opening, averaging one-half inch in its long axis but capable of considerable distention; it is formed by

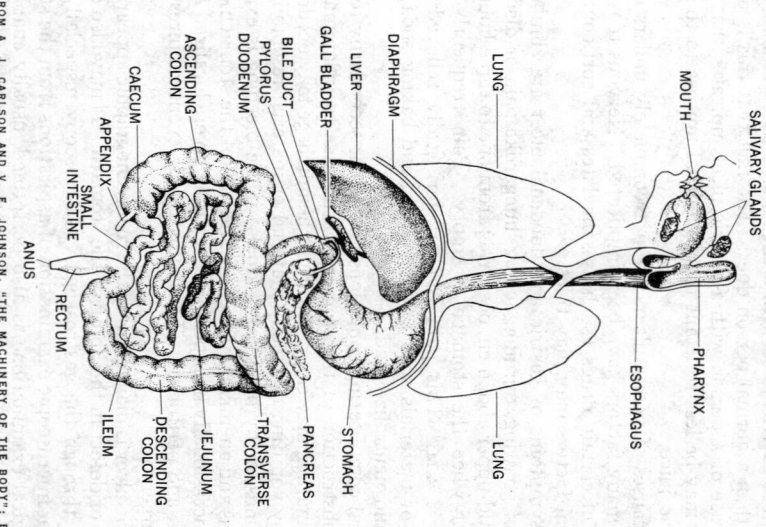

ADAPTED FROM A. J. CARLSON AND V. E. JOHNSON, "THE MACHINERY OF THE BODY"; BY PERMISSION OF THE UNIVERSITY OF CHICAGO PRESS

FIG. 1.—ORGANS AND GLANDS OF THE DIGESTIVE TRACT. PART OF RESPIRATORY SYSTEM IS SHOWN TO INDICATE ITS RELATIONSHIP TO DIGESTIVE TRACT. ORGANS AND GLANDS ARE SPREAD APART FOR CLARITY

GASTROINTESTINAL TRACT

a special development of the circular muscle layer of the stomach, and during life is tightly closed, except during the periodic escape of gastric contents into the duodenum. The mucous membrane of the stomach is thrown into pleats or rugae when the organ is not fully distended.

Superficial to the mucous coat is a submucous, consisting of loose connective tissue, while superficial to this are three coats of unstriped muscle, the inner oblique, the middle circular and the outer longitudinal.

Small Intestine.—The small intestine is a tube, from 22 to 25 ft. long, beginning at the pylorus and ending at the ileocaecal valve; it is divided into duodenum, jejunum and ileum.

The duodenum is from 9 to 11 in. long and forms a horseshoe or C-shaped curve, encircling the head of the pancreas. It differs from the rest of the gut in being retroperitoneal. Its first part is horizontal and lies behind the fundus of the gall bladder, passing backward and to the right from the pylorus. The second part runs vertically downward in front of the hilum of the right kidney, and into this part the pancreatic and bile ducts open. The third part runs horizontally to the left in front of the aorta and vena cava, while the fourth part ascends to the left side of the second lumbar vertebra, after which it bends sharply downward and forward to form the duodenojejunal flexure.

The jejunum forms the upper two-fifths of the rest of the small intestine; it, like the ileum, is thrown into numerous convolutions and is attached by the mesentery to the posterior abdominal wall.

The ileum is the remaining three-fifths of the small intestine, though there is no absolute point at which the one ends and the other begins. Speaking broadly, the jejunum occupies the upper and left part of the abdomen below the subcostal plane, the ileum the lower and right part. At its termination the ileum opens into the large intestine at the ileocaecal valve.

Caecum.—The caecum is a blind sac occupying the right iliac fossa and extending down two or three inches below the ileocaecal junction. From its posterior and left surface the vermiform appendix protrudes, and usually is directed upward and to the left. This wormlike tube is blind at its end and is usually three or four inches long. Its internal opening into the caecum is about one inch below that of the ileum.

On transverse section it is seen to be composed of: (1) an external muscular coat; (2) a submucous coat; (3) a mass of lymphoid tissue, which appears after birth; and (4) mucous membrane. In many cases its lumen is wholly or partly obliterated, though this is probably due to disease. Guarding the opening of the ileum into the caecum is the ileocaecal valve, which consists of two cusps projecting into the caecum; of these the upper forms a horizontal shelf, while the lower slopes up to it obliquely. At birth the caecum is a cone, the apex of which is the appendix; it is bent upon itself to form a U; sometimes this arrangement persists throughout life.

Colon.—The ascending colon (see fig. 1) runs up from the caecum at the level of the ileocaecal valve to the hepatic flexure beneath and behind the right lobe of the liver; it is about eight inches long and posteriorly is in contact with the abdominal wall and right kidney. It is covered by peritoneum except on its posterior surface.

The transverse colon is variable in position, depending largely on the distention of the stomach, but usually corresponding to the subcostal plane. On the left side of the abdomen its ascends to the splenic flexure, which may make an impression on the spleen (q.v.), and is bound to the diaphragm opposite the 11th rib by a fold of peritoneum.

The descending colon passes down in front of the left kidney and left side of the posterior abdominal wall to the crest of the ilium; it is about six inches long and is usually empty and contracted while the rest of the colon is distended with gas; its peritoneal relations are the same as those of the ascending colon, but it is more likely to be completely surrounded.

The iliac colon stretches from the crest of the ilium to the inner border of the psoas muscle, lying in the left iliac fossa, just above and parallel to Poupart's ligament. Like the descending, it is usually uncovered by peritoneum on its posterior surface. It is about six inches in length.

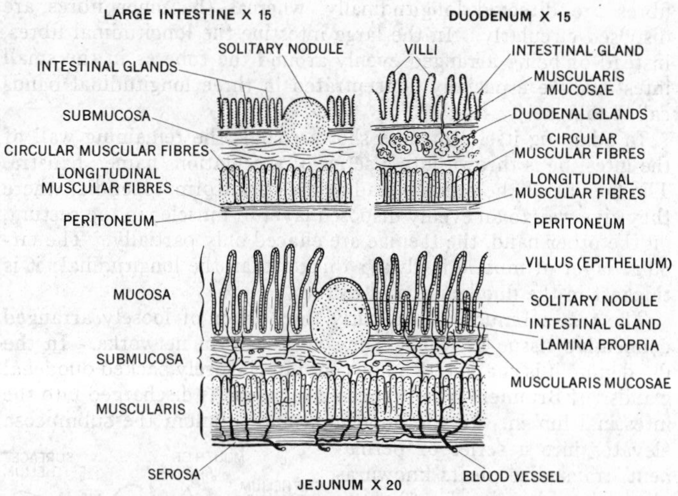

The pelvic colon lies in the true pelvis and forms a loop, the two limbs of which are superior and inferior while the convexity reaches across to the right side of the pelvis. In the fetus this loop occupies the right iliac fossa, but, as the caecum descends and enlarges and the pelvis widens, it is usually driven out of this region. The distal end of the loop turns sharply downward to reach the third piece of the sacrum, where it becomes the rectum. Formerly the iliac and pelvic colons were spoken of as the sigmoid flexure.

Rectum.—The rectum, according to modern ideas, begins in front of the third piece of the sacrum. It ends in a dilatation or rectal ampulla, which is in contact with the back of the prostate in the male and of the vagina in the female and is in front of the tip of the coccyx. The rectum is not straight, as its name would imply, but has a concavity forward corresponding to that of the sacrum and coccyx.

At the end of the pelvic colon the mesocolon ceases, and the rectum is then covered only by peritoneum at its sides and in front; lower down the lateral covering is gradually reflected off and then only the front is covered. About the junction of the middle and lower thirds of the tube the anterior peritoneal covering is also reflected off onto the bladder or vagina, forming the rectovesical pouch in the male and the pouch of Douglas in the female. This reflection is usually about three inches above the anal aperture.

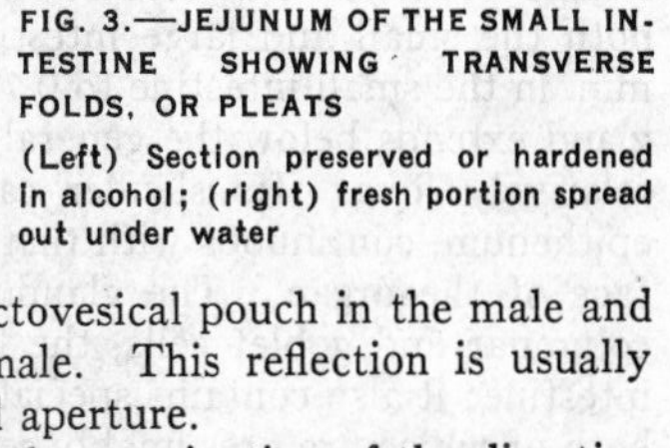

Anal Canal.—The anal canal, the termination of the digestive tract, runs downward and backward from the lower surface of the rectal ampulla between the levatores ani muscles. It is about an inch long and its lateral walls are in contact. Its opening is the anus.

(P. C. M.; X.)

(See also ANATOMY, GROSS.)

Structure of the Intestine.—The intestine conforms to the general structural plan of hollow organs but shows some regional adaptations in agreement with local requirements. There are four coats: serous, muscular, submucous and mucous (see fig. 2). The tunica serosa is an external investment of peritoneum continuous with the mesentery, where present; it is incomplete on those surfaces of the intestine that are pressed against the body wall. Like serous membranes in general, it has a smooth, shiny surface and consists of a single layer of flat epithelial cells (mesothelium) lying upon a bed of connective tissue.

The tunica muscularis is composed of unstriped (involuntary) muscle fibres arranged in two sharply demarcated layers; the outer

LARGE INTESTINE X 15 — DUODENUM X 15 — VILLI — INTESTINAL GLAND — MUSCULARIS MUCOSAE — DUODENAL GLANDS — CIRCULAR MUSCULAR FIBRES — LONGITUDINAL MUSCULAR FIBRES — PERITONEUM — SOLITARY NODULE — INTESTINAL GLANDS — SUBMUCOSA — CIRCULAR MUSCULAR FIBRES — LONGITUDINAL MUSCULAR FIBRES — PERITONEUM — VILLUS (EPITHELIUM) — SOLITARY NODULE — INTESTINAL GLAND — LAMINA PROPRIA — MUSCULARIS MUCOSAE — JEJUNUM X 20 — MUCOSA — SUBMUCOSA — MUSCULARIS — SEROSA — BLOOD VESSEL

FIG. 2.—STRUCTURE OF INTESTINAL WALL AS SEEN IN LONGITUDINAL SECTIONS

(TOWARD PYLORUS)

FROM D. J. CUNNINGHAM, "TEXTBOOK OF ANATOMY," BY COURTESY OF OXFORD MEDICAL PUBLICATIONS

FIG. 3.—JEJUNUM OF THE SMALL INTESTINE SHOWING TRANSVERSE FOLDS, OR PLEATS

(Left) Section preserved or hardened in alcohol; (right) fresh portion spread out under water

GASTROINTESTINAL TRACT

fibres are directed longitudinally, whereas the inner fibres are disposed circularly. In the large intestine the longitudinal fibres, instead of being arranged evenly around the tube as in the small intestine, are especially concentrated in three longitudinal bands called taeniae.

In adapting itself to these shorter bands the remaining wall of the intestine is thrown into a series of sacculations named haustra. The taeniae of the caecum lead to the vermiform appendix, where they give way to an evenly disposed layer of muscle; in the rectum, on the other hand, the taeniae are effaced only partially. The circular layer of muscle is always thicker than the longitudinal; it is thickest in the duodenum and rectum.

The tela submucosa is a fairly thick layer of loosely arranged connective tissue in which many vessels form networks. In the duodenum it is characterized by containing closely packed duodenal glands (of Brunner), whose mucoid secretion is discharged into the intestinal lumen. In the duodenum and jejunum the submucosa elevates into a series of permanent, transverse pleats known as plicae circulares (see fig. 3); over these the mucous membrane drapes.

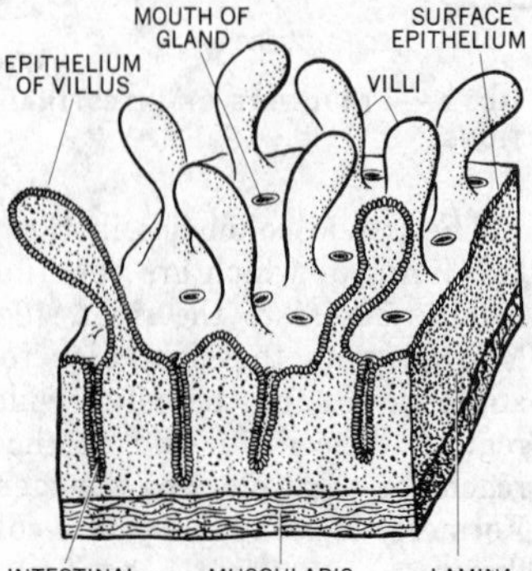

The innermost coat is the tunica mucosa (see fig. 2, 4). The most important component of this membrane is its epithelium, nearest the lumen. This is a single layer of columnar cells, some of which have become specialized as unicellular slime glands (goblet cells). The epithelium rests upon a rather homogeneous basement membrane, beneath which is the lamina propria consisting largely of reticular tissue and lymphocytes. Most externally is a thin layer of unstriped muscle called the muscularis mucosae. The surface of the mucous membrane throughout the entire small intestine has a velvety appearance, due to the presence of closely set, minute, fingerlike elevations named villi. The myriad microscopic villi and the grossly folded plicae increase the secretory and absorptive area enormously.

The entire intestine, large and small, is specifically characterized by simple tubular intestinal glands (of Lieberkühn) that are set close together vertically and extend through the thickness of the lamina propria. There are about 180,000,000 of these glands in both the small and large intestine; their length ranges from 0.1 mm. in the small intestine to 0.7 mm. in the large intestine. Each gland extends below the general surface as a tiny pit, narrow but relatively long. Its slender cavity is enveloped by a tube of epithelium, continuous with that covering the general internal surface of the organ. The glandular epithelium contains ordinary columnar and goblet cells, the latter preponderating in the large intestine; it also contains special Paneth cells and argentaffin cells, both of which are presumably secretory although their exact functions are still obscure.

Scattered throughout the entire intestinal mucosa, and sometimes intruding into the submucosa, are minute masses of lymphoid tissue termed solitary nodules; these are about the size of a pinhead and their number totals tens of thousands. Such nodules are especially abundant in the vermiform appendix. In the small intestine, but mainly in the ileum, they collect in oval groups called aggregate nodules (or Peyer's patches) which may attain a length of an inch or more.

Apposed folds of the mucosa and submucosa produce the ileocaecal valve between the small and large intestine. The rectum bears three shelflike transverse folds that project into the lumen. The anal canal contains a series of permanent longitudinal folds called rectal columns; the circular layer of muscle thickens to produce the internal sphincter of the anus. Outside the canal is an external sphincter of voluntary muscle. Blood vessels reach the intestine by way of its mesentery and

FIG. 4.—SAMPLE BLOCK OF MUCOUS MEMBRANE OF THE ILEUM (MAGNIFIED 35 TIMES)

INTESTINAL GLAND — MUSCULARIS MUCOSAE — LAMINA PROPRIA — EPITHELIUM OF VILLUS — MOUTH OF GLAND — VILLI — SURFACE EPITHELIUM

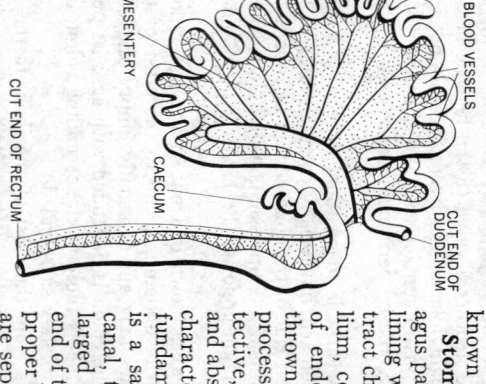

FIG. 5.—INTESTINAL TRACT OF THE FOX, SHOWING RELATIVELY SIMPLE SMALL INTESTINE, ADAPTED TO A CARNIVOROUS DIET

MESENTERY — BLOOD VESSELS — CAECUM — CUT END OF RECTUM — CUT END OF DUODENUM

form an extensive plexus in the submucosa; arterial branches supply the muscular coat and mucous membrane, while venous branches return from the same regions. Lymphatic vessels provide a one-way drainage system for tissue fluids. The intrinsic nerve supply emanates from ganglion cells, located between the muscular layers and in the submucosa; extrinsic fibres come from the vagus nerves (and end on the intrinsic ganglion cells), and from the celiac sympathetic plexus (see NERVE; NERVOUS SYSTEM).

Peritoneum.—For a discussion of the peritoneum, the membrane that surrounds the organs of the abdomen, see COELOM AND SEROUS MEMBRANES.

(L. B. Ay.)

COMPARATIVE ANATOMY

The primitive condition of the vertebrate digestive tract may be described as a straight, simple tube, consisting of an anterior portion, formed by an ectodermal invagination, a long median portion lined by endoderm, and a short posterior portion formed by ectodermal invagination. In the lower vertebrates the primitive tube subserved also the purpose of respiration, and traces of the double function remain in the adult structure of all vertebrates. In fish, the pharynx, or branchial region, suddenly becomes narrower, posterior to the gill slits, to form the esophagus; in adults of higher animals the esophagus is separated from the primitive pharyngeal region and lies dorsal to it. In the primitive vertebrates, the entire digestive tract probably was lined with ciliated cells. Traces of this ciliation persist in many living forms.

Esophagus.—The esophagus is essentially merely a passage, as straight as may be, from the pharynx to the stomach, varying in length with the length of the neck and thoracic regions in different animals, and in calibre with the nature of the food. It is almost invariably lined with a many-layered epithelium, forming a tough coating, readily repaired and not easily damaged by hard food masses. There are only a few exceptions to this structural and functional simplicity. In fishes (see FISH) the swim bladder is developed as a dorsal outgrowth of the esophagus and may remain in open connection with it. In many birds part of the esophagus may be temporarily dilated, forming a "crop," as for instance in birds of prey and hummingbirds. In the flamingo, many ducks, storks and the cormorant the crop is a permanent although not a highly specialized enlargement. Finally, in the vast majority of seed-eating birds, in gallinaceous birds, pigeons, sand grouse, parrots and many songbirds, particularly the finches, the crop is a permanent globular dilatation, in which the food is retained for a considerable time, mixed with a slight mucous secretion, and softened and partly macerated by the heat of the body. Many birds feed their young from the soft contents of the crop, and in pigeons, at the breeding season, the cells lining the crop proliferate rapidly and are discharged as a soft cheesy mass into the cavity, forming the substance known as pigeon's milk.

Stomach.—Where the esophagus passes into the stomach, the lining wall of the gastrointestinal tract changes to a mucous epithelium, consisting of a single layer of endodermal cells, frequently thrown into pits or projecting as processes; from being chiefly protective, it has become secretory and absorbing, and maintains this character nearly to the anus. The fundamental form of the stomach is a saclike enlargement of the canal, the whole forming an enlarged bent tube. At the distal end of the tube the intestinal tract proper begins, and the two regions are separated by a muscular constriction. In fishes the stomach may be a simple bent tube, or an expanded, globular or elongated sac. In amphibians and reptiles it is in most cases a simple sac, marked off from the esophagus only by increased calibre. In the Crocodilia, however, the anterior portion of the stomach is much enlarged and very highly muscular, the muscles radiating from a central tendinous area on each of the flattened sides. The cavity is lined by a hardened secretion and contains pebbles and gravel for mechanical trituration of the food, so that the resemblance to the gizzard of birds is well marked. This muscular chamber leads by a small aperture into a distal, smaller and more glandular chamber.

In birds the stomach exhibits two regions: an anterior glandular region, the proventriculus, the walls of which are relatively soft and contain enlarged digestive glands, and a distal region (gizzard). The distal region is larger and is lined in most cases by a more or less permanent membrane which is thick and tough in birds with a muscular gizzard, very slight in others.

In mammals the primitive form of the stomach consists of a more or less globular or elongated expansion of the esophageal region, forming the cardiac portion, and a forwardly curved, narrower pyloric portion, from which the duodenum arises. The whole wall is muscular, and the lining membrane is richly glandular. In many mammals one, two or three protrusions of the cardiac region occur, while in the manatee and in some rodents the cardiac region is constricted off from the pyloric portion. In the Artiodactyla the stomach is always complex, the complexity reaching a maximum in ruminating forms. In the chevrotains, which in many other respects show conditions intermediate between nonruminant artiodactyls and true ruminants, the esophagus opens into a wide cardiac portion, incompletely divided into four chambers. Three of these, toward the cardiac extremity, are lined with villi and correspond to the rumen or paunch; the fourth, which lies between the opening of the esophagus and the pyloric portion of the stomach, is the ruminant reticulum and its wall is lined with very shallow "cells." The fourth or true pyloric chamber is an elongated sac with smooth glandular walls and is the abomasum, or rennet sac. In the camel the

rumen forms an enormous globular paunch with villous walls and internally showing a trace of division into two regions. It is well marked off from the reticulum, the diverticula of which are extremely deep, forming the miscalled "water cells."

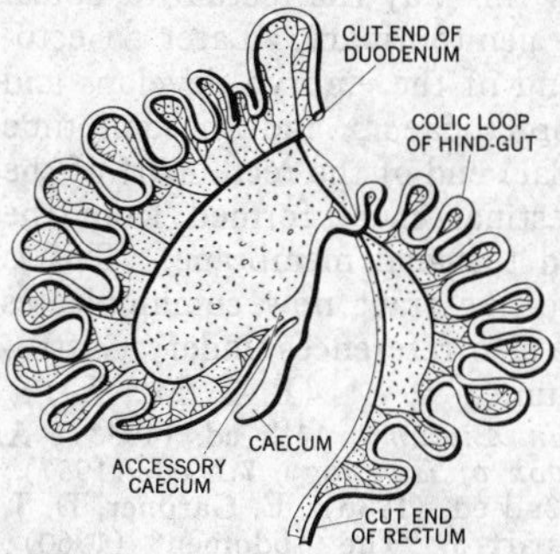

In the true ruminants the rumen forms a capacious, villous reservoir, nearly always, partly sacculated, into which the food is passed rapidly as the animal grazes. The food is subjected to a rotary movement in the paunch, and is thus repeatedly subjected to moistening with the fluids secreted by the reticulum, as it is passed over the aperture of that cavity, and is formed into a rounded bolus. The food bolus, when the animal is lying down after grazing, is passed into the esophagus and reaches the mouth by antiperistaltic contractions of the esophagus. After prolonged mastication and mixing with saliva, it is again swallowed, but is now passed into the psalterium which, in true ruminants, is a small chamber with conspicuous longitudinal folds. Finally it reaches the large abomasum where the last stages of gastric digestion occur.

In the whales the stomach is different from that found in any other group of mammals. The esophagus opens directly into a very large cardiac sac, the distal extremity of which forms a long caecal pouch. At nearly the first third of its length this communicates by a narrow aperture with the elongated, relatively narrow pyloric portion. The latter is convoluted and restricted into a series of chambers that differ in different groups of whales.

In most of the pouched mammals (Marsupialia) the stomach is relatively simple; in the kangaroos, on the other hand, the stomach is divided into a relatively small, caecal cardiac portion and an

FIG. 6.—INTESTINAL TRACT OF THE WALLABY, ADAPTED TO AN OMNIVOROUS DIET OF PLANT MATTER AND INSECTS

CUT END OF DUODENUM — COLIC LOOP OF HIND-GUT — CAECUM — CUT END OF RECTUM — ACCESSORY CAECUM

enormously long sacculated and convoluted pyloric region, the general arrangement of which closely resembles the large caecum of many mammals.

Intestinal Tract.—It is not yet possible to discuss the general morphology of this region in vertebrates as a group. While the modifications displayed in birds and mammals have been compared and studied in detail, those in the lower groups have not yet been systematically coordinated.

Fishes.—In the cyclostomes (lamprey, hagfish), chimaeras and a few bony fishes the course of the gut is practically straight from the pyloric end of the stomach to the exterior, and there is no marked differentiation into regions. In the lungfishes a contracted sigmoid curve between the stomach and the dilated intestine is a simple beginning of the complexity found in other groups. In very many of the more specialized bony fishes the gut is much convoluted, exhibiting a series of watch-springlike coils.

In a number of different groups, increased surface for absorption is given, not by increase in length of the whole gut but by the development of an internal fold known as the spiral valve. A set of organs peculiar to fish, known as the pyloric caeca, is present in numbers ranging from 1 to nearly 200 in the vast majority of fish. These are outgrowths of the intestinal tract near the pyloric extremity of the stomach, and their function is partly glandular, partly absorbing.

In the amphibians the course of the intestinal tract is nearly straight from the pyloric end of the stomach to the cloaca; in the case of the salamanders that retain the gills through life (mud puppy, olm) there are no more than a few simple loops between the expanded "rectum" and the straight portion that leaves the stomach.

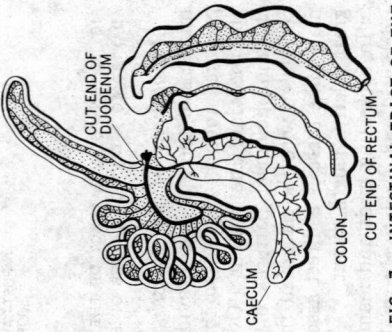

CUT END OF DUODENUM — CUT END OF RECTUM — CAECUM — COLON

FIG. 7.—INTESTINAL TRACT OF THE TAPIR, WITH WELL-DEVELOPED CAECUM, ADAPTED TO A DIET OF SOFT WATER PLANTS

In fishes, amphibians and reptiles the intestinal tract is swung from the dorsal wall of the abdominal cavity by a mesentery which is incomplete because of secondary absorption in places. There are also traces, more abundant in the lower forms, of the still more primitive ventral mesentery.

Birds and Mammals.—The primitive gut must be supposed to have run backward from the stomach to the cloaca suspended from the dorsal wall of the body cavity by a dorsal mesentery. This tract, in the course of phylogeny of the common ancestors of birds and mammals, became longer than the straight length between its extreme points and, consequently, was thrown into a series of folds.

The mesentery grew out with these folds, but the presence of adjacent organs, the disturbance due to the outgrowth of the liver and the secondary relations brought about between different portions of the gut, as the outgrowing loops invaded each other's localities, disturbed the primitive simplicity.

Three definite regions of outgrowth, however, are to be recognized in the actual disposition of the gut in existing birds and mammals. The first of these is the duodenum. The second portion is Meckel's tract. It consists of the part generally known as the small intestines, the jejunum and ileum of human anatomy, and stretches from the distal end of the duodenum to the caecum or caeca. It is the chief absorbing portion of the gut, and in nearly all birds and mammals is the longest portion. It represents, however, only a very small part of the primitive straight gut, corresponding to not more than two or three somites of the embryo. The third portion of the gut should be termed the hind-gut, and lies between the caecum or caeca and the anus, corresponding to the large intestines, colon and rectum of human anatomy. It is formed from a much larger portion of the primitive straight gut than the duodenum and Meckel's tract together, and its proximal portion lies very close to the origin of the duodenum.

Adaptations of the Intestinal Tract to Function.—The chief business of the gut is to provide a vascular surface to which the prepared food is applied so that the nutritive material may be absorbed into the system. Overlying and sometimes obscuring the morphological patterns of the gut are many modifications correlated with the nature of the food. Thus in birds and mammals alike there is a direct association of herbivorous habit with great relative length of gut.

In fish-eating birds and mammals the gut is very long, with a thick wall and a relatively small calibre, while there is a general tendency for the regions of the gut to be slightly or not at all defined. In fruit-eating birds the gut is strikingly short, wide and simple, while a similar change has not taken place in fruit-eating mammals. Carnivorous birds and mammals have a relatively short gut.

The Colic Caeca.—These paired or single organs lie at the junction of the mid-gut with the hind-gut. Meckel's tract and are homologous in birds and mammals although their apparent position differs in the majority of cases in the two groups. The caeca are hollow outgrowths of the wall of the gut, the blind ends being directed forward. They vary in size within very wide limits and there is no invariable connection between the nature of the food and the degree of their development. The caecal wall is in most cases highly glandular and contains lymphoid tissue. In birds and in mammals this tissue may be so greatly increased as to transform the caecum into a solid or nearly solid sac.

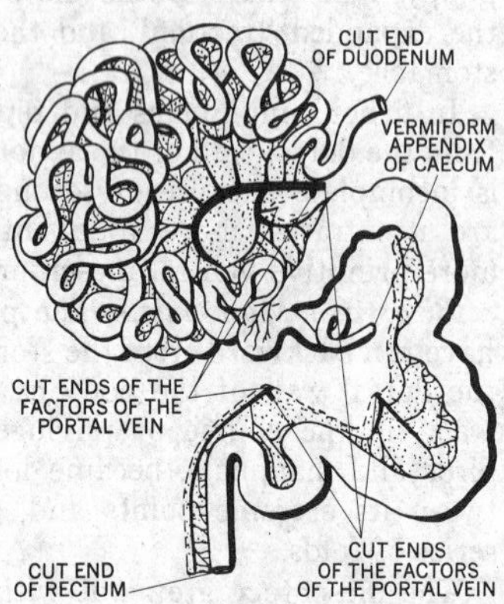

EMBRYOLOGY

The greater part of the digestive tract is formed by the closing in of the entoderm to make a longitudinal tube, ventral and parallel to the notochord.

This tube is blind in front and behind (cephalad and caudad), but the middle part of its ventral wall is for some distance continuous with the wall of the yolk sac, and this part of the tract, which at first opens into the yolk sac by a very wide aperture, is called the mid-gut. The part in front of it, which lies dorsal to the heart, is the fore-gut, while the part behind the aperture of the yolk sac is the hind-gut.

The pharynx, esophagus, stomach and part of the duodenum are developed from the fore-gut, a good deal of the duodenum and the rectum from the hind-gut, while the mid-gut is responsible for the rest. The cephalic part of the fore-gut forms the pharynx, and about the fourth week the stomach appears as a fusiform dilatation in the straight tube.

Between the two the esophagus gradually forms as the embryo elongates. The opening into the yolk sac, which at first is very wide, gradually narrows, as the ventral abdominal walls close in, until in the adult the only indication of the connection between the gut and the yolk sac is the rare presence (about 2%) of Meckel's diverticulum.

The stomach soon shows signs of the greater and lesser curvatures, the latter being ventral, but maintains its straight position. About the sixth week the caecum appears as a lateral diverticulum, and until the third month is of uniform calibre; after this period the terminal part ceases to grow at the same rate as the proximal, and so the vermiform appendix is formed. The mid-gut forms a loop, with its convexity toward the diminishing vitelline duct, or remains of the yolk sac, and until the third month it protrudes into the umbilical cord. The greater curvature of the stomach grows more rapidly than the lesser, and the whole stomach turns over and becomes ventral. This turning over of the stomach throws the succeeding part of the intestine into a duodenal loop, which at first has a dorsal and ventral mesentery. The intestine now grows very rapidly and is thrown into a series of coils; the caecum ascends and passes to the right ventral to the duodenum, and presses it against the dorsal wall of the abdomen; then it descends toward its permanent position in the right iliac fossa.

From the ventral surface on the hinder (caudal) closed end of the intestinal tube the allantois grows to form the placenta and bladder (see URINARY SYSTEM; REPRODUCTIVE SYSTEM; PLACENTA), and this region is the cloaca into which the gastrointestinal, urinary and generative canals or ducts all open. Later, two lateral folds appear which, by their union, divide the cloaca into a ventral and a dorsal part, the former being genitourinary and the latter alimentary or intestinal. In this way the rectum or dorsal compartment is shut off from the genitourinary. Later an ectodermal invagination at the hind end of the embryo develops and forms the anal canal; this is the proctodaeum, and for some time it is separated from the hind (caudal) end of the rectal part of the mesodaeum (or part of the intestinal canal formed from the mesoderm) by a membrane called the anal membrane. This is eventually absorbed, and the digestive tract now communicates with the surface by the anus. See also references under, "Gastrointestinal Tract" in the Index volume.

(P. C. M.; X.)

BIBLIOGRAPHY.—H. Morris, *Human Anatomy*, 11th ed. (1953); A. A. Maximow and W. Bloom, *Textbook of Histology*, 7th ed. (1957); A. E. Barclay, *The Digestive Tract*, 2nd ed. (1936); E. Gardner, D. J. Gray and R. O'Rahilly, *Anatomy*, part 5, "The Abdomen" (1960); *Gray's Anatomy*, "The Digestive System", pp. 1207–1314, 27th ed. by C. M. Goss (1959); T. H. Eaton, Jr., *Comparative Anatomy of the Vertebrates*, 2nd ed. (1960); W. S. Leach, *Functional Anatomy of the Mammal*, 3rd ed. (1961); L. B. Arey, *Developmental Anatomy*, 6th ed. (1954), *Human Histology* (1957); A. S. Romer, *Vertebrate Body*, 2nd ed. (1955).

GASTROINTESTINAL TRACT, DISEASES OF.

Diseases of the gastrointestinal tract are numerous. Only the more important disorders affecting the stomach and intestines are considered in the discussion that follows.

STOMACH

Peptic Ulcer.—A peptic ulcer is a localized loss of tissue in the membrane that lines the stomach or the immediately adjacent portion of the duodenum. This disorder, which occurs much more often in the duodenum than in the stomach, affects from 5% to 10% of all people at some time in their lives. Though there are certain important differences between ulcers in the stomach and those in the duodenum, the two types are considered together here.

The precise cause of peptic ulcer is unknown. It is generally agreed, however, that the hydrochloric acid normally present in the gastric juice plays an important role. The prevailing concept is that the corrosive action of the gastric acid renders the affected area of the stomach or duodenum susceptible to digestion

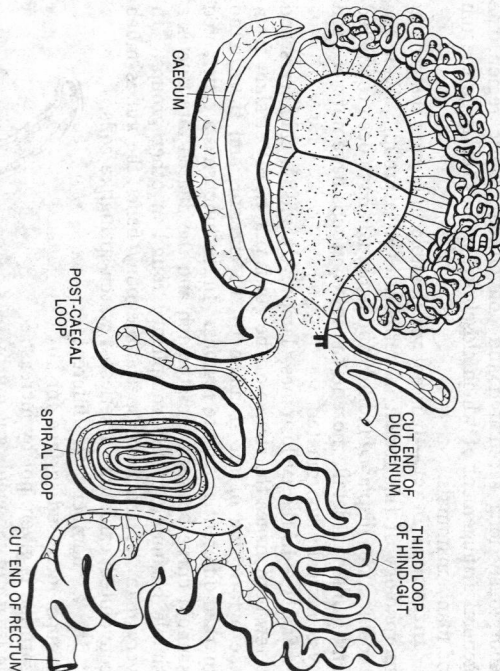

FIG. 8.—INTESTINAL TRACT OF THE GIRAFFE, COMPLEXLY DEVELOPED AND ADAPTED TO A DIET OF LEAVES OF SHRUBS AND TREES

FIG. 9.—INTESTINAL TRACT OF THE GORILLA, ADAPTED TO A DIET OF FRUIT AND LEAVES

by pepsin, a digestive enzyme also found in gastric juice. The fact that ulcer patients, especially those with duodenal ulcer, invariably have free (excess) hydrochloric acid in their gastric juice lends support to the importance attributed to the acid-peptic mechanism.

Many studies have shown that patients with duodenal ulcer are hypersecretors of hydrochloric acid, whereas those with gastric ulcers usually secrete less than normal persons do. There is thus a striking difference between the two kinds of peptic ulcer. Emotional stress also appears to contribute to the formation or recurrence of peptic ulcer. Other factors under investigation in the study of peptic-ulcer disease include the nature of tissue resistance to acid erosion and the protective role of gastric mucus secretion, various genetic factors such as the blood types, the association of other diseases, such as cirrhosis of the liver and chronic lung disease, the use of common ulcer-inducing drugs or dietary moieties, and the role of certain endocrine glands, such as the islet cells of the pancreas, a tumour of which may produce an intractable peptic ulcer.

Recurrent attacks of upper abdominal pain or distress occur periodically in ulcer patients. The pain generally occurs one to two hours after eating or during sleep. Characteristically, relief is temporarily obtained by food, milk, or certain neutralizing drugs known as antacids. Each attack lasts several days or weeks and reappears after several weeks or months. Recurrences are especially frequent in the spring and fall. The ulcer may erode a blood vessel and give rise to hemorrhage; it also may extend through the wall of the stomach or duodenum and cause perforation; or it may form sufficient amounts of scar tissue to obstruct the outlet of the stomach.

The keystone of medical treatment is a program that rests the stomach. This includes physical and mental rest; mild sedation; a bland diet with frequent milk feedings between meals; drugs, such as atropine and belladonna, that reduce acid secretion; and acid neutralizers, such as calcium carbonate and aluminum hydroxide. Surgery is necessary in from 10 to 15% of patients with duodenal ulcer; surgery becomes necessary when patients fail to respond to intensive medical treatment or when they develop some complication of the disease. A gastric ulcer that does not heal in four to perhaps six weeks should be treated surgically, principally because of the possibility that the symptoms may represent an ulcerating cancer rather than a simple benign ulcer. This fear does not apply to duodenal ulcers, which practically never are cancerous. (See also GASTRIC AND DUODENAL ULCER; ULCER.)

Gastritis.—Gastritis is an inflammation, either acute or chronic, of the stomach, principally of its lining membrane. The acute variety is usually a temporary affair and is manifested principally by vomiting and upper abdominal distress. The inflammation usually clears up after removal of the exciting cause, which may be dietary indiscretion, excessive consumption of alcohol, the use of certain drugs, or infection. The cause of chronic gastritis is unknown. Patients with this form of gastritis may experience little or no distress, or they may complain of vague dyspepsia or present symptoms simulating peptic ulcer. Erosive or ulcerative gastritis, whether acute or chronic, may on occasion cause hemorrhage. Inspection of the lining membrane of the stomach through a gastroscope or by intragastric colour photography may disclose one or several changes, such as inflammation, a swollen hypertrophic appearance of the mucosa, or atrophy of the mucosal lining. The latter, designated as chronic atrophic gastritis or gastric mucosal atrophy, is thought to predispose to the development of gastric cancer. The treatment of chronic gastritis consists chiefly of a bland diet and antacids. Liver extract and vitamins have also been reported to be beneficial. (See also GASTRITIS.)

Cancer.—Carcinoma of the stomach is one of the most frequent malignant diseases of the digestive tract, particularly in men over the age of 40 years. It occurs in all races and in all parts of the world. In the 1960s there was a definite but unexplained decline in the incidence of gastric cancer in the U.S. In striking contrast was the very high incidence of the disease in Japan,

China, and Iceland. The disease usually appears in one of three anatomical forms: (1) an ulcer; (2) a projecting tumour; or (3) a diffusely infiltrating and spreading growth. Although the cause of gastric carcinoma is unknown, it is generally agreed, on the basis of present evidence, that a peptic ulcer of the stomach rarely, if ever, turns cancerous. The problem rather is to distinguish an ulcerating cancer from a benign ulcer of the stomach.

The symptoms of cancer of the stomach are often insidious in their development. Indeed, the disease is usually fairly well developed before the first symptoms appear. The patient may initially experience a diminution of appetite, some weight loss, or mild upper-abdominal discomfort or pain. The pain may resemble that of peptic ulcer and may be relieved by eating. Indigestion is especially suspect when it appears for the first time in a middle-aged or older person whose gastric secretion fails to show free acid after appropriate stimulation. The free-acid secretion of the stomach is absent or diminished in most of the patients with gastric cancer. X rays usually give evidence of the disease (80–90% of the cases) when symptoms are present. Additional methods of examination, notably gastroscopy, gastrocamera photography, and the search for cancer cells in gastric washings, increase diagnostic accuracy.

Cure depends upon early diagnosis and early removal of the cancer along with part or all of the stomach. See also CANCER; ABDOMEN, SURGERY OF: Gastrointestinal Surgery.

THE INTESTINES

Regional Enteritis (Ileitis).—This is a chronic inflammatory disease of one or more segments of the small bowel. In its classical form it is confined to the terminal portion of the ileum; i.e., where the ileum joins the colon. In some cases, however, a major part of the small intestine may be affected, either continuously or irregularly with skip areas. In a type of enteritis known as enterocolitis, varying lengths of the adjoining colon also may be involved. In rare cases, the duodenum or even the stomach may be affected by the disease. Consequences of the disease are that the bowel is thickened, its channel is narrowed, and its lining is ulcerated. The cause of regional enteritis is unknown. It affects both sexes of all ages but particularly those between 15 and 30 years. Patients may recover completely from an initial acute attack, but the usual course is one of progression with continuously smoldering disease for many years. Periods of relative freedom from symptoms are interrupted by acute exacerbations; or the patient is never entirely well and complications ensue.

The symptoms are extremely variable. The initial attack may simulate acute appendicitis. The usual picture is that of a continuous or intermittent diarrhea, sometimes bloody, accompanied by painful abdominal cramps. Fever is very common and sometimes overshadows the digestive symptoms. Chronic debility, weight loss, and anemia produce progressive physical deterioration. Grave complications may occur, such as obstruction or perforation of the intestine, the formation of an abscess within the abdomen, or an abnormal communication (fistula) between the diseased gut and adjacent coils of small bowel, the colon, urinary bladder, or vagina. Infections about the anus, particularly a perianal fistula, occur fairly commonly.

Diagnosis is confirmed by X-ray examination of the small bowel and colon. Uncomplicated cases are preferably managed by conservative, nonsurgical measures. These consist basically of physical rest and a bland, nutritious diet with minimal roughage, supplemented with vitamins and iron. Corticotrophin (ACTH), a hormone derived from the pituitary gland, and adrenal cortical hormones, such as cortisone, often produce gratifying improvement. These agents, however, do not cure the disease. Antibiotics are often helpful in the treatment of secondary infection but are not curative. Surgery is reserved for patients who do not benefit from medical treatment or who exhibit the more serious complications. The principle of surgery is to remove the diseased segment or to isolate it from the intestinal stream by connecting normal bowel above the level of the disease to the colon at a point well beyond the diseased segment.

Appendicitis.—Inflammation of the appendix generally occurs as an acute attack; such attacks may culminate in perforation of the appendix with peritonitis or localized abscess formation. Although acute appendicitis is a common disease, there was a sharp decline in both its incidence and death rate in the United States and Western Europe after World War II. The typical picture is one of pain, tenderness, and muscular spasm in the right lower quadrant of the abdominal wall. This is often preceded by pain that is vaguely localized in the middle or upper abdomen. The patient's temperature is usually elevated, and the white blood-cell count is increased. If appendicitis is suspected, nothing should be taken by mouth; laxatives are especially hazardous. Treatment is surgical removal of the appendix as early in the disease as possible.

Chronic appendicitis, a term often used to describe low-grade, recurring pain in the right lower quadrant of the abdomen, is infrequent. Usually the pain is found to result from a disorder other than chronic inflammation of the appendix. (*See also* APPENDICITIS.)

Functional Disorder of the Colon.—Functional disorder of the colon, also known as the "irritable-colon syndrome," is probably the most common cause of abdominal discomfort, pain, and irregular bowel action. The disorder is due predominantly to disturbed motility of the colon, but it may be associated with similar disturbance of function in other parts of the digestive tract. It results from a "nervous" or irritable state of the bowel and not from organic or structural disease. X-ray and other examinations do not disclose organic abnormalities. The terms "mucous colitis" and "spastic colitis" are popularly used to designate this condition. They are undesirable terms, however, because there is no true "colitis" (inflammation of the colon) in this disorder. The disturbed activity of the colon is usually related to nervous tension, worry, and anxiety. The eating of irritant and laxative foods, the overuse of harsh laxatives, allergic response to certain foods, and excessive smoking also may contribute to the irritability of the bowel.

The patient experiences abdominal discomfort, pain, and irregularity of bowel evacuation. Usually the stools are of small calibre, and excessive mucus in the stool is frequently present. Constipation is more common than diarrhea, but both may occur alternately in the same individual. Abdominal distension or bloating, rumbling sounds, and excessive passage of flatus are common symptoms. Usually the digestive complaints are accompanied by general symptoms of nervousness, weakness, and fatigue.

Treatment begins with a thorough examination to exclude organic disease. Reassurance about the nature of the disorder and attempts to alleviate emotional tension are important in treatment. A bland diet free of physically and chemically irritant foods and the use of mild sedatives and antispasmodic drugs are helpful. The patient is urged to discontinue the use of laxatives and enemas and is encouraged to adjust his daily routine so as to provide more rest and relaxation. Development of a regular bowel habit is desirable. Constipation is treated by providing a greater intake of cooked fruits and vegetables and such natural laxatives as prune juice. In addition, the ingestion of a simple hydrophilic colloid may be useful in providing a soft stool.

Constipation.—Constipation is actually a symptom and not a disease. Because of its frequency and the importance attached to it, however, it merits special consideration. Constipation may be defined as the infrequent evacuation of excessively hard, dry stools. Frequency is a less important criterion than the physical character of the stool, since healthy persons vary greatly in the frequency of defecation. The mistaken notion that a daily evacuation is essential for good health has, unfortunately, led to colossal overuse of laxatives and cathartics (*see* CATHARTIC). The commonest cause of functional or simple constipation is the repeated voluntary suppression of the defecation urge in response to the demands of modern civilized life. Social impropriety, inconvenience, the lack of a commode, or other inhibiting reasons lead to a habit pattern in which suppression of defecation becomes simpler than its achievement.

Constipation may be subdivided into functional and organic types. Functional constipation, in which there is no structural abnormality, is a major symptom of the irritable-colon syndrome discussed above under *Functional Disorder of the Colon.* Organic causes are numerous and include such diverse conditions as carcinoma of the colon and rectum, diverticulitis, inflammatory diseases that produce constricting scars in the intestine, a pelvic mass pressing on the colon, and painful diseases of the anus, such as fissure or hemorrhoids. Treatment of organic constipation depends on its cause.

Diarrhea.—Diarrhea, like constipation, is a symptom and not a disease. Diarrhea may be defined as the frequent passage of loose or watery stools. It, too, may be either functional or organic in origin. Diarrhea frequently is a manifestation of the irritable colon and is commonly associated with emotional states, such as fear and anxiety. Laxative foods, cathartics, excessive alcohol, and certain foods to which the individual is sensitive may produce or aggravate diarrhea. Organic causes of diarrhea are numerous. They include infection (*e.g.,* bacillary and amoebic dysentery; *Staphylococcus* food poisoning, cholera, paratyphoid fever, etc.); poisoning, as by mercury, arsenic or other chemical agents; regional enteritis and chronic ulcerative colitis; cancer of the intestinal tract; sprue (*q.v.*) and celiac disease, in which intestinal absorption of foodstuffs is impaired; and overgrowth of fungi or actual organic changes that develop as a complication of antibiotic therapy. Diarrhea is treated basically by physical rest, clear fluids or soft, bland foods, and medication; this treatment is designed to relieve pain, reduce intestinal hyperactivity, and soothe the inflamed or irritated bowel. More specific measures depend on the cause for the diarrhea. (*See also* DYSENTERY; BACTERIA.)

Chronic Ulcerative Colitis.—This is a chronic disease of unknown etiology in which the lining membrane of the colon and rectum is diffusely inflamed and studded with bleeding pinpoint ulcers. The disease affects the left (lower) half of the colon and rectum more often than the right (upper) side of the colon. However, the entire colon is affected in more than 50% of cases. In approximately 5% of all cases, the disorder is confined to segments of the colon above the rectum. Ulcerative colitis most commonly affects persons between 20 and 40 years of age. A few patients recover completely, but most suffer recurrent episodes or are chronically and continuously ill for many years. The disease may at any time become acute and fulminating.

No specific cause is known. It may well be that there are multiple causes, each playing some part. The resemblance of the disease to infection is striking, but no microorganism has been clearly implicated. Emotional disturbance, especially mental depression, is almost invariably present and probably plays an important role. There is some evidence suggesting that the malady may be an autoimmune disease. According to this concept, antibodies injurious to the colon develop as the result of an alteration in the colonic tissue brought about by some noxious agent.

The patient experiences intermittent or continuous diarrhea, with blood commonly present in the stools. Fever, anemia, weight loss, and malnutrition are common symptoms. Serious complications may occur. These include a fulminating progression of the disease, usually associated with a toxic dilation of the colon or even perforation of its wall. Other serious complications include severe hemorrhage, or the development of a perianal fistula or abscess, arthritis, or a variety of skin disorders. In addition to the classical multiple small ulcers, the lining of the affected colon often exhibits projecting tags or islands of tissue referred to as pseudopolyps. The incidence of colonic cancer is decidedly greater in patients who have had this disease for a number of years than it is in the general population. Sigmoidoscopic inspection of the lining membrane and an X ray of the colon ordinarily establish the diagnosis.

Medical treatment is similar to that for regional enteritis. Physical rest and the alleviation or control of emotional factors are essential for good results. Corticotrophin and adrenal cortical hormones are even more helpful in this disease than in regional enteritis. Antibiotics and sulfonamides are used for secondary infection with some benefit.

Surgery is reserved for patients who remain debilitated or incapacitated despite prolonged and intensive medical treatment. The prinor who suffer from certain of the complications. The operation usually employed consists of removing the colon and rectum and bringing the termination of the small intestine to the outside through the abdominal wall. This opening, termed an ileostomy, serves as a substitute for the anus. The fecal discharge from the ileostomy is collected in a rubber or plastic bag. In those few cases in which the rectum is spared, the diseased portion of the colon may be surgically removed and the continuity of the normal bowel reestablished by joining the remaining portions of uninvolved colon.

Diverticulosis and Diverticulitis.—Diverticula (abnormal outpouchings or saccules) are frequently seen in the colons of older persons, especially those who are constipated. When these diverticula are present, a person is said to have diverticulosis. If the diverticula become inflamed, the condition is described as diverticulitis. Diverticula usually cause no symptoms. However, if they become inflamed or complicated by perforation or abscess formation, abdominal pain, diarrhea, bleeding, fever, or intestinal obstruction may occur. Treatment of uncomplicated diverticulosis requires no particular measures other, perhaps, than those directed against constipation. Diverticulitis requires antibiotics and measures designed to keep the bowel at rest; in some cases removal of the inflamed segment of colon is necessary. (*See* also DIVERTICULITIS AND DIVERTICULOSIS.)

Cancer of the Colon.—This disorder occurs even more frequently than cancer of the stomach. Colonic polyps, the benign tumours (adenomas) of the colon and rectum that are found in about 10% of all persons beyond the age of 40, are considered to be potentially precancerous. This has led to the practice of removing polyps of the colon and rectum whenever they are found.

In the lower part of the colon, cancer tends to be constricting in type, producing symptoms of bowel obstruction. The manifestations of this change include abdominal discomfort and an alteration in bowel habit in the direction of constipation. Alternating attacks of diarrhea and constipation may occur. Blood is commonly seen in the stool. (*See* also INTESTINAL OBSTRUCTIONS.)

Cancer situated in the upper part of the colon is less apt to be obstructive and produces poorly defined symptoms. The patient often complains of vague dyspepsia and abdominal discomfort. Diarrhea and constipation are less frequent than in cancer of the lower colon. Weakness and fatigue, caused by anemia, are prominent. A tumour mass may be palpable.

Diagnosis is established principally by X-raying the colon (barium enema) and by direct visualization of the rectum and lower colon through a sigmoidoscope. The treatment of choice is surgical removal of the tumour with restoration of bowel continuity by end-to-end anastomosis of the remaining colon. Growths low in the rectum usually make restoration of bowel continuity impossible, and necessitate the formation of a colostomy, or opening of the colon through the abdominal wall. The feces are collected in a rubber or plastic colostomy bag. It is possible that in addition to surgery, radiotherapy and some new chemotherapeutic means may improve the outlook for patients with the disease. In the mid-1960s, however, the prognosis for curative resection, when the disease is well localized, was the most favourable of all cancers of the digestive tract. *See* also CANCER.

BIBLIOGRAPHY.—W. C. Alvarez, *An Introduction to Gastroenterology* (1948); E. D. Palmer, *Clinical Gastroenterology* (1957); F. A. Jones, *Modern Trends in Gastroenterology*, second series (1958); B. B. Ivy, M. I. Grossman, and W. H. Bachrach, *Peptic Ulcer* (1950); B. B. Crohn and H. Yarnis, *Regional Enteritis* (1958); J. A. Bargen, *Chronic Ulcerative Colitis* (1951); R. Turell, *Diseases of the Colon and Anorectum* (1959); G. Glass, *Introduction to Gastro-intestinal Physiology* (1966); W. S. Blakemore and L. K. Ferguson, *Current Perspectives in Gastroenterology* (1967). (J. E. Bk.; I. A. W.)

GASTROPODA, a large group of invertebrate animals ranked as a class of the phylum Mollusca and represented by such familiar forms as the limpet, whelk, common snail, and slug. *See* SNAIL; MOLLUSK.

GASTROTRICHA, a class of the phylum Aschelminthes, is a group of minute bottom-dwelling (benthic) aquatic animals rang-

ing in size from approximately 0.1 to 1.5 mm. Fresh-water forms occur on pond bottoms and on submerged vegetation. The principal habitat of the marine forms is the space between sand grains in the intertidal and subtidal zones. Of the two orders, the Macrodasyoidea are exclusively marine, as are the families Neodasyidae and Xenotrichulidae of the Chaetonotoidea; the majority of the remaining Chaetonotoidea are in fresh water.

Gastrotrichs are elongate animals that move by means of cilia or cirri on the flattened ventral surface. The body is covered by a cuticle that generally forms scales or spines, or both. The animals are provided with cuticular adhesive tubules that are used for anchorage to the substratum.

Food, which consists of bacteria, organic detritus, and diatoms, is ingested by the sucking action of the muscular pharynx.

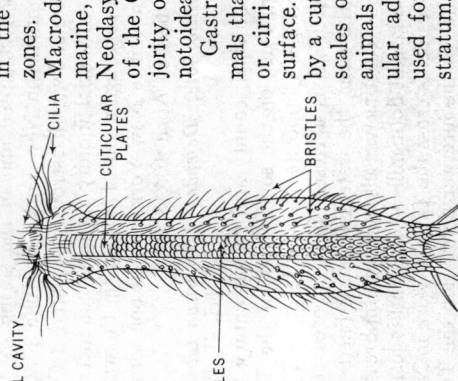

ORAL CAVITY — CILIA — CUTICULAR PLATES — SCALES — BRISTLES

FROM "ZEITSCHRIFT FÜR WISSENSCHAFT"
EXTERNAL FEATURES OF A CHAETONOTID (CHAETONOTUS MAXIMUS)

The pharynx is triradiate, resembling that of the roundworms. The pharynx of the Macrodasyoidea is provided with a pair of pores communicating with the exterior. The intestine is simple. The body cavity, presumably a pseudocoel, contains the excretory organs, the protonephridia.

The Macrodasyoidea are all hermaphroditic, the male and female organs occurring in the same individual. The Neodasyidae, the Xenotrichulidae, and a few species of Chaetonotidae are also hermaphroditic. The remaining Chaetonotoidea, known only as parthenogenetic females, bear eggs that develop without having been fertilized. Gonads are either paired or single. Among Macrodasyoidea, a seminal receptacle and copulatory bursa may be present in the female system and a penis in the male system. Two types of eggs are known for fresh-water gastrotrichs: tachyblastic eggs, which begin cleavage immediately, and opsiblastic eggs, which remain inactive for long periods of time. Opsiblastic eggs can survive drying and freezing. (MN. S.)

GATCHINA, a town of the Leningrad Oblast in the Russian Soviet Federated Socialist Republic of the U.S.S.R., lies 28 mi. (45 km.) south-southwest of Leningrad on the railway and road to Pskov and Riga. Pop. (1969 est.) 57,000. The village of Khotchino was founded there in the 15th century, but the town grew only after the building, between 1766 and 1772, of a summer palace for Catherine II, who presented it in 1783 to her son, later Paul I, by whom it was transformed into a combination of palace, fortress, and barracks. The palace, which had about 600 rooms, including three throne rooms and a theatre, was designed by the Italian architect A. Rinaldi and was surrounded by a fine park; although badly damaged during World War II, it was restored and is now a museum. Gatchina was renamed Trotsk (1923–29) and until 1944 was called Krasnogvardeisk. The modern town is a major railway junction, where the Pskov line is crossed by the Narva–Volkhov outer ring railway of Leningrad. It has factories making machinery for the paper industry and tractor repair shops. (R. A. F.)

GATES, HORATIO (c. 1727–1806), American Revolutionary general, was born in England in 1727. He entered the army and served in America in the French and Indian War. Emerging from the war as a major, he returned to England, but in 1772 migrated to the region that is now West Virginia. Gates sympathized with colonial complaints against the crown and in 1775 was made adjutant general of the continental army. In 1776 he commanded the troops retreating from the unsuccessful invasion of Canada. The next year he superseded Gen. Philip Schuyler in northern New York and in the two battles of Saratoga his army forced Gen. John Burgoyne to surrender, largely, however, because of the previous maneuvers of Schuyler and the initiative of Gen. Benedict Arnold.

Congress elected Gates president of the board of war and at the same time a group of army officers, among them Gen. Thomas Conway, inspired some thoughts of replacing Washington with Gates. The "Conway cabal" soon collapsed and in the spring of 1778 Gates returned to his command in New York. In June 1780 he was transferred to the south and was disastrously defeated at Camden, S.C., on Aug. 16. An official inquiry into his conduct was quashed but Gates did not serve again until 1782. After the war he emancipated his slaves, moved to New York, served one term in the state legislature and died on April 10, 1806.

See S. W. Patterson, *Horatio Gates: Defender of American Liberties* (1941).

(H. H. P.)

GATESHEAD, a municipal, county and parliamentary borough of County Durham, Eng., on the south bank of the Tyne (crossed there by five bridges), opposite Newcastle upon Tyne. Pop. (1971 prelim.) 94,457. It is a closely built-up area rising steeply to 538 ft. above the river, the waterside being lined with wharves and quays used by coasting vessels and for shipbreaking and repairing. One of the largest flour mills in England is located there. Many Gateshead residents cross the Tyne to work in Newcastle, but as a consequence of the interwar depression the Team Valley trading estate, an area of 700 ac., was developed after 1936 in the southwestern part of the borough, where there was established a great variety of small-scale industries including light engineering (pumps, microswitches, light sheet metal), clothing and packaging. Gateshead has iron, steel and engineering works, and coal mines in the vicinity. There is a large technical college specializing in engineering.

Gateshead probably grew up during Saxon times, and Saxon grave covers are preserved in the present church of St. Mary. Except for a short period, the town was under the control of the bishop of Durham, who exercised the right of appointing the keeper of Gateshead tower on the 13th-century stone bridge across the Tyne. The first charter was granted by Bishop Hugh de Puiset (Pudsey) in 1164. The common seal of the borough was mentioned in 1480, but under Edward VI Gateshead was merged for a time with Newcastle. The bishops of Durham incorporated nearly all the trades of Gateshead, and Oliver Cromwell continued this policy. As part of the palatinate of Durham, Gateshead was not represented in parliament until 1832. The county borough was created in 1889 and returns two members to parliament.

St. Mary's church dates mainly from the 14th century, but there was extensive restoration in 1854 after a fire which destroyed much of the town. Holy Trinity church, rebuilt in 1837, incorporates the south aisle of the 13th-century monastic chapel. The Shipley art gallery was opened in 1917. The Saltwell Park museum, opened in 1933, has exhibits relating to local antiquities and industries and a natural history collection.

GATH, one of the five royal cities of the Philistines, the exact location of which in modern Israel has not been determined. The name occurs several times in the Old Testament, especially in connection with the history of David. Goliath, the Philistine champion, hailed from Gath. Rehoboam is said to have fortified Gath, but Uzziah found it still a Philistine city. The records of Sargon II of Assyria show that he took it in 712 B.C. Gath was evidently a place of importance, a walled city (II Chron. xxvi, 6), but its exact location has been lost since the time of Sennacherib. The *Onomasticon* of Eusebius fixes the site near the Roman road five miles from Eleutheropolis (Beit Jibrin) on the way to Diospolis (Lydda). On this road within three miles of the point indicated stands Tell es-Safi, a small mud village on a hill about 300 ft. high. The position of the village at Tell es-Safi has precluded a complete survey, but the excavations carried out there have, on the whole, proved disappointing and rendered the identification with Gath highly questionable. This and the fact that the sister Philistine cities do not occupy sites naturally strong, but are merely mounds on the plain, make it probable that Gath is rather to be sought in the coastal plain west of Judah. Two sites have been proposed: Tell el-Menshiyeh (Sheikh Ahmed el Areini), by W. F. Albright, and more recently Tell en Nejileh farther south. Excavations directed in the former site by S. Yeivin prove the importance of the site but have not yielded clear evidence for its identification with

Gath. Work directed by Ruth Amiran (1962) at Nejileh has directly refuted the identification with Gath.

(W. F. A.)

GATINEAU, a river of southwestern Quebec, Canada, and long a highway for lumber trade, rises in a chain of large lakes due north of latitude 48° N. and continues southwesterly until it merges into the Ottawa river, about one mile below the city of Ottawa. This is one of the main sites of hydroelectric power development in Canada.

GATLING, RICHARD JORDAN (1818–1903), U.S. inventor for whom the Gatling gun was named, was born in Hertford county, N.C., Sept. 12, 1818. He assisted his father in the construction and perfecting of machines for sowing cotton seeds and for thinning the plants. In 1839 he perfected a practical screw propeller for steamboats, only to find that a patent had been granted to John Ericsson for a similar invention a few months earlier. He established himself in St. Louis, Mo., in 1844, and taking the cotton-sowing machine as a basis he adapted it for sowing rice, wheat and other grains. The introduction of these machines did much to revolutionize the agricultural system in the country.

Becoming interested in the study of medicine through an attack of smallpox, he completed a course at the Ohio Medical college in 1850. In the same year he invented a hemp-breaking machine, and in 1857 a steam plow. At the outbreak of the Civil War he devoted himself at once to the perfecting of firearms. In 1861 he conceived the idea of the rapid fire machine gun which is associated with his name. By 1862 he had succeeded in perfecting a gun that would discharge 350 shots per minute; but the war was practically over before the federal authorities consented to its official adoption. Gatling died in New York city, Feb. 26, 1903.

See MACHINE GUN.

GATTY, MARGARET (1809–1873), English writer for children, daughter of Nelson's friend and secretary, the Rev. Alexander John Scott, was born, June 3, 1809, at Burnham, Essex. Her mother died young and her father, a book collector and antiquarian, gave her a sound education. In 1839 she married Alfred Gatty, vicar of Ecclesfield, Yorkshire, where the rest of her life was spent. She died on Oct. 4, 1873. The qualities which gave vitality and charm to Mrs. Gatty's careful etchings, and which made her an exact naturalist, are intermittently apparent in her best-known work, *Parables From Nature* (five series, 1855–71); this was modeled on Hans Christian Andersen's tales and, in spite of uncompromisingly stated "morals," reflects something of his poetry. Her own etchings illustrated the first and second series. Among other publications were *Aunt Judy's Magazine* (1859). In 1866 she began to edit *Aunt Judy's Magazine*, which contained stories and verses; one of the magazine's regular contributors was her daughter, Juliana Ewing (q.v.).

(M. C. Cr.)

GAUCHO, a free-spirited vagabond herder of cattle who flourished in the unfenced *pampa* or grasslands of Argentina, Uruguay and Paraguay from the 18th century until late in the 19th and who remains imaginatively vivid as a lovable, romantic folk hero. Workers on cattle ranches in the region still claim the title and wear the traditional gaucho costume.

Since the earliest Spanish settlements, escaped cattle and horses enjoyed a huge open environment on the pampas, free from predators and competition, and their numbers increased extraordinarily. Soon some of the mestizo (half-breed) offspring of Spaniards and Indians found a way of life, by preying on the wild cattle for meat and hides. In the 18th century herds of half-tamed scrub cattle and mules came to be privately owned as the European market for leather grew and as western South America came to depend on the Argentine supply of mules. The gaucho then became less a primitive nomad and more a skilled employee, somewhat resembling the early North American cowboy.

In the latter part of the 19th century the fertile pampas came under the plow, and the land was fenced into huge *estancias*, farmed by European immigrants who were tenants of the owner. Even the pastoral economy was altered to provide more intensive use of the land as purebred cattle, horses and sheep replaced the scrub or mestizo herds and as alfalfa was grown to feed them. The gaucho was doomed, but the traditions of bravery, honour and astuteness remained even after he became a farm hand or peon.

The untrammeled gaucho is depicted faithfully in *Martin Fierro* by Jose Hernández, and the nostalgic story of his demise is told in an equally fine novel, *Don Segundo Sombra* by Ricardo Güiraldes. *See also* ARGENTINA; PAMPAS. (E. R. Se.)

GAUDEN, JOHN (1605–1662), bishop of Worcester, reputed author of *Eikon Basilike* and editor of Richard Hooker (*q.v.*), was born at Mayland, Essex. He graduated in arts at Cambridge, and later became D.D. of Oxford. He tutored the sons of Sir William Russell, of Chippenham, Cambridgeshire, and married their sister. In 1640 he became vicar of Chippenham and chaplain to the earl of Warwick, the parliamentary general and admiral, who secured for him the deanery of Bocking (1641). Gauden's objective sympathies were with the parliament, before which he preached. He probably took the Solemn League and Covenant, certainly conformed to Presbyterianism, yet wrote a number of books and pamphlets on behalf of the Anglican Church and in 1648–49 published a *Religious and Loyal Protestation* against the trial of Charles I. In this ambiguous position he kept all his preferments until 1660 when Charles II made him royal chaplain and bishop of Exeter. He was translated in 1662 to Worcester, where in September he died.

In 1662 Gauden published the eight books of Hooker's *Laws of Ecclesiastical Polity*. The seventh book had never before been seen. Gauden says that he possessed the manuscript, which lacked only Hooker's "last polishing," but omits to say how he got it. It is in serious conflict with the genuine book iii, and its authenticity is therefore much doubted. Its genuineness can be tested only by internal evidence and by consideration of the character of Gauden, which is shown both by his ambiguous career and by his blackmailing letters to the chancellor, the earl of Clarendon, in 1660. He twice demanded preferment on the ground that he and not Charles I had written the *Eikon Basilike*—published and on sale the day after the king's execution and quickly going through 47 editions—"that great secret" known only to the king and his brother and to Clarendon. He pointed out that the book had begot a pious reputation for Charles I and had been an important factor in re-establishing the monarchy. The evidence of these letters renders any other authorship incredible, reinforced as it is by the statement of James, duke of York (afterward James II), to Gilbert Burnet in 1673 that Gauden did write the *Eikon Basilike*.

BIBLIOGRAPHY.—E. Almack, *Bibliography of the King's Book* (1896); F. F. Madan, *A New Bibliography of the Eikon Basilike* (1949–50); John Shirley, *Richard Hooker* (1949). (F. J. Sy.)

GAUDI, ANTONIO (ANTONIO GAUDÍ y CORNET) (1852–1926), Catalan architect, sculptor and ceramic artist, noted for the great freedom and organic unity of his work, was born at Reus, Tarragona, Spain, on June 26, 1852. He studied at the Barcelona school of architecture. Valued early in the 20th century primarily for his "bizarre" imagination, he became appreciated as a great architectural inventor, as a constructor and as a sculptor of organic form. He studied natural form and developed an expressive *art nouveau* by giving vitality to line, space and volume as well as by original constructions (sloping pillars to take diagonal pressure). Barcelona was the centre of this deeply religious man's steadfast and uncompromising life work. For his patron, Count Güell, he built there a town house (1885–89), the "Palace Güell," and "Park Güell" (1900–02). In this last he made brilliant use of raised ground to create a grandiose children's play terrace. This is bounded by a bench formed of swinging curves, which he encrusted with coloured tile mosaics, carrying out, even at that time, the Cubist "collage" principle in ceramic remainders.

The church of the Holy Family (1883–1926) was the problem of his life, and it remains a huge unfinished building, of significant plan, with brilliant tower construction and ornamental figures. Unfinished also was his best monumental building, the Güell colony church at S. Coloma de Cervelló (1898–1914).

Gaudí deserts the original neo-Gothic elements and embodies new constructive ideas. His apartment houses and office buildings in the Paseo Gracia—Casa Batlló (1905–07) and Casa Milá (1905–10)—expound a style which simultaneously exploits façade and space. His fluid lines, the fantastic sculptural imagination of his chimneys and ventilators and the fluctuating iron trelliswork of gates and balconies here reach their highest expression. Gaudí died at Barcelona on June 7, 1926. (C. G.-Wr.)

GAUDIER-BRZESKA, HENRI (1891–1915), Franco-English sculptor, an outstanding exponent of the Vorticist movement, was born at St. Jean-de-Braye, Loire, Oct. 4, 1891, the son of a woodworker, Joseph Gaudier. (The name Brzeska was that of his devoted Polish companion Sophie Brzeska.) Although he was given a scholarship to study art at Bristol, he was largely self-taught. The poet Ezra Pound became his patron and propagandist; the writer and painter Wyndham Lewis drew him into the Vorticist movement just before World War I. The early carvings of Sir Jacob Epstein affected him, but he showed original attitudes toward form and content. He was an admirable linear draftsman. His letters are deeply moving.

Gaudier-Brzeska was killed in combat in World War I at Neuville-St.-Vaast, June 5, 1915. Much of his work is at the South Kensington museum.

BIBLIOGRAPHY.—Ezra Pound, *Gaudier-Brzeska: His Life and Work* (1916); Harold S. Ede, *Savage Messiah* (1931); Horace Brodzky (ed.), *Gaudier-Brzeska, Drawings* (1946). (L. E. K.)

GAUDIN, MARTIN MICHEL CHARLES, DUC DE GAËTE (1756–1841), French finance minister throughout the consulate and the first empire and again in the Hundred Days, was born at St. Denis on Jan. 19, 1756. From 1773 he worked in the *contrôle général des finances* and rose to be a head of the tax department. In 1791, during the Revolution, he was made a member of the commission in charge of the national treasury, but in 1795 he resigned. The Directory twice offered him the ministry of finance (in 1795 and July 1799), but he accepted it only on Nov. 10, 1799, after Napoleon Bonaparte's *coup d'état*. After the immediate financial crisis had been surmounted Gaudin's task remained hard, even though, from 1801, responsibility for funds and payments was taken over by another ministry (that of the *trésor public*). He wanted to preserve the framework of the financial institutions he knew so well, to make them work better and to reject some of the innovations introduced by the Revolution. He created a body of permanent officials to assess and levy direct taxes; and as early as 1800 he wanted to reimpose certain major indirect taxes, though Napoleon, seeing how unpopular this would be, would not allow it until 1804. Gaudin also proposed a fairer distribution of the land tax and, in 1807, helped to introduce the cadastre, a survey and classified register of all the divisions of the soil (this had been authorized in 1791, but not enforced). Painstaking with his own projects and equally conscientious in carrying out those of others, even though he disagreed with them, Gaudin was highly appreciated by Napoleon, who made him duc de Gaëte in 1809.

Under the second Bourbon restoration, Gaudin represented moderate opinion as a deputy for Aisne in the *chambre introuvable* (1815–16) and in the succeeding assembly (1816–18), speaking and writing on financial topics. He was not re-elected in 1819, but was governor of the bank of France from 1820 to 1834. He died at Gennevilliers (Seine) on Nov. 5, 1841. He published his *Mémoires, souvenirs, opinions et écrits*, three volumes, in 1826–34 (new edition 1926).

See R. Stourm, *Les Finances du Consulat* (1902); F. Latour, *Le Grand Argentier de Napoléon: Gaudin…* (1963). (C. E. Du.)

GAUGAMELA, BATTLE OF (also called BATTLE OF ARBELA), Oct. 1, 331 B.C., in which Alexander the Great of Macedonia decisively defeated Darius III of Persia, often quoted as an outstanding example of the tactics of penetration. For the events leading up to the battle and the composition of Alexander's army *see* ALEXANDER III (The Great).

The plain of Gaugamela, northeast of Nineveh (across the Tigris from the modern city of Mosul, Iraq), was chosen by Darius for a battle with Alexander's advancing force because of its suitability for his cavalry, in which he outnumbered Alexander. The figures given by ancient authorities vary, some being quite fantastic. In any case, the Persians outnumbered the Macedonians, who had 40,-000 infantry and 7,000 cavalry, according to Arrian. In front of the Persian line were the chariots, 50 on the right and centre, 100 on the left; the plain had been specially leveled to give them a clear run. Darius was in the centre of the line, with the Greek mercenary and Persian heavy infantry, archers and Persian and Indian cavalry. On the left wing was Bessus, satrap of Bactria, with Bactrian, Scythian and Arachosian cavalry. Mazaeus, formerly satrap of Cilicia, was on the right wing, with Armenian and Cappadocian cavalry. Inferior troops extended the line between centre and wings. Alexander was thus faced with the problem of striking a decisive blow with his heavy infantry and cavalry without being enveloped by the cavalry of the Persian wings or letting the chariots cut up the phalanx.

He took up position on the right wing with the royal squadron or *agema* of cavalry, heading the rest of the Companion cavalry. In front of him were half the archers and Agrianian javelin men to deal with the chariots. Left of the Companion cavalry were the hypaspists ("shield-bearers"), then the heavy infantry phalanx in six battalions. The left wing was composed of Greek and Thessalian cavalry commanded by Parmenio. Because of the danger of encirclement a second infantry line was formed, prepared to face about if necessary, and reserves were placed on each wing at an angle so that they could either extend the line or double back to meet a flank attack. The right reserve consisted of Greek mercenary and Paeonian cavalry and lancers (*prodromoi*), supported by the other half of the archers and Agrianians and veteran mercenaries, the left reserve of Greek and Thracian cavalry. Well behind the army the Thracian infantry guarded the camp where the baggage and prisoners, including Darius' family, had been left.

Alexander led *en échelon* toward the right, away from the leveled ground. Bessus sent out successive troops of Scythian and Bactrian cavalry. The mercenary cavalry engaged them, supported subsequently by the Paeonians, and though outnumbered they stood their ground. Meanwhile, before the phalanx could get clear of the leveled ground, Darius sent out the chariots but the javelin men and archers shot down most of them before they reached the infantry, who opened ranks to let the others pass through. Ordering the lancers to charge the Scythians and Bactrians, Alexander continued to advance to the right. As more of the Persian left was sent in, a gap opened in the Persian left centre. Alexander promptly wheeled half left with the royal squadron and led the Companion cavalry, hypaspists and four phalanx battalions in a charge at the gap. The Persian centre soon broke, Darius leading the flight.

Pursuit was halted by a call for help from Parmenio. Mazaeus' cavalry had attacked the Thessalians and the other two phalanx battalions had halted to support them. Persian and Indian cavalry had ridden through the gap thus made in the phalanx and on to the camp. The second line had however faced about and attacked them from the rear. The retreating Persians and Indians collided with Alexander's relieving force and were driven off after a sharp fight, by which time the Thessalians had also driven off their opponents. Persian losses were heavy: Arrian gives the Macedonian dead as 100, although Diodorus and Curtius give higher figures. Alexander had finally overthrown the Persian empire.

GAUGES AND COMPARATORS

GAUGES AND COMPARATORS are the means by which industry achieves the necessary dimensional control for interchangeable assembly and mass production. Gauges may be classified as indicating and non-indicating. Indicating gauges provide a direct reading of the actual dimensions of a part. Non-indicating gauges are of standard fixed dimensions against which the part or another gauge is compared. Comparators are devices used to compare an unknown part to a standard that might be a master gauge or simply a sample of the part which is known to fit and function correctly in the final assembly.

Gauges and comparators are available in a large variety of forms corresponding to the size and complexity of the item to be measured, the accuracy required, the time allotted to make the measurement, and the ability of the device to measure a wide range of parts.

Interchangeable manufacture was first introduced on an appreciable scale about 1800. Precision gauges and comparators have been extensively developed since about 1850 when Sir Joseph Whitworth produced an original measuring machine and the system of accurate dimensional standards or master gauges for use with it.

Master Gauges.—Gauges used as standards of comparison for measuring the dimensions of inspection gauges are known as master or reference gauges. Typical master gauges are: (1) Precision gauge blocks or slip gauges, whose dimension between two flat, parallel ends is accurately measured and recorded (available in sets of selected lengths of blocks so that all dimensions, within the range of the set, can be produced in increments as small as 0.00005 in.). (For further discussion see METROLOGY: *End Standards: Mode of Calibration*.) (2) End measuring rods in the form of steel bars having flat or spherical ends. (3) Master disks—accurately lapped steel cylinders—frequently preferred to gauge blocks when pieces to be checked by comparators are round. (4) Gauges having composite surfaces, such as screw thread, profile, or spline gauges. (5) Angle gauge blocks in sets of 13 or 16 selected angles, combinations of which are wrung together to produce any angle to 90°, or with additional blocks to 360°. (6) Interferometers—optical devices using the wavelength of a monochromatic light source as the basic unit length. (See INTERFEROMETER.)

Limit Gauges.—The reproduction of dimensions of mechanical parts within specified limits, or tolerances, is facilitated by checking with gauges, such as a "go" gauge representing the maximum-metal limit and a "no go" gauge representing the minimum-metal limit. Limit gauges are also known as inspection or working gauges.

Dial Indicator Gauges.—Dial indicators provide the measuring contact and the mechanical amplifying mechanism necessary to provide a direct dimensional reading to high precision. A typical dial indicator gauge has a flat, fixed surface, called the anvil or reference contact, at one end of a frame and the sensitive contact and dial mechanism at the other. The sensitive contact is free to respond to the size of the work piece being measured and transmits the response through a network of gears which amplify the motion and turn a dial. For instance, the dial may go through one complete revolution while the sensitive contact has moved only 0.008 in. Mechanical configurations can vary to allow measurement of such dimensions as outside diameter, inside diameter, hole location, hole depth, and screw thread pitch diameter. They can be bench mounted or portable.

Air Gauges.—A precision pneumatic micrometer or air gauge was invented by Marcel Menneson of France in 1928. In its most common form, the air gauge consists of a cylindrical plug which is somewhat smaller than the hole to be measured and which has diametrically opposed orifices through which compressed air is forced. The plug is first inserted in a ring gauge of known size, and then in the piece to be measured. The difference in pressure or in rate of flow of the air in the two cases is indicated by a pressure gauge which is calibrated to yield measurements of differences in sizes as small as 0.000005 in. A useful variation of this technique provides the means for determining clearance or interference of mating parts directly on one dial. In this case, air is forced through a plug and also through a ring. One part is placed in gauging position—e.g., in the ring—and various mating pieces may be checked in turn with the plug until the proper clearance reading is obtained. Air probes operating under the same principle can be used interchangeably with dial indicators where applications require non-contacting probes.

Electronic Gauges.—Electronic gauges provide the capability to measure at very high speeds and to accuracies of 0.000001 in. The gauge head is designed to provide an output voltage which is linearly proportional to the movement of the sensitive contact. This basic signal can be processed electronically to allow one head to provide readings magnified from 500 to 15,000 times and can be used to operate switches, should tolerances exceed predetermined limits.

Automatic Gauging.—Combinations of air and electronic gauges are most frequently found in automatic gauging equipment. One example of an automatic gauging system is one that can make single measurements on as many as 42,000 pieces per hour, measuring differences in increments as small as 0.00001 in. and sorting the pieces into as many as 22 different categories. Another example is a system that can make 11 different measurements to different accuracies on a given part at the rate of 2,000 parts per hour. If any of the 11 dimensions exceeds the prescribed tolerance, the entire part is rejected.

Comparators.—These provide a means to measure the difference between the test object and the standard. Large horizontal comparators, commonly called measuring machines, are built on massive steel or cast-iron beds provided with straight, flat ways on which are mounted a headstock and a tailstock. Devices are provided in the tailstock to ensure constant contact pressure of the anvil to the workpiece. The headstock holds one of the gauging heads that provide magnification of the measurement. Vertical comparators or height gauges use a substantial surface plate as the anvil. The gauge head is adjustably mounted on a vertical column. Both types are made in many sizes and accuracies.

Projection Comparators.—The measurement and comparison of irregularly shaped objects is facilitated by optical projection methods developed during and after World War I by the National Physical Laboratory in London and the National Bureau of Standards in Washington, D.C. Basically, the object to be compared is backlighted by an intense light source and its shadow is projected through a magnifying optical system onto a large viewing screen. The magnified image may be measured directly on the screen or compared against a detailed engineering drawing of the part or a standard part where the drawing or standard is magnified to the same scale and projected on the same screen. Stereo viewing techniques prove helpful in making direct comparisons.

Coordinate Measuring Machines.—Since the advent of numerically controlled machine tools around 1950, complicated parts can be produced at a rapid rate. First-piece inspection is required before production can continue, yet classical measurement techniques take so long that expensive machinery is idle. Thus, the need for a rapid means to measure all dimensional parameters is solved by the coordinate measuring machine (CMM). In the simplest case, the CMM consists of a flat table to support a workpiece and a movable head or carriage. A probe is attached to the head to measure the distance between two points in three dimensions. One merely contacts one point with the probe and then the other. As the head moves between the two points, its displacement along three mutually perpendicular axes is determined. Movement of the head along one axis in the horizontal plane is considered to be along the x-axis. Movement in the horizontal plane perpendicular to the x-axis is considered to be along the y-axis. Movement in the vertical plane is along the so-called z-axis. Readout of the head's motion is provided by dial indicators, scales, or digital displays.

The measuring system for digital display may employ inductive gratings, optical diffraction gratings, master lead screws, or laser interferometers, depending on the accuracies required.

CMM's range in accuracy from 0.001 to 0.000001 in. and in size from 6-in. to 20-ft. travel. Some are manual, some are numerically controlled, and others are operated directly by computers.

BIBLIOGRAPHY.—*Annual Reports of the National Physical Laboratory* (London); F. H. Rolt, *Gages and Fine Measurements,* 2 vol. (1929); International Business Machines Corporation, *Precision Measurement in the Metal-Working Industry,* 2 vol. (1942–44); J. E. Sears, *Precise Length Measurements,* Cantor Lectures, Royal Society of Arts (1923); National Physical Laboratory, *Engineering Dimensional Metrology,* 2 vol. (1955); C. Chandler, *Modern Interferometers* (1950); K. J. Habell and A. Cox, *Engineering Optics* (1948); "Coordinate Measuring Machines: a New Generation of Inspection Equipment," *Quality Assurance,* pp. 18–24 (March 1967); O. W. Ehrhardt, "New Face of Metrology: Its Impact on the Machine Tool Industry. Part 2. Measuring to Millionths," *The Tool and Manufacturing Engineer* (Aug. 1966); P. N. Budziiovich, "Lasers Boost Machine Tool Accuracy," *Control Engineering,* pp. 62–65 (Dec. 1968); C. W. Kennedy, "Inspection and Gauging," *Industrial Press,* rev. ed. (1962); S. Minkowitz, "Industrial Laser in Interferometry," *Optical Spectra* (May/June 1968); D. A. Worth, "How Far and How Straight," *Industrial Research* (Aug. 1969). (Do. A. W.)

GAUGUIN, (EUGÈNE HENRI) PAUL (1848–1903), leading French painter of the Postimpressionist period, was born in Paris on June 7, 1848, the son of a journalist from Orléans and of a mother who was half French and half Peruvian-creole. After Napoleon III's *coup d'état* the Gauguin family moved (1851) to Lima, Peru, and four years later Paul and his mother returned to Orléans. At the age of 17 he went to sea and for six years sailed about the world in freighters or men-of-war. In 1871 he joined the stockbroking firm of Bertin in Paris, and in 1873 married a Danish girl, Mette-Sophie Gad. His artistic leanings were first aroused by his guardian, Gustave Arosa, whose collection included pictures by Corot, Delacroix and Millet, and by a fellow stockbroker, Émile Schuffenecker, with whom he started painting. Gauguin soon took his hobby seriously and started going in his spare time to an *atelier libre* to draw from a model and receive tuition. In 1876 his "Landscape at Viroflay" was accepted for the Salon. He developed a taste for Impressionist painting, and between 1876 and 1881 assembled an impressive group of paintings by Manet, Cézanne, Pissarro, Monet and Jongkind.

Gauguin met Camille Pissarro in 1875–76 and began to work with him, struggling to master the techniques of drawing and painting. In 1880 he was invited to contribute to the fifth Impressionist exhibition, and this invitation was repeated in 1881 and 1882. He spent painting holidays with Pissarro and Paul Cézanne and made visible progress, though his early works are often marred by clumsiness and have drab colouring. Gauguin thus became more and more absorbed by painting until, in 1883, he decided to abandon his job to be free "to paint every day." This was a decision which changed the course of his whole life. He had a wife and four children to look after, but he had no income and no one would buy his paintings. In 1884 Gauguin and his family moved to Copenhagen, where his wife's parents proved unsympathetic and his marriage broke up. He returned to Paris in 1885, destitute and despairing but determined to sacrifice everything for his artistic vocation. From then on he was destined to live in penury and discomfort; his health was undermined by hardship and privation; he became an outcast from the society to which he had belonged and could never establish himself in any other; and he came to despise Europe and civilization.

In 1886 the expressive possibilities of colour were revealed to him in the pictures of Georges Seurat and Paul Signac, and he began to occupy himself with this aspect of painting at Pont-Aven, Brittany. Gauguin then had two decisive experiences: a meeting with Vincent van Gogh in Paris (1886) and a journey to Martinique (1887). The one brought him into contact with a passionate personality who had similar pictorial ideas and tried to involve him in working them out communally; this attempt came to a disastrous end after a few weeks together at Arles in 1888. The other enabled Gauguin to discover for himself the brilliant colouring and sensuous delights of a tropical landscape and to experience the charm of a primitive community living the "natural" life. Gauguin took a great step forward at this time when he decided to seek through painting an emotional release, in consequence of which he reacted against Impressionism. The key to his artistic attitude from 1888 on is to be found in these significant phrases: "Primitive

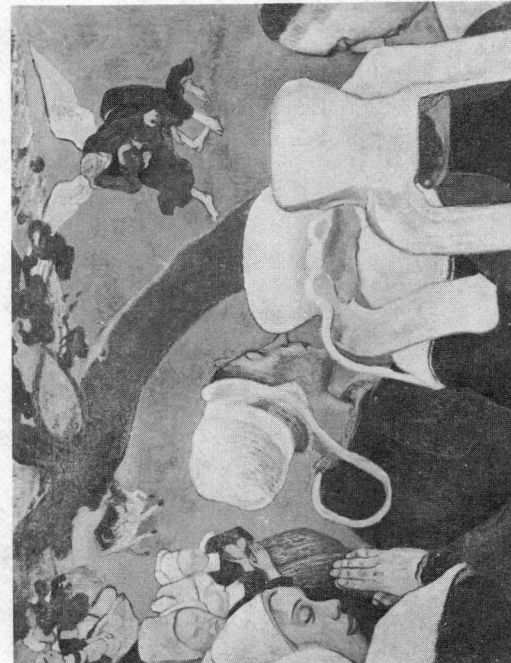

BY COURTESY OF NATIONAL GALLERY OF SCOTLAND, EDINBURGH

"THE VISION AFTER THE SERMON" BY PAUL GAUGUIN; 1888. IN THE NATIONAL GALLERY OF SCOTLAND, EDINBURGH

GAUGUIN

art proceeds from the spirit and makes use of nature. The so-called refined art proceeds from sensuality and serves nature. Nature is the servant of the former and the mistress of the latter. She demeans man's spirit by allowing him to adore her. That is the way by which we have tumbled into the abominable error of naturalism." Gauguin therefore set out to redeem this error by "a reasoned and frank return to the beginning, that is to say to primitive art." A possible method for arriving at a new form of pictorial representation was suggested to him by Émile Bernard, a young artist well acquainted with stained glass, manuscripts and folk art. He pointed out that in these arts reality was generally depicted in nonimitative terms and that the pictorial image was made up of areas of pure colour separated by heavy black outlines. Such was the origin of the style known as *cloisonnisme* or *synthétisme*, which attained its most expressive possibilities in Gauguin's paintings such as "The Vision After the Sermon" (1888), "Bonjour Monsieur Gauguin" and "The Yellow Christ" (1889).

When Gauguin broke with his Impressionistic past he gave up using lines and colours to fool the eye into accepting the flat painted image as a re-creation of an actual scene, and explored instead the capacity of these pictorial means to induce in a spectator a particular feeling. His forms became ideated and his colours suggestive abstractions. Maurice Denis (*Theories*, 1920) describes a small painting executed by Paul Sérusier under Gauguin's direction in 1889. This landscape seemed to "have no form as a result of being synthetically represented in violet, vermilion, Veronese green and other pure colours. 'How does that tree appear to you?' Gauguin had asked. 'It's green isn't it? All right, do it in green, the finest green on your palette. And that shadow? Isn't it blue? Well then, don't be frightened of making it as blue as possible.' Thus (writes Denis) was presented to us for the first time, in a paradoxical but unforgettable manner, the fertile conception of a painting as 'a flat surface covered with colours arranged in a certain order.' "

Gauguin indulged in "primitivism" because he could make a more

BY COURTESY OF THE METROPOLITAN MUSEUM OF ART, GIFT OF WILLIAM CHURCH OSBORN, 1949

"TWO TAHITIAN WOMEN." BY PAUL GAUGUIN. IN THE METROPOLITAN MUSEUM OF ART, NEW YORK

easily intelligible image; his simple colour harmonies intensified this image; and, because he wanted his pictures to be pleasing to the eye, he aimed at a decorative effect. His purpose in all this was to express pictorially an "idea." Gauguin's whole work is a protest against the soul-destroying materialism of bourgeois civilization. "Civilization that makes you suffer. Barbarism which is to me rejuvenation," he wrote (1891) to Strindberg. So Gauguin installed himself in Brittany (Pont-Aven and Le Pouldu, 1889-90, 1894), Tahiti (1891-93, 1895-1901) and the Marquesas Islands (1901-03), where he could paint scenes of "natural" men and women living with their fears, faiths, myths and primitive passions.

Before 1891, Gauguin tended to flatten things deliberately and his effect was often strained, but throughout the 1890s his "primitivism" became less aggressive as the influences of J. A. D. Ingres and Puvis de Chavannes led to increasingly rounded and modeled forms and a more sinuous line. This process can be followed in works such as "Nafea Faa Ipoipo" (When shall we be married?; 1892), "Nave Nave Mahana" (Holiday; 1896) and "Golden Bodies" (1901). Simultaneously Gauguin's images became more luxuriant, and naturally poetic, as he developed his marvellously orchestrated tonal harmonies. His chief Tahitian work is an immense canvas painted in 1897-98 in the belief that he would be dead before its discovery. This is the consummate expression of much that he had painted in the previous six years, and the aura of dreamlike, poetic inconsequence which surrounds this semiphilosophical allegory of primitive life is more powerful than in any other of his canvases.

From 1899 on Gauguin became increasingly ill and was continually in pain; he was also involved in frequent rows with the governing authorities for siding with the natives against them. Yet despite melancholy, his last pictures still have serenity and hope. He died a miserable death at Atuana (Marquesas) on May 8, 1903.

Gauguin was unique in his ability to hold a mysterious balance between idea, perception and visual image, and his pictures make their effect visually, not as a result of literary overtones. He was a great stylistic innovator and, when he rejected the conception of a picture as a mirror-image of an actual scene and turned from an empirical to a conceptual method of pictorial representation, his step was decisive for the developments in art during the first half of the 20th century. In 1889-90 a group of young followers gathered round him at Pont-Aven, including Sérusier, Charles Filiger and Denis, who transmitted Gauguin's ideas to J. E. Vuillard and P. Bonnard, the initiators of the Nabi movement. Edvard Munch too owed much to Gauguin, as did the Fauves—Matisse in particular—who profited from his use of colour. Gauguin's "primitivism" and stylistic simplifications greatly affected the young Picasso, led to the aesthetic appreciation of Negro art and hence to the evolution of Cubism. In Germany, too, Gauguin's influence was very strong, notably on the artists of the Brücke and Blauer Reiter groups.

Gauguin's own writings include: *Les Guêpes* and *Le Sourire*, Tahitian periodicals (1899-1900); *Racontars d'un Rapin* (1902); *The Letters of Paul Gauguin to Georges Daniel Monfreid* (English translation, 1923); *Noa-Noa* (1924); *Letters to Ambroise Vollard and André Fontainas* (English translation, 1943); *Paul Gauguin: Letters to His Wife and Friends* (English translation, 1948); *Ancien Culte Mahorie* (1951); *Avant et Après* (translated as *The Intimate Journals of Paul Gauguin*, new edition, 1952). See also references under "Gauguin, (Eugène Henri) Paul" in the Index.

BIBLIOGRAPHY.—C. Morice, *Paul Gauguin* (1920); J. de Rotonchamp, *Paul Gauguin* (1925); A. Alexandre, *Paul Gauguin . . .* (1930); R. Burnett, *The Life of Paul Gauguin* (1936); Pola R. Gauguin, *My Father, Paul Gauguin* (1937); C. Chassé, *Le Mouvement symboliste . . .* (1947); J. Rewald, *Post-Impressionism* (1956); *Gauguin, Sa Vie, Son Oeuvre*, special number of *Gazette des Beaux-Arts*, series 6, vol. xlvii (1958); H. R. Rookmaaker, *Synthetist Art Theories* (1959); Bengt Danielsson, *Gauguin in the South Seas* (1964); Jean Loize (ed.), *Noa-Noa Authentique* (1966).
(Ds. Cr.)

GAUHATI, headquarters town of Kamrup district, Assam, India, lies mainly on the left or south, but partly on the right bank of the Brahmaputra. Pop. (1961) 100,707. It is picturesquely situated with an amphitheatre of wooded hills to the south. At the foot of Sukleswar hillock are several large tanks and monuments.

Much frequented places of Hindu pilgrimage are the temples of Kamakhya (on a hill 2 mi. W. of the town) and Umananda on a rocky island in the Brahmaputra. Other temples include those of Aswakranta, Nabagraha and the Basistha Ashram.

Gauhati is an important centre of river trade and the largest seat of commerce in Assam. An oil refinery and a state farm are located there. It is the site of Gauhati university (1948) with seven of its colleges, the state high court, state museum and zoological garden. There are air connections with Calcutta (from Borjhar airport) and rail connections with Calcutta and Chittagong.

As Pragjyotishpur, it was the capital of the ancient Hindu kingdom of Kamarupa (c. A.D. 400). During the 17th century Gauhati was taken and retaken by Muslims and Ahoms eight times in 50 years, but in 1681 it became the residence of the Ahom governor of lower Assam, and in 1786 the capital of the Ahom raja. From 1816 it was occupied by the Burmese, but on the cession of Assam to the British in 1826 it was made the seat of the British administration of Assam, and so continued till 1874, when the headquarters were moved to Shillong (67 mi.) with which Gauhati is connected by a good motor road.

GAUL, WILLIAM GILBERT (1855–1919), U.S. artist known for his American Civil War scenes, was born in Jersey City, N.J., on March 31, 1855. He was a pupil of J. G. Brown and L. E. Wilmarth, and he became a painter of military pictures. He was elected an associate of the National Academy of Design in 1880, and in 1882 a full academician, and in the latter year became a member of the Society of American Artists. His important works include "Charging the Battery," "News From Home," "Cold Comfort on the Outpost," "Silenced," "On the Look-out" and "Guerrillas Returning From a Raid." He died in New York city, Dec. 21, 1919.

GAUL (Lat. GALLIA), the name of the two chief districts where Romans encountered the Celts, namely (1) Gallia Cisalpina, that is, the Po valley of northern Italy; and (2) Gallia Transalpina, usually called Gallia simply—i.e., the land bounded by the Alps, the Mediterranean, the Pyrenees, the Atlantic and the Rhine (France and Belgium with parts of Germany, Holland and Switzerland). This article deals with Gallia Transalpina; for Gallia Cisalpina, see GAUL, CISALPINE.

Transalpine Gaul first entered Greco-Roman history about 600 B.C. with the foundation by Greeks from Phocaea of Massilia (Marseilles), from which Greek pottery and other goods were carried up the Rhône and Saône rivers: a startling example is the great 6th-century Greek bronze crater found in 1953 near Châtillon-sur-Seine. From about 400 B.C. Rome was allied with Massilia, which later protected the vital Roman communications with Spain. But the Massiliots found it increasingly difficult to resist raids by tribes of the interior, and in the late 2nd century the Romans intervened more decisively. The Ligurian tribes of the Isère valley were conquered by 123 B.C., when the fortress of Aquae Sextiae (Aix-en-Provence) was founded. Two years later Gnaeus Domitius Ahenobarbus and Q. Fabius Maximus defeated the Allobroges of Savoy and the powerful Arverni of the Auvergnat and formed the province of Gallia Transalpina, the provincia that gave its name to Provence. In 118 Narbo Martius (Narbonne) was founded as a Roman colony, and a vast influx of Roman businessmen began. Trade flowed outside the province across to the Garonne valley and the sea, as well as northward to central and northern Gaul. The provincia was quickly romanized and was consistently loyal to Julius Caesar (q.v.) during his governorship.

Caesar's Commentaries provide fairly full information about pre-Roman Gaul. The provincia apart, Gaul was at that time divided among three more or less distinct peoples, the Aquitani, the Gauls proper "who call themselves Celts," and the Belgae, occupying respectively the south, the centre and the north of the country between the Pyrenees and the Rhine. There were numerous tribes and constant intertribal rivalries and contesting factions within each tribe. It was a faction within Rome's old allies the Aedui (q.v.) and their struggle for primacy among their neighbours which chiefly enabled Caesar to gain a foothold in Gaul; and it was only by a remarkable feat of initiative that Vercingetorix was able to unite the great majority of tribes in his ill-fated attempt to undo the Roman conquest in 52 B.C. (See also CELT and articles on particular tribes; e.g., ARVERNI, HELVETII, SEQUANI.)

The Gallic wars of Caesar brought Roman territory up to the Atlantic, the English channel and the Rhine. The organization was left to Augustus, who established four provinces, namely Narbonensis (the old provincia) together with Aquitania, Lugdunensis and Belgica, these last three collectively called the Tres Galliae ("three Gauls") or Gallia Comata ("long-haired Gaul"). Aquitania extended north to the Loire and east (beyond the Aquitani proper) to take in the Arverni; Lugdunensis (so called from its capital, Lugdunum, Lyons) lay between the Loire and Seine rivers; and Belgica stretched from the Seine to the Rhine, including the Low Countries in the north and the Helvetian territory in the south. (For the adjacent Rhine camps and the later province of Germania Superior see GERMANY: History.) Narbonensis was governed by a proconsul appointed by the senate, and each of the Tres Galliae by an imperial legate of praetorian standing. The only garrison was a single cohort at Lugdunum to guard the imperial mint, but the Rhine army could and did move rapidly into the Tres Galliae if trouble occurred.

Narbonensis, the land between the Alps, the sea and the Cévennes mountains, was in climate and history markedly different from the rest of Gaul. It had attracted a large number of Roman immigrants, both veterans and traders, and under the empire was a land of cities, said by Pliny the Elder to be "Italy rather than a province." Caesar had sent veterans to Arelate (Arles), Augustus to Arausio (Orange); and both Aquae Sextiae (Aix) and Forum Iulii (Fréjus) were colonies of one or the other ruler. But most towns, such as Nemausus (Nîmes; see VOLCAE), Vienna (Vienne; see ALLOBROGES) or Tolosa (Toulouse), received only Latin rights initially, though some, notably Vienna, were promoted later to full Roman status. Splendid public buildings were erected, many of which have left impressive remains. Vines and olives were grown in profusion, and the country's wealth was increased by the development of industries, particularly in timber and specialized metalwork. Narbonensis was the birthplace of several men prominent in Roman public life. Agricola came from Forum Iulii, and it has been conjectured that his son-in-law, the historian Tacitus, was also Narbonese. The high level of culture in the province was famous, particularly the schooling provided at Massilia.

Perhaps the greatest contrast in the Tres Galliae lies in the survival of the old tribal organization. Lugdunum, founded as a Roman colony in 43 B.C., served as common capital of all three provinces, and Augusta Treverorum (Trier) became a colony under Augustus; other towns on the Roman model included Burdigala (Bordeaux), already a flourishing port in Augustus' time), Augustodunum (Autun) and Augustonemetum (Clermont-Ferrand), but these were exceptional. Other urban centres, like Lutetia Parisiorum (Paris), attained some dignity as time went on, but they were not necessarily inhabited by the tribal magistrates.

It is the tribes, not the towns, whose memory is perpetuated in modern place names: compare Bourges, Chartres, Reims, Sens, Soissons, the centres respectively of the Bituriges, Carnutes, Remi, Senones and Suessiones. Hill forts like the Aeduan Bibracte (q.v.) were of course too dangerous to Rome and had to be abandoned; and the ancient power of the Druids was weakened. But there was no interference with religious observance save that human sacrifice was prohibited and that the imperial cult was promoted, notably in the annual meeting of tribal dignitaries at Lugdunum. Roman names were applied to Celtic gods, but local customs and language survived; as late as the 3rd century the Celtic leuga ("league") was reintroduced instead of the Roman mile on local milestones. All opposition to Roman rule disappeared early. A rising led by romanized nobles of the Aedui and Treveri was quickly crushed in A.D. 21. The revolt in 68 by Julius Vindex, the Aquitanian-born governor of Lugdunensis, was directed against Nero rather than against Rome, and the imperium Galliarum proclaimed by the states that joined the movement of Civilis (q.v.) next year was frustrated by the very states that had supported Vindex. Meanwhile Roman citizenship had been conferred on numerous individuals, and in A.D. 48 the emperor Claudius admitted certain Aeduan nobles to the Roman senate, where they were soon followed by men from other tribes.

Economic development owed most to the proximity of the Rhine camps and to the efficient system of communications, based partly on the waterways and partly on the roads radiating from Lugdunum. Winegrowing spread rapidly. In Augustus' day it was confined in Narbonensis, but by the 2nd century vineyards were abundant in Burgundy and along the Moselle river. Equally important was the growth of a pottery industry, which competed successfully against Italian wares both inside and outside Gaul. In south Gaul, La Graufesenque near Rodez put its pottery on the market as early as the reign of Tiberius (A.D. 14–37) and by A.D. 79 was actually exporting to Campania (a crate of La Graufesenque ware was found at Pompeii). More famous later were the products of Lezoux in the Auvergnat, the common ware of the late 1st and 2nd centuries A.D. Livestock products went to Rome from as far as northern Belgica, and Gallic textiles and metal goods found a market not only in the Rhine army but in "free" Germany.

The exactions of the Severan emperors (late 2nd–early 3rd centuries) bore heavily on the Gallic communities, and it was then that the villa, a protection to its owner, began to grow at the expense of towns. The process became more rapid when the frontiers began to break down. In 257 (probably) the Franks crossed into Gaul in great numbers; and when the situation was restored, an independent though romanized state was set up under Postumus, who from Trier exercised authority over Gaul, Spain and Britain. In 268 Spain and Narbonensis fell away and acknowledged Claudius II, but it was not till 273 or 274 that Aurelian recovered the rest of Gaul from Tetricus. The late 3rd century saw the rise of the Bagaudae, brigands who reflect the disorder and economic troubles of the age. Under Diocletian and his colleagues conditions improved. Gaul like other parts of the empire was divided into numerous small provinces, and Constantius Chlorus ruled all of them (together with Britain) from Trier. Fresh invasions of Alamanni and Franks were with difficulty beaten back by Julian, who in 358 allowed the Salian Franks to settle in Toxandria in the Scheldt valley. Yet the frontiers were precariously held till the great invasions of Vandals and other tribes at the end of 406. Even then Gaul remained a bastion of Roman civilization. A Roman general, Aetius (q.v.), led his Gothic and Frankish allies to victory over Attila in 451, and the classical literary tradition was kept alive in this last period of the empire by Ausonius, Symmachus, Sidonius Apollinaris and other Gallic writers, who bear witness to the high level of culture surviving in their days.

See also references under "Gaul" in the Index.

BIBLIOGRAPHY.—The comprehensive work of C. Jullian, *Histoire de la Gaule*, in 8 vol. (1908–26), is still fundamental; as also, on Caesar's campaigns, is T. Rice Holmes, *Caesar's Conquest of Gaul*, 2nd ed. (1911). *See* also M. Rostovtzeff, *Social and Economic History of the Roman Empire*, 2nd ed., ch. 6 (1957); A. Grenier in T. Frank, *An Economic Survey of Ancient Rome*, vol. iii (1937); O. Brogan, *Roman Gaul* (1953); and the detailed bibliography with E. Albertini's chapter in *Cambridge Ancient History*, vol. xi, pp. 501 ff., 905 ff. (1936). For art *see* M. Pobé and J. Roubier, *The Art of Roman Gaul* (1961).
(G. E. F. C.)

GAUL, CISALPINE (GALLIA CISALPINA), the ancient Roman name for the part of northern Italy between the Apennines and the Alps settled by Celtic invaders.

Both the date and the direction of the Celtic invasion of north Italy were disputed in antiquity, and they are still disputed. Livy's account of a crossing of the Mont Cenis or Mont Genèvre pass about 600 B.C. is generally discredited, but the variant tradition of an invasion just before the attack on Rome in 390 is unlikely on the archaeological evidence. The first Gauls probably passed the Alps no later than the early 5th century, and it is possible that their route was as far to the east as the Brenner pass. Mediolanum (Milan) was founded c. 400 by the Insubres after a victory over the Etruscans nearby at Melpum; Bononia (Bologna) did not supplant the Etruscan Felsina until c. 350.

By now Etruscan control over the valley of the Po river had been eliminated. But difficulties with the Veneti of northeastern Italy, which traditionally recalled the Gauls from Rome in 390, made their later southward thrusts less dangerous. In 283 the Boii (q.v.) and Senones were defeated at Lake Vadimo in Etruria, after which the Romans annexed the *ager Gallicus* around Ancona and founded Ariminum (Rimini) as a Latin colony in 268. A major Gallic threat in 225 was completely defeated; the Boii and their allies were crushed at Telamo in Etruria (Talamone) and two years later, making use of the Cenomani in eastern Lombardy as their allies, the Romans received the submission of the Insubres and other tribes. Placentia (Piacenza) and Cremona were founded as Latin colonies in 219 or 218 and were strengthened in 190 after their losses in the Hannibalic war. There followed the Latin colony of Bononia (189) and (183) the Roman colonies of Parma and Mutina (Modena), and then, beyond the Veneti, the Latin colony of Aquileia (181). Major roads were built, especially the Via Aemilia from Ariminum to Placentia (187), and the Via Postumia from Genua (Genoa) to Placentia, Cremona, Verona and Aquileia (begun in 148). Individual Romans received land in great numbers, and Polybius claimed that by his time (c. 150 B.C.) the Gauls had been expelled from the Po valley except from a few settlements near the Alps.

This statement is exaggerated. Celtic nomenclature is obvious on later inscriptions, and the continued predominance of a Celtic population in the lowland towns accounts for the special treatment accorded to the whole region after the Social War (the war of the *socii* or allies; *see* ROMAN HISTORY), when the rest of Italy received Roman citizenship. A province of *Gallia Cisalpina* ("Gaul this side of the Alps") was created, and under a law passed by the father of Pompey the Great in 89 B.C. the native communities acquired "Latin" rights, so that only their magistrates became full citizens. The inferior status of the *Transpadani* ("people living across the Po," for the Latin towns were mainly north of the Po") became an issue of Roman politics, made the more significant, especially during Caesar's governorship (59–50), by the value of the province as a recruiting ground. In 49, soon after the civil war began, Caesar made the desired grant of full citizenship, and in 42 B.C. the triumvirs incorporated the province into Italy.

Gallia Cisalpina was the home of many famous Latin writers: Catullus of Verona in the late republic; Virgil of Mantua and Livy of Patavium (Padua) under Augustus; and Pliny of Comum (Como) in Trajan's time. Under the early principate the prosperity of the district was unrivaled in the empire, and it continued to provide many legionaries and was the home of several Romans of distinction, especially among Pliny's contemporaries. But by that time it was in reality as well as in name a part of Italy, and its economic and social development belong to the main stream of Roman history.

BIBLIOGRAPHY.—Polybius, *Histories*, book ii, 15 ff., with F. W. Walbank's commentary (1957); Strabo, *Geography*, book v, ch. 1. *See* also J. M. de Navarro and L. Homo in *Cambridge Ancient History*, vol. vii, ch. 2 and 17 (1928); J. Whatmough, *The Foundation of Roman Italy* (1937) for the invasions and wars with Rome; U. Ewins in *Papers of the British School at Rome*, vol. xx, pp. 54 ff. (1952) and xxiii, pp. 73 ff. (1955) for the late republic; G. E. F. Chilver, *Cisalpine Gaul* (1941) for the early empire.
(G. E. F. C.)

GAULISH: *see* CELTIC LANGUAGES.

GAULLE, CHARLES ANDRÉ JOSEPH MARIE DE: *see* DE GAULLE, CHARLES ANDRÉ JOSEPH MARIE.

GAULTIER, DENIS (GAULTIER LE JEUNE) (1597 or 1603–1672), French lutenist and composer, whose chief contribution to the music literature of the period is the Hamilton codex of 69 compositions called "La Rhétorique des Dieux" (1664–72). This is a collection of short pieces, mainly dances, in tablature for lute, arranged in groups of suites. The characteristic way in which Gaultier labeled his pieces with fanciful and descriptive titles, a feature later to be found in the music of the clavecinists, stemmed from the group of lutenists called the École de Paris of which Gaultier was the last great exponent. His style explores the full range of the new "French style" of lute playing—ornamentation and broken chords (*style brisé*) are to be found in all his work, again a facet of the lute style later to be transferred to the keyboard. Gaultier was one of the great French virtuosos of the lute. He was enormously popular in his own time and toward the end of his life much of his music was transcribed in staff notation so that it might reach the wider public of keyboard players. Gaultier was the originator of the "tombeau," a small piece written to the memory of a great personage. (B. P.)

GAUR (Lakhnauti), a ruined city of India, in the Malda district of Bengal situated approximately 8 mi. S. of English Bazar and about 163 mi. N. of Calcutta, on the eastern bank of an old channel of the Ganges. It is said to have been founded by Lakshman, the Sena king of Bengal, and its ancient name was Lakshmanavati, corrupted into Lakhnauti. It was the ancient Hindu capital of Bengal. Its recorded history begins with its conquest c. 1203 by Mohammed Bakhtiyar Khalji. Ghiyath ud-din Iwaz Khalji made it his capital c. 1219. The seat of government was transferred c. 1340 to nearby Pandua. Gaur once more became the capital in the mid-15th century. It was besieged and pillaged during the struggle between the Mogul Humayun and the Afghan Sher Shah (1538–39). In 1564 because of a change in the course of the Ganges it was abandoned for Tanda, nearer the main stream. Gaur was temporarily reoccupied in 1575 by Akbar's general Munim Khan, after a struggle with Daud Shah, the last of the Afghan dynasty. This occupation was followed by a virulent epidemic, which depopulated the city. It was, however, the residence of Shah Jahan's son, Shah Shuja', in the mid-17th century. In the 18th century it was little better than a heap of ruins almost overgrown with jungle. In the 1870s, however, the site was partially cleared for cultivation.

The finest ruin in Gaur is that of the Great Golden mosque, also called Bara Darwaza, or "12-doored" (1526). The Small Golden or Eunuch's mosque has fine carving and is faced with stone, fairly well preserved. The Tantipara mosque (1475–80) has beautiful molding in brick, and the Lotan mosque of the same period is unique in retaining glazed tiles. The citadel was entered through a magnificent gateway called the Dakhil Darwaza (1460?–74). At the southeast corner was a palace surrounded by a wall of brick 66 ft. high, of which a part is standing. Nearby were the royal tombs. Within the citadel is the Kadam Rasul mosque (1530), still used, and close outside is a tall tower called the Firoz Minar.

Bibliography.—James Fergusson, *History of Indian and Eastern Architecture* (1876); *Reports of the Archaeological Surveyor, Bengal Circle* (1900–04); article "Gaur" in *Imperial Gazetteer of India*, vol. xii (1908); Sir Jadunath Sarkar (ed.), *The History of Bengal*, vol. ii, *Muslim Period 1200–1757* (1948). (P. H.; X.)

GAUR (*Bibos gaurus*), the wild ox of India, Burma and the Malay peninsula, is the typical representative of an Indo-Malay group of wild cattle characterized by a ridge on the withers, compressed horns and white legs. The gaur, which reaches a height of six feet or more at the shoulder, is characterized by the forward curve and great elevation of the ridge between the horns. The colour is blackish-gray. Except when wounded, the gaur is shy and inoffensive, and stays near the highland forests, where it feeds chiefly on grasses and tree shoots.

GAUSS, (JOHANN) CARL FRIEDRICH (1777–1855), German mathematician and scientist, to whom history has accorded a place with Archimedes and Newton as one of the three greatest mathematicians of all time, is frequently called the founder of modern mathematics. The importance of his work in astronomy and physics is scarcely less than that in mathematics. His full stature became known only in the 20th century since many of his discoveries were published long after his death. During his lifetime he published 155 titles. He was born at Brunswick, April 30, 1777, and died at Göttingen, Feb. 23, 1855.

Gauss was of Nether-Saxon peasant origin. Many anecdotes refer to his prodigious precocity, particularly in mental computation. As an old man he said facetiously that he could count before he could talk. In elementary school he soon impressed his teacher, who is said to have convinced Gauss's father that the son should not learn a trade, but follow a learned profession. In secondary school, after 1788, he rapidly distinguished himself in ancient languages and mathematics. At the age of 14 Gauss was presented to the duke of Brunswick at court, where he was permitted to exhibit his computing skill. On this occasion he was given several mathematical textbooks. Until his death in 1806 the duke generously supported Gauss.

Gauss conceived almost all his fundamental mathematical discoveries between the ages of 14 and 17. In 1791 he gave attention to the arithmetico-geometric mean. Gauss now manifested his outstanding trait of critical analysis and thus began to do creative work. He called this acuteness the *rigor antiquus*. In 1792, the year that he entered the three-year Collegium Carolinum in Brunswick, his interests led him to question the foundations of geometry. Gauss shunned controversy, and though a pioneer he published nothing on non-Euclidean geometry. In 1793–94 he did intensive research in number theory, especially on the frequency of primes. He made this study his life's passion and is regarded as its modern founder. Gauss obtained a copy of Newton's *Principia* in 1794; in that year he discovered the method of least squares. In 1795 he completed important research on quadratic residues.

Gauss studied at the University of Göttingen from 1795 to 1798; there he had access to the works of Fermat, Euler, Lagrange and Legendre, the masters in his field. He soon realized that he too was a master and decided to write a book on the theory of numbers. It appeared in 1801 under the title *Disquisitiones arithmeticae*; this classic work, establishing the theories of cyclotomy and arithmetical forms, usually is held to be Gauss's greatest accomplishment. In studying the roots of the equation $x^n = 1$, Gauss discovered on March 30, 1796, that the regular heptadecagon (polygon with 17 sides) is inscriptible in a circle, using only compasses and straightedge—the first such discovery in Euclidean construction in over 2,000 years. Gauss had been undecided whether to make mathematics or philology his life work; he now resolved to devote his life to the former.

In late 1796 Gauss was busy with research in infinitesimal calculus and algebra and began an investigation of the lemniscate functions; he found a proof of Lagrange's theorem (reversion formula) and discovered the connection between the elliptic quadrant and the arithmetico-geometric mean, as well as its connection with the power series whose exponents are squares. The theories of elliptic functions and of linear differential equations were rediscovered some decades after Gauss had developed them for himself; he discovered double periodicity and operated with the general theta functions.

His interest then turned to astronomy as he developed formulas for the calculation of parallax in April 1799. He went to Helmstedt in Dec. 1799 to live in the home of the mathematician J. F. Pfaff and to use the university library. That month he found the relation of the arithmetico-geometric mean to the elliptic integral of the first order. He returned to Brunswick at Easter in 1800; in May he developed his formula for determining the date of Easter and promptly published it.

The discovery of Ceres, the first planetoid, by Giuseppe Piazzi in Palermo on Jan. 1, 1801, gave Gauss the opportunity of revealing, in a spectacular way, his remarkable mathematical superiority over all his contemporaries. His calculations of the orbit of Ceres began in Nov. 1801; on this problem he succeeded where others had failed. Gauss set up a speedy method for the complete determination of the elements of a planet's orbit from three observations; he elaborated it in his second major work, a classic in astronomy, published in 1809. He said that had it not been for Newton's *Principia* he could not have devised the new method.

Astronomy occupied Gauss's attention the remainder of his life. In 1807 he was appointed director of the University of Göttingen observatory and professor of mathematics, a position he never left in spite of many efforts to lure him away. He trained a considerable number of students who later distinguished themselves and always regarded him as a great teacher. The years 1816–17 marked the close of his work in theoretical astronomy; later he worked in spherical and observational astronomy.

In 1812 Gauss published the first rigorous treatment of the hypergeometric series. He was a pioneer in topology and contributed much to crystallography, optics, biostatistics, mechanics and the study of capillarity and fluids in a state of equilibrium. Gauss was commissioned in 1818 to make a geodetic survey of the kingdom of Hanover; this triangulation occupied him for many years, leading to his invention of the heliotrope and his brilliant work in the theory of surfaces. There he found full application for his method of least squares in solving the problem of determining the earth's figure.

After 1831, Gauss collaborated with Wilhelm Weber in basic research in electricity and magnetism. In 1833 they devised an electromagnetic telegraph. They stimulated others in many lands to make magnetic observations and founded the Magnetic union in 1836, the year that Gauss invented the bifilar magnetometer.

Gauss married twice and became the father of six children; two of his sons emigrated to Missouri in the 1830s. His private life was simple and harmonious although he had his share of grief and trouble. He did not like to travel. Gauss left an estate of 152,892 thalers. His personal and scientific correspondence was voluminous. As a celebrity, he had numerous visitors from abroad. Newton was his ideal. Frequently he meditated on religion and philosophy but was reluctant to talk on these subjects and published nothing on them. His *Collected Works* were published over a long period, from 1863 to 1933; they exhibit the elegant and concise form on which he insisted. He was well versed in the Greek and Roman classics, studied Sanskrit and read extensively in European literature, particularly English and Russian. His library contained 11,424 items. In later years he was showered with honours from scientific bodies and governments everywhere. He was extremely patriotic and politically conservative, though never active beyond watching current events. He served several terms as a dean at the University of Göttingen and always participated wholeheartedly in its affairs. Gauss enjoyed social life but usually limited this in favour of his research. He loved music, especially singing.

Gauss enjoyed good health until the last year of his life. Death came as the result of arteriosclerotic congestive heart failure. His fame lives more strongly than ever, for rarely has the mind of a commanding world figure been so richly furnished.

See also references under "Gauss, (Johann) Carl Friedrich" in the Index.

BIBLIOGRAPHY.—Heinrich Mack, *C. F. Gauss und die Seinen* (1927); G. Waldo Dunnington, *Carl Friedrich Gauss: Titan of Science* (1955); W. Grossmann *et al.*, *Gauss und die Landesvermessung in Niedersachsen* (1955); E. Worbs, *Carl Friedrich Gauss: ein Lebensbild* (1955); W. Klingenberg, H. Salié *et al.*, *Gaussgedenkband* (1957). (G. W. Dn.)

GAUTAMA BUDDHA (c. 563–483 B.C.), the historic founder of the religion known as Buddhism, lived, taught and died in northeast India, but his influence spread throughout central, northern and southern Asia, where it continues to provide a common cultural bond. Traditions of his life were not written earlier than 236 years after his death, but they are preserved variously in the Pali, Sanskrit, Chinese and Tibetan languages. From these, modern historical inquiry has been able to obtain a relatively stable outline of main events in a career still celebrated after 2,500 years.

Buddha was born among the Sakyas, a tribe of the warrior (Kshatriya) caste whose capital, Kapilavastu, was situated in what is now Nepal. (For legends concerning his birth, *see* LUMBINI.) His father, Suddhodana, was ruling noble (or king) of the Gautama clan, whence the name Gautama by which the son was later known, although his given personal name was Siddhartha. His mother, Maya, died soon after he was born. From poetic tales and legends surrounding his birth, infancy and youth, it may be inferred that the prince was a remarkable personality, that although reared in the luxury he was of a serious, meditative turn of mind, and that he was early attracted to a nonworldly religious life. From this neither wife nor the birth of a son could divert him. Actually, in his 29th year, the prince renounced home and secular life to seek the "supreme peace of Nirvana." This goal envisaged deliverance from the painful realities of life's transitoriness, as evidenced by the ceaseless round of birth, old age, sickness and death, repeated according to Indian belief through countless successive rebirths. As a monk he sought instruction under two religious teachers.

Unsatisfied, he next tried extreme ascetic practices for six years, equally fruitless. Returning to a natural regimen, he finally gained his great enlightenment through sitting quietly in concentrated meditation. He detected the cause of suffering in craving due to ignorance, and discovered a path to its removal through right living and mental discipline. Thus he became Buddha, or the Enlightened One.

Feeling compassion for all suffering mortals, he decided to share his wisdom. His remaining 45 years spent as wandering teacher among his own and neighbouring tribes earned him the title Sage of the Sakyas (Sakyamuni). From among his numerous followers he organized a community of monks (the sangha) to carry on after him. In old age he was menaced by a schismatic monk, Devadatta (q.v.), who plotted to seize leadership, but this danger was averted. In his 80th year, still exhorting his disciples to strive earnestly for what is beyond perishing things, Gautama Buddha died. History attests the deep and lasting impression left by his noble spirit and selfless, devoted life. *See also* BUDDHISM.

BIBLIOGRAPHY.—*Extended treatises:* Edward J. Thomas, *The Life of Buddha: as Legend and History*, full bibliography (1927), 2nd ed. (1930); Sir Charles Eliot, *Hinduism and Buddhism; an Historical Sketch*, 3 vol., esp. vol. i (1921), reissue (1954); Hermann Oldenberg, *Buddha: His Life, His Doctrines, His Order*, trans. from German by William Hoey (1882); Maurice Percheron, *The Marvelous Life of the Buddha*, trans. from French by Adrienne Foulke (1960). *Biographical source materials:* Clarence H. Hamilton, (ed.), *Buddhism, a Religion of Infinite Compassion*, selections from Buddhist literature (1952); *The Life of Gotama the Buddha*, compiled exclusively from the Pali canon by E. H. Brewster (1926); *Buddhism in Translations*, passages selected from the Pali canon, trans. into English by Henry Clarke Warren, 10th ed. (1953); *The Road to Nirvana*, selected scriptures trans. from the Pali by E. J. Thomas (1950); *The Quest of Enlightenment*, selected scriptures trans. from the Sanskrit by E. J. Thomas (1950); *The Life of the Buddha and the Early History of His Order*, derived from Tibetan works, trans. by W. Woodville Rockhill (1916); *The Life or Legend of Gaudama, the Buddha of the Burmese*, with annotations, a late noncanonical biography trans. from the Burmese by P. Bigandet, 2 vol. (1880); *The Romantic Legends of Buddha*, from the Chinese-Sanskrit by S. Beal (1875), 2nd ed. (1952). (Cl. H. H.)

GAUTIER, (EMIL THEOBALD) LÉON (1832–1897), French literary historian who rendered great service to the study of early French literature, was born at Le Havre on Aug. 8, 1832, and educated at the École des Chartes (1852–55), and became successively keeper of the archives of the *département* of Haute-Marne and of the imperial archives at Paris under the empire (1859). In 1871 he became professor of paleography at the École des Chartes. He was elected member of the Académie des Inscriptions in 1887, and became chief of the historical section of the national archives in 1893. He died in Paris on Aug. 25, 1897. The most important of Gautier's numerous works on medieval subjects were a critical text (1872), with translation and introduction, of the *Chanson de Roland*, and *Les Épopées françaises* (3 vol., 1866–68; 2nd ed., 5 vol., 1878–97, including a *Bibliographie des chansons de geste*).

GAUTIER, THÉOPHILE (1811–1872), French poet, novelist, critic and journalist, who was largely instrumental in transforming the taste of the early romantic period into the aestheticism and naturalism of the later decades of the 19th century, was born on Aug. 31, 1811, at Tarbes in Gascony. His family moved to Paris in 1814 and he lived there most of his life. At the Collège Charlemagne, he began a lasting friendship with Gérard de Nerval (q.v.). He studied painting, but soon decided that his vocation was poetry. He became a fervent supporter of the romantic movement, with a lifelong admiration for Victor Hugo, its leader, and took a vigorous part in the "battle" between romantics and classicists when Hugo's play *Hernani* was first performed in 1830.

His romanticism was at its height in the 1830s, a period which he remembered with humour and sympathy in his *Histoire du romantisme* and *Portraits contemporains* (both 1874), the latter containing an excellent account of his friend Honoré de Balzac. The extravagances of romanticism, his own included, were amusingly satirized in *Les Jeunes-France* (1833), while in *Les Grotesques* (1834–36) he wrote understandingly about neglected earlier writers whose individualism anticipated that of the romantics.

Gautier's first poems appeared in 1830. In 1832, he published *Albertus*, a long narrative of the macabre, then much in vogue. His apprehensions about death were expressed in *La Comédie de la mort* (1838). Although partly derivative these poems showed descriptive ability and, like some of his later writings, revealed greater poignancy than he is always credited with possessing. Lacking religious faith, he sought consolation in art for his disillusionment and nihilism. His views about "Art for Art's sake," in the preface to *Albertus* and especially in the preface to his novel

Mademoiselle de Maupin (1835–36; Eng. trans. 1948), soon became his fundamental belief, and led him away from romanticism. *Mademoiselle de Maupin* itself caused a considerable stir by its disregard of morality and insistence on the sovereignty of beauty.

In 1840 Gautier spent five months in Spain and here he found the wealth of local colour which exactly suited his acute perception and unerring sense of language. It inspired *España* (1845; ed. by R. Jasinski, 1929), containing some of his best poetry, and his prose *Voyage en Espagne* (1845). Henceforward traveling provided a welcome escape from the incessant journalistic labours by which he earned a living for his dependants and himself. He had a relationship for many years with Eugénie Fort, mother of his son Théophile, and with Ernesta Grisi, mother of his two daughters. He maintained them and also his two sisters.

In 1836 he accepted an appointment from Émile de Girardin as weekly contributor to *La Presse*; he held this post until 1855, when he transferred to *Le Moniteur universel*. In 1851, he became editor of the *Revue de Paris*, and in 1856, of *L'Artiste*: he wrote for many other papers. He often lamented the treadmill existence to which he was committed; he felt that his journalism prevented him from concentrating on creative writing, especially poetry, but in fact he seems to have lacked the sustained creative power possessed by the greatest writers.

Between 1840 and 1859 his journeys to England, Algeria, Italy, Turkey, Greece and Russia yielded material for further writings —*Caprices et zigzags* (1845), *Voyage en Italie* (1852), *Constantinople* (1853), *Voyage en Russie* (1866). His visit to Greece (1852) strengthened his admiration for classical art, already expressed in *Mademoiselle de Maupin*. Art, he declared, should be impersonal, and not concerned with inculcating lessons or doctrines. The artist must concentrate on attaining perfection of form. These views were exemplified in *Émaux et camées* (1852, enlarged ed. 1872; ed. by J. Pommier and G. Matoré, 1947), his finest collection of poetry, and a starting point for Parnassian writers like Théodore de Banville and Leconte de Lisle. (Charles Baudelaire paid tribute to him in the dedication of *Les Fleurs du mal*.) These poems included some of Gautier's most famous *transpositions d'art*, in which he transcribed the exact impressions made by a painting or other work of art. He did not, however, find complete satisfaction in the outward signs of beauty and continued to search (*e.g.*, in his story *Spirite*, 1866) for some spiritual ideal which would transcend material perception.

Gautier's poetry and fantasy were seen to advantage in his fiction. His knowledge of human nature was not profound, but his pictorial qualities gave distinction to *Le Capitaine Fracasse* (1863; Eng. trans. 1933), a novel of the days of Louis XIII, and to the short stories which he wrote throughout his career. These included evocations of ancient Pompeii or Egypt, *Arria Marcella* (1852), *Une Nuit de Cléopâtre* (1845), a modern Arabian Nights theme, *Fortunato* (1836), and stories of the supernatural, *La Morte amoureuse, Avatar* (1857).

Most of his writings first appeared in periodicals and much has never been republished. His output was prodigious, but his art and dramatic criticism alone—partly reprinted in *Les Beaux-arts en Europe* (1855) and in *Histoire de l'art dramatique en France depuis vingt-cinq ans*, six volumes (1858–59)—would ensure his reputation. As a critic of ballet Gautier remains unrivaled. He also wrote plays, perhaps underestimated, and various ballets. These include his masterpiece *Giselle* (1841), written in collaboration with Vernoy de Saint-Georges. Like *La Péri* (1843), this was composed for Carlotta Grisi (sister of Ernesta Grisi), with whom he was greatly in love.

"Le bon Theo," as he was nicknamed, was held in warm regard by many leading figures, including Banville, Baudelaire, Flaubert, Sainte-Beuve and the Goncourt brothers. In his later life he was the friend of the Princess Mathilde and she gave him a sinecure post as librarian to ease his financial strain. He died at Neuilly, Oct. 23, 1872.

BIBLIOGRAPHY.—A. C. J. de Spoelberch de Lovenjoul, *Histoire des œuvres de T. Gautier*, 2 vol. (1887), and editions of separate works by R. Jasinski, A. Boschot, J. Pommier and G. Matoré. *See also* the memoirs of E. Bergerat and Judith Gautier; the *Goncourt Journal*, new ed., 4 vol. (1956–59); A. Cassagne, *La théorie de l'art pour l'art en France* (1906, reprinted 1959); R. Jasinski, *Les années romantiques de T. Gautier* (1929); A. Boschot, *T. Gautier* (1933); A. Bellessort, *Dix-huitième siècle et romantisme* (1941); J. Tild, *T. Gautier et ses amis* (1951); J. Richardson, *T. Gautier, his Life and Times* (1958).
(S. C. GD.)

GAUTIER D'ARRAS (d. c. 1185), French *romancier* and an official of Philippe d'Alsace, count of Flanders; his name occurs in many charters between 1160 and 1185. His romance *Eracle*, a mythical life of the Byzantine emperor Heraclius, was begun in 1176–78 for Marie de Champagne and Thibaut V of Blois, but finished, perhaps in 1179–81, for the young Baldwin V of Hainault. *Ille et Galeron* was undertaken at Besançon in 1178 for Beatrix of Vienne, the wife of the emperor Frederick I (Barbarossa); its theme is the "man with two wives" (*cf.* Marie de France's *Eliduc*).

BIBLIOGRAPHY.—*Œuvres de Gautier d'Arras*, ed. by E. Löseth (1890); *Ille et Galeron*, ed. by W. Foerster (1891) from the inferior Paris manuscript and by F. A. G. Cowper, for the Société des anciens textes français (1956), from the Wollaton Hall manuscript, in Nottingham University library; A. Fourrier, *Le Courant réaliste dans le roman courtois en France au moyen-âge*, I (1960), pp. 179–313, cf. *Romania* xxxii (1961), no. 1,115–28, 1,718, and the 2nd *Supplément* (1961), no. 7,298–7,300.
(C. A. RN.)

GAUZE, a light, open-weave fabric, which when made of cotton is used primarily for surgical dressings; it is also made of silk and other fibres and used for dress trimming. The name is from the middle eastern city of Gaza, where the fabric is thought to have originated. It is made either by a plain weave or by a leno weave, in which the warp threads are arranged in pairs; the filling is then shot across the fabric as in plain weave, but the warp threads are twisted alternately in one direction and then the other, which gives firmness and strength to the cloth.

Other very similar fabrics are cheesecloth, made of cotton, originally used as a wrapping for pressed cheese and now used in bookbinding, as reinforcing in paper where high strength is desired, and for dustcloths and the like; bunting, made of cotton or wool, dyed and used for flags and decorations; scrim, made of cotton and used for curtains; and tobacco cloth, used as shade covering for tobacco plants. All these various terms are used almost interchangeably in many instances, the main differences being in the finishing (for example, cheesecloth that is bleached and stiffened may be called scrim), the quality of the fibre (gauze may be made of very fine yarn, whereas tobacco cloth is made of low grade yarns), and the use to which the material is to be put.

GAVARNI, PAUL (1804–1866), pseudonym of GUILLAUME-SULPICE CHEVALIER, French lithographer and painter, was born on Jan. 13, 1804, in Paris. In early childhood he showed gifts for drawing and at the age of ten was working in the studio of the architect Dutillard and was later employed by a maker of precision instruments. All his life he regretted he could not devote his entire time to his principal interests: drawing, mathematics, literature and the stage. His first lithograph was published in 1824 and attracted the attention of E. Blaisot, who gave him employment. From 1824 to 1828 he traveled in the Pyrenees and at that time he adopted the name Gavarni. Upon his return he worked for the fashion journal *La Mode*, made many contacts in the world of society and art and became the friend of Balzac, M. J. Sue and the duchesse d'Abrantès. About 1831 he began publishing his scenes of everyday contemporary life, and praise from writers such as Balzac gained him popularity in England as well as France. In 1833 he began publication of the *Journal des gens du monde* which failed after 18 numbers and was responsible for Gavarni's imprisonment for debt in 1835 for almost a year. He maintained his cheerful outlook, however, and from 1839 to 1846 he issued his famous series "Les Lorettes," "Les Débardeurs" and "Les Fourberies de Femmes." After the death of his mother and his marriage, about 1845, his style changed, deepening in seriousness and observation. Gavarni then turned his mirror to the grotesque sides of family life and of humanity. While showing the same power of irony as his former works, enhanced by a deeper insight into human nature, Gavarni's compositions of this time generally bear the stamp of a bitter philosophy. In 1847 he left for London, described as "the best-dressed man in France," but spent his time in England observing the life of the poor and producing some of his most compelling work. He traveled in Scotland in 1849 and did much work for English publications. After his return to Paris he devoted more time to water colour and in 1851 met the Goncourt brothers who had long been his admirers and were preparing their book for him. Again Gavarni took up lithography and brought forth another of his great series, "Thomas Vireloque." At the time of his death, on Nov. 24, 1866, he was working energetically in etching, lithography and the new and popular process, electric engraving.

Although Gavarni's work lacks the power of his great contemporary Daumier it can be appreciated for its polished wit, the finesse of his cultured observation and the all-embracing panorama he presents of the life of his time.

BIBLIOGRAPHY.—E. and J. de Goncourt, Gavarni; l'Homme et l'oeuvre (1873); J. Armelhaut and E. Bocher, L'Oeuvre de Gavarni (1873) (the definitive catalogue of Gavarni's prints); P. A. Lemoisne, Gavarni; peintre et lithographe (1924).
(H. Es.)

GAVARNIE, a mountain village in the Hautes-Pyrénées département, France, is situated at an altitude of 4,450 ft. in the valley of the Gave de Pau on the French side of the Central Pyrenees, and is famous for the nearby Cirque de Gavarnie. From the floor of this natural amphitheatre, north-facing, glacially eroded rock walls rise about 5,000 ft. There are three conspicuous terraces in which precipitous faces are succeeded upward by steep slopes of ice and snow. The Grande Cascade plunges about 1,400 ft. from the eastern side. Above are the high summits of the Franco-Spanish frontier ridge: Taillon (10,322 ft.), Marboré (10,672 ft.), and to the southeast Mont Perdu (10,997 ft.). Conspicuous also is the deep cleft of the Brèche de Roland. Near there N. Casteret discovered the Grotte Casteret with its frozen underground stream.

Geologically Gavarnie lies at the southern edge of the axial zone of the Pyrenees (q.v.). Much disturbed Paleozoic rocks of this zone have been thrust southward over a thin layer of Upper Cretaceous limestone (seen as a small scarp in the steep valley sides), which rests unconformably upon a basement of metamorphic rocks. To the south the mountains of the frontier ridge show southward cascade overfolds in Upper Cretaceous and Eocene limestones, initiated by the lateral thrust from the north. The resulting juxtaposition of different rock types is reflected in the scenery, the confused gray summits of the Paleozoics to the north contrasting with the lighter coloured Cretaceous and Eocene rocks which, on the more arid Spanish side, are cut by impressive winding canyons. Gavarnie is a climbing and walking centre and in summer many tourists visit it by motor coach from Lourdes.
(C. H. Ho.)

GAVAZZI, ALESSANDRO (1809–1889), Italian orator of the Risorgimento, was born at Bologna on March 21, 1809. He joined the Barnabite Fathers in 1825 and taught rhetoric in their college at Naples. Dismayed by the social evils of Italy, he was drawn to the movement for Italian independence. His preaching for a united Italy and his criticism of the government of the papal states caused Pius IX to regard him as heretical. After the capture of Rome and the reinstatement of the pope by the French, Gavazzi fled to England in 1849. Disillusioned with papal Catholicism, he associated with the Italian Protestant congregation in London. His lectures against the papacy and his oratorical powers attracted English attention to Italian affairs. Returning to Italy he became chaplain to the army of Garibaldi in 1860. Uncommitted to the theology of the Free Church (Chiesa libera) of Italy, he aided the formation of the Italian Waldensian Church (see WALDENSES), in 1870, seeking to show the simplicity of the primitive church and to avoid the doctrinal emphases of contemporary Protestant churches. Gavazzi taught in the theological college of that church in Rome until his death there on Jan. 9, 1889.

See L. Santini, Alessandro Gavazzi (1955).
(B. H.)

GAVELKIND, a custom formerly presumed to apply to all freehold land in Kent, and capable of applying to land elsewhere in England and Wales. The chief feature of the custom was partibility, whereby on the death of the tenant intestate the land descended to all males of the same degree equally instead of to the eldest male alone. Thus, whereas at common law the eldest son excluded his brothers, by gavelkind all sons shared equally. Gavelkind land in Kent was subject to certain other customs which survived even if the land was disgaveled by statute. These were: (1) the land was always devisable, i.e., disposable by will; (2) there was no escheat (q.v.) on attainder of felony; (3) a tenant could alienate the land by feoffment (q.v.) at 15 years of age; (4) a widow's dower (q.v.) was in one-half of the land dum casta et sola, i.e., while she remained chaste and unmarried, instead of in one-third absolutely; (5) a widower's curtesy (a life interest in his wife's realty) was in one-half of the land until remarriage instead of in the whole absolutely and could be claimed even if no children had been born capable of inheriting the land. Both gavelkind and the Kentish customs were abolished by the Law of Property acts, 1922 and 1925, and the Administration of Estates act, 1925.

Under Irish gavelkind the land was not divided among the sons but was thrown again into the common stock, and redivided among the surviving members of the sept. The equal division of an inheritance in land among children is of common occurrence outside the British Isles. See also INTESTATE SUCCESSION; REAL PROPERTY AND CONVEYANCING, LAWS OF.
(R. E. MY.)

GAVESTON, PIERS (d. 1312), earl of Cornwall, friend and adviser of the English king Edward II, was the younger son of a Béarnais knight and was brought up in the household of Edward, then prince of Wales. In Feb. 1307 Gaveston, whose character was strongly criticized by contemporary chroniclers, was banished by Edward I on account of his friendship with the prince, but he was recalled by Edward II on his accession in July and was created earl of Cornwall in August. Gaveston married Edward's niece, Margaret de Clare, and was made keeper of the realm during the king's absence in France (1308). At Edward's coronation he bore the Confessor's crown. These marks of favour aroused baronial opposition, and in June 1308 Edward was compelled to assent to Gaveston's banishment, appointing him lieutenant in Ireland. After his recall by Edward in 1309, Gaveston's unpopularity, and the favour shown to him by the king, resulted in the formation of a baronial committee of 21, who drafted in 1311 the document known as the ordinances, demanding among other things the renewal of the sentence of banishment on Gaveston. The favourite withdrew briefly to Flanders, but returned by Christmas 1311. In the conflict following his reinstatement, Gaveston was captured at Scarborough castle by a force under the earls of Pembroke and Warenne. Despite a promise of personal immunity, he was seized by forces of the earl of Warwick and executed on Blacklow hill, near Warwick, on June 19, 1312. Edward had Gaveston's body buried in the Dominican church at King's Langley. The execution deepened the conflict between Edward II and the barons and was the first of the many political executions which took place during the 14th century. See also Edward II.

GAVIAL (GHARIAL), a long-snouted fish-eating crocodilian inhabiting northern India. A single species, Gavialis gangeticus, constitutes the family Gavialidae. The snout is extremely slender, with numerous equal-sized teeth. Various crocodiles have relatively slender snouts, and the Malayan false gavial (Tomistoma), a close relative of the true crocodiles, approaches the gavial in this respect. See CROCODILIA.
(J. TA.)

GAVIIDAE, the only family of the order Gaviiformes, which comprises the loons (q.v.; Gavia species), fish-eating diving birds of the northern hemisphere.
(K. P. S.)

GÄVLE (older spelling GEFLE), a seaport of Sweden on an inlet of the Gulf of Bothnia, chief town not only of the län (county) of Gävleborg but also of northern Sweden. Pop. (1960) 54,618. Gävle is the chief port of one of the richest industrial districts in Sweden, and its harbour is kept open all year except for periods during winters of unusually difficult ice conditions. Fredriksskans, the outer harbour, offers facilities for the import of coal, coke and oil and for the export of timber and wood pulp, iron and steel. Export and import traffic, evenly divided, normally amounts to about 2,800,000 tons per year.

The town is an important industrial centre, manufacturing paper, pulp and other wood products, chemicals, leather goods and porcelain; there is also a shipbuilding yard.

The principal buildings of the town—which is first mentioned in the 8th century and was chartered in 1446—are the old castle, in Renaissance style (built in 1568–92 but rebuilt later), and the courthouse, one of Sweden's best-preserved 18th-century buildings. Gävle also has a forestry museum with an arboretum. The Furuvik park nearby is a popular resort. (H. V. H.)

GÄVLEBORG, a Swedish *län* (county), lies on the shores of the Gulf of Bothnia and extends north of the Dal river (Dalälven) for 2° of latitude. The population was 293,070 in 1960. The rivers are not suitable for navigation but are used for floating logs and for power. Agriculture is not of great importance because of poor soil and the severe climate but the *län* has industrial development along the coast, particularly round Gävle its capital, where pulp, paper and cotton textiles are manufactured. Sandviken, which has had a Bessemer steel industry since 1860, is noted for its manufacture of saws. In the extreme west of the *län* is Hamra National park. (A. C. O'D.)

GAVOTTE, originally a sturdy peasants' dance, in brisk 2/2 rhythm, of natives of Gap (Gavots) in the Alpine province of Dauphiné. At the French court in the 18th century it first became stately, and later rococo, with slow walking steps in 4/4 rhythm with upbeats on 3 and 4. In the suite, gavottes are written in their early lusty 2/2 rhythm, but retain the two upbeats. (L. Hr.)

GAVRILO (1881–1950), patriarch of the Serb Orthodox Church of Yugoslavia, was born at Vrujci in Montenegro on May 17, 1881. Educated at Belgrade, he pursued theological studies at Constantinople and Athens. He became metropolitan of Raska i Prizren (1911) and of Pec (1913–20), and served with the Red Cross in World War I. In 1920 he was made metropolitan of Montenegro, and in 1938 became patriarch of the Serb Church. He played a decisive part in bringing Yugoslavia into the war on the side of the Allies in 1940 through his influence with the boy king Peter. When the Germans overran Yugoslavia he was arrested and sent to the concentration camp of Dachau. Rescued by the U.S. army, he remained outside his country at the end of the war until 1946. On his return he encouraged co-operation with the communist government in civil matters but resisted its attempts to interfere in the affairs of the church. He died in Belgrade on May 7, 1950. (H. M. W.)

GAWAIN, one of the most famous heroes of Arthurian romance, the son of King Loth of Orkney and nephew to King Arthur on his mother's side. William of Malmesbury, in his *Gesta Regum Anglorum*, which covers the period 449–1127, records the discovery of the tomb of Walwen in the province of Ros in Wales, and describes Walwen as the noble nephew of Arthur. He also says that he ruled over Galloway but was expelled from his kingdom by the brother and nephew of Hengist.

In the *Historia regum Britanniae* of Geoffrey of Monmouth (*q.v.*) Gawain (Walgainus) plays an important "pseudo-historic" role. He is sent as ambassador to the Romans; and when Arthur, at the news of Mordred's treachery, returns to England, Gawain goes with him and is slain in the battle fought after their landing. Wace (*q.v.*), in his free translation of the *Historia*, the *Roman de Brut*, gives further details about his courtesy and prowess. His name appears on the archivolt of Modena cathedral, which has been placed by some scholars early, by others late, in the 12th century. There the name Galvaginus is carved against one of the figures helping Artus de Bretani to rescue Winlogee from a castle. In the Welsh romances *Gereint, Owein* and *Peredur*, and in the Welsh translation of the *Historia*, Gawain is equated with Gwalchmei who is one of Arthur's warriors in "Culhwch and Olwen" (*c.* 1100) and is there described as son of Gwyar, Arthur's nephew, his sister's son and his first cousin who never came home without the quest he had gone to seek (*see* WELSH LITERATURE: *Early and Medieval Prose*). Gwalchmei also appears in some of the Welsh *Triads*.

Some scholars have suggested that Gawain is a mythological figure with possible connections with sun myths. It is true that in one or two works he has strange adventures. In *Sir Gawain and the Green Knight*, an English anonymous poem of the 14th century, the episode of the beheading challenge is attributed to Gawain but there is no proof that this tale was originally linked with him. It is told of Cuchulain in an early Irish saga, *Bricriu's Feast*, and also in the *First Perceval Continuation*. It is also true that in several French romances, and in Malory, Gawain's strength waxes and wanes with the sun, but not very much is made of this in the romances. He has, on the whole, far less direct contact with the supernatural than, for example, Perceval and Lancelot (*qq.v.*), and although he has Grail adventures in some of the *Perceval Continuations* and is Grail hero in the German romance *Diu Krone* ("the crown of all adventures," *c.* 1220), Jessie Weston's theory that he was the original Grail winner finds little modern support (*see also* GRAIL, THE HOLY).

Nevertheless, he occupies a very important position in Arthurian romance. Although he is not the hero of any of the 12th-century romances of Chrétien de Troyes (*q.v.*), he is always one of the principal characters; for he provides the standard against which all good knights are measured, so that to equal or surpass him becomes the ultimate test of the hero's success. Thus in Chrétien's *Yvain* the culminating point in a series of exploits performed by the hero to win back his lady is an indecisive battle against Gawain fighting incognito. And in his *Le Chevalier de la Charrette* (*Lancelot*), which is both an account of the abduction and rescue of Guinevere and an illustration of the doctrines of courtly love in the person of Lancelot, the ideal lover, Lancelot and Gawain undertake the same adventure. Here the success of Lancelot, set beside the failure of Gawain, does not imply any lack of prowess in Gawain but is rather a testimony to the power of love: prowess alone cannot rise to the heights of chivalry inspired by love. In *Le Conte del Graal*, Chrétien's Perceval romance, Lancelot plays no part; Gawain, still the leading knight of Arthur's court, is again contrasted with the main hero and once more this contrast seems to be related to the underlying theme of the romance. Here the two knights are not directly opposed to one another but undertake a parallel series of adventures which seem to illustrate two different conceptions of chivalry, although, as the poem is unfinished, it is only possible to guess at the author's final intentions. Perceval engages on the quest for the Grail and through this comes to realize that chivalry is more than the seeking of earthly renown through knightly adventures. Gawain does not seek for the Grail itself but for the bleeding lance, and his aspirations remain on a more worldly plane. He is still valiant and courteous, particularly toward ladies, still a model of earthly chivalry, but he seems to lack the spiritual inspiration which drives Perceval, for all his clumsy ignorance, to greater heights.

It is, however, only in the French prose romances of the 13th century that Gawain really begins to sink from his position as the ideal knight against whom all heroes must be measured, and this decline arises directly from a new, austerely spiritual Grail Quest to be found in the prose *Lancelot*, or Vulgate cycle, as it is often called. In the *Lancelot propre*, the third branch of this cycle, Gawain is still the acknowledged leader of Arthur's court, a great warrior and a knight noted for his wisdom, courtesy and moderation. It is only when Lancelot, in another of these battles fought incognito, shows himself superior to Gawain that he proves himself to be the greatest knight of all, just before he gets a seat at the Round Table. But the situation changes with the *Queste del Saint Graal*, when not only is Lancelot displaced by Galahad as the greatest knight but Gawain fails miserably in the Quest and causes the death of a number of good knights. He fails because he relies exclusively on prowess, refuses to seek the help of divine grace through the sacraments and remains blind to the whole spiritual significance of the Grail. In the last branch of the cycle, the *Mort Artu*, when the story returns to a more earthly plane, he resumes his position as chief support of King Arthur and leader of the knights of the Round Table, but although he shows great heroism and dies with tragic dignity, he does not return completely to grace, for it is the bitterness with which he seeks to avenge his brothers' death which is one of the causes of the destruction of the Round Table.

Thus the changing attitude toward the character of Gawain in the Vulgate cycle is connected with a change in attitude to chivalry through the introduction of the Grail theme. Gawain, once again, is the foil for the chief hero and the emptiness of his earthly chivalry is contrasted with the spiritual fullness of Galahad's heavenly chivalry. The deterioration, however, goes far beyond this in later romances such as the prose *Tristan*, where in a number of episodes he appears as treacherous and brutal toward women, and, in contrast with the general tradition of Middle English romances, these darker aspects of his character are also to be found in parts of Sir Thomas Malory's *Morte Darthur* and hence in Tennyson's Arthurian epic, *Idylls of the King*. Nevertheless, Gawain's main role in Arthurian romance is to provide the pattern of chivalry for every young knight.

See also ARTHURIAN LEGEND.

BIBLIOGRAPHY.—A general study of the character is to be found in J. L. Weston's *Legend of Sir Gawain* (1897); but a number of her theories are outdated. For discussion and further bibliography of the large number of works in which Gawain plays an important part *see* J. D. Bruce, *Evolution of Arthurian Romance*, 2nd ed. (1928), and *Arthurian Literature in the Middle Ages*, ed. by R. S. Loomis (1959).
(E. M. K.)

GAWLER, a town of South Australia, lies on the North and South Para rivers, 25 mi. N of Adelaide by rail. Pop. (1966) 5,703. There are four mills, a butter factory, clothing factory, clay and concrete brickworks, and natural sand deposits. Gawler is the centre of a wheat-, fruit-, and flower-growing district. It was named after George Gawler, governor of South Australia from 1838 to 1841.
(A. R. WA.)

GAY, JOHN (1685–1732), English poet and dramatist, author of *The Beggar's Opera*, was born on June 30, 1685, at Barnstaple, Devonshire, and educated at the local grammar school. He was apprenticed to a silk mercer in London, but was released early from his indentures and, after a further short period in Devonshire, returned to London where he lived most of his life. Among his early literary friends were Aaron Hill and Eustace Budgell, whom he helped in the production of *The British Apollo*, a question-and-answer journal of the day. His journalistic interests are clearly seen in a pamphlet, *The Present State of Wit* (1711), a survey of contemporary periodical publications.

From 1712 to 1714 he was steward in the household of the duchess of Monmouth, which gave him leisure and security to write. He had produced a burlesque of the Miltonic style, *Wine*, in 1708 and in 1713 his first important poem, *Rural Sports*, appeared. This is a descriptive and didactic work in two short books dealing with hunting and fishing, but containing also descriptions of the countryside and meditations on the Horatian theme of retirement. Here Gay strikes at once his characteristic note of delicately absurd artificiality. In discussing bait, for example, he tells the reader:

Those baits will best reward the fisher's pains,
Whose polish'd tails a shining yellow stains;
Cleanse them from filth, to give a tempting gloss,
Cherish the sully'd reptile race with moss. . .

He is, of course, aware of the comic disproportion between his language and the subject. But the contrast, while it produces the effect of a *reductio ad absurdum*, does so in a good-humoured way and in a tone of underlying sympathy. This note of sympathetic comedy is the staple one in Gay's poetry. It is strongly marked in his finest poem, *Trivia: or, the Art of Walking the Streets of London* (1716), a work modeled on Virgil's *Georgics* and fully alive today for the detailed observation of urban life which it displays, and for its assured technical dexterity. Something of its flavour can be gained from this couplet, describing a sophisticated lady crossing the street:

Her shoe disdains the street; the lazy fair
With narrow step affects a limping air.

The force of character observation in "disdains," and the way in which the rhythm of the second line echoes the angular movements of the lady, indicate the precision of Gay's craftsmanship. The effect is not to "startle with a fine excess," but to make the reader apprehend one facet of experience more clearly. It is this effect which Gay is constantly achieving. The full significance of a couplet often depends upon a literary parallel and references back to the *Georgics* are common. Virgil, for example, says that the influence of spring is felt throughout the whole of creation, a thought which Dryden renders by the lines:

From hence proceeds the birds' harmonious voice;
From hence the cows exult, and frisking lambs rejoice.

Gay varies the lines in *Trivia*:

The seasons operate on ev'ry breast;
'Tis new that fawns are brisk, and ladies drest,

and the effect is complex, at once satirical, sympathetic and, by its correlation of the animal and human kingdoms, philosophical. It is in this sort of delicate probing of the surface of apparently mundane social life that Gay excels.

Apart from *Trivia* and *Rural Sports*, Gay's most important works are *The Shepherd's Week* (1714), a series of mock classical pastorals, his two series of *Fables* (1727 and 1738) and *The Beggar's Opera* (1728). The *Fables* went through about 350 editions and until the 20th century were the best known of his poems. They are brief octosyllabic illustrations of moral themes, often satirical in tone and frequently directed at the court and courtiers.

Gay's most famous work, *The Beggar's Opera*, was produced on Jan. 29, 1728, at Rich's theatre in Lincoln's Inn fields, where it was said to make "Gay rich, and Rich gay." Its basic idea was to mirror the moral degradation of society by means of a story about thieves and highwaymen, and more particularly to caricature Robert Walpole and his administration. It also makes fun of the prevailing fashion for Italian opera. The play is kept alive, however, not so much by the pungency of its satire as by the effective situations of the plot, and above all by the "singability" of the songs. It ran for 62 nights (not all consecutive) and temporarily drove Italian opera from the stage. Gay wrote a sequel, *Polly*, which is set in the West Indies and in which poetic justice is more clearly seen to be done than in *The Beggar's Opera*, but its production was forbidden by the lord chamberlain, no doubt through the influence of Walpole. The suppression proved an excellent advertisement. Gay's cause found support among his friends and indeed among all who were antagonistic to the government. When it was decided to print the play, subscriptions were canvassed even in the court itself. John Arbuthnot describes the extent of the interest in a letter to Swift (March 19, 1729): "The inoffensive John Gay is now become one of the obstructions to the peace of Europe, the terror of the Ministers, the chief author of . . . all the seditious pamphlets which have been published against the government . . . If he should travel about the country, he would have hecatombs of roasted oxen sacrificed to him." As a result of this uncharacteristic notoriety Gay made well over £1,000 from subscriptions, and *Polly* sold widely. The play was not produced until 1777 when it had a moderate success. Gay's less famous plays include *The What d'ye Call It* (1715), *Three Hours After Marriage* (1717) and *Achilles*, posthumously produced in 1733.

The adjective most often applied to Gay by his friends is "honest," and they agree that this was accompanied by a certain naïveté in the face of practical problems. He lost almost all his money on South Sea stock and suffered disappointments of official patronage. Nonetheless when he died, Dec. 4, 1732, in London, he was worth £6,000, a modest but not negligible fortune. He had been helped by various patrons, including the third earl of Burlington and the third earl of Queensberry; the duchess of Queensberry mourned his death deeply. He was buried in Westminster abbey, next to Chaucer. His monument is by John Rysbrack, his epitaph by Alexander Pope.

Gay's reputation remained high throughout the 18th century; during the 19th he was remembered chiefly as the author of *The Fables* but, following Nigel Playfair's enormously successful revival of *The Beggar's Opera* in 1920, Gay's general reputation gradually rose again and he became valued as a poet of a varied and considerable achievement.

BIBLIOGRAPHY.—The *Poetical Works*, including plays, were edited by G. C. Faber (1926). See also W. H. Irving, *John Gay, Favourite of the Wits* (1940); J. R. Sutherland, in *Pope and His Contemporaries* (1949).
(JN. C.)

GAY, WALTER (1856–1937), U.S. artist who painted scenes of French interiors and French peasant life, was born at Hingham, Mass., on Jan. 22, 1856. Most of his career was spent in Europe.

In 1876 he became a pupil of Léon Bonnat in Paris. He received an honourable mention in the salon of 1885; a gold medal in 1888, similar awards at Vienna (1894), Antwerp (1895), Berlin (1896) and Munich (1897). He became an officer of the Legion of Honour and a member of the Society of Secession, Munich. His works are in the Luxembourg, the Tate gallery and the Boston and Metropolitan museums of art. He died July 14, 1937, in Paris.

GAYA is a city and district of Bihar state, India. The city (pop. [1961] 151,105) is compact but elongated, covering an area of 11.4 sq.mi., and stands largely on the west bank of the shallow, broad-channeled Phalgu river at the junction of the Grand Chord line with the Patna and Kiul branches of the Eastern railway. It is surrounded by a number of quartzitic hillocks, outliers of the Chota Nagpur plateau, and their bare rocks together with the sandy bed of the Phalgu, which is dry for much of the year, make Gaya notoriously hot. A narrow strip of the town is located on the east bank of the river. Gaya is a zone-of-contact town about 55 mi. S. of Patna near the junction of the Gangetic plain and the Chota Nagpur plateau and is an important centre of commerce. It is a celebrated place of Hindu pilgrimage, and about 300,000 pilgrims visit it annually. There are 45 sacred places between Pretsil hill on the north and Buddh Gaya on the south, but most are in Gaya itself. The principal shrine is the Vishnupad temple built by the Maratha princess Ahlya Bai in 1787. Others are on the rocky temple-crowned hills of Ramsilla (715 ft.) and Brahmajuni (793 ft.), the latter being identified as the Gayasirsa hill on which Buddha preached. Buddh Gaya is 6 mi. S. on the western bank of the Lilajan river and connected by two metaled roads. It is famous as the scene of the Buddha's enlightenment. There are modern Tibetan, Burmese and Chinese monasteries, rest houses and a museum.

GAYA DISTRICT (pop. [1961] 3,647,892; area 4,766 sq.mi.) is an alluvial plain bounded on the south by the wooded hilly fringe of Chota Nagpur and having a number of isolated quartzitic outliers, such as the Barabar hills. The principal rivers are the Son, Punpun and Phalgu. The last two shallow-channeled rivers are subject to heavy freshets. Agriculture largely depends on an elaborate indigenous system of irrigation consisting of short channels taking off from rivers or storage reservoirs. The Son canal provides irrigation in the northwest of the district. The population is mainly agricultural, the principal crops being rice, gram, wheat, barley, oilseeds and sugar cane. Some mica is produced. Other manufactures include shellac and black stoneware.
(E. Ah.)

GAYAL, a domesticated breed of the gaur (q.v.), a wild ox of India and southeast Asia. The gayal is heavily built and stands about five feet high at the shoulder. The body is dark brown, and the legs below the knees are white or yellowish. The short diverging horns are thick and massive. Gayal are kept by Indo-Chinese tribes of Assam, Tenasserim and upper Burma solely for food, not for milk and not as draft animals. They roam unattended through the forest by day and return of their own accord to the village of their owner at night.
(L. H. M.)

GAY-LUSSAC, JOSEPH LOUIS (1778–1850), French chemist and physicist, pioneered in the study of the gaseous state. He was born at St. Léonard, in the *département* of Haute-Vienne, on Dec. 6, 1778. His father, Antoine Gay, added Lussac to the name to avoid confusion with others named Gay. (Lussac is an estate near St. Léonard.) He entered the École Polytechnique at the end of 1797; two years later he was transferred to the École des Ponts et Chaussées, and at the same time he assisted Claude L. Berthollet (q.v.) in his researches. In 1802 he was appointed demonstrator to Antoine F. Fourcroy at the École Polytechnique. He succeeded Fourcroy as professor of chemistry on Jan. 1, 1810. From 1808 to 1832 he was professor of physics at the Sorbonne, a post which he resigned for the chair of chemistry at the Jardin des Plantes. In 1806 he was made an academician. In 1831 he was elected to represent Haute-Vienne in the chamber of deputies, and in 1839 he entered the chamber of peers. He died in Paris on May 9, 1850. He lies buried in Père Lachaise cemetery.

Gay-Lussac's earlier researches were mostly physical in character and referred mainly to the properties of gases, vapour tensions, hygrometry, capillarity, etc. His first memoir, published in 1802, dealt with the expansion of gases. In 1804 the French Academy, desirous of securing some observations on the force of terrestrial magnetism at great elevations above the earth, obtained the use of a balloon and entrusted the task to him and Jean B. Biot. In their first ascent from the garden of the Conservatoire des Arts on Aug. 24, 1804, an altitude of 13,120 ft. was attained; Gay-Lussac made a second ascent by himself on Sept. 16, when the balloon rose 23,012 ft. above sea level. At this height, he made observations not only on magnetism but also on the temperature and humidity of the air and collected several samples of air at different heights. The magnetic observations led him to the conclusion that the magnetic effect at all attainable elevations above the earth's surface remains constant; and on analyzing the samples of air he could find no difference of composition at different heights. This work places him among the founders of meteorology. In the same year, in conjunction with Alexander von Humboldt, he read a paper on eudiometric analysis (*Ann. de Chim.*, 1805); it contained the germ of his most important generalization, the law of combination of gases by volumes, which was, however, not enunciated in its general form until after his return from a journey through Switzerland, Italy and Germany.

In 1809 his important memoir on gaseous combination was published. In it he pointed out that when gases combine with one another they do so in the simplest proportions by volume, and that the volume of any gaseous product formed bears a simple ratio to that of the constituents. This is still called Gay-Lussac's law. He was one of the discoverers of the fact that all gases have approximately the same coefficient of expansion (Charles's law).

About this time Gay-Lussac's work became more purely chemical. In 1808, he succeeded, with the collaboration of Louis J. Thénard, in preparing potassium by the action of red-hot iron on fused potash. The properties of the element were studied and in 1809 he used it for the isolation of boron from boric acid. Gay-Lussac carried out some work on chlorine (1809) and iodine (1814) which brought him into direct rivalry with Humphry Davy. He considered "oxymuriatic acid" (chlorine) to be a compound, whereas Davy saw no reason to suppose that it contained oxygen and regarded it as an element, a view which Gay-Lussac was reluctantly compelled to accept.

In 1810 Gay-Lussac published a paper which contains some classic experiments on fermentation, a subject to which he returned in a second paper published in 1815. At the same time he was working with Thénard at the improvement of the methods of organic analysis, and by combustion with oxidizing agents, first potassium chlorate and subsequently copper oxide, he determined the composition of a number of organic substances. His last great piece of pure research was on prussic acid (hydrocyanic acid). In a note published in 1811 he described the physical properties of this acid, but he said nothing about its chemical composition until 1815, when he described cyanogen as a compound radical, prussic acid as a compound of that radical with hydrogen alone, and the prussiates (cyanides) as compounds of the radical with metals. The proof that prussic acid contains hydrogen but no oxygen was a most important support to the hydrogen-acid theory and completed the downfall of Lavoisier's oxygen theory. Gay-Lussac proposed the prefix "hydro" for these oxygen-free acids. He discovered ethyl iodide and chlorcyanogen. The isolation of cyanogen was of importance for the subsequent era of compound radicals in organic chemistry.

As a result of his success as an investigator Gay-Lussac's services as a technical adviser became in great demand. He had been a member of the consultative committee on arts and manufactures after 1805. He was attached to the "administration des poudres et salpêtres" in 1818, and in 1829 he received the lucrative post of assayer to the mint. His services to industry included his improvements in the processes for the manufacture of sulfuric acid (1818) and oxalic acid (1829); methods of estimating the amount of real alkali in potash and soda and for estimating the available chlorine in bleaching powder by a solution of arsenious acid; directions for the use of the centesimal alcoholometer published in 1830 and specially commended by the institute; and the elaboration of a method of assaying silver by a standard solution of common salt. Among his research work of this period may be mentioned the improvements in organic analysis and the investigation of fulminic acid made with the help of Liebig, who gained the privilege of admission to his private laboratory in 1823–24.

The most complete list of Gay-Lussac's papers is contained in the Royal society's *Catalogue of Scientific Papers*, which enumerates 148, exclusive of others written jointly with Humboldt, Thénard, Welter and Liebig. Many were published in the *Annales de chimie*, which, after it changed its title to *Annales de chimie et physique*, he edited, with Arago, up to nearly the end of his life; but some are to be found in the *Recherches physiques et chimiques*, two volumes, published with Thénard in 1811.

See also references under "Gay-Lussac, Joseph Louis" in the Index volume.

For biographical details *see* W. Tilden, *Famous Chemists* (1921); F. Arago, *Éloge de Gay-Lussac* (1854); Biot et Gardem le Brun, *Notice biographique de Gay Lussac* (1850); E. Blanc and L. Delhoume, *La vie émouvante et noble de Gay-Lussac* (1950). (H. S. V. K.)

GAZA (Ghazzah), an ancient city of southern Palestine with a continuous history to modern times, is situated 3 mi. from the Mediterranean coast about 40 mi. S.W. of Tel Aviv-Jaffa. From 1948–67, as the principal city of the Gaza strip (Qita Ghazzah), it was (except for a short period during 1956–57) under Egyptian administration. In ancient times it was the most southerly city of the Philistine Pentapolis and a junction on the coastal road from Damascus and Megiddo to Egypt; gold and frankincense were brought from Arabia to Gaza via Kurnub and Beersheba. Gaza alone stood in the way of the Egyptians as they entered Palestine. Before World War I it was a prosperous town with good bazaars, a considerable manufacture of black pottery and an export trade in barley. It was more than half destroyed by that war, and the population dwindled. It increased again, however, as a result of the influx of Arab refugees during the Arab-Israeli war of 1948.

History.—The Egyptian monarch Thutmose III reached Gaza c. 1468 B.C. at the beginning of his forays into Palestine and established it as a base for operations in Syria. Gaza became one of the main provincial administrative centres of Palestine until 1225 B.C. In Gen. x, 19, Canaan is described as extending from Gaza to Sidon, indicating that Gaza was near its southern border. Joshua captured towns in the vicinity, but Gaza remained outside Israel's borders. In the early 12th century B.C. the Philistines moved into the coastal plain of Palestine and made Gaza the chief city of their pentapolis. Gaza was the scene of the death of Samson. Amos (i, 6–7) denounced the city because of its slave traffic. Assyrian conquest came in 734 B.C. when Tiglath-pileser III stormed the city. Hanun, its king, fled to Egypt but later returned to accept Assyrian rule. Gaza deserted Assyria for Egypt during the reign of Sargon II; this time, Hanun, who had led the revolt, was defeated with his Egyptian allies at Raphia (Rafah; 720 B.C.) and was taken to Assyria in chains. Gaza remained loyal to Sennacherib against Hezekiah of Judah and the Philistines of Ekron. Silibel of Gaza receiving parts of Judah as a reward for loyalty. Silibel remained faithful to Esarhaddon and furnished material for the royal palace in Nineveh. Ashurbanipal also held the city. Gaza resisted the Persian king Cambyses without success. Coins found in Gaza and dated to the period testify to its commercial importance. The town resisted Alexander the Great for two months (332 B.C.). Its ruler, Batis, had hired Arab mercenaries who defended themselves behind the high walls of the mound. Alexander took the city by undermining the walls and forcing their collapse. He was wounded in the campaign, and the city was made a "desert." From the 3rd to the 1st centuries B.C. Egyptian, Syrian and Jewish armies fought for its possession. (J. S. I.)

Captured by Pompey in 62 B.C., Gaza was developed by the Romans as a free "maritime city." It was then known as Gaza Minoa and in 30 B.C. was granted by Augustus to Herod the Great. Upon the latter's death in 4 B.C., it was added to the imperial province of Syria. As a pagan stronghold, it resisted Christianity stubbornly, and remained an important centre for Greek commerce and Hellenistic culture, especially during the 2nd and 3rd centuries A.D. It was not until the opening years of the 5th century that Christianity finally triumphed. With the first sweep of Muslim arms against Palestine in 634, Gaza fell before the invaders and gradually lost its importance as a station along the caravan trade route between the peninsula and Syria. As a city of Palestine, it shared in the process of arabization and islamization that was to transform the ethnic and religious make-up of the entire area. It had a special sanctity for Muslims because Hashim, the great-grandfather of Mohammed, according to tradition was buried there. Its place in Muslim lore was further enhanced by the fact that it was the birthplace of al-Shafi'i (767–820), founder of one of the four schools of law in Islam. In the 12th century, the crusaders found it in near ruins and deserted, and had no trouble in fortifying it, but it never regained its ancient military and strategic importance. After Saladin's victory at Hattin (1187), it reverted to Muslim hands. In 1516 Gaza fell to the Ottoman Turks. In 1799 it was captured by Napoleon Bonaparte. In 1831 it came under the rule of the Egyptian governor Mohammed Ali and his son Ibrahim, but reverted to Turkish rule when the Egyptians were forced to evacuate Syria in 1840. During World War I Gaza was the scene of three battles in 1917 between British and Turkish armies. It was finally evacuated by the Turks when Gen. Edmund (later Field Marshal Viscount) Allenby broke through their line at Beersheba (Nov. 1917). Before the termination in 1948 of the British mandate in Palestine the United Nations general assembly in Nov. 1947 accepted a plan for the partition of Palestine under which Gaza and an area of surrounding territory was to be allotted to the Arabs. (N. A. F.)

The Gaza Strip.—The British mandate ended on May 15, 1948. On the same day the Arab-Israeli war broke out and Egyptian forces entered Gaza, which became the headquarters of the Egyptian expeditionary force in Palestine. As a result of heavy fighting in the autumn of 1948 the area around the town in Arab occupation was reduced in extent to a strip of territory 25 mi. long and 4 to 5 mi. wide, which became known as the Gaza strip. Its boundaries were demarcated in the Egyptian-Israeli armistice agreement of Feb. 24, 1949. The period 1949–54 was relatively quiet except for minor border incidents. In Feb. 1955 Israel launched a heavy raid against the strip, to which Egypt retaliated by organizing commando (*fedayeen*) raids into Israel. Border clashes with heavy loss of civilian life occurred in the spring of 1956. These were followed by a long lull after the nationalization of the Suez canal company, but the area was occupied by Israeli forces during the invasion of Egypt in Nov. 1956. The Egyptian administration returned after the withdrawal of the Israeli forces in March 1957, and units of the United Nations expeditionary force thereafter policed the demarcation line. The population of the strip rose from 70,000 in 1949 to 125,700 in 1962.

After the Arab-Israeli war of 1967, Israel took over jurisdiction of the strip, including the thousands of Palestinian refugees. By the time of the census taken by Israel in 1967, the population had risen to 356,261. Increased emigration caused a decline in 1968, but thereafter, due to a lessening of emigration and to the natural increase, the population again began to rise.

The deplorable living conditions that existed in the strip were somewhat alleviated by aid from the United Nations. Israel instituted a program whereby a number of residents and refugees were sent to work in that country. In 1971 the Israelis began demolishing the houses in three of the more crowded refugee camps, sending families to other places in the northern Sinai or allowing them to make other living arrangements. One of the reasons given was to reduce the threat of the commando raids that have constantly taken place since the Israeli takeover.

See also references under "Gaza" in the Index. (W. A. K.; X.)

GAZELLE, the common name for antelopes of the genus *Gazella*, graceful in build and small to medium in size (24 to 35 in. at the shoulder). Gazelles range the open plains and semideserts from Mongolia through southern Asia to the Atlantic coast of north Africa and throughout east and central tropical Africa. The numerous species differ in body size, coat pattern and size and shape of horns, but the differences are less obvious than the similarities.

In general gazelles are reddish-brown to fawn-coloured above, light below, with a dark streak on the flank separating the colours. A light stripe runs down each side of the face from above the eye to the muzzle, often with a dark streak below it; the forehead and centre of the face between the stripes is generally darker than the body colour. The horns are short to medium in length with numerous raised rings; they may be spreading, lyre-shaped or backwardly curved, and are always slightly upturned at the ends. The horns of the females are smaller and more slender than those of the males, and in one species, the Persian gazelle (*G. subgutturosa*), the females are generally hornless. This species also differs from the others in the development of a goitrelike swelling on the throat in the breeding season. Gazelles run swiftly; Thomson's gazelle of east Africa has been paced from an automobile at 40 m.p.h. over a short distance. See ANTELOPE. (L. H. M.)

GAZETTE, a name given to newssheets or newspapers having an abstract of current events which were forerunners of modern newspapers (*q.v.*). The word came into English from the French, having been adapted from the Italian *gazzetta*, a name given to informal news or gossip sheets first published in Venice in the mid-16th century. Similar sheets soon made their appearance in France and in England. The type of gazette originating from the private newsletter existed in England before the middle of the 16th century, but was confined mainly to detailed accounts of diplomatic maneuvers or to the circulation of courtly verse among a restricted group of readers. Upon the accession of Queen Elizabeth I, however, a far greater variety of such sheets began to appear. Aimed at a wide popular audience, they disseminated gossip, trivia, unofficial news accounts from nongovernment sources, news of recent explorations, commercial advertisements and the more sensational news items of the day—reports of lurid crimes, supposed miracles, witchcraft and the like. The news collected in these sheets was contributed by volunteers, frequently based on the accounts of anonymous witnesses, and was notorious for its inaccuracy. In the 17th century the term was increasingly applied to official government publications, such as the *Oxford, London, Edinburgh* and *Dublin Gazettes.*

See Matthias A. Shraaber, *Some Forerunners of the Newspaper in England, 1476–1622* (1929).

GAZIANTEP, a town and capital of the *il* (province) of Gaziantep in southern Turkey, is situated in limestone hills near the Syrian border about 60 mi. N. of Aleppo. Pop. (1970 prelim.) 329,087, formerly largely Armenian but now Turkoman and Kurdish. Previously known as Aintab, it was renamed by Kemal Ataturk in honour of its resistance to the French in 1920–21 (*Gazi* means "fighter for Islam"); it is, however, frequently referred to by its old name. Well built with stone houses, paved streets and covered bazaars, it is an important market centre and has a meteorological station. It is bordered by gardens, vineyards, olive and nut groves but the surrounding district is barren. In spite of its name (Aintab, "good spring"), the water of Gaziantep is of poor quality. The town has been linked by rail with the Turkish state railway system and is connected by all-weather roads with Adana and Urfa.

The ancient mound of Gaziantep, covered by a medieval castle, is large and the city has probably been occupied since prehistoric times. Its name in Hittite times is unknown but it must have been of strategic importance since it guarded the routes from Syria. In the middle ages it was an important stronghold (Hamtap), and in 1183 it was captured by Saladin. In 1516 it passed to the Ottoman empire and in the early 19th century it served as a base for Ibrahim Pasha before his victory over the Ottoman forces at Nizip (35 mi. E.). In 1921 it was the centre of Turkish resistance to the French attacks and fell in February of that year after a heroic siege of 10 months. It was returned to Turkey in 1922. (See TURKEY: *History.*)

Gaziantep *il* is bounded east by the Euphrates (Firat) river. Pop. (1965) 509,055; area 2,900 sq.mi. It is noted for its wines, and the other chief products are cereals, *baklava* (sweet meats), pistachio nuts, aniseed, *pekmez* (sweet grape paste), tobacco, goatskin rugs and striped cloth. It also supplies remount horses for the Turkish cavalry.

Duluk, ancient Doliche (the site of the famous shrine to Jupiter Dolichenus), lies on the railway several miles northwest of the town and is terraced with vineyards; it has yielded important tombs. (M. V. S.-W.)

GDANSK, one of the three Baltic *wojewodztwa* (provinces) of Poland, was created after World War II from territory around Danzig (parts of East Prussia and Pomerania). Its coastline is 357 km. (222 mi.) in length and its area 10,917 sq.km. (4,215 sq.mi.). Of its 13 counties 5 belonged to Poland before the war (Tczew, Starogard, Wejcherowo, Koscierzyna and Kartuzy). The population (1970) was 1,465,000, of which 70% was urban. The most important towns include Danzig (*q.v.*; or Gdansk), the capital (364,000), Gdynia (190,000), Elblag (89,800), Sopot (47,600), Tczew (40,800), Malbork (30,900). Wejcherowo (33,700), Starogard Gdanski (33,400), Lebork (25,000), and Kwidzyn (23,100).

Three landscape units can be distinguished: the narrow strip of the Baltic coast, with its sand dunes; the Pomeranian lakelands, with a varied morainic surface and their highest point, the Wiezyca, 1,079 ft. above sea level; and the flat (western parts) of the Vistula delta, known as the Zulawy wislane, as much as 6½ ft. below sea level in places. Because of its fertile soil the Zulawy district is the most important centre of agriculture and animal breeding in the *wojewodztwo*. The drainage installations, consisting of many canals, dikes and several hundred pumps, were destroyed by the German forces in 1945, and, although they were rebuilt, productivity has not matched the 1939 level.

The economic life is linked with the sea. The ports of Danzig, Gdynia and Sopot constitute a conurbation which handles about 50% of Poland's ship traffic and more than 60% of the total sea import and export traffic. The shipbuilding industry was revived after World War II, as well as the food industry, which processes products imported by sea. Smaller ports contributing to the fishing industry include Leba, Jastarnia, Hel, Wladislawowo, Puck and Tolmicko as well as two inland ports, Elblag and Tczew. A number of resorts lie along the coast, of which the most frequented are Sopot, Leba, Jastarnia, Jurata, Orlowo. The picturesque lake scenery attracts tourists to the district. (K. M. Wi.)

GDANSK (city): see DANZIG.

GDYNIA, a town of Poland, in the Gdansk *wojewodztwo* (province), one of the three main seaports of Poland, is situated on the Gulf of Danzig 10 mi. N.N.W. of Danzig (Gdansk), with which it is connected by rail. Pop. (1970) 190,100. Gdynia lies on that small sector of the Baltic coast that was returned to Poland by the treaty of Versailles (1919). Difficulties placed in the way of the Polish government by the authorities of Danzig led the former to build a port on its own part of the coast line. The choice fell on Gdynia, a small Kaszuby fishing village, which had natural conditions most suitable for the development of a port. In the period 1924–39 it became the busiest and one of the most modern Baltic ports, the installations including a large cold-storage building, an edible oil plant, shipyards, many stores and railway sidings.

During World War II the Germans occupied Gdynia after a two-week period of stubborn defense. Its name was changed to Gotenhafen, some of the Polish inhabitants were murdered and others were deported and their places taken by Germans. As a base of the German navy, Gdynia suffered from Allied bombing, and the port was almost totally destroyed by the Germans during their retreat in 1945. The installations were rapidly rebuilt after the war.

Since the war Gdynia has formed one port and urban group with Danzig and Sopot (*q.v.*). It is the base of the Polish navy and the main passenger port. Exports include coal, lumber and sugar; iron ore, fertilizers and foodstuffs are imported. Gdynia contains the Technical College for Deep-Sea Fishing, the Sea Fishing institute, the Naval museum and a theatre. (K. M. Wi.)

See also DANZIG: *History.*

GEAR-CUTTING MACHINE: see MACHINE TOOLS.

GEARS are machine parts, operating in pairs, which transmit motion and force from one rotating shaft to another, or from a shaft to a slide (rack), by means of successively engaging projections called teeth. The smaller of a gear pair is called the pinion and the larger is the gear. When the pinion is on the driving shaft, the pair acts as a speed reducer; when the gear drives, the pair is a speed increaser. Gears are more frequently used as speed reducers than as increasers.

The gears in fig. 1 have teeth equally spaced on circles. If the pinion has 10 teeth and the gear 20, the pinion will rotate twice as fast as the gear. The speed ratio will be 20/10 = 2. In general, if a pinion having T_P teeth rotates at N_P r.p.m. and a gear having T_G teeth rotates at N_G r.p.m., the speed ratio R will be

$$R = \frac{T_G}{T_P} = \frac{N_P}{N_G}$$

For gears of the type shown in fig. 1, there are physical limitations to both the minimum number of teeth on the pinion and the maximum number of teeth on the gear.

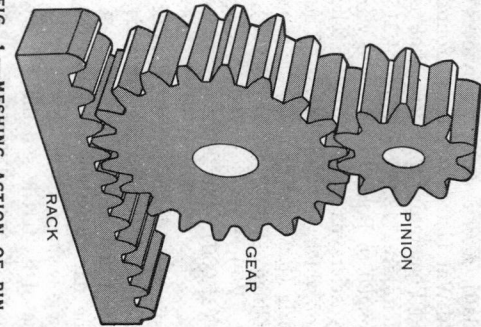

FIG. 1.—MESHING ACTION OF PINION, GEAR AND RACK

PINION · GEAR · RACK

For a large speed ratio, two or more gear pairs may be required. Fig. 2 shows two pairs arranged in a compound train. If $T_A = T_C = 10$ and $T_B = T_D = 20$, the speed ratio will be

$$R = \frac{T_B}{T_A} \times \frac{T_D}{T_C} = \frac{N_A}{N_D} = 4$$

The gears in fig. 1 rotate in opposite directions. If another gear is placed between them, the gear and pinion will rotate in the same direction. The intermediate or idler gear has no effect on the speed ratio. In many cases idler gears (one or more) are used to fill the space when the shafts are too far apart to be connected by one pair.

When the shafts are close together and must rotate in the same direction, a pinion and internal gear may be used, as shown in fig. 3. Teeth on the internal gear are cut on the inside of a cup-shaped member.

If it is required that the input and output shafts be co-axial, the arrangement shown in fig. 4 may be used; this is known as a planetary, or epicyclic, gear train. The sun gear S on the shaft B meshes with two or more planet gears P, which are carried on bearings on a carrier A attached to the shaft C. The planet gears also mesh with an internal gear I.

It can be shown that the speeds of the shafts N_B, N_C and the internal gear N_I are related in the following way:

$$N_C = \frac{N_B}{T_I/T_S + 1} + \frac{N_I(T_I/T_S)}{T_I/T_S + 1}$$

If $T_I = 60$, $T_S = 20$, and the internal gear is prevented from ro-

FIG. 2.—TWO GEAR PAIRS ARRANGED IN A COMPOUND TRAIN

C · D · A · B

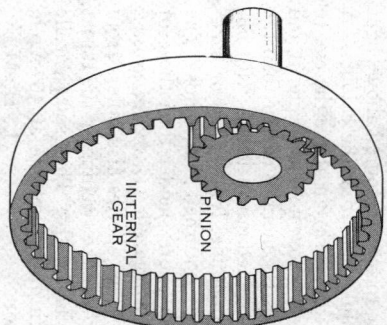

FIG. 3.—INTERNAL GEAR AND PINION

PINION · INTERNAL GEAR

tating by a brake, then $N_I = 0$ and $N_B = 4N_C$. If the sun gear rotates clockwise it will cause the planet gears to roll around on the inside of the fixed internal gear and rotate the arm and shaft C in a clockwise direction. If B is the input shaft and C the output shaft, the unit becomes a compact, symmetrical speed reducer, with a comparatively high-power transmitting capacity, since the load is shared by three planet gears. For this reason planetary transmissions are used on aircraft where space is limited and weight must be kept to a minimum.

Lastly, if the sun gear and the arm are coupled together by means of a clutch so as to prevent gear tooth action and all members are

If the sun gear instead of the internal gear is fixed, $N_B = 0$ and $N_I = 4/3 N_C$. If the gear I is the input, the output shaft C will rotate in the same direction at a slower speed.

If the arm is fixed, $N_C = 0$ and $N_B = -3N_I$, the term -3 indicates that shaft B rotates three times faster than gear I and in the opposite direction.

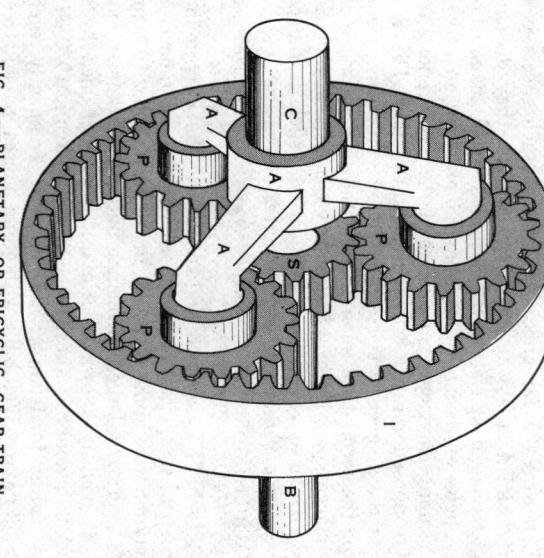

FIG. 4.—PLANETARY, OR EPICYCLIC, GEAR TRAIN

allowed to rotate about the central axis, $N_I = N_C = N_B$.

Thus, with the three-element planetary system of fig. 4, the speed ratio obtained (4, 3, 4/3 or 1) depends on which element is fixed. It is this feature which makes planetary arrangements valuable in the automatic transmissions of automobiles. In these, the fixing and interconnecting of the members is accomplished automatically by brakes and clutches.

The number of ways in which the gears may be arranged in a planetary system is infinite. The planet gears may be compounded (i.e., have more than one gear on the same shaft) and mesh with other sun and internal gears. None of the gears may be fixed. In this case any two (including the arm) may be attached to input shafts and the remainder to output shafts. Speed ratios of 10,000 are easily obtained in planetary transmissions.

All of the gears shown in figs. 1 to 4 are used for connecting parallel shafts. The shapes of the ends of the teeth shown in fig. 1 are involutes—the curve traced by any point on a taut string when the string is unwrapped from a cylinder (fig. 5A). Along their length, the teeth may be either straight and parallel to the shafts, as in fig. 5A, or curved, as in fig. 5B. Gears with straight teeth are called spur gears, while those with curved teeth are called helical gears. The latter may be thought of as twisted spur gears, the teeth curving around the gear like the threads on a screw.

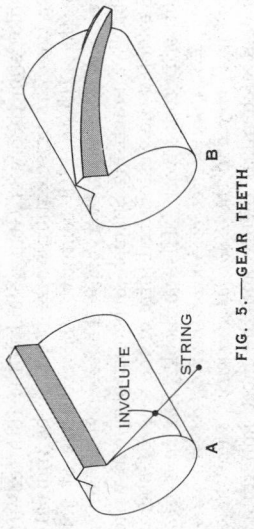

FIG. 5.—GEAR TEETH
(A) Straight or spur; (B) helical

FIG. 7.—CROSSED-AXIS HELICAL GEARS

On account of the overlapping action between the teeth, helical gears are less noisy in operation and have a higher load-carrying capacity than equivalent spur gears. If used singly, however, an axial thrust load is produced as shown in fig. 6(A). This thrust load is ineffective in turning the shaft and results in an undesirable thrust load on the shaft bearings. This may be overcome by having the teeth slope in opposite directions on the two halves of the gear, as shown in figs. 6(B) and 6(C).

On ships, for the transmission of power from high-speed turbines to low-speed propellor shafts, double helical gears are almost universally employed.

Helical gears may also be used to connect nonintersecting shafts at any angle to one another. Fig. 7 shows an arrangement for connecting shafts inclined at 90°. This is the commonest angle for which such gears are used. If the helices sloped in the opposite direction to that shown, the lower shaft would rotate in the opposite direction.

When the shafts are parallel, the contact between the teeth on mating gears is "line contact" regardless of whether the teeth are straight or helical. When the shafts are inclined, the contact becomes "point contact." For this reason crossed-axis helical gears are never used when the power being transmitted is high. However, they are relatively insensitive to misalignment and are frequently employed in instruments and positioning mechanisms where friction is the only force opposing their motion.

There is another aspect in which gears connecting parallel shafts differ from those connecting nonparallel shafts. When the shafts are parallel, there is always one—and only one—pair of imaginary friction disks which would transmit the power with the same speed ratio as the gears. The diameters of these disks are called the pitch diameters of the gears. These diameters must be proportional to the numbers of teeth and fill the space between the shafts, and the gear teeth must be equally spaced on both gears. This spacing is known as the circular pitch and is equal to the circumference of the pitch circle divided by the number of teeth.

On crossed-axis helical gears the circular spacing of the teeth need not be the same on both gears of a pair. It follows that the pitch diameters need not be inversely proportional to the speeds. Consequently, if a large speed ratio is required on one pair of gears—say, 100—this large ratio is more easily obtained when the shaft axes are crossed than when they are parallel. With parallel shafts, the pinion pitch diameter would have to be 1/100 of the gear pitch diameter, which is an impractical proportion. With crossed axes, the pinion could have only one helical tooth (called a thread in this case) and be as large as necessary for adequate strength. The pinion would look like a screw, and the gear would have 100 teeth.

In order to achieve line contact and improve the load-carrying

capacity of the pair, the gear could be made to partially curve around the pinion in somewhat the same way that a nut envelops a screw. The result would be a worm and gear (fig. 8). It is also possible to make worms of an "hourglass" shape, instead of cylindrical, so that they envelop the gear. This results in a further increase in load-carrying capacity.

Worm gears provide the simplest means of obtaining large ratios in a single pair. However, they are usually less efficient than parallel-shaft gears because when the shafts are parallel there is a sliding movement up and down the teeth only; on crossed-axis gears there is also a sliding movement along the teeth.

On parallel-shaft gears, the friction loss in each pair seldom exceeds 5% of the transmitted power and on helical gears it may be as low as 1%. The losses in worm gears may exceed 75% and are seldom less than 5%. They are greatly affected by the diameter of the worm and the number of threads, single thread worms of large diameter having the highest losses (i.e., the lowest efficiencies). When the efficiency of a worm and gear is more than 50%, the gear can drive the worm. With multiple-thread, hardened and ground steel worms meshing with bronze worm gears, efficiencies exceeding 50% are easily obtained, thus providing compact speed increasers that can be used for driving superchargers on aircraft engines.

For connecting shafts whose axes would intersect if extended, bevel gears are used. The pitch surfaces of bevel gears are frustums of cones, and the teeth, which must be tapered, may be either straight or curved (fig. 9). Although curved-tooth bevel gears are called spiral bevel gears, the curve of the teeth is usually a circular arc. The curvature of the teeth results in overlapping tooth action and creates less noise than straight bevel gears. For the transmission of power at high speeds, spiral bevel gears are superior to straight bevel gears, just as helical gears are superior to spur gears for connecting parallel shafts. Spiral bevel gears are invaluable when power is being transmitted at an angle, as on helicopter transmissions.

When adapted for use on shafts which do not intersect, spiral bevel gears are called hypoid gears (fig. 10). On automobiles they are used to connect the engine drive shaft to the rear axles. The offset permits lowering of the centre of gravity of the body. In some respects hypoid gears resemble worm gears. There is more sliding movement than on spiral bevel gears, and the pitch surface diameters are not inversely proportional to the speeds. This permits high-speed ratios, since the pinion may be made as large as necessary for adequate strength.

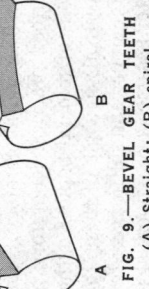

FIG. 9.—BEVEL GEAR TEETH
(A) Straight; (B) spiral

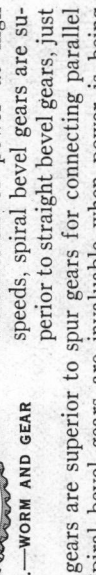

FIG. 8.—WORM AND GEAR

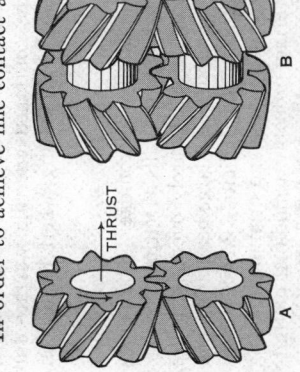

FIG. 6.—HELICAL GEARS
(A) Single helical; (B) double helical; (C) herringbone

An interesting application of a planetary gear arrangement incorporating bevel gears is found in the differential gears of an automobile (q.v.) rear axle. The ring gear, which is driven by the drive shaft pinion, is fixed to the differential carrier which carries the differential gears. Bevel pinions are carried on bearings in the carrier and mesh with bevel gears to which the axle shafts are fixed.

On a straight road, the differential gears revolve as a unit, without meshing action, and the axles revolve as if they were fixed to the ring gear. When turning a corner, the outside wheel (and axle) must turn faster than the inside wheel, and the differential gears rotate relative to one another to permit this. If the angular speeds of the carrier, left axle shaft and right axle shaft are N_C, N_L and N_R respectively, it can be shown that $2N_C = N_L + N_R$. If the rear wheels are jacked up, with the engine stopped, then $N_C = 0$ and $N_L = -N_R$. If the left rear wheel is turned clockwise, the right wheel will turn counterclockwise. Bevel gear differentials are extensively used in computing machines such as adders. If N_L and N_R are the input speeds, N_C will represent one half of their sum. See also references under "Gears" in the Index volume.

(AR. C.)

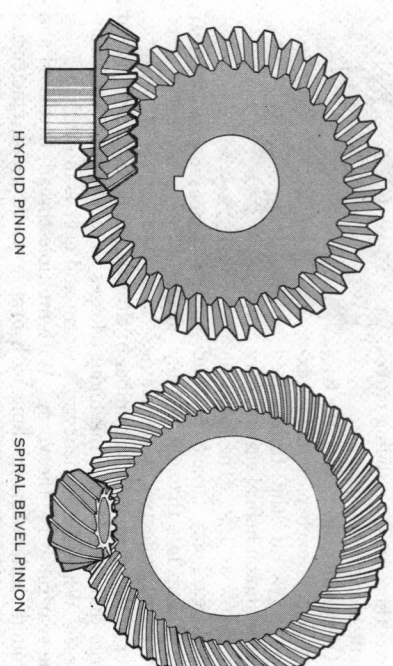

HYPOID PINION

SPIRAL BEVEL PINION

FIG. 10.—SPECIAL GEAR-AND-PINION DESIGNS

GEBER is the name assumed by the author of several books that were among the most influential works on alchemy (q.v.) and metallurgy during the 14th and 15th centuries. The name is a Latinized form of the Arabic name Jabir and was adopted because of the great reputation as an alchemist attributed to a certain Jabir ibn Hayyan, said to have flourished in the 8th century. There may have been an early Arabic alchemist of that name who wrote at least one of the books that bear his name, the *Book of Mercy*. However, the enormous number of works attributed to him, now set at more than 2,000, aroused some doubts as to his existence even among some later Arab scholars. The studies of P. Kraus have shown that the name Jabir was used by writers of the Muslim sect of the Isma'iliya, a brotherhood that was greatly interested in mystical doctrines, astrology, alchemy, numerology and cosmology.

The books ascribed to Jabir apparently were written in the 9th and 10th centuries by a number of different authors. They included many works on alchemy that were based on the Aristotelian idea that matter was composed of four qualities: heat, cold, moisture and dryness. In the Jabirian corpus these qualities are given a more material character than they were by Aristotle; there is even a description of a process by which pure cold can be isolated.

A somewhat quantitative approach was introduced by assuming that the various qualities were combined in definite numerical proportions in the substances with which the alchemist worked. The method of determining these proportions was based, however, on numerology. Some books in the Jabirian corpus described practical laboratory procedures with elaborate classifications of mineral bodies. Other books were highly theoretical and mystical; in some of these, the theory that metals were composed of mercury and sulfur was proposed for the first time. This theory later became very influential in alchemical thought and finally led to the phlogiston theory of Georg Stahl in the 18th century.

By the time Arabic scientific works began to be translated into Latin in the 11th to 13th centuries, the existence of Jabir had been accepted by almost everyone. Thus, when an author who was probably a practising Spanish alchemist began to write about 1310, he adopted the westernized form of the name, Geber, to give added authority to his work. His four books, *The Investigation of Perfection, The Sum of Perfection or the Perfect Magistery, The Invention of Verity* and the *Book of Furnaces*, were the clearest expression of alchemical theory and the most important set of laboratory directions to appear before the 16th century. They were accordingly very widely read and were extremely influential in a field where mysticism and secrecy were the usual rule.

In his theoretical views, Geber accepted most of the Arabic ideas and spread them through western Europe. He assumed the accuracy of the sulfur-mercury theory of metal composition and devoted much space to a description of metallic properties in its terms. He believed in the truth of alchemy and explained the use of an elixir in transmuting base metals into gold. His rational approach, based on apparently valid theories, did much to give alchemy a firm and respectable position in Europe.

At the same time, his practical directions for laboratory procedures were so clear that it is obvious that he was very familiar with many chemical operations. He described the purification of reagents, the preparation of mineral acids, the cupellation method for separating gold and silver, and the construction and use of many pieces of laboratory apparatus, especially furnaces. Although his books certainly owe much to the ideas developed among the Arab alchemists, they are not translations of any known Arabic work. They represent one of the early products of the new learning in Europe and were not equaled in their field until the writings of Vannoccio Biringuccio, Georgius Agricola and Lazarus Ercker in the 16th century.

BIBLIOGRAPHY.—E. J. Holmyard, "An Essay on Jabir ibn Hayyan," *Studien zur Geschichte der Chemie, Festgabe für E. O. von Lippmann* (1927), (ed.), *The Works of Geber, Englished by Richard Russell, 1678* (1928); P. Kraus, *Jabir ibn Hayyan, Contribution à l'histoire des idées scientifiques dans l'Islam*, 2 vol. (1942-43); H. M. Leicester, *The Historical Background of Chemistry*, pp. 63-68, 85-86 (1956).

(H. M. L.)

GEBHARD (GEBHARD TRUCHSESS VON WALDBURG) (1547-1601), archbishop-elector of Cologne from 1577 to 1584, was born on Nov. 10, 1547, of a south German family, his uncle Otto being a cardinal and bishop of Augsburg. A canon of Cologne cathedral from 1561, Gebhard was elected archbishop in 1577 by a narrow majority of votes against the Wittelsbach candidate, Ernest of Bavaria. He had himself consecrated priest in 1578, accepted the creed of the Council of Trent and zealously promoted the Jesuits in Cologne; his election was confirmed by the pope in 1580. From c. 1580, however, he pursued a liaison with the canoness Agnes von Mansfeld, whom he finally resolved to marry. Adopting Protestantism, he married his mistress in 1583, but refused to give up his electorate. He found support only in his duchy of Westphalia (attached to the electorate of Cologne); from the counts of the Wetterau district and from John Casimir, the count Palatine; his opponents, who proceeded to elect Ernest of Bavaria as archbishop, obtained the help of Bavaria and Spain. The ensuing Cologne War devastated the electorate of Cologne. Gebhard, despite occasional successes, was at a disadvantage from the first; and after the loss of his capital, Bonn, in 1584 he retired to the Netherlands, whence he continued guerilla warfare for some time. In 1589 he withdrew to Strasbourg, where he died on May 31, 1601.

See M. Lossen, *Der kölnische Krieg*, 2 vol. (1882-97). (EH. W.)

GECKO is any lizard of the family Gekkonidae. The names gecko, tokay and cheechak are based on the calls of various species. They are small, usually nocturnal reptiles, rarely over six inches in length, with a soft skin, a short, stout body, large head and weak limbs often equipped with suction-padded digits. Most geckos lack movable eyelids, the eyes, usually large and prominent, being protected by a transparent covering, probably a modified nictitating membrane. The family is cosmopolitan in distribution, occurring everywhere in warmer climates, even on the remotest oceanic islands, and is adapted to very diverse habitats. All species are insectivorous.

Most geckos have the digits modified for climbing; the fingers and toes are dilated either terminally or at their bases and the lower surface of the dilation is covered with transverse plates whose arrangement is diverse in the various genera; each plate is beset with numerous tiny, hairlike processes that give the whole surface a velvety appearance. When the feet are placed on any surface the velvety pile accommodates itself to the slightest irregularities and pressure forces the air out from between the hairs; the resulting vacuum gives sufficient adhesion to enable many species to climb absolutely smooth and vertical surfaces and even to run across a whitewashed ceiling or glass surfaces.

Claws are well developed in most species and in a few are provided with a special sheath into which they are retractile. The most remarkable modification of the feet is found in the genus *Palmatogecko* from the deserts of central South-West Africa; they have no adhesive apparatus but the toes are webbed to their extremities to enable the animal to walk over and partially burrow into the loose sand.

Often the tail is peculiar in shape; it may be long and tapering or short and blunt, or even globular; in one species (*Gymnodactylus platyurus*) it is leaf-shaped. It seems highly probable that in many instances, particularly where it is large and globular, the tail serves as a storehouse of reserve nutriment on which the animal can draw during unfavourable conditions. The tail is extremely fragile and if detached is quickly regenerated, the new one having roughly the same shape and scale pattern as the original.

As a rule the skin is soft and delicate, and covered with minute granules; frequently there are large tubercles intermixed with the granules; *Teratoscincus*, a western Asiatic desert dweller, has developed large, overlapping smooth scales, that enable it to slip through the sand with the minimum of friction. Colours as a rule are drab, grays, browns and dirty whites predominating, though one genus, *Phelsuma*, of Madagascar, comprises the bright green day-active geckos.

Although these curious looking lizards are completely inoffensive, in many regions they have been erroneously regarded as being poisonous, probably from their weird and forbidding appearance. They are actually exceedingly useful because of their insect-eating habit.

ERIC HOSKING

NORTH AFRICAN GECKO (TARENTOLA MAURITANICA)

Many species have a voice, the call differing with the species and ranging from a feeble click or chirp to a shrill cackle or bark. All species are oviparous, the eggs being white, hard-shelled and usually laid beneath the bark of trees or attached to the under side of leaves. *See* LIZARD.

GED, WILLIAM (1690–1749), Scottish goldsmith, early developer of stereotyping, was born in Edinburgh in 1690. In 1725 he perfected a system by which printing plates could be cast from type forms but, not being able to interest Edinburgh printers in his venture, he entered into partnership with William Fenner, a London stationer, and Thomas James, a typefounder. They obtained from Cambridge university the privilege of printing Bibles and prayer books by Ged's method, but the partnership was undermined by the typefounder and the process hindered by compositors who saw in it a threat to their trades. Ged returned to Edinburgh where he died on Oct. 19, 1749. A Cambridge prayer book was possibly printed from Ged's plates and certainly an edition of Sallust in Edinburgh. His sons briefly carried on the process but eventually it was abandoned until taken up by others later in the century. (J. C. MN.)

GEDDES, SIR ERIC CAMPBELL (1875–1937), British businessman and administrator remembered for his reforms in economy known as the "Geddes axe," was born at Agra, India, on Sept. 26, 1875. Educated at Merchiston Castle school, Edinburgh, and the Oxford Military college, he went to the United States at 17 and worked in lumber camps, in steel mills and on railways. He also worked on railways in India before returning to England in 1906 to join the North Eastern Railway Co. During World War I Geddes, under Lloyd George as minister of munitions, held several posts in which he brought the British lines of communication in France to a high standard of efficiency. In 1917 he was elected to parliament for the borough of Cambridge and appointed first lord of the admiralty, and in 1919 he became the first minister of transport. Geddes' best-known work was as chairman of the committee on national expenditure, its suggested measures of widespread economy in the nation's finances being called the Geddes axe. In 1922 he left parliament to resume a business career. He died at Hassocks, Sussex, on June 22, 1937.

GEDDES, NORMAN BEL (1893–1958), U.S. designer, particularly influential in the development of theatrical and industrial design, was born in Adrian, Mich., April 27, 1893. Following brief study at the Cleveland Institute of Art and the Art Institute of Chicago, he became interested in the theatre and staged his own first play, *Nju*, and five others for the Los Angeles Little theatre in 1916. In New York in 1918 he did scenic designs for the Metropolitan Opera. He designed, produced or directed some 200 operas, films, plays and musical comedies. His sets included those for Max Reinhardt's *The Miracle* (1924); *Jeanne d'Arc*, produced in Paris with Eva Le Gallienne (1925); and *Dead End* (1935), which were said at the time to have been "more convincing than reality." He changed the whole artistic concept of scenic design from the ornamental to the clean, functional effect —that the audience would "not be conscious of any scenery or background other than the mood in which the characters of the play should move." Toward the end of the 1920s he adapted his ideas to the area of industrial design, gradually building an organization that employed 2,000, and designed such a variety of things as skyscrapers, inkwells, yachts, radios, interiors and refrigerators. He did as much as any U.S. designer to popularize "streamlining" as a style of industrial design (*see* DESIGN). He designed the General Motors Futurama building and exhibit at the New York world's fair (1939–40), which drew greater crowds than any other exhibit. Geddes also designed theatres all over the world, staged circuses, developed equipment and techniques for the armed services and wrote books on a number of subjects. He died on May 8, 1958, in New York city. One of his daughters, Barbara Bel Geddes, gained fame as an actress.
(CD. BN.)

GEDDES, SIR PATRICK (1854–1932), British biologist and sociologist whose pioneer studies of the development of contemporary human communities, an outcome of his biological research, influenced civic and regional planning, was born at Ballater, Scot., on Oct. 2, 1854. He trained in biology in London, under T. H. Huxley, and in France, becoming professor of botany at University college, Dundee, Scot., in 1883 and professor of sociology and civics at Bombay university, India, in 1919. His chief biological work stresses the importance of the role of sex in evolution. In sociology his originality is shown by his thesis, based upon surveys in Scotland, India, Palestine and elsewhere, that the development of human communities presents essentially biological problems whose solutions depend first upon diagnosing the complex interactions between people, their environments and their activities. His works include *The Evolution of Sex* (with J. A. Thomson, 1900), *City Development* (1904) and *Cities in Evolution* (1913). Geddes was knighted in 1931 and died at Montpellier, France, on April 17, 1932.

See A. D. Peacock, "Patrick Geddes: Biologist," *Alumnus Chronicle*, St. Andrews (1955); P. Mairet, *Pioneer of Sociology: Life and Letters of Patrick Geddes* (1957). (A. D. P.)

GEDIMINAS (*c.* 1275–*c.* 1341), grand duke of Lithuania and one of the wisest statesmen in the history of that country, succeeded his brother Vytenis in 1316 and started the Gediminas dynasty. In contemporary documents he was described as "king of the Lithuanians" or "king of Lithuania and Russia." His domain comprised not only Lithuania proper and Samogitia, but also Volhynia, northwestern Ukraine and Belorussia to the Dnieper. The principalities of Kiev, Pskov and Novgorod were for some time under his protection. Gedimas extended the eastern and southern frontiers of Lithuania not by war but through careful diplomacy and through the marriages of his sons and daughters. He became the strongest ruler of eastern Europe and, through his diplomacy, balanced the growing influence of the duchy of Muscovy in northern Russia.

From the west and north, Lithuania was threatened by the Teutonic Order and the Livonian Knights of the Sword under the pretext of converting it to Christianity. After conquering the Prussians, the Teutonic Knights continually attacked the lower Nemunas (Niemen) area, but they did not succeed in occupying Lithuania. Gedimas began negotiating directly with the Holy See. At the end of 1322 he wrote to Pope John XXII, soliciting his protection against the knights, informing him of the privileges already granted to the Dominicans and the Franciscans in Lithuania and desiring that legates should be sent to receive him also into the church. In Oct. 1323 representatives of the archbishop of Riga, the bishop of Dorpat, the king of Denmark, the Dominican and Franciscan orders and the grand master of the Teutonic Order assembled at Vilnius, where Gedimas confirmed his promises and undertook to be baptized as soon as the papal legates arrived. A compact was then signed at Vilnius confirming the promised privileges.

But the christianizing of Lithuania was by no means to the liking of the Teutonic Knights and they strove to nullify Gedimas' designs. Gedimas' chief object was to save Lithuania from destruction at the hands of the Germans. But he was still a pagan ruling over semipagan lands; he was equally bound to his pagan kinsmen in Samogitia, to his Orthodox subjects in Russia and to his Catholic allies in Mazovia. His policy, therefore, was necessarily tentative and ambiguous. Thus his raid upon Dobrzyn, the latest acquisition of the Teutonic Knights on Polish soil, gave them a weapon against him. The Prussian bishops, who were devoted to the knights, at a synod at Elblag (Elbing) denounced Gedimas as an enemy of the faith; his Orthodox subjects reproached him with leaning toward the Latins; while the pagan Lithuanians accused him of abandoning the ancient gods. Gedimas then repudiated his former promises; he refused to receive the papal legates who arrived in Riga in Sept. 1323 and dismissed the Franciscans.

Gedimas saw that the pagan element was still the strongest force in Lithuania and could not be dispensed with in the coming struggle for nationality. Through his ambassador he informed the papal legates in Riga that his difficult position compelled him to postpone his own baptism, and the legates showed their confidence in him by forbidding the neighbour states to make war against Lithuania for the next four years, besides ratifying the treaty made between Gedimas and the archbishop of Riga. Nevertheless in 1325 the Teutonic Order, disregarding the censures of the church, resumed the war with Gedimas, who in the same year by the marriage of his daughter Aldona to Casimir, son of Wladyslaw Lokietek, king of Poland, had improved his own position.

His internal administration bears all the marks of a wise ruler. He protected the Roman as well as the Orthodox clergy, encouraging them both to civilize his subjects; he raised the Lithuanian army to the highest state of efficiency then attainable; defended his borders with a chain of strong fortresses; and built numerous towns including Vilnius, the capital. Gedimas died in the winter of 1341-42. Married three times, he left seven sons and six daughters.

BIBLIOGRAPHY.—V. B. Antonovich, *Ocherk istorii Velikogo Knyazhestva Litovskogo* (1878); J. Jakstas, *Vokiečių Ordinas ir Lietuva Vytenio ir Gedimino metu, Senove*, i-ii (1936-37); H. Paszkiewicz, *Jagiellonowie a Moskwa* (1933) and *The Origin of Russia* (1954).
(Ma. G.)

GEEL (GHEEL), a large village of Belgium, situated 26 mi. E. of Antwerp, in the province of Antwerp. Pop. (1961 est.) 26,611. Geel is served by railroad, canals and highways and has some small industries (tiles, concrete wares, four mills, brewery and cigar factories). Geel is famous for its unique system of family care of the mentally ill. Legend associates this with the Irish St. Dympna, who was beheaded there by her father in the 7th century and around whose tomb miracles soon happened, always in connection with insane persons. A church was built in St. Dympna's honour, and the insane who came to Geel to implore recovery were accommodated in the *Siechenkaemer* built against the wall of the church. As the crowds became too large for this, they were lodged in the houses of the inhabitants. In 1850 this religious-municipal system became a government institution. (A. L. V.)

GEELONG, the second largest city and port of Victoria, Austr., is situated on a landlocked part of Port Phillip inlet, known as Corio Bay, 45 mi. SW of Melbourne by rail. Pop. (1966) 105,059 (urban area). Geelong is an important rail junction and is also linked with Melbourne by the Prince's Highway. It expanded rapidly after World War II. The city is an educational centre with a large modern library that opened in the civic centre in 1959. Among its schools are the Gordon Institute of Technology, specializing in textiles, among other fields. Industries include the manufacture of motorcars, auto castings, safety glass, woolen textiles, cement, phosphatic fertilizers, agricultural machinery, rope and cordage, and spirits. Salt is produced by evaporation, and oil is refined. Geelong is the outlet for the wool-growing area in the state's Western District, and about one-tenth of Australia's wool clip is sold at the wool sales there. The port, which ranks fifth in total trade in Australia, is the terminal for the bulk handling of wheat in Victoria. Ships of 34 ft. draft can be accommodated at low water and there are many all-weather berths. Geelong is a tourist centre and a number of nearby seaside resorts have surfing beaches, including Lorne, Anglesea, Torquay, Barwon Heads, Point Lonsdale, and Queenscliffe.
(F. DE J.)

GEER, DIRK JAN DE (1870-1960), Dutch conservative statesman who defected from Queen Wilhelmina's London government in World War II, was born in Groningen on Dec. 14, 1870. He graduated as doctor in law from the University of Utrecht in 1895 and started his career as parliamentary editor of a newspaper. Entering politics, he became a town councilor of Rotterdam (1901-07) and later a Christian Historical member of the lower chamber (1907-21). From 1921 to 1923 he served as minister of finance, from 1925 to 1926 as minister of the interior and from March 8, 1926, to July 3, 1929, as prime minister and minister of finance. In 1933 he was appointed as minister of state. Having formed a coalition government on Aug. 9, 1939, he was in charge at the time of the German invasion in May 1940 and moved to London with Queen Wilhelmina. After the collapse of France he visited Winston Churchill to propose his mediation of a negotiated peace with Germany. This proposal, based on his long-standing ideas of conciliation in law and politics, was strongly disavowed by Queen Wilhelmina and his fellow ministers, and on Sept. 3, 1940, De Geer resigned. Then, entrusted with a mission to the Dutch East Indies, for which he gave a signed assurance of loyalty, he broke his trust on his way at Lisbon, in Jan. 1941, and went via Berlin to The Hague. For this, on May 23, 1947, he was sentenced to a fine of 20,000 guilders and one year's imprisonment; the latter part of the sentence was suspended because of his age. He died at Soest on Nov. 28, 1960.

GEERTGEN, TOT SINT JANS (c. 1465-c. 1493), Dutch painter active in Haarlem, one of the most interesting Dutch artists of the 15th century and important as representing a school of which very few works have survived destruction. He was surnamed "tot Sint Jans," as he lived with the knights of St. John at Haarlem. According to K. van Mander, the authority on his life, he was a pupil of Ouwater at Haarlem. Neither the year of his birth nor of his death is known, but only that he was 28 years old when he died. Geertgen painted a large triptych for the high altar of the knights of St. John. The central panel with the Crucifixion and one of the wings were destroyed in religious skirmishes; the other wing has been identified with the aid of Van Mander's description. This wing is now in the Vienna gallery, sliced into two separate panels, front and back. The front represents the dead Christ being mourned by His friends. The pathos of the scene is expressed with deep feeling. The influence of Rogier van der Weyden is seen in the Magdalen wringing her hands. In the background is a realistic burial scene on Mount Calvary. Here the artist broke away from the traditional symbolical assemblage of emblematic figures on the altarpieces of his time and felt his way toward the more vivid and dramatic style of the next generation of Dutch painters.

The same is true of the other panel (the back of the wing) on which the emperor Julian the Apostate is directing the burial of the bones of St. John the Baptist. In the mid-distance of this panel is an admirable group of portraits of the knights of St. John at Haarlem among whom the artist lived. They are lifelike studies of individual characters and seem to presage those great democratic portrait groups famous in Dutch paintings of the 17th century.

A number of pictures are ascribed to him on stylistic grounds. Among these is the "St. John the Baptist" of the Berlin museum, where the pensive saint is sitting in beautiful parklike scenery. In the same collection is "Virgin and Child." The Louvre contains the "Resurrection of Lazarus," the Amsterdam museum, "The Virgin's Kindred" and the "Adoration of the Magi." The "Man of Sorrows" at Utrecht is a painful but wonderful picture; a triptych at Prague represents the "Adoration of the Magi" in the centre and "Donors and Saints" on the wings. It is distinguished for the original conception of some of its figures and for its animated background. The National gallery, London, has one of his most attractive pictures. It represents "Nativity," a night scene, remarkable for its rendering of chiaroscuro. One of the most striking of Geertgen's achievements is his harmonious fusion of the elements of the landscape.

BIBLIOGRAPHY.—L. Baldass, *Geertgen van Haarlem* (1921); M. J. Friedländer, *Die altniederländische Malerei, V, G. van Haarlem und Hieronymus Bosch* (1927); J. H. H. Kessler, *Geertgen tot St. Jans* (1930).

GEEZ is the language of an ancient nomadic Semitic race of Ethiopia. *See* ETHIOPIAN LITERATURE; SEMITIC LANGUAGES.

GEGENBAUR, KARL (1826–1903), German anatomist, was born on Aug. 21, 1826, at Würzburg and was educated at the university there. In 1855 he was appointed professor of anatomy at Jena, and in 1873 at Heidelberg, where he was also director of the Anatomical institute until 1901.

In his best-known work, *Grundriss der vergleichenden Anatomie* (1874, Eng. trans. 1878), Gegenbaur laid stress on the high value of comparative anatomy as the basis of the study of homologies. A distinctive piece of work was effected by him in 1871 in supplementing the evidence adduced by Thomas Huxley in refutation of the theory of the origin of the skull from expanded vertebrae. Huxley demonstrated that the skull is built up of cartilaginous pieces; Gegenbaur showed that "in the lowest (gristly) fishes, where hints of the original vertebrae might be most expected, the skull is an unsegmented gristly brain box, and that in higher forms the vertebral nature of the skull cannot be maintained, since many of the bones, notably those along the top of the skull, arise in the skin."

In 1875 he founded the *Morphologisches Jahrbuch*, which he edited for many years. In 1901 he published a short autobiography under the title *Erlebtes und Erstrebtes*. Gegenbaur died at Heidelberg on June 14, 1903.

See M. Fürbringer, "Karl Gegenbaur," in *Heidelberger Professoren aus dem 19ten Jahrhundert* (1903).

GEGENSCHEIN (or COUNTERGLOW) is a slightly oval patch of faint luminosity just opposite the sun in the night sky. As the sun moves in its apparent annual path among the stars, the gegenschein moves along the ecliptic, always in the region where the sun was six months earlier or will be six months later. The patch of light is so faint that it can be seen only in the absence of moonlight, away from city lights and with the eyes adapted to darkness. Most observers use averted vision in order to utilize the peripheral regions of the retina which are relatively sensitive to very faint light. The gegenschein is lost in the light of the Milky Way in the summer and winter. The best observing periods are February, March, April and August, September, October.

The gegenschein and the zodiacal light (q.v.) form a continuous band of light along the ecliptic. The spectrum of the gegenschein is similar to that of the sun, and it is generally believed that it is the result of the back reflection of sunlight from meteoric ma-
terial located in a region of the solar system opposite the sun and, therefore, outside the earth's orbit. The enhanced intensity in the counter-sun direction may be attributed to an increase in the concentration of particles in that direction, to an increased reflecting efficiency for direct back reflection or perhaps to a combination of these two causes.   (F. E. R.)

GEHENNA, in Jewish thought of the New Testament period, was the place set aside for the punishment of the wicked, both those condemned for a maximum of 12 months and those doomed to everlasting torment. "Then the pit of torment shall appear, ... and the furnace of hell [Lat. *gehenna*] shall be disclosed" (Ezra Apocalypse vii. [36]). Some references in the Mishnah are Aiduyoth 6; Aboth 1,5; Rosh Hashono 16. *See* HELL.

GEIBEL, (FRANZ) EMANUEL (1815–1884), German poet and dramatist, the head of the Munich group of formalist poets (which the king gathered round him, including Paul Heyse [q.v.]), was born at Lübeck on Oct. 17, 1815, the son of a Protestant pastor. He studied theology and then classical philology at Bonn and Berlin, and from 1838 to 1840 was a tutor in Athens. After much traveling he returned to Lübeck and taught at the *Gymnasium*, until in 1852 Maximilian II called him to Munich as professor of German literature and aesthetics. In 1868 Maximilian's successor dismissed him because of his incautious support for Prussian hegemony; and he spent the rest of his life at Lübeck, the pension of 300 talers which had been granted by the king of Prussia in 1843 then being increased to 1,000 talers. He died at Lübeck on April 6, 1884.

Geibel was, in both politics and literature, a conservative. He enjoyed great popularity and his *Gedichte* (1840) ran to 100 editions during his lifetime; but his lyrics, despite occasional melodic felicities, now appear derivative and overdecorative. His patriotic poems (*Heroldsrufe*, 1871) are declamatory and vague and of his many plays only the comedy *Meister Andrea* (1855) retains an appeal. His conscientious workmanship appears to greater advantage in his translations, *Spanisches Liederbuch* (1852, with Paul Heyse), made famous by the musical settings of Hugo Wolf, *Fünf Bücher Französischer Lyrik* (1862, with H. Leuthold) and *Klassisches Liederbuch* (1875).

BIBLIOGRAPHY.—*Gesammelte Werke*, 8 vol. (1883–84). Of selections that by W. Stammler, 3 vol. (1920) may be mentioned. *See also* K. Goedeke, *E. Geibel* (1869); C. C. T. Litzmann, *E. Geibel* (1887); K. T. Gaedertz, *E. Geibel* (1897); A. Kohut, *Geibel als Mensch und Dichter* (1915); E. Stemplinger, *Der Münchner Kreis* (1933).   (G. T. HU.)

GEIGER, ABRAHAM (1810–1874), Jewish theologian and orientalist, a leader in the Reform movement in Germany, was born at Frankfurt am Main on May 24, 1810, and educated at the universities of Heidelberg and Bonn. In 1832 he went to Wiesbaden as rabbi of the synagogue, and in 1835 helped to found, and thereafter edited, the *Zeitschrift für jüdische Theologie*. From 1838 to 1863 he lived in Breslau (being after 1843 first rabbi), where he organized the Reform movement in Judaism and wrote some of his most important works. These include *Lehr- und Lesebuch zur Sprache der Mischna* (1845), a translation into German of the poems of Judah Halevi (1851), and *Urschrift und Übersetzungen der Bibel in ihrer Abhängigkeit von der innern Entwicklung des Judentums* (1857). In 1863 Geiger became head of the synagogue of Frankfurt, and in 1870 he moved to Berlin, where he took the principal charge of the newly established seminary for Jewish science. His later works included a history of Judaism, *Das Judentum und seine Geschichte* (1865–71). He died on Oct. 23, 1874, at Berlin.

See the memorial volume, *Abraham Geiger, Leben und Lebenswerk*, prepared by his son Ludwig Geiger in collaboration with others on the 100th anniversary of his birth (1910).

GEIGER, THEODOR (1891–1952), German sociologist, outstanding for his studies of social stratification, was born in Munich on Nov. 9, 1891, and received his early training in law and statistics. The upheavals of the 1920s in Germany led him to inquiries into mass behaviour and the sociology of political movements but the coming to power of the Nazi party in 1933 drove him into exile in Denmark. After some years in Copenhagen, he was appointed to the first chair in sociology in the country in the

University of Aarhus. During the German occupation of Denmark in World War II he again lived in exile, in Sweden, returning to Aarhus in 1945. He then began a series of studies in social stratification and social mobility, culminating in a detailed work on the social origins of the population of Aarhus. Through UNESCO and the International Sociological association, of which he was a founder member, such studies led him to cross-national comparisons in this field. He died on June 19, 1952, at sea while returning from a visiting professorship in the University of Toronto.

His principal works include *Die Masse und ihre Aktion* (1926), *Die soziale Schichtung des deutschen Volkes* (1932) and *Soziale Umschichtungen in einer dänischen Mittelstadt* (1951).

(J. Mv.)

GEIJER, ERIK GUSTAF (1783–1847), Swedish historian, poet and philosopher, the inspiration of the national movement after the political upheavals in 1809, and of liberal thinking in the 1840s, was born Jan. 12, 1783, at Ransäter, Värmland. His father owned a foundry and the home was musical and sociable. A happy childhood instilled in Geijer an independence and harmony which he retained throughout life. Another important influence was a year's stay in England (1809–10). There he listened to parliamentary debates, through which he gained insight into the political life of a great state, and was impressed by the spirit of national unity and freedom.

A collection of his diaries and letters was published as *Geijer i England, 1809–10* (1914; Eng. trans. 1932). The political influence was a "defection" in 1838, when, having long been the leading theorist of Swedish conservatism, he went over to the liberal camp. The political defeat which Sweden suffered in 1809 through the loss of Finland to Russia had led him to abandon his earlier liberalism for nationalism. In 1811 he was one of the founders of Götiska förbundet, which aimed at furthering a deeper national feeling through historical studies. He contributed to its journal *Iduna* (1811) a number of famous poems on national themes, e.g., "Vikingen" and "Odalbonden" ("The Yeoman").

In 1817 Geijer became professor of history at Uppsala. His main historical works are *Svea Rikes Häfder* (1825) and *Svenska folkets historia* (3 vol., 1832–36; Eng. trans., abridged, 1845). Geijer's historical writings are objective, sparing in comment, and show both a grasp of each period's special problems and a sense of the inner continuity of Swedish history in the context of events in Europe. In the posthumously published philosophical *Människans historia* (1856), Geijer interprets historical events as a combination of tradition and creation. His reflections on creation reveal kinship with Henri Bergson's philosophy of half a century later, and his ideas on the unpredictability of events and individual responsibility in historical development are echoed in Isaiah Berlin's *Historical Inevitability* (1954). Geijer developed these ideas in his "philosophy of personality," based on the principle of reciprocity: the "I" and "Thou" develop through reciprocal influence. This led to the conclusion that only in a free community can the social character of the individual fully develop; oppression restricts it.

The isolation which followed Geijer's break with conservative friends led to a new flowering of his lyric poetry. Some of his poems written between 1838 and 1841, and set to his own music, belong to the masterpieces of Swedish verse, expressing the feelings of a farmer, a wanderer and a seeker after truth. They were printed in his collected works (1849–55).

Geijer died at Stockholm, April 23, 1847.

The most comprehensive edition of Geijer's works is that edited by J. Landquist, 13 vol. (1923–31).

BIBLIOGRAPHY.—A. Blanck's introduction to *Geijer i England* (1914); C. A. Hessler, *Geijer som politiker*, 2 vol. (1937 and 1947); E. Norberg, *Geijers väg från romantik till realism* (1944); J. Landquist, *Geijer, En levnadsteckning* (1954); *Geijer-studier* 3 vol., published by the Geijer society (1951–58).

(J. Lt.)

GEIKIE, SIR ARCHIBALD (1835–1924), notable Scottish geologist, was born at Edinburgh on Dec. 28, 1835. He was educated at the high school and University of Edinburgh, and in 1855 became an assistant on the geological survey, under Sir Roderick Murchison. In 1865 he was elected fellow of the Royal society and when a separate branch of the Geological Survey was established for Scotland in 1867 he became director. Geikie was the first holder (1871–82) of the Murchison professorship of geology and mineralogy at Edinburgh. He was a man of great energy, wide interests and vision, gifts which were employed both in his administrative posts and in his writings.

From 1882 until he retired in 1901 he held the joint offices of director-general of the geological survey of the United Kingdom and director of the Museum of Practical Geology, London. Geikie was president of the Geological society of London in 1891–92 and again in 1906–08, of the British association in 1892, and of the Royal society in 1908–13. He was knighted in 1891 and received the Order of Merit in 1914. He died near Haslemere, Surrey, on Nov. 10, 1924.

In addition to many detailed studies published as specialist papers, memoirs, essays and maps, his best-known works have remained in general use: *The Scenery of Scotland* (1865, 3rd ed. 1901); *Life of Sir R. I. Murchison*, two volumes (1875); *Text-Book of Geology* (1882, 4th edition in two volumes 1903); *The Founders of Geology*, lectures at Hopkins university (1897, 2nd ed. 1905); *The Ancient Volcanoes of Great Britain*, two volumes (1897); *Outlines of Field Geology* (1876, 5th ed. 1900).

(W. B. HA.)

GEILER VON KAISERSBERG, JOHANN (1445–1510), "the German Savonarola," noted as an exceptionally forceful and impressive preacher, was born at Schaffhausen on March 16, 1445, but in 1448 went to live at Kaisersberg in Upper Alsace. He studied at Freiburg university, where he afterward lectured until 1478, when he accepted a call to fill an office as preacher, created for him, at the cathedral of Strasbourg. There his sermons—bold, incisive, denunciatory, abounding in quaint illustrations and based on texts by no means confined to the Bible—won for him a wide fame. Although he was much interested in reform, there is no evidence that he ever considered leaving the church. Geiler died at Strasbourg on March 10, 1510.

See L. Dacheux, *Un Réformateur catholique à la fin du XVᵉ siècle* (1876).

GEISHA, the name of a professional class of women in Japan whose occupation is to entertain men, particularly at businessmen's parties in public restaurants (*ryōri-ya*). The word geisha literally means "art-person," and many of the women sing, dance or play musical instruments, but the majority are merely adept in the art of conversation. The main function of the geisha in society is to provide an atmosphere of chic and gaiety. The women are usually exquisitely dressed, delicately mannered and have a knowledge not only of the past and its elegance but of contemporary gossip. The geisha system is a form of indentured labour, although some girls, attracted by the glamour of the life, volunteer. Usually, a girl at an early age is given by her parents for a sum of money to an organization. She is taught, trained, fed and clothed for a period of years. Then she emerges into the society (known as *karyukai*, the "world of flowers and willows") and begins earning money to repay her parents' debt and her past keep. Inadequate geisha may be hired for the equivalent of a few dollars an hour, while famous ones can command as much as several hundred dollars for a single dance. Geisha are often associated with the theatre (many marry actors), and plays frequently dramatize a geisha as a heroine. When a geisha marries, she retires from the profession. If geisha do not marry, they usually retire as restaurant owners, teachers of music or dance, or trainers of younger geisha.

(F. Bs.)

GEISLINGEN AN DER STEIGE, a town of Germany which after partition of the nation following World War II was located in the *Land* (state) of Baden-Württemberg, Federal Republic of Germany, is situated in five valleys in the wooded hills of the Swabian Jura. Pop. (1961) 25,844. Geislingen is a rail junction and manufactures foundry products, machinery, silverware, cutlery, tableware, glass and wood products; there are also craft industries. The town's 14th-century houses and late Gothic church stand near modern schools, industrial buildings and houses. Geislingen was founded and chartered in the 13th century.

(I. V.-B.)

GEL, an elastic coherent mass consisting of a liquid in which ultramicroscopic particles are either dispersed or arranged in a fine network extending throughout the mass. The particles may be large molecules, such as proteins and polymer molecules; or small crystals, such as bentonite; or larger polymer particles, such as polystyrene or latex particles. Gels swell in suitable liquids. Depending on the gel and on the liquid, the swelling (the increase in gel volume) may be minute or very large. Extensive swelling results in a gradual transformation of the gel into a solution. The rheological properties of a gel vary between those of an elastic liquid and a solid. Some gels can be transformed into very fluid colloidal solutions by heat. Others, thixotropic gels, can be liquefied by mechanical action. Removal of the liquid phase, e.g., by evaporation, leads to xerogels. Xerogels are often called aerogels if the air-filled capillaries crisscrossing the system are numerous and wide. For a clearer distinction between gel and xerogel, the presence of liquid in the former may be emphasized by use of the term lyogel instead of the term gel. The terms hydrogel, alcogel, etc., may be used instead, if, in addition, the type of liquid is of interest. Gelatin forms typical lyogels. Dry silicagel is a typical xerogel. The term gel is also used even when it may not be certain whether a second phase such as air or a liquid is present in the system prior to swelling. A typical gel of this type is rubber. The ability of such systems to swell extensively and to change to typical lyogels in the course of swelling, and, in addition, their characteristic elastic properties are considered a sufficient justification to classify them as gels. Precipitates from colloidal solutions are also occasionally called gels. This usage is not recommended since the precipitates do not form a coherent mass. If the individual units of a precipitate conform to the definition of a gel, each unit may be called a microgel. A microgel may represent an aggregate of colloidal particles or a cross-linked complex of macromolecules. (Wi. H.)

GELA, a town on the south coast of Sicily in the province of Caltanissetta, is situated 78 km. (49 mi.) E.S.E. of Agrigento by road. Pop. (1968 est.) 65,289 (commune). The modern town stands on a sand hill near the sea, with a fertile plain (the ancient Campi Geloi) to the north. In the 1950s extensive petroleum deposits were discovered nearby.

The ancient city was founded by Cretan and Rhodian colonists c. 688 B.C., and sent forth colonists to found Akragas (see AGRIGENTO) in 582 B.C. It had a treasure house at Olympia. The town took its name from the river to the east. Gela enjoyed its greatest prosperity under Hippocrates (498–491 B.C.), whose dominion extended over much of the island. Gelon seized the tyranny on his death, became master of Syracuse and transferred his capital there with half the inhabitants of Gela, leaving his brother Hieron to rule over the rest. Gela's prosperity revived after the expulsion of Thrasybulus in 466 B.C. but in 405 it was abandoned by Dionysius' order (see SYRACUSE). The inhabitants returned and rebuilt the town but it was only refortified in the time of Timoleon (d. c. 337 B.C.). In 311 B.C. Agathocles put to death more than 4,000 of its inhabitants and after its destruction by the Mamertines, about 281 B.C., Phintias of Agrigentum transferred the remainder to the new town of Phintias (now Licata). In Roman times they still kept the name of Gelenses or Geloi in their new abode.

Gela has become an archaeological centre of great distinction. The elevation at the eastern end of the site was chosen by the first settlers for the sanctuary of Athena, whose cult they brought from Lindos in Rhodes, and the small primitive edifice was soon replaced by a more impressive one. Vast quantities of fragments of the rich decorative terra-cotta revetments as well as a great deposit of offerings have been recovered. In the 5th century B.C. this temple was dismantled and its cult transferred to another nearby. The adjacent terraces along the northern slope of the ridge were devoted to smaller sanctuaries in the early period, which in the rebuilding of Gela under Timoleon were replaced by a dwelling quarter. At the extreme west of the town, also, a "Timoleontean" quarter arose, protected by fortifications which there consisted of lower courses of admirable stonework and an upper portion of crude brick in almost perfect preservation. Frederick II refounded the town in 1233 and it was called Terranova di Sicilia

until 1928. In World War II Gela was one of the initial landing objectives in the Allied invasion of Sicily. (A. W. V. B.)

GELADA, a large baboonlike animal, *Therophithecus gelada,* differing from the true baboons (q.v.) by the nostrils being situated some distance from the tip of the muzzle. The gelada, sometimes called lion baboon, resembles the Arabian or hamadryas baboon in having a heavy mantle of long blackish-brown hair covering the forequarters of the old males, but differs in having the chest and buttocks bare and bright pink. The gelada inhabits the mountains of southern Ethiopia, where it lives in the steep cliffs of rocky ravines. It seldom climbs trees, preferring to forage for its food—leaves, roots and tubers—on open ground. *See also* PRIMATES.

GELASIUS, the name of two popes.

ST. GELASIUS I (d. 496), pope from 492 to 496, succeeded Felix III in March 492. The date and place of his birth are not known, though it is probable that he was born a Roman citizen in Africa. His pontificate was devoted mainly to combating the Acacian schism which had arisen in the east during the patriarchate of Acacius (471–489) as a result of the Roman see's refusal to accept the Henoticon, a peace formula designed by the emperor Zeno to reconcile the dissident Monophysites (q.v.). During this long bitter struggle with the Eastern Church, Gelasius maintained openly and firmly the primacy of jurisdiction and the apostolic origin of the papacy. This difficult contest, though not settled during his pontificate, earned him the distinction of being one of the great architects of the Roman primacy. His writings, which show clearly the influence of Augustine and Leo I, include various decrees, six theological treatises and some 60 letters, of which the most celebrated is the letter addressed to Anastasius I in 494, in which Gelasius sets forth his understanding of the relation of the church to the empire: "There are two powers by which this world is chiefly ruled: the sacred authority of the priesthood and the authority of kings." Gelasius' doctrine that both sacred and civil power are of divine origin and independent, each in its own sphere, is the most progressive thinking on this subject up to that time and for many centuries afterward. If the Gelasian formula had taken firm root in Christian tradition, it is very likely that the subsequent history of the papacy would have been different. Falsely attributed to Gelasius are the *Decretum Gelasianum* (on the canonical books of the Bible) and the *Sacramentarium Gelasianum.* Gelasius died on Nov. 19, 496. His feast is kept in the west on Nov. 21. *See also* PAPACY: *The First Six Centuries.* (R. E. McN.)

GELASIUS II (John of Gaeta) (d. 1119), pope from 1118 to 1119, was called to Rome from Monte Cassino and created cardinal (c. 1082), then papal chancellor (1089). He was elected pope Jan. 24, 1118, at an advanced age, as successor to Paschal II, whom as leader of the moderate cardinals he had defended against his critics. Gelasius had a reign of unending misfortunes; he was grossly maltreated by the pro-imperial Frangipani, and twice driven from Rome by Henry V, who installed the antipope Gregory VIII. Gelasius died in France on Jan. 28, 1119, as he planned for a council at Reims, leaving the close of the struggle to his successor, Calixtus II.

See H. K. Mann, *The Lives of the Popes in the Middle Ages,* vol. viii, 2nd ed. (1925). (J. J. RN.)

GELATIN, one of the commoner proteins, is most familiar as a food; it has, however, many industrial uses which do not require the high purity of the edible grades. Its name is derived from the Lat. *gelata,* and describes its most characteristic property; *i.e.,* gel formation in water. Contrary to the popular but erroneous concept, gelatin has not been and cannot be prepared from such proteins as horns, hoofs, lungs, muscle tissue and blood. Gelatin is derived from collagen, which is the prime constituent of all white fibrous connective tissue occurring in the animal body. Upon hydrolysis, collagen yields a series of degradation products which are never found in the living animal body and which are called gelatin. This connective tissue is well known in the form of cartilage, sinews, skin or ossein (protein matrix of bone).

Although the relative proportions of constituent amino acids in collagen and gelatin are substantially the same, the physical and chemical properties of these two proteinaceous materials differ widely. Whereas collagen swells and hydrates in dilute acid or alkaline solution, it will not dissolve without hydrolytic cleavage to form the more soluble gelatin. This transformation of collagen into gelatin is rather analogous to the hydrolysis of starch:

Collagen → gelatins → proteoses → peptones → peptides → amino acids
(high viscosity) → dextrins → low viscosity
Starch → → glucose.

Gelatin, like dextrin, can vary in molecular size, and therefore a tremendous number of different qualities of gelatin, as of dextrin, are possible. No definite structure or size has been determined for the gelatin molecule since gelatin is a mixture of degradation products.

Composition.—Both gelatin and its precursor collagen show identical composition when analyzed. The ultimate composition of each is approximately: carbon (50%), nitrogen (18%), oxygen (25%), hydrogen (7%) and sulfur (trace). The constituent amino acids and their relative amounts are approximately: glycine (25%), alanine (9%), leucine (7%), serine (0.5%), phenylalanine (1%), methionine (1%), proline (19%), hydroxyproline (14%), aspartic acid (3%), glutamic acid (6%), histidine (1%), arginine (9%) and lysine (6%). The amino acids valine, isoleucine, tyrosine, tryptophane and cystine are either entirely absent or present only in negligible quantities.

Uses in Foods.—In the food industry advantage is taken of the jellying properties in the manufacture of gelatin desserts, jellied meats and soups, marshmallows, jellied candies and other forms of confectionery. Gelatin exerts a powerful protective colloid action and for this reason is used in commercial ice cream, thereby increasing this product's resistance to "heat shock"; that is, to the formation of ice crystals by sudden changes in temperature. Gelatin has diversified uses in medicine. It is not known to have any therapeutic value beyond that of being a protein food. In pharmacy its most important use is in the manufacture of capsules in which glycerin may be incorporated if a soft capsule rather than a hard one is desired.

Use in Nonfood or Chemical Industries.—Nonfood uses vary from photography to fabric printing. Gelatin is an important ingredient in the preparation of photographic emulsions. For this use it must be particularly free from those impurities which would impair the functions of the silver salts used in the process. Protective colloid uses are found in the dye industry, where gelatin tends to prevent the uneven deposition of colour, and in the manufacture of chemical compounds having a chloramine functional group.

A sheet of flexible jelly, containing seven parts glycerin to one part gelatin, deposited on a paper or fabric back for use as a hectograph or duplicator roll, has the property of absorbing hectograph ink from a master copy and redepositing the impression about 75 times.

Production of Gelatin.—Of the gelatin produced in the United States, 90% is manufactured from hide stock and the remaining 10% is from ossein. According to the U.S. department of commerce the total production is classified as follows: edible (60%–65%); technical (3%–5%); pharmaceutical (15%–20%); photographic (15%–20%).

COMMERCIAL MANUFACTURE OF GELATIN

Preparation of Raw Stock.—The raw material may be hides, skins, bones, sinews or any other suitable collagenous substance. Raw materials preserved by freezing, such as fresh pork skins, must be defrosted prior to processing. Chrome leather waste or similar material which is not suitable to the production of edible gelatin may be processed for technical or industrial gelatin. The raw material, exclusive of bones, is washed to remove surface soil and water-soluble impurities.

Bones are processed somewhat differently in that, after washing, crushing and rewashing, they are subjected to countercurrent treatment with mineral acid (hydrochloric acid). This process, known as demineralization, serves to decalcify, or leach out the calcium phosphates, and to leave a residue consisting of bone protein (ossein).

This concentrated raw material may be processed directly as is other raw stock, or it may be dried and stored. From this preliminary treatment the stock is put in "cure," which is either acid or alkaline depending upon the ultimate use, to which the gelatin is to be put. Acid curing results in gelatin possessing somewhat higher jelly strength but lower viscosity than alkaline curing.

Acid Cure.—In this method the washed hydrated stock is immersed in cold dilute mineral acid (pH 1.5–3.0) and held for 8 to 12 hours depending upon the thickness or degree of comminution of the stock. During this period the protein raw material swells to about two or three times its original volume. After curing, the acidulated stock is washed in running water until excess acid has been rinsed away.

Alkali Cure.—Although alkaline agents ranging from caustic soda to soda ash may be used in the curing of hide or bone proteins, it is conventional practice to use saturated limewater (pH 12.0) as the curing liquor. The washed stock is placed in pits or vats along with the lime liquor and sufficient hydrated lime to maintain saturation. Temperatures are maintained under 75° F. (23.89° C.) and occasional agitation is effected by use of poles or other mechanical means. The curing time may be from three to five weeks, depending upon the thickness of the stock and its type.

When curing is completed, the limed stock is washed with water until excess lime is removed. Then this washing is continued with dilute mineral acid until the external areas are acidic. Washing with pure water is then resumed until the whole lot is approximately neutral.

Extraction.—The cured and washed stock is placed in extraction kettles and covered with hot water. Several extractions are made with consecutive lots of water. A series of 8 to 12 extractions, "runs" or "cooks" may be made, each extraction being somewhat hotter than the preceding one; i.e., 110° F. (43.33° C.), 120° F. (48.89° C.), 130° F. (54.44° C.), etc., until the boiling point is reached. Since the extraction depends upon the conversion of collagen to gelatin by hydrolysis, care must be exercised to avoid excessive hydrolytic breakdown of the gelatin. Highest test gelatin is extracted at the lower temperatures whereas use of higher temperatures produces the lower testing gelatins. Each run of liquor is then removed prior to the addition of fresh water for the subsequent extraction. These liquors, known as "light" because of low solids (2% to 4%) content, are then allowed to settle for a short time, after which more grease may be skimmed. The various runs are then combined according to the quality of gelatin desired and foreign suspended material are removed. Active carbon is sometimes used to minimize high colour. The light liquors, which are sparkling clear and almost water-white, are then continuously evaporated until the increased viscosity makes further evaporation impractical. This situation is reached at concentrations of 8% to 12% in high-test liquors and of 15% to 20% in low-test liquors.

Most high type evaporators tend to break down the jelly strength of gelatin if allowed to concentrate the liquors beyond certain limits. If necessary the heavy liquors from the evaporators may be filtered again and bleached depending upon the quality desired.

Following the evaporating stage the usual drying procedure is based upon the characteristic jelling property of the protein. Heavy liquors are run onto a wide endless belt which conveys the gelatin through a refrigerated chamber. The resultant stiff jelly is placed on metal nets and blown with cold air until it has developed a skin. Hot air is then used to finish the drying process and the final clear sheets are comminuted as required. Other methods of drying, making use of sprays, hot rolls, etc., may be employed. All equipment in the manufacture of gelatin should be so constructed as to avoid contamination by heavy metals. Aluminum for acid-cure processes and nickel or stainless steel for either acid or alkali processes are preferred materials of construction. Certain grades of technical gelatin are preferred in industrial use can be processed in equipment made from iron. Extremely pure grades can be made by dialysis (q.v.), but this procedure is not commercially practical.

Properties.—The protein gelatin, as manufactured, may be marketed as thin, clear flakes or after grinding to various degrees of fineness. In the U.S. a 30-mesh gelatin is considered standard for most uses. Crystal clarity and slight yellow or amber colour are customary. The dry product normally contains from 8% to 12% of moisture, depending upon atmospheric humidity. Commercial gelatins are substantially free from heavy metal and bacterial contamination. Mineral constituents as represented by ash are less than 2%. Specifications of the U.S. *Pharmacopoeia* are satisfactory in general although additional specifications may be required for certain uses (photography, hectography).

Gelatin is insoluble in pure cold water, but will absorb moisture, with swelling. The swollen gel will pass completely into solution when warmed to about 120° F. (48.89° C.), forming a gel again when cooled. The swollen gel will dissolve in hot water, hot aqueous glycerin, hot acids, alkalies and salts. It is insoluble in all organic solvents other than the water-soluble phenols and carboxylic acids. In dilute mineral acid (0.5N HCl) and in dilute alkali (0.15N NaOH), a 1% solution of gelatin can be formed at room temperature. Concentrated mineral acids or alkalies will dissolve larger amounts of gelatin, considerable hydrolysis taking place. Concentrated acetic and formic acids will dissolve gelatin in the cold as will concentrated aqueous solutions of urea, thiourea, calcium chloride, calcium nitrate and other peptizing agents. Aqueous glycerin will swell gelatin slowly in the cold and will dissolve it when heated. The viscous mass will set to a stiff gel when cooled and is the basis for manufacture of printer's rollers, hectograph jellies and capsules.

The isoelectric point of a given gelatin is 4.85 or 7.8 depending upon whether it is derived from acid- or alkaline-cured material. Any gelatin at its isoelectric point exhibits minimum solubility, minimum viscosity, minimum electroconductivity and minimum swelling. Similarly to other water-soluble proteins, gelatin will swell or puff like popcorn when heated dry. At a temperature of 300° F. (148.89° C.), it will polymerize with corresponding increase in viscosity and decrease in solubility.

Tanning agents normally used in leather manufacture will act upon gelatin to produce insolubility in water. Heavy-metal salts, aldehydes and sugars having active aldehydic functions act in the same way. In such cases water insolubility does not mean moisture resistance, since insolubilized gelatin will absorb almost as much water as will the untanned gelatin from the same source.

Two forms of gelatin are believed to exist. These differ only in the specific rotation of plane-polarized light by their solutions. Form A has a specific rotation $[\alpha]_D$ of $-313°$ and is stable above 95° F. (35° C.). Form B has a specific rotation $[\alpha]_D$ of $-141°$ and is stable only below 59° F. (15° C.). Outside the range of 59°–95° F. (15°–35° C.) the specific rotation does not vary with changes in temperature. These two forms are believed to be the sol, 95° F. (35° C.), and gel, 59° F. (15° C.), forms.

For detailed accounts of the more specific physical and chemical properties of gelatin, *see* the references at the end of this article.

Commercial Grades and Tests of Gelatin.—As emphasized, many different qualities of gelatin can be prepared from a given collagenous raw material. The less vigorous the hydrolytic treatment used in its preparation, the higher is the quality of the resulting gelatin.

Uniformity in gelatin of commerce is maintained through process control and by the blending of selected lots of gelatin so that the over-all average molecular weight and other properties remain quite constant.

As a general rule, the product is evaluated on the basis of two colloidal properties, viscosity of solution and stiffness of gel. Viscosity is measured at 6.67% concentration (anhydrous basis) and is expressed in millipoises. Stiffness of gel, or "jelly strength," is determined for the same concentration by the Bloom test; it is expressed as the weight in grams required at 50° F. (10° C.) to impress the jelly surface a given distance. Both determinations are necessary for commercial evaluation since it is quite possible to produce extractions of gelatin of different qualities from the same lot of raw material, one having higher jelly strength and lower viscosity than the other; for instance, 300 g. and 50 millipoises or 240 g. and 60 millipoises. The end use of the gelatin de-

termines which characteristic is of more importance.

High jelly strength is obviously needed for the production of gels. Gelatins are primarily blends of individual lots or extractions. These blends have a jelly strength from 75 g. to 300 g. The higher the Bloom test the greater is the utility, since proportionally less of a high jelly-strength gelatin is required for producing a gel under a given set of conditions.

In the United States the federal government has established specifications for dessert gelatin. The regulations covered such points as strength, clarity, colour, taste, bacterial count and size of the powder crystal.

Additional specifications covering heavy metals and other impurities in foods must be met by all gelatin sold for edible purposes.

In addition to gelatin for desserts or sweets, there are the edible ice cream, marshmallow, confectionery and capsulating gelatins. Hectographic, photographic and other technical gelatins are not required to meet food specifications.

BIBLIOGRAPHY.—British Gelatine and Glue Research Association, *Recent Advances in Gelatin and Glue Research* (1958); J. B. Allison and W. H. Fitzpatrick, *Dietary Proteins in Health and Disease* (1960); H. A. Scheraga, *Protein Structure* (1961). (H. H. Y.)

GELDER, AERT (AERT) **DE** (1645–1727), Dutch painter, was born in Dordrecht Oct. 10, 1645, and spent his life there except for a stay in Amsterdam where he became Rembrandt's pupil around 1661. De Gelder is remarkable in Dutch art as the only artist who kept to the Rembrandt tradition in the late 17th and early 18th century. His biblical scenes especially are full of strong colours and fantastic light effects. He varies Rembrandt's compositional ideas in a personal way (series of the Passion *c.* 1715, Amsterdam and Munich). As a portrait painter he is equally unconventional and the broad character of his painting contrasts strongly with the polished and refined surface paint of his contemporaries. He died in Aug. 1727.

See K. Lilienfeld, *Arent de Gelder, sein Leben und seine Kunst* (1914). (H. K. GN.)

GELDERLAND (GUELDERS), a province of The Netherlands, bounded south by North Brabant, west by Utrecht and South Holland, north by the IJsselmeer (Zuider Zee), northeast by Overijssel and southeast by Germany. Pop. (1960 est.) 1,266,885; area, 1,932 sq.mi. The main portion of Gelderland north of the Rhine and the Oude (Old) IJssel is a formerly glaciated region with a soil of Pleistocene sand; south of this line the soil consists of fertile river-clay. The northern portion is divided by the broad valley of the (Gelderse) IJssel into two distinct regions: the Veluwe on the west and the so-called Achterhoek on the east, the larger part of which is formed by the former countship of Zutphen (the Graafschap). In this last region the ground slopes downward from southeast to northwest (131 to 26 ft.) and is intersected by several parallel streams that flow into the IJssel. Some glacial hills have been preserved, now mainly arable land; pastures are dominant although many patches of wood have been spared. Farming is mixed, with dairy, meat-packing and leather factories. The eastern part has textile works, in particular at Winterswijk. Along the Oude IJssel are a number of foundries. The old town of Zutphen (on the IJssel) and Doetinchem are the chief markets and shopping centres and have some industries. The hill plateau of the Veluwe west of the IJssel is separated from the Utrecht glacial ridge by the Gelderse Vallei, which forms the boundary between the two provinces. This extends from the Rhine along the Grift, and along the Lunterse and the Barneveldse Beek, both tributaries of the Eem (Utrecht), to the IJsselmeer. All over the Veluwe are heaths, scantily cultivated, but there are also woods, especially fir and beech. A large part of the Veluwe is used for military purposes. In the south the Veluwe hills stretch along the Rhine with a rather steep slope, and the wooded part is a residential area. The town of Arnhem (*q.v.*), the provincial capital, is picturesquely situated on this slope. It has important industries (cellulose, artificial silk, metal works, etc.). The other large centre of the Veluwe is Apeldoorn on the eastern border, also with industries including a large number of laundries.

The valley of the IJssel, the Gelderse Vallei and the northern border of the Veluwe are under mixed farming, especially poultry; eggs and chickens are the most important exports. Barneveld is a centre of this trade and around Harderwijk ducks are raised. These districts also have light industries; e.g., bicycles at Dieren, furniture at Nijkerk and artificial silk at Ede.

The southern division of the province is watered by the Rhine, the Waal and the Maas (Meuse) and has a level clay soil, with the higher levels along the rivers and lower lying and somewhat swampy central parts. In the east are some isolated hills and a sandy, wooded stretch south of Nijmegen. The area between the Rhine and the Waal and watered by the Linge is called the Betuwe. This has a denser population, occupied with mixed farming, vegetable growing and orchards (cherries and apples). Along the rivers are many brick factories. Some of the smaller old market towns, such as Culemborg and Tiel, also have industries. The largest town is Nijmegen; it was an important centre in Roman and Carolingian times and now has several industries (electro-technical, shoe, textile and chemical factories). It also has a Roman Catholic university.

(H. J. KE.)

History.—The history of the province of Gelderland begins with that of the countship of Gelre—the Gueldre or Guelders of French and older English writers. There is a legend that a certain Wichard of Pont killed a dragon which shouted "Gelre, Gelre" during the fight and that Wichard therefore gave the name Gelre to the town which he founded (c. A.D. 900) on the site of modern Geldern in the *Land* of North Rhine-Westphalia. In fact the earliest traceable ancestor of the counts of Gelre was Gerardus, surnamed Flamens, who was one of the potentates ruling over the territory between the Rhine and the Meuse rivers in the 11th century. Originally established at Wassenberg castle on the Roer river, he later set himself up at the castle of Gelre on the Niers. His direct descendants acquired during the 11th and 12th centuries parts of the later Gelderland; *i.e.*, the areas of Betuwe and Veluwe. Gerardus IV (c. 1131) married Ermengarde, daughter of Otto; count of Zutphen; and when the male line of the counts of Zutphen became extinct about 1190, Zutphen fell to the Wassenberg-Gelre family, who thus under Otto I (count from 1182 to 1207) obtained an important position among the dynasts of the Low Countries. The counts of Gelre, as they now called themselves, had laid the foundation for a territorial power which, through the control of the larger rivers, Rhine, Waal, Meuse and IJssel, was to play an important role in the later middle ages.

The geographical position of their territory dictated the external policy of the counts during the following centuries: they were committed to the interests of the Holy Roman empire and to expansion in the direction of Brabant, Limburg and Liège and, to the north, in the direction of the "upper diocese" of the bishops of Utrecht. At home, they sought to consolidate the juridical and political system of their dominions.

Under Otto I, his son Gerardus V (1207-29) and his grandson Otto II (1229-71) this policy developed. Otto II's most important gain was the imperial town of Nijmegen, with its environs, which was enfeoffed to him by the German king William of Holland and which linked the northern parts of the countship with the southern part round Gelre and Roermond. Otto II's reign moreover witnessed a notable development of the towns: Arnhem, Nijmegen, Zutphen, Roermond and other smaller towns received their first charters from him.

Otto II's son Reinald I (1271-1326) married Irmingard, the heiress of Limburg, but the possibility of adding this important territory to Gelre did not materialize, because John I of Brabant considered it a threat to his communications with the Rhineland, especially with Cologne. In the War of the Limburg Succession, in which he had the support of the city of Cologne, John defeated Reinald near Worringen (June 5, 1288) and thus acquired the duchy of Limburg. This put an end to the southward expansion of Gelre. The consequences of the defeat bore heavily on Gelre, and only the acquisition of the *jus de non evocando* (whereby the count's subjects were exempted from being brought before tribunals outside his jurisdiction) in 1310 gave the countship more independence. Not till Reinald II's reign (1326-43) did the situation improve. The territory was then enlarged and consolidated through the purchase of smaller estates and titles; river traffic and industry helped to develop the towns, which moreover were capable and willing to assist the count financially; and river tolls brought the count a new source of income. Also Reinald II's first marriage, to Sophia, heiress of Mechelen (Mechlin), improved his financial position; and his second marriage, to Eleanor, sister of Edward III of England, gave him greater prominence among the Netherlands rulers and led to his playing a role in the Hundred Years' War between England and France. He had good relations with the German king Louis the Bavarian, who raised him to the dignity of a duke in 1339. Reinald's early death in 1343 was a misfortune to Gelre, because he left only two infant sons, Reinald III and Edward, who after 1350 disputed each other's claim, supported by factions of the nobility, while the towns made their influence felt as well. In 1361 Edward was recognized as duke, but in Aug. 1371 he died. As his brother Reinald III died in the following December, the male line of the house of Wassenberg then became extinct.

After some years of warfare with other pretenders, William of Jülich, son of Reinald II's daughter Maria, acquired the duchy (1377-1402). His rule was a period of peace and quiet for Gelre, interrupted only by minor wars with Brabant, which brought Gelre some small territorial gains. William's power, however, was greater than his predecessors' because in 1393 he succeeded his father in Jülich. A consequence of the succession was that political and economic relations with the Rhineland and with Westphalia became more important to Gelre than those with the western territories of the Netherlands; but William maintained good relations with England as well and visited London in 1388. He was succeeded by his brother Reinald IV (1402-23). During the latter's reign discontent arose among the nobility and the towns, which united to acquire more influence in the government (1418), so that the duke had to grant concessions. To these can be traced the origin of the later "estates" of Gelre, which developed during the 15th century into a "representative body."

When Reinald IV died childless (1423), Gelre and Zutphen fell to his great nephew, Arnold of Egmond (d. 1473), who was chosen by the nobility and the towns as their ruler, but who was never enfeoffed with these territories by the German king Sigismund. The king enfeoffed instead another member of the family, Adolf of Berg, with Gelre, Zutphen and Jülich, but Adolf could lay hands only on Jülich. Beside the prolonged war caused by this dispute, Arnold's reign was characterized by the ever-growing influence of the towns and nobility, because the duke was in permanent financial difficulties through unfortunate wars. In this period also the expansionist policy of Philip (q.v.) the Good, duke of Burgundy, was felt in Gelre, provoking confusion and continuous change of side and sharpening the differences between Arnold and the majority of his subjects, who did not at once recognize the Burgundian threat. Finally, after a reversal of alliances led by the originally pro-Burgundian town of Nijmegen, a clearly anti-Burgundian movement arose, which not only defended the independence of Gelre, but at the same time accelerated the development of the "estates" as representatives and defenders of the unity of the country. In 1465 Arnold was taken prisoner by his son Adolf, who was then still pro-Burgundian. As soon, however, as Adolf was in power he, too, turned against Burgundy. Then Charles the Bold, duke of Burgundy, intervened, captured Adolf and freed Arnold (1471), from whom he took the duchy in pawn; and in 1473, after having subdued Nijmegen, Charles occupied Gelre. On Charles's death, however, in 1477, the people of Gelre ousted the hated Burgundians and put the government into the hands of Adolf's sister, Catherine, who was to rule first in the name of the imprisoned Adolf. Adolf died the same year and she ruled in the name of his son, the infant Charles of Egmond who in 1492 assumed the government himself, after having been ransomed from the French by his subjects.

In these years 1477-92 the territory of Gelre had to be defended against the attempts of Maximilian of Austria, husband of Charles the Bold's daughter Mary of Burgundy, to conquer it. These failed chiefly because of the resistance of the towns and of the nobility, who in this period acquired so much influence in the government that by 1500 they formed part of it almost by prescriptive right. The reign of Charles of Egmond (1492-1538) was filled by a prolonged war against the Holy Roman emperor Charles V, who claimed Gelre as part of his Burgundian inheritance. Supported by his captain, Martin van Rossum, the duke Charles at the outset battled successfully with the emperor and even temporarily occupied Friesland, Groningen and Overijssel; but his successor, William the Rich of Jülich, who also was duke of Berg and Cleves, could not keep up the unequal fight and in 1543 had to cede Gelre to Charles V by the treaty of Venlo. The country had suffered much and the economy of the towns had declined.

After 1543 Gelre formed part of the Burgundian-Habsburg hereditary lands. It revolted at the same time as the rest of the Netherlands against Philip II of Spain, joined the Union of Utrecht (1579) and until 1795 formed part of the republic of the United Netherlands within the republic. Like the other inland provinces, it was of less importance politically and economically than Holland and Zeeland; it was mainly an agricultural area, with little industry. After the abjuration of Philip II, sovereignty was vested in the "estates" of Gelderland, and the princes of Orange were stadtholders—with more authority in Gelderland than in Holland. In 1672 it was temporarily occupied by Louis XIV; and in 1713 the southeastern part, including Geldern, the ducal capital, fell to Prussia. Gelderland formed part of the Batavian republic from 1795 to 1806, of Louis Bonaparte's kingdom of Holland from 1806 to 1810 and of the French empire from 1810 to 1813. In 1814 it became a province of the kingdom of the Netherlands. The towns of Venlo and Roermond are now part of Limburg province.

BIBLIOGRAPHY.—Gouda Quint, *Bibliographie tot de geschiedenis van Gelderland* (1910-42); W. Jappe Alberts, *De Staten van Gelre en Zutphen*, 2 vol. (1950-56); *Geschiedenis van Gelderland van de vroegste tijden tot het einde der Middeleeuwen* (1966); E. W. de Vries, *De Opkomst van Zutphen* (1960); J. E. A. L. Struck, *Gelre en Habsburg* (1960). (W. J. AL.)

GELDNER, KARL FRIEDRICH (1852-1929), German philologist who edited the Avesta and translated the Rigveda into German, was born on Dec. 17, 1852, in Saalfeld, Thuringia. Geldner studied at a number of universities, but received his doctorate at Tübingen. His first work was a brilliant essay, "Über die Metrik des jüngeren Avesta" (1877). After teaching at Berlin and elsewhere he became professor of Sanskrit at Marburg University where he stayed from 1907 until his death on Feb. 5, 1929. Geldner was a champion of the essentially Indian character of the Rigveda and its relatively late date against those who championed its Indo-European nature and a hoary age before the Aryan migration to India. In both the Avesta and Rigveda he combined the native traditions of Parsees and Indians with European philological methods. (R. N. F.)

GELEEN, a town in the province of Limburg, Netherlands, 11 mi. NNE of Maastricht by road. Pop. (1971 est.) 36,892. The town was an important coal-mining centre. In consequence of the coal crisis, production of coal and coke was stopped. The coke factory was torn down to accommodate chemical plants. Chemicals, fertilizers, concrete, and textiles are manufactured, and there are several engineering works. The town is also the main shopping centre for the surrounding area. It is served by rail, bus, and airlines. The tower of the oldest Roman Catholic church dates from the 13th century, the sheriff's house from 1567, and the Hermitage (where the last hermit died in 1912) from 1699. (L. J. A. M. B.)

GELIMER, the last Vandal king of Africa (A.D. 530-534), was the son of Gelaris and the great-grandson of Gaiseric (*q.v.*). He deposed his pro-Roman cousin Hilderich, probably in 530, disregarding the protests of the eastern Roman emperor Justinian I. In September 533 an east Roman expeditionary force led by Belisarius (*q.v.*) landed in Africa, defeated the Vandal Army 10 mi. from Carthage and occupied the city. Gelimer mishandled the campaign and was defeated again at Tricamaron, 20 mi. W of Carthage. He fled to Numidia, but surrendered in March 534 and was sent to Constantinople. *See also* VANDALS. (E. A. T.)

GELLERT, CHRISTIAN FÜRCHTEGOTT (1715-1769), German poet, author of famous verse fables and of hymns which combined religious feeling with the rationalism of the Enlightenment. He was born at Hainichen, Saxony, July 4, 1715, son of a pastor, one of a family of 13; and food, clothing and education were not easily acquired. He studied at Leipzig, and became *Privatdozent* there in 1745, and in 1751 professor, lecturing on poetry, rhetoric and ethics. His lectures and writings, enforced by his lovable personality, won him influence and friends, many of them of high rank. His *Fabeln und Erzählungen* (1746-48), which made his name, were modeled on La Fontaine, but he drew on his own childhood observation of nature and later experience of urban society. Their charm was well brought out later by D. N. Chodowiecki's illustrations. Gellert also wrote unsuccessful comedies and a conventionally sentimental novel, *Das Leben der schwedischen Gräfin von G.* (1748).

His *Geistliche Oden und Lieder* (1757), though he himself felt that they were inferior to the hymns of Luther, Paul Gerhardt, etc., were unequalled in their day and served the church well at a time when only natural religion was considered worthy of a man of intellect. God, as Father and Creator, was his favourite theme; and doubt has been thrown on his Christology. Nevertheless he is best known to English-speaking readers as the author of the Easter hymn "Jesus Lives!" His hymns were set to music by C. P. E. Bach and Beethoven among others. He died in Leipzig, Dec. 13, 1769.

BIBLIOGRAPHY.—*Sämtliche Schriften*, 10 vol. (1769-74); selection, with introduction, in F. Muncker, *Die Bremer Beiträge* (1899); Eng. trans. of fables, etc., by J. A. Murke (1851); *Briefe*, ed. by K. Blanck (1921). (M. KL.)

GELLERT, in Welsh tradition, was the trusted hound given by King John to his son-in-law Prince Llewellyn the Great of Wales. Being left one day in 1205 to guard his master's infant son, he killed a huge wolf which tried to attack the child. Llewellyn, returning to find the baby missing and Gellert's muzzle stained with blood, assumed that the dog had destroyed his son and stabbed him. He later found the child lying unharmed beneath the overturned cradle, with the wolf's corpse beside him. The remorseful prince caused Gellert to be honourably buried on Mt. Snowdon and named the place Beddgelert; *i.e.*, grave of Gelert. This story, associated now with the historical Prince Llewellyn, is a late Welsh version of an ancient Indian folktale recounted in the Sanskrit *Panchatantra*. The legend is found in various forms in many European countries, and also in Persian, Hebrew and Buddhist tradition. (C. S. HE.)

GELLIGAER, an urban district in the Caerphilly parliamentary division of Glamorgan, Wales, in the heart of the south Wales coal fields. Pop. (1971 prelim.) 33,670. The chief town of the district is Bargoed, about 16 mi. N. of Cardiff, which contains a large public park. Gelligaer takes its name from the Roman fort which lies northwest of the 8th-century parish church of St. Cattwg and is 780 ft. above sea level. Many of the relics found when the fort was excavated are in the National Museum of Wales in Cardiff. Charles I stayed at the 16th-century manor house of Llancaiach when he visited Glamorgan in 1645.

The three coal mining valleys of Taff Bargoed, Deri and Rhymney lie within the district which is bounded on the east by the river Rhymney, there the boundary between Glamorgan and Monmouthshire, and on the west by the river Taff Bargoed. Besides coal mines there are automobile and rubber works.

GELLIUS, AULUS (b. c. A.D. 130), Latin author, who composed a miscellany entitled *Noctes Atticae* in which are preserved many fragments of lost works. He is an interesting source of information about the knowledge and studies of his own day. Both in Rome, where he received instruction in literature (*grammatica*) and rhetoric, and in Athens, where he studied philosophy, his teachers and friends included many distinguished men. He was appointed a judge in private cases in Rome. It was in Athens, during the long winter evenings, that he began his practice of excerpting from authors, and after his return to Rome he continued this work which led to the publication of his *Noctes Atticae*. Written partly for the benefit of his children, it comprised 20 books. The beginning of the preface and the end of the last book are lost and of the eighth book only the chapter headings have survived. It is a miscellany with no systematic order touching on the most diverse matters of language, literature, dialectic, philosophy, arithmetic, geometry, antiquities, law, history and other subjects. Gellius' aim was to provide interesting but not exacting reading. He seems to have been a modest and amiable man. He had neither a profound mind nor much critical power, but he was a diligent and accurate student whose delight was in books and learning.

BIBLIOGRAPHY.—Edition by C. Hosius, "Teubner Series," 2 vol. (1903).; *The Attic Nights of Aulus Gellius*, with Eng. trans., "Loeb Series," 2 vol. (1927–28); H. Nettleship, *Lectures and Essays on Subjects Connected With Latin Literature and Scholarship*, pp. 248–76 (1885).

(G. B. A. F.)

GELMÍREZ, DIEGO (c. 1068–c. 1139), bishop and archbishop of Santiago de Compostela, was the most forceful personality produced by medieval Galicia. His career is described in the *Historia Compostellana*, written by his order to record for posterity his labours to advance the fame of the shrine he ruled. Diego was consecrated bishop of Compostela in 1101 and then devoted himself remorselessly to extending his ecclesiastical and temporal influence. In 1120 Calixtus II promoted him archbishop and appointed him papal legate in Spain. Diego's ambition, arrogance and single-mindedness involved him both in bitter ecclesiastical quarrels and in the civil strife which characterized the minority of Alfonso VII of Castile. On several occasions he narrowly escaped death at the hands of the queen mother Urraca, or the burgesses of Santiago, who found him a tyrannical overlord.

Diego Gelmírez was not an attractive character, but as administrator, financier and rebuilder of his cathedral he did much to develop the reputation of Santiago as a pilgrim shrine. His own wealth and influence were based on it. He reformed what had previously been a lax diocese and, at the Council of Compostela (1124), caused the Peace and Truce of God to be proclaimed for the first time in Castile. In civil war he showed himself to be a competent military commander, and, to defeat Moorish naval attacks on Galicia, he organized a small fleet—the first in medieval Castile. Diego's inordinate desire to extend his power, however, caused Honorius II, the successor of Calixtus II (d. 1124), to deprive him of his legateship and incurred the distrust of his former protégé, Alfonso VII, who managed, by devious methods, to lay hands on some of Diego's great wealth. His influence had, therefore, considerably declined when he died, probably in 1139, but he was to remain as the presiding genius of medieval Santiago.

See Anselm Gordon Biggs, *Diego Gelmírez, First Archbishop of Compostela* (1949).

(P. E. R.)

GELON, son of Deinomenes, tyrant of Gela (491–485 B.C.) and of Syracuse (485–478 B.C.). On the death of Hippocrates, tyrant of Gela (491), Gelon, who had been his cavalry commander, succeeded him. Early in his rule he became involved in inconclusive hostilities with Carthage. He appealed to the Spartans to help him to carry the war into Africa, but no help was sent and the plan was dropped. In 485, taking advantage of an appeal by the *gamoroi* (conservative landowners) of Syracuse, who had been driven out by the people, he made himself master of Syracuse, leaving his brother Hieron to control Gela. Under Gelon Syracuse grew rapidly in population and power. He conquered Sicilian Euboea and Megara Hyblaea, selling their common people into slavery and bringing the oligarchs to Syracuse, which was further swollen by new drafts from Gela and Camarina. Mercenaries were recruited widely and a powerful fleet built up. Gelon controlled the Greek and Sicel communities of east Sicily and was firmly linked by marriage with Theron, tyrant of Acragas (Agrigento, q.v.). When the Carthaginians invaded Sicily in 480 Theron appealed to Gelon, who was primarily responsible for the decisive Greek victory of Himera (see SICILY: *History*). He celebrated the victory by lavish dedications at Delphi, Olympia and Syracuse, and was popular among the Greeks. He died in 478.

See T. J. Dunbabin, *The Western Greeks*, ch. xiv (1948). (R. ME.)

GELSEMIUM (YELLOW JASMINE ROOT), a drug consisting of the dried root of *Gelsemium sempervirens* (family Loganiaceae; q.v.). The plant is a woody twining shrub having a milky juice; opposite, lance-shaped, shining leaves; and clusters of one to five large, funnel-shaped, fragrant yellow flowers. It is native to the southeastern United States, where it is known as wild, yellow or Carolina jasmine and is grown as an ornamental; it is not related in any way, however, to the true jasmine, which is a member of the family Oleaceae. Commercial supplies are collected in Virginia, North and South Carolina, Tennessee and Georgia. The roots and underground stems are dug up in the autumn, washed and dried. The plant was first described in 1640 but was not used medicinally until about 1821.

Three alkaloids have been isolated in crystalline state, gelsemine, gelsemicine and sempervirine. All three have similar pharmacologic properties, gelsemicine being the most potent and the most toxic. Gelsemium depresses the motor nerve cells of the brain and spinal cord, resulting in generalized muscular weakness. Death from action of this drug is caused by respiratory failure resulting from paralysis of the respiratory muscles. The drug is little used medicinally, though formerly it was used in treating various neuralgic conditions.

(V. E.)

GELSENKIRCHEN, an industrial city and inland port of Germany which after partition of the nation following World War II was in the *Land* (state) of North Rhine-Westphalia in the Federal Republic of Germany. Pop. (1961) 382,689. In the mid-19th century Gelsenkirchen was a village with less than 1,000 inhabitants, but because of its favourable location on the Rhine-Herne canal, it developed as a Ruhr mining and industrial town and was chartered in 1875. The neighbouring towns of Buer and Horst were amalgamated with Gelsenkirchen in 1928. Buer, north of the Emscher river which bisects the city, is surrounded by a 1,000-ac. green belt. The moated castles (Schloss Berge, Schloss Horst [restored baroque] and Haus Lüttinghof) survived heavy bombing of the war when more than a third of Gelsenkirchen's public buildings were destroyed. The Hans Sachs house and Buer town hall are the seats of the municipal administration. The city possesses a museum, a zoological garden, several public gardens and two racecourses. The Institute of Hygiene for the Ruhr is situated there. The railway connecting Hamburg with the south and Cologne with the east, the Cologne-Berlin *Autobahn* and two federal highways pass through the town. To the south is the large conglomeration of mines which have made Gelsenkirchen one of the largest coalmining and coking centres of Germany. Its large-scale industry includes steelworks, foundries, chemical plants, armature works, glass and clothing factories.

(P. Z.)

GEM, a mineral used for adornment. The true gem stone is a product of nature and is often referred to as a natural gem to distinguish it from synthetic gems and artificial gems. These terms are discussed at greater length in a later part of this article, which is divided into the following main sections:

I. History
  1. Introduction
  2. Gem Engraving
  3. Mesopotamia
  4. Egypt
  5. Crete
  6. Greece
  7. Greco-Phoenician and Greco-Persian Gems
  8. Etruria
  9. Roman Gems
  10. Late Roman Period
  11. Middle Ages and Modern Times
  12. Gem Cutting
  13. Gem Imitations
II. Natural Gems
  1. Gem Minerals
  2. Colour
  3. Colour Improvement
  4. Brilliancy
  5. Identification of Gems
  6. Trade
III. Synthetic Gems
  1. Methods of Producing Synthetic Gems
  2. Verneuil or Flame-Fusion Process
  3. Corundum (Rubies and Sapphires)
  4. Identification
  5. Spinel
  6. Rutile (Titania)
  7. Emerald
  8. Diamonds
IV. Imitation Gems

I. HISTORY

1. Introduction.—Since ancient times gems have fascinated mankind. They have, of course, long been used in jewelry (*q.v.*); moreover, their hardness, clearness, brilliance and eternal newness caused them to be regarded as miraculous and endowed with mysterious powers. An early document concerned with this subject is a didactic poem by the Greek seer and priest Onomacritus (5th century B.C.), in which the writer, apparently employing ancient Babylonian ideas, discusses the peculiar powers of gem stones. There arose a regular science, codified in lapidaries, which concerned itself with the nature and the miraculous properties of the crystals; this science was transmitted by the Romans to the Germanic north, whose inhabitants had originally been unacquainted with the idea. Such thought persisted through the middle ages and vestiges of it remain, for example, in the modern practice of wearing a birthstone (*q.v.*).

The significance attributed to different stones frequently varied and overlapped. The diamond gave its wearer strength in battle and protected him against ghosts and magic. The sapphire was traditionally a symbol of heavenly bliss and served as a pledge of faithfulness; it also protected its wearer against poverty and betrayal, prevented eye diseases and cured snake bites. The ruby ensured love and happiness, brought bad dreams to naught and gave peace and serenity. The emerald brought riches and fame, broke at the instance of marital infidelity and, when the wearer put it under his tongue, endowed him with the gift of prophecy. The amethyst prevented drunkenness, gave wisdom and invited the favour of the great. The hyacinth gave protection against the striking of lightning, furthered sleep and granted its wearer a happy disposition. The turquoise prevented accidents, especially falls from a horse. The carbuncle lent enthusiasm and could make its wearer invisible; and so on.

As a talisman each stone was bound to its wearer in a special way, but the most effective means of converting to one's own use the powers dwelling in a particular gem was thought to be incorporation. Up to the 18th century gems played a role in popular medicine; before Pope Clement VII died in 1534 he is said to have taken as medicine pulverized gems valued at 40,000 ducats.

In all major civilizations gems were in some way associated with the splendour of the deity. There is, for example, the jade castle of the Chinese ruler of the heavens; and in the Revelation of St. John the "heavenly city," which rests on precious stones, has walls of jasper and gates of pearl.

Tales of adventure surround many large gems, especially diamonds (*see* DIAMOND: *History of Famous Diamonds*). In the course of their more recent existence such historical diamonds were frequently recut, although the irregular basic shape was usually kept in order to change the abnormal weight as little as possible. In most cases such diamonds can be traced back to India, the classic land of precious stones; the gem riches of Indian princes have long been legendary.

(ER. ST.)

2. Gem Engraving.—Gems engraved with designs for sealing (intaglio) or for decoration (cameo) exist in large numbers from the early Sumerian period to the decline of the Roman civilization, and again from the Renaissance to modern times. They exercise a strong appeal in many ways. The inherent beauty of the material, with its rich and varied colours, its lustre and brilliance, gives pleasure at first sight. The hard and durable quality of the stones has made for unusually good preservation, so that in many cases the artist's work can be appreciated in its original state—a rare opportunity in ancient art. Moreover, the smallness and preciousness of the gems invited exquisite workmanship, and in certain periods, when art was at a high level, the achievements in this field were very notable. The best ancient gem engravers combined minuteness and accuracy of detail with a largeness of style that is indeed remarkable. A gem engraving of this class possesses the nobility and dignity of a marble or bronze sculptural work, though it is often confined to the space of less than half a square inch.

In gem engraving, only soft stones and metals can be worked freehand with cutting tools; the harder stones require the wheel technique. This technique was known in Mesopotamia as early as about 4000–3000 B.C., as well as to the Minoans from the Middle Minoan III period (*c.* 1750–1580 B.C.). The method of work seems to have been similar to that in use in the 20th century, to judge by the references in classical literature, especially in the writings of Pliny and Theophrastus, and an examination of the stones themselves. By this method the stones were worked with variously shaped drills ending in balls, disks, cylinders, etc., which were made to rotate by the help of the wheel. In modern practice the stone to be engraved is fastened to a handle, held to the head of the rotating drill and moved as the work requires. It has been suggested that the ancients reversed the process and held the stone stationary while the rotating tools were guided by the hand, as in modern dentistry. The cutting is not actually done by the drills but by the powder which is rubbed on the stone with the drill. This is in modern practice diamond powder mixed with oil; it was known also to the Romans, but in the period before Alexander the Great emery powder was probably used. The wheel used in the 20th century is worked either by foot or by an electric motor lathe. The foot-powered wheel, though more cumbersome, has the advantage of giving the artist more direct control over the speed. On the gravestone of a gem cutter of the Roman empire found at Philadelphia in Asia Minor a tool is represented that looks like the bow used by modern jewelers and which, by being drawn back and forth, could impart a rotating movement similar to that of the wheel. But since the rotating wheel is known to have been used by the ancients in the making of pottery, it is probable that they made use of it in gem engraving also. After the cutting of the gem was complete the surface was often polished, a practice especially popular among the Etruscans and in the later Greek and Roman periods. Naxian stone (*naxium*) was used for polishing, according to Pliny.

It is not known definitely whether the ancient gem cutters made use of the magnifying glass but it is probable that they did. The general principle of concentrating rays was known to Aristophanes. Pliny several times mentions the use of balls of glass or crystal brought in contact with the rays of the sun to generate heat, and Seneca speaks more specifically of this principle applied for magnifying objects.

What seem to be ancient lenses, some going back to the 2nd millennium B.C., were found in Egypt and Crete.

3. Mesopotamia.—The art of engraving stones probably originated in south Mesopotamia. There it attained a high degree of proficiency as early as the 4th millennium B.C.; *i.e.*, during the Elamite and Sumerian civilizations. The engravings were worked on stones mostly of cylindrical shape, which were suspended by a string and used as seals. The materials were petrified shell and marble, and the subjects are chiefly heroes fighting animals, deities with worshipers and decorative motifs. After the Akkadian invasion (*c.* 2800 B.C.) the art of seal engraving reached its greatest height, and such semiprecious stones as rock crystal were cut in masterly fashion. The favourite representation was the mythical King Gilgamesh (*see* GILGAMESH, EPIC OF) performing his great exploits; cuneiform inscriptions began to appear. After the decline of the Akkadian empire the representations became more and more conventionalized. Hematite gradually became the prevailing material. The most frequent subjects were the "introduction scene"—a seated goddess toward whom a second deity leads a worshiper; the Gilgamesh legend; and other mythical representations. During the Amorite dynasty (*c.* 2100–1800 B.C.), to which belonged the famous King Hammurabi, there was a highly artistic period, but probably one of short duration. The representations were mostly the same as during the preceding epoch, and the use of cuneiform inscriptions became important until in the Kassite period (*c.* 1800 B.C.) it constituted the most conspicuous feature.

After the downfall of the Amorites in Babylonia (1758 B.C.), southern Mesopotamia no longer played an important part politically, but the other oriental countries which then came into prominence naturally profited by the older civilization. The Hittites (2nd millennium B.C.), the Assyrians (first half of 1st millennium B.C.) and other peoples of Asia Minor all became conversant with the art of gem engraving and carried on the southern Mesopotamian tradition with some contributions of their own. The favourite subjects were adoration scenes and heraldic groupings of deities and animals. Decorative motifs were popular. The cylinder form remained in vogue, but conical and dome-shaped seals with a flat base for the intaglio were the most popular. The coloured quartzes were the favourite material. When the power of Assyria gave way to that of Persia, the Persian gem engravers followed in the footsteps of their predecessors in both technique and style; but the favourite theme became the exploits of the Persian king Darius the Great.

4. Egypt.—The Egyptians early adopted the art of engraving, employing first the cylinder form, then, from about the 9th dynasty on, the scarab, or beetle, and kindred shapes. As subjects for their engravings they used chiefly symbols, script and ornaments—only occasionally pictorial scenes. Though historically, therefore, these scarabs are of great importance—especially as they have been found in great numbers and form a continuous series—the artistic value is frequently secondary. The great majority lack the interest of subject treatment, though the finish of their execution is remarkable. The commonest materials were glazed steatite and faience, but the coloured quartzes—carnelian, amethyst, jasper, etc.—were also employed.

5. Crete.—From the earliest times Greece took an independent path influenced but not conditioned by its oriental neighbours. In Crete gem engraving occupied an important place. The stones of the Early Minoan period (c. 3000–2200 B.C.) show a great variety of shapes—including cylindrical, pyramidal, conoid, quadrilateral and three-sided, rounded beads—and are engraved with rude pictographs consisting of primitive renderings of human beings, animals, ships and floral and linear patterns. The stone was invariably of a soft variety, i.e., steatite of different colours worked by hand. As time went on—during the Middle Minoan I and II periods (c. 2200–1750 B.C.)—the three-sided, elongated bead became the standardized shape and the pictographs were transformed into less rude, more conventionalized forms. Several symbols generally occurred together, showing that from mere ideographic meaning they had acquired a phonographic value as syllables or letters. In other words, the primitive pictographs had evolved into hieroglyphs. The material was still the soft steatite. During the Middle Minoan III period (c. 1750–1580 B.C.) the hieroglyphic script reached its full development, the symbols appearing in highly systematized form, executed often with great nicety. The stones were no longer steatite but hard varieties, such as carnelian, chalcedony and green jasper. They were worked with the wheel, the use of which was apparently learned from the orient.

In the next period (Late Minoan, c. 1580–1200 B.C.) there was a great change. The Minoan written language had finally evolved into a linear script and concurrently it disappeared from the seal stones. In its stead are found naturalistic designs—animals, cult scenes; i.e., the stock subjects of Cretan art, executed with amazing spirit and vivacity. The stones were regularly the hard quartzes, of lentoid and glandular forms. Similar engraved gems as well as gold rings with engraved bezels have been found at Mycenae and other places within the range of Cretan influence. Toward the end of the Late Minoan period the art deteriorated. The soft steatite again took the place of the harder stones, and the subjects became merely conventionalized representations. Gradually there was established the geometric style in which linear designs were engraved by hand on soft stones of the prevalent oriental forms. In the 7th century B.C. a revival in artistic conceptions is noticeable. Highly decorative animals were carved with considerable feeling for life on steatites of glandular and lentoid forms. This was the prelude to several centuries of a flourishing output, lasting throughout the classical civilizations.

6. Greece.—The study of Greek and Roman gems is the study of classical art in miniature; for the gems reflect faithfully the styles of the various periods to which they belong, so that they represent an accurate picture of the development, the prime and the decadence of classical art. In the gems of the 6th and early 5th century B.C. the dainty charm of archaic Greek art found a happy expression. The chief forms were, the scarab and the scaraboid regularly set in swivel rings. The subjects were the same as in other branches of archaic art. At the beginning of the period the human figure in kneeling posture was the most popular, but soon a greater variety was attempted. Representations of gods and goddesses are comparatively rare, but Hercules was a favourite; and various demons, the Silenus, the Siren and the Sphinx were also common subjects. Among the figures without mythological significance, the commonest were warriors, archers, athletes and horsemen; and among the animals the lion, bull, boar, deer, ram, cock and horse were favoured. The coloured quartzes, such as the carnelian, chalcedony and agate, were the chief materials used.

The second half of the 5th and the 4th centuries mark another climax in the history of Greek gem engraving. In the minute products of the gem cutters as in contemporary statues the same conception of serene beauty is found. The favourite shape employed is no longer the scarab but the scaraboid, generally large and thick, and perforated to be worn on a swivel or as a pendant. With regard to the choice of subjects the chief theme was the daily life of the people, especially of the women. A woman taking a bath, making music, playing with animals, etc., were all favourite representations; animals were likewise common subjects; mythological subjects were less popular. The favourite deities were Aphrodite, Eros and Nike. By far the commonest stone of this period was the chalcedony. Less frequently used were the carnelian, agate, rock crystal, jasper and lapis lazuli.

The inscriptions on Greek gems form an interesting study. They generally give the name of the owner, often only the beginning of his name being recorded. Occasionally they refer to the people represented or they contain a greeting. Sometimes the name of the artist is given. Of the latter the most prominent are Epimenes and Dexamenos. Their works rank among the best which have been produced in Greek gem cutting.

The Greek gems of the Hellenistic period, about 323–30 B.C., reflected the heterogeneous styles of contemporary sculpture; but there were also some notable representations, including a portrait of Philetairos. A change took place in the shape of the stones used. Instead of the perforated scarabs and scaraboids the unperforated ringstone, generally flat on one side and convex on the other, became the accepted form. The stones were often of considerable size and many of the large rings in which they were mounted are preserved. The favourite stones were the hyacinth, garnet, beryl, topaz, amethyst, rock crystal, carnelian, sard, agate and sardonyx, many of them introduced into the Greek world from the east after the conquests of Alexander the Great. Glass, as a substitute for more precious material, was often used. Among the subjects represented the most important is the portrait, which acquired great popularity. Scenes from daily life and mythology both were represented.

A great technical innovation introduced in this period is the cameo, in which the representation instead of being engraved in the surface of the gem is carved in relief. It is therefore the converse of the intaglio. These cameos naturally did not serve as seals, as did the intaglios, but were used purely for decorative purposes. In such work the coloured quartzes were generally employed, their various layers being skilfully and effectively utilized; but imitations in glass paste also occur. The technique was popular in Roman times.

7. Greco-Phoenician and Greco-Persian Gems.—A class of gems in which the influence of Greek art is shown is that of the Greco-Phoenician scarabs, chiefly found in the Carthaginian cemeteries of Sardinia, Carthage and Iviza. The stones discovered there show that at first Phoenician art was strongly subjected to Egyptian influence, but from the 6th century B.C. onward both the Greek style and Greek subjects were adopted. The archaic Greek style prevailed in the Phoenician stones throughout the 5th century and into the 4th, long after a freer style had been introduced in Greece itself—a phenomenon familiar from Carthaginian coins. The shape of stone used is regularly the scarab and the favourite material green jasper. The representations consist chiefly of the favourite Greek types of youths and men, and of mythological creatures. Fantastic combinations of heads and masks probably had significance as a means of averting evil.

The Greco-Persian gems illustrate the influence of Greek art in the east. In Persia the gems of purely Persian style are followed in the second half of the 5th and the first half of the 4th century B.C. by gems in which Persian and Greek elements commingled. They were evidently made by Greeks for Persians. The subjects were taken from the daily life of the Persian nobles, preferably contests of Persians and Greeks, or hunting scenes, or single figures of Persian nobles or ladies. Animals were also favourite subjects. These representations were executed in a broad, spirited style, chiefly on chalcedony stones of scaraboid form. A rectangular shape with one faceted side was also popular.

8. Etruria.—Etruscan gems made their appearance toward the end of the 6th century B.C and remained in vogue until the 4th. They closely copied Greek styles, forms and subjects. At times their execution was excellent, but there is always a certain dryness and stiffness which serve to distinguish even their best products from pure Greek work. The shape used is invariably that of the scarab, worked often with minute care, while to the Greek artist the backs of the engraved gems were of secondary interest. More-over, the edge of the base on which the beetle stands, which in the Greek examples is left plain, is ornamented in the Etruscan gems, except in the earliest period and in the more careless specimens. By far the commonest material is the carnelian. The subjects chosen are chiefly taken from Greek mythology. Homeric and Theban heroes predominate (Peleus, Achilles, Odysseus, Ajax, Tydeus and Kapaneus). Inscriptions sometimes occur; they do not, as in the Greek gems, give the name of the owner or of the artist but of the figure represented.

At the end of the 5th century another class of scarab became prevalent, lasting until the beginning of the 3rd century B.C. It was not confined to Etruria but occurred also elsewhere in Italy. The distinguishing characteristic is that it is roughly worked with the round drill, evidently merely for decorative effect, which is heightened by the brilliant polish. Hercules, Silenus and animals were popular subjects.

9. Roman Gems.—The Etruscan scarabs were superseded in Italy in the 3rd and 2nd centuries B.C. by ringstones in which two styles can be distinguished, according as they imitate Etruscan or Hellenistic art. There are no great artistic achievements among them, but they are nevertheless of interest in that they form an important source of knowledge for the Roman art of the earlier republican period. In the 1st century B.C. the two styles became merged, with Greek elements predominating and growing gradually into the classicist style of the Augustan age.

Engraved gems enjoyed a great popularity in Rome during the late republican and early imperial periods, as evidenced not only from the large number of examples which have survived but also from literary sources. Gem collecting became a passionate pur-suit. Wealthy men vied with one another in procuring fine speci-mens and paid enormous prices for them. The keenness of this rivalry can be gauged by the story that the senator Nonius was exiled from Rome because he refused to give a certain gem (valued at 20,000 sesterces) to Mark Antony. Public-spirited men, after having formed their collections, would deposit them in the temples for all to enjoy. Scaurus, the son-in-law of Sulla, is said to have been the first Roman to have a collection of gems. Julius Caesar was an eager and discriminating collector and deposited as many as six separate collections in the temple of Venus Genetrix. The style of the representations is that of the classicist art of the early imperial period encountered in other contemporary products. Its dominant characteristic is a quiet, cold elegance. The subjects have a wide range comprising mythological and everyday themes, including portraits of distinguished men, copies and adaptations of famous statues, symbols and grylli—fantastic combinations of heads and figures, probably with superstitious import. The preva-lent form throughout is the ringstone. The variety of stones used is large, for at this time of Roman world dominion and increased commercial facilities a wide range of stones could be obtained from all parts of the empire. The commonest were the carnelian, sard, sardonyx, chalcedony and amethyst; especially fine engravings are often found on garnets, hyacinths, beryls, topazes and peridots, more rarely on emeralds and sapphires. The nicolo and red jasper,

which occurred only occasionally in former periods, enjoyed great popularity. The Roman enthusiasm for this wealth of beautiful stones can be gauged from the remarks of Pliny, who declared that some gems are considered "beyond any price and even beyond human estimation, so that to many men one gem suffices for the contemplation of all nature."

Cameos continued in use throughout this period, chiefly of sardonyx, onyx and glass paste. The favourite subjects were portraits and mythological scenes. Among the portraits are valu-able representations of emperors and princes.

Signatures of artists are found rather frequently on both the intaglios and cameos. In fact, by far the majority of ancient gem cutters known by name belong to early imperial times. The most distinguished artist was Dioskourides, who, it is known from Pliny, made the imperial seal ring of Augustus. Other well-known names are Gnaios, Aspasios, Eutyches, Aulos, Apollonios and Agath-angelos. (See ROMAN ART.)

10. Late Roman Period.—By the 2nd century A.D. the art of gem engraving was on the decline. Of the large number of gems of that period which have survived very few have any artistic value. The majority show hasty, careless workmanship and the repre-sentations are lifeless and monotonous. The shape of the gems used is always the ringstone and the materials are very much the same as those in use during the preceding period. Nicolo and jasper became specially common, probably on account of supposed magical properties.

The same deterioration is noticeable in the early Christian and Gnostic gems. The commonest materials were hematite and jasper. More important artistically are the Sasanian gems (3rd to 7th century A.D.) which indeed represent the last important product yet found of gem engraving in the ancient world. The representa-tions are a mixture of oriental traditions and late Roman forms. Especially fine are some of the portraits.

In north India the Hephthalites (White Huns) established a civilization in the latter part of the 5th century A.D. which lasted until about shortly after A.D. 540. That they too practised the art of gem engraving was ascertained by the discovery of a stone with the portrait of an Indian king.   (G. M. A. R.)

11. Middle Ages and Modern Times.—After the period of the early middle ages in which the goldsmiths preferred to re-employ antique cameos, Roman gem engraving flourished with renewed vigour in France from the 13th century onward. But only in the Renaissance did stonecutting on a larger scale become significant again, especially in Italy during the period around 1800 when ancient models were copied as faithfully as possible. The best-known gem cutters, who frequently signed their works in Greek or Roman letters, were the Tyrolese family Pichler, Johann Lorenz Natter, Nathaniel Marchant and Edward Burch. The preponder-ance of cameos at the French court at that time dictated jewelry fashion in the whole of Europe.

12. Gem Cutting.—Of decisive significance for the history of modern jewelry was the kind of cutting known as faceting, which produces brilliancy by refraction and reflection of light (see also section *Brilliancy* below). Until the late middle ages gems of all kinds were cut either *en cabochon* (*i.e.*, rounded, usually with a flat underside), or, especially for purposes of incrustation, into flat platelets.

The first attempts at cutting and faceting were aimed at im-proving the appearance of the stone by covering natural flaws. Proper cutting depends upon a detailed knowledge of the crystal structure of the stone; moreover, it was only in the 15th century that the abrasive property of diamond was discovered and used (nothing else will cut diamond). After this was discovered the art of cutting and polishing diamonds and other gems was de-veloped, probably in France and the Netherlands first. The rose cut (described below) was developed in the 17th century, probably by the gem cutters of Amsterdam and Antwerp. The brilliant cut, now the general favourite for diamonds, is said to have been em-ployed for the first time by the Venetian gem cutter Vincenzo Peruzzi around 1700.

In modern gem cutting, the cabochon method continues to be used for opaque, translucent and some transparent stones, as opal, carbuncle, etc.; but for most transparent gems (especially diamonds, sapphires, rubies and emeralds) faceted cutting is almost always employed. In this method, numerous facets, geometrically disposed to bring out the beauty of light and colour to the best advantage, are cut. This is done at the sacrifice of material, often to the extent of half the stone or more, but the value of the gem is greatly increased.

Cutting can be done in a great variety of ways, but the four most common forms are the brilliant, the rose, the baguette and the step or trap cut. The last-named is used particularly for emeralds and is often called the emerald cut; the general shape is usually oblong, square or octagonal, and the facets above and below the girdle (which divides the upper part, or the crown, from the base) are parallel and horizontal. It is used for rubies, sapphires and larger diamonds, as well as for emeralds. The brilliant and rose cuts are used for diamonds in particular.

The brilliant is essentially a low, double cone, its top truncated to form a large, flat, eight-sided face called the table, and its basal apex also truncated by a very small face known as the culet. The upper and lower slopes are cut into a series of triangular facets, 32 above the girdle, in four rows of 8, and 24 below, in three rows, making 56 facets in all. The rose form is used for diamonds not thick enough to cut as brilliants; it is flat below and has 12 to 24, or sometimes 32, triangular facets above, in three rows, meeting in a point. Stones thus cut are also known as "roses couronnées"; others with fewer facets, 12 or even 6, are called "roses d'Anvers," and are a specialty at Antwerp. Baguettes are flat stones with four, eight, or more facets and a simple top.

Modern gem cutting and engraving are done by means of the lathe, which can be made to revolve with extreme rapidity, carrying a point or small disk of soft iron, with diamond dust and oil. The disks vary in diameter from that of a pinhead to a quarter of an inch. Better than the lathe, also, is the dental engine. The flexibility and sensitiveness of this machine enable it to respond to the touch of the artist and to impart a personal quality to his work not possible with the mechanical action of the lathe, and more like the handwork with the sapphire point. (For diamond cutting see DIAMOND.)

13. Gem Imitations.—From a very early period the imitation of gems was attempted; one of the most common processes employed the backing of dyed glass pastes or crystals with coloured foil. The Romans in particular were very skilful in the production

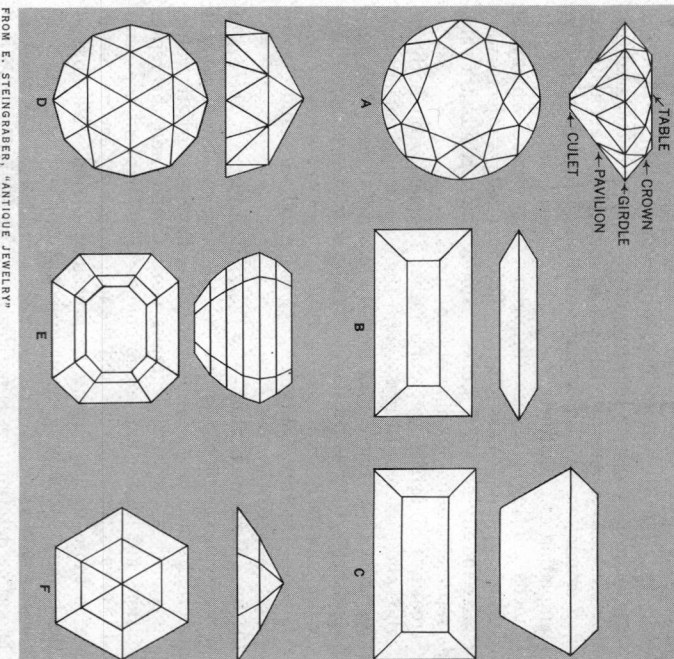

FROM E. STEINGRABER, "ANTIQUE JEWELRY"

POPULAR GEM CUTS: (A) BRILLIANT CUT; (B) THIN BAGUETTE CUT; (C) THICK BAGUETTE CUT; (D) DUTCH ROSE CUT; (E) STEP CUT; (F) ANTWERP ROSE CUT

of coloured glass pastes, which copied especially the emerald and lapis lazuli.

With the increasing demand for jewelry on the part of broader population groups in Europe the number of imitations steadily increased. In 1767 there existed in Paris a guild of 314 Joailliers-faussetiers. In 1758 the Viennese goldsmith Joseph Strasser succeeded in inventing a colourless glass paste which can be cut and which, at a superficial glance, approaches the sparkle of the genuine diamond; the products are called strass stones. This was the beginning of synthetic gem production which has been perfected to a high degree.

(ER. SR.)

II. NATURAL GEMS

1. Gem Minerals.—Of the approximately 2,000 inorganic minerals, only the following 16 achieved importance as gems: beryl, chrysoberyl, corundum, diamond, feldspar, garnet, jade, lazurite, olivine, opal, quartz, spinel, topaz, tourmaline, turquoise and zircon. The quasi mineral pearl completes the list of important gems. All except zircon, which gained widespread popularity in the 1930s, have been worn for centuries. When the same mineral is found in two or more colours, a specific gem name is commonly given to each variety; hence, two gems may be identical in every respect except in the small amount of impurity that acts as a pigmenting agent. Emerald is the green, aquamarine the blue variety of beryl; ruby the red, sapphire the blue variety of corundum. However, in the case of diamond and topaz, individual gem names are not given to the variously coloured stones.

Because wealth can be conveniently concentrated in gems, for which there is a ready market in all parts of the world, persons of wealth have commonly invested portions of their fortunes in gems. Centuries ago, this motive was more compelling than in modern times, but this practice was again demonstrated during the invasion of the Netherlands, Belgium and France in World War II.

The general properties and characteristics of minerals, which are fully discussed in the article MINERALOGY, are applicable to gems. Only those properties which have special significance when attached to gems will be considered here. Gem minerals have certain characteristics that set them apart from nongem minerals—beauty, durability and rarity. No mineral lacking in any of these characteristics has ever achieved distinction. However, beauty only is essential in a gem. Some gem minerals of minor importance, such as satin spar and malachite, are too soft to be durable, and others like rock crystal and pyrope are not uncommon. Among those qualities that give beauty to gems, colour is the most important.

2. Colour.—Only a few gems are idiochromatic; that is, with a colour which is distinctive and inherent in the chemical constitution of the mineral. Most gem minerals are allochromatic; that is, they are colourless when pure, and their colour is dependent upon impurities which act as pigmenting agents. In most instances, allochromatic gems are also transparent or translucent. Gem minerals generally occur in well-developed crystals (see CRYSTALLOGRAPHY). Such crystals are apt to be pure and, therefore, transparent. Opal is the only important gem mineral which is amorphous; that is, not found in the crystalline state. An even distribution of pigment is desirable in transparent gems, but in some translucent stones, such as agate and heliotrope (bloodstone), their mottled appearance, caused by an uneven distribution of pigment, is characteristic.

Because of its other unusual properties, diamond is the only gem which is valuable when colourless. Those varieties which are coloured red, green or blue are, however, much more valuable and are called fancies. Conversely, the colourless variety of topaz is worth little more than the cost of cutting, while the most highly prized topaz possesses a distinct yellow colour faintly tinged with wine. In 1956 the U.S. Federal Trade commission ruled that any colour term, such as blue-white, could not be used in describing a diamond unless the stone had a tinge of the colour mentioned. The so-called blue-white diamond contains no blue pigment.

PLATE I

GEM

Precious stones. *Top row, left and right:* sapphires, or blue corundum (Ceylon). Effect of the star in the sapphire at the left is caused by mineral inclusions and cavities within the stone; *centre:* chrysoberyl, or cat's-eye (Brazil). *Bottom row, left to right:* ruby, the red gem variety of corundum (Burma); diamond (Republic of South Africa); emerald, or green beryl (Colombia)

Precious and semiprecious stones. *Top row:* two forms of gem quartz (left) amethyst and citrine (both from Brazil). *Second row, left to right:* golden or yellow beryl (Brazil); kunzite, a form of spodumene (U.S., California); aquamarine, or blue beryl (Brazil); peridot, a gem olivine (Red Sea area). *Bottom row:* two of the colour varieties of topaz (both from Brazil)

VARIETIES OF CUT AND POLISHED GEM STONES

STONES FROM THE COLLECTIONS OF WALTER C. BLATT, ST. LOUIS, MO., AND WILLIAM V. SCHMIDT, NEW YORK CITY

PHOTOGRAPHS BY JOHN H. GERARD © ENCYCLOPÆDIA BRITANNICA, INC.

PLATE II

Top left: Yellow orthoclase, a gem feldspar (Madagascar); *top right:* apatite (Mexico); *centre left:* topaz (Brazil); *centre:* labradorite, a plagioclase feldspar (Canada); *bottom left:* peridot olivine (U.S., New Mexico); *bottom right:* microcline (U.S., Virginia)

Black opal (Australia)

UNCUT GEM STONES AND CRYSTALS

ALL STONES EXCEPT BOTTOM RIGHT FROM THE COLLECTION OF THE DEPARTMENT OF EARTH SCIENCES, WASHINGTON UNIVERSITY, ST. LOUIS, MO.; (BOTTOM RIGHT) FROM THE COLLECTION OF JOSEPH AND HELEN GUETTERMAN, BELLEVILLE, ILL. PHOTOGRAPHS BY JOHN H. GERARD © ENCYCLOPÆDIA BRITANNICA, INC.

Cluster of amethyst crystals (Mexico)

Moonstone, a feldspar (Ceylon)

Rough emerald crystal (Colombia)

PLATE III

GEM

Varieties of quartz. *Top left:* jasper (U.S., Nevada); *top right:* tiger's-eye (Republic of South Africa); *centre left, bottom right:* smoky quartz (U.S., Montana and Arkansas); *centre right:* citrine, probably heat treated (Brazil); *bottom left:* rose quartz (U.S., Virginia)

Turquoise (U.S., Arizona)

Tourmaline crystals (two rods in the foreground from U.S., California; others from Brazil)

Lapis lazuli, or lazurite (rock from Chile, cut and polished piece from Afghanistan)

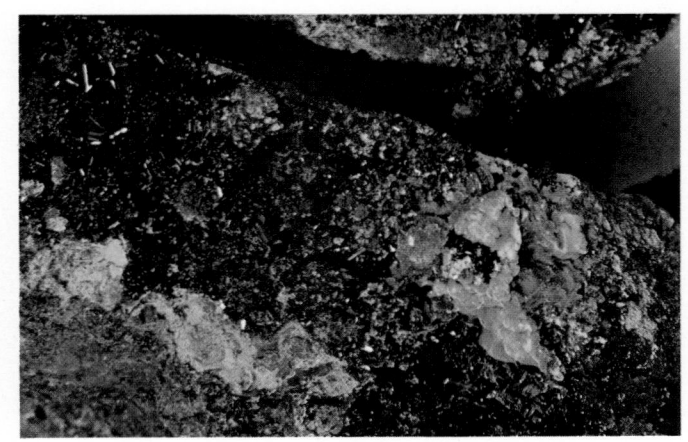

Azurite (blue) and malachite (green) crystals. These minerals are often found together (Mexico)

UNCUT GEM STONES AND CRYSTALS

(TOP LEFT, CENTRE LEFT, BOTTOM LEFT) FROM THE COLLECTION OF JOSEPH AND HELEN GUETTERMAN; (TOP RIGHT AND ROUGH STONE BOTTOM RIGHT) FROM THE COLLECTION OF WALTER C. BLATT; (CUT STONE BOTTOM RIGHT) FROM THE COLLECTION OF WALTER C. BLATT, LECTION OF THE DEPARTMENT OF EARTH SCIENCES, WASHINGTON UNIVERSITY; PHOTOGRAPHS BY JOHN H. GERARD © ENCYCLOPÆDIA BRITANNICA, INC.

PLATE IV

GEM

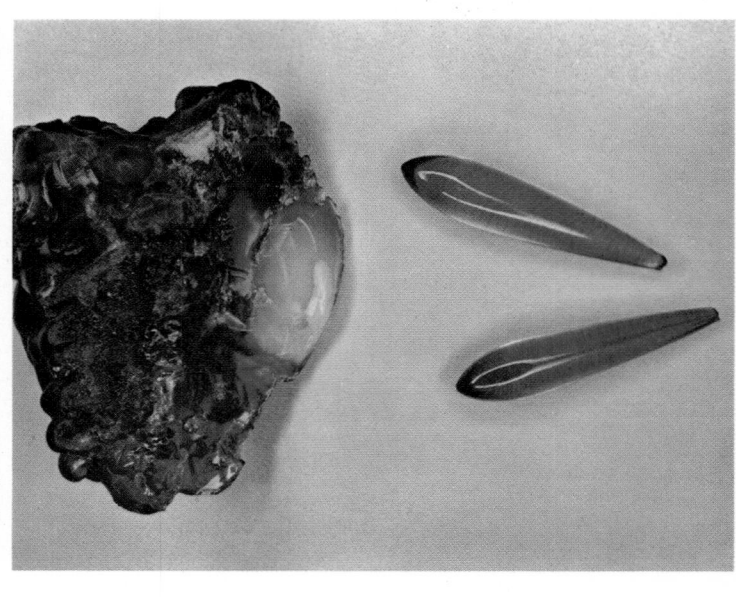

Amber, translucent droplets and a large opaque piece (Baltic sea coast, Poland). Amber is a fossil resin of extinct coniferous trees of the Eocene period

Natural pearls (Persian Gulf). The pearl is an organic concretion formed within the shell of a mollusk

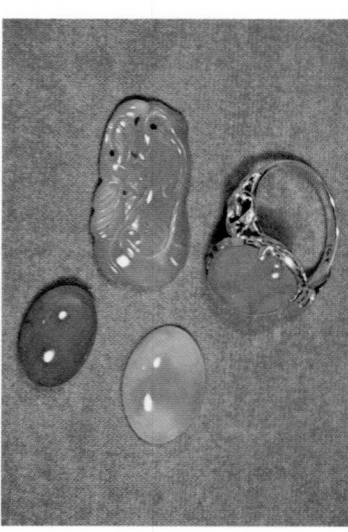

Cut and polished jade in various shades of green (Burma)

OPAQUE CUT STONES AND ORGANIC GEM SUBSTANCES

Polished opaque stones. *Top:* red coral, an organic gem material (Italy); *centre row, left to right:* serpentine (Burma); bloodstone, or heliotrope, a gem quartz (India); malachite (Rhodesia); *bottom row, left to right:* tiger's-eye (Republic of South Africa); carnelian, dyed, a form of chalcedony (Brazil); blue turquoise (Iran)

(TOP LEFT) FROM DEPARTMENT OF EARTH SCIENCES, WASHINGTON UNIVERSITY; (OTHERS) FROM THE COLLECTIONS OF WALTER C. BLATT AND WILLIAM V. SCHMIDT PHOTOGRAPHS BY JOHN H. GERARD © ENCYCLOPÆDIA BRITANNICA, INC.

GEMS: 3000 B.C. TO THE 19TH CENTURY A.D.

First row: (plaster impressions) Contest scene; Akkadian cylinder seal, 1st half of 3rd millennium. Persian seal of Darius, chalcedony; c. 500 B.C. *Second row:* (actual size, plaster impressions) Woman playing harp, rock crystal; Greek, 2nd half of 5th century B.C. Satyr dancing, agate; Greek, late 6th century B.C. Youth and woman, burned carnelian; Greek, 2nd half of 5th century B.C. *Third row:* (actual size, plaster impressions) Portrait of Philetairos, chalcedony sprinkled with jasper; Hellenistic. Two-horse chariot, chalcedony; Greek, c. 400 B.C. Girl writing, chalcedony; Greek, late 5th century B.C. *Fourth row:* (actual size, plaster impressions except left and centre) Bacchic scene, sardonyx cameo; Roman. Mars and Venus with Cupid, onyx cameo; Renaissance, middle of 16th century. Jason and Chiron, inscribed Kromos, carnelian; 19th century

PLATE VI

GEM

ANCIENT GEMS AND THEIR MATERIALS

1. Carnelian. 2. Sard. 3. Chalcedony. 4. Plasma. 5. Nicolo. 6. Moss agate. 7. Banded agate. 8. Peridot. 9. Heliotrope. 10. Black jasper. 11. Green jasper. 12. Red jasper. 13. Yellow jasper. 14. Rock crystal. 15 and 20. Amethyst. 16 and 17. Garnet. 18 and 30. Glass pastes. 19. Hematite. 21. Beryl. 22. Emerald. 23. Topaz. 24. Sardonyx. 25. Turquoise. 26. Lapis lazuli. 27. Onyx. 28. Porphyry. 29. Serpentine. 31. Steatite.
1, Italic, 2nd century B.C.; 2, 4, 5, 7, 8, 9, 12–18, 20, 21, 23, 28, Roman, 1st century B.C. to 2nd century A.D.; 3, 6, 11, Greek, 6th–5th century B.C.; 10, 22, 24, 18–19th century A.D.; 19, Hittite, 2nd millennium B.C.; 25, 30, Hellenistic, 3rd–1st century B.C.; 26, Ephthalite (North Indian), 5th–6th century A.D.; 27, 29, 31 Minoan, 3rd–2nd millennium B.C.; 8, 24, 25, 30 are cameos and the rest intaglio seals

The play of colours characteristic of opal and labradorite is caused by the interference of light waves reflected from successive layers within the stone. It is analogous to the coloured reflections from thin films of oil on water. Similarly, the asterism of star rubies and sapphires and the chatoyancy of cat's-eye, satin spar and tiger's-eye are structure phenomena.

Asterism in the ruby and sapphire is produced by minute inclusions oriented with respect to the hexagonal crystal structure of the mineral; hence, the six-pointed star. Chatoyancy, a single band of light which moves across the surface of the stone as its position is changed, is produced by the parallel orientation of inclusions. The flashes of red and blue which one observes on properly cut diamonds, zircons, rutile, sphenes and demantoid garnets when held in a beam of parallel light are called fire. Like the rainbow, fire is caused by dispersion (see LIGHT).

As recovered from the earth, few gem stones are attractive. Only after the gem cutter has given the stone proper proportions and a high polish to emphasize its pleasing characteristics may it be called a gem. All types of cutting are classified in three general categories: cabochon (curved surfaces); faceted (flat surfaces); and carved, either cameo (relief) or intaglio (engraved). The styles and methods of cutting are described above (see also SEALS).

3. Colour Improvement.—Proper treatment often improves the colour of a gem. This was practised in India centuries ago by heating faintly coloured chalcedony to produce the attractive yellow-red of carnelian. Similarly, amethystine to smoky-coloured quartz may be changed to the yellow citrine, which then is commonly but improperly sold as topaz. The colours of many amethysts and aquamarines and some rubies and tourmalines are the result of heat treatment.

Zircon, when mined, is commonly reddish-brown. Many zircons develop a fine blue colour when heated in a reducing atmosphere at 900° C. to 1,000° C.; an occasional stone becomes red or green, others colourless. Practically all of the zircons marketed are the result of heat treatment.

X-rays, cathode rays, radium emanations and cyclotron bombardment induce many colour changes in gems. Of these, the production of a green colour in diamonds by radium or cyclotron bombardment is the most important. This green colour is only skin deep, and may be removed by heating the diamond at 900° C. Diamonds treated with radium develop a similar green colour and also a secondary radioactivity, which persists for years and serves to distinguish them from diamonds treated in the cyclotron.

Nearly any colour can be produced in chalcedony, agate and onyx by staining with appropriate chemicals or dyes. Agates were first dyed in the Idar-Oberstein district, Germany, in the early part of the 19th century by soaking them in sugar or honey solutions and subsequently placing them in concentrated sulfuric acid. The acid chars the absorbed sugar to carbon, staining the various layers of agate from light brown to black, depending on their porosity. The nonporous layers remain colourless, accentuating the banded structure of the agate.

Red hues are commonly produced by ferric oxide; greens by chromium and nickel compounds; blue by ferric ferrocyanide. Solutions of other inorganic compounds and organic dyes may be used. Practically all agate and onyx of gem quality have been artificially coloured.

4. Brilliancy.—This depends upon the amount of incident light that is reflected from the surface and the interior of the stone. The amount of light reflected by surfaces with equal polish varies with the indices of refraction of the gem. The index of refraction of rock crystal (quartz) is 1.55; sapphire 1.76; zircon 1.95; and diamond 2.42. The percentage of normally incident light reflected from the polished surfaces of these gems is roughly in the ratio of 1:1.5:2.4.

If a gem has been properly cut, the light which enters the stone will be twice totally reflected by the back facets, and will emerge at the front surface. The stone will appear to have a silvered back. The amount of totally reflected light increases with the index of refraction and, therefore, a greater amount of light will be reflected from the interior of the diamond than from any other natural gem; hence, it is the most brilliant.

5. Identification of Gems.—Uncut gem stones may be identified by crystal form, hardness, cleavage, fracture, structure or chemical tests. When cut, many of these properties are not visible, or their determination would damage the gem, though, under the microscope, minute cleavages or fractures and the presence of characteristic inclusions and their distribution may give evidence as to the stone's identity. However, a positive identification is made only after one or more of the physical constants have been determined. In most instances, the determination of the density (specific gravity) and the index of refraction will suffice.

Various methods of determining density are described under the article DENSITY. The Jolly balance is unsatisfactory, except for the larger stones. Accurate determinations can be made on very small stones by suspending the gem in water from the arm of a chemical balance in a spiral coil at the end of a fine wire.

The index of refraction can be conveniently measured by the method of total reflection. Several small, hand-sized refractometers have been specially designed for this purpose. They consist of either a hemisphere or prism of high-index glass, upon which the gem is placed. A beam of light is directed from the under-surface toward the gem. The totally reflected rays fall upon a calibrated ground-glass scale. A numerical value is directly read which is the refractive index of the gem. It is essential that the film of air between the high-index glass and the gem be displaced by a liquid the refractive index of which is greater than that of the gem. A solution of sulfur in methylene iodide with a refractive index of 1.793 is commonly used. Diamond, titanite, zircon, rutile and some garnets have greater indices than this liquid and, consequently, cannot be differentiated by this method.

A determination of the density and refractive index will give a positive identification of an unknown gem, except in those rare instances, such as ruby and almandite, where the values are the same for both gems. However, almandite crystallizes in the cubic system and hence is optically isotropic (singly refractive), while ruby is hexagonal and anisotropic (doubly refractive). Two convenient instruments, the polariscope and the dichroscope, were designed for differentiating gems on the basis of these optical properties. Their use in the determination of gems is discussed under the article CRYSTALLOGRAPHY: *Optical Crystallography.* It has been noted that the refractive indices of diamond, titanite, zircon, rutile and some garnets cannot be determined on the refractometer. However, because garnet and diamond are optically isotropic, and zircon and titanite are strongly anisotropic a positive determination can be made by using the polariscope in conjunction with density determinations.

Of all the diagnostic properties the determination of the index of refraction is the most useful and, at the same time, the most readily determined. Satisfactory readings may often be obtained from the curved surfaces of a cabochon-cut stone by carefully adjusting the position of the stone on the refractometer so that the point of contact with the high-index glass is at the optical centre of the instrument.

6. Trade.—Because of their nearly indestructible character, gems are sold and resold from generation to generation. The available supply is not greatly affected by the production of newly mined gems in any year. However, as with other luxury items, demand fluctuates markedly with business conditions. Hence, price variations are determined largely by demand.

Science and modern industrial processes have had but slight influence on the gem-cutting industry. In the gem-cutting centres of Europe, the family is still the basic business unit. Knowledge and skills are passed on from father to son, and the traditions of the guild survive in many forms. The fine craftsman combines both mechanical and artistic skills.

The Gemmological Association of Great Britain (1931) and the Gemological Institute of America (1931) instituted courses of study based on a scientific approach to gemology. The American Gem society (1934) was organized to maintain and raise professional standards and to promote education and research in its field. The Gemmological Association of Australia (1946) was established for similar purposes. These organizations were founded in the retail trade with which their efforts are primarily concerned, but their influence extends to the producers; manufacturers and wholesalers.

III. SYNTHETIC GEMS

1. Methods of Producing Synthetic Gems.—In the U.S. the Federal Trade commission has restricted the use of the adjective synthetic when applied to gem stones to manufactured materials that possess the same chemical, physical and optical properties as the naturally occurring stone.

In the earliest recorded attempts to produce gems, natural stones were planted in the ground in the hope that they would either reproduce or grow larger. Later, the alchemists attempted to imitate the processes of nature. Microscopic crystals of rubies were produced in 1857 by Marc Antoine Augustin Gaudin by fusing alum to which a little chromium sulfate was added to give the proper red colour. Edmond Frémy and Charles Feil in 1878 produced crystals from which small gem stones were cut by fusing aluminum oxide (Al_2O_3) and lead oxide (PbO). In 1895 Michaud fused fragments of natural rubies to produce larger stones known as reconstructed rubies. For a short time this was a commercially successful process. The method of August Victor Lewis Verneuil (1902) of producing synthetic rubies and sapphires by an oxyhydrogen flame was highly successful and is used today with only slight modification.

This process is also known as the flame-fusion method and is used to produce not only rubies and sapphires but also variously coloured synthetic spinels ($MgO.Al_2O_3$), rutile (titania TiO_2) and the imitation gem, strontium titanate. Chrysoberyl ($BeO.Al_2O_3$) crystals large enough to cut into gems have also been made by this process, but it has not been commercially successful.

Jaeger and H. Espig of the I.G. Farbenindustrie, Bitterfeld, Ger., synthesized emerald ($3BeO.Al_2O_3.6SiO_2$) in 1930 and made crystals, by fusion, large enough to be cut into small gems. The same year Carol F. Chatham of San Francisco, Calif., also synthesized emerald, and in 1935 succeeded in producing crystals large enough to be cut and marketed.

Because of its greater value, many attempts have been made to synthesize diamond. It was generally accepted prior to the 1930s that several of the experimenters had made diamond. Of these, J.B. Hannay (1880) in England, Henri Moissan (1893) in France and Sir William Crookes (1906) in England were most widely credited with success. Hannay heated organic material with water in sealed glass tubes. Moissan dissolved carbon in molten iron in an electric furnace and plunged the molten iron into a brine solution. The cooling and shrinking of the outside layer while the interior was still molten created terrific pressures which supposedly produced diamonds in the interior. Crookes exploded cordite containing excess carbon in a cylinder and momentarily attained calculated pressures of 100,000 lb. per square inch at a temperature of 5,100° C.

In attempts to duplicate the processes no diamonds have ever been produced. Microscopic crystals of metallic carbides that resemble diamond in many ways have been obtained and identified by modern scientific methods not available to those earlier scientists. Edward G. Acheson, while attempting to make diamonds in 1891, produced and identified SiC (carborundum), the second hardest known crystal.

The first synthetic diamonds were produced by the General Electric company at Schenectady, N.Y. The discovery was announced in Feb. 1955. (See DIAMOND: *Synthetic Diamonds*.)

2. Verneuil or Flame-Fusion Process.—Originally developed to manufacture synthetic rubies and sapphires, this method with only slight modifications is used to produce spinel, rutile (titania) and strontium titanate, an imitation gem. It consists essentially of an inverted oxyhydrogen torch which opens into a ceramic muffle and forms the "boule" on a support which can be lowered as the boule grows.

For the formation of a clear single crystal boule it is essential to start with a highly purified alumina. This is prepared by repeated crystallization of ammonium alum and subsequent calcination which leaves pure alumina (Al_2O_3). The alumina is placed in the container which has a fine sieve at the base. When the container is tapped by the mechanically actuated hammer, the alumina sifts down into the enclosed chamber. Oxygen passes into this chamber and carries the finely divided alumina down to the tip of the torch, where it burns with the hydrogen which enters the larger tube which encloses the central tube. The oxygen carries the fine alumina particles into the intense heat of the central part of the flame where they fuse and fall on the molten upper surface of the boule as droplets.

To start the operation a sintered mass of alumina is built up on a fire-clay support using a low heat and a high rate of powder flow. The flame temperature is raised, the rate of powder flow adjusted and the sintered mass lowered at the proper rate until the spine at the base of the boule grows. By controlling the powder flow and the rate of lowering the boule the boule begins to form with a mushroomlike top. When the desired diameter is reached flame characteristics and the rate of powder feed and boule lowering are adjusted to produce a boule of uniform diameter. The temperature of the upper surface of the boule is held just above the melting point, which for colourless sapphire is 2,030° C.

To initiate boule growth the continuous attention of the operator is required. Once started, the boule growth proceeds under automatic control and one operator can attend several furnaces. When a boule reaches the desired size, normally 150–200 carats, the operator shuts off the furnace and allows the boule to cool. During the cooling process the boule develops internal strains which would eventually cause the boule to crack. These are relieved by splitting the boule longitudinally, which is induced by snapping off the elongated stem of the boule. Some residual strain which is not disadvantageous for gem and most industrial uses is left in the half-boule developed by splitting. Strain-free whole boules may be produced by annealing at 1,950° C.

The strain develops during cooling because the outer surface cools faster than the interior, and causes considerable loss from cracking during the manufacturing process. Most successful boule growth takes place when the principal axis of the crystal lies 60° from the vertical axis.

For many scientific and technical uses it is desirable to have boules oriented crystallographically. In the U.S, the Linde Air Products company developed the use of an oriented seed crystal on which boule growth was started. The boule then has the same crystallographic orientation as the seed crystal. The company also developed a semiautomatic process of making rods by continuing the uniform growth of the spine at the base of the boule. Rods 18 in. long and 0.1–2.0 in. in diameter are commercially available. They are ground to uniform diameters and flame polished in an oxyhydrogen flame. Short mushroomlike boules up to 4 in. in diameter are also grown from which circular transparent disks up to 0.2 in. thick are cut and polished.

3. Corundum (Rubies and Sapphires).—Prior to 1940 all synthetic boules were made in Switzerland, Germany and France. For several years after the discovery of the process of manufacture all of the production was used for gem stones. Synthetic ruby was the chief product and was produced by adding chromium sulfate to the purified alum before calcining (at 1,000° C.) in fused quartz dishes, yielding an intimate mixture of aluminum and chromium oxide. Five per cent of Cr_2O_3 gives a pale-pink boule and 6% a deep-red boule. The higher the percentage of chromium oxide the more difficult it is to control boule growth and the greater the loss from boules cracking on cooling.

Blue sapphire was produced by adding iron and titanium, green by cobalt and yellow by nickel and magnesium oxides. Various other colours were produced from mixtures of these oxides.

Star rubies and sapphires, first developed in the U.S. in 1947, are made by adding 1% of titanium oxide to the starting powder and forming the boules in the usual manner. The boules are then heat treated at temperatures between 1,100° C. and 1,500° C. depending on the colour of the "star" to be made. The titanium oxide develops small needlelike crystals of rutile (TiO_2) which are oriented along the hexagonal crystal planes within the boule similar to the same needlelike crystals in natural "stars." After cutting *en cabochon* with the principal crystal axis normal to the base the finished gem has a centred six-ray star. The synthetic gems have sharper and more distinctly developed stars than the natural crystals.

4. Identification.—It is very difficult to distinguish between natural colourless sapphires and synthetic colourless sapphires, but this determination is rarely necessary because these stones have little value. The natural crystals have microscopic irregularly shaped gas and liquid inclusions while the synthetic gems may have minute spherical gas bubbles. The cut synthetic gems usually show microscopic cracks along and normal to the intersection of facets. Coloured gems may be differentiated under the microscope by characteristics of the pigmentation inherent in the processes of growth in addition to the above features present in the colourless gems.

Synthetic coloured boules are purer than the coloured natural stones. The only inclusions seen in synthetics are spherical gas bubbles of microscopic size and rutile needles in "stars." Under the unaided eye. In cut stones they should not be confused with the polishing striations on the surface of the facets often visible under the microscope. Structure lines are only seen when viewing the stones nearly parallel to their plane, and can be followed by focusing the microscope down into the interior of the stone. Unlike polishing striations they are continuous beneath adjacent facets. Some natural stones show straight parallel twinning striations, often in a hexagonal pattern in three directions, which may be confused with the structure lines of synthetics.

On examining faceted gems, reflections from the facets hide the interior features of the stone. It is usually necessary to rotate the stone under the microscope and view it in several directions before evidence of the true nature of the stone is found.

About 1920 the industrial use of synthetic rubies and sapphires began to be of more importance than the gem use when they began to replace the natural stones for jewel bearings in watches and electrical instruments. By 1935 synthetics had replaced natural jewels in both Europe and the United States. Every household electric meter had at least two bearings jeweled with synthetics. Although colourless sapphire is easier to grow, ruby is preferred for industrial jewels because of the greater ease in handling it.

The Linde Air Products company pioneered in the U.S. in other industrial uses which take advantage of the superior hardness of Al_2O_3, second only to diamond. Colourless sapphire rods were introduced as thread guides in the textile industry, followed by the natural sapphire stylus for phonograph needles. Drilled blanks are used as orifices for injection nozzles in oil-fired furnaces because they resist wear and maintain a constant diameter. Small spherical balls of clear sapphire are superior to metal spheres in ball-point pens.

Other industrial uses of sapphire take advantage of its high dielectric constant for electronic devices and of its high melting point for heat resistant windows. Because sapphire transmits not only visible light but ultraviolet and infrared (heat) waves with little absorption loss, it has been used in optical systems needing such characteristics. It resists corrosion by both alkalis and acids. The combination of these properties in a single material has made possible the development of many specialized scientific and technical instruments for high temperature and pressure control and regulation.

5. Spinel.—Spinel boules have a square cross section with round corners, but otherwise are like Al_2O_3 boules in manufacture, size and appearance although they do not develop internal stresses during manufacture. Spinel has a hardness on Mohs' scale of 8 (Al_2O_3 has a hardness of 9; diamond, 10), which gives it adequate durability for gem stone use. Spinels are easier to cut and polish than synthetic rubies and sapphires which can only be worked with diamond powder. They are made in all colours by adding appropriate pigments. The popular "aquamarine" blue is made by adding small amounts of cobalt, nickel, and titanium and vanadium oxides.

The problem of differentiating between natural and synthetic spinels rarely arises because the natural gem is not a popular or valuable one. The natural gems are usually red or blue in colour and have irregular cavities with liquid or gas inclusions and microscopic crystalline inclusions similar to those of natural rubies and sapphires, while the synthetic have only spherical gas bubble inclusions.

Because it is singly refractive, spinel is preferred for some industrial uses, but for most the greater hardness of sapphire is desirable.

6. Rutile (Titania).—Synthetic rutile, first produced in 1948 by the Verneuil process, is far superior to the natural crystals as a gem because natural rutile is dark in colour and was only occasionally cut as a gem stone. The pure synthetic boules have a faint tinge of yellow colour, but may be produced in nearly any colour by the addition of appropriate colorants. The pure titanium oxide used in the flame-fusion process is prepared by calcining hydrolyzed titanium tetrachloride at 500° C. in an oxygen atmosphere for several hours.

The furnace is the same as that used in the manufacture of synthetic rubies, sapphires and spinel although it is sometimes modified by adding a third outer tube through which oxygen passes. The single crystal boules are tetragonal with the principal axis parallel to the boule axis. They have a square cross section similar to the spinel boules, but rarely exceed 100 carats in weight. When removed from the furnace they are black in colour and semiconductors of electricity because some titanium is still unoxidized. On heating in an oxygen atmosphere, oxygen is slowly absorbed, the colour decreases until only a faint yellow tinge is left and the boules become nonconductors.

Because synthetic rutile has a higher index of refraction and greater dispersion than diamond, cut gem stones are more brilliant and show more fire. Its double refraction $\omega_D = 2.616$, $\epsilon_D = 2.903$ exceeds that of any other known substance. Nearly all the titania boules produced are used for cutting into gem stones. They can be readily distinguished from diamond because of the strong double refraction and the prismatic flashes of red and blue due to the strong dispersion. The hardness, 6.5, is much inferior to the diamond.

7. Emerald.—The details of the Chatham process for synthesizing emerald is a closely guarded secret. From the character of the crystals it is thought that the process depends on fusing appropriate chemicals under pressure in the presence of water. Only a small percentage of the emeralds made are suitable for cutting into gems, but several hundred carats are marketed annually. Synthetic emeralds may be distinguished from the natural gems because they fluoresce with a deep red colour under ultraviolet rays while natural emeralds do not.

8. Diamonds.—No synthetic diamonds suitable for gems have been made. Not only is the possible production of crystals suitable for gems fraught with serious technical difficulties, but experience indicates that the public will not buy such synthetic gems unless they are cheap in price.

For industrial purposes, quality and perfection of crystal growth are not important because a major market for abrasive grits and powder is available which needs only the superior hardness of the diamond. At the time diamond was first synthesized, abrasive diamond grits and powder sold for $3 per carat (nearly $7,000 per pound). The better qualities of synthetic diamond are suitable for wheel dressers and for the manufacture of diamond drill bits used in the mining and oil industries.

IV. IMITATION GEMS

Prior to World War II most imitation gems were made from glass, which was usually a special high-lead glass. The word paste was applied to such glasses because the components of the mixture —silica, lead oxide, potassium carbonate, borax and arsenic oxide with appropriate pigmenting materials—were mixed wet to ensure a thorough and even distribution of each.

These glasses were softer than ordinary or crown glass, but had a higher index of refraction and dispersion that gave them greater brilliancy and fire. The cheaper imitations were pressed or molded gems, but on the better qualities the facets were cut and polished. Molded glass imitations can be identified with a hand lens because the edges between the facets are rounded while cut glass has sharp edges.

Glass imitations can be readily identified because they are singly refractive, and the index of refraction and specific gravity, both of which vary with the composition of the glass, are unlike those of the gems they imitate. Most gem stones are doubly refractive. Usually small spherical bubbles are visible in the interior of glass imitations when examined with a lens. Because of the inferior hardness, glass is easily scratched with a file. This test can be applied along the girdle where it will do little damage. Because glass is a poorer heat conductor than natural gems it feels warmer to the touch. Glass imitations that have been worn show under the lens fine scratches on the facets and small conchoidal chips along the edges between the facets.

The finer qualities of imitation gems are made from variously coloured synthetic sapphires or spinels. The superior hardness of these materials makes them much more durable than glass. A new imitation of the diamond was introduced in 1955 that closely resembles diamond in all properties except hardness. Strontium titanate produced in boules by the Verneuil process has an index of refraction of 2.40 while diamond is 2.42. Like diamond it is singly refractive. It has considerably more dispersion that is not noticeable to the layman but which to the trained observer serves to distinguish it from the diamond. Its hardness of only 5.5 as against 10 for a diamond keeps it from being a serious competitor of the diamond as a gem stone.

Before World War II most costume jewelry was made with glass imitations. After World War II glass was displaced by the many newly developed plastics, which are of two kinds. Thermosetting plastics, such as Bakelite, permanently harden when molded and will not soften on reheating. Thermoplastics, such as Lucite and Plexiglas, soften on heating and can be molded and remolded. With proper pigmenting agents both types of plastics can be given any desired colour. Plastic jewelry can be readily identified because it is light in weight and is easily scratched with a knife. Because of their cheapness and easy workability the many new plastics profoundly changed the market for the cheaper forms of jewelry.

See also references under "Gem" in the Index.   (C. B. Sn.)

BIBLIOGRAPHY.—*General:* R. M. Pearl, *Popular Gemology* (1948); R. M. Shipley, *Famous Diamonds of the World,* 5th ed. (1948); A. Austin and M. Mercer, *The Story of Diamonds,* 3rd ed. (1948); A. Pazzini, *Le pietre preciose nella Storia della Medicina e nella Leggenda* (1939); H. Barth, *Das Geschmeide—Schmuck und Edelsteinkunde,* 2 vol. (no date); K. Schlossmacher, *Edelsteine und Perlen* (1954); Michael Weinstein, *The World of Jewel Stones* (1958); Marcus Baerwald and Tom Mahoney, *The Story of Jewelry* (1960).

History: Mesopotamia: H. Frankfort, *Cylinder Seals* (1939) and *Stratified Cylinder Seals from the Diyala Region* (1955); E. Porada, *Corpus of Ancient Near Eastern Seals in North American Collections,* vol. i, *The Collection of the Pierpont Morgan Library* (1948); P. Amiet, *La Glyptique mésopotamienne archaïque* (1961). *Anatolia:* D. G. Hogarth, *Hittite Seals* (1920) (still valuable for stamp seals). *Egypt:* F. Petrie, "Royal Tombs of the First Dynasty," *Egypt Explor. Fund,* XVIIIth *Memoir,* p. 24, pl. xii, fig. 3–7, and pl. xviii–xxix; P. E. Newberry, *Egyptian Antiquities, Scarabs, an Introduction to the Study of Egyptian Scarabs and Signet Rings* (1906); H. R. Hall, *Catalogue of Egyptian Scarabs, Etc., in the British Museum,* vol. i (1913); G. Brunton, *Qau and Badari* (1927–30). *Crete and Mycenae:* A. J. Evans, *Scripta Minoa* (1909) and *The Palace of Minos at Knossos,* vol. i–iv (1921–35); F. Matz, *Die frühkretischen Siegel* (1928); V. E. G. Kenna, *Cretan Seals, With a Catalogue of the Minoan Gems in the Ashmolean Museum* (1960); V. E. G. Kenna, *Cretan Seals* (1960).

Classical Gems: A. Furtwängler, *Antike Gemmen,* vol. i–iii (1900), the fullest and best general account of the subject; M. N. H. Story-Maskelyne, *The Marlborough Gems* (1870); *The Leeves House Collection of Ancient Gems* (1920); G. M. A. Richter, *Catalogue of Engraved Gems in the Metropolitan Museum of Art* (1920; 2nd ed., 1956); H. B. Walters, *Catalogue of Engraved Gems and Cameos in the British Museum* (1926); P. Fossing, *Catalogue of the Antique Engraved Gems and Cameos, Thorvaldsens Museum* (1929); G. Lippold, *Gemmen und Kameen des Altertums und der Neuzeit* (1922); M. L. Vollenweider, *Die Steinschneidekunst und ihre Künstler in spätrepublikanischer und augusteischer Zeit* (1966); G. Sena Chiesa, *Gemme del Museo Nazionale di Aquileia* (1966). For a list of 16th- to 18th-century publications of gem collections, see A. Furtwängler, *Antike Gemmen,* vol. iii, pp. 402 ff.

Sassanian Gems: P. Horn and G. Steindorff, *Sassanidische Siegelsteine* (1891).

Postclassical Gems: O. M. Dalton, *Catalogue of the Post-Classical Gems in the British Museum* (1915); H. Wentzel, "Mittelalterliche Gemmen," in *Zeitschrift des deutschen Vereins für Kunstwissenschaft,* vol. viii (1941), "Mittelalter und Antike im Spiegel kleiner Kunstwerke des 13. Jahrhunderts," in *Studien Tillägnade Henrik Cornell* (1950); E. Kris and F. Eichler, *Die Kameen im Kunsthistorischen Museum in Wien* (1927); E. Kris, *Meister und Meisterwerke der Steinschneidekunst in der italienischen Renaissance* (1929).   (ER. Sr.)

Natural Gems: Jean-Baptiste Tavernier, *Les Six voyages de Jean-Baptiste Tavernier* (1676), Eng. trans. by John Phillips (1677), is the first comprehensive account of the gem industry. Robert Boyle, *An Essay About the Origin and Virtues of Gems* (1672), and David Jeffries, *A Treatise on Diamonds and Pearls,* 2nd ed. (1751), are also of historical importance. Max Bauer, *Edelsteinkunde* (1909), revised by Karl H. Schlossmacher (1932), is the most detailed work on gems. L. J. Spencer, *A Key to Precious Stones* (1937); G. F. Herbert Smith, *Gemstones,* 9th ed. (1940), E. H. Kraus and C. B. Slawson, *Gems and Gem Materials,* 5th ed. (1947), are comprehensive texts. H. P. Whitlock, *The Story of the Gems* (1936), is a popular but authoritative work on the more important gems. G. F. Kunz, *The Curious Lore of Precious Stones* (1913), and C. W. Cooper, *The Precious Stones of the Bible* (1924) contain much interesting information. J. Escard, *Les Pierres précieuses* (1914) and H. Michel, *Die künstlichen Edelsteine* (1926) are authoritative. *The Minerals Yearbook,* U.S. Bureau of Mines, includes a chapter on gem stones giving world-wide annual production figures on gems. A comprehensive survey of the diamond industry appears annually in the *Jewelers' Circular-Keystone.*

Synthetic Gems: H. Sainte-Claire Deville and H. Caron, "Mémoire sur l'apatite, La wagnerite et quelques espèces artificielles de phosphates métalliques," Institut de France, Académie des Sciences, *Comptes Rendus,* vol. lxix, p. 1342 (1869); P. Hautefeuille and A. Perrey, "Sur les combinaisons silicatées de la glucine," *Ann. Chim. (Phys.),* 6 series, vol. xx, p. 447 (1890); C. Friedel, "Sur l'existence du diamant dans le fer météorique de Cañon Diablo," Institut de France, Académie des Sciences, *Comptes Rendus,* vol. cxv, p. 1037 (1892); A. Verneuil, "Production artificielle du rubis par fusion," Institut de France, Académie des Sciences, *Comptes Rendus,* vol. cxxxv, p. 791 (1902); "Sur la nature des oxydes qui colorent le saphir oriental," Institut de France, Académie des Sciences, *Comptes Rendus,* vol. cli, p. 1063 (1910); A. J. Moses, "Some Tests Upon the Synthetic Sapphires of Verneuil," *Amer. J. Sci.,* vol. xxx, p. 271 (Oct. 1910); I. H. Levin, "Synthesis of Precious Stones," *J. Industr. Engng. Chem.,* vol. v, no. 6, pp. 495–500 (June 1913); G. O. Wild, *Praktikum der Edelsteinkunde* (1936).   (C. B. Sn.)

GEM CUTTING: see GEM.

GEMINI (the Twins) is the third sign in the zodiac (*q.v.*), a constellation of stars denoted by the symbol ♊. The Egyptians symbolized this constellation as a couple of young goats; the Greeks altered this symbol to two children, variously said to be Castor and Pollux, Hercules and Apollo or Triptolemus and Iasion; the Arabians used a pair of peacocks. The two brightest stars in Gemini are known as Castor and Pollux; Pollux (β Geminorum) is slightly brighter than Castor (α Geminorum). Castor is a remarkable multiple system consisting of at least six stars. The brightest members are each spectroscopically double and the faint, distant component (Castor C) is an orange-coloured dwarf eclipsing system in which the two stars revolve about each other roughly once every 19 hours. The system of Castor is about 45 light-years from the sun, and its two brightest stars form an interesting double for a small telescope. Pollux is a reddish giant approximately 35 light-years from the sun. There are two bright variable stars in the constellation: the Cepheid variable, ζ Geminorum, whose light varies in a period of about ten days, and the red irregular variable star, η Geminorum. At the time of its discovery (1930) the planet Pluto was in the neighbourhood of the star δ Geminorum. *See also* STAR.

GEMINIANI, FRANCESCO (c. 1687–1762), Italian composer, violinist, writer on musical performance and a leading figure in early 18th-century music. Born at Lucca about 1687, he held posts in his native city and in Naples before going to England in 1714. In London he soon established himself as an exceptionally brilliant performer. His opus 1 sonatas for violin and continuo were published in 1716 and were widely regarded as being on the same musical level as those of Corelli, under whom Geminiani may have studied. They were, however, considered to be almost unplayable because of their technical difficulty. He later published further solo and trio sonatas but was chiefly noted for his *concerti grossi*, of which his opus 2 and opus 3 sets became extremely popular in England and held a place in the concert repertory up to the early years of the 19th century. Later in his life Geminiani spent periods in Paris and Dublin. He died in Dublin in Sept. 1762. His theoretical works, of which *The Art of Playing on the Violin* (1731) is the most important, had considerable circulation and influence in 18th-century England and remain an important source of information on the performance of late baroque music. Geminiani's music has an intensity and nervous energy unusual at the period. He was particularly fond of textural richness and his string writing is always effective and highly idiomatic. (S. J. Sa.)

GEMISTUS PLETHO, GEORGE (c. 1355–1452), the leading scholar and philosopher of the last century of the Byzantine empire, is chiefly notable for his influence upon the Renaissance in western Europe and for the attempt that he made in his principal work, the *Laws* (*Nomoi*), to establish a new polytheistic religion based upon Platonic and Neoplatonic principles, which, he hoped, would supersede both Christianity and Islam. He was born and trained in Constantinople but spent the most important years of his life in Mistra, then an important citadel in the Peloponnese.

During the Council of Ferrara-Florence (1438–39), which, despite his hostility to the proposed union between the Greek and Roman Churches, he attended as lay adviser to the Greek delegation, he fired the humanists with new interest in Plato (who had been ignored in the west during the middle ages because of the preoccupation with Aristotle) and inspired Cosimo de' Medici with the project of founding the Platonic Academy of Florence.

More momentously, in his talks with the astronomer Paolo del Pozzo Toscanelli and others and by his *Excerpts From Strabo*, Pletho introduced the *Geography* of Strabo to the west (where it had hitherto been unknown) and led the way to the overthrow of Ptolemy's erroneous geographical theories. He thus greatly affected the Renaissance conception of the configuration of the earth and so played an important, if indirect, role in the discovery of America by Christopher Columbus, who cites Strabo among his principal authorities.

Besides the *Laws*, Pletho composed orations, two memoirs advocating social and economic reform for the defense of the Peloponnese, numerous excerpts from ancient Greek authors and essays on the differences between Plato and Aristotle, on Zoroaster, on the *Oracula Chaldaica* and on astronomy, music, history, rhetoric, the virtues and various theological subjects. Nearly all his writing is marked by passionate devotion to Greece and a desire to restore its ancient glory.

BIBLIOGRAPHY.—C. Alexandre, *Pléthon: Traité des lois* (1858); S. Lampros, *Palaiologeia kai Peloponnesiaka*, 3–4 (1926–30); J. P. Migne, *Patrologia Graeca*, clx (1866); François Masai, *Pléthon et le platonisme de Mistra* (1956); M. V. Anastos, "Pletho, Strabo, and Columbus," *Annuaire de l'institut de philologie et d'histoire orientales et slaves*, 12:1–18 (1952) and "Pletho's Calendar and Liturgy," *Dumbarton Oaks Papers*, no. 4, pp. 183–305 (1948). (M. V. A.)

GEMMAIL, an art form first conceived by the French artist Jean Crotti in the late 1930s that utilizes layers of coloured glass fragments to reproduce in relief a painting or drawing, and employs light (shining through the glass) as an integral element. Crotti sought a visual technique to use light in a vital and not merely illusory way. He found that glass was the ideal medium: in superposed layers, it added the dimension of depth; permitted the passage of light; and allowed the "mixing" of colours.

A *gemmail* is constructed, piece by piece, on a clear pane of glass on which the picture has been outlined. When all fragments are glued in place, the work is dipped into a transparent enamel and baked until fully fused. It is mounted for exhibition in a metal box frame, and illuminated from behind by soft fluorescent lighting.

Works by Picasso, Braque, and Rouault have been reproduced in this medium, and one of the largest Paris Métro stations is decorated with a series of paintings executed in *gemmaux*.

GEMSBOK (GEMSBUCK), an African antelope (*q.v.*) of the genus *Oryx*; as *Gemsbok*, German for the chamois (*q.v.*).

GENE, the unit of heredity. Genes are the carriers of the genetic information passed on from generation to generation in sex cells of all organisms according to the principles discussed in the article HEREDITY, which the reader might find it profitable to read first.

The evidence is overwhelming that the basic genetic material constituting the gene is fundamentally the same in all living organisms: it consists of chainlike molecules of nucleic acids—deoxyribonucleic acid (DNA) in most organisms and ribonucleic acid (RNA) in certain viruses—and is usually associated in a linear arrangement that, in part, constitutes the chromosome.

The term "gene" no longer stands simply for a discrete structural unit of heredity of definite and invariable length. It is now thought of as an operational entity whose properties depend upon the mode of measurement: mutational capability; recombinational performance; or functional activity. These refinements in definition of genetic material are explained below in the section *Ultrastructure of the Genetic Material*.

An account of the development of the gene concept precedes the discussion of gene structure and function according to the following outline:

I. Development of the Gene Theory
  1. Blood Heredity versus Particulate Heredity
  2. Mendel's Formative Elements or Factors: Units of Segregation
  3. Morgan's and Muller's Conception of Genes in Chromosomes
II. Molecular Level Analysis of the Gene
  1. Bacteria as Experimental Tools
  2. Evidence that the Genetic Material Recombines
  3. Evidence that the Genetic Material is Arranged Sequentially
  4. Evidence that DNA is the Genetic Material
  5. The Watson-Crick Model of the Genetic Material
  6. The Replication of Genetic Material
  7. The Chemical Basis of Mutation of the Genetic Material
III. Ultrastructure of the Genetic Material
  1. Bacteriophages as Experimental Tools
  2. Data Based on the Transduction Phenomenon
  3. Data Based on the Complementation Phenomenon
  4. Extranuclear Genetic Material
IV. Genes and Development
  1. The One Gene-One Enzyme Hypothesis
  2. The Determination of Protein Structure and Synthesis
  3. Translation of the DNA and RNA Codes
  4. The Genetic Code
  5. The Operon and Gene Action
  6. Gene Action and Differentiation

I. DEVELOPMENT OF THE GENE THEORY

1. Blood Heredity versus Particulate Heredity.—Before the time of Gregor Mendel (*q.v.*) it was universally believed that heredity was carried by "blood," and that the "bloods" of the parents are blended in the offspring. Mendel proved that at least some traits that differentiate varieties of peas are inherited through "factors" that do not blend but actually segregate when the sex cells are formed. Although published in 1866, the work of Mendel was unappreciated until 1900. Charles Darwin (*q.v.*) fully realized that understanding the mechanism of heredity was of basic importance for his theory of organic evolution. In 1868, Darwin published *The Variation of Animals and Plants under Domestication*, to which he added an appendix containing his "Provisional Hypothesis of Pangenesis." In this acknowledgedly speculative venture, he surmised that all cells of the body shed into the bloodstream minute particles called gemmules (or pangenes), which assembled to form the sex cells. A gemmule was imagined to be a representative, perhaps a tiny model, of the cell that produced it. When a body cell was altered by some environmental agency, it gave rise to altered gemmules. This detail was important to Darwin because, in common with his contemporaries, he believed in inheritance of acquired characters (*see* LAMARCKISM). The hypothesis of pangenesis seemed to explain adequately at the same time the transmission of inherited and of acquired traits. Francis Galton (*q.v.*) submitted the hypothesis to experimental test. He made blood transfusions between white and black rabbits, reasoning that if the blood carried the gemmules of the cells that produced white and black fur, the offspring of the transfused parents

PANGENESIS

SOMA

GERM CELLS

ACCEPTED RELATION

SOMA

GERM CELLS

1st GENERATION

2nd GENERATION

FIG. 1.—THE CONTINUITY OF THE GERM PLASM

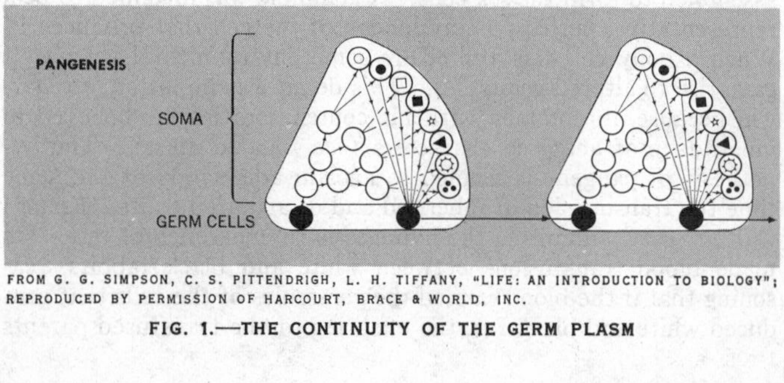

FROM G. G. SIMPSON, C. S. PITTENDRIGH, L. H. TIFFANY, "LIFE: AN INTRODUCTION TO BIOLOGY"; REPRODUCED BY PERMISSION OF HARCOURT, BRACE & WORLD, INC.

should perhaps be spotted white and black. The experiment disproved pangenesis: the offspring were not spotted.

In 1889, H. De Vries (q.v.) advanced the theory of intracellular pangenesis. By then, most biologists no longer regarded inheritance of acquired traits as a well-founded hypothesis, and evidence was rapidly accumulating that the chromosomes of cell nuclei were the carriers of the hereditary materials. De Vries proposed that the pangenes constituted the chromosomes and passed only from the nuclei into the cell cytoplasm, where they became "active." A pangene was defined as a tiny particle consisting of numerous molecules, rather than a single molecule. It was thought of not as a representative or a model of a cell, but as a controlling "hereditary character." Each cell was believed to contain many different pangenes, each of which could become active in different cells (thus explaining why cells become different in the developing organism). The pangenes postulated in pangenes were of two kinds—in relative numbers and in quality. The quantitative variations explained the "fluctuating" variability of the organisms, a feature that Darwin regarded as basic to the operation of natural selection. The qualitative variations of the pangenes were the discontinuous variations that De Vries called mutations.

A. Weismann (q.v.), one of the founders of the chromosomal theory of heredity (1892)—the forerunner of the gene theory—believed that the hereditary materials were composed of "determinants" that specified the characteristics of different cells. The sex cells were thought to contain sets of determinants for all cells, but during the cleavage of a fertilized egg and the cell divisions in a developing embryo, the determinants were gradually sorted out, so that finally every cell retained only the determinants needed to specify the characteristics of a certain tissue or organ. The sex cells were the exception; they had to retain a full set of the determinants, which could be passed on to the offspring. These cells carried the germ plasm, which can be considered potentially immortal, since it may be transmitted from generation to generation without end (fig. 1). In every generation the germ plasm constructs the somatoplasm, the body that is its temporary container and vehicle. The soma is mortal; it dies after it transmits its germ plasm to the progeny. In unicellular organisms, which reproduce by simple fission, the separation of the germ plasm and the soma does not exist; these organisms, themselves, are potentially immortal. Weismann's hypothesis was, thus, an antithesis of Darwin's hypothesis of pangenesis. Instead of the sex cells being compounded of the gemmules shed by the soma, Weismann admitted only the passage of the determinants from the germ plasm to the soma. Quite consistently with this view, Weismann rejected the possibility that characters acquired by the soma may be inherited. He performed a famous experiment that helped disprove the inheritance of acquired characters. He amputated the tails of mice for several generations; the tails did not become any shorter in the offspring of the animals whose tails were cut off.

Alteration of the soma had no apparent influence on the germ plasm.

From the vantage point of present-day knowledge, these pre-Mendelian speculations may appear naive. Their historical importance is, however, unquestionable. They led to the abandonment of the notion that heredity is transmitted by blood, and to the acceptance of the idea that the hereditary materials are particulate. The scientific climate had changed when Mendel's work was rediscovered in 1900, and his approach to the study of heredity was not so strange and unfamiliar as it was in 1866.

2. Mendel's Formative Elements or Factors: Units of Segregation.—Gregor Mendel was by no means the first to experiment on plant heredity, but he did it in a systematic and inspired way (see HEREDITY). Mendel's data revealed to him that each parent contained pairs of factors but contributed only one member of each pair to its offspring. It was also clear that the factors retained their individuality from generation to generation, whether they asserted themselves or not, and united randomly in the offspring.

The gametes (ovules and pollen grains in plants, and egg cells and spermatozoa in animals) of course do not display differentiating characters such as colours or shapes of flowers, seeds, eyes, hair, etc. And yet Mendel's experiments demonstrated that indeed the gametes do contain some formative elements or factors that indeed are responsible for the appearance of characters in the organism. Mendel's results were confirmed and extended in 1900 and thereafter to many species of plants and animals, including man. W. Johannsen proposed in 1909 to call the formative elements, or factors, "genes." He wanted the Mendelian genes not to be confused with the speculative pangenes, determinants, etc. According to him: "The word 'gene' is completely free from any hypotheses; it expresses only the evident fact that many characters of the organism are specified in the gametes by means of special conditions, foundations, and determiners that are present in unique, separate, and thereby independent ways—in short precisely what we wish to call genes."

Mendel's pea varieties with, for example, purple and white flowers carried alternative forms of one gene that allowed the plants to develop flowers of these colours; such alternative states of a single gene were termed by W. Bateson in 1902 allelomorphs (now shortened to alleles). Each "pure" variety contained two similar alleles or a double dose of genes for each trait, and was called a homozygote. Each hybrid variety, which is derived from crossing two pure varieties, necessarily had two unlike alleles for each trait, and was called a heterozygote. When the heterozygote formed sex cells, the alternative alleles segregated and passed into different and equally numerous cells. The sex cells were "pure" since they contained only one allele for a character; for example, either the allele for purple or for white flowers but not both, and not a mixture of the two. These considerations led to Mendel's law of segregation, called by Bateson the law of the purity of the gametes: different alleles of genes do not mix or contaminate each other while they are present together in the body of a heterozygote. Here, then, is a basic difference between the "blood theory" and the gene theory of heredity.

Despite Johannsen's injunction, it proved quite impossible to keep the gene concept purely symbolic and free from any hypotheses. In point of fact, the progress in studying genes came from making a sequence of hypotheses about the genes and submitting these hypotheses to test by experiments. As expected, some of the hypotheses proved to be wrong and had to be abandoned. Thus, it seemed temptingly simple to suppose that each gene represents in the sex cell a certain "unit character," and that the organism is an aggregate, a sort of a mosaic composed of such unit characters. In the development of an organism from a fertilized egg, each gene would add its proper unit character to those produced by other genes, until the body is fully formed. In a sense, this hypothesis was a throwback to something like Weismann's determinants, except that the unit characters were no longer thought of as representing body parts or single cells, but rather as representing qualities, such as colour, pattern, shape, size, etc.

Because of their brevity, expressions such as "the gene for blue eyes" or "the gene for A blood group" are used even now; these expressions are likely to mislead a beginner into believing that there is a one-to-one relationship between each gene and an independent unit-character, or trait, for which a given gene is responsible. This is actually not so. What looks like a trait controlled by a single gene is frequently the result of interaction of several or many genes (fig. 2). For example, the variety of coat colours found in domestic dogs, cats, rabbits, horses, cattle, and other mammals results from often very complex interactions of many genes, some of them represented by several alternative forms (multiple alleles) each. The difference between the skin colours of Negroes and of whites is due to joint action of several genes (the exact number is still in doubt), each of which increases or decreases the skin pigmentation relatively slightly. Conversely, many genes act on constellations of seemingly unrelated traits. Such genes are called pleiotropic. In man, many hereditary diseases are due to single gene changes that produce combinations or syndromes of traits, some structural, others physiological or psychological. Thus, phenylketonuria is inherited as a simple recessive; the afflicted homozygotes have their mental development severely retarded, and their urine contains large amounts of phenylalanine and phenylpyruvic acid. In general, the development of an individual of any species is controlled by all the genes he carries; characters of traits are merely descriptive aspects of this unitary process.

3. Morgan's and Muller's Conception of Genes in Chromosomes.—Although genes were originally simply symbols useful to explain the observable facts of Mendelian segregation, it soon became evident that they had physical reality as component parts of the chromosomes of cell nuclei. A group of brilliant biologists, among them T. Boveri, W. Roux, and A. Weismann in Germany and E. B. Wilson in the United States inferred that the heredity transmitted from one generation to the next must be carried in the chromosomes of the sex cells. This inference had been reached in the closing decade of the 19th century, i.e., before the rediscovery of Mendel's laws. The question of whether the Mendelian genes were also carried in the chromosomes logically presented itself. A positive answer was arrived at independently by W. S. Sutton and T. Boveri in 1902 and 1903. Their argument was simple—the behaviour of the chromosomes during the processes of maturation of sex cells (meiosis) is precisely such that the Mendelian segregation of the genes carried in these chromosomes can be envisaged as a simple and necessary consequence. During meiosis the chromosomes unite in pairs, divide, exchange segments, and then disjoin and pass to different sex cells (gametes). Suppose, then, that the maternal chromosome of a given pair carries an allele of a gene different from that in the paternal member of the chromosome pair. These gene alleles will segregate, one-half of the gametes formed carrying one allele and the other half carrying the other. If female and male gametes unite at random at fertilization, i.e., if there is no tendency for sex cells with similar or with different gene alleles to seek out or to avoid each other, the segregation ratios observed by Mendel necessarily follow (see HEREDITY).

The correctness of the above reasoning was demonstrated experimentally by T. H. Morgan and his co-workers C. B. Bridges, H. J. Muller, and A. H. Sturtevant. Morgan and his colleagues made use of the then new experimental material, the vinegar fly (often called fruit fly) *Drosophila melanogaster*. This fly has four pairs of chromosomes in each of its body cells while its sex cells carry only four chromosomes, one representative of each pair. As shown by E. E. Carothers in 1913 and 1917 (in a species of grasshopper), the chromosomes of maternal and paternal origins in different pairs are distributed randomly at meiosis. The microscopically observed random distribution of the chromosomes is paralleled by the random assortment of genes discovered by Mendel. However, in *Drosophila* more than four, and eventually several hundred, variant genes were discovered. Clearly then, a chromosome may contain several genes. If so, can the random assortment of the genes be an invariable rule? The genes carried on the same chromosomes do exhibit some tendency to remain together in inheritance. As the chromosome is transmitted, so are all its genes transmitted. This tendency, called linkage, was discovered by W. Bateson and R. C. Punnett in crosses of sweet peas in 1906 and 1911, but these investigators did not perceive the parallel between the linkage (which they called coupling) and the chromosome assortment at meiosis. This parallelism was pointed out by Morgan and his colleagues in 1911 and later. H. J. Muller showed in 1914 that the known genes in *Drosophila* belong to four linkage groups, the same number as that of the chromosome pairs. Moreover, one linkage group consists of genes that express themselves in individuals of one sex, that is, they exhibit a sex-linked inheritance; this linkage group is carried in the X chromosome, which is also responsible for the determination of sex. Of the remaining three chromosome pairs, two are large and one very small; correspondingly, there are two linkage groups with many genes and one with relatively few as demonstrated in the progenies of crosses.

The analysis of the relationships between the genes and the chromosomes can be carried further. In the formation of sex cells, genes located in different chromosomes are assorted at random, i.e., by chance they remain together in the original parental combinations in 50% of the sex cells, and, because of crossing-over (see below), form new combinations in the remaining 50%. This expectation, however, is not always realized because genes carried on the same chromosome are linked in various degrees, quite tightly, loosely, or moderately; the frequency of new gene combinations ranging from near 0 to 50%. In 1911, T. H. Morgan advanced a hypothesis that accounts for such variations: the closer together the genes are in the chromosomes, the tighter the linkage and the lower the frequency of recombination; conversely, the farther apart the genes are, the looser the linkage and the higher the frequency of recombination. The degree of linkage may, thus, be used as a measure of the distance between the genes. The members of each chromosome pair twist around each other at meiosis, establishing points of contact called chiasmata (sing. chiasma), and exchange segments. This crossing-over and exchange of chromosome segments was pointed out by Morgan as the explanation of linkage and recombination. A chiasma will be formed less often between neighbouring genes than between genes far apart in the chromosome.

A. H. Sturtevant and H. J. Muller subsequently developed Morgan's idea into a theory of the linear arrangement of the genes in the chromosomes. When the frequencies of recombination (expressed in crossover units) between genes A and B, and B and C are known, the frequency between A and C can be predicted (fig. 3). If crossing-over between A and B occurs 5% of the time and crossing-over between B and C occurs 3% of the time, then when the percentage of crossing-over between A and C is tested, it is either 8% $(AB + BC)$ or 2% $(AB - BC)$. This suggests that the genes are arranged in the chromosome in a linear file, either ABC if crossing-over between A and C is 8%, or ACB, if crossing-over is 2%. When AB and BC are large (say, 10% or more), AC may be less than $AB + BC$. This is explained by the occurrence in the chromosome of more than a single chiasma between the loci of remote genes.

Knowing the degree of linkage of several genes in the same chromosome, it is possible to plot a genetic map of the chromosome. Genetic maps of the chromosomes of *Drosophila melanogaster* were first published in 1915 in *The Mechanism of Mendelian Heredity* by Morgan, Sturtevant, Muller, and Bridges. At present

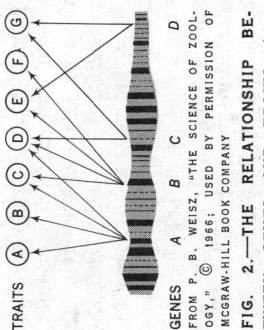

TRAITS (A) (B) (C) (D) (E) (F) (G)

GENES A B C D

FROM P. B. WEISZ, "THE SCIENCE OF ZOOLOGY," © 1966; USED BY PERMISSION OF MCGRAW-HILL BOOK COMPANY

FIG. 2.—THE RELATIONSHIP BETWEEN GENES AND TRAITS (see TEXT)

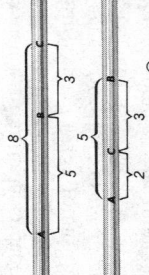

FROM C. A. VILLEE, "BIOLOGY," © 1962; REPRODUCED BY PERMISSION OF W. B. SAUNDERS COMPANY

FIG. 3.—CROSSING-OVER PERCENTAGES USED IN ESTABLISHING THE LINEAR ORDER OF GENES IN A CHROMOSOME (see TEXT)

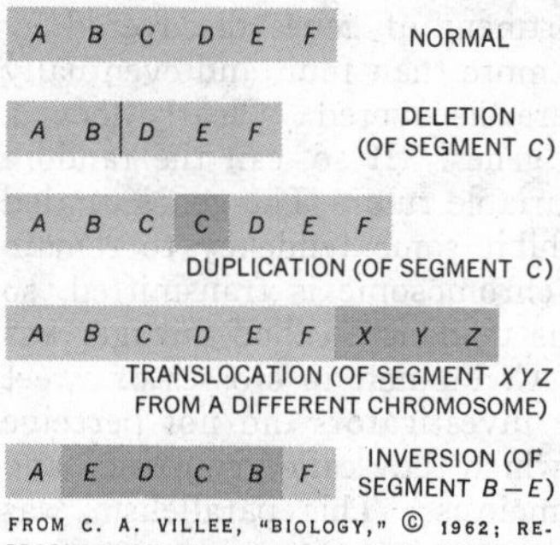

A B C D E F — NORMAL

A B | D E F — DELETION (OF SEGMENT C)

A B C C D E F — DUPLICATION (OF SEGMENT C)

A B C D E F X Y Z — TRANSLOCATION (OF SEGMENT X Y Z FROM A DIFFERENT CHROMOSOME)

A E D C B F — INVERSION (OF SEGMENT B-E)

FIG. 4.—TYPES OF CHROMOSOMAL MUTATIONS

FROM C. A. VILLEE, "BIOLOGY," © 1962; REPRODUCED BY PERMISSION OF W. B. SAUNDERS COMPANY

genetic maps of various degrees of precision exist for several organisms (see HEREDITY).

The genetic, or linkage, maps of chromosomes are constructed entirely on the basis of statistical data concerning the frequencies of recombination between linked genes observed in various crossing experiments. In principle at least, such maps could as well be drawn had the actual, microscopically visible, chromosomes never been discovered. A proof that the linear order of the genes shown on the genetic maps is really the same as their arrangement in the chromosomes became possible owing to the discoveries, mainly by C. B. Bridges, of various chromosomal aberrations in *Drosophila melanogaster*. Sections of chromosomes are sometimes lost (deficiency or deletion), reduplicated (duplication), transferred from one chromosome to another (translocation), or rotated by 180° in the same chromosome (inversion) (fig. 4). Chromosomal aberrations are generally rare, but H. J. Muller showed in 1928 and later that their frequencies are increased in the progenies of parents treated with high-energy radiations. Using techniques developed chiefly in *Drosophila* and in corn, the chromosomal aberrations can be studied genetically. The blocks of genes that are lost, duplicated, translocated, or inverted can be delimited in terms of the sections of the genetic maps. Some chromosomal aberrations can also be discovered under the microscope, because they make certain chromosomes longer or shorter than normal, or fragmented. Extraordinary refinement in the study of the locations of genes in chromosomes became possible owing to the discovery of giant chromosomes in the cells of salivary glands of many flies, including *Drosophila*. They appear to consist of alternating dark (stainable by nuclear dyes) and light bands or discs; because the total length of the salivary gland chromosomes is a hundred or more times greater than that of those in other *Drosophila* cells, it is possible to see chromosomal changes so minute that they escape detection in the normal-sized chromosomes. T. S. Painter and H. J. Muller (1932) and T. Dobzhansky (1932) drew the first cytological maps, showing the location of certain genes of *Drosophila melanogaster* in the microscopically visible chromosomes. This was done at first for the chromosomes in the developing sex cells and nerve cells, and subsequently by C. B. Bridges and others with far greater precision in the giant chromosomes of the salivary glands.

The linear order of the genes as shown on the genetic maps coincides with that on cytological maps, but the relative distances are not always the same. This is explained by the more frequent occurrence of chiasmata in some parts of the chromosomes than in other parts. The salient fact, however, is that the symbolic "genes" finally were shown to be material particles in the chromosomes. The question inevitably arose whether the genes are absolutely discrete particles, or only segments of some kind of a continuum. A chromosome with its genes has sometimes been likened to a string of beads. R. B. Goldschmidt (1938) and others found this simile much too crude, and envisaged genetic variations as generalized changes in whole chromosomes. Molecular level analysis of the genes (*see below*) eventually established that the actual situation lies somewhere between these extremes, but some evidence of interdependence of neighbouring or adjacent genes was obtained through the discovery of position effects. A. H. Sturtevant (1925) found that apparent mutational changes in the "gene" *Bar* in *Drosophila melanogaster* (narrow instead of round eyes) are associated with the occurrence of crossing-over in the chromosome in the immediate vicinity of the *Bar* locus. C. B. Bridges (1936) and H. J. Muller and A. A. Prokofyeva-Belgovskaia (1936) later discovered that *Bar* is actually a duplication for a small section of the chromosome. Let, then, the chromosome of a normal fly be represented as *ABCDE*, and the chromosome carrying the *Bar* mutation as *ABCDBCDE*. Crossing-over between two chromosomes carrying *Bar* gives an *ultra-Bar*: *ABCDBCDBCDE*. Now, a fly with two *Bar* chromosomes, *ABCDBCDE/ABCDBCDE*, has the same genes as one having an *ultra-Bar* and a normal chromosome: *ABCDBCDBCDE/ABCDE*. One expects these two flies to be alike, and yet the latter has appreciably narrower eyes than the former. Repetition of the sections *BCD* in the same chromosome evidently makes the eyes narrower than the presence of the same section in different chromosomes. As more chromosomal aberrations were studied in the 1930s the number of position effects multiplied. For example, flies having two chromosomes with genes *ABCD* and *EFGH* may be fully normal, and flies with the same genes in the order *ABGH* and *EFCD* may be defective. The functioning of a gene apparently depends not only on the intrinsic properties of that gene but on those of the neighbouring genes as well.

II. MOLECULAR LEVEL ANALYSIS OF THE GENE

Perhaps the most impressive and spectacular advance of biology in the 20th century was the discovery of the nature of the genetic material. The way information is encoded in the genes has been clarified, and much has been learned about the mechanisms that translate this information into the developmental processes of the organism.

While the pioneers of genetics used higher plants and animals as experimental materials, much of the work since the late 1940s has been done with microorganisms—bacteria, viruses, and the mold *Neurospora crassa*.

1. Bacteria as Experimental Tools.—The great store of biochemical and physiological data accumulated by bacteriologists has been invaluable for clarifying genetic mechanisms, and the genetic studies have in turn helped to elucidate metabolic pathways in the experimental microorganisms. As seen in retrospect, two misconceptions were responsible for delaying the collaboration of geneticists and bacteriologists. Bacteria were believed to be asexual organisms, reproducing only by simple fission. Their genetic mechanism was thought of as wholly different from the ordered transmission seen in higher organisms. Moreover, bacteria become rapidly adapted to novel and unusual environmental conditions; this rapid adaptation was believed to represent some sort of directed genetic change, rather than the outcome of selection of favourable mutants. In 1947, however, J. Lederberg and E. L. Tatum proved that certain strains of the colon bacteria (*Escherichia coli*, usually abbreviated to *E. coli*) undergo conjugation, a true sexual process in which genetic recombination can occur. Another kind of genetic recombination is transduction, which involves the transfer of sections of a chromosome from one bacterial cell to another by means of attachment to the chromosome of a bacteriophage (bacterial virus). A diagrammatic representation of these processes is shown in fig. 5.

Although *E. coli* is normally the inhabitant of the digestive tract of man and other animals, it is easily cultivated on laboratory media in test tubes or in glass plates (Petri dishes). An individual *E. coli* is a rod-shaped cell about 2 μ in length and 1 μ in width. No discrete nucleus is present, but *E. coli* and other bacteria have genetic materials composed of deoxyribonucleic acid (DNA), organized into a single ring-shaped chromosome (*see below*). Bacteria usually reproduce by fission, and under optimal conditions of food and temperature *E. coli* divides about every 20 minutes. At this rate, a single cell could theoretically produce billions of cells in 24 hours. The discovery of the sexual process (*see below*) was made possible by the availability of mutant strains differing in nutritional requirements. Ordinary strains of *E. coli* grow well on a minimal medium of a simple carbon source, usually the sugar glucose and several simple inorganic elements. Some mutants require particular carbon sources; for example, a mutant may grow well on a glucose medium but not on a medium containing the sugar galactose.

2. Evidence that the Genetic Material Recombines.—Consider two strains of *E. coli* each of which has two different mutants that change the nutritional requirements of their carriers. If the ordinary so-called wild-type *E. coli* carries the genes *ABCD*, the two mutant strains can be represented as *ABcd* and *abCD*, where the lower case letters stand for variant gene alleles that result in the inability of their carriers to grow on the minimal medium. Thus *ABCD* bacteria grow on the minimal medium well, while *ABcd* and *abCD* strains require media with certain chemical substances in addition to those in the minimal one. Cultures of *ABcd* and *abCD* bacteria were mixed together, and after a short period of time, samples of the mixture were taken and placed on solid minimal medium in Petri dishes. Most of the bacteria failed to grow, but some colonies of cells did appear. These colonies consisted of cells carrying the genes *ABCD*, like the wild-type *E. coli*. The appearances of *ABCD* cells were far too numerous to be accounted for by simultaneous mutation. Their appearance in the mixtures must be due to gene recombination.

Certain strains of *E. coli* manifest recombination through conjugation. Two mating types, conveniently referred to as "males" and "females," have been found. Male bacterial cells are determined by the presence of a genetic factor called *F* (for "fertility"), while female cells lack the *F* factor. Male cells are designated *F+*; female cells are designated *F−*. In males the *F* factor can

exist in two states, either as an integral part of the male bacterial chromosome or as a free particle in the cytoplasm. Males with a free *F* factor can conjugate with an *F−* cell but only the *F* factor is transmitted to the *F−* cell. But male cells with an integrated *F* factor always transfer parts of their chromosomes to the female cells. These male, *F+* cells are designated *Hfr* because they yield a *high frequency of recombination* with *F−* cells.

A cross between *F+* and *F−* cells results in conjugation but only the previously mentioned *F* factor is transferred. Only *F+* cells result from such matings. However, in crosses between *Hfr* cells and *F−* cells a portion of the bacterial chromosome is transferred; recombination occurs between the portion of the transferred chromosome and the *F−* chromosome.

3. Evidence that the Genetic Material is Arranged Sequentially.—The observation that the *F* factor is rarely transferred in an *Hfr × F−* cross led F. Jacob and E. L. Wollman to the hypothesis that the *F* factor is the last piece of the chromosome to be transferred. Electron microscope photographs revealed a cytoplasmic tube connecting bacteria of opposite mating types during conjugation of *Hfr × F−* cells. The progress of chromosome transfer can be followed by recording which genes of the male cell appear in recombinants arising from the female cell. Suppose the *Hfr* cell has the genes *ABCDE* so arranged on its chromosome, *A* being transferred first. Suppose further that the *F−* cell has the genes *abcde*. Recombinant bacteria

resulting from this cross can be recognized by the presence of one or more genes originating from the *Hfr* cell. The experiment was performed by artificially interrupting the conjugation between bacterial pairs by violent agitation in a high-speed food blender (fig. 6). When conjugation was interrupted after five minutes, only a small portion of the male chromosome was transferred and inasmuch as the *A* gene was not located at the tip of the transferred portion of the chromosome, no recombinants were observed. When mating was allowed to continue for 20 or 30 minutes, several or all genes were transferred and recombinants were observed. Transfer of the entire male chromosome is a rare event that requires about a two-hour mating. The *F* factor (not shown on the diagram) was transferred last, thus confirming the hypothesis that it is located at the end of the chromosome.

Data derived from the interrupted mating experiment can be used to construct genetic maps of the bacterial chromosome. The length of time needed for a gene to be transferred is a measure of its position along the chromosome. Several *Hfr* strains have been found that transfer their genes in different orders. Analysis of these strains indicates that the bacterial chromosome is a circular structure. The various *Hfr* strains result from the integration of the *F* factor at different points along the circular chromo-

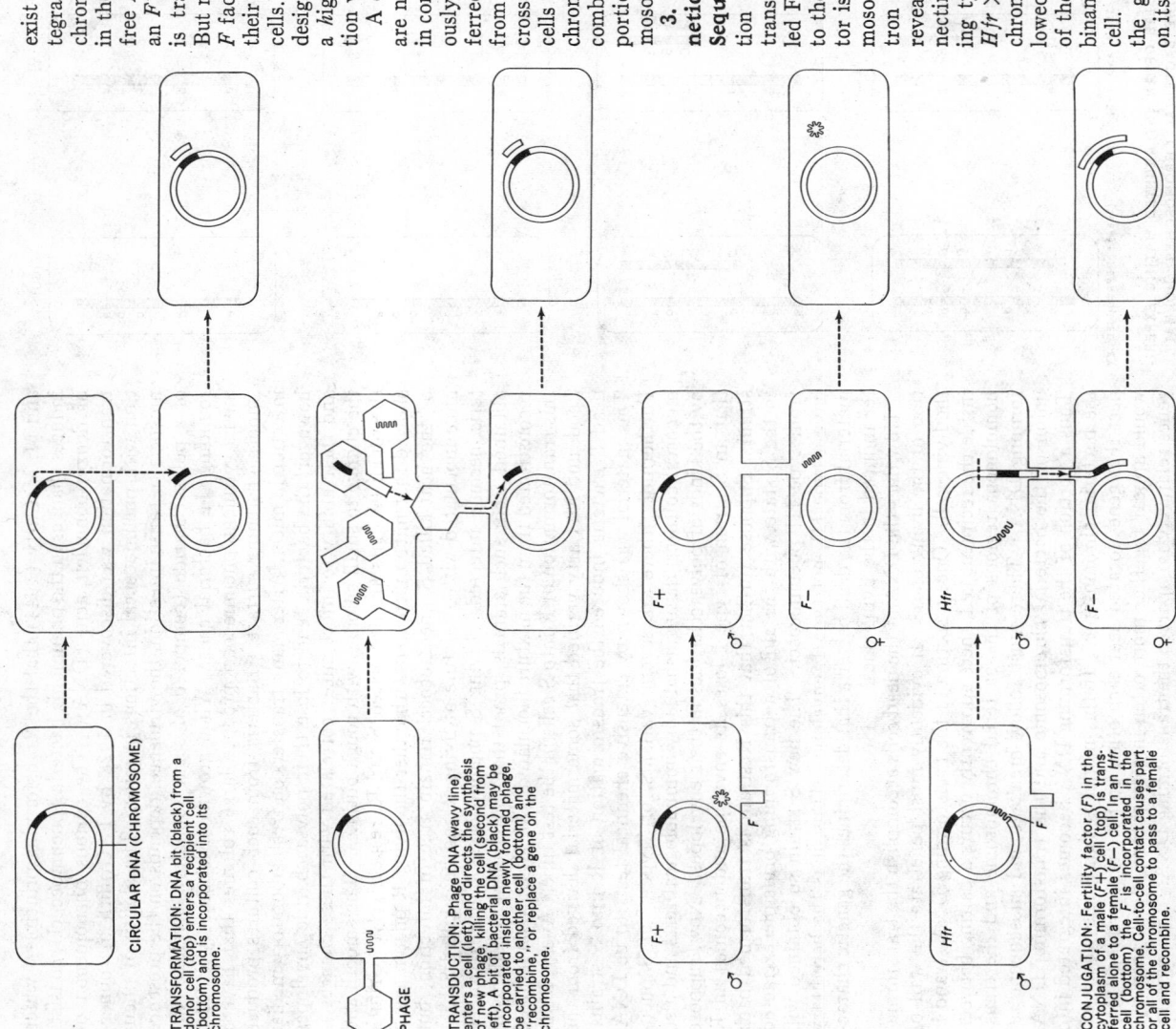

CIRCULAR DNA (CHROMOSOME)

TRANSFORMATION: DNA bit (black) from a donor cell (top) enters a recipient cell (bottom) and is incorporated into its chromosome.

PHAGE

TRANSDUCTION: Phage DNA (wavy line) enters a cell (left) and directs the synthesis of new phage, killing the cell (second from left). A bit of bacterial DNA (black) may be incorporated inside a newly formed phage, be carried to another cell (bottom) and "recombine," or replace a gene on the chromosome.

CONJUGATION: Fertility factor (F) in the cytoplasm of a male (F+) cell (top) is transferred alone to a female (F−) cell. In an Hfr cell (bottom) the F is incorporated in the chromosome. Cell-to-cell contact causes part or all of the chromosome to pass to a female cell and recombine.

FIG. 5.—GENETIC TRANSMISSION IN BACTERIA

GENE

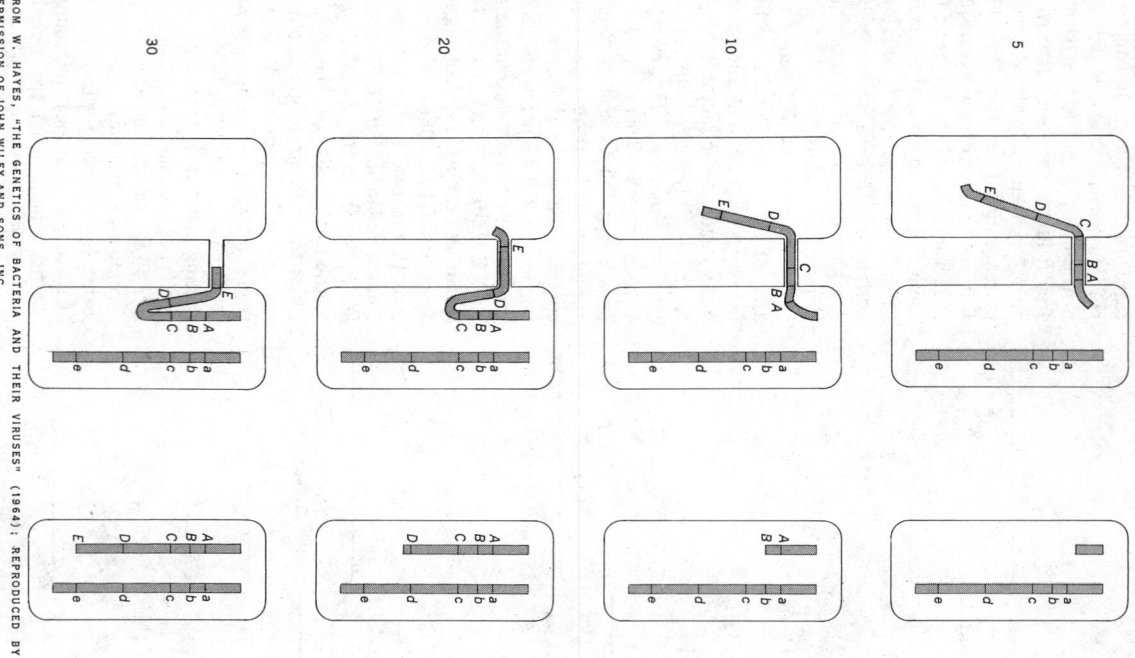

MINUTES   ♂   ♀   ZYGOTES

5

10

20

30

FROM W. HAYES, "THE GENETICS OF BACTERIA AND THEIR VIRUSES" (1964); REPRODUCED BY PERMISSION OF JOHN WILEY AND SONS, INC.

FIG. 6.—DIAGRAM OF THE RESULTS OF AN INTERRUPTED MATING EXPERIMENT IN E. COLI BACTERIA. THE BACTERIAL CHROMOSOMES, NORMALLY CIRCULAR, ARE SHOWN LINEARLY FOR EASE IN REPRESENTATION

some. At the beginning of the conjugation, the chromosome breaks at the location of the F factor; the chromosome tip not containing F is transferred to the F− cell first.

4. Evidence that DNA is the Genetic Material.—The evidence that nucleic acids, especially deoxyribonucleic acid (DNA), act as the carriers of the genetic information came convergently and within a short period of time from several sources. (For the chemistry of these complex molecules, see NUCLEIC ACIDS.) The amounts of DNA per nucleus vary greatly in different sources. The amphibian *Amphiuma* has 168×10^{-9} mg. of DNA per cell, while the jellyfish *Cassiopeia* has only 1.43×10^{-9} mg. DNA per cell. Man is intermediate, with about 6×10^{-9} mg. DNA per cell. There is, however, a remarkable constancy of DNA quantity in the nuclei of cells of different tissues in each species. The only exception to this rule is that the nuclei of gametes, such as spermatozoa in animals, have, within the limits of error of the measurements, one-half of the amount of DNA present in diploid body cells. This is exactly what one should expect, since meiosis results in the gametes being rendered haploid, reduced to one set of chromosomes instead of the two sets present in other cells (see HEREDITY). No other cell constituents show such constancy.

Further evidence involving DNA as the genetic material was provided by the demonstration by O. T. Avery, C. M. MacLeod, and M. McCarty (1944) that the "transforming principle," which induces changes in the pneumonia bacteria (pneumococci), consists of deoxyribonucleic acid (DNA). The curious phenomenon of transformation was discovered in 1928 by F. Griffith in connection with pneumococcal infections in mice. The ability of pneumococci to cause infection, the virulence, depends on the presence of a polysaccharide (composed of sugar subunits) envelope surrounding the pneumococcal cells. When grown on laboratory culture media, virulent pneumococci produce large colonies that have a smooth glistening surface. Bacteria from such cultures produce infection in mice. After many transfers on fresh laboratory media, however, the bacteria tend to lose their polysaccharide envelopes and their ability to infect mice; correlated with these changes is the change to small colonies with rough outlines. The smooth and the rough variants are designated S and R, respectively. Griffith showed that mice inoculated with either the living R pneumococci or the heat-killed S pneumococci remain free of infection, but mice inoculated with a mixture of living R and heat-killed S bacteria become infected. Living S pneumococcal cultures can be obtained from such animals, proof that the virulent S cells were reconstituted from the mixture inoculated. M. H. Dawson induced this transformation of R into S cells in the test tube. Avery, MacLeod, and McCarty verified that some material derived from the dead S bacteria induced the transformation of R into S strains. This material was shown by extensive chemical tests to be DNA. Furthermore, there are several variants, or "types," of S pneumococcal cultures, distinguishable by immunological tests and also by the kinds of polysaccharides in their envelopes. Now, suppose that an S strain of type I loses its envelope and becomes an R strain. Suppose further that this R strain is transformed back to the S state with the aid of a transforming principle extracted from type III pneumococci. The new S strain so obtained will have a type III, not type I, envelope. Thus, it is the hereditary material from the dead bacteria that determines the genetic character induced in the living ones.

How does the DNA of the dead cells accomplish the transformation of the living ones? It evidently must penetrate the wall of the living cell. Once a section of the transforming DNA strand is inside the recipient cell, there apparently occurs a pairing between homologous regions of the bacterial chromosome and the transforming DNA. There must follow breakage and subsequent reunion of the bacterial chromosome and the transforming DNA. Thus a portion of the transforming DNA becomes integrated into the bacterial chromosome. If this model is valid, one would expect that genes located near each other on the transforming DNA would appear together more often in a transformed cell than would genes relatively far apart in the transforming DNA. This expectation is fulfilled, and the principle has been utilized as a means of mapping the donor cell chromosome.

Further evidence that DNA serves as the physical basis of heredity was obtained by A. D. Hershey and M. Chase in the early 1950s, using bacteriophages that attack *E. coli*. The bacteriophage (or simply phage) is an ultramicroscopic tadpole-shaped body, with a hexagonal head, a cylindrical tail, an end plate, and six tail fibres (see VIRUSES). The head contains the DNA; the outer surface and the tail consist of protein. A phage particle attacking *E. coli* attaches itself by its tail plate to the surface of the host bacterial cell. The DNA from the head then passes through the tail and into the body of the host. The metabolic machinery of the bacterial cell is subverted to make phage DNA and phage protein. When a new generation of the phage particles is ready inside the bacterium, destruction (lysis) of the latter takes place, and a hundred or more new phage particles are released into the external medium, where they can attack other bacterial cells. Hershey and Chase obtained phage particles whose protein coats were labeled with radioactive sulfur, and whose DNA contained radioactive phosphorus (fig. 7). These doubly tagged phages were allowed to attach themselves to bacterial cells; some minutes later the culture was subjected to violent agitation in a food blender. The agitation removed the empty protein coats ("ghosts") of the phage particles from the surface of the bacterial cells, but the phage DNA was already inside the bacterial cells. The new phage particles formed inside the cells contained radioactive phosphorus, which could only have come from the phosphorus-labeled DNA of the original phage. The component of the phage that entered the bacteria and became incorporated in the new generation of the phages was evidently their DNA only, and not protein.

5. The Watson-Crick Model of the Genetic Material.—The remarkable properties of the nucleic acids, which qualify these substances to serve as the carriers of the genetic information, have claimed the attention of many investigators (*see* NUCLEIC ACIDS). The groundwork was laid by pioneer biochemists who found that nucleic acids are long chainlike molecules, the backbones of which consist of repeated sequences of phosphate and sugar linkages—ribose sugars in RNA and deoxyribose sugars in DNA. Attached to the sugar links in the backbone are two kinds of purines, adenine (A) and guanine (G); and two kinds of pyrimidines, cytosine (C) and thymine (T) in DNA, or cytosine (C) and uracil (U) in RNA. A single purine or a pyrimidine is attached to each sugar, the compound being called a nucleotide. E. Chargaff discovered an interesting relationship, the significance of which became apparent later in the light of the Watson-Crick model. The nucleic acids extracted from different species of animals and plants have different proportions of the four nucleotides. Some are relatively richer in adenine and thymine, while others have more guanine and cytosine. However, the ratios of A to T, and also of G to C, are equal.

M. H. F. Wilkins and his co-workers (1950) studied the molecular structure of DNA with the techniques of X-ray crystallography. The purine and pyrimidine bases were found to be located along the backbone of the molecule at quite regular intervals, 3.4 Å apart (an angstrom unit is one hundred-millionth of a centimetre). The molecule is, however, not straight but a spiral, forming one complete turn for every ten nucleotides. In 1953 J. D. Watson and F. H. C. Crick proposed their now famous model, which shows DNA as composed of two spirally wound (helical) chains, in which the A's (adenines) in one chain are always linked by hydrogen bonds to T's, and the G's in one chain to C's in the other (*see* NUCLEIC ACIDS). This model fulfills the basic requirements—it makes it possible to envisage how genes replicate their precise structures when their copies are synthesized. It also makes it possible to explain how a gene can carry genetic information written in some chemical code. And finally, it helps to envisage how mutational changes in the genes are produced.

6. The Replication of Genetic Material.—The Watson-Crick model of the genetic material permits an explanation of the

mechanism of precise replication of genes (fig. 8). The paired complementary strands of the DNA molecule may separate owing to a breakage of the hydrogen bonds between the nucleotides. If free nucleotides (base + sugar + phosphate) are present in the medium surrounding the gene, they might pair with the complementary bases on the single strands of DNA. An enzyme, DNA polymerase, functions to form the phosphate bonds between the sugars in the DNA backbone. It has been used in the synthesis of DNA in vitro, in cell-free systems. The enzyme is extracted from rapidly dividing cells of the familiar bacterium, *E. coli.* A supply of the four nucleotides, A, T, G, and C, is provided, as well as a source of energy, adenosine triphosphate (ATP). To start the DNA synthesis another key component is added—a trace of DNA to serve

as a "primer." The kind of DNA that is synthesized depends on the "primer." Even though the enzyme came from *E. coli,* if the "primer" is DNA of some quite different organism, such as cattle, the DNA that is synthesized is not *E. coli* but cattle DNA.

There are at least three possible ways to envisage the mechanism of replication of DNA (fig. 9). One possibility, termed semiconservative replication, would result in two molecules of DNA, each composed of one old and one new strand. Another possi-

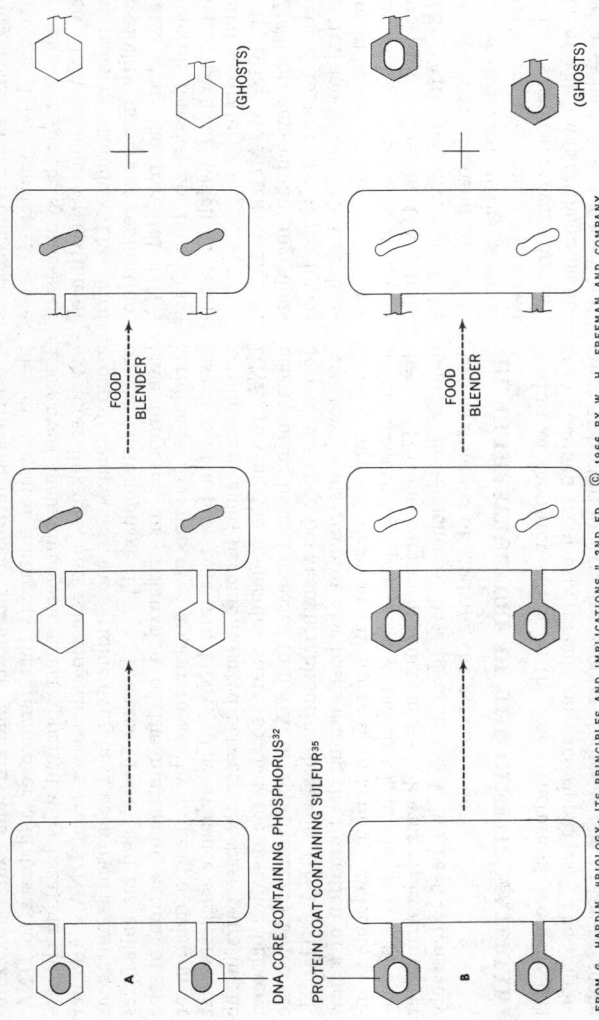

DNA CORE CONTAINING PHOSPHORUS³²

PROTEIN COAT CONTAINING SULFUR³⁵

FOOD BLENDER

(GHOSTS)

A

FOOD BLENDER

(GHOSTS)

B

FROM G. HARDIN, "BIOLOGY: ITS PRINCIPLES AND IMPLICATIONS," 2ND ED., © 1966 BY W. H. FREEMAN AND COMPANY

FIG. 7.—THE HERSHEY-CHASE EXPERIMENT SHOWING THAT ONLY THE DNA CORE OF THE BACTERIOPHAGE IS INJECTED INTO THE BACTERIAL CELL. TONE INDICATES RADIOACTIVE MATERIAL

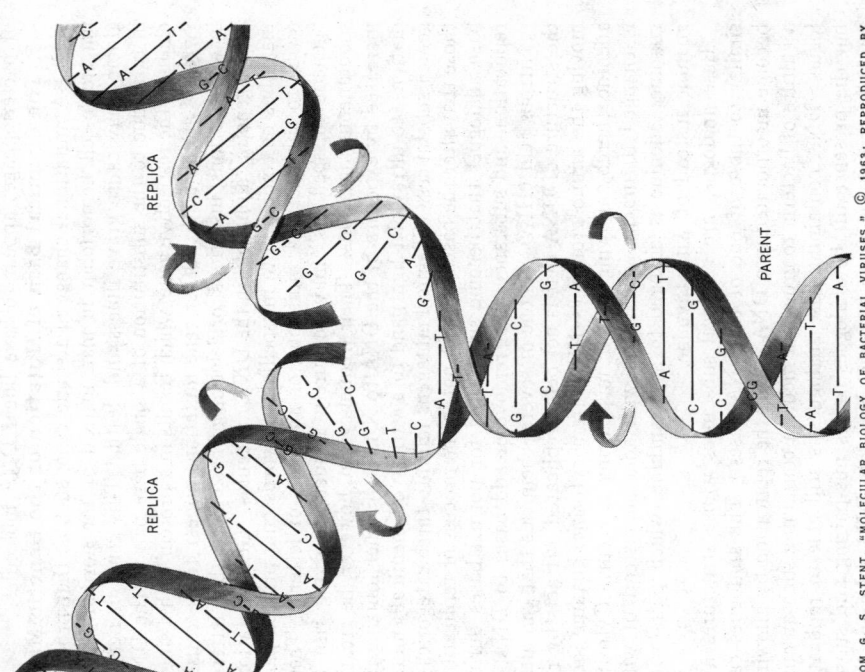

REPLICA

REPLICA

PARENT

FROM G. S. STENT, "MOLECULAR BIOLOGY OF BACTERIAL VIRUSES," © 1963; REPRODUCED BY PERMISSION OF W. H. FREEMAN AND COMPANY

FIG. 8.—A POSSIBLE METHOD FOR THE REPLICATION OF DNA ACCORDING TO WATSON AND CRICK. THE ARROWS INDICATE THE DIRECTION OF ROTATION

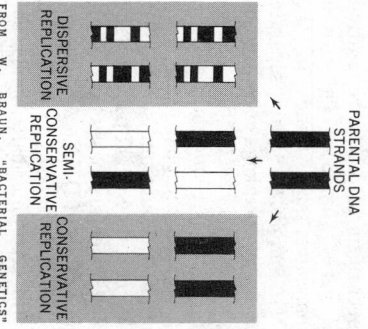

PARENTAL DNA STRANDS

DISPERSIVE REPLICATION

SEMI-CONSERVATIVE REPLICATION

CONSERVATIVE REPLICATION

FROM W. BRAUN, "BACTERIAL GENETICS" (1965); REPRODUCED BY PERMISSION OF W. B. SAUNDERS COMPANY

FIG. 9.—DIAGRAM ILLUSTRATING THREE POSSIBLE MODES OF REPLICATION OF DNA. PARENTAL DNA IS INDICATED IN BLACK; THE NEWLY SYNTHESIZED DNA IS INDICATED IN WHITE. THE DNA STRANDS ARE SHOWN AS STRAIGHT FOR EASE IN REPRESENTATION

bility, conservative replication, is that the DNA molecules serve as templates for the synthesis of new DNA without separation of the pairs of strands. The third possibility, dispersive replication, states that the parental DNA molecule breaks up into fragments, each of which is replicated separately.

In 1958, M. Meselson and F. W. Stahl devised an ingenious method to test the three hypothetical models of DNA replication in bacteria. Their technique utilized high-speed centrifugation to separate different DNA fractions. After one division of the bacteria a single band of DNA, lighter than that of the parental DNA, was observed. After two divisions two bands were present, one of which was at the same po-

sition as the first-division band and a second even lighter band. These results are consistent with the semiconservative model of DNA replication, and rule out the other models. Evidence indicates that the same mechanism of replication of DNA as found in bacteria occurs in higher organisms.

J. Cairns has studied the mechanism of DNA synthesis and the structure of the E. coli chromosome. He demonstrated that synthesis of new DNA occurs while the old chromosome is in the process of uncoiling. Cairns also found that the chromosome of E. coli was a circular structure—a discovery predicted by genetic tests. Several viruses possessing both single and double stranded DNA molecules have since been shown to have circular DNA. This structure is, however, not universal since several other kinds of bacteriophages appear to have linear DNA molecules.

7. The Chemical Basis of Mutation of the Genetic Material.—A mutational change in a single gene, such as that producing sickle-cell hemoglobin in man instead of the normal hemoglobin, may cause grave illness and death. This gene change is, in turn, due to the substitution of a single base pair in the DNA chain of the respective gene, which results in a protein with a single "wrong" amino acid. Other gene mutations appear to be caused by substitutions, insertions, or deletion of base pairs, the "letters" of the genetic "alphabet" in the DNA molecules. Gene mutations may thus be compared to misspellings of words on a printed page owing to substitutions, omissions, or additions of letters. These "genetic misspellings" may be purely accidental, giving rise to spontaneous mutations. Their frequency can, however, be greatly increased by exposure of the DNA to X rays or other ionizing radiations, to ultraviolet light, and to a variety of chemical (mutagenic) substances. Chemical mutagens fall into three categories—those that alter the bases of DNA not in the process of replication, those that become substituted for normal bases during replication, and substances that remove or add bases to DNA.

Nitrous acid (HNO_2) is one of several chemicals that can alter the structure of DNA that is not being replicated. It acts by removing the amino groups ($-NH_2$) from cytosine, guanine, and adenine, thereby allowing cases of mis-pairing to occur. Cytosine is changed to uracil, which pairs with adenine instead of with guanine; adenine is changed to hypoxanthine, which pairs with guanine instead of with thymine.

Base analogues are chemical substances whose structures are similar to those of one of the DNA bases. The analogues can become incorporated into DNA during the replication by allowing a culture of bacteria to grow in a medium containing such an analogue. DNA containing base analogues is still able to replicate, but the presence of the analogues causes mis-pairing and subsequent incorporation of an incorrect base into DNA. Among the mutagenically potent base analogues are 5-bromouracil, an analogue of thymine, and 2-amino purine, an analogue of adenine.

Sulfur and nitrogen "mustards" and ethylene oxides are examples of chemical mutagens that remove or add bases to DNA. They exert their mutagenic effect apparently by breaking the deoxyribose linkages, the acridine dyes, have been used as mutagens on the bacteriophage T4. S. Brenner (1961) and his colleagues have proposed an explanation of the mutagenic action of the acridines. Acridine dyes appear to act by causing a deletion or insertion of a base pair into DNA. The evidence suggests that acridine molecules become inserted between the base pairs in the DNA, forcing the molecules apart, so that the distance between neighbouring bases increases to 6.8 Å, or approximately twice the normal distance between neighbouring bases in DNA. This allows for the insertion of new bases during the formation of a new DNA strand. A deletion will occur if at an acridine molecule is inserted between base pairs in a strand that is in the process of synthesis. This mechanism of mutagenesis, allowing an experimenter to alter the sequence of base pairs in DNA, has been extensively used as a means of studying the genetic code.

III. ULTRASTRUCTURE OF THE GENETIC MATERIAL.

Most of the information on the fine structure of the gene has been obtained from experiments on bacteriophages. The importance of bacteriophages for genetic studies is due to the presence of many mutant forms, the occurrence of recombination among the phage chromosomes, and the phenomenon of transduction. Transduction, discovered by N. D. Zinder and J. Lederberg (1952), consists of transfer by bacteriophages of portions of bacterial chromosomes from one bacterial cell to another.

1. Bacteriophages as Experimental Tools.—There are several techniques to detect mutant bacteriophages. Suppose that a drop of some substance suspected of containing bacteriophages is placed on the surface of a culture medium consisting of agar covered with a layer of E. coli bacteria. If phages are present, they will infect the bacteria and eventually cause their death. The bacterial layer will develop holes, or "plaques," due to the destruction of the individual bacteria by a process termed lysis. Because each plaque develops from a single phage particle, the number of such plaques formed gives an estimate of the abundance of phages in the inoculum. Each type of phage forms a plaque of characteristic appearance, thus mutations can be detected as variations in plaque form. Examples of such mutations are the r mutants of the phage T4, which cause rapid lysis of the bacterial cells, resulting in the formation of larger plaques. Differences in the ability of the phage to attach itself to the host cell form another class of mutations. Some phages are temperature sensitive, and mutants that can grow on certain laboratory strains of E. coli bacteria but not others.

Crosses between mutant phages of different types can be made if a single bacterium is simultaneously infected with two phage mutants. A proportion of the progeny phage will be recombinants for the mutants in question. For example if a bacterium is infected with two types of phages, one having the genes Ab and the other, aB, recombination results in appearance of some phage particles having the genes ab and AB. This method of phage crosses has been utilized to construct a genetic map of the T4 phage (see fig. 10). The map is circular, indicating the physical continuity of the T4 chromosome. The numbered areas are the locations of genes that are lethal (i.e., cause death of the phage) under certain conditions. The dark areas indicate the minimal extent of the gene; gray areas are the locations of genes whose exact length is unknown. Gene e contains the code for the production of the phage enzyme, lysozyme, which causes bacterial cell lysis. The rIIA and rIIB genes control the rapid lysis of bacterial cells and are discussed in detail below.

Bacteriophages do not always cause the destruction of their host cell by lysis. A class of phages termed temperate has the ability to enter into a symbiotic relationship with the bacterial host cell. The chromosome of the temperate phage becomes incorporated into the bacterial chromosome, and is replicated only when the bacterial chromosome replicates. A bacterial cell in this

GENE

FIG. 10.—A GENETIC MAP OF THE CHROMOSOME OF BACTERIOPHAGE T₄. THE NUMBERS INDICATE THE POSITIONS OF GENES. THE BLACK, FILLED AREAS REPRESENT THE MINIMAL LENGTH OF EACH GENE; GRAY AREAS INDICATE A GENE OF UNKNOWN LENGTH. THE SYMBOLS INDICATE INCOMPLETE OR FAULTY VIRUS PARTICLES

state is termed lysogenic for the phage in question. If, however, the chromosome of a temperate phage becomes dissociated from the bacterial chromosome, it is capable of autonomous replication, which results in the lysis of the host cell. A temperate phage can be artificially induced to enter an autonomous state through the action of such stimuli as ultraviolet light.

2. Data Based on the Transduction Phenomenon.—Transduction was discovered in experiments designed to test for gene recombination in the bacterium *Salmonella typhimurium*. Recombination occurred in the usual way in a small number of cells, but it also occurred when one cell culture was treated with a cell-free extract of another. The agent causing recombination proved to be inseparable from the particles of a temperate bacteriophage that occurred symbiotically in one parental strain but infected and lysed the other. When cells lysogenic for a transducing phage produce phage particles, a part of the phage DNA is exchanged for some bacterial genes. Since the transducing phage no longer carries its full complement of genes, it is incapable of multiplying and lysing the host cells. The host bacterium, moreover, now contains the bacterial genes introduced by the phage, and is thus diploid for the genes in question.

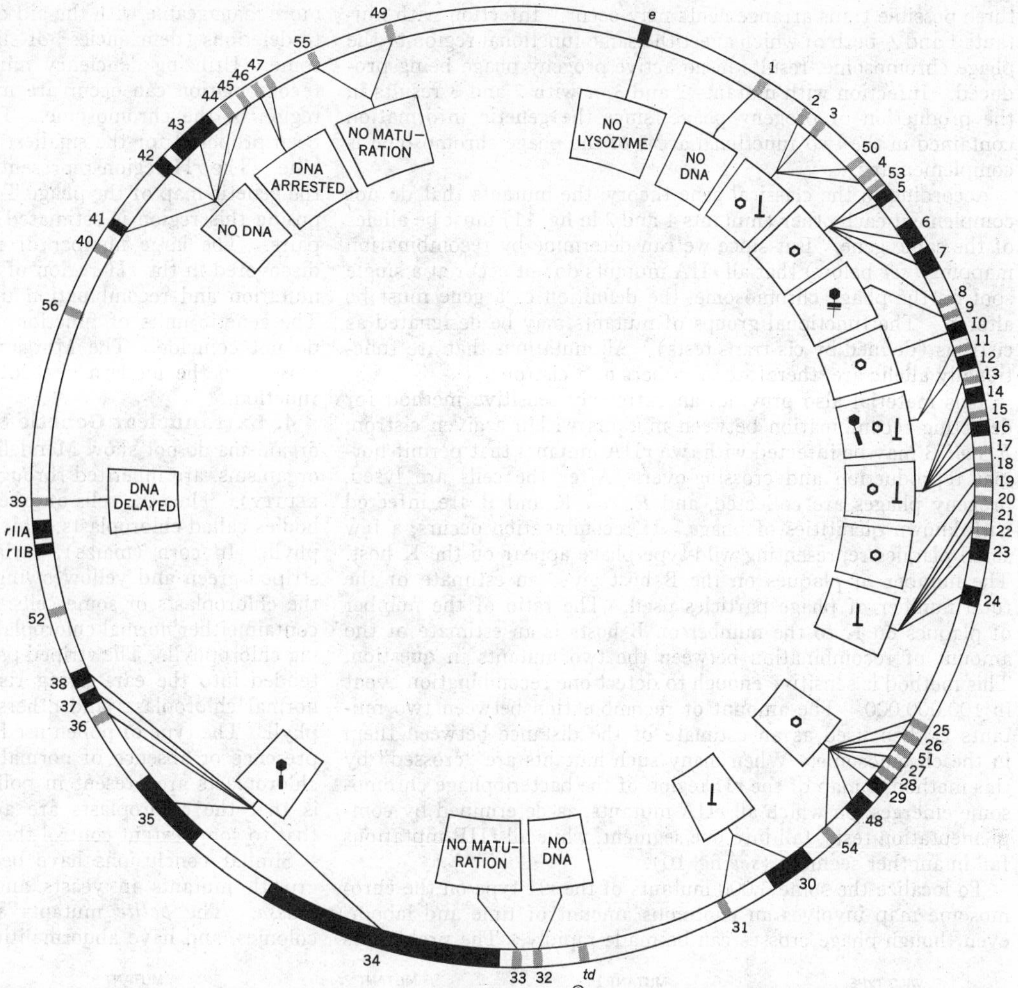

The mechanism of transduc-

tion seems to be as follows. The chromosome of the phage particle is a ring-shaped structure. This chromosome pairs with a certain region of the bacterial chromosome. Both chromosomes then break, and the reunion of the broken ends results in the insertion of the phage chromosomal material into the bacterial chromosome.

Transduction has been utilized to construct a map of the bacterial chromosome. The genes that lie close together in the chromosome will usually undergo transduction together, and if three or four genes are followed simultaneously their order in the chromosome can be determined.

3. Data Based on the Complementation Phenomenon.—The classical Morgan-Muller conception of the gene was defined as a unit of function (its mutants changing, for example, the eye colour, or the wings, or the bristle shape in *Drosophila* flies), a unit of recombination (having a definite position on the genetic map), and a unit of mutation (similar mutational changes arising repeatedly). These three criteria of defining and delimiting the genes usually coincided, and thus gave concordant results. Genetic experiments on *Drosophila* flies deal, however, with numbers of individuals generally several orders of magnitude smaller than are involved in many experiments with microorganisms. Seymour Benzer (1955 and thereafter) has studied in detail a portion of the chromosome of the bacteriophage T₄, called the *r*II region. His experiments indicate that the criteria of the gene as a unit of function, of recombination, and of mutation no longer delimit similar units. Benzer found a mutant (*r*) of the phage T₄ that caused rapid lysis of the strain B of *E. coli* but could not lyse another strain, *E. coli* K 12 (λ). This latter strain, however, was

lysogenic for the phage lambda (λ). This finding led to the development of the so-called complementation, or cis-trans, tests, and to the detection of very small frequencies of recombination. The cis-trans test is made possible by the fact that the bacteriophage *r*II mutants can grow on *E. coli* strain B but not on *E. coli* K. The original, nonmutant, T₄ phages grow equally well on both hosts. If *E. coli* K are infected with an original (*r*⁺) type phage and an *r*II mutant, growth and maturation of both types occurs and mutant progeny are released. The *r*⁺ phages have evidently provided some necessary materials for the reproduction of the mutant. When various combinations of *r*II mutants are used to infect *E. coli* K, two kinds of results are observed. In some combination of mutants normal plaques are formed, while other combinations yield no plaques. The mutants belong consequently to two groups called *r*IIA and *r*IIB, which have altered functionally different regions of the phage chromosome. When two mutants belong to different groups they complement each other, reciprocally compensate for each other's deficiency, and give viable phages that produce normal plaques. Fig. 11 is a diagrammatic representation of the complementation phenomenon in cis-trans tests. The chromosome of the bacteriophage (top row) is shown divided in two functional regions, one of which contains mutants 1 and 2, and the other mutant 3. The strings of squares and circles beneath the phage chromosomes indicate a region of undamaged chromosome. A version of the cis test (middle row) is performed by infecting bacteria with a mutant and a normal, wild-type phage. In all cases this results in the production of active progeny phage and serves as a control experiment for the trans test. When two mutants are used to simultaneously infect a single bacterium (bottom row), three possible trans arrangements may occur. Infection with mutants 1 and 2, both of which affect the same functional region of the phage chromosome, results in no active progeny phage being produced. Infection with mutants 1 and 3 or with 2 and 3 results in the production of progeny phage, since the genetic information contained in the two functional areas of the phage chromosome is complementary.

According to the classical gene theory, the mutants that do not complement each other (mutants 1 and 2 in fig. 11) must be alleles of the same gene. But since we can determine by recombination mapping (see below) that all rIIA mutants do not occur at a single spot on the phage chromosome, the definition of a gene must be altered. The functional groups of mutants may be designated as cistrons (defined by cis-trans tests). All mutations that are functionally allelic are, therefore, members of a cistron.

This material also provides an extremely sensitive method for detecting recombination between mutants within a given cistron. E. coli B may be infected with two rIIA mutants that permit normal reproduction and crossing-over. After the cells are lysed, progeny phages are collected, and E. coli K and E. coli B are infected with known quantities of phage. If recombination occurs, a few small plaques representing wild-type phage appear on the K host. The number of plaques on the B host gives an estimate of the total number of phage particles used. The ratio of the number of plaques on K to the number on B hosts is an estimate of the amount of recombination between the two mutants in question. This method is sensitive enough to detect one recombination event in 100,000,000. The amount of recombination between two mutants is then used as an estimate of the distance between them in the chromosome. When many such mutants are "crossed" by this method, a map of the rII region of the bacteriophage chromosome emerges, on which all rIIA mutants, as determined by complementation tests, fall into one segment, while all rIIB mutations fall in another segment (see fig. 10).

To localize the some 3,000 mutants of the rII type on the chromosome map involves an enormous amount of time and labour, even though phage crosses can be made rapidly. The problem is more manageable with the aid of mutants that are apparently due to deletions (deficiencies) of short sections of the phage chromosome. Utilizing deficiency mutants, sites at which mutation or recombination can occur are more easily mapped within the rII region of the chromosome. The names muton and recon have been proposed for the smallest units that can mutate and recombine. The rII region represents about 2% of the total length of the genetic map of the phage T4 chromosome, and the DNA composing this region is estimated to contain about 4,000 nucleotide pairs. The large number of mutation and recombination sites discovered in the rII region of the chromosome suggests that the mutation and recombination units may be the nucleotide pairs. The genetic units of function, recombination, and mutation thus do not coincide. The Morgan-Muller "gene" corresponds most closely to the modern conception of the "cistron" as a unit of function.

4. Extranuclear Genetic Material.—Some characteristics of organisms do not show Mendelian segregation, and, among higher organisms, are inherited through the maternal line only (see HEREDITY).

Thus the cells of green plants contain in their cytoplasm bodies called chloroplasts, which carry the green pigment, chlorophyll. In corn (maize), variants are known whose leaves are striped green and yellow owing to the absence of chlorophyll in the chloroplasts of some cells. The progeny of the striped corn contain either normal chloroplasts or chloroplasts completely lacking chlorophyll. The striped pattern in the parent presumably extended into the ear, giving rise to some kernels that contained normal chloroplasts and others with chloroplasts lacking chlorophyll. The type of pollen used in such a cross is irrelevant to the presence or absence of normal chloroplasts in the progeny. No chloroplasts are present in pollen grains. The conclusion drawn is that the chloroplasts are autonomous, self-replicating bodies that to some extent control their own characteristics.

Similar conclusions have been drawn from studies of certain growth mutants in yeasts and in the bread mold Neurospora crassa. The petite mutants of yeast grow slowly, form small colonies, and have abnormalities associated with the energy-converting cytochrome enzyme system, found within the cellular bodies termed mitochondria (see CELL). Crosses of normal yeasts to petite yeasts result in the production of all normal yeasts. A similar mutant called poky in N. crassa reduces the growth rate to approximately one-half that of the normal, wild-type fungus. Again crosses between normal and mutant strains give all normal progeny. In both yeast and N. crassa these mutations are linked to deficiencies in the cytochrome systems and to morphological abnormalities in the mitochondria themselves. Cytological examination of petite yeast shows that no identifiable mitochondria are present.

The presence of extranuclear genetic materials suggests that DNA must be present within the cellular bodies in question. The quantity of such DNA might be small, but its presence could be detected if the relative quantities of the four DNA bases were different from those of the nuclear DNA. Centrifugation is used to separate two types of DNA differing in the relative amounts of the bases present. The existence of DNA within

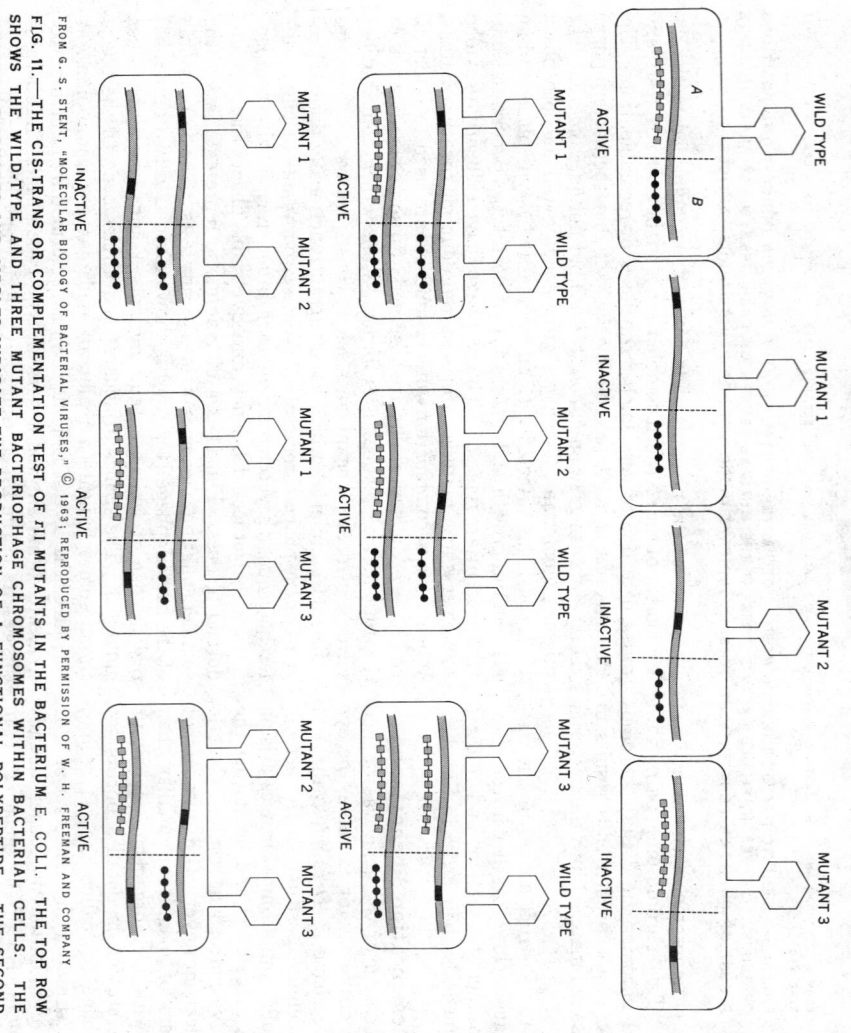

WILD TYPE — A — B — ACTIVE
MUTANT 1 — ACTIVE
WILD TYPE — INACTIVE
MUTANT 2 — ACTIVE
WILD TYPE — INACTIVE
MUTANT 3 — ACTIVE
MUTANT 1 — MUTANT 2 — INACTIVE
MUTANT 1 — MUTANT 3 — ACTIVE
MUTANT 2 — MUTANT 3 — ACTIVE

FIG. 11.—THE CIS-TRANS OR COMPLEMENTATION TEST OF rII MUTANTS IN THE BACTERIUM E. COLI. THE TOP ROW SHOWS THE WILD-TYPE, AND THREE MUTANT BACTERIOPHAGE CHROMOSOMES WITHIN BACTERIAL CELLS. THE SECOND AND THIRD ROWS SHOW THE RESULTS OF SIMULTANEOUS INFECTION OF A BACTERIAL CELL WITH VARIOUS COMBINATIONS OF WILD-TYPE AND MUTANT BACTERIOPHAGE (see TEXT)

chloroplasts was demonstrated in 1963 by E. H. Chun and R. Sager and their colleagues using the large chloroplasts of the green alga *Chlamydomonas*. The chloroplast DNA is different in density from the nuclear DNA; the difference is due to a higher percentage of A–T pairs in chloroplast DNA. DNA has also been demonstrated, by D. Luck and E. Reich (1964), within mitochondria derived from *N. crassa*. The subsequent discoveries of ribosomes, transfer RNA's, and other enzymes within mitochondria and chloroplasts suggest that these cytoplasmic bodies may synthesize part if not all their own proteins.

IV. GENES AND DEVELOPMENT

1. The One Gene-One Enzyme Hypothesis.—The study of mutations that alter metabolic processes has shed light on the mode of action of the genes in the development of the organism. In 1935, G. W. Beadle and B. Ephrussi made a study of certain mutants that change the eye colour of the fly *Drosophila melanogaster*. In the larva there are small patches of tissue, called imaginal discs, from which the body parts of the adult insect later develop. It is possible to take the imaginal disc from which the eye develops from one larva, inject it into the body cavity of another larva, and observe the eye that develops from it in the adult. A mutant called vermilion has red eyes instead of the normal darker red eyes. If a vermilion imaginal disc is injected into a normal (wild-type) larva, the eye that develops is normal red in coloration. This normal eye pigmentation involves a chain of chemical reactions transforming a substance A into B, B into C, C into D, etc. Each transformation is facilitated by a specific enzyme, and each enzyme is a product of a certain gene. A mutation may, then, stand for the absence of an enzyme that transforms A into B; a mutant, such as vermilion, will not develop the normal pigment C. But when a vermilion imaginal disc is implanted into a normal body, the disc will develop the pigment, because the host body does have the enzyme needed for the A → B transformation.

In the early 1940s G. W. Beadle and E. L. Tatum began a series of fruitful studies of biochemical mutants in the bread mold *N. crassa*. Most strains of this mold grow well on a "minimal"

medium" containing sugar, an inorganic nitrogen source, and the vitamin biotin. Some mutant strains do not, however, grow on the minimal medium, and require for growth the addition of certain substances that normal *N. crassa* can synthesize itself. Among many mutants studied in *N. crassa*, those concerned with synthesis of the amino acid tryptophan proved particularly favourable for study. Tryptophan is synthesized as follows: anthranilic acid (A) → indole (B) → tryptophan (C). Mutants were found that blocked the step A → B, others that blocked B → C. Apparently, each step is facilitated by an enzyme produced by a separate gene, and a mutational change in the gene may cause a lack of the enzyme or may make it ineffective.

2. The Determination of Protein Structure and Synthesis.—Proteins, basic components of living organisms, are constructed from nitrogen-containing compounds called amino acids (*see* PROTEINS). Some 20 amino acids are commonly found in naturally occurring proteins. The amino acids are linked together in the proteins by a specific chemical bond, the peptide bond, to form long chains. It is the sequence of the amino acids in a protein that is uniquely determined by the sequence of the four bases in DNA. The amino acid sequence or primary structure of a protein usually determines the three-dimensional structure that the complete protein molecule will take. Interactions between various chemical groups on the amino acid units of protein are responsible for the three-dimensional structure that results. Three groups of proteins can be recognized: (1) enzymes or catalytic proteins, which participate in almost all chemical reactions that take place in cells of living bodies; (2) structural proteins, which form the building blocks of cellular components; and (3) regulatory or control proteins, which interact with genes or their products to control the amounts and presumably the times of production of still other protein molecules.

The amino acid sequence of a protein such as human hemoglobin shows that these molecules are composed of several protein subunits, usually called polypeptide chains, linked together by chemical bonds. Normal hemoglobin A is composed of four polypeptide chains, two alphas (α) and two betas (β), whose amino acid sequences show considerable similarity (fig. 12).

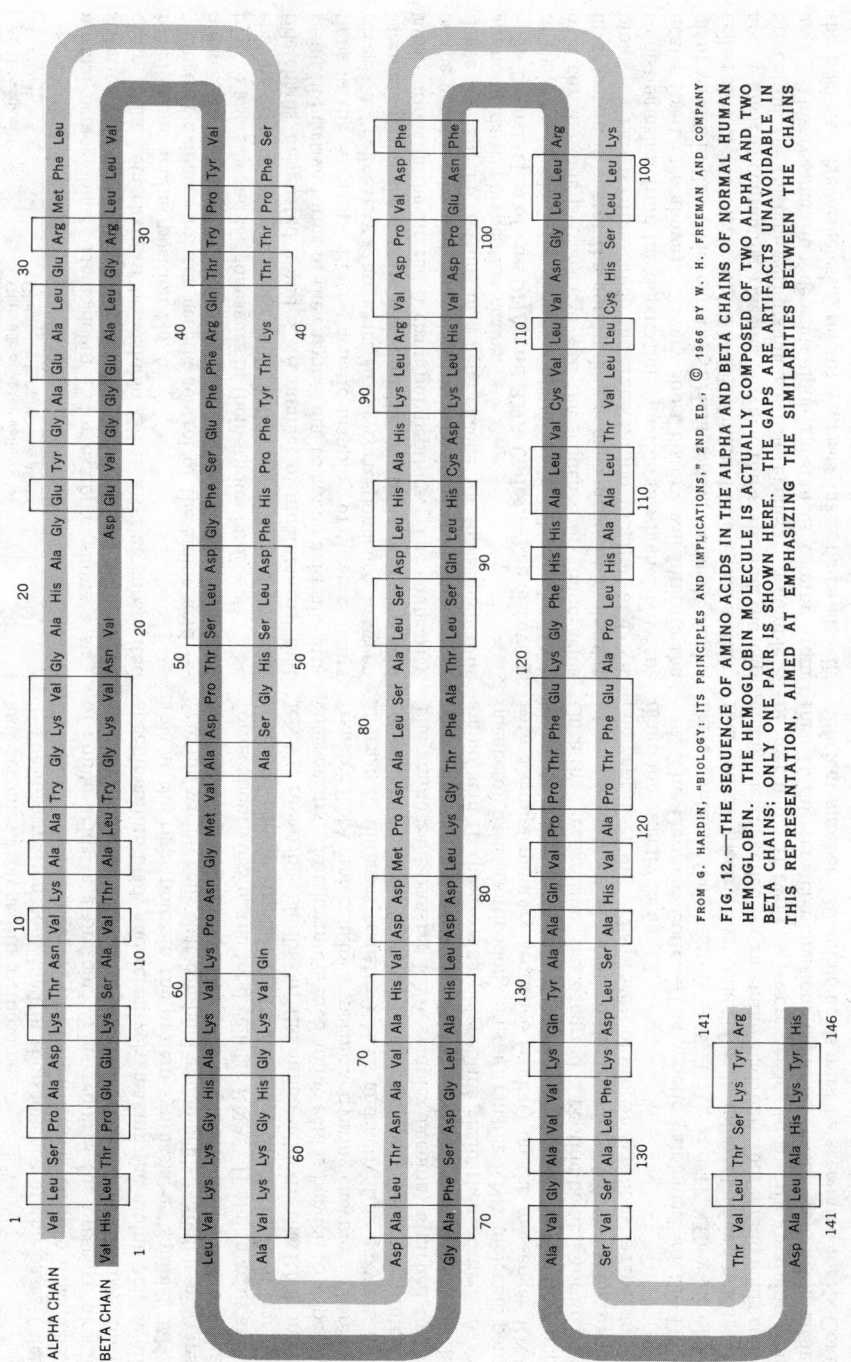

FROM G. HARDIN, "BIOLOGY: ITS PRINCIPLES AND IMPLICATIONS," 2ND ED., © 1966 BY W. H. FREEMAN AND COMPANY

FIG. 12.—THE SEQUENCE OF AMINO ACIDS IN THE ALPHA AND BETA CHAINS OF NORMAL HUMAN HEMOGLOBIN. THE HEMOGLOBIN MOLECULE IS ACTUALLY COMPOSED OF TWO ALPHA AND TWO BETA CHAINS; ONLY ONE PAIR IS SHOWN HERE. THE GAPS ARE ARTIFACTS UNAVOIDABLE IN THIS REPRESENTATION, AIMED AT EMPHASIZING THE SIMILARITIES BETWEEN THE CHAINS

The work of Beadle and Tatum discussed above suggested that genes control the productions of single enzymes. An example of the difficulty encountered by the one gene-one enzyme hypothesis is provided by the variants in the human hemoglobin molecule. Genetic studies of individuals having mutant hemoglobins have shown that the alpha and beta chains of hemoglobin are controlled by two genes located on two different chromosomes. This suggests that the one gene-one enzyme hypothesis should be modified to a one gene-one polypeptide chain hypothesis.

Further studies of mutant hemoglobins have elucidated how the gene might control the specific amino acid sequence of a polypeptide. A hereditary disease in humans, sickle-cell anemia, was first discovered in Africa and the Mediterranean regions of Europe and Asia. Clinical manifestations of this affliction include a change in the form of the red blood cells to a sickle-like shape. Chemical study of the hemoglobins of persons with sickle-cell anemia revealed the presence of an abnormal hemoglobin designated hemoglobin S. Hemoglobin S is composed of two normal alpha chains and two altered beta chains. A study of the amino acid sequence of the mutant beta chain revealed a single amino acid substitution; the glutamic acid at a certain position in the normal chain had been replaced by valine in the mutant chain. Several other mutant hemoglobins were discovered and their analyses showed a single amino acid substitution, compared with the hemoglobin present in "normal" persons. The mutants responsible for these variant hemoglobins evidently alter the genes so that a single amino acid difference appears in the mutant. Table I lists some of these ab-

TABLE I.—Amino Acid Substitutions in Abnormal Human Hemoglobins

Hemoglobin type	Substitution	Position in chain
	IN THE ALPHA CHAIN:	
I-G-Honolulu	Aspartic acid for lysine	16
Norfolk	Glutamine for glutamic acid	30
M-Boston	Aspartic acid for glycine	57
G-Philadelphia	Tyrosine for histidine	58
	Lysine for asparagine	68
	IN THE BETA CHAIN:	
S	Valine for glutamic acid	6
C	Lysine for glutamic acid	6
G-San Jose	Glycine for glutamic acid	7
E	Lysine for glutamic acid	26
M-Saskatoon	Tyrosine for histidine	63
Zurich	Arginine for histidine	63
M-Milwaukee-1	Glutamic acid for valine	67
D-Punjab	Glutamine for glutamic acid	121

normal hemoglobins. Hemoglobin I, for example, shows a substitution of aspartic acid for lysine at position No. 16 in the alpha chain. The beta chain of hemoglobin C has a lysine substituted for glutamic acid at position No. 6.

Further evidence for the genetic control of the amino acid sequences in polypeptide chains of proteins was obtained in 1964 by C. Yanofsky and his colleagues in their studies on E. coli. The enzyme tryptophan synthetase in E. coli consists of two polypeptide chains, designated A and B. A number of mutants exist that result in inactive forms of the enzyme, due to amino acid substitutions in the A chain. Precise genetic mapping of these mutants reveals a "colinearity," an exact linear correspondence between the mutants on the genetic map and the positions of amino acid substitutions in the altered A chain polypeptides. The colinearity of the genetic map and the polypeptide chains is convincing evidence that specific regions of a gene encode for the sequence of amino acids in polypeptide chains.

3. Translation of the DNA and RNA Codes.—The discovery of the ways in which the sequence of the nucleotides in the DNA of a chromosome is translated into the sequence of amino acids in a protein is one of the outstanding achievements of molecular biology. This is often called the transcription function of DNA to distinguish it from the duplication function in which DNA replicates itself (see above). A very short history will indicate the giant strides in this achievement. J. Hämmerling studied a single-celled alga, Acetabularia, which is differentiated into a cap, a stalk, and a nucleus-containing rhizome. When the stalk and the cap are cut off, the rhizome with its nucleus can regenerate a complete alga. This regeneration depends upon substances coming from the nucleus. Nevertheless, protein synthesis takes place also in the parts deprived of their connection with the nucleus, which indicates that the information contained in the nucleus is passed to the cytoplasm to be utilized there. J. Brachet and others found a close correlation between the amount of protein synthesis taking place and the amount of RNA present. Destruction of the RNA by means of the enzyme ribonuclease resulted in complete cessation of the protein synthesis. On the other hand, DNA synthesis was not necessary for protein synthesis.

There are three important chemical differences between RNA and DNA. First, the base thymine of DNA is replaced in RNA by uracil; secondly, the deoxyribose sugar of DNA is replaced by a ribose sugar in RNA; and thirdly, RNA molecules are usually single-stranded while DNA molecules are double-stranded.

The information contained in DNA is first transcribed into an RNA molecule, from which the information is subsequently translated into protein. The hypothesis can be represented thus: DNA→RNA→Protein. Reverse transfer does not occur, i.e., there is no storage of information in the protein molecules, and no transcription of it back into nucleic acids. This is sometimes referred to as "the central dogma" of molecular genetics.

Tiny particles in the cytoplasm of cells have been identified as the sites of protein synthesis. These particles, called ribosomes, consist of both RNA and protein. Besides the ribosomal RNA, another kind of RNA, called messenger RNA (mRNA), found both in the nucleus and in the cytoplasm, serves as a carrier of the genetic information from the nuclear DNA to the ribosomal RNA. The sequence of the genetic "letters," A (adenine), T (thymine), C (cytosine), and G (guanine) in the DNA is first transcribed into the corresponding sequence of the "letters" A (adenine), U (uracil), C, and G in the messenger RNA. This occurs through the action of the enzyme RNA polymerase. This enzyme synthesizes RNA in a test tube from a mixture of the A, U, C, and G bases, but it does so only in the presence of a "primer" DNA. The sequence of the bases in the primer is copied in the RNA. The steps involved in this process are: (1) the DNA double helix unwinds by breaking the hydrogen bonds between the corresponding bases in the paired strands; (2) the RNA polymerase forms the bonds between the RNA bases that are complementary to the bases in the DNA; and (3) the messenger RNA thus formed passes into the cytoplasm and becomes attached to a ribosome.

The information contained in the sequence of the bases ("letters") in the messenger RNA is then translated into a sequence of amino acids in a protein. This requires the presence of still another molecule that is capable of recognizing the code for a specific amino acid, and selectively making the amino acid available at the right point in the protein synthesis, a "soluble" RNA fraction within cells that can bind amino acids. Soluble or transfer RNA (sRNA or tRNA) is a single-stranded molecule that forms about 20% of the total cellular RNA. If amino acids and a source of energy (usually ATP) are added to a mixture of transfer RNA's, reversible binding of the amino acids to the RNA molecules occurs. Furthermore, each amino acid is bonded to a specific transfer RNA molecule by a specific activating enzyme. There are at least 20 different transfer RNA's and activating enzymes that correspond to the 20 amino acids commonly found in proteins. The amino acid-transfer RNA complex becomes attached to the ribosome with its messenger RNA molecule; the addition of the amino acid to the growing polypeptide chain then occurs. A sequence of bases (anticodon) on the transfer RNA molecule pairs with a complementary sequence (codon) on the messenger RNA molecule, which is "held" in the correct position by the ribosome. Once the "recognition" has occurred, a peptide bond is formed between the amino acid bound to the transfer RNA and the growing polypeptide chain. The process of protein synthesis is represented diagrammatically in fig. 13.

4. The Genetic Code.—The genetic "alphabet" of the DNA bases contains four "letters"—A, T, C, and G. How do these four letters specify, or "code," for 20 different amino acids? If a single letter coded for an amino acid, only four amino acids could be specified. If two bases were needed to specify an amino acid, then 16 different combinations could be constructed, again an insufficient number (20 amino acids must be accounted for). Combase mutates to a punctuation mark, the resulting sequence will be complete nonsense functionally.

The third possibility is a nonoverlapping, nonpunctuated code, in which the reading starts from a specific point. In all organisms studied in this respect this is the method of coding used. If the reading of the genetic message begins at a fixed place in a DNA strand, then the addition or the removal of a single "letter" will alter the message read from that point on. Suppose that the DNA message read from left to right reveals the triplets GAC, TCA, and TTA (which are, of course, transcribed in the RNA code as CUG, AGU, AAU).' Deletion of the first T alters the "reading frame" so that triplets GAC, CAT, TA ... will be read. The first triplet is unchanged, but all the remaining triplets may specify wrong amino acids. The chemical addition of a base to the sequence likewise shifts the reading frame; such a mutant will also specify wrong amino acids beyond the point of the base addition. If an original mutant resulted from the deletion of a base from the DNA, the addition of a base at a point beyond the first mutation would restore the "reading frame" of the DNA sequence, and would result in nearly normal function. In the bacteriophage T$_4$, assume the original wild-type phage DNA sequence within the rII region reads ACT GGC TAG CTG TCA TCG .... Deletion of the C in the second triplet results in the following triplets being read: ACT, GGT, AGC, TGT, CAT, CG. ... This is an rII mutant. The subsequent addition of a base (A) between the third and fourth mutant triplets results in the following sequence: ACT GGT AGC ATG TCA TCG.... Note that the first, fifth, and sixth triplets are identical to those in the original wild-type phage. Only the second, third, and fourth triplets are altered, and the reading of the code from the fourth triplet on will be identical to that in the wild-type phage. Frequently suppressor mutations occur in proximity to other mutations and restore the reading frame of the DNA sequence, thereby allowing a sequence of amino acids differing only slightly from the original one to be formed in the protein.

The triplets that actually encode for different amino acids have been discovered by experiments in cell-free in vitro systems of E. coli. In 1961 M. W. Nirenberg and J. Matthaei reported that they obtained ribosomes of E. coli by centrifugation of a suspension of broken-up cells. The ribosomes were added to a solution of transfer RNA's and enzymes, an energy generating ATP system, and radioactively labeled amino acids. After a short time the mixture was found to contain a protein. This protein was analyzed and found to include a high percentage of radioactive amino acids. If the system is treated with ribonuclease, an enzyme that degrades RNA, no protein synthesis occurs. Similarly, if precautions are taken to exclude any messenger RNA from the system, no protein synthesis occurs. Extraneous RNA can be added, and it stimulates the system to produce protein.

In order to decipher the code it was necessary to synthesize messenger RNA's of a known sequence, introduce these molecules into their in vitro protein synthetic system, and determine the amino acid sequence of the resulting proteins. A knowledge of the base sequence in the messenger RNA and the resulting amino acid sequence in protein reveals the code for each amino acid. While determining the amino acid sequence of protein was feasible, the synthesis of a messenger RNA molecule of known sequence was then impossible. The biochemical means for this synthesis of some messenger RNA's were provided by the experiments of S. Ochoa and L. A. Heppel in the late 1950s. They isolated an enzyme, polynucleotide phosphorylase, which randomly couples nucleotides together without the presence of a DNA primer. RNA molecules of a known sequence could be produced in only one way—the enzyme was presented with a solution that contained only adenylic acid or only uridylic acid. Under these conditions RNA chains consisting of only A or U were synthesized. If two nucleotides, C and U, are present in the mixture, an RNA chain will be synthesized with various sequences of C and U whose frequencies will depend upon the initial concentration of the two nucleotides. Addition of poly-U RNA to the in vitro protein synthesizing system resulted in the production of a polypeptide that contained only the amino acid phenylalanine. The triplet UUU

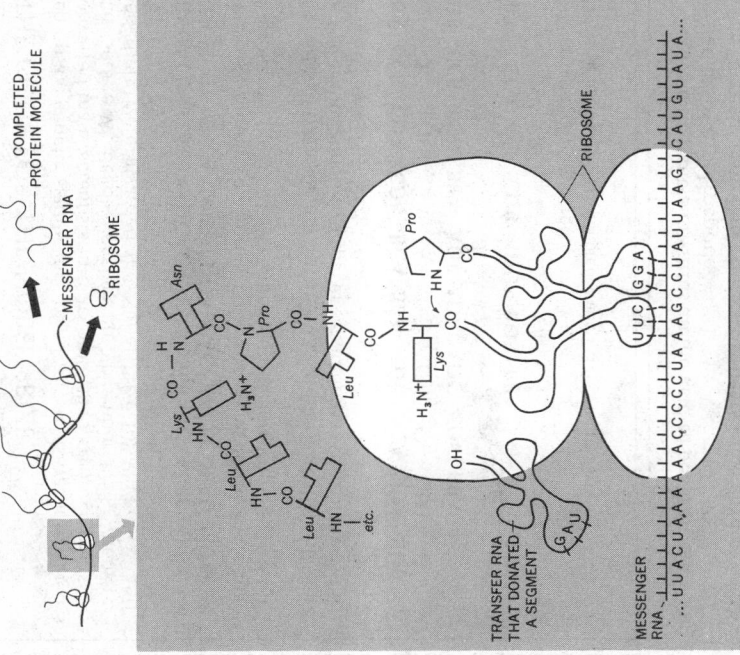

FIG. 13.—SYNTHESIS OF PROTEIN

FROM T. JUKES, "MOLECULES AND EVOLUTION," © 1966; REPRODUCED BY PERMISSION OF COLUMBIA UNIVERSITY PRESS

(Top) The messenger RNA shown with several ribosomes "reading" its message, the translation occurring from left to right, and the polypeptide chain growing as the ribosome proceeds along the messenger RNA. (Bottom) A highly magnified ribosome in the process of "reading" a messenger RNA molecule. The ribosome has just "read" an AAG sequence on the messenger RNA, and a specific transfer RNA molecule moves into place carrying the amino acid lysine which is then added to the polypeptide chain. Next in position is a transfer RNA molecule carrying the amino acid proline to be transferred to the growing polypeptide chain. The ribosome moves from left to right along the messenger RNA molecule. Each ribosome has two binding sites for transfer RNA: one that holds the growing polypeptide chain and a second for positioning a new transfer RNA molecule for processing

binations of three "letters" allow 64 different "words" to be constructed, more than the necessary minimal number. A three-letter, "triplet," code could be constructed in at least three different ways: (1) with "words" overlapping; (2) with words not overlapping and punctuated; and (3) with words not overlapping and not punctuated. An overlapping code is composed of words that overlap each other, i.e., the letters of any given word may belong to one, two, or three "words." For example, the DNA might contain the sequence A G C G T T A C G; the first "word" is AGC, the second CGT, and so on. This type of code is improbable, because of the restrictions it would place upon the possible sequence of amino acids in protein. As the example above shows, if the first word is AGC, the second word must begin with C, etc. Examination of amino acid sequences in a protein such as hemoglobin indicates that any amino acid can follow any other—a possibility not allowed for by an overlapping code.

If the code is nonoverlapping, a problem of distinguishing words from each other arises. DNA contains no spaces separating the words as in written sentences; therefore, there must be other indications of specific starting points for messenger RNA synthesis. The base sequence AGC AGC AGC ... could be punctuated by the presence of a fourth base, T, between each AGC triplet. This would reduce the number of possible triplets to 27. That a punctuated code of this type is not realized is seen from the evidence of the degeneracy in the code for some amino acids. The "degeneracy" means that some amino acids are coded for by more than one triplet, and a punctuated code does not allow enough words. A second objection to this type of code comes from a consideration of the effects of mutation on the coding sequence. If one of the punctuation marks mutates to another base, or a coding

is the code for the amino acid phenylalanine, corresponding to the sequence AAA in the DNA. Poly-A and poly-C messenger RNA's were found to code for lysine and proline, respectively.

Other triplets could be tested for their coding abilities by synthesizing messenger RNA molecules with varying proportions of the two bases. For example, if a mixture of the two bases U and C in a 5:1 proportion are synthesized into RNA, the possible triplets and their probable frequency in the synthetic messenger RNA can be easily determined. The triplet UUU will be most common and appear with the frequency $(\frac{5}{6} \times \frac{5}{6} \times \frac{5}{6})$; the triplets UUC, UCU, CUU will appear in the frequencies of $(\frac{5}{6} \times \frac{5}{6} \times \frac{1}{6})$; the triplets UCC, CUC, CCU will be the next most frequent and appear with a frequency of $(\frac{5}{6} \times \frac{1}{6} \times \frac{1}{6})$; while the triplet CCC should appear only $\frac{1}{216}$ of the time. A messenger RNA of this composition should result in the incorporation into protein of eight different amino acids. In fact only four amino acids were present in the protein produced; this means that several of these triplets encode for the same amino acid, and therefore that the code is degenerate.

The RNA code triplets (or codons) and the amino acids for which they stand are shown in Table II. Triplets have recently been discovered that encode for starting and for stopping the synthesis of protein chains in E. coli. Many proteins of E. coli begin with the amino acid methionine. Two different transfer RNA's for methionine are known to exist, only one of which functions to initiate protein synthesis. After synthesis of the protein, an enzyme may remove a portion of the beginning of the chain to eliminate the obligatory methionine molecule. The second transfer

TABLE II.—*The Genetic Code: Nucleotide Triplets (Codons) Specifying Different Amino Acids in Protein Chains* (after F. H. C. Crick)*

DNA triplet	RNA triplet	Amino acid	DNA triplet	RNA triplet	Amino acid
AAA	UUU	Phenylalanine	ATA	UAU	Tyrosine
AAG	UUC		ATG	UAC	
AAT	UUA	Leucine	ATT	UAA	(Termination: end of specification)
AAC	UUG		ATC	UAG	
GAA	CUU		ACT	UGA	
GAG	CUC		ACA	UGU	Cysteine
GAT	CUA		ACG	UGC	
GAC	CUG		ACC	UGG	Tryptophan
TAA	AUU	Isoleucine (Ileu)	GCA	CGU	Arginine
TAG	AUC		GCG	CGC	
TAT	AUA		GCT	CGA	
TAC	AUG	Methionine	GCC	CGG	
CAA	GUU	Valine	TCT	AGA	
CAG	GUC		TCC	AGG	
CAT	GUA		GTA	CAU	Histidine
CAC	GUG		GTG	CAC	
AGA	UCU	Serine	GTT	CAA	Glutamine (Gln)
AGG	UCC		GTC	CAG	
AGT	UCA		TTA	AAU	Asparagine (Asn)
AGC	UCG		TTG	AAC	
TCA	AGU		TTT	AAA	Lysine
TCG	AGC		TTC	AAG	
GGA	CCU	Proline	CTA	GAU	Aspartic acid
GGG	CCC		CTG	GAC	
GGT	CCA		CTT	GAA	Glutamic acid
GGC	CCG		CTC	GAG	
TGA	ACU	Threonine	CCA	GGU	Glycine
TGG	ACC		CCG	GGC	
TGT	ACA		CCT	GGA	
TGC	ACG		CCC	GGG	
CGA	GCU	Alanine			
CGG	GCC				
CGT	GCA				
CGC	GCG				

*The columns may be read: The DNA triplet is transcribed into an RNA triplet, which then directs the production of an amino acid.

RNA for methionine allows this amino acid to be incorporated into the middle of a polypeptide.

Termination of protein synthesis appears to be effected by three different RNA triplets: UAA, UAG, UGA. These triplets were discovered as mutations that produced premature cessation of protein synthesis in many different genes. The exact mechanism of polypeptide chain termination is not known, although the action of a special transfer RNA molecule is suspected.

5. **The Operon and Gene Action.**—The evidence accumulated in genetics makes it virtually certain that not all the genes present in a cell are active in directing the specific processes of protein synthesis. Gene action can be switched on or off, depending on the position of a cell in the body, the stage of body development, as well as on the external environment.

The control of the gene activity has been elucidated in E. coli by J. Monod and F. Jacob (1961). A culture of these bacteria growing on a minimal medium is able to synthesize the amino acids needed to construct the proteins from carbohydrates and a nitrogen source. The synthesis requires the presence of certain enzymes whose activities can be detected in a growing culture. If the culture of bacteria is supplied with certain amino acids, the synthesis of the enzymes that synthesize these amino acids is quickly arrested. This phenomenon is known as repression, and the enzymes affected are repressible enzymes. The pathway for the synthesis of the amino acid arginine in E. coli is a good example. This synthesis involves three steps and three separate enzymes:

glutamic acid —enz A→ ornithine —enz B→ citrulline —enz C→ arginine

When arginine is present in the medium none of the three enzymes involved in this process are detected, but if arginine is removed all three enzymes rapidly appear. The end product of this pathway, arginine, controls the production of either ornithine or citrulline to the medium has no effect. A related process involves the production of enzymes whose substrates are not always present in cells. E. coli normally utilizes the simple sugar glucose as an energy and carbon source. If a culture is instead supplied with the disaccharide lactose, the latter must be degraded to galactose and glucose before it can be utilized by the cell. The presence of lactose in the medium induces the synthesis of three enzymes: beta galactoside permease, which transports lactose through the cell membrane into the cytoplasm; beta galactosidase, which catalyzes the degradation of lactose into galactose and glucose; and galactoside-transacetylase, the exact function of which is not understood. Lactose is required

---

BREAKING THE CODE FOR THE NOBEL PRIZE

During the 1950s when research on the genetic significance of nucleic acids was intensified, the riddle of the genetic code converted many scientists into accomplished cryptographers.

Among the congratulations that George W. Beadle received in November 1958, when he, Edward L. Tatum, and Joshua Lederberg were awarded the Nobel Prize for Physiology and Medicine, was the following wire from a colleague, the virologist Max Delbrück:

ADBACBBDBADACDCBBABCBCDACBBDBBDBADAAAACBCCBADBBDDCCDAACDADBADDAAAACBBABDC
CDBCCBBDBBBAADBADAADCCDCBBADDCCACAADBBDBDDABBACCAACBCBDBADDBDBBBA

*In the original message, ADC=C erroneously appeared.

From G. W. and M. Beadle, *The Language of Life*, p. 193, Doubleday and Co., Inc., New York, N.Y., 1966.

Divining Delbrück's intent—a message hidden in a triplet code analogous to the molecular codes of DNA and RNA—Beadle broke up the 123-letter communiqué into triplets, like the genetic codons.

A botanist friend of Beadle's, David Smith, observed that the BBA triplet was the only one with a B in the middle, indicating that it functioned as a spacer separating words. That was the key. After considerable effort the message was resolved:

ADB	ACB	BDB	ADA	CDC	BBA	BCB	CDA	CDB	BCA	BBA	ADC	ACA	BDA	BDB
B	R	E	A	K		T	H	I	S		C	O	D	E

BBA	ACA	ACB	BBA	BDC	CCB	BDB	BBA	ADB	ADA	CDC	BBA
	O	R		G	I	V	E	B	A	C	K

DDC	ACA	ADB	BDB	DDA	BBA	CCA	ACB	CDB	ADD*	BDB	BBA
N	O	B	E	L		P	R	I	Z	E	

for the synthesis of these enzymes, which degrade lactose; this phenomenon is termed induction.

An understanding of the mechanisms underlying induction and repression has come from studies of mutants affecting the enzymes and the control of their synthesis. Mutations that result in loss of activity of the beta galactosidase and permease enzymes have been isolated, and their positions on the *E. coli* chromosome map have been determined. The mutant genes (termed z^- and y^-, respectively) proved to be located next to each other on the chromosome. Another class of mutations has been discovered that affects the control of the induction of these enzymes. These mutants synthesize the enzymes even in the absence of lactose and are termed i^-. The i mutants are located close to but not adjacent to the genes for beta galactosidase and permease. The i mutants affect the rate of synthesis of messenger RNA by genes that encode for the structure of the enzymes. Two classes of genes, structural and regulatory, must therefore be recognized. It is believed that the z^+ and y^+ genes encode for the amino acid sequences of the two enzymes. The i^+ gene produces a repressor that prevents the genes z and y from functioning. The i^- gene allows for the continuous (constitutive) synthesis of the enzymes, because of the absence of an effective repressor.

Still another class of mutations, operator mutants, has been identified. They lie in the chromosome very close to the z gene. Operator constitutive (o^c) mutants allow the z^+ and y^+ genes to produce enzymes regardless of the action of the i gene. None of the enzymes is ever produced if an o^o mutant replaces the o^+ or o^c genes. Both types of operator mutants must be located close to the structural genes z and y to exert their effects. The wild-type *E. coli* has the genotype $i^+ o^+ z^+ y^+$ for the genes in question, and the enzymes are inducible. The presence of an i^- or o^c gene results in uninterrupted production of the enzymes.

A scheme explaining these observations is shown in fig. 14. The part of the chromosome containing the genes concerned is divided

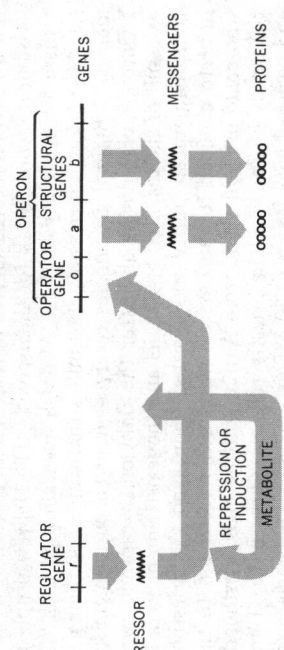

FROM F. JACOB AND J. MONOD, "JOURNAL OF MOLECULAR BIOLOGY" (1961); REPRODUCED BY PERMISSION OF ACADEMIC PRESS, INC.

FIG. 14.—A MODEL OF THE OPERON AND ITS RELATION TO THE REGULATOR GENE (see text)

into two regions, one of which includes the operator and structural genes. This is termed an operon. The other part contains only the regulator gene. The regulator gene need not be located close to the operon. The regulator gene produces some substance, a repressor, which affects a second gene, an operator. There are several lines of evidence that suggest that the repressor substance is a protein molecule. It would be necessary for such a molecule to have at least two areas or sites that interact with the operator gene and/or the metabolite to produce structural changes.

6. Gene Action and Differentiation.—The orderly complexity of the mechanism of cell division insures that a dividing cell will give rise to two daughter cells with exactly similar chromosomes. Yet as a fertilized egg cell gives rise to more and more body cells, these cells differentiate and become distinct from each other. A nerve cell, a muscle cell, a liver cell, and others are strikingly different; if each contains exactly the same chromosomes and genes, how are these differences explained? The same genes are present in all the daughter cells, but different genes become active in different types of cells.

There are at least three mutually reinforcing kinds of evidence for the identity of the gene complements in different cells of the body of an individual, and even in different individuals of the same species. The nuclei of the resting cells and the chromosomes of the dividing cells may look rather dissimilar in different tissues, and yet (with the exception of some polyploid cells) they contain the same amounts of DNA. This amount, of course, doubles in the interval between successive cell divisions. Very interesting, though not quite unambiguous, results were obtained in transplantations of nuclei from cells of developing embryos into eggs of frogs and of toads. The nucleus of an egg cell may be removed by microsurgery, rendering the enucleated egg incapable of normal development. When a nucleus taken from a cell of a blastula is injected into an enucleated egg, normal development ensues. If a nucleus is taken from a cell at a later stage and injected into an enucleated egg, normal development may or may not result. In many organisms a part of the body may regenerate the whole; a single cell from the root of a carrot can give rise to a whole plant.

The operon model (see above) furnishes a plausible explanation of how different genes may be active at different times in different tissues. Very suggestive evidence of such variable gene activity comes from observations on the giant chromosomes present in the cells of larval salivary glands and some other tissues of certain flies. At certain stages of the development of a larva, some of the stainable discs or bands in these chromosomes expand, and at other stages contract again. The expansion is apparently due to a localized uncoiling of the gene strings composing the giant chromosomes. The expanded portions of a chromosome are called "puffs" (fig. 15). There is good evidence that the bands in the giant chromosomes correspond to small groups of genes or even to single genes. Detailed observations on the giant chromosomes in different tissues of the larva of the midge *Chironomus* showed the banding patterns to be identical throughout, but the puffing patterns to vary from tissue to tissue. The puffing patterns of a tissue also varied with the developmental stage of the insect in a precise manner.

More direct evidence that puffs represent specific gene activity was obtained from studies of a glue substance excreted by the salivary glands of *Chironomus* larvae. The ability to synthesize this substance is due to the presence of a single, dominant gene. Fly larvae that possess this gene

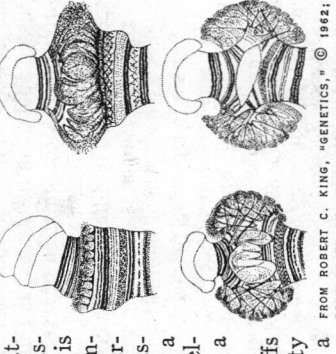

FROM ROBERT C. KING, "GENETICS," © 1962; REPRODUCED BY PERMISSION OF OXFORD UNIVERSITY PRESS, INC.

FIG. 15.—THE DEVELOPMENT OF A CHROMOSOMAL PUFF IN A GIANT CHROMOSOME OF A SALIVARY GLAND CELL OF A MIDGE (CHIRONOMUS) LARVA

have a puff at a specific region of the chromosome while flies homozygous for the recessive allele have no puff and do not secrete the substance. Fly larvae heterozygous for the gene secrete the substance, but an analysis of the salivary chromosomes shows that only half of the chromosomal region is puffed. The molting hormone, ecdysone, causes a specific sequence of puffs to form and regress. The hormone seems to function only to initiate the sequence, since the development of later puffs is dependent upon the synthesis of protein.

The study of the mechanisms of cellular differentiation was advanced by the discovery of nitrogen-rich proteins associated with DNA. These proteins, called histones, have the capability to affect the structure of the genetic material so as to allow or repress the gene activity. The lateral loops of the so-called lampbrush chromosomes (see CELL) in developing amphibian oocytes react to histones by contracting. The rate of RNA synthesis in lampbrush chromosomes is greatest when the lateral loops are fully expanded.

The investigation of histone effects was extended to mammalian cells by A. E. Mirsky, V. Allfrey, and their colleagues (1957 and after). Addition of histones to isolated calf-thymus nuclei inhibits various synthetic reactions, such as ATP and RNA synthesis. The removal of histones from nuclei results in enhanced RNA synthesis. Electron microscopic examination of untreated nuclei shows that the genetic material exists in two discrete states: a compact, darkly staining mass and a diffuse, poorly staining matrix. It has been demonstrated that the overwhelming majority of RNA synthesis occurs in areas of diffuse genetic material. The addition of histones results in an increase in the amount of compact genetic material, while the removal of histones results in the dispersal of the genetic material. This work indicates that changes in the appearance of the genetic material will result in new patterns of RNA synthesis.

The mechanism of the histone effects was studied by examining chemical reactions that affect chemical groups other than the amino acids contained in histones. Measurements of the rate of acetate metabolism showed that as acetyl groups ($CH_3—C=O$) were attached to histone, a corresponding rise in the rate of RNA synthesis by the nuclei was observed. A similar correlation was noted in studies of histone acetylation and RNA synthesis in the salivary gland chromosomes of *Chironomus* larvae. Moreover, both chemical processes could be detected at a single puff site in the chromosomes. The interpretation of these results is that histone acetylation causes some structural change in the genetic material that allows more genes to produce messenger RNA.

Reversible addition and subtraction of acetyl groups in histones may, then, control the gene action in development. Several problems remain to be solved. Histones may control the general gene activity, but development involves the activation and repression of specific gene systems. At present no mechanism is known that would give the needed specificity to histones. The reversible acetylation of histones controls its regulatory activity, but what controls the rate of histone acetylation? The operon model discussed above can be utilized as a first step in an approach to these problems. A combination of several operons into a complex regulatory system gives a system whose properties remotely approach those observed in differentiating cells. The inescapable conclusion is that an organism is a highly complex system, composed of many tissues each of which interacts with the others and with the environment in a precise, predictable manner.

See also references under "Gene" in the Index.

BIBLIOGRAPHY.—See Bibliography in the article HEREDITY. J. Bonner, *The Molecular Biology of Development* (1965); W. Braun, *Bacterial Genetics* (1965); E. A. Carlson, *The Gene: a Critical History* (1966); R. Clowes, *The Structure of Life* (1967); W. Hayes, *The Genetics of Bacteria and Their Viruses* (1964); P. E. Hartman and S. R. Suskind, *Gene Action* (1965); T. H. Jukes, *Molecules and Evolution* (1966); R. Sager and F. J. Ryan, *Cell Heredity* (1961); G. Stent, *Molecular Biology of Bacterial Viruses* (1963).
In *Scientific American, see* W. Beermann and U. Clever, "Chromosome Puffs" (April 1964); S. Benzer, "The Fine Structure of the Gene" (January 1962); J. Cairns, "The Bacterial Chromosome" (January 1966); F. H. C. Crick, "The Genetic Code" (October 1962) and "The Genetic Code: III" (October 1966); R. W. Holley, "The Nucleotide Sequence of a Nucleic Acid" (February 1966); F. Jacob and E. L. Wollman, "Viruses and Genes" (June 1961); M. W. Nirenberg, "The Genetic Code: II" (March 1963); W. B. Wood and R. S. Edgar, "Building a Bacterial Virus" (July 1967).
(T. Dγ., F. H. C. R.; R. C. Rr.)

GENEALOGY is the study of family origins and history and the compilation of pedigrees and lists of ancestors (Gr. *genos*, family, and *logos*, theory). Closely allied to heraldry (*q.v.*), it is also very useful to the general historian. It is international in its scope and interest and, though now principally confined to European and American countries, has been studied in all civilized parts of the world. Wherever there has been a hereditary monarchy or aristocracy (*e.g.*, China and Japan), genealogy has been a necessity as well as a pastime. In Muslim countries descent from the Prophet Mohammed and claims on the caliphate have always had a political as well as a religious significance. In non-Christian countries the frequent practice of polygamy, the legal status given to concubinage and the habit of adoption (as in India) have added problems of their own.

Because genealogy is an international science, attempts have been made to secure a uniform system of signs and abbreviations for universal use in constructing pedigrees. The first International Congress of Heraldry and Genealogy, held in Barcelona in 1928, greatly helped to stimulate interest on a world-wide basis. Many countries now possess societies for promoting genealogical research, and some, for instance Germany, have even established university professorships in it.

The genealogist needs to have some knowledge of paleography, to help him decipher ancient records (*e.g.*, parish registers and rolls, like the so-called Roll of Battle Abbey); and of chronology, so that he can recognize variations in the calendars and assess regnal years, etc. A knowledge of Latin, as well as of the modern languages, is especially helpful. Old deeds, charters, seals, coins, medals, banners, tapestries (for example, the Bayeux tapestry), paintings, tombs, gravestones and monumental tablets such as brasses may also provide valuable information.

Genealogy no longer concerns itself exclusively with the lineage of the highly placed, but has an equal concern for all sorts and conditions of men. It furthermore possesses a genetic interest insofar as certain abilities and characteristics tend to repeat themselves in successive generations.

Ancient Genealogy.—Ancient genealogy probably passed through three stages. At first, knowledge of family relationships was passed on by oral tradition, probably in the form of epic poems (like those of Homer or the Nordic sagas) and songs sung over the campfire. The invention of writing allowed inscriptions to be made which could give more permanent information of kings and their reigns (*e.g.*, the stele of Hammurabi and, for the ancient Egyptian kings, the Palermo stone). Finally the use of papyrus and later parchment made it possible to keep fuller records still. The extent and variety of these records are difficult to estimate, since many of them must have perished.

Scribes in Egypt kept careful records of their kings, queens and priests (as in the Turin papyrus): they divided their rulers into dynasties, each dynasty being a series of rulers descended from the same ancestor and having some family relationship to each other. Herodotus (ii, 143) moreover describes how the priests of Thebes in Egypt had a collection of 345 wooden statues, each one of which they claimed to represent an ancestor of a distinct generation. Assyrian records survive in their *limmu* lists.

The Hebrew people had a taste for genealogy, and the Midrash even affirmed that "God lets his Shekinah dwell only in families that can prove their genealogies." Biblical genealogies received great encouragement (*see* I Chron. i–viii) during and after the Babylonian captivity when, as result of the teaching of Ezekiel and the legislation of Ezra and Nehemiah, racial purity was insisted upon; and the priesthood, hitherto confined to the Levites, was further restricted to those who could prove descent from Aaron, and the high priesthood to the family of Zadok. The priestly rolls were kept in the Temple and perished with it in A.D. 70. This sacerdotal and racial exclusiveness excited some protest—as in the Book of Ruth, where a Moabitess is claimed as an ancestress of David.

The two genealogies of Christ given in the Gospels, tracing his descent from Abraham (Matt. i, 1–16) and from Adam (Luke iii, 23–38), are obviously artificially constructed and hopelessly contradictory. They are inserted to affirm the Davidic descent of the Messiah. In the Christian world, however, the Bible helped to preserve genealogical interest, and printed copies were often the family repository for recording births, marriages and deaths. The custom of setting out family descent in the form of a tree with branches is imitated from ecclesiastical representations of Christ's genealogy inspired by Isa. xi, 1.

Greek genealogies are as lengthy as biblical ones, but it was descent from the gods or heroes that obsessed the Greeks. Thus Solon was supposed to be descended from Poseidon, and Hippocrates claimed to be 20th in descent from Heracles (who is credited with 72 sons and seems to have fathered more genealogies than any other Greek personage) and 19th in descent from the god Asclepius. Asclepius was also supposed to be an ancestor of Aristotle, Zeus of Thucydides (through Ajax), Achilles of Miltiades and Daedalus of Socrates. The poet Hesiod wrote a *Theogonia* or genealogy of the gods; this however was a form of theology rather than genealogy proper. A catalogue of women who married immortals is also attributed to him.

It was in the study of the descent of heroes from gods and of human families from heroes that the historical purpose

GENEALOGY

came to replace the theological. Genealogy had a recognized place in Greek history from the 5th century B.C. when the Ionian Hecataeus wrote his *Genealogiai*, in which he examined critically a number of family traditions, and his *Journey Round the World* (*Periodes Ges*) which also contained genealogical matter. Genealogy as such was subordinate to the main purpose of Herodotus and occurs only incidentally in his history; it may however be inferred that he had access to the pedigrees of many Athenian families, as well as to other sources such as the Spartan king-lists. He could trace the pedigrees of the Alcmaeonidae and the Pisistratidae; and to be so well-informed about Miltiades and Cimon he must have drawn on some copious source for the history of the Philaidae. The pedigree of that family is known to have been traced as far back as Ajax by the Athenian genealogist Pherecydes (mid 5th century?).

Genealogy as the Greeks practised it was, however, unscientific by modern standards: much of it consisted in mere schematization of traditional material (such as was to be found in epic poetry) inspired by an awakened interest in chronology. The Spartan king-lists cannot have been reliable in detail if Herodotus and Ephorus could differ on the question to which of the Spartan royal houses Lycurgus belonged. When the Greeks began to study chronology on a panhellenic scale, the pedigree of local (especially royal) families could be extended to include fictitious members, reckoned in uniformly estimated generations to bring them in line with dates established by other means. Fictions of a more sophisticated kind included names such as Eunomos for the father of Lycurgus (*q.v.*), a reference to Lycurgus law-giving. Royal and noble families took their family names from some heroic or celebrated ancestor (*e.g.*, the Pisistradidae from Pisistratus). The two Spartan royal houses were named after Agis and Eurypontus, and it is doubtful whether all the names preceding these eponyms in the Spartan royal pedigrees are historical figures rather than inventions to fill a chronological hiatus.

The Romans studied genealogy for the distinction between patricians and plebeians (*see* PATRICIANS). When a divine origin was desired, Troy was often the inspiration: thus Julius Caesar boasted of his descent from Aeneas and therefore from Venus. Something of the great Roman families, such as the Fabii, the Cornelii, the Valerii, the Aemilii, the Sulpicii and the Claudii, and the offices that they held is known from the *fasti consulares*. The Claudii, however, were said to have placed their escutcheons in the temple of Bellona; and the Julii possessed a magnificent family shrine at Bovillae.

Roman male children were given at least two names: the *prae-nomen* or forename, which was personal; and the *nomen* or "gentile" name, standing for the clan or family (*gens*). A third name, the *cognomen*, originally an individual's nickname indicating some personal or physical peculiarity, might be transmitted to his descendants and so come to designate a branch of a *gens*. A second *cognomen*, later distinguished as *agnomen*, might indicate either some personal achievement, as an honorific, or the *gens* from which a man had been adopted into another (as when the son of Lucius Aemilius Paullus, adopted by Publius Cornelius Scipio, was named Publius Cornelius Scipio Aemilianus). Roman women, on the other hand, were generally known only by a *nomen* or by some variant of a *cognomen* (*e.g.*, Agrippina, daughter of Marcus Vipsanius Agrippa).

Ancient genealogy suffers from four marked defects: first, it can hardly be disentangled from mythology; secondly, it is fragmentary, frequently unreliable and contradictory; thirdly, it confuses tribal origins with individual names (as in Genesis); and fourthly, it is artificial in that often its main purpose is to offer a descent that would allow a person to qualify for office, priestly or secular. It is in fact easier in ancient history to describe the class system, its rights and privileges, than to give authentic information about those involved in it.

The Feudal World and the Ancien Régime.—When the hereditary transmission of fiefs had become established practice (*see* FEUDALISM; also ENTAIL) questions of descent and kinship became of great political importance. Many of the privileges of the nobility and gentry, moreover, depended on birth: an ennobled commoner, for instance, was less eligible for certain positions than his son or grandson. In Germany, in particular, the notion of *Ebenbürtigkeit* (equality of birth) required the consorts of princes to be themselves of princely descent: otherwise the marriage had to be morganatic and its issue could not accede to the father's dignities. In France proofs of ancient nobility were generally required from candidates for admission to orders of knighthood and chivalry. Apart from these matters, there was also the practice in the middle ages of resorting to genealogists for proofs of consanguinity in order to obtain the annulment of a marriage—as when Louis VII of France wanted to be rid of Eleanor of Aquitaine. In matters of royal succession, pedigrees were submitted by the 13 claimants to the Scottish throne in 1291, and by Edward III of England as claimant to the French crown on the extinction of the male line of Philip IV of France.

Dynastic preoccupations thus to a great extent underlie the great compilations of princely genealogy printed in Europe from the 16th century onward: for instance those of Benvenuto di San Giorgio on the house of Montferrat (1515); of Philibertus Pin-gonius on the houses of Saxony and of Savoy (1521); of Hierony-mus Gebweiler (1527) and of Marquardus Hergott (1737–38) on the Habsburgs; of Jacques de Meyer on the counts of Flanders (1531); and of Edmond du Boulay (1547) and of François de Rosières (1580) on the house of Lorraine. Rosières, indeed, was imprisoned for having traced the descent of the house of Lorraine from the Carolingian kings of France at the moment when the succession to the Valois branch of the Capetians was precarious. An encyclopaedic work, still useful, was the *Histoire généalogique de la maison royale de France* (1674; 3rd ed. 1726–33) by Father Anselme de Ste. Marie (Pierre de Guibours), which covers not only the royal houses of France and their descendants but also peers of France and officers of the crown. The help of Pierre d'Hozier and of Etienne Baluze was eagerly sought by French families anxious to assert themselves as more noble than others for reasons of precedence in Louis XIV's time, and the consequent rivalries sometimes led to allegations of forgery.

Of wider scope were the works of Reinerus Reineck, Hieronymus Henninges and Elias Reusner in the 16th century, of Nicolaus Ritterhusius, Jacob Wilhelm Imhof, Philipp Jakob Spener and Georg Lohmeier in the 17th and of Johann Hübner and Johann Christoph Gutterer in the 18th. The *Almanach de Gotha*, first published in 1763, continued as an annual providing genealogical information on sovereign, princely and ducal families till 1944.

Modern Genealogical Method.—Genealogy, like every other branch of knowledge, must now submit itself to recognized scientific methods and not merely discard the fables of the past but also frankly admit where descents hitherto accepted can no longer be satisfactorily proved. Tradition alone is not valid. Thus the descent of the Belgian princely family of Cröy from Adam (through Attila and Noah); of the French house of Lévis from Levi, son of Jacob; of the Wake baronets from Hereward the Wake; of the Feildings, earls of Denbigh, from the Habsburgs; of the Fitz-geralds, dukes of Leinster, from the Florentine Gherardini; of the Dillons from the Breton house of Léon; and of the numerous Welsh families from David, can no longer be maintained. Likewise numerous families formerly claiming descent from supposed companions in arms of William the Conqueror have had to revise their pedigrees drastically; the number of those whose ancestors' presence at the battle of Hastings can be authenticated does not amount to more than 20.

It became the special task of a school of modern genealogists led by J. H. Round (1854–1928) to separate legend from fact. Mere possession of a name similar to some well-known person or family does not of itself imply consanguinity. Each pedigree has to be carefully scrutinized and each link carefully attested.

For the beginner anxious to construct his own family tree the best method is to begin with himself and work back as far as he can. First he can examine family papers, letters, deeds, journals, diaries and even photographs, study the family Bible where it exists and make himself acquainted with any family traditions (these traditions may suggest from which part of the country his family originally came, but are not conclusive evidence in them-

GENEALOGY

selves). Next he must pass from private to public records, both church and state. The modern techniques of the photostat and the microfilm obviate the need for laborious transcription, and duplicates produced by these methods are invaluable if the originals are destroyed.

State records can be consulted at the public record office in Chancery lane, London. There are not only historic documents such as the Domesday Book (c. 1086–87) and Magna Carta (1215) but also all the exchequer rolls (from 1152), the chancery records (from 1199), the patent rolls, the manor court rolls,

Records and Publications in Great Britain.—The Registration act of 1836 made it compulsory in England and Wales to register births, marriages and deaths (as from July 1, 1837) and provided a central repository where certificates could be consulted. This is the general register office at Somerset house in London. For Scotland, where registration did not become obligatory till 1855, the records are at Edinburgh; for Ireland, where it was not adopted till 1864, at Dublin. Additional information can often be obtained by consulting the census returns, made every ten years (except for the year 1941) since 1801. The first three are purely statistical, but that of 1841, by giving the place of birth as well as the place of residence, have often helped to locate a family that may have moved from its original domicile. Censuses, however, which are less than 100 years old are regarded as confidential, stored at Somerset house and not open to public inspection.

For the centuries before the 19th, recourse to the parish registers is essential. In 1538 Thomas Cromwell made it compulsory for the parish priest to keep registers of baptisms, marriages and burials, and these are the main source of genealogical information to bridge the gulf between 1538 and 1837. These records are sometimes defective (especially during the period of the Commonwealth) and some have been destroyed by civil disturbance or in war, while some have simply vanished. Also they are not stored in one central repository but have to be consulted in the parishes concerned unless they have been copied out. The Society of Genealogists, however, possesses many transcripts of these registers and has also published a national index of copies. Moreover, as the Tudor clergy were not always punctilious or systematic in keeping their records, they were ordered (in 1597 and 1603) to send copies of their registers to the registrar of the diocese in which their parish was; and these "bishops' transcripts," still in the keeping of the diocesan registrars, form a valuable supplement to the registers themselves.

In the 17th and 18th centuries, when dissent became permanently organized outside the confines of the established church, records began to be kept by nonconformist ministers. Most of these, some dating back to 1642, are in the custody of the registrar general. There are also duplicates of the fine records kept by the Quakers from 1655 in the library at Friends' house, Euston Road, London. The Huguenot chapels kept their own records (available at Somerset house) and the Huguenot society has published many of their pedigrees. The Roman Catholics (there is an excellent Catholic Record society) and the Jews (who had been expelled from England in 1290 but who were readmitted during the Commonwealth) also preserved their own records.

The Church of England possesses two further stores of genealogical data of vital importance—marriage licences and wills. Before 1837 many well-to-do people preferred to be married by licence rather than after banns. These licences, usually obtained from the bishop of the diocese or from the vicar-general of the archbishop of Canterbury, remain in the custody of the church and are kept by the diocesan registries. Some have been published by the Harleian society and some by the British Record society.

Since the establishment of the court of probate in 1858 wills have been the exclusive concern of the state and can be consulted at the principal probate registry at Somerset house. Before that they came under the jurisdiction of the ecclesiastical courts where the testator died or held property. If he held property in more than one ecclesiastical jurisdiction, then his will was dealt with by the prerogative courts of Canterbury or York.

the fleet of fines (1190–1833), inquisitions, post mortems, etc. They are invaluable, especially for the medieval period, as most families were involved in litigation at some time or other. For many families the heraldic visitations carried out from 1530–1683 give interesting details, but they have to be regarded with reserve as the pedigrees were supplied by the families themselves and were often, despite obvious fabrications, uncritically accepted. They are kept at the College of Arms (established by royal charter in 1484), but many have been printed by the Harleian society.

Manuscript collections of genealogies extend back to the 15th and 16th centuries—to the days of William Worcester (d. 1482) and John Rous (d. 1491) and to the Elizabethan heralds like William Camden (1551–1623), who helped to found the first society of antiquaries (c. 1586). These and those of later centuries may be found in the College of Arms, in the Bodleian library or in the British museum. Record societies such as the Harleian (founded 1869), the British Record Society (founded 1888) and the Society of Genealogists (founded 1911) also possess manuscripts and collections of original documents.

Miscellaneous information can also be traced from the registers of schools and universities; from the records of the war office, the admiralty and the India office; and, for humbler folk, through indentures of apprenticeship (both the City of London archives and the Society of Genealogists have many original documents here), from churchwardens' accounts and, finally, from the poor law settlement certificates, the rate books, bastardy bonds, workhouse admissions and vagrancy orders.

Sir William Dugdale, who was perhaps the first English genealogist to quote references for the facts that he gave, produced the first peerage book, *The Baronage of England* (1675–76). This was followed by Arthur Collins' *Peerage of England* in 1709 (the prototype of Burke) and by Thomas Wotton's *English Baronetage* in 1727. John Debrett first issued his *Peerage of England, Scotland and Ireland* in 1802, and John Burke his *Peerage and Baronetage* in 1826 (after which he launched many kindred publications, such as the *Landed Gentry*). The greatest achievement in this field, however, was the *Complete Peerage* of G.E.C. (G. E. Cokayne), 1st ed., 1887–98, 2nd ed., 1910, with subsequent revisions under V. Gibbs, H. A. Doubleday and G. White.

Information can also be obtained by consulting the magazine of the Society of Genealogists (published since 1925) and such periodicals as *The Genealogist* (1877–1922) and *Miscellanea Genealogica et Heraldica* (1866–1938), as well as the histories of individual families, provided in ever increasing numbers since the 17th century.

United States and Canada.—In the United States, genealogical interest goes back to the early days of British settlement. The class system in the new world was at first as rigid as in the mother country and families were at great pains to preserve records of their descent. Virginia in particular was the cradle of U.S. genealogy, for there the first families of Virginia constituted themselves a planter aristocracy and used armorial bearings. Massachusetts came a good second (the first Historical society was founded there in 1791), while in Maryland the Catholic family of Calvert (created lords of Baltimore in 1625) established a semifeudal domain. The Puritan middle classes were equally assiduous in maintaining their family records. For humbler emigrants from England, however, there is often some difficulty in tracing ancestors, since the ships' lists, such as that of J. C. Hotten, which covers the period 1600–1700, give only the port from which the emigrant sailed, not the place from which he came.

The break with England added a new interest to U.S. genealogy and made people anxious to establish connection with the heroes of the Revolution—those who had signed the Declaration of Independence, the members of the Boston Tea Party and those who served in the continental forces in 1775–83. Later, with the mass immigration from Europe, genealogical interest once again focused on the old world, still mainly, but no longer exclusively, on Great Britain and Ireland. Census records in the U.S. go back to 1790; and the national archives at Washington are a valuable source of material (e.g., for pension records).
The Daughters of the American Revolution have more than 200,-

000 names recorded and filed in their archives at Memorial Continental hall in Washington and publish lineage books. The United States has been rather rich in this type of society, for, besides the Sons of Confederate Veterans, there are also the Sons and Daughters of the Pilgrims, the Society of the Cincinnati and the Holland Society of New York.

Another important centre of genealogical activity in the U.S. is Utah, where the Mormon community has preserved its records with the same skill and devotion as the Quakers in England. The Genealogical society of Salt Lake city has microfilmed the English census of 1851, and one of the best introductory works on English genealogical method, *Genealogical Research in England and Wales*, was published by two Mormons, D. E. Gardner and F. A. Smith (1956–59).

In the commonwealth the main centre of genealogical study has been Canada. For the French Canadians the standard work of reference is the abbé Cyprien Tanquay's *Dictionnaire généalogique des familles canadiennes*, seven volumes (1871–90 and revised editions); for English settlers, E. M. Chadwick, *Ontarian Families*, two volumes (1894–98). The Hudson's Bay Company Record society (founded 1938) has also published documents from the company's archives. There are also Société Généalogique Canadienne Française (founded 1943) and the Upper Canada Genealogical society (founded 1930).

BIBLIOGRAPHY.—For an elementary introduction to English genealogy see H. G. Harrison, *A Select Bibliography of English Genealogy* (1937); L. G. Pine, *Trace Your Ancestors* (1953); A. J. Willis, *Genealogy for Beginners* (1955); D. E. Gardner and F. A. Smith, *Genealogical Research in England and Wales*, 2 vol. (1956–59); A. R. Wagner, *English Genealogy* (1960); N. Burns, *Family Tree* (1962). For U.S. genealogy see O. Stetson, *The Art of Ancestor Hunting* (1936); (G. H. Doane, *Searching for Your Ancestors* (1948). (S. B.-R. P.)

GENÉE, DAME ADELINE (1878–1970), Danish ballet dancer, first won widespread acclaim and affection in England as the principal ballerina at the Empire Theatre, London, between 1897 and 1907. She was born Anina Jensen at Hinnerup, Jutland, on Jan. 6, 1878, and at the age of eight was adopted by her uncle and aunt, the dancers Alexandre and Antonia Genée, who began to train her for the ballet. Her early appearances took place in Germany and in 1897 she came to London, which she made her home, marrying an Englishman, Frank S. N. Isitt, in 1910. She toured the United States and Canada in 1908 and in subsequent years and appeared for the first time in New York's Metropolitan Opera House in 1912. She retired from dancing in 1917 but continued to play a leading part in English ballet, becoming the first president of the Association of Operatic Dancing of Great Britain (later the Royal Academy of Dancing) in 1920 and retaining that position until 1954. She was created Dame of the British Empire in 1950. Adeline Genée was a dancer in the classical tradition, but it was above all her fine quality of wit and winning personality on the stage, like that of Yvette Guilbert, that made her popular. On April 23, 1970, she died at Esher, Eng.
See Ivor Guest, *Adeline Genée* (1958).

GENELLI, GIOVANNI BUONAVENTURA (1798–1868), German draughtsman, painter, and engraver, of Italian origin, was best known as a draftsman and illustrator of the antique. He was born in Berlin on Sept. 28, 1798, the son of a landscape painter and grandson of a Roman embroiderer employed to found a school of gobelins by Frederick the Great. He studied in Berlin and then went for ten years to Rome, where he became a colleague of, among others, J. F. Overbeck and J. von Führich. In 1830 he was commissioned to decorate a villa in Leipzig with frescoes, but quarrelling with his patron moved in about 1835 to Munich, where he acquired his reputation as a figure draftsman. In 1859 he was appointed a professor at Weimar and died there on Nov. 13, 1868.

Genelli rarely painted in oils. His numerous watercolours, designs for engravings, and lithographs, usually of mythological subjects, reveal the influence of Michelangelo. Though German by birth he was Italian in spirit and his art was deeply rooted in the Italian Renaissance.

GENERAL, a high military rank. Army officers holding this rank usually command units larger than a regiment or its equivalent or units consisting of more than one arm of the service. This applies also to officers commanding comparable units of air forces. In many instances, however, a general is a staff officer who does not command troops but who plans their operations in the field. General, lieutenant general and major general are the first, second and third grades of general officers in most armies. The U.S. army, air force and marines have a fourth general officer grade, brigadier general. The highest U.S. army rank, that of general of the armies of the United States, was created in 1799, presumably for George Washington. There is no record that the appointment was ever made, however, and the office ceased to exist in 1802. In 1919 it was re-established especially for Gen. John J. Pershing, who thus became the only person actually to hold this rank; it lapsed upon his death in 1948. The rank of general of the army was created in 1866 and conferred successively on Gen. Ulysses S. Grant, Gen. William T. Sherman and Gen. Philip H. Sheridan, but ceased to exist with the death of Sherman in 1891. This rank, as the equivalent of field marshal in the British and other armies, was revived during World War II and conferred in 1944 on Gen. Henry H. Arnold, Gen. Dwight D. Eisenhower, Gen. Douglas MacArthur and Gen. George C. Marshall, and in 1950 on Gen. Omar N. Bradley. Following the establishment of the U.S. air force as a separate service, General Arnold's title was changed to general of the air force. (For equivalent ranks in various services see OFFICERS, MILITARY. See also INSIGNIA, MILITARY.)

The term general is also included in the titles of various civil offices of high responsibility such as postmaster general, attorney general and governor general. (LN. MS.)

GENERAL AGREEMENT ON TARIFFS AND TRADE (G.A.T.T.): see TARIFF.

GENERAL STAFF, a military term denoting the staff of officers who assist a commander by performing detailed duties of administration, planning, supply and co-ordination. The general staff concept emerged in European armies during the 19th century, the first and most successful being the general staff of the Prussian army.

The U.S. army created a general staff in 1903, largely resulting from the efforts of the secretary of war, Elihu Root. Soon thereafter, in 1906, the British army also formally established a general staff. In most air forces the counterpart of the army general staff came to be known as the air staff. See STAFF, MILITARY.

GENERAL STORE. In the history of U.S. retailing the general store, or country store, was the successor of the early trading post that served the pioneers and early settlers. Established at a crossroads or in a village, the general store served the immediate community and farmers from the neighbouring countryside. It carried a wide range of goods, including food, clothing, housewares and farm equipment. The storekeeper was frequently the community's leading citizen, for the area looked to him to supply its needs. The store was a popular meeting place where neighbours sat around the potbellied stove and the cracker barrel to discuss politics and the weather. When the storekeeper visited a market centre to obtain supplies he established contacts with other merchants and could report back to his customers on market trends and political events.

In most rural communities money was scarce and exchange was accomplished to some extent by barter. As produce from the land and forest was of a seasonal character the storekeeper extended long-term credit of from six months to a year. Successful operation of such an enterprise called for native shrewdness and the ability to hold the confidence of one's customers.

The general store in the United States flourished throughout the 19th century but declined rapidly in the 20th century, particularly after the 1920s. Some stores survived in isolated communities but their importance in the economy was slight, for they represented less than 1% of the national retail trade. The trend in retailing was in the direction of specialized stores, each handling a particular type of goods. This trend was, in turn, followed by the development of supermarkets, some of which carried as great a variety of items as the old-fashioned general store.

(T. H. S.)

GENERAL STRIKE. A general strike does not necessarily imply a strike of all workers in every industry, but the term does mean that a substantial proportion of workers in each of a number of industries have ceased work in a common endeavour to achieve a certain objective, which may be economic or political. The description may not be properly applied to a strike covering only one industry.

Early Radicals and Chartists.—The idea of the strike as a means of influencing conditions of employment is as old as civilized man and antedates the trade-union movement by centuries. However, as a deliberate part of the tactics of collective bargaining the strike came into regular use with the growth of the trade unions in Great Britain in the late 18th century. The history of the general strike also seems to begin in Great Britain. When the term was first used is not clear, but both the idea and the expression were brought into popular currency during the 1830s. John Doherty, one-time leader of the cotton spinners, used the term in 1834 in a newspaper which he edited, and again when giving evidence before a parliamentary committee in 1838 on the cause of the strikes which had occurred after the repeal of the Combination acts in 1824. Doherty, however, seems to have meant nothing more than a strike which was not confined to a single district, but embraced the whole cotton trade.

In the 1820s and 1830s the idea of a general stoppage of work was advocated by radical orators as a means of securing the reform of parliament and achieving the "rights of labour." The first conception was that of a "national holiday" or "sacred month." In Jan. 1832 William Benbow published a pamphlet entitled *Grand National Holiday and Congress of the Productive Classes*, describing how the workers, if they would act with unity of "thought and action," could by ceasing to work for one month secure "equal rights, equal liberties, equal enjoyments, equal toil, equal respect, equal share of production." The national holiday or sacred month was to be a peaceful affair and achieve its objectives by the simple process of the workers remaining "at leisure."

There was much talk of the sacred month by the Chartists at the time of the great convention in 1839, and a great deal of dispute as to whether it should take the form of a national holiday or an armed insurrection. Little came of the agitation, though it caused considerable apprehension to the government. In 1842 the Chartists tried to turn an outbreak of strikes in Lancashire into a general strike for the charter. They were successful in spreading the stoppage to neighbouring counties, but the strike eventually collapsed in the face of the show of force organized by the government. (See Chartism.)

Syndicalism.—After the failure of the Chartist agitation interest in the general strike declined in Britain until the early years of the 20th century. Discusssion of the theory of the general strike as a method of social revolution was mainly conducted in France, and the doctrines of syndicalism (*q.v.*) developed there gave it a philosophic basis. The question was discussed at the Geneva congress of the International Association of Workingmen in 1866, but it was not until 1893 that the next significant manifestation of the general strike occurred. On the refusal of the Belgian parliament to agree to universal manhood suffrage the Labour party issued orders calling on the workers to stop work immediately, and more than 200,000 workers went on strike, the stoppage being called off only when parliament relented and agreed in a modified form to the workers' demands. Again in 1902 there was another general strike in Belgium that led to riots and to the shooting of some strikers.

In the same year, a large-scale strike took place in Sweden in support of universal suffrage and the reform of parliament, and in 1909 there occurred the most complete general strike for economic ends which had, up to that date, ever taken place in any country. The 1909 general strike in Sweden was largely the result of the high degree of organization and centralized control of both workers' and employers' federations. Falling profits had led the employers to agree among themselves on a nation-wide basis to raise wages and in some instances to cut them. This policy was resisted by the unions, which had also other scores to settle, and they eventually decided to attempt to defeat the employers by calling a general strike.

The stoppage lasted a month and more than 300,000 workers out of a total of 800,000 ceased work. Industry was brought almost completely to a standstill. The strike was entirely peaceful and aroused world-wide interest, large sums of money being subscribed by unions in other countries to assist the striking Swedish workers. Though the results of the Swedish general strike could not be described as either failure or success, it encouraged the growth of the idea in other countries that major economic reforms could be achieved thus without violence necessarily being involved.

Widespread support for the general strike began to develop in Great Britain after the return from Australia of Tom Mann—one of the leaders of the great 1889 dock strike. Mann came back to Britain inspired by the doctrines of syndicalism that had spread from France to America, later being adopted by the Industrial Workers of the World (founded in Chicago in 1905), and re-exported to Europe and Australasia. Mann established in 1911 the Revolutionary Syndicalist league and had a hand in most of the large-scale strikes that occurred in 1910, 1911 and 1912.

The essence of the syndicalist belief was that the workers could not achieve social revolution by democratic political means, but only by the direct overthrow of the capitalist owners of industry through a general strike. Once the power of the capitalists had been destroyed, any re-emergence of centralized authority could be prevented if unions took control of industries and ran each of them for the benefit of the workers. To attain these ends the first essential step was the reorganization of the trade unions on the pattern of industry, since combinations based on craft or occupational differences only weakened the power of the working class.

These ideas were perhaps most brilliantly expressed in the pamphlet published by the south Wales miners in 1913 entitled *The Miners' Next Step*. Between 1910 and 1914 industrial syndicalism gained a considerable following, and on the eve of World War I the road transport, railway and miners' unions came together to form the "triple alliance," to secure, by strike action if necessary, major improvements in wages and working conditions.

The progress of syndicalism was arrested by the war, and the changes wrought by the conflict were such that the syndicalist movement was never able to recapture its pre-1914 attraction. However, the upheaval in social conditions and the problems of social and economic readjustment left by the war to some extent promoted militant ideas. There was much talk of "the day" among shop stewards and other radical elements in the trade-union movement, and when Ernest Bevin organized the councils of action it is almost certain that there would have been a complete stoppage of work throughout the country had not David Lloyd George changed his policy of sending troops to Poland. It was this apparently easily earned victory of 1920 that perhaps led Bevin astray when weighing the situation in 1926.

The General Strike of 1926 in Britain.—The British general strike of 1926 stemmed from the background of developments already sketched and from the conditions of employment in the coal industry. It was not a deliberately planned strike and the policy of the leaders of the trade-union movement was not determined by theoretical considerations, but they and the rest of the active workers did believe that the mineowners and the government could be coerced by a show of peaceful force.

Much had been expected of the triple alliance by militant members of the unions immediately after the end of the war. However, the miners were persuaded not to call upon its aid by the appointment of the Sankey commission, and then, when this proved abortive from their point of view, disagreement between the members of the alliance prevented action. The end of the alliance came in 1921 when the railwaymen and transport workers refused to strike with the miners.

The fundamental weakness of the triple alliance lay in the refusal of each organization to give up final autonomy. The result was that the miners struck alone against wage reductions and a long struggle followed after which they eventually returned to work, bitter at their defeat. The problems faced by the coal industry grew no easier, and with the return of the German, Polish and Belgian coal fields to full production the export market grew even more difficult. The coal owners sought to bring down costs by again reducing the standards of employment of the miners. The conflict came to a head in 1925 and the government staved off another stoppage by granting a temporary subsidy while another royal commission under Sir Herbert Samuel made a further investigation of the industry's sickness.

The report of the commission, which made a number of compromise proposals to tide the industry over its difficulties, was published in March 1926. It was immediately rejected by both sides and a strike appeared inevitable when the government subsidy came to an end on April 30. Meanwhile, the industrial committee of the Trades Union congress had met the prime minister and explored the possibility of getting negotiations restarted. Nothing was achieved, however, in the face of the intransigence of both the miners and the owners. On April 29 the T.U.C. pledged its support to the miners and called a national conference of trade-union executives. The general council then took a roll call of its affiliated unions; 3,653,000 votes were cast in favour of giving the council full powers to act on behalf of the whole movement, and 49,911 against.

Further attempts were made by the Trades Union congress to negotiate with the government, which had invoked the Emergency Powers act passed in 1920 to meet just such a situation as this. Some progress seemed to have been made, but while the general council of the T.U.C. was meeting with representatives of the miners, a summons was received from Downing street. When the T.U.C. delegates arrived they were handed a letter stating that negotiations could not be continued since the machine operators at the *Daily Mail* had refused to print the leading article of the following day's issue. Despite the fact that this action had been taken spontaneously without the knowledge of the T.U.C., the government looked upon it as a sufficient reason for refusing further discussions and insisted that all strike notices be withdrawn before any further talks could be held. Faced with this situation the general council decided that there was nothing further it could do but give the order for the strike to begin.

The unions had talked about making preparations, but in fact little had been done, and a hurriedly improvised organization had to be created. The only possibility of winning the strike lay in frightening the government and so persuading it to intervene, in order to get talks going once again, by the offer of some compromise solution. The government, however, had long made preparations to meet an emergency of this kind, and it was determined to force the unions to capitulate. In spite of the calling out of troops, arming of special constables and the arrest of hundreds of strikers, the whole affair was remarkably peaceful and very few serious incidents were reported.

At this time there were about 5,000,000 trade-union members out of a total wage-earning population of 15,000,000; about 3,000,000 were eventually involved in the strike. The main industries to be stopped included railways, road transport, iron and steel, building and printing; the rest were to be called out later if necessary. The closing of the press prompted the government to produce its own paper, the *British Gazette*; and the T.U.C. also published a strike newspaper, the *British Worker*. In the absence of the daily press many rumours circulated and the effect was to weaken the resolution of the workers and increase the fears of the middle class.

The general council of the T.U.C. rapidly realized that the government was not likely to be stampeded and began to look for a way of ending the strike. Sir Herbert Samuel, who had returned posthaste from the continent, acted as an intermediary on his own initiative, and made certain suggestions to the T.U.C. The miners, however, refused to consider them, and therefore the general council decided to call off the strike as it felt that no solution was possible if the miners would not compromise at all. The general council held that when the miners agreed to give the T.U.C. the responsibility for calling a general strike they also gave the T.U.C. the right to decide on what terms the strike should be settled. This logic the miners vehemently denied. The general strike was thus brought to an end on May 12, having lasted nine days. But the miners refused to return and remained on strike throughout the summer until they were compelled to go back to work by the exhaustion of their resources.

The Legal Issue.—The general strike raised many important issues. How far is it possible for a strike to go before it in fact becomes a revolutionary action directed against the state? Lord Simon held that the strike was illegal since it was not a trade dispute but an attempt "to make the public and parliament and the government do something," and this was not legally permissible under the trade-union acts. On the other hand Arthur Lehman Goodhart challenged this interpretation of the law, holding that the fact that the T.U.C. did not have a trade dispute with the government was irrelevant. The real question was whether the trade unions on strike were furthering a trade dispute, which obviously existed so far as the miners were concerned, in which case the sympathetic strikers were acting legally. This legal dispute was not resolved. The government tried to clarify the issue by passing the Trade Disputes and Trade Unions act in 1927, but after this act was repealed in 1946 the position returned to what it was in 1926.

Later Tendencies.—The effect of the general strike was to make both sides realize the danger to themselves in allowing industrial relations to become so strained. During the following years industrial relations improved considerably and this was to a great extent the result of wise leadership shown by both sides of industry. The *modus vivendi* which unions and employers gradually worked out for themselves in Britain was not achieved in France, which went through a period of bitter industrial unrest involving general stoppages in the 1930s. At the end of World War II there were several instances of general strikes in a number of European countries for both political and economic reasons; however, the syndicalist notion had long been abandoned in most western European countries. In Dec. 1960 an attempt was made by the leaders of the Socialist trade unions in the French-speaking Walloon area of Belgium to organize a general strike against the passing of the *Loi Unique*—a measure designed to help the country recover from the loss of its Congo territories. The main aim of the leaders of the Socialist unions was the overthrow of the Catholic-Liberal coalition government. The strike was also a demonstration of opposition to the Flemish-speaking element in Belgium, who, it was alleged, dominated government and industry and exploited the Walloons.

The strike lasted over a month but, with the refusal of the Catholic unions to join in, the stoppage gradually collapsed, in spite of large sums of money loaned to the Socialist unions by the British T.U.C. and many other trade-union organizations. Unfortunately much malicious damage was done by deliberate sabotage and a number of persons were killed and wounded in pitched battles between strikers and police. This experience illustrated the point that when a general strike occurs, whatever the legal situation may be, it constitutes a challenge to the authority of the state and no government can easily refrain from taking drastic action to bring it to an end.

(B. C. R.)

UNITED STATES

American labour has accepted in principle the inviolability of the collective contract and consequently has in principle always opposed the general strike. A general strike would lead to universal breaches of existing agreements, and would expose weaker unions to reprisals from employers. This kind of opposition by union leaders, based upon pragmatic grounds, has been reinforced by their strong opposition to the use of what is essentially a revolutionary weapon.

There have, nevertheless, been a number of local general strikes, all of which were opposed by the national officers of many of the participating unions. In the period following World War I, mounting radicalism as well as the belief that the employers of the shipyards were out to destroy the newly built unions in their plants led to a strike on Feb. 6, 1919, involving virtually all labour in Seattle, Wash. The walkout lasted five days, and the opposition of the national officers of many of the unions was an important factor in ending it. Local general strikes later took place in Terre Haute, Ind., in July 1935; in Pekin, Ill., in Feb. 1936; and in Oakland, Calif., in 1946; but the most important local general strike took place in San Francisco, Calif., in July 1934. This was caused by the attempt of the stevedores and shipowners to break the maritime strike for union recognition. Violence against the strikers, followed by efforts to carry on stevedoring operations by strikebreakers and the use of the national guard to protect them, precipitated the general walkout. It lasted four days, and the national heads of a number of unions as well as the American Federation of Labor disclaimed any support for this walkout.

General strikes are to be distinguished from industry-wide strikes, which are general as far as the affected industry is concerned. In the period after World War II, there were a number of industry-wide strikes in the bituminous coal and steel industries but only one general strike of a local nature. The reason is that local general strikes can be called only when there is widespread conviction among the organized workers in a community that an attack is being made upon the right of a large body of workers to organize and that united action is necessary. With the acceptance of unions as a normal part of the industrial scene the possibility for local general strikes has been sharply reduced. See also STRIKES AND LOCKOUTS.

(P. Tr.)

BIBLIOGRAPHY.—A. D. Lewis, Syndicalism and the General Strike (1912); J. R. Commons et al., History of Labour in the United States, 4 vol. (1918–35); P. Brissenden, The I.W.W., 2nd ed. (1920); G. D. H. Cole, The World of Labour, 2nd ed. (1915); Lord Askwith, Industrial Problems and Disputes (1920); G. Glasgow, General Strikes and Road Transport (1926); K. Martin, The British Public and the General Strike (1926); A. J. Cook, The Nine Days (1926); R. P. Arnot, The General Strike May 1926: Its Origins and History (1926); E. Burns, The General Strike May 1926: Trades Councils in Action (1926); W. H. Crook, The General Strike (1931); Kenneth G. J. C. Knowles, Strikes—a Study in Industrial Conflict (1952; 1953); Norman Citrine, Trade Union Law (1951); Julian Symons, The General Strike (1957); Anna Louise Strong, Seattle General Strike (1919); Ole Hanson, Americanism and Bolshevism (1920); Paul Eliel, Waterfront and General Strikes, San Francisco, 1934 (1934).

GENERATOR, ELECTRIC, a device in which mechanical power is converted into electrical power, utilizes the principle that a voltage is induced in the turns of a coil of wire while the number of magnetic lines (the flux) linking the turns of the coil are changing. The principle can be illustrated with a horseshoe magnet, a coil of perhaps 50 turns of wire and a galvanometer. Connect the ends of the coil to the terminals of the galvanometer. Then observe the galvanometer pointer as the magnet is placed so that its legs enclose one side of the coil. A pointer deflection in one direction occurs while the magnet is moved toward the coil; a deflection in the opposite direction occurs while the magnet is moved away from the coil. Moving the magnet more rapidly increases the deflection. With the magnet held stationary in any position relative to the coil no pointer deflection is observed. If the magnet is held stationary and the coil is moving, it is found that a deflection occurs only while the coil is moving. If the coil is placed about a leg of the magnet and both are held stationary, and if a piece of steel is now moved to make and break contact with the poles, galvanometer deflection occurs when the steel is being moved—in one direction as the steel approaches the poles and in the opposite direction as it leaves the poles. In some generators the coils are stationary and the magnetic lines are moved across them, in others the coils are moved across the magnetic lines, and in still others both the coils and the source of the magnetic lines are stationary and steel in the magnetic path is moved.

History.—In 1831 Michael Faraday rotated a copper disk edgewise between the poles of a horseshoe magnet and obtained a continuous (direct) voltage between two rubbing contacts, one on the periphery and the other on the shaft of the disk. In this first electric generator the electromotive force was obtained by moving the conductors (i.e., the elements of the disk) across the magnetic flux, not by a change in the amount of flux linking a turn. In this disk generator, of the type now called homopolar or acyclic, the electromotive force generated in any element of the disk maintains a fixed direction with respect to the element for a given direction of disk rotation. Homopolar generators are low-voltage machines; they are not of commercial importance because their efficiencies are lower and their costs of construction are higher for a given power output than for other types of generators.

In 1832 Hippolyte Pixii constructed a generator using permanent magnets and wire armature windings. This type, in which alternate poles have alternate magnetic polarities, is known as heteropolar. In Pixii's generator the electromotive forces generated in the windings are alternating in sign. To obtain a direct current output he contrived the first commutator, a device using moving contacts to reverse the connections at the ends of an armature coil at the instant the voltage in the coil is reversing.

In 1845 Charles Wheatstone replaced the permanent magnets with electromagnets excited with direct current from a battery. In 1857 he added the feature of self-excitation, whereby the field windings received current from the armature terminals. The ring winding of Antonio Pacinotti (1860) and Zenobe Théophile Gramme (1870) made it possible to add the voltages of many conductors of a multipolar generator and thus obtain higher voltages than were feasible earlier. The winding method was such that the conductors were held in place on the surface of the revolving armature. Ring windings were superseded by the more cheaply constructed barrel or drum-type winding of Friedrich von Hefner-Alteneck (1872), a development from the earlier shuttle winding of Ernst Werner von Siemens (1856). Placing an armature winding in slots (first proposed by Pacinotti in 1860) made possible a reduction in the effective length of the air gap in the path of the magnetic lines and a consequent increase in the strength of the magnetic field produced by a given field winding. Rotation of the armature structure causes alternating voltages to be generated not only in the conductors but also in the steel, where circulating or eddy currents cause losses. Eddy current losses were reduced by laminating the armature steel.

Edward Weston and Thomas A. Edison were among the first to recognize all the factors contributing to generator losses, and the latter's bipolar generator raised the standard of generator efficiency from about 50% to the then unheard of value of 90%. This machine had a much greater ratio of copper weight than earlier ones and had the first mica-insulated commutator. In 1886 John and Edward Hopkinson devised the first rational method of generator design. Edison's bipolar generator in 1878, the incandescent lamp in 1879 and the Edison system of central station power production in 1882 gave commercial impetus to electric generator and power development.

In 1881 Charles F. Brush added a second field winding—about the field poles and connected in series with the armature circuit—to form a compound generator. The voltage of this generator automatically remained at a nearly constant value regardless of the amount of current drawn by connected loads.

Brushes used on early generators were of strap copper, copper mesh and metal alloy. Enough sparking occurred to cause burning of the commutator bars and the brushes in addition to friction wear. In 1888 Charles J. Van Depoele invented the carbon brush, which greatly reduced the sparking and the wear on the commutator. In the early 1890s parallel operation of compound generators by means of external equalizer connections was devised, and in 1896 Benjamin Garver Lamme invented internal equalizer connections, which ensure an equal division of the current between parallel armature paths, and made really large generators practical. Thereafter larger and larger multipolar generators, directly connected to reciprocating steam engines, came into use, reaching a peak of development about 1900.

The invention of the first A.C. (alternating current) system of power generation and distribution by Lucien Gaulard and John Dixon Gibbs in Europe and by William Stanley in the U.S. (1885), and of the induction motor by Nikola Tesla (1888), led to A.C. generator developments. Steam engines and, occasionally, water wheels were the early prime movers.

Among the earliest developments was Stanley's inductor generator with stationary field and armature windings which generated voltages from pulsations in a unidirectional magnetic field caused by revolving a toothed rotor. Elihu Thomson's A.C. generator of 1878 was similar to D.C. (direct current) generators, except that a commutator was not required and collector rings were connected to the armature winding in a manner such that alternating voltages were obtained between brushes riding on the rings. Ultimately the advantages of having the armature winding stationary, avoiding high voltages between collector rings, led to universal use of the modern revolving field structure for a synchronous generator.

The frequency of the voltage delivered by early A.C. generators was probably determined by the number of poles that could be readily constructed and the speed of an available prime mover. During the early years of alternating current, installations were made using frequencies ranging from $16\frac{2}{3}$ to $133\frac{1}{3}$ c.p.s. (cycles per second). Changes in the application of alternating current led to changes in the frequencies. The need for a restriction in the number of frequencies led to the almost universal adoption of 60 c.p.s. for lighting and power purposes in the U.S., although 25 and 50 c.p.s. remained in use in some installations.

For a given number of poles and a given speed of rotation, an inductor generator delivers twice the frequency of the present common types of A.C. generators. In the early years of radio telegraphy the inductor generator was the best source of the frequencies required. Generators with a frequency of 100,000 c.p.s. and capacities up to 100 kw. were built. The advent of the electronic tube and the discovery that it could be used to produce a high-frequency output from a D.C. source enabled it to supplant the inductor generator. New applications requiring frequencies ranging from 1,000 to 10,000 c.p.s. for inductive heating and the use of 400-c.p.s. control equipment and motors for aircraft created a demand for which the inductor generator was an economic answer.

Among the first polyphase generators were the three-phase, 100-kw. Lauffen generators designed by C. E. L. Brown (1891) and the two-phase, 5,000-kw. Niagara generators built by the Westinghouse company (1894), both vertical shaft machines with external revolving field structures.

In the late 1890s, when polyphase alternating current was replacing D.C. supply, and before the advent of the steam turbine, steam-reciprocating-engine-driven A.C. generators were built with ratings up to several thousand kilowatts.

The first large steam-turbine-driven A.C. generator in the U.S. was built by the American General Electric company and installed in Chicago, Ill., in 1903. It was of the vertical shaft type and rated at 5,000 kw. Its satisfactory operation led to the almost universal adoption of steam-turbine-driven polyphase generators for central stations. After a few years, turbine-driven generators were designed almost entirely with horizontal shafts and internal revolving field structures. Improved materials and design refinements enabled larger and larger machines to be built, ratings up to 50,000 kw. at 13,200 v. and 3,600 r.p.m. being common. Two-hundred-thousand-kilowatt single-shaft generators at 3,600 r.p.m. have been built, and up to 33,000 v. have been used.

Modern water-wheel generators are almost universally of the salient-pole, revolving field structure type, with drum windings in open slots and welded steel frame structures. Typical of the large machines in modern hydroelectric projects are the 77,500-kva., 88-r.p.m. Dnieprostroi generators, the 82,500-kva., 180-r.p.m. Hoover dam generators and the 108,000-kva., 120-r.p.m. Grand Coulee dam generators.

Some power plants have diesel or other oil engines as prime movers. A.C. generators for this service must have damper or amortisseur windings and often extra flywheels to limit the electric oscillations set up by the pulsating torque of the engine.

Hydrogen cooling of synchronous machines was introduced first in 1928. By the 1950s almost every steam-turbine-driven generator with a rating above 20,000 kw. was hydrogen cooled. An innovation of 1952 was to make the armature conductors hollow so that they could be cooled by blowing hydrogen through them.

DIRECT-CURRENT GENERATORS

A D.C. generator consists of a field structure, a series of alternate north and south magnetic poles equally spaced around a circular periphery and an armature structure built up of laminated steel sections (laminations) with slots in its surface in which a system of electrical conductors (a winding) is placed. A common lamination thickness is 0.025 in. Although either the field or the armature structure can be made the moving part, mechanical considerations cause a D.C. generator to be built with the armature structure as the moving part. An elementary D.C. generator is represented in fig. 1. Here a battery is represented as the source of direct current that flows through the turns of the field winding surrounding the field poles. In this manner the magnetic lines are established in the paths as shown. That the magnetic lines pass through the pole pieces from left to right is determined from the principle that if one coils the fingers of the right hand about an iron core in the direction current flows in turns about the core, the extended thumb is parallel to the lines in the core. The enlarged portions of the poles near the armature are the pole shoes, and the areas facing the armature are the pole faces. The spaces between the pole faces and the armature are the air gaps.

In fig. 1 the number of magnetic lines passing through the armature coil varies from zero when the plane of the coil is horizontal to a maximum when it is vertical. The voltage generated in the coil at a given instant depends not upon the number of lines through the coil but upon the rate at which the number of lines is changing. Just before the plane of the coil reaches the horizontal position the lines are passing through it in one direction; just after it passes that position the lines are passing through it in the opposite direction. At the horizontal position the rate of change of the lines is the greatest and the voltage generated is a maximum. When the plane of the coil is vertical the rate of change of the number of lines through it is zero and no voltage is generated in it at that instant. For nearly one-half revolution, one brush is in contact with the commutator bar attached to one end of the coil and the other brush is in contact with the commutator bar attached to the other end of the coil. Note that the brushes are set so that the left-hand brush makes contact through the commutator bar to a coil side when it is on the left side of the vertical and the right-hand brush makes contact through a commutator bar to a coil side when it is on the right side of the vertical. As soon as a coil side moves from one side of the vertical to the other it ceases contact with one brush and establishes contact with the other. Thus the polarity of a brush remains fixed even though an alternating voltage is being generated in the coil.

The polarities of the brushes in fig. 1 are determined by Flem-

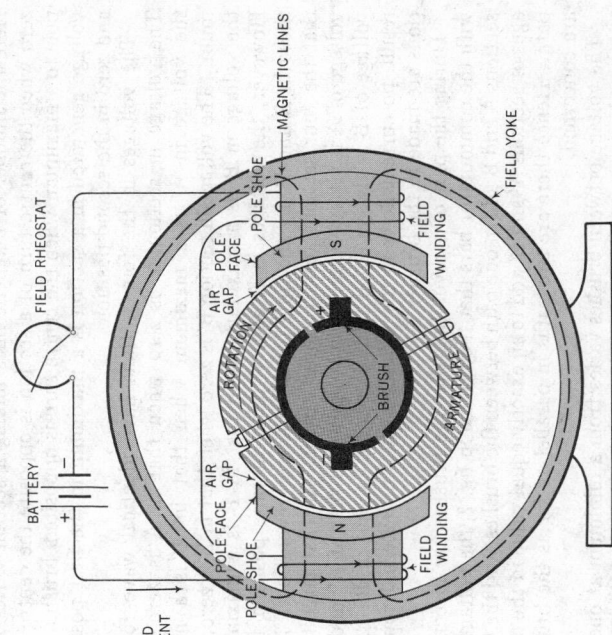

FIG. 1.—ELEMENTARY D.C. GENERATOR WITH ONE-TURN ARMATURE COIL AND TWO COMMUTATOR BARS

ing's right-hand rule. Place the thumb, the first finger, and the second finger of the right hand mutually at right angles, thereby forming the axes of a three-co-ordinate system. Now, while pointing the first finger toward the right in the direction of the magnetic lines from the N pole, turn the hand until the thumb points upward in the direction the left-hand coil side moves in front of the N pole face. Then the second finger points into the page as the direction of the generated voltage in the left-hand side of the coil. The right-hand coil side moves downward in front of the S pole face, so the voltage generated in that coil side is directed out of the page. The right-hand brush is the positive one since it is the one toward which the voltage generated in a coil side acts.

The time variation (wave form) of the voltage between brushes in fig. 1 depends upon the length of the air gap, the contour of the pole face and the percentage of the armature surface covered by a pole face. A D.C. voltmeter between brushes in fig. 1 would read the average value of the voltage. This would probably be more than one-half the maximum voltage, although the exact value would depend upon the wave form.

The voltmeter reading would increase in direct proportion if the speed of rotation were increased. The current in the field circuit could be changed by adjusting the setting of the field rheostat shown. Increasing the field current would increase the voltmeter reading, not in direct proportion with the number of magnetic lines. Starting with zero current, as the current is increased, the number of lines at first increases approximately in direct proportion. As higher values of current are reached, the rate of increase of lines becomes less than that of the current because of magnetic saturation in steel.

If the brushes in fig. 1 were shifted 90° from the position shown, a brush would make contact with a coil side while the side moves from the centre of one pole to the centre of the other. The voltage between brushes would be alternating with an average value of zero, as would be proved by a zero reading on a D.C. voltmeter.

Ring Winding.—If the one-turn coil of fig. 1 were replaced by a coil of more turns wound in the slots and the coil ends connected to the commutator bars, the voltage between brushes would be increased in proportion with the number of turns. For most applications of D.C. generators it is desired that the percentage variation with time of the voltage delivered from the brushes be small. The one-coil generator of fig. 1 would have too great variation for most applications. To reduce the variation, the number of coils and commutator bars is increased. An early means of doing this was with a ring winding such as that shown in fig. 2. This winding has four sections and there are four commutator bars. Here the number of magnetic lines linking a section varies from zero when the centre turn of a section is opposite the centre of a pole to a maximum when the centre turn is opposite a brush. The voltage generated in a section is a maximum in the first position and zero in the second position.

The voltages in the four sections have identical wave forms. The voltage in section A' is zero when that in A is zero, and the voltage in A' is a maximum when that in A is a maximum. The voltage in section B' is zero when that in B is zero, and the voltage in B' is a maximum when that in B is a maximum. However, the voltages in A and A' differ in time position from those in B and B' by the time for one-quarter revolution. Note that the four sections form a closed circuit. In that circuit the voltage of A is always equal to and opposed to that of A', and the voltage of B is always equal to and opposed to that of B'. As a result, no current flows in the windings when no external connections are made to the brushes.

During the part of a revolution that the brushes are in contact with the commutator bars that they touch in fig. 2, the voltages of sections A and B add in one path between the brushes, and the voltages of sections A' and B' add to an exactly equal value in the other path. Hence there are two paths in parallel as far as the brushes are concerned.

The voltage between brushes varies from a minimum at one position of the armature to a maximum at another position. When the armature has turned about one-eighth revolution from the po-

sition shown, two commutator bars touch one brush and the other two touch the other. Then section A is short-circuited by one brush and section A' is short-circuited by the other. At this instant the voltage between brushes is that of section B in one path and that of section B' in the other path. As the armature turns on beyond this position, coil A comes under the influence of the N pole, its voltage reverses from the previous direction and now adds to that of section B' in the right-hand path. At the same time section A' comes under the influence of the S pole, its voltage reverses from the previous direction and it now adds to that of section B in the left-hand path. As rotation continues the transfer of sections from one path to another continues. By using more winding sections and more commutator bars than are shown in fig. 2, the percentage time variation in the voltage between brushes can be reduced to a relatively small value.

When a load (a conducting element) is connected between brushes in fig. 2, the total current drawn divides equally between the two paths, entering the armature at the negative brush and leaving it at the positive brush. As a winding section is being transferred from a path on one side of a brush to a path on the other side, the current in it reverses direction. This reversal occurs during the time a section is short-circuited by a brush, an interval called the time of commutation. Although the generated voltage in a section becomes zero and then reverses during the time of commutation, the current in the section does not become zero and reverse simultaneously. The self-inductance (electrical inertia) of the section causes the current to decrease more slowly to zero than the voltage does.

After the current in the section has become zero, the reversed generated voltage causes the current to increase in the reversed direction. This rate of growth is limited by the self-inductance of the section. If, by the end of the time of commutation, the current in a section has not had time to reverse to a magnitude equal to that of the current in the path in which it is inserted, a spark occurs between a brush and the commutator bar from which it has just parted contact. Some sparking can be tolerated, but excessive sparking causes objectionable heating and pitting of the commutator bars. Most modern D.C. generators have one or more interpoles (commutating poles), which are located midway between the main poles. The winding on an interpole is connected in series with a lead from a brush in order that the number of magnetic lines passing from the interpole to the armature will vary in approximate proportion with the current in the armature coils. The location of an interpole is such that its magnetic lines generate a voltage in an armature coil during the time of commutation. The direction of the voltage is that required to reduce the current in a coil to zero and then establish it in the reverse direction.

Drum Winding.—For economic and mechanical reasons, the ring winding has been superseded by the drum winding. In fig. 3 are represented the form and the connections of coils in a lap type of drum winding. One coil with sides numbered 1 and 10, respectively, is placed so that side 1 occupies the upper half of one slot and side 10 occupies the lower half of another four slot pitches distant. This coil may consist of one or more turns of insulated copper wire taped together as shown. The ends of the coil are

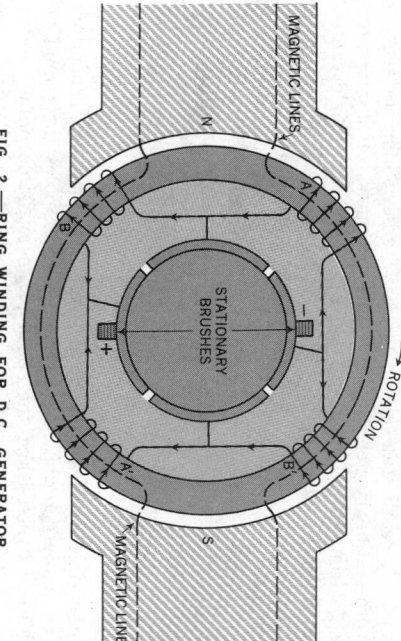

FIG. 2.—RING WINDING FOR D.C. GENERATOR

connected to adjacent commutator bars. A second coil with sides numbered 3 and 12 is displaced one slot pitch from the first with connections to the commutator being advanced by one bar. With this arrangement of coils continued around the armature a closed winding results, having as many commutator bars as there are coils. The ends of each coil connect to adjacent commutator bars.

With a drum winding the number of magnetic lines linking a coil is a maximum when the centre of the coil is opposite the centre of a pole. At that instant the rate of change of lines is zero and the generated voltage is zero. The maximum number of lines would be all those entering or leaving a pole if the span of a coil is equal to the distance from the centre of one pole to the centre of the next. The number of lines linking a coil is zero when the centre of the coil is midway between the centres of two adjacent poles. At that instant the rate of change of lines is a maximum and the generated voltage is a maximum.

Self-Excited Generators.—The generator of fig. 1 is separately excited since its field winding receives current from a source other than the armature terminals. Although the source is represented here as a battery, most separately excited generators receive their field current from a smaller D.C. generator known as an exciter. An exciter is often mounted on a shaft extension from the generator, both being driven by the same prime mover.

After current has been sent through the field winding of a D.C. generator and then removed, some residual magnetic lines remain in the magnetic circuit. As a result, when the generator is driven at rated speed a voltage that may be of the order of 5% of the rated voltage appears between the armature terminals. This voltage is used to produce a build-up to a higher value in a self-

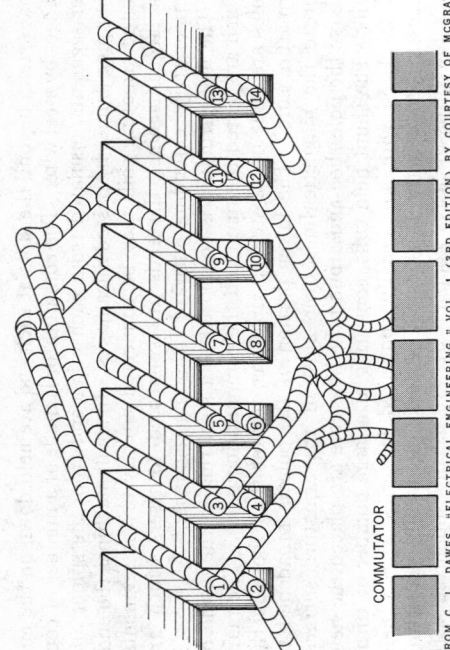

COMMUTATOR

FIG. 3.—LAP WINDING ON ARMATURE OF D.C. GENERATOR

excited generator by using it to send current through the field winding.

In fig. 4 are represented the connections of a shunt-type self-excited generator. Normally no load is connected to the leads coming from the brushes until the voltage has been adjusted to a desired value. With the switch in the field winding circuit open and the armature driven at rated speed, it is assumed that the residual magnetic lines are from left to right as indicated by M_r and that the low voltage between brushes has the polarity indicated. When the switch is closed, current out of the positive brush flows through the field winding in such a direction as to produce an increased number of magnetic lines. This increase causes an increase in the voltage between brushes, which in turn causes a further increase of current. Saturation in the steel in the magnetic circuit prevents the voltage from increasing indefinitely. The value attained can be varied over a wide range by varying the resistance of the field rheostat. When the resistance is a maximum, the voltage may be only slightly greater than that with no current in the field winding. When the resistance is zero, the voltage is likely to be of the order of 50% above rated value. The value of field current required to produce rated voltage is likely to be of the order of 5% of the current rating of the generator.

If in fig. 4 the connections of the field windings to the brushes

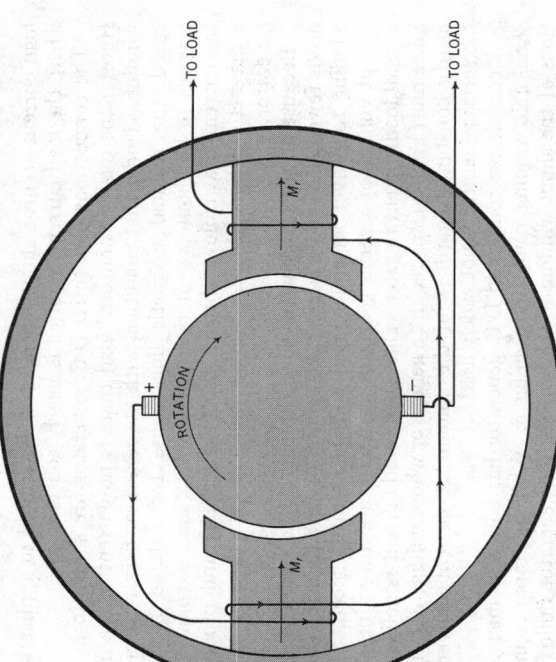

FIG. 5.—CONNECTIONS OF A SERIES-WOUND D.C. GENERATOR

were to be interchanged and if the switch were closed, the current would flow in the field windings in such a direction as to reduce the number of magnetic lines below the residual value. As a result the voltage would reduce.

Consider a shunt generator that is being driven at rated speed with the field rheostat set so that rated voltage is obtained between brushes when no current is being drawn by a load. Under that condition the only current delivered by the brushes is that to the field windings. This is obtained equally from the various paths in the armature winding. When a load is connected it draws additional current from the brushes, and the currents in the armature winding paths increase. These currents cause a magnetic action that in turn causes a reduction (usually small) in the number of magnetic lines and a corresponding reduction in the voltage produced in the winding. In addition, some of the voltage produced is used in sending the current through the resistance of the winding. These two factors cause the voltage between brushes to be reduced below its value when no load is connected. This reduction in voltage causes a reduction in the field current and a further reduction in the number of magnetic lines. Hence the voltage reduces more than it would have if the generator had been separately excited. With a given load current being delivered, it would be possible to bring the voltage back to its no-load value by cutting resistance out of the field rheostat. Because the percentage variations in its output voltage are rather great when changes in the

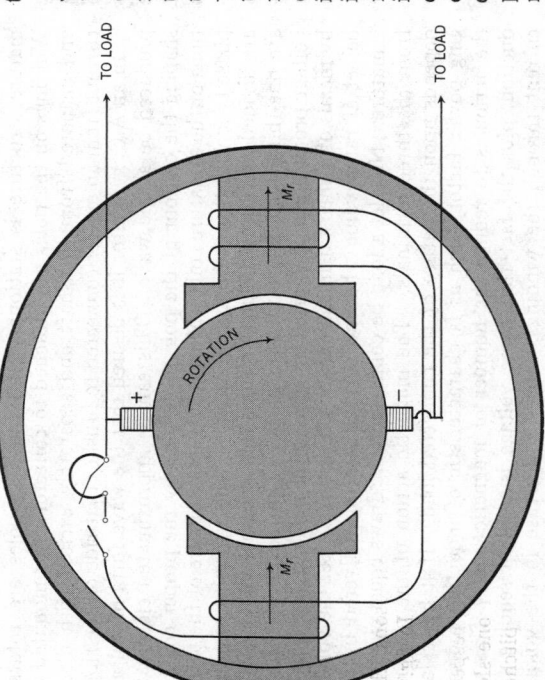

FIG. 4.—CONNECTIONS OF A SHUNT-WOUND GENERATOR

load current occur, a shunt generator is best suited to applications where the load current required is nearly constant.

The connections of a series D.C. generator are shown in fig. 5. Here, if there is no connected load there is no current in the field winding. Under that condition, with the generator driven at rated speed, the residual magnetic lines cause the voltage between brushes to be about 5% of rated value. If a load is connected, the current drawn flows through the field winding and produces a magnetic action to cause voltage build-up just as in a shunt generator.

Because all the load current flows through it, the series winding needs fewer turns and a larger cross section of wire than the shunt winding to deliver an equal rated voltage at rated speed. The output voltage of a series generator varies from a low value with a small load current to rated value when rated current is delivered. Since most applications require a generator whose voltage output is nearly constant, regardless of the amount of current delivered, the series generator is not widely used.

A cumulative compound D.C. generator has both a shunt and a series field winding, connected as in fig. 6. With the proper connections of the shunt winding to the brushes, the generator builds up with no load connected, just as a shunt generator does. The rheostat can be adjusted so that rated voltage is obtained. When a load is connected, the current drawn through the series field winding causes a magnetic action that may increase the number of magnetic lines and consequently the voltage between lines to the load, even though the magnetic action of the current in the armature windings tends to reduce the number of magnetic lines, and some of the voltage produced in the armature windings is used in sending current through the resistance of the armature and series field windings. If the magnetic action of the series field winding is enough to cause a rise in the voltage between brushes when the load current is increased, a rise in the shunt field winding current occurs. As a result the voltage rises more than it would have if no change in the shunt field current had occurred. If the voltage delivered to a load by a generator is greater when rated current is being delivered than with no current, the generator is overcompound. If the magnetic action of the series field winding is such that the voltage delivered at rated current is equal to that with no current, the generator is flat compound.

D.C. Generator Construction.—A typical armature for a D.C. generator has a shaft on which are mounted two spiders, one to support the armature core and the other the commutator. The core is built up of thin steel laminations, insulated from each other and held together by end flanges. In the slots in the core are placed copper conductors which are insulated from the core with treated fabric or paper materials, or pasted mica flakes, and held in the slots by insulating wedges. The portions of the conductors

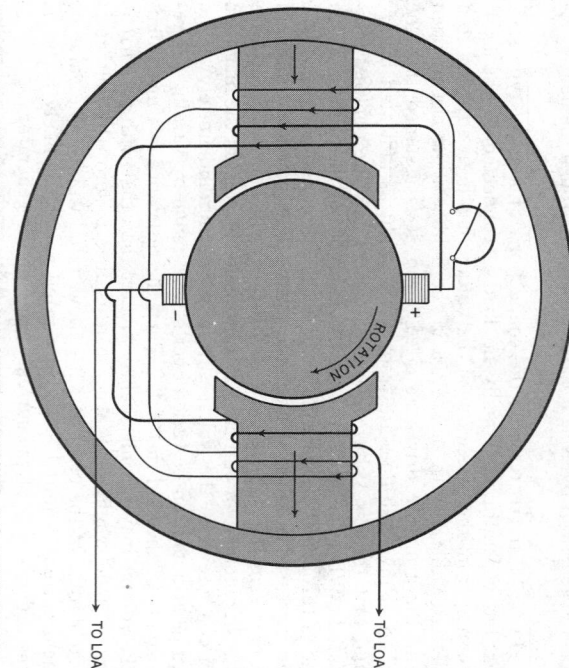

FIG. 6.—CONNECTIONS OF CUMULATIVE COMPOUND D.C. GENERATOR

TO LOAD

ROTATION

TO LOAD

+

that extend beyond the slots at each end are held down on the end flanges by steel wire. The commutator is made of a number of copper segments, insulated from each other and from the spider and clamping flanges by pasted mica flakes. In small machines the ends of the armature coils may be connected directly to the segments. In large machines the ends are connected to risers which are copper strips extending outward from the segments.

The field structure is composed of a steel ring to the inside of which are bolted the main and the commutating poles. The main poles are built up of steel laminations, thicker than those in the armature core. The lower portion of the pole is broadened to spread the magnetic lines over most of the armature surface. Above the pole shoe and around the pole core are placed the field coils. The shunt field coils, consisting of a large number of turns of insulated wire, are usually connected in series with a field rheostat between the brushes. The series field coils, consisting of a few turns of heavy copper wire, are usually supported with the shunt coils.

Graphitized carbon brushes are used with an area such that the normal current density is about 40 amp. per square inch. These are arranged in axial rows, one row for each main pole, equally spaced around the commutator periphery. The brushes fit into metal brush holders and are held against the commutator by spring pressure. The holders are bolted to brackets that are supported by a brush yoke. The centrifugal forces present limit the permissible peripheral speeds of an armature and a commutator to about 10,000 and 6,000 ft. per minute, respectively. The terminal voltage is limited by the commutator segment width and the permissible voltage between segments. Mechanical construction limits the minimum segment width to about 0.1 in. The average voltage between segments is limited to about 20 v. by the sensitivity of the commutator to arcing between brushes at times of sudden load current changes. About 2,000 v. from one commutator is the highest value obtained in normal designs. When higher voltages are needed, two or more commutators are connected in series. D.C. generators are built in capacities up to 300 kw. at 12 v. for electroplating; 5,000 kw. at 600 v. and 240 r.p.m. for industrial power, 1,500 kw. at 1,500 v. and 400 r.p.m. for railways, and 100 kw. at 15,000 v. for radio transmitters. Efficiencies range as high as 94% on the largest units.

ALTERNATING-CURRENT GENERATORS

Let the two commutator bars of fig. 1 be replaced by two continuous rings mounted side by side on, but insulated from, the shaft that rotates the armature coil. Let one end of the coil be attached to one ring and the other end be attached to the other ring. With this arrangement the voltage between rings is alternating and can be obtained externally between brushes riding one on each ring. Few modern generators are constructed in this manner. It is cheaper to brace and insulate the armature winding when the armature structure is stationary and the field poles are rotated. Windings on the poles are attached to collector rings mounted on and insulated from the shaft and separately excited with direct current from an exciter connected to brushes that ride on the rings.

In an A.C. generator it is desired that the wave form of voltage produced be a sine wave. This can be approximated closely by shaping the contour of the pole pieces and by the proper connections of the armature coils. Most A.C. generators are of the three-phase type with three armature terminals. The armature windings are divided into three distinct sections that generate voltages that are one-third cycle apart in time phase. The magnitude of the voltage produced can be varied by varying the field current, usually by means of a rheostat in the exciter field circuit. Let the voltage be set at rated value when no current is being delivered by the armature. Now let a load be connected that draws equal currents from the three terminals. The magnetic action of the currents depends upon the nature of the connected load. If it has a lagging power factor, such as is characteristic of induction motors, the action is to reduce the number of magnetic lines. This reduction, plus the fact that some voltage is used in sending the current through the windings, causes a decrease in the voltage between a pair of terminals. If the load has a leading power factor, the magnetic action may increase the number of magnetic lines enough to cause an increase in the voltage between terminals.

Steam-Turbine-Driven Generators.—High turbine efficiency requires high speed, and high speed produces centrifugal stresses that make it necessary to construct a generator with a large output so that the rotating part (rotor) is long compared with its diameter. To make them rigid, large rotors are usually made from solid steel forgings. In European practice, only the rotor body is made from a forging, and the separate, laminated teeth are inserted in dovetailed slots cut in this body. The field windings are concentric coils of strip copper, insulated with mica and laid in deep radial slots in the rotor. The coil ends are usually held in place by shrunk-on retaining rings of forged nonmagnetic steel. Fans attached to the end of the rotor blow the cooling medium—air or hydrogen—along the rotor surface and out through radial ducts in the stationary portion (stator). Small channels are provided below the rotor slots, or adjacent to the slot walls, through which the cooling medium is driven, leaving the rotor through radial openings. When air is used for cooling, about 100 cu.ft. per minute are required for each kilowatt of loss, or about 200,000 cu.ft. per minute for a 100,000-kva. generator of 98% efficiency. To prevent excessive dirt accumulation, large generators are completely enclosed and the air is recirculated after passing through finned water tube coolers.

Hydrogen has seven times greater thermal conductivity and 30% lower surface temperature drop for a given transfer rate than air and permits about 25% greater output rating for a given machine. The lower density of hydrogen reduces the windage loss to about 10% of that with air and yields about 1% gain in the generator efficiency. Automatic devices control the hydrogen pressure and purity, replacing gas lost by leakage to avoid a possible explosion by admixture of air. Shaft seals hold the loss of hydrogen to low values, usually by means of lubricating oil pumped through the small shaft clearance, the entrapped air and hydrogen being continuously removed by a pumping system through which the oil is circulated.

The stator frame that supports the segmental armature punchings is usually built up of steel plates and ribs welded together. Machines are sometimes made with split frames, or with separate inner and outer frames, to facilitate shipment. The outside of the frame is covered with steel sheeting. The interior space serves as a ventilating passage. The armature punchings are of 2% to 4% silicon steel, 0.025 in. or less in thickness and insulated from each other by thin paper or enamel. Because of the great core length, armature windings usually are made of half coils or bars that are soldered together at the ends after insertion in the slots. To reduce the eddy current losses in them, the armature conductors are made of several insulated strands transposed at regular intervals throughout the length of the core so that each strand occupies each of the possible positions in a slot for equal portions of the length. Armature winding insulation usually is made of mica flakes cemented to paper tape or sheets, a number of layers being taped or wrapped on the conductors and bonded with varnish. The varnish solvent is removed later by vacuum treating and baking processes. Asphalt-base varnishes are commonly used. A layer of asbestos tape and conducting varnish is applied to coil exteriors to prevent damage from electrical discharges that might otherwise occur between a coil surface and slot edges.

Armature coil end connections must be well braced to withstand the forces that may act on them when a short circuit occurs on the system supplied from the generator. The force between two adjacent coil ends is proportional to the square of the current in the coils. The not unusual short-circuit current of 10 times normal value results in 100 times the normal force. The magnitude of the short-circuit current is limited not only by resistance of the winding but also by what is called its reactance. High reactance is undesirable insofar as it affects the change in generator voltage with change in armature current, but it is necessary to hold short-circuit currents to values that can be tolerated. Armature slots are very deep in proportion to their width to increase the reactance and to provide large cooling surfaces.

A steam-turbine-driven generator has a cylindrical or non-salient pole rotor, in contrast to the salient (or projecting) pole rotor used on slower speed generators.

Water-Wheel-Driven A.C. Generators.—Both horizontal and vertical shaft machines are used as water-wheel-driven A.C. generators. In the vertical shaft machine, the weight of the rotor and the downward thrust of the water are carried by a thrust bearing at the upper end of the shaft, while guide bearings above and below hold the rotor in a central position. A thrust bearing carries a load of about 400 lb. per square inch and is cooled by oil. The field structure is usually revolved inside the stationary armature structure. The armature frame ordinarily is built up of welded steel plates. As a water wheel may attain nearly double normal speed before the water can be shut off after a full load is dropped, the generator rotor must pass severe overspeed tests. A pilot exciter at the top supplies the field current of the main exciter below it. That in turn supplies the field current of the generator. As water may leak through closed turbine gates, brakes are provided to stop and hold the rotor when it is taken out of service. These are mounted below the rotor. The generator is cooled by air drawn in between the poles from the ends and blown out through radial ducts in the stator.

In Europe, and to an increasing extent in the U.S., amortisseur windings are used. These consist of copper bars passing through slots in the pole faces and solidly connected by short-circuiting rings at both ends. If a momentary oversupply of water to the wheel should cause the generator frequency to tend to exceed that of the system with which it is connected, currents are induced in the windings in a direction to produce braking action on the rotor. If a momentary undersupply of water should cause the generator frequency to tend to be less than that of the system, the induced currents produce an accelerating force on the rotor.

Water-wheel-driven generators, except for small ones, have a full-load efficiency ranging from 95% to 98%. The Kaplan propeller turbine with adjustable pitch blades yields higher generator speeds in low-head installations than was feasible with fixed blade turbines. These turbines have runaway speeds that may be as great as 280% of rated speed.

Water-wheel generators are so constructed as to make the inertia of the rotating structure high. The high inertia is necessary to reduce to a value that can be tolerated the fluctuations in the speed that accompany sudden changes in the load or the water supply.

Engine-Driven A.C. Generators.—This type of machine is similar to a water-wheel generator. The main differences are that engine-driven generators have horizontal shafts and amortisseur windings (unless the poles are solid). Most of them operate at low speeds and have cast-iron spiders and bolted poles. Some are made with the revolving field structure outside the stationary armature to increase the inertia or flywheel effect. Since the engine torque varies during a revolution, it produces oscillations above and below the uniform speed desired, a phenomenon known as "hunting."

When a generator operates alone, hunting may cause flickering of connected lights or undesirable surges in the speeds of connected motors. When two or more generators are in parallel, it may be that one engine is accelerating at an instant when another is decelerating; and this may cause a large interchange of current between the generators.

In an extreme case, continued parallel operation may be impossible because of the tripping of overcurrent devices in the connecting circuits.

Special Types of Generators.—Although the homopolar generator was the first developed and is the only one that generates direct current without a commutator, it is of no commercial importance because it costs more and has a lower efficiency than a commutator machine of equal rating.

A generator with permanent magnet field poles has some application in measuring speed, for control purposes and as a magneto for an ignition system.

On the automobile, a special type of D.C. generator or control is required so that sufficient current is delivered at low driving speeds and yet not too much is delivered at high speeds. Early third-brush generators made use of a differential magnetizing effect of the armature current to limit it to a permissible value. Modern generators have only two brushes and have a regulator that automatically limits the voltage and current output to permissible values. However, even the most efficient small D.C. generators proved incapable of meeting the demand of many added electrical accessories, and by the 1960s automotive manufacturers were resorting to A.C. generators coupled with converters to provide direct current for ignition and battery charging (see AUTOMOBILE: *Mechanical Operation: Modern Automobiles; Electrical System*).

A D.C. generator mounted under a railway car and belt-connected to a wheel axle is subjected not only to a wide range of speeds but also to a reversal of rotation when the direction of car travel is reversed. One type of generator for this application has the brushes attached to a rigging that will permit the brushes to be shifted through an arc equal to that from the centre of one pole to that of another. When the car is moved in one direction, the friction between them causes the commutator to shift; the brushes to one extreme position at which the generator produces the proper polarity at the armature terminals. If the car is stopped and then started in the opposite direction, the commutator shifts the brushes to the other extreme position, and the generator produces the same polarity at the armature terminals as before.

If an induction motor, when connected to A.C. lines, is driven by a prime mover in the direction it would rotate if the prime mover were not connected, but faster than its synchronous speed, it becomes an induction generator and delivers electrical energy to the lines. This type of generator has only limited applications since another source of A.C. energy is always required.

BIBLIOGRAPHY.—James R. Eaton, *Beginning Electricity* (1952); E. A. Loew, *Direct and Alternating Currents*, 3rd ed. (1946); R. G. Kloeffler *et al.*, *Direct-Current Machinery*, rev. ed. (1948); H. Cotton, *Design of Electrical Machinery* (1934); G. V. Mueller, *Alternating-Current Machines* (1952); M. G. Say and E. N. Pink, *Performance and Design of Alternating-Current Machines* (1936). (G. V. M.)

GENESIS, the name of the first book of the Old Testament, derives its title from the Septuagint rendering of ii, 4: "This is the book of the genesis of heaven and earth." In the Hebrew Bible it is called *Bereshith*, which is its first word and means "in the beginning." Genesis is the first of the five books of the Pentateuch, commonly called the five books of Moses. Beginning with the creation of the world, these books trace the history of the Hebrews down to the time of the death of Moses.

Contents.—The book of Genesis falls into two main parts, i-xi and xii-l. Of these the first deals with the primeval period and the second with the patriarchal period; the second may be divided again into xii-xxxvi, dealing with Abraham, Isaac and Jacob, and xxxvii-l, telling the story of Joseph, but containing the close of the story of Jacob.

Ch. i-xi open with an account of the creation of the world by God and the origin of sin in the serpent's temptation of Adam through his wife to eat of the forbidden fruit in the garden of Eden (i-iii), and proceed to tell of the beginnings of civilization and the moral degeneration of mankind to the time of Noah (iv-vi, 8), when God's patience was exhausted and the flood was sent to destroy all men except for the family of Noah, who was divinely led to prepare the ark in which they escaped (vi, 9-ix,). The divisions of the human race and the confusion of languages which came as a punishment of the overweening pride of men in building the tower of Babel (x-xi) are next described.

Ch. xii-xxxvi tell the story of the three patriarchs, Abraham, Isaac, and Jacob, starting from Abraham's departure from his home in Haran (Harran) and his journey to Canaan with his nephew Lot (xii), and recounting the wanderings of the patriarchs. Of particular interest are the stories of the separation of Abraham and Lot, the latter's settling in the wicked city of Sodom (xiii), the subsequent destruction of Sodom and the neighbouring cities (xix) despite Abraham's noble plea for them to be spared (xviii, 16-35); and the stories of Abraham's rescue of Lot and his fellow captives from the hands of Chedorlaomer and his confederates and payment of tithes to Melchizedek of Salem (xiv), and of Abraham's narrowly averted sacrifice of his son Isaac in the land of Moriah (xxii). Both Isaac and his son Jacob retained their connections with the land from which Abraham came by taking their wives from among their kindred there, Jacob spending many years in the home of his father-in-law, Laban, with Leah and Rachel, the two sisters whom he married (xxviii-xxxi). Here special interest attaches to the story of Jacob's dream at Bethel when he left home (xxviii), and his encounter with the divine assailant by the ford of Jabbok on his return (xxxii, 22-32).

Ch. xxxvii-l tell the immortal story of Joseph, who by his dreams incurred the jealousy and hatred of his brothers, who sold him as a slave into Egypt (xxxvii), where his moral integrity once more brought trouble and imprisonment upon him (xxxix). Subsequently his skill in interpreting dreams (xl) brought him before Pharaoh (xli), who was so impressed by Joseph's interpretations of his own dreams that he promoted him to high office in the state and entrusted important aspects of the administration of the land to him. There follows the story of the coming of Joseph's brothers to Egypt to seek food in a time of famine, and of Joseph's magnanimous forgiveness of their former callous conduct toward him, and the subsequent descent of his father Jacob and the whole family to live in the land of Goshen (xliii-xlvii). This leads on to the story of the oppression in Egypt, with which Exodus opens, and the subsequent deliverance under Moses and the establishment of the covenant of Sinai.

Sources and Purpose.—Since the 18th century much attention has been paid to the evidences of older sources drawn on by the compiler of Genesis, and the reasons for rejecting the tradition that Moses was its author. Three main sources have been distinguished, but there is evidence that material from a variety of older sources has been preserved—mainly in the poetical passages—though some of these may have existed in oral form only (see PENTATEUCH). Some Scandinavian scholars reject the theory of written sources, and hold that the traditions were orally preserved until the composition of the present book.

It is more important to consider the purpose for which the book in its present form was compiled. From whatever source or sources the compiler drew his material, he wished to set forth the beginnings of the history of his own people in terms of the purpose of God for the world. In the story of creation and the flood, his interest is less in the "facts" of the story than in their meaning. God created man for his own fellowship and to obey his will, and only through that obedience could the fellowship be maintained. To miss this through concentration on all the details of the story, which are often characterized as naïve, and on the etiological motifs that may be traced in it, is to miss the author's real aim. The story of the flood is not recounted merely as an event of the past but as something to be understood only in the light of what the author believed to be the purpose of God. Much in the early chapters of Genesis has links with Babylonian traditions. Yet more significant is the quite different use the author makes of it. The puerilities of the Babylonian stories disappear, and the conception of God is quite other than that of the Babylonian authors. Gone is the polytheism, and the author's understanding of the purpose of the only God who figures in his story dominates his work. This is clearly brought out in the major elements of the story on which attention is concentrated.

After the flood the author's interest is limited first to the family of Shem, then to the family of Abraham and finally to the family of Jacob, who is renamed Israel (xxxii, 28). Yet the reader is reminded that there is a wider world to which Israel belongs, including all the nations of the earth known to the author. Abraham is called to leave his father's house not merely to receive the promise of the land of Canaan but in order that in him all the families of the earth should bless themselves (xii, 3; cf. xviii, 18; xxii, 18; xxvi, 4; xxviii, 14). It would be reading too much into these words to find here the conception of the universal sharing of the faith of Abraham. Nevertheless there is the implicit thought that Abraham's obedience to the will of God gave him a universal significance, and his separation from his own people is linked with his meaning for all peoples.

The full meaning of the author's limitation of the story to Jacob in the next stage of his narrative does not appear until the book of Exodus is reached, when the sojourn in Egypt becomes the prelude to the deliverance whereby God reveals his saving power and his compassion, leading to the covenant, whereby Israel pledges herself in gratitude to give him that obedience which alone could give her universal significance.

Historical Value.—That the prepatriarchal section cannot be treated as literal history is beyond question. There are, for instance, discrepancies between the two accounts of creation (in the first, man and woman are created together after all the beasts; in the second, man is created before the beasts and woman after), and within what now appears to be the single account of the flood (in some places a single pair of all species is taken into the ark and in others a single pair of unclean creatures but clean creatures in sevens). Though traditions of a universal flood are found among other peoples, it is impossible to suppose that the whole earth was covered with water to a depth that submerged all the mountains (see FLOOD [IN RELIGION AND MYTH]). On the other hand it can scarcely be doubted that the flood story rests on the memory of some dreadful devastation by water. Archaeological expeditions have revealed deep deposits believed to be the result of flood in some Babylonian cities, and these have been hailed as confirmation of the biblical story. Yet corresponding layers were not found in neighbouring cities, and at Kish evidence that the Babylonian flood story was already known have been found beneath the "flood" layer. But it is quite insufficient to dismiss these stories as historically worthless and based on older Babylonian texts. The compiler of Genesis included them to serve his religious purpose.

The stories of the patriarchs are of a different literary genre. Yet they cannot be treated as strictly historical. For instance, there are references to the Philistines in Genesis (xxi, 32, 34; xxvi, 1, 8, 14, 15, 18); yet the Philistine incursion into Palestine did not take place until after the latest possible date for the age of the patriarchs. This does not mean that these stories preserve no historical memories. Many scholars have regarded them as personifications of tribal histories. It is possible that some such elements are found in the stories. In ch. xxxiv Shechem is a person, and frequently in the Old Testament tribes such as the Midianites, the Ammonites, the Edomites are spoken of under the names of their eponymous ancestors, Midian, Ammon, Edom. The patriarchal stories as a whole cannot be so treated, however. Abraham has always resisted the efforts to dissolve him into a tribe, and the less colourful Isaac cannot be equated with any known tribe. Jacob, the immediate ancestor of the tribes of Israel and their eponymous ancestor under his alternative name of Israel, is a less exalted character than Abraham, and it is hard to escape the conclusion that personal stories as well as tribal traditions have been drawn on.

Excavations at Mesopotamian sites, and especially at Nuzi, have contributed much to bring about the greater respect for these stories that has come to be general. Customs which figure in these stories but which were obsolete at the time when the stories are believed to have been written down are known to have prevailed in the 2nd millennium B.C. (i.e., in the age of the patriarchs) in the Mesopotamia from which the patriarchs are said to have come. From Nuzi there are examples of the adoption of slaves or freeborn persons by childless people, like Abraham's adoption of Eliezer (xv, 3). There, as in the case of Eliezer, the adopted son gave place to the true son if one should subsequently be born. In Nuzi marriage contracts it was often laid down that if the wife should prove childless she must provide her husband with a slave wife to take her place. This custom again is reflected in the biblical stories. Further, in Nuzi if the legal wife should subsequently bear a child, he must take precedence over the slave's child, as was the case with Isaac. It is there laid down, however, that the slave's child must not be expelled. This sheds light on Abraham's reluctance to expel his slave wife Hagar and their son Ishmael until he is divinely told to do so. Rachel's theft of her father's household gods or *teraphim* (xxxi, 19) is illuminated by the same Nuzi texts, in which the possession of such images carried the title to the inheritance of the father's property.

While full weight must be given to the genuine contemporary colour now known to belong to these biblical stories, one must be careful not to go beyond their evidence. If the ancient traditions preserved the memory of obsolete customs, the presumption is strong that they contained true memories in other respects. This does not mean that they can be treated as authentic history in the modern scholarly sense. The fact that Genesis relates two stories of Abraham's passing off his wife as his sister (xii, 10 ff. and xx, 1 ff.) and a similar story of Isaac (xxvi, 6 ff.) probably means that a single story has been differently assigned, rather than that the patriarchs made a practice of this behaviour. Thus, though there is probably a real historical element in the stories, it cannot be recovered with security.

There is but one passage which sets Abraham in the current of world history, and this abounds in problems. Ch. xiv relates the war between Amraphel and his allies and the king of Sodom and his allies. Amraphel has often been identified with Hammurabi of Babylon so that this passage has been used to date Abraham. The biblical chronology would seem to place Abraham in the 21st century B.C., and when Hammurabi was assigned the date 2123–2081 B.C. (as in the *Cambridge Ancient History*, vol. i, 2nd ed., p. 154, 1924), this seemed to tie in nicely. But it is now known from royal synchronisms in the Mari texts that Hammurabi belonged to the 18th or the early 17th century B.C. Many scholars place his reign at 1792–50, or 1729–1686 B.C. Some believe that the general conditions reflected in the stories about him would answer those of the 19th century B.C. Moreover, three or four contemporary kings bore the name Hammurabi. Further, the equating of the name Amraphel with Hammurabi is difficult and is generally given up. It is therefore impossible to date the period of Abraham securely. It should be added that ch. xiv is believed not to be derived from any of the main sources of Genesis. The common view early in the 20th century that it was a late document is no longer held, however, and many scholars date it in the time of David.

The story of Joseph may reasonably be held to preserve more reliable historical memories. There is clear evidence of acquaintance with Egyptian life and customs. The incident of Joseph and Potiphar's wife (xxxix, 7 ff.) is often compared with the parallel Egyptian story of the Two Brothers, but the one is not necessarily derived from the other. It is not hard to suppose that more than one woman may have been guilty of a similar seductive attempt. The rise of a Semite to high office under the Pharaoh is not improbable, even though there is no independent confirmation of this particular incident. Joseph's immovable integrity in prosperity or adversity and his magnanimity toward his brothers make this one of the great stories of the world, and there is no reason to doubt that it rests on actual history. Difficulty arises in attempting to determine the period in which Joseph lived. The biblical chronology would place him long before the time of the Hyksos rulers of Egypt, but many scholars think he should be dated in Hyksos times. In that age it would have been little honour to give Joseph the daughter of the priest of On to wife (xli, 45), since the Hyksos rulers did not respect Ra, the god whose principal temple was at On, or Heliopolis. Other features of the story are hard to connect with this age, and it has been argued that the period of the heretic Pharaoh Ikhnaton (q.v.) would best fit the conditions. This Pharaoh had broken with the Theban priesthood, which had provided many of the chief officers of state, and he would therefore be glad to avail himself of a skilled administrator. He exalted the sun-god to be the sole god whose worship was permitted in Egypt, and worshiped him under the name Aton, whose symbol was the sun disk, so that in no other age would it be a higher honour to marry the daughter of the priest of On.

Characteristics.—Attention has been drawn above to the broad purpose of the compiler of Genesis, and it has been linked with the total purpose of the compilation of the Pentateuch, of which this book forms the first part. It must be recognized, however, that a great variety of interests of the compiler have dictated his choice of some of the material and his use of it. Reference has been made to the etiological motifs which may be traced in many passages. While these must not overshadow the larger aims of the compiler, they should not be overlooked. The subordina-tion of woman to man, the origin of sin and of woman's pains in childbirth, the reason for the variety of languages in the world, the source of the diversity of trades and professions, the explanation of the avoidance of the eating of "the sinew of the thigh" (xxxii, 32), all figure in this book.

The author is much interested in sacred sites, and records a number of theophanies, or divine appearances to men, whereby sites which were marked by shrines where the Israelites later wor-shipped acquired their sanctity. The most notable of these is Bethel, where Jacob had his vision of the ladder reaching up to heaven (xxviii, 12) and where God appeared to him again on his return from Paddan-aram (xxxv, 9 ff.). Other sites where Is-raelite sanctuaries were later found which figure in the stories of the patriarchs are Shechem (xii, 6 ff.); Beersheba (xxi, 31 ff.); Hebron (xiii, 18) and Mizpah (xxxi, 49). Here again, therefore, an etiological element may be found.

A number of blessings are recorded in Genesis, and it is clear that much significance was attached to them. Noah pronounces a curse on Canaan and a blessing on Shem and Japheth (ix, 25 ff.); Abraham blesses Melchizedek (xiv, 19 ff.), Rebekah's family pro-nounces a blessing on her (xxiv, 60), Isaac blesses Jacob (xxvii, 27 ff.) and then pronounces what is probably to be understood as a curse on Esau (xxvii, 39–40), and Jacob blesses the sons of Joseph (xlviii, 15–16). All of these are in poetical form, and in the case of the oracles on Reuben and on Simeon and Levi.

Religious Teaching.

—In the story of creation and of the garden of Eden man is represented as created by God for fellow-ship in obedience to him. By disobedience the fellowship was broken, and it is significant that Adam hid himself from God before he was expelled from the garden. Here in this very early story is found a deep understanding of the character of sin and a clear recognition that man's truest well-being is to be found in doing the will of God. Adam's inner awareness of his disobedience isolates him from God before his punishment falls upon him. His sin is therefore no less against himself than it is against God. His sinful act is sometimes interpreted in terms of sexual ex-perience and the tree of knowledge explained as marital inter-course. In the first account of creation, however, God's com-mand to man is to be fruitful and multiply, and in the second God is at pains to provide him with a suitable partner. It is hard to suppose, therefore, that marital intercourse was thought to be sinful. The forbidden tree is symbolic not of one particular act of disobedience but of all disobedience to the will of God (see also ADAM AND EVE; EDEN).

The following stories contain penetrating insights into the nature of sin. Cain's jealousy of Abel leads to murder and then to Cain's awareness that the hand of every man would be against him. It should not, however, be forgotten that Cain's sin was not merely against God and himself but also against Abel. A man may therefore suffer for the sin of another, and not alone for his own sin. The antisocial nature of sin is further brought out in the subsequent chapters. It spread like a canker through society until God saw that all the imagination of man's heart was evil, and nothing but destruction was adequate to deal with it. Yet even here divine justice was tempered with mercy, and the family of Noah was spared—not wholly for its own righteousness, as can be seen from Noah's conduct after the flood, but in order that it might preserve the species for a new day of opportunity. Here is the beginning of the conception of the remnant, which became so fruit-ful in later prophetic teaching.

The story of the tower of Babel shows how human pride recoils in curse upon men, as later in the story of Lot his cupidity blinds him to his folly in choosing to live in Sodom. In all of this there is profound spiritual teaching, and these chapters are not to be dismissed as childish tales. The simplicity of their form should not distract attention from their depth of penetration, which is the more surprising when their great antiquity is remembered.

The religion of the patriarchs is presented in simple terms. They offer sacrifice, but never employ any priest. In passages ascribed to the latest of the sources of the Pentateuch, which are believed to have a priestly origin, no reference is made to sac-rifice in the time of the patriarchs. This is believed to be due to the fact that in the eyes of the priestly writer no sacrifice could be valid before it was ordained by God and offered by the duly appointed priesthood. In other passages, however, sacrifices offered by the patriarchs figure. The places which appear in the stories are often marked by sacred trees (at Hebron, xiii, 18; xiv, 13; xviii, 1; at Beersheba, xxi, 33; at Shechem, xxxv, 4; at Bethel, xxxv, 8), wells or springs (at Kadesh, xiv, 7, where En-mishpat means "spring of judgment"; at Beersheba, xxi, 29 ff.) or stones (at Bethel, xxviii, 11 ff.). This has led to the supposition that the religion of the patriarchs may be described as animism, according to which these sacred objects were believed to be inhabited by numina, which gave them their sanctity. Such a view is quite inadequate, and it fails to take account of the intimate fellowship between, for instance, Abraham and God, which is quite untypical of what is understood by animism.

The quality of the religion is not to be limited by concentra-tion on the places where sacrifice was offered. It is predominantly a personal religion, consisting not in rites and ceremonies but in a fellowship which leads to exalted character. This is particularly manifest in the case of Abraham, despite the stories of his de-ception in the matter of his wife. The story of his projected sacrifice of Isaac (ch. xxii) is sometimes thought to have a double etiological motif, to explain both why human sacrifice was not demanded by Israel's religion (though there were periods of her history when such sacrifices were offered, under the influence of neighbouring peoples) and why the Temple site was sacred. There is, however, no certainty that Abraham's sacrifice actually took place on the Temple mount, and the story is not merely that of a man who almost offered his son and learned that God did not really want such sacrifices. It is shown in addition that Abraham did not withhold from God what was most precious to him, not because he was making an agonized appeal for some personal advantage, as Mesha did when he offered his son (II Kings iii, 27), but in order to express his obedience to God. Abraham's magnanimity toward Lot in allowing the younger man his choice of country when the two separated (xiii, 8 ff.); his noble intercession for Sodom and Gomorrah (xviii, 22 ff.), which is not to be missed through concentration on the characteristic oriental bargaining which provides the form of the intercession; his unwillingness to accept any personal profit from his rescue of Lot and his fellow captives (xiv, 22 ff.)—all reveal a character of singular exaltation, especially in the setting of the times in which he lived.

Of contemporary Canaanite religion there is considerable knowl-edge through the recovery of the Ras Shamra texts, and it presents a very different picture from the religion of the patriarchs as reflected in Genesis. W. F. Albright, basing himself on these texts and other sources of knowledge of Canaanite religion in the 2nd millennium B.C., speaks of "the extremely low level of Canaanite religion, which inherited a relatively very primitive mythology and had adopted some of the most demoralizing cultic practices then existing in the Near East. . . . The brutality of Canaanite mythology, both in the tablets of Ugarit and in the later epitome of Philo Byblius, passes belief" (in *Studies in the History of Culture*, pp. 28 ff.; 1942). It is not from this source that the character of Abraham, as portrayed in the Bible, is to be explained.

On the other hand, if the ideals of the compiler rather than the character of an individual of the remote past are reflected in Genesis, it is difficult to explain why Jacob is portrayed in less exalted terms, despite the fact that he was believed to be the father of the 12 sons from whom the tribes of Israel sprang. In him are less pleasant traits. His taking advantage of his brother, Esau (xxv, 29 ff.); his deception of his father (xxvii, 5 ff.); his outwitting of Laban, his father-in-law (xxx, 25 ff.); his bargaining with God for his own advantage (xxviii, 20 ff.), put him on a much lower level, and it is hard to suppose that the compiler was not aware of this. Jacob's disappointments and sorrows are the recompense he receives. Chastened perhaps by these, but also transformed by his spiritual struggle at the ford of Jabbok (xxxii, 22 ff.), he rises above his earlier self, though he never attains to the loftiness of Abraham. Nor are the founders of the 12 tribes depicted in a way that leads to the supposition that they and Abraham reflected the ideals of the compiler of the book. For their treatment of Joseph they clearly stand condemned (ch. xxxvii). Moreover, the treachery of Simeon and Levi at Shechem (ch. xxxiv) brings upon them the condemnation of their father, and is generally believed to have been the direct cause of the scattering in Israel which stands as a curse on these two tribes in the blessing of Jacob (xlix, 5–7). Throughout, the compiler is using his material as the vehicle of his teaching rather than reflecting his ideals in his portrayal of his characters.

Reference has been made to the lofty teaching inherent in the story of Joseph. "The Lord was with Joseph" (xxxix, 2, 21 is given as the reason why Joseph came through his misfortunes; but he is also presented as a man who was faithful to his father's God and who rose to high nobility of character no less than to high office. All of this and much more gives to the book of Genesis a profound religious quality, and sets before its readers ideals of character and of faith. *See also* BIBLE.

BIBLIOGRAPHY.—G. J. Spurrell, *Notes on the Hebrew Text of the Book of Genesis* (1887); Commentary on the Hebrew text by J. Skinner, 2nd ed. (1910) in *International Critical Commentary*: Eng. trans. with commentary by S. R. Driver (1904; 12th ed. by G. R. Driver, 1926) in *Westminster Commentaries*, by W. H. Bennett (n.d.) in *Century Bible*, by H. E. Ryle (1914) in *Cambridge Bible* and by C. A. Simpson in *Interpreter's Bible*, vol. i, pp. 437–829 (1952); G. von Rad, *Genesis* (1953; Eng. trans. 1961); E. A. Speiser (1964) in *Anchor Bible*; German trans. with commentary by H. Gunkel, 5th ed. (1922). *See also* S. H. Hooke, *In the Beginning* (1947) in *Clarendon Bible*. For analysis of pre-Deuteronomic elements of Genesis see C. A. Simpson, *Early Traditions of Israel* (1948).
(H. H. Ro.)

GENÊT, EDMOND CHARLES (1763–1834), French diplomat who during the French Revolution tried to bring the United States into the war against England, was born at Versailles on Jan. 8, 1763. He was the son of the head of the translation department at the ministry of foreign affairs, Edmé Jacques Genêt, whom he succeeded in that post in 1781. When the department was suppressed in 1788 he was appointed secretary of the French legation to Russia under Louis Philippe, comte de Ségur. The outbreak of the Revolution in France caused Ségur's departure, and on Oct. 11, 1789, Genêt was made *chargé d'affaires*. His enthusiasm for the Revolution then antagonized Catherine the Great, who slighted him continually, forbade him to appear in court and finally expelled him from Russia (July 1792). On Nov. 14, 1792, Genêt was appointed ambassador to Holland by the Girondin ministry, of which he was regarded as a supporter. In April 1793, however, the ministry transferred him to the United States as *chargé d'affaires*.

Instructed to raise money to set against the U.S. debt to France or at least to obtain credit for purchasing supplies if military aid under the Franco-U.S. alliance of 1778 was not forthcoming, Genêt behaved too impetuously. Hailed as "Citizen" Genêt by Americans who favoured the French cause, he conspired with those who opposed Washington's policy of neutrality. His efforts to bring the United States into the war and his highhanded arming of privateers in U.S. ports to operate against the British brought relations between the U.S. and France to the brink of war and risked the loss of France's sole source of credit abroad. Washington asked for Genêt's recall in August and the French Committee of Public Safety agreed. Genêt, unwilling to face this Jacobin committee, chose instead to settle in the United States, where he married the daughter of George Clinton, governor of New York, and became a U.S. citizen. He devoted himself to farming until his death at Schodack, N.Y., on July 14, 1834.

See P. Mantoux, "Le Comité de salut public et la mission de Genêt aux États-Unis," *Revue d'histoire moderne*, vol. xiii (1909–10).
(A. So.)

GENÊT, JEAN (1910–), French writer who as a novelist transforms his erotic and often obscene subject matter into a poetic and even mystical vision of the universe, and who as a dramatist has become a leading figure in the development of the post-Brechtian "epic" or "open-plan" theatre. Born in Paris on Dec. 19, 1910, Genet was an unwanted child who spent part of his adolescence at a notorious reform school (Mettray), where he lived through many of the nauseating experiences later described in the novel *Miracle de la rose* (1945–46; *Miracle of the Rose*, 1965). His autobiographical *Journal du voleur* (1949; *The Thief's Journal*, 1954) gives an uninhibited account of his life as a tramp, pickpocket, and professional catamite in Barcelona, Antwerp, and various other cities (c. 1930–39); it also reveals him as an aesthete, an existentialist, and a pioneer of the Absurd. It was while imprisoned for burglary at Fresnes in 1942 that he began to write. A series of curiously precious poems (e.g., "Le Condamné à mort," 1942; *The Man Condemned to Death*, 1965), obsessed with sex and death, was followed by an outstanding novel, *Notre-Dame des Fleurs* (1944; *Our Lady of the Flowers*, 1949), vividly portraying the underworld of thugs, pimps, and male prostitutes of the pre-war Butte Montmartre. A prison visitor was struck by his talent; and through her, he became known, first to Jean Cocteau, later to Jean Paul Sartre and to Simone de Beauvoir.

In 1947 Genet burgled once too often, and was condemned to a form of perpetual preventive detention; at the last minute, however, a delegation of famous writers appealed on his behalf to the president of the republic (Vincent Auriol), and he was reprieved. Meanwhile he had written two further novels, *Pompes funèbres* (1947; *Funeral Rites*, 1968) and *Querelle de Brest* (1947; *Querelle of Brest*, 1966), and had begun to experiment with the drama. His early attempts, by their compact, neoclassical, one-act structure, reveal (as does his philosophy at this period) the strong influence of Sartre. *Haute Surveillance* (1949; *Deathwatch*, 1954) continues the themes of *Miracle de la rose*; but *Les Bonnes* (1946; *The Maids*, 1954) begins to explore those complex problems of identity which were soon to preoccupy both Samuel Beckett and Eugène Ionesco (qq.v.). It was this second play (particularly in its revised version, 1954) which established Genet's reputation as one of the outstanding dramatists of the avant-garde theatre. At this point, however, under the impact of Antonin Artaud and Bertolt Brecht, Genet broke free of neoclassicism; and his subsequent plays, *Le Balcon* (1956; *The Balcony*, 1958), *Les Nègres* (1958; *The Blacks*, 1960), and *Les Paravents* (1961; *The Screens*, 1962), are large-scale, stylized, caricatural dramas in the Expressionist manner, designed to shock an audience by playing on its political, racial, and religious prejudices.

Genet is a rebel and an anarchist of the most extreme variety, rejecting all forms of social discipline or political commitment. The violent and often degraded eroticism of his experience leads him, by way of a complex pattern of symbolism, to a concept of mystic humiliation or "sanctity" that owes much to Dostoevski. At the same time, his pornography is never gratuitous. If he explores the furthest limits of shame and abjection, it is to establish the ultimate solitude of man that lies beyond the facade of social solidarity; and his "Theatre of Hatred" represents an attempt to wrest a maximum of emotional and dramatic power from a social or political situation, while at the same time avoiding the platitudes of committed propaganda, whether of the right or of the left.

BIBLIOGRAPHY.—J.-P. Sartre, *Saint Genet, comédien et martyr* (1952; *Saint Genet, Actor and Martyr*, 1963); M. Esslin, *The Theatre of the Absurd* (1961); J. H. McMahon, *The Imagination of Jean Genet* (1963); J. M. Magnan, *Essai sur Jean Genet* (1966); R. N. Coe, *The Vision of Jean Genet* (1968); P. Thody, *Jean Genet, a Critical Appraisal* (1968). (R. N. Co.)

GENETICS, the scientific study of heredity and variation, was so named by William Bateson in 1906, although its origins are traced chiefly to the discovery, about 40 years earlier, by Gregor Johann Mendel (q.v.) of the first general laws of heredity. Genetics is often called the core science of biology. This does not necessarily mean that genetics is the most fundamental among the biological disciplines. It implies only that genetics impinges upon almost every kind of study of life. Anthropology, medicine, biochemistry, physiology, psychology, ecology, systematics, comparative morphology, paleontology; all have borderline considerations with genetics. A geneticist may collaborate with workers in any one, or in several, of the sciences just named.

Genetics is particularly relevant to the understanding of man. Mankind did not cease to be a biological species when it developed culture and civilization. To understand man, both his biological and his cultural-spiritual dimensions must be taken into account. Neglect of either of these dimensions is a sure way to error and misconception. The recognition of this fact does not, of course, preclude the possibility, and indeed the necessity, of studying man by different methods and by specialists in different biological and social sciences. Mankind, as well as all other organisms, is a product of a long history of organic evolution, one that is still going on. Genetics is most relevant to understanding the process of evolution (q.v.) and the causes that bring it about.

Like so many basic, or "theoretical," sciences, genetics has many actual and potential practical applications. Many diseases, malformations, and weaknesses afflicting organisms are conditioned by heredity. Medical genetics is of increasing importance in the understanding and control of the defective heredity. Scientific plant and animal breeding (q.v.) are guided by genetic principles. The need to provide food for the burgeoning population of the world makes the genetics applied to agriculture very important. Most important of all may eventually become the application of genetics for the betterment of the hereditary endowment of mankind, which is the aim of eugenics (q.v.). This endowment must, if possible, be improved; in any event, it should not be permitted to deteriorate.

History.—Even before Mendel's time experimental attempts to analyze the process of biological inheritance had been made by studying the offspring of hybrids between varieties of plants that differed in well-marked traits. Some indications had already been found that certain parental characters, such as seed colour, reappeared as separable traits in the descendants of hybrids. But the crucial demonstration of the hereditary mechanism was the result of carefully planned breeding experiments of Mendel, first reported in 1865 and published the following year.

These epochal experiments revealed that the hereditary material that passes from parents to offspring is particulate in nature and consists of an organization of living units, now known as genes. During the period between 1856 and 1865 Mendel formulated some simple statistical rules describing the transmission of these units in the garden pea, but his observations lay unremarked until 1900, when they were confirmed by several biologists working independently.

Since that time the chief principle that Mendel discovered has been found to be of general validity in all forms of life, from viruses to man. It has been shown that the system of Mendelian heredity, which is primarily responsible for the continuity of living substance through reproduction, is based on a multiplicity of different genes, which separate and recombine as they pass from generation to generation.

Beginning about 1910 additional principles of heredity were established, chiefly by the work of T. H. Morgan (q.v.) and others. These, with the principle discovered by Mendel, formed the groundwork for the modern theory of the gene. Research into the fine structure of genes and into gene action was stimulated by the Watson-Crick formulation, in 1953, of DNA (deoxyribonucleic acid), the molecular basis of the genetic material (see GENE.)

The foundations of genetics have been developed and tested by research carried out in various parts of the world, including the Soviet Union before 1948. In that year, however, a statement issued by the Communist Party of the U.S.S.R. declared the theory of the gene to be in conflict with the party line and declared as official the conception of heredity contained in the writings of the Russian horticulturist I. V. Michurin as interpreted by the Soviet agronomist T. D. Lysenko (q.v.). With the death of Stalin in 1953, Lysenkoism waned, but it was not officially repudiated till after Khrushchev's fall in the autumn of 1964. After more than 20 years as the driving force in Soviet biology, Lysenko was deposed and his theories were discredited. The eradication of Lysenko's doctrines was begun in 1965 with the commemoration of a new Soviet monthly journal, Genetika, published by the Academy of Sciences. Classical genetics once again became respectable in the Soviet Union.

Applications of Genetics.—Although the principles of genetics appear to be coextensive with living matter, their consequences assume human or economic values that vary with different forms of life. Thus human genetics is especially concerned with the interplay of hereditary and environmental factors in determining the physical and mental characters of man, with the effects of heredity on diseases, abnormalities and special abilities and with the biological differentiation of interbreeding groups of man, such as races or subgroups separated by geographic or cultural factors such as language, religion or tradition.

Medical genetics is especially concerned with the influence of heredity on conditions of medical importance, and eugenics (q.v.) with means for the eradication of deleterious genes and for the improvement of human genotypes. Animal breeding (q.v.) and plant breeding (q.v.) utilize genetic principles in programs for improvement of livestock and useful plants. Genetics of microorganisms (bacterial genetics and genetics of fungi, of viruses and of protozoa) has assumed special importance (1) as an applied science concerned with control of pathogenic and parasitic forms, with the utilization of microorganisms in fermentation and with production of antibiotics and of accessory food factors; and (2) as an avenue of approach to the understanding of such fundamental processes as mutation and the manner of effect of genes on metabolic processes.

General Views.—Before discussing any of the special problems of genetics it is necessary to understand the sense in which the terms "heredity" and "hereditary" are used in genetics. An essential act of clarification was that performed by the Danish biologist Wilhelm Johannsen, who first pointed out in 1909 the distinction between "genotype" and "phenotype," a distinction that has proved to be of fundamental importance in genetics. Johannsen, by analyzing results of his breeding experiments with populations of bean plants, discriminated between two sources of variation in such characters as seed weight.

Individual bean plants reproduce by self-fertilization; therefore all such offspring are identical in heredity, forming a "pure line." Continued selective breeding of variants within a pure line (e.g., planting the heaviest or the lightest seeds) resulted in no change in the average weight of seeds; such differences were thus not due to differences in heredity. Selection applied to a mixed population, including seeds characterized by different seed weights, was quickly effective in separating lines characterized by different seed weights. Variation of the first kind, i.e., within a pure line, was called phenotypic; of the second kind, i.e., between pure lines, was called genotypic. The terms are defined as follows: the genotype of an individual is its genetic constitution, the assortment of genes received from the parents; the phenotype is its appearance, the sum total of all the characteristics of the individual, external and internal, structural, physiological and behavioural.

The importance of the distinction is that the genotype is determined by ancestry alone and is kept constant in different conditions and throughout life by the generally faithful reproduction of the genes in all cells of the individual; it can be revealed only by breeding tests or by a record of ancestry. The phenotype, however, is jointly determined by the intrinsic factors received from the parents and by the continuous response of the developing individual to the extrinsic sources of food and energy; it can be revealed by direct examination. The processes of metabolism, growth and development require continuous adjustment of living individuals to their environments. The phenotype is the outcome of this interplay between the intrinsic and extrinsic factors; it changes with age, state of nutrition and health and is influenced by light, heat and other factors of the physical environment.

It follows that "characters," as such, are not inherited; they result from processes of development initiated and modulated by the genotype, which sets limits or ranges to the responses that the individual makes to its environment. The diversity of phenotypes that arises from the interactions between a given genotype and the variety of environments in which it may exist has been called the norm of reaction of that genotype. Thus, what is inherited is the genotype with its norm of reaction, the capacity to respond during development to a range of environmental conditions.

Heredity may consequently be viewed as the repetition in organisms related by descent of genotypic patterns of metabolism and development. This repetition depends, in essence, on the self-reproduction of hereditary elements. In this view, all structures and activities of organisms are due to their heredity, and all at the same time are due to responses to their environments.

It is implicit in this view that while genotypes give rise to genotypes (by replication and transmission of genes to offspring) and to phenotypes (by influencing the ways in which development takes place), phenotypes do not influence genotypes. New hereditary variations, which make new modes or levels of response to environment possible, are due to changes in the genotype and are not effects, as was once thought, of changes in the phenotype. The latter idea, known as the inheritance of acquired characters (see LAMARCKISM), became obsolete with the proof of the existence of self-reproducing units, genes, changes in which are due to a random process, mutation.

Mutation (q.v.) gives rise to a variety of gene forms, which in the course of sexual reproduction are shuffled and recombined in all possible ways. The variety of genotypes thus engendered in the species is winnowed, in the course of generations, by the variety of natural environments in which the species has lived (see EVOLUTION, ORGANIC). Existing genotypes, therefore, have been formed by natural selection acting upon arrays of genes that have the two properties of self-reproduction and mutability.

The Study of Genetics.—The problems with which genetics deals may be grouped under three main heads.

Transmission Genetics.—This is the analytical study of the mechanisms by which genes reproduce, segregate, and recombine; of their spatial arrangements in the chromosomes; and of the occasional cases in which self-reproducing elements are transmitted outside of the nucleus (cytoplasmic inheritance). The principles by which genes are transmitted to descendants all relate to the behaviour of these elements during reproduction, namely during meiosis and fertilization (see CELL).

Physiological Genetics.—This includes phenogenetics, or developmental genetics, and is concerned with the causal relations between genes and the specific characters, chemical, physiological or morphological, that arise during growth, metabolism, and differentiation of living individuals. The chief question with which physiological genetics is concerned is how genes act as regulators of the processes of life as they occur within each individual, first in the cells and then (in multicellular animals and plants) in the tissues and organs whose integrated activities constitute the individual.

Population Genetics.—This is concerned with the arrangements of genes in populations and with the forces such as mutation and natural selection that tend to change the arrays of hereditary variety, leading to formation of races, subspecies, species, and other natural categories. Since the main purpose of population genetics is to analyze the processes by which evolution occurs, it is sometimes called evolutionary genetics. The development of theory in population genetics was stimulated by consideration of evolution as the process by which the genotypes of populations change with time, chiefly under the influence of natural selection, and by the needs of practical plant and animal breeders seeking to improve varieties by artificial selection and other means depending on manipulation of genotypes.

BIBLIOGRAPHY.—J. A. Peters (ed.), *Classic Papers in Genetics* (1959); L. C. Dunn (ed.), *Genetics in the 20th Century* (1951); *The Birth of Genetics*, pub. by Brooklyn Bot. Gardens (1950); R. C. Punnett, "Early Days of Genetics," *Heredity*, 4:1–10 (1950); F. A. E. Crew, *The Foundations of Genetics* (1966).

GENEVA (GENÈVE), a canton of southwest Switzerland situated between the Jura and the Alps and consisting mainly of the city of Geneva. With an area of 282 sq.km. (109 sq.mi.) of which 30 sq.km. (11.5 sq.mi.) are lake, it is, except for Zug, the smallest canton in the Swiss confederation. In the extreme north it borders on Vaud canton for 3½ mi., but is otherwise surrounded by French territory, the *département* of Haute Savoie to the south, and that of the Ain west and north. The Rhône flows through it from east to west and then along its southwest edge. The turbid Arve which flows from the chain of Mont Blanc is its largest tributary and joins the Rhône within the city of Geneva. The climate is healthful, the proximity of the lake regularizing the temperature. Market gardens, orchards and vineyards occupy a large proportion of the soil. Cattle, horses, swine, goats and sheep are kept. Beside building materials, such as sandstone and slate, the only mineral to be found within the canton is bituminous shale.

Geneva was admitted into the Swiss confederation in 1815. In 1815–16 it was increased by adding to the old territory belonging to the city 16 communes (to the south and east) ceded by Savoy and 6 communes (to the north) from the French district of Gex. In 1847 Jean Jacques (James) Fazy instituted a radical regime, but his failure to obtain re-election to the *conseil d'etat* (the executive authority) led in 1864 to disturbances. The radical party in 1870 returned to power and supported the Church of the Old Catholics (q.v.) founded by Père Hyacinthe (Charles) Loyson, against the Roman Catholics. The Roman Catholic bishop of Geneva, Gaspard Mermillod, who later became a cardinal, was exiled in 1873, but a later radical leader, Henri Fazy, was more in sympathy with Roman Catholicism. The separation of church and state was voted in 1907. The conservative party, known as the Democrats, introduced certain reforms such as the referendum, the popular initiative and proportional representation. The Socialist party and other party formations later came into existence. In 1960 the canton adopted women's suffrage in cantonal and commune affairs.

In 1950 the population of the canton was 202,918; in 1959 it was estimated at 247,882; and at the census of 1960 it was 259,234. As to religion, the 1959 population was divided as follows (1950 figures in parentheses): Roman Catholics 110,007 (108,242); Protestants 83,683 (97,877); Jews 3,737 (3,044). By nationality 78,101 (68,623) were Genevese citizens, and 117,748 (99,683) Swiss citizens of other cantons; in 1919 the canton contained 62,611 foreigners, but by 1930 the number had fallen to 51,727 because of emigration during and after World War I, and fell to 40,888 as a result of World War II; in 1959 foreigners numbered 52,033 of whom 12,536 were French, 18,481 Italians, 3,823 Germans and 17,193 citizens of various other countries.

In 1950 there were 138,627 French-speaking people, French being the mother tongue of the Genevese; 24,983 were German-speaking; and there were also 215 Romansh-speaking.

(G. Vr.)

GENEVA (Fr. GENÈVE, Ger. GENF, Italian GINEVRA), a city of Switzerland and capital of the canton of Geneva, lies in the Rhône valley at the extreme southwestern corner of the Lake of Geneva. Pop. (1960) 176,183. To the west of the canton boundary are the Jura mountains while to the south and east are the steep limestone slopes of the Salève. It is of international significance as the classic ground for international conferences and arbitration and has long been a notable intellectual, scientific and theological centre.

History.—In prehistoric times (4th or 5th millennium B.C.) a great lake city built upon piles, some of which may still be seen, existed at the western end of the lake where the waters narrow into the channel of the Rhône. At a later period, the inhabitants established themselves on the hill on the left bank.

Caesar states that Genva was a walled town (*oppidum*) in the extreme north of the country of the Gallic people of the Allobroges; the Rhône separated it from the territory of another Gallic people, the Helvetii, whose invasion Caesar repelled. Later inscriptions refer to Geneva as a *vicus* (community) of the province of Vienna (modern Vienne, Fr.). It had temples, aqueducts, ports and ships and was evidently of some importance judging by the many Roman remains found on the original site of the city (near the former cathedral). About A.D. 400 it is described as a *civitas*. This rise in status was probably connected with the establishment of a bishop's see there. A letter of St. Leo in 450 states that the see was then a suffragan of the archbishopric of Vienne.

In the mid-5th century Geneva came into the possession of the Burgundians; in 534, however, Gundibald was defeated by Clovis, king of the Franks. After the barbarian invasions the city shrank to half its former size. It was then concentrated on the high ground. During the feudal period the Burgundian kings had more to fear from the hereditary counts of Geneva than from the elected bishops; Rudolf III, therefore, conferred estates on the bishops, favouring them at the expense of the counts. The kingdom of Burgundy was bequeathed by Rudolf III (d. 1032) to the emperor Conrad II. Temporal sovereignty of the city was finally granted to the bishop, who, in 1162, was raised to the rank of a prince of the Holy Roman empire. Like many other prince-bishops, the ruler of Geneva had to defend his rights: against powerful neighbours without, and against the rising power of the citizens from within.

The Genevese attempted toward the end of the 13th century to create a municipal organization for themselves, playing off against one another the rival rulers of the district. In Maurienne, a remote district of the country, there presently came to the fore a count, assuming the title of count of Savoy. He tried to win land and power at the expense of both the count of Geneva and the bishop. It was natural, therefore, that the citizens should invoke the aid of Savoy against their bishop. But the count of Savoy, Amadeus V, seized not only the castle of the bishops, but also the office of *vidomne*, the official through whom the bishop exercised his minor judicial rights. By calling in the count of Savoy, the Genevese had succeeded in freeing themselves from the count of Geneva and in defying the bishop; they soon discovered, however, that their "protector," not content with the office of *vidomne*, intended to make himself "prince" of the city. In 1401 Amadeus VIII of Savoy bought the county of the Genevois, the dynasty of its rulers having become extinct, and then attempted to purchase the bishopric of the city. This move was rejected, but Amadeus, having been elected pope under the name of Felix V, named himself to the vacant see of Geneva in 1444. Until 1522 the see was almost continuously held by a cadet of the house of Savoy.

Geneva might soon have become an integral part of the realms of the house of Savoy had it not been for the appearance of new protectors—the Swiss cantons. Early in the 15th century the town of Fribourg negotiated commercially with Geneva, as Fribourg cloth found a market in the long-established Geneva fairs. This took on a political significance in the treaty of *combourgeoisie* (1526) which included not only Fribourg and Geneva but Bern also. The Genevese, wishing to rid themselves of domination by the duke of Savoy, the self-appointed "protector" of the city, turned to the Swiss for help. Swiss armed intervention (1530) forced the duke to sign the treaty of St. Julien by which he engaged not to trouble the Genevese any more, agreeing that if he did so the towns of Fribourg and Bern should have the right to occupy his barony of Vaud. A legal tie was thus established between Geneva and two of the Swiss cantons. The municipal authorities of the city greatly developed and included a *grand conseil* and *petit conseil*.

The Reformation and Independence.—The situation was complicated by the Reformation, in which Fribourg remained loyal to the old faith, while Bern supported the Reformation. In 1535 Geneva formally adopted the Protestant faith. The bishop, Pierre de la Baume, had already left the city (July 14, 1533), never to return. The syndics and the council assumed authority and claimed the sovereign powers of the bishop. The Fribourgeois, who had come to the help of Geneva in 1530, in 1534 seceded from the alliance. The bishop joined forces with the duke of Savoy to attack Geneva. The Genevese were on the point of succumbing in the unequal struggle when, in Jan. 1536, the Bernese at last came to their aid, acquiring the barony of Vaud and the bishopric of Lausanne. They seized the Gex district (pays de Gex), the Chablais, and, in combination with the Genevese, took the castle of

Chillon, from which they delivered François Bonivard, the prior of the Cluniac house of St. Victor. Meanwhile, Guillaume Farel (q.v.) had been advancing the cause of religious reform, which was definitively adopted on May 21, 1536.

In July 1536 a French refugee, John Calvin (q.v.), came to Geneva and was persuaded by Farel to remain. He was not immediately successful, however, and was obliged to leave the town. Later recalled by his partisans (1541), Calvin undertook the task of imposing on the Genevese, intoxicated with their newly won freedom, a severe moral discipline. One of his most lasting achievements was the foundation of the Academy of Geneva, which he set up with the assistance of Théodore Beza (q.v.) in 1559. It was virtually a training school for Protestant missionaries and Geneva became the acknowledged stronghold of Protestantism and the city of refuge for the persecuted from Italy, England and France. Calvin was the virtual ruler of the city from which he directed his disciples in all parts of Europe.

The gains of the war of 1536 were not lasting: Emmanuel Philibert of Savoy recovered his lands; Bern retained only the Vaud; Geneva was once more encircled by enemies; and finally, Calvin died in 1564. On the other hand, Bern renewed the treaty of *combourgeoisie* and Zürich entered the alliance in 1584. Some time before this Henry III of France had made an alliance with Bern and Solothurn for the "conservation" of Geneva (1579). When civil war broke out in France, Henry III's envoy, N. H. de Sancy, brought a Swiss contingent to his aid, and Geneva entered the struggle. Sometimes in concert with Sancy's troops and the Bernese, sometimes alone, the Genevese fought and held their ground. Henry of Navarre, the former Huguenot leader, presently succeeded Henry III. Despite his former friendship with Geneva, he deprived the Genevese of the Gex district, which they had conquered, when he made peace with Savoy (1601).

With complete disregard of treaties, Duke Charles Emmanuel made a final attempt to take Geneva by surprise by scaling the walls with ladders (night of the *escalade*, Dec. 12, 1602). He was repelled with considerable losses, while only 17 Genevese perished. Overjoyed at this victory, the citizens crowded into their cathedral; they sang the 124th psalm which has ever since been sung on the anniversary of this great delivery. The peace of St. Julien (July 21, 1603) marked the final defeat of the duke of Savoy in the long struggle waged (since 1290) by his house against the city of Geneva.

Modern Period.—Geneva then entered on a period of tranquillity. Industry prospered, particularly clockmaking; with the assistance of the refugees who fled to Geneva at the time of the St. Bartholomew's Day massacre (q.v.) and the revocation of the Edict of Nantes (q.v.). There grew up an increasingly inclusive patrician class and several attempts were made by the cultivated middle classes to gain some share in the aristocratic government of the town. Following the French Revolution, Geneva, imitating the example of Paris, had a small version of a "Reign of Terror." An attempt was made to remedy the situation by the egalitarian constitution of 1794, but an end was not put to disorder until shortly before the French occupation of 1798.

On the fall of Napoleon (1814) the city recovered its independence, and finally, in 1815, was received as the junior member of the Swiss confederation. The constitution of 1814 set up a common form of government for the city and the canton, the city not obtaining its municipal independence until the constitution of 1842, which established the *conseil d'état* as the executive authority and the *grand conseil* as the legislative body. A more advanced and liberal constitution was accepted by popular vote on May 21, 1847, after a revolution led by Jean Jacques (James) Fazy.

After World War I Geneva, with its tradition of independence and Swiss neutrality, was chosen as the seat of the League of Nations (q.v.). Although a nucleus of League officials remained after the outbreak of World War II, no meetings of the council or the assembly were held, and the League's activities largely ceased. The International Labour office was at first housed at Pregny, 3 km. (2 mi.) N. of Geneva, and in 1926 in a new building near Ariana park. The departure after 1939 of League officials and Labour office personnel dealt a blow to the prosperity of Geneva. By 1942

GENEVA

more than 11% of its houses were unoccupied.

The situation improved considerably after World War II; the population substantially increased and unemployment disappeared. In 1947 the city was designated as the European centre of the United Nations. In the following year the International Labour office, the secretariat of the International Labour organization, returned to its headquarters in Geneva, and the World Health organization established its headquarters in the Palais des Nations, followed by other international organizations. It was in Geneva that the Asian conference (United States, France, United Kingdom, Soviet Union) took place in 1955 to settle the situation in Vietnam. During that same year the European Organization for Nuclear Research inaugurated its research laboratories at Meyrin, 4 mi. W.N.W. It was the scene of the Geneva "summit conference" in 1955; negotiations between the U.S., the U.S.S.R. and the U.K. on the discontinuance of nuclear weapons tests began there in 1958.

AUTHENTICATED NEWS

AERIAL VIEW OF GENEVA, SWITZ., SHOWING THE OUTFLOWING WATERS OF THE RHÔNE RIVER WHICH DIVIDE THE TOWN INTO TWO PARTS AT THE SOUTHWESTERN END OF THE LAKE OF GENEVA

The City.—The Rhône river, spanned by eight bridges, flows south from the lake and divides the city into two parts: On the left bank, to the south, is the hill where Geneva first stood, surmounted by the town's civic buildings and at the highest point by the former cathedral of St. Pierre (begun in the 12th century). This picturesque area of the old city is reached by a long and narrow street bearing several names, Rue de la Cité, Grand' Rue and Rue de l'Hôtel de Ville, which winds uphill from the Pont de l'Ile. In this street there are some beautiful 17th- and 18th-century houses and the very simple house where Jean Jacques Rousseau was born. The *hôtel de ville* (city hall) is a Renaissance building with 17th-century frontage and cloistered courtyard. An unusual feature is the 16th-century paved slope serving instead of a staircase and leading up to a square tower. Inside are the room of the council of state with its 15th-century paintings and the "Salle de l'Alabama" opening off the court where the arbitration award between Great Britain and the United States was made in 1872 and where the first international convention for the relief of wounded soldiers (Red Cross) was signed in 1864. Parallel with the Grand' Rue is the aristocratic Rue des Granges with its line of beautiful 18th-century mansions built by rich Genevese bankers. The Rue du Puits St. Pierre, facing the city hall, runs along a former corn granary. In it stands the Tavel house, decorated with amusing carved heads, one of the oldest houses of the city. It has an interesting turret and 12th-century cellars. Nearby in the Rue Calvin is the site, now built on, of the house where John Calvin lived and died (1564). This street leads toward the spacious Cour St. Pierre where the former cathedral stands. This 12th- to 13th-century building has a classical frontage added in the 18th century with a columned portico by Benoît Alfieri (1749). Next to St. Pierre, on the Place de la Taconnerie, is the Temple de l'Auditoire (the former 14th-century church of Notre Dame-la-Neuve) where John Knox preached and where John Calvin and Théodore Beza used to teach; to the south is a chapel in flamboyant Gothic style, the Chapelle des Macchabées, built by Cardinal de Brogny, bishop of Geneva (c. 1404). South of St. Pierre is the Place du Bourg-de-Four, a picturesque and irregular square, which was once the Roman forum. Adjoining are the law courts, a fine classical building (1707), formerly a hospital. The Collège de Genève, founded by Calvin in 1559, is nearby. Farther to the southeast is the history and art museum, a large white neoclassic building (1910) housing, in particular, remarkable collections of Genevese and Swiss paintings (Konrad Witz, J. E. Liotard, Alexandre Calame, François Diday, Ferdinand Hodler), collections of lace, watches, ancient vases, enamels and art relics of the old city. Below the hill to the north and close to the lake is the Place du Molard which, in ancient times, was a harbour. The medieval tower formerly standing at its entrance has been restored.

Toward the southeastern part of the city above the Arve river is the Promenade des Bastions with its Reformation monument (1909-17), a 300-ft. wall against which is a central group of statues representing Calvin, Farel, Beza and Knox, flanked by the figures of other great reformers. Nearby are the university buildings (1863-72). Founded by Calvin in 1559, the old academy acquired university status in 1872. Within its walls are the natural history museum and the public and university library containing many valuable books and illuminated manuscripts.

North of the Promenade is the Place Neuve, the finest square in Geneva. In the centre is the bronze equestrian statue of Gen. Guillaume Henri Dufour, commander of the federal army in the Sonderbund War (see SWITZERLAND: *History*). Among buildings in the square are the Conservatoire of music, the Grand Theatre (1879), inspired by the opera house in Paris, and the Rath museum (1824), once the home of the International Agency for Prisoners of War. From the Place Neuve, the Rue de la Corraterie, once flanked by the city wall where the famous *escalade* took place (1602), leads down to the river and the Pont de la Tour l'Ile. On this bridge is the Tour de l'Ile, the remnants of a bishop's castle of the 13th century; across the river is the Place de Coutance in the district of St. Gervais, where the craftsmen of the watchmaking, enamel and jewelry industries established themselves in the 18th and 19th centuries. The 15th-century church of St. Gervais contains wall paintings of the same period. The Quai des Bergues leads along the river bank toward the lake with the Pont des Bergues and the Ile Rousseau with James Pradier's statue of Rousseau (1835) on the right.

In the Quai du Président Wilson along the northern shore is the former Hôtel National which was the first home of the League of Nations. The International Labour office, a massive building completed in 1925, stands near the lake at the end of the wide Avenue de la Paix. This avenue mounts to the Palais des Nations, which is the European office of the United Nations and the headquarters of the World Health organization. Built originally for the League of Nations (1929-37), the Palais des Nations has imposing frontages facing the lake. Among its chief rooms are the assembly hall and the council chamber, adorned with a fresco by the Spanish painter José Maria Sert y Badia. Next to the Palais is the Ariana museum housing a ceramic collection. Across the avenue is the headquarters of the International Red Cross society which was founded at Geneva in 1864 by J. H. Dunant (q.v.). On the right bank of the Rhône, in a district which in the 18th century lay outside the city walls, is the house where Voltaire lived, 1755-58. This house, called "Les Délices," has been restored and contains the Voltaire institute and museum where Voltaire's first publications and manuscripts are kept.

Geneva's parks form a green belt around the city; along the right bank are the Parc Mon Repos, the Parc de la Perle du Lac and the Parc Barton which extends as far as the grounds of the International Labour office. On this bank, too, are the Botanic gardens and the Conservatoire Botanique. On the opposite shore of the lake is the Jardin Anglais or Promenade du Lac with the monument erected in 1864-69 commemorating the entrance of the canton into the Swiss confederation; the Parc des Eaux-Vives and the adjoining Parc de la Grange with its beautiful 18th-century house and rose garden. Offshore on the Jetée des Eaux-Vives plays a fountain the jet of which rises about 425 ft. To the southeast of the old city is the extensive Parc Bertrand.

Trade and Communications.—Geneva, known primarily as a centre of Swiss cultural life and as the headquarters of international movements, is also an industrial city. Watches are the chief product, followed by jewelry and enamels; others include electrical machines and water turbines, medical instruments and precision tools. There are important clothing, food, chemical and printing industries and a prosperous banking business. The hotel trade also contributes largely to the city's income. Geneva is linked by rail with the rest of Switzerland and with France (Lyons, Paris, Marseilles). The station is at Cornavin on the right bank. The station of Eaux-Vives on the left bank connects Geneva with Savoy. The airport at Cointrin, 3 mi. N.W. of the city, is served by international airlines and is one of the largest in Switzerland. The Swiss and French sides of the lake can be reached by steamers.

See also references under "Geneva" in the Index.

BIBLIOGRAPHY.—Société d'histoire et d'archéologie, *Histoire de Genève des Origines à 1798* (1951), *Histoire de Genève de 1798 à 1931* (1956); L. Blondel, *Le développement urbain de Genève à travers les siècles* (1946); F. Gribble, *Geneva* (1908); P. Duparc, *Le comté de Genève, IXᵉ-XVᵉ siècle* (1955); L. Cramer, *La Seigneurie de Genève et la Maison de Savoie de 1559 à 1603* (1912-58); P. F. Geisendorf et al., *L'Escalade de Genève* (1952); M. Peter, *Genève et la Révolution* (1921, 1950); W. Rappard, *L'avénement de la démocratie moderne à Genève* (1942); F. Ruchon, *Histoire politique de Genève, de la Restauration à la suppression du budget des cultes (1813-1907)* (1953); W. Deonna, *Les Arts à Genève* (1942).

GENEVA, LAKE OF (French LAC LÉMAN; German GENFERSEE), the largest Alpine lake in Europe, is situated between southwest Switzerland and Haute-Savoie *département* of southeastern France. It is the Lacus Lemanus of classical writers, but from the 16th century was known as the Lac de Genève, though from the end of the 18th century the name Lac Léman was revived. The lake is 1,220 ft. above sea level, and its area is 224½ sq.mi. of which about 134 sq.mi. are Swiss and 90¼ sq.mi. French; the latter includes the south shore except its west and east ends, which belong respectively to the Swiss cantons of Geneva and Valais.

The lake, crescentic in shape, is formed by the Rhône, which enters it at the east end, between Villeneuve and St. Gingolph, and leaves it at the west end, flowing through the city of Geneva. The only important tributaries are the Drance (south) and the Venoge and the Veveyse (north). The length from the east end to Geneva is 45 mi., the maximum depth 1,017 ft., mean depth 500 ft., average greatest width (between Morges and Amphion) 8½ mi., average width 5 mi. The lake forms two well-marked divisions separated by the strait of Promenthoux, or Nernier, which divides the Grand Lac (east) from the Petit Lac, the special Genevese portion. There is a distinct bar in the strait, the depth of water diminishing to about 100 ft. for a short distance. The water is unusually blue and transparency increases away from the Rhône entry as the river-borne mud sinks to the bottom. The lake level is highest in summer.

There are remarkable temporary disturbances of level known as *seiches* both longitudinal and transverse, in which the whole mass of water in the lake rhythmically swings from shore to shore, causing a rise of 2–5 ft. at Geneva in as many minutes. The principal winds that blow over the lake are the *bise* (northeast), the *vaudaire* or *fölin* (southeast), the *sudois* or *vent de pluie* (southwest) and the *joran* (northwest). The storm winds are the *molan* (from the Arve valley) and the *joran* (northwest).

The lake is not as rich in fish as the other Swiss lakes. There are known to be only 20 indigenous species (of which the *Féra*, or *Coregonus fera*, is the principal) and six that were introduced in the 19th century. Lake dwellings, of varying dates, have been found on the shores.

Steamer services, which have been in operation since 1823 and lakeside railways link the popular resorts. The railway on the northern shore runs from Geneva to Lausanne and Montreux; that on the south from Geneva reaches the shore at Thonon-les-Bains and then runs past Évian les-Bains to Le Bouveret; both lines then ascend the Rhône valley. In the harbour of Geneva two erratic granite boulders project above the water, and are named *Pierres du Niton* (supposed to be altars of Neptune). The lower of the two has been taken as the base of the triangulation of Switzerland. (A. B. M.)

GENEVA CONFERENCE (1954), an international conference called to discuss Far Eastern problems, important chiefly for the signing of the so-called Geneva Accords which ended hostilities between the French and the Vietminh in Indochina. The conference, which had been agreed upon at a meeting of the Big Four (U.S., U.K., U.S.S.R., and France) foreign ministers earlier in the year, opened April 26 and was attended by representatives of the Big Four, of all other nations that had contributed to the UN effort in Korea with the exception of South Africa, and of Communist China and North Korea. This was the first time that Communist Chinese representatives had taken part in such a conference, although the U.S. was careful to insist that their presence did not imply recognition of the Chinese regime. Nothing was accomplished by the conference toward a permanent settlement in Korea, but from the beginning it had been overshadowed by developments in Indochina, where the French position was becoming untenable. Following several weeks of intensive negotiations, internationally guaranteed agreements were signed on July 21 between the French and Vietnamese, Cambodian, and Laotian representatives. They provided, among other things, for a cease-fire line along the 17th parallel, which effectively divided Vietnam into two countries, and for all-Vietnamese elections to be held within two years, a provision which was never honoured and which later became a source of considerable controversy and recrimination.

See further VIETNAM: *History.*

GENEVA CONVENTIONS, a series of four international agreements for the protection of war victims, signed on Aug. 12, 1949, by 58 governments and the Holy See. Convention I, "for the amelioration of the condition of the wounded and sick in armed forces in the field," had a history intimately linked with the founding of the International Committee of the Red Cross. The original convention came out of a conference called by the Swiss federal council in 1864. Twenty-six governments in attendance agreed to respect war wounded, neutrality of hospitals bearing the Red Cross sign and other humanitarian rules. (*See* RED CROSS.)

The development from the convention of 1864 to the comprehensive series of agreements of 1949 reflected the appalling development of naval warfare. The 1864 convention, revised in 1906, was adapted to naval warfare at the second Hague Peace conference of 1907 and, the previous British objections withdrawn, adopted there as Convention X. In its 1949 version, it became known as Convention II (Armed Forces at Sea). Convention III of 1949 (Prisoners of War) was first agreed upon in Geneva in 1929. It reflected the problems of treatment and repatriation of war prisoners, which came to the fore in World War I. (*See* PRISONERS OF WAR.) Finally, the new technology of warfare, which carried its effects among the noncombatants in World War II, resulted in the addition in 1949 of Convention IV (Protection of Civilian Persons in Time of War).

As long as war, though legally outlawed, continued to exist *de facto*, the Geneva conventions were an indispensable part of the effort to keep warfare within some confines. During the Korean War (1950–53), all the parties involved declared themselves bound by the conventions, even if they had not signed or ratified them. The *cause célèbre* of Korea, the repatriation of prisoners of war, involved Convention III. Although tightened in 1949 to favour the prisoners' rights, this convention was susceptible of a literal interpretation that would have supported a forcible repatriation.

This was the drawback of engagements of this type: they responded only to past stimuli instead of looking toward the future. The ideological aspect of contemporary warfare and the desire for international protection of human rights, although extant as factors and likely to increase in prominence, were not positively incorporated into the Prisoners of War convention. Convention IV (Civilians) appeared also outdated in some particulars in view of developments in war technology. Yet it was also true that the fundamental value of the Geneva conventions was their humanitarian spirit, which was ageless and not letterbound. Despite some declarations and conduct to the contrary, this was proved again in the intensive international phase of the Vietnam war.

See also WAR; LAWS OF WAR; HAGUE CONFERENCES; and references under "Geneva Conventions" in the Index.

BIBLIOGRAPHY.—Jean S. Pictet, "The New Geneva Conventions for the Protection of War Victims," *American Journal of International Law*, xliv, 462–475 (1951); Harold C. Gutteridge, "The Geneva Conventions of 1949," *British Year Book of International Law*, xxvi, 294–326 (1949); Jaro Mayda, "The Korean Repatriation Problem and International Law," *American Journal of International Law*, xlvii, 414–437 (1953). (J. MA.)

GENEVIÈVE, SAINT (*c.* 422–*c.* 500), patron saint of Paris, was born, according to tradition, at Nanterre near Paris. At the age of seven she was induced by St. Germain, bishop of Auxerre, to dedicate herself to the religious life, and on the death of her parents she moved to Paris, where she distinguished herself by her benevolence, as well as by her austere life. She is said to have predicted the invasion of the Huns; and when Attila with his army was threatening the city, she persuaded the inhabitants to remain on the island and encouraged them by an assurance, justified by subsequent events, that the attack would come to nothing (451). She is also said to have had great influence over Childeric, father of Clovis, and in 460 to have caused a church to be built over the tomb of St. Denis.

She was buried in the church of the Holy Apostles, popularly known as the church of Ste. Geneviève. In 1793, when the church that had been built in her honour (in 1764) became the Panthéon, her body was removed from it and burned on the Place de Grève; but the relics were enshrined in the church of St. Étienne-du-Mont, where they still attract pilgrims. Her feast is celebrated on Jan. 3.

See C. H. Lesêtre, *Les Saints* (1900); A. D. Sertillanges, *Sainte Geneviève* (1917).

GENGA, GIROLAMO (*c.* 1476–1551). Italian painter and architect, a transitional figure between Renaissance and mannerism, was born in Urbino and studied under Signorelli (working with him on the frescoes in Orvieto cathedral), later under Perugino and at Florence. The "Martyrdom of St. Sebastian" (Uffizi, Florence) exemplifies his style thus formed. Toward 1509 he painted two frescoes in Pandolfo Petrucci's palace at Siena (Siena gallery), and in 1510 the "Transfiguration" (Museo dell'Opera del duomo, Siena). His plastic mature style is seen in the altarpiece painted for the church of S. Agostino, Cesena (1513–18; Brera, Milan, predella panels at Bergamo and Washington), the "Marriage of St. Catherine" (Barberini palace, Rome) and in his masterpiece, the already Mannerist "Resurrection," in the church of Sta. Caterina da Siena, Rome (*c.* 1530). From the 1520s Girolamo Genga was in the service of the dukes of Urbino, and by 1530 was supervising the fresco decoration of the Villa Imperiale near Pesaro and constructing large additions to it. He was architect of S. Giovanni Battista, Pesaro (1543), the work being continued by his son, Bartolomeo (1516–59), a military as well as civil architect. Preparatory drawings by Girolamo for the Cesena altar are in the British museum, London, the Uffizi, and the Louvre. He died in Urbino on Aug. 11, 1551. (P. M. R. P.)

GENGHIS KHAN (also written CHINGHIZ, JENGHIZ, etc.; the form CHINGGIS most nearly represents the Mongol spelling) (d. 1227), khan of the Mongols, was one of the great conquerors of history. But though his armies campaigned from China to Russia, 150 years after his death all the dynasties of his descendants in China, Turkistan, Persia and south Russia had either fallen or declined greatly in power.

Genghis Khan was born in 1155, 1162 or—most probably—1167, the confusion of dates being due to difficulties in reconciling different lunar calendars and 60-year and 12-year cycles of reckoning. He was eight years old (nine by the Mongol and Chinese way of counting age) and already betrothed when his father died. He was about 15 and already a warrior when he married, and 39 when he was acclaimed khan in 1206 (or Jan. 1207). He spent more than 20 years in rising to supremacy in Mongolia and another 20 in conquering other lands. He can hardly be explained as a barbarian genius who swept all before him by sheer ferocity or by force of numbers, for the Mongols and related tribes could not have numbered more than 1,000,-000. He was, rather, skilled in tribal politics, international diplomacy and what is today called psychological warfare.

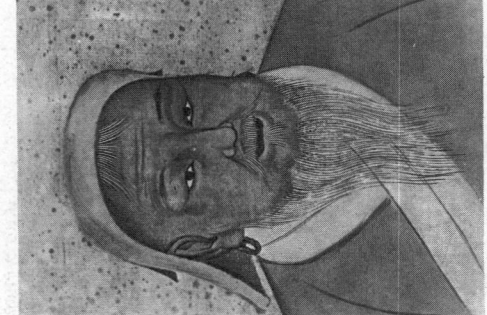

L. CARRINGTON GOODRICH

IDEALIZED PORTRAIT OF GENGHIS KHAN BY A CHINESE ARTIST; IN PEKING

In the 12th century Turkish tribes held much of the west and some of the south of Mongolia. The Mongols themselves were a small group of clans in the northeast corner of Outer Mongolia (the modern Mongolian Peoples Republic). East and south of them were the Tatars, whose name (although Genghis Khan conquered them) came to be frequently used in China and the west to mean Mongols in general. To the east, in Manchuria and Siberia, were Tungus tribes.

This world of pastoral and forest barbarians had for centuries been penetrated by civilized influences. Chinese, Iranian, Indian and Tibetan words, names and titles had been borrowed. Buddhism, Manichaeism and Nestorian Christianity had been partly adopted, especially by the Turks, some of whom were settled and some nomadic. Chinese influences were especially strong. As on the frontier of the Roman empire, whoever held power along the northern frontier of China—sometimes the Chinese, at other times, especially after the 3rd century A.D., barbarians who had conquered parts of China—relied partly on fortifications, including the Great Wall, and partly on using tribal auxiliaries to hold off more distant barbarians. If the auxiliaries became dangerously strong, their subsidy could be cut off and another tribe encouraged to attack them. In this way the barbarians, while remaining barbarians, acquired a sophisticated understanding of great-power politics.

From about 1123 to the time of Genghis, Manchuria and eastern North China were ruled by the Chin (Kin) dynasty, founded by the Jurchen (Jurchit, Nüchen), a Tungusic people. Under Ambahai (Hambaqai), a collateral ancestor of Genghis, the Mongols were auxiliaries of this dynasty on the Manchurian-Mongolian frontier. Then the Chin switched their favour to the Tatars, who delivered Ambahai to the Chin to be put to death. The Mongols therefore had a blood feud with the Tatars and also a sacred duty to take revenge on the Chin.

Genghis was born just when his father, Yesugei Ba'atur, had killed a Tatar chief named Temujin, and the child was given the name of Temujin because of the belief that the valour of a defeated enemy magically entered the newborn. The fact that Temujin (Temurchin) means "iron-worker" accounts for the legend that Genghis was a blacksmith.

When the boy was eight years old he was betrothed to Burte, of the tribe of Onggirat (Konggirat) and left, as was frequently the custom, to grow up in the camp of his betrothed's father. On his way home from the betrothal Yesugei was poisoned by Tatars, and on his deathbed sent for his son. Then began the harried years of the conqueror's boyhood. Left without a chief, the warriors and subjects of Yesugei deserted the mother of Temujin, with her own four sons and the two sons of another wife (or wives) of Yesugei. The family was reduced to living on wild plants, birds, fish and small animals such as mice and marmots—a life of misery for pastoral people. The relatives of Yesugei, who had divided up his possessions, did not want his son to grow up to take revenge for this impoverishment, so they hunted Temujin down and captured him, but he managed to escape. These and other adventures are related in the sagalike chronicle called *Secret History of the Mongols*, first written down in 1241, when many who had known Genghis were still alive.

When he was about 15, having proved by an exploit in recovering stolen horses that he was ready for warrior status, Temujin claimed his betrothed, Burte. Her dowry was a cloak of sable pelts. Temujin made political use of this cloak; he presented it to a former ally of his father's, to seek his patronage. This was Toghril, the "Unc Can" (Ong Khan) or Prester John of Marco Polo, ruler of the Kerait (Keriyet), a tribe that may have been Mongols under an aristocracy of Turks, many of whom were Nestorian Christians.

The political career of Temujin—a career built on the skilful use of well-understood conventions—begins at this point. He sometimes violated the conventions, but never without preparing his case to provide a "higher justification." By benefiting those loyal to him he won more followers than he lost. The first principle was mutual loyalty among men descended from the same ancestor; but this was frequently canceled by blood feuds. Marriage also could lead either to alliance or to feuds. Frequently a man took his wife from his mother's clan, and this made for alliance; but women were also captured, which led to feuds. Temujin's mother, Ö'elun (Hö'elun), had been captured from a man of the Merkit tribe; in due course, Temujin's bride Burte was captured by the Merkit and given to one of their warriors. When she was rescued she gave birth to a son, Juchi (Jöchi), whose father was probably the Merkit; nevertheless Temujin did not hold this mishap against Burte, and treated Juchi as his eldest son.

The principle of blood kinship could be extended by the oath of *anda*, by which two men became brothers. The famous *anda* of Temujin was Jamukha, later his most relentless enemy. They were distant kin, and the kinship was reinforced by the oath, just before Temujin claimed supremacy as Genghis Khan, they led the Mongol war bands together in a dual leadership recalling Romulus and Remus and the later dual Roman consulship. The underlying principle seems to have been a division of the tribe between men on duty in case of enemy attack and men off duty to carry on the daily work.

In contrast to the status of *anda* was that of *nukur* (pl. *nukut*), or "companion," the word now used by Mongol Communists for "comrade." A *nukur* forswore all obligations and loyalties, including kinship, to declare himself solely "the man" of a freely chosen war leader. Several of Genghis' most famous generals were *nukut*.

Temujin's first successes were in hereditary feuds against kinsmen, then in conquering tribes like the Tatars, who were kinsmen in a more distant sense. These victories led to his being acclaimed in 1206 (1207) as "Genghis Khan." In this title "Genghis" is probably from the Turkic *tengiz*, "ocean," with the extended meaning, suitable to the cosmology of the time, of "wide," "encompassing." *Khan*, "chief," is to be distinguished from *Khagan* (*qa'an*), "emperor," a title never used by Genghis. The difference is analogous to that between Chinese *wang*, "king," and *huang*, "emperor," and Persian *shah*, "ruler," and *shah-in-shah*, "king of kings."

The guiding principles of Genghis Khan are unmistakable: to make alliances discreetly and to break them only after preparing arguments to put himself in the right, in order to become undisputed leader of the cavalry élite of all the nomad tribes. Deferring the sacred duty of revenge against the Chin empire, he and his allies, the Kerait, joined a Chin general in crushing the Tatars, and he even accepted a title bestowed by the Chin. Only when he no longer feared tribal attack from the flank or rear did he turn against the settled kingdoms. While gathering his nomad following, he would be generous to a warrior who had fought to the last for his former chief, but merciless to one who, seeking to curry favour, betrayed his chief. Later, when seeking to impose the rule of his small nomad élite on large sedentary populations, he reversed this rule; a city that surrendered without fighting would be spared, but if it resisted the population would be massacred.

Genghis Khan's concern for nomad supremacy is emphasized by the fact that he campaigned in person against the Chin empire (especially in 1211-14) only until he had secured the pasture and mountain approaches from southern Manchuria and Mongolia to Peking, its capital, which he reached but did not attempt to storm. Further conquest in China was left to his generals; the Sung empire, on the Yangtze, was not brought under Mongol rule until the time of his grandson, Kublai Khan (*q.v.*). Genghis himself turned his attention to two kingdoms in the west, whose cavalry armies he feared to leave undefeated.

The empire of Khorezm (*q.v.*), in the region of the Amu-Darya and Syr-Darya (Oxus and Jaxartes rivers), with the great cities of Samarkand and Bukhara, ruled parts of Iran and Afghanistan. Its nobles were Turks, with some Iranians; its town populations and farmers were mostly Iranians; Turkish nomads filled the ranks of its cavalry. Between Genghis Khan and Khorezm lay the ruins of several recently collapsed state of Khara-Khitai, in which remnants of Mongol and Turkish tribes defeated by him had taken refuge. This state had been taken over by a prince of the Naiman, the last powerful tribe to hold out against Genghis in Mongolia, and might be made a rallying point against the spreading Mongol conquest. An expedition under one of Genghis Khan's generals disposed of this threat in 1218. At the same time, all the members of a joint commercial caravan and political embassy sent by the khan to the shah of Khorezm were murdered by a provincial governor, and in his wrath the great conqueror himself took the field.

This, Genghis Khan's most distant and ambitious campaign, lasting from 1219 to 1225, carried Mongol troops through Turkistan into Iran and Afghanistan; to the heights of the Pamirs and the banks of the Indus; into Azerbaijan; the Caucasus and south Russia. While Genghis himself kept the strategic command, columns were sent out in various directions under his sons and generals. It was while on this campaign that he designated Ogadai (*q.v.*), his third son, as his successor; he also had the Muslim religion explained to him by learned divines of Bukhara, had the art of profitably governing cities and settled lands expounded by Khorezmian bureaucrats, and had brought to him from China a Taoist priest, Chang Chun, from whom he hoped to learn the secret of immortality.

These interests are in stark contrast to the ferocity of the Mongol army, the use of civilian prisoners as a living screen in assaulting cities and the deliberate massacres to intimidate cities not yet attacked. The only partly effective commander against the Mongols was Jelal ed-Din, heir of the shah of Khorezm, a good cavalryman but no strategist. The weakness of Khorezm was that its Turkish troops were mercenaries who had no common interest with the sedentary population and did not, like the Mongols, have the thrust of triumph behind them and the lure of booty ahead.

Returning to Mongolia in 1225, the khan had one last strategic objective. The kingdom of Tangut, called by the Chinese Hsia or Hsi-Hsia, stood astride the Yellow river in the Ningsia-Hui Autonomous Region and Kansu. Its Turkish and Tibetan aristocracy ruled a largely Chinese population, and it blocked the invasion route into China from the northwest. It was on this campaign that the khan died, partly from the effects of a fall from horseback while hunting.

Genghis Khan's idea of the state was simple—the nomad warrior élite should remain in the steppes, drawing tribute from the conquered civilized kingdoms. But this concept could not withstand two corrosive trends: the nomads split into groups, each facing toward the subject state (China, Iran, etc.) from which it drew tribute; and in each group those who had to be detached for garrison and administrative service tended to be corrupted (or civilized) by their subjects. When, after several generations, each of Genghis' dynasties fell, some of its adherents retreated into the steppes but others transferred their loyalty to the new, antibarbarian successor-states. See MONGOL; see also references under "Genghis Khan" in the Index.

BIBLIOGRAPHY.—The basic Mongol text (restored from a phonetically transcribed Chinese version) is the *Secret History of the Mongols*. Editions exist in modern Mongol, Chinese, Russian, German (Erich Haenisch, *Die geheime Geschichte der Mongolen*, 2nd ed., 1948), French (Paul Pelliot, *Histoire secrète des Mongols*, 1949; incomplete), and English (Arthur Waley, *The Secret History of the Mongols* . . ., 1964; incomplete). An old Chinese text which preserves original Mongol material overlapping and extending that of the *Secret History* has been translated by P. Pelliot and L. Hambis as *Histoire des campagnes de Gengis Khan*, vol. i only, 1951). There are two Persian texts of exceptional importance, written by Iranian bureaucrat-scholars who knew Mongol and served under Mongol rulers. One, the work of Rashid al-Din, translated into Russian in the 19th century, is appearing in the Soviet Union in a new and much improved edition. The other, the work of Juvaini, has been translated into English by J. A. Boyle as *The History of the World-Conqueror* (1958). The chronological data are critically discussed in Paul Pelliot, *Notes on Marco Polo* (1959), and William Hung, "The Transmission of . . . The Secret History of the Mongols," *Harvard Journal of Asiatic Studies*, vol. 14 (1951).

For the conquest of China, see H. Desmond Martin, *The Rise of Chingis Khan and His Conquest of North China*, ed. by E. Lattimore (1950); of Khorezm, W. Barthold, *Turkestan down to the Mongol Invasion*, 2nd ed. (1928); of Russia, George Vernadsky, *The Mongols and Russia* (1953). The most serviceable biography is R. Grousset, *Conqueror of the World: the Life of Chingis-Khan* (1966). The English translation, edited by D. Sinor, is better than the original French edition of 1944 because of the identification of sources and the excellent bibliography. See also O. Lattimore, "Chingis Khan and the Mongol Conquests," *Sci. Amer.*, vol. 209, no. 2 (1963). Two older biographies, out of date but based on good scholarship, are B. Y. Vladimirtsov, *Life of Chingis-Khan*, trans. by Prince D. S. Mirsky (1930), and Ralph Fox, *Genghis Khan* (1936). Of great supplementary value is *Travels of an Alchemist: the Journey of the Taoist, Ch'ang-ch'un . . . etc.*, trans. by Arthur Waley (1931). (O. L.)

GENIUS, meaning literally in Latin "the begetter," is a word of several meanings derived from and having some relation to the original use of the word in Roman religion.

Roman Usage.—In its earliest meaning in private cult, the *genius* of the Roman housefather and perhaps the *iuno* (see JUNO) of the housemother were worshiped. These certainly were not the souls of the married pair, as is clear both from their names and from the fact that no early document mentions the *genius* or *iuno* of a dead person. As no cult was paid to the *genius* of any other member of the family, it seems reasonable to suppose that they were the male and female forms of the family's, or clan's, power of continuing itself by reproduction, which were in the keeping of the heads of the family or clan for the time being and passed at death to their successors. In this as in all forms of his cult, the *genius* was often conceived as appearing in the form of a snake, although he is also shown in art as a young man, generally engaged in sacrificing. At every wedding a bed, the *lectus genialis*, was made for the *genius* and *iuno* of the husband and wife, and its presence in the house was a sign of matrimony.

Individual Genius.—Because of the rise of individualism and also of the prevalence of Greek ideas concerning a guardian spirit or *daimon*, the *genius* lost its original meaning, and came to be a sort of personification of the individual's natural desires and appetites; hence the phrases *indulgere genio, genium defrudare*, signifying respectively to lead a pleasurable and a stingy life. However, the development did not stop there. The *genius* came to be thought of as a sort of guardian angel, a higher self; and, as the Greek *daimon* was sometimes rationalized into the individual's

character or temper, so also Horace half-seriously in one of his *Epistles* says that only the *genius* knows what makes one person so different from another, adding that he is a god who is born and dies with each one of us. This individual *genius* was worshiped by each individual, especially on his birthday. A few inscriptions even mention the *genius* of a dead person, as Christian epitaphs sometimes speak of the dead person's angel.

Genius of the Emperor.—To show reverence for the *genius* of another, or to swear by it, was a mark of deep respect; hence it is not unnatural that the *genius* of a dead person, and of his successors formed objects of popular cult. Thus to worship the *genius Augusti* avoided the feeling against worshiping any living emperor, which remained fairly strong in Italy; for of course all *genii* were divine and might properly be worshiped.

Further Developments.—As Greek *daimones* were by no means always the guardian spirits of individuals, so also there were a vast variety of *genii*, *i.e.*, guardian spirits, of places, *genius loci*, including buildings (*genius balneorum*, etc.) and corporations of all sorts, from the state (*genius populi Romani*) to small bodies of troops, guilds of tradesmen and so forth. A very curious development is that the *genius* of a god, even of Jupiter, or the *iuno* of a goddess, is sometimes referred to.

Modern English Usage.—The word genius is used in two closely related but somewhat different senses. In the first sense, as popularized by Lewis M. Terman, genius refers to high intellectual ability as measured by performance on a standardized intelligence test. The exact intelligence quotient designating genius varies. Terman set the intelligence quotient for "potential genius" at 140 or over, a level reached by about 1 in 250 of the general population. This seemed to some writers an insufficiently stringent criterion. Leta S. Hollingworth set it at 180 or over, a level reached by perhaps no more than 6 in 1,000,000 of the general population, and this seemed to other writers too stringent. In any event, genius here means simply high intellectual ability and refers to potentiality rather than to attainment. In this sense, the term may be used to characterize children who have not yet had an opportunity to gain eminence by achievement. A growing and probably more practicable usage is to refer to children of this sort as "gifted," and to make a distinction between first-order gifted children, those in the upper 0.1% of the general population, and second-order gifted children, those in the upper 10% of the remaining population.

In the second and more popular sense, as derived from Sir Francis Galton, "genius" is used to designate creative ability of an exceptionally high order as demonstrated by actual achievement. In this sense, men of genius are identified by the eminence of their accomplishment. Although eminence alone may be an imperfect measure of genius, it is held to be the best available, always provided that such eminence is not merely transitory or the result of accident of birth, as in the case of hereditary rulers. To be a sign of genius, eminence must have been won through personal attainment of a superior order.

Genius is distinguished from talent both quantitatively and qualitatively. Talent refers to a native aptitude for some special kind of work. It implies the relatively quick and easy acquisition of a particular skill. Genius is more than this. It involves originality, creativeness and the ability to think and work in areas not previously explored and thus to give to the world something of pre-eminent value it would not otherwise possess. Although men of genius have usually left their unique mark in a particular field, and some writers accordingly include in the term genius persons with special aptitudes independent of more generalized intelligence, studies of the early development of these people appear to show that the general intelligence of the highly talented individual is also exceptionally high. It may very well be that the two senses in which the concept genius has been used represent two sides of the same coin.

There have been a variety of attempts to explain the nature and source of genius. One theory holds that the man of genius belongs to a separate psychobiological species, differing as much from ordinary man in his mental and emotional processes as man differs from the ape. Another theory looks upon genius as closely related to neurosis and psychosis. Cesare Lombroso is perhaps the most widely cited among those who hold or hold this point of view. Although modern psychoanalytic theory would also hold that genius, like neurosis and psychosis, has its source in basic conflict between the self and environment, in the genius these conflicts are resolved in such a way that the symptoms and products are socially useful and valued. Investigations indicate that the man of genius may be classified as "gifted" or "potential genius" are on the average superior to other children in physique and health and in emotional and social adjustment.

Galton, who inaugurated the systematic study of genius, formulated the theory that genius is a very extreme degree of three combined traits—intellect, zeal and power of working—that are shared by all men in various "grades." In his *Hereditary Genius*, which appeared in 1869, he presented the first clear statistical evidence that genius, as measured by outstanding accomplishment, tends to run in families. Since then the extent to which biological heredity, as distinct from education and opportunity, is responsible for the great differences in achievement of different individuals has been the subject of scientific controversy. The question of how much "nature" and how much "nurture" remains unsettled. However, the consensus is that genius is a function of both hereditary and environmental factors. The original potentiality for exceptional achievement comes from heredity, but whether or not this potentiality will be brought to fruition depends, at least to some extent, upon opportunity and training.

Studies of famous men and women show that there is no country and no period of time that has not produced some persons of genius calibre. Perhaps the greatest proportion of men of genius to total population that has ever occurred was found in Athens during the period extending roughly from the 5th to the 2nd century B.C., when the city-state with a population averaging not more than 25,000 gave to the world such men as Pericles, Plato, Themistocles and others of equal or near-equal rank.

In all countries and all periods there have been families, social classes and communities that have produced more than their quota of genius. The chance that men who have themselves achieved prominence will have children who rank in the genius group, either by reason of their exceptional endowment as children or on the basis of exceptional accomplishment as adults, is unquestionably greater than that for the population in general. It is, however, impossible to say with any certainty whether this is due to superior heredity or to superior environment. What must always be borne in mind is that in all places and at all times men of genius have arisen from all ranks of society.

See also GIFTED CHILDREN; INTELLIGENCE; PRODIGY; PSYCHOLOGICAL TESTS AND MEASUREMENTS; ROMAN RELIGION.

BIBLIOGRAPHY.—F. Galton, *Hereditary Genius* (1869); C. Lombroso, *Men of Genius*, Eng. trans. (1891); L. M. Terman *et al.*, *Genetic Studies of Genius*, vol. i–iv (1925–47); E. Ginzberg, *Talent and Performance* (1964); L. S. Hollingworth, *Children Above 180 I.Q.* (1942); V. W. Grant, *Great Abnormals* (1968).
(F. L. G.; J. W. Gs.)

GENIZA, a storeroom, usually attached to a synagogue, in which worn-out sacred books are deposited. This article is concerned with a hoard of Hebrew manuscripts, containing at least a quarter of a million leaves, found in the geniza of an ancient synagogue in Cairo, Egy., in the 1890s. Many of the manuscripts were acquired by various libraries in Europe and the United States. Finally, in 1897, Solomon Schechter (*q.v.*) transferred the bulk of the Geniza to the University Library at Cambridge, Eng.

The Geniza is an invaluable source for both Jewish and Arabic studies. It has preserved many Hebrew writings that had been lost or not even known, the most conspicuous examples being the Hebrew text of ben Sira (Ecclesiasticus; *q.v.*) and the Book of the Covenanters of Damascus (the so-called Zadokite or Damascus Fragment). Both were edited by Schechter. Other important items are ancient versions of both the text and translations of the Old Testament as well as of postbiblical Hebrew literature. The Geniza is particularly rich in medieval Hebrew writings. Thousands of poems, many by previously unknown poets and often of high merit, have been preserved, as well as a great number of *responsa*, or answers of the heads of the Jewish academies in Baghdad and Jerusalem, to questions addressed to them from all over the world. These medieval responsa are a true mirror of the social and cultural conditions of their time.

The Geniza has also preserved much documentary material, such as official, business, and family correspondence, court records, deeds, contracts, accounts, orders of payment, and sundry notes. Although manuscripts of this type were normally written in Hebrew characters, this material is mostly in Arabic, and it constitutes a most precious testimony to the history of the Arabic language, which underwent profound changes during the Middle Ages. Most of these documents date from the 10th through the 13th centuries, and they reflect the life and mind of the middle class in the Arabic-speaking countries of the Mediterranean basin (which then included also most of Spain and Sicily). Since the medieval chronicles usually were reticent about this class, the Geniza documents form a unique source of economic and social history.

BIBLIOGRAPHY.—Solomon Schechter, *Studies in Judaism*, vol. ii (1945); N. Golb, "Sixty Years of Genizah Research," *Judaism*, vol. 6, pp. 3–16, (1957); Paul E. Kahle, *The Cairo Geniza* (1960); S. D. Goitein, "The Documents of the Cairo Geniza as a Source for Islamic Social History," in *Studies in Islamic History and Institutions*, pp. 279–350 (1966), and *A Mediterranean Society: the Jewish Communities of the Arab World as Portrayed in the Documents of the Cairo Geniza*, vol. i (1967), vol. ii (1970); S. Shaked, *A Tentative Bibliography of Geniza Documents* (1964).
(S. D. G.)

GENOA (Ital. GENOVA, Fr. GÊNES, Ger. and anc. GENUA), capital of Genoa province, chief city of the region of Liguria, the greatest port of Italy and the probable birthplace of Christopher Columbus, lies at the head of the Gulf of Genoa, 156 km. (97 mi.) S. of Milan by road. Genoa occupies an amphitheatre on the coastal slope of the Ligurian Apennines between the Polcevera river to the west and the Bisagno river to the east. Greater Genoa, established in 1926, extends along the coast for about 15 mi. between Voltri and Nervi and northward about 6 mi. to Pontedecimo. Pop. (1951) 648,078; (1961) 796,145. Area 91 sq.mi.

The origin of the name Genoa is sometimes identified with the Roman god Janus (*q.v.*, whence *janua*, "gate"), and the port constitutes a major gateway not only to the industrial north of Italy and the Po valley but also (through the Alpine tunnels) to much of central Europe.

Architectural Features.—The old town lies between the water front and the main thoroughfare, which, under various names, leads southeast from the main railway station to the Piazza de Ferrari, the central square. The newer quarters occupy the higher ground to the north and east. The main architectural features of Genoa are its medieval churches, with their striped façades of black and white marble, and its magnificent 16th-century palaces; a modern note is struck by the skyscrapers in the city centre. On the water front the great lighthouse, the Lanterna, rises 380 ft. Among the older churches are Sta. Maria di Castello (11th-century), built on the site of the Roman castle in the Romanesque style with later Gothic additions; SS. Cosma e Damiano, 11th-century Romanesque; S. Donato, also Romanesque (1189), with a polygonal campanile and a beautiful interior; S. Giovanni di Pré (13th-century), with an apse at each end and a campanile with five spires; S. Agostino (1260), a Romanesque church with a fine campanile; and S. Stefano, Romanesque with a tower belonging to an earlier building. S. Matteo, the ancient church of the Doria family, is a small Romanesque building with the characteristic Genoese black and white façade, founded in 1126. The interior dates from 1543, when it was remodeled by Giovanni Montorsoli (1507–63), who designed the tomb of Andrea Doria in the crypt. The small square in front of the church is surrounded by mansions of the Doria family in 13th-century Genoese style.

The cathedral of S. Lorenzo (1100–15), although originally Romanesque, was so much altered that it also presents aspects of Gothic and Renaissance styles. The interior (1307) is carried on the columns of an earlier church, and the nave is covered with a dome erected in 1567 to the designs of the architect Galeazzo

Alessi (q.v.). It contains the chapel of St. John the Baptist (1465), in which are relics of the saint brought from Palestine during the crusades and notable statues of the Madonna and St. John by Andrea Sansovino (q.v.; 1460–1529). In the cathedral treasury is an octagonal bowl, the Sacro Catino, captured by the Genoese at Caesarea in Palestine in 1101 and corresponding to descriptions of the holy grail. It was long regarded as a hollowed-out emerald of matchless value (whence the alternative name Tazza di Smeraldo), but it is actually a remarkable piece of ancient glass; some Genoese assert that glass was substituted for emerald when the bowl was removed to Paris by Napoleon I. Nearby on the southern side of the Piazza de Ferrari is the baroque Jesuit church of S. Ambrogio, of late 16th-century date and with a richly decorated interior that includes an altarpiece by P. P. Rubens and a painting of the Assumption by Guido Reni. One of the largest churches in the city is the sumptuous domed basilica of SS. Annunziata, restored after damage by bombardment in World War II, its interior richly adorned with coloured marble and 17th-century frescoes. S. Siro, a church rebuilt in the 11th century by the Benedictines on the site of the Roman fort, was restored and enlarged at the end of the 16th century and contains frescoes by G. B. Carlone (1592–1677); an inscription marks the spot where St. Siro "destroyed the serpent basilisk" in 580. Sta. Maria di Carignano in the south of the city was designed by G. Alessi in Renaissance style as a small edition of St. Peter's at Rome; it contains statues by Pierre Puget (q.v.; 1622–94) and the highest gallery of its dome commands an excellent view.

The palaces of the Genoese patricians are famous for their sumptuous architecture and their artistic collections. Many of them were built in the latter half of the 16th century by Alessi, whose imposing style displays great ingenuity in using a limited site to the best advantage. Several of the villas on the outskirts are also his work. The Via Garibaldi is flanked by a succession of magnificent palaces, chief among which is the Palazzo Rosso, named for its red colour. After damage in World War II, it was repaired and reopened in 1961. Opposite is the contrasting white Palazzo Bianco. Both these palaces were presented to the city by the Marchesa Maria Brignole-Sale, duchess of Galliera (died 1889), and contain priceless art treasures, including two important picture galleries.

Nearby the Palazzo Municipale, formerly Doria-Tursi (1564), stands on a sloping site, with a magnificent courtyard and a marble stairway leading to the spacious council chamber. In adjacent rooms are preserved autographed letters of Columbus and the Guarnieri violin (1742) of Niccolo Paganini (q.v.), who was also a native of Genoa. Near the Via Garibaldi are the Palazzo Spinola (16th century), housing the National gallery. Its period interior conveys a clear idea of an 18th-century Genoese home. In the Via Balbi are the Durazzo Pallavicini and Balbi-Senarega palaces, both by Genoa's greatest baroque architect Bartolomeo Bianco (1590–1657). The Palazzo dell' Università, built in the first half of the 17th century, is Bianco's finest work; it was designed as a Jesuit college and has been occupied by the university since 1803. Just west of the main railway station is the

Palazzo Doria Pamphily (Palazzo del Principe), bought by Andrea Doria in 1521 and with frescoes by Perino del Vaga (q.v.; 1500–47). The Palazzo Ducale, the former residence of the doges but now the law courts, was modernized after a fire in 1777. The Gothic Palazzo di S. Giorgio, begun in 1260, has been restored and is occupied by the port authority.

Christopher Columbus is reputed to have been baptized in S. Stefano; his supposed birthplace near that church was demolished and the casa di Cristoforo Colombo (house of Columbus) (1700) occupies the site of another where he is said to have resided. The marble statue (1862) of Columbus, in the square fronting the main railway station, shows him leaning on an anchor with a figure representing America kneeling at his feet. The patriot Giuseppe Mazzini (q.v.), also a Genoese, was born at 13 Via Lomellini, now a museum of the Risorgimento. His tomb is in the Staglieno cemetery, 2½ km. (1½ mi.) N., which covers nearly 400 ac. and contains an astonishing collection of modern sepulchral monuments. At Quarto dei Mille, 8 km. (5 mi.) S.E. on the road to Pisa, a monument commemorates the start of Giuseppe Garibaldi (q.v.) on his expedition with "the thousand" in 1860.

From the Piazza de Ferrari, which is the business centre, the wide Via Venti Settembre slopes southeast, famed for its elegant shops. By the Via Dante stands the Porta Soprana (1155), an imposing gateway of the old city wall. The Via Roma leads northeast to the Piazza Corvetto with its bronze equestrian statue of Victor Emmanuel II. North of this square is the Villetta di Negro, a hillside public garden with a marble statue (1882) of Mazzini and busts of famous citizens, and south of it the other main park, the Spianata dell' Acquasola. From the square may be reached the thoroughfare called the Circonvallazione a Monte, which for about three miles follows avenues along the hills at the back of the town and affords excellent views.

The centre of the university, which was founded in 1471, is the palace in the Via Balbi, but the great number of students necessitates the distribution of many faculties in other parts of the city. Other institutions include the academy of arts, the Mazzinian institute for the study of the Risorgimento, the Chiossone Japanese museum, the naval and maritime museum at Pegli (11 km., or 7 mi. W.) and the museums of archaeology and natural history.

Communications.—Genoa is cramped between the sea and the Apennine foothills and was for centuries surrounded by walls. The older parts have thus become a confusion of narrow streets and lanes (caruggi), with stairways climbing the steeper slopes and bridges spanning the deeper valleys. Much of the city is inaccessible to automobiles and trucks and many important streets have little room for traffic. To unite some quarters and to improve access to the harbour a number of road tunnels (gallerie) have been built, and with the same object the lower course of the Bisagno river has been covered in. Communication with the hill suburbs and between different levels in the city is facilitated by three funicular railways and several elevators. Local passenger traffic is mostly by bus and trolley bus. A coastal railway and a coastal road (Via Aurelia) pass through Genoa westward to Nice, France (also a motorway as far as Savona), and southeastward to La

Spezia, Leghorn (Livorno) and Rome. The Polcevera valley northward carries the main roads and railway through the Giovi pass to Turin and Milan and also the express motorway (autostrada) to Milan. Regular shipping services connect with most major ports, and there is an air service between Genoa and Rome.

The inner harbour is protected by the Molo Vecchio or the Old mole (13th century) and has numerous quays. The new harbour extends westward past the suburb of Genova Sampierdarena to the mouth of the Polcevera river and covers a total of more than 1,300

PANORAMIC VIEW OF GENOA, CHIEF PORT OF ITALY, SHOWING A PORTION OF THE HARBOUR AT RIGHT

ac, including about 75 ac. of warehouses and 12½ mi. of quays able to accommodate more than 150 ships.

Trade and Industry.—The ancient saying *Genuensis, ergo mercator* ("a Genoese, therefore a merchant") epitomizes Genoa's age-old prominence in maritime and commercial affairs, and the great power wielded by the famous Banco di S. Giorgio from the 15th to the 18th century is recalled by the observation of the French historian Jules Michelet that Genoa was a bank before it was a city. Genoa is the outlet for the agricultural products of northern Italy (olive oil, wine, macaroni, cheese, fruits, rice and flowers) and also for the finished products of the manufacturing industries. Its main imports are fuels and raw materials (coal, coke, petroleum, iron ore, cotton, wool, hides, metals and grain) and greatly exceed exports. Traditional crafts of the province include filigree and gold and silver inlay work, especially at Campo Ligure; the weaving of velvets and damasks in the neighbourhood of Chiávari (45 km., or 28 mi. E.S.E.) and at Zoagli nearby; the manufacture of tower clocks at Recco, 21 km. (13 mi.) E.S.E.; lacemaking in Rapallo and district; and furniture making at Chiávari. An important concentration of manufacturing industry exists in the suburbs west of Genoa (Genova Sampierdarena, Cornigliano Ligure, Sestri Ponente, Pra, Voltri) and in the Polcevera valley (Rivarolo Ligure, Bolzaneto, San Quirico, Pontedecimo). The principal activities are iron and steel making; shipbuilding and heavy industry (locomotives, marine engines, railroad shops); the manufacture of munitions, chemicals, fertilizers, cement, textiles, paper, soap and rope; canning, brewing, tanning, flour and cotton milling and the refining of oil and sugar.

GENOVA PROVINCE, with an area of 708 sq.mi., has a coast that extends from the city westward to Cogoleto (27 km. or 17 mi.) and eastward to Bracco (66 km., or 41 mi.). It thus contains a large stretch of the Italian part of the Riviera (*q.v.*); popular seaside resorts include Nervi, Portofino, Santa Margherita Ligure and Rapallo, all on the picturesque coast east of Genoa. Inland the Ligurian Apennines rise to about 5,500 ft., their slopes covered with olive trees, firs, pines and scrub. The mild winter climate encourages the cultivation of olives, vines, vegetables and fruits (especially peaches); the growing of flowers for export is of importance. There is some dairy farming and slate and building stone are quarried.

(X.)

HISTORY

Archaeologists have found no trace of settlement in Genoa prior to the 5th century B.C., but their earliest findings already indicate a more advanced civilization than that of the rural and mountainous hinterland (*see* LIGURIANS). What probably began as a Ligurian village on the Sarzano hill overlooking the natural port (today Molo Vecchio) prospered through contacts with the Etruscans and the Greeks. During the Second Punic War, in the 3rd century B.C., it was wrecked by the Carthaginians and rebuilt by the Romans. As a road junction, a military port and a market of the Ligurians, Genoa became a flourishing though not outstanding Roman *municipium*. An episcopal see was installed in the commercial suburb which was slowly growing at the foot of Sarzano and along the shore. After the fall of the Roman empire the Ostrogoths protected the Genoese Jews, and when the Lombards conquered the interior of northern Italy in the 6th century A.D. the archbishop of Milan took shelter in Genoa. Milanese refugees formed a new suburb on the S. Andrea hill, but growth was arrested when Rothari, the Lombard king, conquered the town and razed its walls (c. 641). For three centuries Genoa existed in comparative obscurity as a fishing and agrarian centre with little trade.

The Middle Ages.—By the 10th century, however, the general demographic and economic upswing of Europe brought fresh opportunity and enabled the Genoese to answer the challenge of Muslim raids vigorously. A Fatimid fleet stormed and sacked the town (934 or 935), but the Genoese raised their walls anew and counterattacked under the leadership of their bishop and of the local viscounts. Jointly with the Pisans, they gradually purged Corsica and Sardinia of Saracen marauders; and in 1088, together with other Italian soldiers and sailors, in an enterprise foreshadowing the crusades, they attacked Mahdia, the Zirid capital on the African coast and an important centre of trade, captured the town and extorted from its ruler an indemnity and exemption from tolls. For some time, meanwhile, Genoese merchant ships had been trading briskly in the western Mediterranean and calling at Palestinian seaports.

Before 1100 a voluntary association (*compagna*) of all citizens who would contribute arms, capital or labour to the life of the community generated the independent commune of Genoa. The Holy Roman emperor was still the overlord, and the bishop the honorary president of the commune, but for all practical purposes the executive power was vested in a number of "consuls" yearly elected by a popular assembly (*see* COMMUNE [MEDIEVAL]). The ruling class, sharing with the consuls the government of the city, consisted chiefly of petty noblemen and of affluent bourgeois.

Maritime commerce was the dominant activity. During the 12th and 13th centuries Genoa played a leading role in the commercial revolution that Europe was undergoing. It became a town of about 100,000 inhabitants, a naval power dealing on equal terms with the greatest monarchies and a commercial centre rivaled only by Venice in the Levant trade and competing with other Italian towns in trade with western Europe. Eastern spices, dyestuffs and medicaments, western cloth and metals, African wool, skins, coral and gold were the main articles of a very diversified international commerce. Banking and shipbuilding flourished, and the local textile industry made a good start.

At the same time, the Genoese brought all of Liguria, most of Corsica and northern Sardinia under their direct or indirect control and founded self-governing commercial colonies all around the Mediterranean coast. Many of these colonies were the result of Genoese participation in the crusades (Guglielmo Embriaco of Genoa was especially notable for conveying to Jerusalem the siege machines that helped to capture that city) and of shorter campaigns by the Genoese alone in Spain, Africa and the Levant, but some were set up by peaceful penetration and diplomatic bargaining. They ranged in size from individual buildings to walled suburbs of towns and, eventually, entire islands or districts of coastal land.

The collapse of the crusaders' states, with their Genoese enclaves, in the late 13th century was amply compensated by Genoa's alliance with the Byzantine empire under the treaty of Ninfeo (1261), which paved the way for a great expansion in the Black sea. Pera (modern Beyoglu), the Genoese independent suburb of Constantinople, gradually outstripped the Byzantine capital in economic development if not in artistic or intellectual achievements, and Caffa (modern Feodosiya) became the capital of a broad stretch of the Crimean coast ruled by the Genoese. Many Aegean islands became independent Genoese principalities.

Throughout this period internal political strife in Genoa was almost incessant, but it did not seriously hamper the progress of the community. The state was managed as a business affair, to the common profit of the ruling families—Spinola, Fieschi, Grimaldi, Doria, etc.—and, so far as it was not incompatible, to the advantage of the whole population. Before the end of the 12th century, competition for the office of consul became so bitter that an alternative was sought by inviting someone from outside to be *podestà* or chief magistrate for a year at a time, but this form of government likewise failed to pacify the factions or to cope with the growing political ambitions of the middle class, and in the second half of the 13th century the yearly *podestà* was superseded by native "captains of the people" governing with unlimited tenure and with the support of the guilds. In 1257 Guglielmo Boccanegra, who was not a nobleman, was made captain. Thenceforward, though the richer citizens maintained their economic and political lead, noble birth alone was no longer a guarantee of political supremacy. The living standard of the entire population, including fresh immigrants, constantly improved. Municipal and family pride led to the construction of magnificent buildings in stone, the wharves and the light tower were given special care, streets were paved, bridges were built by public subscription and some fine churches were erected. There were also many schools, some specializing in the humanities, others in commercial subjects (it was in Genoa that double-entry book-keeping and, later, maritime insurance were first developed) and a growing number of Genoese citizens went abroad to study in the universities.

The influx of refugees from southern France after the Albigensian crusade stimulated the growth of a Genoese school of lyric poets, writing first in Provençal, then in the local vernacular. The town government moreover sponsored the writing of historical annals (by Caffaro, Iacopo Doria and others). There were prominent jurists (such as Sinibaldo Fieschi, later Pope Innocent IV), hagiographers (archbishop Iacopo da Varagine), lexicographers (Giovanni Balbi) and map makers (Giovanni di Mauro da Carignano and many others). The brothers Ugolino and Vadino Vivaldi in 1291 tried to reach the far east by sailing through the Strait of Gibraltar and proceeding westward—a daring, though unsuccessful venture. Benedetto Zaccaria was one of the greatest admirals, businessmen and diplomats of his time.

Genoa's political zenith was marked by a crushing naval victory over the Pisans at Meloria (1284) and a less decisive one over the Venetians at Curzola (1298), followed by other successful encounters. At the same period, maritime trade reached its peak: in 1293, sources indicate a total value for incoming and outgoing wares of almost 4,000,000 Genoese pounds—roughly seven times as much as the income of the French monarchy had been under Philip II Augustus.

During the 14th and 15th centuries, however, the whole of Europe was in a profound material and moral crisis. This was sharpened in Genoa by the irrepressible individualism of the citizens. There still was progress in certain fields, for instance in the silk industry and in both private and public banking: the Bank of San Giorgio, in particular, pioneered in the development of joint-stock companies and in colonial expansion through chartered companies. This progress, however, was not enough to offset the decadence of Mediterranean trade and the decline of the population. Moreover, while splendid Renaissance mansions in the town and villas in the surrounding country emphasized the growing difference between the very rich and the very poor, class and party struggle kept the government in perpetual turmoil; and public finances were ruined by war. The election of native doges after the Venetian model, beginning with that of Simone Boccanegra in 1339, was a vain attempt to solve the political problem.

Even military victories often had frustrating results. The colonists of Caffa repulsed a powerful Mongol army, but caught the plague and transmitted the Black Death (q.v.) to Genoa in 1346. The war of Chioggia (q.v.), which brought Venice almost to its knees, ended in a Venetian victory through exhaustion (1379–80). After emerging from a period of French domination (1394–1409), Genoa passed under Milanese overlordship in 1421, and a diplomatic shift by the duke of Milan, Filippo Maria Visconti, made worthless the Genoese naval victory over the Aragonese at Ponza (1435). This provoked a successful rising against the Visconti, but Genoa could no longer be a great power. Corsica was in perennial revolt; Sardinia was overrun by the Aragonese; the Levant colonies, which had become virtually independent of the motherland, were conquered by the Egyptians or the Turks. Only the mainland domain (that is, Liguria proper) was successfully held.

The 16th, 17th and 18th Centuries.—Having accepted the overlordship of Ludovico Sforza, duke of Milan in 1488, Genoa was to be involved in the troubles that ensued when the French king Louis XII began to pursue his claims to the duchy of Milan (1499). In the interval, however, Christopher Columbus (born in Genoa in 1451) had followed the example set by the Vivaldi brothers of seeking a westward route to the Indies and had discovered America for the Spaniards; he assigned one-tenth of his own income from the discovery to the Bank of San Giorgio for the relief of taxation on foodstuffs in Genoa. The Spanish connection was reinforced in the 16th century when Andrea Doria (q.v.) transferred his service from Francis I of France to the Holy Roman emperor Charles V, who was also king of Spain. Andrea Doria, who restored his town to orderly government under biennial doges and an oligarchy of the old and new noble merchants by the constitution of 1528, made Genoa politically a satellite of Spain but ensured that it would be a privileged exploiter of the vast Spanish empire. The result was a partial economic recovery in the 16th and 17th centuries. By chartering ships and extending loans to Spain and to other foreign powers, by daring speculations in foreign exchange and by shrewd management of foreign investments, many Genoese families amassed great fortunes. They generally lived parsimoniously, but often spent lavishly in building houses and endowing charitable institutions. It was still possible for commoners to wax richer and gain admission into the ranks of the privileged aristocracy. In the 17th century there was a brief period of splendid painting by the Genoese school represented by such masters as Bernardo Strozzi and Alessandro Magnasco.

Genoa was heavily bombarded by the French in May 1684, during the Franco-Spanish war over Luxembourg, and was occupied by the Austrians in 1746, during the War of the Austrian Succession (the Austrians were expelled by a popular insurrection, begun accidentally when an unknown urchin, traditionally known as Balilla, threw a stone at an insolent officer). As the fortunes of Spain and Italy declined, Genoa's did so likewise; by the mid-18th century trade had sunk to its lowest level, and the Bank of San Giorgio was in dire straits. In 1768, by the treaty of Versailles, the republic ceded to France its last overseas possession, Corsica.

Later History.—In the French Revolutionary and Napoleonic Wars the republic saw its neutrality violated by both sides. In 1797, under Bonaparte's pressure, it was transformed into an "equalitarian" Ligurian republic, under a French protectorate. The long siege which Gen. André Masséna had to sustain in Genoa in 1800 inflicted great sufferings on the population. Annexation to France in 1805 brought only temporary economic relief, as the British blockade of the continental ports stifled what was left of maritime trade; and amid the blessings of liberty and equality many people longed for the old municipal republic. Lord William Bentinck's empty promise that the republic should be restored stimulated the Genoese to revolt against the defeated armies of Napoleon (April 1814), but the allies already had agreed to yield Genoa to the kingdom of Sardinia—Piedmont under the house of Savoy—whose constant goal for three centuries had been to acquire the town by armed force, by diplomacy, or by promoting conspiracies against the republican government. In Nov. 1814 the congress of Vienna ratified this agreement.

Though the Genoese bitterly resented the authoritarian regime of the house of Savoy, they had everything to gain from union with a large and thriving hinterland. The merchant marine rapidly revived, and Genoese trade blossomed anew, not only in its traditional haunts of the Mediterranean and in the Black sea, but also in the far east and in America. Heavy industry had a promising start. Temporary and permanent emigration to Argentina, Uruguay and Brazil tempted and rewarded men from all walks of life. Genoa nevertheless remained a hotbed of republican and radical opposition, whose last violent expression was a revolt against the armistice concluded in 1848 between King Charles Albert and the victorious Austrians. (See ITALIAN INDEPENDENCE, WARS OF.) Gradually, however, the longing for a local republic gave way to the dream of an Italian republic, such as the Genoese Giuseppe Mazzini envisaged. When Mazzini's plans proved unfeasible, the Genoese accepted the idea of a united kingdom of Italy under the liberalized Savoy dynasty. They gave more than their share to all the battles for independence, and most particularly to Garibaldi's Sicilian venture, which sailed from nearby Quarto in 1860.

The unification of Italy further broadened the scope of Genoese activity. Genoa, then Italy's greatest commercial port, vied with Marseilles for supremacy in the Mediterranean and competed with the ports of the North sea for the trade of Switzerland and central Europe; and when Genoa's share in the latter declined somewhat in the 20th century the difference was counterbalanced by the ever-increasing trade flowing to and from northern Italy. The university, into which pre-existing institutions of higher learning had been fused in 1803, became especially distinguished for its teaching on economic and maritime subjects. In the cultural sphere, 19th-century Genoa experienced a musical awakening, highlighted by the construction of the Carlo Felice opera house and by the activity of Niccolò Paganini, violinist and composer; and later won some reputation in the world of literature through the journalism and fiction of A. G. Barrili and L. A. Vassallo (Gandolin).

Genoa, which harboured a significant underground opposition to Fascism, suffered heavily in World War II from Allied naval and air attacks and from German occupation until, shortly before the final German collapse, local resistance forces liberated the town.

See also references under "Genoa" in the Index volume.

BIBLIOGRAPHY.—For a general survey see V. A. Vitale, *Breviario di storia di Genova* (1955). The series of *Annales Januenses*, ed. by L. T. Belgrano and C. Imperiale (1890-1926), provides a continuous contemporary account of the period between 1099 and 1294. In the series *Monumenta Historiae Patriae* (1938–) and the *Liber Jurium Liguri dei secoli XII e XIII* (1938–) are important collections of medieval documents. Periodical publications include the *Atti della Società Ligure di Storia Patria* (1858–); the *Giornale Ligustico di archeologia, storia e belle arti* (1874-95), the *Giornale storico e letterario della Liguria* (1900-43); and the *Bollettino Ligustico per la storia e la cultura regionale* (1949–).

For particular aspects see E. H. Byrne, *Genoese Shipping in the 12th and 13th centuries* (1930); R. S. Lopez, *Storia delle Colonie genovesi nel Mediterraneo* (1938) and, with I. W. Raymond, *Medieval Trade in the Mediterranean World* (1955); R. Doehaerd, *Les Relations commerciales entre Gênes, le Belgique et l'Oueremont aux XIIIe et XIVe siècles* (1941) and, with C. Kerremans, *Les Relations commerciales entre Gênes, la Belgique et l'Oueremont 1400-1440* (1952); G. Giacchero, *Storia economica del Settecento genovese* (1951); E. Bach, *La Cité de Gênes au XIIe siècle* (1955); P. Revelli, *Il Genovese* (1951); A. L. Rodgers, *Industrial Geography of the Port of Genoa* (1960).
(R. S. L.)

GENOA, CONFERENCE OF (April 10–May 19, 1922), was proposed in Jan. 1922 by David Lloyd George, the British prime minister, at the Cannes meeting of the supreme council of the Allies (*see* CANNES, CONFERENCE OF). Lloyd George argued that a scheme for European economic reconstruction must include Russia. Aristide Briand, the French prime minister, accepted the idea because at the same time Lloyd George offered a British guarantee to France in the event of unprovoked German aggression on French soil. Lloyd George, however, warned Briand that Great Britain would not be willing to incur military commitments in central and eastern Europe. On Jan. 6 the supreme council unanimously voted a resolution summoning to Genoa an economic and financial conference as "an urgent and essential step toward the economic reconstruction of central and eastern Europe."

Accused in French parliament of having accepted a diminution of the rights of France under the treaty of Versailles, Briand resigned on Jan. 12 and was succeeded by Raymond Poincaré. Since the plan of the Genoa conference had been accepted, Poincaré could not reject it altogether, but he sought to interpret the agenda in the narrowest sense and to hedge the participation of Soviet Russia with the fullest possible restrictions.

The Genoa conference was preceded by a not too cordial meeting between Poincaré and Lloyd George at Boulogne (Feb. 25), a meeting of Allied economic experts in London (March 20–28) and two other preliminary meetings of regional character, one between the members of the little entente in Belgrade and another in Warsaw between Poland, Latvia, Estonia and Finland. The parties represented in Warsaw subsequently conferred in Riga with Soviet representatives. In all the three regional conferences the sanctity of the peace treaties was reaffirmed.

Representatives of Great Britain, of the British self-governing dominions and of 29 European states, including not only the Allies and former neutrals, but all the former Central Powers except Turkey, were represented at the conference. The invitation to Genoa was accepted with alacrity by the Soviet government, whose delegation was headed by Georgi V. Chicherin, the people's commissar for foreign affairs. The United States declined to take part on two grounds: that it would not be possible to prevent the conference from trenching on political questions and that the economic recovery of Russia depended less on international action than on the internal policy of the Soviet government.

The conference, solemnly opened at the Palazzo San Giorgio, set up four commissions: the first to examine "conditions under which foreign enterprise and capital could be enlisted for the restoration of Russia," as well as the settlement "of past obligations"; the other three to deal respectively with financial, economic and transport provisions. These three latter commissions all reported before the conference came to an end, but their reports were bound to remain academic unless the first commission achieved positive results. It soon appeared that the labours of the first commission were fruitless because the French and the Belgians insisted on the integral repayment of prewar loans accorded to Russia as well as on integral restitution of foreign-owned private property in Russia. Both of these demands were refused by the Soviet delegation.

The negotiations were dramatically interrupted by the signature at Rapallo, on April 16, by Chicherin and Walter Rathenau, the German foreign minister, of a separate treaty by which, in the published text, the two parties mutually renounced all reparation claims and decided to resume normal diplomatic and consular relations (*see* RAPALLO, TREATY OF). This separate Soviet-German treaty damaged the general prospect of the conference by the fear it instilled into the Allies. It appeared as the first step toward a Soviet-German alliance directed against the territorial stipulations of the treaty of Versailles and other peace treaties. In these circumstances there was little prospect of success for a general treaty of nonaggression which Lloyd George suggested on April 25. But the conference actually broke down through the Franco-Belgian insistence on repayment of loans to and investments in Russia. The Genoa conference was quickly wound up by remitting its agenda to a mixed commission of experts, who duly met at The Hague from June 26 to July 20, 1922; but it also foundered on the rock of foreign-owned private property in Russia.

BIBLIOGRAPHY.—British Blue Book, *Papers Relating to International Economic Conference, Genoa, April-May 1922*, Cmd. 1667 (1922); French Yellow Book, *Documents diplomatiques: Conférence économique internationale de Gênes* (1922); British Blue Book, *Papers Respecting Negotiations for an Anglo-French Pact*, Cmd. 2169 (1924).
(K. SM.)

GENOCIDE. Raphael Lemkin, a U.S. scholar of Polish origin, is credited with having coined the term "genocide." He inspired and promoted action on the international plane to outlaw genocide. The word, as he explained, is a hybrid consisting of the Greek *genos* meaning race, nation or tribe; and the Latin suffix *cide* meaning killing. The realities of European life in the years 1933–45, Lemkin said, called for the formulation of a legal concept of destruction of human groups. (*See* ANTI-SEMITISM.)

In 1946, under the impact of the crimes which had been revealed in the Nürnberg and other war crimes trials, the general assembly of the United Nations affirmed "that genocide is a crime under international law which the civilized world condemns, and for the commission of which principals and accomplices are punishable." Two years later, on Dec. 9, 1948, the general assembly approved the Convention on the Prevention and Punishment of the Crime of Genocide. The convention went into effect on Jan. 12, 1951. By the early 1970s, 70 states had become parties to the convention.

In the words of the International Court of Justice, the convention "was manifestly adopted for a purely humanitarian and civilizing purpose. It is indeed difficult to imagine a convention that might have this dual character to a greater degree, since its object on the one hand is to safeguard the very existence of certain human groups and on the other to confirm and endorse the most elementary principles of morality." In the convention the contracting states confirmed that genocide, whether committed in time of peace or in time of war, is a crime under international law which they undertake to prevent and to punish. The fact that genocide is a crime irrespective of whether it is committed in time of peace or in time of war, distinguishes the idea of "genocide" from that of "crimes against humanity" under the 1945 charter of the international military tribunal (the "Nürnberg tribunal") as interpreted by that tribunal.

Certain inhuman acts are international crimes, *i.e.*, crimes against humanity, only when committed in execution of, or in connection with crimes against peace, or war crimes. Under the definition of genocide, however, the connection with war and crimes committed in preparation of and during a war, is not required. In the convention, genocide means any of the following acts committed with intent to destroy, in whole or in part, a national, ethnical, racial or religious group, as such: (1) killing members of the group; (2) causing serious bodily or mental harm to members of the group; (3) deliberately inflicting on the group conditions of life calculated to bring about its physical destruction in whole or in part; (4) imposing measures intended to prevent births within the group; (5) forcibly transferring children of the group to another group. Conspiracy, direct and public incitement, and attempt to commit genocide and complicity in genocide are also made punishable. Perpetrators shall be punished, whether they are constitutionally responsible rulers, public officials or private individuals. They shall be tried by a competent tribunal of the state in the territory of which the act was committed "or by such international penal tribunal as may have jurisdiction with respect to such contracting parties as shall have accepted the jurisdiction of such tribunal."

During the two decades after the convention was adopted the endeavours to provide for an international criminal jurisdiction had not materialized. It is one of the results of the convention that the parties to it have removed any doubt that genocide, even if perpetrated by a government in its own territory, is not an internal matter of the state concerned ("a matter essentially within the domestic jurisdiction") but a matter of international concern. Any contracting state can call upon United Nations organs to intervene and to take such action under the charter of the United Nations as they consider appropriate for the prevention and suppression of acts of genocide.

BIBLIOGRAPHY.—Nehemiah Robinson, *The Genocide Convention*, has comprehensive bibliography (1960); General Assembly resolutions 96 (I) Dec. 11, 1946, 180 (II) Nov. 21, 1947, and 260 (III) Dec. 9, 1948; "Reservations to the Convention on Genocide, Advisory Opinion," International Court of Justice, *Reports 1951*, p. 15 (1951); R. Lemkin, *Axis Rule in Occupied Europe*, pp. 79–95 (1944); "Genocide as a Crime under International Law"; *American Journal of International Law*, vol. 41, p. 145 (1947); E. Schwelb, "Crimes Against Humanity," *British Yearbook of International Law*, vol. 23, p. 178 (1946).   (E. SB.)

GENOVESI, ANTONIO (1712–1769), Italian philosopher and economist who proposed reforms in the kingdom of Naples in a spirit that sought to combine the ideas of the Enlightenment with an extremely radical Christianity, was born at Castiglione, near Salerno, on Nov. 1, 1712. Ordained priest in 1737, he went to Naples in 1738 and was in 1741 appointed to teach metaphysics in the university there. His *Disciplinarum metaphysicarum elementa* (1743–52) incurred some suspicion of heresy, and in 1748 he decided not to publish the companion work on theology (his treatises on logic and on physics had both appeared in 1745). In 1753, however, he dedicated his *Discorso sopra alcuni trattati d'agricoltura . . . in cui si tratta del vero fine delle lettere* to the influential Bartolomeo Intieri, with the result that in 1754, when Intieri founded at Naples the first European chair of "commerce and mechanics" (i.e., political economy), he stipulated that Genovesi should be its first occupant. Thenceforward Genovesi wrote and lectured mainly in Italian instead of Latin. His subsequent publications included *Meditazioni filosofiche sulla religione e sulla morale* (1758), *Lettere accademiche* (1764) and, most important of all, *Delle lezioni di commercio* (1765; new ed, 1768), the first Italian work on his subject. Genovesi died in Naples on Sept. 23, 1769.

For his metaphysics Genovesi took much from Leibnizian monadism. His theory of knowledge was largely empiricist. His mercantilist system of economics is distinguished by his remarkable analysis of demand, by his high valuation of labour and by his efforts to reconcile protectionism with free competition. In the political field his contention that ecclesiastical authority should be strictly limited to spiritual matters and that the state should dispossess the clergy and religious orders of their lands was most welcome to Bernardo Tanucci's "enlightened" administration in Naples.

See E. Gambini, *Antonio Genovesi* (1910); G. Monti, *Due grandi riformatori del settecento* (1926); A. Tisi, *Il Pensiero religioso d'Antonio Genovesi* (1932).

GENRE PAINTING has primarily to do with a type of subject, but the proper application of the term is limited also by the painter's attitude toward the subject. (*See also* STILL-LIFE PAINTING.) In genre painting, intimate scenes and subjects from ordinary daily life are dealt with. The elimination of imaginative content focuses attention upon the shrewd observation of types, costumes and settings and upon the beauty and appropriateness of colour, form and texture. In true genre painting such subjective qualities as the dramatic, historical, ceremonial, satirical, didactic, romantic, sentimental and religious should be reduced to a minimum. Characteristic works by Jan Steen, Honoré Daumier, Thomas Rowlandson and William Hogarth would thus be too satirical or didactic to be called genre, while those of Francis Wheatley, George Morland and J. H. Fragonard would be too sentimental and those of J. F. Millet too romantic.

In Europe, genre painting does not begin clearly to emerge until the late middle ages, when illuminated calendars showing the occupations appropriate to the months or seasons are found in manuscript books (*see* ILLUMINATED MANUSCRIPTS). These little genre pictures give intimate glimpses of the life of the time. Soon the taste for genre became so keen that Petrus Christus, Pieter Aertsen and Pieter Brueghel painted scenes in shops and kitchens occasionally thinly disguised as religious subjects. The greatest home of genre painting was indeed 17th-century Holland, when Adriaen van Ostade, Gerard Dou, Gabriel Metsu, Jan Vermeer, Pieter de Hooch and Gerard Terborch flourished. Among later exponents are J. B. S. Chardin in France and Pietro Longhi in Italy. Although in modern times colour photography has practically usurped the place of genre painting, the term might include interiors by Jean Édouard Vuillard and Pierre Bonnard, leaders of the French *Intimiste* school, and similar works by Henri Matisse.
(D. L. Fr.)

GENTIAN, botanically *Gentiana*, a large genus of herbaceous plants belonging to the family Gentianaceae (*q.v.*). The genus comprises about 400 species, most of them perennial plants with tufted growth, growing in hilly or mountainous districts, chiefly in the northern hemisphere, but also in New Zealand and South America. The majority of species are remarkable for the deep or brilliant blue colour of their blossoms, comparatively few having yellow, white or, more rarely, red flowers; the last are almost exclusively found in the Andes.

The leaves are opposite, entire, smooth and often strongly ribbed. The flowers have a persistent four- to five-lobed calyx and a four- to five-lobed tubular corolla; the stamens are equal in number to the lobes of the corolla. The ovary is one-celled, with two stigmas, either separate and rolled back or contiguous and funnel shaped. The fruit when ripe separates into two valves and contains numerous small seeds.

About 60 species occur in North America, widely distributed throughout the continent, but most numerous in the Rocky mountain region. Of about 18 species found from the Great Plains eastward, among the best known are the fringed gentian (*G. crinita*), one of the most beautiful American wild flowers; the closed or bottle gentian (*G. andrewsii*), the commonest species; the downy gentian (*G. puberula*), of the prairie region; and the stiff gentian or agueweed (*G. quinquefolia*), which extends southward to Florida. Of the many Rocky mountain species, those with fringed flowers, as *G. elegans* and *G. barbellata*, are among the most conspicuous. Representative of the 12 or more species found in California and northward in the coastal mountains are the single-flowered gentian (*G. simplex*), with slightly fringed flowers, and the explorer's gentian (*G. calycosa*), which throughout the summer forms sheets of intense blue in alpine meadows from California to British Columbia and eastward to Montana.

There are ten species of gentian native to Great Britain. Three of them are perennials belonging to the genus *Gentiana*, while seven, all of which are annuals or biennials, are credited to the genus *Gentianella*, a name preferred by British botanists for annual and biennial gentians but not widely accepted in the United States.

Of the perennial species the marsh gentian (*Gentiana pneumonanthe*), also called the Calathian violet, is six to nine inches high, has blue flowers and is rather rare from Cumberland to Dorsetshire. The spring gentian (*G. verna*) and the small gentian (*G. nivalis*) are much lower plants, have bright blue flowers and are more widely distributed throughout the British Isles.

The annual or biennial gentians of the genus *Gentianella* comprise the felwort (*G. amarella*), often called autumn gentian, which has dull purple flowers and is widely distributed; *G. campestris*, two to nine inches high, with blue or white flowers and found throughout Great Britain; *G. anglica*, confined to southern England, has purple flowers and is only three to five inches high; *G. uliginosa*, a low annual, rare in Pembroke and Glamorgan; and *G. germanica*, a biennial, with blue flowers, rather common on calcareous grasslands throughout Great Britain.

Some of these, but more especially the much finer species from North America, the Himalayas, Burma, Tibet, China and Japan, are much cultivated for ornament in England, where over 150 species are known. Less than 50 of these are much grown in the United States, where the climate is far less suited to gentians than is that of England. None of them is particularly easy to grow, and many of them need the specialized conditions of scree or moraine in the rock gardens. All require coolness and moisture, especially the perennials.

Several preparations obtained from the root of *Gentiana lutea* are used in medicine to stimulate the alimentary tract, thus improving digestion. The chief of these is compound gentian tincture, comprising 100 g. of powdered gentian root, 40 g. of bitter-orange peel and 10 g. of cardamom seed, mixed with glycerin, alcohol and water. In Germany and France other species of gentian, notably *G. purpurea*, *G. punctata* and *G. pannonica*, are sometimes permitted substitutes of *G. lutea*.

G. lutea is a large handsome plant three or four feet high, growing in open grassy places on the Alps, Apennines and Pyrenees, as well as on some of the mountainous ranges of France and Germany, extending as far east as Bosnia and Asia Minor. It has large, oval, strongly ribbed leaves and dense whorls of conspicuous yellow flowers. Its use in medicine is of very ancient date. Pliny and Dioscorides mention that the plant was noticed by Gentius, a king of the Illyrians, living 180–167 B.C., from whom the name *Gentiana* is supposed to be derived. During the middle ages it was much employed in the cure of disease, and as an ingredient in counter-poisons. In 1552 Hieronymus Bock (Tragus), a German priest, physician and botanist, mentions the use of the root as a means of dilating wounds.

The root is tough and flexible, scarcely branched and of a brownish colour and spongy texture. It has a pure bitter taste and faint distinctive odour. The bitter principle, known as gentianin, is a glucoside, soluble in water and alcohol. It can be decomposed into glucose and gentiopicrin by the action of dilute mineral acids. It is not precipitated by tannin or subacetate of lead. A solution of caustic potash or soda forms with gentianin a yellow solution, and the tincture of the root to which either of these alkalis has been added loses its bitterness in a few days. Gentian root also contains gentianic acid, which is inert and tasteless. It forms pale yellow, silky crystals, very slightly soluble in water or ether but soluble in hot strong alcohol and in aqueous alkaline solutions. This substance is also called gentianin and gentisin.

The root also contains 12% to 15% of an uncrystallizable sugar called gentianose, of which fact advantage has long been taken in Switzerland and Bavaria for the production of a bitter cordial spirit called *Enzianbranntwein*. The use of this spirit, especially in Switzerland, has sometimes been followed by poisonous symptoms, which have been doubtfully attributed to inherent narcotic properties possessed by some species of gentian, the roots of which may have been indiscriminately collected with it, but it is quite possible that it may be due to the contamination of the root by that of hellebore (*Veratrum album*), a poisonous plant growing at the same altitude and having leaves extremely similar in appearance and size to those of *G. lutea*. See also HELLEBORE.

(N. TR.)

GENTIANACEAE, the gentian family, includes some of the most beautiful flowering plants of woodlands, meadows and moors.

The fringed gentian (*Gentiana crinita*) is a popular favourite, but the Andean genus *Lagenanthus*, with showy scarlet tubular flowers four to five and a half inches long, is virtually unknown.

J. HORACE McFARLAND CO.

FRINGED GENTIAN (*GENTIANA CRINITA*)

The family contains about 1,000 species in 80 genera; mostly temperate or montane in all continents except Africa, with epicentres in the Alps, Himalayas, western North America and the Andes; mostly annual or perennial herbs of erect tufted habit by the repeatedly dichotomous branching. Less frequent growth forms include vines (Cuban genus *Goeppertia* and Asiatic *Crawfurdia*), rhizomatous perennials (*Menyanthes*, etc.), water lilylike aquatics (*Nymphoides*, etc.), weedy short-lived annuals (*Centaurium*, *Hoppea*, etc.), heathlike subshrubs (*Ericostema*) and shrubs attaining a height of 12 ft. or more (*Macrocarpaea*, *Symbolanthus*). Rock gardeners value low, clump-forming alpines (*Gentiana acaulis*, *bavarica*, etc.) displaying large bell-shaped flowers of intense shades of blue.

The leaves are generally in two-ranked opposite pairs, smooth and shining, the margins without teeth, rarely in whorls (*Curtia* and *Frasera*) or trifoliate (*Menyanthes*). Reduced scalelike leaves occur in anomalous genera of slender nongreen saprophytes (*Voyria*, etc.); these are often confused with species of Burmanniaceae. The inflorescence is generally cymose, but the flowers may be densely spicate (*Coutoubea spicata*) or even solitary (some true gentians). The flowers are perfect and regular with parts in fives (less often in fours), the pistil bicarpellate (uniloculate in *Menyanthes* and allies). The sepals generally form a tubular calyx, but in the primitive neotropical genus *Chorisepalum* they are separate. The corolla varies widely but is plaited or smooth, and most often bell shaped, funnelform or salverform, or sometimes rotate (British genus *Chlora*). Yellow is the primitive flower colour, retained in *Gentiana lutea*, but more numerous are species that have evolved with hues from pale blue to ultramarine. The throat is frequently provided with fringed scales, nectaries, appendages or colour streaks (nectar guides). Stamens, which equal in number but alternate with the corolla segments, are inserted at various levels on the tube, the slender filaments bearing delicate versatile anthers that dehisce by longitudinal slits. In *Centaurium* the stamens coil tightly after flowering. Exceptional variation in pollen grains occurs among genera but this character is evidently not closely correlated with any other floral character although it has been used unsatisfactorily in support of phylogenies. Gelatinous pollen is produced in *Gentiana parryi* and others, where the orientation of the anthers may vary between the closed gentian type and those species with open corollas. The style, which may be short to long, undivided or bilobed, usually terminates in a distinct stigma. Placentation is parietal. The superior ovary contains numerous anatropous (or half-anatropous) ovules; these mature into minute seeds, each provided with copious endosperm in which the small embryo is embedded.

Insect pollination is general in the family. Both oligotropic species (*i.e.*, obligate to specific insects), for example, *Gentiana* subgenus *Cyclostigma* where such long-tongued Lepidoptera as the diurnal hawk moths are vectors, and facultative species (*i.e.*, non-obligate), for example, *Gentiana lutea* where the nectar is accessible to all visitors, are recognized. Although *Centaurium* and *Chlora* are nectarless, they are visited by Lepidoptera; perhaps here the twisting of the stamens, which are easily intercepted by the insect, aids in pollination. Dimorphism obtains in *Menyanthes*, *Nymphoides* and some true gentians. It has been observed in the dimorphic *Menyanthes* that when only long-styled flowers occur in a marsh, ripe fruits fail to be produced.

Bitter principles are widespread in the vegetative parts, especially in the rhizomes and roots, and have fostered their use in medicine; *e.g.*, in *Gentiana lutea* and others. *See* GENTIAN.

(J. A. EN.)

GENTILE, GIOVANNI (1875–1944), Italian philosopher and politician, was born at Castelvetrano (Trapani) on May 30, 1875. He studied literature and philosophy at the University of Pisa and, after a series of university appointments, became in 1917 professor of the history of philosophy in the University of Rome. From 1903 to 1922 he collaborated with Benedetto Croce in editing the periodical *La Critica*. Though he soon developed a philosophy of his own, he remained a friend of Croce until 1924, when they disagreed over fascism. As minister of education in the Fascist government from Oct. 1922 to July 1924, Gentile carried out an organic reform of Italian education; and as president of two commissions for the reform of the constitution he contributed to laying the foundations of the Fascist corporate state (1925). Later, though he was made president of the supreme council of education (1926–28), a member of the Fascist grand council (1925–29) and president of various cultural institutions, his political influence steadily declined. From 1925 to 1943 he planned and edited the *Enciclopedia Italiana*. After Sept. 8, 1943, he adhered to the Fascist government established at Salò and was made the president of the Accademia d'Italia. He was killed in Florence by anti-Fascist partisans on April 15, 1944.

Gentile's philosophy is an extreme form of monistic idealism. He denies the existence of individual minds and of any distinction between theory and practice, subject and object, past and present. Mind is the absolute, and education is the process of revelation of the absolute. In this sense education is always self-education and is ultimately identical with philosophy. Gentile's interest in education and his warm and forceful style of writing explain his great popularity among teachers and educational reformers before 1935. Later his pupils went their own ways; their views continued to be expressed in the *Giornale critico della filosofia italiana*, founded by Gentile in 1920.

Among Gentile's numerous works, which include editions of Giordano Bruno, Tommaso Campanella, G. B. Vico, Vincenzo Cuoco, Antonio Rosmini, Vincenzo Gioberti and Spinoza (with a commentary) and a translation of Kant's *Kritik der reinen Vernunft*, are: *La filosofia di Marx* (1899); *Dal Genovesi al Galluppi* (1903), a volume of the *Storia della filosofia italiana*; *Il modernismo* (1909); *Bernardino Telesio* (1911); *I problemi della scolastica e il pensiero italiano* (1913); *La riforma della dialettica hegeliano* (1913); *Sommario di pedagogia come scienza filosofica*, two volumes (1913–14); *Teoria generale dello spirito come atto puro* (1916; Eng. trans., *Theory of Mind as Pure Act*, 1922); *I fondamenti della filosofia del diritto* (1916); *Sistema di logica come teoria del conoscere* (1917–23); *Le origini della filosofia contemporanea in Italia*, four volumes (1917–23); *Il problema scolastico del dopoguerra* (1920); *La riforma dell' educazione* (1920; Eng. trans., *The Reform of Education*, 1923); *Studi sul Rinascimento* (1923); *Bertrando Spaventa* (1924); *Il fascismo al governo della scuola* (1924); *Che cosa è il fascismo* (1925); *Manzoni e Leopardi* (1928); *La filosofia dell' arte* (1931); *Memorie italiane* (1936); and *La mia religione* (1943). (A. D. Mo.)

GENTILE, a person who is not Jewish. The word stems from the Hebrew term *goi*, which means "a nation," and was applied both to the Hebrews and to any other nation. The plural, *goyyim*, especially with the definite article, *ha-goyyim*, "the nations," is used in the Hebrew Bible in the sense of the nations of the world who are not Hebrews. The translations of the Bible into Latin rendered *goyyim* with *gentes* (sing. *gens*) or *gentiles*, the latter being an adjectival form of *gens*. In general, modern usage has been to reserve the term gentile to the single individual, though occasionally "the gentiles" means the nations; this is the case in English translations of the Bible. In postbiblical Hebrew the term *goi* lost its national application and became instead a term for an individual non-Jew. Since in the western world such an individual was usually a Christian, loose usage among Jews often equates gentile and Christian; strict usage, however, should recognize that a Muslim or a Buddhist would also be termed a gentile. The Mormons (Church of Jesus Christ of Latter-day Saints), regarding themselves as the true Hebrews, use the term gentile for a person, including even a Jew, who is not a Mormon. (S. SL.)

GENTILE DA FABRIANO (*c.* 1370–1427), Italian painter whose few surviving works are among the finest examples of the International Gothic style in Italy, was born in Fabriano in the Marches. An early signed work by him, formerly in the Church of S. Niccolò in Fabriano (now Staatliche Museen, West Berlin), has stylistic affinities with Lombard painting and suggests similar training.

The almost total loss of Gentile's important and influential fresco paintings tends to obscure his very real historical significance. He was in Venice in 1408 and in 1409 was commissioned to decorate the Doges' Palace with historical frescoes; these frescoes, later completed by Pisanello (*q.v.*), were subsequently destroyed by fire. Between 1414 and 1419 Gentile was in Brescia working for Pandolfo III Malatesta; works then executed were studied by Cosimo Tura in 1469 but have since perished. His final important, but again ill-fated, cycle of frescoes was executed in Rome in the Church of St. John Lateran shortly before Gentile's death in Rome in 1427; these frescoes, like those in Venice, were completed by Pisanello, and according to Vasari were admired by Michelangelo. Between 1422 and 1425 Gentile was in Florence. His surviving masterpiece, the "Adoration of the Magi" (now in the Uf-

ALINARI   "ADORATION OF THE MAGI" BY GENTILE DA FABRIANO. IN THE UFFIZI GALLERY, FLORENCE

fizi), was completed there in 1423 for the Church of Sta. Trinita. Its elegant courtly style continued to influence Florentine artists throughout the century and presented a counterattraction to the austere realism introduced by Masaccio (*q.v.*). The central panel with Madonna and Child is in the Uffizi, Florence, known as the Quaratesi polyptych was also executed in Florence (1425). The altarpiece polyptych with Madonna and Child is in the royal collection, London; the wings are in the Uffizi, Florence.

See L. Grassi, *Tutta la pittura di Gentile da Fabriano* (1953).

GENTILESCHI, the family name of two Italian painters:

Orazio Gentileschi (*c.* 1562–*c.* 1647) is commonly named Orazio Lomi de' Gentileschi. He was born in Pisa and studied under his half brother Aurelio Lomi. He afterward went to Rome and painted frescoes in Sta. Maria Maggiore, in the Lateran and in S. Niccolo in Carcere; he was associated with the landscape painter Agostino Tassi, executing the figures for the landscapes of this artist. Among his best works are: "The Circumcision" in the church of Gesu at Ancona; "The Madonna and St. Clara", in S. Siro, Genoa; "The Annunciation" in the Prado, Madrid; "SS. Cecilia and Valerian" in the Brera, Milan; a "Flight Into Egypt" in the Louvre, Paris, and another in the Belvedere, Vienna; and "Joseph and Potiphar's Wife" at Hampton Court. At an advanced age Gentileschi went to England at the invitation of Charles I, being employed in the palace at Greenwich. Van Dyck included him in his portraits of a hundred illustrious men. His works generally are strong in shadow and positive in colour. He died in England about 1647.

Artemisia Gentileschi (1597–after 1651), Orazio's daughter, studied first under Guido Reni, acquired much renown for portrait painting and considerably excelled her father's fame. She was a beautiful and elegant woman; her likeness, painted by her own hand, is to be seen in Hampton Court. Her most celebrated composition is "Judith and Holofernes," Wadsworth Atheneum, Hartford, Conn., certainly a work of singular energy. She went to England about 1638 and painted many portraits there. Artemisia refused an offer of marriage from Agostino Tassi and married Pier Antonio Schiattesi, continuing, however, to use her own surname. She settled in Naples, to which she returned from England, and was commissioned to paint three pictures for the cathedral of Pozzuoli. Her style was violent, characterized by brilliant colour.

GENTILI, ALBERICO (1552–1608), Italian jurist who has great claims to be considered the founder of the science of international law, was born on Jan. 14, 1552, at San Ginesio, Macerata, Italy. After taking the degree of doctor of civil law at the University of Perugia, and holding a judicial office at Ascoli, he returned to San Ginesio and was entrusted with the task of recasting its statutes. In 1579, however, as a result of his Protestant opinions, he was obliged to flee, first to Carniola in Austria and then to England. By the autumn of 1580 he had reached Oxford, and shortly afterward was qualified to teach by being admitted to the same degree which he had taken at Perugia. His lectures on Roman law soon became famous. The dialogues, disputations and commentaries which he then published in rapid succession established his position as a civil lawyer and secured his appointment in 1587 to the regius professorship of civil law. It was, however, by his application of the old learning to the new questions suggested by modern international relations that Gentili produced his most lasting results. In 1584 he was consulted by the government as to the proper course to be pursued with Bernardino de Mendoza, the Spanish ambassador, who had been detected in plotting against Elizabeth I. Shortly afterward he developed his opinion on this question into a book, the *De legationibus libri tres* (1585). In 1588 Alberico published in London the *De jure belli commentatio prima.* A second and a third *Commentatio* followed, and the whole of this material, with many additions and improvements, appeared at Hanau, Prussia, in 1598 as the *De jure belli libri tres.* It was doubtless in consequence of the reputation gained by these works that Gentili became henceforth more and more engaged in forensic practice, resided chiefly in London and left his Oxford work to be partly discharged by a deputy. In 1600 he was admitted to Gray's Inn, and in 1605 was appointed standing counsel to the king of Spain. He died on June 19, 1608, and was buried in the churchyard of St. Helen's, Bishopsgate. His notes of the cases in which he was engaged for the Spaniards were posthumously published in 1613 at Hanau as *Hispanicae advocationis libri duo.*

In contrast with earlier writers who had dealt with various international questions singly and with submission to the decisions of the church, Gentili examined as a whole the relations of states to one another and attempted the solution of the problems involved by principles entirely independent of the authority of Rome. He used the reasonings both of the civil and of the canon law, combined them with the *Jus Naturae* and identified this with the consent of the majority of nations, by which historical precedents were to be criticized and, when necessary, set aside.

His writings have many faults. His style is prolix, obscure and to the modern reader pedantic; but a comparison of the *De jure belli* with the treatises of Pierino Belli, Dominico Soto or even Balthasar Ayala shows that he greatly improved upon his predecessors, not only by the fullness with which he worked out points of detail, but also by clearly separating the law of war from martial law, and by placing the subject upon a foundation independent of theological differences. A comparison of the same work with the *De jure belli ac pacis* (1625) of Hugo Grotius, moreover, reveals the latter's indebtedness to Gentili.

The principal works on international law by Gentili have been republished and translated in the "Classics of International Law Series" on behalf of the Division of International Law of the Carnegie Endowment for International Peace: *De legationibus libri tres,* two volumes, English translation by G. J. Laing, introduction by E. Nys (1924); *De jure belli libri tres,* two volumes, English translation by J. C. Rolfe, introduction by C. Phillipson (1933); and *Hispanicae advocationis libri duo,* two volumes, English translation and introduction by F. F. Abbott (1921). (T. E. Hd.; X.)

GENTILI, LUIGI (Aloysius Bonaventura Francesco Camillus Gentili) (1801–1848), Italian Roman Catholic missionary to England, was born in Rome on July 14, 1801, the son of a Roman lawyer. As a young advocate, Gentili showed strong social ambitions, especially among the aristocratic English colony in Rome, and taught languages privately with notable success. But he suddenly abandoned society to join Antonio Rosmini-Serbati (*q.v.*) in 1830 in his new Institute of Charity, which trained priests dedicated to special duties. In 1835 Gentili went to England, at the request of Bishop P. A. Baines, to assist in organizing the new Roman Catholic college at Prior Park, near Bath. Later (1840) he went to Leicestershire, to undertake missionary work in the district surrounding Grace Dieu, which Ambrose Phillipps had made the focus of a Roman Catholic revival. Through Phillipps, Gentili became acquainted with the leaders of the Tractarian movement at Oxford. Gentili's great gifts as a preacher led to demands for his services all over England, particularly in the new industrial cities, which contained large numbers of Irish immigrants. In 1846 he was appointed an itinerant missionary, to work in England and Ireland. On a mission in the Dublin slums in 1848 he contracted cholera and died on Sept. 28 of that year. In addition to bringing the Rosminians to England and Wales, Gentili was responsible for introducing in England such popular devotions as the Stations of the Cross and the Forty Hours exposition of the Blessed Sacrament.

See D. R. Gwynn, *Father Luigi Gentili and His Mission* (1801–1848) (1951).

GENTLEMAN, in English history a man entitled to bear arms but not included in the nobility. In its original and strict sense the term denoted a man of good family, deriving from the Latin word *gentilis* and invariably translated in English-Latin documents as *generosus.* For most of the middle ages, when the basic social distinction was between *nobiles, i.e.* the tenants in chivalry, whether earls, barons, knights, esquires or freemen, and *ignobiles, i.e.* villeins, citizens and burgesses, the word "gentleman" was roughly equivalent to *nobilis* and there was, in this respect, no distinction between the great earl and the humble freeman. Even as late as 1400 the term still had only the sense of *generositas* and could not be used as a personal description denoting rank or quality, or as the title of a class. Yet after 1413 it was increasingly so used; and the list of landowners in 1431, printed in *Feudal Aids,* contains, besides knights, esquires, yeomen and husbandman, a fair number who are classed as "gentleman."

The immediate cause of this was probably the statute I Henry V cap. v (1413) which required that in all original writs of action personal appeals and indictments which involved the process of outlawry, the "estate, degree or mystery" of the defendant must be stated. More widespread influences were also at work: the profound economic changes of the 14th and 15th centuries, caused partly by the Black Death, made it increasingly difficult and unattractive for the younger sons of the nobility to settle on the land and they tended to seek their fortunes abroad in the French wars, or to become dependents of the court or some great noble house. Such men often chose to describe themselves as gentlemen.

By the 16th century the "gentry" were officially regarded as constituting a distinct order. At the same time the badge of this distinction came to be thought of as the heralds' recognition of the right to bear arms. This view, which was quite unhistorical, for many gentlemen of long descent had never had occasion to assume coat armour and never did, became firmly rooted. The result was the extinction, in England, of the identification of gentry with nobility, for since it was held that a gentleman bore arms, it followed that anyone who bore arms was a gentleman, and in the fluid social conditions of the 16th and 17th centuries many acquired the right to bear arms who were *ignobiles*. Hence the term "nobleman" came to be reserved for members of the peerage, while anyone who could afford, as William Harrison (*Description of England*, 1577) put it, to "live without manual labour, and thereto is able and will bear the port, charge and countenance of a gentleman" could "for money have a coat and arms bestowed upon him by heralds . . . and [be] reputed for a gentleman ever after."

Sought after as an indication of social status, the term gentleman retained a certain value as an index of rank and affluence until the early 19th century, but by 1900, under the influence of the political, economic and social changes of the Victorian era, the word had acquired a variety of usages and meanings which fully reflected the complexity of English society. On the one hand "gentlemen" could be a mere synonym of "men"—used at public places and occasions to distinguish male persons from females; on the other, acceptance by "society" as a gentleman still required an income derived from sources other than manual labour and retail trade.

In England this view, though much weakened by the social upheavals produced by two world wars, to some extent prevailed—preserved, cherished and typified in the rigid distinction on the cricket field between "gentlemen" and "players." In general, however, the modern "gentleman" is well mannered rather than, necessarily, well-bred or well off. The idea of the gentleman as a "gentle man" is found in Chaucer's *Wife of Bath's Tale:*

Loke who that is most vertuous alway
Prive and apert, and most entendeth ay
To do the gentil dedes that he can
And take him for the gretest gentilman.

It gained, perhaps, its highest expression in Richard Steele, who wrote in 1714 that "the appellation of Gentleman is never to be affixed to a man's circumstances, but to his Behaviour in them." In this sense, too, the word gentleman is obviously incapable of strict definition, for "to behave like a gentleman" may mean little or much, according to the person by whom the phrase is used, but at least the rebuke "you're no gentleman" would be generally understood.

BIBLIOGRAPHY.—William Harrison, *Description of England*, books ii and iii, in *Shakespere's England*, ed. by F. J. Furnivall, 4 vol. (1877-1908); Richard Brathwait, *The English Gentleman* (1630), *The English Gentlewoman* (1631); John Selden, *Titles of Honour* (1672); A. Smythe-Palmer, *The Ideal of a Gentleman* (1908); Sir Harold Nicolson, *Good Behaviour* (1955). (W. A. P.; X.)

GENTOFTE, a residential suburb of Copenhagen, Den., with a coast line along the Sound of about 4 mi., is a separate township, developed from the three farm villages of Gentofte, Vangede and Ordrup and the fishing village of Skovshoved. Pop. (1960) 88,308. It is on the railway line from Copenhagen to Elsinore. Gentofte was the site of three royal castles: Ibstrup (demolished 1761), Bernstorff (summer residence of Christian IX) and Charlottenlund (Frederick VIII). The former mansion Øregaard is now a topographical museum. (L. P. Go.)

GENTZ, FRIEDRICH (1764–1832), German political journalist, famous for his writings against the principles of the French Revolution and Napoleon and as the confidential adviser of Metternich, was born in Breslau on May 2, 1764. His father's family came from the Neumark district of Brandenburg, his mother was of pure Huguenot descent through the families of Ancillon and Naudé. Gentz went to Berlin as early as 1779, when his father was appointed director-general of the Prussian mint; was sent to school at the famous Joachimsthaler *Gymnasium;* and then read law for two years at Königsberg university, where he also came under the influence of Immanuel Kant. He entered the Prussian civil service in Berlin in 1785, but only reached the position of counselor in the war office (1793). This slowness in advancement was because of his opposition to civil-service routine and to middle-class standards of life—an attitude which owed much to the philosophical tenets of the later Enlightenment and to theories of natural law.

Gentz hailed the outbreak of the French Revolution and sought to justify it in his first publication (1790); but only a little later discussions with Wilhelm von Humboldt and an interest in Montesquieu, English jurisprudence and Kant's legal theories led him to adopt Burke's condemnation of the Revolution. His translation of Burke's *Reflections on the Revolution in France* (1793), with his commentaries on it, established Gentz as a European celebrity and made him realize that he was destined to be a writer on political matters. Without going through a conversion, but rather on the basis of his unchanged theories of state and society, Gentz henceforth fought against the Revolutionary principles and gradually formulated his own highly conservative conception of the state (1798–99). He rejected the concepts of the sovereignty of the people, of the rights of man, of the right to resist and of political liberty and equality—as well as the general trend toward reform which he had championed as late as 1797 in a *Sendschreiben* at Frederick William III's accession to the Prussian throne. In these years (1794–97) Gentz translated and commented on several more antirevolutionary works, such as those of J. Mallet du Pan, J. J. Mounier and François d'Ivernois; he also founded the *Neue Deutsche Monatsschrift,* which however expired after one year (1795). In 1799–1800 there followed—with the financial support of the Prussian government—two years' issues of the *Historisches Journal,* in which Gentz brought German political journalism to its first summit, thanks not least to his own excellent style. Gentz aroused a great stir, as he expounded not only the dynamics of the Revolution, subject to its own laws, but also its successive phases, its end in the *coup d'état* of 18 Brumaire (1799) and its social aspects, of which he strongly disapproved. He aroused even more attention when, in 1800–01, he denounced the projects of an "eternal" peace and even justified the war against Revolutionary France: Napoleon Bonaparte's militarist policy had turned Gentz, the pacifist opponent of the principles of the Revolution, into a herald of the struggle for the restoration of the basic political order of Europe and the balance of power, which France had destroyed.

Gentz's political realism remained consistent and uncompromising: he did not scruple to denounce the Prussian policy of neutrality; he demanded that the rivalry between Prussia and Austria be overcome; and he praised England as the shield of Europe's liberty. By this attitude he forfeited his special position in Prussia. As he did not want to give up his self-chosen task of political journalism now he had to face a crisis which threatened his private as well as his public life (1801–02). After an attempt to settle in Weimar had failed, he was recommended to Vienna by the Austrian minister in Berlin, Philipp Stadion. He had underrated the strength of the opposition against his entering the Austrian service, but he eventually received the empty title of an imperial and royal privy counselor and a pension from the Austrian government, which thus gave him the social background and the material security needed for free activity as a political writer (Sept. 1802).

A brief visit to London, where he was received with honour

(Nov.–Dec. 1802), decided Gentz's future career. As he was looked upon as a private person in Vienna and was under no obligations with respect either to his foreign connections or to any oath of office, he worked in Vienna from 1803 onward as a free-lance agent of anti-Napoleonic European politics. He therefore could and did accept the financial support which was granted him, particularly by England, in return for his work.

Though Gentz, despite his numerous memoranda, could not directly influence Austria's foreign policy, his influence in Vienna was still considerable. However, his anti-Napoleonic agitation among diplomats and in high society in Vienna, which culminated in the writings later published as *Fragmente aus der neuesten Geschichte des politischen Gleichgewichts in Europa* ("Fragments Concerning the Recent History of the Political Equilibrium in Europe"), was brought to an end in 1805 when the Austrian defeat at Austerlitz obliged him to withdraw to Bohemia and then to Dresden. Finally, after witnessing the collapse of Prussia in 1806, he went in anguish into exile at Prague or at Teplitz to organize, together with like-minded friends, the spiritual and political resistance against Napoleon and to reflect on the reconstruction of Germany and Europe.

Some time passed before Stadion called Gentz back to Vienna—for the composition of the war manifesto in 1809. Not the least of the reasons for this delay was the fact that Gentz, to whom German nationalism was quite uncongenial, fell in only reluctantly with Stadion's plan of making Austria the spearhead of a German rising against Napoleon. Thus Gentz was hit all the harder by the collapse of Austria's struggle for liberation and his forced return into exile in Bohemia (Nov. 1809). He sensed the hopelessness of his fight on the continent and sought to escape to England (1809–10). When he failed in this, he revised his opinion about war and came closer to Metternich's policy of expedients, which was indeed no less anti-Napoleonic than Gentz's old line (*see* METTERNICH, CLEMENS). This led to a limitation of his activities and to a loosening of his connections with England (1810–11). Though Metternich had ordered him to Vienna in Oct. 1810, he did not appoint Gentz to an office in the state chancellery; instead he asked his advice privately in matters of publicity and finance.

For Gentz the wars of liberation that led to the downfall of Napoleon were certainly no occasion for national enthusiasm (this is evident from his celebrated war manifesto of 1813): he sounded notes of triumph only for the restoration of political order in Europe. For the sake of this order and in Austria's interests, he objected to France's being reduced to a second-rate power, to the restoration of the Bourbons in the place of Napoleon (husband of an Austrian archduchess) and to the nationalistic "misuse of superior force" at the second peace of Paris (1815). The Prussians then began the defamation of Gentz as a "time-serving" politician whose shallow pacifism might deprive Germany of the fruits of victory.

The congress of Vienna (*q.v.*), at which Gentz's familiarity with the diplomats of Europe enabled him to officiate in masterly fashion as the principal secretary, marked a turning point in his life. Henceforth he was to be Metternich's indispensable collaborator on basic questions of foreign policy and on all matters concerning the German *Bund* or federation. Gentz acted as secretary-general at Metternich's side at the congresses of Aix-la-Chapelle, Troppau, Laibach and Verona and even more actively at the ministerial conferences in Carlsbad and Vienna (1819–20). His unchanged status as a private person remained in glaring contradiction to these highly creditable performances, but Francis I's antipathy to him precluded him from office, even though the title of court counselor extraordinary had been bestowed on him in 1813. Gentz owed his growing influence exclusively to Metternich's favour and to the effect of his own personality. He was able to maintain an appropriate style of life chiefly because Metternich arranged that, from the end of 1812 onward, he should conduct confidential correspondence with the hospodars of Walachia and Moldavia, for which they paid him a high remuneration.

Because of his opposition to the national and liberal movements after 1815 Gentz was regarded as leader of political reaction. His political creed, however, had not changed since 1798–99. He understood his now somewhat emphatic Austrianism only in the sense of an all-European federative order and solidarity; and therefore he equated national movements with the will to dissolve the bonds of law and order. He considered the demands of early German liberalism as a menacing revolutionary declaration. Two of his countermeasures were always to be remembered against him: his initiative in the matter of political censorship as laid down in the Carlsbad decrees (*q.v.*); and his definition of article 13 of the German federal constitution, on the establishment of state diets—for which he explicitly condemned any interpretation congruent with the doctrine of the sovereignty of the people.

The revolutionary upheavals of 1830 did nothing to alter Gentz's attitude. Even so, a deeper understanding of revolutionary events prompted him to speak against military intervention and to take into consideration the spirit of the age. Metternich then withdrew his favour from Gentz.

The "chevalier de Gentz" (as he was called with reference to a Swedish knighthood of the Order of the North Star bestowed on him in 1804) died, a commoner, in Vienna on June 9, 1832. Defamation by nationalists and liberals followed him beyond the grave. It unjustly dwelled on the weaknesses of his character, as his fight against the revolutionary principles was not understood and his historical merits were not appreciated.

BIBLIOGRAPHY.—P. R. Sweet, *Defender of the Old Order* (1941); A. Haesler, *Die Vertragslehre bei F. von Gentz* (1943); G. Mann, *Secretary of Europe*, Eng. trans. (1946); H. Rumpel, *Friedrich Gentz* (1957). For earlier works and for Gentz's own writings *see* F. M. Kirchdeisen, "Die Schriften von und über F. von Gentz," and F. C. Wittichen, "Zur Gentz-Bibliographie," in *Mitteilungen des Instituts für Österreichische Geschichtsforschung*, 27 (1906).
(H. E. RU.)

GENUS, a category of classification ranking between the family and the species, used in biology to include a group of structurally or phylogenetically related species, or sometimes consisting of an isolated species showing unusual differentiation (monotypic genus, as *Rhoeo discolor*). Thus the species of roses collectively form the genus *Rosa*, of horses and zebras, the genus *Equus*. The genus name is the first word of a binomial scientific name and is always capitalized. *See* SPECIES.
(J. M. BL.)

GÉNY, FRANÇOIS (1861–1959), French jurist and author of the movement for *libre recherche scientifique*, was born at Baccarat, Meurthe-et-Moselle, on Dec. 17, 1861. A university law teacher, he was appointed in 1901 professor of civil law and, in 1919, dean of the faculty of law at the University of Nancy; this office he occupied until 1925. In 1930 he became corresponding member of the Académie des Sciences, Morales et Politiques.

In his principal publications, *Méthode d'interprétation et sources en droit privé positif* (1899) and *Science et Technique en droit privé positif*, four volumes (1915–24), Gény demonstrated the inadequacy of the traditional methods of interpreting the French codes, which assumed that the legislator had provided a solution to every legal question even if it resulted from developments which could not have been anticipated. According to Gény, whenever positive law, written or unwritten, does not yield the answer, the courts are free to make new rules, but must proceed by means of scientific research into the social reality and ideology upon which all law must rest. Gény then developed a theory of law which explains that law results from applying juristic techniques or constructions (*constructs*) to the data (*données*) of science. This theory has exercised considerable influence on modern legal philosophy in many countries and particularly in France, where the emphasis laid by Gény on the creative nature of the judicial function has liberalized the interpretation of codified law and helped to raise the status of the judiciary. Portions of Gény's work were published in English in the Modern Legal Philosophy Series. Gény died at Nancy on Dec. 16, 1959.
See *Science of Legal Method* and *The Theory of Justice* (1921).
(J. U.)

GEOCHEMISTRY. Geochemistry is the study of the chemistry of the earth. Victor M. Goldschmidt formulated the three tasks of geochemistry as follows: (1) to establish the terrestrial abundance relationships of elements; (2) to account for the terrestrial distribution of elements in the geochemical spheres, for instance, in minerals and rocks of the lithosphere and in natural prod-

GEOCHEMISTRY

ucts of various kinds; and (3) to detect the laws governing the abundance relationships and the distribution of elements. Still another task of geochemistry is the study of the chemical evolution of the earth.

C. F. Schönbein, in 1838, was the first to use the name geochemistry. He also mapped out a program for research. K. G. Bischof and J. Roth discussed extensively the field and problems of geochemistry in books published in 1847–54 and 1879–93, respectively. F. W. Clarke and H. S. Washington, V. L. Vernadsky and A. E. Fersman, G. von Hevesy, Ida and W. Noddack and P. Niggli were among the scientists who contributed toward the making of a world-wide interest in the various branches of the science which is closely allied to physics, chemistry, astrophysics, geology and the biological sciences.

Further discussion of theories and concepts involved in the study of geochemistry will be found in the articles CRYSTALLOGRAPHY and MINERALOGY. Crystallization processes which are basic to understanding the geochemistry of the earth's crust are also discussed in PETROLOGY. The various sections of this article are:

I. CHEMISTRY OF THE EARTH
A. METEORITES AND GEOCHEMISTRY

Meteoritics, or the science of cosmic matter captured by the earth, supplies information about the properties and composition of nonterrestrial matter. Because the meteorites are believed by many to be fragments from the interior of a broken planet comparable with the earth in size and in general physical-chemical properties, they are used to give evidence of the internal structure of the earth and of the general geochemical character and abundance of the elements. The meteorites are chiefly composed of three phases—metal, silicate and sulfide.

According to the predominance of the metal or the silicate phase, the meteorites are divided into three principal groups: irons (siderites), stony-irons (siderolites) and stones (aerolites). The tektites, commonly believed to be glass meteorites, make a fourth group. The constituents of the meteorites are called meteorite minerals, and many of them are identical with the minerals found in terrestrial rocks of a corresponding chemical composition. Several meteorite minerals have no terrestrial counterparts.

The most important meteorite minerals are kamacite and taenite (both nickel-iron); olivine, clinoenstatite-clinohypersthene, diopside-hedenbergite, augite, enstatite-hypersthene and plagioclase (silicates); and, as accessory constituents, troilite and oldhamite (sulfides), schreibersite (phosphide), cohenite (carbide) and graphite and quartz.

TABLE I.—Average Chemical Composition of Meteorites
(In weight percentage)

Constituent	Irons	Phase of stones Metal	Phase of stones Silicate
Fe	90.78	88.58	13.25*
Ni	8.59	10.69	0.50 (NiO)
Co	0.63	0.71	0.03 (CoO)
SiO_2			46.26
Al_2O_3			3.45
Cr_2O_3			0.51
MnO			0.38
MgO			27.56
CaO			2.90
Na_2O			1.10
K_2O			0.25
P			0.17
TiO_2			0.15
H_2O			0.59
Total	100.00	99.98	97.10

*From FeO and Fe_2O_3.

The chemistry of the meteorites is of geochemical importance. The average chemical composition of irons, the metal phase of stones and the silicate phase of stones are presented in Table I according to H. Brown and C. Patterson.

The average chemical composition of all meteorites serves as a basis of computation of the relative terrestrial and cosmic abundance of the elements. An uncertainty affecting all such calculations is the difficulty of estimating the relative amounts of meteorite phases.

TABLE II.—Average Chemical Composition of All Meteorites*

Element	Per cent by weight	Element	Per cent by weight
O	32.30	Mn	0.21
Fe	28.80	K	0.15
Si	16.30	Cl	0.10–0.15?
Mg	12.30	Ti	0.13
S	2.12	Co	0.12
Ni	1.57	P	0.11
Al	1.38	C	0.11
Ca	1.33	Cu	0.03
Na	0.60	Zn	0.02
Cr	0.34		0.01

*Based on a ratio silicate phase: sulfide phase: metal phase of 10:1:2.

For Goldschmidt's calculation, based on the ratio of stones to irons equal to 5:1, see Table II. The tektites resemble chemically the aluminum-rich clay sediments. They may represent the uppermost part of the silicate shell of the hypothetical broken planet from which the meteorites proper may have been derived. See also METEORITES; TEKTITE.

B. ABUNDANCE AND ORIGIN OF ELEMENTS

1. Abundance of Elements.—The surface layer of the silicate shell of the earth (the lithosphere) is composed of three groups of rocks of different origin—igneous, sediments and sedimentary, and metamorphic. The last two groups are composed of material ultimately derived from igneous rocks. Consequently, the average chemical composition of the uppermost lithosphere is very nearly equal to the average chemical composition of igneous rocks. Beginning in the 1880s, calculations have been made of the mean chemical composition of igneous rocks. Among the representative ones, the averages of Clarke and Washington, based on 5,159 analyses of igneous rocks from all parts of the world, along with some other computations, are presented in Table III. The averages of J. J. Sederholm and F. F. Grout include also sedimentary and metamorphic rocks. It appears that the areal averages in which the quantitative distribution of the various rock types is considered

TABLE III.—*Chemical Composition of the Uppermost Lithosphere*
(In weight percentage)

Constituent	Igneous rocks*	Cordilleran and Appalachian rocks†	Pre-Cambrian rocks of Finland‡	Canadian Shield§
SiO₂	59.14	61.64	67.45	63.68
Al₂O₃	15.34	15.71	14.63	16.75
Fe₂O₃	3.08	3.08	1.27	2.38
FeO	3.80	3.25	2.38	2.91
MgO	3.49	2.97	1.78	1.78
CaO	5.08	5.06	1.69	1.78
Na₂O	3.84	3.40	3.39	4.07
K₂O	3.13	2.65	3.06	3.64
Subtotal	96.90	97.59	98.17	97.68
H₂O	1.15	1.26	0.79	0.79
TiO₂	1.05	0.73	0.41	0.81
P₂O₅	0.30	0.26	0.11	0.22
MnO	0.12	0.16	0.04	0.02
Total	99.52	100.00	99.52	99.52

*From F. W. Clarke and H. S. Washington. †From F. W. Grout. ‡From A. Knopf. §From J. J. Sederholm.

---

are all more silicic than the world-wide average. Sederholm's and Grout's averages indicate a granodioritic composition, that is, granitic with more plagioclase feldspar than orthoclase, for the rocks of the Pre-Cambrian areas investigated.

The calculations in Table III show that eight elements constitute the bulk of the uppermost lithosphere—oxygen, silicon, aluminum, iron, calcium, sodium, potassium and magnesium. When calculated as elements, the values of Clarke and Washington yield the composition for igneous rocks indicated in Table IV. All other elements, collectively called accessory or minor or trace, make 1.72% of the total mass of the igneous rocks. Table IV also shows the

TABLE IV.—*The Eight Main Constituents of Igneous Rocks*

Element	Per cent by weight	Per cent by volume
O	46.42	91.83
Si	27.59	0.83
Al	8.08	0.79
Fe	5.08	0.58

Element	Per cent by weight	Per cent by volume
Ca	3.61	1.50
Na	2.83	1.64
K	2.58	2.19
Mg	2.09	0.58
Total	98.28	99.94

composition of the igneous rocks in percentage by volume, as recalculated by T. F. W. Barth on a water-free basis. The high oxygen content indicates that oxygen fills out most of the space in the lithosphere; the lithosphere is actually oxysphere.

The trace-element content of igneous rocks is usually determined by means of physical methods used in analytical chemistry, such as spectrochemical and colorimetric analysis and radioactivity methods. The abundance of all elements in them is listed in Table V. The abundance values for several elements are rather unreliable, and some have been determined only in composite

TABLE V.—*Abundance of Elements in Igneous Rocks*
(In parts per million)

Z	Element	Abundance	Z	Element	Abundance	Z	Element	Abundance
0	*	*	34	Se	0.09	68	Er	2.47
1	H	*	35	Br	0.83	69	Tm	0.20
2	He	0.003	36	Kr	1.62*	70	Yb	2.66
3	Li	22	37	Rb	350	71	Lu	0.75
4	Be	2	38	Sr	220	72	Hf	4.5
5	B	3	39	Y	28.1	73	Ta	2.1
6	C	320	40	Zr	185	74	W	1.5
7	N	46.3	41	Nb	24	75	Re	0.05
8	O	466,000	42	Mo	1	76	Os	*
9	F	700	43	Tc	†	77	Ir	0.001
10	Ne	0.00007	44	Ru	1 (?)	78	Pt	0.005
11	Na	28,300	45	Rh	*	79	Au	0.005
12	Mg	20,900	46	Pd	0.01	80	Hg	0.5
13	Al	81,300	47	Ag	0.10	81	Tl	1.3
14	Si	277,200	48	Cd	0.15	82	Pb	15
15	P	1,180	49	In	0.11	83	Bi	0.2
16	S	520	50	Sn	40	84	Po	*
17	Cl	314	51	Sb	*	85	At	
18	Ar	0.04	52	Te		86	Rn	*
19	K	25,000	53	I	0.3	87	Fr	
20	Ca	36,300	54	Xe	*	88	Ra	**
21	Sc	20	55	Cs	6	89	Ac	*
22	Ti	4,400	56	Ba	1,000	90	Th	11.5
23	V	150	57	La	18.3	91	Pa	**
24	Cr	200	58	Ce	46.1	92	U	4
25	Mn	1,000	59	Pr	5.53	93	Np	
26	Fe	50,000	60	Nd	23.9	94	Pu	
27	Co	23	61	Pm		95	Am	
28	Ni	80	62	Sm	6.47	96	Cm	
29	Cu	55	63	Eu	0.91	97	Bk	
30	Zn	40	64	Gd	6.36	98	Cf	
31	Ga	16	65	Tb	0.91	99	Es	
32	Ge	7	66	Dy	4.47	100	Fm	
33	As	5	67	Ho	1.15	101	Md	

*Present. †Presence probable. ‡Presence unsettled.

---

mixtures of argillaceous, or clayey, rocks. The investigation of the abundance relationships of the elements reveals a picture that differs from the conventional opinion of abundance.

In everyday life, the commonness or rarity of an element is usually mistaken for the commonness of its use in technical products and the like, that is, for its apparent abundance. For instance, gold and silver are less abundant in igneous rocks than are the rare-earth metals (lanthanoids, or lanthanides) and hafnium.

There are considerable differences in the abundance of elements in terrestrial igneous rocks (Table V) and in meteorites (Table II). The meteoritic and cosmic abundance values indicate that the chemical composition of the uppermost lithosphere does not agree with the average chemical composition of matter in the universe. The reason for this difference is the manner of formation of the lithosphere by a process of chemical differentiation.

Table V shows that elements with an even proton number (atomic number, Z) are nearly always more abundant than their odd-numbered neighbours. This regularity, known as the rule of Oddo and Harkins, is based on observations made by G. Oddo and W. D. Harkins. The rule is still more evident when the cosmic abundance of elements is considered; this is well illustrated by Goldschmidt's graph in fig. 1. Geochemically coherent elements (*i.e.*, elements accompanying one another in nature) give examples of the rule. The abundance of the lanthanoids is particularly illustrative. (*See* fig. 2, which is based on analyses of E. Minami.)

The abundance values of Table V refer to the elements as natural mixtures of nuclides. Tabulations showing the relative cosmic abundance of the nuclides are based on the cosmic abundance of the elements and on their isotopic constitution. The abundance graph showing the abundance as a function of the mass number of the nuclides describes the general trend in cosmic abundance adequately. It shows a rapid, approximately exponential, decrease in abundance with increasing mass number up to a mass of approximately 100 and its essential constancy thereafter. The rule of Oddo and Harkins is valid also with reference to mass number.

Numerous rules exist correlating the abundance with the proton, neutron and mass numbers of the nuclides; however, they possess a number of exceptions marked by abrupt changes in abundance connected with changes in the structure of the atomic nucleus.

2. Origin of Elements.—The existence of radioactive nuclides indicates that elements have not always existed in their present form. The relationships between cosmic abundance and nuclear properties make the basis of many speculations dealing with the origin of elements and the abundance of nuclides at the time of their formation. It is generally agreed that the relative abundance of nuclides was determined by physical conditions existing in an early stage of the expansion of the universe, when the density of matter and temperature were exceedingly high.

The hypotheses dealing with the origin and abundance distribution are of two principal categories, namely, the equilibrium and the nonequilibrium hypotheses. According to the former, the observed abundance distribution represents a thermodynamic equilibrium between nuclei. The equilibrium hypothesis explains in a satisfactory way only the abundance of the light and heavy nuclides and fails to explain reasonably the whole abundance range. In the nonequilibrium category, the neutron-capture hypothesis explains the abundance distribution chiefly as a result of the radiative capture of neutrons by nuclei, of a number of nuclear reactions among the lightest nuclei, and of radioactive decay among the unstable nuclides that were formed. The neutron-capture hypothesis explains the deficiency of lithium, beryllium, boron and fluorine (fig. 1) and many abundance rules, including the rule of Oddo and Harkins. None of the hypotheses is capable of answering completely the question of the making of the nuclides and the origin of their abundance distribution.

C. GEOCHEMICAL STRUCTURE OF THE EARTH

A. Boisse in 1850 was the first to suggest that the bulk chemical composition of the earth is comparable with the average chemical composition of the meteorites. This qualitative analogy has been used in the construction of various earth models because it is most likely that the meteorites are derived from the different depths of

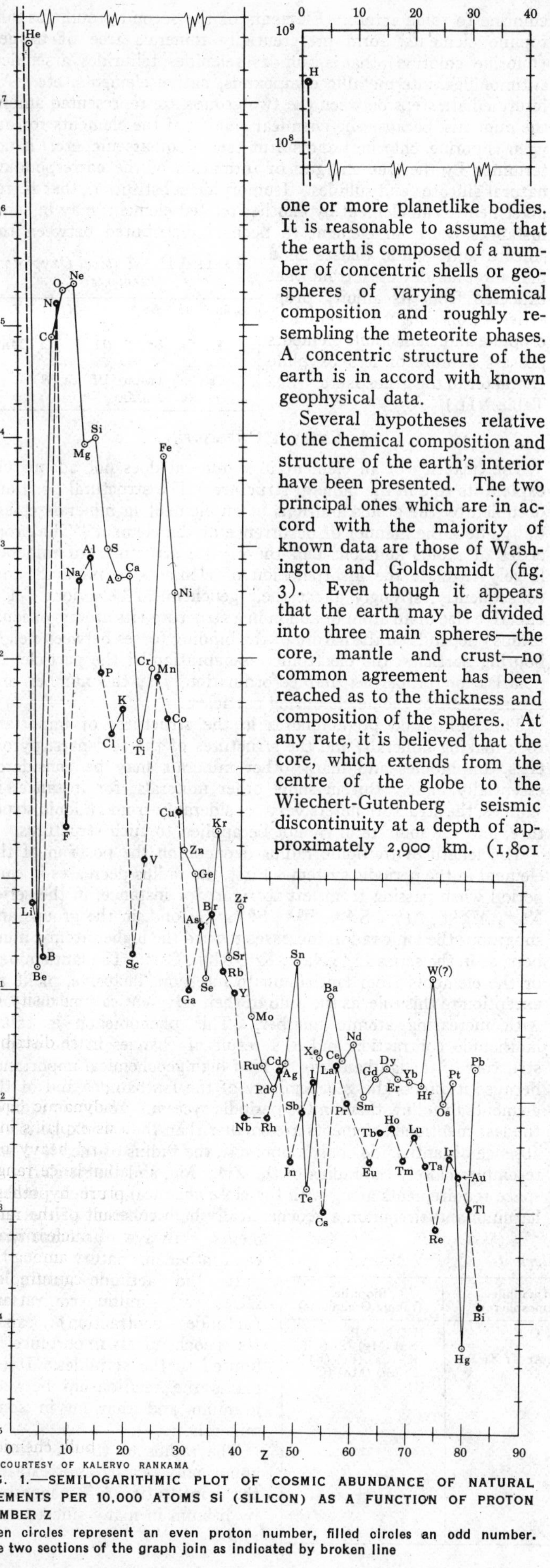

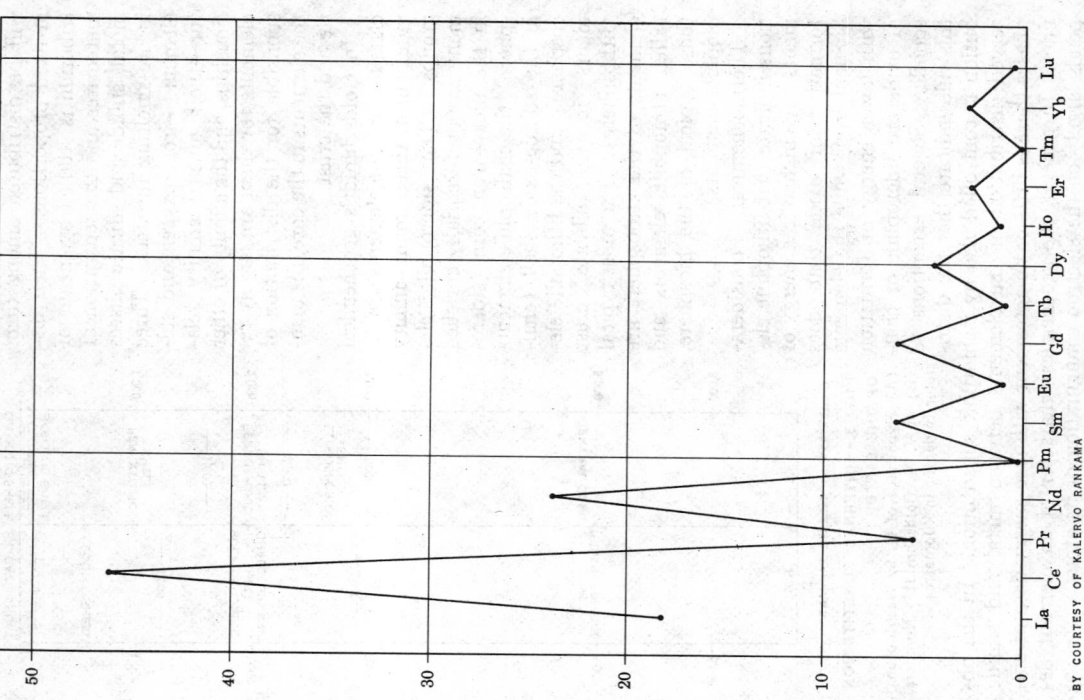

BY COURTESY OF KALERVO RANKAMA

FIG. 2.—ABUNDANCE RELATIONS OF LANTHANOIDS IN SHALES

one or more planetlike bodies. It is reasonable to assume that the earth is composed of a number of concentric shells or geospheres of varying chemical composition and roughly resembling the meteorite phases. A concentric structure of the earth is in accord with known geophysical data.

Several hypotheses relative to the chemical composition and structure of the earth's interior have been presented. The two principal ones which are in accord with the majority of known data are those of Washington and Goldschmidt (fig. 3). Even though it appears that the earth may be divided into three main spheres—the core, mantle and crust—no common agreement has been reached as to the thickness and composition of the spheres. At any rate, it is believed that the core, which extends from the centre of the globe to the Wiechert-Gutenberg seismic discontinuity at a depth of approximately 2,900 km. (1,801

mi.), consists of metallic nickel-iron and corresponds to the pure iron meteorites. Most geophysicists and geologists agree in principle on a mantle composed of silicates and interstitial nickel-iron that increases in amount with depth. The mantle occupies the depth zone between approximately 2,900 km. (1,801 mi.) and approximately 30 km. (18.6 mi.) or 50 km. (31.1 mi.), the Mohorovicic discontinuity, or the upper boundary of the earth's mantle.

In the crust, the continental areas consist of three continental layers, namely: a deep-seated intermediate layer, probably intermediate between basalt and granite in composition; a granitic layer above the intermediate layer; and a sedimentary layer composed of sediments, sedimentary and metamorphic rocks. In the Pacific basin, the continental layers are totally absent, and the uppermost gabbroic (basaltic) layer of the mantle is in almost direct contact with the ocean. (*See also* EARTH; EARTHQUAKE.)

In addition to the shells or geospheres mentioned, three outermost geochemical spheres are distinguished. They are the hydrosphere, which consists of the salt and fresh waters and the continental ice; the atmosphere, or the gaseous outer envelope of the earth; and the biosphere, which comprises the living matter and is the part of the earth capable of sustaining biological activity. The biosphere occupies the lower part of the atmosphere and probably the whole hydrosphere, and makes a thin layer on the lithosphere.

D. DISTRIBUTION OF ELEMENTS

If shells of different composition exist in the earth, the elements

BY COURTESY OF KALERVO RANKAMA

FIG. 1.—SEMILOGARITHMIC PLOT OF COSMIC ABUNDANCE OF NATURAL ELEMENTS PER 10,000 ATOMS Si (SILICON) AS A FUNCTION OF PROTON NUMBER Z

Open circles represent an even proton number, filled circles an odd number. The two sections of the graph join as indicated by broken line

will be distributed among them in fixed proportions. Their distribution is studied by means of meteorites and the separation of metal, sulfide and silicate phases in ore-smelting furnaces. Three elements—iron, oxygen and sulfur—their mutual affinity relationships, and the affinity of other elements for them are largely responsible for the distribution of the elements in the core, the mantle and the crust.

In Goldschmidt's geochemical classification the elements are divided into three main affinity groups. The siderophile elements are preferentially enriched in the nickel-iron core (siderosphere), the chalcophile elements in the sulfide-oxide shell (chalcosphere) and the lithophile elements in the silicate crust (lithosphere). The most typical elements of the atmosphere are called atmophile elements and those typical of the biosphere, biophile elements.

Thermochemical considerations indicate that lithophile elements have higher free energy of formation of oxide than does bivalent iron, while the elements with lower energy of formation of oxide are siderophile or chalcophile. Several exceptions to this rule indicate that the distribution is controlled also by isomorphic substitution. In the observed distribution of the elements between metal and sulfide phases there is little or no agreement with free-energy data of sulfides. In general, the geochemical character of an element depends largely on the electron configuration of its atom.

Used in a purely chemical sense without reference to any supposed distribution among the geochemical spheres, the terms siderophile, chalcophile and lithophile are illustrative and prove useful for many geochemical purposes. The geochemical classification of the elements is shown in Table VI. It appears that the geochemical character is not sharply established for all elements, not even in strictly specified surroundings.

II. GEOCHEMISTRY OF THE LITHOSPHERE

The elements present in the lithosphere are appropriately divided into two groups on the basis of their most important manner of occurrence. The first group comprises the elements that occur largely or exclusively combined with oxygen in oxides, silicates, phosphates, carbonates, nitrates, borates, sulfates, etc. They are called oxyphile elements. Oxygen may be replaced by fluorine and chlorine to some extent. Elements of the second group, the sulfophile elements, form preferentially minerals free of oxygen (fluorine, chlorine), that is, sulfides, selenides, tellurides, arsenides, antimonides, intermetallic compounds, native elements, etc. All intermediate steps between the two groups are represented among the minerals because the chemical affinity of the elements for oxygen (fluorine, chlorine) and sulfur (selenium, arsenic, etc.) is determined by the free energies of formation of the corresponding natural silicates and sulfides. Isomorphic substitution, that is, replacement of an element by another related element, may in some instances cause an element to become distributed between the silicate and sulfide phases in a manner that deviates from that expected from its affinity properties. Consequently several such instances are known in which certain siderophile and chalcophile elements possess a more or less oxyphile character in the lithosphere. (See Table VII.)

A CRYSTAL CHEMISTRY

The quantity of an element in a mineral does not adequately explain its role in the mineral structure. The structural positions occupied by the atoms and ions of an element in minerals essentially affect the manner of occurrence of the element. The properties of atoms and ions and the crystal structures of minerals largely regulate the incorporation of elements in minerals and, consequently, strongly affect their geochemical behaviour. The effective size of an atom or an ion in a structure (its atomic or ionic radius) depends on the nature of the binding forces between neighbouring particles, the electronic configuration of the particle, its polarization properties and co-ordination, i.e., the number and arrangement of the neighbouring particles.

The ionic bond predominates in the structures of important rock-making minerals, and the structures of the feldspars, pyroxenes, amphiboles and many other minerals may be considered essentially ionic. But in some other minerals, for instance, in sulfides, the structure differs very considerably from an ionic structure, and the ionic radii cannot be applied to such structures.

The length of the ionic radius depends on the position of the element in the periodic system. First, the radius decreases in each period when passing from left to right, for instance, in the series Na^+, Mg^{2+}, Al^{3+}, Si^{4+}, P^{5+}, S^{6+}. Second, in the groups and subgroups the ionic radius increases toward the higher atomic numbers, as in the series Li^+, Na^+, K^+, Rb^+, Cs^+. The lanthanides, or the elements from lanthanum to lutetium, inclusive, make an exception to this rule, as the radii of their trivalent cations decrease with increasing atomic number. This phenomenon is called lanthanide contraction and is a result of changes in the atomic structure of the lanthanides. It is of high geochemical importance because it affects the geochemistry of the lanthanides and of the elements to follow them in the periodic system. The ionic radii of the last-mentioned elements are smaller than they would be in the absence of lanthanide contraction, e.g., the radius of the Hf^{4+} ion resembles closely the radius of the Zr^{4+} ion, and the similarity in space requirements along with the close chemical similarity makes hafnium and zirconium a geochemically high coherent pair of elements, always accompanying each other in nature.

In the actinide series a similar contraction (actinide contraction) exists. Its geochemical importance is limited to the actinides. It explains the relationship between uranium and thorium in some minerals.

The radius of the Li^+ ion is abnormally great and explains the substitution of magnesium by lithium in many silicate minerals.

TABLE VI.—*Geochemical Classification of the Elements*

Siderophile (Core)	Chalcophile (Mantle)	Lithophile (Crust)	Atmophile (Atmospheric)	Biophile (Living Organisms)
Au Ge Sn (Pb) C P (As) Mo (W) Re Fe Co Ni Ru Rh Pd Os Ir Pt	Cu Ag Zn Cd Hg Ga In Tl (Ge) (Sn) Pb As Sb Bi S Se Te (Fe Co Ni) (Ru) (Pd) (Pt)	Li Na K Rb Cs Fr Be Mg Ca Sr Ba Ra (Zn) (Cd) B Al Sc Y La Ce Pr Nd Sm Eu Gd Tb Dy Ho Er Tm Yb Lu Ac Th Pa U Np Pu Am Cm Ga (In) (Tl) C Si Ti Zr Hf (Ge) (Sn) (Pb) P V Nb Ta O Cr W Mn (Fe) (Co) (Ni) H F Cl Br I	H C N O I He Ne Ar Kr Xe Rn	H C N O P (Na) (Mg) (S) (Cl) (K) (Ca) (Fe) (B) (F) (Si) (Mn) (Cu) (I)

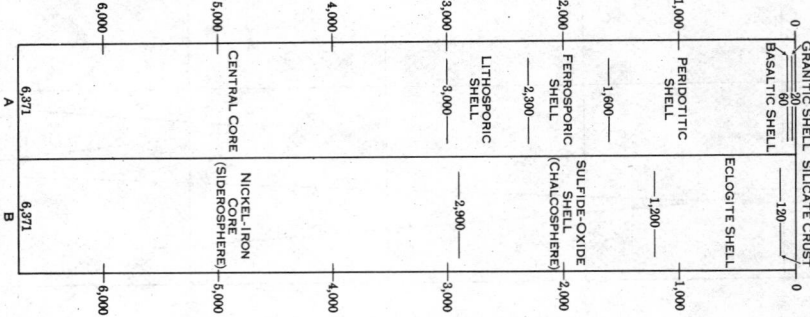

FIG. 3.—INTERNAL CONSTITUTION OF THE EARTH

BY COURTESY OF KALERVO RANKAMA

(A) Hypothesis of H. S. Washington; (B) of V. M. Goldschmidt. Numbers refer to depths in kilometres.

TABLE VII.—*Typical Oxyphile Elements*

H	Li	Be	B	C	N	O	F
	Na	Mg	Al	Si	P	S	Cl
	K	Ca	Sc	Ti	V	Cr	Mn
	Rb	Sr	Y	Zr	Nb		
	Cs	Ba	La-Lu	Hf	Ta	W	
	Ra	Ac-Mn					

1. Co-ordination of Particles.—The most fundamental feature of a crystal structure is the co-ordination of the particles present, i.e., the number and arrangement of particles of one kind surrounding a given particle of another kind as its nearest neighbours. The co-ordination is different for different particles and structures, each particle attempting to occupy the co-ordination into which it fits best. A proper and fitting co-ordination results in strong bonds between the particles and in a stable structure. An ill-fitting and unsuitable co-ordination causes an unstable structure, e.g., the co-ordination of the Zr^{4+} ion in the zircon $Zr[SiO_4]$ structure is not well suited to the space requirements of the ion and causes an unstable structure that is readily disintegrated by the action of alpha radiation (metamict alteration).

In an essentially ionic structure, the co-ordination of the cation, that is, the number and arrangement of the surrounding anions, depends largely on the cation/anion radius ratio. In the important rock-making minerals, oxygen is the principal anion, and such minerals are in fact aggregates of big oxygen ions whose interstices are filled up with the cations.

For instance, in quartz, SiO_2, oxygen makes up 98.7% by volume and silicon, only 1.3%. Consequently consideration of the co-ordination number of the cations with respect to oxygen in minerals is of importance. The co-ordination is variable, as illustrated in fig. 4, in which the cations, arranged according to their size, are plotted against the co-ordination number. The black areas indicate the approximate abundance of the co-ordinations of the ions in the upper lithosphere. The differences in the size of the area illustrate the fact that for big cations the co-ordination number is less definite because of the great size of the cation.

Because the crystal structures of almost all important minerals are known, they form a convenient basis for the classification of minerals. A structural classification of the complicated silicate minerals is particularly useful, and for the silicates the type of linkage of the silicon-oxygen tetrahedra present in their structures is a natural basis of classification. In nesosilicates the separate tetrahedral $[SiO_4]$ groupings do not share any oxygen atoms with neighbouring silicon-oxygen tetrahedra. In sorosilicates the separate groups of tetrahedra share one or more corners with neighbouring tetrahedra of the same group. The sorosilicates may consist of $[Si_2O_7]$ double tetrahedra, five tetrahedra in an open group, rings of three or six tetrahedra. The inosilicates are composed of infinite chains or double chains of silicon-oxygen tetrahedra. In the phyllosilicates there are infinite sheets of the tetrahedra, and in the tectosilicates there are continuous frameworks of linked tetrahedra sharing all four oxygen atoms with neighbouring tetrahedra. (See also CO-ORDINATION COMPOUNDS.)

2. Replacement of Elements.—Because minerals are rarely pure compounds, the chemical formulas usually given for them are idealized. Deviations from the ideal composition are partly a result of structural defects, but their main reason is the presence of impurities, either as mechanically admixed substances or in solid solution (in fixed positions or filling empty spaces in the structure) in the mineral. The solute may not belong to the structure of the solvent, as in the case of the occurrence of helium in beryl, or it forms a complete isomorphic (from the Greek isos, "equal," and morphe, "form") series with the solvent, as does ferrous orthosilicate $Fe_2[SiO_4]$ (fayalite), with magnesium orthosilicate $Mg_2[SiO_4]$ (forsterite), the Fe^{2+} ions occupying the structural positions of the Mg^{2+} ions. Between these two extremes all intermediate types of solid solutions occur in minerals. Isomorphism and related phenomena are of high importance in geochemistry. If atoms and ions occurring in a given structure are considered, such atoms or ions occurring instead of compounds are called diadochic (from the Greek diadochos, "successor") if they are capable of replacing each other, each occupying the position of the other. Consequently, forsterite and fayalite are isomorphic, but the Mg^{2+} and Fe^{2+} ions in their structures are diadochic. Diadochy may be complete or partial.

As a general rule, an ion may replace another ion diadochically if the difference in the size of their radii does not exceed approximately 15% of the radius of the ion to be replaced. Temperature affects the degree of diadochy; high temperature generally favours diadochic substitution. Complete diadochy usually requires a close similarity in ionization potential. The degree of diadochy depends on crystal structure. Finally, ionic charge affects the substitution. The charges may be similar, as in the important Fe^{2+} — Mg^{2+} substitution, or the substitution ion may have lower (e.g., O^{2-} —OH^-—F^-; Ca^{2+}—Na^+) or higher (e.g., K^+—Ba^{2+}—Sr^{2+} —Pb^{2+}) charge than the ion to be replaced. If the charges are different, the electrostatic neutrality of the structure will be disturbed. Consequently, it must be re-established, for instance, by the simultaneous substitution of another ion in the structure, as in the substitution of $Ca^{2+}Al^{3+}$ by Na^+Si^{4+} in the plagioclase feldspars (see FELDSPAR), or by the introduction of balancing ions outside the regular framework of the structure, or by leaving a structural position vacant.

Diadochic substitution in common rock-making minerals regulates the manner of occurrence of almost all elements in the upper lithosphere and is of particular importance for the geochemistry of the trace elements. Some trace elements may form independent minerals that are among the accessory constituents of rocks, among others, sulfur in sulfide minerals, phosphorus in apatite and monazite and fluorine in fluorite. Other trace elements, for instance, manganese, barium and vanadium, seldom, if ever, form independent minerals except in rocks in which they happen to be very strongly enriched. Theirs is a dispersed manner of occurrence. Some elements, such as lead and boron, are intermediate. Three types of diadochy regulate the dispersed manner of occurrence of the trace elements, namely camouflage, when a trace element diadochically replaces a common element of similar valence; capturing, when a trace element replaces a common element with a lower valence and is captured in the structure; and admission, when a trace element replaces a common element of higher valence. Examples are, among others, the substitution of silicon by germanium in silicate minerals (camouflage), of potassium by lead in potassium minerals (capturing) and of oxygen by fluorine in sphene and other minerals (admission).

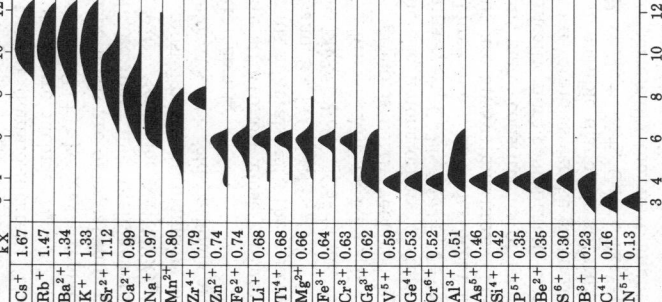

ION	RADIUS kX
Ca+	1.67
Rb+	1.47
Ba2+	1.34
K+	1.33
Sr2+	1.12
Ca2+	0.99
Na+	0.97
Mn2+	0.80
Zr4+	0.79
Zn2+	0.74
Fe2+	0.74
Li+	0.68
Ti4+	0.68
Mg2+	0.66
Fe3+	0.64
Cr3+	0.63
Ge3+	0.62
V5+	0.59
Ge4+	0.53
C6+	0.52
Al3+	0.51
As5+	0.46
Si4+	0.42
P5+	0.35
Be2+	0.35
S6+	0.30
B3+	0.23
C4+	0.16
N5+	0.13

BY COURTESY OF KALERVO RANKAMA

FIG. 4.—CO-ORDINATION NUMBER WITH RESPECT TO OXYGEN OF SOME GEOCHEMICALLY IMPORTANT CATIONS IN UPPER LITHOSPHERE

B. CRYSTALLIZATION OF MAGMA

1. Rock-Making Minerals.—Rocks are called igneous or magmatic if their material has been molten before attaining its present structure and composition. Their material may be primary magmatic or juvenile in the case of true igneous rocks, or secondary, derived by remelting of older rocks in the case of quasi-igneous or pseudoigneous rocks. Phenomena connected with the crystallization of rock melts are geochemically important.

The average chemical composition of igneous rocks approaches the composition of diorites or granodiorites. It indicates only the abundance of the elements and tells nothing about their manner of occurrence as characterized by the minerals in which they are incorporated. The mineralogy of the igneous rocks is illustrated by their average mineralogical composition presented, according to Clarke, in Table VIII. The feldspars, pyroxenes, amphiboles and quartz are geochemically the most important minerals of the igneous rocks, while all other minerals are, both quantitatively and geochemically, of minor importance. The feldspars, the feldspathoids and quartz are the chief salic, or silica-rich, rock-making minerals and contain Na^+, K^+, Ca^{2+} and Al^{3+} as their

Table VIII.—*Average Mineralogical Composition of Igneous Rocks*
(In weight percentage)

Mineral	Content	Mineral	Content
Feldspars	59.5	Titanium minerals	1.5
Amphibole and pyroxene	16.8	Apatite	0.6
Quartz	12.0	Other rock-making minerals	5.8
Biotite	3.8	Total	100.0

most typical cations. The femic, that is, comparatively low in silica, minerals contain Mg^{2+}, Fe^{2+}, Fe^{3+} and, in part, Ca^{2+} and Al^{3+}. The most important accessory minerals of igneous rocks are: zircon, sphene $CaTi[(O,Oh,F)|SiO_4]$, apatite $Ca_5[(F,Cl,OH)|(PO_4)_3]$; and opaque sulfides, such as pyrite FeS_2, pyrrhotite $FeS\text{-}Fe_5S_6$, chalcopyrite $CuFeS_2$, pentlandite $(Fe,Ni,Co)_9S_8$, bornite Cu_5FeS_4; also oxides (ilmenite, $FeTiO_3$; magnetite, Fe_3O_4; chromite, $FeCr_2O_4$).

Among the feldspars the most important are the various potash feldspars $K[AlSi_3O_8]$ and the plagioclase feldspars, mixtures of albite $Na[AlSi_3O_8]$ and anorthite $Ca[Al_2Si_2O_8]$. Structurally they are tectosilicates; chemically, typical aluminosilicates. The cations accommodated in feldspar structure include Na^+, K^+, Rb^+, Cs^+, Ca^{2+}, Sr^{2+}, Ba^{2+}, Pb^{2+} and Tl^+, also Fe^{3+} replacing Al^{3+}. In alkalic rocks, the feldspathoids are of equal importance as are the feldspars in calc-alkalic rocks, but their general geochemical importance is not too great. Nepheline $Na[AlSiO_4]$, and leucite $\beta\text{-}K[AlSi_2O_6]$, are the most important members of this petrographic group. Like the feldspars, the feldspathoids are aluminosilicates with a tectosilicate framework.

The pyroxenes and amphiboles are structurally closely related inosilicates. They consist of numerous minerals with the general formulas $R_2[Si_2O_6]$ for pyroxenes and $R_{14}[(OH)_4|Si_{16}O_{44}]$ for amphiboles. In these formulas R is Mg^{2+}, Fe^{2+}, Ca^{2+} and, in many minerals, Al^{3+}, Fe^{3+}, Ti^{3+}, Mn^{3+}, Mn^{2+}, Na^+, K^+, Li^+, etc. In amphiboles, the OH^- group is partly replaced by O^{2-} or by F^-. Pyroxene species include, among others, enstatite $Mg_2[Si_2O_6]$ and augite, which contains Na^+, Ca^{2+}, Mg^{2+}, Fe^{2+}, Fe^{3+}, Al^{3+} and Ti^{3+} as cations. Three pyroxene series occur in igneous rocks and pyroxene minerals are always mixtures. The augites are among the most important mafic constituents of igneous rocks. The amphiboles are chemically more complicated than the pyroxenes, and no simple structural formulas can be given for them because of the great number of possible diadochic substitutions. The hornblendes, in which R is Na^+, K^+, Ca^{2+}, Mg^{2+}, Fe^{2+}, Fe^{3+}, Al^{3+} and Ti^{3+}, are geochemically the most important amphiboles. In augites and amphiboles, particularly in hornblendes, as much as one-fourth of the Si^{4+} ions may become replaced by Al^{3+}.

Some igneous rocks contain olivines as their principal constituents. The most important olivines are members of the forsterite-fayalite series. Olivines are nesosilicates. Quartz is a tectosilicate. The existence of free silica in igneous rocks is the result of the high abundance of silicon in the upper lithosphere.

Among the micas, which are aluminosilicates with a phyllosilicate structure, biotite $K(Mg,Fe,Mn)_3[(OH,F)_2|AlSi_3O_{10}]$ and muscovite $KAl_2[(OH,F)_2|AlSi_3O_{10}]$ are the most important species. Biotite is the most common mica in igneous rocks. There also exist KMg, NaAl and CaAl micas, and some varieties are known that are characterized by a high content of trace elements, such as lithium, barium, chromium, vanadium, manganese and titanium. The possibilities of diadochic substitution in the micas are numerous, just as in the pyroxenes and the amphiboles.

2. Chemical Differentiation of Rock Melts.—The igneous rocks are chemically widely variable, and rocks with a chemical composition similar to the average composition of igneous rocks are rare. Because it is believed that the original silicate crust of the earth was chemically rather homogeneous, the assumption follows that the igneous rocks are products of an extensive chemical differentiation in the crust. It is believed that the plateau basalts represent the parental magma that differentiated to produce all primary magmatic rocks present in the upper lithosphere. The changes in chemical composition caused by magmatic differentiation are geochemically important.

The general course of crystallization of a calc-alkalic basaltic magma comprises three stages: the early, the main and the late magmatic. Silicates (dunite, anorthosite), sulfides (pyrrhotite-pentlandite assemblage) and oxides (ilmenite, chromite, magnetite) will separate during this stage. The igneous rock series from gabbros through diorites to granites is the product of fractional crystallization during the main stage. The bulk of the volatile constituents of the magma will become enriched in the residual melts and solutions and separate in pegmatites and in pneumatolytic and hydrothermal deposits during the late magmatic stage. Escape of volcanic emanations completes the course of crystallization. The boundaries between the different stages are not very rigid because the processes are continuous.

The early magmatic stage incorporates the separation of much iron and sulfur, and the bulk of copper, nickel, titanium and chromium from the rock melt. Many ore bodies containing these elements are formed during this stage.

3. The Reaction Series.—The course of crystallization of calc-alkalic silicate rocks during the early and the main stage of differentiation may be described by the reaction series that contains both the mafic (dark) and the felsic (light) minerals. The reaction series, introduced by N. Bowen in 1922, is one of the cornerstones of petrology; fig. 5 shows it as a somewhat modified statement of the normal sequence of crystallization of calc-alkalic rocks.

In the right-hand branch containing the light constituents the framework of the Si-O-Al tetrahedra in the mineral structures remains unchanged, whereas in the left-hand branch of the dark constituents the framework changes with proceeding crystallization from independent tetrahedra through chains and double chains to sheets. The stability of the structures decreases in the same order.

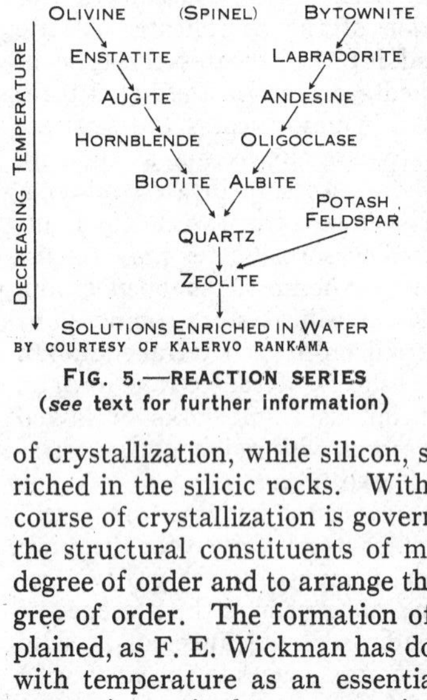

DECREASING TEMPERATURE

OLIVINE (SPINEL)
ENSTATITE
AUGITE — BYTOWNITE
HORNBLENDE — LABRADORITE
BIOTITE — ANDESINE
— OLIGOCLASE
ALBITE
QUARTZ — POTASH FELDSPAR
ZEOLITE

SOLUTIONS ENRICHED IN WATER
BY COURTESY OF KALERVO RANKAMA

FIG. 5.—REACTION SERIES
(see text for further information)

The general course of crystallization proceeds from ultramafic rocks through subsilicic and intermediate types to the silicic rocks largely as a result of fractional crystallization. The principal types of calc-alkalic rocks produced are dunite and anorthosite, gabbro, diorite and granite. Among other chemical changes the Fe/Mg ratio increases toward the later stages of crystallization. Magnesium and calcium are concentrated during the early stages, while silicon, sodium and potassium become enriched in the silicic rocks. With respect to crystal chemistry, the course of crystallization is governed by forces that tend to capture the structural constituents of minerals from the melt with a low degree of order and to arrange them into structures with a high degree of order. The formation of the various minerals may be explained, as F. E. Wickman has done, by means of kinetic reasoning with temperature as an essential function. A given amount of energy is required to move an ion from a position with a given coordination to another position with a different coordination. The energy required is called the migration energy (the activation energy of the migration of the ion) and depends on the coordination, size and charge of the ion, the degree of order in the structure, temperature and pressure. The fact that the migration energy depends on ionic size explains the general separation of Mg^{2+} during an early, and of Fe^{2+} during a late stage of crystallization. Both ions are 6-co-ordinated in the olivine structure, but the size of the Mg^{2+} ion is closer to the optimum size required by 6-coordination, and consequently the migration energy of Mg^{2+} in the olivine structure is greater than the migration energy of Fe^{2+} therein. If two cations are of equal size but of different charge, the cation with the higher charge has the greater migration energy. The difference in migration energy between Na^+ and Ca^{2+} explains the order of crystallization of the plagioclase feldspars. The Na^+ ion with the smaller migration energy is the more mobile of the two ions, and consequently calcic plagioclases separate at higher temperatures than do the sodic plagioclases. The properties of the Si-O framework determine the order of

GEOCHEMISTRY

crystallization of forsterite and enstatite. Enstatite will crystallize before augite because of the absence of Ca^{2+} in its structure and the ensuing higher stability thereof. The separation of the amphiboles after the pyroxenes may be explained by differences in the Si–O framework, chiefly by the linkage differences of the Mg^{2+} ions. Micas crystallize after hornblende because the mica structure is still weaker and more unstable than the amphibole structure. Also, the K^+ ion is rather loosely bound in the structure. In alkalic rocks, the sequence of separation may be entirely different, particularly when certain nepheline syenites are formed. The light constituents may then be the first minerals to separate.

4. Residual Melts and Solutions.—After the close of the main stage of crystallization residual solutions will often remain that are rich in hyperfusible constituents, especially water. Pegmatites are produced during the differentiation of these liquors. Pegmatites of granites and nepheline syenites, or of the last rocks to form during the main stage of crystallization, are rather common. Elements too scarce to make independent minerals and those of ionic size unsuitable for their being incorporated in the rock-making minerals become gradually concentrated in the magmatic residues and separate in the pegmatites. Such elements are, among others, lithium, beryllium, boron, fluorine, rubidium, cesium, niobium, tantalum, uranium and the lanthanides. Uranium, niobium, tantalum and a part of the lanthanides are predominantly concentrated in granite pegmatites, whereas other lanthanides, zirconium and often thorium are enriched in the nepheline syenite pegmatites. The pegmatites may be divided chemically according to the abundance relationships of sodium and potassium *versus* aluminum. In agpaitic pegmatites $Na + K > Al$, while in plumasitic pegmatites $Na + K < Al$ (the names are from locations of occurrences of type specimens in Iceland and California respectively). The different pegmatites have different typical minerals.

Strictly speaking, the formation of pegmatites marks the end of magmatic crystallization. No sharp boundary can be established between the pegmatitic stage and the ensuing pneumatolytic and hydrothermal stages. When a superheated aqueous solution containing dissolved silicates and other substances crystallizes at a temperature higher than the critical temperature of water vapour (374.5° C.), the deposits formed are called pneumatolytic. If crystallization temperature is lower than the critical temperature, the minerals and rocks formed are hydrothermal.

Alkali feldspars, micas, quartz and characteristic minerals containing rare earth elements are the chief minerals formed during the pegmatitic stage; mineral veins are the most important among pneumatolytic and hydrothermal deposits. Many heavy metals separate in the veins and may form ore bodies. The veins contain many sulfophile elements either in the native state or as oxides, sulfides, selenides, tellurides, arsenides, antimonides and various sulfosalts. After deposition of most of their metallic constituents the dilute hydrothermal solutions may deposit quartz and zeolites and minerals containing volatile constituents such as boron compounds and carbon dioxide, if these are present in the solutions.

5. Volcanic Emanations.—In volcanoes the volatile constituents of the magmas escape as volcanic emanations into the atmosphere, dissolve in water, and form volcanic sublimates around the craters and vents.

Water vapour, carbon dioxide, nitrogen and native and combined sulfur are the quantitatively most important constituents of the emanations, but notable local and areal changes in their constitution are observed. Some of the constituents derive from the earth's magma (juvenile constituents), while others come from the earth's surface (superficial constituents) or from the atmosphere (meteoric constituents). The temperature of the emanations and the time elapsed since the start of the volcanic activity also affect the composition of the emanations.

Geochemically, the volcanic emanations are of high importance because of their character as products of the degassing of the earth. They affect essentially the manner of occurrence and the geochemical cycle of many elements. Such elements as chlorine, sulfur and boron (all abundant in volcanic emanations) are directly supplied to the atmosphere and hydrosphere by volcanic emanations and will participate in geochemical processes on the earth's surface.

C. The Exogenic (Minor) Cycle

The upper lithosphere is the seat of numerous geochemical processes that affect its chemical composition both locally and areally. All matter on the surface of the earth and in the uppermost parts of the lithosphere participates in a slow complicated migration, or cycle, that causes more or less pronounced changes in the structure and chemical composition of rocks. New rocks with new properties are produced in this cycle. The migration of matter consists of the exogenic (the product of outside forces), or minor cycle taking place under the direct influence of atmospheric and hydrospheric agents and the major cycle, a material part of which is confined to the uppermost levels of the lithosphere.

In the exogenic cycle the elements behave differently, depending on their individual properties and in accordance with laws that differ basically from the rules valid for the crystallization of rock melts. The migration, consequently, yields products whose formation cannot be explained by the laws of magmatic crystallization. The exogenic cycle starts with solid crystalline rocks and ends in sedimentary rocks. It forms a part of the major cycle. Unlike the major cycle, which is closed, the exogenic cycle, taking place only in one direction, is largely open and is closed only for sedimentary rocks. For all other rocks this cycle is irreversible.

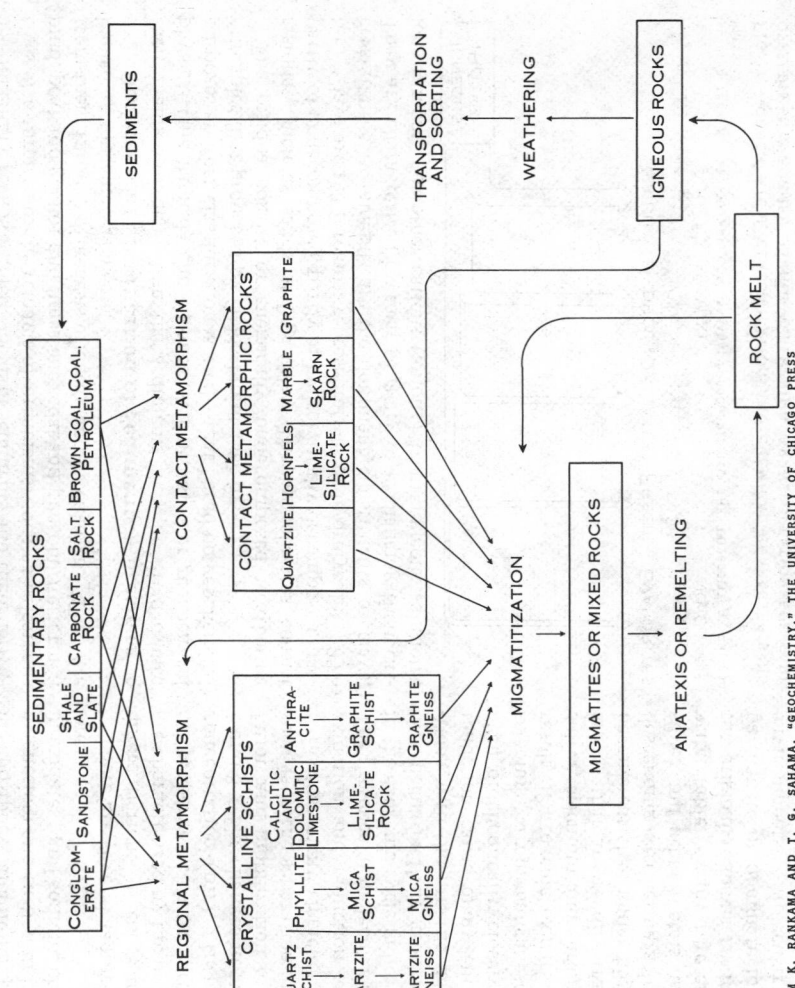

FROM K. RANKAMA AND T. G. SAHAMA, "GEOCHEMISTRY," THE UNIVERSITY OF CHICAGO PRESS

FIG. 6.—THE MAJOR CYCLE OF MATTER

GEOCHEMISTRY

The course of the exogenic cycle as a part of the major cycle is schematized in fig. 6. It consists of the weathering of rocks, transportation of products formed during weathering, and redeposition of material, usually in new surroundings. These processes are in many respects similar to a gigantic semiquantitative chemical rock analysis involving separations on a large scale. Because of its role as a separating and concentrating agent for many elements, the exogenic cycle is of importance for the manner of their occurrence in the uppermost lithosphere and on the surface of the earth.

1. Weathering of Rocks.

—Rock weathering consists of a number of physical and chemical processes that gradually break down the fresh solid rocks into an aggregate of loose material, a part of which is dissolved or changed chemically, while another part remains unchanged. The principal agents of physical (mechanical) weathering are changes in temperature and the action of frost and of crystallizing salts. Chemical weathering is caused by the action of rain, surface and ground water and of the solids and gases dissolved therein. Oxygen, carbon dioxide, nitric acid, sulfuric acid, humic complexes, ammonia and chlorides are the most important chemically active agents in natural waters. The chemical processes taking place during weathering are rather complicated. Oxidation, reduction and action of carbon dioxide are geochemically important weathering processes.

The rock-making minerals are of different stability against weathering, the mafic minerals decomposing more rapidly than the felsic minerals. The stability series of the rock-making minerals proposed by S. S. Goldich is exceedingly similar to the reaction series (fig. 5), the stability increasing from olivine and calcic plagioclase to quartz.

The solid products of completed weathering include substances that are stable under conditions existing on the earth's surface. Clay minerals, the hydroxides of ferric iron and aluminum, and their derivatives are the most abundant weathering products. The loose weathering residues and products are transported and sorted by the action of wind, flowing water, ice and organisms, and a number of chemically and physically different continental and marine sediments are thereby formed. Sorting is according to particle size but includes also chemical separation. In the course of time, deposited loose sediments may change by consolidation, recrystallization and chemical processes in diagenesis (q.v.); thus a sedimentary rock is formed. Several sediments and their derivatives also form from the remains of organisms, such as calcareous mud, peat and guano; and limestone, coal and phosphorite formed from them through diagenesis or decay and incoalation. They are known as biogenic sediments.

2. Geochemical Classification of Sediments.

—According to their manner of deposition the sediments may be divided into physical (mechanical) and chemical sediments. For geochemical purposes another classification is used—that based on geochemical principles first proposed by Goldschmidt (see fig. 7).

The residua consist of chemically undecomposed weathering residues, such as sands and gravels. The hydrolyzates consist partly of undecomposed, partly of hydrolytically decomposed matter. Clays are the foremost representatives of hydrolyzates. The crystalline clay minerals are the dominant constituents of clays. They are characterized by their capacity of exchanging their cations (anions) for other cations (anions) from aqueous solutions.

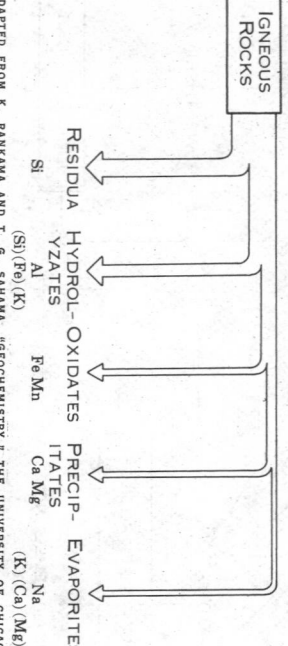

IGNEOUS ROCKS

RESIDUA — HYDROL-YZATES — OXIDATES — PRECIP-ITATES — EVAPORITES

Si — Al — FeMn — CaMg — Na
(Si)(Fe)(K) — (Al) — FeMn — CaMg — (K)(Ca)(Mg)

ADAPTED FROM K. RANKAMA AND T. G. SAHAMA, "GEOCHEMISTRY," THE UNIVERSITY OF CHICAGO PRESS

FIG. 7.—GEOCHEMICAL CLASSIFICATION AND CHEMICAL CHARACTERISTICS OF SEDIMENTS FORMED DURING WEATHERING, TRANSPORTATION AND SEDIMENTATION

The oxidates form by oxidation of Fe^{2+} into Fe^{3+} and of Mn^{2+} into Mn^{3+} and consist chiefly of hydroxides of the two metals. Iron and manganese ores of sedimentary origin belong to this group. The reducites, the opposites of the oxidates, are formed in strongly reducing surroundings. Coal and petroleum, and muds and clays containing sulfides and carbonaceous matter are reducites. The precipitates form by inorganic precipitation from aqueous solutions. Deposits of inorganically precipitated calcium carbonate may occur along with inorganically precipitated calcium carbonate. Because the sedimentation processes are continuous, sediments and their derivatives usually are mixtures belonging to two or three groups, and, consequently, the geochemical division of sediments is not categorical.

The evaporites are deposited from aqueous solutions as a result of evaporation of the solvent. They include extensive salt beds crystallized from sea water. The biolites, or biogenic sediments, often occur together with other sediments, e.g., biogenic calcium carbonate.

3. Chemistry of the Exogenic Cycle.

—The total quantity of rocks decomposed and of sediments formed during the geological history of the earth is of great geochemical importance. The length of the time during which the exogenic agents have operated on the earth's surface is approximately 3.5×10^9 years (3,500,000,000 yr.). Goldschmidt estimated, on the basis of the sodium content of sea water, that 160 kg. igneous rock for each square centimetre of the earth's surface have yielded a total of 169.6 $kg.cm.^{-2}$ (minimum value) of sediments. The argillaceous (clayey) and arenaceous (sandy) sediments are, quantitatively, the most important sediments produced. Another estimate based on the radioactivity of potassium gave 6,462 $kg.cm.^{-2}$ (maximum value) for the total quantity of weathered igneous rock.

The igneous rocks are formed by endogenic (produced by internal forces) differentiation deep under the earth's surface. Another kind of differentiation, called the exogenic differentiation, takes place on the surface and is intimately connected with the exogenic cycle of matter. Some elements become strongly enriched in certain types of sediments, even though a high degree of separation is not always reached. For many elements the exogenic differentiation is the most powerful concentrating and enriching agent. For instance, silicon and zirconium are concentrated in sandstones; aluminum, potassium and boron in shales; calcium, magnesium and carbon in limestones; iron, manganese and barium in oxidates; and sodium, chlorine, magnesium and sulfur in evaporites.

There are several factors of prime importance for the exogenic differentiation. Because most phenomena of the exogenic cycle are characterized by the presence of water, the physical and chemical properties of water are significant, such as the hydrogen ion concentration (pH). In most natural waters the pH is between 6 and 8. The changes in pH play an important role in the precipitation and mobilization of many elements in aqueous solutions, such as in the separation of iron and aluminum.

Because many elements occur in two or more oxidation states, oxidation and reduction are geochemically important processes. The presence of molecular oxygen and of reducing biogenic matter in the exogenic cycle indicates that here both oxidation and reduction occur in their geochemically most important surroundings. Along with the pH, the differences in the degree of oxidation or reduction cause many enrichment processes and the separation even of chemically closely related elements, such as sulfur and selenium. Iron, manganese and cobalt are often precipitated as a result of exogenic oxidation reactions. Many elements, such as sulfur, selenium and chromium, may become oxidized to complex anions that are readily transported in solution. Other elements become enriched under highly reducing conditions. For instance, descending weathering solutions from ore bodies deposit copper, silver and other metals as sulfides in reducing areas below the water table. Many rare elements are concentrated in biolites in the original reducing environments. Biochemical processes may participate or dominate in the creation of oxidizing or reducing environments. Molecular oxygen liberated by green plants in photosynthesis is responsible for the highly oxidizing conditions on the earth's surface. On the other hand, decaying biogenic matter creates reducing conditions.

In the exogenic cycle the two extremes of the oxidizing and reducing conditions are represented by the highly oxidized residua and the strongly reducing bituminous sediments and their derivatives. During weak metamorphism, the degree of oxidation often remains unchanged, and a high degree of oxidation in rocks may afford proof of their superficial origin. With the higher grades of metamorphism, reduction will gradually take place and leads back to the reducing conditions of the rock melts.

During weathering a part of the chemically decomposed material going into solution is present as colloidal particles. A group of phenomena called geochemical sorption largely governs the properties of such particles in sediments and the distribution of elements among various sediments. The sorption of ions by colloidal particles is of high geochemical importance, for example, in the concentration of many elements (such as potassium) in clays.

Goldschmidt did show that a number of phenomena connected with the distribution of elements between sea water and sediments may be explained by considering the ionic potential of elements, that is, the charge of an ion divided by its radius. For instance, preferential adsorption of potassium in argillaceous sediments and preferential migration of sodium to the sea are in accordance with the lower ionic potential of potassium. The fixation of potassium in hydrolyzates may, however, be explained, according to C. S. Ross, by the incorporation of the K^+ ion in the structure of montmorillonite, a clay mineral. Goldschmidt divided the elements on the basis of their ionic potential into three groups, which become separated from one another during sedimentation in the sea. Wickman revised the division and gave a physical explanation to the phenomenon by means of the rules governing hydrogen and hydroxyl bonds in hydroxides. The cations with low ionic potential and ionic bonds in their hydroxides (e.g., the alkali metals) generally remain in ionic solution. The cations with intermediate ionic potential and hydroxyl bonds in their hydroxides, such as aluminum, uranium and tantalum, are readily hydrolyzed and precipitate as hydroxides which are deposited in hydrolyzates. The cations with the highest ionization potential form complex anions with oxygen, and these remain usually in solution. Nitrogen, carbon, sulfur and phosphorus, among others, belong to this group. Their complex anions have hydrogen bonds.

D. THE MAJOR CYCLE

Along with the differentiation by crystallization of rock melts and the cycle of weathering, transportation and sedimentation, processes of still another kind take place in the uppermost lithosphere which cannot be included in either endogenic or exogenic differentiation. These processes, occurring at deeper levels in the crust, tend in part to distribute the elements among various rocks, but their essential role is in the opposite direction, inasmuch as they tend to level off the chemical differences already produced. They form the endogenic cycle of matter. The endogenic and exogenic cycles together form the major cycle.

The processes of the endogenic cycle start from sedimentary or igneous rocks and produce gradually a rock melt. These processes are largely, perhaps almost entirely, based on reactions taking place in the solid state. It is possible that the major cycle actually is the most important process in the chemical modeling of the upper lithosphere.

The course of the major cycle is presented in fig. 6. Unlike the exogenic cycle, the major cycle is closed for all participating rocks. The exogenic cycle, particularly the oceans, however, represents a considerable leak in the cycle because of the (at least) semipermanent accumulation of many elements in sea water and in ocean-bottom sediments. The major cycle begins with molten rock and ultimately winds up with a regenerated rock melt. The melt, on cooling, will crystallize in the form of plutonic or volcanic rocks, according to the level of the seat of crystallization in the lithosphere. The true igneous rocks of juvenile origin must be distinguished from the quasi-igneous rocks that are partly or totally composed of remelted material. On the earth's surface, the rocks participate in the exogenic cycle whereby sediments are ultimately

produced. The sediments and the sedimentary rocks formed from them by diagenesis may reparticipate in the exogenic cycle but may also be removed from immediate contact with the hydrosphere and the atmosphere by continuing deposition of sediments or by tectonic movements. If that is the case, they will depart from the exogenic cycle and, in the course of time, will take part in metamorphic processes.

1. **Metamorphism of Rocks.**—Metamorphism is the physical and chemical adjustment of rocks to conditions existing at the deeper levels of the upper lithosphere. Metamorphic changes are essential for the endogenic processes and may consist of purely mechanical (kinetic) metamorphism, or purely thermal metamorphism, or metasomatism, which is the introduction or removal of material by magmatic gases (pneumatolytic metamorphism), solutions (hydrothermal metamorphism) or molten rock (migmatitization in part). All these processes cause changes in both the mineralogy and chemistry of the rocks affected. Some metamorphic changes are termed autometamorphism when they constitute reactions between a rock and the residual solutions from its crystallization. Complex controlling conditions cause regional metamorphism over wide areas under the combined influence of elevated temperature, variable pressure and high shearing stress, and plutonic metamorphism, which is the deep-seated regional metamorphism at high temperatures and pressures, often accompanied by strong deformation and augmented by injection or infiltration of molten rock or by incipient remelting. At a still greater depth, plutonic metamorphism merges into truly plutonic phenomena. Near the surface, regional metamorphism becomes gradually replaced by kinetic metamorphism. Deformation promotes and accelerates the chemical reactions incorporated in metamorphism.

Because of the complexity of the reacting system, chemical changes involved in metamorphism are usually complicated. When environmental conditions change, the minerals participating in a metamorphic reaction may become unstable and their structures will be gradually torn down, ion by ion. Disorder is thereby created, but finally new structures different from the old ones will form. With reference to stability and composition, the new structures are adapted to new conditions. All these reactions may take place in a liquid phase, called the intergranular film, but structures may also react with one another in the solid state, whereby the ions are simply rearranged to make new structures. But some ions are always present that are not strictly and rigidly bound to

any structure but form a separate phase, called the dispersed phase. The presence of a dispersed phase is the condition of all chemical reactions that take place in rocks. It may be a gas, or a liquid or ions temporarily detached from their original structural positions. Even in solid-state reactions the ions make up the new structure through a dispersed phase.

A process called migmatitization may set in with progressing regional metamorphism to produce migmatites, or mixed rocks, through the migration of the readily mobile elements, such as the alkali metals, and the intrusion of molten rock material into preexisting rocks. The migmatites predominate in the deepest parts of mountain chains. The boundary of the zone of migmatization is called the migmatite front. Many granites and associated rocks are believed to have formed by migmatitization (granitization). Metamorphism may, however, still increase in strength causing the partial remelting (anatexis) of rocks, followed by complete remelting. Thereby a rock melt is produced, and its crystallization, the starting phase of the major cycle, will set in. The most far-reaching and thorough metamorphic changes consequently mean the rebirth, or palingenesis, of rocks.

Regional metamorphism is the most common and petrologically the most important form of metamorphism. It may consist solely of changes that do not affect the bulk chemical composition of the metamorphosed rock. This is isochemical or internal metamorphism. It may also consist of substantial addition or removal of material. This is allochemical or metasomatic metamorphism, and in it the bulk chemical composition will change.

Wholesale diffusion probably is important for the transfer of matter in metamorphism, but diffusion in the solid state, according to laboratory experiments, is insufficient to explain long-distance transport of matter. Migration through liquid and gaseous phases is also possible, and it appears that surface phenomena in the intergranular film are of great importance in controlling metasomatic metamorphism.

Metasomatic changes often pronouncedly affect the chemical composition of rocks. The substances introduced may consist of the alkali metals, calcium, iron with magnesium and silicon, lithium, fluorine, chlorine, sulfur, silicon, tin and carbon dioxide, and the metasomatic changes are accordingly called alkali metasomatism, etc. These processes are little investigated quantitatively, but sometimes amounts of elements calculated in millions of tons are known to have been introduced or removed.

2. Migration in the Lithosphere.—The endogenic migration of matter in the lithosphere is characterized by its selectivity; this means that under given conditions certain elements are able to migrate more readily than others. The elements with high atomic numbers are, in fact, relatively readily mobilized and become enriched in granites and in low-temperature assemblages in general, that is, in rocks and minerals that may be assumed to have formed through a rather notable circulation and migration of matter.

Migration is of importance in molding the chemical composition of the uppermost lithosphere. There is evidence of a global migration affecting many elements. During this migration, the elements become divided into two groups. The granitophile elements are known to be especially enriched in both igneous and quasi-igneous granites. They endeavour to concentrate in the outermost parts of the crust. The granitophobe elements, on the other hand, are pushed down toward the basaltic substratum.

Granitization (or the formation of granite by migration, anatexis and palingenesis) is one of the key processes in the geochemistry of metamorphism. P. Eskola proposed that granitization is caused by a fluid, called the granitic ichor and consisting of truly juvenile residual melts and of the melts first to become squeezed out during the partial remelting of already solidified rocks. The chief constituents of the ichor are silicon, aluminum, sodium and potassium; oxygen and hydroxyl ions also migrate therein. The ichor rises slowly into the superposed rocks giving them a granitic or granitelike composition. But it is probable that both pore solutions and ionic diffusion participate in granitization. The mobility of ions during regional metamorphism and granitization is a function of ionic radius. The Fe^{2+} and Mg^{2+} ions are very mobile and become concentrated in the so-called basic front, the precursor of migmatization and granitization.

All gradations probably exist, from juvenile granites to metasomatic and palingenetic granites. The formation of silicic and other rocks by metasomatic processes implies some loss of significance for the classic theory of differentiation by crystallization. This theory, however, is important as the basis of estimation of the mobility of elements in metasomatic metamorphism. *See also* METAMORPHISM; METASOMATISM.

III. GEOCHEMISTRY OF THE HYDROSPHERE

The lithosphere is partly covered by a water blanket called the hydrosphere; as much as 70.8% of the earth's surface is covered by water. The salt-water bodies, the oceans, with a total volume of $1,370.323 \times 10^6$ km.³ and a mass of $14,060 \times 10^{20}$ g., make by far the greatest and most important part of the hydrosphere. The cavities of rocks and minerals contain salt solutions that may be of primary magmatic origin, while other solutions consist of meteoric water trapped in the rocks.

Fresh water is present in the soil as ground water and in the pores of rocks as hygroscopic water. It flows to the surface of the earth as spring water, fills the ponds and lake basins, and flows in rivers and streams as surface water. The permanent fields of snow, the glaciers, inland ice and permanent ice at high altitudes all consist of frozen water. Ground water, mixed with juvenile water, that is, water that has never been to the surface, enters the volcanic emanations and hot springs. The cavities of water also occurs in some isolated areas on all continents, gathering in depressions to make alkaline or salt lakes.

According to Goldschmidt's estimate there are for every square centimetre of the earth's surface 278.11 kg. of sea water, 0.1 kg. of fresh water, 4.5 kg. of continental ice and 0.03 kg. of water vapour. The absolute amount and relative proportions of the different kinds of water change continuously. Because the bulk of all water present in the hydrosphere consists of sea water, it is appropriate to state that the composition of ocean water. Natural waters in their various states are actually rocks formed by the mineral, water (H_2O), but they are never pure because they contain a number of dissolved gases and solids and particulate matter.

1. Ground Water.—Ground water is, essentially, of atmospheric (meteoric) origin. When the meteoric waters that contain oxygen, carbon dioxide and small amounts of dissolved substances derived from the atmosphere enter soil and rock, they incorporate the soluble inorganic and organic gases, liquids and solids available. The ground water charged with carbon dioxide and oxygen is a powerful weathering agent. Bicarbonates, sulfates and chlorides of the alkaline-earth and alkali metals are the chief constituents of ground water. Its chemical composition is constantly changed by the action of several physical and chemical agents and ranges from that of nearly pure rain water to that found in mineral wells and springs. Another kind of ground water, called connate water, contains substances that were present in solution at the time of deposition of the sediment beds soaked with such a water.

Sulfates and carbonates are the most important constituents of spring water, whereas chloride is usually less important. Some spring waters may be rich in silica. Calcium is the most abundant cation, and consequently spring and well waters are hard. Their chemical composition and salinity depend on local conditions.

2. Surface Water.—Admixture of rain water, surface water and ground water from elsewhere rapidly changes the chemical composition of the spring water flowing to lakes and rivers. Precipitation, solution and pollution by sewage and industrial waste waters will affect the composition of river water, in small rivers in particular. Weathering products and the remaining original constituents of rain water are carried by rivers in their water. The amount of the weathering products and physical properties of rocks and soils in the catchment area. Carbonates dominate in river water and are much in excess over sulfates and chlorides, and calcium is the principal cation. Sulfates and chlorides tend to prevail in waters from arid and semiarid regions. In tropical regions the salinity of river water is remarkably low and the dissolved solids are rich in silicon, the element essentially removed in lateritic weathering (*see* BAUXITE; LATERITE). With dissolved and colloidal inorganic substances, surface waters contain dissolved gases, chiefly nitrogen, carbon dioxide and oxygen, and a number of organic substances.

River waters may be divided into two major groups—carbonate and sulfate. The former are the more common of the two. (*See* Table IX.) While calcium preponderates among the cations in fresh waters, its content in the salts of sea water is rather low, and sodium predominates. Furthermore, carbonate and sulfate preponderates in sea-water salts. These differences result from the precipitation of calcium as carbonate and sulfate in lakes and seas and from incorporation of calcium carbonate in shells and skeletons by marine organisms. Removal of the compounds accounts for the relative enrichment of sodium and chlorine in sea water.

TABLE IX.—*Average Chemical Composition of Dissolved Solids in Lake, River and Sea Waters*

(In weight percentage)

Constituent	Lake and river water	Sea water
CO_3	35.15	0.41*
SO_4	12.14	7.68
Cl	5.68	55.04
NO_3	0.90	..
Ca	20.39	1.15
Mg	3.41	3.69
Na	5.79	30.62
K	2.12	1.10
Fe_2O_3, Al_2O_3	2.75	..
SiO_2	11.67	..
Sr, H_3BO_3, Br	..	0.31
Total	100.00	100.00

*As HCO_3^-

3. **Mineral Springs and Hot Springs.**—Waters in mineral springs and hot springs differ from ordinary well and spring waters in either concentration or composition, or both, chiefly as a result of local conditions. These waters may be classified into chloride, sulfate, carbonate and acid waters as the main types. Furthermore, there are silicate, borate, nitrate, sulfide, phosphate and mixed waters. Many mineral waters contain dissolved gases, such as carbon dioxide, hydrogen sulfide, nitrogen and inert gases. Natural brines of high salinity may contain salts dissolved from salt beds by percolating waters, salt solutions associated with petroleum deposits, or connate waters. Some trace elements are present in mineral waters, partly derived from volcanic emanations and partly leached out from surrounding rocks; the therapeutic value of mineral waters is largely caused by their presence. Juvenile waters or those of deep-seated magmatic origin are usually characterized by a notable content of heavy elements, but in waters originating above the water table or upper level of ground water (*i.e.*, superficial or vadose waters) such elements commonly are totally or almost totally absent. Other differences also exist in the chemical composition of juvenile and vadose waters. Hot springs represent the closing stage of thermal activity in volcanic regions; theirs is largely surface water.

4. **Closed Basins.**—In semiarid and arid regions, the soluble weathering products remain in the soil or are transported to depressions. If the rate of evaporation is too rapid to allow the accumulation of any considerable body of water, great quantities of dissolved matter are deposited in the depressions and finally form alkaline or salt lakes, or even dry salt beds usually consisting of sodium, magnesium and calcium as sulfates, and of some bicarbonate. The basins devoid of an outlet receive water by rivers and streams. In the continental areas of such internal drainage, permanent reservoirs are formed that contain water concentrated by evaporation of incoming water and with a composition entirely different from the composition of sea water. Many salt lakes are in a semisolid state, and the composition of their brines varies according to local conditions. The salt and alkaline lakes are divided, according to the dominant ion, into lakes with chloride waters, characterized mainly by sodium chloride; bittern lakes rich in magnesium salts; sulfate lakes; and carbonate and bicarbonate lakes. In general, alkaline lakes are connected with volcanic areas, and saline lakes, with sedimentary rocks.

5. **The Ocean.**—Sea water contains dissolved salts that have escaped adsorption during the cycle of dissolved substances, and precipitation and crystallization during the history of the ocean. More than 50 elements have been detected in sea water or in marine organisms, and it is probable that all elements are found in

amounts of atmospheric gases are dissolved therein. The bulk of the dissolved gases is made of oxygen, nitrogen and carbon dioxide (chiefly as carbonate and bicarbonate ions).

Sea water is normally alkaline with a pH between 7.5 and 8.4, but variations also occur in pH caused, for instance, by biological activity. Regional changes are observed in the composition of sea water and are mainly connected with biological activity; for instance, the Antarctic ocean is rich in nitrate and the Pacific ocean in silicate. Furthermore, there exists a close connection between the content of phosphate and nitrate and the extent of biological activity in the sea.

The total quantity of carbon dioxide in sea water per square centimetre of the earth's surface is 50 times as high as the quantity of carbon dioxide in the atmosphere. The four forms of carbon dioxide in the sea, namely, free carbon dioxide, carbonate and bicarbonate ions and the undissociated H_2CO_3 molecules, form a buffer system. All these forms are in equilibrium with one another and with the hydrogen ions present in solution, as:

$$\text{Atmosphere} \quad CO_2$$
$$\text{Sea water} \quad H_2CO_3 \rightleftharpoons H^+ + HCO_3^- \rightleftharpoons H^+ + CO_3^{2-}$$

The free (unbound and undissociated) carbon dioxide consists of CO_2 and H_2CO_3 molecules in solution and in equilibrium with each other. The carbon dioxide equilibrium depends on all physical, chemical and biological factors active in the sea. A change in the total concentration of carbon dioxide, caused, for instance, by assimilation and respiration, results in a corresponding adjustment of all concentration constants until a new equilibrium is attained. The adjustments are also observable outside the phase boundary in the atmosphere and in solid carbonate phases. The atmosphere, however, regulates the tension of carbon dioxide in the sea. An exchange of other dissolved gases (certain nitrogen compounds) also takes place between the atmosphere and the sea.

Goldschmidt divided the elements into thalassophile (from the Gr. *thalassa*, "sea," and *philos*, "loved" or "having affinity for") and thalassoxene (from the Gr. *xenos*, "quest" or "stranger") groups according to their distribution between seas and continents. Chlorine, bromine, boron, sulfur (in sulfates), sodium and, partly, iodine are thalassophile, while all such elements are thalassoxene that precipitate in the hydrosphere because of the hydrolytic decomposition of their salts, *e.g.*, aluminum and iron. Some thalassophile elements, such as sodium, have increased in amount in the ocean during its history, while the others are retained in clays. Other elements largely removed from sea water are calcium, aluminum, silicon, iron and manganese. The present content of chlorine, bromine, sulfur and boron in sea water is higher than the content calculated from the amounts actually transported into the sea. The four elements are added to the sea by volcanic emanations and juvenile waters.

Elements forming relatively readily soluble compounds, such as sodium, potassium, magnesium, carbon and nitrogen, remain in sea water in considerable quantities and finally crystallize out in the evaporites. Poisonous elements (mercury, arsenic and lead) are largely removed by incorporation in the hydrolyzates and the oxidates, in a process called depoisoning of sea water.

Particulate matter is carried by rivers into the sea, along with dissolved and colloidal substances. Physical chemical processes may take place between the particles and sea water. *See* also Ocean and Oceanography.

IV. GEOCHEMISTRY OF THE ATMOSPHERE

The atmosphere, or gaseous envelope surrounding the earth, is the outermost geochemical sphere. It consists of a mechanical

TABLE X.—*Major Constituents of Sea Water*

Ion	Content (parts per 1,000)	Ion	Content (parts per 1,000)
Cl⁻	18.9799	Na⁺	10.5561
SO₄²⁻	2.6486	Mg²⁺	1.2720
HCO₃⁻	0.1397	Ca²⁺	0.4001
Br⁻	0.0646	K⁺	0.3800
F⁻	0.0013	Sr²⁺	0.0133
H₃BO₃	0.0260	Total dissolved solids	34.4816

solution in the sea. The constituents given in Table X make up more than 99.9% of the known dissolved solids in sea water. The salt content of ocean water is usually between 3.3% and 3.8%.

The total amount of dissolved elements in sea water is colossal, and the oceans contain vast potential supplies even of many trace elements. The relative abundance of elements in sea water differs pronouncedly from their abundance in igneous rocks. The content of silicon, aluminum and iron in sea water is rather low. Almost all elements have been available in greater quantities than are now present in sea water, and, consequently, have been removed by physical chemical processes and biological activity. Many elements participate in a constant biological cycle in the sea, and their regeneration is relatively complete, even though the marine organisms cause their redistribution in sea water. Many elements, such as iodine, calcium, carbon, phosphorus, silicon and vanadium, are concentrated by marine plants or animals. A small amount of dissolved organic matter is present in sea water, and varying mixture of gases and vapours extending up to approximately 1,600 km. (994 mi.) above the earth's surface and is in contact with the lithosphere and the hydrosphere. Air is present in the spaces between soil particles, in pores of rocks, and is dissolved in water.

The lower limit of the atmosphere is determined by the depth of caves, mines and bore holes. In volcanoes the atmospheric gases are mixed with volcanic emanations. The gases in the cavities in rocks and minerals, occluded gases, petroligenic natural gas and the gases dissolved in the water of mineral springs and thermal springs all add to the atmosphere. Biochemical processes produce great quantities of gases, such as oxygen, nitrogen, carbon dioxide and methane.

1. Composition.—The atmosphere consists of four concentric layers without sharp boundaries. The lowermost layer, the troposphere, extends from sea level to approximately 11 km. (6.8 mi.) at middle latitudes. It is the convection region, and the atmospheric phenomena take place there. The next overlying layer is called the stratosphere, and the boundary between the troposphere and the stratosphere is called the tropopause. The stratosphere extends to an average altitude of 50 km. (31 mi.). In its upper reaches exists a high-temperature region, sometimes called the ozonosphere, caused by a concentration of ozone, which absorbs ultraviolet radiation of the sun. The ionosphere is the ionosphere, which extends to about 600-700 km. (373-435 mi.) above sea level. The ionosphere is characterized by free electrical charges. Some of the gas particles in the ionosphere dissociate into ions and free electrons by the action of ultraviolet radiation. Furthermore, oxygen and nitrogen molecules dissociate into atoms. The temperature in the ionosphere is very high (2,200° C. at the height of 650 km. or 404 mi.). The outermost layer of the atmosphere is called the exosphere and is occupied by relatively freely moving gas particles.

It is believed that the earth's atmosphere is almost entirely of secondary origin and has been produced, like the hydrosphere, by volcanic emanations escaping from the lithosphere during the geological evolution of the earth. The first supply of free atmospheric oxygen formed in the photochemical decomposition of water vapour in the upper atmosphere, while the bulk was derived from water in photosynthesis by chlorophyll-bearing plants.

The total mass of the atmosphere is 51.3×10^{20} g. The average composition of dry air from the troposphere is presented in Table XI. Ozone content increases with height, while radon (a gaseous radioelement) content decreases with height, and the content of water vapour varies from 0.02% to 4% by weight. The composition of the stratosphere is similar to the composition of the troposphere. Other constituents of the atmosphere are carbon monoxide, considerable amounts of which may be present in city air; formaldehyde; nitrogen oxides N_2O, NO_2 and N_2O_5; hydrogen peroxide; heavy waters HDO and D_2O; tritium; sulfur oxides SO_2 and SO_3; hydrogen sulfide; ammonia; iodine; methane; and radionuclides released by nuclear fission. These constituents originate in photochemical, electrochemical, biochemical and nuclear reactions, or are liberated in volcanic emanations or by the industrial activity of man. The composition of the atmosphere changes continuously because of the addition and removal of various substances. For example, helium actually slowly escapes from the atmosphere, as indicated by the fact that the amount of the isotope He^4 present in the atmosphere is much less than the amount generated by the alpha-decay of natural radionuclides during the geological history of the earth.

TABLE XI.—*Average Composition of Dry Air From the Troposphere*

Compound	Per cent by weight	Per cent by volume
Nitrogen (N_2)	75.51	78.09
Oxygen (O_2)	23.15	20.95
Argon (Ar)	1.28	0.93
Water vapour (H_2O)	Variable	Variable
Carbon dioxide (CO_2)	0.046	0.03
Neon (Ne)	0.00125	1.8×10^{-3}
Helium (He)	0.0000072	5.24×10^{-4}
Krypton (Kr)	0.00029	1×10^{-4}
Xenon (Xe)	0.000036	8×10^{-6}
Hydrogen (H_2)	0.0000003	5×10^{-5}
Ozone (O_3) (variable)	0.000002	1×10^{-6}
Radon (Rn) (variable)	4.52×10^{-17}	6×10^{-18}

The elements notably enriched in the atmosphere are called atmophile (having an affinity for, or at home in, the atmosphere) elements (*see* Table VI). Among the elements tabulated, only the inert gases and nitrogen are typically atmophile. Even though oxygen is enriched in the atmosphere, its amount is small compared with the huge amounts bound in the lithosphere and the hydrosphere. Consequently, the atmophile character of oxygen is not too pronounced.

A certain amount of matter other than gaseous constituents is always present in the atmosphere. This matter consists of inorganic substances (*e.g.*, dust of various origin), organic constituents and organisms.

2. Rain Water.—The most important geochemical property of the atmosphere is the chemical disintegration of rocks and minerals caused by atmospheric oxygen and water vapour. Dry oxygen is rather inert, but in the presence of water vapour its reactivity increases. There is a continuous cycle of water from the hydrosphere to the atmosphere and back to the former either directly in the form of rain water or indirectly by drainage. This cycle also includes the transport from sea water of salts, called cyclic salts, consisting chiefly of sodium chloride.

Rain water has a direct solvent action on minerals and, because it contains dissolved substances, it also acts indirectly as an effective carrier of denudation-promoting substances. Both inorganic and organic matter is dissolved in rain water, and particulate matter is often present, especially near cities. The most important among the dissolved inorganic constituents are chlorides, sulfates, nitrates and nitrites of sodium, potassium, calcium and magnesium. Nitrogen occurs also as free and albuminoid ammonia; humus and formaldehyde are frequently present. The gases dissolved in rain water consist of approximately 63% nitrogen by volume, 34% oxygen and 3% carbon dioxide and other gases. The definite enrichment of oxygen and carbon dioxide in rain water over their content in air is the reason for the chemical activity of rain water. The chemical composition of rain water varies greatly and depends on the proximity of sea, character of the landscape, density of population and industrial activity. The purest water is obtained from rain falling after tropical thunderstorms. The average composition of rain water is said to be as follows: chlorides, 3.0 parts per 1,000,000; sulfates, 5.0; nitrates, 0.2; and free ammonia, 0.4. The nitrogen compounds in rain water are of importance as natural soil fertilizers. The composition of the other forms of atmospheric precipitation is similar to the composition of rain water.

See also ATMOSPHERE.

V. GEOCHEMISTRY OF THE BIOSPHERE

The biosphere denotes organic nature as a whole and consists of plants, animals and microorganisms. It occupies the lower part of the troposphere, up to a height of approximately 5 km. (3.1 mi.), probably the whole of the hydrosphere, and a thin layer on the lithosphere, with a lower limit at a depth of approximately 2 km. (1.2 mi.).

The biosphere is the region where reactions caused by solar radiation take place and is the part of the earth capable of sustaining life. It is the youngest among the geochemical spheres.

The branch of geochemistry dealing with the biosphere is called biogeochemistry. Unlike the hydrosphere, the biosphere is rather uniformly distributed over the whole surface of the earth. It is commonly divided into three habitats, or biocycles, which are the terrestrial, the fresh-water and the marine biocycle. The marine biocycle is, quantitatively, the most important of the three. Marine organisms play an important role in the cycle of inorganic and biogenic matter in the sea. The fresh-water biocycle is a small fraction of the terrestrial biocycle. Because of its lack of permanent life, the atmosphere does not form a biocycle.

If the weight of the biosphere is taken as unity, the relative weight of the atmosphere is 300, of the hydrosphere, 69,100, and of the uppermost part of the lithosphere, of the order of 10^6. Notwithstanding the negligible mass of the biosphere, its chemical activity is remarkable, and its geochemical role is important. For instance, most if not all of the free oxygen in the atmosphere is produced in the biosphere by photosynthesis. Chalk cliffs and coral reefs show profuse biological activity. All carbon deposited in the bioliths is collected from the atmosphere containing 0.03% carbon dioxide by volume, and there are mineral deposits of economic importance that are products of migration and concentration of elements in the biosphere.

The green chlorophyll-bearing plants synthesize organic compounds from carbon dioxide and water united in photosynthesis. The compounds synthesized are oxidized in living systems by respiration which is the main source of energy in animals.

1. Composition of Plants and Animals.—The biophile elements listed in Table VI are those occurring typically in the biosphere. Apart from the biophile elements proper, all those present in organisms are called biological elements. They vary considerably in importance, amount and distribution in the organisms. Some are basic elements present in all living matter, while others occur only in certain organisms. Among the basic elements, oxygen is essential for animals, nitrogen and carbon for plants, and hydrogen and oxygen (as water) for all life. Approximately 60 elements are known to occur in the biosphere. Combined, they form all biological matter which is composed chiefly of water, carbohydrates, proteins and lipids, or fats and fatlike substances. The biological elements have a number of important functions in the organisms. Some (carbon and nitrogen) are found in the framework of plant and animal tissue. Others occur in shells and skeletons (calcium, magnesium, silicon, fluorine and phosphorus), as energy-exchange elements (hydrogen, oxygen), as electrolytes and osmotic regulators in cell liquors (sodium, potassium and chlorine as chloride), as catalysts in oxidation-reduction reactions (iron and copper, among others) and as enzyme activators (calcium, magnesium and cobalt). Some elements may be replaced by others in their functions, such as calcium by strontium or barium. The function of some elements is still unknown.

The presence or absence of an element in organisms depends primarily on its physiologic functions. Some elements are temporary constituents, while others are essential for the normal evolution and functions of the organism. The requirements as to essential elements even of closely related species may be different. Some just accumulate in organisms beyond all physiologic requirements, if any. Some nonessential elements may become concentrated in plants because of the defective selection power of the plants, which often cannot distinguish between essential elements and their nonessential fellow travelers.

The classification of the biological elements according to their content in organisms is presented in Table XII. The primary invariable elements make up the bulk of all living matter. They are essential constituents of carbohydrates, lipids and proteins. In addition, some other invariable elements are always present. Among the variable elements, some are found in relatively high concentrations in certain species but are absent in other, even related, species. Plants and animals also differ notably in their composition. In general, the average chemical composition of an organism is reminiscent of the composition of its environment. It is probable that the quantitative chemical composition of an organism is a specific feature.

The principal constituents of organisms are organic material, inorganic skeletal structures and inorganic compounds dissolved in body fluids. Organic material is largely composed of carbohydrates, lipids and proteins. Skeletal material consists mainly of calcium carbonate, calcium phosphate, or silica. Magnesium carbonate may occur as an important constituent of calcareous shells. The average total composition of living matter is presented in Table XIII for man and the alfalfa plant; apparently 11 elements make up this matter. Among the trace elements in man, iron, zinc, copper and manganese are the most abundant. Sodium and calcium are usually microconstituents in plants, but in many animals (vertebrates) calcium is a primary constituent. Compared with animals, plants are usually richer in manganese, nickel, aluminum, titanium and boron but are impoverished in iron, zinc and copper. In general, elements of low atomic number predominate in all organisms. Tables V and XIII indicate that many of the constituents of organisms (e.g., silicon, aluminum and iron) are definitely impoverished with reference to their content in igneous rocks, while many trace elements (such as carbon, hydrogen and sulfur) are concentrated in living matter. The oxygen and calcium contents in igneous rocks and organisms are of a similar degree of magnitude. It appears that organisms select the necessary biological elements irrespective of their concentration in the environment. Tables X and XIII validate this result for sea water also.

According to classic plant physiology, the following ten elements are essential for the healthy growth of plants: carbon, hydrogen, oxygen, nitrogen, sulfur, phosphorus, potassium, calcium, magnesium and iron. The seven last-mentioned elements are called the major nutrients or the mineral nutrients. They are taken up by plants as simple cations, complex cations and anions and as free molecules. Moreover, there is the group of the micronutrient elements known to be essential for plants or to promote their growth when administered in small amounts. Boron, manganese, copper, zinc, molybdenum and, perhaps, gallium are micronutrients. Finally, some elements promote in small quantities the growth of certain plants, among others, lithium, vanadium, fluorine, bromine and nickel. In greater concentrations nearly all of these are poisonous. Some elements, such as aluminum, silicon and chlorine, accumulate at least in some species or genera and may be essential in such instances. The toxicity of elements, in general, increases with increasing atomic number in the groups and subgroups of the periodic system, but the toxic effects depend also on the individual properties of the plants. Also in animals, the major nutrients of plants are indispensable, along with sodium and chlorine. In addition, the following trace elements are essential: iodine, manganese, copper, zinc and cobalt.

2. Accumulation of Elements in Organisms.—Certain organisms are accumulators of definite elements. Some plants tolerate great quantities of elements that, even in small doses, are poisonous to other plants. Many elements, such as aluminum, silicon, sodium and chlorine, even though not essential to the species in question, accumulate in, and are concentrated by, many plants. Their concentration is independent of their value as plant nutrients; they are called ballast elements. Numerous trace elements are present in exceptionally high contents in many coal and brown-coal ashes as compared with their content in igneous rocks. The highest degree of enrichment is observed for boron, germanium, arsenic, molybdenum and bismuth, and the enrichment is independent of the chemical and geochemical character of the element. A

TABLE XIII.—*Average Total Composition of Living Matter*
(In per cent of dry weight)

Element	Adult man (Homo sapiens)	Alfalfa (Medicago sativa)	Element	Adult man (Homo sapiens)	Alfalfa (Medicago sativa)
C	48.43	45.37	P	1.58	0.28
O	23.70	41.04	Na	0.65	0.16
N	12.85	3.30	K	0.55	0.91
H	6.60	5.54	Cl	0.45	0.28
Ca	3.45	2.31	Mg	0.10	0.33
S	1.60	0.44	Total	99.96	99.96

TABLE XII.—*Distribution of Elements in Organisms*
(In per cent of body weight)

Invariable		Micro-constituents <0.05	Variable		
Primary 60-1	Secondary 1-0.05		Secondary	Micro-constituents	Contaminants, among others
H, C, N, O, P	Na, Mg, S, Cl, K, Ca, Fe	B, F, Si, Mn, Cu, I	Ti, V, Zn, Br	Li, Be, Al, Cr, Co, Ni, Ge, As, Rb, Sr, Nb, Mo, Ag, Cd, Sn, Cs, Ba, Pb, Ra	He, Ar, Se, Au, Hg, Bi, Tl

similar concentration of elements is observed in the ashes of many plants, as in those from old forests. Sometimes, as in the case of boron and manganese, the accumulation is biological and takes place in the living plant, but the concentration during decay of biogenic matter is geochemically more important. In this instance the rare elements present in the subsoil are taken up by soil solutions, enter the plants through the roots and are deposited at the sites of strongest evaporation, especially in the leaves, turning yellow and withering the content of most of the major nutrients decreases. The readily soluble compounds of the major nutrients are leached away by rain water, while the sparingly soluble or insoluble compounds of the rare elements, such as hydroxides and protein and humic complexes, are retained, partly by adsorption, in the humus layer. By such simple physical processes as recurrent evaporation and filtration the plants will finally cause the concentration of many elements in the topmost layers of forest soils.

The physical nature of the process is the reason why enrichment is independent of the chemical and geochemical properties of elements. Among others, silver, gold, zinc, thallium, germanium, tin, lead, cobalt and nickel become enriched in humus soils. The concentration principle, called the Goldschmidt enrichment principle, explains the concentration of elements in ashes in a similar way. The degree of enrichment depends on the plant species.

Prospecting.—Many plants are able to become accommodated according to the chemical composition of their substratum, that is, by concentrating certain elements (gold, zinc, copper and others) from soil above or near ore bodies. The ability of plants to indicate the chemical composition of soil is applied to prospecting for metal ores (geobotanical prospecting). The enrichment phenomena are also used for this purpose (biogeochemical prospecting). Compared with plants, animals appear to be able to concentrate only a limited number of trace elements—copper, vanadium, manganese, bromine and iodine. The absence of certain essential elements (cobalt, iron and copper) in the soil may cause regional deficiency diseases in plants, in grazing animals, and even in man. The accumulation of toxic elements, such as arsenic and selenium, by plants may also result in pathological conditions.

3. Photosynthesis.—Most of the energy needed in the functions of organisms is produced by respiration, which is the slow oxidation of organic matter. The ultimate principal products of decomposition is high enough to destroy all biogenic matter in approximately 20 years, except for the fact that a corresponding quantity of matter is concurrently synthesized. This decomposition and regeneration forms a part of the geochemical cycles of the elements present in biogenic matter. The biochemical process by which organic compounds are formed from carbon dioxide and water is called photosynthesis (*q.v.*). It takes place under the action of sunlight and is the fundamental biochemical process. From the first photosynthetic products a number of fats, proteins, nucleoproteins, pigments, enzymes, vitamins, cellulose and other substances are produced. They are oxidized and decomposed before or after the death of the plant. Photosynthesis is an important part in the cycle of oxygen. All oxygen present in the hydrosphere and atmosphere has repeatedly circulated in the cycle from the atmosphere through the biosphere into the hydrosphere and back during the time of existence of chlorophyll-bearing plants on the earth.

4. Geochemical Activity of Bacteria.—Among biogeochemically active agents, bacteria are of great importance in the biosphere and the adjoining geospheres. Their high rate of multiplication and great physiological activity cause their participation in chemical reactions involving considerable amounts of matter. They affect principally the geochemical cycles of carbon, nitrogen, phosphorus and sulfur. They are responsible for many changes in the pH of sediments and in the creation of reducing surroundings. Such surroundings favour the reduction or hydrogenation of organic matter and the formation and preservation of reduced substances, such as the petroleum hydrocarbons. The acids produced by bacteria may dissolve calcium carbonate and other inorganic constituents of sediments, and consequently bacteria affect the cycles of calcium and other elements. Other bacteria favour the precipitation of calcium carbonate and thereby preserve calcareous sediments. Some are able to attack several inorganic substances and almost any kind of organic matter; for instance, sulfate- and nitrate-reducing bacteria are usually abundant in marine sediments. Some are capable of fixing free atmospheric nitrogen, others liberate nitrogen from nitrites and nitrates, still others oxidize ammonia to nitrites and nitrates. Some species produce carbon monoxide, others methane or higher hydrocarbons, while others utilize methane in their metabolic processes. Bacteria may create environments harmful to other forms of life, but they also serve as sources of food and producers of plant nutrients. They are active in rock weathering and may be operative in the formation of sedimentary iron and manganese deposits.

5. Marine Biocycle.—The biosphere and the hydrosphere are closely connected biochemically because water is essential for all life. The marine biocycle is the most important part of the biosphere. Sea water is an especially suitable nutrient for algae, but the content of dissolved phosphate and nitrite regulates marine plant life and consequently affects animal life in the sea as well. The distribution of animals in the sea is also governed by the salinity of sea water.

Plants are the most important consumers of marine inorganic matter and form the supply of food for animal life in the sea. There is a constant life cycle between plants and animals and between the formation and decay of biogenic matter. Changes in chemical composition are produced by the growth and decay of marine organisms. The degree of enrichment of the elements by marine organisms is variable. Nitrogen and phosphorus have the highest degree of enrichment, but the content of carbon, silicon, fluorine, iron and copper is also considerably affected by biological activity.

6. Anthroposphere.—The part of the biosphere inhabited and governed by man is called the anthroposphere. It is increasingly active chemically. Man causes changes in the geochemical cycles of the elements and disturbs the natural balance in the uppermost geospheres. Artificial inorganic and organic compounds, minerals and rocks are produced in the anthroposphere as are metals, such as aluminum and magnesium, that never existed in the native state in the earth. The atmosphere and the hydrosphere are used as sources of raw materials.

Many chemical processes in the biosphere are steered and controlled by man. Noble metals tend to accumulate in the anthroposphere, and new heavy radioactive elements are made artificially by man. The geochemical cycle of carbon, of all elements, is the one that is most strongly affected by the industrial activities of man.

7. Bioliths.—The sediments formed by the geochemical activity of the biosphere are called bioliths. They are divided into caustobioliths (Gr. *kaustikos*, "capable of burning"), which are combustible, and acaustobioliths, which are incombustible. Carbonate, phosphate and siliceous sediments, among others, are acaustobioliths. The caustobioliths consist of humites, liptobioliths and sapropelites, which all are carbonaceous sediments containing native carbon or its oxidizable compounds. Some sulfur deposits of bacterial origin are also included. This group contains all solid, liquid and gaseous sediments used as fuel and is of great technical importance. The humites and liptobioliths are predominantly products of land and marsh vegetation, but the sapropelites contain decay products of many water organisms. The nature of the bioliths formed depends on the presence or absence of oxygen. If an adequate supply of oxygen is present, the decay of biogenic matter will produce carbon dioxide, water, sulfates and nitrogen, nitrates or ammonia. No solid carbon residue (coal) is produced, and only the resins and waxes of low reactivity may remain as liptobioliths. If the supply of oxygen is inadequate, the decomposition is incomplete, and small amounts of carbon-bearing substances will form. If oxygen is deficient at the start and completely absent later during the decomposition, peat will form. Peat is a typical humite sediment of vegetal origin, and humus is the final product of peat formation. If no oxygen is present at all, putrefaction will take place, and sapropel or foul mud and sapropelites are formed as its final product.

ucts. They are typically lacustrine or marine sediments, formed in stagnant water. Putrefaction is a kind of slow distillation in which proteins, fats, oils and waxes are converted into methane and other hydrocarbons, hydrogen sulfide, ammonia, hydrogen, carbon dioxide and many organic compounds. The formation of sapropel affects the cycle of many sulfophile elements by precipitating them as sulfides. If the chemical decomposition of organic matter under reducing conditions is carried still further, petroleum will form as the final product.

Humus.—During the decomposition of biogenic matter some residues are resistant to the action of microorganisms and accumulate, causing the formation of substances called humus. The formation of humus involves the removal, from their cycles, of a part of carbon, nitrogen, phosphorus, sulfur, potassium and other elements which are made available for plants; consequently the formation of humus regulates plant life. It is a highly complex mixture of amorphous organic substances which contains some inorganic compounds of phosphorus, sulfur, iron, calcium and magnesium. It is also in a state of constant decomposition and forms a colloidal system. The colloidal humus-bearing solutions are of importance in weathering because of their dissolving action on detrital minerals; iron and manganese, for instance, are brought into solution as humic complexes. Humus is an important substance of coal. Various types called water humus form under water and may be converted into peat.

Soil.—Humus also plays an essential part in the formation of soil. Soils, composed of a mixture of inorganic and organic substances, support the continental plant life. Their general character depends on the nature of the weathering of their substratum, climate, relief, biological activity and time. Physical, chemical and biological processes are active in their formation. Quartz, clay minerals, limonite, hematite and some carbonate and sulfate minerals are the most important mineralogical constituents of soils. Organic matter greatly affects the physical properties and fertility of soil. The humic complexes are by far their most important organic constituents. Ammonia, carbon dioxide, phosphates and sulfates form during decomposition of soil humus. Ammonia is gradually converted into nitrates. These compounds greatly influence the fertility of soil and form a supply of elements essential for the synthesis of organic substances by plants. (*See also* SOIL.)

Coal, Petroleum and Other Products.—Sapropel (*q.v.*) and peat are accumulations from which coal is formed. Peat, brown coal or lignite and the different varieties of coal are the most important humite sediments. There is no sharp distinction between peat and coal. During coalification, which finally produces anthracite, the carbon content increases, but the content of hydrogen, nitrogen and, especially, oxygen, decreases by the formation and escape of carbon dioxide, water, methane and nitrogen. The coals are divided into humic coals and sapropelic coals according to their origin. Various transitions exist between the sapropelic coals and from them to oil shales and humic coals. The coals are essentially colloidal substances consisting of highly complex compounds of carbon, hydrogen and oxygen. Other more important constituents include nitrogen, sulfur and phosphorus. Sulfides of iron, lead, copper, zinc, nickel and other metals are incidental constituents of coal. Silicon, aluminum and iron are the principal constituents of coal ashes, in which many trace elements are concentrated. The chemical composition of the plant material changes continuously after its deposition, and peat, brown coal, coal and anthracite represent different stages of incoalation or coal formation. The process is materially accelerated by elevated temperatures.

Waxes, resins, fats and oils are able to resist chemical decomposition and may become concentrated to make liptobioliths. They are also responsible for the characteristic properties of sapropel and sapropelic coals, and of some peats. Liptobioliths include resin, wax and spore coals and fossil amber or succinite.

Petroleum is a complex mixture of liquid hydrocarbons in which a number of gaseous and solid hydrocarbons are dissolved. The crude oils also contain small amounts of numerous organic compounds of nitrogen, oxygen, phosphorus, sulfur and some hydrogen sulfide, carbon dioxide and nitrogen. Many metals, notably nickel, vanadium, lead and iron, are present in petroleum, perhaps as metalorganic porphyrin complexes. Many trace elements are constituents of petroleum ashes. Few, if any, of the petroleum hydrocarbons are unsaturated, and all are optically active. The chemical composition of the crude oils varies according to the substances from which they were formed. The mother substance of petroleum consists of plant and animal remains in near-shore marine sapropelic sediments. The remains are partly of marine origin, partly carried to the sea by rivers and deposited under essentially anaerobic conditions. During the formation of petroleum, bacterial action occurred along with the work of physical, chemical and geological factors. The highly reducing environment favoured the hydrogenation of organic matter and the preservation of the petroleum hydrocarbons. Later changes in the composition of petroleum probably were caused by radioactivity. Brines related to petroleum both geologically and genetically occur in connection with most petroleum deposits.

Ozocerite and asphalt are often found together with petroleum and are regarded as solid oxidation and polymerization products of the crudes. Ozocerite is a mixture of solid hydrocarbons. Some asphalts are remarkably rich in nickel and vanadium.

Natural gases are either inorganic gases connected with igneous activity, gases produced by carbonization in the biosphere (marsh gas and gases from coal mines) and gases connected with petroleum deposits, or the natural gases proper. Petroligenic natural gas contains the most volatile constituents of petroleum deposits and is concentrated in the uppermost parts of the oil-bearing beds. Most of its constituents are of biogenic origin. The chief constituents of petroligenic natural gas are highly volatile hydrocarbons. Nitrogen, oxygen, carbon monoxide and dioxide, hydrogen sulfide, helium and hydrogen in varying amounts are its normal constituents; radon and argon are sometimes present. Petroligenic natural gases are divided into hydrocarbon, nitrogen, carbon dioxide and helium types. Many of the rich nitrogen gases are rich in helium also.

See also BIOCHEMISTRY.

VI. GEOCHEMICAL EVOLUTION OF THE EARTH

The study of the chemical evolution of the earth is one of the main tasks of geochemistry. For performing this task, the results of cosmochemistry, or chemistry of the universe, are particularly helpful, partly because of the role of geochemistry as a chapter in universal planetary chemistry and partly because of the close relationships that link nuclear physics, physical chemistry and astrophysics together.

Traditional dogmatic geochemical speculation has dealt with the formation of a once totally molten earth largely according to the processes taking place in ore-smelting furnaces. This dogma, however, was slowly giving ground by the 1950s, and by the 1960s considerable evidence indicated that the earth and other planets were formed by condensation and accumulation from a dust cloud at low temperatures. H. C. Urey developed the new approach in detail, largely on the basis of thermodynamic considerations.

The early stages of the primordial evolution of the earth are usually referred to as the astronomical time in the earth's history. The geological time started when a stable crust had formed and the exogenic processes first started thereon.

According to Urey, the final accumulation of the earth took place, at a temperature of approximately o° C., from small planetesimals containing metallic iron, carbon, iron carbide, titanium nitride and some ferrous sulfide. A gas phase had mainly been lost during the previous, high-temperature stage, and only small amounts of hydrogen, nitrogen, inert gases, water vapour, methane and hydrogen sulfide were left. The iron core of the earth accumulated slowly during the geological history of the earth from an almost uniform mixture of metallic iron and silicates. Consequently, the earth was not molten at the time of the accumulation of its materials.

See also COSMOGONY.

1. **Evolution of the Lithosphere.**—The lithosphere was formed by the separation of the iron and silicate phases and by fractional crystallization in the silicate shell. This differentiation is still going on. Crystallization caused the arrangement of the sili-

cate shell according to the specific gravity of the crystallizing phases. The silicic magmas of low specific gravity and the aqueous residual solutions tend to rise upward. Heavy atoms actually should become concentrated in the lower levels of the lithosphere, but pneumatolytic and hydrothermal phenomena and concentrate these atoms in the uppermost parts of the differentiation counteract the present distribution of the phases of different specific gravity. The modification of the surface layer by endogenic and exogenic processes started with the formation of a stable solid crust. During the earliest phase of geological history volcanic and plutonic activity probably took place on a larger scale than they ever did later. The exogenic cycle has grown in activity with the formation of the hydrosphere and the evolution of an atmosphere containing oxygen. Metamorphic and metasomatic processes are active in the present modification of the composition of the upper lithosphere, just as they were before. Metasomatic processes (see which involve the introduction of new substances into rock (see METASOMATISM) tend to equalize the composition, while exogenic processes cause a chemical differentiation. At present, differentiation predominates over equalization in the earth as a whole. Crystallization and differentiation by crystallization still cause chemical dissimilarity in the upper lithosphere, and light granitic magmas still wander upward through the crust.

The primary distribution of the elements in the various layers of the upper lithosphere may originally have been uniform in all parts of the globe, but at present there are many instances of an inhomogeneity in the upper lithosphere, in particular, among the granites which appear to be the more deficient in certain trace elements the greater their age. A secular migration of the elements on a global scale may take place in the crust causing the chemical inhomogeneity. The explanation of the global migration and differentiation is the continuous self-repeating granitization that is believed to take place in connection with the mountain-building processes. The granitization also enhances the silicic character of the uppermost layers of the lithosphere.

2. Evolution of the Atmosphere.—There is much evidence to indicate that the present atmosphere and hydrosphere of the earth are of secondary origin. It is unlikely that the primordial atmosphere contained free oxygen. According to Urey the primitive reducing atmosphere contained water vapour, hydrogen, ammonia, methane and some hydrogen sulfide. Hydrogen escaped from the gravitational field of the earth, and water was photochemically decomposed into hydrogen and oxygen in the upper levels of the atmosphere. The oxygen formed was consumed in the gradual oxidation of ammonia to nitrogen and water, and of methane to carbon dioxide and water. Finally an excess of free atmospheric oxygen was formed, and an oxidizing atmosphere appeared, perhaps about 700,000,000 or 800,000,000 years ago. The formation of free oxygen is, geochemically, the most important step in the evolution of the atmosphere. Most or all free oxygen present in the atmosphere has been gradually produced from water by photosynthesis taking place in chlorophyll-bearing plants. The small initial supply of oxygen required by plants to make respiration possible was probably a product of the photochemical dissociation of water vapour. Carbon dioxide, like the bulk of water, was gradually added to the atmosphere by volcanic emanations, but its content has not remained stable. At the present time much carbon dioxide is added to the atmosphere as a result of various activities in the anthroposphere. The content of carbon dioxide is bound to increase until the regulating mechanism (i.e., equilibrium between the hydrosphere and the atmosphere) becomes active. All carbon dioxide is finally bound in carbonates during weathering, and chances are small that it will ever be completely released by endogenic processes. Similarly, nitrogen also may be largely produced from weathering. The inert gases are released into the atmosphere by volcanic emanations and weathering of rocks. Helium and argon are constantly produced by radioactive decay. Hydrogen and helium still escape from the uppermost levels of the atmosphere.

3. Evolution of the Hydrosphere.—The present hydrosphere is of secondary origin as is the atmosphere. The primeval hydrosphere must have been much smaller than the present hydrosphere. It is possible that the amount of water in the hydrosphere is still increasing. Even though much water is removed by weathering and sedimentation, it is, at least partly, returned during the slow vertical migration of matter in the upper lithosphere. Much water vapour is given off by the volcanoes, but this water is probably largely of meteoric origin. Changes have occurred in the chemical composition of the oceans during the geological evolution. Many substances, partly produced by rock weathering, accumulate constantly in the ocean. Vast amounts of volatile substances released by volcanic activity are finally transported into the sea. It is possible that all material deposited in the abyssal regions is permanently lost to the cycle.

4. Evolution of the Biosphere.—It is likely that life started soon after the earth had cooled to a proper temperature and that it covered the earth in a geologically short time. The oldest trace of biological activity is finely disseminated biogenic carbon in slates in Manitoba with an approximate age of 2.55×10^9 years. It appears that vast amounts of complex prebiological organic compounds were synthesized during the reducing stage in the atmospheric evolution in thermochemical, photochemical and electrochemical reactions. Life probably started during the change of the reducing atmosphere into an oxidizing atmosphere. Plant life probably could not start until there was some free oxygen in the atmosphere. A landmark in the development of animals is the appearance of the first calcareous skeletons in the Cambrian, about 500,000,000 years ago. The formation of animals is one of the most important processes in the evolution of the biosphere. The anthroposphere as a powerful geochemical agent has been operative but a few hundred years.

The geochemical evolution of the earth did not stop with the formation of a solid crust, the hydrosphere and the atmosphere. Actually, the evolution has continued throughout the geological history of the earth, and new stages have been added, such as the formation of the biosphere. The earth is changeable chemically, and its geochemical evolution still continues.

See also EARTH.

BIBLIOGRAPHY.—F. W. Clarke, *The Data of Geochemistry*, 5th ed., U.S. Geological Survey Bull. 770 (1924); K. Rankama and T. G. Sahama, *Geochemistry*, with bibliography (1952); B. Mason, *Principles of Geochemistry*, 2nd ed. (1958); A A Saukow, *Geochemie* (1953); V. M. Goldschmidt, *Geochemistry*, with bibliography, ed. by A. Muir (1954); K. Rankama, *Isotope Geology*, with bibliography (1954); H. H. Nininger, *Out of the Sky* (1952); S. Glasstone, *Sourcebook on Atomic Energy* (1950); B. Gutenberg (ed.), *Internal Constitution of the Earth*, 2nd ed. (1951); C. W. Stillwell, *Crystal Chemistry*, "International Chemical Series" (1938); R. C. Evans, *An Introduction to Crystal Chemistry* (1939); L. Pauling, *The Nature of the Chemical Bond and the Structure of Molecules and Crystals* (1948); C. Palache, H. Berman and C. Frondel, *The System of Mineralogy of James Dwight Dana and Edwin Salisbury Dana*, 7th ed., vol. ii (1944), vol. ii (1951); H. Strunz, *Mineralogische Tabellen*, 2nd ed. (1949); F. J. Turner and J. Verhoogen, *Igneous and Metamorphic Petrology* (1951); T. F. W. Barth, *Theoretical Petrology* (1952); W. Eitel, *The Physical Chemistry of the Silicates* (1954); F. J. Pettijohn, *Sedimentary Rocks*, "Harper's Geoscience Series," 2nd ed. (1957); H. Ramberg, *The Origin of Metamorphic and Metasomatic Rocks* (1952); H. U. Sverdrup, M. W. Johnson and R. H. Fleming, *The Oceans: Their Physics, Chemistry, and General Biology* (1942); K. Kalle, *Der Stoffhaushalt des Meeres* (1943); G. P. Kuiper (ed.), *The Atmospheres of the Earth and Planets*, rev. ed. (1952); K. Scharrer, *Biochemie der Spurenelemente* (1941); H. C. Urey, *The Planets: Their Origin and Development* (1952). (K. R.)

GEOCHRONOLOGY, a term first used by the geologist H. S. Williams in 1893 to designate studies in which a time scale is applied to the evolution of the earth and its inhabitants. Events are dated by giving the age in years B.P. (before present), though for pre-Pleistocene events the margins of error greatly exceed the difference between the time of the birth of Christ and the present. The number of days in a year may have decreased slowly from, say, 400 days about 400,000,000 years ago to the present 365 days. But in geochronology, units of a year of the present duration are employed.

Seasonal changes may be recorded in the annual organic growth of corals or in tree rings (dendrochronology, q.v., is useful back to 3,000 years). Sedimentation of mud in glacial lakes may show similar seasonal patterns (varves), and estimates of the duration in actual years is then possible (see VARVE ANALYSIS). The greatest duration of time that has been determined by this method is a period of about 8,000,000 years of the nonglacial lacustrine Green River sediments (Eocene) in Wyoming. But these direct count methods are only exceptionally applicable.

Many geological methods have been used to estimate duration by the rate of processes on the earth's surface. These include rate of evolution as revealed by fossil evidence, rate of denudation (or average rate of crustal uplift), and notably rate of sedimentation (or average rate of subsidence). (See FOSSIL; GEOLOGY: *Physical Geology*.) The last gives a useful proportional time scale over long time spans. At the end of the 19th century attempts were made to estimate the age of the earth by the rate of increase in the salinity of the sea and by the rate of cooling of the earth. The results obtained were far too low because, for instance, it was not then realized how much salt is stored as halite (rock salt) deposits in the earth's crust, or that substantial heat might be contributed to the earth by radioactivity.

The principal and most nearly accurate measure of pre-Pleistocene geological time depends on the rate of decay of naturally occurring radioactive isotopes. (See RADIOACTIVITY.) This should be independent of all normal geological conditions and so give an independent (absolute) age. Those with a half-life long enough to be useful in measuring geologic time are few—mainly uranium, thorium, potassium, rubidium, and carbon. Radiometric methods employing these depend on the unstable element being trapped in the material, as on crystallization, and on little, or known, contamination and subsequent loss.

Uranium and thorium as in pitchblende-uraninite and thorianite, after many changes (radioactive decay, or disintegration) give rise to lead and helium, and the methods first used, on E. Rutherford's suggestion in 1903, were intended to measure the lead/uranium or helium/lead ratios. While giving a first reliable indication of the magnitude of geological time, the method has not proved suitable for precise application in geochronology. With the advent of the mass spectrograph and other advances, all modern radiometric work depends on the routine determination of isotopes. Thus, for example, isotopes of uranium give rise to isotopes of lead, plus isotopes of helium, plus a number of beta particles; the number of years required for one-half the atoms of uranium to disintegrate is known as the half-life:

$$U^{238} \rightarrow Pb^{206} + 8He^4 + 6\beta, \text{ half-life } 4,498,000,000 \text{ yr.}$$

The abundant mineral galena (lead sulfide) may be used to determine an age from the isotopes of lead alone (the common lead method). However, lead minerals are not convenient to use stratigraphically. Radium, an intermediate element in the uranium-lead decay series, is distributed in river and sea waters and may be concentrated by organic agency in deep sea deposits. Use of a percent of equilibrium method involving many assumptions may give an estimate of age back to 200,000–300,000 years. Zircon, a common accessory mineral in granites, is widely used for age determination by the measurement of the rate of disintegration of traces of uranium or thorium contained in the crystal lattice.

The rubidium-strontium method depends on the conversion of rubidium-87, half-life about 50,000,000,000 yr., into strontium-87. It has been employed successfully, using common minerals of older metamorphic and igneous rocks, *e.g.*, micas and feldspars.

The potassium-argon method depends on the conversion of potassium-40, half-life 11,850,000,000 yr., into argon-40.

This is complicated by the fact that a proportion of K^{40} also gives rise to Ca^{40}, so the branching ratio must also be known. Potassium is widely distributed in common rocks, for example in the glauconite and sylvite of sedimentary rocks, and the micas, feldspars, and hornblendes of metamorphic and igneous rocks; consequently this has become the most generally used method. Both potassium-argon and rubidium-strontium methods are improving rapidly with better analytical techniques, and the half-lives (or decay constants) which have been difficult to determine except indirectly by comparison with each other and the lead method are also gaining precision. Thus experimental errors of the order of 5% or 10% were, in favourable circumstances, being reduced to 1% or less in the late 1960s.

Radiocarbon, or carbon-14, is the other isotope in general use and differs from the foregoing in having a relatively short half-life (5,568 ± 30 years), which means that it can only be used effectively for ages less than about 40,000 years. Its continued existence on earth depends on continuous generation by cosmic rays ($N^{14} \rightarrow C^{14}$). Steady production and decay rates are assumed without inconsistency, thus providing the atmosphere with a constant proportion of radiocarbon. The carbon of living organisms is derived from the atmosphere, but on death metabolic interchange ceases and the radiocarbon in the tissues slowly decays. Thus the analysis of carbon isotopes in fossil wood, bones, etc., gives results which are invaluable, especially for archaeological studies in late Quaternary stratigraphy (see MAN, EVOLUTION OF: *Estimation of Geological Antiquity*). (See also RADIOCARBON DATING.)

"Apparent ages" are the figures resulting from these isotopic or radiometric methods. They seldom give an unambiguous answer and need careful interpretation and qualification. Ages so determined are used to calibrate the sequence of geological events. Such history may be known in very considerable detail by other stratigraphical methods, but yet may lack a time scale until critical events in the sequence have been dated. Other events may then be fitted by their ages into this sequence, or the rate and timing of various processes may be found. Stratigraphy depends on many methods of correlation, among which radiometric methods are becoming increasingly important, though they are still less precise than paleontological or climatic correlation in favourable circumstances. Precambrian stratigraphy already leans very heavily on radiometric methods (see STRATIGRAPHY).

Examples of methods especially applicable to the Quaternary are the solar radiation method, which depends on recognizing a climatic sequence as revealed, for example, by fossil pollen grains and spores (see PALYNOLOGY), and the exceptional possibility of correlating a sequence of variable seasons, as by varve analysis. Paleomagnetic methods based on the determination of magnetic poles (which have shifted throughout time) from fossil, or remanent, magnetism in rocks provide additional data on the history of the earth (see GEOMAGNETISM); and archeomagnetism, the orientation toward paleomagnetic poles of magnetic particles in fire-hardened clay in ancient pottery kilns and fire pits, has proved useful in dating archaeological finds. Based on data from all these methods a rough time scale of events is now in general use; *e.g.*, earth formed at about 5,000,000,000 years, oldest rocks older than 4,000,000,000 years but only a few examples are known older than 3,000,000,000 years (when primitive algae apparently lived). The base of the Cambrian, marked by the presence of well-organized animal fossils suitable for stratigraphical use, is dated at about 570,000,000 years.

See further GEOLOGY: *Historical Geology*, especially the section *Paleontology and the Scale of Time*, and the chart *Geologic Column and Scale of Time*. For archaeological applications see ARCHAEOLOGY: *The Materials of Archaeology*. See also PALEONTOLOGY; COSMIC RAYS; ISOTOPE: *Naturally Occurring Radioactive Isotopes*; and references under "Geochronology" in the Index.

BIBLIOGRAPHY.—F. E. Zeuner, *Dating the Past*, 4th ed. (1958) discusses the discovery or invention, development, and application of the many and diverse methods of geochronology, with bibliography. *See* also E. I. Hamilton, *Applied Geochronology* (1965); National Academy of Science, *Geochronology of North America* (1965). For surveys of current world literature *see* U.S. Department of the Interior, Geological Survey, *Geophysical Abstracts* (monthly).

GEODE, a hollow nodule of stone formed in sedimentary rock and having walls lined with crystals, among which calcite and quartz are the commonest. Other not uncommon minerals are dolomite, chalcedony, barite and celestite. Exterior surfaces of geodes are usually irregular. The wall minerals may have been deposited by circulating waters as the enclosing sediments became lithified or subsequent thereto.

A common method of origin of the cavities of geodes is by deposition of materials from solution along structural and fracture surfaces of shells, thus producing enlargement of original shell cavities and, at the same time, or subsequently, lining the cavities with crystalline materials.

(W. H. TL.)

GEODESY

GEODESY. Geodesy, one of the oldest sciences of the world, has both scientific and practical purposes. Its scientific mission is to determine the size and shape of the earth and, in co-operation with other sciences, to study the internal structure of the earth. The practical task of geodesy is to carry out the measurements and computations needed for making accurate and reliable maps of the earth's surface.

This article is divided into the following sections:

I. Objectives
II. Early History
III. Ellipsoidal Era of Geodesy
IV. Geodial Era of Geodesy
V. Modern Arc-Measuring Methods
VI. Physical Geodesy
VII. Methods and Achievements of Physical Geodesy
VIII. Measuring Instruments Used in Geodesy
IX. Isostasy
X. Variation of Latitude
XI. International Geodetic Organizations

I. OBJECTIVES

The most important practical objective of geodesy is the determination of the exact co-ordinates of control points on the earth's surface. When two co-ordinates of a control point are known, for instance, its geographic latitude and longitude and, in addition, its elevation above sea level, the exact position of this point on the earth's surface is known. In mapping large areas, such as a whole state or country, not only the curvature of the earth but also its flattening must be considered. The English usage of the word geodesy includes all the measurements, computations and objectives mentioned above.

A reliable control-point system is a prerequisite for accurate maps. It may be compared with a skeleton which has to be covered with flesh and blood, i.e., by a filling-in of details. The filling-in process also belongs to the domain of geodesy, though an essential part of this work can be done on the basis of aerial pictures, by the methods of photogrammetry (q.v.). The elevations of the control points and of other measured points are obtained by precise trigonometric or barometric leveling, methods which are discussed in the article SURVEYING.

Although it may seem easy to determine control points on the earth's surface merely by making astronomical observations of the latitude and longitude at these points, this method is not satisfactory because astronomical observations are not sufficiently accurate, the highest accuracy obtained by the astronomic method being of the order $0''.2$ to $0''.3$ (arc seconds), or 6 to 9 m. along the earth's surface. Furthermore, serious errors will be caused by the irregularities of the earth's figure, to which the astronomical observations refer.

The earth's figure is that of a surface called the geoid, which over the sea is the average sea level and under the continents the imaginary continuation of sea level. The visible and invisible mass anomalies of the earth cause essential irregularities to the geoid and bring about essential errors, sometimes exceeding a mile, when distances between control points are determined astronomically.

Because of these facts we must use as a reference surface a regular mathematical surface that fits the geoid as closely as possible. This surface is an ellipsoid of revolution called a reference ellipsoid. Its surface is in some areas below, in other regions above, the geoid. The angle of tilt between the ellipsoid surface and geoid surface, or between the normal of ellipsoid and the normal of geoid, or plumb line, is called the deflection of the vertical, or deflection of plumb line.

Mathematically speaking the geoid is an equipotential or level surface, characterized by the fact that over its entire extent the so-called potential function is constant. This potential function is a result of the effect of the gravitational attraction of the earth mass, combined with the effect caused by the rotation of the earth about its axis. Since, if air masses are disregarded, there are at the oceans no masses above the sea level, mean sea level is a part of the geoid surface. In the continental areas the geoid is an imaginary sea-level surface defined by spirit level. If small sea-level canals were dug into the interior of the continents or if open-ended pipes, like inverted siphons, were run from the land out into the ocean, the surface sought would be defined physically at various points by the level of the water in these canals or pipes.

To get a system of geodetic control points it is necessary to have the geodetic datum for these points. The geodetic datum is completely determined when we know five quantities: the geographic latitude ϕ and longitude λ of the initial point of the geodetic datum, a direction (azimuth A of the direction between the initial point and some other control point) and finally the equator radius, a, and the flattening, f, of the reference ellipsoid.

In other words, we need a point from which to compute, a direction in which to compute and a surface along which to compute. The co-ordinates of any control point computed in this geodetic system are comparable with one another. Their accuracy depends on the accuracy of the astronomical and geodetic measurements.

If only one of these five quantities changes, the whole geodetic system will also change. Until recent decades most countries had their own initial point of geodetic datum; therefore their geodetic systems were, of course, different even if they used the same reference ellipsoid.

One problem in geodesy is to obtain sufficiently accurate dimensions for the reference ellipsoid. Another difficulty appears in converting the existing geodetic systems to one world system. A third difficulty is caused by the fact that all geodetic observations have to be referred to the geoid, but the computation of the co-ordinates must be carried out along the reference ellipsoid. To get rid of this "dualism" we have to know the distance, N, called warping or undulation of the geoid or the geoid distance, and the tilt between these two surfaces at the initial points of all these geodetic systems. It is also difficult to get the geodetic datum by precise leveling since the sea level is not constant but is affected by geological changes which raise or lower the continents and the ocean beds.

To determine the earth ellipsoid it is necessary to solve two problems, one geodetic and the other astronomical. The length, l, of an arc along the earth's surface must be measured in some direction. In the astronomical problem the central angle, v, corresponding to the measured arc, must be measured. By the aid of l and v the earth radius R can be obtained from the elementary formula $l : 2\pi R = v° : 360°$, or from $R = l/v$, if v is given in radians. The longer the measured arc and the more accurate the astronomical observations, the more accurately R can be obtained. Earlier the arcs l were measured at, or at least close to, the meridian directions, because v was relatively easy to determine in the north-south direction.

II. EARLY HISTORY

It is surprising that ancient civilized peoples, such as the Babylonians and Egyptians, who were interested in astronomy did not realize that the earth is a sphere, since its spherical shape should have been easy to deduce from several phenomena. The earth's shadow during the moon's eclipse has the shape of a circular arc, a shape that only a spherical earth can cause. The stars, while south in meridian, appear much higher in the sky when viewed from Alexandria than from Athens. When a ship approaches port, one first sees the masts and only later the hull. But the significance of these phenomena dawned on mankind only slowly.

The co-ordinates of latitude and longitude were used at the suggestion of Hipparchus (fl. 146-127 B.C.). Because the world known to the ancients was long in the east-west direction from Spain to Persia and relatively short in the north-south direction from the Alps to north Africa, longitude was counted in the east-west direction, latitude in the north-south direction.

Still, Homer, in approximately 900-800 B.C., thought that the earth was a convex disk surrounded by the Oceanus stream. According to the other Greeks of that time the earth plate was supported by four elephants standing on a big turtle. The philosopher Pythagoras (fl. 532 B.C.) was perhaps the first who thought the earth to be a sphere. Hipparchus and Aristotle (384-322 B.C.), however, came to the same conclusion. Eratosthenes (c. 276-c. 192 B.C.), however, is considered the founder of geodesy because he was the man who first measured the size of the earth, assuming that it was a sphere.

With the advent of accurate time signals and perfected clocks it became possible to determine the geographic longitude as accurately as the latitude, and arcs in any direction could be measured with equal accuracy.

This astrogeodetic method was used by Eratosthenes. He knew that in upper Egypt in Syene, now called Aswan, on the Nile, the sun shone at noon in mid-summer vertically down into a well. His measurements showed that in Alexandria the direction of the sunbeams at the same time of the year at noon made with the vertical direction an angle 360°/50 or 7.2° (see fig. 1). Supposing that Syene and Alexandria were at the same meridian, he concluded that the centre angle v_1 between Syene and Alexandria was 7.2°.

As to the measurement of the arc l he was told that a camel caravan needed 50 days to travel from Alexandria to Syene. Assuming that the rather constant speed of camels was 100 stadia a day, the distance between Alexandria and Syene would be 5,000 stadia and the length of the whole meridian circle 50 times larger. So he obtained for a meridian circle the length 250,000 stadia. If the Attic stade, 185 metres, were used, the length of the whole meridian was, according to Eratosthenes, 46,250,000 m. This value is 16% too large, because the real length of the meridian by the definition of metre is, or at least used to be, 40,000,000 m. Fig. 1 also indicates how, by using the same principle, the U.S. army map service (F. W. Hough) determined the value for the equatorial radius of the earth as 6,378,260 m., using also the 100° long arc (central angle v_2) Tornio, Fin.-Cape Town, S.Af., and the best available measuring instruments.

Considering that Alexandria and Syene are not at the same meridian, that the sun 2,200 years ago at noon in mid-summer could not shine in a vertical direction into the well of Syene, and that the measurement of the arc using the camel as a measuring instrument was certainly not accurate, it is surprising that Eratosthenes's result was not more in error. He deserves full credit, however, because his method was right in principle. Modern geodesists follow the same principle but make the astronomical observations with fine observation instruments and measure the length of the arc by triangulation. This important method was conceived by the Dutch scientist, Willebrord Snell (Snellius), in 1615.

The second known determination of the earth's radius was done by Poseidonius (c. 135-50 B.C.), who measured the distance between Rhodus and Alexandria on the basis of the time a boat needed to sail from Alexandria to Rhodus. The corresponding central angle was measured astronomically. He realized that the star Canopus was on the horizon when seen from Rhodus island at the same time that the sunbeams in Alexandria made an angle of 7.5° with the horizon. Consequently, the central angle was, according to his observations, 7.5°. The radius value obtained by him was 11% too large.

Nine hundred years passed before the next measurement of the earth's dimensions was carried out at the suggestion of the caliph Abdullah al Mamun (A.D. 786-833) at the Zinjar plateau close to Baghdad. The Arabs made an actual measurement of the length of the arc by using wooden rods. They also made relatively accurate astronomical observations. According to the Arabs the following relation between the different length units exist:

$$1° = \frac{170}{3} \text{ mi.}$$

1 mi = 4,000 ell
1 ell = 24 in.
1 in. = 6 barley seeds
1 barley seed = 3.526 mm. (according to Snell)

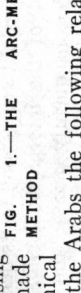

FIG. 1.—THE ARC-MEASURING METHOD

Using these units, the Arabs obtained the meridian quadrant of 10,359 km., only 3.6% too long.

III. ELLIPSOIDAL ERA OF GEODESY

A new epoch began in geodesy with the use of triangulation. The idea of triangulation was apparently conceived by the Danish astronomer Tycho Brahe before the end of the 16th century and was used by him to establish a geodetic connection between Ven Island and the main islands of Denmark. Triangulation was developed as a science, however, by Snell, who also first used it for measuring the dimensions of the earth. The triangle chain of Snell had 33 triangles and rendered for the meridian quadrant a value as much too small (3.4%) as that of the Arabs was too large.

The triangulation of Jean Picard (1620-82), which extended from Paris to north 1°.2 and consisted of 13 triangles, is methodically important because in it the telescope was first used for astronomical observations and logarithm tables were used in computing the results. Picard also measured by wooden rods a base line in the modern sense of this term. This measurement was significant also in that Sir Isaac Newton, when deriving his law of gravitation in 1665-66, used the equator radius value obtained by Picard.

The idea of triangulation is to measure only the angles of consecutive triangles. If in addition, as in fig. 2(A), the length of one side, B_1B_2, of one triangle has been measured, all sides of the other triangles can be computed from the sine theorem. The triangulation points are chosen on hilltops and mountains so that the neighbouring points A, C, D, E can be seen from point B and thus the angles between them can be measured. When the length of the sides is known, the distance between any point (e.g., between A and F) can be computed along the reference ellipsoid, and thus all points of the triangulation can be referred to the same geodetic system. Triangulation can have the shape of a triangle chain as shown in fig. 2(A); or that of an "envelope chain" (fig. 2[B]), much used in the United States; also a triangle net as shown in fig. 2(C).

One side of a triangle is obtained directly by measuring the field base line as accurately as possible. In principle, one base line for every triangulation system would be sufficient. Because of the impossibility of avoiding errors in observation, several base lines, each at an interval of 200 to 300 mi., are measured. Then an adjustment computation is made to take care of the observation errors. For instance, the sum of the angles of every triangle must be 180° + ε; ε is a small quantity called the spherical excess of the triangle in question and is caused by the sphericity of the earth. In a similar way, for every measured base line, computation of its length along the triangles beginning from another base line must give exactly the same length as the measurement itself gives. When computing a closed loop of triangles it is necessary to get for the beginning point its original co-ordinates. So in triangulation there are numerous conditions that the observations must satisfy: the angle control, side control, base-line control and co-ordinate control. All these will be handled in the geodetic adjustment computation based on the "least square" method, which means that the observations have to be corrected so that the sum of the squares of the corrections is a minimum. The main purpose of the adjustment computation is to eliminate the discrepancy in the triangulation net so that exactly the same co-ordinates will be arrived at for any of the triangulation points, regardless of which way they have been computed from the initial point. This does not mean, however, that the errors themselves have been eliminated. The observation errors exist but their effect has been made as harmless as possible.

The best results can be obtained, however, only when the observation errors are as small as possible. Therefore, in triangulation much attention is given to the accuracy of the measurements. For instance, the angles of every triangle are measured not once or twice but as many as 24 times. Similarly the base lines are measured several times and by different measuring wires to reduce the observation error.

Methods of triangulation have been so perfected that the accuracy of the base lines is from 1:2,000,000 to 1:4,000,000 of the length of the base line.

The period from Eratosthenes to Picard may be called the spherical era of geodesy, because the earth was thought to be a sphere. The geodetic problem was then relatively simple. It was necessary only to determine the radius of the sphere. The new era, the ellipsoidal era, began with the theoretical studies of Newton and his contemporary Christian Huygens. The physical proofs of the sphericity of the earth had so far been proofs of its general rotundity. In the Ptolemaic astronomy it had seemed natural to assume—for reasons usually of a metaphysical sort—that the earth was an exact sphere; but with the growing conviction that the Copernican system was true and that the earth rotates about its axis, and with the advance in mechanical knowledge due chiefly to Newton and Huygens, it seemed natural to think of the earth as an oblate spheroid flattened at the poles. There was also the experimental evidence of the astronomer Jean Richer (1630–1696), who found that his clock, regulated to keep time at Paris, lost $2\frac{1}{4}$ min. a day at Cayenne in South America, where he had been sent to make observations.

But the arguments from theory and the evidence of Richer's clock, confirmed by the experience of other observers, seemed to be contradicted by the work of Jean Dominique Cassini and his son Jacques, in France. If the earth is an oblate spheroid, the length of a degree of latitude must increase from the equator to the pole, but the Cassinis, continuing the arc of Picard north to Dunkerque and south to the boundary of Spain, came to the opposite conclusion. They divided the measured arc into two parts, one northward, the other southward of Paris. The length of a meridian degree north of Paris was 111,017 m., or 265 m. shorter than one south of Paris (111,282 m.). This suggested either a prolate (egg-shaped) earth or errors in observation. In any case, their observations contradicted the idea of a flattened earth.

It may seem strange that the length of the meridian degree is longer at the pole than it is at lower latitudes and at the equator. One might think that the reverse would be true, because the pole radius is shorter than the equator radius. Fig. 3 shows, however, why the length of a meridian degree increases with the latitude. The central angles v at the equator and pole are equal, but the radius EC_1 (radius of curvature) of the meridian AE at the equator is shorter than the radius of curvature PC_2 at the pole P. Consequently, the meridian degree PB at the pole is longer than the meridian degree EA at the equator. The pole radius PD and the equator radius ED are quite different from the radii of curvature EC_1 and PC_2.

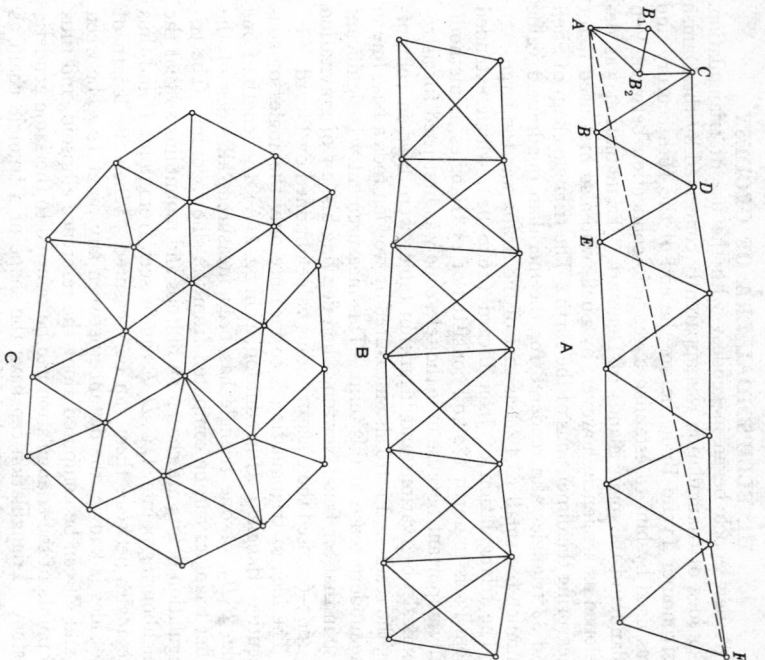

FIG. 2.—THE PRINCIPLE OF TRIANGULATION
(A) single triangulation chain, (B) "envelope" chain, (C) triangulation net

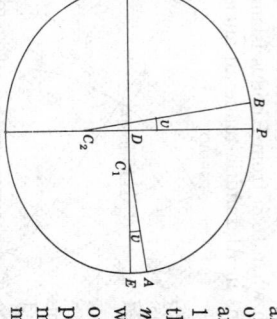

FIG. 3.—THE RELATIONSHIP BETWEEN MERIDIAN DEGREE AND LATITUDE

Because of the Cassinis' results a heated controversy began between the French and British scientists. The British scientists (the "earth flatteners") claimed that the rotating earth must be flattened as Newton and Huygens had theoretically shown. The Frenchmen, particularly the Cassinis, defended their own measurement and continued to believe the earth to be egg-shaped.

To settle this controversy, the French Academy of Sciences in 1735 sent an expedition led by Pierre Bouguer and Charles Marie de la Condamine, to a section of the Spanish province of Peru (which later became Ecuador) to measure the length of a meridian degree close to the equator. Another expedition in 1736, under P. L. M. de Maupertuis, was sent to Lapland to make a similar measurement near the Arctic circle. According to the resulting measurements the length of a meridian degree in Peru is 56,734 toise (French fathom); in Paris 57,060 toise; and in Lapland, 57,422 toise. The meridian degree was found to be longer the farther away from the equator the observations were carried out. These results showed irrefutably that the Cassinis were wrong and that the earth is flattened. The measurements in Peru and Lapland gave for the flattening the value 1:213, quite far from the value 1:297.0, used since 1924.

The general opinion of the geodesists was that the meridian arc measured by the Maupertuis expedition was not as long as the measurement indicated. The control measurements of the Swedish Geodetic Institute (Svanberg) in 1804, in fact, showed that the error was relatively large, according to him, 226 toise or 441 m. In 1928, the Finnish geodesist, Y. Leinberg, discovered that Maupertuis' measurement accumulated a number of errors that totaled 393 m. Unfortunately, all Maupertuis' errors were effected in the same direction, but it was fortunate that they gave him too long a meridian arc. Had his measurement been 441 m. too short, the problem concerning the shape of the earth might not yet have been solved definitely.

18th Century.—During the 18th century there were numerous measurements of arcs. The trigonometric survey of England was begun in 1783, primarily to establish geodetic connection between Greenwich and Paris. More important, however, was the French arc measurement. In 1791 the French national assembly accepted a new length unit replacing the toise. This unit was called a metre, by definition 1:10,000,000 part of the meridian quadrant from equator to pole along the Paris meridian. To get the length of this unit, additional accurate observations were needed. Therefore, a new arc measurement between Dunkerque and Barcelona, Spain, was carried out by Pierre François Méchain and Jean Baptiste Delambre in 1792–98. Their publication in three volumes, *Base du système métrique décimal* (1806–10), in which the measurements carried out in France and Peru were applied, gave for the length of a metre the following value: 1 metre = 443.296 Paris lines; 1 toise = 6 feet = 72 inches = 864 Paris lines. The ratio between toise and metre is therefore 864:443.296, or 1 toise = 1.9490363 metres. Later arc measurements, however, showed that the metre does not correspond to its definition. In fact, the meridian quadrant of the international ellipsoid is 10,002,288.3 m. The metre is consequently 0.02% "too short." The following table may be used for reference:

Fundamental Elements of the International Ellipsoid of Reference
a = semimajor axis (equatorial radius) = 6,378,388 metres
b = semiminor axis (polar radius) = 6,356,911.946 m.

Derived Quantities
e^2 = square of eccentricity = $\dfrac{a^2-b^2}{a^2}$ = 0.006,722,670,022
f = ellipticity (flattening) = $\dfrac{a-b}{a}$ = 1/297 = 0.003,367,003,367
Length of quadrant of the equator = 10,019,148.4 m.

Length of quadrant of the meridian = 10,002,288.3 m.
Area of the ellipsoid = 510,100,934 sq.km.
Volume of the ellipsoid = 1,083,319,780,000 cu.km.
Radius of sphere having same area as ellipsoid = 6,371,227.7 m.
Radius of sphere having same volume as ellipsoid = 6,371,221.3 m.
Mass of the ellipsoid = 5.988×10^{21} metric tons.

19th Century.—Of great significance were the arc measurements carried out in the 19th century by the survey of India under the leadership of the English surveyors general such as Sir George Everest, Sir Andrew Waugh and Sir Sidney Burrard; other scientists included J. H. Pratt, Sir George Airy and, later, F. deGraaff Hunter. In fact, this geodetic work made India the birthplace of isostasy (see below) and yielded detailed shape of the geoid over an area covering nearly all of India.

During the ellipsoidal era, which lasted to the 20th century, several geodesists computed reasonable values for the dimensions of the reference ellipsoid. In addition, the late 18th and early 19th centuries brought to geodesy, through the genius of 18-year-old K. F. Gauss (1795) and of A. M. Legendre (1806), development of the important adjustment computation as well as the definition of the metre and a preliminary value for it. The 19th century introduced the methodologically basic triangulation work of Gauss and F. W. Bessel; the mathematical basis (Stokes' formula) of physical geodesy; and the international co-operation required for the development of geodesy.

IV. GEOIDAL ERA OF GEODESY

The period after 1900 can be called the geoidal era, because after this time it was possible to start the determination of the detailed shape of the geoid and its accurate dimensions to replace the approximations provided by the reference ellipsoid. During this geoidal era new instruments for geodetic, astronomical and gravimetric measurements were devised; the international ellipsoid and international gravity formula to be used in geodetic and gravimetric studies were adopted; extensive isostatic studies of basic significance to physical geodesy were carried out; several long-range triangulations were made; and electronic, celestial and gravimetric methods were applied to geodesy.

In the 19th century, when every country was satisfied with a control-point system of its own, the problems of geodesy were not too complicated. If a country were not too large, any reasonable reference ellipsoid could be used, since the effect of possible errors on its dimensions was quite small and not significant in practical mapping work. The reliability of the co-ordinates of the control points depended mainly on the accuracy of the astronomical, triangulation and traverse measurements. Relatively simple adjustment computation eliminated any inner discrepancy of the geodetic system in question. It did not matter how much the geodetic systems of different countries disagreed with one another. As late as 1947, for instance, the differences of the co-ordinates of the same control point amounted to 95 m. between the Danish and Swedish systems, 250 m. between the Danish and German systems, 171 m. between the Danish and Norwegian systems and 191 m. between the English and French systems. The exact extent of differences among the geodetic systems of the various continents and ocean islands in the 19th century is not known. They may have been as great as 5 mi. or more.

World Geodetic System.—By mid-20th century it was clear that such confusion could not be allowed to continue. The demands of hydrographic surveying and aviation made it of basic importance that the co-ordinates of the different countries and continents be under the same system, that the existing geodetic systems, even across the oceans, be converted as accurately as possible to a single world geodetic system. It did not matter where the initial point of the world geodetic datum was located.

To standardize a world geodetic system the following would be necessary: (1) a common scale or yardstick throughout the world; (2) new arc measurements along the continents and across the oceans; (3) exact localizing of these arcs on the reference ellipsoid; (4) more accurate dimensions of the reference ellipsoid; (5) extremely accurate values of the geoid distances N and the deflections of the vertical components ξ and η at the initial points of the different geodetic systems. As shown in fig. 4, N is the distance between the reference ellipsoid and the geoid at a given point. The tilt of the geoid is given by the angles ξ; the deviation between the plumb line and the perpendicular to the ellipsoid (dotted line) measured in a north-south plane, and η, the deviation measured in an east-west plane (perpendicular to the diagram, fig. 4, and so not shown).

The significance of a common scale is easy to understand. If the length unit obtained by the base-line measurements is different in the various countries and on different continents, the computed geodesic lines to be used in the world-wide computations will not be comparable with one another and will cause systematic errors. Because of this fact it is necessary to measure in the different countries, or at least on every continent, one accurate standard base line on which to calibrate the wires or tapes to be used in the measurement of the field base lines. The light-interference method, invented by the Finnish astronomer Y. Väisälä, and put into practice by the Finnish Geodetic institute, supplies the needed standard base lines.

The United Nations' Regional Cartographic Conference for Asia and the Far East in Mussoorie, India, in Feb. 1955, recommended to the governments of the Asian countries "that a few standard base lines in this region should be established by the Väisälä method for assuring the uniform scale in all networks and for calibrating invar tapes and other equipment." The relative accuracy of the standard base lines of Nummela, Fin., and Buenos Aires, Arg., measured by T. J. Kukkamäki (1948) and T. B. Honkasalo (1953) are 1:17,000,000 and 1:9,000,000, or approximately 0.1 in. per 25 mi.

The Geodimeter.—Designed by E. Bergstrand and developed in Sweden, the United States and Germany, this instrument is based on Armand Fizeau's method for measuring the velocity of light. Instead of using a toothed wheel as the modulator and the human eye as the detector, the geodimeter applies a Kerr cell as the modulating unit and a photomultiplier tube as the detecting unit.

To measure distances the transmitter of the geodimeter sends light impulses at a modulating frequency of 10 mc. The impulses are reflected back from a target and are then detected in the photomultiplier tube of the receiver. If the distance between transmitting and target points is an integral amount of quarters of modulated light waves (about 7.5 m.) a special null detector indicates zero, which can be obtained by alternating the modulating frequency to apply a new unit of measurement. If only one frequency is used the distance must be accurate to ±7.5 m. In practice, however, another frequency deviating 1% from the main frequency is used when the distance must be known only to ±750 m. The instrumental accuracy is mainly dependent on the frequency, which is accurate to 1 or 2 parts in 10,000,000. The practical accuracy is a function of the velocity of light waves *in vacuo* and of the propagation anomalies caused by changing atmospheric conditions. These can be determined with an accuracy of about 1:1,000,000.

To measure the exact dimensions of the reference ellipsoid more and longer geodetic yardsticks (i.e., accurately measured arcs in different parts of the world) are imperative. Up to the late 1950s the classic triangulation method had been commonly used for this purpose. On the basis of astronomical observations of latitude and longitude at or near the end points of these yardsticks, we can locate the arcs approximately at the right places on the earth's surface. This astrogeodetic method can be used on the continents. In fact, the mathematicians of the U.S. army map service in 1956 computed new dimensions for the reference ellipsoid on the basis of the long arcs: Tornio, Fin.–Cape Town, S.Af.; Alaska–Chile; one meridian arc and one longitudinal arc in mainland U.S.; and one Eurasian arc, Atlantic coast–Siberia.

V. MODERN ARC-MEASURING METHODS

Since the old triangulation method cannot operate over the oceans, new methods were needed to connect the continents with one another geodetically. Two modern methods of measuring have been applied: the electronic and the celestial.

Electronic Method.—In the electronic method (Shoran,

Hiran, Loran) it is necessary to know only the velocity of light and relatively short triangulation chains for calibrating the equipment which measures the long distances. Lines up to 880 km. have been measured with a relative accuracy of 1:120,000.

Shoran measurements need two ground stations, A and B, and one or more air-borne stations which carry the transmitting equipment for broadcasting the electromagnetic impulses. The airplane flies in loops over approximately the middle of line AB. The Shoran readings give the time which elapses when the impulses travel from the airplane to the ground station and back. From this time the distance from station A to airplane can be computed. The distance from station B to airplane can be computed. The sum of these distances is different depending on how far the airplane is from the vertical plane through the line AB. Every reading gives a single value for the combined distance A-airplane-B. These values, reduced to the minimum distance, supply the distance between the ground stations A and B.

Celestial Method.—Four celestial methods have been developed: the rocket-star, solar eclipse, occultation and moon camera.

Rocket-Star.—This is a triangulation method invented and developed by Y. Väisälä in 1946. In this method a rocket is launched in an accurately vertical direction to a certain elevation (e.g., 200 km.) and the neighbouring stars are photographed simultaneously from several observatories or other observation points. By measuring the small angular distances between the images of the stars and the rocket, the direction of the rocket from the observation points can be accurately computed. If the rocket were launched to an elevation of several hundred kilometres it would be possible to find distances across the oceans, and for triangulation on the continents.

The advantage of the rocket-star method lies in the large triangles which can be used.

Solar Eclipse.—This once popular method was developed in 1943 by I. Bonsdorff, director of the Finnish Geodetic institute. It is based on the scheme of the Polish astronomer T. Banachiewic and is used for measuring distances across the oceans. The method is simple although technical difficulties appear. With sound-film techniques photographs are made at two stations, A and B (each on different continents), as the totality of the eclipse begins and ends. The exact time, t, elapsing between the beginning (and end) of the totality at A and B is measured from the film, which also contains the tracks of the time signals and chronometer ticks. The time, t, renders with relatively high accuracy the distance between the stations, if the distance of the moon at the observation time is known accurately. For that purpose at least two observation stations, B and C, must be located on the same continent and their distance must have been measured by triangulation. The known distance BC gives the distance of the moon, on the basis of which the unknown distance AB across the ocean can be computed. For intercontinental geodetic ties this method was applied during the total solar eclipses in 1945, 1947, 1948, 1954 and 1955. Unfortunately conditions were so capricious —a cloudy sky too often hindered the observations—that only once was it possible to compute the distance across the Atlantic by this method. The accuracy of this tie, according to Kukkamäki's publication, is of the order of 80 m. An essential part of this error was brought about by the irregularity of the moon's topography.

Enthusiasm for this method has waned since total solar eclipses occur rather seldom, and because of the often inconvenient locations of the observation stations, which are determined by the path of the moon's shadow. Also the irregularity of the moon's limb (outline) decreases the accuracy of the observations, and too frequently "heavenly sabotage" destroys the work of the expedition.

Occultation.—In this method the moments during which a star disappears behind the moon's limb and emerges from behind it are observed. As in the solar eclipse method, the distance between the observation points can be computed assuming that the distance of the moon is known. This method also can be applied only relatively seldom, though more frequently than the solar eclipse method.

Moon Camera.—The moon camera method, invented by William Markowitz at the U.S. Naval observatory, photographs the moon together with the neighbouring stars from observatories on different continents. The moon camera is so constructed that the moon's limb and the neighbouring stars are held stationary during the exposure of the film. The small angular distances of the distinct points of the moon's limb from the neighbouring stars, measured from the film, give the direction to the moon from the observation points. In theory two complete observations of the moon suffice. Analytically considered, two complete observations give four quantities, and only three unknowns have to be found. Considered geometrically, each observation gives a line of sight along which the station lies. Two lines of sight, well separated in direction, will intersect in a point which locates the station. In practice, the use of the moon in the solution of astronomical and geodetic problems is rather difficult from the standpoints of both computation and observation. What is measured is the displacement of the moon from a calculated position. The moon, however, may be displaced for reasons other than that due to the displacement of the station from the centre of the earth. In order to separate all the unknowns involved numerous observations must be made. Moreover, the moon must be observed over a large portion of its orbit, and at each station it must be observed in different parts of the sky. Before mid-20th century this had not been feasible because of the restrictions involved in determining the position of the moon accurately.

The geocentric co-ordinates of these points can, according to Markowitz, be computed, the geocentric radius R with the accuracy of about 40 m. The variation of R with the latitude and longitude of the observation points gives the general shape of the earth with the mentioned accuracy if a sufficient number of observation points exist. Twenty astronomical observatories of different continents agreed to co-operate during the International Geophysical Year 1957–1958 to apply this method on a world-wide scale.

The three moon methods are similar in that the moon is used as one triangulation point of this celestial triangulation. They help in determining the size and general shape of the earth.

All types of arc-measuring methods render the length l of an arc of a great circle of the earth, which is necessary in determining the equatorial radius a.

The flattening f of the reference ellipsoid can be determined also by other astronomical methods utilizing the observed mechanical effects produced by the earth's equatorial protuberance, i.e., by the polar flattening of the earth. This equatorial bulge produces periodic perturbations in the moon's perigee and of the node of its orbit on the ecliptic. The moon in turn acts on the equatorial bulge of the earth and produces the greater part of the slow displacement of the equinoxes known as precession; the sun contributes a fairly large part of the observed precession. Although there are theoretical difficulties in all of the methods mentioned the flattening of the earth may be deduced. From any one of the effects mentioned the precession is as satisfactory as any; it agrees substantially with the flattening, 1:297, of the international ellipsoid. The flattening deduced by the other lunar methods tends to come out a trifle greater than this. The application of these different methods can reduce the errors in calculating the earth's dimensions.

All these celestial methods require land stations and fail over the open oceans. In addition, they are bound to the existing triangulation chains and to the relatively few astronomical observation points. Since the shape of the geoid must be determined point by point, it remained necessary to find a universal method which could be used everywhere in the world. This method will be rendered by physical geodesy.

VI. PHYSICAL GEODESY

There is a difference between geometrical geodesy and physical geodesy. Triangulation, either in the classic or the modern sense, with astronomical observations (i.e., the arc-measuring method), is spoken of as geometrical geodesy because it does not consider the structure of the earth's interior. Solely astronomical observations on, and triangulation along, the earth's surface give the size and general shape of the earth even if its structure is unknown. In this respect geometrical geodesy has had considerable success and has supplied reference ellipsoids that are not too different from the actual geoid.

In the classic computations of the dimensions of the reference ellipsoid physical geodesy played an important role. It had been necessary to make the astronomically observed latitude, longitude and azimuth as representative as possible. In other words, in analyzing the astrogeodetic deflection of the vertical components, ξ and η, we must consider not only the effect of the visible topographic features but also the invisible compensating masses of the earth, and thus consider the internal structure of the earth's crust and of the layers under it. J. F. Hayford's ellipsoid, although based entirely on arc measurements made within the United States, was sufficiently accurate to be adopted in 1924 as the international ellipsoid because he used the topographic-isostatic reduction, i.e., the method of physical geodesy. A similar case was W. A. Heiskanen's derivation of the equator value 978.049 cm. per second per second of the international gravity formula.

Gravity Anomalies.—The main tool of physical geodesy is, however, the gravimetric method. The advantage of this method lies in its use of only one quantity, the gravity anomalies. To get the gravity anomalies it is necessary to reduce in some way the observed gravity from the observation point to sea level. Depending on the reduction method used, different values are obtained for sea-level gravity g_0. Since the earth rotates around its axis and, in addition, is flattened, the g_0 values are smallest at the equator and increase with latitude. The gravity anomalies seem to have a relation not only to latitude but to longitude as well. Therefore, several scientists have derived gravity formulas assuming that the earth is a triaxial ellipsoid instead of an ellipsoid of revolution; in other words, the equator and the parallel circles are ellipses instead of circles. According to them the long axis of the equator would be close to longitudes 0° and 180°; the short axis close to longitudes +90° and −90°. The difference between the large and small semiaxes of the equator is about 120 m.

The triaxiality of the earth is quite difficult to explain geophysically, and even the increasing use of gravimetric methods had not completely proved its existence. It appeared that this problem would best be solved—and in exact form—when the detailed shape of the geoid had been determined gravimetrically. From the geoid map of the world it would be easy to see whether the real geoid is closer to the triaxial ellipsoid or to the ellipsoid of revolution.

The physical basis of physical geodesy lies in the fact that the disturbing masses Δm result in the geoid distances N, the deflection of the vertical components ξ and η, and the gravity anomalies $\Delta g = g_0 - \gamma$, where g_0 is the observed gravity reduced to sea level and γ is obtained from the international gravity formula,

$$\gamma = 978.049 [1 + 0.005 2884 \sin^2\phi - 0.000 0059 \sin^2 2\phi] \text{ cm./sec}^2.$$

Of these quantities, Δg can be measured, and from it the quantities N, ξ and η can be computed. Figs. 4 and 5 show why the geoid is irregular. Fig. 4 indicates that the mass surplus of the mountain pulls the plumb line; the mass deficiency of the ocean pushes it toward the mountain. Consequently, the plumb line (solid line) and the normal of the ellipsoid (dotted line) are not the same but make an angle with one another, the deflection of the vertical, ξ. Because the geoid (as an equipotential surface) is al-

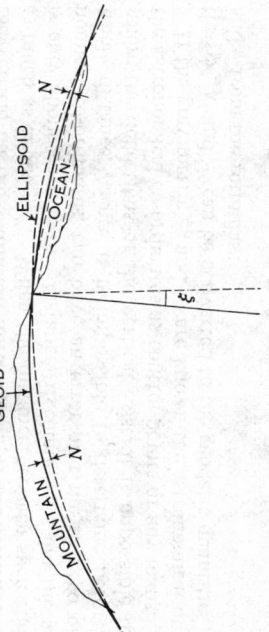

FIG. 4.—THE INFLUENCES OF SURFACE IRREGULARITIES UPON THE SHAPE OF THE GEOID

ways perpendicular to the plumb line, the geoid under the mountains must be above the ellipsoid, and at the oceans it must be below the ellipsoid, if we assume that the mass surplus of the mountains and mass deficiency of the oceans are real and not isostatically compensated. Fig. 5 also shows that the invisible mass anomalies Δm, surplus (+++++) or deficiency (− − − −), bring about the gravity anomalies Δg, geoid distances N and the deflection components ξ and η. In these figures the quantities N and ξ as compared with the size of the earth have been exaggerated greatly to make the picture more clear. In fact, the largest N-values are less than 1:64,000 part of the radius (6,400,000 m.) of the earth, in other words, less than one inch on a sphere of one mile radius.

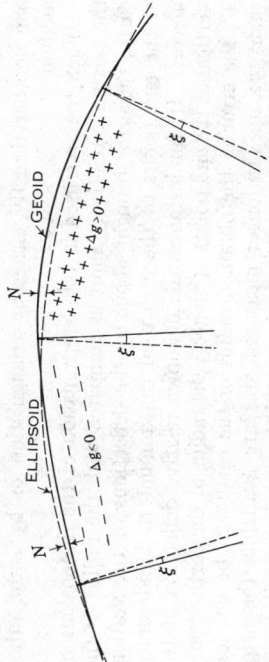

FIG. 5.—THE RELATIONSHIP OF MASS ANOMALIES AND GRAVITY ANOMALIES

VII. METHODS AND ACHIEVEMENTS OF PHYSICAL GEODESY

The mathematical basis of physical geodesy is the Stokes' function, as set forth by Sir George Stokes in 1849, and its derivatives, developed by F. A. Vening Meinesz in 1928. The Stokes' function holds that the shape of the geoid can be determined if the gravity anomalies in the neighbourhood of the computation point are known rather well and those around the world are known in broader terms. The Vening Meinesz formulas indicate that in this case the deflection of the vertical components also can be computed.

Computations.—Fig. 6 shows how the irregular form of the geoid will interfere in the computation of the radius of curvature of the earth. Because of the warping N of the geoid (solid line) and the deflections of the vertical ξ_1, ξ_2 and ξ_3, it is easy to get wrong dimensions for the earth ellipsoid (dotted line). The arc AB, where the geoid is under the reference ellipsoid,

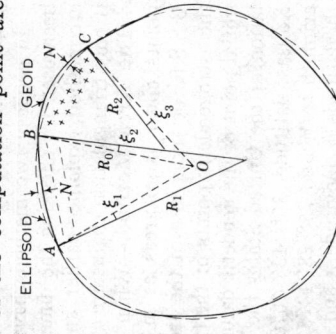

FIG. 6.—THE RELATIONSHIP OF VERTICAL DEFLECTIONS AND DIMENSIONS OF THE REFERENCE ELLIPSOID

gives too large a radius R_1; arc BC, where the geoid is above the ellipsoid, gives too small a radius R_2; the correct value is R_0. Through the isostatic reduction of the astrogeodetic deflections of the vertical the irregularities of the geoid can be "smoothed" and the disturbing effect of the deflections of the vertical on the radius R_0 can be reduced and a better result achieved. The whole effect of the quantities ξ_1, ξ_2 and ξ_3, however, can be eliminated only if they are known and considered. Then both arcs AB and BC give the real radius R_0 of the ellipsoid. To put it more mathematically, the curvature of the geoid along the measured arc is obtained instead of the curvature of the mathematical reference ellipsoid as is the case when the deflections of the vertical ξ are not known. The gravimetric method supplies these quantities ξ.

Figs. 7 and 8 explain the limitations of the arc measuring method. Fig. 7 shows that the fictitious geoid distances N_1, N_2 are obtained if the exact dimensions of the reference ellipsoid are not known. Similarly fig. 8 indicates that wrong N-values also result in the case that at the initial point A of the geodetic datum an unsuitable deflection of the vertical ξ_0 has been used. Therefore, we cannot convert the various geodetic systems to a single world system unless we know the real deflections and the geoid distances at the initial points of these systems, or can connect the initial points with one another directly either by triangulation or by some other method.

When the arcs used in the determination of the dimensions of the earth are relatively short as compared with the deflections of the vertical at the end points of the arcs used can amount to hundreds of metres. If, for instance, the unknown relative deflection of the vertical at the end points of an arc ⅓ the radius of the earth will be not less than 372 m. If longer measured arcs are available, the error caused by the neglected deflections of the vertical is smaller. If, for instance, in South Africa close to the southern end of the meridian arc Cape Town-Tornio, the ξ-component is −10″ and at the northern end, about +2″, neglect of these deflections will produce an error in the radius of the earth, computed by aid of this 100° long arc, of about 220 m. if other astrogeodetic points are not used.

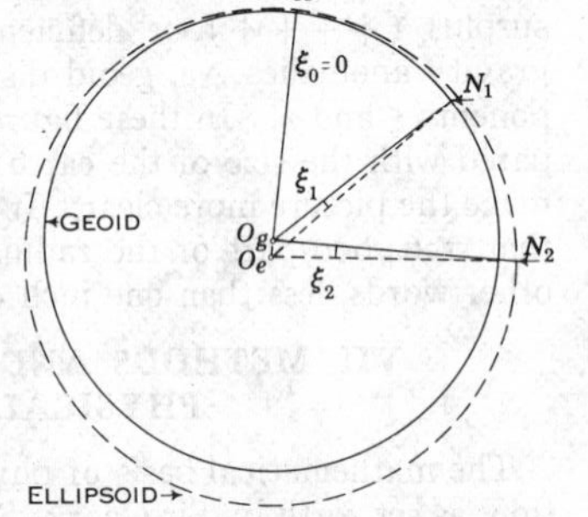

As the examples show, in using measured arcs for checking the dimensions of the earth it is necessary not only to know the length of the yardsticks, but also to be able to localize the arcs at the right places on the ellipsoid to be computed. The central angle of the ellipsoid corresponding to the measured arcs must be determined accurately, considering the vertical at the end points of the arcs, if the arc is to be converted from geoid to ellipsoid.

In geodesy two methods have been used for checking the dimensions of the earth ellipsoid: the arc method, explained earlier, and which comes into consideration if only triangulation chains are available; and the area method.

The Area Method.—When triangulations with astronomical points cover large areas as in the United States, Europe, the U.S.S.R. or India, use of the area method is preferable. One of the astrogeodetic points of the triangulation will be chosen as the initial point of the geodetic datum. For instance, for the triangulation of the United States the initial point is Meades Ranch in Kansas, latitude 39° 13′ 26″.686; longitude 98° 32′ 30″.506, azimuth to Waldo 75° 28′ 14″.52. Beginning at this initial point vertically along the latitude φ, longitude λ and azimuth A are computed geodetically along the chosen reference ellipsoid. The astronomical quantities φ′, λ′ and A′ are referred to the geoid, the quantities φ, λ and A to the reference ellipsoid used. The differences of these quantities give, at all such triangulation points where astronomical observations are available, the deflections of the vertical components ξ and η, as the following classic formulas show:

$$\xi = \phi' - \phi$$
$$\eta = (\lambda' - \lambda)\cos\phi$$
$$\eta = (A' - A)\cot\phi$$

The η-component can be obtained from the longitude observations as well as from the azimuth observations. If both are available, the point will be called the Laplace point and from the two equations for η the famous Laplace equation is obtained: $(A' - A) = (\lambda' - \lambda)\sin\phi$. Because of the observation errors this equation is not satisfied, but becomes instead the equation: $(A' - A) - (\lambda' - \lambda)\sin\phi = w$. The quantity w of the Laplace equation has nothing to do with deflections of the vertical, but is only the measure of the observation errors. The larger the error is w; $w = 0$ means that the error is zero.

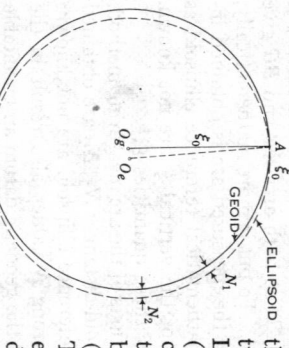

FIG. 8.—THE RELATIONSHIP BE-TWEEN THE DEFLECTION OF THE VERTICAL ξ AT INITIAL POINT AND GEOID DISTANCES N

If the gravimetric ξ_g and η_g are known the astronomical quantities φ′, λ′ and A′ can be converted to the geodetic quantities φ, λ and η from the formulas:

$$\phi = \phi' - \xi_g$$
$$\lambda = \lambda' - \eta_g \sec\phi$$
$$A = A' - \eta_g \tan\phi$$

Among the largest measured deflections of the vertical are the ξ- and η-values found in the Puerto Rican area (43″, according to D. Rice) and in certain of the British islands in the Pacific (54″, according to William Kaula). The relative deflections of the vertical on the south and north coasts of these islands differ as much as about 50″. When the distance between such stations is only about 50 mi, this distance, if computed from the astronomical co-ordinates, can have an error of 1 mi. or 1:50 of the whole distance. Since it is impossible to determine beforehand where the deflections of the vertical exist, it is impossible to use the astronomical co-ordinates as control points of any maps.

The deflections of the vertical average less than 5″; the values over 10″ are exceptional. They have been found for the most part in mountainous regions, and in quite a few cases on islands also, and even in lowlands where abnormally light or abnormally heavy disturbing layers are close to the earth's surface. For instance, in flat land in the neighbourhood of Moscow deflections of even 8″ exist. Similarly in south Finland, in the Åland Islands, between Finland and Sweden, the deflection is 9″, and close to Columbus, O., also in level land, deflections of 10″ have been found.

FIG. 7.—THE RELATIONSHIP BE-TWEEN RADIUS OF THE REFERENCE ELLIPSOID AND THE GEOID DISTANCE N AND DEFLECTIONS ξ

In the area method, of course, the same criterion is used. The astrogeodetic points to be used must be as far as possible from the initial point but not too close to the computation point and to the gravimetrically surveyed areas. The detailed gravity field must be available, say, to 500 km. from the computation point to get reliable gravimetric deflections of the vertical.

If the undulation N_0 at the initial point of the geodetic datum is known or can be guessed, then the warping N of the geoid can be computed with the aid of the obtained ξ- and η-values, along the arc-measuring chain, if it has sufficient astronomical points. If this is combined with the gravimetric method the N-values can be interpolated even when only a few points are available.

In checking the dimensions of the reference ellipsoid based on the arc measurements, the criteria $\Sigma(\xi^2) = $ min, or $\Sigma \eta^2 = $ min, has been used, depending on whether the arc has been measured in the direction of the meridian, or perpendicular to it, or in some other direction. This method is accurate if the astro-measured arcs are long, or if they are short, and if the astrogeodetic points used cover an area where the real deflections of the vertical are systematically either negative or positive. For instance, in Europe the criterion $\Sigma(\xi^2 + \eta^2) = $ min cannot be used because the average value of ξ in that area is of the order +2″ and the average η of the order +2″ to +3″.

The Gravimetric Method.—The gravimetric method makes it possible to obtain essentially more accurate dimensions for the reference ellipsoid merely by making extremely accurate astronomical observations at or in the neighbourhood of the end points of the measured arc. In addition the deflections of the vertical components ξ_a and η_a at both end points of the arc can be computed gravimetrically. On the other hand some arbitrary values have been chosen for the astrogeodetic deflection of the vertical components ξ_a and η_a (e.g., zero) at one end (initial) point of the arc and computed along the arc ξ_a and η_a at the other end point. The computed quantities ξ_a and η_a depend on the reference ellipsoid used while ξ_g, η_g are nearly independent of it. If the differences $(\xi_g - \eta_a)$ and $(\eta_g - \eta_a)$ at both end points of the arc are nearly equal, the reference ellipsoid used is correct. If there is a difference, say, of 10″, the reference ellipsoid must be corrected so that this difference disappears.

Needless to say, if at, or close to, the end point of every measured arc accurate astronomical observations and the best local gravity survey have been carried out, these can be used for checking the dimensions of the earth. By the least square method the different measured arcs of this kind will give, together, the best correction to the equator value of the reference ellipsoid used.

In the area method, of course, the same criterion is used. The astrogeodetic points to be used must be as far as possible from the initial point but not too close to the computation point and to the gravimetrically surveyed areas. The detailed gravity field must be available, say, to 500 km. from the computation point to get reliable gravimetric deflections of the vertical.

The obtained values ϕ, λ and A give the distances and azimuths along the ellipsoid. This is the principle of the astrogravimetric method for determination of the co-ordinates of the control points.

Another example of this principle concerns the western part of the boundary between the United States and Canada, which is the 49th parallel of latitude. For reasons of convenience this parallel was defined astronomically, and the result showed that one bounding station is about 8″ north of where a geodetic determination would have placed it, and another station less than 100 mi. away is about 6″ south. The greatest relative error between two adjacent stations is about 7″ in a distance of 20 mi., which means an error in the direction from one station to the other, as inferred from the latitudes, of about 35 ft. per mile.

When the quantities N, ξ_g and η_g are known they can be used to: (1) compute the distances along the reference ellipsoid between the astronomic points where ξ_g and η_g have been computed; (2) convert the existing geodetic systems to a single world geodetic system; (3) obtain with greater accuracy the dimensions of the earth; (4) check the accuracy of superlong triangulation, which greatly needs checking, especially where the triangulation chains were measured under difficult conditions, e.g., the chain from Alaska to Chile; (5) reduce the geodetic base lines from the geoid to the ellipsoid; (6) compute the error caused by the deflections of the vertical at the triangulation points which in high mountains can be more than 2″; and (7) draft world maps for the geoid distances N, another set of world maps for the deflection of the vertical component ξ_g and a third set for η_g.

These maps have an exceptionally practical geodetic significance; they are also important for geophysics since there is always a close relation between the N, ξ_g and η_g-values and the internal structure of the earth.

By the 1960s several areas, including large parts of the United States, Europe, India, the U.S.S.R., Argentina, Canada and South Africa, had been so well covered by gravity station nets that reliable values, particularly for ξ_g and η_g could be obtained. The enormous progress in this respect was possible because of the following: (1) the invention of very fast, accurate gravimeters which can in three minutes measure a gravity value with 20 to 50 times more accuracy than had been possible to get in two days with pendulum observations; (2) the invention of the Vening Meinesz pendulum apparatus for gravity observations at sea; (3) the invention of the underwater gravimeter for measuring gravity in the shallow shelf areas which cover about 7% of the ocean areas; (4) the interest of the oil companies in carrying out detailed gravity surveys for exploration purposes and universities conducting surveys for scientific purposes.

VIII. MEASURING INSTRUMENTS USED IN GEODESY

For longitude observations in the astronomical part of geodesy the transit instrument has been in general use for a long time. Those used at mid-20th century ordinarily were provided with a self-recording micrometer and were used in conjunction with a chronograph. For latitude determination the same transit, with broken axis, and the zenith telescope (q.v.) are used almost universally. For determination of azimuth and triangulation angles, the modern theodolite is used; this instrument is more accurate than the ordinary surveyor's theodolite but does not differ essentially. In addition, accurate chronometers, crystal clocks and radio receivers are needed for measuring the observation time and taking time signals. The accuracy of the astronomical observations, if observations are made on two or three nights at the same point, are of the order 0″.15 in latitude and 0″.20 in longitude. The standard error of the measurement of one angle in triangulation varies between 0″.3 and 2″.5 in different countries.

Bars and rods were used earlier for the base-line measurements but they were inconvenient. The measurement went slowly and the accuracy was not high regardless of how carefully the observations were made. By mid-20th century bases were measured with tapes or wires made from invar alloy. The coefficient of the temperature expansion of invar is so small (of the order 10^{-7}/°C.) that the temperature need not be determined with high accuracy. The wires and tapes must be calibrated before and after the field work. That can best be done at the standard base lines described earlier.

In principle, the instruments for precise leveling are the same as the usual engineering leveling instruments but are, of course, much more accurate. The development of geodesy as a science closely followed the development of geodetic instruments, as the instruments became handier, more accurate and more rapid, the geodetic observations became more accurate and more convenient.

In modern physical geodesy gravity observations are of basic significance, therefore gravimetric measuring instruments and methods are most important. Gravimetric observations are either absolute or relative. In absolute measurement it is necessary to measure the actual gravity that exists at the observation point. In the relative observation it is necessary to measure only the difference or ratio between the gravity g_0 at the base station and the gravity g at the field stations. When the base-station gravity g_0 is known, the difference $(g - g_0)$ or ratio g/g_0 will give the gravity g at the field stations.

Pendulum Apparatus.—Until about 1935 the pendulum apparatus was used almost exclusively in gravity observations. Its principle is simple. If the length l and period T of the pendulum can be measured the gravity g can be obtained from the formula

$$T = 2\pi\sqrt{l/g}.$$

T is relatively easy to determine, but the measurement of the length of the pendulum l involves difficulties. In addition the length l varies with temperature and other atmospheric conditions. Therefore, absolute gravity observations at one point take many months, and in spite of the utmost care the accuracy is relatively low, rarely more than 3 to 4 mgal. (in geophysics unit g has been named the "gal" [after Galileo]: 1 milligal [mgal.] = 0.001 gal = 0.001 cm./sec./sec.). In relative gravity observations it is necessary to measure only the period T of the pendulum at the base station and the field stations, assuming that l has not changed between the observations. The formula, $g \cdot g_0 = T_0^2 : T^2$, gives the gravity g if T_0 and T have been measured at the base and field stations and g_0 is known.

Pendulum apparatus needs stable support in order to give the best observational results. In the Netherlands, where the land is not stable, Vening Meinesz, after running into difficulties in his gravity measurements, developed in 1923 a pendulum apparatus that could be used not only there but on the oceans as well. Two pendulums of equal length are allowed to swing in the same vertical plane but in different phase angles. By the use of a certain hypothetical pendulum, the phase of which at any instant is the difference between the phases of the two pendulums at that instant, the disturbing effect of the horizontal acceleration of the support can be eliminated. When the apparatus was supported in gimbals in a submarine 30 to 50 m. below sea level, it was possible to eliminate the effect of the horizontal acceleration of the submarine and so to measure gravity on the open sea. The accuracy of these observations is of the order 2 to 3 mgal. or sufficient for thorough studies of the oceans, particularly since the east-west velocity of the vessel which is not known accurately because of the ocean currents can cause an error (Eötvös effect) of 3 to 4 mgal.

Vening Meinesz measured about 900 stations along different oceans. Later, British, French, Soviet, Italian and Spanish scientists continued these observation. However, the greater part of the sea observations between 1945 and 1955 were carried out by Columbia university, New York, under the leadership of W. Maurice Ewing and John Lamar Worzel. More than 4,000 ocean points were observed. Gravity surveys at sea are of basic significance from the geodetic point of view, since without them no application of the Stokes or the Vening Meinesz formulas to geodetic purposes would be possible.

Gravimeters.—Pendulum observations take much time and the results are not very accurate; therefore, various types of gravimeters were devised in the different countries, particularly in the U.S. They are ingenious instruments, working essentially on the principle of the spring balance, and are so accurate that in a few minutes the gravity difference can be read with an accuracy of 0.02 mgal., which is 50 times higher than that obtained earlier by pendulum observations of two days.

As the Vening Meinesz pendulum opened the oceans to gravi-metric survey, gravimeters began a new era in the gravity survey of the continents. Oil companies, universities and geodetic insti-tutes around the world were competing to carry out regional and local gravity surveys that by the latter 1950s covered an essential part of the continental surfaces. Gravimeters, however, must be calibrated, preferably at an accurate pendulum. Gravimeters considered best for geodetic purposes (Worden, Nörgaard gravimeters) have large range (as great as 5,000 mgal.), high accuracy and small weight.

Gravity observations throughout the world can be used for com-puting geoid distances and deflections of the vertical only if they all refer to the same world gravimetric system, regardless of which system it is. Until the latter 1950s all gravity anomalies were computed by the Potsdam system. The absolute gravity observa-tions of this system were done at Pendulum hall, Potsdam, Ger., in 1900–03. The observed gravity value was $g = 981,274$ gal, which, according to later observations, appeared to be about 15 mgal. too high. The error did no harm since the value is used to obtain gravity differences in the formula, $\Delta g = g - \gamma$. If g is 15 mgal. too large, then γ is also 15 mgal. too large and Δg remains the same.

Gravity values can be best changed to the same system if scien-tists use the same type of gravimeters and air transportation and carry out gravity observations at national gravity-base stations. Such a conversion was made over a ten-year period (1947–57), par-ticularly by the University of Wisconsin group under G. P. Wool-lard. This group occupied more than 3,000 base stations all over the world and integrated the essential part of the gravity data with the world gravimetric system, in most cases with an accuracy higher than 1 mgal.

IX. ISOSTASY

The mountains, valleys and oceans make it apparent that the earth is not in hydrostatic equilibrium. But the earth is, in broad terms, in isostatic equilibrium in that, beginning from a certain depth in the earth's interior, the surface units are under the same pressure whether they are beneath mountain, lowland or ocean. The depth of the uppermost surfaces is known as the depth of compensation and this type of equilibrium is called isostasy, at the suggestion of the U.S. geologist, C. E. Dutton, in 1889. This isostatic equilibrium is only possible if the mountains are not abso-lute mass surplus areas nor the oceans absolute mass deficiency areas. In other words, the mean density of the earth's crust must be smaller under the mountains, and larger under the oceans than under the lowlands.

The man who first glimpsed the idea of isostatic equilibrium was Leonardo da Vinci, that many-sided genius of the Renaissance era. Pierre Bouguer and R. J. Boscovich came to the same con-clusion much later (18th century). The principle of isostatic equi-librium was, however, developed in a scientific sense in India, where triangulation with astronomical observations was carried out close to the Himalayan mountains before 1850. The difference between latitudes computed geodetically and observed astronomi-cally at the same point was smaller than the mass surplus of the mountains of Asia would indicate. The observed difference of the deflection of the vertical at the Kaliana and Kalianpur stations was only 5″24 but the value computed from the topographic masses was 15″88. Therefore, J. H. Pratt in 1854 surmised that the mean density of the crust under the mountains of Asia must be smaller than in the lowlands to compensate the attraction of the mass of the mountains of Asia to the plumb-line direction. The astron-omer G. B. Airy came to a similar conclusion in 1855, although he explained the isostatic equilibrium in a different way.

Pratt's isostatic assumption was that mountains rose from the subcrustal area after the manner of fermenting dough, the density of which would be smaller as it rose higher. Airy, on the contrary, reasoned that the high mountains of Asia had sunk in the sub-stratum and would float as timber or icebergs float. The smaller density of the earth's crust under the mountains would, according to Pratt, compensate the effect of the topographic masses and cause the equilibrium. According to Airy the light root formations of the mountains have the same effect.

Pratt contended that if the earth were completely fluid, no mountains or valleys or ocean basins would be possible. But as the earth's crust began to form and gradually grow thicker, contrac-tions and expansions might have taken place in some of its parts which would depress and elevate corresponding areas of the sur-face. Airy thought that there could be no other support than that afforded by the downward projection of a portion of the earth's light crust into the denser lava; and that this downward projec-tion was of an extent to balance the projection above the lava; in much the same manner, when logs float upon the water and the upper surface of one is observed to be higher than that of the others, one assumes that its lower surface lies lower in the water than does that of the other logs.

The isostatic assumptions of Pratt and Airy were completely contradictory; although both were able to explain the discrepancy between the observed and the computed deflections of the vertical and gravity anomalies on the basis of the topography. Both theories have found defenders. The ideas of Pratt were developed in detail by the U.S. scientists, J. F. Hayford and William Bowie. According to them the compensation is complete and local, i.e., every mountain, hill, valley and island is isostatically compensated, however large or small it may be. This assumption was used for practical reasons—to make the mathematical computations as sim-ple as possible. Hayford and Bowie computed needed formulas and tables for the topographic isostatic correction of the deflections of the vertical and gravity anomalies, corresponding to different values of the depth of compensation, D. Every different value of D renders different gravity anomalies (and deflections of the verti-cal) at the observation points. When computing different sets of gravity anomalies, corresponding to different values D, it is pos-sible to discuss which D-value is closest to the real structure of the earth's interior. Computations along these lines carried out by different scientists showed that D is close to 100 km. In geodetic computations the value 113.7 km. obtained by Hayford has been used.

From the geophysical point of view, the Pratt-Hayford assump-tion did not seem suitable; therefore, W. A. Heiskanen made a series of computations (1924, 1931 and 1938) based on Airy's assumption. Heiskanen's method rendered for the normal thick-ness of the earth's crust an average value close to 30 km.

Of course, according to the Airy-Heiskanen system, the actual thickness, T, of the earth's crust is the function of the topography. The higher the topography, the deeper is the root formation; the deeper the ocean, the thicker is the antiroot of heavy material under the ocean (see fig. 9). The light root formation (density

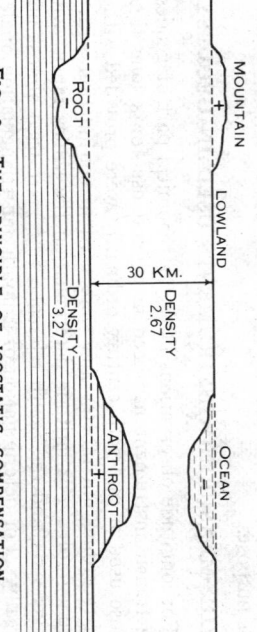

FIG. 9.—THE PRINCIPLE OF ISOSTATIC COMPENSATION

2.67) compensates the mass surplus of the mountains and the heavy antiroot (density 3.27) compensates the mass deficiency of the ocean. Using the density difference 0.6, the real thickness of the earth's crust is 5.5 km. greater for every kilometre of moun-tain elevation and 3.7 km. less under the oceans for every kilometre of ocean depth. In this way, the underboundary of the earth's crust, also called the Mohorovičić discontinuity, is in a way an ex-aggerated mirror picture of the real topography.

For practical reasons it has been assumed in both theories that compensation is complete and local, but in fact, this is not so. Small hills or tiny valleys or islands cannot be in complete isostatic equilibrium. Therefore, Vening Meinesz developed the theory of regional isostatic compensation. This modification of Airy's flo-tation theory claims that every topographical feature has an iso-static effect not only in the vertical direction under it but in the horizontal direction as well, to as much as 100 or 200 km. horizontal distance R. He computed (1931 and 1940) the needed tables for this regional theory according to different T- (normal thickness of the earth's crust) and R-values. Therefore by the 1950s three different systems—the Pratt-Hayford, the Airy-Heiskanen and the Vening Meinesz—existed for the isostatic study of the earth's structure.

Isostatic studies on the basis of gravity material of different countries, continents and oceans have shown that 85% to 90% of the mass deficiency of the oceans and mass surplus of the high mountains is isostatically compensated. Isostatic equilibrium is the rule. Areas such as small ocean islands, the belts of negative gravity anomalies and the postglacial land uplift regions where the isostatic equilibrium is not complete are exceptions. Since isostatic equilibrium prevails the geoid distances N are rather small. Under the leadership of Heiskanen and under the contract of the U.S. air force, the geoid computed in 1951–57 at Ohio State university on the basis of large gravity material of 35 countries revealed that the N-values seldom exceed ±50 m. Without the isostatic compensation N would in some cases even exceed 1,000 m., making the geoid studies more difficult.

(W. A. Hn.)

X. VARIATION OF LATITUDE

The astronomical latitude of every observation point is variable, caused by a displacement of the axis of rotation in the body of the earth. There is in every body, however irregular in shape, an axis of figure, the axis about which the moment of inertia is a maximum. If for any reason the axis of figure and the axis of rotation do not coincide, the pole of the axis of rotation will describe in the body a closed curve about the pole of the axis figure. For a nearly spherical body like the earth, the axis of rotation will retain in space a nearly invariable direction.

The first general rule of variations for a rigid rotating body was stated (1744) by Leonhard Euler. With Euler's theorems in mind astronomers sought to detect by observation a possible variation in latitude, but succeeded only in reaching the conclusion that if any such existed, it must be small. Finally about 1881, S. C. Chandler undertook a careful study apart from any preconceived theory, basing it both on observations of his own and a study of old records, notably those of Greenwich observatory. At about the same time, the reality of a change in latitude due to a motion of the pole was proved by simultaneous latitude observations in Berlin, Ger., and Honolulu, Hawaii, places differing in longitude by almost 180°. It was found that an increase in latitude in one occurred simultaneously with an approximately equal decrease at the other. This could not have resulted from local conditions or from incorrect star locations, but must have been due to a motion of the pole of rotation which in approaching one place receded from the other.

Chandler found that the motion of the pole of rotation about the pole of figure required about 14 months, whereas Euler's theory had led astronomers to expect a 10-month period. Simon Newcomb's explanation, published in 1895, showed that Euler's theory was based on an ideal body absolutely unyielding and unchangeable in shape, a thing unknown in nature. The elastic yielding of the earth and the mobility of the ocean water lengthen the period from 10 months to 14. There is also a motion of the pole of rotation in the body of the earth because the pole of figure itself undergoes a displacement due to seasonal variations in barometric pressure, snow load, etc. The period of these seasonal changes is obviously one year.

The amplitudes of both the annual and the 14-month variations are of the order of magnitude of 0″.1. The quantities sought are small and difficult to measure, but it appears that both components of the polar motion are subject to unpredictable changes. Since the maximum deviation of the pole from its mean position is about 0″.3, which is small in comparison with the usual deflections of the vertical, the reduction of the observed astronomical latitudes to some more or less conventional mean value is not a vital matter in ordinary geodetic work. (It should be noted that the motion of the pole affects longitudes and azimuths also.) The interest of

the subject is more on the astronomical and geophysical side.

The International Geodetic association in 1899 organized an International Latitude service with six special latitude observatories, all on parallel 39° 08′; three have remained in continuous operation. The advantage of having them in the same latitude is that all may use the same stars and uncertainties in the star places do not affect the conclusions. The observations may in fact be used to correct the star places.

XI. INTERNATIONAL GEODETIC ORGANIZATIONS

In 1862 the Central European Geodetic association (*Mitteleuropäische Gradmessung*) was organized on the initiative of Gen. Johann Baeyer of Prussia. Its first general conference was held in 1864 with representatives of 13 states or countries, many of them German states later united into the German empire. General conferences at intervals of three years were arranged, with a permanent committee directing the affairs of the organization between conferences. At the next conference (1867) in recognition of a widening scope, the name was changed to European Geodetic association (*Europäische Gradmessung*).

England and the United States were represented at the general conference in 1883 at which matters of world-wide interest, such as a common prime meridian and an international time system, were discussed. In 1886 the name International Geodetic association (*Internationale Erdmessung*) was chosen to indicate a still wider scope, and a definite international convention was adopted providing for contributions from the member nations. F. R. Helmert, director of the Geodetic institute at Potsdam, Ger., exerted a powerful and beneficent influence on the work of the association. The headquarters, or bureau, of the association remained at Potsdam. The outbreak of World War I prevented the holding of the general conference planned for 1915, leaving that of 1912 in Hamburg the last held by the organization.

In 1919 the International Union of Geodesy and Geophysics was organized at Brussels, Belg., in connection with the newly created International Research council. The International Geodetic and Geophysical union consists of seven semi-independent associations, the largest of which, the International Association of Geodesy, took over the work of the former International Geodetic association. The work of the International Latitude service was taken over jointly by the section of geodesy and the International Astronomical union, since the subject was of interest to both organizations. The general assembly of the union meets every three years.

On the initiative of I. Bonsdorff the Baltic Geodetic commission was established in 1924 at Helsinki, Fin. It included representatives of eight nations bordering on the Baltic sea and dealt with geodetic problems of common interest to them. The triangulation carried out by this commission around the Baltic sea is extremely accurate, the closure error of this nearly 3,000-km.-long triangulation being only 2.5 m. or 1:1,200,000, unparalleled in any earlier studies.

(W. D. LA.)

See also INTERNATIONAL GEOPHYSICAL YEAR.

BIBLIOGRAPHY.—International Association of Geodesy, *Bibliographie Géodésique Internationale*, vol. i-vii (1928-51).

History: G. B. Airy, "On the Computation of the Effect of the Attraction of Mountain Masses as Disturbing the Apparent Astronomical Latitude of Stations in Geodetic Surveys," *Phil. Trans.* B 145, (1855); J. H. Pratt, "On the Attraction of the Himalaya Mountains and of the Elevated Regions Beyond Upon Plumb-Line in India," *ibid.* (1855); G. G. Stokes, "Variation of Gravity and the Surface of the Earth," *Cambridge Phil. Trans.*, 8:672 (1849).

General: William Bowie, *Investigations of Gravity and Isostasy* (1917); C. E. Dutton, "On Some of the Greater Problems of Physical Geology," *Bull. Wash. Phil. Soc.*, B. 11 (1889); J. F. Hayford, *The Figure of the Earth and Isostasy* (1900), and *Supplementary Investigation in 1909 of the Figure of the Earth and Isostasy* (1910); J. F. Hayford and William Bowie, *The Effect of Topography and Isostatic Compensation Upon the Intensity of Gravity* (1910); W. A. Heiskanen, "New Isostatic Tables for the Reduction of Gravity Values Calculated on the Basis of Airy's Hypothesis," *Publ. isostat. int. Ass. Geod. of IAG*, no. 2 (1938), and "On the World Geodetic System," *ibid.*, no. 39 (1951); W. D. Lambert and F. W. Darling, "Tables for Determining the Form of the Geoid and its Indirect Effect on Gravity," U.S. Coast and Geodetic Survey, spec. publ. no. 199 (1936); L. Tanni, "On the Continental Undulations of the Geoid," *Publ. isostat. int. Ass. Geod.*, no. 18 (1948); F. A. Vening Meinesz, *Gravity Observations at Sea*, vol. i-iv (1923-48), "A Formula Expressing the Deflection of the Plumb Line in the "Gravity Anomalies. . . .," *Proc. Kon. Ned. Akad. v. Wet.* (1927), and "Tables for Regional and Local Isostatic Reduction (Airy System) for Gravity Values," *Publ. Netherl. Geod. Comm.* (1941); William Bowie, *Isostasy* (1927); F. A. Vening Meinesz and W. A. Heiskanen, *Earth and Its Gravity Field* (1957).

Serial Publications: Bulletin géodésique (1922 et seq.); *Monthly Notices of the Royal Astronomical Society*; *Geophysical Supplement* (1922 et seq.); *Travaux de la Section de géodésie de l'Union géodésique et géophysique internationale* (1922); *Verhandlungen der Internationalen Erdmessung* (various dates to 1914).

(W. A. HN.)

GEOFFREY MARTEL, (1006-1060), count of Anjou from 1040, was born on Oct. 14, 1006, the son of Fulk (q.v.) Nerra and Hildegarde of Lorraine. During his father's lifetime he was recognized as suzerain by Fulk the Gosling; count of Vendôme, son of Geoffrey's half-sister Adela. On Jan. 1, 1032, he married Agnes, widow of William (Guilhem) V the Great, duke of Aquitaine. In the interests of her children by William the Great, Geoffrey then attacked the latter's son by an earlier marriage, William the Fat, who had succeeded to Aquitaine and who was Fulk Nerra's suzerain for the fiefs of Loudunois and Saintonge, so that Fulk had to take up arms for William. Continually troublesome, Geoffrey even tried to take possession of Anjou during Fulk's last pilgrimage to the Holy Land, but on his return Fulk finally forced him to make peace, pardoning him only after great humiliation (1039).

Having succeeded Fulk in 1040, Geoffrey pursued his father's policy of expansion over neighbouring lordships. His victory at Nouy (Aug. 21, 1044) gave the Angevins possession of Touraine; and from about 1048 he succeeded annexing a large part of Maine. He also resembled his father in having to atone for great misdeeds; hence his foundation of the abbeys of La Trinité in Vendôme (1028) and of L'Esvière in Angers (1040). He died at Angers on Nov. 14, 1060. He had repudiated Agnes (c. 1050) and left no children, so that Anjou passed to the elder of his nephews, Geoffrey the Bearded.

See C. Port, *Dictionnaire historique, géographique et biographique de Maine-et-Loire*, 3 vol. (1874-78); L. Halphen, *Le Comté d'Anjou au XIe siècle* (1906).

(J. LE.)

GEOFFREY PLANTAGENET (1113-1151), count of Anjou from 1129 and the ancestor of the Plantagenet kings of England, was born on Aug. 24, 1113, the son of Fulk V the Young of Anjou (see FULK, king of Jerusalem) and of Eremburge de la Flèche, heiress of Maine. He was called le Bel because of his good looks and Plantagenet allegedly because he wore a sprig of broom (*genista* or *genêt*) in his helmet. On June 17, 1128, at Le Mans, he was married to Matilda (q.v.), daughter of Henry I of England and widow of the Holy Roman emperor Henry V. In 1129 he took over the government of Anjou, Maine and Touraine when his father went to Palestine to marry the heiress of Jerusalem. Subsequently he had to undertake a long struggle to secure part of his wife's inheritance against Stephen of Blois and Eustace IV of Boulogne, but he eventually triumphed and was crowned duke of Normandy at Rouen in 1144. He also had to suppress risings by malcontent Angevin nobles. Geoffrey died on Sept. 7, 1151, and was buried in the cathedral at Le Mans, where a splendid plaque of champlevé enamel from his tomb is preserved. By his marriage with Matilda he had three sons: Henry, the future Henry II (q.v.) of England; Geoffrey (1134-57); and William (1136-63).

BIBLIOGRAPHY.—C. Port, *Dictionnaire historique, géographique et biographique de Maine-et-Loire*, 3 vol. (1874-78); K. Norgate, *England Under the Angevin Kings*, vol. i (1887); L. Halphen and R. Poupardin (eds.), *Chroniques des comtes d'Anjou* (1913); B. Chartrou, *L'Anjou de 1109 à 1151* (1928).

(J. LE.)

GEOFFREY OF MONMOUTH (d. 1155), medieval chronicler and, later, bishop of St. Asaph, whose major work, the *Historia regum Britanniae*, brought the figure of Arthur (q.v.) into European literature. In three passages of the *Historia regum Britanniae*, Geoffrey describes himself as "Galfridus Monemutensis," and since there is no evidence that he had any ecclesiastical connections with Monmouth, the use of the epithet is almost certainly due to the fact that he originally came from this town. Because of his partiality toward the Bretons and the fact that his father's name was apparently Arturus (a name used at that period among the Bretons but not among the Welsh), it has been inferred that he was of Breton descent. He appears as witness to a number of documents relating to the monastic establishments of Osney and Godstow in Oxford during the period 1129-51, sometimes in conjunction with Walter, the archdeacon of Oxford. In 1151, he appears in a Godstow document as "bishop of St. Asaph," although his consecration did not take place until February. Walter was described by a contemporary as an "outstanding rhetorician," and Geoffrey alleges that the *Historia* was translated from a "very old book in the British tongue" brought by Walter from Brittany. This statement seems a pure fabrication, but it is clear that Geoffrey was for most of his life an Oxford cleric, closely connected with Walter the archdeacon and sharing with him a taste for letters. It has been plausibly conjectured that he was an Augustinian canon in the secular college of St. George, Oxford, of which Walter was provost. He appears as a witness in a document of 1153, and this is the last record of him. The Welsh chronicles allege that he died in 1155.

The signature used by Geoffrey in the Oxford documents: "Galfridus Arturus," suggests that his father's name was Arthur, but the view that this Arthur was chaplain to Robert, count of Flanders, and brother of Uchtryd, archdeacon and later bishop of Llandaff, together with the further assertion that Uchtryd provided Geoffrey with his early education, is derived from the *Green-tian Brut*, a document which seems to have been largely forged by Iolo Morganwg (1746-1826), and which, even if it were genuine, could not be earlier than the 16th century.

The *Historia regum Britanniae* was published at some date between the death of Henry I of England (Dec. 1135) and Jan. 1139, when Henry of Huntingdon saw "the great book of Geoffrey Arthur" at the abbey of Le Bec. It was one of the most popular books of the middle ages, although its historical value is almost nil. For its influence on later writers *see* ARTHURIAN LEGEND; LAYAMON; MERLIN; WACE. The work, based on the so-called chronicle of Nennius and a certain amount of native Welsh tradition, the latter freely handled and grossly distorted, owes much to classical models, while the history of Israel, as recounted in the Old Testament, seems clearly to have influenced the general plan. The story begins with the settlement of Britain by Brutus, the great-grandson of Aeneas the Trojan, and by another Trojan, Corineus, the eponymous founder of Cornwall. The giants inhabiting Britain are exterminated by these two, Corineus destroying Goëmagot (Gogmagog). Then follow the reigns of the early kings down to the Roman conquest: here are found such famous episodes as those of Locrin and Sabrina (mentioned in Milton's masque *Comus*), the founding of Bath by Bladud, of Leicester by Leir (Lear), and the division of Leir's kingdom between the two ungrateful daughters. The story of the Saxon infiltration during the reign of the wicked usurper Vortigern, of the successful resistance to the Saxons by Vortimer, and of the restoration of the rightful line, followed by the great reigns of Aurelius and his brother Uther Pendragon, leads up to the account of Arthur's conquests, the culminating point of the work. After Arthur, the fortunes of the Britons decline, until finally in the reign of Cadwallader the land is devastated by a great plague and the king and his surviving subjects emigrate to Armorica, leaving the land to be conquered by the Saxons. In Armorica, Cadwallader receives the divine command to go to Rome and enter religion and it is foretold that he will die a saint. The Britons will eventually return to Britain after long ages, bearing with them the relics of Cadwallader. Chapters 106-111 introduce the prophet Merlin who predicts, in an obscure and apocalyptic manner, the future political history of Britain. These chapters were first published separately, before 1136, and dedicated to Alexander, bishop of Lincoln. They gave rise to the genre of political prophecies attributed to Merlin, which enjoyed an enormous vogue in the middle ages. At some unascertained date, but probably between the end of 1148 and the beginning of 1151, Geoffrey produced a poem in ornate Latin hexameters, the *Vita Merlini*, which portrays Merlin whose adventures are based on genuine Celtic material about a madman with a gift for divination and which ends with a highly classicized account of Avalon (q.v.).

Denounced from the first by sober historians like William of

Newburgh (q.v.), Geoffrey's fictional history nevertheless had an enormous influence on later chroniclers. Romanticized versions in the vernacular, the so-called Bruts (see WACE and LAYAMON), were in circulation from c. 1150. Writers of the later middle ages such as Ralph (Ranulf) Higden, Robert Fabyan, Raphael Holinshed (qq.v.), Warner (Albion's England, 1586) and Michael Drayton (Polyolbion, 1613–22) gave the material a wide currency; and was at its greatest after the accession of the Tudors. It provided themes for writers in the 17th and 18th centuries, although in the 19th, under the influence of the romantic revival, literary artists generally abandoned "the British kings" and turned to such frankly romantic authorities as Sir Thomas Malory (q.v.) and French prose romance tradition (see ARTHURIAN LEGEND) for their themes and treatment of ancient British legend.

BIBLIOGRAPHY.—The Historia and the Vita Merlini are edited in vol. iii of E. Faral's La légende arthurienne (1929). Other editions of the Historia are those by A. Griscom (1929) and J. Hammer, Historia regum Britanniae: a Variant Version (1951). There is an English translation of the Historia by L. Paton, History of the Kings of Britain, Everyman Series (1912), and a separate edition of the Vita Merlini by J. J. Parry (1925). The best short study is by J. J. Parry and R. A. Caldwell, in The History of Arthurian Literature in the Middle Ages, pp. 72–93 (1959). See also E. Faral, La légende arthurienne, vol. ii (1920); J. S. P. Tatlock, The Legendary History of Britain (1950). For biography see J. E. Lloyd, in the English Historical Review, vol. lvii, pp. 460–468 (1942). On the Merlin prophecies see P. Zumthor, Merlin le prophète (1943); on the variant version published by Hammer see R. A. Caldwell in Bulletin Bibliographique de la Société Arthurienne, 9 (1957): Caldwell regards this version simply as an early draft. On the later fortunes of the Historia see R. H. Fletcher, The Arthurian Material in the Chronicles (1906) and Roberta F Brinkley, Arthurian Literature in the 17th Century (1932).   (F. WH.)

GEOFFROY, ÉTIENNE FRANÇOIS (1672–1731), French chemist, whose name is best known in connection with his tables of affinities (tables des rapports), which he presented to the French Academy in 1718 and 1720. Born in Paris on Feb. 13, 1672, he was first an apothecary and afterward practised medicine. After studying at Montpellier he accompanied Marshal Tallard on his embassy to London in 1698 and thence traveled to Holland and Italy. Returning to Paris he became professor of chemistry at the Jardin du Roi and of pharmacy and medicine at the Collège de France, and dean of the faculty of medicine. He died in Paris on Jan. 6, 1731.

The tables of affinities were lists, prepared by collating observations on the actions of substances one upon another, showing the varying degrees of affinity exhibited by analogous bodies for different reagents, and they retained their vogue for the rest of the century, until displaced by the profounder conceptions introduced by C. L. Berthollet. Another of his papers dealt with the delusions of the philosopher's stone, but nevertheless he believed that iron could be artificially formed in the combustion of vegetable matter. Geoffroy's Tractatus de materia medica, published posthumously in 1741, was long celebrated.

His brother CLAUDE JOSEPH, known as Geoffroy the younger (1685–1752), was also an apothecary and chemist who, having a considerable knowledge of botany, devoted himself especially to the study of the essential oils in plants.

GEOFFROY SAINT-HILAIRE, ÉTIENNE (1772–1844), French naturalist whose law of compensation, or balancing of growth, had much influence on contemporary thought, was born at Étampes, Seine-et-Oise, on April 15, 1772. He was originally intended for the church, and studied natural philosophy under M. J. Brisson at the Collège de Navarre in Paris. In 1788 he obtained a canonry of the chapter of Ste. Croix at Étampes, and also a benefice. His preference, however, was for science, so he took up residence at the Collège du Cardinal Lemoine in Paris, where he studied law and became the pupil and friend of the mineralogist abbé R. J. Haüy. Taking his law degree in 1790, Geoffroy began medical studies under A. F. de Fourcroy at the Jardin du Roi and L. J. M. Daubenton at the Collège de France. His studies were interrupted in Aug. 1792 when Haüy and all the professors of the Collège du Cardinal Lemoine and of the Collège de Navarre were arrested by the Revolutionists as priests. Geoffroy had some harrowing experiences when he attempted to save their lives.

At the beginning of the winter of 1792 he returned to his studies in Paris, and in March of the following year Daubenton, through the interest of Bernardin de Saint-Pierre, procured him the office of subkeeper and assistant demonstrator of the Cabinet d'Histoire Naturelle du Roi, vacant by the resignation of B. G. E. Lacépède. By a law passed in June 1793, Geoffroy was appointed one of the 12 professors of the newly constituted Muséum National d'Histoire Naturelle, being assigned the chair of zoology. In the same year he began a menagerie there.

In 1794 through the introduction of A. H. Tessier he entered into correspondence with Georges Cuvier. After Cuvier's appointment as assistant at the Muséum d'Histoire Naturelle, he and Geoffroy wrote five memoirs on natural history, one of which, on the classification of mammals, puts forward the idea of the subordination of characters upon which Cuvier based his zoological system. It was in a paper on lemurs entitled "Histoire des Makis, ou singes de Madagascar," written in 1795, that Geoffroy first gave expression to his views on "the unity of organic composition," the influence of which is perceptible in all his subsequent writings; nature, he observes, has only one plan of construction, the same in principle, but varied in its accessory parts.

In 1798 Geoffroy was a member of Napoleon's military-scientific expedition to Egypt, and on the fall of Alexandria to the British in Aug. 1801, he took part in resisting the British claim to the collections of the expedition. Early in Jan. 1802 Geoffroy returned to his usual work in Paris. He was elected a member of the Académie des Sciences in Sept. 1807. In March of the following year the emperor selected him to obtain collections from the museums of Portugal, and in the face of considerable opposition from the British he eventually was successful in retaining the collections permanently for France. In 1809, the year after his return to France, he was made professor of zoology at the Faculty of Sciences at Paris, and from that period devoted himself more exclusively than before to anatomical study. In 1818 he published the first part of his celebrated Philosophie anatomique, the second volume of which (1822), and subsequent memoirs account for the formation of monstrosities on the principle of arrest of development, and of the attraction of similar parts.

When, in 1830, Geoffroy proceeded to apply to the invertebrates his views as to the unity of animal composition, he found a vigorous opponent in Georges Cuvier, and the discussion between them, continued up to the time of the death of the latter, soon attracted the attention of scientists throughout Europe. Geoffroy, a synthesist, contended, in accordance with his theory of unity of plan in organic composition, that all animals are formed of the same elements, in the same number, and with the same connections; homologous parts, however they differ in form and size, must remain associated in the same invariable order. He held that if one organ takes on an excess of development, it is at the expense of some other part; and he maintained that, since nature takes no sudden leaps, even organs that are superfluous in any given species, if they have played an important part in other species of the same family, are retained as rudiments testifying to the permanence of the general plan of creation. It was his conviction that, owing to the conditions of life, the same forms had not been perpetuated since the origin of all things, although it was not his belief that existing species are becoming modified. Cuvier, who was an analytical observer of facts, admitted only the prevalence of "laws of coexistence" or "harmony" in animal organs, and maintained the absolute invariability of species, which he declared had been created with a regard to the circumstances in which they were placed, each organ contrived with a view to the function it had to fulfill, thus putting, in Geoffroy's consideration, the effect for the cause. In July 1840 Geoffroy became blind. He resigned his chair at the museum in 1841, and died at Paris on June 19, 1844.

See Vie, travaux, et doctrine scientifique d'Étienne Geoffroy Saint-Hilaire, par son fils M. Isidore Geoffroy Saint-Hilaire (1847), to which is appended a list of Geoffroy's works.

GEOFFROY SAINT-HILAIRE, ISIDORE (1805–1861), French zoologist distinguished for his work on anatomical abnormalities in man and animals, was a son of Étienne Geoffroy Saint-Hilaire (q.v.), born on Dec. 16, 1805, at the Jardin des

Plantes, Paris, where he spent most of his life.

In 1824 he joined his father at the Muséum d'Histoire Naturelle as assistant naturalist, and after taking his M.D. in 1829 taught zoology at the Athénée from 1830 to 1833. The end of his first year's course was interrupted by the outbreak of the July revolution, with fighting close to the Jardin des Plantes in the street that bears his family name. He was elected a member of the Académie des Sciences, Paris, in 1833, and in 1837 acted as deputy for his father at the Faculté des Sciences, Paris; the following year he was sent to Bordeaux to organize a similar faculty there. Subsequently he became successively inspector of the Academy of Paris (1840); professor at the museum (1841); a member of the royal council for public instruction (1845); and in 1850 professor of zoology in the Faculté des Sciences, Paris.

He took an active interest in general natural history, teratology and applied zoology, and wrote numerous memoirs in various scientific publications. He died in Paris on Nov. 10, 1861.

His more important works include *Histoire générale et particulière des anomalies de l'organisation chez l'homme et les animaux*, three volumes (1832); *Essais de zoologie générale* (1840); *Vie ... d'Étienne Geoffroy Saint-Hilaire* (1847); and *Histoire naturelle générale des règnes organiques*, three volumes (1854–60).

See R. Knox, *Great Artists and Great Anatomists* (1852).

(ED. HE.)

GEOGRAPHY (ARTICLES ON). The nature of geography as a discipline is discussed in GEOGRAPHY, which surveys the history of geographical exploration; the geographical theories of the ancients; the work of such pioneers of scientific geography as Humboldt and Ritter; the fields of professional specialization that have won general recognition, and the deviant theories. As GEOGRAPHY explains, the scope of the subject is so broad that it touches on many topics that constitute the core of other disciplines.

Many articles written by specialists in these separate areas of study thus have implications of a geographic nature.

In the articles on continents and their subdivisions, the degree of detail increases as the size of the area diminishes. For example, EUROPE in its section on physical geography mentions the Paris basin, the broad lowland crossed by the Seine river; a section on FRANCE is devoted to the geography of the Paris basin; PARIS gives additional detail.

The geographical areas of a general nature to which articles are devoted include ARCTIC, THE; ANTARCTICA; PACIFIC ISLANDS; MELANESIA; POLYNESIA; etc. Articles on oceans, mountains, rivers, lakes, marshes, grasslands, etc., offer additional perspectives. There are also articles on various geographical terms—ATLAS; DELTA; DESERT; LATITUDE AND LONGITUDE; etc., and biographies of geographers, explorers and travelers who have contributed to geographic knowledge.

The article NATURAL RESOURCES gives a world survey, in terms of natural regions, of vegetation, soil, animal products, water supply and minerals. This broad picture is supplemented by separate articles on major raw materials and industries. For example, the fishing industry, discussed in a subdivision of NATURAL RESOURCES, is represented also by the article FISHERIES.

Regional distribution of basic materials is analyzed in articles on the continents and in such articles as PETROLEUM; IRON AND STEEL INDUSTRY; WHEAT; COTTON; FORESTS AND FORESTRY; etc. COMMERCE, HISTORY OF, analyzes the relationship between factors of geography and commerce. TRADE, INTERNATIONAL, emphasizes the relationship between nations, states, cities, etc., and in POPULATION. In the fields of urban and settlement geography, articles of special interest are SOCIOLOGY: *Rural and Urban Sociology*; CITY PLANNING; REGIONAL PLANNING.

Among the articles that may be of interest to the student of military geography, in addition to the articles on wars, battles and campaigns, are MOUNTAIN WARFARE; INTELLIGENCE, MILITARY, POLITICAL, AND INDUSTRIAL; STRATEGY.

ZOOGEOGRAPHY divides the world into zoological regions and traces, in text and maps, the spread of animals throughout the world in the course of the evolutionary process. Population geography is discussed in the articles on nations, states, cities, etc., and in POPULATION. In the fields of urban and settlement geography, contemporary problems and data. There is also an article on SHIPPING ROUTES.

GEOGRAPHY. This article is divided into the following main sections:

I. Introduction
II. Progress of Geographic Exploration
  A. Mediterranean Region
    1. Egyptians and Phoenicians
    2. Greeks
    3. Romans
  B. Norsemen
  C. Asian and African Land Journeys
  D. Opening of the Oceans
    1. Portuguese
    2. Spanish
    3. Voyages by Other Europeans
  E. Search for the Southland
  F. Exploration of the Pacific
III. Completing the Continental Outlines
  A. The Arctic
  B. Antarctic Exploration
  C. Inner Asia
  D. Africa
  E. Australia
  F. The Americas
IV. Problems of Measurement
V. Development of Geographic Concepts
  1. Geographic Ideas of the Greeks
  2. Ideas of the Romans
  3. Muslim Geographers
  4. Revival of 16th-18th Centuries
  5. Kant
  6. Humboldt and Ritter
VI. Geography After Humboldt and Ritter
  A. The Main Stream: Geography as Chorographic Science
    1. French Tradition of Regional Studies
    2. 20th-Century Developments
    3. Surveys and Inventories
    4. Spatial Interchange
  B. Deviants From the Main Stream
    1. Science of Relationships
    2. Study of Landscape
    3. Geopolitics
VII. Geography in the 20th Century
  A. Scope
  B. Subdivisions of Geography
    1. Population Geography
    2. Settlement Geography
    3. Urban Geography
    4. Political Geography
    5. Economic Geography
    6. Physical Geography
    7. Biogeography
    8. Military Geography
    9. Techniques of Geographic Study
    10. Cartography

Map surveys the history and techniques of map making, from the flat world of the ancients to the various types of cartographical projection now in use. The reader interested in modern maps of distribution will find examples in such articles as CLIMATE AND CLIMATOLOGY; OCEAN AND OCEANOGRAPHY; TIDE; TROPICAL STORM.

Among the articles on various aspects of political geography are SPHERE OF INFLUENCE; MONROE DOCTRINE; LAND REFORM.

GEOPOLITICS describes an application of political geography that is generally regarded by geographers as pseudoscientific, but has had a powerful impact on the contemporary world.

The science of ecology, which investigates the relationship of plants, animals and human beings to their environment, has made significant contributions to geography. These are discussed in ECOLOGY and sections on human ecology in SOCIOLOGY and ANTHROPOLOGY.

The relationship between geography and ethnology in various areas of the world is discussed in RACES OF MANKIND. A historical perspective on this subject is presented in MIGRATION, which traces the origin of the connection between various racial groups and the lands with which they are now identified.

Comparative population figures for U.S. cities are given in tables in *Population* sections of the state articles. Readers interested in a specific area or aspect of geography should first consult the Index, which provides information on material throughout the set. Another useful tool is the Atlas section in the Index volume with its own index.

I. INTRODUCTION

Geography is that field of learning in which the characteristics of particular places on the earth's surface are examined. It is concerned with the arrangement of things and with the associations of things that distinguish one area from another. It is concerned with the connections and movements between areas. The face of the earth is made up of many different kinds of features, each the momentary result of an ongoing process. A process is a sequence of changes, systematically related as in a chain of cause and effect. There are physical and chemical processes developing the forms of the land surface, the shapes of the ocean basins, the differing characteristics of water and climate. There are biotic processes by which plants and animals spread over the earth in complex areal relation to the physical features and to each other. And there are economic, social and political processes by which mankind occupies the world's lands. As a result of all these processes the face of the earth is marked off into distinctive areas; geography seeks to interpret the significance of areal likenesses and differences among places in terms of causes and consequences.

In ancient and medieval times geographers could do no more than identify and describe the features that gave distinctive character to different countries. Writers of geography, to be sure, speculated regarding cause and effect processes, sometimes with amazing insight. They made the first attempts to measure things and to place them on maps. During the great age of exploration which began about 1500, the methods of mapping were greatly developed: the continental outlines were plotted with ever-increasing accuracy; the rivers appeared in more and more detail; the positions of mountain ranges were established by survey rather than guesswork. Furnished with all these new data, geographers about the middle of the 18th century started to define broadly homogeneous regions in terms of physical make-up, or in what were conceived to be the major characteristic associations of plants and animals, or in terms of the economic life, or in terms of the political organization of national territories.

As man's understanding of the world increased, more and more attention was given to systematic studies; that is, to those features that were systematically related to each other because they were the result of a single process. Geography has sometimes been called the mother of sciences, since many fields of learning that started with observations of the actual face of the earth turned to the study of specific processes wherever they might be located. These new disciplines were defined by the subjects they investigated. Some of the processes at work on the surface of the earth, notably the physical and chemical ones, were reproduced under laboratory conditions where they could be examined in isolation from the environments of particular places. From these studies there resulted a great increase in the understanding of cause and effect relations, and numerous fundamental principles were formulated to describe the ideal or theoretical sequences of change. In a similar way the biotic processes were examined under controlled conditions, and such important concepts were developed as those of evolution and natural selection. The social sciences, too, have sought to understand the theoretical sequences of economic, social and political change as these sequences were presumed to go on when isolated from the disturbing circumstances of actual places. Since the so-called cultural processes could not be isolated in laboratories, they were isolated symbolically by such phrases as "other things being equal."

Modern geography starts with the understandings provided by the systematic sciences. Unlike these other fields, geography cannot be defined by its subject matter, for anything that is unevenly distributed over the surface of the earth can be examined profitably by geographical methods. Rather geography is a point of view, a system of procedures. It makes three kinds of contribution to understanding: (1) it extends the findings of the systematic sciences by observing the differences between the theoretical operation of a process and the actual operation as modified by the conditions of the total environment of a particular place; (2) it provides a method of testing the validity of concepts developed by the systematic sciences; and (3) it provides a realistic analysis of the conditions of particular places and so aids in the clarifica-

tion of the issues involved in all kinds of policy decisions.

Obviously a large amount of geographic work is done by persons not identified professionally as geographers. Scholars in the various systematic fields do not fail to concern themselves with the applications of their theoretical understandings to the study of conditions in particular situations, and such applications usually involve geographic work. When an economist examines the economic conditions of a country and prescribes remedial measures designed to provide for more production, he is involved in part with the geographic point of view. When a businessman studies the advantages or disadvantages of a specific location for his factory or his retail store, or when he plans for the more efficient operation of a system of transportation or of a marketing organization, he is working in part with geographic data.

Professional geographers can offer certain concepts and methods derived from experience in the analysis of the significance of areal differences on the earth. They play a role similar to that of the professional historian. Many persons who are not historians write accounts of the sequences of events that are called history; but such persons would be severely criticized if they failed to make expert use of historical method. Professional geographers encourage nongeographers to apply geographic concepts and to make use of acceptable geographic method, but they condemn the inexpert use of concepts or method. Unfortunately much work of a geographic nature is done by scholars in other fields, by businessmen and engineers, in a way that reveals an ignorance of the concepts of modern geography and that makes crude and imprecise use of geographic method.

(P. E. J.)

II. PROGRESS OF GEOGRAPHIC EXPLORATION

Exploration, in one form or another, has always been a major concern of geography. Geographic exploration was started long before the beginning of recorded history. As early as it was possible to communicate ideas or experiences, some of these ideas must have been concerned with the nature of the face of the earth, the human habitat. Even if the purpose was to describe the characteristics and arrangement of hunting grounds, or the strange things observed in distant lands, the result was geography of a sort. At first the chief effort was to gather and present facts about places; later the effort was organized around systems of facts, groups of facts related to single processes. Geography was concerned also with the perfecting of methods for selecting and measuring facts. The first phases of this work have been completed: no part of the earth today can be said to be completely unknown; in no part of a map can the cartographer safely draw pictures of Martian monsters or spouting whales. But knowledge of places is a relative matter. There are vast areas of the earth that are not mapped precisely, and the characteristics of many areas are not sufficiently well known to provide a basis for making practical application of geography. The new exploration is no longer concerned with continental outlines; rather it is concerned with filling in those outlines with precise detail relevant to the economic, social, political or military problems with which mankind is faced.

A. MEDITERRANEAN REGION

Geographic exploration, insofar as its record has been handed down as a part of the stream of occidental culture, had its beginnings in the Mediterranean. Even the names Europe, Asia and Africa were first applied to the three shores of the eastern Mediterranean, later to be extended as the geographic horizons were widened.

1. Egyptians and Phoenicians.—The Egyptians had explored and conquered large tracts of land before the 14th century B.C., both southward up the Nile and northeastward to the borders of Assyria; but the first seagoing explorers seem to have been the Phoenicians, who made Sidon a commercial port as early as 1400 B.C. and later raised Tyre to equal fame. The merchant adventurers of Tyre and Sidon explored the whole coast of the Mediterranean, founding the colony of Carthage before 800 B.C. They and other colonizers on the shores of the Iberian peninsula sailed northward along the Atlantic coast, probably trading with Cornwall for tin, and to the south, going far along the west coast of

Africa. With the support of Egypt they traded also on the Red sea, reaching lands yielding gold and ivory, probably on the coast of Africa or Arabia. It is probable that they also reached India from the Red sea. Herodotus heard in Egypt that in the days of King Necho (600 B.C.) a Phoenician fleet, sent from the Red sea, southward along the African coast, had returned to Egypt by the Pillars of Hercules. Herodotus was the earliest of the Greek travelers to give a full and trustworthy narrative of his peregrinations in Asia as far as Persia, in Egypt and north Africa, on the Red sea coasts as far as the Caucasus, and in Italy (c. 464-447 B.C.).

2. Greeks.—The maritime trade of the Greek city-states and their colonies became more important than that of the Phoenicians soon after the 5th century B.C. Greek ships sailed beyond the Mediterranean, opening up the Black sea on the east and the borders of the Atlantic on the west. Massilia (on the site of the modern Marseilles) was a colony of Greeks from Phocaea, and thence a voyage of great importance was made by Pytheas about 330 B.C. His own narrative is lost and the facts have to be gathered from references by Strabo 300 years later to criticisms of the voyage in lost books of the Greek geographers. Pytheas was probably the first navigator to fix the position of the lands he reached by crude astronomical observations, and he seems to have been a keen observer of places and people. He coasted the Bay of Biscay and the east of Britain as far as Orkney, where he heard a report of Thule, a more northern land, and a confused hint of the arctic region. On a later voyage he coasted along the east side of the North sea and probably entered the Baltic. During the same years the conquests of Alexander the Great opened to the Greek world a knowledge of the continent of Asia as far as the northern plain of India, and his general Nearchus conducted a fleet from the mouth of the Indus to the Persian gulf. This was the first voyage in the Indian ocean to be described in a manner comparable with the record of the land journey of Xenophon a century earlier, when, after the death of Cyrus, he led the 10,000 from Mesopotamia across the plateau of Armenia to the Black sea. In the following centuries the Ptolemies, Greek kings of Egypt, encouraged exploration, and about 115 B.C. Eudoxus of Cyzicus under their auspices explored the Arabian sea; he planned to circumnavigate Africa but could not get support for so daring a project.

3. Romans.—The rise and extension of the Roman empire involved scouting expeditions before and surveys after the conquest of each province of the lands bordering on the Mediterranean in Europe, Asia and Africa. Conquering generals described the tribes they subdued and the regions they occupied, and Julius Caesar won renown as a writer no less than as a fighter. Each province of the empire was bound to Rome by the causeways which still form the skeleton of the road map of Europe. Pliny and Seneca say that Nero (about A.D. 60) sent two centuries to follow up the Nile from Egypt, and they were stopped by great marshes, probably those of the Sudan, about latitude 19° N. The practical advantages of discovery appealed to the Roman mentality more powerfully than did the abstract theories which fascinated the Greeks; for example, Hippalus, who, about A.D. 79, learned from the Arabs of the regular seasonal changes of the monsoons, made these winds serve him as the means of establishing a trade route between the Red sea and India across the open ocean, whereas earlier navigators had had to hug the coast. Trade along this route continued to develop, and a century later Pausanias makes it appear that direct communication had even been opened up with China. In the time of Justinian (483-565) two Nestorian monks made the journey from Constantinople overland to China and on their return introduced the first silkworms into the Mediterranean lands.

After the fall of the Roman empire and the incursion of barbarians from the north, a wave of Arab domination surged over the Asiatic and African provinces and swept far into the southern peninsulas of Europe. The geographical learning of the Greeks and Romans enshrined in the writings of Ptolemy of Alexandria (fl. A.D. 150) passed to the Arabs and was forgotten in Christian Europe, where the conception of the globe degenerated to that of a flat disk with Jerusalem at the centre. The Arabs trading with India, China and the east coast of Africa acquired a sound knowledge of the Indian ocean and a fair idea of the interior of Africa before the year 1000. Among the well-known geographical writers of this period were Ibn Khaldun, al-Masudi, Istakhri and Idrisi.

B. Norsemen

Meanwhile the Norsemen from the fjords of Scandinavia were harrying the coasts of northern Europe and even making their way into the Mediterranean. Othar of Helgeland discovered the North cape and, rounding it, proceeded as far as the White sea in the middle of the 9th century. Later he visited the court of Alfred the Great, and it was the English king who first reduced to writing the discoveries of the earliest polar explorer and introduced to literature the midnight sun of the arctic summer. Late in the 9th century Iceland was colonized from Norway, and in 982 Eric the Red, sailing westward, discovered Greenland; soon afterward his son Leif Ericson, sailing thence to the southwest, came on a new land, which he named Vinland, and was thus the first European to reach America.

C. Asian and African Land Journeys

The domination of central Asia from the Caspian to the Pacific by the Mongol emperors made very long overland journeys practicable at the close of the middle ages, and Venetian merchants had thus established contact with China before Marco Polo set out in 1271 for Cambaluc (approximate site of modern Peking), the capital of Kublai Khan. The story of his 17 years' sojourn in the far east and of his journeyings by land and sea in central Asia, China, the Malay archipelago and India was the greatest work on travel of the middle ages, and for the first time it made the venerable civilization and the rich products of the orient familiar to the people of Europe. Many of his statements were derided by contemporaries, but his substantial veracity and remarkable powers of observation have been vindicated by modern travelers and students. Missionaries, whose activity increased as that of the crusaders diminished, pushed far afield in Asia, and their records contain some grains of geographical value among a vast quantity of superstitious and ignorant chaff. One only need be mentioned here, Friar Odoric of Pordenone, who, early in the 14th century, visited India, the Malay archipelago, China and Tibet, where he was the first European to enter Lhasa, not yet a forbidden city. A Muslim contemporary, Ibn Batutah, was the greatest of the Arabian travelers who left accounts of their journeys. Between 1325 and 1355 he explored Arabia and Persia and spent eight years in the service of the Mogul ruler of Delhi, going on to China and the Malay archipelago. He also visited the East African coast as far south as Mombasa and Kilwa and crossed the desert from the Red sea to Syene on the Nile; finally he explored West Africa by land, reaching Tombouctou (Timbuktu) and the Niger.

Many travelers in the early part of the 15th century made notable journeys throughout the mainland of Asia and the eastern archipelago, impelled by the growing demand for the silks, spices and other valuable products of the tropics. From Spain Ruy Gonzáles de Clavijo journeyed to the court of Timur at Samarkand; from Italy Niccolo de' Conti later in the century spent 25 years in the far east, reaching China, Java and Sumatra.

D. Opening of the Oceans

Long voyages out of sight of land began in the 15th century after the use of the magnetic compass had become general. As early as the 13th century portolano charts had been prepared to guide navigators from port to port, and they were quite accurate with regard to the Mediterranean coasts. But whereas latitude could be measured with fair accuracy by the use of the astrolabe, the measurement of longitude remained a matter of guesswork. The first voyages into the open oceans originated in Portugal and Spain.

1. Portuguese.—A large amount of geographical data was collected in Portugal by Prince Henry the Navigator, and under his auspices the earliest great voyages were undertaken. The first objective of the Portuguese was the exploration of the African coast, with the hope that eventually a way would be found to reach India by sea. The Azores, 800 mi. out in the open Atlantic, were rediscovered and settled in 1432, while successive expeditions stimu-

lated by the prince crept by degrees along the Sahara coast to the fertile lands beyond; in 1462, after his death, they reached Sierra Leone and a few years later explored the whole Guinea coast. Then discovery became rapid. In 1481 the equator was crossed, in 1482 Diogo Cam passed the mouth of the Congo, and in 1488 Bartolomeu Dias de Novais, by a splendid effort, fetched a wide sweep far out of sight of land and reached the Cape of Storms. This was the greatest landmark in the history of exploration. The king of Portugal, seeing the wealth of the Indies within his grasp, changed the name to Cape of Good Hope, and Vasco da Gama (q.v.) realized the hope in 1498 by sailing round the cape to the Arab port of Mombasa, whence with the aid of local pilots he reached India and fulfilled the dream of ages. Luis Vaz de Camões, who himself made the voyage half a century later, celebrated the achievement in his epic poem, *Os Lusíadas*.

2. Spanish.—Paolo del Pozzo Toscanelli as early as 1474 had pointed out from Ptolemy's maps that the east coast of Asia might be reached more easily by sailing due west than by going south and then east and north. Christopher Columbus, a native of Genoa who had much experience of navigating the Atlantic and had sailed to Iceland, became possessed with the idea of making this voyage. He spent many years in the endeavour to find a patron, and in 1492 had almost persuaded the king of England and the king of Spain to embark on the enterprise; the king of England hesitated the longer, and Columbus with Spanish ships made an easy passage from the Azores to the islands which he named the West Indies. Following a suggestion of the pope, a meridian line running north and south through the middle of the Atlantic was fixed by treaty between Spain and Portugal, the former country agreeing to restrict exploration to the western hemisphere so marked out and the latter country to the eastern hemisphere. Columbus, after other voyages to the West Indies, died in 1506 in the belief that he had reached the islands off the coast of Asia.

The merchants of Bristol had often sent their ships several weeks' sail to the westward into the Atlantic in search of legendary islands; in 1497 John Cabot, no doubt inspired by the success of Columbus, persevered until he found the coast of Labrador and Newfoundland, thus repeating the old Norse discovery of North America and, though the quest was not then pursued, pegging out a claim to England's oldest colony. The companions of Columbus continued to cruise among the West Indies and quickly traced out the shores of the Spanish Main to the south, and the limits of the Caribbean sea to west and north. In 1513 Vasco Núñez de Balboa caught the first glimpse of an inaccessible ocean to the west from "a peak in Darien" and recognized that Asia was still far off. In 1500 Vicente Pinzón, sent from Spain to explore the coast southward from the Orinoco, first sighted land near Pernambuco and, following it northward round Cape São Roque, discovered the mouth of the Amazon. His shipmate Amerigo Vespucci, a clever man who took part in several voyages of discovery, described this voyage, and by a curious chance his Christian name in its latinized form was attached forever to the continents of America. By making a westward sweep in a voyage to the Cape of Good Hope, Pedro Álvares Cabral lit on the coast of Brazil in the same year. The Spaniards, realizing that America was a solid obstacle between Europe and Asia, pushed forward to discover a passage to the south. In 1516 Juan Díaz de Solís reached the Río de la Plata, which seemed to offer a way through. Four years later Ferdinand Magellan showed that it was only an estuary, and, proceeding southward, he found and passed through the tortuous strait which bears his name, so piercing the barrier of America. Persevering in face of every difficulty which could befall an explorer, he pushed on across the incredible breadth of the Pacific. Although he met his death in the Philippine Islands in 1521, his ship the "Vittoria" under Juan Sebastián del Cano with a handful of survivors returned to Spain in 1522 by the Cape of Good Hope after the first circumnavigation. Among his rewards Del Cano received the proud motto *Primus circumdedisti me.*

3. Voyages by Other Europeans.—The Spanish and Portuguese between them soon completed the rough outlines of Africa and the two Americas. But the 16th century saw their maritime power challenged by the enterprise of France, England and the Netherlands, whose sailors disregarded alike papal bulls and private agreements between Spain and Portugal. These other Europeans established their claim to a share in the new world and in the sea routes to the east. French fishermen following in the track of Cabot early began to frequent the Grand Banks of Newfoundland, and the king of France in 1524 sent out Giovanni da Verrazano, a Florentine, who explored the coast of North America between the lands discovered by Cabot in the north and by the Spaniards in the south. He found no way through, and ten years later a French expedition under Jacques Cartier set out to search the Gulf of St. Lawrence for a way to the far east. In a second voyage in 1535 Cartier ascended the St. Lawrence to the present site of Montreal and, although only the name of Lachine rapids remains of this attempt to reach China that way, he spent two years in the effort to start the French colony of Canada.

Queen Elizabeth I saw a wave of enthusiasm for discovery sweep over England, rousing sailors, soldiers, merchants, parsons, philosophers, poets and politicians to vie with each other in promoting expeditions overseas for the glory of their country and their own fame and profit. The gallants of the court were ever ready to command the expeditions for which the shrewd City merchants found the means, while quiet scholars like Richard Hakluyt promoted the work by recording the great deeds of earlier as well as contemporary adventurers. Hakluyt's *The Principall Navigations*, first published in 1589, is to this day delightful reading, and, supplemented by *Hakluytus Posthumus or Purchas His Pilgrimes*, published in 1625, forms the only record of many great expeditions. On the continent similar compilations such as those of the Italian Giovanni Battista Ramusio (1583–1613) and the splendidly illustrated Dutch volumes of Théodore de Bry (1590–1634) played a similar stimulating part. In England as elsewhere at first the object was to find a westward route to the far east. Richard Chancellor tried for a northeast passage, and though he got no farther than the White sea he went on by land to Moscow and opened up direct trade with Russia, leading to the formation of the Muscovy company, the first of many chartered companies for exploration and trade. In 1576 Martin Frobisher made a spirited attempt to find a northwest passage to China and reached the coast of Labrador at its northern extremity. John Davis, one of the greatest arctic explorers of all time, took up the quest in 1585, and in successive years he navigated the broad strait which bears his name to 72° N., finding open sea to the northward and hope of an ultimate passage westward. Francis Drake, setting out to trace a route from the other side, made the second circumnavigation of the world in 1577–80. He passed the Strait of Magellan, after which he was blown southward to 56° S., and satisfied himself that the Atlantic and Pacific oceans met south of Tierra del Fuego. Drake proceeded northward and explored the Pacific coast of North America to 48° in vain search of a passage to the east. Eventually he returned by the Philippines and the Cape of Good Hope. Thomas Cavendish repeated this voyage in 1586–88, adding to the confidence with which long voyages were undertaken, and Richard Hawkins, though less fortunate, again showed the **English flag** in the Pacific before the end of the century.

Walter Raleigh, Humphrey Gilbert and many more took part in exploring the North American Atlantic coast, and in 1600 Queen Elizabeth I granted a charter to the East India company, which initiated direct trade with India and prepared the way for the British empire in the east. Spanish exploration from the Pacific ports of Spain's American possessions was renewed, partly no doubt in order to anticipate English discoveries. In 1567 Alvaro de Mendaña de Neyra, sailing from Callao, crossed the Pacific and discovered the Solomon Islands. Pedro Sarmiento de Gamboa in 1579 went south from Callao and surveyed the Strait of Magellan with a view to fortifying it and so holding for the Spaniards what they then supposed to be the only entry to the Pacific. The Dutch made many attempts to find a northern passage to China in the last decade of the 16th century. Willem Barents, after discovering Spitsbergen, was icebound on the north coast of Novaya Zemlya, and after wintering there made a heroic journey by boat along the coast, on which he died; his crew returned safely in 1597.

In the 17th century the search for a northern passage to the far east still went on. The work of Davis was followed by that of Henry Hudson, who in 1607 reached a latitude of 81° N. in the Spitsbergen region; in 1610 he discovered the inland sea now known as Hudson bay. William Baffin came later, reaching about 77° 45′ N. in 1616 and naming Smith sound at the north of the great bay called after him at the end of Davis strait. A charter for the Hudson's Bay company was granted in 1670.

E. SEARCH FOR THE SOUTHLAND

A belief in a southern continent surrounding the pole and extending into middle and even low latitudes had found expression on maps since the time of the early Greek geographers. Magellan believed that Tierra del Fuego was a part of this great land mass. Many explorers were drawn by the magnet of this illusion into the unknown parts of the great oceans. Pedro Fernández de Quiros and Luis Váez de Torres were sent out in 1605 by the viceroy of Peru to take possession of the supposed southern continent; on reaching the New Hebrides Quiros believed he had gained his goal and took possession with great ceremony of "Australia del Espiritu Santo," the first appearance of the name "Australia" on the map. In returning Torres passed through the strait which bears his name, discovering the northern end of Australia and exploring part of the coast of New Guinea.

The great period of Dutch voyages began with the formation of the Dutch East India company in 1602, though Dutch merchant adventurers, sailing by the Cape of Good Hope, were active on the coast of Japan by 1600 and soon after were successful rivals to the Portuguese already established in India and the Malay archipelago. The company in 1614 determined to find a way into the Pacific south of the Strait of Magellan and sent out Jacob Lemaire in the "Eendracht" and Willem Schouten in the "Hoorn." These ships passed south of Tierra del Fuego, proving that it was not part of a southern continent, named Staten Land (not recognizing it as an island) and saw and named Cape Horn on Jan. 29, 1616. Lemaire and Schouten crossed the Pacific, sailed along the north coast of New Guinea and reached the Moluccas. Other Dutch mariners working from the north discovered the west coast of Australia, still supposed to be a projection of a vast southern continent, Dirk Hartog reaching 26° S. on that coast in 1616. Antonio van Diemen, governor of the Netherlands Indies, resolved in 1642 to explore the coast of the southern continent and sent Abel Janszoon Tasman to carry out the task. Tasman's voyage was the greatest contribution to exploration since Magellan. He sailed westward across the Indian ocean to Mauritius, then in a great sweep southward and eastward he came on high land which he named after Van Diemen, though it is now known as Tasmania. Sailing farther east he came on the west coast of another lofty land which he named Staten Land, believing it to be part of the southern continent continuous with Schouten's Staten Land off South America. It was really New Zealand. He sailed on to the Fiji Islands and returned along the north coast of New Britain and New Guinea to Batavia. In 1644 he went out again with three ships, when he explored in some detail the south coast of New Guinea and the north and west coasts of Australia, which he called New Holland. In 1699 William Dampier, a noted buccaneer in his early days, made an important voyage in H.M.S. "Roebuck" along the west and north of Australia and the north of New Guinea, rediscovering and naming New Britain. His voyages were remarkable for his extraordinarily keen observations of natural phenomena; in some respects he was the pioneer of scientific exploration. The Dutchman Jacob Roggeveen in 1721 and the Frenchman J. B. C. Bouvet de Lozier in 1739 set out expressly to discover and annex the southland, and the latter took an ice-clad islet of the South Atlantic to be part of it.

F. EXPLORATION OF THE PACIFIC

By the middle of the 18th century the methods of navigation had greatly improved, and the introduction of the quadrant gave new precision to determinations of latitude. The great bugbear of long voyages was scurvy (q.v.), supposed to be an inevitable result of life on board the small craft of those days and often fatal to the larger part of the crew. In the second half of the 18th century scientific geographers in Europe secured a more systematic system of exploration in which adventure, though still encountered, was subordinated to research. Already in the first year of the century the astronomer Edmund Halley had been sent in command of a British warship to the South Atlantic in order to study the variation of the compass. In 1764 John Byron was sent on a circumnavigation voyage for discovery. On his return a larger expedition was dispatched under Samuel Wallis and Philip Carteret; it was absent from 1766 to 1769, discovering Tahiti and many other islands in the Pacific. A French expedition under L. A. de Bougainville followed, and for half a century there was keen rivalry between France and Great Britain in the Pacific.

A new era in exploration, which raised British maritime enterprise to a unique place in the eyes of the world, was introduced with the three great voyages of James Cook. The first of these voyages, from 1768 to 1771, was undertaken in part to observe the transit of Venus of 1769 from a suitable place in the Pacific. This mission was carried out and much more was accomplished. Many island groups in the Pacific were discovered, New Zealand was identified as separate from the southland, and much of the east coast of Australia was surveyed with amazing accuracy. It was on Cook's second voyage of 1772 to 1775 that the chronometer was first used, which for the first time permitted the accurate determination of longitude. Cook sailed far to the south of the Antarctic circle and proved beyond doubt that habitable land did not exist to the south of the known continents. Perhaps the greatest result of this voyage, however, was the proof that scurvy was preventable by proper diet. The third voyage, started in 1776, had the objective of seeking a northern passage from the Pacific to the Atlantic. Cook surveyed the northern part of the Pacific coast of North America and, after passing through Bering strait, pushed northward to 70° N, where he was stopped by ice. In these three voyages Cook not only had sailed completely around the world but had covered more than 140° of latitude. On retiring to Hawaii for the winter Cook was killed by natives in 1779.

Cook's voyage around the antarctic continent was supplemented by a great Russian expedition under Fabian von Bellingshausen in 1819-21, and by a group of hardy American and British sealers in the first third of the 19th century; chief among them James Weddell, who in 1823 reached 74° 15′ S. in the sea named after him, and John Biscoe, who in 1831-32 made a complete circumnavigation, discovering the most southerly land so far known.

Port Jackson, the present Sydney, was founded as the first settlement in Australia in 1788, and the coasts were explored by such daring boat travelers as Matthew Flinders and George Bass, the latter proving that Tasmania was an island in 1798. Cook was followed on the west coast of North America in 1792-94 by George Vancouver, who extended northward from Cape Mendocino the work of Spanish explorers and made exact surveys along the coast. The French expedition of J. F. de Galaup, comte de la Pérouse, in two ships spent the years 1785 to 1788 in crossing and recrossing the widest part of the Pacific; the expedition never returned, and many efforts were made to discover its fate, the most extensive being that made by A. R. J. de Bruni, chevalier d'Entrecasteaux in 1791-93.

III. COMPLETING THE CONTINENTAL OUTLINES

The 18th century saw the completion of the great task of outlining the continental shores. Even those of the Arctic ocean had been traced out by Russian travelers such as Vitus Bering (by birth a Dane), Semen Dezhnev and S. Chelyuskin, whose name remains on the most northerly cape of the old world. The Spaniards had made known the broad lines of the geography of South America, Central America and the southern part of North America, the central and northern portions of which had been penetrated in all directions by French and British pioneers. The interior of Australia remained totally unknown, as were the arctic regions north of 80° N. and the antarctic south of the polar circle. In the old world Asia had been traversed in all directions, although large areas remained unvisited between the trade routes and the tracks of explorers. China was mapped by Jesuit missionaries in the early years of the century, and the accurate mapping of India was under way before its close. Africa was the least known of the continents, and the French geographer J. B. B. d'Anville, despairing of reconciling the conflicting accounts drawn from tradition and the stories of Arab traders, who had undoubtedly penetrated far into the interior, swept the map clear of all features which had not been seen by European travelers and left a blank of "unexplored territory" within the coast line from Morocco and Abyssinia on the north to Cape Colony and Natal on the south. James Bruce explored the Blue Nile from its source in Abyssinia to its junction with the White Nile, and before his death a strong effort was made in England by the founding of the African association, which enabled John Ledyard to make a great journey across the Sudan from east to west and Mungo Park to trace much of the course of the Niger. Scientific geography was powerfully advanced by the measurement of arcs of the meridian near Quito on the equator by a French commission under C. M. de la Condamine in 1735–43 and in Lapland under P. L. M. de Maupertuis in 1736.

A. THE ARCTIC

Only a few outstanding expeditions to the arctic in the 19th and 20th centuries can be mentioned among the hundreds that carried out important work in that area. Sir John Ross in 1818 reached the mouth of Smith sound beyond Baffin bay, and, seeking a northwest passage, his nephew James Clark Ross reached the north magnetic pole on Boothia peninsula in 1831. Sir John Franklin set out in 1845, lured by the fatal fascination of the passage, and when he failed to return there began the rush of arctic exploration known as the Franklin search. Out of much that was weak, foolish and incompetent in direction there arose in execution heroes and geniuses such as Sir Francis Leopold McClintock, who developed the method of man-hauled sledging and stood out among those who explored the coasts and channels of the arctic archipelago. Americans vied with British in the search, and a high place must be given to Elisha Kent Kane, who in 1853 pushed through Smith sound, some of his parties reaching 80° N. In 1873 Karl Weyprecht and Julius Payer on an Austrian expedition discovered Franz Josef Land. In 1875 the last of the oldfashioned British naval polar expeditions in two ships with hundreds of men was sent out under Sir George Nares to reach the north pole. It failed to get through Smith sound, but Albert H. Markham in a sledge journey pushed on to 83° 20′ N. In 1878 Baron A. E. Nordenskiöld in the Swedish ship "Vega" made the long-sought northeast passage along the coast of Siberia and circumnavigated Europe and Asia. In 1882 a series of circumpolar stations for scientific observations was set up by international agreement; the honour of occupying the most northerly point fell to the United States expedition under A. W. Greely, and from his base J. B. Lockwood got to 83° 24′ N. Fridtjof Nansen in 1888 crossed the interior of Greenland for the first time, and by traveling on skis and inventing new devices for camping and cooking revolutionized polar travel. Five years later by a still more daring and original plan he drifted in the "Fram" across the Arctic ocean and got to 86° 13′ N. In 1903–06 Roald Amundsen, another Norwegian, in the "Gjöa," was the first to carry a ship through the half-forgotten northwest passage. Invaluable work was done by American, Italian, British and especially Danish explorers, including Ludvig Mylius-Erichsen, Knud Rasmussen and Lauge Koch in northern Greenland. Robert E. Peary, who had been engaged in polar exploration since 1886, was the first to reach the north pole in 1909. During the 1920s the first air flights to the pole were made. In 1926 Richard E. Byrd flew to the pole from Spitsbergen and returned there. A few days later Roald Amundsen and Lincoln Ellsworth with the Italian pilot Umberto Nobile flew in the dirigible "Norge" from Spitsbergen across the pole to Alaska. After World War II numerous weather stations were established permanently in the arctic regions, and flights to the vicinity of the pole occurred frequently. See also ARCTIC, THE.

B. ANTARCTIC EXPLORATION

The antarctic regions were explored for the last time by sailing ships by three expeditions in the period between 1838 and 1843.

It seems probable that the first to sight the coast of the antarctic continent was an expedition under the command of the U.S. naval officer Charles Wilkes, in 1840. A French expedition under J. S. C. Dumont d'Urville also sighted land at about the same time in the sector south of Australia. A year later a British expedition under James Clark Ross discovered the south-running coast of Victoria Land, with its two great volcanoes, Erebus and Terror, and the great ice barrier that bears his name. The antarctic seas remained largely unvisited, except for a southward dash by the "Challenger" in 1874, until Scottish and Norwegian whalers went in search of new whaling grounds in 1892–95. Scientific expeditions equipped mainly by private enterprise, under the inspiration of the International Geographical congress of 1895, went out from Belgium under Adrien de Gerlache in 1897, spending the antarctic night for the first time drifting in the pack ice south of South America; and from London under C. E. Borchgrevink in the "Southern Cross," spending the winter upon the antarctic continent for the first time in 1898–99. These were succeeded by four simultaneous and purely scientific expeditions in 1901–04. The British national expedition in the "Discovery," under Robert F. Scott of the Royal Navy, initiated antarctic sledging, taking advantage of Nansen's methods, and penetrated far into the frozen continent. The German expedition under Erich von Drygalski in the "Gauss," the Swedish expedition under Otto Nordenskjöld in the "Antarctic" and the private Scottish national expedition under W. S. Bruce in the "Scotia" were all commanded by men of science and did much valuable scientific work.

In 1907–09 Ernest H. Shackleton in a private expedition in the "Nimrod" succeeded, by the innovation of using ponies for transport, in getting to within 97 geographical miles of the south pole and turned only because his provisions were exhausted, while other parties climbed Mt. Erebus and reached the magnetic pole. On Jan. 17, 1912, Scott in the great "Terra Nova" expedition succeeded in reaching the pole by Shackleton's route only to find that he had been anticipated by a month (Dec. 14, 1911) by Roald Amundsen, who had made a dash on skis with dog sledges from a more easterly base. Meanwhile an Australian expedition under Douglas Mawson, with J. K. Davis in command of the "Aurora," explored a great stretch of coast from George V Coast to Queen Mary Coast and penetrated far into the icy interior.

After the addition of air flights and air photography to the techniques of exploration, the antarctic continent was revisited and its character became better known. Among the numerous expeditions sent out for scientific purposes after 1920, the three especially important. The basic purposes were to gather climatic data, to increase the knowledge of antarctic geology and to complete the mapping of the coast line. The first expedition of 1928–30 was followed by a second in 1933–35. A vast amount of meteorological data was gathered, and the coast-line mapping was considerably advanced. A third expedition in 1939–41 established two bases on opposite sides of the continent and carried out numerous exploratory flights back and forth between these bases. The British Graham Land expedition of 1934–37 also brought back important new maps and observations. Thereafter exploration of the interior continued; the International Geophysical year (q.v.) of 1957–58 was a great stimulus to antarctic studies. See also ANTARCTICA.

C. INNER ASIA

In Asia three great areas remained practically unexplored well into the 19th century. These were Arabia, the mountains and tablelands north and east of India and the deserts of central Asia beyond them. The northern half of Arabia was traversed in many directions by European travelers, prominent among them W. G. Palgrave in the middle of the century, followed by Charles Doughty, Wilfrid Scawen Blunt, C. Huber, Gertrude Bell and T. E. Lawrence. To the north of India the great effort was to penetrate the Himalayas and explore Tibet. Most of the work was done by officers of the survey of India, such as George Everest, Sir Richard and Henry Strachey and H. H. Godwin-Austen. Private explorers also had their part: foremost among them were the French missionaries Évariste Huc and Joseph Gabet, who reached Lhasa from China in an expedition of 1844-46; the great botanist Joseph D. Hooker, who explored Sikkim in 1848-49; the great mountaineers, including the three brothers Hermann, Adolf and Robert von Schlagintweit in 1854-57; W. M. (later Baron) Conway, Douglas Freshfield, the duke of the Abruzzi, F. de Filippi, William Hunter Workman and Fanny Bullock Workman. Finally the many attempts to climb the world's highest mountain, Mt. Everest, culminated in the successful British expedition under John Hunt in 1953.

In central Asia north of the great plateau Russian travelers visited the khanates of Bukhara and Samarkand, and many scientific expeditions ranged the vast spaces. Chief among them were those of Nikolai Prjevalsky, who between 1870 and 1885 traversed nearly the whole breadth of the continent and defined the great system of internal drainage and its mountain rampart. His work was supplemented and extended by many of his countrymen and in a high degree by the Swedish scholar Sven Hedin from 1894 onward. Francis Younghusband and other British officers made great journeys in the deserts of Gobi and Takla Makan, and the remains of ancient cities attracted the archaeological survey of India, for which Aurel Stein made important journeys. Of great significance in the history of United States geography was the expedition of 1903 to central Asia under the leadership of Raphael Pumpelly, in which such outstanding scholars as William Morris Davis and Ellsworth Huntington took part.

D. AFRICA

Africa had been left at the end of the 18th century with the map of its interior a blank, the lower course of the Nile, the middle of the Niger, and the mouths of the Congo and Zambezi remaining as openings to the mysteries of the interior. The Niger was traced to its mouth at an early date, and between 1822 and 1827 Dixon Denham and Hugh Clapperton made difficult journeys in the Sahara and Sudan and discovered Lake Chad for the African association. In 1849 David Livingstone, the greatest of all African travelers, began his missionary journeys from Cape Colony and explored the Kalahari desert, discovering the salt Lake Ngami. Convinced that mission work was of little use until the continent was opened up, he spent the rest of his life in settling the puzzling hydrography of central Africa. He traced the course of the Zambezi by 1855. Later he pushed his way northward, discovering Lake Nyasa and exploring Lake Tanganyika, and at the time of his death in 1873 he was intently following the northward-flowing Lualaba in the hope that it would prove to be the ultimate source of the Nile.

The Nile problem, under the encouragement of the Royal Geographical society, attracted many scientific and adventurous explorers. Richard Burton and J. H. Speke in 1858 discovered the vast Victoria Nyanza (Lake Victoria) on the high plateau under the equator, collecting the headwaters which issued from it as the White Nile; and pushing southward they reached Lake Tanganyika in the Great Rift which cleaves Africa from north to south. In 1864 Samuel Baker, exploring the Sudan, discovered the Albert Nyanza, another feeder of the Nile. Details of the geography of the Sudan were worked out by scientific men such as Gerhard Rohlfs, Georg Schweinfurth and Wilhelm Junker between 1860 and 1875. H. M. Stanley, a newspaper correspondent who had been sent out by the New York Herald to "find Livingstone" in 1871, found also that he himself was a born explorer, and in a magnificent journey lasting from 1874 to 1877 he crossed Africa from east to west, proving that Livingstone's Lualaba ran not to the Nile but to the Congo and following that huge equatorial river to the sea. The formation of the Congo Free State under the king of the Belgians led to the rapid exploration of the Congo basin, largely by Belgian officers, and the launching of a German colonial policy in 1884 brought many German explorers and men of science into eastern and western Africa. In the extension of spheres of influence most of the geographical problems of the once "dark continent" were solved before the end of the century, French officers (Gen. Louis Lyautey prominent among them) completing our knowledge of the western Sahara and Sudan.

E. AUSTRALIA

Australia was almost completely explored by white settlers under their own governments within the 19th century. Matthew Flinders was the first to sail around Australia, the coast of which he laid down in 1801-03. The eastern mountain chain shut off the first settlers in New South Wales from the west, but when the range was crossed rivers were found flowing inland and a vague theory of a great inland sea attracted explorers. John Oxley traced part of the Lachlan river in 1817, and the fine pastures of the Darling Downs were discovered in 1827, and the Murray river was followed to the sea in 1829-30. The search for new pastures was the main motive for discovery until after 1850, when prospective new gold fields became a rival lure. The formation of the Swan River settlement in 1829 and of Adelaide in 1836 gave new points of attack on the interior, and in 1840 E. J. Eyre traveled on foot round the shore of the Great Australian bight which separated them. In 1844 Ludwig Leichhardt made a splendid journey of 3,000 mi. across tropical Australia from east to west, including the southern shore of the Gulf of Carpentaria, and in the following year Charles Sturt, leaving the east coast farther south, penetrated to the very centre of the continent. John McDouall Stuart succeeded in crossing the continent from south to north in 1862 after two abortive attempts, and his route was afterward followed by an overland telegraph line. In 1860-61 Robert O'Hara Burke and William John Wills crossed the continent with the aid of camels but perished on the return, a calamity which drew many expeditions into the wilderness to learn their fate. From 1874 for more than 30 years Western Australia was the scene of exploration in search of pasture and of gold, beginning with the journeys of John Forrest, A. C. and F. T. Gregory, P. E. Warburton and Ernest Giles and culminating in the great 5,000-mi. march of David Carnegie in 1895. Journeys of pure scientific research were also made, foremost among them those of Baldwin Spencer.

(H. R. Mr.; P. E. J.)

F. THE AMERICAS

The geographic exploration of the Americas, which resulted in the filling in of the continental outlines with information about the rivers, the mountains, the climate and vegetation and the native peoples, was for the most part carried out by missionaries, gold seekers, fur trappers and adventurers. In any case, they were mostly persons who did not write books. As a result the history of geographic exploration usually omits reference to the Americas. Yet the bandeiras of Brazil, those bands of explorers that pushed out from the chief centres of colonial settlement into the unknown, seeking Indians to Christianize or gold to carry back home or good land to settle on—all these were also explorers who gradually reduced the areas on maps that had to be labeled "unknown." Francisco de Orellana, the Spaniard who was the first European to travel the length of the Amazon, deserves as much of a place among the world's explorers as is accorded to the discoverers of the Nile sources. In North America, the first Europeans to push across the great interior were Spanish missionaries in the southwest and French missionaries and fur trappers in the east and north. There were many pioneers from the English colonies along the eastern seaboard who pushed westward. Some of these, such as Daniel Boone, are well known, but there were many others whose names are not recorded.

After the United States had acquired a vast territory west of the Mississippi as a result of the Louisiana Purchase of 1803, a number of exploring parties and surveys were dispatched to report on conditions in the area between the settled part of the country and the Pacific coast. Some of these expeditions were sent out by the army, some by such civilian agencies of the government as the geographical and geological survey. One of the earliest of these was the expedition headed by Meriwether Lewis and William Clark, which reached the mouth of the Columbia river in 1805. Other exploring parties were headed by Zebulon Pike, John C. Frémont and Stephen H. Long. In 1878 John Wesley Powell, who in 1869 had been the first European to descend the Colorado river through the Grand canyon, published a report on the arid region of western United States, the result of many years of painstaking geographical work. He was perhaps the last of the field men who undertook to prepare inventories of the quality and potential uses of the land.

See also articles on the continents and biographies of explorers.

IV. PROBLEMS OF MEASUREMENT

In the development of geography attention was directed at first to the nature of the observable features that gave distinctive character to particular countries. From the Greeks on, however, geographers have been seeking for more precise ways of measuring things. When Eratosthenes calculated the circumference of the earth in 250 B.C. (*see below*) he understood the theory of measurement but his instruments of observation were poor. New and more accurate means of observation were invented from time to time: the astrolabe, the cross-staff and the sextant in turn made the identification of latitude more exact.

The measurement of longitude could be no more than crude guesswork until John Harrison invented the first practical chronometer in the middle of the 18th century. (*See also* LATITUDE AND LONGITUDE.) But the 20th century has been the era of "gadgetry" and after World War II there was a major advance in the instruments of measurement. Among new instruments of the century are the gyrocompass, the navigational computer, the gravimeter, and chronometers that do not vary as much as a second in thousands of years.

Sooner or later there had to be adopted a standard unit of linear measurement. Yet it was not until 1791 that a comprehensive decimal system was outlined. The metre, the measure of length on which the system is based, was defined as one ten-millionth part of the distance from the equator to the north pole. At that time this distance was calculated to be 39.37 in. Subsequently this was found to be a little short and the definition was revised.

The Cassinis (Giovanni Domenico, 1625-1712; Jacques, 1677-1756) completed the first geodetic survey of a country. They measured a base line on the beach near Dunkerque in France and then ran a grid of triangulation across France to the Mediterranean shore, thus for the first time making possible the accurate measurement of the area of the country. The Cassinis insisted that the earth was a perfect sphere. To disprove this concept the French Academy of Sciences sent expeditions to Peru and to Lapland to measure the arc of the meridian near the equator and at high latitudes.

Before the middle of the 18th century it was proved that the earth was an oblate spheroid, bulging slightly at the equator. In the 1960s, however, observations of the orbits of man-made satellites provided data for further refinements in this understanding. It was then seen that the earth is slightly pear-shaped, being relatively broad and flat in the southern hemisphere and pointed at the north pole. These departures from a perfect sphere would be observable only with the most careful calculations and only become important for map makers when pin-point accuracy is required.

As for measurements of heights, the base is taken as sea level, which in fact is not truly level. The surface of the ocean is about 13 mi. closer to the centre of the earth at the poles than it is at the equator. But in addition the ocean surface is not regularly ellipsoidal. Mean sea level (the mean between high and low tide) is higher in estuaries and bays, or near high mountains, than it is in the open ocean. The Pacific ocean on the western side of Central America is higher than the Caribbean. Furthermore, it is now known that the ocean surface rises to the right of steady ocean currents in the northern hemisphere and to the left of them in the southern hemisphere. Attempts to measure these small differences were made when a large number of observation stations were set up around the coasts of the world during the International Geophysical year.

The measurement of ocean depths was also improved during the 20th century. When H.M.S. "Challenger" sailed the oceans from 1872 to 1876, collecting a wealth of observations of value to the oceanographers (*see* "CHALLENGER" EXPEDITION), depths were measured by sounding at a series of points along the line of the voyage (with a weight on a wire cable). This provided the first measured picture of the profiles of the ocean bottoms. But the sonic depth finder (which measures the time it takes a sound wave to reach the bottom and bounce back; *see* ECHO SOUNDER) makes it possible to prepare a continuous profile of the bottom. By 1960, the shape of the ocean bottoms was known with considerable accuracy. In 1960 explorers descended in a bathyscaphe to one of the greatest ocean depths (35,800 ft. in the Marianas trench off Guam; a depth of 36,201 ft. was determined by sounding).

The measurement of mountain heights is still not easy. The Greeks knew how to measure height by triangulation but even greater accuracy was obtained by the use of leveling devices. In high, rugged mountains such methods are almost impossible to use. The invention of the aneroid barometer (basis for the altimeter in an airplane) made possible the measurement of altitude in terms of decreased air pressure. But variations in pressure associated with weather changes reduce the accuracy of a barometer except for short periods of time. Different climbing parties, at different times, find quite different figures for the elevations of mountains, even when the observations and the instruments are carefully checked later. It is not difficult to understand, therefore, why the elevation of such a peak as Mt. Everest is still subject to correction. Its elevation has been variously given as 29,002, 29,028 (the figure used elsewhere in *Encyclopaedia Britannica*) and 29,141 ft.

V. DEVELOPMENT OF GEOGRAPHIC CONCEPTS

During all the centuries when geography was chiefly concerned with the exploration of unknown areas and with the plotting of continental outlines, geography as a field of scholarship was developing slowly. In the course of its development many concepts regarding the purposes and methods of geography have been formulated, tested, reformulated or abandoned.

1. Geographic Ideas of the Greeks.—The stream of geographic ideas that permeates the western world had its origin in the writings of the early Greeks. The Homeric poems include a strange mixture of fact and fancy concerning the lands and peoples of the Aegean area. However, it is Thales of Miletus (c. 624-c. 545 B.C.) who is commonly recognized as the first Greek geographer. During a visit to Egypt, Thales became acquainted with the practices of abstract geome-

Geographic Measurement

Continent	Area (sq.mi.)	Insular area (sq.mi.)	Altitudes by location (feet) Maximum	Minimum	Longest river and length (miles)	Largest lake and area (sq.mi.)	Largest island (sq.mi.)	Highest waterfall (feet)	Largest desert (sq.mi.)
Africa . .	11,684,000	241,782	19,340 (Kilimanjaro)	-436 (Qattara depression)	Nile (4,157)	Victoria (26,828)	Madagascar (229,906)	Tugela (3,100)	Sahara (3,500,000)
Antarctica .	5,171,000	7,669 (ice-free)	16,863 (Vinson massif)	Sea level	*	*	Alexander †	*	*
Asia . .	17,170,000	1,243,732	29,028 (Everest)	-1,302 (Dead sea)	Yangtze Kiang (3,604)	Caspian sea (143,243)	Borneo (286,971)	Mawsmai (1,148)	Arabian (500,000)
Europe . .	4,056,000	350,657	18,481 (Elbrus)	-92 (Caspian sea)	Volga (2,293)	Ladoga (7,100)	Great Britain (83,698)	Gavarnie (1,384)	—
North America	9,816,000	1,569,759	20,320 (McKinley)	-282 (Death valley)	Missouri-Mississippi (3,892)	Superior (31,820)	Greenland (840,000)	Ribbon falls (1,612)	Mojave (25,000)
Oceania . .	3,291,000	356,206	15,400 (Wilhelm)	-47 (Lake Eyre)	Darling (1,702)	Taupo (238)	Australia (2,944,866)	Sutherland (1,904)	Australian (600,000)
South America	6,878,000	53,505	22,834 (Aconcagua)	-131 (Peninsula Valdez)	Amazon (3,915)	Titicaca (3,141)	Tierra del Fuego (18,605)	Angel falls (3,212)	Patagonia (260,000)

*Not applicable. †Not available.

try as developed in that country for the measurement of land, and he introduced the geometry of lines to Greek thought. His disciple Anaximander (fl. 6th century B.C.) made a map of the world based on information obtained from sailors in Miletus.

One of the fundamental problems with which the Greek geographers wrestled was the form and size of the earth. Before the time of Homer (900 B.C.) the earth had been conceived as a flat disk surrounded by the river Oceanus. Anaximander offered the concept of the earth as a cylindrical mass suspended in a spherical universe. It was Aristotle, however, who first demonstrated the sphericity of the earth by noting: (1) that all matter tended to fall together toward a common centre; (2) that the earth threw a circular shadow on the moon during an eclipse; and (3) that as one traveled from north to south familiar stars disappeared and new ones came above the horizon.

Eratosthenes of Alexandria (c. 276–c. 192 B.C.) calculated the circumference of the earth. He learned of a deep well located at Syene (now Aswan) in Egypt which was completely illuminated by the sun at the summer solstice. Assuming this place to be on the tropic, and assuming Alexandria to be directly north of Syene, he measured the zenith distance of the sun at the latter place at the solstice. Reckoning the distance between the two places to be about 500 geographical miles, he arrived at a figure for the whole circumference of the earth which was within 16% of the figure which is known to be correct.

The Greek geographers, like most of the Greek philosophers, were great believers in the concept of symmetry. Herodotus (c. 484-425 B.C.), who was both a geographer and a historian, held to the view that the inhabitable lands were not circular but were longer from east to west than they were broad from north to south, from which is derived the modern designation of longitude and latitude. He followed the principle of symmetry to fill in the arrangement of lands and the courses of rivers beyond the limits reached by explorers. He insisted that the Nile must flow from west to east before turning north in order to balance the Danube, which flows from west to east before turning south. He also named the three continents that border the eastern Mediterranean: on the northern side, Europe; on the eastern side, Asia; and on the southern side, Africa. The geographical and historical ideas that Herodotus accumulated were derived from the critical examination of a vast number of documents and also from extensive and arduous travels and field observations.

The first geographer to divide the surface of the earth into zones based on latitude (known as *klimata*) was Parmenides (c. 450 B.C.). He conceived of a torrid zone that was too hot to be inhabitable, two frigid zones that were too cold, and two intermediate temperate zones that constituted the inhabitable earth. Aristotle developed the idea of zones of climate and defined the temperate zone as extending from the tropics to the polar circle. Purely on the basis of theory he assumed the existence of a south-temperate zone corresponding to the known world of the Greeks. He, too, believed that the torrid zone was too hot to be inhabitable and that people who lived too close to the equator had been burned black by the sun.

The word "geography" was probably first used by Eratosthenes. The writing of geography, under whatever name, was greatly stimulated by the expansion of Greek culture, partly through the establishment of colonies of Greeks around the coasts of the Mediterranean and the Black sea, and partly through the conquests of Alexander the Great, who extended Greek horizons eastward to India.

2. Ideas of the Romans.—Unlike the Greeks, the Romans were primarily concerned with practical questions. The first of the encyclopaedic descriptive works dealing with the geography of countries came from the Roman geographers. The one whose works are best known is Strabo (c. 64 B.C.–A.D. 20). His 17 volumes describing the whole of the known world, and supported in considerable part by his own field observations, are like a handbook for the guidance of military commanders or public administrators. This work set a pattern for encyclopaedic geographic writing which has been followed ever since.

Claudius Ptolemaus, known as Ptolemy, was a mathematician, astronomer and geographer who lived in Alexandria between A.D. 127 and 141 or 151. In his great work on geography (c. 150–160) he brought together the results of Greek geographical learning. He attempted to provide the data on latitude and longitude by which maps might be constructed, but unfortunately he discarded the estimate of the earth's circumference made by Eratosthenes in favour of a much less accurate one offered by another Greek geographer. He adopted a suggestion of Hipparchus that the equator be divided into 360 parts (later known as degrees). Ptolemy recognized the difference between treatments of the world as a whole, of parts of the world or regions, and of localities; for these different kinds of writings he used the terms "geography," the treatment of the world as a whole; "chorography," the treatment of parts of the earth; and "topography," the treatment of small localities in detail.

3. Muslim Geographers.—The dark age of geography began before the fall of the Roman empire. It resulted in part from the completion of Roman conquests and in part from the rise of Christianity. A narrow interpretation of the Scriptures led certain ecclesiastics to deny the sphericity of the earth and any of the geographical concepts based on it. Greek science gave way to widespread ignorance and bigotry.

Many of the Greek writings, and especially the works of Ptolemy, were translated into Arabic and tested by new observations over a wide area. Such traveling merchants as Ibn Haukal in the 10th century, and Ibn Batutah in the 14th century journeyed far beyond the limits reached by the Greeks. Ibn Batutah (1304–68) went far to the south along the east coast of Africa to a place nearly 10° S. of the equator. He found the temperatures on the equator more moderate than those farther to the north. The idea of uninhabitable torrid zones which appears in the book by Aristotle was thrown in doubt. Yet so simple and persuasive is the idea that the world's climates can be properly grouped in just three zones and that these zones have some effect on the way people live in them that even in the mid-20th century it was still being taught in the schools. This oversimplification has been the cause of much obscurity regarding the relation of man to climate.

The Muslim scholars did much not only to preserve and criticize Greek learning but also to add new knowledge and new concepts of their own. The works in historical geography of al-Biruni, al-Baladhuri and especially of Ibn Khaldun (1332–1406) reach new standards in accuracy of observation and in interpretation of the relations of people to the land. It is apparent, too, that the Muslim geographers had started to formulate ideas concerning the uplift of mountains by folding and the erosion of slopes by running water, and also of the great amounts of time which these processes require. Such advanced ideas were developed by field men, by great travelers; for example, Ibn Batutah, during 30 years of travel, is estimated to have covered 75,000 mi., ranging as far east as India and the Malay archipelago. The Muslims, however, contributed nothing to the progress of cartography.

4. Revival of 16th-18th Centuries.—While the Muslim geographers were making their contributions to the development of geographic thought, the geographic horizons in Christian Europe remained narrow. Roger Bacon, writing in the 13th century and generally credited with originating the modern scientific method, described Ethiopia in terms which Ptolemy would have considered naïve and careless and which were based on information as much as 1,500 years old. Geographic horizons were reopened in Europe first as a result of the crusades and then of the discoveries of the Portuguese and Spanish expeditions.

The revival of geographic thought is recorded in the works of several scholars during the 16th, 17th and 18th centuries. The first of these was Petrus Apianus (Peter Bienewitz), whose book published in 1524 went back to Ptolemy for its inspiration. Gerardus Mercator (Gerhard Kremer) (1512–94) was a student of Apianus and later established a geographical institute at Louvain, where he worked on the development of his well-known projection. Sebastian Münster in 1544 published a descriptive book that followed the example of Strabo. But not until Philipp Clüver (1580–1622) and Bernhardus Varenius (Bernhard Varen) (1622–50) wrote their monumental geographical treatises was the revival of geographic learning well started. Varenius divided the field into general geography (dealing with the earth as a whole) and special geography (dealing with parts of the earth on a chorographic or topographic scale). His early death at the age of 28 prevented him from undertaking his proposed work on special geography, but a century later his general geography was still the accepted standard authority. In 1625 Nathanael Carpenter published the first geographical work in English, in which he showed a remarkable degree of scientific objectivity in his interpretations of observed phenomena. He foreshadowed the point of view of geographers of later centuries by focusing attention on the areal relationships of things on the surface of the earth. In 1686 Edmund Halley produced the first wind chart and presented his theory of the trade winds which related them to the distribution of heat on the earth. In the second half of the 18th century and the early 19th century there was a large amount of geographical writing, bringing together a vast number of new observations concerning physical geography. Some of this was summarized in the works of Philippe Buache (1756), the first geographer to make use of contour lines (1737), and J. R. Forster (1783). At the same time Jedidiah Morse of Charlestown, Mass., published his *American Universal Geography* in 1793; in Britain John Pinkerton's *Modern Geography* appeared in 1802; and on the continent Conrad Malte-Brun started the publication of the first *Géographie universelle* in 1810. This was the period in which there was a wave of new scientific writing, including works by such masters as J. B. de Lamarck, P. S. de Laplace, A. G. Werner, James Hutton, Charles Lyell, Georges Cuvier, William Smith and J. F. Blumenbach. This was the intellectual environment in which Immanuel Kant lived.

5. Kant.—Kant, the great German master of logical thought, gave geography its place in the over-all framework of organized, objective knowledge (science). For a number of years after 1765 he lectured at the University of Königsberg on physical geography, and these lectures were subsequently published. It is possible, according to Kant, to classify all knowledge gained from observation in either of two ways: a classification of things perceived in accordance with some logical system, a logical classification; or a classification of things perceived in terms of the time and space where they occur, a physical classification. From the former method a systematic classification of nature is gained, as when plants or animals are placed in a system of species and genera regardless of where they occur. From the latter a geographic description of nature is gained, as when the plants and animals that occur together in the same area are identified. Description according to time is history; description according to place is geography. History is a report of phenomena that follow one another; geography is a report of phenomena that are beside one another. Geography and history together fill up the entire circumference of our perceptions. This is essentially the concept of the place of geography among the sciences that has guided the main stream of geographic thought since Kant.

Kant regarded physical geography as the summary of nature, the basis not only of history but also of "all other possible geographies." Of the latter he enumerates five: (1) mathematical geography, the measurement of the form, size and movements of the earth and its place in the solar system; (2) moral geography (in the sense of mores), an account of the different customs and characteristics of mankind; (3) political geography, the study of areas according to their governmental organization; (4) commercial geography, dealing with trade in surplus products of countries; and (5) theological geography, the study of the distribution of religions.

6. Humboldt and Ritter.—Until the latter part of the 18th century there were essentially two main purposes of geographic study: there was the study of the shape and size of the earth, represented by Ptolemy and Apianus-Mercator; and there was the compilation of informative descriptions of countries and regions, represented by Strabo and Münster. Kant provided a place in the broad framework of geography for both. Since Kant the mathematical tradition has been carried on by the cartographers, on the border line between geography and geodesy; the tradition of

descriptive writings about places has become the main stream of geographic work.

With Alexander von Humboldt (1769–1859) and Carl Ritter (1779–1859), however, the nature of the main stream itself was changed. When Strabo was writing, and even when Münster was reviving the descriptive tradition, geographers were seeking to identify the phenomena and the associations of phenomena that gave distinctive character to particular places. Understanding of process had not advanced far enough to permit a recognition of phenomena that were systematically related to each other in that they had been produced by the same process. The purpose of descriptive writing had been an essentially practical one: that of providing geographically organized information either for the use of military commanders or public administrators or as a basis for the understanding of history. No scientific principle (that is, no concept of systematically related phenomena) guided the selection of what information to include, what classifications of phenomena to adopt. Such writings have been described as encyclopaedic in that the information included was not necessarily tied together by its relevance to a problem.

By the beginning of the 19th century the systematic sciences, each discipline being devoted to the examination of a particular process (as defined in the introduction to this article), had so far advanced the understanding of physical and chemical processes that no longer could such knowledge be disregarded in the study of particular places. Since the beginning of the 19th century the selection of phenomena to include in a study of the physical aspects of geography and the definition of categories of phenomena to be included in a system of classification have been guided by systematic knowledge of the processes involved. This advance in geographic theory was the result of the work of numerous geographers in the late 18th century who made the first applications of the new knowledge; yet it remained for two men to make the first effective use of these ideas and so to stand out as giants in the development of geographic thought.

It is remarkable that geography all over the world should owe so great a debt to two scholars—Humboldt and Ritter—who worked at the same time, both in Germany, and both for 30 years in the same city, Berlin. They were in many ways quite different in their backgrounds and in their approach to the common subject. Humboldt began his education with the purpose of becoming a diplomat, but stimulating contacts with teachers of science developed the passion and capacity for careful, direct field observations of natural phenomena. During his early 20s he traveled in England and in 1795 he made a geological and botanical tour of Switzerland and Italy. Then for five years (1799–1804) he traveled in South and Central America, amassing a vast amount of recorded and measured data regarding the countries he visited. Later, in 1829, at the age of 60, Humboldt traveled into central Asia. For most of the later years of his life, however, he was engaged in the writing of his great works: the account of his travels in America and his description of the physical geography of the earth in the *Kosmos*. He lived alternately in Paris and Berlin.

Humboldt's great contributions to geographic procedure were two. First, he applied his knowledge of physical and biological processes to the systematic classification and comparative description of the phenomena he and others had observed; second, he devised methods of measuring the phenomena he observed. For example, in his field studies of tropical mountains in America he measured the temperature at different elevations and for the first time showed temperature differences on a map by drawing lines to connect points of equal temperature (isotherms). He made use of census data where they were available, but in the absence of such data he carefully checked estimates of the population of various regions and countries of America. The step from qualitative, encyclopaedic description to quantitative, systematic description was a major one in the history of geography.

Carl Ritter was Humboldt's junior by ten years. He always regarded Humboldt as his master and in many ways based his geographical writings on the ideas of the elder scholar. Perhaps no man had a broader background of preparation for geographic study than did Ritter. He was taught by men who insisted that knowledge of the world could be gained only by the direct observation of nature. Like Humboldt, Ritter was a persistent and careful field observer; unlike Humboldt, he never made long journeys to distant places, but rather confined his field observations to Europe. He received a fine training in the natural sciences, and he was also a student of history and theology. In many of his writings he was more historian than geographer, and opposition to his ideas that developed after his death arose in part from the accusation that he had made geography a handmaiden of history.

Ritter emphasized the importance of comparative studies of different parts of the world and the danger of drawing conclusions or formulating generalizations on the basis of knowledge of one area alone. In his studies he always attempted to show how things existed together in the same areas in mutual interrelationship. He thought of geography as a kind of physiology and comparative anatomy of the features of the earth's surface. Yet his deeply religious attitude led him to adopt a strongly teleological point of view. His monumental work, *Die Erdkunde im Verhältnis zur Natur und zur Geschichte des Menschen*, two volumes (1817–18; 2nd ed., 1822–59), covered only Asia and a part of Africa.

Ritter also made two contributions to geographic method. First, he insisted that one should proceed from observation to observation, not from opinion to hypothesis to observation. He was among the first, for example, to show that Buache's idea of continuous mountain systems separating the drainage basins of the great rivers was contrary to observed facts. In gathering together impressive arrays of data from the reports of others, Ritter's purpose was to let these data speak for themselves in bringing out the coherent relations among things. He was the first to provide a system of subdivisions of the continents based on surface features as a framework for his detailed regional descriptions. Second, Ritter's approach was regional rather than systematic; that is, he focused his attention on particular places and on the phenomena unsystematically associated there rather than on systematically related phenomena wherever they might occur. Yet Ritter himself acknowledged that without the systematic studies of Humboldt his own work could never have been carried out.

VI. GEOGRAPHY AFTER HUMBOLDT AND RITTER

Humboldt and Ritter had gathered together the geographical ideas of the past, and from their writings there emerged a new and unified concept of the nature of geography. The main stream of geographic scholarship since Humboldt and Ritter has been devoted to an understanding of the significance of the likenesses and differences from place to place on the earth and of the meaning of the associations and interconnections among phenomena in particular places. Armchair geography, based on the spinning of elaborate theories in advance of precise observation, is no longer acceptable; in contrast geography has become essentially an out-of-door subject, based in large measure on the direct observation of phenomena in the field. One technical problem has been the method of recording such direct observations. At first such data were recorded only in the form of notes (written or sketched); since 1915 the recording of field data on maps in the field has become standard practice, and since about 1930 the recording of observations on vertical aerial photographs has given a precision to geographical study that it never could have possessed before.

The idea that Humboldt represented a systematic or topical approach to geographic study in contrast with Ritter's regional approach has been overemphasized by some geographers. Clearly both these scholars used both approaches, perhaps with varying emphasis. The modern concept does not recognize the topical and the regional approach as different aspects of geography, but rather recognizes the need for combining them.

In the period since the middle of the 19th century chorographic study (that is, study of areal differentiation and its meaning) has been moving steadily away from the encyclopaedic description of the Strabo-Münster tradition toward an organization of material relevant to a specified purpose or objective. Modern geographic writing starts with a problem and applies the geographic method to the search for answers or for clarification of the issues involved in the formulation of policy.

Meanwhile, however, a number of deviations from the main stream of geographic scholarship have appeared. One such deviation conceived of geography as a science of relationships, specifically those between man and his physical environment. Another conceived of geography as devoted solely to the interpretation of the visible features of the landscape. Still another and widely popular deviation identified geography with geopolitics. Others, such as the identification of geography with geophysics, need not be discussed in this article since they have few if any adherents in the modern period.

A. THE MAIN STREAM: GEOGRAPHY AS CHOROGRAPHIC SCIENCE

Chorographic science is that aspect of learning which treats of the areal arrangements and associations of things on the face of the earth and seeks to understand the causes and consequences of such areal differentiation. As already stated, geography cannot be defined by its subject matter, for anything that is unevenly distributed over the earth can be examined by the methods of geographic study. The continued development of the chorographic approach has led to greater and greater attention to procedures for selecting features to be studied and for rejecting other features as irrelevant. It has also led to great increase in precision of field observation. Both these developments were adumbrated in the writings of Humboldt and Ritter.

Clearly the main stream of geographic scholarship was defined in Germany by two late 19th- and early 20th-century figures. These were Ferdinand von Richthofen and Alfred Hettner. In the modern period the geographers whose contributions have been of the utmost importance, and who have set forth their philosophical ideas regarding the content of geography, are too numerous to permit mention of more than a few. The ideas of Richthofen and Hettner and of many others were discussed and critically analyzed in English in the monumental work of Richard Hartshorne, *The Nature of Geography* (1940).

1. French Tradition of Regional Studies.—No country has contributed more to the development of geography than France. In proportion to the size of the country and the financial resources of its universities the quantity and quality of French geographic work has been outstanding. But France has achieved this status largely during the 20th century.

During most of the 19th century geography was widely taught and geographic writings were in demand. The first chair of geography was established at the Sorbonne in 1809, and in 1821 one of the oldest geographical societies in the world was established at Paris. But the geographical writings of that century were in the encyclopaedic tradition and the teaching was aimed chiefly at a geographic interpretation of history. Two comprehensive series were published under the title *Géographie universelle*: the 8-volume series (1810–29) by Conrad Malte-Brun, and the 19-volume series (1875–94) by Élisée Reclus. The series by Reclus represented in its day the most scholarly kind of descriptive geography; yet it represented no conceptual advance over the work of Ritter since the genetic approach had not yet been applied to the study of population.

French geography was raised to a new level of accomplishment by the great master Paul Vidal de la Blache (1845–1918). In 1899 Vidal de la Blache set the new tone for French geographical studies in his inaugural address at the Sorbonne. He expressed himself as opposed to any strict determinism with regard to the relation of human activities to the physical environment; rather he recognized man as the active agent, operating in a setting that offered both possibilities and obstacles to man's wishes. But he was convinced that the way to go forward in geographical studies was to focus attention on relatively small areas in which to examine in detail the areal differentiation resulting from physical and human processes. Vidal's influence was great, and most of the French geographers after his time were either his pupils or pupils of his

Perhaps Vidal's greatest disciple was Jean Brunhes (1869-1930), whose *Human Geography* is a widely read book in English as well as in the original French.

The French geographers who developed under the influence of Vidal showed a remarkable unity of purpose and achieved a high standard of performance. The French regional monographs, some dealing with parts of France, others dealing with other parts of the world, are a famous and distinctive part of geographic literature. Vidal was responsible for formulating the original plans for another great *Géographie universelle*, and after his death the direction of the project was carried on by his successor Lucien Gallois. The first of these volumes to appear were the ones on the Netherlands (1927) and Great Britain (1928) by Albert Demangeon. The whole series was completed in 1946-48 with the publication of the three volumes on France by Emmanuel de Martonne and Demangeon. No finer books bringing together material on the geography of the whole world had ever been published.

Although all the volumes are of a high standard of accuracy and of literary quality, the outstanding volumes by De Martonne and Demangeon on *La France*, by De Martonne on *Europe Centrale*, by Henri Baulig on *L'Amérique septentrionale* and by Pierre Denis on *Amérique du Sud* should be given special mention. In these the regional descriptions are given focus through the inspired identification of central themes around which the descriptive material is organized.

The French regional tradition was passed, also, to workers in other countries. In Germany Friedrich Ratzel initiated a series of regional monographs dealing with different parts of Germany under the general title of *Forschungen zur deutschen Landeskunde*. The Pan American Institute of Geography and History, a specialized agency of the Organization of American States, undertook to plan and co-ordinate the preparation of a series of volumes dealing with the countries of the western hemisphere. Brazilian geographers were especially active in the writing of regional monographs in the French tradition. They were stimulated, in part, by the presence of several outstanding French scholars, notably Pierre Deffontaines and Pierre Monbeig. The Brazilians were also influenced by the German-American geographer Leo Waibel and by several geographers from the United States who introduced techniques of field mapping and resource inventory.

The French and German chorographic tradition was extended, also, to other parts of the world, where a number of outstanding scholars made contributions to geographic thought. Major geographic work has been done in Australia, New Zealand and South Africa, in Italy, Czechoslovakia, Poland and the Russian S.F.S.R. The Russians were especially important during the 19th century for introducing new concepts in the study of soil geography. Geographical work has also been important in China, Japan and India.

2. 20th-Century Developments.—By the middle of the 20th century the chorographic tradition had been notably advanced by new concepts regarding the focus of geographic objectives and by new techniques of observation and analysis. These changes had their roots in the 19th century, but appeared strongly after World War I. France, Germany, Great Britain and the United States shared in the return to the main stream of geography.

In the first place the need for a central theme or problem around which to organize geographic material became more widely recognized. The encyclopaedic coverage of areas was recognized as important; but it became more and more clearly demonstrated that even an encyclopaedia must be written for a specific purpose or to fill a specific kind of need. This involves, then, a certain amount of selection in the kinds of data to be treated. If the encyclopaedia is to provide background information for the planning of a military campaign, this determines the kind of information required. If the encyclopaedia is to be used as a reference work in schools or colleges, a different selection is required. But there are also many kinds of questions concerning origins and antecedents that may be asked regarding the geographic features of an area, and these questions are problems which in turn provide a means for distinguishing between relevant and irrelevant items. Or there may be an economic, social or political situation which needs to be changed or remedied, and this also provides a problem around which to organize the materials and analyses of geography. By mid-20th century leaders in professional geography were critical of research undertakings not specifically directed toward stated ends.

This trend away from the uncritically encyclopaedic kind of writing gave additional emphasis to direct field observation, again in the tradition of Humboldt. Direct field observation must of necessity be carried out in small areas, for the range of human vision on the curved surface of the earth is small. When the features of the earth are mapped on small-scale maps they must be highly generalized, as when a pattern of specific fields and farms is generalized into a kind of agricultural region. But the agricultural region cannot be seen directly, for it is too big; the details that make it up are the specific features of human settlement, the specific slopes and soils, and these must be mapped on large-scale maps. Geographers still use the adjective "topographic" to define that scale of field mapping which permits the plotting of specific fields and farms or specific blocks and even buildings in a city; a topographic map is one with a scale large enough to permit such specific features to be mapped.

Topographic studies, using the word in this sense, were common in Great Britain even during the 19th century. As early as 1895 Hugh Robert Mill wrote an essay in which he described in detail the characteristics of a small part of Sussex. He urged similar treatment for the area of each of the sheets of the British topographic maps (inch to the mile scale). The numerous essays brought together under the editorship of Alan Grant Ogilvie in 1928 (*Great Britain: Essays in Regional Geography*) dealt with specific kinds of problems or features in relatively small areas. In few of these studies, however, were the physical, biotic and human features of an area treated with the same degree of detail. It was commoner to treat the physical characteristics of an area in detail and then to sketch in the human aspects superficially.

The development of geographic thought and method were greatly advanced when geographers in the United States first developed the procedures for treating all the relevant features of a small agricultural area with the same degree of detail. One of the first geographers to insist on the need for such balance was Wellington D. Jones. With Carl O. Sauer he published an outline for the detailed field study of an agricultural area in 1915. In the summer of 1915 graduate students at The University of Chicago were offered the first field course in which such a balanced approach was taught. Shortly thereafter Sauer made field study a basic part of graduate training at the University of Michigan, Ann Arbor. Thereafter it became standard procedure to examine geographic problems in the field in small areas.

3. Surveys and Inventories.—In the period since 1920 the methods of detailed field study have been applied, with increasing success, to the practical problems of land planning. By mid-20th century it was widely appreciated that an inventory of land quality and existing land use was an essential basis for formulating land-use policy. The first survey with the purpose of providing such background information was the Michigan Land Economic survey undertaken during the 1920s and 1930s to tell the policy makers what actually existed in the cutover lands of the northern part of the state. During the 1930s similar field methods were used by geographers to survey the area of the Tennessee Valley authority. There, for the first time in connection with a large survey, mapping was done on aerial photographs.

At this same time, L. Dudley Stamp introduced the idea of the detailed field survey to Great Britain. In 1930 the British Land Utilisation survey was started with the objective of recording on maps of suitable scale the facts of land use and land quality for every acre of England, Scotland and Wales. The survey was carried out by unpaid volunteers from the universities, colleges and schools under the guidance of professional geographers, using maps of a scale of 1:10,560 (six inches to the mile). This survey proved of inestimable value during World War II, when Britain was forced to make use of every available acre of land for agricultural production. It is not too much to say that the survey was a most important factor in helping Britain to survive the war years. It also provided the material for Stamp's book *The Land of Britain: Its Use and Misuse.*

Two other surveys made use of geographic field methods for resource inventory and land-use mapping as a basis for the formulation of public policy. One was the Puerto Rico Rural Land Classification program (1948–52), done for the government of Puerto Rico, in which the island was mapped on a scale of 1:10,000. From these maps effective plans for the better use of the limited agricultural base were drawn up. Another survey was directed broadly at the resources of tropical Africa under the direction of George H. T. Kimble. It was widely recognized that at mid-20th century there were not enough adequately trained field men to carry on surveys fast enough, even in the world's critical areas. Geographers and others were seeking to perfect the methods of resource inventory through the interpretation of aerial photographs with a minimum of direct field contact. In this development professional geographers in the universities were handicapped by lack of financial support; meanwhile government agencies and private organizations were in some cases proceeding without the benefit of the experience gathered by the geographic profession over centuries of field study.

4. Spatial Interchange.—The study of the movements and communications that connect one area with another has long been an essential aspect of chorographic work. To treat areal differentiation as a purely static phenomenon is insufficient. During the 19th century, especially in Germany and France, there was much interest in transportation as a geographic phenomenon. The study of spatial interchange deals not only with the volumes of movement but also with the facilities, such as railroad equipment, or the capacities of ports and ships to move different kinds of goods. At mid-20th century a tendency had appeared to apply mathematical formulas from the field of physics to the description of the volume and velocity of movements in relation to the factors of location and distance.

B. DEVIANTS FROM THE MAIN STREAM

During the 19th and 20th centuries there were a number of deviant developments in the field of geography. Some of these died out early; for example, the proposal that geography should concern itself wholly with geophysics, abandoning studies of human geography as "unscientific." Other deviants were proposed by individual scholars but attracted few followers; for example, that geography should be defined as human ecology, a field already claimed, if not developed, by sociology. Among the various deviant currents that have appeared, three may be given special attention: (1) geography as the science of relationships; (2) geography as the study of landscape; and (3) geography as geopolitics.

1. Science of Relationships.—The idea of defining geography as the study of relationships appeared during the second half of the 19th century. At that time the understanding of the physical and biotic processes at work on the earth had been much farther advanced than the understanding of the economic, social and political processes. Few geographers have at any time thought of their field as covering only the physical and biotic aspects of the earth or of omitting study of the human or cultural aspects; yet the concepts of causal relationship as developed in 19th-century physical geography and biogeography were quite out of harmony with those of human geography. The theory of evolution applied to the changes in plants and animals had a tremendous influence on the intellectual world. It was reflected in physical geography, especially, by attempts to define ideal sequences of change, such as the cycle of youth, maturity and old age of land forms. These attempts were notably successful. William Morris Davis, professor of geography at Harvard university, was an outstanding leader in this development.

But when the new concepts appeared in physical geography and biogeography, no similar principles were immediately forthcoming to organize the treatment of man and his works. It was in this situation that an attempt was made to relate the human aspects of geography to the better-understood physical aspects and to define geography as the study of the interrelationships between man and his physical environment.

In Germany, Friedrich Ratzel attempted to bring the treatment of man into line with the treatment of physical features. In the first volume of his *Anthropogeographie* (1882 and 1899), he organized his material in terms of the natural conditions of the earth, in relation to which he examined various cultural features. In the second volume (1891 and 1912) he did the opposite, organizing his material in terms of human culture, in relation to which he examined the physical features of the earth. Ratzel, however, was thoroughly in sympathy with the tradition of Humboldt and Ritter; he never lost sight of the need for direct observation of all relevant elements of a situation. Thus in his classic volume on *Deutschland* he pointed out that two physically similar areas, the Black Forest and the Vosges mountains, had developed in quite different ways because of the differences in economy and historical tradition.

Some of Ratzel's disciples were not so careful to observe all the relevant interrelated phenomena. Especially those who were trained chiefly in physical geography insisted that a geographic analysis must show a relationship that crossed the border between physical and human phenomena, thus neglecting the relationships on the same side of the border. Few geographers ever subscribed to such extreme forms of environmental determinism as suggested by the historian H. T. Buckle and others; but many went forth deliberately to seek examples of environmental influence on human activities, and many remained blind to contrary evidence. As a result geography was divided into physical geography (a well-developed field of science) and human geography (a relatively superficial treatment of man's relations to the physical earth). The adjective "geographic" came to refer to the physical character of an area. Thus a "geographic factor" was some condition of the physical environment to which human activities were to be related as "responses" or "adjustments."

Geography as the science of relationships persisted longer in the English-speaking world than elsewhere. It found few adherents in Germany, where Alfred Hettner was developing the ideas associated with the main stream of geography. It was effectively attacked by the French geographers under the leadership of Paul Vidal de la Blache. But it was given persuasive support in the United States by such scholars as William Morris Davis, Ellen C. Semple, Wallace W. Atwood, Ellsworth Huntington, Robert DeCourcy Ward and R. H. Whitbeck. Yet this approach to geographic study proved to be a dead end. As Griffith Taylor, an eloquent supporter of the ideas of environmental determinism, wrote, such relationships between man and his environment are nowhere more clearly seen than when one looks at the world as a whole. Yet when one looks at the world as a whole all the aspects of the face of the earth, physical as well as human, are highly generalized. Only when the earth is examined in topographic detail—that is, on maps large enough to permit the plotting of specific features of human occupance—can generalization be kept to such limits that results can be checked. At mid-20th century detailed field studies had yet to demonstrate through proper historical and comparative methods the validity of the concept of environmental determinism. Modern geographers, on the contrary, insist on the principle that the significance to man of the features of the physical earth is a function of the attitudes, objectives and technical abilities of man himself. In other words, the physical and biotic environment has different meaning for different persons; and further, geography examines the relationships not only between man and the physical or biotic aspects of the environment but also between man and the variety of cultural features resulting from economic, social and political processes. Only thus can the relative significance of areal differences be weighed and evaluated. Geography can no longer be divided neatly into physical and human geography, and a geographic factor is any factor of location or areal association that is relevant to a problem.

2. Study of Landscape.—The idea that geography should be restricted to an examination of the visible character of the landscape appeared as another deviant in 19th-century Germany, especially in the works of Otto Schlüter. In the United States this approach to geography was introduced by Carl O. Sauer in a paper entitled "The Morphology of Landscape" (1925). The immediate popularity of this point of view among the younger geographers of that period represented a reaction against the idea that geography was restricted to a study of the relationships between man and his physical environment. Sauer's paper shows the results of experience in detailed field mapping and field study, the influence of ideas from German geographic literature and the challenge of concepts presented by the rapidly developing field of anthropology. Sauer was concerned with the significance to man of the physical and biotic conditions of a small area or site, and also with man's transformation of the site. Perhaps it was the followers of Sauer rather than Sauer himself who tried to restrict geographic attention to form and structure alone to the neglect of function—in other words, to the anatomy of the visible landscape rather than to its physiology.

As in other attempts to provide a limited definition of the field of geography, this proved to be a dead end. Geography, according to the concepts developed by Kant and restated by Sauer, is one aspect (along with history) of the whole range of perception; Sauer called it a "naïvely-given sector of reality." Geography, then, is not subject to definition or limitation; geography is not what geographers do, for much work in this sector of reality is done by persons who are not professional geographers and who are not especially competent in the use of geographic methods.

3. Geopolitics.—Another deviant from the main stream of geographic science is that known by the popular term "geopolitics." The great popularity of geopolitics as a practical field of study in which human geography and applied political science are used for the examination of certain problems in international relations had its great development as a result of World War II. Karl Haushofer, a German geographer, was credited with the formulation of ideas that had a profound effect on the strategic policy of Adolf Hitler. Whether Haushofer's ideas had the greater influence on Hitler or Hitler's on Haushofer has not been established. The fact is, however, that the German school of geopolitics was used to provide a pseudoscientific rationalization of Nazi policy. In the United States and Great Britain another school of geopolitics was developed which sought to go back to H. J. Mackinder and A. T. Mahan rather than to Haushofer.

Geopolitics, as distinguished from political geography, combines the concepts and techniques of a variety of disciplines for the purpose of formulating strategic policy in international relations. But strategic policy as formulated by the leaders of any one state has the basic purpose of advancing the interests of that state; every state has a somewhat different set of purposes and these are often in conflict with the purposes of other states. Geopolitics, then, is an applied field which would seem inevitably to be divided into as many schools as there are independent states. Geography may be used, along with other disciplines, in working out the plans of geopolitics; but geography is not the same as geopolitics, nor is geopolitics a field of scholarship by itself. See also GEOPOLITICS.

VII. GEOGRAPHY IN THE 20TH CENTURY

A. SCOPE

Geography, like other fields of learning, continues to debate basic questions about scope and method. Is geography purely descriptive, seeking to provide a more and more useful and accurate picture of the face of the earth as the home of man; or is its chief mission to formulate general concepts or theories? In other words, is geography an idiographic or a nomothetic subject? Unfortunately for clarity of thought, many people think of these two objectives as incompatible. Perhaps the more advanced a field of study becomes the easier it is to accept the notion that all science can do is describe. But is description restricted to the reproduction of unique things, or is description to be in terms of theoretical models?

In the 1960s most geographers agreed that the chief purpose was nomothetic, that is, to formulate laws. Formulating and testing general concepts became more effective through the increased use of mathematical procedures. Instead of seeking deterministic concepts of strict cause and effect, geographers discovered that the theory of probability could be applied to the formulation of concepts and forecasts.

These discussions brought out ideas that were not really so new as some thought. A review of the history of geography and of other fields of learning shows how much of this discussion about scope had been argued before. Richard Hartshorne, in The Nature of Geography (1939) and Perspective on the Nature of Geography (1959), presented a discussion of the scope of the field as reflected in the writings of geographers, chiefly in the United States and Europe. In 1954 the Association of American Geographers published American Geography, Inventory and Prospect (edited by Preston E. James and Clarence F. Jones), in which the record of geography in the United States was set forth. Two other important contributions to discussions of scope and method were The Science of Geography, by a committee of the National Research Council in 1965, and Locational Analysis in Human Geography, by Peter Haggett in 1966.

Geography is seen as a single discipline, unified by its general concepts and the kinds of questions it asks about the face of the earth. Geographers ask questions about location and about the interconnections among things that are associated in segments of earth space. The region, as geographers define this term, is still a basic device for identifying the areal spread of spatial systems, that is, systems of interconnected parts occupying specific parts of the earth's surface. Popularly, the word "region" denotes a relatively large area having some general quality of homogeneity, but with boundaries not precisely defined. Geographers define a region as an area of any size that is homogeneous in terms of specific criteria and that is distinguished from bordering areas by a particular kind of association of areally related features. The old distinction between topical (or systematic) geography and regional geography is not considered valid. Topical geography is defined as the study of a particular group of features produced by one kind of process wherever these features may occur in the world (Varenius' general geography); regional geography is defined as the study of many different kinds of features as they occur in particular areas (Varenius' special geography). Insofar as all regions must be defined in terms of specific criteria the approach to regions is a topical one; and since the study of any topic involves the definition of homogeneous areas, all topical study must make use of the regional method.

The new concept of the region stemmed from experience in detailed field studies. It is clear that no two points on the face of the earth are identical. On the other hand, if the complexity of the face of the earth is to be brought within manageable limits for the purpose of examining the causes and consequences of areal differentiation, to examine each spot separately would defeat the endeavour. Geographers must always generalize; they must define categories of phenomena that are meaningful in that they are associated in area with other phenomena; they must seek associations of phenomena, defined as regions, that are significant in that they are related to a particular process or group of processes. In all science, as formulated by Kant, there are two kinds of generalizations: one that deals with the classification of phenomena into categories of greater or lesser degree of generalization; and another that describes the ideal operation of a process, or a sequence of events. Geography traditionally deals with the former; but modern geography classifies phenomena on the basis of systematic knowledge of process.

Conceived in this way the region is a device for illuminating the factors of a problem that otherwise would be less clearly understood. It is not an objective fact; rather it is an intellectual concept. A region is justified if it illuminates the elements of a problem; it is not justified if it obscures these elements. There is no such thing as a "true region"; there are, in fact, as many regional systems as there are problems worth studying by geographic method.

Two important developments after 1954 permitted a much greater precision in the definition of regions, and in the identification of regularities in the location of things on the face of the earth. First was the improvement of remote sensing, that is, deriving a picture of the earth's surface from photographic or electronic images. Satellite images reveal details on the earth's surface never before available for study. In the late 1960s much attention was being given to working out new techniques for the analysis of satellite images. Furthermore, pictures derived from remote sensing could be fed into computers for the analysis of areal associations, and for the preparation of complex maps.

The other development in geographic study was the use of mathematical procedures. Statistical procedures make possible the formulation and testing of hypotheses with much greater precision than could be done with word symbols. In the fields of experimental science, the scholar can retreat to his laboratory and set up an experiment in which outside, disturbing effects are one by one eliminated until the operation of a process in isolation can be observed. The economist does this symbolically by the use of the phrase "other things being equal." But hitherto the procedures for probing complex interconnections among things of diverse origin. By the use of statistical procedures he can identify the elements of spatial systems and discard those elements which are irrelevant to any particular process. By using probability theory he can take account of those "chance" interconnections that are purposely left out of studies in most other disciplines. With the aid of computers it became possible to carry out computations that are far beyond the capacity of the man with a pencil and paper.

Clearly, if one asks a computer to reply to a silly question the answer will be silly. A basic problem in the use of quantitative data is the enumeration area to which the data apply. For example, the population of a city is commonly given by adding the number of individuals within the city limits. But city limits are made for political purposes, and are important for those purposes. In terms of the size of the urban population functionally related to the central city, the political city limits are irrelevant. It is impossible to make a comparative study of urban sizes by using the numbers within political city limits. If data are to be plotted within a grid of rectangles to be fed into a computer, the dimensions of the screen become a very important matter. Too coarse a screen, that is, one with rectangles that are too large, gives less precise information than a fine screen. How fine must the screen be for a particular kind of problem? Mathematical procedures can be of the greatest aid in reaching more precise and useful answers to geographical problems, but they are no substitute for careful observation and logical thinking.

The interconnections among the elements of a spatial system must be traced through time. If two or more phenomena are found to occupy exactly the same segment of earth space, that is no evidence that they are interconnected. Interconnection involves processes, or sequences of events that run through time.

This means that geography cannot be strictly contemporary. All geographic study must be approached historically if it is to be complete. Historical geography is understood to be concerned with the re-creation of past geographies and with geographical changes through time. A full understanding of contemporary geographic phenomena requires the full perspective of past geographies, for the operation of any one process at a particular place and time is to a certain extent modified by the total environment with which the process is involved. The systematic sciences work to unravel all these disturbing connections with the environment and to describe the ideal operation of the process in isolation; geography seeks to put the process back in its earthly setting and to see its connections both in space and time.

B. Subdivisions of Geography

Obviously no one scholar could become thoroughly competent in all branches of so broad a field. In the first place, a considerable amount of geographic work is actually done by persons who are not professional geographers. In the second place, those who hope to become professional geographers must select a group of topical fields and certain areas of the world in which they intend to specialize. There are as many topical fields, at least potentially, as there are kinds of processes acting to differentiate one part of the earth from another. The following brief outline of topical fields is not definitive.

1. Population Geography.—The mapping of the distribution of people, as J. Brunhes pointed out, is one of the primary tasks of geographic study. The data on which maps must be based are numbers of persons, summed up in enumeration areas. But the enumeration areas are usually too large or include arbitrary segments of a national territory that obscure the facts of population distribution. Population geography also includes the study of the movements of people and of such population characteristics as age and sex structure, ethnic composition, religious and linguistic groupings and a variety of other matters. The geographer's contribution consists of finding ways to portray more effectively the patterns of distribution on maps and to analyze more effectively the areal relations of population to other features.

2. Settlement Geography.—This is closely related to population geography in that one of the methods of locating persons within enumeration areas is to observe the distribution of houses. Settlement geography, however, goes beyond this to study all the facilities men build in the process of occupying an area: the forms and functions of buildings, the road and property patterns and the groupings of these things. Much has been done with settlement patterns since August Meitzen in 1895 examined the settlements of eastern Germany. Studies of the rural habitation in France and of house types in the United States have brought to light important relationships not only of houses to building materials but of houses to cultural traditions.

3. Urban Geography.—This topical field includes the urban part of settlement geography, but goes beyond the problems commonly considered in rural areas. Cities are examined not only in terms of their patterns of arrangement, their internal structure and the arrangement of functional areas within them, but also in terms of the services they perform and of the movements of goods and persons that are involved. Urban geography provides an essential background for city planning.

4. Political Geography.—In political geography attention is focused on politically organized areas or political regions. The purpose is to show how the effective administration of a political area is related to the geographic arrangement of the various parts of the state—the capital city, the industrial core, the areas of concentrated settlement, the boundaries, the dependent areas and the sources of raw materials. It is recognized that any successful state operates on the basis of a "state-idea"; that is, a body of principles or traditions which can command the loyal support of a considerable majority of the people. Where the state-idea is poorly developed, or where different state-ideas are held in different parts of the national territory, the effective functioning of the state is imperiled. The arrangement of these nonmaterial aspects of the political life, examined in relation to material aspects such as those enumerated above, offers many problems and opportunities.

5. Economic Geography.—So much attention has been given to the study of the significance of likenesses and differences among places in terms of economic processes that economic geography can no longer be considered as a field of specialization of itself. Among the more important subdivisions of economic geography are the following: the study of resources and the inventory and evaluation of the resource base of an area; the geography of mining and minerals; the geography of agriculture and land utilization; the geography of manufacturing industry, involving the principles of industrial location and the factors in industrial site selection; the geography of transportation, involving not only the movements of goods from place to place but also analysis of the arrangement of facilities such as railroads, docks, airfields or shipping lines; and marketing geography, or the application of geographic methods to the analysis of actual and potential markets, including sales territories, salesmen's routes and all the numerous factors involved in estimating the potential sales of a given site. There are many other topical specialties within the general field of economic geography that might be mentioned, such as the geographic study of recreation, or the geographic study of service occupations, or any number of other ways of making a living.

6. Physical Geography.—Like economic geography, physical geography is a subdivision of the whole field of geography that is too broad to be cultivated as a whole. In each of the topical specialties dealing with physical processes on the earth there have been many important contributions during the 19th and 20th centuries, and in each of these specialties, concerned with areal differentiation, there are close connections with the bordering systematic fields in which study of process is the primary aim. Physical geography is divided into a number of specialties, of which the more important are climatology; geomorphology, closely connected with various aspects of geology; the geographic study of soils, closely connected with studies in agronomy and related subjects; the geographic study of water on the land, closely connected with hydrology; and the geographic study of the oceans, a vast potential field of geographic study only little developed, since most of the work in oceanography has been done from the point of view of physical or biological science. Of these topical fields some have been better developed than others by geographers. Much has been done in climatology, especially in the construction of broad regional systems such as those formulated by A. J. Herbertson, Emmanuel de Martonne, W. Köppen and C. W. Thornthwaite. At the beginning of the 20th century in Great Britain and the United States most of the scholars who called themselves geographers were specialists in geomorphology, the study of land forms. In the United States the geographic profession was established by such notable masters as William Morris Davis, Rollin D. Salisbury and Wallace W. Atwood. Davis' formulation of the cycle of land-form development from youth through maturity to old age stimulated much attention to surface features in America and in Europe and the application of similar ideas to other topical fields. Davis' concepts were challenged by Walter Penck, with the result that by mid-20th century a new and stronger geomorphology was emerging from the co-ordination of the ideas of two quite different approaches: one "life-zone" ideas of C. H. Merriam proved to be too highly generalized to throw much light on the actual arrangements of plants and animals. Yet the classification of vegetation and the preparation of maps of vegetation suitable for geographic uses have been notably advanced, especially by such scholars as F. Shreve, Homer L. Shantz, H. M. Raup, J. W. Harshberger, F. E. Egler and A. W. Küchler. There has been some application of geographic method, also, to the study of animal geography or zoogeography. In the general field of biogeography there is also the topical branch known as medical geography, which deals with the geographic arrangement of diseases and with the factors relevant to the incidence and spread of disease. Notable in this development have been the studies carried on by Jacques M. May at the American Geographical society. During World War II, also, there was a considerable advance in physiological climatology, a field in which the effect of climate on the healthy human being is examined. As a result of experimental studies of human activity under controlled conditions of temperature and humidity, much new light was thrown on human behaviour. The older and stimulating but not always provable suggestions of Ellsworth Huntington regarding climate and man were greatly modified by the new knowledge gained from controlled experiment. A practical result of these studies was the development of new kinds of clothing and new kinds of houses.

8. Military Geography.—A field especially developed during World War II, military geography is the application of all aspects of geographic study to military problems. In no field is precise geographic knowledge regarding particular places more essential than in the field of military planning, whether tactical or strategic.

9. Techniques of Geographic Study.—Much attention has also been given to techniques of geographic study, especially after

about 1920, when the detailed field study of small areas began to bring in striking results. Geographic information is derived from four kinds of sources: documents, including not only written records but also maps, photographs and statistics; vertical aerial photographs; direct observation in the field; and the interview of informants. Geographic data, once brought together, are analyzed in four ways: by expository methods, using word symbols; by statistical methods, using mathematical symbols; by cartographic methods, using map symbols; and by the interpretation of aerial photographs. Most geographic studies require competence in all these methods of gathering and analyzing data. There has been a considerable amount of experimentation, especially in the United States, with the methods of field study in small areas. The methods of recording direct observations in written notes, in field sketches, with ground photography and on maps have all been made vastly more effective. After World War I vertical aerial photography began to play a more and more important role as a geographic technique, and during the 1940s and 1950s the development of new cameras, new film and better planes made this entirely new source of information one of prime importance. It is much less costly and also much more accurate to derive maps of homogeneous areas from the interpretation of aerial photographs than it ever could be from ground observation alone. However, the interpretation of the photographs requires a certain irreducible minimum of groundwork; and the study of all the nonvisible features of an area that cannot be photographed demands actual examination in the field. Aerial photography raises geographic study to a new level of exactness.

10. Cartography.—The art and science of map making is a field that overlaps both geography and geodesy. The traditional interest in mathematical geography, as carried forward by Ptolemy and Apianus, is now to be found among the geographic cartographers, who are still experimenting with new projections, valuable for specific purposes. The actual field construction of detailed maps, once a laborious job carried out with measuring tape and plane table, during the 1940s was greatly speeded and rendered less costly through the application of aerial photography to photogrammetry. Most topographic maps after mid-20th century were made by the methods of photogrammetry. Most of the world had been covered at least once by vertical aerial photographs. The use of such photographs for purposes of map construction involves quite different techniques than does the use of the photographs to bring out the geographic patterns of areal likenesses and differences. Geographic cartography was also enormously advanced during World War II when many new kinds of maps, using different colours or different black-and-white symbols, were tried out. This field included also the construction of detailed terrain models, of which one notable example was the model of the United States at the Babson institute in Wellesley, Mass., made under the direction of Wallace W. Atwood, Jr. As a result of the war new map libraries made their appearance, and the whole new field of map intelligence (the collection of information about map series and the evaluation of maps for different purposes) was developed. Cartography, which is recognized as an essential part of geographic study and which at one time constituted a major interest among geographers, in the mid-20th century was brought back to its proper position as a major geographic interest. *See also* MAP.

See also references under "Geography" in the Index.

BIBLIOGRAPHY.—*History of Geographic Thought:* A. Hettner, *Die Geographie, ihre Geschichte, ihr Wesen, und ihre Methoden* (1927); R. Hartshorne, *The Nature of Geography* (1939), *Perspective on the Nature of Geography* (1959); L. D. Stamp and S. W. Wooldridge (eds.), *London Essays in Geography* (1951); S. W. Wooldridge and G. East, *The Spirit and Purpose of Geography* (1951); T. Griffith Taylor (ed.), *Geography in the Twentieth Century* (1951); J. K. Wright, *Geography in the Making: the American Geographical Society, 1851-1951* (1952), *Human Nature in Geography* (1965); P. E. James and C. F. Jones (eds.), *American Geography, Inventory and Prospect* (1954); E. A. Ackerman, *Geography as a Fundamental Research Discipline* (1958); W. Bunge, *Theoretical Geography* (1962); National Research Council, *The Science of Geography* (1965); P. Haggett, *Locational Analysis in Human Geography* (1966).

General, Regional and Historical Geography: J. K. Wright, *The Geographical Lore of the Time of the Crusades* (1925); P. Vidal de la Blache, *Principes de géographie humaine* (1922; Eng. trans, 1926);

7. Biogeography.—Strictly speaking biogeography is a branch of biology, but geographers have made important contributions, especially in the study of vegetation. To be sure, the 19th-century (Davis') through the study of erosion along valley lines, the other (Penck's) through the study of the development of slopes. In the study of soils, Curtis F. Marbut introduced the concepts developed by the Russian scientists of the 19th century and combined them with an application of the cycle idea of Davis. Geographers made great advances in the whole theory of classification of phenomena on the earth's surface through the study of soils.

E. C. Semple, *The Geography of the Mediterranean Region* (1931); H. C. Darby (ed.), *An Historical Geography of England, Before A.D. 1800* (1936); M. Sorre, *Les Fondements biologiques de la géographie humaine* (1943); R. H. Brown, *Mirror for Americans; Likeness of the Eastern Seaboard, 1810* (1943); E. Huntington, *Mainsprings of Civilization* (1948); G. T. Trewartha, *Japan* (1945); A. Hettner, *Allgemeine Geographie des Menschen* (1947); P. E. James, *Latin America* (1942; 1950, 1959, 1969); L. D. Stamp, *The Land of Britain: Its Use and Misuse,* 2nd ed. (1950); G. East, *An Historical Geography of Europe,* 3rd ed. (1949); P. George, *Introduction à l'étude géographique de la population du monde* (1951); P. Monbeig, *Pionniers et planteurs de São Paulo* (1952); J. Brunhes, *La Géographie humaine* (1910; Eng. trans., abr. ed., 1952); C. O. Sauer, *Agricultural Origins and Dispersals* (1952); W. G. East and A. E. Moodie (eds.), *The Changing World* (1956); G. B. Cressey, *Land and Life in Southwest Asia* (1960); N. Ginsburg (ed.), *Essays on Geography and Economic Development* (1960); R. Murphey, *An Introduction to Geography* (1961); J. O. M. Broek, *Compass of Geography* (1966); W. Zelinsky, *Prologue to Population Geography* (1966).

Political and Economic Geography: D. Whittlesey, *The Earth and the State* (1939); H. J. Mackinder, *Democratic Ideals and Reality* (1942); E. H. Graham, *Natural Principles of Land Use* (1944); R. Capot-Rey, *Géographie de la circulation sur les continents* (1946); R. E. Dickinson, *City, Region, and Regionalism* (1947), *The West European City* (1951); W. Warntz, *Toward a Geography of Price* (1959); J. H. Thompson, *Geography of New York State* (1966).

Physical and Biogeography: W. M. Davis, *Geographical Essays,* a collection of 26 papers (1909); United States Department of Agriculture, *Climate and Man* (1941); C. E. Kellogg, *The Soils That Support Us* (1941); G. Schott, *Geographie des Indischen und Stillen Ozeans* (1935); S. A. Cain, *Foundations of Plant Geography* (1944); R. Hesse, *Ecological Animal Geography,* 2nd ed. by W. C. Allee and K. P. Schmidt (1951); A. N. Strahler, *Physical Geography* (1960); J. E. Van Riper, *Man's Physical World* (1962); S. R. Eyre, *Vegetation and Soils* (1963).

Cartography: W. Chamberlin, *The Round Earth on Flat Paper* (1947); L. A. Brown, *The Story of Maps* (1949); F. J. Monkhouse and H. R. Wilkinson, *Maps and Diagrams: Their Compilation and Construction* (1952); E. Raisz, *Principles of Cartography* (1962); A. H. Robinson, *Elements of Cartography* (1960); D. Greenhood, *Mapping* (1964). (P. E. J.)

GEOGRAPHY, SOCIETIES OF. More than 150 organizations have primary interests in geography and the related fields of exploration and travel. Most are centred in and serve individual cities and their environs. Many are regional, more than 20 are national in scope and 3 are international. They differ greatly in membership, status and objectives.

The predecessor of modern geographical societies is commonly considered to be the Association for Promoting the Discovery of the Interior Parts of Africa (1788). In 1805 the Palestine association was founded in London, and these two organizations were merged into the Royal Geographical society, which originated at London in 1830 and was incorporated by royal charter in 1859. Meanwhile the Société de Géographes was founded at Paris in 1821 and the Gesellschaft für Erdkunde at Berlin in 1828. Gradually other societies came into existence, in Mexico (1839), in Russia (1845) and in the United States (1851). During the latter half of the 19th century the number of geographical societies increased rapidly, and their growth in membership was accelerated during the first half of the 20th century, especially following World Wars I and II.

Of the various types of geographical societies, the most numerous are semiscientific-semisocial organizations composed of merchants, military personnel, government employees, teachers and laymen interested in geography and travel. Among the better known in this category are the National Geographic society (Washington, D.C.), the Canadian Geographical society (Ottawa), and local societies in Berlin, Rome, Paris, Philadelphia and Chicago. They maintain libraries and map collections, sponsor lectures and publish periodicals of mixed popular and professional interest.

Other organizations such as the Alpine club (England) are concerned primarily with organizing expeditions and publishing accounts of exploration and travel in little-known areas.

Some societies, such as the Royal Geographical society (London), have partial support from government sources. Others, such as the American Geographical society (New York city), supplement their income from dues by soliciting gifts, obtaining foundation grants and operating under research contracts. They have employed professional staffs, enlarged their research facilities and produced journals of high scholarly value, among them the *Geographical Journal* and the *Geographical Review.* In addition, they sponsor popular lectures, scientific expeditions and publication of reports, monographs and books.

Societies for teachers of geography, such as the National Council for Geographic Education (U.S.) and the Geographical association (England), are dedicated to the improvement of the techniques and scope of geographical education. Examples of such associations, fundamentally concerned with basic research in geography and its application for the advancement of the profession, are the Association of American Geographers, the Institute of British Geographers, the Association de Géographes Français and the Zentralverband der Deutschen Geographen.

Somewhat more limited in scope but equally professional in character are geographical institutes, usually associated with university departments, or specialized divisions of large associations and scientific bodies such as the Geography and Map division of the Special Libraries association (U.S.), Section E of the American Academy for the Advancement of Science, Section E of the British Association for the Advancement of Science, the Division of Earth Sciences in the National Academy of Sciences-National Research Council (U.S.), and the Institut Géografi Academia Nauk (U.S.S.R.). Government agencies which are primarily geographic, such as the Institut Géographique National (France), the geographic branches of the department of mines and technical surveys (Canada), and of the Commonwealth Scientific and Industrial Research organization (Australia), as well as the Conselho Nacional de Geografia (Brazil), and Institutos de Geografia (or Cartografía) in most Latin-American countries, often support additional research projects in institutes and societies.

International meetings of geographical societies date back to the Congrès International pour les Progrès des Sciences Géographiques at Antwerp, Belg., in 1871. Subsequent congresses were held at London (1895), Geneva (1908) and Rome (1913). In 1922 the International Geographical union was created at Brussels. Member countries are affiliated through their academies of science or their principal geographical organizations. International geographical congresses, held under the auspices of the union, are attended by delegations from member countries and by individual geographers who present and discuss research papers.

The International Society of Geographical Pathology originated at Geneva in 1931. It is composed of national committees and of individual members concerned with the geographical distribution of diseases.

BIBLIOGRAPHY.—John Kirtland Wright and Elizabeth T. Platt, *Aids to Geographical Research,* 2d ed., pp. 63–65 (1947); Chauncy D. Harris and Jerome D. Fellmann (comps.), *A Comprehensive Checklist of Serials of Geographic Value,* mimeographed, part i, (1949); International Geographical Union, *Proceedings,* 8th General Assembly and 17th International Congress, National Academy of Sciences, pp. 58–67 (1952), *Orbis Geographicus* (1960). (A. C. Ge.)

GEOLOGICAL SURVEY (U.S.), a bureau of the U.S. department of the interior, was established by act of congress on March 3, 1879, following recommendations of the National Academy of Sciences, to classify the public lands and to examine the geologic structure, mineral resources and products of the national domain. Additional duties assigned since then require the bureau to supervise mineral lease development and to collect, publish and distribute data concerning the physical features and mineral and water resources of the United States, its territories and possessions. Responsibility for the performance of these functions is distributed among four divisions.

The topographic division is responsible for delineating the physical features of the United States as quadrangles of the National Topographic Map series. These multipurpose three-dimensional maps provide basic information for mineral and water resources studies, engineering projects, national defense and industrial and community planning. The map information office was established by bureau of the budget directive in 1946 as the central source for map information in the U.S. government to answer inquiries and fill requests for maps, aerial photos and related data. During a single year, more than 3,000,000 maps were sold or distributed.

The geologic division maps and studies the surface and bedrock geology of the United States and appraises its mineral and mineral fuel resources, and conducts research in geology, geophysics, geochemistry and allied earth science disciplines with special emphasis on their application to discovery and development of natural resources. The work also includes geologic mapping and research to obtain basic data for engineering construction planning, for military geology, for soils surveys and for advancing the science of geology. The results of investigations have been published in bulletins, professional papers, circulars, and geologic and related map series, in reports printed by co-operative agencies and in trade and technical journals.

The conservation division supervises the development of certain minerals under leases on federal and Indian lands according to the applicable federal laws and examines and classifies federal lands as to mineral and water-power values. In this way the proper development and use of resources on these lands is assured. Early in the second half of the 20th century the value of mineral production on such lands supervised by the geological survey had exceeded $840,000,000 annually, enriching the United States treasury, reclamation fund, Indian beneficiaries and the various states by more than $98,000,000 in annual royalties.

The water resources division investigates and describes the quantity, distribution, chemical and physical quality, sediment content, availability and uses of water.

(H. B. N.)

GEOLOGY (ARTICLES ON). The basic simplicity of geology has been obscured by the giant proportions in which it works—particularly its time scale, in which the whole of recorded history figures as a mere tick of the clock. However, natural processes on so great a scale as, for example, the movement of a continental icecap, the uplift of a submerged land mass or the formation of the sedimentary rock known as coal can hardly fail to leave traces. Some of these were observed in antiquity, but, since they failed to fit in with any pattern of accepted theory, they were dismissed as inscrutable whims of nature. The survey article GEOLOGY summarizes the history of the reduction of these processes to terms of cause and effect, and gives an over-all view of modern earth science.

Individual articles are devoted to the major subdivisions of geology and of geological time. GEOCHRONOLOGY discusses the methods by which the age of the earth's crust as a whole and of various rock strata have been estimated. PALEONTOLOGY explains how fossils are used as keys to the sequence of the sedimentary deposits that encased them in the processes of petrification; it reaches about 500,000,000 years into the past, to fossils of the earliest animals known to have been equipped with bony structures or shells. (*See also* FOSSIL.) PALEOBOTANY traces plant fossils as far back as about 1,500,000,000 years—almost half the estimated age of the earth's crust.

These articles, and sections in the articles on geological epochs, describe forms of life that may seem grotesque but that were adapted to their environment before the occurrence of geological events that involved changes in climate and other factors. Each of these articles includes a survey of a phase of organic evolution. For example, CRETACEOUS SYSTEM tells of "the time of the great dying" of the dinosaurs; the article on the ensuing epoch, EOCENE AND PALEOCENE, reviews the evidence of the rapid advance of mammals from crude and miniature forms to their position of dominance in the animal world. Another example of the articles on geological time units is PLEISTOCENE EPOCH, dealing with the stretch of time in which a large part of the earth's surface was subject to alternate periods of glaciation and interglacially mild climate. It includes a summary of the geological history of man, as written in the strata of this comparatively recent epoch. This subject is developed more fully in MAN, EVOLUTION OF, which links the findings of geology with those of biology and anthropology.

The imprints left on the earth's crust by such geological agents as water, wind and glaciation, and the methods of recognizing these traces, are described in the article which deals with the source of

85% to 90% of the world's mineral wealth—SEDIMENTARY ROCKS. This is supplemented by WIND EROSION AND DEPOSITION. In PETROLOGY the emphasis is on igneous rocks; metamorphic rocks are dealt with in METAMORPHISM. Among other articles closely linked to this subject are MINERALOGY; ORE DEPOSITS; and SOIL. Individual articles are devoted to important rocks and minerals, such as CONGLOMERATE; SANDSTONE; SCHIST; IRON; COPPER; CALCITE; GRAPHITE; etc., and the gems.

Sections of descriptive geology are included in each of the articles on continents, nations and other major geographical units. The basic principles of stratigraphical geology, by which the order of origin of rock strata can be determined in spite of forces that have upset and entangled them, are discussed in STRATIFICATION and STRATIGRAPHY. GEOPHYSICS is devoted to the science that studies the earth as a body of matter subject to the laws of dynamics, gravitation, etc.; the practical applications of some of these theories are treated in GEOPHYSICAL PROSPECTING. The methods by which the size, shape and internal structure of the earth are determined are discussed in GEODESY.

Continents, mountains and oceans, like bodies constructed on a smaller scale, rise and fall in response to variations in their weight and in the strength of counterbalancing forces, although adjustment to a change such as the melting of an icecap is a process measured in many thousands of years. The workings of this principle are explained in ISOSTASY. Various manifestations of it are discussed in GEODESY; EARTH; and EARTHQUAKE.

VOLCANO discusses the geophysical background of volcanoes and volcanic eruptions. TIDE deals with the effects of gravitational pull on the earth's crust and its atmosphere as well as on its waters. GEOCHEMISTRY explores the process of geochemical evolution that prepared the way for organic evolution.

In COSMOGONY, the Brobdingnagian proportions of geology shrink to those of Lilliput. Linking geophysics and geochemistry with astronomy, this science traces the common origin of the chemical elements of our earth and those of the millions of planetary siblings in its galactic family.

See also references under "Geology" in the Index.

GEOLOGY, the study or science of the earth, is a broad and diverse subject with many subdivisions and several closely allied fields. Geologists are concerned primarily with rocks that form the outer part of the solid earth; but an understanding of these materials, and of changes that have occurred and are now going on in their compositions and arrangements, involves principles and techniques of physics and chemistry. Geophysics and geochemistry (*qq.v.*), both important and fast-growing scientific disciplines, are a logical outgrowth of this overlap in interest which extends beyond the visible rocky shell to deeper zones of the earth. Biology also plays an essential role in the study of rocks, great masses of which show profound effects of biologic processes and contain clear records of animals and plants that lived in past ages. Paleontology, the study of this fossil evidence, is an essential part of geology; and the aid of organic chemistry is required for study of the interactions among rock materials and organic substances.

Air and water are major agents in geologic processes; but the atmosphere is the special realm of another science, meteorology, and study of the earth's waters is shared by hydrology and oceanography, two fields closely associated with geology. Inquiries into the origin and formative stages of the earth are a primary concern of cosmogony, a branch of astronomy. Geodesy supplies basic information on the form of the earth, on precise geographic locations, and on values of gravity. Physical geography, concerned with surface features of the globe and giving large attention to maps, likewise has close kinship with geology as another in the group of subjects to which the terms geoscience, geophysical science, and earth science have been applied.

Geology has developed several main branches which for a brief survey may be classified as follows: (1) physical geology, including mineralogy, the systematic study of minerals; petrology, the study of rocks, their physical and chemical properties and modes of origin; geomorphology, the study of land forms and the processes of their development; sedimentation, the origin and deposition of sedimentary materials and their conversion into rock;

structural geology, a study of the geometry of rock masses, with emphasis on crustal deformation, or tectonophysics (*q.v.*); economic geology, including stratigraphy, the systematic study of bedded rocks and their relations in time; paleontology, the study of fossils and their location in the total sequence of bedded rocks; and (3) mapping of bedrock units defined by physical characteristics and geologic age. This general classification does not list specifically a number of important subjects that receive attention below. Moreover, like most brief classifications this one appears to draw sharp boundaries that are not real. For example, stratigraphy is part of the study of sediments, a subject that has both physical and historical aspects. Actually a rigid separation of all geology into physical and historical facets does not bear close analysis. Nearly all geologic study seeks to determine an order of events, and a main objective of the science is to work out the full history of the earth and its inhabitants.

For a guide to the various articles dealing with the science of geology *see* GEOLOGY (ARTICLES ON), above. *See* also articles on the various branches of science referred to, as BIOLOGY; METEOROLOGY; PALEONTOLOGY; etc.; geologic processes, as EROSION OF LAND; METAMORPHISM; etc.; rock bodies, as BATHOLITH; SILL; etc.; eras, systems, periods and epochs, as CENOZOIC ERA; CARBONIFEROUS SYSTEM AND PERIOD; PLEISTOCENE EPOCH; rocks and minerals, as GRANITE; CONGLOMERATE; CASSITERITE; MINERALOGY; CLAY AND CLAY MINERALS; etc.; and CRYSTALLOGRAPHY; MINERALOGY; CLAY AND CLAY MINERALS; etc.; and PETROLOGY. The text cuts and figures accompanying this article illustrate many of the processes and features discussed.

For proper perspective an explanation of geology starts with a summary description of the entire earth and its major physical features. The development of human knowledge and concepts regarding the earth is summarized in a final section of this article. Following are the main divisions of this article:

I. GENERAL VIEW OF THE EARTH

Geodetic studies have determined that the earth has the form of an oblate spheroid with polar radius about 13.3 mi. (21.4 km.) shorter than the equatorial radius. The circumference following the equator measures a little over 24,900 mi. (about 40,000 km.). A pear-shaped theoretical model of the earth was postulated from data provided by geodetic satellites, beginning in the late 1950s (*see* INTERNATIONAL GEOPHYSICAL YEAR). Relief features of the surface, large from the human viewpoint, are relatively small; Mt. Everest, with its summit about 29,028 ft. (8,848 m.) above sea level, would appear to scale on a globe with diameter 16 in. (40 cm.) as a projection only 0.012 in. (0.3 mm.) high. The outer part of the earth consists of three envelopes: atmosphere, hydrosphere, and lithosphere. Though gases of the atmosphere extend outward in detectable quantity through hundreds of kilometers, the major part of the gaseous matter is in a zone 5 to 10 mi. (8 to 16 km.) thick directly above the earth's surface. The great bulk of water making the hydrosphere is in the interconnecting ocean basins covering nearly 71% of the earth's surface; but water is widely distributed on the lands also, in streams and lakes and as ground water filling openings in soil, rock debris, and bedrock. The lithosphere is the solid outer part of the earth.

If all surface irregularities could be leveled off, the sea would be universal with a depth of almost 1.5 mi. (about 2.5 km.). The continental surfaces vary widely in height and configuration; Asia, the highest and most rugged, has average height about 3,200 ft. (1,000 m.) above the sea. All continents have mountainous belts, some youthful and rugged, others old and subdued. The topography of ocean floors, like that of continents, varies from wide plains to high and steep mountain ranges, some of which project above the sea as island chains whereas others are wholly submerged, with shoal water over the highest portions, and ocean floors generally are as uneven as continental surfaces. Conspicuous among major mountain belts rising from deep waters are those forming the islands of Indonesia in the Pacific, and the Antilles in the Atlantic. Many islands have been built up on ocean floors by volcanic eruptions; examples are the Hawaiian Islands in a deep part of the Pacific and Ascension and St. Helena in mid-Atlantic. Some other islands, such as Great Britain and Ireland, are merely parts of continental areas cut off from their mainlands by shallow channels. Many more such islands would be formed if sea level should rise 200 ft. or more, as would result if there were an increase in temperature sufficient to melt the ice caps that cover much of Antarctica and Greenland.

Information on sea floors is building up rapidly through use of echo sounding, magnetic measurement, and other specialized techniques. The bathyscaphe, a deep-sea diving apparatus for reaching great depths without a cable, is used for direct observation and photography of the sea floor. An ingenious device operated by cables from a surface vessel obtains accurate cores, 70 ft. or more long, of deep-sea sediments. Greatest depths of oceans exceed more than 35,000 ft. (10,700 m.). Floors of shallow seas are explored directly by scientific workers in especially constructed diving suits. Such study of modern sea floors is essential for full understanding of deposits laid down on floors of ancient seas and now exposed widely on the continents.

II. PHYSICAL GEOLOGY

A. MINERALOGY AND PETROLOGY

As these subjects are treated at length in separate articles, only a summary of their employment in general geology is appropriate here. Minerals are the basic units in the composition of most rocks, and therefore they are in a real sense the geologist's alphabet. Many hundreds of distinct mineral species are recognized, but comparatively few are important in the kinds of rocks that are abundant in the outer part of the earth. Thus a few related minerals known as the feldspars, together with quartz, are the essential ingredients in granite and its near relatives; and limestones, widely distributed on all continents, consist largely of one mineral, calcite. Many rocks have a more complex mineralogy, and in some the mineral particles are so minute they can be identified only through highly specialized techniques. For example, several clay minerals cannot be resolved by the most powerful optical microscopes. Under favourable conditions mineral substances have grown into nearly perfect crystals that have distinctive external forms. Silicon dioxide forms clear crystals of quartz that are hexagonal prisms with terminations shaped as pyramids; iron sulfide forms perfect cubes of pyrite, the faces marked with parallel lines. But when a substance crystallizes in bulk, crowding of grains growing from neighbouring centres prevents formation of recognizable crystals, though each mineral is formed with its peculiar internal atomic structure. Modern laboratories have varied and highly effective devices for working out the mineral content of rock materials. Standard equipment is the petrographic microscope, constructed for viewing thin sections of rock that are ground uniformly to about .001 in. (.025 mm.) thick. No matter how fine the grain, so long as the rock is crystalline its essential minerals can be determined by their peculiar optical properties as revealed in transmitted light under high magnification. Opaque minerals, such as those with a high content of metallic elements, require a technique that uses reflected light from polished surfaces; this kind of microscopic analysis has particular application to metallic ore minerals (*see also* METALLOGRAPHY). Another device exposes mineral grains to X rays which, on emerging, outline on a photographic film a pattern that represents the atomic structure peculiar to a given mineral species (fig. 1). Substances such as the

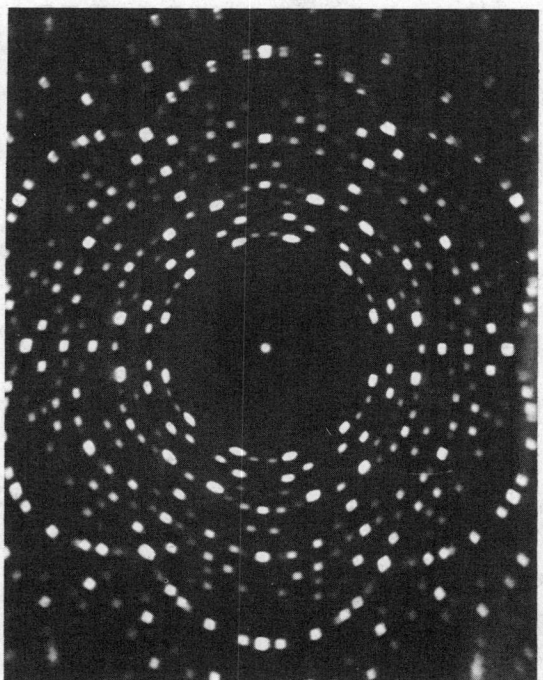

C. S. HURLBUT

FIG. 1.—X-RAY DIFFRACTION PHOTOGRAPH OF BERYL, A MINERAL WITH HEXAGONAL SYMMETRY

clays are made up of particles so minute they are submicroscopic in relation to ordinary petrographic microscopes; but these particles become clearly visible under the electron microscope, which gives images with diameters enlarged by a factor of tens of thousands. The several clay minerals are identified also by a technique known as differential thermal analysis (DTA) which takes advantage of pronounced differences in thermal properties. The instrument used in the analysis automatically draws graphs that are recognized as peculiar to given mineral compositions (*see* MINERALOGY: *Descriptive and Determinative Properties: Heat*).

Analytical chemistry plays a major role in the study of minerals and rocks. An exact quantitative analysis is a valuable supplement to other techniques, and for many specimens the chemical examination plays a major role. Rocks with glassy texture have no atomic organization and therefore give no response to microscopic study. Natural glasses are common in rocks of volcanic origin. In many such specimens small mineral grains scattered through a glassy groundmass can be recognized under a microscope, giving information to supplement the chemical study; but the quantitative analysis is of first importance. Thousands of such analyses made by reliable laboratories are on record for comparative study. Comparing the composition of a glassy specimen with compositions of crystalline rocks whose minerals are known will give much essential information.

Spectroscopic study of rock specimens is an important develop-

ment, and a complex instrument known as the mass spectrometer is used in an increasing number of petrographic laboratories. This device detects the presence of elements in extremely small quantities; it also isolates and measures quantitatively the several isotopes of elements such as lead and carbon. The mass spectrometer is indispensable in analyses used for determining ages of minerals on the basis of progressive atomic changes in such elements as uranium and thorium. (*See also* MASS SPECTROSCOPY.)

1. The Earth's Crust.—The term crust, which geologists commonly apply to the outer part of the solid earth, is inherited from a speculative concept, once widely held, that our globe was once a molten mass which slowly cooled and solidified from the surface downward, and that the major part of the volume is still molten, below a comparatively thin shell of solid rock. This latter view is now untenable, whether or not the earth passed through a molten stage; but, as explained later, we are convinced that an outer part of the earth, no more than a few tens of kilometres thick, differs in physical properties from deeper zones (*see* GEOCHEMISTRY; EARTHQUAKE), though the change is not marked by passage from solid to fluid materials. It is convenient, therefore, to keep the term crust for the distinctive outer zone.

The rocks of the earth's crust are exposed to view only on continents and islands, which comprise almost 30% of the earth's surface. The known rocks are divisible into three main groups: igneous rocks, which have solidified from molten matter called magma; sedimentary rocks, those made up of fragments derived from preexisting rocks, of materials precipitated from solutions, or of organic products; and metamorphic rocks, which have been derived from either igneous or sedimentary rocks under conditions that caused changes in composition, texture, and internal structure.

2. Igneous Rocks.—The igneous rocks are formed as either extrusive or intrusive masses. Extrusive rocks are products of volcanic action; they appear at the surface as molten lavas (fig. 2) which spread in sheets and harden, or they are made up of fragments, large and small, blown from vents by violent gaseous explosions. Intrusive rocks have formed by slow cooling of molten masses below the earth's surface; many such bodies are now exposed to view because long-continued erosion has removed the older rock cover. Some of these bodies doubtless were reservoirs that supplied volcanoes in the past.

The grain size or texture of igneous rocks is closely related to the mode of origin. Lavas generally are fine grained, even glassy, because rapid loss of heat, with resulting solidification, allowed little or no opportunity for mineral grains to grow. But the same kind of magma, under a cover of solid rock thousands of feet thick, has lost heat very slowly; accordingly the grains have had, from the human point of view, long ages for growth, and the re-

BY COURTESY OF U.S. GEOLOGICAL SURVEY; PHOTO, T. A. JAGGAR, JR.

FIG. 2.—TWO "LAKES" OF FLUID LAVA (FOREGROUND AND IN BACKGROUND AT LEFT) ON THE FLOOR OF THE GREAT PIT HALEMAUMAU, KILAUEA VOLCANO, HAWAII

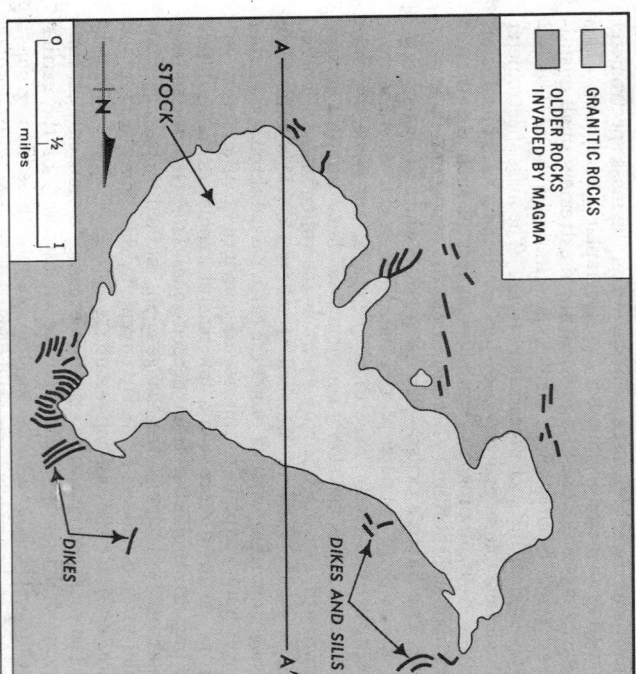

GRANITIC ROCKS

OLDER ROCKS INVADED BY MAGMA

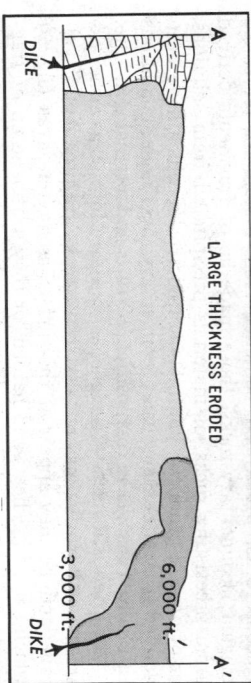

FIG. 3.—MAP OF MARYSVILLE STOCK, NORTH OF BUTTE, MONTANA, AND A VERTICAL SECTION A-A' CONSTRUCTED WITH AID OF MINING SHAFTS AND TUNNELS

sultant rock is coarse grained. Examples are ordinary granites, in which all grains of the essential minerals can be distinguished with the unaided eye. A rock with similar chemical composition that formed in a lava flow may have a uniform appearance, with no distinguishable grains; but magnification up to 50 or 100 times under a petrographic microscope may reveal a texture and mineral composition strikingly like that of the granite. Such a rock, known as rhyolite, is said to have aphanitic (i.e., invisible) texture.

In a general way the textures of igneous rocks vary according to the depth at which the bodies were formed. Deep-seated (abyssal or plutonic) bodies are coarse grained; intrusive bodies that cooled at shallower depths (hypabyssal masses) generally have medium to fine grains; and extrusive rocks are fine grained to glassy. There are, however, some complexities in this general rule. Many sheets of rhyolitic lava have large and well-formed crystals of feldspar and quartz isolated in an aphanitic ground-mass; the rock is called rhyolite porphyry, and the crystals are phenocrysts. Presumably these formed in a quiescent magma body underground, part of which was erupted in a volcanic out-break, whereupon the magma enclosing the crystals cooled quickly to form rock with fine grain. Porphyritic texture is common also in bodies of intrusive rock, of both the shallow- and deep-zone types; in such rocks the groundmass has visible grains which are much smaller than the enclosed phenocrysts. The contrasting grain size in all porphyries suggests an abrupt change in physical-chemical conditions while the parent bodies were forming.

Exposed intrusive bodies are most numerous in great mountain zones for two reasons: (1) the mountain belts have been zones of major deformation, and abundant evidence indicates that ig-neous action is favoured by crustal disturbance; and (2) great uplifts in mountain belts have set the stage for erosion to the depths at which plutonic masses have formed. Logically the best displays of large intrusive bodies are found not in youthful chains

such as the Alps, but in much older mountain units—for example, the Riesengebirge (Giant Mountains) of Germany—where the deep cores have been exposed by erosion through long ages.

Bodies of intrusive rock are classified according to their loca-tions, sizes, and shapes. The general term pluton is used for any large intrusive body. An abyssal mass of major size is appropri-ately called a batholith (literally "deep stone"). Commonly, such a body is exposed over an area measuring hundreds or even thousands of square miles; the Coast Range batholith of British Columbia is more than 1,000 mi. (more than 1,600 km.) long. These large bodies are not simple units with uniform structure and texture; they are complex assemblages of crosscutting and intertwined masses that indicate a long and varied history of de-velopment, with recurrent episodes. The major batholiths com-monly are elongate parallel to the associated mountain belts. Abyssal plutons of smaller scale, many of them probably branches from batholiths, are known as stocks (fig. 3). Intrusive bodies formed at shallow or intermediate depths have varied sizes and forms; most common are dikes, which are tabular, elongate bodies that cut across the enclosing rocks, and sills, generally similar in form to dikes but emplaced parallel to preexisting layers of sedi-mentary or volcanic rocks. Sizes of both dikes and sills have a wide range. Some measure only a few feet in greatest dimension of exposure; but in northern England the Cleveland dike, essen-tially vertical, is traced more than 100 mi. and the Whin sill, nearly horizontal, extends fully 80 mi., with an average thickness about 90 ft.

Knowledge of intrusive igneous bodies has been built up slowly by comparative studies, some in regions where erosion has brought to light only the masses that developed at shallow depths, others in profoundly eroded belts where "only the bones of the extinct mountains" can be seen. Beneath growing mountain chains around the Pacific Ocean igneous intrusive action is doubtless now in progress, though beyond the range of direct observation. Study of extrusive activity and the resulting rocks is more favourable. Active volcanic centres are widely distributed, and some of these are under continuous observation. The behaviour of Vesuvius and other Mediterranean volcanoes has been watched through many centuries; and well-equipped scientific stations have been in operation for some decades at a number of active centres. Study of active volcanoes is supplemented by observations made on great volumes of older volcanic products which, because they accumulated on the earth's surface, are much more accessible than the intrusive bodies which have come into view only through chance exposure by erosion.

Volcanic materials are erupted through openings of two general types—central vents and long fissures. Around a central vent, which is essentially a great vertical pipe, products of eruption are built up to form a cone which may grow into a high mountain with a crater at its top; well-known examples are Vesuvius in Italy, Mayon in the Philippine Islands (fig. 4), and Fujiyama in Japan. Two kinds of products issue from a vent: fragments known as

LARGE THICKNESS ERODED

3,000 ft.

6,000 ft.

DIKE

FIG. 4.—MAYON VOLCANO, AN EXCEPTIONALLY SYMMETRICAL CONE. ALTI-TUDE OF SUMMIT, 7,943 FEET; WIDTH OF BASE, SEVERAL MILES

ash and cinders, which are blasted violently upward by gaseous explosions; and lava or liquid rock, which commonly breaks through the side of the cone and spreads beyond its base. In a fissure eruption, lava wells upward and pours outward along an opening miles or even tens of miles in length. An eruption of this kind was observed in Iceland in 1783. Ancient outpourings of molten rock, in part along great fissures, built up widespread lava fields to form plateaus thousands of square miles in area; outstanding examples are in the Deccan region of India, the Columbia Plateau of northwestern United States and the Paraná Basin of South America. Commonly the outflow along a fissure has become obstructed except at a few favoured points where central eruptions have built up cones along a nearly straight line. The Hawaiian Islands, each constructed by long-continued volcanic eruptions, are arranged along a line that probably represents a great zone of weakness in the floor of the Pacific Ocean. (See also VOLCANO; TECTONOPHYSICS.)

Old volcanic rocks, exposed haphazardly and without relation to vents from which they issued, are distinguished from intrusive rocks by several criteria. Quantities of gas escape freely from molten lava, and in late stages of cooling the gas, expanding under compression in the stiffening fluid, forms rounded openings or vesicles in the upper part of a flow. These vesicles, many of which in old flows have been filled with minerals deposited from solution, serve to distinguish the flow from a sill which may be similar in general form. Moreover, most assemblages of volcanic rocks contain an abundance of distinctive fragmental products of explosive action, and associated glassy materials.

In volcanic rocks the chemical composition, matching that of known intrusive bodies, ranges between wide limits. Silica, the most distinctive ingredient, varies from about 40% to more than 75%. The high-silica rocks are generally light coloured and their excess of silica is expressed in abundant grains of quartz. Low-silica rocks range in colour from gray to brown and nearly black; they are rich in minerals containing iron and magnesium. Intermediate types are numerous, representing a complete gradation between the low-silica, or basic, and high-silica, or acid, rocks. Granite and its near relatives in chemical and mineral composition are commonly grouped as granitic rocks; they are predominant in the continents. Basalt, accepted as typical of the low-silica rocks, appears to be predominant in ocean floors. Basaltic flows that have built up wide plateaus in several continents have remarkably uniform composition. According to a favoured concept these lavas have risen from a zone of dark, heavy rock that extends continuously from the ocean floors beneath the granitic rocks in all the continents.

Igneous rocks yield minerals that are important economically, others that have great scientific value. The most reliable determinations of age are obtained by analysis of certain minerals, notably those containing uranium, that have been sealed in igneous bodies since their formation. From these analyses the oldest igneous masses are known to be more than 3,000,000,000 years old. Such quantitative determinations are in accord with much qualitative evidence in the geologic record, all testifying to the vast length of geologic time.

3. Sedimentary Rocks.—Rock materials exposed to air and moisture are subject to continual change, both physical and chemical. Bedrock is broken into pieces, large and small, which are moved by running water and other agents to lower ground and spread in sheets over lake bottoms, floodplains, and sea floors. Dissolved matter is carried to seas and other water bodies, and some of it is precipitated either chemically or by the action of organisms. The deposited material becomes compacted and in time much of it is cemented into firm rock. Generally the process of deposition is not continuous but sporadic, and sheets of material representing separate episodes come to form distinct layers of rock. As a result the sedimentary rocks are stratified; the individual layers are beds or strata.

Large parts of every continental mass are covered with sedimentary rocks that represent deposits formed during many periods of the earth's history. In part these bedded rocks are nearly horizontal, as they were originally; but in large areas, particularly in mountain belts, they show various degrees of deformation. The principal kinds of sedimentary rocks are conglomerate, sandstone, siltstone, shale, limestone, and dolomite.

Conglomerate, made up of fragments derived from older rocks, more or less rounded by wear and ranging in size from boulders (diameters 25 cm. or more) down to pebbles (minimal diameters 2 mm.); interstices generally are filled with sediments of finer grain, more or less firmly cemented.

Sandstone, consisting of sand grains (diameters 2 to $\frac{1}{16}$ mm.), predominantly quartz. Interstices generally hold still finer particles and cementing material (fig. 5[B]).

Siltstone, consisting chiefly of silt particles (diameters $\frac{1}{16}$ to $\frac{1}{256}$ mm.) more or less well cemented.

Shale, consisting chiefly of clay arranged in thin layers or laminae. If lamination is lacking, the term claystone is appropriate.

Limestone, made up of mineral grains consisting chiefly of the mineral calcite. Commonly has numerous fragments of shells, microscopic or larger, from marine animals.

Dolomite, similar to limestone, but has a high content of magnesium.

Although the kinds of rock listed above are most important quantitatively, many others are recognized, some of large practical value. Among these are beds of common salt, gypsum, phosphate, and iron oxide. Coal, in extensive beds, has developed from plant materials accumulated in swampy areas and later buried under large thicknesses of ordinary sediments.

4. Metamorphic Rocks.—Metamorphism ($q.v.$) means literally transformation, and logically the term might be applied to any profound change. In geology the meaning is restricted; it does not include the decay of rock materials exposed to the weather, nor the fusion of rocks by igneous processes. Metamorphic rocks have been developed from earlier igneous and sedimentary rocks by heat and pressure, at some depth and most effectively in the great mountain zones. Resultant changes are in texture, in mineral composition, and in structural features of the rock. Survival

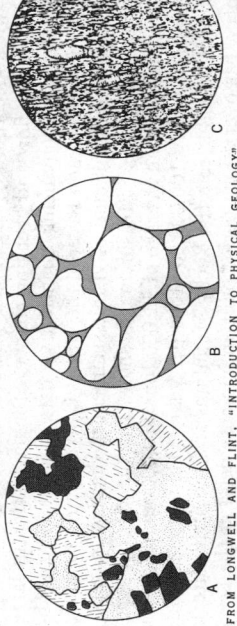

FROM LONGWELL AND FLINT, "INTRODUCTION TO PHYSICAL GEOLOGY"

FIG. 5.—TEXTURES OF ROCKS MAGNIFIED ABOUT EIGHT TIMES. (A) DIORITE (CRYSTALLINE IGNEOUS ROCK); (B) SANDSTONE; (C) PHYLLITE (METAMORPHOSED SHALE)

of some characteristics of the original rock indicates that fusion has not played an essential part in the change.

Two general kinds of metamorphic effects are recognized: (1) dynamic metamorphism resulting from strong compression, perhaps aided by some increase in temperature from friction; and (2) thermal metamorphism caused by high temperature in rocks adjacent to intrusive igneous bodies. Effects are accentuated through introduction of elements by fluids that move from a molten mass into the surrounding rock. Susceptibility of different rocks to either type of metamorphism varies greatly. Thus in part of the Appalachian Mountain belt in Pennsylvania, coal in strongly crumpled beds was changed to anthracite, a type of coal from which nearly all volatile matter has been expelled; but the shale beds adjacent to this coal are unchanged except for the crumpling. By contrast, in a more strongly deformed belt in Rhode Island coal has been changed into graphite, and in the enclosing shale beds shearing has developed thin cleavage plates lined with flakes of mica. Near an intrusive igneous mass in South Africa shale was altered to hornfels, a hard metamorphic rock studded with crystals of minerals that grew during the period of high temperature. Beds of sandstone alongside the altered shale are unchanged except for firmer cementation of the quartz grains.

Extreme metamorphism in some mountain zones has resulted from combined dynamic and thermal effects. Fluids rising from deep-seated plutons have combined with rock material in deformed sedimentary rocks, and the resultant product is indistinguishable from granite that has crystallized from magma. To some extent, therefore, granitic rocks may be a product of metamorphism as well as igneous processes.

Many of the metamorphic rocks consist of flaky minerals, such as mica and chlorite, set in parallel arrangement. These minerals cause the rock to split into thin sheets, and the rocks are said to be foliated (fig. 5[C]).

The commonest kinds of metamorphic rocks are slate, phyllite, schist, and gneiss. Marble and quartzite are nonfoliated metamorphic rocks.

Slate, a rock with remarkably plane cleavage cutting across folded beds of the original rock and dividing it into thin plates. Surfaces of the plates are lustrous, but no minerals are distinguishable without high magnification.

Phyllite, an exceptionally lustrous rock representing a higher stage of metamorphism than slate. The cleavage plates commonly are wrinkled or sharply bent.

Schist, a well-foliated rock in which the flaky minerals, usually mica or chlorite, are plainly visible. Quartz is abundant, and many schists are studded with garnets.

Gneiss, a coarse-grained rock with imperfect foliation. Granite gneiss is a strongly banded rock with the mineral composition of granite.

Marble, recrystallized limestone, wholly granular. Dolomite marble is recrystallized dolomite. Either rock may be studded with minerals formed from impurities.

Quartzite, formed from quartz sandstone by complete filling of all spaces between grains with quartz.

B. GEOMORPHOLOGY

Land forms are features of slow but continuous development. Wide distribution on the lands of sedimentary rocks that had their origin in former seas suggests clearly that the present mountains, plateaus, and other landscape features owe their beginning to widespread uplift. Evidence that these features are being steadily modified is compelling, though parts of this evidence become clear only with special study. Engineers charged with the problem of controlling the flow and checking channels for navigation in large streams supply convincing quantitative data. Even casual observers of the Colorado River in the Grand Canyon of Arizona are impressed with the amount of visible sediment in the stream, especially at flood stage. Measurements show that the river carries past a given point an average of 11,000 tons (10,000 metric tons) per hour, or nearly 100,000,000 tons per year. This annual load, most of it brought from the Rocky Mountains and the high plateau country, has over a long period built an immense delta at the head of the Gulf of California. Many other great rivers, such as the Mississippi, the Amazon, the Niger, the Nile, the Ganges, and the Hwang Ho (Yellow), are carrying vast quantities of rock matter from continents to seas, as indicated by their large and growing deltas. Countless smaller streams that flow directly into the sea swell the total mass of transported sediment, much of which does not go into construction of deltas but is spread widely on sea floors by action of waves and currents. Moreover the water flowing into the seas carries a great total load that is invisible, dissolved from rocks on the lands.

The ultimate forces responsible for wearing down land masses are solar energy and gravity. Heat from the sun evaporates sea water; and, using the atmosphere as its agent, the solar heat causes circulation of water vapour, part of which is precipitated as rain and snow on the lands. The water returns toward the sea, much of it by circuitous routes (fig. 6). This continuous movement of water between sea and land is the hydrologic cycle, which performs a vast amount of work (*see* HYDROLOGY). Water and air react with rock materials, changing them chemically and breaking them into small pieces; this complex action is weathering. Running water moves the loose rock debris and in the process causes further breakup of bedrock. At high altitudes and in polar regions snow is compacted into masses of ice, which move slowly downslope as glaciers and add their energy to that of running water in wearing down the land. Water makes its way underground and slowly moves seaward, dissolving rock material as it goes. Winds and waves join the attack on the lands. All these activities are included in the composite process of erosion, which sculptures the rocks on the lands.

continents in great detail and tends to reduce them toward sea level. Thus gravity, aided by solar energy, strives to establish equilibrium by leveling out all irregularities on the earth's surface. At the present rate of erosion, which is reasonably well known, the continents would be worn to sea level within a small fraction of the time that has elapsed since life on the lands began. This suggests strongly that the work of erosion is opposed by another process; and there is abundant evidence that the lands have been elevated repeatedly, on a large scale. Therefore the landscapes of today represent a stage in the conflict between two sets of forces: one set strives to reduce continents to featureless plains; the other set, within the earth, rejuvenates the lands by forming mountain chains and broad upwarps. The processes of uplift are given special attention in a later section. Weathering and erosion merit further discussion here.

1. Weathering.—Blocks of stone in walls of very old buildings are discoloured, many have irregular surfaces from spalling and some are visibly crumbling. Bedrock in the hills has been exposed to weather vastly longer and shows much greater change unless it is situated where running water or some other agent carries away the products of decay as they are formed. Such a situation is a nearly vertical cliff with a stream near its base; but as a rule even there blocks of rock, fallen from the cliff and in various stages of decay, form great heaps of slide-rock (or rock waste, talus, or scree) (fig. 7, left). Nearly level fields back from the cliff normally have a cover of soil which, as shown by careful study, was produced by decay of the underlying bedrock. Commonly the blanket of soil is several feet or even tens of feet thick; and an artificial shaft penetrating it reveals a gradation from soil downward through decayed rock into unaltered bedrock.

Changes in rock through weathering are partly mechanical, partly chemical. In regions that have cold seasons an effective mechanical agent is frost wedging. Water penetrates crevices in rock, and expansion in freezing, repeated time after time, displaces grains and even large blocks. Growing roots of plants produce similar effects, but rooted plants can grow only where chemical action has made food available to them. The most effective chemical reagent is water that carries in solution carbon dioxide, a gas universally present in the air in minute quantities. Rain carries some of the gas to the ground, and hence much of the water that comes in contact with rocks is a weak solution of carbonic acid, H_2CO_3, which reacts slowly with some of the minerals. Feldspars, the chief minerals in granitic rock, eventually yield clay, which is the basic material in ordinary soils. Clay is a complex mixture of silicate minerals, in themselves a large field for study. Potassium carbonate, another product of weathered feldspar, is a nourishing food for plants. Once a soil with a plant cover is started the chemical breakdown of underlying bedrock is accelerated because decaying plant tissues supply carbonic acid to percolating water. Soils are best developed under warm, humid climates, which favour plant growth and the accompanying chemical decay of bedrock. In Arctic and desert lands chemical weathering is weak, plants are few, and soils are generally poor and nearly

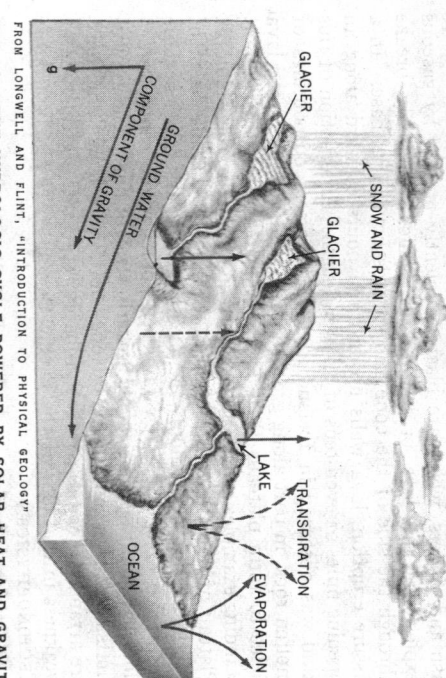

FIG. 6.—THE HYDROLOGIC CYCLE POWERED BY SOLAR HEAT AND GRAVITY

unaltered bedrock is exposed over large areas. (*See* SOIL: *Soil Erosion and Conservation.*)

Large daily variations in temperature, especially pronounced in deserts, were once credited with effective breaking of exposed bedrock. According to this concept expansion from heating during the day, followed by contraction from rapid cooling at night, would explain the separation of thin slabs from large blocks of rock at the surface. This view has been discredited by careful experiments using an electric heating and cooling device equipped with automatic control. Thousands of alternations between temperatures considerably higher and lower than those measured in deserts have failed to produce in samples of rock any fractures detectable even under high magnification. Study of thin shells that separate from rock exposed to the weather reveals as a common cause of the separation the slow development of clay minerals, which involves an increase in volume. The outer surface of exposed rock dries rapidly after wetting; but moisture that penetrates into minor crevices stays until some decay is started, and the resultant swelling causes flaking. Separation of successive thin shells, or spalls, from massive rock such as granite is called exfoliation (fig. 7, right). This is a common form of weathering in regions that have moderate rainfall.

2. Erosion by Running Water.—Rain water falling on a sloping field that has been freshly plowed may wash away quantities of soil. No area of ground is perfectly even, and the water, controlled by gravity, becomes concentrated along local sags in the surface of the field, where stream channels are developed. If the rainfall is of short duration only a few nearly parallel channels may develop, separated by wide, ungullied areas; but if hard rainfall is prolonged, or if the field is left undisturbed through successive rains, channels tributary to those first formed start and grow longer headward; these tributaries in turn become branched, and the process continues until the entire surface is covered with a network of steep-walled gullies. As water continues to flow the gullies are in general continuously deepened. But cutting down of a main channel may be checked where it crosses from the plowed area into a meadow protected by sod; this channel cannot then carry away all the sediment delivered into it by tributary gullies, and the excess material is deposited at the bottom of the main stream to form a widening alluvial flat. With continued growth the alluvial deposit may extend backward into the lower reaches of the tributaries, thus decreasing their gradients and limiting their power to cut down and to carry sediment. Gullies in the higher parts of the slope retain their vigour longest. Every land area with abundant or moderate precipitation has an integrated drainage system. In the Alps, a mountain mass that

was uplifted late in geologic history, a network of deep valleys directs the drainage toward the four points of the compass into four principal streams: northward into the Rhine; westward into the Rhône; southward into the Po; and eastward into the Danube. Each of these major streams has a wide lower valley floored with alluvium which extends downstream to a large and growing delta. Upstream the valley is narrower, with higher and steeper sides; and in the mountains each large tributary is a deep gorge, many with nearly vertical sides. The gradient of the stream bed near the delta is only a few inches per mile; upstream it steepens progressively, and many of the mountain tributaries are raging torrents with stretches of rapids and some vertical falls. Such a stream is actively deepening its valley, though it is floored with bedrock. The swift water is armed with sediment ranging in size from sand grains to coarse rubble; scrubbing of this material over the stream bed breaks and wears the particles themselves, but the constant abrasion also wears the bedrock floor. Moreover much of the bedrock is divided into blocks by intersecting joints, and many such blocks are loosened and dislodged by the force of the swift stream to become part of the abrading load.

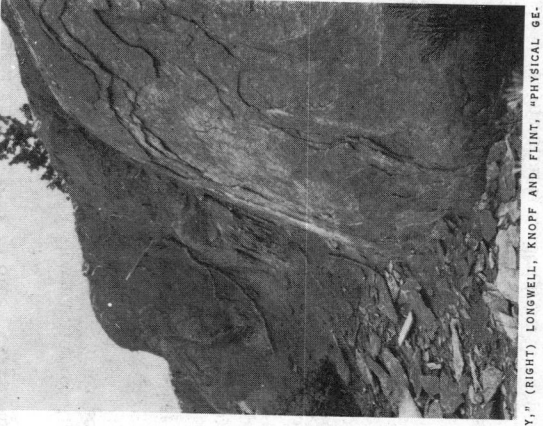

BY COURTESY OF (LEFT, RIGHT) JOHN WILEY & SONS, INC., FROM (LEFT) LONGWELL AND FLINT, "INTRODUCTION TO PHYSICAL GEOLOGY," (RIGHT) LONGWELL, KNOPF AND FLINT, "PHYSICAL GEOLOGY"

FIG. 7.—(LEFT) SLIDE-ROCK ON A SLOPE BELOW A CLIFF IN THE NORTHWEST TERRITORIES, CANADA; (RIGHT) EXFOLIATION OF GRANITE IN A CLIMATE WITH MODERATE TEMPERATURES AND RAINFALL. SIERRA NEVADA, CALIFORNIA

Study of numerous stream valleys in various stages of growth reveals a general progression in development of form, both longitudinally and in cross section. Nearly all large rivers flow into the sea, and sea level limits the depth to which they can cut. In any segment of a valley that is far above sea level the energy of the stream is used mainly in cutting down to establish a graded profile, an ideal slope on which the stream can transport its load of sediment without either cutting or depositing. The large rivers that receive drainage from the western Alps are essentially at grade in their lower courses; but in the high mountain country the profiles are excessively steep, downcutting is active and valleys are deep and narrow. When the profile in a considerable segment of a valley approaches the graded form the stream, deflected from one side to the other, erodes laterally to make the valley floor much wider than the stream channel. This tendency to cut laterally is of course present at earlier stages in valley development; but so long as active downcutting continues the stream is not at a given level long enough for lateral erosion to be effective. After a wide, flat floor is developed the stream at high-flood stage spreads beyond its normal channel and deposits sediment to form a floodplain, which grows in width as the widening of the valley continues. On a well-developed floodplain the sluggish stream characteristically develops a sequence of wide, looping bends, or meanders, many of which impinge against the valley sides (fig. 8).

Deepening of a valley does not end abruptly with the formation

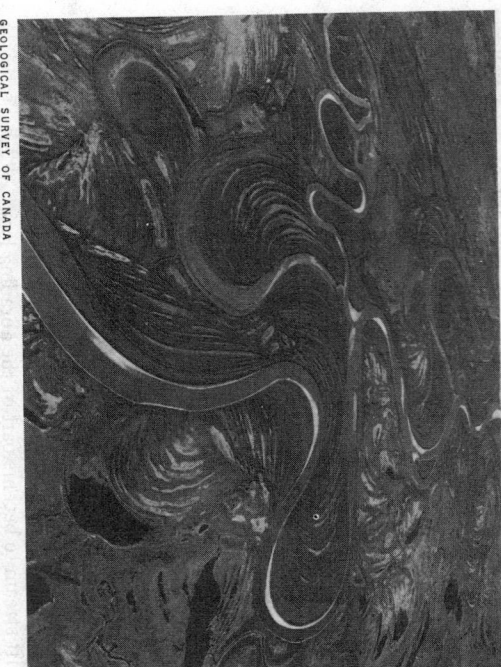

GEOLOGICAL SURVEY OF CANADA

FIG. 8.—STREAM MEANDERING ON ITS FLOODPLAIN. FORMS OF CUT-OFF MEANDERS PERSIST, SOME AS OXBOW LAKES. KOYUKUK RIVER, ALASKA

of a floodplain. Slow downcutting continues; and with lateral shifting of the stream, remnants of earlier valley floors may be preserved as terraces. Commonly these terraces are at different heights on opposite sides of a valley, each being the only remaining part of a former floor. On the other hand some paired terraces, well above the present stream, suggest recent rejuvenation of the stream by uplift of the land or by lowering of sea level. Such terraces in the Mississippi Valley probably indicate downcutting by the stream caused by subtraction of water from the seas in formation of the present ice caps of the polar regions; the river has regraded its valley to the lower sea level.

Lateral cutting by mature streams has been an important factor in the planing down of wide land masses. But the general lowering of a land surface is begun as soon as the surface is occupied by a network of functional stream channels. Streams in the Alps, aided by glaciers, have removed the vast quantity of rock material that once occupied the vacant spaces of the present valleys. Moreover, the divides between adjacent valleys are being reduced slowly as material is eroded from the opposed slopes.

Some wide and high continental areas are not fully covered with stream channels because of deficient rainfall. Permanent streams that cross the Colorado Plateau in western United States receive most of their water supply in the Rocky Mountains to the east and north; and valleys cut into the plateau by these streams are deep, steep-walled canyons that have few large tributaries. Erosion is proceeding far more rapidly in the Alps than in the Colorado Plateau. Many arid regions have no drainage to the sea; examples are the Dead Sea Basin, areas in central and western Australia, and the Great Basin of western United States. The Dead Sea depression is far below sea level and is being filled slowly with sediments brought in chiefly by the Jordan River, which has its source in mountains to the north. The Great Basin, like other regions with interior drainage, receives many streams, some from mountain blocks within its area, others from bordering highlands. Sediments eroded from the high areas are filling the many separate depressions. The tendency is for some depressions, as they are filled, to spill over into lower areas; ultimately the entire region will be reduced nearly to a featureless plain well above sea level unless crustal movements or a change in climate may interrupt the present trend.

3. Erosion by Mass Movements.—Transport of rock debris on land surfaces is not confined to channels of active streams. On every slope a component of gravity exerts a pull which results in large-scale migration of soil, broken rock, and even large masses of bedrock. Abrupt landslides are the most familiar and spectacular example of such movement. Avalanches (snowslides) are large masses of snow or ice, often bearing other materials, that suddenly slide down mountainsides. Every year large numbers of slides and avalanches occur in mountainous country—the Alps, the Himalayas, the Rocky Mountains, and other belts of steep topography; the sliding masses range in volume from a few cubic yards to a cubic mile or more. Some large slides, starting without any warning and moving at high speed, have overwhelmed towns and caused other catastrophes. Commonly a sliding mass blocks a large stream to form a lake, thus complicating the routine of erosive action. In a region subject to strong earthquakes, a sharp shock often has started a number of landslides involving masses that probably were nearing the point of release.

Chronic landslides, which move slowly and intermittently on steep slopes, are more common than the catastrophic kind. Masses of soil and broken rock move partly by slow flowage, partly by slipping over a firmer basement. In cold seasons such masses may be frozen and practically stationary; thawing in spring causes saturation with water and renewed flowage or sliding on a lubricated base. Differential movement creates a hummocky surface; forest trees growing on the slope are tilted at various angles and locally they are uprooted. Chronic slides represent all gradations between regular landsliding and imperceptibly slow downslope movement known as creep, which operates on every slope covered with loose, weathered material. Even soil covered with close-knit sod creeps downslope, as indicated by slow but persistent tilting of poles, gravestones, and other objects set into the ground on hillsides.

The several forms of mass movement on land surfaces are comprised under the general term mass wasting. All such movements tend to bring loose rock material within reach of streams, which continue the transport to lower ground or to the sea. In high country the cutting of deep valleys by streams creates steep slopes on which mass movements are especially effective. Thus stream erosion and mass wasting cooperate in the wearing down of land masses.

4. Erosion by Ground Water.—Of the average annual precipitation on all land areas about 25% runs off directly down slopes into stream channels; a considerable part evaporates; the remainder, half or more of the total, sinks into the ground where it brings about many physical and chemical changes. The weathering processes produce soluble substances which are carried by percolating ground water, some to be deposited in open spaces in bedrock, more to be delivered to streams and carried eventually to the sea. A considerable fraction of the total load carried by rivers is invisible, in dissolved form. One common ingredient, usually in small amount, is sodium chloride, familiar as common salt; another is calcium carbonate, an important part of which is derived from limestone bedrock, another part from decomposed feldspar minerals. Ordinary limestone and dolomite underlie great areas of every continent. Under humid climates with warm seasons the ground water, charged with carbon dioxide

BY COURTESY OF JOHN WILEY & SONS, INC., FROM THORNBURY, "PRINCIPLES OF GEOMORPHOLOGY"

FIG. 9.—CAVITIES IN LIMESTONE CAUSED BY GROUND WATER SOLUTION AND NOW EXPOSED IN A STONE QUARRY

supplied mainly by vegetation, dissolves vast quantities of these carbonate rocks (fig. 9). In Yugoslavia, Kentucky, and many other large areas the subsurface solution has had profound effects on topography. Roofs of caverns have collapsed to form large numbers of steep-walled sinks; streams, large and small, have been drawn into a network of caverns, leaving dry valleys formed at an earlier stage. Remnants of collapsed cavern roofs known as natural bridges are common in such areas. A landscape dominated by the effects of ground-water solution is said to have karst topography, named from a region in Yugoslavia where such effects are prominent.

Whether or not the bedrock of a region is highly soluble, ground water plays a major part in weathering and erosion. It provides the perennial supply for stream flow; immediate surface runoff causes flash floods, whereas the trickling of water from soil and from openings in bedrock continues at a nearly uniform rate. After a period of rainfall the water settles along openings to the water table, a more or less definite surface (higher under hills than under lowlands) at the top of the zone of permanent saturation; wells sunk below this depth are assured a steady flow (fig. 10). Above the water table is a zone of varied thickness known as the zone of aeration because air enters openings after water from the surface settles to the zone of permanent saturation. Weathering is active in the zone of aeration, where air is in contact with rock materials that usually are wet with water bearing carbonic acid from plants. Freezing and thawing of shallow ground water, together with its lubricating effect in soil, play an essential part in movement by creep.

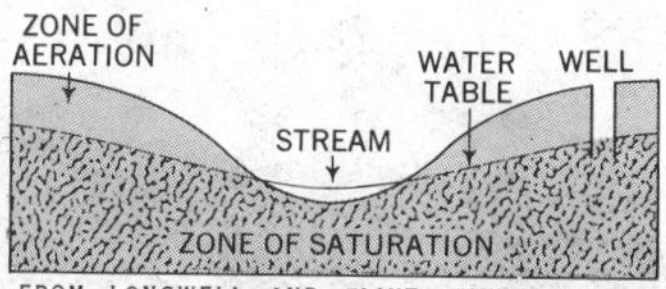

Thus ground water has a major role in weathering and in mass wasting and is the chief agent in delivering to streams vast quantities of dissolved mineral matter. Masses of dripstone formed in many caverns represent local and incidental deposition from the dissolved load in transit. (*See also* CAVE; GROUND WATER.)

5. Erosion by Glacier Ice.—In some high mountains and in large parts of the Arctic regions snowfall exceeds melting. Accumulating snow becomes compressed into ice; and on reaching a critical thickness masses of ice move under their own weight by solid flow; such a moving mass is a glacier (*q.v.*). In the Alps, the Himalayas, the Coast Range of British Columbia, and many other mountain chains the high valleys are filled with glaciers, some of them tens of miles long (fig. 11). Movement of a glacier down its valley is too slow to be seen directly; but accurate instrumental measurements record speeds ranging from a few inches to several

tens of feet per day. At temperate latitudes the lower end of a glacier is at fairly high altitude determined by the balance between rates of movement and of melting. Some glaciers in northwestern Canada flow directly into the sea. Greenland and Antarctica have enormous ice caps in which flowage is radially outward; great masses become separated from the margins and drift away as icebergs.

Information about glaciers as erosive agents comes from study of active glaciers supplemented by observations in valleys from which glacier ice has almost or entirely vanished. At the lower end of a vigorous valley glacier a ridge, or complex group of ridges, extends across the valley. This end moraine is made up chiefly of coarse rubble containing many blocks of rock with one or more faces smoothed and scratched. Similar blocks are frozen in the ice exposed at the glacier front; evidently the morainal ridge was built up slowly by accumulation of rubble as the ice released it by melting along a front that has varied little in position through a long period. Water in streams of meltwater issuing from the glacier is gray-white and has been called glacier milk; it carries in suspension quantities of silt-size particles made of fresh rock ground up by abrasion as the lower surface of the glacier, armed with blocks of rock, grinds over the valley floor. Moraines on top of the glacier are formed of rubble gathered from the valley walls partly as a result of lateral grinding action by the moving ice.

The features of a valley recently cleared of glacier ice testify to vigorous erosive action. Areas of bedrock on the floor are polished and marked with grooves and scratches generally parallel to the axis of the valley (fig. 12). Rugged surfaces, both on the

FROM LONGWELL AND FLINT, "INTRODUCTION TO PHYSICAL GEOLOGY"

FIG. 10.—DIAGRAM OF GROUND WATER ZONES

BY COURTESY OF MCGRAW-HILL BOOK CO., INC., FROM EMMONS, THIEL, STAUFFER AND ALLISON, "GEOLOGY"

FIG. 12.—BEDROCK POLISHED AND GROOVED BY A VANISHED GLACIER. BOULDERS WERE LEFT WHEN THE ICE MELTED. LUCERNE, SWITZERLAND

BY COURTESY OF JOHN WILEY & SONS, INC., FROM FLINT, "GLACIAL AND PLEISTOCENE GEOLOGY"

FIG. 11.—VALLEY GLACIER AND TRIBUTARIES. LATERAL MORAINES OF THE BRANCHES BECOME MEDIAL MORAINES OF THE MAIN GLACIER. BARNARD GLACIER, ALASKA

walls and on the floor, represent forcible removal of blocks bounded by joints. The cross section of the valley suggests a wide U in contrast to the V form of a mountain valley fashioned by a stream. Lateral erosion by the moving ice caused widening by removing not only the points of spurs that normally jut into a main valley between tributaries but also considerable parts of the tributary valleys. Walls of the glaciated valley are remarkably steep and straight and are marked by numerous high falls from tributary streams that would normally join the main stream at grade but now are in hanging valleys (fig. 13). The head of the ice-freed valley has the form of a wide semicircular amphitheatre (cirque), caused by continual plucking action as ice forming in the snowfield became part of the moving glacier. At a divide from which two or more glaciers moved in different directions, the growing cirques partly intersect to form a sharp, jagged ridge (fig. 14). The Matterhorn is a pyramid-shaped mass that has survived destruction between cirques slowly growing together; and numerous similar peaks in the high Swiss Alps testify to the magnitude of erosion by glaciation of that mountain mass. Although the number of glaciers now in the Alps exceeds 1,200, formerly there were many more; and the existing glaciers were much longer than now, as indicated by the glaciated forms of valleys and the abundance of characteristic glacial deposits extending many miles below the present terminal moraines. Long and careful study in the Alps has determined that the valleys were fashioned by stream erosion; onset of a cooler world climate brought development of glaciers that reached to a low level in all Alpine valleys; and increased temperatures have reduced the glaciers to their present status. This general history applies to high mountain valleys in both the Northern and Southern hemispheres.

The deep, steep-walled fjords in Norway, British Columbia, New Zealand, and some other lands are valleys fashioned by glaciers and now occupied by the sea.

Study of modern glaciers has brought realization that at the time of maximum glaciation in the Alps great ice sheets covered wide areas of continents within the temperate zones. In Europe an ice cap extended from the Arctic Ocean to central Germany, and the British Isles were covered with ice; in North America all of Canada and the northern part of the United States were glaciated. Much of the soil was removed from the glaciated areas, and the bedrock was polished, grooved, and locally eroded by plucking action. Wide belts marginal to the ice sheets were mantled with characteristic glacial deposits, including the unassorted and unstratified till (fig. 15) deposited under the ice and in end moraines, and the stratified drift laid down by meltwater flowing from the ice caps during stages of their growth and decay. (See also PLEISTOCENE EPOCH.)

6. Erosion by Waves.—The assault on shore areas by storm waves can be observed at margins of large lakes; and effects of sea waves on open coasts are even more pronounced. Historical records show that wave erosion has made appreciable inroads in some coastal areas; for example, along a 30-mi. stretch of

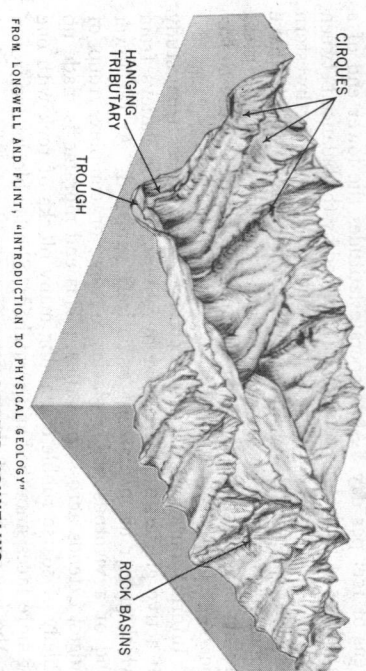

FROM LONGWELL AND FLINT, "INTRODUCTION TO PHYSICAL GEOLOGY"

FIG. 13.—FEATURES IN GLACIATED MOUNTAINS

CIRQUES
HANGING TRIBUTARY
TROUGH
ROCK BASINS

BY COURTESY OF McGRAW-HILL BOOK CO., INC., FROM EMMONS, THIEL, STAUFFER AND ALLISON, "GEOLOGY"

FIG. 14.—RUGGED TOPOGRAPHY IN THE SWISS ALPS BETWEEN VALLEY GLACIERS WHICH HEAD IN CIRQUES. SHARP PEAKS ARE CALLED HORNS

the Yorkshire coast in eastern England waves have cut inland 2½ to 3 mi. since the Roman occupation, sweeping away the sites of many villages. On the other hand some stretches of British and other coasts have been extended seaward through deposition by currents, waves, and streams. Whether wave work is effective in reducing a land area depends on exposure of a shore to prevailing storm winds, kind of bedrock, depth of water near shore, location and direction of currents, relation to streams that carry large volumes of sediment, and other variables. So long as sea level remains constant, the extent to which wave erosion can advance inland is limited. Wave motion extends to a moderate depth in the surf zone, and in the lower part of the layer of agitated water there is little energy. As storm waves plane inland, energy is absorbed by friction on the wave-cut platform. Hence with each advance of the wave-cut surface and the eroded surface slopes upward to an intersection with sea level. If sea level rises slowly, as it did while the great ice sheets of the past were melting, the extent to which waves can plane inland is increased. Northern lands that have been elevated since the ice vanished (see below) have conspicuous wave-cut surfaces on resistant bedrock, terminating inland against unmistakable sea cliffs and remnants of beaches (fig. 16).

Like streams, waves require tools for effective cutting. Blocks dislodged from cliffs by direct impact of the water are then used for abrasion, together with rock fragments brought from the land by streams and shifted along shore by currents. High cliffs commonly are undercut by wave action, and eventually the overhanging parts collapse, to be broken up completely. More resistant parts of the bedrock are bypassed temporarily and stand above water as isolated stacks.

7. Erosion in Arid Regions.—No sharp demarcation can be made between climates classed as arid and humid; but by a common definition, regions with less than 10 in. (25 cm.) average annual precipitation are arid. In these regions the surface of the ground is dry much of the time, there is little or no protective vegetation and strong winds are an effective eroding agent. Coarse particles swept along the ground have sandblast action, wearing and polishing facets on loose stones and on bedrock. Window glass exposed to such storms quickly becomes frosted, and within a short time unprotected wooden telephone poles are worn through near the base. Finer particles are carried away in great quantities and to large distances; during and following strong windstorms in the deserts of North Africa, appreciable amounts of dust settle on decks of ships in the Mediterranean and over wide areas of southern Europe. In grazing and farming regions classed as semiarid, strong winds carry away vast quantities of soil, particularly during periods of exceptional drought. During the early 1930s

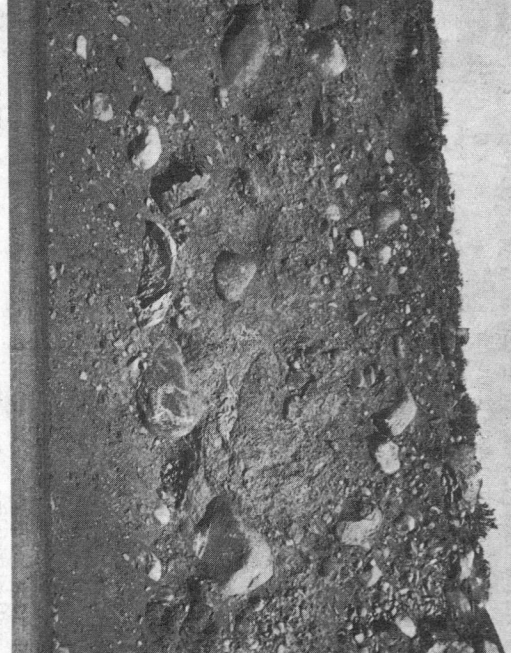

ELIOT BLACKWELDER

FIG. 15.—GLACIAL TILL EXPOSED IN ROAD CUT, EAST SLOPE OF THE SIERRA NEVADA RANGE, CALIFORNIA. LARGEST BLOCKS, ENCLOSED IN FINE-GRAINED MATRIX, ARE THREE TO FOUR FEET LONG

a wide belt east of the Rocky Mountains in the United States lost much valuable topsoil in windstorms known as black blizzards, which carried dust as far east as the Atlantic seaboard.

Although abrasion by windblown sand is important locally, the chief work of the wind is in transportation of rock materials broken up by other agents. In contrast to running water, wind carries quantities of sediment from lower to higher ground. (*See* also DESERT; DUNE; WIND EROSION AND DEPOSITION.)

8. Net Results of Erosive Processes.—Each of the eroding agents—surface water, ground water, glacier ice, wave action, and wind—fashions distinctive landscape features. These land forms are ephemeral, slowly but constantly changing, and the tendency is toward gradual lowering of the lands. The ideal result, if erosion on lands continued without interruption, would be reduction of every continent to a low, featureless surface, or peneplain; and by wave action such surfaces might eventually be brought below sea level. Profound effects of erosion are widespread. Very old mountain chains have been brought to low or moderate altitudes; examples are the Caledonian chains of Scandinavia and Britain, the mountains of eastern Australia and the Appalachian Belt of eastern North America. Still older chains have been entirely destroyed and only their roots remain as evidence (*see* below). In each continent wide surfaces that bevel indiscriminately across resistant and weak bedrock represent close approaches to peneplains; but these surfaces have been uplifted and are now being dissected by streams. The forces causing uplift have been persistent, and erosion keeps refashioning land forms that never are brought to completion.

C. PRINCIPLES OF SEDIMENTATION

An understanding of sedimentary rocks is all-important in geology, and sediments now being deposited provide the essential key. The sedimentary processes are a vast and complex subject for study; kinds of materials are numerous, they are worked on by several kinds of agents, the environments of deposition are diverse and many of them hidden from direct view. Many investigators devote their attention to problems of sedimentation not only by systematic field observations but also in special laboratories equipped with devices for mechanical and chemical analyses. Attack on difficult aspects of the study is made increasingly effective by cooperative pooling of information won by workers in a number of disciplines: for example, soil scientists; engineers concerned with problems of flood control, reclamation, and water-power development; well drillers interested in kinds of material encountered by their tools; companies laying transoceanic cables; and biologists studying the various habitats of organisms that live in swamps; on lake bottoms, or at different depths on the sea floor.

On the basis of environment of deposition, sediments are broadly assigned to the three categories: terrestrial, those laid down on the lands; marine, those deposited on sea floors though they may have come from the lands; and mixed terrestrial-marine, those deposited in transitional environments such as deltas, marine estuaries and areas between high and low tide. In each major group the sediments are further described as clastic (consisting of rock fragments) and chemical (formed either as inorganic precipitates or at least in part through the agency of organisms). Further classifications recognize the particular environments of deposition on land or in the sea, and the several agents that emplace the sediments.

1. Terrestrial Sediments.—Running water is the chief agent for transporting and sorting clastic sediments on land, and vast deposits accumulate in stream valleys. Bars of sand and gravel in stream channels are a familiar example; but such features are ephemeral, shifting with successive floods. Far more important are deposits on floodplains. Maximum loads are carried by a stream at flood stage; in large floods the sediment-laden water spreads beyond the channel, velocity of flow is much decreased and a layer of sediment, chiefly sand, silt, and clay, is spread over the nearly level plain. In a major valley, such as that of the Amazon, the Mississippi, or the Yellow, floodwaters cover a belt tens of miles wide; over much of the area the water, nearly stationary, is present for days or even weeks until the finest clay particles may

settle out. Although floodplain sediments are chiefly fine grained, gravel and coarse sand included locally may represent lateral migration of the channel in the growth and shifting of meanders. Tributaries that enter from hilly country commonly mix coarse deposits with finer sediments of the main valley.

In general the grain size of sediments along a large stream valley decreases steadily downstream. Abundant gravel in headwater areas has angular fragments, many of boulder size. These become smoothed and reduced in diameter by abrasion in transport; careful measurements show a constant increase in average roundness and decrease in average size of grain with distance of travel. The prospective goal of these stream-borne particles is the sea; but there are long delays for quantities of sediment spread over a floodplain. A stream in its slow lateral migration across its valley eventually cuts into these temporary deposits and carries them farther; but they are subject to the chance of redeposition on the wider plain farther downstream. Moreover below a critical point along the course of every major stream the floodplain is steadily building up, burying older deposits to increasing depth, because the grade of the stream adjusts to increasing length as the delta grows seaward. The Mississippi River once entered the sea far north of its present mouth; it has deposited floodplain

FIG. 16.—EVEN TERRACE, CUT BY WAVES ON RESISTANT ROCK, SHOWS BY ITS POSITION 100 FT. ABOVE SEA LEVEL THAT THE LAND WAS UPLIFTED IN RECENT TIMES. ISLAY, INNER HEBRIDES, SCOTLAND

sediments hundreds of feet thick, maintaining a slope of a few inches per mile as the delta front migrates southward.

The profiles of many streams are interrupted by lakes in their paths. Thus the Rhône River flows into the Lake of Geneva, in Switzerland, deposits its suspended load and flows out a clear stream. Eventually the lake will be filled with sediment into which the river will then cut to establish a normal grade. Deposits in lakes generally are coarse grained near the margins, progressively finer grained inward, though preponderant contributions by a large stream make the pattern asymmetric. Known lakes represent various stages in filling by sedimentation; and some old lake deposits have been well exposed to view by erosion. Chemical deposition of calcium carbonate and other mineral substances occurs in the interior parts of some lake basins, especially those in lands with deficient rainfall. In humid regions lakes in the last stages of filling with sediments become swamps in which accumulating plant materials may form beds of peat like those common in Ireland, Scotland, and many other lands. Formation of peat, an early stage in the development of coal, has required accumulation of the plant substances in swampy basins protected from detrital sediments, followed by complex biochemical changes.

Lakes and swamps, with their peculiar kinds of sedimentary accumulations, are especially numerous in the wide continental areas that were covered with glacier ice in the recent past. The unassorted deposits (till) formed by the ice and the stratified drift laid down by meltwater from the icecaps are described briefly above in connection with erosion by glaciers. Other types of unstratified rock waste that are widespread on the lands are the materials moving by creep, landsliding, and other forms of mass wasting, and residual material on low, flat areas where intensive weathering is in progress but there is no appreciable movement. In some tropical countries the deeply weathered residuum has a pronounced red colour from concentration of ferric oxide (see LATERITE).

Distinctive fine-grained sediment accumulated by wind action is called loess (q.v.). In wide areas of China such material, wholly unstratified, is spread over hilly country without regard for topography. The grains are of silt size or smaller, in large part unweathered and with angular shape. Apparently this material was carried by winds from the arid regions of central Asia. Similar loess in many parts of the Rhine and Mississippi valleys evidently had its source on barren plains formed by fine sediments washed from melting ice caps. Another common kind of wind deposit is dune sand, abundant in arid regions but widespread also near sandy shores of seas and large lakes, where a constant supply of sand is provided by the action of waves and currents.

2. Mixed Terrestrial-Marine Deposits.—Great deltas provide the most imposing visible exhibits of waste products moved from lands to seas. Exposed surfaces of the Ganges (Ganga)-Brahmaputra and Nile deltas measure about 50,000 sq.mi. (129,500 sq.km.) and 9,200 sq.mi. (23,800 sq.km.) respectively; that of the Yellow is much larger; and if to these is added the surface area of the deltas of the Amazon, Orinoco, Mississippi, Colorado, Yukon, Indus, Volga, Po, Rhône, Rhine, and other comparable streams, the total is over 386,000 sq.mi. (1,000,000 sq.km.). As all large delta surfaces slope gently outward under water, areas at the bases of marine deltas combine to make a total several times that of the exposed delta plains. Rates at which several great deltas are growing seaward are estimated from frequent measurement of sediments delivered by their streams and from repeated checks on positions of shore lines. The amount of sediment added to the Mississippi delta averages about 2,000,000 tons per day. Locally the exposed surface has grown seaward several miles within 50 years; but in situations exposed to storm waves the shore line has been cut back. Precise geodetic work has determined that in much of its area the delta is subsiding at rates of two or three metres per century, a movement that is partly or wholly compensated by continued upbuilding. Data from deep wells drilled for oil, supplemented by geophysical studies, indicate that the total thickness of the deltaic deposits exceeds 36,000 ft. (11,000 m.); presumably, therefore, crustal subsidence has proceeded as the delta grew.

Streams in crossing their deltas branch into distributary channels which diverge outward in a fanlike pattern. Because of imperfect drainage there are swampy areas and even lakes between adjacent distributaries. Sediments in large deltas are predominantly fine grained; in the Mississippi delta the percentage of clay is high and generally the largest grains are of coarse-sand size, though scattered small pebbles are reported. In parts of the deposit, sand, silt, and clay are mingled in complex fashion because at flood stage the muddy water of the stream mixes with sea water and salt causes flocculation of the clay, which in sinking carries coarser particles with it. Moreover the distributaries continually change their courses, carrying sand and silt into swampy areas to be mixed with clay and decaying vegetable matter. With outward growth of the delta plain, stream deposits of continental type come to overlie marine sediments; later subsidence or a rise in sea level may result in marine deposition over the continental beds. This constant interplay makes deltaic sediments extremely complex.

Most small streams that enter the sea cannot build deltas because waves and currents sweep away the sediments as fast as they are delivered. In some situations areas between the limits of high and low tides—the littoral zone—acquire a mixture of continental and marine deposits. Along some coasts strong waves breaking on a sandy bottom heap the sand into an offshore bar which may grow into an extensive barrier island. Long lagoons protected by such barriers accumulate sediments from the land, as well as sediments brought in by waves during exceptional storms. Another environment for mixture of land and sea deposits is provided by estuaries in which the water changes from salt to fresh with the rise and fall of the tides.

3. Marine Sediments.—Marine basins occupy much more than half the earth's surface. Situated lower than the lands, they have been the receptacles of sediments through long ages. Sediments washed from the lands are continually being spread over sea floors, supplementing vast deposits of directly marine origin. These processes are for the most part concealed from direct human observation. Effective and rapidly improving methods of studying marine sedimentation belong in the field of oceanography (see OCEAN AND OCEANOGRAPHY), but their value in geology justifies a brief summary here. The techniques most essential in geologic study of sea floors are those for determining depths and for bottom sampling. Until well into the 20th century both these operations were slow and inaccurate, and the resulting scattered observations gave little basis for reliable conclusions. The development of equipment for echo sounding made it possible to obtain an accurate continuous profile of the floor beneath a vessel moving at its normal speed.

Until the second half of the 20th century devices used for collecting bottom samples penetrated to very shallow depths and either mixed the sediments indiscriminately or caused distortion and compaction of individual layers. Coring cylinders were developed that have recovered cores up to 75 ft. (23 m.) long in which the layers of sediment are essentially undisturbed. Large numbers of such samples, taken at various depths and representing a wide range in distance from land, are studied in laboratories to determine the physical and chemical compositions of the sediments, thickness and arrangement of layers, content of organic remains, and other significant facts.

Marine sediments commonly are classified according to their depth below sea level, and also according to their origin. Three depth zones are recognized in the first classification; the shallow or neritic zone, the deep or bathyal zone, and the very deep or abyssal zone. These subdivisions are in general those recognized on a profile from a continental margin into an ocean basin. Continents and large islands are bordered by comparatively shallow water on a shelf which slopes gently outward to a depth ranging from 325 to 650 ft. (100 to 200 m.); sediments of this shelf are classed as neritic. At the outer edge of the shelf the grade steepens appreciably on the continental slope, which extends to the deep ocean floor; sediments of this slope are bathyal, and those of the ocean floor are abyssal. A classification according to source of sediments is as follows:

I. Derived from lands and contributed by
  A. Streams
  B. Winds
  C. Wave erosion of coasts
  D. Floating ice
II. Formed in the sea by
  A. Hard parts of marine animals and plants
  B. Chemical precipitation
III. Fragmental material erupted by volcanoes
IV. Particles of meteorites from outside the earth

As the shelf seas border continents and islands, a large part of the neritic sediments is made up of clastic materials derived from the lands. Generally these materials become well sorted according to size; waves agitate the sediments near shore and currents separate fine particles from coarse and carry them to depths below wave action. In a simple system the coarse materials, spread out near shore, would grade seaward into silt and clay. Actually the movements of sea water are extremely complex because of coastal irregularities, varied directions of storm winds, uneven bottom topography, proximity of great ocean currents, and other variables. Accordingly the coarse sediments are carried out much farther in some places than in others. Moreover sea level has not remained fixed and on the gently sloping shelf a moderate shift in the water level results in a large shift of the shore line. During the glacial ages, when vast quantities of water were locked up in ice sheets on lands, sea level was as much as 300 ft. (90 m.) lower than at

PLATE I

GEOLOGY

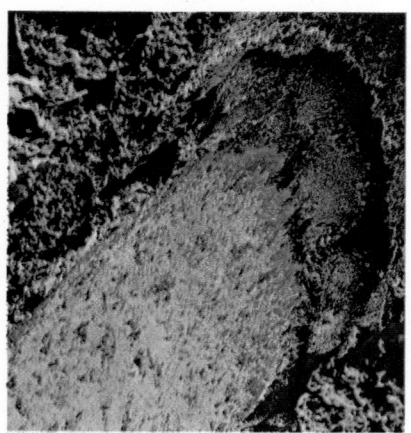

Igneous rocks are products of molten masses generated beneath the earth's surface. When such a molten mass surfaces, either as lava seen (above) flowing down the slope of Mt. Etna, Sicily, or as fragments blown from a volcano's vent, it cools to form a smooth-grained, often glassy, rock (top right). Similar molten magma deep within the earth cools more slowly, to produce a coarse-grained rock, of which granite, shown in Colorado (right), is a well-known example. The products of this process are called intrusive

ROCKS OF THE EARTH'S CRUST

Sandstone, shown (right) on the coast of Prince Edward Island, Canada, is formed of cemented grains of sand. Conglomerate (below), from Long Island Sound, New York, is made up of rock fragments embedded in cemented finer-grained sediments

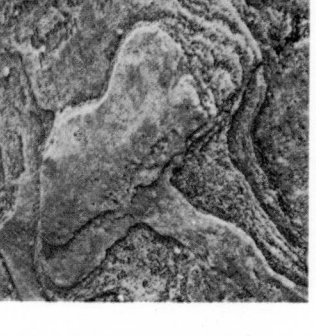

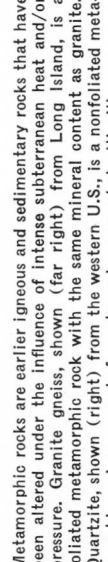

Metamorphic rocks are earlier igneous and sedimentary rocks that have been altered under the influence of intense subterranean heat and/or pressure. Granite gneiss, shown (far right) from Long Island, is a foliated metamorphic rock with the same mineral content as granite. Quartzite, shown (right) from the western U.S., is a nonfoliated metamorphic rock composed of quartz grains cemented with silica

(TOP LEFT, TOP RIGHT UPPER) G. TOMSICH—PHOTO RESEARCHERS, (TOP RIGHT LOWER) ROGER APPLETON—PHOTO RESEARCHERS, (CENTRE LEFT, BOTTOM RIGHT) EDNA BENNETT—PHOTO RESEARCHERS, (CENTRE RIGHT) CHARLES R. BELINKY—PHOTO RESEARCHERS, (BOTTOM LEFT) RUSS KINNE—PHOTO RESEARCHERS

GEOLOGY

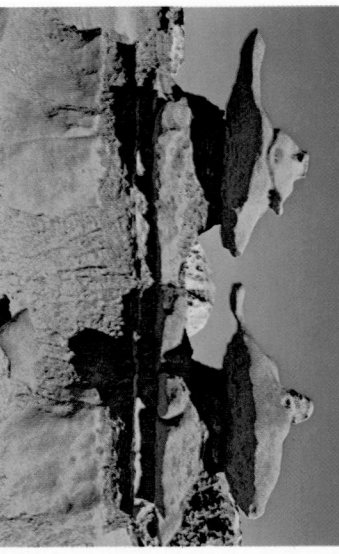

Curious rock formations, produced by centuries of erosion by wind-blown sand on layers of sandstone, Goblin Valley, Utah

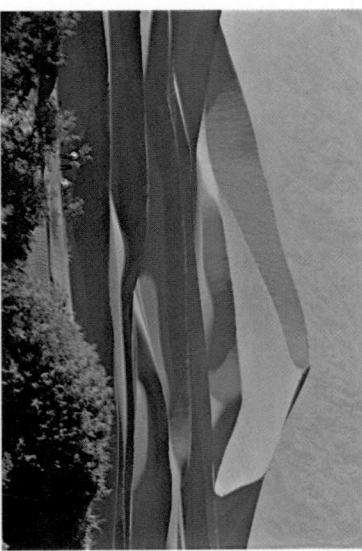

Sand dunes near Stove Pipe Wells, Death Valley, California. Topography of sandy deserts changes constantly as winds shift

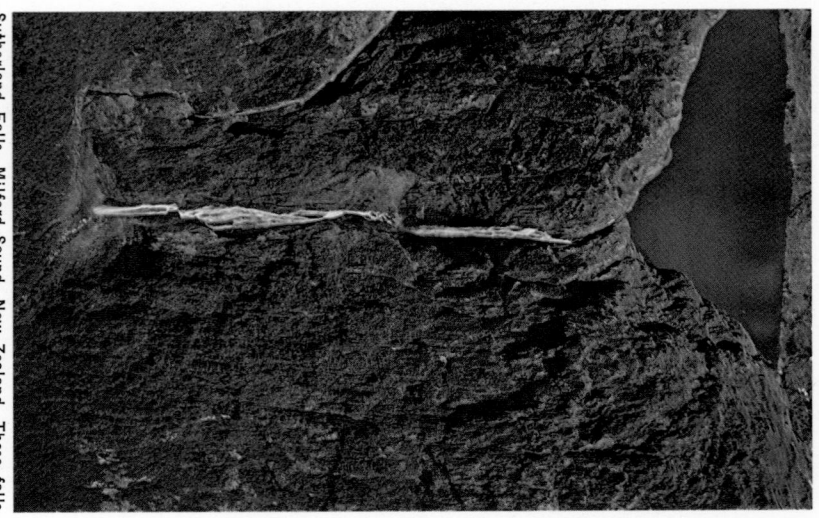

Sutherland Falls, Milford Sound, New Zealand. These falls are characteristic of those in glaciated valleys, emptying a lake that is "trapped" in a hanging valley

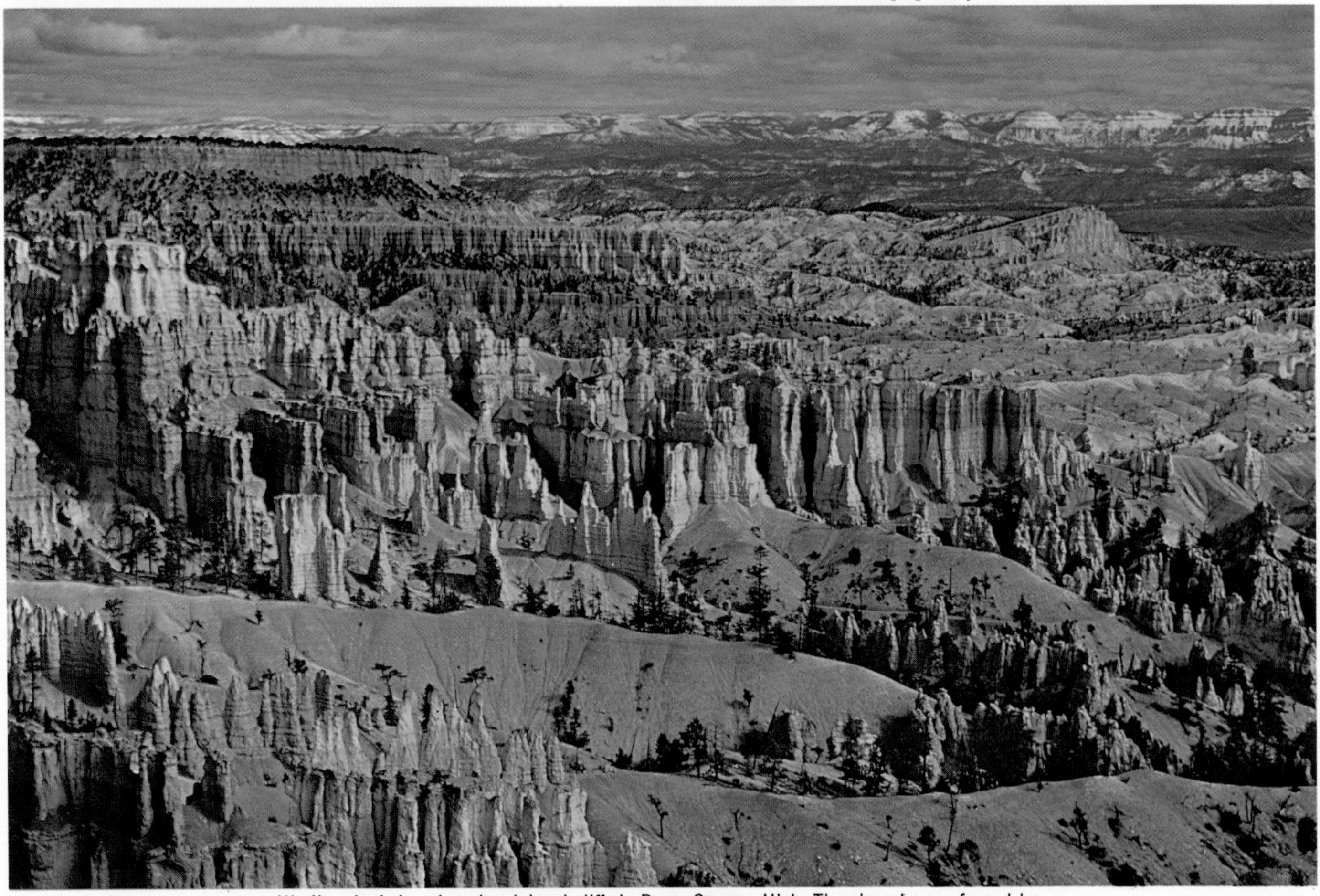

Weathered wind- and sand-sculptured cliffs in Bryce Canyon, Utah. The pinnacles are formed by erosion along vertical joints that cross layers of friable sandstone and limestone

(TOP LEFT AND CENTRE LEFT) WILLIAM BELKNAP, JR.—RAPHO GUILLUMETTE, (TOP RIGHT) ALLYN BAUM—RAPHO GUILLUMETTE, (BOTTOM) ERNST HASS—MAGNUM

PLATE III

GEOLOGY

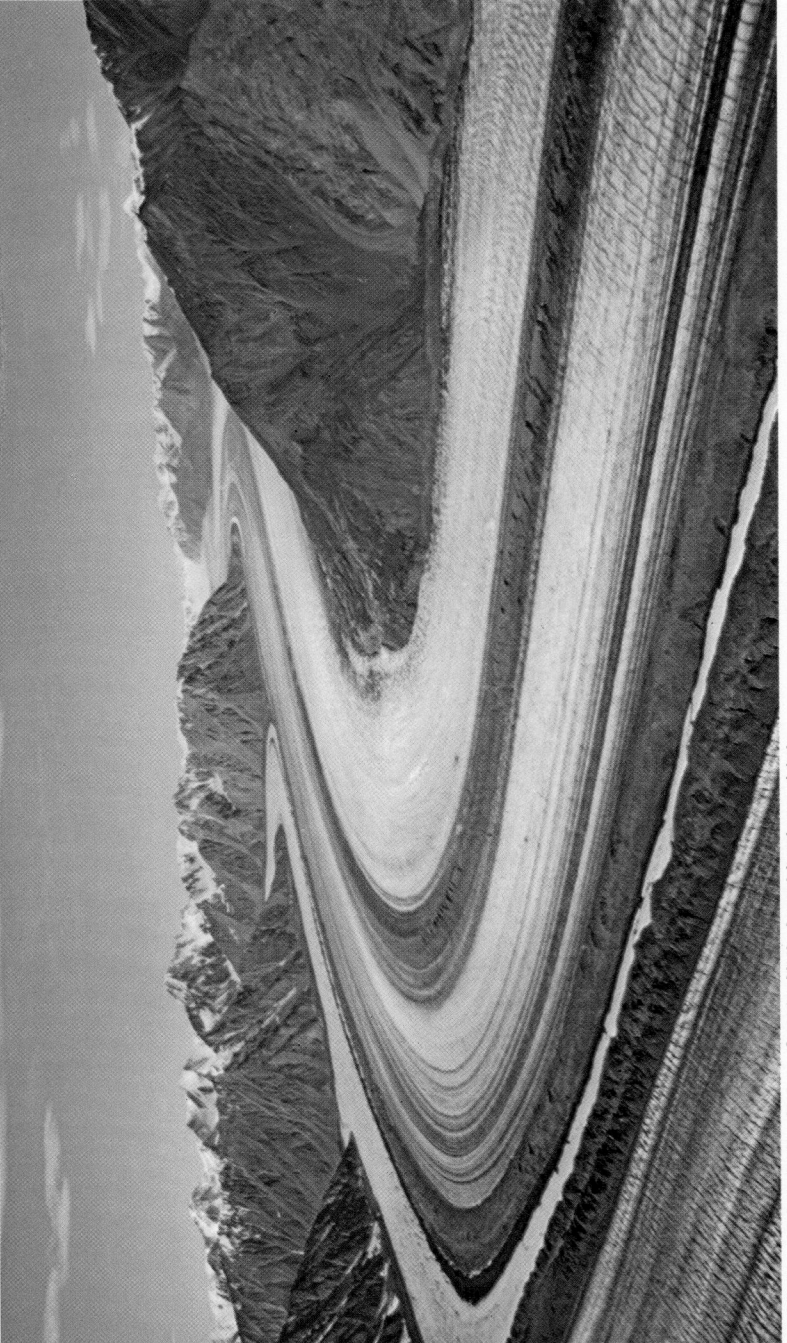

Valley glacier and tributaries, Yukon, Canada. Varicoloured bands are debris-laden ice. Although most glaciers move slowly—their average speed being only inches a day—speeds of up to 150 ft. a day have been recorded

The Matterhorn (foreground), an excessively glaciated peak in the Swiss Alps. The peak has survived the destruction of glacial cirques, or high basins, that once stood on either side. In the background may be seen a small glacier and several similarly formed smaller peaks. Small glaciers are still common in the Alps

GEOMORPHOLOGY

The shape of the land changes constantly. This slow but continuous process is due to several major causes, some of which are shown on these and the following two plates. In regions where snowfall exceeds melting, accumulated snow is compressed into ice. When this ice reaches a certain critical thickness it begins to move of its own great weight and becomes a glacier, capable of powerful erosive action (above and right and Plate II, top right). In arid regions (Plate II, top left and centre left), erosion is often caused by the abrasive and polishing action of wind carrying small particles of sand and rock. Weathering, the actual disintegration and decay of rock itself (Plate II, bottom), may be caused by frost wedging, plant roots, exfoliation, the action on certain minerals of carbonic acid carried by rainwater, or by combinations of any or all of these

BY COURTESY OF (BOTTOM) THE SWISS NATIONAL TOURIST OFFICE; PHOTOGRAPH, (TOP) RUSS KINNE—PHOTO RESEARCHERS

PLATE IV

GEOLOGY

Deeply eroded canyons cut by the Colorado River, Utah. The steep cliffs of the loop (centre) were out after rejuvenation of the entire area by crustal upwarping

Wave-eroded rocks on the heavily glaciated coastline of Bjørnøya (Bear Island), a part of the Norwegian Svalbard archipelago. Inequalities in resistance to wave erosion have produced isolated stacks such as those in the foreground. Eventually, these too will wear away

(TOP) WILLIAM BELKNAP—RAPHO GUILLUMETTE, (BOTTOM LEFT) FRED BALDWIN—PHOTO RESEARCHERS, (BOTTOM RIGHT) H. HAROLD DAVIS—PUBLIX

Natural bridge in the Red River Valley, Kentucky. The bridge is all that remains of the roof of a cavern dissolved out of limestone beds by the action of groundwater

Water is a major erosive force, whether running above or below ground, falling as rain, or battering a coastline in the form of waves. Flowing rivers accumulate sediment and distribute it along their banks (Plate V, top right). Over millennia rivers may cut their way through thousands of feet of rock (above). Underground streams, fed by rainwater and rich with dissolved minerals, erode and alter underground beds of rock (below and Plate V, top left). Lake and ocean shores are under constant assault by the power of wind and waves (left)

PLATE V

GEOLOGY

Extensive alluvial fan in the Yukon, Canada. Alluvial fans, which are made up of stream-carried and deposited sediments, occur when there is a reduction in a stream's velocity or volume or a sudden change in the shape of its bed

Carlsbad Caverns, New Mexico. The caves themselves resulted from long-continued dissolving of limestone by circulating ground water. The thick stalagmites were formed by local deposition as saturated water dripped into the caverns

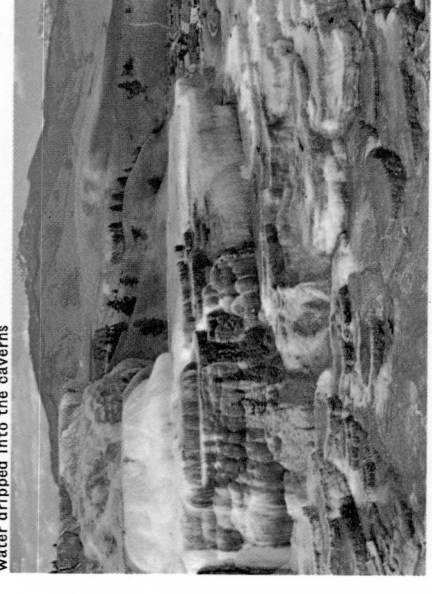

Minerva Terrace, Yellowstone National Park, Wyoming. Formed by hot spring water, the successive pools develop rims of precipitated minerals

Stream meandering on its flat floodplain, Cape Cod, Massachusetts. The sharp bends are characteristic of such streams in the final stage of their erosion cycle

(TOP LEFT) FRED BOND—PUBLIX, (TOP RIGHT) RUSS KINNE—PHOTO RESEARCHERS, (CENTRE LEFT) NORMAN R. LIGHTFOOT—PHOTO RESEARCHERS, (BOTTOM) CHARLES R. BELINKY—PHOTO RESEARCHERS

PLATE VI

GEOLOGY

CRUSTAL MOVEMENTS

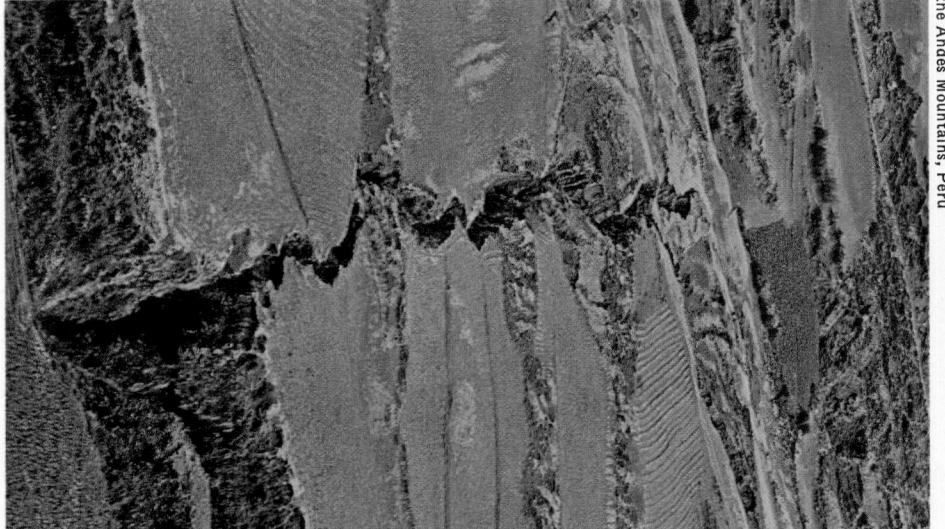

Deep rents in the earth's surface, result of a recent earthquake in the Andes Mountains, Peru

Massive fault in the Wasatch Mountains near Salt Lake City, Utah, had a total displacement of some 10,000 ft. between mountaintops and lowland; thousands of years of weathering and erosion have reduced the difference to about 6,000 ft.

Cleavage layers in a sample of slate from the western U.S.

Folded sedimentary rock layers on an exposed mountainside in the Canadian Rockies, British Columbia

Exposed layers of uptilted sedimentary rock in the Sierra Madre, Mexico

Clearly jointed granite cliffs at Land's End, Cornwall, England

present. As the level shifted gradually, downward and upward with growth and wasting of ice caps, shore lines migrated tens of miles on the wide shelves. As a result coarse clastic sediments were deposited far out at times of maximum glaciation, to be covered with fine-grained deposits when waning glacier ice restored the higher sea level.

Great quantities of land-derived clastic sediments are spread beyond the shelves onto the continental slopes and parts of the deep ocean floors. Geophysical research has determined that thick deposits lie on these floors at the bases of the slopes; probably much of this material is carried out by sliding of loose, water-saturated sediments on the unstable sloping surfaces. Trans-atlantic cables have been broken by such sliding masses; and studies indicate that swift currents generated by the sliding carry loads of clay, silt, and sand far out on the ocean floors. These currents move along the bottom because the exceptional loads of sediments make them turbidity currents, much heavier than the clear water above.

Of the sediments with marine origin an overwhelming percent-age is contributed by animals and plants, for the most part small floating or swimming forms, many of them microscopic or nearly so. In tropical and temperate zones the surface waters teem with myriads of these organisms, some of which form shells of calcium carbonate (commonly called lime), others of silica, extracted from sea water. The discarded shells settle to the ocean floors and slowly build a deposit over wide areas. In warm regions the cal-careous shells are predominant, and great expanses of the ocean floors are covered with calcareous ooze. This deposit is absent from the deeper parts of ocean basins, however, because the cold water at great depth, containing much carbon dioxide, dissolves the slowly settling flakes of calcium carbonate. Siliceous ooze, much less soluble, covers large areas in deep oceans; part of this material may be volcanic dust transported by wind. In wide tracts the siliceous particles are mingled with fine clay, which through oxidation has acquired a distinctive red colour. The red-clay deposits in deep oceans contain more particles of me-teorites than are found elsewhere, probably because accumulation of the clay is so slow the meteoritic materials are relatively con-centrated and conditions on the ocean floors protect these ma-terials from rapid chemical decay.

Some cores brought up from deep ocean floors, far from land, consist chiefly of clastic materials, including fairly coarse sand, with only a thin cover of ooze or of red clay. Probably the clastic sediments were derived by sliding from a continental slope and were carried far out by turbidity currents.

Marine organisms are abundant over the continental shelves, but generally the organic materials are masked by clastic sedi-ments that accumulate more rapidly in most parts of the neritic zone. But there are notable exceptions to this general rule. Along some low coasts that are protected from sediment-laden currents the shells of mollusks and other large shelled animals accumulate in widespread layers. In coastal belts of southern Florida and the Bahama Islands such accumulations are being cemented rapidly into firm rock. On shelves in the tropical zone corals and other reef-forming animals are building immense calcareous deposits, many of them near coasts. Calcareous ooze also is forming on some shelf areas from which clastic sediments are diverted. Pre-cipitation of lime around coasts of some low-latitude islands is explained as the result of oversaturation due to loss of carbon dioxide through increase of temperature or lowering of pressure.

The neritic sediments are of particular interest in geology, be-cause in large part the marine sedimentary rocks now exposed on land have features that indicate their origin in the shelf zone. Some rocks exposed in mountain belts, however, have characteris-tics peculiar to sediments in deeper parts of the oceans.

4. Conversion of Sediments to Sedimentary Rocks.—Ce-mentation and compaction convert deposits of loose clastic sedi-ments and soft oozes into firm rocks, some of them as strong as granite. Layers of clay and fine silt become compacted more and more under the weight of overlying beds, and much water in the original mud is expelled; shale and siltstone are the end products. Calcareous ooze loses excess water in the same way, and slow

crystallization of the carbonate minerals produces firm limestone and dolomite. Water moving through pores between sand grains and pebbles in the coarser clastic layers slowly deposits dissolved mineral matter, such as calcium carbonate, which binds the parti-cles together; layers of sand become sandstone, those made of larger particles—pebbles to boulders—become conglomerate. In the change from loose sediment to strong rock many distinctive features are preserved: tracks of animals made on muddy surfaces; forms of ripples molded in loose sand beneath oscillating waves; cracks formed on muddy surfaces from drying; and, particularly important, shells and bones of animals and tissues and impressions

FIG. 17.—(TOP) ORIGINAL TOP OF A BED CLEARLY INDICATED BY PATTERN OF FILLED MUD CRACKS IN SHALE, MARYLAND. (BOTTOM) FOSSIL FISH ON A SLAB OF SHALE FORMED IN A LAKE DURING EOCENE TIME. SOUTHWESTERN WYOMING

of plants which give reliable information on the environments un-der which the sediments were laid down (fig. 17).

See also STRATIFICATION; SEDIMENTARY ROCKS.

D. STRUCTURAL GEOLOGY

Geometric study of rocks recognizes primary structures—those acquired in the genesis of a rock mass—and secondary structures that result from later deformation. Familiarity with primary features is essential for effective study of deformed masses. The many significant features in sedimentary rocks make them espe-cially valuable for detecting and evaluating later changes in form. Of outstanding importance is the nearly horizontal attitude of true sedimentary beds when they are deposited; such beds that now have steep attitudes clearly record their distortion. In many belts of strong disturbance the beds have been overturned, even com-pletely inverted, as shown by positions of animal tracks, plant roots, mud cracks, and other features that mark tops of sedimentary layers. Volcanic rocks also have distinctive features, such as vesicles in the upper parts of lava sheets, which give them value in structural studies.

Such studies may result in purely factual descriptions of deformed rocks; but a broad view of the subject considers possible causes of deformation, and inquires into the structure of entire continents and of the earth as a whole.

1. Evidence of Crustal Movements.—Within historic time abrupt and large-scale displacements of bedrock have occurred. In 1899 part of the Alaskan coast was raised instantaneously as much as 47 ft. (14.5 m.); the movement was attended by a major earthquake. Other extensive breaks in bedrock, coinciding with earthquakes, have been recorded in Chile, California, Japan, Italy, and many other lands. Movements of another kind, slow and affecting wide areas, are revealed in evidence partly historic and partly older. Marks made at high-tide level along the Norwegian coast more than a century ago are now several feet above the reach of tides. Uplift of Scandinavia has been long continued, as shown by a succession of wide benches bearing marks of shore lines, the highest about 900 ft. (275 m.) above present sea level. Evidence of similar broad uplift is conspicuous in Newfoundland, and in Canada along the St. Lawrence River and around Hudson Bay. A movement of this kind, involving gradual bending of a wide surface, is known as crustal warping. Ancient warping at many dates is recorded in broad bending, both upward and downward, of sedimentary beds; the structural evidence remains though the land surface that must have been deformed has been destroyed by erosion. In addition to broad warps, the principal kinds of structural features that record deformation are folds, joints, faults, cleavage, and unconformities.

Folds occur in a more or less regular sequence of upbends or anticlines and downbends or synclines. In major mountain chains folding has affected belts tens of miles wide and hundreds of miles long; individual folds are continuous for tens of miles and the largest measure several miles between crests of adjacent anticlines. Folds of smaller scale are superimposed on the sides or limbs of the major folds. The general pattern may be imitated in miniature by placing a stack of cloths or of thin paper sheets on a table and compressing from opposite edges. Folding can occur only in layered rocks and is best developed in thick sections of sedimentary beds, although some volcanic rocks consisting of lava flows and beds of volcanic ash also are strongly folded. This kind of deformation indicates large-scale compression.

Joints, or breaks along which no perceptible movement has occurred, are present in nearly all large exposures of bedrock (fig. 18). Only in exceptional places can quarrymen find good stone

FIG. 18.—TWO SETS OF VERTICAL JOINTS, NEARLY AT RIGHT ANGLES, CUTTING HORIZONTAL BEDS OF LIMESTONE. DRUMMOND ISLAND, MICHIGAN

sufficiently free from joints to provide perfect monoliths 50 to 100 ft. long. In igneous rocks many joints have formed by contraction on cooling. Joints cutting rocks of all kinds probably have resulted from stresses set up by warping, folding, and other deformation (fig. 19).

Faults are breaks in bedrock along which displacement has occurred parallel to the fractures. Abrupt slips on active faults

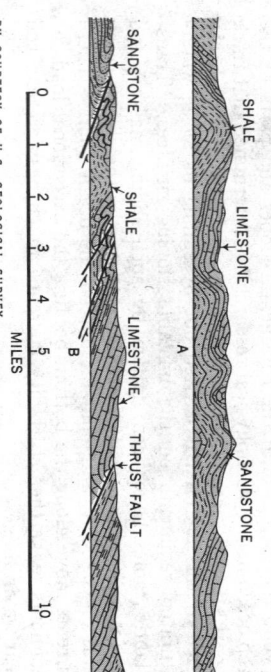

FIG. 19.—(A) FOLDED MARINE STRATA IN WESTERN VIRGINIA; (B) STRATA IN SOUTHWESTERN VIRGINIA, FOLDED AND SLICED BY THRUST FAULTS

cause earthquakes; such movements on a given fault may occur at intervals of years or tens of years to relieve stresses that build up slowly. Dimensions of faults range from inches to hundreds of miles, and amounts of displacement vary widely. The San Andreas fault in California, movement on which caused the earthquake of 1906, can be traced at the surface nearly 600 mi.; displacement in 1906 was horizontal, as much as 21 ft.—roads and fences were sharply offset to that extent. Earlier movements account for a total displacement of many miles. (See Earthquake.) On some other faults the displacement has been chiefly vertical, producing a high cliff or scarp. Most faults are inclined, some steeply, others at a low angle. If displacement is relatively downward on the side toward which the break is inclined, the fault is called normal; if that side has moved relatively upward, the fault is reverse. Reverse faults with low angles of inclination and large displacement are called thrust faults, or simply thrusts. Such faults commonly are associated with folds in mountain belts. In strike-slip faulting the movement is horizontal, parallel to the fault trace. The great majority of known faults are dead—that is, movement on them apparently ceased long ago. (See also Fault; Fold.)

Cleavage has been developed in many large masses of rock under high compressive stress. In nearly all large mountain belts shale in closely folded beds has been transformed into slate. Cleavage, cutting sharply across the original bedding, divides the slate into thin plates with remarkably plane surfaces. In many zones of extreme deformation the slate has passed into lustrous phyllite, or even into mica schist, in which the cleavage surfaces commonly are much crumpled.

Many old crustal movements are recorded by interruptions in sequences of sedimentary beds. For example in the walls of the Grand Canyon of Arizona a thick section of beds containing fossils of marine animals is almost horizontal; but the base of the section rests on the edges of tilted older beds, some of which also are of marine origin. A general succession of events is clearly indicated: the older beds were deposited on a sea floor; they were deformed, lifted above the sea, and partly destroyed by erosion; the region later subsided, a new section of marine beds was laid down and the present land was formed by widespread uplift but with little deformation of the younger beds. The two sequences of beds are unconformable, and because of the angular divergence they are said to be separated by an angular unconformity (fig. 20). Many unconformities represent interruptions in sedimentation by broad warping movements that left the older beds essentially horizontal; successive sequences of beds then have no perceptible angular divergence, though the surface separating them may represent a long history of erosion. Discordant contacts between masses of rock result also from large-scale faulting and from igneous intrusion; but the term unconformity is applied only to a relation that involves erosion followed by deposition of layered rocks, either sedimentary or volcanic in origin.

2. Mountain Structure.—Kinds and structure of rock masses exposed in mountain lands are highly varied; but in every great mountain belt exceptionally thick sedimentary sections have been deformed by folding and faulting. Erosion has truncated folds over wide areas and exposed complete sections of the beds, which have maximum total thicknesses as great as 6 to 8 mi. The beds, consisting of conglomerate, sandstone, shale, and limestone, are largely of marine origin as shown by included fossils, and in considerable part the sediments resemble modern deposits in shallow water and at moderate depths; therefore the basins of deposition must have subsided slowly while the sediments accumulated. In many places the marine beds intertongue laterally with coarse littoral and deltaic deposits. As this relationship extends through large thicknesses, the lands that supplied the clastic sediments must have been rising while the sedimentary basins were sinking. Therefore the site of a mountain belt was a zone of disturbance for a long time before the mountains were formed. Lavas and other volcanic materials commonly are included with sediments in parts of the section.

Generally the zone of subsidence and sedimentation marking the early stages of mountain history was situated near the margin of a continental mass. Much of the clastic sediment, however, has come from land on the seaward side, as shown by the direction of gradation from coarse to fine materials. Thus in parts of the Appalachian Mountains coarse-grained sediments grade westward

BY COURTESY OF C. R. LONGWELL
FIG. 20.—ANGULAR UNCONFORMITY BETWEEN TWO SETS OF SEDIMENTARY BEDS. THE HORIZONTAL BEDS OF TERTIARY CONGLOMERATE (TOP) WERE DEPOSITED AFTER THE BEDS OF PALEOZOIC LIMESTONE HAD BEEN TILTED AND BEVELED BY EROSION. MEADOW VALLEY WASH, NEVADA

through shale to limestone. The land that supplied pebbles, sand, and silt lay east of the present coast, and perhaps consisted of islands in a chain similar to the present island arcs of the Caribbean region and many parts of the Pacific Basin. Modern island arcs are in zones of volcanic activity, with products similar to volcanic rocks found in the deformed sections of mountain belts. The areas of thick sedimentary sections vary in width but generally are no wider than the mountain belt. In the Appalachian Mountains the total section of beds is six to eight times as thick as the section of the same age in the wide Mississippi Valley region directly to the west. Therefore before deformation occurred the base of the thick section curved gently downward in the form of a broad trough, the result of slow subsidence as the sediments accumulated. Because of this troughlike form the area of thick sediments is called a geosyncline—a downbending of global scale —and the long period of sedimentary accumulation before the development of mountain structure is referred to as the geosynclinal stage.

Deformation of a large belt to form mountain structure is called orogeny, literally the genesis of mountains. In a general way orogeny has followed the geosynclinal stage; but the history has

been complex in every great mountain unit. Within parts of the Appalachian Belt angular unconformities record repeated deformation, erosion that beveled the resulting folds and faults, then continued subsidence and sedimentation. But a final paroxysm of deformation ended the geosynclinal stage, mountainous topography became the rule, and later history has been a contest between erosion and renewed uplift. Apparently the Alps and related mountain units, which are much younger than the Appalachians and Urals, are in an early stage of their history following deformation of the geosynclinal deposits. Erosion has proceeded far enough to reveal spectacular effects of folding and faulting. Great folds, overturned toward the north, have repeated the beds in complex fashion; further repetition has resulted from low-angle thrust faults on which great slices of the deformed rock, piled one above another, have been moved many miles northward. Similar structure is found in older mountain belts, where erosion has exposed also great masses of metamorphic rock and large intrusive bodies of granitic rock emplaced during the orogeny.

Sites of the oldest great mountain units are in present lowlands, and are recognized in elongate belts of contorted and faulted sedimentary rocks, much metamorphosed, partly engulfed in large granitic batholiths. Such "roots" of mountains are conspicuous in parts of Canada, Fennoscandia (Baltic Shield), Siberia, central Africa, and Brazil, in areas that through long ages have been above sea level, subject to weathering and erosion. Other well-known mountain belts, forming a sequence from old to comparatively young, have generally similar structure and the heights of the belts increase with decreasing age; examples representing four dates in a long span of time are the northwest Highlands of Scotland, the Appalachian chain, the Rocky Mountains, and the Alps. Some island arcs in the Pacific Basin and in the Caribbean region appear to be mountain units now growing. Therefore orogeny has been continuous or recurrent through much of geologic time. The cause and the mechanism of orogeny and of broad warping movements that repeatedly have lifted and depressed continental areas are matters of much interest and active study; but the subject is too involved and speculative for treatment here. Some physical principles involved in the history of persistent mountain uplifts merit brief attention.

3. Balance in the Earth's Crust.—Old mountain units such as the Appalachian chain, the ranges of South Africa, and the Rocky Mountains of Colorado have been brought to subdued relief by erosion but have regained much of the lost altitude by repeated upwarping. This behaviour is generally similar to that of an iceberg which, though its emerged portion is subject to continuous melting, maintains much of its height by buoyant rise of the greater mass under water. The comparison is a reminder that rocks exposed in the continents are on the average appreciably less dense than the basaltic rocks common in the ocean floors. Though wide continental surfaces have been submerged repeatedly, the resulting seas have been shallow; all known evidence indicates that continents and deep ocean floors never have exchanged places. Therefore a favoured concept regards the continents as the upper surfaces of crustal plates with comparatively low density that are buoyed up on a subcrust of higher density; high mountain chains logically represent thickened parts of the continental plates (fig. 21).

This concept is strongly supported by geophysical data related to the study of earthquakes. Elastic waves traveling from an earthquake centre or from the location of a large artificial explosion move at higher speeds through basaltic rocks than through the granitic rocks common in continental masses. Instrumental

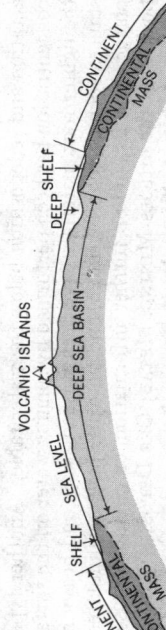

FROM LONGWELL AND FLINT, "INTRODUCTION TO PHYSICAL GEOLOGY"
FIG. 21.—MAJOR FEATURES OF RELIEF ON A SEGMENT OF THE EARTH, WITH VERTICAL SCALE EXAGGERATED ABOUT EIGHT TIMES

records of these waves at many stations indicate that the average thickness of continental plates is 15 to 25 mi. and that beneath a high mountain unit such as the Alps the thickness is 35 mi. or more. Thus the large irregularities of the earth's surface are not haphazard but are controlled by gravity; the general state of balance between segments of the crust that differ in density is called isostasy (equal standing). Figure 22 illustrates the principle involved.

The concept of isostatic balance is in accord with the behaviour of areas that were covered with ice caps during the Great Ice Age, or Pleistocene Epoch. Since the ice disappeared the glaciated areas have been warped upward, as shown by elevated shorelines; in Scandinavia and Canada the highest marine terraces are hundreds of feet above sea level and probably much more uplift occurred while the wasting ice kept the sea from contact with the land. Presumably the ice caps, many thousands of feet thick, disturbed the isostatic balance and caused downwarping; this may have involved slow flowage of rock materials, at great depth, outward from the loaded areas. Wasting of the ice has brought readjustment and rise of land surfaces toward preglacial levels. *See* GEODESY: *Isostasy.*

E. ECONOMIC GEOLOGY

The minerals on which our civilization is heavily dependent are obtained from the earth's crust and therefore have a prominent place in the study and practice of geology. Although the term mineral ordinarily suggests solid substances, water also is a mineral resource of primary importance. A major part of the water supply developed for private, public, and industrial use is obtained directly or indirectly from underground sources; even lakes used in systems of water supply receive their steady replenishment from ground water. Therefore some knowledge of the kinds and structure of local bedrock is essential in plans for developing, conserving, and ensuring the sanitary quality of an adequate water supply, particularly for a large community. Many wide areas on the flanks of highlands are favoured with artesian conditions.

The solid economic minerals are grouped in two general categories: metallic and nonmetallic. Deposits of metallic minerals—those from which are extracted common metals such as iron, copper, zinc, and lead, and many that are less common—are extremely diverse in their occurrence and origin. Many large masses of metalliferous ore are connected, directly or indirectly, with bodies of igneous rock. Masses that apparently separated directly out of molten magmas are illustrated by the magnetic iron ores at Kiruna, Swed. Some metallic ores were formed at contacts of igneous bodies with older rocks; others by hydrothermal action that extended from the bodies of magma far out into the adjacent older rock; still others in veins built up by crystallization from solutions that migrated outward from magmas along joints and faults in older rocks. Important metalliferous deposits of sedimentary origin include the Clinton iron-ore beds that are widespread in the Appalachian region, and the iron ranges of the Lake Superior region. The latter deposits, the largest and richest bodies of hematite discovered by the second half of the 20th century, were enriched by circulating waters which dissolved silica and other substances, leaving a residue with a high content of iron oxide. Many other bodies of metalliferous ores, varied in origin, have been enriched by dissolving of mineral matter in the zone of aeration and redeposition below the water table. Another type of concentration has been performed by running water on the surface; the lighter rock materials have been washed away, and heavy substances such as gold, platinum, and tin oxide have accumulated in placer deposits. (For further information on metalliferous deposits, *see* the articles MINING, METAL; ORE DEPOSITS; and placer deposits.)

Of outstanding importance among nonmetallic deposits are the mineral fuels—coal, petroleum, and natural gas—which are rich

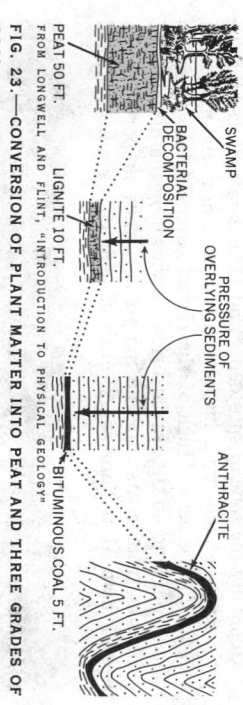

FROM LONGWELL AND FLINT, "INTRODUCTION TO PHYSICAL GEOLOGY"

FIG. 22.—BLOCKS OF COPPER (DENSITY 8.8) FLOAT IN MERCURY (DENSITY 13.6)

MERCURY   COPPER BLOCKS

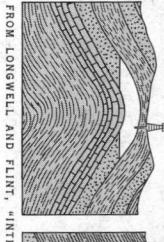
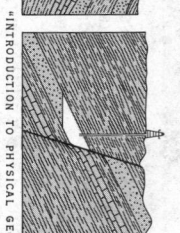
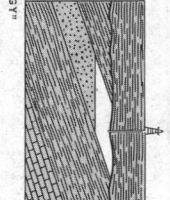

FROM LONGWELL AND FLINT, "INTRODUCTION TO PHYSICAL GEOLOGY"

FIG. 23.—CONVERSION OF PLANT MATTER INTO PEAT AND THREE GRADES OF COAL

SWAMP   BACTERIAL DECOMPOSITION   PRESSURE OF OVERLYING SEDIMENTS   PEAT 50 FT.   LIGNITE 10 FT.   BITUMINOUS COAL 5 FT.   ANTHRACITE

FROM LONGWELL AND FLINT, "INTRODUCTION TO PHYSICAL GEOLOGY"

FIG. 24.—THREE TYPES OF OIL TRAPS. POROUS SANDSTONE IS SHOWN BY DOTS, IMPERVIOUS SHALE BY PARALLEL LINES. OIL FILLS THE ROCK PORES

in solar energy locked up in chemical compounds by plants and animals of past ages. Coal originated in vast swamps; plant material, accumulated in large thickness, were compressed under the weight of sediments deposited over them, and slow chemical changes with attendant loss of gas have resulted in fuels of several grades from peat to anthracite (fig. 23). Petroleum is a product of slow chemical change in organic material, much of it contributed by small marine plants and animals to sediments as they accumulated on sea floors. Oil and gas generated in the source beds have migrated into adjacent porous layers, where generally water has forced the lighter fluids into various kinds of traps, sealed by beds of shale or other impervious rock (fig. 24). Occurrence of some more extensive gas deposits free from oil is explained by escape of the more mobile gas from an earlier common trap to a location under more impervious rock. Exceptionally the migrating oil and gas have come to rest in volcanic rocks, or even in metamorphic rocks that have some porosity; but nearly all oil and gas pools of commercial value are in sedimentary rocks. Geologic principles and information are important aids in the search for new producing localities and large numbers of trained geologists find employment in the petroleum industry. Geophysical principles and techniques for finding favourable structures also are employed extensively in the continuing search for oil. Many important discoveries have been made by drilling to depths considered impractical in earlier exploration; some producing wells are as deep as 20,000 ft. (For further information *see* GEOPHYSICAL PROSPECTING; COAL AND COAL MINING; PETROLEUM; GAS INDUSTRY.)

Other nonmetallic deposits include a large number of mineral concentrates, some of which originated as chemical precipitates in seas and lakes; prominent among these are gypsum, sulfur, and common salt (*see* SALT DOME).

Economic development of deposits in the earth's crust applies principles of geology to practical ends. On the other hand, information revealed in mining operations and in the worldwide search for petroleum has contributed much to the growth of geologic science.

III. HISTORICAL GEOLOGY

A major part of the legible history of the earth is read from sedimentary rocks, which record an order of events, changing environments, developments in animal and plant life, and effects of crustal movements. Important supplements to the record are found (1) in volcanic rocks, which in many places are interlayered with, and grade into, sedimentary deposits; (2) in relations of intrusive igneous bodies to older and younger rocks; and (3) in surfaces resulting from erosion, some of them exhibited in present landscapes, others in large part buried under sedimentary or volcanic accumulations. The highlights of known earth history, viewed in human perspective, make a lively record of a vacillating contest between sea and land; the development, rise, and wasting away of great mountain systems; the waxing, waning, and shifting of volcanic belts; and above all the miracle of evolving life in seas and on lands, leading to modern floras and faunas and the rise of man. Relative dates through a vast lapse of time are clearly indicated in the stratigraphic record and reliable isotopic dates are becoming available from geochemical studies of critical isotopes.

The comprehensive study of stratified rocks is stratigraphy. The study of fossilized plants and animals with regard to their distribution in time is paleontology. These two disciplines are inseparable. In the mentary and in geologic practice they are here introduced separately, though fossils are discussed only in their relation to stratified rocks.

A. STRATIGRAPHY

Study of sedimentary rocks begins logically with consideration of materials that make up the various rock types. This aspect of the subject, sedimentary petrography, is outlined briefly under *Mineralogy and Petrology*, above, though only the commonest kinds of rock are listed. In a descriptive study it becomes clear that the key to an understanding of sedimentary rocks is supplied by the many kinds of sediments now accumulating; this aspect of the subject is discussed above under *Principles of Sedimentation*. The third step in the study considers the overall relations of the stratified rocks in space and time and the history recorded in them; this broad view of the subject is stratigraphy. A fundamental principle in the study, known as the law of superposition, is that in a sequence of layered rocks as they were laid down, any layer is older than the layer next above it. This seems elementary for rocks that have not been disturbed; but commonly in mountain zones very thick sections of strata have been overturned, even completely inverted, and can be correctly understood only through criteria that indicate tops of beds and thus establish the sequence of deposition. Another requirement for useful interpretation of strata is recognition of the physical conditions under which they were laid down. Again comparison is made with sediments now being deposited. Close matching of the diverse kinds of modern sediments with materials in sedimentary rocks representing an immense span of time gives strong support to the uniformitarian principle, which states that processes now acting on the earth have operated continuously and rather uniformly through long ages. This principle, resting on worldwide inductive studies, became one of the most fundamental in geology.

1. **Sedimentary Facies.**—Sediments laid down by a stream on its floodplain are readily distinguished from the unassorted till in the end moraine of a glacier. Each environment of sedimentary deposition puts its stamp on the deposits, and the distinctive marks are preserved in the consolidated sediments. Thus we distinguish marine from terrestrial strata, partly by inherent physical differences and partly by contained fossils. But marine beds are of many kinds: nearshore or littoral deposits of sand and gravel grade outward into muds, which in turn may grade into limy ooze; along many coasts the sand heaped up by breaking surf to form barrier islands grades shoreward into muds rich in black carbonaceous matter from decaying plants. Each distinctive type of sedimentary deposit is a facies (from the Latin for "face"). The term is used flexibly, in relation to broad as well as more specific distinctions in stratified rocks. A littoral facies, representing deposition between high and low tide, differs broadly from a distinctly marine neritic facies deposited below the lowest tides; but within the littoral zone a lagunal facies, common behind the great offshore bars of the U.S. Carolina coast, for example, is very different from a sand-beach facies that is widely developed along the Florida coasts. Moreover the great differences in physical conditions are reflected in the kinds of animals and plants living in the diverse environments. In many sections of sedimentary rocks beds of sandstone are seen to grade laterally into, and interfinger with, beds of shale. Clearly the two types of deposit were formed at the same time; but fossil shells and other remains of animals in the two kinds of rock are very different, indicating that in the past different environments were suited to different forms of life, as is true today. Thus a given biofacies as represented by an assem-

blage of fossils may be recognized as in harmony with a lithofacies represented by rocks in which the fossils occur. (*See also* FOSSIL; SEDIMENTARY ROCKS; STRATIFICATION; STRATIGRAPHY.)

2. **Broad Stratigraphic Patterns.**—Sedimentary deposits of past ages, as of the present, are endlessly complex; but from detailed studies in all continents a few outstanding patterns emerge. Each continent has at least one wide lowland that has been repeatedly invaded by seas and is now mantled with marine strata, little deformed and with small or moderate total thickness. These areas are known as stable platforms; examples are the central part of European Russia, central Siberia, a large part of the Sahara, central and southern Brazil, the central United States and Canada, northern and northwestern Australia. On each of these wide regions the encroaching seas left nearly level beds of limestone, shale, and clean quartz sandstone. Erosion following withdrawals of seas made irregular surfaces on which the next succeeding strata were laid down unconformably but without angular discordance. The total deposit on each platform averages at most a few thousands of feet thick but represents a long span of time. Along one margin of each platform, however, deposits of the same general age are much thicker, more varied in character, and strongly deformed. Thus the strata of the Russian platform thicken eastward into the Ural Mountains, and the little-deformed beds that are widely exposed in the Mississippi Valley pass into the folded, faulted, and far thicker sections of the Appalachian Mountains. These deformed belts went through eventful geosynclinal histories that culminated in mountain-making disturbances.

On the broad platforms the distinctive stratigraphic units can be traced widely and their relations to each other are generally clear. In the geosynclinal belts the relations are more complex because conditions of sedimentation were locally turbulent and deformation has broken the continuity of beds. Many stratigraphic problems in these disturbed belts would be insoluble without the aid of paleontology, which plays a major role in the study and practical use of stratified rocks.

B. PALEONTOLOGY AND THE SCALE OF TIME

Paleontology, in its own right a broad science dealing with the remains of animals and plants preserved in rocks, is treated at length in another article. Its critical importance in geology arises from the use of fossils as time markers in stratified rocks. Near the start of the 19th century independent workers in England and in France discovered that units of sedimentary rocks can be traced over wide areas by means of distinctive fossils in each unit. In England these classical studies involved marine limestones replete with well-preserved shells of clams, cephalopods, and other invertebrates, representing orders and some families common in present-day seas but strikingly different from any known species or genera now living. Moreover some of the fossil species were found only in single beds or a few succesive beds; and those ranging through somewhat greater thicknesses were seen to be replaced in higher beds by different species. Such changes seem commonplace under present concepts of evolution; but the discoverers accepted the facts merely as a rule of thumb to aid in classifying and mapping the thick sections of sedimentary rocks. Within a few decades the work of field classification had progressed widely in Britain and continental Europe and was under way in North America and other continents. The pioneering stages of the study made most rapid strides in Britain, and accordingly many of the widely accepted terms used in stratigraphic classification are of British origin. In its general structure the southern part of Great Britain is rather ideal for an overall view of the stratigraphic sequence; the bedrock is tilted downward to the southeast and long-continued erosion has exposed the strata in general sequence, with progressively older units toward the northwest (fig. 25). (*See also* PALEONTOLOGY.)

The early work on fossil-bearing strata was done northwest of London in the central part of England, where the structure is simple and fossils are fairly abundant. Farther northwest the beds are much folded and faulted, and fossils are scarce in some thick units. Pioneer workers recognized that the deformed strata in western England and in Wales are much older than the beds with simpler

Geologic Column and Scale of Time

(Ages increase from top downward, as in a sequence of sedimentary rocks)

System and Period	Series and Epoch	Distinctive Records of Life	Began (Millions of Years Ago)
CENOZOIC ERA			
Quaternary	Recent (last 11,000 years)		
	Pleistocene	Early man	2+
		Large carnivores	10
Tertiary	Pliocene	Whales, apes, grazing forms	27
	Miocene	Large browsing mammals	38
	Oligocene	Rise of flowering plants	55
	Eocene	First placental mammals	65–70
	Paleocene		
MESOZOIC ERA			
Cretaceous		Extinction of dinosaurs; appearance of floras with modern aspects	130
Jurassic		Dinosaurs' zenith, primitive birds, first small mammals	180
Triassic		Appearance of dinosaurs	225
PALEOZOIC ERA			
Permian		Conifers abundant, reptiles developed	260
Carboniferous	Upper (Pennsylvanian)	First reptiles, great coal forests	300
	Lower (Mississippian)	Sharks abundant	340
Devonian		Amphibians appeared, fishes abundant	405
Silurian		Earliest land plants and animals	435
Ordovician		First primitive fishes	480
Cambrian		Large faunas of marine invertebrates	550–570
PRECAMBRIAN TIME			
No known basis for systematic division		Plants and animals with soft tissues, few fossils	Samples of isotopic dates 1,500* 1,000† 3,200‡ 3,490§

*Schist from Clark County, Nev. †Gunflint chert from Canada. ‡Basement rocks from Minnesota. §Basement rocks from the Congo region.

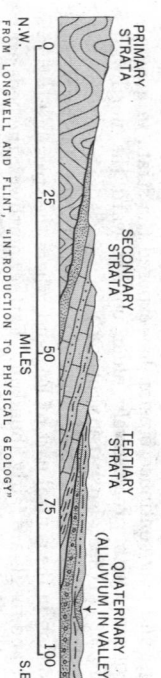

FIG. 25.—DIAGRAMMATIC SECTION ACROSS PART OF WALES AND SOUTHERN ENGLAND TO SHOW GENERAL RELATIONSHIP OF FOUR DISTINCT GROUPS OF SEDIMENTARY ROCKS. FOR DISCUSSION OF NOMENCLATURE see TEXT

PRIMARY STRATA — SECONDARY STRATA — TERTIARY STRATA — QUATERNARY (ALLUVIUM IN VALLEY)

N.W. S.E. MILES 0 25 50 75 100

FROM LONGWELL AND FLINT, "INTRODUCTION TO PHYSICAL GEOLOGY"

structure farther east; and in a first crude classification the deformed rocks of the western sector were designated Primary, the next-youngest series Secondary. The pioneers saw, furthermore, that a distinctive thick sequence in southeast England overlies the Secondary sequence and generally has been less tilted; this third major group was called Tertiary. In more recent years the latest deposits of the region, largely unconsolidated alluvium above the Tertiary rocks, were grouped under the designation Quaternary. But meanwhile research on the older fossil-bearing rocks found that the assemblages of fossil forms are progressively more primitive downward in the total sequence, and three eras were recognized, with names based on the comparative biologic records. The Primary rocks were assigned to the Paleozoic (ancient-life) Era; the Secondary rocks to the Mesozoic (medieval-life) Era; and all younger rocks to the Cenozoic (recent-life) Era.

The contagion of stratigraphic research spread widely; large areas in France, Switzerland, and Germany were studied and mapped, and subdivisions of the eras gradually took form. In Britain the Paleozoic Era was first divided into five periods, each represented by a system of rocks deposited during the time interval. The two oldest of the Paleozoic periods and corresponding systems, named Cambrian and Silurian, had their types in deformed rocks of Wales and the names are of Welsh derivation; the third, Devonian, was named for a section of the rocks in Devonshire; the fourth was called Carboniferous because the section includes widespread beds of coal; the fifth is not well represented in Britain, and its name, Permian, is based on a section in the province of Perm in European Russia. Continued research showed the need for some revisions of the plan for Paleozoic subdivisions. The Silurian System as first defined was disproportionately complex, and the terms Lower and Upper Silurian came into use. Eventually Ordovician, another term derived from Wales, was substituted for Lower Silurian, and this usage met general approval. Likewise Carboniferous was split into Lower and Upper divisions, a usage still followed in many countries, though in the United States, and generally in North America, corresponding terms are Mississippian and Pennsylvanian. Thus the Paleozoic Era has come to have seven recognized subdivisions, each represented by a system of strata.

The section of rocks representing the Mesozoic Era, less formidable than the Paleozoic section, was divided into the three systems, Triassic, Jurassic, and Cretaceous, each representing a period bearing the same name. The term Triassic comes from Germany, where the system is tripartite with a marine unit separating two nonmarine units. The name Jurassic recognizes a prominent development of marine strata in the Jura Mountains of France and Switzerland. Cretaceous, from the Latin *creta*, "chalk," was first applied to the extensive deposits of chalk forming the prominent white cliffs on both sides of the English Channel; eventually the name was applied to the entire thick sequence of strata between the Jurassic beds and those classed as Cenozoic. The Cretaceous is one of the greatest geologic systems, represented by thick marine beds in all continents.

The Cenozoic Era in which we live is commonly divided into two periods, to which the old terms Tertiary and Quaternary are applied. As in human history, the records in the latest geologic periods are best preserved; accordingly each Cenozoic period is divided into epochs, represented by series of deposits in which fossils related to species now living increase steadily in number from the oldest epoch to the youngest.

1. Records Earlier Than Paleozoic.—Every continent has wide exposures of rocks older than Paleozoic; generally the Cambrian beds, the oldest of the Paleozoic, are unconformable on the older rocks, which in large part are much metamorphosed and intruded by igneous bodies. No basis has been found for worldwide systematic classification of these older rocks which are assigned to Precambrian time (*q.v.*). In many places thick sections of unmetamorphosed sedimentary rock are uncomformable below Cambrian beds, but nowhere in these Precambrian sections have any distinctive faunas of megafossils been found. Life existed before Cambrian time, but apparently most of the living forms were simple and without hard parts, such as shell, bone, or woody tissue, that could be readily fossilized. The most abundant Precambrian fossils are deposits of calcareous algae, primitive microscopic plants that grow in moldlike masses and precipitate from sea water calcium carbonate to build up characteristic globular structures with fine lamination (fig. 26). Trails and burrows of wormlike creatures are found in the Precambrian Beltian rocks of Montana; objects resembling sponge spicules and an impression suggesting a jelly fish are reported from beds below the Cambrian in the Grand Canyon; and abundant carbon, some of it metamorphosed to graphite, is disseminated through Precambrian beds in all continents. Geochemical tests of the carbon in rocks of Finland give evidence considered conclusive that the carbon is the residue of organic matter. Apparently life was abundant, at least in the later part of Precambrian time, but few forms had developed the ability to secrete mineral matter for protective parts.

The oldest known structurally preserved evidence of life is reported from black cherts in the Swaziland System in Eastern Transvaal, South Africa. Bacterium-like forms are revealed by study of the chert with an electron microscope. Analysis of rock samples from the section, using the rubidium-strontium whole-rock method, indicates an age greater than 3,100,000,000 years.

Physical processes operated in Precambrian just as in later time. The sedimentary rocks, where they have escaped metamorphism, resemble in all respects the deposits of sediments now forming. Marine, deltaic, and terrestrial facies are clearly distinguished. Crustal movements were similar to those of later eras; thick sedimentary sections were intensely deformed, metamorphosed, intruded and in part engulfed by igneous bodies. Several successive mountain belts, all eroded to low relief, are recognized in Canada,

Finland, and other areas with wide exposures of Precambrian rocks. Dating by radioactive minerals collected in those old mountain zones indicates that four-fifths or more of the earth's history had elapsed at the start of the Cambrian Period.

2. Logic of the Time Chart.—Boundaries between successive eras, periods, and epochs are of course not rigidly fixed. Time runs continuously; we subdivide it, for convenience only, into hours and months, into medieval and modern parts of human history, and into geologic periods. If the subdivisions of the time chart had been designed in southern Africa instead of Europe, doubtless there would be material differences. Rock exposures are restricted to continents, which have had varied histories of submergence, emergence, and orogeny. If the Paleozoic periods had been based solely

larger reptilian forms. The Mesozoic Era was the age of reptiles; dinosaurs appeared in the Triassic Period, developed to huge size through Jurassic time and became extinct before the era ended. Fossils of small mammals are found in Jurassic rocks, and primitive birds with teeth appeared during that period. Forest trees with modern aspect flourished in late Mesozoic time and evolved profusely through the Cenozoic. The Cenozoic Era is the age of mammals; many large forms became extinct during the era, and others—notably the horse, elephant, camel, and several carnivores—reached their zenith in Quaternary time. The development of man began late in the Tertiary Period and proceeded rapidly through the Great Ice Age (Pleistocene Epoch).

4. Isotopic Dates.—The oldest known fossils of fishes are in Ordovician rocks; mammals first appeared late in the Triassic Period; orogeny in the Alpine Belt began near the start of the Cenozoic Era. These statements give relative dates, but how long ago in years did the events occur? Methods have been developed that can give the answer provided suitable materials can be found in critical places. Radioactive elements, notably uranium and thorium, emit helium gas at a uniform rate, and the end product of disintegration is an isotope of lead. If a uranium mineral taken from fresh granite is analyzed precisely, the ratio between the uranium and its lead isotope will give the length of time since the granite crystallized. As many as six methods of age determination that involve the element lead are in use. Another method uses the elements potassium and argon; still another, preferred for dating the older Precambrian rocks, is based on strontium-rubidium ratios. Large numbers of determinations have been made, most of them on minerals in igneous rocks. One rare occurrence of a uranium mineral in a marine sedimentary formation exposed in Sweden dates that formation reliably. The ages of most sedimentary beds can be only approximated by dating igneous bodies older and younger than the beds.

Sample values that fit into the time scale are shown in the time chart. Many granitic bodies cutting Precambrian rocks have supplied exceptionally good material for analyses, and in the research there is particular interest in exploring the earliest available record of the earth's history. As the studies continue the early frontier is pushed steadily back; within a few years the oldest determined dates increased from a little more than 2,000,000,000 to well over 3,000,000,000 years. These values of course apply to local parts of the crust and are minimal for the age of the earth itself.

As more and more isotopic dates have been determined, various modifications in the Geologic Column and Scale of Time have been made. The time spans shown in the accompanying chart may differ with those given in related articles elsewhere in the encyclopaedia; these differences reflect differences in methods of classification and dating, and in the opinions of the various authors concerned.

Because rates of radioactive disintegration are very slow the methods based on these rates are not suitable for determining dates late in the Cenozoic Era. A technique was developed making use

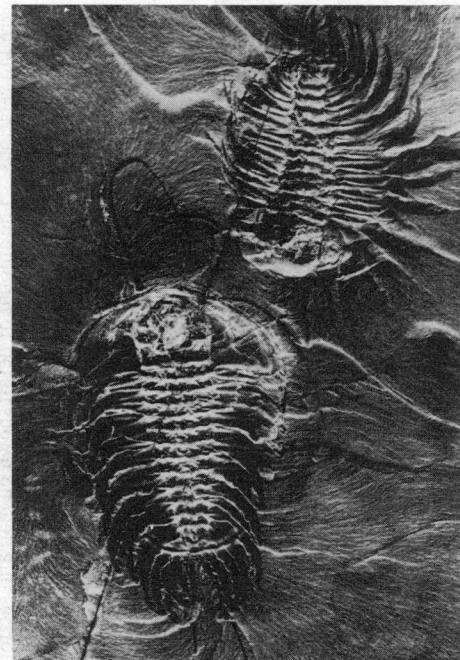

BY COURTESY OF SMITHSONIAN INSTITUTION

FIG. 27.—FORMS OF TWO TRILOBITES ON A SLAB OF CAMBRIAN SHALE. ALBERTA, CANADA

BY COURTESY OF JOHN WILEY & SONS, INC., FROM DUNBAR, "HISTORICAL GEOLOGY"

FIG. 26.—PART OF A LARGE REEF OF MARINE ALGAE IN CAMBRIAN LIMESTONE, EXPOSED ON A SURFACE POLISHED BY GLACIER ICE. SARATOGA, NEW YORK

on evidence found in Great Britain, the limited section there now classed as Permian might have been included with the Carboniferous. In some areas consecutive systems are conveniently separated by unconformities that record uplift and erosion; elsewhere, even on the same continent, rocks of these systems have no sensible physical boundaries and are distinguished only by fossil criteria in comparison with sections taken as standard. Correlation of strata from one continent to another rests in most cases on fossil evidence, which is most trustworthy where sizable groups of fossil forms are available. Floating forms, like some of the tiny foraminifers, are particularly good time markers; the various species had brief spans of life and were widely distributed by ocean currents. One of the most reliable fossils for correlation in Ordovician rocks is the graptolite, a distinctive floating animal. In later geologic time, species of fishes and other swimming forms were distributed more rapidly than bottom-dwelling animals. Most species of animals have been short-lived in a geologic sense, and occurrence of several identical species in widely separated fossil faunas indicates nearly contemporaneous formation of the enclosing rocks.

3. Developments in Life Through Geologic Time.—In the Cambrian Period the seas were populated with invertebrate animals of many kinds, all comparatively small and strikingly different from forms now living, though all major groups were represented. The dominant animal was the trilobite, a swimming arthropod (fig. 27). Primitive plants lived in the seas, but apparently the lands were without plants or animals. Primitive fishes appeared in Ordovician time, and in the Silurian Period lowly plants and animals made a beginning on land. In Devonian time amphibious animals developed, and the first recorded forests were made up of primitive scale trees and large ferns. Thereafter land plants evolved rapidly, and the widespread coal beds of Carboniferous (Pennsylvanian) time are a product of lush forest growth. The first fossils of small reptiles are found in Pennsylvanian beds, and the Permian record shows rapid development of

of the carbon isotope C[14], known as radiocarbon, small amounts of which are present in the carbon dioxide of the atmosphere. Growing tissues of plants and animals incorporate carbon, and durable tissues such as wood retain measurable quantities of radiocarbon long after death of the organism, though the activity of this isotope declines at a known rate. Analyses of carefully selected materials give reliable ages to a range of more than 40,000 years. This method is used for dating events late in the Pleistocene Epoch, involving the declining stages of the great ice sheets and some activities of prehistoric man. *See also* GEOCHRONOLOGY; RADIOCARBON DATING.

IV. GEOLOGIC MAPPING

Programs of geologic study and mapping under way in nearly all countries rest on many practical considerations such as soil conservation, water supply, flood control, development of hydroelectric power, location and recovery of economic mineral deposits. Government bureaus as well as commercial and scientific organizations are active in these geologic programs. In some European countries mapping of the surface geology has been completed to reasonably large scales, though many important details remain for further study. Geologic maps with scale six inches to the mile are available for a large part of Great Britain; but in all continents great areas are still unexplored geologically or have been mapped only in reconnaissance fashion. Preparation of good topographic base maps is a preliminary to satisfactory geologic study of an area. On such a base the geologist plots boundaries of the important bedrock units which on the completed map are shown with distinguishing patterns or colours. Accurate mapping and description of a complex area usually requires cooperative efforts of students with specialized qualifications; for example, petrologists to study the igneous and metamorphic rocks and paleontologists to identify critical fossils in sedimentary strata. A large organization such as a government geological survey has personnel with special equipment for use in the field. A development highly useful to field geologists is a wide coverage of air photographs, both vertical and oblique, which serve as a guide in field study and also help in making accurate locations on maps. Many details of bedrock that are obscure on the ground, especially in wooded country, are shown with remarkable clarity on vertical photographs. A technique known as photogeology uses photographs for constructing preliminary geologic maps, which are then checked and corrected by geologists working on the ground.

A completed geologic map identifies the lithology and so far as possible the geologic age of each important unit of bedrock; it represents also important structural details such as directions and degrees of inclination of strata, locations of faults, and axial traces of folds. Ordinarily the map is supplemented by vertical sections on which structural features seen at the surface are projected to limited depth, thus helping users of the map to visualize the underground relations. The amount of detail shown on map and sections of course depends on the scale. Small-scale maps may represent the sedimentary rocks merely according to the period and system to which they belong; e.g., Cambrian, Jurassic, Tertiary. But generally each distinct lithologic unit large enough to be shown clearly to the scale of the map is represented. A mappable unit is a formation; ordinarily it consists dominantly of one kind of rock—conglomerate, sandstone, shale, limestone, etc.—and represents an episode in the sedimentary history of the region. One geologic period may be represented on a given map by several prominent formations, each with distinctive physical characteristics and with critical fossils that assign it to a lower, middle, or upper position in the parent system.

Thorough study and mapping of the bedrock in a wide region provides a basis for reconstructing physical conditions as they changed from epoch to epoch and period to period of geologic time. Marine strata with distinctive lithologies and fossils reveal the distributions of former seas on modern lands. Margins of those seas are indicated by lateral gradation of marine sediments into littoral or deltaic facies. Advance of a sea across a wide lowland is evident in continuous overlap of littoral and terrestrial sediments by marine deposits; overlap in the reverse order is evidence of a retreating shoreline. Emergence of a land for considerable time resulted in erosion, evident in an unconformity at the base of any younger deposits. Fossil records in beds above and below a surface of unconformity may indicate emergence of the land through a short interval or during geologic periods.

Paleogeographic maps are constructed to show the distribution of seas, lands, and mountain systems at given geologic periods. Such maps cannot be accurate in every detail, but they show with assurance the major geographic elements and a series of such maps is helpful in tracing the evolution of continents from early Paleozoic time to the present. Some maps show, in addition to geographic outlines, the distribution of rock masses and of major structural elements, such as belts of folding, at given geologic dates; these are called paleogeologic maps. Such maps help in reading the history written in rocks of the earth's crust, a chief objective of geologic study.

V. DEVELOPMENT OF THE SCIENCE

A number of ancient scholars did remarkably accurate reasoning about some aspects of geology, but their individual efforts led to no sustained progress. In the 5th century B.C. the Greek philosopher Herodotus deduced from deposits on the floodplain of the Nile that "Egypt is the gift of the river," and from the large number of fossil shells and beds of salt in Egypt that much of the present land had once been under the sea. A century later Aristotle voiced the same conclusion, and offered as an explanation of earthquakes and volcanism the violent escape of winds pent up within the earth. These ideas have the merit that they attribute such phenomena to natural instead of supernatural causes. Another Grecian philosopher who had the scientific attitude was Eratosthenes, who in the 3rd century B.C. announced a first approximation of the earth's circumference and correctly cited the abundance of sea shells on land as proof of earlier extensions of the sea. Similar ideas were voiced by Strabo and other Roman scholars. But these brilliant early views did not rest on a solid foundation of detailed inductive study, and they were all but forgotten in the prolonged intellectual hibernation of the Middle Ages. The world was not yet ready for these advanced ideas. All the fundamentals had to be rediscovered during the intellectual surge that began with the Renaissance. Additional information will be found in biographical entries on persons referred to below.

A. FORMATIVE STAGE

Leonardo da Vinci, the Italian engineer and artist (1452-1519), was an outstanding representative of the formative stage in geologic science. His views are well reasoned and clearly expressed, they concern a wide range of natural phenomena and they are based on original observations. He saw evidence that salt was being carried from lands to the sea, and concluded that "the sea would be more salt in our times than it has been at any time previously." He observed that muddy water flowing into marshy ground emerges clear, and reasoned that the sediment would in time change the marsh into dry ground. Marine shells in bedrock far from the sea and at high altitudes claimed his special attention. In his time a favourite doctrine, dating back to the philosopher Theophrastus (4th century B.C.), held that fossils are merely imitative forms produced by a "plastic force" in the earth. But Da Vinci observed that fossil shells include representatives of several major groups of living marine animals; that individual shells exhibit all minute details, such as muscle scars, found in shells of living forms; and that the rock matrix enclosing fossils consists of sedimentary material identical in all respects with deposits still accumulating. He saw no escape from the conclusion that the layers in which the fossils occur represent deposits on an old sea floor. A tenacious doctrine, of his day and later, recognized that fossil shells are indeed the remains of organisms that once lived, but held they were deposited in their present positions during the Noachian flood. Da Vinci exposed the fallacy of this comfortable view by pointing out that the shells are not related to the surface of the land but lie in many superposed layers that are consolidated and extend underground, beneath the mountains.

Da Vinci's scientific powers were far in advance of his day; but the spirit of original research that he typifies reappeared at intervals and in different lands, and finally became dominant in geology nearly three centuries after his notes were written. Georgius Agricola (1494–1555), a German who studied medicine in Italy, saw evidence that mineral veins had been deposited by rising solutions and on returning to the mining community of Joachimsthal, Bohemia, he made a systematic study of ore deposits as a basis for his published works, *De re metallica* (Eng. tr. by H. C. Hoover and L. H. Hoover, 1912; reprinted 1950). In the following two centuries several able men were concerned with the earth's interior, and speculations in cosmogony became popular. Descartes (1596–1650) published a classical diagram showing the earth with layered structure based on the postulate of an earlier molten stage. A curious feature of the diagram is the representation of vast water bodies in the earth's crust, in keeping with biblical statements about "waters under the Earth"; presumably this common concept arose from attempts to explain the source of springs, the steady flow of streams and the origin of volcanic vapours. Principles of ground-water circulation were not firmly established until the 19th century, although John Ray (1627–1705), an English scientist nearly contemporary with Descartes, published a remarkably accurate treatise on the mechanism of springs. Descartes recognized that great dislocations of the crust had been required to produce the steep inclinations of strata in mountain regions. Though his representation of these movements appears crude from present viewpoints, his interpretation of inclined strata was much more astute than that taught in A. G. Werner's school of mining and geology at Freiberg, Ger., more than a century later.

In spite of difficulties in communication, scholars in several countries of Europe during the 17th century developed geological ideas that were remarkably alike in their modern aspect. The English physicist Robert Hooke (1635–1703) analyzed and discarded the popular doctrine that fossils were "sports of Nature." He demonstrated convincingly that shells in sedimentary rocks are remains of marine organisms and expressed his conviction that Great Britain and Ireland were uplifted from former positions on the sea floor. At almost exactly the same time Nicolaus Steno (1638–86), a brilliant Dane who spent much of his life in Italy, was drawing similar conclusions from his observations in lands bordering the Mediterranean. Steno represents the high-water mark in the development of geologic thought in his century. He went far in the study and description of minerals; he understood clearly the meaning of fossils and the implication of crustal movements given by beds containing marine shells in high mountains; he saw in ancient stratified rocks the analogues of sedimentary deposits then forming (thus he was a pioneer in stating fundamentals of stratigraphy); and he recognized that running water had been the chief agent in sculpturing landscapes.

B. 18th-Century Advances

In the 18th century there were increasing signs of maturity and coordination in thinking about the earth. Reliance on field observation rather than time-honoured speculation was coming to be a basic concept. Improved evaluation of evidence was becoming possible through developments in physics, chemistry, and biology. Comprehension of the real significance of sedimentary rocks was slowly dawning. French mineralogist Jean Etienne Guettard (1715–86) observed that definite bands of these rocks, each with its own peculiarities, are disposed in a roughly concentric pattern in the Paris Basin of France; with patient labour he traced outcrops of these formations, which he called mineral bands, and delineated them on maps. These may be considered the first true geologic maps, though apparently they were constructed without real appreciation of the sequence in formations and were not accompanied by sections to show the geologic structure. In connection with his field work—in which he was assisted for a time by the chemist Antoine Lavoisier—Guettard collected hundreds of fossils, of which he made accurate drawings. So far as we know, however, it did not occur to him that certain fossils characterized each of his mineral bands, or that the fossils were arranged in a sequence according to age.

Guettard found another problem in the course of field work for his map in the Auvergne region of central France, which has a superb exhibit of volcanic rocks. Though he had not seen an active volcano, Guettard had read descriptions of Vesuvius and had seen specimens of its dark lava. With this background he recognized the fresh cinder cones and flows of ropy basalt that are common in the Auvergne landscapes. He identified also older flows, weathered and considerably eroded but still traceable to vents from which they issued. But still he failed to grasp the full implication of the widespread basaltic rocks in central France. Vast quantities of the basalt, older than the cinder cones and forming extensive plateaus, cannot be connected with any visible vents. This older basalt is in nearly horizontal sheets, some of them interbedded with layers of shale and sandstone that contain marine fossils. In accord with an interpretation common in his day, Guettard concluded that basalt was formed primarily by deposition from aqueous solution and that local fusion of the primary rock by subterranean combustion of coal was responsible for the cones and lava flows in Auvergne. Fortunately another French scientist, Nicolas Desmarest (1725–1815), closely followed Guettard in study of the region and compared features there with those in volcanic areas of Italy from Padua in the north to Naples in the south. By this comparative study he demonstrated that all the Auvergne basalt is of igneous origin. But Desmarest also made an error that appears glaring from the present point of view. He found that granitic rocks form the basement beneath the basalts of Auvergne, and suggested that the basalt resulted from fusion of the granite. Analytic chemistry of rocks had not progressed far enough to guide him in this aspect of his problem. Not until much later was it demonstrated that granite and basalt are at opposite poles in a great series of igneous rocks.

Some coordination of efforts in geologic research had begun in the 18th century, but one of the major controversies in the history of the science also raged in that period. The school led by A. G. Werner (1750–1817), known as the Neptunists, maintained that nearly all rocks were formed as precipitates from the water of a primitive universal ocean which held in solution great quantities of mineral matter. According to this theory the first precipitate from the ocean crystallized as granite, which thus was the oldest of the rocks in the visible part of the crust; later precipitates formed gneiss, slate, basalt, porphyry, and syenite, all of which were classed with granite as Primitive rocks, with worldwide distribution. Later the level of the ocean was lowered (by what mechanism is not made clear), and Transition rocks, including limestone and certain kinds of sandstone, were precipitated. Wherever these deposits were laid down against slopes of emerging mountains, the resulting layers were steeply inclined. As the waters continued to subside, rocks called the *Flötz* ("flat," in contrast to the tilted Transition beds) were deposited at lower altitudes. As Werner soon came to recognize basalt in rocks as young as *Flötz*, his theory provided for recurrent precipitation of basalt. This Wernerian theory, which now seems preposterous, was widely accepted for several decades; the author was a magnetic teacher, and students from many lands flocked to his classrooms. The first geologic map of the eastern United States, published in 1809 by William Maclure, represents the rocks in four classes that are essentially Werner's, although Secondary is used instead of *Flötz*.

Geologists in the school opposed to the Neptunists were known as Plutonists because they regarded granite, basalt, and rocks of several other kinds as igneous or plutonic in origin. Desmarest belonged to this school, but the real leader was James Hutton (1726–97) of Edinburgh, whose influence in shaping geologic thought grew as Werner's declined. Hutton spent much of his life making field observations and building inductive concepts which he checked by discussions with acquaintances. The contributions he made to correct understanding of igneous rocks is large, but his outstanding achievement was formulation of the uniformitarian principle, which states that natural agents now at work on and within the earth have operated with general uniformity through immensely long periods of time. This principle, accepted as a basic tenet in geologic thought, was diametrically opposed to the doctrine of

GEOLOGY

catastrophism commonly held in Hutton's day, according to which every major feature such as a mountain chain or a deep chasm was formed abruptly, by catastrophic forces. This concept was taken for granted during centuries dominated by the belief that only a few thousands of years had elapsed since the earth was created. Hutton, reasoning inductively from a wealth of evidence, concluded that the earth dates from the remote past; he could see "no vestige of a beginning—no prospect of an end." He recognized that erosion, which is fashioning the valleys of present landscapes, must have destroyed generations of mountains, and that in the beveled edges of folded strata we view "the ruins of an older world."

The next great advance in geologic thought and method started with discoveries made independently in England and France near the year 1800. William Smith, a surveyor working on canals in central England, observed that in strata now classified as Jurassic any limited group of beds had the same assemblage of fossil forms, in whatever part of England he found it. Higher and lower distinctive units could be recognized in the same way. Using this relationship as a guide, he constructed first (1799) a table of stratigraphic units and later a complete geologic map of England, Wales, and part of Scotland, accompanied by a section showing the general structure. About the same time Georges Cuvier and Alexandre Brongniart, two French zoologists well trained in comparative anatomy, worked together in Guettard's old field, the Paris Basin; there they found that "fossils are generally the same in corresponding beds, and present tolerably marked differences in species from one group of beds to another." By use of this principle they separated the Tertiary strata of north-central France into natural units, arranged these in chronologic sequence and described them (1808). Three years later they represented the distribution of these units and their structural relations by a geologic map and section.

Discovery of a vital scientific principle generally is followed by phenomenal progress in research. At the start of the 19th century geology was ripe for the practical application of paleontology, and the succeeding decades witnessed an amazing development of the science. Christian Leopold von Buch, one of Werner's ablest students, brought out a geologic map of all Germany in 1824; Élie de Beaumont began a similar map of France; an improved map of England and Wales, and maps of Scotland and Ireland, were published within 20 years. During this period the chart of geologic time divisions and systems of rocks was worked out, geological surveys were established in countries of Europe, and work begun in other continents demonstrated that the stratigraphic principle of Smith and Cuvier has worldwide application. Geology had progressed from a field of speculation into a science building solidly on factual data.

The vast field of paleontology continued its development as an ally of stratigraphy, and no doubt the vista into the past revealed by the study of fossils made some contribution to biological researches on which were based the concept of evolution set forth by Charles Darwin in 1859. At least the reverse effect was dynamic; the doctrine of evolution changed paleontology from a rule-of-thumb technique, as practised by Darwin's devotees, into a science with a firm philosophic foundation. The concept was announced, contributed a great store of favourable evidence.

All aspects of physical geology made great progress in the 19th century. Techniques for studying minerals and rocks were steadily improved; as an example, H. C. Sorby's development of thin-section equipment (see PETROLOGY) was a major aid in the system-

C. STRIDES IN THE 19TH CENTURY

Two Germans of the 18th century, J. G. Lehmann and G. C. Füchsel, held advanced views on the meaning of sedimentary rocks. Both realized that the older strata were formed by water action, and that they must have been nearly horizontal at the time of deposition, like their modern representatives. These two workers reasoned correctly that strata now steeply inclined indicate large-scale deformation—a view that contrasts favourably with Werner's concept of the Transition rocks.

D. PROGRESS IN THE 20TH CENTURY

atic analysis and classification of rock materials, leading to fundamental research on problems of their genesis. Swiss students cited evidence that the Alpine glaciers were once much more extensive, and Louis Agassiz went on to demonstrate that Pleistocene ice caps covered great areas in northern Europe and North America. Study of the structure in mountain belts focused attention on the geosynclinal stage in mountain history, first pointed out by James Hall of New York and elaborated by J. D. Dana. Analysis of the complex structure of the Swiss Alps, begun by Arnold Escher von der Linth, was continued by Albert Heim and others. Charles Lapworth, B. N. Peach, and John Horne made their classic study in the northwest Highlands of Scotland. The systematic study of land forms was advanced and stimulated by the explorations of J. W. Powell and G. K. Gilbert in the Colorado Plateau, a region with exceptional exposures of bedrock with comparatively simple structure. This brief list of distinguished workers and achievements could be amplified many times without recording the full century of accomplishment in geology, which included unspectacular but useful exploration and mapping of large areas in several continents, an appreciable start toward the eventual goal—thorough geological study of all land areas.

During the 20th century geology has advanced at an accelerating pace; it has assured foundations, it is aided by growth of kindred sciences and it has the advantage of constantly improving techniques. The discovery of radioactivity and the rapid advances in knowledge of atomic structure have revolutionized some aspects of geologic research. B. B. Boltwood's suggestion in 1905 that lead might be the final disintegration product of uranium started developments in methods for determining ages of minerals. Several independent methods, giving results that can be checked one against another, lead to confident values. X-ray equipment, the mass spectrometer, devices for thermoanalysis and the electron microscope are used for accurate analyses that would have seemed magical to workers in the 19th century. Geophysicists, using seismic, gravimetric, and magnetic equipment, detect important structural elements in the earth (see also GEOPHYSICAL PROSPECTING; INTERNATIONAL GEOPHYSICAL YEAR).

The survey of ocean floors (see OCEAN AND OCEANOGRAPHY), a highly important field in geologic research, is bringing radical changes in some traditional concepts. Continuing advances in geophysical methods have been applied to studies ranging from the deepest trenches to the continental shelves.

International cooperation in earth-science research has accelerated since 1950 and reached a climax in 1957–59, a period known as the International Geophysical Year (q.v.). Within that period cooperative scientific efforts involved about 30,000 scientists and technicians, representing more than 70 nations and operating at more than 2,000 stations. The program included major problems in many parts of the world. Teams of scientists widely distributed in Antarctica studied the great ice sheet and parts of the exposed bedrock. Similar problems were attacked in Greenland and other parts of the Arctic region. The full program included oceanographic explorations, study of solar activity, geomagnetism, seismology, gravity, the size and shape of the earth. Projects begun in the IGY have continued, with many notable results. The International Years of the Quiet Sun (q.v.) also started in 1957–58 during a dazzling display of sunspot activity and culminated in an international program of observations and study when solar activity was at a minimum in 1964–65. The sunspot cycle has large geologic interest and importance; it has left records recognized in sedimentary deposits through a long span of time.

The International Hydrological Decade (q.v.), a sustained and coordinated program of scientific observation and research, began in 1965. The program marked an international approach to the study of hydrology including research on the hydrologic cycle, precipitation, ground-water levels and quality, glaciers, and sediment transport and sedimentation, all of special geological interest.

Within recent years the interest of geologists has been extended from the earth to other parts of the solar system. Space vehicles have contributed some new information on the planets Venus and

Mars, but study is devoted chiefly to our moon on which surface features have been photographed in superb detail. Studies of core samples brought back from manned and unmanned lunar landings have been made to help determine the density, composition, and origins of the moon's crust. A growing branch of geology devoted to study of these features is known as astrogeology. *See* SPACE EXPLORATION: *Space Science: Physical Sciences.*

See also references under "Geology" in the Index.

BIBLIOGRAPHY.—A. Holmes, *Principles of Physical Geology*, new rev. ed. (1965); L. Don Leet and Sheldon Judson, *Physical Geology*, 3rd ed. (1965); A. O. Woodford, *Historical Geology* (1965); Bernhard Kummel, *History of the Earth* (1961); J. D. Dana, *Manual of Mineralogy*, 17 ed., rev. by C. S. Hurlbut (1959); H. Williams, F. J. Turner and C. M. Gilbert, *Petrography* (1954); F. H. Hatch, A. K. Wells, and M. K. Wells, *The Petrology of the Igneous Rocks*, 10th ed. (1949); P. Niggli, *Rocks and Mineral Deposits*, Eng. translation by R. L. Parker of *Gesteine und Mineralagerstätten* (1954); R. A. Daly, *Igneous Rocks and the Depths of the Earth* (1933); F. J. Pettijohn, *Sedimentary Rocks* (1957); C. O. Dunbar and John Rodgers, *Principles of Stratigraphy* (1957); N. M. Fenneman, *Physiography of Western United States* (1931), *Physiography of Eastern United States* (1938); R. F. Flint, *Glacial and Pleistocene Geology* (1957); F. P. Shepard, *Submarine Geology* (1948); P. H. Kuenen, *Marine Geology* (1950); Thomas H. Clark and Colin W. Stearn, *The Geological Evolution of North America* (1960); P. B. King, *The Tectonics of Middle North America* (1951); John S. Shelton, *Geology Illustrated* (1966); A. I. Levorsen, *Geology of Petroleum* (1954); A. M. Bateman, *The Formation of Mineral Deposits* (1951); Charles F. Park and Roy A. MacDiarmid, *Ore Deposits* (1964); E. S. Moore, *Coal* (1940); F. E. Zeuner, *Dating the Past*, 4th ed. rev. (1958); E. S. Barghoorn and J. W. Schopf, "Microorganisms Three Billion Years Old from the Precambrian of South Africa," *Science*, vol. 152, pp. 758–763 (1966); W. F. Libby, *Radiocarbon Dating*, 2nd ed. (1955); Sir A. Geikie, *The Founders of Geology*, 2nd ed. (1905); F. D. Adams, *The Birth and Development of the Geological Sciences* (1938; reprinted 1954); K. A. von Zittel, *Geschichte der Geologie und Paleontologie* (1889; reprinted 1965); George P. Merrill, *The First One Hundred Years of American Geology* (1924; reprinted 1964); Ruth Moore, *The Earth We Live On* (1956). *See also* Georgius Agricola, *De re metallica*, tr. from the first Latin ed. of 1556 by Herbert Clark Hoover and Lou Henry Hoover (1950).

For survey of current publications and reports see *Britannica Book of the Year.*

(C. R. L.)

GEOLOGY, SOCIETIES OF. This article listing selected geological societies in the world also lists geological surveys in various countries. The surveys are agencies of government departments, though in the U.S.S.R. there is a ministry of geology. Societies are free associations of geologists, but in Communist countries they are under government supervision. In some countries there is only a geological survey and no society; in some others there is a society but no survey. The Geological Society of London, founded in 1807, is the oldest association of its kind in the world. The first International Geological congress took place in Paris in 1878, and sessions have been held at intervals ever since. In Britain also was founded the first government geological survey as a result of Charles Lyell's recommendation in 1835. This example was followed by Austria-Hungary (1849), Norway and Sweden (1858) and Italy (1868). In the U.S., the first systematic surveying was started in New York in 1824. The Massachusetts survey of 1830 was imitated by other states, until these schemes were taken over by the U.S. Geological survey in 1879.

Africa.—Egypt has a geological survey which has published reports since 1900; South Africa's survey publishes reports (1910) and its society produces transactions (1896). Surveys in other territories produce similar publications, the Republic of the (former Belgian) Congo since 1945, the countries formerly included in French Equatorial Africa (1943) and French West Africa (bulletin, 1938; also reports, 1946), Ghana (1925; also memoirs since 1929), Kenya (1933), Nigeria (1921), Algeria (publications in six series, since 1885), Mozambique (1937), Federation of Rhodesia and Nyasaland (1917).

Asia.—China has a survey (bulletin and memoirs, 1919) and an institute of geology (bulletin, 1956); India a survey (bulletin, 1950; memoirs, 1856) and a society (journal, 1926); Pakistan a survey (records, 1950); Japan a survey (with reports, 1922; also bulletin, 1950) and a society (journal, 1894); the Philippines also has a society (publishing since 1947).

Australasia and Oceania.—In Australia there is a bureau issuing a bulletin (1932) and reports (1948) and a society issuing a journal (1953). New Zealand has a survey which produces reports (1907) and memoirs (1928).

Europe.—Societies and surveys are to be found in most countries. In Austria there is a geological union with a yearbook (1850) and a society with reports (1908); in Belgium a royal geological society with annals (1874) and memoirs (1898); in Czechoslovakia an institute with bulletin (1921) and transactions (1929). Denmark has a survey (with four series of publications, 1890) and a society (transactions, 1894); France has a survey publishing a bulletin (1889) and memoirs (1893), and a society (bulletin, 1830; memoirs, 1833); the Federal Republic of Germany has an institute (yearbook, 1880) and a society (reports, 1955), and the German Democratic Republic has a service with transactions (1872). In Hungary, the survey publishes annals (1872) and the society journals (1871); Italy's national service and society bring out bulletins (1870, 1882); Norway's survey publishes reports (1891) and its society publishes a journal (1905). Poland has a state institute with a bulletin (1920) and a society with a yearbook (1921); Rumania an institute (annual reports, 1907; also memoirs, 1924); Spain an institute (bulletin, 1874; memoirs, 1873); Sweden a survey, (reports and bulletin, 1868) and a society (proceedings, 1872); Switzerland a commission (reports, 1899) and a society (notes, 1888); Turkey an institute (publications in five series, 1936) and a society (bulletin, 1947). The United Kingdom's survey produces reports (1896), special reports on mineral resources (1915) and a bulletin (1939); its society publishes transactions (1811), proceedings (1834), a journal (1845) and memoirs (1958). The U.S.S.R. has a ministry of geology and an institute which publishes transactions (1938) and journal (1939).

North America.—The Canadian survey and association publish reports (1845) and proceedings (1947) respectively. Mexico has an institute (bulletin, 1895; and annals, 1917) and a society (bulletin, 1905). The United States survey publishes bulletins (1883), water-supply papers (1896), professional papers (1902) and monographs (1890). The Geological Society of America publishes bulletins (1889) and memoirs (1934).

South America.—Argentina's survey publishes a bulletin (1913) and annals (1947), and its society a review (1926). Brazil and Colombia each have a survey with bulletins (1920, 1932). In Peru there is a survey (bulletin, 1945) and a society (bulletin, 1925) and in Venezuela a survey (bulletin, 1951).

GEOMAGNETISM (TERRESTRIAL MAGNETISM) is the natural magnetism of the earth and its atmosphere.

The marvelous property of the magnetism of the earth and its materials has stirred man's imagination since the time of the ancients, when magnetized rocks (loadstones) created wonder and awe as a magical manifestation. Magnets were also an early industrial product of the smithy's forge, since they were made by hammering a piece of steel over an anvil while this steel gradually cooled in the geomagnetic field.

The geomagnetic field is the familiar influence which directs the compass needle. (*See* COMPASS.) The compass was used for the navigation of ships in quite early times. During the period 1200 to 1600 it gradually became clear that the compass needle directed by the geomagnetic field does not in general point true north, nor does it point to the north magnetic pole: instead it tends to orient itself parallel to the lines of force of the field. These facts and their understanding evolved slowly, according to Crichton Mitchell, but were firmly established by the time of the appearance of the first book on terrestrial magnetism in 1600. This book *De Magnete*, by Sir William Gilbert, physician to Queen Elizabeth I, is famous because it was also one of the first modern scientific treatises written on any subject.

The geomagnetic field also bends the rays of the aurora, and changes in the field are accompanied by changes in the quality of radio transmission.

Since the mid-1930s new techniques available for the study of rock or fossil magnetism have renewed interest in geomagnetism. It has been shown that rocks today still retain some of the magnetism acquired at the time of their formation, perhaps several hundred million years ago. The new data thus made available assist in reconstructing the history of the earth. It is argued that some of these data show how the continents drifted and rotated relative to one another, and relative to the earth's axis of rotation during many millions of years. Lava beds laid down one above the other sometimes show alternating directions of magnetization in the geomagnetic field during periods as short as 500,000 years. It has even been suggested on this basis that the earth's magnetic field sometimes reverses itself.

The geomagnetic field may be distorted over mineralized areas, and over oil- or gas-bearing geological structures. This distortion can be measured from low-flying aircraft. The information obtained helps locate new natural resources.

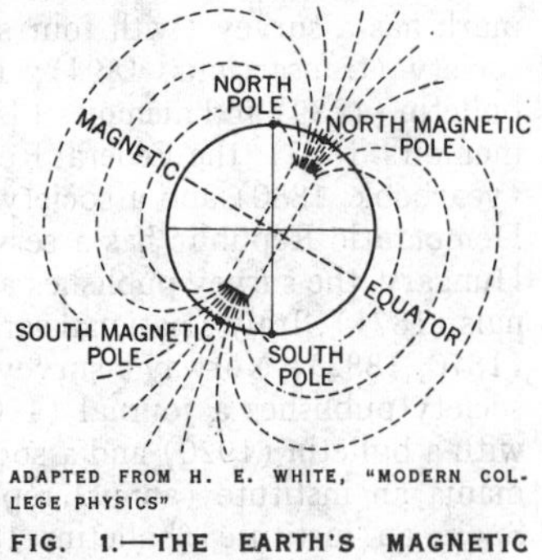

Gilbert showed that geomagnetism arose mainly from inside the earth, and the great German mathematician C. F. Gauss was able to prove this mathematically over 200 years later, about 1830. The character of this field is such as might be expected if it arose mainly from a short, powerful magnet near the earth's centre. The axis of this theoretical magnet is inclined to the earth's axis of rotation, and penetrates the earth's surface at about latitude 78.6° N, and longitude 289.9° E. in the northern hemisphere, and at latitude 78.6° S., longitude 109.9° E. in the southern hemisphere. These points are called geomagnetic poles, and these theoretical poles, of importance to scientists in studies of the aurora and cosmic rays, should be carefully distinguished from the magnetic poles located by compass or other measurements made on polar expeditions. Because of irregularities in the earth's magnetism the actually observed magnetic poles are located 500 mi. or more away from the theoretical geomagnetic poles.

FIG. 1.—THE EARTH'S MAGNETIC FIELD. THE AXIS OF THE FIELD IS INCLINED TO THE EARTH'S ROTATION AXIS

ADAPTED FROM H. E. WHITE, "MODERN COLLEGE PHYSICS"

SOUTH MAGNETIC POLE — MAGNETIC AXIS — NORTH POLE — NORTH MAGNETIC POLE — SOUTH POLE — EQUATOR

The magnetic compass needle tends to align itself vertically at the observed magnetic pole, so that the magnetic force is a region where the compass loses its directive force. The north magnetic pole (1960s) was at about latitude 74° 54′ N, longitude 101° W., near Bathurst Island, North America, and was moving northwest at about 5 mi. per year. The south magnetic pole in 1962 was estimated to be near latitude 70° S, longitude 148° E., on the coast of Antarctica.

At the north magnetic pole the magnetic force is about 0.59 centimetre-gram-second (c.g.s.) unit. Magnetic force has been demonstrated by almost every schoolboy causing a compass needle to move by the action of a steel pocketknife. At the pole this force is directed downward toward the earth's centre. At the south magnetic pole the force is about 0.71 c.g.s. and is directed away from the earth's centre. At the magnetic equator, very roughly about halfway between the magnetic poles, the magnetic force is directed approximately northward, and is roughly half of the polar values, though varying from about 0.30 to 0.40 c.g.s.

The north-seeking end of a compass magnet tends to align itself in the general direction of the north magnetic pole. Local effects caused by magnetic rocks and other irregularities in the earth's magnetism usually are responsible for the fact that the compass direction varies somewhat from magnetic north.

The iron or magnetite content of rocks is highly variable and may produce local distortions of the geomagnetic field called magnetic anomalies. Changes in electric currents flowing deep within the earth produce geomagnetic secular or long-term variations, changing the direction and force of the geomagnetic field slowly over the centuries. Secular changes in direction of the compass as great as 30° in 400 years have been recorded. Small changes of compass direction of the order one-fifth of a degree daily in low latitudes also occur, due to electric currents flowing in the ionosphere (q.v.). These currents acquire their energy from variable winds produced by the heating action of the sun, and from the lunar and solar tides in the upper atmosphere (see ATMOSPHERE). Magnetic storms, which are irregular changes in magnetic field, sometimes appear on a world-wide scale. They occasionally disrupt radio programs and communications, and are associated to some degree with actively changing sunspots or flares on the sun.

Elements of the Geomagnetic Field.—The magnetic elements comprise D, declination (or variation of the compass), the angle between the direction of an ideal compass and true north, measured positively from north around by east; H, horizontal intensity, the maximum strength of the magnetic force in the horizontal plane; Z, vertical intensity, strength of the force in the geographic vertical; F, total intensity, maximum strength of the force, regardless of direction; I, inclination or dip, angle between direction of field and the horizontal plane; X, strength of the force toward geographic north; and Y, strength of the force toward geographic east. X, Y and Z are vectors, since they have both scalar magnitude and direction. H and F are vectors, and D and I are angles. X is reckoned positive when directed toward the north; Y and D when directed toward the east; and Z and I when directed downward. Also $Y/X = \tan D$; $Y/H = \sin D$; $X^2 + Y^2 + Z^2 = F^2$; etc. The elements usually measured are D, I and H, but possibly D, I and F aboard aircraft or nonmagnetic ships.

Declination (D) is measured by noting the deviation from true north of a magnetic needle suspended by a fine fibre. The direction of true north is obtained from observation of the sun to a precision of 0.1′ or less, using observatory or field type instruments.

Horizontal intensity (H) is measured by means of a magnetometer (see MAGNETOMETER) in units of length, mass and time (centimetre-gram-second units). The magnet used for D (see above) may be set in motion and its oscillation timed, and then used to deflect another magnet from a known distance. The period of oscillation $T = 2\pi\sqrt{K/MH}$, where K is the moment of inertia of the oscillating system, M its magnetic moment and H the horizontal intensity. When deflecting, the angle of deflection u is given by $\sin u = 2M/Hr^3$ in which r is the distance between the two magnets. This gives two equations for solving for M and H, and H is expressed in terms of length, mass and time. Laboratory tests determine necessary small corrections so that H is measured fairly readily to about 0.0001 c.g.s. unit or better. The customary unit is the gamma $= 10^{-5}$ c.g.s. unit.

Inclination (I) is measured with an earth inductor (inclinometer) consisting of a coil of wire rotatable about its transverse axis and connected through a commutator to a sensitive galvanometer. The earth inductor is mounted with its axis of rotation in the magnetic meridian, and is rotated. It is then tilted in this meridian into the direction of dip, in which case no deflection of the galvanometer is noted. The angle of tilt, measured downward from the horizontal plane, is the inclination.

Observation Stations.—At about 200 special stations called magnetic observatories measurements are made as described above. Additional measurements may involve accurately mounted and standardized coils in which components of the geomagnetic field may be neutralized and measured. Total intensity F can be measured using a nuclear magnetic-resonance magnetometer. The magnetic moments of the protons in a material precess about a magnetic field F with an angular frequency $\omega = \gamma_p F$, where γ_p, the gyromagnetic ratio of the proton, is equal to $2.67528 (\pm 0.00006) \times 10^4 \text{ sec}^{-1}$ per gauss. A coil carrying a surge of current jolts the protons in the material and the frequency of precession is picked up as a signal in the same or associated coil winding to measure the field F. This type of instrument is preferred for measurements made in motion, such as aboard satellites.

At magnetic observatories widely scattered over the earth, though greatly concentrated in Europe, photographic records of time variations in D, H and Z are obtained by means of magnetic variometers. These are calibrated about once a week by means of magnetometers. The D-variometer consists of a magnet usually suspended by a vertical quartz fibre with negligible torsional restraint. The H-variometer is similar, but uses a vertical fibre which can be twisted so that the magnet is perpendicular to the magnetic meridian. In the vertical or Z-variometer the magnet is balanced against gravity about a horizontal fibre, or consists of a horizontal magnet free to rotate on knife edges about a horizontal axis. Electromagnetic versions of these instruments also exist. Portable observatories in highly compact form measure D, H and Z with accuracy comparable to the permanent observatory type.

Special magnetic survey instruments have been designed and used aboard nonmagnetic survey ships like the "Carnegie," a famous sailing ship destroyed in 1929, and the present-day nonmagnetic ship, the "Zarya," used by the U.S.S.R. Special devices have also been developed to facilitate the search for minerals by magnetic methods of geophysical prospecting. These devices note changes in the magnetic field with distance over the earth's surface both at the ground and in aircraft aloft. Extensive surveys by air have been made over both continental and ocean areas.

The geomagnetic field, as part of our natural environment, has been measured at intervals of from 5 to 20 years at some 2,000 stations, called repeat stations. About 80,000 observations of declination (D) have been made at many thousands of points. Probably several million closely spaced observations of other components of the field have been made in connection with geophysical exploration.

Studies of geomagnetism, as a global phenomenon, are facilitated also by special years in which magnetic observatories are operated at additional and usually less accessible locations, such as in the polar regions. Thus a small network of about 12 stations was added temporarily in 1882–83, the first International Polar year, many more in 1932–33 during the second International Polar year and over 100 additional stations during the International Geophysical year, 1957–58.

The Earth's Main Magnetic Field.—Contour lines drawn on maps of the world are prepared at five- or ten-year intervals by Great Britain, the United States and the Soviet Union, to indicate points of equal magnetic declination, horizontal intensity, vertical intensity, inclination or dip and total intensity. By far the greater part of the magnetic field can be interpreted as due to a short strong magnet at the earth's centre, directed from the north to the

south geomagnetic pole. This magnet is tilted at an angle of about 11.5° to the earth's axis of rotation, so that it lies along the geomagnetic axis intersecting the earth's surface in northwest Greenland, in the meridian 69° W. of Greenwich. The approximation to the earth's surface magnetic field, using the same magnet can be improved by moving the magnet, parallel to itself, toward a point determined to be at about 6.5° N. latitude and 162° E. longitude in 1922. It is known that this eccentric dipole has been drifting slowly westward since 1830. This has sometimes been regarded as indicating that the earth's central metallic core, of radius about 2,900 km., does not rotate as fast as does the surface of the earth. In fact, some irregularities in the rotation of the core have been estimated. These irregularities in core motion may be communicated to the outer solid part of the earth. The changes in angular momentum of the core are adequate to explain irregularities in the rate of rotation at the earth's surface, affecting the length of the day as measured by astronomers.

The strength of the hypothetical short magnet or dipole referred to above is about 8×10^{25} c.g.s. units. On the assumption of uniform magnetization of the entire earth, the intensity of magnetization is about 0.08 c.g.s. unit per cubic centimetre. Such magnetization would result if a saturated steel magnet of volume 80 cc. were imbedded in every cubic metre of the earth's interior. Additional features of the main field can be represented by about 12 radially directed dipoles, each about $\frac{1}{80}$ the strength of the central dipole, and located near the surface of the earth's core.

The anomalies due to crustal rocks are usually associated with deposits of ferromagnetic substances. Anomalies are also caused when relatively highly magnetic igneous extrusions penetrate the weakly magnetic sedimentary rocks. The scale of these anomalies may range in cross section from a few metres to 100 km. or more. They are usually not shown on world maps because they are too small, and the number of magnetic observations are usually too

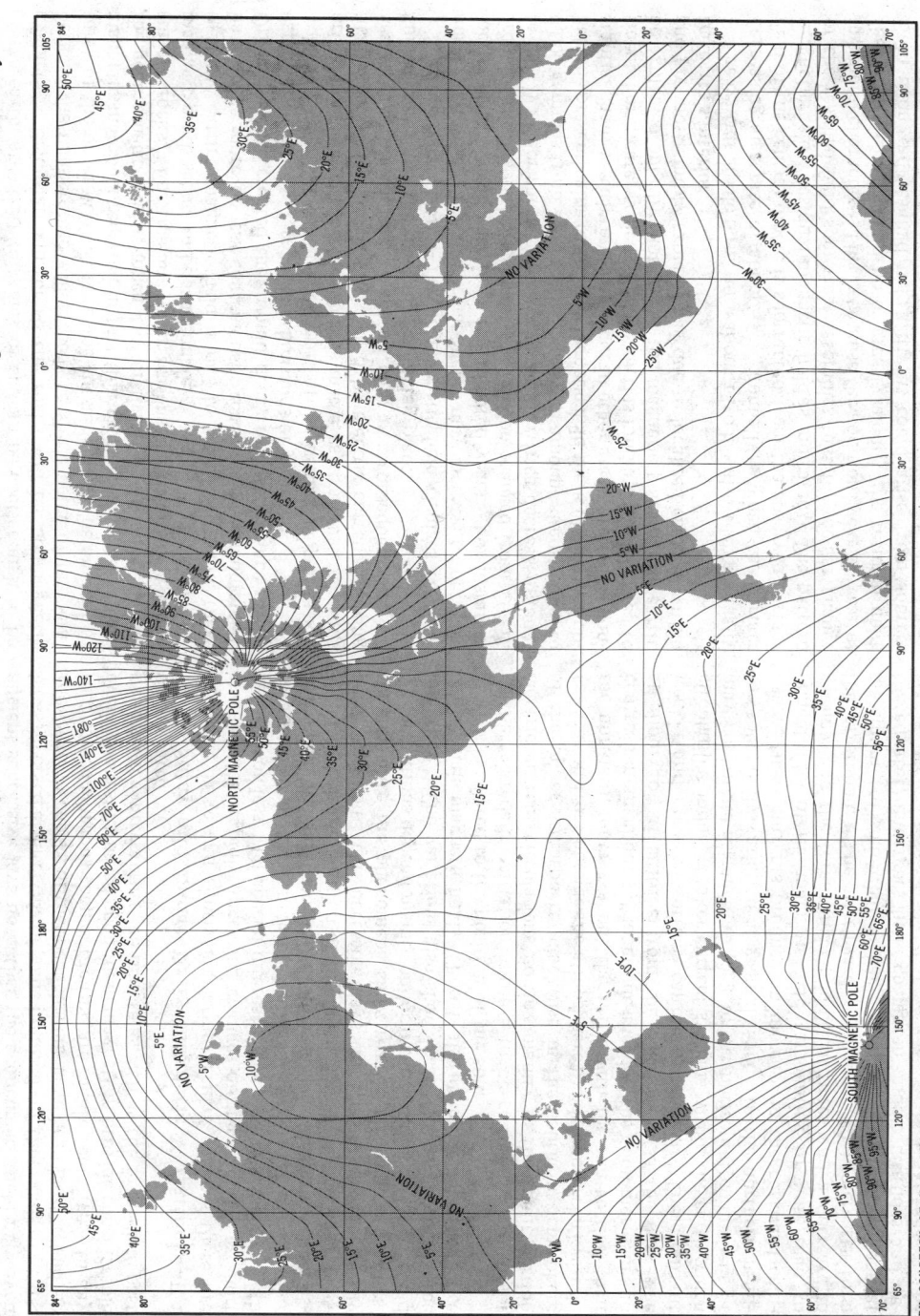

BY COURTESY OF U.S. HYDROGRAPHIC OFFICE

FIG. 2.—WORLD MAP OF MAGNETIC DECLINATION (D); LINES CONNECT POINTS OF EQUAL VARIATION OF COMPASS FROM GEOGRAPHIC NORTH, 1955

few. This fine structure of the earth's surface is about as complicated as the surface topography, to which it is usually not related. Local anomalies due to igneous intrusions or irregularities in basement rocks may range from a few hundred to several thousand gammas. Near deposits of magnetic ore values may rise to several times that of the normal magnetic field.

Origin of the Geomagnetic Field.—Many hypotheses have been brought forward as possible explanations of the origin of the geomagnetic field. These are usually based upon the presence of ferromagnetic material in rocks, electric currents generated within the earth's interior or very tentative suggestions related to the physics of large bodies in rotation.

One of the difficulties of explaining the origin of the geomagnetic field is our lack of knowledge of the earth's interior. From mathematical analysis of the surface field it appears that many of the irregular features of the field are likely to arise from sources no deeper than the outer layers of the field within the earth's central core. According to one prevailing set of ideas the mantle and crust surrounding the core are more or less solid and cannot undergo rapid changes within a century or two. For this reason attempts are made to assign the cause of geomagnetism mainly to energy changes in the outer half of the central core. Elaborate calculations have been made showing that if the fluid motions are of suitable type a magnetic field originally quite small might be built up into a large one. The process is fundamentally similar to that in an ordinary dynamo. Heat necessary to move the fluid is supposed to come from the radioactivity of uranium and other metals, and about 1% of the concentration of these materials known to exist in the earth's crust might suffice. It has also been suggested many times that thermoelectric currents might arise at the junction between mantle and core.

The theory of a ferromagnetic earth, originally proposed by Gilbert in 1600, seems defective because only a thin outer layer of the earth, about 20 km. thick or so, can be cool enough to be magnetic. Below 20 km. or so the rocks will be nonmagnetic because the temperature will exceed the Curie point of temperature (of the order 400° C. for some substances.). The amount of magnetic materials required in this thin crust in order to explain the geomagnetic field is much greater than that found in typical surface rocks. For this and other reasons the theory of a ferromagnetic earth seems to be inadequate.

If the earth's magnetic field is due to electric currents, these have to be more or less continuously generated and maintained. Otherwise once created they would decay to insignificance in the earth's core within a few tens of thousands of years.

Hence it appears that while a part of the earth's magnetism arises from ferromagnetic materials in the earth's crust, it seems likely that the larger part is caused by electric currents flowing near and within the earth's central core as a consequence of the fluid motions and thermal changes taking place.

Secular Variation.—The geomagnetic field changes continuously with time. The field components may increase or decrease locally, a little each year for a few hundred years. For instance, from 1600 to 1800 the declination in London changed from 11° E. to 24° W. Horizontal intensity in South Africa decreased about 6,000 gammas from 1843 to 1943, or by an amount almost equal to half the present value of the geomagnetic field there (1960s). Substantial changes with time also occur in other areas, often on a continental or greater scale. Changes of this kind are too localized to be explained only by motions of the magnetic poles of the earth, and are most simply explained as due to localized changes within the earth's interior.

The central dipole term since about 1830 has also been gradually decreasing at a rate of about $\frac{1}{2,000}$ annually. When the surface field of the central dipole is subtracted from the observed surface magnetic field a residual magnetic field is indicated. The pattern of the residual field somewhat resembles that for secular change in general character. This is because the additions year by year of the secular change build up or greatly modify the residual field. Both main and residual field patterns could arise from sources near the surface of the earth's central core. Since secular change in some components of field may be greater than 100 gammas increase or decrease in one year, it is clear that a substantial residual field can be built up in a few hundred years if the rate of change is maintained. One possible explanation is that the permanent magnetic field in the fluid core is linked to and participates in the motion of the electrically conducting fluid. This could give rise to a residual magnetic field undergoing continuous change in the core, the magnetic field at the surface of the core being able to penetrate the rigid mantle above so that it is observable at the earth's surface.

Secular Variation in the Geologic Past.—Ferromagnetic particles of rock are loosened by weathering and carried in rivers to the ocean, where they are aligned magnetically parallel to the geomagnetic field as they settle to the bottom. As time goes on the layer thickens and the particles become sedimentary rock. Under special and favourable circumstances the direction of the geomagnetic field millions of years in the past may be determined by laboratory experiments on specimens of the rock. Annual bottom layers or varves may also develop, sometimes in glacial lakes, and from them the direction of the geomagnetic field tens of thousands of years ago may sometimes be estimated. A cooled lava bed may also indicate the direction of the geomagnetic field millions of years ago.

If one accepts the results of this fossil magnetism (and many arguments have been urged favouring such acceptance, as well as many to the contrary) it appears that the geomagnetic field has undergone quite substantial changes in the past. According to some of these measurements the magnetic poles have usually remained not far removed from the earth's axis of rotation. In times earlier than 100,000,000 years ago there is some suggestive evidence of motion of the magnetic poles almost to the equator, which has caused some to speculate that the continents may have drifted and rotated relative to the axis of rotation. There are also indications from the directions of magnetization observed in ancient successive lava flows that the geomagnetic field may even have reversed at intervals of some hundreds of thousands of years. Independent checks of these conclusions though exciting are highly tentative. In any event, the results based upon fossil magnetism provide considerable material for interpreting the remote as well as the immediate past of the earth.

The Solar and Lunar Daily Magnetic Variations.—Besides the large and slowly appearing secular changes there are smaller more rapidly appearing changes during intervals as short as a day or less. Of special interest is the change associated with the position of the sun throughout the day, known as the solar daily magnetic variation, and a somewhat smaller similar effect associated with the position of the moon, known as the lunar magnetic variation. On successive days these variations are usually similar, since the phenomena show regular and typical features. The variations also show local features related to the longitude. The variations depend mainly on local time, and upon latitude and earth's main magnetic field. There is also an important dependence on season related to the position of the sun.

The solar daily variation appears to be caused by two major electric current circulations flowing mainly in the sunlit portion of the upper atmosphere, clockwise in the southern hemisphere (as viewed from outside the atmosphere) and counterclockwise in the northern, moving about the earth with the sun so that their centres remain about 15° longitude ahead of the noon meridian and at about 40° of latitude from the equators. On the dark side weaker and reversed vortices can be designated. These current circulations induce weaker current systems within the earth which may contribute as much as 40% to the horizontal component of the solar daily variation at ground level. In the northern hemisphere these currents produce an increase in the eastward component (Y) of the magnetic field (amounting to more than 50 gammas) in the forenoon in middle latitudes and a decrease in the afternoon. The northward component (X) increases to a maximum (of somewhat higher magnitude) just before noon at the equator, undergoes little change in middle latitudes and decreases to a minimum just before noon in high latitudes. The vertical component (Z) shows little change near the equator and

GEOMAGNETISM

in high latitudes but sinks to a minimum just before noon in middle latitudes. In the southern hemisphere these variations are antisymmetric in Y and Z and symmetric in X.

In the northern summer the solar daily variation in the northern hemisphere is about 50% larger in amplitude than the yearly average, this condition being repeated in the southern hemisphere about six months later. At the equinoxes the amplitude is about the same in both northern and southern hemispheres. There frequently appear day-to-day differences which may be as great as 100% in amplitude at any given station and as much as several hours in phase. The amplitude also varies with sunspot cycle and may be as much as 60% greater at sunspot maximum than at sunspot minimum. No connections between fluctuations in the variation field and weather have ever been demonstrated because weather is primarily a local phenomenon and fluctuations in the magnetic variation are more widely manifested.

The solar daily variation also shows irregularities which depend upon regional anomalies of the earth's main field. Because of induced currents differences can probably be detected between effects noted over the oceans as compared with less highly electrically conducting land areas. In addition there are effects related to the position of the magnetic equator and to the general lack of symmetry of the geomagnetic field about the earth's axis of rotation.

The lunar daily magnetic variation is also due to electric current circuits within the ionosphere. These circuits migrate about the earth with the apparent motion of the moon, together with their induced current systems flowing within the earth. Instead of the four current circulations noted for the solar daily magnetic variation, eight are noted in the lunar case, of average strength about $\frac{1}{20}$ that of the solar variations. However, the strength of current flow in the current circuits for the lunar variation is greatest on the sunlit side of the earth.

Magnetic Storms.—Strong and erratic variations in geomagnetism known as magnetic storms may last for from a few hours up to several days. During very great storms the compass direction may change by a degree or more in direction and by as much as 2,000 gammas in intensity in middle latitudes; in the polar regions fluctuations in compass direction may be much greater with changes in horizontal intensity as great as 5,000 gammas in areas beneath intense auroral displays.

Magnetic storms often start suddenly, simultaneously to within a minute or even some seconds over the entire earth. They often start soon after the onset of active solar changes, such as those related to actively changing sunspots. Marked ionospheric storms also occur at times of magnetic storms, and may seriously disrupt radio communications. Polar auroras migrate to lower latitudes and even have been seen from equatorial locations such as India and Samoa. A storm may discharge energy at the rate of more than 2,000,000,000 horsepower for a period of from one to several hours. Field changes at the rate of 10 to 20 gammas per second have been observed. Telegraphic and telephonic communication over long lines is often interrupted. Under extreme conditions electric power lines have become overloaded, and power transformers burned out by the electric currents produced in transmission lines by the magnetic field changes.

Field of Magnetic Storms.—Magnetic field changes minute by minute are recorded photographically as magnetograms at magnetic observatories. During magnetic storms the field changes with time are particularly irregular, complex and erratic. In spite of this, certain main systematic features are noted when departures in field from normal are averaged at a number of stations, grouped in various latitude belts around the earth.

Data averaged for many storms according to time, beginning with the time of sudden commencement of a storm, provide estimates of the storm-time variation in various geographical belts. The same data averaged according to local time give an apparent diurnal effect. This daily variation varies in amplitude with storm time, more or less in unison with the average storm-time variation. The average storm shows an increase in horizontal magnetic intensity during the initial phase of the storm, followed by a much larger diminution to a minimum in about 24 hours. This minimum is called the main or negative phase of the storm. There is then usually a slow recovery to a normal value in the course of a day or two. In the vertical intensity (Z) the changes are smaller, and reversed in sign in low and middle latitudes. The average changes in declination (D) are usually smaller and more localized.

The daily variation of disturbance is associated with opposed current circulations. In the northern hemisphere during storms an electrojet (electric current, limited laterally) is directed westward, centred near an early morning hour meridian, near the auroral zone at 60°-70° north latitude. Another electrojet is similarly centred in south latitude. Roughly diametrically opposite at the other side of the polar cap a weaker eastward-directed electrojet may be in evidence along the auroral zone. Electric currents circulate within the ionosphere completing their current circuits in low latitudes and across the polar caps. The height of current near the auroral zone has been found to be near the 100 km. level; and this has been confirmed directly by rocket by J. A. Van Allen during the International Geophysical year, 1957-58. The height of the storm-time currents may be partly at the same level, and is the subject of further investigation. It is clear from associations with cosmic rays that some substantial electric currents flow at very high levels, and beyond the atmosphere. Some very intense storms have current patterns enduring for only a few hours, and it seems to be established that the very great magnetic storms tend to go through their initial, main and recovery phases more rapidly.

Other Forms of Magnetic Disturbance.—In addition to the daily variations and magnetic storms geomagnetic phenomena include sudden commencements, bays, pulsations and solar-flare effects on the geomagnetic field known as crochets.

Sudden commencements appear more or less simultaneously over the entire earth, within one minute or less. The sudden commencement consists mainly of an abrupt increase of horizontal intensity of from several to several hundred gammas, effects usually being largest in equatorial and especially in the polar regions. Examination of some cases from the Polar year 1932-33 has shown that the effect can be traced or associated with a polar electrojet, at least in part. In equatorial regions, as in the solar daily magnetic variation, an added electrojet at the magnetic equator is sometimes noted on the sunlit side of the earth. In many cases the polar effects are predominant, and in others there may be a preliminary reversed impulse. In some locations, such as the magnetic equator, the average amplitude of sudden commencements is closely related to the amplitude of the solar daily variation. In some cases, at least, polar electrojets seem to provide a fairly localized current distribution during sudden commencements.

Other electrojets appear in the polar regions near or along the auroral zone, where they grow to maximum strength in about an hour and then decay. These current sources produce intensifications of the geomagnetic field lasting a few hours and called magnetic bays. They are often accompanied by local blackout of radio communications, and sometimes but not always appear fairly closely linked with auroral displays.

The geomagnetic field also undergoes sinusoidal or nearly sinusoidal pulsations. Those of higher frequency, of the order several thousand cycles per second, originate in lightning discharges, and are propagated from northern to southern hemisphere, or vice versa, via the lines of force of the geomagnetic field, usually being several earth radii above the earth at the highest point in the plane of the magnetic equator. They are reflected successively from northern to southern hemisphere each time they reach ground level with some reduction in frequency following each reflection. They show a diurnal variation in frequency of occurrence according to universal or Greenwich time, and are believed associated with the world-wide distribution of thunderstorms. When heard as an auditory signal on radio earphones the pitch is reduced after each transmission and return from the opposite hemisphere. For this reason they have been called whistlers. They provide a means of study of regions several earth radii above the earth.

Other pulsations of much lower frequency occur with periods of some seconds to several minutes. The trains of signals may last for minutes or for hours. In some cases these are world-wide and may be manifestations of hydromagnetic waves. In others they appear to correspond to locally intense fluctuations in the intensity or distribution of strongly localized sources such as the electrojets along the auroral zone; in fact, they sometimes precede the appearance of the electrojets of magnetic bays, and depend upon local time. Other pulsations are more frequent at certain hours of universal time, and therefore conditions favouring their occurrence may depend upon the orientation of the terrestrial dipole to the sun.

During solar flares the increased solar radiation augments the electric conductivity of the region in which electric currents producing the solar and lunar daily magnetic variations flow. The resulting pulse in magnetic field, due to strengthening of the current systems, lasts from some minutes to several hours and is called a crochet. It is accompanied by sudden ionospheric changes and by the fade-out of radio communications at some frequencies. Since crochets near the magnetic equator appear to be larger when the solar daily magnetic variation is larger they provide statistical evidence of day-to-day fluctuations in upper air winds, on the basis of the dynamo theory.

Mathematical Analysis of the Field.—Mathematical analysis has shown conclusively that the major part of the magnetic field is due to causes within the earth. It may be assumed that the components of the magnetic field may be expressed to a sufficient degree of accuracy as the appropriate derivatives of a magnetic potential expressed in terms of a spherical harmonic series (see SPHERICAL HARMONICS) of the form

$$V = a \sum_{n=0}^{\infty} \sum_{m=0}^{n} [(a/r)^{n+1}(I_{n,c}^m \cos m\lambda + I_{n,s}^m \sin m\lambda)$$
$$+ (r/a)^n (E_{n,c}^m \cos m\lambda + E_{n,s}^m \sin m\lambda)] P_n^m$$

a being the radius of the earth; P_n^m, the associated Legendrian of degree n and order m; the I's and E's, the coefficients of the particular harmonics; and r and λ, with θ, the spherical co-ordinates, radius, longitude and polar distance, respectively. In this expression the portion containing a/r (and including the coefficients I) satisfy Laplace's equation everywhere outside the sphere $r = a$ and hence must be due to magnetic origins within that sphere. The portion containing r/a (and including the coefficients E) satisfy Laplace's equation everywhere inside the sphere $r = a$ and hence must be due to magnetic origins outside that sphere.

The magnetic elements most frequently used in mathematical analysis, evaluated at the earth's surface where $r = a$, are given by

$$X = (1/a)\partial V/a\partial\theta = \sum_{n=0}^{\infty}\sum_{m=0}^{n}[(I_{n,c}^m + E_{n,c}^m)\cos m\lambda +$$
$$(I_{n,s}^m + E_{n,s}^m)\sin m\lambda]\partial P_n^m/\partial\theta$$

$$Y = -(1/a \sin\theta)\partial V/\partial\lambda = -\sum_{n=0}^{\infty}\sum_{m=0}^{n}[-m(I_{n,c}^m + E_{n,c}^m)\sin m\lambda +$$
$$m(I_{n,s}^m + E_{n,s}^m)\cos m\lambda]P_n^m/\sin\theta$$

$$Z = \partial V/\partial r = \sum_{n=0}^{\infty}\sum_{m=0}^{n}\{[-(n+1)I_{n,c}^m + nE_{n,c}^m]\cos m\lambda +$$
$$[-(n+1)I_{n,s}^m + nE_{n,s}^m]\sin m\lambda\}P_n^m$$

The sums of the coefficients $I_{n,c}^m + E_{n,c}^m$ and $I_{n,s}^m + E_{n,s}^m$ may be obtained by fitting either the observed values of X or of Y by least squares or some other method. If the field is derivable from a potential the values obtained from either the X or the Y data should be identical. Similarly the values of the differences $-(n+1)I_{n,c}^m$ and $-(n+1)I_{n,s}^m$ may be obtained from the observations of Z. Thus, by an analysis of the observations of X or Y and of Z, a means is afforded for separating the field into portions due to internal and external causes by solution of simultaneous equations involving the above-mentioned sums and differences.

Gauss concluded from an analysis of the data available in 1835 that the main field was predominantly, if not entirely, of internal origin. Later analyses by A. Schmidt (1885), L. A. Bauer (1922) and F. Dyson and H. Furner (1922) showed an external field amounting to several per cent of the internal field although the latter investigators attributed the results to uncertainties in the observations. Assumption that the external field is purely a mathematical fiction would require the admission of errors in the magnetic data amounting to about 1° in inclination and consistent with regard to sign. Since external magnetic fields are definitely present in the diurnal variation and magnetic disturbance fields (see below) there is no reason to doubt they may be present in the permanent field as well. However, considerable uncertainty must be attached to the assigned magnitudes of the external field. E. H. Vestine and I. Lange in their analysis of the main field for 1945 found an external part of less than 1% of the whole as did H. F. Finch and B. R. Leaton in 1957.

In the more recent analyses differences appear in the values of the coefficients, accordingly as they were determined from the observations of X or of Y, which appear to be too large to be attributed to errors of observation. But if the earth's field is derivable from a potential the two sets of coefficients should agree to within the accuracy of the observations. This discrepancy is sometimes interpreted as indicating the presence of a nonpotential field, that is, one in which curl $H \neq 0$. Such a field might be due to vertical electric currents flowing between the earth's surface and outer space. Magnitudes of these hypothetical currents are about 0.2 amperes per square kilometre at their maxima, 10⁴ times as great as the normal atmospheric electric currents (see ELECTRICITY, ATMOSPHERIC). Great irregularity exists in the distribution of these currents; in some regions they are directed upward and in others downward. Their existence has not been verified by other physical observations. Present thought is inclined to regard them as mathematical results arising in attempting to fit faulty data to a rigid mathematical frame; in fact, there is a trend among magnetic cartographers to adjust their maps so that curl $H = 0$, thus implicitly denying existence of the so-called nonpotential field, a procedure used in the U.S. hydrographic office charts for 1945.

Other applications have been made of potential analyses to the solar and lunar daily magnetic variations by many writers. Since the number of stations is not great enough to describe the details of the dependence of the solar daily variation upon longitude, dependence upon local time is assumed. The time variations at the available stations are expressed in amplitude and phase by Fourier series. The coefficients found are then conveniently expressed in spherical harmonics as in the case of the earth's main field, using least square methods for obtaining the best fit.

It was found that both the solar and lunar daily variations originate mainly above the earth, with a minor portion, about one-third, originating within the earth. The latter is ascribed to induced earth currents, and its time phase and amplitude used in conjunction with the observed external part derived from the spherical harmonic analysis has yielded estimates of the electric conductivity deep within the earth's interior. At about 250 km. depth this comes out to about 4 × 10⁻¹³ electromagnetic unit. There is an increase with depth, as inferred from similar studies of storm data, so that values are reached as great as 10⁻¹¹, near 1,000 km. depth, and about as conducting as sea water, which is 6.1 × 10⁻⁴ electromagnetic unit.

The first satisfactory explanation of the solar daily variations was offered by Balfour Stewart in his article in the *Encyclopædia Britannica* in 1878, which was a classic in geomagnetism. His ideas have been elaborated further by A. Schuster in 1889 and 1908, and by S. Chapman in 1919, and it appears now certain that upper air winds produce the solar and lunar magnetic variations. (These are partly a consequence of solar heating, and of tidal action (see METEOROLOGY; TIDE). These winds move electrically conducting air across the lines of force of the geomagnetic field, thereby generating currents producing the daily variations. In a narrow belt above the magnetic equator the motion of the ions and electrons is such that the transmission of current is more efficient, thereby giving rise to an electrojet directed from west to east, centred near the 11 A.M. meridian. By firing a rocket carrying a magnetometer through this current layer, the height of the over-

GEOMETRES

185

head current layer near the equator is about 95 km.

At the magnetic equator the day-to-day differences in the solar daily variation are shown to depend mainly upon the size of the solar electrical driving forces in the E-region, and not upon day-to-day differences in electric conductivity. This is because these driving forces are shown to lift the ions upward in unison in higher ionized regions known as the F-region as predicted by the dynamo theory. The day-to-day variability of these generating winds does not seem to vary much with sunspot cycle. A similar but smaller effect of this kind is noted in the E-region itself.

The height of the current layer responsible for the lunar daily variation is not established, but may be near the same level as for the solar case, which is the E-region. The upper more extensive F-region is less suited ordinarily to the generation of electric currents because the geomagnetic field there is able to seriously restrict the flow of current across this field. In the denser E-region the electric current carriers collide so frequently with the gas constituents that continuous effects of the geomagnetic field are much reduced.

It thus appears that the old *Britannica* theory of Stewart is confirmed both qualitatively and quantitatively, though some details of the explanation remain to be worked out. The increase in the amplitude of the variations with local season is due to improved electric conductivity in the ionosphere as the apparent sun moves northward or southward, and probably also in part to the response of the upper air winds to the associated changes in heating action. The changes in amplitude from one day to the next, sometimes as great as 100%, are mainly due to day-to-day changes in wind speed. The dominant influence of the noon-minus-midnight values of the solar daily variation is about 0.99 with the annual means of sunspots. For this reason the magnetic changes, though less frequent at sunspot minimum, are somewhat of interest as a part of our environment in their own right, are continuously monitored as an index of solar activity. Actually, they seem to provide a direct measure of the X-ray and ultraviolet emission by the sun and its corona.

Magnetic disturbance manifests itself over a wide range in intensity; the term magnetic storm designates the more disturbed periods. Magnetic storms are more frequent and intense around or somewhat after the maximum of each sunspot cycle, and are less frequent at sunspot minimum. Various measures of magnetic activity have been devised and extensively studied because they are useful in predicting conditions affecting radio transmission to great distances. For instance, use is made of an international magnetic character figure C. C is 0, 1 or 2 according to whether or not the photographic record or magnetogram for the day is magnetically quiet, slightly disturbed or greatly disturbed, and becomes the international figure when averaged for many stations. A more quantitative measure is the u-measure based on successive day-to-day differences in horizontal intensity averaged for equatorial stations. A third measure is the K-index, introduced by J. Bartels, in which one of a series of numbers from one to nine is given to each three-hour interval of each day at each participating magnetic observatory, according to the departure of any element from smooth undisturbed conditions. A fourth measure is the Q-index, rather similar to the K-index, except for being based upon ranges observed during 15-minute intervals. It is found that K-indices from 0 to 4 show little or no correlation with sunspots, whereas larger K-indices are correlated.

Magnetic disturbance is more marked at the equinoxes, the value being about 30% higher than at the solstices. Storms also tend to recur every 27 days, a consequence of the solar rotation period. Some sequences have persisted for as many as 17 solar rotations.

In 1896 K. Birkeland proposed that magnetic storms and auroras were caused by solar particles penetrating the earth's atmosphere. C. Störmer computed many paths of such solar particles in the earth's neighbourhood. Chapman and Ferraro calculated the magnetic effects of solar streams near the earth, as affected by their motion and interaction with the geomagnetic field. They concluded that the earth's magnetic field would carve out a hollow in the advancing solar stream.

Electric currents induced in the face of the advancing stream would provide geomagnetic effects during the initial phase of a magnetic storm. Later a current ring formed from the solar stream at a distance of several earth radii might contribute during the main and recovery phases of the storm.

It seems to be generally agreed that particles in motion along the geomagnetic field contribute to the aurora and polar disturbances. The polar electrojets show that electrically polarized gases appear in the auroral regions, but the manner in which this electric driving force is generated is obscure. However, it seems likely that positively and negatively charged particles are maintained in a slightly separated state along both a vertical and horizontal direction in the low ionosphere. The electric field produced can contribute substantially to the production of electric currents throughout the ionosphere during storms, and serve to raise, lower and otherwise transport the higher ionosphere as well as contribute to the motion and shifting of auroral rays. Differential penetration of incoming particles, accompanied by X-rays penetrating levels of only a few tens of kilometres is undoubtedly important near the auroral zone, and possibly elsewhere as well; as a very simple partial theory of storms and disturbance the vertical polarization can produce surges of storm-time type, and horizontal polarization can produce many changes in the form of bays or of the diurnally varying type. In addition, there appear to be fields of storm-time variation type originating in regions beyond the atmosphere.

There may also be dynamo effects associated with winds in auroral regions, due to heat transport from solar streams and the hot solar corona.

During the International Geophysical year (*q.v.*) measurements made by earth satellites and lunar probes showed that the earth was encircled by Van Allen radiation belts. An intense equatorial belt about 2,000 km. above the earth is caused by high-energy radiation from space. An outer belt, mainly of energetic electrons, is of greatest strength at about 6 earth-radii. The electrons and protons in these belts undergo spiraling motions along the lines of force of the geomagnetic field, itself believed to be distorted at times by clouds of hot solar gases exerting a dragging action upon the field lines. The electrons and protons also drift across the field and around the earth, and may penetrate into polar regions at times. An explosion of an atomic bomb in the ionosphere confirmed this conclusion. Solar gases also may compress or drag terrestrial field lines to produce an accelerating action upon protons and electrons. This may cause them to leave the radiation belts and penetrate into auroral regions, especially at about the observed local midnight.

See further MAGNETISM; SPACE EXPLORATION; VAN ALLEN RADIATION BELTS; *see also* references under "Geomagnetism" in the Index.

BIBLIOGRAPHY.—S. Chapman, *The Earth's Magnetism*, 2nd ed. (1951); S. Chapman and J. Bartels, *Geomagnetism* (1940); *Terrestrial Magnetism and Electricity*, ed. by J. A. Fleming (1939); E. H. Vestine et al., *The Geomagnetic Field: Its Description and Analysis*, Carnegie Institution Publication 580 (1947), *Description of the Earth's Main Magnetic Field and Its Secular Change, 1905-1945*, Publication 578 (1947); B. M. Ianovskii, *Terrestrial Magnetism* (1953); W. Heiskanen and F. A. Vening Meinesz, *The Earth and Its Gravity Field* (1958); J. W. Chamberlain, *Physics of the Aurora and Airglow* (1961).
(E. H. V.)

GEOMETRES, JOHN (JOHN KYRIOTES) (fl. 10th century), Byzantine poet, official and bishop, is known for his short poems in classical metre. He held the post of *protospatharios* (officer commanding the guards) at the Byzantine court, and later was ordained priest, finally becoming metropolitan of Melitene in eastern Asia Minor. His poems, on both contemporary politics and religious subjects, are distinguished by considerable charm and appreciation of natural beauty. His prose works, largely unpublished, include a life of the Virgin Mary, consisting of a series of sermons for her feast days, and an encomium of the apple.

BIBLIOGRAPHY.—Works in J. P. Migne, *Patrologia Graeca*, vol. 106 (1863). *See also* F. Scheidweiler, "Studien zu Johannes Geometres," in *Byzantinische Zeitschrift* 45:277-319 (1952); K. Krumbacher, *Geschichte der byzantinischen Litteratur*, 2nd ed., pp. 169, 731-737 (1897); G. Moravcsik, *Byzantinoturcica*, 2nd ed., vol. I, pp. 319-320 (1958).
(J. M. Hy.)

GEOMETRIC PERIOD, in architecture, the earlier of the two sections into which the Decorated period (q.v.) of English Gothic (see GOTHIC ART AND ARCHITECTURE) is usually divided, comprising roughly, the last half of the 13th century.

GEOMETRIC SOLIDS: see SOLIDS, GEOMETRIC.

GEOMETRIES, FINITE. The incidence axioms of projective geometry require that every line contain at least three points. If the number of points on one line is a finite number, say $n + 1$, then every other line contains the same number of points and we say that the geometry is of order n. If the geometry is of dimension three or higher, then from the basic theory of projective geometry, it is Desarguesian and may be represented by co-ordinates from a division ring D. In a geometry of order n, the division ring contains exactly n elements. By a well-known theorem of J. H. M. Wedderburn, D must be a finite field, $GF(p^r)$, where $n = p^r$, p being a prime. In the k-dimensional geometry over $GF(p^r)$, designated as $PG(k,p^r)$, a point has a homogeneous representation $(\lambda x_0, \lambda x_1, \ldots, \lambda x_k)$ where $x_0, \ldots, x_k$ are fixed elements of $GF(p^r)$, not all zero, and λ ranges over all nonzero elements of $GF(p^r)$. The points whose co-ordinates satisfy a linear equation

$$c_0 x_0 + c_1 x_1 + \cdots + c_k x_k = 0$$

where the equation is not identically zero, form a subspace of $k - 1$ dimensions; those satisfying m independent linear equations form a subspace of $k - m$ dimensions. (See ALGEBRAS [LINEAR]).

Finite projective planes include the Desarguesian planes $PG(2,p^r)$ but there are also a number of types of non-Desarguesian finite planes. All known planes are of prime power order. These include planes described by O. Veblen and Wedderburn in a paper written in 1907. In these planes there is a system of co-ordinates V with n elements. In V there is an addition $a + b$ and a multiplication ab satisfying the following conditions:

V1. Addition is an Abelian group with a zero element o;
V2. $(a + b)m = am + bm$;
V3. If $a \neq o$, equations $ax = b$ and $xa = c$ have unique solutions for x;
V4. There is a unit 1 such that $1b = b1 = b$ for every b;
V5. If $r \neq s$, then $xr = xs + t$ has a unique solution for x.

From V we may construct a plane π whose points consist of $n + 1$ infinite points designated as (m), m running over the n elements of V and a further point (∞) and also n^2 finite points (x,y) with x and y running over all elements of V. The lines are: L_∞, containing the $n + 1$ infinite points; for each c of V a line containing (∞) and all points (x,y) with $x = c$; for each m and b of V a line containing (m) and all points (x,y) whose co-ordinates satisfy $y = xm + b$. The above conditions imply that $n = p^r$, p a prime, since multiplication induces automorphisms on the additive group permuting all nonzero elements transitively. A nearfield is the special case of a Veblen-Wedderburn system in which multiplication forms a group. Replacement of the distributive law V2', $m(a + b) = am + bm$, by the other distributive law V2, $m(a + b) = ma + mb$, gives the family of planes dual to the Veblen-Wedderburn planes.

The plane of order 2 (known as the Fano plane) contains seven points. If the points are represented appropriately by the numerals 1, 2, 3, 4, 5, 6, 7 then the lines are given as the columns of the following array:

```
1 2 3 4 5 6 7
2 3 4 5 6 7 1
4 5 6 7 1 2 3
```

This is the Desarguesian plane and may be co-ordinatized by $GF(2)$ the field of the residues o and 1 modulo 2. Here we may take
$1 = (\infty)$ $2 = (o)$, $4 = (1)$
$3 = (o,o)$, $5 = (1,o)$ $6 = (1,1)$
$7 = (o,1)$.   The line $y = x + 1$, for example, contains the points 4, 5 and 7. It will be noticed that, permuting the points $1, \ldots, 7$ cyclically in this order, the lines are also permuted cyclically. This permutation is, therefore, a collineation. This is an instance of a general theorem proved by J. Singer, namely, that every $PG(k,p^r)$ possesses a cyclic collineation of order $(q^{k+1} - 1)/(q - 1)$, $q = p^r$, permuting points and hyperplanes regularly.

A nearfield of order 9 exists whose elements are of the form $au + b$, $a, b \in GF(3)$, i.e., a, b residues modulo 3. Addition is given by the rule $(a_1 u + b_1) + (a_2 u + b_2) = (a_1 + a_2)u + (b_1 + b_2)$. The multiplication of the eight nonzero elements is the quaternion group and is determined by the rules $c(au + b) = acu + bc$, $c \in GF(3)$, $(au + b)^2 = -1$, $a \neq 0$ together with the distributive law V2. This yields by the rules above the Veblen-Wedderburn plane (and with the opposite distributive law V2', also the dual plane). This plane and its dual are distinct and are non-Desarguesian.

There is known one other non-Desarguesian plane of order nine, which is self-dual. This was given originally by Veblen and Wedderburn in their 1907 paper and in 1957 Hughes found an infinite family of finite planes including this one. The 91 points are $A_i, B_i, C_i, D_i, E_i, F_i, G_i$, $i = 0, 1, \ldots, 12$ modulo 13. Seven representative lines are:

L_0	A_0	A_1	A_9	B_0	C_0	D_0
M_0	A_0	B_3	B_8	C_0	D_{11}	E_0
N_0	A_0	C_1	C_8	E_7	E_0	F_3
R_0	A_0	D_2	D_{11}	E_9	F_2	G_5
S_0	A_0	E_4	E_7	F_{11}	G_2	B_9
T_0	A_0	F_5	F_6	G_2	B_6	C_{11}
U_0	A_0	G_6	G_5	B_5	D_9	D_1

The rest of the 91 lines are given by adding $1, \ldots, 12$ modulo 13 to the subscripts of both points and lines.

The most striking result known on finite planes, without any further hypothesis, was found by R. H. Bruck and H. J. Ryser in 1949. This asserts that if $n \equiv 1, 2 \pmod 4$, there cannot be a plane of order n unless n can be expressed as a sum of two integral squares, $n = u^2 + v^2$. In particular no plane of order 6, 14, 21, 22 exists and infinitely many other orders are excluded by this rule. In 1956 A. M. Gleason proved that a finite plane, in which every set of four points not on a line lies in a Fano subplane, is necessarily Desarguesian. T. G. Ostrom and A. O. Wagner have shown that if the collineation group of a finite plane is doubly transitive on points, the plane is necessarily Desarguesian.

See also GEOMETRY; PROJECTIVE GEOMETRY; PROJECTIVE GEOMETRY.

BIBLIOGRAPHY.—O. Veblen and J. W. Young, *Projective Geometry*, vol. i (1910), vol. ii (1918); R. D. Carmichael, *Theory of Groups of Finite Order* (1937); Günter Pickert, *Projective Ebenen* (1955); *American Mathematical Monthly*, vol. 62, no. 7 (Aug.–Sept. 1955); Marshall Hall, Jr., *The Theory of Groups*, ch. 20 (1959). (M. H.)

GEOMETRY is a branch of mathematics which deals with the properties of space and of objects in space. The discipline arose in response to such practical problems as those found in surveying, and derives its name from the Greek words meaning earth measurement. Later, it was realized that geometry need not be limited to the classical study of flat surfaces (plane geometry) and rigid three-dimensional objects (solid geometry), but that even the most abstract thinkings and imaginings of people might be represented and developed in geometric terms. Thus, the study of geometry can be most fascinating and personally rewarding, whether it leads immediately to practical applications or not.

What follows is an attempt to provide a historical overview which may help place in perspective aspects of geometry covered in greater detail elsewhere in these volumes. See also ALGEBRAIC GEOMETRY; ANALYTIC GEOMETRY; DIFFERENTIAL GEOMETRY; NON-EUCLIDEAN; GROUPS; GROUPS, TRANSFORMATION; PROJECTIVE GEOMETRY; RIEMANNIAN GEOMETRY; SOLIDS, GEOMETRIC; TOPOLOGY, GENERAL; VECTOR ANALYSIS.

THE BEGINNINGS OF GEOMETRY

Egypt and Babylon.—Geometry is encountered in the first written records of mankind. Fundamental formulas for measurement were known in ancient Egypt and Babylonia, and knowledge of the so-called Pythagorean theorem is shown in clay tablets dating from the end of the 3rd millennium B.C.; there is, however, no evidence for the conjecture, mentioned as a fact in many books, that the Egyptians knew the theorem.

In Babylonia, the language of algebra was often borrowed from geometry. Ancient Babylonians would state an algebraic problem like this: "Length, width. I have multiplied length and width to get the surface. I have added the excess of the length over the width to the surface: 183. I have added the length and the width: 27. Asked length, width, surface."

Today the symbols x and y are used in place of the words length and width, and the problem reads as follows: $xy + x - y = 183$, and $x + y = 27$.

Problems of truly geometrical character can also be found in the cuneiform literature, and were stated in this way: "A beam, long 30, leans against a wall. The top has been lowered by 6. How far has the bottom gone away?"

More abstractly, this problem asks for the third side of a plane right triangle, given the hypotenuse (30) and another side $(30 - 6 = 24)$. From the Pythagorean theorem the third side equals $\sqrt{30^2 - 24^2}$.

The right triangle with sides ratio 3:4:5 occurs most frequently in Babylonian mathematics, which also provides an extensive table of other "Pythagorean" triangles. Good approximations of the ratio of diagonal and side of the square ($\sqrt{2}$) are also found in Babylonian texts. Though theoretical texts on geometry from this period have not been unearthed, some theory probably existed. Empirical methods alone do not lead to ideas like the Pythagorean theorem; some kind of genuine geometrical reasoning is needed (see TRIANGLE).

Greek Geometry.—According to Eudemos of Rhodes (q.v.), the first geometrician was Thales (q.v.), who is said to have predicted the solar eclipse of 585 B.C., and to have proved a number of geometrical theorems. Eudemos' report has often been questioned because it seems improbable that the first geometrician could have proved theorems which suppose deep insight, and which are not mentioned even by Euclid. It is clear from Babylonian excavations that Thales was not the first geometrician. Strong Babylonian influences have been shown in Greek algebra and astronomy, and doubtless reached Thales himself.

Pythagoras, who died about 490 B.C., was known to his contemporaries and even later to Aristotle as the founder of a religious brotherhood in southern Italy, where the Pythagoreans played a political role in the 5th century B.C. (see PYTHAGORAS AND PYTHAGOREANISM). The linking of his name to the Pythagorean theorem is rather recent and spurious. Pythagorean mathematicians developed number theory, music theory and number mystics, and Euclid's arithmetical books (vii and viii) presumably come from a Pythagorean source. An important discovery ascribed to Pythagoras, and in any case due to his school, is that of the incommensurability of side and diagonal of the square; that is, the ratio of diagonal and side of the square is not equal to the ratio of two integers.

In modern notation the proof (in Euclid's tenth book) runs as follows: Let a be the side and d the diagonal of the square; then, according to the Pythagorean theorem, $d^2 = a^2 + a^2 = 2a^2$. Suppose there were integers m and n such that $d:a = m:n$; then, $d^2:a^2 = m^2:n^2$, and hence $m^2 = 2n^2$. The integers m and n may be supposed without common divisor. From $m^2 = 2n^2$ it follows that m^2 is even. This is only possible if m itself is even. Let l be half of m. Then $4l^2 = m^2 = 2n^2$, hence $n^2 = 2l^2$. Thus, n^2 is even and n is even; however, then m and n would have a common divisor. Thus, there are no integers m and n such that $d:a = m:n$. This discovery of irrationality fundamentally influenced the development of Greek geometry (see NUMBER: Irrational Numbers).

In Pythagorean mathematics quadratic equations were formulated and solved by a geometrical procedure, the application of areas with excess or with defect (hyperbole and ellipsis). The quadratic equation $(a + x)x = P$ was interpreted as a problem of applying the given area P as a rectangle ACFD (fig. 1) to the given line segment $a = AB$ such that the excess BCFE is a square. The quadratic equation $(a - x)x = P$ was interpreted as a problem of applying the given area P as a rectangle ACFD (fig.

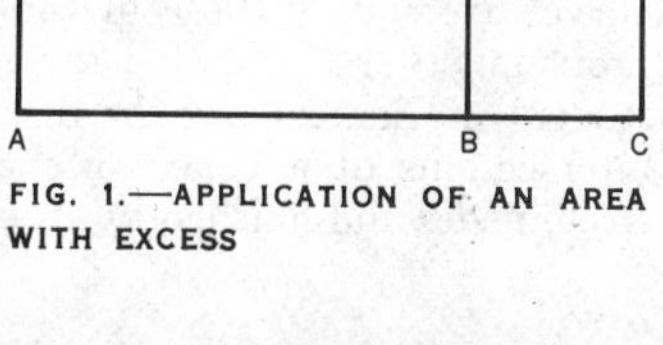

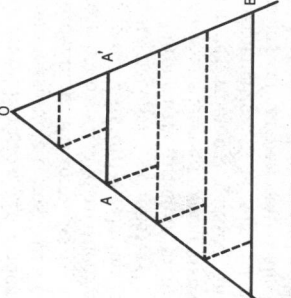

FIG. 1.—APPLICATION OF AN AREA WITH EXCESS

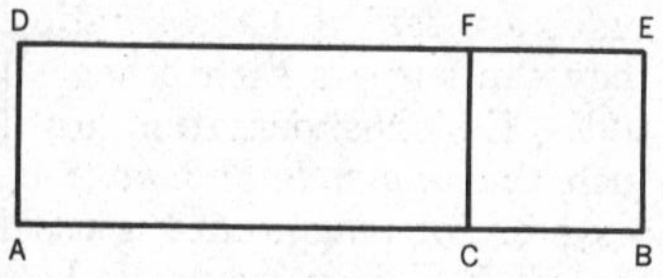

2) to the given line segment $a = AB$ such that the defect (falling short) is square BCFE.

It will now be explained in which way the Pythagorean discovery of incommensurability remodeled Greek geometry.

To prove for rectangles AB-B'A' and ACC'A' with the same altitude the proportionality of areas and bases (fig. 3), ABB'A':ACC'A' = AB:AC, or to prove that proportional segments are cut off by parallel lines upon two fixed lines (fig. 4), OA':OB' , OA:OB , a simple procedure such as indicated in the figures may be applied as long as it is believed that two line segments always possess a common measure of which they are integral multiples.

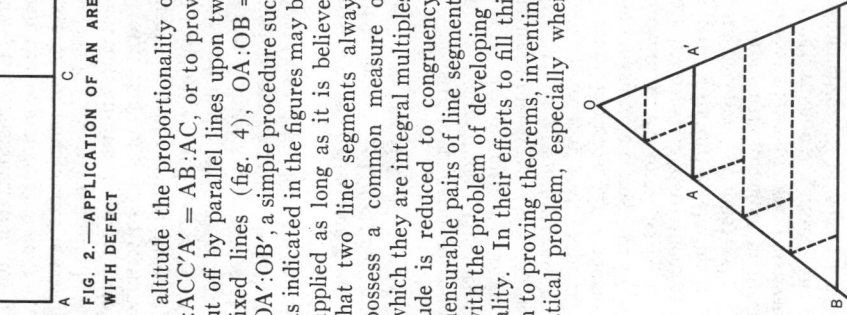

FIG. 2.—APPLICATION OF AN AREA WITH DEFECT

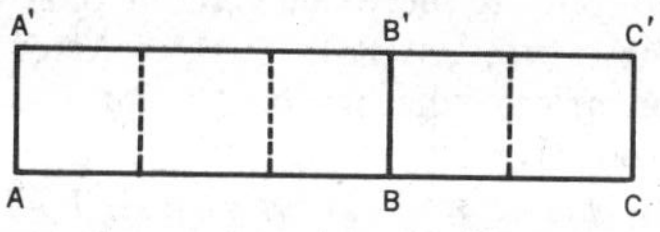

FIG. 3.—THE PROPORTIONALITY OF AREAS AND BASES

By suitable subdivisions similitude is reduced to congruency. Through the discovery of incommensurable pairs of line segments Greek geometricians were faced with the problem of developing a satisfactory theory of proportionality. In their efforts to fill this gap, they realized that, in addition to proving theorems, inventing definitions might be a mathematical problem, especially when some field of empirical experience is to be organized mathematically. It was obvious how to define ratio and proportionality as long as the magnitudes under consideration were commensurable. At a certain moment it was recognized that a suitable definition of ratio and proportionality in the general case would be the clue to proving theorems like those of figs. 3 and 4.

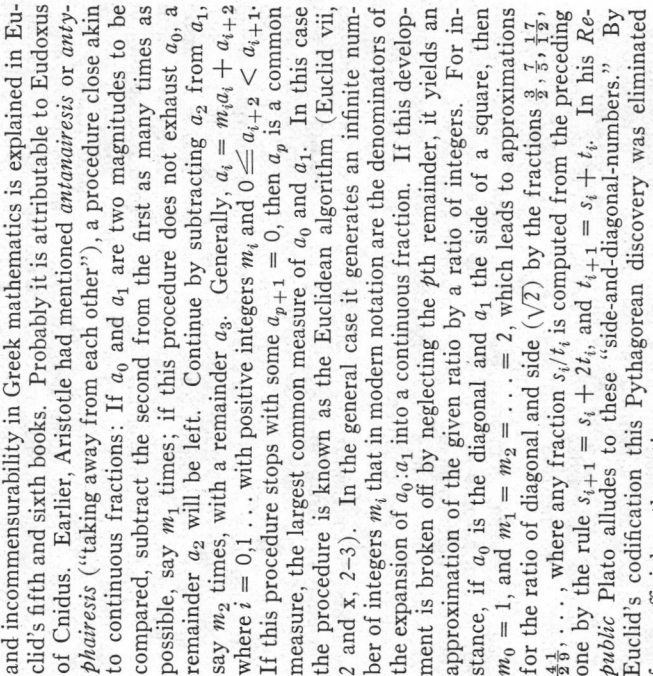

FIG. 4.—PROPORTIONAL SEGMENTS CUT OFF BY PARALLEL LINES

The ultimate procedure for handling ratio, proportionality and incommensurability in Greek mathematics is explained in Euclid's fifth and sixth books. Probably it is attributable to Eudoxus of Cnidus. Earlier, Aristotle had mentioned *antanairesis* or *antyphairesis* ("taking away from each other"), a procedure close akin to continuous fractions: If a_0 and a_1 are two magnitudes to be compared, subtract the second from the first as many times as possible, say m_1 times; if this procedure does not exhaust a_0, a remainder a_2 will be left. Continue by subtracting a_2 from a_1, say m_2 times, with a remainder a_3. Generally, $a_i = m_i a_i + a_{i+2}$ where $i = 0,1 \ldots$ with positive integers m_i and $0 \leqq a_{i+2} < a_{i+1}$. If this procedure stops with some $a_{p+1} = 0$, then a_p is a common measure, the largest common measure of a_0 and a_1. In this case the procedure is known as the Euclidean algorithm (Euclid vii, 2 and x, 2–3). In the general case it generates an infinite number of integers m_i that in modern notation are the denominators of the expansion of $a_0:a_1$ into a continuous fraction. If this development is broken off by neglecting the pth remainder, it yields an approximation of the given ratio by a ratio of integers. For instance, if a_0 is the diagonal and a_1 the side of a square, then $m_0 = 1$, and $m_1 = m_2 = \ldots = 2$, which leads to approximations for the ratio of diagonal and side ($\sqrt{2}$) by the fractions $\frac{3}{2}, \frac{7}{5}, \frac{17}{12}, \frac{41}{29}, \ldots$, where any fraction s_i/t_i is computed from the preceding one by the rule $s_{i+1} = s_i + 2t_i$, and $t_{i+1} = s_i + t_i$. In his *Republic* Plato alludes to these "side-and-diagonal-numbers." By Euclid's codification this Pythagorean discovery was eliminated from official mathematics.

The last pre-Eudoxian theory of proportionality must have consisted in defining two ratios to be equal, if they have the same *antanairesis*, i.e., if the numbers m_i appearing in the above procedure are correspondingly equal. From this definition theorems like those of figs. 3 and 4 can be derived.

Eudoxus' solution (shown in Euclid's books v and vi) was more elegant. Eudoxus did not define ratio. He only said that it is a relation with respect to magnitude. Then he continued: Magnitudes are said to have a ratio if, when multiplied (by integers), they can surpass each other. This means, if a and b are magnitudes, Eudoxus' definition urged the existence of integers m and n such that $ma > b$, and $nb > a$. This property if postulated for a system of magnitudes is usually called the Archimedean axiom, though Eudoxian would be better. By this definition a line segment and an area have no ratio. Eudoxus' definition of equality by the definition $a:b = a':b'$ if and only if there is a pair of positive integers m and n such that $ma = nb$ and $ma' = nb'$ and as well as do $ma < nb$ and $ma' < nb'$. Ratios are compared with each other by the definition: $a:b > a':b'$ if and only if there is a pair of positive integers m and n such that $ma > nb$, but $ma' < nb'$. After these three definitions the question arises whether $a < b$ implies that $a:a > a':b$. This means that positive integers m and n must be sought such that $ma > na$, but $ma < nb$. If $m = n + 1$ is tried, then $(n + 1)a < nb$. In other words, $a < n(b − a)$, which can be fulfilled if a and $b − a$ have a ratio in the sense of Eudoxus' definition.

This is the foundation of Eudoxus' theory of ratio, proportionality and similitude. His method of combining all essential tools into a few definitions foreshadowed the most modern mathematical procedures. His approach was more elegant than that of *antanairesis*. In *antanairesis* an incommensurable ratio is located by comparing it with a special sequence of approximating commensurable ratios. In Eudoxus' approach it is compared with all commensurable ratios. In a certain sense *antanairesis* corresponds to defining real numbers by decimal fractions; Eudoxus' method foreshadowed modern number theories in which a real number is determined by its order relation to any rational number (not only to finite decimal fractions).

Through the problem of incommensurability the Greek mathematicians learned logical analysis and mathematical rigour. These virtues, when exaggerated, finally hampered the progress of Greek mathematics. The view that the existence of incommensurable ratios cannot be granted algebraically, but only by geometry, led them to ban algebra as developed by the Babylonians. By translating algebraic relations into geometry they created geometric algebra, a tool that could be handled by geniuses only.

Another theory that must have been highly problematic before Euclid is that of parallel lines. The uniqueness of the line through a given point and parallel to a given line is required as a postulate in Euclid's first book (whereas the existence of the parallel line is proved). Though enunciated in advance, the application of this postulate is postponed in Euclid's first book as long as possible. This indicates that rather than being spontaneous, the adoption of this postulate as such by Greek mathematics was probably preceded by a thorough exploration of the possibilities. It is probable that at some time before Euclid the need of adopting this postulate was under discussion and, in a comment of Aristotle's, evidence can be found for a competing theory of parallels, using points at infinity.

Euclid's activity (c. 300 B.C.) was mainly that of a compilator. There have been pre-Euclidean *Elements*, which, aside from a few fragments or vague indications, are lost. Euclid compiled pieces of different characters and qualities, and did not succeed in avoiding inconsistencies in terminology and structure. Thanks to these defects the single pieces can be isolated.

Euclid's *Elements* start with definitions, postulates and axioms. The definitions are a strange collection of explanatory statements, loosely connected with the bulk of the work. The famous postulate of parallels is an example of his postulates; the axioms are of the type: "The whole is greater than the part." The *Elements* have become famous as the outstanding example of a deductive theory. The claim, however, that all theorems are derived logically from the definitions, postulates and axioms is unfounded. Modern criticism has shown essential gaps. Order notions, such as the division of the plane by its straight-lines, are never mentioned, though they are implicitly used when proving the existence of parallel lines (eventually the proposition 16 stating that in a triangle an exterior angle is greater than any opposite interior angle). Even

the proof of his first theorem concerning the construction of equilateral triangles is invalid, because the circles used are tacitly assumed to intersect. Postulates of congruency are lacking. The proof of the fundamental congruency theorem actually relies heavily on intuition.

It is, however, not justified to apply modern standards and notions of rigorous deductivity to Euclid's work. The Greek philosophy of mathematics has little in common with the modern ideal of deriving all conclusions from a few fundamental propositions. According to Plato and Aristotle, geometrical subjects are real and knowable; their properties are settled anyhow, whether they are explicitly stated or not; fundamental facts need not be announced explicitly, unless they are controversial.

Nevertheless, as a deductive systematization of a field of knowledge, Greek geometry is much superior to Babylonian and Egyptian geometry. During more than 2,000 years Euclid's *Elements* were a model of deductive approach, often imitated, but never surpassed.

It should be added that after the climax of Greek mathematics the *Elements* were not adequately appreciated. The *Elements* teach geometry with a definitive approach, ignoring prior and alternative approaches, and without motivating highly sophisticated turns. Older works, which could have filled this gap, were completely lost through Euclid's authority. Thus, the problem Eudoxus solved in the theory of proportionality was not understood until R. Dedekind (1871) solved the same problems independently of Eudoxus, but by the same idea. Euclid's sophisticated theory of parallels was not understood until after the invention of non-Euclidean geometry, because the theoretical background of geometrization and the subject matter could be uncovered only by modern historical research.

Euclid's unnatural and artificial methods have been taken over by many textbook writers. Geometrical transformations do not occur in Euclid's work though they were known and applied by his predecessors (especially symmetry, which played an important part in Thales' geometry and some fragments of pre-Euclidean *Elements*). Possibly geometrical transformations were eliminated by Euclid because they seemed to belong to mechanics. Instead, Euclid used artificial auxiliary lines and subdivisions into congruent triangles. In elementary-school geometry his unfortunate method still prevails.

From Archimedes' *The Method* (a palimpsest discovered in 1906), it is known that Archimedes (c. 287–212 B.C.) did not repudiate infinitesimal and mechanical methods. Probably his finest discoveries were made in this way, but in the final editing the heuristic tools were eliminated in order to meet the requirements of Euclidean rigour. There are different levels of mathematical rigour which have their own functions in teaching, learning and exploring. As long as there were written records or oral traditions of unofficial mathematics, Greek geometry could progress. After a sudden break, as by political events, the tradition could not be resumed. The level of sophistication in the surviving literature was too high for it to be used in self-instruction.

Geometric algebra was just sufficient to solve second-degree problems, corresponding geometrically to constructions with ruler and compass. When studying famous higher-degree problems, such as the duplication of the cube and the trisection of the angle, Greek geometricians had to solve the application problems of proportionality with a variable $P = y^2$ (where y was again subjected to a quadratic relation, in order to raise the degree of the whole system). The application problem then runs $(a + x)x = y^2$, or $x^2 − y^2 − ax = 0$, which in modern terms describes an orthogonal hyperbola. After a slight generalization of the application problem, general hyperbolas appear. Other cases of the application problem provide ellipses and parabolas. (The names of these curves are simply those of the different cases of the application problem.) Greek passion for geometrization led Menaechmus, a student of Eudoxus, to the discovery that these curves are plane intersections of a cone. Menaechmus' work was continued by Archimedes and finished by Apollonius of Perga (c. 210 B.C.). In his formidable work he studied conics extensively, using different kinds of co-ordinates, though always in the clumsy language of geometric algebra.

THE ALGEBRAIC APPROACH

In the period coming after the break of the tradition, genuine algebra was resumed and redeveloped by people who were unaware of the Greek scruples. Following the Arabian and "rule of coss" period in the late middle ages, it got its final shape by F. Vieta's (1591) and R. Descartes' (1637) work. Descartes' *Geometrie* is the converse of Euclid's, the algebraization of geometry. Descartes progressed from the point where Apollonius had failed. He did not attach a co-ordinate system to a conic but to the plane, and there he studied different figures in their mutual relations. By Descartes' method (fig. 5) the points in the plane can be described by pairs of co-ordinates, and the figures in the plane by equations between these co-ordinates, the straight lines by linear equations, $ax + by + c = 0$, and the conics by quadratic equations, $ax^2 + 2bxy + cy^2 + dx + ey + f = 0$. Problems of higher degree, and even nonalgebraic problems, can be studied with the same ease. With three co-ordinates the same can be done in space.

y
(x, y)
x

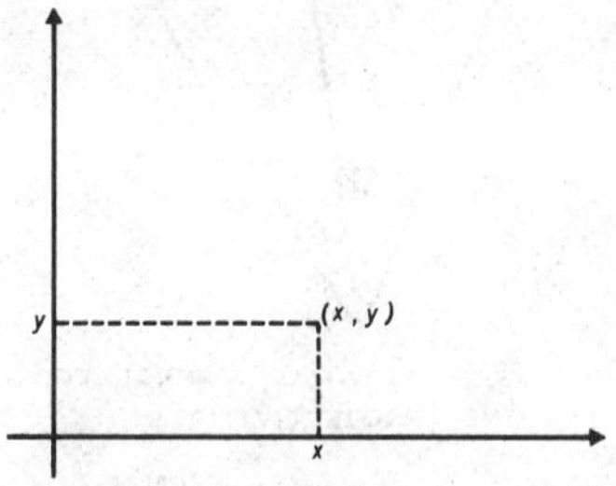

FIG. 5.—CARTESIAN CO-ORDINATES

Descartes' discovery seemed to eliminate geometry theoretically. Practically it was eliminated by the growing importance of calculus. In the 19th century, when geometry revived, a step was taken which had been due during Descartes' lifetime. This was the invention of higher-dimensional space, which found its codification in H. Grassmann's work (1844, 1861) where a system of n numbers is considered as a point of n-space; the n numbers are its co-ordinates. Linear subspaces (corresponding to the straight lines and planes of 3-space) are defined by systems of linear equations between co-ordinates. The distance of two points $x = (\xi_1, \ldots, \xi_n)$ and $y = (\eta_1, \ldots, \eta_n)$ is defined by a higher-dimensional use of the Pythagorean theorem:

$$\sqrt{(\xi_1 - \eta_1)^2 + \ldots + (\xi_n - \eta_n)^2}$$

At the same time, by a slight though fundamental shift of stress, vector algebra changed the intuitive background of geometry in the work of G. Bellavitis (1832) and Sir William R. Hamilton (1845). Under the general name of vector, the arrows (used before in mechanics to represent forces, velocities and accelerations) were introduced in geometry. Formally, addition of points in n-space may be defined by $(\xi_1, \ldots, \xi_n) + (\eta_1, \ldots, \eta_n) = (\xi_1 + \eta_1, \ldots, \xi_n + \eta_n)$. Only if the point x is intuitively replaced by the arrow pointing from the origin to the point x does this "vector addition" get the intuitively significant meaning of the addition of forces, velocities and accelerations in mechanics. The notion of inner product of two vectors, $(x, y) = \xi_1\eta_1 + \ldots + \xi_n\eta_n$ if $x = (\xi_1, \ldots, \xi_n)$ and $y = (\eta_1, \ldots, \eta_n)$ was also borrowed from mechanics. The inner product (x,y) of the force vector x and the path vector y just equals the work done by y through x. Vector inspiration vivified such bloodless algebraic notions as the determinants, a formal tool for solving linear equations. For example, the volume of the parallelepiped (corresponding to a parallelogram as in fig. 6), spanned by n vectors, was found to be equal to the determinant, carrying the given vectors as rows or columns.

AREA = $\begin{vmatrix} \xi_1 & \eta_1 \\ \xi_2 & \eta_2 \end{vmatrix} = \xi_1\eta_2 - \xi_2\eta_1$
(η_1, η_2)
(ξ_1, ξ_2)

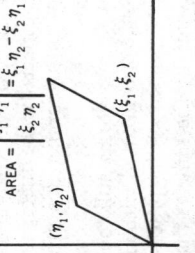

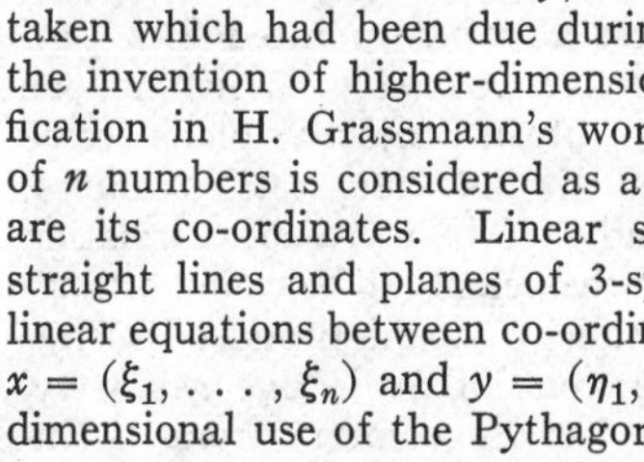

FIG. 6.—AREA OF A PARALLELOGRAM

In the first decades of the 20th century the geometrical spirit of vector algebra was still enforced under the impact of the abstract algebraical school (E. Steinitz, Emmy Noether and F. Riesz, 1913, 1918): Vectors are not to be introduced by their co-ordinates (which have no direct geometrical meaning) but axiomatically by their intrinsic properties. This leads to the definition: The set R is called an (abstract) vector space over the field F of numbers ("scalars") and its elements are called vectors, if two operations are defined in R: adding elements $x,y,z \ldots$ to each other, and multiplying elements $x,y,z, \ldots$ with scalars $\alpha,\beta,\gamma \ldots$ such that the following laws are fulfilled:

(1) $x + y = y + x$
(2) $(x + y) + z = x + (y + z)$
(3) there is one element called 0 such that $x + 0 = x$
(4) for every element x there is one element $-x$ such that $x + (-x) = 0$
(5) $\alpha(x + y) = \alpha x + \alpha y$
(6) $(\alpha + \beta)x = \alpha x + \beta x$
(7) $(\alpha\beta)x = \alpha(\beta x)$
(8) $1x = x$

The underlying field F may be that of the real numbers or complex numbers, or any other algebraic system, which are induced with an addition and a multiplication with the usual properties.

In the (intuitive) plane two vectors e_1, e_2 can be found from which all vectors x may be combined in the form $x = \xi_1 e_1 + \xi_2 e_2$; the numbers ξ_1 and ξ_2 are called the "co-ordinates" of x with respect to this special "basis" e_1,e_2. In the case of ordinary space a basis of three vectors is required. R is called n-dimensional, if a basis of R consists of n elements, and infinitely-dimensional if no such basis is available. Infinitely-dimensional spaces are important in modern analysis, which has fundamentally been influenced by this geometric terminology.

x+y
y
|y|
|x+y|
x
|x|

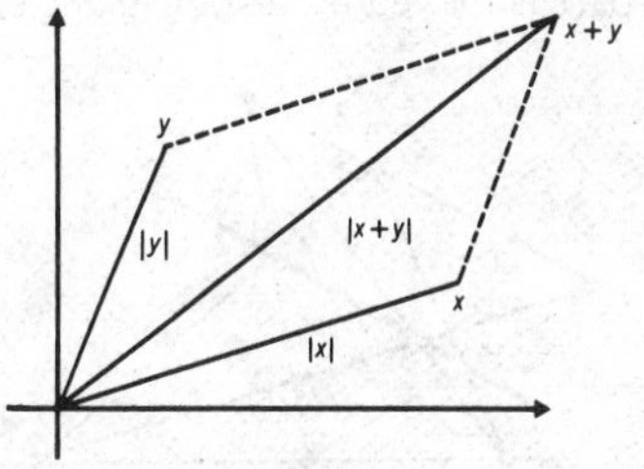

FIG. 7.—PROPERTIES OF VECTOR LENGTH

The notion of vector space is refined by requiring the existence of an inner product of vectors. When F is the field of real numbers, the laws of inner product run as follows:

(1) (x,y) is a scalar
(2) $(x,y) = (y,x)$
(3) $(\alpha x,y) = \alpha(x,y)$
(4) $(x,y + z) = (x,y) + (x,z)$
(5) $(x,x) > 0$, if $x \neq 0$.

By the last law a vector length $|x| = \sqrt{(x,x)}$ can be defined (fig. 7), with the (provable) properties $|\alpha x| = |\alpha| \cdot |x|$ and $|x + y| \leqq |x| + |y|$.

PROJECTIVE GEOMETRY

From the Greek period to the end of the 18th century two momentous geometric discoveries were made, by Girard Desargues (1639) and Blaise Pascal (1640).

Desargues' Theorem: If two triangles (fig. 8) ABC, A′B′C′ are seen perspectively from one point (*i.e.*, AA′, BB′, CC′ intersect in one point), then corresponding sides intersect on one straight

B
C
A
C'
A'
B'

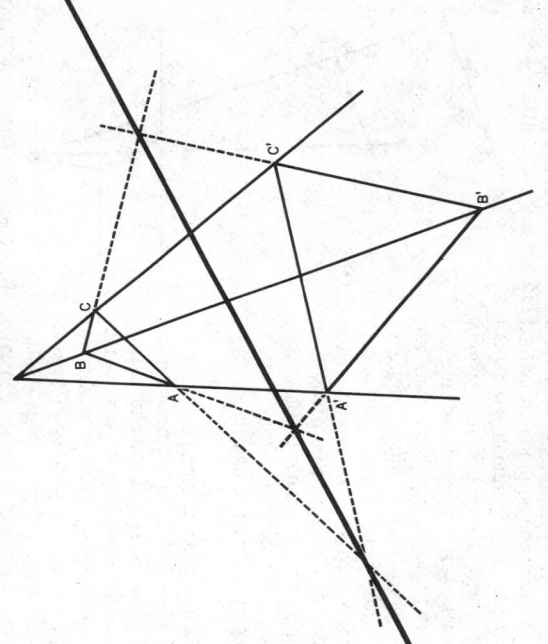

FIG. 8.—DESARGUES' THEOREM

line, and conversely. If the planes of the triangles do not coincide, then the theorem follows from the fact that AB and A'B' are in some plane (because AA', BB' are). The same is true of AC and A'C', and of BC and B'C'. The three pairs of sides intersect upon the intersection of the planes of the triangles. The same holds if ABC and A'B'C' are in the same plane. In the case (fig. 10) of a degenerate conic (a pair of lines) this theorem was known to Pappus of Alexandria (c. A.D. 320).

Till the discovery of projective geometry (J. V. Poncelet, 1813, 1822) Desargues' and Pascal's theorems were like erratic blocks in Euclidean geometry. The only relation that matters in their statements is that of incidence of points and straight lines, and no part is played by distance, angle, congruency or similitude (except in the very definition of conic).

On the other hand, notwithstanding their simplicity, an unusual amount of care must be taken in proving and even formulating these theorems as soon as due regard is paid to what happens when two or more lines in question, instead of intersecting, become parallel. For example, if AB and A'B' are parallel, Desargues' theorem states that the intersection of BC and B'C' lie on a line parallel of AC and A'C' as well as that of BC and B'C' lie on a line parallel with AB; or, AC‖A'C', and BC‖B'C'.

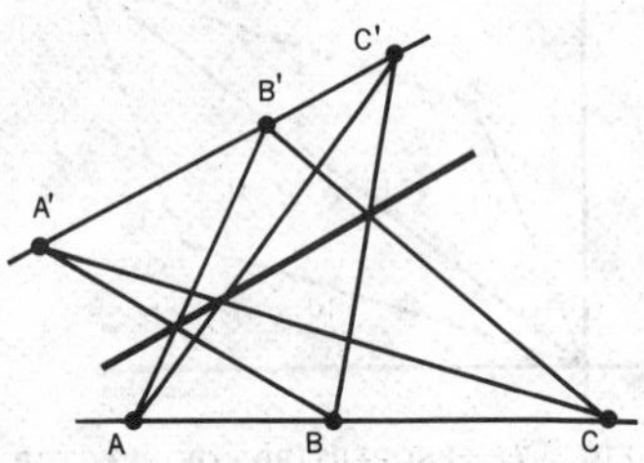

Pascal's Theorem: If (in fig. 9) A, B, C, A', B' and C' are on a conic, then the cross intersections (of AB' with A'B, of BC' with B'C and of CA' with C'A) are on a straight line. In the case (fig. 10) of a degenerate conic (a pair of lines) this theorem was known to Pappus of Alexandria (c. A.D. 320).

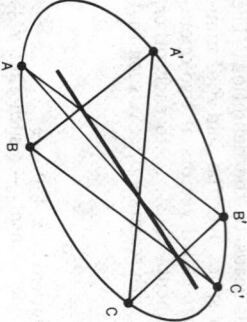

FIG. 9.—PASCAL'S THEOREM IN A CONIC

FIG. 10.—PASCAL'S THEOREM IN A DEGENERATE CONIC

Efforts to overcome these troubles were made by postulating points at infinity, such that every straight line is enriched with a point at infinity, and every plane with a line at infinity; this new point (line) being the same for parallel lines (planes). All infinite elements of space were supposed to lie on the infinite plane of space.

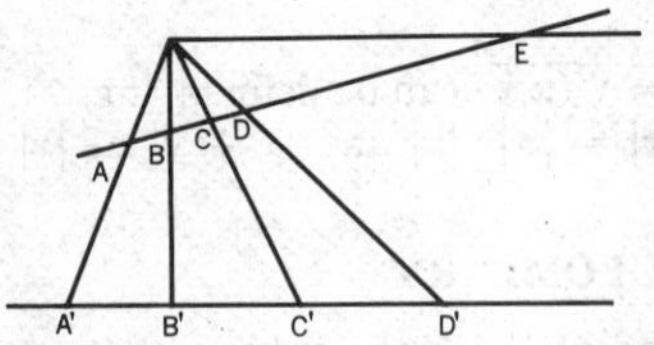

This defined "projective plane" and "projective space" genetically. Afterward the distinction between original and added elements is faded out. Parallelism disappeared as a relation; the only one still left from the variety of Euclid's is that of incidence (lying on). It is a riddle why Poncelet's step was not made centuries earlier. The revival and growth of geometry in the 19th century was psychologically due to the striking simplicity of projective geometry. If simplicity signifies truth, then the new geometry was much more true than Euclid's.

A host of new notions and new "truth," never dreamed of before, were discovered. In ordinary space an intuitively important tool like central projection of one line (plane) upon another (see fig. 11 and 12) was of little use, because of the fact that at a certain point (line) the image vanished into infinity. But in projective geometry the central projection could be considered as a mapping of full lines (planes),

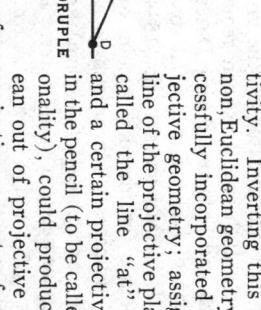

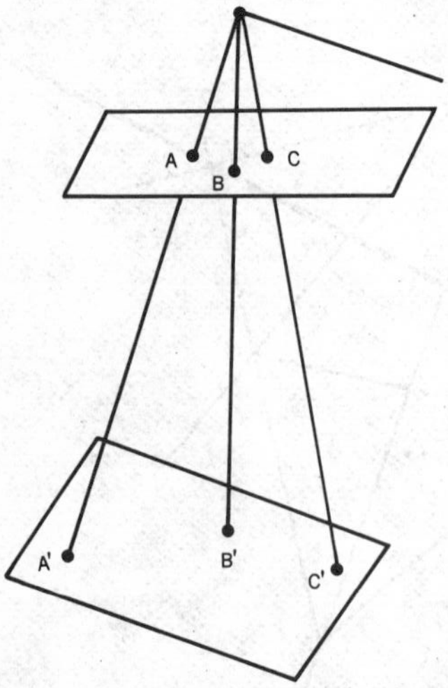

FIG. 11.—CENTRAL PROJECTION OF ONE LINE ON ANOTHER

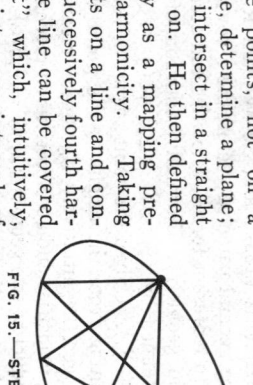

FIG. 12.—CENTRAL PROJECTION OF ONE PLANE ON ANOTHER

The mappings resulting from repeated central projections became important under the name of projectivities (fig. 13). They are dealt with in the following theorems:

Fundamental Theorem of projective geometry: A projectivity of a straight line leaving three points invariant leaves invariant every point of that line. New light spread over large parts of traditional geometry, thanks to the notion of harmonicity; quadruples of points on a line constructed according to fig. 14 are called harmonic.

Theorem of Harmonicity: Three points of a harmonic quadruple determine the fourth uniquely, i.e., independently of the choice of the auxiliary points of the construction. The projective essence of Pascal's theorem was uncovered by *Steiner's Theorem*: The two pencils by which a conic is projected from two of its points (fig. 15) are projectively related in the earlier defined sense of projectivity. By a converse of this theorem a purely projective definition of conics could be given, independent of their generation as plane sections of a cone. The relation of orthogonality in a pencil appeared to be a special kind of projectivity. Inverting this phenomenon, Euclidean geometry was successfully incorporated into projective geometry; assigning one line of the projective plane (to be called the line "at" infinity), and a certain projective relation in the pencil (to be called orthogonality), could produce Euclidean out of projective geometry.

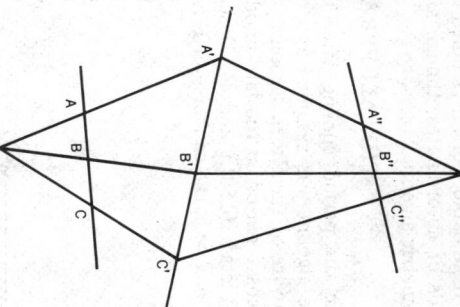

FIG. 13.—REPEATED CENTRAL PROJECTIONS (PROJECTIVITIES)

A major problem was to free projective geometry from its Euclidean substrate and to found it independently. This problem seemed to be solved when K. G. Ch. von Staudt (1847) started with such incidence axioms as: two points determine one straight line; three points, not on a straight line, determine a plane; two planes intersect in a straight line and so on. He then defined projectivity as a mapping preserving harmonicity. Taking three points on a line and constructing successively fourth harmonics, the line can be covered by a "net" which, intuitively, penetrates into any interval of the line. A projectivity leaving the given triple invariant leaves every point of the line. This, von Staudt said, proves the fundamental theorem of projective geometry, especially the theory of conics. Finally, von Staudt showed how to algebraize this projective geometry by geometric means.

Though von Staudt's performance was admirable, he still took the intuitive order relations in line and plane for granted without feeling the need for explicit formulations. Even worse: his process of building up harmonics in succession was essentially the same as that of building up commensurable ratios. His transition from the net to the whole line essentially meant that things proved for commensurable ratios were believed to be valid for all ratios. In 1847 von Staudt had not yet confronted himself with the problems with which Greek geometry had wrestled before Euclid. In 1873 F. Klein discovered the gap in von Staudt's reasoning. Though convinced of the possibility of founding projective geometry independently, he did not succeed in filling the gap.

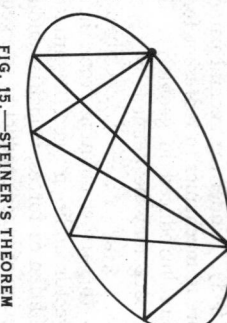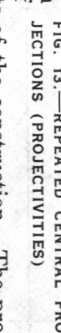

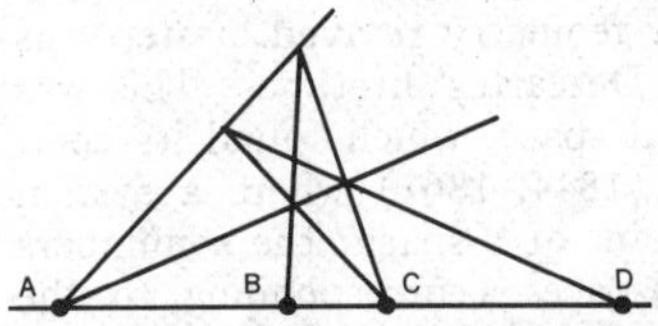

FIG. 14.—A HARMONIC QUADRUPLE OF POINTS

FIG. 15.—STEINER'S THEOREM

A final solution for founding projective geometry independently postulates: (1) the incidence axioms; (2) the cyclical order on the projective line and its preservation under projective mappings; and (3) some kind of Archimedean axiom, which permits the conclusion that a harmonic net penetrates every interval on the line (as the classical Archimedean axiom grants the possibility of fencing in incommensurable ratios by commensurable ratios).

This solution was possible after G. Cantor's (1871) and Dedekind's (1872) re-examination of the ancient problematic. About 1880 M. Pasch and O. Stolz recognized the import of the Archimedean axiom. In 1882 Pasch published the first rigorously deductive system of geometry in history. Through the Italian school of geometry, the formulation of the Archimedean axiom (still too Euclidean in Pasch's system) was better adapted to projective geometry.

A model of the projective plane in ordinary space is obtained by accepting a point O outside the plane and converting a point P of the plane into the line OP and a line l of the plane into the plane through O and l. The system of lines and planes through O, with its relations of incidence, then represents the system of points and lines of the projective plane. Analogously projective n-space may be defined as the system of vector subspaces of an $(n+1)$-dimensional vector space, every $(k+1)$-dimensional vector subspace corresponding to a k-dimensional projective subspace. By this artifice the algebraization of Euclidean geometry immediately applies to projective geometry. On a basis the points of projective n-space can be described by $n+1$ co-ordinates $\xi_0, \xi_1, \ldots, \xi_n$, where two $(n+1)$-tuples represent the same point if they are proportional.

NON-EUCLIDEAN GEOMETRY

Projective geometry toward the end of the 19th century had turned to fundamental research. Yet interest in the foundations of geometry had had an earlier modern awakening. It then centred around the postulate of parallel lines. After a great many attempts in history to prove this postulate, G. G. Saccheri (1667–1733) shifted the standpoint, by deliberately weighing alternative hypotheses and their consequences. Apparently, he was the first to do so, though possibly important work on parallel lines, prior to Euclid, may have been lost. Yet he was still strongly biased in favour of the Euclidean postulate. Carl Friedrich Gauss (1777–1855), who had very early seized upon the idea of non-Euclidean geometry (perhaps before the end of the 18th century), never published his discovery (fearing, he said in personal letters, the clamour of the Boeotians). His fear, however, was unfounded. When, in the early 1830s, N. I. Lobachevski (1792–1856) and J. Bolyai (1802–60) independently made and published the same discovery, nobody was disturbed. After Gauss's death there was gossip that he had pursued non-Euclidean geometry. But even Gauss's name was not strong enough an incentive to invite interest in non-Euclidean geometry.

If a line l is given and a point P is outside l, then in plane Euclidean geometry a line m through P turning around fails to meet l just once. In non-Euclidean geometry as presented by Gauss, Lobachevski and Bolyai, it is assumed that there is an infinity of nonintersecting lines, and among them a first one and a last one. Pursuing the consequences of this assumption they found no trouble in developing a geometry, and they did not hit upon contradictions. Gauss even considered testing the non-Euclidean hypothesis experimentally by surveying large triangles. In non-Euclidean space the sum of the angles of a triangle must be smaller than 180°.

Non-Euclidean geometry was reapproached (about 1868) by G. F. B. Riemann, Hermann von Helmholtz and E. Beltrami in another context. In 1870 Klein discovered a model of non-Euclidean geometry in Arthur Cayley's work. By this model the abstractness of non-Euclidean geometry was mitigated, and non-Euclidean geometry became familiar to mathematicians. However, the discipline was likely to be considered as a strange aberration, often confused with four-dimensional space and projective geometry.

The Cayley-Klein model of non-Euclidean geometry stems from the fact that projective geometry embraces both non-Euclidean and Euclidean geometry. Instead of postulating a line at infinity, a conic K is assigned in the projective plane. Inside K the projectivities of the plane look like the rigid motions in the Euclidean plane. They preserve straightness, and if some point inside K is fixed, they carry the other points around on circlelike curves. They allow a transfer of line segments and angles that obeys the classical Euclidean congruency theorems. But, by the restriction to the interior of K (fig. 16) there is an infinity of lines through P that do not intersect the given line l. (Of course distance and angle measure has to be redefined in this geometry; the line l has an infinite length, though in the model its Euclidean length is finite.)

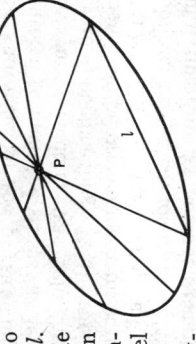

FIG. 16.—IN NON-EUCLIDEAN GEOMETRY THERE IS AN INFINITY OF PARALLEL LINES

Into the same frame Klein fitted another non-Euclidean plane geometry, overlooked by Gauss, Lobachevski and Bolyai, but discovered by Riemann (1854, published 1867). It arises if the real conic is replaced by an imaginary one. But another model of this geometry is still easier: Consider the model of the projective plane mentioned above, where in ordinary space lines through a point O are considered as points and planes through O as lines of a projective plane. Intersect this model with a spherical surface S (O being its centre). Then, to projective points correspond pairs of antipodic points of S, to projective lines great circles of S. In order to avoid ambiguities antipodic points are to be considered as one single point. Then on S through two different points there is one straight line (great circle), and two straight lines (great circles) always intersect in one point. Again the rigid motions in S preserve straightness (as conceived on S) and allow the transfer of line segments (great circle arcs) and of angles under the same congruency laws as in the Euclidean plane. But now the straight lines are closed and finite.

Apart from the identification of antipodes this is just spherical geometry as pursued on the terrestrial or celestial sphere. The analogous model of the first non-Euclidean geometry would use a sphere with imaginary radius.

The two non-Euclidean geometries are distinguished as hyperbolic (the first) and elliptic (the second). In hyperbolic geometry the sum of the angles of a triangle falls short of 180°; in elliptic geometry it exceeds 180°, the excess or defect appearing to be proportional to the area of the triangle.

In this exposition non-Euclidean geometry has been restricted to two dimensions. Spatial elliptic geometry requires a 3-dimensional sphere in 4-dimensional Euclidean space as a model. This has been and still is a difficulty if the intuitive function of a model is not really understood. A model and the thing it represents need not be alike in all aspects. The model of non-Euclidean 3-space in 4-dimensional space does not imply that a non-Euclidean universe actually needs a fourth dimension to be realized. It may be embedded in a higher dimensional space, but its shape does not depend on that embedding.

Even mathematicians felt uneasy as they did not fully grasp the logical status of a model. Klein's model of non-Euclidean geometry, they said, proved nothing. It was constructed in the frame of projective geometry which in turn depended on Euclidean geometry, the mother of all geometries. Klein replied that he had founded projective geometry independently of Euclidean geometry, though his claim was not much better established than von Staudt's had been. People believed that the gap only could be filled in Euclidean geometry; though even in Euclidean geometry it remained unfilled as long as Eudoxus' solution was ignored. But the arguments in this discussion were not to the point. It does not matter whether or not projective geometry depends on Euclidean geometry (though in itself this is an important question). By constructing a model of non-Euclidean geometry in projective geometry (and hence by means of Euclidean geometry) it had been proved that non-Euclidean geometry was as consistent as the Euclidean version. Non-Euclidean geometry had been shown to be noncontradictory unless there were a contradiction in Euclidean geometry. This fact had been exactly proved, and no more could be done by mathematics. But this was a secret to be unveiled later when the logical status of geometry became clear.

PHILOSOPHICAL ASPECTS

History indicates that the philosophical view on geometry had not essentially changed since antiquity. In the realm of knowledge geometry was a peculiar problem. It was reasoned that all knowledge of the physical universe is mere opinion; it had entered through the senses, liable to error, and to be watched by reason. Geometry was held the only exception. Geometrical truth, though dealing with the concrete world and no mere abstractions, can be proved mathematically, and was seen as beyond any doubt. Euclid's long-lasting influence is witnessed by a host of philosophers, theologians, historians, lawyers and physicians who, imitating Euclid's method, attempted to prove their theories *more geometrico* (in the way of geometry). Kant, wondering how we can construct *more geometrico*, with closed eyes as it were, things that prove true as soon as we look into real space, asked the question: How are synthetic judgments a priori possible? He did not doubt that there were synthetic judgments a priori. Geometric judgments *are* synthetic according to Kant; they bring together notions that do not depend on each other by mere analysis. And, he said, they are a priori (earlier to sensual experience) because otherwise they would not be sure.

It does not matter here how Kant answered his question. Philosophical discussions on space and geometry in the 19th century were heavily influenced by Kant's problem and solution. His starting point was never seriously questioned.

Pasch's first rigorous deductive system of (projective) geometry undertook to avoid any surreptitious use of intuition and he scrupulously fulfilled his program: "Whenever geometry has to be really deductive, the process of inferring must be independent of the *meaning* of the geometrical notions as well as of the figures. The only things that matter are the *relations* between the geometrical notions, such as (have been) established in the used theorems and definitions."

Since antiquity an axiom had been considered an evident truth that neither could nor should be proved. Mostly this meant even that axioms need not be formulated. Most people spoke of axioms and never mentioned any one explicitly. If someone pointed out a gap in a geometrical proof, he was likely to be told that this was just an axiom. This was one of the usual contexts of the word "axiom." From Pasch mathematicians learned how to formulate postulates or axioms. They also learned that a complete axiomatic system of geometry must be much more involved than Euclid's, and that there were more axioms than the postulate of parallel lines worthy of special attention. In the Italian school projective planes were discovered where the axioms of order and the Archimedean axiom cannot be satisfied.

The final solution of the philosophical dilemma on geometry was given by David Hilbert in 1899. He starts his *Grundlagen der Geometrie* after a short introduction with the words: "Wir denken uns ..."—"we imagine three kinds of things ... called points ... called lines ... called planes ... we imagine points, lines, and planes in some relations ... called lying on, between, parallel, congruent ...," and then he enumerates the "axioms" to be fulfilled by things and relations imagined.

With "Wir denken uns" the bond with reality is cut. Geometry has become pure mathematics. The question of whether and how to apply it to reality is the same in geometry as it is in other branches of mathematics. Axioms are not evident truth. They are no truth at all in the usual sense.

Hilbert does not define what points, lines, planes are, or what "lying on," "between," "parallel" and "congruent" mean. These undefined notions are presented implicitly through the set of axioms of order." And when stating the axioms he says, "The following axioms define the notion of order." In introducing the axioms he states, "The following axioms define the set of axioms of order." And when stating the axioms "The following axioms define the notion of congruency or motion."

The idea that fundamental notions are defined implicitly by the axioms was the background of Pasch's work too, though he did not say so. But, whereas Pasch still believed that geometry deals with real space and anxiously stuck to what analysis may derive from sense data, in Hilbert's approach geometry was removed from sensory space. It should be remarked that this modern idea on the logical status of geometry occurred a few years earlier to G. Fano, and that it was pronounced with even more emphasis by M. Pieri and A. Padoa one year after Hilbert.

The clean cut between mathematics and phenomenalistic sciences became the paradigm of a new methodology. Through Einstein's booklet of 1916, *Über die spezielle und allgemeine Relativitäts-theorie*, this doctrine made its way in the lobbies of science and philosophy. A few sentences coined by Einstein in his 1921 lecture "Geometrie und Erfahrung" have grown classical: "As far as the mathematical theorems refer to reality, they are not sure, and as far as they are sure, they do not refer to reality. . . . The progress entailed by axiomatics consists in the clean-cut separation of the logical form and the realistic and intuitive contents. . . . The axioms are voluntary creations of human mind. . . . To this interpretation of geometry I attach great importance for should I not have been acquainted with it, I would never have been able to develop the theory of relativity."

THE AXIOMATIC METHOD

The idea on the logical status of geometry is not the only result of Hilbert's *Grundlagen*, and it is not its most important one. For the axiomatic method, which has pervaded mathematics in the 20th century, Hilbert's work was the first specimen, and a manual, in which the method is not explained *expressis verbis*, shows it instead by splendid examples.

Whoever proposes an axiomatic system has to show that it is consistent, *i.e.*, it does not involve contradictions. In most cases consistency cannot be proved directly. It is done by exhibiting a so-called model that fulfills the axioms. Where should a model of the axiomatic system of points, lines, circles and so on be sought? Physical nature or a pre-existent realm of Platonic ideas are no more acceptable as such. Hilbert found his models of geometry in algebra, using Descartes' procedure. Since antiquity the relation between geometry and algebra had been inverted. Greek mathematicians were endeavouring to justify algebra by geometrization; in modern mathematics geometry is justified by algebraization. Another concern in axiomatics is to know whether the different axioms are logically independent (from each other), and what is the exact scope of any one of them. Hilbert showed how to drop axioms or to replace them by alternatives, and to look for the consequences these changes might cause in suitable models.

In this course of thought he resumed the ancient problem of the theory of ratio and proportionality. He succeeded in getting rid of such notions and assumptions of topological character (to use modern terminology) as order and Archimedean axiom. He simply defined proportionality by means of the fundamental theorem which was Eudoxus' first goal. By his definition (fig. 17) OA:OA' = OB:OB' if and only if AB∥A'B'. Of course, a few things must be proved now. First of all it must be proved that OA:OA' = OB:OB' and OB:OB' = OC:OC' imply that OA:OA' = OC:OC', a fundamental property of the equality relation. In other words, it must be proved that (fig. 18) if AB∥A'B' and BC∥B'C', then AC∥A'C'. This, however, is nothing but a special case of Desargues' theorem with one line at infinity.

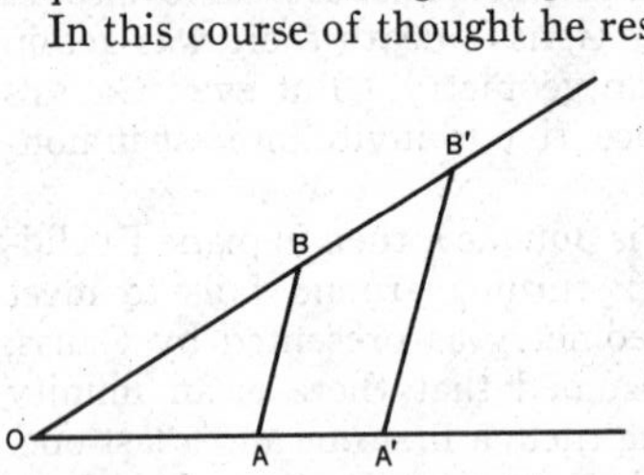

Another thing to be proved (fig. 19) is that OA:OA' = OB:OB' implies that OB:OB' = OA':OA. To this end OB must be transferred to the line OA (yielding

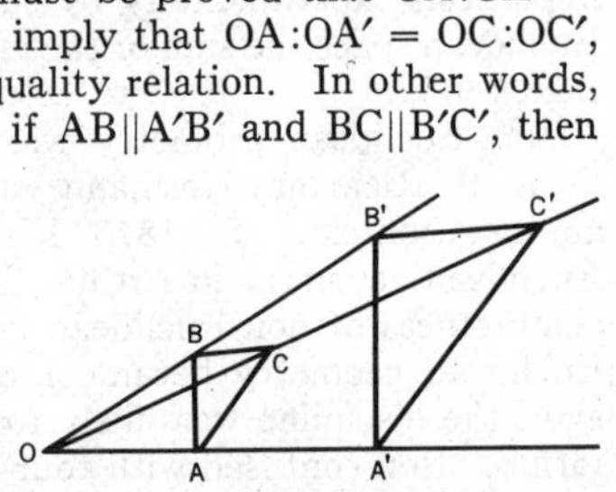

FIG. 17.—PROPORTIONALITY

FIG. 18.—A PROPERTY OF PROPORTIONALITY

OB_0), and OA' must be transferred to the line OB (yielding OA_0'). Then the proportion to be proved then runs $OA:OB_0 = OA_0':OB'$, which by definition means $AA_0' \| B_0B'$. In other words, it must be proved that, if $AB \| A'B'$ and $B_0B \| A'A_0'$, then $AB_0 \| AA_0'$. This, however, is nothing but a special case of Pappus' theorem, known to geometry since about A.D. 340.

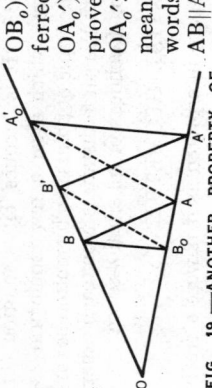

FIG. 19.—ANOTHER PROPERTY OF PROPORTIONALITY

Instead of the Archimedean axiom Desargues' and Pappus' theorems can be used as foundations of the theory of ratio and proportionality. (Actually Desargues' can still be derived from Pappus'.) This is an idea of surprising simplicity, and it may be asked why it did not occur to Greek mathematicians. In fact, it cannot be asserted that it never arose in Greek thinking. But, if it arose, it was apparently rejected, and we even know why, thanks to a remark of Aristotle's.

Greek geometricians probably would not have been satisfied with this theory of ratio and proportionality which applies only to line elements instead of to all kinds of magnitudes. But Hilbert was allowed to stop here, for meanwhile the rest of the problem had been solved by Descartes. Indeed, after some line segment OE is assigned as a unit, the product OC of two line segments OA and OB can be defined by means of the proportion $OC:OA = OB: OE$, and by this geometry can be algebraized (the sum of line segments being unproblematic). But in algebraization all other geometrical magnitudes, such as areas and volumes, are comprehended, and no new theory of ratio is required to deal with them.

Looking to the proportion which defines the product, note that Pappus' theorem actually enforces the commutativity of multiplication, i.e., the law $ab = ba$. Dropping Pappus' theorem as an axiom, geometry can still be algebraized, though over a noncommutative field (see *The Algebraic Approach*, above). Non-Pappian geometries with their algebraic matches, the noncommutative fields, have extensively been studied in modern geometry and algebra.

The algebraic equivalent of Desargues' theorem is the associativity of multiplication, i.e., the law $(ab)c = a(bc)$. The existence of non-Desarguean geometries has been shown by an example of Hilbert's. But there is a still weaker geometrical theorem than Desargues', the theorem of harmonicity. In 1933 Ruth Moufang discovered that its algebraic equivalent is some kind of weak associativity, called alternativity, i.e., $a(ab) = (aa)b$, $(ab)a = a(ba)$, $a(bb) = (ab)b$. By this discovery geometry gave algebra a new notion of major importance.

The fundamental geometric properties (harmonic, Desarguean and Pappian) are matched by the fundamental algebraic properties of multiplication (alternative, associative and commutative). It is remarkable that these properties are just realized by the most important algebraical systems, the Hurwitz algebras, which generalize complex numbers, yet preserving the law $|ab| = |a| \, |b|$, where

$$|a| = \sqrt{a_1^2 + a_2^2}$$

is the norm of the complex number $a = a_1 + ia_2$. It appears that the only Hurwitz algebras are those of the real numbers, the complex numbers, the quaternions (W. R. Hamilton, 1845) and the octaves (J. Graves, 1829; A. Cayley, c. 1875), with 1, 2, 4 and 8 basis units respectively. Real and complex numbers are commutative; quaternions are still associative; octaves are alternative. The outstanding examples of Pappian, Desarguean and harmonic geometries are constructed over these algebras.

GEOMETRICAL TRANSFORMATIONS

It has been mentioned that geometrical transformations, though a quite natural tool, were rejected by official Greek mathematics, maybe because they were reckoned to belong to mechanics. Though this argument was refuted long ago, it is still used to oppose teaching geometrical transformations at the secondary level. Geometrical transformations belong to mechanics as little as functions do. Of course functions are used in mechanics and can be interpreted in a mechanical sense, and so can transformations.

The most perspicuous geometrical transformation (or mapping) is symmetry. Stone Age decorations witness that it was known to early mankind. Symmetry with respect to a plane maps any point of space upon its mirror image. Symmetry with respect to a straight line turns it around this line as an axis over an angle of 180°. Symmetry with respect to a point A maps every point X into the point X' with the property that A is the midpoint of XX'.

In the plane (fig. 20), if first the symmetry with respect to l and then that with respect to m ($\|l$) is applied, any point $X(A, B)$ is first mapped upon its mirror image $X'(A', B')$ with respect to l, and then X' upon its mirror image $X''(A'', B'')$ with respect to m. All the line segments XX'' are equal and parallel. The resulting mapping is a translation. If, however, l and m intersect in O (fig. 21), then the resulting mapping is a rotation around O.

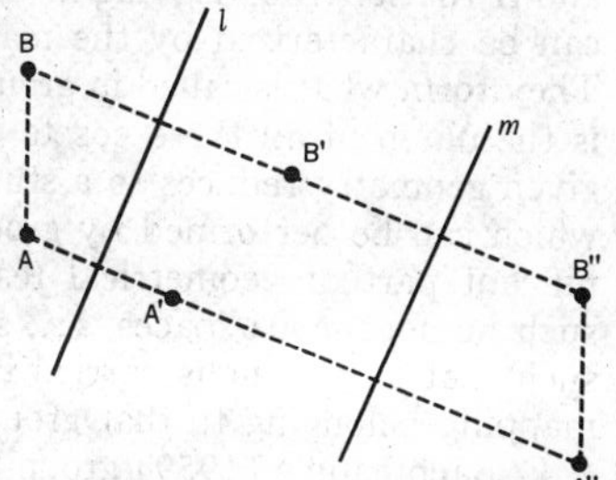

FIG. 20.—SYMMETRIES ON PARALLEL LINES

Notice that another translation or rotation is obtained if the two symmetries are interchanged.

If two translations are applied successively, the result is a translation. Two rotations generally produce a rotation unless the rotation angles are opposite; then a translation results. Symmetries, translations and rotations all are mappings of the plane that conserve distance, hence the rigid structure of the plane.

There are mappings of the plane which multiply all distances by the same factor, e.g., the similitude mapping X upon X' such that all lines XX' go through a fixed point O and X divides OX' in a fixed ratio. These mappings still preserve angles. Parallel projections of one plane upon another preserve parallelism, but generally change angles. Projectivities of projective planes preserve straightness, but not parallelism.

When two mappings are performed, first f and then g, the re-

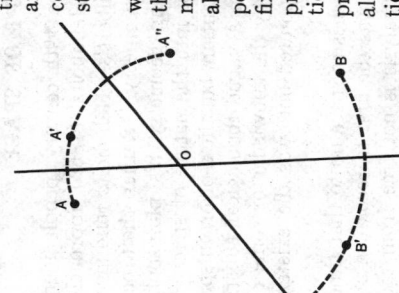

FIG. 21.—SYMMETRIES ON INTERSECTING LINES

sulting mapping is indicated by gf. To any mapping f of the examples given the inverse mapping (called f^{-1}) can be constructed with the property that (for every X,Y) if f maps X upon Y, then f^{-1} just maps Y upon X. A trivial case is the identity mapping i that carries every point into itself. Both ff^{-1} and $f^{-1}f$ are the identity mapping, but generally fg and gf differ from each other.

Examples like these lead to the notion of group (of mappings). A group of G is defined if in the set G a product fg is specified for any couple of elements of G such that: for any f,g,h of G, fg belongs to G and $(fg)h = f(gh)$; there is an (identity) i in G such that for any f in G, $fi = if = f$, and for any f in G there is one f^{-1} in G such that $ff^{-1} = f^{-1}f = i$.

The mappings of the plane conserving distance form such a group, as do the mappings preserving the ratios of distances, the mappings preserving parallelism, the mappings of the projective plane preserving straightness (the projectivities), the projectivities leaving invariant the conic K of fig. 15 or (equivalently) the non-Euclidean distance.

S. Lie and Klein were the first to stress the import of the notion of group in geometry. A geometry is a relational system (e.g., a system of points and lines with the relation of incidence). The mappings of the system which preserve these relations form a group, the group of this geometry. In order to know whether some relation depends on some other, it is useful to determine if the mappings preserving the first one also preserve the other one. Thus, through group theory it can be decided to which kind of geometry some notion belongs, and how different geometries are related to each other. The relationship between the non-Euclidean geometries and projective geometry was settled in this way, and a good many other geometries, discovered in the 19th century, were better understood when they were fitted into projective geometry by group theory methods. This is, in a few words, the purport of Klein's *"Erlanger Programm."*

In the 20th century Elie Cartan stressed the group theory aspect even more. If G is the group of some classical geometry and H the subgroup leaving invariant a point X_0, then any point X can be characterized by the mappings of G carrying X_0 into X. They form what is called in group theory a coset of H in G, and G is the union of all these cosets: By this device the study of this given geometry reduces to a study of the set of cosets of H in G, which can be performed by group theory methods alone. A significant part of geometrical research has since been devoted to such homogeneous spaces, *i.e.*, spaces having an associated group such that any point is carried into any other point by a suitable mapping belonging to that group.

F. Bachmann's (1959) group-theory approach to foundations of geometry can be sketched by the example of plane geometry: Let P and l mean not only a point and a line, but also the symmetries with respect to them. Then, in the sense of group theory, $PP = i$ and $ll = i$. Then clearly $Pl = lP$ means the belonging of P to l, and $l_1 l_2 = l_2 l_1$ means the orthogonality of the lines l_1 and l_2 and so on. In this language of group theory, involved relations and especially fundamental axioms can be formulated.

THE CONCEPT OF SPACE

Throughout the period of the 19th century, people identified foundations of geometry with Helmholtz' (1868) approach that finally was overshadowed by Hilbert's. Helmholtz renounced the conventional attitude toward geometry. Rather than being a logical analysis of some existing geometry his philosophically minded attempt aims at a quest into the nature of space. To a certain degree Helmholtz was Kantian, but the a priori in space he would grant, was no more than a vague topological substratum which is organized a posteriori by the knowledge of some experimental "fact." This fact, he pointed out, was the existence of freely movable rigid bodies.

Indeed, all traditional approaches to space up to that time bore this feature, though Helmholtz was the first to recognize and analyze it mathematically. His analysis is not free from tacit assumptions and arbitrary statements. It is as rigorous as it could have been at that time, though his style, compared with today's, is vague and often admits of alternative interpretations.

Actually, to Helmholtz the whole of space was a rigid body. In modern terminology this means that it is a metric space, *i.e.*, a space in which distance is numerically defined for pairs of points, and that the distance-preserving mappings of space on itself are considered as what should be called motions. These motions form a group. Though Helmholtz did not mention (presumably did not know) the notion of group, he extensively used group theory notions and methods, anticipating Klein and Lie.

The free mobility of rigid bodies or rather of space itself, according to Helmholtz, means: Any point is carried into any other by some motion. If, however, one point P_0 is fixed, then two points at the same distance of P_0 can still be carried into each other by some motion. If two points P_0 and P_1 are fixed, then the same is true of any pair of points at the same distance of both P_0 and P_1. Finally, if three points in a general situation are fixed, no continuous motion is possible. (The last assumption, which means confined rather than free mobility, probably aimed at a restriction of the dimension of space; it is redundant, because this restriction was urged before by topology.)

For n-dimensional space free mobility, according to Helmholtz, goes as far as fixing $n - 1$ points, whereas immobility is reached after an nth point has been fixed. Helmholtz claimed that the only spaces with this property are essentially the classical Euclidean and non-Euclidean spaces, but in 1890 Lie showed that Helmholtz' methods were mathematically unsatisfactory. He improved Helmholtz' proofs, but did not remove differentiability assumptions, which are unnatural to modern taste, and represent a major obstacle. The final formulation and solution of Helmholtz' problem was not found until 1953. It is Jacques Tits's solution (cf. H. Freudenthal, bibliography) which after a few topological assumptions only urges: If some triple of points can by motion be carried into any other triple with the same distances from each other, then space is Euclidean or non-Euclidean or spherical n-space.

DIFFERENTIAL GEOMETRY

The classical concept of space interpreted as if it were a freely movable rigid body had been renounced by Riemann (1854, published 1867) even before it was disclosed by Helmholtz. Riemann, espousing J. F. Herbart's rather than Kant's philosophy, did not accept a general "fact" such as that of rigid bodies to organize the topological substratum into space. Instead he displayed a "hypothesis," the metric structure of space, not subjected to Helmholtz' restrictions, but as general as could be imagined in that time. The metric was supposed to be Euclidean up to the first approximation, with higher-order deviations from Euclidicity, which might vary from point to point.

This had been Gauss's idea earlier when he studied the differential geometry of curved surfaces. Riemann ventured to extend it to space. In order to make things clear here it will be provisionally restricted to the two-dimensional case. Any curved surface is flat in first approximation, *i.e.*, if replaced by its tangent plane in the neighbourhood of any one of its points. In the next approximation it shows deviations from flatness, slight deviations where curvature is small and more significant deviations where curvature is stronger. But, to discover curvature, the outside view is not compulsory. A two-dimensional being can discover its curvature and determine it numerically while performing measurements upon the surface. Interpreting the shortest curves between any pair of points as straight, and surveying triangles, a two-dimensional being will state deviations from the Euclidean structure, such as excessive or defective totals of angles, and defective or excessive hypotenuses (as compared with those calculated according to the Pythagorean theorem). He will explain these deviations, which might vary from point to point, as caused by a positive or negative curvature of the surface he is on, and he will be able to calculate the curvature numerically.

The same train of thought applies in three dimensions. As three-dimensional beings inhabiting a three-dimensional universe men can get information on its curvature by surveying their neighbourhood in the universe, as has been done by 20th-century astronomers. With regard to the terrestrial surface men are happier than two-dimensional beings living on it. They can learn about its curvature also from outside; they can see ships vanish behind the horizon's edge. But they cannot put their heads out of the universe to see its curvature. This inside view of space, though the quintessence of Riemann's theory, was barely considered in the confused discussions of the 19th century, but in the theory of relativity it has been justified in the most splendid way. The disregard paid to Riemann's theory in the 19th century resulted partly from Helmholtz' erroneous criticism. Helmholtz argued that surveying a three-dimensional space requires freely movable rigid bodies as measuring tools. If this were true, Riemann would have derived no more than Helmholtz' theory yields in a more satisfactory way. Riemann's procedure, however, requires freely movable rigid rods only; as it were, one-dimensional rigid bodies. Unless two-dimensional disks are admitted as tools, Riemann's spaces are much more general than Helmholtz'.

In the 20th century Riemann's theory was supplemented by the notion of parallel transport of vectors in a curved space (Tullio Levi-Civita, 1917; Jan G. Schouten, 1918). What this means will again be explained here on a surface, particularly on the terrestrial surface.

A freely suspended pendulum changes its oscillation plane after a while. This is L. Foucault's famous (1851) experiment that verifies the rotation of the earth. Actually the pendulum tends to preserve its oscillation plane in space. Thus, if the earth did not turn, nothing should happen. To explain this phenomenon, replace the Foucault pendulum by a point oscillating in a tangential plane of the earth. As long as this plane rests, the velocity vector of

GEOMETRY, NON-EUCLIDEAN

the oscillation does not change. As soon as the plane is turned around, this vector is forced to change. What happens is that it looses its component orthogonal on the plane. In the same way a being living on a curved surface is transporting his vectors over the surface by having them loose their components orthogonally on the surface. This vector transport is an inner feature of the surface, independent of its embedding, and so it can be defined in curved space too.

In the Foucault case, if a vector is moved around with the moving sphere along a parallel circle of the underlying fixed sphere, what happens can be shown quantitatively by constructing the tangential cone of the sphere along the parallel circle and spreading it upon a plane (see fig. 22; along the two straight lines the cone was cut up; in space they are to be identified). Parallel transport along the parallel circle brings the vector back to A, but then it has undergone a turn equal to the angle of the spread cone.

This is a general feature of parallel vector transport in curved spaces. A vector moved along a closed path may appear to have changed, and the numerical value of this change depends on the value of curvature of the space.

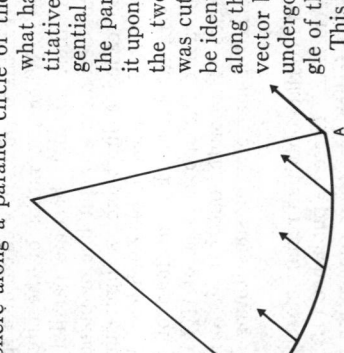

FIG. 22.—TANGENTIAL CONE OF A SPHERE (SPREAD ON A PLANE)

TOPOLOGY

Topology is the youngest branch of geometry but, nevertheless, its most sophisticated. In spite of important but isolated earlier results, its continuous development did not start until about 1911, when L. E. J. Brouwer contributed general methods to topology. Since then it has developed vehemently, closely connected to modern algebra. Here are a few very elementary examples to show what topology means.

Rigidity is the main characteristic of the shapes of elementary geometry. All that Euclid could tell about straight lines, circles, spheres, cones, conics and so on is lost under the slightest deformation of such figures. More arbitrary curves and surfaces are studied in differential geometry. If a curve is smooth enough, its curvature in any point is an important notion to differential geometry. The completely arbitrary curve, however, is an object of topology, and is studied with respect to its roughest intuitive properties. In topology the circumference of a circle is not distinguished from that of an ellipse, of a square or of the leaf of a plant. But all of them are topologically different from the curve suggested by the symbol 8. The capital letters D and O are topologically equivalent (closed simple curves); C, I, J, L, M, N, S, U, V, W and Z are topologically equivalent in the same class (simple arcs); E, F and G do not differ essentially from each other, and among the remaining capital letters there are still a few different types.

The simple arc does not cut the plane. A simple closed curve cuts the plane into exactly two parts. These theorems, though intuitively evident, require sophisticated methods to be proved, and were first proved by Camille Jordan in 1887.

Spheres and potatoes are topologically equivalent. But they are different from a tire or ring (called a torus in topology). Indeed, a spherelike surface is cut into two pieces by any simple closed curve on it. On a ringlike surface, however, simple closed curves which do not cut the surface easily can be drawn. The surface of a ladder is still more involved, becoming more involved with each additional rung. This kind of surface also cuts space (first proved by Brouwer, 1912).

A key theorem of Brouwer's runs in intuitive terms as follows: If a wooden sphere is clothed in thin rubber, then it is impossible to uncover any point of the wooden sphere by deforming the rubber sphere, even if folding is allowed. (Of course, it is forbidden to tear the rubber; deformations should preserve the connection of the parts.)

Two closed curves in space can be located free from each other, or they can be interlaced as the links of a chain. These are topological differences. A simple closed curve can be knotted or not. It is difficult to prove that the clover knot (fig. 23) is topologically different from its mirror image. There are infinitely many topologically different knots, but to know whether two of them are equivalent or not is difficult.

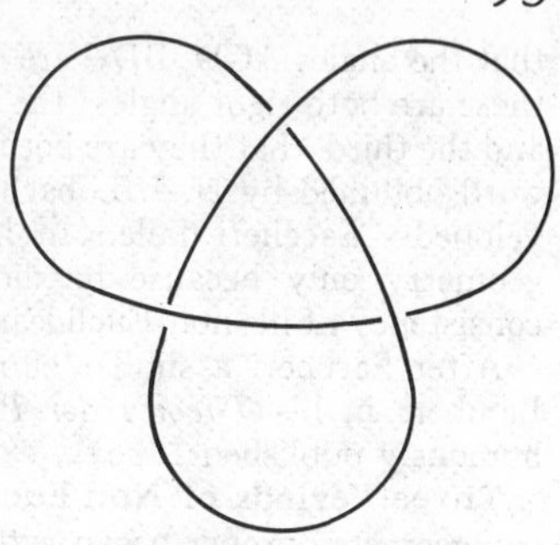

The classifying tool of topology is the so-called topological mapping, which, by definition, is univalent and continuous in both directions. Topology studies those properties which are preserved under these mappings.

See also references under "Geometry" in the Index.

BIBLIOGRAPHY.—E. Artin, *Geometric Algebra* (1957); F. Bachmann, *Aufbau der Geometrie aus dem Spiegelungsbegriff* (1959); R. Baer, *Linear Algebra and Projective Geometry* (1952); H. Freudenthal, "Neuere Fassungen des Riemann-Helmholtz-Lieschen Raumproblems," *Mathemat. Zeitschrift*, 63, 374-405 (1956); T. L. Heath, *The Thirteen Books of Euclid's Elements*, i-iii (1926); D. Hilbert, *Grundlagen der Geometrie* (1899 and 1956); F. Klein, *Vorlesungen über die Entwicklung der Mathematik im 19. Jahrhundert*, i-ii (1926-1927); O. Neugebauer, *Vorlesungen über Geschichte der antiken mathematischen Wissenschaften* (1934); M. Pasch, *Vorlesungen über neuere Geometrie* (1882, 1912); rev. by M. Pasch and M. Dehn (1926); G. Pickert, *Projektive Ebenen* (1955); G. F. B. Riemann, *Über die Hypothesen, welche der Geometrie zu Grunde liegen*, 3rd ed. (1923); O. Schreier and E. Sperner, *Introduction to Modern Algebra and Matrix Theory* (1955); K. G. Ch. von Staudt, *Geometrie der Lage* (1847); O. Veblen and J. W. Young, *Projective Geometry I and II* (1910, 1918); B. L. van der Waerden, *Science Awakening* (1954); H. Weyl, *Raum, Zeit, Materie, Vorlesungen über allgemeine Relativitätstheorie* (1921), *Mathematische Analyse des Raumproblems* (1923).
(H. FR.)

FIG. 23.—CLOVER KNOT

GEOMETRY, NON-EUCLIDEAN. A non-Euclidean geometry is one that is based on postulates other than those offered by Euclid; such geometries are typified by their rejection of Euclid's postulate of parallels.

History.—It was from endeavours to improve the theory of parallels that non-Euclidean geometry arose; and though it has acquired a far wider scope, its historical origin remains instructive and interesting. Euclid's "axiom of parallels" appears as postulate v to the first book of his *Elements*, and is stated thus, "And that, if a straight line falling on two straight lines make the angles, internal and on the same side, less than two right angles, the two straight lines, being produced indefinitely, meet on the side on which are the angles less than two right angles."

To Euclid's successors this had signally failed to appear self-evident, and had failed equally to appear indemonstrable. Without the use of the postulate its converse is proved in Euclid's 17th proposition, and it was hoped that by further efforts the postulate itself could be also proved. First came the discovery of equivalent axioms; Christopher Clavius in 1574 deduced the axiom from the assumption that a line whose points are all equidistant from a straight line is itself straight. John Wallis in 1663 showed that the postulate follows from the possibility of similar triangles on different scales. Giovanni Girolamo Saccheri (1733) showed that it is sufficient to have a single triangle in which the sum of the angles is two right angles. Other equivalent forms may be obtained, but none shows any essential superiority to Euclid's.

A new method that proved immensely fruitful, though it failed to lead to the desired goal, was invented by Saccheri in a work entitled *Euclides ab omni naevo vindicatus* (1733). If the postulate of parallels is involved in Euclid's other assumptions, contradictions must emerge when it is denied while the others are maintained. This led Saccheri to attempt a *reductio ad absurdum* in which he mistakenly believed himself to have succeeded. What is interesting is not his fallacious conclusion but the non-Euclidean results he obtained in the process. Saccheri distinguished three hypotheses (corresponding to what are now known as Euclidean or parabolic, elliptic and hyperbolic geometry), and proved that some one of the three must be universally valid. His three hypotheses were thus obtained: equal perpendiculars AC, BD are drawn from a straight line AB, and C, D are joined. It is shown that the angles ACD, BDC are equal. The first hypothesis is that these are both right angles; the second, that they are both obtuse; and the third, that they are both acute. Many of the results afterward obtained by N. I. Lobachevski and J. Bolyai were here developed, only because he did not perceive the possible self-consistency of his non-Euclidean hypotheses.

After Saccheri a similar effort was made by Johann Heinrich Lambert in his *Theorie der Parallellinien* (written 1766; posthumously published 1786).

Three Periods of Non-Euclidean Geometry.—Non-Euclidean geometry proper began with Carl Friedrich Gauss. He probably was the first to recognize that the postulate of parallels is possibly false, and should be empirically tested by measuring the angles of large triangles. The history of non-Euclidean geometry was aptly divided by Felix Klein into three very distinct periods. The first—that of Gauss, Lobachevski and Bolyai—was characterized by its synthetic method and by its close relation to Euclid. The attempt at indirect proof of the disputed postulate would seem to have been the source of these three men's discoveries; but when the postulate had been denied, they found that the results, instead of showing contradictions, were just as self-consistent as Euclid's. They inferred that the postulate, if at all defensible, can only be verified by observations and measurements. Only one kind of non-Euclidean space was known to them, that now called hyperbolic. The second period was analytical, and was characterized by a close relation to the theory of surfaces. It began with G. F. B. Riemann's inaugural dissertation that regarded space as a particular case of a manifold (*see* MANIFOLDS; RIEMANNIAN GEOMETRY); but the characteristic standpoint of the period was chiefly emphasized by Eugenio Beltrami. The conception of measure of curvature was extended by Riemann from surfaces to spaces, and a new kind of space, finite but unbounded (corresponding to the second hypothesis of Saccheri and Lambert), was shown to be possible. As opposed to the purely metrical second period, the third period was essentially projective in its method. It began with Arthur Cayley, who showed that metrical properties are projective properties relative to a certain fundamental quadric, and that different geometries arise according to whether this quadric is real, imaginary or degenerate. Klein, to whom the development of Cayley's work is due, showed further that there are two forms of Riemann's space, called by him the elliptic and the spherical. Finally, it was shown by Sophus Lie that if figures are to be freely movable throughout all space in ∞^6 ways no three-dimensional spaces other than the above are possible.

Gauss.—Gauss published nothing on the theory of parallels, and it was not generally known until after his death that he had interested himself in that theory from a very early date. In 1799 he announced that Euclidean geometry would follow from the assumption that a triangle can be drawn greater than any given triangle. In 1830 he announced his conviction that geometry is not an a priori science; in the following year he explained that non-Euclidean geometry is free from contradictions, and that, in this system, the angles of a triangle diminish without limit when all the sides are increased. He also gave for the circumference of a circle of radius *r* the formula $\pi k(e^{r/k} - e^{-r/k})$, where *k* is a constant depending upon the nature of the space. In 1832, in reply to the receipt of Bolyai's *Appendix*, he gave an elegant proof that the amount by which the sum of the angles of a triangle falls short of two right angles is proportional to the area of the triangle. From these and a few other remarks it appears that Gauss possessed the foundations of hyperbolic geometry, which he was probably the first to regard as perhaps true.

Lobachevski.—The first to publish a non-Euclidean geometry (1829) was Nikolai Ivanovich Lobachevski, professor of mathematics in the new university at Kazan, Russia. In the place of the disputed postulate he put the following: "All straight lines which, in a plane, radiate from a given point, can, with respect to any other straight line in the same plane, be divided into two classes, the intersecting and the non-intersecting. The boundary line of the one and the other class is called parallel to the given line." It follows that there are two parallels to the given line through any point, each meeting the line at infinity, like a Euclidean parallel. Hence a line has two distinct points at infinity, and not one only as in ordinary geometry. The two parallels to a line through a point make equal acute angles with the perpendicular to the line through the point. If p is the length of the perpendicular, either of these angles is denoted by $\Pi(p)$. The determination of $\Pi(p)$ is the chief problem; it appears finally that, with a suitable choice of the unit of length, $\tan \frac{1}{2}\Pi(p) = e^{-p}$.

Before obtaining this result it is shown that spherical trigonometry is unchanged, and that the normals to a circle or a sphere still pass through its centre. When the radius of the circle or sphere becomes infinite all these normals become parallel, but the circle or sphere does not become a straight line or plane. It becomes what Lobachevski called a limit-line or limit-surface. The geometry on such a surface is shown to be Euclidean, limit-lines replacing Euclidean straight lines. By the help of these propositions Lobachevski obtained the above value of $\Pi(p)$, and thence the solution of triangles. He pointed out that his formulas result from those of spherical trigonometry by substituting ia, ib, ic for the sides a, b, c.

Bolyai.—John Bolyai, a Hungarian, obtained results closely corresponding to those of Lobachevski. These he published (1831) in an appendix to a work by his father, but their conception dates from 1823. The work reveals a profounder appreciation of the importance of the new ideas, but otherwise differs little from Lobachevski's. Both men pointed out that Euclidean geometry is a limiting case of their own more general system, that the geometry of very small spaces is always approximately Euclidean, that no a priori grounds exist for a decision, and that observation can only give an approximate answer. Bolyai gave also a geometrical construction in hyperbolic space for the quadrature of the circle, and showed that the area of the greatest possible triangle that has all its sides parallel and all its angles zero is πi^2, where i is what should now be called the space-constant.

Riemann.—The works of Lobachevski and Bolyai, though known and valued by Gauss, remained obscure and ineffective until, in 1866, they were translated into French by J. Hoüel. But at this time Riemann's dissertation, *Über die Hypothesen, welche der Geometrie zu Grunde liegen*, was already about to be published. In this work Riemann, without any knowledge of his predecessors in the same field, inaugurated a far more profound discussion, based on a far more general standpoint; and by its (posthumous) publication in 1867 the attention of mathematicians and philosophers was at last secured.

Riemann's work contains two fundamental conceptions, that of a manifold and that of the measure of curvature of a continuous manifold possessed of what he called flatness in the smallest parts. There are four points in which this profound and epoch-making work is open to criticism or development—(1) the idea of a manifold requires more precise determination; (2) the introduction of co-ordinates is entirely unexplained and the requisite presuppositions are unanalyzed; (3) the assumption that ds is the square root of a quadratic function of dx_1, dx_2,... is arbitrary; (4) the idea of superposition, or congruence, is not adequately analyzed. The modern solution of these difficulties is properly considered in connection with the general subject of the axioms of geometry.

Beltrami.—The only other writer of importance in the second period was Beltrami, by whom Riemann's work was brought into connection with that of Lobachevski and Bolyai. He gave a convenient Euclidean interpretation of hyperbolic plane geometry and his results will be stated at some length. His paper (1868) *Saggio di interpretazione della geometria non-euclidea* shows that Lobachevski's plane geometry holds in Euclidean geometry on surfaces of constant negative curvature, straight lines being replaced by geodesics. Such surfaces allow a conformal representation (*see* ANALYSIS, COMPLEX) on a plane, by which geodesics are represented by straight lines. Hence if the Cartesian co-ordinates of corresponding points on the plane are taken as co-ordinates on the surface, the geodesics must have linear equations.

Transition to the Projective Method.—The *Saggio* gives a Euclidean interpretation confined to two dimensions. But a consideration of the auxiliary plane suggests a different interpretation that may be extended to any number of dimensions. If, instead of referring to the pseudosphere, distance and angle are merely defined in the Euclidean plane as those functions of the co-ordinates that gave distance and angle on the pseudosphere, the geometry of the plane becomes Lobachevski's. All the points of the limiting circle are now at infinity, and points beyond it are imaginary. If the circle is given an imaginary radius the geometry on the plane becomes elliptic. Replacing the circle by a sphere leads to an analogous representation for three dimensions. Instead of a circle or sphere any conic or quadric may be taken. With this definition, if the fundamental quadric is $\Sigma xx = 0$ and if $\Sigma xx'$ is the polar form of Σxx, the distance ρ between x and x' is given by the projective formula

$$\cos(\rho/k) = \Sigma xx'/\{\Sigma xx \cdot \Sigma x'x'\}^{\frac{1}{2}}$$

That this formula is projective is made evident by observing that $e^{-2i\rho/k}$ is the anharmonic ratio of the range consisting of the two points and the intersections of the line joining them with the fundamental quadric. With this non-Euclidean geometry was brought to the third or projective period. The method of this period is attributable to Cayley; its application to previous non-Euclidean geometry to Klein. The projective method contains a generalization of discoveries already made by E. Laguerre in 1853 as regards Euclidean geometry. The arbitrariness of this procedure of deriving metrical geometry from the properties of conics is removed by Lie's theory of congruence.

The Two Kinds of Elliptic Space.—The projective method leads to a discrimination, first made by Klein, of two varieties of Riemann's space; Klein called these elliptic and spherical. They are also called the polar and antipodal forms of elliptic space. The latter names will be used in this discussion. The difference is strictly analogous to that between the diameters and the points of a sphere. In the polar form two straight lines in a plane always intersect in one and only one point; in the antipodal form they always intersect in two points that are antipodes. The antipodal form may be called a quasi-geometry. Similarly in the antipodal form two diameters always determine a plane; but two points on a sphere do not determine a great circle when they are antipodes, and two great circles always intersect in two points. Again, a plane does not form a boundary among lines through a point: it is possible to pass from any one such line to any other without passing through the plane. But a great circle does divide the surface of a sphere. So, in the polar form, a complete straight line does not divide a plane, and a plane does not divide space, and does not, like a Euclidean plane, have two sides. But, in the antipodal form, a plane is, in these respects, like a Euclidean plane.

Finally, it is of interest to note that, though it is theoretically possible to show, by the methods of empirical science, that a geometry is non-Euclidean, it is wholly impossible to prove by such methods that it is accurately Euclidean. For the unavoidable errors of observation must always leave a slight margin in the measurements. A triangle might be found with angles with certainly greater, or certainly less, than two right angles; but to prove them exactly equal to right angles must always be beyond human powers. If, therefore, any man cherishes a hope of proving the exact truth of Euclid, such a hope must be based, not upon scientific, but upon philosophical considerations.

See ANALYTIC GEOMETRY; CIRCLE; CONIC SECTION; DESCRIPTIVE GEOMETRY; DIFFERENTIAL GEOMETRY; ELLIPSE; GEOMETRY; HYPERBOLA; MENSURATION; PROJECTIVE GEOMETRY; SURFACES; TOPOLOGY, GENERAL.

BIBLIOGRAPHY.—For Lobachevski's writings, *see* F. Engel and P. Stäckel, "Nikolaj Iwanowitsch Lobatschefsky," *Urkunden zur Geschichte der nichteuklidischen Geometrie* (1898). For John Bolyai's *Appendix*, *see* J. Frischauf, *Absolute Geometrie nach Johann Bolyai* (1872), *Elemente der absoluten Geometrie* (1876); M. L. Gérard, *Sur la géométrie non-Euclidienne* (1892).

For expositions of the whole subject, *see* F. Klein, *Nicht-Euklidische Geometrie* (1928); W. Killing, *Die nicht-Euklidischen Raumformen in analytischer Behandlung* (1885); R. Bonola, *La Geometria non-Euclidea* (1906), authorized Eng. trans., with supplement containing translations of works of Bolyai and Lobachevski, by H. S. Carslaw (1955); H. S. Carslaw, *The Elements of Non-Euclidean Plane Geometry and Trigonometry* (1916); J. L. Coolidge, *The Elements of Non-*

Euclidean Geometry (1909); H. S. M. Coxeter, *Non-Euclidean Geometry*, 3rd ed. (1957); H. E. Wolfe, *Introduction to Non-Euclidean Geometry* (1945). A bibliography on the subject up to 1878 was published by G. B. Halsted, *Am. J. Math.*, vol. i and ii; and one up to 1900 by R. Bonola, *Index operam ad geometriam absolutam spectantium ...* (1903); also D. M. Y. Sommerville, *Bibliography of Non-Euclidean Geometry* (1911). (S. S. CH.; X.)

GEOPHYSICAL PROSPECTING (GEOPHYSICAL EXPLORATION, APPLIED GEOPHYSICS) is the application of the principles of physics to the study of subsurface geology, particularly as related to exploration for ore, oil and gas deposits. Geophysical exploration is used for other purposes, including (1) the location of ground-water supplies; (2) the determination of thickness and type of soil; (3) the kinds of rock and their depths and surface configurations; (4) the *in situ* determination of the physical and dynamic properties of soils and rocks; (5) the thickness of ice at sea and on the polar icecaps; (6) the depth of water in oceans and lakes and the nature and thickness of bottom sediments; and (7) the structure and composition of the earth's crust.

The techniques of measurement employed are based on the fundamental principles of those fields of physics represented by gravity, magnetism, electricity, light, sound, heat and radioactivity. The measurements are usually conducted at ground level, but may be made in bore holes or in underground mine workings. In water-covered areas the instruments are either placed on bottom or suspended in the water, and some of the measurements can be made from aircraft.

The success of all geophysical methods depends upon there being a contrast between the physical properties of the material being investigated or sought and those of the surrounding material. The properties exploited are magnetic susceptibility, density, elasticity, electrical conductivity, thermal conductivity and radioactivity. If a substance, such as oil, does not in itself provide a marked enough difference from its surroundings to be detected, then it frequently can be located indirectly through an association with some stratigraphic or structural geologic condition (anticline, fault, buried valley, etc.) which can be geophysically mapped. In the case of disseminated ore minerals where there is no well-defined lode of material, indirect location may be achieved through being able to map the subsurface extent of the host rock, such as an intrusive or associated buried structure. (*See* GEOLOGY.)

METHODS

In accordance with the physical properties of geologic materials that can be utilized for measurements, the methods of applied geophysics can be subdivided into gravitational, magnetic, seismic, electrical, electromagnetic, geothermal and radioactive methods. In nearly all cases the results obtained must be interpreted geologically. Hence, the analysis of the results plays just as important a role in the successful use of geophysical studies as does the choice of measurement used and the care with which the measurements are made.

From the standpoint of interpretation geophysical methods can be subdivided into two groups: (1) methods without depth control; and (2) methods having depth control. In the first group the measurements incorporate spontaneous effects from many sources, both local and distant, over which the observer has no control. For example, a gravity measurement is affected by the change in earth radius with latitude and the earth's rotation, the elevation of the site relative to sea level, the local topography, the thickness of the earth's crust, the configuration of the underlying crystalline rock complex and the density of the intervening rocks, as well as by any abnormal mass variation that might be associated with a mineral deposit. Therefore, the successful interpretation of gravity data depends on: (1) the accuracy with which the effects of known controls related to position and elevation are evaluated; (2) the accuracy with which the residual obtained is subdivided into contributions from regional controls of unknown magnitude related to variations in crustal thickness, basement rock litholity, etc., and those of local origin; and (3) how well knowledge of geologic factors concerning structure or modes of ore deposition can be applied in deducing the significance of the final residual, particularly as to whether this residual represents the effect of a shallow, thin body or a deeper, thicker or more concentrated body. With so many variables it is not possible to make a quantitative analysis leading to an unambiguous solution. In the last stages the interpretation always depends upon the geologic knowledge of the interpreter and his success through trial calculations in finding a reasonable geological model whose gravity effect matches that observed. This in itself, however, is no guarantee that the interpretation is correct. It is a possible interpretation that may even be probable but never unique. The above limitations also apply to the interpretations of magnetic, electrical self-potential, thermal and radioactive measurements.

In the second group of measurements (those with depth control) energy (seismic or electric) is introduced into the ground and variations in transmissibility with distance are observed and interpreted in terms of geologic quantities. The depth of investigation with these techniques is governed by the spacing between the transmitting and reception points. It is thus possible to separate shallow effects from those having a deep origin. By the application of suitable physical theory, depths to geologic horizons having marked differences in transmissibility can be computed on a quantitative basis and the physical nature of these horizons deduced. The accuracy, ease of interpretation and applicability of all methods falling into this group are not the same, and there are conditions, both natural and economic, under which the measurements of the first group are preferable for exploration studies despite their inherent limitations.

In each group (gravity, magnetic, seismic, etc.) there are subdivisions related to variations in technique, instrumentation or quantities measured. A summary of methods and their geologic applications is given in the Table. Details on some of the methods with special reference to rock properties, instruments and interpretation procedures are given in the following sections.

Gravity Methods.—Gravity methods are based upon the measurement of physical quantities related to the gravitational field which in turn are affected by differences in densities and disposition of underlying geologic bodies.

The density values of a few minerals for which gravity prospecting has been done are: Pyrite, 4.9–5.2; pyrrhotite, 4.5–4.7; galena, 7.4–7.6; barite, 4.3–4.5; magnetite, 4.9–5.2; lignite, 1.1–1.2. Concentrations of economic value of these minerals occur in rock materials usually having a density varying from 2.6–2.8 gm/cc. In oil and gas exploration, where there is no direct density control associated with the material being sought, exploration is based on the mapping of geologic structures to determine situations that might localize the material being sought. In such cases the significant density values are: Salt, 2.1–2.2; igneous rocks, 2.5–3.0; sedimentary rocks, 1.6–2.8. The last value increases with depth due to consolidation and geologic age and as a result structural deformation associated with faults and folding can be detected. Compaction of sediments over ridges or knolls on the underlying crystalline rock surface also leads to a local increase in mass, as does the development of calcareous cap rock over the heads of intrusive salt columns. In the latter situation the high density value may be superimposed upon a broader low value related to the deficiency in mass associated with the salt column as a whole. In the early days of gravity prospecting both the Eötvös torsion balance for determining gravity gradient and pendulum apparatus were extensively employed, but these have been supplanted by spring balance systems (gravimeters). The latter can be read in a matter of minutes in contrast to the several hours required for obtaining readings with the earlier instruments. While gravimeters vary in design those in common use consist essentially of a weighted boom that pivots about a hinge point. The boom is linked to a spring system so that the unit is essentially unstable and hence very sensitive to slight variations in gravitational attraction. Deflections of the boom from a central "null" position are measured by observing the change in the tension in the spring system required to bring the boom back to that position. Readings are obtained from a graduated dial on the head of the instrument which is attached to the spring system through a screw. (Gravimeters therefore do not read the force of gravity directly, and only indicate differences in gravitational attraction.) There must be an accurate calibration of the screw, reading dial and spring response for the readings to have gravitational significance. Two methods of calibration are employed: (1) a series of comparative readings is taken between sites for which the change in gravity is known from pendulum measurements; or (2) the instrument is tilted through a known angle and readings are taken for simulated changes in gravity (calculated on the basis that tilting results in an apparent decrease in gravity which varies as the cosine of the angle of tilt).

Relative gravity measurements using a pendulum can be used as a calibration standard, since these are free from side effects so long as the physical dimensions of the pendulum and environment of oscillation remain constant. The only factor having significance then is the change in a period of the pendulum in moving from one site to another.

For discussion of the design, construction, sensitivity and uses of pendulums and gravimeters see GRAVITATION: *Measurements of the Acceleration Due to Gravity.*

By placing gravimeters on bottom in shallow water areas in watertight housings with automatic leveling and electronic recording, it is possible to carry out gravimeter surveys in inundated

SUMMARY OF THE FOUR MAJOR GEOPHYSICAL PROSPECTING METHODS

METHOD		FIELD	GEOLOGIC APPLICATION
SPONTANEOUS ACTION — No DEPTH CONTROL			
I. Gravitational	A. Torsion balance B. Pendulum C. Gravimeter	Oil, mining, salt domes, geodesy	Anticlinal structures; buried ridges; salt domes; faults; intrusions; ore bodies; reefs; major structural trends
II. Magnetic		Oil, mining	Anticlinal structures; buried ridges; intrusions; faults; iron, pyrrhotite and associated sulfide ores; gold placers
REACTION TO ENERGIZING FIELDS			
III. Electrical	A. Self-potential	Mining	Sulfide ore bodies

	B. Galvanic application of primary energy
	 1. Potential distribution of secondary field, measured
	  a. Equipotential line methods
	  b. Resistivity
	  c. Potential drop ratio
	 2. Electromagnetic field, measured
	C. Inductive application of primary energy
		Mining, civil engineering, oil	General stratigraphic and structural conditions; bedrock depth on dam sites; ground water; oil structures; sulfide ore bodies; highway problems; electrical logging

IV. Seismic **(CONTROL OF DEPTH OF PENETRATION)**	A. Refraction	Mining	Iron formation; sulfide ore bodies
		Oil, civil engineering, crustal structure	Faults; anticlinal, etc., structures
		Oil	Salt domes; anticlinal, etc., structures; faults; foundation and highway problems; ground water; marine sediments
	B. Reflection		Low-dip structures; buried ridges; faults; reefs

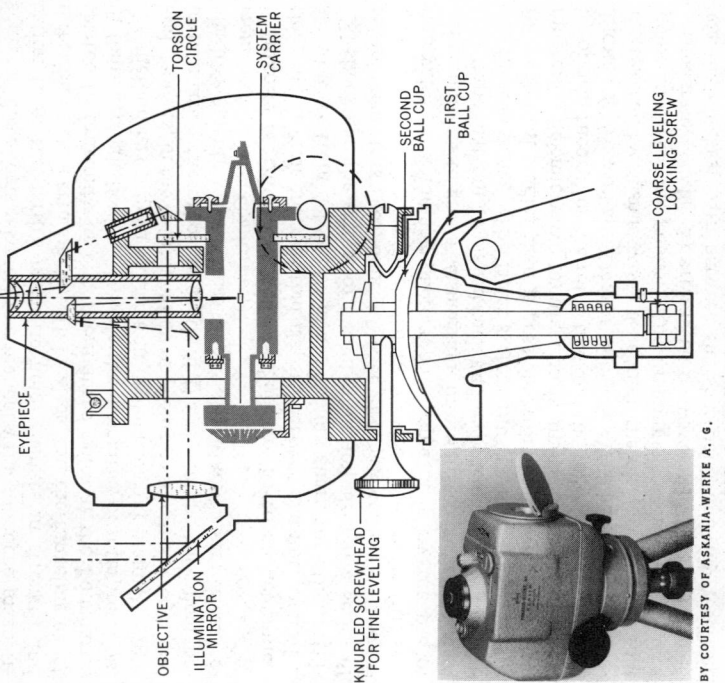

FIG. I.—TORSION MAGNETOMETER

BY COURTESY OF ASKANIA-WERKE A. G.

areas as well as on land. Special gravimeters have been developed for use in submarines and on gyrostabilized platforms on surface ships, and it has been demonstrated that these instruments can be used in aircraft.

With the high sensitivity of modern gravimeters, changes in the length of the springs with time (drift) must be corrected for, as well as the fluctuation in gravity due to the tidal pull of the sun and the moon. The former can be evaluated only by a systematic series of repeat measurements at control bases; the latter can be calculated from suitable tables or determined empirically by direct observation with a stationary instrument. The final observed gravity values are then corrected for latitude, elevation, terrain, etc., to obtain residuals (anomalies) as discussed previously before they can be utilized for evaluating subsurface geologic conditions. In oil prospecting observations usually are made at one-mile intervals; in mineral prospecting observations may be required at intervals of 100 ft.

Magnetic Methods.—Magnetic methods are based upon measuring the magnetic effects produced by varying concentrations of ferromagnetic minerals. Of these, magnetite is the most common mineral and has the greatest magnetic susceptibility, pyrrhotite being appreciably less susceptible and the other common iron minerals are but weakly magnetic.

Instruments used for magnetic prospecting vary from the simple mining compass used in the 17th century to sensitive air-borne magnetic units permitting intensity variations to be measured with an accuracy greater than $\frac{1}{10,000}$ part of the earth's field. It is possible to measure any angular or intensity component, but total intensity and vertical intensity anomalies can be most easily interpreted.

One of the most widely used magnetic instruments is the Schmidt vertical magnetometer. It consists of a pair of blade magnets balanced horizontally on a quartz knife edge.

The balance is oriented at right angles to the magnetic meridian and the deflection from the horizontal observed. Thus magnetic vertical intensity is compared with gravity (assumed to be constant); the deflections of the system are read on an autocollimation telescope (see COLLIMATOR).

Instrument readings are converted into gammas (10^{-5} gauss units) using a calibration factor established by placing the system in a Helmholtz coil and then observing deflections for known electric currents in the coil. The torsion fibre magnetometer (see fig. 1) is another type vertical component instrument that has a greater operating range than the Schmidt type instrument It also has an advantage in that it is easier and quicker to read. The instrument values are referred to a base, corrected for temperature and diurnal variation (see GEOMAGNETISM), and corrected for the normal geographic variation of the earth's magnetic field. Since the end of World War II continuous-recording magnetic instruments have been used. These can be divided into magnetic saturation induction, earth inductor and free proton precession instruments. The magnetic saturation induction instrument has been most widely used. While designs vary, the instrument basically consists of a highly permeable magnetic core of permalloy, mumetal or the like, two opposed identical primary windings, a surrounding secondary winding and an external neutralizing coil. The action of a saturation induction element depends on the core, which becomes completely saturated in magnetic fields of only a few gauss. The core is in the form of a long wire or strip to prevent demagnetizing effect and a primary coil is wound on it; weak currents in the primary carry the core to saturation, and for each cycle of current in the primary the core goes through a so-called saturation or hysteresis cycle. The saturation induction unit measures the change in external magnetic field along the core's length axis. The unit is oriented vertically to record changes on the earth's vertical component. In this position it is subject to an error of 250 γ per degree error in level in the magnetic meridian plane and 16 γ per degree error in level perpendicular to the meridian plane. Aligned along the earth's total intensity vector the error is approximately 16 γ per degree off orientation. The unit, therefore, can best be used to measure changes in total intensity. Recording is done graphically, using a continuous chart recorder. The scale

sensitivity of the resultant magnetogram can be varied by means of a selector switch and set to give a full-scale deflection on the record chart equal to 50, 100, 200, 1,500 or 5,000 gammas. The value of the base line of the record chart can also be changed in steps varying from 50 to 5,000 gammas. When used in aerial prospecting, the detector element is usually housed in a streamlined "bird" which is towed behind and beneath the plane on a cable about 100 ft. long, thus eliminating the magnetic effect of the plane. Wing tip and spar installations of the sensing head have also been successfully used.

As elevation is critical with such measurements, several methods have been used to determine the position of the plane in space. On land surveys a gyroscopically stabilized, continuous-strip camera is used together with a recording radio altimeter. The three records are co-ordinated by an electrical system and marked and numbered simultaneously by a keying device. Another method for use over water or other unmapped areas involves the use of Shoran (short range navigation), a radio navigation aid. With this system the distance from two ground stations is measured electronically and is constantly recorded and co-ordinated with the total magnetic intensity chart. Knowing the position of the ground stations, it is then possible to locate the traverse lines without maps or other information.

The Varian nuclear precession magnetometer is another continuous recording magnetic instrument which measures the earth's total magnetic field by observing the free precession (progressive movement) frequency of the protons in a sample of water. Spinning protons in a sample of water tend to orient their axes parallel to any magnetic field that is present. If the protons are reoriented by a strong magnetic field at right angles to the earth's field and the inducing field is then caused to decay quickly, the protons start to precess around axes parallel to the earth's field. They start in phase and a small electromagnetic force (e.m.f.) is induced in a coil placed near the sample. The frequency of this e.m.f. is proportional to the field causing the precession and inversely proportional to the angular momentum. If this precession frequency is accurately measured, it is possible to determine the total field to an accuracy of 2 gammas.

The interpretation of magnetic measurements is subject to the same fundamental drawbacks mentioned in connection with gravity measurements as regards the contrast in physical properties present, depth of origin and integrated contributions from many sources, plus effects related to permanent versus induced magnetization from the earth's magnetic field, changes in strength and direction from the earth's field with location and the canceling effect related to proximity of opposite induced poles at the boundaries of finite geologic bodies. Despite the difficulties of interpretation, the method has proved valuable in exploration for magnetic mineral deposits, in the determination of geologic structural trends and in estimating the probable depth of the crystalline rock floor beneath sedimentary rock areas. (*See also* MAGNETISM: *Measurement of Magnetic Quantities.*)

Seismic Methods.—Seismic methods are based on determinations of the time interval that elapses between the initiation of a sound wave from detonation of a dynamite charge or other artificial shock and the arrival of the vibration impulses at a series of seismic detectors (geophones). (*See also* SEISMOLOGY.) The arrivals are amplified and recorded along with time marks (.01 sec. intervals) on a moving photographic paper strip by the use of galvanometers to give a seismogram, or are first recorded on magnetic tape that can be played back and recorded as above for various filter systems. The latter system thus permits greater scope for analytical studies than is possible with the conventional seismogram. Seismic wave propagation is analogous to that defined by optical theory for the refraction and the reflection of light (*see* LIGHT: *Refraction and Double Refraction*). The depths and media reached by seismic waves depend on the distance between shot point and receiving points. The first impulses or "breaks" in a seismogram (*see* fig. 2) are caused by waves which have traveled via the quickest path between the shot point and any receiving point. At short distances this is usually also the shortest path, but beyond a certain distance it is quicker for a refracted pulse to travel via a longer path involving underlying layers having a higher velocity. From a plot of travel time as a function of surface distance, data are obtained for determining the velocity of the material and number of layers present. From the distances at which changes in velocity are indicated the depth of each layer can be computed. The method depends upon (1) the velocity within each of the layers penetrated at depth being greater than that in the layers above; (2) the layers are bounded by plane surfaces; and (3) the material within each layer is essentially homogeneous. In areas having sedimentary deposits other than limestone, these conditions are commonly satisfied. As discussed under *Gravity Methods*, above, in general the deeper, older formations have a higher seismic velocity than the overlying material (*see also* EARTH: *Seismic Exploration*; EARTHQUAKES). As the velocity values determined from the travel-time plot are governed by the slope of the underlying surfaces as well as the nature of the material itself, being greater than normal when receiving upslope and less than normal when receiving downslope, it is customary to record in opposite directions over the same surface area. Observed differences in velocity define not only the direction of slope of the rock surfaces, but also provide information for computing the degree of slope present. Where conditions of downward refraction are encountered in the sedimentary column, as is obtained when a high velocity limestone is underlain by a lower velocity sandstone, there may be no direct evidence in the arrivals of this condition and the calculated values for the depth of any horizons below the limestone will be seriously in error. For what might be termed "normal" conditions (increase in velocity with depth) the error in depths determined is usually less than 10% with this method.

For purely qualitative studies for locating marked horizontal discontinuities in transmissibility, such as are occasioned by intrusive bodies or faults of large displacement, the technique of "fan shooting," a variation of refraction shooting, is employed. Here the apparent velocities along several azimuths from a shot point are recorded. Any velocity abnormalities on one or more azimuths will thus give a bearing on disturbed structure. Cross fan recordings across the area will further define the nature and position of the structural abnormality.

Reflection impulses depend upon the reflection of seismic waves from media of greater elasticity at depth. Their time of arrival depends on the average velocity between surface and reflecting surface and the distance between the shot point and receiving points. (*See* SOUND: *Applications: Measurements.*) In essence the method depends upon determining the time for an echo. As in the refraction method, a travel-time graph is obtained. Because of the geometry of the travel path about a central axis defined by the shot point with recording on cross axes portrays the degree of inclination of the buried reflecting horizons. As the travel times for reflected waves are markedly influenced by the low velocity of the near-surface material lying above water table, a correction for the so-called "weathering layer" is important in all reflection studies. This correction can be determined empirically by a short refraction measurement to determine both the velocity and thickness of this layer. The average velocity that is used in computing reflection depths is best determined from velocity measurements in bore holes. Where such control cannot be obtained a value can be derived from a plot of the square of the travel time as a function of the distance. The slope of the resulting graph gives a value that defines the square of the average velocity. Where there is good velocity information and reflecting horizons, the reflection method has been found useful in depicting subsurface structure.

Because the surface distance required for a reflection measurement is so much less than that required for a refraction measurement in exploring to any depth, there are many advantages to be gained from using the method: (1) The short spread of instruments required eliminates the problem of getting permission to work over several routes of land; (2) permits "spot" determination of depths rather than average values over an area as is the case in deep refraction studies; (3) requires small charges of explosives and even allows mechanical methods to be employed as a source of energy; (4) permits rapid observations, since a minimum amount of observational data is required. In general, therefore,

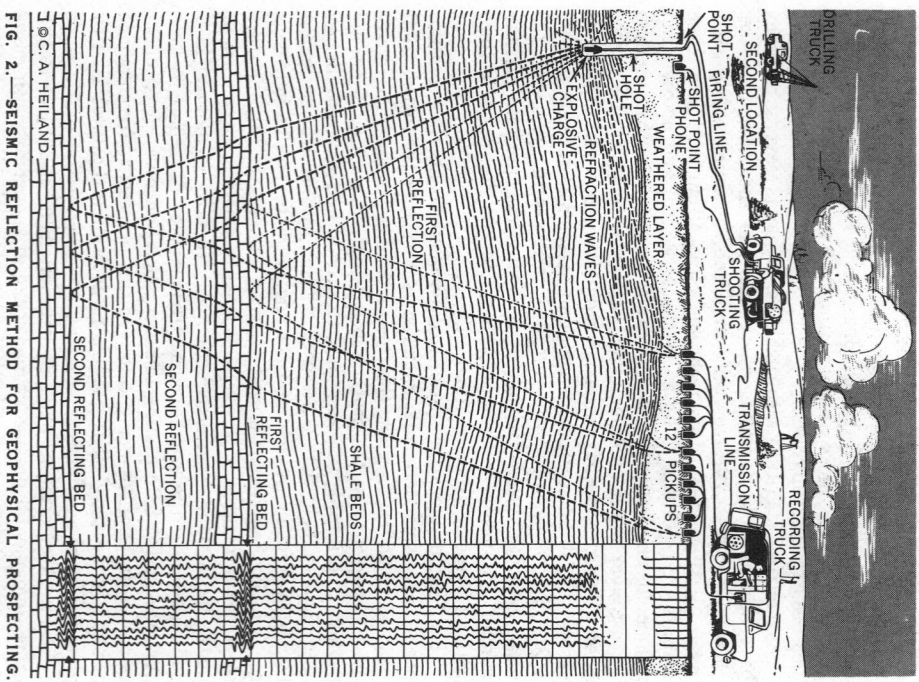

FIG. 2.—SEISMIC REFLECTION METHOD FOR GEOPHYSICAL PROSPECTING. FIELD EQUIPMENT IS SHOWN ABOVE, SEISMIC WAVE PATHS BELOW AND A SEISMOGRAM AT THE RIGHT

the reflection method is employed for all deep exploration work. Resolution at depths shallower than 200 ft. is usually not possible because the time interval between the first refraction arrival and the first reflection arrival at these depths is so short that there is not time enough to damp out the first motion sufficiently for the reflection arrival to be recognized.

The refraction method is therefore commonly used for shallow engineering studies, and has also been found to be useful in deep exploration in certain areas where good reflections cannot be obtained and for studies of crustal structure at depths of 10 to 50 km.

Electrical Methods.—With the exception of the self-potential method, electrical prospecting methods depend upon differences in electrical conductivity between the geological bodies under study and the surrounding rocks. Metallic minerals, particularly the sulfides, range in resistivity from 1.0 to several ohm-cm.; consolidated sediments of low water content average about 10^4 ohm-cm.; igneous rocks range from 10^4 to 10^6 ohm-cm. and saturated unconsolidated sediments, from 10^2 to 10^4 ohm-cm. The resistivity of the latter depends largely on the amount and electrolytic nature (salinity) of the included water.

The self-potential method makes use of the fact that most metallic sulfide minerals are easily oxidized by downward-percolating ground water. Because of the surface oxidation of such ore bodies the elements of a simple chemical battery are established and a spontaneous electric current flows down through the ore body and back to the surface through the surrounding water-saturated ground, which acts as the electrolyte. It is possible to locate these localized electrical fields and hence ore bodies by mapping points of equal electrical potential at the surface using nonpolarizing electrodes and a sensitive ammeter, or a milliammeter, or by measuring potential differences between successive profile stakes forming a grid over an area using a potentiometer.

In all other electrical methods, electrical energy is supplied to the ground either galvanically or inductively. Direct current or alternating current of low frequency is usually used. In the equipotential-line method power is supplied to two points or line electrodes; the equipotential lines are traced by two search electrodes connected through an audio-amplifier with headphones in the output; one of the probes is held stationary and the other is moved until the sound disappears. The presence of a good conductor is indicated by the spreading of the equipotential lines and a poor conductor, by the drawing together of the equipotential lines (*see* fig. 3). Interpretation is largely qualitative and empirical.

FIG. 3.—EQUIPOTENTIAL PATTERN FOR A CONDUCTING ORE BODY. (A, B) ELECTRODES; (C) ORE BODY. SOLID LINES INDICATE EQUIPOTENTIAL; DASHED LINES, CURRENT FLOW

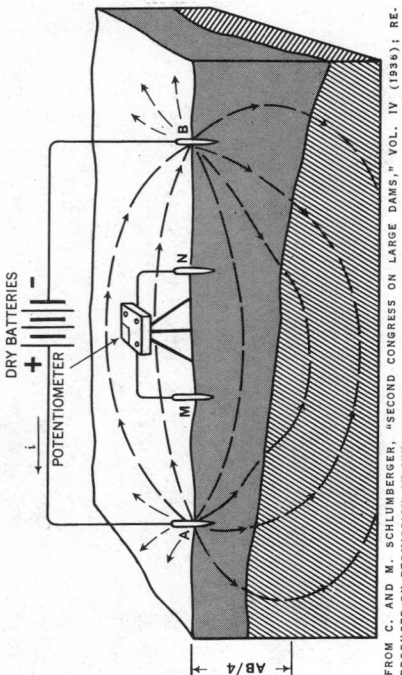

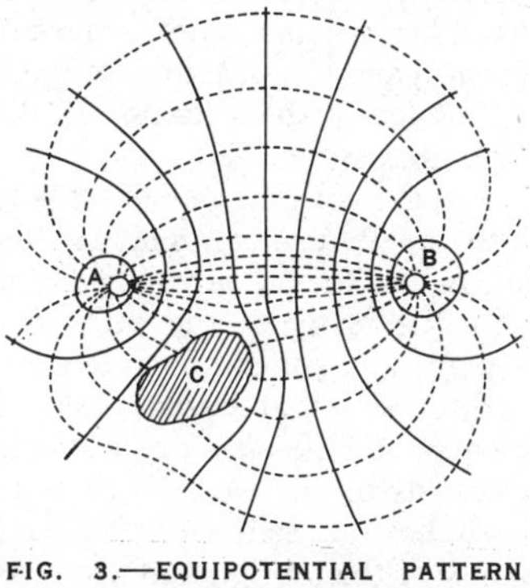

A potential method that is used extensively is known as the "resistivity" method (fig. 4). Four evenly spaced electrodes are driven into the ground; the external pair (A, B) is supplied with current (i) from batteries or an alternating current source that is read on a milliammeter, while the internal pair (M, N) is connected to a potentiometer to determine the voltage difference between them. To avoid polarization effects, nonpolarizing potential electrodes can be used, or a commutator inserted in the circuit so that the current through the ground changes in direction every half cycle but retains the same direction through the instrument. The ratio of voltage and current, multiplied by a factor depending on electrode spacing, gives the true resistivity for homogeneous ground, or the so-called "apparent resistivity" for nonhomogeneous ground. The depth of effective penetration is roughly one-third the distance between the two outer electrodes. If the electrode arrangement is moved over the ground with constant spacing, variation of resistivity in a horizontal direction to a fixed depth is obtained. This method is quite useful for determining the presence of any horizontal discontinuities such as, for example, rock rising

FROM C. AND M. SCHLUMBERGER, "SECOND CONGRESS ON LARGE DAMS," VOL. IV (1936); REPRODUCED BY PERMISSION OF INTERNATIONAL COMMISSION ON LARGE DAMS OF THE WORLD POWER CONFERENCE

FIG. 4.—ELECTRICAL RESISTIVITY METHOD

near the surface along the line of a proposed highway. By keeping the centre of the electrode arrangement fixed and expanding the spacing of the electrodes about this centre point changes in resistivity with depth can be determined and their depth deduced. This method has been extensively used in subsurface engineering studies as, for example, in the determination of the depth to bedrock beneath river bottom alluvium.

Interpretation of resistivity results is handicapped by the marked effects of variations in soil moisture and the chemistry of the interstitial water as well as by vertical and horizontal changes in lithology; the potential differences measured represent accumulative effects from the entire section penetrated. Interpretation techniques employed include the matching of plots of apparent resistivity as a function of electrode spacing against theoretical "type" curves, the location of inflection points, breaks, changes in slope of logarithmic plots of the results, accumulative resistivity value plots and other methods of a somewhat more quantitative nature. Best results in the use of resistivity values for determining depths have been obtained where it has been possible to use well data to establish local empirical correlations between the resistivity plots and geologic depth data.

A special application of electrical methods is in the study of subsurface stratigraphy by measuring the potential differences between the surface and an electrode lowered in a bore hole and by also measuring variations in electrical resistivity with depth. Both measurements must be carried out before a hole is cased. The procedure is known as electrical logging. The potential log gives a measure of porosity and permeability since the measurements are markedly affected by the ability of the drilling fluid to penetrate the formations and the contrasts in electrolytic properties of the formational fluid and the drilling fluid. The resistivity measurements define the position of formational boundaries and the physical character of the lithology. Three resistivity logs usually are taken: one having shallow penetration is used for defining the location of formational boundaries and the other two, having intermediate and deep penetration, are used for determining the extent the drilling fluid has penetrated into the formations and the true resistivity of the formation present. The various measurements taken in conjunction provide a valuable tool for not only studying conditions in a given well but also for carrying out correlation studies between wells and thus defining geologic structure and horizontal changes in lithology.

Electromagnetic Methods.—The electromagnetic methods are based upon the fact that an alternating magnetic field will cause an electric current to flow in conducting material. Since most metallic minerals are good electrical conductors the method is best suited for their exploration. Measurements are carried out by connecting a source of alternating current to a coil of wire which acts as a source for a magnetic field similar to that which would be produced by a short magnet located on the axis of the coil. The magnetic field of the coil alternates in intensity in the same manner that the coil current alternates. A receiving system consisting of a second (search) coil connected to a voltmeter is mounted so as to be free to rotate about a horizontal axis. If the receiving coil is mounted so as to rotate on an axis perpendicular to that of the induced magnetic field then induced voltage will vary from a maximum when the plane of the coil is perpendicular to that of the applied field and to zero when the plane of the coil is parallel to that of the applied field. These are the conditions if no conductor is present. If a conductor is present the induced current in the conductor sets up a secondary magnetic field that distorts the primary field. That is, the inphase portion of the induced current in the meter is used only as a null detector to determine when the receiver coil is parallel to the resultant field. By using an inclinometer to record the angle of the moving search coil when in the null position, the location of a conductor can be determined as the crossover (inflection) point on a profile across the body.

Another variation of this method is to have both the receiver and transmitting coils in the horizontal plane. In this arrangement the voltage developed over nonconducting ground is a function of the construction of the coils which are usually moved across the ground with a constant separation. The presence of a conductor is indicated by changes in the voltage values from the normal values for this configuration. When both coils are outside but adjacent to a conductor the secondary field generated by the induced current in the conductor adds to the normal field and gives an increase in voltage values. When the coils straddle the conductor the secondary field opposes the primary field, giving a decrease in voltage. The conductor is therefore marked by a voltage minimum. Effective depth penetration is about one-half the coil separation. The method is also adaptable for air-borne operations. Here the transmitting coil is mounted on the plane fuselage and the search coil is trailed in a "bird" on a 500-ft. cable.

Radioactive Methods.—In the disintegration of radioactive minerals three spontaneous emissions take place, the ejection of an electron (beta ray), a helium nucleus (alpha ray) and short-wave length electromagnetic radiations (gamma rays) (*see* RADIOACTIVITY). Radioactive measurements are based upon the detection of these natural radioactive emissions, primarily the gamma rays.

The gamma rays correspond to X-rays and have sufficient penetrating power to pass through rock material several feet thick as well as through iron several inches in thickness; it is this property which is utilized in prospecting for radioactive minerals and in radioactive logging in the underground study of oil fields.

The instruments used in radioactive exploration are the Geiger counter and the scintillometer. The gamma rays ionize the medium through which they pass by colliding with nuclear electrons and knocking them out of their orbits, thus leaving the atoms ionized. The Geiger counter is a discharge tube which records the presence of gamma rays by the ionization they produce in a gas in the tube. The gas used is a mixture of argon and some polyatomic vapour. In the centre of the tube is a wire (anode) with an enclosing cylindrical tube serving as a cathode. A difference in potential (about 1,000 v.) is maintained between the anode and the cathode. When the gas is sufficiently ionized by gamma rays passing through the chamber a discharge occurs which is amplified and heard as a click. The number of clicks per minute, which is a measure of the gamma-ray radiation present, is usually indicated on a dial on the counter. Because of cosmic rays in the atmosphere there is a background count which varies with the efficiency of the instrument.

The scintillometer is a gamma-ray detection instrument whose operation depends upon the fact that certain crystal elements emit a flash of light upon absorbing gamma rays. This flash is picked up by a photo multiplier tube and amplified and a visual reading of the emission rate obtained. This instrument is almost 100 times more sensitive than the Geiger counter. Because of the efficiency of this instrument in indicating the presence of gamma rays it is possible to differentiate the emanation from different mineral sources on the basis of the energy levels associated with the source elements. Scintillometers as well as Geiger counter measurements can be carried out both from a moving surface vehicle and from low-flying aircraft.

In addition to prospecting for radioactive minerals the radioactive method is extensively applied in bore hole studies of subsurface stratigraphy. Different sedimentary rocks are naturally characterized by different concentrations of radioactive material. The shales and volcanic ash give the highest gamma-ray count and the limestones the lowest. In addition to the natural gamma-ray log the same technique of measurement is used to determine neutron absorption with a neutron source lowered ahead of a gamma-ray detector. Neutrons are absorbed by hydrogen compounds and as a result a low return indicates the presence of porous formations or those with chemically combined water, as clay and shale. Such ambiguity, however, can be resolved when the neutron log is combined with the gamma-ray log for interpretation.

From the preceding discussion it is clear that geophysical exploration techniques cannot be applied indiscriminately. A knowledge of the geologic parameters likely to be associated with the mineral or subsurface condition being studied is essential both in choosing the method to be applied and in interpreting the results obtained.

For further discussion of geologic principles and concepts used in this article *see* GEOCHEMISTRY; GEOLOGY. *See also* ORE DEPOSITS; PETROLEUM.

BIBLIOGRAPHY.—M. B. Dobrin, *Introduction to Geophysical Prospecting* (1960); J. J. Jakosky, *Exploration Geophysics* (1950); L. L. Nettleton (ed.), *Geophysical Case Histories* (1948), *Geophysical Prospecting for Oil* (1940); C. A. Heiland, *Geophysical Prospecting* (1940). (G. P. W.)

GEOPHYSICAL YEAR, INTERNATIONAL: *see* INTERNATIONAL GEOPHYSICAL YEAR.

GEOPHYSICS, the study of the earth, using the research methods of physics. The areas of interest range from the earth's deep interior where matter is at several thousand degrees centigrade and 3,500,000 atm. pressure, through the crust with its ocean basins and bewildering inhomogeneities, to the tenuous upper atmosphere. The problems are analogous to those of astronomy, in that the subject is seldom under direct observation and handling, forcing conclusions to be drawn primarily by the mathematical and physical interpretation of physical measurements. For discussion of the scientific study of the chemistry of the earth *see* GEOCHEMISTRY.

For the convenience of classification, geophysics may be divided into the following somewhat overlapping branches: geodesy, the study and theory of the earth's figure, including gravity; seismology, the study of the earth's interior layering, lateral variation, and refraction of elastic waves; hydrology, the study of the movements and circulation of water in the uppermost rocks and surface channels of the earth; oceanography, the study of ocean basins, both bottom sediments and current motions; meteorology, the study of the motion and properties of the lower, primarily weather formative atmosphere; upper air physics and cosmic ray research, the study of the electrical and physical properties of the outer fringe of atmosphere and the particle bombardment of the earth from space; terrestrial electricity (geoelectricity), the study of the charge distribution and movement of currents in the atmosphere and earth; terrestrial magnetism (geomagnetism), the study of the source, figure and changes of the earth's magnetic field and the response of matter to it; and volcanology, the study of the origin and properties of volcanoes. In addition, the dating of meteorites and crustal rocks by means of analysis of their radioactive components, as well as the branch of astronomy dealing with the rotational and translational motion of the earth may be included.

For further details on these branches of geophysics, consult the following articles on: ATMOSPHERE; CLIMATE AND CLIMATOLOGY; COSMOGONY; EARTH; EARTHQUAKE; ELECTRICITY, ATMOSPHERIC; GEOCHRONOLOGY; GEODESY; GEOMAGNETISM; HYDROGRAPHY; METEOROLOGY; OCEAN AND OCEANOGRAPHY; PLANETS; RADIOACTIVITY; SEISMOLOGY; SOUND; TIDE: *Bodily Tides*; VOLCANO.

The techniques of geophysics include measurements of gravity, direction and intensity of the earth's magnetic field, electrical potential gradients, movements of fluids and motions of the solid surface, both rapid fluctuations as from earthquakes and long-term events due to gradual shifts relative to sea level. Measurements of the above properties over a period of years permit a determination of properties in the earth's interior. Much laboratory work is also done. The properties of matter are studied under extreme temperatures and pressures. Models of various features of the earth are constructed and tested to ascertain their response to given variation in physical parameters. Many global properties are now determined by using artificial satellites and/or sounding rockets.

The primary international geophysical organization is the International Union of Geodesy and Geophysics formed in Brussels in 1919. The union consists of seven international associations: geodesy, seismology and physics of the earth's interior, meteorology, geomagnetism and aeronomy, physical oceanography, hydrology, and volcanology. Meetings are held every three years. Interrupted during World War II, they were started again in 1948. The United States affiliate of the International union is the American Geophysical union with offices in Washington, D.C.

Many universities throughout the world offer courses in the various branches of geophysics. Since geophysical methods of investigation are primarily mathematical and physical, and in addition demand a knowledge of geology, geophysics is taught chiefly at the postgraduate level. Those who wish to enter this specialty should start their mathematical training at the earliest possible time. Reviews in the various topics of geophysics appear yearly in *Advances in Geophysics* (1955–).

Since geophysics deals with world-wide phenomena, the need for international co-operation is great. This has led to three International Geophysical years, in 1882–83, 1932–33 and 1957–58, the first two being termed International Polar years. The main purpose of these events is to obtain physical measurements simultaneously over large portions of the earth and to inaugurate projects which demand international participation. *See also* INTERNATIONAL GEOPHYSICAL YEAR. (J. C. Jn.)

GEOPOLITICS. The term "geopolitics" was coined shortly before World War I, spread throughout Central Europe between the two wars and came into worldwide use during World War II.

Meaning.—There is no universally accepted definition of the word, and careful analysis is needed in order to distinguish between an objective study of politico-geographical factors and power-political speculations in the realm of geopolitics. Anyone might guess it to be a word combining "geography" and "politics," and wrongly conclude that it is an alternate name for "political geography," one of the oldest branches of earth science. Actually, it is almost never used in this broad sense.

All the usual meanings of "geopolitics" relate to the utilization of geography in the service of national governments. Within this delimitation the term is employed in three senses: (1) As used by some special students of the subject, and sometimes by publicists and editorial writers, the word refers to the power position of the nations, insofar as their power is conditioned by nature. (2) A few careful writers make the term a synonym for "applied political geography," as distinct from the history, principles and theory of political geography. (3) A far larger number of writers and speakers use the term loosely to designate national policy as affected by the natural environment. This is the layman's commonest usage.

The most incisive meaning of geopolitics is very like that last described, but is restricted to conscious special pleading to promote the interests of a particular government or to sway its national policy. This is the sole meaning of the term in Central Europe, where both the name and the restricted definition originated. This narrow geopolitics was best exemplified in the German movement between World Wars I and II which popularized the name. It would be fallacious, however, to look upon geopolitical doctrine and ideology as something exclusively rooted in central European or German soil. Not only did it spread to countries which, like Italy, Spain and Japan, sympathized with the expansionist ambitions of Germany, but it must also be remembered that the U.S. creed of "manifest destiny" between 1830 and 1860 was based on the kind of argumentation typical of geopolitics.

Origin.—The name was coined and defined by Rudolf Kjellén, a Swedish political scientist, who made "Geopolitik" one of the five coordinate aspects of a theoretical system of government, the others being "Ekonomopolitik," "Demo-politik," "Socio-politik" and "Krato-politik." This system he called "The State as an Organism" (*Staten som Lifsform*, definitive edition, 1916).

Kjellén had been profoundly impressed by the work of natural scientists, and especially imbued with the political geography expounded by the German geographer Friedrich Ratzel, who had been trained in the "new" biology of the middle 19th century. Geography, like all the scientific disciplines, was affected by the evolutionary view of the universe. Ratzel restated much of the theory of geography in the light of evolution and natural selection. In particular, he was the first to publish a survey of political geography analyzed as a systematic branch of the subject. In this work Ratzel compared the state to an organism, but he was careful to point out that he was using simile and metaphor.

Kjellén saw in Ratzel's treatise on political geography the logical bridge between natural science and political science. He apparently believed he was incorporating Ratzel's concepts of political geography into his own systematic treatise on the state, but in adapting Ratzel's work, he subtly metamorphosed it. Untrained in the rigorous discipline of natural science, he disregarded Ratzel's cautions and declared flatly that the state *is* an organism, and hence endowed with biological qualities: viz., growth and decay, and differentiation of members and organs.

If the state is an organism, it has powers of action independent of and superior to the human groups or individuals who constitute it. This view coincides with ideas expressed a century earlier by the pre-Darwinian German philosophers Johann Fichte, Georg Hegel and Friedrich von Schlegel. One effect of Kjellén's construction, therefore, was to clothe German political philosophy of an earlier day with the new garment of evolutionary natural science. In an epoch when natural science was conceded by public opinion to have almost the authority of revelation, Kjellén's claim for geopolitics handed a powerful weapon to any state disposed to use it for propaganda and as a mold for national policy. Kjellén's treatise was translated into German in 1917. It was seized upon by certain geographers, political scientists and publicists, who pushed it to the forefront of German attention and kept it there during 20 critical years.

This group was led by Karl Haushofer (1869–1946), who made himself the incarnation of geopolitics. As an officer of the Bavarian army, his career included service on the general staff. Before World War I, he embraced the opportunity to carry his study of geography far beyond the considerable training given to all German army officers. Field studies in the Orient led to the degree of Ph.D. at the University of Munich, with a dissertation on the political and military geography of the Japanese empire as it was in the first decade of the 20th century. On his retirement from the army in 1919 he made his mission in life the regeneration of the German state through the aid of geography. He took over Kjellén's organismal theory of the state, and adopted "geopolitics" as the name for the brand of geography to which he thereafter devoted himself. From facts about the earth, theories of government and items of German history he distilled a powerful propaganda. It was given coherence and direction by the assumption that the German state, which had been continuously growing for centuries, was an organism that must continue to spread until it conquered and absorbed the whole earth.

Methods and Manner.—Haushofer's first platform was in the University of Munich, where he lectured on geopolitics from 1919—after the Nazis came to power in 1933 as professor of geopolitics. There he gathered a group of disciples, including a number of journalists who were instrumental in giving geopolitics wide publicity. In 1924 he extended the range of his influence by launching the monthly *Journal of Geopolitics* (*Zeitschrift für Geopolitik*), of which he became and remained editor in chief and by a long lead the chief contributor. It was supplemented by a steady stream of books.

Haushofer's *Weltanschauung* ("world outlook") was founded on theories of space. Thereby it retained the form of geography, but its content included extensions of geographical space into the realm of the mystical. The drive that made it a practical philosophy was political, springing from the ambitions of German nationalists. The theory and the practice were welded into a national policy that was framed by the nature of Central Europe, rooted in 800 years of German territorial expansion, rationalized by powerful German philosophers of the 19th century, reanimated by the biological (organismal) concept of the state and clothed in the creed of German "racial" superiority.

Nearly all other writers on the subject adhered to their master's views, to the extent of copying his obscure style and cloudy terminology. When the real meaning of the geopoliticians can be discerned their world proves to be a product of environmental determinism, but chauvinistically German, disclosing a pitiless attitude toward non-German society that startles the foreigner. A book by an old-line geographer turned geopolitician created a minor international incident when it was published in an English translation in 1934 (Ewald Banse, *Raum und Volk im Weltkriege*, 1933). For an account of the incident see the British and American editions: *Germany, Prepare for War!* (1934) and *Germany Prepares for War* (1941).

A favourite literary device of the geopoliticians was the slogan. One of the terms they adopted from Ratzel, *Lebensraum* ("living space"), found its way into the English language. Each catchword or phrase refers to the earth, or some part of it, and most of them state or imply a political association with the earth; *e.g.*, boundary consciousness, space policy. Some two-score of these slogans were hammered into the consciousness of the German nation by unceasing repetition.

An important instrument of the geopoliticians was the map, which they used constantly and in novel ways. As geographers they well understood the impressiveness of the map and the ease with which it can be read if simple and neat. Treating it as a "weapon," they published hundreds of maps and pictographs. So far as possible, they restricted each map to a single theme, drawn to show the third dimension, and labeled succinctly. They stretched representation beyond facts to include aspirations, such as territorial goals. They justified omissions, and even falsifications. The *Zeitschrift für Geopolitik* is the principal source of these maps. Reproductions of typical samples are to be found in Derwent Whittlesey, *German Strategy of World Conquest*.

Political Significance.—By gaining the widest possible publicity, the geopoliticians sought ceaselessly to work for acceptance of German plans abroad. Educational propaganda was one of the two roads to the goal of German supremacy that they never lost sight of. The other road was laid out to reach as many responsible officials of the government as possible, and to aid the state in regaining its position as a great power through existing or newly created governmental agencies.

Haushofer made contact with Adolf Hitler very early—during the months of 1923–24 when the future *Führer* was in prison near Munich. That enforced retreat was spent in writing *Mein Kampf*, reportedly with Rudolf Hess as amanuensis. Hess had become an early disciple of Haushofer's, and geopolitics can be credited with a number of the ideas that appear in *Mein Kampf*, especially in the sections on foreign affairs.

Haushofer's long and reputable connection with the army general staff gave him personal access to the men who in the 1920s were undertaking to rebuild *sub rosa* the German military power. The general staff needed no persuasion as to the importance of geography in tactics and in strictly military strategy. The geopoliticians showed the necessity of a comprehensive and thorough knowledge of world geography for successful prosecution of the political strategy, which is an essential component of total war. This they named "geo-strategy" (*Wehr-geopolitik*). In theory a branch of geopolitics, geo-strategy was the resilient core of the larger subject. Haushofer espoused geopolitics as a means of "renovating" Germany and he viewed a state of war as the normal condition of mankind. Geo-strategy treated warfare as total, embracing the entire populations and resources of the contesting states. It recognized the psychological effects of the geography of the war theatre on fighting forces. It helped to make Germany the first country to realize that air power could take a position alongside sea power and land power. It may fairly be said that geo-strategy was the main theme of the geopoliticians and that geopolitics paved the way for modern concepts of total war.

Other branches of geopolitics were geo-medicine, geo-psychology, geo-jurisprudence and geo-economics. None of them was fully formed, as in fact would have been impossible, for the spatial emphasis was not sufficient to create new disciplines. Geo-medicine was concerned chiefly with diseases associated with different natural environments. Geo-psychology appears to have been an attempt to bring mankind's habit of individual thought and action into line with the dominant environmental determinism of geopolitics. Geo-jurisprudence similarly essayed to harmonize law and environmental determinism. Geo-economics covered the fact-finding and planning of agencies set up to guide the government in ordering the destinies of German economic life.

Educational and Operational Centres.—To implement their program, the geopoliticians used established centres of higher education. At the University of Munich, Haushofer organized his Institute of Geopolitics (*Institut für Geopolitik*), the best known, outside Germany, of all the geopoliticians' instruments. It came to be staffed by several score full-time specialists in geography and cognate fields who gathered, compiled and classified detailed information about all parts of the earth—its climate, surface features, natural resources, communication systems, economic production and social and political organization. The work of the institute included both research and planning. Its activities were adopted officially in 1935 by Nazi government agencies.

The University of Heidelberg became the seat of the Association of Workers in Geopolitics (*Arbeitsgemeinschaft für Geopolitik*), an organization of all German university instructors concerned with geopolitics. Haushofer was for some time its president. This association directed the study of geopolitics at the university level, and its members monopolized German publication on their subject. The integration of Haushofer's projects, educational and operational, was signalized by the creation, under the ministry of propaganda, of the National Socialist Teachers' Association (*Nationalsozialistischer Lehrer-Bund*). It included two study groups, one to prepare teachers in the middle schools to present the homeland in geopolitician's terms, the other to prepare teachers in the upper schools to instruct on foreign countries.

In the Advanced School of Politics (*Hochschule für Politik*) in Berlin, Haushofer's son Albrecht was made professor of geopolitics. From 1941 to 1943 he wrote the first volume of a text in political geography and geopolitics (published posthumously in 1951). Albrecht Haushofer, an active member of the German underground opposition, was executed by the Gestapo in April 1945. Karl Haushofer committed suicide in 1946.

Consequences for Germany.—When the Nazi Party took over in 1933, it gave geopolitics official sanction. Almost immediately German geography succumbed to the pressure and lost itself in geopolitics. Members of the profession who would not follow the new leader either withdrew to physical geography, a safe corner removed from political controversy, or were silenced by being refused permission to publish or lecture. Most of those who took their places bore names hitherto unknown to students of geography. Only geopoliticians remained free to publish on aspects of geography that treat of mankind, and they took their cue from Haushofer. What was left of the onetime science of geography became propagandist in tone, intemperate in manner and unreliable as to facts.

The downfall of Nazi Germany erased German geopolitics from the ideological map of the new Germany, although the *Zeitschrift für Geopolitik* was feebly revived in 1951. In fact, the bankruptcy of geopolitics discredited legitimate studies in political geography in Germany following World War II, with the result that Germany failed to match the progress made especially in the United States and Britain in this area.

Sound geography could have placed in correct perspective the relative strength of the nations as to strategic position, natural resources and productive capacity, and it would have warned that the natural environment neither fully measures human capacity nor determines the course of collective human action. The geopoliticians falsely assumed political power to rest wholly on material wealth, statistically computed. They added up the total natural resources of a country and multiplied by the intensity of utilization. Similarly they were content merely to count populations. From these facts they estimated the political and military strength of the nations. So engrossed, they failed to take account of the intangible forces generated in any people by living together as a nation. Furthermore, the myth of German racial superiority blinded them to the latent strength of non-Germans, both as peoples and as individuals.

The martial aims of the geopoliticians became increasingly apparent. They planned to have the revived German nation stride to world supremacy in a single war of conquest. In the slogan "*Blut und Boden*" (race and the land) Germans were taught by the Nazi leaders to vaunt their faith in their racial superiority to all other peoples, and their expectation of territorial supremacy—to be won by one more attack in a centuries-old succession of wars of conquest. While Hitler exploited chiefly the racial aspect of the shibboleth, Haushofer, who was, and remained, married to a woman of Jewish extraction, stressed its territorial aspect. He subscribed to racism only perfunctorily, although he permitted publication of "geographic" articles that embodied the racial "philosophy" of the third *Reich*.

Within its legitimate field geopolitics made itself little more than a formula for justifying Germany in wars of territorial conquest. From Kjellén it borrowed "autarky," the concept of national self-sufficiency. In the contemporary interdependent world, only the very largest and best-endowed nations could hope to approach permanent self-sufficiency. Others might build up stockpiles for or against an anticipated war of aggression. From Ratzel, geopolitics borrowed concepts about space, focusing them in the term *Lebensraum*. This was defined as the *right* of the German state "organism" to expand to the limit of its desires. More important than these loans, it borrowed from a truly outstanding student of political geography, Britain's Sir Halford Mackinder, the concept of "the heartland," a view of the earth as potentially arrayed in two camps—the land power of inner Eurasia and the sea power of the peripheral maritime lands, including all the other continents. By attaching the heartland, the geopoliticians reasoned, Germany could make itself the master of the world.

From the Pan-German movement (*see* PAN-GERMANISM) of the turn of the 19th century, geopolitics borrowed pan-regions, beginning with a German-dominated "Middle Europe" and "Eurafrica" as successive steps toward world conquest. From German political history and Ratzel, Haushofer himself worked out the doctrine that a political boundary marks merely the temporary halt of the nation-in-arms in its march toward unlimited territorial expansion. The geopoliticians advanced a program for world domination, but it was incomplete because they paid no attention to the problem of assimilating the peoples they might conquer. Their preoccupation with war led them to assume that conquest itself would solve the problem.

The contributions of geopolitics to the war that broke out in 1939 were direct and large. The propaganda of geopolitics is generally admitted to have carried most weight with the very classes of German society that were least taken in by Hitler's demagogy. Instruction in geopolitics permeated the school system, and formed part of the training in national fanaticism given to the generation that was destined to bear the brunt of the fighting. The propaganda justified military aggression as "natural," and by implication scientific and inevitable. Geopolitics helped to delude all Germans into accepting an overvaluation of their power as a nation. By the same means it persuaded sympathetic or terrified cliques of collaborators in neighbouring countries to pave the way for conquest.

The information collected by the agencies of geopolitics directly aided German war plans, and the geopoliticians' estimates of relative military preparedness of the nations and the material resources on which each could rely proved accurate through two years of conquest. Germany's first crucial military reverse was also forecast by geopolitics. A persistent disciple of Mackinder's teachings as far as the relationship of Russia and Germany was concerned, Haushofer emphasized time and again the necessity for Germany to join forces with its huge neighbour, and he rejoiced in the treaty of Aug. 1939 as the achievement of a lifelong ambition. Germany's attack on the Soviet Union in 1941 silenced him. Its unsuccessful outcome confirmed his contentions.

Influence Outside Germany.—Beyond the German-speaking world, the dogma of geopolitics was adopted with equal intensity by only one nation—Japan, whose militaristic tradition was reset in a frame of continental or world conquest by the Japanese program of "westernization" after 1868. The objectives of geopolitics were therefore congenial to the Japanese mind, even though Japan and Germany were bound to clash if both persisted successfully in their separate and overlapping plans for conquest. In addition, Haushofer's early enthusiasm for Japan gave his work a very favourable hearing there. Between 1913 and 1938 he wrote six books on Japan alone, besides works covering the Orient more broadly and lengthy commentaries in every issue of the *Zeitschrift*. Some of his work was translated into Japanese, and geopolitics was acclaimed and practised by a vigorous group of Japanese disciples.

Fascist Italy identified its territorial program with geopolitics as far as possible, notably in its claim to the Mediterranean sea as exclusively Italian—"*mare nostro*" ("our sea"). But the German geopoliticians did not hesitate to point out serious inherent weaknesses of Italy as a great power, and also the fact that it lay in the immediate path of German expansion. Presumably geopolitics never seized the imagination of any large section of the Italian people.

In France, the writings of Ratzel exerted considerable influence on such outstanding students of human geography as P. Vidal de la Blache, J. Brunhes and C. Valloux, who incorporated many of Ratzel's ideas in their system of social geography (*géographie sociale*) but refused to follow German geopolitics along the dangerous road of environmental determinism.

Marxist and Leninist theory is bitterly opposed to the recognition of any influence on the life of states and societies by their natural environment, and geographical determinism has no place in its system. It is not surprising to note that Soviet geographers such as J. W. Semjonow in their contemptuous attacks against "Fascist Geopolitics" went far beyond the realm of German geopolitics and included, as alleged representatives of U.S. and British imperialism and colonialism, practically every writer of reputation in these countries who had written on the subject of political geography.

British and U.S. scholars at first dismissed geopolitics without analysis as unscientific and unworthy of study. German geopoliticians had been labouring 20 years when war first brought both geopolitics and Haushofer into full view of the English-speaking public. Beginning in 1940, numerous articles and uncounted comments and editorials made their appearance. In 1942 no fewer than five books traced the origin or analyzed the character of German geopolitics. Under the brilliant, if not always entirely objective, leadership of Nicholas J. Spykman (*America's Strategy in World Politics*, 1942) a new brand of American geopolitics became fashionable. Once geopolitics had been appraised and applied, the spate of commentaries in English abated, but the subject remained very much alive, as was evinced by the continued and frequent appearance of the term in print without explanation or apology. The sudden rise to prominence of the term and its immediate acceptance by all sections of the English-reading public marked it as useful for expressing a concept more universal than the German movement that publicized the name.

Enduring Effects of Geopolitics.—No aspect of geopolitics is wholly acceptable to the world at large, but several of its ideas have been taken over, generally in modified form.

Useful devices embodied in the geopoliticians' maps have been adopted wherever maps are published: among them simplicity, emphasis by means of broad lines or heavy shading, the projection of direction or movement by arrows, and pictorial representation.

The geopoliticians' maps stood as expressions of "global thinking," which Haushofer stressed from the beginning as a necessary preliminary to successful world domination by Germany. Twentieth-century events made global thinking, as a basis for understanding the world, essential to everybody, though that use of the term is very unlike the meaning in geopolitics that gave it currency.

Geopolitics implies a systematic and detailed knowledge of the earth prepared for use by governments. This was the contribution of Haushofer's Institute of Geopolitics at Munich. Similar agencies were set up as a wartime expedient by nations plunged into conflict with Germany, only to find themselves at a dangerous disadvantage through the lack of information. In peace, no less than in war, nations can profit from knowing how the sources of wealth are distributed. The geographic survey, carried on by an agency of government, has permanent and universal utility. It extended the horizon of military procedure in two ways: by adding political strategy to military strategy; by preconditioning the fighting man for each separate natural environment likely to become a theatre of war. Obviously the share of the earth controlled by each nation is a matter involving geography as well as government. Kjellén recognized this in describing the power position of the eight strongest states on the threshold of war in 1914 (*Die Grossmächte der Gegenwart*, 1914), and Haushofer underlined it in the three volumes of his postwar revision and supplement (see *Bibliography*). If the apportionment of the earth's territory and resources among the nations can be measured in advance of war, each will have a true picture of the material foundation of its own power and that of its potential antagonists. So long as the analysis is objective, reliable as to facts, and unbiased by dogma, it can be argued that the study is as likely to lead a nation to shy away from war as to leap into it.

Geopolitics is calculated to aid governments in planning their foreign policy. Planning was conspicuous in German geopolitics. Both Germany and Japan based decisions to launch wars of conquest on geopolitical estimates of the relative power potential of the Axis nations and their adversaries. Their planning was based on a prejudiced estimate of power, however—overvaluation of their own and undervaluation of their rivals'. Bent on war, they prepared themselves to outfight selected opponents who were using equal or richer resources for ends only in small part military. They assumed that the militaristic way of life followed by both nations was mystically determined by the natural environment, instead of having grown up as a result of frequent decisions to fight. Their success in arms lasted only until latent opposition forces could be marshaled.

Planning is a leading objective of those who advocate geopolitics for the world at large. They use the word to mean that a nation should formulate its national policy only after duly appraising the natural environment as an inescapable condition of its power position. They differ from the German geopoliticians in avoiding ambiguous phrasing and in rejecting deliberate falsification. In these stands they take safe ground. Some of them, particularly those who have not been trained in geography, drop into the pitfall of metaphysical philosophy; a still larger number believe the natural environment to be deterministic. Imbued with these ideas, they jeopardize the soundness of their planning and expose their program to risks that proved disastrous to the German and Japanese geopoliticians.

Much of the lumber of geopolitics bids fair to be forgotten. It was used as scaffolding to construct a faulty intellectual edifice. The befuddling phrasemaking was no more than a device for hoodwinking people into accepting as "science" much that is unsound. Its exclusive orientation toward wars of conquest had value only to nations hoping to start such wars. The untenable hypotheses, such as the assumptions that the state is an organism and has a natural right to *Lebensraum*, helped bring on war, but did not show how to win it.

The name "geopolitics" has acquired such odium that many believe it to be unfit to associate with respectable scientific terms. It is the only name available to designate the German pseudo science, and it has been urged that "*Geopolitik*" be reserved for that movement. However, it fits, more exactly than any other title, most of the writing that attempts to apply political geography to the problems of a given nation. The term "applied political geography" is more aptly reserved for studies of the broad values and applications of geography to political life in general, viewed without national bias. Whatever the settled usage turns out to be, the world has been made aware of geography's value to government. *See also* GEOGRAPHY.

BIBLIOGRAPHY.—Principal German works on geopolitics: *Zeitschrift für Geopolitik*, monthly (1924–44; 1951–); Karl Haushofer, *Geopolitik des pazifischen Ozeans* (1924, 1938), *Grenzen in ihrer geographischen und politischen Bedeutung* (1927, 1939), *Wehrgeopolitik* (1932), *Der nationalsozialistische Gedanke in der Welt* (1933, published at the inauguration of the third *Reich*), *Weltpolitik von heute* (1934); Erich Obst, *England, Europa, und die Welt* (1927); Karl Haushofer et al., *Bausteine zur Geopolitik* (1928); Max Georg Schmidt, *Schmidt-Haack Geopolitischer Typen-Atlas* (1929); the following three titles constitute a geopolitics of the contemporary world under the editorship of Karl Haushofer: Rudolf Kjellén et al., *Die Grossmächte vor und nach dem Weltkriege* (1930), Karl Haushofer et al., *Jenseits der Grossmächte* (1932) and *Raumüberwindende Mächte* (1934); Adolf Grabowski, "Das Problem der Geopolitik," *Zeitschrift für Politik*, 22 (1933); Franz Braun and A. Hillen Ziegfeld, *Geopolitischer Geschichtsatlas* (1934); Walther Vogel, "Politische Geographie und Geopolitik," *Geographisches Jahrbuch*, 49 (1934); Otto Maull, *Das Wesen der Geopolitik* (1936). Works expounding, criticizing or reformulating geopolitics: Albert Demangeon, "Géographie politique," *Annales de Géographie*, 41 (1932); Jacques Ancel, *Géopolitique* (1936); Andréas Dorpalen, *The World of General Haushofer* (1942); Johannes Mattern, *Geopolitik* (1942); Raoul de Roussy de Sales, *The Making of Tomorrow* (1942); Nicholas J. Spykman, *America's Strategy in World Politics* (1942), *The Geography of the Peace* (1944); Robert Strausz-Hupé, *Geopolitics* (1942); Hans W. Weigert, *Generals and Geographers* (1942); Derwent Whittlesey et al., *German Strategy of World Conquest* (1942); "Haushofer: The Geopoliticians," in E. M. Earle et al. (eds.), *Makers of Modern Strategy* (1943); Hans W. Weigert and Vilhjalmur Stefansson (eds.), *Compass of the World* (1944); Hans W. Weigert, Vilhjalmur Stefansson and R. E. Harrison (eds.), *New Compass of the World* (1953); Preston E. James and Clarence F. Jones (eds.), *American Geography, Inventory and Prospect* (1954); Hans W. Weigert et al., *Principles of Political Geography* (1957).
(D. Wh.; H. W. Wt.; X)

GEOPOTENTIAL. The geopotential is the potential energy of a unit mass with reference to sea level. Surfaces of constant geopotential or level surfaces are fixed in space and may therefore be used as a scale to measure height. Height measured with reference to the geopotential surfaces is called geodynamic height, and the common unit is the dynamic metre. For the standard value of the gravitational constant the dynamic metre is equal to about 1.02 metric metres.

See ATMOSPHERE; METEOROLOGY; THERMODYNAMICS; UPPER AIR SOUNDINGS.
(H. G. Hn.)

GEORGE, SAINT, patron saint of England, was an early martyr in the east, perhaps at Lydda in Palestine where his alleged tomb is still shown. Nothing is known of his life. There is no reason to suppose that he is referred to, unnamed, in Eusebius' ecclesiastical history (viii, 5), and Gibbon's identification of him with George of Cappadocia, Athanasius' opponent, has been discredited. From the 6th century, legends about him as a warrior saint became very popular and increasingly extravagant. The story of his rescuing a maiden from a dragon, which first appears in the late 12th century and was popularized by the 13th-century *Golden Legend*, may owe something to the fact that the classical legend of Perseus and Andromeda was localized at Jaffa or Arsuf, not far from Lydda. This story is often represented in art, and St. George is frequently depicted as a youth wearing knight's armour with a scarlet cross.

St. George has been known in England at least since the 8th century, but how he came to be looked on as its patron saint is not clear. No doubt returning crusaders popularized his cult (he was said to have been seen in vision helping the crusaders at the siege of Antioch in 1098); but it is probable that he was not recognized as England's patron saint until King Edward III put the newly founded Order of the Garter under his protection. St. George is one of the 14 auxiliary saints, and his feast is April 23; in 1961 it was reduced by the Roman Catholic Church to commemoration.

See H. Delehaye, *Les Légendes grecques des saints militaires*, pp. 45–76 (1909); G. J. Marcus, *Saint George of England* (1929). (D. Ar.)

GEORGE I (1660–1727), king of Great Britain from 1714 to 1727, was born in 1660, the eldest son of Ernest Augustus (elector of Hanover from 1692) and of Sophia, granddaughter of James I of England. By his marriage to his cousin Sophia Dorothea in 1682, George succeeded ultimately in uniting the Hanoverian possessions of the house of Brunswick and so became one of the most important princes in northern Germany. His marriage proved dramatic. He suspected the fidelity of his wife, and her presumed lover, Graf von Königsmark, was assassinated, whether or not by George's orders is not known. George divorced his wife in 1694 and kept her a close prisoner in the castle of Ahlden, where she died 32 years later. He succeeded his father as elector of Hanover in 1698. George's mother, Sophia, became the heir of Queen Anne through the Act of Settlement in 1701.

George greatly enjoyed military life and fought with distinction in the wars against Louis XIV, showing exceptional courage. He sent useful reinforcements to the duke of Marlborough in time for the battle of Blenheim (1704). As his mother grew older and Queen Anne aged, the succession to the British crown seemed likely to devolve on him and British politicians began to court his favour. As some of the Tories, particularly Henry St. John, Viscount Bolingbroke, still flirted with the idea of a Stuart rather than a Hanoverian succession, George I developed strong links with the Whig leaders, who, with Marlborough, obtained in return a guarantee of his succession from the Dutch by the Barrier treaty of 1709. However, both the electress Sophia and the prince avoided taking steps that might have alienated Queen Anne, who viewed the succession of either with some repugnance. A difficult situation was resolved in 1714 by the death first of the electress on June 8 and of Queen Anne on Aug. 1. George succeeded to the throne without difficulty because of the skill of the Whigs in securing the control of the council just before the queen died.

Naturally George I formed a predominantly Whig ministry in which the younger politicians, the earl of Sunderland, James Stanhope, Lord Townshend and Robert Walpole (*see* ORFORD, ROBERT WALPOLE, 1st earl of.) enjoyed high office. This ministry won the general election, which the king's succession had made necessary, by a considerable majority. They immediately used their power to proscribe the Tories. This led to the flight of Bolingbroke, the imprisonment of Robert Harley, earl of Oxford, and to considerable discontent which encouraged the Jacobites to rebel in 1715. They were easily defeated and, although there was another abortive invasion by the Jacobites in 1719 and a further plot in 1722, George's position was never again seriously threatened.

George I was, however, far from popular. He disliked England and the English disliked him. Ugly rumours of his treatment of his wife were widely disseminated; his two middle-aged, rapacious German mistresses, the duchess of Kendal (*q.v.*) and the countess of Darlington, did nothing to improve his popularity, and the constant intrigues of his Hanoverian ministers in London made for difficulties with British statesmen. He personally disliked the trappings of monarchy, and although he was an exceptionally diligent king, possessing shrewd judgment in foreign affairs and very considerable knowledge of European diplomacy, he preferred a retired social life with his friends and mistresses. He was passionately devoted to opera and a good judge of music, but he possessed no interest whatever in architecture, painting or literature.

George's relationship with his son, the prince of Wales, was tempestuous (*see* GEORGE II). It was largely because of their quarrels that the king gave up attending the cabinet in order to avoid meeting the prince. The king saw his ministers personally in his closet and, in consequence, the cabinet, which had largely controlled the business of government in Queen Anne's reign, declined in importance. The violent quarrel between George I and his son in 1717 coincided with a split in the Whig party due partly to personal rivalry and partly to differences on foreign policy. Townshend and Walpole thought that Stanhope and Sunderland had adjusted their policy to the needs of the king's Hanoverian possessions. The king gave his support to Stanhope and Sunderland. In consequence the prince's household at Leicester house became the brilliant centre of the opposition, making a sharp contrast to the king's court. Whenever possible George I re-

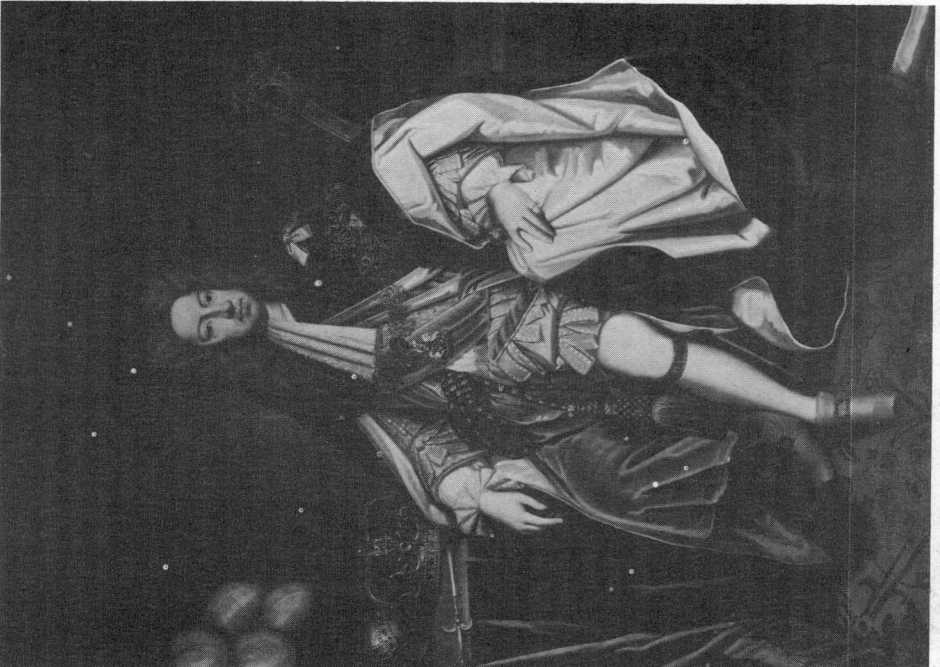

BY COURTESY OF THE NATIONAL PORTRAIT GALLERY, LONDON

GEORGE I: PORTRAIT FROM THE STUDIO OF SIR GODFREY KNELLER

turned to Hanover where the problems of government were simpler. However, contrary to popular belief, his interest in British affairs was always strong, and he gave them his detailed personal interest whether he was in Hanover or London. Nor did the king have the slightest difficulty in communicating with his British ministers; their common language was French, which the majority of British statesmen, including Walpole, understood. Indeed, George I was a far more active ruler than Queen Anne and his indifference to English affairs has been grossly exaggerated.

George himself played an active part in the diplomatic negotiations which led to the quadruple alliance (1718). He was less successful in his attempt to act as mediator in the diplomatic exchanges that led to the treaty of Nystad, 1721, which ended the Northern War. The king was also active in military affairs; he kept the control of the army in his own hands, strongly resented any ministerial interference with military appointments and took a keen personal interest in all details of army organization. In politics, however, the king found it more difficult to get his own way. Sunderland and Stanhope were checked from time to time by the opposition of Walpole and Townshend and on the question of the peerage bill (1719) defeated by them. To overcome these uncertainties, negotiations took place between the ministry and the Whig opposition which resulted in Walpole and Townshend returning to the ministry; one of the conditions for this had been the prior reconciliation of the king and the prince, which neither relished but both consented to.

No sooner had ministerial and family unity been achieved than the country was plunged into a financial crisis through the bursting of the South Sea Bubble (1720). George I, his German mistresses and the Hanoverians had invested largely in South Sea funds and taken part in transactions that were certainly dishonourable and probably illegal. For a time it seemed that the ministry might fall and the dynasty be endangered, but the skill of Walpole in handling the house of commons secured both. Although George I liked neither Townshend nor Walpole, he was forced to give them increased authority. In the following years they gradually pushed out of office ministers unsympathetic to themselves, such as Lord Carteret (afterward Earl Granville), even though they were friends of the king. By 1724 the king had come to accept them personally and to rely completely on their judgment. Townshend, as secretary of state, was careful to pay due attention to the problems of Hanover and pleased George I by his dexterity in handling the complex negotiations that led to the treaty of Hanover (1725). Their ministry gave the country great stability, and, even if it did not make George I popular, at least he became acceptable to the majority of the population.

George I died of apoplexy on June 11, 1727, on his way to visit Hanover. He left two children: his successor, George II, and Sophia Dorothea (1687-1757), wife of Frederick William I of Prussia and mother of Frederick the Great.

BIBLIOGRAPHY.—W. E. H. Lecky, *A History of England in the Eighteenth Century*, rev. ed. (1897); W. Michael, *Englische Geschichte im achtzehnten Jahrhundert*, 5 vol. (1896-1955), partly translated in *The Beginnings of the Hanoverian Dynasty* (1936) and *The Quadruple Alliance* (1939); Basil Williams, *The Whig Supremacy*, rev. ed. (1961), *Stanhope* (1932); J. H. Plumb, *Sir Robert Walpole*, 2 vol. (1956-61), *The First Four Georges* (1956); J. F. Chance, *George I and the Northern War* (1909), *The Alliance of Hanover* (1923).
(J. H. Pl.)

GEORGE II (1683-1760), king of Great Britain from 1727 to 1760, the only son of George I and Sophia Dorothea of Celle, was born in 1683. He married in 1705 Caroline (q.v.) of Ansbach, an attractive woman of strong intellectual interests. Like his father, George II was brought up to a military life, and he fought with some distinction at the battle of Oudenaarde (1708). The Whig ministers persuaded Queen Anne to make him duke of Cambridge in 1706, but he wisely refrained from taking his seat in the house of lords, although subjected to considerable pressure to do so by the Whigs, who saw in his presence in England a guarantee of the Hanoverian succession. He remained, however, in Germany with his father and came to England with George I in Sept. 1714.

Between George I and his son there was a great deal of mutual antipathy. On his first return visit to Hanover in 1716, George I refused to make his son regent and rigorously restricted his authority as guardian of the realm —a title previously unknown in England. The next year a bitter quarrel arose from a trivial misunderstanding with the godparents, whom the king had insisted on naming, on the birth of the prince's son. The prince was placed under house arrest, his children removed from his care, and the king only reluctantly persuaded to restore the prince's freedom. Naturally the prince consorted with the enemies of the king's ministers, and he and his wife maintained a brilliant court at Leicester house that was in marked contrast to the retired, almost secretive, life led by the king. A tepid reconciliation took place in 1720, but so strong was the ill feeling between father and son that, on George II's accession in 1727, everyone expected the immediate dismissal of his father's ministers. In fact, George at once named Sir Spencer Compton as head of affairs. Compton's incompetence and inability to control the house of commons, however, led the king to listen to the advice of his wife, who was strongly in favour of continuing Sir Robert Walpole (see ORFORD, ROBERT WALPOLE, 1st earl of) and Lord Townshend in office. This was done, and in gratitude Walpole obtained the largest civil list ever granted to a British monarch up to that time. Similar crises, caused by the king's initial rashness and overcome later by

BY COURTESY OF THE NATIONAL PORTRAIT GALLERY, LONDON

GEORGE II: DETAIL FROM A PORTRAIT BY THOMAS HUDSON, c. 1737

the good sense and judgment that he usually displayed on reflection, were to mark the reign. Although a man of limited intellectual ability, George II possessed personal characteristics that aided the development of constitutional monarchy. He was a man of narrow vision, restricted interests and strong habits, all combined with a lack of self-confidence.

His major interest in life was military affairs. His own life was regulated with the precision of a drill sergeant. His memory was as exact as his habits and his knowledge of genealogies, regiments and military personnel throughout Europe, most extensive. His courage in battle equaled his addiction to parades—he fought well at Dettingen (1743), the last time a British monarch led his troops in person, and he showed great *sang-froid* at the time of the Jacobite invasion of 1745, when he refused to leave London. Apart from military matters, the king's main interest was music. He loved opera and was the patron of Handel. He also gave his support to the foundation of the University of Göttingen and of Columbia university in New York. Like his father, George II took a great interest in day-to-day decisions about foreign and domestic affairs. He held strong views about men and measures, and, although frequently irascible and always obstinate, he never proved intransigent. Both in 1731 (treaty of Vienna) and again in 1733 (the War of the Polish Succession) George II sacrificed measures which he considered to be in the best interest of Hanover for the sake of British security and neutrality.

Just how much political influence over the king was enjoyed by Queen Caroline is difficult to assess. Certainly she adopted wholeheartedly the policies of Sir Robert Walpole and warmly advocated his cause, but her death in 1737 in no way diminished Walpole's influence with the king. More important than the queen's influence was the king's own sense of his shortcomings; in the last resort he preferred his ministers to take final responsibility, and as he ruled 33 years the result of this attitude was to strengthen greatly the authority of the king's ministers on all political questions, foreign and domestic. Although George II was deeply attached to his wife, he usually maintained a mistress, but not one of these enjoyed the least power of patronage and their financial rewards proved to be excessively modest. His relations with his son were as tempestuous as those with his own father had been, and his intense loathing of his heir, Frederick Louis (q.v.), was shared by Queen Caroline.

After the political crisis created by his accession, George II had resolutely supported Walpole, who pursued a policy of peace and retrenchment. Unable to bear criticism and jealous of his power, Walpole, with the king's support, had driven a number of his colleagues, including his brother-in-law Lord Townshend, out of office. In spite of a formidable press campaign in which neither the king nor his wife had been spared. Walpole had maintained his hold on parliament, partly because his policy pleased many uncommitted members of parliament and partly because the king permitted him to use, whenever he could, crown appointments for political purposes. The effect of this was to draw off many influential men from Toryism and to give powerful aristocratic support for the Hanoverian succession; this was demonstrated by the failure of Prince Charles Edward, the "Young Pretender," to win over any English politician of importance in his bid for the crown in 1745. Nevertheless the quarrel between Frederick Louis and his father gave the opposition a royal leader, increased its power (because the prince of Wales possessed considerable personal patronage), and finally made Walpole's position untenable when he showed himself a lukewarm and disapproving leader in the war against Spain (1739). Opposition politicians, however, displayed more interest in office than in the prince, whose uneasy relationship with his father continued until Frederick's death in 1751.

Although George II deeply regretted the loss in 1742 of Walpole, whom he personally honoured with a pension and title, he quickly found another mentor in Lord Carteret, whose knowledge of European affairs strengthened the king's confidence. For two years the king and Carteret pursued their own foreign policy with little or no consideration of the views of other ministers. Criticism mounted, and when Carteret agreed to take Hanoverian troops into British service and to pay for them the indignation became so forceful and widespread that the king was obliged to dismiss him. The leading antagonist to the use of Hanoverian troops had been William Pitt (afterward earl of Chatham), and George II did his utmost to prevent his promotion to minor office. Finally, threatened by the mass resignation of his ministers (an act which they as well as the king regarded as a most exceptional step and almost unconstitutional), George II yielded. Once more his basic good sense prevailed. As the king aged he took less and less interest in politics and was content to leave offices in the hands of the group of Whigs who could control parliament. Naturally he took an interest in appointments and he never hid his prejudices either about people or policies, but he preferred to leave the main direction of affairs in the hands of his principal ministers—Henry Pelham until his death in 1754 and afterward his brother, the duke of Newcastle, who, in the last years of George II's reign (1757–60), shared the control of the government with Pitt. This proved one of the most brilliantly successful war ministries of the 18th century and much to George II's delight won resounding victories in America, Africa, India and Europe.

George II died suddenly on Oct. 25, 1760, and was succeeded by his grandson, George III. His relations with his daughter-in-law, Princess Augusta, had remained frigid after Frederick's death, and Leicester house had continued to harbour discontented politicians. The king was far more cordial with the rest of his family, particularly his soldier-son the duke of Cumberland (1721–65) and his two unmarried daughters Amelia Sophia Eleonora (1711–86) and Elizabeth Caroline (1713–57). His other three daughters were married: Anne (1709–59) to William, prince of Orange; Mary (1723–72) to Frederick, landgrave of Hesse-Cassell; and Louisa (1724–51) to Frederick V, king of Denmark.

BIBLIOGRAPHY.—There are two excellent memoirs of George II's reign: Lord Hervey, *Some Materials for the Memoirs of the Reign of George II*, 3 vol., ed. by R. R. Sedgwick (1931, abridged ed. 1952); Horace Walpole, *Memoirs of the Reign of George II*, 3 vol. (1947). *See also* W. E. H. Lecky, *A History of England in the Eighteenth Century*, rev. ed. (1897); J. H. Plumb, *The First Four Georges* (1956), *Sir Robert Walpole*, 2 vol. (1956–61); J. B. Owen, *The Rise of the Pelhams* (1957). (J. H. PL.)

GEORGE III (1738–1820), king of Great Britain from 1760 to 1820, enjoyed (perhaps suffered might be the better word) one of the longest reigns in British history. In the course of it Britain changed from a stable squirearchy with a population of about 7,750,000 to a country of almost 14,500,000 in which industrial interests were beginning to agitate for power. The constitution in 1760 was the admiration of all Europe but by 1820 it was condemned even by some of the aristocracy themselves. Religious issues, dormant in 1760, produced anarchic riot in the middle of the reign and at its end were embittering politics and disturbing Ireland. Above all, in those years, the first British empire was lost with the formation of the United States of America. For this loss, the consolidation of control in Canada, the expansion of trade settlements into a government in India, the establishment of a foothold in Australia and the purchase of the Cape Colony in South Africa all seemed an inadequate compensation.

In the economic changes, except for those (not inconsiderable) concerned with increasing productivity by the spread of scientific agriculture, George III was not personally involved, but for the loss of America and for the embitterment of political struggle the king has often been given the major share of the blame. It is certain that George's character was important in all the political events of the reign. His enemies invented the legend that he wished to upset the constitution and to return to the despotism of the Stewarts. This, as study of the working of politics both before and after his accession has proved, is nonsense, but without seeking for new powers the king, in the mid-18th century, was bound to be in a commanding position. His was the responsibility for holding together—and often for holding together—the ministry. Parliament might veto his choice or cause him such difficulty that he had to think again. The circle of men who could ever be made ministers was so small and so interlocked by marriage and friendship that his choice was always limited. Nevertheless, his was the initiative in cabinetmaking and with this initiative went much power. For once a politician had his hands upon the offices and perquisites of government, he could build a

BY GRACIOUS PERMISSION OF H.M. QUEEN ELIZABETH II
GEORGE III; PORTRAIT BY PETER EDWARD STROEHLING (1807), WITH WINDSOR CASTLE IN THE BACKGROUND

considerable political connection by attracting to himself many seekers after place and profit, both noble and humble. When most men had their price, the king could give any chosen leader great bidding power by handing over his treasury patronage.

George III in his youth was more keenly aware of a quite different source of royal strength. Ordinary men disapproved of party politics and in consequence the great politicians pretended to disapprove. The accepted theory was that the king should express the common sense of the country; opposition to him, or his government, could then be dismissed as factious and unpatriotic. For this reason also, therefore, the king's character was of the highest importance for it would influence his effective power. But whatever his character might be, the power would remain considerable.

Early Years.—George III was the son of Frederick Louis (*q.v.*), prince of Wales, and Princess Augusta of Saxe-Gotha. He was born on June 4, 1738 (new style). His father followed the normal Hanoverian practice of heading the party of opposition to the king and to the king's ministers, thus giving that opposition a sort of respectability. From his parents and their entourage, with its headquarters at Leicester house, the young George imbibed an unreasonable dislike of King George II, his grandfather, and of all his policies. George was a child of strong feelings but of slow mental development. This unequal growth of brain and heart produced an appearance of apathy which made him difficult to teach but only too easy to command; he could not read properly until he was 11, while his affection for his immediate family circle dominated his life.

When George was 12 his father died, leaving him heir to the throne and leaving him also to concentrate his love upon his mother and his brother Edward. As the heir began, from his 18th birthday, conscientiously to prepare for his future responsibilities, it is clear that he tormented himself with thoughts of his inadequacy. The curious blend of obstinate determination with self-distrust, which is a feature of his maturity, was already evident. His method of screwing up his courage was to set himself an ideal of conduct. This ideal he thought he had found personified in the earl of Bute (see BUTE, JOHN STUART, 3rd earl of), who became George's inspiration, his teacher and, it was intended, his future chief minister.

George III was potentially a much better politician than Bute, for he had tenacity and, as experience matured him, he could use guile to achieve his ends. But at his accession in 1760 George III did not know his own capacity nor the incapacity of his hero. Even in the matter of marriage George professed that Bute's friendship mattered more to him than the love of women. The prince in 1759 had dutifully sacrificed his desire for Lady Sarah Lennox. As king, in 1761, he asked for a review to be made of all eligible German Protestant princesses "to save a great deal of trouble," as "marriage must sooner or later come to pass." He chose Charlotte Sophia of Mecklenburg-Strelitz and married her on Sept. 8, 1761. The marriage was entered into in the spirit of public duty, but thanks to the king's need for security and to his wife's strength of character it lasted unblemished for more than 50 years. Bute's only other useful contribution to his master was to have encouraged his interest in botany and to have implanted in the court more respect for the graces of life, including patronage of the arts, than had been usual for the past half century.

Political Instability, 1760–70.—Politically, the government of England at this time was weak because it lacked effective executive machinery and because members of parliament were always more ready to criticize than to co-operate with it. Moreover, the ministers were, for the most part, quarrelsome and difficult to drive as a team. The king's first responsibility was that of holding coalitions of great peers together. But he imagined that his duty was to purify public life and to substitute duty to himself for personal intrigue. The two great men in office at the accession were Pitt (see CHATHAM, WILLIAM PITT, 1st earl of) and the duke of Newcastle. Bute and George III disliked both of them, calling Newcastle a knave and Pitt (a renegade from the Leicester house group) "the blackest of hearts" and "a true snake in the grass." Pitt was allowed to resign (Oct. 1761) on the question of war against Spain. Newcastle followed into retirement when his control of treasury matters seemed to be challenged. The two former ministers were at loggerheads with one another but each was dangerous as a focal point for criticism of the new government made up of second-rate men such as the earl of Halifax or the duke of Bedford under the touchy captaincy of Bute. It had two principal problems: to make peace and to restore peacetime finance. It was humiliating to the new king that he was forced to employ Henry Fox, one of the corrupt politicians whom he had dreamed of purging out of public life, to carry through parliament the ratification of the peace treaties and the cider tax, which was intended to remedy the chronic budget deficit.

Though peace was made, it was done in such a way as to isolate Britain in Europe and for almost 30 years the country suffered from the new alignments of the European powers. Nor was George III happy in his attempt to express the agreed purposes of the country which to Bute had seemed so clear. George III might "glory in the name of Briton" but his attempts to speak out for his country were ill-received. In 1765 he was being vilified by the gutter press organized by "that devil Wilkes" while patriotic gentlemen, moved by Pitt or Newcastle, suspected that the peace had been botched and that the king was conspiring with Bute against their liberties. For Bute the way out was easy: he resigned (April 1763). George III, though he often talked of abdication, knew that despite misrepresentation he must battle on.

Too late George III realized that his clumsiness had destroyed one political combination and made any other difficult to assemble. He turned to George Grenville (q.v.), to his uncle the duke of Cumberland, to Pitt and to the duke of Grafton for help. All failed him. George Grenville bullied him and offended his feelings for his mother, the princess dowager. Cumberland's nominee, Lord Rockingham (q.v.), could neither combine with Pitt nor force his own cabinet to agree. Pitt (now Chatham) was frustrated both in his European and his American projects and lapsed into a temporary insanity. As for Grafton, he succeeded only in involving the king in further charges of tyranny over John Wilkes (q.v.). The first decade of the reign was one of such ministerial instability that it was vain to expect any solution to the basic problems of the country. Overseas trade expanded but no method was found of tapping private gains. The riches of India swelled the numbers of retired nabobs but the East India company made no significant contribution to the state. The attempt to make the American colonists meet their own administrative costs only aroused them to resistance. Nor was there consistency in British colonial policy. The Stamp act (1765) was passed by Grenville only to be repealed by Rockingham in 1766. An act declaratory of British right to impose direct as well as indirect taxes was accompanied by declarations that such taxation was inexpedient. Indirect taxes, in the form of the Townshend duties (1767), were imposed without calculation of their probable yield and then repealed (except for that of tea) as a maneuver in home politics.

For this sorry record of profitless squabbling George III was blamed. According to Edmund Burke and his friends, the reason the king could not keep a ministry was that he was faithless; intrigues with friends "behind the curtain" were said to have ruined the king's official ministers. In truth, however, the king was not guilty of causing chaos by intrigue. He had had no political contact with Bute after 1766; the so-called "king's friends" were not his agents but rather those who looked to him for leadership such as his predecessors had given. The king's error was in his tactless expression of his feelings. It was not his fault that no one group was strong enough to control the commons. Much of his inability to unite the groups may be attributed to his inexperience. Furthermore, in this period the issues of Wilkes and of America raised constitutional questions of a profoundly unknown since 1714.

By 1770 George III had learned a good deal. His tightly screwed-up obstinacy was as great as ever. Indeed the misfortunes he had experienced had made him feel more intensely the need to guide the nation. He felt that he had a torturing duty laid upon him by God but he realized by 1770 that he would have to reckon with the realities of political life in doing this duty. He no longer scorned to make use of executive power for winning elections nor did he withhold his official blessing from those of whose characters he disapproved. Lord Shelburne, in a hostile mood, described this metamorphosis—"by the familiarity of his intercourse he obtained your confidence, procured from you your opinion on different public characters, and then availed himself of the knowledge to sow dissension." Put more kindly, this means that George had learned to hold his tongue and to exploit his friendliness to encourage others to talk.

North's Ministry, 1770–82.—In 1770 the king was lucky enough to find a minister, Lord North (see GUILFORD, BARONS AND EARLS OF), who was, as no one had been since Chatham's departure to the house of lords, a leader with power to cajole the commons. North's Walpolean policy of letting sleeping dogs lie lulled the suspicions of independent country members, always so ready to imagine that the executive was growing too strong. North was a good financier and this was appreciated by men of official business and by taxpayers. George III thought North slow and hesitant but he valued his loyalty, his good temper and his skill in debate. Rapidly the king's affectionate nature asserted itself; he gave North, along with many petulant pieces of advice, his warm support. As a result, 12 years of stable government followed the decade of disturbance.

Unfortunately, issues and prejudices survived from the earlier period which North could not muffle but could not cure. Wilkes, in spite of the king's complaints, was allowed to go unharried. India, under the new Regulating act, fell into the background but America was the greatest and the fatal issue. North could not avoid it because the English squires in parliament agreed with their king. America must pay for its own defense and, if possible, for a share of the debt remaining from the war which had given the colonies security. Those who resisted this must be rebels. George III's personal responsibility for the loss of America lies not in any assertion of his royal prerogative. Indeed, Americans were disposed to admit his personal supremacy; their quarrel was with the assertion of the sovereignty of the British parliament. George III was, eventually hated in America because he insisted upon linking himself with his parliament, in being the British constitutional monarch rather than the king of Massachusetts, of Virginia and of New York. North would have had difficulty in ignoring Boston's insults to him in any case; with the king and the house of commons watching to see that he was not weak, he inevitably took the steps that led to war in 1775.

George III was a typical English squire in his feelings about the war as it began, but by 1779 typical English squires had sickened of misfortune and were in a hurry to forget that they had ever believed in the coercion of America. George III was less erratic and therefore less fortunate. He said that no one could believe that the war was defensible on economic grounds but that it still had to be fought; if disobedience were seen to prosper, Ireland would follow along the same path and England would end up insular, insulted and impotent. He argued also, after the French had joined the Americans in 1778, that French finances would collapse before those of Britain. So the king prolonged the war, possibly by two years, by his desperate determination and by his pressure upon Lord North. The period from 1779 to 1782 left a further black mark upon the king's reputation. By 1780 the majority of members of parliament blamed North's government for the calamities which had befallen the country, yet this government remained in power. As yet there was no responsible or acceptable alternative, for the opposition was reputed both unpatriotic and divided, but at the time people believed that corruption alone supported an administration which was equally incapable of waging war or ending it. This supposed increase in corruption was laid directly at the king's door, for North wearily repeated his wish to resign, thus appearing a mere puppet of George III. Hence the passage in April 1780 of Dunning's famous resolution in the house of commons—"That the influence of the Crown has increased, is increasing, and ought to be diminished." When North fell at last in 1782, George III's prestige was at a low ebb. The death of Rockingham in July 1782 after four months in office and the failure of Shelburne's ministry (1782–83) reduced George to the lowest point of all in 1783. North joined with Charles James Fox (q.v.) and the two partners imposed themselves upon the crown; North seemed to accept Fox's aim of giving a stout knock to royal control. The king was not consulted in the making up of a team of junior ministers. The intrigues of politicians in party politics were gaining importance at the expense of royal direction. George admitted that he had to "form a ministry among men who know I cannot trust them ... making me a kind of slave." He concluded that his only honourable course was abdication.

George and the Younger Pitt, 1783–1806.—Yet within a year the king had dramatically turned the tables, carrying out, amid applause, the most high-handed act of royal initiative in the 18th century. When Fox and North produced a plan to reform the East India company, which aroused fear that they intended to perpetuate their power by controlling eastern patronage, the king re-emerged as the guardian of the national interest. He let it be known that anyone who supported the plan in the house of lords would be reckoned his enemy. The bill was defeated. The ministers resigned. The king was ready with a new "patriotic" leader, William Pitt (q.v.), the Younger. This initiative was dangerous. Pitt's government was in a minority in the house of commons and the discarded ministers were in a mood to threaten a constitutional upheaval. Everything depended upon the verdict of the general election in March 1784. The country, moved by real feeling as well as by treasury influence, overwhelmingly endorsed the king's claim to have anticipated their wishes. The king did not go on after his victory to further demonstrations of power. Though many of Pitt's ideas were unwelcome to him he contented himself with criticism and a few grumbles. Pitt could not survive without the king but the king, if he lost Pitt, would have been at the mercy of Fox. They compromised but the compromise left most power, with the king's willing assent, in Pitt's capable young hands. In part this was because George III had no ambitions to raise his own constitutional status but was satisfied to have a minister he could trust to act cautiously and patriotically; in part, it arose from the king's domestic preoccupations.

The king loved his children possessively and with that hysterical force which he had always shown in relations with those close to him. He did not enjoy the prince of Wales's coming of age in 1783, first because it was emancipation from the family, and second because the occupant of the throne must always see in his heir a *memento mori*. The king's ruefulness was soon converted into rage. The prince associated with Fox's Whigs politically and with Fox's gaming friends socially. In contrast to George III's rather strait-laced court (in which Fanny Burney was spiritually at ease though physically cold and uncomfortable), the prince's circle was gay and dissolute. The king's sons, as they grew up, escaped him one by one for loose women and clutching moneylenders. George III in face of any intractable problem, personal or political, was apt to oscillate from excitement to despair. In the crises of his reign he frequently talked of abdication; but in 1788 it was announced that it was his reason which had fled its throne. The stresses endured by this hard-working man seemed sufficient to account for his violent breakdown. Twentieth-century medical investigation, however, indicated that the king had an inherited defect in his metabolism known as porphyria. An excess in purple-red pigments in the blood intoxicated all parts of the nervous system, producing the agonizing pain, excited over-activity, paralysis, and delirium which the king suffered in an acute form, at least four times in his reign.

The king's incapacity produced a political storm. But while Pitt and Fox battled over the powers that the prince of Wales should enjoy as regent, the king suddenly recovered in 1789. He was left with the fear that he might again collapse into the nightmare of madness. On occasion he could even use his mental fragility as a means of getting his own way. A minister who crossed him might receive a hint that unless the king was gratified he might easily go mad again, and his ministers, once they had quarreled with his heir, were influenced by such a threat. But on the whole the king, for the last decade of the 18th century, bothered more about the details than about the main lines of policy. Pitt, whose policies contented him more and more, gradually absorbed in his own following most of North's old connection and even some of Fox's. After the outbreak of war with revolutionary France in 1793, all but the most radical Whigs joined the government, leaving Fox in hopeless, if eloquent, opposition.

The war with France seemed to most of the aristocracy and the upper middle class to be waged for national survival. The king felt this too. In such an atmosphere he became more popular than he had ever been before. The old man, a man who had been the object of compassion in his collapse, an obviously well-meaning man, was soon a symbol of the old English order for which the country was fighting. His potential power in politics was thus greatly increased but his will to use such a power, except in an emergency, was enfeebled. George III enjoyed himself in encouraging farmers to grow more food for a nation at war; or he talked for hours (ending his sentences rhetorically and fussily with the repeated words "what, what, what?") about past conflicts or military tactics or even of the shortcomings of Shakespeare; or he played to himself on his harpsichord; or he regulated the lives of his daughters, who found it so much less easy to escape than did his sons. From such quiet occupations he was roused to activity by Pitt's Irish policy at the turn of the century.

The French war had made the issue of Catholic emancipation urgent. Rebellion in Ireland, in Pitt's view, could not be cured simply by the union of the British and Irish parliaments. Conciliation, by the political emancipation of the Roman Catholics, was a necessary concomitant of union. George III believed this proposal to be radical ruin masquerading as reform and destroyed Pitt's hopes of carrying the emancipation measure on the strength of his own prestige. The king and the country gentlemen revolted together against their overclever prime minister. Pitt resigned

(1801) and George III persuaded the mild Addington (see SIDMOUTH, HENRY ADDINGTON, 1st Viscount) to form a less adventurous cabinet. The collapse of Addington's administration in 1804, after the short peace (1802–03) of Amiens, brought Pitt back into office (1804–06), but he came back at the cost of giving up his emancipation proposals. The king was decisive in this crisis only because it was an issue upon which he felt most deeply and on which he instinctively expressed the feelings of the majority of the backbenchers in the house of commons, though it must be admitted that Pitt never pushed the matter to a real trial of strength.

Last Years, 1806–20.—On the death of Pitt (Jan. 1806), the king accepted Fox as foreign secretary in the "ministry of all the talents" (1806–07). He even came to feel affection for Fox and to lament his death (Sept. 1806) sincerely. During this short period of Whig administration the king allowed his ministers to discuss (abortively) peace with Napoleon and to abolish the slave trade; he asserted himself and forced their resignation only when they dared to propose some amelioration of the laws against Catholics. This second break on the Catholic issue came about in circumstances which witnessed to George's declining abilities. He was still strong in body but had become almost blind. He needed the help of a secretary to help him in the task, which he would not reduce, of reading all the official papers. Lord Grenville thought the king had agreed to a paper which proposed the grant of higher rank in the army for papists. The king thought that his ministers were trying to trick him and that Sidmouth alone had explained to him the significance of the paper. He demanded from his ministers a promise not to bring the subject up again, for he feared he might be deceived into betraying his sworn duty to the Church of England. The perfectly proper refusal of ministers to pledge themselves for the future led to their supersession by the Tories, under Lord Portland (1807–09), Spencer Perceval (1809–12) and Lord Liverpool (1812–27) successively.

Much of the remainder of the king's lifetime was a living death. The death of his youngest child, Princess Amelia, in 1810 was a bitter blow; she had, in part, consoled him for his disappointment about his sons. She had been his companion at Windsor and in those visits to Weymouth when the king, like the prince of Wales, indulged in the new habit of seaside holidays. Worse still was the return of the king's illness.

In 1811 it was acknowledged that he was violently insane. The doctors continued to hope for recovery but parliament enacted the regency of the prince of Wales and decreed that the queen should have the custody of her husband. He remained insane, with intervals of senile lucidity, until his death at Windsor castle on Jan. 29, 1820.

George III's reign on its personal side was the tragedy of a well-intentioned man who was faced with problems too great for him to solve but from which his conscience prevented any attempt at escape. He was incapable of the intellectual effort required to see a situation dispassionately. Thus while he could climb over obstacles with cunning and determination, he could not succeed in any long-term objective. On its constitutional side the reign saw the emergence of party politics. Eventually this was to diminish royal influence but so long as the idea of party was a novelty and so long as the king could express the convictions of the majority of the politically powerful class which as yet was unorganized, he could, on occasion, sweep politicians aside and exercise a power as great as any of his Hanoverian ancestors. See also references under "George III" in the Index.

See J. Steven Watson, *The Reign of George III*, with full bibliography (1960). (J. S. WA.)

GEORGE IV (1762–1830), king of Great Britain and Ireland from 1820 to 1830, was born at St. James's palace, London, on Aug. 12, 1762, the eldest son of George III (q.v.). He became a good linguist, speaking German, French and Italian fluently. Liberated from the harshness, narrowness and restraint of his father's court at the age of 21, when he was given an establishment of his own, he threw decency and self-control to the winds and gave himself up to self-indulgence. By then he was the close friend of Charles James Fox and other dissipated Whigs, and for that reason too, his father regarded him with hatred and contempt.

Before he was 17 he confessed to being "rather too fond of women and wine." After the termination of an intrigue with the Drury lane actress Mary Robinson ("Perdita"), he fell in love with Mrs. (Maria Anne) Fitzherbert (1756–1837), a beautiful and virtuous Roman Catholic who had been twice widowed. She refused to become his mistress, but, after much importunity, consented to marry him. A young Anglican curate, R. Burt, performed the ceremony in secret on Dec. 15, 1785, in the drawing room of Mrs. Fitzherbert's house, and was rewarded with £500 and a promise of preferment. The marriage was illegal, the Royal Marriages act of 1772 prohibiting members of the royal family under the age of 25 from marrying without the king's consent; and by the Act of Settlement (1701) an heir apparent who married a Catholic forfeited his right to the succession. The prince did not do so because the marriage was invalid and in any case was kept secret. There was one child, a son, who later married, and the family emigrated to America.

In order to induce parliament to pay his debts, the prince agreed to take his father's advice and to marry his cousin Caroline (q.v.), daughter of the duke of Brunswick and of George III's sister Augusta. About the same time, in June 1794, the prince broke with Mrs. Fitzherbert, having fallen a victim to the charms of Lady Jersey, whose husband was his master of the horse. The marriage with Caroline (April 1795) was a loveless one. It turned out disastrously, and the blunder cost George 25 years' unceasing humiliation and torture. On Jan. 7, 1796, the princess gave birth to a daughter, Princess Charlotte, and a few weeks later the parents were formally separated. For a time the prince went back to Mrs. Fitzherbert, the only woman he ever deeply loved. He inquired after her on his deathbed and died with her portrait in miniature round his neck.

George III became permanently insane in Nov. 1810 and the prince became regent in 1811 under the terms of the Regency act. As it was thought that the king might recover, his son's powers were limited for one year. During that period he was debarred from creating peers, from granting offices in reversion and from granting offices otherwise than during pleasure (except such as were required by law to be granted for life or during good behaviour). In Feb. 1812, on the removal of these restrictions, he decided to retain his father's ministers and finally broke with his old friends, the Whigs, with whom his connection had become less close since the death of Fox in 1806. That momentous decision was unquestionably in the national interest, though the extraordinary vacillation he now displayed deprives him of much of the merit of his action. It was the right decision because Lord Grey and most of the Whigs had become convinced of the hopelessness of carrying on the war against France. Grey, indeed, was prepared to recommend peace on terms which would have left Napoleon undisputed master of the continent. Moreover, the Whigs would have insisted on the passing of a Catholic relief bill as a *sine qua non*, whereas the prince regent, in spite of former pledges, was no longer favourably inclined to the Catholics; nor was the nation.

George III's death on Jan. 29, 1820, gave his son the title of king without altering the position he had had since the expiration of the regency restrictions. The arrival of Caroline in England (June 1820) from the continent, where she had been living since 1814, caused Lord Liverpool's ministry to introduce into the house of lords a bill to dissolve the marriage and to deprive her of her royal title, the evidence to support a charge of adultery having been collected in Italy two years earlier. But that evidence, though strong, was inconclusive, and, after the bill had been read a third time in the house of lords on Nov. 10 by a majority of only nine, the government, realizing that it would never pass the house of commons, abandoned it. Early in 1821 Caroline accepted a parliamentary grant for her maintenance, and, to everybody's relief, she died on Aug. 7 of that year. Her popularity had been declining, and she was soon forgotten.

George IV's reputation either as a man or as a sovereign has never stood high, and his character is beyond rehabilitation. It is true that he possessed good qualities and accomplishments. Even his enemies admitted that he was one of the cleverest men in the country. He was an excellent judge of pictures. He recognized the genius of Jane Austen and made Walter Scott a baronet. He was one of the most generous of brothers. He hated bloodshed and violence, and loathed deciding, at meetings of the "great cabinet," the fate of prisoners who had been sentenced to death at the Old Bailey; he always leaned to the side of mercy against the opposite inclinations of the lord chief justice. But he deserves little credit for giving his father's library to the British museum: he was with difficulty prevented from selling that magnificent collection to the tsar. Though his wife was a worthless woman, unfit to be queen of England, he treated her shamefully even in the days of her innocence. He twice cast Mrs. Fitzherbert aside after living with her for periods of nine and six years, and repeatedly denied that she was anything but his mistress. He was as faithless to his friends as to his mistresses: with reason, one of the former (the 2nd duke of Northumberland) remarked, "Sincerity and gratitude are certainly plants which do not flourish in a Court." George IV had few friends among the aristocracy, and Viscount Castlereagh was the only cabinet minister for whom he had real affection. He preferred the small circle of his creatures, among whom he could drink and blaspheme without restraint. He habitually indulged in the coarsest language, and some early letters that passed between him and his brothers are so indecent that they will probably never be published. The grand duchess Catherine of Russia, who met him in 1814, declared: "His vaunted amiability really consists of the most licentious, not to say dirty talk, I have heard in my life." One of his ministers said that when he was in Scotland and Ireland he behaved not like a sovereign coming in pomp and state to visit those portions of his dominions but like a popular candidate on an electioneering trip. When he arrived in Dublin in Aug. 1821 he was hardly fit to be received by his subjects, so great was the quantity of drink he had consumed.

His unpopularity with the common people (though they rarely saw him) was associated in their minds with the extravagances of his pavilion at Brighton, with the persecution of his wife and with the general reactionary character of his ministers' policy. He certainly died unlamented. As a sovereign he was inefficient. Boxes of official papers requiring his signature often lay unopened for weeks. He continually thwarted and harassed his prime minister, Lord Liverpool (1822–27), intriguing to undermine his position and sometimes flatly refusing to do business with him. On one occasion he even offered the premiership to Lord Sidmouth behind Liverpool's back.

It was partly because he was always under the influence of a personality stronger than his own that no reliance could be placed on his word. On the question of Catholic emancipation, for instance, he was governed from the grave by his father and his brother Frederick, duke of York. He cared little about the grievances of the Catholics; he did care about his popularity, and he was reluctant to depart from the example of his father and Frederick, who owed much of their popularity to their uncompromising hostility to Catholic emancipation. In 1812, therefore, he would not take the responsibility of choosing Whig ministers who would refuse to accept office unless they were given the right to introduce a relief bill.

He was one of those sovereigns who could not live without a favourite, male and female. Almost throughout the regency the female favourite was Lady Hertford; then in 1819 she was super-

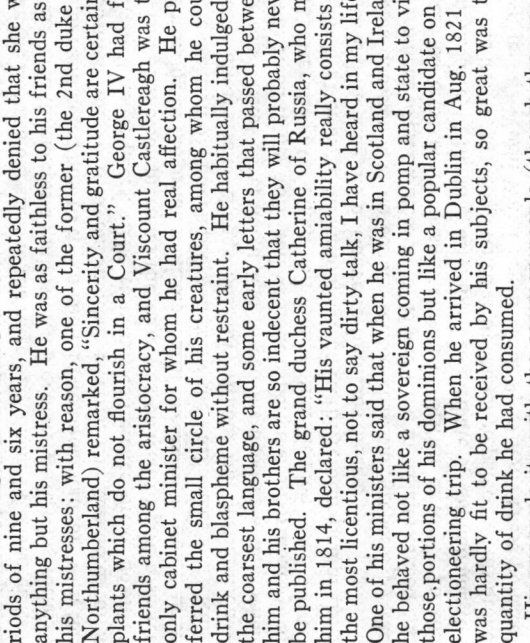

BY COURTESY OF THE NATIONAL PORTRAIT GALLERY, LONDON

GEORGE IV, AS PRINCE REGENT; UNFINISHED PORTRAIT BY SIR THOMAS LAWRENCE, c. 1814

seded by Lady Conyngham, who made a fortune out of her connection with him. Of the males, Sir William Knighton, the physician and keeper of the privy purse, was the most remarkable. It was his ambition to be the king's secret adviser, the power behind the throne. George IV always consulted him in matters of high policy and often deferred to his opinion. It was principally to Knighton that George Canning owed his appointment as prime minister in April 1827, following the physical collapse of Lord Liverpool. Wellington's friend Charles Arbuthnot wrote a frantic letter to Knighton appealing to him to support the duke's claims to the premiership. "If the Duke is to be saved to the king and the country it will be mainly your doing." The king himself wrote to Knighton, "I know I may repose myself in perfect confidence in your hands."

George IV succeeded to a power greater than that of any of his successors. Though tending to decline, it remained substantially unchanged until the Reform act of 1832 transformed the political situation by sweeping away nearly all the rotten and nomination boroughs and extending the franchise, thus destroying the greater part of the elaborate system of patronage and nomination which had enabled the king to change his ministers and to secure for those of his own choice adequate parliamentary support. The growing political consciousness of the people, fostered by the spread of education, by the press and public meetings, made for ultimate change; and the power of public opinion was to be strikingly revealed in Ireland in 1828–29 and in England during the struggle for the Reform bill. Moreover, the personal character of George IV deprived the crown of the support of that moral influence which his father had possessed by reason of his private virtues and which the monarchy was not to recover until Victoria's reign. Also, the decline in the number of political "groups" or "connexions" in parliament had the effect of limiting the king's freedom to choose his ministers. The regent's decision in Feb. 1812 to keep the Tory ministers in office almost entirely destroyed the Carlton house party—the party of "king's friends." The dissolution of a political group that had consisted of some 30 peers and about the same number of members of the commons destroyed a powerful weapon for resisting either ministerial or popular dictation.

In 1820 the king threatened to retire to Hanover because Lord Liverpool would not at first sanction either the introduction of a divorce bill or the provision of a greatly enlarged civil list for the new sovereign. Because he was unable to find alternative ministers he had to make a humiliating surrender to Liverpool's cabinet, with which the Whig opposition was in complete agreement on these points. Similarly, the resignation of more than 40 ministers in April 1827, when they declined to serve under George Canning, compelled the king to acquiesce in the admission of the Whigs to office, with Canning as head of a coalition; and, since the Whigs had always supported Catholic emancipation, George IV had no resource in 1829 but to retain the Wellington cabinet after it decided to avert civil war in Ireland by conceding the Catholic claims.

By speaking disrespectfully of Lord Liverpool to his colleagues and by insinuating that they alone enjoyed his confidence, he sought to undermine the prime minister's position. By seeking advice from nonministerial sources, even from men avowedly in opposition, George IV tacitly encouraged attempts to undermine the authority of the cabinet as a whole. After 1825 Canning, who succeeded Castlereagh as foreign secretary in Sept. 1822, completely won over the king by the success of his foreign policy and by a judicious attention to him and to Knighton. He, in fact, gained an ascendancy at Windsor unrivaled by that of any contemporary minister, and that ascendancy was used in 1827 to foster the king's aversion to the high Tories. By throwing himself wholeheartedly into Canning's hands in April 1827, George IV practically destroyed his connection with the Tories, as, 15 years earlier, he had broken his connection with the Whigs; and consequently the monarchy lost what had been its strongest support. But, as he quarreled with the Tories without abandoning their strongest prejudices, he failed to regain the confidence of the Whigs which he had forfeited in 1812 when he abandoned Whig principles; and after 1827 he ceased to have any personal weight with either of the two great parties.

George IV died at Windsor on June 26, 1830. He was succeeded by his brother, the duke of Clarence, as William IV. His only legitimate child, Princess Charlotte, married Leopold of Saxe-Coburg (1816), afterward king of the Belgians, and died in childbirth on Nov. 6, 1817.

See also references under "George IV" in the Index volume.

BIBLIOGRAPHY.—W. H. Wilkins, Mrs. Fitzherbert and George IV, 2 vol. (1905); Shane Leslie, George IV (1926); Roger Fulford, George IV, rev. ed. (1949). See also A. Aspinall (ed.), The Letters of George IV, 3 vol. (1938), and The Letters of Princess Charlotte, 1811-17 (1949).
(A. Ar.)

GEORGE V (1865-1936), King of Great Britain from 1910 to 1936, was born in London at Marlborough house on June 3, 1865, the second son of the then prince of Wales (afterward Edward VII). His childhood was largely spent in Norfolk at Sandringham, the home to which he was pre-eminently devoted throughout life. His father decided that a naval training was the best preparation for the responsibilities of his two sons, although their grandmother, Queen Victoria, agreed to this only with reluctance. When George was 12 he joined the training ship "Britannia" as a naval cadet with his elder brother Prince Albert Victor and his tutor J. N. Dalton. The two brothers served in the "Bacchante" from 1879 to 1882, their service including a cruise around the world. Throughout the 1880s the prince continued his naval service, being stationed for part of the time at Malta, where he lived on terms of intimate friendship with the family of his uncle Prince Alfred, duke of Edinburgh. It is understood that the duke of Edinburgh started the prince's interest in philately which led to his building up one of the finest private collections of the stamps of Great Britain and its colonies. Prince George was a commander in the navy when his whole career was changed by the unexpected death of his elder brother on Jan. 14, 1892.

As eventual heir to the throne the prince had to abandon his naval career and prepare for the responsibilities of kingship. In 1893 he became engaged to Princess Mary of Teck (q.v.), who had been his brother's fiancée; they were married in the Chapel Royal, St. James's palace, on July 6, 1893. He had been created duke of York on Queen Victoria's birthday in 1892. In the early years of his marriage the duke lived largely at York cottage—a small house on the Sandringham estate—and at York house in St. James's palace. Children were born in rapid succession and during the 1890s the duke and duchess, apart from occasional visits to their relations abroad, devoted themselves to public work at home and, on the duke's part, to study. He always felt that his naval training had placed him at a disadvantage for the throne.

After the death of Queen Victoria on Jan. 22, 1901, Prince George was created duke of Cornwall and set out with the duchess on March 16 on board the "Ophir" to open the first Australian commonwealth parliament in Melbourne. They returned to England by way of South Africa and Canada and at the official luncheon at Guildhall in celebration of the tour the duke said: "The old country must wake up if she intends to maintain her old position of pre-eminence in her colonial trade against foreign competition." He was created prince of Wales on Edward VII's birthday, Nov. 9, 1901.

He was heir to the throne for eight and a half years and during this period he made a number of important visits overseas. In 1905-06 he visited India with the princess and the "wonderful and fascinating country" made a lasting impression on him. In July 1908 he went to Canada to inaugurate the Plains of Abraham as

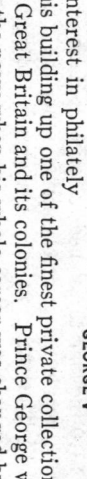

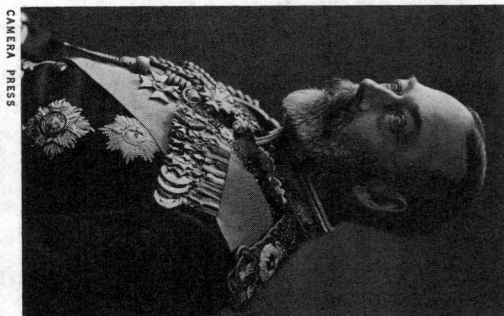

GEORGE V

a national park. On May 6, 1910, his father, King Edward, died and George succeeded to the throne.

George V's coronation took place on June 22, 1911, in Westminster abbey. He described the service as "a terrible ordeal" for, sensitive as he was, he felt the solemnity of having consecrated himself to the service of his peoples. Immediately after the coronation he paid a short state visit to Dublin—the last British sovereign to do this. He was in Wales on July 13, 1911, for the investiture of his eldest son as prince of Wales at Caernarvon castle. At the end of 1911 he went to India for the coronation durbar—an effective tribute to the peoples of India, the idea of which originated with the king himself. The durbar itself took place in Delhi on Dec. 12, 1911.

All these splendid ceremonies could not hide the very formidable difficulties both in home politics and foreign affairs which faced the new king in the early years of his reign. The immediate difficulty after his accession was in the constitutional struggle to curb the powers of the house of lords after they had interfered with Lloyd George's budget of 1909. The Liberal government had been returned at the general election in Jan. 1910 and was determined to proceed against the lords. To do this the government felt that it would need a further mandate from the country and an undertaking from the king that, should the lords not yield, he would create a sufficient number of new peers to overcome opposition. This was a weapon whose use had never been contemplated since the Reform bill crisis in the reign of William IV. George saw H. H. Asquith, the prime minister, immediately after his father's funeral and urged him to try to come to an understanding with the opposition and the need for a guarantee about peers. The resulting conference broke down at the end of the summer and the king was obliged to give a secret undertaking to the prime minister that if necessary he would agree to the creation of enough peers to carry the Parliament act. King George always felt—though possibly without full justification—that the Liberal government had forced his hand at a time when he was fresh to his work and without experience. Fortunately, in 1911, after the government had won another election (Dec. 1910), the lords, after some hesitation, agreed to the reformation of their house and the king did not have to fulfill his pledge.

This question was no sooner settled than the proposal by the government to give a measure of Home Rule to Ireland caused one of the bitterest party clashes known in British history. In the summer of 1914 the king attempted to mediate by summoning the political leaders to a conference at Buckingham palace. This broke down just as World War I began (Aug. 4, 1914). These political troubles, seen as they were against increasing tension in Europe, greatly distressed the king, disturbed his sleep and made him conscious of the gulf between the simplicity of the sailor and the subtleties of politicians which he always found difficulty in understanding.

In these early years of his reign George V did more than any of his predecessors in visiting all parts of the country and seeing at firsthand something of the industrial population outside London and their problems. This was continued throughout the war years when the king, generally accompanied by Queen Mary, visited the centres of the manufacture of munitions and war supplies. He went several times to the front in France and had a serious accident in 1915 when the horse on which he was riding took fright and threw him—a fall which cracked his pelvis.

When World War I broke out the excitement of the London crowds was intense; they found an outlet for their feeling by assembling outside the palace with vociferous cheering which the king described in his private diary as "terrific." On the same evening he wrote "it is a terrible catastrophe, but it is not our fault." In times of extreme national crisis the personal popularity of a constitutional monarch is to some extent inevitably diminished as the full limelight of the press is turned on the politicians and service leaders. But as the result of the war the respect for King George greatly increased in spite of his kinship with many German families. The nation showed that it recognized that his steadfastness and good sense outweighed these chance affinities. In his treatment of the politicians and of the inevitable scares of those times he showed a refreshing detachment from wild or hysterical opinion, though under pressure from Lloyd George he agreed to forgo all alcohol in the royal households for the duration of the war. Many of the ruling houses of Europe were weakened or destroyed by the war; the British monarchy emerged from the conflict stronger and more assured.

After World War I the king was confronted by the appearance of a strong Labour party and an outbreak of serious industrial unrest. The recession in trade in 1920 was followed by a series of strikes and by much hardship. George was faced with a difficult decision on the resignation of Bonar Law in 1923, when he had to find a new prime minister. Both Lord Curzon and Stanley Baldwin had supporters among the elder statesmen George consulted but feeling that Baldwin had more support in the Conservative party and that the prime minister should be in the house of commons, the king selected him. Industrial discontent led to the first Labour government in 1924. The king showed the kindness and sympathy of his character in his handling of the Labour ministers and when, after they had been sworn in, he reminded them that the "happiness of my people is in your hands—they depend upon your prudence and sagacity," they were undoubtedly impressed by his frankness and sincerity. While he may have felt more at ease when Stanley Baldwin was returned with a huge majority at the end of that year, he never forgot his responsibility to all sections of opinion—illustrated by his statesmanlike proclamation to the nation at the end of the general strike in May 1926. On more than one occasion the king wrote to Baldwin urging him to take steps to deal with unemployment and distress, pointing out that he knew something of what this meant through meeting people of all classes and all occupations.

King George was stricken by severe illness at the end of 1928 and it was some time before he could be described as out of danger. For the rest of his reign he had to be extremely careful of his health. In 1931 the collapse of the pound and the consequent financial crisis combined to make the king feel that he should intervene to secure a strong government. J. Ramsay MacDonald's Labour government had collapsed, split by its failure to agree on the steps needed to restore confidence. The king returned from Scotland, where he was on holiday, and was successful in persuading a part of the Labour cabinet to join with Conservative and Liberal ministers in the formation of a national government. There is no doubt that his personal intervention was all-important in forming the coalition; acting entirely constitutionally, he had shown the influence an experienced monarch has in his role of adviser.

In 1932 George inaugurated the World Economic conference; two years before he had opened the round table conference on India. The Statute of Westminster, which defined the relationship between the crown and the dominions and colonies, was passed in 1931. All these constitutional changes—particularly those affecting India—were watched by the king with the closest attention. The closing years of his reign were more tranquil, so far as domestic affairs were concerned, and the celebration of the king's silver jubilee on May 6, 1935, enabled the public to express their feelings of affection and admiration for him. He died, after a short illness, at Sandringham on Jan. 20, 1936. Unlike his father, King George had few social interests. His private friendships were virtually confined to the shipmates of his earliest years. His tastes were those of a country gentleman, with shooting as the recreation he most enjoyed; he was among the best shots of his day. King George had five sons—King Edward VIII (duke of Windsor); King George VI; Henry, duke of Gloucester; George, duke of Kent; and Prince John, who died young—and one daughter, Mary, princess royal, who married the 6th earl of Harewood. See also references under "George V" in the Index.

BIBLIOGRAPHY.—Harold Nicolson, *King George V* (1952); John Gore, *George V: a Personal Memoir* (1941); Sir Charles Petrie, *The Modern British Monarchy* (1961).

(R. T. B. F.)

GEORGE VI (1895–1952), king of Great Britain and Northern Ireland from 1936 to 1952, was born at Sandringham, Norfolk, on Dec. 14, 1895, the second son of the future king George V. He was placed under a tutor at the age of six and entered the Royal Naval college, Osborne, in Jan. 1909, passing to Dartmouth

two years later. From Jan. 1913 until the outbreak of World War I he saw varied naval service at home and abroad. Apart from several long periods ashore because of ill-health, he served in H.M.S. "Collingwood" for the first two years of the war, and as a sublieutenant saw action in the battle of Jutland (1916). Created a knight of the Garter on Dec. 14, 1916, he was appointed to H.M.S. "Malaya," in May 1917, but was obliged to abandon his naval career in August. On Nov. 29, 1917, he was successfully operated on for duodenal ulcer. Later he was appointed to the Royal Naval Air service and in Oct. 1918 was posted to France.

In Nov. 1918, after the armistice, Prince Albert (the name by which he was generally known until his accession) was present, as King George V's representative, at the historic re-entry into Brussels of the king and queen of the Belgians. He returned to England in Feb. 1919 and became, in July, the first member of the royal family to hold a pilot's licence. His commission as a squadron leader in the Royal Air Force was gazetted on Aug. 1, 1919. In October he went up to Trinity college, Cambridge, where he remained until the end of the Easter term, 1920. On June 3, 1920, he was created duke of York, earl of Inverness and Baron Killarney; he took his seat in the house of lords on June 23.

Henceforth the duke of York devoted himself to public duties and began his lifelong interest in the betterment of social and industrial conditions. He had already accepted the presidency of the Boys Welfare association, later to become the Industrial Welfare association, and in the course of the next 16 years he made numerous tours of British industrial areas. On July 30, 1921, he inaugurated the first of his "Duke of York's Camps" where equal numbers of public school boys and boys from the industrial areas spent a week together as his guests. The camps continued until the eve of World War II by which time 7,000 young men had attended them. The duke's close personal association with this unique experiment in social work, which had been entirely his own creation, remained one of his chief interests throughout its duration.

On Jan. 16, 1923, his engagement was announced to Lady Elizabeth Bowes-Lyon, youngest daughter of the 14th earl of Strathmore. They were married on April 26 in Westminster abbey. The following winter the duke and duchess of York went on an extended tour in Africa, returning to England in April in time for the duke to open the second year of the British Empire exhibition on May 10, 1925.

Their first child, Princess Elizabeth (afterward Elizabeth II), was born in London on April 21, 1926. The duke and duchess left England on Jan. 6, 1927, for an official tour of Australia and New Zealand, in the course of which the duke opened the commonwealth parliament in Canberra, the new federal capital of Australia, on May 9. They returned to England on June 27. On Dec. 2, the duke was appointed one of six counselors of state to transact public business of the crown during the illness of his father. He was appointed lord high commissioner to the general assembly of the Church of Scotland in 1929. The second daughter of the duke and duchess of York, Princess Margaret, was born in Scotland at Glamis, on Aug. 21, 1930.

George V died on Jan. 20, 1936, and was succeeded by his eldest son as Edward VIII, but the new king abdicated on Dec. 11 of the same year (*see* EDWARD VIII), and the duke of York then succeeded to the throne as King George VI. He was crowned in Westminster abbey on May 12, 1937. The first years of the new king's reign were clouded by the steady onmarch of German aggression. The king and queen paid a state visit to the president of the French

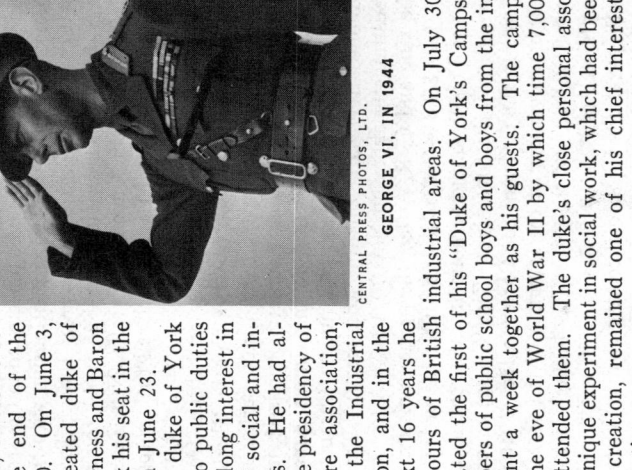

CENTRAL PRESS PHOTOS, LTD.

GEORGE VI, IN 1944

republic in July 1938 and emphasized the solidarity of Anglo-French policy and interests. They sailed for Canada in May 1939 and later paid an official visit to the president of the United States in Washington. The visit was notable for the strong personal friendship which was engendered between the king and Pres. F. D. Roosevelt. The king and queen returned to England on June 22; two and a half months later World War II began.

Throughout the war years the king and queen set an outstanding example of courage, self-sacrifice and devotion. They toured the bombed areas of London and the provinces, and the power and influence of the crown were placed unreservedly in support of Neville Chamberlain and subsequently of Winston Churchill in the great burden which they carried of directing Britain's war effort. The king visited his armies in France in Dec. 1939, in north Africa in June 1943, on the beaches of Normandy in June 1944, in Italy in July 1944 and in the Low Countries in October of the same year. He also paid visits to the fleet on several occasions.

In the postwar years which witnessed the great program of social reforms introduced by the Labour government, the king worked in a remarkable degree of friendship, help and co-operation with his new ministers and accepted with philosophical statesmanship the inevitable changes which occurred in the structure of the commonwealth and its changing relationship with the crown. In 1947 George VI ceased to be emperor of India. Two years later, however, by the declaration of April 27, 1949, the governments of the United Kingdom, Canada, Australia, New Zealand, South Africa, India, Pakistan and Ceylon declared their recognition of the king as head of the commonwealth.

During 1947 the royal family was absent from England (Feb.–April) on a tour of South Africa and the Rhodesias, in the course of which the king opened the Union parliament in Cape Town and the parliament of Southern Rhodesia in Salisbury. Two months after their return to the United Kingdom the king announced the engagement of Princess Elizabeth to Lieut. Philip Mountbatten (later duke of Edinburgh). They were married in Westminster abbey on Nov. 20, 1947. After consultation between the king and C. R. Attlee, the prime minister, it had been agreed on July 23, 1946, that in the future the orders of the Garter and of the Thistle should be nonpolitical in character and in the exclusive gift of the sovereign. King George made his first appointments to the Order of the Garter in Dec. 1946 and he marked the 600th anniversary of the founding of the order by investing Princess Elizabeth and the duke of Edinburgh in full state at Windsor castle on April 23, 1948.

Preparations for a forthcoming visit to Australia and New Zealand had to be abandoned in Nov. 1948 when the king became seriously ill, his condition being diagnosed as one of early arteriosclerosis. He underwent a successful operation on March 12, 1949, and by the end of the year was sufficiently recovered for the plans for the Australian and New Zealand tour to be renewed for 1952. His health, however, deteriorated in the interval. He became seriously ill again during the summer of 1951 and was found to be suffering from cancer of the left lung. An operation was successfully performed on Sept. 23, 1951, and once more the postponement of his visit to the antipodes had to be announced. By the end of the year the king had seemingly made a good recovery. He had renewed to a limited extent his official duties and began again to enjoy shooting at Sandringham. Very early on the morning of Feb. 6, 1952, however, he died there suddenly and peacefully in his sleep from coronary thrombosis.

George VI reigned for only just over 15 years, but these years saw more great happenings and more radical changes than the longer reigns of many of his predecessors. From the moment of his accession his path as a king was beset by grave crises and emergencies. The critical aftermath of the abdication issue was closely followed by the quickly gathering war clouds upon the European horizon and these were but the premonitory symptoms of six years of a life and death struggle for survival and liberty. The conclusion of peace brought with it the immediate problems of postwar reconstruction at home and abroad: the social revolution in Britain, the reshaping of the commonwealth and the problems of relations with the Soviet Union. In all these events King George played his part within the limited scope of his constitutional powers with wisdom, courage and foresight. There have been few more conspicuous examples of a sovereign who grew and developed under the influence and experience of his office from a man almost totally unversed in the affairs of state to the status of one whose advice was willingly and beneficially sought by his ministers. As a husband and father he was greatly beloved by his family. His subjects held him in deep affection and admiration, not only for his leadership in war and peace but also because of his manifest sympathy with them and with their interests and not least also by reason of his heroic and successful struggle with the physical disability of his stammer.

See Sir J. W. Wheeler-Bennett, *King George VI: His Life and Reign* (1958). (Jo. W.-B.)

GEORGE I (1845–1913), king of the Hellenes from 1863 to 1913, second son of Christian IX of Denmark and brother of Queen Alexandra of England, was born in Copenhagen on Dec. 24, 1845. As Prince William of Denmark, he was nominated in 1862 by Great Britain, France and Russia to succeed King Otho I. His nomination was accepted by the Greek national assembly on March 30, 1863, and he acceded to the throne on Oct. 31. His title as king of the Hellenes differed from that of his predecessor, who was king of Hellas. The new title implied an intention that he should reign as a constitutional monarch and operate the monarchical democracy of the constitution promulgated in 1864, which he managed successfully to do for a period of nearly 50 years. It implied also that his subjects were not necessarily confined within the territorial frontiers of the Hellas of 1862, and there was in fact a notable expansion of the country's boundaries during his reign, beginning with the cession of the Ionian Islands by Great Britain (1864), and proceeding with that of Thessaly and Arta by Turkey (1881) to that of Epirus, Macedonia and Crete by Turkey (1913). King George's reign produced the first two Greek statesmen of recognized world importance in Kharilaos Trikoupes and Eleutherios Venizelos (q.v.). The population of the country trebled, and there were notable advances in the economic field with the opening of modern roads and railways. King George was assassinated in the newly occupied city of Salonika on March 18, 1913, by a Greek named Schinas. On Oct. 27, 1867, he had married Olga, daughter of the grand duke Konstantin Nikolaevich of Russia, by whom he had a daughter and five sons, of whom the eldest, Constantine, succeeded him. (B. S.-E.)

GEORGE II (1890–1947), king of the Hellenes from 1922 to 1923 and from 1935 to 1947, eldest son of King Constantine, was born on July 20, 1890, at Tatoi, the royal villa near Athens. Because of his supposed Germanophile tendencies during World War I, he was excluded from the succession by the Allies in favour of his younger brother Alexander on the deposition of his father by the ultimatum of June 11, 1917. After his father's restoration to the throne in 1920, he married on Feb. 27, 1921, Princess Elizabeth, elder daughter of King Ferdinand of Rumania. On the second deposition of his father by the revolution under Gen. Nikolaos Plastiras, his younger brother Alexander I having died in 1920, he succeeded to the throne on Sept. 27, 1922. After the unsuccessful counterrevolution of Oct. 1923, his position became more difficult, although there was no proof that he had been a party to that rising. Republican feeling grew and a number of military and naval officers demanded the deposition of the Glucksburg dynasty. On Dec. 19, 1923, the king and queen left Greece. Next day, Adm. Pavlos Koundouriotis, for the second time, became regent. On March 25, 1924, the assembly deposed the dynasty and forbade its members to reside in Greece; the plebiscite of April 13 confirmed the vote of the assembly.

On Oct. 10, 1935, the assembly declared for the restoration of the monarchy, and after a plebiscite in November showed this to be the popular desire George II returned as king. He gave his support to the right-wing dictatorship of Gen. Ioannis Metaxas (1936–41) and this made the monarchy the subject of political controversy. The German-Italian invasion of 1941 again caused him to leave the country. A plebiscite brought him back on Sept. 27, 1946, for a brief period before his death on April 1, 1947, in Athens. His brother Paul succeeded him. (B. S.-E.)

GEORGE of CAPPADOCIA (d. 361), an Arian bishop who was thrust upon the see of Alexandria in 357 after St. Athanasius' third exile and held it till he was murdered by a pagan mob on Dec. 24, 361. An adherent of the extreme Acacian faction, George was anathema to the semi-Arians as well as the orthodox. Violent and avaricious, he insulted, persecuted and plundered orthodox and pagan alike. The death of Constantius, whose confidence he had, and the accession of Julian as sole emperor gave the pagans of Alexandria the opportunity they needed to wreak a savage vengeance on their oppressor. Edward Gibbon and others have held that George of Cappadocia was the historical figure underlying the legendary story of St. George, patron saint of England and martyr, but the thesis has little to recommend it. (W. J. Br.)

GEORGE of LAODICEA (d. c. 361), a semi-Arian bishop, adversary of St. Athanasius and one of the most active figures in the Arian controversies of the 4th century, was a native of Alexandria. He was ordained there by Bishop Alexander but was excommunicated for his Arian leanings and his immorality. His efforts, probably Arian as they were, to reconcile Arius and Alexander were ineffective. Appointed bishop of Laodicea in Syria c. 335, he attended numerous synods in the following decades and became one of the principal champions of the Homoiousian theology. His literary legacy is small; a defense of his doctrine, which he composed in conjunction with Basil of Ancyra and others, was preserved by Epiphanius. (W. J. Br.)

GEORGE THE MONK (also called HAMARTOLOS, "sinner") (fl. 9th century), Byzantine chronicler, lived during the reign of emperor Michael III (842–867), but nothing seems to be known of his life. His *Chronicon Syntomon* ("Chronicle") in four books covers the period from the Creation to the death (in 842) of the emperor Theophilus, whose widow Theodora restored the use of icons (843). His main attention is focused on religious matters; the iconoclasts are fiercely attacked, and the work is full of theological discussions. It is an important contemporary authority for the years 813 to 842; but the early parts are a compilation based mainly on Malalas, Theophanes and various ecclesiastical works. In the introduction the author declares that his only object is to relate with strict truth such things as are "useful and necessary."

A continuation of this chronicle up to 948 is known as *Georgius Continuatus*. As the continuator is called "a Logothete," in some manuscripts he may have been Simeon Magister. In this continuation more attention is devoted to political history, and the author is clearly biased against Constantine VII and the Macedonian dynasty. This work was frequently used by other historians and the fact that it was subsequently reissued with alterations and interpolations makes it very difficult to arrive at the original text.

BIBLIOGRAPHY.—*Chronicon* ed. by C. de Boor in the "Teubner Series," 2 vol. (1904), and in J. P. Migne, *Patrologia Graeca*, vol. 110 (1863). *See also* K. Krumbacher, *Geschichte der byzantinischen Litteratur*, 2nd ed., pp. 352–358 (1897); G. Moravcsik, *Byzantinoturcica*, 2nd ed., vol. 1, pp. 277–280 (1958). *Georgius Continuatus* is ed. by I. Bekker in the Bonn corpus (1838) and in J. P. Migne, *Patrologia Graeca*, vol. 109, 110, col. 823–984 (1863). *See also* K. Krumbacher (as above) and G. Moravcsik (as above), pp. 269–273. (J. M. Hy.)

GEORGE THE PISIDIAN (GEORGIUS PISIDA or GEORGIOS PISIDES) (fl. 7th century A.D.), Byzantine poet, was a valuable chronicler of contemporary events. Born in Pisidia, he became a deacon and keeper of the records of the church of Hagia Sophia in Constantinople. His works include a poem of 1,088 iambic lines on the campaign of the emperor Heraclius (610–641) against the Persians, apparently the work of an eyewitness; the *Avarica*, an account of the abortive attack on Constantinople by the Avars (626); the *Heraclias*, a survey of the exploits of Heraclius down to the overthrow of the Persian King Khosrau II (628); a didactic poem *Hexaemeron* or *Cosmourgia*, on the creation; a treatise on the vanity of life after the manner of *Ecclesiastes*; a controversial composition against Severus, bishop of Antioch; and a poem on the resurrection of Christ. In his hands the Byzantine 12-syllable iambic verse begins to take shape. This became the principal verse in subsequent learned medieval Greek poetry. Pisides, while adhering faithfully to the rules of ancient metre (which from c. A.D. 200 was no longer distinguishable by ear), normally accentuates the 11th syllable of his iambic verse and rigorously observes the caesura after the fifth or the seventh syllable. He also avoids an accent on the seventh syllable if a caesura follows and is careful to avoid enjambment. By this means he combined the laws of ancient metre (based on quantity) with the new Byzantine metrical system (based on numbers of syllables and place of accents in a line), a real tour de force. Subsequent Byzantine poets as late as the 14th century followed him and even developed this system further when writing iambic trimeters. Although later Byzantines admired his work, and although it has undoubted historical value, modern criticism rightly pronounces it dull.

BIBLIOGRAPHY.—For text see I. Bekkerus (ed.) in *Corpus scriptorum hist. Byz.* (1837); J. P. Migne, *Patrologia Graeca*, vol. xcii (1857–1912). *See also* S. L. Sternbach, *De Georgio Pisida Nonni sectatore* (1893); K. Krumbacher, *Gesch. der byz. Lit.*, 2nd ed. (1897); F. Dölger, *Die byz. Dichtung in der Reinsprache*, p. 19 ff. and p. 39 ff. (1948); P. Maas, *Byz. Zeitschrift*, vol. xii, p. 278 ff. (1903); on the epic encomium see T. Nissen, "Historisches Epos und Panegyricus in der Spätantike," *Hermes*, vol. lxxv, p. 298 ff. (1940). (CE. A. T.)

GEORGE THE SYNCELLUS (d. c. 810), Byzantine chronicler, ecclesiastic and monk. He was the *syncellus* ("cell mate," actually confidential assistant assigned to a high ecclesiastic) of Tarasius, patriarch of Constantinople (784–806). His world *Chronographia* ("Chronicle") goes from Adam to Diocletian (284), and at his request it was continued after his death by his friend Theophanes "the Confessor." It is a chronological table with notes rather than a history, and is valuable, in spite of its dry character, for the fragments of other works preserved in it (*e.g.*, parts of the *Chronicle* of Eusebius). The *Chronographia* was edited by G. Dindorf, in the Bonn corpus, 2 vol. (1829).

See also K. Krumbacher, *Geschichte der byzantinischen Litteratur*, 2nd ed, pp. 339–342 (1897); G. Moravcsik, *Byzantinoturcica*, vol. 1, 2nd ed, pp. 336, 531, 532 (1958). (J. M. Hy.)

GEORGE, HENRY (1839–1897), U.S. economist and land reformer, popularizer of the "single tax" idea, was born in Philadelphia, Pa., Sept. 2, 1839, of a religious, middle-class family. When not quite 14 years of age he left school. After two years as a clerk in the importing house of Asbury and Company, he became a seaman in the "Hindoo" for a voyage to Australia and India. On his return to Philadelphia in 1856 he learned typesetting, and in the following year signed up as steward on the United States lighthouse tender "Shubruck," bound for the Pacific coast service. He quit the ship in San Francisco and joined the gold rush to the Fraser river in Canada, but arrived too late. George spent the next two decades (1858–80) in California in newspaper work and Democratic party politics, developing in the process his gifts for writing and oratory but achieving little worldly success. After eight years of intermittent employment as a typesetter and five years as an editor for several newspapers, including the *San Francisco Chronicle*, he, with two partners, started in 1871 the *San Francisco Daily Evening Post*; four years later, however, a policy of expansion strained the firm's credit and ended the enterprise.

George had failed at several attempts to gain elective office, but in 1876 a Democratic governor appointed him state inspector of gas meters, a job that ended with Republican victory in 1879.

It had enabled him, however, to prepare his most important work, *Progress and Poverty* (1879). This book caught the spirit of discontent that continued to sweep a world just emerging from the great depression of 1873–78. He took as a basis the intricate orthodox, or "Ricardian," doctrine of rent, and in clarifying it for the ordinary reader gave it new meaning. Extending the law of diminishing returns and of a "margin of productivity," but still applying it to land alone, he held that since economic progress entailed a growing scarcity of land, the idle landowner reaps ever greater returns at the expense of the productive factors of labour and capital. The proposal, for which George became famous, was that the state tax away all economic rent—the income from the use of the bare land (but not from improvements)—and abolish all other taxes. (*See* SINGLE TAX.)

He optimistically envisaged that the government's annual income from this "single tax" would be so large that there would be a surplus for expansion of public works, from roads to universities. The economic argument was re-enforced and dominated by a humanitarian and religious appeal. The book had an enormous sale and was translated into many languages. Its vogue was enhanced by his pamphlets, voluminous contributions to the leading popular magazines and his lecture tours both in the United States and the British Isles. George moved to New York in 1880. Such was his reputation that in 1886 he became the mayoral candidate of the reform forces in a spectacular contest, which he barely lost to the Democratic candidate, Abram Hewitt, running substantially ahead of the Republican candidate, Theodore Roosevelt. He died in New York on Oct. 29, 1897.

George's specific remedy had no significant practical result, and economists of reputation who supported it were rare. His economic analysis, though more sophisticated than that of most of his contemporaries, is crude by modern standards. His forceful emphasis, however, on "privilege" and the demand for equality of opportunity, coupled with a systematic economic analysis, proved a stimulus to orderly reform.

BIBLIOGRAPHY.—R. A. Sawyer, *Henry George and the Single Tax* (1926); Anna George De Mille, *Henry George*, ed. by D. C. Shoemaker (1950); C. A. Barker, *Henry George* (1955). (J. Dn.)

GEORGE, STEFAN (1868-1933), German lyric poet who chiefly responsible for the revival of German poetry at the close of the 19th century, was born at Büdesheim, near Bingen, July 12, 1868. He studied philosophy and the history of art in Paris, Munich and Berlin, traveled widely, becoming associated with Mallarmé and the Symbolists in Paris and with the Pre-Raphaelites in London. Returning to Germany, where he divided his time between Berlin, Munich and Heidelberg, he founded a literary school of his own, the *George-Kreis*, held together by the force of his authoritarian personality. Many famous writers—including Hofmannsthal, briefly, Karl Wolfskehl, Friedrich Gundolf and Norbert von Hellingrath—belonged to it, or contributed to its journal, *Blätter für die Kunst*, founded in 1892.

George died at Minusio, near Locarno, Dec. 4, 1933.

George aimed to impose a new classicism on German poetry, avoiding impure rhymes and metrical irregularities. Vowels and consonants were arranged with precision to achieve harmony. The resulting symbolic poem was intended to evoke a sense of intoxication. These poetic ideals were a protest not only against the debasement of the language but also against materialism and naturalism, to which George opposed an austerity of life and a standard of poetic excellence, preaching a humanism inspired by Greece, which he hoped would be realized in a new society. His ideas, and the affectations into which they led some of his disciples, coupled with his claim of superiority and his obsession with power, were ridiculed, attacked and misused by those who misunderstood them; it is necessary to remember that George himself was strongly opposed to the political developments which his ideas are sometimes thought to reflect. It was one of his disciples, Count Claus von Stauffenberg, who attempted to assassinate Hitler on July 20, 1944.

George's collected works fill 18 volumes (*Gesamtausgabe*, 1927-34), including five of translations and one of prose sketches. His collections of poetry, of which *Hymnen* (1890), *Pilgerfahrten* (1891), *Algabal* (1892), *Das Jahr der Seele* (1897), *Der Teppich des Lebens und die Lieder von Traum und Tod* (1899), *Der siebente Ring* (1907), *Der Stern des Bundes* (1914) and *Das neue Reich* (1928) are the most important, show his poetic and spiritual development from early doubts and searching self-examination to complete assurance of his role as a seer and as leader of the coming new society. Personally, and spiritually, he found the fulfilment of his striving for significance in "Maximin"

BY COURTESY OF THE STADTARCHIV, MUNICH

STEFAN GEORGE

(Maximilian Kronberger; 1888-1904) a beautiful and gifted youth whom he met in Munich in 1902. After his death George claimed that he had been a god, glorifying him in his later poetry and explaining his attitude to him in *Maximin, ein Gedenkbuch* (privately published, 1906).

Selections of George's poetry have been translated into English by C. M. Scott (1910) and C. N. Valhope and E. Morwitz (1943).

BIBLIOGRAPHY.—G. Gundolf, *George* (1920); C. M. Bowra, "Stefan George," in *The Heritage of Symbolism* (1943); R. Boehringer, *Mein Bild von Stefan George* (1951); C. David, *Stefan George* (1952); E. K. Bennett, *Stefan George* (1954). (H. S. R.)

GEORGE, LAKE, a long, narrow lake in the eastern part of New York state in the foothills of the Adirondack mountains, which rise more than 2,000 ft. above the lake. Prospect mountain, rising 1,705 ft. above sea level, and Black mountain, 2,732 ft. in height, are the most prominent. Lake George has a maximum depth of about 200 ft., is 317 ft. above sea level and 224 ft. above Lake Champlain, into which it has an outlet to the north through a narrow channel containing many rapids and falls. The lake is about 30 mi. long and varies in width from ¾ mi. to 3 mi. Of glacial origin, it has clear water, coming from mountain brooks and submerged springs. It is noted for its beautiful mountain scenery and its islands, and is a favourite summer resort.

Before the advent of the white man the lake was a part of the natural trail over which the Iroquois Indians frequently made their way northward to attack the Algonkins and the Hurons. Samuel de Champlain explored Lake Champlain in 1609, and at that time heard from the Indians of the beautiful lake, called by them *Andiatarocte* ("place where the lake contracts"); but no records show that Champlain ever visited Lake George. The first white man to see the lake (Aug. 18, 1642) appears to have been Saint Isaac Jogues, a Jesuit missionary, who in company with René Goupil and Guillaume Couture was being taken by his Mohawk Indian captors from the St. Lawrence to the town of the Mohawks. In the spring of 1646 Father Jogues, while on a half-religious, half-political mission to the Mohawks, again visited the lake on the eve of the feast of Corpus Christi. He gave it the name "Lac du St. Sacrement." In 1755, Gen. Sir William Johnson renamed it Lake George in honour of George II of England. James Fenimore Cooper refers to it in his novels as Lake Horicon.

Lake George, on what was still the best route of communication between New York and Canada, was the scene of many engagements during the French and Indian War and during the American Revolution. On Sept. 8, 1755, at the head of the lake, Gen. William Johnson defeated a force of about 1,400 French, Canadians and Indians under Baron Ludwig August Dieskau, who left Canada with the intention of attacking Ft. Lyman (later Ft. Edward). The engagement is known as the battle of Lake George; a monument commemorating the battle was erected in 1903. Following the battle, Gen. Johnson built a fort of logs and earth on the shores of Lake George near the battlefield which he called Ft. William Henry in honour of William Henry, duke of Gloucester. In the meantime the French entrenched themselves at Ticonderoga. Two years later, in March 1757, the governor of Canada sent an expedition of about 1,600 men to capture the fort, but the expedition failed. In August of the same year the garrison, in desperate straits because of lack of ammunition and supplies, surrendered to the marquis de Montcalm. While under escort to Ft. Edward, the Indian allies of Gen. Montcalm massacred or took prisoner a large part of the force. Ft. William Henry was destroyed. Gen. James Abercrombie's large army marched from the lake to its defeat at Ticonderoga in July 1758. Lord Amherst advanced along the lake en route to Ft. Ticonderoga, which he captured in July 1759. Near the site of Ft. William Henry, Gen. Amherst later built a new fort known as Ft. George. Its ruins remain.

During the American Revolution the Green Mountain Boys under Ethan Allen captured Ft. Ticonderoga, including the artillery that Henry Knox (q.v.) transported 300 mi. to Boston where the guns were used to drive out the British.

BIBLIOGRAPHY.—H. Marvin, *A Complete History of Lake George and Lake Champlain* (1853); B. C. Butler, *Lake George and Lake Champlain* (1868); B. F.

Da Costa, *A Narrative of Events at Lake George* (1868); Francis Parkman, *History Handbook of the Northern Tour* (1885); Elizabeth H. Serlye, *Saratoga and Lake Champlain in History* (1898); Caroline H. Royce, *The First Century of Lake Champlain* (1900); W. M. Reid, *Lake George and Lake Champlain* (1910); F. W. Halsey, "The Historical Significance of the Hudson and Champlain Valleys," *N.Y. State Hist. Assoc. Proc.*, vol. ix, pp. 227-236 (1910); E. T. Gillespie, "The War Path," *N.Y. State Hist. Assoc. Proc.*, vol. x, pp. 139-155 (1911); Frederic F. Van De Water, *Lake Champlain and Lake George* (1946). (G. L. F.)

GEORGETOWN, the capital and chief port of Guyana, is on the right bank of the Demerara river at its mouth. Pop. (1969 est.) 97,190. Known during the Dutch occupation as Stabroek ("standing pool"), it was established as the seat of government of the combined colonies of Essequibo and Demerara (now with Berbice forming the country of Guyana) in 1784, its name being changed to Georgetown in 1812. The streets are wide and straight, intersecting each other at right angles, several having double roadways. The city has about 50 mi. of macadamized roads. In Main street, the finest street in Georgetown, the canal which formerly existed in the middle of its dual carriageway has been filled in to form a broad walk with seats beneath its large, overhanging trees, and with gay, tropical flowers in sunken concrete troughs on its parapets. The principal residences, standing in their own gardens, are scattered throughout the town. Most houses and public buildings are constructed of wood, the former generally raised on brick pillars four to ten feet from the ground, with wooden walls, jalousies and roofs in bright colours. As a consequence of two great fires in 1945 and 1951, most buildings in the business section were rebuilt in reinforced concrete.

The public buildings in the centre of the city containing the offices of the government and the hall of the legislature, formerly called the court of policy, were erected between 1829 and 1834. They form a handsome E-shaped, masonry block with deep porticoes and marble-paved galleries carried on cast-iron columns. The law courts, built in the 1880s, have a ground floor of concrete and iron, the upper story being of hardwood. Other public buildings include the town hall, which was designed by a Jesuit priest and built between 1887 and 1889, and the Anglican and Roman Catholic cathedrals, the former a great wooden building and the latter rebuilt in reinforced concrete after a fire in 1913. One of the two hospitals is government owned and the other is run by the Roman Catholic community. There are government-owned secondary schools, the Queen's college for boys and the Bishops' high school for girls, the University of Guyana and a government technical institute which provides basic technical education. The Royal Agricultural and Commercial society has a large reading room and lending library. Its museum is chiefly devoted to the animal life of the area but also contains collections of local economic, mineral and botanical exhibits, and foreign birds and mammals.

There are extensive botanical gardens to the east of the city with a small zoo containing local birds, animals and reptiles, and nurseries devoted chiefly to the raising of plants of economic importance; the collections of ferns and orchids are very fine. The gardens also contain the plots of the board of agriculture, where experimental work is carried on in the growth of sugar cane, rice, cotton, etc. Other places of interest are the sea wall and the promenade gardens in the centre of the city. There are facilities for outdoor sport and recreation including cricket, football, horse racing, rowing and swimming. The city, once malarial, has been free from the disease since 1945. A potable water supply and a sewage disposal system are maintained.

Water street, the main business centre, runs parallel to the river for about two and one-half miles and contains the stores of the wholesale and retail merchants, with wharves projecting into the river. The country is connected by shipping services from Georgetown with the United Kingdom, France, the United States, Canada and other countries. There are public and private tidal berthage facilities with warehouse accommodation. The chief exports are sugar (from the country's large sugar mills), rice, tropical fruits, timber, bauxite, gold and diamonds. (E. A. As.)

GEORGE TOWN, chief port of Malaya in the federation of Malaysia and capital of Penang state, sometimes also called Penang, is on a small triangular plain in the northeast of Penang Island. Pop. (1968 est.) 248,976. It is the first chartered city of the Malayan federation, with a fully elected city council. Along its shores are the wharves, warehouses, business premises and banks serving Penang harbour which lies in the strait between the island and the mainland. The background of forested hills, roads lined with flowering trees and colonial-style residences, makes George Town one of the most attractive ports of Asia, with an atmosphere set by a population more Chinese and Indian than Malay, but so well settled that most of them have forgotten their immigrant origin. Its gay modern residences are occupied by successful Chinese rubber planters and tin miners from the mainland, who have also built spectacular Buddhist shrines and temples. The Chinese are of Hokien and Cantonese origin and the Indians are Tamils from south India. Fort Cornwallis, almost at the easternmost tip of George Town, is preserved for its history as an East India company outpost, acquired in 1786.

The city contains a modern tin smelter run by an English company, which handles ores from Thailand and Perak and exports tin as ingots. International shipping approaches George Town from the north since the southern channel has many shallows. The port function is partly shared with Butterworth and Prai on the mainland, which cannot handle ocean-going vessels. Most of the produce and passengers, therefore, have to be ferried to George Town; some freight reaches the ships by lighter. (E. H. G. D.)

GEORGETOWN, formerly a city of the District of Columbia, U.S., now part of the city of Washington, D.C., is at the confluence of the Potomac river and Rock creek, about $2\frac{1}{2}$ mi. W.N.W. of the national Capitol. The streets are old-fashioned, narrow and well shaded. On the "Heights" are many fine residences with beautiful gardens; the Georgetown Visitation Junior college, a Roman Catholic college for women, founded in 1799; and the college and the astronomical observatory (1842) of Georgetown university.

Georgetown was settled late in the 17th century. It was laid out as a town in 1751, chartered as a city in 1789, merged into the District of Columbia in 1871, and annexed to the city of Washington in 1878. The studio, for two years, of Gilbert Stuart, and "Kalorama," the residence of Joel Barlow, were there. Legislation was passed by the 81st congress in 1950 to preserve the character of this section, to be known as Old Georgetown, by regulating the height, exterior design and construction of private and semipublic buildings in the area. *See also* WASHINGTON, D.C.

GEORGIA is a southern state of the U.S. and youngest of the original 13 states, having been chartered as a colony in 1732 by George II of Great Britain, from whom it derived its name. With a total area of 58,876 sq.mi. (679 sq.mi. of water), it is the largest state east of the Mississippi river and 21st in size of all the states. Until early in the 19th century it comprised nearly all the present area of Alabama and Mississippi. Its size and its agricultural and industrial prominence earned for it before 1860 the popular title of "empire state of the south." The capital has been Atlanta since 1868. The official flower is the Cherokee rose, the state bird is the brown thrasher, and the state tree is the live oak. Georgia is bounded on the north by Tennessee and North Carolina at 35° north latitude, on the south by Florida at 30° 42' 42", on the east by South Carolina and the Atlantic ocean and on the west by Alabama. It lies between 80° 53' 15" and 85° 36' west longitude.

PHYSICAL GEOGRAPHY

Physical Features.—The surface of Georgia is divided into five physical zones. The most prominent of these is the coastal plain of 35,000 sq.mi. It extends from the 100 mi. of Atlantic seacoast, skirted by numerous fertile semitropical islands of the Sea Islands group, northward to the fall line, which extends from Augusta through Milledgeville and Macon to Columbus. North of this line is the Piedmont plateau of rolling foothills that rise gradually in height from 500 ft., until they reach the mountains about 50 mi. N. of Atlanta, to somewhat less than 2,000 ft. Above this plateau lie three small regions, the largest of which is the Blue Ridge in the northeast (part of the Appalachian mountain system), extending south and west into Georgia to a distance of 48 and 92 mi., respectively. In the extreme northwestern corner of the state is the Cumberland plateau (part of the Allegheny system), represented by Lookout and Sand mountains, having an elevation of about 2,000 ft. Between the two regions mentioned lies the Great valley, extending southward to Cedartown. The Georgia mountains are part of a mountain system running from Canada to central Alabama, appearing from Virginia to Georgia in the two separate prongs mentioned above, with a wide valley between. The highest point in the state is Brasstown Bald (4,784 ft.), in the Blue Ridge region. The approximate mean elevation of the state is 600 ft. Near Atlanta, in the upper Piedmont plateau, is Stone mountain, probably the largest piece of exposed granite in the world.

On the Blue Ridge mountains in the northeast corner of the state begins a water parting line (watershed) extending southwest to Atlanta, southeast of which the waters flow into the Atlantic ocean and above which they find their way to the Gulf of Mexico. The Great valley region and most of the western portion of the Blue Ridge mountains are drained by the Etowah and the Oostanaula rivers and their tributaries, forming at Rome the Coosa, which empties into Mobile bay. The Cumberland plateau and the northwestern part of the Blue Ridge mountains constitute a part of the Tennessee basin. The principal rivers of the state are the Savannah, forming the boundary with South Carolina; the Oconee and the Ocmulgee, which unite in the south-central part of the state to form the Altamaha; the Satilla in the southeast; and the Flint and the Chattahoochee, which unite in the southwest corner to form the Apalachicola in Florida. All except the Satilla rise in the upper Piedmont and are navigable only south of the fall line. In the southeastern part of the state is the Okefenokee swamp, covering an area of 600 sq.mi., a national wildlife sanctuary, most of which lies in Georgia. Much of the area in this region of the state is unsuitable for cultivation because of numerous marshes and swamps.

Climate.—The climate of Georgia is mild. Mean annual temperatures range from about 57° to 68° F. (about 14° to 20° C.). January averages are about 40° in the mountains and 54° on the south coast; July averages range from about 74° to 82°. Mean annual rainfall is almost 50 in. a year. Snowfall averages seven to ten inches a year in the mountains, about three in Atlanta and becomes negligible on the coastal plain.

Soil.—Georgia is notable for the variety of its soils, by far the greatest number being found in the upper coastal plain. The dominant pattern is in northern Georgia, loam and clay rich in decomposed limestone and calcareous shales; in the Piedmont, clays and loams, mostly of dark red colour, derived from decomposed hornblende; and in the coastal plain, gray sands and sandy loams.
Vegetation.—There are 250 species of trees native to the state,

more than 90% of which are of commercial importance. The mountains are covered with oak and hickory varieties, with short-leaf pine as a secondary type. Other hardwoods are hemlock, maple and chestnut. Loblolly pine grows abundantly in the Piedmont, while longleaf pine is found in the western and southern portions of the state. White and red oak, yellow poplar, cherry and ash are important hardwoods throughout most of the state. The coastal area is noted for live oaks, cypresses and palmettos. Important flowering trees are magnolia, mimosa, dogwood, redbud, tulip and crepe myrtle, the last being nonindigenous. There are more species of shrubs than of trees. The most common flowering shrubs are yellow jasmine, flowering quince and arbutus, with rhododendron and laurel predominating in the mountains. The Cherokee rose bears a small white blossom with yellow centre. Spanish moss is abundant on the coast and around the streams and swamps of the entire coastal plain.

Animal Life.—There are 79 species of reptiles. Of these 40 are snakes, 23 are turtles, 13 are lizards and 3 are crocodilians. Poisonous snakes are the rattlesnake, of which the eastern diamondback is the most noted, copperhead and cottonmouth moccasin, the last being aquatic and found largely in the coastal plain. The coral snake is rare. Of the 63 species of amphibians 35 are salamanders and 28 are frogs and toads.

There are 160 species of birds that breed in Georgia and a greater number of migratory fowl. The largest family is the sparrow, of which 67 varieties have been identified. The bobwhite, or Virginia quail, is widely distributed and is the most popular game bird. Second in popularity and distribution is the dove. Marsh hens are abundant on the coast, and wild turkeys are found in the mountains and on the coast. Migrating geese and ducks are found on inland lakes, as well as on the coast. The Okefenokee swamp has many interesting and rare waterfowl, including the water turkey. Virginia deer are found in every county, the population in the late 1960s being estimated at 100,000. The black bear is found in 13 counties being most abundant in Ware and Charlton. Other prominent wildlife include the rabbit, squirrel, opossum, fox, raccoon, muskrat, mink, otter and weasel. Less prominent are the beaver, badger, wildcat, civet cat, mole, panther and skunk. The most popular fresh-water game fish are trout, bass, bream, shad and catfish; all except the last are produced in state hatcheries for restocking. Off the coast are dolphins, porpoises, edible shrimps, blue crabs and tidewater oysters.

Parks and Monuments.—The 45 state parks range in area from the Jefferson Davis Memorial park (less than 5 ac., near Irwinville) to Jekyll Island (an 11,000-ac. sea island, near Brunswick). The parks are distributed throughout the state but are more numerous in the mountain area, where Vogel State park ranks high in tourist popularity. Nearly all state parks contain

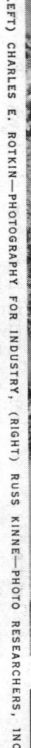

(LEFT) CHARLES E. ROTKIN—PHOTOGRAPHY FOR INDUSTRY, (RIGHT) RUSS KINNE—PHOTO RESEARCHERS, INC.

(LEFT) FISHING BOAT WINDING ITS WAY THROUGH MARSHES IN THE COASTAL PLAIN REGION NEAR SAVANNAH. (RIGHT) AERIAL VIEW OF STONE MOUNTAIN IN THE STONE MOUNTAIN CONFEDERATE MEMORIAL AREA NEAR ATLANTA

lakes or are adjacent to large bodies of impounded water. The Georgia Veterans Memorial park in Crisp county borders on the 13,000-ac. Lake Blackshear. The federal government administers about 12 historical and recreational areas in Georgia, the largest being the Chattahoochee National forest in north Georgia, comprising 691,977 ac. Others of unusual interest are Oconee National forest, Kennesaw Mountain National Battlefield park near Marietta, Chickamauga and Chattanooga National Military park in Walker and Catoosa counties, and Ocmulgee, Ft. Pulaski and Ft. Frederica National monuments. The most important cemetery park is at Andersonville in Sumter county, where about 13,000 Union prisoners died in 1864 and early 1865.

HISTORY

Colonial.—Georgia's formation was the result of a desire of the British government to protect South Carolina from invasion by the Spaniards from Florida, and by the French from Louisiana, as well as of the desire of James Edward Oglethorpe (q.v.) to found a refuge for the persecuted Protestant sects and for the unfortunate but worthy indigent classes of England. The charter was granted to "the trustees for establishing the colony of Georgia in America," giving the colony a unique type of control, yet somewhat like the proprietary form. Parliament gave £10,000 to the enterprise, and the trustees encouraged the settlers to grow silk, grapes, hemp, olives and medicinal plants, for which England was dependent upon foreign countries. The sale of rum' and the introduction of Negro slaves were forbidden, and severe limitations were placed on land tenure. Oglethorpe, as resident trustee, accompanied the first colonists, who settled at Savannah in 1733. The early settlers were English, German Lutherans (Salzburgers), Scottish Highlanders, Portuguese Jews, Piedmontese, Swiss and others; but the main tide of immigration came from Virginia and the Carolinas after 1750.

As a bulwark against the Spanish and French the colony was successful, but as an economic and philanthropic experiment it was a failure. The industries planned for the colony did not thrive, and because sufficient labour could not be obtained, the importation of slaves was permitted, under certain conditions, in 1749. About the same time, parliament directed the trustees to end the prohibition on the sale of rum, and the restrictions on landholding were gradually removed. In 1753 the charter of the trustees expired and Georgia became a royal province, its character rapidly changing to resemble that of other southern colonies.

Under the new regime the colony was so prosperous that Sir James Wright (1716–85), the last of the royal governors, declared Georgia to be "the most flourishing colony on the continent." The people were led to revolt against the mother country through sympathy with the other colonies rather than through any grievance of their own. The centre of revolutionary ideas was St. John's parish on the coast (settled by New Englanders, chiefly from Dorchester, Mass.) and the area north of Augusta (settled by Carolinians and Virginians). Loyalist sentiment was so strong that only 5 of the 12 parishes sent representatives to the first provincial congress, which met on Jan. 18, 1775, and its delegates to the continental congress therefore did not claim seats in that assembly. Six months later all the parishes sent representatives to another provincial congress that met on July 4, 1775.

The war that followed was a severe civil conflict, with the Loyalist and Revolutionary parties being almost equal in numbers; a large number of moderates preferred a neutral course. In 1778 the British seized Savannah, which they held until 1782, mean-

while reviving the British civil administration, and in 1779 they captured Augusta and Sunbury; but after 1780 the Revolutionary forces were generally successful in the upcountry in bloody guerrilla fighting. Civil affairs also fell into confusion, partly because of a schism among the revolutionists. While a state constitution was adopted in 1777, harmony did not prevail until 1781.

Early Statehood.—In the Constitutional Convention of 1787 Georgia's delegates almost invariably gave their support to measures designed to strengthen the central government. Georgia became the fourth state to ratify the federal constitution (Jan. 2, 1788), and one of the three that ratified unanimously. Afterward a series of conflicts between federal and state authority caused the growth of states' rights theories. Because of these conflicts a majority of Georgians adopted the principles of the Democratic-Republican party, and early in the 19th century the people were virtually unanimous in their support of Jeffersonian ideas.

The position of congress and of the supreme court with regard to Georgia's policy in the Yazoo land frauds aroused distrust of the federal government. In 1795 the legislature granted, for $500,000, the territory extending from the Alabama and Coosa rivers to the Mississippi river, and between 35° and 31° N. lat. (almost all the present state of Mississippi and more than half of the present state of Alabama), to four land companies, but in the following year a new legislature rescinded the contracts, on the ground that they had been fraudulently and corruptly made. In the meantime the U.S. senate had appointed a committee to inquire into Georgia's claim to the land in question, and as this committee pronounced that claim invalid, congress, in 1800, established a territorial government over the region. The legislature of Georgia remonstrated but expressed a willingness to cede the land to the United States. In 1802 the cession was ratified, it being stipulated, among other things, that the United States should pay to the state $1,250,000, and should extinguish "at their own expense, for the use of Georgia, as soon as the same can be peaceably obtained on reasonable terms," the Indian title to all lands within the revised limits of Georgia. In 1824 the state protested in vigorous terms against the dilatory manner in which the national government was discharging its obligation, with the result that in 1825 a treaty was negotiated at Indian Springs by which a small and unrepresentative group of friendly (Lower) Creeks agreed to exchange their remaining lands in Georgia for $5,000,000 and equal territory beyond the Mississippi. But Pres. John Quincy Adams, convinced that this treaty was accompanied by bribery and learning that it was not confirmed by the entire Creek nation, authorized a new one, signed at Washington in 1826, by which the Creeks kept a small tract within the recognized limits of Georgia. Gov. George M. Troup (1780–1856) proceeded to execute the first treaty, and the Georgia legislature declared the second treaty illegal and unconstitutional. In reply to a communication of President Adams, early in 1827, that the United States would take strong measures to enforce its policy, Governor Troup asked his legislature to pre-

L. TAGER—BLACK STAR

RUINS OF FORT FREDERICA, WHICH WAS BUILT BY JAMES EDWARD OGLETHORPE ON ST. SIMONS ISLAND IN 1736 AS A DEFENSE AGAINST SPANISH ATTACK

pare to resist to the utmost any military attack that the U.S. government should think proper to make. A final treaty, in 1827, ended the Creek controversy.

The controversy with federal authorities over Indian removal then focused on the Cherokees. In 1828 the legislature extended the jurisdiction of Georgia law to the Cherokee lands lying in the northern part of the chartered limits of Georgia. Andrew Jackson, then president, sided with Georgia, informing the Cherokees that their only alternative to submission to Georgia was emigration. Thereupon the chiefs resorted to the U.S. supreme court, which in 1832 declared that the Cherokees formed a distinct community "in which the laws of Georgia have no force" and annulled the decision of a Georgia court that had extended its jurisdiction into the Cherokee country (*Worcester v. Georgia*). But the governor of Georgia declared that the decision was an attempt at usurpation that would meet with determined resistance, and President Jackson refused to enforce the decree. He did, however, work for the removal of the Indians, which was completed in 1838.

Politics and Slavery.—Despite early national political unity, local partisanship had been represented by two factions. One, led successively by William H. Crawford and George M. Troup, represented the interests of the coastal element and the upcountry slaveholding communities; the other, formed by John Clark (1766-1832) and his father Elijah, found principal support among the nonslaveholders and the frontiersmen. At the same time there was a sectional cleavage between the older communities along the coast and the newer upcountry communities, in which the latter early gained a dominant position, as a result of which the capital was removed to the upcountry, where it became fixed at Milledgeville in 1807, and in the creation of numerous counties throughout the rapidly expanding cotton belt of middle Georgia.

The Troup faction, under the name of the States' Rights party, after 1832 endorsed the nullification policy of South Carolina against federal tariff laws. The Clark faction, calling itself the Union party, opposed South Carolina's conduct, but on the grounds of expediency rather than of principle. Because of its opposition to President Jackson's stand on nullification, the Troup party was affiliated with the new Whig party, while the Clark party was merged into the Democratic party led by Jackson. The anti-slavery and nationalistic views of the Whig party during the 1850s caused most of its members in Georgia to shift to the Democratic party.

The activity of Georgia in the slavery controversy was important. Popular opinion at first opposed the Compromise of 1850 (*see* COMPROMISE OF 1850), and some politicians demanded immediate secession from the union. Others contended that the compromise was a great victory for the south and in a campaign on this issue secured the election of such delegates to the state convention (at Milledgeville) of 1850 that that body adopted, on Dec. 10, by a vote of 237 to 19, a series of conciliatory resolutions, since known as the Georgia platform. The approval in other states of the Georgia platform in preference to the Alabama platform (*see* ALABAMA) caused a reaction in the south against secession, which was followed for a short period by a return to approximately the former party alignment. But in 1854 the Whig leaders went over to the Democrats. The Know-Nothing party was nearly destroyed by its crushing defeat in 1856, and in the next year the Democrats, by a large majority, elected as governor Joseph Emerson Brown (1821-94) who, by three successive re-elections, was continued in that office until the close of the American Civil War.

Secession and the Civil War.—The Kansas question and the attitude of the north toward the decision in the Dred Scott case were arousing the south when Brown was inaugurated the first time. In his inaugural address he clearly indicated that he would favour secession in the event of any further encroachment on the part of the north. On Nov. 7, following the election of Pres. Abraham Lincoln, the governor, in a special message to the legislature, recommended the calling of a convention to decide the question of secession. Alexander H. Stephens and Herschel V.

Johnson contended that Lincoln's election was insufficient ground for such action. On Nov. 17 the legislature passed an act directing the governor to order an election of delegates on Jan. 2, 1861, and their meeting in a convention on Jan. 16. On Jan. 19 this body passed an ordinance of secession by a vote of 208 to 89. Already the 1st regiment of Georgia volunteers, under Col. Alexander Lawton (1818-96), had seized Ft. Pulaski at the mouth of the Savannah river, and Governor Brown proceeded to Augusta and seized the Federal arsenal there. Toward the close of 1861, however, Federal warships blockaded Georgia's ports, and early in 1862 Federal forces captured Tybee Island, Ft. Pulaski, St. Marys, Brunswick and St. Simons Island. Georgians responded freely to the call for volunteers, but when the Confederate congress, in April 1862, passed the conscript law, Governor Brown, in a correspondence with Pres. Jefferson Davis, offered serious objections. Brown also quarreled with Davis on other Confederate policies that he considered as infringements on the rights of a sovereign state.

In 1863 northwest Georgia was involved in the Chattanooga campaign. In the following spring Georgia was invaded from Tennessee by a Federal army under Gen. William T. Sherman. The resistance of Gen. Joseph E. Johnston and Gen. J. B. Hood proved ineffectual, and on Sept. 2 Atlanta was taken. On Nov. 15 Sherman burned Atlanta and began his famous march to the sea, taking Savannah late in December. In the spring of 1865, Gen. J. H. Wilson, with a body of cavalry, entered the state from Alabama, seized Columbus and West Point on April 16, and on May 10 captured Jefferson Davis, president of the Confederacy, near Irwinville.

Reconstruction.—In accord with Pres. Andrew Johnson's plan for reorganizing the southern states, a provisional governor, James Johnson, was appointed on June 17, 1865, and a state convention reformed the constitution to meet the new conditions, rescinding the ordinance of secession, abolishing slavery and formally repudiating the state debt incurred in the prosecution of the war. A legislature and other officials were elected in Nov. 1865. The legislature ratified the 13th amendment on Dec. 9, and five days later Charles J. Jenkins was inaugurated governor. But both the convention and legislature incurred the suspicion and ill will of congress. Georgia was placed under military government, as part of the 3rd military district, by the Reconstruction act of March 2, 1867.

Under the auspices of the military authorities, registration of electors for a new state convention was begun, and 95,168 Negroes and 96,333 whites were registered. The acceptance of the proposition to call the convention and the election of many conscientious and intelligent delegates were largely the result of the influence of former Governor Brown, who was strongly convinced that the wisest course was to accept quickly what congress had offered. The convention met in Atlanta on Dec. 9, 1867, and by March 1868 had revised the constitution to meet the requirements of the Reconstruction acts. The constitution was duly adopted by popular vote, and elections were held for a governor and legislature. Rufus Brown Bullock, Republican, was chosen governor; the senate had a majority of Republicans; and in the house of representatives, by a vote of 76 to 74, a Republican was elected speaker. On July 21, the 14th amendment was ratified, and, as evidence of the restoration of Georgia to the Union, its representatives in congress were seated on July 25, 1868.

In Sept. 1868 the Democrats in the state legislature, being assisted by some of the white Republicans, expelled the 27 Negro members and seated their defeated white contestants. In retaliation congress excluded the state's representatives on the technicality that their credentials did not state to which congress they were accredited, and, on the theory that the government of Georgia was a provisional organization, passed an act requiring ratification of the 15th amendment before Georgia's senators and representatives would be seated. The department of war then concluded that the state was still subject to military authority and placed Gen. A. H. Terry in command. With his aid and that of congressional requirements that all members of the legislature must take the test oath of nonsupport to any pretended government, i.e., the

THE CIVIL WAR IN GEORGIA

(Above) Andersonville Confederate military prison where nearly 13,000 Federal prisoners died; photograph by A. J. Riddle, 1864. (Left) Damage done by Federal cannons at Ft. Pulaski; photograph by T. O. Sullivan, 1862. (Below) Federal troops ripping up railroad tracks at Atlanta during Sherman's march to the sea; photograph by George Barnard, 1864

Confederacy, and that none be excluded on account of colour, a Republican majority was secured for both houses, and the 15th amendment was ratified. On July 15, 1870, Georgia was finally readmitted to the union.

Reconstruction in Georgia was comparatively moderate, largely because a number of conservatives under the leadership of former Governor Brown supported the Reconstruction policy of congress. The election of 1870 gave the Democrats a majority in the legislature; Governor Bullock, fearing impeachment, resigned, and at a special election James M. Smith was chosen to fill the unexpired term. After that the control of the Democrats was complete. Georgia, however, did not frame its home-rule constitution until 1877, when the threat of further military intervention had ended.

Post-Reconstruction.—The history of Georgia since Reconstruction has been one of nominal social and economic progress, with the state firmly Democratic in politics until 1964. The 18-year interval following 1872 was dominated by the Bourbon triumvirate of Joseph E. Brown, Alfred H. Colquitt and John B. Gordon, who stood for low taxes and limited public services and who maintained a close liaison between business and political interests. The leasing of convicts to private concerns was the most criticized of their policies. The Independent movement, later backed by the

Farmers' alliance, challenged Bourbon control throughout most of the period, but by 1892 the Populist threat, with its greater appeal to rural voters, became more serious. All factions sought the Negro vote, and political corruption was widespread. The waning of Populism at the beginning of the 20th century was accompanied by the adoption of several new measures. Virtual disfranchisement of the Negro was effected by registration requirements in 1908 ("grandfather" laws, which placed restrictions on registration which were difficult for Negroes to meet but not for white registrants), and the convict-lease system was abolished. A state-wide prohibition law of 1907 proved unpopular, and this issue remained prominent until adoption of the 18th amendment to the U.S. constitution in 1919 brought national prohibition. Laws seeking to protect labour in the state's growing industries and reforms in educational policy, with additional appropriations for public schools, were other notable measures adopted in the first quarter of the 20th century.

County Unit System and Apportionment.—The Neill act of 1917 placed primary elections under legal control, establishing the county unit system for determining winners in such elections. In 1920 a constitutional amendment fixed the number of first-class counties at 8 and the number in the second classification at 30, while those remaining were in the third class. First-class counties were the most populous, and each had three representatives in the legislature and cast six unit votes. The second group of 30 counties had two representatives each and was entitled to four unit votes. The remaining 122 counties were the least populous, and each cast one representative and cast two unit votes. Thus first-class counties had a total of 48 votes; second-class, 120 votes; and third-class, 244 votes; the total of all votes being 412. Subsequently the number of counties was reduced to 159 and the total of county unit votes to 410. Since nomination in the Democratic primary in Georgia was tantamount to election, county unit voting, together with the three-class system of representation, placed political control in the hands of the smaller counties dominated by rural voters. This inequality of representation led in 1962 to a suit in the federal courts, the result of which was the voiding of the county unit system. A short time later the court ordered that one of the two legislative branches be apportioned on a population basis. Subsequently the 54 senate seats were reapportioned, with 23 going to the urban areas. In 1964 the court ruled that both houses be apportioned on a population basis and rejected as invalid a new constitution framed by the existing legislature. In 1964 the U.S. supreme court ruled that the Georgia apportionment for the U.S. house of representatives was unfair to urban voters and that congressional districts must be established on the basis of "equal representation for equal numbers of people." Congressional districts were reapportioned in 1965, as was the Georgia house of representatives. The plans were accepted as interim measures, but a federal court ordered both houses and the districts reapportioned again. A new plan was drawn up in 1967 and, with minor amendments ordered by the court, went into effect in 1968.

Issues of Integration.—In 1930 Richard B. Russell was elected governor on a platform of revamping governmental machinery to effect economy and efficiency. The Reorganization act of 1931 reduced 102 administrative units to 18 and established a board of regents to administer the public colleges and the university. Russell was succeeded in 1933 by Eugene Talmadge, who for four years opposed most aspects of the national administration. The Roosevelt administration was popular in Georgia, however, and Eurith D. Rivers after 1937 brought the state into the orbit of the New Deal, although his failure to finance expanded state services brought Talmadge back to power four years later on a platform of economy. He now attacked the more subtle effects of the New Deal, and the promotion of social equality for all races, and launched a white supremacy offensive. He caused the dismissal of several university-system officials thought to be advocating mixing of the races in public colleges and schools; the dismissals in turn causing the colleges to lose accreditation. Ellis Gibbs Arnall defeated him in 1942 and introduced a program of reform, restored college accreditation, lowered the voting age to 18, abolished the poll tax and promoted the adoption of a new constitution in 1945, embracing approximately 50 changes.

In the Democratic primary of July 1946, Talmadge, backed by rural voters and supported by some industrialists, again received the nomination for governor under the county unit system, although losing the popular vote to James V. Carmichael. In the following November Talmadge was formally elected governor without opposition, but he died before his inauguration. The general assembly convened in January and according to law canvassed the election returns to find that about 700 write-in votes had been cast for the governor-elect's son, Herman E. Talmadge, whom they then declared governor. Because the constitution of 1945 was not clear on the question of succession in such a case, confusion followed. Arnall and the lieutenant governor-elect, Melvin E. Thompson, each claimed the succession. On March 16 the state supreme court ruled in favour of Thompson, but in the special primary of 1948 young Talmadge won over Thompson in a county unit vote of 312 to 98.

A federal court decision in 1945 ordered the Democratic (white) primary in Georgia open to Negro voters, causing the registration of Negroes to increase more than 700% by the end of the following year and providing new impetus to the white-supremacy issue. A registration act in 1949, containing literacy, character and citizenship tests, and aimed at minimizing the Negro vote, proved unsatisfactory and was repealed after one year. In 1950 (and again in 1952) a proposed amendment extending the county unit system to general elections was defeated. In the meantime a sweeping 3% sales-tax levy enacted by the Talmadge administration, most of which went for educational purposes, resulted in a rapid upgrading of Negro schools. What promised to prove the most serious issue since Reconstruction was provided in May 1954, when the U.S. supreme court announced its unanimous decision that racial segregation in public schools was unconstitutional.

In November an amendment was ratified enabling the state to abolish public education but granting subsidies to private schools. Marvin Griffin campaigned for governor on the Talmadge position of continued segregation and was elected. In 1955, the legislature passed a stand-by private-school law to go into effect if the court ordered a specific school to desegregate.

The administration of Gov. Ernest Vandiver, who succeeded Griffin, abandoned the previous policy of 'massive resistance' and in effect placed the closing of public schools to prevent integration under local option. The board of regents was given similar power to close public colleges. Early in 1961 two Negro students were admitted with police protection to the University of Georgia under a federal court order. In the next several years seven public and two private colleges were integrated with a total of less than 40 Negro students. In the meantime the Atlanta school board, under court mandate, on Aug. 30, 1961, enrolled nine Negro students in four previously all-white high schools. Lester G. Maddox, who was elected governor by the legislature in Jan. 1967, continued the fight against school integration and a December report showed that 90% of the Negro pupils still attended all-Negro schools. Maddox was legally unable to succeed himself as governor, and in 1970 Jimmy Carter, a Democrat, was elected. In 1964, when Democratic Pres. Lyndon B. Johnson supported the Civil Rights bill, Georgia voted for a Republican presidential candidate for the first time in its history. In 1968 the state gave its presidential vote to George C. Wallace.

GOVERNMENT

Constitutions.—Georgia has had a total of eight constitutions, that of 1877 having the longest continuous history although amended 301 times. In 1945 a new constitution was adopted, about 90% of which was taken from the preceding document. Revision was largely confined to form and organization although important changes were made. The amendment of 1941 increasing the governor's term from two to four years was continued in (1943). The governor was made ineligible to succeed himself until four years from the date of leaving office. The membership of the state senate was increased from 52 to 54, bringing the total membership of the legislature to 259. The membership was reduced to 251 (56 senate seats and 195 house seats) in 1968. The office of lieutenant governor was added along with several new boards, all being constitutional offices. The number of justices of the supreme court was increased from six to seven.

Gov. Eugene Talmadge had obtained legislative endorsement of his plans to give the governor, functioning along with the state auditor as the budget committee, power to transfer funds from one purpose to another. This executive subsequently exercised such power over the purse as to give him unusual control over every aspect of state government and to open the way for administrative abuses, which in turn crystallized a movement led by Governor Arnall to weaken the powers of the governor and to improve administrative efficiency. Arnall's proposals to make the board of regents, board of education, board of pardons and paroles, game and fish commission, and public service commission constitutional agencies were ratified by the people in 1943.

The 1877 constitution placed severe limitations on finance, taxation and debt, although amended many times to meet requirements of changing circumstances. In June 1937, 26 constitutional amendments were ratified, liberalizing the powers of the legislature, particularly with respect to the state's co-operating in the social program of the New Deal. A clause limiting the debt of a minor civil division to 7% of the assessed valuation of its property was amended 135 times before 1945. The new constitution raised the limit to 10%, but the additional debt had to be approved by a majority vote, as against a two-thirds vote in the old constitution, and had to be paid in five years. A significant new provision required that all tax moneys for state purposes be paid into the state treasury and that appropriations be made by the legislature to departments and agencies in specific sums. The new provision removed the old principle of allocating certain revenue to specific objectives, a practice which at one time removed as much as 60% of all state funds from legislative control. A determined effort by highway interests to amend the new constitution so that most of the gasoline taxes and license-tag fees would be earmarked for construction and maintenance of roads succeeded in 1952.

Finances.—In the late 1960s, Georgia's total annual revenue exceeded $1,300,000,000, much of it derived from taxes that were nonexistent at the beginning of the century. The 3% general sales tax, begun in 1951, accounted for about 37% of the amount collected through taxes. Motor-vehicle license taxes and gasoline taxes, begun in 1910 and 1921, respectively, provided 20%; while the income tax, introduced in 1929, accounted for slightly more than 16%. State taxes on land and real estate, once an important source of state revenue, were reduced to one-fourth of a mill in 1951 and thereafter contributed only a negligible part of the state's income but remained the most important source of revenue for local government. Of the state's total general revenue nearly one-half was being spent for education; about one-fifth for highways; and more than one-fifth for public welfare, health and hospitals. By 1950 Georgia's fixed debt had been paid off.

POPULATION

In 1760 Georgia's population was less than 10,000, with Negro slaves forming one-third of the total. By the end of the colonial period the number of settlers had grown to 33,000, of whom 15,000 were slaves. The state continued to grow throughout the American Revolution and by the first census in 1790 had reached 82,548, concentrated in the L-shaped corridor along the Savannah river and thence down the coast to the Altamaha. By 1800 the population had almost doubled, having increased to 162,686, 90% of the increase occurring in the up-country, where land grants had become available. The population reached 691,392 by 1840, resulting from the freeing of land by removal of Indians, free grants of the state's western lands and rapid expansion of cotton planting. The 1860 population of 1,057,286 was 44% Negro and was con-

centrated in the newer middle Georgia counties. In 1900 the population was 2,216,331, with 46.7% Negro and 15.6% urban. Throughout the 20th century there was a steady decline in the proportion of Negroes and a sharp rise in the percentage of urban inhabitants.

In 1970 the total population was 4,589,575 (an increase of 646,-459 over 1960), or 77.9 persons per square mile. The entire urban population, including the urban fringe adjacent to the five larger cities (and six unincorporated places of 2,500 or more elsewhere), was 2,768,074, or 60.3% of the state total. There are seven standard metropolitan statistical areas—Albany, Atlanta, Augusta, part of Chattanooga, Tenn., Columbus, Macon and Savannah. With the exception of the nonwhites (practically all Negro), who comprised 26.2% of the total population, Georgia's people were largely of Anglo-Saxon origin. The foreign-born comprised only a small fraction of 1%. South Georgia was heavily populated with Negroes, while a few north Georgia counties had none. All groups were predominantly Protestant in religion. In both the native white and the Negro population males were outnumbered, the ratios being 96.7 (per 100 females) and 88.6, respectively, in 1970. The rural population was declining more rapidly than in the past because of crop-reduction programs and other changes in the agricultural pattern. Farm tenancy was also declining, 40% of the farmers belonging to that category, as opposed to 55% in 1940. Many Negroes were moving from farms to urban communities outside the state.

EDUCATION

State School System.—As early as 1742 the Georgia trustees provided free tuition for children of poor families to attend a school at Savannah, and various forms of educational subsidy have continued throughout the state's history. After the American Revolution, academies were established in several counties with funds from confiscated Loyalist estates and by gifts of public land. By 1860 over 500 academies had been chartered, many by private, civic and religious groups. The academy system, essentially aristocratic, remained the general pattern of education throughout the pre-American Civil War period. Tuition was not free until 1817 and then only for children of indigent parents.

The constitution of 1868 authorized free public education on the elementary level for all children, and a school law was enacted in 1870. Appropriations reached $1,000,000 in 1893. Supplementary local taxes for elementary schools were permitted by a constitutional amendment in 1904, but counties were not required to levy such a tax until 1919. In 1911 the state board of education became a professional one, and uniform schoolbooks were adopted; in the following year high schools became a part of the public-school system. In 1937 a seven-month elementary-school term was guaranteed by the legislature. The compulsory school law as amended in 1919 required attendance between the ages of 8 and 14 at least through the seventh grade.

School consolidation on a local experimental basis was begun in 1903, but not until 1919 did the legislature appropriate funds to encourage this movement. Simultaneously an adult illiteracy commission was established, followed by local taxation for adult schools, resulting in noteworthy progress in the eradication of illiteracy, dropping from 18.4% in 1920 to 9.4% in 1930.

In 1933 the budget for elementary and secondary education was approximately $16,000,000. By the late 1960s it was more than $500,000,000. Free textbooks, a retirement system and a twelfth grade had been added. The average teacher's salary was $7,000. Vocational education was expanded and library services added, including one of the largest film libraries in the U.S.

Colleges and Universities.—The University of Georgia, at Athens, the oldest institution of higher learning in the state, was chartered in 1785 but did not open until 1801. In 1828 a medical college was established at Augusta. During the latter half of the 19th century the state established many other colleges, including the Georgia Military Institute at Marietta (destroyed by Federal military forces in 1864); the Georgia Institute of Technology at Atlanta, Woman's College of Georgia (renamed Georgia College at Milledgeville and co-educational, 1967), a teachers' college

Georgia: Places of 5,000 or more Population (1970 census)*

Place	1970	1960	1950	1940	1900
Total state	4,589,575	3,943,116	3,444,578	3,123,723	2,216,331
Albany	72,623	55,890	31,155	19,055	4,606
Americus	16,091	13,472	11,389	9,281	7,674
Athens	44,342	31,355	28,180	20,650	10,245
Atlanta	496,973	487,455	331,314	302,288	89,872
Augusta	59,864	70,626	71,508	65,919	39,441
Bainbridge	10,887	12,714	7,562	6,352	2,641
Blakely	5,267	3,580	3,234	2,774	—
Brunswick	19,585	21,703	17,954	15,035	9,081
Cairo	8,061	7,427	5,577	4,653	690
Carrollton	13,520	10,973	7,753	6,214	1,998
Cartersville	9,929	8,668	7,270	6,141	3,135
Cedartown	9,253	9,340	9,470	9,025	2,823
Chamblee	9,127	6,635	3,445	1,081	—
Cochran	5,161	4,714	3,357	2,464	517
College Park	18,203	23,469	14,535	8,213	17,614
Columbus	154,168	116,779	79,611	53,280	3,473
Cordele	10,733	10,609	9,462	7,929	2,062
Covington	10,267	8,167	5,192	3,900	4,315
Dalton	18,872	17,868	15,968	10,448	2,926
Dawson	5,383	5,062	4,411	3,681	1,418
Decatur	21,943	22,026	21,635	16,561	—
Dock Junction	6,009	5,417	4,160	—	—
Doraville	9,039	4,437	472	—	—
Douglas	10,195	8,736	7,428	300	617
Douglasville	5,472	4,462	3,400	2,555	—
Dublin	15,143	13,814	10,232	7,814	2,987
Eastman	5,416	5,118	3,597	3,311	1,235
East Point	39,315	35,633	21,080	12,403	1,315
Elberton	6,438	7,107	6,772	6,188	3,834
Fitzgerald	8,015	8,781	8,130	7,388	1,817
Forest Park	19,994	14,201	2,653	577	—
Fort Benning	27,495	—	—	—	—
Fort Gordon	15,589	—	—	—	—
Fort Valley	9,251	8,310	6,820	4,953	2,022
Gainesville	15,459	16,523	11,936	10,243	4,382
Garden City	5,741	5,451	1,557	—	—
Griffin	22,734	21,735	13,982	13,222	6,857
Hapeville	9,567	10,082	8,560	5,059	430
Jesup	9,091	7,304	4,605	2,903	805
La Fayette	6,044	5,588	4,884	3,509	491
La Grange	23,301	23,632	25,025	21,983	4,274
Lawrenceville	5,115	3,804	2,932	2,223	—
Macon	122,423	69,764	70,252	57,865	23,272
Marietta	27,216	25,565	20,687	8,667	4,446
Midway-Hardwick	14,047	16,909	14,774	—	—
Milledgeville	11,601	11,117	8,835	6,778	4,219
Monroe	8,071	6,826	4,542	4,168	1,846
Moultrie	14,302	15,764	11,639	10,147	2,221
Newnan	11,205	12,169	8,218	7,182	3,654
Perry	7,771	6,032	3,849	1,542	650
Rome	30,759	32,226	29,615	26,282	7,291
Roswell	5,430	2,983	2,123	1,622	—
St. Simons	5,346	3,199	—	—	—
Sandersville	5,546	5,425	4,480	3,566	2,023
Savannah	118,349	149,245	119,638	95,996	54,244
Smyrna	19,157	10,157	2,005	1,440	238
Statesboro	14,616	8,356	6,097	5,028	1,197
Summerville	5,043	4,706	3,973	3,575	—
Swainsboro	7,325	5,943	4,380	3,575	895
Thomaston	10,024	9,336	6,580	6,396	1,714
Thomasville	18,155	18,246	14,424	12,683	5,322
Thomson	7,001	4,522	3,489	3,088	—
Tifton	12,179	9,903	6,831	5,228	1,384
Toccoa	6,971	7,303	6,781	5,494	2,176
Valdosta	32,303	30,652	20,046	15,595	5,613
Vidalia	9,507	7,569	5,819	4,109	503
Warner Robins	33,491	18,633	7,986	—	—
Waycross	18,996	20,944	18,899	16,763	5,919
Waynesboro	5,530	5,359	4,663	6,793	2,030
Winder	6,605	5,555	4,604	3,974	1,145
Windsor Forest	7,288				

*Populations are reported as constituted at date of each census.
Note: Dash indicates place did not exist during reported census, or data not available.

and a college of agriculture at Athens, an agricultural college at Dahlonega and a number of small branches colleges in southern Georgia. In the first half of the 20th century five senior colleges and eight junior colleges (including a technical school) were established, all for white students. In addition, three public Negro colleges were provided, all in the southern part of the state, at Albany, Fort Valley and Savannah.

Before 1931 the public colleges each had its own board of trustees and operated independently under separate fiscal systems. The creation of the university system of Georgia brought them and three agricultural experiment stations under one board of regents, the chief administrative officer being the chancellor, with his office in Atlanta. Seven of the existing institutions were immediately discontinued, and one new college was established in western Georgia, a populous area where four institutions were abolished. The regents controlled all the institutions as one fiscal unit. They set up a council of the university system, comprising administrative officers and some members of the teaching staffs of the schools, and some progress was made in defining the function of higher education. The regents, however, did not halt the trend of various units and integrating them into a more logical system early manifested in Georgia of developing area or regional colleges. In 1970 the state system included the University of Georgia, Georgia State university, Georgia Institute of Technology, and the Medical College of Georgia, all with doctoral programs; 11 senior colleges; and 11 junior colleges.

Private schools include Agnes Scott college, Decatur (for women; 1889), Berry college, Mount Berry (nonsectarian; 1926), Tift college, Forsyth (Baptist; 1847; for women), Emory university, near Atlanta (Methodist; 1836), La Grange college, La Grange (Methodist; 1831), Mercer university, Macon (Baptist; 1833), Oglethorpe college, near Atlanta (nonsectarian; 1835), Piedmont college, Demorest (Congregational; 1897), Shorter college, Rome (Baptist; 1873), Wesleyan college, Macon (Methodist; 1836; for women), and Brenau college, Gainesville (nonsectarian; 1878; for women). Atlanta is the largest centre in the south for the higher education of Negroes, having four undergraduate private colleges: Spelman (nonsectarian; 1881; for women), Morris Brown (Methodist; 1881), Clark (Methodist; 1869), and Morehouse (Baptist; 1867; for men); the Interdenominational Theological center (created in 1957, incorporating four existing seminaries); and Atlanta university (nonsectarian; 1865), for graduate study. Paine college (Methodist; 1883) in Augusta is the only other private college established for Negroes in Georgia.

CORRECTIONS AND WELFARE

In 1811 Georgia began construction at Milledgeville of a state penitentiary that had a number of workshops and by 1820 had inaugurated a program of penal and criminal reform unusually progressive for the times. The rapid increase of the prison popu-

PHOTOGRAPH, UNIVERSITY OF GEORGIA

THE OLD COLLEGE BUILDING, COMPLETED IN 1804, WAS THE FIRST PERMANENT BUILDING AT THE UNIVERSITY OF GEORGIA, ATHENS

lation following the emancipation of the Negro in 1865, there being no Negro prisoners before emancipation, brought a reversal of the earlier policy, resulting in the bulk of prisoners being leased to private businesses or assigned to county chain gangs. The former practice ended in 1908. The constitution of 1945 established a board of corrections that assumed operation of a large central penitentiary at Reidsville, and the use of convicts on county roads practically disappeared. By the late 1960s about 15 prison branches had been established, and these, together with the Reidsville facility, usually contained over 4,500 prisoners.

All of Georgia's charitable institutions were administered by a single board of control from 1931 to 1940 and by a public welfare department from 1940 to 1943. In the early 1970s, after several subsequent organizational changes had occurred, most of these institutions were under the control of three state agencies. The department of education directed both the Georgia Academy for the Blind at Macon and the Georgia School for the Deaf at Cave Spring. Under the supervision of the department of public health were the tuberculosis sanitarium at Rome, Gracewood State school and hospital for mentally retarded children, and ten psychiatric institutions, the largest of which, Central State hospital at Milledgeville, could accommodate as many as 10,000 patients. The department of family and children's services had been delegated responsibility for a factory for the blind at Bainbridge and three youth development centres for delinquents, located at Milledgeville (boys), Atlanta (girls) and Augusta (co-educational). This last department also administered the state's public assistance program.

THE ECONOMY

Agriculture.—Agriculture was the principal occupation of the people of Georgia until after World War II, when acceleration of mechanized farming reduced the farm population and the state underwent rapid industrialization. The most significant trend in Georgia agriculture in the second half of the 20th century was away from cotton, the principal money crop for 150 years, to a wide diversification. The largest cotton crop was in 1911, when 2,768,000 bales were produced on approximately 5,000,000 ac. A marked decline in cotton was noted in the early 1920s as a result of boll weevil infestation, the 1923 crop dropping to 588,000 bales. Diversification began at this point, and, after 1933, federal crop control programs accelerated the movement. In the second half of the 20th century the soil-bank program had removed 380,000 ac. from production, of which only 10% was cotton; and the value of the state's corn crop in 1957 exceeded that of cotton for the first time since the American Civil War.

Loss of income from cotton was more than replaced by income from such new crops as tobacco, peanuts, poultry, livestock and forestry products. Tobacco, grown in Georgia since colonial times, came into demand for cigarettes during World War I, and by the late 1960s about 60,000 ac. annually were harvested. The state ranked first in the nation in peanut and in pimiento production, more than 500,000 ac. of peanuts being planted annually and harvested for nuts in addition to 150,000 ac. for hog grazing and other purposes. The pimiento (Spanish paprika) industry began in 1912, when a superior plant was imported from Spain and was found to be adaptable to the cotton belt. The peppers came to be grown under contract to commercial packers.

The most spectacular development in Georgia agriculture was the rapid rise of the poultry industry. While the initial emphasis in the 1920s had been on egg production, the most outstanding results were later achieved in growing broilers, production increasing 600% from 1950 to 1969. Tributaries to the broiler industry were processing plants, hatcheries, feed mills and supply houses. Livestock and livestock products were in the late 1960s responsible for almost 60% of the state's cash income. Georgia played a leading role in developing herds of improved breeds, the greatest expansion being in the former cotton belt. Free range grazing in southern Georgia did not completely disappear until the second half of the 20th century. Other income from diversified agriculture was in valuable peach and watermelon crops in middle and southern Georgia, respectively; apples in northeast Georgia; and

BILL MAHAN—LEVITON, ATLANTA

PRELIMINARY PROCESSING OF KAOLIN AT A MINE IN GORDON

pecans, produced in nearly every county in the state, with large commercial orchards in its middle and southern portions.

Woodlands covered about 26,000,000 ac., comprising two-thirds of the state's total area; under fire-protection measures, they were one of the state's greatest natural resources. After 1933 over 360,000,000 ac. of Georgia land were replanted with more than 1,000,000,000 trees, and the total annual value of raw timber and pulpwood after harvesting rose to $200,000,000, its processed value being $800,000,000. In lumber products Georgia ranked high in the nation and produced about 80% of the nation's naval stores.

Industry.—The total annual value of Georgia's manufactured goods in the second half of the 20th century was more than twice that of agricultural products. More than half of the state's rural population commuted daily to urban jobs. The mill village, once common everywhere, had almost disappeared. The largest single product manufactured was textiles. Transportation equipment ranked second followed by food products. Wood processing and wood products plants increased more than sixfold after 1935, employees in this industry quadrupling in number. The manufacturing of pulpwood began in 1936, much of this going into the production of paper bags. About 40% of Georgia's new manufacturing plants were located in towns of fewer than 5,000 persons and utilized local labour and raw materials, but many large national concerns also located in Georgia near urban centres and were engaged in the manufacture of a wide range of products.

Minerals.—The most important mineral, sedimentary kaolin, found largely in the coastal plain just south of the fall line, is used in making whiteware and as filling and coating for paper. Other products of the region are limestone, fuller's earth, portland cement and bauxite. The crystalline rocks of the Piedmont and mountain region provide granite, marble, talc, feldspar, asbestos, ochre and barite, of which granite is the most important, being used principally for monuments. The granite industry is mainly around Elberton in northeast Georgia. Marble from the Tate quarries is widely noted for its quality and beauty and is second in importance in this region. In the Paleozoic area of northwest Georgia the principal products are portland cement, crushed limestone and ochre. Metal mining is confined to Bartow, with barite, ochre and brown iron ore the leading products. Small quantities of coal are mined on Lookout and Sand mountains. The Dahlonega district, once famous as a gold-mining region, produces only negligible quantities of this metal.

Transportation.—Atlanta, long an important rail centre for the southeastern U.S., became a major air and motor transportation hub in the second quarter of the 20th century. Georgia by the late 1960s had about 67,000 mi. of surfaced highways with about 17,400 in the state system, about 190 airports, and a motor vehicle registration of about 2,324,000. Rail mileage was about 5,000. Other means of transportation were navigable rivers below the fall line, and ocean vessels having piers at St. Marys, Brunswick, Darien and Savannah.

See also references under "Georgia" in the Index.

BIBLIOGRAPHY.—The most complete bibliography of the materials of Georgia history is *The Catalogue*, the W. J. De Renne Georgia library, 3 vol. (1931), compiled by Leonard L. Mackall. *See also* Ella M. Thornton, *Finding-List of Books and Pamphlets Relating to Georgia and Georgians* (1928); R. P. Brooks, "A Preliminary Bibliography of Georgia History," *University of Georgia Bulletin*, vol. x, no. 10a (1910).

Works Covering All of Georgia History: E. M. Coulter, *A Short History of Georgia* (1933); Amanda Johnson, *Georgia as Colony and State* (1938); James C. Bonner, *The Georgia Story* (1958).

Works Devoted to Special Periods or Subjects: W. B. Stevens, *History of Georgia to 1798*, 2 vol. (1847); C. C. Jones, *Antiquities of the Southern Indians, Particularly of the Georgia Tribes* (1873); Horace Montgomery (ed.), *Georgians in Profile* (1958); R. H. Shryock, *Georgia and the Union in 1850* (1926); U. B. Phillips, "Georgia and State Rights," *American Historical Association Annual Report for 1901*; Kenneth Coleman, *American Revolution in Georgia, 1763-1789* (1958); Milton S. Heath, *Constructive Liberalism: the Role of the State in Economic Development in Georgia to 1860* (1954); T. Conn Bryan, *Confederate Georgia* (1953); R. P. Brooks, *The Agrarian Revolution in Georgia, 1865-1912* (1914); *Financing Government in Georgia, 1850-1944* (1946); James C. Bonner, *A History of Georgia Agriculture, 1732-1860* (1964); Willard Range, *A Century of Georgia Agriculture, 1850-1950* (1954); C. M. Thompson, *Reconstruction in Georgia* (1915); Alex M. Arnett, *The Populist Movement in Georgia* (1922); J. R. McCain, *Georgia as a Proprietary Province* (1917); Frederick Doveton Nichols, *The Early Architecture of Georgia* (1957); Albert B. Saye, *A Constitutional History of Georgia, 1732-1945* (1948); C. B. Gosnell and C. D. Anderson, *The Government and Administration of Georgia* (1956).

Source Material May Be Found in: The Colonial Records of the State of Georgia (1904-13); *The Confederate Records of the State of Georgia* (1909-10); and *The Georgia Historical Society Collections* (1840-1916).

Current statistics on production, employment, industry, etc., may be obtained from the pertinent state departments; the principal figures are summarized annually in the States Statistical Supplement of the *Britannica Book of the Year.* (Js. C. B.; X.)

GEORGIA, STRAIT OF. The Strait of Georgia lies between the central east coast of Vancouver Island and the southwestern mainland of the province of British Columbia, Canada. Its length is about 140 mi., and its greatest width about 20 mi. The northern part of the strait is almost closed off by a group of islands lying northeast of the town of Campbell River. The southern end of the strait is blocked by the San Juan Islands of Washington state. Depth of water in mid-channel is about 150 to 200 fathoms, but there are deeper, submerged valleys, and also numerous shoals which indicate the tops of submerged islands. There is a general counterclockwise movement of surface water in Georgia strait, aided by the large outflow of fresh water from the Fraser river. Tidal streams are complicated because tidal currents from Juan de Fuca strait to the southwest, and from Queen Charlotte strait to the northwest, both penetrate into Georgia strait. (J. L. R.)

GEORGIAN ARCHITECTURE, the style of the 18th century in England and in the English colonies in America. There are slight differences in usages of the term in the two countries. In England, Georgian refers to the mode in architecture and the allied arts of the reigns of George I, II and III, extending from 1714 to 1820. The last decade of this era is often distinguished as Regency. The English Georgian style was strongly influenced by the work of the Italian Andrea Palladio (1518-80). Introduced to England during the reign of James I, the Palladian style became even more admired in the 1720s under George I. Classical, formal and elegant, it esteemed "correctness" more than comfort.

In America, Georgian refers to the architectural style of the English colonies from about 1700 to the Revolution. Also formal and aristocratic in spirit, it was at first based on the baroque work of Sir Christopher Wren and his English followers in the late Stuart period, but after 1750 it became more severely Palladian. Typically, houses were of red brick with white-painted wood trim and sliding-sash windows. Interiors had central halls, elaborately turned stair balustrades, paneled walls painted in warm colours and white plaster ceilings. All of these features were new to the colonies in 1700. Some of the earliest Georgian buildings were at Williamsburg, capital of Virginia from 1699 to 1780; other notable examples are Independence hall, Philadelphia (1745), and King's chapel, Boston (1754). The style was followed after the Revolution by the Federal style, 1780-1820. *See also* BAROQUE AND POST-BAROQUE ART AND ARCHITECTURE; GEORGIAN STYLES.

See Hugh Morrison, *Early American Architecture* (1952). (HH. M.)

GEORGIAN BAY, the northeast section of Lake Huron, lies entirely within the Canadian province of Ontario. The bay is separated from the lake by Manitoulin Island and the Saugeen (or Bruce) peninsula. It is 120 mi. (193 km.) long and 51 mi. (82 km.) wide. Depth of water in the bay is generally between 100 and 300 ft.; the maximum depth is 540 ft. (165 m.) at a point near the main channel leading to Lake Huron. The bay also is connected with the north channel of Lake Huron, which lies north and west of Manitoulin Island. The principal tributary rivers are the French, draining Lake Nipissing on the northeast; the Maganatawan; the Muskoka, draining the Muskoka chain of lakes; the Severn, draining Lake Simcoe; and the Nottawasaga, which enters from the south. Small boats may pass from Georgian bay to the Bay of Quinte, on Lake Ontario, by traveling through the Trent Valley waterway, which includes the Trent canal built in 1918.

The Georgian Bay Islands National park, at the southeastern corner of the bay, was established in 1929 and includes 30 of the bay's more than 20,000 small islands. The region is forested and thousands of tourists visit the shore resorts in summer. The bay was the first part of the Great Lakes seen by white men, who reached it by way of the Ottawa and French rivers in 1615.

For a discussion of origin, geologic setting, history and commerce *see* GREAT LAKES, THE; HURON, LAKE.   (J. L. HH.)

GEORGIAN LANGUAGE, together with Svanian, Mingrelian and Lazian, the southern or Kartvelian group of the Caucasian languages (*q.v.*). For the speakers of Svanian and Mingrelian it serves as the language of literature and of instruction. Among the Caucasian languages, only Georgian has an ancient literary tradition. The oldest inscriptions date from the 5th century, at which time also parts of the Bible were translated from Armenian into Georgian. The language of the 10th and 11th centuries differs in some points from classical Old Georgian of the 10th and 11th centuries still in use in religious services. Old Georgian is somewhat difficult to understand but by no means incomprehensible to the Georgians of today; it was used in liturgy and for theological writings until the end of the 18th century. Old Georgian abounds in loan words from Armenian and especially from Greek; with the help of Greek the foundations were laid for a philosophical terminology. The language of medieval poetry, largely influenced by Persian, stands nearer to the contemporary language. But only in the middle of the 19th century did the literary language become definitively adapted to the living language of the people. The vocabulary of New Georgian is very extensive as compared with that of Old Georgian, every author drawing from his vernacular and even coining new expressive words. The dialects of modern Georgian show but slight differences, the most aberrant being those of the northeastern mountain tribes (Khevsurs, P'shavs).

The phonemic system of Georgian comprises the five cardinal vowels and 28 (Old Georgian, 2 more) consonant phonemes. This system is notably simpler than that of the North Caucasian languages; it shares with them some characteristic traits, *e.g.*, the division of the stops and affricates into three modes of articulation: voiced *b, d, g, dz, j,* voiceless with aspiration *p', t', k', ts, ch* and voiceless glottalized *p, t, k* or *q, ds, tch.* Diphthongs were current in Old Georgian, but have been reduced to single vowels. There is no phonemic vowel length. The first syllable of the word, or in longer words frequently the antepenultimate, is marked by very slight stress.

Georgian has roughly the same parts of speech as the Indo-European languages. The opposition between noun and verb is distinctly marked. The noun has seven cases: nominative, vocative, genitive, dative, ablative-instrumental, terminative-adverbial and a special case called ergative which in some constructions denotes the agent with a transitive verb. Because of fusion with postpositions there arose in New Georgian some secondary local cases. In Old Georgian the plural was formed in the nominative by *-ni,* vocative *-no,* oblique cases *-t'a;* this plural is seldom used in New Georgian, the regular plural being formed with a suffix *-eb-* to which are added the case endings used in the singular. There are no articles and no gender, even in pronouns. The attributive adjective, standing in New Georgian habitually before the noun, agrees with the noun in case but not in number. It is also the verb which shows fundamental differences from Indo-European languages. The Georgian verb is multipersonal: (1) The person of the agent is denoted in the third person by endings,

The Georgian Alphabet

No.	KHUTSURI (Ecclesiastical script)	MKHEDRULI (Modern alphabet)	Transliteration	Numerical value
1			a	1
2			b	2
3			g	3
4			d	4
5			e	5
6			v	6
7			z	7
8			ey	8
9			t'	9
10			i	10
11			k	20
12			l	30
13			m	40
14			n	50
15			y	60
16			o	70
17			p	80
18			ž [zh]	90
19			r	100
20			s	200
21			t	300
22			u	400
23			w [vi]	400
24			p'	500
25			k'	600
26			g [gh]	700
27			q	800
28			š [sh]	900
29			č [ch]	1,000
30			c [ts]	2,000
31			dz	3,000
32			ç [ds]	4,000
33			ç [tch]	5,000
34			x [kh]	6,000
35			q' [kh]	7,000
36			j	8,000
37			h	9,000
38			ho [oy]	10,000

GEORGIAN SOVIET SOCIALIST REPUBLIC

in the first and second persons by prefixes most of which are not connected etymologically with the independent personal pronouns: *me v-dser* "I write," *shen dser* (in oldest Georgian *kh-dser*) "thou writest," *igi dser-s* "he writes." (2) Another set of personal prefixes refers to an object: *m-dser* "thou writest to me," *g-dser-s* "he writes to thee." (3) Relations between agent and objects are denoted by called "versions" by Georgian grammarians are denoted by vowels inserted between the personal prefixes and the verbal root: *a-dser* (in oldest Georgian *kha-dser*) "thou writest on it," *vi-dser* "I write for me," *vu-dser* "I write for him," *e-dser-ebis* "it is written on it/for him." (4) The tenses of the verb are distributed according to three systems: present, aorist and perfect. In verbs present the agent is put into the nominative, both direct and indirect objects into the dative: *kats-i dser-s dseril-s* "the/a man is writing the/a letter." In the aorist the object is put into the nominative, the agent into the ergative: *kats-man da-dser-a dseril-i* "the/a man wrote the/a letter." This construction which resembles the passive construction of other languages is characteristic of all Caucasian languages. In the perfect which denotes an action in the past not witnessed by the speaker, the object is put into the nominative, the agent into the dative: *kats-s da-u-dser-ia dseril-i* "it appears (it is said) that the man wrote the letter."

The Georgian alphabet was probably composed by Christian missionaries during the 5th century under the influence of and with some loans from the Greek alphabet. The bulk of the signs might have been derived from a form of the Aramaic script used in inscriptions dating from the 2nd century which have been discovered at Armazi, an ancient capital of Georgia. From the oldest form of the Georgian script arose in the 10th century an angular book script; from this developed the round form called *mkhedruli* on which are based the modern printed characters.

BIBLIOGRAPHY.—*Grammars:* N. Y. Marr and M. Brière, *La Langue géorgienne* (1931); A. Shanidze, *K'art'uli gramatika* (1930 *et seq.*); Franz Zorell, *Grammatik zur altgeorgischen Bibelübersetzung* (1930); H. K. Vogt, *Esquisse d'une grammaire du géorgien moderne;* reprint from *Norsk Tidskrift for sprogvidenskap,* ix–x (1938); K. Tchenkeli, *Einführung in die georgische Sprache,* 2 vol. (1958). *Dictionaries:* D. I. Chubinov, *Dictionnaire Géorgien-Russe-Français* (1840) and *Gruzinsko-russki slovar* (1887); E. Cherkesi, *Georgian-English Dictionary* (1950).
(GD. D.)

GEORGIAN LITERATURE. The literary history of Georgia, like that of neighbouring Armenia, begins with the conversion of the country to Christianity in the 4th century and the resulting need to invent an alphabet for the propagation of the Scriptures in the vernacular. The Gospels were translated in the 5th century from an Armenian version, itself deriving from the Syriac; the Acts and Psalms were translated soon afterward, and also works of early Greek Fathers (*e.g.,* Gregory of Nyssa, Gregory of Nazianzus, John Chrysostom, Basil the Great).

Original Georgian literature begins with lives of saints, the first surviving one being that of St. Shushanik (composed *c.* 480). Other early works include an account of the conversion of Georgia by St. Nino (*q.v.*), and semilegendary stories of the exploits of King Vakhtang Gorgaslani, a hero of the 5th century. Much of this material was subsequently woven into the Georgian annals (*K'art'lis tskhovreba*). The Georgians were the first to give a Christian colouring to the Buddhist legend of Barlaam and Josaphat (*q.v.*), which reached them in the 9th century via the Arabic. The beginnings of a philosophical school in Georgia were laid by the Neoplatonist Ioane Petridsi (d. *c.* 1125; a pupil of the Byzantine scholars Michael Psellus and John Italus), who strove to impart to Georgian Orthodoxy a deeper metaphysical content.

Whereas much of Georgian ecclesiastical literature has its roots in Byzantine Greek culture, Georgia's medieval romance and epic are impregnated with the civilization of Persia, blended with original elements of Caucasian folklore. Important prose romances are the *Visramiani* (Eng. trans. *Visramiani: the Story of the Loves of Vis and Ramin,* by O. Wardrop, 1914), adapted in the 12th century by Sargis of T'mogvi from an original Iranian romance going back to Parthian times, and *Amiran-Darejaniani* (Eng. trans. by R. H. Stevenson, 1958), a cycle of fantastic tales of adventure, at-tributed to Moses of Khoni. The foundations of secular poetry were laid at the same period by Ioane Shavt'eli and Chakhrukhadze, who respectively wrote formal odes in honour of King David II "the Builder" (1089–1125) and Queen Tamara (1184–1213). The supreme literary achievement of Georgia's golden age is Shot'a Rust'aveli's epic *Vep'khis-tqaosani* (Eng. trans. *The Man in the Panther's Skin,* by M. S. Wardrop, 1912), in which the themes of ideal comradeship, courtly love and heroic endeavour are treated in a sublime and sophisticated manner. Whether Rust'aveli was a real personage living during the reign of Queen Tamara, or a pseudonym cloaking a poet of some later period, remains controversial. His poetic tradition, broken by the Mongol invasions, was renewed in the 17th century by the royal poets Teimuraz I (1589–1663) and Archil (1647–1713).

Belles-lettres revived in Georgia during the 18th century with the lexicographer Sulkhan-Saba Orbeliani (1658–1725), who wrote a book of fables, *Dsigni sibrdzne-sitsruisa* (Eng. trans. *The Book of Wisdom and Lies,* by O. Wardrop, 1894); King Vakhtang VI (1675–1737), who founded a printing press in Tiflis and had the Georgian annals edited and completed; and his son Vakhushti (*c.* 1695–1772), the historian and geographer. The main poets of the period were David Guramishvili (1705–92) and Besarion Gabashvili, called Besiki (1750–91).

The Russian occupation of 1801 brought Georgia into the orbit of European intellectual life. Romantic poetry flourished with the work of Alexander Tchavtchavadze (1786–1846) and the Byronic lyrics of the youthful bard Nicholas Barat'ashvili (1817–45). Satirical comedy developed under the lead of Giorgi Erist'avi (1811–64), founder of the modern Georgian theatre. Exponents of the realistic novel were Lavrenti Ardaziani (1815–70) and Ilia Tchavtchavadze (1837–1907), the latter being Georgia's most distinguished man of letters of modern times, renowned as an essayist, publicist and poet. The life of the Georgian mountaineers is brilliantly portrayed in the stories of Alexander Qazbegi (1848–93) and the ballads of Vazha P'shavela (1861–1915). Even more famous was the patriotic poet and man of letters Akaki Dseret'eli or Tsereteli (1840–1915). Several of Shakespeare's plays were translated by Ivane Machabeli (1854–98).

Under the tsarist regime Georgian literature often assumed a propagandist, moralistic tone. Even the romantic story *Suramis tsikhe* ("Suram Castle") by Daniel Tchonk'adze (1830–60) contains implied criticism of contemporary serfdom. Under the Soviet regime a number of leading writers, including the novelist Mikheil Javakhishvili and the poets Paolo Iashvili and Titsian Tabidze, perished in the Stalin purge of 1937. However, poets of the stature of Ioseb Grishashvili (1889–1965), dramatists such as Shalva Dadiani (1874–1959) and novelists such as Konstantine Gamsakhurdia (1891–) succeeded in maintaining a high standard of creative originality.

BIBLIOGRAPHY.—J. Karst, *Littérature géorgienne chrétienne* (1934); A. Baramidze *et al., Istoriya gruzinskoi literatury,* new ed. (1958); M. Tarchnishvili, *Geschichte der kirchlichen georgischen Literatur* (1955); V. Urushadze, *Anthology of Georgian Poetry,* 2nd ed. (1958); D. M. Lang, *Lives and Legends of the Georgian Saints* (1956).
(D. M. LA.)

GEORGIAN SOVIET SOCIALIST REPUBLIC (GRUZINSKAYA SOVETSKAYA SOTSIALISTICHESKAYA RESPUBLIKA; commonly called GEORGIA, Georgian SAKARTVELO, Russ. GRUZIYA), one of the 15 constituent union republics of the U.S.S.R., is in western Transcaucasia and includes the Abkhaz and Adzhar Autonomous Soviet Socialist Republics (*qq.v.*) and the South Ossetian (Yugo-Osetinskaya) Autonomous Oblast (*see* OSSETIA). It is bounded to the north by the Russian Soviet Federated Socialist Republic, to the east by the Azerbaijanian Soviet Socialist Republic, to the south by the Armenian S.S.R. and Turkey, and to the west by the Black sea. Its area is 26,911 sq.mi. (69,719 sq.km.).

Physical Features.—Georgia falls into three main structural regions which originated in the vast earth movements of the Alpine folding period. In the north is the Greater Caucasus range, in the centre a tectonic depression or trough, and in the south the mountains of Transcaucasia. All the southern flank of the Greater Caucasus range, usually regarded as the boundary of Europe and Asia, lies in Georgia, as far east as Mt. Diklos-Mta. Although the high-

GEORGIAN SOVIET SOCIALIST REPUBLIC

est peak, Elbrus, lies just over the boundary of the republic, many high summits are on the crest line: Shkhara, 17,063 ft., Dzhangi-Tau, 16,565 ft., Kazbek, 16,558 ft., Ushba, 15,453 ft. Many of the peaks have extensive glaciers. Toward the west, approaching the narrow coastal strip along the Black sea, the range becomes lower. South of the main range is a series of lower ranges, usually roughly parallel to it and separated from it and from each other by deep valleys and gorges. From west to east the chief of these ranges are the Gagrinsky, Bzybsky, Abkhaz, Kodorsky, Svanetsky, Metrelsky, Lechkhumsky and Rachinsky. Farther east, the Suramsky, Kartalinsky and Nakhetinsky ranges are perpendicular to the Greater Caucasus. The rivers, which mostly rise in the ice fields, are many and fast-flowing, the largest being the Bzyb, Kodori, Inguri, Tskhenis-Tskali and Rioni (q.v.), flowing to the Black sea, and the Kura tributaries, Aragvi, Iori and Alazani, flowing to the Caspian. In the extreme northwest is the picturesque Lake Ritsa, formed by a landslide, a popular tourist centre.

The tectonic trough is divided in two by a saddle formed by the Suramsky range. To the west is the wedge-shaped lowland of Kolkhida, the legendary land of the Golden Fleece. Into this level plain the Rioni and other mountain rivers bring enormous volumes of water and silt, and widespread swamps have been formed. The central part of the swamps, between the Rioni and the Khobi, has been reclaimed and further reclamation took place in the 1960s. East of the Suramsky saddle the trough continues as a series of high, level plains, notably those of Gori and Rustavi, drained to the east by the Kura and its tributaries. The third region, in the south, consists of ranges and plateaus, often called the Lesser Caucasus. Much lower than the main range, it rises to 10,830 ft. in Mt. Bol Abul. The chief ranges are the Adzharo-Imeretinsky and the Trialetsky. A narrow, swampy coastal plain fringes the Lesser Caucasus (see also CAUCASUS).

The climate of Georgia is varied. The western part has the highest rainfall of the U.S.S.R., from 40 in. a year on the plains to more than 100 in. on the mountains. The temperature regime is almost subtropical, with mild winters and hot summers, modified only by the proximity of the sea and by height. Batumi has a January

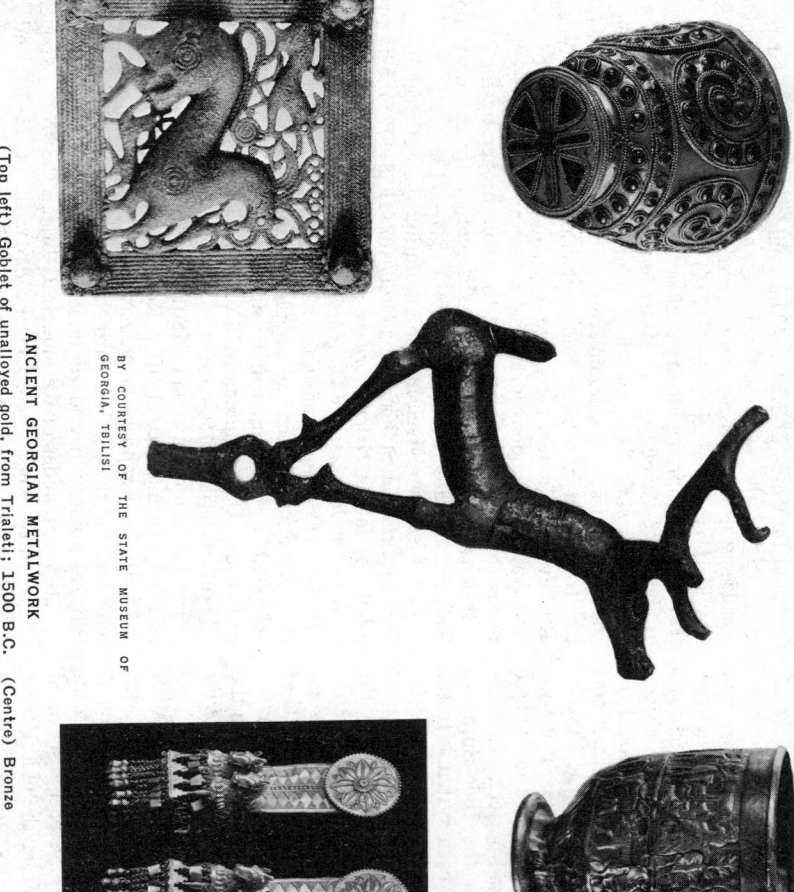

ANCIENT GEORGIAN METALWORK

(Top left) Goblet of unalloyed gold, from Trialeti; 1500 B.C. (Centre) Bronze standard in the form of a sculptured deer, from Tianeti; 500 B.C. (Top right) Silver goblet with ritual scenes, from Trialeti; 1500 B.C. (Bottom left) Bronze belt plate with fantastic animals, from Racha; 1st century B.C. (Bottom right) Gold pendants with figures of horses, from Akhalgori; 5th century B.C.

average of 43° F. (5.56° C) and a July average of 73° F. (22.78° C.). In the Kura (q.v.) valley, a rain-shadow area, rainfall drops to under 20 in., although temperatures remain high. Relief naturally imposes wide variation locally and conditions become increasingly severe with height. The great variety of relief and climate brings about a similar variety of soil and vegetation. In the Kolkhida lowland, apart from reed and grass swamp, vegetation is subtropical, with many exotics, such as palm, bamboo and eucalyptus. The lower slopes are in dense lianoid forest of oak and beech, with creepers, especially ivy and clematis. Higher up this gives way to coniferous forest of Caucasian fir and some spruce; higher still are thickets of rhododendrons and azaleas with birch and juniper, which yield in turn to alpine meadow and eventually to rock and ice. In the drier east steppe vegetation is found on the plains. Soils range from bog and alluvial soils in the Kolkhida lowland to terra rossa and brown forest earths on the slopes and black earths and chestnut soils in the east. (R.A.F.)

The People.—The Georgian nation, as far as can be judged from available historical and archaeological evidence, represents a fusion of local, autochthonous inhabitants with tribes infiltrating from Asia Minor in remote antiquity. There has also been an admixture of Greek, Scythian, Iranian and Armenian elements.

The characteristic physical type is dark-haired, slim, tall, robust and athletic; fair skin, a strong growth of beard, dark eyes (about 30% gray or blue), and a prominent nose either of Armenoid type, with curved or hooked outline, or else straight and aquiline, are common features. There is also a short, squat, swarthy physical type. The women are noted for beauty, intelligence and modest demeanour. The Georgians have been Christians since the 4th century, and belong to an autocephalous national church within the Greek Orthodox communion. Survivals of pagan practices have lingered on into modern times in more remote regions. The kindred people of Lazistan (now within Turkey) and Adzharia (round Batumi) adopted Islam under Ottoman influence.

The inhabitants of each region of Georgia have their own special characteristics; but in general the Georgians are a convivial, easy-going, amiable race, fond of sport, hunting and martial pursuits. They are great wine drinkers. Generally tolerant and broad-minded, they are intensely jealous of the honour of their women and proud of their national heritage. They show marked talent for poetry, music, ballet, opera, painting, and every form of artistic, literary, scientific and scholarly activity. (See GEORGIAN LANGUAGE; GEORGIAN LITERATURE.)

History.—*Prehistoric Period.*—The latest findings of archaeology make it possible to trace the origins of human society on the territory of the modern Georgian S.S.R. back to the early Paleolithic and Neolithic periods. A number of Neolithic sites have been excavated in the low-lying Kolkhida (Colchian) basin, in the Khrami valley in central Georgia and in South Ossetia; they were occupied by settled tribes engaged in cattle raising and agriculture. The cultivation of grain in Georgia during the New Stone Age is attested by finds of saddle-querns and flint sickles; the earth was tilled with stone mattocks. The Caucasus was regarded in ancient times as the primeval home of metallurgy. The start of the 3rd

NOVOSTI PRESS AGENCY

BRONZE STATUE COMMEMORATING VAKHTANG GORGASLANI, 5TH-CENTURY RULER OF GEORGIA, ON A ROCK ABOVE THE KURA RIVER AT TBILISI. THE MONUMENT IS A MODERN WORK BY GEORGIAN SCULPTOR ELGUDZHA AMASHUKELI

ished the Iberian monarchy. For the next three centuries, local authority was exercised by the magnates of each province, vassals successively of Iran, of Byzantium, and, after 654 A.D., of the Arab caliphs, who established an amirate in Tbilisi (Tiflis).

Then came a national revival leading ultimately to the unification of all the lands inhabited by peoples of Georgian and related Ibero-Caucasian stock. This movement was led by the Bagrationi (Bagratids), a princely dynasty long prominent in the affairs of Armenia (*q.v.*). Toward the end of the 8th century, the Bagratid Ashot I the Great settled at Artanuji in Tao (southwestern Georgia) receiving from the Byzantine emperor the title of *kuropalates* ("guardian of the palace"). In due course, Ashot profited from the weakness of the Byzantine emperors and the Arab caliphs and set himself up as hereditary prince in Iberia. King Bagrat III (975–1014) later united all the principalities of eastern and western Georgia into one state. Tbilisi, however, was not recovered from the Muslims until 1122, when it fell to King David II Aghmashenebeli ("the Builder"; reigned 1089–1125).

The zenith of Georgia's power and prestige was reached in the reign (1184–1213) of Queen Tamara, whose realm stretched from Azerbaijan to the borders of Cherkessia, from Erzurum to Gandzha (Kirovabad) forming a pan-Caucasian empire, with Shirvan and Trabzon as vassals and allies.

The invasions of Transcaucasia by the Mongols from 1220 onward, however, brought Georgia's golden age to an end. Eastern Georgia was reduced to vassalage under the Mongol Il-khans of the line of Hulagu, while Imeretia, as the land to the west of the Suram range was called, remained independent under a separate line of Bagratid rulers. There was a partial resurgence during the reign (1314–46) of King Giorgi V of Georgia, known as the Brilliant, but the onslaughts of Timur between 1386 and 1403 dealt blows to Georgia's economic and cultural life from which the kingdom never recovered. The last king of united Georgia was Alexander I (reigned 1412–43), under whose sons the realm was divided into squabbling princedoms.

Turkish and Persian Domination.—The fall of Constantinople to the Ottoman Turks in 1453 isolated Georgia from western Christendom. In 1510 the Turks invaded Imeretia and sacked the capital, Kutaisi. Soon afterward, Shah Ismail I of Iran invaded Kartalinia. Ivan the Terrible and other Muscovite tsars showed interest in the little Christian kingdoms of Georgia, but the Russians were powerless to stop the Muslim powers partitioning the country and oppressing the inhabitants. In 1578 the Turks overran the whole of Transcaucasia and seized Tbilisi, but were subsequently driven out by Shah Abbas I (reigned 1587–1629), who deported many thousands of the Christian population to distant regions of Iran. There was a period of respite under the viceroys of the house of Mukhran, who governed at Tbilisi under the aegis of the shahs from 1658 until 1723. The most notable Mukhranian ruler was Vakhtang VI, regent of Kartalinia from 1703 to 1711, and then king, with intervals, until 1723. Vakhtang was eminent as a lawgiver and introduced printing to Georgia; he had the Georgian annals edited by a commission of scholars. However, the collapse of the Safavid dynasty in 1722 led to a fresh Ottoman invasion of Georgia. The Turks were expelled by the Persian conqueror Nadir Shah who gave Kartalinia to Teimuraz II (1744–62), one of the Kakhian line of the Bagratids. When T'eimuraz died, his son Erekle II reunited the kingdoms of Kartalinia and Kakhetia, and made a brave attempt at erecting a Caucasian multinational state based on Georgia. Imeretia under King Solomon I (reigned 1752–84) succeeded in throwing off Turkish domination.

Annexation by Russia.—Raids by Lezgian mountaineers from Dagestan, economic stringency and other difficulties impelled Erekle to adopt a pro-Russian orientation. On July 24, 1783, he concluded with Catherine the Great the treaty of Georgievsk, whereby Russia guaranteed Georgia's independence and territorial integrity, while Erekle accepted Russian suzerainty. Russia soon left her new ally in the lurch. Erekle and his Georgians had to face alone the fierce hordes of the Persian eunuch Agha Mohammed Khan Kajar. Tbilisi was sacked in 1795 and Erekle died brokenhearted in 1798. His invalid son Giorgi XII sought to hand over the kingdom unconditionally into the care of the mad emperor

millennium B.C. witnessed the beginning of Georgia's Bronze Age. Remarkable finds made by the late B. A. Kuftin in Trialeti show that central Georgia was inhabited during the 2nd millennium B.C. by cattle-raising tribes whose chieftains were men of wealth and power. Their burial mounds yielded up finely wrought vessels in gold and silver; a few are engraved with ritual scenes suggesting Asianic cult influence.

Origins of the Georgian Nation.—Early in the 1st millennium B.C., the ancestors of the Georgian nation emerge in the annals of Assyria and, later, of Urartu (Armenia). Among these were the Diauhi (Diaeni) nation, ancestors of the Taokhoi, later domiciled in the southwestern Georgian province of Tao, and the Kulkha, forerunners of the Colchians, who held sway over large territories at the eastern end of the Black sea. The fabled wealth of Colchis (*q.v.*) early became known to the Greeks, and finds symbolic expression in the legend of Medea and the Golden Fleece.

Other names encountered in connection with the early history of the Georgian people are those of the tribes known to the Assyrians as the Tabali and Mushki. These are the Tubal and Meshech of Ezekiel, the Tibareni and Moskhoi of classical writers.

Following the influx of tribes driven from the direction of Anatolia by the Cimmerian invasion of the 7th century B.C. and their fusion with the aboriginal population of the Kura valley, the centuries immediately preceding the Christian era witnessed the growth of the important kingdom of Iberia, the region which now comprises modern Kartalinia and Kakhetia, with Samtskhe and adjoining regions of southwestern Georgia. Colchis to the west was colonized by Greek settlers from Miletus, and subsequently fell under the sway of Mithradates the Great, king of Pontus. The campaigns of Pompey led in 65 B.C. to the establishment of Roman hegemony over Iberia, and direct Roman rule over Colchis and the rest of Georgia's Black sea littoral.

Medieval Georgia.—Georgia embraced Christianity about the year 330; its conversion is attributed to a holy captive woman, St. Nino (*q.v.*). During the next three centuries, Georgia was involved in the conflict between the Byzantine and Persian empires. Lazica on the Black sea (incorporating the ancient Colchis) became closely bound to Byzantium. Iberia passed under Iranian control, though toward the end of the 5th century, a hero arose in the person of King Vakhtang Gorgaslani, a ruler of legendary valour who for a time reasserted Georgia's national sovereignty. However, the Sasanian monarch Khosrau I (reigned 531–579) abol-

Paul I, but both rulers were dead before this could be formally implemented. In 1801 Alexander I reaffirmed Paul's decision to incorporate Kartalinia and Kakhetia into the Russian empire. Despite the treaty of 1783, the Bagratid line was deposed and replaced by Russian military governors, who deported the surviving members of the royal house and behaved in such a way as to provoke several popular uprisings. The western Georgian kingdom of Imeretia was annexed in 1810, while Guria, Mingrelia, Svanetia and Abkhazia were finally swallowed up in 1829, 1857, 1858 and 1864 respectively. The Black sea ports of Poti and Batumi, and areas of southwestern Georgia long under Ottoman rule, were wrested from Turkey in successive wars, culminating in the campaign of 1877–78.

National Revival.—By waging war on the Lezgian clansmen of Dagestan, and on Iran and Turkey, the Russians ensured the corporate survival of the Georgian nation. Under Prince M. S. Vorontsov who served with distinction as viceroy (1845–54), commerce and trade began a rapid upswing, and a theatre and other institutions and amenities were opened in Tbilisi. Following the liberation of the Russian serfs in 1861, the Georgian peasants also received freedom from 1864 onward, though on terms regarded as burdensome. The decay of old patriarchal ways was accelerated by the spread of education and European influences. A railway linked Tbilisi with Poti from 1872 and mines, factories and plantations were developed by Russian, Armenian and western entrepreneurs. Peasant discontent, the growth of an urban working class and the deliberate policy of russification and forced assimilation of minorities practised by emperor Alexander III (1881–94) fostered radical agitation among the workers, and nationalism among the middle-class intelligentsia. The tsarist system permitted of no organized political activity, but social issues were debated with verve in journals, works of fiction and local assemblies.

The leader of the national revival was Prince Ilia Tchavtchavadze (or Chavchavadze; 1837–1907), leader of a literary and social movement dubbed *Pirveli dasi*, or "the First group." The *Meore dasi* or "Second group," led by Giorgi Tsereteli (1842–1900), was more radical in its convictions, but it paled before the *Mesame dasi* or "Third group," an illegal Social-Democratic party founded in 1893 and led by Noe Zhordania (1868–1953), Karlo Chkheidze and others. The "Third group" professed Marxist doctrines; from 1898 it numbered among its members Joseph Dzhugashvili (Stalin). When the Mensheviks under Zhordania gained control of the group Stalin left the Caucasus and threw in his lot with Lenin.

The 1905 revolution in Russia led to widespread disturbances and guerrilla fighting in Georgia, later suppressed by Cossacks with indiscriminate brutality. After the Revolution of March 1917 the three Transcaucasian nationalities, Georgians, Armenians and Azerbaijanis, were ruled by a committee controlled by Petrograd and known as the Ozakom. The Bolshevik coup later in the year forced the predominantly Menshevik politicians of Transcaucasia to secede from Russia, though with reluctance, and form a new body, the Transcaucasian commissariat. The stresses of local nationalisms, combined with a Turkish advance from the west, brought about the breakdown of the federation. On May 26, 1918, the Georgians set up an independent state and placed themselves under German protection, but the collapse of the Central Powers at the end of 1918 led to a British occupation. The Georgians viewed Anton Denikin's White Russians, who enjoyed British support, as more dangerous than the Bolsheviks themselves. They refused to co-operate with a movement designed to restore the tsarist imperial order and British forces evacuated Batumi in July 1920.

Although the independence of Georgia had been recognized *de facto* by the Allies in Jan. 1920, the country's fate was now sealed. The Russo-Georgian treaty of May 7, 1920, enabled a Soviet mission under S. M. Kirov to be sent to Tbilisi in order to undermine the Georgian regime and prepare the way for a Bolshevik coup there.

Incorporation in the U.S.S.R.—In Jan. 1921 the Georgian republic was recognized *de jure* by the Allies, after having been refused admission to the League of Nations. Within a month the Red army, acting under the orders of two Georgian Bolshevik leaders, Stalin and G. K. Ordzhonikidze, entered Georgia, and on Feb. 25 a Soviet regime was installed in Tbilisi.

After the establishment of a Soviet republic in their native country, Stalin and Ordzhonikidze incorporated Georgia in a Transcaucasian Soviet Federated Socialist Republic, abolishing the country's autonomy. A period of the severest repression began, with the aim of destroying "the hydra of nationalism" and consolidating the country within the Soviet framework. Active nationalists and others were executed, the Georgian Church was subjected to persecution and even the Georgian Communist party itself had to be vigorously purged of local patriots.

The transition to the new order was to some extent eased by the Socialist policies pursued by the Georgian Mensheviks, who had nationalized all important industries. But the Georgian peasantry rose against the Communists on several occasions. Particularly violent was the rising which broke out in 1924 under the leadership of Kaikhosro Cholokashvili which had to be put down by the Red army.

On Dec. 5, 1936, the Transcaucasian Federated Republic was dissolved. The Georgian Soviet Socialist Republic became a full-fledged member of the U.S.S.R. Under the Stalin constitution, the country and its citizens enjoyed numerous rights including that of seceding from the Soviet Union at any time. Many of the original local Bolshevik leaders were executed as Trotskyite deviationists during the purges of 1936–37. L. P. Beria, a Georgian who had played a prominent part in bringing his fellow countrymen to heel, became head of the Soviet secret police, N.K.V.D. Industrialization and collectivization of agriculture were pressed on apace. Public institutions, including a Georgian Academy of Sciences, were set up and much progress was made in public health and education. In spite of social regimentation and political conformity, Georgia has shared in the growing material prosperity of the U.S.S.R. (D. M. LA.)

Population, Administration and Social Conditions.—The 1970 (prelim.) census enumerated 4,688,000 inhabitants of Georgia, of whom 2,447,000 (52%) were rural and 2,241,000 urban. The population comprised mostly Georgians (64%), Armenians (11%) and Russians (10%) with smaller minorities of Adzhars, Abkhazians and Ossetians. There are 44 towns and 54 urban districts ("settlements of town type"), of which the largest are the capital, Tbilisi ([1970] 889,000); Kutaisi (161,000); Batumi (101,000), the capital of the Adzhar Autonomous Soviet Socialist Republic; Sukhumi (102,000), capital of the Abkhaz Autonomous Soviet Socialist Republic; Rustavi (1969 est. 102,000); and Tskhinvali, formerly Stalinir (30,000), the administrative centre of the South Ossetian (Yugo-Osetinskaya) Autonomous Oblast.

The constitution of the Georgian S.S.R. was adopted in 1936 (see *History* above). The Supreme Soviet, elected in 1959, comprises 368 deputies. The republic is divided administratively into independent cities and *rayony* (districts). Since the Revolution modern social conditions have been introduced into Georgia, with universal education and literacy and medical and other welfare services. By the late 1960s the number of hospitals exceeded 600 and there was a high ratio of doctors (more than 35 per 10,000 inhabitants). All along the subtropical coast are many sanatoriums and rest homes catering to people from all parts of the U.S.S.R. Traditionally a highly artistic and imaginative people, the Georgians prize education greatly. There is an academy of sciences and an academy of agricultural sciences at Tbilisi. Throughout the republic are 155 other scientific institutions, 18 higher educational foundations and over 4,500 schools.

Although national costume has largely disappeared from ordinary life, it is still preserved for festive occasions. There are many ensembles which keep alive traditional Georgian folk music and folk dances, some of which groups have established a reputation beyond the frontiers of the U.S.S.R. Tbilisi has a theatre of Georgian opera and ballet.

The Economy.—Because of its climatic peculiarities Georgia is one of the most important agricultural areas of the U.S.S.R., and it is the major area for many subtropical crops, especially tea. The terra rossa hillsides facing the Black sea have been cleared over wide areas for tea plantations, and 95% of the tea produced in the U.S.S.R. comes from the republic. Much of the tea-picking is now done by machinery. In the Kolkhida lowland (especially the drained parts) and the coastal strips to north and south citrus fruits are grown—oranges, lemons, tangerines and grapefruit. Of these Georgia supplies 98% of U.S.S.R. production. There are vineyards on the hillsides of western Georgia and on the plains of the east, and Georgian wines, such as Tsinandali, are considered the best in the Soviet Union. Olives, figs, persimmons, pomegranates and loquats are also grown in the west, while apples, peaches, pears, plums, cherries and apricots are widespread. Tung trees have been introduced as a source of vegetable oils and mulberries for silk worms. Of the field crops grains are dominant—winter wheat in the drier east, where irrigation is essential (several large irrigation projects have been established in the Kura and Alazani valleys), and maize (corn) in the west. In higher areas spring wheat and barley are grown. Among industrial crops tobacco holds first place. Plants for perfume-making, such as geraniums, roses, sorghum, jasmine and basil, are grown, especially in the Abkhaz republic. Other crops include sugar beet and vegetables, and especially melons. The high mountain pastures are much used for raising stock, sheep and goats being predominant in the east and cattle in the west. Transhumance is widely practised. Poultry farming is well developed.

Among industries mining is very important. Chiatura (q.v.) in the Kvirila valley, with the port of Poti (q.v.) as its outlet, is one of the world's largest sources of manganese. Coal is mined round Tkibuli and Tkvarcheli and although quantities are small they are very valuable because of the distance of other coal fields. In the east, near Mirzaani, some oil is obtained. Batumi is an oil-refining centre, the terminus of three pipelines from Baku. Heavy industry in Georgia has been increased since the opening in 1950 of the Rustavi combined iron and steel plant, making in particular steel pipes, largely used in the oil industry of Baku. Zestafoni, near Chiatura, uses electric hearths to make ferroalloys. Engineering is concentrated in Tbilisi (machine tools), Kutaisi (trucks), Batumi (tea-picking and other machinery) and Poti (suction dredgers). The chemical industry is rapidly developing in Batumi, Tbilisi and Rustavi. Extensive forests form the basis of the important timber industry, which makes use of exotic trees such as bamboo and eucalyptus. Paper is made at Inguri, veneer at Tbilisi, matches at Mtskheta, and furniture, musical instruments and parquet elsewhere. The textile and food industries are widespread. Hydroelectric power is abundant and by the early 1960s more than 200 stations were in operation. Tbilisi receives its power from the Zemo-Avchala plant on the Kura.

The main axis of communication is the railway along the Black sea coast from Tuapse to Sukhumi and then inland to Tbilisi and on to Baku. From this there are many branch lines, notably to Yerevan in Armenia, with links to Turkey and Iran, and to Batumi, Poti, Tkvarcheli and Chiatura. Three motor roads, all originally built during the Russian conquest of Caucasia in the 19th century, cross the Greater Caucasus range—the Georgian Military highway from Tbilisi to Ordzhonikidze by the Krestovy pass, the Ossetian Military highway from Kutaisi to Ordzhonikidze by the Mamisonsky pass and the Sukhumi Military highway from Sukhumi to Cherkessk by the Klukhorsky pass. The main airport is at Tbilisi.

The favourable climate, especially in winter, the rich variety of scenery and vegetation, and the long, sandy beaches of the coast have made Georgia one of the most popular resort areas of the U.S.S.R. The coast is lined with resorts, of which Sukhumi (q.v.) is the best known. See also references under "Georgian Soviet Socialist Republic" in the Index. (R. A. F.)

BIBLIOGRAPHY.—M. Tamarati, L'Église géorgienne des origines jusqu'à nos jours (1910); W. E. D. Allen, A History of the Georgian People (1932); Zourab Avalishvili, The Independence of Georgia in International Politics (1940); A. Sanders (i.e., A. Nikuradze), Kaukasien: Geschichtlicher Umriss (1942); F. Kazemzadeh, The Struggle for Transcaucasia (1917–1921) (1951); D. M. Lang, Studies in the Numismatic History of Georgia in Transcaucasia (1955); The Last Years of the Georgian Monarchy, 1658–1832 (1957); and The Georgians (1966). (D. M. La.)

GEORGIAN STYLES, in architecture and the decorative arts, developed during the 18th century in Great Britain and its colonies. During the reign of the Georges (1740–1830), urban aristocrats and merchants preferred the sober models of Andrea Palladio and Inigo Jones to the grandeur of continental baroque, and they built entire city squares of uniform, symmetrical town-houses, the façades of which were characterized by classical pilasters, pedimented doors and windows and graceful moldings. Their interiors—with paneled walls, quiet colours, Roman stucco ornamentation and Chippendale, Hepplewhite or Sheraton furniture—made elegant settings for the works of Reynolds and Gainsborough. Under the influence of the Adam brothers, the later style veered toward more authentic neoclassicism.

See BAROQUE AND POST-BAROQUE ART AND ARCHITECTURE; GEORGIAN ARCHITECTURE; NEOCLASSICAL ART AND ARCHITECTURE. See John Gloag, Georgian Grace (1956); A. E. Richardson, Georgian England (1931). (Wm. F.)

GEORGIUS CONTINUATUS: see GEORGE (the Monk).

GEOSTROPHIC WIND. When air moves horizontally without friction or acceleration, there is a balance between the deflecting force of the earth's rotation—Coriolis force (see MOTION, PRINCIPLES AND LAWS OF)—and the force arising from the horizontal variations of pressure. The wind blowing under this balance of forces is called geostrophic wind.

The magnitude and direction of geostrophic winds are given by the direction and spacing of isobars (lines of constant pressure) on a horizontal surface. In the figure, two such isobars are drawn. The pressure P_1 along one isobar is less than the pressure P_2 along the other. The pressure-gradient force acts at right angles to the isobars and toward lower pressure. The Coriolis force acts at right angles to the wind, to the right in northern hemisphere. In order that these two forces balance, the wind, indicated in the figure by the white arrow, must be parallel to the isobars, with lower pressure to its left. The smaller the distance between isobars, the faster the wind. Geostrophic wind is also proportional to the slope of isobaric surfaces and directed along contours of such surfaces, with high elevations to the right of the geostrophic wind (in the northern hemisphere).

In the southern hemisphere, the Coriolis force acts to the left of the wind, and therefore the relations between direction of the geostrophic wind and pressure field are opposite to those in the northern hemisphere.

In general, the geostrophic wind represents the actual wind with an error of about 10%, provided the actual winds are averaged over areas of 100 mi. or more. But the geostrophic wind is generally a poor approximation close to the surface (see EKMAN SPIRAL), in regions of fast winds and large trajectory curvature and near the equator.

The geostrophic wind relation is useful in the analysis of weather maps because it aids in the construction of streamlines in regions of scant wind observations and in the construction of isobars where pressure data are poor, particularly in the stratosphere (q.v.). (H. A. A. P.)

LOW PRESSURE

ISOBAR (P_1)

PRESSURE-GRADIENT FORCE

VELOCITY

CORIOLIS FORCE

ISOBAR (P_2)

HIGH PRESSURE

DISTANCE

THE BALANCE OF FORCES FOR GEO-STROPHIC AIR FLOW IN THE NORTH-ERN HEMISPHERE

GEPHYREA, an obsolete phylum of small to microscopic wormlike animals, which was broken down into four groups: Echiurida (spoon-worms), Sipunculida (peanutworms), Priapulida (priapulid worms), and Phoronida (beardworms) (qq.v.).

GERA, a town of Germany which after partition of the nation following World War II became capital of the Bezirk (district) of Gera, German Democratic Republic. Pop. (1964) 106,838. Gera, located about 43 mi. W. of Karl-Marx-Stadt (Chemnitz), on the Weisse Elster river, is a railway junction. Manufactures include cloth, metal products, machinery, fats, oils and furniture. Near the city are mines producing uranium ore. It received its municipal charter in the 13th century and in 1550 became part of the principality of Meissen. The town was burned by the Swedes in 1639 during the Thirty Years' War and fires destroyed large areas in 1686 and 1780, but it was always rebuilt. The town hall dates from the 16th century and Trinity church from the early 17th.

GERALDTON, a town and seaport of Western Australia, lies 312 mi. by road NNW of Perth to which it is also connected by rail. Pop. (1966) 12,125. It is a seaside resort and the centre of an extensive mining, agricultural, and pastoral area. There is an important crayfishing industry and the chief exports are wheat, wool, manganese, lead, and horticultural produce.

GERANIACEAE, a family of herbaceous plants (rarely shrubs or small trees), of limited importance, in the dicotyledonous order Geraniales. It includes more than 600 species in 11 genera distributed on all continents (except Antarctica) but is best developed in temperate and subtropical climates. Some species are grown as ornamentals. The well-known garden and greenhouse "geraniums" are species of *Pelargonium* (*see* GERANIUM) from southern Africa. The crane's-bills, or wild geraniums (*Geranium* species), and the heron's-bills (*Erodium* species) are sometimes cultivated in the wild garden. Although a few species of *Erodium* are grown for forage in dry areas or as bee plants, most of them are considered weeds; they are an important winter host for the beet leafhopper in the western U.S., and their seeds may injure livestock by penetrating the animals' flesh.

The family consists of annual, biennial or perennial plants, whose leaves are mostly lobed, dissected or compound, more rarely entire. The bisexual, regular or irregular (*Pelargonium*) flowers may be solitary or in clusters. The flower parts are usually arranged in whorls of five (rarely four; eight in *Dirachma*, which by some is placed in a separate family, *Dirachmaceae*). The distinct or partially united sepals are generally overlapping, the dorsal one being spurred in *Pelargonium*; the petals (absent in *Rhynchotheca*) are alike or differ in size and shape, distinct and overlapping in bud, and borne below or slightly surrounding the ovary. Of the stamens, two to three times the number of sepals, only two to seven bear anthers in *Pelargonium*, and in *Erodium* those opposite the petals lack anthers; the filaments are more or less united basally, and the anthers open by lengthwise slits. The carpels, which sometimes number only two or three, are united in a lobed ovary. In ripe fruit, the one-seeded (rarely more) carpels often roll outward and upward or twist spirally away from the central axis in releasing the seed.

For a synopsis of the family, see R. Knuth, "Geraniaceae," in Engler and Prantl, *Pflanzenfamilien,* 2nd ed., vol. 19a, pp. 43–66 (1931).
(H. E. Mo.)

GERANIUM, a genus of plants, the typical representatives of the family Geraniaceae (*q.v.*), commonly called crane's-bill; the name, sometimes as "florist's geranium," is also popularly applied to the showy garden and greenhouse plants belonging to the genus *Pelargonium.*

The more than 300 species of *Geranium* consist mostly of annual, biennial or perennial herbs, though some in Hawaii and South America have woody stems. These woodland plants are found mostly in temperate regions, but some species occur in tropical mountains. The generally opposite leaves are for the most part palmately lobed, rarely ternately divided or entire. The flowers are regular, consisting of five overlapping petals, alternating with five small glands at their bases; ten stamens; and a beaked ovary (hence the name crane's-bill). Many species are cultivated as hardy perennials in borders or rock gardens, three of the more common being: *G. sanguineum,* with reddish-purple to white flowers; *G. pratense,* with robust stems and large purple to white flowers; and *G. robertianum* (herb Robert), with numerous small reddish-purple flowers. Others, such as *G. molle, G. pusillum* and *G. pyrenaicum* of Europe, tend to become naturalized elsewhere as weeds.

Pelargonium, though agreeing with *Geranium* in certain points of structure, differs in that the flowers are irregular, the two petals that stand uppermost being different—larger, smaller or differently

marked—from the other three, which are occasionally wanting. This irregularity the modern florist has done much to annul, for selective breeding for larger flowers has usually been accompanied by the disproportionate enlargement of the smaller petals. Another well-marked difference, however, remains: the back, or dorsal, sepal in *Pelargonium* has a hollow spur, which is joined for its whole length with the flower stalk, while in *Geranium* there is no spur. This peculiarity is best seen by cutting through the flower stalk just behind the flower; in *Pelargonium* there will be seen the hollow tube of the spur.

Most of the cultivated pelargoniums are of hybrid origin, having been derived from species early introduced from the Cape of Good Hope. They may be placed in four main groups: (1) The older show-flowered cultivars (horticultural varieties) belong to the hybrid species *Pelargonium domesticum* (a mixture of perhaps as many as seven species) and are best for indoor or greenhouse use (*see also* HOUSE PLANTS). Variable in size and habit, all are characterized by colourful, often ornamented flowers sometimes belonging to the hybrid *P. hortorum,* are thought to have arisen as hybrids between *P. inquinans* and *P. zonale,* with an admixture of other species; they are grown indoors or in the garden. (3) The ivy-leaf geranium, derived from *P. peltatum,* has given rise to an important class of both double- and single-flowered forms, adapted especially for pot culture, hanging baskets and window boxes; they are grown in the greenhouse or used on walls and in patios in warm, dry regions. (4) The scented-leaved geraniums consist of several species and many hybrids, which are fragrant of lemon, rose, apple, mint or spices when the foliage is touched or bruised.

Geranium oil, important in perfumery, is processed from *P. asperum,* a presumed hybrid between *P. graveolens* and *P. radens,* and from the parental and perhaps a few other species. Réunion Island, and to a lesser extent north Africa, are chief oil-producing regions. Other species are sometimes cultivated for odd or unusual stems, leaves or flowers.

The best soil for pelargoniums is a mellow fibrous loam enriched with good well-rotted stable manure or leaf mold in about the proportion of one-fifth; the manure or leaf mold should not be sifted but pulled to pieces by hand, and as much sand should be added as will allow water to drain freely. Pelargoniums are readily increased by cuttings made from the shoots when the plants are cut back after flowering or in the spring. Cuttings will root freely in a temperature of 65° to 70° F. (18° to 21° C.); they should not be kept too close, and should be very moderately watered. The common household geranium can be wintered-over by hanging the plant upside down in a cool, frost-free place.
(H. E. Mo.)

GERARD (d. 1108), archbishop of York who played an important part in the Investiture conflict in England (*see* ENGLISH HISTORY: *The Normans [1066–1154]*), was a Norman clerk who became royal chancellor about 1085. He was made bishop of Hereford (1096) and was present at the coronation of Henry I, who promoted him to the see of York (1101). Gerard objected

(LEFT) J. E. DOWNWARD; (RIGHT) ROCHE
(LEFT) GARDEN GERANIUM (PELARGONIUM); (RIGHT) WILD GERANIUM (GERANIUM)

to making a profession of obedience to Anselm, archbishop of Canterbury, and strongly supported the king in the Investiture contest, representing him at the papal *curia* (1102). But he became a vigorous supporter of Anselm (1105) and was perhaps influential in bringing about a settlement of the dispute (1107). The attribution to Gerard of authorship of some or all of the tracts defending royal prerogative and the sacerdotal nature of kingship, usually ascribed to the "Anonymous of York," remains uncertain. He died on May 21, 1108.

See N. F. Cantor, *Church, Kingship and Lay Investiture in England, 1089–1135* (1958); V. H. Galbraith, "Girard the Chancellor," *English Historical Review*, vol. lxvi (1931). (G. W. S. B.)

GERARD OF CREMONA (*c.* 1114–1187), medieval translator of Arabic into Latin, was born at Cremona in Lombardy. Little is known of his life. He went to Toledo to learn Arabic in order to read the *Almagest* of Ptolemy (not then translated into Latin) and remained there for the rest of his life. About 80 translations from the Arabic have been attributed to him, but it has been suggested that he was in charge of a school of translators which was responsible for some of the translations. Many early printed editions of them omit the name of the translator. His translation of the *Almagest* (printed in 1515) was finished in 1175; it became more popular than that made from the Greek text about 15 years earlier in Sicily. Among other Greek authors translated from Arabic versions traditionally by Gerard are Aristotle, Euclid and Galen.

Translations of original Arabic texts attributed to him include works on medicine (*e.g.*, Avicenna's "Canon"), mathematics, astronomy, astrology and alchemy.

See B. Boncompagni, *Gherardo Cremonese e Gherardo da Sabbionetta* (1851); G. Sarton, *Introduction to the History of Science,* vol. 2, pp. 338–344 (1931).

GERARD, FRANÇOIS, BARON (1770–1837), French painter, who executed portraits of the most celebrated men and women of Europe, was born on May 4, 1770, at Rome, where his father occupied a post in the house of the French ambassador. At the age of 12 he obtained admission into the Pension du Roi at Paris, and from there passed to the studio of the sculptor Augustin Pajou; he subsequently studied with the painter Brenet and with David. In 1791, on his return to Paris after a stay in Rome, David availed himself of Gérard's help, and one of that master's most celebrated pictures—"Le Pelletier de St. Fargeau"—may owe much to the hand of Gérard. In 1793, at David's request, he was named a member of the Revolutionary tribunal, from the fatal decisions of which, however, he invariably absented himself. In 1794 he obtained the first prize in a competition, the subject of which was "The Tenth of August," and in 1795 produced his famous "Bélisaire." A portrait of his generous friend Isabey made the miniaturist (in the Louvre) obtained undisputed success in 1796, and the following year he executed his "Psyché et l'Amour" (also in the Louvre). A portrait of Madame Bonaparte in 1799 established his position as a portrait painter. All the leading figures of the first empire and the Restoration sat for Gérard. This extraordinary vogue was due partly to the charm of his manner and conversation; Madame de Staël, Canning, Talleyrand and the duke of Wellington all bore witness to this. Gérard died on Jan. 11, 1837.

GERARD, JAMES WATSON (1867–1951), U.S. lawyer and diplomat, was born at Geneseo, N.Y., on Aug. 25, 1867. Educated at Columbia university and at the New York law school, he was admitted to the bar in 1892 and began to practise in New York city. In 1908 he became associate justice of the supreme court of New York, resigning in 1913 on being appointed ambassador to Germany. At the outbreak of World War I, he assumed the care of British, Japanese, Rumanian and Serbian interests in Germany. On Feb. 3, 1917, diplomatic relations were broken off by the U.S. and he was recalled. On his return he resumed the practice of law in New York city. He died in Southampton, N.Y., Sept. 6, 1951.

Gerard wrote *My Four Years in Germany* (1917); *Face to Face With Kaiserism* (1918); and *My First Eighty-three Years in America* (1951).

GERARD, JEAN IGNACE ISIDORE: *see* GRANDVILLE.

GERARD, JOHN (1545–1612), English herbalist and surgeon best known for his catalogue of plants entitled *Herball,* was born at Nantwich, Cheshire. He was educated at Willaston and, setting up in London, acted as superintendent of the gardens of Lord Burghley, chief secretary of state under Elizabeth I. Gerard's *Herball* (1597) was really an adaptation of the *Stirpium historiae pemptades* (1583) of Rembert Dodoens. Its style makes it the most famous of English herbals, though not the best. Its illustrations are mostly impressions from the wood blocks employed by Johann Teodor Tabernaemontanus in his *Icones plantarum,* published at Frankfurt in 1590. In addition to the factually correct entries, Gerard's *Herball,* like the other herbals, contains much that is sheer fancy. One of the woodcuts represents the potato, and is thought to be the first figure of the plant published. But there is also a figure of the "goose tree."

Gerard died in London in Feb. 1612.

See A. Arber, *Herbals,* 2nd ed. (1938).

GERARD, JOHN (1564–1637), English Jesuit missionary in England under Elizabeth I, was born at Etwall hall, Derbyshire, Oct. 4, 1564. After studying at the English college in Rome, where he was ordained priest, he entered the Society of Jesus in 1588, and returned secretly to England. Starting in Norfolk and then working south into Suffolk and Essex, Gerard established several centres with resident Catholic priests in the houses of the gentry. Dressed as a country gentleman he traveled unmolested and made many converts. He was a born leader, a man of commanding stature, great vigour of constitution, fluent in several languages, with a natural courtliness of manner. In July 1594 he was captured and spent three years in prison. He escaped from the Tower of London in 1597, and subsequently worked in Northamptonshire, Oxfordshire and Buckinghamshire. After the Gunpowder plot he managed to leave England in disguise in 1606. The rest of his life was spent in English colleges on the continent. In 1607 he wrote a history of the Gunpowder plot and his autobiography, a vivid and accurate account (in Latin) of his experiences in England. He was spiritual director of the English college in Rome (1627–37), where he died, July 27, 1637.

See The Condition of Catholics Under James I (*Father Gerard's Narrative of the Gunpowder Plot*), ed. with his life by J. Morris (1871) and P. Caraman's trans. of the Autobiography, 2nd ed. (1956). (P. CN.)

GERASA (modern JARASH), an ancient city of Palestine in the highlands of Gilead, about 23 mi. N. of Amman and 20 mi. E. of the Jordan river, in the modern kingdom of Jordan. It lies in the valley of the Chrysorrhoas (Barada) river, a tributary of the Jabbok (Nahr az Zarqa), about 1,750 ft. above sea level, in the midst of a fertile and well-watered agricultural area. Gerasa is the best-preserved Palestinian city of Roman times, excavated by the British School of Archaeology in Jerusalem, Yale university and the American School of Oriental Research in Jerusalem.

History.—Nothing is known of the history of the city in Old Testament times or earlier, although pottery remains of the Iron Age and Early Bronze Age discovered in the area testify to its occupation. Iamblichus asserts that it was originally colonized by veterans of Alexander the Great. Josephus states that it was captured by Alexander Jannaeus (*c.* 83 B.C.), rebuilt by the Romans (*c.* A.D. 65) burned by the Jews and subsequently destroyed and burned by Vespasian's captain, Annius. From the time of Trajan it belonged to the Roman province of Syria, but about A.D. 160 it was allotted to the province of Arabia, and during the peaceful reign of the Antonines in the 2nd century it was adorned with magnificent buildings and rose rapidly in importance and prosperity. It was the second city of the Decapolis (*q.v.*), and early in Christian times became the see of a bishop.

The "Gerasenes" mentioned in some versions of Matt. viii, 28 seem not to have been native of Gerasa, since it is too far from the Sea of Galilee to suit the account. They may have been from a village (modern Kersa) on the east shore of Galilee, five miles from the entrance of the Jordan into the lake.

Archaeology.—Gerasa offers an outstanding example of a rich Greco-Roman city. It was surrounded by a wall, about 2¼ mi. in length, enclosing an area of about 210 ac. The wall was about ten feet thick, broken regularly by towers, of which 101 were observed by the excavators. The city was bisected, from north to south, by a colonnaded street, whose well-preserved pavement has been cleared for almost its entire length. The street led to the circular colonnaded forum, almost 300 ft. in diameter, most of the columns of which still stand. The monumental north gate of the city was built by Trajan (A.D. 115), and at the south end of the city Hadrian built a triumphal arch (A.D. 130). The temple of Artemis was the principal building of Gerasa, in honour of the patron goddess of Gerasa. Work on it must have continued for decades before and after A.D. 150, when the propylaea of the temple were dedicated. Second to it was the temple of Zeus, erected about A.D. 163. Several other major temples have also been discovered. Three theatres of varying sizes, the largest seating 3,000–4,000 persons, provided for amusement. Slightly south of the city was a stadium, large enough for 15,000 persons. However, it seems likely that the stadium was never completed, and later the northern third was made over into an amphitheatre. There are two half-ruined baths, and two or three bridges crossed the Chrysorrhoas, which flows approximately parallel to the north-south street. Many other remains add to the impressiveness of the Roman city.

A number of early Christian churches have also been investigated. A three-aisled basilica with an inscribed apse faced on a paved court. It was probably built about A.D. 365. A second basilica, dedicated to the martyr Theodore, was built in 494, and other churches dating from the 5th, 6th and 7th centuries have been found. The city was shattered by earthquakes in the 8th century and left deserted for most of the next 1,000 years.

See C. H. Kraeling (ed.), *Gerasa, City of the Decapolis* (1938).
(E. D. GR.)

GERBIL, a small, jumping rodent of the deserts of Asia and Africa. The typical genus *Gerbillus,* along with *Meriones, Tatera* and others, form a special subfamily, Gerbillinae, of the family Cricetidae. Gerbils have unusually large eyes and ears, elongated hind limbs and long hairy tails; they progress by leaps, in the same manner as jerboas (*q.v.*).

These sandy-coloured herbivores live in burrows furnished with numerous exits and containing large grass-lined chambers. Some species are active during the day, others at night.

GERENUK, a gazellelike antelope, also known as Waller's gazelle (*Litocranius walleri*), having exceptionally long limbs and a long, slender neck. It ranges in east Africa from the Somali region to Kilimanjaro, being found in family groups. The gerenuk is noted for its ability to stand on its hind limbs while browsing on branches and leaves of trees and shrubs. The buck's horns are heavy and have a peculiar forward curvature at the tips; the coat is reddish-brown with a broad darker band down the back.

See ANTELOPE.

GERGOVIA (modern GERGOVIE), the chief settlement of the Arverni (*q.v.*), situated in Auvergne, 8 mi. from the Puy de Dôme, France. Julius Caesar attacked it in 52 B.C. but was beaten off; some walls and earthworks survive, probably of that period. It continued to exist as a small Gallo-Roman settlement at least until the time of Nero, but some of its inhabitants resettled four miles away in the plain at the new Roman city of Augustonemetum (modern Clermont-Ferrand).

GERHARD, JOHANN (1582–1637), German Lutheran theologian, chairman of every major Lutheran theological assembly of his period, biblical and patristic scholar of the first rank and a formidable polemicist, was born of a prominent Quedlinburg family on Oct. 17, 1582. Profoundly influenced in his youth by the great Lutheran theologian-mystic Johann Arndt (*q.v.*), Gerhard studied philosophy, medicine and theology at the universities of Wittenberg, Marburg and Jena (D.Th., 1605.) He became superintendent of the churches of Heldburg in the duchy of Coburg (1605); in 1615 he was appointed general superintendent of all churches in the duchy. The next year he rejoined the Jena theological faculty, where he remained until his death, Aug. 17, 1637.

Gerhard's theological system—most fully set forth in his monumental nine-volume *Loci theologici* (1610–22), the most important dogmatic work of the era of Lutheran orthodoxy—is deliberately designed to be both catholic and evangelical. Though constructed, after the fashion of the times, on a neo-Aristotelian framework, it recognizes the Sacred Scriptures as its only "principle" and breathes a profoundly practical and ethical concern throughout.

His other major works are the four-volume *Confessio catholica* (1634–37), a defense of the catholicity of the Lutheran position; *Meditationes sacrae* (1606), a small devotional manual that has been translated into almost every European language; *Harmonia evangelistarum* (1626–27), a harmonization of and commentary on the Gospels, completing the earlier work of Martin Chemnitz (*q.v.*); and Polycarp Leyser; and his posthumous *Patrologia* (1653).

BIBLIOGRAPHY.—E. R. Fischer, *Vita Ioannis Gerhardi* (1723); B. Hägglund, *Die Heilige Schrift und ihre Deutung in der Theologie Johann Gerhards,* with detailed bibliography (1951); Robert P. Scharlemann, *Thomas Aquinas and John Gerhard* (1964); Herman A. Preus and Edmund Smits (eds.), *The Doctrine of Man in Classical Lutheran Theology,* pp. 27–68 (translation of the *locus* on the image of God from the *Loci theologici;* 1962).
(A. C. PN.)

GERHARDSEN, EINAR HENRY (1897–), Norwegian statesman, leader of the Arbeiderparti (Labour Party) from May 1945 and thrice prime minister, was born at Asker, near Oslo, on May 10, 1897, the son of a road worker. Between the ages of 11 and 18 he worked as an errand boy, after which he found employment on the roads. His active association with the Labour Party began during World War I at a critical stage of the party's existence. There was a bitter struggle for control between a moderate Social Democratic element and a section, which included Gerhardsen, advocating revolutionary methods. The radical section was victorious, and the Social Democrats withdrew after the party had joined the Third (Communist) International. In 1920 Gerhardsen attended the Comintern conference in Moscow and was unfavourably impressed. Many of the radicals now reacted against the central control of Moscow. In 1923 Gerhardsen became secretary of the Labour Party, the party withdrew from the Comintern, and its orthodox Communists broke away.

A member of the Oslo municipal council from 1932, Gerhardsen became mayor of Oslo in 1940. During the German occupation in World War II he was imprisoned (1941–44). In May 1945 he resumed office as mayor and was elected leader of the Labour Party.

Gerhardsen was prime minister of Norway from June 26, 1945, to Nov. 13, 1951 (when he resigned for reasons of health); again from Jan. 21, 1955, to Aug. 23, 1963 (when the *Storting* passed a motion of no confidence, 76 votes to 74); and then from Sept. 24, 1963, to Oct. 11, 1965 (when the elections favoured his opponents). For events during his aggregate of 17 years of government *see* NORWAY: *History.*
(G. M. G-H.)

GERHARDT, CHARLES FRÉDÉRIC (1816–1856), French chemist and theorist on organic compounds, was born at Strasbourg on Aug. 21, 1816. After attending the *Gymnasium* at Strasbourg and the polytechnic at Karlsruhe, he was sent to the school of commerce at Leipzig, where he studied chemistry under Otto Erdmann. Later he worked for some time with Liebig at Giessen. At Liebig's recommendation he was appointed demonstration assistant to Dumas in Paris. In 1841 he received the doctorate at the University of Paris. He became professor of chemistry at Montpellier in 1844, and in 1855 at Strasbourg, where he died on Aug. 19, 1856.

Although Gerhardt did some noteworthy experimental work—for instance, his preparation of acid anhydrides in 1852—his contributions to chemistry consist not so much in the discovery of new facts as in the introduction of new ideas that vitalized and organized an inert accumulation of old facts.

In 1839 he revived the old radical theory of organic compounds under the title of the "theory of residues." In 1845 he invented the theory of homologues, which proved very useful in determining what members were still missing in the various series of compounds. Gerhardt first suggested that many organic substances were "conjugated" or "copulated" compounds formed by the union of two residues. In 1842 he attempted the first definite classification of organic compounds, but owing to the obscurity of some of his concepts, little progress was made until he cooperated with Auguste Laurent (*q.v.*).

Eventually Gerhardt introduced the idea that all substances were based on four main types; viz., hydrogen, hydrochloric acid, water and ammonia. Although these ideas were later abandoned they play an important part in the development of structural organic chemistry.

His chief works were *Précis de chimie organique* (1844-45), and *Traité de chimie organique* (1853-56).

GERHARDT, ELENA (1885-1961), German mezzo-soprano who was the finest singer of German *Lieder* of her time. Born in Leipzig on Nov. 11, 1885, she studied with Carl Rebling and Marie Hedmont at the Leipzig conservatory, whose principal, Arthur Nikisch, helped to launch her as recitalist and opera singer. Nikisch accompanied her at her debut at Leipzig on Nov. 11, 1903, and frequently thereafter. Having early decided against an operatic career, she made an international reputation as an exponent of German song, her interpretation of Hugo Wolf being unsurpassed in her day. She first appeared in London in 1906 and in New York in 1912. In 1934 she settled in London, where she developed her career as a teacher. She gave her last recital at Liverpool on March 15, 1947. She died in London on Jan. 11, 1961.

See Elena Gerhardt, *Recital* (1953). (Wr. S. M.)

GERHARDT, PAUL (1607-1676), the greatest of German hymn writers, was born at Gräfenhainichen, Saxony, March 12, 1607. He studied theology at Wittenberg, then the home of the rigid Lutheranism of the *Formula Concordiae* (see CONCORD, Book OF). From Wittenberg he went to Berlin and, after six years in the little church in Mittenwalde, was called in 1657 to the St. Nikolaikirche there. He became involved in the religious troubles of the time which, like war and plague, formed the background to his life. In 1664 the Calvinist elector of Brandenburg issued a decree forbidding anti-Calvinist polemic in the pulpit and commanding pastors to baptize with exorcism if they were asked to do so. Gerhardt refused to sign this edict and lost his office. Petitions for his restitution were made and the elector agreed to reinstate him on the ground that he had probably misunderstood the edict. Gerhardt felt unable to take advantage of this loophole and he remained out of office until in 1668 he was called to Lübben, Saxony. He died there, Jan. 7, 1676. He had lost his wife and three of his four children by 1668.

The first 18 of Gerhardt's hymns were published by his friend Johann Crüger in *Praxis pietatis melica* (1648). He wrote 120 hymns in all and a remarkably large number have remained in use. He left none of the great Christian festivals uncelebrated: to mention only a few, "Ich steh an deiner Krippe hier" (Christmas), "Auf, auf, mein Herz" (Easter), "O du allersüsste Freude" (Whitsun). His Good Friday hymn "O Haupt voll Blut und Wunden" ("O Sacred Head, Sore Wounded") is particularly well known. But his characteristic note is joy: "Geh aus, mein Herz, und suche Freud"; "Soll ich meinen Gott nicht singen"—such openings are typical. It is the joy of the Lutheran doctrine of justification by faith—deeply personal yet extrovert and unmystical. His richness of imagery is largely drawn from the Bible; and indeed more than half his hymns are based on biblical passages or earlier hymns. His commentary on Romans, 8, "Ist Gott für mich," however, is an example of his original and personal treatment of his models. His hymns have deservedly held their place in Protestant worship.

BIBLIOGRAPHY.—E. von Cranach-Sichart (ed.), *Wach auf mein Herz. Die Lieder des Paul Gerhardt* (1949); Eng. trans. of hymns by J. Kelly, *Gerhardt's Spiritual Songs* (1867); monographs by H. Petrich (1914); K. Hesselbacher (1936) and F. Seebass (1951); T. B. Hewitt, *Gerhardt . . . and His Influence on English Hymnody* (1918). (M. KL.)

GERIATRICS: see GERONTOLOGY AND GERIATRICS.

GÉRICAULT, JEAN LOUIS ANDRÉ THÉODORE (1791-1824), French painter who influenced the romantic and realist movements, was born at Rouen on Sept. 26, 1791. He studied under Carle Vernet, who introduced him to the traditions of English sporting art, and then under Pierre Guérin, absorbing the methods of classicist figure construction and composition. At the Salon of 1812, he attracted notice with his "Charging Chasseur" (Louvre, Paris), executed in an impetuously dynamic, colourist style inspired by Gros and Rubens. Already he had begun to develop along two divergent lines shown in the visual realism of his many small studies of horses and soldiers, as against the grander more severe style of his mythological compositions and landscapes (*cf.* the two "Heroic Landscapes," Chrysler collection). At the Salon of 1814, his "Wounded Cuirassier" (Louvre) shocked critics with its ponderous forms and sombre colours. Géricault spent 1816-17 in Florence and Rome, where his chief project was the unfinished "Race of the Riderless Horses," a huge, heroic frieze composition, surviving in a series of studies (Baltimore, Md.; Lille; Louvre; Rouen).

Returning to France in 1817, Géricault drew a group of military lithographs reckoned among the early masterworks in this

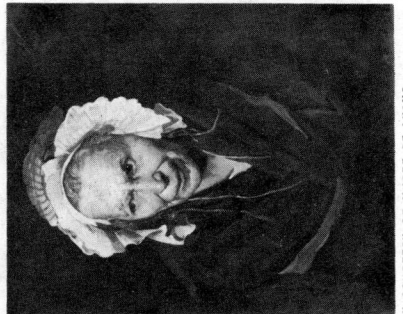

"A MAD WOMAN WITH A MANIA OF ENVY," ONE OF A SERIES OF FIVE PORTRAITS OF THE INSANE BY GÉRICAULT, IN LYONS MUSEUM

BY COURTESY OF MUSEE DE LYONS

medium. His sensational "Raft of the Medusa" (Louvre) was suggested by a contemporary shipwreck. In this enormous canvas he tried to raise a contemporary event beyond the triviality of reportage to the dignity of monumental art. The two aspects of his style here became united: starting with a close inquiry into its visual aspects (*cf.* the portraits of cadavers), he developed his theme into a carefully constructed dramatic composition. This controversial work marked the beginning of the struggle between the classicist and romantic movements. Disappointed by its hostile reception, Géricault left for England (1820) where, again influenced by British genre art, he produced lithographs, water colours and oils ("Epsom Downs Derby," Louvre) of superb colour and grandly simple forms. The most significant of his last works are the portraits of the insane (Louvre; Lyons; Ghent; Winterthur and Springfield, Mass.). He died from the consequences of a fall from his horse on Jan. 26, 1824, in Paris.

See C. Clement, *Th. Géricault*, 2nd ed. (1879); G. Oprescu, *Géricault* (1927); K. Berger, *Th. Géricault* (1952), Eng. trans. by Winslow Ames (1955); D. Aime-Azam, *Mazeppa* (1956). (L. E. A. E.)

GÉRIN-LAJOIE, ANTOINE (1824-1882), Canadian writer, librarian and leader in the early literary movement of French Canada, was born at Yamachiche, Aug. 4, 1824. He was educated at the Collège de Nicolet, where he wrote the first French-Canadian play, *Le jeune Latour*. In 1844 he joined the staff of the Montreal newspaper *La Minerve*, of which he soon became editor. At the same time he studied law and he was called to the Quebec bar in 1848, but he never practised law. In 1852, he was appointed translator to the legislative assembly of Canada; four years later he was made assistant librarian of parliament, a post which he held until 1880. He died at Ottawa on Aug. 4, 1882.

Gérin-Lajoie was one of the founders of the Montreal club, Institut Canadien and of the literary magazines *Les Soirées canadiennes* (1861-65) and *Le Foyer canadien* (1863-66). He was the author of *Catéchisme politique* (1851); *Dix Ans au Canada, de 1840-1850* (1888), the history of the advent of responsible government in the colony; and of a novel in two parts, *Jean Rivard, le défricheur* (1862) and *Jean Rivard, l'économiste* (1864), a portrayal of rural life in French Canada in mid-19th century. (J. G. SE.)

GERIZIM, MOUNT (JABAL AT TUR), a mountain in the Israeli-occupied sector of Jordan about 2,890 ft. above sea level, is the southern of a pair of mountains between which lie Nablus (*q.v.*) and Balatah mound, site of ancient Shechem (*q.v.*). The northern mountain, Ebal (Jabal 'Aybal), is the higher. This is a strategic location since travel routes from all directions converge in the pass between the mountains; most of Palestine can be seen from the peaks. Shechem figures prominently in patriarchal accounts in Genesis. A patrician villa of the 16th century B.C. stood on the slope of Mt. Gerizim above Shechem, consisting of a small central court, surrounded by rooms. It was on Ebal and Gerizim that the tribes assembled under Joshua to hear the curses and the blessings connected with the violation and observance of the law (Deut. xi.). Jotham addressed his parable to the treacherous elders of Shechem from Gerizim (Judg. ix.). It is the holy place of the Samaritans (q.v.) and the scene of their traditional Passover rites. About 432 B.C., after the Jews who had returned from exile refused to recognize the Samaritans, the latter erected on Gerizim a temple as rival to that in Jerusalem; it was destroyed by John Hyrcanus I (c. 128 B.C.) and never rebuilt. The Samaritan woman, who spoke to Jesus of her fathers' worshiping "on this mountain" referred to Gerizim (John iv, 20, 21). The Samaritans were expelled from Gerizim by the emperor Zeno, who built a church (A.D. 484) on the ruins of the temple. In the course of his struggle with the Samaritans Justinian surrounded the church with a fortress. The site of the church was uncovered by the German Archaeological Institute.

(E. D. GR.)

GERLACH, HELLMUT VON (1866-1935), German pacifist, radical journalist and political leader, a courageous opponent of German nationalism under William II, the Weimar republic and the Hitler regime, was born on Feb. 2, 1866, at Mönchmotschelnitz in Silesia. The descendant of a family of Prussian administrators, Gerlach held the conservative views of his class; but during his studies at Geneva, Strasbourg, Leipzig and Berlin he was influenced by Christian Socialism and Lord Randolph Churchill's "Tory democracy" won his admiration. In 1887 he entered the Prussian civil service but left it for journalism, working for Adolf Stöcker (who combined Christian Socialism with anti-Semitism) on the newspaper *Das Volk.* Gerlach's political ideas were too radical for the paper, however, and Stöcker dismissed him in 1896. In the same year Gerlach was a co-founder, with Friedrich Naumann, of the National Social association (Nationalsozialer Verein) and, after visiting England and the Balkans, joined the staff of Naumann's new paper *Die Zeit.* In 1901 he became editor of the Berlin democratic newspaper *Die Welt am Montag,* and from 1903 to 1906 he represented the National Social party in the *Reichstag.* After losing his seat he visited Africa, where he became an admirer of British colonial methods.

During World War I Gerlach openly championed pacifist views. After the revolution he was undersecretary of state in the Prussian ministry of the interior (Nov. 1918–March 1919), where his conciliatory and liberal policy toward Poland earned him the hatred of the German nationalists. He remained, however, an active supporter of pacifist and radical-democratic organizations. In 1933 he emigrated, becoming the recognized head of German exiles in Paris, where he died on Aug. 2, 1935. His books include *Der Zusammenbruch der deutschen Polenpolitik* (1919); *Erinnerungen eines Junkers* (1924); *Von Rechts nach Links,* ed. by Emil Ludwig (1937).

GERLACH, LEOPOLD (1790-1861) and **ERNST LUDWIG VON** (1795-1877), brothers, were leading figures in the movement of romanticism and reaction that determined Prussian politics from the Napoleonic Wars to the end of Frederick William IV's reign, after which Ernst Ludwig lived on to represent conservative opposition to Bismarck's power politics. Leopold was born in Berlin on Sept. 17, 1790, Ernst Ludwig on March 7, 1795. Leopold served as an officer in the war of 1806 and again in that of 1813-15, in which his brother also served as a volunteer. The romantic and conservative spirit of the Wars of Liberation against the French inspired both brothers with a lifelong belief in a greater Germany, with Revolutionary France as its hereditary enemy; and therefore also with a readiness to side with Austria. In 1811, together with the poets Achim von Arnim and Heinrich von Kleist, Leopold joined the Christlich-Deutsche Tischgesellschaft (Christian-German Dining club); and from 1816 to 1819 both brothers were members of the Christlich-Germanische Tischgesellschaft favoured by the crown prince, the future Frederick William IV. Both identified themselves with the strict pietism of the postwar years, taking their political principles from Albrecht von Haller and, above all, from Friedrich Julius Stahl. After Frederick William had come to the throne (1840), Leopold, who had formed a close friendship with him, rose to be his adjutant general (1849) and became the most influential man of his entourage. In the fight against the revolution of 1848 he was the moving spirit of the "Camarilla" at court which, though it had to put up with the constitution of Nov. 1850, did its utmost to revise it in a conservative direction.

Meanwhile Ludwig, who in 1844 had been appointed president of the Magdeburg appeal court; founded the conservative newspaper *Kreuzzeitung* in 1848, in which his monthly commentaries appeared until 1857. Even more dogmatic than Leopold, he was second only to Stahl as a leader of conservative thought. In 1849 the brothers, uncompromisingly opposed to the liberal idea of a German nation, persuaded Frederick William IV to refuse the imperial dignity offered to him by the Frankfurt assembly. Both vigorously fought the German politics of J. M. von Radowitz, welcomed the Olmütz agreement (1850) and vainly sought to persuade the king to join Russia during the Crimean War. Leopold's correspondence with Bismarck, in its discussion of Napoleon III as a potential ally, shows that the early opposed his young friend's *Realpolitik,* though he had himself recommended Bismarck as Prussia's representative at the federal diet in Frankfurt. However, the brothers' narrow dogmatism, which regarded the movement toward German unity only as a "nationalist swindle," represented a lost cause even before Frederick William IV was dead. Leopold died at Potsdam on Jan. 10, 1861, eight days after Frederick William IV. His memoirs, in two volumes, were published in 1891-92 and his correspondence with Bismarck, ed. by H. Kohl, in 1896.

During the decade after 1862 Ludwig lived to see Bismarck completely abandon the ideas of traditional conservatism. His protest against the Prussian annexations of 1866 completed the breach between the former friends. Ludwig joined the Centre party as guest member, since throughout his life he had combined a firm Protestant conviction with respect for the ordered authority of the Roman Catholic Church. He died in Berlin on Feb. 18, 1877. There are *Aufzeichnungen aus seinem Leben und Wirken,* ed. by his son (1903).

See G. Ritter, *Der preussische Konservativismus und Bismarcks deutsche Politik, 1858-66* (1913); H. J. Schoeps, *Das andere Preussen* (1952).

(Ha. H.)

GERLACHE, ÉTIENNE CONSTANTIN, BARON DE (1785-1871), Belgian Catholic statesman and historian, was born at Biourge, Luxembourg, on Dec. 26, 1785. He studied law in Paris and practised there for some time, but he settled in Liège after the establishment of the kingdom of the Netherlands. As a member of the estates-general, he was an energetic leader of the opposition. He supported the alliance of the Belgian Catholics with the Liberal party, which paved the way for the revolution of 1830. On the outbreak of the insurrection in Aug. 1830 he still, however, thought the Orange-Nassau dynasty and the union with the Dutch provinces essential; but his views changed, and after holding various offices in the provisional government, he became president of the national congress and brought forward the motion inviting Leopold of Saxe-Coburg to become (on July 21, 1831) king of the Belgians. In 1832 he was president of the chamber of representatives, but on Oct. 4, when Pope Gregory XVI, in the encyclical *Mirari vos,* condemned H. F. R. de Lamennais's conception of liberty, he resigned, accepting the Holy See's ultramontane ideas. On Oct. 13, 1832, the king appointed him president of the *cour de cassation* (supreme court of appeal), and he kept that office for 35 years. He was created a baron on Jan. 16, 1844. He also presided over the Catholic congresses held at Malines between 1863 and 1867. That his early liberal views underwent some modification was plain from the conservative principles enunciated in his *Essai sur le mouvement des partis en Belgique* (1852). As a historian his work was strongly coloured by his anti-Dutch feelings and his Catholic predilections. His *Histoire du royaume des Pays-Bas de 1814 jusqu'en 1830* (1839), published in two volumes, was a piece of special pleading against the Dutch domination. A complete edition of his works, six volumes (1874-75), includes a biography by J. J. Thonissen. He died in Brussels on Feb. 10, 1871.

See Pierre de Gerlache, *Gerlache et la fondation de la Belgique* (1931).

(C. VE.)

GERMAN CONFESSING CHURCH (BEKENNENDE KIRCHE), the name of the movement for revival within the German Protestant Church, which developed out of resistance to Adolf Hitler's attempt to turn the church into an instrument of National Socialist propaganda and politics. The German Protestant tradition of close co-operation between state and church, as well as dislike of the Weimar democracy, at first caused the church to take a favourable attitude toward Hitler. But the latter's church party, the Deutsche Christen, gained control of the church by unlawful means, and Ludwig Müller, who under strong Nazi pressure had been elected *Reichsbischof*, threatened the authoritative position of the Scriptures and the confessional writings of the Reformation by tolerating the Nazi doctrine of race.

In opposition to this the Jungreformatorische Bewegung (Young Reforming Movement) was formed within the church under the leadership of Hanns Lilje, Martin Niemöller (*q.v.*) and W. Künneth. In Nov. 1933 Niemöller founded the Pfarrernotbund (Pastors' Emergency league), which rejected, among other things, the church's *Arierparagraphen* (laws concerning Jewish Christians). At Barmen, in May 1934, was held the synod whose famous theological declaration, strongly influenced by Karl Barth, transformed the defensive movement against Nazi control of the church into an organized revival especially where territorial churches were subject to Nazi administration. (*See* BARMEN, SYNOD OF.)

At the end of 1934, at the second synod of Dahlem, the church proclaimed its *Notrecht* (emergency law): the true church was that which accepted the Barmen declaration, and where church leadership was no longer faithful to the true confession, ministers and parishes were to follow the orders of the Confessing Church. Thus, in practice two Protestant churches developed in Germany: that under state control and the church of the Confessing synods, which the state did not recognize. The latter, together with the churches of Bavaria, Württemberg and Hanover (which were independent of Nazi rule), formed the Vorläufige Leitung der Evangelischen Kirche (provisional government of the Evangelical Church) with a synodal committee known as the Reichsbruderrat (Council of Brethren).

Internal confessional and political differences, however, led to the secession of the majority of Lutheran churches. The Reformed and united sections of the Confessing Church, the Dahlemer Flügel (Dahlem wing), remained particularly active in protesting against euthanasia and the persecution of the Jews. Nazi pressure was gradually intensified, and increasingly the Confessing Church was forced underground. In 1937 Niemöller, Heinrich Grüber and other clergy were arrested.

After the outbreak of World War II the Confessing Church continued, though seriously handicapped by the conscription of clergy and laity (the latter being very important in the life of the Confessing Church). In 1948 it handed over its leadership to the reorganized German Evangelical Church, though Niemöller's "Confessing Church Group" continued as a movement within the church.

BIBLIOGRAPHY.—W. Niemöller, *Die Evangelische Kirche im Dritten Reich* (1956); D. Bonhoeffer, *Gesammelte Schriften* (1958–61); S. W. Herman, *It's Your Souls We Want* (1943); E. Wolf, *Barmen* (1957). (H. KG.)

GERMANDER, the name given to plants of the genus *Teucrium*, mint family (Labiatae), comprising about 100 species distributed all over the world, a few of which are grown for ornament or fragrance. The common North American forms (*T. canadense* and *T. occidentale*) and the common British species (*T. scorodonia*) are often called wood sage. The plants are small, with small flowers remarkable for the slight development of the upper lip.

GERMANIC LANGUAGES are a group of related languages comprising the modern and earlier forms of English, Frisian, Netherlandish (Dutch, Flemish), German (High and Low), Icelandic, Norwegian, Danish, Swedish and a number of extinct languages, notably Gothic. The earliest recorded Germanic consists of mere fragments: from the 3rd to the 1st century B.C., a single inscription in North-Etruscan letters on a helmet unearthed near Negau, southern Austria: *harigasti teiwa* "Harigasti (owner of the helmet?) Teiwa (name of a god)"; and, beginning in the 1st century B.C., isolated Germanic words and names recorded by classical authors (Caesar, Tacitus, Pliny and others). The earliest extensive Germanic text is the (fragmentary) Gothic Bible translated by the Visigothic bishop Ulfilas (*c.* A.D. 350) written in a 27-letter alphabet of his own invention. From *c.* 200 to 800 there are scattered early Norse inscriptions written in the 24-letter runic alphabet; *e.g.,* the inscription on a golden horn found in Gallehus, Denmark, dating from *c.* 400: *ek hlewagastiʀ holtijaʀ horna tawido* "I, Hlewagast of Holt [Holstein], made [this] horn." Derivatives of this runic alphabet were used sparingly in England, Germany and particularly in Scandinavia. All extensive later texts use adaptations of the Latin alphabet. Old English (Anglo-Saxon) texts date from the early 7th century; Old High German from the middle 8th; Old Low German (usually called Old Saxon) from the early 9th; Old Norse (Old Icelandic and Old Norwegian) from the middle 12th (though many poems preserve an older form of the language); Old Netherlandish (Old Dutch) from the late 12th; Old Frisian from the early 13th; Old Swedish and Old Danish from the end of the 13th. The following abbreviations will be used: Gmc., Germanic; Got., Gothic; ON, Old Norse; OE, Old English; OF, Old Frisian; OS, Old Saxon; OHG, Old High German. *See* GOTHIC LANGUAGE; RUNE.

Proto-Germanic.—The statement that the languages named are related is based on the technical linguistic usage: related languages are variant historical developments of a single earlier language. Thus the Romance languages (French, Spanish, Italian, etc.) are said to be related because they can be shown to be variant developments of a single earlier language, Latin, of which there are extensive written records. In the case of Germanic, no written records of the parent language exist; but much of its structure can be deduced by the comparative method of reconstruction. (A reconstructed language is called a proto-language; reconstructed forms are marked with an asterisk.) For example, a comparison of Runic -*gastiʀ*, Got. *gasts*, ON *gestr*, OE *giest*, OF *iest*, OS and OHG *gast* "guest" leads to the reconstruction of the Proto-Germanic (PGmc.) form *$*gástiz$. Similarly, a comparison of Runic *horna*, Got. *haurn*, ON, OE, OF, OS and OHG *horn* "horn" leads to the reconstruction of PGmc. *hórnan.

Such reconstructions are in part merely formulas of relationships: the $\ʒ$ of *gástiz is the particular phoneme of PGmc. which by regular phonetic change gave Got., ON, OS and OHG *g*, but (before an *a* which had changed to *e*) OE *gi-* and OF *i-*. Likewise, the *o* of *hórnan is the particular phoneme of PGmc. which, in this environment, gave *au* in Gothic, *o* in the other languages. In other environments, *e.g.,* when followed by nasal plus consonant, the same phoneme gave *u* in all the languages: PGmc. *dumbaz, Got. *dumbs*, ON *dumbr*, OE, OF and OS *dumb*, OHG *tumb* "dumb." What may be deduced is that in some environments the phoneme sounded more like *o*, in others more like *u*. It may be written $u\sim o$, indicating that it varied between these two pronunciations.

The example of PGmc. $u\sim o$ shows that the reconstructions are more than mere formulas: they also give some indication of how PGmc. actually sounded. Sometimes the correctness of these deductions is independently confirmed. For example, OE *cyning* and OS and OHG *kuning* "king" are the basis for the reconstruction of PGmc. *kúningaz; this is confirmed by Finnish *kuningas*, which must have been borrowed from Gmc. at a very early date.

As reconstructed, PGmc. had the following system of vowels and consonants:

$$i\sim e \quad u\sim o \quad \bar{\imath} \quad \bar{u} \quad iu\sim eo$$
$$\bar{e} \quad \bar{o} \quad ai \quad au$$
$$a \quad \bar{a}$$

$$p \quad f \quad b\sim ƀ \quad s \quad z \quad m \quad n$$
$$t \quad þ \quad d\sim đ \qquad w \quad j \quad l \quad r$$
$$k \quad h\sim x \quad g\sim ɣ$$

The *þ* represents the *th* of *thin*, *x* the *ch* of German *ach*, *j* the *y* of *yes*. To the above should perhaps be added long nasalized $\tilde{\bar{\imath}}\ \tilde{\bar{u}}$, which resulted when *inx anx unx* changed to *īx ūx ūx*. The phonemes noted as *b~ƀ*, *d~đ*, *g~ɣ* were the stops *b d g* in some environments, the spirants *ƀ đ ɣ* in others. (This type of alternation is not unusual; it occurs, for example, in modern Spanish.) The distribution seems to have been: all were stops after nasal (mb nd ng) and when doubled (bb dd gg); d→ð was also a stop initially and after l (d-ld); b→ð was also a stop initially (b-); in other environments all three were spirants. The phoneme noted as h~x seems to have been h initially (h-), but x elsewhere.

Development.—By pushing the comparative method still farther back, relationships can be established between Germanic and other language groups, notably Celtic, Italic, Greek, Baltic, Slavic, Iranian and Indic. All of these can be derived from a still earlier parent language, Proto-Indo-European (PIE). A comparison of PGmc. with the PIE from which it developed reveals the many changes that occurred.

Consonants.—PIE had the spirant s, a few obscure consonants called "laryngeal," and at least the following stops (perhaps more): p t k kʷ, b d g gʷ, bh dh gh gʷh. By a change known as the Gmc. consonant shift (Grimm's law), the stops developed as follows:

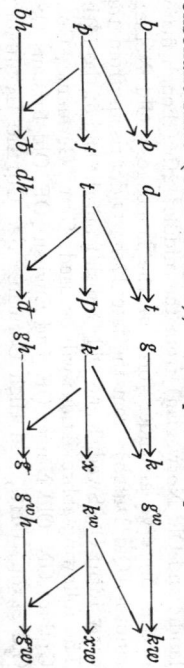

Examples of b d g are: Lithuanian *bald* and Latin *decem* and *genus* but p t k in English *pool, ten* and *kin*. Examples of bh dh gh are: Sanskrit *bhṛ-, dhā-, hā-* (from *ghē-) but b d g in English *be, do, go*. As for p t k, in the clusters sp st sk pt kt they gave PGmc. sp st sk ft xt: Greek *spáthē, stásis, skiá, skápton* and *oktō* and also English *spade, stead, shine* (OE *scinan*), *shaft* (OE *sceaft*) and *eight* (OE *eahta*). (By a special development, tt gave ss: Sanskrit *sattá-*, OE *sess* "seat.") Elsewhere, p t and k seem to have first become the voiceless spirants f þ and x. They remained so initially and after an accented vowel: Latin *piscis, tenuis* and *centum* but f þ h in English *fish, thin,* and *hund(red)*; but, by a change known as Verner's law, after an unaccented syllable all voiceless spirants became voiced. Thereby f þ x coalesced with the new ð ð and s became z: Sanskrit *upári, mātár-, śvaśrū-* (from *sueḱrú-) and *śaśá-* (from *ḱasó-) but OE *ofer* (from *obar, cf. OHG *obar*) "over," *mōdor* "mother," *sweger* "mother-in-law" and *hara* (from *χaza-) "hare." PIE gʷ kʷ gʷh developed parallel to g k gh; but whereas they were separate phonemes in PIE (contrasting with the clusters and gave kʷ xʷ gʷ, Gmc. they coalesced with these clusters and gave kʷ xʷ gʷ.

These changes gave the 11 stop and spirant phonemes assumed for PGmc. Reconstructions from the individual Gmc. languages then indicate that some of these began to undergo further changes: ð ð g changed from spirants to stops in certain positions; and x changed to h initially.

Vowels.—Besides the above obstruents (stops and spirants), PIE had two other classes of phonemes: vowels and resonants. The vowel of any given root was not necessarily fixed, but varied in an alternation termed ablaut. Thus the root "sit" was alternately *sed-, *sod-, *sēd-, or *sōd- (Eng. "sit" is from *sed-, "sat" from *sod-, "seat" from *sēd-); and the root "do" was *dhē-, *dhō-, or *dhā- (Eng. "deed" is from *dhē-, "do" from *dhō-). Other vowels were a, ā, i, ī, u, ū. The PIE resonants were i~į, u~u̯, m~m̥, n~n̥, l~l̥, r~r̥. They were syllabic in some environments, nonsyllabic in others. Thus *bhṛtó- (Sanskrit *bhṛtá-* "the bears") had nonsyllabic ṛ, but *bhéreti (Sanskrit *bhárati* "he bears") had syllabic r. (Eng. "bear" is from *bher-, "bier" from *bher-.) *bhor-, "burden" from *bher-.

This PIE system of vowels vs. resonants was reshaped by a number of changes. Syllabic i u m n l r gave the vowels i u and the sequences um un ul ur; nonsyllabic m n l r gave the consonants m n l r; nonsyllabic į u̯ before vowels gave the consonants j w, though after vowels they continued to form diphthongs (ei ai oi, eu au ou). The resulting vowels and diphthongs then developed as follows:

```
i→e   e   a   o
ī     ē   ā   ō   ū
o→u   i   u̯   ī̆   ū̆
ō→u   ū̆
i~e   a   o   ō~u   ū
ei    ai  oi      eu   au   ou
iu~eo           au   on
```

These changes gave the PGmc. system of three short vowels, five long vowels, and three diphthongs (counting i~e, u~o as one each), five long vowels and three diphthongs (counting iu~eo as one). The variants e, o, o occurred before a low vowel in the following syllable; the variants i, u, iu occurred before a high vowel (or j, w) in the following syllable, or before nasal plus consonant. Compare the following: PGmc. *beranan, OE *beran* "to bear," but *birþi, OE *bir(e)þ*, "beareth"; PGmc. *gʊlþan, OE *gold* "gold," but *gʊlþjanan, OE *gyldan* "to gild"; PGmc. *leoxtan, OE *leoht* "light," but *liuxt-janan, OE *liehtan* "to give light."

Accent.—The PIE pitch accent which could fall on any syllable of a word was replaced in PGmc. by a stress accent on the first syllable. This seems to have led to a progressive reduction of unstressed syllables, e.g., PIE *sodéionom, PGmc. *sătjanan, OE *settan*, Middle Eng. *sette(n)*, modern *set*. Strong initial stress is also reflected in the basic unit of old Gmc. poetry: two half lines, each with one of a small number of stress patterns, linked by the alliteration of stressed initial consonants or vowels (e.g., *Beowulf*, li. 18: *Bēo-wülf wæs brēme / blǣd wīde sprǎng* "Beowulf was famous, his renown went far").

Declensions.—PGmc. kept the PIE system of three genders (masc., neut., fem.) and three numbers (sing., dual, plur.), though the dual was obsolescent. It reduced the PIE system of eight cases to six: nominative, accusative, dative, genitive, instrumental, vocative (though the last two were obsolescent). In the adjective declensions it made two innovations: (1) To the PIE vocalic types (o-, ā-, i-, u-stems) it added some pronominal endings to give the Gmc. "strong" adjective declension. (2) The PIE n-stem endings were extended to all adjectives to give the Gmc. "weak" adjective declension (e.g., mod. German, strong: *gutes Bier* "good beer," but weak: *das gute Bier* "the good beer").

Conjugations.—The PIE verb seems to have had five moods (indicative, imperative, subjunctive, injunctive and optative), two voices (active, mediopassive), three persons (first, second, third), three numbers (sing, dual, plur.) and several infinitives and participles. In Gmc. these were reduced to: indicative, imperative, subjunctive-optative (usually called subjunctive, but containing the functions of both and actually derived from the PIE optative); a full active voice, plus an obsolescent passive (found only in Gothic); three persons; full singular and plural forms, plus an obsolescent dual (found only in Gothic); and one infinitive (present) and two participles (present and past). The PIE tense-aspect system (present, imperfect, aorist, perfect) was reshaped to a single tense contrast: present v. past. The past showed two innovations. On the one hand, in the "strong" verb, PGmc. transformed the ablaut of PIE into a specific tense marker, e.g., PIE bher-, bhor-, bhēr-, bhṛ- in OE *beran* "bear," past singular *bær*, past plural *bǣron*, past participle *boren*. On the other hand, in the "weak" verb, it formed a completely new past and past participle, e.g., OE *fyllan* "fill," past *fylde*, participle *gefylled*. Weak verbs fell into three classes depending on the syllable preceding the endings, e.g., OHG *full-e-n* (from *full-ja-n*) "fill," *maþk-ō-n* "make," *sag-ē-n* "say." Gothic also had a fourth type: *full-nō-da* "it became full."

Many PGmc. strong verbs showed a consonant alternation ("grammatical change") between f/b, þ/d, x/g, s/z. This was the result, through Verner's law, of the alternating position of the PIE accent:

PIE	PGmc.	OE	
*preisomom	*frèosanan	frèosan	"to freeze"
*prôuse	*fráus	frēas	"(it) froze"
*prusñt	*fruzunþ	fruron	"(they) froze"
*prusénos	*fróʒenaz	froren	"frozen"

In this particular word, English has generalized the s (now z): *freeze, froze, frozen*; German has generalized the z (now r) *frieren, fror, gefroren*; Dutch still shows the alternation: *vriezen, vroor, gevroren*. English has preserved grammatical change only in *was, were* and in a few isolated forms such as *sodden, (for)lorn*, the old past participles of *seethe, lose*.

Germanic Dialects.—Archaeological evidence suggests a relatively uniform Germanic people c. 750 B.C. located in southern Scandinavia and along the North sea and Baltic coasts from Holland to the Vistula. By c. 250 B.C., they had spread farther south and five general groups were distinguishable: (1) along the North sea coast and in Jutland; (2) along the middle Rhine and Weser; (3) along the middle Elbe; (4) along the Oder and Vistula; and (5) in Scandinavia (excluding Jutland).

Another 500 years later (A.D. 250) the division was much the same, though the Elbe group had spread southward to the Danube and the Oder-Vistula group southeast into the Carpathians and beyond.

Then came the great tribal migrations: part of the North sea group (Bede identifies them as Angles, Saxons and Jutes) conquered much of England; the Rhine-Weser group (Franks) conquered northern France; the Elbe group (Alemannians, Bavarians, Lombards) vacated the north and spread south; the Oder-Vistula group (Goths, Burgundians, Vandals) left to begin their many wanderings.

This five-way division of the Germanic peoples is based on nonlinguistic evidence; but it agrees well with the linguistic picture derived by the comparative method from earliest texts. Five groups were indeed distinguishable, though they were linked in sets of two, three or four through common linguistic innovations. Thus the East Gmc. group (Oder-Vistula) shared innovations with the North Gmc. group (Scandinavian): there PGmc. *jj, ww* (e.g., *twajji-, *trewwj-*, cf. OHG *zweiio* "of two," *triuwi* "faithful") developed to long stop plus semivowel (cf. ON *tueggja, tryggr*, Got. *twaddjē, triggws*). On the other hand, North Gmc. and three West Gmc. groups (North sea, Rhine-Weser, Elbe) shared certain later innovations: coalescence of *z* with *r* (Got. *maiza* "more," but ON *meire*, OE, OF *māra*, OS *mēro*, OHG *mēro*) and the loss of the reduplicative past of certain strong verbs (Got. *lailōt* "let," but ON, OE, OF, OS *lēt*, OHG *liaz*). The West Gmc. groups also showed innovations of their own: replacement of the *d~ð* alternation by simple *d* (PGmc. *blōðan* "blood," Got., ON *blōþ*, but OE, OF, OS *blōd*, OHG *bluot*); the loss of final -*z* after unstressed vowels (PGmc. *dǣgaz* "day," Got. *dags*, ON *dagr*, but OE *dæg*, OF *dei*, OS *dag*, OHG *tag*); and the doubling of consonants in certain positions, especially before *j* (Got. *satjan* "set," ON *setia*, but OE *settan*, OF *setta*, OS *settian*, OHG *setzen*; though ON also showed the doubling of *g* and *k*: Got. *lagjan* "lay," but ON *leggia*, OE *lecgan*, OF *ledza*, OS *leggian*, OHG *leggen*). Within West Gmc., the North sea group showed innovations of its own: a single ending in the plural of verbs (where the others have one for each of the three persons); loss of the reflexive pronoun; loss of -*z* in certain pronoun forms (PGmc. *wiz* "we," Got. *weis*, ON *vēr*, OHG *wir*, but OE *wē*, OF, OS *wī*). The North sea group also shared some innovations with North Gmc.: loss of nasals before spirants (Got. *fimf, munþs, uns*, OHG *fimf, mund, uns* "five," "mouth," "us," but OE, OF, OS *fīf, mūþ* or *mūth, ūs*; in ON, only before *f* and *s*: *fīf* from **fimfill* "giant," *ōs* "us") and *i*-umlaut, *i.e.*, the raising or fronting of stressed vowels before unstressed *j, i, ī* (cf. the words "sit" and "lay" above; umlaut was just spreading into OHG at the time of the earliest texts). Within the North sea group, OE and OF showed still further innovations of their own: raising of *a* to *æ* and *e* (*dæg, dei* above) and palatalization of *gg* before *j* (*lecgan, ledza* above). Finally, to complete the circle, the Elbe group (from which came southern OHG) shared a few innovations with North and East Gmc.: the spread of the nominative and accusative singular neuter pronoun ending **-at(a)* to strong adjectives (OE, OF *hāl* "whole," OS *hēl*, but Got. *hailata*, ON *heilt*, OHG *heilaz*); and it shared certain forms with East Gmc. (PGmc. **iz* "he," in Got. *is*, OHG *ir, er*, but **h-* forms in ON *hann*, OE, OF, OS *hē*). *See also* the articles on individual languages.

BIBLIOGRAPHY.—E. Prokosch, *A Comparative German Grammar* (1939); A. Meillet, *Caractères généraux des Langues Germaniques* (1949); W. Streitberg, *Urgermanische Grammatik* (1896); Hermann Hirt, *Handbuch des Urgermanischen*, 3 vol. (1931–34); J. Fourquet, *Les Mutations Consonantiques du Germanique* (1948); W. G. Moulton, "The Stops and Spirants of Early Germanic," *Language*, vol. 30, pp. 1–42 (1954); W. F. Twaddell, "Prehistoric Germanic Short Syllabics," *Language*, vol. 24, pp. 139–151 (1948); J. W. Marchand, "Germanic Short **i* and **e*: Two Phonemes or One?" *Language*, vol. 33, pp. 346–354 (1957); Friedrich Maurer, *Nordgermanen und Alemannen*, 3rd ed. (1952). (W. G. MN.)

GERMANIC LAWS, EARLY. In Germanic tradition, law was either customary from time immemorial, a set of fixed rules reflecting the convictions of those subject to it, or it was constituted at a time still remembered and thus derived its force from a known act of legislation. The two did not have the same standing: the Franks demanded special decrees to invest newly established *capitula* with the authority enjoyed by the old *leges*; while in Scandinavia a new law held either for a set time only or had to be proclaimed afresh at a popular assembly, failing which it would lapse. The assembly, made up of those fit to bear arms, was the legislator; but one man alone put forward the legal clauses in words, which, through acclamation, became law. More vital still was the role of the Scandinavian "law man" or "law speaker," who had to recite the whole law at the annual assembly and thus attained a unique position. In Sweden he counterbalanced the king, who was the political ruler, thus foreshadowing the modern division of powers. In Iceland he became the sole guardian of tradition; if strife threatened to uproot the community (as in A.D. 1000, when Christianity was first introduced), he preserved national unity. For many centuries the law was thus handed down by word of mouth alone. A simple society, where noble differed from free peasant only by lineage and wealth, had no need of learned lawyers and written codes. The runic script, though widely used for diverse inscriptions, hardly lent itself to recording laws, all the more since proper writing materials were scarce. A great change came when these tribes collided with Greco-Roman culture and with Christianity. When they set up Teutonic kingdoms within the Roman empire, they had to codify and write down their ancestral laws; the Visigoths, Burgundians and Salic Franks recorded theirs around A.D. 500, the Lombards about 650. The tribes of central Europe owe their codes to the influence of their Frankish masters: the Alemans and Ripuarian Franks to Clotaire II; the Bavarians to Pepin III; the Chamavic Franks, Saxons, Thuringians and Frisians to Charlemagne.

These *Leges Germanorum* are codifications mainly of parts of criminal law and of procedure, combining traditional laws with newly constituted laws (*capitularia*) that survived sometimes as amendments (*novellae*) to older laws, sometimes as special laws. The most important capitularies were those of Charlemagne and of his son Louis. Though *leges* and *capitularia* are in Latin, most of them contain some Germanic legal terms as well. Fragments of the Salic law and of a Carolingian capitulary survive in an Old High German translation.

Leges Visigothorum.—Indirect evidence points to a law promulgated by Theodoric II (reigned 453–466), probably for the Romans under Visigoth rule. Chapters 276–336 of the code of his brother and successor Euric (d. 484), largely extant (in a palimpsest manuscript at Paris), deal with Gothic quarrels and with cases between Goths and Romans. The law of the Bavarians, covering similar ground, helps partly to fill in the gaps. Leovigild (d. 586) produced a version (now lost) of Euric's code. After his reign, new laws made by the king were declared binding on all his subjects of whatever race; the law thus became territorial, a principle gradually extended to the older code. Moreover, when his son Reccared I (reigned 586–601) turned from Arianism to Roman Catholicism, the religious split among his subjects vanished; as Christians, all of them had to abide by the conciliar canons enforced by the kings. Reccesvinth (reigned 649–672) set up a new code which contained 87 laws of his own and 99 of his father's (Chindasvinth, reigned 642–653), and took over 324 constitutions from Leovigild as well as a few laws of Reccared and Sisebut.

Lex Burgundionum.—The "book of constitutions," or *Lex Gundobada* issued by King Gundobad (d. 516), with later additions by himself or by his son Sigismund (d. 524), was applied among Burgundians and to their dealings with Romans. It was still in use in the 9th century, as evidenced by the protest against it by Agobard, bishop of Lyons.

Leges Langobardorum.—The so-called edict of the Lombards, in 388 chapters, was promulgated by King Rothari at a diet at Pavia on Nov. 22, 643. The compilers borrowed form and language from Roman law, but the content is Teutonic. Later kings added further provisions, many of them ecclesiastical. When the

Lombards and Franks united, their joint capitularies were applied to Italy; of those valid for Italy alone some were appended to Rothari's edict.

In Italy, lawyers and jurists early compiled codes. Eberhard, duke and margrave of Rhaetia and Friuli, had the edict and its additions arranged into a *Concordia de singulis causis* (829–832). The 10th-century *Capitulare Langobardorum* is a collection of capitularies in use in Italy. The *Liber legis Langobardorum* (*Liber Papiensis*) and the *Lombarda*, early and late 11th century respectively, were influenced by the law school at Pavia.

Alamannic Codes.—Two texts survive. The earlier *Pactus (legis) Alamannorum* was compiled by King Clotaire II between 613 and 623, and promulgated by a Frankish assembly. The later *Lex Alamannorum* was an edict of duke Lantfrid, probably in 724–725; later, with borrowings from the *Pactus*, it became Frankish law.

Lex Baiuvariorum.—The law of the Bavarians seems to date from a time when their dukes were vassals of the Frankish kings. Compiled in 743–744, it draws on Euric's code, on the Salic law and on the later form of the Alamannic law.

Lex Saxonum.—This was written down probably at the Diet of Aachen (802–803), after Charlemagne had conquered Saxony. It is headed by two of his capitularies: the very severe *Capitulare de partibus Saxoniae* (782 or 785), dealing death for any infringements of the Christian religion; and the less brutal *Capitulare Saxonicum* (promulgated in 797, probably at Alcuin of York's instance), which allows composition of previously capital offenses.

Thuringian Laws.—This survives in manuscript as *Lex Thuringorum* and in an old edition entitled *Lex Angliorum et Werinorum, hoc est Thuringorum*. In the 8th century the Angles lived south of the river Unstrut, and the Werini east of them, between the Saale and Weisse Elster rivers. The compilations are probably coeval with those of Saxon law.

Lex Frisionum.—This is a mixed collection. Some of its items are pagan: one paragraph allows a mother to kill her new-born child, another orders that whosoever defiles a temple shall be sacrificed to the gods. Other sections, such as those that forbid incestuous marriage, or Sunday work, are purely Christian. This compilation, too, goes back to the intense legislative period at Charlemagne's court at Aachen in the early 9th century.

See also ANGLO-SAXON LAW; CAPITULARY; SALIC LAW; GERMANIC PEOPLES: *Form of Government*; GOTHS.

BIBLIOGRAPHY.—*Monumenta Germaniae historica, sectio leges* (1888–1967), *Germanenrechte* (1934–66); K. von Amira, 2nd ed. (1906); H. Brunner, *Deutsche Rechtsgeschichte*, I, 2nd ed. (1906); Alvaro d'Ors (ed. and trans.), "Codex Euric," *Estudios Visigóticos*, II (1960); F. Beyerle (ed. and trans.), *Lex Burgundionum* (1936), *Leges Langobardorum* (1962); K. A. Eckhardt (ed. and trans.), *Pactus Alamannorum* (1958), *Lex Alamannorum* (1962), *Lex Baiuvariorum* (1934); *Leges Saxonum, Thuringorum, Chamavorum* (1934), *Lex Frisionum*, based on J. Herold's edition of 1557 (1934). (K. A. ECK.)

GERMANIC MYTHOLOGY AND HEROIC LEGENDS.

This article is designed as an outline of the mythology and the heroic literature which are a common heritage of the German, Anglo-Saxon and Scandinavian peoples.

GERMANIC MYTHOLOGY

The Germanic peoples probably developed their legends of the gods and the nature of the cosmos from a common Indo-European mythology; there are illuminating parallels with Indian and Hellenic mythology that seem to spring from similar conceptions. There is also, however, great diversity and independence of detail. The fullest sources for modern knowledge of Germanic mythology are the Icelandic *Eddas* (see ICELANDIC LITERATURE; EDDA). Sufficient record remains from other Germanic nations (*e.g.*, names of deities and sacred objects, accounts of rites banned by the church, ancient charms) to make it possible to regard Scandinavian legends as an acceptable index to Germanic mythology in general. No picture of the beliefs of (for example) the heathen Anglo-Saxons could be derived from Old English sources alone; although these preserve the names of Woden, Tiw, Þunor, Ing, Frigg (and possibly Baldr), the occasional allusions to the powers or rites of these gods can only be elucidated by reference to Scandinavian sources. In the following consecutive account, where confusion might arise separate legends will be numbered; unless otherwise stated, names are given in their Norse forms.

Cosmology.—Tacitus (*Germania*, 2) states that the Germans sing of a god, Twisto (? "Twofold"; *i.e.*, "Androgynous One"), born of the Earth, who had a son, Mannus, originator of the human race. Norse legends place at the head of creation a giant, Ymir (*cf.* Sanskrit Yama, "Twin," the first mortal, and Latin Ianus geminus), formed magically by a conjunction of elements in a vacuous abyss, Ginnunga gap, "Magic Void." (1) Like Twisto, Ymir reproduced creatures from himself alone: a son and daughter were born from his armpit, a six-headed giant from his feet. (2) Ymir was fed by a cow, who herself licked a man into being from a salty block of ice. From this man the god Oðinn (Odin) and his two brothers were descended. They killed Ymir and created the world from his body: "earth from his flesh, mountains from his bones, sky from his skull and sea from his blood." The legend in the *Prose Edda* that Ymir's blood drowned all the giant race except one is thought to be an invention by Snorri Sturluson, author of the *Prose Edda*, on the analogy of the biblical flood. (3) Oðinn and two fellow gods endowed with life and faculties the first human beings, a man and woman formed from two pieces of driftwood (Askr, "Ash"; and Embla,? "Elm" or "Vine").

The earth on which men live was conceived of as a central enclosure, Miðgarðr (O.E. Middangeard; Midgard), surrounded by the sea, in which the cosmic serpent Miðgarðsormr lies, his teeth biting his tail. Within Miðgarðr is the realm of the gods, Asgarðr (Asgard), reached by the bridge of the rainbow, Bifröst, "Coloured Way." Utgarðr, "Outer Realm," home of the giants, lies far to the east. Sometimes it is said to be in the north, which is the direction also of Hel (*q.v.*), the world of the dead, and in some legends the giants have the character of chthonic powers (*cf.* their immense age and wisdom and their repeated efforts to capture the goddesses of fruitfulness, as Hades captures Persephone in the Greek legend). The universe is supported by a great ash tree, Yggdrasill, the "Horse of Yggr" (*i.e.*, the Terrible One, Oðinn); *cf. Irminsul*, "Mighty Pillar," which, according to Rudolf of Fulda (9th century), the Saxons revered as "the universal pillar sustaining all things." The axle pin on which the heavens revolve is the Pole Star. The roots of the tree Yggdrasill grow through every world of living and dead. It is watered from a sacred well at its foot, where Urðr (O.E. *wyrd*), "Destiny," decides the fates of men. Life-giving, meadlike dew falls on the earth from its branches, and a goat that pastures on its leaves gives mead for the gods to drink. The tree also suffers: a winged dragon, Niðhöggr, "Malicious Striker," gnaws at the roots; in the branches an eagle sits; and a squirrel runs up and down the tree stirring up strife between eagle and dragon.

This world is not imagined as lasting forever. The cyclic conception of history found in other mythologies has its counterpart in Norse legends: (1) of a monstrous winter in which all life will perish, except for a man and woman who live on inside a tree to re-people the earth; and (2) of a heroic conflict at the end of the world, Ragnarök (*q.v.*), "Doom of the Gods," when monsters—the fire demon Surtr, the sons of Muspell (? "Destruction"), the cosmic serpent Miðgarðsormr, the chained wolf Fenrir (*q.v.*) who swallows the sun, and Loki (*q.v.*), evil genius of the gods—break loose and overwhelm gods and men. The stars fall, the earth sinks into the sea, flames rage to the skies. But from the destruction a new earth rises, and the gods return to a hallowed peace and plenty. Eschatological legends were probably common to the heathen Germanic peoples and would be readily reformed and moralized on biblical lines by Christian poets (*cf.* the recurrent theme of the crumbling of the world in Old English verse; and, in the Old High German poem *Muspilli*, the fight at the end of the world between St. Elias and Antichrist, when Elias will be killed and the earth will burst into flames).

The Gods.—Four deities are known to have been common to the Germanic nations: Oðinn, Týr, Þórr (O.E. Woden, Tiw, Þunor; O.H.G. Wuotan, [no form for Tiw], Donar), equated by Tacitus with Mercury, Mars and Hercules, respectively; and Frigg (O.E.

Frig; O.H.G. Frija), equated in the names of the days of the week with Venus. In Norse they are called Æsir (singular Ás; O.E. Os, most common in personal names; Gothic Anses, according to the historian Jordanes, the ancestors worshiped by the Goths). The one-eyed Oðinn, chief of the gods, is also the most complex (see ODIN). From his seat, Hliðskjálf, "Gate Tower," he can see into all worlds. He is master of magic who can restore the dead to life; god of wisdom and rhetoric who has exchanged his eye for a draught of the well of knowledge, stolen from the giants the mead of poetry and enacted in his own person a rite of initiation, hanging for nine nights in hunger and thirst on Yggdrasill, wounded with a spear like a victim sacrificed to himself, until he won power over runes, symbols of magic knowledge (cf. the Eddic poem *Hávamál*; the O.E. Nine Herbs Charm and Runic Poem). He is deceptive, often disguised, a breaker of oaths, inspirer of lawless fury, of the possessed state of poets and warriors. His name, Woden, cognate with *vates*, means "Furious, Excited One," and he has attracted to himself some of the characteristics of shamanism (*q.v.*). It is probable that the turbulent life of the southern Germanic tribes in the centuries of their invasions upon the Roman world made Woden their chief god, a god of battle and of the slain, to whom human sacrifices were offered (*Germania*, 9). This cult spread to Scandinavia and in Viking times inspired a savage heroism and scorn of death and a macabre poetry rich in images of battle, in which to die was to dwell with Oðinn; the Valkyrjar, "Choosers of the Slain," led the heroes to feast with him in Valhöll, "Hall of the Slain" (*see* VALHALLA).

Of Týr less is known, though his cult must once have been widespread. He appears to have been the god who presided over the formalities of war (especially treaties) and of law (in an early inscription he is called Mars Thincsus, "Mars of the Assembly"); he bears a spear as sign of his judicial function. He is one-handed: when the gods, as if in sport, tried to chain the wolf Fenrir, Týr heroically placed his hand as a pledge in the wolf's mouth; when the wolf could not break the chain, Týr paid for the gods' deception (*cf.* the legend of the Irish hero Nuadu). In the O.E. Runic Poem, Tiw is said to "keep faith well with princes."

Þórr, most beloved by the Scandinavian farming communities, was the red-bearded personification of strength, the Thunderer (hence *dies Iovis*, "Jove's day," became Thursday), armed with his hammer, as Hercules with his club. Because strength is his main attribute, myths often show him teased or outwitted, but it is he who defends Miðgarðr against the giants, warring perpetually upon them, and when he falls at Ragnarök the dissolution of the world begins (*see also* THOR).

Frigg, wife of Oðinn and mother of the most beautiful of the Æsir, Baldr, has no clearly defined function save that of divine wife and mother. She strives to preserve the life of her son by taking an oath from all created things to spare him (*see below*). Little is known of her worship, but her name probably means "Loved One" or "Noble Kinswoman," and in parts of Germany her day (Friday) was regarded as especially favourable for marriage.

A second race of gods, the Vanir (a name found only in Norse), were deities of wealth, fertility and peace. Incest and sorcery were practised among them. Njörðr, associated especially with the harvests of the sea, dwelling in Nóatún, "Home of Ships," is male counterpart of the goddess Nerthus, *Terra Mater*, who was worshiped by tribes along the south Baltic shore (Tacitus, *Germania*, 40). The ritual of her worship is similar to that of Freyr, son of Njörðr, which is described in Norse sources, and that of Ing, which is referred to in the O.E. Runic Poem. The effigy of these deities was borne about the land on a car, a symbol of the car of the sun, which brought fertility. Freyr, "Lord," or Yngvi (O.E. Ing)" divine ancestor of the Ingvæones, was called "God of the World" and invoked for rich harvests and peace; in a Norse love poem he woos Earth with gifts of perpetual fruitfulness. Associated with him (as with, *e.g.*, Tammuz and Adonis) is the motif of death and renewal and of slaying by a tusk or horn. The boar especially is sacred to Freyr and one of the names of his sister and concubine, Freyja, is "Sow." She is the goddess "beautiful in weeping," for, like the Egyptian Isis or the Greek Aphrodite, she seeks a lost husband throughout the world, and her tears are gold.

The Vanir are warred upon by the Æsir but are eventually reconciled to them by treaty; thus it is suggested (especially in the works of G. Dumézil) that deities representing the functions of priest, sovereign and warrior (Oðinn, Týr, Þórr) are united with those who provide fertility and wealth, and that this divine community reflects the structure of human society, the proper functioning of which depends upon a similar union. When the pact between Æsir and Vanir is made, they mingle their spittle in a bowl (an ancient method of fermentation) and form from it a man, Kvasir (*cf.* Russian *kvass*, a fermented drink), the wisest of all creatures. He is killed by two dwarfs who are bored by his learning; his blood is mixed with honey and becomes the mead of poetry.

Just as southern Germanic records refer to deities not found in Norse (*e.g.*, Saxnot of the Saxons, Fosite of the Frisians and numerous variants of the goddess of fertility), Norse mythology also includes many not found elsewhere; *e.g.*, Heimdallr, whom nine sisters gave birth to, sleepless sentinel of the gods with fabulous powers of seeing and hearing, who, it is thought, may represent the World-Tree itself, and Iðunn, the goddess who keeps the apples that the gods eat to preserve their youth (*see* HEIMDALL; IDUN). Among the Æsir the most problematical figure is Loki. He is blood brother of Oðinn and frequently assists Þórr, but he is also father of the cosmic serpent, of the wolf Fenrir and of the goddess Hel of the underworld, and in his deliberate acts of mischief or malice (cutting off the golden hair of Sif, Þórr's wife; almost selling Freyja and Iðunn into the power of the giants) he seems to menace the security and self-satisfaction of the gods. His one irreparable act is to cause the death of Baldr (*see* BALDER), whom all things had promised to spare, save only the mistletoe, which Frigg had not asked. Hel offers to surrender Baldr if all creatures will weep for him, but Loki, in disguise, refuses. As a punishment, he is chained in torment by the gods (his anguished writhing is the cause of earthquakes), until at Ragnarök he breaks loose against them. Loki may owe some of his evil character to Christian conceptions of the Devil, but the complexity of his satirical and disastrous nature must already have been well-developed in heathen times.

THE HEROIC LEGENDS

Sources and Nature of the Legends.—The heroic legends told by the early Germanic peoples became part of the European inheritance of story and survive in many different literary forms, reflecting the conventions and tastes of different periods and tellers: (1) in vernacular heroic lay (the O.H.G. *Hildebrandslied*; the fragmentary O.E. *Waldere* and *Finnsburg*; the O.N. lays of the *Edda*); (2) in Latin epic (*Waltharius* [*q.v.*], written probably in Germany in the 9th century); (3) in Latin chronicles, where the legends are incorporated as history (Paulus Diaconus, *Historia Langobardorum*; Saxo Grammaticus, *Gesta Danorum*; etc.); (4) in M.H.G. epic romance (*Nibelungenlied* [*q.v.*]) and Icelandic and Norwegian prose saga (*Völsunga Saga*, *Þiðreks Saga* [*Thidreks Saga*], all from the 13th century, and even later in ballads.

The great legends are of two kinds. Some can be traced to historical happenings and have historical persons as their heroes (Ermanaric the Ostrogoth, Attila the Hun and the emperor Theodoric). Others go back to myth and folk tale and have dateless heroes such as Wayland the Smith (*q.v.*); monster-killers such as Beowulf (*q.v.*), Sigurðr in the *Edda*, and Grettir; releasers of spellbound maidens (Sigurðr); and tamers of princesses fierce to their wooers (Offa in *Beowulf*, Sifrit in the *Nibelungenlied*). The two kinds of legend lived for centuries side by side in oral tradition, so that by the time a cycle of legends attained literary form (as in *Beowulf* or the *Nibelungenlied*) it might be a complex of stories of both kinds.

Spread of the Legends.—The historical figures in Germanic heroic legend belong to the age of the great Germanic migrations from the 4th to the 6th centuries A.D. Events of this period lived in popular memory and became the most cherished themes of Germanic poets, not only in the countries to which the heroes belonged but in any land where a Germanic language was spoken. The stories, like news, spread orally, for not until several centuries after the establishment of Christian learning were any of the legends recorded in writing. Verse was the medium in which historical knowledge was most effectively preserved, as the fixed form aided the memory. The custom common to the Germanic nations of reciting tales for entertainment (in the early centuries, at least, accompanied by the harp), in the common Germanic alliterative metre and archaic poetic diction, made communication of legends easy. Tales from foreign lands were received with avidity, and a poet prided himself on the range of legend on which he could draw. That this might be considerable is shown by the wealth of allusion in the O.E. poem *Widsið* to ancient continental kings and the tribes they ruled and warred with. Skilled poets were maintained by kings and chieftains in their households (*cf. Deor*) and might accompany their patrons to foreign courts, taking their stock of legends with them (as the poet *Widsið* accompanied the princess Eahhild to the court of Ermanaric).

The recital of tales, however, was not confined to professional poets or royal courts. At any gathering of men even a cowherd, such as the Northumbrian Caedmon (*q.v.*), would be expected to take up the harp and recite. So venerable and widespread was the custom that in the early centuries of Christianity even monks would recite in the refectory ancient lays of heathen kings, as Alcuin complained in a letter to the bishop of Lindisfarne in 797. Any traveler might carry the legends he had heard in his own country to a foreign land: the Dane Saxo Grammaticus (*q.v.*), for example, whose heroic legends are found (the Christian epic *Beowulf*, for example, was built from Germanic heroic material). learned many poems, which he used as sources for part of his *Gesta Danorum*, from an Icelander, Arnold, who was accompanying a Danish embassy into Saxony; and German merchants in Bergen c. 1230 may have told the primitive version of the Nibelung story upon which the Norwegian *Þiðreks Saga* was based.

From the earliest times legends might pass from one country to another. A feud between Frisians and Danes in the 5th century and wars in Denmark and Sweden in the 6th were themes of poetry in Anglo-Saxon England. South German stories of Ermanaric, Gundicarius the Burgundian and Attila were retold by poets in Norway, Iceland and even Greenland before they were written down in Iceland in the 13th century. The fantastic and savage story of Wayland the Smith, which is probably German in origin, was known in Anglo-Saxon England and was carved there in pictures on a whalebone casket in the 8th century (the Franks casket, in the British museum). A Norwegian poet, who seems to have known Old English as well as German traditions, composed an Eddic lay of Wayland (*Völundarkviða*), placing the story in a northern setting. Still later, German tales of Wayland, some of which contain the closest parallels to incidents carved on the Old English casket, were incorporated in legend in the *Þiðreks Saga*. Sometimes the character attributed in legend to a historical king reflects the political sympathies of the early tellers: Attila is a powerful but kindly ruler in east Germanic tradition (and so represented in *Waltharius* and the *Nibelungenlied*) but a treacherous villain in the west (as the tradition is preserved in the *Edda*).

History and Legend.—The stages by which a narration of historical happenings developed into the extant poetic versions cannot be determined precisely, but it seems clear that within a few generations the history of events might be altered in the telling. In tradition some facts remained fixed, while less determinate elements—character, motive, dialogue—were subject to the teller's interpretation as he dramatically unfolded his tale. As the events became more distant in time, the account of them probably tended to follow the pattern of more ancient traditional lays in the teller's repertory and to reflect the notions of honour, justice, transience and fate dominant in Germanic society.

So a legend acquired an ideal structure that belonged to art rather than history. Ermanaric (O.E. Eormenric, O.N. Jörmunrekkr, M.H.G. Ermenrich) is said by the contemporary (4th-century) historian Ammianus Marcellinus to have killed himself before his imminent defeat by the invading Huns. Historians in the 6th century state that Ermanaric was severely wounded by two brothers (Sarus and Ammius); they avenged their sister (Sunilda), whom Ermanaric had had torn to death by wild horses because her husband had deserted him; Ermanaric died of the double misfortune of his wounds and the incursions of the Huns (see also ERMANARIC). Norse poetic tradition (based on German tradition and most fully preserved in the *Edda*) presents a close-knit tragic story: Jörmunrekkr (Ermanaric) had his own wife (Svanhildr) trampled to death by horses, because she had been accused by an evil counselor of adultery with Jörmunrekkr's son. He has his son hanged. As her brothers (Sörli and Hamðir) set out to avenge her, their bastard half-brother offers to help them. They mock him; he answers them scornfully, and they kill him for his insolence. They reach the hall of the Goths, beat them back, cut off Jörmunrekkr's hands and feet (a detail preserved also in a German chronicle of the early 11th century) and taunt him. He shouts to the Goths to stone these men whom weapons will not bite, and they are stoned to death, acknowledging the cause of their failure: had their half-brother been with them, Jörmunrekkr's head would not have been on his shoulders to shout that order. From the story of Ermanaric the historical and political elements have been lost; it has become a tale of domestic tragedy and revenge. Perhaps because Ermanaric was not, historically, killed outright by attackers, a later poet attributed guilt and failure to the avenging brothers.

Similarly, the history of Gundicarius the Burgundian (O.E. Guðere, O.N. Gunnar, M.H.G. Gunther), who was killed in battle against the Huns (not led by Attila) in 437, and of Attila (O.E. Ætla, O.N. Atli, M.H.G. Etzel), who died in 453, drunk, in his bed, choked by nosebleeding on the night of his wedding to Ildico (probably a German woman), is transformed in heroic legend (preserved in the *Edda*); Gunnar is flung to his death in a snake-pit by Atli, who wishes to extort from him the hiding place of his treasure. In revenge Atli's wife, Guðrun, the sister of Gunnarr (Kriemhild in the *Nibelungenlied*), kills her children by Atli and serves them to him as food; then, when he is drunk, she murders him in his bed and sets fire to the hall over the sleeping Huns. As in the tale of Jörmunrekkr, certain pivotal facts are preserved from history, and the horror and tension of the story spring from the violation of bonds of blood and marriage.

In later German and Norse tradition this legend is linked with that of Brunhild (*q.v.*; O.N. Brynhildr, M.H.G. Brünhilt), who though she may be ultimately traceable to the Visigothic princess Brunichildis of Toledo, wife of Sigyberthus of the Franks, becomes in legend either a spellbound princess (*Edda*) or an Amazonian queen intractable to wooers (*Nibelungenlied*). Gunnarr the Burgundian wins her as his bride with the help (though she does not know it) of Sigurðr (Sifrit in the *Nibelungenlied*), the most famous hero and dragon-slayer of Germanic legend (see SIEGFRIED). He is the first husband of Gunnarr's sister Guðrun. When later, at Brynhildr's instigation, Gunnarr has caused Sigurðr's death, he inherits the dragon's treasure hoard. For this hoard Gunnarr is murdered by Atli. The chain of guilt and retribution is extended as one legend is linked with another.

The final extension of this cycle is the inclusion of the story of Jörmunrekkr. Svanhildr becomes the daughter of Sigurðr and Guðrun; Sörli and Hamðir are Guðrun's sons by a third marriage, and it is she who dispatches them on their fatal journey to avenge their sister. Guðrun is now the central figure of the cycle: all griefs accumulate on her head; she suffers as wife, sister and mother (*Edda*). In the *Nibelungenlied* the romantic taste of a later age makes Guðrun (Kriemhild), remarried to Etzel, betray her brother Gunnar (Gunther) to his death in revenge for her peerless husband Sifrit (Siegfried).

No versions of the stories of Attila, Gundicarius and Ermanaric survive in Old English, though the names Ætla, Guðere, Hagen in *Widsið* and the reference in *Beowulf* to Sigemund (in O.N. and M.H.G. the father of Sigurðr-Sifrit) suggest that the Nibelung story may once have been known in England, and the allusions to Eormenric in *Deor* and *Beowulf* shows that cruel legends of his tyrannies were also current there.

Heroes and Gods.—While the legends of dragon-slaying heroes may ultimately be traceable to myths of the god who contends with the serpent of Chaos and Death (*see* DRAGON), in Germanic legend the tales of heroes and those of the gods have little to do with each other. Only in late Viking tradition does Oðinn become lord of the heroes; they feast with him in Valhöll and will fight on the side of the gods at Ragnarök.

See also articles on the literatures of the Germanic peoples and on other mythologies and such related articles as HERO, etc.

BIBLIOGRAPHY.—*The Gods*: J. Grimm, *Teutonic Mythology*, Eng. trans. (1880–83); V. Rydberg, *Teutonic Mythology*, Eng. trans. (1889); P. D. Chantepie de la Saussaye, *The Religion of the Teutons*, Eng. trans. (1902); R. Jente, *Die mythologischen Ausdrücke im altenglischen Wortschatz* (1921); E. A. Philippson, *Germanisches Heidentum bei den Angelsachsen* (1929); J. A. MacCulloch, *The Mythology of all Races, II. Eddic* (1930); V. Grönbech, *The Culture of the Teutons*, Eng. trans. (1932); F. Ström, *Loki* (1956); J. de Vries, *Altgermanische Religionsgeschichte*, 2nd ed., and bibliography there cited (1956–57); G. Dumézil, *Les Dieux des Germains* (1959), *La Saga de Hadingus* (1953) and *Loki*, rev. ed. (1959); H. Ellis-Davidson, *Gods and Myths of Northern Europe* (1964); G. Turville-Petre, *Myth and Religion of the North* (1964).

The Heroes: W. P. Ker, *Epic and Romance* (1897; 2nd ed., 1908) and *The Dark Ages* (1904); A. Heusler, *Lied und Epos in germanischer Sagendichtung* (1905) and *Die altgermanische Dichtung*, vol. xi of *Handbuch der Literaturwissenschaft*, ed. by O. F. Walzel (1924); R. W. Chambers, *Widsið* (1912); H. M. Chadwick, *The Heroic Age* (1912); A. Olrik, *The Heroic Legends of Denmark* (1919); H. Schneider, *Germanische Heldensage* (1928); H. de Boor, *Das Attilabild in Geschichte, Legende und heroischer Dichtung* (1932); H. M. and N. K. Chadwick, *The Growth of Literature*, 3 vol. (1932–40); C. Brady, *The Legends of Ermanaric* (1943); P. Courcelle, *Histoire littéraire des grandes invasions germaniques* (1948); G. Zink, *Les Légendes héroiques de Dietrich et d'Ermrich dans les littératures germaniques* (1950); C. M. Bowra, *Heroic Poetry* (1952); H. Kuhn, "Heldensage vor und ausserhalb der Dichtung," in *F. Genzmer Festschrift* (1952); O. Höfler, *Siegfried, Arminius und die Symbolik* (1961); J. de Vries, *Heroic Song and Heroic Legend*, Eng. trans. (1963). (U. M. D.)

GERMANIC PEOPLES. The Germanic, or Teutonic, peoples are a branch of the Indo-Europeans; that is, the peoples of Asia and Europe whose original common language was Indo-European (q.v.). Their origin is a problem of profound obscurity and discussion of it is riddled with doubt and dispute. A major cause of the difficulty is the paucity of archaeological finds relating to them in northern Germany and southern Sweden between the end of the Bronze Age (c. 500–400 B.C.) and the 2nd century B.C. It may be supposed, however, that in the Late Bronze Age Germanic peoples inhabited southern Sweden, the Danish peninsula and northern Germany between the Ems and Oder rivers and the Harz mountains. The Vandals, Gepidae and Goths migrated from southern Sweden in the closing centuries B.C. and occupied the area of the southern Baltic coast between the Oder and the Vistula and even beyond to the Passarge (Pasleka) river. At an early date there was also migration toward the south and west at the expense of the Celtic peoples who then inhabited much of western Germany: the Helvetii, for example, who were confined to Switzerland in the 1st century B.C., had once extended as far as the Main river.

By the time of Julius Caesar Germans were established west of the Rhine and toward the south had reached the Danube. Their first great clash with Romans came at the end of the 2nd century B.C., when the Cimbri and Teutoni (Teutones) invaded southern Gaul and northern Italy and were annihilated by Marius in 102 and 101. But although individual travelers from the time of Pytheas onward had visited Teutonic countries in the north, it was not until the 1st century B.C. was well advanced that the Romans learned to distinguish precisely between the Germans and the Celts, a distinction that is made with great clarity by Julius Caesar. It was Caesar who incorporated within the frontiers of the Roman empire those Germans who had penetrated west of the Rhine and it is he who gives the earliest extant description of Germanic culture. In 9 B.C. the Romans pushed their frontier eastward from the Rhine to the Elbe but in A.D. 9 a revolt of their subject Germans headed by Arminius (q.v.) ended in the destruction of the occupying army of P. Quinctilius Varus in the Teutoburg forest and in the withdrawal of the Roman frontier to the Rhine. In this period of occupation and during the numerous wars fought between Rome and the Germans in the 1st century A.D., enormous quantities of information about the Germans reached Rome, and when Tacitus published in A.D. 98 the book now known as the

Germania, he had reliable sources of information on which to draw. The book is one of the most valuable ethnographical works in existence; archaeology has in many ways supplemented the information Tacitus gives but in general it has tended only to confirm his accuracy and to illustrate his insight into his subject.

Tacitus relates that according to their ancient songs the Germans were descended from the three sons of Mannus (perhaps "Man"), the son of the god Tuisto, the son of Earth. Hence they were divided into three groups: the Ingaevones, the Herminones and the Istaevones. The first of these groups embraced the peoples of the northwest, the second those of the interior and the third the remainder (those near the Rhine?). These names, which are also mentioned by the elder Pliny and in a 6th-century Frankish document, are clearly of great antiquity but Tacitus gives no further information about them, and what this grouping amounted to in practice or what it was originally based on is unknown. Indeed the historian records a variant form of the genealogy according to which Mannus had a larger number of sons, who were regarded as the ancestors of the Suebi, the Vandals and others. At any rate the existence of these poems suggests that in Tacitus' time the various Germanic peoples were conscious of their relationship with one another. But although individual Germans in Roman service would sometimes refer to themselves as *Germani*, the free Germans beyond the Rhine had no collective name for themselves until the 11th century A.D., when the adjective *diutisc*, "popular" (modern *deutsch*), came into fashion. A famous sentence in which Tacitus attempts to account for the origin of the word *Germani* as a generic term has been interminably discussed. Its general sense is that *Germani* was originally the name of one Germanic people, the people later known as the Tungri. When the Tungri first crossed the Rhine at an unknown date into the Meuse valley (where they have given their name to Tongeren or Tongres in Belgium) and expelled the Gauls there from their habitations, their name, which was *Germani* at that time, was applied to all their fellow countrymen. (Similarly, the Hellenes were called *Graeci* by the French call the Germans *Allemands* after the Alamanni.) The meaning of the word *Germani* and the language to which it belongs are unknown.

Distribution.—The principal Germanic peoples were distributed as follows in the time of Tacitus. The Chatti lived in what is now Hesse. The Frisii inhabited the coastlands between the Rhine and the Ems. The Chauci were at the mouth of the Weser and south of them lived the Cherusci, the people of Arminius. The Suebi, who have given their name to Schwaben, were a group of peoples inhabiting Mecklenburg, Brandenburg, Saxony and Thuringia; the Semnones, living around the Havel and the Spree rivers, were a Suebic people, as were the Langobardi (Lombards) who lived northwest of the Semnones. Among the seven peoples who worshiped the goddess Nerthus were the Angli (Angles), centred on the peninsula of Angeln in eastern Schleswig. As for the Danubian frontier of the Roman empire, the Hermunduri extended from the neighbourhood of Regensburg northward through Franconia to Thuringia. The Marcomanni, who had previously lived in the Main valley, migrated during the last decade B.C. to Bohemia (which had hitherto been occupied by a Celtic people called the Boii), where their eastern neighbours were the Quadi in Moravia. On the lower Danube were a people called the Bastarnae, who are usually thought to have been Germans. The Goths, Gepidae and Vandals on the Baltic coast have already been mentioned. Tacitus mentions the Suiones and the Sitones as living in Sweden. He also speaks of several other peoples of less historical importance than those listed here but he knows nothing of the Saxons, the Burgundians and others who became prominent after his time.

By the end of the 3rd century A.D. important changes had taken place. East of the Rhine there now lived three great confederacies of peoples unknown to Tacitus. The Roman frontier on the lower Rhine now faced the Franks. The Main valley was occupied from c. 260 by the Burgundians, while the *agri decumates* (q.v.) were held by the Alamanni. The Burgundians appear to have been immigrants from eastern Germany. The Franks and the Alamanni may have been confederacies of peoples who had lived in these respective areas in Tacitus' day, though perhaps with an admixture of immigrants from the east. The peoples whom Tacitus mentions as living on the Baltic coast had moved southeastward in the second half of the 2nd century. The Goths now controlled the Ukraine and much of modern Rumania; the Gepidae were in the mountains north of Transylvania with the Vandals as their western neighbours.

By the year 500 further striking changes had taken place. The Angles and Saxons were in England and the Franks controlled northeastern Gaul. The Burgundians were in the Rhône valley with the Visigoths as their western neighbours. The Ostrogoths were established in Italy and the Vandals in Africa. In 507 the Franks expelled the Visigoths from most of their Gallic possessions, which had stretched from the Pyrenees to the Loire river, and the Visigoths thereafter lived in Spain until their extinction by the Muslims in 711. In 568 the Lombards entered Italy and lived there in an independent kingdom until they were overthrown by Charlemagne (774). The areas of eastern Germany vacated by the Goths and others were filled up by the Slavs, who extended westward as far as Bohemia and the basin of the Elbe. After the 8th century the Germans recovered eastern Germany, lower Austria and much of Styria and Carinthia from the Slavs.

Material Civilization.—According to Julius Caesar the Germans were not primarily agriculturists; they were pastoralists and the bulk of their foodstuffs—milk, cheese and meat—came from their flocks and herds. But agriculture was not unknown and Caesar's description of their system of land tenure has been much debated. His words are:

No one has a fixed measure of land as a private property; but the magistrates and leading men distribute every year to the clans and groups of kinsmen [what follows in the Latin text is corrupt: the words further defined the kinsmen] as much land and in such place as has seemed right to them, and in the following year force them to move on.

It does not follow from this description that any given piece of land was tilled for one year only and was thereafter deserted by the community; it cannot be inferred that the entire community abandoned its dwellings and moved on each year to completely new habitations after reaping their crops. Such a type of migratory agriculture had almost completely disappeared from Europe at a far earlier date; and such a hypothesis could hardly be reconciled with the archaeological evidence, which shows German settlements continuously inhabited for very long periods of time. The correct inference would seem to be that the same piece of land was used by the same community indefinitely but that the arable land was redistributed annually so that the one kindred did not till the one piece of land for more than a year. A further inference is that land was not privately owned in the middle of the 1st century B.C., but was in some sense the property of the community: in the case of the Suebi, Caesar emphasizes this point. What exactly is to be understood by the "community" in this context Caesar does not make clear. Is he speaking of villages or of *pagi* (these appear to have been adjacent groups of kindreds but information about them is very meagre) or of some other unit? At all events, it seems certain that the leading men distributed each piece of arable land not to individual cultivators but to kindreds, which tilled their allotment in common. This system of annual redistribution ensured the general equality of the kindreds insofar as agriculture was concerned, and Caesar comments that it guaranteed that the masses of the warriors would be contented and disinclined to engage in factional strife and revolt.

As regards Tacitus' description of Germanic land tenure, it must be remembered that he is discussing the situation as it existed more than 100 years after Caesar had been on the Rhine and at a date when the proximity of Roman civilization had possibly brought about considerable changes in Germanic society. His words are:

Lands proportionate in extent to the number of cultivators are occupied in turn by the whole body of them, and these they then divide among themselves according to social standing: distribution is easy owing to the wide expanse of ground. They change their arable every year and yet there is land in abundance.

Whatever is to be made of this, one point seems clear: although the annual redistribution mentioned by Caesar was still practised, the arable land was now allotted not to kindreds but to individuals—

the term "social standing" (*dignationem*) makes this certain. In other words, although the private ownership of land was not yet known in Germany, it had come perceptibly closer than it had been in Caesar's day. The kindred, at any rate in matters relating to agriculture, was no longer the basic unit of Germanic society; its place had been taken by the individual. When Tacitus goes on to say that grain alone was grown by the Germans, he is in error; a great variety of root crops and vegetables was known to them, though of fruits only the apple was cultivated by them in the Roman period. As for the techniques of agriculture, Caesar and Tacitus are silent on these, but even the Bronze Age rock carvings at Bohuslän in southern Sweden include a picture of an ox-drawn plow.

It must be stressed, however, that cattle were the main source of food for the Germans. There is no reason to think that in the historical period cattle were owned by the clan collectively; they were the private property of individuals and a man's status was reckoned on the basis of the number of cattle he owned. Both the cattle and the horses of the Germans were of poor quality by Roman standards.

The Iron Age had begun in Germany about four centuries before the days of Caesar but even in his time metal appears to have been a luxury material for domestic utensils, most of which were made of wood, leather or clay. Of the larger metal objects used by them, most were still made of bronze, though this was not the case with weapons. Pottery was for the most part still made by hand and pots turned on the wheel were distinctly unusual. On the problem of whether writing existed among them at this date *see* RUNE.

The degree to which trade was developed in early Germany is very obscure. There was certainly a slave trade and many slaves were sold to the Romans. Such potters as used the wheel—and these were very few—and smiths and miners no doubt sold their products. But in general the average Germanic village is unlikely to have used many objects that had not been made at home. Foreign merchants dealing in Italian as well as Celtic wares were active in Germany in Caesar's time and supplied prosperous warriors with wine, bronze vessels and so on. But from the reign of Augustus onward there was a huge increase in German imports from the Roman empire. The German leaders were now able to buy whole categories of goods—glass vessels, red tableware, Roman weapons, brooches, statuettes, ornaments of various kinds and other objects—that had not reached them before. These Roman products brought their owners much prestige but how the Germans paid for them is not fully known. The amber trade, however, became important after the middle of the 1st century B.C., though for the most part it affected eastern Germany alone.

Form of Government.—No trace of autocracy can be found among the Germans whom Caesar describes. The leading men of the *pagi* would try to patch up such disputes as arose but they acted only in those disputes that broke out between members of their own *pagus*. When disputes arose between persons belonging to different *pagi* there appears to have been no mediatory body at this date. In fact in peacetime there seems to have been no central authority that could issue orders to, or exercise influence over, all the *pagi* of which any one people (*civitas, Stamm*) was composed. Evidently the clans or groups of clans were more or less independent of one another in internal affairs and on at least some occasions they could act independently even in their foreign relations. Some clans or *pagi* could, for example, negotiate with the Romans without reference to the other clans of which their people was composed. Caesar relates, however, that in wartime a number of confederate chieftains were elected and he gives no indication that any one of them had greater authority than the others; they were joint leaders and they held office only in time of war. It was still the case among some Germanic peoples in the 4th century A.D. and even later there was normally no one over-all peacetime chieftain. Nor was the multiple war leadership quick to disappear in all parts of Germany; it could still be found among the Franks, Burgundians and Alamanni in the 4th and 5th centuries.

A new type of military chieftainship had come into being by the time Tacitus wrote. This type of chieftain was also elective but not all the warriors were eligible for election. The office was confined to the members of a recognized "royal clan," such as is known to have existed among the 1st-century Cherusci and Batavians, the 6th-century Heruli (q.v.) and others. Any member of this royal clan was eligible for election and the chieftainship was in no way hereditary. There is no conclusive evidence that any Germanic chieftain of the 1st century A.D. was followed as leader of his people by his son. A chief of this type held office for life and had religious as well as military duties. But he was in no sense an autocrat. He could be overruled by the council of the leading men and the proposals he laid before the general assembly of the warriors might be rejected by them. On the battlefield, too, he had no powers of coercion; he could only set an example and give advice. The degree of his influence, in fact, depended largely on his own personal qualities. Among the peoples who retained the type of chieftainship described by Caesar, it became very common to appoint two leaders to hold office simultaneously but the chief of the type mentioned by Tacitus had no colleague.

The council of the leading men (principes) dealt with matters of minor importance affecting the people as a whole, while the most weighty business was decided by the general assembly of the warriors, though this too received preliminary consideration in the council of the leading men. Little is known of how these leading men were appointed, or of their numbers or whether each pagus necessarily had one or more representatives on the council. As for the general assembly, all the warriors had the right to attend its meetings except those who had thrown away their shields in battle. The assembly could not initiate measures nor does it seem to have had the right to debate any proposals put to it by the chief or the leading men; it could only adopt or reject their proposals, but its decision was final. It is not known what happened when opinion was divided in the assembly but there were certainly no means by which a substantial minority of the warriors could have been coerced into a course of action of which they strongly disapproved. The assembly exercised judicial functions in cases that were felt to affect the community as a whole. Tacitus lists treachery, desertion, cowardice and homosexuality as examples and for all these offenses the penalty was death.

As for the administration of justice in general, it has been seen that in Caesar's day the leading men of each pagus tried to settle disputes that arose within the pagus. There is no evidence that they could oblige the disputants to appear before them or that they could enforce their decisions; they could, it seems, only use their influence. But in Tacitus' time the general assembly elected a number of the leading men to act as judges and these judges traveled through the villages to hear private suits. Each of them was accompanied by 100 attendants to lend authority to his decisions. That is to say, the judge now came into the community from outside and he might well be a stranger to those among whom he was to adjudicate. A rudimentary judicial apparatus had come into existence. A person who was found guilty by these judges had to pay a number of horses or cattle proportionate to the gravity of his offense. But many disputes—e.g., those arising from homicide, wounding or theft—continued to be settled by the kindreds themselves, and the blood feuds to which they gave rise might continue from generation to generation. Long after the conversion to Christianity the German rulers found it difficult to stamp out the blood feud.

It is possible, then, to detect a considerable development in Germanic society between the time of Caesar and that of Tacitus. In the 1st century A.D. the Germans were less primitive than they had been in Caesar's day. The rudiments of the state had now made their appearance. Power, insofar as it existed at all, was tending to become concentrated and wealth to accumulate in private hands. Perhaps the most remarkable development concerns the "retinue" (comitatus). In Caesar's day one of the leading men would announce in the assembly that he proposed to undertake a foray and would call for followers. Whoever was attracted by the proposal would volunteer his services and when he had done so the relationship between the leader and his followers was a purely temporary one, lasting only for the duration of the raid, and the followers could not be described as dependents of the leader. But in the time of which Tacitus speaks the relationship between the leader and his "companions" (comites) had become a permanent one. The leader fed them and kept them about him in peacetime as well as in war. He supplied them with their weapons and horses and with a share in the booty taken during their raids, though in these early times he could not supply them with land, for full private ownership of land did not yet exist. The retinue leaders thus acquired a military force over which the other warriors had little or no control and his followers were prepared to fight for him to the death—it was a disgrace for them to survive their leader. The members of the retinues seem nearly always to have been drawn from among the more well-to-do warriors, so that in Tacitus' time the tribal aristocracy appeared to be well on the way to overthrowing the primitive democracy described above and to establishing something like state power among the various peoples. But in fact only one Germanic chieftain is known who was able before A.D. 100 to set up a personal tyranny over his people. This was Marobodus, who led the Marcomanni from their homes in the Main valley c. 9 B.C. and settled them in Bohemia. From there he conquered a considerable number of other Germanic peoples between the Elbe and the Vistula, including the Semnones, the Lombards and the Lugii. But the Cherusci, joined by some of the king's subjects, attacked him in A.D. 17, overthrew him and drove him into the Roman empire. All other chiefs who attempted in this period to establish monarchies were, so far as is known, defeated.

Many of the peoples who had been prominent in western Germany in the days of Tacitus disappeared from history during the 2nd century and their place was taken by the Franks, Burgundians, Alamanni and others. Sources for their internal and social history during the 3rd and later centuries are very fragmentary and uninformative. In general it is not easy to detect any substantial difference in their material civilization or social organization from what Tacitus had described, except that there is now little or no evidence for the existence of the general assembly of the warriors among any of the great peoples living along the Rhine and the Danube. Thus information about the Visigoths is more abundant than information about any of the other peoples but nothing is ever said by any ancient authorities about the Visigothic warriors having the right to assemble together in order to approve or veto the recommendations of their leaders. This suggests that in the 4th century the rank and file of the population had less control over their own affairs than they had had 300 years earlier. Even so, there are few reports in this period of the overthrow of such democratic institutions as still existed or of the establishment of monarchies. The only certain example is that of Ermanaric (q.v.), who ruled the Ostrogoths in the Ukraine as a king in the middle of the 4th century. The monarchy did not become fully established in the Germanic world until German peoples had settled as federates inside the Roman empire, and the leaders of the Ostrogoths in Italy, the Visigoths in Gaul and Spain, the Vandals in Africa and so on are the first Germanic kings. Other famous German chieftains in this period, such as Athanaric and Alaric (q.v.), who either lived outside the Roman frontier or whose peoples were not federates settled in the provinces under a treaty (foedus) to defend the frontier, seem to have had little more personal authority than the war leaders described by Tacitus.

Warfare.—In the period of the early Roman empire German weapons, both offensive and defensive, were characterized by shortage of metal. The warrior, whether mounted or on foot, had as his chief weapon a long lance with one end hardened by fire or else fitted with a short, narrow iron point, which could be hurled or used for thrusting. But very few of them carried swords. Helmets and breastplates were almost unknown and the German went into battle naked or wearing a short cloak. His only defensive weapon was a light wooden or wicker shield, sometimes fitted with an iron rim and sometimes strengthened with leather. This lack of adequate equipment explains the swift, fierce rush with which the Germans would charge the ranks of the heavily armed Romans. Their only hope of overwhelming a Roman army in open country was to break it by the impetus of their first attack, for if they became entangled in a prolonged, hand-to-hand grapple, where their light shields and thrusting spears were confronted with Roman arms and armour,

GERMANIUM

they had little hope of success. Their best plan was to catch the Romans on an open plain surrounded by woods and then to launch incessant, short, sharp attacks on them from all sides, using the woods as cover.

In the period of the later Roman empire the equipment of the German warriors does not seem to have improved very much. In the 3rd century they began to use bows and arrows extensively, which they had not done before, but their armies were still mainly infantry. Even in the 6th century there is no reason to think that helmets and breastplates were not something of a rarity in the armies of the Germanic peoples who were now living in what had been the Roman provinces. The Ostrogothic army in Italy which fought against Belisarius was an army of mounted spearmen supported by unmounted archers. Such, too, was the army of the Vandals (q.v.) in Africa in the 6th century and the army of the Visigoths in Spain in the 6th and 7th centuries. These peoples seem to have had a higher percentage of cavalry in their armed forces than the Germans had had in Tacitus' day, but in defensive armour little progress had been made. The Frankish army was different. Its main strength lay not in mounted spearmen but in its infantry, whose characteristic weapon was a short-handled, double-headed ax used as a missile weapon. The Frankish infantry, too, wore little defensive armour. None of these peoples evolved a military force adequate to deal with the heavily armed mounted archers of Justinian I. Nor did they master the art of siege warfare; throughout the first six centuries A.D. there is no report of a Roman town skilfully and successfully besieged by a German army (the fall of Philippopolis in 250-251 was due to the treachery of the governor).

Conversion to Christianity.—For primitive Germanic paganism see GERMANIC MYTHOLOGY AND HEROIC LEGENDS. Christianity was first brought to the Visigoths by some of the prisoners whom they took during their raids on Asia Minor in the mid-3rd century (see ULFILAS). But the Visigoths do not seem to have been converted to Christianity until they were living as federates in the Roman province of Moesia (south of the lower Danube) in the years 382-395. The evidence suggests that before the fall of the Western Roman empire in 476 none of the great Germanic peoples was converted to Christianity while still living outside the Roman frontier but that all the Germanic peoples who moved into the Roman provinces before that date were converted to Christianity within a generation of their arrival on Roman soil. The Vandals seem to have been converted when in Spain in 409-429, the Burgundians when in eastern Gaul in 412-436, the Ostrogoths when in the province of Pannonia c. 456-472 and so on. The only certain exception is the people known as the Rugi, who were already Christian before 482 while living north of the Danube in lower Austria; in what circumstances they had been converted is not known. In all these cases it seems likely that the conversion was carried through by German-speaking and not by Roman missionaries, and Visigothic priests are likely to have played a major part in the process.

In all these cases the Germans embraced the Arian form of Christianity: none of the major Germanic peoples became officially Catholic until the conversion of the Franks under Clovis (496) and of the Burgundians under Sigismund. The reason for their adoption of Arianism rather than Catholicism is very obscure. Unhappily, the books produced by the Arian Germans have all disappeared with the exception of the fragments of Ulfilas' Bible, some leaves of an anonymous Gothic commentary on St. John's Gospel and a fragment of a church calendar written in Gothic. It is clear, however, that their theology was peculiarly arid, depending on a literal interpretation of the Scriptures and refraining from drawing practical lessons from the texts. But although the pagan Germans living outside the Roman frontier once or twice persecuted the Christians in their midst, the Arian German kings, with the exception of the Vandal kings of Africa, were extraordinarily tolerant both of Catholics and of Jews.

The last Germanic people on the continent to be converted to Christianity were the Old Saxons (second half of the 8th century), while the Scandinavian peoples were converted in the 10th century, though several districts there remained pagan until late in the 11th century. England had been converted in the 7th century, while Christianity obtained public recognition in Iceland in the year 1000. (See also GOTHS.)

See also references under "Germanic Peoples" in the Index, and separate articles on the various tribes.

BIBLIOGRAPHY.—For the archaeological evidence see especially the excellent bibliography to G. Ekholm, Cambridge Ancient History, vol. xi, ch. 2 (1936); for current finds consult the periodical Germania. On Roman objects of trade imported into Germany, H. J. Eggers, Der römische Import im freien Germanien (1951), is fundamental; i det fria Germanien (1926). On German weapons and armour see M. Jahn, Die Bewaffnung der Germanen (1916). The best commentaries on Tacitus' Germania are those of J. G. C. Anderson (1938); see also E. Norden, Die germanische Urgeschichte in Tacitus Germania (1920), Alt-Germanien (1934). On early Germanic history to the end of the migration period see L. Schmidt, Geschichte der deutschen Stämme (1934-38); for their wars with the Romans see the relevant chapters of the Cambridge Ancient History, especially those by R. Syme in vol. x-xi (1934, 1936). For the period of the later Roman empire see O. Seeck, Geschichte des Untergangs der antiken Welt (1921); J. B. Bury, History of the Later Roman Empire (1923), The Invasion of Europe by the Barbarians (1928); E. Stein, Histoire du Bas-Empire (1949-60). For the conversion to Christianity see K. D. Schmidt, Die Bekehrung der Germanen zum Christentum (1939); H. E. Giesecke, Die Ostgermanen und der Arianismus (1939). (E. A. T.)

GERMANIUM, a chemical element notable for its remarkable electrical properties, is a silvery gray solid with a metallic appearance; however, it is generally regarded as a metalloid with properties somewhere between a true metal and a nonmetal. It is in the fourth group of the periodic table (see PERIODIC LAW) between silicon and tin. It is brittle and nonductile; it crystallizes in the diamond lattice. Its symbol is Ge, atomic number 32, and its atomic weight 72.59. It has five stable isotopes with masses from 70 to 76, and nine radioisotopes, the latter with masses from 65 to 78, having relatively short half-lifes.

In 1871, D. I. Mendeléyev predicted the existence and properties of a hypothetical element between silicon and tin that he called eka-silicon. In 1886, C. Winkler, in analyzing the sulfide mineral argyrodite, found a previously unknown constituent that he succeeded in isolating and to which he gave the name germanium after his native country. Further investigation definitely fixed the position of germanium in the periodic table between silicon and tin, confirming Mendeléyev's predictions.

Even though germanium had been known for many years, it attained importance only after 1945 when it may be said to have initiated a revolution in electronics. This application is based upon the fact that being a metalloid it belongs to a class of materials known as semiconductors; i.e., with electrical conductivity midway between a metal and a nonmetal. This characteristic permits the use of germanium devices as replacements for many of the former applications of vacuum tubes and rectifiers, as well as in newer electronic devices, such as transistors, used for a variety of purposes. (See Uses below.)

Sources and Preparation.—Germanium is a rare element, its occurrence in the Earth's crust being estimated at about 0.0004 to 0.0007%. This occurrence exceeds the content of such elements as beryllium, boron, arsenic, silver, gold, platinum, and uranium but is somewhat lower than that of such elements as lead, zinc, and tin. The problem of recovery is complicated by the fact that there is very little natural concentration such as occurs with the other elements mentioned.

Germanium is never found in the free state. It is a constituent of the following uncommon minerals: argyrodite ($4Ag_2S \cdot GeS_2$ 6 to 7% germanium); germanite ($7CuS \cdot FeS \cdot GeS_2$—8.7% germanium); and renierite (a Cu, Fe, Ge, As sulfide with about 5-7% germanium). The last two minerals have been found in South West Africa and the Democratic Republic of the Congo.

The three chief sources of germanium are: (1) the zinc sulfide concentrates of the Tri-State zinc-lead mining district of Missouri, Kansas, and Oklahoma, which contain about 60% zinc and 0.010 to 0.015% germanium; (2) certain metallurgical residues resulting from treatment of copper-zinc ores from the Democratic Republic of the Congo; as well as (3) residues coming from the treatment

GERMANIUM

of copper-lead-zinc ores from South West Africa, the latter two now being the world's largest single sources of germanium. In all cases, after preliminary steps suitable to the particular source, the resulting low-grade germanium residues are treated with strong hydrochloric acid and the germanium chloride is distilled off. This crude chloride is purified by successive distillations. The highly pure product is hydrolyzed in water to form germanium dioxide, which is then reduced to powdered metal by hydrogen in graphite boats at a temperature of about 650° C. After reduction, the powdered "metal" is melted into ingots or billets in an inert atmosphere at about 1,100° C.

Germanium also occurs in minute amounts in bituminous coals from many parts of the world, including the United States. Under certain conditions of combustion, germanium will concentrate in the flue dusts, from which it can be extracted. As far as is known, however, this source of germanium has been exploited only in Japan and England, and possibly in Russia. With new sources coming on the market, material of this type probably is no longer utilized. The process was rather complicated, but eventually a crude germanium tetrachloride was distilled off and purified in much the same way as described above.

Properties.—Germanium has valences of both two and four, but compounds of the latter valency are more stable and more numerous. The metal is quite stable at atmospheric temperature. At 600° to 700° C oxidation in air or oxygen proceeds. Germanium reacts readily with the halogens to form corresponding tetrachlorides. Of the common acids, only nitric acid and aqua regia will attack germanium appreciably. Caustic solutions have little or no effect on germanium, but it will quickly dissolve in molten sodium or potassium hydroxide, forming the germanates.

Some Physical Properties of Germanium

Crystal Structure	Diamond cubic
Ductility	Frangible
Hardness, Mohs' scale . .	6.0
Melting point, °C . .	937.4
Boiling point, °C . .	2,832 (approx.)
Vapour pressure at 27° C, atm. .	1.1×10^{-9}
Density at 25° C (g./c.c.) .	5.323
Specific heat (0–100° C) (cal./g./°C) .	0.074
Intrinsic resistivity at 25° C, ohm-cm^2 .	53.0
Index of refraction, n_o . .	3.994

Compounds.—The two most important compounds are the dioxide (GeO_2) and the tetrachloride ($GeCl_4$), both intermediate products in the processing of raw materials to metal. The dioxide is a white crystalline material, the exact crystal structure depending upon conditions of formation and the subsequent treatment. The common or hexagonal form, sometimes called "soluble" because it is sparingly soluble in water (0.45% at 25° C), is moderately reactive chemically; while the insoluble (0.00045%) tetragonal is quite unreactive, requiring the use of an alkali fusion to get it into solution.

Germanates analogous to silicates exist and can be formed by heating the dioxide with basic oxides. One of these, zinc germanate (Zn_2GeO_2) is used as a phosphor. Germanous monoxide (GeO) is a black powder that oxidizes readily to the dioxide upon heating in air. Germanium tetrachloride is a volatile colourless liquid, freezing at about −50° C and boiling at 83° C. Tests indicate that neither germanium nor germanium dioxide are toxic, although the tetrachloride causes irritation when inhaled, undoubtedly because of hydrolysis that frees hydrochloric acid.

Analysis.—Spectrographic methods having a range of 0.002 to 1% germanium and an accuracy within 10% are usually employed for the analysis of most raw materials because of their low germanium content. Germanium (over a range of 0.01 to 100%) may be determined gravimetrically by first distilling off as the tetrachloride in a closed system, then precipitating the germanium as the sulfide in an acid solution, followed by conversion to the dioxide under carefully controlled conditions, and weighing. A titrimetric method (also satisfactory over a range of 0.01 to 100%) may be used. The germanium is distilled off as tetrachloride (as above) and reduced to the germanite ion by boiling with sodium hypophosphite. The reduced germanium (in solution) is reoxidized to germanate ion by titration with a standard potassium iodate solution in a closed system.

Analysis of the purer grades of germanium and germanium dioxide offers serious problems because of the minute amounts of impurities. Spectrographic methods were being used in some cases in the late 1960s but had their limitations as did chemical methods. To determine the suitability of germanium for specific semiconductor applications, use of an electrical resistivity method was the preferred procedure.

Uses.—The availability of germanium of an extraordinarily high degree of purity was responsible for the revolution in electronics that began toward the close of World War II. This application is by far the major use of germanium. A succession of devices such as diodes, transistors, and rectifiers were developed to perform most of the functions of vacuum tubes, as well as other functions that a tube will not handle. These devices are characterized by simplicity and ruggedness, long operating life, low power consumption, and little heat emission. They begin to function immediately since there is no filament to heat. Germanium electronic devices in the late 1960s seemed to be evolving in two main directions: (1) high-performance, low-cost units for audio, radio, and high-fidelity applications, and (2) high-voltage, high-peak power capability units for television ignition and computer applications.

The germanium diode consists of a thin waferlike disk of correctly prepared germanium with a fine wire of a suitable conductive material "spotted" to it. The germanium disk and the wire are soldered to separate electrical conductors and the unit is embedded in plastic or enclosed in glass to inhibit sensitivity to moisture and ambient temperatures (which in use should not exceed 125° C). The complete assembly is smaller than a kernel of corn (maize). An interesting property of germanium diodes is their photoelectric characteristics, commercially utilized in the photodiode, that are said to have definite advantages over the electric eye.

In 1948 the germanium triode or transistor (point-contact type with two wires in contact with the germanium wafer) was announced (see TRANSISTOR: *Materials for Transistors: Control of Conductivity and Carrier Lifetime*). Since then further developments, particularly that of the diffused-junction transistor, have taken place. Transistors have proved of immense value in many applications; *e.g.*, in hearing aids, where their use has resulted in smaller and more dependable units. The use of transistors has also tremendously simplified the construction of computers and at the same time notably increased their range of applicability. Still later, large germanium junction rectifiers, both air- and water-cooled, were developed, permitting much higher current densities than selenium and copper oxide devices.

While opaque to visible light, germanium, whether mono- or polycrystalline, is transparent in the infrared region, thus making it extremely useful in infrared equipment both as a detector and as a window or lens. Lens elements and windows have been fabricated with diameters ranging from $\frac{1}{4}$ to 15 in. and in thickness from $\frac{1}{16}$ to $\frac{1}{2}$ in. The high index of refraction of germanium also renders it useful in the design of refracting optical elements.

The silica content of glasses may be replaced wholly or in part by germanium dioxide. Optical glasses so constituted show an extension in range of properties, particularly in index of refraction and dispersion. Glasses of high refractive index are used in wide-angle camera lenses, in microscope objectives, and for various military purposes. Also, germanium dioxide-containing glasses have a high infrared transmission, making them suitable for use as windows for the protection of new infrared ultrasensitive detectors developed for the space program. One such glass is made by fusing germanium dioxide (about 6%) with lead monoxide (37%) and titanium dioxide (3%). Another glass containing MgGeO₄ transmits infrared radiation over a broad spectral range and has use in infrared spectroscopes and other infrared optical instruments. Germanate glasses exhibit considerable chemical durability, will withstand thermal shock, do not soften below 400° C, and can be easily fabricated. The melting temperature of many of the germanium glasses is about 1,500° C.

The chemistry of germanium, as would be expected from its position of proximity to carbon in the periodic table, has certain similarities to the chemistry of carbon, thus stimulating much research in the field of organic germanium compounds. Such compounds seem to have possibilities as catalysts for various organic reactions such as polyester manufacture.

Germanium forms alloys with many elements, but the commercial uses of such alloys were limited in the late 1960s. Because of the similarity of the two elements, it forms a continuous series of solid solutions with silicon characterized by low thermal conductivity with consequent high efficiencies for thermoelectric power generation, resulting in devices with important commercial applications. A germanium-magnesium phosphor has been used commercially in fluorescent lights. Also, an alloy of the two elements in the ratio represented by the formula Mg_2Ge reacts with dilute acids to give a mixture of volatile hydrides (germanes) similar to the methane series of hydrocarbons. Germanium, like bismuth (and water), has the peculiar property of expanding upon freezing; even when it is alloyed with as much as 92% gold, this property persists, suggesting the use of this alloy for precision castings such as dental alloys, the colour being that of 18 k. gold.

The demand for germanium was high in the 1960s and early 1970s, due to its increased use for radiation-detection devices, thin-film glassy semiconductors, catalysts, and infrared lenses. In the mid-1960s, factory shipments of germanium diodes and transistors had reached an annual rate of about 800,000,000 units, with a value of more than $250,000,000. Although the price of germanium had decreased previously, in 1969 there were price increases for both the purified ingot and the electronic grade of germanium dioxide amounting to about 15 and 20%, respectively.

BIBLIOGRAPHY.—A. P. Thompson and J. R. Musgrave, "Germanium, Produced as a Byproduct, Has Become of Primary Importance," *Journal of Metals*, 4:1132–37 (Nov. 1952); in C. A. Hampel (ed.), *Rare Metals Handbook*, "Germanium" by H. R. Harner, pp. 188–197 (1961); Germanium Information Center, Midwest Research Institute, *Germanium* (1962–); J. R. Musgrave, "Germanium," in I. M. Kolthoff et al., *Analytical Chemistry of the Elements*, part 2 of *Treatise on Analytical Chemistry* (1964); H. R. Harner, "Germanium," in R. E. Kirk and D. F. Othmer (eds.), *Encyclopedia of Chemical Technology*, 2nd rev. ed. (1966); U.S. Department of the Interior, Bureau of Mines, *Mineral Facts and Problems*, bulletin 585, section on germanium by F. L. Fisher, pp. 341–346 (1960), *Minerals Yearbook* (published annually).
(A. P. TN.)

GERMAN LANGUAGE.

German is spoken throughout a large area in Central Europe, where it is the national language of Germany and of Austria, and one of the four national languages of Switzerland. From this homeland it has been carried by emigration to many other parts of the world: there are German-speaking communities in North and South America, South Africa, and Australia. Altogether, it is the native language of some 100,000,000 persons, and is thus the sixth largest language of the world (after Chinese, English, Hindi-Urdu, Spanish, and Russian). German is widely studied as a foreign language and is one of the main cultural languages of the Western world.

As a written language (*Schriftsprache*) German is quite uniform; it differs in Germany, Austria, and Switzerland no more than written English does in the U.S. and the British commonwealth. As a spoken language, however, German exists in far more varieties than English. At one extreme is Standard German (*Hochsprache*)—used in radio, television, public lectures, the theatre, schools, and universities—which is based on the written form of the language and is relatively uniform except that speakers often show by their accents the general areas from which they come. At the other extreme are the local dialects (*Dialekte, Mundarten*), which differ from village to village—more in some areas, less in others. Between these extremes there is a continuous scale of speech forms which, in cities, are often close to the standard and are called Colloquial German (*Umgangssprache*).

SOUNDS AND SPELLINGS

Vowels.—The vowels, in phonemic notation, are:

Short and lax	Long and tense	Diphthongal	Unstressed
i ü	i: ü:	ai	ə
e ö	e: ö:	oi	
a o	a: o:	au	

Short Vowels.—These are short and lax, *i.e.*, pronounced with relatively little muscular tension. Unlike the remaining vowels, they are also checked, *i.e.*, they occur only before consonants. The short vowels /i e a o u/ of German *mitt, Bett, hat, Gott, Busch* /mit 'bet 'hat 'got 'buš/, "with, bed, has, god, bush" are much like the vowels of English *mitt, bet, hut, bought, bush.* (The symbol /ˈ/ marks the beginning of a stressed syllable; *see* below.) Short /ü ö/ are pronounced with the tongue position of /i e/ but with the lip rounding of /u o/: *Stücke, Stöcke* /'štükə/ 'štökə/ "pieces, sticks."

Long Vowels.—These are long when stressed (less so when unstressed) and tense, *i.e.*, pronounced with relatively great muscular tension. The long vowels /i: e: a: o: u:/ of German *sie, See, sah, so, Schuh* /'zi: 'ze: 'za: 'zo: 'šu:/ "she, sea, saw, so, shoe" are much like the vowels of English *see, say, spa, so, shoe.* However, whereas the vowels of English *see, say, say, so,* tend to be lax and diphthongal (with a more or less strong upward glide), the vowels of German *sie, Schuh,* and *See, so,* are tense and steady (with no upward glide). Long /ü: ö:/ are pronounced with the tongue position of /i: e:/ but with the lip rounding of /u: o:/; as in *früh, schön* /'fru: 'šö:n/ "early, beautiful."

Diphthongs.—The diphthongs /ai oi au/ of German *bei, Heu, Bau* /'bai 'hoi 'bau/ "by, hay, building" are much like those of English *buy, boy, bough,* though shorter and tenser.

Unstressed /ə/.—The unstressed /ə/ of German *beginnen, geredet* /bə'ginən gə're:dət/ "to begin, spoken" is much like the unstressed *e* of English *begin, raided.*

Nasalized Vowels.—Four nasalized vowels /ẽ ã õ œ̃/, not listed above, are often used in loanwords from French. Examples: *Teint, Chance, Pardon, Verdun* /'tẽ 'šãsə par'dõ ver'dœ̃/ "complexion, chance, pardon, Verdun." Less elegantly, these are pronounced as vowel plus /ŋ/ as in /'teŋ 'šaŋsə par'doŋ ver'doŋ/.

Vowel Alternations.—The "plain" vowels /a o u a: o: u: ai/ often alternate with the "umlaut" vowels /e ö ü e: ö: ü: oi/, respectively, as in the following examples with plain singular but umlauted plural: *Gast, Gäste* /'gast 'gɛstə/ "guest(s)," *Götter* /'göt 'göter/ "god(s)," *Mutter, Mütter* /'mutar 'mütar/ "mother(s)," *Vater, Väter* /'fa:tar 'fe:tar/ "father(s)," *Söhne* /'zo:n 'zö:na/ "son(s)," *Brüder* /'bru:dar 'brü:dar/ "brother(s)," *Braut, Bräute* /'braut 'broita/ "bride(s)."

Spellings.—Though the spelling does not always indicate the difference between short and long vowels, the following devices are used more or less consistently. (1) A vowel is always short if followed by a double consonant letter: *still, wenn, Rasse, offen, Hütte* /'štil 'ven 'rasə 'ofan 'hütə/ "still, if, race, open, hut"; contrast the long vowels of *Stil, wen, Straße, Ofen, Hüte* /'šti:l 've:n 'štra:sa 'o:fan 'hü:ta/ "style, whom, street, stove, hats." (2) A vowel is always long if followed by an (unpronounced) *h*: *ihnen, stehlen, Kahn, wohnen, Rahm* /'i:nan 'šte:lan 'ka:n 'vo:nan 'ru:m/ "to them, to steal, barge, to live, fame"; contrast the short vowels of *innen, stellen, kann, Wonne, dumm* /'inan 'štelan 'kan 'vona 'dum/ "inside, to place, can, bliss, dumb." (3) A vowel is always long if written double: *Beet, Staat, Boot* /'be:t 'šta:t 'bo:t/ "bed, state, boat"; contrast the short vowels of *Bett, Stadt, Gott* /'bet 'štat 'got/ "bed (for sleeping), city, god." In this respect, *ie* counts as the doubled spelling of *i*; contrast the long /i:/ of *Miete* /'mi:ta/ "rent" vs. the short /i/ of *Mitte*

/'mitə/ "middle." (4) A vowel (except unstressed e) is long when it stands at the end of a word: *Schi, je, ja, so, zu* /ʃiː 'jeː 'jaː 'zoː 'tsuː/ "ski, ever, yes, so, to," and also *Nazi, Sofa, Otto, Zulu* /'naːtsi 'zoːfaˑ'oto: 'tsuːluː/ "Nazi, sofa, Otto, Zulu."

Though /e eː oi/ are usually spelled *e, e(h), eu,* they may also be spelled *ä, ä(h), äu;* and they are always spelled this latter way when they represent the umlaut of /a aː au/, respectively. Noun examples already given: *Gast, Gäste, Vater, Väter, Braut, Bräute.* Verb examples: *fallen, fällt* /'falən 'felt/ "to fall, (he) falls"; *tragen, trägt* /'traːgən, treːkt/ "to carry, (he) carries"; *laufen, läuft* /'laufən 'loift/ "to run, (he) runs." Where the letter *ä* represents a long vowel, the *Siebs* (the authority on pronunciation; see *Bibliography* below) prescribes a special long vowel /ɛː/, much like the vowel of English *fair,* e.g., *Väter, trägt* /'fɛːtər, trɛːkt/. But many German speakers use instead the ordinary /eː/, e.g., *Väter* /'feːtər/ *trägt* /'treːkt/.

Consonants.—The consonants, in phonemic notation, are:

	Labial	Apical	Palatal	Velar
Obstruents { stops	p,b	t,d		k,g
fricatives, sibilants	f,v	s,z	[ç / š,ž]	x
nasals	m	n		ŋ
liquids		l r		
glides			h j	

Twelve of the 13 obstruents occur in pairs, separated above by commas: /p t k f s š/ are fortis (pronounced with strong muscular tension) and voiceless (pronounced without simultaneous vibration of the vocal cords); /b d g v z ž/ are lenis (pronounced with weak muscular tension) and usually voiced (pronounced with simultaneous vibration of the vocal cords).

Obstruents.—German /p,b t,d k,g f,v s,z/ are pronounced much like the English sounds spelled with these letters. German /š/, as in *Schiff* /ʃif/ "ship," is pronounced much like English *sh* in *ship,* though with more lip rounding. German /ž/, which occurs only in loanwords such as *Journal* /žuːrˈnaːl/ "journal" and *Garage* /gaˈraːžə/ "garage," is pronounced much like the *z* of English *azure,* though again with more lip rounding. German /x/ is a voiceless velar fricative, like the *ch* in Scottish *loch*; German /ç/ is a voiceless palatal fricative, like the *h* that many English speakers pronounce in *hue, huge, human.* Both sounds constitute a single phoneme, spelled *ch.* This is velar /x/ after /a aː o oː u uː/, e.g., *Bach, Buch, Brauch* /bax 'buːx 'braux/ "brook, book, custom"; but it is palatal /ç/ otherwise, e.g., *Bäche, Bücher, Bräuche* /'beçə 'büːçər 'broiçə/ "brooks, books, customs," and also *manch, solch, durch, China* /'manç 'zolç 'durç 'çiːnaː/ "many a, such, through, China," as well as in the diminutive suffix *-chen,* e.g., *Mädchen* /'meːtçən/ "girl."

Nasals.—German /m n ŋ/, as in *kommen, rennen, singen* /'koman 'rɛnan 'ziŋan/ "come, run, sing," are pronounced like the nasals in English *come, run, sing.* Words like *Finger, länger, Hunger* /'fiŋər 'leŋər 'huŋər/ "finger, longer, hunger" have only /ŋ/ rather than the /ŋg/ of English *finger, longer, hunger.*

Liquids.—German /l/ is never the "dark" (velarized) *l* of English *mill,* but always the "bright" (nonvelarized) *l* which many English speakers use in *million.* German /r/ has two pronunciations. When followed by a vowel it is the voiced uvular fricative or trill [ʀ]; but when not followed by a vowel it is usually the vowel [ʌ], much like the *a* of English *sofa.* These two sounds thus alternate: [ʀ] in *lehren, Leere, bessere* ['leːʀan 'leːʀə 'besəʀə] "to teach, emptiness, better ones"; but [ʌ] in *lehrt, leer, besser* ['leːʌt 'leːʌ 'besʌ] "teaches, empty, better." Instead of uvular [ʀ], some speakers use a tongue-tip [r].

Glides.—German /h/ is like English *h,* e.g., *Haus* /'haus/ "house." German /j/ is like English *y,* e.g., *ja* /'jaː/ "yes."

Consonant Alternations.—Voiced /b d g v z/ do not occur (1) at the ends of words, (2) at the ends of parts of compound words, (3) before suffixes beginning with a consonant, or (4) before endings in /s/ or /t/. In these positions they are replaced in pronunciation (though not in spelling) by the corresponding voiceless consonants, namely /p t k f s/. Examples: /b/ in *leben* /'leːbən/ "to live," but /p/ in *leblos* /'leːploːs/ "lifeless," *lebt* /'leːpt/ "(he) lives"; /d/ in *Räder* /'reːdər/ "wheels," but /t/ in *Rad* /'raːt/ "wheel," *Radfahrer* /'raːt.faːrər/ "bicyclist"; /g/ in *Tage* /'taːgə/ "days," but /k/ in *Tag* /'taːk/ "day," *täglich* /'teːklɪç/ "daily"; /v/ in *Motive* /moˈtiːvə/ "motifs," but /f/ in *Motiv* /moˈtiːf/ "motif," *des Motivs* /mo:'tiːfs/ "of the motif"; /z/ in *lesen* /'leːzən/ "to read," but /s/ in *lesbar* /'leːs-baːr/ "legible," *er liest* /liːst/ "he reads," *er las* /laːs/ "he read." The one irregularity in this unvoicing of voiced obstruents concerns the /g/ of the suffix *-ig.* Though speakers in the south (southern Germany, Austria, Switzerland) unvoice this regularly to /-ik/ and hence say *König* /'köːnɪk/ "king," etc., the *Siebs* prescribes that it should be unvoiced to /-iç/. Examples: /g/ in *König, reinigen* /'köːnɪgə 'rainɪgən/ "kings, to clean," but /ç/ in *der König, des Königs, er reinigt* /'köːnɪç 'köːnɪçs 'rainɪçt/ "the king, of the king, he cleans."

Spellings.—Special remarks need to be made concerning the spellings (1) *w* and *v*; (2) *sp* and *st*; (3) *ss* and *ß* ; (4) *tz* and *z*.

(1) German *w* always spells /v/: *Winter, Löwe* /'vintar 'löːvə/ "winter, lion." German *v* spells /f/ in native words: *Vater, vier* /'faːtər 'fiːr/ "father, four"; but it spells /v/ in foreign words: *Vase, November* /'vaːzə noˈvembar/ "vase, November." (2) German *sp, st* spell /šp/, /št/ in most positions: *Wespe, Liste* /'vespə 'listə/ "wasp, list"; but they spell /šp/, /št/ at the beginnings of words or word stems: *sprechen, besprechen, stehen, verstehen* /'ʃpreçən beˈʃpreçən 'ʃteːən fer'ʃteːən/ "speak, discuss, stand, understand." (Otherwise /š/ is spelled *sch*: *Schiff, waschen, Busch* /'ʃif 'vaʃən 'buʃ/ "ship, to wash, bush.") (3) Medial *ss* marks a preceding vowel as short, medial *ß* marks it as long: short *Masse, Busse* /'masə 'busə/ "mass, busses," but long *Maße, Buße* /'maːsə 'buːsə/ "measurements, penitence." (But medial *ss* changes to *ß* word-finally and before consonant: medial *hassen, küssen* /'hasən 'küsən/ "to hate, to kiss," but word-finally *Haß, Kuß* /'has 'kus/ "hate, kiss," and before consonant *er haßt, er küßt* /'hast 'küst/ "he hates, he kisses.") (4) German *z* always spells /ts/: *Zeit, heizen, schwarz, Holz* /'tsait 'haitsən 'ʃvarts 'holts/ "time, to heat, black, wood." The spelling *tz* marks a preceding vowel as short, simple *z* marks it as long: short *putzen* /'putsən/ "to polish," long *duzen* /'duːtsən/ "to call a person *du*."

Stress.—German, like English, has two types of stress: sentence stress and word stress. Neither is indicated in spelling.

Sentence Stress.—This type of stress (marked here as /°/) is part of the structure of sentences. It is used to place some particular word at the centre of attention. For example, the sentence *Hans wohnt hier* may be /°hans 'voːnt 'hiːr/ "*Hans* lives here," or /'hans °voːnt 'hiːr/ "Hans *lives* here," or /'hans 'voːnt °hiːr/ "Hans lives *here*."

Word Stress.—This type of stress is part of the structure of words. German, like English, has three degrees of word stress: (1) primary stress /'/, e.g., *Bad, baden, badete* /'baːt 'baːdən 'baːdətə/ "bath, to bathe, bathed"; (2) secondary stress /ˌ/, especially in compounds, e.g., *Badetuch* /'baːdəˌtuːx/ "bath towel," *Nordwesten* /ˌnortˈvestən/ "northwest"; and (3) weak stress (unmarked), as in the unmarked syllables of the above examples. Most native German words are stressed on the first syllable: *Arbeit, Arbeiter, arbeitslos, Arbeitslosigkeit* /'arbait 'arbaitər 'arbaitsloːs 'arbaitsloːziçkait/ "work, worker, unemployed, unemployment." But prefixes are generally unstressed: *gearbeitet, besprechen, verstehen* /gəˈarbaitət bəˈʃpreçən ferˈʃteːən/ "worked (past participle), discuss, understand." Loanwords are often stressed on some syllable other than the first: *Demokrat, Demokratie, demokratisieren* /deːmoˈkraːt deːmoˈkraːtiː deːmoˈkraːtiˈziːran/ "democrat, democracy, democratize."

PARTS OF SPEECH

Major Word Classes.—These include verbs, nouns, and adjectives.

Verbs.—These are inflected for three moods: indicative, subjunctive, imperative. In the indicative there are two tenses: present and past, e.g., *er spricht* "he speaks," *er sprach* "he spoke." There are two subjunctives, often called type I or special: *er spreche,* and type II or general: *er spräche.* All these forms are inflected for three persons: first, second, third; and for two numbers: singular and plural. There are three second person imperative forms: familiar singular *sprich*, familiar plural *sprecht*, polite singular-plural *sprechen Sie*. Verbs also have three nonfinite forms: infinitive *sprechen*, present participle *sprechend*, past participle *gesprochen*.

Nouns.—These are classified for gender: masculine *der Mann, der Löffel* "the man, the spoon"; feminine *die Frau, die Gabel* "the woman, the fork"; neuter *das Kind, das Messer* "the child, the knife." Nouns are inflected for four cases: nominative, accusative, dative, genitive, and for two numbers: singular and plural.

Adjectives.—When used attributively, adjectives are inflected to agree with the noun they modify in gender, number, and case. They take weak endings when preceded by an inflected determiner: *der heiße Kaffee* "the hot coffee"; otherwise strong endings: *heißer Kaffee* "hot coffee," *kein heißer Kaffee* "no hot coffee." Adjectives are uninflected when used predicatively: *der Kaffee ist heiß* "the coffee is hot," and when used adverbially (corresponding to English adverbs ending in -ly): *heiß umstritten* "hotly contested." Adjectives may be compared: *heiß, heißer, heißest* "hot, hotter, hottest"; if uninflected, the superlative has a special form: *am heißesten*.

Minor Word Classes.—These include all other types of words: auxiliary verbs, pronouns, determiners, prepositions, coordinating conjunctions, subordinating conjunctions, adverbs (other than adjectives used as adverbs), and interjections. The following deserve particular mention:

Auxiliary Verbs.—*Haben* "to have" and *sein* "to be" are the perfect auxiliaries. *Haben* is used with most verbs, including all transitive verbs: *Er hat geschlafen* "He slept, has slept"; *Er hat es gesehen* "He saw it, has seen it." *Sein* is used with verbs meaning change of position: *Er ist nach Hause gegangen* "He went home, has gone home," or change of condition: *Er ist eingeschlafen* "He went to sleep, has gone to sleep," as well as with *bleiben*: *Er ist hier geblieben* "He stayed here, has stayed here," and with *sein* itself: *Er ist hier gewesen* "He was here, has been here." (The perfect is generally used in isolated statements referring to past time, the past tense in narrative statements referring to past time.) *Werden* "to become" is the future auxiliary: *Er wird es tun* "He will do it." *Werden* is also the passive auxiliary: *Es wird jetzt getan* "It is now being done"; *Es wurde gestern getan* "It was done yesterday." Further auxiliaries are the modals: *dürfen, können, mögen, müssen, sollen, wollen* "may (be allowed to), can, like to, must, be supposed to, want to."

Determiners.—These include (1) the definite article *der* "the" (which, when stressed, means "that"), the indefinite article *ein* "a, an" (which, when stressed, means "one"), the negative indefinite article *kein* "no, not a, not any"; (2) such demonstratives as *dieser* "this," *jeder* "each, every," *welcher* "which"; and (3) the possessives *mein, dein, sein, ihr, unser, euer, ihr, Ihr*. Determiners are inflected to agree with the noun they modify in gender, number, and case.

Prepositions.—Some prepositions govern the accusative: *um den Garten* "around the garden"; others the dative: *aus dem Garten* "out of the garden"; others the genitive: *innerhalb des Gartens* "inside the garden"; still others both the accusative (indicating place to which): *in den Garten* "into the garden," and the dative (indicating place where): *in dem Garten* "in the garden."

SYNTAX

Sentences.—Any German sentence must contain at least three elements: (1) a subject, e.g., *der Mann* "the man"; (2) a predicate, e.g., *den Hut kaufen* "to buy the hat"; and (3) a tense and/or mood marker, attached to a full or auxiliary verb to give the so-called finite verb of the sentence. Depending on the nature of these three elements, and the order in which they occur, German has four basic sentence types:

Statement.—The finite verb is in second position:
Der Mann *kauft* den Hut. "The man buys the hat."

General Question.—The finite verb is in first position:
Kauft der Mann den Hut? "Does the man buy the hat?"

Specific Question.—A question word is in first position, the finite verb in second position:
Wer kauft den Hut? "Who buys the hat?"
Was kauft der Mann? "What does the man buy?"

Command.—The finite verb is in the imperative, and the subject (if expressed) follows it:
Kauf den Hut! "Buy the hat." (familiar singular)
Kauft den Hut! "Buy the hat." (familiar pl)
Kaufen Sie den Hut! "Buy the hat." (polite sing-pl)

Obligatory Word Order.—In addition to the elements illustrated above which must occur in first position or second position, there are three types of elements which must occur in last position; these are the separable prefixes (e.g., the *auf* of *aufziehen* "to wind up"), infinitives, and past participles. Examples:

Er *zieht* die Uhr *auf.* "He winds up the clock."
Er *wird* die Uhr *aufziehen.* "He will wind up the clock."
Er *hat* die Uhr *aufgezogen.* "He has wound up the clock."
Er *wird* die Uhr *aufgezogen haben.* "He will have wound up the clock."
Er *muß* die Uhr *aufziehen.* "He must wind up the clock."
Er *hat* die Uhr *aufziehen müssen.* "He has had to wind up the clock."

Optional Word Order.—Within the limits set by obligatory word order, the elements in a German sentence may occur in various positions with different stylistic emphases. A few examples:
(1) Ich *habe* diesen Hut gestern in New York *gekauft*.
(2) Gestern *habe* ich in New York einen Hut *gekauft*.
(3) Diesen Hut *habe* ich gestern in New York *gekauft*.
Approximate translations: (1) "I bought this hat yesterday in New York." (2) "As for yesterday, I was in New York and bought a hat." (3) "As for this hat, I bought it yesterday in New York."

Subordinate Clauses.—A different type of obligatory word order is used in subordinate clauses. Here the finite verb must be in last position. Examples: daß er den Hut *kauft* "that he buys the hat"; daß er den Hut *gekauft hat* "that he has bought the hat"; daß er den Hut gekauft haben *wird* "that he will have bought the hat"; daß er den Hut kaufen *muß* "that he must buy the hat." The one exception concerns the perfect auxiliary *haben* when it occurs together with a full verb plus a modal auxiliary; it then precedes these latter two: daß er den Hut *hat* kaufen müssen "that he has had to buy the hat."

DIALECTS

The Netherlandic-German Dialect Area.—Within the area outlined on the accompanying map, two standard languages have

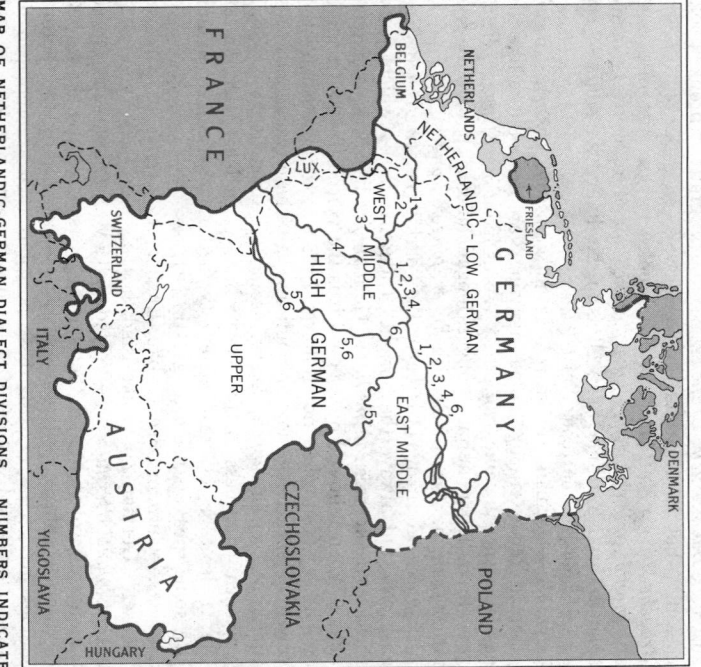

arisen out of the local dialects: in the northwest, Netherlandic (often called Dutch in the Netherlands, Flemish in Belgium); elsewhere, German. From the point of view of local dialects, however, this is a single speech area. One can start in the Alps of Austria, northern Italy, and Switzerland, go into the Netherlands, Belgium, and a bit of adjacent France, and never encounter a village where the local speech is suddenly different. The only sharp breaks occur in the French-speaking parts of France and Belgium, or the Frisian-speaking part of the Netherlands (the province of Friesland). (Until the end of World War II, the German speech border extended farther to the east—particularly in the northeast, as far as East Prussia. The inhabitants of these areas were expelled immediately after the end of the war.)

In the south of this German-speaking area, nearly everyone grows up speaking the local dialect (though he is taught Standard German in school), and he continues to use it with family, friends, and neighbours. In the north, on the other hand, many city dwellers grow up speaking only the local variety of Standard German and never learn the local dialect.

Low and High German.—The most striking dialect differences within this large area are those which divide it into Netherlandic-Low German in the lowlands of the north, v. High German in the highlands of the south. When the Germanic tribes migrated into southern Germany during the early centuries of the Christian era, their speech had the voiceless stops *p t k* in much the same distribution as modern English. Then, probably during the 6th century, in what is called the "High German consonant shift," these stops when initial (*p- t- k-*) or long (*pp tt kk*) came gradually to be pronounced as affricates; and when following a vowel (*Vp Vt Vk*) to be pronounced as long fricatives. The modern results, compared with related English words, are:

p-	pound	Pfund	*pp*	apple	Apfel	*Vp*	hope	hoffen
t-	ten	zehn	*tt*	sitting	sitzen	*Vt*	bite	beissen
k-	can	khann*	*kk*	lick	lekchen*	*Vk*	make	machen

*khann and lekchen, with affricates, are southern dialect forms; Standard German has stops: kann, lecken.

It is not known just where these changes originated, though it was most probably in southern Bavaria and adjacent Austria. Once the new pronunciations had arisen, they spread rapidly, though not uniformly. The situation at the end of the 19th century was that indicated on the map. Line 2, *maken/machen*, is generally chosen as the Low German/High German boundary, since it is typical for the shift of *Vp Vt Vk* (*hopen/hoffen, biten/beissen, maken/machen*) and of *t-* (*ten/zehn*) and *tt* (*sitten/sitzen*). Where exceptions occur, they are usually at the western or eastern ends of the line. Thus line 1, *ik/ich* "I," shows that shifted *k* spread unusually far to the northwest in this word. Line 3, *Dorp/Dorf* "village" (*cf.* archaic English *thorp*) shows that shifted *p* after *r* and *l* spread less far than usual. And line 4, *dat/das* "that," shows that shifted *t* spread still less far in this word (and in a few others: *dit/dies* "this," *it/es* "it," *wat/was* "what"). The striking way in which these lines radiate in the west has led to their being called the "Rhenish fan."

Shifted *p-* and *pp* spread still less far than other sounds. Line 5, *Appel/Apfel*, lies wholly within the High German area and is customarily used to subdivide it into Middle German (*Appel*) v. Upper German (*Apfel*). Line 6, *Pund/Pfund*, largely coincides with this in the west, but then runs north to join the *maken/machen* line; it is customarily used to distinguish West Middle German (*Appel, Pund*) from East Middle German (*Appel/Pund*—the latter being commoner than Upper German *Pfund*).

HISTORY

Preliterary Period (to c. A.D. 750).—German belongs to the family of Germanic languages (*q.v.*), whose recorded history begins with the first contact with the Romans, starting in the 1st century B.C. At that time and for several centuries thereafter there was only a single "Germanic" language, with little more than minor dialect differences. Only after the consonant shift are we justified in speaking of a "German" (*i.e.*, High German) language, distinct from Netherlandic-Low German, Frisian, English, etc. Nevertheless, two matters from this early period deserve mention because of their importance for the later "German" language.

Starting around the beginning of the Christian era, Germanic speakers were in close contact with the Romans especially in the area of the lower Rhine. In this and the following centuries they borrowed many Latin words, *e.g.*, English *pound*, German *Pfund*, from Latin *pondō* "in weight"; Eng. *pepper*, Ger. *Pfeffer*, from Lat. *piper*; Eng. *tile*, Ger. *Ziegel*, from Lat. *tēgula*; Eng. *street*, Ger. *Straße*, from Lat. (*via*) *strāta* "(paved) road"; Eng. *kettle*, Ger. *Kessel*, from Lat. *catillus*; Eng. *cook*, Ger. *Koch*, from Lat. *coquus*. These words must have been borrowed before the consonant shift, since they show its effects.

Starting toward the end of the 4th century there began the great migrations of Germanic tribes, resulting in a considerable expansion of the Germanic-speaking territory. Angles, Saxons, and Jutes crossed the channel to England; Franks moved southwest into northern France and south into southern Germany; and Alamannians, Bavarians, and Langobards moved south into southern Germany, Switzerland, Austria, and northern Italy. At the same time, the area east of the Elbe and Saale rivers was largely vacated, and Slavic speakers moved in.

Old Period (c. 750–1050).—In the southern area settled by Franks, Alamannians, and Bavarians, the first written records (Old High German) begin to appear during the second half of the 8th century. Their language is best described as a collection of monastery dialects: there is a certain uniformity in the writings of any given monastery, but little for the area as a whole. The documents show the monks struggling to express new concepts in German, first through translations of Latin word lists, then in prose translations —some highly skilful (Isidore, *c.* 800), others less so (Tatian, *c.* 835)—and in a new verse form with end rhyme (Otfrid, *c.* 870); they culminate in the able translations and interpretations of the Swiss monastery teacher Notker Labeo (d. 1022). From the north (Old Low German, but usually called Old Saxon), the most extensive documents preserved are a life of Christ in alliterative verse (*Heliand, c.* 830) and a fragment of a similar Genesis translation.

In this period also there were many borrowings from Latin, nearly all connected with the Christianization of the Germans. Since they were made after the consonant shift, they do not show its effects. Examples: *predigōn* (modern *predigen* "to preach"), from Lat. *praedicāre*; *tempal* (modern *Tempel* "temple"), from Lat. *templum*; *spiagal* (modern *Spiegel* "mirror"), from Lat. *speculum*. On the other hand, borrowings of this period reflect sound changes that had occurred in popular Latin; *cf.* the change of Lat. *c* before *e* to *ts* in *cella, crucem* "cell, cross," OHG *zella, kriuzi*, modern *Zelle, Kreuz*; or the change of Lat. medial -*b*- to -*v*- in Lat. *tabula* "table," OHG *tavala*, modern *Tafel*.

Middle Period (c. 1050–1350).—Several developments justify the usual assumption of a new period (Middle High German) beginning around 1050. First, there were changes in the language itself. A consonant change was the unvoicing of final *b, d, g; cf.* OHG *grab, rad, tag* "grave, wheel, day," but MHG *grap, rat, tac* (now again spelled *Grab, Rad, Tag*, but pronounced with final /p t k/). A vowel change was the reduction of the "full" vowels of unstressed syllables to /ə/, usually spelled *e*; *cf.*, in the plural of the word for "day," OHG nominative-accusative *taga*, genitive *tago*, dative *tagun*, but MHG *tage, tage, tagen* (and modern *Tage, Tage, Tagen*). Second, there were great changes in the geographical area in which German was spoken. In the west the Franks of northern France had become romanized, and the French-German language border had assumed approximately its present course; in the east, on the other hand, German now began to spread into Slavic territory, a process that was to continue for many centuries and to be reversed only at the end of World War II. Finally, writing now became independent of the monasteries, and the number of written documents soon increased greatly in both north and south. In the south especially, a remarkable literature developed (courtly epic, *Minnesang*). There is clear evidence of a trend toward a standard MHG literary language, though it seems to have had no influence on ordinary speech. This literature was based largely on French models, and many French words were borrowed into German.

Early Modern Period (c. 1350–1650).—Four events—the

growth of trade, the rise of a middle class, the invention of printing, and the Reformation—were of great influence on the development of the language. In the north, because of the prosperity of the Hanseatic League, a standard Low German written language began to develop, though it never reached full growth and probably had little influence on everyday speech. In the south, the dialects which developed in the recently settled East Middle German area were relatively uniform and contained elements from both West Middle and Upper German. Gradually they came to be used as the official languages of the chancelleries of the area, including that of Saxony; and on this latter Martin Luther based the language of his widely read Bible translation (1522–34). This type of German then grew gradually into modern Standard German. Its growth was aided by the fact that printers preferred it as a means of making their books appeal to the widest possible audience.

Three striking vowel changes are characteristic of this period. (1) In the southeast, as early as the 12th century, long /iː/, /uː/ ü:/ began to be diphthongized to /ei ou oü/; this is the "New High German diphthongization." By the 15th century these new diphthongs had spread to East Middle German, and in the standard language they merged with old /ei ou oü/. Compare MHG *mîn, hîs, hiûsar* /miːn 'huːs 'hiːsar/ "my, house, houses" v. *ein, troum, troüme* /ein 'troum 'troümə/ "a, dream, dreams"; but modern standard *mein, Haus, Häuser* /main 'haus 'hoizar/ with the same diphthongs as *ein, Traum, Träume* /ain 'traum 'troimə/. (2) By a specifically Middle German development, /ia ua iä/ (still preserved in the south) were monophthongized to long /iː uː üː/. This is the "New High German monophthongization"; cf. MHG *tief, guot, güete* /'tiəf guət 'güətə/ "deep, good, goodness," but modern standard *tief, gut, Güte* /'tiːf guːt 'güːtə/. (3) Short vowels remained short in closed syllables before long fortis consonants; cf. MHG *mit-te, of-fen* /'mitə 'ofən/ "middle, open;" modern *Mitte, offen* /'mitə 'ofən/. But they were lengthened in open syllables before a short lenis consonant plus unstressed vowel; cf. MHG *ni-der, o-fen* /'nidər 'ofən/ "down, stove," modern *nieder, Ofen* /'niːdər 'oːfən/. This is "lengthening in open syllable."

Modern Period (c. 1650 to the Present).—The outstanding developments of the modern period have been the increasing standardization of Standard German and its increasing acceptance as the supradialectal form of the language. In writing, it is almost the only form used; in speech, it is the first or second language of nearly the entire population.

Though Standard German is clearly based on the East Middle German dialects, it is not identical with any one of them. It has accepted and standardized many forms from other areas, notably Upper German *pf* (*Pfund, Apfel*), and also large numbers of individual words in the form of other dialect areas. Since it is the only type of German taught in schools, its spoken form is based to a large extent on its written form; and the spoken form that carries the greatest prestige (that of stage, screen, radio, etc.) uses largely a Low German pronunciation of this written form. As a result, Standard German has been called—and not only facetiously—"High German with Low German sounds."

BIBLIOGRAPHY.—Pronunciation: William G. Moulton, *The Sounds of English and German* (1962); Theodor Siebs, *Deutsche Hochsprache, Bühnenaussprache,* 17th ed. (1958); *Duden: Aussprachewörterbuch* (1962). Spellings: *Duden: Rechtschreibung der deutschen Sprache und der Fremdwörter,* 15th ed. (1961). Grammar: Herbert Lederer, *Reference Grammar of the German Language* (1969), translated and adapted from Heinz Griesbach and Dora Schulz, *Grammatik der deutschen Sprache,* 4th ed. (1966); Herbert L. Kufner, *The Grammatical Structures of English and German* (1962); *Duden: Grammatik der deutschen Gegenwartssprache,* 2nd ed. (1966). Dialects: R. E. Keller, *German Dialects* (1961); Adolf Bach, *Deutsche Mundartforschung,* 2nd ed. (1950); V. M. Zhirmunski, *Deutsche Mundartkunde* (1962). History: W. B. Lockwood, *An Informal History of the German Language* (1965); John T. Waterman, *A History of the German Language* (1966); Adolf Bach, *Geschichte der deutschen Sprache,* 8th ed. (1965). (W. G. MN)

GERMAN LAW

GERMAN LAW. The present article is concerned with the development and content of the law of the Federal Republic of Germany. For the legal system of the German Democratic Republic, much sovietized since 1952, *see* GERMANY: *Constitution and Government.* The law of the early Germanic or Teutonic peoples is discussed in GERMANIC LAWS, EARLY.

INTRODUCTION

German law "received" Roman law as embodied in the *Corpus juris* from the 15th century onward and with this "Reception" (*see* CIVIL LAW) came a legal profession and a system of common law developed by lawyers (*Juristenrecht*). Roman law provided both the theoretical basis for legal progress, culminating in the 19th century in the work of the Pandectists (the commentators on the *Pandectae; see* ROMAN LAW) who, following Kant, worked out on the basis of the autonomous moral person the concepts of a subjectively conceived legal system. The influence of the *Corpus juris* is also partly responsible for the codified form of the law of the Pandectists, constructed on the model of Justinian's *Digest.* Thus in Germany the legal process consists in applying the legal principle to the individual case and the courts have not been so dominant as in a case-law system, such as that of England. Another effect of Roman law in Germany was to strengthen the conception of national sovereignty, the idea that the legislative function is a state monopoly and that the responsibility for the development of law rests with a legally trained state-controlled bureaucracy rather than with the unpaid and legally untrained leading men of the old estates (nobility, clergy, *bourgeoisie*). The supremacy of the ruler's will over the life of the community was thereby established, even if limited by prevailing Christian and customary conceptions of political ethics. This union of the sovereign state with Roman law gave rise to a bureaucracy and to a type of judge who was a university-trained official, giving his opinion as an expert under the authority and anonymity of the court.

Modern German law assumes that the proper form of society is that of a social democracy, not merely conferring individual rights but also involving the responsibility of the state for social welfare and the duty of individuals to behave in a socially responsible way. The former concern of German law with abstract concepts has given place to a more sociological approach with the aim of applying the scale of values laid down by the legislator to the varying problems of community life.

CIVIL LAW
HISTORY

Codification.—The movement toward codification began with the Bavarian *Codex Maximilianeus Bavaricus Civilis* (*Kurbayerisches Landrecht*) of 1756, but it is the Prussian Code of 1794 (*Preussisches Allgemeines Landrecht*) which displays most clearly the union of the law of reason with the state planning of the Enlightenment. Its 17,000 paragraphs aimed at laying down a final solution for every legal situation, thus seeking to avoid judicial interpretation by judges. More practical were the 1,502 sections of the Austrian Civil Code of 1811 (*Allgemeines Bürgerliches Gesetzbuch*) which, with amendments, has remained in force. In 1814 A. F. J. Thibaut, a law professor, under the influence of the War of Liberation, demanded a unified civil code for the whole of Germany; F. K. von Savigny (*q.v.*; 1779–1861), the outstanding German jurist of the 19th century, replied in a famous article rejecting codification on two grounds: that law grows only out of the inner convictions of the people, the *Volksgeist*; and that, in his age, it would be pointless or harmful to codify. German law since few had the requisite skill or vocation.

Because states remained sovereign within Germany no unified civil law arose. Meanwhile, a general German law on bills of exchange (*Allgemeine Deutsche Wechselordnung*, 1848) was brought into force by the individual states of the German confederation; the general German Commercial Code (*Allgemeines Deutsches Handelsgesetzbuch*, 1861) was similarly enacted. With the foundation of the German Empire in 1871, imperial laws on judicial administration were passed; in 1874 the first commission for drafting a unified civil law was set up; the Civil Code was promulgated on Aug. 18, 1896, and came into force on Jan. 1, 1900.

German "Legal Family."—The German Civil Code and the attendant laws of procedure have had an important influence on other systems of law. The Japanese Civil Code of 1898 was based on the first draft of the German Civil Code; the Civil Code of Siam of Jan. 1, 1925, and of China of 1929–31 followed the same pattern. The Swiss Civil Code of 1907–12, in spite of numerous original ideas, also owes much to the German Civil Code, and it was adopted by Turkey. Together with the German Civil Code, the Swiss Civil Code influenced the legislation supplementing the Austrian Civil Code, the Soviet Civil Code of Oct. 31, 1922, the Polish Law of Obligations of Oct. 27, 1933, the Czechoslovakian law of Oct. 25, 1950, and the legislation of Hungary, Yugoslavia, the Scandinavian countries, Peru, and other states. In 1946, in spite of World War II, the makers of the Greek Civil Code turned to the German Civil Code. The latter, either directly or through the Swiss Civil Code, has thus engendered a "legal family" which takes an honourable place beside the legal families of the Anglo-Saxon and French traditions.

Civil Code

General Character.—The Civil Code (*Bürgerliches Gesetzbuch*) begins with a "general part," consisting not of basic political and ethical principles but of the fundamental elements of civil law; that is, in accordance with Gaius' "persons, things and actions," of those generalizations which can be made about subjects, objects, and transactions over the whole field of civil law. Four parts follow: law of obligations; property law; family law; and succession. The law of obligations has itself a general part, containing the rules common to all obligation (BGB, ss. 241–432), followed by a special part (BGB, ss. 433–853).

This arrangement is characteristic of a code made by competent legal technicians rather than by a single outstanding jurist, such as Eugen Huber who formulated the Swiss code. The German Civil Code thus is logically clear and precise, but not intuitive. It does not try to emphasize ethical imperatives, except that it forbids breaches of customary morals (*gute Sitten*), abuse of rights, and underhand legal transactions (*Schikane*). Nor does it lay down a new pattern of society; but its "general clauses," leaving the making of specific norms to the judge, have allowed it to become adapted to modern needs, particularly in the economic and cultural spheres. These general clauses use such words as "good faith" (*Treu und Glauben*), "customs of social intercourse" (*Verkehrssitte*), "important reason" (*wichtiger Grund*), "lack of proportion" (*Unverhältnismässigkeit*), "exploitation" (*Ausnutzung von Notlagen*), "inexperience" (*Unerfahrenheit*).

The Code's General Part.—Every natural person acquires on birth the capacity to exercise rights and to fulfill duties (*Rechtsfähigkeit*), slavery and civil death being unrecognized by the law. Full capacity is acquired at 21 (*Geschäftsfähigkeit*). A minor's interests are guarded by a representative in the name of the child, German law not knowing the English trust; but an infant from seven years of age may enter into legal transactions, provided they are profitable to him (ss. 106 ff.).

A general personal right (*allgemeines Persönlichkeitsrecht*), protected by an action for damages and, if the defendant has been negligent or acted intentionally, by an injunction (*allgemeine Unterlassungsklage*), covers many aspects of human personality; among them are freedom from personal injury and from attacks on individual dignity, the right to possess a recognized name, and freedom to develop one's abilities. The courts may extend protection to other unspecified expressions of human personality. They give compensation in increasing amounts, even for pain and suffering, in spite of BGB, s. 253.

As to legal personality (ss. 21–89) the Civil Code deals only with associations (*Vereine*, ss. 21–79) and foundations (*Stiftungen*, ss. 80–88), leaving other groups to the commercial code or special laws. Associations have a general assembly of members (*Mitgliederversammlung*), a board (*Vorstand*), and a statute (without the distinction of English law between the memorandum and articles of association). The general assembly elects the board which is the agent of the *Verein*, and the capacity of which is not limited by any doctrine of *ultra vires* (acts in excess of statutory rights), as in Anglo-American law. The *Verein* may be incorporated by regis-

tration at the district court (*Amtsgericht*), subject to conditions in the interests of the community and its own members.

Under the heading of voluntary legal transactions (*Rechtsgeschäfte*) the code requires only two corresponding declarations of intention (*Willenserklärungen*), without necessity for either consideration (English law) or a justifying interest (Italian law) to constitute a contract. Such a declaration of intention becomes effective (s. 130) on receipt even without actual knowledge on the part of the recipient, where, in accord with ordinary business usage, he might be expected to have such knowledge. Unless there is special provision for writing (*Schriftform*), or for public certification of the signature by a court or notary (*öffentliche Beurkundung*), or for public authentication (*öffentliche Beurkundung*), voluntary legal transactions require no special form. While a legal transaction may be void by statute (*e.g.*, for immorality), mistake, unlike English law, renders it only voidable (s. 119). The mistaken party is more readily excused than in English law, and fraud (with a wider duty to disclose facts than in English law) and threats are also grounds for avoidance. But a party who has relied on a declaration made by the other party under a mistake can recover damages from the latter to the extent of his loss by such reliance.

After dealing with interpretation, which must not be too literal (s. 133) and which must observe good faith in the light of ordinary usage (s. 157), the code (s. 164 ff.) treats the "grant of authority" as part of the general rules about agency, as distinguished from the resulting contract (*e.g.*, mandate or the contract of employment), which is to be found in the law of obligations. Unlike English law, in principle there is no undisclosed agency; either the agent or the person in whose name he contracts alone is bound.

Limitation (*Verjährung*) and exercise of rights (*Rechtsausübung*) conclude the general part. Limitation is substantive, not merely procedural. Thirty years is the general rule but there are many exceptions. Restrictions on the exercise of a right cannot be imposed for longer than 30 years; the entail (*fideicommissum*) was abolished after World War I.

Law of Obligation.—Of cardinal importance is s. 242 in the general part of the law of obligations: the debtor is bound to effect performance according to the requirements of good faith, ordinary usage being taken into consideration. This rule parallels the wide power given by s. 1 of the Swiss Civil Code to the judge to assume a legislative function where there are "gaps" in the law. It has been particularly necessary in the rapidly changing conditions of the 20th century and may be compared with equity (*q.v.*) in English law, though giving wider scope in the interpretation of contract.

Specific performance (unlike English law) is the normal remedy for breach of contract, and compensation (s. 249) is in principle in kind rather than in money. Contributing fault and negligent failure to mitigate damage is specifically dealt with in s. 254.

Time and place of performance, forms, content, and types of contract are then dealt with, as well as the various kinds and consequences of breach, delayed performance (*Verzug*), and subsequent impossibility of performance (*Unmöglichkeit*). There follow ways of discharge of obligation (ss. 362–397) and of assignment (ss. 398–413) from one creditor to another.

The special part of obligation covers the law of sale (ss. 433–515), in principle both as regards chattels and real property; to both of these the law relating to letting also applies, although subject to emergency legislation (authorizing subletting, exchange of dwelling, fixing rents, etc.) in respect of real property. Next come loan, contract of employment and contract to perform a work, mandate, gaming and betting, suretyship and liability of innkeepers, etc.

The important topic of unjust enrichment follows (ss. 812–822). Section 812 says: "Anyone who through an act performed by another or in any other way acquires something at the expense of that other without legal justification is bound to return it to him"; but it has been restrictively interpreted by the courts and legal writers. The ensuing sections deal with special cases.

Finally there is the topic of delicts (ss. 823–853). General clauses concerning delict are: s. 823 i, by which any person who intentionally or negligently injures unlawfully the life, body, health, property, or any other absolute right of another person is bound to compensate him for any damages arising therefrom; s. 823 ii, imposing a civil remedy for violation of a statutory duty; and s. 826 which reads: "A person who intentionally causes damage to another in a manner *contra bonos mores* is bound to compensate him for such damage." There are a small number of special delicts.

Important statutes, introducing liability without fault, are the *Reichshaftpflichtgesetz* of June 7, 1871 (railways), the *Strassenverkehrsgesetz* of Dec. 19, 1952 (road traffic), and the *Luftverkehrsgesetz* of Aug 1, 1922, as amended on Jan. 10, 1959 (aircraft). Strict liability in respect of motor accidents, according to the *Strassenverkehrsgesetz*, is limited to DM 50,000 for damage to property and DM. 250,000 for personal injury, but a higher sum may be claimed in respect of negligence under the Civil Code. Third-party insurance for motorcars and aircraft is compulsory.

Law of Property.—Under the law of property, transfers are valid even if the relevant contract of sale is invalid (*e.g.*, because of error or immorality); third parties are thus protected and adjustments are made by the rules of unjust enrichment.

Sections 854-872 deal with possession, ss. 903-1007, with ownership. The unqualified character of the latter is qualified by the principle of the 1919 constitution: "Ownership entails obligations. Its use should be of service to the common weal," a statement approved in all German constitutions since 1945. Agricultural reform also belongs here. The *Flurbereinigungsgesetz* of July 14, 1953, seeks to pool farms consisting of small parcels of land, redistributing to the members of the pool unified coherent holdings equivalent to their contribution. This makes for better use of machinery, more efficient production, and an increased yield.

By s. 873 every creation, transfer, encumbrance, or cancellation of a right in real property requires, in addition to the agreement of the parties, registration in the register (*Grundbuch*) kept by the district court (*Amtsgericht*). The general principles of real property are contained in ss. 873-902.

With movable property what counts is possession. If the owner-transferor and the transferee agree that property should pass, it does so on delivery. Corresponding rules apply to the creation of a pledge (ss. 1204 ff.). The transferee in good faith of chattels from the possessor, or of real property from the person registered in the land register, is protected, but not if the transferor has acquired against the will of the true owner, as in the case of a finder or thief; this important rule of German law, although far-reaching, is cautiously applied by the courts.

Hypothecs (rights against the debtor's real property given to a creditor without transfer of possession), land charges, and annuity charges are dealt with in ss. 1113 ff. There being nothing comparable to the equity of redemption of English law, the creditor in a German hypothec or land charge has a restricted legal right. Through the court he can satisfy his claim by foreclosure or sequestration. Other sections deal with ownership of flats (*Gesetz über Wohnungseigentum*, March 15, 1951,), servitudes over land (ss. 1018 ff.), limited personal servitudes (ss. 1090 ff.), rights of preemption over land (ss. 1094 ff.), heritable building rights (*Verordnung über das Erbbaurecht*, 1919), and homesteads (*Reichsheimstättengesetz*, 1920).

Law of Domestic Relations.—Since 1875 marriage has required civil celebration by a registrar who cannot be a priest, the celebration in church following the civil ceremony. The current regulations are to be found in *Ehegesetz* of Feb. 20, 1946, Control Council Law no. 16, ss. 11 ff. Marriages can be declared null and void (*nichtig*) on application of one of the spouses or by the public prosecutor on various grounds (*Ehegesetz*, ss. 16 ff.), such as lack of form or affinity, but the consequences of such nullity approximate to those of divorce, the children being not necessarily illegitimate. Annulment (*Aufhebung*; see *Ehegesetz*, ss. 28 ff.)—for example, for lack of consent of parents—has similar results. The grounds for divorce (*Ehegesetz*, ss. 42 ff.), which have been relaxed, involve either (1) a matrimonial offense (adultery or violation of a matrimonial duty leading to disruption of the marriage), (2) factors such as the physical or mental condition of a spouse or, (3) by the important s. 48 of the *Ehegesetz*, a deep-rooted incurable disruption of marital relations without expectation of restoration of common life, with the parties not having lived together for three years. Custody of children on divorce is decided mainly on the basis of their own welfare. The lower courts have final and exclusive jurisdiction with wide discretion in questions relating to furniture and living accommodations following divorce.

Articles 3 (ii) and 117 of the Basic Law (GG; see *Public Law: After World War II*, below) annul all rules contradicting the principle of equality (*Gleichberechtigung*) between husband and wife. Their implementation was left at first to the courts but has since been effected by the Equal Rights Act (*Gleichberechtigungsgesetz*) of 1957, although the Federal Constitutional Court has declared part of this act (BGB, ss. 1628-29) void because it violates the principle of equality (insofar as it favours the father in decisions affecting children). The right to determine questions relating to the matrimonial home must be decided by both spouses. But the wife, and not the husband, has the right to pledge the other spouse's credit as an agent of necessity (s. 1357), she too being liable if the husband is insolvent. The "ordinary statutory regime" when the husband administering and using the wife's estate has been replaced by the regime of separation of goods with a subsequent equalization of the surplus (*Zugewinngemeinschaft*, ss. 1363 ff.). By s. 1371 of the BGB (as amended by the Equal Rights Act) the surviving spouse may get half the estate if there are children, or 75% if there are none, which is somewhat at odds with the principle of equality. Care for the person and property of the child and power of representation belong to both spouses. The Court for the Protection of Wards may take steps to prevent dangers to children threatened by parental neglect (s. 1666). Article 6 of the GG puts legitimate and illegitimate children on an equal footing but this constitutional requirement was not given practical effect until January 1969. In contrast to earlier law an illegitimate child now in principle inherits from his father but has claim in substitution for his rights as her expressed in equivalent monetary terms. Furthermore, the illegitimate child has the special possibility, when between the ages of 21 and 27, of claiming in the lifetime of his father a sum by way of compensation for his rights on succession; this sum is three times the average annual maintenance provided by the father for the child over the last five years in which he was completely dependent on such maintenance. While the mother has parental authority and care of the child, the father is responsible for the maintenance of the child when living with the mother; the amount of the maintenance payments is determined by reference to the position in life of both parents.

Law of Succession.—Succession (BGB, bk. v) is no longer based on the idea of family or community but merely on the distribution of goods *mortis causa* ("by reason of death"). An heir, appointed by will or taking under intestacy, assumes automatically all the rights and liabilities of a person on his death (s. 1922). A testator may appoint an executor (*Testamentsvollstrecker*, ss. 2197 ff.), but unlike the English executor he does not assume the rights and liabilities of the deceased and acts only for the heirs, disposing of the estate according to the law and the will and exercising other powers given in the will. The heir can disclaim (ss. 1942 ff.), but only within a limited time; otherwise he is usually liable personally for the debts of the estate.

Wills are private or public. Private wills may be in handwriting; they only require signature and are liberally interpreted; they are opened at a special hearing of the lower court which issues an inheritance certificate (*Erbschein*, ss. 2353 ff.). Public wills are either made orally before a notary, who records them, or they are set down in a document which the testator hands to a notary with a declaration that it is his last will. A near relative not appointed heir can claim from the heirs a sum equal to half of what he would have received on intestacy (ss. 2303 ff.).

On intestate succession (ss. 1924 ff.) the deceased's relatives are divided into groups (*Parentelen*): the first, his descendants; the second, his parents and their descendants; the third, his grandparents and their descendants; and so on. Even one surviving member of a group excludes all the next group. The testator's spouse has a share in the capital of the estate (ss. 1931 and 1371), varying with the degree of nearness of the surviving relatives. In the matrimonial property regime of *Zugewinngemeinschaft* (*see* above) the surviving spouse as against the children gets a half of the estate; where there has been separation of goods and one or two children she gets an equal share with them; in other cases she gets one-quarter of it.

Although not hindering testate succession, special laws govern intestate succession to farms to avoid their being split up.

COMMERCIAL CODE: OTHER COMMERCIAL LAWS

Principles.—Unlike modern Swiss law, German law maintains separate civil and commercial codes. The Commercial Code (*Handelsgesetzbuch*) supplemented by later laws, dates from the General German Commercial Code of 1861; it applies to commercial questions. If there is no special commercial rule, the appropriate section of the BGB becomes applicable (HGB Introductory Law, s. 2). Whereas the French Commercial Code is based on an "act of commerce," in Germany the central concept is a merchant who "exercises his commercial profession" (HGB, s. 1). Some undertakings are by nature commercial, some by virtue of their organization (as companies limited by shares, private limited companies, and cooperative societies), and some by registration in the *Handelsregister* (kept by the district courts), in which the seat and the civil and commercial name (*Firma*) of an enterprise, whether of a single merchant, partnership, or company, must be registered. The *Handelsregister* aims at showing the legal position of merchants with reference, for example, to bankruptcy and the appointment of general agents called *Prokuristen*.

Book ii of the HGB (ss. 105 ff.) deals with ordinary commercial partnerships (*offene Handelsgesellschaften*), limited partnerships (*Kommanditgesellschaften*), and associations with silent partners (*stille Gesellschaften*) which in German, unlike French and Italian law, are not legal persons but belong to all the partners in common (*Gesamthand*). Members of an *offene Handelsgesellschaft* are liable without limit personally to partnership creditors; in the *Kommanditgesellschaft* one or more members have limited and the others unlimited liability; the silent partner in a *stille Gesellschaft* is not liable to the creditors directly but only, within limits, to the other partners.

The substantive rules of the HGB (bk. iii), mostly developed by mercantile custom, aim at reconciling freedom of trade with the public interest. Book iv covers maritime law, in particular associations of part owners of seagoing ships (*Reedereien* or *Partenreedereien*) and marine insurance.

Company Law.—The *Aktiengesellschaft*, corresponding to the English company limited by shares, has capital (*Grundkapital*) divided into shares (*Aktien*). With a minimum capital of DM. 100,000 the *Aktiengesellschaft* is confined to major undertakings; the form of private company (*Gesellschaft mit beschränkter Haftung*) is available to smaller enterprises. Shareholders must contribute at least the nominal value of the shares. Bearer shares, transferable by informal agreement and delivery of the certificate, and registered shares are possible but, unlike in England, the former are common and the latter rare.

Aktiengesellschaften have a general assembly of shareholders (*Hauptversammlung*), a supervisory board (*Aufsichtsrat*), and an administrative board (*Vorstand*). The last runs the company and corresponds most closely to the English board of directors. The general assembly decides only on the distribution of profits; the balance sheet, profit-and-loss account, and profits held in reserve are decided by the supervisory and administrative boards. The supervisory board appoints the administrative board, supervises them through auditors, and receives their report. The new Company Law of 1965 tightens up the provisions regarding publicity and reforms the law governing associated companies.

The important law relating to the organization of undertakings (Oct. 11, 1952) gives employees' representatives, elected by secret ballot, one-third of the seats on the supervisory board, two seats being reserved for employees of the company, the others being

open to outsiders; *i.e.*, to representatives of the German Trades Union Federation. The law on workers' participation in the coal and steel industries (May 21, 1951) gives the workers equal representation (five seats) with the shareholders on the supervisory board, trade unions being allowed to fill three-fifths of the workers' seats and to control nominations made by the works councils. A complicated system, sometimes involving appeal to the labour courts, decides the 11th neutral member. The supervisory board in the coal and steel industries must appoint a labour manager, who is responsible for social and personnel problems, to the administrative board on which he has equal rights with the other members.

The *Gesellschaft mit beschränkter Haftung* has a minimum capital of DM. 20,000 in shares (*Stammeinlagen*); the members have the right to participate (*Geschäftsanteil*). Shares are not negotiable on the stock exchange and transfer, somewhat complicated, is by agreement before a notary. A member is liable to the amount of his share. One or more managers (*Geschäftsführer*) correspond to the *Vorstand* of the *Aktiengesellschaft*. An *Aufsichtsrat* is optional. This type of company, dating from 1892, is a theoretical rather than practical product. Restricting risk, in contrast to the individual merchant or partnership, it is difficult to reconcile with free competition, especially in the case of the "one-man company".

F. H. Schulze-Delitzsch, in 1849, organized the first German cooperative society (*Erwerbs- und Wirtschaftsgenossenschaft*) on the English model, a form since developed very successfully. A legal person with no fixed capital or predetermined number of members or shares, its voting rights are equal irrespective of financial interest. Some societies have limited, others unlimited, liability; the members' liability is to the society and arises only when it goes bankrupt.

Negotiable Instruments, Patents, Copyright.—A law of 1933 governs negotiable instruments such as bills of exchange, checks, and promissory notes. German law accepts the International Convention of Geneva (1930–31), without special peculiarities. Patents, copyright, and designs are based on international conventions dating from the conventions of Paris (1833) and Berne (1886).

PUBLIC LAW
CONSTITUTIONAL

From 1849 to 1945.—In Germany the revolutionary movements of 1848–49 culminated in the Frankfurt constitution (March 27, 1849). It aimed at a Federal Constitutional Empire, a parliament with two houses, manhood suffrage, and a responsible ministry. Western conceptions of separation of powers, parliamentary institutions, and guaranteed personal freedom prevailed over the autocratic traditions of most of the states. However, it was rejected by the princes of the constituent states (*Länder*) and never became effective (*see* GERMANY: *History*). Unlike that of 1848, Bismarck's constitution of 1871, concise, clear, and practical, was based on agreement between the rulers of states and fitted an autocratic empire. Prussia dominated through the traditional authority of its constitutional monarch, civil service, and army. Individual liberties (*e.g.*, regarding arrest, movement, press, trade, and assembly) were not contained in a separate bill of rights but regulated by special laws subject to legislative alteration; the constitution was mainly concerned with relations between the states (with enumerated and residual powers) and the empire (with enumerated and delegated powers), ensuring real power for the empire, the legislative authority of which rested with the Federal Council (*Bundesrat*) and the Federal Assembly (*Reichstag*).

The Weimar constitution of 1919 provided for a directly elected president who nominated the cabinet and the chancellor, a *Reichsrat* representing the *Länder* and a *Reichstag* the people; the *Reichstag* had real legislative power and the chancellor was responsible to it. There were human-rights provisions in the constitution but how far these were binding on the legislature, executive, and courts, or merely declaring future policy, required decision in each case. Thus, although advanced in many of its social provisions, the Weimar constitution failed to circumscribe the state's authority. The legislature, unlike the U.S. federal legislature, could change the constitution; the president appointed the chancellor and could dissolve parliament and order new elections; he also could, together with the chancellor, legislate by decree (the famous art. 48). After Hitler's rise to power the Weimar constitution was completely undermined by an Enabling Act (March 23, 1933) which allowed him to legislate and even change the constitution without reference to the *Reichstag* or *Reichsrat*.

After World War II.—Not unlike the Weimar constitution and the constitutions of the *Länder* after World War II were those of the *Länder* (1946), which were drafted by Germans and approved by the occupying powers. The British zone *Länder* followed (1950). The constitutions of Bavaria and the French zone's *Länder* reveal religious influence. The *Länder* constitutions contained some innovations, especially in economic and social matters.

The Basic Law (*Grundgesetz*) of Bonn in 1949 avoids the term "constitution," which might suggest a permanently divided Germany; according to its last article it lapses when a new constitution is approved by a free vote of the German people. The German-prepared draft was modified mostly in favour of greater federalism to meet objections of the military governors; it existed alongside the Occupation Statute, which remained in force until May 5, 1955.

The *Grundgesetz*, or GG, is considered to be prior to the state and binding on the legislature, executive, and judiciary. "In no circumstances may the substance of any fundamental right be interfered with" (art. 19).

More federal than the Weimar constitution, the GG places state authority with the people (art. 20). The *Bundesversammlung*, consisting of the *Bundestag* (Federal Assembly) and a certain number of members elected by the parliaments of the *Länder*, elects the president, who has but modest powers. The chancellor, appointed by the president, dominates the cabinet; without his countersignature the president cannot act. To promote stable rule, art. 67 requires the election of a new chancellor before a vote of no confidence compels the government to resign. The *Länder* take part in federal legislation and administration through a Federal Council (*Bundesrat*).

The Federal Constitutional Court (*Bundesverfassungsgericht*), consisting of the *Bundestag*, controls the legislature, the executive, and the judiciary. Due process and judicial independence are guaranteed (art. 97, 101, 103, 104). Judicial review, much extended, gives even an individual the right of complaint (*Verfassungsbeschwerde*) concerning violated human rights.

Local government codes (*Gemeindeordnungen*) after World War II took account of the medieval traditions of the 13th to 15th centuries, and of the Stein-Hardenberg Reforms in Prussia (from 1807 onward), which provided the basis of modern municipal self-government throughout Germany. This allows the individual to cooperate at a practical level within his grasp while the state acts as a kind of umpire.

The communes (*Gemeinden*) have full powers of local self-government and carry out work for which the federal and *Länder* governments are responsible, except where the law expressly provides otherwise. Most larger units have a *Magistratsverfassung* whereby the *Gemeindevertretung* (popularly elected council) legislates and a *Kollegium* of officials (*Magistrat*) administers. The *Magistrat*, elected by the council, consists of the *Bürgermeister*, one professional, and one nonprofessional group of officials.

ADMINISTRATIVE

Administrative law regulates communes, municipalities, and public corporations concerned with social insurance, public health, welfare, housing, road traffic, public services, taxes, education, and the like. It is only partially codified; for instance, federal tax law, Police law is codified by the *Länder*. Influenced by French law, it distinguishes between the administrative act and the juristic act of private law; the former, even when illegal, may yet be binding until withdrawn by the issuing authority or quashed by a higher authority or an administrative court. Nevertheless, some rules of civil law are applied *mutatis mutandis* to administrative law.

To prevent the weakening of administrative courts such as occurred under Hitler, the law controls administrative discretion more strictly than before 1933. Intentional or negligent excess of official duty may make the state or public corporation (but not the official) liable in damages (GG, art. 34), above all where dangerous activities are involved; the state can claim indemnity against the official for gross negligence or intentional misconduct.

LABOUR

The early German labour laws, unlike their English counterparts, did not seek to develop collective bargaining but to protect workers. Going back to the time of Bismarck (*q.v.*), they covered such matters as industrial accidents, factory inspection, Sunday work, and social insurance, and forbade wages in kind and excessive deductions from wages. The *Kündigungsschutzgesetz* (Aug. 10, 1951) forbade socially unjustified dismissals and dealt with mass discharges, dismissed workers being also favoured by unemployment insurance and labour-exchange laws.

The Weimar constitution recognized trade unions and stimulated collective bargaining. After World War II the right to organize trade unions and to strike was constitutionally guaranteed. The *Tarifvertragsgesetz* of 1949 gave extended effect (*Allgemeinverbindlichkeit*) to collective wage-scale contracts, automatically applying to all individual employment contracts (*Unabdingbarkeit*). Minimum wages and holidays are settled by statutory machinery but ministers of labour may intervene or refer disputes to voluntary or compulsory arbitration. The *Betriebsverfassungsgesetz* of Oct. 11, 1952, concerns compulsory works council, which now have wide comanagement rights, especially social and personnel. Their agreements with individual employers are not only wage-scale contracts but also important sources of labour law.

CRIMINAL

Early Criminal Codes.—Written collections of criminal law date from the 6th century (*Lex Salica*) and comprehensive codifications existed in some German states from the 15th and 16th centuries (so-called *Halsgerichtsordnungen*). The first country-wide Criminal Code was the *Constitutio Criminalis Carolina* of 1532 (Charles V's *peinliche Halsgerichtsordnung*). Reasonable and excellently written in the vulgar tongue, it combined German with Italian ideas and remained in force for three centuries. Advocates of reform included Benedikt Carpzov (1595–1666), J. S. F. Böhmer (1704–70), and P. A. von Feuerbach (1775–1833) (*q.v.*), the author of the Bavarian Criminal Code of 1813. With the Enlightenment, criminal law became more humane, the inquisitorial procedure being abolished at the time of the French Revolution, and even earlier in Prussia (1740).

Federal Criminal Code.—After Hitler's abolition of the rule of law and of the principle of *nullum crimen sine lege* ("no crime without law," which goes back to the Enlightenment and French Revolution), the original Federal Criminal Code of 1871 was again in force. Special amendments have somewhat tempered the individualistic tone of the criminal law; for instance, it is an offense not to give assistance normally expected in accidents and in cases of public danger or emergency, especially when asked to help by the police (*Strafgesetzbuch*, s. 330c). General systems of reform have, however, considerably influenced Switzerland (1942 onward) and Scandinavia (20th-century criminal codes). The general part of a new Criminal Code was passed in 1969; making no striking break with the past, the new Criminal Code incorporates modern juristic theories on such matters as culpability, intention, and negligence which have since received general acceptance.

The general part of the Criminal Code explains the nature of offenses and punishments, the objective and subjective elements of a crime, exemptions from punishment, circumstances excluding guilt (particularly mistake), and methods of participation (for instance, attempts and aiding and abetting; but not conspiracy, which as such is unknown to German law, see however the special case of *Strafgesetzbuch*, s. 49b). Jurists distinguish in the subjective element direct and indirect intent and unconscious and aggravated negligence (*i.e.*, recklessness) but there are scarcely any presumptions of guilt. The solving of problems of negligence, particularly regarding error, have been assisted by H. Welzel's "doctrine of final action" (*Finale Handlungslehre*), which distinguishes causality and finality. Punishments (StGB, ss. 14–42) have varied with the political and economic background of the country. The "conditional suspending of sentence on probation" (*Strafaussetzung auf Bewährung*) of 1953 had been worked out by Franz von Liszt (1882). The GG (art. 102) abolished capital punishment. The new Criminal Code of 1969 has made imprisonment the only punishment involving deprivation of liberty; shorter prison sentences have to a large extent been replaced by fines; the possibility of imposing a suspended sentence has been considerably widened. Additional special security and reform measures may be imposed, such as confinement in an asylum, an institution for alcoholics and drug addicts, or a workhouse. Young persons (between 14 and 18, or 18 and 21 if the court so decides) under the *Jugendgerichtsgesetz* of 1953 are subject to an educational sanction involving reprimand or an order to follow a particular way of life (for instance, regarding residence, work, or habits); reformatory schooling; disciplinary measures, such as seeking pardon of the victim or attendance at a weekend juvenile detention centre; probation and punishment by a specified or indeterminate sentence in a juvenile prison not involving contact with adult prisoners.

The special part of the Criminal Code (StGB, ss. 80–370) deals with particular offenses; other penal laws cover taxation, economic matters, and police regulations. Work on the reform and redrafting of the special part of the Criminal Code is now proceeding.

LAW OF PROCEDURE

CIVIL

Development.—Since 1871, the gap between English emphasis on remedies and German attention to rights and duties has lessened. A romanized canon and Germanic law of procedure, taken from Italy to Germany at the time of the Reception, was transformed by the states' laws and court decisions into the *Gemeine Prozess*, later influenced by the Enlightenment and French *Code de Procédure Civile* (1806). Uniform procedure (more urgently demanded than uniform substantive civil law) was achieved in 1877 by four major acts (*Reichsjustizgesetze*) covering the court organization (*Gerichtsverfassungsgesetz*), civil procedure (*Zivilprozessordnung*), criminal procedure (*Strafprozessordnung*), and bankruptcy (*Konkursordnung*). A Supreme Court (*Reichsgericht*) was established at Leipzig in 1879; its predecessor, the *Reichskammergericht*, founded in 1495, had disappeared with the Holy Roman Empire in 1806.

Organization of the Courts.—Judges, university trained and having passed two state examinations, are appointed by the government at the outset of their career. They are not bound by precedent. At the first instance in the local court (*Amtsgericht*) they sit alone; at the next instance, the *Landgericht*, there are a number of courts (*Zivilkammern*) for civil cases, each presided over by a *Kollegium* of three judges. The *Landgericht* also has first-instance jurisdiction in civil cases where the amount in issue is over DM. 1,500. The *Oberlandesgericht*, sitting in senates of up to three judges, hears appeals from several *Landgerichte*. The three instances are part of the judicial system of the *Land*. The Federal Supreme Court (*Bundesgerichtshof*) sits at Karlsruhe. Lawyers (*Rechtsanwälte*) prepare the cases and appear in court, combining the functions of the English solicitor and barrister.

Principles of Procedure.—Except in questions of status (for example, divorce), the courts in principle consider only those facts presented by the parties and do not proceed inquisitorially. There must be a public oral hearing, though it may become less important where written pleadings are necessary. The principle of free assessment of evidence (ZPO, s. 286) allows the courts discretion in admitting and evaluating any kind of evidence. Special courts have additional procedural rules; *e.g.*, the labour courts (with a three-tiered hierarchy of *Arbeitsgerichte*, *Landesarbeitsgerichte*, and the *Bundesarbeitsgericht* at Kassel) dealing with individual or collective agreements between employer and employee and wrongful acts connected with industrial disputes.

ADMINISTRATIVE

Since World War II the *Länder* have provided the main laws of administrative courts (*Verwaltungsgerichte*, *Oberverwaltungsgerichte* and *Bundesverwaltungsgericht*) and of special bodies such as taxation courts (*Finanzgerichte* and *Bundesfinanzhof*), social insurance courts (*Sozialgerichte*), and the patent tribunal (*Bundespatentgericht*). The Law of Administrative Procedure was unified in 1960 by a federal act, the *Bundesverwaltungsgerichtsordnung*. Any administrative act (not merely those enumerated by statute) is justiciable before one of these courts which, though relying on specialized knowledge, seek to develop general conceptions applicable to all of them. They decide on the legality of administrative acts (*Anfechtungsverfahren*), the validity of subordinate legislation (*abstraktes Normprüfungsverfahren*), and other types of public-law disputes. Failing a remedy, the individual may lodge a complaint in the Federal Constitutional Court, charging that administrative acts, statutes, and ordinances do not conform with the rights of the GG.

CRIMINAL

Criminal procedure, as in English law, is accusatory: the judge does not initiate proceedings but hears a case presented by the prosecutor. The same courts function as in civil cases but the *Amtsgerichte* may sit with lay assessors (*Schöffengerichte*) and the *Landgerichte* with three professional judges and two laymen (*grosse Strafkammer*), or in certain matters with three professional judges and six laymen (*Schwurgerichte*) deciding together on guilt and punishment. The judge (unlike his English counterpart) himself interrogates the witnesses and experts, although he must on request allow the prosecutor, defendant, or his counsel to put questions to them. There is nothing equivalent to the cross-examination of Anglo-American procedure. The court must do everything necessary to ascertain the truth, but the accused has the benefit of the doubt.

Unlike judges, public prosecutors are subject to their superiors' instructions, a principle borrowed from the French *Code d'instruction criminelle* (1806). The minister of justice is the head of the public prosecutor's department (*Staatsanwaltschaft*), with offices attached to every court. The public prosecutor must investigate the circumstances of the alleged offense (StPO, s. 160); if convinced of the guilt of the accused, he must initiate proceedings (the "legality" principle, StPO, s. 152). At the trial he has an equal right with the accused to be heard, to produce evidence, and to appeal; but unlike the accused he may call on the police to assist him and may arrest suspected persons where delay in issuing a warrant would hamper the prosecution, provided the reasons would have justified a warrant. Persons so arrested must within 24 hours be brought before a judge who must issue a warrant or release them.

See also references under "German Law" in the Index.

BIBLIOGRAPHY.—English texts of German laws: Chung Hui Wang, *German Civil Code* (1907); W. Loewy, *German Civil Code* (1909); Press and Information Office of the German Federal Government, *Basic Law for the Federal Republic of Germany* (1966); The American Series of Foreign Penal Codes, *German Penal Code of 1871* (1961), *German Code of Criminal Procedure* (1965), and *The German Draft Penal Code E 1962* (1966). *See also* E. J. Cohn, *Manual of German Law*, vol. i, 2nd ed. (1968), vol. ii (1952); P. Koschaker, *Europa und das römische Recht*, 4th ed. (1966); F. Wieacker, *Privatrechtsgeschichte der Neuzeit*, 2nd ed. (1967); G. Radbruch and K. Zweigert, *Einführung in die Rechtswissenschaft*, 11th ed. (1964); J. von Staudinger, *Kommentar zum BGB*, 5 vol., 11th ed. (1957 *et seq.*); *Das Bürgerliche Gesetzbuch, Kommentar, hrsg. von Reichsgerichtsräten und Bundesrichtern*, 11th ed. (1959 *et seq.*); O. Palandt, *Kurzkommentar zum BGB*, 28th ed. (1969); W. Erman, *Handkommentar zum BGB*, 2 vol., 4th ed. (1967); L. Enneccerus, T. Kipp, and M. Wolff, *Lehrbuch des bürgerlichen Rechts*, 15 vol., new ed. (1959 *et seq.*); *Grosskommentar zum Handelsgesetzbuch*, 5 vol., 3rd ed. (1967 *et seq.*); T. Maunz and G. Dürig, *Das Grundgesetz, Kommentar*, 2nd ed. (1963 *et seq.*); K. A. Bettermann, H. C. Nipperdey, F. Neumann, and U. Scheuner, *Die Grundrechte*, 5 vol. (1954 *et seq.*); H. J. Wolff, *Verwaltungsrecht*, vol. i, 7th ed. (1968), vols. ii and iii, 2nd ed. (1967); A. Schönke and H. Schröder, *Strafgesetzbuch, Kommentar*, 14th ed. (1969); H. Welzel, *Das deutsche Strafrecht*, 10th ed. (1967); R. Bruns, *Zivilprozessrecht. Eine systematische Darstellung* (1968); A. Baumbach and W. Lauterbach, *Kurzkommentar zur ZPO*, 29th ed. (1966).

(W. M.-F.; N. S. M.)

GERMAN LITERATURE.

The literary history of the German-speaking peoples of Europe is here considered as a whole, since its development in general transcended national frontiers.

GERMAN LITERATURE

There are articles on AUSTRIAN LITERATURE and SWISS LITERA-TURE, which consider the special characteristics of German litera-ture in these countries. Many of the writers mentioned in the article below have separate articles which provide biographical in-formation and further critical comment; these articles may be found most conveniently by consulting the Index. There are also separate articles on many general subjects, *e.g.*, AUTOBIOGRAPHY; BIOGRAPHY; CLASSICAL SCHOLARSHIP; COMEDY; DRAMA; GER-MANIC MYTHOLOGY AND HEROIC LEGENDS; HUMANISM; NOVEL; REFORMATION; ROMANTICISM; SATIRE; THEATRE; which should be consulted as well as specialized aspects of German literature to which references will be found in the text. For medieval and Renaissance German literature in Latin *see* LATIN LITERATURE. This article is divided into the following sections:

I. OLD HIGH GERMAN PERIOD

The first written records of the continental German tribes date from the second half of the 8th century. There is, however, evi-dence of an earlier "literature" which lived by oral transmission. This consisted of short *Heldenlieder*, songs celebrating the exploits of famous heroes, ritual hymns connected with pagan religious rites, battle songs and laments for the dead. None of these was recorded but much of their substance formed the basis of later popular heroic epics.

The earliest records are glosses and are of interest only to the philologist tracing the development of the German vernacular. As in the other Germanic areas the first significant texts in German were a product of the efforts to spread Christianity. These are didactic in character and often evangelical in purpose. Many are translations from Latin; of these the more notable are the Alaman-nic version (c. 800) of Isidore of Seville's *De Fide Catholica* which was probably used as a clerical textbook, and an east Franconian rendering (c. 835) of Tatian's *Diatessaron*, a life of Christ made up of selected passages from the Gospels. Toward the end of the period Notker Labeo, a teacher in the monastery school of Sankt Gallen (St. Gall), added to the range of these works with his trans-lation (c. 1000) of the *De Consolatione* or "Consolations" of Boethius and of parts of the Bible, notably the Psalms and the Revelations of St. John.

More original are the few extant verse works. Of these the most extensive is the *Evangelienbuch* (c. 870) of the monk Otfrid of Weissenburg. This presented the life of Christ in a form to rival the pagan *Heldenlieder* or heroic lays, but it was handicapped by the didactic introduction of passages of commentary and expla-nation. Formally the poem is of interest as the first German work to use the end rhyme of medieval Latin verse as opposed to the alliteration of Germanic tradition. (*See* also ALLITERATIVE VERSE.) A more successful heroic treatment of the life of Christ was achieved by the unknown author of the earlier Old Saxon *Heliand* (*q.v.*; c. 830), which both in form and in spirit remains closer to the popular tradition. Some shorter Christian *Helden-lieder*, notably the *Ludwigslied* (881) and the *Georgslied* (c. 900), celebrate the exploits of kings or saints in the service of God. Other interesting fragments of largely Christian inspiration are the *Wessobrunner Gebet* (c. 800), which includes a brief picture of the creation, and the *Muspilli* (c. 830) which presents a vivid picture of the Last Judgment.

In spite of the attempts of churchmen to discourage, even eradi-cate, interest in pagan works, a few survived. Some are slight but of anthropological interest: such are the *Zaubersprüche* associated with Merseburg, Trier, Vienna, Lorsch and Strasbourg—spells to be used against prisoners and as a cure for the common cold. The most significant and interesting of all the records is however the *Hilde-brandslied* (c. 800), a fragment which recounts a grim Germanic version of the theme made familiar to English readers through Matthew Arnold's *Sohrab and Rustum*. The somewhat corrupt text which has survived by happy accident reveals a High German poem modified for a Low German audience.

Throughout the Old High German period the vernacular strug-gled for recognition as a valid literary language but scholars still preferred to write in Latin. As a result a number of the notable works by German writers of the period were written in Latin. Of special interest are the *Waltharius* (*q.v.*), an exercise (c. 930) by the young monk Ekkehard of St. Gall, an epic writing on a Ger-manic legendary theme, and a number of short plays celebrating saintly women by the 10th-century nun Hrosvitha of Bad-Ganders-heim. These have respectively a place in the development of the heroic epic and of the drama of Germany.

II. MIDDLE HIGH GERMAN PERIOD

1. The Transition.—In the first half of the 10th century a movement of ascetic reform spread over western Europe from the Burgundian monastery of Cluny. One of its results was that churchmen were dissuaded from writing for a secular public, so that there is little recorded literature in German for about a cen-tury thereafter. By the time works in the vernacular were written again, important changes in the form of the language had taken place and the old ecclesiastical didacticism had been replaced by the new spirit of courtly feudalism which was first developed in the courts of Provence. The knight replaced the cleric as the main poet and it is his interests and ideals that form the substance of the new writing. These changes mark the transition from Old to Middle High German.

The early works of this period still show traces of the previous clerical tradition. The *Ezzolied* (1063) by a Bamberg monk cele-brates the miracles and the death of Christ, while the *Annolied* (c. 1080) combines fanciful history and symbolic moralizing in praising Bishop Anno of Cologne. But there is already a hint of the new order in Heinrich von Melk's *Von des tôdes gehugede*, or ("Remembrance of Death"; c. 1160). In illustrating the main vanities of the day and reminding his contemporaries of the immi-nence of death he points to the 'spiritual and social folly of the feudal knight's love of combat.

The main literary forms of the Middle High German period were the love lyric (*Minnesang*) and the epic. In these the poets, mainly noblemen, expressed their love according to courtly convention or told traditional tales of combat and romance to the glory of God and for the edification and entertainment of their peers. In this they continued popular oral traditions of long standing but in addition they imported the most characteristic elements from west of the Rhine, namely a new conception of social behaviour and new metrical forms.

2. The Epic.—In the epic the local tradition had been created by the wandering minstrel (*Spielmann*), the successor of the Germanic *Skop*, as entertainer at court or in castle. He collected and recited heroic songs drawing on popular national legends and began to link up the shorter *Heldenlieder* to form longer epic narratives treating the exploits of famous heroes. He loved spectacular detail and incredible incident, his taste, if crude, matching that of his public. The *Spielleute* have left a number of interesting, sometimes amusing, commentaries on the life of their times. An early example, *König Rother* (c. 1160), like many others a repetitive tale of violent bride abduction, is of interest more for the detail than any general central theme, and is noteworthy historically as probably the earliest epic compilation of shorter heroic songs. *Salman und Moralf* is concerned not with the stealing of a bride but of a wife, and it introduces an additional conflict between Christian and pagan communities, a reflection of the interest aroused by the crusades. This is also evident in two similar tales, *Orendel* and *Sankt Oswald*, as well as in the lengthy, rambling *Kaiserkronik* (c. 1150) which turns to the national past for its subject matter. With the *Alexanderlied* (c. 1130) and the *Rolandslied* (c. 1175) German poets began to draw on successful French epics, since these are free renderings of the *Chanson d'Alexandre* and the *Chanson de Roland* respectively. (*See also* ALEXANDER ROMANCES; ROLAND, CHANSON DE.)

The culmination of the *Spielmann's* art is seen in the *Nibelungenlied* (*q.v.*), the greatest of the national German epics. Its author, an anonymous Austrian minstrel, showed his unusual skill, dramatic imagination and poetic ability in telling an astonishingly well-integrated story of Siegfried, his death at the hands of Hagen and the Burgundians and Kriemhild's revenge on her brothers. It combines songs of heroic legend based on historical events not only with tales linking the mythical representation of natural phenomena and Siegfried but also with an epic recounting the destruction of the Burgundians. This remarkable epic, handicapped by its four-line stanza form, has fired the imagination of German poets ever since and its survival in no fewer than 36 complete and fragmentary versions (the earliest c. 1200) testifies to its medieval popularity. The *Nibelungenlied* is largely a product of the south; the other important heroic epic, *Gudrun* (c. 1210), is based on Baltic coast legends, though it was also composed by an Austrian poet. Less dramatic and less popular than the *Nibelungenlied*, *Gudrun* is concerned with the brave loyalty of the young betrothed heroine, Gudrun, in the face of the humiliation and hardship inflicted on her by suitors who abduct her. The *Spielleute* also composed a number of minor romances, loosely connected with the life of Theodoric the Great, who as Dietrich von Bern was one of the favourite heroes of south Germany. These include *Die Rabenschlacht, Dietrichs Flucht, Alpharts Tod* and *Laurin* and they form part of a collection known as *Das Heldenbuch* (*q.v.*).

Alongside the national heroic epics, which seem to have appealed most in the south and southeast, where the German tradition was in conflict with the Slavic, there developed farther west, under strong influence from France, a form of courtly epic, in rhymed couplets, dealing with Arthurian subjects. The work of Chrétien de Troyes was the main model but most of the more successful French epics were remodeled into German versions. The forerunners in this genre were Eilhart von Oberge, whose *Tristant und Isolde* (c. 1170) was the first notable Arthurian poem in German; Herbort von Fritzlar, who composed a *Liet von Troye* (c. 1210); and Heinrich von Veldeke, a nobleman from the neighbourhood of Maastricht who based his *Eneit* (c. 1175–86) on a French source and is usually considered as the father of the German court epic. (*See also* ARTHURIAN LEGEND.)

The prestige of the Middle High German court epic rests, however, on three poets who composed most of their works between 1190 and 1210, namely Hartmann von Aue, Wolfram von Eschen-

bach and Gottfried von Strassburg. They handled their themes to illustrate the knightly virtues of moderation, constancy and loyalty and to stress the need for service of man and God in fearlessness, humility and faith. Hartmann, a minor Swabian nobleman, discussed in his poems *Erec* and *Iwein* the conflict between private inclination and public responsibility as it affected the medieval knight. He used the corresponding poems of Chrétien as his sources, displaying his poetic craftsmanship in his clarification of obscurity and in his ordering of the narrative. In *Gregorius* and *Der Arme Heinrich* he illustrates man's relationship with God.

WOLFRAM VON ESCHENBACH (FL. EARLY 13TH CENTURY). FROM THE MANESSE MANUSCRIPT

His poems are models of lucidity and he was noted among his contemporaries for his delicate artistry in storytelling. Wolfram von Eschenbach, whose *Parzival* is probably the greatest of the court epics, was a Bavarian who gloried in his unorthodoxy as a poet and reveals his unusually original personality especially in his imagery, which however often suffers from obscurity. *Parzival*, which tells of the innocent simpleton's eventful and dramatic progress to mature and wise responsibility as keeper of the Holy Grail, is the most subtle and ambitious courtly treatment of man's search for truth in his relationship with God. (*See also* PERCEVAL; GRAIL, THE HOLY.) Gottfried von Strassburg, less nobly born than the other two, wrote his Tristan epic using the chronicles of Thomas of Brittany as his source. He is less concerned with other-worldly considerations and shows the ideal primacy of love in this life in his treatment of the fortunes of Tristan and Isolde. Gottfried, who criticized Wolfram for his obscurities and his wild tales, was, like Hartmann, a careful craftsman and a master of form. (*See also* TRISTAN.)

The success of these three great poets inspired efforts to emulate them in the next two generations. Heinrich von dem Türlin followed in the footsteps of Hartmann but his epic *Die Krone* (c. 1220) is excessively long and ill-composed; Konrad Fleck's model on the other hand was Gottfried, but his account of the romance of *Flore und Blanscheflur* (c. 1220) is hardly more successful. More important were the two poets of the second generation, Rudolf von Ems (d. 1254) and Konrad von Würzburg (d. 1287). Rudolf, a most prolific poet, had strong didactic tendencies of a somewhat schoolmasterly type; he reveals the weakening of the courtly tradition in his choice of more abstruse subjects as in *Barlaam und Josaphat*. More significant and almost equally productive was Konrad. Among his shorter poems *Otte mit dem Barte* reveals an unusual sense of humour in relating a doubtless apocryphal incident in the life of the emperor Otto II, while the last of his longer works, the *Trojanerkrieg*, links him with an earlier tradition. The latter, like most of the late epics, is notable more for its length than its excellence. Konrad also initiated heraldic poetry in German with his shorter moral tale *Der Turnei von Nantheiz*.

An outstanding later epic is *Meier Helmbrecht* (c. 1250) by Wernher der Gärtner. This shorter poem describes movingly and uncompromisingly the lawlessness and violence of decadent feudal society. Its hero, the rascally son of a law-abiding peasant, illustrates the seamy side of a social order where strength was paramount, but he suffers a suitably cruel fate as punishment for his own brutality. In the social level of its subject and the realism of its approach, *Meier Helmbrecht* announces the end of courtly literature.

Similar characteristics are also to be found in the short didactic poems of the poet known as *Der Stricker*, of which even titles such as *Der nackte Bote* ("The Plain Messenger") and *Pfaffe Amis* ("Priest Amis") give sufficient hint. And by the mid-15th century the tone and spirit of the court epics had disappeared entirely, to be replaced by the satirical and realist didacticism of the middle classes.

3. The Lyric.—The other important literary form of the courtly period was the love lyric or *Minnesang* (see MINNESINGER). There had been simple love songs in German before the courtly period, and a few anonymous ones (*trällieder*) survived. *Minnesang*, like the court epic, owed its main characteristics to French influence. The new code of courtly love (*q.v.*) with all its conventions and conventional situations supplied the subject, the themes and the sentiments, while the new tripartite stanza form became the only one permissible. The increasing impact of the new ideas can be seen throughout the early phase, usually referred to as *Des Minnesangs Frühling* ("the springtime of Minnesang"). The poems have been recorded in particular in a magnificent early 14th-century manuscript known either as the *Grosse Heidelberger Liederhandschrift* or as the *Manessische Handschrift*. The earliest named poet, the Kurenberger, still shows nothing of the coming trend: he uses a simple four-line stanza form and expresses a virile independent spirit in his treatment of highborn ladies. Already in the songs of Dietmar von Aist and Friedrich von Hausen, however, the new form and the new artificial sentiments of *Minnesang* have been introduced. Most of the *Minnesänger* were noblemen, though of all levels of nobility from emperor to knight, and they lived or traveled widely in the Rhine and Danube valleys. A little more personal and original than most was the Saxon Heinrich von Morungen, but the most accomplished of all was Reinmar von Hagenau, who was born near the Rhine but achieved fame as the official court poet in Vienna in the last decade of the 12th century. He was recognized by his contemporaries as the most technically accomplished of all the *Minnesänger* but his range was narrow, being restricted to the plaint of long-suffering, unrequited love. In the eyes of his successors and in modern assessment he was far surpassed, however, by one of his pupils, Walther von der Vogelweide (*c.* 1170–*c.* 1230), who extended the range of subject, tone and form with masterly skill and lively enthusiasm. He not merely expressed conventional and unconventional sentiments of love but also wrote religious poetry and in the contemporary conflict between the popes and the emperors composed spirited patriotic and political poems, attacking the secular ambitions of the popes and supporting the emperors Otto IV and Frederick II. Walther represents the *Blütezeit* ("high summer") of *Minnesang*.

Among his successors the most significant lyricist was the Bavarian Neidhart von Reuenthal (*c.* 1180–*c.* 1250), in whose courtly rustic poetry the satirical realism of the declining feudal society can be seen. The interest in poems of satire and worldly wisdom (*Sprüche*) had of course existed before Walther. It had been exploited by singers like Spervogel and was developed by Walther's political poems but it now became much more widespread as is seen in longer poems of this nature like the anonymous *Der Winsbeke* (*c.* 1230), Freidank's *Bescheidenheit* (*c.* 1230) and Hugo von Trimberg's *Der Renner* (*c.* 1300). The two last mentioned were highly popular in succeeding generations, being frequently reproduced or copied, and they lead on to the more middle-class writing of the 15th and 16th centuries. This was already apparent with the *Ritterspiegel* (1416) of the Thuringian priest Johannes Rothe in which nothing of the old spirit is left and only a commoner's view of the externals of knightly honour takes its place.

4. Prose and Drama.—The prose literature of the Middle

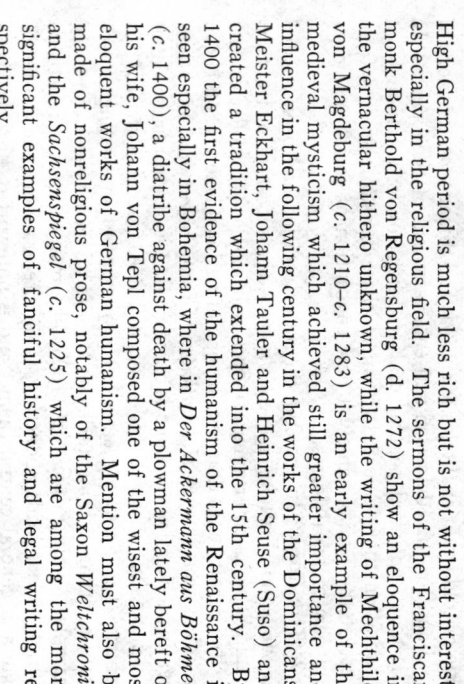

THE BETTMANN ARCHIVE

WALTHER VON DER VOGELWEIDE (ABOUT 1170–ABOUT 1228). FROM THE MANESSE MANUSCRIPT

High German period is much less rich but is not without interest, especially in the religious field. The sermons of the Franciscan monk Berthold von Regensburg (d. 1272) show an eloquence in the vernacular hitherto unknown, while the writing of Mechthild von Magdeburg (*c.* 1210–*c.* 1283) is an early example of the medieval mysticism which achieved still greater importance and influence in the following century in the works of the Dominicans, Meister Eckhart, Johann Tauler and Heinrich Seuse (Suso) and created a tradition which extended into the 15th century. By 1400 the first evidence of the humanism of the Renaissance is seen especially in Bohemia, where in *Der Ackermann aus Böhmen* (*c.* 1400), a diatribe against death by a plowman lately bereft of his wife, Johann von Tepl composed one of the wisest and most eloquent works of German humanism. Mention must also be made of nonreligious prose, notably of the Saxon *Weltchronik* and the *Sachsenspiegel* (*c.* 1225) which are among the more significant examples of fanciful history and legal writing respectively.

In the drama there are also historically interesting beginnings to note. The 13th-century Christmas and Easter plays of Benediktbeuern, composed in Latin verse, the fragmentary Easter play of Muri, in German, and the St. Gall passion play (*c.* 1330) lead on to a growing volume of popular morality and miracle plays which form part of the church's campaign to educate and inspire the lower orders. Toward the beginning of the 15th century a more popular form of the drama still appears in the carnival plays or *Fastnachtsspiele*, farces often of a very crude nature, written purely for secular entertainment. Hans Rosenplüt of Nürnberg (a town which was already beginning to achieve the fame which distinguished it in the heyday of the Meistersinger) and his younger contemporary, the barber Hans Folz of Worms, who also settled in Nürnberg, were the more notable purveyors in the mid-15th century of this popular type of formless and uninhibited comedy which in the 16th century reached a level of greater respectability and artistic form in the works of Hans Sachs.
(W. W. Cs.)

III. FROM MIDDLE HIGH GERMAN TO BAROQUE, 1450–1600

1. The Transition.—The fall of Constantinople (1453) opened the way for a Turkish threat to western Europe which lasted more than two centuries; fear of the hated Turk was a common literary theme in the 16th and 17th centuries. At home, territorial rulers —lay and ecclesiastical princes and free imperial cities—asserted their independence at the expense of the empire. Nicolas of Cusa (*c.* 1400–64), strongly influenced by Renaissance Platonism, dominated the intellectual field, while Johann Gutenberg's invention of printing from movable type (*c.* 1440) marked an epoch in European letters. Yet the established genres continued to entertain and instruct without apparent change. Meistersingers such as Hans Rosenplüt, and those like Michael Beheim who stood close to them in outlook and technique, became ever more involved in deadening rules during the 15th century until Hans Folz introduced into the new *Singschule* at Nürnberg more liberal rules which led to a revival of the art (see MEISTERSINGER). The folk song flourished; songs of love and nature, war and death, drinking and conviviality, religious lyrics, legendary and historical ballads survive in great profusion in various collections (Klara Hätzlerin's songbook, 1471; *Bergreihen*, 1531; Georg Forster's *Frische teutsche Liedlein*, 1539–56). In the south the *Fastnachtspiel* became a vehicle of satire and of broad, often coarse humour in the hands of writers such as Rosenplüt and Folz; in the north its more patrician devotees produced a more restrained type. Collections of comic anecdotes (*Schwänke*), often grouped round a single "hero," as in Philipp Frankfurter's *Pfarrer vom Kalenberg* (printed 1473), found a ready audience; *Till Eulenspiegel* (*q.v.*) acquired a European reputation. *Des Spiegels Abenteuer* and *Die Mörin* (1453; on the subject of Venus and Tannhäuser) by Hermann von Sachsenheim, represent medieval allegory. Elaborate religious mystery and morality plays continued to be performed at the main Christian festivals, and despite continued opposition from the reformers the genre survived until well into the 16th century.

2. The Courtly Renaissance.—At certain princely courts,

notably Rottenburg and Innsbruck, the Burgundian courtly "renaissance" fostered a revived, though often misinformed, interest in medieval chivalry. At Innsbruck, Duchess Eleonore of Austria (1433–80), in emulation of the prose romances of Countess Elisabeth of Nassau-Saarbrücken (1397–1456), wrote a prose version of a French chivalrous romance, *Pontus und Sidonia* (printed 1483); at Rottenburg, Jacob Püterich von Reichertshausen's *Ehrenbrief* (1462) fostered a cult of Wolfram von Eschenbach. Medieval poems were printed, either in their original verse form (*Parzival, Heldenbuch,* 1477) or—more characteristically of an age which valued subject matter as a means of education or entertainment far more than literary form—in prose versions of little literary distinction (*Wigoleysz*; printed 1493, after Wirnt von Grafenberg; *Tristant,* 1484, after Eilhart von Oberge). Ulrich Füeterer in his huge *Buch der Abenteuer* (finished 1478) retold the Arthurian stories yet again. In the next generation the allegorical works of the emperor Maximilian I, *Weisskunig* (1514, prose) and *Theuerdank* (1517, verse), represent probably the last attempt to live by medieval chivalrous ideals.

3. Humanism.—In sharp contrast to this courtly renaissance —though often sharing the same princely patronage—stands the new element in German literature after 1450: the humanist movement. Early Bohemian humanism had been an isolated episode; the humanists of the decades between 1450 and 1480 drew their inspiration afresh from Italy. Though they wrote a little in Latin, Albrecht von Eyb, Heinrich Steinhöwel, Niklas von Wyle, "Arigo" (Heinrich Schlüsselfelder?) and Antonius von Pforr were chiefly translators who, in seeking to introduce into German the linguistic ideals of humanistic Latin, produced versions of many Latin classics, as well as of some Greek and Indian ones, and of outstanding Italian works including the *Decameron.* This remarkable group of translations marked an important stage in the development of German prose and introduced welcome new subjects for later writers.

After 1480, and throughout most of the 16th century, German humanism presented quite a different picture. More exclusive than their predecessors, Conradus Celtis, Euricius Cordus, Eobanus Hessus, Crotus Rubeanus and Beatus Rhenanus, to name but a few, were closely associated with university circles and wrote almost entirely in Latin. A strong patriotic and political strain was not lacking, witness the *Germania* (1501) of Jacob Wimpfeling, Celtis's edition of Tacitus' *Germania* (1500) and the diplomatic activities of Konrad Peutinger; nor was a lively interest in German history, a field in which German was used alongside Latin, e.g., Beatus Rhenanus' *Rerum germanicarum libri III* (1531), the *Chronik der Abte von St. Gallen* (1533) of Joachim Vadianus or the *Bayerische Chronik* (1533) of Aventinus. But their writings had little direct influence on the mass of the people; they belong to the wider movement of European humanism. This is eminently true of the Christian humanism of Erasmus, and perhaps even of Johann Reuchlin, the distinguished Hebrew scholar whose defense of Jews and Jewish studies led to the brilliant satire on monkish life and letters, *Epistolae obscurorum virorum* (1515–17).

In one field, however, the humanist impact was more direct: the drama. While mystery plays and *Fastnachtspiele* continued to edify and amuse the general populace, the humanists established a lively dramatic tradition as part of their school and university curricula. Roman comedies, especially those of Terence, and Latin plays by modern authors—Wimpfeling's *Stylpho* (composed 1480), criticizing the clergy, and Reuchlin's *Henno* (1497), with a plot similar to the French *Maître Pathelin,* were two of the first—were performed as a vehicle of moral instruction and to teach deportment and eloquence. These plays, with their concern for form, small casts, division into acts and classical chorus, contrasted sharply with the medieval dramatic types; from them, rather than from the medieval tradition, 16th-century German drama developed. Later this Latin drama was turned to the service of the Reformation by Wilhelm Gnaphaeus with his *Acolastus* (1529), Georgius Macropedius with *Hecastus* (1539) and Thomas Naogeorgus with *Pammachius* (1538) and *Mercator* (1540).

The concentration on Latin by the most gifted writers of the age goes far to explain why, in contrast to the brilliance of the

plastic arts (Lucas Cranach, Mathias Grünewald, Hans Holbein and especially Albrecht Dürer), vernacular literature between 1490 and 1520 is so scarce. (This division between learned Latin and popular German persists until at least the 17th century, when the two streams begin to merge.) Apart from the patriotic *Tell* play from Uri (after 1511), satirical or didactic works predominate, reflecting a decline in moral standards and general discontent with conditions in church and state. The most famous work of the 15th century, the *Narrenschiff* (1494) of Sebastian Brant, which reviewed all the major and minor vices of the age, provided material for sermons by the Strasbourg preacher Johann Geiler von Kaisersberg. It acquired a European reputation—though admittedly in Latin translation—and set a fashion for "fool literature" which was ably followed by, among others, the Franciscan Thomas Murner in his own hard-hitting moral satires (1512–19). In the Low German *Reynke de Vos* (printed 1498), a descendant of the medieval beast epic, the verse of the text is accompanied by an extensive prose commentary applying the satirical episodes to contemporary evils. In Basel, Pamphilus Gengenbach adapted the popular southern *Fastnachtspiel* for moral teaching (*Spiel von den zehn Altern,* 1515) and political satire (*Der Nollhart,* 1517).

4. The Reformation.—From a purely literary point of view, the Reformation brought little change in the old forms and genres; indeed the vigour of the protests which Martin Luther raised against ecclesiastical abuses (and later against certain doctrines), and the variety and violence of the reactions he evoked, deeply affected the whole political and social life of Germany and left little room for purely aesthetic considerations. The humanists, who favoured reform of abuses but opposed doctrinal changes, mostly held aloof, though with certain notable exceptions: Ulrich von Hutten hoping for a political reformation to complete the ecclesiastical one, supported Luther's cause with embarrassing vigour, particularly in a series of pamphlets first written in Latin and translated into German (*Gesprächbüchlein,* 1521); Philipp Melanchthon, the Greek scholar, made valuable contributions to the scholarship of the new church and introduced the humanist tradition into Protestant schools. But apart from the humanists, almost every writer of note was preoccupied with the Reformation. From the torrent of printed works of every description which swept over Germany a few stand out as having some literary merit: Luther's own many and various writings, all with the directness and vigour of good popular preaching, his eloquent Reformation pamphlets of 1520, for example, or his appeal for the foundation of municipal schools (*An die Ratherren aller Städte deutschen Lands,* 1524), his terrible condemnation of the peasants' revolt (*Wider die räuberischen und mörderischen Rotten der Bauern,* 1525) or his lively defense of his own Bible translation (*Sendbrief vom Dolmetschen,* 1530); the dialogue *Karsthans* (1521), with the honest peasant supporting Luther; the *Fünfzehn Bundesgenossen* (1521–23), in which Johann Eberlin von Günzburg attacks

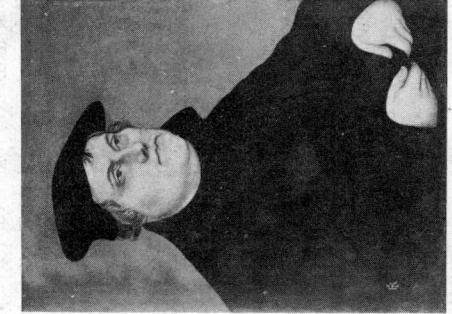

THE BETTMANN ARCHIVE

MARTIN LUTHER (1483–1546). A PAINTING BY LUCAS CRANACH. IN THE UFFIZI GALLERY, FLORENCE, ITALY

abuses and commends an inward religion of the heart; the most ruthless of all Thomas Murner's satires, *Vom grossen lutherischen Narren* (1522), in defense of the old religion; the *Wittembergisch Nachtigall* (1523) of Hans Sachs and his Reformation dialogues (1524) with their gentle, kindly satire; the fierce anti-Catholic satire in the *Fastnachtspiele* of Niklas Manuel of Bern, *Vom Papst und seiner Priesterschaft* (1523), *Der Ablasskrämer* (1526); the rational, humanist sermons of Huldreich Zwingli and his poems expressing his faith in the involved metres of the Meistersinger; the *Paradoxa* (1534) and *Germaniae Chronicon* (1537) of the independent radical thinker Sebastian Franck.

In three respects the Reformation had a lasting effect on German literature. First, Luther's Bible translation (New Testament, 1522; Old Testament complete, 1534), though not the first—the translation printed by J. Mentel in Strasbourg about 1466 had been the first of several printed versions—was not only based for the first time on the Hebrew and Greek texts (Erasmus' New Testament appeared in 1516) but also achieved a vigorous, popular German style. It has exercised an incalculable influence on the ideas—to say nothing of the language—of later German writers. Moreover, its widespread use made it a rallying point and a standard of reference in the long, complex struggle for a standard literary language. (*See also* BIBLE, TRANSLATIONS OF.)

Secondly, Luther, a great music lover, established congregational hymn singing as an essential part of the Protestant service and himself wrote several hymns still in regular use: *Vom Himmel hoch da komm ich her* ("From Heaven Above to Earth I Come"); *Aus tiefer Not schrei ich zu dir* ("From Depths of Woe I Cry to Thee"); and especially *Ein feste Burg ist unser Gott* ("A Mighty Fortress Is Our God"). His example was followed during the period by Paulus Speratus, Nikolaus Herman, Bartholomaeus Ringwaldt, Philipp Nicolai and others, who established a tradition of hymn writing which continued far beyond the 16th century and has been a major (but often unacknowledged) German contribution to the whole Christian world. (*See also* HYMN.)

Thirdly, Luther, while condemning the medieval mysteries, had commended certain biblical subjects as suitable for plays. With this in mind, many dramatists—of whom Sixtus Birck, Paul Rebhuhn, Joachim Greff, Burkhard Waldis and Jörg Wickram are the most outstanding—wrote plays in German as vehicles of Lutheran teaching. Favourite subjects, treated again by different dramatists, were the stories of Susanna (Birck, 1532; Rebhuhn, 1536), Judith (Birck, 1534; Greff, 1536), the marriage at Cana (Rebhuhn, 1538) and the Prodigal Son (Waldis, 1527, in Low German; Wickram, 1540). Modeled more or less closely on the Latin school drama, these plays marked a break with the medieval types of drama.

The Reformation, however, despite its importance, does not account for all the vernacular literature after 1520. In scholarly works, for example, German was gradually beginning to replace Latin. Prose chronicles have been mentioned; there may be added the *Vier Bücher von menschlicher Proportion* (1528) of Albrecht Dürer and some of the treatises of the Swiss doctor, alchemist and scientist Paracelsus (Theophrastus von Hohenheim, 1493–1541). Otherwise, as throughout the century, satirical or didactic works remain predominant. This is clear in the collection of proverbs (1528) by Johann Agricola. The fable, too, with its unambiguous and explicit moral, enjoyed revival. Luther's own translations from Aesop first appeared in his collected works (1557) and have no special merit; but Erasmus Alberus in his *Fabeln* (1534; 2nd ed. 1550, renamed *Buch von der Tugend und Weisheit*) and Burkhard Waldis in his *Esopus* (1548) turned the fable into a lively minor genre. And in *Grobianus* (1549) by Friedrich Dedekind, a satirical Latin guide to table manners, translated into German boorishness, appeared as a dreadful commentary on contemporary manners.

Apart from Luther, the most prolific—and probably the most characteristic—writer of the century was Hans Sachs (1494–1576). His works, didactic in aim but—after his earliest years—entirely unpolemical, reflect the ideals of the devout, upright, industrious Lutheran townsman and artisan. By common consent the greatest of the Meistersingers, he brought the genre to perfection and virtually to an end, despite attempts at revivals by later poets, among them Adam Puschmann, whose *Gründlicher Bericht des deutschen Meistergesangs* (1571) contains a valuable account of the movement. Sachs was at his best in the comic verse anecdote and the *Fastnachtspiel*; but here, too, he had no adequate successors. Jakob Ayrer's *Fastnachtspiele*, for instance, lacked Sachs's compactness of plot. (His *Singspiele* were more successful.)

5. Light Literature.—As the tide of Reformation polemics receded—and even before the peace of Augsburg (1555) brought a respite in the religious conflict—works of pure entertainment came into greater prominence. The popular chapbooks (so-called *Volksbücher*) had various origins; some were prose versions of medieval verse romances, some were adapted from foreign sources. But whatever their origin the stories of *Fortunatus*, *Die vier Haimonskinder*, *Kaiser Oktavian*, *Magelone*, *Melusine* and many others were favourite reading far beyond the 16th century. Men which went back at least to found distraction also in collections of anecdotes, a type of work influenced by humanist collections such as Heinrich Bebel's *Facetiae* (1509–12). The *Schimpf und Ernst* (1522) of Johann Pauli had didactic aims; but entertainment was the sole aim of Jörg Wickram's *Rollwagenbüchlein* (1555) and of similar collections by others which followed in quick succession. About this time, too, Wickram's more substantial prose narratives (*Knabenspiegel*, 1554; *Der Goldfaden*, printed 1557; *Von guten und bösen Nachbarn*, 1556) and in the German translation of the Spanish *Amadis de Gaula* (a new influence in German literature), 24 volumes of which appeared between 1569 and 1595.

6. The Close of the Century.—The Council of Trent (1545–63) and the advent of the Jesuits gave religious controversy a new turn. The Jesuits adopted the Latin school drama for their own educational purposes, developing it into elaborate spectacular presentations which are one of the roots of baroque drama. But no outstanding dramatists appeared until the 17th century. Meanwhile the Protestant academy in Strasbourg, especially under the Christian humanist Johannes Sturm (1507–89), developed a rich educational and dramatic tradition; Kaspar Brülow (1585–1627) is only the most distinguished of many playwrights who worked there.

In the last quarter of the century the sole outstanding author was Johann Fischart, many of whose works were directed against the Jesuits, the Counter-Reformation and notably the brilliant Franciscan preacher Johannes Nas. But in all his writings, even including the huge expanded version of Rabelais' *Gargantua*, the *Geschichtschrift* (1575, later renamed *Geschichtklitterung*), the didactic and satirical aims characteristic of the age were combined with something long missing from German literature, an interest in literary form. *Das glückhaft Schiff* (1576) is, formally and stylistically, one of the most distinguished poems of the century. Fischart's contemporary Philipp Nikodemus Frischlin was the last notable Latin dramatist of the century; otherwise the last years of the century saw only minor figures. *De düdesche Schlömmer* (1584), a Low German play by Johann Stricker, points clearly back to medieval drama; the pseudo-Homeric battle between frogs and mice, *Froschmeuseler* (1595), by Georg Rollenhagen, ends the beast epic tradition; the anonymous *Lalebuch* (1597; 2nd ed. renamed *Die Schildbürger*, 1598) is the last collection of comic anecdotes. On the other hand, the versions of psalms (1572 and 1573) by Paul Schede-Melissus and Ambrosius Lobwasser on the Calvinist model of Clément Marot add a new element to Protestant hymn writing, while the anonymous chapbook, *Historia von Dr. Johann Fausten* (1587), bears within it the seeds of the whole European Faust tradition from Marlowe onward. (*See also* FAUST.)

The most noteworthy feature in the last years of the century, however, was the arrival in Germany of troupes of English actors (*Englische Komödianten*) whose repertoire included versions—often crude and sensational, but theatrically effective—of contemporary English plays. Their influence on Jakob Ayrer was considerable; and they also found a ready welcome at the court theatre—the first of its kind—of Duke Heinrich Julius of Brunswick who himself learned much from them in the composition of his own 11 plays (all but one printed in 1593–94). This new influence from England, which promised to revive the German drama —though indeed the promise was only partially fulfilled—marks an epoch in the history of German literature; with it German literature moves into the baroque age.

(J. R. WE.)

IV. THE 17TH CENTURY

1. The Character of the Period.—German 17th-century literature, widely known as baroque literature, is very much the product of its times and of the conditions obtaining in Europe, but particularly in Germany, during the period. It is ushered in against a background of witch burning, religious strife, changing social conditions and political uncertainty. It is dominated in the first half of the century by the Thirty Years' War and the shadow this cast over all walks of life. It is located against a background of princely absolutism and the cultural centre of the court, where every German ruler strove to emulate the court of Versailles. It is concerned, directly or indirectly, with the struggle between the champions of the Reformation and the Counter-Reformation for the souls of men in an age that still believed in religious values and for which the battle between good and evil was a metaphysical reality. But it reflected as well the dawn of a new age, where the frontiers of science and learning and of the physical world were being pushed back by a series of brilliant scholars and explorers. The cultural temper of the age is overshadowed by formative influences from the preceding century, by Martin Luther and Ignatius of Loyola, by Machiavelli, the exponent of modern statecraft, by Justus Lipsius, with his doctrine of neostoicism, and, belatedly, by the Petrarch and the Renaissance ideals which, submerged by the religious polemic of the 16th century, exerted their influence on the cultural values of the 17th century. The century witnessed the rise of baroque art, with its startling blend of sensual extravagance and formal precision, of emotion and mathematics, qualities that are reflected in the literature to which the term baroque is often applied.

This literature has only recently been properly appreciated. This is partly because the 20th century has many affinities with the baroque world, with its wars, social upheavals, political opportunism, cultural experimentation and scientific progress, partly because our evaluation of baroque literature is no longer so dominated by Goethean and post-Goethean concepts of the importance of the confessional element in literature and by romantic ideals which have nothing in common with the world of the baroque. For baroque literature is dominated, not by the *Erlebnis*, the experience, but by the *occasio*, the occasion; and the writers, of whom there are many, do not express themselves subjectively but through the medium of conventional images and conceits. They avail themselves of strict formal patterns, a curious intellectual geometry, against which the emotional tensions reflected in the prevailing themes are not repressed but rather heightened.

German baroque literature is dominated by certain themes which appear throughout in the lyric, the epic and the drama. These are the common currency of European 17th-century literature. Some examples may suffice. In a world of uncertainty apparently ruled by chance the goddess Fortuna presides and is continually referred to as *das wanckelmüthige Glück* ("fickle fortune"). The theme of time is all-important, life is precarious, all earthly things are transitory, nothing lasts, behind everything looms the shadow of death. The world is a *Jammerthal* ("a vale of tears"), and the illusory nature of worldly pleasures is contrasted unfavourably with the eternity beyond the grave. While on this earth, however, man must fill the role allotted to him; the theme of the world as a stage and of man as an actor playing a role is rarely absent. The literature presents such roles, as examples of how man may escape the toils of fortune and cheat the ravages of time. The baroque martyr scorns the world and aspires to eternity; the baroque statesman makes use of the passing moment to further his advantage; the stoic bears the trials of the world with exemplary *Beständigkeit*, or "steadfastness," the hermit flees from them; the shepherds and shepherdesses of the pastoral escape into their own world of make-believe, the mystic seeks for union with God; through his work the poet hopes for the fame that will secure for him a relative immortality.

2. Lyric Poetry.—These themes are expressed above all in the works of the lyric poets. There were many of them, and they tended to congregate in particular areas, notably in Heidelberg, Königsberg, Nürnberg, Hamburg and above all Silesia. At first their efforts were tentative and hardly to be compared with the neo-Latin poetry that was so abundantly produced and which reached a peak in the work of Jakob Balde (1604–68). But in a very short time the quality of the lyric poetry improved out of all recognition;

MARTIN OPITZ (1597–1639). FROM A PAINTING BY JACOB VON HENDEN. 1631

and it is primarily the lyric poetry which makes such an impact on 20th-century readers. Much of the credit for this must go to Martin Opitz. In his critical works (*Aristarchus*, 1618, and *Buch von der deutschen Poeterey*, 1624) Opitz showed how a suitably purified German language was capable of elevated literary expression, laid down rules, such as the observance of stress in poetry instead of mere syllable counting, for emerging poets, and made suggestions, such as the adoption of the alexandrine, which his contemporaries were quick to seize on; and he was a sufficiently able poet to give practical examples (*e.g.*, in his *Teutsche Poemata*, 1624) of what he meant. The result was that the pathfinding efforts of gifted poets such as Georg Weckherlin and Andreas Tscherning could be viewed against the background of Opitz' reforms and a new generation of poets soon arose who far outshone their master.

The variety of German baroque verse, given the basic similarity of theme already referred to, is astonishing. There is the lyric power, emotional depth and manly independence of Paul Fleming, revealed in his love poems and sonnets; there is the deep pessimism and intense religious fervour of Andreas Gryphius, who, with great technical virtuosity and a sovereign command of language, gives expression to the existential problems of the age in the *Angst*-laden lines of poems such as *Es ist alles eitel, Menschliches Elend* and the *Kirchhofsgedanken*. The formal dexterity of a Philipp von Zesen and the verbal exuberance of the Nürnberg poets Johann Klaj and Georg Philipp Harsdörfer are examples of the urge to experiment which, for all its flashy cleverness, can communicate a sense of creative spontaneity. The baroque poet wears many masks; the intellectual mannerisms, rhetorical exaggerations and lascivious undertones of Christian von Hofmannswaldau as he dwells on the charms of the beloved can give place to the sober sincerity of the same poet as he reflects on the transitoriness of life in *Wo sind die Stunden*. It is, perhaps, above all in the religious lyric that German baroque poetry reaches the greatest height, understandably enough in an age so concerned with ultimate values. All the leading poets wrote religious as well as secular lyrics. Among those who concentrate on religious verse the outstanding writer is the Lutheran Paul Gerhardt, whose hymns, many of which are still in use, show a quiet simplicity and a warm humanity whose appeal is timeless. Other religious writers, of widely differing character, are the Catholic Friedrich von Spee, with his religious pastoral lyric, Angelus Silesius (pseudonym of Johannes Scheffler), and the mystic visionary Quirinus Kuhlmann. A genre that admirably reflected the intellectual temper of the age and gave full scope to its tendency to precise antithetical formulation was the epigram, and the writing of epigrams was developed to a fine art by such poets as Daniel Czepko, Angelus Silesius and Friedrich von Logau.

3. Drama.—For an age which witnessed the development of modern stagecraft and the rise of opera, the achievements in the field of German drama are modest and their influence does not extend beyond the 17th century. Heinrich Julius, duke of Brunswick, as has been mentioned, ushered in the century with plays that reflect the influence of the English players, but while such plays as *Vincentius Ladislaus* and *Von einem ungeratenen Sohn* are of some literary interest they only serve to show how backward vernacular German drama was, particularly when compared with the neo-Latin drama written at the same time. Very different is the picture presented in the second half of the century, when the baroque dichotomy between excess of feeling and acuteness of intellectual perception culminates in the fulsome rhetoric that dominates the plays of Daniel Caspar von Lohenstein. Yet the age did produce two dramatists of outstanding merit. The Jesuit Jakob Bidermann wrote during the first two decades of the century neo-Latin dramas (*Cenodoxus, Philemon Martyr, Cosmarchia* and others) which deal in a highly artistic and dramatically effective way with the baroque themes of mutability, the vanity of this world, and the urgency of individual salvation, and which met with great popular success wherever they were staged. The Silesian Andreas Gryphius wrote tragedies and comedies in which the themes of stoicism and the preservation of personal integrity stand out against a sombre background of deceit and uncertainty that mirrors the age in which Gryphius lived. The situations in his plays are more dramatic than is often allowed, the language is stately and impressive and often highly moving, and the resources of the alexandrine metre are exploited to the full. Yet his dramas, remarkable though they are, belong essentially to the category of school drama. Such drama was literary, rather than popular, in character; and its influence on succeeding generations was slight. For as the century wore on people turned increasingly from the world of straight drama to that of the masque, of ballet, court spectacle and opera; and the drama that eventually flourished in the following century was to develop along very different lines.

4. The Novel.—German baroque literature owes much to foreign influences, and this is particularly so in the case of the novel, which draws considerably on Spanish, French and neo-Latin sources. Translations provided an impetus; Aegidius Albertinus translated Mateo Alemán's *Guzmán de Alfarache* (1615) and inaugurated the German picaresque novel, Opitz translated John Barclay's *Argenis* (1626) and adapted Sir Philip Sidney's *Arcadia* (1629), and a whole host of translations soon flooded into Germany. The result was that a considerable number of novels were written, and the German novel as such began to take shape. Many of the novels are sprawling and diffuse, an amalgam of didactic and moralizing elements on the one hand and fantastic, exotic and diverting elements on the other, designed to meet the insatiable *Stoffhunger* of the age. It is not always easy to enthuse over the satirical works of a Philipp von Zesen, the political and courtly novels of Caspar von Lohenstein and Anton Ulrich von Braunschweig. Two writers stand out above their contemporaries. One is Johann Beer (1655–1700), a gifted novelist whose distinctive realist style points forward to the next century; and the other is H. J. C. von Grimmelshausen, whose novel *Der abenteuerliche Simplicissimus* (1668–69) stands head and shoulders above all other novels of the age and deserves to rank as one of the great novels of German literature. Outwardly picaresque in form, in a great measure autobiographical in content, it depicts with uncompromising realism the Germany of the Thirty Years' War. It incorporates all the principal themes of the age, and with its metaphysical depth and religious insight represents probably the greatest achievement of German baroque literature.

5. Philosophy and Criticism.—The outstanding thinker at the beginning of the century is the Silesian mystic Jakob Boehme, a highly original philosopher who directly influenced such writers as Daniel von Czepko and Angelus Silesius and whose doctrines helped to inspire several religious separatist movements throughout western Europe. At the century the achievements of the age are summed up in the figure of Gottfried Wilhelm Leibniz, who points forward to the 18th century, where a very different type of literature was to be evolved. For J. C. Gottsched and his contemporaries most baroque literature was anathema. They had little understanding of the problems and aims of the preceding century; and it was not until the 20th century that baroque literature was to be rediscovered and properly appreciated.

(D. G. D.)

V. THE AGE OF ENLIGHTENMENT

1. The Climate of Opinion.—If religion was the dominant factor in German intellectual and spiritual affairs in the 17th century, and thoughts of the hereafter were uppermost in men's minds, the Enlightenment brought about a reaction. Its outlook reposed upon the acceptance of the primacy of reason. Man now claimed to be able to understand the universe independently of supernatural revelation by virtue of his possession of the divine gift of reason. Dogmatic religion gave way to natural religion, or deism (*q.v.*), belief to knowledge, concern for the hereafter to concern for life in this world. Empirical and idealist thinkers alike were united in rejecting traditional authority. In a harmonious, rational universe, governed by the mathematical law of cause and effect, there was no room for mystery. There was no room either for the doctrines of original sin and predestination. Evil was no more than the result of irrational conditions of life, and man had it in his power to improve his lot by the pursuit of science and education. An egalitarian creed was inherent in this new philosophy since reason was the possession of all men. An optimistic belief in human perfectibility was generally held; the way toward it lay in the cultivation of reason and tireless effort in the service of human improvement. The baroque exaggerations were thus bound to be condemned. The new age had more practical objectives. The man of the world being more highly regarded than the devout Christian, good taste and common sense came to be demanded. Literature possessed a markedly didactic character. The fable, satire, epigram and idyl were highly favoured modes, but the didactic element was equally important in other genres. Nature was treated as the manifestation of the Creator's wisdom and as the embodiment of harmony, order and purpose.

2. Rationalism.—The intellectual life of Germany recovered rapidly from the social upheavals of the Thirty Years' War. The foundations of rationalism were laid by Samuel Pufendorf (1632–94), Christian Thomasius (1655–1728), Christian Wolff (1679–1754), and, above all, by Leibniz (1646–1716), the first of the great German philosophers. With him the relationship of God and man to each other ceased to be considered within the limits of Christian dogma; the universe came henceforth to be apprehended not in religious but in secular terms. Leibniz' theory of monads, his doctrine of pre-established harmony and his acceptance of this as the best of all possible worlds affected the thought of the whole of the century. German religious life was marked by a revival of pietism not in conformity but in the individual's spiritual experience. At the same time Gottfried Arnold (1666–1714) undermined the authority of organized religion by his theory that those whom the church called heretics were really endowed with the true basis of religious feeling.

In literature the new ideas soon began to emerge. Mediocre though they were, the so-called "court poets," Friedrich von Canitz, Johann von Besser and Benjamin Neukirch, substituted the "good taste" of Nicolas Boileau-Despreaux for the extravagance of Giambattista Marino; from their midst sprang one lyric poet of high gifts, Johann Christian Günther. In Hamburg, Barthold Heinrich Brockes, who was deeply impressed both by Wolffian rationalism and by English nature poetry, gave the artificiality of poetic expression its deathblow. Ubiquitous translations and imitations of the English *Spectator, Tatler* and *Guardian*—the so-called *Moralische Wochenschriften* or moral weeklies—helped to regenerate literary taste and strove to improve the morals of the German middle classes. Indeed, one of the most marked features of German literature in the 18th century was the progressive influence of English literature; first, of Joseph Addison, Jonathan Swift, Daniel Defoe, Alexander Pope and Lord Shaftesbury; later, of James Thomson, who nourished the rising interest in nature poetry; then, as the importance of the imagination came to be recognized, of John Milton and Edward Young. George Lillo (and others) and Samuel Richardson exercised much effect upon the growth of the domestic tragedy and the moral novel respectively, while Young's *Conjectures on Original Composition* heralded a new epoch in German literature that was to be profoundly affected by James Macpherson's *Ossian*, Thomas Percy's *Reliques* and Shakespeare—the epoch of the *Sturm und Drang*. Laurence Sterne, Henry Fielding and Oliver Goldsmith had many echoes, mainly, but not exclusively, in the sphere of the novel. The

GERMAN LITERATURE

principal centres through which English influence reached Germany included, as might be expected, Hamburg, with its important overseas commercial connections, Leipzig, the headquarters of the book trade, and Göttingen, the seat of the university founded by George II.

3. The Reaction Against Rationalism.—Between 1724 and 1740 the critic Johann Christoph Gottsched succeeded in establishing in Leipzig, then the metropolis of German taste, literary reforms in accord with French 17th-century classicism. He purified the stage by abolishing irrelevant buffoonery and provided it with a repertory largely of French origin; and, in his *Kritische Dichtkunst* (1730), he laid down the principles according to which good literature was to be produced and judged. Reform was necessary, but the francophile limitations of Gottsched soon encountered resistance, and important opponents arose in the Swiss scholars J. J. Bodmer and J. J. Breitinger. Basing their arguments on *Paradise Lost*, which Bodmer had translated into prose, the Swiss demanded room for the play of genius and inspiration; they insisted that the imagination should not be dominated by reason. The effects of the controversy appeared toward the middle of the century in a group of Leipzig writers of Gottsched's own school, the *Bremer Beiträger*, as they are usually called after the paper in which they published their work. These men—C. F. Gellert, the author of graceful fables and tales in verse, hymns, moralizing comedies and a sentimental novel; G. W. Rabener, a mild satirist of Saxon provincialism; the dramatist J. E. Schlegel; and a number of minor writers—were in sympathy with many of the views which the Swiss critics had advocated. And in the *Bremer Beiträge* there appeared anonymously in 1748 the first installment of an epic in hexameters by F. G. Klopstock, *Der Messias*, which the author had planned while still at school. Its theme created a sensation when the first cantos appeared, and numerous imitations were soon produced. Klopstock's genius was, however, more suited to the lyric, and his odes, in which both patriotic and sentimental themes were prominent, gained an immense reputation. He also wrote dramas on biblical and teutonic subjects. His rising interest in Germanic antiquity, accompanied by the enthusiasm that was awakened in Germany for James Macpherson's *Ossian*, aided the growth of the so-called "bardic" movement which was led by H. W. von Gerstenberg, F. F. Kretschmann and Michael Denis, the translator of *Ossian* into German (1768–69).

Signs of growth were also noticeable elsewhere. At Halle, before Klopstock's name was known at all, two young poets, J. I. Pyra and S. G. Lange, wrote in rhymeless metres such as Klopstock advocated. After the middle of the century the Prussian poets J. W. L. Gleim, J. N. Götz and J. P. Uz, who were associated with Halle, and K. W. Ramler in Berlin, cultivated mainly the anacreontic lyric and the horatian ode, Gleim acquiring fame also in the field of the patriotic lyric inspired by the campaigns of Frederick II. At the same time Friedrich von Hagedorn in Hamburg showed to what perfection the lighter *vers de société* could be brought. The Swiss anatomist Albrecht von Haller, in *Die Alpen* (1729), was the first who gave expression in German to the beauty and sublimity of alpine scenery and the moral purity of its inhabitants, admiring always the great wisdom of the Creator; while a Prussian officer, Ewald Christian von Kleist, author of *Der Frühling* (1749), wrote admirable sentimental nature poetry. The Swiss Salomon Gessner became a European figure with his prose pastoral idylls.

4. The Influence of Lessing.—As Klopstock had been the first of modern Germany's inspired poets, so Gotthold Ephraim Lessing was the first critic who brought credit to the German name through-

F. G. KLOPSTOCK (1724–1803)

out Europe. Like his predecessor Gottsched, whom he vanquished more effectually than Bodmer had done, he had unwavering faith in classicism, but classic meant for him, as for his contemporary J. J. Winckelmann, Greek art and literature not French pseudo-classicism. He went, indeed, still further, and asserted in his *Litteraturbriefe* (1759–65) and *Hamburgische Dramaturgie* (1767–68) that Shakespeare, with all his irregularities, was a more faithful observer of the spirit of Aristotle's laws than were the French dramatists, though the French knew of these laws and Shakespeare did not.

It is true, however, that Lessing's own exposition of Aristotle's theory of tragedy was full of the moral preoccupations of the Enlightenment. He looked to England and not to France for the regeneration of the German theatre. His own dramas were pioneer works in this direction. *Miss Sara Sampson* (1755) was a *bürgerliches Trauerspiel* on the English model; *Minna von Barnhelm* (1767), a comedy in the spirit of George Farquhar; in *Emilia Galotti* (1772) Lessing remolded the "tragedy of common life" in a form that came to be acceptable to the *Sturm und Drang*; and finally in *Nathan der Weise* (1779) he won acceptance for iambic blank verse as the medium of the higher drama. His two most promising disciples, J. F. von Cronegk and J. W. von Brawe, unfortunately died young; but another of his friends, C. F. Weisse, was the most successful playwright of his day. Lessing's name is associated with Winckelmann's in *Laokoon* (1766), a treatise which defines the boundaries between plastic art and poetry, and with those of the Jewish philosopher Moses Mendelssohn and the Berlin bookseller C. F. Nicolai (*qq.v.*) in the famous *Literaturbriefe*. The last years of Lessing's life were embittered by conflict with Lutheran orthodoxy and bigotry, and his *Nathan der Weise* was a plea for rational understanding and toleration.

GOTTHOLD EPHRAIM LESSING (1729–1781)

Because of Lessing, German literature made a great leap forward beyond the feeble achievements of the first half of the century. The time of the fumbling imitations of the French drama was over and German literature could hold up its head among its European neighbours. The domestic tragedy, its plot centred upon the problem of class distinction, foreshadowed plays involving marked political and social criticism in the *Sturm und Drang* period, while *Nathan* was an important forerunner in style and content of the "drama of ideas" of Weimar classicism, and *Minna* has remained unsurpassed in the field of comedy. Lessing's theoretical work, with its wide range of interest, its pugnacity and its convincing argumentation, placed criticism in the forefront of affairs in literary Germany. His sharp rejection of descriptive poetry and his insistence that, whereas painting is restricted to a single moment in time, poetry deals with a succession of moments and should be concerned with action, exercised a great effect upon the writing of the next generation, while his attack upon the literary authority of France prepared the way both for a greater attention to English examples and for the search for native originality.

To the widening of the German imagination C. M. Wieland contributed by introducing remote and exotic literary settings, largely under French inspiration. With the exception of his verse-romance *Oberon* (1780), his work fell into neglect; he did excellent service, however, to the development of German prose fiction with his psychological novel *Agathon* (1766), insisting upon the cultivation of wisdom, virtue and happiness, and with his humorous epic *Die Abderiten* (1774). He also translated 22 plays of Shakespeare. Wieland had a considerable following, including M. A. von Thümmel; the Austrians Aloys Blumauer and J. B. von Alxinger, who wrote travesties and epics under his influence; and K. A. Kortum, author of the most popular comic epic of the time, the *Jobsiade* (1784), but the groundwork and form were borrowed from English models; Gellert had begun by imitating Samuel Richardson in his *Schwedische Gräfin* and he was followed by Sophie von La Roche, A. von Knigge and J. K. A. Musäus, the last-mentioned being, however, better known as the author of a famous collection of *Volksmärchen* (1782–86). Meanwhile rationalism was spreading rapidly. Men like Knigge, Mendelssohn, J. G. Zimmermann, T. G. von Hippel, Christian Garve, J. J. Engel, as well as the educational theorists J. B. Basedow and J. H. Pestalozzi, wrote books and essays on popular philosophy which were as eagerly read as had been the *Moralische Wochenschriften*. In this context must also be mentioned the most brilliant of German 18th-century aphorists, G. C. Lichtenberg.

VI. THE AGE OF GOETHE

1. The New Outlook.—The period of classicism and romanticism, the greatest epoch in German literature, fell within the lifetime of Johann Wolfgang von Goethe. The age of Goethe went beyond the Enlightenment's substitution of science for religion, inasmuch as it ascribed to science only a relative position in relation to the ultimate questions of life. It insisted upon the value of feeling in face of the limitations of reason. Impulse, instinct, emotion, fancy and intuition acquired a quasi-religious significance, being regarded as the links which connected man with divine nature. Those things which were held to conflict with feeling—the conventions and ordinances of social, political or religious life—were rejected as though partaking of blasphemy. Culture, it was felt, must accordingly not base itself upon reason alone but give full scope to man's emotional character. The ideal of the classical age, soon to be called *Humanität*, was that of the fully developed personality in which intellect and feeling should be harmoniously balanced. Because art was held to express a synthesis of these two complementary aspects of man's nature it came to play a paramount role as an instrument of civilization. Three phases may be distinguished in the evolution of this new outlook: *Sturm und Drang*, classicism, and romanticism, the first two being represented by one and the same generation of writers, the last by a new generation.

Sturm und Drang.—The youth and early manhood of Goethe belonged to, and profoundly affected, the movement known as *Sturm und Drang* ("Storm and Stress"), which aimed at overthrowing the cult of rationalism. Seeds of the new growth were to be found in Klopstock, in the spiritual force of pietism and in the rising resistance to French classical taste, while the influence of Rousseau, Edward Young and James Macpherson, and of the recently translated Shakespeare, was of prime importance. Nature, genius and originality were the slogans of the new epoch. An increasingly oppressive sense of dissatisfaction with the civilization of the day, because it seemed to be at loggerheads with these new subjects of belief, assailed the new generation and, being without the consolation of normal religious faith, it fell victim to *Weltschmerz* in varying degrees of intensity. Some of its members, like Goethe, were assisted by their own practical efforts in the task of accommodating themselves to life; others, like Herder and Schiller, by historical and philosophical studies; some, like J. M. R. Lenz, failed entirely. Nature was deified as a restlessly growing and changing thing; indeed it was called the "living garment of God" and the cult of nature completely replaced orthodox religion. No law was recognized as being above the individual conscience, and conscience must behave according to the teaching of this dynamically conceived nature. The standard outlook thus demanded un-

THE BETTMANN ARCHIVE

JOHANN WOLFGANG VON GOETHE (1749–1832). PAINTING BY GERHARD VON KÜGELGEN. 1810

ceasing effort, like that of Faust; and this in turn projected immense problems into the foreground. The types of character who believed they embodied nature in themselves needed to adjust themselves somehow to the unsatisfying realities of the world; those who did not, required to strive in search of nature. In either case the path was not easy. Strain, protest, revolt, yearning, disillusion were obvious on all sides, and egotism became a dominating feature in literature and thought.

The critical writings of H. W. von Gerstenberg (*Briefe über Merkwürdigkeiten der Litteratur*, 1766–67) stressed personal feeling in matters of taste, but the chief impetus came from the oracular utterances of Johann Georg Hamann, the "Magus im Norden," who observed that the basic verities of existence were to be apprehended through faith and the experience of the senses, emphasized the inspirational and symbolical function of language and pointed out the value of primitive poetry, such as that of the Bible. Poetry, he declared, was the mother tongue of the human race and not the product of learning and precept. His pupil was Johann Gottfried von Herder, who grasped, as no thinker before him had done, the idea of historical evolution. Beginning with literary criticism, which engendered the main current of the *Sturm und Drang*, he ended as a philosopher of history and religion, writing on biblical interpretation, aesthetics, history of literature and many other fields, allied to his great objective, the history of mankind. His doctrine of *Humanität* is fundamental to German classicism. He stressed the value of historical continuity in literature, finding therein the reason for the greatness of other literatures; he rejected imitation, discussed the essentials of a poetic language, explained original genius and pointed to the folk songs, ballads and romances of the middle ages as sources of inspiration, to which Percy's *Reliques* had recently drawn attention. Among his many works may be mentioned his *Fragmente über die neuere deutsche Litteratur* (1767), *Über den Ursprung der Sprache* (1772), *Kritische Wälder* (1769), *Von deutscher Art und Kunst* (1773), *Volkslieder* (1778), *Ideen zur Philosophie der Geschichte der Menschheit* (1784–91). Percy's *Reliques* also affected the poets who, adoring Klopstock and hating Wieland, founded in 1772 the *Göttinger Musenalmanach*. With the exception of the two brothers, Christian and F. L. Stolberg, the members of this coterie belonged to the peasant class or the lower bourgeoisie; J. H. Voss, the leader of the *Bund* and author of the famous idyl *Luise* (1784), was a typical peasant. L. H. C. Hölty and J. M. Miller excelled in simple lyrics in the tone of the *Volkslied*. Closely associated with the Göttingen group were Matthias Claudius, a poet and prose writer of an unassuming religious character, and G. A. Bürger, author of the famous ballad *Lenore*.

The *Sturm und Drang* was intimately associated with Goethe. As a student in Leipzig, Goethe had written lyrics in the anacreontic vein and dramas in alexandrines; but in Strasbourg, where he continued his studies in 1770–71, he made the acquaintance of Herder, who interested him in Gothic architecture, the *Volkslied* and Shakespeare. The pamphlet *Von deutscher Art und Kunst* (1773), to which, besides Goethe and Herder, the historian Justus Möser contributed, was a kind of manifesto of the *Sturm und Drang*. The new ideas seemed at once to set Goethe's genius free, and from 1772 to 1775 he was extraordinarily fertile in poetic ideas. His *Götz von Berlichingen* (1773), the first important drama of the *Sturm und Drang*, was followed within a year by the first novel of the movement, *Die Leiden des jungen Werther* (1774), which made the author world famous. He dashed off *Clavigo* and *Stella* —not to mention matchless lyrics. In all forms of literature he set the fashion for his time; the Shakespearean restlessness of *Götz von Berlichingen* found imitators in J. M. R. Lenz, F. M. von Klinger, J. A. Leisewitz, H. L. Wagner and Friedrich Müller, better known as "Maler" Müller. The dramatic literature of the *Sturm und Drang* was its most characteristic product; indeed, the very name of the movement was borrowed from a play by Klinger, the title of which was inspired by the desire to present upon the stage figures of Shakespearean grandeur impelled by gigantic passions, all considerations of plot, construction and form being subordinated to character, and all accepted authority, literary, social, political or moral, being rejected. The fiction of the *Sturm und Drang* was in its earlier stages dominated by Goethe's *Werther*, as seen in the novels of F. H. Jacobi and of J. M. Miller, mentioned above. Later, it was developed in a broader and less turbulent spirit by J. J. W. Heinse, author of *Ardinghello* (1787), Klinger, and K. P. Moritz, whose *Anton Reiser* (1785-90) foreshadowed *Wilhelm Meister*.

With the production of *Die Räuber* (1781) by Johann Christoph Friedrich von Schiller, the

THE BETTMANN ARCHIVE

JOHANN CHRISTOPH FRIEDRICH VON SCHILLER (1759-1805)

drama of the *Sturm und Drang* entered upon a new phase. Schiller's tragedy was more skilfully adapted than those of his predecessors to the exigencies of the theatre; it and the succeeding dramas, *Fiesco* and *Kabale und Liebe*—all three in prose—were masterpieces of high promise. In his fourth drama, *Don Carlos* (1787), he abandoned prose for iambic blank verse. In Swabia, however, the *Sturm und Drang* had also been displayed in the writings of the irritable C. F. D. Schubart (1739-91). Other eminent dramatists of this time were O. von Gemmingen, an imitator of Diderot; F. L. Schröder and A. W. Iffland, the two latter being the greatest actors of their time. Germany owed to the *Sturm und Drang* period its national theatre; permanent theatres were established in these years at Hamburg, Mannheim and Gotha, and the Hofburgtheater was founded at Vienna in 1776.

2. Classicism.—Self-discipline was lacking as a *Sturm und Drang* theme, and the movement soon exhausted itself. Its spirit of revolt always ended in tragedy. In classicism is found a positive form of moral idealism. This appeared in the poetry of Goethe and Schiller, as well as in the philosophy of Kant. Freedom still remained an ideal, but the idea was of freedom within the law, the law of nature, which could be ascertained by scientific study, or the moral law, the subject of philosophy. These were not necessarily in conflict. The problem of freedom was rendered acute by the impact of the French Revolution, which German literature generally regarded as a warning. The problem of freedom, the antagonism between duty and inclination, could be resolved, Schiller believed, once morality became "second nature" and this could only be achieved through the contemplation and production of beauty. Art thus acquired an educational function and aesthetic education was one of the major objectives of classicism. Goethe added more practical considerations in the writings of his last period.

For Goethe a new phase in his development began with his departure for Weimar in 1775, while after *Don Carlos* Schiller turned aside from poetry to study history and philosophy; not until the very close of the century did he, under the stimulus of Goethe's friendship, return to the drama. The first ten years of Goethe's life in Weimar were marked by his renewed friendship with Herder, whose ideal of *Humanität* was now maturing, by an interest (which was to be lifelong) in scientific research, by his public service as a minister of state and by his emotional attachment to Charlotte von Stein. He did not achieve greater clarity in his ideas until after his sojourn in Italy (1786-88). Italy was, in the first instance, a revelation of the antique. In Italy he gave *Iphigenie auf Tauris* its final form, he completed *Egmont*—like the exactly contemporary *Don Carlos* of Schiller, a kind of bridge from *Sturm und Drang* to classicism—and replanned *Torquato Tasso*. *Wilhelm Meisters Lehrjahre*, Goethe's most important novel, which had been originally concerned only with the theatre, had become, by the time it appeared in 1795-96, a book on the conduct of life. It is an outstanding example of the *Bildungsroman*, or "educational" novel, a characteristic German novel form, and profoundly affected future practitioners of the genre.

Before *Wilhelm Meister* appeared, however, German thought and literature had arrived at that degree of stability in form and ideas essential to a great literary period. In the year of Lessing's death (1781), Immanuel Kant, the great philosopher, had published his *Kritik der reinen Vernunft* (*Critique of Pure Reason*) and this, together with his two later treatises on practical reason and judgment, placed the Germans in the front rank of philosophy. Under the influence of Kant, Schiller turned to the study of aesthetics, the first fruits of which were his wonderful philosophical lyrics, and his treatises *Anmut und Würde* (1793), *Ästhetische Erziehung des Menschen* (1795) and *Über naive und sentimentalische Dichtung* (1795-96). Schiller's histories (*Geschichte des Abfalls der vereinigten Niederlande* and *Geschichte des dreissigjährigen Krieges*) show much literary quality but scarcely entitle him to rank alongside Johannes von Müller, the greatest historian of the time in Germany.

The years 1794-1805, when in Jena and Weimar Goethe and Schiller were united in close friendship, mark the culmination of literary classicism. Schiller's treatises provided the theoretical basis; his new journal *Die Horen* and his *Musenalmanach*—in which the two poets published their magnificent ballad poetry—were its literary organs. Goethe, as director of the ducal theatre, influenced the whole dramatic production of Germany. Under his encouragement Schiller turned from philosophy to poetry and between 1798 and his death in 1805 wrote a series of classical dramas which are Germany's greatest and which placed the German drama well ahead of that of contemporary Europe: the trilogy *Wallenstein*, *Maria Stuart*, *Die Jungfrau von Orleans*, *Die Braut von Messina*, *Wilhelm Tell*, closing with the fragment *Demetrius*. To Goethe we owe the idyllic epic *Hermann und Dorothea*. His severely classical plays *Die natürliche Tochter* and *Pandora* are less important. It was chiefly because of Schiller's stimulus that in those years Goethe brought the first part of *Faust* (1808) to a conclusion.

Although acknowledged leaders of German letters, Goethe and Schiller met with considerable opposition, especially from representatives of the once dominant rationalist movement. But, apart from the two great poets, literature was in no very healthy condition; the stage was dominated by the extraordinarily popular plays of A. von Kotzebue; and there is a wide gap between Moritz's *Anton Reiser* or the philosophical novels which Klinger wrote in his later years and Goethe's *Meister*. In lyric and epic poetry, it is impossible to regard poets like the gentle F. von Matthisson, or the less inspired G. L. Kosegarten and C. A. Tiedge, as worthy of an age that produced Goethe and Schiller. Georg Forster, however, who accompanied Capt. James Cook round the world, provided a model of lucid descriptive writing.

The supreme work of Goethe's latter years is *Faust*, Germany's greatest contribution to the literature of the world. In Part I (1808) is set out Faust's despair, his pact with Mephistopheles and his love for Gretchen; Part II (1832) covers the magician's life at court, the winning of Helen of Troy and Faust's purification and salvation. The doctrine of the fulfillment of life by striving and selfless activity, with the problems contained within it, was fundamental to Goethe's mature wisdom. *Wilhelm Meisters Wanderjahre*, with its social utopianism and teaching of restraint, offered a criticism of the rise of industrialism. The tragic novel *Die Wahlverwandtschaften* (1809) had insisted upon the theme of renunciation. The autobiographical *Dichtung und Wahrheit* (1811-33) affirmed the causality existing within individual development. Dramatic pieces, a periodical *Über Kunst und Altertum*, scientific writings, the *Italienische Reise* and *Campagne in Frankreich*, lyrics (especially *Der Westöstliche Divan*) of an intensely personal and philosophical kind, indicate the many-sidedness of Goethe's achievement. Letters, diaries and conversations afford an unusually complete picture of his old age. His house at Weimar became a place of pilgrimage; his visitors and correspondents belonged to all countries, and his influence was widespread inside and outside Germany, Thomas Carlyle being an ardent disciple.

3. The Romantic Movement: First Phase.—The romantic movement began not so much as a protest against the classicism of

Weimar, with which many romantics were in sympathy, but as a radical extension of some of its beliefs and interests; especially, at first, its emphasis upon Greek antiquity, longed for like some lost paradise. Romanticism saw Greece and the modern age in historical perspective and discovered unsuspected possibilities in both. Yearning was the romantic characteristic, the object of yearning being infinite and therefore unattainable. The individual ego, romanticism emphasized, mirrors actuality and is the only means of apprehending it; apprehension is thus subjective. Indeed, actuality has no existence independent of the individual ego, each such ego as it were creating its own actuality. The ego should, as J. G. Fichte thought, or should not, as F. D. E. Schleiermacher believed, be bound by the limits of reason. More than the intellect was involved; the emotions, the imagination, the subconscious in all its operations, even the state of ecstasy or trance, whether or not deliberately stimulated, had a part to play. The romantic poet could thus project himself into actuality and create his own world from within the realm of the seen or the unseen, of reality or of fancy, often in a highly capricious manner; he could turn whatever he liked into poetry. The nature of individuality and its modes of approach being infinitely varied, the range of literature was immensely expanded beyond the achievements of the earlier generation, and there was to be no end to the innovations made in content and style by the great wealth of literary talents who now emerged all over Germany and from various strata of society. It was an age of new beginnings. The rising generation felt free and able to revise all accepted representative values, not only in art and literature but in other spheres as well, the whole of contemporary civilization coming under scrutiny as war was declared upon one-sidedness and limitation and the yearning to attain completeness of vision and understanding, to grasp the infinite through the finite, grew ever more powerful. Between poetry, philosophy, scholarship, music, politics and religion there was henceforth to be no separation. In the belief that completeness was equal to the sum of the infinity of individual phenomena, all things came to be seen not only in their local but also in their historical setting. Philology, with the attendant interest in medievalism and nationalism, came to be extremely important, and translation to be regarded as a fine art. The subconscious became a subject of serious study. The realm of the wonderful, the supernatural, the fairy world came into vogue. In religion, romantic subjectivism led to mysticism, until later a markedly Catholic tendency supervened.

It was inevitable that disappointment and disillusion should result from this new brand of egotism in thought and literature. Friedrich Hölderlin, one of Germany's greatest lyrical poets and author of the novel *Hyperion* (1797–99), grew up as an admirer of Schiller; he sank into despair on realizing the impossibility of his longing for an age of heroic idealism and beauty such as that of ancient Greece. The hellenic interests of the age were linked by him with an intense patriotism. Jean Paul Friedrich Richter, known as Jean Paul, was a disciple of Herder. His sentiment, ingenuity, whimsical style and lavish detail gained for his shapeless novels a vast degree of popularity; his sustained attention to contemporary life, rather than antiquity or the middle ages, and particularly to the smaller problems of life, was a new feature, and his work foreshadowed the *Dorfgeschichte* of later decades. His principal novels, written between 1795 and 1804, were *Hesperus*, *Quintus Fixlein*, *Siebenkäs*, *Titan* and *Flegeljahre*; his *Vorschule der Ästhetik* (1804) revealed a historical grasp of literary growth and *Levana* (1807) was a treatise on education.

The first romantic school proper was founded at Jena in 1798, appropriately near Weimar. Johann Ludwig Tieck, a leading member of the school, early developed a lifelong enthusiasm for Shakespeare and the Elizabethan and Spanish drama. Gruesome plays and fairy tales, novels and fantastic comedies full of wit and mockery were his earliest works. The short stories of his later period were more valuable. The theoretical basis of romanticism was laid down by the two brothers August Wilhelm and Friedrich Schlegel, who, accepting in great measure Schiller's aesthetic conclusions, adapted them to their own needs. These romantic critics maintained that the first duty of criticism was to understand and appreciate; the right of genius to follow its natural bent was sacred. The *Herzensergiessungen eines kunstliebenden Klosterbruders* (1797) by Tieck's school friend W. H. Wackenroder contained the romantic theory of art. The greatest imaginative achievement is to be found in the lyrics and fragmentary novels of Novalis (Friedrich von Hardenberg), in which Christian mysticism, romantic medievalism, and symbolism transfer the reader into the realm of the *Märchen*; this is particularly so in *Heinrich von Ofterdingen* (1802). The novel was the romantic art form par excellence and was attempted by almost every one of the romantics. The universal sympathies of the movement were exemplified by many admirable translations, of which the greatest was A. W. Schlegel's translations of Shakespeare's plays (1797–1810), and by his courses of lectures at Berlin and Vienna. The critical essays and aphorisms of F. Schlegel are among the most important features of the movement; they argued that modern (or romantic) literature, as distinct from ancient (or classical), should deal with modern life in all its manifestations without any restriction, and they put forward *Wilhelm Meister* as the model to be followed. The literary organ of the school was the *Athenäum* (1798–1800). J. G. Fichte and to a much greater extent F. W. J. von Schelling were the exponents of the romantic doctrine in philosophy, while the theologian F. D. E. Schleiermacher demonstrated how vital its individualism was for religious thought.

4. The Second Romantic School.—The first romantic school had dispersed by 1804. Two years later, however, another phase of romanticism was initiated in Heidelberg. The leaders of this second romantic school were Clemens Brentano, Achim von Arnim and J. J. von Görres; their organ was the *Zeitung für Einsiedler*, or *Tröst-Einsamkeit*, and their most characteristic production the collection of *Volkslieder* published under the title *Des Knaben Wunderhorn* in 1805–08. Compared with the earlier school, the Heidelberg writers were more practical; they wrote historical works, not stories of an imaginary medieval world as Novalis had done, and they collected *Volkslieder* and *Volksbücher*. Their immediate influence on German intellectual life was consequently greater; they stimulated the interest of the German people in their history; and to them is attributed the foundation of the study of German philology and medieval literature, the brothers Jakob and Wilhelm Grimm having been in touch with the circle in their early days. The Heidelberg poets strengthened the national and patriotic spirit; they prepared the way for the rising against Napoleon, which produced an outburst of patriotic song, the chief voices being those of E. M. Arndt, K. T. Körner and M. von Schenkendorf.

When, c. 1809, the Heidelberg school broke up and Arnim and Brentano settled in Berlin, the romantic movement followed two clearly marked lines of development, one north German, the other associated with Württemberg. In the north Heinrich von Kleist, Prussia's greatest dramatic poet, created a romantic drama and short story of high poetic achievement; he was a leading writer in the patriotic movement against Napoleon. His plays, such as *Amphitryon* (1807), *Der zerbrochene Krug* (1808), *Das Käthchen von Heilbronn* (1810), *Die Hermannsschlacht* and *Der Prinz von Homburg*, express the belief that the only security in life is to be found in the unconscious voice of feeling and instinct. Zacharias Werner, an undisciplined and unbalanced dramatic genius, sounded depths of mysticism and fatalism. There were at the same time some elements of decadence; Friedrich de la Motte Fouqué, for instance, showed how easy it was for the medieval tastes of the romantics to be satisfied with mediocre novels and plays. During the same period E. T. W. Hoffmann, a novelist of genius, cultivated a preference for a morbid supernaturalism and gave European currency to German romanticism. The north German romantic circle could point to one lyric poet of the first rank, the Silesian J. von Eichendorff; while A. von Chamisso, a French émigré, developed into an outstanding German poet. Others, like Friedrich Rückert, sought new inspiration in the poetry of the east; and Wilhelm Müller, following Byron's example, stirred up German sympathy for the oppressed Greeks and Poles.

The last phase of romanticism was represented by the Swabian school. Its chief representative, Ludwig Uhland, a disciple of Schiller, as a ballad poet was second only to Schiller in his popular esteem. One might say that the mission of the Swabian circle, the chief members of which were J. Kerner, G. Schwab, W. Waiblinger, W. Hauff and, most gifted of all, E. Mörike, was to preserve in both poetry and prose the romantic traditions from the disintegrating influences to which their north German contemporaries were exposed in the next generation. (A. Gs.)

VII. THE 19TH CENTURY

1. The Mood of the Period.—Goethe's death marks the end of an epoch. The literature of the 19th century is informed by a mood quite different from the cosmopolitan humanism so characteristic of the 18th. Goethe had been the last great representative of German classical culture; furthermore, romanticism, the movement of the generation after Goethe, was in decline; the writers who were now coming to the fore belonged to another age. Although some of the leading romantics—A. W. Schlegel, Ludwig Tieck, Clemens Brentano and Eichendorff—survived Goethe by a decade or more, the movement as a whole had lost its impact. Only the Swabian school clung to a romantic mode of writing. In more conservative spheres than literature, romanticism proved more tenacious and fruitful; the study of philology, of history and of law was promoted by romantic ideas. In politics, however, the alliance between romantic thought and the rising nationalism was forged, which was to colour German thinking for over a century. Indeed, the romantic mode of thinking, despite some violent, but ineffective, attacks on it, permeated a wide area and in many ways differentiated German from other European thought. In imaginative literature, however, few writers were unaffected by his work, though the effect sometimes took the form of rebellion against his olympian predominance.

The rule of conservative governments under the leadership of Metternich in Austria occasioned much frustration among German intellectuals since it often repressed liberty of thought. The dark shadows of political storms to come, the social unrest arising from the beginning of industrialization, were keenly felt; the efforts of writers to prescribe solutions for these ills were foiled by a severe censorship. It had become only too evident that earlier political and cultural ideals were not being realized. A sense of disillusionment with man's capacity to achieve lofty ends and a pessimistic appraisal of man's role in the universe dominated imaginative literature and entirely changed its tone, which once had been imbued with buoyant hope or at least reflected a solidly constructive attitude. Gradually, as writers sought to free themselves from the bondage of classical and romantic thought, they struck out on new paths.

2. Grillparzer and the Drama.—The greatest poet of this post-Napoleonic era, Franz Grillparzer, consciously cast his dramas in the tradition of classicism. Yet his work is of a different hue; it lacks self-confident vigour and assurance. His tragedies have as their theme weakness of will. His heroes and heroines founder because the individual's effort is of no avail against the overwhelming power of circumstance. The world cannot give contentment to man; only cultivation of his inner resources and self-abnegation are able to grant inner peace. To aspire beyond the narrow orbit of individual action is to court disaster. In his first play, *Die Ahnfrau* (1817), written in trochaic metre and influenced by the popular romantic fate-tragedies (*Schicksalstragödien*) of Zacharias Werner, fate is still an external force; but in his trilogy *Das goldene Vliess* (1822) it is the combination of character and circumstance. In *Medea*, the last and most powerful play of this trilogy, cast in the form of German classical drama, the breakdown of a marriage leads to an extreme catastrophe where both partners stand in isolation, incapable of reconciliation because of their burden of guilt.

THE BETTMANN ARCHIVE
FRANZ GRILLPARZER (1791-1872)

The dramatic action is interrupted by reflective passages which emphasize the weakness of will of the two chief characters.

This element pervades Grillparzer's plays: *Sappho* (1819), modeled on Goethe's *Torquato Tasso*, depicts the tragedy of a poetess seeking in vain to hold her younger lover; *Des Meeres und der Liebe Wellen* is the tragedy of a priestess' love for a young man, ended by hostile circumstances; *Der Traum; ein Leben* shows the folly of ambition. Among them, *König Ottokars Glück und Ende* is the tragedy of a great ruler's downfall through overweening ambition, while in *Ein Bruderzwist in Habsburg* (written c. 1848) untimely action is the source of evil. The failure in 1838 of his comedy *Weh dem, der lügt* caused Grillparzer to withdraw from the stage and public life, and three of his dramas were published only posthumously.

The sombre mood of Grillparzer's dramatic work, which was matched by his own personal difficulties and disappointments, also prevails in other plays of the period, notably in those by C. D. Grabbe and Georg Büchner; it invades even the popular comedies of F. Raimund, J. N. Nestroy and E. E. Niebergall. In Raimund's fairylike comedies there is an undercurrent of tragic pessimism. Nestroy, another Viennese, who ousted the more profound Raimund from the Viennese stage, even more savagely satirized Viennese middle-class society. From Hesse comes Niebergall's *Datterich* (1841), another satirical comedy. Niebergall expresses a sense of disillusionment with high ideals which, in turn, he parodies. The heritage of classicism and romanticism appeared discredited, but no new faith had yet grown out of the resulting disillusionment. In the new drama, therefore, established values were questioned and disparaged. Grillparzer's doubts of his creative capacity and his conflicting aspirations gave rise to contradictions in his work, but they were held in check by the overriding impulse to create an almost classical form. Grabbe, however, did not aim at formal perfection; the chaos of a meaningless world is stronger than the effort of the individual who strives to impose an order upon it. The tragic error of his heroes springs from the mistaken belief in their ability to control the course of history. The inert mass described in realistic scenes is stronger than the great men—Hannibal, Marius, the Hohenstaufen emperors, Napoleon—whose failure was Grabbe's theme. In *Don Juan und Faust* (1829) he attempted to fuse two myths in a powerful confrontation of the two heroes, although the play as a whole, as always with Grabbe, is not very skilfully composed. For Büchner, too, the world appeared meaningless; but he was a much more incisive dramatist than Grabbe, for his was a more radical vision. As a student, this young man, who died at 23, anticipated Marx in his pamphlet *Der Hessische Landbote* (1834), a clarion-call for political and economic revolution, but he had been disappointed by the political ineffectiveness of would-be revolutionaries. Politics appeared a mixture of lofty ideas and ineffectual action, ruthless tyranny and senseless suffering. In his writings he wages war against unrealizable ideals and sham rhetoric. His comedy *Leonce und Lena* is a satire on romantic drama and on the nebulousness of romantic ideas; *Dantons Tod* (1835) is a tragedy of heroic pessimism; and in the fragmentary drama *Woyzzeck* he exposes the exploitation of an uneducated half-idiot by the powers that be. In Büchner's world the individual is caught in the net of hostile social forces and his work is an indictment of the social and cosmic order. His succession of snapshot scenes anticipates 20th-century Expressionist drama, but also recalls the *Sturm und Drang*. Crispness of speech and stark realism, combined with precise historical documentation, alienated his age (his plays were not performed until after his death) but give his work a striking modernity.

3. Lyric Poetry.—Extremes of melancholy were conveyed in the lyric verse of Nikolaus Lenau, a Hungarian by birth, whose melodious, though sometimes rather monotonous, verse speaks of Byronic discontent. From this morbid subjectivity he was able to escape only very rarely. The great tradition of classical and romantic poetry made it, on the whole, relatively easy for poets to achieve formal excellence, but they found it more difficult to strike a note of their own. This is particularly true of Friedrich Rückert and August Platen-Hallermünde, two of the most con-

GERMAN LITERATURE

summate formal lyricists. Rückert was a scholar and poet of no mean importance, but his large output tends to obscure his genuine poetic achievement, his portrayal of the conflict between reason and will. His *Kindertotenlieder* (1872), his *Liebesfrühling* (1844) and many proverbs in alexandrines from *Die Weisheit des Brahmanen* (1836–39), a collection of didactic verse, come to life by their rhythmic power. In Platen-Hallermünde's *Sonette aus Venedig* (1825) the German language is skilfully adapted to what is essentially an alien verse form. His carefully chiseled verses symbolize his inner struggle for purity.

For Eduard Mörike, too, classical poetry is the model; Mörike's formal excellence never grates, but is matched by his idyllic and often melodious portrayal of nature and country life. His classicism has different strands. Simple lyrics in the *Volkslied* manner alternate with verse in classical metres. His range is limited; he deliberately turned from grand themes to find fulfillment within a restricted sphere. In *Mozart auf der Reise nach Prag* (1856) the problems of an artist in a world basically uncongenial to art are portrayed with humorous sympathy which stems from a serene rather than from a tragic view of life. Nature is also the source of inspiration of Annette von Droste-Hülshoff. A powerful rhythm and a sombre language express her apprehension of the irrational forces of life, as in *Das geistliche Jahr* (1851), but her poetry greater maturity so that wisdom and humour rather than apprehension became the keynote. In *Die Judenbuche*, a masterly *Novelle*, she blended psychological realism with a sense of mystery.

On none of the poets of this period did romanticism exert so strong an influence as on Heinrich Heine, and none attacked it so ruthlessly. His German literature remains in dispute, mainly because he dared to subject German national susceptibilities and romantic nationalism to scathing criticism, but his *Buch der Lieder* (1827) is one of the best-known anthologies of love poetry. Heine describes his dreams and yearnings, but his sense of realism makes him show that they are only dreams and yearnings; he pricks the bubble of illusion by a cruel ironic twist. His creation of melodious verse and of theatrical effects is masterly. Although the collection is uneven it contains some of the best-known lyrics in the German language, often more appreciated outside Germany than within it. In later, more mature work—the *Romanzero* (1851) and the posthumously published poems—his self-pity and overdramatization are gone; his poetry conveys the hopes and anguish which were so real during his last long drawn-out illness. His early Saint-Simonian belief in the "rehabilitation of the senses" had given way to a belief in God. His awareness of the perils lurking beneath the gay surface of life, his sense of the carnival of human existence with its masquerades, is most strikingly transmuted into art in his ballads. His poetry is better known, but his prose, *Reisebilder* (1826–31); *Lutetia* (1854), a collection of reports on life in France; his analysis of German intellectual life and history in *Die Romantische Schule* (1836) and *Geschichte der Philosophie und Religion in Deutschland* (1834) reveal him as a master of ironic prose, who, dissatisfied with the solemnity and pretension of his literary predecessors, sought to convey truth by means of satire. His most effective political satire is contained in his verse epic *Deutschland, ein Wintermärchen* (1844), a savage attack upon his personal enemies and upon the political conditions of his time.

4. Young Germany.—In 1835 an edict of the federal diet had banned Heine's writings, together with those of Ludolf Wienbarg, Karl Gutzkow, Heinrich Laube and Theodor Mundt. Since Wienbarg's *Ästhetische Feldzüge* (1834) were dedicated to "Young Ger-

HEINRICH HEINE (1797–1856)

CULVER PICTURES, INC.

many," this name was given to these writers, supposing a movement of mean importance, but the name, even if inappropriate, survived. The radicalism of the Young Hegelians and political liberals frustrated by severe censorship and authoritarian government influenced these writers, who preached individualism. Wienbarg, in his theoretical writings, proclaimed the need for a new literature which was to deal with political and social problems. K. F. Gutzkow criticized conventional morality and orthodoxy in his novel *Wally die Zweiflerin* (1835) and later in his drama *Uriel Acosta* (1846). In his later cycle of novels *Die Ritter vom Geiste* (1850 et seq.) he sought to create the social novel of the age. Theodor Mundt, in his novel *Madonna eine Heilige* (1835), advocated a fuller conception of personal life, while Heinrich Laube is mainly known as theatre director; his own dramas are conventional. *Graf Essex* (1856) is written in the style of Schiller, but his novel *Das junge Europa* (1833–37) provides a fine analysis of social life. Exile was often the fate of those who dared to criticize the established political and social order. Ludwig Börne was a highly talented prose writer who went to a self-imposed exile in Paris. His *Briefe aus Paris* (1830–33) are valuable social documents. Two important lyric poets, Georg Herwegh and Ferdinand Freiligrath, had to flee, one to Switzerland, the other to London. Herwegh's *Gedichte eines Lebendigen* (1841–43) have a strong rhetorical pattern which made them very popular. Freiligrath's poems are more vivid in style.

5. The Conservatives.—Other poets of the period were conservative in politics. The patriotic lyrics of Emanuel Geibel, collected in *Zeitstimmen* (1841), *Juniuslieder* (1848) and *Heroldsrufe* (1871), are polished, but language and imagery remain conventional. His popularity was extreme; "Der Mai ist gekommen" is the most widely known of his songs. Geibel was the leading figure of the Munich school, which had come together under the patronage of Maximilian II of Bavaria. Of other lyrical poets—Hermann Lingg, Graf Adolf Friedrich von Schack, Friedrich von Bodenstedt—only Heinrich Leuthold rises beyond virtuosity. Paul Heyse, a master of formally perfect *Novellen*, rarely rouses the reader, since his treatment is on conventional lines. Joseph Victor von Scheffel's verse-tale *Der Trompeter von Säckingen* (1854) and his novel *Ekkehard* (1855) were very popular at the time, but today their romanticism sounds unconvincing.

6. Realism and Regionalism.—During this period real strength was found in realistic literature, often of regional inspiration. Poetic realism, a term coined by Otto Ludwig, has as its aim the portrayal of life, but only insofar as life is artistically significant and appears to possess intrinsic value. Attention is focussed on social reality, but not, as in the later Naturalism, on its ugly, pathological side. The main concern of the realist writer is to discover positive values in everyday life without reference to transcendental ideas. The impetus to realism in literature corresponded to changes in social life; the beginning of urbanization and industrialization had become perceptible; the railways were changing the tempo of life. The development of scientific thought and the rise of technology were accompanied by a literature critical of the social order and in revolt against idealistic classicism and romanticism. Karl Marx is only the best known of a host of social critics; the antirealistic philosophies of A. Schopenhauer and L. Feuerbach also show this tendency to a more sober appraisal of man's capacity. It was accompanied by positivism in many branches of intellectual inquiry, which, by way of analogy, sought to apply to the study of literature and society methods which they mistakenly believed to be those of the natural science. Nonetheless, a fruitful study of sources and texts resulted which was formalized by the first important organized school of literary history in Germany, that of Wilhelm Scherer (1841–86) who, together with his successors Erich Schmidt and Jakob Minor, established the criticism of modern literature as an academic discipline; Jakob Grimm and Wilhelm Grimm and Karl Lachmann had already given academic respectability to German medieval studies. In the field of imaginative literature Berthold Auerbach was often acclaimed as the creator of the peasant *Novelle*, but his *Schwarzwälder Dorfgeschichten* (1843–53) appear artificial compared with the masterpieces of realism. Karl Immermann, whose work was still greatly influenced by classicism, in *Der Oberhof* (1839) portrays peasants deeply rooted in their work and in their countryside. The Low German novels *Ut de Franzosentid* (1859) and *Ut mine Stromtid* (1862–64) by Fritz Reuter are humorous and humane in conception, with a wealth of individual character made more convincing by the lively dialect style. With *Quickborn* (1853), his collection of lyrical poetry, Klaus Groth became the prototype of the regional poet; his dialect clearly links his work to colloquial speech and shows the roots of his poetry which, in its sincerity and simplicity, recalls the folk song. Another dialect writer was the Swiss novelist Albert Bitzius, who wrote under the pseudonym Jeremias Gotthelf. A close knowledge of the life of the Swiss peasants and their problems is reflected in his novels, of which *Uli der Knecht* (1846) and *Uli der Pächter* (1849) are the best known. Concerned for the moral welfare of the peasant community, he preaches against liberalism in politics and against the loosening of moral sanctions and seeks to advocate a life of probity based on communal responsibility. His works convince the reader because of his shrewd insight into the mind of the peasants, his realistic assessment of their motives and his faithful description of the peasant community. In *Die schwarze Spinne* (1842) the events and persons, though realistically described, assume almost symbolical importance.

Adalbert Stifter, too, drew much strength from his native Bohemian forest; some of his tales, collected in *Studien* (1844–50) and *Bunte Steine* (1853), are set there, but his language is classical, reflecting his quest for stylistic perfection. For Stifter the world of everyday events is a symbol of emotional significance; he therefore carefully portrays it and can thus rightly be called a poetic realist. In *Nachsommer* (1857), a *Bildungsroman* or "pedagogical" novel influenced by Goethe's *Wilhelm Meister*, Stifter stresses the power of art to educate; he seeks to show how the gentle law of humane action, based on justice, simplicity, self-control, restricted activity and admiration of the beautiful, is effective in bringing about an exemplary life true to nature. Renunciation of violence is the major theme of *Witiko* (1865–67), a historical novel about the growth of culture in the 12th century; humane restraint is also the message of his story *Die Mappe meines Urgrossvaters* (1841–67).

The realism of Otto Ludwig has a psychological flavour. "Die Heiterethei" and "Aus dem Regen in die Traufe," the two tales making up his collection *Thüringer Naturen* (1857), are a humorous exploration of life in his native land, while in his novel *Zwischen Himmel und Erde* (1856) a conflict within an artisan family is explored with striking objectivity and careful characterization. His *Erbförster* (1849) is a domestic tragedy of a forester obsessed by a sense of justice who finally shoots his own daughter in mistake for the son of his enemy. While Ludwig's *Shakespeare-Studien* (1871) reveals a fine understanding of dramatic art, his own *Die Makkabäer* (1854) is a failure.

With Gottfried Keller the pinnacle of poetic realism in prose narrative is reached. The scene of his works is his native Switzerland. All his writings reveal his attempts to differentiate between those characters whose thought and conduct allow their personalities to mature and those who, ignoring the voice of nature, fail to develop their inner potentialities. *Der Grüne Heinrich* (1854–74), a semiautobiographical *Bildungsroman*, is the story of the lively struggle and development of a Swiss painter. Keller portrays a romantic personality seeking to come to terms with life and shows how youthful dreams may become mutilated and how the artist's vision has to be readjusted to the demands of everyday life. *Die Leute von Seldwyla*, a collection of *Novellen* (1856–74), reveals his humour at its best. He resists the flights of a romantic imagination and cautiously consolidates his appraisal of everyday life. *Martin Salander* (1886) is political in tone and its strictures on the liberalism of the day do not enhance its artistic value.

Another important realist was Theodor Storm, whose work is stamped by the atmosphere of his native Schleswig-Holstein. In his work romantic elements were gradually subordinated to realistic description. The elegiac, often sentimental, tone of his earlier writing prevailed less and less, though both his prose-tales and his lyric poetry were permeated by his sense of the ephemerality of life. Romantic preoccupation with the past had stimulated his-

torical thought and writing. Some of Storm's and Keller's *Novellen* had dealt with the past, but other writers, such as Willibald Alexis, C. F. Meyer, Wilhelm Hauff, Gustav Freytag and W. H. Riehl, made history their main theme. The stories of Alexis—of which *Die Hosen des Herrn von Bredow* (1846) are the best known—are imbued by a delicate sense of humour and a feeling for the landscape of Brandenburg. Freytag was less successful in his historical novel *Die Ahnen* (1872–81) than in portrayal of social and economic changes of his age in *Soll und Haben* (1855) and in his comedy *Die Journalisten* (1854). Friedrich von Spielhagen describes social conditions more amply in a series of novels written after 1861—*Problematische Naturen, Reih und Glied, Hammer und Amboss, Die Sturmflut*—which were very popular at the time; they contain political criticism, but are spoiled by their sentimentality.

Wilhelm Raabe's analysis of social life is more profound. His writings appear complex; he anticipates 20th-century methods of storytelling in focusing attention not only on the story but on the way in which the story is told. He attacked the narrowness of the bourgeois philistinism and the nationalism of Bismarck's empire. His humour helped him to overcome the pessimism of his early work, of which *Der Hungerpastor* (1864), *Abu Telfan* (1868) and *Der Schüderump* (1870) are striking examples. In his later work —*Alte Nester* (1880), *Das Horn von Wanza* (1881) and *Stopfkuchen* (1891)—he depicted eccentric characters with a rich inner life who achieve spiritual freedom. His pessimism and humour is paralleled by Wilhelm Busch, whose laughter over human imperfection savagely exposes hypocrisy and illusion.

In Austria gentler moods prevailed toward the end of the century. Ferdinand von Saar and Marie Ebner von Eschenbach provided realistic accounts of both bourgeois and peasant Austrian society. The novelist Peter Rosegger and the dramatist Ludwig Anzengruber wrote about peasant life. Anzengruber's humour, as seen in his plays *Der Pfarrer von Kirchfeld* (1871), *Der G'wissenswurm* (1874) and *Das vierte Gebot* (1878), softens his polemical didacticism.

Conrad Ferdinand Meyer, a Swiss, through his understanding of history, achieved a rare fusion of poetry and realism. He describes in chiseled prose the downfall of great men through the lust for power. The best of his *Novellen*, written after 1870, such as *Jürg Jenatsch, Das Amulett, Angela Borgia* and *Die Versuchung des Pescara*, are inspired by an insight into the life of the Renaissance which had been stimulated by the work of the Basel historian Jacob Burckhardt. In *Der Heilige* he goes further back to the days of Thomas (à) Becket. His lyrical poetry showed, like his prose, a rare sense of form. It is symbolical poetry; his personal feelings are subordinated to the image, but his symbolism points to a lack of natural affinity with the world.

The plays of Friedrich Hebbel reveal poetic realism at its most powerful. His work is a synthesis of psychological analysis and metaphysical beliefs. Deep inner impulses drive his characters to doom. Tragedy is inevitable since individuality by its very attempts at self-expression and self-assertion clashes with the world in which it must perish. Of his dramas, *Judith, Herodes und Mariamne* and *Gyges und sein Ring* (all between 1840 and 1856) depict the tragedy of those who suffer defeat because their outraged individuality does not allow them to compromise. In *Maria Magdalena* (1844) Hebbel showed the disastrous effects of the tyranny of petty bourgeois life, while in *Agnes Bernauer* the unusual individual, here an exceptionally beautiful woman, is sacrificed to uphold political tradition. The more individuality perfects itself the more likely tragedy becomes, for assertion of individuality against the inevitable process of history is futile. In his last play, *Die Nibelungen*

FRIEDRICH HEBBEL (1813–1863). PAINTING BY KARL RAHL

(1862), he interprets an old legend in terms of his own psychological and metaphysical ideas. His lyrical poetry is sombre. Its power depends on a close identification with the growth and decay of nature. Theodor Fontane is a more sober-minded though also more delicately realist writer. He was already 60 when he began his novels about life in Brandenburg. They are characterized by psychological insight and by an understanding of social problems. He uncovers the crack in the social fabric produced by industrialization and urbanization. In *L'adultera* (1882), *Irrungen, Wirrungen* (1888), *Frau Jenny Treibel* (1892) and *Effi Briest* (1895) human relationships clash with society and survive or break down according to their innate strength, while in *Schach von Wuthenow* (1883) the weakness of the Prussian ruling class allows us to foresee Napoleon's victory over Prussia in 1806. Fontane portrays a limited section of Prussian life, mainly its upper class, but his power of observation is sharp, his characterization is skilful and the action is carried on by a superb handling of conversation and by a detached and suffused irony.

7. Wagner and Nietzsche.—Since Richard Wagner wrote the texts of his own operas his work also belongs to the history of literature. His operas express romantic aspiration: the distinctions between the genres are not observed and German myths and legends are popularized. At first he was hailed by Friedrich Nietzsche as successor to the Greek dramatists, but Nietzsche turned against Wagner when he forsook the pessimism of Arthur Schopenhauer for Christianity. Nietzsche's subsequent attack was a violent exposure of what he believed to be Wagner's morbidity, vulgarity and fanaticism. Nietzsche was one of the harbingers of 20th-century literature. His distinction (in *Die Geburt der Tragödie aus dem Geiste der Musik*, 1872) between the Apollonian and Dionysiac elements of art, although criticized by classical scholars, was of considerable consequence. The view that classical art was not only calm but could also be ecstatic, and that the origins of Greek drama sprang from the orgiastic intoxication of Dionysian religious mysteries. Nietzsche's emphasis on the need to liberate his personality from the shackles of conventional Christian morality, his skepticism as to the validity of the artist's statements and his place in society, and his prophecy of the nihilism to come provided an arsenal of ideas and intellectual ferment for the next generation of writers.

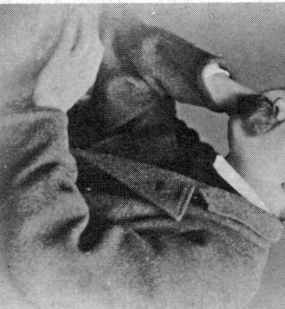

FRIEDRICH NIETZSCHE (1844-1900)

THE BETTMANN ARCHIVE

8. Naturalism.—If Nietzsche's ecstatic, but wayward, writings provided some of the high lights for 20th-century writing, Naturalism supplied much of its solid base, especially for its prose. As so often in German literature, the Naturalist movement was heralded by pamphlets demanding a new manner of writing. Their keynote was scientific objectivity. Their principal model was Émile Zola and their organs were the journals *Kritische Waffengänge* (1882–84) edited by the brothers Heinrich and Julius Hart in Berlin and, in Munich, M. C. Conrad's *Die Gesellschaft* (1885–1902). An anthology of lyric verse, *Dichtercharaktere*, appeared in 1884, in which urban life was the theme. The real revolution was made by the writings of Arno Holz, who in *Buch der Zeit* (1886) revealed himself as the first important poet of Naturalism. Together with Johannes Schlaf he developed, in the *Sekundenstil*, three tales published under the title *Papa Hamlet* (1889), which was to make the representation of the minutiae of life possible. Many of his poems, often cast in startlingly free rhythm, deal with the life of the poor (*Armeleutepoesie*). "Consistent Naturalism," in the wake of Zola, made even the smallest details of life the subject of literature; hence the preference of these writers for the pathological and even sordid. Their work started as a criticism of the Munich school in lyric verse; Holz experimented with form,

substituting the natural rhythm of speech for the polished metre of his formalist predecessors. In drama the triumph of Naturalism was assured by Gerhart Hauptmann's *Vor Sonnenaufgang* (1889), a play primarily memorable for its novel technique, for it is a drama without a hero and without a proper plot; Hauptmann's exposure in it of the sordid effects of alcoholism on a peasant family made it a *succès de scandale*. Social criticism was powerful in *Die Weber*, another play without a plot. It depicts the misery of the weavers and is an indictment of the dire poverty caused by industrialization, and tolerated by the powers that be. *Der Biberpelz*, one of the few successful German comedies, is a satire on Prussian officialdom outwitted by the common sense of a clever washerwoman. Hauptmann's attempt to create Naturalist historical drama in *Florian Geyer* was adjudged a failure. Hauptmann soon found the bond of Naturalism too constricting, although later, in *Fuhrmann Henschel, Der rote Hahn, Die Ratten* and *Rose Bernd*, he returned to the Naturalist manner, and began to experiment with Symbolist drama in *Hanneles Himmelfahrt* (1894). *Die versunkene Glocke* is a more thorough exploration of this genre. Verse drama along more traditional lines supplants extreme realism as Hauptmann portrays the problems of the artist in his lonely struggles. His later plays did not enjoy the popularity of his early social drama. Of his many plays some were based on German legends, others were romantic dream-plays, while in others he treated themes from classical antiquity. Hauptmann was a prose-narrator of considerable force. The tale *Der Narr in Christo Emanuel Quint* describes a spiritual pilgrimage, while *Der Ketzer von Soana* portrays the sensual awakening of a priest who forsakes his calling.

In the wake of Hauptmann several writers wrote in the straightforward Naturalist manner. The best known among them are Hermann Sudermann, notable for *Ehre* (1889) and *Heimat* (1893), plays criticizing middle-class morality; and Max Halbe, whose *Jugend* (1893) is a drama of adolescent love. Carl Hauptmann, like his brother Gerhart, also turned away from Naturalism after having written plays in this manner and in *Einhart der Lächler* (1907) he depicted the spiritual struggles of an artist.

In the course of the 19th century German literature had increasingly abandoned an idealistic conception of man and turned to a more down-to-earth and deprecating appraisal of reality, reflecting the rise of positivist and materialist thought in science. This proved too narrow; and in consonance with the new relativist scientific cosmology of the 20th century, the artistic imagination began to portray a more complex vision of the world.

VIII. THE 20TH CENTURY

1. The Turn of the Century.—The rise of urban civilization, the increasing abuse of language, and the inadequacy of conventional methods of literary presentation encouraged a change of consciousness in those writers and poets who felt that prevailing literary traditions were inadequate to express new ideas. To maintain their creative freedom writers often experimented with traditional literary forms. Experiment, in itself nothing new, took many forms and produced many literary schools, linked by a conscious concern with experimentation. The quest for the new reflected an endeavour to assert independence from the past. It seemed imperative to avoid sterility and to strike forth on new paths in order to avoid sterility and to vindicate the vitality of language. This experimentation was, however, built on the solid achievement of the 19th century, and emerged only slowly as the dominant force of the 20th. Much of this new writing still had a Naturalist basis. Indeed, the first important movement of the 20th century, Impres-

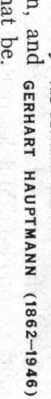

GERHART HAUPTMANN (1862-1946)

THE BETTMANN ARCHIVE

GERMAN LITERATURE

273

sionism, which began to emerge in the last decades of the 19th, was closely allied to Naturalism, though it differed from it in important respects. Hermann Bahr (1863–1934), who tried his hand at many styles, defined its aims. As in painting, Impressionism attempts in literature to evoke a mood by suggesting states of mind. In lyric poetry Detlev von Liliencron led the way with *Adjutantenritte* (1883), in which brief but vivid impressions conveyed by sound-painting and a fresher vocabulary than that of other poets of the period created a new poetic style. A more powerful lyrical poet was Richard Dehmel (1863–1920). Influenced by Impressionism and Naturalism, his style—evoking mood through a pattern of sound—is impressionistic; but his subject matter is often Naturalist, whether frank portrayal of sex or of social distress in modern city life. His poetry is exuberant but is controlled by the power of its rhythms. Dehmel's experience of life was too earthy and vigorous to agree with the nebulous poetic speculations of Alfred Mombert (1872–1942), who called himself a cosmic Impressionist, although Dehmel was loosely connected with the same group. The metaphysical nonsense verse of Christian Morgenstern (1871–1914) stands apart from any school.

Much more influential was Stefan George (1868–1933), whose austere sense of poetic mission expressed in measured verse makes him a poet of very different calibre. For him poetry is a sacred trust, and it is the poet's task to regenerate society; to achieve this aim it is necessary first to regenerate poetry. By his solemn, carefully composed, majestic verse he aims at asserting the lofty stature of poetry which, for him, has a religious character. A successor of French Symbolism, he wrote poems which, because of their obscurity, are intelligible only within the framework of the cycle to which they belong. George appears as prophet and priest of an esoteric faith; his poetry reveals his spiritual struggles as well as his convictions. He surrounded himself with a group of disciples; to publish their poetic work he founded in 1892 the journal *Blätter für die Kunst* ("News of the Arts"). Although a stern master, he attracted a group of talented men, among them at least two important literary critics, Friedrich Gundolf and Ernst Bertram, and one poet of rank, Karl Wolfskehl (1869–1948), whose verse develops the note of prophecy found in George, although his style is less formal. Wolfskehl's letters from exile in New Zealand, where he spent the last ten years of his life, are a moving testimony by a European separated from his native culture and re-creating it in his mind.

Hugo von Hofmannsthal (1874–1929), whom George had tried to persuade to join his circle, was a sensitive poet, delicately analyzing his own sensibilities. His lyrical poetry is small in bulk and was written mainly when he was very young. He was the heir of Romanticism, and his poetic language is melodious; but his poetry is haunted by a sense of the ephemerality of life and by an obsession with the inadequacy of language to convey feeling. In his essay *Ein Brief* (the so-called *Chandos Brief*, 1902; trans. as *The Letter of Lord Chandos*, 1952) he records his sense of inability to put into words the whole of his thought and feeling. In his plays of the early 1890s—*Gestern* (1891; *Yesterday*); *Der Tod des Tizian* (1892; *The Death of Titian*, 1913) and *Der Tor und der Tod* (1893; *Death and the Fool*, 1913)—he treats the problem of the aesthete who comes to realize his inadequacy in face of reality. Later dramas—e.g., his adaptation of the medieval morality play *Everyman* as *Jedermann* (1911) and *Das Salzburger grosse Welttheater* (1922; *The Great Salzburg Theatre of the World*, 1966)—strike a religious note and show indebtedness to medieval and baroque drama. His comedies convince by subtle analysis of character. *Der Schwierige* (1921; *The Dif-*

ficult Man*, 1966) is a profound study of a sophisticated mind inhibited by the weight of social tradition. Conscious of the heritage of European culture, of ethical responsibility, his writings convey a strong awareness of moral issues. The libretti he wrote for Richard Strauss (q.v.) introduced his work to a wider public. Their most successful achievement, *Der Rosenkavalier* (1911; *The Cavalier of the Rose*, 1966), presents a felicitous fusion of words and music.

The *fin-de-siècle* mood of Hofmannsthal's early writings also prevails in the work of Arthur Schnitzler (1862–1931), the penetrating analyst of man's inner life. His characters are mainly drawn from the Viennese upper-middle class, whose decadence he portrays. By means of an Impressionist technique—in his *Novelle*, *Leutnant Gustl* (1901), he uses the stream-of-consciousness style of narrative—he succeeds in evoking the atmosphere of Vienna before 1914. A host of less-known but talented authors made Vienna a centre of literary activity. Among them were Richard Beer-Hofmann (1866–1945), a writer of ornate poetry; Richard von Schaukal (1874–1942), a gifted traditional lyricist; Anton Wildgans (1881–1932), a dramatist with leanings toward Naturalism and Expressionism; Felix Salten (1869–1945), a narrative artist of great delicacy; and Karl Kraus (1874–1936), a vehement critic and satirist. The most searching analysis of Austrian culture was made by Robert Musil (1880–1942), whose reputation became established only after World War II. In his monumental novel *Der Mann ohne Eigenschaften* (1930–42; *The Man Without Qualities*, 1953–64) he examines modern incertitude of mind and relentlessly exposes sham values.

2. Symbolism: Rilke and Thomas Mann.—Another focal point of Austrian culture was Prague, from which came many important poets and prose writers: Rainer Maria Rilke, Franz Kafka, Franz Werfel, Max Brod, and Gustav Meyrink. The mood informing the work of these writers is more esoteric. Rilke's ability to create melodious verse full of imaginative power gave his idiosyncratic vision a compelling character. His fame was established by the lyric anthology *Das Stunden-Buch* (1905; *The Book of Hours*), which describes his search for the spiritual life amidst a hostile urban civilization. Rilke's conception of God is unorthodox; his quest for artistic fulfillment determined his vision of everything, even of God and death. *Die Aufzeichnungen des Malte Laurids Brigge* (1910; *The Notebooks of Malte Laurids Brigge*) is an imaginative portrayal of the neurotic obsession and spiritual anguish that stem from his sense of isolation. In *Neue Gedichte* (1907–08; *New Poems*) he finds meaning in an external world exemplified by the objects which he describes in a detached, yet often extremely personal, manner. In the *Duineser Elegien* (1923; *Duino Elegies*), his spiritual struggles are summed up in complicated, severe verse, while the *Sonette an Orpheus* (1923; *Sonnets to Orpheus*) are a joyful tribute to the power of poetry, of which Orpheus is the symbol, to transmute the problems of existence. These later poems are more direct: through powerful images he conveys the anguish of the poet's loneliness and the assurance which poetic creation bestows.

Rilke's work, like that of most of the great 20th-century lyrical poets, drew its strength from the heritage of Symbolism. Symbolism also influenced prose writers. The most representative was Thomas Mann (1875–1955), whose work increasingly became an attempt to use symbol and myth in narrative. He started from a realist basis, a clinical analysis of the diseases afflicting the mind and body of modern man; but his characterization is Impressionist: he makes impressions into leitmotivs, thus conveying the power of the subconscious. His masterly narrative art remains paramount as he handles complex ideas, for his work has a philosophical flavour influenced by Schopenhauer and Nietzsche. His portrayal of social change and of the impact of ideology on society is penetrating, but it is always an organic part of his story, so that the reader's interest does not flag. Throughout his work Mann is occupied with the status of the artist in society. In his early work art appears as the symbol of decadence, indicating a pathological overrefinement which is no longer viable; but from *Der Zauberberg* (1924; *The Magic Mountain*, 1927) onward the emphasis is rather on the constructive qualities of art and humanism.

THE BETTMANN ARCHIVE
HUGO VON HOFMANNSTHAL (1874–1929)

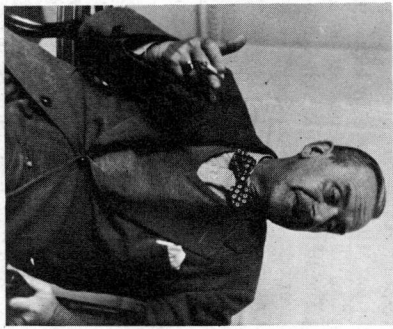

FELIX H. MAN–PIX, INC.

THOMAS MANN (1875-1955)

even though his fascination with disease and death never lessens. The milestones of his work are his great novels: *Buddenbrooks* (publ. 1900, dated 1901; trans. 1924), a portrayal of 19th-century bourgeois society; *Der Zauberberg*, an investigation into the corroding intellectual diseases of our time; the four-part novel, *Joseph und seine Brüder* (1933-43; *Joseph and His Brothers*, 1935-45), an attempt to make biblical myth the basis of literature; *Doktor Faustus* (1947; trans. 1949), an analysis of the German mind and character, of the rise of Nazism and of the re-lation between genius and disease; *Die Bekenntnisse des Hochstaplers Felix Krull* (1954; *The Confessions of Felix Krull, Confidence Man*, 1955), a fragmentary picaresque novel parodying the progress of a rogue who is half-criminal, half-artist. In his *Novellen*—e.g., *Tonio Kröger* and *Tristan* (both 1903); *Der Tod in Venedig* (1912; *Death in Venice*, all trans. in *Three Tales*, 1928)—he treats the same themes in a masterly but more concise way. His all-pervasive irony makes ambiguity a central characteristic of his work; it allows him, through parody, to be indebted to, and yet independent of, tradition; while his increasingly complex style reflects his study of the history of ideas and the complexity of his mind. As a whole his work is the testimony of a humanist who, inspired by the example of Goethe, wishes to safeguard values in the face of the forces of unreason; and who in his later work seeks to point the way toward a synthesis of the conflicting forces of mind and life, art and society, the man of genius and the normal citizen, that threaten to destroy the balance of man's personal and social life.

In his essays and philosophical writings, some political, Mann ranges over large areas of the history of thought. He adopted a nationalist conservatism during World War I, but after 1933 became the leading German champion in exile of liberal democracy. His brother Heinrich (1871-1950), on the other hand, was always a political radical. Many of his novels are savage attacks on the social and political abuses of pre-1914 Germany: *Professor Unrat* (1905) and *Der Untertan* (1918; *The Patrioteer*, 1921) are the best known. His satire is often shrill and sensational; other novels (e.g., *Die kleine Stadt*, 1910; *The Little Town*, 1930) reflect quieter moods.

In contrast, Hermann Hesse (1877-1962) concentrates on the inner life. A Neoromantic, he portrays in a series of delicate novels written in the first three decades of the century—*Peter Camenzind* (1904), *Demian* (1919), and *Der Steppenwolf* (1927), his way in a world hostile to sensitivity. In *Narziss und Goldmund* (1930; trans. as *Death and the Lover*, 1932) and *Das Glasperlenspiel* ("The Bead Game," 1943; trans. as *Magister Ludi*, 1949) he explores the significance of the subconscious and seeks to steer a course between the demands of the flesh and the spirit.

A romantic view of history and contemporary society characterizes the novels of Ricarda Huch (1864-1947) who, like Heinrich and Thomas Mann, is concerned to safeguard the independence and dignity of the individual.

3. Expressionism.—The often ecstatic style of Heinrich Mann anticipated Expressionism (*q.v.*), the dominant literary movement in Germany during and immediately after World War I. Expressionism was a revolt against traditional valuations; it aimed to convey ideas by means of a new style. Its concern was with general truth rather than with the particular situation. It was not the psychology of the individual but the predicament of symbolic types that was explored. Emphasis was laid not on the outer world but on the inner life; as a result, imitation of life was replaced by ecstatic evocation of states of mind. A forerunner of Expressionist drama was Frank Wedekind (1864-1918), who, on the basis of Naturalist description, created plays full of fantastic scenes which, often by a cinematic snapshot technique, caricatured conventional reality. He appeared obsessed with sex and violently attacked conventional morality. The first full-fledged Expressionist drama, however, was Johannes Sorge's *Der Bettler* ("The Beggar," 1912). Here the characters appear not as individuals but as abstract functions in each other's lives. Their speech too is functional. This play, like the dramas of Walter Hasenclever, Paul Kornfeld, Fritz von Unruh, Ernst Barlach the sculptor, and Oskar Kokoschka the painter, is characterized by a quest for the essence of things, for the ideas behind personality and for a spiritual meaning in life. The comedies of Carl Sternheim (1878-1942), though close to Expressionism, have also a strongly Naturalist character. His criticism of middle-class attitudes is enlivened by humour. Ernst Toller's *Masse Mensch* (1920; *Man and the Masses*, 1924) and *Die Maschinenstürmer* (1922; *The Machine Wreckers*, 1923) are openly political. The latter has a historical setting. For Georg Kaiser, Expressionism was only a phase, although *Von Morgen bis Mitternacht* (1916; *From Morn to Midnight*, 1922), *Die Koralle* (1917; *The Coral*, 1931), *Gas I* (1918) and *Gas II* (1920; both trans. 1924), indictments of the social order, made him the leading playwright of the movement. He began his career as a Naturalist, and his later, more mature plays, on subjects from Greek mythology—collectively called the *Griechischer Dramen*—are written in a traditional manner. The coherence of Expressionist poetry, too, is nonreferential. The poem does not reside in its conceptual thought, but in its musical composition. The leading Expressionist poets were Ernst Stadler, Georg Heym, Georg Trakl, Franz Werfel, Johannes Becher, August Stramm, Theodor Däubler, Gottfried Benn and Else Lasker-Schüler. Heym (1887-1912), Trakl (1887-1914) and Stadler (1883-1914) died young, yet they were the leaders of the movement. Heym's apocalyptic vision of doom was embodied in often grotesque verse of great concentration. Trakl was a gentler poet, obsessed by disgust with modern civilization. That the world seemed to him atomistic is reflected in his language, in which disconnected words and images are bound together only by rhythm. Fears erupting from man's urban existence dominate his work; and also that of Stadler and Stramm. In the poetry of Heinrich Lersch (1889-1936) these fears are expressed in a staccato verse representing a radical departure from accepted tradition. The early verse of Gottfried Benn (1886-1956) is macabre because of the clinical objectivity with which he regards human suffering. His realistic descriptions conceal an underlying lyricism. The nihilism of his later poetry takes the form of obscurity in language. Hans Arp (1887-1966) and Yvan Goll (1891-1950) also abandoned their Expressionist beginnings; like Benn, they turned to Surrealist poetry.

Powerful as was the impact of Expressionism, its greater figures did not stay within its orbit. Although there are Expressionist features in the work of Benn, Brecht, Kafka, Kaiser and Werfel, their work has a distinct personal note. Kafka, who became famous only after his death in 1924, depicts the world of anxiety in which the individual appears crushed by unfathomable forces. In his great novels *Der Prozess* (1925; *The Trial*, 1937) and *Das Schloss* (1926; *The Castle*, 1930), and in his tales, a mainly grotesque humour exposes the incongruities of human aspiration and the weakness of reason, but also points to the ambiguity of the situation in which his characters find themselves. It is never certain whether their sense of guilt or their protest against the

THE BETTMANN ARCHIVE

FRANZ KAFKA (1883-1924). SKETCH BY HANS FRONIUS

social and cosmic order is justified. Bertolt Brecht (1898–1956) is Expressionist in his insistence on the gap between art and reality, and in his ecstatic manner of writing, but his incisive social criticism, stemming from Marxist ideology, gives his work its distinctive character. His sense of theatre, masterly handling of crowd scenes, powerful evocation of the clashes of personality, probing into human convictions and the energy of his poetry—he was also a most gifted poet—make his major plays striking parables of man's corruption and yearning for a better order. Brecht's pessimistic appraisal of man, however, shows his difference from the Expressionists' contention that man is essentially good, a belief that inspired Leonhard Frank in his choice of title for his collection of short stories, *Der Mensch ist gut* ("Man is Good," 1919). Franz Werfel, whose early poetry and play—*Der Spiegelmensch* (1920)—were Expressionist, followed more conventional paths in his later novels. In *Das Lied von Bernadette* (1941; *The Song of Bernadette*, 1942), an account of the saint of Lourdes, he expresses profound religious conviction.

4. Post-Expressionism and Social Realism.—With the return to normality after the war and the ensuing period of inflation, desire to reform the world subsided and Expressionism was replaced by a movement called "*Die neue Sachlichkeit*." An attempt at this "new objectivity" coloured novels about both the war and society. Arnold Zweig's *Der Streit um den Sergeanten Grischa* (1927; trans. as *The Case of Sergeant Grischa*, 1927) and Erich Maria Remarque's *Im Westen nichts Neues* (1928; *All Quiet on the Western Front*, 1929) present a harrowing indictment of the evils of war. Description of the social and political situation in Germany in the 1920s is found in the novels of Hans Fallada (pseudonym of Rudolph Ditzen), *Bauern, Bonzen und Bomben* ("Boors, Bosses and Bombs," 1930) and *Kleiner Mann, was nun?* (1932; *Little Man, What Now?* 1933), as well as in the satirical verse and humorous novels of Erich Kästner. Some of the dark undercurrents of German society that came to the surface with the rise of Nazism are here detected. Novels of social documentation written later are Anna Seghers' *Das siebte Kreuz* (1939; *The Seventh Cross*, 1942) and Bruno E. Werner's *Die Galeere* ("The Galley," 1949). Carl Zuckmayer's ability to convey social criticism in realistic scenes drawn from observation of contemporary life makes *Der Hauptmann von Köpenick* (1931; *The Captain of Köpenick*, 1932) a successful satire on Prussian society, and *Des Teufels General* (1946; *The Devil's General*, 1947), a vigorous portrayal of the predicament of those German officers in World War II who were torn between their sense of duty and their awareness of the evil of the regime. Social reality was also explored by Alfred Döblin, who in his novel *Berlin Alexanderplatz* (1930; trans. as *The Story of Franz Biberkopf*, 1931) uses the stream-of-consciousness technique for social documentation and psychological analysis.

In Herman Broch's *Der Tod des Vergil* ("The Death of Virgil," 1945) this technique was used to depict the poet's reaction to his work and to the external world. In his trilogy *Die Schlafwandler* (1931–32; *The Sleepwalkers*, 1932) he not only depicts social changes in 20th-century Germany but seeks, by the insertion of an essay on the values of our age, to analyze the intellectual background of modern civilization—an indication of his strong interest in the social, political and philosophical problems that make up the bulk of his essays.

Another writer with philosophical leanings, Ernst Jünger (1895–), is concerned with the decline of bourgeois culture and the social impact of technology. He extols heroism in war in his war diary *In Stahlgewittern* (1920; *Storm of Steel*, 1929); nonetheless he soon became a critic of the Third Reich, as is shown by his symbolical tale *Auf den Marmorklippen* (1939; *On the Marble Cliffs*, 1947), and by his later diaries and prose.

His brother Friedrich Georg Jünger (1898–) shows a more developed lyrical and narrative talent. Both his poetry and prose reveal formal mastery and a strong sense of tradition. This feeling for tradition also shaped the work of two other poets, Josef Weinheber (1892–1945) and R. A. Schröder (1878–1962) who, though different in outlook, both attempted to re-create classicism in the modern age.

Conversion to Catholicism forms the main inspiration of Gertrud von Le Fort (1876–1971) and can be discerned in the symbolism of her novels. The work of Werner Bergengrün (1892–1964) is also imbued with Catholic values. His sense of the grotesque makes his writings often startling, but also attractive.

5. The Third Reich.—The Third Reich disrupted the continuity of literary life in Germany. Many authors, among them some of the most famous—Heinrich and Thomas Mann, Remarque, Wolfskehl—emigrated, and some, like Mann and Stefan George, chose not to return. Of those who remained in Germany, some found it impossible to publish their works; others were exterminated, and their work was recognized only posthumously. The less said about Nazi writers the better. Of its much vaunted school of blood and soil the talent of E. G. Kolbenheyer, Friedrich Blunck and Hans Grimm was limited. Under Hitler the life of the mind was smothered and Germany was cut off from contact with other countries. A few nonpolitical writers were able to continue publication. The autobiographical novels of Hans Carossa (1878–1955) must be singled out for their emphasis on the need to develop curative powers within the individual by following traditional and developing inner resources.

6. Literature After World War II.—The end of World War II meant a breakdown in social and economic life, and it took some time for organized literary life to revive. Much of the writing that first came to the fore was ephemeral. Established writers continued to publish their work, often abroad, and for some time dominated the scene. Posthumous publication of works banned by the Nazi regime rescued important figures from neglect or oblivion. The most outstanding poet among them was Gertrud Kolmar (1894–?1943), who had been murdered in a Nazi extermination camp. The powerful cadences and imagery of her verse spring from profound emotional turbulence. Other lyric poets, such as Jesse Thoor (1905–52), Max Hermann-Neisse (1886–1941), Else Lasker-Schüler (1876–1945) and Franz Baermann Steiner (1909–52), also became widely known only after the war. Other reputations, such as that of Kafka, were definitely established. Kafka influenced several writers, of whom Hermann Kasack (1896–1966) was the most important. The war cut short the lives of several writers of promise. Among them were Felix Hartlaub (1913–45), a prose writer of great sensitivity; and Wolfgang Borchert (1921–47), whose *Draussen vor der Tür* ("Outside in Front of the Door," 1947) recalls Expressionism.

Of lyrical poets who survived, Bergengrün, R. A. Schröder, Hermann Hesse, H. Leifhelm (1891–1947), Marie Luise Kaschnitz (1901–), Rudolf Hagelstange (1912–) and F. G. Jünger sought to appeal to man's desire for spiritual harmony; others were influenced by Oskar Loerke (1884–1941), who in his nature lyrics attempts to grasp reality in a moment of significance. Wilhelm Lehmann (1882–1968), an older poet who became known only after the war and who continued linguistic experimentation, was another influence. This tendency to free lyric language from convention produced almost a new tradition, that of unconventionality of expression. Ingeborg Bachmann (1926–), Günther Eich (1907–), Carl Magnus Enzensberger (1929–), Walter Höllerer (1922–), Karl Krolow (1915–) and Heinz Piontek (1925–) are among those who try to express the chaotic experience of their age, often through experiments with form. Their images, metaphors and sentences are disconnected; they rely on rhythmic coherence and association of impressions and ideas rather than on a logical and syntactical sequence. The most important poet who follows this trend is Paul Celan (1920–70) who uses visionary language and has a rare sense of aesthetic and moral values. Of a different character is the poetry of the Austrian Christine Lavant (1915–), who conveys spiritual anguish in more conventional, melodious verse. The poetry of the East German Peter Huchel (1903–) has a simplicity akin to that of Greek poetry, matched by his feeling for nature and peasant life. In drama the most important contribution after World War II came from Switzerland (*see* SWISS LITERATURE: *German Swiss Literature*). Carl Spitteler, the most important Swiss poet at the turn of the century, created in *Olympischer Frühling* ("Olympian Spring," 1900–10) an epic in alexandrines in which ancient mythol-

GERMAN LITERATURE

ogy was reset in an ideal Switzerland, the scene of a struggle between good and evil. Two other Swiss writers, Robert Walser (1878–1956) and Albin Zollinger (1895–1941), gained full recognition only after 1945. Walser was admired by Kafka for his style; he conveys a similar anguish. Zollinger's tales and lyrical poetry contain sensitive social criticism and self-analysis. The comedies of the Swiss Curt Goetz (1888–1900) show little regional influence, and provide polished entertainment enlivened by keen wit. The two best-known modern Swiss writers are Max Frisch (1911–) and Friedrich Dürrenmatt (1921–); both have made bold experiments with dramatic form. Dürrenmatt's *Besuch der alten Dame* (1955; trans. as *The Visit*) and *Die Physiker* (1961; *The Physicists*) and Frisch's *Nun singen sie wieder* ("Now Sing Again," 1946) and *Andorra* (1961) are modern morality plays; and his novels, *Stiller* (1954) and *Homo Faber* (1957), are investigations into the place of the intellectual in the modern world. Both writers criticize the emotional sterility of modern life. Dürrenmatt has also experimented with the radio play. Other practitioners of this new genre were Günther Eich (1907–) and Ingeborg Bachmann; the latter's *Der Gute Gott von Manhattan* (1958) was a moving outcry against modern spiritual sterility.

In the mid-1960s political drama began to dominate the German stage. Among playwrights whose work became internationally famous was Rolf Hochhuth (1931–), whose *Der Stellvertreter* (1963; *The Representative*; U.S. title, *The Deputy*), a documentary drama posing the question of how the world could tolerate Hitler's extermination of the Jews without rising in protest, and accusing Pope Pius XII of guilt by silence, caused a fierce debate. His *Soldaten* (1967; *Soldiers*), in which aerial bombing and Winston Churchill are attacked, was equally controversial. Heinar Kipphardt (1922–) based his dramas *In der Sache J. Robert Oppenheimer* (1964) and *Joel Brand* (1965) on documentary evidence, as did Peter Weiss (1916–) in his play about the Auschwitz trial of 1964–65, *Die Ermittlung* (1965; *The Investigation*), and his quasi-historical *Die Verfolgung und Ermordung des Jean-Paul Marat...* (1964; better known as *Marat/Sade*). Martin Walser (1927–), in *Eiche und Angora* ("Oak and Angora," 1962), deals with the attempt of former Nazis to conceal their past, while Günter Grass, in *Die Plebejer proben den Aufstand—ein Deutsches Trauerspiel* (1966; *The Plebeians Rehearse the Rising: a German Tragedy*, 1967), makes use of Brecht's attitude to the East Berlin rising of 1953.

There were many novelists, but few had real distinction. Heinrich Böll (1917–) seeks to fathom the origins of the forces molding public life. In *Haus ohne Hüter* (1954; *Unguarded Home*, 1957) he analyzes the psychological problems of fatherless children after World War II. His *Irisches Tagebuch* ("Irish Journal," 1957) and *Dr. Murkes gesammeltes Schweigen* ("The Collected Silences of Dr. Murke," 1958) show him as an accomplished humorist. Gerd Gaiser (1908–) explores experimentalism in the novel, most adventurously in *Schlussball* (1958; *The Last Dance of the Season*, 1960). Heimito von Doderer (1896–1966) in a series of novels, of which *Die Strudlhofstiege...* (1951) and *Die Dämonen* (1958; *The Demons*, 1962) are outstanding, depicts Austrian society on several levels. Edzard Schaper (1908–) takes his themes from Baltic countries and from Christian mysticism. Probably the most widely acclaimed novelist is Günter Grass, whose *Die Blechtrommel* (1959; *The Tin Drum*, 1962) and *Hundejahre* (1963; *Dog Years*, 1965) are disturbing and bizarre, but vigorous, satirical novels, exploring the luxuriant undergrowth of the German lower middle-class imagination. Uwe Johnson, in *Mutmassungen über Jakob* (1959; *Speculations About Jakob*, 1963), analyzes in an experimental style problems raised by the political division of Germany. Other prose writers of talent included Hans Erich Nossak, Rudolf Hagelstange, Siegfried Lenz, Klaus Röhler, Martin Walser, Herbert Heckmann and Johannes Bobrowski.

Literary criticism also became more complex during the 20th century. The positivist school was followed by a variety of groups treating literature in the context of contemporary problems or of the history of ideas. Approaches differ; and there are considerable divergences of method. W. Dilthey, F. Gundolf, J. Petersen, F. Strich, and H. A. Korff are the best-known literary critics. Common to all is the attempt to establish a study of literature that can claim the status of a science, and a tendency to see literature in a nonliterary perspective. After World War II stylistic analysis, which made the work of literature rather than the writer the focus of inquiry, emerged as the most popular tendency. Its leading critic is Emil Staiger. The widespread, growing complexity of literary studies helped to further both the impulse toward rationality and the high consciousness characterizing fictional literature—a consciousness which reflected the writer's need to come to terms with a more sophisticated vision of life than had past writers and his desire to modify the conventional picture of reality.

See articles on many writers cited; DRAMA; ROMANTICISM; etc.; *see also* references under "German Literature" in the Index.

BIBLIOGRAPHY.—*General Works*: H. de Boor and R. Newald, *Geschichte der deutschen Literatur* (1949–); H. O. Burger (ed.), *Annalen der deutschen Literatur* (1952); F Martini, *Deutsche Literaturgeschichte*, 10th ed. (1960); F. Mossé, *Histoire de la littérature allemande* (1959); T. Stockum and J. van Dam, *Geschichte der deutschen Literatur*, 5th ed., rev. by E. Purdie (1967); W. Stammler (ed.), *Deutsche Philologie im Aufriss*, 2nd ed. (1957–); G. Waterhouse, continued by H. M. Waidson, *A Short History of German Literature* (1959); J. Bithell, *Germany*, 2nd ed. (1955); R. D. Gray, *An Introduction to German Literature* (1965); *Introductions to German Literature*, 4 vol. (1967–), vol. i, *The 16th and 17th Centuries* (1968), with bibliographies of authors, etc.

Collected Texts and Anthologies: J. Kürschner (ed.), *Deutsche National-literatur* (1882–99); H. Kindermann et al. (eds.), *Deutsche Literatur: Sammlung literarischer Kunst- und Kulturdenkmäler in Entwicklungsreihen* (1930 et seq.); *Bibliothek des literarischen Vereins in Stuttgart* (1843 et seq.); H. G. Fiedler (ed.), *The Oxford Book of German Verse*, 3rd ed. by E. Stahl (1967).

Old and Middle High German: G. Ehrismann, *Geschichte der deutschen Literatur bis zum Ausgang des Mittelalters*, 4 vol. (1922–55); H. de Boor, *Die deutsche Literatur von Karl dem Grossen bis zum Begin der höfischen Dichtung* (770–1170) (1955) and *Die höfische Literatur. Vorbereitung, Blütezeit, Ausklang* (1170–1250), 3rd ed. (1957); C. von Kraus, *Deutsche Liederdichter des 13. Jahrhunderts* (1952–58); W. Stammler, *Die deutsche Literatur des Mittelalters, Verfasserlexikon* (1933); J. Schwietering, *Die deutsche Dichtung des Mittelalters* (1941); H. Schneider, *Heldendichtung, Geistlichendichtung, Ritterdichtung* (1943); M. Richey, *Essays on the Mediaeval Love Lyric* (1943); A. Moret, *Les Débuts du lyrisme en Allemagne* (1951); H. Kuhn, *Minnesangs Wende* (1952); M. OC. Walshe, *Medieval German Literature* (1962); *Poets of the Minnesang*, ed. by O. Sayce (1967). (W. W. Cs.)

The 16th and 17th Centuries: G. Müller, *Deutsche Dichtung von der Renaissance bis zum Ausgang des Barock, 1400–1600*, 2nd ed. (1957); P. Hankamer, *Deutsche Gegenreformation und deutsches Barock*, 2nd ed. (1947); A. Taylor, *Problems in German Literary History of the 15th and 16th Centuries* (1939); E. Hederer, *Deutsche Barocklyrik* (1956); R. Newald, *Die deutsche Literatur vom Spälhumanismus zur Empfindsamkeit, 1570–1750* (1951); R. Stamm (ed.), *Die Kunstformen des Barockzeitalters* (1956); various authors, *Aus der Welt des Barock* (1957). See also *Neudrucke deutscher Literaturwerke des XVI. und XVII. Jahrhunderts*, ed. by W. Braune (1876 et seq.). (J. R. WE.; D. G. D.)

The 18th Century: H. Hettner, *Geschichte der deutschen Literatur im 18. Jahrhundert*, 7th ed. by E. A. Boucke, 3 vol. (1925–26); F. J. Schneider, *Die deutsche Dichtung der Aufklärungszeit*, 2nd ed. (1949), and *Die deutsche Dichtung der Geniezeit* (1952); A. Köster, *Die deutsche Literatur der Aufklärungszeit* (1925); W. H. Bruford, *German Culture and Society in Classical Weimar, 1775–1806* (1962); R. R. Heitner, *German Tragedy in the Age of Enlightenment, 1724–68*, 2 vol. (1963–64); O. Walzel, *Deutsche Dichtung von Gottsched bis zur Gegenwart* (1927); E. Ermatinger, *Deutsche Dichter, 1700–1900* (1949); K. Viëtor, *Deutsches Dichten und Denken von der Aufklärung bis zum Realismus* (1949); H. M. Wolff, *Die Weltanschauung der deutschen Aufklärung* (1949); R. Benz, *Deutsches Barock. Kultur des 18. Jahrhunderts* (1949); R. Pascal, *The German Sturm und Drang* (1953), and *The German Novel* (1956); H. B. Garland, *Storm and Stress* (1952); F. Schultz, *Klassik und Romantik der Deutschen*, 2nd ed. (1952); H. A. Korff, *Geist der Goethezeit* (1923–57); L. A. Willoughby, *The Classical Age of German Literature*

(1926), and *The Romantic Movement in Germany* (1930); F. Strich, *Deutsche Klassik und Romantik*, 4th ed. (1949); F. Martini, *Die Goethezeit* (1952); G. Krüger, *Die Religion der Goethezeit* (1931); M. Colleville, *La Renaissance du lyrisme dans la littérature allemande aux xviii° siècle* (1936); S. S. Prawer, *German Lyric Poetry* (1952); B. von Wiese, *Die deutsche Lyrik* (1957), and *Die deutsche Tragödie von Lessing bis Hebbel*, 2nd ed. (1952); W. Kayser, *Geschichte der deutschen Ballade* (1936); H. H. Borchardt, *Der Roman der Goethezeit* (1949); F. Gundolf, *Shakespeare und der deutsche Geist*, 11th ed. (1959); P. Grappin, *La Théorie du génie dans la préclassicisme allemand* (1952); R. Haym, *Die Romantische Schule*, 5th ed. by O. Walzel (1928), 6th ed. by E. Redslob, vol. 1 (1949); O. Walzel, *Deutsche Romantik*, 5th ed. (1923–26); P. Kluckhohn, *Die deutsche Romantik* (1924); J. Petersen, *Die Wesensbestimmung der deutschen Romantik* (1926); R. Huch, *Die Romantik*, rev. ed. (1951); R. Benz, *Die deutsche Romantik*, 4th ed. (1940); A. Béguin, *Le Romantisme allemand* (1949); E. Ruprecht, *Der Aufbruch der romantischen Bewegung* (1948); R. Tymms, *German Romantic Literature* (1955); B. Seuffert and A. Sauer (eds.), *Deutsche Literaturdenkmale des 18. und 19. Jahrhunderts* (1881–1924); W. D. Robson-Scott, *The Literary Background of the Gothic Revival in Germany* (1965).

The 19th Century: Ernst Alker, *Geschichte der deutschen Literatur von Goethes Tod bis zur Gegenwart*, 2nd ed. (1962); E. K. Bennett, *A History of the German Novelle From Goethe to Thomas Mann* (1934); H. Bieber, *Der Kampf um die Tradition* (1928); G. Brandes, *Hovedstrømninger i det 19de aarhundredes Litteratur*, vol. vi, *Det unge Tyskland* (Eng. trans. *Main Currents in 19th-Century Literature*, vol. vi, *The Young Germany*, 1901–05); E. M. Butler, *The Saint-Simonian Religion in Germany; a Study of the Young German Movement* (1926); W. Höllerer, *Zwischen Klassik und Moderne* (1958);

The 20th Century: F. Bertaux, *Panorama de la littérature allemande contemporaine* (1931); J. Bithell, *Modern German Literature*, 3rd ed. (1959); H. Böschenstein, *The German Novel, 1939–44* (1949); A. Eloesser, *Modern German Literature* (1933); V. Lange, *Modern German Literature, 1870–1940* (1945); O. Mann and H. Friedmann, (eds.), *Deutsche Literatur in 20. Jahrhundert* (1954); *Christliche Dichter der Gegenwart* (1955) and *Expressionismus* (1956); F. Lennartz, *Dichter und Schriftsteller unserer Zeit* (1955); H. Naumann, *Deutsche Dichtung der Gegenwart* (1933); M. Rychner, *Zur europäischen Literatur zwischen zwei Weltkriegen* (1943); R. Samuel and R. H. Thomas, *Expressionism in German Life, Literature and Theatre* (1939); A. Soergel, *Dichtung und Dichter der Zeit* (1928); W. H. Sokel, *The Writer in Extremis* (1959); H. M. Waidson, *The Modern German Novel* (1959).

GERMANOS (LOUKAS STRENOPOULOS) (1872–1951), Greek archbishop of Thyateira and a leader of the ecumenical movement (*q.v.*), was born at Delliones in eastern Thrace on Sept. 15, 1872. He was educated in Constantinople and at the theological college at Halki, and in 1900 went to Germany for further study. He returned to be a professor at Halki (1904) and was ordained priest, later becoming also the director of the college (1907). In 1912 he was made metropolitan of Seleucia, but retained his position at Halki until 1922, when he became metropolitan of Thyateira and exarch of western and central Europe with his headquarters in London. In 1924 he was also named special representative of the patriarch of Constantinople to the archbishop of Canterbury, and in 1942 was awarded the Lambeth cross for his services to Anglican-Orthodox understanding. He played an important part in the formative years of 20th-century Christian co-operation, becoming a first president of the World Council of Churches on its establishment in 1948. His guidance helped bring the Orthodox churches into fuller association with the Western churches.
He died in London, Jan. 23, 1951. (H. M. W.)

GERMANTOWN, a section of Philadelphia, Pa., which before 1854 was a separate borough, is one of the most historic communities in the state. It lies 6 mi. N.W. of the centre of Philadelphia and extends for more than a mile along Germantown avenue, formerly High street. Its first settlers were part of the vanguard of the great Germanic invasion of colonial Pennsylvania. William Penn's promise that his colony would offer an asylum where men might worship God as they chose early attracted Pietists from the Rhineland, and in 1683 a group of such people, chiefly from Frankfurt and Krefeld, founded Germantown. The principal figure among them was Francis Daniel Pastorius. Germantown quickly became a prosperous settlement, developing various handicraft industries. Weaving, tanning and wagon building were especially noteworthy. On the Wissahickon creek William Rittenhouse in 1690 built the first paper mill in the British colonies. In 1738 Christopher Sauer and his son established in Germantown a printing press which became perhaps the largest in colonial America. Sauer's German Bible was the first to be printed in a European language in America. One of his employees, Jacob Bey, was the first manufacturer of type in the British colonies.

Germantown soon ceased to be a wholly German community, and especially after the 1750s the English influx was great. Most of the fine buildings for which Germantown avenue is famous, symmetrical stone houses characterized often by the Germantown pent roof and by inviting benches flanking the doorway, date from the middle and late 18th century. Outstanding among them is Cliveden (1763), planned by Chief Justice Benjamin Chew, an especially good example in stone of the monumental late Georgian style of the Philadelphia area. Grumblethorpe (1744) is lighter in style and a more typical Germantown home. The Morris house (1772) once served as the presidential mansion of the United States and is a graceful Pennsylvania Georgian town house. The original building of the Germantown academy (1760) still stands. From an earlier period (1690 and later) Wyck survives, and from a later period (1798) there is Upsala, an example of the delicate Federal style in Pennsylvania. Various organized groups are dedicated to the preservation of these buildings and of whole neighbourhoods of the colonial village.

On Oct. 4, 1777, several of the Germantown houses figured in military history, when Washington's continental army fought the battle of Germantown among them in an effort to break the defenses of British-occupied Philadelphia. (R. F. WE.)

GERMAN VOLGA REPUBLIC was from 1924 to 1941 one of the ten autonomous soviet socialist republics of the Russian federation and was situated between latitude 49° 50′ N. and 52° N. and longitude 44° 45′ E. and 48° 5′ E. It was bounded west, north and east by the Saratov *oblast* and south and southwest by the Stalingrad (now Volgograd) *oblast*. Its area was 10,888 sq.mi. and it lay on both banks of the Volga river.

About 27,000 German colonists were settled on the Volga river in 1760 and 1761 at the invitation of Catherine II by special manifesto. The climatic difficulties of their new environment, lack of capital, oppression by officials and attacks by Kirgiz and Kalmyks diminished their numbers by 50% in the first ten years. They were at first given special privileges, including exemption from army service, but in the mid-19th century these privileges were annulled. About 1870 the small measure of autonomy remaining to them was canceled and the colonies broken up.

When World War I broke out the German colonists were persecuted, and in Feb. 1915 an imperial ukase ordered the destruction of their settlements in frontier areas. In Feb. 1917 another ukase prescribed the transportation of the Volga Germans to Siberia. Before this was carried out the 1917 Revolution took place. In early 1918 a commission was set up at Saratov to organize Soviet rule among the Volga Germans, and at that town in June 1918 the first Soviet congress of the Volga Germans expressed a wish for autonomous government. On Oct. 19, 1918, the Autonomous German Workers' commune was created by decree, and it became a republic on Feb. 20, 1924. Engels became the capital. Of its 12 cantons, 5 had purely German inhabitants, 4 mixed German-Russian or German-Ukrainian inhabitants and 3 were predominantly Russian or Ukrainian. By 1939 the republic's population was 605,542 of which 67% was German, 20% Russian and 12% Ukrainian. The republic was abolished on Sept. 24, 1941; its territory was divided between the Saratov and Stalingrad (Volgograd) *oblasts* and its German inhabitants deported to Siberia.

GERMANY (DEUTSCHLAND), a country of central Europe bordering on the Netherlands, Belgium, Luxembourg, France, Switzerland, Austria, Czechoslovakia, Poland and Denmark. The year 1949 saw the emergence of two separate republics in Germany: the Federal Republic of Germany (Bundesrepublik Deutschland; West Germany) consisting of the area of the former three western zones of occupation; and the German Democratic Republic (Deutsche Demokratische Republik; East Germany) consisting of the eastern zone. Berlin was similarly

GERMANY

divided into a western and an eastern section, East Berlin acting as the capital of the German Democratic Republic. The capital of the Federal Republic of Germany is Bonn. Because of its isolation, West Berlin could not become a constituent part of the Federal Republic of Germany but close ties were maintained between the two areas.

The Federal Republic of Germany (including West Berlin) has an area of 95,929 sq.mi. and a population of (1961) 56,174,826—an increase of 30% over 1939. The German Democratic Republic, referred to by the West Germans as central Germany as distinct from the eastern territories annexed by Poland, has an area of 41,816 sq.mi. and a population of 17,011,931 (1964), an increase of over 15% since 1939. The former German eastern territories cover 39,370 sq.mi. and had in 1957 a population of 6,500,000, representing a decrease of one-third since 1939, and a complete change from German to Polish occupants.

In 1945, with cities in ruins and millions of people uprooted and destitute, with the country divided in such a way that the western zones of occupation had millions of extra people to employ and feed, with foreign trade at a standstill, and with the east separated from the west and subjected to the rigorous policies of the Soviet Union, the prospects for the German people seemed to be grim indeed. Contrary to all expectations, both West and East Germany underwent a remarkable recovery, though there were great contrasts in the social and economic developments of the two portions of the country. East Germany experienced profound changes in its social and economic structure through the imposition of Communist policies and centralized and directed economic planning. It underwent a two-year plan (1949–51) and two five-year plans during the 1950s, the aims of which were to increase agricultural production and to develop the heavy industries. Population slightly decreased during the 1950s and housing construction was far below the level of West Germany. Agricultural production did not seem to have reached the headway that was planned, but industrial production, with 1953 as 100, reached 136 in 1957, as compared with 146 in West Germany. This is a record of remarkable achievement in both east and west, but in the former it was accompanied by a lag in other spheres of economic growth.

The divergence between West and East Germany after partition lay not only in the differences between the two sections of a country that had evolved in the closest interdependence but also in the development of two contrasted ideologies—that of democracy and private enterprise in the west and a communistic regime with a controlled economy in the east.

This article contains the following sections and subsections:

I. PHYSICAL GEOGRAPHY

1. Geology.—Germany consists of a floor of Paleozoic rocks upon which rest unconformably the comparatively little-disturbed beds of the Mesozoic system, while in the north German plain a covering of glacial deposits conceals the whole of the older strata from view, excepting some scattered and isolated outcrops of Cretaceous and Tertiary beds.

The rocks that compose the ancient floor are thrown into folds, which in the western half of Germany run approximately from west-southwest to east-northeast. They are exposed, on the one hand, in the neighbourhood of the Rhine, and, on the other hand, in the Bohemian massif. With the latter must be included the Frankenwald, the Thüringer Wald and the Harz. The oldest rocks, belonging to the Archean system, occur in the folds. Along the Vosges and the Black Forest (Schwarzwald) in the south, forming the greater part of the Bohemian massif, including the Erzgebirge, in the east. They consist chiefly of gneiss and schist, with granite and other eruptive rocks. Farther north, in the Hunsrück, the Taunus, the Eifel and Westerwald, the Harz and the Frankenwald, the ancient floor is composed mainly of Devonian beds. Other Paleozoic systems are, however, included in the folds. Along the northern border of the folded belt lies the coal basin of the Ruhr in Westphalia, which is the continuation of the Belgian coal field, and bears much the same relation to the Rhenish Devonian area as the coal basin of Liège bears to the Ardennes. The Permian, as in England, is not involved in the folds which have affected the older beds, and in general lies unconformably upon them. It occurs chiefly around the masses of ancient rocks, and one of the largest areas is that of the Saar.

Between the old rocks of the Rhine highlands on the west and the ancient massif of Bohemia on the east a vast area of Triassic

PLATE I

GERMANY

Hamburg Harbour, seen from St. Pauli *Landungsbrücken*

The Karlsplatz in Munich, capital of Bavaria. The two 320-ft. towers of the Late Gothic Frauenkirche are seen beyond the Karlstor, an old city gate

Street scene in Rothenburg ob der Tauber, medieval town in Bavaria

(Top left) The monorail suspension railway at Wuppertal. (Top right) One of the Rhine harbours of Düsseldorf, capital of North Rhine-Westphalia. (Bottom left) Ernst Reuter Platz, West Berlin, looking toward the Europe Centre and the Kaiser Wilhelm Memorial Church. (Bottom right) The city of Cologne's twin-spired Gothic cathedral and the Late Romanesque church of Gross-St. Martin

PHOTOGRAPHS, (TOP, BOTTOM RIGHT) RAY MANLEY FROM SHOSTAL, (BOTTOM LEFT) BILDARCHIV H. V. IRMER, (OTHERS) ZFA—PUBLIX

PLATE II

GERMANY

Coblenz, Rhineland-Palatinate, at the confluence of the Moselle and Rhine rivers

Heidelberg, on the banks of the Neckar River in Baden-Württemberg. About 300 ft. above the town itself is the Heidelberg Castle

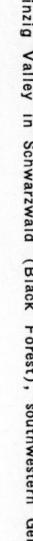

Kinzig Valley in Schwarzwald (Black Forest), southwestern Germany

(Top left) Leer, an inland port in Lower Saxony, northwest Germany. (Top right) Berchtesgaden, a resort of southeastern Bavaria, lying in a deep valley on the northern side of the Alps. (Bottom left) The Sieg Valley, North Rhine-Westphalia. (Bottom right) Vineyards along the hills at Lorchhausen on the banks of the Rhine River

PHOTOGRAPHS, (TOP, CENTRE LEFT) FRED BOND—PUBLIX, (CENTRE RIGHT) THOMAS HOLLYMAN—PHOTO RESEARCHERS, (BOTTOM RIGHT) H. ADAM—BAVARIA-VERLAG, (OTHERS) ZFA—PUBLIX

beds extends from Hanover to Basel and from Metz to Bayreuth. These beds, as the name suggests, fall into three series; the Lower Bunte sandstones, the middle shelly limestones (*Muschelkalk*) and the Keuper marls and sandstones. Over the greater part of central Germany the Triassic beds are free from folding and are nearly horizontal. The Triassic beds must have covered a large part of the old rock masses, but they have been preserved only where they were faulted down to a lower level. Along the southern margin of the Triassic area there is a long band of Jurassic beds dipping toward the Danube. At its eastern extremity this band is continuous with a syncline of Jurassic beds, running parallel to the western border of the Bohemian massif, but separated from it by a narrow strip of Triassic beds. Toward the north, in Lower Saxony and North Rhine-Westphalia, the Triassic beds are followed by Jurassic and Cretaceous deposits, the latter being there the more important. As in the south of England, the lower beds of the Cretaceous are of estuarine origin and the Upper Cretaceous beds overlap the Lower, lying in the valley of the Ruhr directly upon the Paleozoic rocks. In Saxony also the Upper Cretaceous beds rest directly upon the Paleozoic or Archean rocks. The Eocene system is unknown in Germany except in the foothills of the Alps; but the Oligocene and Miocene are widely spread, especially in the northern plain and in the depression of the Danube. The Oligocene is generally marine. Marine Miocene occurs in northwest Germany and the Miocene of the Danube valley is in part marine, but in central Germany it is of fluvial or lacustrine origin.

The horizontal sediments of the Mesozoic that lay on the old peneplain were gently folded or rippled by the earth movements of the Tertiary period and vale, scarp and upland have been formed through differential erosion from the three main strata of the Triassic series. Especially important in Germany is the so-called Saxonian folding. This affected the Mesozoic and more especially the Cretaceous strata on the northern edge of the Hercynian land mass, between the Rhine plateau and the Harz. This folding began in the Upper Jurassic and continued through the Miocene. Anticlines and synclines have been eroded to form scarped ridges and vales, some of these taking the form of an "inverted" relief, in which the rocks of the synclines stand out as ridges with outward-facing scarps. These folds trend from northwest to southeast and have the same direction as the faulted highland of Thuringia. The Westphalian uplands are an eroded anticline. A variety of north-west to southeast ridges, some of them with inverted relief, rising from loess-covered plains, lies between the Leine and Weser and also on the northern border of the Harz.

Vulcanicity accompanied the Tertiary earth movements and continued until the glacial period. Basalt lava flows, like those of central France, form the Rhön and Vogelsberg in central Germany. Crater lakes, cones and residual plugs of more recent date occur in many parts of the central highlands. The trachytes of the Siebengebirge are typical. The precise age of the volcanoes of the Eifel, many of which are in a perfect state of preservation, is not clear, but they are certainly post-Tertiary.

The greater part of north Germany is covered by Quaternary deposits. These are in part of glacial origin and contain Scandinavian boulders; but fluvial and aeolian deposits also occur. The latter, called loess, occur on the northern border of the central highlands, and in the sheltered lowlands and on the river terraces in the highlands and in southern Germany. Quaternary beds also cover the floor of the broad depression through which the Rhine meanders from Basel to Mainz and occupy a large part of the plain of the Danube. The depression of the Rhine is a trough lying between two series of faults. The broader depression of the Danube is associated with the formation of the Alps and was flooded by the sea during a part of the Miocene period.

2. Geographical Regions, Relief and Drainage.—The physical features of Germany—rock types, land forms, climate and vegetation—are associated with each other in such a way as to permit the recognition of distinct physical or natural units. In spite of human interference, these remain as the fixed framework of human occupancy of the country. A detailed division of Germany into physical units has been undertaken by a specially appointed government authority in order to provide a standard

basis of reference. From detailed map studies on a scale of 1:200,000, several hundred units have been mapped and these in turn are grouped into 88 larger units which are grouped into the four major physical divisions of Germany—the northern lowland (north German plain), the central or mid-German highlands, the scarplands and lowlands of southern Germany, and the Bavarian Alps and plateau. These divisions are used in the articles elsewhere on the individual *Länder* (states), to which reference should be made for further detail.

The North German Plain.—This area is flat to the west of the Berlin area, but to the east it consists of morainic hills more or less parallel to the Baltic coast and usually less than 600 ft. high, separated by wide, flat valley floors.

In the western section the land is low-lying, with reclaimed coastal marshes providing rich pasture land behind which lie bogs and sandy heaths. In the eastern section (beyond and including the Lüneburg heath [*see* LÜNEBURGER HEIDE]) there are two main belts of morainic hills. These are the Baltic uplands (strewn over large areas with numerous lakes and patches of marsh) extending from Schleswig to East Prussia, and the Lüneburg-Altmark-Fläming-Lusatian heath lands to the south. Between these two belts are marshy valley floors and the raised diluvial platforms of old glacial rivers.

On the southern border of the plain, and bordering on the mid-German highlands to the south, there is a belt of rolling country called the Börde. The subsoil is largely loessic, making it very fertile. From prehistoric times this area has been inhabited. Running into the hills from the plain are great bays of lowland, the two biggest being the Cologne and Leipzig bays.

There is a great difference between the coast of the North sea and that of the Baltic. On the former, where the sea has broken up the ranges of dunes formed in bygone times and divided them into separate islands, the mainland has to be protected by massive dikes, while the Frisian Islands (*q.v.*) are being gradually washed away by the waters. There are now only seven of the East Frisian Islands, of which Norderney (*q.v.*) is the best known; of the North Frisian Islands, on the western coast of Schleswig, Sylt (*q.v.*) is the most considerable. Besides the ordinary waste of the shores, there have been extensive inundations by the sea within the historic period, the Gulf of the Dollart having been so created after 1276. Sands surround the whole coast of the North sea to such an extent that entrance to the ports is not practicable without the aid of pilots. Heligoland is a rocky island, but it also has been considerably reduced by the sea. The tidal range is 12 to 13 ft. in Jadebusen (Jade bay) and at Bremerhaven, and 6 to 7 ft. at Hamburg.

The coast of the Baltic, on the other hand, possesses few islands, the chief being Alsen and Fehmarn off the coast of Schleswig-Holstein, and Rügen off Pomerania (Polish Pomorze). It has no extensive sands, though on the whole it is very flat; it has no perceptible tides; and a great part of its coast line is covered with ice in winter which also blocks up the harbours so that navigation is interrupted for several months of every year. The eastern coast of Schleswig-Holstein is penetrated by long embayments (*Förden*). The coast line farther east is smooth, since the eastward drift of the currents has formed long sand spits (*Nehrungen*) with enclosed haffs or shallow lagoons behind them at the mouths of the rivers.

The rivers of the great lowland, the Ems, Weser, Elbe and Oder, are naturally navigable and need very few locks. Post-Pleistocene land sinking has brought the sea up the river mouths so that most of Germany's ports are river ports and have developed outports, as Bremerhaven below Bremen on the Weser, Cuxhaven below Hamburg on the Elbe, and Warnemünde below Rostock on the Warnow. The east-west sections of the rivers in different parts of the same low area between morainic hills have been linked together in many cases by canals, so that a system of river and canal communication crosses Germany from its eastern to its western border. This system converges upon Berlin and helps to account for the phenomenal growth of the city from its insignificant position in the middle of the 17th century. The Oder from Ratibor (Raciborz) in Poland and large sections of the Havel, Spree and Saale

GERMANY

are navigable. The Elbe itself can be navigated right up into Bohemia, and its tributary, the Moldau (Vltava), as far as Prague.

The Mid-German Highlands.—This is a west-east belt of high-land blocks crossed from south to north by rivers, either in gorges like that of the Rhine, or in lowland troughs, like those of the Weser and the Leine rivers. In the western half is the great rectangular block of the Rhine plateau. This is composed of pre-dominantly impervious rocks, slates, sandstones and quartzites, though there are more productive and closely settled areas on limestone rocks and loess deposits. The plateau is crossed by the gorge of the Rhine from Bingen to Bonn and by the similar valleys of several of its tributaries, notably the Moselle. Between this block and the Thüringer Wald is the complicated zone of uplands and lowlands that is drained by the Weser and the Leine and gives easy routeways from north to south. At the southern end of this trough are the great volcanic massifs of the Rhön (3,117 ft.) and the Vogelsberg (2,539 ft.). The trough is itself composed of hori-zontal strata of the Triassic series, forming areas of wooded sand-stone uplands, rolling plateaus of cultivated limestone and the

main valley troughs cutting right through. This trough connects Frankfurt am Main, Kassel, Hanover and other intermediate cities and has been a most important factor in their historical develop-ment. East of the Weser basin is the northwest-southeast Thü-ringer Wald, which together with the Harz mountains beyond have long been associated with the mining of metals.

The southeastern end of the Thüringer Wald and the northeast-ern end of the Franconian Jura and the highlands farther east (the Erzgebirge) approach one another in the Fichtelgebirge (3,448 ft.). Rivers radiate from this plateau. The Naab flows south between the Franconian Jura and the Bohemian plateau to the Danube, the Main flows west to the Rhine between the Thüringer Wald and the Jura, the Saale and its tributaries flow north between the Thüringer Wald and the Erzgebirge, while in Bohemia the Eger flows east on the south side of the Erzgebirge. Highlands trend northeast-ward to the Erzgebirge (4,082 ft.), which is the northern edge of the Bohemian block, as far as the sharp break by which the Elbe passes from Czechoslovakia to Germany. Beyond the Elbe the hills trend southeastward as the Riesengebirge (5,266 ft.) and

THE CHIEF PHYSICAL REGIONS OF GERMANY WITH THEIR MAJOR SUBDIVISIONS

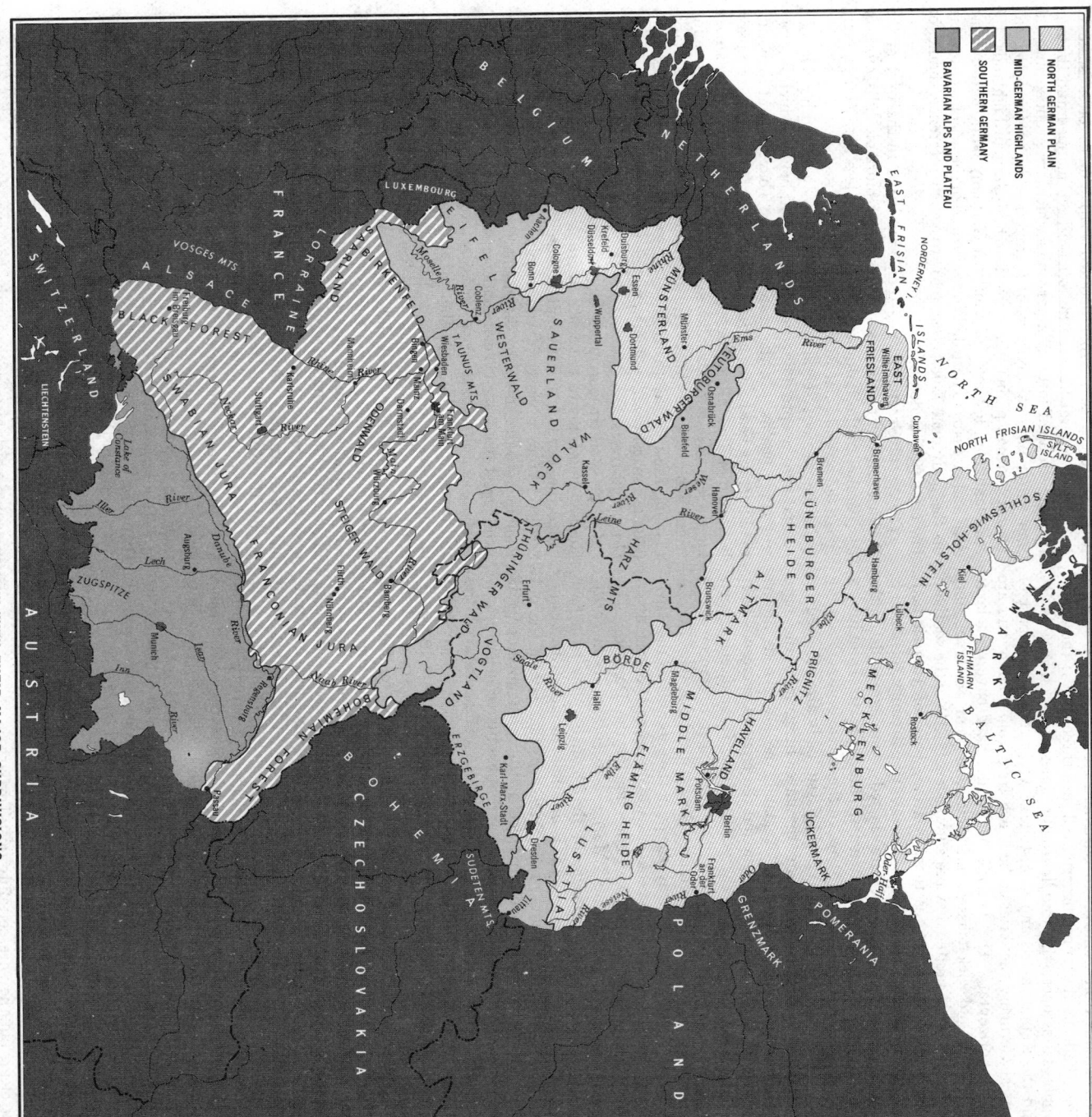

NORTH GERMAN PLAIN
MID-GERMAN HIGHLANDS
SOUTHERN GERMANY
BAVARIAN ALPS AND PLATEAU

the Sudeten, forming the northeast side of the Bohemian block.

Southern Germany.—This area stretches from the Vosges to the Bohemian forest (Böhmer Wald), and from the mid-German highlands in the north to the Alps in the south. The Main and Neckar are right-bank tributaries of the Rhine. Their basins are framed by the Swabian Jura (Schwäbische Alb) and Franconian Jura (Fränkische Alb) on the south and east, the Black Forest on the west and the mid-German highlands on the north. The Neckar and Main lands are made up of rolling limestone uplands, wooded sandstone hills and cultivated plains on marls and clays. There are extensive areas of fine loess. The climate in these lowlands is warm and dry and these lowlands are among the most fertile lands in Germany, growing mainly vines and grain. The Neckar escapes to the Rhine south of, and the Main north of, the Odenwald. In the valley of the Neckar basin Stuttgart is the chief city. In the valley of the Main, Nürnberg, Bamberg, Würzburg and Frankfurt are the chief centres.

The Swabian and Franconian Jura are built mainly of porous, limestone rocks dipping southward and eastward and the drainage is in many parts in deep-cut valleys. The Swabian Jura is higher and less broken than the Franconian, and from the rawness of its winters, a large part is known as the Rauhe Alb. The strata of the Swabian Jura dip gradually to the left bank of the Danube, and those of the Franconian Jura to the Rednitz valley, and this is the direction of the drainage. The scarp slopes face north or northwest and are steep and deeply dissected where they face the Neckar lowland, and present very beautiful scenery.

The Bavarian Alps and Plateau.—The plateau is framed on the south by the Lake of Constance and the Bavarian Alps, and on the north by the Swabian-Franconian Jura and the southwest border of the Bohemian massif. It is drained by the Danube, which rises in the Black Forest and flows near the northern side of this area, following the edge of the Jura down to Regensburg, beyond which it flows beneath and parallel to the granite edge of the Bohemian block and then onward past Passau. The main tributaries of the right bank are the Iller, Lech, Isar and Inn. On the left bank the Wörnitz, which joins the Danube at Donauwörth, flows from the Franconian Jura and through the fertile lowlands of the Ries. The Altmühl and its feeders also cross the Franconian Jura in a deep and wide valley. Linking the Danube and the Main and using the lower valley of the Altmühl, a canal was built after 1960 from Bamberg through Nürnberg to Kelheim. Much land on the south of the Danube is poor and wooded, but some areas toward the centre and east, where the subsoil is loess, are fertile and mainly under arable farming. Strips of meadow occur along the many river plains.

Only the northern fringe of the Alps, from the Lake of Constance to near Hallein, is in Germany and the Austrian frontier there lies along the northernmost of the east-west ridges of the Alps; the highest point in Germany, the Zugspitze (9,720 ft.), stands on the border of the Tirol. The Bavarian Alps are of great beauty, with some exquisite mountain lakes, and, farther down the northward valleys, long lakes have been formed behind morainic dams.

From Basel to Mainz the Rhine flows through a remarkable rift valley. On the east the upstanding edge is the sharp western slope of the Black Forest (the Feldberg is 4,898 ft. high) as far north as the latitude of Karlsruhe; recognizable again farther north is the Odenwald (about 1,700 ft.). West of the Rhine the upstanding edge is the Vosges (in France), becoming lower and smoother north of Saverne but rising again in the Hardt (highest point, Donnersberg, 2,254 ft.). The continuous block that once included the Vosges and the Black Forest was a Hercynian massif, and the rift (a fault trough) has formed a broad valley floor with parallel sides. A volcanic mass, the Kaiserstuhl, stands out in the middle of the plain. The banks of the rapid river have few towns in the south, but many from Speyer northward. From Mainz to Bingen the Rhine flows from east to west, from the rift valley to the gorge through the mid-German highlands. From Worms through Mainz to Bingen the land is relatively low and has loess subsoil, making it one of the best agricultural parts of the country; it is especially important for vine cultivation.

3. Climate.—The climate of Germany is intermediate between the oceanic and continental climates of western and eastern Europe respectively. The differences in the range of temperature and the amount of rainfall throughout Germany are accentuated by the elevated plateaus and mountains in the south, while the north is occupied by low-lying plains. In the northwest, no chain of hills intercepts the warmer and moister winds which flow from the Atlantic, and these accordingly influence at times even the eastern regions of Germany. The mean annual temperature of south-western Germany is about 12° C. (53° F.), that of central Germany 9° C. (49° F.) and that of the northern plain 8° C. (47° F.). The difference in the mean annual temperature between the southwest and northwest of Germany amounts to about 2° C. (3° F.). The valley of the Rhine above Mainz has the mildest winters and the warmest summers. The Baltic has the lowest spring temperature, and the autumn there is not much warmer. In central Germany the high plateaus of the Erzgebirge and Fichtelgebirge are the coolest areas.

In south Germany the Bavarian plateau experiences a harsh winter and a cool summer. The warmest district is the Rhine valley from Karlsruhe northward, less than 300 ft. above sea level and protected by high land. The same holds true of the valleys of the Neckar, Main and Moselle. Hence the vine is everywhere cultivated in these districts. The mean summer temperature there is 19° C. (66° F.) and upward, while the average temperature of January is above 0° C. (32° F.). The climate of northwestern Germany is oceanic, with cool summers (mean summer temperature 16° C. [61° F.]), and snow in winter remains but a short time on the ground. West of the Weser the average temperature of January exceeds 0° C. (it is about 2° C. at Cologne [Köln]. To the east it sinks to −2° C., and the Elbe is generally covered with ice during several months of the year, as are also its tributaries. The farther one proceeds to the east the greater are the contrasts of summer and winter.

Rain falls at all seasons, but chiefly in summer. The rainfall is greatest in the highlands of western Germany. In the Eifel, Sauerland, Harz, Thüringer Wald, Rhön, Vogelsberg, Spessart, the Black Forest, the Vosges, etc., the annual average rainfall is 34 in. or more, while in the intermediate altitudes of southwestern Germany and in the Erzgebirge it is about 25 to 30 in. The same average obtains on the humid northwest plain of Germany as far as Bremen and Hamburg. In the low-lying, sheltered parts of western Germany it amounts to less than 25 in. In the wine districts, *i.e.*, in the valley of the Rhine below Mannheim and also in the valley of the Main, no more than from 16 to 20 in. fall. Eastern Germany as far south as the Thüringer Wald has an annual rainfall of only 16 to 20 in. Thunderstorms are most frequent in July.

The soils of Germany are usually of low quality. Those of the north German lowland are predominantly sandy, though clays occur in the coasts and loams on the morainic upland. The loess soils of the Börde are the richest. In central and south Germany the soils of the highlands are thin on impervious bedrock. The loess of the lowlands and the limestone bedrock yield fertile loams, and loams are characteristic of wide areas of the Bavarian plateau.

(R. E. Di.)

4. Vegetation.—More than a quarter of the whole area of Germany is covered with forest. About 45% of this forest is pine, about 40% beech and about 8% oak. Though plantations are extensive, there is still a certain amount of natural forest.

Beech (*Fagus sylvatica*) forest is found on all well-drained soils in the temperate regions, from sea level up to 2,000 ft. in the Harz mountains and 4,500 ft. in the Bavarian Alps. Associated with beech are silver fir, spruce, pine and oak. Where there is enough light and good soil the ground flora consists of dog's mercury, sweet woodruff, violets, etc; higher up in wet places it includes balsam, willow herb and monkshood; on acid soils bilberry, foxgloves and wavy hair grass are found.

On poorer, lighter soils, especially in the northeast and the Palatinate, the forests are of Scots pine (*Pinus sylvestris*). They ascend to 4,000 ft. in the Black Forest mountains and 5,000 ft. in the Bavarian Alps. Most of these forests are planted, often also with Austrian pine (*Pinus nigra*), and there are many plantations on inland sand dunes, for example, along the Rhine valley floor between Karlsruhe and Mainz. The plantations have a poor ground flora, but the native forests often contain juniper, bilberry and heather, mosses and lichens. Many are mixed with oak, beech and hornbeam.

Extensive plantations of spruce (*Picea abies*), or spruce mixture, make up 20% of the productive forest of Germany. More tolerant of extreme cold than beech, it grows as a native tree on the upper slopes of the central and southern mountain areas where it is found up to the highest limit of trees. This limit is higher in the south than it is in the north. There are vast areas of spruce in the Black Forest and the Bayerischer Wald. The oak woods on the light, sandy, acid soils of the northwest are generally mixed with birch. In the adjacent heath lands grow broom, juniper, heather, bilberry, bracken, etc. The oak forests in the west are mixed with hornbeam with a well-developed shrub layer and ground flora. The northern and eastern oak woods are mixed with pine. The two oaks found most in Germany are common oak (*Quercus robur*), which occurs everywhere, and Durmast oak (*Q. petraea*), which occurs more in the east. Alder (*Alnus glutinosa*) dominates the peaty fen woods and is the characteristic tree of river valleys, often with willow and poplar where it is very wet, or oak, ash, elm and hornbeam where it is drier. Willows, poplars, elms, sweet chestnuts, walnut, maples and ash are locally common.

The silver fir (*Abies alba*) is indigenous in the central and southern mountains, being especially abundant on the western slopes of the Black Forest. In the Thuringian forests it grows at elevations up to 2,600 ft. and in the Bavarian Alps it reaches 5,000 ft. Above the silver fir is the European larch (*Larix decidua*), which grows up to 6,500 ft., mixed with spruce and Arolla or Swiss stone pine (*Pinus cembra*). Above the timber line the mountain pine (*Pinus mugo*) occurs as a prostrate shrub and beyond this rhododendrons (*Rhododendron ferrugineum* and *R. hirsutum*) and alpine plants.

Heath land is characteristic of the northwest with heather (*Calluna vulgaris*), whins, grasses, mosses and lichens where it is dry, and cross-leaved heath (*Erica tetralix*), club mosses, sundews and cotton grass in the wetter parts. Much land from the saltings and estuarine marshes of the North sea coast has been reclaimed and is now grassland. Reclamation of fens and marshes in areas where the soil contains lime has turned these into rich pasture. In places where the soil is acid, especially in the wide coastal belt, are many bogs containing *Sphagnum*, cotton grass, sundews, etc. The peat of those bogs is often exploited as fuel or for horticultural purposes. In the north German plain and in southern Bavaria sandy heaths, moors and bogs are being reclaimed.

(H.-H. HE.)

5. Animal Life.—Germany's central position in Europe means that while the fauna is broadly the same as that of continental Europe as a whole, invasion by species from all directions is a particular feature. The birds illustrate this well. The birds of Germany are similar to those in Britain but with notable additions. The lesser gray shrike and the woodchat shrike are there although they belong more to southern and western Europe. Germany also shares a number of birds with northern and eastern Europe, such as the thrush nightingale and the bluethroat, the nutcracker and the fieldfare. It is, however, noticeable that so many species of birds seen in Germany are more familiar in the extreme east of Europe or the Balkans. These include the pygmy owl and Ural owl, Tengmalm's owl, the gray-headed and the black woodpecker, the river warbler and the icterine warbler.

Much the same pattern may be seen in the mammals, especially in the smaller rodents. As compared with Britain, Germany has three kinds of dormouse, the common, fat-tailed and garden dormice, but no water vole. Three notable eastern species of mammals found in Germany are the parti-coloured bat, the suslik and the common hamster. Beaver still live in the valley of the Elbe. Roe and red deer are well represented, the latter reaching finer proportions than in Britain because their true habitat is the woodlands and forests, where they get a richer food. Introduced fallow deer are also numerous. The pine forest shelters wildcats, pine martens and, in the wilder parts, wolves, and on the lower ground to the north the wild boar is not uncommon. Germany is one of several European countries in which the introduced muskrat has established itself.

The country offers a wide variety of habitat, with the plains to the northeast, where the great bustard survives, and the pine forests to the south sheltering the capercaillie.

There are a number of nature parks and reserves; the first national park, the Bavarian Forest National Park, adjoining Czechoslovakia's Bohemian Forest, opened in 1970.

(MA. BU.)

II. THE PEOPLE

German is the name that has prevailed since the 8th century for the principal Germanic stocks. Thereafter the language came into prominence as a unifying characteristic of the peoples in the realm of Charlemagne. In the 9th century this common consciousness grew stronger, tending toward a separate existence in contrast to the Slavic peoples of the east Frankish realm. Since the 10th century, following the division of the Frankish realm (843), the term Diutisk-German has comprised the stocks of the Franks, Saxons, Bavarians, Alamanni (Swabians), Thuringians and Frisians. It is historically significant that the name and the concept of the Germans, alone in Europe, derives not from an older tribal or territorial name but from the mother tongue and has continued to exert emphasis on linguistics and civilization.

1. Early Settlement Patterns.—The history of the German people was decisively determined by the great migrations during the 6th to 4th centuries B.C. and by the great migration of peoples in the Christian era. Both those epochs were also linguistically characterized through two great sound-shifting processes. The first and more embracing process affected almost all Germanic languages, while the second, following the 6th and 7th centuries A.D., influenced only the middle and upper German dialects. This linguistic loosening of the stocks, did not, however, affect political and cultural development. From the manifold migrations and widespread colonizations of numerous stocks the German nation arose, through the political achievements of the Frankish kings (above all, Charlemagne), of the Saxon emperors and the Hohenstaufens.

In the Carolingian period the Germans, in order to find room for the growing population, began to make new settlements by clearing and cultivating land hitherto virgin and unoccupied. This internal colonization was driven forward energetically into the mountains and woods by the Frisians and Saxons of lower Germany, by the Franks of middle Germany and by the Swabians and Bavarians of upper Germany. At the same time colonization of districts outside the Frankish realm by partly peaceable and partly warlike acquisition began. As the Germanic-Roman ethnic frontier could only be pushed forward to the east, settlement was renewed in regions that, once German, had been abandoned in the migration period and thereafter thinly settled by Slavs. This German settlement took place in various waves, beginning in the 8th and continuing until the 13th century. Hand in hand with the colonization went an admixture of the several peoples, which proceeded with increasing pace. The distribution of stocks found today was created at that time. The Frisians were masters of the North sea coast and of the off-lying islands, the Saxons between the Elbe and lower Rhine, and later also in eastern Germany, where they almost completely drove out the Slavs. The Franks remained in middle Germany to settle in a wide zone from the Fichtelgebirge along the Main and Rhine to the sea, and also in northern Baden and Württemberg. They were the chief element in the southeastward expansion. In the 5th century the High German group—initially the Alamanni and then the Bavarians—pushed forward against the Roman lands. The Alamanni spread over Alsace and the Alps. The Bavarians in the 6th century pushed forward from Bohemia to the Danube and spread out over the south bank as far as the Alps, and crossed the Inn into Austria. These stocks continue to live within the borders they occupied in the Frankish period but neither now forms a political entity. The modern German *Länder* (states) have no longer any connection with individual stocks. They are arbitrary structures, dynastically formed since the 13th century, sometimes comprising fragments of several stocks (as for

GERMANY

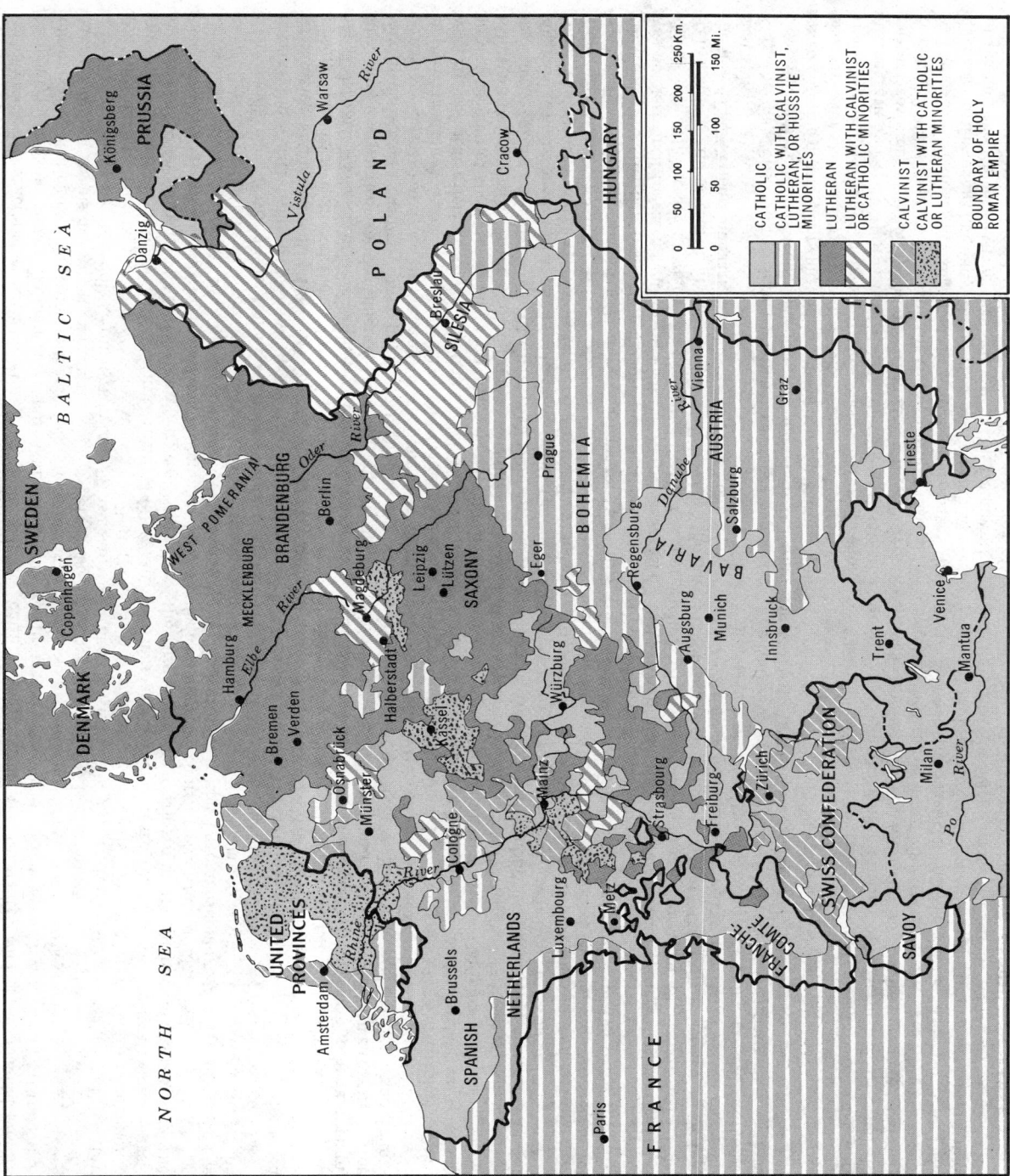

Legend:

- CATHOLIC
- CATHOLIC WITH CALVINIST, LUTHERAN, OR HUSSITE MINORITIES
- LUTHERAN
- LUTHERAN WITH CALVINIST OR CATHOLIC MINORITIES
- CALVINIST
- CALVINIST WITH CATHOLIC OR LUTHERAN MINORITIES
- — BOUNDARY OF HOLY ROMAN EMPIRE

RANGE OF CONFESSIONS IN GERMANY (1650) AS A RESULT OF THE THIRTY YEARS' WAR

---

instance Bavaria with part of the Swabians, Franks and Rhenish stock, as Franks) and sometimes only with a fraction of a single stock, as in Thuringia. Easternward settlements were brought to a sudden end by the great mortality, through plague, in Germany after about 1350.

The Germans adopted many methods of settlement. At first the only towns were those founded by the Romans; German settlements were weak and widely scattered. By progressive division of the labour and concentration of the populations they agglomerated in continually larger settlements and became an increasingly urban community. The layout of the settlements shows Celtic, Romance and Slavonic influences. The oldest and most important form is the *Haufendorf* (clustered village), found among northern and southern German stocks. Likewise in the oldest tradition are the detached or individual farms of the Saxon and Frisian regions and of all mountain districts. The villages arranged with the houses in a row are a colonization type, which had already begun to prevail in Frankish and Swabian districts under Charlemagne. In the border districts between Germans and Slavs are villages of circular or radial form, arranged round a market place in a defensive pattern rather like a wagon stockade.

The oldest German form of dwelling is certainly that of the Lower Saxon house and that of the Swabian-Bavarian *Einhaus*, or unit house, accommodating people and livestock under the same roof. Between these *Einhaus* regions is a wide zone of the middle and upper German farmsteads, specially notable for their rooms with stoves. The space for husbandry is specifically divided from the living quarters, an advance probably attributable to Romance influence and necessitated by the increased requirements for space posed by a more intensive mode of agriculture—barns, stables and the like. There arose the Frankish layout of farm premises, with a three- or four-sided farmyard. More than two-thirds of the German settled area have this sort of farmyard. Within these groups exists a great variety of types and mixtures of dwellings.

The domestic arrangements and household furniture also differ. In the north there is a close relationship with Scandinavian practice: built-in furniture, heating apparatus, shape of hearth, fire irons, type of container and the predominance of woodwork. All indicate an earlier common German origin. The very different disposition of the household furniture in the upper German house is distinct and migrated with the Franks.

2. Racial Characteristics.—The Germans are not racially pure. They have in the course of their history mixed plentifully with other peoples; in southern and western Germany, in Switzerland and in Tirol with the residues of the Celts and Romance Celts who settled there in pre-Christian times; in the east beyond the Elbe and Saale, as well as in the upper Main region and in Austria, with Slavs. The least mixed were the Germans in Lower Saxony.

The physical characteristics have therefore been molded from the many Germanic stocks. Blond hair, fair skin and light-coloured eyes distinguish the true Germanic folk from the Romance peoples. As history would indicate the highest percentage of the blond type is met in middle Germany (up to 54% as against 31.8% throughout Germany and 19.79% in Austria) and of the brunet type in west and south Germany (in Germany 14.05%, in Austria 23.17%, in Switzerland 25.7%). As a people of the centre the Germans have continuously been laid open to influence by the surrounding populations. As a peasant people, they have preserved the core of the race with tenacious inertia. As the founder in the middle ages of world-wide trading ventures (the Hanse, the Fuggers, the Welsers) they have shown themselves to be adaptable, far-thinking and masterful. The shift of industry in the 19th century considerably altered the national character.

3. Customs.—The stocks were, at the time of the Frankish mastery, complete political entities differing from one another markedly in dialect and custom. They possessed their own law (*see* GERMANIC LAWS, EARLY). In the army of the king they fought in separate groups under their own dukes and frequently led a separate political existence too. The branch duchies were split only at the end of the 12th century (Saxony, Bavaria) and in the 13th century (Swabia). After 939 the Franks came directly under the king. Through the creation of the new High German literary language, whose spread was assured by Luther's translation of the Bible, the cleavage in dialect was substantially bridged, although differences exist even now.

In the mid-20th century German national costumes were fast disappearing. Garments from ancient graves show how the troussered costume of the Germanic and eastern peoples in Europe won the day over the southern type of cloak garment. Modern costumes are of no great age, deriving at the earliest from the fashions of the 18th and early 19th centuries. Notable survivals are the peasant costumes of the Schwalm district in Hesse, the Bückeburg region, the Black Forest valleys and the German Alpine district.

The course of life is accompanied by customs and usages that go back to Germanic antiquity. The customs in Swabia, Westphalia and the Rhineland have survived well. The framework of the marriage customs is old Germanic, with the character of a family festival that is at the same time a parochial celebration (the *Polterabend*, the conveyance by wagon of the bride's goods, the barring of the way, the discharge of firearms, the outriders, the musicians, the bridal procession, the bridal dance, the "stealing" of the bride, the wedding banquet, etc.). The birth of a child is surrounded by numerous customs signifying life (the birth tree, the *Glückshaube*, the preservation of the umbilical cord, the burial of the afterbirth, etc.). For the dead a wake is held, mourning is worn, a funeral feast is given, the bier is set up, etc.

The joy of the pagan festivals of nature (summer solstice, the celebration of Walpurgis on the eve of May day) at the peak period of work on the land became in the course of time associated with the major feasts of the church. In the dark months mummers appear: Klaus, Krampus, Knecht Ruprecht (Santa Claus), bell ringers and masked figures. Shrove Tuesday is celebrated with dancing and tumbling. Christmas is the great family feast. In the pagan era the winter solstice was celebrated: the Yule feast or feast of newly rising light. Christianity transformed it into the feast of Christmas: the feast of the heavenly light, of the birth of Christ. The character that it bore as a pagan feast, falling at the period for slaughtering, was retained in the Christmas fare and feasting, the Christmas confectionery in special forms (loaf-shaped cakes, marzipan, springerle, biscuits of almonds and butter, gingerbread). A double amount of fodder is given to the cattle, Cribs, midnight Masses, singing beneath the stars and the burning of incense are connected with the belief in the visit of the supernatural beings during the 12 nights (wild chase, magical powers of protection, the oracle of New Year's Eve). The Christmas tree took the place of the former customary pyramid of candles about the beginning of the 19th century.

The egg customs at Easter, the blessing of palms and the May tree are symbolic of growth. Harvest customs are uncommonly rich and include the harvest wreath, harvest festival, vintage feast, the driving of the cattle from the mountain pastures and the dedication of the church or the church fair. (H. PL.)

4. Religion.—In the Federal Republic freedom of religion is guaranteed under the Basic law (constitution). According to the 1961 census 51.1% of the population was Protestant and 41.1% Roman Catholic. The Protestants, who are in the majority in northern Germany and West Berlin, are members of the Evangelische Kirche in Deutschland (Evangelical Church in Germany or E.K.D.), an association of Evangelical-Lutheran, other Lutheran, Reformed and unified churches. Its legislative organ is the Synod with headquarters at Hanover (ecclesiastical) and Frankfurt am Main (external affairs). (*See also* LUTHERANISM.) Catholics are dominant in the west and south, particularly in Bavaria. The Federal Republic has five ecclesiastical provinces, and the official representation of German Catholics is at the Bishops' Conference at Fulda.

In the Democratic Republic it is estimated that 82% of the population is Protestant and 12% Roman Catholic. Both churches strive to be a unifying force in a divided country, and the number and organization of Catholic dioceses have remained substantially unchanged regardless of the political events that followed World War II.

The charitable work of the churches is carried on by the Catholic Caritas association and the Protestant Innere Mission. During the immediate postwar years the valuable social work performed by these organizations was widespread.

For languages *see* GERMAN LANGUAGE; GERMANIC LANGUAGES. For culture *see* GERMAN LITERATURE and the appropriate sections in GOTHIC ART AND ARCHITECTURE; etc.
(X.)

III. HISTORY

A. ANCIENT HISTORY

Classical writers from the time of Thales (*c.* 600 B.C.) were acquainted with the amber of the north German coasts, and the traveler Pytheas (*c.* 300 B.C.) certainly visited Germany and may have reached the Vistula. But there seem to have been few contacts between the classical and the Germanic world before the Cimbri and Teutoni, who probably came from the Danish peninsula, invaded the Mediterranean regions and Italy itself (113–101 B.C.). The distinction between Germans and Celts was not clearly recognized until the Gallic campaigns (58–51 B.C.) of Julius Caesar brought more exact knowledge. (*See* GERMANIC PEOPLES for an account of the prehistoric Germans.)

Caesar's conquest of Gaul halted the German pressure on the Celts, which had virtually driven them from the eastern bank of the Rhine and had led to Ariovistus' settlements on the upper Rhine, perhaps in 71 B.C., and to extensive infiltration (attested by archaeology and by Caesar himself) on the middle and lower Rhine by the Treveri, Nervii and others. An invasion of Usipetes and Tencteri, repressed in 55 B.C., led Caesar to undertake two punitive expeditions across the Rhine in 55 and 53 B.C., neither intended to penetrate far. The province of Gaul as created by him in 51 B.C. extended to the Rhine, which he regarded as an ethnic frontier.

Augustus (31 B.C.–A.D. 14) seems at first to have held Caesar's view of the Rhine frontier, but in 12 B.C. his stepson Nero Claudius Drusus undertook what was evidently understood as a combined campaign of Gaul and Roman against the traditional enemies of both. It is not clear, however, how far Augustus intended annexation to go. Drusus himself died soon after reaching the Elbe (9 B.C.), but his work was resumed by his brother, the future emperor Tiberius, from 8 to 7 B.C. Meanwhile the growth of a German empire under Marobodus in the territory of the Boii was engaging Roman attention: between 7 B.C. and A.D. 4 a series of expeditions penetrated into Germany across the Danube; and in

GERMANY

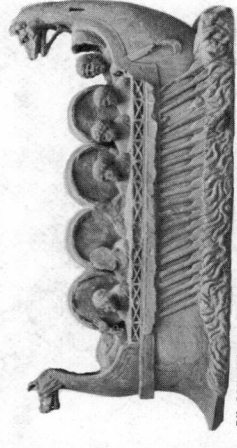

BY COURTESY OF (ABOVE) THE LANDESMUSEUM TRIER; PHOTOGRAPH, (LEFT) FOTO MARBURG

(ABOVE) RHENISH WINE SHIP, A ROMAN SCULPTURE OF ABOUT A.D. 250 FOUND AT NEUMAGEN. (LEFT) PORTA NIGRA, THE FORTIFIED NORTH GATE OF THE ROMAN TOWN OF TRIER, POSSIBLY 4TH CENTURY A.D.

A.D. 5 Tiberius subdued the Cimbri in the Danish peninsula. A grand campaign in A.D. 6 was forestalled, however, by a revolt in Pannonia, and in A.D. 9 there was a revolt in the west under Arminius: the governor P. Quinctilius Varus perished with three legions in the battle of the Teutoburger Wald. Augustus, who now appreciated the insuperable difficulties of conquering a wild country with a backward political organization, bequeathed to his successors the doctrine that the Rhine and the Danube were the frontiers of the empire. Only along the North sea coast (Frisii) and in the region of the upper Weser river and Taunus mountains, where the Chatti, the most civilized German tribe, commanded the trade route, did Rome have interests beyond the Rhine; and the campaigns of Germanicus (A.D. 14–16), described by Tacitus, are to be regarded as determined by this fact and by the need of re-establishing prestige. All garrisons across the Rhine were withdrawn under Claudius (emperor 41–54), and the Romans confined themselves to diplomatic intrigue, a method that had proved successful against Arminius (slain by his own kin in 19).

A new approach to the German problem was seen under the Flavian dynasty (Vespasian, Titus and Domitian, 69–96). Roman control of the territory of the Frisians was reasserted, and the Chatti were subdued in two campaigns of Domitian (83 and 88). To shorten the line of the Rhine-Danube re-entrant, the defenses enclosing the area conquered from the Chatti up to the crest of the Taunus were extended southward and eastward to join the Danube near Regensburg, and the frontier works (limes) were improved and extended by Hadrian (emperor 117–138) and Antoninus Pius (138–161), bringing Roman dominion and even the outward signs of Roman civilization up to the central German or Hercynian forest. An accompaniment of the policy was the creation by Domitian of the two provinces of Lower and Upper Germany, the former (carved out from Gallia Belgica) consisting of the more or less germanized tribes along the western stretches of the lower and middle Rhine, the latter comprising in the main the new conquests. Meanwhile a changed attitude to the nature of German dangers was seen in the disposition of the legionary garrisons. Whereas under Tiberius (emperor 14–37) there had been eight legions on the Rhine and five on or near the Danube, a century later the proportion was four to nine.

Western and Eastern Germans.—Tacitus' study of the Germans, published in A.D. 98, divides them into three groups, the Ingaevones of the northwest, the Herminones of the interior and the Istaevones of the Rhine. These names are not fitted by Tacitus into his description of individual tribes and clearly derive from an earlier period during which Germans had hardly penetrated across the Elbe; they prepare for the distinction, only slightly blurred by tribal migrations, between western and eastern Germans, a distinction of great importance in their subsequent relations with Rome. (For details of the distribution of tribes in Tacitus' time see GERMANIC PEOPLES.)

Most of the individual tribal units eventually disappeared, to be replaced by greater political units, the Saxons, the Franks and the Alamanni. These confederacies were becoming a menace to Rome in the 3rd century: in 276, Franks and Alamanni overran the whole of Gaul; and c. 260 the limes was finally abandoned. Attacks on Britain by the Saxons then began in earnest and the *Litus Saxonicum* may even commemorate their settlements as well as the defense against them. Diocletian (emperor 284–305) and his successors Constantine (emperor 306–337), Julian (who was in Gaul from 355 to 360) and Valentinian (emperor 364–375) encouraged campaigns and fortification, and a frontier along the Rhine was maintained, though Julian had to agree to a treaty allowing the Franks to settle in much of modern Flanders. The Marcomanni and the Quadi gave trouble to Rome under

Domitian (88–89) and Nerva (97). In 167 they took advantage of a plague and a Persian war to burst the frontier and penetrate into Italy itself. They were pacified by Marcus Aurelius only after a series of exhausting campaigns lasting until his death (180). Commodus (emperor 180–192) entered into treaty with them and fortified the Danube yet more intensively.

These tribes continued to be dangerous neighbours to the empire, but their place as its principal assailants was taken in this sector by the Goths, who reached the Black sea in the second half of the 2nd century A.D. and attacked the Danube frontier in 238. A succession of emperors (one of whom, Decius, met his death at their hands in 251) failed to check their forays, which extended over Greece and Asia Minor until Claudius II, surnamed Gothicus, defeated them in 269. His successor Aurelian (emperor 270–275), however, abandoned Dacia to them, and about this time the distinction between Visigoths and Ostrogoths begins to appear, the former in Dacia, the latter still in southern Russia. Warfare and fortification along the Danube frontier are attested notably in the reigns of Constantine and his sons and of Valentinian I.

The *Völkerwanderung* or Great Migrations.—Germans had for two centuries been infiltrating into the empire as soldiers and as captives settled in groups for agriculture; but their permanent entry in mass was part of the great migration precipitated in Europe by the westward movement of the Huns. About 370 the Ostrogothic kingdom was destroyed and soon after both branches of the Gothic nation requested asylum within the empire. Dissension with their hosts soon broke out, and the Romans were decisively defeated at Adrianople (modern Edirne) in 378, after which the Goths were never expelled. Under their king Alaric (c. 365–410) and his successors, the Visigoths wandered over the empire seeking lands and political privileges and sacking Rome on the way (410). By the end of the 5th century their kingdom embraced southwestern Gaul (with its capital at Toulouse) and also most of Spain. In the early 5th century the principal general of the western Roman empire, Stilicho, himself of Vandal origin, was compelled to remove the garrisons of the Rhine for the defense of Italy, and the Rhine frontier was crossed at the end of 406 by a mixed host of Germans who penetrated first into Spain and then into Africa, where their leader, Gaiseric, founded a kingdom at Carthage in 439.

The first half of the 5th century is marked by complicated military and diplomatic maneuvering between the rulers and generals of the eastern and western empires, the German tribes and the Huns, whose empire under Attila (434–453) embraced virtually all Germany. It was probably not least in order to escape this rule that the Saxons and kindred tribes from the seaboard in the next generation invaded Britain, which had been denuded of its Roman troops in 410. But Attila himself was defeated by Romans and Visigoths on the Catalaunian Plains (451), and the whole Hunnish empire broke up after the defeat of the Nedao river (455). During this period the situation of German tribes in the west begins to crystallize. Franks, Alamanni and Burgundians appear in Gaul, their areas of extensive settlement (as opposed to conquest) being still on the whole discernible from the linguistic frontier between German and French. In the eastern empire, the Goths

BY COURTESY OF (LEFT) WÜRTTEMBERGISCHES LANDESMUSEUM, STUTTGART, (RIGHT) LANDESMUSEUM FÜR VORGESCHICHTE, HALLE

(LEFT) GOLD-LEAF CROSS, PROBABLY FROM ULM, WITH PORTRAIT OF A RULER, 7TH CENTURY. (RIGHT) GRAVESTONE FROM HORNHAUSEN WITH RELIEF OF A GERMAN WARRIOR ON HORSEBACK, 7TH–8TH CENTURIES A.D.

GERMANY

revolted under Gainas in Asia Minor (399) and attempted to act as emperor-makers in Constantinople. But the eastern emperors succeeded in eliminating them; the most important incident was the emperor Zeno's transference in 488 from the Balkans to Italy of the Ostrogothic bands under Theodoric, who was to gain the mastery (489–493) over the mixed body of mercenary Germans that had already ejected the last western Roman emperor in 476. This process left a vacuum in the Danube basin, subsequently filled by Slavs and Ugrians, so that only enclaves—remnants for instance of the Gepidae—survived there of the eastern Germans.

The ancient period of German history may be said to close with the gradual extension of Frankish rule under Clovis (king 481–511) and his sons. Of the great confederacies only the Saxons and Alamanni remained in Germany, to be absorbed eventually in the new Germanic empire of Charlemagne. In Italy, Theodoric's successors failed to hold their ground against the generals of Justinian (emperor 518–565), under whom Africa too was regained for the eastern empire. A last phase of the *Völkerwanderung* was the entry of the Langobardi (Lombards) into Italy in 568. The ethnic pattern observable in the Germany of the middle ages was then completed.

These tribal movements did not usually involve large numbers (the total of Vandals invading Africa is given as 80,000) and the Germans came more as conquerors than as settlers. They accepted the late Roman social structure of landlord and serf, the varying relationships being regulated by individual codes of law. There is virtually no archaeology of the migrations, the vestiges even of such settling migrants as the Rhineland Franks following late Roman typological developments. The long contacts with Rome had had their effects, not least in the conversion of principal tribes to Christianity, which followed rapidly on the mission of Ufilas to the Goths (c. 341–c. 347). The majority of German tribes (the Franks, being the notable exception) accepted Arianism.

(C. E. S.)

B. MEROVINGIANS AND CAROLINGIANS

When the original western empire came to an end, the German tribal lands lying east of the Rhine had no unity, geographical or political. Divided from each other by forest or water, the German tribes were further subdivided by the varying degrees of romanization that they had experienced. Archaeology suggests that their social habits followed the same general pattern, and philology confirms that, despite dialectal differences, they spoke the same language. Nevertheless, "Germania" meant nothing to them, and their drawing together to form a medieval state was not an inevitable process but the outcome of a series of unpredictable accidents.

Merovingian Germany.—The Franks (*q.v.*), settled for the most part in romanized Gaul, were nevertheless drawn toward the Rhineland and thus into the feuds and rapidly shifting alliances of the Germans on the eastern bank. Of these interventions we have intermittent literary evidence from the 6th century onward. They may be said to start with the wars of Clovis, during which the Merovingian dynasty of the Salian Franks established its authority over the Ripuarian or Rhineland Franks in part of what was later to be called Austrasia. With much less success, Clovis and his successors attempted to dominate the Thuringians of central Germany and the Alamanni and Bavarians of southern Germany. The latter in particular could often look for help from the masters of Italy; and thus the Catholic Franks found that their raiding and counter-raiding across the Rhine helped to embroil them with the Arian Goths. However, it would be folly to elevate these clashes to the rank of wars of religion; no serious attempt seems to have been made to convert the Germans; rather, the intention was to exact tribute from them (in the case of the Saxons this usually took the form of cattle), to use them as mercenaries and to trade with them when possible. Certainly the spirit of tribal or national independence was unaffected, and the threat to the Rhineland remained. Meanwhile, the eastern borders of Germania became the prey of the land-seeking Slav peoples; and occasionally, as in the reign of Dagobert I, the Germans were glad enough of Merovingian help against their supplanters in the east. In the course of the 8th century, Frankish occasions of intervention tended to increase, and chieftains were deposed or, as occasion offered, imposed on recalcitrant tribes. But this relationship was too spasmodic to justify thinking that the Germans were subjected to any effective Frankish high kingship.

The Rise of the Carolingians and Boniface.—The Carolingian dynasty, which with papal backing supplanted the Merovingians at the end of 751, was Austrasian and drew its strength from extensive estates in the lands between the Meuse and the Rhine (*see* CAROLINGIANS). It had grown up in the atmosphere of Rhenish prosperity and likewise of Rhenish insecurity and was directly interested, in a way in which the Merovingians had never been, in the fate of the Rhineland and the behaviour of the German peoples beyond. It also saw clearly that effective control over them would necessitate their conversion to Christianity, and hence from the earliest days of their power the Carolingian mayors of the palace supported missionary work, both Irish and Roman. The pattern of Frankish penetration was always the same: small communities or churches were settled upon land newly won from forest or marsh; granted them by their Carolingian protectors. Thus, from Frisia in the north to Bavaria in the south, religious and economic penetration went hand in hand. A distinguished part was played by Anglo-Saxon missionaries, who linked the Frankish world not only with the high culture of the churches (notably York) from which they set out but also with Rome, the ultimate source of their inspiration. Chief among them were Willibrord (658–739), who worked among the Frisians and later the Thuringians, and St. Boniface (c. 673–754), the real founder of the German church. Supported by Charles Martel against the growing influence of aristocratic Frankish clergy, who perhaps feared the growing influence of Rome, Boniface led missions into Franconia, Thuringia and Bavaria, where he founded or restored a primitive diocesan organization. In 742 he played a large part at the first council of the new German church. However, all this work was a mere beginning; the surface of paganism had scarcely been scratched, and the north, where the Saxon tribes lived, was untouched and hostile. But when Boniface finally left his beloved monastery of Fulda to seek martyrdom, with a few companions, among the northern Frisians, he had made a vital and doubtless unintentional contribution to the political unification of the German peoples.

All except the Saxons had now begun to pass under the yoke of Rome.

Charlemagne.—What Boniface began Charlemagne (*q.v.*; *see* also HOLY ROMAN EMPIRE) took one stage further. Contemporary writers were vastly impressed by the great warrior's almost ceaseless German campaigning. Both the East Frisians and the Saxons (whom archaeologists find difficulty in distinguishing) now came within the orbit of his missionary enterprise, and both resented it. In the wake of the missionaries, Frankish counts and other officials moved into northeastern Frisia, raising contingents for the royal host and doing the other business of secular government. One unforeseen effect of this subjugation of Frisia was the crippling of the only independent sea power that could protect the Frankish and English coasts from the marauding Norsemen. As for the Rhineland, the richer it grew the more necessary it became to protect its hinterland, Franconia (Hesse) and Thuringia, from Saxon raids. But this was a hard task, since east of the Rhine there was no natural barrier to hold. Thus, each of Charlemagne's punitive expeditions bit deeper than its predecessor into the heart of Germany, leaving behind it bitter memories of forced conversion, deportations and massacre. It should not, however, be thought that Charlemagne's treatment of the Saxons sprang only from political considerations. He was as sincerely resolved to fulfill with fire and sword his missionary duty as a Christian ruler as were the Saxons to resist conversion and to uphold the bloodthirsty pagan rites of their ancestors. Whenever Charlemagne's attention was distracted to some other part of his dominions, the Saxons could be counted on to revolt, to slaughter the Frankish officials and priests in their midst and to raid as far westward as they could manage. Charlemagne, in his turn, would punish the

offending tribes and garrison the defense points abandoned by the Saxons. (These defense points, *werfs*, or *burgs*, must have been centres for trade as well as defense, for coin hoards have often been found in their vicinity.) The most famous leader of Saxon resistance was Widukind. Widukind, for longer than any other Saxon, succeeded in keeping together a majority of the chieftains in armed resistance to the Franks. His difficulty was not that they tolerated the Franks but that their own feuds were too deep and complex to permit of serious political coherence. Resistance gave the Saxons a certain sense of racial unity that never deserted them; but they were not yet politically united among themselves, let alone with other Germans. They continued to live, much as in the days of Tacitus, upon their estates among the forest clearings—*edhelingi* (nobles), *frilingi* (freeman) *lazzi* (half-free) and unfree—a hierarchized society bound to the soil and little interested in common means of action. Widukind finally surrendered and was baptized; the Rhineland and the East Frankish church were saved, but at the cost of most savage repression in Saxony, which is reflected in the *Capitulatio de partibus Saxoniae.* The extreme north, looking to the Baltic and enjoying Danish support, was impossible to control; but finally, in 797, Charlemagne negotiated a form of peace with the remaining Saxons, the terms of which were embodied in the *Capitulare Saxonicum,* a statesmanlike measure. The battle for the north continued, but Saxony as a whole was slowly becoming integrated with the other national areas of Germany under Frankish control and had become part of the great march protecting the Frankish world from Danes, Slavs and Avars.

BY COURTESY OF THE STAATLICHE MUSEEN, BERLIN

CHARLEMAGNE, PORTRAIT ON A COIN (PFENNIG), AFTER 804

In the Bavarians Charlemagne found a people as independent as the Saxons but more civilized. They had commercial and dynastic contacts with Lombardy that made them (and to some extent the Alamanni of Swabia also) a southward-looking people. Italian preoccupations were, as much as anything, responsible for Charlemagne's decision to end the spasmodic control exercised by the Franks over the powerful Bavarian ducal dynasty of the Agilolfings and to establish a direct supervision. This was achieved. Bavaria was not frankified, but Carolingian rule replaced Agilolfing, and Frankish churchmen and officials (such as the counts and *missi dominici*) moved as freely about Bavaria, seeing to the enforcement of the royal will, as they did in Saxony. But, as northern Frisia became the Frankish march against the Danes and Saxony that against the Slavs, so did Bavaria, together with Lombardy, become the march against the Avars. Only Christianity did as much to draw the regions of Germany together as did the powerful administrative measures taken by the Franks to weld them into a protective march against the central European threat. But it was Francia, not Germany, that was protected.

The Kingdom of Louis the German.—Charlemagne's successor as emperor, Louis I the Pious, was not unpopular with his German subjects; on two occasions he owed his restoration to power largely to their support. In 825 one of his sons, Louis (*q.v.*) the German, was entrusted with the government of Bavaria, whence he was gradually to extend his power over all Carolingian Germany. This was the first time that the German nations had had a ruler whose authority was confined to their own lands, and whose time was largely taken up with defending them from Slav penetration; but this was by no means the sum of ambition for Louis the German, who tended, like all his house, to regard the whole of Francia as a partible family inheritance of which each member, in each generation, should take for himself and his followers what he could get. Louis was thus satisfied neither with the partition treaty of Verdun (843) by which he obtained the bulk of the lands east of the Rhine together with the districts round Mainz, Worms and Speyer on the left bank, nor with that of

BY COURTESY OF THE STAATLICHE BIBLIOTHEK, BAMBERG

ST. BONIFACE, FOUNDER OF THE GERMAN CHURCH, DEPICTED BAPTIZING CONVERTS IN A 10TH–11TH CENTURY MANUSCRIPT FROM FULDA ABBEY; THE SCENE OF HIS MURDER IS SHOWN BELOW

Mersen (870), by which he and his half brother the West Frankish king Charles the Bald came to terms over Lotharingia, the middle kingdom of their nephew Lothair (see LORRAINE). Under the latter treaty Louis's dominions reached almost the proportions of medieval Germany. On the east they were bounded by the Elbe and the Bohemian mountains; on the west, beyond the Rhine, they included the districts afterward known as Alsace and Lorraine. Ecclesiastically they included the provinces of Mainz, Trier, Cologne, Salzburg and Bremen. But Charlemagne's capital at Aachen and the rich family estates in Lotharingia were never finally abandoned by either branch of the Carolingian dynasty, although the bulk of the lands that they controlled increasingly assumed the separate outlooks of France and of Germany. An example of this increasing separation is provided by the oaths sworn at Strasbourg in 842 by Louis and Charles, the former swearing in his brother's language, Romance, the latter, conversely, in German; but this drifting apart is in some ways less significant than the things that still held France and Germany together.

The ceaseless external blows from Danes, Saracens and Magyars that fell upon the Carolingian world in the 9th century did not have the effect of uniting it in resistance. Not only the Carolingians themselves but their followers also were prepared to take advantage of each other, to compromise with the enemy and to carve out even more dominions from each other's lands. The motives that led them to behave thus, however, were not so simple as they may now at first look. So, in 887, Arnulf (q.v.), an illegitimate son of Louis the German's son Carloman, led an army of Bavarians against Charles the Fat, in part because Charles was not defending the Rhineland from the ravages of the Danes, in part because his aim was the full Carolingian inheritance. But Arnulf was not equally successful in defending his eastern possessions. After his death in 899 the German kingdom came under the nominal rule of his young son, Louis the Child, and in the absence of strong military leadership became the prey of the Magyar horsemen and other invaders from the east.

Rise of the Duchies.—The rise of the German duchies was a direct outcome of the Carolingian decision, avoidable or not, to leave defense in the hands of those who were attacked; in other words, to decentralize military command and with it, inevitably, something else of the royal authority. The new *duces* were not, as was once thought, appointed by the peoples concerned, nor were they the descendants of the tribal chieftains of the postmigration period. It seems more likely that they were Carolingian counts who took the initiative in organizing defense on a local basis, without thereby seeking to shake men's loyalty to the house of Charlemagne, of which the German church was a natural champion. All the same, their initial success established them in the hearts of those whom they protected. This was particularly the case with the Saxons, whose dukes, the Liudolfings, were descended from the military commanders first sent by Louis the German to defend eastern Saxony. Similarly, the Swabian dukes began with a military title (*duces Raetianorum*); so did the Bavarian ducal family of Liutpold. The origins of the short-lived duchy of Thuringia are less easy to determine. Franconia naturally remained the German duchy most intimately associated with the East Frankish kingship. How, in practice, the lives of the German landowning or land-renting freemen were affected by these changes is a matter largely of guesswork. Perhaps it is true that political insecurity and its economic consequences tightened the lord-man relationship, as in France and elsewhere (see FEUDALISM). However, nothing is more striking than the variety, between region and region, of German social organization. Perhaps much more of the tribal ways of local government survived the Carolingians and the Magyars than was once thought possible.

C. THE 10TH AND 11TH CENTURIES

Conrad I (911-918).—When in 911 Louis the Child, last of the East Frankish Carolingians, died without leaving a male heir, it seemed quite possible that his kingdom would break into pieces. In at least three of the four stem lands, Bavaria, Saxony and Franconia, the ducal families were established in the leadership of their tribes. In Swabia (Alamannia), it is true, two houses were still fighting for hegemony; but only the church, fearing for its endowments, had an obvious interest in the future of the monarchy, its ancient protector. Against the growing authority of the dukes and the deep differences in dialect, in customs and in social structure between the tribes there stood only the Carolingian tradition of kingship; but, with Charles the Simple as holder of the West Frankish kingdom, its future was uncertain and not very hopeful. Only the Lotharingians put their faith in the ancient line and did homage to Charles, its sole reigning representative. The other component parts of the East Frankish kingdom did not follow suit.

We can only guess at the motives of the Saxon and Frankish tribal hosts who on Nov. 10, 911, elected Conrad, duke of the Franks, as their king at Forchheim in Franconia (see CONRAD I, German king). At the opening of the 10th century the Germanic peoples settled in the lands east of the Rhine and west of the Elbe, the Saale and the Bohemian forest, rude and thinly spread though their settlements were, had to face even more savage and pagan races pressing in from farther east, especially the Magyars. The Saxons, headed by their duke Otto, of the house of the Liudolfings, were threatened by more enemies on their frontiers than any other tribe; Danes, Slavs and Magyars simultaneously harassed their homeland. A king who commanded resources farther west in Franconia might therefore prove to be of help. The Rhenish Franks on the other hand, having hitherto given their royal house, the Carolingians, to the other tribes, did not wish to abdicate from their position as the leading and kingmaking people, which gave them many material advantages.

Conrad, elected by Franks and Saxons, was soon recognized also by Arnulf, duke of Bavaria, and by the Swabian clans. In descent, honours and wealth, however, he was no more than the equal of the dukes who had accepted him as king. To gain a lead over them, to found a new royal house and to acquire those wonderworking attributes which the Germans venerated in their rulers long after they had been converted to Christianity, he had yet to prove himself able, lucky and successful. The reason why the relations between the German kings and a few score families of magnates seemed eventually to make up the sum of political events was that, at the very foundation of the German kingdom, circumstances had long favoured those men whom birth, wealth and military success raised well above the ranks of the ordinary free members of their tribe. Their estates were cultivated in the main by half-free peasants, slaves who had risen or freemen who had sunk. The holdings of these dependents fell under the power of the lord to whom they owed service and obedience. Already they were tied to the lands on which they laboured and already they received justice for many offenses at the hands of their protectors. For many reasons ordinary freemen tended generally to lose their independence and had to commend themselves to more fortunate and powerful neighbours and thus lost their standing in the assemblies of their tribe. Everywhere except in Friesland and parts of Saxony the nobles wedged themselves between king or duke and the rank and file. They alone could become prelates of the church, and they alone could command the possession and enjoyment of governmental rights. Besides the dukes of the stem lands who owed nothing in their position to the crown the bulk of administrative authority, jurisdiction and command in war lay with the margraves and counts whose hold on their charges developed gradually into hereditary right. The commended men and the half-free disappeared from the important functions of public life. In the assemblies of the county they could no longer be doomsmen but came only to pay dues and to receive orders, justice and penalties. Their political role was passive. Those lords whose protection was most worth having also had the largest throng of dependents and thus became more formidable to their enemies and to the remaining freemen. Lordship and submission to it were hereditary, and thus the horizon of the dependent classes narrowed until eventually the lord and his officials filled the place of all secular authority and power in their lives. Military strength, the possession of arms and horses, and tactical training in their use were decisive. Most dependent men were disarmed; that being part of their degradation.

(J. M. W-H.)

The Accession of the Saxons.—Conrad I was quite unequal to the situation in Germany. According to the beliefs of contemporaries his failure meant that his house was luckless and without the prosperity-bringing virtues which belonged to true kingship. On his deathbed in 918 he therefore proposed that the crown, which in 911 had remained with the Franks, should now pass to the leading man in Saxony, the Liudolfing Henry (later called the Fowler). Henry I (see HENRY I, German king) was elected by the Saxons and Franks at Fritzlar, their ancient meeting place, in 919. With a monarch of their own race the Saxons now took over the burden and the rewards of being the kingmaking people. The centre of gravity shifted to the east, where the Liudolfing lands and their power lay.

The transition of the crown from the Franks to the Saxons for a time enhanced the self-sufficiency of the south German tribes. The Swabians had kept away from the Fritzlar election. The Bavarians believed that they had a better right to the Carolingian inheritance than the Saxons (who had been remote outsiders in the 9th century) and in 919 elected their own duke Arnulf king. They too wanted to be the royal and kingmaking people. Henry I's regime rested in the main on his own position and family demesne in Saxony and on certain ancient royal seats in Franconia. His kingship was purely military. He hoped to gather authority by waging successful frontier wars and to gain recognition in the first place by concessions rather than to insist on the sacred and priestlike status of the royal office which the church had built up in the 9th century. At his election he refused to be anointed and consecrated by the archbishop of Mainz. In settling with the Bavarians he abandoned the policy of supporting the internal opposition that the clergy offered to Duke Arnulf, a plank to which Conrad had clung. To end Arnulf's rival kingship he formally surrendered to him the most characteristic privilege and honour of the crown: the right to dispose of the region's bishoprics and abbeys. Arnulf's homage and friendship entailed no positive obligations toward Henry, and the Bavarian duke pursued his own tribal interests—peace with the Hungarians and expansion across the Alps—as long as he lived.

From these unpromising beginnings the Saxon dynasty not only found its way back to Carolingian traditions of government but soon got far better terms in its relations with the autonomous powers of the duchies, which had gained such a start on it. However, the constitution that it bequeathed to its Salian successors was self-contradictory; while seeking to overcome the princely aristocracies of the stem lands by leaving them to themselves, the Saxon kings came to rely more and more, both for the inspiration and for the practice of government, on the prelates of the church, who were themselves recruited from the ranks of the same great families. They loaded bishoprics and abbeys with endowments and privileges and thus gradually turned the bishops and abbots into princes with interests not unlike those of their lay kinsmen. These weaknesses, however, lay concealed behind the personal ascendancy of an exceptionally tough and commanding set of rulers up to the middle of the 11th century. Thereafter the ambiguous system could not take the strain of the changes fermenting within German society and even less the attack on its values that came from without—from the reformed papacy.

The Liudolfing kings won military success, and with it they gained that respect for their personal authority which counted for so much at a time when the great followed only those whose star they trusted and who could reward services with the spoils of victory. In 925 Henry I brought Lotharingia back to the East Frankish connection (see LORRAINE). Whoever had authority in this half French-speaking, half German-speaking region could treat the neighbouring kingdom of the West Franks as a dependent. The young Saxon dynasty thus won for itself and its successors a hegemony over the west and the southwest which lasted at least up to the middle of the 11th century. The Carolingian kings of France and the great feudatories who sought to dominate if not to ruin them became in turn petitioners and even vassals of the German court during the reign of the Ottos. The kings of Burgundy, whose suzerainty lay over the valleys of the Saône and the Rhône, the western Alps and Provence, likewise fell under the

tutelage of the masters of Lotharingia. Rich in ancient towns, this region, once the homeland of the Carolingians, was more thickly populated and wealthier than the stem lands east of the Rhine. What little international trade came their way entered the Rhine valley through Lotharingia.

The Eastern Policy of the Saxons.—Greater prestige still and a claim to imperial hegemony fell to the Saxon rulers when they broke the impetus of the Hungarian invasions against which the military resources and methods of western European society had almost wholly failed for several decades. In 933, after long preparations, Henry routed a Hungarian attack on Saxony and Thuringia. In 955 Otto I (q.v.; king 936–973), at the head of a force to which all the tribes had sent mounted contingents, annihilated a great Hungarian army on the Lech river near Augsburg. The battle again vindicated the efficiency of the heavily armed man skilled in fighting on horseback.

With a Saxon dynasty on the throne, Saxon nobles gained office and power with opportunities for conquest along the eastern river frontiers and marches of their homeland. Otto I indeed had an eastern policy which aimed at getting more than slaves, loot and tribute. Between 955 and 972 he founded and richly endowed an archbishopric at Magdeburg which he intended to be the metropolis of a large missionary province beyond the Elbe, among the heathen Slavs. This would have brought their tribes under German control and exploitation in the long run; but the ruthless methods of the Saxon lay lords clashed with the church's efforts at peaceful penetration. In the 10th century there was little or no German agricultural settlement beyond the Elbe. Far too much forest clearing remained to be done in all the regions of western and southern Germany. The Saxon conquests up to the Oder were secured by military strongholds, called burgwards, and lasted only as long as their garrisons had the upper hand. Behind the Slav peoples of Brandenburg and Lusatia, moreover, new powers rose: the Poles under Mieszko and, to the south, the Czechs under the Premyslids received missionaries from Passau and Magdeburg without falling permanently under the political and ecclesiastical domination of Bavarians and Saxons. The heathen Elbe-Slavs, kept under by the Saxon margraves, rose in 983 when the military occupation collapsed and with it the missionary bishoprics which had been founded at Oldenburg, Brandenburg and Havelberg. Farther south the defenses of the Thuringian marches between the Saale and the middle Elbe remained in German hands, but only after a long and fierce struggle against Polish invaders early in the 11th century. The northern part of the frontier reverted to what it had been before Otto's trustees, Hermann Billung and Gero, opened their wars. Missionary enterprises directed from Bremen and Magdeburg achieved little before the 12th century. The Saxon ruling class, bishops and margraves, must bear the responsibility for the fiasco of eastward expansion in the 10th century. The prelates, too, saw their missions as means to found ecclesiastical empires with subject dioceses and tithes on Slav soil. The tribes across the Elbe therefore remained unconverted and implacable foes, a standing menace to the nearby churches. The wars also left a legacy of savagery on both sides so that from c. 1140 onward the substitution of German settlers for the native Slavs became the common policy of both the church and the princes.

Dukes, Counts and Advocates.—Conrad I's and Henry I's kingships rested on the will of the tribes or rather on that of their leaders and of the higher aristocracy. It was in the first place an arrangement between the Franks and the Saxons which the Bavarian and Swabian dukes recognized at a price by acts of personal homage. But the German kings, of whatever dynasty, had to live under Frankish law. After the death of Conrad I's brother Eberhard in 939 Otto I kept the Franconian dukedom vacant and the Franconian counts henceforth stood under the immediate authority of the crown. In Saxony too Otto kept in his hands the dukedom of his ancestors. The march-duchy of the Billungs, a bulwark raised against the Danes and the northern Slav tribes, did not give that family authority over the other Saxon princes. In the south the Ottonians sought to turn the dukedoms of the stem lands into offices held of the crown as fiefs and to supplant native dynasties by aliens and members of their own clan. When even that did

GERMANY

ROMA, GALLIA, GERMANIA, AND SCLAVINIA RENDERING HOMAGE TO THE EMPEROR: ILLUSTRATION FROM A GOSPEL OF OTTO III

not stop rebellions under the banner of tribal self-interest, they began to break up the ancient Bavarian stem land by creating a duchy in Carinthia to cut off the spearhead of Bavarian expansion southward. The first two Salians, Conrad II (king 1024–39) and Henry III (sole king 1039–56), also bestowed vacant duchies quite freely on their own kin and on men from outside the stem boundaries. They competed against ducal power but could neither abolish nor replace it. In the 11th century as before, the dukes held assemblies of their folk, led the tribal host in war and enforced peace.

The counts, who were the ordinary officers of justice in serious, criminal cases, obeyed the ducal summons, but for the most part they received their "ban," the power to do blood justice, from the king himself. The fiefs and the customary rights attached to their office, and indeed the office itself, not only became hereditary but also came to be treated more and more as a patrimony to which they had an inherent right against all men, king and duke included. Even so, however, a good many comital families died out and their counties fell back into the king's hands. From Otto III's reign (983–1002) onward it became not at all unusual to bestow these on bishoprics and certain great abbeys rather than to grant them out again to other lay magnates. The bishops, however, could not perform all the functions of the counts; in particular their holy orders forbade them to pass judgments of blood. They needed officials called advocates (Vögte; sing. Vogt) to take charge of the higher jurisdiction in the counties and franchises that their churches possessed by royal grant. In the 10th and 11th centuries these advocates had to be recruited from the aristocracy, the very class whose greed for hereditary office was to be checked, because ordinary freemen could not enforce severe sentences or defend the privileges of the church against armed intrusion. Dangerous neighbours of bishoprics and abbeys in any case, the nobles as advocates and protectors of ecclesiastical possessions were anything but reliable servants of their ecclesiastical overlords.

Thus there arose in nearly all German lands, whether the ducal office survived or not, powerful lines of margraves, counts and hereditary advocates who enriched themselves at the expense of the church (which meant also the crown) and in competition with one another. From the abler, more fortunate and long-lived races among these dynasts sprang the territorial princes of the later 12th and 13th centuries, absorbing and finally inheriting most of the rights of the original government.

The king was the personal overlord of all the great. His court was the seat of government and it went with him on his ceaseless journeys. The German kings, even more than other medieval rulers, could only make their authority respected in the far-flung regions of their kingdom by traveling ceaselessly from duchy to duchy, from frontier to frontier. Wherever they stayed their jurisdiction superseded the standing powers of dukes, counts and advocates and for a brief while they could collect the profits of local justice and wield some control over it. As they came into each region they summoned its leaders to attend their solemn crown wearings, deliberated with them on the affairs of the Reich and the locality; presided over pleas, granted privileges and made war against peacebreakers at home and on enemies abroad.

The Promotion of the German Church.—The royal revenues came from the king's demesne lands and from his share of the tributes that Poles, Czechs, heathen Slavs and Danes had to pay whenever he could enforce his claims of overlordship. The king's demesne was his working capital. He and his household lived on its produce during their wanderings through the Reich, and it also served to provide for his family, to found churches and to reward faithful services done to him, especially in war. To swell the hosts, vassals had to be enfeoffed, and alienations were inevitable. The Salians, though they inherited the remains of Ottonian wealth as imperial demesne, brought little of their own to make up for its diminution. Already the last Saxon, Henry II (1002–24), and after him Conrad II therefore took to enfeoffing vassals with lands commandeered from the monasteries. But the beneficiaries often enough were already powerful and wealthy men in their own right, so that no class of freeborn mounted warriors, linked permanently with the crown, sprang from the loyalties and rewards of one or two reigns. In any case the lion's share of grants went to the German church.

From the Carolingians the German kings inherited their one and only institution of central government: the royal chapel, with the chancery that does not seem to have been distinct from it. Service there became a recognized avenue of promotion to the episcopate for highborn clerks. In the 11th century bishops and abbots conducted the affairs of the Reich much more than the lay lords, even in war. They were its habitual diplomats and ambassadors. Unlike Henry I, Otto I and his successors sought to free the prelates from all forms of subjection to the dukes. The king appointed them, and to him alone, as to one sent by God, they owed obedience. Thus there arose besides the loose association of stems in the German kingdom a more compact and uniform body with a far greater vested interest in the Reich: the German church. By ancient Germanic custom, moreover, the founder of a church did not lose his estate in the endowment that he had made; he remained its proprietor and protecting lord. The bishoprics, it is true, and certain ancient abbeys such as St. Gallen, Reichenau, Fulda and Hersfeld did not belong to the king; they were members of the kingdom but under his guardianship. The greater churches therefore had to serve the rulers with mounted men, money and free quarters. Gifts of royal demesne to found or to enrich bishoprics and convents were not really alienations but pious reinvestments, as long as the crown controlled the appointments of bishops and abbots. But the church did not merely receive grants of land, often waste, to settle, develop and make profitable: it was also given, as has been shown, powers of jurisdiction over counties and to some extent even duchies. Nor did the kings stint the prelates in other regalian rights, such as mints, markets and tolls. These grants broke up counties and to some extent even duchies, and that was their purpose: to disrupt the secular lord's jurisdictions which escaped royal control.

This policy of fastening the church, a universal institution, into the Reich with its well-defined frontiers is usually associated with the name of Otto I. But it gathered momentum only in the reigns of his successors. It reached a climax under Henry II, the founder of the see of Bamberg in the upper Main valley; but Conrad II, though less generous with his grants, and his son Henry III continued it. Bishops and abbots became the competitors of lay princes in the formation of territories, a rivalry which more than any other was the fuel and substance of the ceaseless feuds, the smoldering internal wars in all the regions of Germany for centuries. The welter and the confused mosaic of the political map of Germany until 1803 is the not so remote outcome of these 10th- and 11th-century grants and of the incompatible ambitions that they aroused.

The Ottonian Conquest of Italy and the Imperial Crown.—Otto I's marriage with Adelaide (Adelheid), daughter of Rudolph II of Burgundy, and the Italian rivalries between his brother Henry, duke of Bavaria, and his (Otto's) son Liudolf, duke of Swabia, drew him southward. After 951, expeditions into Italy were a matter for the whole *Reich* under the leadership of its ruler and no longer just an outlet for the expansion of the south German tribes. For the Saxon military class too the south was more tempting than the primeval forests and swamps beyond the Elbe. With superior forces at their back the German kings gained possession of the Lombard kingdom in Italy. There too their overlordship in the 10th and the 11th centuries came to rest on the bishoprics and abbeys and a handful of great abbeys.

After his victory over the Magyars in 955, Otto I's hegemony in the west was indisputable. By the standards of one chronicler, the Saxon Widukind, he had already become emperor because he had subjected other peoples and enjoyed authority in more than one kingdom. But the right to confer the imperial crown, to raise a king to the higher rank of emperor, had fallen to the papacy, which had crowned Charlemagne and most of his successors. The Carolingian order in the west was still the model and something like a political ideal for all its ruling families in the 10th century. Otto had measured himself against the political tasks which had faced his East Frankish predecessors and more or less mastered them. To be like Charlemagne, therefore, and to clothe his newly won position in a traditional and time-honoured dignity he accepted the imperial crown and anointment from Pope John XII in Rome in 962. The substance of his empire was military power and success in war; but Christian and Roman ideas were woven round the Saxon's throne by the writers of his own and the next generation. Although the German kings as emperors did not give the law to the Roman Church in matters of doctrine and ritual, they became its political masters for nearly a century. The imperial crown enhanced their standing even among the nobles and knights who followed them to Italy and can hardly have understood or wanted all its outlandish associations. Not only the king but also the German bishops and lay lords thus entered into a permanent connection with an empire won on the way to Rome and bestowed by the papacy. (See HOLY ROMAN EMPIRE.)

HENRY II RECEIVING A BOOK FROM A MONK: MINIATURE FROM AN 11TH-CENTURY MANUSCRIPT OF THE HOMILY ON EZEKIEL BY GREGORY THE GREAT, WHO IS SHOWN ABOVE

BY COURTESY OF THE STAATSBIBLIOTHEK, BAMBERG

Otto II (sole king 973–983) and above all Otto III (983–1002) were strongly drawn toward their new Mediterranean sphere of action but Henry II returned to a sober regime centred on Germany and contented himself with three brief Italian expeditions.

The Salians, the Papacy and the Princes, 1024–1125.—Under Conrad II (1024–39), the first member of the Rhine-Frankish house known as the Salians, the kingdom of Burgundy fell finally under the overlordship of the German crown and this tough and formidable emperor also renewed German authority in Italy. His son and successor Henry III (1039–56) treated the empire as a mission which imposed on him the tasks of reforming the papacy and of preaching peace to his lay vassals. Without possessing

any very significant new resources of power he gave to his authority an exalted and strained theocratic complexion. Yet under him, the last German ruler to maintain his hegemony in western Europe, the popes themselves seemed to become mere imperial bishops. He deposed three of them, and four Germans held the Holy See at his command; but lay opposition to the emperor in Germany and criticism of his regime over the church were on the increase during the last years of his reign.

The Papal Reforms and the German Church.—More than any other feudal society in early medieval Europe, Germany was divided and torn by the revolutionary ideas and measures of the reformed papacy. From the pontificate of Leo IX onward—he was one of Henry III's nominees—the most determined and inspired spokesmen of ecclesiastical reform placed themselves at the service of the Holy See. Only a few years after Henry III's death (1056) they agitated against lay authority in the church, founded on proprietary rights. They regarded the laity as passive partakers of the sacraments and denied the supernatural status of kingship. Priests, including bishops and abbots, who accepted their dignities from lay lords and emperors at a price committed a sin, nor could earthly powers could not rightly confer churches at all, nor could they own them. They believed moreover that thorough reforms could only be brought about by the exaltation of the papacy so that it commanded the obedience of all provincial metropolitans and was out of the emperor's and the local aristocracy's reach. The endless repetition of these teachings in brilliant pamphlets and at clerical synods spread agitation in Italy, Burgundy and Lotharingia, all parts of the empire. Their new program committed the leaders of the movement to a struggle for power, because it struck at the very roots of the regime to which the German church had grown accustomed and on which the German kings relied. The vast wealth that Henry IV's predecessors had showered on the bishoprics and abbeys would, if the new teaching prevailed, escape his control and remain at the free disposal of prelates whom he no longer appointed. Under Roman authority the churches were to be freed from most of the burdens of royal protection without losing any of its benefits. The most fiery spirits in Rome did not flinch from the consequences of their convictions. Their leader Hildebrand, later Pope Gregory VII (1073–85), was ready to risk a collision with the empire.

Henry IV was not yet six years old when his father died in 1056. The full impact of the Gregorian demands, coming shortly after a royal minority, a Saxon rising and a conspiracy of the south German princes, has often been regarded as the most disastrous moment in Germany's history during the middle ages. In fact the German church proved thoroughly unreliable as an inner bastion of the empire even before Rome struck. Its leaders, Anno and Adalbert (*qq.v.*), archbishops of Cologne and of Hamburg-Bremen respectively, shamelessly exploited their hold over the young king by hunting for spoils out of the imperial demesne. When Gregory VII launched his decrees against simony and clerical marriage, humiliated the aristocratic episcopate by summonses to Rome and sentences of suspension and, in 1075, forbade rulers to invest bishops and abbots with their churches, the German hierarchy was demoralized and shaken. The prelates' return to their customary support of the crown was neither disinterested, wholehearted nor unanimous.

The Discontent of the Lay Princes.—Henry IV's minority also gave elbowroom to the ambitions and hatreds of the lay magnates. His mother Agnes of Poitou's feeble regency faltered before the throng of princes who respected only authority and forces greater than their own. The ruling influence of the higher clergy at the court of Henry III and the renewed flow of grants to the church had estranged them from the empire. It is likely also that these eternally belligerent men were lagging behind the prelates in the development of their agrarian resources. The prelates had a vested interest in peace and under royal protection improved and enlarged their estates by turning forests into arable land and also by offering better terms to freemen in search of a lord. The bishops' market and toll privileges brought them revenues in money, which many of the lay princes lacked. So far, however, the princes' military power, their chief asset, had remained unchallenged. Now for the first time they had also to face rivals within their own sphere of action. Henry III and the young Henry IV began to rely on advisers and fighting men drawn from a lower tier of the social order, the poorer freeborn nobility of Swabia and above all the class of unfree knights, known as *ministeriales*. The latter had first become important as administrators and soldiers on the estates of the church early in the 11th century. Their status and that of their fiefs was fixed by seigniorial ordinances, and they could be relied on and ordered about, unlike the free vassals of bishops and abbots. The Salian kings, beginning with Conrad II, used *ministeriales* to administer their demesne, as household officers at court and as garrisons for their castles. They formed a small army which the crown could mobilize without having to appeal to the lay princes whose ill will and antipathy toward the government of the *Reich* grew apace with their exclusion from it.

Having come of age, Henry IV used petty south German nobles and his *ministeriales* to recover some of the crown lands and rights which the lay princes and certain prelates had acquired during his minority, particularly in Saxony. There, however, his recuperations went further and a great belt of lands from the northern slopes of the Harz mountains to the Thuringian forest was secured and fortified under the supervision of his knights to form a compact royal territory, where the king and his court could reside almost continuously. The south German magnates were thus kept at a distance when Henry and his advisers struck at the neighbouring Saxon princes, especially Otto of Nordheim and the Billung family.

The storm broke in 1073. A group of Saxon nobles and prelates and the free peasantry of Eastphalia who had to bear the brunt of statute labour in the building of the royal strongholds revolted against the regime of Henry's Frankish and Swabian officials. To overcome this starting combination and to save his fortresses, the king needed the military strength of the south German princes, Rudolf of Rheinfelden, and Berchtold of Zähringen, duke of Carinthia. Suspicious and hostile at heart, they took the field for him only when the Eastphalian peasantry committed outrages which shocked aristocratic caste feeling everywhere. Their forces enabled Henry to defeat the Saxon tribal rebellion near Langensalza in June 1075. But when the life-and-death struggle with Rome opened only half a year later, the south German malcontents deserted Henry and, together with the Saxons and a handful of bishops, entered into an alliance with Gregory VII. Few of them at this time were converted to papal reform doctrines, but Gregory's daring measures against the king gave them a chance to come to terms with one another and to justify a general revolt.

The Civil War Against Henry IV.—On Feb. 22, 1076, the pope had absolved all men from their oaths to Henry and solemnly excommunicated him. In October his legates met the German lords at Tribur (modern Trebur) to decide on the future of the king, whom his last adherents now abandoned. Although Henry was absolved by Gregory at Canossa in Jan. 1077, the princes two months later nonetheless elected Rudolf of Rheinfelden to rule in his place.

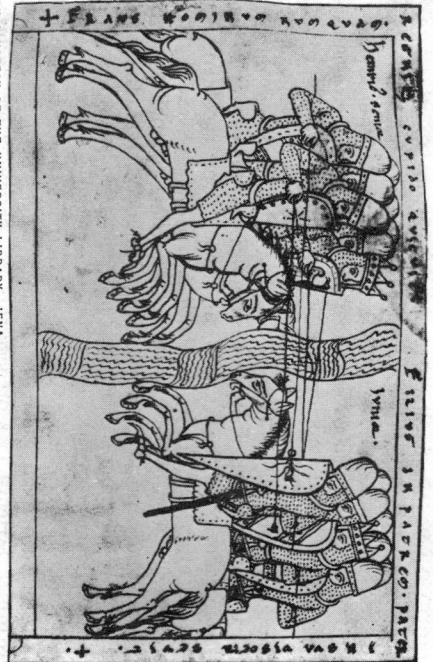

BY COURTESY OF THE UNIVERSITY LIBRARY, JENA

HENRY IV IN BATTLE WITH HIS SON HENRY; DRAWING FROM A MANUSCRIPT OF THE "CHRONICA" OF OTTO OF FREISING, c. 1170

The war which now broke out lasted for almost 20 years. A majority of the bishops, most of Rhenish Franconia (the Salian homeland) and some important Bavarian and Swabian vassals sided with Henry. He thus held a central position dividing his south German from his Saxon enemies, who could not unite long enough to destroy him. With the death in battle of Rudolf of Rheinfelden (1080) and the demise in 1088 of another antiking, Hermann of Salm, the war in Germany degenerated into a number of local conflicts for the possession of bishoprics and abbeys. It almost died down in 1098, when the south German adherents of the papacy came to terms with Henry for the time being, but without recognizing his antipope Clement III. Throughout these years the crown, the churches and the lay lords had to enfeoff more and more *ministeriales* in order to raise mounted warriors for their forces. Though this and frequent devastations strained the fortunes of many nobles, they knew how to recoup themselves by extorting more fiefs out of neighbouring bishoprics and abbeys. The divided German church thus bore the brunt of the costs of civil war and needed peace almost at any price. Henry, since 1080 once again a vulnerable excommunicate, could not protect it.

Henry V and the Results of the Conflict.—The Salian dynasty and the rights it fought for were saved because Henry IV's son and heir himself seized the leadership of a last and pitiless rising against his father (1105). This cold-blooded maneuver enabled Henry V (1106–25) to continue the struggle for the crown's prerogative over the empire's churches against the inexorable demands of the papacy. The conflict now shrank into a legalistic dispute over the right to invest bishops and abbots with their dignities and the secular possessions attached to them (see INVESTITURE CONTROVERSY). In the course of it the princes became the arbiters and held the balance between their overlord and the pope. In 1122, acting as intermediaries and on behalf of the *Reich*, they forced the temporary concessions known as the Concordat of Worms out of the Holy See and its German spokesman, Archbishop Adalbert of Mainz (1109–37), the bitter personal enemy of Henry V and the territorial rival of the Hohenstaufen sons of Henry's sister Agnes. But by then they had for the most part defeated efforts to restore royal rights in Saxony and to stem the swollen jurisdictions and territorial powers of the aristocracy elsewhere. When Henry V, the last Salian, died childless in 1125, Germany was no longer the most effective political force in Europe. The brilliant conquest states of the Normans in England and in Sicily and the patient, step-by-step labours of the French monarchy were achieving forms of government and concentrations of military and economic strength which the older and larger empire lacked. The papacy had dimmed the empire's prestige, and Rome now became the true home of universalistic interests. When Pope Urban II preached the first crusade in 1095, Henry IV, cut off and surrounded by enemies, lived obscurely in a corner of northern Italy. The Holy See by its great appeal to the militant lay nobility of western Europe thus won the initiative over the empire. At this critical moment the *Reich* also lost control in the Italian bishoprics and towns just when their population, trade and industrial production were expanding fast. Germany did not even benefit indirectly from the crusaders' triumphs although some of their leaders (e.g., Godfrey of Bouillon and Robert II of Flanders) were vassals of the emperor. The civil wars renewed for a time the relative isolation of the southern and central German regions.

Internally the crown had saved something of the indispensable means of government in the control over the church, but it was a bare minimum and its future was problematic. The ecclesiastical princes henceforth held only their temporalities as imperial fiefs, for which they owed personal and material services. As feudatories of the empire they came to represent the same interests toward it as did the lay princes; at least their sense of a special obligation tended to weaken. The king's jurisdiction continued to exist side by side and in competition with that of the local powers. The great tribal duchies survived as areas of separate customary law. Each developed differently, and the crown could

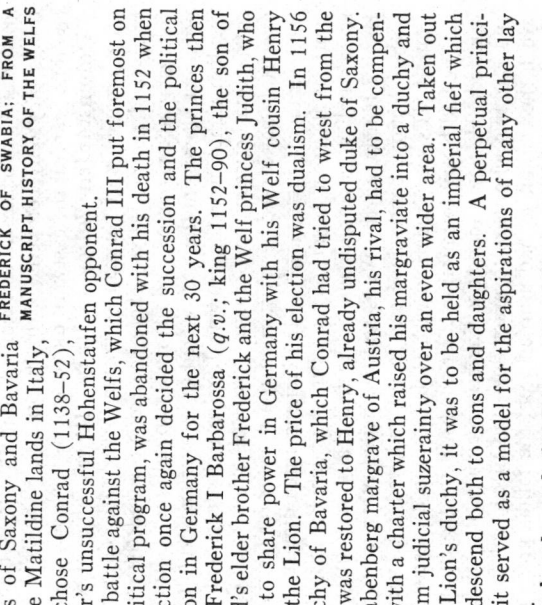

BY COURTESY OF THE HESSISCHE LANDES-
BIBLIOTHEK, FULDA

EMPEROR FREDERICK I WITH HIS
TWO SONS, KING HENRY VI AND
FREDERICK OF SWABIA: FROM A
MANUSCRIPT HISTORY OF THE WELFS

not impose its rights on all alike or change the existing social order. The most tenacious defenders of this legal autonomy had been the Saxons; but in Swabia, where distinct territorial lordships grew fast, it prevailed also. The Gregorian reform movement therefore aggravated the age-old contradictions in Germany's early medieval constitution. But its monastic culture and its intellectual interests were anything but barren. Both sides fought with new literary weapons to work on public opinion in cathedrals and cloisters and perhaps also in the castles of the lay aristocracy. In their hard-hitting polemical writings they attempted to expound the fundamental theological, historical and legal truths of their cause. The agitation did something to disturb the cultural self-sufficiency of the German laity. It drove many of the south German nobles to maintain direct connections with the Holy See and, whether they wanted it or not, they had to fall in with the aspirations of the religious leaders. The reform movement of the 11th and 12th centuries, one might almost say, very nearly completed the conversion of Germany which had begun five centuries before.

D. GERMANY AND THE HOHENSTAUFEN, 1125–1250

Dynastic Competition, 1125–52.—The nearest kinsmen of Henry V were his Hohenstaufen nephews, Frederick, duke of Swabia from 1105 to 1147, and his younger brother Conrad, the sons of Henry's sister Agnes and Frederick, the first Hohenstaufen duke of Swabia. Some form of election had always been necessary to succeed to the crown, but before the great civil war nearness to the royal blood had been honoured whenever a dynasty failed in the direct line. By 1125, however, the princes, guided by Archbishop Adalbert of Mainz, no longer respected blood right. Affinity with Henry V was no recommendation to them, and hereditary succession seemed to lower their authority in the government of the *Reich*. Instead of Frederick they chose the duke of Saxony, Lothair of Supplinburg, king from 1125 to 1137 and emperor as Lothair II (*q.v.*) from 1133. Like the Hohenstaufen, he had risen by a lucky marriage and a successful career of continuous fighting into the first rank of dynasts but, unlike them, had served the cause of the Saxon opposition to the Salians.

With the enormous Nordheim and Brunonian inheritances behind him, Lothair II could humble the Hohenstaufen brothers (1134) after marrying his only daughter and heiress to a Welf, Henry (*q.v.*) the Proud. The Welfs, already dukes of Bavaria and possessors of vast demesnes, countships and ecclesiastical advocacies there and in Swabia, were even without this dazzling alliance somewhat better off than their Hohenstaufen rivals. In 1137, however, the fears of the church and a few princes turned against them. Instead of Henry the Proud, who now held the duchies of Saxony and Bavaria and the Matildine lands in Italy, they chose Conrad (1138–52), Lothair's unsuccessful Hohenstaufen opponent.

The battle against the Welfs, which Conrad III put foremost on his political program, was abandoned with his death in 1152 when an election once again decided the succession and the political situation in Germany for the next 30 years. The princes then chose Frederick I Barbarossa (*q.v.*; king 1152–90), the son of Conrad's elder brother Frederick and the Welf princess Judith, who agreed to share power in Germany with his Welf cousin Henry (*q.v.*) the Lion. The price of his election was dualism. In 1156 the duchy of Bavaria, which Conrad had tried to wrest from the Welfs, was restored to Henry, already undisputed duke of Saxony. The Babenberg margrave of Austria, his rival, had to be compensated with a charter which raised his margraviate into a duchy and gave him judicial suzerainty over an even wider area. Taken out of the Lion's duchy, it was to be held as an imperial fief which might descend both to sons and daughters. A perpetual principality, it served as a model for the aspirations of many other lay princes.

Colonization of the East.—The history of Germany in the 12th and 13th centuries is one of ceaseless expansion. A conquering and colonizing movement burst across the river frontiers into the swamps and forests from Holstein to Silesia and overwhelmed the Slav tribes between the Elbe and the Oder. Every force in German society took part: the princes, the prelates, new religious orders, knights, townsmen and peasant settlers. Agrarian conditions in the older lands of Germanic occupation seem to have favoured large-scale emigration. With a rising population, there was much experience in drainage and wood-clearing but a diminishing fund of spare land to be attacked in the west. Excessive subdivision of holdings impoverished tenants and did not suit the interests of their lords. Sometimes also seigniorial oppression is said to have driven peasants to desert their masters' estates. They certainly found a better return for their labour in the colonial area: personal freedom, secure and hereditary leasehold tenures at moderate rents and in many places quittance from services and the jurisdiction of the seigniorial advocate. The colonists brought with them a disciplined routine of husbandry, an efficient plow and orderly methods in siting and laying out their villages. Very soon even the Slav rulers of Bohemia and Silesia competed for immigrants. First and foremost, however, the Saxon and Thuringian marcher princes sought to attract settlers for the lands that they had conquered and the towns that they founded to open up communications and trade routes. The older regions of the *Reich* moreover had not only peasants but also men of the knightly class to spare—soldiers who needed fiefs and lordships to uphold their rank. Both could be gained beyond the Elbe under the leadership of successful princes. The germanized east thus became the home

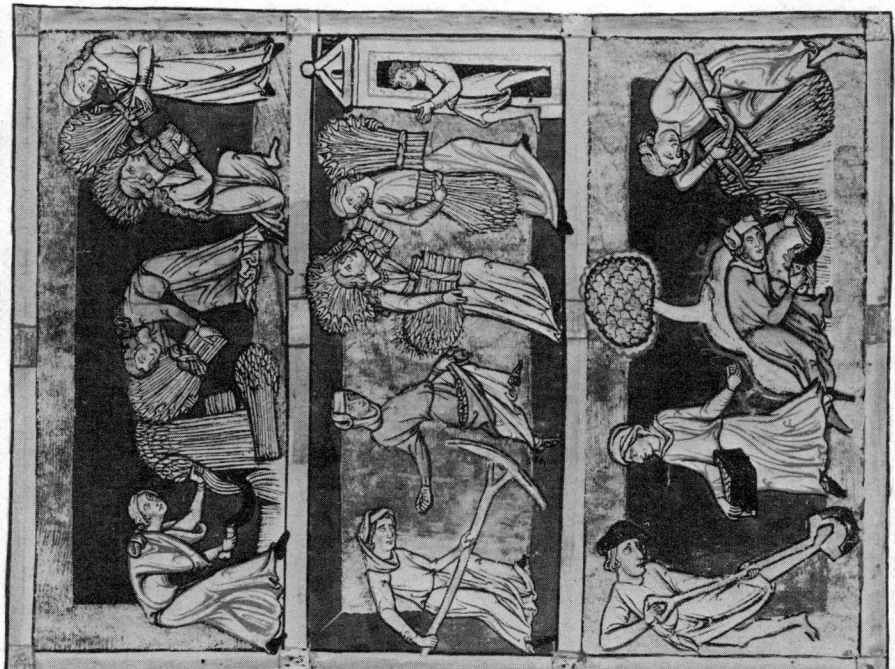

BY COURTESY OF THE RHEINISCHES LANDESMUSEUM, BONN

AGRICULTURAL WORK DEPICTED IN A 12TH-CENTURY GERMAN MANUSCRIPT

of fair-sized principalities in the 13th century, while all along the Rhine valley the rights of government were scattered over smaller and less compact territories. The Ascanian dynasty for instance, which under Albert (*q.v.*) the Bear began to advance into Branden-burg, by 1250 not only ruled over a broad belt of land up to the Oder river but had already established itself on the eastern banks ready for further advances. Farther south the Wettin (*q.v.*) margraves of Meissen busied themselves with settlements and town foundations in Lusatia.

For a time Henry the Lion, as duke of Saxony (1142–80), over-shadowed all these rising powers, and the Welf profited as much by his ruthless use of his resources against weaker competitors as by his own efforts in northeastern Germany. As his protection was alone worth having in Mecklenburg, the newly established Baltic bishoprics were at his mercy and he alone could attract the traders of Gotland to frequent the young port town of Lübeck, which he extorted from one of his vassals in 1158.

The *Reich* too possessed demesnes in the east, notably the Eger-land, Vogtland and the land of Pleissen in the Thuringian march. The Hohenstaufen kings therefore took some part in opening up these regions. They too founded towns and monasteries on their thickly wooded lands and established their *ministeriales* as bur-graves and advocates over them. But in this as in many other things they only competed with the princes. They did not and could not control the eastward movement as a whole.

Hohenstaufen Policy in Italy.—It was different with the other great field of German expansion in the 12th century, Lom-bardy and central Italy. There the emperors and their military following alone counted, and the rural population of Germany had no direct interest in the wars waged to recover and exploit ancient regalian rights over the growing Lombard city communes. The connection between the German crown, the empire and dominion over Italy has indeed been regarded as a disaster for Germany and the ever increasing concern of the Hohenstaufen dynasty with the south as its most tragic phase. But although Frederick Barba-rossa's policy was opportunistic he had really very little choice. Having bought off the Welfs and reconciled other great families with yet more concessions and lastly endowed his own cousin, Conrad III's son Frederick, with Hohenstaufen demesnes in Swa-bia, he had to try to mobilize their good will for the empire while it lasted. He now aimed at setting up a regime of imperial officials and captains who were to exact dues and to control jurisdiction which the communes had usurped from the failing grasp of their bishops. The Germans in Italy did not bring valuable accomplish-ments to poor and savage tribesmen, but they attacked econom-ically advanced and better developed communities to which they demanded. Military power was their chief asset in Lombardy and they used it ruthlessly.

For the Hohenstaufen *ministeriales* the rule of their masters in northern and central Italy was a career. They could be deployed continuously and became therefore the backbone of the imperial occupation. A handful of minor dynasts also served Barbarossa for many years in the powerful and profitable commands that he established. The German bishops and certain abbots still had to supply men and money, and some of them threw themselves whole-heartedly into the war: for instance Rainald of Dassel and Philip of Heinsberg, archbishops of Cologne from 1159 to 1167 and from 1167 to 1191 respectively, who as archchancellors for Italy had a vested interest in it. But the support of the lay princes was fitful and sporadic. Even at critical moments they could not be counted on unless they individually agreed to serve or to send their much-needed contingents for a season. The refusal of the greatest of them, Henry the Lion, in 1176 brought about the emperor's defeat at the battle of Legnano and in the long run spoiled many years' efforts in Lombardy.

The Fall of Henry the Lion and the Estate of Princes.—Forced to retreat before the Lombard league in 1177, Barbarossa cooled toward his Welf cousin, whom he could justly blame for some of his setbacks. Dualism in Germany had outlived its pur-pose. Hitherto the enemies of Henry, the princes, bishops and magnates of Saxony, had been unable to gain a hearing against him

at the emperor's court days. By 1178, however, the emperor was ready to help them. Outlawed (1180), beaten in the field and deserted by his vassals, the Welf had to surrender and go into exile in 1182. His duchies and fiefs were forfeited to the *Reich*.

His fall left a throng of middling princes face to face with an emperor whose prestige, despite reverses, stood high and whose resources had greatly increased since he began to reign. They were nonetheless the chief and ultimate gainers by the events of 1180. The final judgment by which Henry the Lion then lost his honours was not founded on folk law but on feudal custom. The princes who condemned him regarded themselves as the first feudatories of the empire, and they also decided on the redistribution of his possessions among themselves. During the 12th century the stem duchies of the Ottonian period finally disintegrated. Within their ancient boundaries not only bishops but also lay lords succeeded in eluding the authority of the dukes. In their large immunities they themselves wielded stem-ducal powers. To enforce the im-perial peace laws became both their ambition and their justifica-tion. Everywhere the greater lay dynasties and even some bishops tried to acquire a ducal or an equivalent title which would enable them to consolidate their scattered jurisdictions and if possible force lesser free lords to attend their pleas. These highest dynasts had interests in common, and they closed their ranks not only against threats from above but also against fellow nobles who had been less successful in amassing wealth, counties and advocacies for in feudal custom the superior jurisdiction of a duke, a mar-grave, a count palatine or a landgrave. They and they alone were now called princes of the empire. To lend a certain cohesion to their varied rights they were willing to surrender their households to the *Reich* and receive them back again as a princely fief. For the emperor it was theoretically an advantage that men so power-ful in their own right should owe their chief dignity and most valued privileges to his grant. It opened the possibility of escheats, and who did not possess the superior jurisdiction of a duke, a mar-stem law. But in Germany the political misfortunes of rulers brought it about that, by and large, ancient caste feeling and no-tions of inalienable right conquered the principles of feudal law. By 1216 it was established that the emperor could not abolish principalities, nor could he create princes at random.

The "heirs" of Henry the Lion had to fight a ceaseless battle to establish and maintain themselves. In Bavaria the Wittelsbachs (*q.v.*) had received the vacant duchy but they were not recognized as superiors by the dukes of Styria or by the dukes of Andechs-Meran. In Saxony the archbishop of Cologne was enfeoffed with Henry the Lion's ducal office and all his rights in Westphalia, while an Ascanian prince, Bernard of Anhalt, received the eastern half of his duchy. Neither he nor the archbishop, however, could make much out of their dukedoms, except in those regions where they already had lands and local jurisdictions. All over the *Reich* these and regalian rights, such as mints, fairs, tolls and the right of granting safe-conducts, were the substance of princely power, and to possess them as widely as possible became the first goal of the abler bishops and lay lords.

The Hohenstaufen Conflict With the Papacy, 1159–1215.—The attempt to establish a direct imperial regime in Italy antago-nized the papacy once again and led to a new struggle with Rome, the ally of the Lombard communes. Political and territorial rather than ecclesiastical interests were at stake in this quarrel; but the popes could only fight it as heads of the universal church defending its liberty against a race of persecutors and had to employ their characteristic weapons, excommunication, propaganda and intrigue. Nonetheless the German bishops stood by Barbarossa and for the most part followed him in maintaining a prolonged schism against Pope Alexander III. Unsuccessful in Lombardy, the centre of Hohenstaufen ambitions after 1177 shifted to Tuscany, Spoleto and the Romagna. This redoubled the fears and the resentment of the popes, particularly when Frederick's son and chosen successor, Henry VI (king 1190–97), became after 1189 the legitimate claim-ant to the Sicilian kingdom through his wife Constance, the sole surviving legitimate heiress. With their backs to the wall the popes had to make what use they could out of any opposition to the Hohenstaufen. Their chance came in 1197 when Henry VI died prematurely, leaving a three-year-old son, Frederick, to succeed him. To escape the chaos of a minority regime, the bulk of the German princes and bishops in 1198 elected the boy's uncle, Philip of Swabia (d. 1208); but an opposition faction in the lower Rhenish region, led by the archbishop of Cologne and financed by Richard I of England, raised an antiking in Otto IV (q.v.), younger son of Henry the Lion. Pope Innocent III had to enlarge on his rights over imperial coronations and become a partisan in the German electoral feud if he wished to defend his recuperations in Italy against Hohenstaufen claims. Territorial interests in the empire's constitution, the uncertainties of electoral custom and the lack of strict legal norms in Germany. During the war for the crown much hard-won demesne and useful rights over the church had to be sacrificed by the rivals to bribe their supporters.

Frederick II and the Princes.—Frederick II (q.v.) entered Germany to regain his own against Otto IV in 1212 and secured the crown in 1215. Despite promises to divide his inheritance, he kept the kingdom of Sicily and the empire together and thus he also shouldered the inevitable life-and-death struggle with the papacy. The Hohenstaufen demesne in Swabia, Franconia and Alsace and on the middle Rhine was still very considerable, and Frederick even recovered certain fiefs and advocacies which had been lost during the recent civil wars. Their administration was improved, and they provided valuable forces for his Italian wars. The great peace legislation of 1235 moreover showed that the emperor had not become a mere competitor in the race for territorial gain. But except for brief intervals the princes and bishops were left free to fight for the future of their lands against one another and against the intractable lesser dynasts who refused to accept their domination. The charters that Frederick had to grant to the ecclesiastical princes (*Privilegium in favorem principum ecclesiasticorum*, 1220) and later to all territorial lords (*Constitutio* or *Statutum in favorem principum*, 1232) gave them written guarantees against the activities of royal demesne officials and limited the development of imperial towns at the expense of episcopal territories. But they were not always observed, and until 1250 the crown remained formidable in southern Germany, despite the antikings Henry Raspe and William of Holland whom the papacy caused to be elected by the Rhenish archbishops in Germany in 1246 and 1247.

The Reich After the Hohenstaufen Catastrophe.—Frederick II died in 1250, in the midst of his struggle against Pope Innocent IV. His son Conrad IV (d. 1254) left the north in 1251 to fight for his father's Italian possessions. William of Holland, antiking from 1247 to 1256, was thus without a rival in an indifferent Germany which had lost interest in its rulers. But the princes were not ready to become the sole residuary legatees of imperial authority. The bishops' cities and the towns, many of them founded on royal demesne, could not be absorbed. Their economic power challenged the age-old aristocratic order in German society. Deprived of royal protection they banded together to defend their autonomy. Within the nobility moreover each rank tended to acquire some of the personal rights of its betters. The princes could not mediatize the free lords and counts or turn their vassalage into effective subordination. The Hohenstaufen breakdown after 1250 left a gap in Swabia which no rising territorial power was able to fill. Countless petty lords and imperial *ministeriales* of the southwest succeeded in holding their seigniories as immediate vassals of the *Reich*. Their independent territories often survived for centuries. The *ministeriales* elsewhere too ceased to be the dependable servants that they once had been. Many free nobles voluntarily joined their ranks, and the knights thus assimilated the rights of the free aristocracy. They became the governing class of the territorial principalities, the standing councilors of their masters whose household offices and local justice they monopolized and held in fee for many generations. Without the consent of this territorial nobility the princes could neither tax nor legislate. Even the less important *ministeriales*, who only administered manors for their lords, entrenched themselves as hereditary bailiffs who kept surplus produce for themselves and usurped seigniorial dues, so that it paid the owners to commute the labour services of their villeins into money rents and to lease out those portions of the demesne which the unfree peasants had cultivated for them. Even then, however, the hereditary officials could not be easily dislodged. Lastly the ambitions of the princes themselves did not aim above the patrimonial policies of the past. They were acquisitive, and attempted to build up their territories by usurpation, inheritance, marriage treaties and escheats. They also tried where possible to administer their lands with officials whom they could depose at will. Yet they did this not to found sovereign states but chiefly to provide for their families. Again and again they divided their dominions among sons who in turn founded cadet lines and set them up on a fraction of the principality.

By 1250 there was thus no really effective central authority left in Germany. The prince-bishoprics had become fiercely contested prizes between neighbouring dynasties, often vassals of the Holy See. But constant feuds, disorder and insecurity did not by any means frustrate the immense energies of the Germans in the 13th century. Eastward expansion continued under the leadership of the princes and, above all, of the knights of the Teutonic Order. Their advance into Prussia went hand in hand with the opening up of the Baltic by the merchants of Lübeck. It is possible that three centuries of complete security from foreign invasion made it unnecessary for the German aristocracy to learn the virtues of political self-discipline and subordination; but it would be a great mistake if Hohenstaufen Germany were to be judged solely by its failure to achieve political and administrative unity. (K. J. L.)

E. THE RISE OF THE HABSBURGS, 1254–1493

The Great Interregnum.—The period from the death of Conrad IV to the election of Rudolf of Habsburg in 1273 is generally called the Great Interregnum. It was used by the princes to increase their authority, although Richard, earl of Cornwall, who was crowned in 1257, enjoyed some authority in the Rhineland, thanks to his wealth, until his death in 1272. The interregnum established the electors, who from then on possessed vested interest in the maintenance of the royal title.

Until this time the territories of a prince were rarely divided among his descendants, the reason being that, although the private fiefs of the nobles were hereditary, their offices—margraviate, countship and the like—were in theory at the disposal of the king. There was now a tendency to set this principle aside. Otto II, duke of Bavaria, a member of the Wittelsbach family, had in 1214 become by marriage ruler of the Rhenish Palatinate. For two years after his death (1253) his extensive inheritance was ruled in common by his two sons; but in 1255 a formal division took place and the territory of the Wittelsbachs was divided into the duchies of Upper Bavaria and Lower Bavaria (in the next generation the Palatinate was in turn detached from the Upper Bavarian branch of the family). About the same time Saxony (i.e., the small eastern portion of Henry the Lion's powerful duchy, which the Ascanian princes had acquired) was divided into two duchies, those of Wittenberg and Lauenburg.

The First Habsburg Kings and Adolf.—The end of the interregnum was brought about by the pope, who realized the necessity for some power which could protect the church in Germany. In Oct. 1273, at the instigation of Pope Gregory X, the electors raised to the throne a Swabian noble, Rudolf, count of Habsburg. The situation on the eastern border was critical, because of the aggressive policy of Otakar II, king of Bohemia. The victory won by Rudolf I over Otakar at Dürnkrut (Aug. 26, 1278) saved eastern Germany from disintegration. By the annexation of all Otakar's possessions except Bohemia, Rudolf suddenly became one of the chief territorial princes in the empire. His policy of territorial aggrandizement was justified by the condition of the German kingdom, the ruler of which had little strength save that which he derived from his hereditary lands. Four years after the fall of Otakar, Rudolf obtained from the princes a reluctant assent to the granting of Austria, Styria and Carniola to his own sons, Rudolf and Albert. In 1286 Carinthia was given to Meinhard, count of Tirol, on condition that when his male line became extinct it should pass to the Habsburgs. (*See* AUSTRIA, EMPIRE OF.)

After Rudolf's death (July 1291) the electors, fearing the new power which he had founded, passed over his son Albert and elected

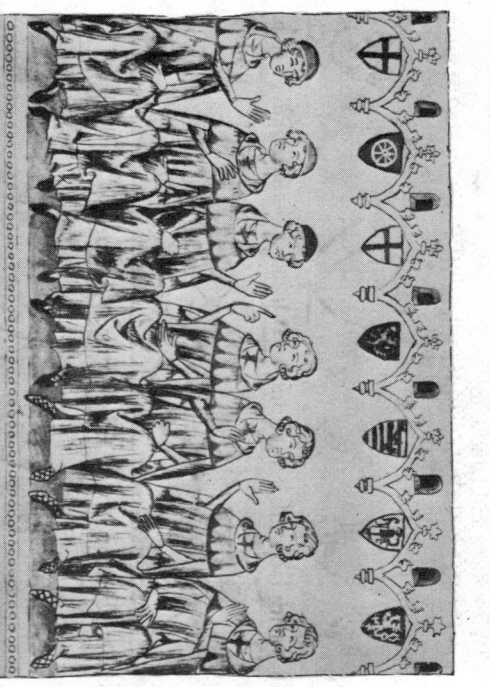

Adolf, count of Nassau (May 5, 1292). Like his predecessor, Adolf wished to secure an extensive territory for his family. Meissen, which he claimed as a vacant fief of the empire, and Thuringia, which he bought from the landgrave Albert II, seemed to offer a favourable field for this undertaking; and he spent a large part of his short reign in a futile attempt to carry out his plan. Naturally he sought to isolate Albert of Habsburg, who was treating with Philip IV of France, and this led to an alliance with Edward I of England. But many of the princes were disgusted with him, and at Mainz in June 1298 Adolf was declared deposed. He resisted the sentence, but Albert of Habsburg, who had been chosen his successor, marched against him, and on July 2, 1298, at Göllheim near Worms, Adolf was defeated and killed.

Albert was crowned at Aachen on Aug. 24, 1298. As his father had done, the new king Albert I made it the principal object of his reign to increase the power of his house, but he failed in his attempt to add Bohemia and Thuringia to the hereditary lands of the Habsburgs, and he was equally unsuccessful in his endeavour to seize the counties of Holland and Zeeland as vacant fiefs of the empire. He recovered some of the lost crown lands, however, and sought to abolish unauthorized tolls on the Rhine; he encouraged the towns and took measures to repress private war; he befriended the serfs and protected the persecuted Jews. His greatest danger came from a league which was formed against him in 1300 by the four Rhenish electors, who disliked his pro-French policy and resented his action with regard to the tolls. Albert, however, supported by the towns, was victorious; and the electors soon made their peace.

The Luxembourg Dynasty and the Wittelsbachs.—After King Albert's murder in May 1308, Henry, count of Luxembourg, a brother of Baldwin, archbishop of Trier (1307–54), was elected king as Henry VII in November. Since 1273 the material conditions of Germany had improved because the Habsburg kings had confined their activities to north of the Alps; but in 1308 as in 1291 the electors preferred a weak ruler. Henry was an ideologue who felt himself obliged to restore imperial rule in Italy; but he did not lack shrewdness, as witness his seizure of Bohemia for his son John in 1310. At the end of 1310 he crossed the Mont Cenis into Italy but died there (Aug. 1313) when, superficially, success seemed within his grasp. Dante (cf. especially Paradiso, xxx, 137–139, 142–144) conferred on him a reputation in excess of his ability.

After a year's delay there was a double election to the empire when one group of electors chose Louis of Wittelsbach, duke of Upper Bavaria, and another chose Frederick, duke of Austria, the son of Albert I. After a war of eight years, Frederick was defeated at Mühldorf on Sept. 28, 1322. The success of Louis IV was to some extent due to the imperial cities which supported him from the first; but he was perhaps still more indebted for his victory to the outbreak of war between the Swiss and the Habsburgs; the

position of the Habsburg family had been somewhat weakened by the defeat of Frederick's brother Leopold I of Habsburg, duke of Austria, at Morgarten on Nov. 15, 1315. Northern Germany, where emperors were usually ignored, had been unconcerned in the struggle, which was an episode in the feud between the powers of Wittelsbach and Habsburg that lasted to the 17th century. Until the battle of Mühldorf, Pope John XXII was ostensibly neutral, but the appointment by Louis of an imperial vicar in Lombardy in 1323 caused the pope to arraign and later to excommunicate Louis. Louis insisted that the vote of the electors sufficed to make a German king and that the approval of the papacy was not essential.

Thus Louis retained the support of most electors until 1346. In a diet at Frankfurt (1338) the papacy was declared excluded from any share in the choice of an emperor. The higher clergy and princes were alarmed at papal aggression; but there was no national opposition to the pope. Foreign scholars, William Ockham, Marsilius of Padua, Jean de Jandun and the Spiritual Franciscans were more valuable to Louis than his own countrymen. He added Brandenburg, Tirol, Holland and Hainault to the lands of his family, which however soon proved incapable of keeping them. The death of Louis. (Oct. 1347) forestalled civil war with Charles of Luxembourg, margrave of Moravia and king of Bohemia, a papal candidate accepted by four electors in July 1346.

Charles IV, who has an important place in the history of Bohemia (q.v.), was crowned in 1349 amid the visitation of the Black Death, which in Germany led to attacks on the Jews exceeding in violence similar attacks elsewhere. In the Golden Bull (q.v.) of 1356, Charles, who had been crowned emperor in April 1355, gave the German kingdom a firmly defined electoral college and a law of succession. For several generations the princes had regarded themselves as a caste rather than as ter-

ritorial rulers, and their lands were subdivided to support all the sons of a family. By asserting the indivisibility of electoral lands Charles encouraged reconsolidation. The cities, despite the prohibition of the Golden Bull, formed new associations for mutual defense or strengthened those which already existed. The Hanseatic league (*q.v.*) carried on a successful war with Valdemar VI of Denmark, while it extended its commerce. In 1376 some Swabian towns formed a league which in spite of the imperial prohibition soon became powerful in southwestern Germany and defeated the forces of Eberhard II of Württemberg, led by his son Ulrich, at Reutlingen in May 1377 (*see* SWABIA). Meanwhile the emperor who, unlike his predecessor, avoided conflict with either the papacy or the princes was steadily increasing the power of his house chiefly at the expense of the Wittelsbachs and Habsburgs. When he died in Nov. 1378, he wore the crowns of the empire, of Germany, of Bohemia, of Lombardy and of Burgundy (Arles); he had added lower Lusatia and parts of Silesia to Bohemia; he had secured the mark of Brandenburg for his son Wenceslas in 1373; and he had bought part of the Upper Palatinate. Learned and systematic, he was responsible for the foundation of Prague university, an international but also a German seat of learning. By his reform of the imperial chancery he created a court and a centre of scholastic jurisprudence, which for the next 150 years was to exert an influence over Germany out of proportion to the power of the crown.

Such was the ascendancy of Charles IV that his son Wenceslas succeeded him peacefully in 1378, although for 200 years no son had followed his father on the throne unchallenged. For several years Wenceslas proved a successful king of Bohemia; but by 1385 anarchy aggravated by the schism in the church (*see* PAPACY) prevailed in Germany. The Swabian league allied itself with the Swiss cantons; and, though only the Swiss were victorious in the field, it became impossible to prevent the towns from receiving external burghers, *Pfahlbürger*, as a means of extending municipal interests in the countryside and of undermining the jurisdiction of neighbouring lords. The chief sufferers were the knights holding their fiefs of the empire; except in parts of southern Germany where their confederation, the Shield of St. George, successfully bargained with princes and towns, these knights became a distressed class prone to lawlessness. Intellectual development suffered little, and the foundation of universities was even promoted by the schism, which cut off Germany from France; *e.g.*, Vienna (1384, second foundation), Heidelberg (1385), Cologne (1388), Erfurt (1392, second foundation) and, after the expulsion of Germans from Prague by the Czech Hussites, Leipzig (1409). In Aug. 1400 the Rhenish electors set up the able Rupert of Wittelsbach, the elector palatine, as a rival king. But Rupert had no large patrimony to sustain his dignity and, intervening in Italy (1401), was defeated by the Visconti and their mercenaries; he died in May 1410 having failed to establish himself.

Sigismund, a brother of Wenceslas, was elected king in Sept. 1410. He gained standing for himself and for the empire by his part in the Council of Constance (1414-17); but he proved unable to defend Germany against the Hussites or to recover Bohemia.

He was mainly preoccupied in Hungary. Bohemia recognized him after negotiation with the Council of Basel in 1435. From 1434 to his death in Dec. 1437 he concerned himself with imperial reform; and his proposals for the division of the country into circumscriptions and for the regulation of currency and justice set the program for many schemes until Maximilian's time.

The Habsburgs Established.—In March 1438 the electors chose Albert V of Habsburg to be king as Albert II, in the hope that he would defend the eastern frontier. He was universally respected but died after a single campaign against the Turks in Oct. 1439. Then Frederick V of Habsburg, duke of Styria and the senior prince of his house, was elected king as Frederick III in Feb. 1440. His reign was a series of crises for Germany and particularly for the Habsburg lands. From 1438 to 1448 the electors preserved neutrality in the rivalry between the papacy and the Council of Basel. Habsburg territories were jeopardized by the counts of Cilli until Ulrich of Cilli was murdered in 1457; and then by Frederick's brother Albert VI of Habsburg until 1463. Peasant revolts in the southeast and feuds among the lesser nobility were acute examples of social troubles besetting all Europe at this time. Frederick's greatest success was the securing for his family of the succession to the Burgundian Netherlands in 1477. He died in Aug. 1493.

The Estates in the 15th Century.—In defense of order Germany was compelled to rely on local organs of government. One of these, the *Fengericht* Feme or Fehmic court, which spread from Westphalia, had a brief period of general usefulness before its venality led to its repression (after 1450). Elsewhere the estates in a particular area, assembled in a *Landtag*, would by means of a *Landfriede* restrain private wars when they became intolerable. Disintegration had reached its extreme, and although the unity of the *Reich* was farther than ever from realization, the 15th century witnessed a slow consolidation of the territories ruled by princely dynasties. The estates, normally composed of nobility, towns and clergy, played their part in effecting unity on a local scale and preventing it on a national scale. At the same time as the Hohenzollern margrave and elector Albert Achilles was enacting the *Dispositio Achillea* (1473) to introduce primogeniture into Brandenburg, the estates of Württemberg were participating in the reunion of territories formerly partitioned among members of the reigning house. As feudal revenues declined, the princes were driven to depend on grants from the estates of their territories, and those of Saxony gained an exclusive right to impose taxation. The local estates throughout Germany wrecked the national taxation on which hung all plans for the reform of the *Reich*; and those of Bavaria, Saxony and Austria removed foreigners (*e.g.*, Styrians in Austria) from the administration. The economy and civilization of Germany were sustained by the towns, and the stand of Nürnberg against Albert Achilles did much to save the independence of imperial cities; but the majority of other towns were submitting to the government of princes.

German Society in the 15th Century.—Meanwhile technical discoveries and improvements were transforming society. These included not only printing and the glazing of stoneware but also

NÜRNBERG, PANORAMIC VIEW BY HANS WURM IN PEN AND WATERCOLOUR, ABOUT 1520

GERMANY

THE "TRIUMPHAL CAR" OF THE EMPEROR MAXIMILIAN I BY ALBRECHT DÜRER, 1522; THIS DRAWING WAS TO FORM PART OF THE GREAT SERIES OF WOODCUTS COMMISSIONED BY MAXIMILIAN FROM LEADING GERMAN ARTISTS TO COMMEMORATE THE HABSBURG DYNASTY AND HIS OWN ACHIEVEMENTS

advances in metallurgy and mining, as well as the instrument manufacture of Nürnberg without which the Portuguese voyages of discovery could hardly have been made. A wave of piety swept Germany in the 15th century but ecclesiastical conditions were uneven and mainly unsatisfactory. A large number of monasteries were reformed. In the north the Augustinian congregation of Windesheim was the chief agency, in the south the Benedictines of Melk. Notwithstanding the efforts of the cardinals John Carvajal and Nicholas of Cusa (legate 1451–52) the reform of the church, such as it was, owed most to the participation of the princes.

(C. A. J. A.; A. Lн.)

F. THE REFORMATION, TO 1555

Maximilian I and the Beginning of Lutheranism.—Maximilian I, emperor from 1493 to 1519, the "last knight," has exercised German imagination as few other emperors have done. Dignified, affable and showy, famous as a leader of the mercenary *Landsknechte*, as a hunter and as a patron of the arts, he hatched the most fantastic plans to escape his unceasing financial embarrassment. In spite of all his failures, luck and chance continued to deal him winning cards. His favourite project was to lead a European army against the Turks, but this could not be realized. Charles VIII of France invaded Italy in 1494; and this endangered not only the imperial fief of Milan but also the communications with Rome which the emperor valued as he considered himself the protector of Christendom. Maximilian was not able to maintain his rights, despite the long series of wars and the continually changing alliances with the Italian states, the papacy, the Swiss, Spain, England or France against whoever held Milan at the time. The German princes refused to follow Maximilian as they feared that the would use them only to strengthen Habsburg interests. It is true that the estates in the diet of Worms, guided by the archbishop of Mainz, Berthold (q.v.) von Henneberg, in 1495 granted a uniform and general tax, the "common penny," for the establishment of an imperial army and agreed to the erection of a supreme court to supervise the execution of the "permanent public peace" forbidding private feuds; but in return Maximilian had to agree to the setting up of a council of regency which was to supervise the emperor. However, the estates were neither organized nor resolute enough to impose their will for long on the emperor, while the empire, without an imperial civil service, was too weak to secure its own revenue by taxation. The war with the Swiss league, which refused to tolerate Habsburg territorial possessions on its soil, virtually severed the connection between Switzerland and the empire in 1499, though Swiss independence was not formally recog-

JAKOB FUGGER "THE RICH," BANKER TO THE HABSBURGS, AND HIS CHIEF ACCOUNTANT MATTHÄUS SCHWARZ; A PAINTED MINIATURE OF 1519

nized till the peace of Westphalia in 1648. In order to strengthen the material basis of his power Maximilian was forced to expand the hereditary Habsburg territories.

He never forgot this necessity, not even when he had to mortgage important sources of income such as the Tirolese silver mines to his creditors, mainly the banking house of Fugger (q.v.). The marriages (1496 and 1497) of his son Philip the Fair to Joan the Mad and of his daughter Margaret to Joan's brother John, heir to the Spanish crowns (who however died within a few months of his marriage), brought about that linking of Spain, the Netherlands and Austria which formed the basis for the world-wide empire of Charles V. Likewise the marriage of his grandson Ferdinand in 1516 to the Jagiello princess Anna created a claim on the succession not only to Hungary (where the rule of the Jagiello dynasty was weakened militarily and financially by the wars with the Turks and by the opposition of the Magyar nobles) but also to Bohemia, since her father was king of both. In return, however, Maximilian had to agree that the Order of the Teutonic Knights should do homage for Prussia to Anna's uncle Sigismund I of Poland, which they had refused to do since 1466. His arbitration between Bavaria-Munich and the Palatinate for the disputed succession to Bavaria-Landshut was paid for by his acquisition of the towns of Kitzbühel, Rattenberg and Kufstein and the bailiwicks of Hagenau and Ortenau (1504). The territory around Lienz, which escheated to him after the death of the last count of Görz, linked Tirol and Austrian Swabia in the west with Austria proper in the east.

Maximilian's reign saw the beginning of the Reformation. Criticism of the church had continued unabated since the great reforming councils of the 15th century. The western European states had long ago made concordats with the Holy See permitting them to draw on the rich property of the church for government expenditures and forming in fact state churches largely independent of Rome. Similar moves on behalf of the *Reich* were unsuccessful as long as its rulers did not give up their pretension to the secular universal empire and therefore could not afford to renounce the power of the universal church. The only gainers were the territorial princes and the towns: they used the emergency powers of all secular authorities to reform the church in their territories, but still allowed the papacy's complicated financial demands. Hence, from 1456, the imperial and territorial diets repeatedly formulated the "grievances (gravamina) of the German nation." They complained bitterly that the church was but an enormous financial institution which, down to its least branches, administered the means of grace essential to salvation only with an eye to material profit. Complaints were also made against the privileged social and economic position of the clergy. In its higher ranks the church had become a welfare organization for the younger sons and daughters of the nobility. In some districts one-third of the soil was ecclesiastical property. The radical sermons of the mendicant friars glorified the ideal of a poor church, but the lower clergy, an ecclesiastical proletariat, could only live if its members accumulated benefices from among the mass of pious foundations without fully executing the duties associated with them. Many prebendaries, monks and nuns lived the pleasant life of drones, enjoyed special legal status, were free of all civic burdens and, when they competed in economic life, possessed an unfair advantage. This criticism found new food as the lives of high and low

MARTIN LUTHER PREACHING: DETAIL FROM THE PREDELLA OF THE ALTARPIECE IN THE TOWN CHURCH, WITTENBERG, BY LUCAS CRANACH

ecclesiastics became more secular and less edifying. The harm done was deeply felt, for life was still permeated by religious concepts: quiet devotion and the sanctity of labour as well as the need for pomp and circumstance, the belief in witches and miracles as well as apocalyptic imaginings.

Martin Luther (q.v.) gave to this public criticism of the church a voice that could not be quieted and thus compelled a complete reconstruction of the church. The young monk and theologian had, after many solitary struggles, learned from his study of the Bible that men are justified not by the accumulation of pious works but by trusting in the mercy of God. His opposition to the traditional customs of the church became public because of the abuses connected with the sale of indulgences. Albert of Brandenburg (1490–1545), son of the elector John Cicero, was a pluralist, holding the archbishopric of Magdeburg and Mainz and the administration of the bishopric of Halberstadt; and this breach of canon law had to be paid for by increased dues to Rome. In order to reimburse the Fuggers and to obtain some additional income, he permitted a clever salesman, the Dominican Johann Tetzel, to sell indulgences in his dioceses by every dirty trick; the indulgence in question had been promulgated by Julius II in 1506 on the occasion of the papal jubilee and had been renewed by Leo X to obtain funds for the rebuilding of St. Peter's. Luther, a professor of theology and having cure of souls in Wittenberg, affixed 95 theses to the door of the palace church on Oct. 31, 1517. This was the usual way of inviting an academic discussion concerning a doctrine which was not yet a dogma of the church and which, according to Luther, endangered the sacrament of penance. Within a few weeks the theses were printed and distributed all over Germany by businesslike publishers; against Luther's wish they were interpreted as an attack on the Roman Catholic Church. The papacy opened proceedings against him, but he was protected by his territorial prince, the elector Frederick the Wise of Saxony, a key figure in the contemporary struggle for the imperial crown.

The Election of Charles V.—Maximilian's succession was contested by his grandson Charles I of Spain, by Francis I of France and for a short period by Henry VIII of England. Charles had been in Spain since 1517; after the death of his father Philip the Fair (1506) he united Burgundy with the kingdom of Castile and its newly discovered lands in America; after the death of his maternal grandfather Ferdinand II of Aragon (1516) he joined Aragon, Naples and Sicily to his realms; and after the death of Maximilian (1519) he and his brother Ferdinand I (q.v.) shared the Austrian hereditary lands together with claims on Bohemia and Hungary. Francis I of France, threatened by this extension of Habsburg power into the area of the Meuse and Scheldt and across the Pyrenees, did not intend to give up France's claim to lead Europe. Pope Leo X, as the temporal ruler of the papal states, wished neither for a renewal by the Habsburgs of the Hohenstaufen combination of the empire and Naples nor for the foundation by Francis I, who held Milan, of a French imperial line. He therefore advocated the candidature of Frederick the Wise, who was, however, too clearly aware of his own limitations and those of his power to agree to this. Both the French and the Habsburgs offered enormous bribes to the electors, but the contest was decided unanimously in favour of Charles, who became emperor as Charles V. German public opinion was also in his favour. The princes insisted on a series of solemn promises on the emperor's part, contained in a "capitulation," both in order not to be drawn into the imminent war between him and France and in order to limit his rights by means of an oligarchic constitution for the *Reich*. If he broke the capitulation, the estates were to have the right to oppose him by force. For the remainder of his life Charles tried to fuse the dynastic and the imperial ideals; but he was pushing both ideas beyond their limit in the very period which saw the rise of the national states in western Europe.

The Diet and Edict of Worms (1521).—In the meantime the Lutheran affair assumed the proportions of a national movement. The Leipzig disputation with Johann Eck (1519) and his study of ecclesiastical history confirmed Luther in his opinion that the Church of Christ according to Holy Writ was not a visible external organization but a small group of people separated from the mass of nominal Christians by their belief in the divine revelation witnessed by the Bible. Luther felt called to a reform of the existing church, not to its complete reconstruction. The humanists, fighting against the schoolmen and the friars, believed him to be their partisan. Erasmus counseled moderation but Ulrich von Hutten (q.v.) hoped to win both Luther and the young emperor over to his fight against Rome after the Swabian league had driven the quarrelsome Duke Ulrich from Württemberg and transferred the administration of Württemberg to Austria. Public opinion felt certain that the long-awaited reform of church and state would at last be realized. Luther, the most popular professor at Wittenberg university, where he allied himself with Philipp Melanchthon in an attempt to reform the curriculum, symbolized his formal separation from the church by burning a copy of the papal bull excommunicating him. He used the printing press for an extensive literary agitation; his three great reforming pamphlets, published in 1520, were widely distributed: *To the Christian Nobility of the German Nation*; *On the Freedom of a Christian Man*; and *On the Babylonian Captivity of the Church*.

Charles came from Spain to be crowned at Aachen in Oct. 1520 and to open his first diet at Worms in 1521. He left Spain in a state of revolt. The regency, led by Cardinal Adrian of Utrecht

THE SALE OF INDULGENCES IN CHURCH; WOODCUT FROM THE TITLE PAGE OF LUTHER'S PAMPHLET "ON APLAS VON ROM," PUBLISHED ANONYMOUSLY IN AUGSBURG, 1525

(the future pope Adrian VI), managed only slowly to gain the upper hand. Charles's aim, instilled by his chancellor Mercurino Gattinara, was to renew the universal empire on the basis of the universal Habsburg power. At the diet the estates obtained the agreement of the self-confident emperor to the establishment of a *Reichsregiment* or council of regency, which however was to function only during his absence from the *Reich*, was to be led by an imperial viceroy and was to be barred from dealing with foreign affairs. Since the capitulation that had secured Charles's election had stipulated that no subject of the empire could be declared an outlaw—a procedure which normally followed papal excommunication—without public trial, Luther's case had to be heard. When Luther steadfastly refused to recant, the Edict of Worms was promulgated outlawing him and forbidding the reading and sale of his books. On his way home to Wittenberg he was secretly taken to the Wartburg castle on the elector Frederick's order. There, far from the quarrels of the day, he translated the New Testament into German in ten weeks.

Immediately after the diet of Worms, Charles made alliances against France, first with Pope Leo X, then with Henry VIII of England. He reconquered Milan and Genoa and defeated and captured Francis at Pavia in 1525. The peace of Madrid, which the imprisoned king signed to secure his release, did not last long, since the new pope, the vacillating Clement VII, formed the League of Cognac with Milan, Venice and France in order to obtain small territorial gains. The sack of Rome by German and Spanish mercenaries in 1527 forced the pope and France to make peace (treaties of Barcelona and Cambrai, 1529). Charles received the imperial crown at the pope's hand in Bologna before he left again for Germany, the last elected king to be so crowned.

Lutheran Church Organization and the Peasants' Revolt.—Germany had seen far-reaching changes while Charles was absent. Luther's doctrines of the priesthood of all believers and of the Bible as the sole norm of life had shaken the bases of society as it had formerly been constituted on Catholic principles. Wherever the authorities did not interfere, Evangelical congregations were formed, independent in doctrine and discipline. This demonstrated at once how dangerous it was to have no agreed authority for the interpretation of the Bible. For while Luther stayed in the Wartburg, his Wittenberg congregation listened to the "prophets of Zwickau," led by Nikolaus Storch, who taught, as did Thomas Münzer in Thuringia, that the true authority was not the Bible but the inner light given by God to those who were his. Luther restored order in eight days by his sermons. Other men, appealing to Luther's writings as their authority, used the general insecurity to further their own egotistic ends. The rich Franz von Sickingen (*q.v.*), a friend of Hutten and, like all knights, hemmed in between the rising cities and the territorial princes, hoped that the impending changes would bring him a principality between the Nahe river and Alsace. He made war against the archbishop of Trier but was himself besieged and killed in his castle of Landstuhl. The Swabian league razed the castles of the knights allied with him throughout Franconia and the Odenwald (1523). The greatest upheaval was caused by the peasants' revolt, which began in 1524 in the southern area of the Black Forest and spread in 1525 through southern Germany (except Bavaria), Hesse, Thuringia, Saxony and Tirol. Citing Luther's plea for the "liberty of their Christian men," the peasants demanded the restoration of their customary rights and destroyed abbeys and manor houses. Luther, however, attacked them in passionately worded pamphlets. The individual peasant bands, badly led, were easily defeated with enormous loss of life by the armies of the territorial princes.

When the Reformation began Luther had avoided any formulation of his doctrines (except for the *Loci communes* published by Melanchthon in 1521), trusting in the power of "the Word alone"; he had abolished the Mass but had not created a new order of service or united the congregations in a central body. The experience of the peasants' revolt proved that the Reformation could not advance by itself outside the cities. Ecclesiastical visitations, however, showed that the common man was rude and hostile to all religiosity while the clergy were ignorant, negligent wasters of church property. With Luther's encouragement each territory

now established its own state church; they all differed according to the character of the prince concerned and according to the changing political circumstances. Unsuitable priests were dismissed; inventories of ecclesiastical property were drawn up; consistories supervised the clergy with the prince as *summus episcopus* ("supreme bishop") and judge of appeal; the monasteries were made to bear the cost of schools and churches; and provision was made for education, for church discipline and for a uniform development of dogma. Nobody was to be forced to believe, but all were to be taught and exhorted alike: liberty of conscience meant free access to the Scriptures, compulsion of the conscience meant burdening it with papal laws. As none of the rulers wanted to give up uniformity of public service or of dogma, their subjects who differed from them on grounds of conscience had to emigrate.

The Diets of Speyer (1526, 1529) and Augsburg (1530).—During the long absence of the emperor none of the estates tried to find a political solution of the religious differences, but Charles refused to call a German national council. Some of the Roman Catholic territories, united in the Regensburg convention (1524) and in the Dessau league, promised one another mutual succour in the execution of the Edict of Worms, but this provoked the formation of the Torgau league of Evangelicals. At the diet of Speyer of 1526 Luther's followers were willing to uphold the union with Rome if they were permitted to treat institutions and ceremonies based on the Bible as essential and only to regard those that were man-made as not essential and only to be settled by a council until the calling of a general council. Charles objected again, for he wished all ecclesiastical changes only to be settled by a council called by both emperor and pope. As these two powers were actually in a state of war, the estates bound themselves to follow only their conscience until the next council.

Besides the state churches based on Lutheran doctrines there arose another type of Reformed organization, the Zwinglian, in which the civil community was itself identified as the legal embodiment of the church and in which the citizen was equated with the Christian and strictly supervised by the *Ehegericht* (marriage court). Huldreich Zwingli (*q.v.*) had abolished the Mass and removed the sacred images in the Swiss city of Zürich. Zürich thus had to face the hostility of neighbours who had remained Roman Catholic and, for economic reasons, were not prepared to follow Zürich's example in cancelling their treaty for the provision of Swiss mercenaries to France. In Switzerland also there arose the Anabaptist movement, which substituted adult baptism for pedobaptism. Small Anabaptist congregations rapidly spread through out southern Germany, Thuringia, Hesse, Silesia and Moravia, into the Alpine valleys and down the Rhine into the Netherlands; everywhere they were cruelly persecuted by both Roman Catholic and Reformed authorities. The extent of the feeling of insecurity can be gauged by the measures taken by the landgrave Philip (*q.v.*) of Hesse in 1528 to forestall an apparently imminent Roman Catholic attack. He had been tricked by the Saxon secretary Otto von Pack, but a general war of religion was avoided only with difficulty. The diet of Speyer of 1529 failed to produce any recess to which all the estates could agree: the Roman Catholic majority resolved to leave the solution of the religious quarrel to a future council, to oppose Zwingli's doctrines and to keep the Edict of Worms; the "protesting" minority appealed to the emperor and to the council and in the meantime did not wish to do anything against their conscience. Philip of Hesse invited Luther and Zwingli to Marburg in the hope of reconciling their differences about the Eucharist so as to make possible a political alliance with the Swiss, but the attempt failed. Lutherans and Zwinglians presented to

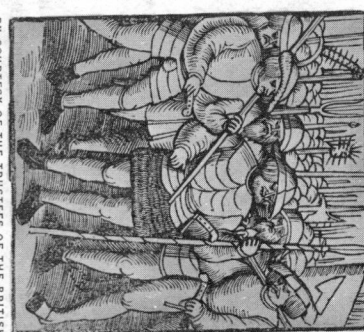

"THE PEASANTS' REVOLT." WOODCUT FROM THE TITLE PAGE OF A PAMPHLET ISSUED BY THE REBELS, 1525

the emperor different formularies of faith at the diet of Augsburg (1530): the *Confessio Augustana* drawn up by Melanchthon and the *Confessio Tetrapolitana* of the south German cities. Though drawn up in a conciliatory spirit, they did not lead to any compromise, since the Evangelicals remained firm on all questions of conscience. Yet the calling of a council could not be expected from the contemporary papacy, which had grown up in opposition to the conciliar movement of the 15th century and could only foresee a diminution of its power as the likely result. Thus failed the attempts to reform the church in the empire. Those who wanted to recover the lost areas for Roman Catholicism had to use force.

The League of Schmalkalden.—To be prepared against force, Philip of Hesse and the elector of Saxony John the Steadfast formed the League of Schmalkalden, consisting of the north German Protestant princes, Strasbourg and a number of south German cities (1531). It proved impossible to form a counterleague, as the political interests of the Roman Catholic princes concerned were too divergent. Ferdinand, Charles V's brother, had been made his successor in part of Hungary in 1526 after the death of his brother-in-law King Louis II in the battle of Mohacs against the Turks (who advanced as far as Vienna in 1529); and in 1526 also a quarrel about the succession to Louis II's other kingdom, Bohemia, had ended with Ferdinand's victory over his rivals, the Bavarian dukes. In 1531 Charles saw to it that Ferdinand was elected king of the Romans, despite strong Roman Catholic and Lutheran opposition; this made him Charles's heir presumptive in the imperial dignity. In the same year the south German cities lost their Swiss backing when Zwingli was killed in the battle of Kappel against the Roman Catholic cantons (Heinrich Bullinger, however, continued Zwingli's work). When the Turks invaded Hungary again in 1532 Ferdinand was forced to buy the indispensable Protestant support by the religious peace of Nürnberg: a truce was called in doctrinal matters until the meeting of a council (now very far distant) or the next *Reichstag*. Philip of Hesse succeeded, with the help of French subsidies, in restoring Duke Ulrich to Württemberg, where he immediately introduced the Reformation (1534). Such successes gained new members for the Schmalkaldic league. The Reformation, in the form of strictly regulated state churches, spread along both shores of the Baltic, into Silesia and to the lower Rhine.

Charles, full of the dream of a universal empire, held it his highest duty to fight infidels and heretics. He was victorious against the Barbary corsairs of north Africa, but this led to a renewal of hostilities with France. After futile campaigns in Provence and in the Netherlands the ten-year truce of Nice was mediated by Pope Paul III (1538). Paul, however, refused Charles's demand for a council. Consequently Charles extended the religious truce to all the new adherents of the Augsburg Confession (Frankfurt agreement, 1539), for he needed the aid of the Protestants against the Turks and now moreover had to compete not only with France but also with William, duke of Cleves-Jülich-Berg, heir to the rich duchy of Gelre (*see* GELDERLAND). Religious colloquies at Hagenau, Worms and Regensburg came to nothing. All that Charles achieved was an agreement with Philip of Hesse promising him that he would not be punished for his bigamy if he refused alliances with foreign powers and prevented the admission of Cleves to the Schmalkaldic league. King Ferdinand had to watch impotently while the Ottoman sultan Suleiman I occupied Hungary. Charles failed in his attempt to relieve the Turkish pressure by an attack on Algiers.

In 1542 Francis I of France felt strong enough to make his fourth war against Charles V. The Schmalkaldic league remained inactive while Charles occupied Cleves and reintroduced Roman Catholicism; but Philip of Hesse and the elector John Frederick I (*q.v.*) of Saxony together expelled the emperor's firmest partisan, Henry II of Brunswick-Wolfenbüttel, from his duchy and proceeded to evangelize it. At the same time Hermann (*q.v.*), of Wied, archbishop-elector of Cologne, attempted to introduce Protestantism in his diocese with the advice of Melanchthon and the Strasbourg reformer Martin Bucer. The Protestant faith was openly accepted in the bishoprics of Münster, Osnabrück, Pader-

born and Minden and was professed by Maurice (*q.v.*), of the then ducal line of Saxony, and by Otto Henry of Palatinate Neuburg.

The peace of Crépy-en-Laonnois (1544) between Charles V and Francis of France created the preconditions for a thorough overhaul of German affairs. While the Protestants were fooled by renewed religious talks at Regensburg, Charles got ready for war. The papacy had called a general council to Trent for 1545 but hoped to escape this irksome promise by actively supporting the emperor with money and troops. Charles obtained the neutrality of Bavaria and of Duke Maurice by vague promises. There was no doubt about the emperor's purpose, yet the Schmalkaldic league proved unable to reform its cumbersome organization. The em-

BY COURTESY OF THE MUSEO DEL PRADO, MADRID

EMPEROR CHARLES V AS VICTOR OF THE BATTLE OF MÜHLBERG ON APRIL 24, 1547: PAINTING BY TITIAN, 1548

peror took the field in the summer of 1546. Hesse and electoral Saxony could not bring themselves to risk the effective army which they and their allies had quickly assembled; consequently the emperor was able to reinforce himself from Italy and the Netherlands. Impatient, Duke Maurice brought the decision when he, together with King Ferdinand, invaded unprotected Saxony in order not to lose the electoral dignity which had been promised to him. John Frederick fled but was caught near Mühlberg on April 24, 1547, and Philip of Hesse was made prisoner in July at the moment of asking the emperor for mercy on bended knees. Charles V had reached the zenith of his power, ready, with the help of the council, to lead back the strayed sheep into the fold of the church. Luther, the enemy of all compromise, Henry VIII and Francis I were dead.

The Augsburg Interim.—The papacy, however, was not willing to see the emperor all-powerful. Charles V had asked the pope to consider and redress first the "grievances," but when the long-awaited council had at last met it had begun by redefining the creed and the apostolic traditions of the church. Indeed, Paul III had withdrawn his troops even before the battle of Mühlberg and transferred the council to Bologna in order to withdraw it from imperial influence (*see* TRENT, COUNCIL OF). Thus it was without papal backing that Charles V forced the Interim on the estates at the diet of Augsburg (1547–48). This conciliatory formula restored Roman Catholic ritual in general but conceded the eucharistic cup to the laity and allowed priests who were already married to keep their wives pending the final decision of the general council. The Roman Catholic princes refused to accept this before the council had actually decided, and Roman Catholic priests were reintroduced by force in the Protestant areas and towns of southern Germany, but the common people either remained faithful to the expelled ministers (unless they went into exile) or renounced sermons and sacraments altogether where the authorities did not find a means of circumventing the Interim. The city of Magdeburg was put under the ban of the empire but despised all threats of force and satirized in numerous pamphlets the timorous Melanchthon, who had retreated from his original Lutheran position and was fumbling to find weak compromise formulas.

Pope Julius III recalled the council to Trent in 1551, but the Protestant envoys, now admitted to its sessions, had to limit themselves to the mere presentation of their confessions of faith and to protests against decrees which had already been settled and could no longer be revised. Deeply disappointed, the emperor had to recognize that the general council was unable to provide a viable solution for the religious conflicts in Germany.

Maurice of Saxony's War (1552).—All the estates agreed in opposing the imperial absolutism, the "beastly Spanish servitude," as long as the emperor, contrary to his election capitulation, kept Spanish troops in the *Reich*. The soul of the resistance movement was the ambitious Maurice of Saxony, whose Protestant faith was chiefly a means of affirming his princely independence and rise to power. His treaty of Chambord with Henry II of France (1552) provided him with large subsidies for his war against the emperor in exchange for the cession to France of the imperial cities of Metz, Toul, Verdun and Cambrai. Taken by surprise, the emperor fled from Innsbruck to Villach pursued by the troops of Saxony. Hesse and Brandenburg-Kulmbach; the Council of Trent disintegrated out of fear of the approaching army. Yet in the negotiations at Passau the opposition achieved only a renewed truce until the calling of the next diet, which was to decide whether the religious conflict was to be ended by decision of the council, by a recess of the diet or by a religious colloquy. Maurice was killed in the battle of Sievershausen in July 1553, against Albert Alcibiades of Brandenburg-Kulmbach, who had continued the war on France's order, burning and killing as he pleased.

Charles V's Abdication and the Peace of Augsburg (1555). —Charles besieged Metz unsuccessfully, but his hopes for a universal empire were revived again by the marriage of his son Philip with the English queen Mary I (1554); by combining the resources of the Netherlands, England, Spain and the *Reich*, he hoped to encircle and defeat France. The marriage, however, remained childless, so that the emperor's expectations came to nothing. When Henry II of France found a supporter in the new pope, Paul IV (elected 1555), Charles abdicated, worn out by all his failures. He handed over the Netherlands to his son Philip in 1555, Spain to Philip in 1556 and his imperial authority to his brother Ferdinand in 1556 also. He then withdrew to Estremadura, near the monastery of San Yuste. Thus he admitted that the medieval ideal of the unity of Christendom was no longer valid.

In 1555, despite Charles's protests, the diet of Augsburg sanctioned the existing state of affairs. The peace of Augsburg (*q.v.*) acknowledged the coexistence of Roman Catholicism and Lutheranism and promised no toleration for Zwinglians, Calvinists or Anabaptists. Lawyers later elaborated the formula *cujus regio ejus religio* (the prince's religion is the religion of his dominions) to be applied to the individual territories. The so-called "ecclesiastical reservation" stipulated that if an ecclesiastical prince became Lutheran, he had to renounce his office: thus his change of religion would not affect his subjects as a secular prince's change would. Church property secularized before 1552 was to remain so. The cities that had accepted the Interim had to tolerate both Roman Catholicism and Lutheranism within their boundaries. The peace of Augsburg was a deep disappointment to the high hopes entertained at the beginning of the Reformation. Its authors held it to be only a temporary solution, but nobody could really believe that a final religious reconciliation would be brought about in the future. The idea of one Christian Church had to be given up now that two creeds were legally established side by side.

The recess of the diet of 1555 also decided the conflict between emperor and estates in favour of the estates. By its "executive ordinance," the "imperial circles" (administrative districts established by Maximilian) were given powers to administer law and order within their areas and execute the decisions of the imperial chamber or *Reichskammergericht*. In the southern and western areas, where there was the greatest number of quasi-independent authorities, this "circle" organization provided at least some safeguard against the religious wars threatening to spill over into Germany from the west. The vital forces making for a renewal of political life were now to be found in the individual territories of the empire rather than in the empire as a whole. They were not active in foreign affairs. Within the territories, however, newly created administrative organizations, centrally directed and staffed with trained lawyers, began to issue numerous laws covering every aspect of life. Economic policy was especially affected by a mixture of paternalist welfare legislation and rationalizing utilitarianism which aimed both at increasing the princes' revenue and at keeping the subjects happy and contented. The subjects were treated as uniformly as possible within the boundaries of each state, and the habit of obedience to orders was instilled: the territorial estates, composed of nobility and towns, gradually saw their rights severely curtailed, especially that of deciding taxes. As regards ecclesiastical policy the territorial princes, "vicegerents of God," felt responsible for maintaining uniformity of belief: whatever their momentary belief might be, it was to be the only truth recognized, upheld and propagated in their states. Regarded by contemporary opinion as an essential safeguard against heresy and revolution, the doctrinal unity thus enforced was used as an instrument of state policy to strengthen the unity of the territory and so to augment its power. The religious struggles in Germany came to be settled on the territorial plane; and the resultant territorial distribution of the various creeds survived, by and large, into the 20th century.

The independence of the numerous though varied states was hardly called into question any more, so that emperor and empire faded into the background, having shed their universal claims. The emperors had to co-operate with independent institutions of the *Reich* and to reach an agreement with the diets and the representatives of imperial "circles." The emperors' power was not enough to stop the centrifugal forces or to inaugurate that development toward the formation of a national state which had already affected the other European monarchies. True, the princes had not the power to subordinate the Habsburg wearers of the imperial crown, who retained their European connections. While Austria remained the strongest upholder of the imperial tradition, still not quite extinct, despite the other princes' misgivings. Indeed, the Austrian rulers used their imperial dignity to further their interests as territorial princes, fully incorporated in the *Reich*; on the Austrian hereditary lands, Ferdinand I based his power on the lands of the Bohemian crown, which were not represented in the *Reichstag* or incorporated in the circles; and on the kingdom of Hungary, entirely outside the *Reich* and largely in the hands of the Turks and their vassal Transylvania.

G. THE COUNTER-REFORMATION AND THE THIRTY YEARS' WAR

Ferdinand I and Maximilian II.—The partition of Charles V's dominions meant that henceforth there were two Habsburg lines, the Austrian and the Spanish, but both were still Roman Catholic and they were closely linked with one another despite occasional tension and opposition. Ferdinand I was no less devoutly Roman Catholic than Charles V had been, but reasons of state found him readier to make necessary concessions. His son and successor Maximilian II, emperor from 1564 to 1576, was still readier for compromise as he leaned toward Protestantism, though he never confessed it publicly. During their reigns, however, the leadership in the world of ideas, which Luther and the proponents of universal empire had combined to give to Germany, passed to the new spiritual forces which took advantage of the peace that now prevailed in the *Reich*. The Roman Catholic Counter-

Reformation, inaugurated by the Council of Trent and promoted by Spain, Rome and Italy, put forward the idea of the hierarchical structure of the church, led by the papacy, against the Protestant doctrine of the priesthood of all believers. The Tridentine Creed (1564), the Roman catechism (1566), the breviary and the missal (1570) were the instruments of an internal renewal as well as the offensive weapons of the Counter-Reformation. The reformed papacy, moreover, possessed in the Society of Jesus its most reliable army, which turned its attention immediately to the most threatened spot, Germany: Jesuit settlements had been founded as early as 1544 in Cologne, Vienna, Ingolstadt and Prague, that is, in areas where the religious decision was still in the balance. Moreover, the relationship between the Habsburgs and the Bavarian dukes created a Roman Catholic bloc in southern Germany with its political and intellectual centre in Munich; and this reimposed the old belief by force in Bavaria, in the archbishopric of Salzburg and in the bishoprics of Bamberg and Würzburg. Though support from the rest of Germany was always most readily forthcoming for the defense of the empire against the Turks, which bore most heavily on Austria, Ferdinand and Maximilian nevertheless avoided offensive war in order not to have to make further religious concessions to the Protestant Austrian estates.

The Lutheran princes east of the Weser river, meanwhile, received effective help from Denmark. Electoral Saxony, Brandenburg and Pomerania not only secularized ecclesiastical property and established Lutheran state churches within their territories but also began, from 1555, to absorb neighbouring bishoprics and abbeys when chapters sympathetic to Lutheranism elected Protestant administrators to supersede the Catholic prelates. Despite endless disputes, which paralyzed the diets, this proved a successful method of circumventing the "ecclesiastical reservation" that had been meant to protect such ecclesiastical principalities. Disunity, however, grew among the German Protestants when French and later Dutch land refugees brought Calvinism first to the Palatinate (1559) and then to Nassau, Hesse and the lower Rhine valley. Soon after Luther's death (1546) doctrinal strife had broken out between the followers of the old radical Lutheranism and those who preferred Melanchthon's compromise formulas. As the princes could decide what form of religion they wished to establish, this theological quarrel had political consequences. By order of the elector palatine Frederick III, the Heidelberg catechism was drawn up in 1563—though it became the official doctrinal statement of the Reformed (that is, Calvinist) Church only in 1619. This catechism is the most important German contribution to the doctrines of international Calvinism. Electoral Saxony, Württemberg and Brunswick-Wolfenbüttel were eventually to end the constant doctrinal disputes among the Lutherans by accepting, after a long struggle, the *Formula concordiae* of 1577, after Rudolf II's accession as emperor. This did not prevent them from regarding the Calvinists as more serious opponents than the Roman Catholics. When the Calvinist John Casimir of the Palatinate tried to form a Protestant league, Saxony wrecked the plan. John Casimir was the foremost of the German princes to intervene on the Huguenot side in the wars of religion in France.

Wherever Austrian power proved ineffective, the empire suffered great losses. As the Teutonic Order had been secularized as early as 1525, its calls for help were ignored, so that Courland became a Polish fief in 1562, while Livonia was divided between Poland and Russia and Estonia passed under Swedish rule. On the western frontier the French kept the cities of Metz, Toul and Verdun even after the peace of Câteau-Cambrésis (1559) and extended their influence over Lorraine. When the revolt of the Netherlands broke out against Spanish rule, the empire did not intervene, though the Netherlands belonged to the Burgundian circle of the empire and though the leader of the revolt, William the Silent, was himself a prince of the empire (Nassau and Orange). Only the Calvinist Palatinate gave William direct support: otherwise the Protestant estates merely appealed for Maximilian II's mediation, which Spain rejected. Finally Spain and the rebel provinces came to act as sovereign powers in the Netherlands, independently of the empire. (See NETHERLANDS: *History*.)

Rudolf II, the Cologne War and Matthias.—Maximilian was

succeeded by his eldest son, Rudolf II, emperor from 1576 to 1612. By this time the conflict in the Netherlands was having its effect on the strife of the creeds in the Rhineland. The fluctuating religious position there was decided by events in the archbishopric of Cologne (Köln), where Archbishop Gebhard (*q.v.*) wanted to marry and so, in order to circumvent the "ecclesiastical reservation," tried to secularize the diocese (1582–83). Cologne's conversion to Protestantism would have given the Protestants a two-thirds majority in the electoral college, with far-reaching repercussions on the election of an emperor, and would probably have led to the conversion of the vacillating duchy of Cleves-Jülich-Berg and the Westphalian bishoprics. Ernest of Bavaria, bishop of Freising, Hildesheim and Liège, was consequently put forward by Bavaria, Spain and the papacy to take Gebhard's place. Gebhard put his troops under the leadership of John Casimir of the Palatinate but received no help from the Lutheran princes. Defeated in 1584, he withdrew to the Netherlands and then to Strasbourg. The Spaniards and the Dutch, however, continued the war for years, devastating the country; Münster and the other Westphalian bishoprics fell to Ernest of Bavaria, as well as Cologne. A sequel to the Cologne War was a double election to the bishopric of Strasbourg in 1592; after long conflict, the Catholic candidate prevailed (1604).

Rudolf II had been educated in Spain; he was devoutly Roman Catholic, interested in intellectual matters, of good political judgment but of an odd nature. He fled from human contact, was afraid to act and lived alone in his castle in Prague till his reason gave way and he became incapable of making political decisions. The violent means by which Catholicism was being restored in all the Austrian territories and in Hungary provoked the opposition of the Protestant territorial estates everywhere and fanned the discord between Rudolf and his brother Matthias, who in 1606 was

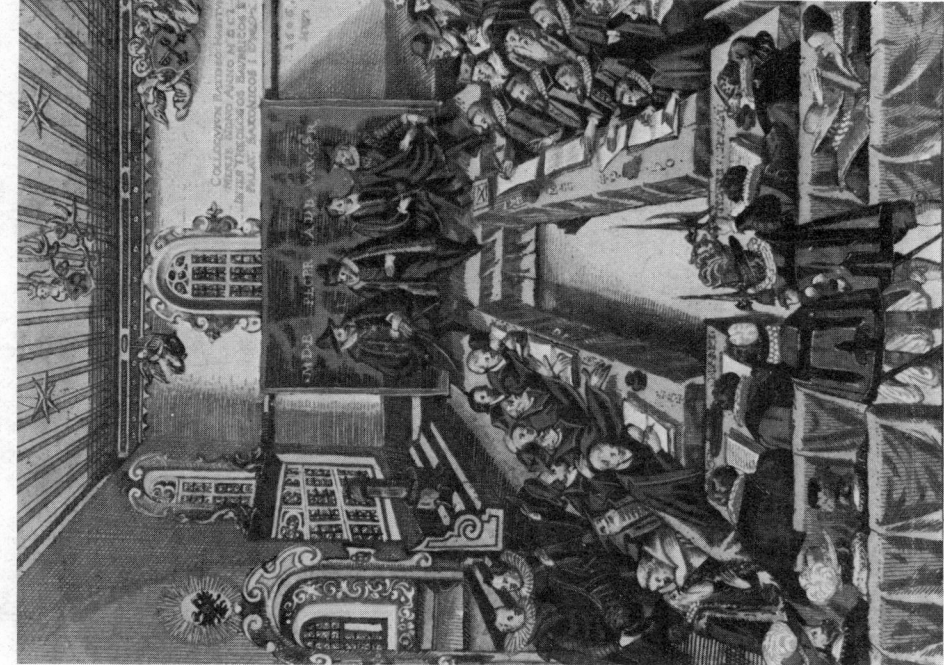

CATHOLIC AND PROTESTANT THEOLOGIANS MEET FOR DISCUSSIONS IN REGENSBURG, 1601; FROM A MINIATURE OF 1606

declared the head of the house of Habsburg in Rudolf's place. It seemed as if the Habsburg dominion would disintegrate into separate small territories, each controlled by its estates, thus completely paralyzing Austria's capacity for action. As Rudolf, the wearer of the imperial crown, was thus incapacitated, imperial institutions slowly ceased to function. The new state of affairs, arising from the divergent interpretations of the religious peace of Augsburg, could not be undone, and existing disputes could be solved neither in the diets of the circles nor by special commissions of the imperial chamber or of the imperial diet. The threat of the ban of the empire was unavailing. Help was not even forthcoming for war against the Turks. The religious groupings neutralized one another and hence were not able to oppose the Spanish interventions in the lower Rhineland and Westphalia. The strict Lutherans for conscience's sake refused to act against the emperor. The activist Protestants known as the "corresponding princes" were led by the elector palatine, who, as a Calvinist, was not even included in the religious peace. Maximilian, duke of Bavaria, who forced his Protestant subjects either to submit to the Roman Catholic Church or to emigrate, rose to be the leader of the Roman Catholic party.

The absolute paralysis of emperor and empire revived the old plan to form religious associations. Two such groupings soon opposed one another: the Protestant union led by the Palatinate (1608); and the Catholic league led by Maximilian of Bavaria (1609). The former looked for help to France, the latter to Spain, and both armed themselves, as France and Spain seemed about to begin a European war over the succession to Cleves-Jülich-Berg and its undecided religious allegiance (see JÜLICH). The assassination of Henry IV of France (1610) prevented the outbreak of war, and Matthias (emperor from 1612 to 1619) tried to ease the tension by his policy of "compositions," that is, of small concessions. Finally, in 1614, the duchy of Cleves-Jülich-Berg was peacefully partitioned, without imperial mediation, by the late duke's heirs: John Sigismund of Brandenburg, who had just turned Calvinist, and Wolfgang William of Palatinate Neuburg, who had just turned Catholic.

Ferdinand II and Bohemia.—Since neither Matthias nor his surviving brothers had legitimate heirs, it was planned that the Habsburg and the imperial succession should pass to their cousin Ferdinand of Styria, a pupil of the Jesuits and a convinced champion of the Counter-Reformation who had just recatholicized inner Austria by force. Philip III of Spain renounced his own claims and offered help to Ferdinand in exchange for the cession of the Austrian territories in Alsace and Ortenau, which would link the Spanish Netherlands with the Spanish Franche-Comté and the routes to Italy and thus extend the arc of encirclement round France. The Protestant Bohemian estates, however, objected strongly to recognizing Ferdinand as their future king, and in 1618, during a dispute over local grievances, some radical nobles in Prague threw the imperial governors out of the windows of the Hradcany palace. The Bohemians then prepared for war, and after the death of Matthias, proceeded to elect the Calvinist Frederick V, elector palatine, as king of Bohemia on Aug. 26, two days before the Habsburg candidate was elected emperor as Ferdinand II. Ferdinand had the support of Spain, Poland, the papacy and, especially, the Catholic league. Their combined armies defeated the isolated Frederick at the battle of the White Hill near Prague in Nov. 1620. Draconic measures destroyed Protestantism in Bohemia and the remaining Austrian territories, and the influence of the estates was abolished. The army of the Catholic league pursued the last partisans of the "winter king" on their flight to the Netherlands. Maximilian of Bavaria was granted the electoral dignity, which had been the condition of the help that he gave to the emperor.

The Thirty Years' War.—The Bohemian revolt and its suppression are conventionally regarded as the beginning of the complex European struggle designated as the Thirty Years' War (q.v.). The surprising resuscitation of the power of the German Habsburgs, the occupation by the Spaniards of the Rhenish Palatinate and the resumption of war between Spain and the United Provinces after a 12-year truce (1621) called the European powers into the arena, for they did not wish a revival of the empire of Charles V. Thus the warfare in Germany became a general European war. Christian IV of Denmark wished to acquire the bishoprics of Verden, Bremen, Osnabrück and Halberstadt, which were under Protestant administrators and surrounded by secular principalities. Against him Ferdinand put a new army into the field under the leadership of Albrecht von Wallenstein (q.v.). This soldier of fortune had acquired an enormous compact mass of lands in Bohemia by a rich marriage and augmented it from the confiscated estates of Protestant nobles. After his elevation to the dukedom of Friedland (1625) he turned this property into a huge armaments factory. Basing himself on this and holding to the principle that war must feed war, Wallenstein became independent of the imperial treasury and thus, at first, indispensable to Ferdinand. Johann Tserclaes, Graf von Tilly (q.v.), the general of the Catholic league, defeated Christian near Lutter (1626); Wallenstein occupied Jutland, Mecklenburg and Pomerania; only the city of Stralsund, supplied by sea from Denmark and Sweden, withstood siege (May–July 1628). Christian was forced to make peace at Lübeck (1629), regaining his lands but renouncing his alliances with the north German princes and his claims on the bishoprics in Lower Saxony.

Now at the height of his power, Ferdinand issued the Edict of Restitution (1629), enforcing again the "ecclesiastical reservation," the most debated of all the provisions of the religious peace of 1555, and ordering all bishoprics and abbeys secularized since 1552 to be restored to the Roman Catholic faith. This edict showed the emperor determined to revolutionize all existing political conditions: the independent and aggressive spirit that he revealed provoked even the opposition of the Catholic league and especially that of Maximilian of Bavaria. At a meeting at Regensburg (1630) the electors, backed diplomatically by France, forced Ferdinand to dismiss Wallenstein (whom he had made duke of Mecklenburg and thus a prince of the empire), to reduce the imperial army and to accept the electors' control of foreign and military policy. Wallenstein's dismissal made it easier for the Swedish king Gustavus II Adolphus to decide to land in Pomerania. The king of Sweden was brought to this decision by Sweden's struggle for the *dominium maris Baltici* (supremacy in the Baltic sea), for which he had fought Russia, Livonia and Poland and which was endangered by the successes of the imperial army. It was also motivated by his desire, based on his deep religious convictions, to liberate the north German Protestants and to obtain the large subsidies offered by France. Of the Protestant states only Hesse-Kassel voluntarily joined the Swedish king; Saxony was forced into an alliance because of counterpressure from Vienna. The princes feared for their freedom and dreaded the emperor's revenge. In 1631, in the first of the battles of Breitenfeld, Gustavus Adolphus defeated Tilly, who had taken Magdeburg: the victory was so complete that the Catholic party collapsed completely in northern Germany, the Catholic league dissolved itself, Munich was occupied and even Vienna appeared to be falling prey to the Swedes.

In this danger Ferdinand asked Wallenstein to recruit another army and made him its generalissimo. Wallenstein proceeded very cautiously, since he wanted both to demonstrate his indispensability and to avoid hazarding his new army. Gustavus Adolphus restored Protestantism in large areas of Germany, but fell mortally wounded in the battle of Lützen (1632). The Swedes however, under the chancellor Axel Oxenstierna, continued the war, united in the League of Heilbronn and again threatened the Austrian hereditary lands after the conquest of Regensburg. The Vienna court began to distrust Wallenstein because of his hesitant strategy. Indeed, since his dismissal, Wallenstein was torn between thoughts of a general pacification, the need for revenge and more egotistic aims. He negotiated with Saxony and Sweden without, however, following a clear line of policy. Suspected of high treason, he was murdered with Ferdinand's consent by some of his officers (1634). The imperial army, still intact, and the newly arrived Spanish auxiliary troops defeated the Swedes at Nördlingen and again occupied southern Germany to the Rhine. Peace was made at Prague between the emperor and Saxony

(1635), and most German states joined this in course of time. The peace of Prague fixed the religious divisions as they had existed in 1627 (an arrangement originally limited to 40 years and not applicable to Calvinists); renounced the Edict of Restitution; and gave the emperor the supreme command over a new imperial army to be provided by the estates and to be used against the foreign powers.

Despite this renewed effort German strength did not suffice to enforce peace. War ravaged the country for another 13 years; it was no longer fought for German questions but to divide the spoils between Sweden and France. After the victory of the French crown over the malcontent nobility and the Huguenots alike, the cardinal duc de Richelieu declared war against the Spanish world power on all fronts in 1635, regardless of doctrinal considerations but simply following the dictates of French reason of state. France gained footholds in Savoy, Mantua and Parma and thus controlled Spanish Milan and the passes over the Alps into southern Germany. The United Provinces and those states of the empire which stood aside from the war were strengthened by subsidy treaties. Along the western frontier of Germany, Richelieu occupied Lorraine and pushed his occupation troops through Alsace to the Rhine. In order to keep the Swedish army in the German theatre of war, he mediated a prolongation of the Swedish-Polish truce for another 26 years and granted annual subsidies for the Swedish armies fighting in the empire. There were meetings of the electors and of the diet, but neither the emperor nor the estates were able to bring about a general pacification. One after another made separate treaties with the foreign powers.

The Peace of Westphalia (1648).—Ferdinand II was succeeded by his son Ferdinand III, emperor from 1637 to 1657. Nine years after his accession, with Spain's power sapped by the revolts in Catalonia and Portugal (1640), the enemies of the house of Habsburg won the upper hand in Germany. In 1648 the French had crossed Bavaria and reached the Inn river and the Swedes were again attacking Prague when the news of the peace of Westphalia at last arrived.

Earlier peace feelers had been in vain, but from 1644 onward serious negotiations had been taking place among the interested powers. First Spain concluded a separate peace with the United Provinces of the Netherlands, whose sovereignty was recognized (though the Franco-Spanish war was to go on for 11 more years, till the peace of the Pyrenees in 1659). The conditions offered by the emperor and the states of the empire to the Swedes at Osnabrück and to the French at Münster were accepted, and peace was signed in Oct. 1648: in addition to 5,000,000 thalers to pay off their troops, the Swedes obtained the archbishopric of Bremen, the bishopric of Verden, the town of Wismar and western Pomerania; the French obtained the Habsburg rights in Alsace and the Lorraine bishoprics of Metz, Toul and Verdun, together with the fortress of Breisach and the right to occupy the fortress of Philippsburg. The Swiss and the Dutch, now sovereign powers, severed all links with the empire.

Within the empire, Bavaria retained the electoral dignity and the Upper Palatinate; the elector of Brandenburg received the bishoprics of Kammin, Halberstadt and Minden, with the reversion to that of Magdeburg, in compensation for what he had had to cede to Sweden; and the dukes of Mecklenburg received the

bishoprics of Ratzeburg and Schwerin, likewise in compensation. Otherwise the territorial *status quo* of 1618 was restored. The religious *status quo* of 1624 was acknowledged, except for the Austrian hereditary lands and Bavaria, and Calvinism was recognized as one of the creeds of the empire. Constitutionally, the emperor's power was considerably reduced in favour of the estates or members of the empire, even in matters of foreign policy. To prevent majority decisions in denominational disputes, the estates were divided between a *Corpus Evangelicorum* or Protestant group and a *Corpus Catholicorum*, both of which had to be in agreement if a decision was to be valid for the empire as a whole. Finally, the fact that France and Sweden were guarantors of the peace laid Germany open to foreign intervention.

(W. P. F.)

H. THE EMPIRE IN DECAY, 1648–1721

Emperor and Empire After 1648.—After the peace of Westphalia, the expression emperor and empire (*Kaiser und Reich*) ceased to mean the whole body politic with its monarchical head but emphasized the contrast between the emperor, who had no power in the empire, and the empire, which had little use for the emperor. Free to form associations among themselves or with foreign princes (provided that they were not directed against empire or emperor), the rulers of the member states had become nearly fully sovereign and independent in international law. The emperor was reduced to the rank of an honorary president of an aristocratic republic; he was unable either to make laws or to levy taxes for the *Reich* without the consent of the imperial diet or *Reichstag*. On the other hand, the territorial diets declined nearly everywhere—with the special exceptions of Mecklenburg and Württemberg, where the dukes were almost powerless. Therefore the territorial princes could now build up their military power and finances without interference from above or below and so consolidate the basis not only for increasing independence but also for absolute government within their own territories.

The *Reichstag*, which from 1663 was to be permanently established at Regensburg, was composed of three chambers: the college of electors (*Kurfürstenkollegium*); the council of, princes of the empire (*Reichsfürstenkollegium*); and the college of imperial cities (*Reichsstädtekollegium*). The electors were the archbishops of Mainz, Cologne and Trier, the king of Bohemia, the dukes of Saxony and Bavaria, the margrave of Brandenburg and the count

BANQUET IN NÜRNBERG CELEBRATING THE PEACE OF WESTPHALIA, 1648:
ENGRAVING BY W. KILIAN

palatine (*Pfalzgraf*) of the Rhine, with a ninth, Hanover, added in 1692 (recognized by the *Reichstag* as late as 1708). The number of entities represented in the council of princes is less easy to state because of recurring divisions within dynasties and reunions through inheritance, as well as the varying readiness of the *Reichstag* to admit transfers or new creations. The estimate therefore varies between 170 and 200 secular principalities and countships in addition to about 50 ecclesiastical principalities (archbishoprics, bishoprics, abbeys and orders of knighthood). The 59 greater princes, however, had each a separate vote in the council (*Viril-stimme*), while the lesser counts of the empire voted collectively through representatives of the four "benches" or colleges among which they were grouped (*Kuriatstimme*). Similarly, 35 eccle-siastical princes had *Virilstimmen*, while the remaining abbeys, etc., were grouped in two *Kurien*. The imperial cities (*q.v.*) had two

votes, one for the 14 cities of the "Rhenish bench" and one for the 37 of the "Swabian bench"; their right to a casting vote was disputed. There were thus about 300 entities with practically sovereign rights and the quality of *Reichsstandschaft*; *i.e.*, that of being represented in the *Reichstag* as an estate of the empire. In addition to these quasi sovereignties there were nearly 1,500 other minor lordships which, without having *Reichsstandschaft*, enjoyed *Reichsunmittelbarkeit*, or "immediate" dependence on the *Reich*, with no suzerain other than the emperor.

Besides the *Reichstag*, there were three other general organs for the empire. The *Reichskammergericht* or imperial chamber (*q.v.*), which sat at Speyer and later at Wetzlar, was the supreme judicial body, but it was hampered in its effectiveness by the pro-lixity of its procedure (61,233 suits were found to be awaiting judgment in 1772) and was moreover in perpetual rivalry with the *Reichshofrat* or aulic council (*q.v.*) in Vienna. In Vienna also was the *Reichskanzlei* or imperial chancery, which dealt with all ques-tions of rights, privileges, pardons, etc., depending on the emperor. When the Austrian court chancery was detached from it in 1620, the imperial chancery had faded into the background, but at the end of the 17th century it regained a certain importance as the great European wars strengthened the bond between emperor and *Reich*. Under Friedrich Karl, Graf von Schönborn, as vice-chancellor (1705–34), this revival was especially marked.

The Territorial Powers in the 17th Century.—The greatest of the secular powers in the *Reich* was the house of Habsburg, which ruled over a vast area in the southeast, comprising Bohemia, Austria, Styria, Carinthia, Carniola, Istria, Trieste and Tirol and held also numerous hereditary possessions in southern Swabia ex-tending to the banks of the Rhine (Breisgau). These lands, how-ever, had from time to time been distributed among various branches of the house and were not finally reunited until 1665 (after the extinction of the Tirolese branch). Moreover, the cen-tral authority for the Habsburg possessions, which Maximilian I had tried to set up, exercised little control, as many of the com-ponent territories kept their own administrations and diets. (*See* AUSTRIA, EMPIRE OF; HABSBURG.) The kingdom of Hungary was a Habsburg territory outside the *Reich*.

From the middle of the 17th century the house of Hohenzollern (*q.v.*) was outpacing the houses of Wittelsbach and Wettin in the struggle for the second place in the *Reich*. The Hohenzollern

margraves of Brandenburg had inherited Cleves in western Ger-many, together with Mark and Ravensberg in Westphalia, in 1614 and the duchy of Prussia, which was a Polish fief outside the *Reich*, in 1618; and had secured eastern Pomerania, as well as the former bishoprics of Kammin, Minden and Halberstadt, together with the reversion to Magdeburg, in 1648. Next, in the course of the so-called First Northern War (1655–60), Poland under the treaty of Wehlau (1657; confirmed by the peace of Oliva in 1660) renounced suzerainty over the duchy of Prussia, which thus became sovereign. When Prussia was raised to the rank of kingdom in 1701, the elec-tor of Brandenburg thus became king of a realm independent of the *Reich*, just as the head of the Habsburgs was in respect of Hungary. The individual districts under Hohenzollern rule, how-ever, maintained their own institutions to a considerable extent. (*See* BRANDENBURG; PRUSSIA.)

The house of Wettin (*q.v.*) was divided into so many branches that its head, the elector of Saxony, ruled only a portion of its lands. The same was true of the house of Wittelsbach (*q.v.*); its largest and most compact territory was Bavaria, whereas its scat-tered lands in the Palatinate were distributed among junior branches of the family. The house of Welf (*q.v.*), which had the leading role in northwestern Germany, also divided its lands in Brunswick and Hanover between various branches (seven or some-times even more); and the house of Hesse was likewise divided. In the extreme southwest the house of Zähringen, with the mar-graviate of Baden, and the house of Württemberg were the most important dynasties.

Most of these great princes in the course of the 17th and 18th centuries succeeded in reducing the old-established powers of the diets in their territories, though they did not dare to suppress them outright. Government and justice, however, in the hands of paid officials, were far more efficiently administered in the greater principalities than they were in the lesser ones. The lesser secular princes ruled their subjects patriarchally, but employed quan-tities of officials out of all proportion to the size of their miniature territories and maintained sumptuous courts, for the upkeep of which they were ever preoccupied with devising new taxation or obtaining "pensions" from foreign monarchs, chiefly France. The ecclesiastical princes in general governed no better than the secular ones, since their lack of legitimate issue made them sometimes careless of the future well-being of their countries. Elected by the chapter with which he was to share the administration and which was composed largely of younger sons of the local nobility, a bishop or abbot would often use his position to further the in-terests of his family by settling his brothers, cousins and nephews on church property or bringing them into the chapters.

Some of the imperial cities were towns of major importance with a long-standing commerce, such as Lübeck, Hamburg, Bremen, Nürnberg, Augsburg, Ulm, Frankfurt am Main and Strasbourg. The majority, however, were little country towns in southwestern Germany, with 3,000 inhabitants or less, which had long ago lost any significance. Overshadowed by the capitals rising round the princely residences, the imperial cities were for the most part gov-erned by a few patrician families who monopolized all positions of influence and profit and used them to their personal advantage.

Finally, there were the dominions of the "immediate" knights of the empire (not to be confused with the knights of orders, whose master was an ecclesiastical prince), nearly all in southwestern Germany. These knights were no more than large landowners who exercised sovereign rights over their manor and perhaps some ad-jacent village.

Leopold I and the French and Turkish Wars to 1699.—Ferdinand III, emperor from 1637, had secured the election of his eldest son Ferdinand as king of the Romans, or successor designate to the emperor, in 1653; but the young king had died in 1654, and the emperor died in April 1657, before securing the election of his second son, Leopold I, as king of the Romans. After 15 months' interregnum Leopold was elected emperor (July 1658), but not be-fore he had signed a capitulation whereby the emperor's rights were still further reduced. Leopold had originally been destined for the church, and his deeply religious nature would have justified such a calling. When he came to rule he always protected the interests of the church and completed the work of the Counter-Reformation. The high moral tone of his life and conduct gave an example to others. Peaceful by nature, he had to make almost continual war on several fronts, which again and again interrupted the economic reconstruction of his territories. He was interested in the arts and sciences (the theatre, music, political science), though his reign did not witness such magnificent works as did that of his cousin Louis XIV of France. His greatest fault was his lack of energy and of decisiveness—of which even his spiritual advisers (Emmerich Sinelli and Marco d'Aviano) complained. Yet his firm conviction that he was an instrument of the divine will endowed him with an almost unshakable spiritual equanimity which saved him in the extremely critical situations so frequent during his reign. Though benevolent and even weak by nature, Leopold was unyielding on all matters involving either the interest of the church or his own sovereign rights.

In the first decade after the peace of Westphalia, the primary concern of all the estates was the maintenance of peace. As the war between France and Spain lasted until 1659 and as grave issues were arising in the north and in the east, Germany could easily have been involved again in a general war. As no one believed in the ability of the emperor to safeguard the empire from this danger, there grew up a network of alliances between the different territories for mutual defense. The elector of Mainz, Johann Philipp von Schönborn, succeeded in uniting the most important Catholic and Protestant princes in a great defensive alliance. This first *Rheinbund* or Confederation of the Rhine was signed in Aug. 1658, for three years, and had for its object the full execution of the peace of Westphalia, the prevention of foreign wars and the defense of its members' own territories; but in fact into an understanding with Poland and the emperor. This warfare, however, was waged for the most part outside the territory of the empire. Germany was far more deeply disturbed by the course of events on its western frontier.

During the so-called First Northern War (1655-60), the emperor, in the Catholic interest, supported the Catholic king of Poland, John Casimir; and the elector of Brandenburg, Frederick William, who at the outset had supported Sweden, later entered the alliance, which the emperor regarded as directed against France. It was frequently renewed and lasted until 1667.

The continuing Spanish possession of the southern Netherlands and of Franche-Comté was an obstacle to the traditional French policy of advancing the frontier into Flanders and toward the Rhine, which Louis XIV was determined to pursue. After his War of Devolution (1667-68) against Spain had been brought to an abrupt end because of intervention by the triple alliance of England, Sweden and the Dutch, Louis decided that the Dutch would have to be crushed. When he induced the archbishop of Cologne (Maximilian Henry of Bavaria) and the bishop of Münster (Bernhard von Galen) to co-operate with his invasion of the United Provinces, the neighbouring states, fearing that they would be involved in the war, invoked the assistance of the emperor and the empire. Moreover, Louis XIV had, without any legal grounds, driven the duke of Lorraine, Charles IV, who was a prince of the empire, out of his duchy. The empire thus had good cause to intervene. (*See* DUTCH WARS.)

Yet Leopold hesitated to take any action against Louis XIV. Foreseeing the extinction of the Spanish branch of the Habsburgs, his main policy was to assure its succession for his own branch. This would require the French king's acquiescence, for which Louis let him hope, so that Leopold did not feel himself at liberty to oppose him. Hence the Dutch found their sole support in the elector of Brandenburg, Frederick William, who had grown up in Holland and whose first wife had been a princess of Orange. By cutting the dikes and flooding their country the Dutch were able to avert the French attack in 1672. At the urgent request of the estates, Leopold determined to send an army, under Raimund Montecuccoli, for the defense of the imperial frontier on the Rhine, but with instructions to maintain the defensive. Finally, having allied himself with Spain, the emperor secured the declaration of war by the *Reich* against France in 1674.

The war was chiefly waged in the Austrian Netherlands and on the Rhine. The Swedes, in alliance with Louis, invaded Brandenburg from Pomerania to restrain Frederick William, who was participating in person in the war against France. At the same time Louis entered into relations with Poland, with Turkey, and also with the Hungarians, who were discontented with Habsburg rule. The emperor then found himself threatened in the rear. By his victory at Fehrbellin on June 28, 1675, Frederick William drove the Swedes out of his territory and occupied nearly the whole of Swedish Pomerania. The French on the other hand were for the most part victorious on the western front, and eventually Louis was able to induce first the Dutch and then Spain to conclude a separate peace (1678). When the emperor could no longer hope to win anything by continuing the war, he acceded to the peace of Nijmegen in Feb. 1679. The elector of Brandenburg, who was required by the peace to give up his new acquisitions in Pomerania, was unwilling to do so and fought on forlornly till the following year, when he too had to conclude peace.

Convinced by these experiences that the *Reich* was too weak to withstand encroachments on its territory, Louis next proceeded to set up, at Metz, at Breisach and at Besançon, the so-called "chambers of reunion" for the purpose of determining what lands had at any former time belonged to districts already ceded to him. On the strength of these investigations, he declared that the countship of Mömpelgard (Montbéliard), the whole of Alsace and certain districts in the Palatinate and in the electorate of Trier belonged by right to France. French armies occupied the territories; and the imperial city of Strasbourg was seized on Sept. 28, 1681, and at once erected into a powerful French fortress. The emperor and the *Reichstag* contented themselves with ineffectual protests.

The emperor's failure to safeguard the integrity of the *Reich* at this crisis is partly to be explained by his preoccupation with the dangers threatening his own territories. The Turks in Hungary were planning an invasion of Austria; and in the spring of 1683 they appeared with a powerful army before the walls of Vienna. Charles V, duke of Lorraine, and Ernst Rüdiger, Graf von Starhemberg, managed however to hold off the attack; and finally John Sobieski of Poland and the electors Maximilian Emanuel of Bavaria and John George III of Saxony arrived with an army to defeat the Turks and free the city.

When Louis XIV sought to bring the Palatinate within his grasp, claiming it as the inheritance of Elizabeth Charlotte, the wife of his brother Philippe, duc d'Orléans, war once more broke out in the west. French armies invaded the Palatinate, and the emperor allied himself with England and the Dutch. The War of the Grand Alliance inflicted severe losses on the French but did not result in any decisive victory (*see* GRAND ALLIANCE, WAR OF THE). Once more Louis was able to sow dissension among his enemies and to isolate Germany, and the emperor had to conclude the peace of Rijswijk in 1697, with but small gain to himself. Louis restored Lorraine to the rightful duke, Leopold Joseph, and abandoned his claims to the Palatinate and to the districts outside Alsace that had been declared to have once formed part of it; but he retained the whole of Alsace and also Strasbourg.

Meanwhile the war between the emperor and the Turks continued in the east; two-thirds of Hungary remained in Turkish hands. Prince Eugene of Savoy, in command of the Austrian army, won a decisive victory at Zenta (Aug. 29, 1697), invaded Serbia and Bosnia and forced the Turks to conclude the peace of Carlowitz on Jan. 26, 1699. By this peace all Hungary except the banat of Temesvar (modern Timişoara) was restored to the emperor. It was the conquest of Hungary that paved the way to the later Habsburg monarchy and its position as a great power.

The War of the Spanish Succession (1700-14).—The last Habsburg king of Spain, Charles II, died childless on Nov. 1, 1700. The question of succession, which had already occupied the European diplomats for decades, had now to be settled. Both Leopold I and Louis XIV were the sons of Spanish Habsburg infantas and had also both been married to infantas; but whereas at the time of Leopold's marriage (his first, to the infanta Margarita Teresa) it had been agreed that her children should inherit Spain if the Spanish male line should die out, at the time of the French marriages the infantas concerned had renounced their rights to Spain, Louis, however, argued that these renunciations were invalidated because the infantas' dowries had not been paid in full; and he had tried to come to terms with Leopold for a partition of the Spanish inheritance. Charles II of Spain, meanwhile, had in 1698 designated as his heir the child Joseph Ferdinand, electoral prince of Bavaria, son of Leopold's daughter Maria Antonia by the elector of Bavaria, Maximilian II Emanuel; but Joseph Ferdinand died in 1699. Finally, Charles, under pressure from the French party in Spain, drew up a second will in favour of Philippe, duc d'Anjou, one of Louis XIV's grandsons. When Louis, on Charles II's death, recognized this grandson as Philip V of Spain, the War of the Spanish Succession broke out (see SPANISH SUCCESSION, WAR OF THE).

Leopold maintained the right to the Spanish inheritance of the archduke Charles, the younger son not of his first marriage but of his third (to Eleanor of Palatinate Neuburg), yet still the grandson of Leopold's Spanish mother. Great Britain and the Dutch, led by Louis XIV's old enemy William III of Orange, stadholder of the Netherlands and from 1689 also king of England, supported the archduke's claim, while the French had the help of the Hungarians, of the English Jacobites and of a number of German princes, chief of whom was Maximilian Emanuel of Bavaria. In the first years of the war the advantage lay with the French, who might have struck a deadly blow at Austria by a concerted attack from the Rhine and Italy. This danger was averted by the great Anglo-Austrian victory in the battle of Blenheim (q.v.) on Aug. 13, 1704. Bavaria was occupied by the imperial troops, and Maximilian Emanuel fled to Brussels.

Leopold I died in May 1705. His eldest son, Joseph I, who succeeded him as emperor (1705-11), had a character quite different from his father's: he was eager for fame and glory and the renewal of the imperial idea. He aimed at regaining the Spanish territories in Italy, especially in Lombardy; and obsolete imperial rights were refurbished to supply a legal basis to these ambitions. From this there followed a long quarrel with the papacy, since the lines of communication between southern and northern Italy led across the papal states.

The war against France was pursued with great successes throughout the reign. The archduke Charles landed in Catalonia and by the summer of 1706 was in Madrid. After French defeats in the Netherlands and in Italy, Louis XIV in 1708 expressed his readiness to renounce on behalf of his grandson all claims to the Spanish throne and to agree to a restoration of the Franco-German frontier on the line laid down in the peace of Westphalia in 1648, which would have meant restoring Strasbourg. The allies, however, demanded that French troops should help them to expel Philip V from Spain; and when Louis refused this, they broke off negotiations. Likewise, after the battle of Malplaquet (1709), when Louis even offered to give up his acquisitions in Alsace and the three bishoprics, Metz, Toul and Verdun, together with money to be used for driving Philip V out of Spain, the allies stood by their former demands, so that negotiations once more broke down.

The death of the emperor Joseph I (April 1711) changed the situation. As he left no son, his younger brother the archduke succeeded him as the emperor Charles VI (1711-40). Now, if Austria, the empire and the Spanish inheritance were all to be united under one ruler there was danger that such a disproportionate concentration of power would threaten the European balance of power more seriously than the establishment of a French dynasty in Spain; and neither England nor the Dutch now wished to prosecute the war for such an object. A peace congress met at Utrecht in 1712 and the chief treaties were signed in 1713. These awarded only a portion of Lombardy, the Neapolitan mainland and the former Spanish Netherlands to Charles VI; and no mention was made of a restoration of the old Franco-German frontier. Meanwhile the emperor and the Reich were still at war with France, but when Landau and Freiburg im Breisgau had been lost they were forced in the treaties of Rastatt and Baden (March and September 1714) to assent to the terms of Utrecht. The frontiers of the German Reich remained as laid down in the treaty of Rijswijk; the elector of Bavaria recovered his territories; and the prospect of winning back the old German territories in the southwest had completely vanished. Thus the War of the Spanish Succession had overthrown the supremacy enjoyed by France in Europe in the early years of Louis XIV's reign without yielding any profit to Germany.

The Northern War (1700-21).—At the same time another long-standing quarrel was being fought out in the north and the east. In 1697 the elector Frederick Augustus I of Saxony, after conversion to Catholicism, had been elected king of Poland as Augustus II. In alliance with Denmark and with the Russian tsar Peter the Great, he began a war against Charles XII of Sweden in the summer of 1700, with the object of breaking the power that the Swedes had been exercising in the Baltic area since the Thirty Years' War. By the spring of 1706, however, Charles XII was in possession of the greater part of Poland and, in agreement with a section of the Polish nobility, had set up Stanislaw Leszczynski as king in opposition to Frederick Augustus. He then marched through Silesia into his enemy's German territories, occupied a great part of Saxony and established his headquarters during the winter of 1706-07 in Altranstädt near Leipzig. But the peace which Frederick Augustus had to sign, renouncing the Polish throne, did not long remain in force. When Peter the Great threatened to occupy Poland, Charles marched against him and was completely defeated at Poltava (1709). The Swedes were driven from Poland, and their allied enemies invaded Swedish territory on all sides. The elector Frederick III of Brandenburg, who with the emperor Leopold I's consent had assumed the title of king in Prussia as Frederick I, in 1701, also took part in the attack. Pomerania, Bremen and Verden, Sweden's possessions in Germany, were seized.

After Charles XII's death (1718), the conclusion of peace was possible. Sweden had to surrender Bremen and Verden to Hanover (1719) and western Pomerania south of the Peene to Prussia (peace of Stockholm, 1720). Of greater importance for future Russo-German relations, however, was the peace of Nystad (1721), whereby Sweden ceded Estonia, Livonia and Ingria to the tsar, thus giving Russia a firm foothold on the shores of the Baltic and thereby a position that became more and more threatening to Germany. Sweden meanwhile retained the northern part of western Pomerania and Rügen. (See NORTHERN WAR.)

Imperial authority in Germany, meanwhile, was based both on the imperial constitution and on the territorial power of the emperor and his house; and as the various Austrian lands grew into a political organism the interests of the Reich and the interests of the house of Austria diverged more and more. This is clearly visible in the disputes between the aulic chancery led by Ludwig Philipp, Graf von Sinzendorf, and the imperial chancery under Friedrich Karl, Graf von Schönborn, nephew of the archbishop of Mainz, Lothar Franz von Schönborn. The smaller secular and ecclesiastical states of the Reich were concerned to retain and to strengthen imperial power, but the larger states, especially Hanover and Brandenburg, which wanted to expand, were opposed to this. Four of the most powerful electors were now sovereign rulers: the elector of Brandenburg was king in Prussia, the elector of Hanover king of Great Britain, the elector of Saxony king of Poland and the emperor himself king of Hungary. Moreover, the kings of Denmark and of Sweden were also princes of the empire, the greater Whereas the smaller states regarded the imperial power as the only guarantee of their "liberty" against aggression, the greater

I. THE AUSTRO-PRUSSIAN CONFLICTS IN THE 18TH CENTURY

Charles VI and the Pragmatic Sanction.—From his early youth the emperor Charles VI had been regarded by the emperor Leopold as a future king of Spain and had been brought up in the spirit of Spanish Jesuitism. In his reign (1711-40) Austrian policy became more and more obviously inspired by the desire to strengthen Habsburg influence in Italy and also to win more territory along the lower reaches of the Danube. In this latter aim he was at first successful, through the war that he entered in 1716 in support of Venice against the Turks. By the peace of Passarowitz (1718), thanks to Prince Eugene's victories, Austria obtained the Banat, Little Walachia, northern Serbia (with Belgrade) and part of Bosnia.

states regarded that power as a danger to their own "liberty," fearing that the emperor might erect a "despotic" or truly monarchical regime. Whenever the interests of the more powerful states were involved the emperor found few means at his disposal to render effective legal and constitutional decisions. Indeed the evolution of the territorial states undermined the imperial constitution and the feeling for the unity of the *Reich*. There was no common political history for Germany in this period, though Germany's destiny as a whole was to be deeply influenced by international affairs.

When Charles had gone to Spain to enter into his inheritance there, a secret family compact had been made to regulate the succession, the *Pactum Mutuae Successionis* (1703). After Spain had been lost and Charles had succeeded to Austria, it became necessary to adapt the precedence of the heirs and the order of their succession to the changed circumstances if Austria was to remain a unitary state (*Monarchia Austriaca*) and to be saved from partition among the various claimants. This was done not only in the interest of Austria and of the dynasty but also in that of Germany and indeed of Europe, since the European balance of power depended on the survival of the undivided Austrian state. Charles spared no effort to ensure that after his death his wishes respecting the succession would be carried out. These wishes he embodied in a special law, the Pragmatic Sanction, for which he secured the approval of the diets in all his territories. (See AUSTRIA, EMPIRE OF.)

Charles did not consider this security enough: he sought to have the Pragmatic Sanction recognized by the great powers and approved by the *Reichstag*. The approval of the *Reichstag* was especially difficult to obtain because two of the most important princes in Germany, the future electors Frederick Augustus II of Saxony and Charles Albert of Bavaria, had, in 1719 and 1722 respectively, married the emperor Joseph I's daughters and so had an immediate personal interest in frustrating the execution of Charles VI's wishes. In these circumstances, the emperor particularly desired Prussia's consent to his plan. Frederick William I of Prussia was quite willing to fall in with the emperor's wishes but demanded in return that the emperor should help him to pursue his claim to part of the inheritance of the duchies of Jülich and Berg on the lower Rhine. The emperor appeared to assent to this and so secured Frederick William's agreement to the Pragmatic Sanction by the treaty of Berlin (Dec. 23, 1728). Soon, however, it became clear that the emperor had made contrary promises to the rival claimants to Jülich and Berg. This estranged Prussia from Austria, and Frederick William allied himself with the emperor's enemies.

The War of the Polish Succession (1733-35).—In 1733 Augustus II of Poland (that is, Frederick Augustus I of Saxony) died. While Austria and Russia declared themselves in favour of

BY COURTESY OF THE STAATLICHE GEMÄLDE-GALERIE, DRESDEN; PHOTOGRAPH, DEUTSCHE FOTOTHEK DRESDEN

ELECTOR FREDERICK AUGUSTUS I OF SAXONY AND KING FREDERICK WILLIAM I OF PRUSSIA: PAINTING BY LOUIS SILVESTRE, 1730

the succession of his son Augustus III (Frederick Augustus II), a number of Polish nobles, who were in relations with France, chose Augustus II's former opponent, Stanislaw Leszczynski, whose daughter was married to the young French king, Louis XV. When the War of the Polish Succession (*q.v.*) broke out, the French used the opportunity to acquire at last the long-disputed duchy of Lorraine. The Spanish Bourbons also entered the war in order to realize their claims to the Italian duchies of Parma and Piacenza. Though the *Reich* as a whole took the emperor's side, the Wittelsbach rulers of Bavaria, the Palatinate and Cologne refused to do so. Old and ill, Prince Eugene of Savoy could only hold the defensive with a small army; and he advised the emperor to make peace. As the French minister, Cardinal Fleury, also wanted peace, the preliminary agreements of 1735 became the basis of the final treaty of Vienna (1738). The emperor had to abandon Sicily and Naples, which were placed under the rule of one of the Spanish princes, Don Carlos, though the duchies of Parma and Piacenza were ceded to Austria. Of special significance to Germany was the emperor's consent to the cession of Lorraine, which was made over to Stanislaw Leszczynski as compensation for his renunciation of the Polish crown but was to revert to France after his death. The reigning duke of Lorraine, Francis Stephen, who was married to Charles VI's heiress Maria Theresa, was compensated with the grand duchy of Tuscany. France, in return, recognized the Pragmatic Sanction—with the important reservation that it only did so insofar as it did not conflict with established third-party rights.

In the closing years of his life, from 1737, Charles VI undertook a new war against Turkey, this time in support of his Russian ally. The war ended disastrously for him. By the peace of Belgrade (1739), he had to restore a great part of the conquests won in his war of 1716-18, and a frontier was laid down for Serbia and Walachia that was to remain essentially the same until the outbreak of World War I.

The War of the Austrian Succession (1740-48).—When Charles VI died on Oct. 20, 1740, his daughter Maria Theresa at once assumed the government of the countries belonging to the house of Habsburg. The interests of power politics, however, proved stronger than the treaties by which her father had sought to secure the succession for her. Though Germany and even Europe required that the integrity of her inheritance should be maintained, the electors Frederick Augustus II of Saxony (Augustus III of Poland) and Charles Albert of Bavaria protested against her accession and were supported by the French, who desired to see a partition of the Austrian territories; and a still more pressing danger threatened Maria Theresa when the new Prussian king joined her opponents. Frederick II the Great of Prussia at first offered Maria Theresa his help against her enemies if she would cede to him a part of Silesia to which Prussia had some claim by virtue of old dynastic agreements. When she rejected his proposal, he determined to occupy the disputed Silesia territory by force.

Frederick crossed the Silesian frontier in Dec. 1740, advanced as far as Breslau and defeated an advancing Austrian army near Mollwitz in April 1741. At the same time the Bavarians, supported by a French army, advanced as far as Linz and even seized Prague with the help of the Saxons. Next the German electors, under French and Prussian influence, elected as emperor not Maria Theresa's husband, Francis Stephen, but the elector Charles Albert

ULLSTEIN BILDERDIENST

"TABAKSKOLLEGIUM" ("TOBACCO CLUB") OF KING FREDERICK WILLIAM I OF PRUSSIA: CONTEMPORARY PAINTING BY AN UNKNOWN ARTIST

of Bavaria (Jan. 24, 1742), who assumed the name of Charles VII. When Frederick, having occupied all Silesia and invaded Moravia, won the battle of Chotusitz against an Austrian army, Maria Theresa thought it prudent to open negotiations—though her troops had regained Linz and even invaded Bavaria. Great Britain, also at war with France over colonial questions, acted as intermediary and thus the peace of Breslau (June 11, 1742) was concluded between Austria and Prussia. Austria ceded the greater part of Silesia along with the countship of Glatz to Prussia and retained only the principalities of Troppau and Teschen. In return Frederick promised his neutrality. The First Silesian War, which ended with this peace, established the military reputation of Frederick the Great. It was the first armed contest between the two greatest German states that had developed out of the old *Reich*—states which had long regarded each other with distrust and jealousy.

The struggle for the inheritance of Charles VI continued. The Austrian army captured Prague, freed Bohemia from the invaders and even captured Munich, the Bavarian capital. A British army, led by George II in person, defeated the French at Dettingen and advanced from Hanover as far as the Rhine. Then, when the Austrians, led by Prince Charles of Lorraine, were advancing from southern Germany with the intention of crossing the Rhine, Frederick the Great decided to intervene again, lest Maria Theresa, after a complete victory over her other enemies, should try to wrest back Silesia. Having signed a new alliance with France, he invaded Bohemia in Aug. 1744 but had to withdraw because the expected simultaneous advance of the French army did not take place. Then Charles VII died (Jan. 20, 1745), and his son, the elector Maximilian III Joseph of Bavaria, at once made peace with Maria Theresa, recovering his ancestral domains in return for the renunciation of all his claims to the Austrian inheritance. Frederick Augustus II of Saxony had already abandoned his claims and made peace with Austria, and, as the French were fully occupied in Flanders, Frederick found himself alone opposed to the main force of Austria. Strengthened by Saxon troops, the Austrians attacked Silesia but were defeated near Hohenfriedeberg on June 4, 1745. Once more Frederick invaded Bohemia, and by the end of the year a great part of Saxony was in his possession. On Dec. 15, his chief general, Leopold of Anhalt-Dessau, won a fresh victory over the Austrians and Saxons at Kesselsdorf, near Dresden.

The majority of the electors had in the meantime, at Frankfurt am Main, elected Francis Stephen of Lorraine as emperor. As Francis I he was nominal head of the *Reich* from 1745 to 1765. Maria Theresa, who now saw that it would not be so easy to retake Silesia and who laid great stress on the recognition of her husband as emperor by Frederick, was ready to reopen negotiations. On Dec. 25, 1745, the Second Silesian War was brought to a close by the peace of Dresden, by which Frederick retained Silesia and recognized Francis I as emperor.

The war against France lasted nearly three years more, but French victories on land were more than offset by the British victories at sea. Finally, by the peace of Aix-la-Chapelle (1748), Maria Theresa was recognized as her father's sole heiress, but gave certain frontier districts in Lombardy to Savoy and the duchy of Parma to the Spanish prince Philip. Maria Theresa had to come to terms mainly because Great Britain wanted to end the war. The peace negotiations were conducted by Wenzel Anton von Kaunitz, who represented her as queen of Bohemia and Hungary. She had made her husband Francis Stephen coruler in her hereditary Austrian lands. (*See* AUSTRIAN SUCCESSION, WAR OF THE.)

The Seven Years' War (1756-63).—Though peace was thus outwardly restored, tension between Austria and Prussia remained, since Maria Theresa had never abandoned her hopes of regaining Silesia. These hopes were shared by her chief minister, Kaunitz (now prince von Kaunitz-Rietberg), who looked on Prussia as the natural enemy of Austria. Neither party, however, wished to resume the contest without the help of powerful allies. Kaunitz had already established relations with Russia, and his special concern was to induce France, Austria's old enemy, to support his schemes. The French meanwhile, viewed the growing power of Prussia with dislike and feared lest their influence in western Germany should be prejudiced. Frederick, for his part, was convinced that he would have to defend Silesia against an Austrian attack and so was anxious to detach the British from their traditional support of Austria if he could do so without impairing his formal friendship with France, Great Britain's principal rival.

In 1755, when French and British settlers in North America had already come to blows and the Austrian government showed itself unwilling to undertake the protection of Hanover in the event of Anglo-French hostilities in Europe, the British government sought a promise of help from Prussia. Since it was to be a purely defensive agreement, Frederick considered that he could enter into it without breaking faith with France and, on Jan. 16, 1756, concluded the convention of Westminster, which stipulated that Prussia should help Great Britain if the French attacked Hanover and that Great Britain should support Frederick if the Austrians attacked Silesia. The French, however, saw this convention as a detection by Frederick from his French commitments; and on May 1, 1756, at Versailles, the defensive alliance for which Kaunitz had so long laboured was concluded between France and Austria. Kaunitz, with the zealous support of Russia, set to work in Paris to turn the Austro-French defensive alliance into an offensive one for the complete destruction and partition of Prussia; and Frederick the Great learned that an attack on Prussia by Austria, Russia and France was being planned for the following spring. Having received an evasive answer when he asked Maria Theresa for assurances about her intentions, Frederick resolved to anticipate his enemies and gave the order to his troops to cross the Saxon frontier. Thus began the Seven Years' War (q.v.), in which Prussia fought against Austria, France, Russia, Saxony and Sweden. Frederick's sole ally was Great Britain-Hanover, whose support consisted mainly in a subsidy of 4,000,000 thalers a year. It was only his generalship and his determination not to consent to any diminution of his territory that made it possible for him to survive.

In the autumn of 1756 Frederick occupied Saxony and, after defeating a relieving Austrian army at Lobositz, compelled the Saxon army to surrender at Pirna. In 1757 he invaded Bohemia and besieged Prague but was himself heavily defeated at Kolin on June 18 and forced to withdraw. At the same time Russian troops threatened East Prussia, one French army overran Hanover, and a second French army, in conjunction with an imperial army, advanced from Thuringia on Berlin. Frederick defeated the French and imperial forces at Rossbach on Nov. 5 and then hastened to Silesia where by the battle of Leuthen (Dec. 5) he recovered Breslau from the Austrians. The moral effect of Rossbach (where Frederick owed his victory mainly to the Prussian cavalry under Friedrich Wilhelm von Seydlitz and to the lack of co-ordination between the imperial army and the French) was even greater than its military effect, for it brought many members of the *Reich* to "a Fritzian way of thinking" (Goethe): it was not only a victory over the French but also a victory over the *Reich*, which, notwithstanding the smaller states' leadership in cultural matters, had declined in political importance while Austria and Prussia rose to power.

Despite these defeats Maria Theresa remained convinced of the justice of her cause. When in 1758 the Russians resumed their attack on East Prussia and occupied Königsberg (modern Kaliningrad), the Austrians advanced to join them and laid siege to Küstrin. Frederick, who had again attempted an attack on Moravia, returned to prevent a junction of the enemy armies and defeated the Russians at Zorndorf on Aug. 25, whereupon they retreated into Pomerania and besieged Kolberg. The Austrians, however, had entered Lusatia, and Frederick was defeated at Hochkirch, near Bautzen, on Oct. 14. Yet he was able, on the whole, to maintain himself in Silesia and Saxony, while in the west Ferdinand of Brunswick, who commanded the British and Prussian forces, held the line of the Rhine.

The following years brought Prussia to the verge of disaster. While the French advanced as far as the Weser, Austrian and Russian armies together defeated Frederick at Kunersdorf on Aug.

BATTLE OF LEUTHEN, DEC. 5, 1757: FROM A CONTEMPORARY ENGRAVING

12, 1759. With his army well-nigh exterminated, Frederick thought that Prussia was bound to fall; but disunity among leading Russian and Austrian commanders gave him time to recruit a new army. The imperial army entered Dresden and occupied a part of Saxony, but the illness of the empress Elizabeth hindered the operations of the Russians, since it was common knowledge that the sympathies of the heir apparent, the future Peter III, were with Frederick. However, a Russian advance guard did on one occasion reach Berlin (Oct. 1760); and in 1761 the Austrians captured Schweidnitz (Swidnica) and the Russians Kolberg. It became daily more difficult for Frederick to obtain reinforcements and money. After the fall of the elder William Pitt's ministry, the British government began to negotiate for peace with France and ceased its financial support of Prussia from April 1762.

By this time, however, Frederick's position had been decisively improved by the death of Elizabeth of Russia on Jan. 5, 1762: her successor, Peter III, made peace with Frederick and entered into an alliance with him. Though Peter was murdered a few months later, his successor, Catherine the Great, also thought that neither a strengthening of Austria nor the destruction of Prussia would serve Russia's true interests. She withdrew her military support from Frederick but did not renew the alliance with Austria.

Furthermore, after signing the preliminaries of peace with Great Britain (Nov. 1762), the French lost all interest in the war with Prussia and withdrew their troops from Germany. Hence Maria Theresa gave up all hope of a decisive victory and entered into negotiations. Peace was signed at Hubertusburg on Feb. 15, 1763. Frederick evacuated Saxony but retained Silesia. Both parties renounced all claims to a war indemnity.

The importance of the Seven Years' War in German history lies in the failure of Austria's attempt to destroy Prussia before Prussian power was consolidated. The hostility between the two greatest German states continued to exist and to influence powerfully the whole future political development of Germany.

Joseph II (1765–90).—Francis I died in 1765 and was succeeded as emperor by his son Joseph II, who was appointed coregent in the Austrian possessions by Maria Theresa. As long as his mother was alive, Joseph's influence on internal Austrian policy

was limited. His ambition therefore led him to invest the imperial position with new significance, to reform the aulic council and the imperial chamber and to restore many imperial rights that had fallen into disuse. He was steeped in the ideas of the Enlightenment and strove to bring them into public life. He had the best intentions to raise his country to power and prosperity, but in the belief that general principles could be applied regardless of circumstances he proceeded without taking into account the great differences in the social structure of the various peoples over whom he ruled. His noble desire for reform, which made him subordinate everything to the service of the sovereign state, failed because of the violent opposition provoked by the despotic methods which he used to impose his innumerable decrees. Frederick the Great said of him that he invariably took the second step before he had taken the first; and from the beginning his projects aroused the deep distrust of the German princes. Moreover, Joseph was very desirous of securing some compensation for the loss of Silesia and indeed sought to extend the frontiers of his realm on all sides. This was first evident when Polish affairs called for interference on the part of the neighbouring powers.

The First Partition of Poland.—When Augustus III died in 1763 he was succeeded on the throne of Poland by a king of Polish birth, Stanislaw Poniatowski. Stanislaw had made enemies in Poland, however, and the Russian empress Catherine sought to use these internal disputes to make herself mistress of all Poland. Though Frederick the Great believed it impossible to prevent Russia's expansion into Poland, he hoped that at least Austria and Prussia might obtain a share in the spoils; and when Joseph on a visit to Frederick at Neisse in 1769 expressed his readiness for an understanding with him, concerted action by Austria and Prussia seemed to be possible. Joseph turned his energies to bringing this about, despite Maria Theresa's disapproval, and even took the initiative of occupying Szepes.

This action was followed by the first partition of Poland in 1772 (see POLAND: *History*): Russia took an area in the northeast; Prussia, which had the smallest share, secured what came to be the province of West Prussia, establishing a territorial link between East Prussia and the Hohenzollern possessions in Germany; and Austria obtained Galicia and Lodomeria.

The War of the Bavarian Succession.—Joseph II had designs in Germany also. In 1777 the elector Maximilian III Joseph of Bavaria died, and with him the Bavarian branch of the Wittelsbachs came to an end. According to the family compacts of the Wittelsbach house, Bavaria fell to the head of the younger branch, Charles Theodore, the elector palatine; but the emperor, who maintained that he himself had claims on Bavaria, induced Charles Theodore to cede Lower Bavaria to Austria in return for recognition of his right to the rest of the inheritance. The other German princes, however, especially Frederick the Great, saw themselves threatened by this extension of the Habsburg power. The emperor's action seemed especially questionable because his claim was difficult to prove; moreover, Charles Theodore was childless, and the next heir after him, Charles of Zweibrücken, protested to the *Reichstag* against the injury done to his rights. When the emperor sought to extend his claim to include Upper Bavaria and proposed to compensate the elector palatine with the scattered Austrian possessions in Swabia and the upper Rhineland, Charles of Zweibrücken again protested to the *Reichstag*. Frederick the Great promised his protection to Charles of Zweibrücken and, after assuring himself of the co-operation of Frederick Augustus III of Saxony, invaded Bohemia in June 1778. The War of the Bavarian Succession (*q.v.*) came to an end without a decisive battle. Maria Theresa, who from the beginning had disapproved of Joseph's transactions, at once initiated negotiations with Frederick, which led to the peace of Teschen (May 13, 1779). Austria received only a small district in Bavaria, the so-called Innviertel, and renounced all claims to the Bavarian inheritance.

The League of Princes.—Maria Theresa died on Nov. 29, 1780. Joseph II now became sole ruler in Austria, Bohemia and Hungary. While he sought by far-reaching laws to transform these states into a more centralized state under German rule, to free the peasants and to reduce the influence of the church, he pursued his old schemes in foreign policy. He purchased Catherine the Great's support by promising to help her to realize her eastern policy, and he resumed afresh his negotiations with Charles Theodore for the cession of the whole of Bavaria to Austria. This time he offered him as compensation the Austrian Netherlands and the title of king of Burgundy. Charles Theodore was not unwilling to accept the offer; but once again Charles of Zweibrücken raised objections and appealed to Frederick the Great, who seized the opportunity to put into execution a long-cherished plan. Disillusioned with foreign alliances, Frederick now thought to raise the status of Prussia by an alliance with the more powerful German princes. As these all felt themselves threatened again by the emperor's action, Frederick found them more sympathetic to his idea than previously. On July 23, 1785, the League of Princes or *Fürstenbund* was concluded between Prussia, Saxony and Hanover, to which were later added Saxe-Weimar, Saxe-Gotha, Palatinate-Zweibrücken, Brunswick, Baden, Hesse-Kassel, Anhalt, Ansbach, Mecklenburg, the electorate of Mainz and some other smaller states. The preservation of the integrity of the imperial constitution was the ostensible aim and object of this anti-Habsburg league. When the emperor saw that the majority of the German princes had united to oppose his projects, he was obliged to abandon them.

The League of Princes was the first occasion on which the majority of the German states allied themselves under the leadership of Prussia and in opposition to Austria. However, it was not regarded by Frederick the Great or by most of its members as a permanent institution. Of all its members, only Charles Augustus of Saxe-Weimar sought to give it a purpose beyond that of restraining Joseph II from his expansionist policy; he thought to endow it with a permanent constitution and to establish a common legal, financial and customs administration, supported by a joint army. The league would then have taken the place in German political life of the old *Reich* now crumbling into ruins, but this plan awakened no response in the other members.

The establishment of the League of Princes was the last political act of Frederick the Great. He died on Aug. 17, 1786, feared and admired by his contemporaries but not loved. The emperor Joseph II in the last years of his reign threw himself into vast undertakings in the east. The war against Turkey (1787–91), into which he entered in alliance with Russia, proved unfortunate for Austria and was threatening to involve Germany in a European war when Joseph died, on Feb. 20, 1790.

J. THE FRENCH REVOLUTIONARY AND NAPOLEONIC PERIODS

As Joseph II's successor the electors chose his younger brother, Leopold II, grand duke of Tuscany, who ruled for only two years. A peaceable and farsighted man, Leopold at once sought to end the war in the east, to bring about friendly relations with Prussia, to overcome the mistrust aroused in the German princes by Joseph's adventurous schemes and to quiet the disorder that had arisen within his dominions in consequence of the hasty reforms.

The French Revolution.—After the outbreak of the French Revolution in 1789, the ideas of liberty, equality and fraternity became popular among the educated classes in Germany. The proceedings of the first French National Assembly were regarded as an attempt to put into practice in political life the great principles of reason; but public opinion was sobered and disillusioned when the Reign of Terror followed. As yet the lower classes were not sufficiently independent to take a lively interest in these questions. Only in the Rhineland, which was soon afterward invaded by the French, was there any real agitation.

There was at first friction between the new rulers in France and the neighbouring German princes when the National Assembly wished to put its decree abolishing feudal rights into practice in Alsace, where many German princes had extensive lands. The princes appealed to the emperor Leopold II and the *Reich* for help, but Leopold had little desire to be involved in a war with France for such a cause. Day by day, however, more French *émigrés* arrived in Germany, and the Rhineland princes permitted them to enlist and arm volunteers. Though the French demanded the disbandment of these troops, war would probably still not have broken out if the course taken by the Revolution and the attempted flight of Louis XVI in 1791 had not placed the lives of the French royal house in danger. Queen Marie Antoinette was the sister of the emperor, and she had long entreated him to support her and her husband, but Leopold considered that this would only be possible if concerted action were taken by all the great European powers. He invited the sovereigns of Europe, in a circular note of July 6, 1791, to make common cause with him on behalf of the French king and queen; and Frederick William II of Prussia, who met Leopold at Pillnitz (Aug. 25–27), energetically supported this proposal. Accordingly the declaration of Pillnitz was made, assuring the French *émigrés* of intervention by Austria and Prussia in France provided that the non-German powers also promised their support. When Louis XVI, however, accepted the National Assembly's constitution, Leopold declared, in a circular note of Nov. 12 addressed to all the great powers, that he considered the French king's acceptance to have been a voluntary act and that the necessity for intervention by the great powers no longer existed.

Meanwhile the declaration of Pillnitz had aroused fierce resentment in France, where threatening speeches were made in the Legislative Assembly and the influence of extreme elements increased. Leopold then thought of summoning a European congress, concluded a defensive alliance with the king of Prussia for the maintenance of the integrity of their own dominions and sent a sharply worded note to the French government in which he announced that the growing disorder and the ascendancy of the war party in France obliged him to take precautions on the frontiers of the *Reich*. The Girondins, who had now taken control of the French government, demanded in reply that he should cease all military preparations immediately and abandon explicitly the European congress, but when this answer reached Vienna the emperor had just died (March 1, 1792). His son, the emperor Francis II, at once returned the answer that he could not grant either request until the complaints of the Alsatian princes had been settled and a government had been set up in France able and willing to carry out treaty obligations. On receipt of this reply the French government declared war on April 20. (*See* FRENCH REVOLUTIONARY WARS.)

The Austro-Prussian campaign against France did not begin until the autumn of 1792. From the very outset its progress was crippled by the fear that Catherine the Great would seize the opportunity presented by the allies' preoccupation in France to annex the whole of Poland to Russia. The chief command was entrusted to the duke Charles William Ferdinand of Brunswick, who increased the resentment of the French by issuing a menacing manifesto to his armies. The German armies succeeded in capturing Verdun and advancing as far as the passes of the Argonne, but there Brunswick delayed his attack so long that the French were able to bring up reinforcements. The bombardment of the heights of Valmy (Sept. 20) had no decisive result. Brunswick did not dare to attempt a general assault or to advance any farther. Since, moreover, differences of opinion had meanwhile arisen between the Austrian and Prussian commanders and news had arrived that a Russian army had, in fact, marched into Poland, Frederick William II, who was present with the army, decided to order a retreat. The

GERMANY

The attack on France was thus frustrated. As Goethe rightly observed on the day of the battle, Valmy marked the beginning of a new epoch.

While it was yet winter the French took the offensive and occupied Speyer, Worms and Mainz, but failed to obtain more than a temporary grip upon Frankfurt am Main. Wherever the French troops came, they set up Jacobin clubs and sought to win over the population to revolutionary ideas. In this they were at first partially successful; but it was soon clear that the Paris government was more concerned with plundering than with liberating the occupied districts, so that public opinion turned against the French. The threatening advance of the French on the Rhine again forced the two German powers to take vigorous steps. During 1793 the French were again driven out of the Austrian Netherlands, the greater part of which they had occupied. Mainz was recaptured and the German troops entered Alsace. It was not until 1794 that the French were able by their victory at Fleurus to reconquer the Austrian Netherlands, to regain possession of Alsace and to advance on the lower Rhine as far as Aachen and Cologne. They were able to do this chiefly because Prussia had virtually retired from the war in order to concentrate on Polish affairs.

Second and Third Partitions of Poland.—In the autumn of 1792 negotiations were initiated between Russia and Prussia for a new partition of Poland. On Jan. 23, 1793, a treaty was signed between these two powers by which Prussia was to have Gdansk (Danzig), Torun, Poznan (Posen) and nearly all Great Poland, while Russia was to have the eastern provinces. Austria was merely promised assistance in reconquering the Austrian Netherlands. The emperor felt that he had been cheated, and his distrust of Prussia steadily increased from that time.

The Polish diet was forced to agree to the partition on Sept. 23, 1793. Then the patriotic insurrection of 1794 convinced Russia and Prussia that in order to secure their gains they would have to partition what remained of Poland. This time, however, Austria had to be given a share of the plunder, and after long negotiations a series of treaties, that of 1795, was achieved. Prussia got Warsaw with the district up to the Bug and Memel; Austria got the so-called West Galicia, with Cracow; and Russia got the rest. The partition was an act of violence characteristic of the *Kabinettspolitik* of the 18th century.

Basel, Campo Formio and Lunéville.—Meanwhile Frederick William II of Prussia had signed at Basel (April 5, 1795) a separate peace with France. By this treaty the left bank of the Rhine was given over to France, while Frederick William reserved the right to demand, in compensation for Prussia's cessions, that Germany north of a line drawn from the Rhine to Silesia should be declared neutral. French troops were not to enter this area, and in return Prussia promised to use its influence to prevent the north German princes from supporting the emperor against France. Thus Prussia once more resumed the anti-Austrian policy that it had temporarily abandoned to make common cause with Austria against France.

Austria fought on, with British financial support, for two more years until Napoleon Bonaparte's Italian campaign forced the emperor to conclude the peace of Campo Formio (Oct. 1797), whereby he surrendered Lombardy and the Austrian Netherlands to France, and received in return Venetia, Istria and Dalmatia. He also had to agree, however, to the cession of the left bank of the Rhine to France; and the German princes thus dispossessed were to be compensated on the German right bank of the Rhine. A congress was to meet at Rastatt to settle these princes' claims individually.

This congress met, but before it had completed its labours war had broken out anew, with Austria, Russia and Great Britain in a new coalition against France. The allied army under the Russian general Aleksandr Suvorov drove the French out of Italy in 1799, but the Austrian army that was trying to expel them from Switzerland was defeated near Zürich. The French were also victorious over the British in the Netherlands; and when Napoleon Bonaparte returned from Egypt in the autumn of 1799 and took over the supreme command, the French resumed the offensive. By their victory at Marengo (June 1800) they won back Italy. They also advanced victoriously into southern Germany. Thereupon the allies decided to treat for peace with Napoleon, who had in the meantime become head of the French republic as first consul. By the peace of Lunéville (Feb. 9, 1801) the cession of the left bank of the Rhine to France was confirmed. Peace between France and Great Britain was signed in the following year at Amiens.

Napoleon and the Confederation of the Rhine.—Negotiations now began in Germany for the compensation of the German princes who had incurred losses on the left bank of the Rhine. The *Reichstag* appointed a special commission, the *Reichsdeputation*, for this purpose, but the settlement really lay in the hands of the great powers, especially France. Napoleon came to an understanding with the Russian emperor Alexander I and with Frederick William III, king of Prussia from 1797, to divide up the ecclesiastical states and the majority of the imperial cities among the injured princes. Bavaria, Württemberg, Baden and Hesse were won over by promises of especially large compensation; finally the Austrian government assented also, despite its reluctance to admit such a diminution of the Catholic elements in the *Reichstag*. On Feb. 25, 1803, the results of the negotiations were embodied in the commission's final decision, the *Reichsdeputationshauptschluss*: 112 states were apportioned, out of which in the first place certain foreign princes who had sustained losses elsewhere had to be compensated. Thus the hereditary stadholder of the Netherlands, who had been driven from his dominions, was given the abbacy of Fulda and certain adjoining districts; the duke of Modena the Breisgau; and the grand duke of Tuscany the archbishopric of Salzburg. Prussia was indemnified by the bishoprics of Münster, Paderborn and Hildesheim in addition to Erfurt and the imperial cities of Dortmund and Goslar; Bavaria received the bishoprics of Würzburg, Bamberg, Augsburg and Freising, with a number of south German imperial cities; and Württemberg, Baden, Hanover and Oldenburg were similarly greatly increased in area. The map of Germany was entirely altered by these political changes, which yet marked only the beginning of a transformation to be carried still further three years later.

Meanwhile war had again broken out between France and Great

DEUTSCHE FOTOTHEK DRESDEN

KING FREDERICK WILLIAM III OF PRUSSIA WITH HIS FAMILY; ENGRAVING BY J. F. KRETHLOW AFTER A PAINTING BY H. A. DÄHLING

Britain. Russia and Austria made common cause with the British; Prussia remained neutral. Napoleon's great victory in the battle of Austerlitz (*q.v.*) on Dec. 2, 1805, decided the war in his favour. The Russian emperor withdrew; and Prussia, on the point of declaring war because French troops had violated Prussian territory, again entered into an understanding with Napoleon. Austria had to sign the peace of Pressburg on Dec. 26, 1805, surrendering Venetia to the new kingdom of Italy, Tirol to Bavaria and the remainder of the Habsburg lands in Swabia to Württemberg and to Baden and receiving in compensation only the archbishopric of Salzburg (the grand duke of Tuscany was given Würzburg instead). The emperor also had to recognize the elevation of Bavaria and Württemberg to the status of kingdoms: the Bavarian elector Maximilian IV Joseph thus became king as Maximilian I; and Frederick II, duke of Württemberg, king as Frederick I. Napoleon set up in the Rhineland a new grand duchy of Berg for his brother-in-law Joachim Murat.

Napoleon now resolved to unite the states that he had created or enlarged in a permanent confederation; and on July 12, 1806, he founded the second Confederation of the Rhine or *Rheinbund*, which included Bavaria, Württemberg, Baden, Hesse-Darmstadt, Nassau and Berg as well as some smaller states. The territories of the counts and knights of the empire (*Reichsgrafen* and *Reichsritter*) which lay between these states were divided up among them. The states of the Confederation of the Rhine remained independent in internal administration but could not pursue an independent foreign policy and were required to place their troops at any time at the disposal of Napoleon, who had been nominated the official protector of the confederation. The members of the confederation informed the emperor Francis II and the diet at Regensburg that they regarded themselves as having ceased to be members of the *Reich* and that this had ceased to exist (Aug. 1, 1806).

Francis II had already assumed the title of emperor of Austria, as Francis I, in Aug. 1804, in anticipation of Napoleon's making himself emperor of the French (Dec. 1804). The last recess of the imperial diet and the declaration of the Confederation of the Rhine virtually terminated the Holy Roman empire. Since the title of Holy Roman emperor had no real meaning any longer, Francis accordingly renounced it on Aug. 6, 1806, declaring at the same time that the Holy Roman empire was now extinct. He did this mainly to prevent Napoleon from assuming the first crown in Christendom and from declaring himself the successor of Charlemagne. Thus the Holy Roman empire disappeared entirely, and the complete independence of the individual states that had grown up on its territory was legally recognized. Germany became a geographical expression without any political or national unity.

Prussia's Collapse and Resurgence.—Napoleon now thought that his day of reckoning with Prussia had come. Thanks to his too cautious and wavering policy, Frederick William III could now look for support only to Russia (with which he concluded a de-

NAPOLEON ENTERING BERLIN THROUGH THE BRANDENBURG GATE, 1807; DRAWING BY LUDWIG WOLF

BY COURTESY OF THE STAATLICHE MUSEEN, BERLIN

fensive alliance), to electoral Saxony and to certain small north German states. When Napoleon occupied some Prussian districts on the Rhine on behalf of the grand duchy of Berg and demanded that Prussia should recognize this act of violence as valid and disarm completely, Frederick William replied with an ultimatum requiring the French to evacuate southern Germany. Napoleon naturally refused to comply with this demand, and war broke out between France and Prussia in Oct. 1806.

The battles of Jena and Auerstädt (*qq.v.*) on Oct. 14, 1806, decided the fate of the Prussian kingdom. Napoleon entered Berlin in triumph and Frederick William fled to Königsberg. All northern Germany was occupied by the French, and only a few Prussian fortresses put up a successful resistance. The elector Frederick Augustus III of Saxony made peace with Napoleon and entered the Confederation of the Rhine with the royal title as Frederick Augustus I. If Russia had not at this moment intervened, Prussia would have been wholly destroyed. The bloody fighting in West and East Prussia during the early months of 1807 failed to bring about a decisive victory, and Napoleon therefore entered into the peace negotiations with the Russian emperor Alexander. Under the peace of Tilsit (July 7, 1807), Prussia continued to exist as a kingdom but had to renounce all territory west of the Elbe and most of that acquired in the last partition of Poland; to consent to the occupation of its most important fortresses by French troops until a vast war indemnity had been paid in full; and to limit its army to 42,000 men. Napoleon merged the former Prussian territory between the Elbe and the Weser with Hesse-Kassel and other areas to form the kingdom of Westphalia for his brother Jérôme.

The originator of the Prussian reforms was Karl Freiherr vom Stein (*q.v.*). Stein had pressed for alterations in the government before 1806, but without success. After Jena, however, Frederick William III saw that desperate measures were needed. Partly on Napoleon's suggestion—ironically enough, since Stein was strongly anti-French and wanted to make Prussia the nucleus of a free and united Germany—the king appointed Stein as his chief minister on Oct. 4, 1807.

Stein and Hardenberg.—French rule in Germany brought about, directly or indirectly, important changes. In the states belonging to the Confederation of the Rhine a French administrative system and code of laws was directly imposed. In Prussia, on the other hand, the changes came from within, though there too they were conceived and carried through by a few men with power and were not the outcome of a popular movement.

In his 14 months of office Stein produced domestic reforms which might have given Prussia a new life if they had not been allowed to disappear later under Junker pressure. The system whereby power was divided between the ministers of state and the cabinet, a body of the king's private advisers, was abolished; instead the administrative heads of the various departments of state. Towns were freed from the jurisdiction of men appointed by the crown and were made self-governing, a reform which was to have been extended later to country districts, where government was in the hands of the Junker manorial courts. Moreover, Stein struck at the caste system which ran through Prussian society. He placed himself behind the land reforms already recommended by the king's "Immediate" commission; and on Oct. 9, 1807, he issued the edict abolishing serfdom in Prussia. The laws whereby land could not pass from one class of owner to another were annulled; the Junkers were now permitted to sell their land, and the middle classes, which had the money to cultivate it, could buy it. Further, by the same edict, all the regulations confining particular occupations to particular classes were abolished. Meanwhile Gerhard von Scharnhorst was making changes in the army, trying to create a national rather than a purely professional force, and Stein supported these reforms also. Unfortunately an intercepted letter showed Napoleon where Stein's policy was designed to lead; an imperial decree was issued against him on Dec. 6, 1808, and he fled to Bohemia. His place was taken by Karl August von Hardenberg (*q.v.*), who had been associated with him and pursued a similar policy of reform.

The Austrian War of 1809.—While Napoleon's attention was engaged in Spain (*see* PENINSULAR WAR), Austria made another attempt in 1809 to regain its old position. Count von Stadion, the archduke John and the archduke Charles, commander in chief of the Austrian army, showed great eagerness for reform and inaugurated successfully a far-reaching patriotic propaganda. Besides the standing army, a popular militia was introduced, joined by volunteers from all classes of the people. As in Spain, so in Germany, the war against Napoleon's rule was to be the concern not only of the state and the dynasty but of the whole nation. The patriotic elements in Germany were to join Austria's standard and there was to be a general war against the foreigner. But the German princes who had benefited from Napoleon's reorganization of Germany did not dare to leave his side, and the German people were not yet ready for a general revolt. Only the Tirolese followed enthusiastically their emperor's call and had had some successes (*see* HOFER, ANDREAS). Austria was too weak to stand alone against Napoleon, whose armies comprised not only Frenchmen but also contingents sent by his devoted German princely allies. Russian aid was small and came too late; and Prussia could not bring itself to help Austria. Austria's offensive toward southern Germany failed, and Napoleon moved again down the Danube toward Vienna. The battle of Aspern-Essling (May 21–22, 1809) ended in a notable success for the archduke Charles; but Napoleon managed to extricate himself from his precarious position, was joined by his reserve troops, crossed the Danube and won at Wagram (July 6) one of the greatest and bloodiest battles of his career. The Austrian army, however, was not completely destroyed. Hence Napoleon gave up his original plan of dividing Austria and concluded the peace of Vienna (Oct. 14, 1809): Austria had to cede Salzburg, Tirol, Galicia and the south Slav provinces, which left the emperor Francis only with Upper and Lower Austria, Styria, part of Carniola and the kingdoms of Bohemia and Hungary. The emperor had also to agree to the payment of a large war indemnity and to a reduction of his army. Thenceforward Metternich (*q.v.*), the Austrian foreign minister, pursued a policy of appeasement until circumstances made it possible for him to act differently. The Polish lands taken from Austria were added to the duchy of Warsaw, which Napoleon had created after the peace of Tilsit for the king of Saxony.

The War of Liberation.—A change came over the scene with Napoleon's Russian campaign in 1812. In this the French army

was almost entirely destroyed, and a miserable remnant alone survived to reach Germany in the winter. Though Germany was now anxious to shake off Napoleon's rule, there was still no single directing will, since the country was in part governed by princes who were vassals of France and in part occupied by French garrisons. The population of the north, where foreign rule had been most oppressive, was filled with a wild hatred against the French; but in the south, where German princes still ruled and no foreign troops or officials had penetrated, there was not so much anti-French feeling. For the first time the educated classes in Germany learned to understand the importance of a national state in the common life of a people. The rulers of the greater states, however, still hesitated. The emperor Francis did not wish to fight against his son-in-law, and Frederick William III of Prussia feared that he might lose the rest of his kingdom if the new war should prove unsuccessful. Only when the Russians seemed determined to pursue the French into Germany were the German princes forced to make up their minds.

At Napoleon's bidding, Austria and Prussia had sent contingents to help him against Russia. The commander of the Prussian contingent, Johann Yorck von Wartenburg, acting on his own responsibility, concluded a treaty of neutrality with the commander of the Russian forces opposing him (convention of Tauroggen, Dec. 30, 1812), but it was only in March 1813, under pressure from the Russian emperor Alexander, that Frederick William III finally issued from Breslau the "Appeal to my People" and declared war against France. The Prussian proclamation gave the signal for a general rising in northern Germany against Napoleon. Volunteers enthusiastically rushed to arms and the Russian and Prussian troops advanced to the Saxon frontier. Austria remained neutral at first but secretly made preparations for military intervention while Metternich began diplomatic negotiations to draw the German princes away from Napoleon.

Napoleon hastened to the defense of his German allies, defeated the Russians and Prussians at Lützen and at Bautzen and forced them to retreat to Silesia. Then he concluded an armistice, during which peace negotiations were opened at Prague through the intermediary of Austria. Napoleon, however, was unwilling to surrender any of his conquests, and after much hesitation the emperor Francis made common cause with the allies and declared war on France on Aug. 11, 1813. The campaign in Germany finally ended in the defeat of Napoleon at the battle of Leipzig (Oct. 16–19). The French army had to retreat over the Rhine; and on New Year's Eve the allied forces crossed it also and advanced into northern France. By the end of March 1814 the allies were in possession of Paris. Napoleon was compelled to abdicate his throne, and by the first treaty of Paris the French were forced to abandon all the conquests made since 1792. (*See also* NAPOLEONIC WARS.)

The Congress of Vienna (1814–15).—With the removal of French rule the difficult question of Germany's future organization arose. Austrian policy, now inspired by Metternich, aimed at preventing Prussia from becoming too powerful and tried to attract the German princes who had been allied with Napoleon. By the

treaty of Ried the emperor Francis recognized the full sovereign rights of the king of Bavaria, Maximilian I; and similar treaties were concluded with Württemberg, Baden and other states in the former Confederation of the Rhine. Hanover, whose ruler was the king of England, also remained intact. Meanwhile, if the vassal states created by Napoleon were to be preserved, it seemed unjust to exclude from their territories the princes whom Napoleon had exiled. Consequently it was very difficult to find a means of giving expression to the political unity of Germany.

GERMAN SATIRICAL PRINT BY G. SCHADOW ON NAPOLEON'S RETREAT FROM MOSCOW, 1812

...demand for constitutional reform. The establishment of the German confederation at the congress satisfied neither the demand for German unity nor the demand for constitutional reform. The history of the next 50 years in Germany showed the difficulty of reconciling these two demands and determined the form that German unification was to take.

(E. BRA.; HU. HH.)

K. THE GERMAN CONFEDERATION, 1815–66

The 1815 Settlement.—The Napoleonic Wars had broken the old political structure of Germany. At the same time the administrative changes brought about by the French and the patriotic emotions of the war of 1813 had led many Germans to demand a measure of German unity and also constitutional reforms in the individual states.

At the congress of Vienna, which sat from Sept. 1814 to June 1815, the German question was one of the most difficult problems considered. Finally it was agreed that Austria should recover Tirol, Vorarlberg, Salzburg and the Innviertel from Bavaria; Venetia and Lombardy in the south; and also Dalmatia and the former Illyrian provinces of the Napoleonic empire. Austria also kept most of Galicia, but the southern Netherlands and Austrian possessions in Swabia were given up. Thus Austria withdrew from western Germany, and the task of safeguarding the western frontier was passed on to Prussia, which was given a large area in the Rhineland and in Westphalia; i.e., lands which on the east of the Rhine had belonged to members of the Confederation of the Rhine and which on the west had formed part of Napoleonic France. These lands were entirely separate from Prussia's other possessions and a corridor joining them was refused. Even so, other powers, and especially Great Britain, hoped that Prussia would now provide a bulwark against possible French aggression and also be a safeguard to the new kingdom of the Netherlands. Prussia also received the Swedish province of Pomerania and about two-fifths of Saxony: the Saxon king, Frederick Augustus I, had now to pay the penalty for having remained loyal to Napoleon to the last. Of its Polish lands, Prussia kept only Posen (Poznan), Danzig (Gdansk) and what it had gained in 1772. In compensation for the territory handed back to Austria, Bavaria was given Würzburg and the Palatinate lands on the left bank of the Rhine, together with the south German districts of Ansbach and Bayreuth, which were renounced by Prussia. Hanover gave up Lauenburg to Prussia, but was enlarged by East Frisia, Hildesheim, Goslar and some smaller lands.

After the settlement there remained in Germany 39 different states, of which 4 were the free cities of Hamburg, Bremen, Lübeck and Frankfurt; the rest had monarchical constitutions. The idea of restoring the Holy Roman empire was abandoned and the 39 states formed a union, the *Deutscher Bund*, whose constitution was laid down in the Federal act of June 8, 1815. (*See* VIENNA, CONGRESS OF.)

BY COURTESY OF THE MUSEUM FÜR GESCHICHTE DER STADT LEIPZIG

ENTRY OF THE ALLIES INTO LEIPZIG FOLLOWING THE DEFEAT OF NAPOLEON, OCT. 1813; PRINT BY R. BOWYER

...the middle states—Bavaria, Hanover, Württemberg, Baden and Saxony—was confirmed, and their rulers were reluctant to give up their new power to any central body. In the circumstances, the German confederation set up in June 1815 left few powers to the federal diet, or *Bundestag* established at Frankfurt am Main. The federal diet was a meeting of plenipotentiaries and not a legislative assembly able to make decisions directly binding on individual citizens. It consisted of representatives of 39 states, some of whose sovereigns ruled over territory not included in the confederation; much of the Austrian empire and the eastern provinces of Prussia were excluded; the king of Hanover was also king of England; the duke of Holstein and Lauenburg was king of Denmark; and the grand duke of Luxembourg was king of the Netherlands. The individual states retained full sovereignty over their internal affairs. Even the establishment of a supreme court of justice for the confederation could only be effected by a unanimous vote, an extension of its competence was practically impossible. The avowed purpose of the confederation was "to uphold the external and internal security of Germany and the independence and integrity of the individual German states." During the following years it was to demonstrate its inability to do either.

The establishment of the confederation in this form was largely the work of Metternich, the Austrian chancellor, and it was his influence that predominated in Germany until 1848. The working of the confederation depended on agreement between the two German great powers, Prussia and Austria. During the reign of Frederick William III of Prussia this peaceful dualism worked successfully. Frederick William was a timid, skeptical, unimaginative man with an unremitting dislike of liberalism, and he was quite ready to follow Metternich's lead both within the German confederation and by opposing domestic reforms in Prussia. Under his influence the changes introduced by Stein and Hardenberg in the stress of defeat before 1813 were never completed, although Hardenberg remained chancellor until his death in 1822. The promises of a representative assembly that Frederick William had made in May 1815 remained unfulfilled until 1847, and a long struggle was carried on in the new Prussian provinces of western Germany in an attempt to remove the French influence on the administrative and judicial systems.

Metternich hoped to use both the German confederation and the Holy alliance (*q.v.*) of Prussia, Austria and Russia (1815) as a means of fighting revolution wherever it might threaten. In a series of congresses between 1818 and 1823 (Aix-la-Chapelle, Troppau, Laibach, Verona) he tried to establish the principle that the great powers had the right to intervene to suppress revolution elsewhere; e.g., in Spain and Italy. This policy was only partially successful since Great Britain refused to associate itself with it. Inside Germany, however, Metternich with Prussian support was able to use the federal diet to pursue the same ends. Some of the middle and smaller states, notably Bavaria, Baden and Württemberg, had adopted constitutions based on representative assemblies, and liberals in the other states were demanding similar measures. In the universities the *Burschenschaften* (see BURSCHENSCHAFT) were agitating for German unity, while papers like Joseph von Görres' *Rheinischer Merkur* expressed liberal discontent with the settlement of 1815. In Oct. 1817 these sentiments found expression in a great gathering at the Wartburg in commemoration of Luther's tercentenary and of the fourth anniversary of the battle of Leipzig. Within two years, however, Metternich found the excuse he needed for attacking the whole of this liberal and national movement. On March 23, 1819, August Friedrich Ferdinand von Kotzebue, a writer and a propagandist in Russian pay, was murdered by a student named Karl Sand, who had been associated with one of the most radical of the student organizations, the *Unbedingten*, led by Karl Follen. Metternich at once summoned a conference, which met at Carlsbad in August and was attended by representatives of most of the German princes. A series of decrees (the Carlsbad decrees) was drawn up and passed by the federal diet in September. The governments of the German states undertook to introduce press censorship, to remove university teachers suspected of subversive doctrines, to forbid the *Burschenschaften* and to establish a central commission to investigate the revolutionary movement.

The Carlsbad decrees began a decade of reaction when it seemed that Metternich had succeeded in halting the demand for national unity and constitutional change. The decrees were executed with various degrees of severity in the different states, for while some, such as Baden, had a genuine constitutional life, others, such as the two Mecklenburg duchies, had preserved an almost medieval feudal system, and in Brunswick, Hesse-Kassel and others the most capricious and unenlightened despotism prevailed. In Prussia the most prominent of the leaders of the national and liberal movement were arrested or driven into exile.

The Zollverein.—Yet the political inactivity of the 1820s was accompanied by economic developments of the greatest importance. The end of the war had brought serious economic difficulties in most of the countries of Europe, and not least in Germany. Other countries were imposing tariffs that excluded German grain; British manufactured goods were flooding the German market. All over Germany there was an agitation for some measure that would remove the differences of tariffs, currencies, weights and measures and of general economic policy between the individual German states. The economist Friedrich List led the movement in southern and western Germany, but efforts at action through the federal diet were unsuccessful. Similarly, negotiations between the governments of the southern states broke down because of particularist feeling and jealousy. By 1825 the initiative in forming a customs union lay with the one state prepared to take

In June 1816 all internal customs barriers inside Prussia had been abolished and in 1818 the tariff was revised and a moderate protectionist system was introduced. Both these measures aimed at restoring order in the state's finances and at the integration of the newly won provinces into the Prussian state. From 1819 onward the independent principalities of Schwarzburg and Anhalt, which were surrounded by Prussian territory, interrupting communications and serving as centres for smuggling, were absorbed into the Prussian economic sphere, so that by 1829 a large part of northern Germany was included within a single customs system. In 1825 a new Prussian finance minister, Friedrich von Motz, began to extend this area. On Jan. 11, 1828, Hesse-Darmstadt adhered to the Prussian system, and by May 1829 agreement had been reached with Bavaria, whose new king, Louis I, was anxious for a customs union, and whose government had already succeeded in coming to an agreement with the neighbouring German states of the south. The remaining states were rapidly obliged by their own interests to join, and neither the attempt made in Sept. 1828 to form a mid-German commercial union (*Mitteldeutscher Handelsverein*), nor the effort to secure economic co-operation between Hanover, Oldenburg, Brunswick and Hesse-Kassel (treaty of Einbeck, March 1830) was long successful. By Jan. 1, 1834, a customs union (*Zollverein*) was in being, including all the states of Germany except Austria, Hanover, Brunswick, Oldenburg and the Hansa cities. An attempt by the latter to form a rival union, the *Steuerverein*, did not long survive in the face of the changing economic situation and the attractions of membership of the *Zollverein*; Brunswick agreed to join in 1844, Hanover in 1851, Oldenburg in 1852 and Lübeck in 1867; only the great ports of Hamburg and Bremen remained outside until after the foundation of the empire. The *Zollverein* was a triumph for the Prussian

officials who planned it. The inadequacy of the machinery of the federal diet had been demonstrated, and a step had been taken in the substitution of Prussian for Austrian leadership in Germany, since Austria was excluded from the *Zollverein* and the economic developments that resulted from it. Above all, a fresh impetus was given to trade and industry all over Germany, preparing the way for the great developments of the German economic system after 1850.

The Liberal Movement.—The prevailing political conditions in Germany prevented many attempts to follow the example of the French revolution of July 1830. The particularly arbitrary rulers of Hesse-Kassel and Brunswick were deposed, and there were minor revolutionary outbreaks elsewhere. On May 27, 1832, a demonstration (similar to the 1817 Wartburg demonstration) was held at Hambach in favour of the liberal and national cause. Its sole effect was to enable Metternich to persuade the members of the confederation again to declare their support for conservative principles and to agree on further measures of repression (the Six Articles, June 1832).

Nevertheless, the death of the emperor Francis I in 1835 and the accession of his feeble-minded son Ferdinand began to weaken Metternich's influence inside the Austrian government. At the same time new movements in Germany began to make themselves felt. In spite of the ban imposed in 1835 on the writings of Heinrich Heine and the writers of the Young Germany movement, in spite of the suspension of seven Göttingen professors in 1837 by the new king of Hanover, Ernest Augustus (the former duke of Cumberland, who succeeded to the throne when the crowns of England and Hanover became separated on the death of William IV), the movement for national unity and constitutional government continued to gather strength. An opportunity for demonstrating this national feeling occurred in 1841, when an international crisis gave rise to rumours of a possible French attack on Germany; it was at this time that "The Watch on the Rhine" ("Die Wacht am Rhein," the title of a song written in 1840 by Max Schneckenburger") first became a national slogan.

Moreover the accession in June 1840 of a new king of Prussia, Frederick William IV, aroused hopes that Prussia might take the lead both in constitutional reform and in national unification. These hopes were to be disappointed. The new king had, it is true, a romantic feeling for a common German past, its traditions and monuments, but this included a respect for the house of Habsburg as the traditional imperial dynasty in Germany so that he was unwilling to break the peaceful dualism that had been established in 1815. He had been brought up on the ideas of the conservative political philosophers of the romantic age, and he looked back to an idealized medieval state very unlike the system of government at which the liberals were aiming. Nevertheless his imagination, eloquence and enthusiasm, coupled with such measures as a relaxation of the censorship and the rehabilitation of some of those teachers and writers who had suffered for their liberal views, meant that in Prussia political activity of all kinds began to revive. New

DEUTSCHE FOTOTHEK DRESDEN

SATIRICAL PRINT ON THE RHINE QUESTION, ABOUT 1840, WHEN GERMAN NATIONAL FEELING WAS STIRRED BY RUMOURS OF A POSSIBLE FRENCH ATTACK

leaders of the liberal movement were emerging from the new industrial and commercial middle class of the Rhineland, men such as Ludolf Camphausen, David Hansemann and Gustav von Mevissen, and they joined with the liberals in other parts of the kingdom in pressing for the fulfillment of Frederick William III's promise of a representative assembly, given in 1815 and not kept in his lifetime. After long hesitations and delays the king eventually summoned in Feb. 1847 an assembly composed of all the diets of the various Prussian provinces, and this united diet met on April 11, 1847. It soon became clear, however, that Frederick William's conception of a medieval system of estates (*Ständestaat*) grouped together under a king whose position derived from divine right was incompatible with the beliefs of even the mildest of liberals, and in June 1847 the diet was prorogued.

In most of the other states of Germany there were similar movements although their nature depended on the prevailing political conditions, which differed widely among the various states. In the towns artisans and apprentices were anxious to be rid of the last medieval restrictions on their professional freedom; in the country the peasants in the south and west and in the German provinces of Austria wanted to be freed from their remaining feudal obligations. The intellectual classes—lawyers, professors, students—wanted freedom of speech, trial by jury and a representative system of government as well as the satisfaction of their desires for a German national state. In Austria the non-German nationalities were stirring, while the diets of the German provinces, especially that of Lower Austria, were voicing liberal demands. Liberal leaders in the individual states of Germany were beginning to meet one another and to draw up common programs expressing their liberal and national aims. The meeting in Lübeck of the German philologists, the "intellectual diet of the German nation," in 1847, was of special significance.

The Year of Revolution.—It needed only the example of the Paris revolution of Feb. 1848 to bring these discontents in Germany to a head. Within a few weeks the governments in most of the middle and small states had yielded to popular agitation, promised a constitution and appointed liberal ministers. In Bavaria, where dislike of the king's mistress, Lola Montez, had confused the political situation, Louis I was forced to abdicate in favour of his son Maximilian II on March 20. The revolution scored equally easy and surprising successes in Vienna and Berlin. On March 13 Metternich was forced to resign and then went into exile; the emperor promised a constitution, and a national guard was formed. At the same time the non-German nationalities in the empire were demanding autonomy and constitutional government. On March 18, encouraged by the events in Vienna, the workers and artisans of Berlin, not content with the promises the king had already made of summoning the united diet again, started riots in

BY COURTESY OF THE STAATLICHE MUSEEN, BERLIN

STREET BARRICADES IN FRONT OF THE TOWN HALL, BERLIN, MARCH 18–19, 1848: LITHOGRAPH BY L. ELSHOLTZ

the streets. The king, with characteristic impetuosity, issued a long-winded sentimental proclamation "to my dear Berliners" and later even consented to salute the corpses of those killed in the street fighting. On March 19, on his orders, the troops were withdrawn from the city although they could easily have suppressed the disturbances. A constituent assembly was summoned, and a ministry headed by the Rhenish liberals Camphausen and Hansemann was appointed.

These easy revolutionary successes in the individual states were accompanied by plans for establishing a measure of national unity. On March 5 a meeting of the leading academic liberals at Heidelberg had declared in favour of a national representative assembly, while the Hessian statesman Heinrich, Freiherr von Gagern, sent his brother Maximilian on a mission to the courts of Germany to try to secure common action. These efforts were overtaken by the revolutions in Berlin and Vienna. The initiative now lay with the liberals rather than with the princes. The Austrian government was distracted by the revolutions in Hungary and in Milan and by the war with the kingdom of Sardinia for the possession of Lombardy. In Prussia, Frederick William appeared to be prepared to co-operate in the work of German unification and declared on March 21 that Prussia would merge itself in Germany.

The Frankfurt Assembly.—A preliminary parliament (*Vorparlament*) met in Frankfurt am Main at the instigation of the liberal leaders who had assembled at Heidelberg early in the month, and it established a committee of 50 to prepare for the election of a national assembly (*Nationalversammlung*). The elections were duly held, though the electoral laws and methods varied considerably from state to state, and on May 18 the national assembly met in the Paulskirche in Frankfurt. The success of the moderate liberals in the elections to the diets of the individual states and to the Frankfurt assembly, together with the defeat of a radical rising in southwestern Germany in April, led liberals all over Germany to hope that a constitution for a united Germany might emerge without difficulty.

The Frankfurt national assembly devoted a great deal of its time to the discussion of general principles and of the basic human rights that it was necessary to guarantee in the new united Germany. But it also had to decide on immediate practical problems, such as the nature of the executive power and Germany's territorial extent. As a temporary answer to the first problem the archduke John, an uncle of the emperor Ferdinand and the most liberal-minded member of the Habsburg family, was appointed regent on June 29, and a government was formed under Charles, prince of Leiningen, the half brother of Queen Victoria. Yet it soon became

BY COURTESY OF THE TRUSTEES OF THE BRITISH MUSEUM; PHOTOGRAPH, JOHN R. FREEMAN

THE NATIONAL ASSEMBLY MEETING IN THE PAULSKIRCHE, FRANKFURT, 1848, AN ILLUSTRATION FROM THE "LEIPZIGER ILLUSTRIERTE ZEITUNG"

clear that the executive appointed by the Frankfurt assembly had no power except such as was granted to it by the governments of the individual states. The Frankfurt assembly took over the conduct of a war with Denmark about the duchies of Schleswig and Holstein. Frederick VII of Denmark wished to separate Holstein from the German confederation and treat both duchies like the other provinces of the Danish kingdom. (*See* SCHLESWIG-HOLSTEIN QUESTION.) The war had broken out in April and was being waged by Prussian troops under a Prussian commander in chief, Friedrich, Graf von Wrangel. The Prussian government alone decided when the war should end and signed the peace of Malmö on Aug. 26. The war had been the object of great national enthusiasm, and Prussia's decision to end it (under pressure from Russia, Great Britain and Sweden) became a source of such dissatisfaction at Frankfurt that Leiningen was forced to resign on Sept. 5, 1848. He was succeeded by Anton von Schmerling, a moderate liberal from Austria, who held office until December when he was succeeded by Heinrich von Gagern.

The Counterrevolution.—In September and October, during the political crisis caused by the end of the war with Denmark, revolutionary outbreaks by radical republicans in Frankfurt itself and in the southwest of Germany had to be suppressed. These risings were defeated only with the help of Prussian and Austrian troops. In October a similar revolt in Vienna was also suppressed and the city was bombarded by Alfred, prince von Windischgrätz. By the end of the year the counterrevolution had triumphed in both Austria and Prussia. The emperor Ferdinand abdicated in favour of his 18-year-old nephew, Francis Joseph, on Dec. 2, and the new Austrian minister, Felix, prince zu Schwarzenberg, was prepared to reassert the authority of the central imperial government both inside the Austrian monarchy and in the rest of Germany. In Prussia, too, Frederick William IV had lost all the sympathy with the liberals that he had shown in the spring and was relying increasingly on extreme conservative advisers such as the brothers Gerlach. On Dec. 5 the Prussian national assembly was dissolved and a new constitution issued by royal proclamation. A new ministry with conservative sympathies had already been formed in November under Friedrich Wilhelm, Graf von Brandenburg. Although it contained certain concessions to the liberals, these were largely undone in the subsequent months when a restricted franchise was imposed.

The re-establishment of conservative governments in the two great states of Germany was inevitably reflected in the discussions of the Frankfurt assembly about the nature of the sovereign power in Germany and its territorial extent. By the end of 1848 the assembly had completed its discussions about the basic rights to be included in the constitution, and in Jan. 1849 the proposed constitution was circulated to the individual states for their comments without any decision having been taken about the person or nature of the central executive. The second reading was concluded and the constitution adopted on March 27. The final decision was that the executive power should be in the hands of a hereditary emperor, although to obtain this the radicals had to be soothed with the promise of universal suffrage. The next stage was to elect an emperor.

Meanwhile, the territorial extent of the new Germany had been partially decided by the proclamation of a new Austrian constitution on March 4. By this, the Austrian empire was treated as a single whole, and it was made clear that the whole empire or none of it would have to enter the new Germany. This was a blow to all those south German and Austrian liberals who had hoped for a "great German" (*grossdeutsch*) settlement that would include at least the German provinces of Austria and meant that the initiative passed to those who believed in a "little German" (*kleindeutsch*) settlement under Prussian leadership. Accordingly, when the election of an emperor took place in the national assembly on March 28, 290 votes were cast for Frederick William against 248 abstentions. On April 3 the king received a deputation headed by Eduard Simson, the president of the assembly, which came to offer him the crown. The offer was refused. Frederick William was too deeply conservative to receive a German imperial crown from any hands except those of the other German princes. On April 21, in spite of last-minute efforts by Camphausen and the governments of some of the smaller states, the king formally declared that Prussia could not accept the proposed constitution.

Without the support of either Prussia or Austria the Frankfurt assembly could not now survive. By May Gagern's ministry had broken up and the majority of the deputies were ordered home by the governments of their respective states. The rump that remained was forced to move to Stuttgart and was finally dispersed on June 18 by Württemberg troops and police. In May and June final risings by the left in Baden and Saxony were suppressed with the help of Prussian troops. The revolutions were over.

The Prussian Union Project (the Erfurt Union).—With the failure of the Frankfurt assembly to achieve German unification the opportunity for action passed back to the two great powers, Prussia and Austria. In the spring of 1849 Frederick William IV was listening to the advice of Gen. Joseph Maria von Radowitz. Radowitz was a Catholic conservative who believed that if Germany was to be saved from revolution, some concessions must be made to the social and national demands of the liberals. He devised a plan for setting Prussia at the head of a union of the states of northern and central Germany that should be linked with the existing German confederation. On May 26, 1849, an "Alliance of the Three Kings" was concluded between Prussia, Hanover and Saxony to further the project, and in June a congress was held at Gotha attended by some of the former members of the Frankfurt assembly—moderate liberals willing to accept Prussian leadership in a little Germany—who gave Radowitz' plan somewhat reluctant support. In spite of opposition from many of the Prussian nobility, who (again led by the Gerlachs) suspected what they held to be Radowitz' leanings toward liberalism, it was agreed that a conference should meet at Erfurt in March 1850 to discuss a new constitution for Germany.

Meanwhile, Austria too had embarked on a positive policy. The king of Sardinia, Charles Albert, had been finally and decisively defeated at the battle of Novara in March 1849. The Hungarian revolt had been crushed with Russian assistance, and the Hungarian forces had capitulated at Világos on Aug. 13, 1849. The national movement in Bohemia had already been put down in June 1848. The danger of the disintegration of the Habsburg empire had gone, and Schwarzenberg was determined to follow up his attempt to consolidate and centralize the monarchy by a reassertion of Austria's predominance in Germany. He was aided in this task by Karl Ludwig, Freiherr von Bruck, his minister of commerce, who had a grand design of uniting the whole of central Europe into a single economic sphere of 70,000,000 inhabitants, a scheme which some of the liberals in south Germany were prepared to support. By the end of 1849 Austrian diplomacy had succeeded in drawing many of the small and middle states away from Prussia; Saxony and Hanover withdrew from the union project before the Erfurt congress assembled. Meanwhile Austria had announced its support for an alternative plan of constitutional amendment put forward by Brunswick, Hanover and Württemberg and, as the presiding power, had summoned a meeting of the federal diet for May 1850 to re-establish and revise the old federal constitution.

In spite of the relative failure of the Erfurt meeting, inevitable under these circumstances, Radowitz continued to work for the formation of the Prussian union. In the autumn of 1850 an internal conflict in Hesse-Kassel brought Prussian and Austrian troops face to face. The elector Frederick William I had appealed to the federal diet for support in his struggle with the liberals and on Oct. 31, 1850, Austrian and Bavarian troops entered Hessian territory in response to the elector's appeal; shortly afterward Prussian troops marched in to assert Prussia's right to defend the military roads that linked the parts of the Prussian kingdom lying on either side of Hessian territory. Radowitz urged the reluctant king to mobilize and prepare for war against Austria, and Brandenburg had been to Warsaw to try to gain the support of the Russian emperor. But Nicholas I's sympathies were with Austria, and indeed most Prussian conservatives (Otto von Bismarck among them) were opposed to a breach between the two traditionally conservative powers in Germany. The influence of the conservatives prevailed, for Frederick William IV was reluctant to embark on a war between Germans and in any case was never capable of pursuing a consistent policy for long. Radowitz was obliged to resign on Nov. 3 and Brandenburg died suddenly on Nov. 6. A new ministry was formed under Otto, Freiherr von Manteuffel. The new government decided to negotiate with Austria, and with Nicholas I's encouragement an agreement between the two governments was signed by Manteuffel and Schwarzenberg at Olmütz (Olomouc) on Nov. 29. By this convention, long remembered by many of the Prussian supporters of Radowitz' policy as the "humiliation of Olmütz," Prussian troops were withdrawn from Hesse, and the question of the future constitution of Germany was referred to a conference which met at Dresden in Dec. 1850.

The Confederation Restored.—At the Dresden conference (Dec. 1850–March 1851), Schwarzenberg was unable to secure for Austria the position in Germany for which he had hoped. Prussia, moreover, was able to win some support from the smaller states against the idea of a strong executive in Austrian hands. As a result, the only solution was a compromise that restored the old federal constitution of 1815 unchanged. It was as if the revolutions of 1848 had never been. Nor were the Austrians any more successful in using their political success at Olmütz to force their way into the *Zollverein*; the most that they secured was a commercial treaty with Prussia in 1853. Schwarzenberg's plans for the establishment of Austrian political power in Germany and Bruck's plans for an "empire of 70,000,000" in central Europe had both been disappointed. Thus the restoration of the position as it had been before 1848 pleased nobody and opened a period of political reaction and dull discontent. Many liberals went into exile (one, Carl Schurz, even became secretary of the interior in the United States), while those who remained behind began to realize that the unification of Germany could only come about by the action of those actually in possession of political power.

In Prussia, Austria and nearly all the smaller states every attempt was made to return to the constitutional position of the years before 1848. The Prussian constitution promulgated in Dec. 1848 was given its final form on Jan. 31, 1850; though it still made concessions to some liberal ideas, it was based on a restricted franchise by which two-thirds of the votes were held by those citizens whose taxes were rated in the two highest groups, while only one-third of the votes were held by the majority of the population. In 1849 was replaced by a patent of Dec. 1851 which made up the majority of the population. The Austrian constitution of 1849 was replaced by a patent of Dec. 1851 which imposed a centralized bureaucratic system of government on the whole empire. In 1855 this was followed by a concordat with the pope, which restored the Roman Catholic Church to a position such as it had not enjoyed since before the reign of the emperor Joseph II. Yet the unimaginative bureaucracy that ruled in the largest states of the confederation and the general political stagnation were accompanied by considerable economic developments. Capital was being more widely invested; the railway network was being extended and the main railway system completed; coal production was rising, so that by 1860 Germany produced more coal than France and Belgium combined. At the same time the urban population, especially in Prussia, was increasing, so that a new industrial working class was coming into being, creating new problems with which economists such as Franz Hermann Schulze-Delitzsch, the founder of the co-operative movement in Germany, and agitators such as Ferdinand Lassalle were becoming concerned. (Lassalle began his agitation in 1861 and founded the Allgemeiner Deutscher Arbeiterverein in 1862.)

Moreover, events outside Germany made it increasingly clear that the restored machinery of the confederation was inadequate. The rise of Napoleon III and the re-emergence of France as a great military power, the Crimean War and the growth of the movement for Italian national unity all influenced developments inside Germany. In the Crimean War no common policy was followed by Austria and Prussia. Austria had hesitated between Russia and the west, but had, by mobilization, forced Russia to evacuate the principalities of Moldavia and Walachia. Prussia remained strictly neutral, although the opinion of the governing class was deeply divided and the king himself, as so often, was unable to make up his mind. The situation of the confederation was even more serious in 1859 when Austria was involved in a war with France and Sardinia in defense of the Austrian possessions in northern Italy. Francis Joseph appealed in vain to the Prussian government for support. The most that Prussia was prepared to do was to order a partial mobilization so as to enforce an armed mediation if necessary. After the Austrian defeat and the armistice of Villafranca (July 1859), Francis Joseph publicly complained that he had been deserted by his natural allies. The period of peaceful dualism in the German confederation was clearly drawing to an end.

The many projects for the reform of the confederation that were put forward after 1859—the attempts to overhaul the federal machinery or to restore co-operation between the two German great powers—were based on a deep division in the beliefs of Germans about the kind of united Germany that they wished to see. The war of 1859 had given an opportunity for the expression of these different views. There were some who regarded Austria as taking the lead in a common German cause against the traditional enemy, France. Others regarded the Italian movement for national unity with sympathy and as an example which Germany must soon follow; to them Austria was a reactionary power hampering the free national development of Germany. The latter section of opinion began to find expression in a new political organization, the Nationalverein, founded in Sept. 1859. This body soon had branches in most of the states in northern and central Germany and conducted a vigorous agitation for a united and liberal Germany from which Austria should be excluded. Its leaders, such as Rudolf von Bennigsen and Johannes von Miquel, were to play important parts in the foundation and consolidation of the North German federation and the empire after 1866. It was inevitable that such a project should look to the unification of Germany under the leadership of Prussia, yet the political situation in Prussia was such as to make it difficult for liberals to accept its leadership.

The "New Era" in Prussia.—In Sept. 1858 Frederick William IV, whose mind had been growing increasingly deranged, finally became incapable of carrying on the government, and a regency was formed under his brother William, prince of Prussia (the future emperor William I). The regent had a personal dislike for his brother's ministers, and the Manteuffel government was replaced by one headed by Karl Anton, prince of Hohenzollern-Sigmaringen. Because the new government included one or two moderate liberals such as Rudolf von Auerswald, who had been a member of the liberal ministry of 1848, and because most of its members belonged to the group that had criticized Manteuffel in their journal the *Wochenblatt*, the rival of the extreme conservative *Kreuzzeitung*, the new administration was hailed as inaugurating a new era of liberal rule.

In fact, the regent had no intention of making concessions to the liberals. He was a simple, practical man whose main interest was in the army in which he had served since his early youth, and it was over the question of military reforms that he was to come into conflict with the liberal elements in the Prussian diet. The mobilization in the summer of 1859 had shown that the Prussian army needed overhauling and in Dec. 1859 the regent appointed the general Albrecht von Roon as war minister. Early in 1860 Roon brought his proposals for reform before the Prussian diet and asked for funds to put them into practice. The two points that aroused the most political discussion were a proposal to increase the active strength of the army by making every recruit serve a full three years, and a proposal to link the *Landwehr*, the militia, more closely with the regular army. It was the latter suggestion that especially aroused the anger of the liberals, for the *Landwehr* had been a preserve of the middle class and was connected with the ideals of a "people in arms" dating from the war of 1813. The liberal opposition to the military budget put an end to the idea of a new era in Prussia and involved the regent in increasing hostility to the liberals. For the year 1860 a compromise solution was found, and a military budget was voted so that Roon's reforms could be started; but the conflict was repeated the following year when the military budget was passed by only a small majority. In the autumn of 1861 a new party, the Deutsche Fortschrittspartei (the Progressive party), was formed by those liberals who saw the importance of retaining parliamentary control of finance and who wanted to unite Germany under the leadership of a liberal Prussia. In the elections of Dec. 1861 the new party had considerable success, and in March 1862 the diet rejected the military budget. The diet was dissolved but in spite of attempts to influence the elections a new parliament was returned with a majority opposed to the military budget.

The king (the regent had succeeded to the throne on the death of Frederick William IV on Jan. 2, 1861) was unable to find a government that could resolve the conflict and win parliamentary support. The generals were talking of a coup d'état. Finally, on Sept. 18, 1862, Roon summoned Otto von Bismarck (q.v.), from Paris, where he had recently become ambassador, and on Sept. 22, Bismarck agreed to become minister president of Prussia.

The Establishment of Bismarck.—It was only with reluctance that William had agreed to approach Bismarck. Bismarck had been closely associated with the extreme conservatives of the *Kreuzzeitung* group, with whom the king had broken in 1858, and his violent temperament and his ruthless methods made him a figure of alarm. He had served as the Prussian representative with the federal diet from May 1851 to Jan. 1859, and then as ambassador in St. Petersburg until March 1862, when he was appointed to Paris. In his diplomatic career he had learned the necessity of making Prussian policy independent of that of Austria, and he was a firm believer in the necessity of friendship with Russia. He had used his influence in favour of neutrality during the Crimean War, and in Feb. 1863 he sent Gen. Gustav von Alvensleben to Russia to sign an agreement by which the Prussian government promised to help the Russians to suppress the revolt that had broken out in Russian Poland. When Bismarck assumed office he not only had to solve the Prussian constitutional deadlock; he had also to decide on the policy Prussia should follow in the face of the various plans for reform of the confederation and the growing popular demand for national unity. For four years he solved the constitutional problem by governing without a budget.

Austrian Plans for Reform.—The rifts in the federal system revealed by the war of 1859 caused several plans of reform to be put forward. The minister president of Saxony, Friedrich Ferdinand, Graf von Beust, and the Bavarian minister, Ludwig von der Pfordten, tried to revive the idea of a triple division of power in Germany, in which the middle and small states would play a role equal to that of Austria and Prussia. The suspicions felt by the middle states for each other prevented these plans from coming to anything. At the same time the Austrian government was taking the initiative both in constitutional change inside the empire and by attempting to reform the German confederation. The failure of the war of 1859 had obliged Francis Joseph to reform his methods of government. The first attempt in the October diploma (Oct. 20, 1860) was an attempt to establish a quasi-federal system based on the conservative landlords in the historic provinces. It soon failed and the patent of Feb. 26, 1861, restored a centralized form of government with a central parliament whose members were elected indirectly by the provincial diets. (See AUSTRIA, EMPIRE OF.) To Germans, if not to the other peoples of the empire, the February patent could be represented as a step in a liberal direction. Many liberals in southern Germany still had the hope that Germany might be united under Austrian leadership and be a greater Germany that included the Germans inside the Austrian empire. In Oct. 1862 the Reformverein was founded in Munich to promote these aims. Its most important member was Julius Fröbel, a former member of the left in the Frankfurt assembly, who had taken part in the rising in Vienna in Oct. 1848. Now, however, he was reconciled with the Austrian government and even exercised an influence on some members of it; for while Johann, Graf von Rechberg-Rothenlöwen,

the foreign minister, was a disciple of Metternich and believed in a peaceful dual control of Germany by Prussia and Austria. Anton von Schmerling, the minister of the interior, believed in the formation of a greater Germany under Austrian leadership.

In the summer of 1863 the emperor Francis Joseph took the initiative and summoned a congress of the German princes to meet at Frankfurt am Main on Aug. 18. Early in August the emperor met the king of Prussia at Gastein and invited him to attend, but without success. When the princes met, amid considerable enthusiasm in southern and western Germany, another attempt was made to persuade the king of Prussia to come, and the king of Saxony was sent to make a personal appeal. However, Bismarck with some difficulty succeeded in persuading William to stay away. This absence prevented the congress of princes from having any serious significance and made its discussions on reform of the confederation purely academic. The Austrian plan, by which the confederation was to be headed by a directory of five advised by an assembly of delegates from the individual states, was only to come into effect if Prussia agreed. But Bismarck put forward, on Sept. 15, an alternative plan including the alternation of the presidency between Austria and Prussia, a Prussian right of veto against any declaration of war if federal territory was not attacked (i.e., Prussia would not defend Austria's Italian dominions) and the creation of "a true national representation based on the direct participation of the whole nation." Although the liberals were still too suspicious of Prussia's conservative internal policy to give Bismarck's proposals a warm welcome, the Austrians had lost their initiative and the next move lay with Prussia.

Schleswig-Holstein.—It was the revival of the Schleswig-Holstein question (q.v.) that presented the confederation with its next crisis. After the Prusso-Danish war of 1848 the constitutional position of those two duchies had become a matter of international concern. The London protocol of May 8, 1852, had ruled that if Frederick VII of Denmark died without male heirs and the throne of Denmark passed to the line of Holstein-Glücksburg, the new king should also inherit the duchies of Schleswig, Holstein and Lauenburg. It was provided, however, that the duchies should be governed autonomously and not fully incorporated in Denmark. Holstein and Lauenburg remained as before within the German confederation. At the same time Christian, duke of Augustenburg, the other claimant for the succession in the duchies, renounced his claims. The federal diet had, however, become increasingly anxious because the king of Denmark was not fulfilling his obligations and was asserting that the Danish constitution was valid in Holstein. In March 1863 the king of Denmark had issued a royal patent that applied the Danish constitution to Schleswig and left the position of Holstein unsettled. This move aroused great popular disapproval in Germany because it appeared to separate Schleswig from Holstein definitively, dividing territory that all German liberals regarded as German. On Oct. 1, 1863, the federal diet decided on action against Denmark.

The situation was complicated still further on Nov. 15 by the death of King Frederick VII, so that the question of succession to the duchies was added to that of their constitutional position. Christian of Glücksburg ascended the throne of Denmark as Christian IX and at once declared himself duke of Schleswig, Holstein and Lauenburg. At the same time Frederick of Augustenburg announced that he did not recognize his father's renunciation of his claims to the duchies and declared himself duke. His claim was widely supported inside Germany, for he was believed to have liberal leanings, and it was hoped that he would enable the duchies to be incorporated in the confederation. While the federal diet was supporting Frederick of Augustenburg's claims and sending federal troops into Holstein (Dec. 1863), Bismarck was acting with Austria independently of the confederation. He was anxious about international complications, and he was still in conflict with the Prussian diet; he was therefore careful to associate Austria with every step he took, a course which Rechberg, the Austrian foreign minister, was very ready to support. An Austro-Prussian alliance was signed on Jan. 16, 1864. An ultimatum presented to the Danes on Jan. 16 was rejected, and on Feb. 1 Austrian and Prussian troops invaded Schleswig under the command of Friedrich von Wrangel. The German forces stormed the fortifications of Düppel on April 18 as a preparation for crossing to the islands of Als and Fyn. Meanwhile the great powers were asked by the Danish government to mediate, and a conference was held in London from April 25 to June 25, accompanied by an armistice. The conference failed to reach an agreed solution since the Danes refused to accept either the Austrian suggestion that the duchies should be linked to the Danish crown purely by a personal union or the suggestion that they should form a separate state under Frederick of Augustenburg. Hostilities were resumed and the Prussians were successful in landing on Als on June 29. The Danes, all hopes of British and Swedish assistance having vanished, sued for peace, and an armistice was signed, which took effect on July 20. Preliminaries of peace were signed in August and the peace treaty was formally signed in Vienna on Oct. 30, 1864. Denmark gave up all rights to the duchies and they were handed over to Austrian and Prussian occupation.

The question at once arose of how the duchies should now be administered. The bulk of German opinion still supported the claims of Frederick of Augustenburg. Austria had little direct interest in the territories but hoped to be able to use them as a bargaining point that would make Prussia agree to support Austria's position in northern Italy and might possibly even make Prussia cede some territory in Silesia. Bismarck, on the other hand, had already determined that the duchies should come under Prussian control. His position in Prussia had been strengthened by the successful war. The conservatives were given fresh confidence in him by the triumphs of the Prussian army and he had demonstrated his independence of the diet by fighting a war for which it had not voted any credits. The other members of the German confederation were still hoping for the establishment of Frederick of Augustenburg, but these hopes were rendered vain by Bismarck's hostility to him and by the refusal of Prussia to allow the other states to participate in the occupation of the duchies. (The Saxon troops, the last to leave, departed from Holstein in Dec. 1864.) At the same time the Prussians were beginning to make use of their position in the duchies, and in March 1865 the Prussian naval base was moved from Danzig to Kiel.

Convention of Gastein.—By May 1865 the differences of policy between Austria and Prussia were becoming acute. Bismarck had stated in Feb. 1865 that he was prepared to recognize Frederick of Augustenburg as duke only if Frederick were prepared to give Prussia control of the economic and military life of the duchies. These conditions were unacceptable both to Austria and to the federal diet, which continued to recognize Frederick's claims. On May 29, 1865, a Prussian crown council discussed the means by which the duchies might be annexed, but no firm decision was taken. Bismarck does not seem to have been ready for war, and in Aug. 1865 the king of Prussia and the emperor of Austria met at Gastein where a convention about the duchies was signed on Aug. 14. The convention of Gastein laid down that Austria should administer Holstein and Prussia Schleswig. The port of Kiel and the fortress of Rendsburg came under Prussian control, nominally in the name of the confederation. In fact, the other members of the confederation were not consulted, and the convention not only put an end to Frederick of Augustenburg's chances but also made it harder afterward for Austria to claim to be the champion of the federal constitution against Prussia. Bismarck himself regarded the convention as a "papering over the cracks" and not as a lasting settlement. However, before a final breach with Austria he needed to ensure that Prussia would not be faced with a hostile coalition of foreign powers; he also needed a measure of popular support both in Prussia and in the other states of the confederation. A conversation with Napoleon III at Biarritz on Oct. 11, 1865, did not make France's intentions any clearer. Then, on Feb. 28, 1866, a Prussian council decided to strengthen Prussia's position by offering an alliance to Italy, which was signed on April 8. Italy undertook to support Prussia against Austria on the understanding that the

treaty would lapse if there were no war within three months.

The Austro-Prussian Diplomatic Struggle.—Bismarck also surprised everyone on April 9, 1866, by proposing at a special meeting of the federal diet that a German parliament should be elected by universal suffrage and should meet to discuss constitutional reform of the confederation. This offer of universal suffrage, which was an attempt to gain popular support, was only partly successful in winning the liberals, but it showed that reform of the federal constitution was Prussia's aim and not just the annexation of Schleswig and Holstein. During the next two months, too, Bismarck was in touch with the leaders of the Nationalverein in the other states of northern Germany; among them Bennigsen and Miquel in Hanover, in the hope of winning their support. They at least were prepared to support a policy of neutrality in an Austro-Prussian war and declared their belief in this policy at a liberal meeting at Frankfurt on May 20. Bismarck was not successful in eliminating the constitutional crisis in Prussia at this stage. Although after the success of the war with Denmark some of the Prussian liberals were prepared to vote Bismarck an indemnity for the period during which he had governed without a budget, the king was opposed to any such compromise and a suggestion made by Karl Twesten at the end of May 1866 for a solution of the conflict had to be refused.

The Austrians saw the Prussian preparations with alarm and began to strengthen their military forces in Bohemia. Alexander, Graf Mensdorff-Pouilly, Rechberg's successor as foreign minister, was anxious for a peaceful solution, but other members of the Austrian administration were eager to assert Austria's rights against Prussia by war if necessary, notably Ludwig, Freiherr von Biegeleben, the head of the German department in the Austrian foreign office. Austria's finances were in a bad state. The cost of the mobilization during the Crimean War in 1854–55 and of the war with Italy in 1859 had left its credit weak and it had been persistently excluded from the *Zollverein*. In 1862 a commercial treaty between Prussia and France gave France the most-favoured-nation treatment hitherto accorded to Austria under the treaty of 1853, and the *Zollverein* had been renewed in 1863 without Austria on the basis of the acceptance of the French treaty by the other members.

Nor did Austria succeed in welding the middle and small states of Germany into a solid anti-Prussian bloc. The two most important, Bavaria and Saxony, had ministers who still believed that the middle states could play a role of their own independently of Prussia and Austria. Moreover, Louis II of Bavaria was a neurotic young man who gave little of his time to the affairs of state. Many of the small states of central and northern Germany had been forced by their geographical position to sign military agreements with Prussia and the most that they could hope for in an Austro-Prussian struggle was neutrality. Hanover and Hesse-Kassel had rulers ready to support Austria but the liberals in both states wanted at least neutrality even when they did not actively desire a Prussian victory.

On April 21, 1866, the emperor Francis Joseph ordered the mobilization of Austria's southern army under the archduke Albert, and the army of the north under Ludwig von Benedek was mobilized between April 27 and May 5. Prussian mobilization was complete by May 8. Last minute attempts at mediation were unsuccessful. Napoleon III proposed a European congress (May 24) but, although Bismarck was ready to accept, the Austrians were prepared to do so only if the congress did not discuss any territorial increases for any of the participating states, and the proposal was dropped. Inside Germany an attempt was made by Anton von Gablenz, brother of the Austrian governor of Holstein, to mediate, but equally without success. By May 28 his proposals had been put aside. At the last minute Napoleon concluded a secret treaty with Austria by which it won, to receive Venetia, which was then to be handed over to Italy, while Austria was to receive compensation in Germany.

The Seven Weeks' War.—Early in June Austria summoned the diet of Holstein to meet on the 11th of the month and this step was immediately denounced by Prussia as a breach of the Gastein and other earlier agreements. Prussian troops entered Holstein on June 7. The last meeting of the federal diet took place on June 14, and at it Austria moved that troops of the confederation should be mobilized against Prussia. Bismarck denounced this step as unconstitutional and said that he would regard any states that voted for the Austrian proposal as being in a state of war with Prussia. Bavaria introduced a motion calling for the mobilization of contingents other than those of Austria and Prussia. This was carried by nine votes to six, Luxembourg, the Mecklenburg duchies and three groups of the smallest states of the north and centre voting against. The Prussian representative then left.

Prussian troops crossed the frontiers of Hanover, Saxony and Hesse-Kassel on the night of June 15-16. One army marched through Hesse toward the Main river; on June 29 the Hanoverian army was forced to capitulate despite their victory at Langensalza two days before. The Prussian army captured the king of Hanover and the elector of Hesse, crossed the Main and entered Bavaria.

In the south the Italians had engaged the Austrians but were defeated on land at Custoza (June 24) and at sea in a battle off Lissa (July 20). The main theatre of war, however, was Bohemia, where the Prussian armies advanced from Saxony and Silesia in accordance with the plan of Helmuth von Moltke. On July 3 Benedek's position at Sadowa (Königgrätz) was attacked by two Prussian armies, and they were joined by the third under the crown prince of Prussia at a critical moment. The Austrian army was utterly defeated. (*See* SEVEN WEEKS' WAR.)

King William and the generals would have liked to march on Vienna, but they were restrained by Bismarck supported by the crown prince. Rejecting an offer of mediation by Napoleon III, Bismarck began negotiations with the Austrians, and a preliminary peace was signed at Nikolsburg (Mikulov) on July 26 and embodied in the final peace of Prague on Aug. 23. The Austro-Italian peace treaty was signed on Oct. 3. Treaties with the southern states were negotiated during the same period. The terms were extremely mild. Austria paid an indemnity and surrendered Venetia to Italy but lost no other territory. Bavaria, Saxony, Württemberg, Baden and Hesse-Darmstadt paid indemnities but remained intact. Prussia annexed Schleswig-Holstein, Hanover, Hesse-Kassel and Frankfurt am Main. The southern states agreed that their armies should come under Prussian command in the event of war. The states north of the Main, together with the kingdom of Saxony, joined a new North German federation under Prussian leadership. The old confederation was at an end; and Austria had been finally excluded from Germany. (J. B. JL.)

L. THE GERMAN EMPIRE, 1866-71 AND 1871-1918

The Compromise of the Prussian Liberals.—The peace of Prague cleared the way for a settlement both in Prussia and in the wider affairs of Germany. The Prussian parliament had been dissolved at the beginning of the war, and new elections were held on the day of the battle of Sadowa. The liberals had a reduced majority, and they were now split in their attitude to Bismarck; his success had shaken their liberal principles. The moderates broke away from the Progressives (Deutsche Fortschrittspartei) to form the National Liberal party, a party in which liberalism was subordinated to nationalism. Bismarck, on his side, made a conciliatory gesture by asking for an act of indemnity for the unconstitutional collection of taxes since the beginning of the parliamentary struggle in 1862. This act was passed on Sept. 3, 1866, by 230 votes to 75. It was a decisive step in German history. The Prussian liberals, hitherto genuine opponents of Bismarck, dropped their insistence on parliamentary sovereignty in exchange for the prospect of German unity and for an assurance that united Germany would be administered in a "liberal" spirit. Instead of a struggle for power there was henceforth compromise. The capitalist middle classes ceased to demand control of the state; the crown and the Junker governing class conducted the state in a way which suited middle-class needs and outlook. Since the middle classes ceased to be liberals, the Prussian Junkers had to become "Germans." Neither side kept its bargain fully, and there were renewed alarms of constitutional struggle throughout the period of the empire. But the decision of Sept. 3, 1866, was not undone;

Germany did not become a constitutional monarchy of the western type.

North German Federation.—With the decisive defeat of Austria, Prussia was now the sole power in Germany. Bismarck was limited only by the promise given to Napoleon III that the states south of the Main should have "an internationally independent existence." All Germany north of the Main had been virtually conquered by Prussia, but Bismarck was anxious to conciliate south German opinion. Besides, he dreaded the radical nature of a unitary German state. Therefore he tried to change as little as possible, and the North German federation which he created in 1867 had curious echoes of the despised German confederation which had vanished in 1866. Indeed Bismarck still thought of German unification as primarily an affair of foreign policy; *i.e.*, to represent a united power abroad. For him the only difference with the period before the war of 1866 was that, instead of being balanced by Austria, Prussia now dominated, but since this domination was exercised in the interests of conservatism he expected little change. The federal constitution which he hastily drafted early in 1867 was not a sham. It contained genuine federal guarantees for the individual states. Nevertheless it was a pretense in that the reality on which it rested was not federal. A federation must be an association of states more or less equal in power; in the North German federation Prussia overshadowed the others so decisively that Prussian will was always likely to prevail.

The federal constitution was adopted by the North German *Reichstag* on April 17, 1867. Four years later it became almost without change the constitution of the German empire. Two principles were balanced against each other—the sovereignty of the German states and the national unity of the German people. In constitutional theory the first carried the day. The *Bundesrat* (federal council), its members nominated by the state governments, initiated laws, conducted the federal government and could alter the constitution by a two-thirds majority. (Prussia, which had 17 members out of 43, could thus veto any constitutional change.) The king of Prussia, as president of the federation, nominated the chancellor who was to carry out federal affairs under the direction of the *Bundesrat*. The *Reichstag*, on the other hand, elected by direct universal suffrage, was strictly limited to legislative activities; there was no provision by which it could interfere with the activities of the federal government. Even its control of finance was limited to an approval of expenditure, other than that permanently authorized by the constitution (court expenses, chancellor's salary, etc.); and since the member states were expected to supplement the regular federal revenue by "matricular" contributions, the *Reichstag* did not possess the usual parliamentary sanction of being able to cut off the government's income. Yet despite these provisions the *Bundesrat* soon lost all importance and the German government became in as much need of a parliamentary majority as though Germany were a thoroughly liberal state. The federal element counted for more in the sphere of administration where there was a real division of duties. The federal authority controlled foreign affairs, the army and economic affairs, and there was to be a single judicial system and a single legal code. The states conducted ordinary administration and remained in control of educational and religious matters.

The war of 1866 had destroyed the *Zollverein.* In July 1867 Bismarck offered to all German states a new customs union on condition that they accepted a customs parliament. As this parliament was to consist of the members of the North German *Reichstag* with members from southern Germany added, this was a way of smuggling in German unity by a side door. Thus the "line of the Main" was weakened, though not removed, within a year of its establishment as an international boundary. The North German federation was regarded by many, including Bismarck, as a halfway house to German unification which would stand for a long time. Indeed between 1867 and 1870 the movement for German unity lost ground in southern Germany. Early in 1870 the pro-Prussian government of Chlodwig, prince von Hohenlohe-Schillingsfürst, in Bavaria, was replaced by a clericalist government under Otto Camillus Hugo, Graf von Bray-Steinburg, and this gov-

GERMANY

ernment pushed ahead with plans for a separate South German confederation, predominantly Roman Catholic and under the protection of France and Austria. This underlined the precariousness of the existing situation, and the deciding question between 1867 and 1870 was not German opinion but whether France and Austria would come together in order to oppose Bismarck's policy or even to undo his work.

Tension With France (1867–70).—The first alarm came in 1867 when Napoleon III raised the question of Luxemburg. This had been a member of the old confederation and a Prussian garrison still remained there. Napoleon III proposed to buy the grand duchy from its ruler, the king of the Netherlands. There was an outcry in Germany and questions in the *Reichstag*. Bismarck held that no essentially German issue was at stake and probably held too that Prussia was not ready for a new war. But there was an uproar in Germany; and other European powers protested. After a conference in London, Luxembourg became an independent neutral state with its fortifications dismantled. Thereafter Napoleon sought more actively for an alliance with Austria but without effect. The Austrian government would not risk a new defeat and its real interest in the French alliance was to resist Russia in the near east —a concern far removed from Napoleon's preoccupation with Germany and the Rhine.

Early in 1870 Bismarck made a move against France which has been variously interpreted; he hinted unofficially to the provisional rulers of Spain that they should offer the throne to Leopold, prince von Hohenzollern-Sigmaringen, a member of the Roman Catholic branch of the Hohenzollern family. It has often been argued that Bismarck gave this advice in order to provoke France into war, and that he was driven to provoke war by the trend of opinion hostile to Prussia in southern Germany. There is little evidence for this. It is just as likely that he promoted the candidature to increase the prestige of the Hohenzollern dynasty or to keep out some ultramontane prince. At all events he could not have foreseen the folly of the French government which deliberately forced a crisis when it had already received satisfaction. Bismarck's intention had been to present the French with a *fait accompli*. They were to know nothing until Prince Leopold was actually elected. By the blunder of a cipher clerk the Spanish *Cortes* adjourned before Leopold's answer of acceptance arrived and the French government had to be told on July 3 why the *Cortes* was being recalled. There were wild protests in Paris and an immediate demand that Leopold be ordered to withdraw. On July 12 his father, Prince Karl Anton, renounced the Spanish candidature on Leopold's behalf. This was not enough for the French government; it insisted that King William, as head of the Hohenzollern family, should promise that the candidature be never renewed. This demand was presented to the king at Ems by Vincent Benedetti, the French ambassador, on July 13. Though the king refused to give a promise, he dismissed Benedetti in a friendly enough way. But when the 'Ems telegram' reached Bismarck, he shortened it in such a way as to imply that the king had refused to see the French ambassador again. This version provoked a French declaration of war on July 19. But though the Ems telegram gave the occasion for

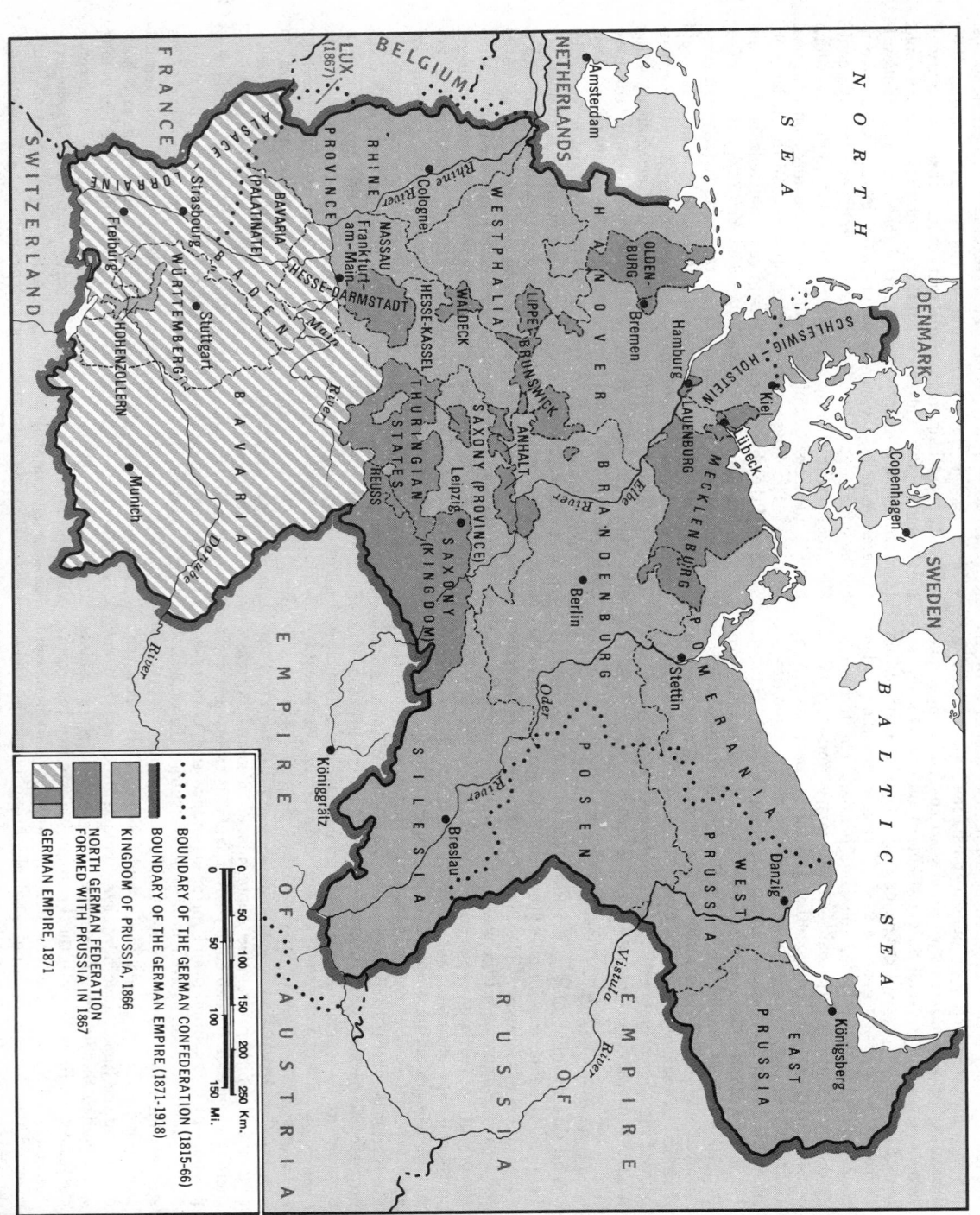

GERMANY IN THE 19TH CENTURY

········· BOUNDARY OF THE GERMAN CONFEDERATION (1815–66)

BOUNDARY OF THE GERMAN EMPIRE (1871–1918)

NORTH GERMAN FEDERATION FORMED WITH PRUSSIA IN 1867

KINGDOM OF PRUSSIA, 1866

GERMAN EMPIRE, 1871

rate treaties of union, which were concluded at the end of November. Some Bavarian wishes were fulfilled. Bavaria and Württemberg kept their own postal and telegraph services and were able to levy taxes on beer and brandy; Bavaria further kept its own army in peacetime. As a particularly meaningless concession, a committee of the *Bundesrat* under Bavarian chairmanship was to advise the chancellor on questions of foreign policy; the advice was seldom sought and never taken.

There remained the question of a name for the new state. Bismarck wished to revive the title of emperor, a proposal most unwelcome to William. It was equally unwelcome to Louis II of Bavaria, the one important German sovereign. With great adroitness Bismarck maneuvered one against the other and actually induced Louis to press the imperial title on William. The proposal was seconded by the other German princes and supported by the North German *Reichstag*; the leader of the *Reichstag* deputation was Eduard Simson, who had offered the imperial crown to Frederick William IV in 1849 on behalf of the Frankfurt assembly. William could hold out no longer; he was proclaimed German emperor at Versailles on Jan. 18, 1871.

war, the cause of it was to be found in the French determination to check Prussia's greatness and to restore the fading glory of Napoleon III's empire by a renewal of prestige in foreign policy.

The Franco-German War.—Though the war was perhaps not planned by Bismarck, it was certainly not unwelcome to him. It solved at a stroke the problem of south Germany, since all the south German states at once acknowledged their treaty obligations to Prussia and placed their troops under William's command. Austria dared not join France, Russia was won to benevolent neutrality by Bismarck's support of Russian designs in the Black sea, and Great Britain cared only for the neutrality of Belgium. The French had supposed that they would take the offensive. Instead, after a trivial victory at Saarbrücken, the French armies under Patrice de MacMahon were defeated on the frontiers at Wörth and Wissembourg (Aug. 4 and 6). One French army under Achille François Bazaine was driven into Metz and failed to break out in the two fierce battles of Mars-la-Tour and Gravelotte (Aug. 16 and 18). The main French army under MacMahon at first retreated and then attempted to pass the flank of the German forces in order to relieve Metz. This army was surrounded at Sedan and on Sept. 2 forced to surrender. That brought the overthrow of Napoleon and the establishment of a provisional government in Paris. The new government was resolved not to surrender any French territory, and the war was therefore continued. Strasbourg surrendered on Sept. 28, Metz on Oct. 27. The German armies were then free to press the siege of Paris throughout the winter. Though the French, under the inspiration of Léon Gambetta, made an amazing recovery, they were unable to relieve Paris which was compelled to capitulate on Jan. 28, 1871. An armistice was then concluded and a French national assembly elected which had to authorize the conclusion of peace. Preliminary terms were agreed to by Jules Favre on Feb. 26, and the final peace treaty was signed at Frankfurt am Main on May 10. France had to cede Alsace and most of Lorraine including Metz, its capital. Bismarck seems to have doubted the wisdom of such excessive demands, but was overborne by the German generals. On their prompting he also demanded Belfort, but abandoned this demand in exchange for a victory march by the German army through the streets of Paris. France had also to pay an indemnity of 5,000,-000,000 fr., and the Germans remained in occupation of part of France until the indemnity was paid. (*See also* FRANCO-GERMAN WAR.)

The Making of the Empire.—During the war, negotiations were pushed on for the uniting of all Germany outside Austria. In September a conference of Prussia, Bavaria and Württemberg met at Munich to discuss the terms of unification. Bray, the Bavarian prime minister, held out against any real union and demanded special treatment for Bavaria. Bismarck turned his flank by securing the incorporation of Baden in the North German federation. Bavaria and Württemberg then negotiated sepa-

The remaining formalities were few. A *Reichstag* was elected from all Germany, and this *Reichstag* accepted the constitution of 1867, with the concessions to Bavaria, as the imperial constitution on April 14, 1871. The new *Reich* consisted of 4 kingdoms, 5 grand duchies, 13 duchies and principalities and 3 free cities (Hamburg, Lübeck and Bremen). Alsace-Lorraine was treated as a conquered province. It was made a *Reichsland* and ruled by an imperial governor or *Statthalter*. In theory this was a temporary settlement, but Alsace-Lorraine never developed the German loyalty which would have qualified it for autonomy. The constitution left open the great question of the powers of the *Reichstag* over the executive. The question was symbolized in two forms: the position of the imperial chancellor and the method of authorizing expenditure on the army. The chancellor was defined as "responsible" but it was not stated to whom; Bismarck contended that he was responsible to the emperor, while the politicians tried to insist that he was responsible to the *Reichstag*. As to military credits, Bismarck tried to include the sums necessary for an army of 400,-000 men as a permanent grant in the constitution, and thus exempt from parliamentary criticism or control. He failed to carry this and had to agree to a compromise, the *Septennat*, by which military credits were voted for seven years—hence the political crises which occurred every seven years, when artificial alarm had to be created in order to renew the army grant.

Bismarck's Liberal Period and the Kulturkampf.—Bismarck had been on bad terms with the Prussian Junkers or conservatives ever since 1866, and the estrangement was completed by the creation of the empire. Only a small group, the Reichspartei, composed mainly of officials, remained loyal to him. On the other hand, the National Liberals were more enthusiastic for Bismarck than ever before, and from 1871 to 1879 they formed almost a government party. Bismarck discussed proposals for legislation with their leader, Rudolf von Bennigsen, and the National Liberals supported his general conduct of policy. Moreover, in the first years, the National Liberals managed to win more votes than any other single party despite universal suffrage; only in 1879 did it become clear that a purely middle-class party could not keep its hold on peasant and working-class voters. Thus the first period of the empire was the great age of liberal reform. Germany was given at a stroke uniform legal procedure, uniform coinage and uniform administration. An imperial bank was created, most restrictions on freedom of enterprise and freedom of movement were removed, and limited companies and trade combinations were allowed. Freedom of the press was secured in 1874. Work was begun on an imperial civil code, which finally extended to all Germany in 1900. Particularly important was the establishment of municipal autonomy in 1873; this freed the towns from the control of the *Landrat* (usually a large landowner) and cleared the way for the development of local government, in which Germany led the world.

Bismarck's alliance with the National Liberals naturally led him into conflict with the Roman Catholics, who made up more than a third of the population of the new empire. The conflict began after the Vatican council of 1870 had declared the infallibility of the pope. Some leading German Roman Catholics, known as Old Catholics, opposed these decrees; and the church demanded that the German states should dismiss all Old Catholic teachers. Thus a struggle began over the independence of the Roman Catholic Church. The conflict was also political. The German Roman Catholics were anti-Prussian both by tradition and by geography; they were at once particularist and "great German," in that they favoured both the small states and the German Austrians. As the struggle developed, the Roman Catholics strengthened their political organization, the Centre party, and this party cut across class and state lines. The Centre was, in fact, its confessional nature, it could never win a majority. But it was strong enough to menace the stability of Bismarck's political system.

The conflict with the Roman Church, the so-called Kulturkampf, was fought by Bismarck with all his usual exaggeration and violence. He abolished the special section in the Prussian ministry which dealt with Roman Catholic affairs, made marriage an exclusively civil proceeding and insisted on a state degree before a priest was appointed to a benefice. When the church excommunicated all Old Catholic teachers, Bismarck answered by expelling the Jesuits from Germany. The clergy refused to appear before the state courts or to pay the fines which were imposed. The archbishops of Posen and Cologne were imprisoned and the former deposed. These penal measures were expressed in the "May laws" which the Prussian *Landtag* passed in 1873, and were by further measures promoted by Adalbert Falk, the Prussian minister of cults, in 1874 and 1875. By then it was clear that Bismarck would not achieve victory. The Old Catholics carried no weight and even many Protestants, particularly among the Junkers, disliked this attack on religious teaching. Though Bismarck still allowed the struggle to continue, he put increasing responsibility on Falk and thus made it easy for himself to repudiate responsibility when the time came for a change of course. The conflict also served a purpose in foreign policy. It was a move against the Roman Catholic powers, France and Austria-Hungary, and a gesture in favour of Protestant England and Orthodox Russia. By 1877 the needs of Bismarck's foreign policy were changing. The danger of an ultramontane bloc had disappeared, if it had ever existed; and here too the way was open for a change of course.

The Breach with the National Liberals.—The first Bismarckian system broke down between 1877 and 1879. In 1877 Bismarck, still at odds with the Centre, offered to make Bennigsen, the leader of the National Liberals in the *Reichstag*, a Prussian minister. Bennigsen thought that this was the preliminary to a fully parliamentary ministry and insisted on bringing in two Liberal colleagues with him. Bismarck refused and, from that moment, was determined on a reconciliation with the Conservatives and the Centre in order to escape from National Liberal control. He had also pressing financial motives for this breach. The revenues allotted to the empire by the constitution were from the first inadequate, and Bismarck disliked the dependence on contributions from the separate states which this involved. The National Liberals wished to create direct imperial taxation, in order to increase the power of the *Reichstag*; for the opposite reason Bismarck was determined to institute indirect taxes. He attempted to introduce a tobacco monopoly but was defeated by National Liberal opposition. Later he had still more urgent reasons for action. Toward the end of the decade German agriculture faced the challenge of American wheat for the first time, and Bismarck was determined to protect German agriculture for reasons of social conservatism and also because he regarded the agricultural workers as the best element for the army in time of war. But it was not only agriculture that needed protection. German industry, too, was hard hit by the great economic crisis of 1873 and there, also, Bismarck was determined to protect a great iron and steel industry so as to ensure German strength in wartime. Thus every motive combined to thrust him over into

a policy of protection—agricultural protection to satisfy the Junkers; industrial protection to satisfy the capitalists; and an escape from the interference of the *Reichstag* by the increase in custom dues.

The last of the old duties, inherited from the *Zollverein*, were repealed in 1877 and a new protective tariff was introduced in 1879. This tariff was opposed by the National Liberal party, which in 1880 broke into two. One group, which retained the party name, hoped to renew the alliance with Bismarck; the other formed the Liberal Union party, which in 1884 joined the Progressives under Eugen Richter to form the German Radical party (Deutsche Freisinnige Partei). In return Bismarck struck a bargain with the Centre. He agreed that the conflict with the Roman Catholic Church should be called off and that any increase in the customs yield beyond 130,000,000 marks (M.) a year should be divided among the individual states—a striking illustration of the Centre's particularism. The new tariff was then passed on June 12, 1879, and Germany became a protectionist country.

Bismarck kept his bargain with the Centre. Falk resigned after being repudiated by Bismarck in the *Reichstag*. In 1880 Bismarck got power to suspend the May laws in individual cases and the secular examination for candidates to the priesthood was abolished. Pope Leo XIII, more conciliatory than his predecessor Pius IX, made Bismarck's task easy; he induced the two recalcitrant archbishops to resign. Peace was finally concluded in 1887. The peace was a compromise, not a defeat for Bismarck as sometimes suggested. The Roman Catholic Church preserved intact the education of priests for which it had been contending. In exchange the Roman Catholic party of the Centre accepted Bismarck's *Reich* and tacitly agreed to support his policy when confessional issues were not at stake. In fact the Centre became purely a party of tactics, once its religious concerns were secured.

The Attack on the Social Democrats.—Bismarck always believed that every political system needed an enemy or whipping boy. The Centre had been the whipping boy of the liberal era; the Socialists were now chosen to take its place. Bismarck genuinely believed that the Social Democrats, as the followers of Karl Marx called themselves, represented a grave social peril; he took them as seriously as Metternich had taken the threat from "the revolution." In 1877 the Social Democrats won 12 seats at the general election. Bismarck then introduced exceptional legislation against them, but was thwarted by the National Liberal majority. An attempted assassination of the emperor on June 2, 1878, gave Bismarck the opportunity to dissolve the *Reichstag* and to win the election on the cry of "the social peril." The Liberals lost some seats and the Conservatives gained some. The so-called exceptional laws were then carried, on Oct. 19, 1878; the Social Democratic party was declared illegal and its press and its meetings were forbidden. In practice these laws amounted to little. Social Democrats were still candidates at elections and still sat in the *Reichstag*; their journals were easily smuggled in from Switzerland; and in all, between 1878 and 1890, only 1,500 persons were imprisoned. But as a political maneuver the attack on the Social Democrats secured a Conservative majority in 1879. Bismarck's other weapon against the Social Democrats was his social policy. Bismarck had never shared the laissez faire views of the Liberals and his breach with them freed his hands for measures of social security. The workers, too, were to be made to feel that they had a stake in the greatness of the German *Reich*. In 1881 he proposed a system of compulsory accident insurance, supported in part by subsidies from the *Reich*. This met with opposition from the Liberals, who in 1881 recovered in part from their defeat of 1878, and the Industrial Accident Insurance act was not enacted until June 1884. The previous year the German Sickness Insurance act had been effected, and a system of old-age pensions also was subsidized by the *Reich*. Though the Social Democrats remained theoretically revolutionary, Bismarck's aim was achieved; the workers came to believe they were benefiting not from their own efforts but from the state.

Foreign and Colonial Policy (1879-87).—The year 1879 also

GERMANY

marked an epoch in Bismarck's foreign policy. Once the empire was founded, Bismarck's sole aim was peace and security. This aim never varied, though methods changed. In the first years of the *Reich* Bismarck had aimed at peace by avoiding foreign commitments and he was resolutely impartial during the great eastern crisis of 1875-78 (see EASTERN QUESTION; also BERLIN, CONGRESS OF). Thereafter Bismarck came to see that he must take a more active line if Europe was to be kept at peace. On Oct. 7, 1879, he concluded a defensive alliance with Austria-Hungary against Russia; though this guaranteed Austria-Hungary's survival as a great power, it did not provide German support for its Balkan ambitions. Indeed Bismarck always advocated a partition of the Balkans between Austria-Hungary and Russia. The Austro-German alliance, far from estranging Russia, won it back to the side of peace and conservatism, and the League of the Three Emperors (June 18, 1881) was a revival, in more modern terms, of Metternich's Holy alliance. But its precondition was that neither Russia nor Austria-Hungary should have Balkan ambitions, a condition almost impossible of fulfilment. To give Austria-Hungary greater security, Bismarck also concluded the triple alliance between Germany, Austria and Italy (May 20, 1882), by which Germany guaranteed Italy against France in exchange for Italian neutrality in the event of a war between Austria-Hungary and Russia. The triple alliance was not a vital part of Bismarck's diplomatic system; it seemed to become essential to Germany only when his successors failed to keep on good terms with Russia.

Bismarck's diplomacy became increasingly elaborate in method when a new eastern crisis arose over Bulgaria in 1885. His aim remained the same—to avoid being drawn into a war between Russia and Austria-Hungary and if possible therefore to prevent such a war. Since Russia and Austria-Hungary would not agree, each side had to be strengthened so as to maintain the balance between them. On the Russian side Bismarck concluded the Reinsurance treaty (June 18, 1887), promising Russia diplomatic support in Bulgaria and at the straits (Bosporus and Dardanelles) and agreeing to stay neutral unless Russia attacked Austria-Hungary. On the other side Bismarck promoted the Mediterranean naval agreements between Italy, Great Britain and Austria-Hungary (likewise in 1887), which virtually created a triple entente opposed to Russia in the near east. These complicated arrangements subsequently led men of lesser understanding to accuse Bismarck of duplicity, but they served their purpose of averting a new Balkan war. Since Germany occupied the centre of Europe, its policy was bound to be two-faced.

Bismarck was long sternly opposed to German expansion overseas; he believed that Germany ran enough risks in Europe without also challenging the imperial interests of Great Britain and France. But when he had to choose between satisfying German national feeling by supporting German expansion in southeastern Europe and thus identifying himself with Austro-Hungarian ambitions or by launching colonies overseas, he chose the less provocative course. He had also a subsidiary motive in considerations of foreign policy. Between 1883 and 1885 he strove actively for a reconciliation with France, and he believed that this reconciliation would be easier if Germany were in conflict with Great Britain, France's colonial rival. Bismarck deliberately chose areas which were on the fringe of British colonial interests in the hope of provoking a violent British reaction: thus South-West Africa trampled on the toes of Cape colony, and New Guinea on the toes of Australia. His two tropical colonies, the Cameroons and East Africa, cut across the British plans that were just developing for a new empire in central Africa. The French, however, remained suspicious, and the colonial conflict with Great Britain failed to mature, for the British were too conciliatory. In 1885 Bismarck called off the conflict, especially as he needed British support for Austria-Hungary, and he would have been glad to get rid of the German colonies except for the pressure of colonialist feeling inside Germany. The German colonial empire was never a serious factor in German economic life; the colonies were an embarrassment, not a source of strength, and important only as an emotional outlet for the growing sense of German power. Though Bismarck had made the German empire in 1871

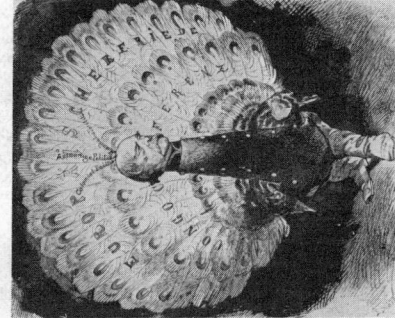

"HOW DO WE STAND IN THE WORLD NOW?": CARICATURE OF BISMARCK FROM "KLADDERADATSCH," BERLIN, 1884

by evoking national feeling, he was anxious thereafter to arrest German expansion. His social and political conservatism made him dread a Germany that would dominate all Europe. Hence he sought to divert German nationalism into harmless channels. With this purpose, he took up the struggle with the Poles in eastern Germany. This struggle began in the days of the conflict with the Roman Catholic Church and was continued in 1886 by an economic war to eliminate Polish landowners and to establish German colonists in the eastern marches. The conflict had the great advantage of being directed against a Slav people and yet being welcomed by Russia, itself in conflict with the Poles. For similar reasons, Bismarck exacerbated the conflict in the *Reichsland*, Alsace-Lorraine. This estranged even German liberals from France and made them tolerate Bismarck's policy of friendship with tsarist Russia. In essence, Bismarck wished to keep up hostility with France as being less risky for conservative Germany than a struggle for existence in eastern Europe.

This was well shown in the so-called war crisis of 1887. Bismarck had tried to win the general election of 1884 solely on the issue of colonies, but this cry had strengthened the left-wing parties, instead of the conservatives, who were opposed to colonial expansion. By 1887 the time for a new army grant was approaching; and Bismarck knew that he could not carry it through the existing *Reichstag*. Bismarck therefore deliberately raised the alarm of a French "*revanche*," and his maneuver was successful. The *Reichstag* threw out the army bill and was dissolved in Jan. 1887. Bismarck fought the election on the cry "the fatherland in danger" and won a majority for his coalition of agrarian and industrial supporters. The reconstituted National Liberals, the party of capitalist interest, became the largest single party in the *Reichstag* for the last time (122 members). The Bismarckian coalition carried the army bill on March 11, 1887. It was Bismarck's last triumph.

The Fall of Bismarck.—Bismarck's impregnable position had a weak spot; he must be regarded by the emperor as indispensable. The old emperor, William I, remained faithful until his death on March 9, 1888; he never forgot that Bismarck had saved him from "liberalism" in 1862. Frederick III, his son and successor, was bound to Bismarck by memory of the triumphs of 1870. Liberal in phrase, he was at best National Liberal and, like the other National Liberals, would have made his peace with Bismarck in exchange for a few concessions. But he was already a dying man and his reign of 99 days ended on June 15, 1888. William II (*q.v.*), third and last German emperor, had no memory of past dangers or past victories to bind him to Bismarck. He represented the new Germany which knew no moderation, the self-confident Germany which recognized no limits to German power. At the same time, he was impatient with Bismarck's social conservatism, which seemed to estrange the emperor from the mass of his subjects.

The dispute came to a head after the general election of 1890. Bismarck had failed to hit on a national cry and failed to carry the election. The Bismarckian coalition of Conservatives and National Liberals fell from 220 to 135; the Radicals, Centre and Social Democrats rose from 141 to 207. Bismarck wished to tear up the imperial constitution which he himself had made and to set up a naked military dictatorship. William II was determined to continue on the path of demagogy, appealing still more strongly to German national sentiment. There were, of course, also elements of personal conflict. Bismarck objected to the emperor's interference on questions of policy; William objected to Bismarck's attempts to maneuver with the party leaders, especially with Ludwig Windthorst, the leader of the Centre. But essentially it was a conflict between the old Junker Germany which tried to maintain moderation for reasons of conservatism and the new imperialist Germany which was without moderation. Once Bismarck had quarreled with the emperor, he had no real support, for he had always fought the parties of the German masses. He tried without success to engineer a strike of Prussian ministers. Finally he was opposed even by the leaders of the German masses. Finally he was opposed even by the leaders of Prussian ministers. He tried without success to engineer a strike of Prussian ministers. Finally he was opposed even by the leaders of Prussian army. On March 18, 1890, he was forced to resign.

Caprivi.—Bismarck's successor was Leo von Caprivi (q.v.), a military administrator who, despite his conservatism, accepted William II's policy of winning over the parties of the masses. Caprivi inaugurated the four years of the "new course," an attempt to follow a more democratic line without changing the social or economic foundations. Caprivi's first act was to refuse to renew the Reinsurance treaty with Russia, thus breaking the partnership between tsardom and the Junkers which had been the basis of Bismarck's policy. Caprivi promised German support for Austro-Hungarian plans in the Balkans, and he dreamed of bringing Great Britain as a fourth partner into the triple alliance. The symbol of this hope was the treaty of July 1, 1890, by which Germany received Heligoland in exchange for concessions to British interests in East Africa. In economic affairs Caprivi lowered the Bismarckian tariffs and looked forward to a free-trade era, in which German trade would expand overseas under the protection of the British navy.

Caprivi refused to renew the anti-Socialist laws and viewed without dismay the increase in the Socialist vote. He carried measures of social security and of factory inspection, which offended the great capitalists as much as his free-trade policy offended the agrarians. To please the Centre, Caprivi promoted an education bill which gave the church control of religious instruction. This led to a revolt of Prussian ministers, headed by Johannes von Miquel, now Prussian minister of finance and a former National Liberal. In the outcome the bill had to be withdrawn and the Centre party returned to opposition. At bottom Caprivi's problem was the same as Bismarck's; i.e., how to carry the septennial army grant. But Caprivi meant to carry it with the support of the Centre and of the left-wing parties, the Radicals and the Socialists. It was symbolical of his opportunist policy that in 1892 he ceased to be Prussian prime minister; in theory the Prussian Junkers ceased to dominate the *Reich*. Caprivi introduced an increased army grant in the autumn of 1892; in view of his "liberal" foreign policy, he had to invoke the danger from Russia, not from France, and this led the conservative parties to oppose

the bill. As the Centre also opposed it because of the education bill, it was rejected. Caprivi dissolved the *Reichstag* and tried the line of more social concession to please the Social Democrats and a reduction of the period of the army grant from seven to five years to please all the parties of the left. The Radical party split, a minority (the Freisinnige Vereinigung) supporting the army bill and being joined by some of the Centre party. The Centre members supported Caprivi purely as a matter of tactics; the Radicals supported him from the conviction that even radical Germans should favour war against Russia, a conviction shared by the Social Democrats.

The split in the Radical party was the end of German radicalism, an event as decisive as the split between the Progressives and the National Liberals in 1866. Caprivi's anti-Russian line led even the Polish deputies to support the army bill, a unique event in the history of the *Reich*. With this miscellaneous support the army grant was renewed on July 13, 1893.

Caprivi, though a conservative, tried to behave as if Germany had passed through a liberal revolution. He played for the support of the parties of the left and, in political and economic matters alike, ignored the interests of the Junkers and of the great capitalists as though they no longer held the keys of power. He had claimed that this would lessen the appeal of the Social Democrats; instead they increased their representation to 44 in the general election of 1893. William II was now disillusioned with the policy of social concessions and began to advocate most of the violent measures that Bismarck had been dismissed for supporting in 1890. Moreover Botho, Graf zu Eulenburg, the Prussian prime minister, also advocated a revival of the anti-Socialist laws. Caprivi answered by proposing that the Prussian franchise should be revised in a democratic spirit. The struggle between Junker Prussia and democratic Germany, which Bismarck had avoided, seemed to be approaching; but democratic Germany was not fighting for itself. Its cause was merely being promoted by Caprivi, an enlightened general.

Caprivi's fall was hastened by the failure of his foreign policy. He had counted on winning Great Britain for the triple alliance but the British would not commit themselves. In June 1894 Caprivi's subordinates, Adolf von Marschall von Bieberstein, the secretary of state, and Friedrich von Holstein (q.v.), the real adviser on foreign policy, tried to blackmail Great Britain into friendship by joining with France to oppose British schemes in central Africa; this was the first open dispute with Great Britain since 1885. The British, far from being won over, were estranged and repudiated their earlier promises of support for Austria-Hungary. Germany had consequently to try to restore good relations with Russia. Thus foreign policy, too, dictated a return to conservatism. In Oct. 1894 William II "solved" the conflict between Caprivi and Eulenburg by abruptly dismissing both. There was neither anti-Socialist law nor revision of the Prussian franchise; merely a prolongation of the Bismarckian compromise or deadlock.

Hohenlohe.—Hohenlohe-Schillingsfürst (q.v.), the new chancellor, had been prime minister of Bavaria before 1870 and subsequently *Statthalter* of Alsace-Lorraine. His greatest qualification was that he was 75; he was to revive the glories of the age of Bismarck without the personal difficulties of the great man's temper. Hohenlohe at first found it easy to get on good terms with the Conservatives. Moreover, his Bavarian experience had made him less hostile to the

STAATSBIBLIOTHEK BERLIN BILDARCHIV (HANDKE)

THE OPENING OF THE REICHSTAG BY EMPEROR WILLIAM II AFTER HIS CORONATION, 1888: A PAINTING BY ANTON VON WERNER

Centre than Bismarck had been, and he won the support of the Centre by agreeing to many of their confessional demands.

In foreign policy Hohenlohe renewed German friendship with Russia, a task made easier by the shift of Russian interest to the far east. He refused to support Bismarck's land legislation against the Poles. The Social Democrats were again treated as a subversive force but Hohenlohe made no serious effort to pass new anti-Socialist laws. In fact, his short period of effective rule, from 1894 to 1897, was an attempt to repeat the era of Bismarck without its troubles. Hohenlohe tried to behave like a good-tempered Bismarck, and William II modeled himself on his grandfather. The most striking event of this period was the flagrant dispute with Great Britain over the Boer republics which culminated in the Kruger telegram (Jan. 3, 1896) congratulating the president of the Transvaal on having defeated the Jameson raid. Like many of Bismarck's demonstrations in foreign policy, this was an attempt to satisfy German feeling by a display of power, proof that Germany now counted for something even in South Africa. The Kruger telegram did not affect British policy in South Africa, but it had a lasting effect on German feeling; it taught the Germans, for the first time, to regard the British as their principal rivals in imperial greatness.

Bülow and "World Policy."—Hohenlohe was too old to inaugurate a new policy or even to revive an old one; he could not even control the demagogic enthusiasms of William II. Philipp, Graf zu Eulenburg, the emperor's only personal friend, wished to bring his erratic behaviour under some control and in June 1897 persuaded him to appoint Bernhard von Bülow (*q.v.*) secretary of state. Bülow became at once the leading man, a position openly acknowledged on Oct. 17, 1900, when he displaced Hohenlohe as chancellor. Bülow's task, in Eulenburg's words, was "to satisfy Germany without injuring the emperor"; in other words, to display imperial power without allowing William to make a fool of himself. In home affairs Bülow depended on Miquel, Prussian minister of finance since 1891 and vice-president of the Prussian ministry in 1898. Miquel was a former Radical, once a friend of Karl Marx, and now intent on reviving the partnership between Junker agrarianism and pan-German industrialism which had been broken in the days of Caprivi. All through the 1890s the Junkers had threatened to "bolt," as they did when they brought down Caprivi, thus displaying too openly the artificial Prussian control of the *Reich* which Bismarck had cloaked in national phrases. Miquel bought the Junkers anew for the *Reich*, not, as Bismarck had done, with arguments of high conservative principle, but literally by high tariffs on grain and by favouritism in fiscal policy. Tariffs on food would make the *Reich* self-sufficient in time of war, and easy credits for the Junkers were to enable them to defend the "national" cause against Polish encroachments. Miquel's financial policy, culminating in the high and rigid tariff of 1902, made the Junkers economically dependent on the *Reich*. Though they might still dislike the policy of limitless expansion, the mortgages which weighed on every estate east of the Elbe made them unwilling accomplices in pan-Germanism.

Bülow's own contribution was "world policy," the pursuit of grandeur abroad in order to stave off reform or conflict at home. The new generation of Germans wished to experience anew the glories of the age of unification without its risks or dangers and such organizations as the Colonial society, the Navy league and the Pan-German league existed more for the purpose of boasting than anything else. Nevertheless it was impossible to continue boasting without coming to believe that the boasts were true, and in time the demagogic organizations of imperialism took the government prisoner. There was some foundation for their boasts. Thanks to the iron and steel of the Ruhr, Germany had become the greatest industrial power of Europe, and there was nothing to stop its economic domination of the continent if it pursued a cautious foreign policy, relying on peaceful penetration, not on armed force. This was the justification for Bülow's policy of "the free hand," keeping Germany free from foreign alliances except its virtual protectorate over Austria-Hungary. Even the Austro-German alliance seemed without risk, since Russia was now absorbed in the far east. Bülow's great object was to avoid being drawn into the far eastern conflict between Russia and Great Britain. He repeatedly rejected the British offers of an alliance, made most positively by Joseph Chamberlain in March 1898 and by Lord Lansdowne, British foreign secretary, in the spring of 1901. This British attempt is often treated as a turning point in the relations of the great powers, but this is to misunderstand its meaning. The British were concerned solely with China and were incapable of giving the Germans any support in Europe; the Germans were thus being asked to fight a war for existence against both Russia and France for the sake of British investments in the far east. Nor did the failure of the alliance negotiations lead to an estrangement between Great Britain and Germany. Bülow was as careful not to offend Great Britain in Africa as not to offend Russia in China. In Aug. 1898 he concluded an agreement with the British for a hypothetical partition of the Portuguese colonial empire and in exchange abandoned German patronage of the Boer republics. Moreover, during the South African War, official German policy remained strictly neutral, though public opinion in Germany (as elsewhere in Europe) was strongly on the side of the Boers.

Tirpitz and the German Navy.—Far more decisive in its effect on Anglo-German relations was the building of a great German navy, first sketched in the Navy law of 1898 and fully launched by the Navy law of 1900. The protagonist of this policy was Alfred von Tirpitz (*q.v.*), secretary of state for the navy since 1897. The essence of Tirpitz' naval policy was a great battle fleet, and he justified this by various strategical arguments. At times he spoke of a "risk theory," that Great Britain, on bad terms with Russia and France, would not risk a conflict with a German navy even smaller than its own; at others he envisaged a "decisive battle" with the British fleet. At bottom, Tirpitz, like the other supporters of the great navy, simply held that a great navy was essential to a great power; or, in the words of Theobald von Bethmann Hollweg, that it was necessary "for the general purposes of imperial greatness." Tirpitz insisted that the navy must be planned on a long-term basis, and the Navy law of 1900 laid down the lines on which the German navy should develop until 1917. This made it difficult or impossible to modify German building plans when the British later sought a naval agreement. Here again it would be a mistake to put too early a significance on the German navy. So long as the German plans were merely plans, they did not alarm British opinion much; the great naval scare came only after 1908 when the German navy seemed to be approaching British strength.

The naval projects played an essential part in German home policy. In 1897, when the plans were first drafted, German industry was going through a period of depression, and one object of the great navy was to provide a stable demand, at the taxpayers' expense, for German iron and steel. It was a concession to the German steel magnates which balanced Miquel's favouritism of the Junker landowners. But the navy had a wider appeal. Unlike the army, which retained its Prussian character, the navy was essentially German, an affair of the *Reich*, and now Tirpitz' plans won the support of many liberals who would have opposed an anti-British policy on any other issue. Most striking of all, the Centre voted solidly for the second Navy law (1900) though it drew most of its support from peasants and artisans in areas far from the great ports. With this vote the Centre openly joined the government coalition. It tried to make one condition—that the navy should be paid for by direct taxation. This was the old demand that the Liberals had made in regard to the army. The Centre, too, was unsuccessful; the conservative agrarians had supported the navy only on condition that it should be financed by increases in the taxes on food or by an increase in the national debt. Direct imperial taxation was the vital issue on which the landed classes maintained a veto almost until the outbreak of World War I. In fact, the navy, like the army before it, was largely paid for by state borrowing. Thus inflationary finance, by which Germany conducted World War I, was the basis of the fiscal policy of the *Reich* long before the outbreak of war. Implicit in it was the argument, based on the French indemnity of 1871, that the army and navy would in time pay for themselves by imposing terms of conquest on the other nations of Europe.

The First Moroccan Crisis (1905–06).—The policy of "the free hand," which Bülow conducted on Holstein's advice, assumed that Great Britain, France and Russia would always remain on bad terms, because of their conflicts in Africa and the far east. So long as these conflicts continued, Germany could ignore such a triviality as Italy's reconciliation with France (1902), which was upset by the Anglo-Japanese alliance of 1902, which enabled the British to check the Russians in the far east without becoming involved themselves; this was shown in 1904 when the Russo-Japanese War broke out. The Germans would have welcomed a conflict between Russia and Great Britain, but they were far from willing to join in the war on the Russian side. The most they were prepared to offer was an alliance with Russia which would become operative when the war in the far east was over. This offer was made in Nov. 1904 and repeated by William II in theatrical terms when he met the Russian emperor Nicholas II at Björkö in July 1905. The offer had no attractions for the Russians; once they had been defeated in the far east, their enemy would be Austria-Hungary, not Great Britain. Bülow and Holstein, however, believed that the principal opposition to a "continental bloc" against Great Britain came from France. They therefore decided to use the opportunity of Russia's preoccupation in the far east to force France into dependence on Germany, the more so as the Anglo-French entente (April 8, 1904) had been concluded without inquiring into Germany's position. The result was the first Moroccan crisis.

On March 31, 1905, William II landed at Tangier and announced German support for Moroccan independence. The French sought to negotiate. They were answered by a German demand for the resignation of Théophile Delcassé, French foreign minister, and faced, as they supposed, by a threat of war, gave way. Delcassé resigned and on the same day William II created Bülow a prince. This was the reward for success on a Bismarckian scale. But thereafter things went wrong for Germany. Holstein had launched the Moroccan crisis in the old style of cabinet diplomacy without making any attempt to prepare German opinion, which was indifferent to Moroccan affairs. The French received strong diplomatic support from the British, including even military conversations against a possible German aggression, and recovered their nerve. At the conference of Algeciras (Jan.–April 1906) the Germans were compelled to acquiesce in French predominance in Morocco and to content themselves with a shadow recognition of its independence. Holstein resigned in protest against this compromise and the German foreign ministry was left without any guiding intelligence until Alfred von Kiderlen-Wächter (q.v.) became secretary of state in 1909. The crisis had been the first for almost 20 years; and it had ended in failure for Germany. The Bismarckian system had been accepted by Germans because it had offered them success abroad; now this capital of success had been exhausted. The German government would either have to make political concessions at home or seek success abroad by more violent means.

The Bülow Bloc.—In 1906 it still seemed possible that Germany might follow the path of liberal reform. Until 1906 Bülow had controlled the *Reichstag* by a coalition of Conservatives and the Centre. This coalition was held together by concessions to the agrarian interest of the one and the confessional interest of the other. In 1906 the Centre put their price too high; they demanded a large share of government appointments for Roman Catholic officials and special privileges for Roman Catholic missionaries in the German colonies. When these terms were refused, they voted against the military grants for suppressing a native revolt in South-West Africa (Oct. 1906). Since the colonies were a popular cause, Bülow seized the opportunity to break with the Centre and organized instead a coalition between the Conservatives and the non-Socialist parties of the left; even the two Radical groups, which had held out against the government until now, joined the Bülow bloc. Bülow believed that this coalition, in which the left predominated, would enable him to solve the financial problem; he would be able to carry direct taxation over Conservative opposition. The bloc was successful at the general election of 1907, principally at the expense of the Social Democrats. Bülow now followed a progressive policy in colonial administration and revived the struggle against the Poles, which had always been a popular cause. But he was still the prisoner of the Conservatives; he failed to reform the Prussian franchise, and he was unable to introduce direct taxation.

The logical consequence of the swing toward liberalism in home affairs should have been a *rapprochement* with England and an estrangement from Russia, as in the days of Caprivi. Bülow certainly attempted to improve relations with Great Britain, but his hands were tied by Tirpitz' naval plans, which after the development of the dreadnought or all-big-gun ship reached their most dangerous point. In fact Anglo-German relations took a sharp turn for the worse in 1908 and reached a crisis in March 1909, with the great naval scare in Great Britain. In order to get a yearly program of six dreadnoughts against Germany's four, Reginald McKenna, the first lord of the admiralty, had exaggerated Germany's building rate. This frightened the public into demanding more than McKenna himself wanted and "We want eight and we won't wait" became the slogan. On the other hand Bülow certainly accomplished the

"PERHAPS WE OUGHT TO HAVE A BRAKE," CARTOON BY T. T. HEINE IN "SIMPLICISSIMUS," JUNE 1907, ON THE ERRATIC COURSE OF THE EMPEROR'S FOREIGN POLICY

estrangement from Russia. In Oct. 1908 Russia and Austria-Hungary fell out over the Balkans, when Austria-Hungary annexed Bosnia-Hercegovina. Despite the criticism expressed by William II, the German government decided to support Austria-Hungary unreservedly and in March 1909 settled the crisis by a virtual ultimatum to Russia. The Bismarckian attitude of indifference in Balkan affairs was decisively abandoned, and later attempts to return to it proved ineffectual. Yet Bülow condemned his own policy when he said, on his resignation, "No more Bosnias."

The high-water mark of Bülow's pose as a liberal statesman came in the autumn of 1908. In the "liberal" atmosphere of the Bülow bloc it became fashionable to blame William II for the erratic course of German policy and for all the failures of the preceding years. Criticism of the emperor became stronger in 1907 after Eulenburg was driven from public life by charges of immorality. In Oct. 1908 the English *Daily Telegraph* published an interview with William II on Anglo-German relations. This interview, in the usual rhapsodical style of imperial utterances, naïvely expressed the bewilderment which most Germans felt at the British resentment against German "world policy." Ordinarily it would have passed unnoticed; in the autumn of 1908, with isolation abroad and liberal stirrings at home, it became the focus of every German discontent. William II had in fact submitted the interview to the German foreign ministry before passing it for publication but Bülow made out that he had been too busy to read it. While ostensibly accepting responsibility, he encouraged the uproar in the *Reichstag* (Nov. 10–12) and public opinion was satisfied only when Bülow announced that in future William II would "respect his constitutional obligations." This seemed a great victory for liberal principles and for Bülow personally. He seemed to have broken the imperial authority which had been too much for Bismarck. But this was true only if Bülow remained in control of the *Reichstag* and that soon escaped him. The Conservatives resented Bülow's quarrel with Russia at the time of the Bosnian crisis (Oct. 1908–March 1909); they resented still more his proposal to introduce death duties on landed estates. They returned to their alliance with the Centre and defeated the death duties by a narrow majority. Bülow wished to dissolve the *Reichstag*; but this made him again dependent on the emperor, and William II eagerly seized the chance to dismiss him on July 14, 1909. This ended the Indian summer of liberalism in Germany. Bülow was the last effective chancellor. After him Germany was administered, not governed, as Metternich's Austria had been in its days of decay.

Bethmann Hollweg.—Theobald von Bethmann Hollweg (*q.v.*), the new chancellor, was a perfect symbol of the decline in the authority of the *Reich*. He had no experience either in politics or foreign affairs; he was content to administer. Cultured and honest, he ran over with good intentions, and his high character often put William II and even the *Reichstag* on their best behaviour. But he had no sense of power; he put forward sensible proposals and when these were defeated acquiesced in the wild policy of his opponents. This was early shown in his negotiations with Great Britain over the limitation of naval armaments. In March 1909, during the naval scare in Great Britain, the effect of an agreement would have been enormous on British opinion. Bethmann saw this clearly and tried to negotiate but he was resisted by Tirpitz, overruled by the emperor and gave way without protest. Again Bethmann was led by Kiderlen, his secretary of state, into a second conflict with France over Morocco (July–Nov. 1911).

The Second Moroccan Crisis, 1911.—Kiderlen's object was to restore good relations with France but, with German heavy-handedness, he chose the way of threats and bullying. A German warship, the "Panther," was sent to the Moroccan port of Agadir in order to stake out a claim against the French; and Kiderlen demanded the French Congo as compensation for surrendering German rights in Morocco which did not exist. Pan-German feeling was aroused and Kiderlen received more support in Germany than he had bargained for. Against his will he had to create a war crisis, and in this war crisis Germany was defeated by Anglo-French resolution. The Agadir affair ended with a settlement in which Germany received only a fragment of the French Congo. In the ensuing *Reichstag* debate Bethmann and Kiderlen were furiously attacked for their timidity, attacks openly patronized by the crown prince William. Bethmann would not make a frank defense of his pacific policy, yet was resolved against a policy of violence. Hence, as usual, he fell back on a policy of routine.

In the two and a half years between the Agadir crisis and the outbreak of World War I, Bethmann made sincere, though ineffectual, attempts to lessen the tension in international relations. He tried vainly to take advantage of Lord Haldane's visit to Berlin (Feb. 1912) to improve Anglo-German relations, an attempt once more wrecked by Tirpitz' refusal to restrict his naval plans. Again, Bethmann worked with Sir Edward Grey to limit the Balkan Wars and successfully prevented their turning into a conflict between Russia and Austria-Hungary. Finally he negotiated with the British agreements settling the Baghdad railway and devising a new hypothetical partition of the Portuguese empire. These seemed both signs of a policy of appeasement. But Bethmann was the prisoner of German opinion and of the great general staff. He was engaged in postponing a European war, not in preventing one, and even the improved relations with Great Britain aimed partly at detaching the British from France and Russia so that Germany would have more chance of winning a continental war.

Bethmann and the Reichstag (1912–14).—In home affairs also Bethmann kept things at a standstill. Like Bülow and even Bismarck before him, he recognized that the only secure future for Germany was as a democratic monarchy with a government based on a solid *Reichstag* majority. But, like his predecessors, he had no idea how this could be brought about and regarded himself as a "caretaker," administering affairs on a day-to-day basis until the politicians of the *Reichstag* somehow accomplished the miracle which was beyond him. Yet the democratic majority was only just round the corner. The Progressives of the Fortschrittliche Volkspartei (in which the Radicals had come together again), the Centre and the Social Democrats would provide a more or less permanent majority in the *Reichstag*, if they could only coalesce. This was impossible as long as the Social Democrats retained in theory the revolutionary principles which they had long discarded in practice; yet they could not drop these principles until they were faced with the responsibilities of office. Hence the incipient democratic majority never became a reality until after the defeat of Germany in war. Bethmann's solution for every problem was to do nothing. Thus, in order not to annoy the Poles he did not

enforce Bülow's anti-Polish laws; but in order not to annoy national feeling he did not repeal them. The general election of 1912 returned the Social Democrats as the largest single party. Bethmann did not attempt to renew Bismarck's battle against the Social Democrats. On the other hand he did not bring them over to the government side. As usual he made gestures without action. He consulted the Social Democratic leaders but did not act on their advice. He promised a reform of the Prussian franchise but was unable to redeem his promise.

Bethmann's helpless position was clearly shown in Nov. 1913. The officers of the garrison at Saverne (Zabern) in Alsace provoked quarrels with the townspeople and arrested some of them in defiance of the law. Bethmann thought the military authorities in the wrong, but thought it his duty to defend them. The *Reichstag* revolted, and Bethmann was censured by a vote of 293 to 54. It was a vote without a sequel. Bethmann did not resign; the military authorities were not punished; and the "progressive" *Reichstag*, which had condemned the military, voted an enormous capital levy for the further increase and equipment of the army. Thus, to the end, the German people tried to combine the rule of law at home and the rule of German military power abroad. It was certainly a great achievement that Germany remained a *Rechtsstaat* (a state of law) throughout the period of the empire; but it was an achievement that had to be paid for by the other peoples of Europe.

The Outbreak of World War I.—The diplomatic crisis of July 1914 was not, like the two Moroccan crises, manufactured by the German foreign office. There is little or no evidence that the Germans deliberately planned war in the summer of 1914; the strongest argument against this view is that there was probably no one in the government capable of planning anything. The crisis caught the German statesmen unawares. They had now to answer the question which Bismarck had evaded: were they to abandon Austria-Hungary or must they fight for its sake a war against the other great powers? The rulers of Germany determined to stand by Austria-Hungary, but they did not at first appreciate that this was a decision for war; they supposed that a firm line would lead the other powers to give way. On July 5, William II and Bethmann authorized Austria-Hungary to act against Serbia and promised German support if Russia attempted to intervene. The promise was given without serious consideration and in the belief that it would not be called upon.

Three weeks later Germany warned Russia against mobilization. The warning was in vain. Helmuth von Moltke, the chief of the general staff, then lost his head. He believed that Germany's only chance of victory lay in defeating France before Russia was ready. Therefore he insisted that the Russian mobilization gave the German government no choice: it must at once declare war on both France and Russia. Bethmann could find no answer to this military argument. Not only did he acquiesce: he finished up by defending the German march through Belgium which he knew to be indefensible and which brought Great Britain into the war against Germany. It was claimed subsequently that "mobilization meant war" for all powers and that this was universally known. Hence Russia was supposed to have started the war by mobilizing first. The argument was unsound. For the other powers mobilization meant simply mobilization; it did not make war inevitable though it made it easier. Mobilization meant war only for Germany; and this not from some inscrutable decision

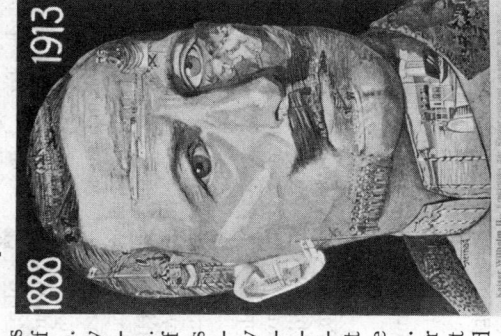

of providence but as a deliberate calculation made long beforehand, in order to exploit Germany's speed of mobilization and thus to solve the problem of war on two fronts. In this sense the man most responsible for the war was Alfred, Graf von Schlieffen, the former chief of the general staff, who had died in 1913; for it was his strategical plan of attack on France through Belgium which led Moltke to insist on declaring war in Aug. 1914. (*See* World Wars: *World War I: The Schlieffen Plan.*)

The outbreak of war accomplished something which social concessions had failed to do; it brought the Social Democrats over to the support of the imperial government. The German Socialists had always been the leading spokesmen in the Socialist international of the general strike against war. When it came to the point, they were won over by the argument that Germany was being attacked by tsarist Russia. At the meeting of Socialist members, a minority opposed the war; but when the *Reichstag* met, the entire Socialist party voted for war credits, in the name of party unity. The Socialists went further. They joined the other parties in declaring *Burgfrieden*, a civil truce, by which they agreed to criticize neither each other nor the government. In other countries at war, the party politicians formed a coalition or otherwise established control over the government. In Germany the members of the *Reichstag* abdicated to the imperial government, though it remained unchanged and beyond their control. No wonder that William II declared, "There are no more parties; I see only Germans." This was, of course, an exaggeration. The Social Democrats had always some doubts about supporting the war without reserve, and they had to devise increasingly elaborate arguments in order to satisfy their consciences. In the autumn of 1914, after the battle of Tannenberg, it became obvious that Russia was not a menace to Germany. The Social Democrats then made out that Germany was becoming a Socialist country under the pressure of war and that they were fighting a war of defense against "Entente capitalism."

For Germany, as for other belligerent countries, World War I fell into two distinct phases: the first, old-style conventional war which lasted until 1916; the second, a war of desperate expedients when both sides fought a struggle for existence. The German war plan was a plan for a short war. France was to be overrun within six weeks, Russia within six months; Great Britain would be excluded from Europe. This plan met disaster at the battle of the Marne (Sept. 1914). The Germans missed the capture of Paris on which they had pinned their hopes; lines of trenches stretched to the French coast, and the Germans were left in occupation of Belgium and of northern France. Yet at the same moment the defeat of the Russians at Tannenberg gave Germany the security which was its ostensible war aim and at any time between Sept. 1914 and the summer of 1917 the Germans could have had peace on the basis of the *status quo.* Such a peace, however, was impossible for Germany. It would have destroyed the prestige of the German armies; it would have arrested the expansion of German industry; above all, it would have led to a political revolution at home. The Bismarckian compromise between the demands of the middle classes and those of the Junkers had been created by him in order to restrain German ambitions and to make a moderate policy possible; now the Germans had to wage a war of conquest and to abandon all moderation in order to preserve the Bismarckian compromise.

The defeat at the Marne brought a change in the high command. Helmuth von Moltke, nephew of the great commander of 1866 and 1870, disappeared and was succeeded by Erich von Falkenhayn, an organizer rather than a strategist. He determined to stand on the defensive in the west, while breaking Germany's enemies in the east. This plan was, in its limited aim, successful. Anglo-French offensives on the western front achieved nothing. Meanwhile the Russians were driven out of Galicia, and the way was prepared for the conquest of Poland. In the autumn of 1915 Serbia was overrun, and with the entry of Bulgaria into the war the Central Powers had a secure land route to Turkey and beyond it to the Persian gulf. Turkish efforts to threaten the Suez canal failed but this was more than offset by the Allied failure to break through the Dardanelles. The Allies had counted on great advantage from bringing Italy into

EMPEROR WILLIAM II (CENTRE) WITH MARSHAL VON HINDENBURG (LEFT) AND GENERAL LUDENDORFF STUDYING A MAP

the war (May 1915); but their hopes were disappointed. The Italian armies were no more than a match for the Austro-Hungarian army; and in any case they had to attack on a very narrow front where no decisive victory could be obtained.

In home affairs the second year of the war saw the first effort to mobilize German resources for a serious war. No preparations had been made for this, and the inspiration of the program came from Walther Rathenau (*q.v.*), an industrialist who convinced Bethmann and the high command of the need for an economic plan in the winter of 1914. It may be said without exaggeration that Rathenau alone made it possible for Germany to wage war for four years. Politically, too, the second year of the war saw the beginning of an effort to think in war terms. The conquest of Belgium shifted Germany's interests, as it were, west. Throughout the war Germans of every party, including the Social Democrats, made the annexation of Belgium, in whole or in part, or at least German control of Belgium, an essential condition of peace. This was sometimes justified by strategic arguments, disguised as the need for security, sometimes by arguments of economic union. The basic fact was that German plans of conquest had moved to the west and for a simple reason: Germany had become the greatest industrial power. The plans for extending German territory in the Baltic—the only plans with which the Prussian Junkers sympathized—were plans for the benefit of landowners; the plans for controlling southeastern Europe, also of long standing, were the plans of German magnates; both were eclipsed by the ambition of the German magnates of the Ruhr to control the industrial resources of northeastern France. Against these plans, there was a stirring of German liberal sentiment, some of it roused merely by the hope that Germany might make peace with the entente if it demanded less territory in western Europe or was even content with its territory in the east. But there was also a movement among a minority of the Social Democrats against a war of conquest, and soon against any war at all. In Dec. 1914 Karl Liebknecht, a left-wing Socialist, first voted against the war credits; in 1915 some Social Democrats began to move against their party and to form an "independent" group, largely pacifist in tone.

In 1916 Falkenhayn, still without a constructive strategy, attempted to "bleed the French white" by the prolonged battle of Verdun (Feb.–June) which exhausted the Germans almost as much as it did the French. At the same time an attempt to break British naval power by direct assault failed at the battle of Jutland (May 31, 1916), the only serious engagement fought by the German high seas fleet in the course of the war. It became clear that new men and new methods were necessary if Germany was to continue the war. The decisive change came on Aug. 29, 1916, when William II dismissed Falkenhayn and appointed Paul von Hindenburg (*q.v.*) chief of staff with Erich Ludendorff (*q.v.*) as his quartermaster general. Hindenburg had achieved a somewhat spurious fame as the victor of Tannenberg. Elderly, stolid, imperturbable, he symbolized for Germans "the will to victory." Wooden statues of him were erected; and Germans paid to drive nails into them as a contribution to war charities. Ludendorff, a man of middle-class origin, had a wider strategic vision and combined this with an obstinate belief that Germany could achieve total victory.

The Political Crisis of 1916–17.—The appointment of Hindenburg and Ludendorff ushered in the political crisis of the German empire. Until then the Bismarckian balance had been maintained. Falkenhayn and Bethmann were agreed that Germany could hope, at best, for a compromise peace; and each worked for this in his own sphere without interfering in the other's. Falkenhayn aimed to wear down the French at Verdun. Bethmann negotiated with tsarist Russia for a peace without victory and tried to enlist the sympathetic mediation of the United States. These moderate policies did not satisfy the confident ambitions of most Germans. In Oct. 1916 the *Reichstag* passed a motion, proposed by the Centre, that it had confidence in Bethmann so long as he possessed the confidence of the high command. This resolution cut the ground from beneath Bethmann's feet; he could no longer sustain civil authority against the demands of Hindenburg and Ludendorff. In Nov. 1916 Ludendorff insisted on the proclamation of an independent kingdom of Poland, in the hope of winning Polish recruits for the German army; this effectively ended the peace negotiations with Russia, though it brought little Polish support to the armies of the Central Powers. On Jan. 9, 1917, after prolonged debate, a crown council resolved, much against Bethmann's opinion, to inaugurate unrestricted submarine warfare, in the hope of bringing the British to their knees. Though this campaign, announced on Feb. 1, came within sight of success, it was ultimately defeated by the British system of convoys; and it had the far graver consequence of bringing the United States into the war against Germany.

The spring of 1917 saw the growth of war-weariness in Germany. The hard winter was accompanied by a shortage of food; it was long remembered in Germany as "the turnip winter." Ludendorff had taken over a difficult strategic situation and had to conduct a defensive war, with dispiriting results, throughout 1917. The first Russian revolution (March 1917) encouraged left-wing feeling in Germany, and on April 7 Bethmann once more promised a democratic reform of the Prussian franchise, though as usual the promise was not fulfilled. In July there was a mutiny in the German navy, which was confined to its base at Kiel. Hitherto the attacks on the war had come from the Independent Social Democrats and from the Spartacists, as the revolutionary followers of Liebknecht were coming to be called. But in the spring of 1917 Matthias Erzberger (*q.v.*), leader of the Centre, visited Gen. Max Hoffmann, who had succeeded Ludendorff on the eastern front, and learned from him that the war was lost. Erzberger returned to Berlin, determined to secure for the Centre the position of leading antiwar party; after all, it was the only party that could survive any change of regime. On July 6 he launched an attack on Bethmann, accusing him of advocating a policy of conquest and demanding the enunciation of defensive peace terms. Ludendorff had long regarded Bethmann as weak and too pacific, but he nonetheless welcomed this attack by Erzberger as a way of getting a chancellor more to his taste. Thus the high command and Erzberger worked hand in hand, though for exactly opposite reasons. Both wanted to get rid of Bethmann: Ludendorff in order to secure a puppet chancellor who would acquiesce in a more aggressive conduct of the war; Erzberger and the politicians in order to impose a compromise peace on the high command by calling Bülow in as chancellor. For Bülow enjoyed an undeserved reputation as a liberal, because of his clash with the Conservatives in 1909. His parting words to the Conservatives had been: "We shall meet again at Philippi." Bülow and the politicians of the *Reichstag* thought that Philippi had now come. When Ludendorff renewed his complaints against Bethmann, William II sent his son, the crown prince William, to Berlin, in order to sound political opinion. The leaders of the political parties duly reported that they had lost confidence in Bethmann, and he resigned. At this point Erzberger's grotesque scheme broke down. William II, with the humiliation of the *Daily Telegraph* still rankling, refused to hear Bülow's name mentioned; the politicians had no other candidate to suggest, and Ludendorff then nominated out of hand Georg Michaelis, an unknown official who had acted competently as Prussian food controller. Thus ended the great crisis that was to give Germany parliamentary government with the backing of the high command.

The *Reichstag* had to be given some satisfaction. Having failed to make a chancellor, the politicians were allowed to make a policy. The "peace resolution" of July 19 was a string of innocuous phrases, expressing Germany's will to peace, but without a clear renunciation of indemnities or annexations. Most of the politicians who supported it, including Erzberger himself, were still in favour of annexing Belgium and part of northeastern France. Later in the year the *Reichstag* received a further acknowledgment from the high command. Ludendorff admitted that Michaelis had proved incompetent as chancellor and ordered him out of office (Oct. 31, 1917). The next chancellor, Georg, Graf von Hertling, was 75 years of age and had been prime minister of Bavaria. He was appointed principally to please the Centre, as he was a Roman Catholic. As a further concession, Friedrich von Payer, the leader of the Progressives, became vice-chancellor. Neither Hertling nor Payer had any influence on policy, which was determined by the high command. Only Richard von Kühlmann, the secretary of state, tried to assert some civilian control, but he too was ordered out of office by the high command when he ventured to suggest in the *Reichstag* that a peace based on complete victory was no longer possible.

The Last Year of the German Empire.—Bismarck's *Reich* was to have a last year of illusory success before defeat. In 1917 Ludendorff met and routed the Allied offensives on the western front. More important, the Russian forces on the eastern front fell to pieces, particularly after the failure of A. F. Kerenski's offensive (July 1917) and the Bolshevik revolution in Nov. 1917. The Bolsheviks believed that they could cause revolution also among the German workers by offering a peace "without indemnities or annexations." Hence they negotiated with the German high command at Brest-Litovsk. The Bolshevik calculation proved false. Though Germany was swept by a wave of strikes in Jan. 1918, these sprang simply from grievances against the hard domestic conditions, and in any case they collapsed without producing any political result. The German working class, through the mouths of the Social Democrats, had announced that they were fighting a war of defense against tsardom; but they continued to fight when tsardom had disappeared. On March 3, 1918, the Bolsheviks had to sign the peace treaty of Brest-Litovsk, by which Russia lost 56,000,000 inhabitants, 79% of its iron and 89% of its coal production. This annexationist treaty was not opposed by the parties that had voted for the "peace resolution." The Centre and the Progressives voted for the treaty, the bulk of the Social Democrats abstained and only the Independent minority of Social Democrats voted against. When it came to the treaty of Bucharest with Rumania (May 7, 1918), which made Germany the economic master of that country, the majority of the Social Democrats actually voted for the treaty. Thus, for a few brief months, Germany achieved the dream of having all Europe east of the Rhine under its economic domination.

The decisive battle had, however, still to be fought in the west. On March 21, 1918, Ludendorff launched the "emperor's battle" (much against the emperor's wish). On April 9 he won a battle against the British and at the end of May against the French. Decision eluded him. On July 18 the French struck back, and on Aug. 8—"the black day of the German army"—the British broke through. Ludendorff remained confident that he could fight a defensive war. At the end of September Bulgaria collapsed and the collapse of Austria-Hungary was near. On Sept. 29 Ludendorff lost his nerve and declared that an immediate armistice was necessary. Further, to make the approach to the Allies easy, he ordered that Germany should become a constitutional monarchy overnight. Prince Max of Baden, who had long enjoyed a happy reputation as a liberal and an international conciliator, became chancellor (Oct. 3). The same day the political leaders were told by Ludendorff's representatives that the war was lost. Ludendorff had never studied the fourteen points; and when he understood their implications he wished to continue the war. He was overruled and resigned on Oct. 26. Hindenburg remained at the head of the general staff with Wilhelm Groener as quartermaster general.

The Revolution of 1918–19.—The change to constitutional monarchy had been carried through peacefully, at the order of the high command. At the end of October the *Reichstag* resolved that the chancellor must henceforth possess the confidence of the *Reichstag* and this resolution was approved by the emperor. But the German people were now growing impatient. On Nov. 3 mutiny broke out in the fleet at Kiel and revolt soon spread to Berlin. On Nov. 9 Liebknecht, the Spartacist leader, prepared to proclaim a soviet republic. Prince Max's cabinet tried to counter this by proclaiming the abdication of the emperor. When this failed, Philipp Scheidemann, one of the two Social Democrats in the cabinet, proclaimed the republic in order to anticipate Liebknecht, much to the fury of Friedrich Ebert (*q.v.*), his colleague. Prince Max handed over his office to Ebert, who thus became for 24 hours the last imperial chancellor.

Meanwhile at Spa, the seat of the high command, where William II had taken refuge, the emperor tried to defend his position. He was told by Groener that the army would not support him and on Nov. 9 he fled to the Netherlands. Thus the Social Democrats and the high command, much against their will, combined to create

MEMORIAL WOODCUT TO THE MURDERED SPARTACIST LEADER KARL LIEB-KNECHT, BY KÄTHE KOLLWITZ, 1920

the German republic. On Nov. 10 the workers' and soldiers' councils of Berlin, which had been set up in imitation of the Russian soviets, gave a revolutionary blessing to Ebert's regime; it was more important for him that the high command blessed it at the same time. It remained to establish a government for the state.

Ebert, last imperial chancellor, became chairman of the Council of Peoples' Commissars, a body dominated by Majority Socialists who were opposed to revolution. His first act was to strike a bargain with the high command; Hindenburg would retain his command, and Ebert would resist the revolution. This had already lost its mass appeal with the signature of the armistice (Nov. 11). On Dec. 19 Ebert persuaded the Congress of Soldiers' and Workers' Councils to fix elections for the constituent assembly for Jan. 19, 1919. On Dec. 23 revolutionary sailors answered by occupying the chancellery and taking Ebert prisoner. He was rescued on Dec. 24 by troops from the Potsdam garrison. On Dec. 29 the three Independent Socialists resigned from the government in protest against Ebert's counterrevolutionary policy; this left him with a free hand. Gustav Noske, another Majority Socialist, organized a volunteer corps with which to defeat the revolution. He said:

"Someone must play the bloodhound; I am not afraid of the responsibility."

On Jan. 4, 1919, Robert Emil Eichhorn, an Independent Socialist and police president of Berlin, was dismissed. Mass demonstrations of protest followed, but the government was not overthrown. On Jan. 11 Noske's Volunteers entered Berlin. Heavy street fighting took place, which ended with Noske's victory on Jan. 15. The same evening the two Spartacist leaders Karl Liebknecht and Rosa Luxemburg were arrested and murdered by Volunteer officers. Elections for the national assembly were duly held on Jan. 19. The social revolution had been defeated and the way was clear for a democratic republic to preserve the economic order and the military values of imperial Germany. Ebert and Hindenburg, the two presidents of the Weimar republic, were also the partners who brought it into existence.

(A. J. P. T.)

M. THE GERMAN REPUBLIC, 1919–33

The Weimar Constitution.—The national assembly met at Weimar on Feb. 6, 1919. Friedrich Ebert's opening speech underlined the breach with the past and urged the Allies not to cripple the young republic by the demands imposed on it. On Feb. 11 the assembly elected Ebert as president of the *Reich*, and on Feb. 12 Philipp Scheidemann (Social Democrat) formed a ministry with the Centre and the Democrats.

The principal task of the assembly was to provide a new constitution, which was promulgated on Aug. 11, 1919. The government's draft was drawn up by Hugo Preuss, of the Democratic party. Preuss, however, was not able to secure a unitary *Reich* in which Prussia would have been broken up and the old states (*Länder*) abolished in favour of a new division by provinces. The republic, like the empire that it replaced, was to have a federal basis. The powers of the *Reich*, however, were considerably strengthened and it was now given overriding control of all taxation. National laws were to be superior to the laws of the states, and the *Reich* government was given the power to supervise their enforcement by the local authorities. Under the republic there were 17 *Länder* in all, ranging from Prussia with a population (in 1925) of 38,000,000 and Bavaria with 7,000,000 to Schaumburg-Lippe with 48,000. The only new *Land* was that of Thuringia, formed in 1919 from the amalgamation of seven small principalities.

The *Länder* continued to be represented in the *Reichsrat*, which replaced the imperial *Bundesrat*, but the new chamber became subordinate to the *Reichstag*, to which alone the government was made responsible. All men and women over the age of 20 were to have the right to vote for the *Reichstag*, and the elections were to be conducted on the basis of proportional representation. Provision was also made for popular initiatives in legislation and for referenda.

As a counterweight to the *Reichstag*, the president as the chief executive was endowed with strong powers. He was to be elected independently of the *Reichstag* by the nation itself, was to hold office for seven years and was to be eligible for re-election. He was to make alliances and treaties; he was the supreme commander of the armed forces, with the right to appoint and remove all officers; he could dissolve the *Reichstag* and submit any law enacted by it to a referendum. Finally, under the famous article 48, he had the right to suspend the civil liberties guaranteed by the constitution in case of emergency and to take any measures required to restore public safety and order. These provisions reflect the insecurity, bordering on civil war, with which Germany was faced at the time; they were to prove of great importance in the final stages of the history of the Weimar republic. Under the president, political responsibility was to rest with the chancellor. The government was made dependent upon the confidence of a majority of the *Reichstag*; with the withdrawal of this confidence the government had to resign.

The Weimar constitution has been subjected to considerable criticism, notably for the system of proportional representation which it introduced and the large powers which it conferred on the president. For the first time in German history, however, it provided a firm foundation for democratic development. The fact that within 14 years this ended in a dictatorship was due far more to the course of events and to the character of social forces in Germany than to constitutional defects.

The German *Reich*, as it was re-established in 1919, was a democratic but not a socialist republic. A number of measures (*e.g.*, the socialization of certain parts of the national economy (*e.g.*, the coal, electrical and potash industries) were introduced but proved ineffectual. German industry continued to be marked by cartels and other combines of a monopolistic character, control of which was increasingly concentrated in the hands of a small number of men. The fact that, after the hopes aroused in 1918–19, no far-reaching plan for securing public control over industry or for breaking up the big landed estates was carried through had two consequences. Although the German working class undoubtedly improved its political and economic status under the republic, a considerable section was embittered by the failure to effect a drastic reform of the social and economic systems. This was to provide the left-wing opposition with strong working-class support which weakened both the Social Democratic party and the republic. Secondly, economic power was left in the hands of classes who were either irreconcilable opponents of the republic from the beginning or equivocal supporters with a preference for authoritarian forms of government.

The position of the trade unions, the eight-hour day and the right of collective bargaining were safeguarded under the republic, but the attempt to extend democracy to the industrial sphere met with powerful opposition from the industrialists. A system of works councils set up early in 1920 enabled the workers in each factory to elect representatives to share in the control of management. This experiment, however, soon disappointed the hopes entertained of it, largely because of the stubborn resistance of the employers. The attempt to establish an economic parliament (*Reichswirtschaftsrat*), with equal representation for employers and workers, proved equally disappointing.

For an analysis of the voting for the *Reichstag* at the nine elections between 1919 and 1933 *see* Table I.

TABLE I.—*Elections to the Reichstag in the Weimar Republic, 1919–33*
(Percentages of valid votes)

Parties	Jan. 1919	June 1920	May 1924	Dec. 1924	May 1928	Sept. 1930	July 1932	Nov. 1932	March 1933
Communists	—	2	12	9	11	13	14	17	12
Independent Socialists	—	18	—	—	—	—	—	—	—
Majority Socialists or Social Democrats	38	22	21	26	30	25	22	20	18
Centre	20	14	13	14	12	12	12	12	12
Bavarian People's party	—	4	3	4	3	3	3	3	3
Democrats	19	8	6	6	5	4	1	1	1
People's party	4	14	9	10	9	5	1	2	1
Nationalists	10	15	20	21	14	7	6	8	8
National Socialists	—	—	7	3	3	18	37	33	44
Other parties	2	3	7	8	14	14	3	3	2

The Treaty of Versailles.—The government's instructions to the German peace delegation that went to Versailles at the end of April 1919 show how wide was the gap between German and Allied opinion. In German eyes the break with the past was complete, and the Wilsonian program of self-determination and equality of rights as set out in the fourteen points was binding on both sides. The fact that the Allied powers refused to permit negotiations and the character of the terms presented on May 7 provoked bitter indignation throughout all classes in Germany.

Germany was called on to cede Alsace-Lorraine to France; the big industrial area of upper Silesia, most of Posen and the so-called West Prussia to Poland; north Schleswig to Denmark, and three small frontier districts to Belgium. Danzig was to become a free city, independent of Germany; East Prussia was separated from the rest of the *Reich* by Polish Pomorze, and Memel was handed over to Lithuania. In Europe alone (without counting the German colonies, all of which had to be handed over to the Allies) Germany lost about 27,188 sq.mi. of territory, with a total population of over 7,000,000. The union of Austria with the *Reich*, which was advocated in both countries, would have compensated for these losses, but was expressly forbidden by the treaty.

The left bank of the Rhine was to be occupied by Allied troops from 5 to 15 years to ensure the execution of the treaty's terms.

The left bank, and the right bank to a depth of 50 km., were to be permanently demilitarized. Germany was to lose the rich coal fields of the Saar for 15 years: at the end of this period a plebiscite was to be held. Until then the Saar was to be governed by the League of Nations and its coal mines administered by France.

A decision on reparations was deferred until 1921, but the Germans were to make a provisional payment of 20,000,000,000 M. in gold as well as deliveries in kind. Prewar commercial agreements with foreign countries were canceled; German foreign financial holdings were confiscated and the German merchant marine reduced to less than one-tenth of its prewar size. At the same time the Allies were to enjoy most-favoured-nation rights in the German market for five years.

The German army was to be limited to 100,000 officers and men; conscription was forbidden; the German general staff was to be dissolved; great quantities of war matériel were to be handed over, and the future manufacture of munitions rigidly curtailed. German naval forces were to be reduced to a similar scale, while the possession of military aircraft was forbidden. Inter-Allied control commissions were set up with wide rights of supervision to make sure that the disarmament clauses were carried out. A list of those accused of violating the laws and customs of war was to be prepared, and those named were to be handed over to the Allies for trial. Finally, as justification for their claims to reparations, the Allies inserted the famous war-guilt clause, article 231: The Allied governments affirm and Germany accepts the responsibility of Germany and her allies for causing all the loss and damage to which the Allied governments and their nationals have been subjected as a consequence of the war imposed upon them by the aggression of Germany and her allies.

All the German parties united in a solemn protest against these terms. The Allies were declared to have flagrantly violated the principles of a just peace proclaimed by Wilson, while the belief that Germany had been tricked into signing the armistice was widespread. The only concession of importance that the German delegation was able to secure was the promise of a plebiscite in upper Silesia. In June the Allies presented an ultimatum, and the German government had to face the alternatives of signing the peace treaty or submitting to an invasion of their country. Scheidemann, who was personally opposed to acceptance, resigned when his cabinet was unable to agree, and was succeeded by Gustav Bauer, who formed an administration supported by the Social Democrats and the Centre, but without the Democrats, most of whom joined the Nationalists (Deutschnationale Volkspartei) and the People's party (Deutsche Volkspartei) in opposition. On June 23 a majority of the assembly, persuaded that there was no alternative, voted in favour of acceptance, and the treaty was signed at Versailles on June 28.

The Allies' insistence that the republic should accept a peace settlement universally regarded in Germany as unjust and humiliating contributed powerfully to weakening the new regime. The republic never succeeded in breaking its association with the capitulation of 1918 and the signature of the peace treaty in 1919. For neither of these could the republic's leaders justly be held responsible, but the legend that the German army had never been defeated but was stabbed in the back by the Republicans, the Socialists and the Jews, "the November criminals," was assiduously repeated by the enemies of the republic and, in the mood of resentment created by the treaty, was readily accepted by many Germans. The Republican leaders, to whose sense of responsibility the nation owed the preservation of its unity and the avoidance of far worse disasters in the critical year which followed the request for an armistice, had to endure a campaign of vilification which represented them as traitors to the fatherland.

Years of Crisis (1920–23).—The "Weimar coalition" of the Social Democrats, Centre and Democrats which had been the basis of Scheidemann's ministry (Feb.–June 1919) was re-established by Bauer when the Democrats joined his government in Oct. 1919 and maintained by Hermann Müller (also a Social Democrat) when he took Bauer's place as chancellor at the end of March 1920. The elections of June 6, 1920, however, showed a marked swing against the parties most closely identified with the republic—the Social Democrats and the Roman Catholic parties, that is, the Centre and the Bavarian People's party. The opposition parties, the Nationalists and the People's party on the right, the Independent Socialists on the left, all showed heavy gains. Thus the year 1920 marked the end of the brief period during which the Social Democrats were the dominant party in the republic. At the end of June the Weimar coalition was replaced by a new combination under Konstantin Fehrenbach (Centre), representing the Centre, the Democrats and for the first time the People's party, whose left wing, led by Gustav Stresemann (q.v.), was willing to co-operate in the development of the republic on the pattern of a bourgeois and capitalist democracy.

The plebiscite held in upper Silesia on March 20, 1921, resulted in a majority for remaining with Germany. Disregarding the treaty provisions for the partition of the area according to the wishes of the inhabitants expressed by communes, Germany claimed that the whole territory should remain German. The Poles retaliated by organizing an armed revolt and attempting a seizure by force. After a division of opinion among the Allies, with France supporting the Poles, the dispute was referred to the League of Nations, which gave two-thirds of the territory to Germany, but left the coal mines, the principal industrial areas and a considerable German minority on the Polish side of the frontier. The decision was hotly resented in Germany.

On April 27, 1921, the Allied reparation commission fixed the total to be paid by Germany at 132,000,000,000 gold marks. Regarding this as far in excess of the country's capacity to pay, the Fehrenbach government at once resigned (May 4). The Allies retorted with an ultimatum calling on Germany to announce its unconditional acceptance of the figure within six days, under threat of the occupation of the Ruhr. The Nationalists again took the easy way out by demanding the rejection of the Allies' demand, but Karl Joseph Wirth (Centre), the new chancellor of another "Weimar coalition," secured a reluctant vote from the

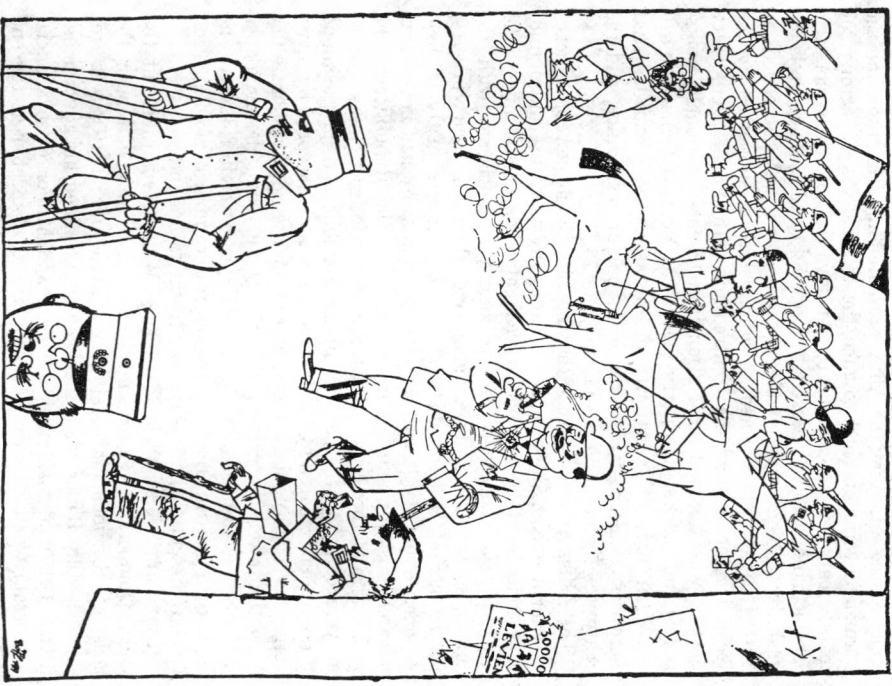

Reichstag in favour of accepting. Once again the Republican parties were saddled with the responsibility for carrying out decisions forced on a resentful country by the Allies. The German government, however, found it impossible to pay the sums required on time. Relations with France had in any case remained bad. The French had twice already marched troops into German cities on the grounds that Germany was not carrying out its obligations under the treaty. French attempts to develop a separatist movement in the Rhineland failed, but strengthened German impressions of an inflexible hostility and determination to break up the *Reich* on the part of France. Then, in Jan. 1923, on the pretext of a technical default by Germany in its deliveries of timber, the French occupied the Ruhr.

The Rapallo Treaty.—One way of breaking the hostile ring with which the Germans felt themselves encircled was to make common cause with the other outcast among the European nations, the Soviet Union. This idea was attractive not only to many on the left but to some on the right, who believed that another war with France was inevitable and were looking for allies. Economic negotiations with Russia in 1921 proved successful, and support for a *rapprochement* between the two countries came from Gen. Hans von Seeckt, the commander in chief of the army. On April 16, 1922, a treaty of friendship was signed between Germany and Russia at Rapallo, waiving reparations claims by both sides and promising the expansion of Russo-German trade. The French and British were surprised and angry. No counteraction was taken, but Rapallo no doubt helped to harden French opinion. The most important practical consequence was the conclusion of secret agreements between the German and Russian armies, which allowed German officers and units to acquire experience with the Red army and provided opportunities for experiments with the design of forbidden weapons such as tanks and aircraft.

Political Disturbances at Home.—At home, the republican regime was challenged from both right and left. A workers' rising led by Communists took place in the Ruhr in the spring of 1920, and there was fierce fighting with the army and with the volunteer *Freikorps* before it was suppressed at the beginning of April. When miners in the Mansfeld district of central Germany took up arms against the police in March 1921, the Communists called for a general strike, but without success, and order was rapidly restored.

There was still widespread fear of a German revolution on the model of Russia's. Against this the powerful and moderate Social Democratic party and the trade union movement proved an effective barrier. After the left wing of the Independent Socialists joined the Communists (Dec. 1920), the majority of the Independents drew closer to the Social Democrats and a union of the two parties was achieved in Sept. 1922.

The greater danger to the republic came from the right. As early as March 1920, a *coup d'état* was attempted by Gen. Walther von Lüttwitz, who commanded the troops in the Berlin area, and Wolfgang Kapp, an East Prussian official. With the help of the Ehrhardt brigade, one of the *Freikorps* formations, they assumed power in Berlin for a few days. The Kapp *Putsch* however failed to receive the support anticipated from the army or from the parties of the right (who regarded it as premature), and it was met by the solid resistance of the working-class organizations, led by the trade unions, which called a highly successful general strike and forced Lüttwitz and Kapp to abandon their attempt.

Inside the *Reichstag*, the Nationalists kept up an unrestrained campaign against the republic and its leaders. But even the Nationalists were not sufficiently extreme for groups like the German Racial Freedom party in the north or Adolf Hitler's National Socialists in Munich, which combined anti-Semitism, antisocialism and inflammatory nationalism with open demands for the overthrow of the republic. Closely linked with these groups were paramilitary organizations under a variety of names, drawing their membership largely from ex-servicemen (many of whom had served in the *Freikorps* after the war), and in close touch with officers in the regular army who provided them with arms and looked upon them as a reserve for the day when they would

MIDDLE-CLASS DEMONSTRATION IN THE LUSTGARTEN, BERLIN, AGAINST INFLATION. 1922

rise to destroy the republic and avenge the defeat of 1918. From this underworld of conspiracy, which was a breeding ground of the Nazi movement, were recruited gangs like the notorious *Organisation Konsul* which assassinated among others Matthias Erzberger (Aug. 26, 1921) and Walther Rathenau (June 24, 1922). One of the most disturbing features was the marked leniency shown by the courts toward political terrorism when practised by the right.

The stronghold of these counterrevolutionary forces was Bavaria. The most powerful party in southern Germany, the Catholic Bavarian People's party, made no secret of its antirepublican and particularist views or its sympathy with proposals to restore the Wittelsbach monarchy in Bavaria. Relations between the state government in Munich and the *Reich* government in Berlin were continually strained by the refusal of the Bavarian authorities to proceed against the extremist organizations which found shelter in their territory, including Hitler's National Socialists who throughout the 1920s were predominantly a Bavarian movement.

The Ruhr and Inflation.—During these immediate postwar years the value of the mark steadily deteriorated. This was due to a number of factors, among them reparation payments, the flight of German capital abroad, the obstacles to the revival of German foreign trade and a consequent adverse balance of payments. Faced with budgetary deficits, the German government followed a practice already begun during the war; that of issuing more money to meet its expenses. The result was a runaway inflation more severe than in any other part of postwar Europe. This process was well under way in 1922, during which the value of the mark in terms of the dollar (pre-1914 relation: $1 = 4.20 M.) fell from 162 M. to more than 7,000 M. The culmination of the inflation, however, came in 1923, the year which also saw the climax in the protracted crisis of internal disorder and disunity.

The occupation of the Ruhr by French troops in Jan. 1923 soon led to what was virtually a state of undeclared war between the French and the Germans in the Rhineland. The government formed by Wilhelm Cuno (Centre, People's party and Democrats), which succeeded that of Wirth in Nov. 1922, ordered passive resistance to French and Belgian attempts to get the mines and factories working and a ban on all reparation deliveries. The occupation forces retorted with mass arrests, deportations and an economic blockade which cut off not only the Ruhr but the greater part of the occupied Rhineland from the rest of Germany. This was a most serious blow to the German economy in view of the economic dependence of the rest of the country on the west, especially after the loss of upper Silesia. On the German side there was resort to sabotage and guerrilla warfare.

The blockade enforced by the French dislocated the whole economic life of the country and gave the final touch to the depreciation of the currency. The mark fell to 160,000 to the dollar on July 1; 242,000,000 to the dollar on Oct. 1; and 4,200,-000,000,000 to the dollar on Nov. 20, 1923. Barter replaced other commercial dealings, food riots broke out and despair seized hold of large sections of the population. The heaviest losers were the middle classes and pensioners, who saw their savings completely wiped out; the drop in real wages however hit the working classes hard. On the other hand, many businessmen and industrialists made large profits, speculation was rife, and everyone with debts to pay off, such as farmers and landowners with mortgages on their land, gained immensely.

Threats of Disintegration and Civil War.—The extremist parties hastened to exploit the situation. In Saxony and Thuringia the Communists joined the local Social Democrats in the *Land* governments with the intention of carrying out a seizure of power in the *Reich* (Oct. 1923) and in Hamburg a Communist-led rising occurred on Oct. 23. At the same time the *Land* government in Bavaria, where a coup seemed imminent, openly defied the orders of the *Reich* government, while Hitler and the small National Socialist movement were urging the Munich authorities to stage a march on Berlin.

In August the Cuno government had been forced to resign in face of a Social Democratic demand for a stronger policy. A new ministry was formed by Gustav Stresemann with the support of the People's party, the Centre, the Democrats and (until November) the Social Democrats. On Sept. 26 Stresemann courageously called off the campaign of passive resistance in the Rhineland, ordered the immediate resumption of work in the occupied areas and lifted the ban on reparation deliveries. A state of emergency was declared under article 48 of the constitution; the army was used to suppress the danger of a Communist coup in Saxony and Thuringia, the Hamburg rising was put down by the police, and the *Reich* government threatened drastic action if the Bavarian authorities did not fall into line. In a last effort to force the hand of the Bavarian government, Hitler attempted to stage a *Putsch* in Munich on Nov. 8–9 without success; the Munich authorities were glad enough to suppress the Nazis and make their peace with Berlin.

Toward Stabilization.—Having mastered the threat of civil war, Stresemann turned to face the problem of the mark. A new currency, the Rentenmark, was introduced on Nov. 20, 1923, in strictly limited quantities; cover was provided by a mortgage on the entire industrial and agricultural resources of the country. The process of stabilization was painful but was pushed through with determination by Hjalmar Schacht, who was made president of the Reichsbank on Dec. 22, 1923.

The drastic action taken by Stresemann to end the crisis proved successful, but his critics on the left and right combined to defeat a vote of confidence on Nov. 23, and he promptly resigned. He was succeeded by Wilhelm Marx (Centre); Stresemann himself retaining the key post of foreign minister. In Feb. 1924 Marx felt secure enough to end the state of emergency.

The Dawes Plan.—The Ruhr was still occupied by the French, and the question of reparations remained unsettled. Thanks to the efforts of the British and U.S. governments, however, a committee of experts, presided over by a U.S. financier, Charles G. Dawes, produced a report, which was accepted by the Allies and by Germany on Aug. 16, 1924 (*see* Reparations). No attempt was made to determine the total amount to be paid, but payments were to be resumed on a scale beginning at 1,000,000,000 gold marks in the first year and rising to 2,500,000,000 in 1928 and subsequent years. Detailed arrangements were made for raising and transferring these sums, under foreign supervision, while a foreign loan of 800,000,000 RM. was secured to help the German government.

These proposals led to further bitter attacks on Stresemann's foreign policy of "fulfillment." But, despite the success of the extremist parties at elections held in May 1924, Marx succeeded in finding a majority for the legislation embodying the Dawes proposals, and in return Stresemann secured the withdrawal of the French troops from the Ruhr.

On Aug. 30, 1924, the Reichsbank was made independent of the government and introduced the new reichsmark currency with the exchange rate of 1 RM. = 1,000,000,000 M.

The year 1925 saw further progress toward stabilization. In

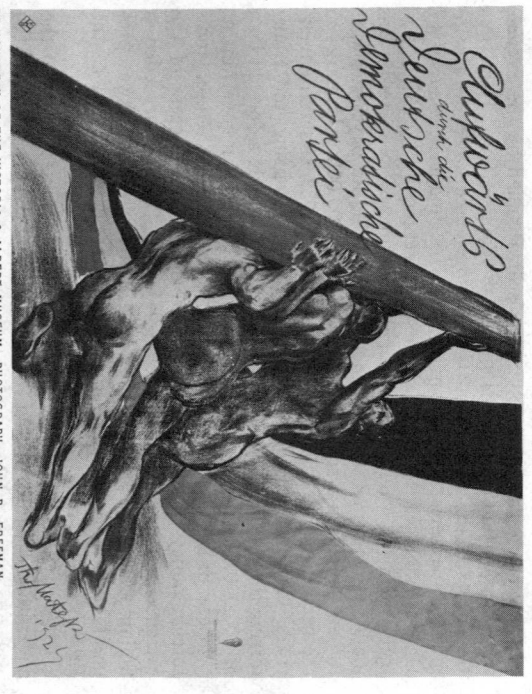

GERMANY

Feb. 1925 President Ebert died, and Field Marshal Paul von Hindenburg was elected in his place. The election of Hindenburg, a monarchist and the candidate of the right, was opposed by the republican parties and aroused considerable concern abroad. But Hindenburg, by his loyalty to the constitution during his first five years of office, in fact strengthened the republic and did something to reconcile the more moderate members of the monarchist right to the regime.

Locarno Pact.—In foreign policy, helped by the more conciliatory attitude of Edouard Herriot and Aristide Briand in France, Stresemann followed the Dawes agreement by the conclusion of the treaties of Locarno (*q.v.*) on Oct. 16, 1925. By this, Germany reaffirmed its renunciation of Alsace-Lorraine and undertook not to attempt any alteration of its frontiers with France and Belgium by force, which frontiers were guaranteed by the signatory powers, including Great Britain and Italy. The treaties of Locarno were followed by the Allies' evacuation of the first (Cologne) zone of the occupied Rhineland, and by Germany's entry into the League of Nations with a permanent seat on the council in Sept. 1926.

The Locarno pact was regarded with grave suspicion by the Russians who feared that Germany might join an anti-Soviet bloc. To reassure them, Stresemann signed a new Russo-German treaty in Berlin on April 24, 1926, confirming and extending the friendly relations established at Rapallo. Unlike Stresemann's agreements with the western powers, the treaty of Berlin received the unanimous approval of the German parties, including the right. A series of commercial treaties, completed in these years, began to restore German foreign trade. At the end of Jan. 1927, the Allied military control commission was withdrawn and, urged on by Stresemann, the League of Nations began to examine the problem of general disarmament. When the Kellogg-Briand pact to outlaw war was proposed, the German foreign minister went to Paris for the ceremony of signature and was warmly received in the French capital (Aug. 27, 1928). In the five years since the crisis of 1923 Germany had thus made considerable progress toward regaining a position in Europe corresponding to its size and importance. This was almost entirely due to Stresemann.

Following the Dawes plan and the treaties of Locarno, large foreign investments were made in Germany, mostly in the form of short-term loans. As a result, the period from 1925 to the end of 1928 was one of remarkable prosperity in Germany. German industry was re-equipped, production boomed, wages were high, and in 1927 unemployment fell to 1,000,000. Moreover, large public works were undertaken and reparation payments were promptly met.

Party Politics and the Elections of 1924 and 1928.—Throughout the years from 1924 to 1928 Germany was governed by a succession of coalition cabinets based on the three bourgeois parties,

the Centre, the Democrats and the People's party. From the end of 1923 to the end of 1924 the office of chancellor was held by Marx (Centre); from Jan. 1925 to May 1926 by Hans Luther, a former minister of finance; and from May 1926 to June 1928 again by Marx. Elections were held twice in 1924, on May 4 and on Dec. 7. On the first occasion, the effects of the crisis and inflation were reflected in the marked gains of the extremist parties. Democrats and the Centre, supporting the republic, held their ground. In December the Nationalists registered further gains, but the Nazis and their allies and also the Communists lost votes. The Social Democrats and the three bourgeois parties regained many of the votes they had lost.

Opposition, apart from that of the Communists and the extreme right, came principally from the Social Democrats and Nationalists. The Social Democrats supported Stresemann's foreign policy and were loyal to the republic, but opposed the social and economic policies of governments which in their opinion were too much under the influence of industrial and business circles and too lenient toward the antirepublican forces on the right. The Nationalists, violently critical of Stresemann's foreign policy, were sharply divided in their attitude to the republic; representatives of the more moderate section were brought into their cabinets by both Luther and Marx, but were forced out again by the opposition of the party's irreconcilables led by Alfred Hugenberg.

In 1926 the question of compensation for the deposed princely houses excited prolonged controversy. A bill to provide generous compensation was challenged by the left, which demanded a plebiscite. More than 14,000,000 people voted in favour of expropriation without compensation, but this fell short of the majority required by the constitution and the compensation bill was passed by the *Reichstag*. Social Democratic criticism of the army administration and clandestine rearmament roused another storm in the same year. General von Seeckt, the commander in chief of the army, was obliged to resign, but the independent position of the army in the state was not impaired. The following year, Marx's government was responsible for two of the major achievements of the Weimar republic in social legislation, a comprehensive scheme of unemployment insurance covering 16,000,000 people and the extension of state arbitration in labour disputes.

On May 20, 1928, the German people again went to the polls. The most striking feature of the results was the swing to the left. On June 28, 1928, Hermann Müller, a Social Democrat, formed a cabinet with the People's party, the Democrats and the Centre; Stresemann remained at the foreign ministry.

The Young Plan.—The first tasks of the new government were to secure a definitive settlement of the reparation question and

GUSTAV STRESEMANN ADDRESSING DELEGATES TO A PEACE CONFERENCE IN GENEVA. SEPT. 1929

GERMANY

the complete evacuation of the Rhineland. On Feb. 11, 1929, a new committee of experts under the chairmanship of another American, Owen D. Young, set to work to fix the total of reparations. This time, the Germans themselves were represented in the discussions. An agreed report was accepted with certain modifications at the two Hague conferences (Aug. 1929 and Jan. 1930) and came into force on Sept. 1, 1930. Total reparations were fixed at 121,000,000,000 RM., to be paid in 59 annuities, the present value of which was 39,000,000,000 RM. The foreign controls over German economic life established by the Dawes plan were abolished, and the Bank of International Settlement was set up to handle the financial problems involved in transferring these amounts.

Under the leadership of Hugenberg the Nationalist party now joined forces with the Nazis in organizing a plebiscite in favour of a bill refusing all further obligations to pay reparations and declaring the chancellor and his ministers to be punishable for treason if they accepted new financial commitments. It was during this campaign that the Nazis, financed by the Nationalists and their friends among the industrialists, made their first appearance on the national political scene. The campaign, however, failed completely, and a revolt against Hugenberg's leadership led to a break away from the Nationalist party. Stresemann had secured from the Allies, at the same time that he accepted the Young plan, a promise to evacuate the whole of the Rhineland by June 1930. This was a decisive argument and the bills embodying the Young legislation were passed by the *Reichstag* in March 1930. By then Stresemann, the outstanding political figure of the Weimar republic, was dead (Oct. 3, 1929), worn out by the double strain of negotiating with the Allies and defending his policy against the attacks made on it by the right in Germany.

The End of the Republic.—The basis of German prosperity in the later 1920s was precarious: it was dependent on foreign credits. When these dried up and the loans already made were called in, Germany was plunged into a slump which was more severe than that experienced by any other country. Signs of this were already apparent at the beginning of 1929. With the crash on the New York Stock exchange in Oct. 1929 and the beginning of the world depression, German unemployment figures shot up; foreign trade was drastically curtailed; wages fell and the number of bankruptcies increased daily. The effects of the slump were felt by all sections of the community, nor were they limited to the economic field and to the hardship suffered by millions who only a few years before had experienced the rigours of the inflation. The depression had immediate political repercussions, undermining the foundations of the republic and producing a notable increase in the support for the extremist parties both on the left and on the right. Within two years the Nazis shot up to the first and the Communists to the third place among the German parties. In 1933 Hitler told a Munich audience: "We are the result of the distress for which the others are responsible." The depression was the indispensable condition for the Nazis' rise to power.

The immediate consequence of the slump was the breakup of the coalition government under Müller. Sharp differences of opinion divided the parties on the share of the burden to be borne by the different classes they represented. The particular issue in dispute was a proposal to cut unemployment benefit payments. To this the Social Democrats were strongly opposed, and on March 27, 1930, the Müller cabinet resigned.

Brüning and Schleicher.—The man selected by Hindenburg to form the next government was Heinrich Brüning (*q.v.*), of the Centre, a man who had not previously held high office. His first concern was to pass the budget, but he was unable to secure a majority in the *Reichstag* for his proposals, the Social Democrats combining with the Communists, Nationalists and Nazis to make up the hostile majority. Faced with a parliamentary deadlock, Brüning resorted to the use of the president's emergency powers under article 48 to put his program into effect by decree (July 16, 1930). Such a possibility had been envisaged at the time of Brüning's appointment to the chancellorship by a small group of men round the president, prominent among whom was Gen. Kurt von Schleicher, head of the ministerial office in the ministry of defense, a man who exercised great influence behind the scenes. It was Schleicher who had suggested Brüning to Hindenburg as chancellor, and Brüning, although sincerely attached to parliamentary institutions, accepted the view that the economic situation called for the use of emergency methods. His action was promptly challenged by the Social Democrats who defeated him for the second time in the *Reichstag*. Brüning thereupon dissolved the chamber and fixed new elections for Sept. 14, 1930. Both at the time and subsequently Brüning's decision to resort to the methods of presidential government over the head of the *Reichstag* has been the subject of much controversy.

The elections were held in an atmosphere of public disorder for which the Nazis, with the organized violence of their brownshirted storm troopers, and also the Communists were chiefly responsible. The results were disastrous. The impact of the depression on German society was reflected in the sensational rise of the Communist and more especially the Nazi vote.

Despite these results Brüning decided to remain in office. He had to face the noisy opposition of the Nazis and the Communists who attacked his government as unconstitutional and proceeded

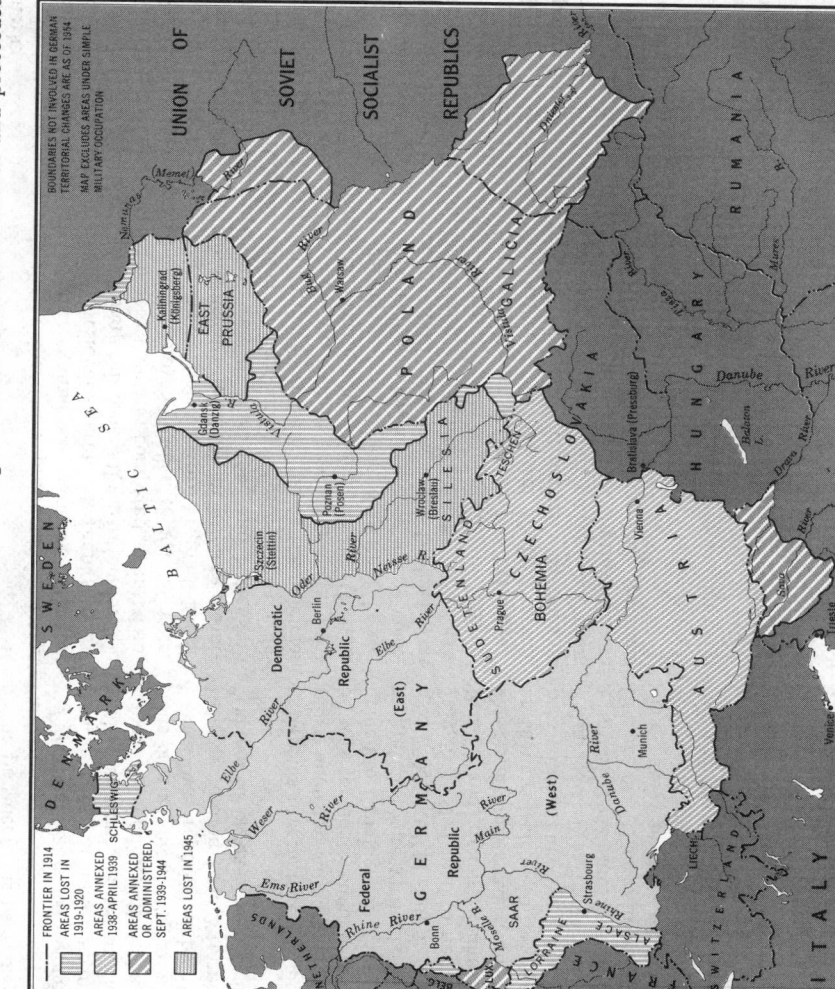

GERMAN TERRITORIAL CHANGES 1914-1957

to reduce parliamentary procedure to a prolonged brawl. The Social Democrats, however, alarmed at the threat to the republic from the rising power of the two extremist parties, rallied to the chancellor's support, although they were critical of the deflationary policy he was pursuing. This provided Brüning with sufficient votes to defeat the frequent motions of no confidence, while he put his program into effect by presidential decree. The measures introduced by the government failed to check the slump, which was a world-wide phenomenon. In an effort to break through the economic barriers separating the nations, Julius Curtius, the foreign minister, proposed an Austro-German customs union (March 24, 1931) which would also have placated the large body of opinion in both countries in favour of the combination of the two German states. But France and Italy forced the German government to abandon its plan.

In July 1931 a severe financial crisis led the big Darmstadt and National bank to close its doors, and in September the figure for registered unemployment reached 4,300,000. On Oct. 3 Brüning reconstructed his cabinet, assuming the office of foreign minister himself. His dour struggle to master the economic situation continued, and he displayed unusual courage and integrity in standing up to unscrupulous opposition, but in the early months of 1932 unemployment passed the 6,000,000 mark.

In these circumstances the prospect of a presidential election when Hindenburg's term of office expired was alarming. Brüning sought a prolongation of the president's term, but thanks to the opposition of Hitler and Hugenberg this proposal was rejected. On March 13 Hitler and three other candidates competed against Hindenburg, and the old field marshal, now 84, polled 18,661,736 votes to Hitler's 11,328,571. A second election, on April 11, made necessary by Hindenburg's failure by 0.4% to secure an absolute majority, raised the field marshal's vote to 19,359,642 and Hitler's to 13,417,460. The chief reason for Hindenburg's success was the decision of all the republican parties to vote for him as the defender of the constitution. This trust was soon to be disillusioned.

The political struggle in Prussia, the largest of the German *Länder* or states, was scarcely less important than that in the *Reich.* Since 1920, Prussia had been governed by a stable coalition of the Social Democrats and Centre under the leadership of two Social Democrats, Otto Braun and Karl Severing. The Prussian government was regarded as the principal bulwark of German democracy and as such was a special object of the extremists' hatred; in particular, they wished to get control of the Prussian police force out of the hands of Severing. At the state elections on April 24, 1932, the Nazis scored another big success, becoming with 162 seats out of a total of 428 the largest party in the Prussian *Landtag;* and the Social Democrat-Centre coalition only remained in office as a caretaker ministry.

Brüning hoped to offset his setbacks at home with successes abroad. He sought to secure the abandonment of reparation payments and the recognition of Germany's right to equality of armaments. There was considerable support for the cancellation of reparations on the Allied side, but Brüning's hopes were dashed by the postponement of the proposed conference until June 1932. Although the disarmament conference opened in February, French opposition rapidly brought it to a standstill.

DR. ERICH SALOMON—PETER HUNTER/AMSTERDAM

A SESSION OF THE REICHSTAG IN 1931: ALTHOUGH IT WAS AGAINST PARLIAMENTARY REGULATIONS, NAZI PARTY MEMBERS (RIGHT) WEAR FULL UNIFORM

Meanwhile intrigue among the president's camarilla, in which Schleicher played a leading part, led Hindenburg to withdraw his confidence from Brüning (May 30, 1932), an event which may be regarded as decisive for the fate of German democracy. Brüning's program had raised powerful enemies among the industrialists and Junker landowners, and once Brüning had secured the re-election of the president, his usefulness in Schleicher's eyes had been exhausted.

Papen and Schleicher.—One of the last acts of Brüning's government had been to impose a ban on the Nazi SA (*Sturmabteilungen*). Schleicher secured Nazi tolerance for his new nominee, Franz von Papen, on condition that the ban should be lifted and new elections held at once. Papen, although nominally a member of the Centre, was repudiated by that party, which remained loyal to Brüning, and on June 2 formed a nonparty cabinet, known as the "cabinet of barons," in which Schleicher became minister of defense.

Papen's government was highly unpopular in the country, but he relied upon the support of the president (and of the army), and he was fortunate enough to secure the success in foreign policy denied to Brüning. At the Lausanne conference on June 8, 1932, reparations were virtually abolished in return for a payment of 3,000,000,000 RM. into a fund for European reconstruction. On July 20, 1932, Papen turned out the Braun-Severing government in Prussia and appointed himself *Reich* commissioner for Prussia. The Social Democrats, hamstrung by the attacks of the Communists on them as traitors to the working class, allowed Papen's action to pass without effective challenge.

Immediately afterward elections to the *Reichstag* were held (July 31, 1932) and resulted in a Nazi triumph, giving them 230 seats in the *Reichstag.* Papen agreed with Schleicher that it was necessary to make the Nazis share the responsibility for governing the country, but he hoped to force Hitler to accept office on his and not Hitler's terms. When the *Reichstag* met in Sept. 1932, the Nazis succeeded in massing an overwhelming vote against Papen, but he promptly dissolved the chamber and fixed new elections for Nov. 6, governing in the meantime by emergency decree.

At the elections the Nazis lost nearly 2,000,000 votes, but Schleicher, alarmed at the prospect of continued deadlock and at the further increase in the Communist vote, forced Papen's resignation and took office himself (Dec. 3, 1932). Hindenburg, however, had been alienated by Schleicher's intrigues, and when Schleicher in turn failed to win the support of the other parties or to bring the Nazis into his government, Hindenburg declined to give him the power to dissolve the *Reichstag*. In the meantime, Papen had made contact with Hitler and the Nationalists and was able to offer the prospect of a coalition which had a chance of securing a majority in the chamber.

Hitler was driven by the declining fortunes of the Nazi party to accept considerably less than he had demanded earlier in 1932, but he secured the chancellorship for himself. Papen, for his part, was convinced that he had tied Hitler's hands by forcing him into a coalition in which the Nazi ministers were heavily outnumbered and held no key posts and in which he himself became vice-chancellor as well as *Reich* commissioner for Prussia. On Jan. 30, 1933, the coalition assumed office, and Adolf Hitler became chancellor of Germany, legally as he had been determined to do and not by revolution.

N. THE THIRD REICH, 1933-39

The Nazi Revolution.—In the coalition cabinet the Nazis held only 3 out of 11 seats. They had Hitler as chancellor, Wilhelm Frick as *Reichsminister* of the interior and Hermann Göring (who became Prussian minister of the interior) as a *Reichsminister* without portfolio. The ministry of economy and that of food and agriculture, both in the *Reich* and Prussia, were held by Hugenberg, the leader of the Nationalists; the foreign ministry by Konstantin von Neurath, a career diplomat of conservative views; the ministry of defense by Gen. Werner von Blomberg. As vice-chancellor, Papen claimed the right to be present on all occasions when the chancellor saw the president and as *Reich* commissioner for Prussia he controlled the principal administrative machine in Germany. In this way Papen believed that he had effectively blocked any threat of extremist action by the Nazis. He was soon to be disillusioned.

Hitler's first step was to persuade the cabinet to agree to new elections in order to provide a majority in the *Reichstag*; he overcame their doubts by a categorical promise that, whatever the results, no change would be made in the composition of the coalition. The elections were fixed for March 5, 1933, and the Nazis made full use of the power that they now possessed over the apparatus of the state, including the radio, to launch a whirlwind campaign. Although the other parties were still allowed to function, their meetings were broken up, their speakers assaulted and their newspapers continually suppressed. Göring, in control of the Prussian police force, displayed great energy in carrying out a purge of the police which placed the force under Nazi control; in addition, he called up 50,000 auxiliary police, the majority of them SA and SS (*Schutzstaffel*). The police were forbidden to interfere with the many acts of intimidation carried out by the SA who were given the "freedom of the streets."

On the night of Feb. 27 the *Reichstag* building was destroyed by fire. On the pretext of a Communist plot to seize power the constitutional guarantees of individual liberty were suspended and the *Reich* government given emergency powers. It was in this atmosphere of fear and insecurity that the elections were held a week later. Nevertheless the Nazis failed to secure an outright majority, and both the Centre party and the Social Democrats held firm. It was only with the help of his Nationalist partners that Hitler secured a bare majority of 288 plus 52 seats in a house of 647 deputies.

Hitler's next step was to secure the passage of an enabling act which would give the government the power to issue decrees independently of the *Reichstag* and of the president. For this he required a two-thirds majority in the *Reichstag*. The 81 Communist deputies were either arrested or excluded; the support of the Nationalists and of the Centre party (73 seats) was obtained by assurances and promises, and the Social Democrats who alone opposed the bill (March 23) were outvoted by 441 to 94. The Enabling act remained the constitutional basis of Hitler's dictatorship. No new constitution was ever introduced to replace that of the Weimar republic; fresh laws were promulgated as they were required. Thus the third *Reich* (empire) was created. (The second *Reich* was that formed by Bismarck in 1871; the term first *Reich* denoted the Holy Roman empire of 962-1806.)

Armed with overriding powers, which he had been careful to obtain without formally infringing on the principle of legality, Hitler proceeded to carry out a revolution with the authority of the state on his side. A series of decrees culminating in the Law for the Reconstruction of the *Reich* (Jan. 30, 1934) abolished the *Land* diets and transferred the sovereign powers of the *Länder* to the *Reich*. In May 1933 the trade unions organization was suppressed and the unions merged into a German labour front under Robert Ley. This was followed in the course of the summer by the suppression or "voluntary" dissolution of the other political parties, and on July 14, 1933, the Nazi party was formally declared to be the only political party in Germany.

Opposition to these measures in the cabinet crumpled before the wave of revolutionary violence which swept over the country. Papen was shorn of his authority as *Reich* commissioner for Prussia, being replaced by Göring, and Hugenberg was unable to prevent the dissolution of his own party and was forced to resign. The Nazi group in the cabinet was strengthened by the inclusion of Josef Goebbels as minister of public enlightenment and propaganda (March 14, 1933), but in fact the cabinet had ceased to count, and all decisions were taken by the Nazi leaders on their own authority.

There was, however, a point beyond which the process of *Gleichschaltung* (co-ordination), the current euphemism for Nazi seizure of control, could not be carried without seriously endangering the efficiency of the state and of the German economy. During the summer of 1933 Hitler began to call a halt. The plans of the radical wing of the party to replace the capitalist economy by some form of corporate organization under state control were abruptly repudiated. Hitler could not afford to quarrel with the big industrialists and financiers, and from June 28 Hugenberg's successor at the ministry of economy was Kurt Schmitt, director-general of the biggest insurance company in Germany, while Schacht, the new president of the Reichsbank (appointed on March 16), set his face firmly against radical anticapitalist experiments.

The Röhm Affair.—There was considerable opposition to Hitler's new policy of stabilization, both from the more radical section of the Nazi movement and from those who had been left out in the scramble for positions and wanted no end to the revolution until they had been provided for. This opposition found its focus in the SA and its leader in the SA chief of staff, Ernst Röhm. From the summer of 1933 to the summer of 1934 this question of the so-called "second revolution" formed the dominant issue in German politics.

During the first half of 1934 the conservative forces in Germany came to look to the army with its particular claim to the loyalty of Hindenburg. The army leaders were inflexibly opposed to Röhm's plans for the incorporation of the SA into the army. Hitler for his part could not afford an open clash with the army which still remained the most powerful independent institution in the country. He needed the help of the generals in carrying out the rearmament of Germany, and he was anxious to secure their support for his succession to the presidency (which included the supreme command of the armed forces) when Hindenburg, now in his 87th year, should die.

The crisis was touched off by Papen, who on June 17, 1934, delivered a speech in which he gave expression to the anxieties of the whole nation. Hitler now knew that Hindenburg had only a few weeks to live, and on June 21, when he flew to see the president, he was met with an uncompromising demand, presented by the minister of defense, General von Blomberg: either the government must bring about a relaxation of the state of tension or the president would hand over power to the army.

Röhm had powerful enemies inside the party, notably Göring and Heinrich Himmler, the *Reichsführer* of the SS, the party *corps d'élite*. When Hitler reluctantly made up his mind to take action against Röhm and the SA leadership, it was Göring and Himmler who carried out the preparations for the purge. Röhm and his chief lieutenants were seized on the weekend of June 30, 1934, and executed without trial. The opportunity was also taken to settle other

GERMANY

accounts in this "night of the long knives"—among those murdered were Schleicher and the former Nazi leader Gregor Strasser. A month later, on Aug. 2, President Hindenburg died. Then with the agreement of the army leaders the office of president and supreme commander was merged with that of chancellor, and Hitler assumed the title of *Führer und Reichskanzler*. On Aug. 19 a plebiscite confirmed his new office by 88% of 43,529,710 votes cast.

The crisis of June 1934 was the turning point of the regime. Although the army leaders congratulated themselves on the outcome, it was Hitler who after a period of hesitation had triumphantly reasserted his authority. Forced to choose, he had

struck at the radicals and repudiated the "second revolution" but in doing so had used methods which only underlined the radical and revolutionary character of the regime he had established.

The Totalitarian Police State.—The years between 1934 and World War II saw the steady elaboration of the totalitarian police state. The principal instrument of control was the unified police, security and SS organization under the direction of Himmler and his chief lieutenant, Reinhard Heydrich. Schools, universities, the press, the theatre and the arts were forced to follow the pattern of Nazi regimentation, and the most determined efforts were made to indoctrinate the younger generation with the Nazi ideology through the schools and the compulsory Hitler Youth. The concordat which the Vatican had signed with the new German government on July 20, 1933, did not protect the Catholic community in Germany from constant interference and persecution by the Nazi authorities. The refusal of the Nazi-sponsored German Protestants to accept the authority of the Nazi-sponsored German Christian movement led to an equally bitter conflict between the Protestant churches and the state, in the course of which many Protestant pastors, including Martin Niemöller (July 1937), were arrested and ill-treated.

Treatment of Jews.—The regime showed particular hostility toward the Jews, who were singled out for attack from the first day of Hitler's chancellorship. A law of April 7, 1933, decreed the dismissal of the Jews from government service and the universities; they were also debarred from entering the professions. Under the Nürnberg laws of Sept. 15, 1935, marriages between Jews and persons of "German blood" were forbidden, and the Jews were virtually deprived of all rights. Their persecution reached its climax in the pogrom of Nov. 9-10, 1938, carried out under the direction of the SS. The greater part of all Jewish property was confiscated, and the surviving Jews were restricted to a ghettolike existence until the war when they were systematically put to death. Altogether, in German-occupied Europe, out of a total of about 8,300,000 Jews, 6,000,000 were killed or died in extermination camps of starvation or disease.

Rearmament.—By an extensive program of expenditure on public works—afforestation, land improvement, road building, etc.—the Nazi government succeeded in reducing the number of registered unemployed from more than 6,000,000 in Jan. 1933 to

BOYCOTT OF JEWISH-OWNED STORES, 1933; THE PLACARDS WARN, "GERMANS, BE ON YOUR GUARD. DON'T BUY FROM JEWS"

2,600,000 in Dec. 1934. From 1935 onward rearmament on a massive scale rapidly changed the problem from one of mass unemployment to one of an acute labour shortage. This remarkable recovery however did not lead to any comparable rise in the standard of living, which was deliberately held down by wage and price stabilization in order to permit the diversion of the greatest possible proportion of the national resources to the creation of a powerful military force.

All other considerations were sacrificed to Hitler's demand for the rearmament of Germany at double the rate which the military and economic experts thought possible. In Sept. 1936 Hitler proclaimed a four-year plan and gave Göring plenipotentiary powers to execute it. Schacht, who became minister of economic affairs on Aug. 2, 1934, and to whom Hitler owed the expert planning of the finances of German rearmament as well as the elaborate network of controls over German foreign trade, became increasingly critical of the reckless arms program and on Nov. 26, 1937, resigned. Although Schacht remained minister without portfolio at Hitler's insistence and until Jan. 20, 1939, president of the Reichsbank as well, from the end of 1937 Göring was able to carry out Hitler's economic plans in preparation for war without hindrance. Germany's expenditure on armaments is estimated at more than 51,-000,000,000 R.M. in the six years before 1939, rising from less than 2,000,000,000 R.M. in 1933-34 to 10,000,000,000 R.M. in 1936-37 and 16,000,000,000 in 1938-39.

Shortly after Schacht's final resignation, Hitler proceeded to reorganize the two principal institutions which had so far escaped the process of *Gleichschaltung*—the army and the foreign service. He used the pretext of Field Marshal von Blomberg's *mésalliance* and a trumped-up charge of homosexuality against the minister of defense, Gen. Werner von Fritsch, to secure their removal, assuming Blomberg's office of commander in chief of the armed forces himself and abolishing the ministry of defense and replacing it by a separate high command of the armed forces (*Oberkommando der Wehrmacht*, O.K.W.) which in fact acted as his personal staff. Sixteen of the senior generals were retired, others were transferred to different posts.

In Feb. 1938 Neurath was relieved of his post as foreign minister and replaced by the subservient Joachim von Ribbentrop, while the insignificant Walther Funk assumed office at the ministry of economics. Henceforth until the end of the war Hitler's arbitrary power over Germany was complete.

Hitler's Early Foreign Policy.—From the time that Hitler came to power his unswerving aim was to overthrow the peace settlement of 1919 and establish a German hegemony in Europe. These aims had, however, to be disguised until German rearmament had made progress, and Hitler showed great skill in soothing the anxieties of the other powers by his constant talk of peace.

On Oct. 14, 1933, Germany withdrew from the League of Nations and the disarmament conference. This was represented as a protest against the hypocrisy of the victor nations in refusing to keep their promise to follow Germany's example after they had forced it to disarm. The nonaggression pact with Poland, signed on Jan. 26, 1934, was used by Hitler as further evidence of his eagerness for peace, and when a Nazi rising in Austria on July 25, 1934, failed to secure power, he was quick to repudiate his followers and send Papen to Vienna on a mission of conciliation.

With the reunion of the Saar with Germany, following the plebiscite of Jan. 13, 1935, which had shown a 90% vote in favour of a return to the *Reich*, Hitler declared that all causes of dispute between Germany and France had been removed; but he evaded British and French schemes for a general European settlement and on March 16, 1935, announced that Germany was reintroducing conscription with the aim of creating a peacetime army of 35 divisions. This open repudiation of the treaty of Versailles involved a considerable risk, but the gamble came off: the other powers contented themselves with protests, and Hitler was encouraged to take bigger risks in the future.

During the next few years Hitler played with remarkable success upon the divisions between the other European powers. He persuaded the British to sign an Anglo-German naval treaty (June 18, 1935) which was much resented in France, and he soon

GERMANY

became the principal beneficiary of the quarrel between Italy and the western powers over Ethiopia. The outbreak of the civil war in Spain in 1936 enabled him to establish close working relations with Mussolini (Oct. 20–24, 1936). Using the Spanish civil war as his text Hitler now redoubled his propaganda campaign against the dangers of communism with very considerable success in dividing and confusing public opinion in the western countries.

The ratification of the Franco-Soviet treaty of mutual assistance of May 2, 1935, provided Hitler with a convenient pretext for the denunciation of the Locarno pact and the remilitarization of the Rhineland (March 7, 1936). The fact that this second open breach of the Versailles treaty was allowed to pass without effective challenge not only increased Hitler's confidence but had immediate repercussions in the alignment of the smaller powers. The alliance system which the French had built up in eastern Europe after 1919 began to show signs of strain.

On Nov. 25, 1936, Ribbentrop concluded the anti-Comintern pact with Japan, which gave a strong fillip to Hitler's anti-Bolshevik propaganda campaign, and a year later (Nov. 6, 1937) he secured the adhesion of Italy to the pact after Mussolini's state visit to Germany in Sept. 1937. By the end of 1937 Hitler was ready to take the offensive in foreign policy. German rearmament had already made considerable progress; he was convinced that France and Great Britain would never fight; he had driven a powerful wedge between the Soviet Union and the western powers; and he had won Italy away from the Anglo-French camp to close co-operation with himself.

Peaceful Annexations.—Hitler's first objective was the annexation of Austria. After the unsuccessful *Putsch* of 1934, Hitler for a time had to go carefully, but then closer co-operation with Mussolini, who had hitherto been the most determined opponent of an *Anschluss*, opened up new possibilities. On July 11, 1936, a so-called gentlemen's agreement was concluded between Germany and Austria, which was used by the German government as a means of exercising pressure on Kurt von Schuschnigg's government in Vienna. Hitler sought to preserve the façade of legality while applying political pressure under the threat, but without the overt use, of force. On Feb. 12, 1938, Schuschnigg, the Austrian chancellor, was bullied into accepting far-reaching demands during an interview with Hitler at Berchtesgaden. Schuschnigg's subsequent decision to hold a plebiscite, however, forced Hitler to act quickly and on March 12, 1938, German troops occupied Austria, 24 hours before the plebiscite was due to be held. Once again the other powers failed to do more than utter solemn protests, and Hitler rapidly turned toward his second objective, the disruption of the Czechoslovak republic. The demands of the Sudeten German minority in Czechoslovakia for greater autonomy were skilfully used by Hitler to create a situation in which Czechoslovakia's ally, France, and Great Britain brought heavy pressure to bear on the Prague government. This situation culminated in Neville Chamberlain's direct intervention to secure Czech acceptance of Hitler's ultimatum for the cession of the Sudetenland to Germany (Munich conference, Sept. 29–30, 1938). Hitler in fact aimed at far more than this and soon came to look upon the Munich settlement as a mistaken concession which had balked him of his entry into Prague. In March 1939 he used the smoldering quarrel between the Slovaks and the Czechs to create a further crisis which served as his pretext for the occupation of the whole of Bohemia and Moravia (March 15). Also, on March 22, he secured the return of Memel from Lithuania to the *Reich*.

Poland's Refusal.—Shortly after the Munich settlement, Ribbentrop had opened yet another claim by suggesting that Poland should agree to the return of the free city of Danzig to the *Reich* and the construction of a German extraterritorial road and railway across Polish Pomerania to link East Prussia with the rest of Germany (Oct. 24, 1938). These demands were renewed in sharper terms after Prague. They met with an uncompromising refusal from the Polish government, and on March 31, 1939, the British government, which had abandoned its policy of appeasement after the occupation of Bohemia-Moravia, announced its guarantee to Poland in the event of any act of aggression.

Hitler's immediate retort was to denounce on April 28 the German-Polish nonaggression pact of 1934 and the Anglo-German naval treaty of 1935. In May, the understanding with Mussolini was converted into the public "pact of steel," but Hitler's attention was directed above all to Moscow where the British and French were negotiating with the Russians to build up a common front of resistance to German aggression. The difficulties encountered in these talks encouraged Hitler to make a secret counterproposal. Stalin agreed to a visit by Ribbentrop and the Nazi-Soviet pact was signed in Moscow on the night of Aug. 23–24. To the public pact of nonaggression was appended a secret treaty dividing the whole of eastern Europe into spheres of influence and partitioning Poland. Hitler was convinced that the signature of the Moscow pact would lead the British and French to withdraw their guarantees to Poland. When the British government replied with the signature of the pact of mutual assistance between Great Britain and Poland (Aug. 25), Hitler attempted to avert British intervention by further negotiations. The British, however, refused to bring pressure to bear on the Poles, and on Sept. 1 the German army invaded Poland. Two days later Great Britain and France, after delivering an ultimatum demanding the immediate withdrawal of the invading forces, declared war on Germany.

WIDE WORLD

ADOLF HITLER (STANDING IN FIRST CAR) IS GREETED BY THOUSANDS OF HANDS RAISED IN THE NAZI SALUTE AS HE DRIVES THROUGH NÜRNBERG. SEPT. 1938

O. WORLD WAR II

The Years of Easy Conquests.—Hitler began World War II (see WORLD WARS) with the intention of waging a localized war against Poland and following this with the quick offer of a peace settlement. The campaign, however, lasted only 35 days, and the ease of his conquest tempted Hitler to take the initiative in extending the war to the west.

During the course of the winter of 1939-40, Adm. Erich Raeder, commander in chief of the navy, won over Hitler to the idea of occupying Norway and Denmark, partly to safeguard the vital iron-ore supply route from northern Sweden through Narvik, partly to guarantee the inviolability of the Baltic and partly to prevent the dispatch of British and French troops to the aid of Finland (then at war with the U.S.S.R.) through Norwegian ports. The operation was launched on April 9 and proved highly successful without disturbing the main concentration of German forces.

The invasion of the Netherlands, Belgium and France was begun on May 10, 1940. The German armoured forces concentrated on breaking through the hilly and lightly defended Ardennes sector of the front. The success of this advance through Sedan to the Channel coast, which cut off the French and British troops fighting in Belgium, proved the key to victory. The Dutch and Belgian armies surrendered before the end of May, the British were driven into the sea at Dunkerque, and by the middle of June the French had requested an armistice.

Hitler had no plans at all for the next stage of the war, but when the British showed no disposition to consider a compromise peace, he ordered preparations to be made for the invasion of Britain. How far he seriously intended to embark on so difficult an undertaking has been questioned, but in any case the failure of the German air force to win air supremacy over the Channel and their defeat in the battle of Britain meant that the essential preliminary conditions were lacking, and in Oct. 1940 Operation "Sea Lion" was postponed indefinitely.

Russian economic collaboration had been of great value to Germany in reducing the pressure of the British blockade, and in the first half of 1941 the Soviet government showed a marked disposition to avoid a breach with Germany. Hitler, however, had long envisaged German expansion eastward and now rapidly convinced himself that Germany was threatened by Russian ambitions. On Dec. 18, 1940, he signed the directive for Operation "Barbarossa," to crush Soviet Russia in a quick campaign.

At this point, Hitler's plans were complicated by the action of Mussolini (who had entered the war on June 10) in attacking Greece (Oct. 28, 1940). The effect of this was to open up a Balkan front, of which the British might take advantage. The situation was made worse by the total failure of the invasion of Greece and by the rapid retreat of the Italians in north Africa before Sir Archibald Wavell's advance (Dec. 1940). Hitler was obliged to come to the aid of his Axis partner. He sent German reinforcements to north Africa (where Erwin Rommel succeeded in driving the British back in the spring of 1941) and prepared for a German invasion of Greece. Hungary and Rumania were already German satellites and allowed German troops to move toward the Greek frontiers. In March 1941 the Germans proceeded to occupy key positions in Bulgaria, after a sharp diplomatic contest with the Russians, and also induced Yugoslavia to accede to the tripartite pact, but the Yugoslav government was overthrown by a palace revolution in the name of the young king Peter. Thereupon Hitler ordered drastic measures to make an example of Yugoslavia. In April 1941 German forces invaded and occupied both Yugoslavia and Greece, the former operation being accompanied by air attacks on the defenseless city of Belgrade, and in the last half of May German parachute troops completed the conquest of the Balkans by the capture of Crete.

Invasion of the Soviet Union.—With the occupation of Crete and Rommel's success in driving back the British to the Egyptian frontier, Raeder and others who hoped to make the main German effort in the Mediterranean called for a decisive blow against the whole British position in the middle east. But Hitler was set upon attacking and defeating the U.S.S.R., a task which he confidently expected to accomplish within six or eight weeks.

The invasion began on June 22, 1941, and though in the opening stages of the campaign the German army drove deep into Soviet territory, Hitler left the frontal assault on Moscow until late in the year. At the beginning of Dec. 1941, the onset of the dreaded Russian winter and the unexpected Soviet counteroffensive faced the German high command with a major military crisis. This brought to a head the strained relations between Hitler and the army leaders. In Dec. 1941 he assumed the direct command of the field armies himself. The fact that by drastic measures he succeeded in holding the Soviet attacks during the winter greatly increased his confidence in his own military genius. Henceforward he refused to listen to any views, or even information, which ran counter to his own conception of how the war should be conducted.

Germany Declares War on the United States.—The Japanese attack on Pearl Harbor in Dec. 1941 now extended the war to the whole world. Hitler promptly declared war on the United States, whose resources he underestimated as grossly as those of the U.S.S.R. Hitler failed to grasp the importance of seapower and it was not until 1942 that Karl Dönitz (who succeeded Raeder as commander in chief of the navy in Jan. 1943) was able to persuade him of the importance of the U-boat war. Great efforts were then made to build up Germany's submarine forces, and the U-boat attacks taxed the Allies' shipping resources to the limit, but by the end of 1943 the British and Americans had established a superiority in methods of defense and the Germans had lost the battle of the Atlantic, largely through Hitler's neglect of its possibilities at an earlier stage.

Hitler had shown an equal blindness to the importance of the Mediterranean theatre of operations. At the close of 1942, the advance of the British 8th army from the east and the joint Anglo-U.S. landings in northwest Africa were driving the German and Italian forces under Rommel into a trap. Hitler now hurriedly sent reinforcements, but the only result was to increase the size of the forces captured in Tunisia, where more than 250,000 German and Italian troops surrendered in May 1943.

Meanwhile Hitler had embarked on still more ambitious operations for the eastern campaign of 1942, aiming at the occupation of the Caucasus oil fields and a drive to the Volga. The invasion of the Caucasus fell short of its objective, while the drive to the Volga turned into a desperate contest for the city of Stalingrad (Volgograd), where Hitler's obstinate refusal to withdraw in time led to the encirclement and capitulation of the German armies at the end of Jan. 1943.

The double defeat of Stalingrad and Tunisia represented the turning point of the war. By mid-1943, the German forces everywhere stood on the defensive.

The Nazi Empire.—At the height of his success, Hitler was the master of the greater part of the European continent. German rule in the east was extended to wide areas of the Baltic states, Belorussia, the Ukraine and European Russia; Poland and the protectorate of Bohemia-Moravia; Serbia and Greece (where the occupation was shared with the Italians); and the nominally independent, satellite states of Slovakia, Croatia, Hungary, Rumania and Bulgaria. In the west, Norway, Denmark, the Netherlands, Belgium and France were all under German occupation, part of France from the summer of 1940 and the whole country from Nov. 1942.

German economic exploitation of these territories was ruthless. In eastern Europe, German policy treated the population, in accordance with Nazi teaching, as inferior races fit only to serve as slaves. Those classes of the population which on account of their education or position might be expected to provide leadership, together with the Jews and any who showed signs of resistance, were put to death. At Mauthausen, one of the extermination camps in Austria, close to 2,000,000 people, mostly Jews, were exterminated between 1941 and 1945; at Oswiecim (Auschwitz) in Poland, as many as 4,000,000 were reported to have died in the gas chambers as well as from starvation and disease. Frequent manhunts were carried out to round up labour for deportation to Germany; at the end of 1944, about 4,795,000 foreign workers had been recruited in this way, the three largest groups being Russians (1,900,-000), Poles (851,000) and French (764,000). Those from the east were treated entirely as slave labour and the conditions under which they lived were often appalling, though Hitler's and Himmler's plans for the new order that they meant to build in eastern Europe were only partially carried out.

In certain parts of the occupied territories (especially where the terrain was favourable) the Germans encountered partisan movements; *e.g.*, in Yugoslavia, Poland and the U.S.S.R. In almost all there was some form of resistance movement, in Norway, France and the Netherlands as well as in the east. The German measures for stamping out this opposition were often brutal and included the shooting of hostages.

In Germany itself the impact of war was not sharply felt until 1942. Casualties in the early campaigns were comparatively light and not until the winter of 1941–42 in Russia did they reach the scale of World War I. The effects of the blockade were reduced by the plundering of the occupied countries.

After the crisis of 1941–42 on the eastern front Hitler demanded total mobilization. Fritz Sauckel took over the recruitment of foreign labour, while Albert Speer was appointed minister of armaments. By a remarkable feat of organization and improvisation Speer succeeded in maintaining and even raising German war production despite the heavy Allied bombing of industry and communications. By 1944 he had 14,000,000 workers under his direction and was virtually the economic dictator of the country.

In the early stages of the war, Göring was the second man in Germany and was named by Hitler as his successor. But by 1942 Göring suffered total eclipse with the failure of the air force to check the Allied raids or make effective retaliation. His place was taken by Himmler, who extended the functions of the SS until it became virtually a state within the state. Not only was Himmler put in charge of the resettlement of the occupied territories in the east but in the *Waffen* (armed) SS divisions, 500,000 strong by 1944, he created a rival army to the *Wehrmacht*.

The Beginning of Defeat.—By the end of 1943 at the latest Germany's defeat seemed certain to many of its own military leaders. The fact that the war continued for another 18 months, at terrible cost, was due to the refusal of Hitler to admit defeat and his determination to drag down Germany and half of Europe with him rather than repeat the capitulation of 1918.

During the course of 1943 Mussolini was overthrown, Anglo-U.S. forces invaded Italy, and the Russians began the series of massive attacks which were to carry them deep into central Europe. In the east Hitler insisted that the German troops must defend everything they held and obstinately refused to allow the strategic withdrawal which his generals considered the better course. In the summer of 1944 the German front in Poland broke and the Russians pressed forward toward the frontiers of the *Reich*.; on June 4 Rome was liberated and on June 6 the British and Americans made their landings in Normandy.

Since the beginning of 1942 the Allied air forces had steadily increased the weight of their bombing attacks on Germany. The first 1,000-bomber raid, on Cologne, took place on the night of May 30–31, 1942. In July 1943 Hamburg was devastated in a series of such raids, while between mid-Nov. 1943 and mid-Feb. 1944 the R.A.F. dropped 22,000 tons of high explosives on Berlin. In March, the United States army air force carried out its first day raids on the German capital. These combined attacks continued without respite for three years and did enormous damage. (*See* Air Power.)

The Plot Against Hitler.—Realizing that Hitler's refusal to consider surrender would do irreparable harm to Germany, a group of German patriots had for some time been plotting to assassinate him. The German opposition was composed of a number of loosely connected groups, fluctuating in membership, with little common organization or common purpose other than their detestation of the Nazi regime. The two senior members, who had been engaged in conspiring to overthrow Hitler from before the war, were Gen.

Ludwig Beck, chief of staff of the army until 1938, and Karl Goerdeler, a former *Oberbürgermeister* of Leipzig. The only institution in Germany able to stage a successful *coup d'état* was the army, and one of the principal centres of the plot was the *Abwehr* (the counterintelligence service of the armed forces). This was broken up by Himmler during 1943 but was replaced by a small group in the command headquarters of the reserve army, whose outstanding personality was Col. Graf Claus von Stauffenberg.

On July 20, 1944, Stauffenberg placed a bomb concealed in his brief case under the table during a conference at Hitler's headquarters in East Prussia. By chance, however, Hitler, although injured, was not among those killed. The attempt of the conspirators to seize power in Berlin and bring the army over openly to their side failed, and both there and in Paris the coup was suppressed before the morning of July 21.

The End of the Third Reich.—By the end of 1944 the western Allies reached the Rhine, and six months' fighting in the west alone had cost the Germans 1,000,000 men killed, wounded and captured. The Russians swept through the Balkans and by Dec. 1944 were besieging Budapest and threatening East Prussia. Nazi propaganda foretold a terrible fate for the German people if they failed to hold off the enemy, while extravagant hopes were placed in the secret weapons (guided missiles, jet planes and new U-boats) and in a split between the western powers and the U.S.S.R. Ignoring the danger of a Soviet breakthrough in the east, Hitler persisted in gambling his last resources on an attempt to disrupt the Allies' front in the west by the abortive Ardennes offensive of Dec. 1944. In Jan. 1945, the Russians launched an attack along the whole line from the Baltic to the Carpathians and broke into Germany from the east, while in March the British and Americans crossed the Rhine and poured in from the west. At Hitler's command Germany was turned into a battlefield in a senseless campaign to delay the inevitable defeat.

Although there had been talk of the creation of a national redoubt in the mountainous country of Bavaria, which was the birthplace of the Nazi party, Hitler finally refused to leave Berlin. In a political testament to the German nation, he laid the blame for the disastrous war on others, principally on the Jews, and expressed neither regret nor remorse for what had happened. He appointed Admiral Dönitz his successor as head of state and Goebbels as chancellor. In the early hours of April 29, he married his mistress, Eva Braun, and so far as is known shot himself on the afternoon of April 30. Goebbels committed suicide the following day and Himmler shortly afterward. Göring, Speer, Ribbentrop and most of the other Nazi leaders were captured and subsequently tried by the Allies as war criminals at Nürnberg.

Admiral Dönitz attempted to negotiate with the western powers, but the Allies insisted upon an unconditional surrender and this was signed at Reims on May 7, 1945, to take effect at midnight May 8–9.

P. GERMANY AFTER WORLD WAR II, 1945–49

With the unconditional surrender the German state ceased to exist and the responsibility for the government of the German people was assumed by the four occupying powers, the United States, Great Britain, the U.S.S.R. and France. On June 5, the four original members of the Allied Control council (Gen. Dwight D. Eisenhower, Field Marshal Sir Bernard Montgomery, Marshal G. K. Zhukov and Gen. J. de Lattre de Tassigny) published in Berlin a declaration stating that the governments of the four powers "will hereafter determine the boundaries of Germany or any part thereof and the status of Germany or of any area at present being part of Germany." Berlin (*q.v.*), although situated in the Soviet zone, was to be occupied by all four powers and to be governed by an inter-Allied authority or, in Russian, *Kommandatura*.

The Potsdam Agreement.—At the Potsdam conference (July 17–Aug. 2, 1945), attended by Stalin, Harry S. Truman, Winston Churchill and Clement Attlee (but not by a French representative), it was agreed, though a program of decentralization was to be carried out, not to partition Germany but to treat the country as a single economic unit with certain central administrative departments. Great Britain and the United States agreed to support

GERMANY

at the peace settlement the Soviet annexation of the northern half of East Prussia (including Königsberg). The conference also agreed "pending the final delimitation of Poland's western frontier" to leave the "former German territories" east of the rivers Oder and Neisse (Pomerania, including Stettin [Szczecin] and Swinemünde; Silesia; and the southern part of East Prussia,) as well as the former free city of Danzig, under Polish administration, stating that these territories "should not be considered as part of the Soviet zone of occupation in Germany." These changes in the east meant the loss of occupation of 23% of German territory as constituted by the treaty of Versailles.

The Potsdam conference also decided that "the transfer to Germany of German populations, or elements thereof, remaining in Poland, Czechoslovakia and Hungary, will have to be undertaken." On Nov. 20, 1945, the Allied Control council agreed on a plan to move the entire German population from Poland, including the territories east of the Oder-Neisse line, to the Soviet and British zones of occupation, and the entire German population from Czechoslovakia, Austria and Hungary to the U.S., Soviet and French zones. In all, during 1946 and 1947, about 6,650,000 Germans were transferred to the four zones of occupation. This total does not include about 6,200,000 Germans who had fled in 1944-45 westward from Poland, Czechoslovakia and the Danubian countries at the time of the advance of Soviet armies.

The Failure of Joint Allied Control.—The Allied plans for a common policy in Germany and for the treatment of the country as a single economic unit proved abortive. There were three principal reasons for this failure. The first was the opposition of the French, who had not been represented at Potsdam and who wanted a partition of the *Reich* to prevent the reappearance of a unified German state. The second was the growing divergence between the policies pursued by the powers in their zones. The third and most important was the breakdown of the alliance between the United States and Great Britain on the one side and the U.S.S.R. on the other. Their differences covered the whole field of Allied policy, but so far as Germany was concerned, the most important issues were the functions and powers of the future German government, the economic unity of Germany, reparations, frontiers and the future of the Ruhr. Prolonged negotiations between the four powers, culminating in four meetings of the Council of Foreign Ministers (London, Sept.–Oct. 1945; Paris, July 1946; New York, Nov.–Dec. 1946; Moscow, March–April 1947), produced no agreement. On March 1, 1947, however, the Allied Control council promulgated a law declaring that "the Prussian state, which from its early days had been promoter of militarism and reaction in Germany, has *de facto* ceased to exist."

The deadlock on the Allied Control council had already driven the British and U.S. authorities to act on their own initiative in dealing with the problems of their own zones of occupation. These were particularly severe in the British zone which contained the densely populated and heavily bombed industrial centres of the Rhineland, the Ruhr, Hanover and Hamburg.

The Allies undertook the occupation of Germany with the purpose of rooting out the Nazi regime and destroying the basis of German military power. Hence their original directives laid great stress on political and economic decentralization, disarmament, the arrest of war criminals, denazification, the dismantling of German war industries and reparations. They rapidly found themselves forced to deal with quite a different set of problems: economic stagnation, the dislocation of communications, famine, a desperate shortage of housing, an unstable currency and rampant black market and the influx of millions of refugees expelled from eastern Europe.

In 1946 the British accepted the offer of the U.S. government to merge their two zones for economic purposes and the bizone came into existence on Jan. 1, 1947. This development was attacked by the Soviet government and was disliked by the French. The British and U.S. authorities had already handed over much administrative responsibility to the Germans and had set up state (*Länder*) governments. State parliaments (*Landtage*) were brought into being by elections in the U.S. zone in November and December 1946, in the British in April 1947 and in the French in

May 1947. The three largest parties to emerge were the Christian Democratic Union (Christlich-Demokratische Union, C.D.U.), the Free Democratic party (Freie Demokratische Partei, F.D.P.) and the Social Democratic party (Sozialdemokratische Partei Deutschlands, S.P.D.), the last-named being closely bound up with the revived trade union movement. In the bizone, on Jan. 1, 1947, a German economic council of 52 members elected by the *Landtage* assumed responsibility, under Allied supervision, for economic reconstruction.

Alongside this rebuilding of the German economy and frequently at variance with it, the Allies continued their measures to disarm Germany and reduce the industrial basis of its military power. This led to confusion in Allied policy which already suffered from major differences between the western powers; *e.g.*, between the British Labour government and the United States over the socialization of the Ruhr industries; between the French and the other two western powers over the creation of centralized organs of administration and government. The resulting sense of insecurity added to German demoralization and apathy. Apart from the hardships of life in ruined and hungry towns, other factors weighed heavily on the Germans; *e.g.*, the large numbers of prisoners of war still held abroad, especially in the U.S.S.R., and the difficulties of absorbing the refugees.

The turning point in the postwar history of Germany was the year 1948. The U.S. and British were determined to press ahead with their plans for the reorganization of western Germany. On Jan. 7, 1948, the powers and composition of the German Economic council for the bizone (meeting in Frankfurt am Main) were changed to create the nucleus of a future German government. The Economic council was expanded from 52 to 104 members and a second chamber, a *Länderrat* consisting of two representatives from each state, was set up. To meet French objections, a six-power conference in London (United States, Great Britain, France, Belgium, the Netherlands and Luxembourg) produced on June 7 an agreed program for the future development of the three western zones. Its main features were: a constituent assembly and federal German government for all three zones (without the Saar, which at the end of 1947 became an autonomous territory economically attached to France); an Allied occupation statute governing relations between the Allies and the German authorities; an economic merger of the French with the British and U.S. zones; the establishment of an Allied military security board to enforce demilitarization; and an international Ruhr authority to control the coal and steel industries of the Ruhr basin.

The Soviet government reacted strongly to these developments. It attacked the new policy in western Germany, withdrew its representative from the Allied Control council (March 20) and began to place obstacles in the way of communications between western Germany and Berlin. After the much-needed currency reform in the western zones (put into operation on June 20) the Soviet authorities proceeded to enforce a blockade of the Allied garrisons in Berlin and of about 2,500,000 inhabitants of West Berlin, with the intention of driving out the western powers. This blockade lasted from the summer of 1948 to the summer of 1949. The answer of the western powers was to institute a counterblockade of the Soviet zone and to organize the supply of Berlin by air. By Sept. 30, 1949, when the airlift ceased, 2,323,738 tons of food, fuel and raw materials had been

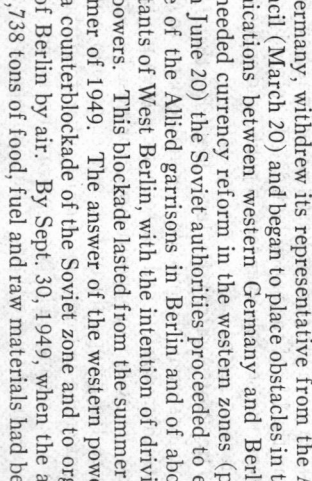

WIDE WORLD

WORKERS UNLOAD COAL FROM A U.S. AIRPLANE DURING THE AIRLIFT THAT SUPPLIED WEST BERLIN DURING THE SOVIET BLOCKADE, 1948

brought into the beleaguered city in this way. Meanwhile the Allied governments pressed ahead with the execution of the decisions made in the summer of 1948. On Sept. 1, a parliamentary council of 65 members, elected by the *Landtage*, met at Bonn under the chairmanship of Konrad Adenauer (*q.v.*), of the C.D.U., to draft a constitution. Pending a decision by a future German government on the question of public or private ownership, the coal, iron and steel industries of the Ruhr were placed in the hands of German trustees and an international Ruhr authority set up with powers to allocate supplies between internal and export needs, as well as to fix quotas, tariffs and prices.

After the Marshall offer of U.S. aid to Europe, further economic aid on a large scale (the European Recovery program) was made available to western Germany, and this, combined with the currency reform, led to a remarkable economic recovery. In the second half of 1948 industrial production rose from 45% to nearly 75% of the 1936 level, while steel production doubled during that year. The economic policy of free competition pursued by the German authorities under Ludwig Erhard's guidance was criticized by the S.P.D. and the trade unions on the grounds that it led to a steep rise in prices and hardship for the poorer classes, but revival in German confidence was marked.

In May 1949 the U.S.S.R. finally agreed to lift the blockade of Berlin. In the same month the western powers put into operation a new occupation statute for West Berlin which gave greater freedom and responsibility to the city administration under its mayor, Ernst Reuter (S.P.D.). When the Soviet authorities made further attempts to interfere with freedom of communication, the Allies continued the airlift. Finally a tacit working agreement was reached which left Berlin divided into western and eastern sectors under separate administrations, but with the garrisons of the western powers still *in situ*.

Two meetings of the Council of Foreign Ministers held in London (Nov.-Dec. 1947) and in Paris (May-June 1949) succeeded no more than earlier meetings in reaching agreement on a unified policy for the whole of Germany; and, in the meantime, the measures for the organization of separate west and east German states had gone on. On Jan. 17, 1949, an Allied security board had been set up to supervise the demilitarization of Germany. Strong German protests continued to be made against the dismantling of German factories. A new program for demilitarization agreed on by the U.S., British and French foreign ministers in Washington in April made considerable concessions to the German attitude, but this did not stop the agitation, which led to a number of incidents with the British authorities in the course of the year. The three foreign ministers at their Washington meeting completed the arrangements for the merger of the French with the Anglo-American bizone and on April 10, 1949, published the promised occupation statute. This guaranteed full powers of self-government to the new West German state except for certain reserved subjects (see *Constitution and Government*, below).

(A. Bk.; U. W. K.)

Q. FEDERAL REPUBLIC OF GERMANY

With the Occupation Statute published, the parliamentary council at last concluded its discussions on the Basic Law of the new state. This was passed by the council on May 8, 1949, by 53 votes to 12 and approved by the Allied military governors on May 12 with certain reservations, the most important of which was the exclusion of West Berlin, the proposed 12th *Land* of the federation. The 11 *Länder*, then, were Schleswig-Holstein, Hamburg, Bremen, Lower Saxony, North Rhine-Westphalia, Rhineland-Palatinate, Hesse, Bavaria, Baden, Württemberg-Baden, and Württemberg-Hohenzollern (the last three were in 1952 merged to form Baden-Württemberg). In 1957 the Saar, returned by France, became the 10th *Land*. The Basic Law was ratified by the legislatures of all the *Länder* save Bavaria (which had hoped for a decentralized distribution of power) and came into force on May 23, 1949. For the constitution of the new Federal Republic of Germany thus established *see* below, *Administration and Social Conditions: Constitution and Government*.

The first federal election was held on Aug. 14, 1949. Led by

Konrad Adenauer (*q.v.*), the Christian Democrats, with the Christian Socials (Christlich-Soziale Union, or CSU, the Bavarian sister party of the CDU), won 7,359,084 votes, or 31% of the poll, and obtained 139 seats out of 402 in the *Bundestag*. The Social Democrats, led by Kurt Schumacher (1895-1952), won 6,934,975 votes (29.2%) and obtained 131 seats. Of the other eight parties which entered the *Bundestag* the most important was the Free Democratic (2,829,920 votes), with 52 seats, followed by the conservative German Party (Deutsche Partei) and by the federalist Bavarian Party (Bayernpartei), with 17 seats each. The Communists obtained 15 seats, the Centre (Zentrumspartei, occasionally allied with the Bavarian Party) 10. An alliance with the Free Democrats and with the German Party enabled Adenauer to be elected chancellor by an absolute majority of one vote in the *Bundestag* and to form a coalition government, taking eight ministers from the CDU-CSU, three from the FDP, and two from the German Party. Theodor Heuss, of the FDP, was elected president of the Republic on Sept. 12. By a vote of Nov. 3, Bonn was retained as the seat of the *Bundestag* and of the government, despite the Social Democrats' pressure for a move to Frankfurt.

On Sept. 21, 1949, the Occupation Statute came into force. The Allied military government was then replaced by an Allied High Commission, which on Nov. 24, by the Petersberg Agreement, made further concessions to the Germans on dismantling and demilitarization, allowed the building of a merchant fleet, and permitted the Federal Republic to become a direct member of the Ruhr Authority and of the Council of Europe and to establish consular and commercial relations abroad.

Foreign Policy under Adenauer (1949-63).—For Adenauer, foreign policy took precedence over all other concerns. When the Allied High Commission, in a revision of the Occupation Statute, authorized the establishment of a West German Foreign Office (March 6, 1951), he took the post of foreign minister for himself in addition to the chancellorship; and even after Heinrich von Brentano's appointment as foreign minister in 1955, major decisions were clearly reserved to Adenauer.

In tune with public opinion, Adenauer deplored the division of Germany. Reunification was his avowed aim, but he consistently maintained that the responsibility to bring it about rested with the Allies. Therefore, he based his foreign policy on the Western alliance under U.S. leadership and, within that alliance, on a federalist concept of West European unity. He had himself for years looked forward to a united Europe, and the ideal now appealed very strongly to Germans disillusioned with the effects of nationalism and afraid of Communist expansion. Also, while their neighbours seemed determined that German national institutions should never regain powers which the Nazi regime had criminally abused, membership in a supranational institution offered to the Germans a way back to equality with the other members.

The Social Democratic opposition was in principle not unfavourable to European integration, but in practice (partly for tactical reasons) until 1956 condemned the particular forms which it took. Schumacher objected to the entry of the Federal Republic to the Council of Europe in 1950 largely on the grounds that the Saar was admitted to the council simultaneously—a move which he feared would appear to sanction its political separation from Germany. When the French proposed a coal and steel pool between France and Germany, the SPD saw in this a device to exploit German heavy industry for France's benefit and a confirmation of the economic integration of the Saar with France.

Most hotly debated of all were the issues of German rearmament, first raised in 1950. The Western powers had allowed Germany a security police force as a counterpart to the "People's Police" of the Soviet zone, but after the outbreak of the Korean War it was felt in Washington that 12 German divisions were required to help defend Europe. To prevent the emergence of a new German national army, both Sir Winston Churchill and René Pleven (of France) proposed a European army, in which German units would be integrated under European command. But the SPD waged a long battle against rearmament, in which they were aided by Gustav Heinemann, lay president of the synod of the Evangelical Church and Adenauer's first minister of the interior, who voluntarily resigned from the government in 1950, and by Martin Niemöller, president of the Evangelical Church of Hesse. This battle was not finally lost until after the election of 1953, when the government secured a two-thirds majority in both houses and thus made the constitutional question whether rearmament involved amendment of the Basic Law irrelevant in practice.

The federalists hoped that an apex for the European Coal and Steel Community and for the European Defense Community would be formed by a European political community, the details of which were worked out in 1952-53 as a basis for governmental discussions by a constitutional committee of which Brentano was the *rapporteur*. But the defeat of the EDC in the French National Assembly in August 1954, which held up the restoration of German sovereignty, made an alternative solution necessary both for the problem of German rearmament and for the further progress of European unification.

Accordingly, by the Paris agreements of Oct. 23, 1954, which came into force on May 5, 1955, the Federal Republic became a sovereign state and a full member of the North Atlantic Treaty Organization (NATO), pledged to set up its own armed forces within the NATO framework. Great Britain and the six countries of the Coal and Steel Community joined in a Western European Union which was to supervise German rearmament and ensure the maintenance of a sufficient British force on the continent. The Saar was to be given a European statute after a referendum; but when the local population rejected this settlement on Oct. 23, 1955, the Saar returned to Germany politically to become a *Land* when the local population rejected this settlement on Oct. 23, economically on Jan. 1, 1957, and to be integrated into the Federal Republic on July 6, 1959.

But neither NATO nor the Western European Union was a tight enough framework to satisfy Adenauer's federalist conception of European unity, and in 1955 the Federal Republic massively supported the plans for two further supranational communities to integrate the member states of the Coal and Steel Community: a European Atomic Energy Community and a European Economic Community (EEC). In the negotiation of these schemes the Federal Republic made major concessions to France; nevertheless the two treaties, signed in Rome in March 1957, were ratified with the votes of the Social Democratic opposition, and a German, Walter Hallstein, previously secretary of state in the Foreign Office, was appointed president of the EEC commission. Adenauer had gone to meet General de Gaulle in September 1958, and for the next year the two men worked in a close harmony.

A certain coolness developed at this period between the Federal Republic (which viewed with distrust Harold Macmillan's gestures to Moscow) and the United Kingdom (left out of continental arrangements). The Germans felt that the popular reception given to President Heuss on a state visit to London in October 1958 had been too cool, and Adenauer in 1959 made an impromptu statement on "wire-pullers" operating against Germany in the British press. In Great Britain there was anxiety over the influential positions held by many former Nazis in the German government and judiciary. It was not until after the failure of the Summit Conference of May 1960, when Adenauer had in the meantime grown impatient of President de Gaulle's attitude toward European integration (which to the chancellor seemed a continuation of nationalist aggrandizement by other means), that a *rapprochement* was initiated and Macmillan was invited to come to Bonn.

Beyond Europe, the foreign policy of West Germany paid particular attention to the emergent states of Asia and Africa. Israel was a special case; and as an attempt to make partial material atonement for the death of 6,000,000 Jews, the Federal Republic in March 1953 ratified an agreement with Israel for reparations amounting to DM. 3,450,000,000 over 12 years. But in the Arab world also, and in non-Arab Africa, the Federal Republic was anxious to establish itself as a noncolonial power which could supply capital goods and technicians, and even some export credits (insured by the German government), to facilitate economic development.

U.S.-German relations were cordial throughout the 1950s. After 1956, especially, when it had differed from Great Britain and from France over the Suez crisis, the U.S. Department of State felt that in Adenauer's Germany it had a firm European ally on whose partnership it could count. Adenauer was able to carry a good deal of weight in Washington when, before the Summit meeting of 1960, he feared that Western policy, in the course of negotiating with the U.S.S.R., might lose sight of Germany's special position.

With the U.S.S.R., relations were much more complicated, the Federal Republic seeming, at times, to be stalling in the face of alternating blandishments and threats. The U.S.S.R. offered diplomatic relations in 1955, which Adenauer, visiting Moscow in September, agreed to establish in return for the release of nearly 10,-000 German prisoners of war still in Russian hands. Soviet policy was to recognize two German governments and to insist that only by negotiations between these two could German unity be restored. The Federal Republic, on the other hand, would not acknowledge East Germany as foreign territory. Regarding the government of the Democratic Republic as a temporary dictatorship on German soil, it adopted the Hallstein Doctrine (formulated in 1955) of regarding it as an unfriendly act for any state —except the U.S.S.R.—to recognize that government.

In particular the Federal Republic's government, in contrast to the SPD and sometimes also to the FDP, denied that its policy of rearmament jeopardized the chances of German reunification. It likewise rejected proposals for an "atom-free" zone in Central Europe and the plan (endorsed by Khrushchev in 1957) for a confederation between the two German political units with a consultative all-German council to prepare for the withdrawal of all foreign troops.

A trade agreement between the Federal Republic and the U.S.S.R. was signed in April 1958. In November, however, Khrushchev demanded the withdrawal of all Allied troops from Berlin within six months, under threat of his transferring to the East German authorities the control of the routes of access. The Western powers stood firm and, in December, rejected his proposal for a "free city."

The Conference of Foreign Ministers (in Geneva, May-August 1959), which was attended by West German and East German observers, failed to produce agreement on the German question or on Berlin in particular. The Summit Conference in Paris (May 1960) and Khrushchev's meeting with U.S. Pres. John F. Kennedy in Vienna (June 1961) failed likewise. Berlin, however, was the gap through which the main stream of East German refugees escaped to the West (*see* below); and finally, to stop this drain on the German Democratic Republic's manpower, Khrushchev in August 1961 authorized the building of the Berlin Wall (*see* BERLIN).

The outstanding event in foreign affairs for the Federal Republic in 1962 was the establishment of closer relations with France. Adenauer's state visit to France in July was a resounding success, and President de Gaulle's return visit in September was welcomed with enthusiasm. On Jan. 22, 1963, in Paris, a Franco-German Treaty of Cooperation was signed, at the end of another visit by Adenauer.

Relations with the United States, which had become noticeably cooler during 1962, were much improved after Kennedy's visit to Germany in June 1963. Whereas De Gaulle had avoided going to West Berlin, Kennedy went there and proclaimed himself *ein Berliner*. On Aug. 18, after much hesitation, the Federal government decided to sign the Nuclear Test-Ban Treaty of Aug. 5. Soon afterward in October, Adenauer resigned the chancellorship.

Domestic Affairs under Adenauer (1949–63).—The most urgent of the internal problems which Adenauer's first administration had to face was the resettlement of refugees. About 8,000,000 Germans had been expelled at the end of World War II from Poland's territories east of the Oder-Neisse line or from the Sudeten lands; there were others from the Balkans; and tens of thousands of additional fugitives were arriving every year from East Germany (more than 1,000,000 in the period 1949-53, to be followed by nearly 1,700,000 more before the erection of the Berlin Wall in 1961). The presence of these refugees put a social burden on the Federal Republic, but their assimilation proved surprisingly easy (except in certain rural areas and for people of advanced years). Many of the refugees, indeed, were skilled, enterprising, and readily adaptable, and ultimately the "economic miracle" of West Germany's speedy recovery could not have happened without them.

Politically the refugees were strongly anti-Communist; and the occupying powers, fearing that they might provide a reservoir of votes for a new nationalistically orientated social radicalism, had refused to license any "refugee party" for the elections of 1949. In 1950, however, the Bund der Heimatvertriebenen und Entrechteten (League of the Expelled and Dispossessed) was founded in Schleswig-Holstein, where in the local elections it won 23% of the votes. Quickly spreading to other Länder, it reorganized itself as the All-German Bloc (Gesamtdeutscher Block) in 1952, to contest the Federal elections next year.

Meanwhile organizations perpetuating certain ideals of the Nazi movement caught the public eye. The Sozialistische Reichspartei (one of whose leaders, Otto Remer, had shot many of the anti-Nazi plotters of July 1944) won 11% of the poll in Lower Saxony in 1951, but was banned by the Constitutional Court as antidemocratic and therefore unconstitutional in October 1952, in response to the government's application of November 1951. Similar anxiety was caused by reunions of ex-soldiers' organizations and by the discovery that Werner Naumann (whom Hitler had nominated as Goebbels' successor) and his friends were trying to infiltrate other parties, including the Free Democrats, and to weave a web of international connections. Naumann, who was arrested in January 1953 on the orders of the British High Commission but was released in July, subsequently joined the Deutsche Reichspartei (extreme nationalists and for persons aggrieved by denazification). The Communist Party, on the other hand, against which the Federal government had also applied to the Constitutional Court in November 1951, was not finally banned as unconstitutional till August 1956.

The first legislative period (1949–53) was marked by the struggle over the Law of Codetermination, demanded by the Trade Union Federation. "Labour directors" nominated by the trade unions were made compulsory in the coal and steel industries under a law passed on April 10, 1951. But in spite of disagreements over the distribution of the national product, the German trade unions were extremely moderate in their wage demands throughout the postwar decade, thereby facilitating economic growth.

A great consolidation of domestic politics took place through the elections of Sept. 6, 1953, when the CDU-CSU won 12,444,799 votes (45.2% of the total poll) and obtained 244 seats out of 487 in the Bundestag. Economic progress, and the desire to remain close to the protection of the West were the chief reasons for this success. The Social Democrats, now led by Erich Ollenhauer (1901–63), increased their poll to 7,939,774 votes; but this represented only 28.8% of the total and gave them only 151 seats. The Free Democrats, who as junior partners in Adenauer's coalition could neither attack its record nor claim much credit for its achievements, dropped to 2,628,146 votes and to 48 seats. While the German Party obtained 15 seats, the All-German Bloc, contesting a Federal election for the first time, obtained 27. Adenauer formed a second coalition government, in which his own followers held 9 posts, the Free Democrats 4, the German Party 2, and the All-German Bloc 2. Heuss was reelected president of the Republic on July 4, 1954.

Strains and stresses soon developed. The Trade Union Federation, claiming to speak for its 6,000,000 members, came out clearly on the side of the SPD against rearmament and conscription and in favour of further efforts to negotiate for German reunification: the "German manifesto" issued from the Frankfurt Paulskirche in 1955 was supported by the SPD, the Federation leaders, and prominent Protestant churchmen. But on July 15 a law for the formation of a volunteer army (in preparation for conscription) was passed by the Bundestag, special provisions being inserted in the bill to ensure civilian control and to attempt to exclude from the higher ranks of the army those whose political past was suspect. The Conscription Bill was passed on July 21, 1956, and the first recruits were called up on April 1, 1957.

During 1955, the All-German Bloc split, and when Adenauer retained its two ministers in his cabinet, the majority of its deputies went into opposition. Early in 1956, after a bitter conflict over the terms of the next electoral law, the Free Democrats also broke with the chancellor. In North Rhine-Westphalia some young Free Democrats coalesced with the Social Democrats to swing the five votes of the Land in the upper house against Adenauer. Only 16 FDP Bundestag members (including four ministers) split off from the FDP to remain loyal to the government.

The end of Adenauer's supremacy, however, was not yet at hand. The U.S.S.R.'s suppression of the Hungarian rising in November 1956 put an end to the "Geneva spirit" in which reunification plans of the type envisaged by the Social and Free Democrats had appeared realistic. In the spring of 1957 a major reform greatly increased pensions and tied future pension rates not only to the cost of living but to the growth in national income. Insisting on the Federal Republic's phenomenal economic progress since 1949, for which much of the credit was due to Ludwig Erhard as minister of economics, the chancellor's party launched an efficient campaign for the elections of Sept. 15, 1957. Backed by business finance and by the Catholic Church's moral influence, it won a massive victory.

With 15,008,399 votes (50.2% of the poll), the CDU-CSU obtained 270 out of 497 seats in the Bundestag. The Social Democrats, who had discarded socialism from their election appeals and had concentrated on denouncing conscription and atomic weapons, got 9,495,571 votes (31.8%) and obtained 169 seats. The Free Democrats, who had declared that they would not bind themselves to either major party before the election, were reduced to 2,307,135 votes (7.7%) and 41 seats. The All-German Bloc got 4.6% of the poll but no seats, whereas the German Party, with only 3.4%, got 17 seats by grace of the CDU. Adenauer formed his third government with 15 ministers from the CDU-CSU and 2 from the satellite German Party.

The Social Democrats, with the aid of trade unions, launched a "campaign against atomic death" (i.e., atomic armament) in March 1958 and once more called for the withdrawal of foreign troops. The Trade Union Federation, however, refused to call a general strike in favour of the campaign, and the Constitutional Court prevented the holding of referenda on the question in the Länder Bremen and Hamburg (which had Social Democratic governments). The Federal armed forces in 1958 received dual-purpose missiles capable of carrying atomic warheads; and by the end of 1960 these forces numbered more than 290,000 men, making seven divisions under NATO command and four in process of formation.

The year 1959 saw the first attempt to challenge Adenauer's leadership within the CDU. The crisis was provoked at the end of Heuss's second term as president by Adenauer's proposal to have Erhard elected as president of the Republic, thereby eliminating him from the succession to the chancellorship. When Erhard, prompted by party colleagues who feared that the CDU would thereby lose a major electoral asset, refused to stand, the CDU in a surprise move induced Adenauer himself to accept nomination (April 7). But when the party seemed determined to nominate Erhard for the chancellorship, Adenauer on June 7 reversed his decision. Though he had cast severe aspersions on Erhard's political experience and reliability in foreign policy, he was able to scotch an incipient revolt in the party immediately and without difficulty. The candidate finally elected president, on July 1, 1959, was Heinrich Lübke, of the CDU.

In November 1959 the Social Democrats adopted the first "Program of Principles" since that agreed upon in Heidelberg in 1925. This Bad Godesberg Program marked a complete aban-

GERMANY

donment of Marxism, scarcely mentioned socialization, and advocated an economic policy of "as much freedom as possible, as much planning as necessary." On June 20, 1960, after the failure of the Summit Conference, the party proceeded to abandon its opposition to the chancellor's foreign policy and called for a common reappraisal of the situation and a common foreign policy. Then at Hanover, in November 1960, the party conference confirmed Willy Brandt, the mayor of West Berlin, as its candidate for the chancellorship. Brandt reversed the party's remaining major stand against the government by accepting both conscription and the possibility that German troops might be equipped with atomic weapons. The party thus aligned itself in policy matters very closely with the CDU and evidently hoped to fight the electoral campaign of 1961 chiefly by contrasting Brandt with the octogenarian chancellor.

The elections of Sept. 17, 1961, returned only three parties to the *Bundestag*: the CDU-CSU, with 14,298,372 votes (45.4% of the poll), obtained 242 seats; the Social Democrats, with 11,427,353 votes (36.2%), obtained 190; and the Free Democrats, with 4,028,765 votes (12.8%), obtained 67.

Having lost their absolute majority, the Christian Democrats decided to form a coalition keeping the Social Democrats out of the government. Erich Mende, leader of the Free Democrats, wanted a chancellor other than Adenauer; but after protracted negotiations Adenauer was reelected chancellor on Nov. 7, 1961. Fifteen portfolios in his new cabinet went to the CDU-CSU and 5 to the FDP, which also secured the departure of Brentano from the Foreign Ministry and an undertaking from Adenauer that he would resign the chancellorship before the end of the legislative period. Brentano's successor was Gerhard Schröder (CDU); Erich Mende remained vice-chancellor and minister of economics. Mende refused to serve in the cabinet.

Erhard (1963-66).—On Oct. 15, 1963, Adenauer resigned the chancellorship; on Oct. 16 the *Bundestag* elected Erhard chancellor; and on Oct. 17 Erhard formed a coalition cabinet on the same lines as the outgoing one, but with Mende now included as vice-chancellor and minister for all-German affairs. Lübke was reelected president of the Republic on July 1, 1964.

The government's announcement, on Nov. 5, 1964, that it would not extend beyond May 1965 the time-limit (20 years) for initiating judicial proceedings against suspected criminals of World War II aroused widespread criticism; and on March 25, 1965, the *Bundestag* extended the limit by four years and eight months. While this was a matter of domestic policy in which foreign opinion was greatly interested, the conduct of foreign relations in the stricter sense caused more lasting difficulties.

As political tension over West Berlin was gradually eased, the possibility of a dialogue between the Federal Republic and the U.S.S.R. came to be considered in the autumn of 1964, notwithstanding the U.S.S.R.'s treaty of June 1964 with East Germany. Schröder's policy had reached the point where Khrushchev expressed willingness to visit Bonn for political talks; then in October Khrushchev fell from power.

Meanwhile the Federal Republic's relationship with the Western powers was complicated by the problem of reconciling "Atlanticism," European unity, and the Franco-German treaty, as France became progressively estranged from NATO and sought to impose the French interpretation of Europe, with the exclusion, moreover, of Great Britain from the Common Market of the EEC.

Erhard and Schröder were "Atlanticists" and favoured British membership of the EEC, whereas Franz Josef Strauss was the chief spokesman of the "Gaullist" view, with the support of Adenauer. (Strauss had been forced to resign from the government in 1962 after the so-called *Spiegel* affair, in which he had denied intervening to have several journalists and the owner of the opposition news magazine *Der Spiegel* arrested for alleged publication of official secrets concerning a NATO exercise.) Further difficulties arose over problems of West German equality of status in any plan for a "multilateral nuclear force" within NATO: De Gaulle wanted to keep the deterrent for France alone, and the British Labour government declared its opposition to allowing a German "finger on the nuclear trigger." The 12th German division, however, was delivered to the NATO command in Europe in April 1965, completing the Federal Republic's quota under the protocol of 1954; and the state visit of Queen Elizabeth II to West Germany and to West Berlin in May 1965 was acclaimed as a major contribution toward improving German-British relations.

ASSOCIATED PRESS—WIDE WORLD
FEDERAL PRES. HEINRICH LÜBKE (LEFT) AND CHANCELLOR KONRAD ADENAUER AT A RECEPTION IN BAD GODESBERG, 1961

In the general elections of Sept. 19, 1965, the CDU-CSU won 15,524,067 votes (47.6% of the poll) and obtained 245 seats in the *Bundestag*; the Social Democrats 12,813,185 votes (39.3%) and 202 seats; and the Free Democrats 3,096,736 votes (9.5%) and 49 seats. After recent successes for the Social Democrats in provincial and local polls, the Christian Democrats' relative majority came as a surprise, and the victory was regarded as a personal one for Erhard. Erhard, however, had to face a challenge from Strauss when he began to form his new government, again in coalition with the Free Democrats. Having tried unsuccessfully to prevent the "Atlanticist" Schröder from being reappointed foreign minister, Strauss sought the exclusion of Mende from the Ministry for All-German Affairs, on the ground that Mende was dangerously conciliatory toward the East German regime. On the threat of the Free Democrats to go into opposition, Erhard finally overruled Strauss and was reelected chancellor on Oct. 20. Twelve seats in his cabinet went to members of his own party, the CDU; five to CSU; and four to the Free Democrats. Strauss remained without a cabinet post.

The controversial plan for a "multilateral nuclear force" was abandoned in December 1965, when Erhard had talks in Washington with U.S. Pres. Lyndon Johnson. German-French relations, however, remained at a stalemate, and German-British relations were clouded by financial embarrassments about paying for the upkeep of British troops in Germany.

On his visit to Washington in September 1966 Erhard obtained nothing new on reunification, but gave a promise that the Germans would spend $700,000,000 on American arms to offset U.S. forces' support costs in Germany.

Meanwhile, however, the German economy, hitherto so buoyant, ceased its fast growth for the first time since the currency reform of 1948. Industrial production actually fell in 1967 and unemployment rose to 500,000—a figure unprecedented in the 1960s. The lack of clear political leadership coupled with widespread fear of large the National Democratic Party—a neo-Nazi right-wing opposition formed in the mid-1960s—attracted attention and support; though they only polled 2% in the Federal elections of 1965, they polled between 7 and 8% in the provincial elections held Nov. 20 in Bavaria and Hesse. In Bonn the Free Democrats, worried about their own political future as junior partners in a government in difficulties, on Oct. 27 withdrew from Erhard's cabinet over the proposals for a tax increase in the 1967 budget.

Kiesinger (1966-69).—This left the cabinet without a parliamentary majority, and the CDU without a leader who could command sufficient parliamentary support to head the next government. On Nov. 11, after three ballots, the CDU chose the minister-president of Baden-Württemberg, Kurt Georg Kiesinger (who was strongly supported by Strauss), as their candidate for the chancellorship in preference to Gerhard Schröder, who was known to oppose any coalition with the Social Democrats. (Kiesinger's former formal membership of the Nazi Party was regarded as a handicap, but no disqualification.) After complicated negotiations between the three parliamentary parties, an unprecedented coalition resulted between the CDU and the SPD: Herbert Wehner, the former Communist official who had thrown his political weight behind the Godesberg Program seven years earlier, was the moving spirit in this "grand coalition" on the Social Democrat side as Strauss was on the Christian Democrat side. On Dec. 1, the *Bundestag* elected Kiesinger chancellor by 340 votes to 109, with 23 abstentions; Brandt became vice-chancellor and foreign minister, while Strauss as minister of finance was paired with Karl Schiller of the SPD as minister of economics.

In his policy declaration Kiesinger stressed Germany's historic role as a link between Eastern and Western Europe and his government's desire to seek a *détente* with the East; while reaffirming Germany's place in the Western alliance, he also laid special emphasis on its relationship with France. Neither of these trends two years of his chancellorship. The *rapprochement* with Eastern Europe, begun by an exchange of ambassadors with Rumania in 1967, was cut short by the Russian occupation of Czechoslovakia in summer 1968; and friction between France and the Federal Republic subsisted, coming to a head for the second time particularly over Brandt's warm support for Britain's bid to join the EEC (vetoed by President de Gaulle in December 1967) and over the currency crisis of November 1968, in which Strauss (having, with Schiller, resisted pressure from France and other countries to revalue the Deutsche Mark) went so far as to recommend a devaluation of the French franc which President de Gaulle announced he would not carry out.

Domestically the Kiesinger government presided over a revival of economic growth and a return to full employment; but like other Western governments in the period it encountered vociferous opposition from both right and left. On the right the National Democrats polled around 6–7% in the three *Landtag* elections it fought during 1967 and then in April 1968 polled nearly 10% in Kiesinger's own *Land* of Baden-Württemberg. On the left many Social Democrats felt themselves betrayed by their leaders' joining in a coalition with the CDU, and the SPD lost votes in the *Landtag* elections: moreover, unrest broke out among students, partly in revolt against university overcrowding and conditions, partly against the pattern of West German society and its power structure as a whole, particularly after one student was shot dead by a policeman in Berlin in 1967 and again after an assassination attempt on Berlin student leader Rudi Dutschke in spring 1968. (U. W. K.; X.)

On Oct. 14, 1968, President Lübke announced his resignation, and the subsequent decision to hold the 1969 presidential elections in West Berlin on March 5, 1969, provoked a storm of protest from the East Germans, and reprisals in the form of travel restrictions in the Democratic Republic on all members of the Federal Assembly. Nevertheless, elections were held and on July 1 Gustav Heinemann, the SPD nominee, was elected president.

The election of the sixth *Bundestag* took place on Sept. 28, 1969. The Christian Democrats won 242 seats, the Free Democrats only 30, while the Social Democrats gained 224 seats (22 more than in 1965). Though they were in the governing coalition, the Social Democrats fought the election as an opposition party. On the morrow of the poll Brandt made his bid for the chancellorship as he had known since July that a left-centre coalition was probable.

Brandt's Administration (1969–).—On Oct. 21 Willy Brandt became West Germany's first Social Democratic chancellor. He received 251 votes of the *Bundestag's* 496 members, two more than the number required to see him safely in. Kai-Uwe von Hassel, elected president of the *Bundestag* in February 1969 (when Eugen Gerstenmaier was forced to resign), was reelected on Oct. 20. The new cabinet comprised 12 Social Democrats, 3 Free Democrats, and one nonparty member. Walter Scheel, the leader of the Free Democrats, became foreign minister; Helmut Schmidt, a Social Democrat, succeeded Schröder as defense minister, while Alex Möller, another Social Democrat, took over the Ministry of Finance; Schiller remained minister of economics. On Oct. 24 the new cabinet announced a 9.29% revaluation of the Deutsche Mark, for which the Social Democrats had argued unsuccessfully for many months with their Christian Democrat partners.

WIDE WORLD
WILLY BRANDT ADDRESSING A PARTY MEETING IN KARLSRUHE, 1964

On Oct. 28, in his inaugural policy address to the *Bundestag*, Chancellor Brandt said that the international recognition of the German Democratic Republic by the Federal Republic was out of the question because although there existed "two states in Germany," they were not foreign countries to each other. He called for negotiations between Bonn and East Berlin aimed at contractually agreed cooperation and welcomed the upsurge of intra-German trade. Brandt promised to take up Poland's offer of talks, made on May 17 by Władysław Gomułka, who suggested the establishment of full diplomatic relations on condition that the Federal Republic follow the German Democratic Republic in recognizing the Oder-Neisse frontier as final.

West German readiness to open negotiations with East European states with a view to establishing good relations on a realistic basis had been gladly accepted by the U.S.S.R., Poland, and the German Democratic Republic. The West German-Soviet talks began in February 1970 in Moscow between Andrei Gromyko, the Soviet foreign minister, and Egon Bahr, state secretary in the chancellor's office. After more than a dozen meetings, a tentative draft agreement was ready by the end of May and became the basis of 11 days' negotiation between Gromyko and Scheel. The draft treaty was initialed by the two ministers on Aug. 7 and signed in Moscow on Aug. 12 by Chancellor Brandt and Premier Aleksei Kosygin. In the treaty the Federal Republic of Germany undertook to respect the territorial integrity of all states in Europe within their existing frontiers, including the Oder-Neisse line, which formed the western frontier of Poland, and the frontier between the two German republics.

Polish-West German talks began in February between Józef Winiewicz, deputy foreign minister, and Georg Ferdinand Duckwitz, state secretary at the Bonn Foreign Office. After six preliminary meetings, final negotiations began in Warsaw between the two foreign ministers, Scheel and Stefan Jędrychowski. Initialed by them on Nov. 18, the Polish-West German treaty was signed on Dec. 7 by Brandt and Premier Józef Cyrankiewicz. In this historic document likewise, the West German government declared that the existing border line along the Oder and Neisse rivers formed the western state frontier of Poland and affirmed its inviolability.

The U.S., British, and French governments, informed in advance by the West German government of the contents of the Moscow and Warsaw treaties, welcomed and approved both of them. At the NATO foreign ministers' meeting in Brussels on Dec. 3, Scheel declared that ratification of all the treaties concluded by the Federal Republic with the East European states presupposed a settlement of the question of Berlin (*q.v.*).

R. GERMAN DEMOCRATIC REPUBLIC

For the East German zone, a Soviet Military Administration (SMA) was formed on June 9, 1945, with Zhukov at its head. Its chief concerns were to provide for the future security of the U.S.S.R. by setting up a pro-Soviet regime in Germany and to begin the collection of reparations, for which a total of $10,000,000,-000 was demanded. The blocking of all bank accounts, from which no one was allowed to withdraw more than RM. 300, reduced everybody to an equal footing and to an equal need to find work; and on July 26 all private banks were closed, and all firms, organizations, and individuals were ordered to hand over, within five days, all gold and silver currency, bullion bars, foreign bank notes, deeds, and valuables. Factories were dismantled by way of reparation, and rolling stock and in some cases the rails themselves

WALTER ULBRICHT, CHAIRMAN OF THE DEMOCRATIC REPUBLIC'S COUNCIL OF STATE, INSPECTING EAST BERLIN FACTORY MILITIA DURING A MASS RALLY, 1961

were transferred to the U.S.S.R. On June 10, 1945, the political freedom of all "anti-Fascist" parties was proclaimed. Besides the Communist Party of Germany, there emerged Social Democrats, Christian Democrats, and Liberal Democrats.

The Soviet-occupied zone was divided into five *Länder* (provinces): Saxony, Brandenburg, Mecklenburg (including part of Pomerania), Saxony-Anhalt, and Thuringia. On Sept. 12, 1945, a central administration for the zone, comprising 12 departments headed by Germans, with Zhukov as chairman, was created.

A far-reaching land reform was completed by Dec. 8, 1945: all estates of more than 100 ha. (247 ac.) were expropriated without compensation. About one-third of the country's agricultural land, previously belonging to about 3,000 big landlords, thus passed into the hands of 544,000 farm workers, smallholders, and refugees from Poland and Czechoslovakia.

In April 1946, after four months' negotiation, the Communists and the Social Democrats of East Germany were merged into a single Socialist Unity Party of Germany (Sozialistische Einheitspartei Deutschlands, or SED); Wilhelm Pieck and Otto Grotewohl were elected joint chairmen, and Walter Ulbricht (1893–) became secretary-general. (The title was changed to "first secretary" in 1953.) This fusion was strongly condemned by the Social Democrats of West Germany, where the Allied authorities did not recognize the SED. In September 1946 elections for municipal and local councils took place, the SED winning most votes. In the elections of Oct. 20 to the provincial councils, or *Landtage*, the SED won 47.5% of the poll, the Liberal Democrats 24.5%, and the Christian Democrats 24.4%.

In 1948, when the U.S. and British authorities set up the German Economic Council in their bizone of West Germany (Jan. 7), the Soviet authorities in the east retorted by creating a 25-member Economic Commission (Feb. 13), which assumed control of the central administrative departments. Its chairman was a veteran Communist, Heinrich Rau. Then the SED, which had already held one "People's Congress" in East Berlin (Dec. 6–7, 1947), held a second one (March 17–18), attended by about 2,000 delegates. This congress set up a *Volksrat* (People's Council) of 400 members, which in autumn 1948 was set to work to draft a constitution for a German Democratic Republic (G.D.R.).

The constitution was adopted on May 30, 1949, by a third People's Congress of 1,525 elected members. A new *Volksrat* of 400 was appointed. This *Volksrat* was transformed into a *Volkskammer* (People's Chamber) on Oct. 7; a *Länderkammer* (Chamber of the Provinces) was appointed on Oct. 10; and on Oct. 11 the two chambers elected Pieck president of the Republic. A government was formed, with Grotewohl as premier and Walter Ulbricht as first deputy premier. The SMA then formally transferred power to the new government and was replaced by a Soviet Control Com-

mission. On July 6, 1950, a treaty recognizing the Oder-Neisse line as the permanent frontier between Poland and Germany was signed at Zgorzelec (Görlitz).

In May 1952 the East German government announced measures to isolate its territory from that of the Federal Republic: a police-guarded cordon of land, 3 mi. wide, was created along the whole frontier in the west. Meanwhile the land reform of 1945 had left about 1,900,000 ha. (4,700,000 ac.) of agricultural land in the possession of individual farmers owning 20 to 100 ha. each. Collectivization of these farms began in July 1952. On July 23, 1952, moreover, the *Länder* were dissolved into 15 new *Bezirke* (administrative districts), East Berlin being one of them.

In May 1950 Stalin had announced a reduction by 50% of the reparations which would still be due from 1951 onward; and in October 1950 the G.D.R. had been admitted to the Council for Mutual Economic Assistance (Comecon), which comprised the U.S.S.R. and its European satellites. In May 1953, after Stalin's death in March, the Soviet Control Commission was abolished and a Soviet high commissioner appointed, to inaugurate a new policy of concessions to German public opinion. Already, however, the Germans had been exasperated by persecution of the churches, by collectivization, and by a serious food shortage. When the norms of production required from workers were raised, a wave of strikes led to a great popular rising on June 17, 1953. Whole towns were temporarily taken over by the insurgents till Soviet troops intervened to help restore order.

On Jan. 1, 1954, the U.S.S.R. ceased the collection of reparations; and on March 25 it announced that the G.D.R. was sovereign. On May 14, 1955, the G.D.R. became a founder-member of the Warsaw Treaty Organization (*q.v.*). When Pieck died, in September 1960, the office of president of the Republic was abolished and a Council of State was formed, with Ulbricht as chairman. He remained the SED first secretary.

There remained the vexed problem of Berlin (*q.v.*). West Berlin was an aperture through which refugees from East Germany could escape to the West. The total number of people from East Germany who between the collapse of the Third Reich and mid-August 1961 took refuge in West Germany amounted to about 4,000,000. This massive ebb included not only fugitives from agricultural collectivization but also industrial workers and professional men; and it continued, albeit in decreased volume, after the Western powers' rejection of the Soviet proposal for a demilitarized "free city" of West Berlin in 1958. The exodus gravely impaired the economy of the G.D.R. Finally, the *Volkskammer* on Aug. 12, 1961, adopted a decree, prompted by Moscow, for the sealing-off of West Berlin. A barbed-wire barrier, erected in the night of Aug. 12–13, was later replaced by a concrete wall topped with barbed wire.

The closing of the "Berlin gap" between the two German states marked the beginning of an economic revival of the G.D.R. Rebuilding of East Berlin, Leipzig, Dresden, Magdeburg, Halle, and other cities was rapid and spectacular. Everything of historical and architectural value was preserved and restored, but otherwise these cities changed almost beyond recognition.

Economically speaking, 20 years after its formation the G.D.R. was a going concern, and this was due both to painstaking work and intelligent planning. The *Neue Oekonomische System* of management of the national economy had been adopted in 1963 and introduced a year later. It had three aims: to adjust industrial prices to levels reflecting the true costs of production; to transfer investment decisions from the State Planning Commission to the managers of industrial enterprises; and to rely on credit control through the banks in place of the former direct control by the Planning Commission.

In external affairs the G.D.R.'s position improved considerably. To the bilateral 20-year treaty of alliance signed for the first time between the U.S.S.R. and the G.D.R. on June 12, 1964, four other similar treaties were added in 1967: with Poland, Czechoslovakia, Hungary, and Bulgaria. All these treaties contained a special article stipulating that the contracting parties were determined to defend the inviolability of existing frontiers in Europe, including "the state frontier between the G.D.R. and the G.F.R." In the

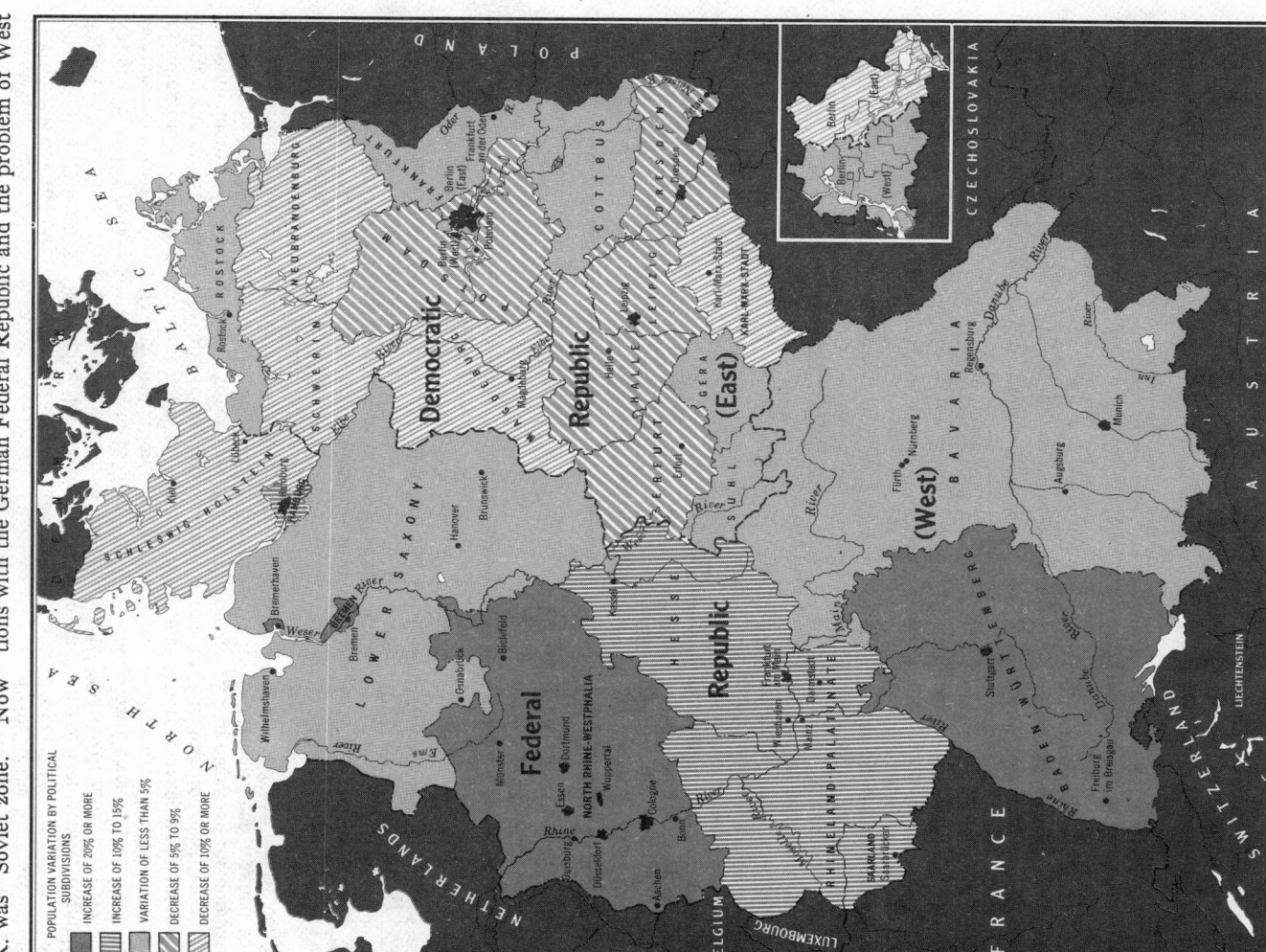

POPULATION VARIATION BY POLITICAL SUBDIVISIONS, 1950-69

POPULATION VARIATION BY POLITICAL SUBDIVISIONS
INCREASE OF 20% OR MORE
INCREASE OF 10% TO 15%
VARIATION OF LESS THAN 5%
DECREASE OF 5% TO 9%
DECREASE OF 10% OR MORE

late 1960s, East German foreign representation comprised 13 embassies in socialist states (including Yugoslavia), 5 embassies in Arab states (including the U.A.R.), an embassy in Cambodia, 5 consulates-general and 12 consulates in the states of the "third world," and 11 commercial missions in other states of the latter group. In addition the Chamber of Foreign Trade of the G.D.R. had official delegations in an additional 16 countries (including France and Great Britain).

The East German claim to recognition by the West was strenuously opposed by the West German government who claimed that they alone had the right to speak in the name of the whole German nation. At the end of 1966, when the Christian Democrats and Social Democrats formed the "grand coalition," a new Ostpolitik was formulated by the Bonn government. As they proclaimed their readiness to establish diplomatic relations with all Communist states of Central and Eastern Europe, they had also to introduce a new tone in their relations with East Germany. Commercial relations between the two German states amounted in the late 1960s to DM. 2,800,000,000. Before 1966 the name given in Bonn to the G.D.R. was "Soviet zone." Now it became "the other part of Germany."

Willi Stoph, the East German prime minister (Grotewohl, his predecessor, died in September 1964), decided to use this opportunity and on May 10, 1967, sent a letter to Kurt Georg Kiesinger, the Federal chancellor, proposing that the heads of the two German governments should meet to discuss the next move in the German question. Kiesinger replied on June 13, agreeing only to meetings of high ranking civil servants with the aim of removing human hardship caused by the country's division. Stoph replied on Sept. 18 by sending Kiesinger a draft of a treaty to establish normal diplomatic relations between the two German states, and to recognize all the existing frontiers in Europe.

To reinforce their claim to sovereignty the East German government took on June 11, 1968, far-reaching measures to control traffic and communications between the two German states and West Berlin, including transit visas and liability to transit tax.

A new constitution, defining the G.D.R. as "a socialist state of the German nation," and proclaiming Berlin its capital, was unanimously adopted by the Volkskammer on March 26, 1968, and ratified on April 6 by a plebiscite, with 11,536,265 (94.54%) votes in favour and 409,329 against. (See below.)

On the night of Aug. 20-21, 1968, an East German -division took part in the occupation of Czechoslovakia by the armed forces of the five Warsaw Treaty Organization countries.

On Dec. 18, 1969, Ulbricht initiated a discussion with the Federal government about the full sovereignty of the Democratic

Republic, by addressing a message to Gustav Heinemann, president of the Federal Republic of Germany, and submitting a draft treaty between the two republics establishing their relations on "the basis of the generally accepted principles and norms of international law." Premier Stoph and Chancellor Brandt met on March 19, 1970, at Erfurt, East Germany, and again on May 21, at Kassel, West Germany. Nothing positive was achieved. Stoph insisted on immediate recognition of the Democratic Republic as a sovereign and independent state. Brandt, while ready to respect the existing frontier, held that there was one German nation—the two states were not "foreign" to each other—and that relations had to be established on a unique "inner German" basis.

Dissatisfied, Ulbricht proceeded no farther, but at the demand of the Soviet Union the talks were restarted at the end of November between Egon Bahr, state secretary in Brandt's chancellery, and Michael Kohl, state secretary in the East German ministerial council.

On Dec. 2, 1970, the Political Advisory Committee of the Warsaw Treaty powers met in East Berlin to discuss their future relations with the German Federal Republic and the problem of West

Berlin. The NATO foreign ministers, at their meeting in Brussels on Dec. 3, formally confirmed that there would have to be a satisfactory conclusion of the talks with the Soviet Union on Berlin before such a European security conference was held.

On May 3, 1971, Ulbricht resigned as first secretary of the SED because of age. The party's Central Committee unanimously elected Erich Honecker to the post.

(K. Sм.)

IV. POPULATION

The changes in area and population from 1871 are given in Table II. The population of the German Empire at its establishment was about 41,000,000. Between 1871 and 1914, a period of rapid industrial expansion, the birthrate in Germany was unusually high. It rose to more than 39 live births per 1,000 population in the 1870s and then fell steadily to 27.5 in 1913. By 1914 the population exceeded 67,000,000. World War I severely reduced the population in three ways: the loss of men from all war causes was estimated at 2,870,000; the birthrate fell to the lowest point in history—14.3 in 1918; and, by the Versailles Treaty, Germany had to surrender territories containing nearly 7,000,000 persons.

After the war the birthrate rose to 25.9 per 1,000 in 1920 but fell again to 14.7 in 1933. Regarding the low birthrate as an obstacle to the industrial and military expansion of the *Reich*, the National Socialist leaders adopted between 1933 and 1939 several measures designed to increase the population. These measures, including the system of government marriage loans of which one-quarter was remitted for each child born alive, brought about a moderate increase in the birthrate. At the end of 1937 the population of nearly 69,000,000, bringing the grand total for greater Germany to a figure in excess of 86,000,000.

World War II reduced the population of Germany in much the same way as World War I: losses from war causes were estimated at 4,700,000; the birthrate fell from 20.6 per 1,000 in 1939 (in terms of Germany's 1937 frontiers) to 15 in 1942; and the loss of German territories to the east of the Oder-Neisse line brought about a further reduction of about 9,600,000. Nevertheless, based on the combined area of the two postwar republics, the population

TABLE II.—*Germany: Area and Population*

From 1871 to 1945

Date	Territorial changes	Area (sq.mi.)	Population
May 10, 1871	—	208,825	41,059,000
July 1, 1914	Alsace-Lorraine annexed	208,825	67,800,000
June 28, 1919	Losses resulting from the Treaty of Versailles*	180,934	59,800,000
Jan. 13, 1935	Saar returns to Germany	181,677	66,871,000
March 12, 1938	Incorporation of Austria	214,052	75,300,000
Sept. 21, 1938	Annexation of the Sudetenland	225,287	79,350,000
March 15, 1939	Annexation of Bohemia and Moravia	244,117	86,250,000
March 22, 1939	Annexation of Memel (Klaipeda)†	245,258	86,400,000
Aug. 2, 1945	Losses resulting from the Potsdam agreement‡	136,557	

The two republics and Berlin

Division	Area (sq.mi.)	Population 1939 est.	Population 1946 census	Population 1967 est.
Federal Republic of Germany§	95,778	40,248,000	43,694,000	57,698,000
West Berlin	185	2,750,500	2,012,500	2,173,300
German Democratic Republic	41,610	15,157,100	17,313,700	16,001,500
East Berlin	156	1,588,300	1,174,600	1,080,800
Total	137,729	59,743,900	64,194,800	76,954,300

*Alsace-Lorraine was returned to France; Saar was created as a territory administered by the League of Nations and incorporated within the French customs regime; Eupen-et-Malmédy was acquired by Belgium; northern Schleswig was returned to Denmark; Danzig (Gdansk) was created a free city; Memel (Klaipeda) was given to Lithuania, while Pomorze (Pomerania) and Poznania (Poznan) were incorporated with restored Poland; Upper Silesia was partitioned between Germany and Poland.
†German wartime annexations to the detriment of Poland (western part of the country incorporated with the greater German *Reich* and the so-called Warsaw *General-Government* created; France (Alsace-Lorraine), Luxembourg (included into "Gau Moselland"), Belgium (Eupen-et-Malmédy), and Yugoslavia (northern Slovenia) were created.
‡Austria and Czechoslovakia regained independence, Memel returned to Lithuania, all the lands east of the Oder-Neisse line, together with the free city of Danzig, were included into Poland, the only exception being the northern half of East Prussia which was incorporated with the U.S.S.R.: Saar was again created a separate territory united with France by a customs union.
§Including Saar, politically reunited with Germany on Jan. 1, 1957; area 991 sq.mi.
∥Including Saar.
1 sq.mi. (1967 est.) 1,131,800.
1 sq.mi.=2.59 sq.km.

increased from 59,743,900 in 1939 to about 76,954,300 in 1967 (*see* Table II). This increase was concentrated in the territory of the Federal Republic of Germany (West Germany) and was largely accounted for by the influx of German refugees expelled from Poland (in its new frontiers), Czechoslovakia, and other countries of Eastern and southeastern Europe. In 1950 the Federal Republic included 4,500,000 Germans from the territory east of the Oder-Neisse line; 3,400,000 from Czechoslovakia, prewar Poland, and Eastern European countries; and 1,548,000 from the German Democratic Republic (see *The Refugees*, below).

Although war losses in the postwar German area were more than made good by the influx of German refugees, women still outnumbered men. In 1950, for example, there were 113.4 women for every 100 men in the Federal Republic and 124.2 women per 100 men in the Democratic Republic. By 1967 this disproportion became smaller; for every 100 men there were 111 women in the Federal Republic and 118 in the Democratic Republic.

The disparity of population changes between the Federal Republic and the Democratic Republic reflects, besides the movement of refugees, the respective birth and death rates. During 1946–50 the birthrate in the Federal Republic remained at about 16 per 1,000, while the death rate decreased from 12.4 to 10.4. In the Democratic Republic in 1948 the birthrate was 12.8 and the death rate 15.1. By 1965 the excess of births over deaths in East Germany was only 3.1 per 1,000, compared with 6.2 in West Germany. Nowhere is the difference between the two republics more marked than in the population of large towns and cities. The wartime destruction of western centres like Hamburg and Essen dispersed the population for a time, but by 1959 the prewar totals had been reached and surpassed, whereas the large towns in the east had mostly continued to decrease in size.

TABLE III.—*Population of Principal Towns: Federal Republic*

Town	1961 (census)	1967 (est.)	Town	1961 (census)	1967 (est.)
Bremen	564,517	602,500	Hamburg	1,832,346	1,839,600
Cologne (Köln)	809,247	856,700	Hanover	572,917	535,200
Dortmund	641,480	651,400	Munich	1,085,014	1,242,900
Duisburg	502,993	473,600	Nürnberg	454,520	467,600
Düsseldorf	702,596	692,300	Stuttgart	637,539	617,600
Essen	726,550	710,100	West Berlin	2,197,408	2,173,300
Frankfurt am Main	683,081	670,300	Wuppertal	420,711	416,300

*The only towns in the G.D.R. with populations exceeding 200,000 in 1967 are: East Berlin (1,082,000); Leipzig (591,500); Dresden (500,200); Karl-Marx-Stadt (294,900); Halle (266,000); and Magdeburg (268,100).

In the first years after World War II the East German authorities made no effort to check the drastic population developments in their territory, influenced, no doubt, by the overcrowding and chaos which prevailed. Then there was a tendency to introduce population measures reminiscent of the Nazi era. Measures against abortions were tightened up, and in 1950 a law "for the protection of mother and child and the rights of women" was introduced, with the dual aim of increasing the employment of women in industry and encouraging the production of large families. Such measures, however, were largely offset by an increasing exodus to the Federal Republic of members of the most fertile age groups during the ensuing years.

The density of population in Germany (including the Saar, but not later annexations) increased steadily from 322 per sq.mi. (124 per sq.km.) in 1910 to 382 (148) in 1939. The most rapid increase in density was in the cities and the industrial areas, while the countryside was becoming gradually depopulated. The absorption of refugees in West Germany by the least populated areas has helped to spread the pressure but the concentration in the cities and industrial areas remains. By 1967 the density of population was 624 per sq.mi. (241 per sq.km.) in the Federal Republic and 409 (158) in the Democratic Republic.

The Refugees.—Under the 1945 Potsdam Agreement about 6,500,000 persons of German origin in former German territory east of the Oder-Neisse line, in Czechoslovakia, Hungary, and Poland, were to be returned to Germany (2,750,000 to the Soviet zone and 3,900,000 to three western zones). By the end of 1953 there were 8,451,000 expelled persons living in the Federal Republic and an additional 2,153,000 political refugees from the

Democratic Republic who together formed about 22% of the population of the Federal Republic. In the Democratic Republic the refugee population in August 1950 was 4,312,000, 24% of the population. This number, however, was reduced to 3,800,000 by mid-1953 as many continued their flight to the west. Until Aug. 13, 1961, when East Berlin was sealed off from the west, there had been a steady stream of refugees from the Democratic Republic to the west, varying in intensity with the political situation and the economic conditions in the Democratic Republic. It was estimated that between 1949 and Aug. 13, 1961, when East Berlin was sealed off, about 2,700,000 inhabitants of the Democratic Republic found refuge in the west. By June 1961 it was estimated that more than 12,500,000 Germans in the Federal Republic were refugees. As the average age of the refugees was lower than that of the nonrefugee population, the former have helped to redress the balance, disturbed by the war, between the more fertile and the less fertile age groups.

(R. A. A. C. DE S.; K. SM.)

V. ADMINISTRATION AND SOCIAL CONDITIONS

Since Germany's unconditional surrender in 1945 there has been no central government for the whole country. The evolution of the two German Republics after partition is discussed in *History* above. Their political systems are now completely divided, and each is treated separately below.

A. FEDERAL REPUBLIC OF GERMANY

1. Constitution and Government.—Efforts to establish a central German government by quadripartite agreement at successive conferences of the four foreign ministers having failed, the three Western powers eventually decided that governmental development in West Germany could be held up no longer. At a series of talks between the three Western powers in London in the spring of 1948, principles were enumerated for the formation of a central government in West Germany, for the international control of the Ruhr, and for the establishment of a Military Security Board. The ministers president of the western German *Länder* were authorized to convene a Constituent Assembly for the drafting of a democratic and federal type of constitution which would combine adequate central authority with a proper degree of self-government for the participating *Länder*. The constitution was to make possible the accession of the *Länder* of East Germany, and to remain in force until the Constituent Assembly of a united Germany could draft a more permanent instrument. For this reason the German ministers president insisted on calling the constitution the Basic Law (*Grundgesetz*). It was adopted by the Parliamentary Council at Bonn on May 8, 1949.

At first sight, the Basic Law closely resembles the Weimar constitution in being a federal, republican type of constitution, weighted in favour of the central authority. It contains, however, a number of provisions aimed at strengthening German democracy and avoiding some of the most dangerous practices of the Weimar constitution. The latter did not guarantee the participation of the people in making the laws nor make individual basic rights legally binding. The Basic Law not only laid down these basic rights as binding and not subject to the amendment procedure but also set up a Constitutional Court with the specific task of ensuring respect for them. Moreover, the Basic Law reversed the relative positions of the president and the chancellor within the state. Under the Weimar constitution, the president had to be elected directly by an absolute majority of the popular vote. He was, therefore, in a political position superior to that of the chancellor, who owed his office to an uneasy coalition of representatives elected under proportional representation. The Basic Law provides for the indirect election of the president for five years by a Federal Assembly (*Bundesversammlung*) composed of both legislative chambers, *i.e.,* the *Bundestag* or lower house and the *Bundesrat* or upper house, and transfers his former emergency powers, in a severely curtailed form, to the chancellor and his cabinet. The chancellor is nominated by the president but must be elected by an absolute majority of the *Bundestag*, and he cannot be dismissed except through the election of a successor by the same method.

Like the Weimar constitution, the Basic Law provides for a two-chamber legislature: a *Bundestag* (composed of 496 members plus 22 representatives from West Berlin who, however, cannot vote), representing the nation as a whole and elected by direct universal suffrage for four years; and a *Bundesrat*, formed from members of the *Land* governments. The *Bundestag* (which has 41 members plus 4 deputies from West Berlin) acts mainly in an advisory capacity, but its consent is required for a large number of laws and for the issue of regulations affecting the *Länder*, as well as for amendments to the Basic Law.

The Basic Law was approved by the American, British, and French military governors with certain reservations and came into force on May 23, 1949. The exercise of sovereign powers in the new Federal Republic was restricted by the Occupation Statute, by which the three Allied powers reserved to themselves powers of control in a number of fields relating to questions already the subject of wider agreements or of special interest to them. A reservation concerned the position of Berlin. It was decided that, in view of the quadripartite occupation of the city, West Berlin could not be included in the new Federal Republic.

TABLE IV.—*Federal Republic of Germany: Länder (States)*

Land	Area (sq.mi.)	Pop. (1967 est.)	Capital	Population (1967 est.)
Baden-Württemberg	13,803	8,547,800	Stuttgart	617,600
Bavaria (Bayern)	27,239	10,256,200	Munich (München)	1,242,900
Bremen	156	750,500	Bremen	602,500
Hamburg	288	1,839,600		
Hesse	8,151	5,249,700	Wiesbaden	258,900
Lower Saxony (Niedersachsen)	18,303	6,981,600	Hanover	535,200
North Rhine-Westphalia (Nordrhein-Westfalen)	13,145	16,832,200	Düsseldorf	692,300
Rhineland-Palatinate (Rheinland-Pfalz)	7,657	3,620,400	Mainz	146,600
Saar	991	1,131,800	Saarbrücken	133,900
Schleswig-Holstein	6,045	2,488,900	Kiel	269,900
Berlin (West)†	185	2,173,300		
Total	95,963	59,872,000		

*1 sq.mi. = 2.59 sq.km.
†Not a constitutional part of the Federal Republic of Germany.

The Länder.—The ten *Länder* of the Federal Republic of Germany, together with areas, populations, and capitals, are shown in Table IV. Each of them has its own written constitution and each has an Assembly (*Landtag*) elected for four years by popular vote according to proportional representation. The *Land* governments are usually composed of a minister president chosen by the Assembly together with four or five ministers. Each *Land* can legislate on any subject concerning its territory and inhabitants which is not expressly allocated to the federation by the Basic Law; *i.e.,* in practice, mainly education, local government, cultural affairs, and the police. All the *Länder*, except Schleswig-Holstein, Saarland, and the city-states, are divided into administrative areas (*Regierungsbezirke*), in turn subdivided into *Landkreise* and *Gemeinden. See also* separate articles on the *Länder*.

Political Parties.—Since 1949 West German parliamentary life has tended increasingly toward the two-party system. This tendency toward the gradual elimination of the small parties is largely caused by the adoption of an electoral system under which half the deputies are elected directly by the people in constituencies and the remaining half are chosen from party lists on the basis of proportional representation. In this allocation of seats, however, the law provides that no consideration will be given to any party which fails to get a candidate elected directly in a constituency or does not obtain 5% of the total votes.

The Christlich-Demokratische Union (Christian Democratic Union or CDU) is a postwar development in German party politics. It was established as a centre party to which Protestants as well as Roman Catholics could belong. At the same time it appealed to the workers as well as the middle classes, and in 1947 it went so far as to recommend the nationalization of heavy industry. Since then, however, its policy has been modified, and by the late 1960s the CDU could best be described as a broad-based conservative party with a religious bias. Its social policy stresses the right of the churches to play a part in education and emphasizes the importance of the family as the basic unit of society and the necessity for wide and generous social services. It believes in a minimum of state interference in economic affairs.

346

(LEFT) UPI COMPIX. (RIGHT) CAMERA PRESS—PIX FROM PUBLIX

(LEFT) EAST GERMAN WORKERS REINFORCING THE BERLIN WALL BY BUILDING A SECOND WALL BEHIND THE OLD ONE.
(RIGHT) MEMBERS OF THE GERMAN NATIONAL PEOPLE'S ARMY PATROLLING THE BORDER BETWEEN THE TWO GERMANYS

GERMANY

In foreign policy the CDU has consistently maintained that the problem of reunification can be solved only by close alliance of the Federal Republic with the Western powers, and it keenly supports the movement toward European integration. The party was the mainstay of each government from 1949 until the late 1960s. It has the tacit support of the Roman Catholic Church, and its Protestant and undenominational following increased in the 1950s. It is also supported by business corporations, which subscribe heavily to its funds.

The Christlich-Soziale Union (Christian Social Union or CSU) is the Bavarian counterpart of the CDU, but organizationally separate, and has strong support in that *Land*. It emphasizes Bavarian state rights, is more predominantly Catholic in membership, and opposes centralism.

The Sozialdemokratische Partei Deutschlands (Social Democratic Party of Germany or SPD) is the postwar successor of the German Social Democratic Party founded in 1875, which became the largest single party in the *Reichstag* until the Nazi Party worsted it in 1932. The SPD quickly reconstituted itself after World War II and was in 1949 the second largest party in the *Bundestag*. Its limited appeal was largely caused by its continued adherence to the policy of nationalization, its tradition of anti-clericalism, and its pacifist and antimilitarist tendencies. In 1958, however, it adopted a policy favouring the maintenance of "a large variety of economic forms of enterprise" and specifically restricting nationalization to coal, oil, and atomic power. It also began to advocate the strengthening of private property "of the millions of small and medium-sized enterprises." Moreover, although from the beginning the SPD opposed the rearmament policy, particularly conscription and atomic weapons, in 1958 party leaders advised local SPD officials to establish friendly contact with the armed forces in their districts and encouraged their members to enlist in the *Bundeswehr* (Federal Armed Forces). This tendency to abandon classical socialism and to adapt policy to changing circumstances was maintained at the extraordinary party conference held at Bad Godesberg in November 1959. According to the program adopted at this conference, protection had to be given to owners of means of production who did not hinder the development of a just social order, although the political and economic power of large-scale enterprises had to be contained. The party supported a free market with "as much competition as possible, as much planning as necessary." In addition the tradi-tions of anticlericalism and pacifism were abandoned for the ad-vocacy of freedom of conscience and of cooperation with the churches, and the support of national defense. The party, however, still maintained its opposition to the production and use of nuclear weapons.

The Freie Demokratische Partei (Free Democratic Party or FDP) was formed from a merger during 1945–46 of various liberal-democratic groups. In February 1956 the party withdrew from the federal coalition government because of disagreement over foreign policy and a proposed electoral law. In the social and economic fields its policy is the exponent of free enterprise and the determined opponent of socialism in any shape or form. It goes farther than the CDU in supporting unrestricted private enter-prise; it also tends to be a "secular," as distinct from a "Christian," party (thus, for example, opposing denominational influence in education). With regard to problems such as reunification and relations with the Eastern bloc, it favours a more elastic policy.

At the 1965 general election for the first time the new extreme right-wing Nationaldemokratische Partei Deutschlands (NPD) took part. It also fought the 1969 election. As it polled only 2% of the national vote in 1965, and 4.3% in 1969, it gained no seats in the *Bundestag*. Led by Adolf von Thadden (1921–), who had been a member of the Hitler Youth from 1933 and of the Labour Service from 1939, the NPD stood for the restoration of Greater Germany comprising the G.D.R., the new Polish western territories, the Sudetenland, Austria, and South Tirol.

In September 1968 a Deutsche Kommunistische Partei (DKP) was formed in Frankfurt am Main. The new party, allegedly in-dependent from the old Kommunistische Partei Deutschlands (KPD) which had been banned in 1956, declared itself for the respect of the existing frontiers and friendly relations between the two German states.

2. Taxation.—In West Germany after the currency reform in 1948, fiscal measures were applied much more frequently than before World War II to influence the level of economic activity. There was a steady reduction of rates of taxation and an increase of personal and child allowances. In this way, income tax rates (levied on a progressive scale) declined by more than 50% and, in the main, were lower than those levied in 1936. To stimulate industrial investment, tax exemption was granted for new and re-placement plants, and undistributed profits and accumulated reserves received preferential treatment; many of these very con-siderable concessions were reduced or abolished by subsequent legislation.

But most measures favoured the medium- and higher-income groups, especially those deriving their incomes from company profits, and made it easier for them to accumulate capital. Lower-income groups, too, benefited through the reduction of the tax on salaries and wages and through successive cuts in excise duties. Improved social insurance benefits resulted in higher deductions, and for these groups compulsory social insurance contributions were, in fact, more important than the payment of wage tax. In the late 1960s there were three major sources of federal revenue amounting to DM. 78,167,000,000: the turnover tax bringing 30%, wage tax 25%, and income tax 20%.

3. Employment and Trade Unions.—As a result of World War II losses, the German labour force as a whole decreased as a proportion of the population. The position in 1946 was abnormal in that a large part of industrial life was at a standstill; accommodation in the industrial areas was severely limited, and more than 7,000,000 refugees from the east were living in predominantly agricultural areas. By 1950 the occupational distribution of the German population was gradually reverting to its prewar structure, the drift away from agriculture into trade and industry being particularly noticeable. By the late 1960s the number of employed persons in the Federal Republic far exceeded the total in the same area for the late 1930s, when German economic resources were being used to the fullest. Although unemployment after the war never reached the dimensions witnessed in Germany during the world economic crisis (in February 1932 more than 6,000,000 persons were unemployed), the problem in West Germany was serious enough in the years immediately following the currency reform enacted in June 1948.

Currency reform in West Germany brought about a return to more efficient standards in business and industrial life; economies were introduced into the running of both public administration and private firms, and the production of inessential goods was gradually reduced. The real extent of unemployment then became apparent, and by 1950 it had reached a monthly average of 10%. High unemployment resulted from the disruption of the economic structure, from the destruction and dismantling of industrial plants, from Allied prohibitions on industry and shipping, from an increase in population from 35,000,000 in 1936 to 47,700,000 in 1949, and from the division of Germany.

In 1950 the federal government embarked on a plan to create jobs which involved the expenditure of DM. 3,400,000,000 on such schemes as housing, credits to Länder with large refugee populations, the movement of unemployed persons from distressed areas, and credits to industry. As a result of this plan, coupled with the general economic improvement as industrial conditions expanded, assisted by the setting up of the European Economic Community (EEC—the Common Market), unemployment in the Federal Republic in the late 1960s was reduced to 1% of the 26,700,000 active population. At the same time more than 1,000,000 foreign workers were employed there, including 288,000 Italians, 139,000 Turks, 136,000 Greeks, 112,000 Spaniards, and 99,000 Yugoslavs.

Trade Unions and Industrial Management.—After World War II the growth of a democratic trade union movement was encouraged in the western zones, but, on the general principle of replacing democratic institutions from the lowest levels upward, the trade unions were at first authorized to form only locally. The result was a great variety of types of unions, organized in some places according to industries, in others by professions, and in yet others in comprehensive associations. In no case were they subdivided into political groupings, however. Gradually these unions federated, first at Land and later at zonal levels, and in 1950 a single federation, the Deutscher Gewerkschaftsbund, was established for the territory of the Federal Republic; its membership in the late 1960s amounted to 6,408,000. After the establishment of the federal government in 1949 the trade union movement asserted an appreciable influence over the government's industrial policy. It was consulted over the decentralization of heavy industry, and its plans for copartnership between employers and workers (Mitbestimmung) in the management of the reconstituted coal, iron, and steel concerns were accepted.

4. Wages and Cost of Living.—During the two decades after World War I, wages and the standard of living fluctuated widely as Germany passed through first the inflation period and then, after a short-lived return toward economic prosperity, the economic depression following 1929. By 1933 wages had declined to a very low level. Although full employment was reached by 1938 and both wages and prices were in general pegged from that time onward, the standard of living on the whole deteriorated as the quality and quantity of consumer goods decreased and taxation and contributions to the National Socialist organizations increased.

Shortly after the occupation in 1945, the Allies directed that existing controls over wages be maintained, subject to the removal of certain inequities and discriminatory measures and to the variations of rates and allowances within the average wage levels. In West Germany there was a general removal of price and rationing controls after the currency reform of June 1948, and an initial 15% wage increase was permitted. This was followed in October 1948 by the complete abolition of the wage control legislation and by a return to the recognized measures of collective bargaining between the trade unions and the employers' associations which had been current during the Weimar Republic.

For a few years after World War II the rise in the cost of living far outstripped the rise in average gross weekly earnings. But the 1948 currency reform soon corrected this trend, and by 1950 the increases in the cost of living and in gross weekly earnings in industry were practically identical when compared with 1938. Between 1950 and 1960 earnings almost doubled whereas the cost of living increased by only about one-fifth. At the same time the average weekly hours worked in industry fell from 49 in 1950 to 41.8 in 1967. By the late 1960s, in these circumstances, it was hardly surprising that wage claims by organized labour were based on the demand for a larger share in the increased prosperity rather than on hardship arising from cost-of-living increases.

5. Health and Welfare Services.—In the Federal Republic, a Ministry of Health was formed in 1961, taking over a department which had formerly been controlled by the minister of the interior. There are three main types of hospitals, state, free, and private. The free hospitals are mainly religious or charitable foundations. City corporations are represented on the board of many hospitals; they appoint physicians and are the hospitals' chief source of revenue. Three classes of treatment are provided, the difference being in conditions rather than in medical attention. Social insurance covers the cost of basic treatment.

An extensive system of compulsory, mainly contributory, social insurance had been built up in Germany during the second half of the 19th century, and in the 1930s unemployment insurance was introduced. In 1945, under Allied supervision, the system began to function again, but the aftermath of the war imposed an increasing burden of expenditure in this field. The importance attached in West Germany to the social services was shown in the establishment, in 1953, of a Ministry for Family Affairs, and by the coming into force, on Jan. 1, 1955, of a law on family allowances, by which DM. 25 was payable each month for the third and further children of a family. Other social insurance benefits include pensions, sickness and accident, unemployment relief, war disablement, etc. In 1958 pensions ceased to be paid on a flat rate, being based instead on the average earnings of a lifetime at the rate of 1.5% of each year's wages. Pensions would be annually reassessed by parliament to ensure against loss of purchasing power. Contributions of both workers and employers rose accordingly to cover the extra costs, in addition to a large government grant.

National insurance is compulsory for all but those in the highest income groups. Benefits include unemployment allowance, treatment, sick pay or leave allowance, maternity and child allowances, death payments, and old-age and disability pensions. Employees contribute 20% of the first DM. 600 monthly of their taxable income (30% for mine workers); an equal amount is contributed by the employer.

6. Housing.—The housing situation in Germany was already serious before World War II. In 1946, in West Germany the number of destroyed or heavily damaged dwellings represented nearly one-quarter of the total number in existence in 1939, the proportion for Berlin being as high as two-fifths. Over the same period the average number of persons per dwelling had risen from 3.8 to 5.5 in West Germany, and from 2.8 to 3.4 in Berlin.

By 1950 there were nearly 10,000,000 dwellings in the Federal Republic, more than 500,000 being emergency constructions. But although the total number was not far short of the prewar figure, the population of West Germany had increased greatly as a result of the influx of refugees from the east, and the housing shortage remained acute. Between 1945 and 1954 about 3,000,000 new dwelling units were constructed in the Federal Republic, and by the late 1960s that figure amounted to more than 6,000,000.

7. Education.—In the Federal Republic the school system reverted largely to the traditional Weimar structure, with considerable variations from one *Land* to another. In 1959 it was decided to add a ninth year to the *Volksschule* (free elementary school for children between 6 and 15) where this was not already the case. More than half of all West German children receive only *Volksschule* education, followed by part-time attendance at vocational schools. *Mittlere* (intermediate) and *Gymnasium* (secondary) schooling is not everywhere free, but where fees are charged the number of scholarships has risen. The oldest and best-known form of secondary education was the classical *Gymnasium*, which, modeled upon the ideas of Wilhelm von Humboldt (*q.v.*), gave a thorough grounding in Greek, Latin, and the humanities; next the *Realgymnasium* was instituted, in which classical and modern subjects were more evenly balanced, and finally the *Realschule*, teaching mathematics, science, and modern languages. (See EDUCATION, HISTORY OF.)

The universities were faced with great problems at the end of World War II. Not only were the teaching staffs curtailed by denazification and many of the buildings destroyed but the number of prospective entrants was abnormally high as a result of neglected studies during the war. Even after certain categories of Nazis and regular officers were excluded, it was found necessary to restrict entry (by means of examination) during the early postwar years. Apart from the introduction of a system of state grants to needy and gifted students in 1957, other proposals for university reform were frustrated by the continuing influx of students. By the late 1950s the ratio between teaching staff and students was approximately 1 to 50 and a number of the technical colleges were forced to adopt a *numerus clausus* (restricted number). As a means of dealing with this problem, the West German Council of Arts and Sciences proposed in 1960 that 12,000 new chairs be created in the existing universities and that three new universities and one technical university be founded. The Federal Republic has universities at Bonn (founded 1818), Düsseldorf (1965; formerly the Academy of Medicine), Erlangen (1743), Frankfurt am Main (1914), Freiburg (1457), Giessen (1607), Göttingen (1736), Hamburg (1919), Heidelberg (1386), Kiel (1665), Cologne (1388), Mainz (founded 1477, closed 1816, reopened 1946), Marburg (1527), Munich (1472), Münster (1780), Saarbrücken (1948), Tübingen (1477), and Würzburg (1582). The Free University in West Berlin was founded in 1948. Other educational establishments of university status are the Mining Academy at Clausthal, the College of Veterinary Medicine at Hannover, the Agricultural Academy at Hohenheim, the Academy of Economics at Mannheim, and the College of Social Sciences at Wilhelmshaven. There are also technical colleges at Aachen, Brunswick, Darmstadt, Hanover, Karlsruhe, Munich, Stuttgart, and West Berlin (technical university). (See also UNIVERSITY; LIBRARY; MUSEUM.)

8. Justice.—Judges and public prosecutors in Germany have always been civil servants. They are appointed for life (subject to the age limit) after university studies, a first examination, three years of basic practice in the courts, in public prosecutors' offices, and in private legal practice, and a final examination.

At the base of the structure of courts as established in 1879 is the local court (*Amtsgericht*) with jurisdiction over minor civil and criminal matters and such other matters as land registry and bankruptcy. Above the local court is the district court (*Landgericht*), which is both a court of appeal from the local court and a court of first instance for more serious civil and criminal matters and divorce cases. Above the district courts are the courts of appeal (*Oberlandesgerichte*), of which there is normally one in each *Land*. The Supreme Court of the *Reich* (*Reichsgericht*) was established at Leipzig in 1879. It acted as the final court of appeal in matters of civil and criminal law, as the court of first and only instance in cases of treason, and also served the purpose of guaranteeing the uniform application of the law. The courts of appeal and the Supreme Court were entirely composed of professional judges. Certain cases before local courts were heard and tried by a single professional judge assisted by law assessors, and some criminal and civil cases before district courts by a jury under the chairmanship of a professional judge. Special tribunals were also set up to deal with labour disputes, taxation, and pension appeals.

Under the Nazi regime the *Länder* were deprived of their prerogatives in the administration of justice, which was made the exclusive concern of the *Reich*. A special supreme court, the People's Court (*Volksgerichtshof*), was established, competent for political cases, which were withdrawn from the *Reichsgericht*. At local and district levels, special courts for those and similar cases were established. After World War II the occupation powers cleansed the whole legal system—law, procedure, and organization—of Nazi features. The division between West and East Germany resulted in the separate development of both after 1946.

In West Germany authority over the legal system was gradually handed back to the administration of the *Länder*, and German jurisdiction over this field was finally restored in 1949. The Basic Law reestablished conditions very largely as they were in the *Reich* before 1933, although it abolished capital punishment. Competence over legal matters rests with the legislative authorities of the Federal Republic. The organization, the appointment of judges, and the budgetary provisions of the administration of justice are the concern of the *Länder*. The structure of the system of courts was maintained. The *Reichsgericht* was replaced by the Federal High Court (*Bundesgerichtshof*) at Karlsruhe. There are also federal high courts for administration, financial jurisdiction, labour, social questions, and civil service. The Federal Constitutional Court (*Bundesverfassungsgericht*), also at Karlsruhe, decides in litigations between the federation and the *Länder*, on the interpretation of the Basic Law, and on the constitutionality of federal and *Land* law. It is called upon to decide whether a political party pursues any aims or methods conflicting with the spirit or letter of the Basic Law. The federal president and federal judges can be impeached before the Constitutional Court. (See also GERMANIC LAWS, EARLY; GERMAN LAW.)

9. Police.—Traditionally, the police in Germany were responsible not only for the preservation of public peace, security, and order but "for the general welfare of our loyal subjects from the negative, as well as the positive, point of view" (King Frederick William III of Prussia, 1808). Almost every act of internal administration was thus a "police" act. Under the Weimar Republic, the task of the police was limited to warding off "dangers through which the public security and order were threatened." This was still a wide conception, as "public order" was considered the expression of the social opinion of the society which at the time formed the state, about what was consistent with its own best interests. Thus, with little change, the police could be made to serve the Nazi state.

Before 1933, the police were the responsibility of the *Länder*; there was no *Reich* police force and little control from the *Reich*. In the *Länder* the leading official at each level of internal administration was also the police authority for the area under his jurisdiction and was responsible for the issue of police ordinances. Police forces were either state (*Gendarmerie*) or municipal (*Schutzpolizei*), although in some large cities the police force was also controlled by the *Land*. There were also criminal police, administrative police, and other specialized bodies. All these police officials were civil servants and could act only on the basis of, and in accordance with, the law. Their acts could be challenged before the administrative tribunals.

Hitler created the post of *Reich* chief of police and brought the police forces of the Länder under the control of the minister of the interior. The Gestapo (*Geheime Staatspolizei*) and the security services had been placed above the law and they permeated all police forces, which they used as instruments to reshape the life of the German people.

After World War II the occupying powers completely reorganized the police, different systems being applied in each zone of occupation in accordance with the experience of the occupying power. After the creation of the Federal Republic, the various *Länder* resumed control of their own police forces and largely returned to the prewar organization. The police forces—*Ordnungspolizei*, *Gendarmerie*, and *Kriminalpolizei*—were, however, once more subordinated to the detailed provisions of the Basic Law concerning individual rights and liberties. The control of the Federal government over the police was still indirect, although, in September 1950, it was authorized by the Western powers meeting in New York to create a frontier protection police (*Bundesgrenzschutzpolizei*) of 30,000 men to patrol the frontier between the Federal Republic and the Democratic Republic.

10. Defense.—Although strictly speaking the German Army was founded in 1871, its origins and traditions may be traced back to a much earlier period (*see* ARMY). Before unification of the German Empire several of the German states possessed independent armies, the best and the largest of which was the Prussian. As Prussia acquired hegemony in the second *Reich*, Prussian methods and spirit dominated the creation of the imperial German Army. They survived in the republican *Reichswehr* created after the 1918 defeat and became much alive in Hitler's *Wehrmacht*. After the total collapse of 1945, Germany was completely disarmed and demilitarized, but in 1949 two German republics came into being. Both soon began to organize armed forces of their own. In the *Bundeswehr* of the Federal Republic great importance is attached to the old German military tradition.

Soviet policy in Germany, aiming at the formation of a Communist satellite state, and Communist aggression in Korea in June 1950 caused the Western Allies to review the question of German disarmament and demilitarization. In September 1950 the U.S., British, and French foreign ministers agreed that German participation in an integrated force for European defense was desirable. In October the French National Assembly adopted a plan providing for a European Defense Community (EDC), in which Germany would play an active part, and in December this was approved by the council of the North Atlantic Treaty Organization (NATO). In February 1952, by 209 votes to 156, the *Bundestag* declared its support for the government's policy of assuming a fair share of the burden of defense, provided that it was on a basis of complete equality.

In May a treaty instituting the EDC was signed in Paris by France, the Federal Republic of Germany, Italy, Belgium, the Netherlands, and Luxembourg. It defined the EDC as an organization of supranational character, with common institutions and common forces composed of 43 divisions, including 12 German. The EDC was to be defensive, within the NATO framework.

Although ratification of the EDC treaty was completed in the Federal Republic, as well as in Belgium, the Netherlands, and Luxembourg, the French National Assembly in August 1954 rejected it, and the whole scheme fell to the ground. The British government immediately proposed that the Federal Republic enter NATO as an equal partner; that France accept German rearmament only in a framework where the size of the German contingent was fixed by international agreement and German troop movements were controlled by the supreme Allied commander in Europe; and that the United Kingdom be committed to keeping its forces permanently on the continent. In October the United Kingdom, the United States, Canada, and the six EDC powers signed in Paris a new series of agreements. A protocol specified that German federal armed forces should not exceed the numbers fixed in the EDC treaty of May 1952. The Paris agreements were approved by the French National Assembly in December, and on May 9, 1955, the Federal Republic was formally inducted as the 15th member of NATO.

On July 22, 1955, the first West German armament act, the Volunteer Act, was passed, empowering the government to prepare for the establishment of armed forces authorized by the Paris agreements. In 1955 a German general assumed command of the NATO land forces in Central Europe; in 1960 another German general was appointed chairman of the NATO military committee in Washington; in 1966 a third German general became commander in chief of the Allied Forces, Central Europe.

Planned in 1952, West German rearmament was practically completed in 1964. By the late 1960s the *Bundeswehr* comprised 456,000 men, namely 326,000 in the Army or *Heer* (including 20,-000 territorials or *Heimatschutztruppen*), 98,000 in the Air Force (*Luftwaffe*), and 32,000 in the Navy (*Marine*).

The Army was organized in three corps and 32 brigades, namely 12 armoured, 16 armoured infantry, 2 mountain, and 2 airborne. Their armament included 1,500 Patton and 1,400 Leopard tanks, 1,500 heavy guns, and 1,000 tank-destroyers (with 90 mm. guns or antitank missiles). In addition the Army had 12 battalions with Honest John and 4 battalions with Sergeant surface-to-surface missiles.

The Air Force had 500 combat aircraft (McDonnell F-4 Phantoms, Lockheed F-104G Starfighters, and Fiat G-91). It also had 6 battalions of Nike-Hercules and 9 battalions of Hawk surface-to-air missiles, as well as 3 battalions of Pershing surface-to-surface missiles.

The Navy comprised 8 destroyers, 6 destroyer-escorts, 9 submarines, and a large number of minelayers, minesweepers, and fast patrol boats—160 armed seagoing ships in all.

By the late 1960s the *Bundeswehr* had 215 generals and admirals, 25,600 officers, and 111,600 noncommissioned officers. There were 750,000 trained reservists. The defense budget (1968) amounted to DM. 20,435,000,000 ($5,108,000,000) or 4% of the estimated gross national product.

(I. L. G.; P. G. Rs.; R. A. A. C. DE S.; T. C. PE.; K. SM.)

B. GERMAN DEMOCRATIC REPUBLIC

1. Constitution and Government.—After the Potsdam Agreement, the Soviet zone of occupation was submitted to a regime radically different from that in the three western zones. By 1946 three political parties were in existence, the Sozialistische Einheitspartei Deutschlands (SED), the Christlich-Demokratische Union (CDU), and the Liberal-Demokratische Partei Deutschlands (LDPD). In May 1948 the National-Demokratische Partei Deutschlands (NDPD) was created to group the reformed members of the ex-Nazi Party; in June 1949 the Demokratische Bauernpartei Deutschlands (DBD) was organized to rally the farmers.

The first constitution, adopted on May 30, 1949, bore a superficial resemblance to the Weimar constitution, but whereas the constitution of the G.F.R. amended it in the direction of greater *Land* autonomy, that of the G.D.R. strengthened the powers of the central government, although there was ostensibly a two-chamber legislature, the *Länderkammer* and the *Volkskammer*. The first president of the republic was elected on Oct. 11, 1949, by the joint assembly of the two houses and had purely representational powers. The upper house disappeared on July 23, 1952, when the five *Länder* had been subdivided into 15 districts or *Bezirke* (*see* TABLE V). Each district comprises from 8 to 24 *Kreise* or counties (216 in all, including 24 urban ones); each *Kreis* is subdivided into *Gemeinden* or communes (9,190 in all).

The first *Volkskammer* was elected on Oct. 15, 1950, by the single list system prepared by the *Nationale Front* grouping all the five political parties and five mass organizations. Its composition was as follows: SED 120 members; CDU 60; LDPD 60; NDPD, DBD, and the mass bodies 160 in all. The composition of the second (1954), third (1958), and fourth (1963) People's Chambers were similar. When the fifth *Volkskammer* was elected on July 2, 1967, each list in all the 67 constituencies contained more candidates than there were places to fill: 583 candidates for 466 seats. The SED was allocated 117 seats, and the other four parties 52 seats each; in addition there were 53 members of the Trade Union Federation, 29 of the Free German Youth, 29 of the German Women's Federation, 18 of the German League of Culture, and 12 of the Peasants' Mutual Aid Association.

On April 8, 1968, a new constitution was promulgated. The *Volkskammer* of 500 members, elected for four years, is the supreme organ of state power. Every citizen of the G.D.R. of 18 has the right to vote, and can be elected to the *Volkskammer* when 21. The *Volkskammer* elects the Council of State (*Staatsrat*), the Council of Ministers (*Ministerrat*), the National Defense Council, the Supreme Court, and the prosecutor general. The Council of State operates between sessions of the *Volkskammer* and is composed of the chairman, 6 vice-chairmen, 16 members, and the secretary. The Council of Ministers organizes, on behalf of the *Volkskammer*, the execution of the political, economic, cultural, social, and military tasks of the state.

The constitution does not define the role of the SED in the state, but as the strongest party it naturally supplies the chairmen of the Council of State and Council of Ministers. The Politburo of the SED is the policy-making body. Ulbricht was its first secretary from 1946, and as such he was the dean among the first secretaries of the socialist camp.

SED had 1,769,912 members and candidates. Its seventh congress (April 1967) elected a Central Committee of 131 members which elected a Politburo of 15.

2. Taxation.—Taxes in East Germany are both sources of revenue for the state budget and a means of fulfilling political as well as economic tasks. At first, industrial enterprises transferred to public ownership paid the same taxes as private firms. In 1955, however, the Soviet "two-channel" system was intro-

TABLE V.—*German Democratic Republic: Bezirke (Districts)*

Bezirke*	Area (sq.mi.)†	Population (1967 est.)
Cottbus	3,190	843,058
Dresden	2,602	1,885,517
Erfurt	2,837	1,253,937
Frankfurt an der Oder	2,775	667,891
Gera	1,546	734,944
Halle	3,386	1,933,266
Karl-Marx-Stadt	2,320	2,077,503
Leipzig	1,917	1,510,066
Magdeburg	4,450	1,335,869
Neubrandenburg	4,167	637,164
Potsdam	4,853	1,133,403
Rostock	2,730	847,614
Schwerin	3,348	598,171
Suhl	1,489	552,096
Total	41,610	16,001,249
East Berlin	156	1,080,754
Total	41,766	17,082,253

*The *Bezirke* are named after their chief towns.
†1 sq.mi.=2.59 sq.km.

duced: publicly owned industry and trade (and after 1957 agriculture) pay production or trade levies to the budget account as well as their net profits. The rates of the levy vary; they are lowest in the case of essential capital goods but reach high proportions for consumer goods. By changing the rate the state influences the selling price and, in the final analysis, the allocation of resources and the volume of purchasing power in circulation.

The public sector of the East German economy contributes the bulk of the funds of the state budget. In the late 1960s it accounted for more than 60% of total revenue, compared with about 3% for the remaining private firms. In the virtual liquidation of private enterprise, taxation played a significant role through high rates of progression (up to 90% in the case of income tax compared with a 20% maximum for wage and salary earners), a ban on the formation of tax-free reserves, and restriction of depreciation allowances and of claimable expenses. Private firms in which the state had become a partner, however, enjoyed certain concessions.

While private firms and craftsmen are liable to trade tax, inheritance tax, and vehicle tax as well as income and corporation taxes, agricultural producer cooperatives and craft cooperatives are wholly or partly exempt. Private traders and innkeepers who entered into special arrangements with the state trading organizations to work on a commission basis also received preferential treatment.

3. Trade Unions.—In the Soviet zone the trade union movement was reorganized from the top downward. As early as June 1945 an executive committee of the Freier Deutscher Gewerkschaftsbund (Free German Trade Union Federation or FDGB) was established; by the late 1960s it comprised 9 industrial unions and 6 professional associations. With the rapid reduction of private enterprise in the G.D.R., the trade unions dropped their original function of representing the workers' interests as against the employers', becoming instead agents for the administration of social insurance, for the organization of technical training and political indoctrination, and for ensuring execution of the various economic plans. The FDGB was now under the leadership of the Communist-dominated SED and its members lost the right to strike. The FDGB claimed a membership of more than 6,800,000 by the late 1960s.

Following an order of June 8, 1950, general collective agreements were to be drawn by the trade unions and the competent ministries for the various branches of industry, and within these framework agreements the nationalized undertakings, and private concerns employing more than 20 persons, were to draw up works collective agreements.

4. Wages.—In September 1967 a five-day week was introduced for the vast majority of the population. Hitherto there had been one free Saturday every second week. The minimum monthly wage was increased from DM. 220 to 300. Between 1955 and 1965 the average monthly earnings of full-time workers and office employees in nationalized enterprises (82% of the total labour force) rose from DM. 459 to 655. With the possible exception of Czechoslovakia, the standard of living in the G.D.R. was the highest in the socialist camp.

5. Health and Welfare Services.—In the Democratic Republic the nationalized health system resembles that of the U.S.S.R., embodying a comprehensive scheme of prevention and treatment, with emphasis on the former. In 1954 the organization was changed so that each district became the health centre for its own district with the duties of prevention, treatment, and aftercare. In addition to the main hospitals there are cottage hospitals, polyclinics, dispensaries, and consultation and treatment centres.

By a government decree of April 26, 1951, the responsibility for the control and administration of the system of compulsory social insurance was transferred to the Trade Union Federation (FDGB). Unemployment insurance, workmen's compensation, and sick leave benefits are paid. Employed prospective mothers receive maternity leave with pay and there is a system of children's allowances.

6. Housing.—Between 1950 and mid-1961 the number of dwellings in the G.D.R., excluding East Berlin, rose from 4,671,500 to 5,506,900. Until that time East German building had lagged behind the rate in West Germany. Later it improved considerably; by 1965 there were 350,000 new dwellings and in the late 1960s the monthly average of new completed dwellings was 12,000.

7. Education.—Following the partition of Germany the comprehensive type of school became fully established only in the G.D.R. This *Grundschule* provided for an eight-year compulsory elementary stage followed by four years' secondary education in one of two types of polytechnic *Oberschulen* (high schools). By 1955 the period of compulsory education was extended to ten years. Higher education was provided in seven universities (at Leipzig [1409], Rostock [1419], Jena [1558], Greifswald [1456], Halle [1694], Berlin [1809], and Potsdam [1948]), and 12 other academic establishments.

8. Justice.—The legal tradition of the former German *Reich* is summarized in the *Justice* subsection of *Federal Republic of Germany*, above.

In the Democratic Republic the legal system underwent considerable changes. Large parts of the Civil and Commercial Code became obsolete by the abolition or restriction of private property in agriculture, industry, and trade. The Criminal Code was extended by that type of offense falling under the heading of economic crimes and sabotage. In 1952 the *Volkskammer* passed a new criminal procedure law in which great importance was attached to making criminal procedure lead to respect for the socialist law, for socialist property, for labour discipline, and for the protection of democracy. In August 1952 the system of courts was reorganized to fit in with the new administrative pattern. The new Law on the Constitution of Courts provided for only three kinds of courts: district courts (*Kreisgerichte*, replacing the *Amtsgerichte*), regional courts (*Bezirksgerichte*, replacing the *Landgerichte*), and the Supreme Court. The *Oberlandesgerichte* were eliminated. The underlying principle of the new legal system was the formation of a new class of "people's judges" who would ensure that the courts acted as guardians of the new social and economic order of the state. All criminal and civil matters dealt with by the new district and regional courts in the first instance were to come before a senate consisting of one professional judge and two law assessors (*Schöffen*), who would exercise full judicial functions. The Supreme Court hears appeals only on behalf of the state. The *Volkskammer* is nominally the supreme authority in the administration of justice and holds the functions of a Constitutional Court.

9. Police.—The evolution of German police systems is summarized above in the *Police* subsection of *Federal Republic of Germany*.

In the Democratic Republic the *Volkspolizei* was under central control and was adapted to all police requirements.

10. Defense.—East German armed forces were at first organized by the Department for Internal Affairs of the Soviet military administration. The first *Bereitschaften* (alert units or battalions) were formed in September 1948, shortly after the Soviet authorities had started the so-called Berlin blockade. At the end of 1950 the force officially known as the *Kasernierte Volkspolizei* (barracks people's police) comprised 39 *Bereitschaften* organized as military formations of a particular arm or service. In June 1952 the *Volkskammer* approved the establishment of a *Nationale Volksarmee* (national people's army). On May 14, 1955, a treaty of mutual defense was concluded by the U.S.S.R. and the seven European people's republics, including the German Democratic Republic (*see* WARSAW TREATY ORGANIZATION). In September 1955 the *Volkskammer* approved the addition of two amendments to the constitution declaring conscription a national duty and authorizing the necessary legislation.

By the late 1960s the National People's Forces comprised 126,000 men including 85,000 in the Army (2 tank and 4 motorized rifle divisions), 25,000 in the Air Force (270 combat aircraft and an anti-aircraft division), and 16,000 in the Navy (4 destroyer escorts, 25 coastal escorts, 45 minesweepers, and 110 smaller craft). Para-military forces included 20,000 security and 70,000 border troops. The armed workers' units (*Betriebskampfgruppen*) numbered 250,000. A conscription law, permitting the induction of men between 18 and 26 for 18 months' active duty in the Army, and two years' in the Air Force and the Navy, was promulgated in September 1961. An estimated 20 Soviet divisions were stationed on the territory of the G.D.R.

VI. THE ECONOMY
A. THE BACKGROUND

Germany went through a profound transformation in its economic and social structure between the date of the establishment of the second *Reich* in 1871 and the years immediately preceding World War I. In 1871 two-thirds of the population lived in the country and one-third in the towns. Within one generation this situation was reversed. In 1871 industry consisted mainly of handicrafts pursued in homes and small workshops. The Germany of 1910 was based upon coal and iron and factory production. Germany rivaled Great Britain in both industry and foreign trade. Production of coal in 1860 was 12,500,000 tons, and of lignite 4,500,000. In 1914 production reached 191,000,000 tons of coal and 87,000,000 tons of lignite (292,000,000 tons in Great Britain). In 1871-75 production of pig iron was 2,000,000 tons per year, in 1911-13, 17,000,000 tons per year (10,000,000 tons in Britain). Within one generation Germany became a powerful industrial state. It also experienced a great increase in agricultural production and a rapidly expanding foreign trade and became a colonial power. In spite of the losses of two subsequent world wars, Germany twice made phenomenal recoveries in production and levels of living. This is to be attributed above all to the extraordinary skill and

persistence with which the German people have utilized their relatively meagre natural resources and the poor quality of the soils in order to increase production of industrial goods and foodstuffs.

After World War I Germany lost about 12% of its area of population, 12% of its agricultural production, 10% of its manufacturing production, and 75% of its iron ores.

A shortage of raw materials and an inadequate food supply was always evident and the country's existence therefore has depended upon its ability to export manufactured goods to pay for the import of these necessities. Between 1913 and the outbreak of World War II the relative importance of the principal groups of goods comprising Germany's imports remained fairly constant, despite great changes in the total volume of trade, but this was not true of exports. Thus, although food steadily averaged about two-fifths of total imports and raw materials about one-third, by 1937 food had vanished from the list of exports, and raw materials had also declined as a proportion of exports. Correspondingly, the proportion of total exports represented by finished goods increased from less than two-thirds to nearly four-fifths between 1913 and 1937.

1. Interwar Period.—Germany's industrial transformation during the half century before the outbreak of World War I was checked for a time after that conflict. The Treaty of Versailles dislocated some of the leading industries, inflation upset the home market, and the scarcity of capital following inflation hampered industrial reorganization. However, in 1925 Germany started forward again in a great industrial recovery which continued during the next four years. The adoption of the Dawes Plan for reparations (*see* DAWES, CHARLES GATES) reestablished German credit and allowed Germany to borrow heavily abroad. Part of the money borrowed was spent in prompt payment of reparations obligations, but part was spent in public welfare improvements and much of the remainder in the "rationalization of industry"; that is, in the modernization of old plants and the construction of new ones with up-to-date machinery.

The excessive rationalization of industry, or replacement of hand labour by machines, affected Germany adversely in two ways. It saddled the nation with an intolerable foreign debt at high rates of interest which could not be met when the world depression began in 1929. It also tended to increase the chronic unemployment situation in Germany which was at its worst in 1932.

In 1933 another great industrial recovery began. It was stimulated by the National Socialist policy of reducing unemployment by spreading out work at short hours and giving fixed low wages to as many persons as possible. The National Socialists also reduced unemployment by great government expenditure on rearmament and public works. By 1939 the feverish effort at rearmament had completely wiped out unemployment and even created a severe labour shortage. As German exports were insufficient to pay for all the raw materials needed from abroad, Germany also began to feel a severe shortage of these. As the nation also aimed at self-sufficiency in case of a future war and blockade, it developed a policy of autarchy. Instead of manufacturing goods from imported raw materials it began to manufacture them as far as possible from its own domestic resources. These substitute products, such as oil from coal, textiles from wood fibre or cellulose, and artificial rubber or buna, required more labour, capital investment, horsepower, and domestic materials, such as coal and timber, than goods formerly made from imported raw materials. The severity of the shortage of labour and raw materials was thus further intensified.

Coal mining, one of Germany's basic industries, had lost about one-sixth of the production capacity of 1913, the ceded part of Upper Silesia having an output of 32,000,000 tons of the total German output of 193,000,000 tons. Moreover, 13,000,000 tons a year from the Saar were not available from 1919 to 1935. These losses could not be completely overcome even by 1939. The world's coal situation had changed; lignite (brown coal) had become of great importance, and oil and electricity became serious competitors. German coal production increased to 163,000,000 tons in 1929, sank to 105,000,000 in 1932, and then rose again to

184,500,000 in 1937. Lignite production increased rapidly after World War I until it almost exactly equaled coal production in weight. It was largely used in the form of briquettes for domestic use, and also for generating energy in electric power plants and for the production of heavy chemicals. About one-third of the total coal production was used for coking and distillation. The coking process produced coke for smelting iron ore, gas which was piped for hundreds of miles, oil, coal tar, dyes, and thousands of other derivatives invaluable for the chemical industry and for the manufacture of many substitute products.

Iron and steel, another of Germany's basic industries, suffered an even greater dislocation as a result of World War I and the cession of Alsace-Lorraine to France. The production of iron ore had been 28,600,000 tons in 1913; of this output the districts remaining to Germany produced but 7,300,000 tons—a reduction of three-quarters. This production even dropped in 1932 to 1,300,000 tons. The number of separate undertakings fell from 328 to 115, and the number of persons employed from about 43,000 to 14,000. After 1933, however, iron and steel production recovered rapidly. Its great lack was iron ore to make up for the ores lost in Lorraine. To overcome this Germany in 1937 imported 20,600,000 tons, mostly from Sweden and France, but also from Belgium, Luxembourg, Spain, Newfoundland, Algeria, Norway, and other countries. Its own domestic production of iron ore rose from 2,600,000 tons in 1933 to 9,700,000 tons in 1937. The total of imported and domestic iron ore in 1937 (30,300,000 tons), however, was not enough for Germany's rearmament and other needs, so there was formed, as part of the four-year plan, the Hermann Göring Reich Company for Ore Mining and Iron Smelting to exploit Germany's low-grade ores in the area of Salzgitter, south of Brunswick.

2. Post-1945.—World War II brought grave damage to German industry, and the victorious powers had to frame a policy for a German industrial system that had collapsed. The policy was set down in the Potsdam Agreement of Aug. 2, 1945, which was designed, in the economic sphere, to eliminate or control any branches of industry which could be used for military production; to ensure payment of reparations claims; but also to ensure that Germany, after all claims had been met, should be left with a self-supporting economy. The Potsdam Agreement therefore provided for the total prohibition of armaments, aircraft, and seagoing ships, and industries that had potential war importance were to be strictly controlled in order to ensure that production was limited to Germany's legitimate peacetime needs. Surplus productive capacity was to be removed or destroyed. The agreement also required that German industry be decentralized by the elimination of all excessive concentrations of economic power.

In March 1946 the Allied Control Council published a provisional level-of-industry plan in implementation of the Potsdam Agreement. This plan, if carried out, would have restricted Germany's industrial capacity to little more than half the 1938 level. It was based, however, on various assumptions which were not fulfilled, such as the treatment of Germany as an economic unit, the pooling of resources between the four zones of occupation, and the use of the proceeds from current German production in the first place to pay for necessary German imports. Disagreements arose between the U.S.S.R. and the three Western Allies on all these points and, though right up to 1947 the Western Allies tried to ensure that Germany should be treated as an economic unit by the four occupying powers, circumstances forced them ultimately, in their own as well as Germany's interests, to organize industry in the western zones independently of what the Soviet occupation authorities were doing in their own zone. On Jan. 1, 1947, the British and U.S. zones were fused, for economic purposes, into a bizone, and later the French zone also joined the merger so that a uniform economic policy for the whole of West Germany became possible.

On Aug. 29, 1947, in default of a wider agreement, an Anglo-U.S. plan for a revised level of industry in the bizone was published. This provided for reparations claims and also for security considerations, but it allowed German industrial capacity, including a permitted level of steel production of 10,700,000 metric tons (11,100,000 metric tons including the French zone), to be retained at roughly the 1936 level. As a corollary to this revised plan, a dismantling list was published on Oct. 17, 1947, which enumerated 682 plants that were to be removed as reparations or destroyed as surplus to the requirements of the new level of industry.

A Divided Economy.—The postwar division of an integrated state created problems of structural readjustment, but by the early 1960s these had evidently been overcome. In 1936 western Germany accounted for about seven-tenths of the total national product and it produced almost all the hard coal, petroleum, and iron ore. After the war there were surpluses of these products in West Germany and deficits in East Germany. Brown coal and potash production, on the other hand, were heavily concentrated in the east and in these commodities the west had deficits. The processing of iron and steel was sited in the Ruhr coal field which, together with Upper Silesia, supplied eastern Germany with these products. The production of textile and office machinery was mainly concentrated in East Germany but agricultural machinery (much in demand in the eastern sector) was mainly produced in the west.

The problem of surplus industries was more easily overcome than was expected, because of the rapid rate of expansion at home and in foreign markets. The deficit industries in each area raised bigger difficulties, but gaps were filled quickly by the application of technical skills and a high rate of capital formation. Structural adaptation in West Germany was complete by the mid-1950s. There was full employment, industrial products were competitive in foreign markets, and there was a favourable balance of payments. Though big strides had been taken in East Germany, the readjustment was not complete even by the early 1950s. This was because, first, there had been heavy demands for reparation payments; second, East Germany was markedly deficient in heavy industries and investment goods; third, consumer-goods industries were underutilized for lack of markets and raw materials; and fourth, centralized and controlled economic policies had laid down a set of planned priorities.

Industry accounts for about two-fifths of the output of both West and East Germany. It has expanded faster than all other sections of the economy, though individual industries have had particular problems of readjustment. The number of persons employed in industry considerably increased in both East and West Germany. The increase was mainly in producer-goods rather than consumer-goods industries. In East Germany the increase was outstanding in the heavy industries, whereas in West Germany it was largely in the metal-using industries. In both areas almost two-thirds of the industrial workers are engaged in heavy and metal-using industries, and little more than one-third in consumer-goods and food industries.

The division of Germany (into the Federal Republic of Germany and the German Democratic Republic) has, however, entailed substantial modifications in the economies of both republics which are discussed separately in sections below.

B. FEDERAL REPUBLIC OF GERMANY

1. Agriculture.—Up to the end of World War II, two main systems of landholding formed the basis of German agriculture. The east, especially east of the Elbe, was a land of big properties, some tracts such as East Prussia and parts of Silesia being in the hands of comparatively few owners. Little of the agricultural land was farmed by tenants, the rest being run by the owners or their administrators with hired labour. In the west, south, and most parts of central Germany the land was mainly held by peasant proprietors. Some of them, especially in the northwest, owned larger farms and employed hired labour. Others, especially in the Rhine Valley, were smallholders, running their plots of land with the help of their families and often engaging in some secondary industrial occupation. Agrarian Germany was thus a kind of peasant democracy in the west and a type of estate-owning aristocracy in the east.

After World War II measures of land reform were carried in the Federal Republic which considerably changed the structure of agricultural industry there. In the late 1960s more than half of the total land area (*i.e.,* 24,740,000 ha.) was arable. Between

1949 and 1968 the number of holdings fell from 1,939,600 to 1,376,900 because the smallest and uneconomic farms were sold to the largest ones. In 1968 there were only 2,800 holdings of more than 100 ha. The average farm area rose between 1949 and 1968 from 6.95 ha. to 9.34 ha. At the same time the number of people employed in agriculture fell from 3,800,000 to 1,620,000, which meant that more than 2,100,000 found employment in industry and trade. The Federal Republic produces from its own resources nearly four-fifths of its food requirements.

In the early years after World War II the shortage of fertilizers, seeds, equipment, and machinery, as well as skilled agricultural labour, badly affected the harvests. By 1949, however, both the harvests and the yields per hectare were approaching, and in some cases outstripping, the prewar averages for the same areas. Between 1949 and 1968 agricultural production of the Federal Republic rose by two-thirds. Annual averages of the main crops for the years 1961-65 were as follows (in metric tons; yields in quintals per hectare in brackets): wheat 4,607,000 (33.1); rye 3,028,000 (26.6); barley 3,461,000 (30.1); oats 2,185,000 (28.8); potatoes 22,219,000 (2.47); and sugar beets 10,938,000 (370). For the years 1964-67, on the average, the Federal Republic imported yearly 1,677,000 tons of wheat and 1,445,000 tons of barley. Viticulture has long been important in southwest Germany. The main areas lie on the better-drained sloping lands with a southerly exposure in the valleys of the Rhine above Bonn, and in the Neckar and Main valleys, as well as the edges of the upper Rhine valley. The largest area is in the Rhineland-Palatinate, southwest of Mainz. Production is mainly in the hands of small peasant cultivators and holdings are normally extremely fragmented. The cultivated area decreased substantially after World War II but recovered during the 1950s; average annual production in the late 1960s (nearly 5,000,000 hl.) was roughly double that of the late 1930s. Hops are also cultivated in the sheltered and warmer areas of the southwest. Bavaria is responsible for 90% of the total production.

Livestock.—The early postwar food shortage in West Germany caused farmers to slaughter livestock and convert their grassland to edible crops. This trend was gradually reversed after 1948 as supplies of foodstuffs became available through the European Recovery Program and as crop yields improved. By 1954 West Germany was practically self-sufficient in meat and dairy products, and by the late 1950s animal husbandry accounted for three-quarters of the total food production. In the late 1960s the number of cattle amounted to 14,000,000 head, an increase of 2,000,000 head on figures for 1938 in the same territory; there were also more than 19,000,000 pigs, a one-third increase on 1938.

2. Fisheries.—Seafood forms an important supplementary source of food supply. In the late 1960s West German craft were landing more than 650,000 metric tons of fish annually in domestic ports. The total figures were of the same order of magnitude as prewar ones. About 40% of the catch (in value) consists of herrings. The principal fishing grounds are in the North Sea, whence comes half of the catch. The remainder are caught in the North Atlantic, especially in Icelandic waters (25%) and off the Norwegian coast (10%). In order to satisfy consumption more than 200,000 tons of fish were imported annually. Half of the West German trawler landings are at Bremerhaven, one of the largest fishing ports in Europe. Others are at Cuxhaven, Hamburg, and Kiel. The herring catch is mainly landed at the smaller ports on the lower Weser and at Emden.

3. Forestry.—Forests, consisting mostly of fir, spruce, beech, oak, and pine, cover 7,200,000 ha. (30% of the Federal Republic area). Even before World War II Germany had been obliged to import about one-third of its timber requirements. Not only did imports cease in 1945 but the great demand for timber for reconstruction purposes reduced supplies needed for paper, wood fibre, cellulose, *Ersatz* products, pit props, and railway sleepers (ties). However, with the restoration of normal trade conditions, timber felling in the Federal Republic was reduced from nearly 40,000,000 cu.m. in 1948 to an annual average of about 27,000,000 cu.m. in the late 1960s. After 1949 over 3,700,000 ac. were replanted—more than one-fifth of the area under timber. Nearly

one-third of the forests is owned by the federal government, the *Länder,* or communes.

4. Industry.—The new phase of West German industrial development began in 1948 as a result of the Allied intention to associate the country in the economic revival to be fostered by the ERP (European Recovery Program). The United States, Great Britain, and France, in collaboration with the three Benelux countries, began discussions which resulted in an agreement to set up an international authority for the Ruhr to control Germany's heavy industries, and a Military Security Board to watch over German industry in general to see that it did not infringe Allied controls. The association of West Germany in the ERP, however, made it essential to reconsider the level-of-industry plan and the dismantling list of 1947. Consequently in April 1949 the United States, Great Britain, and France agreed on a substantial reduction of the dismantling list, and many prohibitions and restrictions on German industry were removed. In September 1950 the foreign ministers of the three powers agreed to a further revision of Allied controls. The remaining restrictions on industry in the Federal Republic were abolished on May 5, 1955, when the Paris agreements giving sovereignty to the Federal Republic came into force. On the same date the functions of the Military Security Board came to an end.

On May 16, 1949, the occupying powers in West Germany promulgated Law no. 27 to redefine Allied policy on the decartelization of German industry. During the inflation of the 1920s the concentration of industry in a few hands in combines or cartels had been common in Germany and most of the basic industries (coal, lignite, pig iron, steel, potash, and many others) adopted this highly centralized form of organization, thus securing a kind of cooperative monopoly for their members. The law passed by the Western Allies to deal with this state of affairs transferred the heavy industries (coal, iron, and steel) to German trusteeship for the period of the planned decartelization. The first decartelization orders were issued on July 10, 1951, and transferred property from the former great steel combine, known as Vereinigte Stahlwerke, and the firm of Otto Wolff, Cologne, to five specially created, smaller "unit companies."

The European Coal and Steel Community came into being on July 25, 1952, and, in accordance with the Allied undertaking, all the postwar restrictions imposed by the Western occupying powers on German steel production were formally abolished, and the progressive liquidation of the International Authority for the Ruhr, set up by the Western powers in 1949, was announced.

Iron and Steel.—Germany before World War I emerged as one of the chief steel-producing countries of the world. This industry was based primarily on coal from the Ruhr and iron ore from Lorraine and abroad. The loss of the Lorraine ore field in 1918 drastically reduced Germany's iron-ore production, and since then the country has imported most of the iron ore it needs. By the late 1960s production of iron ore in the Federal Republic (including the Saar) was about 6,600,000 metric tons (32% iron content). Production of pig iron and blast-furnace ferroalloys was 30,000,000 metric tons and that of crude steel 41,000,000 tons (7.5% of world production; after the U.S., the U.S.S.R., and Japan, the Federal Republic is the fourth world steel producer). The best deposits of iron ore are in the Lahn, Sieg, and Dill valleys in the plateau to the east of the Rhine. These ores, which are deep mined by shafts, are good but costly, and resources and production are small. Especially important are the low-grade iron ores that occur at Salzgitter. There an iron- and steelworks, which utilizes coal from the Ruhr brought in by the Mittelland Canal, has an annual output of about 2,000,000 metric tons.

5. Manufacturing Industries.—Roughly 27% of industrial workers are in the basic industries (energy, mining, metallurgy, chemical, and building materials); a little more than one-third in the metal-using industries (engineering, electrical industries, precision instruments, and optics); 29% in the light industries (woodwork, textiles, paper and printing, and other consumer goods); and a little less than one-tenth in the food industries.

Engineering.—This major group of industries includes steel constructional work, and the production of machinery and vehicles.

These account for about one-fifth of all industrial workers. The semifinished products of iron and steel plates, rails, girders, wires, etc., are located with the blast furnace and the steel converter and rolling mills. Passenger and freight cars are made at Essen, Kassel, and Mannheim; diesel and electric locomotives at Berlin and Mannheim. Cutlery, nails, bolts, screws, and hardware, etc., are manufactured in the Solingen district south of the Ruhr. Most of the fabricating industries are carried on near the seats of iron and steel production or in the cities. Production of motor vehicles has increased rapidly since the early 1950s, and production was controlled by a few firms in a few large plants located at Rüsselsheim, Stuttgart, Cologne, and Frankfurt. The growth in the late 1950s was largely due to the vast Volkswagen plant at Wolfsburg (east of Brunswick, alongside the Mittelland Canal).

The electrical industries were mainly concentrated in Berlin before 1939. Following World War II the industry was reestablished in West Berlin and in other cities of the Federal Republic.

Shipbuilding.—The Federal Republic occupies a leading place in the world in shipbuilding, competing with Japan and the U.K. Shipbuilding and marine engineering are concentrated in the North Sea ports, notably in Hamburg.

Chemical Production.—Germany's share of the world production reached 21.9% in 1938. The Federal Republic's share now exceeds 6%; the main seats of heavy chemical production are situated in the Ruhr and in several great complexes on the navigable waterfront of the Rhine—notably at Leverkusen, Ludwigshafen, and Höchst (near Frankfurt am Main). The district around Cologne facing on the Rhine witnessed a great growth in the mid-20th century of petroleum chemicals, and downstream, as far as the Ruhr, there are rayon and man-made fibre and heavy-chemical plants.

Textiles.—Employing about 9% of the workers, the textile industry is dominant in the lower Rhinelands, both south of the Ruhr (Wuppertal) and west of the Rhine (Krefeld); also in the southwest in the Neckar Valley and between Constance and Augsburg. A more balanced industry has resulted from the increased production of man-made fibres.

Other Industries.—Glassmaking is located in the Ruhr and the Saar. Precision instruments and electrical apparatus are manufactured in major cities, especially West Berlin. Optical and precision instruments are produced in small towns in Baden-Württemberg, while clocks, toys, jewelry, and footwear are made in several small towns in southwest Germany; e.g., jewelry at Pforzheim and boots and shoes at Pirmasens. Many skilled industries, such as the making of harmonicas, are to be found in the country villages and small towns of this area.

6. Mining.—For iron ore see *Iron and Steel*, above.

Coal.—As far as industrial resources are concerned, Germany's greatest natural assets are hard coal (deep mined) and brown coal or lignite (mostly surface mined). Small bituminous coal fields are scattered along the northern edge of the central highlands, but the Ruhr is the main seat of production and, in fact, the greatest coal field in Europe. In the mid-1960s it accounted for about three-quarters of the 125,000,000 metric tons produced annually in the Federal Republic, including the Saar. At that rate of production its reserves should last for another 400 years.

Lignite.—Lignite beds lie in the southern portion of the northern lowland. In the Federal Republic the main area is the Ville to the southwest of Cologne, while a much smaller field lies near Helmstedt. Annual production in the late 1960s averaged about 100,000,000 metric tons. The lignite is surface mined to depths of several hundred feet using gigantic excavators and very little labour. Though low in calorific value, its large-scale production and utilization on the spot as a fuel, or its fabrication into coal bricks for wider distribution, have been the basis of a 20th-century industrial revolution. Thermoelectric plants, together with chemical plants producing synthetic nitrates and oils, are located near the workings. However, it was estimated that the accessible reserves in the Ville district, for example, would last only about 70 years.

Other Mineral Resources.—Apart from coal and iron ore, the only other natural mineral resources of which Germany has large quantities are potash and rock salt. Before World War II Germany had almost a world monopoly of potash, which is used as a fertilizer and as a basis for chemical industries. The Federal Republic has supplies that yield about 2,300,000 metric tons of potash annually, a sixth of the world production. The Federal Republic meets 90% and 60% of its requirements of zinc and lead respectively. Copper production is small and aluminum production depends entirely on imports; for Germany has no bauxite deposits.

There are crude petroleum deposits in the Emsland, in the extreme northwest of the Federal Republic. Production rose rapidly from 1,100,000 metric tons in 1950 to about 8,000,000 metric tons in 1968, which was meeting almost a third of the domestic demand.

7. Power.—In the Federal Republic, of the electricity capacity in 1968, about one-half consists of hard-coal plants, one-quarter of hydroelectric undertakings, and the rest of brown-coal stations. About one-sixth of the total consumption of electricity is derived from water resources, the hydroelectric stations being located mainly in the Bavarian Alps. Between 1950 and 1968 generation of electric power in the Federal Republic more than quadrupled, rising from 47,500,000,000 to 197,750,000,000 kw.-hr.

From 1956 the nuclear power industry, enjoying considerable support from the government, made rapid progress toward assuming a position commensurate with its great technical and other resources. In 1960 an experimental nuclear power station with a boiling-water reactor came into operation. The following year the federal government placed an order for a 15,000-ton nuclear-powered merchant vessel, named "Otto Hahn" after the celebrated German nuclear physicist; in 1968 this ship underwent successful sea trials. In 1965 a full-scale nuclear power plant of 240 Mw. capacity started production at Gundremmingen (Bavaria). In 1968 three other nuclear power stations, at Lingen, on the Ems River, at Kahl (Hesse), and at Obrigheim (Baden-Württemberg), joined the grid, increasing the nuclear installed capacity to 900 Mw. Construction of two new nuclear power stations started in 1967: at Stade, near Hamburg, of 630 Mw. capacity, and at Würgassen, on the upper Weser River, of 612 Mw. From 1956 to 1968 the Federal Republic spent DM. 6,300,000,000 on nuclear research and industry.

Gas derived from one-third of the coal production is an important source of power in the Federal Republic. Most of the production is from coking plants at the pits and the rest from steelworks and municipal gasworks. Between 1950 and 1961 manufactured gas output trebled to 24,828,000,000 cu.m., but by 1968 fell to 19,200,000,000 cu.m. However, extraction of natural gas rose between 1950 and 1968 from 67,000,000 to 5,200,000,000 cu.m.

8. Location of Industry.—The chief industrial areas of the Federal Republic are summarized below.

North Rhine-Westphalia.—This *Land* has as its heart the Ruhr coal field and the Ville coal field, together with the industries associated with them. To the southwest and northwest is a zone in which the textile, metalware, and machine industries are dominant. The industrial area of the Ruhr—the series of towns reaching from Duisburg on the Rhine through Essen to Dortmund in the east—is the hub of this complex and, indeed, of the West German economy. North Rhine-Westphalia accounts for about two-fifths of the industrial workers of the Federal Republic. The Ruhr produces nine-tenths of Germany's bituminous coal and is, in consequence, the main seat of production in Germany, and in Western Europe, of iron and steel, gas, electricity, and distillation products.

Middle Rhine Region.—This area has its chief centres at the northern end of the upper Rhine plain in Frankfurt am Main, Mainz, and Wiesbaden and, farther south, in Ludwigshafen and Mannheim. It has a great variety of industries, some of which are old established ones, such as leatherworking and the production of boots and shoes, based originally on local raw materials. But modern growth has been particularly due to the transport facilities offered by the Rhine for bulky raw materials. This accounts, for example, for the vast heavy-chemical industries at Ludwigshafen and at Höchst, west of Frankfurt am Main.

Baden-Württemberg.—This *Land* developed skilled domestic crafts in the 18th century, particularly those that involved the

there are many places where tourism is the primary source of livelihood. There are about 240 inland spas, while the shores of the North Sea provide sandy beaches and bathing facilities on a major scale, including the islands of Sylt and Norderney. The lakes of the south are much frequented and the Germans flock to the Bavarian Alps. The highlands of West Germany, particularly the Black Forest, attract visitors in winter and summer. Apart from the scenic areas, the numerous small historic towns and the great cities also attract many visitors, especially in the Rhineland.

10. Trade.—After World War II Germany was poorer than ever in raw materials and food supplies, with its economy unbalanced and suffering great losses from war damage, reparations, and controls. At the same time its shipping resources had almost vanished and its capital reserves were heavily mortgaged by prewar and postwar debts. Nevertheless, largely as a result of the European Recovery Program (ERP), most-favoured-nation treatment from the United States and Great Britain, and the various measures that were taken by the Organization for European Economic Cooperation (OEEC) to revive western trade in general, the foreign trade of West Germany recovered to a remarkable degree.

From 1948 onward West Germany began to play a major role in the expansion of Western European trade. By 1953 the total volume of imports and exports of the Federal Republic was already half as large again as that for the same area before World War II. The Federal Republic achieved its first postwar surplus of visible exports over imports in 1952. In 1968 its exports amounted to DM. 99,500,000,000 with a surplus of DM. 18,400,000,000.

By the late 1960s the structure of the Federal Republic's imports had changed compared with the prewar position of the *Reich* as a whole. The share of food in total imports had fallen from about two-fifths to less than a third, and that of raw materials from more than a third to about a quarter, the share of semifinished and finished goods having increased correspondingly. The structure of exports had changed little, however, the main items being finished and semifinished manufactures. The direction of trade had altered. Trade with the member states of OEEC and their associates had increased in importance compared with that for the prewar *Reich*, while more than a quarter of the Federal Republic's imports were from the western hemisphere compared with less than a fifth before. Membership in the European Economic Community (EEC) in 1958 and in the planned integration of the economies of the member countries was a landmark in West German economic history (see EUROPEAN UNITY). In 1970 the U.S.S.R. and West Germany completed negotiations to allow the Soviet Union to trade natural gas for West German steel pipe.

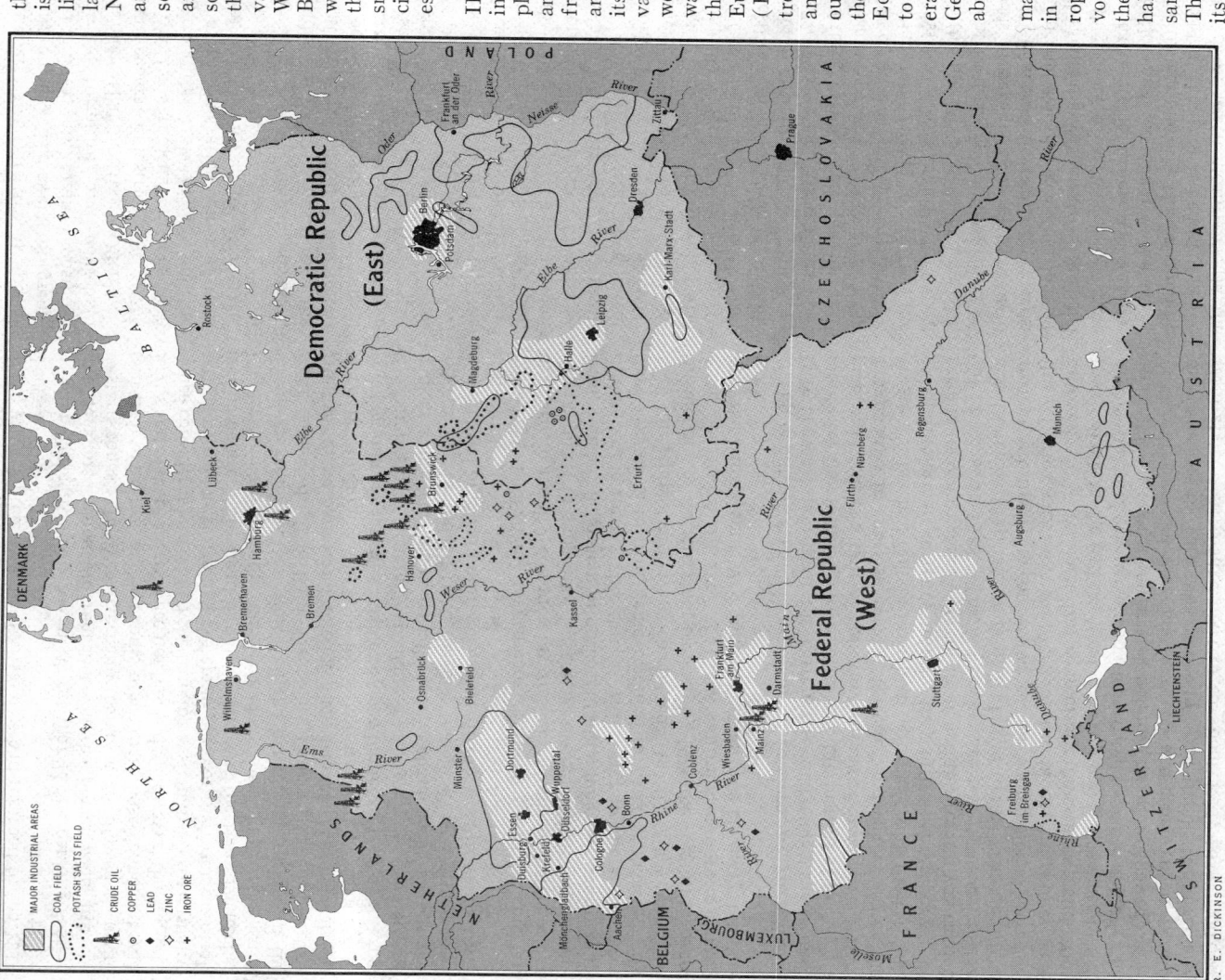

INDUSTRIAL AND MINERAL RESOURCES OF GERMANY

R. E. DICKINSON

treatment of textiles and metals. Skilled manipulative industries are located in the environs of Stuttgart as well as in the small towns and villages. In this area a large number of workers travel many miles each day from remote villages to places of work in both big cities and small towns. Great skills and small quantities of raw materials characterize the industries in the area.

Other Industrial Centres.—Several of the great cities are outstanding as seats of industry. West Berlin is the greatest of them. Before the war it employed 1,000,000 persons in industry, or 8% of the total for the *Reich*. In the late 1960s the skilled steel and metal industries of West Berlin were especially important, and electrical supplies were among its chief products. Clothing industries, building trades, foods, and printing are its other main industries. Hamburg and Bremen owe their strong concentration of industry to their functions as ports. The other major regional capitals outside the main industrial areas are also important seats of industry, particularly Munich, Nürnberg, Hanover, and Kassel.

9. Tourism.—In West Germany the various forms of tourism yielded about 8% of the national income in the late 1960s, and

Trade Fairs.—Annual international trade fairs are of special significance. The most important are held at Hanover (representing West German industries), Frankfurt am Main (consumer goods), Cologne (mostly hardware, furniture, and household goods), Nürnberg (toys), Munich (handicrafts), Offenbach (leather goods), and West Berlin (general industries).

11. Finance.—Before World War I government functions were divided between three authorities: the *Reich,* the *Länder,* and the local authorities, but the burden of administration remained with the *Länder.* Each level of administration levied its own taxes, often on the same basis, but by 1910 the percentage which the local authorities could add to the *Land* rate of income, turnover, and other taxes was limited. Under the Weimar constitution the *Reich* took over more administrative services than it had previously been responsible for, but police, education, justice, public health, and supervision of industry continued to be within the competence of the *Länder.* These had tax collecting services of their own, though some of the smaller ones entrusted the *Reich* authorities with the collection of their taxes. The *Reich, Länder,* and local authorities shared certain sources of revenue but the proportion going to the *Reich* increased gradually as the burdens of the latter increased. This raised the question of equalization of the burden of expenditure in the different *Länder,* but it was not until 1938 that, in Prussia, a proper financial equalization based on need and taxation capacity was evolved. By 1939, as a result of the centralizing policy of the Nazis, the central government had become the chief taxing authority in Germany, and the *Länder* had been ousted from their former privileged position. The central government controlled not only customs and excise but also income tax, corporation tax, and the inheritance and property taxes.

After World War II the financial system in the Federal Republic was based on the principles laid down in the Basic Law. By these the federal government acquired exclusive legislative rights over some taxes (*e.g.,* customs and excise, except beer, and financial monopolies) and concurrent legislative powers with the *Länder* in the case of certain other taxes (*e.g.,* income and property taxes). The revenue from beer and various other taxes accrued to the *Länder.* Similarly there was a division of competence with regard to the actual administration of the taxes. The Basic Law also authorized the federal government to draw upon an equalization fund provided from the proceeds of various *Land* taxes, and to make grants to the poorer *Länder* in accordance with their needs. As more of the burdens of reconstruction and compensation for war damage were assumed by the federal government, its financial requirements increased, and the Basic Law was accordingly amended during 1955–56. The shares of the income and corporation taxes flowing to the federation and the *Länder* were to be changed in or after 1960 by federal law, requiring the consent of the *Bundesrat.* Principles were laid down which meant that, in the long run, the federation would draw in the revenue and share it out on the basis of need and the remaining taxation capacity of the *Länder.* By the late 1960s the total annual revenue of the federation and the *Länder* exceeded DM. 80,000,000,000.

Banking and Currency.—The first commercial bank was established in Germany in 1619, but it was not until the late 19th century that a modern, coordinated banking system developed. By the 1930s German banking was dominated by the Reichsbank and five other big banks, two of which were purely Berlin institutions, while the "big three" (the Deutsche Bank, Dresdner Bank, and Commerz- und Privatbank) had branches throughout the country. After the inflation of 1923 the Reichsbank was reorganized under the Dawes Plan and managed to preserve some semblance of independence until 1939, when a decree placed it directly under the control of Hitler, who exercised the control through Walther Funk, *Reich* minister of economics and president of the Reichsbank. There were also in prewar Germany public banks maintained by the *Land* governments, provinces, and municipalities, and these were important as savings banks. Savings, however, suffered because of the 1923 inflation and in 1924 they were only one-fifteenth of what they had been in 1914. Later, confi-

dence was restored, and by 1937 savings had returned to the 1914 level.

After Germany's collapse in World War II the banking system was developed along different lines in the Soviet zone and the western zones. In West Germany banks were allowed to maintain their existence, and accounts other than those connected with *Reich* and Nazi property were not blocked. However, the Western Allies considerably modified the banking system in place of the former centralized structure. The head of this system was the Bank Deutscher Länder, and each of the *Länder* had its own autonomous bank (*Landeszentralbank*) on which all the banking operations in the *Land* depended. The Bank Deutscher Länder derived its funds from the *Land* banks and acted as their banker. Although it was the only bank allowed to issue notes, and was to that extent a centralizing influence, it was unable to open branches or to do internal German business, generally speaking, except with the *Land* central banks. Moreover, the essentially federal character of the postwar system may be judged from the fact that no West German bank was allowed to maintain branches outside the *Land* in which it was registered.

In 1951 the Federal government approved a new banking law designed to modify considerably this decentralized system. The law proposed to substitute for the 30 or more small banks functioning under the system of decentralization nine successor organizations to the former "big three," with power to operate in three large regions instead of being confined to *Land* boundaries. By 1954 this reorganization was completed. In 1956 a law permitted the merging of the successor banks. By 1958 the "big three" were again operating. In 1957 the *Land* central banks were merged with the Bank Deutscher Länder to become the Deutsche Bundesbank.

The dominant economic requirement in Germany after World War II was a reform of the currency so that money could once more play its essential part in economic life instead of finding its place usurped, as a unit of value and means of exchange, by such commodities in short supply as cigarettes and coffee. After the Western Allies had failed to reach an agreement with the U.S.S.R. on an all-German currency reform, they instituted a separate reform in their own zones of occupation, and this reform was carried out in stages in 1948. The old reichsmark was converted to the new Deutsche Mark at a rate of RM. 10 to DM. 1, and half the amount resulting from conversion was placed in a blocked account. By a further currency law 70% of the blocked accounts were canceled, 10% retained for compulsory investment, and 20% freed. Thus in the end the West Germans had the free use of 6% of their holdings (though a provision existed by which a later claim up to 10% of former reichsmark holdings might be allowed).

The reform was severe, but necessary and beneficent in its ultimate effects. By July 1948 money in circulation had been reduced from about RM. 65,000,000,000 to about DM. 10,000,000,000, and this restoration of the purchasing power of the mark and of people's confidence in it was the indispensable foundation of the Federal Republic's subsequent economic recovery. By August 1957 the position of the Deutsche Mark was strong enough to allow the lifting of all external currency restrictions, for by then the balance of payments was showing a large surplus. In March 1961 the exchange rate of DM. 4.20 = $1 was revalued at DM. 4 = $1. In 1962 the current account was in deficit for the first time since 1950, but in 1963 exports rose by 10% while imports rose by only 6%, leading to a substantial surplus in the balance of payments. In the late 1960s the persistent strength of the Deutsche Mark and the large trade surpluses of 1966, 1967, and 1968 led to speculation that there would be a second revaluation, especially as there was international pressure for this from the U.K., U.S., and France, whose currencies were facing difficulties. However, the Federal government resolved to maintain the existing parity of the Deutsche Mark and took various alternative measures to ward off inflation. Nevertheless, on Oct. 24, 1969, the Deutsche Mark was revalued by 9.29%, that is, DM. 3.66 = $1.

12. Transport and Communications.—*Railways.*—Prussia nationalized its railways during 1876–79, and the other German

Länder followed suit. In 1919 the *Reich* took over the various railways but failed to run the unified system at a profit. Later, with the help of funds made available through the Dawes Plan, the railways were reorganized and their financial position improved. World War II, however, put an intense strain on rail transport, and Allied bombing did enormous damage to rolling stock, tracks, and marshaling yards. After the war the railways felt the competition of road services and were thus in a weak financial position. The bulk of the railway system (now the Deutsche Bundesbahn) in West Germany was formally designated as federal property in 1951. By 1968 the length of the Federal railway system was 18,580 mi. (29,900 km.), of which 5,016 mi. (8,075 km.) were electrified; there were also 2,641 mi. (4,250 km.) of privately owned railways. Only 10% of traction on Federal railways was by steam locomotives, while 52% was assured by diesel electric and 38% by diesel engines. Traffic on Federal railways amounted in the late 1960s to 34,356,000,000 passenger-km., and about 55,000,000,000 ton-km. annually.

Roads.—By 1938 the new Autobahnen (highways) totaled about 1,900 mi. Plans for extending the Autobahnen in the Federal Republic were not approved until 1955, when a bill was passed to increase taxation on gasoline and diesel oil both to assist in financing new Autobahn construction and also to help the Federal railways. In 1968 classified roads totaled 100,153 mi. (161,181 km.), including 2,464 mi. (3,966 km.) of Autobahnen.

Shipping.—Very little tonnage was left to Germany in the immediate postwar years, most having been set aside for reparations. Moreover, for security reasons the German shipbuilding industry was severely limited, and many dock and shipbuilding installations were destroyed or dismantled. Afterward, Allied restrictions on the industry in West Germany were progressively removed. Between Dec. 31, 1949, and Dec. 31, 1968, the gross registered tonnage of merchant shipping rose from 331,000 to 7,068,976 BRT, the last figure exceeding by some 2,500,000 tons the total owned by the *Reich* in 1939. Hamburg handled nearly half the total overseas freight, and Bremen nearly a quarter; the other chief ports were Emden and Lübeck.

Inland Waterways.—Before World War II about one-fifth of German inland traffic was waterborne. But the inland shipping system suffered great damage during the war, both from Allied bombing and from the demolition of bridges and locks on canals by the Germans themselves. For example, at the end of the war the important Dortmund-Ems Canal was completely out of action. After 1945, however, rapid progress was made in both East and West Germany in repairing war damage and in extending the inland waterways. The Rhine is navigable for 4,000-ton barges to Duisburg and for 2,000-ton barges to Basel; it dominates the waterborne traffic of Western Europe. Duisburg receives ores, grain, oil, and timber. Some of this traffic moves to the upstream parts, together with Ruhr coal and Rhenish brown-coal briquettes. The Mitteland Canal, completed in 1938, carries 1,000-ton barges from the Ruhr to the Elbe, and serves, among other areas, the industrial complex of Salzgitter (iron and steel), Wolfsburg (automobiles), and around Brunswick. The Weser is navigable for 600-ton barges almost to Kassel, with improvements to Minden (at the junction with the Mittelland Canal) to take 1,000-ton barges. Bremen's waterborne traffic has doubled since World War II, whereas that of Hamburg is below prewar figures, since East Germany favours its own ports, while Czechoslovakia uses the Polish ports to a great extent. In the Federal Republic by 1960 the Neckar had been made navigable as far as Stuttgart for 1,200-ton barges, and the canalization of the middle Weser was completed by 1966. The canalization of the Moselle, agreed jointly with France in 1956, was completed in 1966 as far as Metz. In 1968 the first 32-km. stretch on the Bamberg-Nürnberg section of the canal that would link the Rhine to the Danube via the Main river was opened. Completion of this canal would make a new water connection between Rotterdam and the Black Sea, usable by ships of up to 1,500 tons. Freight traffic on the Federal inland waterways reached in the late 1960s 232,000,000 metric tons, of which 120,300,000 tons represented international trade while 10,-200,000 tons passed the Federal Republic in transit.

Air Transport.—For ten years after World War II Germany was served exclusively by foreign aircraft, but in 1955 the Allied High Commission gave permission for the newly constituted airline Lufthansa to begin both internal and external services. It soon operated regular flights to many European capitals, North America, South America, and the Middle and Far East. By 1969 the Lufthansa had an all-jet fleet of 71 aircraft, maintaining a total of 185,800 mi. (299,000 km.) of regular air services; its air traffic amounted in 1968 to 6,000,000,000 passenger-km. and to 328,540,-000 ton-km. of freight.

Postal Services and Telecommunications.—The postal services in West Germany are federally operated, and the federal government also has a monopoly of telephone, telegraph, radio, and television systems. In 1968 West Germany had 11,250,000 telephones, 18,900,000 radio receivers, and 14,900,000 television receivers. In the same year 9,220,000,000 letters and 288,000,000 parcels were handled.

C. GERMAN DEMOCRATIC REPUBLIC

1. Agriculture.—There is a brief historic discussion of German "peasant" agriculture in the *Agriculture* subsection of *Federal Republic of Germany* above.

A drastic system of land reform was introduced in the Soviet zone in 1945, affecting all holdings of more than 100 ha. (247 ac.). Farms and estates with a total area of 7,207,000 ac. were expropriated, being mostly parceled out in peasant holdings of between 7 and 9 ha. (17.3 and 22.2 ac.). The recipients were mostly agricultural labourers and small peasants, together with many refugees from the east. By 1949, holdings of more than 250 ac. formed only 3.6% of all agricultural land, compared with 28.3% in 1939, although the latter percentage was more than restored by the subsequent policy of collectivization.

Collectivization.—In the early postwar years, farming in the German Democratic Republic suffered from a shortage of both labour, which was being attracted into industry, and technical equipment. Agricultural costs were much higher than in the Federal Republic, and compulsory deliveries at low fixed prices were graded progressively steeper for the "larger" farmer, who was gradually squeezed out. The Communist-dominated Peasants' Mutual Aid Organization soon began to control every aspect of farm life. In 1949 the state agricultural machinery pools were set up and acquired a virtual monopoly of larger agricultural machinery. By 1960 East German collectivization had been completed. Though the establishment of the agricultural production cooperatives (*Landwirtschaftliche Produktionsgenossenschaften*) was one of the most disputed measures taken by the G.D.R., the abundance of good agricultural machinery and artificial fertilizers, and, paradoxically, the partial depopulation of the countryside, contributed to the success of the experiment, the main success of this kind among the countries of the socialist camp. The "socialized sector," comprising nearly one-half of the productive agricultural land, is now under some form of collective ownership—state farms, other publicly owned farms, or agricultural production cooperatives.

Crops.—Between 1960-67, the wheat harvest rose by 50%, and its yield per hectare by 20%; the production of rye and potatoes remained stationary, that of barley doubled, and that of sugar beets increased by one-fifth.

Livestock.—Special attention was given to the increase of livestock and milk production in East Germany, but it still lagged behind the west. The number of cattle rose (1960-67) from 4,675,300 to 5,018,500, and of pigs from 8,316,100 to 9,253,900, which meant that by the late 1960s there were 40% more cattle and 66% more pigs in East Germany than before 1939.

2. Fisheries.—Although sea and coastal fishing had reached over 220,000 metric tons by the late 1960s, supply remained far below domestic demand. The catch is landed mainly at Rostock and Sassnitz, which are canning and preserving centres.

3. Forestry.—As in West Germany, after World War II the timber supply situation was difficult. Afforestation in East Germany amounted to about 65,000 ha. a year in the late 1950s. From 1966 to 1968 almost 101,000 ha. were forested. The production of sawn timber declined annually from 1950-68.

4. Industry.—Industry in East Germany was severely hampered during the first two years after the end of World War II by the extensive dismantling of equipment and its removal as reparations to the U.S.S.R. Factories, mining equipment, railway lines, and overhead electricity wires were among the items removed on a large scale, and in addition many thousands of skilled workers were deported to the U.S.S.R. In the industries left in their zone of occupation the Russians followed a policy of eliminating private ownership and enterprise as far as possible. Socialization of industry formally ended on April 17, 1948. At that time about half of the East German industrial production was under state or public ownership, about a quarter in the hands of the 126 industrial Soviet-owned enterprises known as Sowjet Aktiengesellschaften (SAG), and the rest in private hands.

As soon as the initial policy of dismantling and removal of equipment and installations to the U.S.S.R. had ceased, the Soviet authorities embarked on a more positive economic policy in their zone, and one aspect of this was a consistent effort to raise the level of industrial production. An expedient to this end was the adoption, as in the U.S.S.R., of concerted "plans." On June 30, 1948, a two-year plan was drawn up; and this was replaced, on Jan. 1, 1951, by the five-year plan, which was designed to double industrial production in the Democratic Republic by 1955.

The pressure on the population of the Democratic Republic to achieve the objects of the five-year plan led to much hardship and discontent, which formed one cause of riots in Berlin and elsewhere in June 1953. A few days earlier the government had decided to slacken the tempo, and the disturbances caused this "new course" to be emphasized still further. It involved concessions to private industry, a policy of labour incentives, and efforts to increase the quantity and reduce the prices of consumer goods. Also, the Soviet government in August 1953 announced the end of reparations from the Democratic Republic as from Jan. 1, 1954, cancellation of the republic's debts to the Soviet Union, a reduction in the costs of the Soviet forces of occupation, an increase in deliveries of goods from the Soviet Union, large credits, and finally the transfer of the 33 remaining SAGs to the republic. In March 1954 a second five-year plan was prepared, to follow the first at the end of 1955. Production was later geared to a seven-year plan (1959–65) which replaced the second five-year plan.

The seven-year plan had ambitious objectives. It was expected that industrial production would double in value as a result of an 85% increase in the productivity of labour. Continued emphasis was to be placed on basic materials and producer goods, the production of which was to be doubled, but it was also planned to increase the production of consumer goods by three-quarters in order to raise the standard of living. By the early 1960s total industrial production was four times as large as it had been ten years earlier, an increase comparable with West German production, which was twice as large as before World War II.

The total value of industrial production in the late 1960s amounted to more than DM. 100,000,000,000 ($24,700,000,000) annually, which placed the G.D.R. fifth in Europe and ninth in the world in terms of output. Calculated per capita, industrial production amounted to 85% of that of West Germany. About 80% of the gross national product fell to about 182,000 nationally owned industries.

Comparative production figures for East and West Germany are shown in Table VI above.

Manufacturing Industries.—Compared with the Federal Republic, the Democratic Republic had the major share of the production of textile machinery, electrical apparatus, and optical instruments. Heavy industry is located at Karl-Marx-Stadt, the lignite fields of Lower Lusatia, and East Berlin. A large part of the engineering products of East Germany is exported to the Soviet bloc. Steel construction and electrical industries have made big strides. Shipbuilding is of minor importance, although there is some development at Rostock.

Chemical production is based on lignite, plus potash and salt mined around the Harz, chiefly the Leunawerke near Merseburg. The principal heavy-chemical products are caustic soda, sulfuric acid, chlorine, synthetic ammonia, phosphate, nitrogen products, and calcium carbide. Pharmaceutical products, photographic supplies, perfumes, soaps, plastics, etc., are rather widely distributed in many of the major towns. The chemical industry accounted for more than one-sixth of total industrial production in the early 1960s, and there was subsequently a big increase in the production of plastics and artificial fibres. These industries were hard hit through their separation from the sources of prewar imports, and the clothing industry in East Berlin suffered from being cut off from Western markets. Cotton textiles have the biggest share of the total production. The production of man-made fibres is receiving high priority.

Metalworking industries accounted for nearly one-third of industrial production in the early 1960s, and the engineering industry provided nearly two-thirds of total exports. Machine tool production was to be increased by 150% during the seven-year plan.

5. Location of Industry.—The middle Elbe region is the main industrial area of East Germany. The predominantly industrial character of the hill country of Saxony is due in origin to the early development of handicrafts. It has a great variety of highly skilled machine and metalworking industries and is also a main seat for the production of textiles. Thuringia is also a seat of skilled industries, such as the making of hardware, toys, musical instruments, and porcelain. The lowland to the north of Saxony is an area of recent development, based entirely on the production of brown coal, together with salt and copper. It is mainly an area of new heavy industries. Close to the brown-coal workings are thermoelectric plants, chemical works, and glass production in Lower Lusatia.

Before World War II the middle Elbe area accounted for one-fifth of the industrial workers in the *Reich*, and in this respect it was as important as North Rhine-Westphalia. Eisenhüttenstadt on the Oder was a new and modern steel city with more than 40,-000 inhabitants. Schwedt on the Oder, which before 1939 was a provincial town with a population of 10,000, had risen by the late 1960s to a town with 30,000 inhabitants because it had become the terminal of the huge Kuibyshev (U.S.S.R.) pipeline; a large refinery converted the crude petroleum into its derivatives, and with Leuna, near Halle, Schwedt was now an important centre of the chemical industry.

The old and picturesque cities of Rostock and Stralsund on the Baltic, which had populations of 121,000 and 53,000 respectively in 1939, by the late 1960s had increased to 190,000 and 70,000 with the erection of large new shipyards.

6. Mining.—There are small bituminous coal fields in Saxony, notably near Zwickau, but by the early 1960s the whole production amounted to less than 3,000,000 metric tons annually. Brown coal was the main source of energy and its annual extraction in the late 1960s amounted to 250,000,000 metric tons, or two and one

TABLE VI.—*Industrial Production, 1950–68*

	East Germany		West Germany	
	1950	1968	1950	1968
Coal	2,805	1,584	110,755	112,012
Lignite	137,050	247,113	75,841	101,515
Metallurgical coke	259	2,921*	27,333	35,245*
Gas, manufactured	1,498	3,868	13,266	19,284
Gas, natural	—	—	68	5,787
Electricity	19,466	63,228	44,466	203,934
Iron ore (metal content)	100	360	2,900	2,300
Pig iron	337	2,333	9,473	30,305
Crude steel	1,257	4,695	12,121	41,159
Sulfuric acid†	300	1,078	1,446	4,210
Phosphate fertilizers‡	25	346	350	905
Nitrogen fertilizers§	231	351	440	1,567
Potash salt‖	1,336	2,293	912	2,561
Cement	1,412	7,551	10,877	33,443
Automobiles	7.2	114.6	216	2,862
Commercial vehicles	1.0	23.6	82	225

*1967. †In terms of 100% H_2SO_4. ‡In terms of pure P_2O_5. §In terms of pure N. ‖In terms of pure K_2O.

Sources: *Statistisches Jahrbuch für die Bundesrepublik Deutschland* (1969) and *Statistisches Jahrbuch der Deutschen Demokratischen Republik* (1969).

Figures are given in 000 metric tons, except for gas (000,000 cu.m.), electricity (000,000 kw.-hr.), and motor vehicles (000 units).

GERMANY

half times more than in 1936. By the late 1960s lignite production in the Democratic Republic had increased to more than 242,400,000 metric tons annually.

Production of iron ore increased between the late 1950s and the late 1960s, but it was still only about 490,000 metric tons annually. The output of pig iron increased sevenfold to about 2,500,000 metric tons and that of crude steel more than doubled, reaching about 4,500,000 metric tons annually; and, in the face of higher industrial output generally, the degree of self-sufficiency in metals had not improved.

The main fields of potash (2,006,000 metric tons annually) and rock salt lie east of the Harz around Stassfurt. Resources of copper (from the Harz), lead, and tin (the fields in upper Silesia were lost to Poland) are small. All mining operations are state controlled.

7. Power.—All producing and distributing enterprises were nationalized in 1946. The potential sources of hydroelectric power in East Germany are limited to the Erzgebirge (Ore Mountains) and the Sudeten (Sudeten Mountains). However, the Democratic Republic utilizes its large quantities of lignite, and in the mining areas mammoth thermoelectric plants are located. By the late 1960s capacity had increased more than four times since before World War II, and was over 60,000,000,000 kw.-hr. Nevertheless, the shortage of power was still one of the chief industrial bottlenecks in East Germany. The operation of a 70-Mw. prototype nuclear reactor began in 1966.

8. Trade.—The foreign trade of East Germany after World War II concentrated largely on the export of industrial goods of high quality, including textiles and chemicals, in return for food and raw materials. This trade became a state monopoly and was diverted mainly toward the U.S.S.R. and other Communist states. The decisive change in the direction of East German trade took place after 1948, the first year of ERP.

During the two-year plan of 1949–50 and the five-year plans which followed, the tendency was to integrate the economy of the Democratic Republic more closely with the Soviet bloc and gradually to make the republic independent of trade with the West.

After 1948 there was a rapid expansion in the trade of the Democratic Republic, which within a few years had the largest total trade turnover of any Eastern European country and was the most important trading partner of the U.S.S.R. By the late 1960s the total trade turnover of East Germany was equivalent to $6,-700,000,000, of which three-quarters was with other Communist countries. More than four-fifths of the imports consisted of vegetable products, minerals, foodstuffs, textiles, and metallurgical products, while chemicals and machinery of all kinds accounted for more than half the exports. The most important international trade fair takes place every autumn at Leipzig.

9. Finance.—The central administrative organs of the Soviet zone, which were the precursors of the ministries of the Democratic Republic, had no tax revenues of their own and were financed from contributions from the railways and postal services and from the various *Land* governments. However, in 1950 the financial system of the Democratic Republic was centralized. The authority to raise revenue and the right to receive the revenue were taken from the *Land* authorities and given to the central Ministry of Finance, which made allocations to the *Länder, Kreise,* and *Gemeinden* to enable them to carry on their necessary work of local administration. By the late 1960s annual government revenue was more than DM. 63,200,000,000.

Banking and Currency.—In 1948, after a separate currency reform had been carried out, the Deutsche Emissions- und Girobank was set up as a central bank for controlling the new currency. Its title was soon changed to Deutsche Notenbank, and from that time the new institution began to exercise an ever greater control over banking activities throughout the G.D.R. In 1951 the Deutsche Notenbank became the official state bank with functions enabling it to control the carrying out of long-term economic planning besides controlling note circulation and foreign exchange transactions. On Dec. 1, 1967, its name was changed to Staatsbank der Deutschen Demokratischen Republik and a woman, Grete Wittkowski, was appointed its president.

In 1953 the eastern Deutsche Mark was "revalued" at an exchange rate of 1 DM. Ost = 1.80 rubles. The third postwar currency reform took place in 1957, when old notes were exchanged at par but only in limited amounts. Officially at par with the western Deutsche Mark, the eastern Deutsche Mark was being exchanged in West Berlin at a rate far below its par value.

10. Transport and Communications.—After 1945 the railway network in East Germany suffered severely as a result of wholesale removal of rolling stock and tracks by the U.S.S.R. as reparations. They remained state owned and operated and had been largely reconstructed, completing more than 17,000,000,000 passenger-km. and a freight tonnage of 38,500,000,000 ton-km. annually. There are more than 10,000 mi. of railway track. The road network is highly developed and there are about 30,000 mi. (48,270 km.) of classified roads. There are about 1,650 mi. (2,675 km.) of navigable waterways. By the late 1960s the *Deutsche Seereederei* (DSR), founded in Rostock in 1952, had 300 ships of 100 tons and totaling over 642,000 gross register tons.

A new harbour was opened in Rostock in May 1960, and by 1969 goods loaded and unloaded there reached 7,300,000 metric tons. The G.D.R. was 11th in the world as a producer and 7th as an exporter. A canal from Niederneuendorf to Paretz, to the northwest of Berlin, designed to enable East German inland shipping to avoid using waterways of West Berlin, was opened to traffic in 1952. The East German Interflug (state airline) operates services to Moscow and the capitals of Eastern European and Arab countries.

All telephone, telegraph, radio, and television facilities are government owned and operated

See also references under "Germany" in the Index. (K. Sm.)

BIBLIOGRAPHY.—Current history and statistics are summarized annually in *Britannica Book of the Year. Physical Geography:* R. E. Dickinson, *Germany: a General and Regional Geography* (1953) with biblio.; F. Ratzel, *Deutschland,* 5th ed. (1945); E. de Martonne, *L'Europe Centrale,* 2 vol. in *Géographie Universelle* (1930–31); *Handbuch der Geographischen Wissenschaft,* ed. by F. Klute, *Das Deutsche Reich,* 2 vol. (1941); Publications of the *Bundesamt für Landeskunde* and of the *Institut für Raumforschung,* Bad Godesberg, including many volumes of regional studies of the *Forschungen zur deutschen Landeskunde* and the quarterly periodical *Raumforschung und Raumordnung;* Georg Müller, *Die Stadt- und Landkreise in der Statistik, Institut für Raumforschung,* with a series of maps of the Federal Republic of Germany (1959); E. Meynen (ed.), *Geographisches Taschenbuch: Jahrweiser zur deutschen Landeskunde* (annual 1949–)

The People: M. Haberlandt, *Die Völker Europas und des Orients* (1920); R. Much, *Deutsche Stämme,* 3rd ed. (1920); A. Haberlandt, "Die volkstümliche Kultur Europas in ihrer geschichtlichen Entwicklung," and M. Haberlandt, "Die indogermanischen Völker des Erdteils Europa," *Illustrierte Völkerkunde,* ed. by G. H. T. Buschan, 2nd ed. part 2 (1926); R. Beitl, *Wörterbuch der deutschen Volkskunde,* 2nd ed. (1955).

History: Ancient History: The classical sources on the ancient Germans are Caesar, Tacitus, Ammianus Marcellinus and Jordanes (qq.v.). See further T. Mommsen, *The Provinces of the Roman Empire,* ch. 5, Eng. trans. (1886); E. Gibbon, *Decline and Fall of the Roman Empire,* vol. i–vi, ed. by J. B. Bury (1909–14); J. B. Bury, *History of the Later Roman Empire From the Death of Theodosius I to the Death of Justinian,* vol. i (1923); *The Invasion of Europe by the Barbarians* (1928); Nils Aberg, *Archäologie der Völkerwanderungen* (1922); L. Schmidt, *Geschichte der deutschen Stämme bis zum Ausgang der Völkerwanderungen,* 2nd ed. (1934); E. A. Thompson, *History of Attila and the Huns* (1948).

Merovingians and Carolingians: The fundamental documents (diplomas, capitularies, cartularies, canons of councils and formularies) are printed in the various series of the *Monumenta Germaniae Historica* (1826–   ). See further L. Schmidt, *Geschichte der deutschen Stämme :...*, 2nd ed. (1934); W. Levison, *England and the Continent in the Eighth Century* (1946); *Aus rheinischer und fränkischer Frühzeit* (1948); L. Halphen, *Charlemagne et l'empire carolingien* (1947); J. Calmette, *L'Effondrement d'un empire* (1941). On the German Church see A. Hauck, *Kirchengeschichte Deutschlands,* 5 vol., vol. i–iv in 3rd and 4th ed. (1887–1920). For economic and social aspects see A. Dopsch, *The Economic and Social Foundations of European Civilization* (1937); *The Cambridge Economic History of Europe,* vol. i and ii (1941–52); E. Salin, *La Civilisation mérovingienne,* vol. i (1950). For further bibliography see W. Wattenbach, *Deutschlands Geschichtsquellen im Mittelalter,* rev. ed. by W. Levison, vol. i (1952); Boyd H. Hill, *The Rise of the First Reich: Germany in the Tenth Century* (1969); F. H. Bäuml, *Medieval Civilization in Germany* (1969). *German Kingdom From 911 to 1254:* J. W. Thompson, *Feudal Germany* (1928); G. Barraclough (ed.), *Mediaeval Germany 911–1250: Essays by German Historians* (1938), *The Origins of Modern Germany,*

2nd ed. (1948); F. Kern, *Kingship and Law in the Middle Ages*, Eng. trans. (1939); G. Tellenbach, *Church, State and Christian Society at the Time of the Investiture Contest*, Eng. trans. (1940); R. Holtzmann, *Geschichte der sächsischen Reiches*, 3rd ed. (1943); K. Hampe, *Deutsche Kaisergeschichte in der Zeit der Salier und Staufer*, 10th ed. (1949), K. Bosl, *Die Reichsministerialität der Salier und Staufer*, 3rd ed. (1955); K. Bosl, *Die Reichsministerialität der Salier und Staufer*, 2 vol. (1950–51).

Rise of the Habsburgs; T. Lindner, *Deutsche Geschichte unter den Habsburgern und Luxemburgern*, 2 vol. (1890–93); V. von Kraus and K. Kaser, *Deutsche Geschichte im Ausgang des Mittelalters*, 2 vol. (1888–1912); C. C. Bayley, *The Formation of the German College of Electors in the Mid-Thirteenth Century* (1947); F. L. Carsten, *The Origins of Prussia* (1954).

The Reformation to 1555: For the first half of the 16th century see J. Janssen, *History of the German People at the Close of the Middle Ages*, Eng. trans., 17 vol. (1896–1925); L. von Ranke, *Deutschland im Zeitalter der Reformation*, 6 vol., rev. ed. (1925–26); W. Andreas, *Deutschland am Vorabend der Reformation* (1932). For the later period, to the peace of Westphalia, see *Deutsche Geschichte im Zeitalter der Gegenreformation und des dreissigjährigen Krieges*, 3 vol. (1889–1908). See further works cited under CHARLES V and under the articles on the succeeding emperors; and THIRTY YEARS' WAR.

From 1648 to 1815: B. Erdmannsdörfer, *Deutsche Geschichte, 1648–1740*, 2 vol. (1892–93); K. T. von Heigel, *Deutsche Geschichte, 1786–1806*, 2 vol. (1899–1911); G. P. Gooch, *Germany and the French Revolution* (1920); H. Nicolson, *The Congress of Vienna* (1946); P. Rassow, *Deutsche Geschichte* (1953); and works cited in the bibliographies to articles on the emperors, kings, statesmen and wars cited in the text above, as well as under AUSTRIA, EMPIRE OF and PRUSSIA.

The German Empire. For general surveys of the period between 1815 and 1918 see F. Meinecke, *Weltbürgertum und Nationalstaat*, 7th ed. (1928); E. Vermeil, *L'Allemagne du congrès de Vienne à la révolution hitlérienne* (1934); H. von Srbik, *Deutsche Einheit*, 4 vol. (1935–42); J. H. Clapham, *The Economic Development of France and Germany, 1815–1914*, 4th ed. (1937); R. Pascal, *The Growth of Modern Germany* (1946); F. Schnabel, *Deutsche Geschichte im XIX. Jahrhundert*, 4 vol., new ed. (1948–51); also *The Zenith of European Power*, being vol. x of *The New Cambridge Modern History* (1960); T. S. Hamerow, *Restoration, Revolution, Reaction* (1958). For the revolution of 1848 in particular see V. Valentin, *Geschichte der deutschen Revolution von 1848–49*, 2 vol. (1930–31); J. Droz, *Les Révolutions allemandes de 1848*; abridged Eng. trans.; *1848: Chapters on German History*, 1940). For Bismarckian Germany see E. Brandenburg, *Die Reichsgründung* (1922); J. Ziekursch, *Politische Geschichte des neuen deutschen Kaiserreiches*, 3 vol. (1925–30); H. Goldschmidt, *Das Reich und Preussen im Kampf um die Führung; von Bismarck bis 1918* (1931); E. Eyck, *Bismarck*, 3 vol. (1941–44); A. J. P. Taylor, *The Struggle for Mastery in Europe, 1848–1918* (1954); *Bismarck: the Man and the Statesman* (1955); F. Darmstaedter, *Bismarck and the Creation of the Second Reich* (1948). For Germany under William II see E. Eyck, *Das persönliche Regiment Wilhelms II: politische Geschichte des deutschen Kaiserreiches von 1890 bis 1914* (1948). For the parties see L. Bergsträsser, *Geschichte der politischen Parteien in Deutschland*, 3rd ed. (1924); K. Bachem, *Vorgeschichte, Geschichte und Politik der deutschen Zentrumspartei*, 9 vol. (1927–32); T. Eschenburg, *Das Kaiserreich am Scheideweg: Bassermann, Bülow und der Block* (1929). For colonial policy see M. E. Townsend, *The Rise and Fall of Germany's Colonial Empire, 1884–1918* (1930); A. J. P. Taylor, *Germany's First Bid for Colonies, 1884–1885* (1938; reprinted 1967). For World War I see A. Rosenberg, *Birth of the German Republic*, Eng. trans. (1931); F. P. Chambers, *The War Behind the War, 1914–1918* (1939); H. W. Gatzke, *Germany's Drive to the West* (1950); J. W. Wheeler-Bennett, *Brest-Litovsk, the Forgotten Peace, March 1918* (1938).

The Weimar Republic (1919–33): Adolf Hitler, *Speeches, April 1922–1939*, ed. by N. H. Baynes, 2 vol. (1943); Alan Bullock, *Hitler: a Study in Tyranny* (1952); A. and V. M. Toynbee, *Hitler's Europe* (1954); W. L. Shirer, *The Rise and Fall of the Third Reich* (1960); B. A. Carroll, *Design for Total War: Arms and Economics in the Third Reich* (1968); E. B. Wheaton, *Prelude to Calamity: the Nazi Revolution, 1933–1935* (1969). On special aspects see C. W. Guillebaud, *The Economic Recovery of Germany From 1933 ... to 1938* (1939); E. Wiskemann, *The Rome-Berlin Axis* (1949); Georg R. Bluhm, *Détente and Military Relaxation in Europe: a German View*, in Adelphi Papers no. 40, Institute for Strategic Studies (1967); Joachim C. Fest, *The Face of the Third Reich*, trans. (1970).

Since World War II: W. H. Chamberlin, *The German Phoenix* (1963); W. W. Schütz, *Rethinking German Policy: New Approaches to Reunification*, trans. (1967); R. Flenley, *Modern German History*, with additional chapters covering 1939–45 and postwar years to 1968 by R. Spencer, 4th ed. (1968); David Childs, *East Germany* (1969).

ersten deutschen Demokratie (1946); G. Scheele, *The Weimar Republic: Overture to the Third Reich* (1946); E. Vermeil, *L'Allemagne contemporaine*, vol. ii (1954); J. W. Wheeler-Bennett, *The Nemesis of Power: the German Army in Politics, 1918–45* (1953).

The Third Reich: Adolf Hitler, ... S. W. Halperin, *Germany Tried Democracy* (1946); N. Stampfer, *Die 14 Jahre der ersten deutschen Demokratie*.

Administration and The Economy: J. K. Pollock and H. Thomas, *Germany in Power and Eclipse* (1952); Ralf Dahrendorf, *Society and Democracy in Germany* (1967); H. W. Flannery and G. H. Seger, *Which Way Germany?* (1968); T. H. Elkins, *Germany* (1968); R. B. Tilford and R. J. C. Preece, *Federal Germany: Political and Social Order* (1969); R. F Bunn, *German Politics and the Spiegel Affair* (1968); F. C. Hunnius, *Student Revolts: the New Left in West Germany* (1968); ... of each *Land*; N. J. G. Pounds and W. N. Parker, *Coal and Steel in Western Europe* (1957); J. Chardonnet, *Les Grandes Puissances: Étude Économique, Tome I, L'Europe*, 2nd ed. (1957); L. Erhard, *Germany's Comeback to the World Market* (1954); Gustav Stolper, *The German Economy; 1870 to the Present*, trans. by Toni Stolper, rev. ed. (1967). The standard geographical monographs are *Forschungen zur deutschen Landeskunde*, 70 vol. (1945–). Statistical Sources: *Statistisches Jahrbuch der Deutschen Demokratischen Republik* (annual); *Wirtschaft und Statistik* (monthly 1949–); *Statistisches Jahrbuch für die Bundesrepublik Deutschland*; Statistisches Bundesamt (annual).

GERMFREE LIFE

GERMFREE LIFE, the existence of plants and animals in the absence of all demonstrable living microorganisms. It is an extension of the pure culture concept of microbiology wherein one species can be isolated from all other species. The terms "germfree," "axenic," and "sterile" are all included in the term "gnotobiotic," derived from the Greek meaning "known life." Gnotobiotics includes the study both of germfree life and of life in which known microorganisms are present either naturally or by experimental introduction. The component parts of a living system may be treated as integral units after separating the host from its normal load of microorganisms, its microflora. When one or more known species of microorganisms are added to a germfree plant or animal, the host is of course no longer germfree, but both the host and the introduced species are gnotobiotic since they are the only species present that are known to the investigator.

Historical Background.—Before germfree animals were obtained, germfree plants were used to resolve the controversy concerning nitrogen fixation by legumes. In 1858 J. B. Boussingault found nitrogen fixation occurred in lupines grown on unsterile soil but not in those grown on sterile soil. He attributed this action to the "organic corpuscles," or nodes, on the roots of the plants grown on unsterile soil. These nodes were shown to harbour bacteria by H. Hellriegel and H. Wilforth when they repeated the experiment in 1888. Pasteur thought that animal life without bacteria was impossible because bacteria were needed for the digestion of natural foodstuffs. In early experiments, in the 1890s, germfree animals did not grow or survive beyond two weeks. Within two decades, success was obtained when M. Cohendy (1912) raised germfree chicks and E. Küster (1911–15) raised germfree goats for two months. Following G. Glimstedt's publication (1936) of a monograph on the underdeveloped lymphatic system in germfree guinea pigs, three laboratories began rearing germfree animals. The methods and momentum developed by J. A. Reyniers and associates in the United States, B. E. Gustafsson in Sweden, and M. Miyakawa in Japan elucidated the characteristics of germfree animals and laid the foundation for further progress. The establishment of germfree animal colonies and the development of inexpensive plastic isolators provided a base for new industries and easy access to both animals and equipment. Predictably, much future work will involve studies of the reactions of germfree animals to inoculation with specific microorganisms.

Methods and Techniques.—Germfree chicks, turkeys, and Japanese quail can be obtained by passing surface sterilized eggs through a germicidal trap into a sterile isolator where they are allowed to hatch. The eggs must be obtained from flocks free from microorganisms that invade the egg in the oviduct. Germfree plants can be obtained from seeds that have been surface sterilized. The fetus of mammals is normally bacteriologically sterile, and germfree young can be obtained by Caesarian operation, under germfree conditions, with transfer of the mature embryo into a sterile isolator. These young must be fed by hand to avoid contamination by the mother. Subsequent reproduction

phological differences, such as the small liver in many germfree animals, are not always apparent in individual cases but can be shown statistically. Most germfree animals show a histologic regularity that has been described as textbook perfect in its lack of flaws. This clarity of germfree tissues contrasts with the mildly inflammatory digestive and respiratory tissues of conventional animals.

Growth rates are faster in germfree animals than in conventional animals. The average number of viable young at birth and at weaning is higher in germfree colonies than in most conventional colonies. Germfree animals share with conventional animals a variety of stress reactions, such as radiation sickness, hemorrhagic shock, and anal block, with similar symptoms and pathology, with the exception of terminal infection. Carcinogenesis follows a similar route when chemical carcinogens are applied to germfree and conventional animals. Spontaneous tumours are rarer in germfree animals. Transmissible tumours, such as mammary tumours, do not occur spontaneously in germfree mice. The respiratory exchange and circulation of germfree rats seem to be lower than that of conventional animals. Although longevity has not been studied systematically, the lifespan of germfree mice has been observed to be about one-fourth longer than that of conventional mice.

Nutritional studies reflect the morphological and physiological finding that germfree animals have more efficient food utilization. Apparently the germfree animal, requiring less energy for defense mechanisms, puts relatively more energy into growth. Intestinal microorganisms produce some vitamins that are utilized by the conventional host; lacking such assistance, germfree rats require dietary folic acid, biotin, and vitamin K. On the other hand, germfree rats may require lower quantities of amino acids than do conventional rats. This suggests that the intestinal microflora may compete with the host for scarce nutrients. Iron salts are poorly absorbed by germfree rodents while calcium is more readily absorbed. Germfree mice and rats have more calculi ("stones") in the kidney and bladder. Dietary antibiotics stimulate growth to a lesser extent in germfree chicks and turkeys than they do in conventional animals; the direct action of dietary antibiotics is of less importance than the indirect action via the intestinal microorganisms. Germfree animals have more digestive enzymes in the lower tract and excreta than have conventional animals, suggesting that intestinal bacteria degrade these products.

A variety of immunological studies hinge upon the underdeveloped lymphatic system, the negligible antibody production, and the absence of bactericidal serum lysozyme. The blood has almost no gamma globulins. Plasma cells and secondary reaction centres are missing in lymphatic and thymic tissues in germfree guinea pigs. Since these defense mechanisms can be readily activated, the machinery is not defective.

The Exploitation of Germfree Life.—Germfree life is useful in theoretical biology for understanding the role of the intestinal microflora in the host and for learning the characteristics of animals living free of microorganisms. Germfree animals are essential to the study of physiological diseases in the absence of infection. Germfree animals are especially valuable for standards for studies in toxicology and pollution and in vaccine testing, because their decreased variability gives increased assay reliability. The noticeable effects of an external force such as radiation or a noxious gas are easily distinguishable from secondary effects and infection.

The germfree animal is a useful tool in the search for life on other planets. Space rockets, effectively sterilized to avoid contaminating other planets with earth's microorganisms, will someday bring back extraterrestrial material in isolation chambers. Samples of these celestial bodies will be inoculated into germfree animals to culture whatever can be nourished within a gnotobiote.

New industries have arisen to produce germfree animals and accessory equipment. Germfree techniques also have been used for sterile surgery. A plastic isolator is glued onto the germicide-treated skin and the operation proceeds with both patient and doctor outside; only the instruments are actually inside the iso-

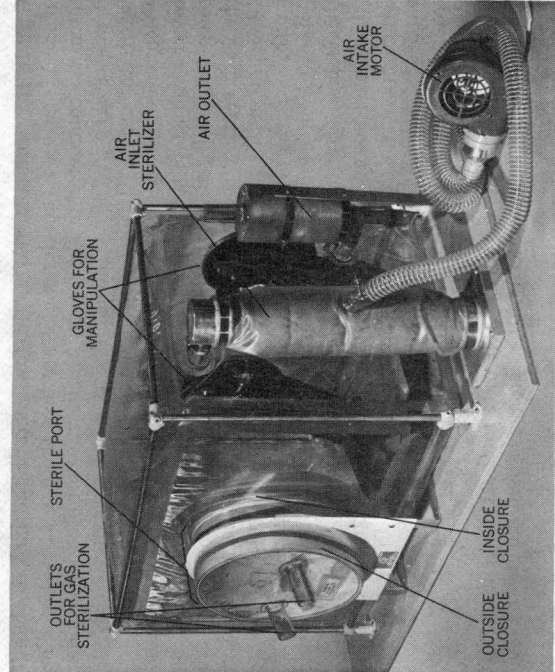

GERMFREE CHAMBER

G-F SUPPLY DIVISION, STANDARD SAFETY EQUIPMENT CO., PALATINE, ILL.

of hand-reared germfree mammals allows routine production of germfree colonies. Germfree rats or mice can be purchased from breeding companies and simply transferred aseptically from the animal colony isolator into a shipping isolator; after shipment, the animals are transferred from the shipping container into the experimental isolator.

The isolator is a physical barrier through which no living microorganisms can pass. It may be a small or large container, usually made of glass and steel or plastic, with plastic or rubber gloves. A sterile room may also serve as an isolator. The laboratory isolator has an entry for the organism, food, and utensils; a source of air with exhaust; and most have arm-length gloves. Food and utensils are sterilized and taken into the isolator through an adjoining area called the sterile lock. Special attachments may be a liquid dip tank, a shipping cage, a bacterial filter for liquids, or a second isolator. The most widely used isolator is a soft plastic sacklike container that comes in many shapes and sizes. Sterilization of metal isolators and most utensils is accomplished with steam under pressure. Germicidal vapour sterilization (2% peracetic acid) is used for plastic isolators, which cannot endure the heat of steam sterilization. Air for the isolated organism is sterilized by mechanical filtration through fine glass wool. Eggs are surface treated with mercuric chloride and seeds with peracetic acid or formalin. Food and water are sterilized by steam, irradiation, or filtration, depending upon the requirements of the investigation.

Diets fed to germfree animals are comparable to those fed conventional animals (often termed "classic" animals) with the following exceptions. Certain vitamins are added to supplement chemically defined, synthetic diets and some natural diets. Additional fibre is recommended in diets for germfree rodents and rabbits.

Microbiological tests for living microorganisms are the key to all aspects of theoretical and practical germfree life. The criterion of germfreeness—no contaminating microorganisms—is established by direct examination and exhaustive laboratory tests. These, plus symptomatic data from the organisms themselves, take two weeks to establish that a given plant or animal is germfree.

The Appearance and Condition of Germfree Animals.—Germfree chicks, turkeys, Japanese quail, guppies, dogs, cats, pigs, sheep, goats, and monkeys have a normal general appearance. In germfree rodents and rabbits an enlarged caecum may show as an overfull abdomen. (Inoculation of certain bacteria reduces the contents of these caeca dramatically within 24 hours.) Lymph nodes of germfree animals are one-third as large as those of conventional animals. (Injection of antigen causes a two-fold increase in the lymph node size within 24 hours.) Other mor-

lator. Larger germfree units are being used to house patients under specific pathogen-free conditions for heavy irradiation therapy or for treatment of severe and extensive burns. By maintaining pathogen-free conditions the patient has a better chance for survival.

Gnotobiological research has begun to clarify certain long-standing questions regarding many common health problems. Germfree studies on tooth decay have implicated certain infectious bacteria. Similarly, it has been shown that the protozoan responsible for amoebic dysentery and the distemper virus do not give classic clinical or histopathologic syndromes unless certain bacteria are present.

Articles on germfree life and gnotobiotic research appear in many different journals. Reviews of the state of knowledge in this field appear frequently in *Advances in Applied Microbiology* and in *Annals of Surgery*, among other annual reviews. Reports of symposia and meetings are listed in *Biological Abstracts, Index Medicus,* and in *Applied Science and Technology Index.* Popular writings on these subjects are listed in *Readers' Guide to Periodical Literature.*

(T. D. L.)

BIBLIOGRAPHY.—M. Miyakawa and T. D. Luckey (eds.), *Advances in Germfree Research and Gnotobiology* (1968); M. Coates (ed.), *The Germ-free Animal in Research* (1968); E. C. Dougherty, "Axenic Culture of Invertebrate Metazoa," *Ann. N.Y. Acad. Sci.,* vol. 77 (1959); T. D. Luckey, *Germfree Life and Gnotobiology* (1963), includes an extensive bibliography and chronology of important events in gnotobiological research.

GERONA, a maritime frontier province and its capital city, situated in northeastern Spain. The province was formed in 1883 from parts of Catalonia. It is bounded on the north by France and the Pyrenees, east and southeast by the Mediterranean sea, southwest and west by Barcelona and northwest by Lérida. Pop. (1960) 351,369. Area 2,273 sq.mi. The region is rich in historical associations (*see* CATALONIA), and it has acted as the guardian of the passes through the Pyrenees at the eastern end, performing the same service as Roncesvalles in the west. The three main rivers, the Ter, Muga and Fluviá, rise in the Pyrenees, flow in a southeasterly direction to the Mediterranean, draining the fertile coastal plain of Ampurdán. The lower slopes of the Pyrenees are well wooded with oak, pine and chestnut. Cape Creus, a marked feature of the coast line, is the most easterly point of the Iberian peninsula. The climate varies locally. The high valley of Cerdaña and other mountainous tracts are cold for most of the year, while features. The coastal fisheries are important especially at Llansá, Rosas, Palamós and Blanes. The cork industry flourishes at San Feliu de Guixols (with fisheries), Palafrugell and Cassá de la Selva. There is also a little metalliferous mining. Much use is made of water power, and the linen, cotton and general textile manufactures are important. Figueras was long a most important frontier fortress. Gerona was held by government troops during the civil war of 1936-39 until after the capture of Barcelona on Jan. 26, 1939.

(X.)

The city of GERONA is built on a plain adjoining the foothills of the Angeles mountains. Pop. (1960) 32,784. It is crossed from south to north by the Oñar river, which enters the Ter on the urban boundary. Gerona can be divided into three zones: the interior (which includes all the old part of the town), the town extension and the part outside this. Main roads passing through the town include that from Madrid to France, via La Junquera; others originate in the town. The international railway line of the Red Nacional de Ferrocarriles Españoles (RENFE) passes through Gerona, which is also on the line to Olot and to San Feliu de Guixols.

Industrially Gerona is important. Milk pasteurization, filtering, freezing and preserving are carried on at the municipal central dairy; there are two flour mills, a biscuit factory, a confectionery factory, two distilleries and several mineral water factories. Textile manufacture is considerable, and, in addition, there is a paper mill, a publishing house, several chemical factories, a soap factory, and factories making detergents, machinery, electronic equipment and motorcycles.

Gerona was a fortified site of the Iberians (remains of walls of the 4th or 5th centuries B.C. are preserved) and of the Romans (Oppidum Gerundae), because of its position on the route from Gaul to the peninsula. After the town had passed into the hands of the Visigoths, a church council was held there in 516-517. The town was conquered in 714 by the Muslims, who called it Jerunda; it was retaken in 785 by the Franks, who lost it again in 793. It was recaptured by Louis of Aquitania in 797. In the 11th century a Romanesque cathedral was built, of which the cloisters and tower (known as the Charlemagne tower) still exist. In 1285 the town was besieged by the French king Philip III the Bold. In the 15th century the first bank was formed; printing appeared in 1483, and in this period also the work of the town's gold and silversmiths was highly regarded. The university was founded by Alfonso V in 1446. The city has three museums. Parks include the Dehesa, granted in the 15th century.

Gerona took an active part in the 17th-18th-century wars between Spain and France, and was besieged several times by both parties. It was beleaguered several times also by Napoleon's troops, the siege of 1808-09 being particularly memorable. The War of Independence left the town's fortunes at a low ebb, and their revival was hindered by civil wars in the 19th century. It has completely recovered from the damage caused during the civil war of 1936-39.

(J. T. Ca.)

GERONIMO (c. 1829-1909) was a leader but not chief of the Chiricahua tribe of Apache. (*See* APACHE.) Geronimo gave June 1829 as the date of his birth and stated that the place was No-doyohn canyon, Arizona. His mother taught him tribal legends. Geronimo said that when a boy he "would practise stealing" and "feats of war." He rose to leadership of a faction of braves by exhibiting extraordinary courage, determination and skill in successive raids of vengeance upon Mexicans, by whom his mother, wife and children had been killed in 1858. Devastating Apache raids and massacres in Arizona and New Mexico brought action by the U.S. army under command of Gen. George F. Crook which placed offenders, including Geronimo, on reservations. In 1876 Geronimo fled to Mexico. During the following decade he led outlaw bands in intermittent raids against American settlers. In 1886 General Crook finally succeeded in bringing Geronimo to a meeting wherein he and his Apache warriors agreed to surrender if they would be taken to Florida where their families were being held. The terms were agreed to, but on the way the Indians escaped. General Crook was replaced by Gen. Nelson A. Miles, who after months of pursuit finally secured another conditional surrender of the elusive Geronimo and followers. During this final campaign, which lasted 18 months, no fewer than 5,000 troops and 500 Indian auxiliaries had been employed in the apprehension of a band of Apaches comprising only 35 men, 8 boys and 101 women, who operated in two countries without bases of supply. Army and civilian losses totaled 95; Mexican losses were heavy but unknown. Geronimo's losses were 13 killed, but none from direct U.S. army action.

By orders from Pres. Grover Cleveland, and contrary to terms agreed upon by Miles, Geronimo and 14 companions were placed under military confinement, finally, at Ft. Sill, Okla. There Geronimo was allowed to carry on stock raising and farming. Before his death on Feb. 17, 1909, this most cunning of Indian fighters dictated to S. M. Barrett *Geronimo's Story of His Life* (1906).

See Britton Davis, *The Truth About Geronimo,* ed. by Milo M. Quaife (1951). (O. W.)

GERONTOCRACY, government by old men. The degree to which the old are accorded prestige and status varies greatly from society to society and from one social class to another. Yet in both primitive and highly developed societies and in many, particularly religious, organizations it frequently works out that major policy determination, executive and administrative responsibility, and judicial authority rest in the hands of older people.

In advanced societies outstanding creative works in the arts and sciences are most frequently produced by men in their 30s. The qualities and conditions that make for governmental leadership, however, seem to develop more slowly and to combine in such a way that outstanding leaders as a group are notably older than outstanding scientists are at the time they produce their greatest work.

Among primitive societies the vast majority have older men

serving as chieftains, as counselors and in judicial roles. Among Australian tribes, especially, aged men have great authority, and it is here that the best examples of what approaches a "true" gerontocracy—rule by the old men as a class—exist. The Dieri, e.g., are reported to have had, within a general assembly made up of all men fully initiated into adulthood, a great council made up of aged men. This council made the major decisions, administered justice, and regulated the ceremonies and movements of the group.

Relevant facts for more highly developed societies are often a matter of public record, thus permitting a clearer assessment of the role of the aged in governmental matters than is possible in the instance of primitive groups. But surveys in both primitive and advanced societies indicate that, strictly speaking, gerontocracy as a form of government seldom exists. Rather there is often a disproportionate representation of older men in governmental activities. Successful candidates for president of the United States are most frequently nominated and most frequently serve when between 55 and 59 years of age. Notable exceptions were Theodore Roosevelt and John F. Kennedy, who became president at the ages of 42 and 43 respectively. Peak years of service of prime ministers of England and of presidents of republics other than the United States have also been between 55 and 59. Members of the U.S. presidents' cabinets have most often served when between 50 and 54 years of age, members of the British cabinet, 55 and 59. Where electoral terms are long (as in France) or where appointment is for life, or continued tenure is contingent upon personal desire of the incumbent, a much greater age during service is recorded. Thus, appointments to the U.S. supreme court are most frequently made at ages 55 to 59, but over 85% of the service rendered is by men beyond 65. A variety of evidence suggests that new movements are more frequently started by young men, but as the organization becomes established and stable, older men dominate in the government. In the United States, the passage of time has brought an increased emphasis upon older leadership. For example, the mean ages of representatives and senators in 1799 were 43.5 and 45.25 years respectively. By the mid-1920s mean ages had increased to 53.46 years for representatives and 57.5 for senators. Along with increased age of the groups as a whole, considerable weight is given to seniority in committee and other assignments through which power is wielded.

In general, there appears to be no uniform or even clearly defined pattern of gerontocracy in either primitive or modern societies, though in both there is a strong tendency in this general direction. Rarely is advanced age in itself a sufficient qualification for an important post; usually old leaders had attained prominence in some way in their prime and have maintained their prominence into old age. Old men occupy influential positions in overwhelming numbers compared to old women. And, finally, the old are more likely to have governmental responsibility in the more stable societies with advanced economies and more complex organizations.

A number of reasons for the widespread political power of older people suggest themselves. It may be that the qualities required for leadership emerge more slowly than other capacities, that the reputation and broad personal contacts necessary for vote getting and the experience needed to function effectively require years to develop or that older persons, being more conservative and ...ence more interested in the maintenance of the *status quo*, are ...ore highly motivated to seek and retain office. On the other ...and, the reasons may lie in the characteristics of the groups which ...ppoint or elect leaders. It has been suggested that a basic con...ervatism of the mass of the party membership results in the re-...eated nomination and election of those who by virtue of previous ...fficeholding have served a long "apprenticeship" to the party

and represent familiar faces in whom the general population can have confidence. Moreover, the organization of the political group may be a factor in determining the ease with which younger men are introduced into positions of leadership. In groups autocratic in structure vigorous action by the central figures may force a certain mobility of younger talent, not so possible under the election systems of democratic parties. Of interest in this connection is the fact that in the French national assembly of 1946 about 33% of the deputies from the Communist party (a highly centralized party) were under 36 years of age whereas only 8% of the deputies from the Socialist party were under 36. The latter party, although characterized by a strong organization, is highly decentralized and has a highly democratic system for the appointment of leaders. The rules, procedures and customs of political parties may thus play a significant role in determining the relative influence of the young and the old. (R. G. Kn.)

GERONTOLOGY AND GERIATRICS. Gerontology is the scientific study of the phenomena of aging. By aging is meant the progressive changes that take place in a cell, a tissue, an organ system, a total organism or a group of organisms with the passage of time. All living things change with time in both structure and function, and the changes that follow a general trend constitute aging. Aging is part of the developmental sequence of the entire life span. Beginning with conception, this developmental sequence includes prenatal growth and development, birth, infancy, childhood, adolescence, maturity and senescence. Aging is a normal part of this total process. However, gerontology is concerned primarily with the changes that occur between the attainment of maturity and the death of the individual and with the factors that influence these changes. These factors may range from heredity to climate and they may include social customs and attitudes. Some investigators believe that aging results from the accumulation of random trauma, such as disease and malfunction, during the lifetime. Others believe that aging is due to an intrinsic process that is fundamental, inevitable and irreversible. Both views agree that aging can, in general, be represented as a progressing inability to cope with environmental demands and is reflected in an increasing probability of death as individuals age.

The problems of gerontology fall into four major categories: (1) social and economic problems precipitated by the increasing number of elderly people in the population; (2) psychological aspects of aging, which include intellectual performance and personal adjustment; (3) physiological bases of aging, along with pathological deviations and disease processes; and (4) general biological aspects of aging in all animal species.

Gerontology, a relatively new science, utilizes the methodologies of many other scientific disciplines, such as biology, genetics, biochemistry, physiology, psychology, medicine and the social sciences. The goal of research in gerontology is to learn more about the aging process—not for the purpose of extending the life span but so that the disabilities and handicaps of old age can be minimized.

Geriatrics is the branch of medical science concerned with the prevention and treatment of diseases in older people; it is thus a part of the broader field of gerontology.

Social and Economic Aspects.—The social and economic problems of elderly people in the United States centre around employment, income maintenance after retirement, compulsory retirement because of age, housing, adequate utilization of the talents of aged people, and methods of financing adequate medical and hospital care. Although these problems have always been present, they became especially acute after 1950 because of the increase in the actual and also in the relative number of elderly people in the population.

Between 1900 and 1970 the population of the United States nearly tripled, but the number of persons aged 65 years and over increased seven times. In 1900 only about 4.1% of the United States population was 65 years of age and over; the percentage increased in 1940 to 6.8, in 1950 to 8.1, in 1960 to 9.2, and in 1970 to 9.9. In 1970 there were 20,000,000 people in that age category. Similar shifts in the proportion of older people in the population were taking place throughout the world. In highly developed countries such as France the percentage of the population over age 65 in the mid-1960s was as high as 12%, whereas in underdeveloped countries it was only 3% or 4%. The cultural pattern, economic level, public health status, birthrates and the death rates for the various age groups play a major role in determining the proportion of older people in a population.

The average life expectancy in the United States increased from about 47 years in 1900 to 71 years in 1960, largely because of a reduction in the deaths of infants and children. The average life span for females in 1970 in the United States was seven years greater than for males (74 years to 67 years). One important social result of this difference in longevity is that with increasing age there is a greater proportion of females in the population. At birth there are approximately 104 males per 100 females. At age 65 and over, however, there were in 1950, 1,115 women for every 1,000 men; in 1960, 1,207 women, and in 1970, 1,385 women for every 1,000 men. In the age groups over 65, 18% of the men were widowers, whereas 54% of the females were widows. These facts have important implications for housing, community programs and retirement plans.

There was a general trend in the U.S. in the late 1960s toward reduction of employment among the elderly. Many surveys have shown that older workers are at a disadvantage in the labour market and a number of suggestions for improving their work opportunities were made. These proposals included legislation prohibiting discrimination in employment because of age and the establishment of special counseling and placement facilities for elderly workers. In 1890, 68.2% of the male population aged 65 and over was employed, compared with 38.7% in 1954 and about 25% in 1969. After age 70, only 18% of the males were working. The adoption of policies of forced retirement at a given chronological age significantly reduced employment among the aged. Studies of physiological or psychological capacities indicate that performance ability does not decrease suddenly at any specific age. Furthermore, the 65-year-old person of today is probably healthier than his counterpart of 50 or 60 years ago. Hence, many individuals who are forced into retirement are still capable of working effectively.

Although the income of the aged improved markedly between 1950 and 1970, older persons still had less than half the income of their younger counterparts. In 1948 approximately 3,500,000 (32%) of the 11,500,000 persons aged 65 and over in the United States had no money income of their own. By 1954 only about 24% of that group received no income and by 1963 only about 5% were in that category. The improvement in the economic status was brought about by the benefits provided by the federal Old Age, Survivors, Disability and Health Insurance program (Social Security). About 98 out of every 100 jobs are covered by this insurance on a contributory (tax) basis. Even so, in 1970 about 150,000 families headed by a person over 65 had incomes of less than $1,000 a year, and 1,100,000 older people living alone or with nonrelatives had incomes of less than $1,000.

Although elderly people who are maintained in institutions are often regarded as the aged in the U.S., they represent only a small proportion of the elderly. In 1970, for instance, 95% of the persons aged 65 or over were living in households of some kind. About 66% of older men live in families with their wives but only about 33% of older women live in families that include their husbands. Only 5% of the older population live in institutions for the aged or in mental hospitals.

Although no single formula is adequate for describing the housing preferences of the elderly, privacy and independence without segregation or isolation are the qualities most commonly desired. The healthy aged usually want housing of an appropriate type that is situated close to community services, members of their families and their friends. Most want above all freedom to choose their own living arrangements. The federal government recognized the need of elderly people for improved housing and in the 1960s encouraged the construction of specially designed units for the elderly in connection with many low-cost housing projects. In addition to

such federally subsidized housing projects, a number of communities for aged were developed. Church and fraternal groups also sponsored low-cost housing for the elderly.

Psychological Aspects.—Aging usually is accompanied by a gradual impairment of a number of sensory functions. However, many individuals live to an old age without substantial impairment. Quantitative measurements of auditory acuity have demonstrated that hearing loss with increasing age is greater in males than in females and is more severe for high-pitched tones than for low tones. The impairment for the higher tones in persons over 50 is of psychological significance since the perception of higher frequencies is important in the understanding of conversation. Similarly, visual acuity diminishes with increasing age but is more closely related to the development of diseases of the eye than to age itself. Losses in hearing acuity because of aging are readily corrected by hearing devices and vision can be improved by corrective lenses or by simply increasing the brightness of the illumination.

Perhaps the most outstanding feature of aging is the gradual slowing of responses. However, when the elderly individual is given ample time he is able to discriminate almost as well as a young person. Although early studies indicated that intelligence declines as age advances, the tests used in these studies were developed primarily for school children and young adults. When the aged are given all the time they wish on tests that are not heavily dependent upon school skills, their performance is only slightly poorer than that of young adults. Performance change because of age varies considerably in different types of tests. For instance, decrement is very small on tests that depend on vocabulary, general information and well-practised activities. Decrement is largest on tests in which associations formed early in life must be superseded or displaced by new ones.

Experimental evidence indicates that older people can continue to learn throughout their lives. However, their rate of acquisition of a new skill may be somewhat slower than in young adults and is greatly influenced by the degree of motivation. In older people, learning is also apt to be slower than in the young because of interference from previously learned material.

Historical evidence supports the view that age in itself is no deterrent to creativity; many examples of major achievements in the arts and sciences have been reported for people of advanced age. Systematic surveys indicate, however, that outstanding achievements, particularly in the physical and biological sciences, are more apt to occur at an early than at a late age. In other areas of activity, e.g., politics and administration, the maturity and experience of a lifetime are important factors in determining achievement.

Many studies indicate the influence of different factors on personal adjustment in old age. Among them, health and income play important roles. Although high income does not assure good adjustment, an adequate income is essential. Health status is a source of concern to many elderly people, but the social and economic results of ill health are perhaps more important to them than is physical status itself. Older people who live in a community are more apt to be well adjusted than those living in institutions. It seems apparent that the maintenance of a broad spectrum of activities and interests is the best insurance against maladjustment in old age.

Other studies have shown that the conception of increased rigidity and conservatism among older people has little basis in fact. It has also been found that industrial workers are much more willing to accept retirement than are professional people. Such findings have important implications for the organization of programs in the field of aging.

Physiological Aspects of Aging.—Since the probability of death increases with age, it is assumed that changes must take place within the individual with the passage of time. However, the general pattern of change is a gradual reduction in the performance of an organ system; this reduction begins by the age of 30 or 35 and continues throughout life. There is no evidence that aging begins precipitously at any given chronological age. There are wide individual differences in aging among different people, so that some individuals of 70 may possess the performance capacities of the average 50-year-old. Age also reduces the ability of the individual to deal with physiological stresses. Even abilities that show no age change in the resting state show significant differences in the degree of displacement and rate of recovery following a stimulus.

For example, when the blood sugar level is raised experimentally it requires more time to return to normal in an elderly person than in a young person, even though fasting blood sugar levels are the same in young and old. Experimental evidence indicates that aging is accompanied by loss of reserve capacities in many organ systems.

Although aging and disease are often mistakenly regarded as synonymous, no disease is limited solely to the later years of life. Certain disorders, however, are common in senescence; they include arteriosclerosis (hardening of the arteries), hypertension (high blood pressure), diabetes, arthritis, gout and cancer. Of these, the disorders involving the circulation (arteriosclerosis and hypertension) and therefore the heart are by far the most important. These diseases, along with cancer, are the leading causes of death in elderly people. Their causation is largely from within the body rather than from obvious external sources such as infection. They arise as a result of the summation of many superimposed insults and in no two instances are the causative factors necessarily identical.

Biological Aspects of Aging.—Aging is a biological process that occurs in all organisms; the length of life is one index of the rate of aging. Life spans differ greatly among different species; some insects, such as the May fly, live only one day, whereas some tortoises have been known to live 177 years. The greatest plausible record of human longevity is 113 years. Aging and life span are influenced by genetic characteristics, body temperature, nutrition, radiation and disease. Offspring of long-lived parents generally live longer than those of short-lived animals. Raising the temperature of cold-blooded animals shortens their life span. Excessive food shortens the life span, as does exposure to sublethal amounts of radiation. Diseases also shorten the life span in all animals.

The loss of performance and reserve capacities because of age may be explained in large measure by progressive loss of functioning cells. In many tissues this loss can be detected by examining the cells under a microscope. Other evidence for cell loss comes from physiological and biochemical data.

The key question in gerontology therefore is: "Why do cells die?" Some cells in the body undoubtedly die from disruptions in their supply of oxygen or other nutrients. It is known, for example, that heart muscle cells may die when branches of the coronary artery are blocked. Hardening of the arteries may be responsible in part for reducing blood supply and thus causing cell death. However, aging and cell death occur in many animals that do not have hearts or blood vessels. Cell death also may be caused by interference of the supplies of oxygen and other nutrients by the accumulations of fibrous connective tissue, which develops at a progressive rate with aging.

At least three hypotheses may be advanced to explain the phenomenon of cell death: (1) exhaustion, (2) eversion and (3) error.

The exhaustion hypothesis assumes that aging is due to the depletion of some essential material in the cell. Not many biochemical data support this theory.

According to the eversion theory, aging may be due to alterations in essential molecules after they have been formed. These are large protein molecules such as collagen and many complex enzymes that are important in tissue structure and cellular function. There is some support for the hypothesis that with the passage of time structural changes occur in these molecules so that they no longer are capable of carrying out their cellular function and thus the cell dies. For example, highly insoluble granules accumulate in the heart muscle cells and may impair their function.

The error theory suggests that the master information code in the complex deoxyribonucleic acid (DNA) molecule is obscured, if not, as time passes. When this occurs the cell is no longer able to form new molecules of the enzymes that are essential for existence.

Whatever the ultimate cause of aging, it is known that at the present time humans do not die of old age; they die of diseases. As more knowledge accumulates about biology and physiology it is not unreasonable to expect that within the next 50 or 100 years many humans will approach their full life potential, which may be as long as 100 to 120 years.

See also ANATOMY, GROSS: *Changes Incident to Old Age;* DEATH (BIOLOGICAL); LIFE SPAN.

BIBLIOGRAPHY.—J. E. Birren, *Handbook of Aging and the Individual* (1959); A. I. Lansing (ed.), *Cowdry's Problems of Ageing: Biological and Medical Aspects,* 3rd ed. (1952); A. Comfort, *Aging: The Biology of Senescence,* 2nd ed. (1964); E. J. Stieglitz, *The Second Forty Years* (1946); N. W. Shock, *Trends in Gerontology,* 2nd ed. (1957); C. Tibbitts (ed.), *Handbook of Social Gerontology* (1960). (N. W. S.)

GEROUSIA, the council of elders at Sparta. It no doubt began as a council of nobles advising the kings in the Homeric manner, but at an early date the ordinance called the Great Rhetra, quoted by Plutarch (*Lycurgus* 6), redefined its functions and fixed its numbers at 30, including the two kings. (The date of the Great Rhetra is still disputed; both the 9th and 7th centuries B.C. have been widely accepted.)

In the classical period the ephors sat with the council and probably presided (*see* EPHOR). Members held office for life, being elected by the full assembly, as vacancies arose, from candidates over age 60. The council (like the *boule* at Athens) prepared the business to be submitted to the assembly. The Rhetra gives the final decision to the latter, and, though a rider to the Rhetra empowers the council to set aside "crooked" decisions of the people, major issues were in fact regularly decided by the assembly.

It had extensive judicial powers, and was the only Spartan court that could pronounce sentence of death or exile; for the trial of a king the court was composed of the council, the ephors and the other king, though here too the decision sometimes went to the assembly.

Classical Greece was more familiar with councils elected annually and answerable for their actions while in office, so that the power and influence of the *gerousia* seemed one of the stranger features of the Spartan constitution. (*See also* GREECE: *History: The 9th and 8th Centuries B.C.;* LYCURGUS; SPARTA.)

Aristocratic councils elected for life existed in other Greek states; *e.g.,* the *timochoi* at Massilia (Marseilles). The Areopagus at Athens, though deprived of political power in 462 B.C., is another example. (A. As.)

GERRY, ELBRIDGE (1744–1814), signer of the Declaration of Independence and vice-president of the United States, was born in Marblehead, Mass., July 17, 1744, the son of a prosperous merchant. He graduated from Harvard college in 1762 and entered his father's business. He was a member of the Massachusetts general court in 1772–73, served on the committee of correspondence (which became one of the great instruments of intercolonial resistance) and became a member of the Massachusetts provincial congress in 1774–75. From 1776 to 1781, Gerry was a delegate to the continental congress in Philadelphia, Pa., where he early advocated independence.

Gerry was a member of the congress under the Articles of Confederation from 1783 to 1785 and in 1787 was chosen as a delegate to the constitutional convention in Philadelphia. He opposed the adoption of the proposed new constitution, but after it was ratified he gave it his support and was elected a representative to congress for two terms (1789–93). In 1797 Pres. John Adams sent

BY COURTESY OF THE FOGG ART MUSEUM, HARVARD UNIVERSITY, LOUISE E. BETTENS FUND

GERRY, PORTRAIT BY AN UNKNOWN ARTIST, COPIED AFTER PORTRAIT BY JOHN VANDERLYN

him on a mission to France (with John Marshall and Charles Cotesworth Pinckney) to negotiate a treaty that would settle several long-standing disputes. The discourteous and underhand treatment of the American negotiators by Talleyrand and his agents resulted in the speedy departure from Paris of Marshall and Pinckney.

Gerry remained in Paris for some time in the vain hope that Talleyrand might offer him, a known friend of France, terms that had been refused to Marshall and Pinckney, whose anti-French views were more than suspected. This action brought down upon Gerry from Federalist partisans a storm of abuse and censure from which he never wholly cleared himself.

After four unsuccessful attempts, 1800-03, to win election as governor of Massachusetts, Gerry succeeded in 1810 and was re-elected in 1811. His administration was especially notable for the enactment of a law by which the state was divided into new senatorial districts in such a manner as to consolidate the Federalist vote in a few districts, thus giving the Democratic-Republicans an unfair advantage. The outline of one of these districts, which was thought to resemble a salamander, gave rise in 1812, through a popular application of the governor's name, to the term "Gerrymander." In 1812 Gerry, who was an ardent advocate of the war with Great Britain, was elected vice-president of the United States on the ticket with James Madison. He died in office at Washington, D.C., Nov. 23, 1814.

See J. T. Austin, *Life of Elbridge Gerry, With Contemporary Letters,* 2 vol. (1828-29); S. E. Morison, "Elbridge Gerry, Gentleman-Democrat," *By Land and by Sea* (1953). (N. E. Cu.)

GERRYMANDER: see GERRY, ELBRIDGE.

GERS, an inland *département* of southwestern France, comprising parts of Armagnac and other districts of Gascony, and bounded north by Lot-et-Garonne, northeast by Tarn-et-Garonne, east and southeast by Haute-Garonne, south by Hautes-Pyrénées, southwest by Basses-Pyrénées and west by Landes. Pop. (1962) 182,264. Area 2,415 sq.mi.

The *département* consists of an inclined platform at the foot of the Pyrenees, grooved by the valleys of the river Adour and its tributaries, and by tributaries of the river Garonne, diverging fanwise. The Gers river flows from south to north through the centre of the *département.* The whole area is essentially agricultural, almost devoid of mineral wealth, and with little manufacturing industry. It is a rural backwater off the main routes, and the only towns are small market centres; Auch is the only one with more than 10,000 inhabitants. Much of the soil is gravelly, especially in the south. There are tracts of poor woodland, but much land is occupied by vineyards, Armagnac being one of the main products of the *département.*

The river valleys are often fertile, but the rivers have very irregular regimes and are liable to cause extensive floods, so that their proximity is avoided by settlements. Wheat and maize (corn) are widely grown, and green fodder crops are also important. A wide variety of livestock is kept, including large numbers of poultry.

Auch, the ancient capital of Gascony and seat of an archbishopric, is the largest town (16,109 in 1962) and prefecture, centrally situated on the Gers river, and focus of the roads and railways that serve the *département.* It has a fine 16th-century cathedral, especially noted for its Renaissance stalls and stained glass. The *département* comes under the *académie* of Toulouse and the court of appeal of Agen. Auch, Condom and Mirande are the centres of the three constituent *arrondissements.* (AR. E. S)

GERSHOM BEN JUDAH (c. 950-c. 1028), known as RABBENU GERSHOM, and "the Light of the Exile," was the greatest rabbinical authority of the Jews of western Europe. As the brilliant teacher of the rabbinic academy at Mainz in Germany, he was one of the first to transplant the talmudic learning of Babylonia and Palestine to the schools of the west. A consummate scholar, he attracted students from all parts of Europe, and was the mentor, guide and appellate judge of the autonomous and democratically governed Jewish communities of Germany and France, helping to mold their political, social and co-operative institutions. At synods of community leaders he proposed and guided the adoption of legal enactments that shaped the organized life of European Jewry. These enactments prohibited polygamy and limited the husband's right of arbitrary divorce, strengthened the jurisdiction of courts of law and extended the use of the principle of majority rule in community legislation. He wrote many *responsa,* worked on a critical text of the Talmud and on the Masora, and transmitted to his students an extensive oral commentary on the entire Talmud. All rabbinic scholars of Germany and France of the subsequent generations considered themselves the students of his students, and followed faithfully his teachings, his customs and his legal enactments. (I. A. A.)

GERSHWIN, GEORGE (1898-1937), U.S. composer whose songs, orchestral and stage works derived from jazz created a new type of urban American music. Born on Sept. 26, 1898, in Brooklyn of Jewish-Russian immigrant parents, he took music lessons in New York city and was employed as a pianist in a music publishing house. In 1919 Gershwin achieved his first popular success with the song *Swanee,* its nervous energy already characteristic of his style. He subsequently collaborated with his brother Ira Gershwin, a gifted writer of lyrics, and together they produced popular musical comedies on Broadway, among them *Lady, Be Good* (1924), *Strike up the Band* (1927) and *Of Thee I Sing* (1931), the last a political satire that was awarded the Pulitzer prize.

In his *Rhapsody in Blue,* commissioned by Paul Whiteman and orchestrated by Ferde Grofé, Gershwin originated a novel type of symphonic jazz in which popular American rhythms and melodic patterns provide thematic material for works in traditional forms. The *Rhapsody in Blue* is in effect a one-movement piano concerto based on the rhapsodic forms of Liszt and derived thematically from the "blues" and jazz. Gershwin was the soloist at its first performance in New York city on Feb. 12, 1924. The following year a sequel to the *Rhapsody in Blue* was produced with the *Concerto in F* for piano and orchestra, following the traditional piano concerto form. It was commissioned by Walter Damrosch, who conducted it with the composer as soloist in New York city on Dec. 3, 1925. In 1928 Gershwin wrote the symphonic poem *An American in Paris* (New York, Dec. 13), in which quotations from popular French music alternate with original dance tunes, the score including parts to be played by Paris taxi horns.

The *Second Rhapsody* for piano and orchestra, which Gershwin played with the Boston Symphony orchestra, conducted by Serge Koussevitzky, on Jan. 29, 1932, fell below the spontaneous inspiration of the *Rhapsody in Blue* and remained unsuccessful.

Gershwin's last and finest work was the opera *Porgy and Bess,* with a libretto based on Negro life by DuBose Heyward and written for Negro singers. It was first staged in Boston on Sept. 30, 1935, and subsequently in New York city, Europe and the U.S.S.R. Although its initial reception was not enthusiastic, the opera grew in popularity and became especially known for its songs, "Summertime," "I Got Plenty o' Nuttin'" and "It Ain't Necessarily So."

Gershwin died in Hollywood, Calif., on July 11, 1937.

See I. Goldberg, *George Gershwin* (1931); D. Ewen, *A Journey to Greatness: the Life and Music of George Gershwin* (1956). (N. Sv.)

GERSON, JEAN DE (1363-1429), French theologian, chancellor of the University of Paris and a leader of the conciliar movement for church reform, called *doctor christianissimus.* He was born at Gerson (from which his surname is derived) near Reims on Dec. 13, 1363; the family name was Charlier. He was educated at the College of Navarre in Paris, studying theology under Pierre d'Ailly (*q.v.*), who remained his lifelong friend. At the university he was elected procurator for the French "nation" in 1383, and in 1387 was sent with the chancellor and others to Clement VII to procure the condemnation of Jean de Montson, a Dominican who had rejected the Immaculate Conception. When D'Ailly was made bishop of Le Puy in 1395, Gerson was elected chancellor of the university, then at the height of its fame and attracting students from all the lands of Christendom.

In theology Gerson was a follower of the nominalist William Ockham (*see also* NOMINALISM; OCKHAM, WILLIAM). Impatient with the merely verbal subtleties of decadent scholasticism, he turned away from the whole medieval tradition that had emphasized the value of reason in the discernment of divine truth. For Gerson the good or evil of an action depended solely on the will of God, which human reason could not fathom. He urged students to apply themselves to the study of the Bible and the church fathers instead of indulging in finespun arguments on points of speculative theology. It seemed an attractive program to many, but the rejection of human reason as a key to theological truth could as easily lead to religious skepticism as to the purer and simpler faith at which Gerson aimed.

His own theological writing was influenced by the mystical tradition of the Victorines and of St. Bonaventura. He had a great reputation as a preacher and a moralist; one of his moral treatises was a work warning university students against the obscenity and skepticism of the then very popular *Roman de la rose*. Some scholars have credited Gerson with the authorship of the famous mystical treatise *The Imitation of Christ*, but it is most probably not his work.

Gerson is especially remembered for his part in healing the Great Schism which began in 1378 when two rival candidates, Urban VI and Clement VII, disputed the papal throne. (*See also* PAPACY: *The Great Schism, 1378–1417.*) At first his attitude was moderate. He deprecated the views of zealots on both sides who held that all members of the opposing party were in a state of excommunication and lacked valid sacraments; but as the schism grew more embittered Gerson came to propound really radical doctrines on church government as the only means of restoring unity. He taught that although the papacy was divinely established as the head of the church, nevertheless the authority of the whole universal church was greater than that of any individual pope. The practical consequence was that a general council could judge and depose a pope. Gerson supported the Council of Pisa (1409) which claimed to depose the two existing "popes" and elect a third. After it became apparent that this had merely produced three "popes" instead of two, the Council of Constance assembled in 1415.

Gerson attended this council and played a leading part in its deliberations (including those that led to the condemnation of John Huss). His views on conciliar authority were accepted, and the schism was ended by the forced resignation of two "popes" and the deposition of the third. Gerson, however, had one major defeat at the council. In 1408 he had taken the lead in condemning a work of the theologian Jean Petit, who had defended the assassination of the duc d'Orléans by partisans of the duke of Burgundy as justifiable tyrannicide. The case of Jean Petit was reconsidered at Constance, but the council refused to condemn him explicitly. When Gerson left Constance in 1418 he was prevented from returning to France by the threats of the duke of Burgundy, and he went into exile in Germany.

In 1419, on the death of the duke, he returned to France and settled at Lyons. Gerson had always showed a tenderness toward small children, and he spent his last years teaching children and writing hymns and works of devotion. He died with a reputation for exemplary piety on July 12, 1429.

The best editions of his collected works, those of Paris, four volumes (1606), and Antwerp, five volumes (1706), are both very imperfect.

BIBLIOGRAPHY.—J. B. Schwab, *Johannes Gerson* (1858); J. L. Connolly, *John Gerson, Mystic and Reformer* (1928). (B. Ty.)

GERSONIDES (LEVI BEN GERSHON) (1288–c. 1344), known from his initials, with the title Rabbi, as RALBAG and also called LEO DE BAGNOLAS, LEO HEBRAEUS or MAESTRO LEON, Jewish mathematician, astronomer, philosopher and biblical commentator, was born at Bagnols in Languedoc, of a family distinguished for piety and learning. He lived at Avignon (where the rule of the Angevin counts of Provence and later of the popes was comparatively tolerant), at Orange and at Perpignan. His *De Numeris* (written in Hebrew but extant only in the Latin version) was composed at the instance of Philip of Vitry, bishop of Meaux. Other mathematical works of his include a treatise called *De Sinibus, chordis et arcubus*, one of the first European writings on trigonometry. He invented (or improved) an astronomical instrument, which he called Jacob's staff (*baculus Jacob*), for meas-

uring heights and used the camera obscura. These inventions enabled him to correct the astronomical tables of the time. His importance as an astronomer is undisputed but cannot easily be assessed, as the astronomical part of his philosophical work *Milhamot Adonai* ("The Wars of the Lord"; partial Ger. trans. by B. Kellermann, *Die Kämpfe Gottes*, 2 vol., 1914–16) was unfortunately omitted both from the *editio princeps* (1560) and from the second edition (1868), although it had been translated into Latin in 1342. As a philosopher Gersonides develops the synthesis of Aristotelianism and Judaism which Maimonides (*q.v.*) had effected. On account of his familiarity with Averroës' commentaries, he is more firmly grounded in Aristotle than his illustrious predecessor. He himself wrote supercommentaries on the six books of the Aristotelian *Organon* and on Porphyry's *Isagoge*, some of which were printed, with the commentaries of Averroës, in the Latin edition of Aristotle (1550). His pronounced rationalism is in evidence also in his commentaries on the Bible. His orthodox contemporaries mockingly called his main work "Wars *against* the Lord." *See also* JEWISH PHILOSOPHY. (A. An.)

GERSTÄCKER, FRIEDRICH (1816–1872), German traveler and author of popular travel books, was born at Hamburg on May 10, 1816, the son of a famous singer. From 1837 to 1843 he led an adventurous life in America, studying local customs and traveling widely throughout the United States. On his return he described his experiences in a number of sketches, *Streif- und Jagdzüge durch die Vereinigten Staaten Nordamerikas*, two volumes (1844; Eng. trans., *Wild Sports in the Far West*, 1854). In the next year he published a novel, *Die Regulatoren in Arkansas*, three volumes (Eng. trans., *Feathered Arrow*, 1851), incorporating similar material, and thereafter produced a stream of travel sketches and novels. He made journeys to South America, California, Australia and the Dutch East Indies (1849–52), to the German colonies in South America (1860–61) and to Mexico, Ecuador, Venezuela and the West Indies (1867–68), as well as smaller expeditions. His impressions of South America are recorded in *Achtzehn Monate in Südamerika*, three volumes (1862), and he later campaigned effectively for the interests of the German emigrants and for proper national representation overseas. He died at Brunswick on May 31, 1872.

Gerstäcker's works attained enormous popularity, answering to the widespread interest in far-off countries. His novels have no particular formal or stylistic qualities, nor do they go very deep, but they tell exciting stories with liveliness and exotic detail, being set most frequently in passionate tropical lands. His observation is rarely detailed or accurate enough to be of scientific value, and his books are no longer widely read. Apart from the one mentioned above, his novels *Die Flusspiraten des Mississippi* (1848; Eng. trans., *The Pirates of the Mississippi*, 1856) and *Tahiti* (1854) are among his best. His collected works appeared in 44 volumes (1872–74). (W. D. Wr.)

See F. Seyfahrt, *Friedrich Gerstäcker* (1931).

GERSTENBERG, HEINRICH WILHELM VON (1737–1823), German poet, critic and theorist of the *Sturm und Drang* movement, was born at Tondern, Schleswig, Jan. 3, 1737. After studying law at Jena he entered the Danish military service and took part in the Russian campaign of 1762. He spent the next 12 years in Copenhagen, where he was a friend of the poet Klopstock. From 1775 to 1783 Gerstenberg was official Danish representative at Lübeck, and in 1786 received a judicial appointment at Altona, where he died, Nov. 1, 1823. The text of his cantata *Ariadne auf Naxos* (1767) was set to music by J. A. Scheibe and J. C. Bach (these scores were lost) and later adapted for a famous duodrama by Georg Benda. Gerstenberg also translated Beaumont and Fletcher's *Maid's Tragedy* (1765), and himself wrote a gruesome but powerful tragedy, *Ugolino* (1768). His chief service to the new literary movement was his *Briefe über Merkwürdigkeiten der Literatur*, three volumes (1766–67), in which the critical principles of the *Sturm und Drang*—and especially its enthusiasm for Shakespeare—were first definitely formulated. As a musician Gerstenberg, a pupil of Scheibe, formulated theories on instrumental and dramatic music opposed to those of Jean Jacques Rousseau.

BIBLIOGRAPHY.—Gerstenberg's *Vermischte Schriften* appeared in 3 vol. (1815–16). The *Briefe über Merkwürdigkeiten der Literatur* were republished by A. von Weilen (1888–89). *See also* A. M. Wagner, H. W. *von Gerstenberg und der Sturm und Drang*, 2 vol. (1920); J. W. Eaton, *Gerstenberg and Lessing* (1938). For Gerstenberg's musical influence *see* A. Schering, "C.P.E. Bach und das 'redende Prinzip' in der Musik," in *Jahrbuch der Musikbibliothek Peters* (1939).

GERVAIS, (FRANÇOIS LOUIS) PAUL (1816–1879), French paleontologist and zoologist most noted for his work on fossil vertebrates, was born on Sept. 26, 1816, in Paris, where he obtained doctorates in science and medicine. He studied paleontology as assistant to H. M. D. de Blainville, Cuvier's successor as professor of comparative anatomy in the Museum of Natural History. In 1845 Gervais was appointed to the chair of zoology and comparative anatomy in the faculty of sciences at Montpellier of which he was appointed dean in 1856. He returned to Paris in 1865 with professorships in anatomy, comparative physiology and geology at the Sorbonne. Three years later he achieved his ambition of succeeding to the chair of Cuvier and Blainville in the museum. Most important of Gervais' earlier works were his *Zoologie et paléontologie françaises* (1848–52), essentially a continuation of Cuvier's and Blainville's publications on the same subject. Among his major later works were *Zoologie et paléontologie générales* (1867–75) and, with Van Beneden, a series of important studies on whales—*Ostéographie des cétacés vivants et fossiles* (1868 et seq.). He also published numerous papers on vertebrates brought back by French expeditions abroad, and was the author of such general zoological works as *Histoire naturelle des mammifères* (1855) and, with Van Beneden, *Zoologie médicale* (1859). Gervais died in Paris on Feb. 10, 1879.

(A. S. RR.)

GERVASE OF CANTERBURY (GERVASIUS DOROBORNENSIS) (c. 1141–c. 1210), English monk and chronicler, who championed the Canterbury monks in their struggle with the archbishops. Perhaps of a Kentish family, he entered the monastery of Christ Church, Canterbury, at an early age, and was professed (1163) and ordained by Thomas Becket. He took a prominent part in the disputes between the monks of Christ Church and Archbishop Baldwin (1185–91) and was made sacrist (after 1190, until 1197).

About 1188 he undertook the compilation of his *Chronica* (from Stephen to the death of Richard I, usually an independent authority for the years 1188–99). A second history, the *Gesta regum*, on a smaller scale, traces the fortunes of Britain from the days of Brutus to about 1210; the latter part only, from 1199, deserves much attention.

See Gervase's *Historical Works* ed. by W. Stubbs with notes, "Rolls Series," no. 73, 2 vol. (1879–80); *see also* D. Knowles, *The Monastic Order in England*, pp. 316–324 and 331–333 (1949).

(Pr. GN.)

GERVASE OF TILBURY (c. 1152–c. 1220), scholar and courtier, is a striking representative of the cosmopolitan society of the 12th century. A kinsman of Patrick, earl of Salisbury, he presumably spent his childhood in England. He was, however, in Rome by 1166, studied at Bologna and afterward taught canon law there. He returned to England about 1180 and entered the household of Henry II's eldest son, Henry, "the young king," after whose death in 1183 he passed into the service of William, archbishop of Reims, and from there into that of William II of Sicily. Gervase made an advantageous marriage in the early 1190s with a kinswoman of Humbert, archbishop of Arles. It was doubtless this connection that led later to his appointment by the emperor Otto IV as marshal of the kingdom of Arles. He appears to have remained in the imperial service until Otto's death in 1218, but soon afterward returned to England where, his wife being dead, he retired from the world to an unnamed house of regular canons. Gervase's claim to fame rests upon the *Otia Imperialia*, dedicated to Otto IV. The work was still in progress in 1215 and cannot have been presented to the emperor until near the end of his life. Intended as a compendium of geography, history and natural history, it is above all a book of marvels. Extracts have been published from the 17th century onward and an edition of the whole work was published by Leibniz in 1707 and 1710. Apart from a single anecdote by Ralph of Coggeshall, all that is known of Gervase is to be gathered from his book.

(H. G. Rr.)

GERVINUS, GEORG GOTTFRIED (1805–1871), German historian and Shakespearean commentator, was born on May 20, 1805, at Darmstadt, and died on March 18, 1871, at Heidelberg. In 1835 he became professor of history at Göttingen. His *Geschichte der poetischen Nationalliteratur der Deutschen*, five volumes (1835–42), subsequently entitled *Geschichte der deutschen Dichtung*, 5th ed. by K. Bartsch (1871–74), was the first comprehensive and scholarly history of German literature. In 1837 he was one of the seven Göttingen professors dismissed for their protest against the violation of the constitution by the king of Hanover. After some years in Heidelberg, Darmstadt and Rome, Gervinus settled in Heidelberg, where in 1844 he was appointed honorary professor. In the following year he espoused the cause of the German Catholics, hoping for a union of all the Christian confessions and the establishment of a national church. In 1846 he came forward as a champion of the Schleswig-Holsteiners. With other patriotic scholars he founded the *Deutsche Zeitung*, one of the best-written liberal journals published in Germany in the 19th century. Between 1849 and 1852 Gervinus published his important work, *Shakespeare*, in four volumes (4th ed., 2 vol., 1872; Eng. trans. by F. E. Bunnett, 1863, new ed., 1877). During this period he also sketched his *Geschichte des neunzehnten Jahrhunderts*, eight volumes (1854–60). His parallel study of Handel and Shakespeare appeared in 1868.

See M. Rychner, G. G. *Gervinus. Ein Kapitel über Literaturgeschichte* (1922).

(A. Gs.)

GESENIUS, (HEINRICH FRIEDRICH) WILHELM (1786–1842), German biblical critic and a highly important figure in Hebrew and other Semitic language studies, was born at Nordhausen, Hanover, on Feb. 3, 1786. He was educated at Helmstedt and at Göttingen and in 1811 became professor of theology at Halle, where he attracted many students. Though accused of rationalism, he was never dismissed from his post. He published little that was controversial, his chief theological publication being a commentary on Isaiah (1821–29). Gesenius inaugurated in Semitic language studies a modern philological approach such as had been developed in Indo-Germanic linguistics. His Hebrew grammar (1813; edited and enlarged by E. Kautzsch; 2nd English edition revised according to the 28th German edition by A. E. Cowley, 1910) and his Hebrew and Chaldee (i.e., Aramaic) dictionary (1810–13) taught generations of scholars, and have been kept alive to this day through the labours of editors and translators. Gesenius also laid the basis for Semitic epigraphy, collecting and deciphering the Phoenician inscriptions then known. He died on Oct. 23, 1842.

See E. F. Miller, *The Influence of Gesenius on Hebrew Lexicography* (1927).

GESNER, ABRAHAM (1797–1864), Canadian geologist and inventor, noted for his early processes for distilling kerosene, was born in Nova Scotia on May 2, 1797. He qualified as a doctor of medicine in London in 1827. Returning to Canada, he published in 1836 *Remarks on the Geology and Mineralogy of Nova Scotia*, and in 1843 brought before the Geological society of London "A Geological Map of Nova Scotia, With an Accompanying Memoir." In 1849 he issued a volume on the industrial resources of the country. He dealt also with the geology and mineralogy of New Brunswick and Prince Edward Island. In 1854 Gesner established a New York company at Newton Creek, L.I. to manufacture kerosene from petroleum. Devoting himself later to the economic side of geology in various parts of North America he published in 1861 *A Practical Treatise on Coal, Petroleum and Other Distilled Oils*, which was translated into a number of languages. He died at Halifax, N.S., on April 29, 1864.

GESNER, KONRAD VON (1516–1565), German-Swiss writer and naturalist whose monumental *Historia animalium* is considered the starting point of modern zoology, was born at Zürich. He took his M.D. at Basel in 1541 and then practised at Zürich, where he became lecturer in physics at the Carolinum. Gesner was a versatile intellect, knowledgeable in many fields; Cuvier called him "the German Pliny." He illustrated his many works with figures outstanding for their freshness and, with few exceptions, their trueness to life—this in an age known for its stylized and often fanciful depiction of animals and plants. He was elevated to the nobility in 1564 and died of plague on Dec. 13, 1565, when he refused to desert his patients during an epidemic in Zürich.

To his contemporaries he was best known as a botanist, though most of his botanical manuscripts were not published till 1751–71, at Nürnberg. In 1545 he published his remarkable *Bibliotheca universalis* edited by J. Simler (1574), a catalogue (in Latin, Greek and Hebrew) of all past writers with the titles of their works, etc. A second part, under the title of *Pandectarum sive partitionum universalium Comradi Gesneri Ligurini libri xxi*, appeared in 1548, only 19 books being then concluded. The 21st book, a theological encyclopaedia, was published in 1549, but the 20th, intended to include his medical work, was never finished. His great zoological work, *Historia animalium*, appeared in four volumes (quadrupeds, birds, fishes) folio, 1551–58, at Zürich, a fifth (snakes) being issued in 1587 (there was a German translation entitled *Thierbuch*, of the first four volumes, Zürich, 1563).

Not content with such vast works, Gesner put forth in 1555 his book entitled *Mithridates de differentiis linguis*, an account of about 130 known languages, with the Lord's Prayer in 22 tongues, while in 1556 appeared his edition of the works of the early Roman writer Aelian.

To nonscientific readers, Gesner is probably best known for his love of mountains and for his many excursions among them, undertaken partly as a botanist, but also for the sake of exercise and enjoyment of the beauties of nature. In 1555 Gesner issued his narrative (*Descriptio Montis Fracti sive Montis Pilati*) of his excursion to the Gnepfstein (6,299 ft.), the lowest point in the Pilatus chain, and therein explains at length how each of the senses of man is refreshed in the course of a mountain excursion.

See *Lives* by J. Hanhart (1824) and J. Simler (1566); *see also Papers Bibliog. Soc. Amer.*, x, pp. 53–86, ed. by J. E. Bay (1916).

GESNERIACEAE, a family of dicotyledonous plants, consisting of herbs, vines and shrubs, chiefly tropical, a few found in temperate regions. It includes the popular house plants African violet (*Saintpaulia* species) and gloxinia (*Sinningia speciosa*). Over 80 genera are recognized, with about 1,200 species, the tropical genera being sharply limited geographically as between the tropics of the two hemispheres. Large genera in the old world are *Cyrtandra*, *Didymocarpus* and *Aeschynanthes*, and in the new world *Columnea*, *Kohleria*, *Corytholoma* and *Gesneria*. Many species representing various other genera are cultivated for ornamental purposes. These include *Ramonda* and *Haberlea*, rock garden subjects; Cape primrose (*Streptocarpus*) and *Episcia*, showy house plants.

See AFRICAN VIOLET; GLOXINIA.

GESSI, ROMOLO (1831–1881), Italian explorer and administrator in the Sudan, was born at sea on April 30, 1831, of an Italian father (in the British Levant consular service) and an Armenian mother. He was an interpreter with the British army in the Crimean War during 1854–55 and a volunteer in the Sardinian army that fought against Austria (1859). Later an Italian citizen, he set up in business at Tulcea in Rumania. In 1873 the khedive Ismail appointed Col. (later Gen.) C. G. Gordon governor of the Egyptian Equatorial province, and Gordon, who had met Gessi in the Crimea and again at Tulcea, invited him to the Sudan. Under Gordon's direction Gessi and C. Piaggia circumnavigated Lake Albert. Then, disappointed by the lack of official recognition, Gessi resigned the Egyptian service. During 1877–78, with P. Matteucci, he vainly attempted to penetrate western Ethiopia from the Blue Nile valley. Gordon, now governor general of the Sudan, re-employed him as governor of the Bahr el Ghazal province and commander of an expedition against the rebel Suleiman wad al-Zubayr. After a hard campaign he caught and killed Suleiman, an action which, though approved by Gordon, was criticized by Gordon's successor, Mohammed Rauf Pasha, who dismissed Gessi. Racked by fever he left for Europe but died at Suez on April 30, 1881. Gessi's memoirs, unfinished at his death, were published as *Sette anni nel Sudan egiziano* (1891; Eng. trans. by L. Wolffsohn and B. Woodward, *Seven Years in the Soudan*, 1892; abridged Italian ed. by A. A. Michieli, 1930). (R. L. HL.)

GESSLER, OTTO KARL (1875–1955), German minister of war for nearly five years when the Versailles treaty was imposing disarmament, was born at Ludwigsburg on Feb. 6, 1875, and entered the legal department in Bavaria in 1904. He was burgomaster of Regensburg in 1911, and of Nürnberg in 1913–19. A founder of the German Democratic party, he was minister of reconstruction in the *Reich* from 1919 to 1920. On March 24, 1920, he became minister of war. As such he was faced with the necessity of allaying the suspicion of the Allies. He had as his colleague Gen. Hans von Seeckt and in spite of difficulties succeeded in reorganizing the *Reichswehr*. Gessler became increasingly unpopular with the parties of the left, and the Social Democrats asserted that relations were maintained between the patriotic unions and the *Reichswehr*. He resigned on Jan. 19, 1928. Always a royalist, Gessler kept contact with Bavarian royalists after 1933 and was imprisoned for seven months in 1944–45. He became head of the Bavarian Red Cross in 1949 and of the German Red Cross in 1951, remaining its president until his death at Lindenberg on March 24, 1955.

GESSNER, SALOMON (1730–1788), Swiss writer, painter and etcher, was born at Zürich on April 1, 1730, and died there on March 2, 1788. With his pastoral prose *Idyllen* (1756–72) and his epic poem *Der Tod Abels* (1758), he was the most successful and typical representative of a literary rococo movement. In the melodious rhythms of his prose, the playful dream of a new Arcadia goes hand in hand with keen observation and love of nature. His pastorals were translated into 20 languages including Welsh, Latin and Hebrew. The English version ran through about a score of editions, was appreciated by Sir Walter Scott, Lord Byron and William Wordsworth, and is mentioned by Thomas Hood in his "Dream of Eugene Aram." He translated some of Alexander Pope's *Pastorals* and two tales of Denis Diderot. His works were published in his own important publishing house, illustrated with excellent etchings by himself. He served his town as a town councillor and was an efficient forestry superintendent. The final collection of his works was published at Zürich in 1841.

BIBLIOGRAPHY.—P. Leemann van Elck, *S. Gessner* (1930), a biography with register of the literary and artistic works. *See also* J. J. Hottinger, *S. Gessner* (1796); H. Wölfflin, *S. Gessner* (1889); *S. Gessner, 1730–1930, Gedenkbuch zum 200. Geburtstag* (1930); Bertha Reed, *The Influence of S. Gessner on English Literature* (1905). (M. WE.)

GESTA FRANCORUM (in full, *Gesta Francorum et aliorum Hierosolymitanorum*, "Deeds of the Franks and of the Others of Jerusalem"), a short and anonymous chronicle of the first crusade, one of the best sources and consequently much exploited by historiographers. The author (sometimes mistakenly identified with Alexander, chaplain to Stephen, count of Blois) was an eyewitness, apparently a Norman knight who set out with Bohemund I from southern Italy but went on, after the capture of Antioch, with Raymond IV of Toulouse to Jerusalem. The narrative, which ends with the battle of Ascalon (1099), seems to have been composed for the most part while the crusade was actually in progress. Its chronology is exact, and it gives information about the army's *morale* and about material conditions in the course of the warfare. It has a bias in Bohemund's favour. An account of the origins of the crusade (omitting the council of Clermont) and some passages in the epic manner, such as those describing what was going on in the Turkish camp (with the speeches of the Turkish leaders), may have been added by a cleric rewriting the authentic chronicle.

Completed by 1101, the work soon became widely known in western Europe. It was copied by Tudebodus, a priest of Civray in Poitou, who may have been in Palestine between 1102 and 1111; and it was rewritten, in a more pretentious style, by Baudry de Bourgueil in his *Historia Iherosolimitana* (c. 1108). It likewise provided the substance of the *Historia Hierosolymitana* of Robert, a monk of Marmoutiers (c. 1122); and Guibert of Nogent used it as his chief source for his *Gesta Dei per Francos* (c. 1104), though he added other elements, as Robert did. Other writers who drew very largely upon the *Gesta* were Ekkehard of Aura (or von Urau), who accompanied the expedition of 1101, found the chronicle in Jerusalem and used it for the first crusade in his *Hierosolymita*; Raoul of Caen, for his *Gesta Tancredi*; and the poet Graindor, for the *Chanson d'Antioche*.

First printed by Jacques Bongars in his *Gesta Dei per Francos* (1611), the *Gesta Francorum* is included in the *Recueil des historiens des croisades*, section *Historiens occidentaux*, vol. iii (1866), under the title *Tudebodus abbreviatus*, as it was once wrongly supposed that Tudebodus was the original source. There are separate editions by H. Hagenmeyer (1890), with French trans., and by L. Bréhier, with French trans., *Histoire anonyme de la première croisade* (1924). (J. B. R.)

GESTALT PSYCHOLOGY. The word *Gestalt* is used in modern German to mean the way a thing has been *gestellt*, *i.e.*, "placed" or "put together." There is no exact equivalent in English. "Form" and "shape" are the usual translations; in psychology the word is often rendered "pattern" or "configuration." Gestalt theory began toward the close of the 19th century in Austria and south Germany as a protest against the piecemeal analysis of experience into atomistic elements that was characteristic of the associationist school in north Germany and that reached its climax in the influential teaching of Wilhelm Wundt. It ended its independent existence as a distinct school by absorption into the main stream of mid-20th-century psychological and philosophical thought, with ramifications in biology, chemistry, aesthetics, economics and other disciplines.

The Gestalt Principle.—The chief tenet of the Gestalt approach is that analysis of parts, however thorough, cannot provide an understanding of the whole. Rather, to comprehend the full nature of the whole, it is necessary to analyze "from above down," from the structure of the whole to the characteristics of its constituent parts. The whole may have attributes that require a certain place, role and function for each part in the whole; these attributes are not deducible from analysis of the parts in isolation.

A whole that is a Gestalt is not simply the sum of its parts. A soap bubble, for example, has a structure that imposes certain characteristics on each "part" of the film composing it; change of one part results in a dramatic change in the entire structure. On the other hand, a sum of money or a pile of poker chips is not different from the sum of its parts, and hence is not a Gestalt but merely an additive aggregate; changing one part has no effect on the others.

In a Gestalt, the nature of the parts is required by the characteristics of the whole, and the parts are fused and interdependent, interacting in a specific structural manner. This is not true of a conglomerate in which the parts are readily separable and functionally isolated; they are arbitrarily hooked together and indifferent to one another. Parts of a Gestalt have no meaningful identity independent of their place, role and function in the whole.

Antecedents.—The Gestalt approach was, in many ways, radically new. Yet many aspects of what later became Gestalt theory had been anticipated by philosophers since antiquity. Aristotle included "form" and "matter" among his four causes: form (which for him meant intelligible structure rather than perceptible shape) holds together matter (*i.e.*, the material or substratum) and converts it into a meaningful object. John Locke provided a demonstration of the Gestalt principle of relational determination in his famous experiment on temperature perception. If the left hand is first held in a bucket of warm water while the right is in cold, and both hands are then plunged into tepid water, the tepid water feels cool to the left hand and warm to the right. Not only the immediate stimulus of the tepid water's temperature but also its relation to preceding stimulation determines the quality of the sensation. Kant partly anticipated the doctrine of Gestalt by emphasizing the organized nature of experience in his doctrine of apperceptive synthesis. The objects of experience form integrated wholes perceived in terms of the categories of time and space. John Stuart Mill, in arguing that the qualities of water cannot be predicted from knowledge of the properties of its constituents, hydrogen and oxygen, provided a clear illustration of what later writers called the principle of emergent quality. Christian von Ehrenfels, a student of Franz Brentano at Vienna (where he was appreciably influenced by Ernst Mach's doctrine of space-Gestalt and time-Gestalt) published in 1890 an epoch-making paper, *Über Gestaltqualitäten*, in which he argued that form is a quality immediately experienced. A square is not merely a combination of sensory elements.

composed, as Wundtian analysis might lead one to expect, of four equal straight lines and four right angles; in addition to these there is another element, squareness. Like squareness, other perceptual qualities—angularity, slenderness, roundness and in music such characteristics as the major or minor mode—are elements over and above the elements constituting the whole. Such Gestalt qualities, as Ehrenfels called them, can be transposed to an entirely different set of elements without affecting the Gestalt quality of the whole. When presented in a different colour, place or size an object remains as square, angular or round as before; the same melody can be transposed to a different key, using as elements an entirely different set of tones.

While the Wundtian psychologists used an introspective method for the analysis of consciousness, specifying that observation must reduce experience to its elements, Gestalt studies made use of an alternative method, phenomenology. This method, with a tradition going back to Goethe, involves nothing more than the description of direct psychological experience, with no restrictions on what is permissible in the description.

Meanwhile, G. F. Stout had been led by his introspective studies of apperception (or, as he preferred to call it, "noetic synthesis") to a doctrine that was the same in essence as that of the later Gestalt school, on the basis of which he put forward drastic criticisms of the associationist theories prevalent in Great Britain during the greater part of the 19th century. His main conclusion was that a form of combination (*i.e.*, the shape of a triangle, the melodic outline of a tune, the rhythmic pattern of a movement) is itself "a material constituent of consciousness" apprehended quite as directly as the sensory constituents that are so combined.

Founding and Early Development of Gestalt Theory.—Max Wertheimer (*q.v.*) in 1912 published the paper generally considered to mark the founding of the Gestalt school. In it he reported the result of an experimental study done at Frankfurt with two colleagues, Wolfgang Köhler and Kurt Koffka (*qq.v.*); these three formed the core of the Gestalt school for the next decades.

Wertheimer's paper dealt with the perception of apparent motion. If the reader holds a finger before his face, and looks at it first with the right eye and then with the left, opening one eye as the other is closed, the finger will appear to move from left to right. As a feature of certain toys, such as the stroboscope, the phenomenon had been familiar since 1830 if not earlier, and it forms the essential principle on which the modern motion picture is based. Using the familiar apparatus of the psychologist's laboratory, Wertheimer exposed in rapid succession two stationary stimuli (*e.g.*, points of light in a darkroom), varying the intervals of time and space. If the time interval is less than 3/100 sec., the flashes seem simultaneous; at about 6/100 sec. the observer sees a single point moving from one position to the other; with an interval of 20/100 sec. or more the stimuli are seen for what they are—two successive flashes at different places.

This appearance of continuous movement when there is no corresponding physical movement Wertheimer called the phi phenomenon. Evidently the effect is inexplicable on the old assumption that the sensations of perceptual experience stand in a one-to-one relation to the physical stimuli. The perceived motion is an emergent experience, not present in the stimuli in isolation but dependent upon the relational characteristics of the stimuli. The nervous system of the observer and the observer's experience do not passively register the physical input in a piecemeal way. Rather, the neural organization as well as the perceptual experience springs immediately into existence as an entire field with differentiated parts. In later writings this principle was stated as the law of *Prägnanz*: The neural and perceptual organization of any set of impinging stimuli forms as good a Gestalt or whole as the prevailing conditions allow.

Not only are sensory elements not considered primary, as they were in associationist psychology, but the existence of sensory elements as parts of perceptual experience is explicitly denied. Things, objects, parts of the perceptual field arise from a differentiation and segregation of the total input, not from an additive combination of sensory elements.

Major elaborations of the new formulation occurred within the next decades. Wertheimer, Köhler and Koffka and their students extended the Gestalt approach to problems in other areas of perception, in problem solving, learning and thinking.

Perception.—Much of the early work was directed against the brick-and-mortar interpretation of perception (*q.v.*) as corresponding one-to-one with the mosaic of stimulation. Many experiments demonstrated that the local stimulus can remain constant while the experience changes, and that the local stimulus can be altered without affecting the perception. Locke's demonstration and Ehrenfels' analysis had pointed in this direction, but the new research went far beyond these.

The perceptual constancies provided rich ground for demonstrations of relational determination. The illumination of an object and its immediate environment can be greatly decreased, for example, without appreciably affecting the apparent brightness of the object. As a person moves away from the observer, his image on the observer's retina decreases in size, yet the person hardly appears to shrink.

Contrast effects in perception also showed that the percept is not tied point for point to the local stimulus but is dependent upon the interaction of stimulus and background. If two small circles are cut from the same piece of gray paper, and one is placed on a black background and the other on white, the former looks noticeably lighter than the latter.

Movement perception yielded further evidence. If an object and its surroundings are moved relative to one another, the object is seen as moving irrespective of whether it is the object or the framework that is actually in motion; the moon may be perceived as moving while the clouds appear to be stationary.

Work on the Ehrenfels qualities was extended to dependent part qualities: the attributes of a part depend upon its place, role and function within the whole of which it is a part. Thus middle C may acquire quite different perceptual characteristics when played as part of a C7 chord, a melody in C or an A minor sequence; the word "well" means different things in different settings.

Among the most influential new formulations were Wertheimer's principles of perceptual organization (1923), which aimed to answer the question of how the perceptual field becomes grouped into wholes. Parts that are similar and near each other tend to form units, as do parts that move together or that form a "good" Gestalt or a closed form. When such stimulus factors are equivocal, the observer's set, motivation, habits or attention may influence unit formation. Borrowing from Edgar Rubin, the Gestalt theorists noted that the units perceived as objects are more "thing-like" than their background and stand out from the ground perceptually and in memory.

Learning and Thinking.—The Gestalt approach to the study of learning was radically different from that of Wundtian elementism and that of the behaviouristic stimulus-response associationism that flourished contemporaneously with the Gestalt school. The elementists held that the connection between remembered items is indifferent to the nature of the connected items; elements are hooked together much as objects can be connected with strings. The elementists also believed that perception is intimately affected by past experience of this arbitrary hooking-up variety. The Gestalt psychologists disagreed vigorously with these formulations. Associations, according to the Gestalt view, vary with the characteristics of the items; all interaction depends on the nature of the interacting objects. Experimental work demonstrated that factors that make for strong perceptual grouping of items do indeed also make for strong associations. In recall and recognition, present experience reactivates past experience in a highly selective way, with similarity as the basic principle; the present experience can make contact with the trace of the past event only if the two are similar in some way. The basic process in learning is conceived not as a series of automatic arbitrary hookups but as discovering the structural, organized characteristics of the environment. This leads to important educational consequences; not drill and repetition but insight and understanding must be emphasized.

Problem Solving.—The study of problem solving by Wertheimer (1912) emphasized the difference between the psychology of problem solving and its logic. Wertheimer showed that traditional logic does not describe the way men actually think but rather prescribes criteria that guarantee the precision, validity and consistency of such products of thought as general concepts, propositions, inferences and syllogisms. Köhler's investigations of problem solving and insight in chimpanzees showed that animals tend to behave with insight if the problem permits a meaningful solution lying within their powers, and that they act blindly only if the problem is too complex or beyond their ordinary range. Karl Duncker showed that human problem solving typically involves a perceptual or cognitive reorganization of the problem material.

Dissemination and Later Developments.—By the 1920s the Gestalt school was a forceful voice in psychology. Koffka in 1922 wrote an article in English for the *Psychological Bulletin* introducing the Gestalt approach to the United States, in 1929 Köhler's book *Gestalt Psychology* appeared and in the 1930s the three leaders and many of their students moved to the United States. Among the books published in that decade, the most ambitious was Koffka's *Principles of Gestalt Psychology* (1935). Two American psychologists, Harry Helson and W. D. Ellis, aided the spread of Gestalt psychology in the United States and in England; the former writing a series of articles in the *American Journal of Psychology* in 1933, the latter publishing in 1938 a book of condensed English translations of some of the basic Gestalt writings.

In the 1920s, '30s and '40s new fields were explored. The Gestalt principles were applied to motivation, social psychology and personality by Kurt Lewin, Muzafer Sherif and Solomon E. Asch; to aesthetics by Rudolf Arnheim; and to economic behaviour by George Katona. Wertheimer demonstrated that the Gestalt concepts of relational determination and requiredness can also be used to shed light on problems in ethics, political behaviour and the nature of truth.

The principles of problem solving, from the modest process of learning how to compute the area of a parallelogram to the major scientific insights of Galileo and Einstein, were further developed by Wertheimer in a small book, *Productive Thinking*, published posthumously. Productive thinking involves going from a situation whose structure hides the solution to a state in which relations that at first were unrecognized become central; with appropriate reorganization, the solution emerges.

During the 1920s and '30s Köhler elaborated on Wertheimer's brain theory of 1912 with his concept of psychophysical isomorphism, the identity of the field structure of psychological experience and the underlying brain process. This formulation led in the 1940s and '50s to studies of figural aftereffects, a class of perceptual illusions. Prolonged exposure to a figure subsequently presented in the same place. Such an illusion is presumed to be the isomorphic reflection of the change in the brain medium produced by the prolonged stimulation with the preceding figure. Köhler also studied the implications of his field-theoretical view of brain function by direct experimental investigation of the electrical properties of the brain.

Dissolution as a School.—By the middle of the 20th century, the Gestalt movement had so influenced the entire field of psychology that it, in effect, died of success; the movement could no longer be considered to have an independent existence as a school. This is not to say that all the issues had been resolved. A wide range of problems raised by Gestalt theorists—the role of learning in perception, the nature of learning, the organization of brain function, characteristics of personality structure and motivation—remained as foci of psychological interest and controversy. At the centre of all of these is the basic Gestalt issue, by no means resolved by the middle of the 20th century, of empty hookups versus meaningful organization.

BIBLIOGRAPHY.—K. Koffka, *Principles of Gestalt Psychology* (1935); W. D. Ellis, *A Source Book of Gestalt Psychology* (1938); W. Köhler, *Gestalt Psychology* (1947); R. S. Woodworth, *Contemporary Schools of Psychology* (1948); G. Murphy, *Historical Introduction to Modern Psychology* (1949); E. G. Boring, *A History of Experimental Psychology* (1950); M. Wertheimer, *Productive Thinking* (1959). (M. M. WR.)

GESTA ROMANORUM, a Latin collection of anecdotes and tales, probably compiled early in the 14th century, very possibly in England. It was one of the most popular books of the time, and the source, directly or indirectly, of much later literature, being used by Chaucer, John Gower, Thomas Occleve, Shakespeare and many others. Of its authorship nothing certain is known, but its didactic nature and the allegorical explanations attached to the stories in the early versions suggest that it was intended as a manual for preachers.

The name, *Deeds of the Romans*, is only partially appropriate, since it contains, in addition to stories from classical history and legend, many others from a variety of sources, oriental and European. The compiler, whose style is very uneven, clearly aimed to please and to edify; the collection is full of the sort of story beloved in the middle ages—tales of magicians and monsters, ladies in distress, escapes from perilous situations, all unified by their moral purpose and made real by details drawn from observation of nature and everyday life. He brought together a variety of excellent material—the germ of the romance *Guy of Warwick*; the story of "Darius and His Three Sons," versified by Occleve; part of Chaucer's *Man of Law's Tale*; and a tale of the emperor Theodosius, the same in its main features as that of *King Lear*. The loose structure of the book made it possible for a transcriber to insert additional stories into his own copy, and therefore the manuscripts show considerable variety. The earliest printed editions were produced at Utrecht and Cologne, late in the 15th century, but their exact dates are unknown.

Three English versions were made during the 15th century, two of them about 1440, the third later. This last, probably based directly on Harleian manuscript 5369 (British museum, London), was re-edited by W. Hooper (1877) and reissued with preface by E. A. Baker (1905). The English versions were edited by Sir F. Madden for the Roxburghe club (1838), and by S. J. H. Herritage for the Early English Text society (1879; reprinted 1932 and 1962), both with valuable introductions. *See also* T. Warton's "Dissertation" prefixed to his *History of English Poetry*, vol. 1 (1824); H. S. Bennett, *Chaucer and the 15th Century* (1947), vol. iii of the *Oxford History of English Literature*. (N. D.)

BIBLIOGRAPHY.—On the manuscripts *see further* M. Krepinski, in *Le Moyen Age*, 2nd series, xv (1911). The Latin text was edited by H. Oesterley (1872) and W. Dick (1890). A translation by C. Swan (1824) was published by Wynkyn de Worde about 1524; the only known copy is in the library of St. John's college, Cambridge. In 1577, Richard Robinson published a revised edition of De Worde, which proved extremely popular. The first volume of a translation by "B. P." (probably Bartholomew Pratt) "from the latin edition of 1514" appeared in 1703.

GESTATION PERIOD.

The period of gestation, or pregnancy, in mammals is usually defined as the time, between conception and birth, in which the embryo or fetus is developing in the uterus. This definition raises occasional difficulties since in some species (*e.g.*, in monkeys and man) with long periods during which intercourse may be performed, the exact time of conception may not be known. In these cases it is customary to date the beginning of the period from some well-defined point in the reproductive cycle, such as the beginning of the previous menstrual period. However, as knowledge of the time of ovulation becomes more precisely known correction is made for this factor.

The length of the gestation period varies from species to species, and each has its characteristic average duration. The shortest known gestation is that of the Indian elephant, about 22 months. Very little is known of the causes of this species variation but in most mammals the time of birth is determined by the length of life of the *corpus luteum*, a glandular organ that replaces the ovum in the ovary. The *corpus luteum* secretes a hormone, progesterone, that is essential for the maintenance of pregnancy. When it degenerates and no longer secretes progesterone, birth follows. The length of life of the *corpus luteum* is, therefore, a determining factor in the length of the gestation period. Pregnancy may be extended by the injection of progesterone and the young continue to grow, but they do not live for more than a few days under this treatment. However this is not the only mechanism, since in the mare and the East African bat *Nycteris luteola*, the *corpora lutea* (plural) degenerate early in pregnancy, yet pregnancy continues. Probably in these species some other organ takes over the secretion of progesterone. Removal of the *corpora lutea* during pregnancy produces variable results. In the monkey and in man they may be removed early, *i.e.*, soon after uterine implantation of the embryos, without interruption of gestation; in other species (*e.g.*, mice, cattle and goats) the *corpora lutea* appear to be essential throughout, since abortion or resorption of the embryos follows their excision.

Evolutionary Factors.—In the course of evolution the duration of gestation appears to have become adapted to the needs of the species. The degree of ultimate growth is a factor, for smaller animals usually have shorter periods of gestation than do larger forms. Main exceptions to this rule are found in the guinea pig and related South American rodents, in which gestation is prolonged (averaging 68 days for the guinea pig and 111 days for the chinchilla), in comparison with the 20-30 days gestation period usual for rodents. The young of these species having a prolonged gestation period are born in a state of greater maturity than are those of the rat with its period of 22 days. Another factor is that, in many species with restricted breeding seasons, the gestation period is adjusted to cause birth at the season when food is most abundant. Thus the horse, a spring breeder with 11 months' gestation, has its young the following spring, while the sheep, a fall breeder with a 5 months' gestation, lambs also in the spring. Animals that live in the open tend to have longer gestations, and the young are born in a state of greater maturity, than those that can conceal their young in underground burrows or in caves. This applies to rodents generally, and to the bear, whose young are born very immature, while the she-bear is in her period of winter sleep; these animals have short gestation periods. The Virginian opossum and other marsupials generally have short gestations; *e.g.*, 40 days only for the largest kangaroos. The young are born in an extremely immature state and immediately transfer to the pouch in which gestation may be said to continue.

Delayed Implantation.—Embryos of some species experience an arrest in development at the blastocyst (hollow sphere of cells)

Animal	Gestation Periods (in days)	
	Average	Variation
Ape, Barbary	210	
Ass	365	
Baboon, sacred	183	
Bat, Common European	50	
Bear, American black	210	
Buffalo (Bison)	275	
Camel	406	370-440
Cat	63	55-69
Cattle	284	260-300
Chimpanzee	237	216-261
Chipmunk	31	
Coyote	60-65	
Deer, Virginia	215	
Dog	61	58-63
Dolphin	276	
Elephant, Asiatic	645	520-730
Ferret	42	
Fisher	338-358	
Fox	52	49-55
Giraffe	395-425	
Goat	151	145-157
Ground squirrel	28	
Guinea pig	68	
Hamster	16.5	
Hedgehog, European	35-40	
Horse	337	320-355
Hyena	110	
Kangaroo, giant	38-40	
Lion	108	105-113
Marten, pine	267	250-285
Mink	50	39-76
Monkey, capuchin	185	
Monkey, grivet	215	
Monkey, rhesus	164	146-180
Mouse	19	18-20
Opossum, Virginian	12.5	
Otter, Canada	62	
Orangutan	245-275	
Pig, domestic	113	110-120
Rabbit	31	30-32
Raccoon	63	
Rat	22	
Rat, cotton	27	21.5-22
Reindeer	215-245	
Seal, northern fur	350	
Sheep	148	143-159
Skunk	63	
Squirrel, gray	44	
Tiger	105-109	
Whale	365	
Woodchuck	28	

stage, thus greatly prolonging the gestation period. This is especially true of the fur-bearing carnivores, the martens and weasels. Thus, the European badger and American marten breed in July and August; the embryo develops for a few days, then lies dormant in the uterus and is not implanted in the uterus until January. After implantation, however, development is normal and birth occurs in March. The total gestation period is thus about 250 days, but only 50 are actually taken up by growth. The dormant period can be reduced by at least three months if the pregnant females are exposed to artificial light during autumn and winter in order to increase daily amounts of light, a result that suggests that the pituitary gland, by its regulation of the *corpus luteum*, may be involved in prolongation. This type of gestation has also been observed in the armadillo and the roe deer; there is reason to suspect that it occurs in bears and seals.

Delayed implantation also occurs in mice and other small rodents that become pregnant while they are still suckling a litter. Under such circumstances gestation in these animals may be prolonged by 10 to 20 days. The prolongation results from the drain on the mother caused by lactation, since the degree of lengthening is directly related to the number of young that are being suckled. Delayed implantation is shown less in larger rodents, such as the common rat (gestation 22 days) and the cotton rat (27 days) than it is in mice.

Minor Variations in the Gestation Period.—If a large series of gestations of one species are plotted as a curve, the distribution is found to be normal (a bell-shaped curve); *i.e.*, there are few periods of short length, then the daily frequency increases rapidly to a maximum, and the number of longer gestations falls off rapidly until there are very few greatly prolonged ones. This distribution suggests that either a single factor or a great number of minor factors, all culminating at or near one date, determine the length of gestation. The latter is probably nearer the truth, as several minor variations are known to occur: in man, the gestation period for males is three to four days longer than that for females; and in cattle, bulls are carried about one day longer than heifers. In both species the gestation period of twins is five to six days less than it is for singlets. In animals such as the rabbit or pig, which bear many young at a time, gestation is shorter for larger litters than it is for smaller ones. Heredity also influences gestation; in cattle the mean gestation period for Holstein-Friesians is 279 days, while that for Brown Swiss is 290 days, with other breeds falling between these extremes. The same tendency is noticeable in horses, where draft horses tend to have a shorter gestation than saddle horses, though Percherons fall into the longer group.

The season of year affects gestation in a few species. This effect is most marked in the horse, in which gestations terminating in winter average about 20 days shorter than those ending at any other time of year. The cause of this has not been explained. The age of either parent seems to have no influence on the duration of gestation.

When hybrids are produced by crossing of two species that have different gestation periods, the hybrid is carried for a period that lies somewhere between those of the two parents. Thus a mare carries a mule foal (fathered by a jackass) about 10 days longer than the normal period for the horse (about 337 days), while a jenny ass carries a hinny foal (fathered by a stallion) about 10 days less than the normal for the ass (about 365 days). In either case the gestation period of the hybrid is not exactly midway between those of the parents, but is a little toward the mother's species, suggesting that maternal physiology is an influence as well as that of the hybrid.

See EMBRYOLOGY AND DEVELOPMENT, ANIMAL; REPRODUCTION; REPRODUCTIVE SYSTEM; BIRTH, HUMAN; PREGNANCY; *see also* references under "Gestation Period" in the Index.

For a more complete discussion *see* L. B. Flexner's *Gestation* (1955); the gestation periods of many species may be found in J. H. Kenneth's *Gestation Periods* (1943). (S. A.)

GESUALDO, DON CARLO, PRINCE OF VENOSA (c. 1560–1613), Italian composer and lutenist whose musical fame rests on his six sets of five-part madrigals, was born in Naples. Gesualdo seems to have lived most of his life in or around that city; he

died there on Sept. 8, 1613. He won notoriety by ordering the murder of his first wife for her unfaithfulness. His madrigals were published between 1594 and 1611 in the usual partbooks and in 1613 were printed in score—one of the first publications of its kind. The madrigals in the first four books are conventional pieces of competent workmanship, typical of their age. The astonishing madrigals in the last two books, with their dramatic exclamations, discontinuous texture and harmonic licence, are not "progressive," as has often been said. They are, rather, the work of a highly individual composer and, as such, lacked any successors in this bizarre vein.

See C. Gray and P. Heseltine, *Carlo Gesualdo, Prince of Venosa, Musician and Murderer* (1926). (N. Fo.)

GETA, PUBLIUS SEPTIMIUS, joint Roman emperor 209–212, was born in Milan in 189, younger son of the emperor Septimius Severus and Julia Domna. He was styled *Caesar* in 198, when his elder brother Caracalla became joint emperor (*Augustus*) with their father, and was himself promoted *Augustus* in 209. The furious rivalry between the brothers made each the focus of opposing groups within the empire. After their father's death at York early in 211, both brothers openly sought each other's murder until, in Feb. 212, Caracalla succeeded in having Geta murdered in their mother's arms, in her apartments in the palace. (JN. R. M.)

GETAE, an ancient people of Thracian origin, closely akin to the Daci (*see* DACIA). They inhabited lands on both banks of the lower Danube, and to the north of the river extended far into south Russia, where Thracian personal and place names can be traced as far east as the Crimea. The Getae are first noted in literature by Herodotus, recounting the invasion of Scythia by Darius I about 513 B.C.; and a century later, as remarked by Thucydides in his *History* (ii, 96), certain Getae were under the suzerainty of Sitalces, king of the Odrysae. When the Odrysae were subjected by Philip II of Macedonia in 342 the Getae made overtures to him, and their king's daughter became his wife. Alexander the Great on his accession decided to make his power felt in the north and, after defeating the Triballi of the Balkans, crossed the Danube and burned the Getic capital (335); but about 326 Zopyrion, the Macedonian governor of Thrace, was killed in an expedition against the tribe. In 292 Lysimachus penetrated to the Bessarabian plain but was forced to surrender, though the Getic king Dromichaetes allowed him to depart unharmed. From the late 3rd century onward the military power of the Getae was broken by the mass invasions of the Bastarnae (*q.v.*) and other tribes. The Romans occupied all the country up to the Danube by Augustus' day, and about the beginning of the Christian era the Sarmatians finally conquered south Russia. From then on the Getae disappear from history.

Later writers gave the name Getae to the Goths, who had no connection whatever with the people described above. The Getae were Thracians subjected to Scythian influence, expert as mounted archers and devotees of Zalmoxis, a deity translated by Porphyry as "bearskin" and "strange man." The Greeks were greatly impressed by the Getae's belief in man's immortality, and Greek rationalizers in the Black sea colonies identified Zalmoxis as a pupil of Pythagoras.

BIBLIOGRAPHY.—Herodotus, *History*, iv, 93 *et seq.*; Strabo, *Geography*, vii, 295–305; *Cambridge Ancient History*, vol. xi, pp. 77 (reprint 1954). (G. E. F. C.)

GETHSEMANE (GETHSEMANI; "oil press"), the place to which Jesus withdrew with his disciples on the evening before the crucifixion (Matt. xxvi, 36; Mark xiv, 32). Luke xxii, 39 locates it on the Mount of Olives, which was across the brook Kidron east of Jerusalem. John xviii, 1 says that Jesus withdrew to a garden, presumably enclosed, across the brook Kidron and so on the western slope of the Mount of Olives. The name suggests that the "garden" was a grove of olive trees in which there was an oil press. The exact spot to which Jesus went cannot be determined with certainty, but the Armenian, Greek, Latin and Russian churches have all claimed to mark the site by the olive groves on the lower western slope of the Mount of Olives, and this area would suit well the meagre details given by the Gospels. An ancient tradition locates the scene of Jesus' Gethsemane prayer and betrayal at the spot now called the Grotto of the Agony, near the bridge that crosses the Kidron. A little farther south, in a garden containing very old olive trees, the Latin church built by the Franciscans is located on ruins of a 4th-century church that attest an alternate tradition. *See also* JERUSALEM. (F. V. F.)

GETTYSBURG, a borough of southern Pennsylvania, U.S., 35 mi. S.W. of Harrisburg; it is the county seat of Adams county. It lies in a beautiful rolling country of fertile farms. Named for James Gettys, to whom the site was granted by William Penn, it was settled about 1780, became the county seat in 1800 and was incorporated as a borough in 1806. Gettysburg college (originally Pennsylvania college) was established in 1832 with Lutheran affiliation. It is a coeducational liberal arts college. Dedication of the national cemetery at Gettysburg in Nov. 1863 was the occasion of Lincoln's Gettysburg Address. The battlefield became a national park in 1895; jurisdiction passed to the national military park service in 1933. For comparative population figures *see* table in PENNSYLVANIA: *Population.*

Battle of Gettysburg.—This three-day battle, which started July 1, 1863, at a place where neither opponent expected a major engagement, is generally regarded as the turning point of the American Civil War. It has probably been more intensively studied and analyzed than any other battle in U.S. history. (For background, *see* AMERICAN CIVIL WAR.)

After defeating the Federal forces under Gen. Joseph Hooker at Chancellorsville in May 1863, Gen. *Robert E. Lee* had decided to invade the North. The morale of his troops was high while defeatist sentiment was spreading in the North. He hoped that a bold thrust into Pennsylvania might cause further discourage-

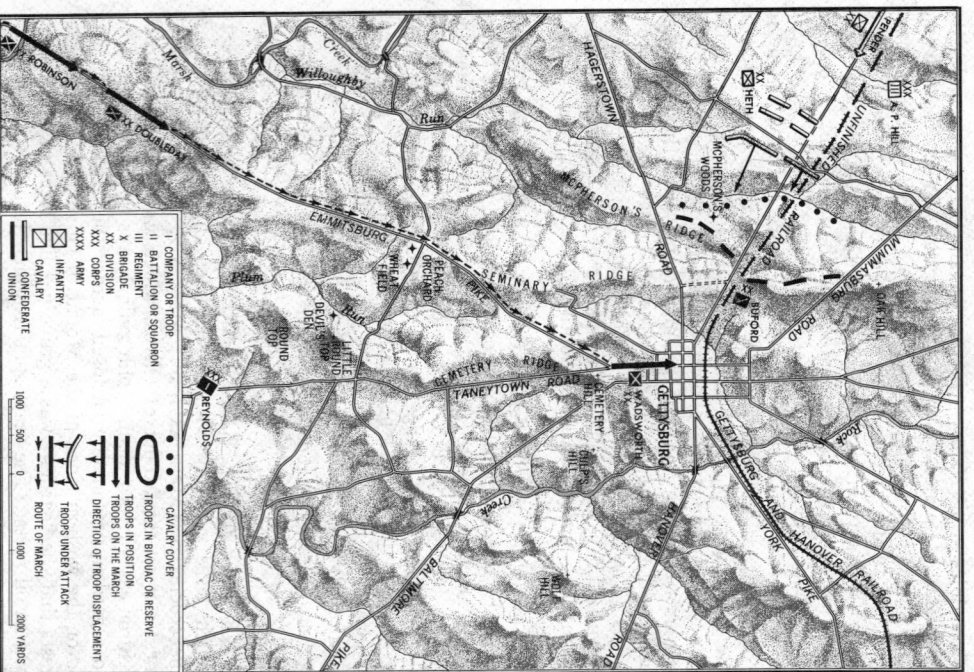

FROM "THE WEST POINT ATLAS OF AMERICAN WARS," VOLUME 1, PUBLISHED BY FREDERICK A. PRAEGER, INC. (1959)

FIG. 1.—SITUATION ON THE FIRST DAY OF THE GETTYSBURG BATTLE, JULY 1, 1863, AT 10 A.M.

ment in the North and at the same time induce European powers to give diplomatic recognition to the Confederacy. In preparation for his invasion *Lee* reorganized his army of about 75,000 men into three corps under Gen. *A. P. Hill*, Gen. *James Longstreet* and Gen. *R. S. Ewell.* The cavalry was led by Gen. *J. E. B. Stuart.* During the last week in June, *Stuart* made a bold and, in the opinion of some, ill-advised cavalry sweep completely around the Federal forces, passing between them and the national capital.

On June 28, when his army of northern Virginia was extended deep into Pennsylvania, *Lee* was out of touch with his cavalry under *Stuart*, which should have served as the eyes of the army. Through a spy *Lee* received a report that Hooker's army of the Potomac was at Frederick, Md., under a new commander, Gen. George G. Meade, who had just replaced Hooker. *Lee* took immediate steps to meet this unexpected threat. *Ewell*, whose corps had been preparing to carry the offensive across the Susquehanna from positions at Carlisle and York, was ordered to move either to Cashtown or Gettysburg. *Longstreet's* corps at Chambersburg and *A. P. Hill's* corps at Greenwood, both of which had been preparing to move north, were to march east to Cashtown. This concentration east of South mountain would put *Lee* in an excellent strategic position to defend or attack.

Early on June 29, Meade started north with Gen. John Buford's two cavalry brigades scouting ahead of the army. While maneuvering to keep between *Lee* and the Federal capital, Meade intended to make *Lee* turn and fight before he could cross the Susquehanna. On June 30, Buford's troopers met and drove back a Confederate brigade from *Hill's* corps that was approaching Gettysburg to seize a reported supply of badly needed shoes. *Hill* then authorized Gen. *Henry Heth* to lead his division into Gettys-

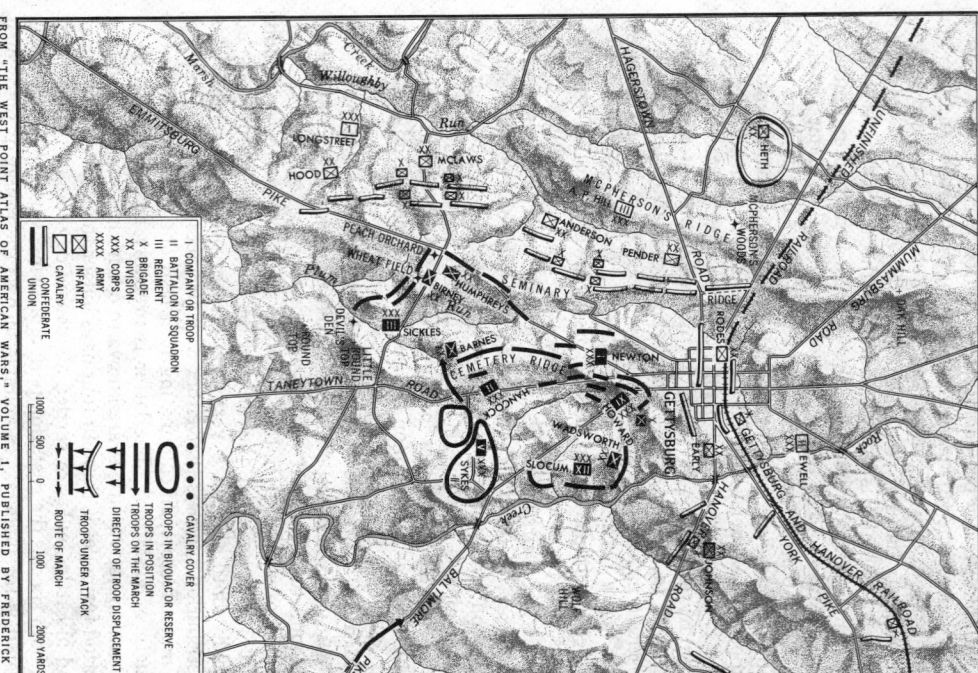

FROM "THE WEST POINT ATLAS OF AMERICAN WARS," VOLUME 1, PUBLISHED BY FREDERICK A. PRAEGER, INC. (1959)

FIG. 2.—SITUATION ABOUT 3:30 P.M. ON SECOND DAY OF BATTLE OF GETTYSBURG

burg the next day. Buford, meanwhile, had immediately recognized the strategic importance of Gettysburg as a road centre and prepared to hold the town until reinforcements arrived.

First Day's Battle.—On July 1, one of Buford's brigades, armed with the newly issued Spencer repeating carbine, delayed *Heth's* division until J. F. Reynolds' I corps began to arrive at about 11 A.M. A vigorous counterattack drove *Heth's* two leading brigades back with heavy losses on both sides. Reynolds was killed by a sharpshooter. By 1 P.M., all three divisions of the I corps were deployed along Seminary ridge and two divisions of the XI corps had arrived to defend the northern approaches to the town. A third division of the XI corps was posted on Cemetery hill. Gen. O. O. Howard reached the field about noon, turning his XI corps over to Gen. Carl Schurz and succeeding Gen. Abner Doubleday in over-all command of the battlefield. The Federals resisted on both fronts until about 2:30, but an attack by Gen. *Jubal Early's* division against the northeast flank of the XI corps led to collapse of their entire position. The XI corps was routed, exposing the flank of the I corps and forcing it to retreat. Before the defenders could rally on Cemetery hill the two Union corps had sustained more than 50% casualties. *Lee* now had superior strength available, but, being in the dark as to the enemy's true dispositions, he did not want to bring on a general engagement until *Longstreet's* corps arrived. About 4 P.M., Gen. W. S. Hancock arrived to examine the situation for Meade and decide whether to drop back to previously prepared positions along Pipe creek, 15 mi. S.E. After recognizing the importance of Culp's hill and ordering it occupied, Hancock studied the terrain and reported that Gettysburg was the place to fight. Meade, having reached the same conclusion, had already ordered the III and XII

corps forward. *Lee* told *Ewell* to attack Cemetery hill "if possible," but *Ewell* did not elect to take the risk. Whether this decision was correct remains a moot point.

The Second Day, July 2.—By dawn, Meade's troops occupied a line along Culp's hill, Cemetery hill and Cemetery ridge. Both opposing commanders recognized that a Confederate success on the Federal right would jeopardize Meade's entire position by threatening his line of communications along the Baltimore pike. *Lee* wanted to exploit this strategic weakness, but *Ewell* argued that *Longstreet* should make the main attack on the opposite flank. *Longstreet*, on the other hand, contended that *Lee* should make Meade attack. Delayed by the opposition of his corps commanders, *Lee* did not issue his orders until 11 A.M. *Longstreet* was to envelop the Federal south flank and attack north along the Emmitsburg pike, where *Lee* erroneously believed Meade's main line to be; *Hill* and *Ewell* were to make secondary attacks.

When *Longstreet's* artillery started preparatory firing at 3 P.M. Meade rushed to the heretofore neglected south flank and found that Gen. D. E. Sickles had not positioned his III corps along Cemetery ridge as directed but had moved forward to higher ground; this created a dangerous salient and weakened the south flank, but it was too late to pull him back. Gen. J. B. *Hood's* division attacked at 4 P.M. About this time Gen. G. K. Warren, Meade's chief engineer, reached Little Round Top and found it undefended; but before the 500 Alabama troops who had scaled (Big) Round Top could continue their attack from that hill, Warren had diverted sufficient Federal reserves to defend Little Round Top. While Warren's action secured the main battle position, the Federal III corps was driven from "Sickles' salient" with crippling losses. There was desperate fighting at Little Round Top, Devil's Den, the Wheat field and the Peach orchard. Both *Hood* and Sickles were seriously wounded. Confederate secondary attacks were so poorly timed, however, that Meade could shift strength from quiet parts of his line and move reserves to meet each new threat. *Hill* attacked too late to achieve significant results, and not until 6 P.M. did *Ewell* launch the assault that should have started with *Longstreet's*. Some of *Ewell's* troops reached Cemetery hill but were driven off; others were stopped on the southeast slopes of Culp's hill.

The Third Day.—In spite of *Longstreet's* objections, *Lee* was determined to attack again on the third day. Meade, on the other hand, was less confident and it was only after a formal council of war that he decided to stay and fight. While *Ewell* made a secondary attack against Culp's hill, *Lee* planned to hit the Federal centre with ten brigades, three of which were fresh troops of Gen. G. E. *Pickett's* division. Although this attack has been immortalized as "*Pickett's* charge," that general's only over-all responsibility was to form the divisions of J. J. *Pettigrew* and I. R. *Trimble* as they reached their attack positions on his left; *Longstreet*, not *Pickett*, was in command of the operation. Shortly after 1 P.M., the Confederates started a tremendous artillery preparation, which was answered immediately by Federal counterfire. At 3 P.M., the infantry moved out of the woods in parade ground order and started across the 1,400 yd. of open fields toward Cemetery ridge. The Federals watched in awed silence as 15,000 Confederate troops moved toward them. Then the Federal artillery, which had ceased fire an hour earlier to save ammunition, went back into action with devastating effect at a range of 700 yd. Almost unscathed by the Confederate artillery preparation, most of which had gone over their heads, the 10,000 Federal infantry against whom the attack was directed waited coolly behind stone walls and held their fire until the Confederates were within effective range. The southern spearhead broke through and penetrated onto Cemetery ridge, but there it could do no more. Critically weakened by artillery during their approach, formations hopelessly tangled, lacking reinforcement, and under savage attack from three sides, they marked "the high tide of the Confederacy" with the bodies of their dead and wounded. Leaving 19 battle flags and hundreds of prisoners, the southerners retreated, demoralized but without panic. Part of one Union brigade advanced to hasten their retreat, but the army of the Potomac had been too roughly handled to mount a counterattack.

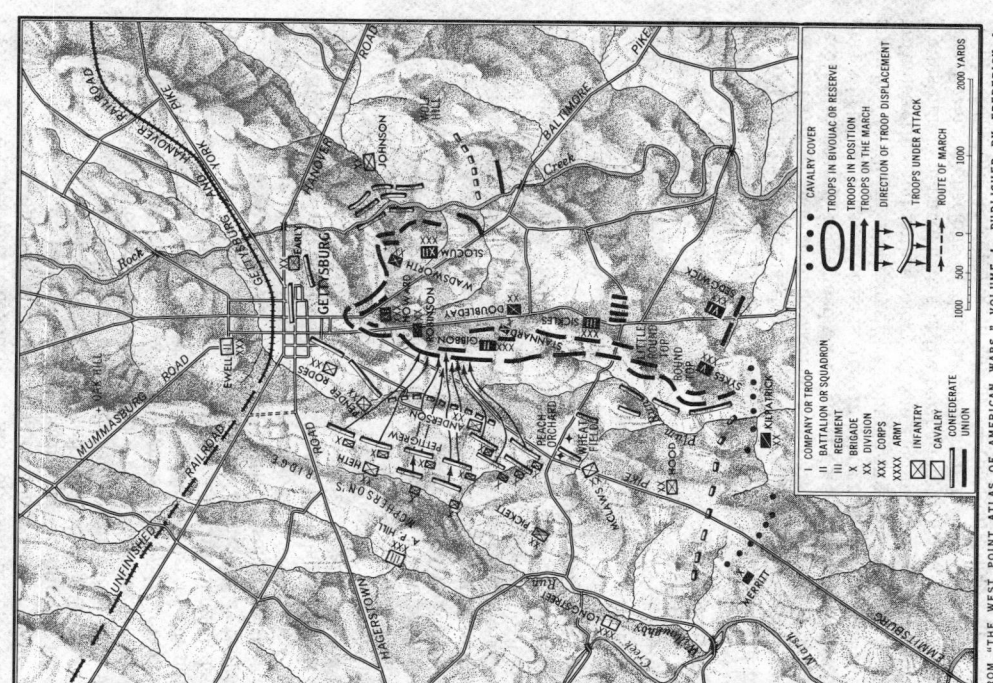

FROM "THE WEST POINT ATLAS OF AMERICAN WARS," VOLUME 1, PUBLISHED BY FREDERICK A. PRAEGER, INC. (1959)

FIG. 3.—GETTYSBURG BATTLE, SITUATION ABOUT 2:30 P.M. ON THIRD DAY

Early in the day, *Ewell* had attacked Culp's hill without success. *Stuart*, whose bone-tired brigades had arrived the previous evening, was driven back by three Federal cavalry brigades when he tried to envelop Meade's strategic north flank. At the other end of the lines Federal cavalry was foolishly employed in futile and costly charges across rough terrain against *Hood's* infantry.

Lee waited during July 4 to meet an attack on Seminary ridge that never came. That night, taking advantage of a heavy rain, he started retreating to Virginia. After the war, when Gettysburg was recognized as the turning point, southern sentiment charged *Longstreet* with "losing the war" by not properly co-operating with his commander on July 2 and 3. *Longstreet* was unenthusiastic about the invasion of Pennsylvania and advocated forcing the Federal army to attack. Confederate successes at Bull Run, Antietam and Fredericksburg had convinced him the war could be won by a policy of strategic offensive and tactical defensive. However, according to Lee's biographer, D. S. Freeman, "Lee never gave any intimation that he considered Longstreet's failure at Gettysburg more than the error of a good soldier. To Longstreet's credit was the belief that Cemetery ridge, on July 2–3, was too strong to be stormed successfully. If, when the balance of Longstreet's account is struck, it still is adverse to him, it does not warrant the traditional accusation that he was the villain of the piece." (*Lee's Lieutenants*, vol. iii, pp. 188–189; copyright 1944, Charles Scribner's Sons, New York, N.Y.) Lee's defeat stemmed from overconfidence in his troops, Ewell's inability to fill the boots of Gen. Thomas J. ("Stonewall") Jackson, and faulty reconnaissance. The latter cannot be attributed entirely to *Stuart's* unfortunate raid; *Lee* was so dependent on *Stuart* personally that he failed to employ properly the four cavalry brigades left at his disposal. Meade has been criticized for not destroying the army of northern Virginia by a vigorous pursuit. But it must be said to his credit that only five days after taking command, Meade had stopped the Confederate invasion and won a three-day battle. Coming the day before Grant's triumph at Vicksburg, Meade's victory meant that destruction of the Confederacy was only a matter of time.

Numbers and Losses.—According to T. L. Livermore, Union losses at Gettysburg were 23,049 out of 88,289 engaged; Confederate losses were 28,063 out of 75,000. Another Northern authority, W. F. Fox, puts Confederate losses at 20,448, which agrees almost exactly with the official Confederate figure of 20,451.

BIBLIOGRAPHY.—U.S. Department of Interior, National Park Service, *Gettysburg National Military Park, Pa.* (May 1961); D. S. Freeman, *R. E. Lee, a Biography*, 4 vol. (1935), *Lee's Lieutenants: a Study in Command*, 3 vol. (1942–44); Frank A. Haskell, *The Battle of Gettysburg*, (1908 and 1958); K. P. Williams, *Lincoln Finds a General*, 5 vol. (1949–56). (M. M. Bo.)

GEULINCX, ARNOLD (1624–1669), like Spinoza, was among the most notable philosophers of the golden age of the Netherlands. Baptized a Catholic at Antwerp on Jan. 31, 1624, Geulincx studied philosophy and theology at the University of Louvain, where he received his first professorships in 1646 and 1652. Probably because of Jansenist tendencies he was dismissed in 1658 and took refuge at Leiden, where he became a Calvinist. He became doctor of medicine on Sept. 16, 1658, and in 1659 he was authorized for a few months to lecture privately in philosophy. He lived in penury, an exile. In 1662, however, through the recommendation of his protector, the theologian A. Heydanus, he obtained a lectureship in logic. In 1665 he was made professor extraordinary of philosophy and ethics. He died of the plague in Nov. 1669.

During his lifetime had been published *Quaestiones quodlibeticae* (1653), re-edited at Leiden under the title *Saturnalia* in 1665; *Logica restituta* (1662); *Methodus inveniendi argumenta* (1663); an ethical dissertation *De virtute et primis ejus proprietatibus* (1665). After his death, his pupil C. Bontekoe, a doctor, published under the pseudonym "Philaretus" the six treatises of the *Gnothi seauton, sive Arnoldi Geulincx Ethica* (1675). Other posthumous works include *Metaphysica vera et ad mentem peripateticam* (1691); *Physica vera* (1688); *Annotata praecurrentia ad R. Cartesii principia* (1690); *Annotata majora* (1691); *Collegium oratorium* (1696).

The work of Geulincx usually appears in the history of philosophy as a mere signpost on the road opened up by the *Meditationes Metaphysicae* of Descartes. If his place be among the epigones of French philosophers, however, what sets him apart at once is the intention of completing Cartesianism with a definitive ethics, to which Descartes had aspired as the supreme goal of philosophic inquiry. Through Philaretus, Geulincx proclaims his loyalty to Descartes. He writes on morals according to his master's principles; for him, to reduce Cartesianism, as some did, to a physics, and not to see that it must issue in wisdom, is to misrepresent it. Thus Geulincx takes the main tenets of Cartesian metaphysics as established: there is the same passage from doubt to *cogito*, from *cogito* to God; the same duality of thought and extension; the same conception of the will's dominant role in determining the judgment. Yet the disciple's preoccupation is quite different from his master's and belongs to a different climate. Whereas Cartesian wisdom expects metaphysics to found a science which would give us mastery of matter, life and mind, in the *Metaphysica vera* Geulincx aims to deepen the relations of the ego and of things with God: he reveals the enigma of man's condition, his ontological impotence before the ineffable transcendence of his creator. The perspectives of conquest which Cartesian metaphysics opened give way to an ethics of humility and of submission of the will (which alone is our own possession) to the order of reason.

Jansenist at Louvain, Calvinist (at least officially) at Leiden, Geulincx always drew his inspiration in metaphysics and ethics from Augustine. The opposition between God, creator, transcendent, incomprehensible, and his quite powerless creation: this is the key idea giving new life to the Cartesianism of the *Metaphysica vera*, and to the neo-stoic, even Spinozist formulas of the *De Virtute*. Here lies the real source of his "occasionalism."

Among the corollaries of the disputation *De incendio Aetnae*, defended by P. Romeyn under the presidency of Geulincx in June 1669, are the following three axioms, vital for grasping Geulincx' wisdom: (1) *Quod nescis quomodo fiat, id non facis* ("one cannot do that which one does not know how to do"); (2) *Facimus semper quod Deus vult* ("we always do what God wills"); (3) *Deus neque peccati neque erroris causa est* ("God is cause neither of sin nor of error"). The first axiom displays his conception of knowledge and being. In the *cogito*, I have the intuition of myself as thinking being, which gives me the certainty of the absolute existence of God, infinite and creator, of whom my thought is but a mode. As man, composed of body and soul, I depend both in my being and action on God, for God is the unique cause of all he knows, to wit, of all that occurs in the universe. I cannot know the being of things because I have not made them, and because the divine action is beyond my grasp. Whether it be the world of thought or the world of matter or their reciprocal action, I can know them only in so far as God reveals them to me, and according to my human capacity. God, unique source of all causality, disposes of mind and matter as of instruments of his infinite power. All activity flows from the creator; in creatures it can therefore be only immanent. I am not the author of my thoughts, no more than of extension, the "brutum," which borders on nothingness, cannot really act on me either. The enclosed world of my sense experience is only a world of appearances, a subjective reflection of the world of extension, in itself unknowable. God uses the "occasion" of the body to produce my various thoughts; what I think I do is really his making my will effective. Instrumentalism is a better name for this than occasionalism. The link between the first and second axiom now becomes apparent: man, like things bereft of causality, is confined within strict determinism: he always does what God wills. Yet he is free, and thus responsible for error and sin. Geulincx' metaphysics of human impotence issues in an optimist ethic and anthropology. Man's nothingness is not total. By his mind, he participates in the perfection of his creator, *Deus sive Ratio*. Conscious of this reason that is in him, he can conform to the divine will, not in his acts—these are operations of God—but in his intention, his voluntary submission to the divine will. This is where man acts freely, and this is the whole of virtue: it establishes man in a bond of love with God, who for Geulincx the philosopher is doubtless identical with the God of his faith as a Christian.

Geulincx' works have been edited by J. P. N. Land, *Arnoldi Geulincx Antverpiensis Opera Philosophica*, 3 vols. (1891–93).

BIBLIOGRAPHY.—V. van der Haeghen: *Geulincx, études sur sa vie, sa philosophie et ses ouvrages* (1886); J. P. N. Land, *Arnold Geulincx und seine Philosophie* (1895); M. Paulinus, *Die Sittenlehre Geulincx* (1892); E. Terraillon, *La Morale de Geulincx dans ses rapports avec la philosophie de Descartes* (1912); H. J. De Vleeshauwer, "Les antécédents du transcendentalisme: Geulincx et Kant," *Kantstudien*, XLV (1953–54), pp. 245–273 and "Occasionalisme et conditio humana chez Arnold Geulincx," *Kantstudien*, L (1958–59), pp. 109–124. (P. Di.)

GEYSER, an intermittent hot spring which, at more or less regular intervals, spouts its contents of water and steam into the air to heights varying from mere inches to, in exceptionally vigorous geysers, hundreds of feet. The word stems from "Geysir," the Icelandic proper name, meaning gusher or spouter, which has been applied since 1647 to a particular geyser in southwestern Iceland. In 1847 the German chemist Robert Wilhelm von Bunsen used the word as a technical term for all hot springs similar to "Geysir" in action; the English spelling is geyser.

Geysers are a rare natural phenomenon that occurs mostly in regions of relatively recent volcanic activity. The three areas of highest development are at Yellowstone National park in the United States, and in Iceland and New Zealand. Geysers have also been reported from Alaska, Tibet, Japan, the Malay archipelago, South and Central America and Nevada. Cold-water springs exhibiting geyser action occur at Kane, Pa., and Soda Springs, Ida.

Yellowstone National park in northwest Wyoming possesses the world's greatest concentration of geysers. Whereas all of Iceland contains only 30 known active geysers, Yellowstone's boundaries include some 200 active geysers, almost 10% of the hot springs being geysers. The hot springs and geysers tend to be concentrated along the drainage basins of streams, such areas then being called "geyser basins." This local usage conflicts with the earlier and preferred use of geyser basin to denote the bowllike depression or crater containing the geyser's pool during quiescence.

The two major geyser basins of Yellowstone National park, the upper basin and the lower basin, are located along the rather level valley floor bordering the Firehole river. The upper basin, the most spectacular of its type on the globe, possesses a myriad of hot springs and geysers, some with pools containing water above the boiling temperature of 93° C. for that elevation yet, for unknown reasons, not boiling. Old Faithful, the most renowned of the upper basin's 70-odd geysers, erupts to heights of 100 to 150 ft. at intervals of about an hour and for durations of about five minutes. Grand geyser, which erupts irregularly at intervals varying from once to twice a day, majestically expels its water to heights approaching 160 ft.; the eruption, punctuated by short periods of quiescence, may last from 18 to 50 min. and results in the discharge of over 9,000 cu.ft. of water. Castle geyser, whose eruptions may be accompanied by earth tremors, sometimes steams for two hours after the eruption. Beehive geyser, an infrequent performer, was observed to erupt to a height of 219 ft., the highest measured in the park.

The great geyser district of New Zealand, located near the upper basin of the Waikato river in the south of the province of Auckland, presents a striking profusion of boiling springs, steam jets and mud volcanoes. The geysers were inactive in 1880 but revived after the Tarawera volcanic eruption of 1886; seven gigantic geysers then came into existence, discharging water, steam, mud and stones to heights up to 800 ft. for four hours before quieter conditions prevailed. Waimangu, the greatest of all geysers, was active from 1900 to 1904, occasionally spouting jets to 1,500 ft.; draining nearby Tarawera lake in 1904 caused Waimangu's water level to drop about 35 ft., whereupon geyser action ceased.

Iceland's geysers are mostly concentrated within two areas, one 30 mi. N. of Reykjavik, the second extending eastward from Reykjavik toward the active volcano Hekla. Geysir itself is 30 mi. N.W. of Hekla in a broad valley at the foot of a range of hills. During its calm periods Geysir appears as a sea-green

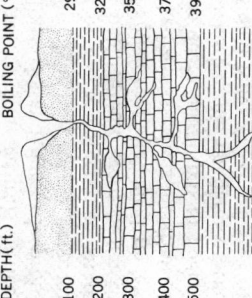

DEPTH (ft.)	BOILING POINT (°F.)
100	291°
200	329°
300	356°
400	377°
500	394°

FROM H. BROWN, V. MONNETT AND J. STOVALL, "INTRODUCTION TO GEOLOGY," 1958

DIAGRAMMATIC REPRESENTATION OF A GEYSER TUBE

Geyser action presumably results from constricted portions of the tube interfering with the formation of convection currents and permitting water to accumulate in the lower parts of the tube until heated far above the normal boiling point. The boiling points indicated for the different depths assume the tube to be completely filled with water, which would be true only toward the end of each period

pool 60 ft. in diameter and 4 ft. in depth, filling and gently overflowing a bowllike depression or basin on the summit of a mound of siliceous mineral deposits, or sinter (*q.v.*). Extending downward from the basin's centre is a 10 ft. diameter, 70 ft. deep, welllike shaft whose water temperatures, at various depths, were first measured by V. Lottin in 1836. Ten years later Bunsen and A. L. O. des Cloizeaux observed that: (1) Geysir's temperature increased steadily from its surface downward to the mid-point of its well whereupon, for greater depths, it increased at a lesser rate; and that (2) Geysir's temperature at all depths, except for minor fluctuations, steadily increased as the time for the next eruption drew near. Conclusions drawn in Bunsen's classic (1847) paper were: (1) the steady temperature increase for all depths would, Geysir's temperature-depth relationships being as observed, cause boiling conditions to be most closely approached at mid-depths; (2) an upward movement of the water column in the tube sufficient to cause overflow from the basin would trigger the eruption by elevating the deeper, high-temperature waters to shallower levels of reduced pressure such that the water at mid-level would, during one of these upward surges, exceed the boiling temperature of its new site; (3) the volumes of steam consequently formed at mid-depths would increase the upward surge of the water column to accelerate overflow; and (4) in turn, this accelerated overflow would cause more levels within the geyser column to boil, the chain reaction ultimately producing a full-scale eruption.

Bunsen's theory, conceived to fit only Geysir, was widely accepted and extended, perhaps unduly, to cover all geysers. Subsequent work revealed features of geyser action unaccounted for by the theory. For example, H. O. Lang in 1880 noted the necessity of an influx of relatively cooler water to terminate an eruption, otherwise all geysers would simply become steam vents. T. Thorkelsson in 1940 cited evidence in support of his theory that bubbles formed by dissolved gases in the water, principally nitrogen, carbon dioxide, oxygen and argon, could cause eruptions without boiling conditions being attained at depth.

See E. T. Allen and Arthur L. Day, *Hot Springs of the Yellowstone National Park*, Carnegie Institution of Washington, D.C. (1935); T. F. W. Barth, *Volcanic Geology, Hot Springs and Geysers of Iceland*, Carnegie Institution of Washington, D.C. (1950). (F. D. B.)

GEZELLE, GUIDO (1830–1899), Flemish priest and poet, one of the masters of modern European lyric poetry, was born at Bruges, May 1, 1830. He spent his youth in Bruges, at that time almost a medieval town, studying the humanities there and at Roulers (1846–49), and philosophy and theology at Bruges (1850–54). At Roulers were awakened his combative Flemish nationalism and his poetic genius; there too companionship with English students aroused his sympathy for Britain, which lasted all his life. He was ordained in 1854 although already a teacher at Roulers, where he remained until 1860. His own personality developed to the full and he worked to inspire his students with his religious, poetic and Flemish nationalistic idealism. His romantic views on education, friendship, aesthetics, language and poetry clashed with conservative opinion, however, and in 1860 he was transferred to Bruges where he became professor of philosophy and vice-principal of the Anglo-Belgian seminary (1861–65) and curate (1865–72).

Meanwhile he revealed himself as a lively, sometimes reckless political journalist, writing with startling facility in his weekly, *'t Jaer 30*, and edited a cultural weekly, *Rond den Heerd* (1865), for which he wrote on his main interests—philology, folklore, local history and natural science. Overwork, disappointments, political attacks and domestic problems reduced his poetic output and brought him to the verge of a nervous breakdown. In Sept. 1872 he was transferred as curate to Courtrai, where he recovered his balance and again began to write poetry. In 1881 he founded *Loquela*, a philological review edited by himself, and in 1886 published a masterly translation of *Hiawatha*. From about 1877 until his death his output of poetry continued constant. In March 1899 he became chaplain of the English convent at Bruges, where he died Nov. 27.

During his first period (1850–70), Gezelle's poetry (*Kerkhofblommen* and *Dichtoefeningen*, 1858; *Kleengedichtjes*, 1860; *Gedichten, gezangen en gebeden*, 1862) was the untrammeled expression of a sensitive, passionate and versatile personality, illadjusted to life, enthusiastic yet shy, egocentric, yet delighting in sentimental friendship and the beauty of nature and finding its spiritual exaltation in love of God. The poetry of his second period (1877–99), collected in *Tijdkrans* (1893), *Rijmsnoer* (1897) and *Laatste verzen* (1901), was more mature and controlled in construction, and, although the poet still longed for liberation from earthly bonds, he attained greater harmony with the outer world. Almost from the beginning he had shown great technical originality in his use of language and imagery, rhythm and rhyme, developing a style highly individual yet rooted linguistically in the west Flemish dialect. His work as philologist and folklorist is also interesting, and his influence on 19th-century Flemish intellectual life was great. His originality in writing poetry of great lyrical purity and intensity, liberating the secret forces of the word at a time when positivism prevailed, has caused him to be considered a forerunner of their art by modern poets.

BIBLIOGRAPHY.—*Jubileumuitgave van Guido Gezelle's Volledige Werken*, 18 vol. (1930–39); G. Gezelle's *Dichtwerken*, ed. by F. Baur, 4 vol., 3rd ed. (1950–51); *Lyra Belgica*, I, Eng. trans. by C. and F. Stillman (1950); G. L. van Roosbroeck, G. Gezelle: the Mystic Poet of Flanders (1919); A. Walgrave, *Het leven van G. Gezelle, Vlaamschen priester en dichter*, 2 vol. (1923–24); U. van de Voorde, G. Gezelle (1926); F. Baur, *Uit Gezelle's leven en werk* (1930); R. F. Lissens, *Het Impressionisme in de Vlaamsche letterkunde* (1934); A. Vermeylen, De Vlaamse letteren van Gezelle tot heden (1949); H. Bruning, Guido Gezelle de andere (1954). Eng. trans. of selections from his poems by M. Swepstone (1937). (R. F. Ls.)

GEZER, once a royal Canaanite city, now a small village and agricultural settlement about 6 mi. S.S.W. of Lydda in Israel. It was described in the Old Testament as on the boundary of Ephraim, in the maritime plain and near the Philistine border. According to Jerome, Gezer was 4 Roman mi. N. of Nicopolis ('Amwas). At this point, near the village of Abu Shusha, stands Tell Jezer, whose identification with Gezer was suggested by Clermont Ganneau in 1871 and later confirmed by the discovery of boundary inscriptions on rock outcroppings around the site.

History.—Gezer is often mentioned in the Egyptian records of the New Kingdom, from Thutmose III (15th century) to Merneptah (late 13th century B.C.). Among the clay tablets in Babylonian cuneiform which were found at Tell el-Amarna in Egypt, from the reigns of the Egyptian Pharaohs Amenhotep III and IV (early 14th century B.C.), were 11 official letters, ten written by princes of Gezer with biblical names and one written by Pharaoh in reply. A fragment of another Egyptian letter to the prince of Gezer was discovered at Gezer itself. Gezer was abandoned about 900 B.C. and was little occupied thereafter.

Archaeology.—The site was excavated systematically by R. A. S. Macalister for the Palestine Exploration fund during 1902–05 and 1907–09. The excavations disclosed a whole series of strata covering most periods from the Neolithic Age to the time of the Maccabees, together with a long series of structures and objects illustrative of a corresponding variety of cultures and cults. Among the discoveries of special interest are two cuneiform tablets of the 7th century B.C., an alignment of monoliths (*mazzeboth*) of presumed infant sacrifice, a water tunnel cut to a vertical depth of 94 ft., and an agricultural calendar from the 10th century B.C., written in Hebrew. Excavations were resumed at Gezer in 1923 and have continued intermittently. In 1957 Y. Yadin identified the Solomonic wall and gateway of Gezer, referred to in I Kings ix, 15–17; these fortifications are identical in construction with the corresponding Solomonic remains excavated at Megiddo and Hazor.

BIBLIOGRAPHY.—R. A. S. Macalister, *Bible Sidelights From the Mound of Gezer* (1906), *The Excavations of Gezer*, 3 vol. (1912); Y. Yadin, "Solomon's City Wall and Gate at Gezer," *Israel Exploration Journal*, vol. viii, pp. 80–86 (1958). (W. F. A.)

GEZIRA (Arabic for "island"), a triangular area in the Republic of the Sudan, lying between the Blue and White Niles south of their confluence at Khartoum as far as latitude 13° 30' N., is a clay plain about 1,300 ft. above sea level. Its irrigation works known as the Gezira scheme depend for their water on the Sennar (formerly Makwar) dam, built 1922–25. Canalization irrigates about 1,000,000 ac. yielding valuable crops of long-staple cotton, millet and fodder. The scheme incorporates an agreement between the Sudanese government, the Gezira board and the Sudanese cultivators. The government, which provided and maintains the dam and principal canals, receives 40% of the proceeds of the cotton crop, 20% being paid to the board (which supervises cultivation, transport, ginning and marketing) and 40% to the tenants who cultivate and pick the crop. The tenants (about 25,000) each farm about 40 ac. under a prescribed rotation. They are mostly descended from those formerly cultivating the area under uncertain and sporadic rainfall. They also receive rent from the government for their ancestral holdings. The Managil extension (about 830,000 ac.) was completed in 1962, its water duty being provided from Sennar. There tenant holdings are smaller and the crops more diversified. The dam at Er Roseires (Ar Rusayris), assisted in 1960 by a World bank loan of $15,500,000, opened in 1965, providing supplies both for Managil and for the Kenana (Kinanah) plan (1,200,000 ac.) west of Singa. The yield of cotton varies from about 4 to 18 cwt. per ac. The chief town of Gezira is Wad Medani, which is the capital of Blue Nile province. (J. H. G. L.)

GHANA (ANCIENT). The ancient West African empire after which the modern Ghana (q.v.) is named was centred in the regions of Aukar, Hodh, and Bakhunu, between the Sahara and the headwaters of the Senegal and Niger rivers, partly in the southeastern sector of the Islamic Republic of Mauritania and partly in modern Mali. It was peopled predominantly by Soninke clans of the Mande-speaking Negroes. Its origins are obscure, though traditions recorded in Tombouctou (Timbuctu) *Tarīkhs* (chronicles) of the 16th and 17th centuries suggest that the first kings may not have been Negro and, possibly, that the kingdom may have originated about A.D. 300. The first written references to the empire are those of Arab geographers and historians from the 8th century. Contrary to common belief, it was probably not visited by Ibn Hawqal, and the fullest description of the empire in its maturity is that written by al-Bakri in the years 1067–68. By then the rulers as well as the people were pagan Negroes, and al-Bakri's account of the court and customs of Ghana suggests interesting parallels with more recent and better-known West African Negro states. The name Ghana was properly the title of the ruler, and the empire was ruled through tributary princes who were probably the traditional chiefs of subject clans. There were probably a number of successive capitals, also known as Ghana; that of the 11th century has been identified by archaeologists with the ruins at Koumbi Saleh, 200 mi. (322 km.) N of modern Bamako.

The principal *raison d'être* of the empire was the desire to control the Sudanese end of the trade, principally in alluvial gold, which had attracted Moroccan merchants to the Sudan and had led the pastoral nomad Berber tribes of the desert, such as the Sanhaja, to develop the western trans-Saharan caravan road. Gold was secured, often by mute barter, from Negroes at the southern limits of the empire and conveyed to the capital, where a Muslim commercial town developed alongside the native city. There the gold was exchanged for commodities, the most important of which was Saharan salt, imported by the North African caravans.

The empire began to decline with the emergence of the Muslim Almoravids (q.v.), a confederation of the Sanhaja and other desert Berber tribes. After some years of warfare, the Almoravids overran Ghana in 1076. Almoravid domination of Ghana lasted only a few years, but their activities had upset the trade on which the empire depended, and the irruption of their flocks into an arid agricultural terrain had initiated a disastrous process of desiccation. The subject peoples of the empire began to break away, and in 1203 one of these, the Sosso, occupied the capital. Eventually in 1240 the city was destroyed by the Mande emperor Sundiata, and what was left of its empire became incorporated in the new and greater empire of Mali which he founded.

See R. Mauny, "The Question of Ghana," in *Africa*, vol. xxiv (1954); J. D. Fage, "Ancient Ghana; A Review of the Evidence," in *Transactions of the Historical Society of Ghana*, vol. iii (1957).   (J. D. F.)

GHANA, a nation of West Africa, consists of the former British colony of the Gold Coast and of that portion of Togoland formerly under United Kingdom trusteeship, which on March 6, 1957, were formed into a self-governing dominion. Ghana became a republic with the president as head of state on July 1, 1960, remaining a member of the Commonwealth of Nations. Its first president was Kwame Nkrumah.

The country, which is a portion of Upper Guinea, lies between latitudes 4°45′ and 11°10′ N and longitudes 1°12′ E and 3°15′ W and is bordered on the west, north, and east by the Ivory Coast, Upper Volta, and Togo republics. On the south it faces the Atlantic Ocean along a coast of 334 mi. (537 km.). Its area is 92,100 sq.mi. (238,539 sq.km.). The population in 1970 was 8,545,561. Ghana is divided into eight administrative regions. The capital district is Accra, which is in the eastern sector of the coast.   (Er. A. B.)

This article is divided into the following sections and subsections:

I. PHYSICAL GEOGRAPHY

1. Geology.—About half the surface area is composed of Precambrian rocks. Most of the remainder is a platform of Paleozoic sediments. From southeast to northwest, in the region northeast of Accra, the Precambrian consists of: (1) *Dahomeyan* schists, granitic gneisses, hornblende-garnet-gneisses, pyroxenites, and eclogites. Tremolitic marble and nepheline-syenite also occur; (2) *Akwapimian* (Togo series) quartzites, phyllites, and, locally, garnetmica-schists; (3) *Buemian* (northward from near Koforidua) quartzites, conglomerates, shales, and lavas. Westward from the Akwapimian the Precambrian consists of: (4) *Birrimian* graywackes, phyllites, pillow lavas, tuffs, and epidiorites; (5) granites and migmatites; (6) *Tarkwaian* gold-bearing conglomerates, sandstones, flags, and phyllites.

The sandstones, conglomerates, and shales of the Voltaian are probably of Lower Paleozoic Age. Mid-Devonian sandstones and shales form the coastline east and west of Accra. Somewhat similar rocks with boulder beds and felspathic grits extend along the coast from Cape Coast to beyond Takoradi. Fossils suggest an Upper Paleozoic Age.

Upper Cretaceous and Tertiary sediments occur in the Volta Delta area and along the extreme western strip of coastline. Lake Bosumtwi, with fossiliferous lacustrine sediments, is thought by some to be a meteoritic crater. Laterite with lesser bauxite and manganese ore form thick surface coverings over much of the country.   (W. J. M.)

2. Physiography.—Relief throughout the country is generally low. The southwestern, northwestern, and extreme northern parts consist of a dissected peneplain rising up to 1,000 ft. (304 m.), above which stand a number of peneplain residuals of up to 2,000 ft., with a northeast-southwest trend. In the vast basin of the Volta occupying the central part of the country the land rarely exceeds 500 ft., but the Kwahu and Gambaga plateaus marked by bold erosional scarps, which form the southern and northern borders of the basin, attain heights of 1,500–1,750 ft. (457–533 m.). In southeast Ghana, trending northeast from Accra to the Togo boundary, lie the Akwapim-Togo ranges averaging 1,500 ft. and containing the highest mountains in the country (Mt. Djebobo 2,873 ft. [876 m.]; Mt. Afadjato 2,905 ft. [889 m.]). These ranges separate the Voltaian Basin on the west from the Accra plains on the southeast. The coast is generally flat, sandy, and fringed with lagoons, but between Cape Three Points and Accra extends a succession of bays and rocky headlands. East of Accra the main feature is the Volta Delta and its associated lagoons. The drainage is dominated by the Volta, the middle section of which above Akosombo is now occupied by an artificial lake 3,275 sq.mi. (8,482 sq.km.) large and 250 mi. long. South of the Kwahu Plateau smaller rivers such as the Pra (160 mi. [257 km.]), Ankobra (130 mi. [209 km.]), and Tano (250 mi. [386 km.]) drain directly into the sea. The rivers exhibit seasonal variation and are interrupted by rapids, thus restricting navigation.

3. Climate.—This is governed by the tropical continental air mass, or harmattan (*q.v.*), consisting of hot, dry, dust-laden air from the northeast across the Sahara and the tropical maritime air mass consisting of moist and relatively cool monsoonal air from the southwest across the Atlantic. The two meet along a broad front known as the Inter-Tropical Convergence Zone (ITCZ), where their contrasting effects produce violent thunderstorms or line squalls. Seasonal variation in weather is caused by the oscillation, following the overhead sun, of the ITCZ, which reaches its most northerly position north of Ghana in August and its most southerly near the Guinea coast (latitude 7° N) in January. Rains occur where the dominant air mass is monsoonal, while the harmattan is associated with drought.

In the savanna country north of the Kwahu plateau the year falls into two seasons; a dry season from November to March with hot days and cool nights and a wet season reaching a peak in August–September. The mean annual rainfall diminishes generally northward from about 45 to 35 in. and heavy, violent storms are usual. In the southern forest country two rainy seasons with peaks in May–June and October are separated by two relatively dry periods during the harmattan from December to February and in August, which along the coast is a cool and misty month. The mean annual rainfall there varies from 86 in. in the west around Axim to 45 in. in the east. Around Accra anomalously low figures of 40 in. to less than 30 in. occur, and the rainfall variability resembles that in the northern savannas.

Temperatures show much more uniformity; the annual mean is 26°–29° C (79°–84° F) and the daily range is only 6.7°–7.2° C along the coast and 10°–16.7° C in the north. Relative humidity is high (90–100% in the south and 65% in the north), producing with the high temperatures enervating conditions—though during the harmattan relative humidities as low as 12% occur in the Accra plains. Locally, conditions are moderated by high altitudes and by regular land and sea breezes. In most places the hottest months are February and March, just before the start of the rains, while the lowest temperatures occur in January, or along the coast in August.   (Er. A. B.)

4. Vegetation.—The natural vegetation is high forest in the south and savanna woodland in the north. Most virgin forest has been replaced by a mosaic of permanent cocoa farms and more or less temporary mixed farms where banana, plantain, oil palm, maize (corn), and market-garden crops are cultivated. Shifting cultivation frequently results in overcropping and loss of fertility, and cassava is extensively grown in poor soils. When forest farms are abandoned a fallow of thicket reverts to a secondary type of forest and fertility is eventually restored. Citrus and other fruit trees are planted around villages.

The most luxuriant vegetation is in the statutory reserved forests which are mainly of mature secondary type. There isolated emergent trees of silk cotton (*Ceiba pentandra*), wawa (*Triplochiton scleroxylon*), utile (*Entandrophragma utile*) and African mahogany (*Khaya ivorensis*) overtop successive canopies of smaller trees and shrubs, and robust climbers reach to the upper strata. Epiphytic ferns, lichens, mosses, and inconspicuous orchids clothe the high branches. On the shaded ground broad-leaved herbs abound amid saplings and low shrubs, but grasses are few. In swampy parts of the forest *Raphia*, climbing palms, bamboo, and scrambling herbs and ferns are characteristic.

In the drier coastal regions, particularly near Accra, scattered thicket clumps with *Elaeophorbia* surround old termites' nests in an open-grass savanna. Savanna grasslands are subjected to regular dry-season burning and thus are not truly natural. Guinea savanna, a thin woodland of small widely spaced trees and abundant tall grass, occurs in the lower Volta and Afram river areas and over most of the transitional zone between forest and savanna. In northern Ghana, yams, groundnuts (peanuts), and Guinea corn (sorghum) are widely grown. Wild trees and shrubs such as dawadawa (*Parkia clappertoniana*), shea butter (*Butyrospermum parkii*), rubber-vine (*Landolphia*); etc. are preserved for various uses, and baobab, akee apple (*Blighia sapida*), *Acacia albida*, neem (*Azadirachta indica*), mango, and *Khaya senegalensis* (the dry-zone African mahogany) are commonly planted for shade, fruit, or firewood.

(C. D. A.)

5. Animal Life.—As in other tropical countries the fauna of Ghana is very rich in species, particularly in the south of the country. In the high forests there is little variation in rainfall and food resources. Animals involved in processing dead vegetation are, therefore, active at all times in the moist litter. These include oligochaete worms, giant snails (*Achatina*), millipedes, termites, ants, and many species of wingless insects. The majority of the remaining species are herbivorous with rather narrow niche requirements, thus allowing many species to coexist. They include insects, many of which are pests of cocoa (the major economic crop) and other agricultural crops grown under the forest canopy; limbless amphibia, tree frogs, giant toads (*Bufo superciliarius*), green mambas, gaboon vipers, rhinoceros vipers, the small forest crocodile (*Osteolaemus*), hornbills, plantain eaters, sunbirds, the rock fowls (*Picathartes*), the potto, the black and white colobus, various species of *Cercopithecus*, mangabeys, chimpanzees, the bongo (*Boocercus eurycercus*), the royal antelope, several duiker species, the bush pig, the small forest elephant (*Loxodonta cyclotis*), the forest genet, and leopard.

In contrast, the savanna area which covers about two-thirds of Ghana, north of the forest and along much of the coastal region, has a well-defined wet and dry season. Oligochaete worms and mollusks tend to be rare or absent. Their ecological niche is taken by the termites which culture the microorganisms and fungi concerned with decomposition either in the termitaria or in their alimentary canal. The commonest species is *Macrotermes natalensis* whose large, cone-shaped termitaria are scattered in a matrix of tall, tussocky, perennial grass. These grasses are subject to one or two annual burns during the dry season, and as the fire-resistant shrubs and trees occur either on or in the vicinity of the savanna termitaria, the inorganic and organic wealth of the savanna tends to accumulate in these regions. During the dry season there is little food for the herbivores, particularly grazers. It is not surprising, therefore, that an increase in metabolic activity, reproduction, and dispersive activity is synchronized with the appearance of lush, green vegetation, intermittent pools, streams, and swollen rivers during the wet season. Dominant herbivores include crickets, grasshoppers, ants (including tree ants [*Oecophylla*]), weaver-birds, pin-tailed wydahs, bishop birds, waxbills, fire finches, green fruit pigeons, Senegal parrots, gray plantain eaters, cutting grass *Thryonomys swinderianus*, Togo hare *Lepus capensis*, the domestic sheep, and the cow. The larger indigenous mammalian herbivores, including the western hartebeest, the Senegal hartebeest, Buffon's kob, the bushbuck, crown duiker, Maxwell's duiker in the drier areas, the waterbuck, and reedbuck in the vicinity of water, and the aquatic chevrotain, hippopotamus (including the pigmy hippopotamus), and the manatee, are rare or very rare as a result of the depredations of man. In consequence large concentrations of game can be seen only in the 900 sq.mi. (2,330 sq.km.) Mole Game Reserve in northwest Ghana. The rate of production of meat and milk by domestic animals is very low. Chickens and pigs compete with humans for staple foods and in the rural areas they live mainly as scavengers. Horses are rare. Common carnivores include the praying mantis, scorpions, a variety of frogs including *Kassina senegalensis*, *Rana galamensis*, *Phrynomerus microps*, *Hemisus marmoratus*, Bosc's monitor, the Nile monitor, the black kite, the cattle egret, the Senegal coucal, bulbuls, and many species of kingfishers, flycatchers, warblers, and shrikes. The larger mammalian carnivores such as the leopard, lion, hyena, hunting dog, serval, and golden cat are rare.

Water is the focus of major parasitic diseases, important vectors of which include the mosquito, the black fly *Simulium*, and mollusks such as *Bulinus*. The recent construction of many man-made lakes and the development of irrigation schemes have resulted in increased yields of fish protein. In contrast, such schemes have thus increased health hazards. Important fishes include the bichir, lung fish, species of cichlids including *Tilapia*, catfishes of many families including *Clariidae*, snakeheads, elephant fish, characins including the tiger fish, *Citharinidae*, the electric catfish, and the Nile perch. Many of the important food fish in the sea undergo seasonal migrations and are seasonally abundant. They include the herring (*Sardinella*) and the cassava fish (*Sciaena* and *Cynoscion*).

(J. D. Th.)

II. THE PEOPLE

Ghanaians are Negroes. In the north they speak Mossi-Grussi languages and in the south Kwa languages; both subfamilies of the widespread Niger-Congo family. The two linguistic areas, between which the Black Volta forms an approximate boundary, correspond to distinguishable culture areas. But throughout Ghana some values are shared, particularly an insistence on the duality of the physical and spiritual worlds. Amid a rich diversity of ritual practice and doctrine a remote supreme being is generally recognized, approachable through manifestations of the spirit or through minor deities to whom libations and sacrifices are offered. The earth is sacred and ancestors are respected.

More than 70% of the population subsist primarily by cultivating the soil, and have their homes in small towns, villages, or hamlets. Workers and professional men maintain farming interests, and the welfare of the land is a primary value. Men hunt, fish, clear the bush, and pursue handicrafts; women engage in petty trade and domestic chores. Both sexes farm and either may practise as herbalists and diviners. Most people live among their kinsfolk, and widespread family and lineage obligations condition social intercourse and economic endeavour. Regular invocations of ancestors renew lineage solidarity, while wider ties are reinforced by ceremonies linking localized groups.

Most of southern Ghana is occupied by groups of the Kwa language subfamily (Akan, Ewe, Ga-Adangme [*qq.v.*], and Guang). Of the Akan, who are numerically and culturally dominant, the best-known groups are the Ashanti and Fanti (*qq.v.*), and the Akim, Akwapim, Ahanta, and Nzima. Another group of the Kwa subfamily are the Gonja of northwest Ghana. (*See* AFRICAN LANGUAGES: *The Niger-Congo Family*.)

The rule of matrilineal descent is the key to Akan social organization. Inheritance to office, status, and most property descend within the matrilineage. Certain spiritual and personal qualities pass through the paternal line. Each lineage has at its head an elder responsible for its internal peace and relations with other lineages. He is custodian of the lineage's "stools," which embody the spirits of the ancestors, and is thereby mediator between the living and dead members. Within a town stools are hierarchically ordered, and each lineage has specific military, political, and ritual duties. One stool is the town stool, and its occupant is the "chief," who always has sacerdotal as well as secular functions. Town stools are grouped in a similar hierarchy within a "state." The most illustrious chiefs are gazetted "paramount" chiefs. States vary in population from a few thousand to the great Ashanti confederacy of states, which, at its height, contained more than 800,-000. Other Kwa speakers are traditionally organized into numerous politically independent subtribes, consisting of a group of related patrilineages. Links with maternal kin are important.

In the north broad cultural similarities are concealed by local variations, with differently based descent systems, virilocal and uxorilocal residence patterns, and varying rules of exogamy. Moreover the subcultures have no sharp boundaries. Dagomba, Gonja (qq.v.), and Mamprusi are "states," with rulers selected from chiefs of specified lineages. Outside these states, and even to some extent within them, authority is traditionally vested in clans and their segments. Political stability depends on the maintenance of equilibrium within the lineage system. Chiefship is the prerogative of certain primarily immigrant clans. Chiefs do not rule, though they are respected and enjoy economic privileges. They are principally custodians of shrines and the ritual guardians of their communities.

At the 1960 census 42.8% of adult Ghanaians were enumerated as Christians (13.4% Catholic; 10.3% Methodist; 9.9% Presbyterian; 2.6% Anglican; 2.4% Apostolic; and 4.2% members of small missionary or "spiritual churches"). Only 38.2% declared themselves as adherents to indigenous religions, but most Ghanaians maintain some traditional rituals. Twelve percent are Moslems.

One-eighth of the population is of foreign origin, but of this proportion less than 0.25% is of European descent and some 0.08% of Asian or Levantine stock. Most are engaged in commerce, education, or technical services. Since 1948 the European population has more than doubled.

III. HISTORY

1. **Prehistoric Era.**—As elsewhere in Africa, the climate of Ghana varied during the Pleistocene Epoch. With greater rainfall forest spread northward and man retreated toward the Sahara; when rainfall diminished, man occupied even the present forest. Correlations with Europe are established by raised beaches.

Apart from some pebble tools from high river terraces, the first industry is Late Chellean in the southeast, in middle river gravels corresponding to the 23-metre beach. In the succeeding pluvial era, the Acheulean culture is lacking save from the extreme north. With increasing aridity, man reappeared, bringing Late Acheulean and Sangoan cultures, probably successively. He moved along the Togo mountain range from the Niger River. Sangoan tools abound in Transvolta and around Accra and extend to Kumasi; the west remained forest and was rarely visited. Late Acheulean is associated with the 14-metre beach and the lower terraces; a developed Sangoan with the 8-metre beach.

The Sangoan culture waned in the Gamblian pluvial era. At its close there appears a Lupemban culture, probably from the desiccating Sahara; it occurs in basal gravels of valleys carved during the preceding pluvial period. In central Ghana its tools are shapely, near the coast crude and formless.

Degenerate Middle Stone Age traditions lingered into the succeeding subpluvial era. Thereafter excavations at Legon yielded quartz microliths made on small pebbles. Upcountry these occur on silt terraces deposited in the preceding wet phase as far as the Niger. This culture is independent of the Saharan mesolithic.

The latest Mesolithic Age has stone hoes, quartz beads, and other Congo types; pottery seems absent. This stage dates to the post-Flandrian marine regression (? end of 2nd millennium B.C.).

Several Neolithic cultures seem identifiable. They contain polished axes and usually coarse pottery. The most distinctive appears around Kintampo and in the Accra plains; it had clay houses, Saharan chert microliths, shale armrings, and scored terra-cottas like flattened cigars. A neolithic culture more in mesolithic tradition was excavated near Abetifi.

Evidence lacks for the introduction of iron. Polished stone was commonly used until the 16th century, especially in the forest. Trade in greenstone for ax manufacture flourished. In Transvolta and the west greenstone hoes are common. No satisfactory chronology has been established, nor can existing tribes be identified before the 17th century. Of excavated sites, Nsuta, with decorated pottery and bobbin beads, should be early medieval; Sekondi village and cemetery, with fine pottery, stone axes, and quartz and shell beads, lasted until Portuguese times. In the north heavily decorated pottery continued later on open sites and mounds indicating clay houses. Associated European imports are unknown before the 17th century.
(O. D.)

2. **Early Traditions.**—The modern state of Ghana is, named after the ancient Negro empire that flourished until the 13th century and was situated close to the Sahara in the western Sudan. The centre of ancient Ghana (q.v.) lay about 500 mi. to the northwest of the nearest part of the modern state, and it is tolerably certain that no part of the latter lay within its borders. The claim that an appreciable proportion of modern Ghana's people derive from emigrants from the ancient empire cannot be unequivocally substantiated with the evidence at present available. Written sources relate only to the period since European contact with the Gold Coast, i.e., modern Ghana, began in the 15th century, or to Muslim contacts with ancient Ghana from about the 8th to the 13th century. Many modern Ghanaian peoples possess well-preserved oral traditions, but even though some of these may reach as far back as the 14th century, this is after the final disappearance of ancient Ghana, and such very early traditions often present considerable problems of interpretation. Little progress has so far been made in linking the surviving traditions with the available archaeological evidence.

More archaeological research, especially into the Iron Age, will undoubtedly do much toward resolving present uncertainties about the early history of modern Ghana, but for the moment little more can be said than that the traditions of many of the states into which the country was divided before it came under British rule refer to their people having immigrated within the last 600 years either from the north or northwest or from the east or northeast. Such traditions link up with other evidence to suggest that the area which is now Ghana was for many centuries a meeting place for two great streams of west African history. Ultimately these streams stemmed from the existence of two major trans-Saharan routes, a western one linking the headwaters of the Niger and Senegal rivers to Morocco and a more central one linking the region between the Niger bend and Lake Chad with Tunisia and Tripoli. At the end of the western route arose the great Mande states, notably ancient Ghana and Mali, while around the more easterly termini developed Songhai, the Hausa states, and Bornu. There is evidence that parts of modern Ghana north of the forest were being reached by Mande traders (seeking gold dust) by the 14th century, and by Hausa merchants (desiring kola nuts) by the 16th century. In this way the inhabitants of what is now Ghana were influenced by the new wealth and cross-fertilization of ideas which arose in the great empires of the western Sudan following the development of Islamic civilization in northern Africa.

It is against this background that the traditions of origin of the Ghanaian states must be viewed. It would seem that the first states of the Akan-speaking peoples who now inhabit most of the forest and coastlands were founded, c. the 13th century, by the settlement, just north of the forest, of migrants coming from the direction of Mande; that the dominant states of northern Ghana, Dagomba, Mamprussi, and their satellites were established by the 15th century by invaders from the Hausa region; that a little later the founders of the Ga and Ewe states of the southeast began to arrive from what is now Nigeria by a more southerly route; and that Gonja, in the centre, was created by Mande conquerors about the beginning of the 17th century.

Tradition tends to present these migrations as movements of whole peoples. In certain instances, for example Dagomba, Mamprussi, Gonja, it can be shown that the traditions relate in fact to

CHRISTIANSBORG CASTLE, ACCRA, ORIGINALLY BUILT BY THE DANES IN THE 17TH CENTURY, WAS TRANSFERRED TO THE BRITISH IN 1850. IT IS NOW THE OFFICES OF GHANA'S HEAD OF STATE

comparatively small bands of invaders who used military and political techniques acquired farther north to impose their rule on already established Negro populations whose own organization was based more on community of kin than on allegiance to political sovereigns. It is probable that the first Akan states, e.g., such influential states as Bono and Banda north of the forest or the smaller states founded on the coast by migration down the Volta River, were also established in this way. The later Akan infiltration into the forest, which then was probably sparsely inhabited, and the Ga and Ewe settlement of the southeast may have been more of mass movements, though in the latter case it is known that the immigrants met and absorbed earlier inhabitants.

3. Contact With Europe and Its Effects.—A revolution in Ghanaian history was initiated by the establishment of direct sea trade with Europe following the discovery of the coast by Portuguese mariners in 1471. Initially Europe's main interest in the country was as a source of gold, a commodity which was readily available at the coast in exchange for such European exports as cloth, hardware, beads, metals, spirits, arms, and ammunition. This gave rise to the name Gold Coast, by which the country was to be known until 1957. In an attempt to preserve a monopoly of the trade, the Portuguese initiated the practice of erecting stone fortresses (Elmina castle dating from 1482 was the first) on the coast on sites leased from the native states. In the 17th century the Portuguese monopoly, already considerably eroded, gave way completely when traders from the Netherlands, England, Denmark, Sweden, and Prussia—Protestant seapowers antagonistic to Iberian imperial pretensions—discovered that the commercial relations developed with the Gold Coast states could be adapted to the export of slaves, then in rapidly increasing demand for the American plantations, as well as of gold. By the mid-18th century the coastal scene was dominated by the presence of about 40 forts controlled by Dutch, British, or Danish merchants.

The presence of these permanent European bases on the coast had far-reaching consequences. The new centres of trade thus established were much more accessible than were the Sudanese emporia, and this, coupled with the greater capacity and efficiency of the sea-borne trade compared with the ancient overland routes, gradually brought about the reversal of the direction of the trade flow. The new wealth, tools and arms, techniques and ideas introduced through close contact with Europeans initiated political and social as well as economic changes. The states north of the forest, hitherto the wealthiest and most powerful, declined in the face of new combinations farther south. At the end of the 17th century the Akan state of Akwamu created an empire which, stretching from the central Gold Coast eastward to Dahomey, sought to control the trade roads to the coast of the whole eastern Gold Coast. The Akwamu empire was short-lived, but its example soon stimulated a union of the Ashanti (q.v.) states of the central forest, which union, after establishing its dominance over other neighbouring Akan states, expanded north of the forest to conquer Bono, Banda, Gonja, and Dagomba.

Having thus engrossed almost the whole of the area which served as a market and source of supply for the coastal trade, Ashanti turned toward the coastlands. Here traditional ways of life were being increasingly modified by contact with Europeans and their trade, and when, beginning in the latter part of the 18th century, Ashanti armies began to invade the coastal states, their peoples tended to look for leadership and protection to the European traders in the forts. But between 1804 and 1814 the Danes, English, and Dutch had each in turn outlawed their slave trades, and the gold trade was declining. The political uncertainty following the Ashanti invasions and the development of new trades, and in these circumstances the mutually suspicious European interests were not always keen to embark on new political responsibilities. However, during 1830-44, under the outstanding leadership of George Maclean, the British merchants began to assume an informal protectorate over the Fanti states, much to the commercial benefit of both parties. As a result of this the British Colonial Office finally agreed to take over the British forts, and in 1850 it was able to buy out the Danes. However, trade declined under the new regime, which was averse to assuming formal control over the territory influenced from the forts, and in the 1860s onward, of Christian missionary education, the Fanti states attempted to organize a European-style confederacy. Further Ashanti incursions and the final evacuation of the coast by the Dutch (1872) combined to reverse this negative British policy, and in 1874 a punitive expedition destroyed Kumasi, the Ashanti capital, and the Gold Coast was declared a British colony.

4. Colonial Period.—French and German activity in adjacent territories and the demand of British mining and commercial interests for better protection led to a further active period of British policy during 1895-1901, during which Ashanti was finally conquered and its northern hinterland formed into a British protectorate. The 50 years of British rule that followed went far toward welding into one state the three elements of the territory, the colonies of the Gold Coast and Ashanti and the protectorate of the Northern Territories, to which after World War I was added a fourth, under mandate from the League of Nations, the western part of former German Togoland (see Togo, Republic of). But this was hardly the result of deliberate policy. The ever increasing assimilation of European ways by the people on the Gold Coast had already made possible there the introduction of such organs of government as a legislative council (1850) and a supreme court (1853), but for many years Ashanti and the Northern Territories remained the sole responsibility of the governor, whose officials were from the 1920s onward encouraged to work with and through the authorities of the indigenous states. Attempts to introduce similar elements of indirect rule in the Gold Coast served mainly to stimulate a nationalist opposition among the educated professional classes, especially in the growing towns, which aimed at converting the legislative council into a fully responsible parliament.

What really brought the country together was the great development of its economy following the introduction and rapid expansion of cocoa-growing by local farmers in the forest. By the 1920s, the Gold Coast, while continuing to export some gold, was producing more than half of the world's supply of cocoa: timber and manganese later became additional exports of note. With the wealth created by this great increase of trade, it was possible to provide modern transport facilities—harbours, railways, roads—and social services, especially education (to the university level), all of which tended toward the conversion of the traditional social order, of groups bound together by kinship, into one in which individuals were linked principally by economic ties.

5. Independence.—Political advancement tended to lag behind economic and social development, especially in the south (for the role of the Northern Territories was principally the supply of cheap labour for the Gold Coast and Ashanti). World War II and its aftermath tended to accentuate this lag, and in 1948 there were riots in the larger towns. The Watson Commission of Inquiry reported that the Burns constitution of 1946, which had granted Africans a majority in the legislative council, was "outmoded at birth." An all-African committee under Justice (later Sir Henley) Coussey was appointed to work out a new constitution in which some executive power would be transferred to African ministers responsible to an African assembly; but, under Kwame Nkrumah, the new Convention People's Party (CPP) arose and demanded immediate self-government and entered on measures of "positive action" to enforce its will. In 1952 Nkrumah became prime minister. The Gold Coast passed rapidly through a period of transition in which government was transferred by stages to an all-African cabinet responsible to a national assembly elected by adult suffrage. On Dec. 13, 1956, following a plebiscite held under UN auspices, the British Togoland trust territory was integrated with the Gold Coast. Securing over 70% of the seats in the assembly in 1954 and 1956, Nkrumah and his CPP government were able in 1957 to obtain recognition of their country, renamed Ghana, as an independent, self-governing member of the Commonwealth and a member of the UN.

Nkrumah saw independent Ghana as a spearhead for the liberation of the rest of Africa from colonial rule and the establishment of a socialist African unity under his leadership. After the establishment of a republic in 1960, the state became identified with a single political party (the CPP), with Nkrumah, as life president of both, taking ever more power for himself. By 1966 his dream of African socialism was foundering under haphazard and corrupt administration, massive foreign debts, and declining living standards. On Feb. 24, while he was in Peking, army and police leaders rose against him, and his regime was replaced by a National Liberation Council (NLC), chaired by Lieut. Gen. Joseph A. Ankrah. In April 1969 Brig. Akwasi A. Afrifa succeeded to the chair. A complete overhaul of the administration and judiciary followed, with the aim of restoring democratic government, and conservative financial policies were initiated.

On Aug. 22, 1969, the Constituent Assembly enacted and promulgated the constitution of the Second-Ghanaian Republic, and the NLC became a provisional caretaker government pending the general elections. The result of the elections, held on Aug. 29, was an overwhelming victory for Kofi Busia's Progress Party (PP). On Sept. 3 Busia was sworn in as prime minister and a three-man presidential commission was appointed. On Sept. 30 the NLC was dissolved, to be followed in August 1970 by the dissolution of the presidential committee. On Aug. 31, 1970, former chief justice Edward Akufo-Addo was elected as the first civilian president since the ending of military rule. Ghana's return to a democratic system of government did not last, however. Its economy remained geared to cocoa, the price of which in 1970–71 fell from £330 to £230 a ton, and added to Nkrumah's foreign debts were £82,000,000 of short-term debts. On Jan. 13, 1972, while Busia was in London, his government was overthrown in a military coup led by Col. I. K. Acheampong, who accused Busia of malpractice and economic mismanagement. The constitution was withdrawn and Parliament dissolved, and Acheampong announced that the country was to be run by a National Redemption Council. The new government repudiated the huge external debt left from the Nkrumah period; canceled the 44% devaluation of the currency by Busia; and lowered prices of many staples. Population increase is estimated at 2.5% annually.

(J. D. F.; X.)

1966, Ghana was a republic within the Commonwealth of Nations. The president of the republic was the head of state. All powers were vested in a parliament consisting of the president and a single-chamber national assembly, the president having power of veto on bills passed by the assembly. The assembly had a speaker and not fewer than 104 members, elected every five years by adult suffrage in single-member constituencies; and ten women members, elected by simple majority vote by assembly members, to represent the eight regions and the one capital district. The president selected his ministers from the assembly, presided over the cabinet, and appointed envoys, senior civil servants, and supreme court judges. After the coup of February 1966, the country was governed by the National Liberation Council of police and army officers. The coup of January 1972 by the military set up the National Redemption Council, which ruled by decree after dissolving Parliament and suspending the constitution that had been approved and promulgated in August 1969.

The 1969 constitution provided for a strongly democratic government and contained many elaborate safeguards against such authoritarian practices as election-rigging, press censorship, and tribalism. Certain entrenched provisions may not be amended, but of those that remain, some may be amended by a two-thirds majority vote.

The president, who is elected every four years by an electoral college of 164 members, may serve for two terms without executive power. He appoints the prime minister, on whose advice he also designates such key officials as the chief justice, the auditor general, the ombudsman, and the governor of the Bank of Ghana. He supervises professional bodies and may delay parliamentary bills for up to two weeks. The Council of State, by which he is assisted, is made up, among others, of the chief justice, the prime minister, the leader of the opposition, the attorney general, and the commander in chief of the armed forces.

The prime minister appoints a cabinet that is collectively responsible to him and is himself responsible to parliament in all matters of general policy. Should a vote of no-confidence be returned against him, he would have to resign. (X.)

The regional subdivision was reorganized in 1960. Each region has a house of chiefs, which assembles three times a year to discuss matters of customary law and questions referred to it by the central government. There are about 60 local and urban councils elected by adult suffrage. The four major towns of Accra, Cape Coast, Sekondi-Takoradi, and Kumasi have municipal councils.

2. Taxation.—Taxes on export goods and on imports, excise duties on drinks and tobacco, and purchase taxes are the main source of central government revenue. Personal income tax contributes less than 2% and company tax about 10%. A property tax (similar to local authority rates but payable to the central government) and a compulsory saving plan repayable in ten years with low interest were introduced in 1961. The heavy reliance upon outlay taxes on general consumables and the burden of taxation on while the high cost of collection of a generalized scheme of income tax discourages any rapid change to progressive taxation. But as education, roads, and health are among the main items of central government expenditure, a fair amount of income redistribution on progressive lines does take place.

3. Justice.—The judiciary system is based chiefly on the English pattern. The supreme court is divided into a court of appeal and a high court, and there are also magistrates' courts. The former native courts have been superseded by local courts in which part-trained magistrates administer local customary law. Under Nkrumah, a special three-member court might be appointed by the president to try offenses against the state; there was no appeal from its decisions. The government might imprison any Ghanaian citizen for up to five years without reference to the courts. The minister of justice is a cabinet member and has under him an attorney general and a solicitor general. The central police department under the minister of the interior is highly mechanized and equipped with rapid-communication systems and is used throughout Ghana in criminal cases and for the defense of law and order, although district police systems are maintained by local authorities.

IV. POPULATION

The 1970 census gave a total population of 8,545,561, corresponding to an average population density of 92.8 persons per square mile. However, the population is rather unevenly distributed. A triangular area with a base 250 mi. long on the coast from Axim to the Togo frontier and with its apex about 150 mi. inland north of Kumasi covers only about one-fifth of Ghana's territory but contains about two-thirds of its population, with an average density approaching 300 per square mile. A similar but much smaller high-density area extends along the northeast frontier. At the other extreme, a belt of land 100–150 mi. broad stretching from south of Wa in a southeasterly direction has a density below 10 per square mile.

V. ADMINISTRATION AND SOCIAL CONDITIONS

1. Constitution and Government.—Under the 1960 constitution, suspended by the National Liberation Council in February

4. Living Conditions.—The great majority of workers are self-employed, employed within a family group or working on profit-sharing arrangements. By the early 1960s fewer than 10% of the population of working age were recorded as in receipt of wages or salaries, and 95% of those in regularly paid posts were males. Many wage earners are seasonal or longer term immigrants (mostly single) from neighbouring territories. The proportion of wages (including those of nonrecorded employees) to gross national product was estimated at 25% in 1960. The first trade unions were formed in 1942; 16 national units were federated in the Ghana Trade Unions Congress, which was reconstituted in 1958. Unskilled wages are too low to maintain a family, but petty trading by women adds substantially to family incomes.

5. Welfare Services.—Hospitals and clinics provided by the government and by the Christian missions exist in most parts of Ghana; other clinics, health centres, dispensaries, and dressing stations are managed by local authorities. Government programs of rural community development are assisted in every region by village improvement projects undertaken with the active participation of the inhabitants. In urban communities welfare services concentrate more on case work, probation work, youth activities, and guidance of the numerous voluntary organizations.

6. Education.—Schooling in Ghana was pioneered in the 19th century by the missionaries. Following the colonial system of grants to schools achieving certain standards (1882), numerous schools were opened by the central government and local authorities. Most schools are now owned or heavily subsidized by the state, and free primary education (introduced in 1952) is available to about three-quarters of the population—the main deficiency being in the Northern and Upper regions, where there is a shortage of teachers and some reluctance on the part of the parents. After 1961 primary and middle school education between the ages of 6 and 16 was made free and compulsory. English is the language of instruction. The University of Ghana at Legon (near Accra) was founded in 1948 as a university college preparing students for the degrees of the University of London; it acquired university status in 1961. The University of Science and Technology at Kumasi, founded as a college of technology in 1952, reinforces a system of technical education including a number of government technical institutes and trade schools. Enrollment in all educational establishments in the early 1960s was reckoned at one-tenth of the population, and substantial state and voluntary effort was devoted to overcoming rural adult illiteracy. There were several thousand Ghanaian students studying abroad, mainly in the U.K. and U.S.

7. Defense.—The Ghana Army, formed from the Gold Coast Regiment of the former Royal West African Frontier Force, is an independent force with its own ancillary services and military academy. Ghanaians have largely replaced British officers. The Navy has detachments at Takoradi and Accra and is equipped with minor war vessels transferred from the Royal Navy. British and Canadian instructors staff the flying school, and a number of Air Force pilots have been trained in Britain.

(B. M. N.)

VI. THE ECONOMY

Ghana is basically a country of small farmers with a population density low enough for the land to support the people in moderate comfort. On this and the proceeds of Ghanaian exports the apparatus of a modern state is being erected.

1. Production.—The principal food crops are cassava, yams, maize (corn), millet, and plantain, but little meat is produced and the main local source of animal protein is fish, which is caught extensively along the coast. Most of Ghana is not a natural rearing zone for livestock, but by the early 1960s the cattle population (largely white Fulani zebu cows) was about 500,000, a fivefold increase since 1930. Cocoa, grown in the forest areas by small farmers on plots of two or three acres, dominates all other cash crops with a yield in excess of 300,000 tons annually. The Ghana Cocoa Marketing Board is the statutory body responsible for grading, exporting and selling the entire cocoa crop. Minor export crops include copra, kola nuts, palm kernels, bananas, tobacco, coffee, and rubber. Forest reserves total about 8,500 sq.mi. and logs and sawn timber are significant export items. Gold mines

produce an annual average of 880,000 oz. fine gold. Mining occupies about 30,000 workers, and average annual production figures for other minerals are: diamonds (more than half obtained by individual diggers) 3,225,000 carats; manganese 563,000 tons; bauxite 193,000 tons. There is no coal and by the early 1960s electricity (mainly for domestic use) from diesel-powered generating stations was available only in the larger towns; the mines are the biggest industrial users. Manufacturing plays a small part in the economy, and there are few factories (cigarettes, canning, biscuits, matches, nails, plywood, furniture, vehicle assembly).

The Volta River Project.—With the object of expanding the economy and lessening the dependence on cocoa, the Volta Plan based on damming the lower river was launched in 1961, when the Italian firm that built the Kariba Dam (Rhodesia) obtained the contract for the main Volta Dam at Akosombo, about 70 mi. (113 km.) from the sea. The dam, financed by the Ghanaian government and by loans from the World Bank, the U.S., and the U.K., was completed in 1965. The lake behind it, with an area of 3,275 sq.mi. (8,482 sq.km.) and a capacity of 120,000,000 ac.ft., is planned to become a freshwater fishery, the terminus of an inland waterway system, and an irrigation source for rice growing in the surrounding basin and for livestock on the Accra plains. The electricity generated will supply an aluminum smelter of about 200,000 tons annual capacity, to be built at Tema by U.S. and U.K. aluminum interests, and to furnish power for secondary industries and new towns. *See also* VOLTA RIVER.

2. Trade and Finance.—There is an extensive domestic trade in food. Much of the import and internal trade is handled by overseas firms; the chief imports are textiles, food, drink, tobacco, and commodities such as cement, trucks and vehicles, industrial machinery, and petroleum oils. Except for some timber and a small amount of gold, the whole of the cash crop and mining production is exported.

Ghana currency is based on the new cedi, first introduced in 1967 (2.45 cedis = £1 sterling = U.S. $2.40). The Bank of Ghana (1957) is the central bank of issue. Commercial banks include the state-owned Ghana Commercial Bank and two large British banks. An agreement with the U.S.S.R. in 1960 provided for a Soviet loan, economic and technical aid, and the supply of machines and equipment in exchange for cocoa and other primary products. A consortium of West German manufacturers in the same year agreed to provide credits of £G150,000,000 toward in-

FISHERMEN ARRANGING THEIR NETS AND CLEANING THEIR BOATS AT TEMA

dustrial projects in Ghana, and the Italian state-controlled oil corporation agreed to build a refinery at Tema.

3. Transport and Communications.—Ghana had in the early 1960s about 4,420 mi. of trunk roads, of which 1,900 mi. were tarred. The railways, of 3 ft. 6 in. gauge and with a route mileage of about 620, are confined to the southern half of the republic and serve mainly for carrying export commodities. Most local passenger traffic is by bus, and modern "tro' tro'" motor coaches are replacing the old-style "mammy wagons." The Black Star Line, founded in 1958, is the state mercantile marine. Until 1961 the main port was Takoradi, but in that year the eight-berth deepwater harbour at Tema opened. Ghana Airways operates international and local services, with main airfields at Accra, Takoradi, Kumasi, and Tamale. The postal service handles about 60,000 inland items annually. There are over 30,000 telephones. The national broadcasting service has transmitters at Accra and Tema. See also references under "Ghana" in the Index. (J. W. WI.)

BIBLIOGRAPHY.—P. B. Redmayne, *Gold Coast to Ghana* (1957); F. Wolfson, *Pageant of Ghana* (1958); R. Raymond, *Black Star in the Wind* (1960); *Physical Geography:* R. J. H. Church, *West Africa* (1957); E. A. Boateng, *A Geography of Ghana* (1959); H. O. Walker, *Weather and Climate of Ghana* (1957). *The People:* M. Manoukian, *Akan and Ga—Adangme Peoples of the Gold Coast* (1950), *The Ewe-Speaking People of Togoland and the Gold Coast* (1952); D. Westermann and M. A. Bryan, *The Languages of West Africa* (1952); K. A. Busia, *The Position of the Chief in the Modern Political System of Ashanti* (1951); E. L. R. Meyerowitz, *Akan Traditions of Origin* (1952); J. B. Christensen, *Double Descent Among the Fanti* (1954); J. H. Greenburg, *Studies in African Linguistic Classification* (1955); J. R. Goody, *The Social Organization of the Lowiili* (1956); F. M. Bourret, *Gold Coast*, 2nd ed. (1952), *Ghana, the Road to Independence* (1960); *Colonial Reports on the Gold Coast* (annually to 1954); Central Office of Information, *The Making of Ghana* (1956); Kwame Nkrumah, *Ghana* (1957); W. E. F. Ward, *History of Ghana*, 2nd ed. (1958); J. D. Fage, *Ghana: a Historical Interpretation* (1959); J. G. Amamoo, *The New Ghana* (1958); D. Warner, *Ghana and the New Africa* (1960); T. E. Hilton, *Ghana Population Atlas* (1960), *The Economy: Economic Survey* (annually); K. A. Akwawuah, *Prelude to Ghana's Industrialisation* (1960); J. B. Wills (ed.), *Agriculture and Land Use in Ghana* (1962); current history and statistics are summarized annually in *Britannica Book of the Year.*

GHARBIYAH, AL and **KAFR ASH SHAYKH**, governorates of the Nile in lower Egypt, are bounded north by the Mediterranean, northeast by Dumyat (Damietta) governorate, east by the Damietta branch of the Nile, south by Al Minufiyah governorate and west by the Rosetta (Rashid) branch of the Nile. Formerly Al Gharbiyah included all the delta north of Al Minufiyah, but in 1949 a new province, Fouadiya, was created, renamed Kafr ash Shaykh in 1955. Kafr ash Shaykh comprises the northwest part of the old province. Area 1,330 sq.mi. Pop. (1966) 1,118,495. The population of Al Gharbiyah in 1966 was 1,905,226, with an area of 770 sq.mi. Northern Kafr ash Shaykh consists of Lake Burullus, about 200 sq.mi., separated from the sea by a narrow sand bar 35 mi. long and bordered southward by extensive saline marshes under reclamation. Rice is an important crop on the reclaimed land. About 62% of the occupied population work at agriculture; the level, fertile land is intensively cultivated and the principal crops are cotton, rice, maize (corn) and wheat. Fishing in Lake Burullus is done from Baltim. The capitals are Tanta and Kafr ash Shaykh; other important towns are Al Mahallah al Kubra and Zifta, Bilqas Qism Awwal, and (in Kafr ash Shaykh) Disuq and Biyala. All are market towns having industries connected with agriculture (cotton ginning, flour and rice milling). Al Mahallah al Kubra is the chief centre of Egypt's textile industry and Kafr az Zayyat has one of the country's largest ginneries and soap and chemical works. A barrage at Zifta raises the level of the Damietta branch to supply canals irrigating the north and northeastern parts of the delta. Southern Gharbiyah has a density of population exceeding 2,000 per square mile. Sa al Hajar or Sais (*q.v.*), Bahbit al Hijarah (Iseum) and Samannud (Sebennytos) are notable sites of antiquity. (A. B. M.)

GHATS, a word which, in its Anglicized plural form (formerly ghauts), is applied particularly to the Eastern and Western Ghats which form the eastern and western edges respectively of the great plateau of peninsular India, having been transferred from the mountain passes to the mountains themselves.

Ghat is a Hindi word signifying "landing stairs from a river" and "a pass through a mountain," and hence any steep road or rail incline. The word is also used of the artificial terracing of river banks, as in bathing and crematory ghats at Varanasi (Benares) and other Indian cities, and to ferry landings.

The term Eastern Ghats is applied to several discontinuous and dissimilar hill areas (there is a 100-mi. gap across the lower Godavari river and the Krishna river). In the north they are dissected blocks of ancient Peninsular rocks, in the centre (the Cuddapah ranges) worn-down stumps of loftier ancient mountains, and in the south mainly rounded masses of gneiss. In Orissa they sometimes exceed 3,000 ft., but they are lower elsewhere. Local names are given to the separate parts.

The Western Ghats are the crest of the western edge of the plateau, possibly a great fault scarp. Their seaward slopes are very steep and dissected by canyonlike valleys, but on the landward side slopes are gentle and valleys wide and mature. The scarp begins south of the Tapti estuary and for its first 300 mi. rises to 3,000–5,000 ft. In this section the plateau is capped by the Deccan lavas, which give it a wall-like face and tabular upper surface. From near Goa southward the ancient gneisses and granites of the plateau form the escarpment. For more than 200 mi. summit levels are below 3,000 ft. Hill forms are more rounded, and several of the coastal streams have cut their valleys inland beyond the crestline and captured headwaters of plateau rivers. Beyond the 13th parallel summit levels rise again until the Ghats culminate in the Nilgiri hills. This great dome of gneiss reaches a height of 8,760 ft. in Mt. Dodabetta. It overlooks the wide Palghat gap which is usually regarded as the southern limit of the Ghats though continued through the lofty Anaimalai, Palni and Cardamom hills to the southernmost tip of India in Cape Comorin. The westward face of the Ghats receives a heavy monsoon rainfall and is clothed with dense evergreen forest. The streams of the Western Ghats are important sources of power, notably at Gersoppa falls and in the Nilgiris.
(T. HER.; L. D. S.)

GHAZIPUR, a municipality and district in the Varanasi (Benares) division, Uttar Pradesh, India. The town stands on the left bank of the Ganges, 45 mi. E. of Varanasi. Pop. (1961) 37,147.

The ancient town Gadhipur was renamed Ghazipur in about A.D. 1330, traditionally after the title of a Muslim ruler. During early British rule it enjoyed great strategic significance and a cantonment was established; it also served as an important river port. The cantonment is occupied by the civil lines, comprising Gora bazar, a church, the mausoleum of Lord Cornwallis, viceroy of India who died there in 1805, and a college of Gorakhpur university. The town is stretched out along the high bank of the Ganges. It is served by two stations of the North-Eastern railway and one of the Eastern, on the opposite bank. Ghazipur is an administrative and business centre and the headquarters of the dwindling opium department. Perfume distilling, flour and oil milling and hand-loom cloth are local industries.

GHAZIPUR DISTRICT (area 1,308 sq.mi.; pop. [1961] 1,321,578) forms part of the great alluvial plain of the Ganges which divides it into two unequal portions. The main crops are rice, barley, gram, millets, sugar cane, wheat and opium. Subject to frequent floods and droughts, it is a "deficit" district. (R. L. SI.)

GHAZNI, once a famous city in central Afghanistan and the seat of an extensive empire under two medieval dynasties, and now the capital town of the province of Ghazni, is situated on both banks of the Ghazni river on a high tableland (altitude 7,300 ft.), 224 mi. N.N.E. by road from Kandahar and 94 mi. S.S.W. from Kabul. It lies at the base of the terminal spur of a ridge of hills which forms the watershed between the Arghandab and Tarnak rivers. Pop. (1969 est.) 43,423.

The old city on the left bank of the river, still completely walled and topped by a citadel used as a military fort, stands at the northern angle (about 150 ft. above the plain) next to the hills. Its high walls, built partly of stone or brick laid in mud and partly of clay built in courses, and incorporating numerous towers, present a remarkable spectacle to the observer below. This is the only walled town surviving in Afghanistan. Entrance to the old city which contains narrow and picturesque bazaars is through two gates. The present restricted walls could not have contained the vaunted city of Mahmud of Ghazni; but the existing site may have formed the citadel of his city. A considerable area to the northeast is covered with ruins, a vast extent of shapeless mounds which are referred to as Old Ghazni. The most prominent remains are two remarkable towers rising to about 140 ft. and about 400 yd. apart. They are similar to each other and belong on a smaller scale to the same class as the Kutb Minar at Delhi. Arabic inscriptions in Kufic characters show the northern tower to have been the work of Mahmud himself and the other that of his son Mas'ud. The outline of many larger buildings can be clearly seen from air photographs. One of these, believed to be the mosque of Mas'ud, was excavated by the Italian archaeological mission working on the site. The shape of the courtyard, its flagstones and decorative carvings are plainly visible. Several dwelling houses on the slope of the hill have also been excavated. In the plain to the south a prominent mound, called Tepe Sardar, has yielded interesting Buddhist remains.

On the old road to Kabul, one mile beyond the minaret of Mahmud, is a village called Rowza, where lies the tomb of the famous conqueror, a prism of white marble standing on a plinth of the same material and bearing a Kufic inscription praying for the mercy of God. The tomb itself stands in a chamber covered with a clay dome and set in a small garden. The village is surrounded by many gardens and orchards, watered by an aqueduct, and has a library and archaeological museums (one founded in 1835) containing objects found in various excavations by French and Italian archaeologists. There are a number of elementary schools, a high school for boys, a school for girls and a cinema, and a model town was developing in the 1960s on the right bank of the river.

Ghazni contains many other holy shrines, such as that of the poet Sana'i, which make it a place of Muslim pilgrimage. The town

The city, once one of the most glorious in Asia containing countless riches plundered from India by Mahmud of Ghazni, was long in decay. Its strong walls did, however, play an important role in the Afghan wars of the 19th century. It is now an agricultural and commercial centre having revived since the opening of the Kabul-Kandahar road. Many of the well-known Afghan sheepskin coats (*pushtin*) are manufactured there. The chief trade is in corn, fruit, madder and in the sheep's wool and camel's-hair cloth that is brought from the adjoining Hazarajat country to the north. The population consists mainly of Tadzhiks (Tajiks) though the nomadic Afghan tribe of Ghilzais lives in the surrounding villages.

(X.)

History.—The city's early history is obscure and identification of it with the Gazaca of Ptolemy or with the Gazos of Greek poets remains conjectural. It was, however, probably the same city as the Ho-si-na of the Chinese traveler Hsian Tsang which, about A.D. 644, he described as the capital of Tsao-kin-to, a powerful kingdom deeply influenced by Buddhism. In works by the early Arab and Persian geographers and chroniclers the area around Ghazni, called Zabulistan, was regarded as part of Hindustan and was the object in the second half of the 7th century A.D. of many abortive Arab raiding expeditions operating up the Helmand valley from their base at Zaranj in Seistan. The area of Ghazni itself was conquered by the Saffarid Yakub ibn Laith c. 871. A Persian source, the *Ta'rikh-i-Sistan*, actually attributes the foundation of the city to Yakub ibn Laith, but this is inconsistent not only with the Chinese evidence, but also with that of the 10th-century Persian geographical work, the *Hudud al-'Alam*.

Ghazni's political importance in Islamic times begins with its conquest, in 962, by the Turk Alptigin, former captain of the guard to the Samanid amirs of Samarkand and Bukhara. Alptigin himself was seeking a refuge from his enemies at the Samanid court, but he and his successors, Abu Ishaq Ibrahim, Bilkatigin Piritigin and Subuktigin acknowledged the sovereignty of the Samanids. Ghazni became completely independent with the capture in 999 of the Samanid family by the Qara-Khanids of Turkistan and under Mahmud, who reigned from 998 to 1030, rose to be the centre and the capital city of a great but, as it proved, evanescent empire stretching at its height, in varying degrees of subordination, from Lahore in the east to Ray and Isfahan in the west, and from the Oxus river (Amu-Darya) in the north to the coast of Makran in the south. It was from Ghazni that Mahmud launched his famous plundering raids into Hindustan, the loot from which was used, in part, to beautify the city. Under his son Mas'ud (1030–41) the power of Ghazni was eroded by the nomad Seljuks. After the battle of Dandanqan in 1040, Ghazni lost its possessions in Khurasan and its effective power was confined to the area of Afghanistan and the Punjab. During the reign of Bahram Shah (1117–57) Ghazni was sacked by 'Ala-ud-din (Jahansuz) of Ghor (q.v.) and never recovered the splendour which was then destroyed. Between 1161 and 1173 it was occupied by a horde of Ghuzz Turkmen nomads while the last of the Ghaznavid rulers, Khosrau, took refuge in the Punjab. The Ghuzz were expelled by the nephews of 'Ala-ud-din Jahansuz, Ghiyath ud-din Mohammed ibn Sam and Mu'izz ud-din Mohammed ibn Sam (Mohammed of Ghor), the latter making Ghazni a headquarters between 1175 and 1206 for campaigns in Hindustan which led eventually to the foundation of the Delhi sultanate (*see* DELHI, SULTANATE OF).

The death of Mohammed ibn Sam in 1206 was followed by a struggle among his relatives and former slaves for the possession of Ghazni, the most notable contestants being Taj ud-din Yilduz and Qutb ud-din Aibak. In 1215, however, following Yilduz's re-capture by the Turkish ruler of Delhi, Iltutmish, Ghazni was occupied by the Turkish forces of the Khwarizmshah, 'Ala ud-din, who conferred it upon his son, Jalal ud-din. In 1221 it fell to the Mongols and was occupied by Genghis Khan's son, Ogadai. The seizure was not at first secure, for about 1225 Ghazni appears to have been under a Turkish chief, Sayf ud-din Hasan Qarlugh who had earlier served under the Khwarizmshah. By 1238 however, he had submitted to Ogadai but was soon expelled east of the Indus into Sind. Ghazni thereafter provided a base for occasional Mongol raids into the Punjab. After the death of Ogadai in 1241, the Mongol empire was divided, the Ghazni area going to the Il-khans in Persia. Toward the end of the 13th century they were replaced at Ghazni by the Jagatai Mongols of Transoxiana who proceeded, during the reign (1296–1316) of the Delhi sultan 'Ala ud-din Khalji, to embark on major incursions into India. In the 14th century there are few references to Ghazni. Passing through the area in 1333, the Moroccan traveler, Ibn Batutah, noted that the greater part of the city was in ruins. At the end of the 14th century, Ghazni fell under the rule of Timur (q.v., Tamerlane). In 1397 he left his grandson, Pir Mohammed, as governor of Kabul, Ghazni and Kandahar before himself leading his destructive expedition into Hindustan (1398–99). A century later, Ghazni was still in the possession of a descendant of Timur, namely Ulugh-Beg, an uncle of Babur (q.v.), the first Mogul ruler in India. Ulugh-Beg died in 1501 and in 1504 Babur acquired Kabul and its then appendage, Ghazni. For more than 200 years Ghazni remained under the overlordship of the Indian Moguls. In 1738 it passed under Nadir Shah (q.v.). Under Ahmad Shah Durrani it became part of the new Afghan kingdom created by him, being occupied by Durrani's forces in 1747.

In 1839 Ghazni was thrust upon the attention of the western world when captured by the British under Gen. Sir John Keane. It was recaptured by the Afghans in 1842 only to be reoccupied by the British in the autumn of the same year. Ghazni and the great Ghaznavid empire of Mahmud's day again emerged into the view of the outside world with the discovery, in 1948–49 by M. D. Schlumberger, leader of a French archaeological expedition, of the remains of Mahmud of Ghazni's palace at Lashkari-Bazar near Bust (Qala Bist) on the Helmand river.

GHAZNI PROVINCE lies at the centre of the eastern frontier of the country and is bordered northwest by Kabul province, northeast by Paktia, south by Kandahar and southeast by Pakistan. There is a mountainous region in the north, but to the south it is largely a bare plateau rising to the Shinkai hills in the southeast, to the north of which is the Ab-i-Istada lake. The climate in winter is intensely cold and snow lies 2 to 3 ft. deep for about three months. Fuel consists chiefly of prickly shrubs. The sum-

(P. H.)

mer is not so hot as that in Kabul or Kandahar but the evenings are oppressive and constant dust storms occur. Wheat, barley, alfalfa and madder are grown, besides minor products. The province had an estimated population in 1960 of 790,000 ([1954 census] 424,221). In the mountains to the north of the Kandahar road, notably in the Jaghuri valley, live the Mongolian Hazaras, whereas the main part of the province is inhabited by the Ghilzai Afghans. The largest and most powerful subtribe of the Ghilzais, the Suleiman Khel, most of whom spend their winters in Pakistan, live in the southernmost part of the province. Apart from Ghazni the most important settlements are Mashaki and Mukur; all three towns lie on the Kabul-Kandahar road which traverses the province. (X.)

See V. Minorsky's Eng. trans. and commentary on *Hudud al'Alam,* (1937); article "Afghanistan" in *Encyclopaedia of Islam,* vol. i, 2nd ed. (1954-60).

GHAZZALI, AL- (ABU-HAMID MOHAMMED IBN MOHAMMED AL-TUSI AL-SHAFII AL-GHAZZALI; Lat. ALGAZEL) (1058-1111), Islamic theologian and philosopher, was born at Tus, 15 mi. N.W. of Meshed, of Iranian stock. In theology he belonged to the school of al-Ash'ari (*q.v.*), which in his time supported the Seljuk regime, and in 1091 he was appointed professor in Baghdad by the vizier Nizam al-Mulk. After a physical and psychological crisis, he left his professorship in 1095 and spent ten years in seclusion cultivating the mystical life, first for two years in Damascus and then, after a pilgrimage to Mecca, probably again in Baghdad. He was prevailed upon by the sultan to accept a professorship at Nishapur in 1105 but soon left it and lived in retirement at Tus with a few disciples.

Most of al-Ghazzali's numerous works have survived, but not all have been published. Several works appear to have been falsely ascribed to him (see the *Journal of the Royal Asiatic Society,* pp. 24-45, 1952). His chief book, *The Revival of the Religious Sciences* (*Ihya' 'Ulum al-Din*), contains the insight he gained from the crisis of 1095 and subsequent meditations, combining theological orthodoxy with mystical experience. Though few followed him exactly, his work partially reconciled theologians and mystics (Sufis), who had often been violently opposed to one another.

If al-Ghazzali is sometimes called "the Proof of Islam" (*Hujjat al-Islam*), this is less for that reconciliation than for his defence of orthodoxy against the propaganda of the revolutionary Isma'ili movement and against the Arabic Neoplatonism of al-Farabi and Avicenna. Al-Ghazzali, by his own reading, mastered the logical technique of these philosophers and then, in his *Incoherence of the Philosophers* (*Tahafut al-Falasifa*), used it against their metaphysical positions where these were opposed to Islamic orthodoxy. Since his time most Islamic theology has had a Greek philosophical basis.

BIBLIOGRAPHY.—For manuscripts and editions *see* C. Brockelmann, *Geschichte der arabischen Literatur* (1937). For translations, books and articles *see* P. J. de Menasce, "Arabische Philosophie," *Bibliographische Einführungen in das Studium der Philosophie,* part 6 (1948). The chief studies are: D. B. Macdonald, in *J. Amer. Orient. Soc.,* vol. xx (1899); F. Jabre, article in *Mélanges de l'Institut Dominicain d'Études Orientales,* vol. i (1954); J. Obermann, *Der philosophische und religiöse Subjektivismus Ghazalis* (1921); A. J. Wensinck, *La Pensée de Ghazzali* (1940); M. Smith, *Al-Ghazali: the Mystic* (1945); W. Montgomery Watt, *Muslim Intellectual: a Study of al-Ghazali* (1963). Much of al-Ghazzali's *Ihya* is reproduced by M. Asin Palacios, *La Espiritualidad de Algazel y su sentido cristiano* (1934-41); and there is an analysis and index edited by G. H. Bousquet (1955). W. Montgomery Watt, *The Faith and Practice of al-Ghazali* (1953), includes a translation of his spiritual autobiography. The *Tahafut* is mostly translated in *Averroës' Tahafut al-Tahafut* by S. van den Bergh (1954). (W. M. Wt.)

GHEE (CLARIFIED BUTTER) is the most valued food in India, apart from wheat and rice. It is used not only by all classes and castes for cooking and in medicine but also by Hindus in their religious ceremonies. The word is derived from the Sanskrit *ghrita* through the Hindu *ghi.*

Ghee is produced as follows: butter made from cow's milk is melted over a slow fire and then heated slowly until the separated water boils. The final traces of water are removed by short, intense heating and the vessel is allowed to cool slowly. The precipitated protein settles to the bottom and the semifluid, clear fat, which is the best ghee, is carefully decanted through cloth. The sedimented protein, which still contains 50% or more of fat, may be reworked with addition of peanut oil or buffalo milk fat to make inferior grades of ghee. A major portion of the ghee consumed in India is made from buffalo butter, but only ghee made from cow's butter has religious or medical significance.

In early Sanskrit writings ghee is said to have powers of improving a person's appearance, voice and mental powers, as well as being efficacious in disorders of the stomach and digestion. It also used to be applied externally to wounds and to diseased skin and eyes. A Hindu believes that ghee is more curative when old, and it is often kept for ten or more years; examples that were even 100 years old have been known.

In the numerous rites that followers of Vishnu or of Siva must observe at different moments of their lives, the use of ghee is prescribed in almost every one—at birth (ghee is a symbol of fertility), at the cutting of hair, at the piercing of the ear, at the initiation into manhood, as part of the wedding sacrifices and as gifts at death. Images of the gods are washed in ghee and it is frequently used to light holy lamps or is thrown upon an altar fire in sacrifice. (C. C. H. F.)

GHENT (Flemish GENT, Fr. GAND), the capital of East Flanders, Belg., stands at the junction of the Lys and the Scheldt. The population of the city proper was 149,265 in 1970. Including the suburbs of Ledeberg, Gentbrugge, St. Amandsberg, Marisherke and Wondelgem, the population was 229,305 and the total area about 30 sq.mi. Ghent has retained more traces of its past than any other Belgian town. Among the old buildings grouped at its centre is the Gothic cathedral of St. Bavon (Sint Baafs), begun in the 12th century and finished in 1531, when the tower (262 ft.) was completed. It contains, among many works of art, the great polyptich altarpiece "The Adoration of the Lamb" by Hubert and Jan van Eyck. The original 12 panels, which had been dispersed since 1816, were eventually brought together again under the treaty of Versailles in 1920. The picture was removed by the Germans in World War II but restored in 1945. Other old churches include St. Nicholas (13th century), St. Jacques (12th-14th centuries), St. Michel (15th-17th centuries), and St. Pierre, at one time the oratory of the abbey of the same name, which is also an imposing building. Among other notable abbeys are the abbey of St. Bavon, founded in the 7th century, and the abbey of the Byloke, with its splendid 14th-century gable.

Ghent is famous for its Béguines (*q.v.*), the name given to members of lay sisterhoods founded in the 12th century who live in enclosed districts known as *béguinages.* One of the most attractive of these is the Béguinage of Ter Hoyen, which has entirely preserved its original appearance.

In the centre of the city stands the Belfry (14th century), a massive, rectangular construction about 300 ft. high. Its bell tower, frequently altered in the course of centuries and entirely rebuilt 1912-13, is surmounted by a gilded copper dragon, forged in Ghent in 1377. The carillon (mid-17th century), one of the most important in the country, is composed of 52 bells. The town hall comprises two buildings of different styles, the diversity of which is a reflection of the diversity which once reigned in the administrative and judiciary organization of the city: the Schepenhuis van de Keure (an alderman's house), which faces north, was built between 1518 and 1535 and is a magnificent example of Flamboyant Gothic; the Schepenhuis van Ghedeele (also an alderman's house), which faces east, was completed in 1620 in Renaissance style. The interior of the town hall is no less imposing, with its splendid Gothic staircase and its vast chapel. Not far away is the moated castle of the counts of Flanders ('s Gravensteen), which was begun in 1180 by Philip of Alsace in order to humble the troublesome townspeople. Restored at the beginning of the 20th century, this warlike structure with its great keep and circular walls stands in striking contrast to the buildings that surround it. Other historical buildings include the Cloth hall (14th century), the Groat Vleeshuis (meat hall, 15th century), and the castle of Gerard the Devil, built in the 13th century, which now houses state archives. Ghent is also well known for its large public squares and market places, of which the principal one is the Vrijdagmarkt (Friday market), the centre of the life of the medieval city. Of Ghent's many public parks the two chief ones are the Parc de la Citadelle (57 ac.) and the Parc Albert (22 ac.), both in the southern quarter of the town. By the Parc de la Citadelle stands one of the city's numerous museums, the Museum of Fine Arts. It contains two famous paintings by Jerom Bosch, "Christ Carrying the Cross" and "The Penitence of St. Jerome." The Museum of Archaeology, housed in the abbey of the Byloke, and the Lapidary museum, in the ruins of the abbey of St. Bavon, both have important collections. Ghent possesses a state university, founded in 1816 by William I, and also an agricultural college. The university library, which has been housed in a new building since 1941, has a large collection of books and manuscripts. The city of Ghent is also the seat of a bishop.

Ghent is a road and rail junction, and is connected to the mouth of the Scheldt by the Terneuzen canal (built in 1822–29), thus giving it direct access to the North sea. The seaport, which lies north of the city on the canal, is the basis of its industrial activity, and extensive alterations made to the canal and its lock will make the port accessible to the largest vessels. Near the city, and particularly toward the east, there is a vast horticultural region where azaleas, palms, orchids, begonias and many other plants are grown, and every five years a great flower show, the "Floralies," is held, attracting visitors from all over the world. Ghent's principal industries are textiles (cotton and linen), metallurgy, including the making of machines, and chemicals. The making of paper is the chief of the secondary industries. The city is also a centre of commerce and banking.

History.—Ghent was with Bruges and Ypres one of the chief towns of the county of Flanders. It owes its origin to the economic developments which took place in Flanders in the 10th century, and the city itself sprang up on the banks of the Lys, under the protection of the castle which the counts of Flanders had built nearby. The growth of Ghent in the 12th century was rapid, and by the 13th century it was one of the largest towns in northern Europe. Its astonishing prosperity was due largely to the cloth industry. Ghent cloths, which were luxury products made from English wool, were famous all over the known world up to the 15th century. The city's wealth gave it great political power, which it defended fiercely. It also had considerable privileges and was autonomist and republican, which aroused the hostility of the counts of Flanders and often led to open conflict. At the beginning of the Hundred Years' War, Louis de Nevers, count of Flanders, remained a faithful vassal to the king of France, whereas the city, fearing that the wool trade would suffer unless it continued to be friendly to England, ranged itself on the side of Edward III under the energetic leadership of Jacob van Artevelde as king of France in Jan. 1340, Edward III was given public acknowledgment as king of France in the Vrijdagmarkt. In March, the same year, John of Gaunt (i.e., Ghent), duke of Lancaster, was born in the abbey of St. Bavon. The end of the 14th century saw a terrible insurrection against another count of Flanders, Louis de Male. In the following century the policy of the dukes of Burgundy provoked fresh uprisings. The army of Ghent was massacred by Philip the Good at Gavere in 1453, and the city rose in revolt against the emperor Charles V in 1539 (who was born in the city in 1500) as a protest against the crippling taxes they were forced to pay. This rebellion was sternly repressed. Ghent was stripped of its privileges, and the emperor imposed a new constitution which practically ended its communal autonomy, together with its social and economic structure, which had been largely democratic. In the 16th century, too, the cloth industry disappeared, unable to compete with the English cloth trade. During the second half of the century Ghent came into prominence again at the time of the religious troubles and the uprisings against Philip II of Spain. Within its walls was signed the famous Pacification of Ghent in Nov. 1576 (see NETHERLANDS, THE). From 1577 to 1584 the city was under Calvinist domination. Ghent continued to decline in importance despite the linen trade which began in the 17th century. However, at the beginning of the 19th century cotton spinning was begun there and in 1827 a port was constructed. Since then Ghent has become the centre of the Belgian textiles industry. During World War I, Ghent was under German occupation from Oct. 9, 1914, until Armistice day, Nov. 11, 1918. During World War II, German troops again occupied the city from May 1940 until its liberation by Allied forces in 1945.

Famous men born in Ghent include Lambert Quetelet (*q.v.*), the astronomer, meteorologist and statistician, and Maurice Maeterlinck (*q.v.*), the dramatist and poet. *See also* references under "Ghent" in the Index volume.

BIBLIOGRAPHY.—V. Fris, *Bibliographie de l'histoire de Gand*, 2 vol. (1907–21), *Histoire de Gand*, 2nd ed. (1930); H. van Werveke, *Gand, esquisse d'histoire sociale* (1946); Y. Dhondt and P. de Keyser, *Gent* (*Les Monuments*) (1947); M. E. Dumont, *Gent, een stedenaardrijkskundige studie*, 2 vol. (1951)
(M. E. Dr.; H. Nɛ.)

GHERARDESCA, DELLA, an Italian noble family, reputedly of Lombard origin, who ruled for a time in medieval Pisa. They are first recorded during the 10th century as lords in the Tuscan Maremma, where their fiefs included La Gherardesca and Donoratico. Their relations with the bishop and later with the commune of nearby Volterra were embittered, and it was in Pisan war and politics that they first achieved distinction. One of them, TEDICO, was the first attested *podestà* of Pisa (1190). For long they led the aristocratic Ghibelline interest, but in 1275 Ugolino DELLA GHERARDESCA, count of Donoratico, joined the Guelphs, with whose support he tried to make himself lord of the city. In 1284 he was created *podestà* and in 1285 *capitano del popolo*, for the space of ten years. In fact, however, his power did not last so long. He quarreled with the Guelphs but failed to form any durable alliance with the Ghibellines, who, under Archbishop

GUILD HOUSES ON THE QUAI AUX HERBES. THE OLD PORT OF GHENT. THE HOUSE ON THE LEFT DATES FROM ABOUT 1200, THE OTHERS FROM THE LATE 17TH CENTURY

Ruggieri degli Ubaldini, preferred to revive the old republican regime. Ugolino was charged with treason and imprisoned (July 1288) and then shut up and left to die of starvation (March 1289). His cruel death is immortalized in Dante's *Inferno*, xxxii, 124 ff.

The Della Gherardesca recovered authority in the 14th century and for about 30 years (1316–47) were almost continuously dominant in Pisa. They then lost power to the Gambacorta. In the 16th century part of the family moved to Florence, where they retain a place among the aristocracy.

BIBLIOGRAPHY.—P. Litta and L. Passerini, *Famiglie celebri italiane*, vol.ix (1868); G. Volpe, *Studi sulle istituzioni comunali a Pisa* (1902); G. Rossi-Sabatini, *Pisa al tempo dei Donoratico (1316–47)* (1938).
(P. J. J.)

GHETTO, formerly a street or quarter of a city in which all Jewish people were compelled to reside. The term sometimes is used loosely for any close settlement of a minority group, even if the compulsory character of such a settlement is merely indirectly indicated.

Distinction must be made between a settlement in which conationals or coreligionists voluntarily congregate and a segregated settlement imposed by force. Historically, in the cities of the Roman and the neo-Persian Sassanian empires, people of various ethnic backgrounds lived in separate quarters, but intermingled without legal interference. Thus, large Jewish communities existed in Alexandria, Antioch, Rome and the major cities of Babylonia and Persia. St. Paul found numerous unsegregated Jewish communities on his apostolic travels. Likewise, in the early middle ages, groups of Jewish families settled in the cities of Europe under special charters and in specifically designated quarters (Juderia, Judaca, Juiverie, etc.), without compulsory concentration or restriction of activities.

However, throughout this period the church, fearing undue influence of Jews on Christians, agitated for segregation and found support among the merchant and craft guilds who were bent upon restricting Jewish economic activities. In addition, murderous mob attacks on Jewish quarters starting at the time of the first crusade (1096) made more effective control a necessity. The third and fourth Lateran councils (1179 and 1215) prohibited Christians from lodging among Jews and from entering into the service of Jews; they also imposed on Jews the requirement of wearing a distinctive badge. But these and other stipulations were not rigorously observed until the period of the Counter-Reformation, when the bull *cum nimis absurdum* of Pope Paul IV (1555) enjoined for the first time the consistent enforcement of the medieval principles of segregation. The ghetto of Rome, to which all Jewish inhabitants of the eternal city were forcibly transferred, was established in 1556. The name ghetto, probably derived from an iron foundry in the neighbourhood, was first used in Venice in 1516. In that year, an area for Jewish settlement was set aside, shut off from the rest of the city and provided with Christian watchmen. The Venetian ghetto became the model for other ghettos in Italy.

Comparable developments took place in other countries. In north Africa the first compulsory transfer of Jews to segregated quarters, ostensibly for protection, is reported from Fez in Morocco (1280), but widespread deterioration of living conditions in Jewish quarters in Muslim countries dates from the 17th century. The Moroccan institution is called Mellah; other names used (in Tunisia, Persia, etc.) are Hara and Qa'at al-Yahud. Especially in Shi'ite Muslim countries (*see* SHI'ISM) a rigid ghetto system was enforced, with restrictions regarding the sizes of houses and doors. In the Germanic countries, closed-in Jewish streets, or Judengassen, became the rule after the bloody persecutions in the period of the Black Death (1348–49). The ghetto of Frankfurt am Main, described by Goethe, and the Prague Judenstadt were renowned. In Poland, King John I, under pressure from Florentine merchants and the general populace, ordered the Jews of Cracow to take up residence in the suburb of Kasimierz in 1495. Similar moves in other cities (Lublin, Vilnius, etc.) followed. In Poland-Lithuania, however, Jews were numerous enough to constitute a majority of the population in many cities and towns, in which they occupied entire quarters.

Within the ghettos the Jews enjoyed a considerable degree of autonomy under short-term contracts. The Jewish street or quarter formed an independent corporation, with its own religious, judicial, charitable and recreational institutions. Local pride was not absent. But economic activities were frequently restricted to pawnbroking and other despised occupations and the tax burden was oppressive. Since lateral expansion, as a rule, was impossible, houses tended to be of unusual height, with consequent congestion, fire hazards and the spread of unsanitary conditions. Since Jews could not hold real estate, the rabbinic institution of *hazakah*, forbidding a Jew to bid for the rental of a house occupied by another Jew, was used to prevent exploitation by gentile landlords. The ghettos were enclosed with walls and gates and kept locked at night and during church festivals, *e.g.*, Holy Week. Even so, looting and pogroms were not always prevented. Venturing outside invited harassment and bodily harm at all times.

The ghettos in western Europe were opened in the wake of the French Revolution, but permanently abolished only in the course of the 19th century. The last vestige disappeared with the occupation of Rome by the French in 1870. In Russia, until the overthrow of the tsarist regime in 1917, a Pale (*q.v.*) of Settlement was imposed, with Jews being restricted on the whole to the western provinces of the empire, extending from the Baltic to the Black sea. Within this Pale, they were prohibited from living in villages. Outside the Pale only certain categories of "privileged" Jews were permitted to reside. Ghettos continued in some Islamic countries, *e.g.*, Yemen, until the large-scale emigration to Israel in 1948. Compulsory ghettos were revived by the Nazis during World War II, but without the redeeming features of internal autonomy. These ghettos were corrals, preliminary to extermination (*see* GENOCIDE). The Warsaw ghetto during World War II is a foremost example.

The ghetto denotes a way of life, in addition to being a habitat. It promotes human warmth and mutual help, but also jealousy and narrowness of outlook. Its inhabitants are torn between the desire to escape its confines and the fear of being exposed to discrimination once they have cut themselves loose from its sheltering institutions. They are lured by opportunity, but kept captive by prejudice.

Formerly, a sense of belonging to a particular community neutralized these conflicting forces, but cultural corrosion has brought the inherent contradictions to the fore. In the United States immigrant groups and Negroes have been compelled to live in "ghettos," not so much by legal devices but by economic and social pressures. The fact that these ghettos are slums or blighted areas encumbers them with a social stigma while escape from them is made difficult by the resistance of status fears and real estate interests elsewhere.

See also ANTI-SEMITISM; JEWS; SEGREGATION, RACIAL.

BIBLIOGRAPHY.—Salo W. Baron, *A Social and Religious History of the Jews* (1937); David Philippson, *Old European Jewries* (1894); Israel Abrahams, *Jewish Life in the Middle Ages* (1896, 2nd ed. 1932); Heinrich Heine, *The Rabbi of Bacherach* (1947); M. Lowenthal, *The Jews of Germany* (1936, 2nd ed. 1940); Cecil Roth, *History of the Jews of Italy* (1946); Israel Zangwill, *Children of the Ghetto* (1894), *Dreamers of the Ghetto* (1923); Leon Poliakoff, *Harvest of Hate* (1954); Philipp Friedman, "The Jewish Ghettoes of the Nazi Era" in *Jewish Social Studies*, vol. xvi, no. 1 (1954); Louis Wirth, *The Ghetto* (1928); Horace R. Cayton and St. Clair Drake, *Black Metropolis* (1945); Robert C. Weaver, *The Negro Ghetto* (1948); Kenneth B. Clark, *Dark Ghetto* (1965).
(W. J. C.)

GHIBERTI, LORENZO (1378–1455), Italian sculptor, who executed the second and third pairs of bronze doors of the baptistery in Florence, was born in Florence in 1378. Trained as a goldsmith under his stepfather, Bartolo di Michele, called Bartoluccio, he was active in 1400 as a fresco painter at Pesaro, whence he returned in the winter of 1400–01 to take part in the competition for the second bronze door of the Florentine baptistery. The seven competitors (who included Filippo Brunelleschi and Jacopo della Quercia) were required to prepare bronze trial reliefs of the sacrifice of Isaac. According to Ghiberti's own account, "the palm of victory," was unanimously awarded to him and in 1403 he received the contract for the bronze door. Work on the door occupied him for 21 years and it was set in place in April 1424.

Each wing of the door contains ten scenes from the New Testament and four reliefs, of church fathers and evangelists. The scenes, like the trial relief, are set in quadrilobe frames imitated from those on the first bronze door by Andrea Pisano and the exposed surfaces are gilt. In the *Commentarii* Ghiberti expresses admiration for the work of a German goldsmith, Gusmin, and the style of the trial relief is influenced by French rhythms of the composition are, however, personal to Ghiberti and recur in the later reliefs on the bronze door. In the later reliefs, *e.g.*, the "Christ Before Pilate" and "Christ Carrying the Cross," use is made of more complex and ambitious schemes.

The success of the door led to the commissioning in 1425 of the third bronze door of the baptistery, generally known, from a comment of Michelangelo, as the "Gate of Paradise." The panels of this door were cast by 1437, and the door was completed in June 1452. Each wing of the door, the Porta del Paradiso contains five rectangular reliefs of scenes from the Old Testament between figurated borders containing statuettes in niches and medallions with busts. The entire surface of the door is gilt. The change in the shape of the relief field between the earlier and later doors made it necessary to include in the latter a number of separate incidents in each relief, and this in turn involved compositional and spatial problems not present in the earlier door. Especially in the beautiful scene of the "Story of Isaac" these were solved by Ghiberti with remarkable success. The poetic rendering of landscape throughout the reliefs is also notable. Before executing the "Gate of Paradise" Ghiberti produced for the baptismal font at Siena two reliefs of the "Baptism of Christ" and "St. John the Baptist Before Herod" (commissioned 1417, completed 1427), which mark the transition from the style of the earlier to that of the later bronze door, and concurrently with the bronze door he designed the shrine of St. Zenobius for the *duomo*, or cathedral, in Florence (commissioned 1432, completed 1442). Ghiberti revived the classical practice of bronze casting on a monumental scale, and for the guildhall of Or San Michele cast three bronze statues of St. John the Baptist (1412–16), St. Matthew (1419–22) and St. Stephen (1425–28). He also designed a number of stained-glass windows for the cathedral in Florence and has been credited with many terra-cotta sculptures. He died at Florence on Dec. 1, 1455.

Ghiberti's *Commentarii* are a document of major importance for the study of Italian art. The first of the three commentaries gives an account of ancient art (based in the main on Pliny); the second describes the course of Italian art from the late 13th century to Ghiberti's own time, and includes the sculptor's autobiography; and the third deals with optics and art theory.

BIBLIOGRAPHY.—R. Krautheimer, *Lorenzo Ghiberti* (1956); J. von Schlosser, *Lorenzo Ghibertis Denkwürdigkeiten* (1910); J. von Schlosser, *Leben und Meinungen des Florentinischen Bildners Lorenzo Ghiberti* (1941).
(J. W. P-H.)

GHICA (GHIKA or GHYKA), a Rumanian family of Albanian origin that settled in Moldavia in the middle of the 17th century. GHEORGHE GHICA was appointed by Vasile Lupu (prince of Moldavia from 1634 to 1653 and also an Albanian) as his representative at the Ottoman Porte. The Turks appointed him first prince of Moldavia (1658–59) and then prince of Walachia (1660–64). He was succeeded in Walachia by his son GRIGORE I GHICA (1659–60) who, when forced by the Turks to take part in the war against Austria, joined the imperial forces at the battle of Leva (Levice in Slovakia, 1664). However, when peace was concluded, he came to terms with the Turks who reappointed him prince of Walachia (1672–73), but this time he had to fight an internal struggle against the Cantacuzinos, a rival boyar family. During the battle of Hotin (Chocim, 1673), won over the Turks by Jan Sobieski, Grigore I deserted the Turks once more to join the Poles. He finally returned to Constantinople, where he died.

GRIGORE II GHICA, a grandson of Grigore I, ruled during three different periods over Moldavia (1726–33, 1735–39, 1747–48) and twice over Walachia (1733–35, 1748–52). During his second reign in Moldavia the Russo-Turkish war broke out; Grigore II raised a small army with which he tried, unsuccessfully, to prevent his country from being occupied by the Russians. Throughout his periods of administration, both principalities were subjected to heavy taxation. Grigore II died in Bucharest, being succeeded in 1752 on the Walachian throne by his son MATEI who, a year later, was appointed ruler of Moldavia (1753–56). Both principalities were shaken during this period by revolts against the Greek coteries swarming round the ruling prince. SCARLAT GHICA, Matei's brother, ruled over Moldavia for one year (1757–58) and twice over Walachia (1758–61, 1765–66). He died in Bucharest and was succeeded in Walachia by his son, ALEXANDRU I GHICA (1766–68).

At the outbreak of a new Russo-Turkish war Alexandru I was in his turn replaced by his uncle, GRIGORE III GHICA, a nephew of Grigore II. Grigore III ruled at first over Moldavia (1764–67), distinguishing himself by taking steps toward easing taxation and by reorganizing the Greek academy at Iasi, the capital. During his reign in Walachia (1768–69) Rumanian volunteers rebelled against Turkish domination and, joining forces with the Russians, occupied Bucharest, arresting Grigore III. Taken to St. Petersburg, he was well received at the court of the empress Catherine II. After the conclusion of the Kuchuk Kainarji peace treaty (1774), Grigore III returned to Moldavia, where he was reappointed prince (1774–77). During this reign he regulated by law (1775) the position of the peasantry *vis-à-vis* the landowners on the basis of a fixed number of working days free of remuneration. This reign, however, having mediated the treaty of 1774, demanded in compensation Bukovina, a Moldavian province, and in 1775 the Turks agreed to this.

Grigore III raised a protest on behalf of the whole country but was murdered in Iasi on the sultan's orders.

After the Phanariotes were removed from the thrones of Rumanian principalities in 1821, as a consequence of the popular uprising led by Tudor Vladimirescu, the Turks appointed as prince of Walachia GRIGORE IV GHICA (1822–28), a nephew of Grigore III, protecting Rumanian culture and education. The treaty of Adrianople (1829) decided that future princes of the Rumanian principalities, was inaugurated a more patriotic regime, should be constitutionally elected on the basis of the *Règlement organique*, promulgated under Russian supervision in Walachia (1831) and Moldavia (1832).

ALEXANDRU II GHICA, a brother of Grigore IV, was elected prince of Walachia and during his term (1834–42) a national democratic movement took shape. The Russian emperor Nicholas I became suspicious and dethroned him. Some time later, however, while merely ruling as a deputy-prince of Walachia (1856–58), Alexandru contributed to the union with Moldavia. The last Moldavian prince, before the union of both principalities, was GRIGORE V GHICA (1849–56), a great-grandson of Grigore III, who also supported the popular movement toward union.

Among other members of Ghica family worth mentioning is ION GHICA (1817–97), a descendant of Grigore III, a prominent man of letters who was twice Rumanian prime minister (1866 and 1870–71) and later minister plenipotentiary in London (1881–89). ELENA GHICA (Princess Koltsov-Massalska) became known under her *nom de plume*, Dora d'Istria (1829–88), as the author of numerous essays on the Rumanian and Albanian peoples.

See Dora d'Istria, *Gli Albanesi in Rumania: Storia dei principi Ghica* (1873); D. Russo, *Cronica Ghiculeastilor, 1695–1754* (1916). (A. Or.)

GHILZAI, one of the largest of the Afghan (Pashto-speaking) tribes in Afghanistan, whose traditional territory extended from Ghazni and Kalat-i-Ghilzai eastward into the Indus valley. They are reputed to be descended at least in part from the Khalaj or Khilji Turks, who entered Afghanistan in the 10th century. The Lodi, who established a dynasty on the throne of Delhi in Hindustan (1450–1526), were a branch of the Ghilzai, and in the early 18th century Mir Vais Khan, a Ghilzai chieftain, captured Kandahar and established an independent kingdom there (1709–15). From this capital his son Mahmud conquered Persia. Some of the Ghilzai had long been nomadic merchants, buying goods in India (West Pakistan) where they wintered, and in summer transporting these by camel caravan for sale or barter in Afghanistan. In the late 19th century Afghan nomads began to enter the central mountains of Afghanistan, and several summer trading camps were established in the western mountains. Also, former stockbreeding nomads, who had always obtained grain and other necessities from villagers along their route, increased their trading activities. Some acquired land, and in summer moved from one tenant-cultivated property to another. In eastern Afghanistan many Ghilzai have become settled cultivators. *See also* PATHAN; AFGHANISTAN: *History; The People.*

See Ferdinand Klaus, "Nomad Expansion and Commerce in Central Afghanistan," *Folk* (Copenhagen), vol. 4, pp. 123–159 (1962). (EL. B.)

GHIRLANDAJO (GHIRLANDAIO, GRILLANDAJO, originally DOMENICO DI TOMMASO BIGORDI) (1449–1494), one of the finest of the Florentine painters of frescoes, and master of Michelangelo, was born in Florence in 1449. He probably began his career as a goldsmith, but was certainly active as a fresco painter by the early 1470s, his earliest works being influenced both by Andrea del Castagno and by such ceremonial portrait cycles as the Medici chapel frescoes by Benozzo Gozzoli. Three saints at Cercina, near Florence, may be his earliest works, but the "Mater Misericordiae" and the "Pietà," with members of the Vespucci family introduced as mourners (Ognissanti, Florence), probably date from about 1473. They already show his characteristic style in that they have likenesses of the donors introduced rather incongruously into the sacred scenes, which are themselves depicted with a minute realism influenced by Flemish art. This may be seen most clearly in the "St. Jerome," also in Ognissanti, dated 1480, which may even be copied from an original by Jan van Eyck; the contrast between it and the more sensitive realism of the companion "St. Augustine" by Botticelli is very marked and clearly reveals the fundamentally pedestrian character of Ghirlandajo's art. Before that date, he had already painted the scenes from the life of Sta. Fina (San Gimignano, Pieve; almost certainly 1475), and he had begun to use assistants, a practice he was to carry to great lengths. In 1475 he was also working in the Vatican, but the first surviving fresco

there is one of the two which formed part of the scenes from the lives of Christ and Moses, commissioned from several painters by Pope Sixtus IV for his Sistine chapel; there is a contract of Oct. 27, 1481. The important fresco is the "Calling of the First Apostles," which is chiefly noteworthy as being stylistically old-fashioned in its reminiscences of Masaccio and as having many portraits of members of the Florentine colony in Rome.

On his return to Florence, Ghirlandajo began in 1482 to paint the "Roman Heroes" in the Sala dei Gigli of the Palazzo Vecchio. Many details from classical antiquity occur in his later works, and it is clear that he had spent much time in Rome in the study of the remains (a sketchbook in the Escurial, Madrid, is attributed to his workshop and contains numerous drawings of the antiquities). During the last years of his life he and his helpers produced two major fresco cycles and a large number of altarpieces, but for all his panel paintings he remained faithful to the old-fashioned tempera technique and never painted in oil himself.

The frescoes and altarpiece in the Sassetti chapel, SS. Trinità, were painted between about 1482 and 1485 for Francesco Sassetti, an agent of the Medici bank. The ceiling has representations of the four sibyls and the walls are devoted to scenes from the life of St. Francis. The "Pope Authorizing the Rule of the Franciscan Order" contains a large number of portraits of the Medici, the Sassetti and other dependents of the Medici, and there can be little doubt that these were intended to show Francesco Sassetti's close ties with the ruling family. The decoration was completed by the altarpiece of the "Adoration of the Shepherds," dated 1485,

GIRAUDON

"OLD MAN WITH HIS GRANDSON" BY GHIRLANDAJO. IN THE LOUVRE, PARIS

and showing a blend of interest in classical antiquity in the treatment of the subject, and in contemporary Flemish painting—such as the Portinari altar by Hugo van der Goes—in its handling of detail.

On Sept. 1, 1485, Ghirlandajo signed a contract with Giovanni Tornabuoni (also a Medici banker) to decorate the choir of Sta. Maria Novella with frescoes depicting the lives of the Virgin and the Baptist; the fresco of "Zaccharias and the Angel" bears the date 1490, but the altarpiece was still incomplete at Ghirlandajo's death in Florence on Jan. 11, 1494. This cycle was Ghirlandajo's major work and for it he employed many assistants, among whom was very probably the boy Michelangelo, who certainly served a short apprenticeship under him.

Ghirlandajo's main claim to fame may well lie in his having taught the technique of fresco painting to Michelangelo. The lack of imagination in his works has led to his being ranked well below Botticelli, in spite of the great appeal his realistic detail made to the 19th century. It may be observed that he never received a commission from the Medici themselves, but only from their supporters—wealthy but not perhaps highly sensitive.

(P. J. MX.)

BIBLIOGRAPHY.—G. Vasari, *Lives of the Most Eminent Painters, Sculptors and Architects,* vol. iii, Eng. trans. by G. de Vere (1912); J. A. Crowe and G. B. Cavalcaselle, *A History of Painting in Italy,* iv, ed. by L. Douglas (1911); J. Lauts, *Domenico Ghirlandajo* (1943); *see also* G. Marchini in *Burlington Magazine,* vol. 95, pp. 320 ff (1953) for attributions of some figures in Sta. Maria Novella to Michelangelo.

(P. J. MX.)

GHIRLANDAJO, RIDOLFO (1483–1561), Florentine painter, was the son of Domenico Ghirlandajo. He was born in Florence on Jan. 4, 1483, and, since his father died in 1494, he was brought up by his uncle David and presumably received his first training from him in the family shop; but G. Vasari, who knew him, says he was a pupil of Fra Bartolommeo, and it is likely that he was also influenced by F. Granacci and others, in particular Raphael. The two were close friends when Raphael was in Florence between 1504 and 1508, and both were in close contact with Fra Bartolommeo, so that all three must have influenced each other. Ridolfo, however, did not really live up to his early promise and he settled down to enjoy his Florentine fame, producing much decorative work and going into local politics. He and his assistants arranged the decorations for such ceremonial occasions as the entry of Pope Leo X (1515) or of the Emperor Charles V (1536). He also painted many religious pictures and many excellent portraits, his earliest datable work being either the "Madonna and Saints" (1503; Accademia, Florence), which is reasonably attributed to him, or the "Coronation of the Virgin" (1504; Louvre museum, Paris). Other works by him are in London, New York, Philadelphia (Johnson collection) and several museums and churches in Florence. He died in Florence on Jan. 6, 1561.

See G. Vasari, *Lives of the Most Eminent Painters, Sculptors and Architects,* vol. viii, Eng. trans. by G. de Vere (1914); C. Gamba in *Dedalo,* ix (1929) II, pp. 463 ff. and 544 ff.

(P. J. MX.)

GHOR (GHUR), a mountainous territory in western Afghanistan, to the southeast of Herat and northwest of the Helmand valley, which gave its name to a medieval dynasty whose members and military officers founded a Muslim sultanate in Hindustan (*see* INDIA-PAKISTAN, SUBCONTINENT OF: *History*). In modern Afghanistan Ghor is a minor province (pop. [1961 est.] 326,426). The small town of Qala-i-Ghor (Taiwara) lies near the ruins of the ancient capital.

In the 10th century A.D. the area of Ghor was said to be under two rival families of Tajik (Iranian) origin, one of whom, the Darmishi-Shahs (probably identical with the Shanaspids), had the princely power, and the other, the Ghur-Shahs, the military command. The inhabitants were mainly non-Muslim. In 1009 and 1020 the area was conquered by the forces of Mahmud of Ghazni and paid tribute to the Ghaznavids until the mid-12th century. In the reign of Saif ud-din Suri (c. 1145–49) a division of power occurred, the present-day Taimani country going to Qutb ud-din, Suri's half-nephew, and Bamian and Tukharistan to another half-nephew, Fakhr ud-din. The latter's descendants remained rulers of Bamian until the Khwarizmshahi invasion in 1215. It was the other line of the family that destroyed the Ghaznavids. In 1149,

Bahram Shah of Ghazni poisoned Qutb ud-din, who had fled to Ghazni after a family quarrel. In 1151 in revenge 'Ala ud-din (Jahansuz) sacked and burned Ghazni. Although he did not hold Ghazni, his triumph enabled his nephews Ghiyath ud-din Mohammed ibn Sam and Mu'izz ud-din Mohammed ibn Sam [q.v.] of Ghor) to retake it from Ghuzz nomads in 1173. Between 1173 and 1202 Ghiyath ud-din, the senior and suzerain, with his headquarters at Firuz Kuh, and Mu'izz ud-din, his loyal *frère-cadet* with headquarters at Ghazni, raised Ghorid power to its peak. Ghiyath ud-din struggled with the Khwarizmshahs for the division of the Seljuk empire in Khurasan. In 1176 the Ghorids occupied Herat, in 1198 Balkh, in 1200 Nishapur, Merv, Sarakhs and Tus. Meanwhile, Mohammed ibn Sam and his lieutenants were extending Ghorid sway in India from Multan in Sind to Gaur in Bengal.

But the glory of Ghor proved short-lived. In 1202 Ghiyath ud-din died. In 1204 Mohammed ibn Sam was defeated at Andkhud by the Qara-Khitay of Turkistan who had come to support the Khwarizmshah, 'Ala ud-din. By 1206, when Mohammed ibn Sam was assassinated, in Khurasan the Ghorids retained only Herat and Balkh. A confused struggle then ensued among the remaining Ghorids and their officers, with Taj ud-din Yilduz and Qutb ud-Din Aibak (q.v.) contending for Ghazni and Ghiyath ud-din Mahmud, son of Ghiyath ud-din Mohammed, seizing Firuz Kuh.

In 1215 the Khwarizmshah destroyed Ghor as a power by occupying both Firuz Kuh and Ghazni. In 1221 most of Afghanistan suffered the invasion of Genghis Khan (q.v.), Firuz Kuh being completely destroyed. Under the overlordship of the Mongol Il-khans, a Tajik dynasty, the Karts, descended in the maternal line from the Ghorid sultans, ruled over Ghor from about 1245 to 1379, when Timur (q.v.) captured their capital, Herat. Thereafter, Ghor relapsed into obscurity. In 1958, however, a minaret erected about 1170 by Ghiyath ud-din Mohammed was discovered in a remote defile of the Hari Rud valley by a French archaeological expedition.

A satisfactory explanation of the meteoric rise and fall of the Ghorids in the 12th century has yet to be made. Possibly they benefited from the decline of the Seljuk empire to attract a strong military following of Turks, Khaljis and Afghans and their early successes in India no doubt enhanced their ability to finance their central Asian ambitions. The unjealous relationship between the two brothers was a contributory factor unusual in Muslim dynastic annals.

BIBLIOGRAPHY.—"Tabaqat-i-Nasiri," Eng. trans. by H. G. Raverty, in *Bibliotheca Indica*, vol. 78 (1873–97); B. Spuler, *Die Mongolen in Iran* (1939); *Hudud al-'Alam: The Regions of the World*, Eng. trans. by V. Minorsky (1937). (P. H.)

GHOST DANCE.

In 1870 there started among the Paiute Indians (Paviotso) of western Nevada a new faith—the Ghost Dance religion—which in most cases spread rapidly because of wide feeling, founded on solid fact, that the westward movement of white culture was destined to destroy the native culture. In some cases the new cult was encouraged by the chiefs as a check to the rival powers of the shamans or medicine men. Although the Modoc war of 1873 (*see* Modoc) saw the immediate disappearance of the cult, in 1890 the appointment of inexperienced men as heads of the reserves led to widespread discontent, notably among the Sioux of Pine Ridge, S.D. Pledges had been broken. Messianic ideas of a deliverer who would restore the world to the godly and punish the transgressors of his ordinances had long existed in Indian thought, and there is discernible a continuity of idea, inspired by, and probably based on, political conditions, unifying the ideals of Pontiac; the Paiute dreamer of 1870 named Tä'vibo; Smohalla, the dreamer of the Columbia region whose oratory, activities and personality made him a man of wide influence; the Shaker teachers of Puget sound; and the doctrines of Wovoka the Messiah, the Paiute who is known as Jack Wilson.

Toward the end of 1888, already known among his people as a gifted medicine man, Wovoka became seriously ill with some sort of febrile disease. In his delirium, Wovoka seems to have experienced what he called a visit to the world of the spirits. During his stay among the ghosts, he reported having received a message from the deity, revealing a momentous change that soon was to better the lives of all Indians. According to the revelation the ancient dominion of Indians over lands that had been taken over by white men was to be restored.

In addition, there was to be a great reunion of the living with their relatives and comrades who had been taken in death. Wovoka instructed the Paiutes that to make themselves ready for the imminent miracle they were to become skilful in the ritual singing and dancing he prescribed. Especially impressive to those who heard him was the fact that during his illness a great darkening of the sun came to pass. (Undoubtedly this was the eclipse of the day on Jan. 1, 1889, that was photographed on the North American continent by teams of astronomers in the states of California and Nevada.)

At any rate, the new teaching—in reality it seems to have been the old teaching—reached the Sioux in 1889 and took the form of a prophecy of a new world. Even progressive and intelligent Indians believed in the close advent of a liberator who would restore the Indian race, living and dead, to a regenerated earth where the pristine conditions of life would prevail. Administration of Indian reserves had been adequate, intelligent, sympathetic and satisfactory in many cases, and the prophecy sometimes allowed the white man to share the predicted felicity. The movement took hostile expression among the discontented Sioux, whose leaders, Sitting Bull (q.v.) and Red Cloud, were irreconcilable enemies of the whites. Sitting Bull was killed on Dec. 15, 1890. By Jan. 16, 1891, the outbreak ended, as a result of the military and political operations conducted by Gen. Nelson Miles, who put the agencies in charge of military officers who were known and respected by the Indians. However, this was not until the occurrence of a massacre of hundreds of Sioux who peacefully were attempting to return home after having given their pledge to authorities that they would do so. On Dec. 29, 1890, in the state of South Dakota at Wounded Knee creek, troops of the U.S. 7th cavalry slaughtered by gunfire more than 200 Sioux (children included).

The Ghost Dance ceremony began in the middle of the afternoon or later. No musical instrument was used except by individual dancers. The Sioux wore a "ghost shirt," almost always made of white cloth, tailored in Indian fashion. No metal was allowed to be worn. The ghost stick carried by the leader was a staff about six feet long, with red cloth and red feathers. Other articles used were arrows with bone heads, a bow, a gaming wheel and sticks. The ground was consecrated. The priests were ordained by the confinement of a consecrated feather, either of a crow, the sacred bird of the Ghost Dance, or of the eagle, sacred in Indian lore, given to the candidates by the apostle. The feathers were painted. The dancers were ceremonially painted on the face with elaborate designs, in red, yellow, green and blue, suggested in trances, and were thus strengthened in spiritual vision and physical health. All went to bathe—to wash away all evil, spiritual and material. Attendance was compulsory, as those who stayed away would be turned to stone or punished. Songs, adapted to the simple dance step, were carefully rehearsed. Participants fell into trances and on regaining consciousness narrated their visions. Significantly, the sexual display characteristic of much primitive dance was sternly and successfully suppressed in the Ghost Dance, in which the whole attention of the performers was successfully concentrated upon the purpose of the dance and upon the message of salvation which it conveyed. *See also* NATIVISTIC MOVEMENTS.

BIBLIOGRAPHY.—James Mooney, *The Ghost Dance Religion and the Sioux Outbreak of 1891* (1896); A. L. Kroeber, "A Ghost Dance in California," *Journal of American Folklore*, vol. 17 (1904), and *Handbook of the Indians of California* (1925); Leslie Spier, *The Ghost Dance of 1870 Among the Klamath of Oregon* (1927); A. H. Gayton, *The Ghost Dance of 1870 in South-Central California* (1930); Cora du Bois, "The 1870 Ghost Dance," *Anthropological Records*, vol. 3 (1939); D. H. Miller, *Ghost Dance* (1959); R. M. Utley, *The Last Days of the Sioux Nation* (1963).

GIACOMETTI, ALBERTO

(1901–1966), Swiss-born artist, sculptor, painter and poet, pursued in Paris one of the loneliest and most important paths of development in modern sculpture. He was born in Stampa in 1901, and studied in Geneva and Italy before settling in Paris. Although a student of older art, by the late 1920s Giacometti had joined with the surrealists, and later created

"The Palace at 4 A.M." (1932-33) and "Slaughtered Woman" (1932).

Working from images and emotions evoked from within himself, Giacometti did not deal with the exterior reality of the human figure and objects until after 1935. After a long illness, ending in 1945, Giacometti produced his famous elongated solitary figures, whose elusive silhouettes and rough unsensual surfaces recreate the mystery of the human figure when seen from afar. Giacometti sensed a fundamental human spiritual isolation. His portraits of his brother Diego and figures in "City Square" (1948-49) and "Man Pointing" (1947) unite the human only with space. He died in Chur, Switz., on Jan. 12, 1966.

See J. P. Sartre, *Giacometti* (1949); C. Giedion-Welcker, *Contemporary Sculpture*, 3rd ed. (1960). (A. E. EL.)

GIAMBONO (MICHELE DI TADDEO BONO), Italian painter and mosaicist, was active in Venice from 1420 to 1462. He was a representative of the old Gothic tradition in Venice, but was much influenced by Gentile da Fabriano and Pisanello and the new International Gothic introduced by them into Italy. Among the few signed works by him are a large polyptych in the Accademia, Venice, a "Madonna" in the Galleria Nazionale, Rome, and the mosaics of the Mascoli chapel in St. Mark's at Venice. The mosaics represent an attempt to introduce three-dimensional representation in a technique dominated by the two-dimensional Byzantine tradition, but it is not certain that the architectural settings are his. Other works include a copy, of 1447 (in the Accademia), of an altarpiece by Vivarini in S. Pantaleone, Venice, and an altarpiece of 1441 in S. Daniele del Friuli, near Udine. The National gallery, London, and the Metropolitan museum, New York, are among those having works attributed to him.

See E. Sandberg-Vavala in *Journal of the Warburg and Courtauld Institutes*, pp. 20 ff. (1947). (P. J. Mx.)

GIANNINI, AMADEO PETER (1870-1949), U.S. banker, founder of regional branch banking in America, was born in San Jose, Calif., May 6, 1870, the son of an Italian immigrant. He established the Bank of Italy in San Francisco in 1904, after retiring from active participation in his stepfather's produce business. He offered liberal terms for loans to farmers and small businessmen and aggressively solicited small depositors and borrowers. After the San Francisco earthquake and fire of 1906, Giannini salvaged the gold and securities from his bank and began making loans for rebuilding the city.

Giannini's first move toward regional branch banking occurred in 1909 when the Bank of Italy opened a branch in San Jose, Calif.. By the end of 1910, he had doubled the size of his bank by mergers and purchases. In 1928 he organized Transamerica corporation as a holding company for the stock of all the Giannini banks. In 1930 the banks owned by Transamerica were consolidated into the Bank of America National Trust and Savings association. By 1948 it had become the largest bank in the United States, with 517 branches and assets of more than $6,000,000,000. Giannini died at San Mateo, Calif., on June 3, 1949, after giving away half of his $1,000,000 estate.

See Marquis James, *Biography of a Bank* (1954). (J. R. LR.)

GIANNINI, VITTORIO (1903-1966), U.S. composer of Italian extraction known for his operas written for radio production. Born in Philadelphia, Oct. 19, 1903, he studied in Milan and in 1925 in New York city under Rubin Goldmark and Hans Letz. In 1932 he won the music prize of the American Academy in Rome

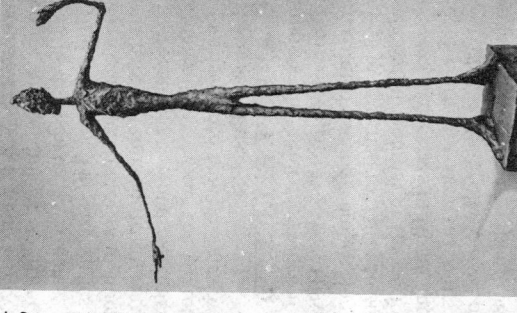

COLLECTION, THE MUSEUM OF MODERN ART, NEW YORK, GIFT OF MRS. JOHN D. ROCKEFELLER III

"MAN POINTING" BY ALBERTO GIACOMETTI, COMPLETED IN 1947. THE ORIGINAL SCULPTURE IS BRONZE AND STANDS 70½ IN. HIGH

and in 1939 was appointed teacher of composition at the Juilliard school in New York. Two of his early operas were first performed in Germany: *Lucedia* (Munich, 1934) and *The Scarlet Letter* (Hamburg, 1938), based on the novel by Nathaniel Hawthorne and with Giannini's sister Dusolina (b. 1902) in the principal part. He wrote two operas for radio production, *Beauty and the Beast* (1938) and *Blennerhasset* (1939), and his grand opera *The Taming of the Shrew* was the first produced in colour television (1954). Between 1936 and 1959 he also wrote symphonies, a requiem (1937), chamber music, songs and concertos for piano, violin and organ. He died in New York City on Nov. 28, 1966. (N. Sy.)

GIANNONE, PIETRO (1676-1748), Italian historian, who opposed the papal interference in Naples, was born at Ischitella, Capitanata, May 7, 1676. He graduated in law (Naples, 1698), became interested in the New Learning and wrote the *Istoria civile del Regno di Napoli* (1723)—a polemical survey of Neapolitan history in which he espoused the side of the civil power in its conflicts with the Roman Catholic hierarchy. As a result of this the *Istoria* was placed on the *Index* and Giannone excommunicated. In Vienna, where until 1734 he received a pension from Charles VI, Giannone prepared his most important work, *Il Triregno, ossia del regno del cielo, della terra, e del papa* (3 vol., ed. by A. Parente, 1940). On the transfer of the Neapolitan crown to Charles of Bourbon, Giannone left Vienna for Venice. Unhappily there arose a suspicion that his views on maritime law were not favourable to the pretensions of the republic, and this, together with clerical intrigues, caused him finally to seek refuge in Geneva (1735). But while visiting a village in Piedmont, he was kidnaped by agents of the Sardinian government and taken to the castle of Miolans (1736). There he wrote his *Autobiografia* (ed. by F. Nicolini, 1905). Giannone was incarcerated for the last 12 years of his life in the fortresses of Ceva and of Turin, where he died March 17, 1748.

BIBLIOGRAPHY.—F. Niccolini, *Gli scritti e la fortuna di P. Giannone* (1914) and *Le teorie politiche di P. Giannone* (1915); C. Caristia, *P. Giannone giureconsulto e politico* (1947); L. Marini, *P. Giannone e il giannonismo a Napoli nel Settecento* (1950). (D. M. WE.)

GIANT. The giants of Greek and Norse mythology were primeval beings who existed before the gods, and were overcome by them in battle (*see* GIGANTES; GERMANIC MYTHOLOGY AND HEROIC LEGENDS). In folk tradition the term was usually applied to a supposed race of mortals, akin to humans but of immense size, who inhabited the world in early times. Stories of aboriginal giants are common to many countries. In Num. xiii, 32-33, it is stated that Israelite spies in the land of Canaan saw there giants, "the sons of Anak, men of great stature . . . and we seemed to ourselves . . . [and to them] like grasshoppers." According to a legend told by Geoffrey of Monmouth in his *Historia regum Britanniae* (c. 1136), when Brutus came to Cornwall after the fall of Troy, he found it inhabited by giants. These his followers destroyed, the last and greatest, Goëmagot (Gogmagog), being slain in single combat with Corineus.

In most European folk tales, giants appear as cruel and stupid savages, given to cannibalism, often one-eyed, and sometimes hardly distinguishable from monsters. Individual heroes who killed them, like Grimm's Valiant Tailor, or the English Jack the Giant-Killer, often succeeded in doing so more by wit than by strength. Kindly giants occur in a few stories (e.g., Rübezahl, a giant who lived in the Bohemian forest), but the majority were feared and hated, although marriages between their daughters and the hero of the story were not impossible. All this suggests that these tales may be derived in part from dim traditions of primitive races living alongside more advanced peoples who had conquered the land but had not succeeded in extirpating the aborigines.

Belief in giants was probably strengthened by discoveries of fossil bones of extinct animals, and also by hill figures, like the giant of Cerne, cut in the chalk near Cerne Abbas, Dorset, which were thought to represent real beings. Megalithic monuments and long barrows also seemed to presuppose giant builders to those who had no knowledge of primitive burial customs, barrows often being thought to be the graves of giants. There was also at one time a tradition that people had once been taller and stronger, but had degenerated after the close of the Golden Age. There are, however, no rational grounds for this belief. The word giant is commonly used in describing unusually tall men and women. (For medical aspects see DWARFISM AND GIGANTISM.)

In the middle ages, towns often had tutelary giants whose effigies were carried in procession on great occasions. In London the figures of Gog and Magog (see GOG), which used to stand at the entrance to the City and are now in the Guildhall, are supposed to represent two Cornish giants brought by Brutus to act as doorkeepers in his palace. The 40-ft. effigy of Antigonus at Antwerp and the 22-ft. figure of Gayant at Douai preserve similar traditions.

See also FOLKLORE.

GIANT MOUNTAINS (Czech. KRKNOŠE, Ger. RIESENGEBIRGE), the highest of the ranges bounding the Bohemian massif on the northeast. The covering name for these mountains is Sudetes, and the western part of the Czechoslovak-Polish frontier runs through them. The ranges show the effect of pressure from the south during the period of Tertiary mountain building, and the features of tilting, fracturing and faulting are emphatic; hence, probably, the breaking of the rim of the massif there into six sets of mountains.

The ranges contain a variety of rock series: the crystalline blocks are the most conspicuous and are ringed around with metamorphic schists. In the centre, in the Glatz depression, some covering of Cretaceous sandstones and limestones has survived. The Giant mountains are a formidable mass: Snezka (Schneekoppe) is 5,259 ft. and the highest summit in Bohemia, and Sisak (Hohes Rad) is 4,968 ft. The height of the mountains is accentuated by the fault-line features on the inner and outer sides. Yet the northeast highland is so much fragmented and indeterminate in configuration that traditionally the details of frontiers are influenced by the direction of river drainage patterns. The Elbe river (Czech. Labe) rises on the Bohemian slope. The forest covering is substantial; beech grows up to 3,000 ft. with pine and fir above; the high ridges and summits are often alpine meadowland and give fine skiing.

The complication in place names rightly suggests the German past, though the German character of the area was more uneven than in the Erzgebirge or Ore mountains (q.v.); it appeared by the 1960s to have recovered from population changes after World War II and a part of it, from Liberec (Reichenberg) in the northwest to Trutnov (Trautenau) in the southeast, showed increases in settlement. The most conspicuous feature in industry is the tradition and range of textile industries—wool, cotton and linen—with Liberec (pop. [1961] 67,180) as the main centre. In some of the southern foothills is the arenaceous quartz used for the production of Bohemian glass. The commercial centre for this industry is Jablonec (pop. 27,533), both for magnificent craftsmanship of costly pieces and for skill in cheap products and costume jewelry. The industry is typified by small units reaching high up the slopes of the Giant mountains, and the forge chimneys attached to cottages are prominent. Together with machine production and timber working, these occupations explain the employment of a high percentage of the population in industry. Rail connections from Prague to Wroclaw and from Prague to Görlitz cross the ranges. The main road from Prague to Wroclaw crosses near Nachod.

(C. S. HE.)

GIANT'S CAUSEWAY, a promontory of columnar basalt, extending along the northern coast of County Antrim, N. Ire., between Portrush and Ballycastle. Local folklore ascribes its formation to a race of giants who built it as a roadway to Staffa (q.v.), where a similar structure occurs. The prismatic forms were caused by the rapid cooling of the lava flows where they entered the sea. The thousands of pillars composing the Giant's causeway are mostly irregular hexagons. In diameter they vary from 15 to 20 in., and some are 20 ft. in height. The great causeway is in places nearly 40 ft. wide and is highest at its narrowest part. It extends outward into a platform and for nearly 100 yd. is above water. Other cliffs to the east exhibit similar columns. The most remarkable of the cliffs is the Pleaskin, the upper pillars of which are 400 ft. high; beneath these is a mass of coarse black amygdaloidal rock, of the same thickness, underlain by a second range of basaltic pillars, from 40 to 50 ft. high.

(H. G. S.)

GIANT'S KETTLE (GIANT'S CALDRON), a glacial pothole, a deep cylindrical hole in solid rock drilled out by eddying currents of water of subglacial streams, bearing stones, gravel and other detrital matter. The size varies from a few inches to several feet in depth and diameter, and upon the retreat of the ice the hole frequently contains the sand, gravel or boulders which have assisted in its formation. Good examples occur in the Alps (Lucerne), in Germany, Norway and the United States. Giant's kettles must not be confused with true potholes, which occur in river beds and at the bases of sea cliffs.

GIARDINI, FELICE DE' (1716–1796) Italian violinist and composer who influenced musical development in England, was born in Turin on April 12, 1716. He was a chorister at Milan cathedral, then studied singing, composition and the harpsichord with A. Paladini. He returned to Turin to study the violin under G. B. Somis, a celebrated violinist of the period. As a youth Giardini played in the opera orchestras in Rome and Naples. In 1748 he set out on a tour of Germany, then made his way to London, where he arrived about 1750. His brilliant style of playing won him a great reputation in England, and he spent the greater part of his life in London as a composer, violinist, concert director, leader at the opera and sometimes even impresario. With his younger colleagues, J. C. Bach, K. F. Abel and J. C. Fisher, he was one of the acknowledged leaders of the new *galant* style, which they introduced and established in Britain. Giardini was long accepted as the greatest violinist in England, a position he held without dispute until the arrival of W. Cramer and J. P. Salomon in the latter part of the century. In 1784 Giardini left England to retire to his native Italy, but he returned again to London and about 1790 was directing operas at the Haymarket. He then went to St. Petersburg (c. 1793), where he died on June 8, 1796. As a composer Giardini was prolific, but his music lacks the spontaneity and melodic warmth of Bach and Abel.

(Cs. Ch.)

GIAUQUE, WILLIAM FRANCIS (1895–), U.S. physical chemist, was winner of the 1949 Nobel prize in chemistry for his studies of the properties of matter under conditions approaching absolute zero. Born May 12, 1895, in Niagara Falls, Ont., of U.S. parentage, thus acquiring U.S. citizenship, he was educated at the Niagara Falls Collegiate institute and the University of California (Berkeley). Upon receiving the Ph.D. degree in 1922 he was appointed to the faculty of the department of chemistry at Berkeley. By comparing entropies of gases obtained from experimental low temperature calorimetric measurements with those calculated theoretically from spectroscopic data, Giauque established a firm experimental basis for quantum statistics and the third law of thermodynamics (q.v.) and led to an understanding of the apparent exceptions to this law. In 1929, with H. L. Johnston, he discovered the oxygen isotopes of mass 17 and 18 and thus disclosed the difference between the physical and chemical atomic weight scales. In 1926 he proposed the adiabatic demagnetization method for obtaining temperatures well below $1°$ K., and in 1953, with D. P. MacDougall, performed the first successful experiments making use of this method. Giauque's adiabatic demagnetization method is basic to numerous experiments which have since been made in the temperature range below $1°$ K. He also has received the Chandler, Cresson, Gibbs and Lewis awards.

(J. W. SR.)

GIBBET, a primitive form of gallows. It was a custom at one time—though not part of the legal sentence—to hang the body in chains, this being known as gibbeting. See HANGING; CAPITAL PUNISHMENT.

GIBBON, EDWARD (1737–1794), English historian, whose outstanding work was *The History of the Decline and Fall of the Roman Empire*, was born at Putney, Surrey, on April 27, 1737. After the reform of the calendar in 1752 his birthday fell on May 8. His grandfather, Edward, had made a considerable fortune and his son, also Edward, the historian's father, lived an easygoing life in society and parliament. He married Judith, a daughter of James Porten (pronounced Porteen) whose family had originated from Germany. The historian succeeded eventually to an embarrassed estate but he too had independent means throughout his life. He was the eldest and the only survivor of seven children, the rest dying in infancy. His own childhood was a series of illnesses and more than once he nearly died. He was neglected by his mother and owed his life to her sister, Catherine Porten, whom he also called "the mother of his mind." After his mother's death in 1747 he was almost entirely in his aunt's care. He early became an omnivorous reader and could indulge his tastes the more fully since his schooling was most irregular. He attended a day school in Putney and in 1746 Kingston grammar school. In 1749 he was admitted to Westminster school. He was taken in 1750 to Bath and Winchester in search of health and after an unsuccessful attempt to return to Westminster was placed for the next two years with tutors from whom he learned little. His father took him on his visits to country houses where he had the run of libraries filled with old folios. He noted his 12th year as one of great intellectual development, and says in his *Memoirs* that he had early discovered his "proper food," history. By his fourteenth year he had already covered the main fields of his subsequent masterpiece, applying his mind as well to difficult problems of chronology. The keynote of these early years of study is self-sufficiency. Apart from his aunt's initial guidance Gibbon followed his intellectual bent in solitary independence. This characteristic remained with him throughout his life. His great work was composed without consulting other scholars and is impressed with the seal of his unique personality.

In his *Memoirs* Gibbon remarked that with the onset of puberty his health suddenly improved and remained excellent throughout his life. It must be noted that he was never a strong or active man. He was of diminutive stature and very slightly built, becoming corpulent in later years. This improvement in health apparently accounts for his father's sudden decision to enter him as a gentleman-commoner at Magdalen college, Oxford, on April 3, 1752, about three weeks before his 15th birthday. He was now privileged and independent. Any expectations of study at Oxford were soon disappointed. The authorities failed to look after him intellectually or spiritually or even to note his absences from the college. Left to himself, Gibbon turned to theology and read himself into the Roman Catholic faith. It was a purely intellectual conversion. Yet he acted on it, being received into the Roman Catholic Church by a priest in London on June 8, 1753. His father was outraged by this step, since under the existing laws his son had disqualified himself for all public service and office. Gibbon's father acted swiftly. On June 19 the youth was dispatched to Lausanne and lodged with a Calvinist minister, the Rev. Daniel Pavillard. The change was complete. Gibbon was now under strict surveillance, in great discomfort and with the scantiest allowance. Yet he always spoke of this period with gratitude. To Pavillard he owed kindly and competent instruction and the formation of regular habits of study. He mastered the bulk of classical Latin literature, and studied mathematics and logic. He also became perfectly conversant with the language and literature of France which exercised a permanent influence on him. These studies made him not only a man of considerable learning but a stylist for life. He began his first work written in French, *L'Essai sur l'étude de la littérature*. Meanwhile the main purpose of his exile had not been neglected. Not without weighty thought, Gibbon at last abjured his new faith and was publicly readmitted to the Protestant communion at Christmas 1754. "It was here," Gibbon says somewhat ambiguously, "that I suspended my religious enquiries, acquiescing with implicit belief in the tenets and mysteries which are adopted by the general consent of Catholics and Protestants." In the latter part of his exile Gibbon entered more freely into Lausanne society. He attended Voltaire's parties. He formed an enduring friendship with a young Swiss, Georges Deyverdun, and also fell in love with and rashly plighted himself to Suzanne Curchod, a pastor's daughter of great charm and intelligence.

In 1758 his father called Gibbon home shortly before his 21st birthday, and settled an annuity of £300 on him. On the other hand he found that his father and his second wife were implacably opposed to his engagement, and he was compelled to break it off. He never again thought seriously of marriage. After a natural estrangement Mlle Curchod, later Mme Necker, remained a devoted friend. During the next five years Gibbon read widely and considered many possible subjects for a historical composition. He published his *Essai* first in French (1761) and later in English (1764). From May 10, 1760, until the end of 1762 his studies were seriously interrupted by his service on home defense duties with the South Hampshire militia. With the rank of captain he did his duty conscientiously and later claimed that his experience of men and camps had been useful to him as a historian.

The Seven Years' War being over, Gibbon left England on Jan. 25, 1763. He spent some time in Paris, making the acquaintance of Denis Diderot, Jean d'Alembert and others. During the autumn and winter spent in study and gaiety at Lausanne he gained a valuable friend in John Baker Holroyd (created Lord Sheffield in 1781), who later took over the management of his affairs. In April 1764 Gibbon crossed the Mt. Cenis pass into Italy and, going by leisurely stages, arrived in Rome in October. There he made an exhaustive study of the antiquities and it was on Oct. 15, 1764, while musing amid the ruins of the Capitol that he was inspired to write of the decline and fall of the city. It was to be some time yet before he decided on the history of the empire. After visiting Naples he returned through Italy and Provence and was home by June 1765. The next five years were the least satisfactory in Gibbon's life. He was dependent on his father and although nearly 30 had achieved little in life. Although bent on writing a history he had not settled on a definite subject. Impressed by the supremacy of French culture in Europe he began in that language a history of the liberty of the Swiss, but was dissuaded from continuing it. He and Deyverdun published two volumes of *Mémoires littéraires de la Grande Bretagne* (1768–69). In 1770 he sought to attract some attention by publishing *Critical Observations on the Sixth Book of the Aeneid*.

His father died intestate in 1770. After two years of tiresome business Gibbon was established in Bentinck street, London, and concentrated on his Roman history. At the same time he entered fully into social life. He joined the fashionable clubs and was also becoming known among men of letters. In 1775 he was elected to The Club, the brilliant circle which Sir Joshua Reynolds had formed round Dr. Johnson. Although James Boswell openly detested Gibbon and it may be inferred that Johnson disliked him, Gibbon took an active part in The Club and became intimate with Reynolds and David Garrick. In the previous year he had entered parliament, and was an assiduous, though silent, supporter of Lord North.

The first quarto volume of his history was published on Feb. 16, 1776. It immediately scored a resounding if somewhat scandalous success. This no doubt was not without the author's intention since the last two chapters were the 15th and 16th in which he dealt with the rise of Christianity. At the same time he was recognized by the historians David Hume and William Robertson as their equal if not their superior.

Gibbon went on to prepare the next volumes. Meanwhile he was assailed by many pamphleteers and subjected to much ridicule. His ugliness and elaborate clothes made him an easy target. For the most part he ignored his critics. Only to those who had accused him of falsifying his evidence did he make a devastating reply in *A Vindication of Some Passages in the XVth and XVIth Chapters of the Decline and Fall of the Roman Empire* (1779).

In the same year he obtained a valuable sinecure as a commissioner of trade and plantations. Shortly after that he composed *Un Mémoire justificatif* (1779), a masterly state paper in reply to continental criticism of the British government's policy in America. In 1781 were published the second and third volumes of his history, bringing the narrative down to the end of the empire in the west. Gibbon paused at this point to consider continuing his history. In 1782, however, Lord North's government fell, and soon Gibbon's commission was abolished. This was a serious loss of income. To economize he left England and joined Deyverdun in a house at Lausanne. There he quietly completed his history in three more volumes, writing the last lines of it on June 27, 1787. He soon returned to England with the manuscript and these volumes were published on his 51st birthday, May 8, 1788. The completion of this great work was acclaimed on all sides. Returning to Lausanne, Gibbon turned mainly to writing his memoirs. His happiness was broken first by Deyverdun's death in 1789, quickly followed by the outbreak of the French Revolution and the subsequent apprehension of an invasion of Switzerland. He had now become very fat and his health was declining. In 1793 he returned to England suddenly on hearing of Lady Sheffield's death. The journey aggravated his ailments, and he died in a house in St. James's street, London, on Jan. 16, 1794. His remains were placed in Lord Sheffield's family vault in Fletching church, Sussex.

Gibbon's Achievement as a Historian and Writer.—The *Decline and Fall* presents a continuous history from the 2nd century A.D. to the fall of Constantinople in 1453. The work is in two divisions, equal in bulk but inevitably different in treatment. The first half covers a period of about 300 years to the end of the empire in the west, about 480. In the second half nearly 1,000 years are compressed. Yet the work is a coherent whole by virtue of its conception of the Roman empire as a single entity throughout its long and diversified course. Gibbon imposed a further unity on his narrative by viewing it as an undeviating decline from those ideals of political and still more intellectual freedom that he had found in classical literature. The material decay which had inspired him in Rome was the effect and symbol of the moral decadence. However well this attitude suited the history of the west, its continuance constitutes the most serious defect of the second half of Gibbon's history, and involved him in obvious contradictions. For example, he asserted that the long story of empire in the east is one of continuous decay, yet for 1,000 years Constantine stood as a bulwark of eastern Europe. The fact is that Gibbon was not only out of sympathy with Byzantine civilization, he was less at home with Greek sources than with Latin and had no access to vast stores of material in other languages which subsequent scholars have assembled. Consequently there are serious omissions in his narrative as well as unsatisfactory summaries.

Nevertheless this second half contains much of Gibbon's best. With all its shortcomings, it marshals with masterly lucidity the successive forces which eventually overthrew Constantinople. Many of his most famous chapters occur there, such as those on Justinian, on the Trinitarian controversies, the rise of Islam and the history of Roman law, and there is the brilliant and moving story of the last siege and capture of Constantinople and finally, the epilogue of chapters describing medieval and Renaissance Rome, which gives some hope that the long decline is over and that mankind has some prospect of recovering intellectual freedom. The vindication of intellectual freedom is a large part of Gibbon's purpose as a historian. When toward the end of his work he remarks, "I have described the triumph of barbarism and religion," he reveals epigrammatically his view of the causes of the decay of the Greco-Roman world. They can hardly be disputed. But there is the further question whether one regards the changes brought about as ones of progress or retrogression. Writing as a mid-18th-century "philosopher" Gibbon saw the process as retrogression, and his judgment remains of perpetual interest.

Reactions to his treatment of Christianity have displayed various phases. In his lifetime and after he was attacked and personally ridiculed by those who feared that his skepticism would shake the existing establishment. In the 19th century he was hailed as a champion by militant agnostics. Gibbon himself was no cry with Voltaire, "*Écrasez l'infâme!*" because in his England and Switzerland he saw no danger in the ecclesiastical systems. His concern was past history. One may say with confidence that he had no belief in a divine revelation and little sympathy with those who had such a belief. While he treated the supernatural with irony, his main purpose was to establish the principle that religions must be treated as phenomena of human experience. In this his successors have followed him and added to the collateral causes of Christianity's growth those that he had overlooked or could not know of, such as the various mystery religions of the empire and particularly the Mithraic cult. Although Gibbon's best-known treatment of Christianity is found mainly in the 15th and 16th chapters, not less significant are those later chapters where he traces the developments of theology and ecclesiasticisms in relation to the breakup of the empire. The touchstone of his treatment lies in the observation that "ambition is a weed of quick and early growth in the vineyard of Christ."

Yet he is always fair to honest opinion and true devotion, for he was a man of probity and honour, as well as of great humanity. Those who sought to discredit his history by assailing his character were pursuing a path of twofold error. Our knowledge of history in Gibbon's field alone has increased conspicuously. Economic, social and constitutional history have grown up. The study of coins, inscriptions and archaeology generally has brought in a great harvest. Above all, the scientific examination of literary sources, so rigorously practised now, was unknown to him. Yet Gibbon often exhibits a flair and an acumen which seem to anticipate these systematic studies. He had genius in large measure, as well as untiring industry and accuracy in consulting his sources. These qualities, expressed with his command of historical perspective and his incomparable literary style, justify a modern historian's dictum that "whatever else is read Gibbon must be read too," or J. B. Bury's conclusion, "That Gibbon is behind date in many details and in some departments of importance, simply signifies that we and our fathers have not lived in an absolutely incompetent world. But in the main things he is still our master above and beyond 'date.'"

The *Memoirs of My Life and Writings* (edited by Lord Sheffield from manuscript drafts, 1796), commonly known as the *Autobiography*, is thought by some critics to be superior in style to the *Decline and Fall*. It is a fascinating if not very intimate record, and many famous phrases such as "I sighed as a lover, I obeyed as a son" by which he dismissed his abortive engagement, or the reference to his school days, "at the cost of many tears and some blood I purchased a knowledge of the Latin Syntax," are unforgettable.

BIBLIOGRAPHY.—*Works*: *The Decline and Fall*, original ed., vol. i (1776), vol. ii–iii (1781), vol. iv–vi (1788). Numerous later editions, especially W. Smith's reissue of Dean Milman's ed. with Guizot's notes, 8 vol. (1854 and 1872), and J. B. Bury's ed. 7 vol. (1896–1900 and 1909–14), with valuable introduction and commentaries. Abridged in 1 vol. by D. M. Low (1960); *Miscellaneous Works*, ed. by Lord Sheffield, 2 vol. (1796), 5 vol. (1814 and 1815) containing the *Memoirs*, by J. Murray (1896) and J. B. Bury (1907, 1923); *Manuscript Drafts*, ed. by J. E. Norton (1956). *Letters*, ed. by R. E. Prothero, 2 vol. (1896); *Correspondence*, minor works and unpublished material, ed. by J. E. Norton, 3 vol. (1956).

Journals: *Gibbon's Journal to January 28, 1763*, ed. by D. M. Low (1929); *Le Journal de Gibbon à Lausanne, 1763–1764*, ed. by G. A. Bonnard (1945); *Gibbon's Journey from Geneva to Rome 1764*, ed. by G. A. Bonnard (1961).

Bibliography: H. M. Beatty in vol. 7 of J. B. Bury's ed. of the *Decline and Fall* (1914); J. E. Norton, *A Bibliography of the Works of Edward Gibbon* (1940).

Biography and Criticism: J. C. Morrison, *Gibbon* (1878); G. M. Young, *Gibbon* (1932); D. M. Low, *Edward Gibbon, 1737–1794* (1937); G. Giarizzo, *Edward Gibbon e la cultura europea del settecento* (1954); E. J. Oliver, *Gibbon and Rome* (1958); H. L. Bond, *The Literary Art of Edward Gibbon* (1960).
(D. M. Lo.)

GIBBON, any one of the several species of small manlike apes (anthropoids) of Indo-Malayan countries, constituting the family Hylobatidae (sometimes considered a subfamily of the family Pongidae). The group comprises two living genera, *Hylobates* and *Symphalangus* (*see* PRIMATES). Gibbons differ from the larger anthropoids in having small calliosities on the buttocks and a greater relative length of the arms. Their voices are characteristic both in volume, musical quality and carrying power.

Highly arboreal, their mode of progression typifies that known as brachiation, the body being swung like a pendulum from the extended arms. On the ground they walk erect without assistance from the arms, which are held aloft or behind. Bamboo jungles at high altitudes constitute their most favoured environment. There they feed on young

W. SUSCHITZKY
WHITE-HANDED GIBBON OR MALAYAN LAR (HYLOBATES LAR LAR)

shoots, nuts, fruit, insects, birds' eggs and occasional young birds, which they catch by hand. A single young is produced after seven months' gestation. Sexual differences are slight, the canines of females being enlarged as in males.

The webbing of the interval between index and middle fingers and the presence of a dilatable air sac in the throat distinguish the large, wholly black siamang (*Symphalangus syndactylus*) of Sumatra. A dwarf siamang (*S. klossi*) inhabits the mountains of Selangor, Malaya. A vocal sac is present in the male only in the concolour gibbon (*Hylobates concolor*) of Hainan and Indochina. Of the remaining gibbons the hoolock (*H. hoolock*) of Assam is black except for a white browband. The Malayan lar (*H. lar*) may be black or buff, but has white extremities. Closely related are the dark-handed *H. agilis* of Sumatra and the gray *H. moloch* of Java and Borneo. *See also* APE. (W. C. O. H.)

GIBBONS, GRINLING (1648–1721), the most famous English decorative wood-carver, responsible also for much stone ornamentation at Blenheim, Hampton Court, and St. Paul's Cathedral, and for church monuments, doorcases, and chimneypieces in marble. Born in Rotterdam on April 4, 1648, of an English father, he settled at Deptford, Eng., in or about 1667 and was discovered there by John Evelyn in 1671. Evelyn, impressed by Gibbons' carved relief of Tintoretto's "Crucifixion," introduced him to Charles II. Soon after, Gibbons was commissioned to carve limewood festoons of fruit, flowers, and game for the new suite of royal apartments being built by Hugh May at Windsor Castle. His work for William and Mary at Kensington Palace and Hampton Court was to be still more elaborate. William appointed him master carver in 1693.

At St. Paul's Cathedral Gibbons carved the choir stalls, thrones, and the great organ screen. The latter was removed in 1860. For Wren's exterior he carved in stone most of the panels below the lower windows. In Wren's St. James's, Piccadilly, London, one may still see Gibbons' carved wood reredos and organ case and his marble Adam and Eve font. His Carved Room at Petworth, Sussex, is enough in itself to convince the visitor that Gibbons' skill as a wood-carver has never been equaled. Horace Walpole declared it "much the finest carving of Gibbons that ever my eyes beheld. There are birds absolutely feathered; and two antique vases with bas-reliefs, as perfect and beautiful as if they were carved by a Grecian master." Other excellent examples of his wood carving for country houses are to be seen at Badminton, Gloucestershire, Burghley, Northamptonshire, Hackwood, Hampshire, Kentchurch, Herefordshire, and Luton Hoo, Bedfordshire. Few craftsmen can have been more versatile than Gibbons: Drumlanrig and Dalkeith in Scotland have marble chimneypieces by him; Chatsworth, Derbyshire, Cullen, Banffshire, and the Victoria and Albert Museum have point-lace cravats carved in limewood; his marble monuments are in Westminster Abbey and in many country churches, notably Badminton, Gloucestershire, and Exton, Rutland; his statues include the bronze of Charles II at Chelsea Hospital and that of James II in front of the National Gallery, London. Much wood carving has been falsely attributed to him, and the peapod is not, as was once thought, his exclusive sign manual. He died at his house called the King's Arms in Bow Street, on Aug. 3, 1721, and is buried in the crypt of St. Paul's, Covent Garden, London.

See David Green, *Grinling Gibbons: His Work as Carver and Statuary, 1648–1721* (1964); H. Avray Tipping, *Grinling Gibbons and the Woodwork of His Age (1648–1720)* (1914). (D. B. G.)

EDWIN SMITH

DETAIL OF CARVED WOODEN PANELING AT PETWORTH HOUSE

GIBBONS, JAMES (1834–1921), U.S. Roman Catholic cardinal and archbishop, called by Theodore Roosevelt in 1917 the most respected, venerated and useful citizen of the U.S., was born in Baltimore, Md., July 23, 1834. Gibbons was ordained priest on June 30, 1861, and after four years as a pastor and volunteer chaplain to the Civil War troops in the military hospitals of Baltimore, he became secretary to Archbishop Martin J. Spalding. In 1868 he was consecrated bishop and appointed to organize the new vicariate apostolic of North Carolina, in which capacity he attended the first Vatican council in 1869–70. In 1872 he was promoted to be bishop of Richmond, and in 1877 he was named co-adjutor to the archbishop of Baltimore. His experiences as a missionary bishop brought home to him the need for a simple and concise statement of Roman Catholic doctrines, and during his time in Richmond he wrote *The Faith of Our Fathers* (1876), which proved to be the most popular work on Catholic apologetics ever published in the U.S.; it is still widely sold. In Oct. 1877 Gibbons succeeded to the premier see of Baltimore, and in that office he presided as apostolic 'delegate over the Third Plenary council of the American hierarchy (1884). In 1886 Pope Leo XIII made him the second American cardinal.

Cardinal Gibbons was a fairly frequent contributor to periodicals on questions of national interest, and besides *The Faith of Our Fathers* he wrote four other volumes dealing with religious subjects. Upon the opening of the Catholic University of America in Washington (1889) he became its first chancellor and was its powerful protector during the first difficult years.

The spirit in which the cardinal always viewed his native land and its institutions is illustrated by his remark that the constitution of the United States was the greatest instrument of government that ever issued from the hand of man. His sermon upon taking possession in Rome of his titular Church of Santa Maria in Trastevere (March 25, 1887) was in high praise of the practical workings of the U.S. system of separation of church and state. The nation, in turn, felt a deep affection for him, and at the civic celebration of his golden jubilee as a priest and his silver jubilee as a cardinal (Baltimore, June 6, 1911) the United States witnessed the most distinguished gathering that it had ever seen in honour of a private citizen, led by President Taft. Cardinal Gibbons died on March 24, 1921, loved and esteemed by Americans of every walk of life and of every religious belief.

See John Tracy Ellis, *The Life of James Cardinal Gibbons, Archbishop of Baltimore, 1834–1921*, 2 vol. (1952). (J. T. E.)

GIBBONS, ORLANDO (1583–1625), English composer, one of the last great figures of the English polyphonic school. He was the most illustrious of a large family of musicians. His father, WILLIAM Gibbons (c. 1540–95), was appointed one of the waits at Cambridge in 1567. Four of William's sons were accomplished musicians. EDWARD (1568–c. 1650) was a priest vicar at Exeter cathedral and a few of his compositions have survived. Only two works by ELLIS (1573–1603) are extant. These are the madrigals that he contributed to Thomas Morley's collection, *The Triumphs of Oriana* (1601). FERDINANDO (1581–?), William's fourth son, is mentioned in the records of Lincoln for June 8, 1611, as being one of the city waits. ORLANDO was born in Oxford in 1583. At the age of 12 he became a chorister at King's college, Cambridge, where he took the degree of bachelor of music in 1606. Records of the college show that in 1602 and 1603 he received sums of money in payment for works composed for special occasions. At the age of 21 he was made organist of the Chapel Royal, a post he retained for the remainder of his life, receiving many marks of royal favour. In 1619 he was appointed one of the "musicians for the virginalles to attend in his highnes privie chamber" and in 1622 he was made honorary doctor of music of Oxford university. The following year he became organist at Westminster abbey, where he later officiated at the funeral service of James I. Gibbons was part of the retinue attending Charles I when the king traveled to Dover to meet his bride, Henrietta Maria, on her arrival from France. On the journey back Gibbons succumbed to apoplexy at Canterbury on June 5, 1625, and was buried in the cathedral there.

Gibbons had seven children, one of whom, his son CHRISTOPHER (1615–76), was a distinguished composer of keyboard music as well as a notable contributor to the stage music of his time.

Of the considerable amount of church music written by Orlando Gibbons, only two anthems were published in his lifetime. After Gibbons' death J. Barnard in his *First Book of Selected Church Musick* (1641) included both of Gibbons' services for the English rite, his first pieces and psalms and five anthems. The first service and three of the anthems were reprinted in W. Boyce's *Cathedral Music* (1760–73) and these works remained for a long time in the English cathedral repertory. Of the 40 or so anthems that survive only 15 are purely polyphonic; the remainder are "verse anthems" (*see* ANTHEM) in which the solo voice, accompanied by organ or viols, alternates with the chorus. Gibbons' full anthems are among the most distinguished works of any British composer of any age, as are the "little" anthems of four parts. His *Madrigals and Motetts of 5 parts* . . . was published in 1612. This collection contains deeply felt and very personal settings of texts that are, for the most part, of a moral or philosophical nature. It shows Gibbons' mastery of the polyphonic idiom of his day and contains many undisputed masterpieces of late madrigalist style, among them the well-known "The Silver Swan" and "What Is Our Life?" Two years previously there appeared *Fantasies in Three Parts Compos'd for Viols* (c. 1610), said to be the first music printed in England from engraved copperplates. This, together with a quantity of viol music preserved in manuscript, shows Gibbons to be one of the foremost composers at a time when English viol music was in its prime. Gibbons was famous as a keyboard player and toward the end of his life he was said to be without rival in England as an organist and virginalist. Several of his virginal pieces were published in *Parthenia* (c. 1612) and more than 40 others survive in manuscript. Gibbons lived at a time when the polyphonic and basically vocal styles of the 16th century were becoming modified by a more markedly instrumental and harmonically conceived idiom. These changes left him almost untouched; his music, rather, sums up the achievement of the past generation.

BIBLIOGRAPHY.—*Vocal music: Tudor Church Music*, vol. iv, ed. by P. C. Buck *et al.* (1925); *English Madrigal School*, vol. v, "Orlando Gibbons. First Set of Madrigals and Motets of Five Parts," ed. by E. H. Fellowes (1921). *Viol music: Orlando Gibbons—9 Fantasies for Strings in Three Parts*, ed. by E. H. Fellowes (1924). *Keyboard music: Orlando Gibbons: Complete Keyboard Works*, ed. by M. H. Glyn (1925). Biography: E. H. Fellowes, *Orlando Gibbons* (1925).
(B. P.)

GIBBS, JAMES (1682–1754), British architect, designer of St. Martin-in-the-Fields, London, was born in Aberdeen on Dec. 23, 1682. In 1703 he entered the Pontifical Scots college in Rome to train for service as a Catholic missionary in his native land, but soon left it to study the arts, first painting and then architecture. In 1709 he went to England, where a sinecure granted by the earl of Mar enabled him to set up as an architect in London.

Gibbs was appointed one of the surveyors to the commissioners for building 50 new churches in London, and in 1714 designed St. Mary-le-Strand, his first public building. Among his most famous buildings were St. Martin-in-the-Fields, London (1722–26), the Senate house at Cambridge (1722–30) and the Radcliffe library at Oxford (1737–49). He was an architect of great ability whose Roman training kept his style outside the Palladianism that then dominated English architecture. His books, especially *A Book of Architecture* (1728), were influential in Britain and America well into the 19th century. Gibbs died on Aug. 5, 1754, in London.

See Bryan Little, *The Life and Work of James Gibbs 1682–1754* (1955), with a bibliography; and John Summerson, *Architecture in Britain 1530–1830* (1954), for the best discussion of his architectural style.
(Ms. W.)

GIBBS, JOSIAH WILLARD (1839–1903), U.S. mathematical physicist who developed the application of thermodynamics to chemistry, was born at New Haven, Conn., on Feb. 11, 1839. He graduated from Yale in 1858 and later studied in Europe. Returning to New Haven in 1869, he was appointed professor of mathematical physics at Yale in 1871 and held that position till his death in New Haven on April 28, 1903. His most important publication was his famous paper "On the Equilibrium of Heterogeneous Substances" (1876–78), which, it has been said, founded a new department of chemical science. He printed some notes on the elements of vector analysis for the use of his students;

these were never formally published, but they formed the basis of a textbook, *Vector Analysis*, which was published in 1901. Between 1882 and 1889 a series of papers on certain points in the electromagnetic theory of light and its relation to the various elastic solid theories appeared. His last work, *Elementary Principles in Statistical Mechanics*, was issued in 1902. In 1901 the Copley medal of the Royal society of London was awarded him as being "the first to apply the second law of thermodynamics to the exhaustive discussion of the relation between chemical, electrical and thermal energy and capacity for external work."

Gibbs's original scientific papers were assembled in 1928 and published in two volumes by the Yale University Press as *The Collected Works of J. Willard Gibbs*, *A Commentary on the Scientific Writings of J. Willard Gibbs*, written by a group of distinguished authors. An extensive bibliography of books and articles about Gibbs can be found in *Josiah Willard Gibbs, The History of a Great Mind* (2nd ed., 1952), written by L. P. Wheeler, a former student of Gibbs. This book should be consulted for further biographical information, and for letters and short manuscripts not in *The Collected Works*.
(B. B. On.)

GIBBSITE (HYDRARGILLITE), aluminum hydroxide or trihydrate, is an important mineral of many bauxites. Commercial trihydrate bauxite, a major source of aluminum, may contain 60% or more aluminum oxide, or alumina (Al_2O_3), but rarely does this all represent gibbsite. Gibbsite is prominent in bauxites of Arkansas, Jamaica, the Guianas, Brazil, west Africa, India and many other locations. In bauxites, gibbsite is usually fine grained and may be cryptocrystalline, or occasionally relatively coarse in small cavities, or vugs, or veinlets.

Gibbsite in significant deposits is of secondary origin, but small-scale hydrothermal sources are known. Under extreme weathering conditions, it may develop from any aluminous mineral, especially feldspars or feldspathoids. It may form directly from these or with the intermediate formation of clay mineral, or from boehmite.

Synthetic gibbsite is made from bauxite or high-alumina materials for production of aluminum metal and alumina chemicals. High temperature calcination yields corundum (*q.v.*) but partial calcination may yield a variety of near-anhydrous alumina types of difficulty analyzed structures.

The formula is α-$Al_2O_3 \cdot 3H_2O$ or structure cell formula $8[Al(OH)_3]$. Bayerite, a dimorph of gibbsite, is not known in nature. Gibbsite, which is monoclinic prismatic, frequently occurs in tabular crystals of hexagonal aspect. Cleavage is perfect, hardness 2.5 to 3.5, specific gravity 2.4 or slightly less. Refringence is moderate (1.568–1.587). It is soluble in strong mineral acids and alkalies. The theoretically pure mineral contains 65.4% Al_2O_3 and 34.6% H_2O, but natural specimens are generally contaminated by ferric oxide, silica and other impurities. *See also* ALUMINA; ALUMINUM; BAUXITE; CORUNDUM. ARTIFICIAL.
(W. K. Gr.)

GIBEAH, a town of the Israelite tribe of Benjamin, now Tell el-Ful, 3 mi. N. of Jerusalem, in Jordan. The site was partially excavated by W. F. Albright in 1922 and 1933. The hilltop on which the town stood had been so denuded by wind and rain over the past 2,000 years that house remains had virtually disappeared except along the edge of the hill, but a summit fortress was cleared. It had originally been built in the Middle Bronze Age, was reconstructed in the 12th–11th centuries B.C., and was replaced by an imposing citadel at the end of the 11th century (time of Saul, c. 1020–1000 B.C.), when it served as the first "royal" residence of Israel. After an insignificant later history, it was destroyed at the time of the first Jewish revolt, c. A.D. 68.

See L. A. Sinclair, "An Archaeological Study of Gibeah (Tell el-Ful)," in *Annual of the American Schools of Oriental Research*, xxxiv-xxxv (1960).
(W. F. A.)

GIBEON, an important town of ancient Palestine, now Al Jib, 5 mi. N.W. of Jerusalem in Jordan. Its inhabitants submitted voluntarily to Joshua (Josh. ix) at the time of the Israelite conquest of Canaan. In the time of Solomon a well-known sanctuary ("high place") was located at Gibeon by very ancient tradition.

Archaeological work was undertaken at Al Jib in 1956 by a U.S. expedition headed by J. B. Pritchard, with excellent results. The site had been occupied during parts of the Early and most of the Middle Bronze Age (first half of the 2nd millennium B.C.), to which remains of several city walls and a great many tombs belong. Occupation in the latter part of the Late Bronze Age is attested by a number of tombs and scattered potsherds of the 14th–13th centuries B.C. This was the age just before Joshua's conquest of Canaan, during which the town was a dependency of the city-state of Jerusalem and does not seem to have been fortified at all. The city was surrounded by an earlier wall and by a much stronger later wall during the Iron I period (12th–10th centuries B.C.). Being located north of the northern boundary of Judah, it does not seem to have been destroyed by the Babylonians in the early 6th century but continued to be occupied during the exile. To this period belong a large number of characteristic wine cellars excavated in bedrock. The vintner's trade is further illustrated by a large number of inscribed jar handles belonging to the 6th century B.C., among them over 30 which contained the name "Gibeon" in Hebrew characters of that period. The sometimes disputed identification of the site with Gibeon is thus confirmed beyond doubt.

BIBLIOGRAPHY.—J. B. Pritchard, "The Water System at Gibeon," *Biblical Archaeologist,* 19:66–75 (1956), "Hebrew Inscriptions and Stamps from Gibeon," *Bulletin of the University of Pennsylvania Museum* (1959), *Gibeon, Where the Sun Stood Still* (1962), *The Bronze Age Cemetery at Gibeon* (1963).
(W. F. A.)

GIBRALTAR, the only town on the Rock of Gibraltar, lies, with most of its buildings crowded together, at the northwestern corner of the Rock. Pop. (1961) 21,785; area is about 0.2 sq.mi. The modern town was built after most of the older buildings had been destroyed in the great siege (by the Spanish) of 1779–83. Some of the buildings are on reclaimed land, but elsewhere the foundations lie upon the shales below the surface sands. Much of the population is concentrated in the area first used by the Moors, for the problem is to find space in areas suitable for building. Within the older tenement houses, dwellings often consist of only one or two rooms, but modern flats have provided some relief from overcrowding. In the eastern part the rows of houses rise one above the other on the steep slope, although the streets are mostly narrow. The business quarter of the town is, however, situated on lower and more level ground. The barracks for the military garrison lie to the south of the town and these, together with training grounds, sports fields and areas reserved for amenity reasons, have imposed a further limitation on the area of the town itself.
(P. W. C. D.)

GIBRALTAR, ROCK OF, a limestone mountain standing at the eastern end of the Strait of Gibraltar, is connected to the Spanish mainland (Andalusia) by a low-lying sandy isthmus which divides the Bay of Gibraltar (Algeciras Bay) from the Mediterranean. The promontory itself is about 3 mi. long and ¾ mi. wide (4.8 by 1.2 km.) and rises to a height of 1,396 ft. (426 m.). There is a lighthouse on Europa Point at the southern end. The Rock of Gibraltar is a British fortress and naval and air base which, with the southern half of the isthmus, constitutes a colony, known since 1969 as the City of Gibraltar. Area 2¼ sq.mi. (5.8 sq.km.), including reclamations.

Physical Geography.—The dominant physical feature of Gibraltar is the limestone mass of the Rock. In the north this rises in a precipitous cliff from the sandy isthmus to a height of 1,330 ft. (405 m.) at Rock Gun. From there a sharp jagged arête runs southward, dominant points being Signal Station (1,260 ft.), Middle Hill (1,195 ft.), a point just above Monkeys' Alameda (1,398 ft.), and O'Hara's Tower (1,380 ft.).

The axis of the Rock is bow-shaped and curves from northeast to south-southeast. On the eastern side the slope is nearly vertical at the northern and southern extremities, but in the centre it is tempered by blown sands. On the western side the slope is fairly steep down to about 400 ft. (120 m.) above sea level. Below that there are gently sloping shales and sands, on which the town is built. South of O'Hara's Tower the ridge is abruptly truncated and falls steeply for about 900 ft. to Windmill Hill Flats, 300–400 ft. above sea level. The area constitutes a small plateau which terminates in precipitous cliffs at the southern end. Below these cliffs lie Europa Flats, about 100 ft. above the sea. This small plateau likewise ends in steep cliffs, which fall to the sea. Marine deposits indicate that Europa Flats constitute a raised beach.

The limestone of the Rock is of Lower Jurassic age. It is of a grayish-white colour, of compact structure and sometimes finely crystalline. North of the great main fault, which lies toward the southern end of the Rock, the limestone beds dip steeply westward, but south of the fault the dip is reversed. There is well-marked jointing in the limestone, and large caves have been eroded in many places by the action of water in the joints; these contain some fine stalactite formations. North of the great main fault, and on the western side of the Rock, shale beds overlie the limestone, but south of the fault the shales dip beneath it. The Alameda Sands lie on the shales of the western side, while limestone conglomerate and calcareous sands lie directly upon the limestone on the eastern side.

Bone breccias mixed with other debris have collected in caves and fissures, and remains found indicate the presence at some time of at least 25 species of mammals including the elephant, rhinoceros, and panther. Tunneling operations in 1944 led to the discovery of Gorham's Cave, in which excavations in 1948 revealed four levels of occupation from Neanderthal to Roman times.

Although the erosion of caves by the action of water percolating through limestone has produced much of interest in the Rock, the porous nature of the limestone has caused great difficulties regarding water supplies. Some potable well water can be obtained from the Windmill Hill area, where shale underlies the limestone, but most fresh water has to be obtained from catchment areas on the Rock. This water is stored in large reservoirs built inside the Rock during tunneling operations, but supplies are inadequate and brackish water has to be used for some domestic purposes.

Gibraltar has hot and almost rainless summers; comparatively warm winters during which there is abundant rain; and warm and rainy transition seasons. August is the hottest month, with a mean daily maximum temperature of 85° F (29° C) and a mean daily minimum of 69° (21°). The prevalence of a moist wind (levanter) from the Mediterranean at this season makes the heat oppressive at times. January is the coolest month, with mean maximum and minimum temperatures of 61° (16°) and 49° (9°), respectively. The average annual rainfall is 35 in. (889 mm.), but there is considerable annual variation.

Although large trees do not flourish on the Rock, there are many small flowering plants, more than 500 species having been identified; one of these, the Gibraltar candytuft (*Iberis gibraltarica*), is not found elsewhere in Europe. The only mammal is an imported species of Barbary ape, but the Rock provides a resting place for many species of migrant birds.
(P. W. C. D.)

History.—Gibraltar derives its name from a corruption of the Arabic Jabal al-Tarik ("Mt. Tarik"), so called in honour of Tarik ibn Ziyād, the Muslim commander who captured it in 711. The Rock, called Mons Calpe by the Romans, is generally considered to have been one of the celebrated Pillars of Hercules (the other being Mt. Hacho, on the North African coast opposite)

A. F. KERSTING
THE ROCK OF GIBRALTAR AND PARTIAL VIEW OF THE TOWN AS SEEN FROM THE HARBOUR

that for centuries were regarded as the limits of seafaring enterprise by the peoples of the Mediterranean.

The Muslim occupation was finally ended in 1462 and Isabella I annexed Gibraltar to the Spanish crown in 1501. During the reigns of Charles I (the emperor Charles V) and Philip II the fortifications were so improved that the fortress was regarded throughout Europe as impregnable. Under the later Habsburgs, however, the military installations were allowed to fall into serious decay.

British Occupation.—Gibraltar came under British occupation in 1704 during the War of the Spanish Succession; but possession did not follow automatically, for Gibraltar had been taken by Dutch as well as British troops, and both nations were acting, ostensibly, on behalf of the archduke Charles of Austria, whom they then recognized as king of Spain. Great Britain in fact acquired Gibraltar by coming to an agreement with France during the secret peace negotiations of 1711 and then presenting the Dutch and Spanish with a *fait accompli.* The Spanish garrison withdrew in March 1713, and the cession was accepted by Spain in the Treaty of Utrecht the following July.

British-Spanish Relations, 1714-79.—Until 1720 there was little esteem for Gibraltar in England, and by 1718 English ministers were prepared to offer restitution of the Rock as a *douceur* to secure Spanish adherence to the proposed Quadruple Alliance. This condition Spain refused to accept and went to war. Forced by military defeat to come to terms in 1720, Spain still demanded restitution. By this time, however, public opinion in England had become hostile to the idea, and the most Spain could obtain in the settlement of 1721 was a promise that the matter would be raised in the English Parliament at the first opportunity.

In December 1726 Spain began an armed assault on Gibraltar. Although the British successfully defended the fortress, diplomatic rather than military motives prompted the truce of May 1727 and the British commander confessed to being apprehensive of the outcome had the siege continued. Diplomatic considerations likewise impelled the Spanish, in the Treaty of Seville with Britain in 1729, to pass over in silence the question of Gibraltar. Later in the 18th century, however, Spain took advantage of British involvement in the American Revolutionary War first to seek Gibraltar as the price of continued neutrality and then, in 1779, to launch another siege.

The Great Siege.—The great siege of Gibraltar began in June 1779 and lasted for almost four years. At first the fortress was only blockaded; supply problems sometimes became serious, but the garrison was twice relieved, first in January 1780 by Adm. Sir George Rodney, and second in April 1781 by Adm. George Darby. At this point, however, the Spanish siege batteries opened fire for the first time, inflicting serious damage. A British sortie in November 1781 put them largely out of action. Defense galleries were excavated in the Rock, but the most novel feature of the siege came in 1782 when the Franco-Spanish attacking force prepared ten floating batteries armed with more than 200 cannon. When the assault was launched on Sept. 13 it proved a complete failure. Less than a month later (Oct. 11) the third relief of the garrison was effected by Lord Howe. Spanish determination secured the continuation of the siege, though somewhat half-heartedly, until Feb. 5, 1783, when news arrived of the signature of the peace preliminaries.

Later Spanish Claims to Restitution.—The European situation before, and the internal condition of Spain after the Peninsular War put an end to serious Spanish attempts at recovery for many years. In 1830 Gibraltar attained the status of crown colony. By the time that Spanish agitation for restitution next became acute (in the 1880s) the opening of the Suez Canal had made the question, from a British point of view, quite unthinkable. Successive Spanish governments found it convenient to keep the issue alive, and in this respect the administration of Gen. Francisco Franco has been particularly active. Proposals for the conquest of Gibraltar were discussed by Spain and Germany after World War II had broken out, but these plans came to nothing in the face of Spanish unwillingness to enter the war.

Gibraltar's main problem has always been lack of land space. Early in the 20th century the Rock was tunneled to facilitate communication between the east and west sides and the excavated material was used to reclaim 64 ac. (26 ha.) from the sea. During World War II all civilians, except about 3,000 men engaged on essential work, were evacuated. Additional defenses were constructed on the land side to guard against possible invasion through Spain, a canal was cut across the isthmus, and the length of tunneling was increased from two to ten miles. Material excavated was used to extend the air runway on the isthmus. After the war the strategic role of Gibraltar was changed, but a military garrison of slightly less than 1,000 men was maintained there in the late 1960s plus a naval headquarters and an RAF contingent.

In May 1954 Queen Elizabeth II, the duke of Edinburgh, and their children visited the Rock. This event provoked numerous anti-British demonstrations in Spain and led the Spanish government to impose restrictions on frontier traffic. These continued intermittently until October 1964, when the Spanish government introduced measures designed to impede frontier communications, culminating in the downgrading of the La Linea customs post in October 1966. This last step made virtually impossible the movement of any vehicular traffic or merchandise across the frontier. The Spanish actions were initiated by the administration in August 1964 of a new constitution for Gibraltar. The changes then introduced were intended to effect a greater measure of internal self-government but were regarded by Spain as an abrogation of the terms of the Treaty of Utrecht.

In July 1966, during the course of negotiations with Spain along the lines recommended by the UN Special Committee of 24 on the ending of colonialism (which had considered Spanish complaints in 1963 and 1964), the British government proposed that self-government should be exercised by the municipal authorities rather than by the executive and legislative councils and that Spain should have some share in the dockyard and airport facilities. In October 1966 when the talks were resumed the British government further proposed that the legal issues involved be referred to the International Court of Justice. Spain rejected this proposal in December. In November Britain had announced a grant of £600,000 ($1,680,000 U.S.) to the colony to permit the launching of a development plan intended to make its economy independent of Spain.

In compliance with a UN resolution of December 1966, calling on Britain and Spain to resume negotiations for the "decolonization" of Gibraltar, a British note was sent to the Spanish government asking for the resumption of talks. It was announced that the talks would be held in London in April 1967. On April 12, however, just before the talks were due to start, the Spanish government prohibited all flights by foreign aircraft, civilian or military, over an area around Algeciras immediately contiguous to Gibraltar. The ban, issued for "national security reasons," also extended to adjacent Spanish territorial waters. Britain appealed to the International Civil Aviation Organization, which declined to express any definite opinion in the matter, and there was an exchange of notes between the British and Spanish governments. Britain threatened to put the matter before the International Court of Justice. Spain replied that the question could be solved "only within the framework of negotiations for the decolonization of Gibraltar," and negotiations broke down.

In June 1967 Britain announced that a referendum would be held in Gibraltar early in September and that the colony would be given the choice of opting for Spanish sovereignty, or for continued close association with Great Britain. In spite of strong Spanish opposition, the referendum was held on Sept. 10 and was attended by a team of observers from the Commonwealth. The result was an overwhelmingly pro-British vote, and the referendum was characterized by enthusiastic demonstrations of loyalty to Great Britain. In October, Britain sent a note to Spain offering further talks on improving Spain-Gibraltar relations but emphasizing that there could now be no further discussion of Spain's claim to sovereignty. Spain rejected the offer, and further frontier restrictions were imposed in 1968.

A new constitution was introduced in May 1969 (see *Administration and Social Conditions,* below). The constitution was denounced by the Spanish authorities as a violation of the Treaty of

Utrecht and as a flagrant disregard of the UN resolution on Gibraltar. In June they closed the border between Spain and Gibraltar at La Línea and stopped the ferry service from Algeciras, thus effectively depriving Gibraltar of about one-third of its normal labour force. Later, Gibraltar's telephone links via Spain were cut. After an election held on July 30, 1969, Major Robert Peliza, leader of the Integration with Britain Party, became chief minister in place of Sir Joshua Hassan, leader of the Gibraltar Labour Party.

(B. J. R.; V. E. I.)

Population.—When the Rock was captured by the British in 1704 most of the civilian population left and reestablished themselves in the Spanish towns of San Roque and Algeciras. There was then a gradual process of repopulation by immigration from Spain, and Genoese and Jews were attracted to the Rock after Queen Anne had declared it a free port. By 1791 the population was only 2,890, but the situation changed rapidly during the Napoleonic Wars when prize cargoes were sold in the port, and it was used for supplying the duke of Wellington's armies during the Peninsular War. By 1824 the population had reached 17,000, but an outbreak of yellow fever resulted in some reduction and a restriction of immigration. The population declined until the Suez Canal was opened in 1869, after which it rose to 20,355 by 1901. The 1931 census showed a decline to 17,405. During World War II most civilians were evacuated from Gibraltar, but the majority returned. By 1961 the population had increased to 24,502 and it was estimated at 26,007 in 1969.

Only Gibraltarians have a right to reside on Gibraltar, and others, even British subjects, may do so only by special permission. Briefly, Gibraltarians are defined as persons whose names are on the register for which the main qualification is birth before July 1925 or descent from persons so born. They are mostly of Spanish, Italian, Maltese, or Portuguese descent, but they have become assimilated as Gibraltarians. The fishing village of Catalan Bay on the east side of the Rock is exceptional in that the inhabitants are almost entirely of Genoese descent and have tended to marry among themselves.

Almost all the people belong to the Roman Catholic Church, and Gibraltar has been a Catholic bishopric since 1910. The Anglican bishopric of Gibraltar was created in 1842 to minister to Anglican congregations throughout southern Europe; apart from the garrison and civil officials, there are few members of the Anglican Church. Spanish is the language normally used and thousands of Spanish workers still enter daily from La Línea.

Administration and Social Conditions.—Following a referendum in 1967 in which 12,138 votes were cast for retaining links with Britain with only 44 against it, constitutional talks were held between the British government and the Gibraltar government in 1968. These resulted in the introduction of a new constitution in 1969, replacing a constitution of 1964. Gibraltar's link with Britain was reaffirmed and an Assembly of 15 members replaced the former Legislative Council and City Council. Ministers were to be responsible to this Assembly, the governor remaining responsible for defense, external affairs, and internal security.

The courts of law consist of the Supreme Court, the Court of First Instance, and the Magistrates' Court. The Supreme Court has original jurisdiction in both civil and criminal cases similar to that exercised in England by all divisions of the High Court of Justice and Assize Courts. It also has appellate jurisdiction, but this can be expected in the future to be vested in a new Court of Appeal. The Court of First Instance is subordinate to the Supreme Court and has jurisdiction comparable to that of County Courts in England. The substantive law consists of the English law contained in statutes enacted up to Dec. 31, 1883, more recent acts expressly applied to the colony, the English common law, orders in council, and locally enacted ordinances and subsidiary legislation.

Education is compulsory between the ages of 5 and 15 years. It is free in the 14 primary and 8 secondary government schools. There are also some private schools.

Housing is a major problem owing to the lack of building land. Apartments are the only practicable dwellings and about 2,000 of these have been built since World War II.

The government maintains four hospitals including specialist units for heart, chest, and mental illnesses.

The Department of Labour and Social Security is responsible for social insurance and welfare services, the registration of trade unions, and the enforcement of the law relating to factories and hours of work. There is also a Control of Employment Ordinance designed to give Gibraltarians protection in employment from persons entering from outside.

(X.)

The Economy.—Owing to the infertility of the soil there is no agricultural production; all food supplies have to be imported. This also applies to nearly all manufactured products, since there are only a few small-scale industries. These include coffee processing, mineral water manufacture, and canning. Over one-third of the imports consist of foods, drink, and tobacco. Exports consist almost entirely of reexports, among which fuel for ships is an important item. For many years the economy has been largely dependent upon services to the armed forces and upon the activities of the port.

Restrictions on the passage of goods and traffic imposed at La Línea from 1964 onward had some substantial effects on the economy, but toward the end of 1968 nearly 6,000 workers were still crossing the frontier daily to work in Gibraltar. In the year after the restrictions were imposed, the volume of trade was reduced by about 40%. Annual imports were valued at more than £8,000,000 ($19,200,000 U.S.) in the late 1960s and exports at about £2,500,000 ($6,000,000 U.S.). Food supplies were obtained mostly from the Netherlands and Morocco. After World War II the tourist trade assumed increased importance. In 1964 more than 738,000 tourists visited Gibraltar, but this figure became reduced by about 30% as a result of the Spanish frontier restrictions. In developing the tourist trade attention has been given to hotel accommodation and to opening up places of interest such as St. Michael's Cave, Moorish Castle, and the Upper Galleries used in the great siege.

After World War II a commercial port was developed, but the closing of the Suez Canal in 1967 resulted in passenger liners, on routes to the Far East, ceasing to call at the port. Many cruising liners, however, visit the port and an annual total tonnage in excess of 13,000,000 is normally cleared at the port.

Gibraltar was a free port from 1705 until 1955, but import duties were thereafter imposed on a few items including gasoline, alcoholic beverages, perfumed spirits, and cigarettes. The reduction in imports resulted in lower revenue from duties, so it was necessary to increase other taxes and to obtain aid from the United Kingdom. In the late 1960s about half the government expenditure was concerned with social services. British currency has been in use since 1898 and the government of Gibraltar issues notes in £5 and £1 (U.S. $2.40) denominations.

Gibraltar has about 18 mi. (29 km.) of roads suitable for motor vehicles. There are regular air services to London, Madrid, and Tangier from the airport, which is operated by the Royal Air Force in conjunction with Gibraltar Airways. There is a worldwide cable communication service.

See also references under "Gibraltar, Rock of" in the Index.

(P. W. C. D.)

BIBLIOGRAPHY.—The best general history is Ignacio López de Ayala's *Historia de Gibraltar* (1782) translated and abridged in James Bell, *History of Gibraltar* (1845). W. C. Abbott, *An Introduction to the Documents Relating to the International Status of Gibraltar, 1704–1934* (1934); E. R. Kenyon, *Gibraltar Under Moor, Spaniard and Briton* (1938); G. T. Garratt, *Gibraltar and the Mediterranean* (1939). The diplomatic question is fully treated in S. Conn, *Gibraltar in British Diplomacy in the Eighteenth Century*, with full bibliography (1942). *See* also B. Larsonneur, *Histoire de Gibraltar* (1955); Allen Andrews, *Proud Fortress* (1958); J. Russell, *Gibraltar Besieged 1779–1783* (1965); *Colonial Report* (annual) and *Gibraltar Directory and Guide Book* (annual). For Spanish claims to Gibraltar *see* J. de Areilza and F. Castiella, *Reivindicaciones de España*, 2nd ed. (1941); W. C. Atkinson, "Gibraltar: the Spanish Case," *Fortnightly* (Feb. 1951); current history and statistics are summarized annually in the *Britannica Book of the Year*.

GIBRALTAR, STRAIT OF (ancient FRETUM HERCULEUM, "Strait of Hercules"), the channel connecting the Mediterranean sea with the Atlantic ocean, lies between southernmost Spain and northwesternmost Africa. It is 36 mi. long and, at its narrowest point, south of Tarifa, only 9 mi. wide. Its eastern extreme lies between the ancient "Pillars of Hercules"—the Rock of Gibraltar and (probably) Mt. Acho just east of Ceuta—and there the width is 14 mi.

Fossil evidence suggests that the strait was formed in Pliocene times. Faulting may have taken some part in the formation, but the strait probably originated as a low sill over which water passed from the Atlantic to the Mediterranean. Both sides of the strait are clearly part of the same geological feature.

The flow of water from the Atlantic still continues. Except when affected by easterly winds, a two-knot surface current flows eastward through the channel, the rate being greatest in autumn and least in winter. This eastward surface movement exceeds a westward flow of heavier, colder and more saline water which takes place below a depth of about 68 fathoms. Thus only the existence of the strait prevents the Mediterranean from becoming a shrinking salt lake.
(P. W. C. D.)

GIBSON, CHARLES DANA (1867–1944), U.S. artist and illustrator, creator of the "Gibson girl," was born at Roxbury, Mass., on Sept. 14, 1867. After a year's study at the schools of the Art Students' League, he began with some little drawings for the humorous weekly *Life*.

These he followed up with more serious work, and soon made a place for himself as the delineator of the American girl, at various occupations, particularly those out-of-doors. The "Gibson girl" obtained an enormous vogue, being later published in book form. Some book illustrations followed, notably those for *The Prisoner of Zenda*.

Gibson was imitated by many of the younger draftsmen, copied by amateurs, and his popularity was shown in his engagement by *Collier's Weekly* to furnish weekly for a year a double page, receiving for the 52 drawings the sum of $50,000, said to have been the largest amount ever paid to an illustrator for such a commission.

These drawings covered various local themes and were highly successful, being drawn with pen and ink with masterly facility and great directness and economy of line. So popular was one series, "The Adventures of Mr. Pipp," that a successful play was modeled on it. In 1905, although besieged with commissions, Gibson withdrew from illustrative work, determining to devote himself to portraiture in oil, in which direction he had already made some successful experiments; but in a few years he again returned to illustration. He published a number of books of sketches. In 1932 he became a member of the National Academy of Design. Gibson died in New York city on Dec. 23, 1944.

See Fairfax Downey, *Portrait of An Era* (1936).

GIBSON, EDMUND (1669–1748), English theologian and jurist who played a prominent part in the controversies concerning the position and authority of convocation at the beginning of the 18th century, was born at Bampton, Westmorland, where he was baptized on Dec. 19, 1669. He entered Queen's college, Oxford, as "a poor serving child" (1686), and became a fellow of his college and took holy orders (1694). While at Oxford he brought out (1692) an edition of the *Anglo-Saxon Chronicle*, with a Latin translation, and one of Quintilian's *De Institutione oratoria* (1693). He also translated Camden's *Britannia* (1695). He was made chaplain to Thomas Tenison, archbishop of Canterbury, and began to catalogue the library of Lambeth palace. He became rector of Stisted, Essex (1700) and of Lambeth (1703) and was appointed archdeacon of Surrey (1710). During this period the convocation controversy caused him to compile the works on which his fame in the Church of England chiefly rests. In opposition to Francis Atterbury (q.v.), Gibson maintained that the archbishop had authority over both houses of convocation; his studies on these questions led to the publication of his *Synodus Anglicana, or the Constitutions and Proceedings of an English Convocation* (1702) and of his *Codex Juris Ecclesiae Anglicanae* (1713).

Gibson was made bishop of Lincoln (1716) and was translated to London (1723). From this time until his quarrel with Sir Robert Walpole over the Quaker relief bill (1736), he was the chief ecclesiastical adviser to the government. As bishop of London Gibson censured court masquerades, and wrote and preached against deists, freethinkers, Methodism and popery. He died at Bath on Sept. 6, 1748.

See N. Sykes, *Edmund Gibson* (1926).

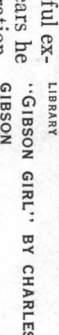

BY COURTESY OF RADIO TIMES HULTON PICTURE LIBRARY

"GIBSON GIRL" BY CHARLES DANA GIBSON

GIBSON, JOHN (1790–1866), English neoclassical sculptor, whose attempt to revive polychromed sculpture caused much controversy, was born on June 19, 1790, at Gyffin, Conway, Caernarvonshire. In 1804 he was apprenticed to a monumental mason in Liverpool, in which city he remained until 1817, latterly enjoying the patronage of the writer William Roscoe.

One of his first Royal Academy submissions, "Psyche Borne on the Wings of Zephyrus" (1816), was praised by John Flaxman, under whose persuasion he went to Rome in 1817. There he was befriended by Antonio Canova, leader of the neoclassicists; he was also instructed after 1822 by Bertel Thorwaldsen. His commissions from Rome (he did not return to England, even for visits, until 1844) included "Mars and Cupid" (1819), "Hylas and the Water Nymphs" (1826) and "Hunter and Dog" (1844); he was elected an associate of the Royal Academy in 1833 and a full member in 1838.

In face of opposition, but invoking Greek precedent, he introduced colour into a statue of Queen Victoria done for Liverpool in 1847, tinting only diadem, sandals and robe hem. A repetition of the 1833 "Cupid Tormenting the Soul" was, however, completely coloured—Gibson said at the behest of the god in a vision—and the best-known example of this polychromy was the "Tinted Venus" of 1851–55.

His commemorative sculpture included the Queen Victoria group for the princes' chamber, houses of parliament, London (1850–55), statues of George Stephenson (1844) and Sir Robert Peel (1851) and portrait busts. Gibson died in Rome on Jan. 27, 1866. The Gibson gallery, Burlington house, contains his bequest to the Royal Academy of casts and a few works in marble.

GIBSON, THOMAS MILNER (1806–1884), English statesman, was the leading associate of Richard Cobden and John Bright (qq.v.) and became prominent as a persuasive exponent of their doctrines. He was born at Port of Spain, Trinidad, on Sept. 3, 1806. By birth and marriage an East Anglian landowner, he was elected Conservative member for Ipswich in 1837; converted to free trade, he turned Liberal two years later and lost his seat. He was member for Manchester from 1841 to 1857, when his opposition to the Crimean War led to his defeat, and for Ashton-under-Lyne from 1857 to 1868. Vice-president of the board of trade under Lord John Russell from 1846 to 1848, he became president in 1859 upon Cobden's refusal to enter Lord Palmerston's ministry, relinquishing the presidency of the poor law board. During his long tenure on the board of trade, which ended in 1866, Milner Gibson gave valuable support to W. E. Gladstone's fiscal and financial reforms at the exchequer, and was himself largely responsible for the repeal of "taxes on knowledge." He withdrew from politics in 1868 and died at Algiers on Feb. 25, 1884.

Milner Gibson was an effective propagandist for the Anti-Corn Law league, a respected and popular figure in parliament and an adequate administrator. His wife's *salon*, for long a noted meeting place of English and European intellectuals, added to his influence in Liberal society. Consistently loyal to Cobden and Bright, he lacked their reluctance to take office as well as their stature, and found a place in the variegated cabinets of Russell and Palmerston primarily as the best available representative of the "Manchester school."
(A. F. T.)

GIBSON, WILLIAM HAMILTON (1850–1896), U.S. illustrator, author and naturalist, was born in Sandy Hook, Conn., on Oct. 5, 1850. He had sketched flowers and insects when he was only eight years old, had long been interested in botany and entomology and had acquired great skill in making wax flowers. His first drawings, of a technical character, were published in 1870. He rapidly became an expert illustrator and a remarkably able wood engraver, while he also drew on stone with great success. He drew for many periodicals, his most popular works being a long series of nature articles published in *Harper's*, *Scribner's* and *Century*. Gibson died July 16, 1896, at Washington, Conn.

Gibson was an expert photographer, and his drawings had a nearly photographic and almost microscopic accuracy of detail. He was perfectly at home in black and white, but rarely (and feebly) used colours.

GICHTEL, JOHANN GEORG (1638–1710), German Protestant mystic, the distinctive emphasis of whose mysticism was his doctrine of the heavenly marriage between the spiritual man and the divine Wisdom, which he regarded as somehow personal. He was born at Regensburg on March 14, 1638, and studied theology, history and law in Strasbourg. Early in his life he developed leanings toward a mysticism that alienated him both from the clergy of the Lutheran Church and from the Lutheran doctrine of justification by faith. These mystical leanings influenced him to become a disciple of Jakob Böhme (*q.v.*), and in 1682 Gichtel published his doctrine of the heavenly marriage, Gichtel nevertheless urged those who were already married to remain so. In his break with traditional forms of ecclesiastical organization Gichtel was more Protestant than the Reformers, as is evident also from his influence upon the radical historian and critic of orthodox Christianity Gottfried Arnold; but in his asceticism Gichtel was closer to the early church and to the middle ages. He died at Amsterdam on Jan. 21, 1710. His *Theosophia practica* was edited by Arnold in 1701 and by J. W. Ueberfeld in 1722.

See Fritz Tanner, *Die Ehe im Pietismus* (1952).   (J. J. Pn.)

GIDDINGS, FRANKLIN HENRY (1855–1931), U.S. sociologist and one of the founders of systematic sociology in the U.S., was born in Sherman, Conn., on March 23, 1855. He studied engineering at Union college, Schenectady, N.Y., and after graduating in 1877 was a journalist in Springfield, Mass. He succeeded Woodrow Wilson as professor of politics at Bryn Mawr college in 1888 and was professor of sociology at Columbia university from 1894–1928. He died at Scarsdale, N.Y., on June 11, 1931.

Giddings' idea of sociology as the basic social science, formulated in his *Principles of Sociology* (1896), was derived from A. Comte and L. F. Ward. In his psychological analysis of society he was influenced by Adam Smith, from whom he derived his doctrine of "the consciousness of kind," through which the integration of society is achieved. This was further developed in his conception of social behaviour as "differential responses to stimulation" in his *Studies in the Theory of Human Society* (1922), the best statement of his mature sociological theory. Giddings was stimulated by the theories of Herbert Spencer, Charles Darwin, Ludwig Gumplowicz, Gabriel Tarde, Emile Durkheim, Karl Pearson and others, welding their doctrines into a well-integrated system. In such later works as *The Scientific Study of Human Society* (1924), he emphasized the importance of a statistical approach to sociological problems. On public affairs he wrote *Democracy and Empire* (1900), *Western Hemisphere in the World of Tomorrow* (1915) and *The Responsible State* (1918). *The Mighty Medicine* (1930) and a posthumous volume, *Civilization and Society* (1932), summarized his theory and its applications.

See J. L. Gillin, ch. 7, *American Masters of Social Science*, ed. by H. W. Odum (1927); F. H. Hankins, "Franklin Henry Giddings (1855–1931)," *American Journal of Sociology*, pp. 349–67 (Nov. 1931); C. H. Northcott, ch. 38, in *Introduction to the History of Sociology*, ed. by H. E. Barnes (1947); R. G. Hoxie et al. (eds.), *A History of the Faculty of Political Science, Columbia University* (1955).   (H. E. Bar.)

GIDDINGS, JOSHUA REED (1795–1864), U.S. congressman, prominent in the antislavery movement for more than 20 years, was born at Tioga Point in northeastern Pennsylvania, Oct. 6, 1795. When ten years of age he moved with his parents to the Western Reserve in Ohio. There he received a little schooling, worked on the family farm, fought briefly in the War of 1812, taught school, studied law and entered politics.

He served in the Ohio legislature from 1826 to 1828 and in the U.S. house of representatives from 1838 to 1859, first as a Whig, then as a Free-soiler and finally as a Republican. In congress he championed freedom of debate in all slavery matters, opposed the annexation of Texas and the Mexican War as conspiracies of the slave interests, demanded the exclusion of slavery from all national territories, and at every opportunity attacked slaveholders with vigour and bitterness. His basic desire was to abolish slavery but he recognized that congress had no authority over slavery in the states. In 1842 his radical stand in behalf of slaves who seized the brig "Creole" on the high seas and sought freedom in a British port resulted in formal censure by the house of representatives. He promptly resigned, appealed to his constituents and was immediately re-elected by a large majority. From 1861 until his death, in Montreal, Que., May 27, 1864, he served as U.S. consul general in Canada.

See George W. Julian, *The Life of Joshua R. Giddings* (1892); Robert P. Ludlum, "Joshua R. Giddings, Radical," *Mississippi Valley Historical Review*, 23:49–60.   (B. Dv.)

GIDE, ANDRÉ PAUL GUILLAUME (1869–1951), French man of letters, humanist and moralist, winner of the Nobel prize for literature in 1947, who, by the untiring exploration of his own nature, posed the claims of the civilized individual in the modern world, was born in Paris on Nov. 22, 1869. His father was of southern Huguenot stock, his mother a Norman heiress who, although Protestant by upbringing, belonged to a family that was originally Catholic. Gide was later to attribute to this mixed heredity the conflicting elements in his character. His uncle was the economist Charles Gide; his father, professor of Roman law at the University of Paris, died at the age of 48 when Gide was 11.

Gide was educated at the École Alsacienne in Paris and, for one term only, at the Lycée Henri IV; his schooling was much interrupted because of his delicate health. He passed most of his holidays in Normandy where he had many uncles and aunts, the summers at La Roque where his mother had inherited a castle dating back to the 16th century and which he used as a setting in two of his tales: *L'Immoraliste* (1902) and *Isabelle* (1911). Other holidays were spent at Cuverville, the home of his Rondeaux cousins, and which was later to be his own home for many years while his wife was alive. It is a pleasant 18th-century house which he used as a setting for his most perfect work, *La Porte Étroite* (1909).

When Gide was 13 he underwent the emotional experience which altered his life and gave it a new meaning. One day he came upon his cousin Madeleine weeping as she knelt at prayer. She alone of her family had discovered the infidelity of her mother and had to keep the secret to herself. He fell in love with her on the spot and realized that he had found the devotion of his whole life. He used the scene twice, first in *La Porte Étroite* and later in his autobiography, *Si le Grain ne meurt* (1926).

After he passed his *baccalauréat* Gide determined to devote his life to literature—he was not obliged to earn his living. His first work was the autobiographical *Les Nourritures Terrestres*, published anonymously, at his own expense, in 1891. That same year he became a member of Mallarmé's "Tuesdays," and thereafter, for some years, was much influenced by the aesthetics of the Symbolist movement. Such works as *Voyage d'Urien* and *La Tentative Amoureuse* (both, 1893) belong to this phase: *Le Traité du Narcisse* (1891) formulates one of the clearest definitions of Symbolist aims.

In 1893 Gide paid the first of his many visits to north Africa. He fell ill while he was there, and it was when recovering his health that he composed part of *Les Nourritures Terrestres* (1897), a hymn in praise of the full life. But he was obliged to return to what he called the stifling atmosphere of the Paris *salons*, and found relief from despair in treating it ironically in *Paludes* (1895). In 1894 he returned to Africa where he met Oscar Wilde and Lord Alfred Douglas, who encouraged him in his revolt against traditional morality. As a result he composed the largest part of *Les Nourritures Terrestres*, which is an answer to the problem set out in *Paludes*, and preaches escape from accepted conventions. However, before he had completed it, he was obliged to return home on account of his mother's illness, and she died shortly afterward. Grief shattered his recent joy in life, and he wrote *Saül* (1928) which is in diametrical opposition to *Les Nourritures Terrestres*.

In Oct. 1895 Gide married his cousin Madeleine Rondeaux, who had earlier refused him. When he returned from his honeymoon, in May 1896, he was elected mayor of La Roque, the youngest mayor in France. In April 1897 he published *Les Nourritures Terrestres* which fell completely flat, although it was to become his most influential work—especially during the years which followed World War I.

During the next ten years Gide composed many works which enjoyed a limited *succès d'estime*—*El Hadj* (1899), *Le Prométhée mal enchaîné* (1899), *Oscar Wilde* (1910) and so forth, and his most original work up to date, *L'Immoraliste* (1902). In 1908 he was foremost among those who founded *La Nouvelle Revue Française* which, until World War II, united the most progressive writers in France. In 1909 he published *La Porte Étroite*, the pendent to *L'Immoraliste*, which was the first of his works to reach a large public. *Isabelle*, published in 1911, closes the first part of his main creative phase, and *Les Caves du Vatican*, which appeared in 1914, marks the transition to the next. This was the first of his works to be severely attacked for its alleged immorality.

During World War I Gide worked first with the Red Cross, then in a convalescent home for soldiers and finally was director of the Foyer Franco-Belge. The war was a period of psychological crisis for him and *Numquid et tu?* (1926) records his anguished search for faith. He emerged from this crisis with the resolution to turn his back on the past and achieve his own personal ethic; he cast aside his self-torturing sense of guilt to become, as he believed, his true self. Then, in a desire to liquidate the past, he wrote his autobiography, *Si le Grain ne meurt* (1926), his life up to his marriage.

A great change now took place in Gide and his face assumed the serene expression of his later years—perhaps the birth of his daughter in 1923 gave him ground for hope in the future. His first task was to finish *Corydon* (his justification of homosexuality), and he published it in 1924. This was disastrous to him and he was violently attacked on all sides—even by his close friends. His next work was what he called his only novel, *Les Faux Monnayeurs*, published in 1926 which, like *Les Caves du Vatican*, is a transition work. It is a very deliberate composition and he declared that his aim had been to attempt, in fiction, what Bach had achieved in the *Art of Fugue*. After he had finished it he set off for French Equatorial Africa and returned a year later with two works which attacked the French colonial system, *Voyage au Congo* and *Retour du Tchad* (1927). His journey to Africa released Gide from his personal obsessions, giving him the energy to attack the problems of the world outside himself. He became the champion of social outcasts; he protested against the inhuman treatment of criminals, the exploitation of natives in the colonies, antifeminist prejudice, the lot of the underprivileged. His enthusiasm for communism impelled him to visit the U.S.S.R. He set out for the Soviet Union in June 1936 full of hope. His subsequent disillusionment was expressed in the two books (*Retour de l'U.R.S.S.*, 1936, and *Retouches à mon Retour de l'U.R.S.S.*, 1937) which he wrote on his return.

Between the entries in his *Journal* for April and Aug. 1938, a thick black line is ruled across the page. This symbol of mourning marks the death of his wife, the great love of his life.

Gide was almost 70 when World War II broke out. It was then that he began to appreciate the value of tradition and the past, when they seemed in danger of being lost. In 1942 he went to north Africa where he spent the remaining years of the war. He founded a literary magazine, *L'Arche*, the title of which is self-explanatory. While in north Africa he composed *Thésée*, his last great work, his literary testament, which was published in 1946. In June 1947 he received the first honour of his life, the degree of D.Litt. of the University of Oxford, which was followed in November by the Nobel prize for literature. In 1950 he published the final volume of his *Journal*, bringing it up to his 80th year.

He resolved to write no further works however long he lived but he kept a notebook in which he recorded his random thoughts, published posthumously under the title *Ainsi soit-il, les jeux sont faits* (1952). He died on Feb. 19, 1951, and was buried in the country cemetery at Cuverville beside his wife.

Gide was not only one of the greatest European writers of his time but was also a considerable force, whose influence extended to countries as far distant as Japan. He produced novels, plays and essays, but it is probably in his *Journal*, that unique work of almost 1,000,000 words, that he is seen at his most characteristic, with all his interests and passions, and especially with his perfection of style. The final impression that he leaves is that of a moralist, psychologist and stylist rather than that of a novelist or dramatist, for he was more interested in humanity than in individuals. But he is a moralist in the French 17th-century tradition, whose integrity and nobility of thought, whose purity and harmony of style, give him a permanent place among the great masters of French—indeed European—literature.

BIBLIOGRAPHY.—*Editions*: *Oeuvres Complètes*, 15 vol. (1932-39). The most convenient edition of the *Journal* is the one in 2 vol. in the *Bibliothèque de la Pléiade*: *Journal 1889-1942* and *Journal 1939-1949 et Souvenirs* (1954). Collection of letters with Francis Jammes, 1893-1938 (1948), Paul Claudel, 1899-1926 (1949), and with Paul Valéry, 1890-1942 (1955); *Lettres de Charles Gide et réponses d'André Gide* (1950). Most of his works have been translated into English. *Biography and Criticism*: C. du Bos, *Le Dialogue avec André Gide* (1929); J. Hytier, *André Gide* (1938); K. Mann, *André Gide, the Ethics of Modern Thought* (1948); D. L. Thompson, *André Gide and the Crisis of Notes sur Gide* (1950); A. Guerard, *André Gide* (1951); L. Pierre-Quint, *Portrait of André Gide* (1953); G. Brée, *André Gide, l'Insaisissable Protée* (1953); J. Schlumberger, *Madeleine et André Gide* (1956); J. Delay, *La Jeunesse d'André Gide*, 2 vol. (1956-57); H. Watson-Williams, *André Gide and the Greek Myth* (1967). (E. St.)

GIDE, CHARLES (1847-1932), French economist and supporter of the co-operative movement, was born on June 29, 1847, at Uzès (Gard). Educated at the Collège d'Uzès, he entered the faculty of law of the University of Paris. He early became professor of political economy, first at Bordeaux, then at Montpellier and from 1898 to 1920 at the University of Paris. He was the author of one of the best introductory treatises on political economy, *Principes d'économie politique* (first published in 1884 and later translated into English and other languages), and joint author with Charles Rist of a work on the history of economic theory, *Histoire des doctrines économiques* (3rd ed., 1920). Gide devoted a great deal of time and energy to the encouragement and furtherance of the co-operative movement in France, and wrote largely on this question. He unremittingly endeavoured to maintain and promote harmonious international relations and especially to preserve co-operation among intellectual workers in different countries. He died in Paris on March 13, 1932.

GIDEON, surnamed JERUBBAAL (in the Douai version of the Bible, GEDEON JEROBAAL), a liberator, reformer and "judge" of Israel who delivered Israel from hordes of desert raiders—Midianites and others (Judg. vi-viii). He is called Jerubbaal also in the narrative, and it is possible that the exploits of two heroes have been combined in the passage. There are, as a matter of fact, at least two narratives combined in the relevant chapters of Judges. According to one account Gideon is visited by the angel of Yahweh as he is threshing corn in a wine press, to hide it from the Midianites, and is greeted as the future saviour of Israel. A portion of this narrative has been lost, but it must have told of a raid on Tabor by the Midianites, in the course of which Gideon's brothers were killed. Gathering 300 of his clansmen, Gideon first attacked the raiders by night and drove them away in flight, and then, pursuing them beyond Jordan, captured and slew their two chiefs, Zebah and Zalmunnah. He was then offered the throne, but refused it, and made an image from the Midianite spoil, thus leading Israel into idolatry. In the other narrative Gideon is summoned at night by Yahweh to overthrow the altar of Baal and to establish an altar to Yahweh in its place. This is discovered in the morning, and Gideon is saved from the anger of his fellows only by the pleading of his father, who argues that since Baal has been insulted, Baal must take vengeance—if he can. Gideon then gathers all Israel, his force is reduced to 300 in number, and with these, encouraged by a dream which he hears told in the camp of Midian, he assaults the enemy by night. They flee in panic, but find that the fords of Jordan are held against them by Ephraimites, who capture and kill the two chiefs Oreb and Zeeb. The Ephraimites then complain that Gideon, a Manassite, had not summoned them to follow him, and he appeases their anger by pointing to the honour they have won in killing Oreb and Zeeb.

The story is important as illustrating the danger of raids from the desert to which Palestine was subject, and it prepared the way for Abimelech (q.v.), Gideon's son, who made the first effort to establish an Israelite monarchy. *See also* JUDGES, BOOK OF.

(S. A. C.; T. H. R.)

GIDEONS. The Gideons, the Christian Commercial Men's Association of America, International, was organized by three traveling men at Janesville, Wis., on July 1, 1899. In Nov. 1908 the organization began to place copies of the Bible in hotel rooms, later into hospitals, penal institutions and schools as well. During World War II the Gideons supplied the U.S. armed forces with service Testaments. The work is supported through freewill offerings. The organization's emblem is a two-handled pitcher and torch, in memory of Gideon's victory over the Midianites in Judg. vii.

GIEDION, SIGFRIED (1888–1968), Swiss art historian and among the first to apply scholarly methods of analysis successfully to 20th-century architecture, was born in Lengnau, Switz., on April 14, 1888. He was influenced by scholars such as Jacob Burckhardt, Alois Riegl, August Schmarsow and his teacher Heinrich Woelfflin. Giedion's initial training in engineering stood him in good stead when he set out to clarify origins and directions of modern architecture, which he was able to observe closely in his capacity (from 1928) as secretary-general to the International Congresses for Modern Architecture (CIAM) and through his friendship with such leading architects as Walter Gropius and Le Corbusier.

Giedion taught at the Federal Institute of Technology, Zürich, and at Harvard university and wrote a number of books. His *Space, Time and Architecture* (1941; numerous later editions and translations) is indispensable for an understanding of 20th-century architecture. *Mechanization Takes Command* (1948) dealt with the consequences of industrialization. *The Eternal Present: the Beginnings of Art* (1962) and *The Eternal Present: the Beginnings of Architecture* (1964) marked a new stage in his development; he turned to prehistory and preclassical antiquity in an attempt to reinterpret such basic concepts as abstraction, symbolization, constancy and change. His work was characterized by unorthodox approaches and strength of perception; in his historical studies he tried to see the past in its relevance for the present and future. He died in Zürich on April 10, 1968.

(E. F. SR.)

GIERKE, OTTO VON (1841–1921) was a leader of the German school of historical jurisprudence second only to F. K. von Savigny (1779–1861). Born at Stettin on Jan. 11, 1841, he studied at the universities of Berlin and Heidelberg and was professor of law at Breslau (1871–84), Heidelberg (1884–87) and Berlin (1887–1921). His first researches, on the history of associations in German law, culminated in *Das Deutsche Genossenschaftsrecht*, four volumes (1868–1913). This major work was partly translated into English by F. W. Maitland under the title of *Political Theories of the Middle Age* (1900). Its "realist" doctrine of corporations profoundly influenced legal theory. From about 1888 Gierke turned more to private law, commenting on the German civil code then newly drafted, and published *Deutsches Privatrecht*, two volumes (1895–1905) and *Das Recht der Schuldverhältnisse* (1917). Gierke died at Berlin on Oct. 10, 1921.

His son JULIUS (1875–   ), born at Breslau on March 5, 1875, wrote several works on commercial, insurance and maritime law, and was professor at Göttingen from 1925.

See the introduction by F. W. Maitland to *Political Theories of the Middle Age* (1900); S. Mogi, *Otto von Gierke* (1932).

GIERS, NIKOLAI KARLOVICH (1820–1895), Russian statesman and foreign minister during the reign of Alexander III, a supporter of a policy of peace through alliance with Germany and Austria-Hungary, was born at Radzivilov (now Chervonoarmeisk), in Volhynia, on May 21 (new style; 9, old style) 1820, the son of a postmaster of Swedish origin. He began his career in 1838 in the Asiatic department of the foreign ministry and from 1850 held subordinate posts in Jassy (Iaşi), Constantinople, Alexandria and Bucharest. He then served as minister in Persia, Switzerland and Sweden. He received his first major assignment in 1875 when he was appointed director of the Asiatic department and deputy minister of foreign affairs under Prince A. M. Gorchakov. In April 1877, despite strong resistance from the foreign ministry, Russia was drawn into war with Turkey over the Balkan Slavs. As a consequence of military victories, Russia gained from Turkey the drastic peace of San Stefano, which gave Russia dominance in the Balkans and at the straits through the creation of a large Bulgarian state. Faced with this upset of the balance in the Balkans, the powers forced Russia to surrender the greater part of these gains at the congress of Berlin in 1878.

Because of the increasing senility of Gorchakov, Giers for all practical purposes became foreign minister after 1878, although he did not formally assume office until April 9 (N.S.; March 28, O.S.), 1882, working always in subordination to Alexander III. Giers' principal concern as minister was to secure a period of peace and tranquility in which Russia could recover from the War of 1877–78 and concentrate on internal reforms. Believing that this condition was best assured through alliance with the conservative monarchies, Austria-Hungary and Germany, Giers favoured the renewal of the *Dreikaiserbund* which had been broken by the congress of Berlin. In June 1881 a new agreement was reached based on mutual guarantees of neutrality and the protection of Austrian and Russian particular interests in the Balkans and at the straits. The agreement was renewed in 1884 despite growing Austro-Russian tension over Bulgaria. In Sept. 1885 a major Balkan crisis was precipitated by the union of Eastern Rumelia with Bulgaria and the subsequent Serbo-Bulgarian War. Although these events did result in the shattering of the *Dreikaiserbund*, Giers was able to continue Russia's connection with Germany through the Reinsurance treaty of June 18, 1887.

The traditional ties between St. Petersburg and Berlin, strongly supported by Giers, were broken at the accession of the German emperor William II, who preferred agreement with Austria-Hungary and Great Britain. Faced again with the danger of diplomatic isolation, Giers was forced to consider French approaches. Although with few interests in common beyond a mutual concern over Germany, Russia and France in Aug. 1891 concluded an entente; and in Jan. 1894 a military alliance came into force. This reorientation of Russian policy, the major event in Giers' ministry, thus did not come about with the minister's wholehearted approval. Giers died in St. Petersburg on Jan. 26 (N.S.; 14, O.S.), 1895, soon after the death of Alexander III. His *Memoirs* appeared in English in 1962.

(B. J.)

GIESEBRECHT, (FRIEDRICH) WILHELM (BENJAMIN) VON (1814–1889), German historian, author of the first general history of the medieval empire based on modern critical methods, was born in Berlin, March 5, 1814, and studied under Leopold von Ranke. In 1857 he became professor at Königsberg and in 1862 succeeded Heinrich von Sybel at Munich, where he died, Dec. 18, 1889. In *Geschichte der deutschen Kaiserzeit* (6 vol., 1855–95; completed by B. von Simson), Giesebrecht concerned himself with political and religious aspects, ignoring legal, social, economic and constitutional history. His romantic view of the emperors aroused controversy, notably with Sybel. Other works include *Jahrbücher des deutschen Reichs unter Otto II* (1840) and the restoration of the important monastery records *Annales Altahenses* (1841).

GIESSEN, a town of Germany, which after partition of the nation following World War II was included in the *Land* (state) of Hesse, Federal Republic of Germany. It stands 540 ft. above the Lahn, 41 mi. N.N.W. of Frankfurt am Main, and is an important traffic centre between Westerwald and Vogelsberg. Pop. (1961) 66,291. The town came, in 1203, into the possession of the count palatine who sold it in 1265 to the landgrave Henry of Hesse. It was fortified in 1530 but in 1805 the walls were demolished. In the old part of the town the streets are narrow and irregular. The ruins of the old castle date from the 14th century, while the so-called new castle was built in the 16th century. In Giessen university (Justus-Liebig-Universität), founded in 1607, the chemical laboratory of Justus von Liebig may still be seen. There are schools of agriculture, veterinary science and medicine, and the university runs an experimental farm. The Upper Hessian museum and the botanical gardens are also noteworthy. The industries include metal founding and the manufacture of rubber articles, machines, leather, tobacco and beer.

GIFFARD, WALTER (d. 1279), chancellor of England and archbishop of York, was a son of Hugh Giffard of Boyton, Wiltshire. He became canon and archdeacon of Wells and was elected bishop of Bath and Wells in May 1264. After the royalist victory over Simon de Montfort and the barons at Evesham (Aug. 4, 1265) Giffard was made chancellor (Aug. 10). He helped draw up the *Dictum de Kenilworth* (1266), by which peace terms were arranged with the remaining rebels. In that year he was replaced as chancellor, but was appointed archbishop of York by Pope Clement IV. He was one of the three regents of the kingdom between the death of Henry III (Nov. 1272) and the return of Edward I from crusade (Aug. 1274). He died at York on April 22, 1279.

GIFFARD, WILLIAM (d. 1129), bishop of Winchester, received his see from Henry I (1100). He was one of the bishops elect whom Anselm refused to consecrate (1101) as having been nominated and invested by the lay power. During the investitures dispute Giffard was on friendly terms with Anselm, and drew upon himself a sentence of banishment through declining to accept consecration from the archbishop of York (1103). He was, however, one of the bishops who pressed Anselm, in 1106, to give way to the king. (*See also* ANSELM, SAINT.) He was consecrated after the settlement of 1107. He founded at Waverley, Surrey, the first English Cistercian house (1128) and restored Winchester cathedral with great magnificence.
(D. H. W.)

GIFFORD, ROBERT SWAIN (1840-1905), U.S. painter and etcher, best known for his coastal views and north African scenes, was born at Naushon, Mass., Dec. 23, 1840. He was a late product of the Hudson river tradition. He worked mainly in New York city, where he was long a teacher in the Woman's Art School of Cooper Union and its director from 1896 until his death, Jan. 15, 1905. He was also an etcher and water colorist of considerable reputation.

GIFFORD, WILLIAM (1756-1826), English man of letters who, as first editor of the *Quarterly Review*, attacked Leigh Hunt and what he called the Cockney school of poetry, was born in Ashburton, Devonshire, in April 1756. Orphaned at 12, he was harshly treated by his godfather who resented paying for his schooling and sent him first to a farm, then to sea and finally to a shoemaker as apprentice. Through the kindness of an Ashburton surgeon, William Cookesley, he was sent back to school and to Exeter college, Oxford. He took his degree and in 1782 became tutor to Lord Grosvenor's son and began to publish verse. *The Baviad* (1794) is a satire, after Persius, on the Della Cruscan coterie led by Hester Lynch Piozzi (*q.v.*), and *The Maeviad* (1795) is an attack on the corruptions of the drama. In 1802 he published a translation of Juvenal's *Satires*, prefaced by a short autobiography. An admirer of the classics, he was also interested in post-Shakespearean dramatists and edited the plays of Philip Massinger (1804-13), Ben Jonson (1816) and John Ford (published posthumously, 1827).

Meanwhile, with George Canning's support, Gifford had founded the *Anti-Jacobin* (1799), and in 1809 he became editor of the new *Quarterly Review* founded by Canning and his friends to counterbalance the Whig *Edinburgh Review*. For the next 15 years he made it the vehicle for his hatred of radicals and also of most rising authors, upon whom, according to Southey, he looked as Izaak Walton did upon worms. Although ultimately responsible for it, he almost certainly did not write the famous attack on Keats's *Endymion* (1818); but his habitually malevolent reviews provoked Hazlitt into writing *A Letter to William Gifford, Esq.* (1819) in which he called him "the Government Critic... the invisible link, that connects literature with the police." He resigned from the *Quarterly Review* in 1824, and died in London on Dec. 31, 1826.

See R. B. Clark, *William Gifford* (1930).

GIFT, a present or thing bestowed gratuitously. In American law the term is restricted to mean *inter vivos* gratuitous transfers of chattels personal; *i.e.,* voluntary transfers of personal property (movables) between living persons (*see* PERSONAL PROPERTY). A valid gift requires: (1) a competent donor; (2) an eligible donee; (3) an existing, identifiable thing or interest; (4) an intention to donate; (5) delivery, *i.e.,* a transfer of possession to or for the donee and a relinquishment by the donor of ownership, control and (except in gifts *causa mortis, i.e.,* those made by someone believing himself near to death and that become final only if the giver dies) power to revoke; and (6) acceptance by the donee. Formal acceptance is necessary under French law, but Anglo-American law rebuttably implies acceptance of beneficial gifts. *See also* LEGACY.
(E. M. M.)

GIFTED CHILDREN. "Giftedness" has been variously defined. In its broadest sense the word covers all who are naturally endowed with a high degree of mental ability, either general or special. Since little is known about special abilities, the term is usually confined in psychological and educational writings to children whose innate general ability rises above a certain specified borderline. The borderline itself is largely a matter of administrative convenience. In the United States the commonest cut-off point is an I.Q. of 130-135. This corresponds to the borderline generally adopted in Britain for scholarships to secondary (grammar) schools in the early days of scholarship examinations. Some

The term "genius" denotes a somewhat different category. In psychology it is commonly applied to those who, in addition to an exceptional degree of intellectual ability, are also endowed with character traits that tend to ensure exceptional performance in adult life, often in the face of adverse circumstances. In his well-known study of *Hereditary Genius*, Francis Galton gives a "classification according to natural gifts"; geniuses are defined as those who are among the ablest 0.25%—*i.e.,* 1 in 4,000, a figure equivalent to a borderline of about 150 I.Q. The main sources of information about children in the groups thus defined are L. M. Terman's elaborate studies of 1,000 gifted children attending the schools of California; here the line was drawn at 140 I.Q., a figure that would select about 1 in 400. *See* PSYCHOLOGICAL TESTS AND MEASUREMENTS.

Identification of Gifted Children.—In countries that make special provision for educating gifted pupils, the commonest method of selection consists of written tests taken by the children sitting in groups. In Great Britain the traditional plan has been an examination in the basic school subjects: reading (*i.e.,* the understanding of printed matter), writing (*i.e.,* English composition) and arithmetic. The scholastic examination is supplemented or even superseded by written tests of all-round ability or intelligence. However, the purpose of such examinations as usually conducted is not so much to estimate innate potentiality as to determine whether, at the time of the examination, the child is suitable for transference to some higher type of education. Unless carefully checked, the marks obtained are liable at times to be misleading. The best indications of the pupils' relative merits are, or should be, those provided by the teachers themselves, supplemented by the data contained in cumulative school records. Teachers, however, differ in their ability to make such assessments, particularly when classes are large and pupils newly promoted. They are too inclined to attach excessive importance to sheer mechanical memory and actual scholastic attainments. Above all, each has his own subjective standards and his own method of scaling. Hence some objective type of examination, common to all the schools in the area, is essential. The marks so obtained should always be submitted to the teacher for comment or criticism, and doubtful or borderline cases should be retested individually. Early identification within the school is urgently desirable, even though the actual selection is not to be made till the age of 11 or later. To leave it until the children are old enough to sit for a written examination is too late.

Incidence of Superior Ability.—Galton's studies of the families of the most gifted individuals in British history and J. McK. Cattell's statistical study of eminent men in the United States furnished strong *prima facie* evidence for the view that both general and specific abilities are inherited. As ordinarily defined, the term inheritance is taken to mean "the tendency of like to beget like." There is, however, ample evidence to show that mental ability, like most other graded characteristics, is transmitted in accordance with Mendelian principles. This accounts for the fact that the distribution is approximately normal and explains why in so many instances "like begets unlike." One of the most surprising yet well-established phenomena is the emergence from time to time of extremely bright individuals in families where the low intellectual level of the parents and the adverse conditions of the home would, it might be supposed, condemn every child to failure. On the Mendelian hypothesis of multifactorial transmission these anomalies are what should be expected (*see* HEREDITY).

The rise and progress of civilized societies depend largely on the active presence of able individuals, and this, as the geneticist R. A. Fisher showed, has nearly always involved class differentiation. In general each class obeys strict rules of inbreeding, yet there is usually a varying amount of interchange—the abler and more energetic members born in the lower social and economic classes work their way up to the higher, and vice versa. As a result the proportion of gifted individuals differs widely from one class to another. In London surveys where the borderline was set at 135 I.Q., the percentages found in the various socioeconomic classes were as follows: higher professional, 19%; lower professional, etc., 11%; clerical or highly skilled, 6%; skilled, 3%; semiskilled or below, 1.5%. Since in the higher social and economic classes the total numbers are comparatively small, the absolute numbers of gifted children differed little in the first three classes. In Terman's survey, among the fathers of 1,000 gifted children 33% were in professional occupations, 32% in semiprofessional and higher business and 21% in clerical occupations or skilled trades. In Britain, surveys carried out during 1930–40 revealed that nearly 40% of those capable of profiting by a university education failed to gain entrance.

Other investigations have shown that a large fraction of this potential talent remains undiscovered or undeveloped. This seems due not so much to financial handicaps (as in the past) but rather to lack of efficient ascertainment and guidance in the schools and of adequate motivation in the children and their parents. In

Characteristics of the Gifted.—As a scientific theory, the notion that genius is something abnormal and that "great wits to madness sure are near allied" is due chiefly to C. Lombroso (*q.v.*); the biographies analyzed by Galton and Havelock Ellis show that such cases are exceptional. Among the gifted children studied by Terman "the incidence of physical defects and abnormal conditions generally was well below that reported in the general school population": the children were on the whole taller, stronger, healthier and better adapted socially than the majority of their fellows. By the age of 35, 80% had posts in the highest occupational groups (semiprofessional or higher business) as contrasted with 14% of the ordinary population; 20% were already mentioned in *Who's Who in America* or *American Men of Science*; and some had achieved international reputations.

Educational Provision.—In theory there are two main ways of meeting the educational problem: (1) the "method of acceleration," whereby the gifted child is promoted more rapidly through the ordinary series of grades or classes; (2) the "method of enrichment," whereby he works through the usual grades at the usual pace but the curriculum is supplemented by a variety of cultural activities. In practice the arrangements made must depend largely on the way the school system is organized. In England under the majority of education authorities the brightest 20% (or thereabouts) are transferred at age 11 or after (11+) to grammar or technical schools, while the remainder go to a secondary modern school. In the remaining districts all children are classified in streams according to ability and aptitude. A few authorities have introduced special experimental schemes of their

own. A high proportion of the ablest children, however, obtain entrance, often by scholarship, to one or other of the so-called public schools.

In the United States only about 30 cities appear to have organized special schools or classes for gifted children. The first was instituted in 1901 at Worcester, Mass. The best-known and most typical scheme is that started in 1920 at Cleveland, O.

The advantages usually claimed for special schools or classes are as follows: (1) The gifted child is able to develop at his own accelerated pace and undertake work commensurate with his own high ability. (2) The instruction, method and materials can be adapted to the needs of each individual. (3) Working with others who are quick and bright, each child is encouraged to put forth his best efforts; left to work in the ordinary class with average pupils of his own chronological age, he soon becomes bored and restless; on the other hand, if promoted to work with those of his own mental age, he finds himself sitting side by side with children three or four years older, so that either way he tends to feel peculiar and ill-adjusted. (4) In the special class he can be trained for the future responsibilities that will be his lot in later life.

The following are the commoner criticisms: (1) The segregation of children in special schools tends to create an intellectual aristocracy that is quite as objectionable as an aristocracy based on birth, wealth or political power. (2) Since the majority of the gifted are found in the higher economic classes, segregation exaggerates class distinctions and is therefore undemocratic. (3) All existing methods of selection are imperfect and encourage teachers and parents to press children of moderate ability to achieve a transference for which they are not really fit. (4) The inevitable rejection of a large proportion of candidates generates resentment not only among pupils who are of average or inferior ability but also among their parents. (5) In most areas the cost of special classes, additional books and apparatus, and adequately trained examiners and teachers would be prohibitive. In each of these criticisms there is a large element of truth. But the opinion of the majority of impartial educationists and psychologists, in both the United States and Britain, appears to be that with further experience it should be possible to reduce such dangers to a minimum.

See also GENIUS; *Modern English Usage*; PRODIGY; CREATIVITY; CHILD PSYCHOLOGY: *Individual Differences.*

BIBLIOGRAPHY.—F. Galton, *Hereditary Genius* (1869); L. M. Terman, *Genetic Studies of Genius*, vol. i and ii (1925–26); L. S. Hollingworth, *Gifted Children* (1926); White House Conference, *Special Education: The Handicapped and the Gifted* (1931); L. M. Terman and M. H. Oden, *The Gifted Child Grows Up* (1948); *The Yearbook of Education: The Gifted Child* (1962).
(Cx. B.)

GIFT EXCHANGE refers to a type of exchange in which the transfer of an item is made in the form of a gift and a corresponding item is returned (as a countergift). Such exchanges are met with in every society (as in present-giving in western societies), but they are particularly important in nonliterate societies, where social anthropologists have studied their effects. The phrase "gift exchange" may seem contradictory, since in ordinary usage a gift suggests something for which no precise return is expected or something not offered in fulfillment of an obligation. Legally, the principle *debitor non praesumitur donare* implies that where indebtedness exists the transfer of an item (*e.g.*, as countergift) cannot ordinarily be assumed to be a gift even if alleged to be so. In the case of nonliterate societies, however, the following elements have been taken to justify the use of the term "gift": (1) the first offering is made in a generous and disinterested manner and there is no haggling between donor and recipient; (2) the initiation of a cycle of gift exchange is made as an expression of an existing social relationship or to establish a new one that differs in nature from the impersonal contacts between participants in an ordinary market transaction; (3) the profit in gift exchange may be in the sphere of social relationships and of the acquisition of prestige and moral virtue rather than in the sphere of material advantage. Some or all of these criteria distinguish gift exchange from other types of exchange or trade.

An analysis of the form of a gift-exchange cycle reveals three requirements that must be fulfilled: (1) the obligation to give;

(2) the obligation to receive; and (3) the obligation to return. Without the first obligation the cycle would obviously not exist, but more important is the fact that in simpler societies, sanctions may exist that induce people to offer gifts to others. People in certain social positions (such as kin or friends) may have a duty to do so and failure may meet with disapproval and loss of prestige. The obligation to receive implies that if an offering is made, there is an obligation on the part of the person for whom it is intended to accept it. If the gift is refused, this is tantamount to refusing social relations and can act almost as a declaration of open enmity. The obligation to return the gift represents the reciprocity inherent in the exchange cycle. Immediately, or after some time, a return must be made such that there is not too great a disparity between the value of the offering and that of the return. The value of the return is kept up, in the absence of haggling, by the prestige attached to apparent generosity. During the course of a gift-exchange cycle, links are established between those concerned. The initiator of the cycle is in a position of social superiority, and the recipient, until he returns the gift, is under an obligation and therefore in a position of inferiority. This may act as a sanction for return. In some societies, the prestige gained by extravagant giving determines the whole society's hierarchy of status. The Kwakiutl Indian potlatch (*q.v.*)—a ceremonial destruction or dispersion of property to demonstrate superior riches, power and generosity in one of two opponents—is usually taken as the classic type of such conspicuous consumption.

Many applications of the analysis of gift exchange to various aspects of social life in technologically primitive societies have been made. It is evident that the notion does not rule out the possibility of the purely disinterested gift lacking any suggestion of reciprocity. But when it is realized both that what may appear at first sight to be gifts may in fact be exchanges and that what may be transferred in exchanges vary from tangible objects to social support and spiritual virtue, and from consumers' goods to women, the field of applications becomes wide. The first extended use of the idea was made in 1925 by Marcel Mauss, a French anthropologist interested in comparative studies of gift exchange seen as contract. He looked at gift exchange as a phenomenon that should be studied in its totality and saw it as having aspects that touched every facet of social life. He observed that a thing given still had links with its original owner and this formed a bond between original and existing owners. He stressed the social concomitants of gift exchange rather than its economic functions. In the course of his study he drew on the research of others including B. Malinowski, who had described gift exchanges of the Trobriand islanders of southeast Melanesia. These islanders were best known for maintaining an elaborate form of exchange (the *kula*) in which traditional valuables (necklaces and bracelets) were given and accepted as gifts, following an established, ceremonial pattern and trade route. The valuables were not producers' capital, directly consumable or media of exchange outside the ceremonial system; but they were highly prized. The widespread *kula* trade ring necessitated trading expeditions to other islands and linked together as semipermanent partners people who might otherwise have been enemies. Under protection of the gift-exchange partnership, ordinary trading transactions were conducted with a strict eye to profit and individual advantage. In this way the *kula* had an effect on the wider economy. But Malinowski further revealed that a great deal of the distribution of all types of goods in a simple economy may be in the form of a gift exchange rather than in the form of a market (in the actual or conceptual sense) and that reciprocity in gift exchange permeated Trobriand social life. The important conclusion suggested by Malinowski and Mauss and borne out by subsequent inquirers is that in primitive societies economic transactions may have more effect in the social sphere than they do in complex, industrialized societies. A gift exchange may not only provide a recipient with what amounts to credit for a period (to be returned with interest); it also validates, supports and expresses a social relationship in terms of the status of the persons concerned. This does not apply to other forms of exchange. Natives may distinguish between goods suitably exchanged as gifts and goods that may be bought, bartered and haggled over with no wider social repercussions than those occasioned by the immediate event.

The notion of reciprocity lying behind gift exchange may be extended into the field of ritual and religion. Some sacrifices, for example, may be considered as types of gift exchange, in which an apparently free and generous offering is made to the supernatural powers, but the expectation among members of the society may be of a return in the form of supernatural approval and aid. Gift exchange may also throw light on reciprocal social relationships. Many societies differ from the individualistic, western type in that marriages may join groups of persons together (as relatives-in-law) through strong and clearly defined social bonds. The offering of a woman in marriage by a group of kinsmen to a member of another group is in some ways cognate in terms of obligations and types of relationship to a gift exchange. C. Lévi-Strauss studied the implications of widespread exchange or transfer of women as wives in societies in which kinsfolk form important units and attempted to show the general significance of bonds thus set up in the total structure of simple societies. Some students of behaviour have been so impressed by the way in which it is possible to discern gift exchange and reciprocity in many aspects of social life that they see here the basis of social organization. George Homans emphasized the usefulness of interpreting all behaviour in society in terms of transactions, and in this he draws his main inspiration from Mauss. *See also* TRADE, PRIMITIVE.

BIBLIOGRAPHY.—B. Malinowski, *Argonauts of the Western Pacific* (1922); M. Mauss, *The Gift*, Eng. trans. by I. Cunnison (1954); C. Lévi-Strauss, *Les Structures élémentaires de la parenté* (1949); H. Codere, *Fighting With Property* (1950); R. Firth, *Primitive Economics of the New Zealand Maori* (1929); G. Homans, "Social Behaviour as Exchange," *American Journal of Sociology* (May 1958); C. Kaut, "Utang Na Loob: a System of Contractual Obligation Among Tagalogs," *Southwestern Journal of Anthropology*, vol. 17 (1961); P. Tournier, *The Meaning of Gifts* (1963).

(L. F. B.)

GIFU, landlocked Japanese prefecture of central Honshū, is dominated by mountains except for a small southern portion, which is the inner part of the Nōbi plain. The plain section has most of the agriculture, the capital Gifu, other leading cities (Ogaki, Seki, Mino) and most industry—textiles, pottery, paper, cutlery, automobiles, machinery, wood products and chemicals. Forestry is the main occupation in the mountain districts. Economic ties with Nagoya are strong and many industries are either branches or subsidiaries of Nagoya firms. Railways link Gifu with Pacific coast cities and Toyama on the Sea of Japan. Area 4,046 sq.mi. Pop. (1965) 1,700,265.

(J. D. EE.)

GIFU, capital and largest city of Gifu prefecture, central interior Honshū, lies at the foot of Mt. Kinka along the Nagara river in the Nōbi plain. Once a feudal period castle town, it achieved prosperity as a textile centre with strong commercial ties with Nagoya. Many large, modern factories house silk, cotton and wool textile, metals and machinery manufacturing. At the same time, Gifu is well known for its paper umbrellas, lanterns, fans and other traditional handicraft products that are made in hundreds of small household workshops. It serves as the regional commercial centre for the inner Nōbi plain and has the prefectural offices and university, many fine parks, temples and libraries. A summer tourist attraction is nighttime cormorant fishing on the Nagara river, where tame cormorants, with rings around their necks to prevent swallowing, catch and disgorge small trout. Pop. (1960) 304,492.

(J. D. EE.)

GIGANTES, the Giants of Greek mythology, monstrous, savage creatures, often depicted with men's bodies terminating in serpentine legs. They are mentioned by Homer (in the *Odyssey*) and by Hesiod, who makes them sons of Ge (earth) and Uranus (heaven). It is not certain, however, that either poet knew of the Gigantomachy (*i.e.*, the battle between the Gigantes and the Olympians), though this variant of the age-old myth of a war between the powers of heaven and earth must have been a theme of early epic. After a desperate struggle the gods prevailed, through the aid of Heracles the archer, and the Gigantes were slain. Many of them were believed to lie buried under mountains and to indicate their presence by volcanic fires and earthquakes; when bones of prehistoric monsters came to light, they also were often regarded as the remains of dead giants. The Gigantomachy became a popular artistic theme, especially in sculpture and vase painting, being interpreted as a symbol of the triumph of Hellenism over barbarism and of good over evil. Its most celebrated appearance in sculpture is on the frieze adorning the great altar at Pergamum.

See Waser, "Gigantes," Pauly-Wissowa, *Real-Encyclopädie der classischen Altertumswissenschaft,* supplementary vol. iii (1918).
(D. E. W. W.)

GIGANTISM: *see* DWARFISM AND GIGANTISM.

GIGLI, BENIAMINO (1890–1957), the greatest Italian operatic tenor of his day, was born at Recanati, near Ancona, on March 20, 1890. He made his operatic debut at the age of 15 in the operetta *La Fuga di Angelica* at Macerata. He studied in Rome with Agnese Bonucci, Antonio Cotogni and Enrico Rosati. After winning a competition at Parma in 1914 he made his professional debut in *La Gioconda* at Rovigo, followed by engagements in Naples, Rome and Milan. In 1917 he sang in Spain and two years later in South America. He made his debut at the Metropolitan Opera, New York city, in 1920 as Faust in Boito's *Mefistofele* and remained with the company for 12 seasons. In 1930 he first appeared in London at Covent Garden in Giordano's *Andrea Chénier.* Between 1935 and 1951 he made numerous films in Germany and Italy. His lyric tenor voice was remarkable for its power, its mellow quality and smoothness of production. His musical taste was not flawless and his acting never lost a primitive stiffness, but his natural musicianship and the lively charm of his vocal personality continued to hold operatic audiences. From 1946 he often appeared in opera with his daughter, the soprano Rina Gigli. He last sang in opera in *Cavalleria Rusticana* and *Pagliacci* in 1954 at the arena named after him in his native village and gave his last concert at Washington, D.C., the following year. He died in Rome on Nov. 30, 1957.

See The Memoirs of Beniamino Gigli, Eng. trans. by Darina Silone (1957).
(WI. S. M.)

GIGLIO (Lat. IGILIUM), an island in the Tyrrhenian sea, about 10 mi. off the coast of Italy, in Grosseto province. It is 8 km. (5 mi.) long, 5 km. (3 mi.) wide, with an area of 21 sq.km. (8 sq.mi.). Pop. (1961) 2,067. The island is mountainous, its highest point reaching 496 m. (1,627 ft.). There are terraced vineyards producing excellent wine, and considerable offshore fishing. The village of Giglio Castello, surrounded by medieval walls, is the principal inland settlement; Giglio Porto on the east coast is the only landing place. Pisa and then Florence controlled the island during the middle ages; later it was owned by the Piccolomini and by Eleanor of Toledo, wife of Cosimo I, grand duke of Tuscany. There is daily steamer service to Giglio from Porto Santo Stefano, on the Tuscan coast.
(G. Kн.)

GIGUE, the courtly version of the English jig from which it derived its name when entering the court circles of continental Europe during the 17th century. Whereas true Scottish and Irish jigs were quick and wild and of indefinite form and rhythm, *gigues* were danced by couples in formal, ballet style and generally in 6/8 or 12/8 time as the melodic lines were fashioned of rapidly moving groups of three eighth-notes. In musical literature the *gigue* attained importance as the final movement of the suite (*q.v.*). Invariably written in fugal style, the contrapuntal lines retained the rapid groups of three eighth-notes.
(L. Hт.)

GIJÓN, a town of Oviedo province, Spain, the maritime capital of Asturias, located on the Bay of Biscay at the foot of the Santa Catalina peninsula. Pop. (1970 prelim.) 187,612 (mun.). Railroad and bus lines unite Gijón with other towns of the province and with Madrid, Santander, Irún and La Coruña. At its seaport call ships en route to other coastal ports as well as to the Canary Islands and to America. Radio broadcasting stations serve air and sea traffic. Gijón's seaport, El Musel, is a splendid shelter and leads Spain in the coasting trade, visited by about 6,000 ships annually. Coal, mined in the vicinity, is the chief item of freight exported, but iron ore also is important. There are in addition fishing and liner ports. Industries include iron and steel and chemical manufactures, oil refining, tobacco manufacture, brewing and food processing.

As ancient monuments, Gijón has Roman hot baths and 14th-, 15th- and 16th-century palaces. It has modern commerce and industrial schools, and, on the southeast edge of the city, the Labour university, for the sons of workers, noted for its gigantic proportions and its boldly conceived theatre and church. The town's main park is the Parque de Isabel la Católica. A long sandy bathing beach lies within the city, and other beaches and beautiful surroundings have made Gijón an important summer resort.

Gijón is usually identified with the Roman Gigia, captured by the Moors early in the 8th century and one of the first cities to be retaken (about 737). It was capital of the kingdom of Asturias till 791. In 1244 Gijón successfully resisted a Norman raid; in 1395 it was burned down, and in the 16th and 17th centuries it suffered many attacks by corsairs. The remnants of the Spanish Armada took refuge there in 1588. In the civil war of 1936–39 it was the last northern port to fall to the insurgents.
(J. O. A.)

GILA CLIFF DWELLINGS is a U.S. national monument located about 47 mi. N of Silver City in the southeastern part of Caton County, New Mexico. The monument was established on Nov. 16, 1907, to protect a group of caves containing the well-preserved ruins of cliff dwellings of the Pueblo people. A half-mile trail leads to and through the cliff dwellings, which are about 180 ft. above the canyon floor in the west fork of the Gila River. The 533-ac. area is administered by the U.S. Department of the Interior and is within the Gila National Forest.

GILA MONSTER (*Heloderma suspectum*) and its relative the Mexican beaded lizard, or escorpión (*H. horridum*), are the only existing truly venomous lizards. The Gila monster (pronounced *he′-la*), so named because it was once relatively common along the Gila River basin, occurs from the southern tip of Nevada and adjacent Utah southeastward through Arizona (where it is now protected by law) into New Mexico and the state of Sonora, Mex. *H. horridum* ranges from Sonora southward into Guatemala.

The Gila monster is a stout-bodied lizard with black and pink blotches or bands across the beadlike scales. Maximum length is 21 in. The escorpión is darker and reaches a greater size. Although sometimes abroad during the day in spring, the Gila monster is mostly nocturnal. In winter and periods of drought it remains inactive in burrows, depending on fat stored in the tail and abdomen for nourishment. Prey includes young mammals, fledgling birds, and birds' and reptiles' eggs. As in many snakes, food is apparently located more by chemical than by visual senses; the flicking tongue carries odours to sensory pits (Jacobson's organ) in the roof of the mouth. No natural enemies are known. Except that eggs are laid, little has been recorded of the reproductive habits.

Generally slow moving, the Gila monster displays agility when annoyed, and its bite is tenacious. Most of the teeth have two grooves, which presumably conduct venom into a wound through capillary action. The venom comes from specialized salivary glands beneath the skin of the lower jaw; its biochemical structure has not been investigated, but the venom is known to be primarily neurotoxic, with strong effects on the respiratory centre. Bites to humans, usually inflicted when the animals are being handled or teased, have been deadly in exceptional cases. *See* LIZARD.

See also C. M. Bogert and R. Martin del Campo, "The Gila Monster and Its Allies," *Bull. Amer. Mus. Nat. Hist.,* 109, art. 1: pp. 1–238 (1956).
(G. B. R.)

GILAN, an *ostan* (province) of Iran constituted in 1938, comprises the old Caspian province of Gilan, enlarged by the neighbouring *shahrestans* (districts) of Astara and Rudsar, taken from East Azerbaijan and Mazanderan *ostans,* respectively. It is bounded on the northeast by the Caspian Sea, on the north by the U.S.S.R., on the west by East Azerbaijan and Kurdistan, on the south by Zanjan *farmandarikol* (general governorate) and Central *ostan,* and on the east by Mazanderan. The province contains ten *shahrestans:* Astara, Bandar-e Pahlavi, Fumen (Fowman), Hashtpar, Lahijan, Langerud, Rasht, Rudbar, and Sumelehsara. Its area is 5,679 sq.mi. (14,709 sq.km.).

The physiographic division is into the coastal plain, including the large delta of the Safid Rud and the adjacent parts of the Elburz chain. The coastal plains and slopes are humid throughout the year, annual precipitation exceeding 50 in. (1,270 mm.), but fluctuations occur. The water supply from the Safid Rud may be deficient in early summer (when it is most needed) as it is drawn from a large subhumid or semiarid basin. Winters are wet and mild, snowfall and frost being not unknown. A foehnlike warm and dry wind blowing from the highland is a feature. The soil is a fertile dark loam, or sandy loam, largely leached by paddy growing. There are dunes and marshy stretches along the lower parts of the plain. The luxuriant junglelike forest, with oak, ash, hornbeam, box, and other partly endemic species (such as Caucasian wingnut [*Pterocarya fraxinifolia*], *Gleditsia caspica*, silk tree [*Albizzia julibrissin*], Persian parrotia [*Parrotia persica*]) still covers part of the plain, especially in Tavalesh, but otherwise has been transformed into fields or worthless thorny brushwood. On the mountain slopes the ravages of charcoal burners and shepherds are visible. Waterfowl, whether migrant or resident, abound in the coastal stretches.

Gilan proper remained independent after the Arab conquest of Persia and a stronghold of the old faith and of local rulers. It was the original home of the Buyids, who were masters of most of the Caliphate during the 10th century. Conquered by Hulagu in the 13th century, it was formed into the two principalities of Lahijan and Fumen.

The population in 1966 was 1,291,159, mainly Persian-speaking Gilaki, with a large Turkish element. The average population density in the plain of Gilan is 227 to the sq.mi., compared with 55 in nearby Zanjan *farmandarikol*. Most of the cultivated land is reserved for rice, a substantial surplus of which is exported to the U.S.S.R. The paddy area, irrespective of the water deficiency, has been constantly enlarged because of the rise in population in Iran. Broad beans, melons, and vegetables are grown for subsistence; cash crops are tobacco and kanaf (a local form of hemp) as well as tea and peanuts, mostly grown in Lahijan. Sericulture, once an important industry, was badly hit by disease in the 19th century. A little sugarcane is grown and some citrus and other fruits. Olives are grown at Rudbar in the Safid Rud valley. Fishing is important; formerly organized by a joint Soviet-Iranian company, it was taken over by the government in 1953. Most of the catch (sturgeon, salmon, whitefish) is exported, as is the caviar, which, at 100-160 tons annually, is about 20% of world production. Gilan has a few modern factories mainly for tea and rice processing; a silk mill and a kanaf plant are at Rasht. Modern developments include a dam at Manjil, at the upper entrance of the Safid Rud gorge, which was designed for irrigation and electric power.

The capital and the main commercial centre of the *ostan* is Rasht (pop. [1966] 143,557). Other centres in Gilan proper are Lahijan (25,725), Langarud (20,668), and Bandar-e Pahlavi (41,785), the busiest of the Caspian ports of Iran.

BIBLIOGRAPHY.—H. L. Rabino, *Les provinces caspiennes de la Perse, Le Guilan* (1917), reprinted from *Revue du Monde musulman*, vol. xxxii; J. B. L. Noel, "A Reconnaissance in the Caspian Provinces of Persia," *Geogr. Journal* (June 1921); L. S. Fortescue, "Les provinces caspiennes de la Perse," *La Géographie*, xliii (1925); H. Bobek, "Die Landschaftsgestaltung des Süd-Kaspischen Küstentieflands," *Festschrift N. Krebs* (1936); C. Sahami, *Le Guilan*, Institut de Géogr. (1965).
(H. Bo.)

GILA RIVER. The Gila river rises in southwest New Mexico in Grand and Catron counties near the Gila Cliff Dwellings National monument. The river, 630 mi. long, flows west-southwest over the hot, dry desert land of southwestern United States into the Colorado river at Yuma, Ariz. (elevation 141 ft.). Near Clifton, Ariz., the Gila receives its main charge of water from the San Francisco river. On the San Carlos Indian reservation, near Globe, Ariz., the Gila is dammed by the Coolidge dam completed in 1928. The dam's capacity is 1,250,000 ac.ft. of water, which is used for irrigation in the Casa Grande valley. From Coolidge dam the river flows west about 125 mi. to a point 20 mi. W. of Phoenix, where it receives the Salt river, its major tributary from the northeast. Roosevelt dam on the Salt and Coolidge dam on the Gila store all available surface water and the Gila river bed is a dry, desolate, barren wasteland to its confluence with the Colorado river near Yuma. Other major tributaries include the San Pedro and Santa Cruz rivers. Important towns on or near the river are Yuma, Florence, Safford, Hayden and Coolidge, all in Arizona.
(M. J. L.)

GILBERT, SAINT, OF SEMPRINGHAM (c. 1083-1189), founder of the Gilbertines, the only medieval religious order of English origin, was born at Sempringham in Lincolnshire. He studied in France, was ordained in 1123 and was presented by his father to the living of Sempringham. In 1131 he succeeded his father as lord of the manor. The new religious order began there by his giving a rule of life, inspired by the Benedictine rule as interpreted by Cîteaux, to seven girls, his parishioners, who were under his spiritual direction. To perform the heavy work and cultivate the fields, he formed a number of labourers into a society of brothers attached to the convent, like the *conversi* of Cîteaux. There were also serving nuns in the domestic offices, and later a fourth division, canons regular, the rule of St. Augustine. Alexander, bishop of Lincoln, favoured Gilbert's work and helped him to find resources. Similar establishments sprang up elsewhere and after failing, in 1147, to get them incorporated in the Cistercian order Gilbert received papal encouragement to continue as before. The order of Sempringham was double, the communities of men and of women living side by side but separately, the property belonging to the nuns and the superior of the canons being the head of the whole establishment. There were also houses for canons only, all under the master of Sempringham. Gilbert died at Sempringham in 1189, on Feb. 4, his feast day from the very beginning and his date in the Roman martyrology (though the dioceses of Nottingham and Northampton keep the feast on Feb. 16), and was canonized in 1202. The order never spread beyond England, except for one Scottish house. At the dissolution, there were 25 monasteries.

BIBLIOGRAPHY.—Between Oct. 13, 1202, and July 13, 1205, a canon, the sacrist of Sempringham, probably Ralph de Lille, gathered a whole dossier on Gilbert including a formal life (printed in W. Dugdale, *Monasticon Anglicanum*, vol. vi, part 2, 1830; 2nd ed. 1846), miracles and correspondence about the canonization, etc.; some are printed in Dugdale, the rest by R. Foreville, *Un Procès de canonisation à l'aube du XIIIe siècle. Le Livre de Saint Gilbert de Sempringham* (1943). See also R. Graham, *St. Gilbert of Sempringham and the Gilbertines* (1901); D. Knowles, *The Monastic Order in England*, pp. 205-207 (1949); D. Knowles and R. N. Hadcock, *Medieval Religious Houses, England and Wales*, pp. 122-125 (1953).
(Pt. Gn.)

GILBERT, SIR ALFRED (1854-1934), British sculptor and goldsmith, whose best-known work is the "Eros" memorial fountain in Piccadilly Circus, London, was born in London on Aug. 12, 1854. His first training in art was at Heatherley's art school, London, and he also studied at the Royal Academy schools and under Sir Joseph Edgar Boehm. From 1875 to 1878 he attended the École des Beaux-Arts in Paris under P. J. Cavelier. He then went to Italy, where he produced his first important works, including "The Kiss of Victory" and "Perseus Arming." In 1884 he returned to England and his "Icarus," commissioned by Lord Leighton, was exhibited at the Royal Academy that year.

In 1885 Gilbert began the memorial (known as "Eros") to the philanthropic earl of Shaftesbury, which was unveiled in 1893. In 1888 he produced the statue of Queen Victoria at Winchester and also made the first sketches for the silver gilt and enamel mayoral chain for Preston, a good example of his talent for delicate craftsmanship. In 1892 he was elected royal academician and began his memorial to the duke of Clarence (one of his most important works), which was placed in the Albert chapel, St. George's, Windsor. In 1904 he became bankrupt and settled in Bruges, Belg., where he remained until 1926 when, at the wish of King George V, he returned to England to finish the Clarence memorial. Gilbert's last important work was the Queen Alexandra memorial opposite St. James's palace, London, unveiled in 1932, in which year he was knighted. Gilbert died in London on Nov. 4, 1934.
(R. Gs.)

GILBERT, CASS (1859-1934), U.S. architect, designer of the Woolworth skyscraper and the U.S. supreme court building, was born at Zanesville, O., on Nov. 24, 1859. He studied at Massachusetts Institute of Technology and in 1883 began his career as an architect in St. Paul, Minn, but later moved to New York. He became most widely known as the architect of the Woolworth building in New York (1913), which, with its 60-story tower rising to a height of 792 ft., lacily ornamented in modified Gothic, is regarded as one of the best designed of early skyscrapers. He utilized the neoclassical style characteristic of the national capital for the treasury annex (1919) and the supreme court building (completed 1935) in Washington, D.C.

Gilbert's other buildings include the Minnesota state capitol at St. Paul; the Endicott building, the Dayton avenue church and St. Clement's Episcopal church in St. Paul; the U.S. customhouse and the Union club, New York; the Brazer building and the Suffolk Savings bank in Boston; Art building and Festival hall (for the Louisiana Purchase exposition) and the Central Public library, St. Louis; Ives Memorial library, New Haven (Conn.); and the Public library, Detroit. He drew the plans for the University of Minnesota and for the University of Texas. Gilbert died on May 17, 1934, at Brockenhurst, Eng.

GILBERT, GROVE KARL (1843–1918), U.S. geologist, was born at Rochester, N.Y., on May 6, 1843, and graduated at the University of Rochester in 1862. He began the study of geology and in 1869 went as a volunteer assistant on the second Ohio State survey. In 1871 he was assigned to the G. M. Wheeler survey west of the 100th meridian and during his three years' service took a remarkable trip by boat up the lower canyons of the Colorado river, by pack train through central Arizona and down the valley of the Gila, and again by boat down the Colorado to the Gulf of California. As a result of this trip he published two papers characterizing the basin range and plateau provinces and naming and describing ancient Lake Bonneville. He was transferred to the John Wesley Powell survey in 1875 which took him to Utah, and with the formation of the U.S. geological survey in 1879 he was placed in charge of the Appalachian division of geology and in 1889, upon the creation of the division of geologic correlation, he was placed at its head. After 1892 he relinquished most of his administrative duties and his position as chief geologist in order to return to the fuller study of some of his earlier problems. The *Bonneville Monograph*, which he himself regarded as his magnum opus, was published in 1890. His report on the *Geology of the Henry Mountains*, in which the intrusive igneous structure known as a laccolith (q.v.) was first described, and his *History of the Niagara River* (1890) were of particular importance. He had much to do with planning the federal survey's bibliographic work and the adoption of principles of nomenclature and cartography which form the basis of the survey's geologic map work. He died at Jackson, Mich., on May 1, 1918.

See *Bull. Geol. Soc. America*, vol. xxxi, pp. 26–64 (March 1920), which includes a complete bibliography of Gilbert's publications; and W. M. Davis, *American Journal of Science*, 4th ser, vol. xlvi, pp. 669–681 (Nov. 1918).

GILBERT, SIR HUMPHREY (c. 1537–1583), English soldier and navigator, who spent most of his life devising and carrying out projects of colonization, was the second son of Sir Otho Gilbert of Compton, near Dartmouth, Devon, and half brother of Sir Walter Raleigh. According to John Hooker, he was educated at Eton and Oxford. He entered the service of Princess Elizabeth in 1544 or 1545. Wounded at the siege of Le Havre (1563), he was concerned in 1565–66 with Anthony Jenkinson in projects for discovering a northward passage to Cathay, and wrote a *Discourse* in support of the northwestern route. Gilbert went to Ireland as a captain under Sir Henry Sidney in July 1566, but returned in November. In Dec. 1566 he put forward a proposal for an expedition to explore the northwest passage, but abandoned it in the face of opposition from the Muscovy company. He spent most of the three years after May 1567 in Ireland, where he and other west countrymen began to elaborate projects for colonization, at first in Ulster and then in Munster. From Sept. 1569 Gilbert was in charge of operations against the Munster rebels, whom he suppressed with great vigour and ruthlessness. He was knighted in 1570, but his colonizing schemes fell through and he returned to England, sitting as member of parliament for Plymouth in 1571

and again in 1581. He commanded, with more energy than skill or success, the English "volunteers" sent in 1572 to assist the Netherlands' revolt against Spain.

Gilbert was living at Limehouse from 1573 to 1578. He drew up an interesting plan for reforming the practice of wardship and establishing an academy in London. His interest in the northwest passage revived in 1575, and the printing of his earlier *Discourse* in 1576 probably encouraged the voyages of Martin Frobisher (1576–78). Gilbert did not subscribe to them, however, for he was now beginning to think of applying the ideas of colonization, evolved in Ireland, to parts of the American continent. He put forward a plan in 1577 for seizing the Spanish, Portuguese and French Newfoundland fishing fleets, occupying Santo Domingo and Cuba and intercepting the ships that carried American silver to Spain. The following year the queen granted him a patent for six years, in very vague terms, to discover and settle "heathen lands not actually possessed of any Christian prince or people." He strained his means to the uttermost, even pledging the estates of his wife, Anne Aucher, of Otterden, Kent, to fit out an expedition which sailed from Dartmouth on Sept. 26, 1578. His exact objective remains obscure and his ill-equipped, ill-disciplined force broke up and drifted home or into piracy by the spring of 1579. During that summer he and some of his ships were employed against Fitz-Maurice's rebellion in Ireland.

Four years later, after many struggles to raise funds, he managed to equip another expedition for a more ambitious project of "western planting." He sailed from Plymouth on June 11, 1583. One of his five ships turned back on June 13, but on Aug. 3 he arrived at St. John's, Newfoundland, and took possession of it in the queen's name. Moving southward with three ships, he lost the largest of them on Aug. 29 and two days later turned homeward with the "Golden Hind" (40 tons) and the "Squirrel" (10 tons). Obstinately insisting upon sailing himself in the tiny "Squirrel," he was last seen, according to Hayes, captain of the "Golden Hind," during a great tempest "sitting abaft with a book," shouting to the "Golden Hind" that, "we are as near heaven by sea as by land." In the night the "Squirrel's" lights disappeared as she, and Gilbert with her, were "swallowed up of the sea."

See D. B. Quinn, *The Voyages and Colonising Enterprises of Sir Humphrey Gilbert*, 2 vol. (1940). (R. B. Wm.)

GILBERT, SIR JOHN (1817–1897), English painter and illustrator of the works of Shakespeare and other dramatists, both English and foreign, was born at Blackheath, London, on July 21, 1817. He received some rudimentary training from the still-life painter George Lance, and in 1837 began exhibiting oils of historical and romantic subjects at the British institution. From 1838 he sent regularly (except for a break of 16 years) to the Royal Academy, becoming a full academician in 1876. A prolific watercolourist, Gilbert became an associate of the Old Water Colour society in 1852, a full member in 1854 and president in 1871, shortly after which he was knighted. His imaginative designs enhanced the popularity of the *Illustrated London News*, his drawings being notable for their breadth of scale and dramatic chiaroscuro. He died at Blackheath on Oct. 5, 1897. (D. L. Fr.)

GILBERT, RUFUS HENRY (1832–1885), U.S. surgeon and transit expert who played a major role in the development of rapid transit in New York city, was born in Guilford, N.Y., Jan. 26, 1832. He attended the College of Physicians and Surgeons in New York city and then served as a surgeon in the Union army in the Civil War. He had become interested in the development of rapid transit in large cities as a means of allowing movement of population from crowded downtown tenements, with their high incidence of illness, and left the army to pursue that work. After gaining experience with the Central Railroad of New Jersey, he incorporated the Gilbert Electric Railway company in 1872 to build elevated lines in New York utilizing pneumatic tubes set on elevated structures, with cars propelled by air pressure in the tubes. Financing difficulties prevented construction until 1876, however, and forced adoption of the more conventional type of elevated railroad, with trains drawn by steam locomotives. The Sixth avenue line, from Trinity church to Central park, was completed and placed in operation in April 1878. But financiers forced Gilbert from the company and he died July 10, 1885, broken financially, physically and mentally. (J. F. D.)

GILBERT (GYLBERDE), WILLIAM (1544–1603), the most distinguished man of science in England during the reign of Queen Elizabeth I, was a member of an ancient Suffolk family, long resident in Clare, and was born on May 24, 1544, at Colchester, where his father, Hierome Gilbert, became recorder. Educated at Colchester school, he entered St. John's college, Cambridge, in 1558, and after taking the degrees of B.A. and M.A. in due course, graduated M.D. in 1569, in which year he was elected a senior fellow of his college. He traveled in Europe, and in 1573 settled in London, where he practised as a physician. He was admitted to the College of Physicians probably about 1576, and he held several important offices. In 1589 he was one of the committee appointed to superintend the preparation of the *Pharmacopoeia Londinensis* which the college in that year decided to issue, but which did not actually appear until 1618. In 1601 Gilbert was appointed physician to Queen Elizabeth I, with the usual emolument of £100 a year. On the death of the queen in 1603 he was reappointed by her successor; but he did not long enjoy the honour, for he died on Dec. 10 (new style; Nov. 30, old style), 1603, either in London or in Colchester. He was buried in the latter town, in the chancel of Holy Trinity church, where a monument was erected to his memory. To the College of Physicians he left his books, globes, instruments and minerals, but they were destroyed in the Great Fire of London.

Gilbert's principal work is his treatise on magnetism (q.v.), entitled *De magnete, magneticisque corporibus, et de magno magnete tellure* (London, 1600; later editions—Stettin, 1628, 1633; Frankfurt, 1629, 1638). This work, which embodied the results of many years' research, was distinguished by its strict adherence to the scientific method of investigation by experiment, and by the originality of its matter. It contains an account of the author's experiments on magnets and magnetic bodies and on electrical attractions, and also his great conception that the earth is nothing but a large magnet, and that it is this which explains, not only the direction of the magnetic needle north and south, but also the dipping or inclination of the needle. A posthumous work of Gilbert's was edited by his brother from two manuscripts; its title is *De mundo nostro sublunari philosophia nova* (1651). He followed the astronomer Thomas Digges in supporting the views of Copernicus, and adopted Digges' theory (1576) of an infinite universe.

GILBERT, SIR WILLIAM SCHWENCK (1836–1911), English playwright and humorist, best-remembered as the writer of witty librettos for the comic operas of Arthur Sullivan (q.v.), which were performed mainly at the Savoy theatre. The son of William Gilbert (himself a novelist and a descendant of Sir Humphrey Gilbert), he was born in London on Nov. 18, 1836. Educated at Boulogne, at Ealing and at King's college, London, he became a clerk in the education department of the privy council office in 1857. He had already entered the Inner Temple as a law student in 1855; a legacy in 1861 enabled him to leave the civil service for a legal career. He was called to the bar in Nov. 1863 and joined the northern circuit in 1866. His practice was inconsiderable, and his military and legal ambitions were eventually satisfied by a captaincy in the volunteers and appointment as a magistrate for Middlesex (June 1891). In 1861 he began to contribute comic verse to *Fun*, with his own humorous illustrations, over the signature of "Bab." These were collected in 1869 under the title of *Bab Ballads*, followed by *More Bab Ballads* (1873). The two collections and *Songs of a Savoyard* were united in a volume issued in 1898.

Early in Dec. 1866 the dramatist T. W. Robertson (q.v.) was asked by Miss Herbert, lessee of the St. James's theatre, to find someone who could turn out a bright Christmas piece in a fortnight, and suggested Gilbert who promptly produced *Dulcamara or the Little Duck and the Great Quack*, a burlesque of *L'Elisir d'amore*, written in ten days, rehearsed in a week and duly performed at Christmas. He sold the piece outright for £30, a rash action which he had cause to regret, for it turned out a commercial success. In 1870 he was commissioned by J. B. Buckstone to write a blank verse fairy comedy, based upon *Le Palais de la*

vérité, the novel by Madame de Genlis. The result was *The Palace of Truth*, produced by Kendal in November at the Haymarket. This was followed in 1871 by *Pygmalion and Galatea*, and in 1873 by *The Wicked World*, and *The Happy Land*, written in collaboration with Gilbert à Beckett. Gilbert's next dramatic ventures inclined more to the conventional pattern—*Sweethearts* (Prince of Wales's theatre, Nov. 7, 1874); *Tom Cobb* (St. James's, April 24, 1875); *Broken Hearts* (Court, Dec. 17, 1875); *Dan'l Druce* (Haymarket, Sept. 11, 1876); and *Engaged* (Haymarket, Oct. 3, 1877). *Gretchen*, a verse drama in four acts, appeared in 1879 and a one-act piece, called *Comedy and Tragedy*, was produced at the Lyceum on Jan. 26, 1884. Two dramatic trifles of later date were *Foggerty's Fairy* (1881) and *Rosenkrantz and Guildenstern* (1891).

In the autumn of 1870 the composer Fred Clay introduced Gilbert to Arthur Sullivan and they started to work together in the following year. The first two comic operas, *Thespis, or the Gods Grown Old* (Dec. 26, 1871) and *Trial by Jury* (Royalty, March 25, 1875), were followed by four productions at the Opéra Comique —*The Sorcerer* (Nov. 17, 1877); *H.M.S. Pinafore, or The Lass That Loved a Sailor* (May 25, 1878); *The Pirates of Penzance, or The Slave of Duty* (April 3, 1880). In Oct. 1881 *Patience* was moved to a new theatre, the Savoy, specially built for the Gilbert and Sullivan operas by Richard D'Oyly Carte (q.v.). *Patience* was followed on Nov. 25, 1882, by *Iolanthe, or The Peer and the Peri*; and on Jan. 5, 1884, by *Princess Ida, or Castle Adamant*, a recast of *The Princess*, a fantasia which Gilbert had written in 1870 and had then described as a "respectful perversion of Mr. Tennyson's exquisite poem." The impulse reached its fullest development in the operas that followed—*The Mikado, or The Town of Titipu* (March 14, 1885); *Ruddigore, or The Witch's Curse* (Jan. 22, 1887); *The Yeomen of the Guard* (Oct. 3, 1888); and *The Gondoliers* (Dec. 7, 1889). After the appearance of *The Gondoliers* a coolness occurred between the composer and librettist; Gilbert thought that D'Oyly Carte had not supported him in a business disagreement with D'Oyly Carte. But the estrangement was not final. Gilbert wrote several more librettos and of these *Utopia Limited* (1893) and *The Grand Duke* (1896) were written in conjunction with Sullivan. The music for Gilbert's last opera, *Fallen Fairies* (1909), was written by Edward German. His last play, *The Hooligan*, was performed in 1911.

Gilbert began to write in an age of rhymed couplets, puns and travesty, and his early works exhibit the facetiousness of all writers of extravaganza. His importance lies in the fact that he turned his skill away from these tedious arts and developed instead a general burlesque of contemporary behaviour. A different age is ignorant of many of his original targets—pre-Raphaelite aesthetes, women's education, Victorian plays about Cornish pirates, or the long theatrical vogue of the "jolly jack tar"; but Gilbert's burlesque was replaced by a more ironical humour, but it is a mistake to believe that Gilbert was a satirist. None of his works are angry; not even *Patience* is designed as punishment.

As a writer of words for music Gilbert is important not only because of a natural ability for casting words in musical shapes but also because he was able to suggest to his composer many opportunities for the burlesque of musical conventions.

Gilbert was knighted in 1907. He died on May 29, 1911, from a heart attack brought on by saving a woman from drowning in a lake at Harrow Weald, Middlesex.

BIBLIOGRAPHY.—Sidney Dark and Rowland Grey, *W. S. Gilbert: His Life and Letters* (1924); Hesketh Pearson, *Gilbert and Sullivan* (1935); Reginald Allen, "William Schwenck Gilbert: an Anniversary Survey," *Theatre Notebook*, vol. xv, no. 4. (1961).
(T. S.; V. C. C.-B.)

GILBERT AND ELLICE ISLANDS, a British colony consisting of 37 coral atolls and islands spread over more than 2,000,000 sq.mi. of the western Pacific Ocean. Pop. (1968) 53,517. Total land area 283 sq.mi. There are 16 Gilbert islands, 9 Ellice islands, 8 Phoenix islands, and 3 of the northern Line islands, with Ocean Island as an outlier from the Gilbert Islands. The Gilbert Islands lie between 4° N and 3° S and 172° E and 178°

E. They are Makin or Butaritari, Little Makin, Marakei, Abaiang, Tarawa, Maiana, Abemama or Apamama, Aranuka, Kuria, Nonouti, Tabiteuea, Onotoa, Beru, Nikunau, Tamana, and Arorae.

Ellice (Lagoon) Islands lie between 5° S and 11° S and 176° E and 180° E. This group consists of Nanumea, Niutao, Nanumanga, Nui, Vaitupu, Nukufetau, Funafuti, Nukulaelae, and Niulakita.

Phoenix Islands are situated between 2° S and 5° S and 171° W and 175° W. They are Gardner, Hull, Sydney, McKean, Phoenix, Birnie, Enderbury, and Canton islands, the last two under joint Anglo-American administration.

Line Islands. The three islands of this group lie between 1° N and 5° N and 157° W and 161° W and are Fanning, Washington, and Christmas islands.

Ocean Island is located at 0° 52' S, 169° 35' E.

With the exception of Ocean Island, which is a coral and phosphate mass of 1,500 ac. thrown up by volcanic action to a height of about 265 ft., the colony consists of low-lying coral islands or atolls of coral islets surrounding lagoons of irregular shape. The islands seldom rise more than 12 ft. above high water, but they are protected from heavy seas by outlying coral reefs. Most of the islands are densely covered by coconut palms and to a lesser extent by the pandanus or screw pine, but undergrowth is scanty. Rainfall ranges from 120 in. annually in the Ellice Islands and 80–100 in. in the northern Gilbert Islands to 50 in. in the Phoenix Islands and 40 in. in the southern Gilberts, the two latter groups being subject to severe droughts. The daytime temperature varies between 26.7° and 33.9° C (80° and 93° F) and seldom drops below 21.1° C (70° F) at night.

Nikunau was discovered by Commodore John Byron in 1765; others of the Gilbert Islands by the British shipmasters Thomas Gilbert and John Marshall in 1788; and the remainder by the masters of trading vessels (usually British) between 1799 and 1824. Some of the Ellice Islands were probably seen by the Spanish explorer Alvaro de Mendaña in 1568 and 1595 and by his compatriot Francisco Maurelle in 1781; the others were discovered by trading or whaling vessels between 1809 and 1825. Some of the Phoenix Islands were also sighted by the early Spanish navigators and others discovered in the early 19th century. Christmas Island is believed to have been sighted in 1537 by Hernando de Grijalva and was charted by James Cook in 1777. The other Line islands were discovered in 1798 by Edmund Fanning in the U.S. trading vessel "Betsey." Great Britain established a protectorate over the Gilbert and Ellice groups in 1892 and annexed them as a colony in 1915. The Phoenix Islands, peopled by emigrants from the Gilberts, were included in the colony in 1937. The Japanese seized the Gilberts in December 1941 and Ocean Island the next year. They were expelled from the Gilberts by Allied forces in 1943 and from Ocean Island in 1945. (*See* WORLD WARS: *World War II: The Aleutians, Rabaul, and the Gilberts.*)

The people in the Gilbert Islands are Micronesians, while the smaller number of Ellice islanders are Polynesians. The people live in villages of native huts built of coconut and pandanus timbers thatched with pandanus leaves. Most of them are Christians, having been converted from tribalism.

A new constitution that became effective April 14, 1971, granted virtual self-government to the Gilbert and Ellice Islands. The British high commissioner for the Western Pacific relieved of responsibility for the islands, and the British resident commissioner was required to get the consent of an elected legislative council in all matters except those pertaining to defense and security.

Education is compulsory up to the age of 16 and there are many primary and a few secondary schools, mostly run by missionary societies. There is a large central hospital on Tarawa and each inhabited island has a native hospital.

Exports from the colony normally exceed £1,000,000 annually, of which more than half is accounted for by the high-grade phosphate rock which is mined on Ocean Island by native labour and of which about 300,000 tons are exported annually by the British Phosphate Commission. The only other export is copra, gathered from the scattered islands and shipped from Tarawa. Most families engage in subsistence fishing. Imports, largely from Australia and New Zealand, consist chiefly of cotton goods, fuel oils, tobacco, soap, building materials, and foodstuffs. Apart from Ocean Island, trading is in the hands of native cooperative societies and a government-controlled wholesale cooperative society. The islands are off the normal shipping routes, and interisland communications are maintained by a few small vessels owned by the government, the cooperative society, and the missions. Mails into and out of the colony are usually carried by ships visiting Ocean Island for phosphate. Apart from Ocean Island, the ports of entry are Tarawa, Funafuti, and Fanning and Christmas islands. A central radio station at Tarawa maintains contact with branch stations in the other islands. There is a weekly air service between Fiji (Suva) and Tarawa, maintained by Fijiair. Canton Island has an international airport on the southern route from North America to Fiji, Australia, and New Zealand, while Fanning Island has a relay station on the transpacific cable from Australasia to Canada. With the aid of substantial grants from the Commonwealth Development Fund much progress has been made in education, in medical care, and in government services generally.

BIBLIOGRAPHY.—C. Wilkes, *Narrative of the United States Exploring Expedition, 1832–42* (1845); C. Hedley et al., *A General Account of the Atoll of Funafuti* (1897); F. Lenwood, *Pastels From the Pacific* (1917); P. S. Allan, *Stewart's Handbook of the Pacific Isles* (1923); *Gilbert and Ellice Islands Colony Blue Book, 1940–41* (1944); Sir Harry Luke, *From a South Seas Diary* (1945); Sir Arthur Grimble, *A Pattern of Islands* (1952); *Gilbert and Ellice Islands Colony* (biennial report, H.M.S.O.).
(G. H. EA.)

GILBERT DE LA PORRÉE (*c.* 1075–1154), scholastic logician and theologian, was imbued with Platonic realism and familiar with Aristotelian logic. After studies under Bernard of Chartres and Anselm of Laon, he taught for several years at Chartres, where he became chancellor. About 1139 he went to Paris to lecture "on logical and divine subjects," and in 1142 he became bishop of his native Poitiers. Although accused by Bernard of Clairvaux of heretical doctrines concerning the Trinity, Gilbert escaped formal condemnation at the Council of Reims (1148) by agreeing to correct his writings. Proceeding from the idea that the conceptual universal is prior to the actual individual, he attempted to compromise between Plato and Aristotle in the controversy over universals. According to Gilbert, "native forms" are created examples of an eternal exemplar in the mind of God, while there is a distinction between the "subsistence" or common essence that makes beings members of a class and the "substance" that makes them particular individuals. As applied to the Trinity in his *Commentary on ... Boethius*, Gilbert's tendency to identify the logical and ontological led him to distinguish between an abstract divine nature (*Deitas* or *Divinitas*) and the actual God of Three Persons (*Deus* or *Trinitas*). This and similar conclusions were rejected at Reims as contrary to generally accepted doctrinal formulas. Gilbert apparently also wrote *The Six Principles*, which distinguishes among the ten categories of Aristotle four essential ones and six subsidiary ones, and comments upon the latter. This treatise enjoyed great authority during the middle ages. His aforesaid works and various scriptural commentaries are published in vol. lxiv and clxxxviii of J. P. Migne's *Patrologia latina*.
(D. D. McG.)

GILBERT FOLIOT (d. 1188), bishop of Hereford and of London, is first mentioned as a monk of Cluny, whence he was called in 1136 to plead the cause of the empress Matilda against Stephen (*q.v.*) at the Roman court. Shortly afterward he became prior of Cluny; then prior of Abbéville, a house dependent upon Cluny. In 1139 he was elected abbot of Gloucester. The appointment was confirmed by Stephen, and from the ecclesiastical point of view was unexceptionable. But the new abbot proved himself a valuable ally of the empress, and her ablest controversialist. Gilbert's reputation grew rapidly. He was respected at Rome and in 1148 was nominated by the pope to the see of Hereford. He was an Angevin at heart, and after 1154 was treated by Henry II with every mark of consideration. He was Thomas Becket's rival for the primacy, and the only bishop who protested against the king's choice. Becket endeavoured to win his friendship by procuring for him the see of London (1163). But Gilbert evaded the profession of obedience to the primate, and apparently aspired to make his see independent of Canterbury. On the questions raised by the Constitutions of Clarendon (q.v.) he sided with the king, whose confessor he had now become. He urged Becket to yield and, when this advice was rejected, encouraged his fellow bishops to repudiate the authority of the archbishop. Gilbert was twice excommunicated by Becket, but on both these and other occasions he showed great dexterity in detaching the pope from the cause of the exile. It was chiefly due to his influence that Henry avoided an open conflict with Rome of the kind which John afterward provoked. Gilbert was one of the bishops whose excommunication in 1170 provoked the king's knights to murder Becket, but he cannot be reproached with any share in the crime. His later years were uneventful, though he enjoyed great influence with the king and among his fellow bishops.

BIBLIOGRAPHY.—Gilbert's letters were edited by J. A. Giles in *Patres Ecclesiae Anglicanae*, 2 vol. (1845). *Materials for the History of Thomas Becket*, ed. by J. C. Robertson, "Rolls Series" (1875-85); K. Norgate, *England Under the Angevin Kings* (1887); D. Knowles, *The Episcopal Colleagues of Archbishop Thomas Becket* (1951).
(H. W. C. D.)

GILD: see GUILD.

GILDAS (GILDUS) (d. 570?), British saint, author of the *De excidio et conquestu Britanniae* ("The Ruin of Britain"), one of the few sources for the confused and uncertain history of Britain in the 6th century, was born, if a late biography is to be trusted, in Strathclyde. He probably studied under St. Illtyd in Pembrokeshire and made a journey to Ireland; an alleged visit to Rome is hardly credible. He certainly founded a monastery in Brittany, called after him St. Gildas de Rhuys, near which he is said to have died. Gildas' own writings mention Maelgwn, king of Anglesey (d. c. 547), as still alive; but a certainly corrupt sentence in chapter 26 of the *De excidio* cannot be used to date his own birth.

Fragments of correspondence, a penitential manual and a magical poem (called *Lorica*) against attacks from demons have been attributed to him, the last probably wrongly. His most famous work, however, is the *De excidio*, a historical and moralistic tract. It is written in very euphuistic, but for the time and the place remarkably grammatical, Latin, and catalogues the sins of five British kings who can be located in Cornwall and Wales, and of priests generally. The charges are supported by a mass of scriptural quotations of some value as their text is not that of the Vulgate. These denunciations are preceded by a summary of British history up to the battle of Mons Badonicus (c. 500). It is the earliest authority for the British appeal to the Roman general Aetius, *i.e.*, the letter called the "Groans of the Britons," sent probably between 446 and 453; for the invitation of the English by the British king Vortigern (though names are not given), and for the battle of Mons Badonicus itself, in connection with which Ambrosius Aurelianus is mentioned but not Arthur. Gildas considered that the Britons deserved their fate—to be "slaughtered in heaps" or forced into emigration.

Since the historical summary of the *De excidio* seems to date the building of both Hadrian's Wall and the Antonine Wall (qq.v.) to about A.D. 400, historians have tended to dismiss it as valueless. But it is possible to argue that Gildas was making a blundering effort to correlate certain casual references to Britain in continental sources such as Orosius with native traditions of some value.

BIBLIOGRAPHY.—Gildas' works (excluding *Lorica*) are ed. by T. Mommsen in the *Monumenta Germaniae historica* series, *Chronica minora*, vol. iii (1898) and (including *Lorica*) with Eng. trans. by H. Williams, *Gildae de excidio Britanniae*, "Cymmrodorion Record Series," vol iii (1899-1901)..The historical portions of the *De excidio* have been trans. by A. W. Wade-Evans, *Nennius* (1938). See also C. F. C. Hawkes (1956); C. E. Stevens, "The Jutes of Kent," in J. D. B. Harden (ed.), *Dark-Age Britain*, vol. xxxv (1956); C. E. Stevens, "Marcus, Gratian, Constantine," *Athenaeum*, vol. xxxv (1957); P. Grosjean, "Notes d'hagiographie Celtique," *Analecta Bollandiana*, vol. lxxv (1957); C. E. Stevens, "Gildas sapiens," *English Historical Review*, vol. lvi (1941).
(C. E. S.)

GILDERSLEEVE, BASIL LANNEAU (1831-1924), U.S. philologist, who was recognized by many as the greatest classical scholar in America, was born in Charleston, S.C., on Oct. 22, 1831. He studied at Princeton, Berlin, Bonn and Göttingen, was professor at the University of Virginia from 1856 to 1876, and in 1876 became professor of Greek at the newly founded Johns Hopkins university, from which he retired in 1915. In 1880 *The American Journal of Philology* was established under his editorial charge, and he contributed many articles, particularly on grammar.

He published a *Latin Grammar* (1867) marked by lucidity of order and mastery of grammatical theory. He edited *The Olympian and Pythian Odes of Pindar* (1885), with a brilliant and valuable introduction. His edition of *The Apologies of Justin Martyr* (1877)—to use his own words—he used unblushingly as a repository for his syntactical formulas. A collection, *Essays and Studies, Educational and Literary*, appeared in 1890. His mastery of Greek syntax could scarcely be equaled, though unfortunately he did not cover the field thoroughly; the largest portion is in his *Syntax of Classical Greek From Homer to Demosthenes* (with C. W. E. Miller, Part I, 1900; Part II, 1911). He died in Baltimore, Md., on Jan. 9, 1924.
(S. Ln.)

GILDING, the art of decorating wood, metal, plaster, glass or other objects with a covering or design of gold in leaf or powder form. The term also embraces the similar application of silver, palladium, aluminum and copper alloys.

The earliest of historical peoples had masterly gilders, as evidenced by the overlays of thin gold leaf on the royal mummy cases and furniture of ancient Egypt. From early times, the Chinese ornamented wood, pottery and textiles with beautiful designs in gold. The Greeks not only gilded wood, masonry and marble sculpture but also fire-gilded metal by applying a gold amalgam to it and driving off the mercury with heat, leaving a coating of gold on the metal surface. From the Greeks the Romans acquired the art that made their temples and palaces resplendent with brilliant gilding. Extant examples of ancient gilding reveal that the gold was applied to a ground prepared with chalk or marble dust and an animal size or glue.

Beating mint gold into leaves as thin as $\frac{1}{280000}$ in. is done largely by hand although machines are utilized to some extent. After being cut to a standard $3\frac{3}{8}$ in. square, the leaves are packed between the tissue paper leaves of small books, ready for the gilder's use. (*See also* GOLDBEATING.)

The many substances to which the gilder can apply his art, and the novel and beautiful effects he can produce, may require special modifications and applications of his methods and materials. Certain basic procedures, however, are pertinent to all types of gilding. For example, the ground to be gilded must be carefully prepared by priming. Flat paints, lacquers or sealing glues are used, according to the nature of the ground material. Metals subject to corrosion may be primed, and protected, by red lead or iron oxide paints. With pencil or chalk the gilder lays out his design on the ground after the ground has been prepared and is thoroughly dry. Patterns may also be laid down by pouncing powdered chalk or dry pigment through paper containing perforations made with pricking wheels mounted on swivels; the swivel arrangement permits the attainment of the most intricate of designs.

To create an adhesive surface to which the gold will be securely held, the area to be gilded is sized. A variety of sizes and appropriate brushes for applying them are available to the gilder. The substances used include oils, glues, varnishes, commercially prepared japanner's gold sizes and water size; the latter consists of isinglass or gelatin in aqueous solution and is used particularly in connection with gilding on glass. The type of size used depends on the kind of surface to be gilded and on whether it is desirable for the size to dry quickly or slowly. When the size has dried enough so that it just adheres to the fingertips it is ready to receive and retain the gold leaf or powder.

Gold leaf may be rolled onto the sized surface from the tissue book. Generally, however, the gilder holds the book firmly in his left hand with the tissue folded back to expose as much leaf as is needed and detaches that amount with a pointed tool, such as a sharpened skewer. He then picks up the leaf segment with his gilder's tip, a brush of camel's hair set in a thin cardboard holder, and carefully transfers it to its place in his design. The leaf is held to the tip by static electricity, which the gilder generates by brushing the tip gently over his hair. For some gilding operations the gilder uses a cushion to hold his pieces of leaf. This is a rectangular piece of wood, about 9 x 6 in. in size, that is padded with flannel and covered with dressed calfskin; a parchment shield around one end protects the delicate leaf from disturbance by drafts of air. When the gilding is completed, the leaf-covered area should be pounced with a wad of soft cotton of surgical grade. Rubbing with cotton burnishes the gold to a high lustre. Application of a gilder's burnisher, i.e., a highly polished agate stone set in a handle, also imparts a fine, high finish to the metal. Loose bits of gold, or skewings, may be removed from the finished work with a camel's hair brush.

Leaf gold may be powdered by being rubbed through a fine-mesh sieve. Powdered gold is so costly, however, that bronze powders have been substituted almost universally for the precious metal. Thin pieces of bronze, usually of the type comprised of copper and zinc, may be very finely flaked by being struck on an anvil by hammers that rise by cam action and fall by gravity, rotating on their axes as they fall to exert a burnishing as well as a flaking action on the metal. Bronze powders are produced in a variety of colours, including various shades of gold.

Metallic powders may be pounced on a sized surface with a soft material such as velvet or plush, or they may be combined with a lacquer or with a chemical base and then applied as metallic paint. A finishing coat of clear lacquer prevents discoloration of the metallic surface by oxidation.

When gold leaf is employed in the gilding of domes and the roofs of buildings, it is used in ribbon form. (E. L. Y.)

GILDO, the name of a Moorish potentate who rebelled against Rome in A.D. 397-398. He had in 375 helped the Romans to crush his brother Firmus. As a reward he was eventually appointed count of Africa and master of the soldiers. He refused to help Theodosius I in his struggle with the usurper Eugenius, and in 397 he prevented the African grain ships from sailing to Rome. The senate declared Gildo a public enemy and in the spring of 398 sent a force to Africa under the command of Mascezel, a brother of Gildo. Little effort was required to crush the rebel; between Theveste (Tebessa, in northeastern Algeria) and Ammaedara (Haidra in Tunisia) Gildo's forces, said to number 70,000, melted away. Their leader tried to escape by sea but was driven ashore at Thabraca (Tabarka, on the north coast) and executed. The swiftness of Mascezel's victory was unwelcome to Stilicho, at that time the effective ruler of the west; and when Mascezel was drowned shortly after his return to Italy, Stilicho was believed to have had him murdered. Gildo's property was so vast that after his death the Roman government had to appoint a special official to administer it. The war against Gildo forms the subject of one of the poems of Claudian, in which the achievements of Mascezel are played down. (E. A. T.)

GILEAD, an area of ancient Palestine east of the Jordan river, corresponding to the northwestern sector of the modern kingdom of Jordan. The region is bounded in the north by the Yarmuk river and in the southwest by what were known in ancient times as the "plains of Moab." It is about 35 mi. long from north to south and 25 mi. from east to west. To the east there is no definite boundary. The decreasing rainfall gradually makes cultivation and finally even grazing impossible. It is a highland area, averaging 2,500 ft. and reaching over 3,300 ft. in the "Gilead dome." Gilead is divided into northern and southern sections by the Jabbok river (Nahr az Zarqa), the valley of which is deep and steep-sided. The territory receives excellent rainfall and heavy summer dew. In ancient times it included rich forest areas, fine grazing lands and good vineyard and grain districts. Sometimes "Gilead" is used in a wider and more general sense for all the region east of the Jordan river.

The first appearance of the name Gilead is in the account of the last meeting of Jacob and Laban, in "the hill country of Gilead" (Gen. xxxi, 21-22). After Israel had defeated Sihon and Og, the tribes of Reuben and Gad were attracted by the good grazing land there, so this area was assigned to them and to the half-tribe of Manasseh. Reuben was in the south, Gad in the centre and half-Manasseh in the north, although the boundaries, uncertain in any case, fluctuated with the relative strengths of the tribes and with the changing fortunes of Israel and its enemies. Ammon was located southeast of Gilead, generally east of the north-south section of the Jabbok river. However, when Ammon was prosperous, it expanded to include good sections of southern Gilead. Moab, usually well to the south, also on occasion occupied southern Gilead. Gilead likewise felt the shock of Syrian onslaughts and the rolling tide of Assyrian invasion; Tiglath-pileser III established the Assyrian province of Gal'azu (Gilead) about 733 B.C.

Gideon swept back the hosts of Midian apparently on the soil of Gilead (Judg. viii). Jephthah the Gileadite smote the Ammonites from Aroer to Minnith (Judg. xi, 33) and then, using the key word shibboleth, detected and slaughtered the Ephraimites at the fords of the Jordan (Judg. xii). In Gilead, Saul's son Ishbosheth was made king by Abner. To Gilead fled Absalom from the anger of his father, David, as did David later flee from Absalom. Gilead was the home of Elijah, and Jesus at least twice visited the area of Peraea, the land beyond the Jordan. There are extensive remains in Gilead from Roman and later periods.

The "balm of Gilead" is probably to be identified with mastic, the resin furnished by Pistachia lentiscus; it is mentioned in the Amarna tablets (14th century B.C.). (E. D. GR.)

GILES, SAINT, patron of Saint-Gilles, a town in southern France (département of Gard) on the site of an ancient abbey claiming his relics and protected by Charlemagne. One of the 14 Holy Helpers, or auxiliary saints, Giles was venerated throughout Europe as patron of cripples, beggars and blacksmiths; and pilgrims to his tomb contributed much to the prosperity of the medieval town and abbey. The saint's symbols, the hind and arrow, refer to famous but conflicting legends based upon a 10th-century uncritical biography which claims that he, a young Athenian aristocrat, after visiting St. Caesarius of Arles (d. 543) lived as a hermit until wounded by Flavius, king of the Goths, who was pursuing a hind that had fled to Giles for safety. Later Flavius built an abbey, making Giles abbot. His feast day is Sept. 1.

See F. Brittain, Saint Giles (1928); H. Thurston and D. Attwater, Butler's Lives of the Saints, vol. iii, pp. 457-458 (1956). (A. B. WR.)

GILES OF ROME (Lat. AEGIDIUS ROMANUS) (c. 1245-1316), Italian theologian and philosopher, known honorifically as doctor fundatissimus ("the best-grounded teacher"). The intellectual leader of the Augustinian hermits, Giles was probably a pupil of Thomas Aquinas in Paris, and for eight years refused to submit to the ecclesiastical condemnation of Aquinas' philosophical doctrines (1277). Giles was general of his order from 1292 to 1295 and archbishop of Bourges from 1295 to 1316. Developing in an original way Augustinian and Thomistic doctrines, he maintained that God's existence is both directly evident to the human mind and demonstrable from sense experience; that essence and existence are distinct (his polemic with Henry of Ghent became famous), both being "things" at the same level, that is, by participation in God's ideas and in God's existence respectively; and that the pope must have direct political power over the whole of mankind. His vast literary production includes commentaries on Aristotle, on the De causis, on Peter Lombard's Sentences and on parts of the Bible; theological works (Quodlibeta and Theoremata, notably the Theoremata de esse et essentia, ed. by E. Hocedez [1930]); political treatises (De ecclesiastica potestate against Philip IV of France, ed. by R. Scholz [1929], and the very popular De regimine principum); and Errores philosophorum, edited by J. Koch with English translation by J. Riedl (1955). Numerous editions of collected and individual works of Giles appeared in the 15th, 16th and 17th centuries; for a catalogue see G. Bruni, Le opere di Egidio Romano (1936).

BIBLIOGRAPHY.—E. Hocedez, introduction to the Theoremata de esse et essentia (1930); B. Geyer, Die patristische und scholastische Philosophie, new ed. (1951); E. Gilson, History of Christian Philosophy in the Middle Ages, Eng. trans. (1955). (L. M.-PO.)

GILES, PETER (1860-1935), Scottish comparative philologist, who was master of Emmanuel college, Cambridge, from 1911 until his death, was born near Aberdeen on Oct. 20, 1860. He was educated at the local parish school, the University of Aberdeen, Freiburg im Breisgau, and Gonville and Caius college, Cambridge, where he took a first class in the classical tripos, won a large number of scholarships (including two for New Testament and international law) and was appointed reader in comparative philology in the university in 1891. He was the author of a *Short Manual of Comparative Philology for Classical Students* (1895) and of many articles in works of reference. A man of strict integrity, Giles managed the affairs of Emmanuel college in a businesslike way and raised its status in Cambridge by securing only good appointments among its fellows. He died on Sept. 17, 1935, at Cambridge.

(J. WH.)

See an appreciation by J. Whatmough in *Word Study*, vol. 30, no. 1, pp. 1–3 (1954).

GILGAL ("stone circle"), the name of several places in western Palestine (modern Jordan and Israel) mentioned in the Old Testament. The most important is that located near Jericho (Josh. iv, 19; xv, 7), which served as an encampment for the 12 tribes upon entry into Palestine. Josephus recorded that it was ten stadia and Jerome that it was two Roman miles from Jericho, but neither identified the site. F. M. Abel placed Gilgal at Khirbet en-Netheleh 3 mi. S.E. of Jericho; James Muilenburg placed it near Khirbet el Mefjer, north of modern Jericho. The exact location remains uncertain. A shrine of the God of Israel was located there. Another Gilgal, mentioned in the Hebrew text of Josh. xii, 23, has been identified as modern Jiljulieh in the neighbourhood of Shechem (Nablus). A third Gilgal may have been in the foothills of Samaria, an important site at the junction of the great coastal route and the road to Shechem (Deut. xi, 30). Numerous Old Testament references to a Gilgal (cf. Amos iv, 4; Hos. xii, 11) are not sufficiently specific to locate the site of an important cult centre.

See F. M. Abel, *Géographie de la Palestine*, vol. ii, p. 337 (1938); J. Muilenburg, *Bulletin of the American Schools of Oriental Research*, 140:11–27 (1935).

(J. S. I.)

GILGAMESH, EPIC OF, one of the most important literary products in the Akkadian language (*q.v.*), relates the story of Gilgamesh, the best known of all Sumerian heroes. More tales are told of him than of any other. None lived so long in local memory and none dared so mightily as he and his friend Enkidu. Each adventure, however imaginary, makes a good tale. The whole has been described as an Odyssey, but an Odyssey of a king who did not want to die. The storyteller takes his audience not only to danger spots on earth but also to the final rendezvous of kings and commoners. He provides one of the very rare indications of local beliefs as to the state of the dead. To Bible students the account of the deluge is of particular interest. Students of comparative literature admit the possibility that the Gilgamesh story, current in Asia Minor in Hittite and Hurrian languages, may have influenced the Greek *Odyssey*. Similarities are noted especially between the Calypso and Siduri episodes. Themes from the Gilgamesh epic are said to occur also in the folklore of the Pacific.

The Text.—The fullest text extant is that of the 12 incomplete tablets in the Akkadian language found at Nineveh, in the library of Ashurbanipal, king of Assyria (669–630? B.C.). Long before this date, however, Gilgamesh was celebrated in story. Five short poems in the Sumerian language are known from tablets which were written sometime in the first half of the 2nd millennium B.C. To these have been given the descriptive titles: Gilgamesh and the land of the living; Gilgamesh and the bull of heaven; Gilgamesh and Agga of Kish; Gilgamesh, Enkidu and the underworld; the death of Gilgamesh. There is no echo of the third and fifth poems in the Nineveh version. A tablet of about 1800 B.C., in the Akkadian Old Babylonian language, found at Sippar in Babylonia, contains parts of tablets ii, iii and x of the 7th-century Nineveh version. From the Boğazköy Hittite archives (c. 1400 B.C.) have come a text in Akkadian, some fragments in Hittite and a fragment in Hurrian. This last is useless because largely unintelligible, but the others help to fill gaps in the final versions. In about 1200 B.C., the poet Sin-leqe-unnini, who lived in Uruk (biblical Erech, *q.v.*), made an Akkadian version of the traditions concerning Gilgamesh. Of this the Nineveh version may well be a copy. Such gaps as occur in this final version can be partly filled by use of the fragments mentioned from the 2nd millennium B.C., and from other fragments of the 7th and 6th centuries B.C. found at Uruk itself, at Ashur (Assur), one-time capital of Assyria, and at Sultantepe, near Harran in northern Mesopotamia. There are differences where these tablets overlap with the Ninevite version, but the essentials of the story are not in doubt.

Gilgamesh and Enkidu.—The Gilgamesh of the poems and the epic was probably the Gilgamesh who ruled at Uruk sometime during the first half of the 3rd millennium B.C. at the same period as Agga of Kish, and is mentioned in the much later Sumerian list of kings as reigning after the flood (*see* BABYLONIA AND ASSYRIA). The name Gilgamesh is Sumerian and is variously translated by scholars as "father, hero" and "the old one, the hero." There is no historical evidence for the exploits narrated in poems and epic.

Enkidu, in Sumerian texts the servant, but in the epic the friend and companion, of Gilgamesh, is not otherwise known. His name also has been variously interpreted: as identical with the deity Enkimdu ("lord of the dike and the canal"), and as meaning "lord of the reed-marsh" and even "Enki (*i.e.,* Ea) has created."

The Story.—Tablet i of the Nineveh version of the epic begins with a prologue in praise of Gilgamesh, part divine and part human, the great builder and warrior, who knows all things on land and sea. In order to curb his oppressive rule the god Anu causes the creation of Enkidu, a wild man who at first lives among animals. Soon, however, he is initiated into city-going ways by a courtesan and goes to Uruk, where Gilgamesh awaits him. Tablet ii, known chiefly from an Old Babylonian text, describes a trial of strength between the two men in which Gilgamesh is the victor. In Tablets iii–v they set out together against Humbaba (Huwawa), the divinely appointed guardian of a remote cedar forest, but the result of the engagement is not recorded in the surviving fragments. Tablet vi tells how Gilgamesh, now returned to Uruk, rejects the marriage proposal of Ishtar, the goddess of love, and then, with Enkidu's aid, kills the divine bull that she sends to destroy him. Tablet vii begins, according to the Hittite version, with Enkidu's account of a dream in which the gods Anu, Ea and Shamash decide on the instigation of Enlil that of the two friends it is Enkidu who must die for slaying the bull. Enkidu then falls ill, and dreams of the "house of dust" which awaits him. Tablet viii relates Gilgamesh's lament for his friend and the state funeral of Enkidu. Tablets ix and x describe Gilgamesh's dangerous journey in search of Utnapishtim, the survivor of the Babylonian flood, in order to learn from him how to escape death. In Tablet xi Utnapishtim tells Gilgamesh the story of the flood and shows him where to find a plant which renews youth. But after Gilgamesh has obtained this plant it is seized by a serpent, and he returns saddened to Uruk. Tablet xii, which is an appendage to the epic, relates the loss of objects called *pukku* and *mikku* (perhaps "drum" and "drumstick") given to Gilgamesh by Ishtar according to a Sumerian legend. The epic ends with the return of Enkidu, who promises to recover these objects and gives a grim report on "the ways of the underworld."

BIBLIOGRAPHY.—Eng. trans. by R. C. Thompson, *The Epic of Gilgamesh* (1930), by A. Heidel, *The Gilgamesh Epic and the Old Testament Parallels* (1946), and by E. A. Speiser in J. B. Pritchard (ed.), *Ancient Near Eastern Texts Relating to the Old Testament*, 2nd ed. (1955). German trans. by Albert Schott, *Das Gilgamesch-Epos* (1958); Italian trans. with exhaustive bibliography down to 1956 by G. Furlani, *Miti Babilonesi e Assiri* (no date).

(T. FH.)

NATIONAL MUSEUMS OF FRANCE

GILGAMESH HOLDING CAPTURED LION. BAS-RELIEF FROM KHORSABAD, 8TH CENTURY B.C. IN THE LOUVRE

GILGIT, a territory in the northwest of Kashmir containing Gilgit town, gives its name also to (1) the Gilgit river; (2) the Gilgit *wazarat* lying to the south; and (3) the Gilgit agency now comprising four political districts of Gupis, Punyal (Punial), Ashkuman (Ishkuman) and Yasin, two subdivisions of Gilgit and Astor, two states of Hunza and Nagar and the subagency of Chilas. These territories extend toward Chitral, Afghanistan, the U.S.S.R. and Sinkiang (China). Since 1947 the whole area has been administered by Pakistan.

Physical Characteristics.—The terrain is extremely mountainous, being near the junction of the Hindu Kush and Karakoram ranges. The glaciers of Nagar are enclosed between the spurs of the Muz Tagh Ata range on the northeast and the frontier peaks of Kashmir (terminating with Rakaposhi, 25,550 ft.) on the southwest, and mass themselves in an almost uninterrupted series from the Hunza valley to the base of those gigantic peaks which stand about Mt. Godwin Austen (K2). From its utmost head to the foot of the Hispar, overhanging the valley above Nagar, the length of the glacial ice bed known under the name of Biafo is said to measure about 90 mi. Throughout the mountain region of Hunza and Nagar the valleys are deeply sunk between mountain ranges which are nowhere less than 15,000 ft. in altitude and average above 20,000 ft. As a rule these valleys are bare of vegetation.

One of the oldest recorded routes through this country is that which connects Mastuj on the Chitral valley with Gilgit, through the Shandur pass, and now forms the high road between Gilgit and Chitral. Each of the northern affluents of the main Gilgit stream is headed by a pass, or a group of passes, leading either to the dumbash Pamir and the Gilgit basin. They are all about the same height, 15,000 ft. All are passable only for short seasons.

The Gilgit river joins the Indus a few miles above the little post of Bunji. Just below Bunji the Astor river joins the Indus from the southeast, and this deep pine-clad valley indicates the continuation of the highroad from Gilgit to the south, via the Tragbal and Burzil passes. Another well-known route connecting Gilgit with Pakistan lies across the Babusar pass (13,690 ft.) linking the picturesque Hazara valley of Kagan to Chilas, Chilas (4,150 ft.) being on the Indus, 50 mi. below Bunji. This is a more direct connection between Gilgit and the plains of Pakistan than that afforded by the Kashmir route via Gurais and Astor, which involves two considerable passes—the Tragbal (11,586 ft.) and the Burzil (13,775 ft.). Like the Kashmir route, it is now defined by a good military road by which Gilgit is within 250 mi. of the railway at Hasan Abdal.

The People.—Within the wider limits of the Gilgit agency are many mixed races, speaking different languages, but usually classed together under the name Dard. One of the most distinctive tongues is the Burushaski language (q.v.). Between Chitral and the Indus the Dards of Dardistan are chiefly Ashkuns (or Yeshkuns) and Shins, and it would appear from the proportions in which these people occupy the country that they must have primarily moved up from the valley of the Indus in successive waves of conquest, first the Ashkuns and then the Shins. The Shins are of Hindu origin and spread northward and eastward as far as Baltistan, where they abutted the aboriginal Tatar population of the Asian highlands. The *wazarat* of Gilgit had a population (1961) of 176,242. The Shins are the dominant race whose language Shina is widely spoken. This is one of the so-called Pisacha languages, an archaic Aryan group intermediate between the Iranian and the Sanskritic (*see* DARDIC LANGUAGES).

In general appearance and dress all the mountain-bred peoples extending through these northern districts are very similar. They are well built and of a fair complexion. Thick felt coats reaching below the knee, loose "pajamas" with cloth puttees and boots are almost universal, the distinguishing feature in their costume being the felt cap worn close to the head and rolled up round the edges. They are fond of polo and dancing.

History.—The Dards (Daradae) were located by Ptolemy with surprising accuracy on the west of the upper Indus, beyond the headwaters of the Swat river (Gr. Soastus), and north of the Gandarae, *i.e.*, the Gandharans, who occupied Peshawar and the country north of it. This region was traversed by two Chinese pilgrims, Fa-Hsien, coming from the north about A.D. 400, and Hsüan Tsang, ascending from Swat, in A.D. 629, and both left records of their journeys. Gilgit, as far back as tradition goes, was ruled by rajas of a dynasty called Trakane. When this family became extinct the valley was desolated by successive invasions of neighbouring rulers, and in the 20 or 30 years ending with 1842 there had been five dynastic revolutions. The Sikhs entered Gilgit about 1842 and kept a garrison there. When Kashmir was made over to Maharaja Gulab Singh of Jammu in 1846 by Lord Hardinge the Gilgit claims were transferred with it, and a boundary commission was sent that included the first Englishmen to visit Gilgit. The Dogras (Gulab Singh's people) in 1860 were driven out for eight years and 2,000 of their men were exterminated. In 1860 they returned to Gilgit and took Yasin twice, but did not hold it. They also, in 1866, invaded Darel, one of the most secluded Dard states, to the south of the Gilgit basin, but withdrew again. In 1889, in order to guard against the advance of Russia, the British government, acting as the suzerain power of Kashmir, established the Gilgit agency. On the British withdrawal in 1947 the place of the political agent was taken by a Kashmiri governor. In Nov. 1947 the Gilgit scouts rose in revolt, imprisoned the governor and proclaimed Gilgit's accession to Pakistan.

Administration and Economy.—When the fighting between India and Pakistan ceased in Jammu and Kashmir (q.v.) in 1949, a cease-fire line was established. The whole of Gilgit, including the agency and the *wazarat*, lay north of this line and from that date it has been administered directly by the government of Pakistan which appoints a political agent as head of the administration. There are assistant political agents for Gilgit and Astor subdivisions and Chilas subagency. The two states are administered by the respective rulers in accordance with tribal custom through local elective assemblies and are under the direct control of the political agent. The four political districts are administered by governors who are also under the control of the political agent.

There are a high school and a girls' high school at Gilgit and middle schools at Astor, Gupis and Hunza, and more than 60 primary schools in the agency. There is a hospital at Gilgit and a number of dispensaries in other areas.

The population is Muslim, mainly of the Shi'ah sect.

The fields are carefully tilled and irrigated. Rice, wheat and other food grains are grown. Fruits are plentiful. In Astor cultivation is precarious because of the high altitude. Weaving of woolen cloth (*pattu*) is the chief industry. Essential commodities are carried by air from Rawalpindi to Gilgit.

GILGIT TOWN. The little hill station of Gilgit (4,890 ft. above sea level), the headquarters of the agency, spreads itself in terraces above the right bank of the river nearly opposite the opening leading to Hunza. It nestles under the cliffs of the Hindu Kush which separates it on the south from the savage mountain wilderness of Darel and Kohistan. Mountain roads radiate into the surrounding valleys and its geographical position now, as in ancient times, has made Gilgit the nodal point for the area. A suspension bridge connects Gilgit with the left bank of the river. The climate is cool and dry. The ancient name of the site under its Hindu rulers was Sargin. Later it was known as Gilit, which the Sikhs and Dogras corrupted into Gilgit. To the country people it is familiar still as Gilit or Sargin Gilit. The remains of ancient stone buildings and Buddhist carvings suggest that Gilgit was once a centre of Buddhism.

The old Buddhist route between Gilgit and the Peshawar plain passed through the gorges and clefts of the unexplored Darel valley to Thakot under the northern spurs of the Black mountain.

BIBLIOGRAPHY.—G. W. Leitner, *Dardistan* (1895); J. Biddulph, *The Tribes of the Hindu Kush* (1880); E. F. Knight, *Where Three Empires Meet* (1892); W. Lawrence, *The Kashmir Valley* (1895); A. G. A.

Durand, *Making a Frontier* (1899); Government publication, Delhi, *Memorandum on Indian States* (1936). (K. S. AD.)

GILIA, a genus of about 100 species, chiefly of the family *Polemoniaceae*, a few of which are used in the flower garden. *Gilia* species are mostly native to western North America, a few to South America; they include annual, biennial and perennial sorts that show much variation in growth habit, inflorescence and flower colour.

The following are popular garden plants: *G. capitata*, an annual of about two feet with dense globose heads of light-blue flowers; *G. rubra*, commonly known as standing cypress, a common, leafy-stemmed garden perennial, three to five inches high, with a narrow panicle of externally bright scarlet flowers that are yellowish and dotted with red on the inside; *G. aggregata*, known as scarlet or skyrocket gilia, a biennial, one to three feet high with showy scarlet to white flowers; and *G. tricolor*, known as bird's-eyes, an annual one to three feet, with loose clusters of fragrant flowers with yellowish tubes, purple throats and lilac or violet roundish corolla lobes. All are of easy culture, and even the biennials and perennials will often flower from seed within a single season.

(J. M. BL.)

GILL, SIR DAVID (1843–1914), British astronomer, skilful observer of solar and stellar parallax and pioneer in the use of photography for mapping the stars, was born at Aberdeen, Scot., on June 12, 1843, and educated at Marischal college and at the University of Aberdeen. In 1872 he became director of Lord Lindsay's private observatory at Dunecht near Aberdeen, whence he undertook expeditions to observe the transit of Venus at Mauritius in 1874 and the close approach to the earth of Mars at Ascension Island in 1877.

In 1879 Gill was appointed H.M. astronomer at the Cape of Good Hope in succession to E. J. Stone. In 1888 and 1889 he carried out, with the co-operation of many astronomers, a program of intensive observation with the heliometer of selected minor planets. This led to the first determination (1901) of the solar parallax with modern accuracy ($8''.804 \pm 0''.0046$). While at the Cape observatory Gill completed a series of photographic observations (1885–89), introduced observations of stellar parallax with the heliometer, and served as one of the original council for the International Astrographic Chart and Catalogue. He was made knight commander of the Order of the Bath in 1900.

Gill died in London on Jan. 24, 1914.
(O. J. E.)

GILL, (ARTHUR) ERIC (ROWTON) (1882–1940), English sculptor, engraver, typographical designer and essayist, was born on Feb. 22, 1882, at Brighton, Sussex. The family moved in 1897 to Chichester, where Eric spent two years in an art school. In 1899, he was articled to a London architect but in 1902 he turned to letter carving after studying in his spare time at the new Central School of Art with Edward Johnston, a pioneer in the revival of lettering. From then until 1910, he earned his living as a carver of tombstones, although by 1909 he had turned to figure sculpture. A "Madonna and Child" (1910) brought him into public notice through the efforts of Roger Fry. On Jan. 20, 1911, Gill held his first exhibition at the Chenil gallery, London; its success established him as a sculptor. On his 31st birthday in 1913, Gill and his wife were received into the Roman Catholic Church and he was commissioned to carve the stations of the cross for Westminster cathedral (1914–18), London. These bas-reliefs, each 5 ft. 8 in. by 5 ft. 8 in. in size, were cut in Hoptonwood stone, a stone he helped make fashionable in the 1920s and 1930s. It was in this material that he carved his most famous figure, the torso "Mankind" (1928; Tate gallery). In 1931 he won a commission to do the reliefs "Prospero and Ariel" over the main entrance of Broadcasting house, London, and in 1935–38 he was commissioned by the British government to provide the three bas-reliefs entitled "The Creation of Adam" in the lobby of the council hall of the Palace of Nations at Geneva; the lobby was the British government's contribution to the League of Nations.

Gill was equally successful in his work for printers, particularly in his partnership with H. D. C. (Douglas) Pepler in their founding of the St. Dominic's press in 1915. Gill not only contributed wood engravings and lettering for the press but also began his pro-vocative writings on the relationship of religion to the workman and art. In 1924 he was asked to do engravings for the Golden Cockerel press, and his work there brought him international fame. The best remembered of his hundreds of engravings and dozens of books is the "Four Gospels" (1931), printed from type expressly designed by him for the "Four Gospels". At this time he formed, with his son-in-law René Hague, a private press, at his home at Pigotts, Buckinghamshire, and there in 1931 he printed his controversial essay on printing, "Typography."

Type faces he designed included Perpetua, his most notable book face, in 1925; Gill Sans, a popular printers' type, in 1927; Joanna, designed for his own use in 1930 and recut for popular use in 1958; and Bunyan, designed in 1934 but recut for machine use and renamed Pilgrim in 1953.

Gill was made an associate of the Royal Academy in 1937 and of the Royal Society of British Sculptors in 1938. He died at Uxbridge Nov. 17, 1940, and is buried in the country churchyard of Speen near Pigotts.

BIBLIOGRAPHY.—J. K. M. Rothenstein, *Eric Gill* (1927); J. Thorp, *E.G.* (1929); E. Gill, *Autobiography* (1940); W. Shewring (ed.), *Letters of E.G.* (1948); Evan R. Gill, *Bibliography of Eric Gill* (1953), *A List of Eric Gill's Inscriptional Work* (1963).
(A. SN.)

GILL (BRANCHIA), the name given to any structure specially adapted for aquatic respiration. The essential features of gills are thinness and large surface of exposure to facilitate exchange of respiratory gases; hence they are generally filamentous, feathery or plate-shaped body projections. Gills occur in some annelids (*e.g.*, tube-dwelling marine worms), most mollusks (*e.g.*, oysters, squid), the larger crustaceans (*e.g.*, crayfish), aquatic larvae of insects, almost all fishes, most larval and a few adult amphibians (*e.g.*, salamander) and perhaps some aquatic arachnids. Gills often have accessory functions, as producing food-concentrating currents and brooding of young (as in certain fresh-water bivalve mollusks). (*See* ANNELIDA; CRUSTACEA; FISH; MOLLUSK.)

The word is also applied to structures resembling the gills of fishes, such as the wattles of a fowl or the radiating films on the underside of a mushroom.

See also references under "Gill" in the Index.

GILLES LI MUISIS (LE MUISET) (*c.* 1272–1352), French chronicler, was born probably at Tournai, and in 1289 entered the Benedictine abbey of St. Martin in his native city, becoming prior of this house about 1329, and abbot two years later. Gilles wrote two Latin chronicles, *Chronicon majus* and *Chronicon minus*, dealing with the history of the world from the creation until 1352. This work, edited by J. J. de Smet, in *Corpus chronicorum Flandriae, tome* ii (1841), and by H. Lemaître for the Société de l'Histoire de France (1906), is valuable for the history of northern France and Flanders during the first half of the 14th century.

Gilles also wrote some French poems, and these *Poésies de Gilles li Muisis* were published by Baron Kervyn de Lettenhove (1882).

GILLESPIE, GEORGE (1613–1648), one of the leading Scottish covenanting ministers, was born at Kirkcaldy on Jan. 21, 1613, where his father, John Gillespie, was parish minister, and was educated at the University of St. Andrews. As private chaplain to the earl of Cassillis he wrote his first work, *A Dispute Against the English Popish Ceremonies Obtruded Upon the Church of Scotland* (1637), which was burned by order of the privy council; his later publications were also highly controversial and hostile toward state domination of the church. In 1640 he was ordained minister of Wemyss (Fife) and in the same year was a member of the Glasgow general assembly, before which he preached (Nov. 21) a sermon against royal interference in matters ecclesiastical. In 1640 he accompanied the commissioners of the peace to England as one of their chaplains and was one of the first systematically to expound Presbyterian ideals to the English Puritans. As a result he was moved to Edinburgh in 1642 and helped to frame the covenant. In 1643 he was appointed one of the four Scottish commissioners to the Westminster assembly, where he displayed great debating power. In 1645 he drafted the Act of Assembly sanctioning the directory of public worship, and in London he also contributed to the Westminster confession of faith. Gillespie was elected moderator of the assembly in 1648, but died at Kirkcaldy a few months later on Dec. 17, 1648.

See W. M. Campbell, *The Triumph of Presbyterianism* (1958).

GILLESPIE, THOMAS (1708–1774), Scottish minister and one of the founders of the Relief Church, was born at Clearburn, Duddingston, in 1708. He was ordained at Northampton in Jan. 1741, having studied for a time in England. In Sept. 1741 he was inducted to the parish of Carnock, Fife. In 1752 he was a victim of the controversy, following the Patronage act of 1712 (see Scot-LAND, CHURCH OF), over the right of congregations to approve the choice of ministers. Having absented himself from the meetings of presbytery held in order to induct an unacceptable presentee as minister of Inverkeithing, he was deposed by the assembly for maintaining that the refusal of the local presbytery to act against the wish of the parish was justified. The case was used by the assembly finally to subordinate inferior to superior church courts, and marked the collapse of resistance to patronage. Gillespie continued to preach at Carnock, and afterward in Dunfermline, where a large congregation gathered round him. In 1761 with Thomas Boston of Jedburgh and Thomas Colier of Colinburgh, he formed a separate communion under the name Presbytery of Relief. Its distinctive mark was liberality toward other churches, by contrast to the Secession (see UNITED PRESBYTERIAN CHURCH). Gillespie died at Dunfermline on Jan. 19, 1774.

See G. Struthers, *History of the Relief Church* (1843); J. H. S. Burleigh, *A Church History of Scotland* (1960).   (H. WA.)

GILLETTE, WILLIAM HOOKER (1853–1937), U.S. playwright and actor, most successful in portraying the cool, resourceful man of action and associated particularly with the character Sherlock Holmes, was born at Hartford, Conn., on July 24, 1853. After graduation from Hartford high school, he studied at various times at New York university, Massachusetts Institute of Fine Arts and Boston university.

Gillette served with a number of stock companies and made his first appearance as an actor at the Globe theatre in Boston, Mass., in 1875 in *Faint Heart Ne'er Won Fair Lady*. His play *The Professor*, a light comedy in which he appeared in the title role, was produced at the Madison Square Garden theatre in New York city in 1881. *Esmeralda*, his second successful play, produced later in 1881, ran for a year and was later revived from time to time. *Held by the Enemy*, a Civil War spy story (produced in Brooklyn, N.Y., in 1886), and *Secret Service* (Philadelphia, 1895) are considered among his best original works. His famous play *Sherlock Holmes*, first produced in New York in 1899 and later in England, was frequently revived in both countries with Gillette in the leading role. His only motion-picture appearance was as Sherlock Holmes in a production of 1915. He died at Hartford, Conn., on April 29, 1937.

GILLINGHAM, a municipal and parliamentary borough of Kent, Eng., stands on the Medway next to Chatham with which it and Rochester form the three "Medway towns." Pop. (1971 prelim.) 86,714. The church of St. Mary Magdalene dates from Norman to Perpendicular. There was formerly a palace of the archbishops of Canterbury covering a large area surrounding the church, which has therefore been described as "an archbishop's peculiar," that is, at one time outside the jurisdiction of the diocesan bishops. A prominent landmark for many years, and an architectural and religious curiosity, was the Jezreel tower, begun in 1885 as a temple (New and Latter House of Israel) for the Jezreelites. Building ceased in 1889 when funds ran out and it was finally demolished in 1960 to make way for industrial development. Before the establishment of the royal dockyard of Chatham a portion of the town, then known as Grench, was a limb of the Cinque port of Hastings. Sir Francis Drake's father was vicar at nearby Upchurch. Will Adams, the Gillingham sailor who served under Sir Francis Drake when the Armada was defeated, was the first Englishman in Japan. He rendered distinguished service to that country where he died in 1620 and he is commemorated in Gillingham by a memorial. Among famous soldiers who received their early training as royal engineers' officers at Brompton barracks were General Gordon and Lord Kitchener. Gillingham was incorporated in 1903, and in 1929 the boundaries were ex-

tended to include Rainham parish. Until 1903 a court leet (*q.v.*) existed, one of the last to function in the country. The population is largely industrial, employed in the royal dockyard, the greater part of which actually lies within the borough, and in numerous local light industries. Some residents are attached to the services in local establishments, notably the royal engineers.   (N. T.)

GILLOT, CLAUDE (1673–1722), French painter and engraver, best known as the master of Watteau and Lancret, was born at Langres on April 27, 1673. His sportive mythological landscape pieces, with such titles as "Feast of Pan" and "Feast of Bacchus," opened the Academy of Painting at Paris to him in 1715; and he then adapted his art to the fashionable tastes of the day. He was connected with the opera and theatre as a designer of scenery and costumes. He died in Paris on May 4, 1722.

GILLRAY, JAMES (1757–1815), English caricaturist, who lampooned the political figures of his day, was born at Chelsea. Gillray began by learning letter-engraving and later was admitted as a student to the Royal Academy, supporting himself by engraving and perhaps by caricatures signed with fictitious names. William Hogarth's works were a source of study and delight for him in these years. Soon his own caricatures began to appear; the first that is certainly his is "Paddy on Horseback," published in 1779. The name of Gillray's publisher and print seller, Miss Humphreys, is inextricably associated with his. He lived in her house during all the years of his fame and his prints were shown in the windows of her shop.

A number of his most trenchant satires were directed against

"THE PLUM PUDDING IN DANGER" BY JAMES GILLRAY

"Farmer George"—King George III—and his court. After the French Revolution, Gillray became a conservative and he issued caricatures ridiculing Napoleon and the French and glorifying John Bull. His last work, from a design by Bunbury, is entitled "Interior of a Barber Shop in Assize Time" and is dated 1811. While engaged on it he became mad, although he later had occasional intervals of sanity. He died on June 1, 1815.

Gillray's caricatures may be divided into two classes: the social and political. The political caricatures form a historical record of the latter part of the reign of George III. They were circulated not only over Britain but throughout Europe and exerted a powerful influence. In this series George III, the queen, the prince of Wales, Fox, Burke, Pitt and Napoleon are the most prominent figures; the latter two are satirized in "The Plum Pudding in Danger." Among Gillray's best satires on the king are: "Farmer George and His Wife," companion plates, in one of which the king is toasting muffins for breakfast, and in the other the queen is frying sprats; "The Anti-Saccharites," where the royal pair propose to dispense with sugar to the great horror of the family; "A Connoisseur Examining a Cooper"; "Temperance Enjoying a Frugal Meal"; and "Royal Affability." "The First Kiss This Ten Years," a satire on the peace, is said to have greatly amused Napoleon.

Like most of the English caricatures of the time, Gillray's plates were executed in etching with stipple and coloured by hand.

They were produced for popular consumption and perhaps this is one of the reasons for that hurried vitality and spontaneity which make them so lively and timely. The injustices and pretensions which they depict as ridiculous absurdities are always present in some form or other, and in the work of Gillray they are leveled to the ground of truth by combination of conviction, vitality, acute human observation, fantasy and artistic naïveté. Unlike Daumier, Gillray does not situate the caricature in the realm of great art, but he does bring it to the threshold.

See Thomas Wright and R. H. Evans, *Historical and Descriptive Account of the Caricatures of James Gillray* (1851); Mary Dorothy George, *Catalogue of Political and Personal Satires . . . in The British Museum*, vol. v–ix (1935–49). (H. Es.; X.)

GILLYFLOWER (GILLIFLOWER), a name applied to various clove-scented flowers, especially the carnation (*q.v.*), or clove pink (*Dianthus caryophyllus*), and stock (*q.v.*; *Matthiola incana*), but also given to the wall-flower (*Cheiranthus cheiri*). The name is derived ultimately from the Greek word for clove tree, *karyophyllon* (literally, "nut-leaf") and was given originally, in Italy to plants of the pink family (Caryophyllaceae). The gillyflower of Chaucer, Spenser and Shakespeare was the carnation. Other plants that have the name gillyflower in their names are dame's violet (*Hesperis matronalis*), or dame's gilly-flower; the soapwort, or bouncing bet (*Saponaria officinalis*), called mock gillyflower; the grass, or sea gillyflower; and the thrift (*Armeria maritima*), called sea pink, or sea gillyflower. (J. W. Tr.)

H. SMITH
WALL GILLYFLOWER OR WALL-FLOWER (CHEIRANTHUS CHEIRI)

GILMAN, DANIEL COIT (1831–1908), U.S. educator, first president of Johns Hopkins university, was born in Norwich, Conn., on July 6, 1831. After his graduation at Yale in 1852 he went to St. Petersburg, Russia, as attaché, then studied at Berlin (1854–55). For 17 years he worked at Yale as assistant librarian, professor of physical and political geography and secretary of the governing board. From 1872 to 1875 he was head of the University of California at Berkeley. In 1875 he became first president of Johns Hopkins. This post he filled until 1901, after which, until 1904, he served as the first president of the Carnegie institution at Washington, D.C. He died at Norwich on Oct. 13, 1908.

Gilman's influence upon higher education in the United States was great, as was his contribution to the organization of the Johns Hopkins hospital, of which he was made director in 1889. Under him Johns Hopkins had an immense influence, especially in the promotion of original and productive research. Through his services on numerous foundations and boards devoted to education, and as president of the National Civil Service Reform league, he further aided in educational and social betterment in the United States.

See Fabian Franklin, *Life of Daniel Coit Gilman* (1910); John Thomas Faris, *Men Who Conquered* (1922).

GILMORE, PATRICK SARSFIELD (1829–1892), Irish-American bandmaster and organizer of music festivals, was born in County Galway, Dec. 25, 1829. He emigrated to the U.S., and in 1859 formed the Gilmore band, for which he wrote much music. He organized the National Peace jubilee (1869) and the World Peace jubilee (1872) in Boston with choruses of thousands of voices and large instrumental groups including an *Anvil Chorus*, consisting of 100 firemen beating anvils to mark the rhythm. Gilmore traveled with his band throughout the U.S. and Canada, and in 1878 brought them to Europe. He died in St. Louis, Mo., Sept. 24, 1892.

See M. Darlington, *Irish Orpheus: the Life of Patrick Gilmore* (1950). (N. Sv.)

GIL POLO, GASPAR (c. 1530–1585), Spanish pastoral novelist and poet of Valencian origin, is known only as the author of *La Diana enamorada* (Valencia, 1564), a charming continuation of the *Diana* of Jorge Montemayor (*q.v.*), which it surpasses in readability. The numerous interpolated verses include metrical innovations and constitute, together with the delightful evocation of the Valencian countryside, the chief attraction of the novel, which was praised and imitated by Cervantes and early translated into various languages. A Latin version (*Eroto-didascalus*, 1625) by the eccentric Kaspar Barth achieved a certain celebrity, and Bartholomew Young's English translation, current in manuscript in the 1580s (published 1598), is said to have suggested the Felismena episode in *The Two Gentlemen of Verona*. Gil Polo died at Barcelona in 1585.

See J. B. Avalle-Arce, *La novela pastoril española* (1959). (F. S. R.)

GIL ROBLES, JOSÉ MARÍA (1898–), Spanish politician and leader of the Catholic party during the second republic, was the son of an eminent professor of law. He was a journalist on the staff of the Catholic newspaper *El Debate* when, in 1931, he was chosen to lead the newly founded Catholic party, *Acción Popular*. By 1933 he had organized a combination of right-wing parties, C.E.D.A. (*Confederación Española de Derechos Autónomos*), which became the most powerful political group after the elections of Nov. 1933, when women voted for the first time. Nevertheless, the president, Niceto Alcalá Zamora, asked the radical Alejandro Lerroux to form a government. This was because Alcalá Zamora feared left-wing reactions if the administration were entrusted to Gil Robles, who was accused of wishing to re-establish the monarchy and set up a Catholic corporative state on the Austrian model. C.E.D.A. supported, but did not join, the Lerroux's government and that of his successor Ricardo Samper until Oct. 1934. Lerroux then formed another government in which

GILPIN, BERNARD (1517–1583), one of the most conscientious and broadminded upholders of the Elizabethan church settlement, was born at Kentmere, Westmorland, in 1517, and educated at Queen's college and Christ Church, Oxford. He was ordained in 1542, and associated with the conservative supporters of the Reformation. He defended the doctrines of the church against John Hooper (*q.v.*) and Peter Martyr, and in 1552 preached before Edward VI a sermon on sacrilege, in which he denounced the expropriation of church property. He became vicar of Norton in the Durham diocese in 1552 and obtained a licence, through William Cecil, secretary of state, as a general preacher throughout the kingdom during Edward VI's lifetime. Just before Mary's accession he went to study at Louvain, Antwerp and Paris, returning in 1556 to be rector of Easington and archdeacon of Durham. He was the friend of both Erasmus and Cardinal Reginald Pole and frankly refused to accept definitely either Calvinism or the decrees of the Council of Trent. Charged with heresy, he was defended by his great-uncle, Cuthbert Tunstal, bishop of Durham, who gave him the rich living of Houghton-le-Spring, Durham. An accident prevented Gilpin's complying with a royal warrant for his apprehension in London, and Mary's death saved him from further danger. He joined the majority of the lower clergy in subscribing to the Elizabethan supremacy, despite his personal doubts of contemporary Puritan trends, in order not to be "a means to make many others to refuse, and so consequently hinder the course of the word of God." However, he declined several offers of promotion and concentrated on pastoral work throughout the north, helped poor scholars to attend universities and visited prisons. Austere in private life, Gilpin was highly esteemed for his generosity to all classes of his parishioners, founded a grammar school, remained celibate and retained other characteristics of the Catholic tradition, although many of his pupils became Puritans. He died at Houghton on March 5, 1583.

See C. Wordsworth, *Ecclesiastical Biography*, vol. 3, 4th ed. (1853); G. Every, "Letters of an Elizabethan Saint," *Church Quarterly Review*, vol. 124 (1937).

C.E.D.A. ministers were included. This provoked the left-wing risings of the autumn of 1934. A governmental crisis in March 1935 was resolved by the formation of a new administration, still under Lerroux, in which Gil Robles became, significantly, minister of war. He continued in office under Joaquín Chapaprieta, but resigned, with the other C.E.D.A. ministers, in Dec. 1935 over the budget and the *estraperlo* scandals.

In the ensuing elections of Feb. 1936, Gil Robles led an alliance of C.E.D.A. and other right-wing parties in a national front, but although C.E.D.A. became the largest single party in the new *Cortes*, the majority was won by the left-wing popular front. Gil Robles' supporters now became impatient with his policy of gaining power through peaceful means: he lost the support of the middle classes, and his extremist adherents followed his youth leader Ramón Serrano Súñer into the Falange. He remained chief opposition spokesman in the *Cortes*, but was increasingly eclipsed there by the monarchist José Calvo Sotelo. He was an intended victim of the plot responsible for Calvo Sotelo's murder (July 1936). Soon after the outbreak of the civil war, he went to Lisbon to set up a mission with Nicolás Franco for the purchase of arms for the rebels. After the war he largely retired from public life. In June 1962 he chose to go into exile rather than comply with an order from Gen. Francisco Franco's government forcing him to reside outside Madrid.
(J. C. J. M.)

GILSONITE is a native bitumen (*q.v.*), an asphaltite, found near the Colorado–Utah border in the Uinta basin. It is named after S. H. Gilson, one of its discoverers; the alternative names uintaite or uintahite are derived from its location. Gilsonite is a lustrous, jet-black solid bitumen exhibiting conchoidal fracture. It gives a brown streak, ranges in specific gravity from 1.03 to 1.10 and is soluble in carbon disulfide. The melting point varies from 110° to 260° C., depending on chemical composition.

Gilsonite occurs as veins filling parallel, vertical fractures. The largest veins are several miles long, thousands of feet deep and about 20 ft. thick. Maximum annual production before 1950 was about 75,000 tons, when it was used largely in manufacturing paints and other coating materials. Gilsonite production increased after 1957, when it was mined hydraulically and transported as a water slurry by pipeline to refineries for conversion to coke and gasoline.
(S. R. Sn.)

GILYAK (NIVKH), an east Siberian people, about 4,000 in the 1960s, who inhabit the lower course of the Amur river, the coast of the Okhotsk sea and the Pacific, and northern parts of the nearby island of Sakhalin. Their homeland has a severe subarctic climate. They had no definitely known linguistic affiliation, but it has been suggested that they form part of a larger family together with the Ainu (*q.v.*). Their closest geographic neighbours are the small Manchu-Tungusic tribes of the Amur basin, who are more closely related to the Mongols and Koreans linguistically. The Gilyaks have undoubtedly occupied their territory for a very long time.

They are a prime example of a hunting, fishing and gathering economy and live almost exclusively by the products of the sea and river. They fish for salmon and sturgeon and hunt sea mammals (seal and white whale). Hunting of land animals is of minor importance, and the women do a limited amount of wild-plant gathering.

They have domesticated the dog, but no other animal, and have no domesticated crops. The dog, in harness to a sledge, is their most important means of transportation; the dog is also a source of food and pelts. They have little idea of ethnic unity or identity. The social organization has been best described by the great Russian ethnologist, L. Y. Sternberg, who was exiled to their territory during tsarist times. Their chief social unit is the village, and they are formed into clans which live together, work together and own fishing territories in common. The core of the kinship organization is a group of siblings and cousins, who bear a common kinship designation, the *tuvn* or *ruvn*. Men related as *tuvn* have certain rights over each others' wives and property.

The bear plays an important role in their religion. Each clan has an annual ceremony in which a bear that has been captured for the occasion is sacrificed. Shamanism is practised among them, but not at the time of the bear ceremony, a phenomenon indicative of the coalescence of two different religious practices. *See also* PALEO-ASIATIC LANGUAGES.
See M. Czplicka, *Aboriginal Siberia* (1914).
(L. K.)

GIN, a potable distilled spirit, deriving its principal flavour from the juniper berry (*juniperus communis*). The origin of gin was medicinal and is attributed to Franciscus de la Boe (1614–72), professor of medicine at the University of Leiden, Holland, who distilled spirits in the presence of the juniper berry in order to prepare a specific with known diuretic properties. The juniper berry was known by its French name of *genièvre*, which the Dutch altered to *genever*, and the English to gin.

By 1792 Holland was producing 14,000,000 gal., of which 10,000,000 were exported. British soldiers returning from the wars on the continent brought the taste for gin to England. However, it was Queen Anne who gave gin distilling its impetus during her reign (1702–14), when she raised the duties and taxes on imports and lowered the excise on home products.

There are two basic types of gin, those produced in the Netherlands and those produced elsewhere, principally in England and America. The difference derives from the fact that the Dutch utilize very rich, full-bodied spirits and distill their gin at a very low proof, usually below 100, while the English and American distillers use highly purified spirits, distilling their gins off at about 160 U.S. proof.

Dutch gins are known as Geneva, Genever, Schiedam or Hollands. Low-proof spirits distilled from a mash of at least one-third barley malt are rectified. The resultant spirits, together with the flavouring agents, are redistilled, coming off at between 94 and 98 proof. Dutch gins are malty in flavour and have a very full body. Other "botanicals" are included with the juniper berries, but not in the variety employed in England and the United States.

English gin is produced by rectifying high-proof grain whisky or spirits to assure complete purity and flavour-free spirits. These are then reduced with water to proof strength (114.2 U.S. proof), placed in a pot still together with the flavouring agents, and the whole redistilled. The resultant gin is reduced to 80, 86 or 94 U.S. proof, depending on the market for which it is intended, and allowed to rest for a very short period before bottling.

The "botanicals" used to flavour gin in England and the United States are juniper berries, preferably from Germany and Italy; orris, angelica and licorice roots; bitter almonds, caraway, coriander, cardamon, anise and fennel seeds; calamus, cassia bark, lemon peel, sweet and bitter orange peels, etc. Each gin producer has developed his own secret formulas, using some or all of the foregoing.

American gin producers follow the English method, usually employing solely 190 proof grain spirits. Their gin stills often have a tray or gin head in which the botanicals rest and through which the alcoholic vapours swirl as they rise.

Usually, gin is not aged. Some U.S. producers do age their gin although under U.S. regulations no claim of age may be made for gin. Such aged gins have a pale golden colour.

English and American gins are dry gin. The term London Dry gin is used in the United States and has lost its geographical significance. Old Tom gin is a slightly sweetened gin, while fruit flavoured gins are produced by adding such flavors as orange, lemon, raspberry or pineapple to finished gin.

Sloe gin is a gin in name only. It is a sweet liqueur with the acid tang of the sloe berry.

Hollands gin is generally drunk neat or mixed with water, while dry gins are consumed in a variety of fashions—neat, in cocktails such as the dry martini and long drinks such as the Tom Collins, or mixed with tonic water. *See also* ALCOHOLIC BEVERAGES, DISTILLED.
(H. J. GN.)

GINDELY, ANTON (1829–1892), Austrian historian, noted for his work on Bohemian history and on the period of the Thirty Years' War, was born in Prague, Sept. 3, 1829, the son of an Austrian father and a Czech mother. He studied at Prague and in 1855 made the first of his journeys investigating archives in Bohemia, Poland and Germany. There he gained access to the records of the Moravian Brethren, which led him to write several works, including *Geschichte der böhmischen Brüder* (1857). In 1862 he became professor at Prague and in 1867 official Bohemian archivist. He was also the editor of *Monumenta historiae bohemica* (5 vol., 1864-90). Gindely died in Prague, Oct. 24, 1892. His *Geschichte der Gegenreformation in Böhmen* was edited by T. Tupetz (1894). Gindely's other important works include *Geschichte des 30-jährigen Krieges* (1869-80), *Rudolf II und seine Zeit* (1863 and 1868) and a criticism of Wallenstein, *Waldstein während seines ersten Generalats* (2 vol., 1885-86), which caused controversy.

GINER DE LOS RÍOS, FRANCISCO (1839-1915), Spanish professor of the philosophy of law and educational reformer, was born at Ronda, in Andalusia, on Oct. 10, 1839. After graduating in law at Granada, he went to Madrid in 1863 and obtained employment in the archives of the ministry of state. Frequenting university circles, he came under the influence of Julián Sanz del Río, the leading Spanish exponent of the philosophy of Karl Krause (*q.v.*), which he adopted.

In 1866 Giner won nomination as professor of the philosophy of law at Madrid; but he had hardly taken possession of his chair, in 1867, when Sanz was dismissed from his university post for refusing to swear an oath of loyalty to church and monarchy. Giner then renounced his chair in sympathy with Sanz and tried to practise as a lawyer, which he found distasteful. Restored to his chair after the revolution of 1868, he showed himself favourable to radical reforms in education without concerning himself with political activity. On the restoration of the Bourbon monarchy a new attempt was made to restrict the freedom of teaching, and Giner protested so forcefully that he was imprisoned for a time at Cádiz (1875).

Released but excluded from the university, he inspired other chairless professors to join with him in founding the Institución Libre de Enseñanza in 1876. This was to stand for teaching in complete independence of confessional, philosophical or political prejudices. Restored again to his chair in 1881, Giner eventually decided that the Institución should be concerned mainly with development in educational method. He sponsored coeducation and organized excursions for his pupils from Madrid to the countryside and provincial towns. An admirer of English methods, he was welcomed by Benjamin Jowett on a visit to England in 1884. He also visited France, the Low Countries and England again in 1886 and France again in 1889.

His pupils, with whom his personal relationship was no less important than his teaching, came to know him affectionately as "the Grandfather." He died in Madrid on Feb. 17, 1915. A collected edition of his writings, in 20 volumes, appeared between 1916 and 1936.

GINGER, an economically important spice, consisting of the rhizome (underground stem) of *Zingiber officinale* (family Zingiberaceae; *q.v.*), a perennial reedlike plant. Although not known with certainty in the wild, the ginger plant is considered to be a native of tropical Asia, whence it was carried by man throughout the warmer parts of the world. The use of ginger in India and China has been known from very ancient times. By at least as early as the 1st century A.D., the spice had travelled in trade to the Mediterranean region, and by the 11th century was well known in England. It was brought to the West Indies and Mexico by the Spaniards soon after the conquest and by 1547 was being exported from Jamaica to Spain.

Jamaica, India, Nigeria, Sierra Leone and China are important producers of ginger. The plant is propagated by cuttings of the rhizome. When the leafy stems turn yellow and wither (usually in nine or ten months after planting) the ginger is ready for harvesting, which is done simply by digging the rhizomes from the soil. The cured, or dried, ginger of the spice trade is prepared in two major ways, coated and uncoated. Pieces of the rhizome, called races, or hands, may simply be dried in the sun after they are washed; ginger so prepared is coated, because its epidermis is still intact. In the preparation of uncoated ginger the rhizomes are washed, the epidermis is partially or completely removed by peeling, scraping or trampling and the rhizomes are then dried.

To improve its appearance, ginger of some grades may be bleached, either with lime or with sulfur fumes. In some regions ginger is scalded or boiled before it is dried, without peeling, to produce the so-called "black" ginger.

Ginger is added, usually ground, to many kinds of food and beverages. Medicinally it is used chiefly for its carminative, stimulant, rubefacient and counterirritant properties. Essential oil of ginger, to which the odour of the spice is due, is isolated from the rhizomes by distillation and is extensively used in the food industry. It is also employed in some perfumes. Oleoresin of ginger, to which the pungency of the spice is due, is obtained by percolating ground ginger with acetone, alcohol or ether and then evaporating away the solvent; it finds some use as a carminative and in the treatment of certain gastrointestinal disorders. Preserved ginger is the peeled young rhizomes, carefully boiled in syrup. Green ginger, used in cooking, is the fresh rhizome. Candied ginger forms an agreeable sweetmeat.

The leafy stems of ginger grow three to four feet high. The flowers, borne on leafless stems from 6 to 12 in. high, are in dense conelike spikes. The spikes are about one inch thick and from two to three inches long and are composed of overlapping green bracts, which may be edged with yellow. Each bract encloses a single, small, yellow-green and purple flower. The elongate leaves are alternate on the stem, arranged in two vertical rows, and are 6 to 12 in. long. The leaf blade arises from a sheath that enwraps the stem.

The generic name of ginger, *Zingiber*, is derived from the Greek *zingíberi*, which in turn comes from the Sanskrit name of the spice, *singabera*.

(J. W. Tr.)

GINGER ALE, a sweetened, carbonated beverage, the predominating flavour and pleasant warmth of which are derived mainly from the underground stem, or rhizome, of *Zingiber officinale*. Though originally carbonated by fermentation, modern ginger ales are artificially saturated with carbon dioxide gas. The Jamaican and African varieties of ginger rhizome yield the finest-flavoured beverages, the flavour and pungency of the rhizome being dependent upon the essential oil and oleoresin, which are its principal active constituents.

Other flavouring materials are frequently added; for example, spices, citrus essences, fruit juices, foam-producing substances, etc., and occasionally peppery materials, such as capsicum, to increase the pungency of the beverage.

There are two general types: pale dry ginger ales tend to be less sweet, more acid, lighter, milder and highly carbonated; golden, or aromatic, ginger ales tend to be sweeter, less acid, darker and generally more pungent. The joint committee of definitions and standards of the U.S. department of agriculture in 1922 defined ginger ale as the carbonated beverage prepared from ginger ale flavour, sugar syrup, harmless organic acid, potable water and caramel colour. Ginger ale flavour, or ginger ale concentrate, was defined as the flavouring product in which ginger is the essential constituent, with or without the addition of other aromatic and pungent ingredients, citrus oils and fruit juices.

In preparing a carbonated ginger ale, a sirup is first made, this being compounded from water, sugar, ginger ale flavour or extract, citric or tartaric acid, caramel colour and possibly foam essence. Such a sirup is employed in making the carbonated beverage in the manner which is described under SOFT DRINKS.

(R. W. Me.)

GINGER BEER is the generic term for three classes of nonexcisable (less than 2% proof spirit) ginger-flavoured beverages: brewed fermented ginger beer, beverages made by the artificial carbonation of brewed ginger beer, and non-brewed ginger beers.

The principal differences between ginger beer (also called ginger-ade) and ginger ale lie in the rather higher gravity and greater proportion of extractive matter in ginger beer; in the appearance, ginger beer usually being cloudy while ginger ale is brilliantly clear; and also in the fact that ginger ales frequently contain certain capsicum extracts which increase the sharpness of the beverage.

Until about 1850, brewing and fermenting of mixtures of ginger, other spices and bitter vegetable substances constituted the only known method of making ginger beers, many of which had alcoholic contents in the region of 10%-12% proof spirit. The restrictions created in Great Britain by the Excise act of 1855 led to the manufacture of ginger beer by the dilution of brewed concentrates with carbonated water. Nonbrewed ginger beers later became popular, although many of these beverages have a pronounced lemon flavour; they frequently contain a foam-producing extract—usually an extract of quillai bark.

The production of ginger beer by fermentation is carried out by first making an aqueous infusion of a mixture of vegetable products among which ginger predominates. The following is a suitable mixture: bruised Jamaica ginger 6 parts, licorice extract 2 parts, hops 3 parts, cloves 3 parts, gentian ¼ part. Five parts of such a mixture are boiled in 200 parts of water for 20 to 30 min.; the extract is strained and sweetened with 6 or 7 parts of sugar. Caramel colour is added as desired, the extract cooled to about 70° C. and, after adding 1 fl.oz. of brewer's yeast, the liquor according to the taste of the manufacturer, and the beverage is bottled after standing for a few days to permit the mucilaginous matter to settle out. The bottled product is pasteurized by some manufacturers. (W. P.-D.)

GINGHAM, a fabric usually made with a plain weave; it originally was made completely of cotton fibres but later much of it was made of man-made fibres. The name comes from the Malayan word *gingan,* meaning striped, and thence from the French *guingan,* a term used by the Bretons to signify cloth made from striped colouring.

Medium or fine yarns of varying quality are used to obtain the plain, check or stripe effects. The cloth is yarn- or skein-dyed or printed, and it runs to about six yards to the pound. Texture thread counts average 64 x 56 per square inch. The warp and the filling may be the same, even-sided and balanced.

Gingham is strong, rather stout, substantial and serviceable. It launders easily and well, but lower-textured fabric may shrink considerably unless preshrunk. Prices of gingham have a wide range; designs or patterns run from the conservative to gaudy, wild effects.

Uses include dress goods, trimming, kerchiefs, aprons, children's wear and beachwear. It is very popular in summer dress wear for women and children. Ginghams on the market in the early 1960s included chambray gingham, nurses' gingham, Scotch, tissue and zephyr. (G. E. L.)

GINKGO or **MAIDENHAIR TREE** (*Ginkgo biloba*), a tree grown since ancient times about temples in China, where it is considered a sacred plant. Although reported as native in western China, it is not positively known to occur in a truly wild state.

It is a smooth, sparingly branched tree, sometimes 120 ft. high, with deciduous fan-shaped leaves, 2-4 in. broad and nearly as long, which in form, veining and aspect resemble those of the maidenhair fern. Botanically, the closest allies of the ginkgo are the cycads. Like them, it is dioecious, *i.e.,* the pollen and seed cones are on male and female trees respectively.

As the sole survivor of a numerous group of plants with a very long geological ancestry the ginkgo may be legitimately regarded as a "living fossil." It has existed essentially unchanged for millions of years, tracing back directly to the fossil Cordaitales of the Permian period. Fossil species occur in the Triassic, Jurassic and Tertiary formations in the British Isles, and forms with leaves very similar to those of the living ginkgo are abundant in Triassic and Jurassic rocks of the Pacific coast of North America, especially in Oregon and Alaska.

The ginkgo, especially the male

JOHN H. GERARD
LEAVES AND FRUIT OF THE GINKGO (GINKGO BILOBA)

tree (the fruit, borne by the female tree, has a very disagreeable odour), is cultivated as an ornamental in temperate countries, growing without protection in many parts of Europe and also in North America as far north as the Great Lakes.

For its structural peculiarities see GYMNOSPERMS: *Ginkgoales.*

GINNING: see COTTON; COTTON MANUFACTURE; WHITNEY, ELI.

GINSBURG, CHRISTIAN DAVID (1831-1914), Hebrew and biblical scholar, who was the foremost authority in England on the Masorah, was born a Jew in Warsaw on Dec. 25, 1831, and emigrated to England not long after his conversion to Christianity in 1846. There while working as missionary among the Jews (until 1863) he made a name as a biblical scholar, publishing translations with commentaries on the Song of Solomon (1857), Ecclesiastes (1861) and Leviticus (1882) as well as brief treatises on the Karaites (1862), the Essenes (1864; reprinted 1955) and the Kabbalah (1865). He republished Jacob ben Chajim's introduction to the Rabbinic Bible (first printed in 1524-25) with an English translation (1867), edited the Masorah, without the biblical text (4 vol., 1880-86), and wrote a learned but not always correct *Introduction to the Massoretico-Critical Edition of the Hebrew Bible* (1897). This volume served as introduction to his critical edition of the text of the Hebrew Bible according to the Masoretic tradition (1894). A further edition which began to appear in 1911 but was finished only after his death in Palmers Green, Middlesex, on March 7, 1914, showed little critical sense. He was a member of the committee for the Revised version of the Old Testament. See MASORETES. (C. R.)

GINSENG (SANG) is the common name of two species of *Panax* (family Araliaceae), herbs whose roots constitute a drug in China. *Panax quinquefolius* is the American ginseng, which is native of rich cool woods from

JOHN H. GERARD
AMERICAN GINSENG (PANAX QUINQUEFOLIUS)

Quebec and Manitoba southward to Florida, Alabama, Louisiana and Arkansas. Approximately 150 ac. are cultivated in America. Almost all of the carefully dried root of ginseng is exported to Hong Kong, from where it is distributed in southeast Asia. The export from America amounts to about 100,000 lb. annually. *Panax ginseng,* Asian ginseng, native of Manchuria and Korea and cultivated in Korea and Japan, is more appreciated in some markets than is the American ginseng.

The Chinese from time immemorial have considered ginseng to be a cure for most diseases and infirmities. In fact the generic name of the plant, *Panax,* is derived from Greek words translated as "panacea," a cure-all. The continued demand for ginseng roots, and especially those roots that may resemble a man in form, is probably due to a belief widely held among the Chinese that ginseng is an aphrodisiac. There is no evidence, however, to indicate that ginseng has any value, either as a drug or as an aphrodisiac.

The export of wild ginseng root from America to the orient began in the early 1700s. In 1773 the sloop "Hingham" sailed from Boston for China with 55 tons of ginseng aboard. Shipments have continued from that time until the present. The greatest amount shipped in any year was 622,761 lb. in 1862. The price of ginseng varied from 49 cents to $27 a pound during the century 1858-1958.

Ginseng has been in cultivation in America since about 1870, and in Korea since at least the early years of the century. In the years 1895 to 1903 or 1904 a ginseng "boom" took place in America. Extravagant and sometimes fraudulent representations were made concerning the fortune to be made from ginseng culture. Hundreds of gardens were started and stock companies were formed to grow ginseng on a grander scale. A leaf disease of ginseng became prevalent in 1904, ruining many plantations and discouraging growers.

Most ginseng gardens are small, less than one acre. Intensive cultivation is practised and nearly all labour involved must be done by hand. Rich soil, woodlands with adequate natural shade, or rich farm land with artificial shade, is necessary. Ginseng requires five to seven years to mature from seed. The value of the crop depends on the care with which the root was prepared and the market when it is sold. The grading of ginseng root is a highly subjective art. The value of cultivated ginseng root is about 60% of a comparable grade of wild root.

BIBLIOGRAPHY.—Herber W. Youngken, *Textbook of Pharmacognosy*, 6th ed. (1948); Louis O. Williams, "Ginseng," *Econ. Bot.*, 11:344-348 (1957); U.S. Department of Agriculture, "Ginseng," 9 pp. (1957).
(L. O. W.)

GINZBERG, LOUIS (1873-1953), talmudic scholar and teacher, was born at Kovno, Lithuania, on Nov. 28, 1873, and was educated in the Lithuanian rabbinical schools of Kovno and Telshe and at various German universities. He mastered the Talmud in his youth, and his secular studies gave him command also over western methods of research. Moving to the United States in 1899, he became editor of rabbinical literature of the *Jewish Encyclopedia*. In 1902 Ginzberg became professor of Talmud at the Jewish Theological Seminary of America, remaining there until his death on Nov. 11, 1953.

Ginzberg's best-known works are *Legends of the Jews* and the *Commentary on the Talmud of Jerusalem* (in Hebrew). Into the first he gathered all the folklore in Jewish tradition bearing on Scripture, and in two volumes of notes, with enormous erudition and remarkable insight, he traced these legends to their sources. In the second work, of which only the commentary on the first treatise of the Talmud was completed, Ginzberg included discussions bearing on the whole rabbinic system and showing the scope and development of rabbinic theology and ritual. His massive studies in the development of *halaka* (Jewish religious law) demonstrated that sociological and economic factors influenced the evolution of Jewish law in its creative periods.
(L. F.)

GIOBERTI, VINCENZO (1801-1852), Italian philosopher and writer who played an important part in shaping Italian national feeling in the *risorgimento* and was, briefly, prime minister of Piedmont. He was born at Turin, April 5, 1801, of poor parents. After graduating in theology (1823) he was ordained priest (1825) and began to teach theology at Turin university. His brilliance was soon remarked; his students admired him and he became famous, although his ideas were already showing traces of romantic unorthodoxy. At Charles Albert's succession he was appointed a court chaplain, but soon afterward his career was cut short by disgrace and exile. He had already been indiscreet in the expression of his radical political views and he was accused of participation in a republican plot. He was arrested (1833) and, after a short imprisonment, went to Paris and Brussels, remaining abroad until 1845 and living by teaching while writing his first major works—*Teorica del sovrannaturale* (1838) and *Introduzione allo studio della filosofa* (1839-40). Gioberti was the first major Italian philosopher to attack the Cartesian foundations of the Enlightenment and these books were also important in their day for the reaction they expressed against the teaching of Antonio Rosmini-Serbati (q.v.). As the introduction into Italian philosophy of the implications of the work of Kant and the exposition of the metaphysical and ontological foundations of Gioberti's social and political thinking, they are still interesting, primarily to historians of philosophy.

Gioberti's political thinking had a more abiding interest. As early as 1833 he published in the Mazzinian journal *Giovine Italia* an essay on republicanism and Christianity. This was the extreme position of his political evolution; he never joined Mazzini's organization, and by 1840 he was violently criticizing the democratic republican belief in insurrection as a way of uniting Italy. In exile Gioberti came to believe that there was a role in Italy for constitutional monarchy and in 1840 defined his position in moderate terms as the search to create a state 'as far removed from demagogy as it is from despotism." His most famous book, *Del Primato morale e civile degli Italiani* (1843), was from one point of view an attempt to find a practical means of realizing this ambition for Italy. Its central conception was that of the spiritual and moral primacy of the Italian race and of the unique contribu-

tion it could make to civilization. The primacy was to be given an appropriate political form by the creation of an Italian federation under the leadership of the pope. A practical identification of the cause of Italy and the cause of Christianity thus resulted. The *Primato* created a great sensation: it seemed both to make possible a reconciliation between patriotism and the papacy, hitherto regarded as impossible by the radicals, and to unite religion and liberalism. Its tone and demands were moderate; it preserved the particularist interests of the individual states and avoided criticism of the Austrians by finding a place for their provinces in the federal scheme. It was more acceptable than any earlier patriotic program. When Pius IX was elected he was called "Gioberti's pope" because he was believed to be sympathetic to these neo-Guelph ideas.

The heightening of tension after the papal election resulted among other things in an amnesty in Piedmont under which Gioberti returned to Paris just after the battle of Novara. This was a form of disguised exile and he resigned soon afterward, remaining in Paris until he died (Nov. 26, 1852). By that time his views were held in great disfavour at Rome. In 1847 he had published an attack on the Jesuits for which he had not been forgiven, and the *Rinnovamento civile d'Italia* (1851), his second major political book, showed more sympathy for a unitarist answer to Italy's difficulties than had the *Primato*. His hopes had now been transferred from the papacy to Piedmont and the risings of 1848 in Venice and Milan had made him more hopeful of democracy. It was not surprising, therefore, that his works were placed on the *Index Librorum Prohibitorum*.

BIBLIOGRAPHY.—For bibliographical information *see* A. Bruers, *Gioberti* (1924). Gioberti's works are available in the *Edizione Nazionale*, ed. by E. Castelli (1938); *Epistolario*, ed. by G. Gentile, 11 vol. (1927-37); *Carteggi di Vincenzo Gioberti* (1935-37). See also A. Anzilotti, *Gioberti* (1922); A. Omodeo, *Vincenzo Gioberti e la sua evoluzione politica* (1941); G. Saitta, *Il pensiero di Vincenzo Gioberti*, 2nd ed. (1927).
(J. M. Rs.)

GIOLITTI, GIOVANNI (1842-1928), Italian statesman, five times prime minister between 1891 and 1921, a supreme architect of coalitions to hold the balance between left and right in parliament, was born at Mondovi, in Piedmont, on Oct. 27, 1842. A lawyer by training, he graduated in Turin in 1860. For a short time he was king's procurator in Turin, but thereafter for 20 years his career was that of a civil servant. He reached high rank in the ministries of justice and finance. This experience developed in him the administrative ability for which he was to become famous, and even after entering parliamentary politics his instinct was always to turn issues of principle where possible into uncontroversial matters of mere administration. Elected a deputy for Cuneo in 1882, Giolitti immediately showed his skill as a highly effective committeeman. He led an attack against Agostino Depretis and Francesco Crispi for competing with each other in reducing taxes for electoral purposes while the government was financed out of credit. In 1888 the fall of the finance minister Agostino Magliani was largely due to Giolitti, and in 1889-90 he himself became minister of the treasury in the second Crispi cabinet.

Giolitti's first ministry was from May 15, 1892, to Nov. 24, 1893, with a predominantly left-of-centre government. This was a brief administration, partly because his policy of legalizing strikes and trying to redress the social balance seemed highly shocking to many people. A more important reason for failure was his involvement in certain dramatic bank scandals, which he had tried but failed to conceal. Misguidedly he proceeded to confer senatorial rank on the director of the Banca Romana even though he knew of this man's peculations. A public commission finally exposed the improper connection between high finance and parliamentary politics, and Giolitti, though not deeply implicated personally, had to leave the country for a period. He again became important in 1899, when his group on the centre left of politics lined up with the extreme left and just managed to arrest the movement toward a monarchical autocracy. In 1901–03 he was minister of the interior under Giuseppe Zanardelli; and on Nov. 3, 1903, he became prime minister again. Once more he began introducing a few moderate social reforms and trying to bring the Radicals and Socialists inside a governmental coalition for the first time. But he failed to win over this extreme left, and on March 4, 1905, feeling his majority insecure, he resigned temporarily in favour of one of his own party, Alessandro Fortis.

Giolitti was prime minister a third time for the unusually long period of three years between May 29, 1906 and Dec. 2, 1909. By now he had perfected his art of "managing" elections, and in 1909 he obtained a large majority in the chamber. Nevertheless it was becoming ever harder to keep a broad coalition together now that Socialists had arrived to challenge and weaken the old Liberal centre grouping which hitherto had held a monopoly of power. For instance, the conservative Liberals, led by Sidney Sonnino, were alarmed by Giolitti's notions of social reform, and in 1909, despite this electoral victory, they managed to defeat his measures to introduce a progressive income tax. He came back into office for the fourth time on March 27, 1911, and was successful in introducing a national insurance act and in widening the electorate. But universal manhood suffrage in effect made his coalition even harder to keep in balance, for a new type of deputy was coming into politics, and at the extremes there were Catholics, Syndicalists and a Socialist party under Benito Mussolini, all of them opposed to Giolitti's form of liberalism.

In an attempt to patch these internal cleavages, Giolitti in Oct. 1911 declared war on Turkey (see ITALO-TURKISH WAR). Italian nationalists had been insisting on the conquest of Turkish Libya in order to balance French intervention in Morocco and Austrian penetration in the Balkans. But this search for prestige defeated itself, for the war proved much more difficult than expected, and Italy emerged from it weakened at the same time as Italian nationalist feelings became more injured and frenetic. In 1913 Giolitti used an even greater degree of force and corruption in the parliamentary elections, but this time the result was to leave his majority less compact and the extremes stronger. Once again, on March 10, 1914, he decided that a temporary retreat from politics was desirable in order to reassess and regroup his coalition. He was succeeded by Antonio Salandra and the Conservatives.

When World War I broke out Giolitti was aware of Italian weakness and advocated neutrality. Salandra, too, decided not to join the Central Powers, to whom Italy was tied by the triple alliance. But in 1915, partly in order to keep Giolitti out of power, Salandra secretly committed his country to fight against its officially established allies, ignoring Giolitti's argument that Italy could gain a great deal by staying neutral between two groups of combatants. Since a majority of deputies agreed with Giolitti, Salandra organized violent popular demonstrations in favour of intervention, and parliament was kept in recess and confronted with a *fait accompli*. War was declared on Austria in May 1915. Giolitti's fear that Italian resources were unequal to such a war was justified by the event. For several years he did not appear in parliament, though in 1917, after the disaster of Caporetto, he made an eloquent appeal to Italians to stand firm and united.

Giolitti had his fifth and last term of office as prime minister from June 16, 1920 to June 27, 1921, at a time of great turbulence in Italy. The suffering and loss caused by the war, the disappointments over Italy's failure to profit much by the peace, together with the growth in antiparliamentary feelings on both right and left, made the country almost ungovernable. Giolitti was the most experienced man in politics, but was perhaps too old to check the revolution that was imminent. He had made a number of overtures to both Socialists and Popolari (Christian Democrats), but he had failed to bring them into his coalition, and from 1919 these two groups became the largest parties in parliament. His policy of sweet reasonableness was no longer effective before outbursts of violence. When in Sept. 1920 a large number of factories

were taken over for several weeks by strikers, his moderation proved momentarily successful, but the manufacturers wanted something much more drastic against this threat of Communist revolution. Giolitti also annoyed the nationalists in 1920 by giving up occupation of Valona on the Albanian side of the Adriatic and by trying to win the friendship of Yugoslavia by waiving the Italian claim to Dalmatia in the treaty of Rapallo (Nov. 12, 1920). At the same time his tax policy antagonized the church, and his modest plans for social reform and land distribution made him enemies among men of property. When he saw the prevalent trend toward more reactionary government, Giolitti changed tack and decided to weight his coalition toward the right. He even gave the Fascists tacit permission to use violence against the Socialists and to exercise many of the functions pertaining to government, apparently thinking that he could stand above the melee without compromising himself too far with either extreme. In May 1921 new elections were held, and Giolitti even included the Fascists in his own coalition list; by this means Mussolini and 34 other Fascists at last entered parliamentary politics, which they could then undermine from within. Giolitti tried to get full powers from parliament in order to deal with the emergency, but even Mussolini deserted him and he had to resign.

Giolitti in 1922 did not oppose the accession to power of Mussolini, but he commanded his followers to accept it as the only remedy for the existing political anarchy. In the elections of 1924 he did not join Mussolini's list of candidates, but he still continued to support the dictator until all means of opposition were destroyed. Giolitti died at Cavour, Piedmont, on July 17, 1928.

BIBLIOGRAPHY.—Giovanni Giolitti, *Memoirs of My Life*, Eng. trans. (1923); A. W. Salomone, *Italian Democracy in the Making*: *the Political Scene in the Giolittian Era, 1900–1914* (1945); D. Mack Smith, *Italy: a Modern History* (1959).
(D. M. Sᴍ.)

GIONO, JEAN (1895–1970), French novelist, whose works are set in Provence, and whose rich and diverse imagery has been widely admired, was born in Manosque, Basses-Alpes, on March 30, 1895; he died there on Oct. 8, 1970. He was largely self-taught, reading Homer, Virgil, Herman Melville and Walt Whitman. He was a soldier in World War I and hated it: he saw in war mainly its horrors, and described them in *Le Grand Troupeau* (1931). He made himself known by regionalist, anti-intellectual novels such as *Colline* (1928), *Un de Baumugnes* (1929), *Regain* (1930; Eng. trans. *Harvest*, 1939); short, moving stories of primitive but noble people. Loosely constructed but written in a poetic style reminiscent of Virgil's *Bucolics*, they were the protest of a sensitive man against modern civilization. This tendency was even more apparent in the trilogy *Le Chant du monde* (1934; Eng. trans. *The Song of the World*, 1937) and in *Que ma joie demeure* (1935) and *Batailles dans la montagne* (1937), longer works with a prophetic quality which developed Giono's ideal of blending man with nature.

Giono, still a pacifist, did not publish much during World War II, but devoted most of his time to writing. After the war, a new Giono emerged. Instead of writing pages filled with imagery and torrential descriptions of nature, he had developed a concise, almost bare style and concentrated on storytelling. His new novels were more in the tradition of Joseph Conrad and Stendhal than in his former pantheistic, allegoric, pagan vein. He still condemned society as wedded to evil, but was on the whole more optimistic about man. His best works in the new manner were *Le Hussard sur le toit* (1952; Eng. trans. *The Hussar on the Roof*, 1953) and *Le Bonheur fou* (1957), with the same hero, a young Italian adventurer of 1830–48, reminiscent of Stendhal's Fabrice Del Dongo.

Jean Giono also wrote plays, including *Le Bout de la route*, *Le Lanceur de graines*, *La Femme du boulanger*, later successful as a film (collected 1943), and *Le Voyage en calèche* (1947).

BIBLIOGRAPHY.—R. de Villeneuve, *Jean Giono, ce solitaire* (1955); J. Pugnet, *Jean Giono* (1955); H. Chonez, *Giono par lui-même* (1956).
(P. E. B.)

GIORDANO, LUCA (1632–1705), the most celebrated and prolific Neapolitan painter of the late 17th century, was born in Naples in 1632. His nickname *Luca fa presto* ("Luke, work quickly") is said to derive from his father's admonitions, which were certainly heeded. He probably learned his technical virtuosity at a very early age, since he was the son of a painter-copyist. His other nickname, Proteus, was due to his skill in producing pastiches in the style of almost any other artist, including even Dürer and Rembrandt, but it seems that he never made any copies in the strict sense of the word. Since he is said to have painted a complete high altarpiece in one day, it is no wonder that his output was huge, both in oil and in fresco. His range of subject matter was equally great, although most of his pictures naturally deal with religious or mythological themes.

Giordano's earliest dated work is of 1651, but he is not recorded in the painters' guild until 1665. He was very much influenced at the beginning of his career by the work of Jusepe de Ribera, the major Neapolitan artist of the first half of the century, and it is likely that he was actually Ribera's pupil. His style underwent a profound change as a result of journeys to Rome, Florence and Venice. The lightness and brightness of Veronese's decorative works in Venice and the recent work by Pietro da Cortona in Rome and Florence induced him to abandon the gloom and drama of Ribera in favour of a more decorative approach; and the influence, is particularly evident in Luca's huge ceiling fresco in the ballroom of the Medici-Riccardi palace, Florence, begun in 1682 and completed in the following year. In 1682 he also painted the ceiling of the Corsini chapel in Sta. Maria del Carmine, Florence.

He went to Spain in 1692 as court painter to Charles II, returning via Genoa to Naples in 1702. The frescoes in the Escorial are often held to be his best works, but nearly 50 pictures in the Prado museum, Madrid, all painted in Spain, testify to his unflagging energy.

Much the greater part of his output nevertheless remained in Naples, particularly in the churches, but many of his frescoes were destroyed or damaged in World War II. The great St. Benedict cycle of 1677 in the abbey of Monte Cassino was entirely destroyed, but the "Christ Expelling the Traders from the Temple" (1684) in the Gerolomini (S. Filippo Neri) in Naples survived the damage to the church. His last great work in Naples was the ceiling of the Cappella del Tesoro in S. Martino, begun on his return in 1702 and completed in April 1704. Giordano died in Naples on Jan. 12, 1705. His usual signature was "Jordanus," and this has led to confusion with Jacob Jordaens, with whose work Luca's has very little in common.

BIBLIOGRAPHY.—G. P. Bellori, Le vite de' pittori . . . , 2nd ed. (1728); B. De Dominici, Vite de' pittori . . . napoletani (1742-43); R. Wittkower, Art and Architecture in Italy, 1600-1750 (1958). (P. J. Mv.)

GIORDANO, UMBERTO (1867-1948), Italian opera composer, a follower of P. Mascagni and known for his opera *Andrea Chénier*. The son of an artisan, he was born at Foggia on Aug. 27, 1867, and studied music first in his native town and then at the Naples conservatory. He reached manhood when Mascagni was startling the world with the realism of *Cavalleria Rusticana* (1890); Giordano's early operas, among them *Mala vita* (1892), were written in the same forceful, melodramatic style. In *Andrea Chénier* (1896), based on the life of the French revolutionary poet, he tempered violence with gentler characteristics and scored a lasting success. Neither *Fedora* (1898), nor its chief successors, *Siberia* (1903) and *Madame Sans-Gêne* (1915), achieved a similar popularity. In *La Cena delle Beffe* (1924) Giordano reverted to a sensational manner with a story set in medieval Florence. He died in Milan on Nov. 12, 1948.
(Dv. H.)

GIORGIO, FRANCESCO DI: see FRANCESCO DI GIORGIO.

GIORGIONE (1477 or 1478-1510), Italian painter of the Venetian Renaissance, was born at Castelfranco. Contemporary documents call him Zorzo or Zorzi da Castelfranco. The form of Giorgione or Zorzon (meaning tall or great George) cropped up 40 years after his death. Because of an unfounded tradition, appearing about 1650, of his illegitimate descent from the local gentry family of Barbarella or Barbarelli, he is often referred to as Giorgione Barbarella or Barbarelli. Giorgio Vasari, writing before 1550, states that Giorgione was of very humble origin.

Giorgione presents a fascinating problem in the history of Renaissance art. The few documents available and the contemporary literary sources show that he was held in high esteem at a relatively young age, and that his work was regarded as a sort of turning point in art between the 15th and the 16th centuries and as the beginning of a new, "modern," style based on the effects of colour and light; they also show that his fame was not limited to Venice. The number of his documented works is exceedingly small, even allowing for the short span of his active life, a mere 12 to 13 years. By the 17th century, a Giorgione myth based on anecdotes had come into existence, of which the writings of Ridolfi are a telling expression. Giorgione was erroneously claimed as ancestor of a romantic trend in Venetian painting after 1600 (e.g., Pietro della Vecchia), which displayed dramatic accents and violent contrasts of light and shade.

The Giorgione literature since 1870 shows such a lack of consensus that a great Italian art historian (A. Venturi) could exclaim: "Everybody makes his own Giorgione." Two opposite tendencies, however, can be distinguished among the critics of that period: one "expansionist" (H. Cook, Monneret de Villard, L. Justi), attributing to Giorgione more and more pictures, especially those displaying a softly emotional, moody character; the other "restrictive" (Gronau, Lionello Venturi, Hourticq) trying, among this welter of mostly very subjective attributions, to go back to the facts securely established by the earliest sources. About 1870-80, G. B. Cavalcaselle and G. Morelli did great service in dispelling this fog. The Giorgione exhibition in Venice in 1955 provided an opportunity for putting some order into chaos, but his early work proves that his compositions were influenced more by Vittore Carpaccio (q.v.) and by the classicism of Francesco Francia and Lorenzo Costa. Also, the treatment of light on shining surfaces as introduced in Venice by Antonello da Messina in his altarpiece of S. Cassiano (1475) must have impressed the young artist.

The contemporary inscription on the back of a painting entitled "Laura" (Vienna) mentions its completion, on June 1, 1506, by Giorgione, who is described as a colleague of Vincenzo Catena. On Aug. 14, 1507, and Jan. 24, 1508, the Council of Ten ordered payment to Giorgione for a painting for the audience room of the Ducal palace; by May 23, 1508, this painting was certainly completed. On Aug. 1, 1508, the frescoes on the façade of the German Merchants' hall were underway. In Sept. or Oct. 1510, Giorgione died of the plague that raged in Venice. Shortly after his death, Isabella d'Este, marchioness of Mantua, wrote to her agent T. Albano, entreating him to secure a nativity scene by Giorgione. Albano replied that Giorgione had done this subject twice, but that neither of the owners wished to sell. Count Baldassare Castiglione, writing in Rome not later than 1524, mentioned Giorgione among the "most excellent" painters, together with Leonardo, Mantegna, Raphael and Michelangelo. The most valuable source, however, consists of the notes written by the Venetian patrician Marcantonio Michiel between 1520 and 1543, each entry being carefully dated. He mentions 12 paintings and one drawing by Giorgione; also one painting of which he is not quite sure and two copies after Giorgione. Most of these works are lost, as is the picture of an armoured St. George mirrored in a pond and in two looking glasses, described by Paolo Pino in 1548. Two of the paintings mentioned by Michiel, however, can be identified: the "Three Philosophers" (or magi), in the Vienna gallery; and the landscape with the thunderstorm (tempesta), depicting a young man and a woman nursing her baby, in the academy in Venice. To these should be added the portrait of a woman called "Laura," in the Vienna gallery; the altarpiece in the parish church of Castelfranco; and the fresco-fragment of a female nude in the academy in Venice—the only fragment that has survived, though in an appalling state of preservation, of Giorgione's decoration of the German Merchants' hall. These five pictures, and especially the four oil paintings, dated between 1505 and 1508, are the hard core on which the knowledge of Giorgione's art rests. Giorgione's technique is the contrary of a "sweeping movement." His brush stroke consists of very fine disconnected lines and dots. The modeling is achieved by a sort of hatching that resembles the technique of water-colour miniatures and is related to what was later called pointillism. Its effects are to make the entire surface seem to vibrate, so that the atmosphere between individual objects, permeated by light, becomes the subject of artistic rendering.

This new feeling for nature is the source of the charm and the peculiar mood emanating from Giorgione's paintings. It has been aptly called pantheistic. This feeling, though not caused by, is intimately related to the philosophical "naturalism" informing the contemporary Venetian and Paduan humanists grouped around Barbaro and Pietro Pomponazzi.

On the criterion of this unmistakable "trembling" brush stroke, the following additional pictures can be confidently attributed to Giorgione: "The Testing of Moses" (Uffizi, Florence), but only the nine figures on the left and the distant part of the landscape (the rest, as also the companion piece, the "Judgment of Solomon," is clearly by an assistant, possibly G. Campagnola); the "Adoration of the Magi" (National gallery, London); the "Judith" (Leningrad); the three exquisite little mythological panels (two in Padua and one in the Philipps memorial, Washington, D.C.); the little "Madonna With Child" (Leningrad; the head is badly repainted); the "Madonna With SS. Catherine and John" (Academy, Venice); the ex-Benson "Nativity" (Kress collection, National gallery, Washington, D.C.) and the ex-Allendale "Adoration of the Shepherds" (same collection). The only extant drawing is a landscape with a seated man (ex-Koenig, Museum of Rotterdam). The "Boy With Arrow" (Vienna) is doubtful (possibly a studio picture with partial collaboration of the master). All these should be dated before 1505; likewise, the so-called "Vendramin" portrait (Berlin); the original parts of the portrait of a young woman (Duveen, New York, much restored); the "Old Woman" ("Col Tempo," Academy, Venice); and the heads and a few other parts of the two youths in the "Concert champêtre" (Louvre), the rest being completed by the young Titian (q.v.), who

BY COURTESY OF KUNSTHISTORISCHES MUSEUM

"THREE PHILOSOPHERS" BY GIORGIONE. IN THE KUNSTHISTORISCHES MUSEUM, VIENNA, AUSTRIA

was an assistant in Giorgione's workshop about 1508 and possibly later (Titian's collaboration is proved by the statuary conception of the standing woman and the broad, sweeping, dramatic brushwork). To the end of Giorgione's short life belong the unfinished "Madonna With SS. Anthony and Roch" (Madrid) and the fragment of a self-portrait (Braunschweig); X-rays have revealed that it is painted over an earlier, unfinished Madonna by Giorgione. However, Giorgione's development after 1508 (the year of the frescoes) is very dim and not likely to become clearer, because of lack of material.

Among many, the following paintings that have been variously attributed to Giorgione should be rigidly excluded from his work: "The Dresden Venus" and the "Concert," both by Titian; the "Boy With Flute," possibly by Titian; the "Three Ages," possibly by G. Bellini; the "Concert," possibly by Lotto; the "Judgment of Solomon," by Sebastiano del Piombo; the "Adulteress," probably by D. Mancini; the double portrait (Venezia palace, Rome); the "Knight and Page" (Uffizi); the so-called "Broccardo" (Budapest); and the two pictures of singing men (Borghese, Rome). The last six paintings belong to a later development.

Giorgione did not form a school, properly speaking. But his influence was colossal and decisive—on Titian, Sebastiano del Piombo and Bellini, and on the entire tradition of Venetian painting and its derivations, through Velázquez to Manet.

BIBLIOGRAPHY.—A. Morassi, Giorgione (1942); P. Zampetti, Giorgione e i Giorgioneschi (catalogues of Giorgione exhibition in Venice), with bibliography, 2nd ed. (1955); Ludwig von Baldass und Günther Heinz, Giorgione (1964).   (E. H. Bu.)

GIOTTINO (GIOTTO DI MAESTRO DI STEFANO), an early Florentine painter, whose name occurs in 1368 in the records of the guild. His father is sometimes identified with a pupil of Giotto, who attained some fame. In 1369 Giottino was called to Rome to assist in paintings in the Vatican. To his early period are ascribed the frescoes in the lower church of Assisi representing the "Coronation of the Virgin" and two scenes of the legend of St. Nicholas. They differ somewhat in style from his later work—the frescoes in the chapel of the Bardi family in Sta. Croce in Florence representing the miracles of Pope St. Silvester.

These works are animated and firm in drawing, luminous in colour, with naturalism carried further than by Giotto. They are among the most important paintings of Giotto's school. A "Descent From the Cross," in the Uffizi at Florence, also has been ascribed to Giottino.

Much confusion has arisen because Vasari identified Giottino with the painter Maso, who was active between 1320 and 1350, and to whom Ghiberti ascribed the frescoes of the St. Silvester legend.

GIOTTO (GIOTTO DI BONDONE) (1266/67?–1337), Italian painter, was born at Vespignano near Florence. For more than six centuries he has been revered as the father of modern art and the first of the great Italian masters. He certainly achieved great personal fame in his own lifetime; as Dante says in the Divine Comedy (Purg. xi, 94–96), "Cimabue thought to hold the field in painting, but now Giotto has the cry, so that the fame of him is "obscured." The mere fact that he was mentioned in Dante, even though not in a particularly flattering context, was sufficient to establish and maintain this fame in 14th- and 15th-century Italy and legends soon began to crystallize around his name. When, in 1550, Giorgio Vasari published the first modern history of art, he naturally began with Giotto as the man who, even more than his master Cimabue, broke away from the dark ages and ushered in the "good modern manner."

As early as the middle of the 15th century the story was told of Giotto as a shepherd boy drawing his father's sheep on a piece of flat stone and being discovered by Cimabue, who took him to Florence. Still earlier, however, the Anonymous Dante Commentator (of c. 1400) had told an entirely different story, for, according to him, Giotto was apprenticed to the wool trade in Florence but spent all his time in Cimabue's shop, so that finally his father transferred his apprenticeship. Both stories agree in making Giotto Cimabue's pupil and this tradition is probably largely correct. Nevertheless, whatever he may have learned from Cimabue it is certain that, like Niccolò Pisano about 30 years earlier, he was truly a reviver of classical ideals and a great innovator at the same time, bringing the new humanity, which St. Francis had brought to religion, into painting.

In Giotto's works the human beings who are his exclusive subject matter act with dedicated passion their parts in the great Christian drama of sacrifice and redemption. By comparison, all his predecessors and most of his immediate successors painted a puppet show with lifeless manikins tricked out in the rags of the splendid, hieratic and impersonal art of Byzantium, which was to be entirely superseded by the urgent emotionalism of the Franciscan approach to Christianity.

The Date of Giotto's Birth.—The date of Giotto's birth can be taken as either 1266/67 or 1276, but the 10 years' difference is of fundamental importance in assessing his early development and is crucial to the Assisi problem (see below). It is known that Giotto died Jan. 8, 1337 (new style; 1336, old style); this was recorded at the time in the Villani *Chronicle*. About 1373 a rhymed version of the Villani *Chronicle* was produced by Antonio Pucci, town crier of Florence and amateur poet, and in this it is stated that Giotto was 70 when he died. He was thus born in 1266/67, and it is clear that there is 14th-century authority for the statement (possibly Giotto's original tombstone, now lost). Vasari, however, gives 1276 as the year of Giotto's birth and it may be that he was copying one of the two known versions of the *Libro di Antonio Billi*, a collection of notes on Florentine artists. In this version, the *Codex Petrei* (Biblioteca Nazionale, Florence), the statement that Giotto was born in 1276 at Vespignano, the son of a peasant, occurs at the very end of the 'Life' and may have been added much later, even, conceivably, from Vasari. In any case, whether Vasari or "Antonio Billi" first made the statement, it cannot have the same authority as attaches to Pucci, who was about 27 when Giotto died. Certainty of the date of Giotto's birth, if settled by new documents, could help to solve the problem of his work at Assisi and the question of the origins of his style.

The Assisi Problem.—This, the central problem in Giotto studies, may be summed up as the question whether Giotto ever painted at Assisi and, if so, what? There can be no reasonable doubt that he did work at Assisi, for there is a long literary tradition which goes back to the *Chronicle* of Riccobaldo Ferrarese who wrote in or before 1319; *i.e.*, when Giotto was alive and famous. Later writers down to Vasari expanded this and made it clear that Giotto's works were in the great double church of S. Francesco. By Vasari's time several frescoes in both upper and lower churches were attributed to Giotto, the most important being the cycle of 28 scenes from the life of St. Francis of Assisi in the nave of the upper church and the "Franciscan Virtues" and some other frescoes in the lower church.

In the 19th century it was observed that all these could not be by the same hand, and the new trend toward skepticism of Vasari's statements led to the position adopted by F. Rintelen in which he rejected all the Assisi frescoes and dated the St. Francis cycle to a period after Giotto's death. This extreme view has been

generally abandoned, and indeed a dated picture of 1307 can be shown to derive from the St. Francis cycle. Nevertheless, many scholars prefer to accept the idea of an otherwise totally unknown "Master of the St. Francis legend" on the grounds that the style of the cycle is irreconcilable with that of the Padua frescoes, which are universally accepted as Giotto's. This involves the idea that the works referred to (in Giotto's lifetime) by Riccobaldo cannot be identified with anything now extant and must have perished centuries ago, so that Ghiberti, Vasari and others mistakenly transferred the existing St. Francis cycle to Giotto. Five hundred years of tradition are thus written off.

Still more difficult, the St. Francis frescoes, major works of art, must be attributed to a painter who cannot be shown to have created anything else, whose name has disappeared without trace although he was of the first rank and, odder still, was formed by the combined influences of Cimabue the Florentine and P. Cavallini the Roman, influences which coalesce at Assisi and may be taken as the influences which formed Giotto himself. Arising out of the fusion of Roman and Florentine influences at Assisi, there was later a tendency to see the hand of Giotto, as a very young man, in the works of the "Isaac Master," the painter of two scenes of "Isaac and Esau" and "Jacob and Isaac" in the nave above the St. Francis cycle. If this theory is accepted it is easy to understand that Giotto, as a young man, made such a success of this commission that he was entrusted with the most important one, the official painted biography of St. Francis based on the new official biography written by St. Bonaventura. In fact, the whole of our mental picture of St. Francis stems largely from these frescoes. Clearly, a man born in 1276 was less likely to have received such a commission than one ten years older, if, as was always thought, the commission was given in 1296 or soon after by Fra Giovanni di Muro, general of the Franciscans. (For reasons why this date is not necessarily binding, see bibliography, P. Murray.) The works in the lower church are generally regarded as productions of Giotto's followers (there are, indeed, resemblances to his works at Padua) and there is real disagreement only over the "Legend of St. Francis." The main strength

MANSELL-ANDERSON
"SAINT FRANCIS RENOUNCING HIS PATRIMONY" BY GIOTTO; ABOUT 1296. FRESCO FROM THE UPPER CHURCH AT ASSISI, ITALY

of the non-Giotto school lies in the admittedly sharp stylistic contrasts between the St. Francis cycle and the frescoes in the Arena chapel at Padua, especially if the Assisi frescoes were painted 1296–c. 1300 and those of the Arena c. 1303–05; for the interval between the two cycles is too small to allow for major stylistic developments. This argument becomes less compelling when the validity of the dates proposed and the Roman period c. 1300 are taken into account. As already mentioned, the Assisi frescoes may have been painted before 1296 and not necessarily in or before 1309, although probably painted c. 1305–06; clearly, a greater time lag between the two cycles can help to explain stylistic differences, as can the experiences which Giotto underwent in what was probably his second Roman period.

Roman Period c. 1300.—Three principal works are attributed to Giotto in Rome. They are the great mosaic of "Christ Walking on the Water" (the "Navicella") over the entrance to St. Peter's; the altarpiece painted for Cardinal Stefaneschi, in the Vatican gallery; and the fresco fragment of "Boniface VIII Proclaiming the Jubilee" in S. Giovanni Laterano. Giotto is also known to have painted some frescoes in the choir of Old St. Peter's but these are lost. It is known from the *Necrology* (1343) that Cardinal Stefaneschi was a great benefactor of St. Peter's and that he employed Giotto to make the "Navicella" but the date 1298 for this commission does not occur in the actual text, although it is often said to occur, on the authority of F. Baldinucci, who saw another version in the 17th century.

It is known, however, that the religious jubilee of 1300 was very largely unpremeditated and the "Navicella" is most probably a commemoration of its success, and therefore commissioned at almost any date after 1300. In any case, it was almost entirely remade in the 17th century except for two fragmentary heads of angels (in the museum of St. Peter's and in Boville Ernica), so that old copies must be used for all stylistic deductions.

The fresco fragment in S. Giovanni Laterano was cleaned in the 20th century and was tentatively reattributed to Giotto on the basis of its likeness to the Assisi frescoes. The original attribution cannot be traced beyond the 17th century, but, on the other hand, the "Stefaneschi Altar" (Vatican), with its portrait of the cardinal himself, must be one of the works commissioned by him. It is, nevertheless, so poor in quality that it cannot be by Giotto's own hand. It may be observed that several works bearing Giotto's signature, notably the "St. Francis" (Paris, Louvre) and the altarpieces in Bologna and Florence (Sta. Croce), are generally regarded as school pieces bearing his trade-mark, whereas the "Ognissanti Madonna" (Uffizi, Florence), unsigned and virtually undocumented, is so superlative in quality that it is accepted as entirely by his hand.

The Crucifix in Sta. Maria Novella and the "Madonna" in S. Giorgio sulla Costa (both in Florence) may be possibly identifiable with works mentioned in very early sources and if so they throw light on Giotto's early style (before 1300). It is also possible that, about 1305, Giotto went to Avignon but the evidence for this is slender.

Paduan Period.—There is thus no very generally agreed upon picture of Giotto's early development and many of the surviving documents and pictures are capable of more than one interpretation. It is some relief, therefore, to turn to the fresco cycle in the chapel in Padua known as the Arena or Scrovegni chapel. Its name derives from the fact that it was built on the site of a Roman amphitheatre by Enrico Scrovegni, the son of a notorious usurer mentioned by Dante. The founder is shown offering a model of the church in the huge "Last Judgment," which covers the whole west wall. The rest of the small bare church is covered with frescoes in three tiers representing scenes from the lives of SS. Joachim and Anna, the life of the Virgin, the Annunciation (on the chancel arch) and the Life and Passion of Christ, concluding with Pentecost. Below these three narrative bands is a fourth containing monochrome personifications of the Virtues and Vices. The chapel was apparently founded in 1303 and consecrated on March 25, 1305. It is known that the frescoes were completed in or before 1309 and they are generally dated c. 1305/6, but even with several assistants it must have taken at least two years to complete so large a cycle.

The frescoes are in relatively good condition, and all that has been said of Giotto's power to render the bare essentials of a setting with a few impressive and simple figures telling the story as dramatically and yet as economically as possible is usually based on the narrative power which is the fundamental characteristic of these frescoes. These dominating figures, simple and severe, are the quintessence of his style, and anatomy and perspective were used—or even invented—by him as adjuncts to his narrative gifts; he never attained to the skill which so often misled the men of the 15th and 16th centuries. In the Padua frescoes the details are always significant, whereas it is a characteristic of the Assisi cycle that there occurs from time to time a delighted dwelling on details that are not absolutely essential to the story.

Sta. Croce Frescoes.—Documents show that Giotto was in Florence in 1311–14 and 1320 and it was probably during these years, before going to Naples (c. 1329?), that he painted frescoes in four chapels in Sta. Croce belonging to the Giugni, Tosinghi-Spinelli, Bardi and Peruzzi families. The Giugni chapel frescoes are lost as are all the Tosinghi-Spinelli ones, except for an "Assumption" over the entrance, not universally accepted as by Giotto. The Bardi and Peruzzi chapels contained cycles of St. Francis and the two SS. John, respectively, but the frescoes were whitewashed and were not recovered until 1852, when they were damaged in the process of removing the whitewash and then heavily restored. Much the same happened to a portrait of Dante in the Bargello, also in Florence, for which there is a traditional attribution to Giotto. The account taken of the restorations to the Bardi and Peruzzi chapel frescoes and of the similarities and dissimilarities between the Bardi St. Francis frescoes and those at Assisi tends to vary according to the writer's views on the Assisi problem, but most students would agree that it would be imprudent to ascribe much of the actual handling (as distinct from the design) to Giotto himself in either chapel. There is no evidence for the dating of the chapels, nor is it certain which came first, but they are probably approximately contemporary. The date 1317 is often advanced as a terminal point for the Bardi chapel, since it contains a representation of St. Louis of Toulouse, who was canonized in that year. This is inadmissible since his halo may well have been added, and in any case it is not unknown for holy personages to be represented as haloed before their formal canonization.

Naples and the Last Florentine Period.—On Jan. 20, 1330, King Robert of Naples promoted Giotto to the rank of "familiar" (member of the royal household), which implies that he had been in Naples for some while, possibly since 1328, and he remained there until 1332/33. All the works he executed there have been lost, but traces of his style may be distinguished in the local school. On April 12, 1334, he was appointed *capomaestro*, or surveyor, of the Cathedral of Florence and architect to the city. This was a tribute to his great fame as a painter and not on account of any special architectural knowledge. On July 19 of the same year he began the campanile, or bell tower, of the cathedral. It was later altered but is known, in part at least, from a drawing in Siena. He may have designed some of the reliefs carved by Andrea Pisano on the campanile; certainly the bronze doors of the baptistery by Andrea show clear traces of Giotto's frescoes in Sta. Croce. Indeed the whole course of painting in Tuscany was dominated by his pupils and followers—by Taddeo Gaddi, Bernardo Daddi, Maso, Orcagna and the Lorenzetti in Siena—but none of these really understood all of his innovations and it was not until Masaccio (b. 1401) and Michelangelo (b. 1475) that his true successors arose.

See also references under "Giotto" in the Index.

BIBLIOGRAPHY.—R. Salvini, *Giotto Bibliografia*, with full bibliography up to 1937 (1938); *Giotto*, ed. by C. H. Weigelt, "Klassiker der Kunst" Series (1925); the large commemorative catalogue of the 1937 exhibition, G. Sinibaldi and G. Brunetti, *Pittura italiana del Duecento e Trecento* (1943). *See* also articles in *Burlington Magazine* by R. Offner, "Giotto," "Non-Giotto," 74:259 ff. (1939) and 75:96 ff. (1939), by C. Brandi, 94:218 (1952) and by J. White, "The Date of "The"

Legend of S. Francis' at Assisi," 98:344 ff. (1956); in the Journal of the Warburg and Courtauld Institutes, by C. Mitchell, 14:1 (1951) and P. Murray, "Notes on Some Early Giotto Sources," 16:58 ff. (1953); W. Paeseler in Römisches Jahrbuch für Kunstgeschichte ("Hertziana Jahrbuch"), vol. v, pp. 51 ff. (1941); R. Salvini, Tutta la Pittura di Giotto (1952); C. Gnudi, Giotto (1959).

GIOVANNI DI PAOLO (c. 1403-1482), the name commonly given to Giovanni di Paolo di Grazia, a long-lived, enormously productive Sienese painter of great individuality. He probably was a pupil of Taddeo di Bartolo, whose style is reflected in his earliest dated work, the "Madonna" of 1426 at Castelnuovo Berardenga. In that year Giovanni fell under the influence of the art of Gentile da Fabriano, who was then active in Siena. The earliest example of Gentile's influence, dominant for a decade, is the "Madonna" of 1427 in the Robert von Hirsch collection, Basel, Switz. During the 1440s and early 1450s Giovanni produced his most important works. These include the monumental altarpiece of the "Presentation of Christ" of 1447-49 in the Siena gallery, the somewhat later altarpiece of "St. John the Baptist," only ten scenes of which work are known, and 12 splendid miniatures in an antiphonary in the public library, Siena. The brooding "Madonna" altarpiece of 1463 in the Pienza cathedral marks the beginning of Giovanni's late period, of which the coarse "Assumption" polyptych of 1475 from Staggia is the last important example.

Giovanni's tormented spirituality and expressionist style were little appreciated before about 1920, but from that time his tense, often highly dramatic art aroused constantly increasing interest. Not only the coloristically and formally attractive figures and landscapes of the painter's early and middle period, but also the harsh, ugly forms of the 1460s and especially the 1470s are of interest, as they illustrate the artist's changing vision of the world during the course of his development.

BIBLIOGRAPHY.—John Pope-Hennessy, Giovanni di Paolo (1937); Cesare Brandi, Giovanni di Paolo, in Italian, with a comprehensive bibliography (1947); Pèleo Bacci, Documenti e commenti per la storia dell'arte, an important study of the documents, pp. 63-94 (1944).
(G. M. Cr.)

GIOVIO, PAOLO: see JOVIUS, PAULUS.

GIPPSLAND: see VICTORIA.

GIRAFFE, the tallest of all mammals, reaching an over-all height of more than 18 ft., forms with the okapi (q.v.) the family Giraffidae in the suborder Ruminantia, order Artiodactyla. Two sub-species are usually recognized: Giraffa camelopardalis camelopardalis, the common or blotched giraffe; and G. c. reticulata, the reticulated or Somali giraffe. "Giraffe" comes from the Arabic word zarafa, meaning, among other things, "one who walks swiftly." It is said that Julius Caesar was the first to import a giraffe to Europe, exhibiting it in Rome about 46 B.C. To the Romans the animal was "camelopardalis," a term that survived for some time in English as "cameleopard."

The giraffe's body is comparatively short, but the legs and neck are very long. In spite of its length, the neck, as in almost all mammals, contains only seven vertebrae. The forequarters stand higher than the hind, and the tail tuft reaches below the hocks; there are no lateral toes on the feet. The short thorns on the head, present in both sexes, are covered with skin and end with short tufts of hair. There is always at least one pair and a central swelling on the forehead, between the eyes, which in some races is almost as long as the horns. In some races, too, there is a second smaller pair of horns behind the main ones, making five in all. The horns are not used in defense, which is effected instead by powerful kicks from the fore- or hind legs, but they are used in sparring, when rival males are engaged in "necking" combats. The ground colour of the coat is pale sandy, covered to a greater or

CAMERA PRESS LTD.
RETICULATED GIRAFFE (GIRAFFA RETICULATA)

lesser extent with darker spots, which may be diffuse and pale (G. c. camelopardalis) or very clear-cut and richly coloured (G. c. reticulata). In the latter type the spots predominate so that the ground colour looks like a light-coloured net thrown over a dark background. Many subspecies have been described, based on variation of coat pattern and the size and number of horns, but it is not certain that they are really distinct.

Giraffes are native to most of Africa south of the Sahara, and live in savanna or open bush country, but do not penetrate into the forests. They browse upon trees, but do not habitually graze, for they have to spread the forelegs widely to reach the ground or to drink. The gait of the giraffe is a pace (both legs on one side move together) and, because of the long stride, is swifter than it appears; more than 30 m.p.h. may be reached at a full gallop. One young is produced at a birth, after a gestation of about 14 months; the calf can follow its mother within two hours of its birth. The voice, ranging from low call notes to a hoarse roar, has so rarely been heard that giraffes are popularly supposed to be completely dumb. Giraffes are still numerous in east Africa, where they are protected, but elsewhere they have dwindled in number because of injudicious hunting by man: the tribesmen seek them for food; the big game hunters, for trophies.

See also ARTIODACTYL; RUMINANT.
(L. H. M.)

GIRALDI, GIAMBATTISTA (known also as CINZIO, the Italian form of his "academic" name, CYNTHIUS) (1504-1573), Italian novelist, poet and dramatist, a typical representative of mid-16th-century Italian literary ideals, was born in Ferrara. He studied under Celio Calcagnini and succeeded him in the chair of rhetoric there (1541), later moving to the universities of Turin and Pavia. He died in Ferrara.

Giraldi was influenced both by the Paduan reintroduction of Aristotelian literary principles and by the Catholic reaction to it. In his Discorso intorno al comporre de' romanzi (1549) he defended the legitimacy of the romantic epic, and in his poem Ercole (1557) he tried to reconcile the Aristotelian rules with modern taste. In his Discorso sulle commedie e sulle tragedie (1543) he reacted against the austerity of the classical tragedies and in his own tragedies—Orbecche (1541); Selene; Eufimia; Arrenopia; Epitia, from which Shakespeare's Measure for Measure derives; and Antivalomeni (1549)—he included new dramatic elements while conforming to the Aristotelian rules. His Ecatommiti (1565), 112 stories collected according to the pattern of Boccaccio's Decameron, aims at stylistic distinction as well as showing a liking for direct narrative, in the manner of Matteo Bandello. They are moralistic in tone and were translated and imitated in France, Spain and England: Shakespeare's Othello derives from Giraldi's story of the Moor of Venice. He tried to renew the pastoral drama with his Egle (1545).

In spite of his ambition toward erudition, all Giraldi's literary attempts are amateurish: they remain interesting examples of the transition from Renaissance to Counter-Reformation ideals.

BIBLIOGRAPHY.—Scritti estetici di G. B. Giraldi (1864); C. Guerrieri-Crocetti, G. B. Giraldi ed il pensiero critico del sec. XVI (1932); R. Piccini, "Vita di G. B. Giraldi," in Atti e memorie per le provincie modenese e parmense, xviii (1886); G. Perale, Sul valore morale degli "Ecatommiti" (1907); A. Milano, Le tragedie di Seneca del '500: G. B. Giraldi (1901); L. Dondoni, "Un interprete di Seneca del '500: G. B. Giraldi," in Rendiconti Istituto Lombardo, Classe di Lettere, etc., xciii (1959).
(G. A.)

GIRALDUS CAMBRENSIS (GERALD OF WALES, also called GERALD DE BARRI) (c. 1146-c. 1223), archdeacon of Brecon from 1175 to 1204, author and vigorous opponent of Anglo-Norman authority over the church in Wales, was born in Manorbier castle near Pembroke, the youngest son of William de Barri, the Norman castellan of Pembroke. More significantly, Gerald's grandmother was Nesta, a descendant of the princes of south Wales; hence his pride of ancestry and race, though he was not Welsh-speaking. A precocious child, early destined for the church, he was educated in Paris, returning to Wales in 1175, when he was appointed archdeacon of Brecon. Though a man of the world and proud of his literary ability, Gerald was primarily an ecclesiastic and he rapidly distinguished himself by his reforming zeal. He was nominated as bishop of St. David's (1176) but was not elected, and returned to Paris to study canon law and theology. He entered the royal service, probably in July 1184, and two journeys undertaken during this period led to the compilation of his best-known and, indeed, indispensable books, those on contemporary Ireland and Wales. He visited Ireland (1185-86) with Henry II's youngest son (afterward King John) and as a result wrote his *Topographia Hibernica* (c. 1188) and the *Expugnatio Hibernica* (c. 1189). His tour of Wales (1188) with Baldwin, archbishop of Canterbury, undertaken to raise soldiers for the third crusade similarly provided material for his *Itinerarium Cambriae* (1191) and *Descriptio Cambriae* (1194). He left the king's service in 1195, retiring to Lincoln to study theology.

Gerald's later life was clouded by his frustrated ambition to succeed to the see of St. David's and to make it a metropolitan see independent of Canterbury. This ambition, according to his autobiography, *De rebus a se gestis* (c. 1204-05), led him to reject four Irish and two Welsh bishoprics. He was again nominated for St. David's in 1199; but Hubert Walter, archbishop of Canterbury, promoted a rival candidate and although showing some sympathy for Gerald's cause, Pope Innocent III quashed both elections (1203). Gerald resigned his archdeaconry in 1204 and died probably in 1223.

Gerald's learning, of which he was vain, was old-fashioned; he was uncritical and violently emotional, venting his spleen in scandalous and unwarrantable charges against those who offended or slighted him. But his writings are full of admirable descriptions of both the high life and the everyday life of his own time; they sparkle with vivid anecdotes about the church, especially in Wales, about the growing universities of Paris and Oxford and about notable clerics and laymen. Above all, they provide a lively and incomparable portrait of one of the most engaging figures of the 12th century, Gerald de Barri himself.

BIBLIOGRAPHY.—J. S. Brewer *et al.* (eds.), *Giraldi Cambrensis opera* (1861-91); W. S. Davies (ed.), *Giraldus Cambrensis: de invectionibus* (1920); F. M. Powicke, *Gerald of Wales* (1928); H. E. Butler (ed.), *The Autobiography of Giraldus Cambrensis* (1937). (H. G. Ri.)

GIRARD, JEAN BAPTISTE (known as PÈRE GIRARD or PÈRE GRÉGOIRE) (1765-1850), French-Swiss educationalist, hailed in Switzerland as a second Pestalozzi, was born at Fribourg on Dec. 17, 1765, and educated for the priesthood at Lucerne. In 1804 he began his career as a public teacher, first in the elementary school at Fribourg (1805-23), then, on being driven away by Jesuit hostility, in the *Gymnasium* at Lucerne until 1834. In that year he retired to Fribourg and devoted himself to the production of his books on education, *De l'enseignement régulier de la langue maternelle* (1834; Eng. trans., *The Mother Tongue*, 1847) and *Cours éducatif* (1844-46). Girard's books influenced educational methods elsewhere. He abandoned the system of cramming children's minds with rules and facts, seeking instead to stimulate their intelligence. He died March 6, 1850.

GIRARD, STEPHEN (1750-1831), U.S. financier, philanthropist and founder of Girard college, Philadelphia, Pa., was born in Bordeaux, France, May 20, 1750. Before he was 14 he went to sea as a cabin boy, and at 24 was captain of a vessel in the American coastal trade. In 1776 he settled in Philadelphia, where he married and devoted himself to foreign trade. He developed a world-wide trading fleet which laid the foundation of his fortune.

During the yellow fever plague in Philadelphia in 1793 he volunteered to act as manager of the hospital, and again in the epidemic of 1797 he took the lead in caring for the sick. In May 1812, he bought the building and other assets of the Bank of the United States and established the Bank of Stephen Girard in Philadelphia, which was known as the "sheet anchor" of government credit in the War of 1812. In 1814 his bank subscribed for 95% of the government war loan issue. At his death on Dec. 26, 1831, most of his fortune was bequeathed to the city of Philadelphia for a school or college for "poor, white, male orphans," and for municipal improvements.

See J. B. McMaster, *Life and Times of Stephen Girard*, 2 vol. (1918); C. A. Herrick, *Stephen Girard, Founder* (1923). (J. R. Lт.)

GIRARDIN, DELPHINE DE (1804-1855), French writer, the wife of Émile de Girardin (*q.v.*), and a leading figure in Parisian literary society in the early 19th century, was born at Aix-la-Chapelle (Aachen), Jan. 26, 1804. Her mother, Sophie Gay, was also a writer. As a girl Delphine was the centre of attraction at her mother's *soirées* and became a society favourite, wooed by fashionable editors to provide poems for their periodicals. Her early works were published as *Essais poétiques* (1824) and *Nouveaux Essais poétiques* (1825). On a tour of Italy in 1826-27 she was elected to the Academy of the Tiber at the Capitol in Rome. Her 68 poems show snatches of brilliance but she was unable to sustain her inspiration. In 1831 she married Émile de Girardin and from 1836 to 1848 produced sketches for his journal *La Presse*, collected as *Lettres parisiennes* (1843 and 1853). To her famous *salon* came all the literary celebrities of Paris, including Théophile Gautier, Honoré de Balzac, Alfred de Musset and Victor Hugo. Her novels, brilliant in style but often somewhat lacking in invention, include *Le Canne de Monsieur Balzac* (1836) and *Il ne faut pas jouer avec la douleur* (1855). She also wrote several one-act comedies in prose and verse including *C'est la faute du mari* (1851), *Le Chapeau d'un Horloger* (1855) and *Une Femme qui déteste son mari*, published in 1856, a year after her death in Paris on June 29, 1855.

BIBLIOGRAPHY.—G. d'Heilly, *Mme de Girardin, sa vie et ses oeuvres* (1868); Imbert de Saint Amand, *Mme de Girardin* (1875); H. Malo, *Une Muse et sa mère, Delphine Gay* (1924) and *La Gloire du vicomte de Launay* (1925); Maurice Reclus, *Émile de Girardin* (1934).

GIRARDIN, ÉMILE DE (1806-1881), French writer, a pioneer of modern popular journalism, known as the Napoleon of the press, was born at Paris on June 21, 1806, the illegitimate son of Comte Alexandre de Girardin and of Mme Adelaide-Marie Dupuy, the wife of a lawyer. He left the Inspectorat des Beaux Arts to take up journalism and in 1828 founded *Le Voleur*, a monthly review of arts and science. In 1831 he married the writer Delphine Gay (see GIRARDIN, DELPHINE DE). He was elected deputy for Bourganeuf in 1834 and gained popular success by founding a new newspaper, *La Presse* (1836), for which the annual subscription was only 40 fr., but which made a profit because of excellent publicity. After a private and political dispute with Armand Carrel, director of the *National*, he killed him in a duel (July 22, 1836), and Girardin's popularity declined. He was excluded from the chamber of deputies on April 13, 1839, because of his doubtful nationality, but by April 23 his French birth had been officially established and he was readmitted in 1842. His political ideas followed the fluctuations of public opinion; he was a middle-class conservative who occasionally showed progressive tendencies. In 1848 he advised Louis Philippe to abdicate and hand over the regency to the duchess of Orléans, and at first supported the second republic, but after the risings of June 1848 he declared his support for Louis Napoleon. His waverings persisted under the second empire; in 1856 he gave up editorship of *La Presse*, but returned in 1862, joined the liberal party and pressed for war with Prussia. In 1866 he took control of *La Liberté*, an almost forgotten journal, which after a few weeks had a sale of 16,000 at 10 centimes a copy. After 1870 he became a Republican and in 1872 bought *Le Petit Journal*; its sale quickly rose to 500,000, and in 1874 he became political editor of *La France*. Both journals played a great part in the Republican triumph in the elections of 1877. After his wife's death in 1855, he married Mina Brunold de Tieffenbach, said to be the illegitimate daughter of Prince Frederick of Nassau. They separated in 1872. Girardin died on April 27, 1881, in Paris.

His writings include *De la presse périodique au XIXe siècle* (1837), *De la liberté de la presse* (1842), *Le droit au travail* (1848) and *Questions de mon temps, 1836 à 1856* (1858).

See C. A. Sainte-Beuve, *Nouveaux Lundis* (VII) (1861-66); M. Reclus, *Émile de Girardin* (1934). (J. L.-D.)

GIRARDON, FRANÇOIS (1628-1715), French sculptor, the most purely classical of the sculptors employed at Versailles, was born at Troyes, where he was baptized on March 17, 1628. He attracted the attention of Chancellor Pierre Séguier who brought him to Paris to study under François Anguier, and afterward sent him to Rome. He returned about 1650 and became a member of the academy in 1657. He worked for Nicolas Fouquet at Vaux-le-Vicomte and after the minister's fall was extensively employed under Charles Le Brun on the decoration of the royal palaces. In 1663 he was working under Charles Le Brun on the Galerie d'Apollon at the Louvre, and in 1666 received the commission for his most famous work, the "Apollo Tended by the Nymphs," for the Grotte de Thétis at Versailles. The inspiration for this elaborate work (later moved and its grouping altered), seems to derive partly from Hellenistic sculpture (particularly the Apollo Belvedere), and partly from Nicolas Poussin's paintings. Of his other works for Versailles the most notable are the relief on the Bain des Nymphes (1668–70), perhaps inspired by Jean Goujon's Fontaine des Innocents, and "The Rape of Persephone" (pedestal completed 1699), in which he challenges comparison with Giovanni Bologna's "Rape of the Sabines." The effect of this group is marred by its present situation in the centre of the colonnade at Versailles where it can be seen from all sides instead of from a fixed viewpoint as originally intended.

Although superficially a baroque artist, Girardon's deep-seated classical tendencies emerge in the careful relating of sculpture to site. This is evident in his two principal works outside Versailles, the equestrian statue of Louis XIV in the Place Vendôme (1683–92), which was destroyed during the Revolution, and his tomb of Richelieu in the Sorbonne (1675–77). He undertook comparatively little portrait sculpture, but the classical bias of his mind and his abilities as a decorator made him the ideal collaborator with Le Brun (who designed many of Girardon's numerous works for Versailles), just as Antoine Coysevox (q.v.) was with Le Brun's successor, Jules Hardouin Mansart. As Coysevox's star rose, that of Girardon sank, and he received few royal commissions after 1700. He died in Paris on Sept. 1, 1715.

See P. Francastel, *Girardon* (1928) and *La Sculpture de Versailles* (1930); M. Oudinot, "François Girardon: Son rôle . . . à Versailles et aux Invalides," *Bulletin de la Société de l'Histoire de l'Art Français*, pp. 204 ff. (1937). (F. J. B. W.)

GIRAUD, HENRI HONORÉ (1879–1949), French army officer, was born in Paris on Jan. 18, 1879. After graduating from St. Cyr in 1900, he served in French Morocco until World War I. Captured by the Germans in 1914, he successfully escaped—a feat he repeated in World War II, 28 years later. He returned to Morocco in 1922 and participated in the Rif war. In World War II, Giraud commanded the 7th army and, for a few days before his capture in May 1940, the 9th army. His second escape occurred in April 1942.

Seven months later, after secret negotiations with the Allies, he was whisked to north Africa in the wake of the Anglo-American landings. Appointed commander in chief of the French forces, he raised and equipped, largely with American matériel, 250,000 combat troops. From June to Oct. 1943 he was co-president (with Charles de Gaulle) of the French Committee of National Liberation. Differences with De Gaulle resulted in his retirement in April 1944.

After the war, Giraud was elected to the constituent assembly. He also served as vice-president of the Conseil Supérieur de la Guerre. He died in Dijon on March 11, 1949, and was buried at the Invalides, in Paris. His publications include two memoirs: *Mes Évasions* (1946) and *Un seul but, la Victoire* (1949). (M. V.)

GIRAUDOUX, (HIPPOLYTE) JEAN (1882–1944), French essayist, novelist and playwright who created an impressionist form of the drama by emphasizing dialogue and style rather than realism, was born in Bellac, Haute-Vienne, on Oct. 29, 1882. Educated at the École Normale Supérieure, he made the diplomatic service his career. He became known as an avant-garde writer when Émile Paul (who also published the work of Rainer Maria Rilke and Jean Cassou, and Alain-Fournier's *Le Grand Meaulnes*) first published his poetic novels: they were thought difficult, indeed far-fetched—in short, precious—an example of this being *Suzanne et le Pacifique* (1921). But other works soon appeared: in *Siegfried et le Limousin* (1922) Giraudoux depicts in silhouette, as it were, the hostility existing between a pair of enemies, France and Germany, as a background to his story of a man who has lost his

memory; *Bella* (1926) is a love story behind which there can be glimpsed the insurmountable rivalry between two statesmen—the nationalist Dubardeau (*i.e.*, Raymond Poincaré) and the internationalist Rebendart (Aristide Briand)—and between two conceptions of the nature of the state.

Thus it became clear what was to be the central theme of Giraudoux's plays: a pair of opposites, whatever they might be—man and God, as in *Amphitryon 38* (1929), man and woman, as in *Sodome et Gomorrhe* (1943) at the other end of his literary career, or indeed, as in *Judith* (1931), the world of paganism and the world of the Old Testament. It is this fixed idea of his that remembering Heraclitus' famous remark, "The road from above and the road from below are one and the same," he should try to resolve conflict between opposites by bringing them into contact, which gives substance to the reproach of preciosity sometimes leveled against his work.

In fact, the springboard Giraudoux used for the "leap in the dark" he made when he began to write for the theatre was *Siegfried* (1928), a dramatization of his own novel, in itself an ambiguous work. *Siegfried* introduced Paris to a great new dramatist, its success being due in part to the actor Louis Jouvet (q.v.), who was always Giraudoux's good genius.

It is noticeable that apart from *Intermezzo* (1933), Giraudoux never worked on a directly imagined subject: having reworked *Siegfried et le Limousin* in dramatic terms, he sought inspiration in tradition, first a pagan one in *Amphitryon 38* and later in *Électre* (1937), then a biblical one. Meanwhile he had adapted Margaret Kennedy's novel *The Constant Nymph* as *Tessa* (1934) and Baron Friedrich de la Motte-Fouqué's *Undine* as *Ondine* (1939). In his extraordinary essay *Racine* (1930) he explained the purely literary reasons which had led the great playwright from *Phèdre* to *Esther* and *Athalie*: the Judaic tradition had offered the power to condemn his enemies to everlasting torment. This play may have also given Giraudoux, the author of *Le Cantique des cantiques* (1938), a means of truly "eternizing"—as one can prolong a musical note in time—his relentless investigation and discussion of the conflict between a pair of opposites with which his works were most profoundly concerned, demonstrating as it does the fact of the fundamental duality of existence. Many of his works have been translated into English, the best-known being *La Folle de Chaillot*, adapted as *The Madwoman of Chaillot* by Maurice Valency in 1947, and *La Guerre de Troie n'aura pas lieu* (1935), adapted by Christopher Fry as *Tiger at the Gates*. Giraudoux died in Paris on Jan. 31, 1944.

BIBLIOGRAPHY.—*Le Théâtre complet de Jean Giraudoux* (1945-53); C. E. Magny, *Précieux Giraudoux* (1945); J. Toussaint, *Jean Giraudoux* (1953); M. Mercier-Campiche, *Le Théâtre de Jean Giraudoux* (1954); L. L. Sage, *Metaphor in the Nondramatic Works of Jean Giraudoux* (1952), *L'Oeuvre de Jean Giraudoux* (1957, Eng. trans. 1959); D. Inskip, *Jean Giraudoux* (1958); A. G. Raymond, *Jean Giraudoux: the Theatre of Victory and Defeat* (1966); R. Cohen, *Giraudoux: Three Faces of Destiny* (1968). (C.-E. MA.)

GIRDLE (BELT), a band that encircles or girds the waist either to confine the loose and flowing outer garments so as to allow freedom of movement or to fasten and support the garments of the wearer. Girdle in this sense is now a literary word and may connote a more elaborate item of dress than does the term belt, although strictly speaking this is not a point of distinction between them.

Among the Romans the girdle was used to confine the *tunica* and formed part of the dress of the soldier and the matron. Although girdles and girdle buckles are not often found in Gallo-Roman graves, they are almost invariably present in the graves of Franks and Burgundians and are often ornamented with bosses of silver or bronze, chased or inlaid. In Anglo-Saxon dress the girdle was unimportant, and Norman knights generally wore belts under their hauberks. After the Conquest, however, the artificers gave more attention to a piece whose buckle and tongue invited the work of the goldsmith.

In the latter part of the 13th century the knight's surcoat was girdled with a narrow cord at the waist, while the great belt, which became the pride of the cavalier, looped across the hips, carrying the heavy sword aslant across the hips of the wearer.

In the second half of the 14th century the knightly belt took its most splendid form. The belt was then worn aslant, as a rule, girdling the hips at some distance below the waist and was probably supported by hooks. The end of the belt, after being drawn through the buckle, was knotted or caught by a tongue (as in a conventional modern buckle). Ornament covered the whole belt, commonly seen as an unbroken line of bosses enriched with curiously worked roundels or lozenges, which, in instances where the loose strap-end was abandoned, met in a splendid clasp. About 1420 this fashion tended to disappear, the loose tabards worn over the armour in the jousting-yard hindering its display. The belt never regained its importance as an ornament, and in illustrations showing clothing worn at the beginning of the 16th century sword and dagger are sometimes seen hanging at the knight's side without visible support.

In civil dress the belt of the 14th century was worn by men of rank over the hips of the tight, short-skirted coat, and in that century and in the 15th and 16th centuries there were laws to check the extravagance of rich girdles worn by men and women whose stations made such display unseemly. Even priests were rebuked for their silver girdles with baselards (short swords). Purses, daggers, keys, pens and inkhorns, beads and even books dangled from girdles. After the early 16th century the girdle continued as a mere strap for holding up clothing or as a sword belt. During the Restoration the men of the court wore a light rapier hung from a broad shoulder belt (a continuation of the style seen in the well-known portrait of Charles I by Anthony Van Dyck) while the men from the countryside wore a heavy weapon supported by a narrow waist belt. Soon afterward both fashions disappeared. Sword hangers were concealed by the skirt, and the belt, except in certain military and sporting costumes, was no longer in sight in England. Even as a support for breeches or trousers the use of braces (suspenders) supplanted the belt, whereas in the United States the reverse largely obtained.

In women's clothing a belt is often used to give the garment a finished appearance and, especially if it is in a contrasting material or colour, to provide part of the decoration; there is a great variety of styles. Sashes, broad folded bands of material tied around the waist, began to be worn by women in the latter part of the 18th century; prior to that time they sometimes formed part of a military uniform worn by men. The cummerbund, a similar item, originated in India, where it was worn by men; it was widely adapted for men's dress clothes and also for women's wear. In parts of the world where peasant costumes are maintained, the belt or girdle is frequently a conspicuous part of the clothing and is often decorated with embroidery and other forms of needlework. Folklore and ancient custom are much concerned with the girdle. Bankrupts at one time took it off in open court; French law refused courtesans the right to wear it; an earl has been "belted" since the days when putting on a girdle became part of the ceremony of his creation; and many fairy tales concern girdles that give invisibility to the wearer.

In modern usage, the word "girdle" is used, especially in the United States, in referring to an undergarment, whose purpose is much that of a corset, but not so restricting. It is generally made of material (mainly nylon) that has been woven to give it a two-way-stretch quality. See DRESS: Post-World War I.
(M. B. K.; X.)

GIRI, VARAHAGIRI VENKATA (1894–   ), Indian statesman, became president of India on Aug. 24, 1969; he was born of Telugu parentage on Aug. 10, 1894, in Berhampur in what is now the state of Orissa. He began his education at the nearby Kallikota College and then went to Dublin to pursue his studies in law. There he became engaged in the Sinn Fein movement and was expelled from Ireland in 1916. Returning to India, he joined the infant Labour movement and soon showed that he had marked organizational gifts. He became general secretary and president of the All-India Railwaymen's Federation and was twice vice president of the All-India Trade Union Congress, an influential organization closely linked with the Congress Party. He attended the International Labour Conference in Geneva in 1927, and the second Round Table Conference (on Indian independence) in London in 1931.

When the Congress Party formed a government in Madras in 1937 Giri became minister of labour and industries. With the resignation of the Congress governments and launching of the anti-British "quit India" movement in 1942, he returned to the Labour movement, and was imprisoned with his colleagues.

After India became independent he was appointed high commissioner in Ceylon and in 1952 was elected to the *Lok Sabha* (House of the People) and made minister of labour in the central government. The early 1950s was the period of Jawaharlal Nehru's greatest dominance, and independence in the Cabinet was accordingly rare; but in 1954 Giri resigned on a policy question concerning his ministry, upholding trade unionists against a decision which, he suggested, reflected the influence of the rightists in the government. After this Giri was appointed successively to the largely ceremonial governorships of Uttar Pradesh, Kerala, and Mysore. In 1967 he was elected vice-president.

At the death of Pres. Zakir Husain in 1969, Giri became acting president and announced his intention to stand for the presidency. By that time the office, until then not much more than ceremonial, had become a prize in the developing faction struggle within the Congress Party. The party's nomination went to another candidate; Mrs. Indira Gandhi, the prime minister, supported Giri, however, and by a narrow majority he was elected. The immediate impression was that Giri would be Mrs. Gandhi's man, and his election much strengthened her position; but the independence he had shown in the days of Mrs. Gandhi's father, Nehru, suggested that if political forces in India worked to enlarge the initiative and influence of the presidency, Giri would be ready to respond.   (NE. M.)

GIRL GUIDES, an organization for girls in the United Kingdom aiming to educate in its widest sense through enjoyment. The biggest youth movement in the country, it was founded in 1910 by Sir Robert (later Lord) Baden-Powell in response to the demands of girls who were enthusiastic about his Boy Scout Movement. When the Scouts held their first rally in 1909, some girls arrived uninvited, announcing that they too wanted to be Scouts. Sir Robert enlisted the help of his sister Agnes and set up a training scheme designed to help the girls become good citizens.

The movement is open to girls of all races and religions and is nonpolitical. The only requirement is that girls who want to join should be prepared to make the "promise."

There are three sections of the movement: Brownie Guides, Guides, and Ranger Guides. In Britain, each member promises to do her best to do her duty to God, to serve the queen, to help other people, and to keep the Guide (Brownie Guide) Law. In addition a Ranger Guide undertakes to be of service to the community.

The Guide Law requires a conscious effort to be loyal and honest, trustworthy, polite, thoughtful, hardworking, careful of her own and others' possessions, respectful of all living things, and self-controlled in thought as well as deed and word. Every guide is encouraged to actively practise her own religion.

Development.—In 1923 the association was incorporated by royal charter and in 1928 the World Association of Girl Guides and Girl Scouts (*q.v.*) was formed. This is a loose federation of autonomous member countries, for Guiding in all countries must develop according to local conditions and need. In order to be a member of the World Association, a country must be willing to accept the principles contained in the promise and to keep the movement independent of any political organization. It must also be open to every girl regardless of race, colour, or religion.

In 1966 a modern approach was made to the unchanging basics of Guiding. The Eight Point Program is designed to bring out the best ways of developing mental and physical qualities, creative talent, character, relationships with others, service, home skills, and enjoyment of the outdoors. Each guide possesses her own personal handbook that is designed to motivate her interest, enthusiasm, and ambition. The award of badges for progress made is planned to encourage the widening of interests and development of each of the eight points. Projects such as organizing a camp, putting on a show, and doing a good turn are important parts of the program. The out-of-doors plays a large part in Guiding. Brownie Guides are aged between 7 and 11; Guides, 10 to 16; Ranger Guides 14 to 20. Handicapped girls and those living too far from a company to attend its meetings regularly can join any section. Adult leaders in all three sections are called guiders and assistant guiders.

Olave, Lady Baden-Powell, widow of the founder, was appointed chief commissioner of the movement in 1916, chief guide in 1918, and world chief guide in 1930 at one of the first international conferences of the World Association. These conferences are held regularly in different countries.

The queen and queen mother are patrons of the movement and Princess Margaret is its president. The Girl Guides Association is a recognized part of the Youth Service and has been a member of both the Standing Conference of National Voluntary Youth Organizations for England, Wales, and Northern Ireland and the Scottish Standing Conference of Voluntary Youth Organizations since their inception.

Organization.—The chief commissioner and the Executive Committee are elected by the Council. The commissioners of the U.K. countries, through their county, division, and district commissioners, ensure that the organization does not become too centralized and allow training to be carried out and the needs of the girls to be represented. This method establishes a direct channel from the Executive Committee to the girls and vice versa.

Interested adult nonmembers can join local associations whose aim is to support the movement and enlist public interest. Former members who can no longer play an active part in Guiding but would like to support it and carry its ideals into their own communities are able to join the Trefoil Guild.

Training.—Adult leaders receive training in a variety of ways. There are two residential training centres in England run by Commonwealth headquarters: Foxlease in Hampshire and Waddow Hall in Lancashire. Scotland, Wales, and Northern Ireland also have training centres.

The girls themselves are trained through their membership of a unit. Brownie Guides learn to express themselves and voice their views at the Pack Council or "Powwow." Guides discuss in small groups (patrols) and the patrol leaders meet as a committee to decide company affairs. In the Ranger Guide Service Section, affairs are arranged to give the girls an understanding of democratic government and personal responsibility. There are opportunities for meeting members from other countries, traveling abroad, and attending international gatherings, camps, and conferences.

There are four World Guide Centres: in Switzerland, the United Kingdom, Mexico, and India.

(J. M. J.)

GIRL SCOUTS is a voluntary organization dedicated to the purpose of "inspiring girls with the highest ideals of character, conduct, patriotism, and service that they may become happy and resourceful citizens" (preamble to the constitution of the Girl Scouts of the U.S.A.) The informal educational program through which the organization achieves its purpose is carried out in small groups with adult leadership and provides a wide range of activities developed around the interests and needs of girls.

Girl Scouting is open to all girls 7 through 17 years old who are willing to subscribe to the promise and laws of the movement. Adult membership, also requiring acceptance of the promise and law, is open to both women and men. Girl Scouts are part of the world-wide movement founded by Sir Robert (later Lord) Baden-Powell in 1910; the organization in the United States is a member of the World Association of Girl Guides and Girl Scouts.

Juliette Gordon Low of Savannah, Ga., formed the first Girl Scout troop in the United States in 1912, following the pattern set up for Girl Guides, sister organization of the Boy Scouts of Great Britain. Mrs. Low was a native of Georgia, but she had lived in Great Britain and had helped to organize Girl Guide troops. She became the first president of the U.S. organization; when she retired from office in 1920 she received the title of founder, and her birthday (Oct. 31) was set aside as a special day for the Girl Scouts. At the time of her death in 1927 the Girl Scouts had troops in every state of the union and had more than 140,000 members.

The Girl Scout promise is: "On my honor, I will try: to do my duty to God and my country; to help other people at all times, to obey the Girl Scout Laws." These laws are as follows:

1. A Girl Scout's honor is to be trusted.
2. A Girl Scout is loyal.
3. A Girl Scout's duty is to be useful and to help others.
4. A Girl Scout is a friend to all and a sister to every other Girl Scout.
5. A Girl Scout is courteous.
6. A Girl Scout is a friend to animals.
7. A Girl Scout obeys orders.
8. A Girl Scout is cheerful.
9. A Girl Scout is thrifty.
10. A Girl Scout is clean in thought, word and deed.

These laws are an understandable code for growing girls and are substantially the same in all countries in which Girl Scouting or Guiding is organized; they have been recognized as a standard of conduct and an expression of friendship regardless of race, nationality or religion. The trefoil emblem of the Girl Scouts, which symbolizes the three parts of the promise, is used in various versions throughout the world-wide movement.

Girl Scouting in the United States is divided into four age groups: Brownie Girl Scouts, 7 and 8 years old; Junior Girl Scouts, 9 through 11; Cadette Girl Scouts, 12 through 14; Senior Girl Scouts, 15 through 17. Girl Scouting presents a single, continuing program for girls as they progress through these age levels. The design of the program is based on six foundation elements which have been characteristic of Girl Scouting since its inception: The Girl Scout promise and laws, service to others, troop management by the girls themselves, citizenship, international friendship, and health and safety are embodied in activities related to the arts, the home and the out-of-doors.

Girl Scouting is "girls and adults working together" in basic units called troops, which usually consist of 16 to 32 girls and an adult leader or leaders. Except for the Brownie Scouts, troop business is transacted and decisions arrived at through a representative system of government whereby smaller subunits known as patrols elect their representatives to a "court of honour" which also includes the elected troop officers and the adult leaders.

Activities of girls in Scouting are designed to foster good social attitudes, broadened interests, development of individual capacities, growth of a sense of responsibility. Girls undertake projects which are progressively challenging. Community service is basic to the program, and may range from making simple gifts for invalids or singing Christmas carols to beautifying the grounds of public buildings. Scouts learn to know and appreciate the out-of-doors through games, nature study and camping.

The activities of the Brownie Girl Scout appeal to her curiosity, spontaneous creativity and desire to be helpful. By learning skills appropriate to her age group, a Brownie works toward fulfilling her promise "to help other people every day, especially those at home."

The Junior Girl Scout develops her skills in a wide variety of activities represented by various proficiency badges. As she advances she may earn one or both of the Signs of Junior Scouting, the Sign of the Arrow and the Sign of the Star.

The badges earned by the Cadette Girl Scout are more complex and specific. She may select from a number of badges covering such diversified areas as Aviation, Child Care and Interior Decoration. Earning badges and working toward a series of challenges placed before her, a Cadette progresses toward First Class, the highest award of her age group.

The Senior Girl Scout devotes much of her time to community service and vocational exploration, often combining them by working as a volunteer hospital aide or a museum aide, or by assisting at a public playground. Many Seniors take part in visits exchanged among girl members of the various associations in the world-wide Scout-Guide movement.

Adapting itself to the changing needs of girls, the organization grew from the first troop of 12 girls to a membership in the early 1970s of more than 3,235,000 girls and 669,000 adult volunteers. Administrative and executive workers in Girl Scouting account for less than 0.5% of adult membership.

The Girl Scout council is the organization which makes Scouting available to girls in the community. It is established, developed, maintained and financed by local volunteers. Clubs, schools, church groups and other private organizations assist local councils by providing meeting places, leadership, financial help, volunteer support and other co-operation. The Girl Scout national organization is financed principally by nominal annual membership dues. The governing body is the National council, consisting of delegates elected by local Girl Scout councils and meeting at regular intervals.

The national organization publishes *The Girl Scout Leader*, *The American Girl* and various handbooks. It also produces a variety of audio-visual materials for training of volunteers and interpretation of the program. The headquarters are in New York city. For the British equivalent of Girl Scouts, see GIRL GUIDES.
(CA. M. B.)

GIRODET-TRIOSON (ANNE LOUIS GIRODET DE ROUCY) (1767–1824), French painter typical of the first phase of the romantic movement, known as Girodet-Trioson after his guardian, M. Trioson, was born at Montargis, Loiret, on Jan. 29, 1767. A pupil of J. L. David, his "Joseph reconnu par ses frères" ("Joseph Recognized by His Brothers") won him the Prix de Rome at the age of 22. He submitted to the Salon of 1792 "Le Sommeil d'Endymion" ("Endymion Sleeping") (Louvre), a cold, sensual crepuscular work, nearer in feeling to the troubled romanticism of Chateaubriand than to the Spartan ideal of David. Girodet was also a poet, and his interest in literature is given full reign in the curious "Ombres des guerriers français recues par Ossian dans le palais d'Odin" ("Ossian Receiving the Generals of Napoleon in the Palace of Odin"), done for Malmaison in 1801, "Fingal" (Leningrad), painted for Napoleon in 1802, and above all, the famous "Atala au Tombeau" ("The Burial of Atala") (Louvre) of 1808. This, together with his windswept portrait of Chateaubriand meditating in front of the Coliseum (1809, Versailles), is Girodet's most typical work. In "La Révolte du Caire" ("The Revolt in Cairo") (1810, Versailles), he made a determined effort to copy the swirling compositions of Antoine Gros, for whom he had a deep affection. His landscape sketches and book illustrations, notably for Pierre Didot's *Racine* (1801–05), have a freshness that is missing from his more elaborate works. He died in Paris on Dec. 9, 1824.

Girodet's poem *Le Peintre* and essays on *Le Génie* and *La Grâce* were published after his death with a biographical notice by his friend M. Coupin de la Couperie (1829); E. J. Delécluze, in his *Louis David, son école et son temps* (1855), gives a brief life.
(AA. B.)

GIRONDE, a coastal *département* of southwestern France, astride the Gironde estuary and the lower valleys of the rivers Garonne and Dordogne, with the tongue of land (Entre-deux-Mers) between, consists of parts of ancient Guienne (q.v.) and was under the allegiance of the English kings for three centuries before the end of the Hundred Years' War. The modern *département* has an area of 4,141 sq.mi. and a population (1962) of 935,448. It is bounded north by Charente-Maritime, east by Dordogne and Lot-et-Garonne, south by Landes, and west by the Bay of Biscay.

The great rivers Garonne and Dordogne, flowing in wide, alluvium-floored valleys with ancient gravel terraces and steep flanking hills, enter the tidal estuary, which widens from two to six miles at its mouth in the Bay of Biscay. Bordeaux, the great commercial port, on the convex left bank of a curve in the wide river channel, lies 60 mi. from the ocean, and the estuary is encumbered by islands and sandbanks that make navigation difficult, so that in modern times outports have been developed, notably at Pauillac. At Ambès, in the confluence fork of the Dordogne and Garonne, 16 mi. below Bordeaux, there is a modern oil-refining plant. At the mouth of the Gironde is the famous lighthouse tower of Cordouan, built between 1585 and 1611. Extensive marshes fringe the low-lying estuary shores and have been partly reclaimed by diking. The western portion of the long peninsula between the Gironde and the straight dune-fringed coast of the Bay of Biscay is the northernmost prong of the Landes, and was extensively planted with forests of maritime pine after the middle of the 19th century. There are large lagoons and in the south the almost landlocked Bay of Arcachon, with extensive oyster beds. In the southwest of the *département* electricity is generated on the small lignite field of Hostens.

The *département* has a humid climate, with long, hot summers and very mild winters. Although polyculture, with maize (corn) especially important, is practised in some parts, agriculture is generally dominated by the cultivation of the vine. The district round Bordeaux, the Bordelais, has long been a specialized area of viticulture, exporting its produce through the port. The vineyards occupy terraces of old, coarse, river gravels (*graves*) and flanking hills, and have also spread on to low-lying tracts of modern alluvium (*palus*), though there the wine is of inferior quality. Médoc, on the left bank of the Gironde north of Bordeaux, was the source of clarets much esteemed in England in the middle ages. The Médoc vineyards occupy a strip of country as far south as Blanquefort. The true Graves country lies round Bordeaux itself. Sauternes come from a small district farther south, flanking the Ciron tributary. On the right bank of the Garonne are the Côtes de Bordeaux and Entre-deux-Mers districts, and vineyards are also extensive beyond the river Dordogne.

Bordeaux (q.v.), is the great market centre of the industry. It grew and flourished in the colonial period of the 17th and 18th centuries and is still one of France's major ports and leading provincial cities. It dominates the *département* as an administrative and service centre. Other centres of *arrondissements* are Blaye, Langon and Libourne. The last, founded by Edward I of England, is noteworthy as a medieval planned town, laid out as a regular grid. Cadillac and Ste. Foy-la-Grande are other bastide towns of the period of medieval town planning.
(AR. E. S.)

GIRONDINS, members of a political group, collectively known as the Gironde, which played an important role in the French Revolution (q.v.). By their contemporaries they were usually called BRISSOTINS, after J. P. Brissot (q.v.), or sometimes BUZOTINS, after F. N. L. Buzot, a deputy for Eure, or again ROLANDINS, after J. M. Roland (q.v.). The name Girondins, which owes its currency to Alphonse de Lamartine's use of it in his *Histoire des Girondins* (1847), refers to the strength that the group derived from deputies for the Gironde *département*.

Since the Constituent Assembly had forbidden the re-election of its members, the Legislative Assembly, which met in Oct. 1791, consisted of entirely new men. Among these were 136 deputies who joined the club of the Jacobins or that of Cordeliers (qq.v.) and from whom the Girondin group evolved. Most of these deputies were professional men, barristers or journalists, well educated and moderately rich, unquestionably enthusiastic for the Revolution and ambitious for themselves. As representatives of the ports (Marseilles, Nantes and, especially, Bordeaux), they were connected with the middle-class businessmen, shipfitters and bankers who supported the reforms of 1789 and wanted to stabilize them against the threat of counterrevolution but were ready to consider a continental war, which would naturally benefit the arms suppliers without damaging France's sea trade. Their social background and their philosophy inclined the Girondins to political but not to social democracy; they wanted political institutions to protect wealth and to favour ability.

The Girondins met in Paris in the houses of Madame Roland (Manon Philpon) and of Madame Dodun (Louise Julie Bourgeois), the friend of P. V. Vergniaud (q.v.). Brissot, already a famous journalist with experience of foreign countries, was their diplomatic expert, but his ill-considered conduct earned them a reputation for unreliability. Vergniaud was their greatest orator but was temperamentally incapable of translating into action the measures that he proposed.

From the end of 1791 the Gironde advocated war. This policy implacably opposed Brissot and Robespierre. Brissot was convinced that an attack on Austria would succeed, for the appeal to downtrodden nations would be answered: "The moment has come," he declared on Dec. 30, 1791, "for a new crusade, a crusade for universal liberty." In this, as Marie Antoinette saw, they were unwittingly playing the court's game. With two members of their group in the government (Étienne Clavière as minister of public contributions and Roland as minister of the interior) the Girondins secured the declaration of war on Austria on April 20, 1792.

The war, however, did not fulfil the expectations of the Girondins. Though at first their offer of liberation to sister nations served to consolidate their popularity in France, the reverses suffered by the French armies in the spring of 1792 (see FRENCH REVOLUTIONARY WARS) provoked an unforeseen upsurge of national feeling that led to a new phase in the Revolution. After the failure of the demonstration that they organized on June 20, 1792, in the hope of forcing Louis XVI to approve new decrees on national defense, the "statesmen" of the Gironde, as J. P. Marat sarcastically called them, began to hesitate for fear of the *sans-culottes*, whose insurrectionary movement now seemed likely to escape from their control and to endanger the influence of wealth and property. The attack on the Tuileries palace, on Aug. 10, which resulted in the fall of the monarchy, was made without the participation of the Girondins and was the first step toward their overthrow.

Thenceforward conflict between the Girondins and the architects of the insurrection became overt. It was aggravated by the massacres of Sept. 1792 and by the beginning of the Terror. The Girondins, frightened and resentful at being pushed aside, blamed the Parisian *sans-culottes* for their troubles, especially after the election of the Montagnards to the Convention. The idea of a guard to be recruited from the *départements* for the protection of the new assembly was put forward by Madame Roland, who now hated Robespierre bitterly and Danton even more so; it was she who inspired the intransigent Girondin faction to which Buzot, C. M. Barbaroux and J. B. Louvet de Couvrai belonged.

Against the centralized dictatorship of the Montagnards, based on Paris, the Girondins appealed to the regional particularism of the moderate *bourgeoisie* entrenched in local administration: they relied less on the more extreme "federalism," though some sympathized with it. The social aspect of the conflict became clear when the Girondins—and Roland in particular—defended economic freedom against demands by the *sans-culottes* for more rigorous taxation. In the Convention, and even more in the *départements*, the Gironde was the screen behind which the *bourgeoisie* rallied to protect its interests.

The trial of the king intensified the antagonism between Girondins and Montagnards in the Convention. The Girondins wished to spare his life and adopted obstructive tactics, demanding first the banishment of all the Bourbons, then maintaining that the Convention's decision should be ratified by the people and lastly proposing a reprieve. After the execution of the king (Jan. 21, 1793), the reverses sustained by the French in the Netherlands led to the final ruin of the Girondins. The Convention's foreign policy, conducted by Brissot, provoked a general coalition against France, and the defeat at Neerwinden on March 18, followed by the treachery of C. F. Dumouriez in April, exasperated the patriotic feelings of the masses. Since the Girondins obstinately refused to take emergency measures, they seemed to be preventing any effective defense of France and of the Revolution. The Montagnards of the Convention had the support of the Paris commune and of most of the Paris *sections* against the Girondins, and the struggle culminated in the popular rising of May 31–June 2, 1793. On June 2 the Convention, surrounded by 80,000 armed insurgents, capitulated and ordered the arrest of 29 Girondin deputies.

Most of these deputies managed to escape. They tried to rouse Normandy, Brittany, the southwest, the south and Franche-Comté in their favour, but these "federalist" risings failed for lack of popular support. The trial of 31 Girondins took place in Oct. 1793, before the Revolutionary tribunal; a special decree stifled their defense, and they were guillotined on Oct. 31, Brissot and Vergniaud among them. The trial of Madame Roland followed. Other Girondins, including Buzot, Clavière, J. Pétion de Villeneuve and Roland committed suicide. Louvet de Couvrai and Maximin Isnard, who escaped the purge, returned to the Convention after the Thermidorian reaction of July 1794.

BIBLIOGRAPHY.—The 19th-century works dealing with the Girondins as a group, such as A. de Lamartine, *Histoire des Girondins* (1847), J. Guadet, *Les Girondins*, 2 vol. (1861), and E. Biré, *La Légende des Girondins* (1881), are obsolete or unduly biased. *See* rather A. Aulard, *Les Orateurs de la Législative et de la Convention*, 2 vol. (1885), and *Histoire politique de la Révolution* (1901), together with biographies of individual Girondins.
(A. So.)

GIRTIN, THOMAS (1775-1802), English landscape painter in water colour, was born in London on Feb. 18, 1775, the son of a brushmaker. He was apprenticed to Edward Dayes, the watercolourist, with whom he later quarreled. While still boys he and J. M. W. Turner were employed by the connoisseur Thomas Monro in copying works by J. R. Cozens. Girtin went on numerous sketching tours, chiefly in the north of England, and founded a sketching club for young artists. During 1801-02 he visited Paris and produced a series of etchings of that city. His gigantic panorama of London, the "Eidometropolis," was exhibited just before his premature death, probably from tuberculosis, on Nov. 9, 1802.

Girtin's earlier landscapes are in the 18th-century topographical manner, but in his last years he evolved a bold, spacious and romantic style, in spirit akin to the contemporary poetry of Wordsworth, which greatly influenced English landscape painting. The increasing power of his last works at least tempers the exaggeration of Turner's supposed remark: "If Tom Girtin had lived, I should have starved." The British museum and the Victoria and Albert museum, London, are rich in examples of his work.

See J. Mayne, *Thomas Girtin* (1949); T. Girtin and D. Loshak, *The Art of Thomas Girtin* (1954).
(D. Lx.)

GIRVAN, a small burgh and fishing town of Ayrshire, Scot., at the mouth of the River Girvan, 54½ mi. SSW of Glasgow and 22 mi. SSW of Ayr by road. Pop. (1971 prelim.) 7,405. The principal industries—besides catering to visitors and fishing (herring and whitefish)—are the manufacture of woolen goods, tweeds, and knitwear, the building and repairing of fishing boats and the processing of seaweed. In the town centre is a green plot (Knockusion or "hill of justice") where Robert Bruce granted a charter in the 14th century. It is the port of communication with Ailsa Craig (q.v.).

GIRY, (JEAN MARIE JOSEPH) ARTHUR (1848-1899), French historian, who made a considerable contribution to the study of the origins and significance of the urban communities in France. He was born at Trévoux (Ain) on Feb. 28, 1848, and studied at the École de Droit, the École des Chartes and the École des Hautes Études. He held posts at the Bibliothèque Nationale and the Archives Nationales before being appointed lecturer at the École des Hautes Études in 1877. He became lecturer at the faculty of letters of the Sorbonne in 1881 and professor at the École des Chartes in 1885. He died at Paris on Nov. 13, 1899.

His *Manuel de diplomatique* (1894) secured his election to the Académie des Inscriptions.

Giry's works include *Histoire de la ville de Saint-Omer et de ses institutions jusqu'au XIVe siècle* (1877); *Les Établissements de Rouen*, two volumes (1883-85); *Documents sur les relations de la royauté avec les villes de France de 1180 à 1314* (1885); and *Étude sur les origines de la commune de Saint-Quentin* (1887).

GISBORNE, a seaport of New Zealand and administrative centre of the Poverty Bay district on the east coast of North Island. Pop. (1970 est.) 29,500. The port is connected with Wellington by road and rail. Gisborne land district embraces the hilly and mountainous easternmost projection of North Island from Opotiki and the Mahia Peninsula to East Cape. Apart from Gisborne the only town of any size is the small port of Opotiki (2,590) on the Bay of Plenty. The rest of the population is overwhelmingly rural and largely Maori. The chief economic activity is extensive sheep rearing on hill pastures in country often seriously affected by soil erosion. Captain Cook landed near the site of Gisborne in 1769 and gave Poverty Bay its name because of his inability to obtain supplies from the hostile natives.
(K. B. C.; X.)

GISORS, a town of northwest France, Eure *département*, lies in the pleasant valley of the Epte, 42 mi. (68 km.) N.W. of Paris by road. Pop. (1962) 5,952. It is dominated by an 11th- and 12th-century stronghold of the kings of England. The central tower, the choir and parts of the aisles of the church of St. Gervais date from the middle of the 13th century and the rest from the Renaissance. Gothic and Renaissance styles mingle in the west façade, adorned with a profusion of sculpture; there is fine carving on the wooden doors of the north and west portals. Gisors is on the main railway from Paris to Dieppe. Its industries include the manufactures of felt, electrical machinery, electric lamps and batteries.

In the middle ages Gisors was capital of the Vexin. Its position on the frontier of Normandy caused its possession to be hotly contested by the kings of England and France during the 12th century, when with the fortresses of Neaufles and Dangu it was ceded by Richard Cœur de Lion to Philip Augustus. During the wars of religion of the 16th century it was occupied by the duc de Mayenne on behalf of the League, and in the 17th century, during the Fronde, by the duc de Longueville. Gisors was made a duchy in 1742 and afterward came into the possession of the comte d'Eu and the duc de Penthièvre. The town was badly damaged during World War II but has since been rebuilt.

GISSAR (Hissar) is the name of a mountain range (Gissarski Khrebet) and valley (Gissarskaya Dolina) in the western part of the Tadzhik Soviet Socialist Republic and the southern part of the Uzbek Soviet Socialist Republic of the U.S.S.R., and also of a small town 15 mi. W. of Dushanbe, the capital of the Tadzhik S.S.R. The valley is thickly populated, and cotton and other subtropical crops are grown. It is watered by the Gissar canal built during World War II, which is part of the extensive new irrigation systems constructed to increase the production of cotton in the Fergana (q.v.), Vakhsh and Gissar valleys. The town, at the head of a defile carved out by the Kafirnigan river, a tributary of the Amu-Darya, was once the capital of an independent region which was finally incorporated in the former emirate of Bukhara. It was formerly famous for silks and damascened swords. (G. E. Wr.)

GISSING, GEORGE ROBERT (1857–1903), English novelist, noted for the unflinching realism of his novels about the poorer middle classes, was born at Wakefield on Nov. 22, 1857. Exceptionally precocious, he was educated at the Quaker boarding school of Alderley Edge and at Owens college, Manchester, where his academic career was brilliant. His personal life was, until the last few years, mostly unhappy. His two marriages—the first to a prostitute and the second to a servant girl—brought him little but misery and the need to live the life of near poverty and constant drudgery—writing, reading and coaching—described in the novels *New Grub Street* (1891) and *The Private Papers of Henry Ryecroft* (1903). Before he was 21 he had conceived the ambition of writing a long series of novels, somewhat in the manner of his admired Balzac. The first of these, *Workers in the Dawn*, appeared in 1880, to be followed by 21 others, of which *Demos* (1886), *Thyrza* (1887), *The Nether World* (1889), *Born in Exile* (1892), *The Odd Women* (1893), *In the Year of Jubilee* (1894) and *Eve's Ransom* (1895) are, with the two mentioned above, the most notable. He also published several books of stories and sketches and *Charles Dickens: a Critical Study* (1898), a remarkably able and perceptive piece of literary criticism.

His friend H. G. Wells justly described Gissing as "a highly respected, but never very popular or prosperous writer." His work is serious—though not without a good deal of comic observation—interesting, scrupulously honest and rather flat. It has a good deal of documentary interest, for he wrote in detail of aspects of lower-middle-class London life seldom described so accurately elsewhere. On the social position and psychology of women he is particularly acute. He did not lack human sympathies, but his obvious dislike of and contempt for so many of his characters leaves a bitter taste and reflects an artistic limitation. Although not committed to a specific philosophical or political position (his cast of mind was independent to the point of eccentricity), Gissing was deeply critical, in an almost wholly negative way, of contemporary society. The vulgarity, ugliness and frustration of the life he is describing emerge powerfully; his delineation of character and of individual moral dilemmas is often penetrating; yet the total effect is somewhat lacking in artistic vigour. Often he seems "got down" by the philistinism he is describing. Yet there is little doubt that he has been, in his lifetime and since his death, an underestimated writer deserving a more exalted reputation. Of his novels *In the Year of Jubilee* gives perhaps the most impressive evidence of his powers. He was also a good classical scholar and kept up his studies in late Roman history and Italian antiquities.

In the last years of his life Gissing established a happy relationship with a Frenchwoman, Mlle Gabrielle Fleury, with whom he lived. He died at St. Jean de Luz on Dec. 28, 1903.

BIBLIOGRAPHY.—F. Swinnerton, *George Gissing* (1912); M. Yates, *George Gissing* (1922); M. Evans, *George Gissing* (1951); M. C. Donnelly, *George Gissing, Grave Comedian* (1954); A. C. Ward, *George Gissing* (British Council pamphlet, 1959); *Letters of George Gissing to Members of his Family*, ed. by A. and E. Gissing (1927); *George Gissing and H. G. Wells, Their Friendship and Correspondence*, ed. by R. A. Gettman (1961); Arthur C. Young (ed.), *The Letters of George Gissing to Eduard Bertz* (1961). (AD. C. K.)

GITTERN, a small medieval stringed instrument played with a plectrum. Early drawings and carvings and the sole surviving example (c. 1300) suggest that the body, neck and pegbox were usually carved from one solid block of wood. In the 16th century the name seems to have been used for the four-course guitar. *See* GUITAR. (E. HA.)

GIULIO ROMANO: *see* ROMANO, GIULIO.

GIUNTA PISANO (d. 1255–1267), Italian painter, a native of Pisa and according to some critics a pioneer who, coming from Tuscany to Assisi, influenced the development of Umbrian art. It is said that he painted in the upper church of Assisi, notably a "Crucifixion" dated 1236, with a figure of Father Elias, the general of the Franciscans, embracing the cross. This painting no longer exists. Three large Crucifixions are ascribed to the same master, whose signature can be traced on them. One is in SS. Raineri e Leonardo in Pisa and was formerly in the convent of St. Anna; the other, in the Museo Civico at Pisa, is completely overpainted; the third is in Sta. Maria degli Angeli at Assisi. In these paintings Christ is represented with his head leaning on one side with an expression of pain, and his body bending forward in agony—a conception differing from "the triumphant Christ" of the preceding age.

GIURGIU, a town in the Bucharest *regiunea* (administrative region) of the Rumanian People's Republic, the administrative centre of Giurgiu district, stands on the left bank of the Danube 40 mi. S.S.W. of Bucharest. Pop. (1960) 34,248. Giurgiu is an old Danube port tracing its origin to the ancient Genoese commercial settlement of San Giorgio founded during the decline of the Byzantine empire. The first written reference to the town dates from 1394, during the reign of Mircea the Old. The ruins of a fort of this period can still be seen. In 1417 the town was conquered by the Turks, and its inhabitants were made rayahs (i.e., non-Muslim Turkish subjects). Not until 1829, by the peace of Adrianople, was it returned to Wallachia. It was severely damaged during World War I. The main industries are shipyards, reconstructed during the late 1950s, and food and light industries; the town is also important as a rail terminus and as a junction for Ploesti oil pipe lines. In 1954 a bridge was completed over the Danube between Giurgiu and Ruse, connecting Rumania and Bulgaria.

GIUSTI, GIUSEPPE (1809–1850), Italian poet whose satires on Habsburg rule in Italy in the early years of the Risorgimento are still enjoyed for their literary merits, was born at Monsummano in Tuscany on May 13, 1809. After two periods as a law student at Pisa (1826–29 and 1832–34), he led an inconspicuous life until the revolution of 1848. He then sat as a deputy in the two Tuscan legislative assemblies and in the short-lived constituent assembly (till April 1849). He died in Florence on March 31, 1850.

Giusti's satirical poems were at first circulated only in manuscript, and the first collections of them, *Poesie italiane* (unauthorized, 1844) and *Versi* (1845; to be distinguished from the innocuous Leghorn edition, *Versi di Giuseppe Giusti*, 1844), had to be printed outside Italy, at Lugano and at Bastia, without the author's name. His first notable satire, *La ghigliottina a vapore*, dates from 1833. Other satires were *Lo stivale* ("The Boot," in allusion to the cartographical shape of the Italian peninsula); *La terra dei morti*, in protest against Lamartine's description of Italy as the land of the dead; *Il brindisi di Girella*; *Gingillino*, denouncing opportunist officials; *Il dies irae*, on the death of the Austrian emperor Francis I; and *Per l'incoronazione*, on the coronation of the succeeding emperor. His masterpiece, however, is

Sant' Ambrogio (1847), a poem describing a company of Austrian soldiers at Mass, in which the poet begins by deriding them but gives way to sympathy with them, as they join in a chorus by Verdi. Popular in their day because of their liberal, anti-Austrian ideas, their satire against the Tuscan grand duke and his agents and their patriotic expression of faith in Italy's resurgence, Giusti's satires can still be read with pleasure for their wit, their humorous turns of phrase and their power of ridicule in characterization. His complete works, including some previously unpublished material, were edited by F. Martini (1924); selections were edited by P. Carli (1912).

BIBLIOGRAPHY.—E. Bellorini, *Giuseppe Giusti* (1923); M. Parenti, *Bibliografia delle opere di Giuseppe Giusti*, 2 vol. (1951-52); B. Croce, *Poesia e non poesia* (1923).
(F. Dr.)

GIUSTINIANI, an Italian family name represented in Venice, Genoa, Naples, Corsica and various Greek islands. A Venetian branch first became prominent and gave a doge to the republic in the 17th century. A Genoese branch, probably unrelated to the Venetian line, became rich and powerful in the late 14th century, when it amalgamated with other families sharing with it the government and exploitation of the island of Chios.

In the Venetian line the following are most worthy of mention:

LORENZO (1380-1456) entered the congregation of the canons of St. George in Alga and in 1433 became general of that order. Eugenius IV made him bishop of Venice; the removal of the patriarchate from Grado to Venice in 1451 made him the first patriarch of the town. He was canonized by Alexander VIII (St. Laurence Giustiniani; feast day Sept. 5). His works, remarkable for their mystical fervour, were reprinted by the Benedictine P. N. A. Giustiniani (2 vol., 1751).

LEONARDO (1388-1446), brother of Lorenzo, was for years a senator of Venice and in 1443 was chosen procurator of St. Mark. His fame rests on his translations and original writings in Latin and Greek and more especially on his popular poems, amatory and religious, in Italian (with a fresh, lively Venetian strain). The songs, set to music by him, became known as *Giustiniane*. B. Wiese published *Poesie edite e inedite di Leonardo Giustiniani* (1883).

BERNARDO (1408-1489), son of Leonardo, entered the Venetian senate and served on diplomatic missions to France and Rome; about 1485 he became one of the Council of Ten. He wrote a history of Venice, *De origine urbis Venetarum rebusque ab ipsa gestis historia* (1492; Ital. trans. 1545). It is to be found in vol. i of the *Thesaurus* of Graevius.

PIETRO, also a senator, lived in the 16th century and wrote a *Historia rerum Venetarum* in continuation of Bernardo. He also wrote chronicles *De gestis Petri Mocenigi* and *De bello Venetorum cum Carolo VIII* (*Rer. Ital. Script.*, vol. xxi).

ORSATTO (1538-1603), Venetian senator, translator of the *Oedipus Tyrannus* of Sophocles and author of a collection of *Rime* in imitation of Petrarch, was one of the latest representatives of the classic Italian school.

Of the Genoese branch of the family the most prominent members were the following:

AGOSTINO (1470-1536) was born at Genoa and, after joining the Dominicans in 1487, studied Greek, Hebrew, Chaldee and Arabic; in 1514 he began the preparation of a polyglot edition of the Bible. As bishop of Nebbio, Corsica, he took part in the earlier sittings of the Lateran council (1516-17) but, in consequence of party complications, withdrew to his diocese and ultimately to France, where he became a pensioner of Francis I and was the first to occupy a chair of Hebrew and Arabic in the University of Paris. He became acquainted with Erasmus and More and returned to Nebbio about 1522. He bequeathed his fine library to the republic of Genoa. Of his projected polyglot only the Psalter was published (*Psalterium Hebraeum, Graecum, Arabicum, et Chaldaicum*, Genoa, 1516). Besides an edition of Job, containing the original text, the Vulgate and a new translation, he published a Latin version of the *Guide of the Perplexed* of Maimonides (*Director dubitantium aut perplexorum*, 1520) and also edited in Latin the *Aureus libellus* of Aeneas Platonicus and the *Timaeus* of Chalcidius. His annals of Genoa (*Castigatissimi annali di Genova*) were published posthumously in 1537.

POMPEO (1569-1616) was a native of Corsica, who served under Alessandro Farnese and under Ambrogio Spinola in the Low Countries, where he lost an arm and hence came to be known by the sobriquet Bras de Fer. He defended Crete against the Turks, fought the Austrians and was killed in Friuli. He left in Italian a personal narrative of the war in Flanders, repeatedly published in Latin (*Bellum Belgicum*, 1609).

GERONIMO, a Genoese (16th century), translated the *Alcestis* of Euripides and three of the plays of Sophocles; he wrote two original tragedies, *Jephte* and *Christo in Passione*.
(R. S. L.)

VINCENZO, who built the Roman palace in the beginning of the 17th century, made the art collection associated with his name. The collection was removed in 1807 to Paris, and in 1815 all that remained of it, about 170 pictures, was purchased by the king of Prussia and removed to the Berlin royal museum.

GIZA (GIZEH; AL JIZAH), a town of upper Egypt and capital of Giza governorate, stands on the west bank of the Nile opposite Cairo, with which it is connected by bridges across the islands of Rawdah (Roda) and Al Zamalik (Gezira). Pop. (1957) 208,667. Giza, which is the seat of Cairo university and has extensive zoological and botanical gardens, grew rapidly after 1945 as a dormitory town of Cairo. Its industries include the manufacture of cotton textiles, footwear, beer and bricks. Giza is also the principal seat of the Egyptian motion-picture industry. A wide straight five-mile motor road and tramway lead westward to the famous pyramids of Giza.

GIZA GOVERNORATE consists of the narrow strip of cultivated land flanking the Nile, bounded north by the Rosetta branch and south by Bani Suwayf governorate. Pop. (1960 census) 1,337,000. Area 387 sq.mi. This strip contains many antiquities, particularly the chain of pyramids west of the Nile between Giza and Dahshur, and includes the great sphinx, the Giza and Abu Sir pyramids, the great necropolis are the limestone quarries of Tura (10 mi. S. of Cairo) from which much of the building material was obtained. Limestone is still quarried nearby for large cement works (Tura, Ma'sarah, Hulwan) but the principal occupation is agriculture, which occupies about 55% of the employed population and all the irrigable land. The population density of 2,900 per square mile is one of the highest in Egypt.

The chief crops are maize (corn), cotton, wheat and millet. At Al Hawamidiyah, just south of Tura, is a large sugar refinery (the only one in Egypt), and the by-product molasses is distilled for alcohol. (For the antiquities *see* EGYPTIAN ARCHITECTURE.)
(A. B. M.)

GJELLERUP, KARL ADOLPH (1857-1919), Danish poet and novelist who shared the Nobel prize for literature with Henrik Pontoppidan in 1917. Born at Roholte, Zealand, on June 2, 1857, he studied theology, although already an atheist; and, strongly influenced by Georg Brandes and Darwinism, wrote novels expressing optimistic radicalism—*En Idealist* (1878) and *Germanernes Laerling* (1882). Travel broadened his outlook and he reacted against naturalism, developing an idealistic philosophy incorporating elements derived from Schiller, Schopenhauer, Wagner and Buddhism. He settled in Germany in 1892 and wrote many of his later works in German, often using Germanic and classical or Indian themes and settings. His works include novels—*Die Opferianer* (1903), *Pilgrimen Kamanita* (1906; Eng. trans. by J. E. Logie, *The Pilgrim Kamanita*, 1911); plays—*Brynhild* (1884), *Wuthhorn* (1893); and verse in Danish. He died at Klotzsche near Dresden, Oct. 11, 1919.

GJIROKASTËR (GJINOKASTËR; Gr. ARGYROKASTRON), a town of southern Albania and centre of an administrative division, lies about 1,150 ft. above sea level on the eastern slope of the Mali Gjere ("broad mountain"), overlooking the wide Dhropull valley, 66 mi. S.E. of Vlore by road. Pop. (1960) 14,000, part Muslim and part Orthodox. Its picturesque latticed houses sprawl across the spurs of the mountainside and are dominated by the fortress built by Ali Pasha after his capture of the place in 1811. The fortress is well preserved and has latterly been used as a prison. After the Balkan Wars (1912-13), the town was claimed by Greece until the occupation by Italian forces (1915-

20). Seized, like the rest of Albania, by Italy in 1939, it was captured by the Greek army on Dec. 8, 1940, and held until Germany's Balkan campaign the following April. The town is a centre of the Bektashi Muslims. It stands near the site of the Roman town Hadrianopolis. (D. R. O.-H.)

GLABER, RADULFUS (c. 985–c. 1047), French monk and chronicler, was born near Auxerre. He entered the monastery of St. Léger at Champeaux as an oblate, but he had little inclination for religious life and his notable instability took him from monastery to monastery. He was befriended by William of Volpiano, abbot of St. Bénigne at Dijon, who took him to Italy (1028–29). After William's death, however, Glaber went to Cluny, and it was to Odilo, abbot of Cluny, that he dedicated the five books of his *Historiae*. Finally, about 1035 he returned to St. Germain d'Auxerre, where he had already spent some time at an earlier stage. He died there about 1047. Glaber's work is of scant historical value since he paid no regard to chronology. Nevertheless, by its wealth of curious detail it provides useful colour and is the only source for much of the 11th-century history of Germany, of Italy and, especially, of France. (J. DE.)

GLACE BAY, a town, port, and coal-mining centre in Cape Breton County, Nova Scotia, on the Atlantic Ocean. The town is 14 mi. E of Sydney, with which it is connected by railway. Coal mining dates from 1720 and major operations from 1858, but these declined after 1960 because of deteriorating markets and the high cost of mining in seams which dip for more than four miles under the sea. The population of the municipality, including the town of Glace Bay and its suburbs, was 37,246 in 1961. Large fishing fleets, particularly for swordfishing, are stationed there. Marconi sent a transatlantic wireless message from Glace Bay in 1902. (C. W. RD.)

GLACIAL EPOCH: *see* PLEISTOCENE EPOCH.

GLACIER, a body of ice originating on land by compaction and recrystallization of snow and showing evidence of present or past movement. Glaciers occur where snowfall in winter exceeds melting in summer, conditions which prevail only in high mountain areas and polar regions at present. Because they are restricted to cold, remote places, glaciers are less familiar to most persons than are rivers, lakes, and other kinds of hydrologic phenomena. Nonetheless, glaciers are extremely important features because of the direct and indirect effects on the earth and its inhabitants resulting from the presence of extensive ice-covered areas.

Glaciers occupy a total of 5,800,000 sq.mi., or 10% of the earth's land surface, an area nearly as large as South America. Of the present area of glaciers 96% is concentrated in Antarctica and Greenland, and the remainder is widely scattered on all continents, except Australia, and on many islands in high latitudes. The exact volume of glaciers is not known, but conservative estimates suggest that there is enough ice to incase the entire earth in a mantle between 100 and 200 ft. thick. Variations in the existing amount of glacier ice are highly critical to man because appreciable changes, either increases or decreases, would adversely affect the distribution of people and their economic relationships. For example, if all existing glacier ice were to melt, the resulting rise in sea level of about 200 ft. would submerge every major coastal city in the world.

Types of Glaciers.—*Ice Sheets.*—The largest glaciers, which are called ice sheets or icecaps, cover huge areas and in many cases are thick enough to bury entire mountain ranges except for the highest peaks. Practically all of Antarctica, an area of more than 5,000,000 sq.mi. is covered by an ice sheet locally 8,000 ft. or more in thickness. The Greenland ice sheet covers about 650,000 sq.mi. and has a maximum measured thickness of nearly 11,000 ft. Smaller ice sheets occur on Iceland, Spitsbergen and several other arctic islands, and still smaller ones in the highlands of Norway.

Valley Glaciers.—Ice streams which flow down mountain valleys are valley glaciers. The Alps, Rockies, Himalayas and other high ranges of the world contain many glaciers of this kind. The smallest valley glaciers are thin patches of ice covering only a fraction of a square mile. And at the other extreme is Beardmore glacier in the antarctic which is about 120 mi. long and 25 mi. wide.

Hubbard glacier in Alaska is about 75 mi. long. Many large valley glaciers are 1,000 to 3,000 ft. thick.

Piedmont Glaciers.—A third and more rare type, intermediate between valley glaciers and ice sheets, are piedmont glaciers. They are valley glaciers which spread laterally over the lowland at the foot of a mountain range. The Malaspina and Bering glaciers in Alaska, each of which covers about 1,500 sq.mi., are splendid examples.

Differences in size between these three types of glaciers depend on climatic factors which determine the amount of snow that accumulates. Differences in form result from the fact that glacier ice flows and thus can mold its form according to the topography.

How Glaciers Form.—Glaciers originate in snow fields. The lower limit of perennial snow fields is called the snow line. The snow line is at sea level in polar regions and rises gradually toward the equator. The maximum altitude of the snow line (about 20,000 ft.) occurs not at the equator but in the dry horse latitudes between 20° and 30° north and south of the equator. Climatic conditions, which are determined by geographic position and altitude, affect both winter snowfall and summer melting, and thus are the major factors affecting locations of snow fields and glaciers. It is for this reason that some very cold but dry areas have no glaciers whereas other warmer areas with abundant snowfall support large glaciers.

As snow fields grow in thickness, solid ice is formed through gradual recrystallization of the accumulated snow. In the first step, which takes place near the surface, melting, evaporation and compaction transform fluffy flakes of new-fallen snow into a porous mass of small, rounded granules called firn or névé. This stage in the change of snow to solid ice can be seen in any melting snowdrift. The weight of snow which accumulates year after year buries the firn of previous years to greater and greater depths. The increasing pressure causes melting and recrystallization at the edges of grains until all air space is gone, and solid crystalline ice is formed.

The thickness of snow, firn and ice can continue to increase only until the strength of ice is exceeded by the pressure exerted by the weight of the accumulation, at which point movement begins. As a result of the pressure from above, ice at the bottom moves in much the same way that cold molasses or tar will flow. Although ice in small pieces is a brittle substance incapable of flowing, ice under sufficient pressure behaves as a plastic material and flows readily though quite slowly. The thickness required to initiate movement varies somewhat depending on slope of the land surface, temperature of the ice and other factors, but some flow occurs in ice masses as little as 50 ft. thick.

Flowage causes a glacier to move downward or laterally into a zone where losses exceed annual accumulation of snow. If the glacier descends below the snow line, losses are due mostly to melting and evaporation, but where a glacier extends into the sea much of the wastage may result from breaking off of icebergs which float away. Thus, the size of a glacier and also variations in its size depend on the degree of balance between accumulation and wastage rates. A glacier which is in equilibrium (a rare condition) does not fluctuate in size because flowage from the zone of accumulation exactly compensates for losses sustained in the zone of wastage.

Glaciers move so slowly that the motion cannot be seen, but the speed of movement can be estimated in various ways. For example, there are many records of the bodies of mountaineers buried by avalanches in the Alps having been carried several miles to a glacier terminus in a few decades. Likewise, the movement of large rocks or other objects on a glacier surface can be determined by successive observations or measurements from some fixed point off the ice. Somewhat more precise ways of measuring glacier speeds include drilling deep holes in the ice and inserting pipes which are progressively deformed, or by setting up rows of stakes and measuring their movement by surveying techniques. Maximum velocities up to 150 ft. per day have been recorded, but a few inches or a few feet per day are more typical.

The various parts of a glacier move at different rates. Movement of a valley glacier is similar to the flow of a river in that velocities are greater in the centre than near the edges, as is shown by the fact that a straight row of stakes soon becomes curved. Ordinarily flow is more rapid in the middle part of a glacier than near its head or terminus. The upper 100 to 200 ft. of a glacier is composed of rigid, brittle ice which does not flow but is carried along by the mobile ice underneath. This brittle zone fractures easily and is characterized by long cracks called crevasses, which are caused by forces that result from different rates of flow in various parts of the glacier. Especially at places where the gradient of the bedrock floor changes abruptly, the upper surface of the glacier may be broken into a jumbled maze of ice pinnacles called *séracs*.

Effects of Glaciation.—Glaciers are the most powerful of all erosional agencies and their special effects on land features commonly are both distinctive and spectacular. Glaciated mountains are much more rugged than nonglaciated mountains. Sharp, pointed peaks like the Matterhorn in Switzerland and deep, U-shaped valleys like Yosemite in the Sierra Nevada of California owe their form mainly to glaciation. The fjords of Norway, Patagonia and Alaska are glaciated valleys now partially submerged by the sea.

A glacier abrades and polishes the bedrock floor over which it passes; rocks and sand pushed along by the ice have the effect of a giant rasp or piece of sandpaper. Frost action, landsliding and avalanching carry rock debris onto a glacier surface from the land protruding above it. The material carried by a glacier ranges from house-sized boulders to clay particles. When the glacier melts all of this material is laid down as an unsorted deposit called till or boulder clay. At the terminus of a glacier the melting ice drops its load in the form of mounds and ridges referred to as a terminal moraine. Valley glaciers also commonly have lateral moraines between the edge of the ice and the valley walls, and medial moraines formed by confluence of tributary glaciers that have lateral moraines.

Drumlins are clusters of elongate hills oriented parallel to the direction of ice movement; they are composed of till laid down near the margins of large ice sheets.

Much of the material laid down by glaciers is reworked by melt-water streams, which build outwash plains and outwash terraces composed of stratified sand and gravel. Kettles are depressions on outwash plains formed by melting of ice blocks buried in the outwash deposits. Eskers are winding ridges of stratified gravel and sand believed to have been deposited by subglacial streams.

Former Periods of Glaciation.—Present-day glaciers are in part remnants left over from the Ice Age or Pleistocene epoch (*q.v.*), when the ice-covered area of the earth was three times its present size (*see also* MAN, EVOLUTION OF; *Estimation of Geological Antiquity*). The antarctic and Greenland glaciers were not much larger then than now, but large areas in North America and Europe were covered by ice sheets. Exactly when Pleistocene glaciation began is not known, but probably less than 1,000,000 years ago. Available evidence indicates that there were at least four major glacial periods, separated by intervals when the climate was warmer than at present. So far as can be determined by use of the radiocarbon method for dating wood and other organic matter found in glacial deposits, the last major ice advance in North America and Europe culminated about 18,000 years ago. At this time the snow line was 1,200 to 1,400 ft. lower than at present and mean annual temperature may have been about 14° F. cooler. Final shrinkage of the North American and European ice sheets began about 11,000 years ago, and by 3000 B.C. glaciers were less extensive than at present. After 2000 B.C. glaciers again expanded slightly and in most parts of the world attained sizes slightly greater than during the 17th and 18th centuries. Warmer climate during the last half of the 19th century, and especially the first half of the 20th century, caused extensive shrinkage of glaciers throughout the world. Although recession has been the general rule during this period, a few glaciers have either advanced or remained essentially stable.

Not only are remnants of Pleistocene glaciers still present, but also the landscape over wide areas bears the direct or indirect imprint of glaciation. Areas that were covered by ice are strewn with till and characterized by typical glacial land forms, including moraines, drumlins and eskers. Drainage features reflect influences of glaciation in that the courses of some rivers, as the Missouri, were determined by the position of the glacier margin; furthermore, the thousands of lakes and swamps in Canada and the northern United States and in northern Europe occupy basins formed by glacial erosion and deposition. Indirect effects of the Pleistocene glacial episode extend far from the areas actually covered by ice. Belts of sand dunes and blankets of wind-blown silt, called loess (*q.v.*) occupy large areas south of the boundaries of the former North American and European ice sheets.

Terraces caused by variations in stream load accompanying glaciation and deglaciation are prominent features in many valleys. Terraces were also formed along the coast as a result of sea level fluctuations during glaciations and interglacial periods. Large lakes developed in regions now arid, as a result of greater precipitation and less evaporation during glacial times; Great Salt Lake (*q.v.*) is a remnant of a formerly much larger body referred to as glacial Lake Bonneville (*see also* UTAH).

Before the Pleistocene Ice Age, there were two earlier major glaciations. Both of these occupied large areas in belts which are now tropical. One glaciation occurred during late Pre-Cambrian time (about 600,000,000 years ago) and the other during the Permian period (roughly 235,000,000 years ago). Apparently, all three of the known major glacial episodes were rather brief, and during the long intervals between them glaciers were not present even in high mountain and polar regions. This means that we are living during an unusual period, because during most of geologic time climate was considerably warmer than at present, and trees of subtropical types grew even in polar areas that are now covered by ice.

Glaciological Research.—Although an impressive amount is known about glaciers, many important problems await solution. Much remains to be learned about the physical properties and behaviour of glaciers, especially the large ice sheets. Flow speeds of many glaciers have been determined, but there is no satisfactory explanation of the mechanism by which flow of ice occurs. Relations between glacier fluctuations and climatic variations are highly complicated and poorly understood. The ultimate cause of world-wide climatic changes which during geologic time have resulted in three major glaciations is still an unsolved mystery. Variations in astronomic, atmospheric, oceanic and continental tectonic factors have been considered, and recently migration of the poles was suggested. All of these and many other related problems are the subjects of intensive study by glaciologists all over the world. Apart from purely scientific interest, there is a practical aspect to such investigations because of potential effects on man that would accompany changes in the present amount of glacier ice. Studies of past behaviour of glaciers have been too limited in scope to be of significant value in forecasting future trends.

See GEOLOGY; *see also* references under "Glacier" in the Index volume.

BIBLIOGRAPHY.—Among the older works are: J. Tyndall, *The Glaciers of the Alps* (1896); A. Penck and E. Brückner, *Die Alpen im Eiszeit-alter* (1909); W. H. Hobbs, *Characteristics of Existing Glaciers* (1911). Later work includes: H. W. Ahlmann, *Glacier Variations and Climatic Fluctuations* (1953); A. E. Vial, *Alpine Glaciers* (1952); F. E. Matthes, "Glaciers" in *Physics of the Earth*, vol. ix (1942); R. F. Flint, *Glacial and Pleistocene Geology* (1957); R. P. Sharp, "Glacier Flow: a Review," *Bull. Geol. Soc. Amer.*, 65:835–838 (Sept. 1954); the latter two references contain extensive bibliographies. The *Journal of Glaciology* and *Zeitschrift für Gletscherkunde* are devoted almost entirely to results of glacier research; in addition, articles on glaciers appear in many other geological and geographical journals.
(J. P. Mr.)

GLACIER BAY NATIONAL MONUMENT is approximately 100 mi. N.W. of Juneau in southeastern Alaska. Its ice fields terminate in more than 20 glaciers. Muir glacier, the best known, has a face 2 mi. wide and more than 200 ft. high. Glacier bay lies in a basin whose high western boundary culminates in 15,300-ft.-high Mt. Fairweather. Many glaciers funneling into a single narrow channel produce dramatic ice movements.

The region has been known since about 1700. Around 1750 the ice filled practically the entire bay; it had begun to retreat by the time of Capt. George Vancouver's visit in 1794. Since then

PLATE I

GLACIER

East ridge of the Doldenhorn in the Bernese Alps, Switz., showing packing of new snow on old snow to create firn that avalanches into the valley to begin an alpine valley-type glacier

Franz Josef glacier, Westland, South Island, N.Z., showing crevasses and jagged ice formations

Commonwealth glacier, McMurdo sound, Antarctica, upper centre, after its narrow passage into Taylor Dry valley becomes a pancakelike piedmont glacier

MOUNTAIN GLACIERS

An alpine glacier, the Greater Aletsch, Switz., showing crevasses and the medial moraine formed by a tributary glacier as seen from the Aletsch forest in the Valais

BY COURTESY OF (CENTRE LEFT) THE NEW ZEALAND HIGH COMMISSIONER, (BOTTOM LEFT) SWISS NATIONAL TOURIST OFFICE, (RIGHT) U.S. NAVY; PHOTOGRAPH, (TOP) BRADFORD WASHBURN

PLATE II

GLACIER

A glacier pushed out from the thick interior ice sheet north of Thule, Greenland, has formed a distinctive glaciated nunatak

Glacier du Géant in the French Alps spills out of a valley in a maze of séracs to merge into the Mer de Glace on the northern slope of Mt. Blanc, in the centre background

Malaspina glacier in the St. Elias mountain range, Alaska, a piedmont-type glacier showing accumulated deposits of till or boulder clay (dark areas)

FLOWAGE OF GLACIERS

BY COURTESY OF (TOP) U.S. NAVY, (CENTRE) INSTITUT DE GÉOGRAPHIE ALPINE; PHOTOGRAPH, (BOTTOM) BRADFORD WASHBURN

the ice front usually has been in retreat. The U.S. naturalist John Muir visited and reported on Glacier bay in 1879 and 1880. Thereafter it was intensively studied by glaciologists, climatologists and plant ecologists.

Glacier bay was made a national monument in 1925; a unit in the U.S. national park system, it comprises 2,274,595 ac. It may be reached by ship, small boat or air. (J. E. Cl.)

GLACIER NATIONAL PARK, in northwestern Montana, U.S., was established in 1910 to protect a highly scenic part of the Rocky mountains. Traversed from north to south by the continental divide, the park is a wilderness of more than 1,000,000 ac.

The mountains constitute a fault-block range. Faulting of the earth's crust along the eastern slope has resulted in rock of ancient origin being forced eastward for 15 mi. on rock of a later geologic period, a formation referred to as the Lewis overthrust.

Mountains, lakes, cirques and U-shaped valleys all show the effect of glacial action that took place during a more recent period, when the region was covered by an ice sheet hundreds of feet thick. A few remnants of the glaciers still cling to the higher peaks.

West of the continental divide, rainfall is heaviest, so that forest growth is more luxuriant there. Characteristic trees are western red cedar, hemlock, larch, white birch, lowland white fir and western white and ponderosa pine. East of the divide, lodgepole pine and Engelmann spruce predominate, while Douglas fir occurs on both sides. At high elevations, groups of limber pine, whitebark pine and alpine fir grow in meadows that are bright with wild flowers in the summer.

The white mountain goat attracts the attention of visitors by its ability to traverse sheer cliffs. Other mammals of the sanctuary are black and grizzly bear, mountain lion, coyote, elk, moose and deer. Some of the park's birds are Rocky Mountain jay, water ouzel, Clark's nutcracker, white-tailed ptarmigan and grouse.

Adjoining the international border, Glacier is contiguous to Canada's Waterton Lakes National park. The two comprise the Waterton-Glacier International Peace park. (Dx. B.)

GLACKENS, WILLIAM JAMES (1870–1938), U.S. painter, a member of the group known as The Eight, was born in Philadelphia on March 13, 1870, studied at the Pennsylvania Academy of the Fine Arts and at the same time worked as an illustrator for the *Philadelphia Record*, the *Public Ledger* and the *Press*. In 1895 he spent a year in Paris and then settled in New York where he continued as an illustrator for the *New York Herald* and the *New York World*. *McClure's Magazine* sent him to Cuba in 1898 to cover the Spanish-American War. At about the turn of the century he took up painting seriously; "Hammerstein's Roof Garden" (1901) was his first important picture. As an illustrator he had dealt with all aspects of contemporary life; he was a sure draftsman and had a keen visual memory, which gave an authentic quality to his work.

He joined with a group of artists who were also interested in depicting contemporary life, and they united to oppose the stodgy, old-fashioned viewpoint of the National Academy. Robert Henri was the leader, and around him gathered John Sloan, George Luks and Everett Shinn as well as the more romantic painters Ernest Lawson, Maurice Prendergast and Arthur B. Davies. Known as The Eight (later, known as the "Ash Can school" because of their honest rendering of city scenes) they held one memorable exhibition in 1908 at the Macbeth gallery, but, due to diversity of viewpoints, the group did not hold together.

One of Glackens' major early works was "Chez Mouquin" (1905) showing a gay New York restaurant in a vivid and robust manner. Later he became interested in Impressionism and very consciously tried to imitate Renoir. He died in Westport, Conn., on May 22, 1938.

See I. Glackens, *William Glackens and the Ashcan Group* (1957); G. P. Du Bois, *William Glackens* (1931). (F. A. Sw.)

GLADBACH, the name of two towns in Germany, both in the *Land* (state) of North Rhine-Westphalia which after partition of the nation following World War II was included in the Federal Republic of Germany. They are distinguished as Bergisch Gladbach and Mönchengladbach (*qq.v.*).

GLADDEN, WASHINGTON (1836–1918), U.S. Congregational minister and religious journalist, the foremost early advocate of the social gospel (*see* CHRISTIAN SOCIALISM) in the U.S., was born at Pottsgrove, Pa., Feb. 11, 1836. He grew up on a farm and received early newspaper training in a small city newspaper office. He attended Williams college, Williamstown, Mass., and later held pastorates at North Adams and Springfield, Mass. He was religious editor of the *New York Independent* for four years from 1871. In 1882 he became pastor of the First Congregational church of Columbus, O., which he served until his death (becoming emeritus pastor in 1914).

Gladden was attracted to the ministry by "a religion that laid hold upon life with both hands, and proposed, first and foremost, to realize the Kingdom of God in this world" (*Recollections*). As acting editor of the *Independent* he aided in the exposure of the Tweed ring. He opposed both socialism and classical economic theory and sought to apply the "Christian law" to social problems; he was probably the first U.S. clergyman of note to approve of unionization. A popular speaker, he appeared before universities and theological schools, twice giving the Beecher lectures at Yale. The titles of his 40 books often conveyed their messages: *Applied Christianity* (1887), *Who Wrote the Bible?* (1891), *Ruling Ideas of the Present Age* (1895), *Social Salvation* (1901). His poem "O Master, Let Me Walk With Thee" became a familiar hymn.

Gladden advocated church union, stimulating the formation of many federations by his fictional account of *The Christian League of Connecticut* (1883). He was a charter member of the American Economic association and served two years on the Columbus city council. In 1904 he was elected moderator of the National Council of Congregational Churches and shortly afterward startled the country with a proposal to reject a $100,000 gift from John D. Rockefeller to the denomination's foreign missions board, on the ground that it was "tainted money." He died at his home in Columbus on July 2, 1918.

See his autobiography, *Recollections* (1909), which contains a bibliography of his works; C. H. Hopkins, *The Rise of the Social Gospel in American Protestantism, 1865–1915* (1940). (C. H. Hs.)

GLADIATORS ("swordsmen"; from Lat. *gladius*, "sword"), professional combatants in ancient Rome. They originally performed at Etruscan funerals, no doubt with intent to give the dead man armed attendants in the next world; hence the fights were usually to the death. At shows in Rome these exhibitions became wildly popular and increased in size from three pairs at the first known exhibition in 264 B.C. (at the funeral of a Brutus) to 300 pairs in the time of Julius Caesar. Hence the shows extended from one day to as many as a hundred, under Titus; while the emperor Trajan in his triumph (107) had 5,000 pairs of gladiators. Shows were also given in other towns of the empire, as can be seen from the traces of amphitheatres.

There were various classes of gladiators, distinguished by their arms or modes of fighting. The *Samnites* fought with the national weapons—a large oblong shield, a visor, a plumed helmet and a short sword. The *Thraces* ("Thracians") had a small round buckler and a dagger curved like a scythe; they were generally pitted against the *mirmillones*, who were armed in Gallic fashion with helmet, sword and shield, and were so called from the name of the fish which served as the crest of their helmet. In like manner the *retiarius* ("net man") was matched with the *secutor* ("pursuer"); the former wore nothing but a short tunic or apron and sought to entangle his pursuer, who was fully armed, with the cast net he carried in his right hand; if successful, he dispatched him with the trident he carried in his left. There were also the *andabatae*, who are believed to have fought on horseback and to have worn helmets with closed visors—that is, to have fought blindfolded; the *dimachaeri* ("two-knife men") of the later empire, who carried a short sword in each hand; the *essedarii* ("chariot men"), who fought from chariots like the ancient Britons; the *hoplomachi* ("fighters in armour"), who wore a complete suit of armour; and the *laquearii* ("lasso men"), who tried to lasso their antagonists.

The shows were announced several days before they took place by bills affixed to the walls of houses and public buildings; copies were also sold in the streets. These bills gave the names of the chief pairs of competitors, the date of the show, the name of the giver and the different kinds of combats. The spectacle began with a procession of the gladiators through the arena, after which their swords were examined by the giver of the show. The proceedings opened with a sham fight (*praelusio, prolusio*) with wooden swords and javelins. The signal for real fighting was given by the sound of the trumpet, those who showed fear being driven on to the arena with whips and red-hot irons. When a gladiator was wounded, the spectators shouted "*Habet*" ("He is wounded"); if he was at the mercy of his adversary, he lifted up his forefinger to implore the clemency of the people, to whom (in the later times of the republic) the giver left the decision as to his life or death. If the spectators were in favour of mercy they waved their handkerchiefs; if they desired the death of the conquered gladiator they turned their thumbs downward. (This is the popular view; the opposite view has been held by J. E. B. Mayor and others, that those who wanted the death of the defeated gladiator turned their thumbs toward their breasts as a signal to stab him and those who wished him to be spared turned their thumbs downward as a signal to drop the sword.) The reward of victory consisted of branches of palm, sometimes of money.

If a gladiator survived a number of combats he might be discharged from further service, the sign of this being the presentation to him of a wooden sword (*rudis*). He could however re-engage after discharge.

On occasion gladiators became politically important, as many of the more turbulent public men had bodyguards composed of them. This of course led to occasional clashes with bloodshed on both sides. Gladiators acting on their own initiative, as in the rising led by Spartacus (*q.v.*) in 73-71 B.C., were still more of a menace.

A gladiator had by way of documentation a little ivory tablet (*tessera*) with his name, that of the head of the school (*patronus, dominus*) and the date of issue. The men were drawn from various sources, but were chiefly slaves and criminals. Discipline was strict, but a successful gladiator not only was famous but, according to the satires of Juvenal, enjoyed the favours of society women. A curious addition to the ranks of gladiators was not uncommon under the empire. A ruined man, perhaps of high social position, might engage himself as a gladiator, thus getting at least a means of livelihood, however precarious. One of the freaks of the emperor Domitian was to have grotesque gladiators (dwarfs and women), and the half-mad Commodus appeared in person in the arena, of course winning his bouts.

To be the head of a school (*ludus*) of gladiators was a well-known but disgraceful occupation. To own gladiators and hire them out was, however, a regular and legitimate branch of commerce.

With the coming of Christianity, gladiatorial shows began to fall into disfavour. Constantine I actually abolished gladiatorial games in A.D. 325, but apparently without much effect since they were again abolished by the emperor Honorius (393-423), and may perhaps even have continued for a century after that.

The continued popularity of gladiatorial shows, like the equally common fights of *bestiarii* with wild beasts of various sorts, was a symptom of the bloodthirsty tastes of the Roman mob, which crowded the theatres at these exhibitions of bloodshed and death.
(H. J. R.)

GLADIOLUS (from Lat. *gladius*, a "sword," in allusion to the sword-shaped leaves), a large genus of showy herbs belonging to the iris family (Iridaceae), and prized as summer-blooming garden plants for their rich glowing colours. They grow from a solid fibrous-coated corm (bulblike enlargement of the base of the stem) and have long, narrow, plaited leaves and a terminal one-sided spike of generally bright-coloured irregular flowers blooming from the bottom upward.

There are about 250 known species, a large number of which are South African, but the genus extends into tropical Africa, forming a characteristic feature of the mountain vegetation, and as far north as central Europe and western Asia. One species, *G. illyricus*, though very rare, is found wild in England, in the New forest and the Isle of Wight. Several of the species have long been cultivated in flower gardens, where both the introduced species and the modern varieties bred from them are very ornamental and popular.

The modern varieties of gladioli have almost completely driven the natural species out of gardens, except in botanical collections. The most attractive groups are those of hybrid origin, most of which have been derived from *G. blandus, G. cardinalis, G. dracocephalus, G. psittacinus, G. gandavensis, G. oppositiflorus* and *G. primulinus*. The beginning of the modern cultivated gladioli was probably the introduction of *G. gandavensis* (itself a hybrid) in 1841. The flowers of the best varieties are of great size and substance, often measuring seven to nine inches across; the range of colour is wide, with shades of gray, purple, scarlet, salmon, crimson, rose, white, pink, yellow, etc., often beautifully mottled and blotched in the throat. The plants are vigorous in growth, often reaching a height of three to four feet.

A deep and rather stiff sandy loam enriched with well-decomposed manure is the best soil for gladioli. The corms should be planted in succession at intervals of two or three weeks, after warm weather arrives, about three to five inches deep and at least one foot apart. The gladiolus is easily raised from seeds, which should be sown in March or April in pots of rich soil placed in slight heat, the pots being kept near the glass after they begin to grow, and the plants being gradually hardened to permit their being placed out of doors in a sheltered spot for the summer. The time occupied from the sowing of the seed until the plant attains its full strength is from three to four years. Because few of the seeds come true to type, approved sorts are multiplied by secondary corms, which form around the principal corm; however in this they vary greatly, some kinds furnishing abundant increase, while others fail to yield offsets.

Gladioli are also very desirable and useful flowers for room decoration, for while the blossoms themselves last fresh for several days if cut early in the morning or late in the evening, the undeveloped buds open in succession so that a cut spike will go on blooming for some time.
(N. Tr.)

GLADKOV, FËDOR VASILEVICH (1883-1958), Soviet writer whose novels dealing with social and economic aspects of Russian life have earned him distinction, was born in Chernavka, June 9, 1883. After working as a schoolteacher and (in 1920) joining the Communist party, he scored a success with *Tsement* (1925; Eng. trans. *Cement*, 1929), the first notable Soviet novel devoted to the restoration of industry. A later novel, *Energiya* (1932-38; "Energy"), continues this theme into the period of more intensive industrialization and describes the building of the Dneprostroi dam with the wealth of technical detail typical of the Soviet "Five Year Plan novel." Outstanding among his other work is *Povest o detstve* (1949; "Story of Childhood"), a volume of reminiscences.
(R. F. Hr.)

GLADSTONE, WILLIAM EWART (1809-1898), the greatest British statesman of the 19th century and four times prime minister, was born in Liverpool on Dec. 29, 1809. His mother, formerly Anne Robertson of Dingwall, came of good Highland family; and his father, John (1764-1851), was descended from the Gledstanes of Lanarkshire, once bailies to the earls of Douglas. His father's father had been a merchant corn dealer at Leith; John Gladstone made himself a merchant prince by trading with the East and West Indies and became a

A GARDEN GLADIOLUS

J. HORACE McFARLAND CO.

leading citizen of the great slaving port of Liverpool. He was a Canningite member of parliament from 1818 to 1827, was made a baronet in 1846, and died worth about £600,000. William Ewart Gladstone, named after a friend of his father's, was the fifth of six children. He was sent to Eton, where Arthur Hallam, the subject of Tennyson's *In Memoriam*, was his closest friend. Eton he always afterward described as the queen of all schools; he did not particularly distinguish himself there. He first displayed his considerable powers of intellect at Christ Church, Oxford, where he secured two first classes in 1831, in Greats (classics) in November and in mathematics in December.

His father dissuaded him from his original intention to take orders in the Church of England; yet he devoted his life, as he saw it, to serving the principles of the gospel in politics. As a disciple of Edmund Burke and George Canning, he mistrusted parliamentary reform; his speech against it in May 1831 at the Oxford union, of which he had been president, made a strong impression and was indeed regarded as the finest so far delivered there. One of his Christ Church friends, son of the duke of Newcastle, persuaded the duke to support Gladstone as candidate for Newark in the general election of Dec. 1832; thus the "Grand Old Man" of Liberalism began a parliamentary career of more than 60 years as a Tory member for what was little better than a pocket borough.

His abilities were noticed early; his maiden speech on June 3, 1833, defending the treatment of slaves on a plantation his father owned in Demerara, made a decided mark. He held minor office in Sir Robert Peel's short government of 1834-35, first at the treasury under Peel himself, then as undersecretary for the colonies under Lord Aberdeen. After two other women had refused him, in July 1839 he married Catherine (1812–1900), daughter of Sir Stephen Glynne of Hawarden near Chester. She was a woman of lively wit, complete discretion and exceptional charm, utterly devoted to her husband, to whom she bore eight children. This marriage gave him a secure base of personal happiness for the rest of his life. It also established him in the aristocratic governing class of the time; his wife's mother had been Pitt's first cousin. His first book, *The State in Its Relations With the Church*, had been published in 1838. He outgrew while he wrote it its strong and narrow doctrines, to the effect that the Church of England must act as the conscience of the state, which in its turn can distinguish religious truth and falsehood—doctrines already obsolescent when the book appeared.

The Influence of Peel.—Macaulay, in a too celebrated afterthought, in reviewing this work referred to Gladstone as the rising hope of stern and unbending Tories. His early parliamentary performances were indeed strongly Tory; but time after time actual contact with the effects of Tory policy forced him by the evident justice of each particular case to take a more liberal view. His conversion from the conservatism in which he was brought up to the liberalism which gave him lasting fame was prolonged by stages over a generation. He took his first steps in a liberal direction during Peel's second ministry (1841-46). By 1840 he was attending meetings of what would now be called the shadow cabinet and had hoped to be included in the new cabinet from the start as secretary for Ireland; however, Peel rightly judged that he was too strong an Anglican for immediate contact with a country part Roman Catholic and part Presbyterian, and that the son of so successful a merchant would be useful at the board of trade. Gladstone, made vice-president of the board under the ineffective Lord Ripon, complained privately that "the science of politics deals with the government of men, but I am set to govern packages"; yet the wisdom of Peel's choice was soon apparent. The vice-president's powers of application astonished even his hardworking colleagues; Sir James Graham said of him that he could do in four hours what would take any other man 16, and that he worked 16 hours a day.

Under Peel's supervision he embarked on a major simplification of the tariff; the duties on no fewer than 750 articles were removed or reduced in 1842. While mastering the complexities of this subject Gladstone became indeed a more thoroughgoing free trader than Peel himself. The prime minister felt that Gladstone was outstanding among all the promising young men in the government; said that a more admirable combination of ability, knowledge, temper and discretion had never before been exhibited in parliament; and in May 1843 invited him into the cabinet as president of the board of trade.

Gladstone accepted, after characteristic hesitations about a proposal to amalgamate two Welsh bishoprics, and continued the work of improving the commercial structure of the country. The Railway act of 1844, prepared under his direction, compelled all lines to carry passengers in covered coaches, once a day at least, at a charge of not more than 1*d.* a mile and made provision for eventual state purchase of railway lines. Among other useful tasks, he much improved working conditions for coal heavers in the London docks. Early in 1845, when the cabinet proposed to increase the state grant to the Irish Roman Catholic college at Maynooth, Gladstone resigned—not because he did not approve of the increase, but because it went against the views he had published seven years before. Plain men found his reason for resigning pernickety. At the end of the year he rejoined the cabinet as secretary of state for the colonies. This legally involved the resignation of his seat at Newark. As he was by now a convinced free trader, and the duke of Newcastle was a protectionist, he could not win it again, and for various reasons he did not contest any of the half-dozen possible seats suggested to him by the Conservative whip. For six months, till Peel's government fell in June 1846, he was in office, but not in parliament—a position of doubtful constitutional propriety. Absence from the commons had an effect of importance to him: he was unable to make any personal reply to Disraeli's onslaughts on Peel. While he was at the colonial office he was led nearer to liberalism by being forced to consider the claims of English-speaking colonists to govern themselves, but he was there too short a time to make any useful mark on colonial policy.

Private Preoccupations.—The Glynne family estates were deeply involved in the financial panic of 1847. For several years Gladstone was concerned with extricating them, devoting his customary energy to the intricacies of industrial investment and land tenure; dull as this work must have been at the time, it gave him a still fuller insight into practical economics, which helped him later when he was chancellor of the exchequer. In the course of these operations he became the largest landlord in the county of Flint. At about the same time he began, with singular simplicity, a habit of charitable work which was open to a great deal of misconstruction; he often tried, in the streets of London, to persuade prostitutes to enter a home which he and his wife maintained, or in some other way to take up a different way of life. He spent much time and money on these efforts till well past his 80th birthday. Another private matter that absorbed a great deal of his attention was the conversion of his younger sister to the Roman Catholic church; this pained him even more acutely than any of the political separations that befell him.

Several of his closest Oxford friends were among the Anglicans who left the Church of England for the Church of Rome under the impact of the Oxford movement and the Gorham judgment (see MANNING, HENRY EDWARD; OXFORD MOVEMENT). Gladstone had been brought up by an evangelical mother; he had moved over to a high Anglican position when in Italy just after leaving Oxford, and once he had reached it he retained it. Neither affection nor argumentative skill could ever persuade him to become a Roman Catholic himself, but the suspicion that he was one dogged him, and was used against him from time to time by political and clerical adversaries. Of these he had many in the University of Oxford, for which he was elected M.P. in Aug. 1847. He scandalized many of his new constituents at once by voting for the admission of Jews to parliament, and many more by his tolerant opposition to Lord John Russell's Ecclesiastical Titles act of 1851.

Gladstone made his first weighty speech on foreign affairs in June 1850, opposing Lord Palmerston in the Pacifico debate. That autumn he paid a private visit to Naples and called on a learned friend, who turned out to be in prison. Already an experienced prison visitor, he was so appalled by the conditions that when he returned to London next

February he could talk of little else. Brushing aside a request to join a proposed protectionist government, he appealed to Lord Aberdeen, the leader of his Peelite friends, to use his influence to help the many thousands of starving political prisoners Gladstone had seen living chained to criminals in underground dungeons. Aberdeen took time in consulting powerful acquaintances in Vienna; nothing was actually done. So in July 1851 Gladstone published two trenchant *Letters to Lord Aberdeen* which described what he had seen and appealed to all Conservatives to set an iniquity right. The results were far from what he had desired. For the time, the Neapolitan prisoners were treated even worse than before, and most Conservatives, all over Europe, were deaf to his appeal. But Palmerston circulated the *Letters* to all the British missions on the continent, and they delighted every liberal who heard of them.

Financial Policy.—For nine years after Peel's death in 1850 Gladstone's political position was seldom comfortable and sometimes embarrassing. One of the most eminent of the dwindling band of distinguished Peelites, he was mistrusted by the leaders of both the main parties, and distrusted some of them—particularly Palmerston and the protectionist Disraeli—in his turn. He refused to join Lord Derby's government in 1852. At the end of that year, by a brilliant attack on Disraeli's budget, he brought the government down; and he took a long stride forward in public estimation as a result, for he joined Aberdeen's coalition as chancellor of the exchequer. His first budget speech on April 18, 1853, gave the country in Greville's words "the assurance of a *man* equal to great political necessities, and fit to lead Parties and direct Governments." In his bold and comprehensive plan he made further large reductions in duties, propounded the eventual elimination of the income tax, and with considerable political courage revived and carried a scheme that Pitt had not been strong enough to carry in 1796 for the extension of the legacy duty to real property. Every other member of the cabinet at first opposed this proposal, and he converted them all.

His budget provided the backbone of the coalition's success in 1853, a year in which he spent much time in arranging for competitive entry into the civil service. He was also busy preparing the Oxford University act passed in the following year; this local preoccupation kept him from taking any detailed interest in the events which led up to the Crimean War. He defended the war, then and thereafter, as necessary at its inception for the defense of the public law of Europe; but of course its outbreak deranged his financial plans. He determined to pay for it as far as possible by taxation, and doubled the income tax—from 7d. to 1s. 2d.—in 1854. When Aberdeen fell in Jan. 1855 Gladstone agreed to join Palmerston's cabinet, but resigned three weeks later with two other Peelites, Sir James Graham and Sidney Herbert, sooner than accept J. A. Roebuck's committee of inquiry. This action was no more readily explicable to ordinary men than his resignation ten years earlier had been, and he was for a time unpopular in the country. He made himself more unpopular still by speeches in parliament in the summer of 1855 in which he held that the war was no longer justified, as its proper objects had already been attained. Meanwhile his imagination was still haunted by the horrors of Naples. He helped finance a quixotic project, which Palmerston aided with £500 from secret service funds: a steamer with an armed crew was dispatched to rescue some Neapolitan prisoners confined on a Mediterranean island. The good and the harm that might have come of this voyage were alike averted when the vessel sank on the way.

Gladstone always kept up his reading in classical studies, as well as in theology and Italian poetry; and used his leisure out of office to prepare a long book, *Homer and the Homeric Age* (3 vol., 1858), which suggested that ancient Greek life had been designed by providence to show men how they should behave to each other. He helped to defeat Palmerston in the commons by a speech on China in March 1857; and later that year opposed the Divorce bill on religious grounds with such persistency that he was accused long afterward of having invented parliamentary obstruction himself. He twice refused to join Disraeli, but accepted in 1858, in spite of a generous letter from Disraeli, an offer to visit the Ionian Islands protectorate as lord high commissioner in the winter of 1858–59, a journey that produced no useful results.

In June 1859 Gladstone gave a silent, unavailing vote for Derby's Conservative government on a confidence motion, and caused surprise by joining Palmerston's Whig cabinet as chancellor of the exchequer a week later. His sole, but overwhelming, reason for joining a statesman he neither liked nor trusted was the critical state of the Italian question. The triumvirate of Palmerston, Russell and Gladstone did indeed help over the next 18 months to secure the unification of almost all Italy, but on other matters the cabinet was much divided.

Gladstone was constantly at issue with his prime minister over spending on defense. By prolonged efforts, he managed to get the service estimates down by 1866 to a lower figure than that for 1859. He took little other part in the government's foreign policy, except for an unfortunate and unauthorized reference to the seceding American states as "a nation" in Oct. 1862. The national economy responded well to his policies at the exchequer, which included the abolition of a further 370 duties by the celebrated budget of 1860. Two other financial measures of that year were important: the Anglo-French trade treaty, a project of Richard Cobden's which Gladstone warmly supported, and which shortly doubled the value of Anglo-French trade; and Gladstone's proposal to abolish the duties on paper, which to Palmerston's ill-concealed delight the house of lords rejected. Next year Gladstone repeated the proposal, this time including it with all the other budget arrangements in a single finance bill which the lords dared not amend, a procedure that has been followed ever since. Another particularly useful step was the creation of the post office savings bank. These measures brought him into increased contact, and increased popularity, with the leaders of working-class opinion; journeys round the main centres of industry did the same. A few words of his in the commons on May 11, 1864, were widely interpreted outside as a declaration of belief in practically universal suffrage; seen in their context, they are not quite so extreme. They are worth quoting, with their context, as an example of his characteristic tendency to qualification:

I venture to say that every man who is not presumably incapacitated by some consideration of personal unfitness or of political danger is morally entitled to come within the pale of the Constitution. Of course, in giving utterance to such a proposition, I do not recede from the protest I have previously made against sudden, or violent, or excessive, or intoxicating change.

In the general election of July 1865 Gladstone was defeated at Oxford, but just secured a seat in south Lancashire; the sadness of the defeat was atoned for in some degree by a contact with a popular constituency which he found refreshing. When Palmerston died in October and Russell became prime minister, Gladstone took over the leadership of the house of commons, while remaining at the exchequer. He was not well suited for the new post; he was too busy to spend much time in making himself agreeable to backbenchers, and while Whigs distrusted him as a former Conservative, Conservatives distrusted him as a renegade, and radicals as a churchman.

By now quite convinced of the need for a further reform of parliament, he introduced a bill for the moderate extension of the franchise in March 1866. Violently attacked by Robert Lowe, it foundered in committee in June, and the whole government resigned. Next year Disraeli introduced another moderate Reform bill; and this passed, but not until John Bright and Gladstone had transformed it in committee into a stronger one that gave a vote to most householders in boroughs. Disraeli became prime minister early in 1868. Gladstone, two months later, carried against him in the commons three resolutions calling for the disestablishment of the Protestant church in Ireland. That autumn in *A Chapter of Autobiography* he explained the reasons that had led him so far from the conclusions of his first book. Russell had by now retired from active politics, and it was to Gladstone that the Liberal whips looked for instructions during the general election at the end of the year. Though Gladstone lost his Lancashire seat, he was returned for Greenwich; and the Liberal party won handsomely in the country as a whole. His abilities had made him its indispensable leader, and Queen Victoria called on him to form a government when Disraeli resigned.

First Administration.—Gladstone's first cabinet (1868–74) was perhaps the most capable of the century. Its prime minister tried, like Peel and unlike Palmerston or Disraeli, to supervise the work of each department, while giving close attention to church appointments and devoting his main efforts to Irish and foreign policy. The Irish church was successfully disestablished in 1869, and a first attempt to grapple with Irish land was made in 1870; but the Land act of that year almost broke up the cabinet, and was emasculated by the lords. Abroad, an attempt to promote disarmament in 1869 failed, as Bismarck refused to consider it. The Franco-German War took the government completely by surprise, and the cabinet would not allow Gladstone to propose to Prussia the neutralization of Alsace and Lorraine. The principal achievements of 1871 and 1872, the London declaration by the great powers that they would not in future abrogate treaties without the consent of all the signatories, and the settlement by arbitration of the "Alabama" claim of the United States, look well in retrospect but were thought pusillanimous at the time. The most useful reforms at home were administrative, except for the Education act of 1870 and the Ballot act of 1872; these measures supplemented the work of parliamentary reform, but antagonized opposite wings of the Liberal party. When an Irish University bill failed by three votes to pass the commons in March 1873, Gladstone resigned, but was forced back into office by Disraeli. In August he had to reshuffle his cabinet, and again took on the chancellorship of the exchequer himself. Fascinated by another plan to abolish income tax altogether, he dissolved parliament suddenly in Jan. 1874, but his party was heavily defeated, and his government resigned. As far back as 1855 he had written: "Public life is full of snares and dangers, and I think it a fearful thing for a Christian to look forward to closing his life in the midst of its (to me at least) essentially fevered activity." So he gave up the Liberal party leadership, though he remained M.P. for Greenwich; and retired to Hawarden, to write pamphlets attacking papal infallibility and articles on Homer.

Bulgarian Atrocities.—The indifference of Disraeli's government to the brutality of Turkish reprisals against risings in the Balkans in 1875–76 brought Gladstone back to active politics. For many years he had held that the only just solution to Balkan problems was to hand the peninsula over to its indigenous inhabitants. Now, in Sept. 1876, he published a famous pamphlet on *Bulgarian Horrors and the Question of the East* which demanded that the Turkish irregulars should remove themselves, "one and all, bag and baggage, ... from the province they have desolated and profaned." He took the lead in stirring popular indignation against the government's bellicose eastern policy; but it was uphill work. London society and the London mob were both against him; the queen, under the blandishments of her prime minister, strongly disapproved; the Whiggish elements in his own party were lukewarm or indifferent at first; and only some radicals, with whom he had little in common, supported him hotly. He paid too little attention to the embarrassment he was causing the Liberal party leader, Lord Granville. Yet in the end he triumphed.

He gave up his Greenwich seat, and stood for the Scottish county of Midlothian against a sitting Conservative who was heir to the greatest local magnate. In two tremendous outbursts of oratory in Nov. 1879 and March 1880, Gladstone secured his own return to parliament, but he also did much more: he overthrew a government.

The general election of March and April 1880 had more, and on the whole more ardent, contests than any before, and it was this one man's eloquence that decided the result and secured a large Liberal majority. The feat is unique. . Gladstone was able, by manifest sincerity and skill of argument combined, to convince a majority of the electorate all over the kingdom that recent Conservative policy had been morally wrong, and the Conservative government had to resign.

Second Administration.—In his second administration (1880–85) Gladstone foolishly combined again for two and a half years the duties of prime minister with those of chancellor of the exchequer. Party lines had not yet set firm, and his large apparent majority in the commons was unruly; for example, he was dogged by the tiresome controversy over Charles Bradlaugh; and it was not till 1884 that he could introduce the measure for which most Liberals had been pressing, a third Reform act that nearly doubled the electorate by giving votes to householders in country districts. This measure was passed only after a stiff quarrel with the house of lords. Gladstone had hoped to settle the eastern question quickly, and then retire. As it was, he and Granville, the foreign secretary, did manage by a brusque naval threat to compel Turkey to cede Thessaly to Greece; yet Granville would not let him go on to give up Cyprus, as the government had already been weakened by other questions and had vital work still before it. There was, again, an appearance of weakness in what can now be recognized as Gladstone's magnanimous attitude to the Transvaal Boers after Majuba (see SOUTH AFRICA, REPUBLIC OF: *History*); and there were still graver troubles in Ireland, in the throes of agricultural catastrophe. The exceedingly complicated Irish Land act of 1881, largely Gladstone's own work, did promote in the long run the prosperity of the Irish peasant; but violent crime continued, culminating in the murder on May 6, 1882, of Gladstone's close friend and nephew-in-law Lord Frederick Cavendish, whom he had just sent to Dublin as chief secretary in the hope that a settlement could be reached. No alternatives were left to strong police powers in Ireland and measures to restrict the freedom of Irish members to obstruct the work of the commons; Gladstone hated both, but had to sanction them.

A third imperial imbroglio came to overshadow the other two, when a series of unavoidable decisions compelled the cabinet to authorize the occupation of Egypt in 1882. Gladstone's settlement of the Egyptian debt question (1885) was honourable to his belief in the concert of Europe, but had the unintended effect of tying British foreign policy to German. The worst mistakes he ever made were to allow Gen. C. G. Gordon, whom he never met, to go to Khartoum, and then to fail to rescue him; Gordon was killed in Jan. 1885, and his death cost Gladstone much in popularity. Firm handling of a dispute with Russia over the northern borders of Afghanistan did something to restore his prestige; but when the government was defeated on the budget in June 1885 he was glad to resign. He refused a gracefully worded offer of an earldom from the queen.

Irish Home Rule.—Though he had only spent three weeks in Ireland in his life (in 1877), Gladstone had historical insight and imaginative sympathy enough to appreciate the full force of Irish nationalism. For many years he had looked favourably on the case for Irish Home Rule, that is, for a subordinate parliament in Dublin, as his close colleagues knew. In the autumn of 1885 he believed the time for it was ripe; but as a combination of Irish with Conservative votes had defeated him in June, he waited silently to see what an Irish-Conservative combination would produce. Before the general election of Nov.–Dec. 1885 the radical leader Joseph Chamberlain, whom Gladstone never much liked or understood at all, secured the allegiance of enough of the new voters in the countryside for his "unauthorized program" to produce a paradoxical result: in the new parliament the Liberal members exactly equaled the total of Conservatives plus Irish. At this moment an indiscretion by Gladstone's youngest son revealed his father's conversion to Home Rule, and most Conservatives therefore turned against it. Lord Salisbury's government was defeated when parliament met, and Gladstone formed his third cabinet in Feb. 1886. His Home Rule bill was rejected in parliament in June by a large secession of Whigs under Lord Frederick Cavendish's brother Lord Hartington, and in the country at a general election in July, and Gladstone resigned office.

He had kept his Midlothian seat, unopposed, and carried with him into the new parliament a personal following 190 strong, supported by the National Liberal federation, the most powerful political machine in the country. He devoted the next six years to an effort to convince the British electorate that to grant Home Rule to the Irish nation would be an act of justice and wisdom. This policy was abhorrent to the English upper classes, and for the first time a marked class division between the leading parties opened. At the jubilee of 1887 Gladstone was cheered from the pavements but hissed from the balconies. The act was symbolic of the position he had now reached of the great popular hero of the age. His reputation stood higher with Scotsmen, Irishmen and Welshmen than with Englishmen, except for the English Nonconformists, to whom his tendency to regard and describe great political questions as moral ones made a strong appeal; portraits of him were far commoner in poor men's cottages than those of any other political leader. He spoke at many great meetings, and cooperated with the Irish leader C. S. Parnell (q.v.). But his judgment did not improve as he got older, and in 1890, when he was over 80, momentary excitement led him into a dangerous quarrel with Parnell about the political consequences of the O'Shea divorce. (Gladstone had not believed the rumours about Parnell's liaison, holding that Parnell would never "imperil the future of Ireland for an adulterous intrigue.") He never sought to correct the errors about him which Parnell spread in Ireland. He sanctioned an extensive program of Liberal reforms drawn up at Newcastle in 1891, because it was headed by Home Rule, and on this platform the Liberals won in the general election of 1892 a majority of 40—if the Irish voted with them.

Gladstone, an "old, wild, and incomprehensible man of 82½," as the queen called him in a letter at the time, formed his fourth cabinet in Aug. 1892. Its members were only held together by awe of him. He piloted another Home Rule bill through 85 sittings of the commons in 1893; the lords rejected it on Devonshire's motion by the largest majority ever recorded there, 419-41, but the full discussion in the commons brought Ireland eventual benefit. The cabinet rejected Gladstone's proposal to dissolve.

He could not agree with his colleagues that a large increase in the naval estimates was necessary, and finally resigned—ostensibly because sight and hearing were failing—on March 3, 1894. He was much mortified by the coolness of his last official interview with the queen he had served loyally all her reign; by now she frankly detested him, and had to struggle to conceal the fact in his presence. He retired to Hawarden, and busied himself with a critical edition of the works of Bishop Joseph Butler (3 vol., 1896), whom he used to name with Homer, Aristotle and Dante as his "four great teachers" besides the Gospels. Humanitarian to the end, in his last great speech, at Liverpool in Sept. 1896, he denounced Turkish atrocities in Armenia. After a painful illness, he died of cancer of the palate at Hawarden on May 19, 1898. His body lay in state in Westminster hall for three days, and was buried in Westminster abbey. (See also ENGLISH HISTORY.)

Character.—As a young man Gladstone was handsome. As he grew older his face grew more formidable, with deep lines from beside the nostrils to the corners of the mouth, and was much wrinkled in old age. His spare and upright figure, well proportioned, was just below middle height. His voice was clear, deep and sonorous, with a touch of Lancashire accent; and none who saw it soon forgot the flash of his dark eyes.

His truly extraordinary vigour far exceeded that of other men, and was coupled with no less extraordinary powers of self-control and an iron devotion to duty. Training and natural ability led him to qualify statements and subdivide arguments; his thoughts indeed were often complicated, but his character was fundamentally simple. It was a simple sense of duty that took him into politics, a career in which he never felt really at home and for which he was in some ways unfitted, not least by his tendency to believe that other men's motives were invariably as disinterested as his own, and by his excessive anxiety to maintain the consistency of his own conduct. Political courage and personal magnanimity he had in abundance, and he was the most efficient administrator of his age. His gift for concentration was remarkable; this helped people who did not know him well to think him hard or even hypocritical. But no one who knew him intimately doubted his entire sincerity or failed to be captivated by his delightful manners, the warmth of his human sympathies and the range of his mind. He was combative by instinct, and combined a magical quickness of understanding with an unusually retentive memory and an inexhaustible fund of phrase; these qualities made him a fearsome adversary in debate. In his prepared speeches he was able to communicate to his hearers a full sense of the significance of the subject he was discussing, and of their responsibility for seeing that it was decided rightly. Purely as an orator, he had two or three equals in his own day; as a statesman, only Peel came near him. A few British prime ministers—Walpole, Chatham, Pitt, Churchill—have been leaders as great; none has been more inspiring. Lord Acton, indeed, assessing for Gladstone's daughter in 1879 her father's standing among the world's statesmen of the past two centuries, concluded that ("in the three elements of greatness combined—the man, the power, and the result—character, genius, and success—none reached his level." See also references under "Gladstone, William Ewart" in the Index volume.

BIBLIOGRAPHY.—Gladstone's official *Life* is by John, Viscount Morley, 3 vol. (1903). It should be supplemented for personal details by *The Diary of Lady Frederick Cavendish*, ed. by J. Bailey, 2 vol. (1927); Herbert, Viscount Gladstone, *After Thirty Years* (1928); Lord Kilbracken, *Reminiscences* (1931); Sir P. Magnus, *Gladstone* (1954); and Georgina Battiscombe, *Mrs. Gladstone* (1956), R. W. Seton-Watson, *Disraeli, Gladstone and the Eastern Question* (1935) and J. L. Hammond, *Gladstone and the Irish Nation* (1938) are the only satisfactory full-length monographs on him.

Among the British Museum Additional Manuscripts are 750 volumes of Gladstone papers which await full research. A little of his correspondence has been published: selected *Correspondence on Church and Religion*, ed. by D. C. Lathbury (1910); *Gladstone and Palmerston* (1928) and *The Queen and Mr. Gladstone*, 2 vol. (1933), both ed. by P. Guedalla; *Gladstone to His Wife*, a selection, ed. by A. Tilney Bassett (1936); *The Gladstone-Granville Political Correspondence, 1868-1886*, ed. by Agatha Ramm, 4 vol. (1952-62). He made two selections himself from his numerous articles in magazines: *Gleaning of Past Years*, 7 vol. (1879) and *Later Gleanings* (1897). Of a projected edition of his *Speeches* by A. W. Hutton and H. J. Cohen only 2 vol. appeared (1891-92). A. Tilney Bassett, *Gladstone's Speeches* (1916) contains, besides the texts of 14 of his best speeches, complete lists of all of them and of all his publications.

(M. R. D. F.)

GLAGOLITIC ALPHABET.

According to tradition, when St. Cyril of Thessalonica undertook his mission to Moravia in the middle of the 9th century A.D., he invented an alphabet for his Slavonic translations of essential religious texts. This alphabet was, almost certainly, the Glagolitic, in which some of the earliest extant manuscripts of Old Church Slavonic are written. After the failure of the Moravian mission, it was quickly superseded among the Orthodox Slavs by the so-called Cyrillic alphabet, and it remained in use principally among those Catholic Croatians who persevered in their loyalty to the Slavonic liturgy. The name of the alphabet is, in fact, probably derived from the Old Church Slavonic *glagola* ("he) said," which would be frequently heard in the chanting of the liturgical Gospels. The origin of the individual letters cannot be said to be well established, despite several, often conflicting, attempts to derive them from contemporary Greek forms or from oriental sources that would have been familiar to such an accomplished linguist as St. Cyril. See ALPHABET.

See J. Vajs, *Rukověť hlaholské paleografie* (1932); V. Jagić, *Glagoličeskoe pis'mo* (*Ènciklopedija slavjanskoj filologii* 3); III (1911). (F. J. WD.)

GLAMIS,

a village and civil parish in Angus (Forfarshire), Scotland, 5 mi. S.W. of Forfar. Pop. (1951) 876. The name (pronounced Glaams) is derived from the Gaelic, *glamhus*, "a wide gap," "a vale." In the village is a sculptured stone, supposed to be a memorial of Malcolm II, although a statement by John of Fordun, the Scottish chronicler, that the king was slain in the castle is now rejected.

Glamis castle, the seat of the earl of Strathmore and Kinghorne, is a fine example of the Scottish baronial style, enriched with certain features of the French château. In its present form it dates mostly from the 17th century, but the original structure was as old as the 11th century, for Macbeth was thane of Glamis. Robert II bestowed the thanedom on John Lyon, who had married the king's second daughter by Elizabeth Mure and was thus the founder of the existing family. Patrick Lyon became hostage to England for James I in 1424. When, in 1537, Janet Douglas, widow of the 6th Lord Glamis, was burned at Edinburgh as a witch for conspiring to poison James V, Glamis was forfeited to the crown, but it was restored to her son six years later when her innocence had been established. The 3rd earl of Strathmore entertained the Old Pretender in 1715 and fell on the battlefield at Sheriffmuir. Sir Walter Scott spent a night in the "hoary old pile" when he was about twenty years old, and gives a striking relation of his experiences in his *Letters on Demonology and Witchcraft*. The castle was the early home of Lady Elizabeth Bowes-Lyon, who became consort to King George VI. In 1930 it was the birthplace of Princess Margaret Rose, the first royal baby to be born in Scotland for 300 years.

GLAMORGAN (Welsh, SIR FORGANNWG), a county of southern Wales, is bounded northwest by Carmarthenshire, north by Carmarthenshire and Brecknockshire, east by Monmouthshire and south and southwest by the Bristol channel and the Loughor estuary. The word Glamorgan is a corruption of the Welsh *Gwlad Morgan*, meaning the land of Morgan, a 10th-century Welsh prince. Area 817.6 sq.mi. Structurally it falls into two sections: (1) the northern upland section of barren moorland, part of the south Wales coal field; (2) the rural southern section comprising the Vale of Glamorgan and the Gower peninsula.

Physical Features.—The body of the county forms a quarter circle between the rivers Taff and Neath. Near the apex of the angle formed by these rivers is the highest ground in the county, the great Pennant scarp of Craig-y-Llyn (1,969 ft.). To the south and southeast extends the south Welsh coal field, its surface forming an irregular plateau with an average elevation of 1,000 ft., but with higher ground of 1,500 ft. or more, Mynydd-y-Caerau being 1,823 ft. Out of this plateau have been carved, to the depth of 500 to 800 ft. below its general level, three distinct series of narrow river valleys, those in each series being more or less parallel. The Cynon, the Rhondda Fach and the Rhondda Fawr (tributaries of the Taff) and the Ely flow to the southeast, the Ogwr or Ogmore (with its tributaries the Garw and Llynfi) flow south through Bridgend, and the Avon brings the waters of the Corrwg and Gwynfi to the southwest into Swansea bay at Aberavon. To the east of this region and divided from it by high ground culminating in Carn Bugail (1,570 ft.) is the Rhymney, which forms the county's eastern boundary. On the west, similarly, high ground divides the Neath from the Tawe and the Tawe from the Loughor, which, with its tributary the Aman, separates the county on the northwest from Carmarthenshire. The rivers are all comparatively short, the Taff, the chief river, being only 40 mi. long.

To the south of this country, which is wet, cold and sterile, and whose slopes form the coal field's southern edge, there stretches to the sea the undulating plain known as the Vale of Glamorgan, rising in places to more than 400 ft. The floor of the vale is of New Red Sandstone and Lias. On the faces of the perpendicular cliffs can be seen the strata of coloured rocks—red and green marls, black shales and blue and yellow limestones. Stretching westward from Swansea is the Gower peninsula, a low plateau with some hills rising to 600 ft. Cefn-Bryn, an anticline of Old Red Sandstone, forms its prominent backbone.

Most of the southern part is of Carboniferous Limestone covered inland by boulder clay. The limestone cliffs are of great beauty. The Gower peninsula was officially designated by the national parks commission as an "area of outstanding natural beauty" in 1956.

After the local measures forming the north of the county had been deposited, the southern part was subjected to powerful folding; the resulting anticlines were worn down, and then submerged slowly beneath a Triassic lake in which accumulated the Keuper conglomerates and marls which spread over the district west of Cardiff and are also present on the coast of Gower. The succeeding Rhaetic and Lias of the coastal plain of the vale were laid down by the Jurassic sea. A well-marked raised beach is traceable in Gower. Sand dunes are present locally around Swansea bay and between the rivers Ogmore and Neath where the medieval town of Kenfig lies buried. Moraines, chiefly formed of gravel and clay, occupy many of the Glamorgan valleys and are glacial in origin. Between the vale and the coal field is a succession of ridges of Old Red Sandstone, Carboniferous Limestone and gray-green Pennant Sandstones. The uplands of the coal field are of Pennant Sandstone. The soil of the uplands is dry and sandy, with oc-

casional patches of peat. In the lower areas of the north there is more boulder clay and gravel. The Vale of Glamorgan has the best soil of the county, a rich loam, extensively cultivated. Gower has a large area of boulder clay and gravel, but the Carboniferous Limestone covering more than half its surface supports an infertile soil, lacking depth and uncultivated.

The climate is mild, influenced largely by the long coast line and the westerly winds. The temperature falls and rainfall increases as the land rises to the north. The average rainfall at the coast is 35 in., rising to 60 in. on the higher ground, and 90 in. near Craig-y-Llyn.

History and Antiquities.—The earliest traces of man within the county are remains of the Paleolithic period discovered in the caves of the south coast of Gower (*q.v.*). Flint implements have been found on the coast particularly at the mouth of the river Ogmore. Cairns and tumuli are found on the uplands. There is a well-preserved stone circle at Carn Llechart, near Pontardawe, and fine cromlechs at Cefn-y-Bryn in Gower, at St. Nicholas and St. Lythan's near Cardiff, and elsewhere. Beakers have been found in the vale; the valley ways, especially that of the Taff, have yielded Late Bronze Age socketed axes. The Llyn Fawr hoard, discovered when the lake was drained, is important. Strategic sites on the coast and along the inland valleys were guarded by hilltop forts. At the time of the Roman invasion the county was inhabited by the Silures, whose conquest began about A.D. 75. Roman roads, linking military forts, were built from Caerleon in Monmouthshire through Cardiff and the vale to Neath (Nidum), from Cardiff through Gelligaer and Penydarren to the Gaer near Brecon, and from Neath through Capel Coelbren to Brecon.

In Glamorgan there were important centres of Celtic Christianity. Llandaff is associated with St. Dubricius or Dyfrig and St. Teilo (6th century), and the establishment of the great monastic settlements of Llancarfan, Llandough and Llantwit Major also belongs to this period. There are Ogham inscribed stones at Loughor and Kenfig. Saxons and Scandinavians raided the coasts of Glamorgan, which were left without protection after the withdrawal of the Romans.

The Norman conquest was effected at the end of the 11th century by Robert FitzHamon, lord of Gloucester, who began the building of Cardiff castle. His followers introduced manorial feudalism into the vale, while in the hill country the Welsh retained their customary laws and much of their independence. Glamorgan, extending between the rivers Neath and Rhymney, became a marcher lordship with its centre at Cardiff, which was granted municipal privileges. In time Cowbridge, Kenfig, Llantrisant, Neath and Aberavon became chartered market towns. Cistercian abbeys were founded at Neath (1129–30) and Margam (1147), the Benedictine priory of Ewenny in 1141, and that of Cardiff about 1100. Dominican and Franciscan houses were established at Cardiff in the next century.

The lordship, held first by the earls of Gloucester, passed by descent through the families of De Clare, Despenser, Beauchamp and Neville to Richard III, in the right of his wife. Attacks from the Welshries, with local or even wider support, characterize the turbulent history of medieval Glamorgan. The building of Caerphilly (*q.v.*) castle, a fine extant example of concentric military architecture and one of the many castles of Glamorgan, was begun in 1271 to counter a threat to the lordship supported by Llewelyn ap Gruffydd, the last Welsh prince of Wales. Its importance declined, however, a few years later with the loss of Welsh independence in 1282–83. Caerphilly castle was besieged by Queen Isabella's army, after Edward II's capture nearby, in 1326. In the early years of the 15th century the forces of Owen Glendower ravaged the county.

By the Act of Union (1536) the modern county of Glamorgan was created by the addition to the old county of the lordship of Gower and Kilvey (which had a separate history, see GOWER) west of the river Neath. The lordship of Glamorgan, shorn of its quasi-regal status, was granted by Edward VI to Sir William Herbert (c. 1506–70), afterward 1st earl of Pembroke, from whom it has descended to the present marques of Bute (see CARDIFF). The rule of the Tudors promoted the assimilation of the inhabitants of the county, and by the reign of Elizabeth I the descendants of the Norman knights had largely become Welsh both in speech and sentiment.

In the Civil War the county was at first mainly royalist, but later dissatisfaction caused it to declare for parliament. A subsequent royalist revolt in Glamorgan in 1648 was crushed by Colonel Thomas Horton at the battle of St. Fagan's. Nonconformity, appearing in the mid-17th century, gained strength with the Methodist revival of the following century and became an important influence in religious and political life.

Industrial Development.—Toward the middle of the 18th century the coal, which underlies practically the whole surface of the county, began to be worked on a large scale for use in smelting iron, a process hitherto performed with charcoal. The ironworks that arose were concentrated along the northern fringes of the county, at Hirwaun, Merthyr Tydfil and Dowlais, spreading eastward along the outcrop of the coal field where ironstone, limestone, coal and water were all readily available. The wars with Revolutionary and Napoleonic France lent impetus to the manufacture of iron in the region; the number of furnaces grew, and the output, despite periods of fluctuation, continued to increase until well into the third quarter of the 19th century, stimulated by the demands of home and overseas markets, especially during the great era of railway construction. Following the development of the Bessemer process in the 1850s, there was a great expansion in the output of steel, produced mainly from imported ores. At first these ores were transported to the works at the heads of the valleys, but by the end of the 19th century the cost had compelled the transfer of many of the steelworks to sites on the coast, while the older manufacturing centres closed down.

Coal had been worked in Glamorgan in small quantities since medieval times, but from the middle of the 18th century its exploitation increased to satisfy the needs of the new iron foundries. As a result, the larger collieries were owned initially by the ironmasters, and were worked primarily for their needs. About 1850, in the area north of Cardiff, the suitability of the lower seams for steam purposes was realized, and an export trade sprang up which rapidly made Cardiff the greatest coal port in the world. Later, however, the modernizing of power plant and equipment led to a sharp drop in the demand for south Wales steam coal in the years following World War I, and by the 1930s this decline, with a decline in the demand for Welsh iron and steel, had produced a serious depression, during which many collieries became derelict.

In the southwest of the county the metallurgical industries focused on Swansea were concentrated in the triangle formed by Port Talbot, Ystalyfera and Loughor, where the emphasis has been on nonferrous metals, copper, spelter (zinc), silver, lead and tin. The copper-smelting industry dates back to 1584 at Neath, and to 1717 at Swansea. The nickel works at Clydach-on-Tawe were of considerable importance. During the 19th century the tin-plate industry rose to prominence in the area, and toward the end of the century the development of the neighbouring anthracite coal field made Swansea an important coal exporting port.

Population and Administration.—The rapid exploitation of mineral resources and the industrial development of the 19th century made Glamorgan the most populous county in Wales. In the years between 1801 and 1901 the population rose from 70,879 to 860,510. By 1921 the figure had increased to 1,253,728. The 1971 census (preliminary report) gave a total for the county of 1,255,374, which represents 46% of the population of Wales and Monmouthshire. Well over one-third of this total live in Cardiff (278,221), Merthyr Tydfil (55,215) and Swansea (172,566). Other populous townships are Rhondda (88,924), Port Talbot (50,658), Barry (41,578), Aberdare (37,760), Caerphilly (40,689), Pontypridd (34,465), Gelligaer (33,670) and Neath (28,568).

The area of the geographical county, which includes the three county boroughs (*see below*), is 817.6 sq.mi., of which the administrative county comprises 732.5 sq.mi. The county has seven parliamentary divisions—Aberavon, Barry, Caerphilly, Gower, Neath, Ogmore and Pontypridd—each returning one member. In addition there are three members for Cardiff, two each for Swansea and Rhondda, and one each for Aberdare and Merthyr Tydfil. The city of Cardiff (capital of Wales), Merthyr Tydfil and Swansea are county boroughs; Barry, Cowbridge, Neath, Port Talbot and Rhondda are municipal boroughs. There are in addition 12 urban and 7 rural district councils.

Glamorgan is in the Wales and Chester circuit and assizes are held alternately at Cardiff and Swansea. The three county boroughs are quarter sessions boroughs and have their own commissions of the peace and police forces. Of the municipal boroughs only Port Talbot has its own commission of the peace.

The county lies in the diocese of Llandaff, except for the extreme west which is in the diocese of Swansea and Brecon. There are university colleges at Cardiff (1883) and Swansea (1920), constituent members of the University of Wales. The oldest educational establishment in the county is Cowbridge Grammar school, founded in 1608 by Sir Edward Stradling of St. Donat's. There are more than 500 primary and 125 secondary schools administered by the county.

Economy.—Although primarily an industrial county, Glamorgan retains an extensive agricultural character, more than 60% of its total area being given over to rough grazing and crops. The northern hills are suitable only for the raising of sheep and cattle, and the upland farmsteads concentrate on the production of mutton, lamb, wool, cattle and milk. The fertile Vale of Glamorgan remains largely rural in character producing a high milk yield as well as wheat, dairy cattle and sheep. The farms of the county are small, averaging no more than 60 or 70 ac. and are largely family concerns. Since the beginning of World War II a feature of local farming has been the production of early vegetables and fruit in the Gower peninsula. The forestry commission had more than 53,600 ac. under plantation in the early 1970s, much of the timber produced being used locally for pit props.

In Glamorgan, economically the most important of the Welsh counties, the acute depression of the 1930s resulted in serious efforts to diversify the economy. New light industries were introduced and the Special Areas (Improvement and Development) act of 1934 led to the establishment of the Treforest Trading estate in the lower Taff valley, with the object of attracting light industry to the area. World War II promoted further economic recovery and other trading estates have been set up at Bridgend, Hirwaun and Fforest Fach, which, with light industrial development along the fringes of the coal field, resulted in the following being numbered among the county's products: aluminum, bedding, clothing, bicycle equipment, zip-fasteners, furniture, hosiery, paint, paper, pencils, washing machines and television sets.

In addition to these projects an attempt has been made to develop the old-established steel and tin-plate industries. In this respect the most important undertaking has been the pooling of resources by four major Welsh firms to form the Steel Company of Wales, which has modernized the local tin-plate industry by establishing a strip-mill plant at Port Talbot, with complementary cold-reduction plants at Trostre, near Llanelli (Carmarthenshire), and Velindre near Swansea. The company subsequently brought into operation a new plant designed to increase the ingot capacity of steel produced to 3,000,000 tons a year with further expansion projected. Six 100-Mw. and three 500-Mw. generating sets were commissioned at Aberthaw, which, by the mid-1970s was the site of the largest power station in south Wales.

Another important industrial enterprise was the construction at Llandarcy of a big oil refinery. Built in 1922, large sums were spent on modernizing the plant and a pipeline was built to link Llandarcy with the new deepwater oil-tanker terminal at Milford Haven in Pembrokeshire.

By the early 1970s the volume of trade entering the ports of Cardiff, Penarth, Barry, Port Talbot and Swansea had greatly increased over the 1938 figure of 3,500,000 tons. The export tonnage, however, fell to a little over 4,000,000 tons in the same period.

At Cardiff, where the chief imports are iron and other ores, building materials and grain, the export of coal has dwindled from a peak of 8,500,000 tons in 1923 to less than 200,000 tons. Farther west at Barry petroleum is the principal import, although attempts have been made to develop the importation of fruit and vegetables. Grain, pitwood, chemicals and building materials also enter south Wales through Barry. The development of trade through Port Talbot has coincided with the creation and growth of the Steel Company of Wales. Imports have increased fivefold since 1938, the principal commodity being iron ore, of which more than 3,000,000 tons entered the port annually in the early 1970s. Iron and steel are its main exports. The commercial prosperity of Swansea, the port carrying the largest volume of trade in the county, rests largely upon the proximity of oil refineries, crude oil forming the principal import and the refined product the chief export. More than 1,000,000 tons of coal still pass outward through Swansea annually, and there is an expanding export trade in tin plate.

At the end of the 18th century iron was brought by canal along the river valleys to Cardiff, Neath and Swansea. The second quarter of the 19th century saw the development of railway communication. The physical features of the county aided transport to the ports, the railways taking advantage of the gradient to bring coal trucks from the high ground of the coal field to the vale and thence to the coal-exporting ports on the coast. Railway lines ran down from the coal valleys to Cardiff, Barry, Port Talbot and Swansea, all well provided with dock accommodation. Gradually the small railway companies amalgamated and after 1923 they were all owned by the Great Western railway. After 1946 they became part of the Western region of the nationalized British railways. The main line (London-Fishguard) running between the uplands and the sea, passes through Cardiff, Llantrisant, Bridgend, Port Talbot, Neath, Swansea and Loughor.

Cardiff is served by Rhoose airport (12 mi. W. by road) from which airline services have been established with Bristol, the Channel Islands, Dublin, Belfast, Manchester, Glasgow and Paris. The headquarters of the Welsh region of the British Broadcasting corporation is in Cardiff, and there are television transmitters at Wenvoe and St. Hilary.

BIBLIOGRAPHY.—G. T. Clark, *The Land of Morgan* (1883), *Limbus Patrum Morganiae et Glamorganiae* (1886); W. Rees, *South Wales and the March, 1284-1415* (1924); C. J. O. Evans, *Glamorgan: Its History and Topography*, 2nd ed. (1953). (P. CR.; W. A. L. S.)

GLANDERS (FARCY) is primarily a specific infectious and contagious disease of solipeds (the horse, ass and mule). Secondarily, man may become infected through contact with diseased animals or by inoculation while handling diseased tissues and making laboratory cultures of the causal bacillus. As a disease of solipeds, glanders was recognized at an early period. In 425 B.C. it was mentioned by Hippocrates in his writings. In 1797 Erill Viborg, a Danish veterinarian, first published a systematic description of glanders and farcy. He rightly described them as one and the same disease, capable of being transmitted by contact. In 1882 Friedrich Löffler and Johann Schütz in Germany isolated and identified the causal agent, which they named the *Bacillus mallei*, now designated technically as the *Pfeifferella mallei* or *Malleomyces mallei*. Ordinarily it is spoken of as the glanders bacillus and described as a gram-negative bacterium, non-spore forming and nonmotile, growing readily in laboratory culture media. In the affected animal, the bacillus is present in the nasal discharges, secretions from pustules and ulcers on the skin or from diseased nodules in the lungs, bronchial and submaxillary lymph glands.

The infection can be disseminated through the medium of both clinical and nonclinical (latent) cases. Close contact between the affected and nonaffected always results in an increasing spread of the disease. Natural infection may take place through one of the following channels: by ingestion into the digestive tract through the consumption of infection-contaminated feed or water; by inoculation through slight abrasions of the skin or mucous membrane, or by inhalation into the respiratory tract. After infection, the disease usually follows a chronic course with a variable period of incubation extending from several weeks to several months. Horses that are kept closely stabled and worked hard or debilitated usually develop clinical symptoms in a shorter period than those kept outdoors on open range. The period of incubation appears to be relatively shorter in the mule and donkey.

Clinical cases are manifested either by a chronic nasal discharge from one or both nostrils, with or without visible ulceration of the nasal septum; chronic enlargement and hardening of the submaxillary lymph glands without outward suppuration or the presence of pustules and ulcers (farcy buds) on the skin of the hindlegs or other parts of the body. Nonclinical or latent cases are essentially pulmonary in type and the lesions remain in a concealed state (occult) in the lungs as tuberclelike nodules and suppurating foci. In many latent cases, the affected animal shows slight signs of lung trouble (altered breathing). These occult cases frequently spread infection through the respiratory secretions for a variable period of weeks or months before showing clinical symptoms and can be detected only by the use of the mallein test. The agent used for this test is an extract or toxin produced from pure cultures of the bacillus, and its use as a diagnostic agent for glanders was first demonstrated in 1891 by O. Kalning and C. Helman in Russia and by Leonard Pearson in the U.S. There are three recognized types of mallein test: (1) the subcutaneous mallein test, a hypodermic injection of mallein under the skin on the side of the neck, which in from 10 to 12 hr. produces a definite rise in temperature (thermal reaction) and a distinct painful swelling at the site of injection; (2) the ophthalmic mallein test, in which the mallein is placed in the fornix of the eye and the reaction is manifested in from 6 to 12 hr. by the development of a purulent discharge from the eye; (3) the palpebral intradermic mallein test in which the mallein is injected into the loose fold of skin below the margin of the lower eyelid and the reaction is manifested in from 24 to 48 hr. by marked swelling of the eyelid and a muco-purulent discharge from the eye. In addition to these allergic mallein tests, several laboratory methods can be used, especially in the diagnosis of human glanders: the agglutination, precipitin and complement-fixation tests and laboratory culture examinations.

The post-mortem appearances of glanders comprise one or more of the following gross lesions: skin lesions, consisting of nodules, pustules and ulcers especially of the hindlegs; respiratory lesions, consisting of nodules and ulcers on the nasal septum, turbinated bones, larynx and trachea; pulmonary lesions consisting of tuberclelike nodules embedded in the lungs; lymphatic lesions, involving the submaxillary, bronchial and inguinal lymph glands. Lesions also may occasionally be found in several of the body glands such as the liver, spleen and kidney. The treatment of glanders in animals is not recognized as a cure for the disease.

The only effective policy for the control and suppression of the disease is compulsory notification of all cases, slaughter of all reactors to the mallein test and proper cleaning and disinfection of the affected premises. Under this policy, glanders was almost completely eradicated in the U.S., Great Britain and Canada. The disease is still known to prevail in some parts of Europe, Asia and Africa.

Glanders in Man.—A specific description of glanders as a disease of man was first definitely recorded in 1830. Since then many cases of glanders in man have been reported. In 1900 Otto von Bollinger in Germany published an account covering 120 cases. In 1906 George D. Robins in Canada published a report of 156 cases. In 1908 William Hunting in England reported 10 cases which he observed personally. Following World War I (1914-18) the incidence of human glanders in Russia was appallingly high for a time because of lack of control over the disease in horses. Fewer than 15 cases of glanders in man have been reported since the late 1930s in the United States.

Glanders most frequently occurs in many through occupational contact with diseased horses, from making an autopsy on a diseased animal or from making laboratory cultures of the bacteria. In man the period of incubation averages from one to five days. The onset and manifestations of the disease are fairly typical. Within a few days following infection, constitutional disturbances develop, manifested by fever, malaise, fatigue, loss of appetite, jaundice, nausea, headache and rheumatic pains. More definite signs develop rapidly in the form of an erysipelaslike swelling of the face and the limbs or a painful nodular eruption which is soon followed by a general pustular eruption. There is also nasal involvement accompanied by a purulent nasal discharge and ulceration of the septum. The final stage of the disease is characterized by profuse suppurating pustules covering the body, intramuscular abscesses, pneumonia, diarrhea, emaciation and eventually death.

The average duration of acute cases is from two to four weeks. In chronic cases, the symptoms are quite similar in character but are prolonged over a period of several months. The treatment of human glanders has included the use of many drugs, largely tonic and palliative, combined with surgical treatment. In selected cases, the use of certain antibiotics has shown promising results. Favourable results were also reported in several cases following the use of serum from hyperimmunized horses. The prevention of glanders in man depends essentially on the eradication of the disease in horses, asses and mules.

See R. L. Cecil and R. F. Loeb, *A Textbook of Medicine*, 10th ed., pp. 239–240 (1961).

(C. D. Mc.; X.)

GLANDS. Glands are structures which secrete fluids. They are classified according to their mode of secretion, the behaviour of the secretory gland cell and the organization of the gland. The mode of secretion may be toward the outside of the body (exocrine) or toward the blood and lymph vessels (endocrine). The secretion may be characterized as cellular (as in the testis) or noncellular (prostate, thyroid or salivary glands).

The gland may be composed of a single cell or of a simple or complex organization of cells. The gland cells produce their characteristic secretions either through cellular activity without any direct contribution of the protoplasm (merocrine type, as in salivary glands) or through cellular disintegration (holocrine type, as in sebaceous glands), or apocrine type, as in mammary glands).

Anatomy.—The unicellular glands in mammals are limited entirely to goblet cells. These secrete mucus, a lubricating fluid widely distributed in the body, especially in the intestinal tract. The multicellular glands consist of four components: (1) secretory gland cells; (2) ducts which convey the secretory product from the gland cells to an external surface; (3) connective tissue elements which provide a framework to maintain the preceding two elements; and (4) blood vessels, lymphatics and nerves which supply the nutrients and raw materials of the secretion, carry away the waste products, and in some places control the activity of the gland cells and blood vessels. All four parts are intimately interwoven anatomically and integrated functionally.

The gland cells may be arranged as a folded sheet (as in the choroid plexuses of the brain). They may be arranged as punched-out projections, generally toward the connective tissue framework. These projections may be simple (as in intestinal glands) or branched (as in gastric glands), and each is further subclassified according to whether the projection is tubular (as in the intestine), coiled (as in sweat glands), or acinar or grapelike in shape (as in the sebaceous glands of the skin). In the simple glands each secretory projection pours out its secretion directly into an unbranched duct. In the compound glands the ducts are branched and the secretion passes from the secretory portion to a series of progressively larger ducts which finally empty onto an outer surface (as in salivary glands, pancreas, liver).

All compound glands are enclosed in connective tissue capsules. The glands are partly broken up into grossly visible lobes (as the liver, which has five lobes) in relation to major branchings of the duct system. These are further partly separated into smaller units, the lobules, which are also visible with the naked eye. These are branched further divided into microlobules which are visible only with the microscope. All four components of glands (secretory, ductular, connective, and vascular and neural) consist of cells and a cellular cement or binding substance. Embedded in the latter only in the connective tissue are microscopically visible fibres. In the connective tissue the cement substance with its fibres is the most prominent feature, the cells being sparse. In the other three gland components the cells are most conspicuous, the cement substance being small in amount.

Histology.—As stated above, there are four components of glands: secretory portion (whence the secretion originates), the duct system (which conducts the secretion to a surface), the connective tissue (which is the sustaining framework of the gland) and the blood vessels and nerves. The last two components are present in all glands and differ in their microscopic structure in no essential way from their counterparts in nonglandular organs. The ducts may be absent from certain glands in later embryos and fetuses and in adult life. Such organs are endocrine and secrete directly into the circulating blood. Some endocrine glands (the islets of Langerhans of the pancreas, producing insulin) frequently retain a relationship to ducts; the secretion is nevertheless passed directly into the blood just as in other endocrine glands.

There are certain glands which have no true ducts and are not endocrine. Their secretion passes directly onto the surface of the organ (as for example, goblet cells, choroid plexus). The necks of these glands are all of the nature of cylinders whose walls consist of cells. These may occur as a single layer of cells which may be flat (as in intercalary ductuli), cuboidal (as in the pancreas), columnar (as in the kidney); or they may be arranged in layers two or more cells thick (as in salivary glands).

It is possible that certain ducts not only conduct the secretion but also alter its composition. Gland cells, like other cells, consist of a cell membrane, the nucleus and the cytoplasm, including the ground substance, a basophilic substance (called chromophile), mitochondria and Golgi apparatus. In addition, the cytoplasm frequently contains specific granules, watery vacuoles and fat droplets. The specific granules are believed to contain the specific protein in some form resembling that which is characteristic of the secretion.

Some gland cells show little or no detectable change in structure whether they are secreting or not. Others, both exocrine and endocrine, pass through cyclic morphological changes during strong secretion and then revert to the normal or relatively inactive state. These changes include: reduction in the number of specific granules, increase in the number of watery vacuoles, increased prominence of the chromophile substance, increased number and size of the mitochondria, and hypertrophy of the Golgi apparatus. In addition, the nucleus increases in volume with an apparent decrease in stainability of the chromatin, an increase in size and stainability of the nucleolus and a displacement of the nucleus as a whole toward the secretory surface. The cell as a whole becomes smaller. All of these structures revert to normal in the absence of marked secretory activity.

Gland cells, like all other cells, must be considered to be in a state of continual activity. Even "resting" cells are active, performing work in maintaining their integrity and internal organization, and in synthesizing and secreting their specific substances or secretions at minimum levels.

See ENDOCRINOLOGY; HORMONES: *Vertebrate; see also* references under "Glands" in the Index.

(I. GH.)

GLANVILL (GLANVIL), **JOSEPH** (1636–1680), English philosopher, an apologist for witchcraft and for the Royal society, was born at Plymouth, of Puritan stock. He was educated at Exeter and Lincoln colleges, Oxford, where he developed a deep distrust of Puritan sectarianism and "enthusiasm." After being successively rector of Frome Selwood, Somerset, and rector of the Abbey church, Bath, in 1666, to which he conjoined in 1678 a prebendaryship of Worcester cathedral; he acted as chaplain in ordinary to Charles II from 1672. He died at Bath on Nov. 4, 1680. His philosophical ideas derive, especially in his earlier writings, from Descartes and from Henry More; he was also greatly influenced by the development of experimental science within the Royal society. His first publication, *The Vanity of Dogmatizing, or Confidence in Opinions* (1661; modern reprint, 1931), is particularly directed against scholastic dogmatism, to which Glanvill opposes the experimental method. Such a method, he admits, can never lead to a complete knowledge of nature; for no experiment can demonstrate that the conformities which it reveals will hold under all circumstances. So far Glanvill, like Hume after him, is prepared to describe himself as a skeptic. But the experimental method is the best way available to us of achieving knowledge of, and control over, nature and, insofar as it reveals the workings of God to us, is the firmest foundation for piety. He praised and defended the Royal society in his *Plus Ultra or the Progress and Advancement of Knowledge Since the Days of Aristotle* (1668), which has been described as the first history of modern science. What Glanvill hoped for from the Royal society is revealed in the title of his *Philosophia Pia: or a Discourse of the Religious Temper and Tendencies of the Experimental Philosophy, Which is Profest by the Royal Society* (1671). Much of his work is devoted to a defense of the reality of ghosts and witchcraft. Thomas Hobbes had denied that "witchcraft is any real power"; Glanvill, like Henry More, thought that the rejection of witches and ghosts led straight to atheism and hoped to demonstrate their reality scientifically by serious research into reported cases of witchcraft and apparitions. His *A Philosophical Endeavour Towards the Defense of the Being of Witches and Apparitions* (1666)—variously renamed in revised editions and best known under the title of the posthumous edition *Saducismus Triumphatus* (1681)—exerted a great influence for more than a decade. Some regard Glanvill as a pioneer of psychical research. In his *Lux Orientalis* (1662) he expounded and defended More's doctrine of the pre-existence of the soul. He also published *Essays on Several Important Subjects in Philosophy and Religion* (1676).

BIBLIOGRAPHY.—F. Greenslet, *Joseph Glanvill* (1900); H. S. and I. M. L. Redgrove, *Joseph Glanvill and Psychical Research* (1921); B. Willey, *The Seventeenth Century Background* (1934); J. I. Cope, *Joseph Glanvill, Anglican Apologist* (1956). (JN. A. P.)

GLANVILLE (GLANVIL or GLANVILL), RANULF DE (d. 1190), chief justiciar of England and reputed author of the first classical text on the common law, was born at Stratford, Suffolk, date unknown. In 1180 Glanville, who had served as sheriff of Yorkshire and Lancashire, succeeded Richard de Lucy as chief justiciar. For the remainder of the reign of Henry II he was the king's principal adviser, and during the king's frequent absences was, in effect, viceroy of England. He was removed from office in 1189 by Richard I and imprisoned until, it is said, he paid a ransom of £15,000. He subsequently accompanied King Richard I on the third crusade, dying at Acre, in Palestine, in 1190.

Glanville, a man of great energy and versatile talent, was useful to Henry II in many ways, chiefly in the great legal changes that mark Henry's reign. The common law was greatly strengthened by the re-establishment of the *curia regis*, by the increased use of itinerant justices and by new remedies and improved methods of procedure, including the inquest, from which the right of trial by jury was ultimately developed.

Glanville is best known for the *Tractatus de legibus et consuetudinibus regni Angliae* ("Treatise on the Laws and Customs of the Kingdom of England"), the earliest of the classical texts on the common law. This treatise, attributed to Glanville, but probably written by his nephew and secretary Hubert Walter (*q.v.*), was an accurate, lucid description of the procedure in the king's court. It was soon accepted as the authoritative statement of the law of the period and did much to establish and to extend the common law in competition with the canon and the feudal systems of law. Largely because of the *Tractatus* this period in the common law came to be known as the age of Glanville.

Written about 1188, the *Tractatus* was first printed in London in 1554. An annotated edition by George E. Woodbine was published in New Haven, Conn., in 1932. John Beames' English translation of 1812 was reprinted in Washington, D.C., in 1900, with an introduction by Joseph Henry Beale. *See also* ENGLISH LAW; COMMON LAW. (S. Tr.)

GLAPTHORNE, HENRY (c. 1610–c. 1643), English poet and dramatist whose poetry resembles that of his "noble Friend and Gossip, Captaine Richard Lovelace," to whom he dedicated his poem *Whitehall* (1643). He was presumably born in 1610 at Whittlesey, Cambridgeshire, where he was baptized on July 28 of that year. His plays included *Argalus and Parthenia* (1639), a pastoral tragedy, and *Albertus Wallenstein* (1639), his only attempt at historical tragedy. His plays, although undistinguished, contain isolated passages of merit. He also published *Poems* (1639), many in praise of an unidentified "Lucinda," and edited the *Poems Divine and Humane* of his friend Thomas Beedome (1641). He was living in London in 1643 when he published an unofficial royalist pamphlet, but nothing further is known of him.

GLAREOLIDAE, a family (order Charadriiformes) of old-world shore birds comprising the coursers and pratincoles.

GLARUS (GLARIS), a town and canton in east central Switzerland. The town, capital of the canton, is situated 36 mi. E. of Lucerne and 42½ mi. S.E. by rail from Zürich. Pop. (1960) 5,852. It lies 1,578 ft. above sea level on the left bank of the river Linth, at the northeastern foot of the Vorder Glärnisch (7,648 ft.), while on the east rises the Schild (7,543 ft.). In May 1861 practically the whole town was destroyed by a fire fanned by a violent south or *föhn* wind rushing down the Linth valley. The Kunsthaus (art gallery) contains a permanent collection of 19th- and 20th-century art and a collection of natural history. The parish church is used by both Roman Catholics and Protestants. Glarus is linked with the international railway from Basel and Zürich to Graubünden and to Austria.

GLARUS CANTON comprises the upper valley of the river Linth (*q.v.*) which rises in the glaciers of the Tödi (11,876 ft.) at the southwestern extremity of the canton. Pop. (1960) 40,148, about 70% Protestant and 30% Catholic, all German-speaking. Area 264 sq.mi., of which 173.1 sq.mi. are classed as productive, forests covering 41 sq.mi. The river has carved out a deep valley with a comparatively level floor now occupied by a number of villages. There are glacier passes and a rough footpath over the Kisten pass to the canton of Graubünden, while a road goes over the Klausen pass to Uri canton. The Sernf valley, which joins the Linth at Schwanden a little above the town of Glarus, has a track leading to Graubünden over the Panixer and Segnes passes. Just below Glarus the Klön joins the Linth from the southwest; the Klön valley is separated from the main valley by Glärnisch (9,560 ft.), while the Sernf valley is similarly cut off from the Grosstal by the high ridge running northward from the Hausstock (10,361 ft.) over the Kärpfstock (9,167 ft.). In the east the Rieseten pass leads to the Weisstannen, and the Widersteinerfurkel to the Murgtal, both being valleys in the canton of Sankt Gallen. There is a sulfur spring at Stachelberg, near Linthal, and an iron spring at Elm; there are slate quarries in the Sernf valley at Plattenberg and at Tschingelberg. The slate industry (in existence since the 17th century), cotton spinning (introduced in 1714), cotton printing (established in 1740) and weaving are the important industries of the canton. There are hydroelectric plants along the river Linth, two factories for electrical devices, metal and machinery works and paper and cardboards mills. There is little agriculture, but the breeding of cattle is important in this region of mountain pastures. The canton produces green cheese made of skimmed milk of goats or cows mixed with buttermilk and coloured with powdered *Trigonella caerulea*, a cloverlike plant.

After the capital the largest villages are Näfels, Ennenda (almost a suburb of Glarus on the opposite bank of the Linth), Netstal, Schwanden and Linthal. A railway runs through the canton from north to south, past Glarus to Linthal village; from Schwanden there is a line (opened in 1905) to Elm. High up on an alpine terrace almost opposite Mt. Tödi is Braunwald, a wintersports resort, accessible only by a funicular railway from Linthal.

The district of Glarus is said to have been converted to Christianity in the 6th century by the Irish monk St. Fridolin (*q.v.*). He founded the Benedictine nunnery of Säckingen on the Rhine between Constance and Basel, and about the 9th century the district was owned by the convent. The Habsburgs gradually claimed all rights over the convent so that in 1352 Glarus joined the Swiss confederation. It did not gain complete freedom until the battle of Näfels in 1388 (*see* SWITZERLAND: *History*). Huldreich Zwingli (*q.v.*), the reformer, was priest in Glarus from 1506 until 1516, and Glarus early adopted Protestantism, but the Zwinglians were eliminated by 1554. There were many struggles between Roman Catholics and Protestants, and to secure peace it was arranged that besides the common *Landsgemeinde* (democratic assembly) each party should have its separate *Landsgemeinde* (1623) and tribunals (1683). In 1798, in consequence of the resistance of Glarus to the French invaders, the canton was united to other districts under the name of canton of the Linth. The old system of government was restored in 1814, but in 1836, by the new liberal constitution, only one *Landsgemeinde* was retained.

Under the present constitution, which dates from 1887, the canton forms a single administrative district and contains 28 communes. It sends representatives elected by the *Landsgemeinde* to the *Ständerat* (council of states) and *Nationalrat* (national council). The canton still keeps its original form of *Landsgemeinde*, meeting annually in the open air at Glarus on the first Sunday in May, composed of all male citizens of 20 years of age or over. It acts as the sovereign body so that no "referendum" is required, while any citizen can submit a proposal. It elects the executive of six members, besides the *Landammann*, or president, who all hold office for three years. The communes (forming 18 electoral circles) elect for three years the *Landrat*, a standing committee of members in the proportion of 1 for every 500 (or fraction over 250) inhabitants.

GLAS (GLASS), **JOHN** (1695–1773), Scottish Presbyterian minister, founder of the Glasite Church, was born at Auchtermuchty, Fife, where his father was parish minister, on Sept. 21, 1695. After graduating in arts at St. Andrews and training in theology in Edinburgh he became minister of Tealing, Dundee, in 1719. At first loyal to the national church, he was soon led, in reaction to certain overzealous parishioners, to question its scriptural basis. From the doctrine of the essentially spiritual nature of the kingdom of Christ, Glas concluded that there is no warrant in the New Testament for a national church; that national covenants are as such has no function in the church; and that the church of Christ cannot be built or upheld by political and secular weapons but by the word and spirit of Christ only. This argument is most fully expounded in Glas's chief work, *The Testimony of the King of Martyrs* (1729). He maintained that churches should be gatherings of true believers rather than parochial congregations, a view approximating to that of the Congregationalists, who partially derived their ideas from him. He organized a society within the church from his own and neighbouring parishes.

In 1726 Glas was summoned before his presbytery, was suspended in 1728 and finally deposed in 1730 by the commission of assembly. His society became the Glassite, or Glasite, Church, soon transferring its seat to Dundee where Glas officiated as elder. He next worked in Perth where he was joined by Robert Sandeman, who married Glas's daughter. Sandeman came to be recognized as the leader and principal exponent of Glas's views; these he developed in a direction that laid them open to the charge of antinomianism. In 1738 Glas returned to Dundee where the remainder of his life was spent. In 1739 the general assembly removed his sentence of deposition and restored him to the character and function of a minister of the gospel of Christ but not that of full minister of the established Church of Scotland. He died in Dundee in 1773. *See also* GLASITES.

See J. T. Hornsby in *Records of the Scottish Church History Society*, vol. vi (1937); H. Escott, *A History of Scottish Congregationalism* (1960).
(H. Wa.)

GLASER, DONALD ARTHUR (1926–   ), U.S. nuclear physicist who was awarded the 1960 Nobel prize in physics for his invention and subsequent development of a research instrument known as the bubble chamber (q.v.), was born in Cleveland, O., on Sept. 21, 1926. After graduating from Case Institute of Technology, Cleveland, in 1946, he attended California Institute of Technology, Pasadena, where he received his Ph.D. in physics in 1950, specializing in cosmic ray studies and nuclear physics. He conceived the idea for the bubble chamber while at the University of Michigan, where he taught from 1950 to 1959, when he joined the faculty of the University of California at Berkeley. At age 34 he was one of the youngest scientists ever to be awarded a Nobel prize.

GLASGOW, ELLEN ANDERSON GHOLSON (1873–1945), U.S. novelist who wrote vividly of life in the upper south, was born April 22, 1873, in Richmond, Va., and died there on Nov. 21, 1945. In 1941 she received the Pulitzer prize for fiction for *In This Our Life*. A sequel to that novel, *Beyond Defeat*, was published in 1966.

From *The Descendant* (1897) to her posthumously published memoirs, *The Woman Within* (1954), she brought out 19 novels and a volume of critical essays, *A Certain Measure* (1943), besides other articles, short stories and poems. With *The Voice of the People* (1900), Ellen Glasgow began her social history of Virginia. Most of her succeeding novels, such as *Virginia* (1913), contributed to this study, but her work after 1925 represents an altered emphasis. In *Barren Ground* (1925) and *Vein of Iron* (1935) she created fiction of epic and, occasionally, tragic depth and fullness. In *The Romantic Comedians* (1926), *They Stooped to Folly* (1929) and *The Sheltered Life* (1932) she wrote novels of manners unsurpassed for brilliant style, penetrating ironic vision, and sympathetic, though sometimes malicious, shaping of people through their inner lives and in their social relationships.

BIBLIOGRAPHY.—*Letters of Ellen Glasgow*, ed. by Blair Rouse (1958); William W. Kelly, *An Ellen Glasgow Bibliography* (1963); Frederick P. W. McDowell, *Ellen Glasgow and the Ironic Art of Fiction* (1960); Blair Rouse, *Ellen Glasgow* (1962); *The Collected Stories of Ellen Glasgow*, ed. by R. K. Meeker (1963).
(H. B. Ro.)

GLASGOW, a city, and county of a city, royal and parliamentary burgh, port and university city of Lanarkshire, Scot., is on both banks of the Clyde (20 mi. from its mouth), 44 mi. W.S.W. of Edinburgh and 396 mi. N.W. of London. Pop. (1961) 1,054,-913; (1971 prelim.) 896,958. Area 62.1 sq.mi. The largest city in Scotland and its industrial and commercial capital, Glasgow almost fills a section of the Clyde valley from north to south. Its southern boundary is, at one point, beyond the range of hills which forms the natural boundary of the valley. Glasgow is, historically, in Lanarkshire but many of its suburbs are in Renfrewshire and Dunbartonshire.

The city's commercial and administrative centres, with most of its important buildings, are on the north side of the Clyde, the banks of which are lined with shipbuilding, engineering, shipping and commercial installations. Industrial and commercial undertakings of all kinds and sizes are to be found in the many districts of Glasgow. Near the city are the industrial burghs of Paisley, Rutherglen and Clydebank. Immediately outside Glasgow's boundaries are the residential areas like Giffnock and Milngavie, while there are many residential burghs of Bearsden, Newton Mearns, Burnside, Uddingston and Bishopbriggs in the adjoining county areas, the populations of which are largely composed of people who work in Glasgow. The working-class districts of Glasgow have hitherto tended to remain in the central district or in the inner suburbs but post-World War II housing developments have removed many of their residents to estates on the outer fringes; e.g., Castlemilk on the southern boundary, Drumchapel in the northwest and Easterhouse in the east. Efforts are being made to stabilize Glasgow's population by moving some of it into towns outside. Three New Towns have taken much of Glasgow's overspill—East Kilbride, 8 mi. S.S.E., Cumbernauld, 15 mi. N.E., and Glenrothes in Fife—while many established towns like Haddington have arranged to accept a proportion of Glasgow's population.

Buildings.—Nineteenth-century industrial development and the operations of the City Improvement trustees caused most of Glasgow's ancient buildings to be removed and there are now few of dates earlier than the 18th century. The oldest buildings are the cathedral, "Provand's Lordship" (the manse of the 15th-century St. Nicholas hospital although mostly of later building), the Cross or Tolbooth steeple (1627), the Tron steeple (1637) and the steeple of the old Merchants' house in the Bridgegate (1655). The Trades' hall in Glassford street (1791) was designed by Robert Adam and there are Adam-style buildings in its vicinity. David Hamilton (1767–1843) designed many Glasgow buildings of the early 19th century, including the Royal exchange (1829), now Stirling's library, Hutcheson's hospital in Ingram street (1803) and Gorbals parish church (1803). Alexander Thomson, known as "Greek" Thomson from the classical nature of his designs, was the architect of St. Vincent street church (1859), Caledonia road church (1857), Moray place (1862) and Great Western terrace (1870). The City chambers in George square (1883–89) designed by William Young is a large block of offices and council rooms in Italian Renaissance style with marble corridors and ornate reception rooms. A large office extension was built in 1923 on the eastern side of it. The General Post office (1877) is on the south side of George square and the Merchants' house (architect John Burnet, Sr.; 1880) is on the west side. The terraces above Kelvingrove park (built c. 1854) make a fine example of Victorian house architecture and street planning. Charles Wilson was the architect for most of these and for Trinity college with its twin towers and high campanile. Charles Rennie Mackintosh (q.v.; 1868–1928) was the most important Glasgow architect of late Victorian and Edwardian times. He designed the Glasgow School of Art in Renfrew street (completed 1909), Queen's Cross church (1899–1909), Scotland Street school (1904–06) and many dwelling houses in and around Glasgow. He created a new style, widely adopted in England and on the continent of Europe. Many of the solid stone buildings of 19th-century Glasgow have decayed and are unsuitable to modern conditions (particularly tenement buildings) and an extensive plan of city redevelopment has been formed to include 29 city districts. During World War II Glasgow suffered less from air raids than did many other cities. The most important building destroyed was the "Greek" Thomson Queen's park St. George's church. Air raids, particularly in 1941 and 1943, caused some damage in the west end and in the Tradeston district. The Hampden Park football stadium, scene of the Scottish Cup final and international matches, is the largest in Britain (maximum capacity about 150,000 spectators).

Churches.—Because of competition in church building among various denominations in the 19th century, Glasgow's churches are numerous but of varying architectural quality, perhaps the best being Wellington (architect T. L. Watson; 1883), the Barony church (architect Sir John J. Burnet; 1886–1900) and the Barony North church (architect John Honeyman; 1880). There are two notable 18th-century churches: St. Andrew's-by-the-Green Episcopal church (1750), the earliest post-Reformation church built in Glasgow, and St. Andrew's parish church (architect Allan Dreghorn; 1756), the design of which was based upon St. Martin in the Fields, London. The Roman Catholic cathedral of St. Andrew was formally opened in 1816.

Glasgow cathedral is in the oldest part of the city on a slope facing the Necropolis, the old Fir park of the bishops. It is of Early Pointed and Transition architecture and has a nave, a choir and a lower church or crypt. It is surmounted by a central spire rising to 220 ft. The original intention may have been that the cathedral should be cruciform but the only structure which projects beyond the aisles is a part of the crypt known as "the Fergus or Blacader Aisle" built by Robert Blacader, archbishop from 1484 to 1508. The cathedral measures about 283 ft. in length and 61 ft. in breadth with eight bays in the nave and five in the choir. A chapter house occupies the northeastern angle of the choir. The beautifully molded rood screen (or choir screen) dividing nave and choir is attributed to Archbishop Blacader. The lower church is unusual in that it is entirely aboveground because of the sloping nature of the site. It contains the oldest part of the cathedral and the reputed grave of St. Mungo. The cathedral stands on the probable site of a church built by St. Mungo in the 6th or 7th century. (See *History*, below.) The wooden cathedral of Bishop John Achaius was destroyed by fire and rebuilt by Bishop Jocelin (1175–99). Part of his work remains in the lower church of the present building. William de Bondington (bishop 1233–58) commenced the cathedral as it is today with the building of the choir and most of the lower church. The tower and chapter house were the work of William Lauder (bishop 1408–25) although they were finished by John Cameron (bishop 1426–46). After the Reformation the church was used for the new form of worship by three separate congregations. In 1570 an attempt was made to demolish it while the altars and images were being removed but this was prevented by the craft guilds of Glasgow. The building was alternately abused and neglected during the 17th and 18th centuries but in the 19th century various local societies and individuals interested themselves in restoring and maintaining the fabric and beautifying the church. In 1854 the town council, which was then responsible for the cathedral, was advised that the two western towers (a bell tower and a consistory house) ought to be removed, being of a later date than the rest of the church and of

an inferior style. This was done, to the regret of many architects and friends of the cathedral. The cathedral (or St. Mungo's High church as it is officially known) is now used for worship by one congregation of the Church of Scotland (Presbyterian) and the fabric is under the care of the ministry of works. Surrounding the cathedral is the High Kirk burying ground which contains some interesting 17th-century tombstones and monuments. Early memorials preserved inside the cathedral include a recumbent effigy of Bishop Robert Wishart (1276–1316), some portrait bosses of Bishop Bondington and others in the crypt and a memorial brass to the Stewarts of Minto, 17th-century provosts of Glasgow.

University, Colleges and Schools.—Glasgow university was founded in 1451 by a bull of Pope Nicholas V on the petition of King James II of Scotland. William Turnbull, bishop of Glasgow (1447–54), was the first chancellor. Its classes in theology and arts were probably held in the cathedral and the Black Friars' monastery at first but were soon removed to a *paedagogium* in the Rottenrow. About 1460 lands granted by Lord Hamilton on the east side of High street formed the site of the university until its removal to the west end of Glasgow in 1870. The Reformation caused the university to decay greatly but Andrew Melville, the great Presbyterian scholar, revived it and drew up a new constitution entitled the *Nova Erectio*, which was confirmed in 1577. The religious disputes of the 17th century again lowered its standards but, despite a falling off then, a new building was erected for it between 1632 and 1660. Another revival took place in the 18th century, partly because Glasgow university had a wider freedom of teaching and student entrance than Oxford and Cambridge. Glasgow gained a national reputation, having among its teachers men like Adam Smith, William Cullen and Joseph Black. Among its assistants were James Watt and the famous printers Robert and Andrew Foulis. In the 19th century Glasgow university's medical school (associated with the Royal infirmary opened in 1794) became famous internationally with teachers like Lord Lister, professor of surgery who carried out his pioneer work in antiseptic surgery there. Sir William Thomson (later Lord Kelvin), the celebrated physicist, was professor of natural philosophy for many years. By mid-19th century the old college in High street had become surrounded by slums and was sold by the university to the Glasgow City Union Railway company, which turned it into a railway station and later demolished the building. The university removed to a new building, designed by Sir George Gilbert Scott, at Gilmorehill in the west end of the city in 1870. Under acts of parliament of 1858 and 1889 the university is now governed by the senate for academic matters and the university court for finance and general administration. There are seven faculties— arts, divinity, law, medicine, veterinary medicine, science and engineering—in each of which degrees are conferred. The rector, often a person chosen apart from academic considerations, is elected triennially by the students. The Students' Representative council forms a liaison between the student body and the university authorities.

The Royal College of Science and Technology, which was Britain's oldest and largest technical college, grew out of Anderson's college, founded in 1796 by John Anderson, which later amalgamated with the Glasgow Mechanics' institution (founded in 1823) and with the Atkinson institute (1861) to form the West of Scotland Technical college. From 1912 it was known as the Royal Technical college and was affiliated with Glasgow university in 1913. In 1956 it was renamed the Royal College of Science and Technology, Glasgow, and in 1964 it was amalgamated with the Scottish College of Commerce to form the University of Strathclyde, with the student proportions of one-third arts and social studies and two-thirds science, technology and engineering. The Glasgow School of Art has diploma courses in the various branches of art and in architecture.

The Royal Scottish Academy of Music, founded originally in 1874, prepares students for recognized certificates and diplomas in music. Allied to it is the College of Dramatic Art. The West of Scotland Agricultural college (1899) trains students for university degrees in agriculture and for its own diplomas at the college in Glasgow and at the college estate at Auchincruive in Ayrshire.

Trinity college is the theological college of the Church of Scotland. It was founded in 1856 as the Free Church college and prepares students for university degrees in divinity. The Glasgow and West of Scotland College of Domestic Science (founded 1875) gives full-time diploma instruction for those entering the fields of cookery, catering, dietetics, household management or the making of clothing.

Two boys' senior secondary schools in Glasgow are of some antiquity. The High School of Glasgow (the Grammar School of Glasgow until 1834) was founded before 1450. It is now under the Glasgow corporation education department. Hutcheson's Grammar school is an independent school managed by Hutcheson's Educational trust. It was founded about 1643 under the will of George and Thomas Hutcheson, writers (solicitors) in Glasgow. Each of these schools has a counterpart for girls—Glasgow High School for Girls (1894) and Hutcheson's Girls' Grammar school (1869). Allan Glen's school (1853) was originally a primary school for sons of craftsmen, becoming later a secondary and technical institution. It is now under the Glasgow corporation education department and specializes in science and technology. Glasgow academy (1846) and Kelvinside academy (1877) are independent schools resembling English "public schools." St. Aloysius college (for boys), founded in 1643, and Notre Dame High School for Girls (1897) are the principal Roman Catholic schools in Glasgow.

Libraries, Museums and Art Galleries.—Glasgow corporation's public-library service consists of the Mitchell (Reference) library in North street (700,000 vol.); more than 30 branch libraries with home-reading and children's departments and reading rooms; the Commercial library of books on business and industry, directories, maps, reports and statistical material; and the Rankin Reading room, a small establishment in the east end of the city. The Commercial library also has a library of patents containing many British, American and foreign specifications. The Mitchell library was founded in 1874 under the will of Stephen Mitchell, a Glasgow tobacco manufacturer. It has reference books on all subjects with several special collections, notably on Glasgow, Robert Burns and Scottish poetry and music. The Jeffrey Reference library, bequeathed in 1901 by Robert Jeffrey, a Glasgow manufacturer, housed in a separate room in the Mitchell library, has many rare and beautiful works. Stirling's library, in the Old Royal Exchange (which also houses the Commercial library), is the central home-reading library but was founded originally as a subscription library in 1791. Baillie's Institution Free library is a small reference library in Blythswood square, catering for students especially in local and Scottish history. Glasgow university has a large library for the use of the students and teaching staff with many rare and valuable works. Among its collections are those made by William Euing (15,000 vol.), with its rare Bibles, and the library of Sir William Hamilton, the philosopher (8,000 vol.). Other large special libraries are those in the Royal College of Science and Technology and in Trinity college.

Glasgow's principal museum and art gallery is in Kelvingrove park and was opened in 1901. It contains an art collection which is among the best owned by a municipality in the United Kingdom, as well as departments of antiquities, engineering and shipbuilding and natural history. The art collection, founded upon the pictures collected by Archibald McLellan, a Glasgow coachbuilder, and purchased by the corporation in 1854, contains such famous works as Rembrandt's "Man in Armour," Jean Baptiste Corot's "Souvenir d'Italie," James McNeill Whistler's "Portrait of Thomas Carlyle" and Salvador Dali's "Christ of St. John of the Cross." In 1944 Sir William Burrell, a Glasgow shipowner, presented his collection of paintings, tapestries, sculpture and other objects of art, representing all ages and types, adding to it until his death in 1958. Other corporation museums are in the People's palace at Glasgow green (the Old Glasgow museum), Tollcross park (a children's museum and a branch of the schools' museum service, supplied by the museums and art galleries and education departments of Glasgow) and Old Camphill house in Queen's park. The Hunterian museum of Glasgow university was bequeathed to his university by William Hunter (1718–83), the famous physician. It includes collections of material relating to medicine, natural history and antiquities as well as a valuable collection of coins and a fine art collection with many important items of British and European art. A special feature is the collection of paintings, drawings, etchings and lithographs by James McNeill Whistler presented by the artist's relatives with some personal relics.

Government.—Glasgow is administered by the corporation of the city of Glasgow directed by the town council, which consists of 111 elected members for the city's 37 municipal wards with 2 nominated members—the deacon convener, who is president of the Trades' house, and the dean of guild, who is president of the Merchants' house. The civic head is the lord provost, an elected councilor, and there are 23 bailies, whose status is analogous to that of aldermen of English cities, undertaking magistrates' duties and other municipal work. The civic centre is the City chambers in George square which contain the principal corporation offices, although there are departments which have their chief offices in other parts of the city.

Glasgow has many parks and open spaces; more than 20 are spacious parks including Glasgow green in the centre of the city, which has been owned by the city since the 17th century, the Royal Botanic gardens along the Great Western road and Loch Lomond park on the shore of the famous loch. The Zoological gardens at Calderpark, Uddingston, are privately owned.

Transport and Communications.—Northern and southern Glasgow are separated by the Clyde. On the north side, adjacent to the river, runs what is in effect one long road from the eastern boundaries to the western extremity of the city at the boundary of the burgh of Clydebank. This road is composed of Gallowgate and London road which run almost parallel for many miles and join at Glasgow cross to form Trongate. At Stockwell street this becomes Argyle street until it joins Sauchiehall street at Kelvingrove to become Dumbarton road which it remains to the city boundary. A similar road runs from Rutherglen to Paisley on the south side of the river. This road branches at Paisley Road Toll to become Paisley Road West and Govan road, the latter joining a road which runs to the boundary of the burgh of Renfrew. Roads run north and south through the city leading to the northern suburbs and the central Highlands and to the southern boundaries of the city, joining the main roads to southern Scotland and England. The centre of the city is concerned with administration, trade, commerce and business and has relatively few residents, most of those working there travelling to and from their homes in the suburbs.

The suburban districts vary in character. Some show all the characteristics of the independent towns they were; some, like Knightswood and Mosspark, were created as housing programs; others were shaped by social and economic circumstances—like Gorbals, which has since the mid-19th century attracted immigrants, first from eastern and central Europe and after World War II from India and Pakistan.

Glasgow corporation owns and operates a large network of transport routes served by buses. A short underground railway, opened in 1896, runs on a circular route of 6½ mi. through the city and the inner suburbs. There are two railway terminals—Central station, with main lines to London and the southwest of Scotland; and Queen Street station, with service to the west Highlands to Edinburgh, and the north and east of Scotland. Suburban lines run from both stations. Prestwick airport, 28 mi. S.S.W. is served by international airlines; Glasgow airport at Abbotsinch, 7 mi. (11 km.) west of the city centre and linked to it by a motorway extension, is served by British and European airlines.

Commerce and Industry.—Glasgow's first industry was probably salmon fishing, but its geographical position gave it an advantage as a market town for the west of Scotland. By the 17th century Glasgow merchants were trading with many parts of Britain and with Ireland, France and Norway, exporting coal, plaiding and herrings. The union of parliaments with England gave Scottish merchants parity with those of England in American trade and the Americas. Glasgow became very prosperous as the tobacco-importing centre of the world until the tobacco supplies stopped with the American Revolution when the merchants transferred their commercial activities to other goods and to the manufacture of textiles, wooden and metal goods, pottery and rope and to brewing and sugar processing. With the Industrial Revolution came coal mining, iron founding and chemical manufacture and shipbuilding was undertaken with increasing success from the early years of the 19th century. The prosperity of the heavy industries was shaken by the aftereffects of World War I and, although these are still the basis of Glasgow's livelihood, the pattern of industry after 1920 shows a much wider variety. Manufactures include textiles, clothing, foodstuffs, brewing, tobacco, paper, printing and chemicals, while machinery of all kinds is made. Abundance of skilled labour in the Glasgow area has encouraged firms from other parts of the United Kingdom, from the United States and from the European continent to establish factories in and around Glasgow. Many small industrial firms have been accommodated in Glasgow's five industrial estates—Hillington, Queenslie, Carntyne, Craigton and Thornliebank. The city's development plan makes provision for industrial installations and for the avoidance of their confusion with residential areas, while several important industrial concerns have established themselves in Glasgow's New Towns and in neighbouring industrial burghs, while their administration is based on Glasgow.

The Clyde and the Port of Glasgow.—The Clyde in its westerly course through Glasgow is almost entirely industrial and commercial. It is administered by the Clyde Navigation trust from Albert bridge, Glasgow, to Newark Castle, Port Glasgow (an independent burgh although initiated by Glasgow in 1667). The port of Glasgow consists of the quays and docks lining the river from Albert bridge to Rothesay dock, Clydebank, a distance of six miles. There are five docks (Kingston, Queen's, King George V, Prince's and Rothesay) capable of accommodating all types of ships except the largest ocean liners. There are also basins at Yorkhill and quays which cover a water area of 255 a.c. (103 ha.). The river is crossed by several bridges within the Glasgow area. Farthest upstream is Rutherglen bridge from Bridgeton to the Rutherglen boundary, built in 1893; next is the Richmond park footbridge and the James street (or Ballater street) bridge, both terminating on Glasgow green. The St. Andrew's suspension bridge was built in 1856 for the convenience of weavers traveling from Hutchesontown to Bridgeton. The Albert (or Saltmarket) bridge, built in 1871, replaced a bridge damaged by floodwater. The Victoria (or Stockwell) bridge, from Stockwell street to Gorbals (opened in 1854), succeeded Glasgow's oldest stone bridge, the so-called "Bishop Rae's bridge," probably built in the 14th century and demolished in 1850. The Portland street suspension bridge was built by the heritors of Laurieston in 1853. Glasgow bridge (also known as Jamaica bridge and Broomielaw bridge) connects Union street and the western part of central Glasgow with the southwestern suburbs. It was opened in 1899 and replaced a bridge completed by Thomas Telford in 1836. Telford's bridge succeeded the original Jamaica bridge or New bridge built in 1767-72. Adjacent is a railway bridge from the Central station and west of this is the bridge farthest downstream, King George V bridge, built in 1927-28 to ease the strain of traffic borne by the older bridges. Farther downstream a number of passenger and vehicular ferries cross the river. The Clyde tunnel, connecting Whiteinch and Linthouse, three miles downstream from the city centre, and consisting of twin tunnels for vehicles and a subway for pedestrians and cyclists was opened in 1963. A smaller tunnel from Finnieston on the south bank to Plantation on the north bank was made in 1895 but closed in 1943. There are coastal and packet services for England, Ireland, the Hebrides and the continent. Passenger steamers (curtailed in winter) depart from Bridge wharf to various places along the Clyde.

History.—The origin of the name Glasgow is uncertain. Historians agree that it is probably derived from Celtic words *gleschu* (*glas ghu*) meaning "the green glen" or "the dear green glen," a reference to the valley of the Molendinar, a stream associated with St. Mungo and his evangelization of Glasgow in the 6th and 7th centuries. There are earlier evidences of settlements in Glasgow. Relics of the Late Stone Age and the Early Bronze Age have

been found in and around the city. A prehistoric village appears to have been formed on one of the 37 drumlins—low boulderclay hills left on the passing of the Ice Age—on which central Glasgow is founded. The village (named in ancient British times Cathures) seems to have been fortified and to have been a trading centre for the local tribes and the Highland clans. Two great roads—between Edinburgh and the Lowlands—crossed at or near the present-day junction of High street and Rottenrow. The Clyde was famed in ancient days for its large catches of salmon and the area surrounding the primitive village was covered with heath and forest which held game. Although the Antonine wall (*q.v.*) is only about 4 mi. from the city centre and actually within the boundary at some points, the Romans seem to have made little impact on the centre of Glasgow, although Roman relics have been found in some districts of the modern city. St. Kentigern (Celtic, "High Lord"), usually known as St. Mungo (Celtic, "my dear friend," a name said to have been given to him by his teacher St. Serf), came to Glasgow from his native Culross in Fife about 550 to convert the British tribes of the district. He formed a Christian community and built the first Glasgow cathedral and, after his death in 603, was canonized. Glasgow appears again in history in 1115 when King David I of Scotland ordered the compilation of the "Notitia" or "Inquisitio," an account of the church's ancient possessions in Scotland to be used in the king's plan of religious revival in the land. The king's tutor John Achaius, appointed bishop of the reconstituted see, rebuilt the cathedral about 1136.

Glasgow was created a burgh of barony, under the bishop, by William the Lion about 1180 and about 1189 was granted the right to hold an annual fair. Sir William Wallace is said to have fought the battle of the Bell o' the Brae with the English in 1300 and John McUre, the city's first historian (1736), states that Glasgow's first stone bridge over the Clyde was built by Bishop William Rae in 1350. In 1450 the city was created a burgh of regality by James II of Scotland. In 1560 the Reformation caused Archbishop James Beaton to seek refuge in France taking the cathedral plate and archives; the archives are now in private hands in Scotland; the plate was given to a religious order in France. In 1568 the troops of Mary, queen of Scots, were defeated by the regent James Stuart, earl of Moray (Murray), at Langside a few miles outside the city. The Glasgow Faculty of Physicians and Surgeons was founded in 1599 and the trades incorporations were organized in a "Letter of Guildry" by King James VI of Scotland (James I of Great Britain and Ireland) in 1604. In 1636 King Charles I extended the charter of a royal burgh that was granted in 1611 by James VI, although with reservations to the authority of the bishop. The general assembly of the Church of Scotland met in Glasgow in 1638 and proclaimed Presbyterianism as the Scottish system of church government. In connection with this assembly the first book to be printed in Glasgow was issued in the same year. Oliver Cromwell, after defeating the Scots at Dunbar, visited Glasgow in 1650 and in 1689 the revolution settlement, by ending the powers of the bishop of Glasgow, gave Glasgow an independent town council. In 1695 Glasgow lost £3,000 in the Darién scheme (see DARIÉN). Glasgow's first newspaper, the *Glasgow Courant*, was published in 1715 and, in 1745, Prince Charles Stuart, on his retreat northward, spent ten days there and levied contributions that nearly ruined the city financially. In 1750 Glasgow's first banks, the Ship and the Glasgow Arms, began business and in 1755 the deepening of the Clyde was investigated by John Smeaton. James Watt came to Glasgow in 1757 and by the end of the century the expansion of Glasgow was shown by the opening up of George square (1782) and the foundation of the chamber of commerce (1783). In 1812 the first passenger-carrying steamboat in Britain, the "Comet," was launched by Henry Bell (*q.v.*) on the Clyde. Glasgow's town council was changed by the Burgh Reform act of 1833. In 1857 the Western bank failed owing a large sum of money and ruining many depositors and investors, while a much more serious bank failure was that of the City of Glasgow bank in 1878. In 1859 the water of Loch Katrine was supplied to the city by aqueduct for the first time and in 1866 the City Improvement trustees obtained powers to demolish old slum

GLASITES

GLASITES (SANDEMANIANS), a Christian sect, founded c. 1730 in Scotland by John Glas (q.v.). It spread into England and America, where the name Sandemanians was more commonly used. Glas dissented from the Westminster Confession only in his views as to the spiritual nature of the church and the functions of the civil magistrate. But his son-in-law Robert Sandeman added a distinctive doctrine as to the nature of faith which is thus stated on his tombstone: "That the bare death of Jesus Christ without a thought or deed on the part of man is sufficient to present the chief of sinners spotless before God." In their practice the Glasite churches aimed at a strict conformity with primitive Christianity as understood by them. Each congregation had a plurality of elders, pastors or bishops, who were chosen according to what were believed to be the instructions of Paul, without regard to previous education or present occupation; the Lord's Supper was observed weekly; between forenoon and afternoon service every Sunday a love feast was held at which every member was required to be present; the ceremony of washing each other's feet was at one time observed; new members, on admission, were received with a holy kiss. The accumulation of wealth was held to be unscriptural and improper.

Churches of this order were founded in Paisley, Glasgow, Edinburgh, Leith, Arbroath, Montrose, Aberdeen, Dunkeld, Cupar, Galashiels, Liverpool and London, where the scientist Michael Faraday was long an elder. The Glasites' exclusiveness in practice, neglect of education for the ministry, and the antinomian tendency of their doctrine contributed to their dissolution. Most Glasites gravitated into other denominations, and the sect is now practically extinct. The last of the Sandemanian churches in America ceased to exist in 1890.

See James Ross, *History of Congregational Independency in Scotland* (1900); H. Escott, *A History of Scottish Congregationalism* (1960).
(D. M.; X.)

GLASS, CARTER

GLASS, CARTER (1858–1946), U.S. publisher, congressman, senator and secretary of the treasury, was born in Lynchburg, Va., on Jan. 4, 1858. A lifelong Democrat in the strict Jeffersonian tradition, he served in the house of representatives from 1902 to 1918. His most notable contribution as congressman was the framing and sponsoring of the Federal Reserve act (1913). Pres. Woodrow Wilson appointed him secretary of the treasury in 1918, and he supported Wilson's fight for the League of Nations. In 1920 he accepted an interim appointment as senator from Virginia and remained in the office by election until his death on May 28, 1946.

As senator, Glass's principal role was one of opposition. He supported F. D. Roosevelt for president in 1932 but afterward became a sharp critic of the New Deal. With his fellow senator from Virginia, Harry F. Byrd, Glass led the conservative southern Democratic bloc. His position rested upon certain dogmatic and inherited principles of Virginia politics: states' rights, racial segregation, sound money, government economy, noninterference with private enterprise and strict construction of the federal constitution. His bitterest assault on Roosevelt came during the controversy over "packing" the U.S. supreme court in 1937.

Glass was in the main self-educated, having left the public schools of Lynchburg at the age of 13. He followed his father's path into journalism, serving as printer's devil, reporter, editor, and finally proprietor of the *Lynchburg Daily News* and the *Daily Advance*. He was of notable independence of mind and had a rare talent for forceful and logical expression. He wrote one book, *An Adventure in Constructive Finance* (1927), which tells his story of the enactment of the Federal Reserve legislation.

See Rixey Smith and Norman Beasley, *Carter Glass* (1939).
(T. H. GR.)

GLASS

GLASS has from very early times been used for various kinds of vessels, and in all countries where the industry has been developed there has been produced a great variety of forms and kinds of decoration, much of it of great beauty. This aspect of glass is the subject of this article. For the use of glass in jewelry see GEM; *Imitation Gems*. For the composition and properties of glass and the manufacture of various glass products such as glass containers, window glass, plate glass, optical glass and glass fibres, see GLASS MANUFACTURE. The manufacture of bottles is described separately under BOTTLES.

This article is divided into the following main sections:

I. Ancient Times to the 19th Century
  1. Early Glass
  2. The Roman Empire
  3. Islam
  4. Venice and the *Façon de Venise*
  5. Germany
  6. England
  7. The Far East
  8. United States
II. Modern Glass from 1850
  1. Great Britain
  2. United States
  3. Czechoslovakia, Austria and Germany
  4. France
  5. The Scandinavian Countries
  6. Belgium and the Netherlands
  7. Italy

I. ANCIENT TIMES TO THE 19TH CENTURY

1. Early Glass.—It is not certain in which of the riverine civilizations of the ancient near east glass was first made. The earliest wholly glass objects from Egypt are beads dating from after c. 2500 B.C. Possibly earlier than these is a green glass rod, found at Eshnunna in Babylonia, that may go back as early as 2600 B.C. A small piece of blue glass found at Eridu dates from before 2200 B.C. There can be little doubt that the first vessels of glass were manufactured in Egypt under the 18th dynasty, particularly from the reign of Amenhotep II (1448–20) onward. These vessels are distinguished by a peculiar technique: the shape required with sand formed of clay (probably mixed with sand) fixed to a metal rod. On this core the body of the vessel was built up, usually of opaque blue glass. On this, in turn, were coiled threads of glass of contrasting colour, which were pulled alternately up and down by a comblike instrument to form feather, zigzag or arcade patterns. These threads, usually yellow, white or green in colour, and sometimes sealing-wax red, were rolled in (marvered) flush with the surface of the vessel. Finally, if desired, handles—often of translucent glass and sometimes of patterned "canes"—were added. The vessels so made were nearly always small, being mainly used to contain unguents and the like. Occasionally glass was decorated on the lapidary's wheel. Glass is known to have been made on the palace site of Tell el-Amarna, the residence of Ikhnaton (c. 1375–54 B.C.), and the number of fragments found in and near the palace of Amenhotep III (c. 1408–1375 B.C.) at Thebes suggests that it was made there also. This palace activity seems then to have died down and after the 21st dynasty (about 1000 B.C.) to have ceased altogether.

In Mesopotamia the Nineveh tablets of the reign of Ashurbanipal (668–c. 626 B.C.) and the remains of glass in various forms excavated by M. E. L. Mallowan at Nimrud (Kalakh) indicate that glassmaking was carried on there during the 8th to the 6th centuries B.C. It is possible that certain vase-shaped vessels of palish green glass, cut from the solid mass as if from stone, may be Mesopotamian and may date from as early as the 2nd millennium B.C., although none has been found in controlled excavations. A vase of this type, contrasting completely with the core-wound glass of Egypt, bears the cartouche of the Assyrian king Sargon (722–705 B.C.), and it is possible that glass treated in this way was manufactured over a long period in Mesopotamia.

---

houses and rebuild and replan parts of the city. In 1891 Glasgow extended its boundaries and population by annexing several suburban burghs and made a similar annexation in 1912. The city was made a county of a city in 1894.

Glasgow has had four major exhibitions—the International exhibitions of 1888 and 1901 and the Scottish National exhibition of 1911, all in Kelvingrove park, and the Empire exhibition of 1938 in Bellahouston park. See also references under "Glasgow" in the Index.

BIBLIOGRAPHY.—G. Eyre-Todd and R. Renwick, *History of Glasgow*, 3 vol. (1921–34); C. A. Oakley, *The Second City* (1946); J. M. Reid, *Glasgow* (1956); J. House, *The Heart of Glasgow* (1965); A. Gomme and D. Walker, *The Architecture of Glasgow* (1968).
(G. C. EM.)

Glass was made in Greece in Mycenaean times, usually in the form of small molded architectural details, but a few pieces suggest that perhaps some vessel glass also was made in the Egyptian technique, though not in Egyptian forms. Other glass of this period found throughout the Aegean may have been imported from Egypt.

In general, glass of the first half of the 1st millennium B.C. is scarce and displays little homogeneity. From the 6th century B.C., however, glass begins to appear in great quantities once again, particularly on the Greek-inhabited islands of the Aegean, in Greece itself, in Italy and Sicily and even farther west. This contrasts with the meagre contemporary finds on Egyptian soil. Although in the old Egyptian core-wound technique, these later glasses were probably made in Syria or some part of the Greek world. The vessels were still small but differ in shape from the earlier Egyptian dynastic work. They were usually decorated with light-coloured threads on a dark, usually blue, ground (familiar from the Egyptian 18th dynasty) but a notable variation is to be found in pieces decorated with dark purple threads on a white ground. In the Hellenistic period (roughly from the 4th century B.C.) the shapes of glass degenerated. The technique of decoration, however, remained the same; new colour combinations were used, and indeed continued into the era of blown glass.

2. The Roman Empire.—In Egypt during the Ptolemaic period (323–330 B.C.) Alexandria came to the fore in glassmaking; about the 1st century B.C., which saw the beginnings of glass as known today, it had become pre-eminent in certain glass techniques. Alexandria inherited and perfected the manipulation of coloured glass rods to make composite canes which, cut across, revealed a design (mosaic glass). Slices from such canes could be arranged side by side to produce repetitive patterns. When, as often happens, the cane slices show starry or flowerlike designs, the resultant glass is called millefiori ("thousand flowers"). An Alexandrian technical advance more important for the future, however, was mold pressing. A combination of this with the millefiori technique enabled bowls to be produced with variegated designs in infinite variety. Sometimes glass of various colours was irregularly compounded to give the effect of a natural veined stone; occasionally enclosures of gold leaf in the glass simulated the glitter of natural pyrites (aventurine glass). Bowls were often finished round the rim with a cordon made of a clear glass thread twisted with one of opaque white; sometimes such cable threads were themselves coiled round and round from a centre to make a bowl of lacy appearance, with the opaque white glass threads apparently set in a clear colourless matrix.

All these pieces might be finished with a fire polish by returning them to the furnace, but many mold-pressed glasses were, in fact, given a rotary polish, either by means of a spinning wheel fed with abrasives or by a process similar to lathe turning, where the object spins and the tool is stationary. Similar equipment probably was used for the numerous pieces that give every appearance of having been cut from a solid block of glass or at least from a thick, mold-pressed blank. Such pieces (usually flat dishes or two-handled cups) follow current forms of pottery and metalwork. Wheel engraving appears to have become an Alexandrian specialty around the 1st century B.C. and probably continued so throughout the two succeeding centuries. Alexandrian wheel engravers produced not only the massive cut shapes described but also intaglio and relief surface decoration, the latter by laboriously grinding back the surface of the glass to form a background for the design. Simple motifs such as lotus buds or lotus flowers were produced in this way and occasionally more elaborate figural compositions were also done. Other specialties attributed to Alexandria were enamel painting (pigments mixed with a glassy flux were fused to the surface of the glass vessel by a separate firing in a muffle kiln) and an extraordinary technique of sandwiching a gold leaf etched with a design between two layers of clear glass.

The most important innovation in the whole history of glass manufacture was blowing. Perhaps by a stroke of pure inventive genius it was perceived that glass on the end of a hollow metal tube could be blown into a mold as easily as it had theretofore been pressed in. The next stage was to use molds for forms, such as flasks, that could not be made by pressing. Finally, it was realized that the glass bulb on the end of the blowpipe could be shaped freehand to any form desired, and handles, feet and decorative elements could be added at will. This liberating discovery, probably made during the 1st century B.C., gave rise to the astonishing growth of the glass industry in Roman imperial times. Not only were luxury vessels of types already described produced with an elaboration of skill which astonishes, and often baffles, the modern technician, but commercial containers in great variety were mass-produced in common greenish glass on a scale unmatched until the 19th century.

The discovery of glass blowing may well be credited to the Syrian glassworkers, since the first mold-blown glasses bear the signatures of Syrian masters and since the readily ductile Syrian soda glass was especially apt for this purpose. Syrian glassworkers, however, seem to have migrated wherever demand promised a ready market, and some masters of mold blowing appear to have moved to Italy early in the 1st century A.D.; in the course of that century Italy became an important glass-producing area. Glass engraving especially seems to have flourished there and particularly one form of the art—grinding through an opaque white layer to a darker ground (cameo glass). The most famous example of this exacting technique is the Portland vase, in the British museum, London. The capacity of the Italian glass craftsman to surpass all earlier masters in work of the most complex character is seen in the so-called cage cups (diatreta), on which the design—usually a mesh of tangent circles with or without a convival inscription—is so undercut that it stands completely free of the body of the vessel, except for an occasional supporting strut. These cups were made perhaps at Aquileia and date from the 3rd and 4th centuries A.D.

Parallel to the pottery industry, glassmaking spread from Italy to northern Gaul, in particular to the valleys of the Rhône and the Rhine. In Britain the industry was probably not of great importance. The Rhineland, however, became one of the great glassmaking areas of the Roman world (partly due, it is thought, to successive migrations of near eastern workers) and although Rhenish glass is always recognizably Roman, several types of decorated glass were specialties of the district. Glasses decorated in serpentine patterns by threads trailed on and then pressed flat and notched are perhaps the most important and typical (Schlangenfadengläser). A considerable school of glass engraving also seems to have flourished, probably around Cologne. Although some engraving shows an impoverished linear style eked out by lines scratched with a hard stone point, some is executed by means of wheels sufficiently thick to permit rounded cuts corresponding to the modeling of the human figure, and simulating it when the piece is seen against the light. Both types of decoration flourished in the 3rd and 4th centuries A.D.

In Egypt in the later centuries of the Roman epoch glass was in frequent use for tableware, but artistic standards were not high. Plain dishes, cups, bowls and lamps are frequently met with, the glass of the tablewares ranging from an almost colourless "metal" of good quality to a greenish-brownish substance full of bubbles and impurities. Decoration in this late period is mainly restricted to a few rough-cut lines, an occasional group of coloured glass blobs on, for instance, the lamps, or a zigzag trail of glass thread running between the lip and the shoulder of a vase. In Syria during the same period, however, this trailing technique, which was particularly suitable to the ductile Syrian material, was carried to extreme lengths, circuits of threads round the body or neck of a vessel, zigzags and fantastically worked handles being favoured. Here too the quality of the material eventually degenerated.

With the breakdown of the Roman empire glassmaking fared differently in different parts of the world. In the east urban life continued relatively undisturbed, and glassmaking evolved in an unbroken progress into Islamic times. In the northern provinces, however, from being a centralized industry, glassmaking became an affair of small, often isolated, glasshouses working in the forests that supplied them with fuel. Relatively simple shapes were made of an impure greenish or yellowish material, their decoration restricted to simple trails of thread. Considerable virtuosity, however, was displayed in the manufacture of elaborate and fantastic "claw beakers" (*Rüsselbecher*) from c. A.D. 500 onward. On these, two superimposed rows of hollow trunklike protrusions curve down to rejoin the wall of the vessel above a small button foot.

In the eastern parts of the empire Syria appears to have continued its predilection for trailed and applied ornamentation. In Egypt the art of glass suffered a catastrophic decline; only small, rough vessels of impure green or blue material were manufactured. In Byzantium itself the position of glassmaking is obscure. A distinction between *vitriarii* ("glassmakers") and *diatretarii* ("glass cutters") in edicts of Constantine the Great, Theodosius and Justinian suggests that cutting played an important part in Byzantine glass decoration. This is borne out by the fact that the greater part of the glass brought back from the sack of Constantinople by the crusaders, and placed in the treasury of St. Mark's in Venice, is, in fact, cut. Apart from a few pieces of obviously Roman glass, presumably kept as heirlooms in Byzantium, these glasses are decorated either with tessellated patterns of overlapping round or oval facets or with round bosses in relief. These same two forms of cutting are observable in glass of the 5th century excavated at Kish in Mesopotamia; it is a fair assumption that Byzantine taste in glass, as in some of the other arts, was strongly influenced by the east. It is probable, however, that some enameled and gilt glass also was made in the Byzantine provinces (*e.g.*, in Corinth), if not in Byzantium itself. The position of glassmaking in Venice in the 10th century, is obscure but it was already practised in Italy.

3. Islam.—In the 7th century A.D. the whole near east was overrun by the Arabs and, although a number of rival dynasties were established in different parts of the conquered territory, there was created an Islamic civilization comparable to the preceding area of Greco-Roman culture. In these conditions a distinctively Islamic glass style evolved. Although often it is not possible to say where a particular glass was made, different parts of the Islamic world seem to have shown predilections for one or another type of glassmaking. In Syria pieces more or less heavily decorated with trailed threads or applied blobs, and pieces blown in molds, patterned with ribs or other allover designs, were still made. In Mesopotamia glassmaking and, in particular, engraving flourished, especially under the Abbasids (A.D. 740–1258), who attracted many of the best artists in the Islamic world. A great school of glass engraving appears to have been established in Mesopotamia. Not only were the earlier modes of facet- and boss-cutting continued, but (perhaps deriving from them) two splendid new styles were created, one of linear intaglio, the other of relief cutting (outlines were left in relief by cutting back the ground and were then enlivened by crosshatching). Bowls, bottles and ewers of remarkable sumptuousness were decorated with forms of running animals and plant scrolls. The quantity of engraved glass of these types found in Persia suggests that such work may have been done there also.

In Egypt there was both innovation and, after the post-Roman period, a notable revival of earlier techniques. Among the innovations was the stamping of glass by means of tongs, one jaw of which was patterned. The technique, however, is found in other lands and one extension of it, by which the upper and lower halves of bottles, made separately in contrasting colours, were decorated by the tongs and then joined together, was probably a Syrian innovation. More important was the Egyptian invention of lustre painting. In its simplest form this consisted of painting with a pigment containing silver that, when fired in a smoky atmosphere varying in colour from pale yellow to brown. Intact bowls and a bottle decorated by this technique exist, but whole classes of much more elaborate lustre-painted glass are represented only by fragments. A very wide variety of sumptuous polychrome effects are represented, many probably not produced by lustre properly so-called; the technical secrets of these are not yet understood.

Egyptian Islamic revivals in glass included millefiori effects, mainly in plaques for wall decoration, and white fern and feather patterns produced on dark glass vessels by combed and imbedded glass threads. Glass cutting was also practised in Egypt, mainly for the production of deeply incised small perfume bottles of

square section, the bases of which were often cut into four tapering feet ("molar tooth" bottles). Egypt probably also perfected the techniques of gilding, decisive for the next phase in Islamic glassmaking. Glassworkers migrating from Egypt to Syria after the fall of the Egyptian Fatimite dynasty in 1171 may have laid the foundation of the Syrian art of enameled and gilt glass.

Although earlier phases of this art are incompletely understood, the first group of enameled and gilt glasses seems to be one in which thick enamels are used (particularly white and turquoise-blue), often in series of beadlike drops. This class is tentatively associated with the origins of two broad families into which Syrian glass of the 13th century is divided. One, characterized by the use of thick, jewellike enamels, is connected with the town of Aleppo; the other, notable for its exquisitely painted small-scale figural decoration, is attributed to Damascus. Both cities were famous for their glass at this time, but it is uncertain what each produced. Wherever made, these two types of glass represent one of the high lights in the history of the art, whether one considers the rich green, red, yellow, white and turquoise-blue enamels of the "Aleppo" group, or the masterly red outline drawing of the "Damascus" group. Toward 1300 Chinese influences, infiltrating by way of the Mongols and Tatars, makes itself felt in the decoration of these glasses, as is apparent in the series of great mosque lamps which then began to be inscribed with the names of rulers and great officers of state in Egypt. From a peak of excellence at the beginning of the 14th century a decline set in, greatly precipitated by Timur's sacking of the chief Syrian cities at the end of the century. Damascus fell finally in 1400, and it is recorded that the glassworkers of that city were carried into captivity in Samarkand. Nevertheless, some enameled glass of inferior quality continued to be made in the 15th century, perhaps in Egypt. By the end of that century, however, there is evidence that mosque lamps were being made in Venice for the oriental market and the great near eastern tradition of enameled and gilt glass was clearly moribund.

4. Venice and the *Façon de Venise*.—A glass industry was already established in Venice in the 10th century and vessel glass was made there by the third quarter of the 13th century. In 1291 the glass furnaces were removed to the neighbouring island of Murano to obviate the risk of fire in the city. Although Venice had constant contact with the east, there is no evidence that it was indebted to that source for its skill in glassmaking. Venetian enameled glasses appear in the second half of the 15th century, and although their technique is essentially similar to that of the Syrian glasses just mentioned, it is clear that they are of independent development. Little is known of the vessels made before this period, but it is evident from representations in pictures that they were mainly footed flasks and low beakers. The Venetians attributed the introduction of enameling to a member of the glass-making family of Barovier. The earliest pieces known, commencing with a goblet referable to the year 1465, certainly show no signs of outside influence. These, like most Venetian glass of this period, were inspired by the artistic ideals of the Italian Renaissance. The decorations, drawn from contemporary woodcuts and *Niello*, represent triumphs, allegories of love, grotesques and so forth, with borders of dots of enamel laid on a ground of gold etched in scale pattern. Many of these pieces were of richly coloured glass, blue, green or purple. The Venetians were keenly aware of Roman achievements in glassmaking as in the other arts; they reproduced mosaic, millefiori and aventurine glass, and miscalled *Schmelzglas*), and they even copied a Roman form of bowl with vertical, external ribs. All these types of glass were Venetian specialties, probably developed as a part of the extensive local bead industry.

The greatest achievement of Venice, however, and that upon which its great export trade came to be based, was the manufacture of clear, colourless glass, the secret of which had apparently been lost during the middle ages. From its resemblance to natural crystal, this material was called *cristallo*, although in fact it often has a not unpleasing brownish or grayish cast. Being fluxed with soda, it was very ductile and cooled quickly. It therefore demanded of the workmen great speed and dexterity and this in turn affected the nature of the glasses made. Although in the first half of the 16th century the Venetian glass blowers produced glasses of an austere simplicity, as the century proceeded (and more markedly still in the 17th century) there was a tendency to produce elaborate and fantastic forms. Enameling on glass went out of fashion in Venice (except on pieces for export) in the first half of the 16th century, its place being taken to some extent by the use of opaque white glass threads for decorative purposes (latticinio). This form of decoration became progressively more complex, opaque threads being embedded in a matrix of clear glass and then twisted into cables which were themselves used to build up the wall of a vessel. The height of complexity was reached when a bulb of glass decorated with cables or threads running obliquely in one direction was blown inside a second bulb with threads twisted in the other direction, the composite globe thus formed then being worked into the desired form. This resulted in a vessel completely covered with a lacy white pattern (vetro di trina). Other methods of decoration at this time were mold blowing, and dipping a vessel while hot into water or rolling it on a bed of glass fragments to produce a crackled surface (ice glass). Cristallo was also found suitable for engraving with a diamond point, which produced spidery opaque lines especially suitable for delicate designs. The technique seems to have come into use about 1530.

The glassworkers of Murano were forbidden to leave Venice or to teach their secrets to outsiders, under dire penalties both to themselves and their families. Such was the demand for Venetian glass in the rest of Europe, however, and such was the desire of kings and nobles to control and reap the profits of its manufacture, that many Venetian workmen in the course of the 16th century were tempted to abscond to other countries, where they helped to set up glassworks. Furthermore, there was at L'Altare, near Genoa, a second great centre of glassmaking, where glass was made so like the Venetian in style and material that it is nowadays impossible to distinguish between the two. The glassworkers at L'Altare, moreover, were governed by no such laws as the Venetians and rather made it their policy to supply their men and teach their methods wherever there was a demand for them. By these two agencies, therefore, the Italian art of glass spread to the rest of Europe, and glasshouses were established in France, Spain, Portugal, Austria and Germany, while in the north Antwerp seems to have been a secondary source of diffusion. Italian glassworkers were to be found as far north as England, Denmark and Sweden. Their labour was necessarily diluted by that of native workmen to whom they were often required to teach their methods; changed raw materials modified the quality, and local taste the form and ornaments, of the glass they made. Nevertheless, in the late 16th and the 17th centuries there was an international style in glass, wholly Italian in origin and inspiration (façon de Venise).

Although there was everywhere a family likeness among glasses of the façon de Venise, certain countries developed types peculiar to themselves that are worthy of mention. Thus in Spain not only were fantastic and even bizarre shapes evolved in green metal, both in the south and in Catalonia, but in Barcelona a characteristic kind of enameled decoration was developed, the peculiarities of which include a light leaf-green colour and a constantly recurring lily of the valley motif (late 15th-16th century). At Hall, in the Tirol, a characteristic decoration with the diamond point, often supplemented by cold painting, was favoured in alternating broad and narrow upright panels containing symmetrical scrollwork or coats of arms and other devices. Almost equally stiff and formal diamond-point work is to be seen on glasses probably made at the London glasshouse of Jacopo Verzelini (examples dated between 1577 and 1590). A more promising development of diamond-point engraving occurred in the Netherlands. There too the work of the 16th century was relatively formal and stiff, linear and clear, with simple hatching only. In the succeeding century, however, diamond-point engraving became initially more supple and pleasing, only to degenerate eventually into overelaboration.

Diamond-point engraving was there practised widely by talented amateurs, among them the humanists such as Maria Tesselschade Roemers Visscher (1595-1649), her even more famous

sister Anna Roemers Visscher (1583-1651) and Anna Maria van Schurman (1607-78). The latter two decorated their glasses with flowers and insects drawn with a gossamer touch, often accompanied by epigrams in Latin or Greek capitals scratched with severe precision or in the free scrolled style of the Italianate writing masters of the time. A similar calligraphy was practised at a later date by the amateur Willem Jacobsz van Heemskerk (1613-92), with notably beautiful results. Engraving in the first half of the 17th century gradually abandoned linear clarity in favour of crosshatched chiaroscuro effects, the high lights being formed by sometimes completely opaque spots. Many artists worked in this manner; two are worthy of special mention. One was an accomplished engraver signing "C. J. M.," whose earliest dated glass is of 1644; the other was Willem Mooleyser, of Rotterdam, who worked in the last two decades of the 17th century with a scribbled freedom and vigour that raised his work above the average. By the end of the century this type of diamond-point work was superseded in popularity by wheel engraving.

5. Germany.—In Germany toward the end of the 17th century a reaction to Venetian glass styles seems to have set in. In that country there had been a continuous survival, probably from late Roman times, of a local type of green glass, made in forest glasshouses and fluxed with potash obtained by burning forest vegetation, and called therefore *Waldglas* ("forest glass"). From this material, often of great beauty of colour, were made shapes peculiar to Germany, notably a cylindrical beer glass studded with projecting bosses, or prunts (*Krautstrunk* or "cabbage stalk") and a wineglass (*Römer*) with cup-shaped or ovoid bowl set on a similarly prunted hollow stem. This became the classic German shape of wineglass which survived into the 18th century and, with modifications, to the present day. Apart from these indigenous forms, made in a native metal, German glass in Venetian-type *cristallo* developed local characteristics of its own in the latter part of the 17th century. In Nürnberg, for instance, the tall-stemmed Italianate goblet underwent a transformation into a severe glass with stem composed of no more than a baluster-shaped element and a bulb, joined together by a number of disk-shaped elements or *mereses* and attached to foot and bowl by the same means. On such goblets is to be seen some of the most accomplished glass engraving ever practised.

The leader and founder of the Nürnberg school of engravers was Georg Schwanhardt (1601-67), a pupil of Caspar Lehmann. Lehmann had been gem cutter to the emperor Rudolf II in Prague and there had taken the decisive step of transferring the art of engraving from precious stones to glass. His first dated work is a beaker of 1605; in 1609 he obtained an exclusive privilege for engraving glass. Although he is the first great personality in glass engraving, he was not the first to practise the art in the German area. On Lehmann's death in 1622 Schwanhardt inherited his patent and moved to his own native city, Nürnberg, where a whole school of glass engraving grew up around him and his family. Schwanhardt's work is characterized by delicate, tiny landscapes, often accompanied by bold formal scrollwork. His son Heinrich excelled in minute landscapes but also engraved inscriptions of fine calligraphic quality. Other notable Nürnberg engravers of the late 17th century were Paul Eder, Hermann Schwinger (1640-83), a master calligrapher, and H. W. Schmidt and G. F. Killinger, both notable for the delicacy with which they rendered landscapes. Somewhat similar work was done at Frankfurt am Main by members of the Hess family.

In Bohemia, after Lehmann's death, little engraving of high quality was done. Just before 1700, however, with the perfection of a massive, crystal-clear, potash-lime glass that allowed cuts of considerable depth, the engravers of the Bohemian-Silesian area came into prominence. The harnessing of water power in the Riesengebirge enabled engravers (those of the Hirschberger Tal in particular) to practise relief engraving, which demands immense energy for grinding down the background of the design. Massive covered goblets were decorated with powerful acanthus scrolls in the contemporary baroque taste. Relief engraving (*Hochschnitt*) was only occasionally used by itself in the Bohemian-Silesian area in the 18th century, being more often employed in conjunction with intaglio (*Tiefschnitt*). By the turn of the 18th century the engravers of this area—anonymous workmen regarded as artisans rather than as artists—had acquired great technical skill; this enabled them to adapt to glass all the changing fashions of the 18th century in the decorative arts. Glass engraving, often of fine quality, was also practised in many parts of Germany—notably Thuringia, Saxony and Brunswick—but the most significant work of the late 17th and early 18th centuries was that done in Brandenburg. There, the glassworks at Potsdam (moved to Zechlin in 1736) produced massive goblets and beakers that were engraved—usually to order for the court—in Berlin, where a water-powered engraving shop had been installed in 1687. Both relief and intaglio engraving were practised, the latter being favoured. This workshop, indeed, produced perhaps the greatest of the German intaglio engravers, Gottfried Spiller (d. after 1721), whose deep cutting on the thick Potsdam glass has seldom, if ever, been surpassed in the history of glass engraving. A notable, if lesser, engraver from the same shop was Heinrich Jaeger (working before 1694 until after 1701); and later, in the 1730s and 1740s, work of high quality was done by Elias Rosbach (d. 1765). Another workshop of great significance was set up toward the end of the 17th century at Cassel, in Hesse. There worked perhaps the greatest of all the relief engravers, Franz Gondelach (b. 1663, still working 1716), who handled glass with a truly sculptural feeling.

In the second half of the 18th century engraved glass declined in favour, although the technical skill required for its production never died out in the Bohemian-Silesian area. It experienced a great revival in the second quarter of the 19th century when the taste of the newly prosperous *bourgeoisie* favoured elaborate decoration. The engraving of this period is often skilful in the extreme, although marred by excessive naturalism. Striking innovations of the period were the use of a casing (normally ruby-red or opaque white) through which the design was cut down to the colourless glass. A yellow coating (the silver stain of the stained-glass artist) was often used in the same way. Notable engravers of this epoch were Dominik Biman (1800–57), August Böhm (1812–90), A. H. Pfeiffer (1801–66) and members of the Pelikan and Simm families.

Second in importance only to engraving as a method of decorating glass in Germany was enameling. Germany had proved a profitable market for enameled Venetian glass during the 16th century and in the latter part of that century glass enameling began to be practised in the Germanic lands themselves, the most notable centre being Bohemia. This enameling, in bright opaque colours, was much favoured throughout the 17th century, chiefly on the cylindrical drinking glasses, often of great size, known as *Humpen*. The glass of which they were made was frequently impure and of a greenish or yellowish cast, while the painting itself was the simplified repetitive work of artisans rather than of original artists. Nevertheless, the gaiety of colour of these glasses and a certain naïveté in their painting give them an authentic unsophisticated charm. The most favoured types of decoration include a representation of the imperial double-headed eagle (*Reichsadlerhumpen*); representations of the emperor with his seven electors, either seated or mounted on horseback (*Kurfürstenhumpen*); subjects from the Old and New Testaments; and allegorical themes such as the Eight Virtues and the Ages of Man. These were painted between borders of multicoloured or white dots or intersecting ellipses, often on a gold ground. This general style continued into the 18th century, but in the course of that century the levels of artistic and technical competence sank and the tumblers and spirit bottles which were the main types produced can be regarded only as objects of peasant art.

A far more sophisticated type of enamel painting was carried on during the third quarter of the 17th century at Nürnberg. Here, painting in black or sepia (*Schwarzlotmalerei*)—a technique borrowed from the stained-glass artist—was used to decorate the small cylindrical beakers (often resting on three hollow ball feet) which were a locally favoured shape. Other colours, notably red used in touches with the black, were also occasionally employed. The greatest and most original artist of this school was Johann Schaper (1621–70), who painted delicate architectural and landscape compositions in which a fine point was used to etch in details. The

best of Schaper's followers were J. L. Faber, Hermann Benkert (1652–after 1681), Johann Keyll and Abraham Helmhack, but none of them equaled him in artistic competence. Comparable work appears to have been done, although on a more restricted scale, in the Rhineland, notably by Johann Anton Carli (d. 1682) of Andernach. At the beginning of the 18th century *Schwarzlot* painting, often with touches of gold, was practised in Bohemia and Silesia and reflected the changing fashions in the decorative arts. Daniel Preissler (1636–1733) and his son Ignaz are known to have done this work.

In the first half of the 19th century the decorators of vessel glass once again borrowed from the stained-glass artist. Samuel Mohn (1762–1815), his son Gottlob Samuel Mohn (1789–1825) and Anton Kothgasser (1769–1851) painted the beakers typical of this 'Biedermeier' period in transparent enamels and yellow stain.

A technique peculiar to Bohemia in the 18th century was that of the "gold sandwich glasses" (*Zwischengoldgläser*). These were beakers, or less often goblets, made of two layers of glass, exactly fitting one over the other, between which was sandwiched a gold leaf previously etched with a steel point to the desired design. The earliest work in this technique was anonymous, but at a later date J. J. Mildner (1763–1808) employed it with notable success, making gift tumblers decorated with medallions of etched gold or silver leaf (often backed with red pigment) and sometimes also engraved on the wheel or with the diamond point.

6. England.—Glass was certainly made in England during the later middle ages, but most of it was used for church windows. (*See* STAINED GLASS.) The vessel glass of the period has not been much studied and is only imperfectly understood. It is only when the 16th century is reached, and particularly the second half of it, that the picture becomes clearer. Two lines of development may be traced in this period. One is the glass of German *Waldglas* type, made in the woods that supplied the furnaces with fuel and a source of potash. These glasses were made by glassworkers whose traditions were those of Lorraine and of Flanders. Much of their production was of window glass but they also made vessels in a modest variety of shapes and modes of decoration. Chief among the forms made was a tumblerlike drinking glass with a low doubled-foot rim produced by pushing in the bottom of the bulb from which the glass was made; this might be decorated either by mold-blown diaper patterns, by swirled ribbing imparted by mold blowing and subsequent twisting or by a zone of trailed threading below the rim. Applied notched ribbons or small circular motifs also were used. Small bottles of mold-blown hexagonal section or of flattened ovate form with diagonal ribbing also were made. The second line of development was that of the international Venetian style brought by immigrant Italians; this, however, in time acquired an English idiom. This work was done mainly in London.

In the 17th century these two traditions were welded into one, the main factor in the process being the proclamation of 1615 forbidding the use of wood in glass furnaces, as in certain other industries, in an effort to prevent the deforestation of the country. Thereafter coal was the sole means of fusing glass, and glasshouses tended to be located where coal deposits (and the frequently concomitant fire clays for making glass pots) were abundant. These areas were for the most part those where industrial development has been continuous ever since (*e.g.*, the Stourbridge area and Tyneside) and excavation on these sites has seldom been practicable. Little, therefore, is known of provincial glassmaking in England in the 17th century, but it is clear that Venetian influences gradually replaced the earlier *Waldglas* tradition. Some idea of the new style may be gained from the fragments of glasses often excavated in London and other cities. It is frequently difficult to distinguish between an English glass and an imported European one, although a certain coarseness may be taken as symptomatic of English make.

During the first half of the 17th century glassmaking was among the English industries for which monopoly rights were granted by the crown; the greatest of a series of monopoly holders was Sir Robert Mansell (1593–c. 1656), who effectively controlled the industry from 1623 until his death. After the Restoration, al-

PLATE I

GLASS

Bowl of millefiori glass. Roman; 1st century A.D. Diameter: 5 in.

Beaker with cut lines. Roman; 1st century A.D. Height: 5 in.

Pillar-molded bowl. Roman; 1st century A.D. Diameter: 6¾ in.

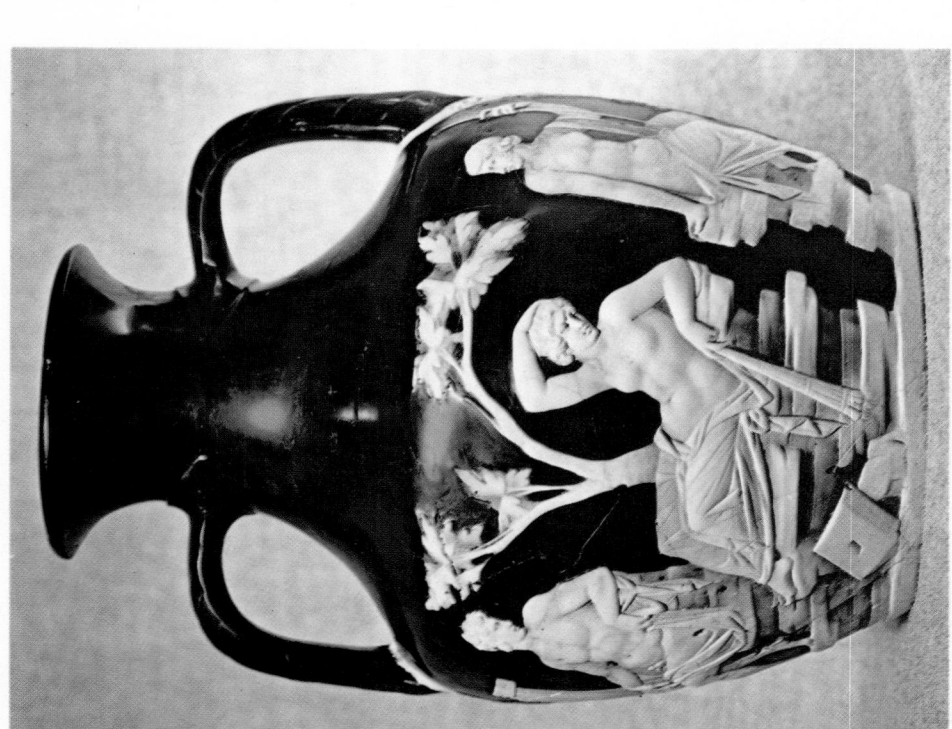

The Portland vase, blue glass cased with white and carved. Roman; 1st century A.D. Height: 9¾ in.

Toilet jug. Probably Egyptian; 3rd–1st centuries B.C. Height 5½ in.

ANTIQUE GLASS

PLATE II

GLASS

Beaker of smoky topaz-coloured glass, cut in relief (Hedwig glass). Egyptian; 11th or 12th century. Height: about 6 in.

Beaker, crystal glass cut in relief, Persian or Mesopotamian; 9th or 10th century. Height: about 3½ in.

Mold-blown bottle, probably Syrian; 2nd or 3rd century. Height: 3¾ in.

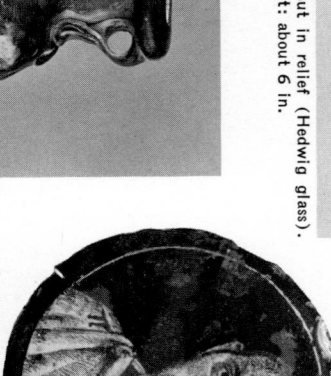

Beaker of green glass with pinched decoration. Egyptian; 8th–9th centuries. Height: 4½ in.

ROMAN, TEUTONIC AND ISLAMIC GLASS

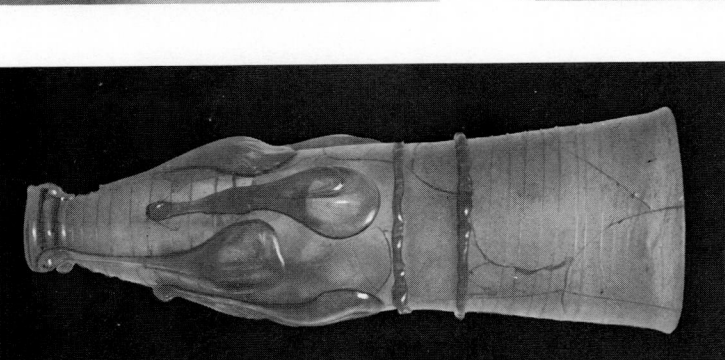

Claw beaker, Frankish; probably 7th century. Height: about 12 in.

Portrait head, etched gold leaf between layers of glass. Roman; 2nd or 3rd century. Diameter: 1¾ in.

Jug with coloured applied threads (*Schlange fadenglas*). Rhenish; probably 3rd century. Height: 5½ in.

Cage cup (*diatreton*). Roman; 3rd century. Height: about 4 in.

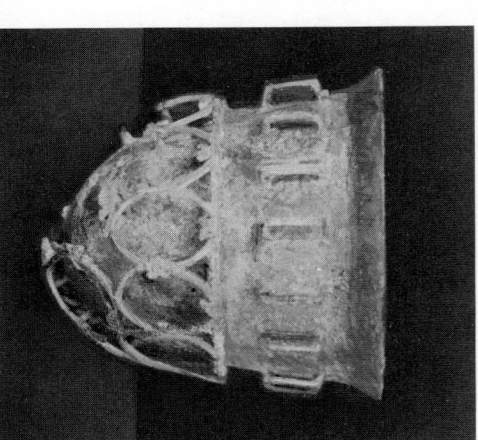

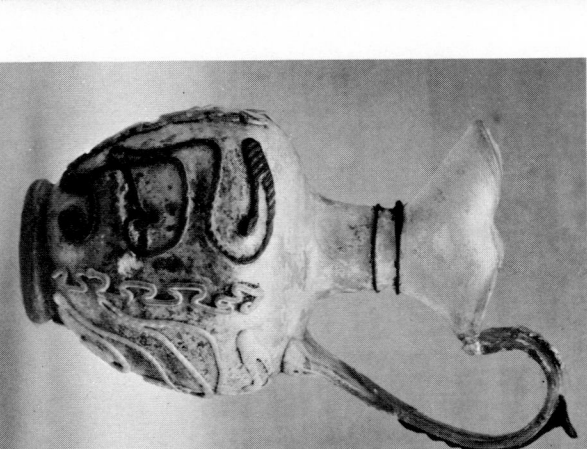

PLATE III

GLASS

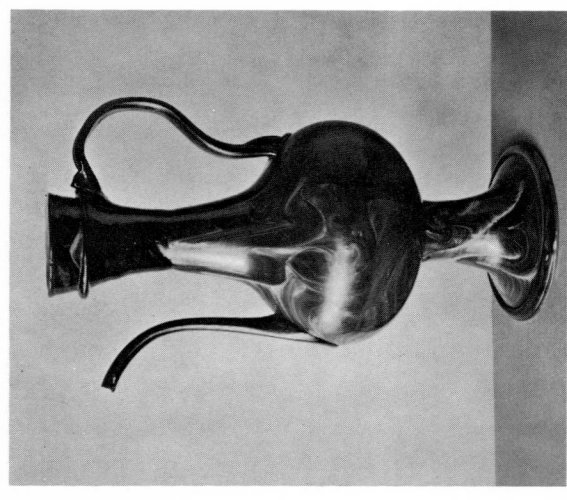

Ewer of agate glass (*calcedonio*), Venice; about 1500. Height: 12 in.

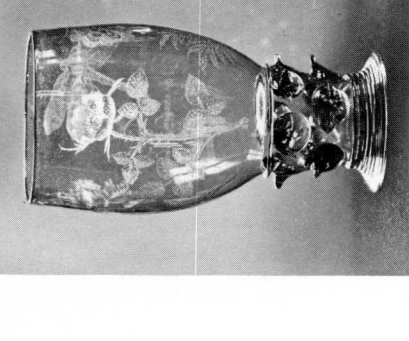

Römer, engraved with diamond point by Anna Roemers Visscher, Dutch; 1621. Height: 6 in.

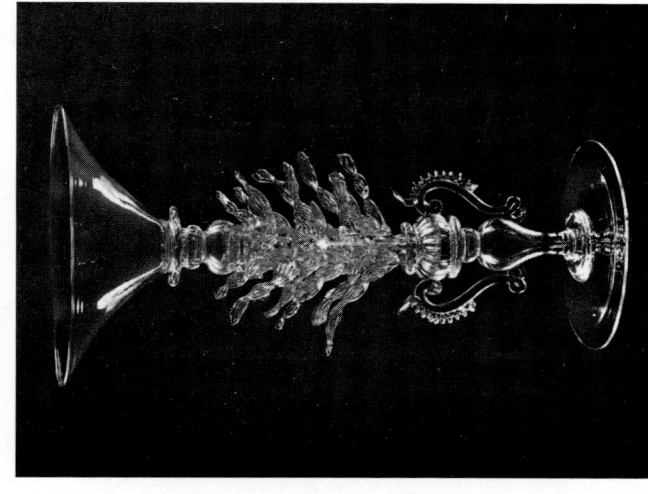

Wineglass, probably Venice; 16th century. Height: 8⅝ in.

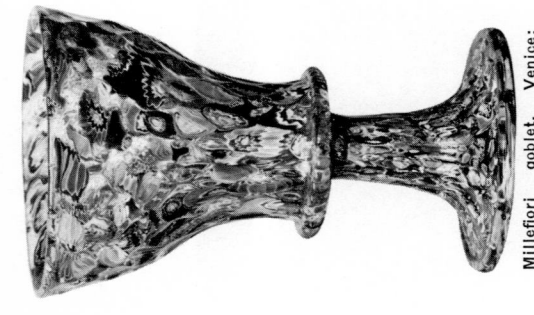

Millefiori goblet, Venice; about 1500. Height: about 6 in.

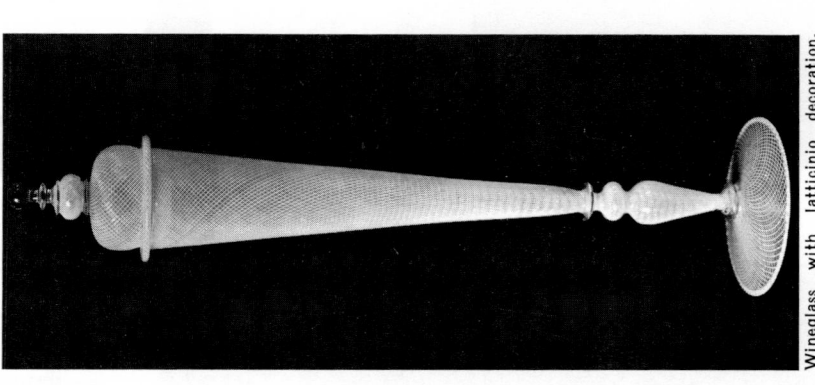
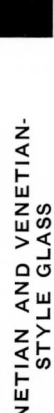

Wineglass with latticinio decoration, probably Venice; 17th century. Height: 16 in.

VENETIAN AND VENETIAN-STYLE GLASS

Vase, Spanish (Andalusia or Castile); 17th century. Height: 8 in.

Kuttrolf of clear glass; probably German; 16th or 17th century. Height: 8⅝ in.

Vase of enameled glass, Barcelona, Spain; early 16th century. Height: 10¾ in.

PLATE VIII

GLASS

AMERICAN GLASS BEFORE 1850

"Tobias and the Angel," covered flip glass. John Frederick Amelung, New Bremen Glassmanufactory, Maryland; 1788. Height: 11⅞ in.

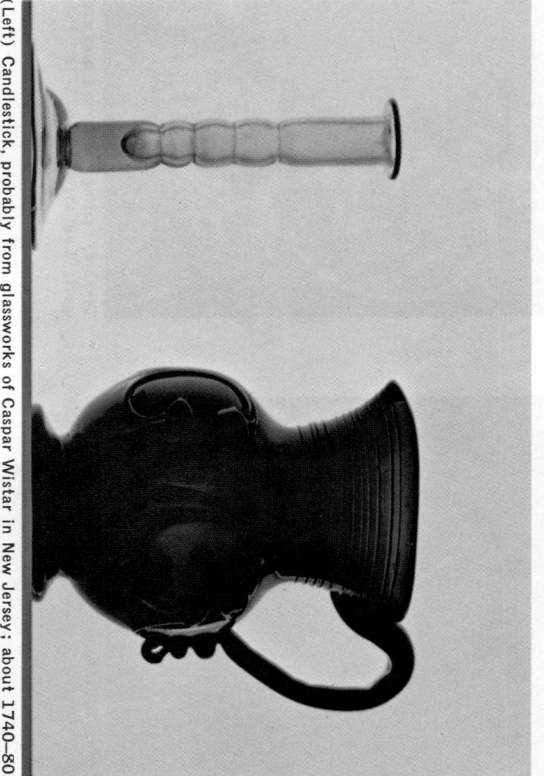

(Left) Candlestick, probably from glassworks of Caspar Wistar in New Jersey; about 1740–80. Height: about 6¾ in. (Right) Lily-pad pitcher, blown by Matthew Johnson, Stoddard, N.H.; about 1846–72. Height: 7¾ in.

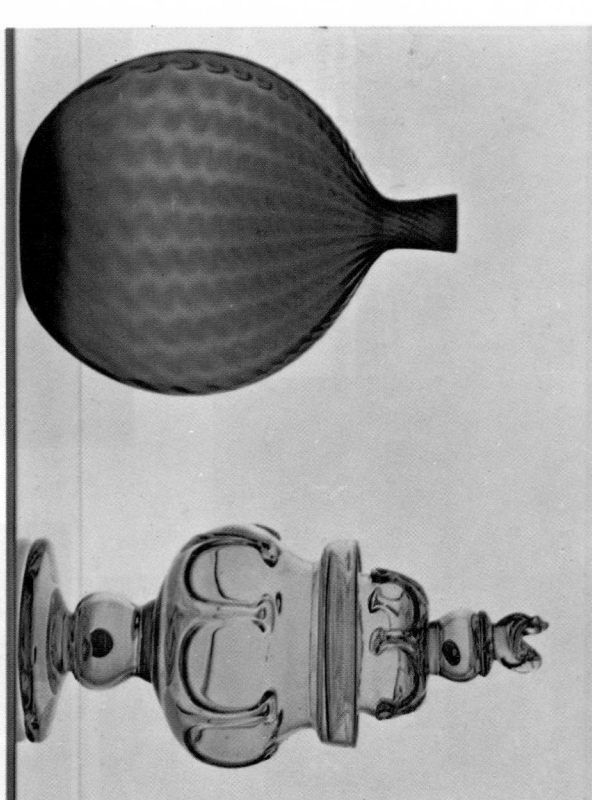

(Left) Midwestern flask, probably Zanesville glassworks, Zanesville, O.; 1815–35. Height: 8¹³⁄₁₆ in. (Right) Lily-pad sugar bowl, attributed to Redford or Redwood glassworks, New York; about 1835–50. Height: 10⅝ in.

Lily-pad pitcher, attributed to Lancaster or Lockport glassworks, New York; about 1840–60. Height: 7⅞ in.

Sugar bowl with cover, attributed to glassworks of Henry William Stiegel, Manheim, Pa.; about 1764–74. Height: 6⅛ in.

BY COURTESY OF THE CORNING MUSEUM OF GLASS

Tumbler, probably from glassworks of Henry William Stiegel, Manheim, Pa.; about 1764–74. Height: 4¼ in.

Sugar bowl, Wistar glassworks, or the factory at Glassboro, N.J.; probably last quarter of the 18th century. Height: 6⅛ in.

PLATE IX

GLASS

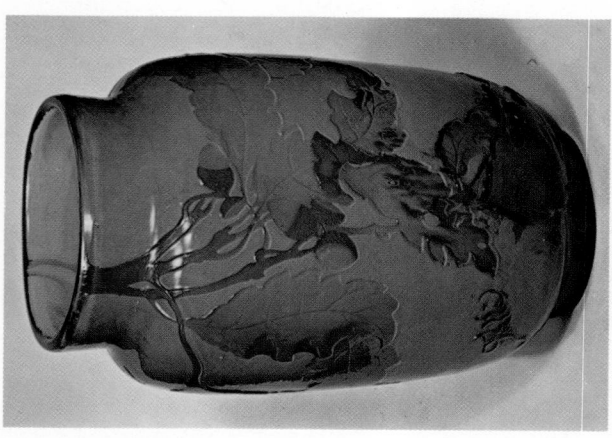

Vase with relief decoration made by Émile Gallé, France; probably about 1895. Height: 9¾ in.

Bowl, produced by J. and L. Lobmeyr, Vienna, from designs by August Kühne and Josef von Storck, engraved by Karl Pietsch, Kamenicky Senov (Steinschönau), Bohemia; 1875. Length: 10½ in.

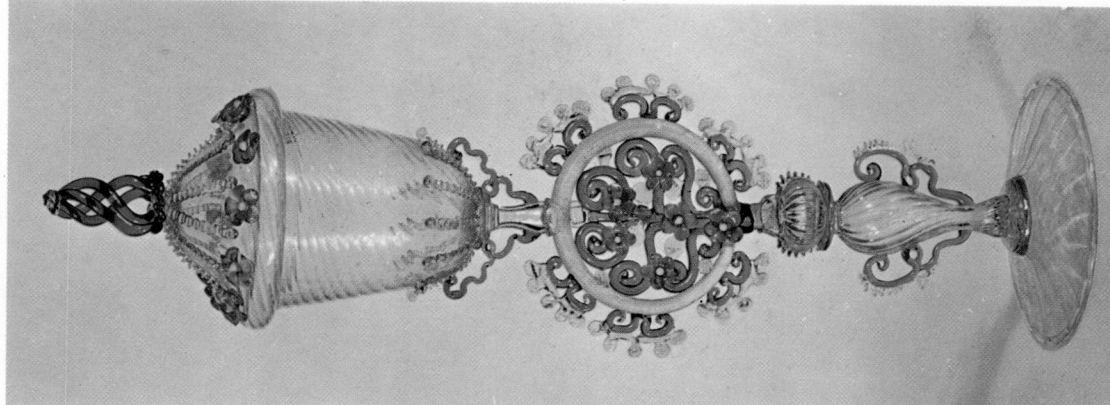

Covered goblet made by the firm of Salviati, Venice; 1869. Height: 21¼ in.

Bohemian layered-glass vase, painted and gilt, probably of the 1850s, (Wilhelm Hoffmann, Prague and Vienna). Height: 16½ in.

MODERN GLASS: 1850–1900

The "Pegasus" vase, carved in cameo relief by John Northwood of Stourbridge, Eng.; 1876–1882. 21½ in.

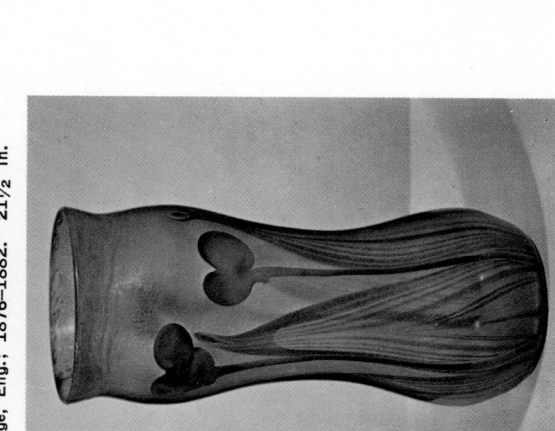

...ase of Favrile glass made by Louis Comfort Tiffany, New York; 1896. Height: 12⅞ in.

PLATE X

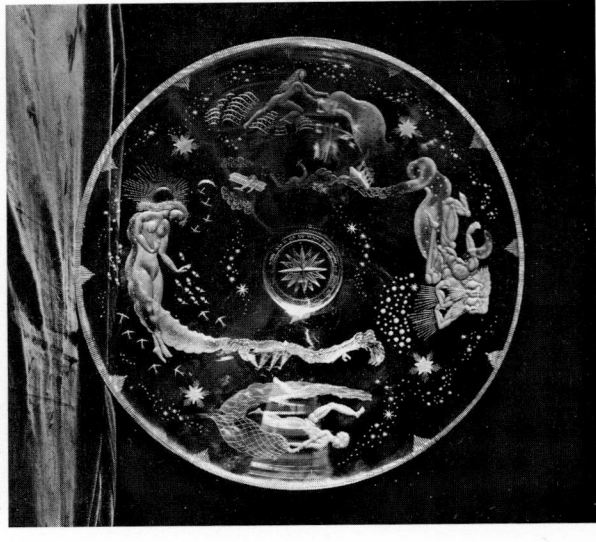

Engraved bowl designed by Edward Hald at Orrefors glassworks, Sweden; 1925. Height: approximately 12 in.

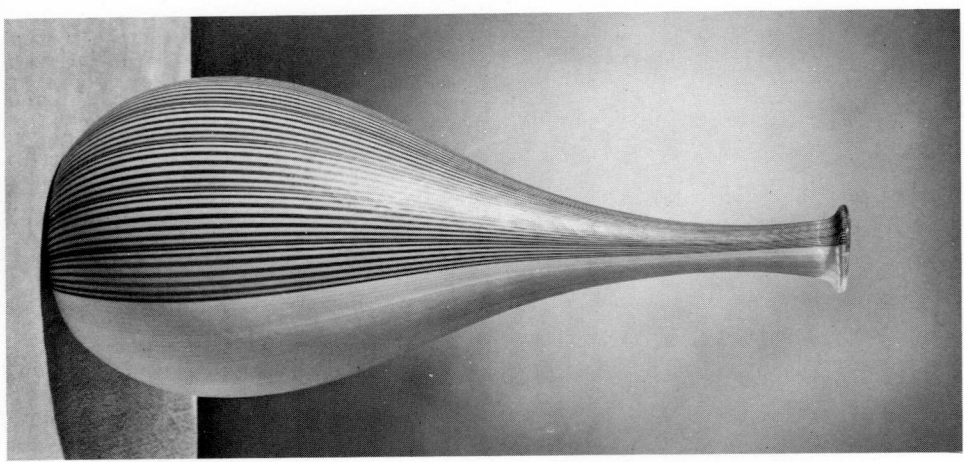

Vase with coloured threads designed by Carlo Scarpa for Venini, Venice, Italy; 1940. Height: 13½ in.

Cut glass bowl designed by Keith Murray for Stevens & Williams, Brierley Hill, near Stourbridge, Eng.; 1935. Diameter: 8½ in.

Partly coloured vase, designed by Timo Sarpaneva for the Karhula-Iittala glassworks, Finland; about 1961. Height: 4 in.

The "Merry-go-round" bowl, a wedding gift presented in 1947 to Princess Elizabeth by Pres. and Mrs. Harry S. Truman, designed by Sidney Waugh and made by the Steuben glass company, Corning, N.Y. Height: 10 in.

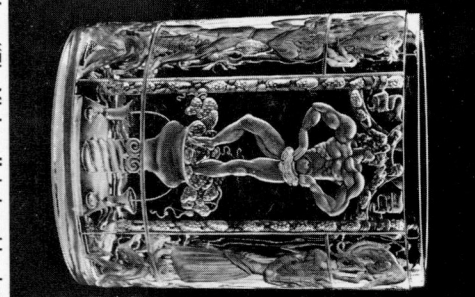

Vase, "The Vintage," designed by Jaroslav Horejc and engraved at the Lobmeyr studio, Kamenicky Senov (Steinschönau), Czech.; 1922. Height: 7 in.

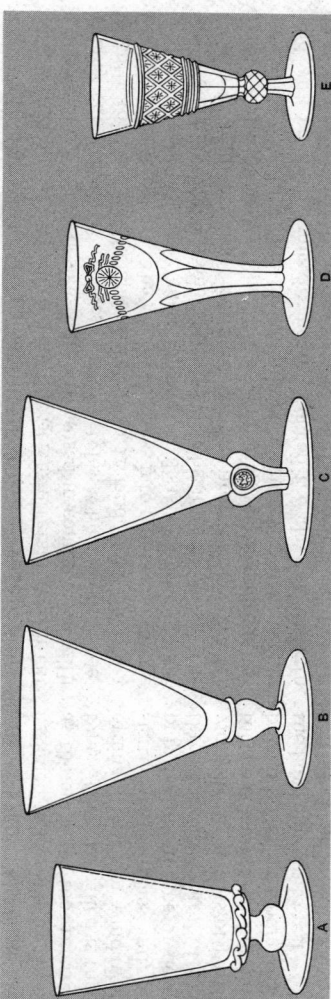

(A) MANSELL GLASS: ABOUT 1660. (B) JOHN GREENE FORM: ABOUT 1660. (C) RAVENSCROFT GLASS. IDENTIFIED BY SEAL BEARING RAVEN'S HEAD: ABOUT 1675. (D) WINEGLASS WITH STEM CUT IN FLUTES AND BOWL ENGRAVED: MID-18TH CENTURY. (E) ELABORATELY CUT WINEGLASS: EARLY 19TH CENTURY

though some monopolies were granted for certain categories of glasswares, an increasingly important role in the English industry was played by the Worshipful Company of Glass Sellers (reincorporated in 1664), which was able to keep closely in touch with the needs of the English market. Its members seem to have laid stress on simplicity of shape and durability of material, as appears from the correspondence of one of them, John Greene, with his suppliers in Venice. Dissatisfied with the quality of glass supplied to them and no doubt also anxious to make England independent of foreign sources of both finished glass and raw materials, they commissioned George Ravenscroft (1618–81) to make experiments with native materials in the hope of evolving a more solid metal than the Venetian and one which more closely resembled rock crystal.

Ravenscroft was completely successful, his crucial discovery being the use of lead oxide as a flux. His "glass of lead," evolved about 1675, was perfected toward the end of the century and set a standard for the rest of Europe. It was solid and heavy and more durable than the Venetian-type glass which it progressively displaced. It was also characterized by brilliance and dark shadow paradoxically combined. It was slower to work than the Venetian glass and gradually the Venetian idioms were dropped from English glassmaking in favour of a genuine native style. This style is best seen in the drinking glasses that, at the end of the 17th century and beginning of the 18th, constituted the chief glory of the English industry. These often massive baluster glasses were composed of a usually funnel-shaped bowl and a stem compiled of any of a large variety of pear-shaped and bulbous knops. In their simplicity and the harmony of their proportions they rank among the classics of the Queen Anne style.

Toward the middle of the 18th century taste in the arts generally inclined to lighter forms, and in the case of glass this tendency was given additional impetus by the passing in 1745–46 of an excise levied on glass by weight. Drinking glasses became slighter, the bowls smaller and the stems taller and more slender. The loss in architectural values was often offset by extraneous decoration. At first this tended to be concentrated in the stem. Bubbles of air had sometimes previously been enclosed in a knop forming part of the stem of a wineglass and these bubbles were now drawn out and twisted so that they formed a cable of air ribbons inside a cylindrical stem. Stems of this type were popular about the middle of the century. Just before 1750 a stem came into favour which was decorated with threads of opaque white glass instead of the air twists. These stems were made by much the same techniques as the Venetian latticinio glass. They remained in fashion during the third quarter of the century, their lapse from favour perhaps being hastened by the second Glass Excise act in 1777, which imposed a tax on the opaque white "enamel" glass, previously exempt.

These forms of ornament had been restricted to the stems of glasses, but other methods of decoration were simultaneously evolved to embellish the whole glass. First of these was engraving, which had been sporadically practised in England as early as the end of the 17th century. This work, and the inscriptions, coats of arms and arabesque borders in German style which were engraved during the first 20 years or so of the 18th century, were undoubtedly the work of immigrant (probably German) artisans. By 1735, however, at least one English engraver was capable of executing such commissions and from about this time engraving on glass began to take on a more English character. An artless use of floral motifs, chinoiseries and scenes from country life is typical of the engraving of the third quarter of the 18th century, and in this period also falls the frequent representation on glasses of Jacobite themes—portraits of the Old and Young Pretenders, the

rose with buds, the honeysuckle and the other flowers used in the symbology of the Stuart cause, together with the mottoes of such "loyal" societies as the Cycle club. Engraving never reached great heights in England, but English glasses were in demand by engravers in Europe, particularly in the Netherlands, where the work of at least one notable artist—Jacob Sang, of Amsterdam—was almost exclusively done on imported English drinking glasses. English lead glass also seems to have been particularly sympathetic to the Dutch diamond-point engravers, whose work in this period was executed almost exclusively in stipple. The chief masters of this delicate art, in which the design seems no more than a bloom on the surface of the glass, were Frans Greenwood (1680–1761) of Dordrecht, the originator of the style, and David Wolff (1732–98) of The Hague, whose work, if uninspired, is of high technical accomplishment.

The second decorative technique of foreign inspiration to be used on English glass in the 18th century was enameling. It was used for embellishing opaque white glass in imitation of china about the middle of the century—a type of work usually associated with the name of Michael Edkins (1734–1811), a Bristol artist, but in fact done in many parts of the country. Perhaps the most original work in this medium was done on clear glass by members of the Beilby family of Newcastle upon Tyne during the 1760s and 1770s. Their rendering in pink- or blue-toned white enamel of ruins, trophies of arms and rural pastimes, often framed in scrollwork or the utmost delicacy, is one of the best things in English rococo glass. Gilding was also used at this time to decorate glasses, usually with simple designs of vine and grapes.

These ornamental techniques, however, were of ephemeral growth in England. Far more significant than any of them, because more firmly rooted in the very nature of English glass, was the art of cutting. Although literary references to cut glass occur before 1720, the earliest known pieces extant can hardly be dated much before 1730. On them the cutting is mainly confined to brims and feet, which are scalloped or notched; or, in the case of wineglasses, to the thicker parts of the glass, such as the stem, which might be fluted or cut in an allover pattern of flat diamonds. Throughout the period from about 1745 to 1770, shallow cutting was the norm, diamonds, hexagons, flutes and scale pattern being combined with segmental lunate cuts (produced by holding the glass at an angle to the cutting wheel) and with triangular and diamond motifs in very low relief. These elements could be combined to produce designs of great complexity and richness and this period is the golden age of English cutting. About 1770 a plainer style, employing mainly flutes, responded to the rising neoclassical fashion in the other arts. The flutes were sometimes combined with diamonds in relief and when further taxes were imposed on glass in 1777 and 1781, and in 1780 trade between England and Ireland was freed, it was this relief-diamond style which was taken up in the latter country by the glasshouses founded under these favourable economic conditions. The Irish glassworkers could afford to be more lavish with their metal and on this thicker glass increasingly deeply cut diamonds and other relief motifs could be produced. About the turn of the century the diamonds began to be reduced in size and to be used as a diaper pattern covering whole areas, often alternating with fields of larger truncated diamonds, the surfaces of which were themselves diversified with crosshatching. Such designs were often used in combination with deeply cut horizontal grooves. These styles, which were subsequently followed in England as well as in Ireland, finally led to a complete breaking up of the face of the glass into points and ridges, with increased prismatic effect but with a disastrous loss of that surface quality which is one of the peculiar beauties of glass. The prismatic brilliance was enhanced by the progressively greater purity and whiteness of the glass made during the second quarter of the 19th century, and the temptation to cut ever more deeply and with greater complexity finally seduced the glassmakers into producing the "prickly monstrosities" of the Great exhibition of 1851.

Throughout the 18th century there was great admiration in Europe for English lead "crystal," and in the second half of it some of the European glasshouses, by the use of lead oxide, had contrived to produce a comparable material. English cut glass was admired and exported and the styles of cutting of the late 18th and early 19th centuries were much imitated abroad.

7. The Far East.—Glass has never been truly at home in China. Records suggest that it was brought there from the west as early as the 3rd century A.D., but finds of small glass objects of typical Chinese shapes dating from as early as the Han dynasty (202 B.C.–A.D. 221) suggest that, even if the material was brought from the west, it could be worked on the spot to conform to Chinese usage. It was no doubt regarded as a cheap substitute for jade. The Chinese themselves do not claim to have made glass before the 5th century A.D., and even then it is very doubtful if they knew more than how to make beads and other similar small objects. The vessels of glass occasionally found in burials of the T'ang (618–906) and later dynasties although perhaps locally made are more likely imports. Of the extant glass vessels typically Chinese in form, none can be shown to be of a date earlier than the reign of K'ang-Hsi (1662–1722), and there is every likelihood that glassmaking was in fact introduced in this period when, through the Jesuits, China became vividly aware of western culture. To this period probably belongs a series of bowls and vases of which the blown character is manifest. They are often of a decayed metal which appears to suffer from the same deficiencies as European glass of the same epoch. During the reigns of the emperors Yung Chêng (1723–35) and Ch'ien Lung (1736–96) the emphasis on natural forms is subordinated to the desire to make glass a surrogate for natural stones. Although the colours used are often not such as are found in nature, the glass is handled as though it were jade, the foot in particular being fashioned as though cut from stone. This lapidary treatment is further emphasized in the cased glass bottles cut on the wheel in such a way that the design stands in one or more colours on a ground of a contrasting tone.

(R. J. C.)

8. United States.—Glassmaking was apparently the first industry to be transplanted from Europe in the wake of the Spanish conquerors. As early as 1535 glass was being made at Puebla de los Angeles in Mexico, and in 1592 a glasshouse was located in the territory of the Río de la Plata in the town of Córdoba del Tucumán, Arg. Broken glass, undoubtedly of European origin, was remelted at the latter and fashioned into various objects including thick, semitransparent flat glass.

The London company of Virginia set up a glasshouse in Jamestown in 1608 for the manufacture of "glasses" and beads. A "tryal of glasse" was sent off to England before the winter of 1609, the "starving time" during which 440 of the colony's 500 inhabitants died. In 1621 the company tried again and, although the second attempt was more carefully planned, it too failed. Excavation of the site has revealed that glass was melted in considerable quantities though no evidence of bead manufacture has been found.

For more than a century after Jamestown, there was little American glass. The earliest successful glasshouse was begun in 1739 by Caspar Wistar. The fact that his works produced only humble utilitarian vessels and windowpanes saved him from extermination by the "lords of trade." Wistar died in 1752, after which the factory was operated by his son Richard. It was offered for sale in 1780. Although few, if any, objects exist which can be assigned to the Wistar Glass works with certainty, it is important as the cradle of the American glass known today as South Jersey type. Glass so-called is the work of individual glass blowers using an ordinary bottle or window glass to make objects of their own design. Applied glass and, occasionally, pattern molding were the only feasible means of decoration and the resultant loopings and threadings are typical of European traditions. One decorative device, the lily pad, is of particular importance as no European prototype is known. A hot gather of glass applied to the base of the bowl is pulled up around the sides in a series of projections in which the bowl appears to rest.

The second great name in early American glass is Henry William Stiegel. In 1763, 13 years after his arrival in America and after several years in the iron business, he built his first glasshouse. Like Caspar Wistar, Stiegel was concerned with the manufacture of bottles and windowpanes but, with the founding of his second house at Manheim, Pa., in 1765, he ventured into the table glass business. No longer beneath the notice of the "lords of trade," he reported to them in 1767 that the glass he made was both inconsiderable in quantity and ordinary in quality. This report is in sharp contrast to the many advertisements in which he favourably compares his wares with English imports. Encouraged by the patriotic adoption of the nonimportation agreement, Stiegel built a third glasshouse, the American Flint Glass works, also located at Manheim and completed in 1769. Adverse economic conditions, caused by approaching war and colonial preference for imported tablewares, brought final failure in 1774.

Few pieces can be attributed with confidence to the Stiegel factories and, like that of Wistar, his name survives as the founder of a tradition. Stiegel-type glass is characterized by the use of clear and artificially coloured glasses; by extrinsic decoration such as engraving, enameling and pattern molding; and, in general, by two distinct styles, one involving English and the other German techniques and decorative devices. Certain mold-blown patterns, such as the diamond-daisy and daisy in hexagon, are believed to have been originated at the Stiegel houses, no European prototypes having been identified.

Before the turn of the century, several other glassworks were founded, but few survived the Revolution. These houses were devoted largely to the manufacture of bottles and window glasses and, with the notable exception of the New Bremen Glassmanufactory, most of the offhand pieces which can be tentatively assigned to them are of the South Jersey tradition. Three of these enterprises are of particular importance. First, the New Bremen Glassmanufactory, founded by John Frederick Amelung and company, is of special interest as many of its presentation pieces are both signed and dated as well as being among the finest produced in the U.S. before 1800. Originally from Bremen, Ger., Amelung was persuaded to go to America, Maryland in particular, for the express purpose of founding what he believed to be a much-needed industry. By 1785 his works offered green and white hollow ware for sale; by 1795 the glassworks themselves were offered for sale. One of the most famous pieces in the history of American glass is the Bremen *Pokal*, blown and engraved in 1788 and sent back to Amelung's financiers in Bremen, probably the only return they ever received on their investment.

The second factory of importance, later known as the Olive Glass works, was completed in 1781 by former employees of the Wistar Glass works, the Stanger brothers. In addition to the many fine South Jersey pieces attributed to this house, it is of interest because of its long history, eventually becoming part of the Owens Bottle company, a forerunner of the Libbey-Owens-Ford Glass company.

The third notable venture begun before 1800 is the well-known works associated with the name Pitkin. Erected near the Connecticut river in 1783, it was intended for the manufacture of crown window glass, but need and foresight converted it in 1788 to a manufactory of bottles and flasks. The factory thrived until 1830 and is best known for the half-post ribbed flasks in natural browns, ambers and greens. Today the word "Pitkin" denotes a type of flask and not a specific glassworks.

The few houses which survived the 1790s and the depression following the War of 1812 multiplied to more than 90 by 1830. This high rate of increase is partially explained by the false prosperity which preceded the War of 1812 and later by the employment of a special sales agent, extensive paid advertising and adequate tariff regulations finally achieved in 1824. For convenience, they are divided into three geographical groups: New England, the middle Atlantic states and the midwest.

Until about 1830 U.S. glasshouses produced little more than simple imitations of European glasses, at best interesting and often very handsome combinations of various decorative devices and traditions. The big change occurred between 1830 and 1840 with the production of fine lead glass, the use of the full-size incised mold and, finally, the pressing machine.

The glasshouse known as Bakewell's was synonymous with the finest achievements of the revived industry. Originally established in 1808 in Pittsburgh, Pa., the first city to use coal for fuel in glassmaking, the company survived under several different firms until 1882. Glass cutting, introduced to Pittsburgh by William Peter Eichbaum, glass cutter to Louis XVI, was an important part of Bakewell's operation. In addition to being the first U.S. company to supply the White House, serving Pres. James Monroe in 1817, Bakewell's produced such specialties as lead glass tumblers with "sulphides" (cameo insertions of white fireproof material in an envelope of glass) in the bases portraying Marquis de Lafayette, Andrew Jackson, George Clinton, Benjamin Franklin and George Washington. This company also held the first patent on mechanical pressing, granted in 1825 for a device to make knobs.

Fine lead glass was first successfully made in the New England area in the south Boston works of the Boston Crown Glass company. Thomas Cains, first employed by this firm in 1812, was making flint glass there in 1813. He left the firm in 1824 to found the Phoenix Glass works, which survived until 1870. One particular glass device usually associated with the Boston manufactories of this period is the guilloche or chain, employed in the decoration of a large variety of tableware.

The New England Glass company, founded in 1818, maintained the same high standards as Bakewell's, even to the point of making glass for President Monroe. This factory held the second patent on a device for mechanical pressing, granted in 1826, and produced quantities of pressed glass of all types before it was moved to Toledo, O., in 1888. The New England Glass company was also famous for its very fine free-blown and engraved glass. In addition vessels were made there in the so-called blown three-mold technique in which decorative designs adapted from cut glass patterns of the period were impressed in the glass by blowing in molds hinged in two, three or more sections. More than 400 different molds have been determined and grouped according to pattern under three primary headings: geometric, arch and baroque. By 1830 this type of production was being replaced by the much more efficient pressing machine.

Deming Jarves, one of the founders of the New England Glass company, founded the Boston and Sandwich Glass company in 1825. Because of his Reminiscences, extensive advertisements and thorough excavations of the factory site, more is known about this particular factory than any other of the period. Consequently, "Sandwich" has become a generic term for pressed glass even though many other factories used identical machinery and, in cases, identical molds. Jarves' first patent on a pressing device, the fifth to be granted, was received in 1828 after the Boston mold maker Hiram Dillaway entered his employ. Before the fires were drawn at Sandwich in 1888, Jarves had founded the Mount Washington Glass works in 1837 and the Cape Cod Glass works in 1857.

Among the outstanding makers of fine lead glass in the middle Atlantic states were the Brooklyn Flint Glass works of John L. Gilliland and company and the Dorflinger Glass works. Gilliland, a partner in the Bloomingdale Flint Glass works, sold out in 1823 and founded his own works in Brooklyn. In 1864 two members of the Houghton family acquired controlling interest and in 1868 the works was moved by barge to Corning, N.Y., to form part of the now famous Corning Glass works.

Perhaps the most fascinating aspect of American glass is that series of pictorially molded bottles known as historical flasks, produced between 1815 and 1870. Three hundred and ninety-eight different examples have been divided into the following groups: (1) Masonic; (2) emblems and designs related to economic life; (3) portraits of national heroes and designs associated with them and their deeds; and (4) portraits of presidential candidates, emblems and slogans of political campaigns. In the second group are a number of interesting designs encouraging the U.S. system of better internal transportation and high protective tariffs. Among the 16 celebrities portrayed in the third and fourth groups are Jenny Lind, the Swedish singer; Lajos Kossuth, the Hungarian patriot; Marquis de Lafayette; and the notorious Thomas W. Dyott, a patent medicine vendor and bottle manufacturer. These containers were used also as propaganda during political campaigns. William Henry Harrison is pictured in this connection with other impedimenta relative to the "log cabin and hard cider" campaign of 1840.

The first 25 years of pressed glass, 1825 to 1850, are referred to by collectors as the "lacy period." A milestone within this brief span occurred in 1830 with the development of the cap ring, a device which ensured uniform thickness at the edge of each piece regardless of the amount of glass forced into the mold. Before this date most impressed designs were inspired by Anglo-Irish cut glass, often coupled with popular U.S. devices such as the sheaf of wheat. Between 1830 and 1840 the objects were thinner and more lavishly decorated, often including elaborate motifs based on the classic and Gothic revivals. Because of the unpleasant surface left by the mold and in an effort to imitate the brilliance of cut glass, unstippled areas were filled in with over-all lacelike patterns; hence the term "lacy." About 1840 economic conditions forced glassmakers to revert to cheaper molds and simpler geometric forms and to abandon the stippled patterns. During this period the mechanical press became firmly established and by 1850 glassmaking was one of the United States' new mass production industries.

(T. S. B.)

II. MODERN GLASS FROM 1850

The modern history of glass can be said to begin in the middle of the 19th century with the great exhibitions and with the new self-consciousness in the decorative arts which they expressed. Glassware was being publicly discussed in art journals and collected in museums, and this new spirit of awareness led to a greatly increased exchange of ideas among the leading glass centres and to the borrowing of ideas from the past.

In some degree the established glass-producing centres were still concerned in the modern period with the styles of glassware for which they had achieved an earlier reputation. The English glasshouses continued their production of deeply cut crystal; engraved glass and to a lesser extent coloured and painted glass were given the greatest attention in central Europe; the Venetian glasshouses at Murano were the leading exponents of furnace-manipulated glass. But alongside these traditional methods of using and decorating glassware can be discerned the development of a renewed interest in the beauty of the material itself. Expressed in various ways, in the use of thick masses and in internal figuring and patterning, this interest has been the keynote of the most significant modern contributions to the art of glass.

Pressed glassware, which had been first made with great promise in the first half of the 19th century, was being widely made in the middle of the century, and later, as a cheap imitation of cut crystal. The decorative possibilities of the process continued, however, to be exploited in a variety of popular wares; and in the 20th century a series of new simple forms of pressed glassware appeared which had been expressly designed in relation to the

1. Great Britain.—The Great exhibition of 1851 was the culmination of a period of intense activity in the British glasshouses. The excise duty on glass had been removed in 1845 and the British glassmakers were determined not only to excel in their traditional deeply cut crystal but also to rival the Bohemians and the French in coloured, layered and enamel-painted wares. Probably the most enterprising of the English glassmakers of the period was Benjamin

Richardson, of Wordsley near Stourbridge; surviving pieces of this period from the Richardson firm include some admirable painted and engraved pieces as well as crystal wares deeply cut in elaborate patterns.

Probably in reaction against the banality of pressed-glass imitations of cutting, the most sophisticated work in crystal during the later 1850s, 1860s and 1870s was decorated by engraving, and this was often carried out by immigrant Bohemian craftsmen.

The Venetian style of furnace-manipulated glass was also exerting a strong influence. It can be seen, for instance, in the development of the elaborate Victorian centrepieces in the 1860s and 1870s. In some degree the Venetian style was also an influence, alongside that of the far east, in the fashioning of the fancy wares that were made in Great Britain, as in the United States and elsewhere, during the 1880s and 1890s. These wares, in fancy colours and shapes, were often given specific trade names and were mostly made in the English midlands by firms such as Thomas Webb & Sons of Stourbridge and John Walsh Walsh of Birmingham.

A striking form of mid-Victorian virtuosity was the cameo glass produced by Stourbridge glassworkers. This work, which was inspired by the Portland vase, required a lengthy process of etching and carving, normally through an opaque white glass layer to leave a white carved design in relief on a dark-coloured glass body. The first important pieces were produced in the 1870s by John Northwood, and in the later part of the century the most distinguished cameo work was carried out by George Woodall.

The influence of the arts and crafts movement was toward the use of plastic forms and furnace decoration, which John Ruskin had advocated in *The Stones of Venice* (vol. ii, 1853). In 1859 Philip Webb designed for William Morris some simply formed tableware which was made at the London glassworks of James Powell & Sons. From about 1880 this glassworks was under the control of Harry J. Powell who, working until World War I, developed a simple, dignified style of handmade blown glass, which was subsequently continued in designs by Barnaby Powell, James Hogan and others.

During the 1930s and after World War II other firms produced work in which a restrained and distinctively modern approach was made to the cutting of faultless crystal glass. Notable designs were produced by Keith Murray for Stevens & Williams shortly before World War II and by David Queensberry (12th marquess of Queensberry) for Webb Corbett in the 1960s. Among the more distinguished engraved work may be mentioned the diamond-point fantasies of Laurence Whistler and the movable-wheel engraving of John Hutton who was responsible for the great screen in the new Coventry cathedral. The appearance of new factories in the 1960s, concerned primarily with form and colour, widened the scope of British glass design; and at this time the glass-teaching schools were especially significant as centres for original work by individual artists.

2. United States.—By the middle of the 19th century American pressed glass was already a disturbing influence on the design of the finer wares. Its decoration was by that time mostly designed in imitation of cut glass, and the process of fire polishing was being used to give a surface almost as smooth as that of blown glass. During the succeeding decades pressed-glass designs became increasingly complicated and this tendency was accentuated in the soda-lime glass which William Leighton began to use for pressed work at Wheeling, W.Va., in the 1860s and which was later widely used in the western glasshouses for the cheapest coloured wares.

In general the finer wares of the early part of the period were similar to those of the Biedermeier and later styles of Europe. The New England Glass company at Cambridge, Mass., was employing many European craftsmen and was producing a wide variety of richly decorated layered and engraved wares. At the Boston and Sandwich Glass company layered glass was extensively used for large kerosene lamps. The effect of the competition of pressed glass on cut-crystal work can be seen in the appearance of fine-line cuttings, and during the period up to the Philadelphia Centennial exhibition of 1876 the most significant crystal work was decorated by engraving. Louis Vaupel and Henry S. Fillebrown were two notable engravers employed by the New England company from 1856 and 1860, respectively.

At the time of the Centennial exhibition cut-crystal work began to revive and by 1880 a considerable boom in its production had developed—a boom which was to continue throughout the 1880s and 1890s. New industrial methods contributed to the production of crystal glass of flawless quality and to its deep cutting with mathematical accuracy in elaborate designs. Among many others, a noteworthy producer of this type of glass in the 1890s and later was the Libbey Glass company, which was the successor to the New England Glass company in Cambridge and had moved in 1888 to Toledo, O. Later, in the early years of the 20th century, intaglio cutting in crystal became popular, and work in this expensive process was carried out in a number of cut glass factories such as the T. G. Hawkes Glass company at Corning, N.Y.

As in Great Britain and elsewhere a great amount of glass was made in fancy forms and colours in the 1880s and 1890s which, although undisciplined and often tasteless, nevertheless preserves perhaps more than any other glass the flavour of the period. These wares, often bearing specific names such as pomona, Burmese and peachblow, were made by such firms as the New England Glass company, the Mount Washington Glass company at New Bedford, Mass., and the Hobbs, Brockunier company at Wheeling.

Although belonging essentially to the category of the fancy glasses, the Favrile glass of Louis Comfort Tiffany represented an altogether higher level of achievement both in its shapes and in the colouring and figuring of the glass. It was first shown to the public in 1893, and in pieces that were produced a few years later Tiffany achieved an outstanding expression in glassware of the *art nouveau* style. Much of his work was in a heavily lustred glass that was considerably admired abroad, especially in central Europe where it created a new fashion.

From the period of World War I onward new forms of pressed glassware appeared in simple, satisfying designs appropriate to their purpose and the process of manufacture, such as the Pyrex ovenware shapes of the Corning Glass works. The Steuben Company of Corning was known for fancy glasses designed by Frederick Carder, until in 1933 the company was given a change of direction by Arthur Amory Houghton, Jr., who, with the help of John Monteith Gates and the sculptor Sidney Waugh, aimed to produce glass with intaglio engraving which would rank as fine art. Other noteworthy modern American work included simple designs in blown glass by the Blenko Glass company of Milton, W.Va., and enamel patterned bowls by the independent artist Maurice Heaton. The appearance of new factories in the United States of studio glass, produced by individual artists, was a development of international significance. It was initiated in the 1960s notably by Harvey Littleton and Dominick Labino, and included work such as that produced personally by Joel P. Myers at the Blenko Glass company.

3. Czechoslovakia, Austria and Germany.—In the middle of the 19th century the glasshouses of central Europe were producing a great variety of the layered and coloured wares that had become particularly associated with Bohemia in the preceding Biedermeier period. They were also producing a great amount of cut crystal glass in the deeply cut English style, and indeed work of this nature continued with little change throughout the modern period.

A revival of the indigenous art of engraving was initiated by Ludwig Lobmeyr, who from 1864 was in control of the Viennese firm of J. and L. Lobmeyr. His first opportunity came at the Paris exhibition of 1867, and his reputation was firmly established at the Vienna exhibition of 1873. He commissioned designs for his glasses from the leading Viennese architects and painters of the time and his work was carried out by the finest craftsmen in Bohemia and Austria.

The *art nouveau* style, which went under the name of *Jugendstil* in central Europe, made a deep impression on central European glassware. The work which was made around the turn of the century abounds in slender shapes and flowing organic motifs. Glasses designed by Karl Koepping in Berlin, with long, waving stems and tuliplike bowls, were perhaps the extreme instance of the art nouveau style applied to glassware. In 1897 an exhibition of the museums in the area. Not only the forms of the Tiffany glasses but also their figured and heavily lustred material attracted great interest. Several factories started making a similar heavily lustred glass, and the firm of J. Lötz' Witwe of Klášterský Mlýn (Klostermühle) won a grand prix at the Paris exhibition of 1900 with glassware in this type of material.

From around 1900 onward a movement toward a modern purist approach to glass was largely fostered by the work of designers connected with the Vienna Kunstgewerbeschule. Men such as Kolo Moser and Josef Hoffmann, who were also closely associated with the Wiener Werkstätte, were designing glasses in simple rational forms, and much initiative in this movement was shown by the firms of E. Bakalowits Söhne of Vienna and J. Lötz' Witwe. The Czech architect Jan Kotěra was influential in the modern design of glass, and in the early years of World War I the Czech Artěl organization of artists and architects was concerned with the design of glass, as of other decorative art objects, in a forward-looking cubist manner.

After World War I the outstanding figure in Czech glass art was Josef Drahoňovský, who was professor at the Prague School of Industrial Art. He was essentially a sculptor and most of his glass designs were for sumptuously engraved glass of a monumental quality. His colleague in Prague, Jaroslav Horejc, designed for engraved work of a broadly similar character, some of it for the Lobmeyr firm of Vienna. The decades after World War II saw considerable activity in glass design. Notable artists in the 1960s were Stanislav Libenský, René Roubíček, Pavel Hlava, and Vaclav Cigler.

In Austria after World War I the Lobmeyr firm under the control of Stefan Rath produced many admirable engraved and relief-carved pieces designed by artists such as Ena Rottenberg, Lotte Fink and Vally Wieselthier. Lobmeyr also produced some of the best designs of Michael Powolny, who had his own workshop and had designed for the firm of J. Lötz' Witwe.

In Germany the outstanding engraver and glass carver of the period after World War I was Wilhelm von Eiff, who was professor at the Stuttgart Kunstgewerbeschule, while Bruno Mauder of the glass-teaching school at Zwiesel in Bavaria was a strong influence for the use of natural and appropriate glass forms. Some fine tablewares were produced, especially in the decades after the middle of the century, by designers such as Wilhelm Wagenfeld, Richard Süssmuth and Heinz Löffelhardt. An interesting development was that of the Rosenthal firm which used the Finnish designer Tapio Wirkkala and the Dane Björn Wiinblad to effect in each case matching glass and porcelain suites of the firm's own manufacture.

4. France.—In France, as in central Europe and in England, the production of fine glassware in the middle of the 19th century was mainly divided between cut crystal and coloured wares. The "opalines," the semiopaque white and coloured wares, often with elaborately painted and gilt decoration, were especially popular; and it was during these years that the French paperweights, containing coloured patterns, became internationally known and admired. The larger factories, particularly Baccarat and St. Louis, continued to participate in the international fashions of the rest of the century and beyond. But in France inventive genius manifested itself mainly in the work of individual artists and thereby a new spirit was introduced into the modern conception of glass.

In the late 1860s and 1870s three individual artists were experimenting in glasswork and all of them were represented in the Paris exhibition of 1878. The first was Joseph Brocard, who was studying the enameling of glass and whose main ambition was to reproduce medieval Syrian glass. The second was Eugène Rousseau, a commissioning dealer in ceramics who had turned to glasswork at the end of the 1860s and was at the height of his achievement in the years c. 1880. Typically his glasses were thick-walled and translucid, often with interior crackling and shot with random streaks of colour. In 1885 he associated with E. Léveillé, who continued to work in a similar style after Rousseau's death in 1891.

The third of the individual artists at the 1878 exhibition, and the best known of them, was Émile Gallé of Nancy, who had been experimenting in glasswork since about 1867. His earliest work was in clear glass, lightly tinted and decorated with enamel and engraving; but he soon developed the use of deeply coloured, almost opaque glasses in heavy masses, often layered in several thicknesses and carved or etched to form plant motifs. His work reflected the prevailing interest in Japanese art and with its frequently asymmetrical form contributed largely to the art nouveau of the end of the century. In this period much of Gallé's manner was reflected in ranges of industrial glassware made by the firm of Daum Frères of Nancy.

A number of French artists explored with success the use of pâte de verre, which is powdered glass fired in a mold; the pioneer in its use was Henri Cros, who was working near the end of the 19th century. It was later the medium for important work by Albert Dammouse and François Décorchemont.

Among the later leaders of French glass art was René Lalique, who was producing his most typical work around the 1920s. Lalique's work is characterized by relief decoration produced by blowing into molds or by pressing. He was a leading advocate of the use of glass in architecture and much of his work was in the form of lighting equipment and other details of interior decoration. The work of his contemporary, Maurice Marinot, was more in the tradition of Rousseau, with heavy, thick-walled vessels in strong forms often with boldly cut-away abstract decoration; and Henri Navarre in the 1930s was producing work of a similar monumental nature.

The most significant work of Jean Luce and Marcel Goupy, designers of glass and ceramics, was in the production of elegant tablewares. For a long period André Thuret made glasses in thick plastic forms; and Jean Sala worked in bubbled glass. The firm of Daum was distinguished, after World War II, by its thick clear glass vessels manipulated into flowing shapes to designs by Michel Daum.

5. The Scandinavian Countries.—Up to the time of World War I the Swedish glass industry produced little original work. The sudden development of modern Swedish glass in the 1920s was attributable mainly to the initiative of the Swedish Arts and Crafts society that resulted in the employment of the painters Simon Gate and Edward Hald by Orrefors glassworks and Edvin Ollers by Kosta glassworks from the years 1916-17. The first results were exhibited in Stockholm in 1917 and consisted of handblown, undecorated tablewares, together with the luxury "Graal" glass with internal stained decoration which had been so rapidly developed under Gate's inspiration at Orrefors. It was however engraved glasswork, chiefly that designed by Gate and Hald at Orrefors, on which the reputation of Swedish glass was established in the 1920s and particularly at the Paris exhibition of 1925.

In the 1930s came a change of direction whereby the Swedish factories took less interest in engraving and followed the initiative of the French artists in making thick tinted and figured glasses. In this mode they found their greatest success and this can be attributed largely to their having achieved a system of intimate association between the artists and the glassmaker craftsmen.

At Orrefors additional artists were added to the establishment from 1929 onward, including Vicke Lindstrand, Sven Palmqvist, Nils Landberg, Edvin Öhrström, John Selbing and Ingeborg Lundin. Each of them worked in an individual style, and in addition to decorative pieces many of them designed tablewares for the subsidiary Sandvik factory. At Kosta important work was produced by Elis Bergh and later by Lindstrand. Gerda Strömberg designed for both Eda glassworks and for Strömbergshyttan. In the 1960s many new methods of forming and decorating glass were explored by young designers; and an element of the current "pop art" was discernible, such as in the work of Gunnar Cyrén at Orrefors.

In Denmark the Holmegaard glassworks and in Norway the Hadeland glassworks both followed in some respects the example of Swedish glass. At Holmegaard the movement began in the late 1920s with the appointment as art director of Jacob E. Bang,

GLASS MANUFACTURE

whose designs included an amount of striking engraved work, and was continued in the clean forms of his successor, Per Lütken. At Hadeland some distinctive glass was designed by a number of artists including Sverre Pettersen, Willy Johansson and Arne Jon Jutrem.

In Finland original modern work of great significance has been carried out. Following the example of the Swedish factories, the artist Henry Ericsson was appointed designer at the Riihimäki glassworks in the late 1920s, and Göran Hongell was employed in a similar capacity at the Karhula glassworks in the 1930s. At this time the well-known Finnish artists Arttu Brummer and Alvar Aalto (q.v.) were also concerned in glass design. Shortly after World War I the influential designer Gunnel Nyman (d. 1948) was producing tall asymmetrical shapes freely modeled in clear un-tinted glass. Other important designers were Tapio Wirkkala and Timo Sarpaneva working for Karhula-Iittala, Kaj Franck for the Wärtsilä-Notsjö glassworks and Helena Tynell and Nanny Still for Riihimäki. In the 1960s Timo Sarpaneva struck a new note with his sculptures formed in wooden moulds, while Oiva Toikka designed for Wärtsilä-Notsjö objects of a markedly "pop art" nature.

6. Belgium and the Netherlands.—In Belgium the Val St. Lambert factory was an important producer of heavily cut crystal throughout the period. It is also associated with layered work and was particularly prominent with original work of this nature around 1900. Later Charles Graffart designed for it wares made in a variety of techniques, some of them with engraved decoration.

The Dutch glassworks at Leerdam played an important part in the modern movement and followed a line of development distinct from that of the Scandinavian factories. In 1915 the decision was made to invite designs from artists, and by the early 1920s excellent simple tablewares were being made to designs by the architects K. P. C. de Bazel and H. P. Berlage and by the decorative artist C. de Lorm. From the early 1920s onward special pieces called Unica were made; some of the earlier examples were by Chris Lebeau, but most were produced by Andries D. Copier. Later decorative work included interesting designs by Floris Meydam and Willem Heesen.

7. Italy.—By the middle of the 19th century Italian glass-making had partially revived. In the 1860s the Museo Vetrario was founded at Murano (Venice) and Antonio Salviati began to produce the glasses that attracted much attention at the Paris exhibition of 1867. These were variations of the traditional Venetian style with elaborate furnace decoration, and the production of glasses of this nature continued at Murano throughout the remainder of the 19th century and beyond.

The 1920s saw the development of a more conscious spirit of artistry in Italian glasswork. Paolo Venini was concerned in producing simple elegant glasses designed by the decorative artist Vittorio Zecchin, and G. Balsamo Stella and his Swedish wife Anna were producing engraved work. In later years, both before and after World War II, much research was done in new methods of colouring and figuring glass; the results were seen in the glasses designed by Ercole Barovier for the firm of Barovier & Toso and in those designed by Giulio Radi for the firm Arte Vetraria Muranese.

From the Venini firm, presided over by Paolo Venini until his death in 1959, came many interesting innovations such as the colourful glasses designed by Carlo Scarpa and by Fulvio Bianconi and an interesting series by the Finn Tapio Wirkkala. For the firm of Vistosi some striking modern glasses were designed by artists such as Peter Pelzel and Alessandro Pianon. Some of the work, such as a series of vases designed by Flavio Poli for Seguso Vetri d'Arte, showed some influence from the thick-glass techniques of the north, but the modern Italian glass mostly retained a distinctly Venetian volatile character. An experiment of interest was the production of a series of glass sculptures from sketches and models commissioned by the dealer Egidio Constantini from internationally prominent painters and other artists.

See also references under "Glass" in the Index.

(H. W.)

BIBLIOGRAPHY.—*Early Glass:* A. Kisa, *Das Glas im Altertume* (1908); P. Fossing, *Glass Vessels Before Glass-Blowing* (1940); W. B. Honey, *Glass: a Handbook and a Guide,* ch. ii and iii (1946); W. Morin-Jean, *La Verrerie en Gaule sous l'empire romain* (1913); F. Fremersdorf, *Römische Gläser aus Köln* (1928); D. B. Harden, *Roman Glass From Karanis* (1936).

Islam: C. J. Lamm, *Das Glas von Samarra* (1928), *Mittelalterliche Gläser und Steinschnittarbeiten aus dem Nahen Osten* (1929–30), *Glass From Iran in the National Museum, Stockholm* (1935); W. B. Honey, *Glass: a Handbook and a Guide,* ch. iv (1946).

Venice: B. Cecchetti and V. Zanetti, *Monografia della vetraria veneziana e muranese,* (1874); R. Schmidt, *Das Glas,* ch. v and vi (1922); A. Gasparetto, *Il Vetro di Murano* (1958).

Germany: R. Schmidt, *Das Glas,* ch. vii (1922); G. E. Pazaurek, *Gläser der Empire- und Biedermeierzeit* (1923); R. Schmidt, *Die Gläser der Sammlung Mühsam* (1914 and 1926); F. Rademacher, *Die deutschen Gläser des Mittelalters* (1933); W. B. Honey, *Glass: a Handbook and a Guide,* ch. xi (1946).

England: A. Hartshorne, *Old English Glasses* (1897); H. J. Powell, *Glass-Making in England* (1923); F. Buckley, *A History of Old English Glass* (1925); W. A. Thorpe, *A History of English and Irish Glass* (1929), *English Glass* (1949); M. S. D. Westropp, *Irish Glass* (1920); S. E. Winbolt, *Wealden Glass; The Surrey-Sussex Glass Industry* (1933); *Far East:* W. B. Honey, *Glass: a Handbook and a Guide,* (1946).

United States: A. W. Frothingham, *Hispanic Glass* (1941); J. Harrington, *Glassmaking at Jamestown* (1952); G. S. McKearin and H. McKearin, *American Glass* (1950), *Two Hundred Years of American Blown Glass* (1950); H. McKearin, *American Historical Flasks* (1953); J. H. Rose, *American Pressed Glass of the Lacy Period, 1825–1850* (1954).

Modern Glass: A. Polak, *Modern Glass* (1962); G. Beard, *Modern Glass* (1968); H. Wakefield, *Nineteenth Century British Glass* (1961); H. J. Powell, *Glass-Making in England* (1923); R. W. Lee, *Victorian Glass* (1945); D. Daniel, *Cut and Engraved Glass* (1950); L. W. Watkins, *American Glass and Glassmaking* (1950); G. E. Pazaurek, *Moderne Gläser* (1901), *Kunstgläser der Gegenwart* (1925); L. Rosenthal, *La Verrerie française depuis cinquante ans* (1927); C. G. Janneau, *Modern Glass* (1931); H. Seitz, *Glaset förr och nu* (1933); E. Steenberg, *Modern Swedish Glass* (1949); A. Gasparetto, *Il Vetro di Murano* (1958).

GLASS MANUFACTURE. The common article of commercial manufacture known as glass is normally a transparent, hard, brittle substance. Glasses are formed from certain liquids that have the property of cooling below their freezing point without crystallizing, thus becoming liquids of increasingly high viscosity until eventually they are so stiff that by all ordinary definitions they have the properties of a solid. The scientific definition that regards glass as a "supercooled" liquid thus includes such materials as toffee, which is a supercooled sugar solution, and the higher alcohols (such as the sterols), which can be frozen into glasses by cooling well below the freezing point of water. On the other hand, many of the new organic high polymers from which transparent materials can be prepared are not necessarily glasses by this definition. Such materials have been described as organic or polymeric glasses. The definition accepted in the United States by the American Society for Testing Materials (ASTM) recognizes as glasses only those that are made of inorganic substances, stating: "Glass is an inorganic product of fusion which has cooled to a rigid condition without crystallizing." This article is confined to inorganic glasses and is arranged as follows:

I. Introduction
   1. Chemical Composition of Various Glasses
   2. Physical Structure of Glass
   3. Fluorescence
   4. Historical Outline of the Industry
II. Properties
   1. Chemical Durability
   2. Viscosity
   3. Surface Tension
   4. Density
   5. Thermal Expansion
   6. Thermal Endurance
   7. Thermal Conductivity
   8. Mechanical Properties
   9. Electrical Properties
   10. Optical Properties
   11. Ultraviolet Ray Transmission
III. Manufacture
   1. Raw Materials
   2. Glass-Melting Furnaces
   3. Glass-Forming Processes
   4. Drawing Processes

I. INTRODUCTION

1. Chemical Composition of Various Glasses.—Commercial glasses may be divided conveniently into soda-lime-silica glasses and special glasses, over 95% of the tonnage produced being of the former class. Such glasses are made from three main materials—sand (silicon dioxide, or SiO_2), limestone (calcium carbonate, or $CaCO_3$) and sodium carbonate (Na_2CO_3).

Fused silica itself is an excellent glass but, as the melting point of sand (crystalline silica) is above 1,700° C and as it is very expensive to attain such high temperatures, its uses are restricted to those in which its superior properties—chemical inertness and the ability to withstand sudden changes of temperature—are so important that the cost is justified. Nevertheless the production of fused silica glass is quite a large industry; it is manufactured in various qualities and when intended for optical purposes the raw material used is rock crystal rather than quartz sand.

In order to reduce the melting point of silica it is necessary to add a flux; this is the purpose of the sodium carbonate (soda ash, mostly obtained from the Solvay process), which makes available the fluxing agent sodium oxide. By adding about 25% of the sodium oxide to silica the melting point is reduced from 1,723° to 850° C and thus the melting difficulty is very considerably reduced. However, such glasses are easily soluble in water (their solutions are known as water glass, which has various domestic uses; e.g., egg preserving). The addition of lime (calcium oxide, or CaO), supplied by the limestone, renders the glass insoluble once again, but too much lime makes a glass prone to devitrification; i.e., the precipitation of crystalline phases in certain ranges of temperature. The optimum composition is approximately 75% silica, 10% lime, and 15% soda, but even this is too liable to devitrification during certain mechanical forming operations to be satisfactory.

In making sheet glass it is customary to use 6% of lime and 4% of magnesia (magnesium oxide, or MgO) in bottle glass about 2% alumina (aluminum oxide, or Al_2O_3) is often found to be present. Other materials are also added, some being put in to assist in refining the glass (i.e., to remove the bubbles left behind in the melting process), while others such as selenium and traces of cobalt oxide are added to improve its colour. For example, sand always contains iron as an impurity, and, although the material used for making bottles is specially selected for its low iron content, the small traces of impurity still impart an undesirable green colour to the container; by the use of selenium and cobalt oxide together with traces of arsenic trioxide and sodium nitrate it is possible to neutralize the green colour and produce a so-called white (decolourized) glass. (*See also* Bottles: *Raw Materials and Composition*.)

Glasses of very different, and often much more expensive, compositions are made when special physical and chemical properties are necessary; for example, in optical glasses, where a wide range of compositions is required to obtain the variety of refractive index and dispersion needed if the lens designer is to produce multi-component lenses that are free from the various faults associated with a single lens, such as chromatic aberration.

Another disadvantage of ordinary glass is that when it is subjected to a sudden change of temperature, stresses are produced in it that render it liable to fracture; however, by reducing its coefficient of thermal expansion it is possible to make it much less susceptible to thermal shock. The glass with the lowest expansion coefficient is fused silica. Another well-known example is the borosilicate glass used for making domestic cookingware, which has an expansion coefficient only one-third that of the typical soda-lime-silica glass. In order to effect this reduction, much of the sodium oxide added as a flux is replaced by boric oxide (B_2O_3)

and some of the lime by alumina. Another familiar special glass is the lead crystal glass used in the manufacture of superior tableware; by using lead monoxide (PbO) as a flux it is possible to obtain a glass with a high refractive index and, consequently, the desired sparkle and brilliance. Lead crystal glass is also used for the pinch of electric lamps (the small piece of glass tubing through which the lead-in wires are conveyed) because, owing to its low soda content, it is a much better electrical insulator than the soda-lime-silica glass used for the bulb of the lamp.

Other familiar special glasses are those made to resist the attack of various chemicals; for example, a special "neutral" glass, about halfway in composition between soda-lime-silica glass and the borosilicate glass used for ovenware, is made for ampules to contain pharmaceutical preparations. Special glasses (*see* Table III) are also needed for the street lighting lamps that operate by causing an electrical discharge in sodium or mercury vapour, since these vapours attack most types of glasses. One phosphate glass (British patent 585,257 of Feb. 3, 1947) has remarkable resistance to hydrofluoric acid solution, which rapidly attacks all ordinary glasses. Another phosphate glass is the heat-absorbing glass commonly used in slide projectors.

2. Physical Structure of Glass.—In the mid-20th century the scientific study of glass was being intensively pursued and some of its properties were beginning to be understood in terms of the structure and properties of the ions that compose it. As glass is a liquid-like material there is no regular long-distance order of the arrangement of atoms on a lattice as there is in a crystal. However, the densities of glasses and of crystals of the same composition are very similar and therefore the atoms must be about the same distances apart in both substances. While the special properties of liquids and glasses arise from this very lack of long-distance order, if one were to judge the structure of the glass merely by the next nearest neighbours to any particular atom, the appearance would be very much that of a crystal. As long ago as 1932, W. H. Zachariasen, a crystallographer, showed that the silicon and oxygen atoms in silicate glasses were arranged in a kind of irregular network, each silicon being surrounded by four oxygens and each oxygen being shared between two silicons. The introduction of sodium oxide weakens this network by bringing in more oxygens per silicon so that some silicons could not be joined to other silicons by the oxygen bridges. This "random network theory" found much favour for 20 years or so. However, in the mid-1960s, it was recognized that besides the silicate glasses many other glasses exist and that the real criteria of glass formation are not concerned so much with the final structure of the substance as with the conditions in which it can be cooled from a liquid to a solid without precipitation of crystals; i.e., with the conditions that make crystallization difficult.

There is always a certain amount of energy resident in the surface of any body and this energy manifests itself in various phenomena usually described as being due to surface tension. For example, oil will spread on water because the surface energy of the water-air surface is greater than the energy of the oil-air surface and, by spreading, the oil decreases the energy. As a crystal gets smaller the surface energy makes a greater and greater contribution to the total energy of the crystal. This results in very tiny crystals being more soluble than large crystals, and so it is impossible for the smallest crystal to grow. This apparent impasse is the problem of nucleation; it is overcome either by a crystal growing on some foreign group of atoms, when it is called heterogeneous nucleation, or by a momentary local departure from the equilibrium conditions where the small nucleus of a crystal exists long enough for growth to take place; this is homogeneous nucleation. Nucleation and crystal growth are therefore the controlling processes of crystallization or, in the parlance of glass technology, of "devitrification."

Glass-forming liquids are those in which the barriers to nucleation and crystal growth are high. In the silicate glasses the very high viscosity at the liquidus temperature makes crystal growth slow. Also, even in the common silicate glasses, the initial difficulty of nucleation helps to prevent devitrification.

Since the 1950s crystallization has been employed commercially.

Suitable glasses are first melted and shaped by the usual glassmaking techniques; a subsequent treatment nucleates crystals and as the temperatures increase these crystals grow until the glass is completely changed into crystals. Such a substance is known as a glass-ceramic and is very much stronger than ordinary glass, particularly at high temperatures. The process was patented by the Corning Glass Works of Corning, N.Y., and the first product made in this way (patented 1960) is called Pyroceram. In order to provide nucleation centres some more easily precipitated material such as titanium dioxide is added. In order to obtain materials with special properties, such as almost zero thermal expansion, the composition of the parent glass has to be adjusted so that certain crystals are precipitated. The parent glasses are usually mixtures of the oxides of silica, lithium, aluminum, titanium, and sometimes phosphorus.

3. Fluorescence.—New uses for glass arise continuously, as also do new developments in the glasses themselves. In the mid-1960s a glass was developed for use in the laser (light amplification by stimulated emission of radiation). In this device it is necessary to have certain ions in surroundings that will permit them to be excited by incident light so that they will emit radiation of longer wavelength through the process known as fluorescence. When certain critical conditions associated with the electronic processes in the ion are satisfied it is possible to produce in this way very intense and highly homogeneous beams of light. Such beams have been reflected from the surface of the moon and detected again on earth; they can also be made of such intense energy that they can produce a small hole in a coin. A glass containing 5% of the rare-earth element neodymium has proved particularly suitable for some of these applications. This glass has to be specially prepared and to be particularly free from iron, which would interfere with the radiative processes.

4. Historical Outline of the Industry.—Soda-lime-silica glasses have been known for at least 2,000 years, lead glass for perhaps 400 years, and all the others for not more than 75 years, indeed many of them for less than 35 years. The modern advances have followed the application of chemistry to the problem of producing glasses with the desired physical and chemical properties, and have been made effective by the development of new technologies. The processes for shaping glass remained much the same in principle from the early Christian era until nearly the end of the 19th century, when the development of machines, at first semi-automatic, began in the United Kingdom and the U.S. The regenerative furnace, patented in 1856 by F. and W. Siemens and adopted by the glass industry, made large supplies of molten glass available to feed the new machines. In the 20th century epoch-making advances took place—especially in the U.S. but also in Belgium and the U.K.—in the invention of fully automatic machinery. The Corning ribbon machine, for example, can make more than 1,000,000 electric light bulbs a day. At least 95% of the total weight of glass manufactured in the U.S., the U.K., and other industrialized countries is fashioned by automatic machinery. These great advances were rendered possible by clever inventors backed up by systematic scientific research and control. The first university department for research and teaching in glass technology was established in 1915 at Sheffield, Eng., and the first Society of Glass Technology in 1916, also in Sheffield. Similar institutions soon followed in the U.S., then in 1922–23 in Germany, and later in several other countries. In glass as a decorative material, notable advances were made after 1920 in purity, range of colouring, form, and decorative surface treatment. These innovations were pioneered mainly by individual glassworks or by individual artists.

Table I.—*Glass Production 1900 to 1965 in the Largest Manufacturing Countries* (in 000s)

Country	1900 Pop.	1900 Tons	1950 Pop.	1950 Tons	1965 Pop.	1965 Tons
United Kingdom	38,000	220	50,000	1,230	48,000	2,290
United States	76,000	1,000	151,000	5,460	195,000	10,270
Germany†	39,000	400	50,000	800	59,000	2,400

*Figures not available for the U.S.S.R.
†Figures for 1950 and 1965 refer to the Federal Republic of Germany.

To the long-established schools for training in glass craftsmanship at Zwiesel in Bavaria, at Kamenicky Senov (Steinschönau) and at Novy Bor (Haida) in Czechoslovakia there were added others at Zelezny Brod (Eisenbrod) in Czechoslovakia, at Rheinbach in the Federal Republic of Germany, and in Great Britain at London, Edinburgh, and Stourbridge. An International Commission on Glass maintains contact with all institutions engaged in promoting the study of glass in all its aspects.

The expansion of the glass industry in the 20th century is illustrated in Table I. The number of glass containers sold per head of population was, in 1966, 150 in the U.S., 94 in the U.K., and 82 in West Germany. Among other countries the figure was 92 (Denmark), 84 (Belgium), 82 (Sweden), 40 (Italy), 31 (Austria), 23 (Spain), and 15 (Portugal). (W. E. S. T.; R. W. Do.)

II. PROPERTIES

The general compositions of the simpler types of commercial glass have been mentioned already, and since chemical and physical properties are controlled largely by composition, it follows that these can be varied over a wide range. Indeed, it has been claimed that in the making of glass-to-metal seals, for instance, when the expansion characteristics of glass and metal must be matched quite closely, it is easier for the glass manufacturer to adjust his glass to match a given alloy than for the alloy maker to produce his alloy to match a given glass. In such an ancient craft as glassmaking, trial and error has resulted over the centuries in the development of certain glass compositions that are particularly suited to certain processes (e.g., lead crystal glass for lengthy hand-forming operations), but the introduction of mechanical methods of forming and the need for glasses for electrical and other special purposes resuited in demands that could scarcely have been met without the systematic research on the effect of composition on glass properties that has been carried out in the 20th century.

Properties that are particularly important are chemical durability; viscosity; surface tension; density; thermal properties, including thermal expansion, endurance, and conductivity; mechanical properties, such as compressibility and tensile strength; electrical properties, including conductivity and dielectric constant; optical properties; and ultraviolet ray transmission.

1. Chemical Durability.—Chemical durability is the resistance of the glass to attack by weather or by whatever solid, liquid or gaseous material is in contact with it. The alkali content of the glass is the most important, though not the only, factor: high alkali causing poor durability. Boric oxide, aluminum oxide (alumina), zinc oxide, and zirconium oxide (zirconia) all improve glass durability in certain cases. The extent of attack and the order of resistance of different glasses depend on both the nature of the reagent and the temperature. Since the weathering and chemical corrosion of commercial glasses are usually extremely slight and noticeable only after a considerable time interval, the methods of testing durability exaggerate the severity of the conditions either by reducing the glass to the form of small grains of controlled size, thus greatly increasing the surface exposed to attack, or by raising the temperature; or both methods may be united in one test. Table II gives results of tests carried out on crushed glass particles, carefully sieved to control their size, using boiling water or other reagents for one hour.

It is very necessary that certain types of glass, e.g., blood stor-

Table II.—*Comparative Durabilities (Powder Method)*

Glass	Water % loss	Constant boiling hydrochloric acid % loss	Approximately 2.5% sodium carbonate solution % loss	Approximately 2% caustic soda % loss
Bottle glass, good	0.09	0.08	0.53	1.42
Bottle glass, bad	0.27	0.18	1.78	1.99
Lead crystal glass (22%PbO)	0.31	0.37	2.10	3.36
Lead crystal glass (28%PbO)	0.16	0.26	1.98	3.20
Chemical ware	0.02–0.06	0.06–0.11	0.22–0.6	1.6–3.9
Gauge glass tubing	0.01–0.02	...	...	...
Ample tubing	0.01–0.05	...	...	...
Soft soda tubing	0.1	...	...	...

age vessels and ampules for injection solutions, should not give up sufficient material to affect the liquids stored in them. This necessitates careful choice of composition.

2. Viscosity.—Viscosity, and, particularly, the rate at which viscosity changes with temperature, has an important effect on the forming of glass while hot and plastic. Since such operations often proceed step by step, it is necessary that the glass remain soft enough to yield to formative pressure over a considerable range of temperature, ending at a viscosity high enough to retain the final shape. Alteration of the forming process thus quite often means alteration of composition in order to secure the required viscosity. The lead crystal glass used for hand working remains soft over much too wide a range of temperature to suit an automatic bottle-forming machine, and again the glass suitable for the latter would not be suitable for flat glass-drawing machines. The unit of viscosity is the poise (see VISCOSITY); the viscosity of water at room temperature is .01 poise but the viscosity of glass is so high that it is generally given in powers of ten. Important viscosities in the manufacture of glass are the "working point," i.e., 10^4 poises; the "softening point," at which a glass rod of specified dimensions elongates at 1 mm. per minute under its own weight, $10^{7.6}$ poises; "annealing point," 10^{13} poises; and "strain point," $10^{14.5}$ poises. These "points" are specified by temperatures determined by following a closely controlled technique using apparatus of specified construction (ASTM specifications C. 336 and C. 338). At the softening point glass deforms rapidly and will adhere to other bodies, at the annealing point internal stress is relieved in 15 minutes, while at the strain point it takes 4 hours to do this. When annealing glass, the rate of cooling from just above the annealing point to a little below the strain point is kept quite low, the precise value depending on the glass thickness. (For a fuller discussion of annealing see Annealing, below).

3. Surface Tension.—This property plays a part in forming operations and prevents glass from penetrating into minute crevices in molds. Values for silicate glasses are about 300 dynes per centimetre.

4. Density.—Ordinary bottle and window glasses have densities in the region of 2.5. That of lead crystal glass is approximately 3.1, of "densest flint" optical glass 7.2, and of fused silica 2.2.

5. Thermal Expansion.—This is important as a factor in the resistance of glass to heat shock and in determining the stresses set up in windows under alternating heating (solar radiation) and cooling (sleet and rain). A very powerful factor is alkali content, since both sodium and potassium oxides markedly increase the expansion. Values range from 5.6×10^{-7} to 140×10^{-7} cm. per centimetre per degree centigrade. (Silica glass 5.6×10^{-7}, Vycor glass 8×10^{-7}, Pyrex glass $32-36 \times 10^{-7}$, bottle glass $82-88 \times 10^{-7}$, lead crystal glass 88×10^{-7}.) In glass-to-metal seals the expansions of glass and metal must match closely over the range of temperature in which glass cannot yield to stress.

6. Thermal Endurance.—Thermal expansion, mechanical strength, the dimensions of the article, and the rate at which heat is spread all affect thermal endurance. Glass rods of Pyrex type in one test withstood, when dropped into cold water, a shock of 325° C, while soft lamp-working glass withstood only 112° C and a commercial soda-lime glass 131° C. Tests to detect faulty ware are routine practice in many glassworks as thermal endurance is very sensitive to departures from normal technique.

7. Thermal Conductivity.—Values range from 0.0012 to 0.0033 cal. per centimetre per °C per second at room temperature. High soda, potash, and lead oxide contents decrease thermal conductivity while high silica and boric oxide increase it.

8. Mechanical Properties.—Glass is very strong in compression. When it breaks it does so in tension. Compressive strength ranges from 90,000 to 180,000 lb. per sq.in. (psi). tensile strength from 4,000 to 1,500,000 psi (depending on the surface condition of the specimen); Young's modulus averages 6,500,000 psi; Poisson's ratio (σ) is 0.14-0.271 (ordinary glass about 0.22). The strength determined from practical tests is always considerably lower than that predicted by theory, the discrepancy being due to the presence of microscopic unavoidable flaws in the surface. Considerably greater strength is obtained from simple shapes by a controlled sudden chilling instead of the normal annealing. Such "toughened" glass, which is used as automobile windows, will withstand an impact roughly eight times that needed to break ordinary glass of the same thickness (see Safety Glass, below).

Containers such as milk bottles make many trips between factory and consumer. The improvement in mechanical and thermal properties achieved is illustrated by the fact that whereas 20 trips was regarded as average in the 1920s, the figure in the 1960s was nearer 60. Improved design of the containers also helped.

9. Electrical Properties.—Conductivity.—The electrical conductivity of glass varies with composition and increases with temperature; therefore, though most glasses are good insulators at room temperature, having resistivities in the range from 10^8 to 10^{18} ohm cm., it is possible when it is raised to red heat to pass sufficient current through the material to raise the temperature to 1,400° C and continue melting by electrical energy. In most glasses the current is carried by alkali metal ions moving through the material, but semiconducting glasses have recently been discovered in which the current is carried by electrons. These glasses may have resistivities as low as 10^4 ohm cm. at room temperature. Lead glasses of good working properties have high resistivity and so are used in electric lamps to support the filament.

Dielectric Constant.—This value depends on composition and on the temperature and the frequency. It varies from 3.7 to 16.5. Pyrex-type glass has the low value of 4.1-5.0. Dielectric loss varies with frequency. For Pyrex-type glass the value changes from 1.9×10^{-2} to 4×10^{-2} as frequency falls from 10^6 to 10^3 cycles. Values for most glasses are around $1-2 \times 10^{-2}$.

10. Optical Properties.—Refractive Index.—The refractive index (for sodium D line) varies from 1.458 (fused silica) through 1.478 for fluor crown, 1.517 for hard crown, 1.613 for dense barium crown, 1.613 for dense flint, 1.668 for dense barium flint to 1.717 for double extra dense flint.

Dispersion.—The dispersion (difference between refractive indexes for wavelengths in different parts of the spectrum) varies between (Fraunhofer lines C-F) 0.007 for fused silica and 0.024 for double extra dense flint glass.

Stress Optical Coefficient.—Under stress glass becomes doubly refracting, i.e., the velocity of propagation of a beam of plane-polarized light through the glass depends upon the orientations of the light path and the polarization direction relative to the direction of the stress. On this property, demonstrated by D. Brewster, depends the working of the strain viewer used to test whether an article is properly annealed or not.

Absorption and Transmission.—When "white" light falls on a glass plate at right angles to the surface, some is reflected, some is absorbed, and some emerges at the other surface. The absorption is not the same for all wavelengths, so the emerging light is relatively stronger in some wavelengths than others in comparison with the incident light so that instead of being ordinary white light it is coloured. The extent of the absorption in the various wavelengths depends upon the composition, thickness, and temperature of the glass. Specially interesting are (1) glasses very low in iron content, which transmit ultraviolet light (quartz glass is best); (2) glasses of high ferrous iron content, which cut off both ultraviolet and heat radiation, as that used in spectacles for furnace workers; and (3) glasses containing nickel oxide, which transmit ultraviolet but no visible light.

11. Ultraviolet Ray Transmission.—The most active rays that affect the photographic plate have a wavelength shorter than 400 mm. (that is, shorter than the visible violet of the spectrum, the symbol $m\mu$ representing 1 millimicron, or $\frac{1}{1,000,000}$ mm.). Fused silica or quartz glass transmits rays down to 190 $m\mu$ and other glasses transmitting more or less in this range have been known for many years. E. Zschimmer in 1907 and, at about the same time, O. Schott at Jena produced a number of them, including "Uviol." They are important in photography, especially that of the stars.

Just after World War I much flat glass with high ultraviolet transmission was made for windows in sanatoriums, factories, and private dwellings as a result of studies of the good effect of high alpine sunlight in tuberculosis treatment. In 1925 E. Lamplough

GLASS MANUFACTURE

developed Vita-glass and several other similar products were made. Their chief characteristics were low iron and titanium contents; they usually contained a little boric oxide, which, like silica, favours ultraviolet transmission.

One, Corex D, was designed more particularly for use in ultraviolet "sun" lamps (mercury vapour arc lamps) and had a transmission at 302 mμ of 64%, falling only to 62% after stabilization. Unfortunately, many of the commercial glasses as a result of solar radiation suffered a considerable reduction in ultraviolet transmission, and as they are only effective if kept very clean they are no longer used for ordinary glazing purposes. See also SPECTROSCOPY; PHOTOCHEMISTRY.

III. MANUFACTURE

1. Raw Materials.—The oxides shown in the conventional expressions of glass compositions are not always present as such in the mixture, or "batch," charged into the melting furnace. In many cases the material furnishing them to the glass is a carbonate; sometimes it is a nitrate or sulfate or possibly a hydroxide. Materials may be chosen for their cheapness or for some property in addition to their capacity to yield a desired constituent. Thus alkali nitrates, which are much more expensive than the carbonates, per unit of oxide contributed to the glass, are sometimes employed because they assist melting and provide an oxidizing atmosphere that is desirable when melting lead glasses and certain coloured glasses. Sundry fluorides are used, primarily because they can be made to opacify the glass, if added in sufficient quantity, or to speed up melting and refining when used in small quantities.

Colours in glasses are produced in two ways: (1) by solution, in which case the colour is due to ions; (2) by the separation from the clear melt under appropriate conditions of finely divided particles of material; for example, gold, copper or cadmium selenide or sulfoselenide in the case of ruby glasses, and cadmium selenide in the case of some yellow and orange glasses. Of the solution colours, copper and cobalt compounds are used to produce blue glasses, green is produced by chromium compounds, and amber is produced by carbon and sulfur or by iron and manganese compounds. Nickel oxide gives a purple colour in a potash glass but a relatively large amount is used, when the purple colour is again apparent.

Sand is a most important material. It must possess a reasonably uniform grain size with no large grains and little dusty material and, for colourless glass, must contain very little iron oxide (0.03% maximum for good-quality containers, 0.013% for lead crystal tableware, and not more than 0.008% for optical glass; window-glass sands may contain as much as 0.10%, obtained by blending good sands with poorer ones); other colouring materials should not be present in great enough amounts to give rise to detectable colour. Other natural materials used to furnish glass constituents include limestone (which provides calcium oxide), dolomite (calcium and magnesium oxides), feldspar, lepidolite, nephelite-syenite (alumina, silica, and alkali metal oxides). Cryolite also contains aluminum but is used only when its fluorine content is required to produce opal glasses. Other raw materials used consist mostly of the carbonates, nitrates, or oxides of the elements involved.

Batch Preparation.—The raw materials are stored in bins, "silos," or sacks, and are weighed out, mixed, and sent to the furnace. In large installations the weighing may be automatic, the material being fed in predetermined sequence to a weighing machine so interlocked that further use is impossible until correct weight is shown. When weighed out, the batch is tipped into a mixer, frequently of the well-known concrete-mixer type, and is either discharged to a hopper that holds one "mixing" or is elevated and conveyed to a storage bin. Very special batches (e.g., for optical or coloured glass not made in quantity) are sometimes mixed by hand and shovel in wooden tubs. The batch is conveyed by bucket or belt conveyor, by "unit mix" hopper on a monorail, or by compressed air along a tube. Segregation by vibration or "free fall" is of course a danger. Such segregation troubles are said to be avoided if the batch is briquetted (compressed into blocks) before conveyance. It is customary and in general beneficial to include in the mixing a proportion of broken glass of the same composition as that to be made. This is supplied from the waste glass incidental to manu-

TABLE III.—Percentage Compositions of Typical Commercial Glasses

Glass type	Flat glass window glass — Colburn type	Flat glass window glass — Fourcault type	Plate glass	Container Glass — British	Container Glass — U.S.: 1960	Container Glass — Amber (U.S.)	Container Glass — Amber	Container Glass — Dark blue	Container Glass — Dark green	Cheap tumbler and electric lamp bulb	Lead crystal (pot-melted)	Lime (pot-melted)	Soda for lamp working	Machine-made	Colour-less	Fused silica	Vycor (U.S.)	Pyrex brand	Monax	Amber (Fiolax) Ampule	Gauge glass	Clinical thermometer bulb	Sealing to Fernico alloy	Sealing to tungsten	Television tube screens	Mercury-vapour lamp (H.P.)	Sodium-vapour lamp	Projector lamp
Silica	71.7	71-72.5	72.2	72-74.5	71.5-71.9*	70.5	67.8	71-72	67.2	70.1	56.6	70.0	72.2		67.2	100	96.3	80.1	76.7	69.4	71-77	55.7†	65.5	77.0	65.3-69.1	58.7	22.4	75.0
Boric oxide				0-0.2	0-0.15					0.7	0.2	0.6					2.9	12.0	11.1				24.1	15.4		3.0	25.7	18.2
Alumina	0.7	1-2	0.14	0.4-1.5	1.7-2.1	2.1	1.1	1.1	1.9	2.6	0.8	2.5	2.5	5.0	3.7		0.4	3.1	2.7	3.2-6.2	7-12	0.2	2.2		22.4	24.4	2.2	
Iron oxide	0.05			trace-0.4		0.14			2.6					3.5	0.07			0.08	0.4		3-9	0.02			0.1	0.1		0.1
Lime	9.7	7-9	11.2	8-11.3	8.8-9.4	8.9	8.6	11.5-12.5	8.1	5.4		5.0	3.7	6.5	9.2			0.1		0.2-0.5	7-12		5.9	1.1	8.0	5.9	0.4	0.3
Magnesia	4.3	2.5-4.5	2.1	0.1-3.5		1.4	1.3		1.5	3.6		3.5	3.5	0.1	0.1			0.1		0-1.5								
Soda	13.0	14.5-15.5	13.7	13.8-14.3	16.0	16.0	13.9	11.5-12	14.8	16.8	5.1	17.2	10.85		13.8			4.1	12.0	0-5	0-5	31.4	4.1	4.6	4.1		8.4	3.4
Potassium oxide		0.2-0.8		0-0.2		0.6	0.4	0.3-0.8	1.0	0.3	7.2	0.2	6.0						0.1		1.2-5.1	0.1			6.6-7		1.1	1.9
Manganese oxide							3.8 (barium oxide 3.1)		2.5												0.8-5.2	12.0			0-0.1	0.3		
Zinc oxide																									2.4			
Lead oxide											30.2																	
Cobalt oxide								0.1-0.3																				
Chromium oxide									0.5-0.8																			
Fluorine				0.1-0.17		0.1-0.4																						

facture and is called cullet. It should consist of small-sized pieces.

Batch Feeding.—Large furnaces are generally fed automatically by screw or pusher feeding device, or by discharging a thin stream across the furnace to form a "blanket" of batch. Pots are usually filled by shovel.

2. Glass-Melting Furnaces.—Meltings in early times were carried out in clay pots heated by wood. The process, on more modern lines, still persists, but producer gas from coal or lignite, oil, coke-oven gas, and natural gas are the common fuels. Electric heating is employed where electricity is cheap and other fuels expensive (as, for example, in Switzerland) and its use as a boost to the other methods of heating was, in the mid-1960s, becoming common in the U.K. and the U.S. The advantage of the all-electric melting furnace is that it gives off much less heat to its surroundings and the heat is generated where it is most needed—in the material to be melted. Special glasses and those made in small quantity are generally melted in pot furnaces containing 1–20 pots (most often 8–12). The pots may be open or "closed"—*i.e.*, covered with a hooded side opening that abuts on a hole in the furnace wall in such a way that the flame gases have no access and cannot affect the glass. Their capacity ranges from a few pounds to 30 cwt., and their shapes vary. A common one has an egg-shaped horizontal section so that the maximum amount of floor space of a circular furnace may be used. The clay mixture of which the pots are made contains raw clay with a percentage (30 or more) of carefully graded prefired clay ("grog"), sometimes composed of so-called sillimanite. The pots are formed either by hand from rolls of plastic mixture or by casting a fluid slip in plaster molds as in the pottery industry. Drying must be slow and very carefully controlled and, before being placed in the melting furnace, pots are heated in a "pot arch" to a temperature in excess of 1,000° C and are transferred hot. A ring of clay is placed in each to define a clean area from which molten glass will be gathered. The flames come from ports, generally in the floor of the furnace but sometimes in the end walls in the case of rectangular furnaces (pots in two parallel rows), and, circulating over the pots, pass out by flues in the pillars supporting the crown or by a port at the opposite end. When the pot has been brought to the correct temperature (1,350°–1,450° C) in the furnace, the batch is "filled on." When melted down, a second filling, and generally a third, is made to produce a full pot when all the batch has melted (see *The Melting Process*, below). Larger amounts of glass are melted in tank furnaces, based on the Siemens invention, in which the walls define the glass-melting area and the flame passes over the glass surface.

Those of small size, *i.e.*, with a capacity of from 2 to 10 tons, may be "day tanks" in which glass is melted overnight and worked

out during the day, or their contents may be melted one day and night and then worked out. Bigger tanks are continuous, the batch being charged at one end into a "doghouse" and removed at the other as reasonably homogeneous glass for feeding to forming machines. Except for tanks melting sheet or plate glass, they are divided into melting and working ends by a bridge wall. Communication is either through a "doghole" in the bridge or by a submerged "throat" that connects holes in the floor of each compartment. The flames may pass from side to side (crossfiring) or, entering at the back wall, pass down to the bridge and return (horseshoe firing) or, in small tanks, pass down from the back walls and out through ports at either side of the bridge. In yet another form the furnace crown is hollow and the flame from the back wall returns from near the bridge between the false crown and the outer one to pass to a heat recovery system. Such systems may be (1) regenerative, in which the waste gases heat stacks of brickwork, which then, by reversal of flame direction, are used to preheat the combustion air and fuel gas, or (2) recuperative, in which the gas flow through the system is constantly in one direction and the waste gases pass over tubes through which the combustion air is led for preheating. Large tanks of the window-glass type are around 150 ft. long and 30 ft. wide and hold an approximately 5-ft. depth of glass; *i.e.*, about 1,200 tons. Gas consumption for such a tank is about 50,000,000 cu.ft. per month.

By the 1960s many furnaces had been converted to the use of oil from producer gas. The Glass Manufacturers' Federation estimated that in 1966 85–90% of the British industry's production was melted by oil, consumption being around 725,000 tons. An oil-fired furnace needs only one set of regenerators to preheat the air at each side of the furnace. A similar construction holds for furnaces fired by natural gas since it is not customary to preheat this gas on account of its high hydrocarbon content.

Unit Melter.—The unit melter was developed in an attempt to provide the optimum conditions for supplying one forming machine. It consists of a narrow channel (6 ft. wide and 36 ft. long), at one end of which the batch is fed in, being melted and conditioned on its way to the feeding device supplying the machine at the other end.

Refractories.—The life of glass-melting tanks was much increased, and the output raised, because of the higher melting temperatures made possible by the use of blocks cast from electrically fused high alumina melts (Corhart) or high zirconia (Zirconium dioxide) ones (ZAC). These blocks are much more resistant to attack by the glass.

The Melting Process.—During the melting, carbonates, sulfates, nitrates, etc. in the batch decompose, with evolution of the corresponding acid gases (CO_2, SO_3, etc.). In addition, water is driven off from wet sand and from some crystalline salts; *e.g.*, borax. The more easily fusible materials form a glaze, which speeds up reaction by increasing surface contact, and the proportion of molten matter increases. Finally even the grains of silica disappear. The resultant melt is full of bubbles, a state referred to as "seedy."

Refining.—The temperature is now raised somewhat to reduce viscosity and to complete decomposition so that the bubbles disappear. After this the temperature is slowly reduced from the 1,400°–1,500° C (1,600° for Pyrex-type glass) at which melting was carried out to the working temperature of around 1,250°–1,400° C. This temperature gradient from end to end of the tank is achieved by using the proper location and size of burners and by screening the working end in some cases by a "shadow wall" built on the bridge.

3. Glass-Forming Processes.—*Hand Processes.*—These glass-blowing processes are generally applied to pot-melted, good-quality glass, frequently lead crystal because its working properties suit the leisurely sequence of manipulations involved. After the glass within the ring in the pot has been skimmed clean, an amount of glass is gathered on the blowpipe and withdrawn, the tail of glass being dropped outside the ring at the instant of separation so that it does not contaminate the next gather. By blowing, rolling on a polished iron plate (marver), swinging, etc., the glass is formed into a hollow, pear-shaped bulb. The blowpipe may be rolled up

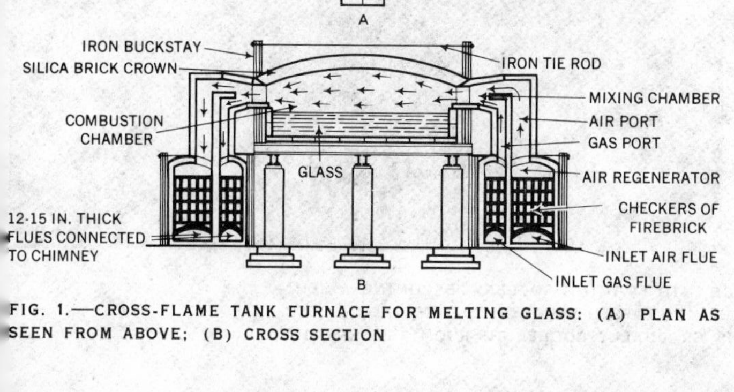

FIG. 1.—CROSS-FLAME TANK FURNACE FOR MELTING GLASS: (A) PLAN AS SEEN FROM ABOVE; (B) CROSS SECTION

WORKING END OF TANK

DOUBLE-WALLED BRIDGE

SUBMERGED CONNECTING PASSAGE (DOGHOLE)

REFINING ZONE

OUTGOING PORTS CONNECTED TO CHIMNEY

FIRE-CLAY TANK BLOCKS 12-15 IN. THICK

DOGHOUSE INTO WHICH RAW MATERIALS ARE FED

INCOMING GAS PORT

INCOMING AIR PORT

MELTING ZONE

A

IRON TIE ROD

MIXING CHAMBER

AIR PORT

GAS PORT

AIR REGENERATOR

IRON BUCKSTAY

CHECKERS OF FIREBRICK

COMBUSTION CHAMBER

GLASS

SILICA BRICK CROWN

INLET AIR FLUE

12-15 IN. THICK

INLET GAS FLUE

FLUES CONNECTED TO CHIMNEY

B

and down the long arms of the glassmaker's chair while he works on it with shearlike tools (pucellas or procellas) to construct it, draw it out, flatten the base with a wooden "battledore" and so on. Extra glass may be cast on to form stems, bases, handles, etc. The glass is then attached at the base to a rod (punty) and is cracked off the pipe so that the other end of the article may be finished, using the rod as axis of rotation. Production can be speeded up by blowing the body of the article in a mold and then finishing at the chair. Large articles such as illuminating globes are mouth-blown in molds, and the excess glass is cracked off, after annealing, by heating at a diamond scratch. An alternative method of removing the waste cap of glass is to rotate the blank upside down and melt off the waste by very intense pinpoint flames applied at the line of separation. This is done for tumbler and some electric lamp blanks.

Lamp Working (Bench Glass Blowing).—This is carried out using glass tubing or rods of various diameters. They are heated in the flame of a gas-air blowpipe, the air being enriched with oxygen when borosilicate glass is worked. The articles made include chemical and other scientific and surgical apparatus (*e.g.,* glass eyes, ampules, syringes, thermometers), egg timers, decorative figures and animals, beads and Christmas tree ornaments.

The making of such items as electric lamps, electron tubes, and television tubes is a development of these processes, but it has been largely mechanized, while massive components of glass pipelines and heavy chemical apparatus are handled by semimechanical processes. Some use has been made of high-frequency electric welding.

Molds.—Molds for glass are mostly of fine-grained gray cast iron. When extra-high polish is required or conditions are very exacting, special heat-resisting alloys of the stainless steel or Nichrome type are used. Molds for most purposes are used hot, sometimes at temperatures approaching 600° C; but for thin-walled hollow ware they are used wet and are coated with a paste (comprising carbonizable material with a binder) to retain the water so that a cushion of steam is provided between glass and mold when the former is rotated. Usually the molds are of two or more sections in the body, together with a base and in some cases (for example, for pressing) a ring to define the upper edge of glass and to locate the plunger in proper relation to the mold body.

Molds used for automatic machines present problems in cooling. This factor largely controls the rate of working.

Mechanical Methods.—These include pressing, blowing, drawing, casting, rolling, either individually or in combinations of two or more processes. Thus bottles may be made by press and blow or blow and blow (or suck and blow) methods as described in the article BOTTLES: *Methods of Manufacture.*

Feeding Glass to Machines.—In the semiautomatic processes, which are still operated to deal with special shapes, this is done by hand. The glass is gathered on an iron rod with a ball-shaped end and is allowed to run off the latter into the mold. The machine operator shears through the stream when sufficient glass has been supplied. Fully automatic container-forming machines either receive separate charges extruded from a feeder channel running from the working end of a tank furnace and cut off by mechanically or pneumatically operated shears. Very accurate control of glass level, glass homogeneity, temperature and feeder mechanism is needed to deliver charges of constant weight to make articles of constant capacity.

Pressed Glass.—The molds may be "block" (*i.e.,* the body in one piece), with a movable base to eject the pressed article, or, for heavily decorated pieces, the body may be in three, four, or more sections hinged to swing open to clear projections. For ware of precise dimensions, or when a number of articles are desired at one pressing, font molds are used, with cavities fed from a central reservoir at which the pressure is applied by plunger and in which excess glass remains to form a means for removing the pressing from the mold. Automatic presses carry a number of molds on a circular table, rotated step by step to bring each in turn below a charging device (feeder), then to a pressing station and, after a sufficient interval for cooling, to a take-out point. Pressure in automatic machines is generally exerted by compressed air through a cylinder and piston and a toggle linkage. Hand presses operate as a rule by lever and crank.

Glass blocks for light-transmitting walls are made by welding together at the edges two rectangular cup-shaped pressings. They have good thermal- and sound-insulating properties, and when prismatic ribs are formed on the inside surfaces considerable spreading of the transmitted light results.

Light-Blown Hollow Ware.—Blanks for making tumblers, electric lamp envelopes, and the like are made on Westlake-type machines or on the Corning ribbon machine. The former machine uses shorter pipes and gathers by suction. The Corning machine takes a continuously rolled ribbon of glass bearing thickened hot portions spaced by thinner cold ones and from the hot "blobs" blows the blank, using blowheads on one continuous belt above the

(LEFT) MOLTEN GLASS FLOWS FROM THE FURNACE INTO FORMING ROLLERS, BECOMING A SEMI-SOLID, CONTINUOUS RIBBON OF GLASS. (RIGHT) HAVING PASSED THROUGH THE ANNEALING LEER, THE GLASS ENTERS A COOLING AREA WHERE IT IS GRADUALLY COOLED TO ROOM TEMPERATURE

ribbon and molds on another belt below it. Speeds of up to 1,000 or more bulbs per minute are attainable.

4. Drawing Processes.—*Tubing*.—When tubing is drawn by hand a parison (a rounded mass of molten glass blown at the end of the pipe into a thick-walled "bubble") of suitable shape is attached at the free end to a punty and is then drawn out. The drawn tube (or rod if not blown out) is rested on a ladderlike rack and is cut up into lengths. There is much waste glass attached to both pipe and punty.

In one mechanical drawing process (Danner), a stream of glass flows as a flat ribbon onto a revolving, hollow, downwardly inclined mandrel, blends thereon to a uniformly thick coating, and is drawn off the lower end as a tube if air is blown into the upper end at relatively low pressure (up to 5 in. water gauge). The size of mandrel nose, temperature and rate of feed, and removal of glass together with the pressure of air determine tubing dimensions. Drawing speeds range from about 20 to 850 ft. per minute. Removal is controlled by a drawing device, located 100–200 ft. away, consisting of two endless caterpillar belts whose asbestos-faced shoes engage the tubing or rod, which is by that time almost cold. Various devices on the machine are used to cut the glass into lengths depending on its thickness and diameter.

Precision-Bore Tubing.—Suitable tubing is passed round a sizing mandrel while hot and plastic, and a very accurate bore is produced by exhausting the glass round the mandrel. The tubing is then used to form barrels for hypodermic syringes and other precision instruments without the need for internal grinding, which would much reduce its strength and increase its liability to attack by chemicals and sterilizers.

Glass Fibres.—See below.

Sheet Glass.—Early sheet glass was handmade (1) by blowing a large parison, attaching it to a punty, cracking it off from the pipe, and reheating and spinning the punty so that centrifugal force caused the glass to spread out to form a disk attached at its thickened centre to the punty; (2) by blowing and swinging the parison so that it elongated to form a long cylinder, which was then, after its ends had been cracked off, split longitudinally and opened out after transferring to a flattening kiln. The first step in mechanization, attributable to J. H. Lubbers, was the production of glass cylinders approximately 40 ft. long by 30 in. in diameter, which were treated by the latter method. Present methods are two. In the first the sheet is drawn upward from a pool of glass, the line of draw being located either by a slot in the bottom of a long fire-clay boat (Fourcault process) or by a cooling bar placed a little below the surface (Slingluff or Pittsburgh process). When the sheet is a few feet above glass level it is rigid enough to be engaged by the first of a series of pairs of asbestos-faced rollers, which continue to draw it upward. The ribbon is cut into sheets, which are removed as they emerge and are stored after washing in dilute acid to remove surface deposit.

The second method is horizontal drawing (Colburn or Libbey-Owens process). Here, although the sheet is drawn vertically from the pool, it is bent horizontally over a Nichrome roller and passed between two endless belts, which draw it forward into a 200-ft.-long roller annealing furnace (leer, or lehr), at the cold end of which it is cut into sections. The speed depends on the thickness of the sheet and is of the order of 100 in. per minute. Production per machine is much greater with the Colburn than with the Fourcault or Slingluff processes.

Rolled Glass.—Originally the demarcation between sheet and plate glass was sharp. One was blown, the other was cast, rolled, and (generally) ground and polished to a flat surface on each side. The demarcation is not so clean-cut now. The first cast and rolled plate is ascribed to Lucas de Nehou in 1688. A process for casting molten glass onto an inclined table feeding a pair of rolls was developed by Chance Brothers and E. F. Chance in 1890 to produce figured (i.e., patterned surface) glass. The discontinuous process reached its peak development in the Bicheroux process (1918). The glass was rolled from the teemed contents of a pot and was received on a train of cars that moved past the inclined rolling table, where shears cut between them to enable each in turn to be

hauled away to the annealing leer. Continuous methods for making rolled plate are typified by those of the Ford Motor Co. and Pilkington Brothers Ltd. In the first the glass passes from the melting furnace through a channel where temperature and quantity are closely controlled. It then flows in a widening stream down an inclined spout to feed a large-diameter bottom roll working with a small-diameter top roll. The 40-in.-wide rolled ribbon passes directly into a leer 440 ft. long, which it traverses in about two and one-half hours. The glass is then cut into lengths, ground and polished. In the Pilkington process, the ribbon may be much wider, and in one form it passes directly without cutting from the leer to the grinding and polishing section in which it is operated upon on both upper and lower surfaces at once (twin plate process).

5. Grinding and Polishing of Plate Glass.—The old discontinuous process involved setting sheets of glass in plaster on huge 30-ft.-diameter, circular, cast-iron tables. Spaces between sheets were filled with waste glass. The tables were then taken to the motor and rotated below a "spider" carrying a number of cast-iron "tools," which had "nogs" on their undersurfaces to engage the glass, with spaces through which sand or emery could be carried by water as a slurry to do the abrading. Starting with fairly coarse sand, the size of abrasive was reduced stage by stage until a very smooth gray surface was obtained. The tools were then changed for polisher disks faced with felt, which was charged with rouge and water. This brought about the final polish. The irregularity of the surface of cast and rolled rough plate made necessary the removal of much material and encouraged the development of later methods, which employed pairs of rollers instead of a casting table and "rolling pin." The continuous grinding and polishing methods of Ford and others involve bedding the glass on fabric and conveying it on carefully leveled cars beneath a series of independent

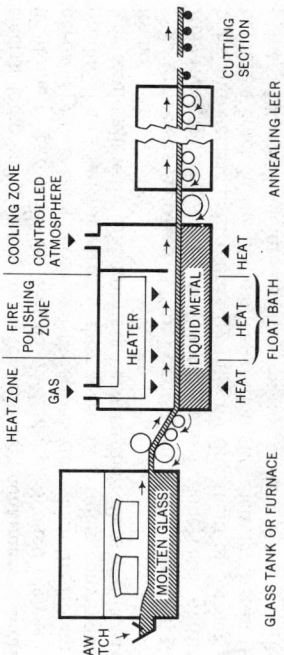

FIG. 2.—FLOAT GLASS PROCESS: FROM THE GLASS TANK OR FURNACE, THE GLASS RIBBON IS DELIVERED ONTO THE SURFACE OF LIQUID METAL IN THE FLOAT BATH. THE RIBBON IS COOLED WHILE STILL ON THE MOLTEN METAL, WITH THE RESULT THAT THE SURFACE OF THE GLASS, AFTER ANNEALING, IS SMOOTH AND POLISHED

motor-driven heads that operate tools supplied with successively finer abrasive. After a space for cleaning and inspection, the glass is then passed beneath similarly driven polishing heads supplied with rouge paste. Elaborate arrangements for collecting, regrading, and returning abrasive to the system may be provided. The glass, polished on one face, is rebedded and the process repeated, on a second line, on the opposite face. The Pilkington twin-plate process saves cars and double track.

6. Float Glass.—A great saving of space is effected by the float glass process of Pilkington Brothers Ltd. (British Patent 797,101/2, June 25, 1958), a major development in the production of "polished" flat glass. After rolling (fig. 2), the glass ribbon passes into a heated compartment where it floats on the surface of a molten metal (e.g., tin) maintained at such a temperature that the surface irregularities of the glass are smoothed out and the sheet becomes quite flat. The temperature is reduced until the glass is rigid before the glass ribbon leaves to pass to the leer for annealing. Since the glass has not been chilled on its surface by contact with cooler metal it retains its high polish.

7. Foam Glass.—Molds are packed with a mixture of crushed grains and a substance (for example, limestone) that will give off a gas at a temperature at which the grains are soft enough to cohere. The molds are then suitably heated and the porous mass so obtained is cooled and used for some thermal- and sound-insulating purposes. It is light enough to float in water and is rotproof. It has been used as a substitute for cork.

8. Annealing.—When glass cools freely from the molten state it solidifies first on the outside. Such material, being rigid, resists the inward pull of the hotter glass inside, which, in cooling down to room temperature, needs to contract more than the surface. Such a piece of glass is left when cold with the surface in compression if of simple shape (*e.g.*, a sphere) and as such it strongly resists mechanical shock. Surfaces with sudden changes of contour, on the contrary, are in similar circumstances very prone to disruption by the application of slight additional stress, mechanical or thermal. To make commercial glassware safe to use it must, after receiving its final shaping, be cooled very slowly from a temperature at which it is soft enough for stresses to be relieved in a few minutes to a lower temperature below which it is not possible to introduce permanent stress by sudden cooling. This process is known as annealing. From the latter point the limit to the rate of cooling is the ability of the article to withstand the temporary stresses set up by the thermal gradient at the moment. The process may be carried out (1) batchwise, in kilns that are charged with the hot, newly formed glass, heated and then cooled slowly. This method is usually reserved for optical glass and certain very thick-walled goods. (2) Most often, the ware is passed on a conveyor belt down a tunnel leer, 2 ft. 6 in. to 11 ft. wide and 30 ft. to 440 ft. long, in which a suitable temperature gradient is established. The atmosphere in the leer may be controlled to affect the surface of the glass and improve durability. Heating is by gas, oil, or electricity.

Modern leers, because of good insulation and rapid transfer of ware from machines, need little additional heat above that taken in by the hot glass itself. The time to anneal depends upon the wall thickness of the article. Very thin ware, such as electric lamp bulbs, needs only a few minutes; containers generally need one to two hours in leers 65–75 ft. long. Rolled plate glass needs very long leers because of the speed with which the ribbon is produced and fed forward; a slow speed in a roller conveyor or leer would allow the ribbon to sag between the rollers and destroy its flatness.

9. Processes Applied After Formation and Annealing.—

Removing Waste Caps From Blanks.—This is done (*e.g.*, of tumblers and electric light bulbs) by (1) cracking them off, either by making a crack in the plane of separation and then heating in this plane with needle-pointed flames, or by heating first and then scratching; or (2) melting off. (*See also Glass-Forming Processes*, above.)

Edge Grinding.—Dishes, globes, illuminating bowls, tumblers, etc., are held down on a horizontally rotating iron disk fed with abrasive and water. Alternatively, a fine-grit sandstone wheel is used.

Fire Finishing.—The ground edges are heated first in a soft flame and then in a high-intensity flame till fusion rounds them and removes the grayness. Slow cooling follows. With tumblers less bead is produced this way than by melting off.

Decorative Cutting (Grinding.)—The design is roughed out on the article in a water-resistant paint and is then cut on an abrasive wheel. Formerly this was an iron disk with a mitred edge that was fed with sand and water. The process, repeated with emery and water, gave a smoother finish, which was further improved by the addition of powdered pumice and finally by brushing with putty powder (tin oxide).

The modern method employs a silicon carbide wheel of, say, 80 to 100 grit followed by an alumina wheel of, say, 150 to 180 grit. The article is then immersed in an acid polishing bath containing strong sulfuric and hydrofluoric acids, worked warm. Cheap ware, mass-produced in molds to standard dimensions, may be cut in machines that index the ware step by step and present it to the wheel at each step.

Other Abrasive Processes.—Intaglio is similar to decorative cutting, but the spindle is overhanging and the wheels are much smaller. The depressions are shallower and the process is intermediate between cutting and engraving. The latter process uses an overhanging spindle with copper wheels of various diameters (*e.g.*, from pinhead size to around four inches), thicknesses, and edge contours. These are fed with a mixture of oil and abrasive (emery, generally) and in the hands of the expert can be made to turn out the most artistic "drawings" on glass. In sandblasting, sand grains entrained by a blast of air at pressures usually of 2–25 psi will obscure the surface of glass with a pattern rather like that given by grinding. The portions to remain clear are protected by paper backed with a resilient sticky substance such as glue and glycerin. Designs can be produced quickly by this method. Metal stencils are used in sandblasting trademarks and the like on glassware. Sandblasting in stages, changing the pattern of the resist (the protected area) at each stage as the depth of excavation increases, produces some very striking relief effects. In glass sculpture, hand tools operated by flexible drive or a motor of the Bosch type are used to execute designs *in situ* on large sheets of glass.

Etching.—Hydrofluoric acid attacks most glasses readily but the visual effect varies according to whether the material removed remains in solution or is left in the surface. This in turn depends partly on the acid strength and partly on what other substances are present in the etching mixture. Clear etching is produced by either dilute hydrofluoric acid alone or in some cases (*e.g.*, on lead glasses and some low silicates) by strong acid used with strong sulfuric acid. In the case of lead glass there is a deposit but it brushes off in warm water.

In other circumstances, rough mat or translucent surfaces can be produced; *e.g.*, with potassium fluoride and a mineral acid a delicate satin finish is obtained, with ammonium bifluoride mixtures a "white" finish. The internal surface of a "pearl" electric light bulb is produced in two stages: first a coarse etch is achieved with an internal spray of a strong ammonium bifluoride mixture, secondly a spray rinse with a more dilute solution that smooths the too-sharp contours of the first etched surface and largely restores the original strength of the bulb. Ammonium bifluoride is the active constituent of inks for writing on glass and of pastes for badging glassware through a wax resist.

Enamelling.—(1) A design cut in a brass or glass plate is charged with a mixture of enamel colour and medium (*e.g.*, lithographic varnish). A sheet of transfer tissue paper is gently applied and then peeled off, bringing with it the design in enamel. The paper is applied to the clean glass surface, damped and peeled off, leaving enamel only on the glass, which is then heated carefully until the enamel fuses to it. The same transfer method is used for applying wax resists to glass to be etched. (2) A silk or other mesh screen carrying light-sensitive material is exposed behind a negative and developed so that a design is produced in the apertures (the background is composed of the closed spaces). The screen is then placed on the glass and an enamel mixture is brushed over it with a squeegee. The mixture is forced through the apertures and the design emerges on the glassware. For circular containers the ware is rotated below the screen. (*See Silk Screen Printing.*)

Silvering, Coppering, Gilding.—Mirrors, once made with tin amalgam, have, since the discoveries of Michael Drayton and Justus von Liebig, been made by the chemical reduction of silverammonia compounds to metallic silver. Modern developments include processes in which the "silver" and "reducer" solutions meet in a spray above the cleaned glass, which is passing on a conveyor, and deposit the silver immediately the spray falls on the glass. Copper and gold may also be deposited by chemical reduction. Gold films of controlled thickness may be obtained by heating an organic gold compound. Dark-coloured mirrors are made by depositing films of lead sulfide on the glass. Films may be produced not only by chemical deposition but also by "sputtering" (high-voltage discharge between electrodes) *in vacuo* or by evaporating *in vacuo*; the latter process is used to make aluminum or rhodium mirrors and, with certain fluorides, the "bloomed" lens that has a very high light transmission. Two kinds of film allow the passage of sufficient electric current to warm the glass: first, the rather thick sprayed aluminum grid that enables the glass plate to be used as a radiator; and, second, the film of tin oxide that can be heated to preserve clear vision through a windshield (glass screen) in vehicles.

Some compounds of silver and other metals, if applied as liquid suspensions to glass coming hot from the forming process, give a surface that may be soldered to metal. "Lustres" are produced by painting glass with organic sulfur compounds of gold, platinum, or other precious metals in an essential oil (a volatile odoriferous vegetable oil; e.g., lavender). Gentle heating smokes off the medium and decomposes the sulfur compound, leaving a bright metallic mirror surface on the glass. Glass stained with silver or copper compounds yields the yellow or red colours seen in stained glass windows.

Photosensitive Glass.—Certain glasses (U.S. patent 2,515,275 of July 18, 1950) containing small amounts of gold, silver, or copper are sensitive to light. When exposed to ultraviolet radiation no obvious change occurs until the glass has subsequently been heated to a temperature a little below that at which it softens. The characteristic colour (yellow or ruby) then develops. Some of the glasses are of such a composition that the "nuclei" produced initiate devitrification and produce an opal effect. By exposure to the radiation behind a negative or stencil, very decorative effects may be produced.

The first of these nucleating processes was called the Fotolite process. It was followed by the Fotoform, in which the glass composition was so chosen that, after exposure behind a negative to ultraviolet light, the heat treatment caused a separation from the rest of the glass of a phase that could be dissolved away by suitable solutions (U.S. patents 2,515,937 to 2,515,943; July 18, 1950) to give a very precisely "machined" outline, e.g., patterns of minute holes to form screens for various purposes. If the Fotoform process is applied to remove developed material, and the remainder is then heavily exposed again to radiation, further heat treatment at a high temperature produces a dense, hard, strong ceramic with good high-temperature properties. This material is called Fotoceram.

10. Safety Glass.—This has been defined as glass so treated or so combined with other materials as to reduce the likelihood of injury to persons by objects entering from exterior sources or by the glass itself when it is cracked or broken. Two types are available.

Laminated Glass.—The first commercially successful patent was taken out in France by Edouard Benedictus in 1909. He took a sheet of celluloid and bonded it between two pieces of glass. On fracture the glass fragments remained adhering to the celluloid where they were unlikely to produce severe injuries.

Celluloid has the disadvantage of turning brown on continued exposure to sunlight. Several other plastics were tried but in 1936 polyvinyl butyral (PVB) was developed and this had so many desirable properties that its use became universal. It does not discolour, retains its elastic properties even at 0° F (−17.7° C), and it sticks to glass of its own accord.

In manufacture the glass and interlayer are washed, dried, and assembled in a dry air-conditioned room since the moisture content of PVB must be kept low. Alternate rolling and heating bring about preliminary adhesion and the bonding is completed by further application of heat and pressure in an autoclave.

For use in automobiles the interlayer thickness is generally 0.030 in. but for special applications, such as the windows of aircraft, the thickness may be 0.25 in. with glass components of 0.5 in. thickness or more. Bullet-resistant glass is frequently built up to a thickness of 1.5 in. by the use of several glass and plastic components.

Heat-Treated Glass.—In manufacture, sheets of glass of the correct shape are suspended in a furnace, heated to about 650° C, withdrawn and suddenly but uniformly chilled with compressed air. This produces a skin of compressive stress of over 30,000 psi in the glass and increases its strength about six times. When such a glass does break, it shatters into granules with blunt rectangular edges incapable of causing more than minor scratches. Because of the harmless nature of these fragments and of its much en-

hanced strength, this glass is accepted as a safety glass and is very generally used in automobile door lights and rear windows.

Its use in windshields is more controversial and certain countries (notably the U.S.) will not permit its use in this situation because, should a heat-treated windshield shatter and the fragments remain in position, a frosted appearance instantly covers the whole windshield and robs the driver of vision. The drawback has been largely overcome by retarding either the heating or cooling over that area of the windshield through which the driver normally looks. After fracture the fragments in this zone are much larger and adequate vision is still possible.

Curved Safety Glass.—Improved aerodynamic shape of automobiles led to a demand that the windows be curved to correspond with the general shape of the body; nevertheless generally accepted standards of safety and clarity of vision had to be maintained.

Since, during heat treatment, glass is taken to its softening point, advantage may be taken of this to bend it by pressing between dies when first withdrawn from the furnace and before chilling. In another process the glass rests horizontally on a curved peripheral mold and is allowed to soften and sag into shape in a furnace; when the required curvature is attained, the glass and mold are withdrawn from the furnace and chilled.

Curved laminated glass is more difficult since the two glass components have to be bent together (usually on a peripheral mold), annealed, and laminated. (G. B. WA.; A. C. WE.)

11. Chemcor Process.—The Fotoceram process led to the development of others in which nucleation was initiated without exposure to ultraviolet or X radiation. The Pyroceram one (U.S. patent 2,920,971, Jan. 12, 1960) has been mentioned already (see *Physical Structure of Glass*, above).

Later the Corning Glass Works patented, with S. D. Stookey and others, two processes for imparting enhanced strength to glass surfaces. The first (U.S. patent 2,998,675, Sept. 5, 1961) is applied to lithia-alumina-silica glasses with a catalyst (e.g., titanium dioxide, boric oxide, lead oxide, or sodium carbonate) and consists in heat treatment for a specified time within a specified temperature range. A film of crystals is developed on the surface, with the result that the outer surface is left in strong compression when cold.

The second process involves the immersion of an alkali-titanium dioxide-alumina-silica glass in a fused lithium sulfate-sodium sulfate bath (e.g., 95% Li_2SO_4, 5% Na_2SO_4 by weight) at 860°–900° C. Lithium ions diffuse from the bath into the glass, displacing sodium ions and producing an opaque material of lower thermal expansion than the main glass, so that again the outer surface is in strong compression when cold. These are known as the Chemcor processes. The bending strength of glass so treated may be as much as five times that of toughened (tempered) glass.

12. Glass Fibres.—The possibility of drawing hot glass into threads was recognized very early in the history of glassmaking and such threads were wound around vessels as a decoration, for example in ancient Egypt and in the Rhineland of the late Roman Empire (see GLASS). In the 18th century finer fibres were prepared by drawing a thread from a heat-softened glass rod onto a spinning wheel. This method proved economic only when the spinning wheel was replaced by a large drum drawing a number of fibres simultaneously. In 1908 G. von Pazsiczky invented the "Gossler" process, drawing several fibres from holes in the bottom of a refractory glass melting chamber. In the 1920s W. Schuller revived the use of rods, drawing from 100 electrically or gas-heated rods onto one drum. Both processes are still in use.

As early as 1911 E. Pick obtained a patent to draw fibres by centrifugal force, Harford and Stafford experimented in the U.S., but it was F. Rosengarth together with the Hager brothers who developed in 1929 a method which for many years remained the main glass wool process in Europe. In this "Hager" process, a stream of molten glass fell on a fire-clay disk with radial serrations, rotating rapidly about a vertical axis, and throwing fibres off tangentially, unfortunately together with a number of unattenuated slugs of glass.

Modern Manufacturing Methods.—In the U.S. the Owens-Illinois Glass Co. and Corning combined their separate glass-fibre research facilities to form Owens-Corning Fiberglas. Under G. Slayter, J. H. Thomas and others developed some fundamental new principles allowing fibres to be mass produced, forming the basis for the industrialization of glass-fibre production between 1936–50.

To subdivide the molten glass coming from the forehearth of a glass tank "bushings" were used. These are precious metal troughs with a number of perforated nipples, each issuing a fine stream of molten glass. Electric heating of the bushings provides the high accuracy needed for temperature control.

To draw these streams of glass into fine fibres "blowers" were developed, in which they passed through the blower slot between two converging, downward directed, blasts of high-speed air or steam. They are thereby attenuated into much finer fibres, 0.00035-in. diameter against the 0.00080 of the older processes. If the turbulence in the blower is great the streams are broken into short "wool" fibres (about 1–5 in. long). These can then be sprayed with a binder (a thermosetting resin), collected on a conveyor, and compressed to the desired density. After cure in an oven, rolls or slabs of wool are cut to convenient size. By keeping turbulence in the blower low, longer fibres (25–30 in.) are produced, and these can either be formed on a conveyor into thin sheets (the "staple tissue" process), or they can be sucked onto a rotating perforated drum forming a web. This is drawn off the drum as fast as it forms and is elongated into a sliver (a loose collection of interfelted parallel fibres). The silver can be drafted, twisted, and plied as in ordinary textile manufacture, resulting in a staple fibre yarn ("staple fibre" process).

In the same period Owens-Corning Fiberglas developed the "continuous filament" process. In this the bushing is fed with glass marbles at a rate to maintain a constant liquid glass level in it, while practically endless lengths of fibres are drawn from the tips at the bushing base. Strands of several hundred fibres are drawn simultaneously from bushings of this type and after application of a size are wound onto fast-moving winding heads (fibre diameters 0.00012 to 0.00060 in.). Continuous filament has a silky lustrous appearance, while staple fibres are mat owing to the many free fibre ends. Another OCF process developed later was the "superfine fibre" process. In this, coarse fibres are drawn from a continuous filament bushing by a pair of rollers and fed into the high-speed, high-temperature exit flame of an internal combustion burner. Wool fibres of 1–4 microns in diameter are produced.

In the 1950s the centrifugal process was considerably improved by the Cie de St. Gobain and by OCF (the "TEL" or "Rotary" process). In this the refractory disk is replaced by a metal spinner carrying thousands of fine holes in its cylindrical vertical wall. From each hole a fibre is drawn by centrifugal force and immediately deflected down and further attenuated by a blowing ring. The fibres are again bonded with resin and collected on a conveyor. Because products made by this method have finer fibres (0.00015–0.00030 in.) and greater uniformity, the rotary process has come to replace most other earlier wool-making methods.

Properties of Glass Fibres.—Glass fibres have the characteristic properties of glass; that is, they are incombustible, inorganic, non-absorbent, are not hygroscopic, and chemically are quite stable. Their small diameter, however, results in an exceedingly large surface area in relation to their volume (one glass marble ¾ in. in diameter yields about 97 mi. of single filament). The surface properties thus become of paramount importance and compositions have to be adjusted to ensure that, for example, attack by weathering does not impair the performance of the fibres, particularly of those used for electrical insulation. For this purpose a glass substantially free from alkali is used, e.g., of composition 55% silica, 10% boric oxide, 14% alumina, 17% lime, 4% magnesia by weight. Fine fibres are remarkable for their tensile strength, which is much greater than that of bulk glass. In ordinary production, strengths of approximately 200,000 psi are common; in laboratory tests as much as 350,000–500,000 psi have been reached as compared with values as low as 4,000 for bulk glass.

The excellent heat and sound insulating properties of glass wool are due to the ability of keeping small volumes of air still. Higher densities or finer fibres result in a reduction in the size of these air pockets and an improvement in the insulating properties. In British thermal units, the conductivity (K) is 0.27 for a 1½ lb. per cubic foot density. Woven materials are closer packed and therefore conduct more heat, which is useful in electrical insulation (e.g., motor windings), apart from their ability to withstand much higher temperatures, and to pack into small thicknesses. It is difficult to bond to a glass surface but pigments can be adhered by carrier resins, and adhesion to plastics effected through "linking" agents (e.g., silanes).

Uses of Glass Fibres.—By far the largest tonnage of glass fibres is sold as wool. This is particularly suited for the thermal insulation of buildings (e.g., attic insulation in private houses) and acoustic insulation in concert halls or in floating floors to prevent sound transmission. Wool is also widely used in the insulation of equipment (pipes, tanks, boilers, refrigerators) and transport.

Coarse fibred mats are used in air filters and washers and in rectifying towers of distillation plants. Staple tissue reinforces bitumen in pipe wrapping and roofing felt, or acts as a separator in storage batteries. Staple fibre fabrics are used in filtration, and glass fabrics with a crimp-setting ("coronizing") treatment are glass fibre bundles felted into "glass papers." For a long time the main application for continuous filament has been in electrical insulation. Today the fastest growing market is in the reinforcement of thermosetting and thermoplastic resins. Reinforced plastics are remarkably strong; large and complicated shapes can be produced with ease. The main uses of reinforced plastics are in boats, automobile bodies, building panels, translucent sheets, containers, jigs, tools, and aircraft parts. The reinforcement of rubber in tire manufacture promises well. Printed glass fabrics with a crimp-setting ("coronizing") treatment are much used as curtains because they are fireproof.

Medical uses include the making of splints for maximum support to limbs, and sutures in surgery. Glass fibre bundles when embedded in a medium of different refractive index can transmit images over a distance and around corners. A medical use for this is in "gastroscopes." *See also* references under "Glass Manufacture" in the Index.

(T. S. R.; A. DE D.; M. PN.)

BIBLIOGRAPHY.—H. Schulz, *Das Glas* (1923); B. Long, *Les Propriétés physiques et la fusion du verre* (1935); H. Jebsen-Marwedel, *Glastechnische Fabrikationsfehler*, 2nd ed. (1959); R. Macgrath and A. C. Frost, *Glass in Architecture and Decoration*, 2nd ed. (1961); G. O. Jones, *Glass* (1956); J. E. Stanworth, *Physical Properties of Glass* (1950); F. Franceschini, *Il Vetro, Trattato Generale* (1954); C. J. Phillips, *Glass, the Miracle Maker*, 2nd ed. (1948); C. J. Phillips and D. J. Duffin, *Get Acquainted with Glass* (1950); J. H. Partridge, *Glass-to-Metal Seals* (1949); W. A. Weyl, *Coloured Glasses* (1951); W. A. Weyl and E. C. Marboe, *The Constitution of Glasses* (1963); S. R. Scholes, *Modern Glass Practice*, 2nd ed. (1952); F. V. Tooley (ed.), *A Handbook of Glass Manufacture*, vol. 1 (1953), vol. 2 (1960); R. Günther, *Glasschmelzwannenöfen* (1954); Eng. trans., *Glass-Melting Tank Furnaces* (1958); W. H. J. Eitel, *Physical Chemistry of the Silicates* (1954); G. W. Morey, *The Properties of Glass*, 2nd ed. (1954); H. Rawson, *Inorganic Glass-Forming Systems* (1967); J. de Jong, *Transmission of Glass in the Ultraviolet* (1952); M. B. Volf, *Technical Glasses*, Eng. trans. (1961); M. C. Nokes, *Modern Glass Working*, 4th ed. (1958); A. de Dâni, *Glass Fibre Reinforced Plastics* (1960); G. L. Steele, *Fiber Glass* (1962); F. R. Mills, *Potters and Glassblowers* (1963); R. H. Slavin, *The Pressed and Blown Glassware Industry* (1963); American Society for Testing and Materials, *ASTM Standards on Glass and Glass Products*, 5th ed. (1963); T. C. Barker, *Pilkington Brothers and the Glass Industry* (1960); E. W. Fairchild, *Fire and Sand; the History of Libbey Owens Sheet Glass Co.* (1960); M. K. Berlye, *The Encyclopaedia of Working with Glass* (1968); F. J. Terence Maloney, *Glass in the Modern World* (1968).

The following are the most important technical periodicals: *J. Soc. Glass Tech.* (1917–59), now *Physics and Chemistry of Glasses* and *Glass Technology* (1960 et seq.); *Glastech. Ber.* of the Deutsche Glastechnische Gesellschaft (1923 et seq.); *J. Amer. Ceram. Soc.* (1918 et seq.); *Bull. Amer. Ceram. Soc.* (1922 et seq.); *J. Ceram. Ass. Japan* (1924 et seq.); *Verres et Réfr.* (1946 et seq.); *Glastekn. Tidsskr.* (1946 et seq.); *Glass Ind.* (1920 et seq.); *Sprechsaal* (1867 et seq.); *Silicates Industr.* (1930 et seq.); *Szkło i Ceram.* (1950 et seq.); *Skláři a Keram.* (1951 et seq.); *Steklo i Keramika* (*Glass & Ceramics, Moscow*) (1956 et seq.); *Glas-Email-Keramo-Technik* (1950 et seq.); *Cen. Glass Ceram. Res. Inst.* (1954 et seq.).

(X.; M. PN.)

GLASTONBURY, a market town and municipal borough of Somerset, Eng., lies 6 mi. S.S.W. of Wells and 26 mi. S.W. of Bath by road. Pop. (1968 est.) 6,280. The town lies on the slopes of a group of orchard-clad hills that rise abruptly from the level meadowland of the Brue valley and culminate in the Tor (522 ft.), a green conical height crowned by the tower of St. Michael's church (c. 1400). Excavations on the hilltop in 1964-66 revealed remains of what was probably a 6th-century stronghold.

The Benedictine abbey of St. Mary (see below) was perhaps the oldest and certainly one of the richest in England. The chief buildings in the town, apart from the abbey ruins, are the churches of St. John the Baptist (c. 1470) and St. Benedict (c. 1520); the George hotel, built by the abbey to house pilgrims (c. 1470); the Abbey Tribunal, the abbot's law court (15th century); and the Abbey barn (14th century), a beautiful cruciform building still used as a barn. The town hall was built in the early 19th century and extended in 1930. Sharpham park, where the last abbot, Richard Whiting, was arrested in 1539 and where the novelist Henry Fielding was born in 1707, is now a farmhouse.

The Lake Villages.—The level meadowland running northwest from Glastonbury toward the Bristol channel was once a peat bog with winding watercourses, reedy pools and oak, willow and alder thickets. In 1892 low mounds in a field 1½ mi. N. of Glastonbury were found to contain remains of dwellings of the prehistoric Iron Age; these were excavated between that date and 1907 by A. Bulleid and H. St. George Gray, who began work in 1908 on two groups of similar mounds at Meare, 3¾ mi. N.W. of Glastonbury. At the Glastonbury lake village the peat has a depth of 15 ft. A substructure of timber and brushwood was laid and held in position by sharpened piles driven down into the peat, and on this foundation a floor of clay was spread and a hut, usually circular, built with a hearth of baked clay; these floors tended to sink in the soft peat and new floors and hearths were laid over them. Some huts had only one floor, but one had as many as ten.

At Meare some of the huts were built without the timber substructure, the peat being drier, and there are few traces of the postholes of circular huts, suggesting that many may have been of lighter construction. A few huts at Meare were built on a rectangular mortised framework, and fragments of similar timbers at Glastonbury suggest that rectangular huts preceded the round ones. The Glastonbury village was surrounded by a timber palisade, a feature not found at Meare.

The occupation of the villages dates from the 2nd or 1st century B.C. At Glastonbury it ended, possibly with a massacre, a few years before the Romans came; at Meare the village continued a few years longer and part of the site was reoccupied in the 4th century. Otherwise the pottery types found are similar in the lower and higher levels and in the Glastonbury and Meare villages.

The discovery of parts of wooden looms, loom weights, weaving combs and spindle whorls show that cloth was manufactured; the people were skilled workers in wood; their cutting tools were of iron. Many bronze objects were found, fibulae (of the La Tène III type), finger rings, brooches, harness parts and, at Glastonbury, a bowl of excellent design ornamented with rounded rivets. The discovery of similar rivets, crucibles and slag shows that this bowl was actually made in the village. Wheat, barley, peas and beans were grown and cattle, sheep, pigs, horses and dogs kept. Dugout canoes have been found and a broken axle shows that wheeled carts were used. Their trade goods included amber from the Baltic, jet from Whitby, Kimmeridge Shale for bracelets from Dorset and tin from Cornwall.

Pottery of the same types has been found in Wookey Hole cave and in excavating Ponters Ball, an earthwork protecting the high land at Glastonbury from the east. The objects from the Glastonbury village are exhibited in the Glastonbury museum, now in the Tribunal, and those from Meare at Taunton. Several timber causeways crossing the peat marsh have been located, some Neolithic and others of Bronze age or later.

The Benedictine Abbey of St. Mary.—William of Malmesbury wrote his De Antiquitate Glastoniensis Ecclesiae between the years 1125 and 1130, when he was staying at the abbey, basing his work on the documents and other evidence that he was able to study there. His book has been added to by later Glastonbury writers, but the original sections can be distinguished. He says that "annals of good authority" state that the old church of the Blessed Virgin was built by missionaries sent from Rome at the request of King Lucius, a legendary hero reputed to be the first Christian king in Britain, in A.D. 166; he would not commit himself to earlier stories of which he was aware. This church built of timber and wattles, and later enclosed in wood, was still in existence when William wrote; on either side of the altar were the tombs of St. Patrick and St. Indract. Other places claim the tomb of St. Patrick, but there is no doubt that there was a Celtic monastery with strong Irish associations at Glastonbury before the time of the Saxon conquest. Excavations between 1951 and 1959, under the direction of C. A. Ralegh Radford, have shown that there was a Roman settlement, presumably a villa, on the site of the abbey from the 1st to the 3rd century A.D. Almost certainly pre-Saxon are traces of a great bank and ditch that may have surrounded the monastery and, to the south of St. Mary's chapel, an extensive burial ground that once contained little timber and wattle buildings, probably chapels. At Beckery, on what was a small island in the marsh, excavations in 1887-88 and in 1967 exposed the foundations of a late medieval chapel and those of a Norman chapel within it, standing in a Christian cemetery of earlier but uncertain date; the name Beckery is Irish, meaning "Little Ireland."

The Anglo-Saxon Chronicle states that Ine, king of Wessex from 688 to 726, founded the abbey of Glastonbury. Apart from the evidence of a Celtic monastery on the site, the charters that William of Malmesbury was able to study confirm an earlier date than Ine. In 678 King Centwine granted the Island of Glastonbury to Hemgisl the abbot, free of all service, with six hides, and in 681 Baldred gave Hemgisl six hides on Pennard hill. These two grants made up Glaston XII hides, the manor and hundred in which later abbots established wide privileges. None of the early charters granting land to the abbey has survived in the original, and many are only known in much altered copies of the 13th century or later; nevertheless they tell a consistent story; no later grant of Glastonbury itself to the abbey is recorded.

Ine is said by William of Malmesbury to have built the church of St. Peter and St. Paul as an appendix to the old church. Excavations carried out between 1927 and 1929 by C. R. Peers and A. W. Clapham revealed the foundations of Ine's church and its later enlargements beneath the west end of the 13th-century nave. The proportions of the aisled plan correspond with churches at Canterbury, Rochester and Reculver built a few years earlier. At some date before the time of St. Dunstan (909-988) a narthex or porch was built joining Ine's church to the old church of St. Mary.

Dunstan was made abbot of Glastonbury by King Edmund about 943 and was chief minister of state under Edred; exiled in 955 by Edwig, he returned to power as archbishop of Canterbury under Edgar. He extended Ine's church eastward with a tower and chapels. The importance of the abbey at this time was shown by the burial there of three kings, Edmund the Magnificent, Edgar and Edmund Ironside.

As a result of the Norman conquest, Glastonbury abbey lost several estates, but Domesday Book shows that it remained one of the wealthiest churches in the country, holding rich manors in Somerset, Wiltshire, Dorset, Gloucestershire and Berkshire. Turstin (1078-1100), the first Norman abbot, was active in recovering lost properties and began rebuilding the church of St. Peter and St. Paul, but he fell foul of the monks, who refused to change their Gregorian chant in favour of new music attributed to Abbot William of Fécamp. Turstin called in archers who shot arrows from an upper gallery at monks clustered round the altar, killing 3 and wounding 18. The long and vivid account in the Anglo-Saxon Chronicle under the year 1083 shows how deeply the English resented this incident. Herlewin (1101-20) pulled down Turstin's partly built church and began afresh on a grander scale, but in 1184 a disastrous fire destroyed his church (molten lead from the roof was found between its reddened paving stones). With it were burned most of the monastic buildings, whatever was left of the Saxon church and the wattle church of St. Mary.

King Henry II appointed Robert Fitz Stephen to rebuild the abbey and a new chapel of St. Mary, of the same dimensions as the old church and on its site, was dedicated by Bishop Reginald of Bath in 1186. The contrast between the rich but archaic style of this building, with roundheaded windows and interlaced arcading, with Bishop Reginald's work then in progress at Wells, with pointed arches, may have been due to the venerable antiquity of the church it replaced. The rebuilding of the church of St. Peter and St. Paul on a vast scale, in a Gothic style that retained some features of Romanesque and in particular began before St. Mary's chapel was completed. In 1193 Savaric became bishop of Bath and Glastonbury; the monks refused obedience, and a costly struggle continued with varying fortunes. In 1205 Jocelin (Jocelin) succeeded him as bishop of Bath and Glastonbury and made a settlement with the monks in 1218; four manors were surrendered to the bishop, and the monks were allowed to choose an abbot. Building was resumed 20 years later, but the church of St. Peter and St. Paul was not completed for another 80 years. The galilee, linking the nave with St. Mary's chapel, was built before the end of the 13th century in a mature Early English style.

Abbot Monington (1342–74) extended the choir, built the retrochoir, using the chevron ornament over the windows to harmonize with the earlier work, and refaced the interior of the choir with paneling in stone (as at Gloucester, 1337–40). Abbot Richard Bere (1493–1525) built the Edgar chapel east of the retrochoir, and hollowed out a crypt under St. Mary's chapel and part of the galilee, probably to provide a shrine for St. Joseph of Arimathea; in so doing the floor of the chapel was raised.

Excavations south of the nave have revealed the foundations of the later monastic buildings and traces of buildings that preceded them, forming parts of the Saxon and Norman monasteries. The discovery of small glass furnaces of the 9th or 10th centuries shows a considerable glass industry in the monastery of that period. The abbot's lodging was pulled down in the 18th century, but the abbot's kitchen stands. Probably early 14th century, but based on the design of the Romanesque kitchen at Fontevrault-l'Abbaye in Anjou, W. France, it is square in plan with huge corner fireplaces making the square an octagon; the stone roof rises to a central louvered octagon containing a ventilating shaft.

Richard Whiting (abbot from 1525 till 1539) signed with his monks the declaration of royal supremacy in 1534. In 1539, however, he refused to surrender the abbey and was arrested and convicted of treason on a trumped-up charge of concealing the abbey treasure. He was executed on Tor hill with two monks; the abbey was forfeited to the king.

The annual value of the abbey estates in 1539 was £4,228. A comparison between the values in Domesday Book and in 1539 shows the extent to which the abbey had improved land drainage near Glastonbury. A process which began with straightening and deepening watercourses led to the deposit of flood soil over new areas and the conversion of peat bogs and alder thickets into rich meadows.

In 1550 the duke of Somerset installed a party of French and Flemish weavers in the abbey buildings, but as Protestant refugees they were forced to leave the country on Mary's accession. Her government considered restoring the monastery, but the difficulties were too great. From that time the abbey was used as a quarry for building and road stone; the beautiful ruins of St. Mary's chapel remain, with enough of the galilee and of the choir, nave and transepts of the church of St. Peter and St. Paul to give some idea of the whole. Since 1909 the abbey has been the property of the Church of England.

King Arthur and Avalon.—William of Malmesbury, who was fully aware of Glastonbury records and traditions as they were known in 1135, refers to the many fanciful tales told of King Arthur and adds that his burial place is unknown. His contemporary, Geoffrey of Monmouth, in his romantic *Historia Regum Britanniae*, describes Arthur's many victories. After the last he retired to Avalon (*q.v.*), the "Island of the Blest" of Celtic tradition, to cure his wounds. In 1191 a grave said to be that of Arthur and Guinevere, his queen, was discovered between two pyramids in the cemetery at Glastonbury; the bones were reinterred in the great church before the altar in the presence of Edward I. From that time the Isle of Avalon has been identified with Glastonbury and romances connecting Arthur and Glastonbury are still being written.

St. Joseph of Arimathea.—The saint was supposed to have brought the chalice of the Last Supper or, according to another tradition, phials holding blood of the Crucifixion (see GRAIL, THE HOLY). The earliest mention of the medieval legend that St. Joseph (*q.v.*) of Arimathea came to Glastonbury is in a mid-13th-century addition to William of Malmesbury's book. The story was fully told before the end of that century by John of Glastonbury, who quoted from a book called the *Holy Grail*. The monks, however, ignored the Grail legend but claimed possession of St. Joseph's cruet. The story connecting the Grail with Chalice well or the "blood spring," whose waters gave Glastonbury a brief period of fame as a spa after 1751, seems to have originated early in the 19th century. Chalice well (the name is derived from "Chalk" well) is in a garden, now in trust, in a valley below the Tor. A shrine in the crypt of St. Mary's chapel, which itself came to be known as St. Joseph's, was a place of pilgrimage where miracles are said to have occurred in the early 16th century. The Glastonbury thorn (*Crataegus monogyna praecox*), reputed to have blossomed miraculously at Christmas, is first mentioned in a poem of 1502; later a legend asserted that it sprang from the staff of St. Joseph. It is probably a perpetual sport from the common thorn obtained by grafting; trees raised from its seeds revert to type. The original thorn grew on Wyrral (Wearyall) hill outside the town where a new specimen has been planted.

The Town.—The name of Glastonbury has been the subject of speculation from Saxon times. A. G. C. Turner rejects previous theories and derives the name from Old Cornish *glastann*, "an oak."

The dissolution of the abbey left the town with few resources other than agriculture, a weekly market and an annual fair. Some stocking making and worsted and silk spinning struggled on into the 19th century. Then the improved drainage and enclosure of the common moors increased prosperity. The borough was incorporated in 1705. The chief local industries, apart from dairy farming, are dressing and dyeing wooled sheepskins and the manufacture of sheepskin rugs and coats and of sheepskin-lined boots and slippers.

BIBLIOGRAPHY.—Thomas Hearne (ed.), *Adami de Domerham Historia rebus gestis Glastoniensibus . . .*, 2 vol. (1727), which includes William of Malmesbury's *De Antiquitate Glastoniensis Ecclesiae*, *Johannis contrairis et monachi Glastoniensis chronica . . .*, 2 vol. (1726); R. Warner, *An History of the Abbey of Glaston and of the Town of Glastonbury Abbey* (1826); T. S. Holmes, *Wells and Glastonbury* (1866); R. Willis, *The Architectural History of Glaston-bury Abbey* (1866); T. S. Holmes, *Wells and Glastonbury* (1908); A. Bulleid and H. St. George Gray, *The Glastonbury Lake Village . . .*, 2 vol. (1911, 1917); *The Meare Lake Village . . .* (1948, 1955, 1967); J. A. Robinson, "William of Malmesbury 'On the Antiquity of Glaston-bury,'" in *Somerset Historical Essays* (1921), *Two Glastonbury Legends* (1926); F. Bligh Bond, *An Architectural Handbook of Glastonbury Abbey* (1926); Reports of excavations, etc., in the *Proceedings of the Somersetshire Archaeological and Natural History Society* and in *Somerset and Dorset Notes and Queries*.
(S. C. MD.)

GLATIGNY, JOSEPH ALBERT ALEXANDRE (1839–1873), French minor poet of the Parnassian school, whose adventures as journalist, playwright and strolling actor earned him a legendary reputation, was born at Lillebonne (Seine-Inférieure), May 21, 1839. He was apprenticed to a printer, but, inspired by reading Théodore de Banville's *Odes funambulesques*, began to write poetry. Verses written in 1857 were published as *Les Vignes folles* in 1860; later collections included *Les Flèches d'or* (1864) and *Gilles et Pasquins* (1872). Specializing in little poems of satirical comment on current affairs and personalities, he became a regular contributor to *Le Rappel*. For a time he exploited his talent for extempore composition by giving public recitals and then joined a traveling company of actors with whom he went to Corsica. There a misunderstanding with the police led to temporary imprisonment: he used his experiences in a one-act comedy in verse, *L'illustre Brizacier* (1873); the hero, a disillusioned actor, is a self-portrait. Other plays were *Le Singe* and *Les Folies-Marigny* (both 1872).

Glatigny died at Sèvres, April 16, 1873. His life formed the subject of a book and a play, *Glatigny, drame funambulesque* (1906), by Catulle Mendès.
(R. DL.)

GLAUBER, JOHANN RUDOLF (1604–1668), German

chemist, who because of his wide knowledge is sometimes called the German Boyle (father of chemistry). Born at Karlstadt, in Bavaria, he settled in Holland, where he made his living chiefly by the sale of secret chemical and medicinal preparations. Though his writings abound in universal solvents and other devices of the alchemists, he made many real contributions to chemical knowledge. He clearly described the preparation of hydrochloric acid by the action of sulfuric acid on common salt; he pointed out the manifold virtues of the residue, sodium sulfate—*sal mirabile*, Glauber's salt; and he noticed that nitric acid was formed when potassium nitrate was substituted for common salt. He prepared many substances, including salts of lead, tin, iron, zinc, copper, antimony and arsenic.

He also made a number of useful observations on dyeing and gave a clear description of the preparation of tartar emetic (antimony potassium tartrate). One of his most notable works was his *Teutschlands Wolfarth* in which he urged that the natural resources of Germany should be developed for the profit of the country, giving various instances of how this might be done. He died in Amsterdam on March 10, 1668. His more important works are contained in *Opera omnia*, which was reissued under the title *Glauberus concentratus* in 1715.

(R. E. O.)

GLAUCHAU, a town of Germany that, after partition of the nation following World War II, became a regional capital in the *Bezirk* of Karl-Marx-Stadt, German Democratic Republic. Pop. (1961 est.) 33,361. The town is about 19 mi. W. of Karl-Marx-Stadt (Chemnitz) on the Zwickauer Mulde. It is a railway junction and adjoins the industrial town of Meerane; it has many textile plants and machinery factories. North of the town, near Callenberg, are extensive deposits of nickel, the exploitation of which has been undertaken; the building of a nickel foundry southeast of Glauchau, near St. Egidien, was begun in 1955. The remains of a 12th-century castle are to be seen in Glauchau.

GLAUCOMA: see EYE, HUMAN: *Diseases of the Eye and Visual Disorders; Surgery of the Eye.*

GLAUCONITE is a green, fine-grained crystalline mineral, a hydrous silicate of iron and potassium found in marine sedimentary rocks of all geologic ages since the Pre-Cambrian, and still in process of formation. Glauconite occurs commonly as globular to lobate bright green grains or pellets a millimetre (0.03937 in.) or less in diameter. It may also occur as irregular grains or flakes, or as clay. It may be confused with the minerals chamosite, celadonite, chlorite and greenalite. Some glauconite has natural bleaching qualities and can be used as a fuller's earth (*q.v.*) and glauconite marls, because of their base-exchange properties, have been used in water-softening units (*see* MARL).

Glauconite is composed of clay minerals and the name has been used interchangeably both as a mineralogic and a morphologic term. It has been defined as a specific micaceous mineral, although it is commonly described as small green pellets of heterogeneous mineral content. It forms in waters of normal salinity on continental shelves, swells and banks off coasts of crystalline land areas that lack important rivers. It is not known to form in fresh water deposits. The formation takes place principally in the upper part of the 10- to 400-fathom interval. The temperature range of formation is apparently wide but markedly warm water is not favourable. Very slow or interrupted sedimentation in more or less agitated water, and at least slightly reducing conditions, which may be facilitated by decaying organic matter, are conducive to glauconite formation. Source materials are principally bottom muds and clays of terrigenous origin, although biotite, feldspars, volcanic glass and other materials may contribute. Under the necessary physiochemical environmental conditions, glauconitization occurs as a marine alteration of terrigenous matter to glauconite. Formation of glauconite from a colloidal state may also occur, as this process tends toward the same crystallochemical equilibrium as that obtained in the alteration of clay. Common coagulation of all these amorphous and cryptocrystalline products with selective absorption of potassium from the sea water leads to the formation of grains of glauconite.

Glauconite grains are common in calcareous sediments but rare in pure clay rocks, pure quartz sandstones or chemically precipi-

tated carbonates. Glauconite is commonly found associated with remains of fecal pellets of sediment-ingesting organisms or as internal fillings of foraminifera. It is rare or absent in beds rich in algae, corals or bryozoans.

Sediments rich in glauconite grains are known as greensand (*q.v.*).

(H. D. G.)

GLAUCOPHANE, a group of rock-forming minerals consisting of the iron-free sodium amphiboles (*see* AMPHIBOLE). The glaucophane group have all the characteristics of the rest of the amphiboles but are distinguished by their distinct blue colour, especially in thin slices.

Glaucophane occurs exclusively in certain metamorphic schists. These schists present a problem in petrology. They contain sodium-rich amphiboles which form in a rock not especially enriched in sodium. In short, the sodium is present in the amphiboles rather than in the plagioclase feldspars where it is usually concentrated (*see* FELDSPAR). Because of this peculiarity and because they are dense rocks and associated with other dense minerals, glaucophane schists have been thought to represent high pressure mineral assemblages. Other workers have shown that localized introduction of sodium, magnesium and iron into sedimentary rocks has caused the formation of glaucophane without the presence of relatively high pressures. Thus, glaucophane schists might form at high pressures and, on the other hand, might represent a peculiar sequence of sodium introduction into pre-existing mineral assemblages. Glaucophane schist is used by some writers as a separate metamorphic facies. Glaucophane schists are widely distributed over the coast range of California but are unusual elsewhere in the United States.

The members of the glaucophane group vary in composition from $Na_2Mg_3Al_2Si_8O_{22}(OH)_2$ to $Na_3Mg_3Al_2Si_8O_{22}O(OH)$ to $Na_2CaMg_3Al_2Si_8O_{22}O_2$.

(G. W. DEV.)

See also METAMORPHISM.

GLAUCUS ("gleaming") is the name of several figures in Greek mythology, the most important of whom are the following:

1. Glaucus, surnamed Pontius, a sea divinity. Originally a fisherman and diver of Anthedon in Boeotia, he ate a certain magical herb and leaped into the sea, where he was changed into a god and endowed with the gift of prophecy. Another story makes him spring into the sea for love of the sea god Melicertes, with whom he was often identified. He was worshipped in most parts of the Greek world by fishermen and sailors. In art he is depicted as a merman covered with shells and seaweed.

2. Glaucus, of Potniae near Thebes, son of Sisyphus by Merope and father of Bellerophon. According to one legend he fed his mares on human flesh and was torn to pieces by them.

3. Glaucus, the son of the Cretan king Minos and his wife Pasiphae. When a child, he fell into a jar of honey and was smothered. His father, after a vain search for him, consulted the oracle, and was referred to the person who should suggest the aptest comparison for one of his cows, which had the power of assuming three different colours. The seer Polyidus likened it to a mulberry (or bramble), which changes from white to red and then to black. Polyidus soon discovered the child, but on confessing his inability to restore him to life was shut up in a vault with the corpse. There he killed a serpent and, seeing it revived by a companion which laid a certain herb upon it, brought the dead Glaucus back to life with the same herb.

4. Glaucus, son of Hippolochus, grandson of Bellerophon, and great-grandson of Glaucus of Potniae, above. He was a Lycian prince who, along with his cousin Sarpedon, assisted Priam in the Trojan War. When he found himself opposed to Diomedes, his guest-friend, they ceased fighting and exchanged armour. Since the equipment of Glaucus was golden and that of Diomedes bronze, the expression "gold for bronze" (*Iliad*, vi, 236) came to be used proverbially for a bad exchange.

See Larousse Encyclopaedia of Mythology (1959).

GLAZE: *see* GLAZING; POTTERY AND PORCELAIN.

GLAZING. In its simplest context, glazing means the fitting of panes of glass into suitable frames in order to form a window which will admit light into a building. In the middle ages and up to the end of the 17th century this meant the use of leaded lights, small areas of glass fastened together with specially formed strips of lead ("calms") and held in a frame of wood or wrought iron. From the end of the 17th century until the end of the 19th century this principle was followed, but developing skill in the making of large sheets of glass saw a gradual increase in the size of the panes and window areas, while the leaded light was replaced by sashes of wood in which the glass was held with wood beads or putty. Until the end of the 19th century the architectural conception of a window was that of a comparatively small area of glazing placed in a thick load-bearing wall and restricted to the provision of daylight in a building, but the development of steel and reinforced concrete framing in the 20th century considerably altered this. In framed structures the loads of floors and roof are concentrated on to comparatively slender columns, thus leaving large areas of walling which can as well be filled by glazing as by the more traditional materials such as brick or stone. Further technical development in the glass industry provided the means to fill these large areas, so that glazing is not only concerned with the transmission of light into a building but can also provide the whole external surface.

Method.—The normal process of glazing small windows into wooden or metal frames has changed little. The tools generally used are the diamond for cutting, laths or straightedges and T square for accurate measurement and setting out, glazing knife, hacking knife and hammer. The materials used in addition to the glass are putty, priming or paint, glaziers' sprigs (small headless nails), wash leather or synthetic rubber strip. Putty is made of whiting and linseed oil and it should be stored so that it is kept moist and workable. Wood sashes must be primed before glazing, i.e., given a thin coat of paint usually containing red lead; this enables the putty to adhere to the sash. When each square of glass is cut to size, allowing about $\frac{1}{16}$ in. tolerance all round, the glazier with his hands runs the putty round the rebate in the frame into which the glass is to fit, pressing it firmly against the wood. He then beds the glass into it by pressing it down firmly on all the edges and the glass is further secured by the glaziers' sprigs, knocked in on the rebate side. He then trims off the protruding putty and fills the remainder of the rebate, bevelling it off on the outside of the sash with the putty knife. When a broken pane is to be replaced the hacking knife is employed to cut out the old putty and remaining broken glass. Metal sashes are glazed in a similar way, although the putty used is usually modified by the addition of a dryer to enable it to set satisfactorily, as there is no absorption of the oil by a metal sash. Proprietary glazing compounds are manufactured for this purpose also and some sashes incorporate spring clips and other devices for securing the glass. In glazed doors and sashes used internally the panes of glass are generally fixed with wood beads, held in place with screws. In doors subject to vibration or slamming the panels are usually bedded in wash leather or synthetic rubber strip and secured by wood beads.

Types of Glass.—For all common glazing in small sizes sheet glass is used. It is available in several qualities and thicknesses and in sizes depending on the thickness up to 80-100 in. length and width combined. For larger areas and for work where a high degree of transparency is required, polished plate glass is used. This can be supplied in very large sizes, but the practicable size for any particular job is governed more by problems of cutting, transporting and fixing than by manufacturing difficulties.

For work requiring specially strong glass, armour plate is used. This glass is specially toughened by heat treatment after cutting to size and is therefore supplied by the manufacturers ready for fixing and must not be subsequently cut. Where resistance to fire or danger of breaking makes ordinary glass a potential hazard, wired glass is used. A wire mesh is rolled into the glass during manufacture and even if large areas are shattered the glass adheres to the wire and is not broadcast. This makes it suitable for roof glazing and skylights, where generally the building regulations make its use obligatory. Prismatic glass, designed to refract light, is of use in increasing the light to rooms overshadowed by adjacent buildings. Antisun glass, which absorbs heat without reducing unduly the light transmission, is used in the glazing of schools, offices and airport control towers and where unusual climatic conditions make it especially suitable. An amber tinted antifly glass is an effective deterrent against houseflies and is therefore used for glazing the windows of buildings storing or manufacturing food.

Special Problems.—The design tendency for the elimination of the load-bearing wall in favour of a framed construction and the introduction of ever-larger window areas presents some special glazing problems. The highest standards of heat insulation are demanded in modern buildings to save both in cost of heating and in actual fuel consumption, but large areas of thin sheet or plate glass cannot satisfy these conditions because large windows mean high heat loss and consequent problems such as excessive condensation. The solution is the use of double glazing, in which two sheets of glass are fixed instead of one so that there is a confined space between them. This may be done either by fixing the two sheets of glass in one frame or by having each in a separate frame. The use of two windows in double glazing has been practised for many years particularly to improve sound insulation, but it is cumbersome and expensive. However, manufacturers are now offering factory-made double glazed window units, simply fixed into a single frame, which consist of two sheets of glass separated by a suitable spacer at the edges, usually metal or plastic strip. This unit is hermetically sealed against the external atmosphere, the cavity being filled with clean dry air at the time of sealing. Experiment has shown that an efficiency of 90% can be obtained if the space is as little as $\frac{1}{4}$ in. The smaller spacing is therefore generally used as the resulting unit is more easily accommodated in a sash of normal dimensions. The operation of assembly and sealing calls for skill and accuracy, so that such units made under factory conditions are relatively expensive, but the extra cost is soon offset by the saving in fuel consumption and there are a number of additional advantages such as the fact that condensation is eliminated, there is no "misting" of the glass and there is a significant reduction in sound transmission.

Where large areas are to be lighted, particularly in industrial buildings, it is usually necessary to provide areas of glazing in the roofs. Although it is not easy to measure the relative amount of light obtained from a unit of roof glazing as compared with the same area in a vertical plane, it is probably as much as three times. Almost all roof glazing, or patent glazing as it is more usually called, is of special design and patent manufacture. There is a wide range of types but basically the systems consist of a bar, usually of steel or aluminum of special section which incorporates fixing clips on the upper part to hold the glass and condensation channels at the bottom. Steel bars are usually covered with a thin lead sheathing to protect them against rusting. The bars are normally placed at about 2 ft. centres and spans up to about 10 ft. can be obtained without extra support. Special devices are incorporated in each design to ensure that the roof remains watertight in spite of widely varying atmospheric conditions and most systems can be fixed at any desired angle.

BIBLIOGRAPHY.—Raymond McGrath and A. C. Frost, *Glass in Architecture and Decoration* (1937); J. E. Gloag, *The Place of Glass in Building* (1943); E. Molloy, *Windows and Window Glazing* (1943).
(A. Rd.)

GLAZUNOV, ALEKSANDR KONSTANTINOVICH (1865-1936), the chief Russian symphonic composer of the generation after Tchaikovsky, was born at St. Petersburg on Aug. 10, 1865. His family had been book publishers for three generations. His mother, a piano pupil of Balakirev, took her obviously talented son to her teacher who nicknamed him "the little Glinka" and advised a course of study with Rimski-Korsakov. This began in 1880 and the following year the boy wrote his First Symphony, which was publicly performed by Balakirev early in 1882; it was, however, revised several times before the millionaire timber merchant M. P. Belyaev printed it in 1886 and thus began Belyaev's famous music-publishing firm, which Glazunov later helped to direct. By that time Glazunov had also written two string quartets, two overtures on Greek folk tunes and the symphonic poem *Stenka*

Razin. In 1886 he finished his Second Symphony. At this period he was the recognized heir of the great nationalist group and naturally composed in their styles; he also absorbed the influence of Liszt, whom he visited at Weimar in 1884. But other influences, notably Wagner's and Tchaikovsky's, later made themselves felt and Glazunov's music gradually deteriorated into a weak, though pleasant, eclecticism. Most of his best works—the Fourth, Fifth and *Les Saisons*—date from the 1890s. He finished his last complete symphony, the Eighth, in 1906 just after he had become director of the St. Petersburg conservatory, where he had been professor of orchestration since 1899. Glazunov, who became more and more involved in teaching and administration, wrote few large-scale works after 1906: two piano concertos (1911 and 1917), two string quartets (1920 and 1930) and a Concerto-Ballata for cello and orchestra (1931). After the Revolution Glazunov remained at his post until the summer of 1928, when, feeling completely isolated, he left Russia. After an unsuccessful concert tour in America in the winter of 1929–30 he made his home in Paris, where he died on March 21, 1936.

See M. O. Yankovski *et al.*, *A. K. Glazunov: Issledovaniya, materialy, publikatsii, pisma*, 2 vol. (1959–60); M. A. Ganina (ed.), *A. K. Glazunov: Pisma, statii, vospominaniya* (1958).
(G. Ab.)

GLEIG, GEORGE (1753–1840), Scottish churchman, bishop of Brechin (1808–40), and primus of the Episcopal Church of Scotland (1816–37). As fourth editor (1793–1801) of the *Encyclopaedia Britannica*, he wrote much of the two supplementary volumes (1801) to the third edition. He was born at his father's farm, Boghall, Arbuthnot, Kincardineshire, on May 12, 1753, entered King's College, Aberdeen, at the usual age of 13, and took holy orders in 1773. A contributor to reviews and magazines, he wrote for the third edition of the *Britannica*, then being edited by Colin Macfarquhar (*q.v.*). On Macfarquhar's death (1793) he was asked to edit the final volumes and the two supplementary volumes. His dedication to George III is remembered for its reference to the "French *Encyclopédie*" as "that pestiferous Work," and his advertisement in vol. ii of the Supplement for his disarming appraisal of his "labour and industry" as "great" notwithstanding that "perfection" seemed "to be incompatible with the nature" of encyclopaedic works. His admiration for Dr. Johnson, whose biography he wrote for the third edition, was sometimes reflected in his style: "For the omission of the life of Soame Jenyns," he wrote, "I can make no apology: it was the consequence of forgetfulness."

Though thrice elected bishop of Dunkeld, the opposition of one powerful bishop nullified the support of the other clergy, but election to Brechin was soon followed by elevation to primus. He spent much time in fostering a spirit of greater tolerance, and greatly improved relations with the Church of England. Forced to resign by ill health, he died at Stirling on March 9, 1840.

See also ENCYCLOPAEDIA: *Encyclopaedia Britannica.* (J. AE.)

GLENCOE, a glen in the north of Argyll, Scot., contains the river Coe or Cona, traditionally associated with Ossian, legendary Gaelic warrior and bard. Its name is probably derived from the Gaelic *gleann-cumhann*, "narrow glen." From a relatively low valley watershed and pass to Glen Etive at 1,011 ft. the glen runs eastwest for about 5 mi., straight-sided, with steep walls, heavily glaciated and about ½ mi. wide, amid glowering dark hills of andesite lavas, rising to 3,000 ft. or more; it then turns northwest as a rather broader glen amid softer hills and the river Coe enters the sea in Loch Leven at Invercoe near the slate-quarrying town of Ballachulish. The summits include on the south side Buachaille Etive, Bidean-nam-Bian (3,766 ft.), Meall Mor and Sgorr Dhearg (southwest of Ballachulish) while to the north are the Pap of Glencoe (only 2,430 ft. but a striking landmark) and the Devil's Staircase, a steep boulder-strewn path, strikes north for the river Leven and Fort William. Ossian's cave, by tradition his birthplace, is near Loch Triochatan midway along the glen. A motor road follows the glen, but it is almost without permanent human habitation. A few green patches in the valley bottom, grazed by sheep fed mostly on the rough pasture round, may mark what was once the arable land

of clansmen's townships. A Celtic cross erected by a Macdonald in 1884 recalls the tragedy of Feb. 13, 1692, when anti-Jacobite measures became involved in clan strife, being made the occasion of a treacherous massacre of many of the able-bodied men of the Macdonalds of Glencoe. The slaughter was decreed at the instigation of the earl of Breadalbane by soldiers under Campbell of Glenlyon (*see* BREADALBANE, JOHN CAMPBELL, 1st earl of). About 13,000 ac. in and around Glencoe belong to the Scottish National trust.
(A. T. A. L.)

GLENDALE, a city of Los Angeles county, at the southern extremity of the San Fernando valley in southwestern California, U.S., is 8 mi. N. of the civic centre in the city of Los Angeles.

The land known as Glendale was first taken in a private land grant by José María Verdugo in 1784 as the Rancho San Rafael. Portions of the old rancho still remain as Glendale city shrines. The Verdugo title to Rancho San Rafael was confirmed by Mexico and again by the new state of California. In 1869, after the owners' failure to pay a mortgage, the rancho was sold at public auction.

During the early 1880s, portions of the private holdings were pooled and a survey was ordered for a townsite, completed early in 1887. In March of that year, the town of Glendale was recognized by Los Angeles county. The name was chosen in 1884 from six others by local residents. Glendale absorbed much of the population influx of the 1880s into the Los Angeles basin. During the boom, several buildings were constructed, including a hotel and a newspaper plant. Although its 1910 population was only 2,700, it had grown to 75,000 by the outbreak of World War II. It is part of the Los Angeles standard metropolitan statistical area. The population of Glendale was 95,702 by 1950 and 132,752 in 1970.

Industries include the manufacture of airplanes and aircraft products, optical instruments, pharmaceuticals and clay and plastic products. Glendale (junior) college was established as a public school in 1927. Forest Lawn Memorial park is a cemetery publicized for its elaborate statuary (which includes reproductions of famous works of art) and other special attractions. Glendale was incorporated as a city in 1906 and in 1914 adopted the council-manager form of government. (J. M. Wo.)

GLENDALOUGH, VALE OF (GLEANN DA LOCHA), in County Wicklow, Republic of Ireland, is about 20 mi. W. of Wicklow town by road. There are frequent tours from Dublin along the road through the Wicklow mountains. The valley's monastic traditions date back to the 6th century, when St. Kevin (*q.v.*) settled there as a hermit. Though remote, Glendalough became the centre of a diocese until 1216, when it was united to Dublin. The series of churches scattered through the valley probably date from the 11th and 12th centuries, with earlier stone relics. Most of them have features of interest, such as fine Celtic carving; all are in ruins except for the small church known as St. Kevin's Kitchen, which has a splendid high-pitched roof of stone and a round belfry. Close by is the cathedral, 73 ft. long and 51 ft. wide; St. Kevin's cross (an 11 ft. high granite monolith); and the Round tower, 110 ft. high. Such towers, built as refuges from the Norse invaders, were entered by doorways at least 12 ft. from the ground. The Church of Our Lady is the legendary site of St. Kevin's grave. The original monks settled in a wild and desolate place, but one of majestic beauty. The valley has two lakes, with very limited farmland. Extensive areas on the valley sides are covered with woods, partly the natural oak-birch type and partly modern plantations supplied from a forest nursery between the two lakes. Visitors may be rowed across the upper lake, allegedly bottomless, to see a cleft in the rocks where St. Kevin may have spent many uncomfortable hours. (T. W. FR.)

GLENDOWER, OWEN (in Welsh, OWAIN GLYN DWR, OWAIN AP GRUFFYDD) (*c.* 1354–*c.* 1416), the last independent prince of Wales, was lord of Glyn Dyfrdwy and Sycharth in north Wales and also possessed lands in Cardiganshire. Owen's father, Gruffydd Vychan, represented the line of princes of Powys Fadog, and his mother, Helen, was descended from the royal house of Deheubarth. Little is known of his early career but he was educated at the Inns of Court in London. He married, *c.* 1383, Margaret, daughter of Sir David Hanmer of Maelor, and he fought in the Scottish campaign of 1385. In the political struggles of Richard II's reign, his sympathies were apparently with the king's opponents; he is said to have been sometime in the service of Richard, earl of Arundel, and also in that of Henry of Lancaster (later Henry IV).

Owen's rebellion, which began in Sept. 1400, resulted from a personal feud with his neighbour Reynold, Lord Grey of Ruthyn. The rebels are said to have proclaimed Owen prince of Wales, but the rising collapsed in north Wales after a defeat near Welshpool on Sept. 24. However the insurrection spread in 1401 to south Wales, where the king's campaign in October was largely ineffective, as were similar expeditions in the autumn of 1402 and 1403. Perhaps unwittingly, Owen had put himself at the head of a movement that became a Welsh national rebellion, provoked by the oppressiveness of English rule. Henry IV's many troubles, especially baronial disloyalty in England, explain Owen's triumphs in the next few years. He had the good fortune, in April 1402, to capture Lord Grey of Ruthyn; his ransom was 10,000 marks. Owen's victory at Bryn Glas, near Pilleth, in Radnorshire on June 22 gave him another notable prisoner, Sir Edmund Mortimer, whose nephew, the infant earl of March, was a potential claimant to the English throne.

In Nov. 1402 Mortimer came to terms with his captor and married Glendower's daughter Catherine. This alliance probably enabled Owen to make contact with the discontented Percies, the earl of Northumberland and his son Hotspur (Mortimer's brother-in-law). Serious reverses followed in 1403; in May Prince Henry ravaged Sycharth and Glyn Dyfrdwy unopposed, the Percy rebellion failed to overthrow Henry IV, and Hotspur was killed at the battle of Shrewsbury on July 21, ten days after Owen's defeat near Carmarthen. Despite these checks, 1404 marked the climax of his fortunes. The capture of Aberystwyth and Harlech castles gave him the status of a *de facto* ruler, controlling most of Wales between Anglesey and Glamorgan. Owen now formally styled himself prince of Wales, dating his reign from 1400. According to Adam of Usk, he summoned a "parliament" to meet at Machynlleth and concluded an alliance with Charles VI of France in July 1404. Ecclesiastically as well as politically, he was aiming at complete independence; the terms on which he was prepared to transfer allegiance to the Avignon pope, Benedict XIII, in 1406, included the establishment of a separate province of Wales, with St. David's as an archbishopric, and the founding of two Welsh universities.

The tide began to turn in the spring of 1405. The Welsh were defeated at Grosmont in March and at the disastrous battle of Pwll Melyn, near Usk, in May, when Owen's eldest son, Gruffydd, was captured. It was probably in Feb. 1405 that the alliance between Owen, Mortimer and the earl of Northumberland was embodied in the tripartite indenture, by which a partition of England was agreed. Archbishop Scrope's Yorkshire rebellion, the last serious threat to Henry IV's position, was put down in June, and Northumberland fled to Scotland. Thenceforth only foreign intervention could save Owen from ultimate defeat; a French force of a few thousand men landed at Milford Haven in Aug. 1405, and Owen was able temporarily to threaten Worcester. His French allies withdrew from Wales early in 1406. The reconquest of the principality was the achievement of the future Henry V, and the recovery of Aberystwyth and Harlech in 1408 destroyed the main basis of Owen's power. He was still active as a rebel as late as 1412, and he probably died in 1416. Owen had several sons and daughters, but, of his sons, only Maredudd appears to have survived his father. Glendower's rebellion was destructive in its consequences; but in modern times he has come to be regarded as a national hero.

BIBLIOGRAPHY.—Contemporary sources include *Chronicon Adae de Usk*, ed. by E. M. Thompson (1904); *Original Letters Illustrative of English History*, 2nd series, vol. i, ed. by Sir H. Ellis (1827). *See also* D. R. Phillips, *A Select Bibliography of Owen Glyndwr* (1915). For the Welsh church and Glendower's rebellion, *see* G. Williams, *The Welsh Church from Conquest to Reformation* (1962).
(T. B. P.)

GLENN, JOHN HERSCHEL, JR. (1921–), first U.S. astronaut to make an orbital space flight, was born July 18, 1921, in Cambridge, O. Commissioned in the U.S. Marine Corps in 1943, Glenn flew 59 missions during World War II and 90 during the

BY COURTESY OF SCHWEIZER AIRCRAFT CORP.

HIGH-PERFORMANCE, TWO-PLACE SAILPLANE

Korean War. Oldest of the seven astronauts selected in 1959 for Project "Mercury" space-flight training, he served as "back-up" pilot for Alan B. Shepard, Jr., and Virgil I. Grissom, who made the first U.S. suborbital flights. Glenn was selected for the orbital flight on Nov. 29, 1961, and on Feb. 20, 1962, his space capsule, "Friendship 7," lifted off and went into an orbit that ranged from approximately 100 to 162 mi. in altitude. He made three orbits in 4 hr. 55 min. at about 17,545 m.p.h., landing in the Atlantic near the Bahamas. In January 1965 he retired from the Marine Corps and subsequently entered private business.

GLIDING AND SOARING. Gliding, narrowly defined, is that phase of flight in which a bird or aircraft descends on an inclined path toward the ground. Soaring is the term applied to unpowered flight that uses the upward motion of the air or shifts of wind velocity with small changes in altitude to maintain or gain altitude. Soaring permits unpowered flight over long distances, at high altitudes and for extended periods of time.

When applied to the sport that has developed around motorless flight, the two terms become essentially synonymous. Thus, in Great Britain and most parts of the Commonwealth, the sport is called gliding, and the aircraft, a glider; in the United States the sport is called soaring, and the aircraft, a sailplane. A glider is a motorless, winged aircraft made for either gliding or soaring, and the term may include everything from troop-landing gliders of World War II to the most highly refined modern competition soaring plane. A sailplane is designed and built for soaring. (*See* AVIATION, HISTORY OF: *Prehistoric Period*.) Not until the mid-19th century did men seriously attempt to learn how to fly by using gliders rather than by trying to flap birdlike wings.

Important contributors to aviation before Otto Lilienthal (*q.v.*; 1848–1896) achieved predictable and controlled glider flights include Leonardo, closely succeeded by the mathematician Giovanni Battista Danti, who realized that to achieve flight, wings with an area proportionate to the combined weight of the pilot and the aircraft would be necessary. Giovanni Borelli (1608–1679) first realized that man's chest muscles were a very much smaller proportion of his total body weight than is the case with birds and concluded that man would never be able to achieve powered flight by flapping attached wings.

Early History.—A longing for human flight goes back to the times before history was recorded.

Vast steps forward were taken by Sir George Cayley (1773–1857), father of English aeronautics, who developed a scientific engineering view of aeronautics and by 1809 was studying airfoil sections. He realized the importance of streamlining and built a full-sized aircraft by 1850 and a man-carrying glider which flew and crashed in 1853. Between 1850 and 1880 Alphonse Pénaud and even identified and described slope lift, atmospheric waves, and thermal air currents. Louis Mouillard published *L'Empire de l'air* in 1881, a work that greatly inspired Otto Lilienthal and the Wright brothers, Orville and Wilbur.

Capt. Jean Marie le Bris, a French sailor, allegedly made a number of successful glides in the 1860s. In the late 1850s and during the 1860s he built gliders with wings shaped like those of an albatross and with bird-shaped bodies. He did not employ stabilizing tail surfaces, and it was more luck than scientific skill that permitted him to survive his experiments. John J. Montgomery, the first American to use gliding to study aerodynamics in flight, in 1883 is reported to have made a flight of 600 ft.

The most famous pioneer of gliding, Otto Lilienthal, with his brother Gustav, began to experiment in 1867. They did basic research on the buoyancy and resistance of air, and Otto investigated camber and wing sections and studied ways to increase the stability of the gliders he built, finally incorporating stabilizing tail surfaces on them. In 1891 he built his first man-carrying ship and established the era of the hang-glider. He would take off by running downhill into the wind. One of his first gliders weighed only 44 lb. Lilienthal even built a conical hill of earth 50 ft. high from which he could launch himself and his gliders no matter which way the wind was blowing. He established glider flight as practical and predictable; he made painstaking observations and recorded them. His name is memorialized in the Lilienthal Medal, the world's highest soaring award.

In 1896, at 64, Octave Chanute (*q.v.*), U.S. civil engineer, began making gliding flights. He discarded Lilienthal's method of securing control by stabilizing the tail surfaces and substituted a rudder and articulated wings. So stable did he make his gliders that they made 2,000 flights without a single accident. Chanute introduced the bridge-builder's Pratt truss (*see* TRUSS) to biplane glider structure. The Pratt truss consists of vertical struts combined with diagonal bracing wires and was used on all the Wright biplane gliders and the Wright "Flyer." The first Englishman to fly a glider was Percy Pilcher, a disciple of Otto Lilienthal, who began flying in 1895. He was interested in slope soaring and made successful slope-soaring flights, during some of which he actually gained altitude. Pilcher introduced wheels on his hang-glider, a contribution that saved many a crash landing when the pilot landed at speeds faster than he could run.

In 1900 Wilbur and Orville Wright first planned to construct a craft which could be used as a man-carrying kite in a sea breeze. For their flights they selected the Kill Devil sand hills near Kitty Hawk, N.C., which provided a reasonably steady onshore wind. Their first glider, although a biplane, differed in many respects from the Chanute glider. The pilot lay prone on the top surface of the lower wing to reduce air resistance. The vertical rudder was discarded, and the horizontal rudder was placed forward in front of the pilot. Lateral control was secured by warping the wings. Control wires were arranged in a manner which would twist the trailing outboard edge of one set of wings down while simultaneously twisting the trailing edge of the opposite wings upward, thus giving the effect of modern ailerons. The Wrights' most successful early glider was built in 1902. From previous experiments, they decided to use a vertical rudder and later made the rudder adjustable. In September and October nearly 1,000 flights were made, several of which covered distances of more than 600 ft. The great early achievement of the Wright brothers was in securing complete control by using a horizontal rudder (soon to be called the elevator), then combining an adjustable vertical rudder with the wing-warping mechanism. This perfect control made their gliding safe and allowed them to proceed to the building of the first successful powered plane. In 1911 the Wrights returned to gliding and soaring because Wilbur had made some studies of dynamic soaring and wished to test his theories. With more powerful controls, and with the elevator moved to the rear, the brothers made many long flights, one a remarkable slope-soaring flight of 9 min. 45 sec., which remained the world duration record until 1921.

In Germany, where sport soaring was born in 1909, an architect, Frederic Harth, in 1910 designed the first modern glider. Like the Wright brothers, he spent his effort designing a true aircraft, not an imitation bird. His glider was designed to use atmospheric power rather than motor power. In 1911, boys from the Darmstadt Technical High School camped and flew their gliders from the Wasserkuppe, a great round-sloped hill in the Rhön Mountains. That same year Hans Gutermuth glided 1,000 yd. in 1 min. 52 sec.

In 1920 the first postwar glider meeting at the Wasserkuppe was attended by the youthful Wolfgang Klemperer, Peter Riedel, and Wolf Hirth, who were to become soaring immortals. In 1921 the shape of the coming sailplane was introduced in the "Vampyr" of Arthur Martens, an aircraft more advanced than Klemperer's "Black Devil" of 1920 or "Blue Mouse" of 1921. The "Vampyr" was a high-wing monoplane with longer and more slender wings than the "Blue Mouse" and a cockpit fully enclosed except for the pilot's head. It had a sinking speed of only 2.6 ft. per sec. An understanding of streamlining and the advantages of the high aspect ratio wing were soon to come. In 1921, Frederic Harth increased the world duration record to 21 min. 30 sec. with true hill soaring, landing only 40 ft. below takeoff point.

In 1922, a dramatic year in world soaring history, hill soaring came to be widely understood and practised, and in August of that year Martens slope soared his "Vampyr" over the Wasserkuppe for 1 hr. 6 min., the first soaring flight ever to exceed an hour. The next day Heinrich Hentzen increased the record to 2 hr. 10 sec. and within a week had raised the record to 3 hr. 7 min., only to be beaten in October by A. Maneyrol of France during a contest at Itford, Eng., where the record was set at 3 hr. 21 min. In 1922 the first experimental gliding congress was held in France. Flying at Combergrasse, one pilot circled and gained altitude in a thermal air current, but this kind of lift was not yet understood or pursued.

In Germany after World War I, many factors contributed to the popularity of gliding: the Versailles Treaty limited construction of powered aircraft; meteorological conditions in the Rhön Mountains provided upcurrents favourable to soaring; and a number of pilots, aerodynamicists, and glider-builders all came together.

New Techniques and Records.—Until 1926 soaring was strictly topographical, using air currents deflected upward by hills, thus limiting the flights to the extent of the range of hills. An increased knowledge of meteorology gave rise to several methods of soaring by which long-distance flights could be made. Of these, thermal soaring and the use of thunderstorms were the most important early discoveries. Thermal currents are formed by heated air rising from the ground under such conditions as frequently exist on a hot summer afternoon. On reaching the cooler upper atmosphere, the moisture in the thermal current often condenses, forming a cumulus cloud which marks the thermal current. Soaring flights can be made by circling in this updraft. In time pilots learned the techniques of blind flying and were able to continue their spiral climb right into the cloud. Advanced pilots even attempted flying in the towering cumulonimbus clouds called thunderheads. Pilots learned frontal soaring, accomplished by keeping near the boundary or front between two masses of air in which the cold air mass wedges under and lifts the warm air, a condition often accompanied by thunderstorms.

In 1926 Max Kegel of Germany astonished the aeronautical world by flying 34 mi. in a thunderstorm, a happy accident which Kegel was lucky enough to survive (he made the flight without planning) in a sailplane built only for smooth-air flying. He had neither the instruments nor the experience necessary for blind flying in clouds. From 1926 to 1928, however, Robert Kronfeld explored and learned the complexities of thermal soaring under clouds, and on July 20, 1929, soaring up from the Wasserkuppe, he guided his sailplane under the leading edge of a thunderstorm which he rode for the record distance of 85.5 mi. In the same flight he established an altitude record of 7,525 ft. After 1929 constant refinement in the design of sailplanes and improved pilot techniques resulted in continually improved performances.

In the United States, interest in soaring was reawakened in 1928 when a group of German pilots came to the United States to set up a soaring camp on Cape Cod. They brought with them the first modern sailplane seen in the U.S., the "Darmstadt." In it they made a flight of four hours. Lieut. Ralph S. Barnaby, a young naval officer in this camp, became the first American to qualify for the newly established "C," soaring emblem. R. E. Franklin of the University of Michigan developed his Franklin PS-2 utility glider. Hawley Bowlus, well known in aviation circles for the major part he had had in building Charles A. Lindbergh's "Spirit of St. Louis," turned his attention in the late 1920s to designing and building modern sailplanes. In October 1929 the first motorless flight to exceed one hour in an American-built sailplane was made at Point Loma, Calif. By February 1930, the U.S. record had risen to more than nine hours, and within two months an unofficial world duration record of 15 hr. had been set in California. Wolfgang Klemperer had come to the U.S. With Jack O'Meara he explored the soaring possibilities in Elmira, N.Y. In 1930 the first U.S. National Soaring Contest was held there, and on Oct. 4 Wolf Hirth made the first long flight on dry thermals, covering 54 mi. without slope wind and without any clouds guiding him toward his thermals.

Before the early 1930s, a majority of soaring records were held by Germany and Austria with limited competition from other countries. Then, however, Great Britain, the U.S.S.R., the United States, France, and Poland all took an active interest in soaring, and records moved back and forth between countries with great rapidity. In 1932 the Soaring Society of America was established under the leadership of Warren E. Eaton to promote gliding and soaring in the U.S., bringing to an end the lethal days when the primary glider was ascendant, and untutored enthusiasm brought many fatalities and a bad repute to soaring in the U.S. In 1934 Richard du Pont brought the world distance record back to the United States for a short time, flying 158 mi. By 1937 soaring had become sufficiently international that the first world championship contest was held in Germany on the Wasserkuppe.

In Poland and, especially, in Russia during the late 1930s, flat country thermal soaring for distance was practised widely and competitively. On July 6, 1939, the world distance record was increased to 465.5 mi., the flight by Olga Klepikova being over the flat Russian steppes.

A flight of 21 hr. 34 min. by Lieut. William Cocke, Jr., established a new duration record in Hawaii in 1931. Although considered an unbreakable record at the time, it was exceeded many times in later years, the last official international duration record being made by a Frenchman, Charles Atger, in April 1952, a solo sailplane flight of 56 hr. 15 min. Later pilots were killed going to sleep while trying to exceed this record, and duration was eliminated as an official record category by the Fédération Aéronautique Internationale, the international controlling body of sporting aviation. In the summer of 1961, however, the Hungarian pilot Geza Vass and the American copilot Guy Davis flew a Pratt-Read sailplane over the Nuuanu Pali in Hawaii for 71 hr. 5 min.

World War II.—Troop-carrying gliders of World War II flew with as many as 130 men aboard. During the German attack on Belgium, the Netherlands, and Luxembourg in May 1940, the German Army, in order to take certain bridges and the Albert Canal in Belgium, used trains of gliders towed by transport planes, each containing six fully armed soldiers. The Ger-

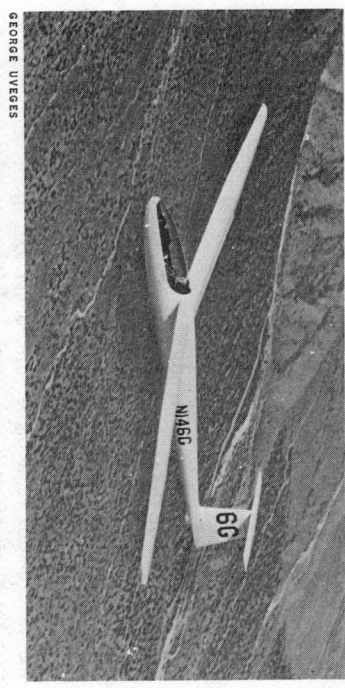

GEORGE UVEGES

FIBRE GLASS SAILPLANE, MADE IN SWITZERLAND

mans also used gliders to take Belgian forts, and brought fame to this method of landing troops during their conquest of the island of Crete in May 1941. During the Burma campaign, British Maj. Gen. Orde Wingate commanded a glider-supplied operation far behind the Japanese lines. In 1943 the U.S. landed combat troops in Sicily by gliders, and large numbers of men and an important number of light guns were landed in Normandy by gliders during the critical hours of the cross-channel invasion. One of the nearly perfect operations later in the war was using gliders for ferrying supplies and fresh troops across the Rhine River and bringing out wounded.

Research.—The sport of soaring was stimulated to improve performance by the return of technically trained students after World War II. During the late 1940s August Raspet, at Mississippi State College, made revolutionary contributions to the development of low-drag sailplanes by application of laminar-flow airfoils and advanced boundary layer control techniques.

From 1935 onward the sailplane had gained in reputation as a tool for meteorological and aeronautical research. Sailplanes equipped with radio and recording instruments were used in thunderstorm research sponsored by the United States Weather Bureau. Paul Tuntland, Wally Wiberg, and others flew heavily instrumented World War II training sailplanes into the core of thunderstorms to collect data on the strength and nature of cumulonimbus clouds. As a result of these studies, a project to study the airflow over the Sierra Nevada Mountains of California by means of sailplanes was sponsored by the U.S. Air Force in 1950–51, during which Lawrence Edgar and Harold Klieforth reached an altitude of 44,255 ft. above sea level and established two world altitude records: one for absolute altitude and one for altitude gained. This flight surpassed the single-place altitude record of William S. Ivans, who in December 1950 had climbed in a Schweizer 1–23 to 42,100 ft. above sea level in the Sierra Wave.

Modern Sailplanes and Records.—As soaring became a more widely practised international sport, progressively higher achievements were recognized with a series of emblems, the requirements for which were the same all over the world. In ascending order of difficulty, the emblems were called C, Silver C, Golden C, and Diamond C. One of the leading figures in U.S. soaring during the years just before World War II and immediately thereafter was John Robinson, who in 1950 became the first Diamond C pilot in the world.

Richard H. Johnson ushered in the era of modern soaring in 1951 with the first flight to exceed 500 mi., flying 535 mi. from Odessa, Tex., to Salina, Kan., in 8 hr. 40 min. In 1953 the Russian Victor Ilchenko and a passenger extended to 515.6 mi. the world distance record flight for a pilot with a passenger.

Modern sailplanes owe their high-performance characteristics to refined aerodynamic shapes, very accurately contoured, low-drag laminar-flow airfoil sections in wings of high aspect ratio (long, narrow wings) and the progressive reduction of drag-producing bumps such as wheels, landing skids, antennae, thermometers, and even towing mechanisms. Thus such planes are highly streamlined and "clean" aerodynamically. Wingspans are generally from 50 to 60 ft. with chord lengths at the wing root running from 3 to 4 ft. Early ships of wood and fabric in some instances gave way to welded steel tube fuselages with wing ribs of built-up wood construction and in other instances were replaced by plywood. During the mid-1960s, many high-performance European sailplanes were made of molded fibre glass, which is easy to form to the very close tolerances and aerodynamic shapes that involve compound curves.

The Schweizer Aircraft Corporation, which had made large contributions to the production of training gliders during World War II, developed all-aluminum sailplanes. Their sailplanes are noted for exceptional strength, and Schweizer has set the world standard for safety in the construction of sailplanes. In England after World War II, Slingsby Sailplanes became the most important English sailplane manufacturer. Philip A. Wills, who had begun soaring in 1932, emerged as a figure of international proportions, becoming the best-known soaring writer in the English-speaking world and one of the few pilots to be a world soaring champion, winner of the Lilienthal Medal, and holder of the Diamond C Emblem. Both in England and on the Continent after World War II, almost all soaring was done in factory-built sailplanes. Soaring in the U.S. developed with a strong similarity to the early days in Germany. Among the many important individual builders of sailplanes were Harland C. Ross, Richard E. Schreder, Leonard A. Niemi, and Irving O. Prue, all of whom designed and built sailplanes which set world records.

In 1956 Paul B. MacCready, Jr., became the first U.S. world soaring champion. In 1958 Ross, one of the discoverers of the famed Sierra Mountain Wave near Bishop, Calif., set three world multiplace triangular speed records in three consecutive days in a sailplane of his own design and construction. The following year Schreder won the Lilienthal Medal for setting three world triangular speed records in a sailplane he designed and built. In 1961 Paul F. Bikle made an altitude flight to 46,266 ft., setting the world single-place altitude record and altitude gained record for which he was awarded the Lilienthal Medal in 1962.

From the early 1950s, after the 535-mi. flight by Richard H. Johnson, the soaring world looked forward to the first 1,000 km. (622 mi.) flight as it seemed within reach of existing technical and meteorological knowledge. The first such flight was made on July 31, 1964, by Alvin H. Parker of Odessa, Tex., who flew an American Sisu 1-A from Odessa, Tex., to Kimball, Neb., the official distance being 647 mi. He was airborne more than 10 hr. He was awarded the Lilienthal Medal for the flight.

Controls and Instruments of gliders and sailplanes are similar in action to those of powered airplanes. Flight instruments most commonly fitted are the air speed indicator; a turn-and-bank indicator; an altimeter; and the variometer, a fast-acting and sensitive rate-of-climb indicator. The variometer is the one indispensable instrument for soaring. True sustained thermal soaring flight by humans was not possible until the variometer was invented and perfected. The reason is that the human ear, unlike the inner ear of a soaring bird, is not highly sensitive to slight reduction of air pressure and thus cannot immediately sense a gain of altitude. This deficiency is made up for by the variometer, invented by A. Lippisch and Robert Kronfeld in 1928 and continually refined since then.

Launching Techniques.—To fly, a glider must be accelerated to flying speed, the speed at which wings generate enough lift to overcome the force of gravity. In most of the early gliders flying speed was very low and normal practice was to fly into a wind, so the actual acceleration required was not great. Some kind of forward propulsion, or the force of gravity, or a combination of both was called upon to launch the aircraft.

By the mid-19th century a number of small gliders were actually flying, launched by hand. Sir George Cayley launched one of his passenger-carrying gliders by shoving it down a steep hill. Other gliders were pulled into the wind by ropes, and Captain Le Bris launched his "Albatross" from a farmer's cart. A coachman drove the specially rigged cart down a beach into the wind. During the hang-glider era the universal method of launch was to run down a windward slope while hanging in the wings. In 1920 Wolfgang Klemperer brought shock-cord or bungee launching into the world. Shock-cord launching works on the principle of a rubber slingshot. In the United States, automobile towing and the winch tow gained importance during the early 1930s. In auto tow a rope or cable from 500 to 2,000 ft. long connects the nose of the sailplane to a car. Upon acceleration, the aircraft rises much like a kite. In winch tow, the winch, generally driven by a powerful car engine, reels in towline from 40 to 70 mph, giving very fast takeoff and climb. Winch tow works like a gigantic fish reel in which the sailplane is the fish. Either of these launching methods can work on windless days.

The modern launching technique is the airplane tow in which a sailplane is actually towed into the air by a powered plane. Normally the towrope used is 200 ft. long with a steel ring attached at each end, one fitting the towhook of the towing aircraft, the other attached to the sailplane's towhook. After World War II airplane tow eclipsed all other forms of towing in the U.S. It reduces the strain put on sailplanes during launch, and has the great advantage that rising or sinking air is dramatically shown to the sailplane pilot by the relative position of the towplane while the tow is actually going on.

Once launched, the pilot must immediately search for a rising air current if he wishes to soar. Updrafts may be found along the windward slopes of hills and mountains; beneath and within cumulus clouds; in clear-air dry thermals, the base of which is often indicated by a whirlwind or "dust devil" in-arid country; along a cold front; in a shearline formed by the convergence of two air masses; or in mountain lee waves. Great distance flights are sometimes achieved by using several types of upcurrents.

BIBLIOGRAPHY.—Philip A. Wills, *On Being a Bird*, 2nd ed. (1953); Ann and Lorne Welch and Frank Irving, *New Soaring Pilot* (1968); Ann and Lorne Welch, *The Story of Gliding* (1965); Derek Piggott, *Gliding: a Handbook on Soaring Flight* (1958); C. E. Wallington, *Meteorology for Glider Pilots* (1961); Joseph C. Lincoln, *Soaring for Diamonds*, 2nd ed. (1967); *Soaring*, journal of The Soaring Society of America (1937–).   (J. C. Li.)

GLINKA, KONSTANTIN DIMITRIEVICH (1867–1927), Russian soil scientist whose work had a tremendous influence throughout the world, was born in Smolensk in August 1867. While working for a degree in geology at the universities of Moscow and St. Petersburg, he became a student of V. V. Dokuchaiev, the founder of modern soil science (pedology). For the next 18 years he served as lecturer and professor at the Novo-Alexandria Institute. In 1911 he returned to St. Petersburg and developed the first course in soil science there. Between 1908 and 1914 Glinka organized more than 100 soil-survey parties. He directed the soil survey of Siberia and of a part of European Russia, and published about 123 scientific books and papers.

Although the general theory of soils as independent natural bodies had been proposed by Dokuchaiev and developed further by N. Sibirtsev, it was Glinka who organized the subject. His textbook, *Soil Science*, was first published in 1908 and went through three subsequent editions. Because of the language barrier, few outside Russia read it. A German version, *Die Typen der Bodenbildung, ihre Klassifikation und geographische Verbreitung*, was published in 1914, and Curtis F. Marbut's English translation appeared as *The Great Soil Groups of the World and Their Development*, 2nd ed. (1937).

Glinka's influence reached its climax just before his death when he took an active part in the First International Congress of Soil Science held in the U.S. in 1927. Glinka died on Nov. 2, 1927.   (Ch. E. K.)

GLINKA, MIKHAIL IVANOVICH (1804–1857), the first Russian composer to win international recognition and the acknowledged founder of the Russian national school, was born in the village of Novospasskoe (Smolensk government) on June 1, 1804. He was 10 or 11 years old before his interest in music was aroused by his uncle's private orchestra. From 1817 to 1822 he studied at the Chief Pedagogic institute at St. Petersburg, also taking piano lessons from John Field and Charles Mayer. From 1824 to 1828 he served in the ministry of communications, but was too indolent and unambitious for an official career. As a dilettante he composed songs and a certain amount of chamber music. Three years in Italy brought him under the spell of Bellini and Donizetti,

BY COURTESY OF SCHWEIZER AIRCRAFT CORP.

TRAINING GLIDER BEING TOWED ALOFT BY A POWERED PLANE

though ultimately "homesickness gradually led me to the idea of writing music in Russian."

First he studied composition seriously for six months with Siegfried Dehn in Berlin, where he began a *Sinfonia per l'orchestra sopra due motive russe* (1834). Recalled to Russia by his father's death, he married and settled down to the composition of the opera that first won him fame, *Life for the Tsar* (originally named, and since the Revolution re-named, *Ivan Susanin*); this was produced at St. Petersburg on Dec. 9, 1836, in the presence of the tsar. A month later he was appointed master of the Imperial chapel, though he resigned this post in 1839. At this period Glinka composed some of his best songs and in 1840 the music to N. V. Kukolnik's play *Prince Kholmsky*. In 1842, on the sixth anniversary of *Life for the Tsar*, his second opera, *Ruslan and Lyudmila*, was produced; the fantastic-oriental subject and often boldly original music of *Ruslan* won neither imperial favour nor popularity, though Liszt was at once struck by the novelty of the music.

Disgruntled, and with his marriage broken though not finally dissolved, Glinka left Russia in 1844 and consoled himself with a succession of mistresses. He had the satisfaction of hearing excerpts from both his operas performed in Paris under Berlioz (March 16, 1845—the first performance of Russian music in the west) and others. From Paris he went to Spain, where he stayed for two years (until May 1847) collecting the materials used in his two "Spanish overtures," the *Capriccio brillante on the Jota aragonesa* (1845) and *Summer Night in Madrid* (1848). Glinka returned to Russia for a short period but spent most of his time until Oct. 1851 in Warsaw, where he wrote *Kamarinskaya*, an orchestral piece on two Russian folk tunes (1848). Between 1852 and 1854 he was again abroad, mostly in Paris, until the outbreak of the Crimean War drove him home again. He then wrote his highly entertaining memoirs (first published in St. Petersburg, 1887), musical, social and amorous, which give a remarkable unconscious self-portrait of his indolent, amiable, hypochondriacal character. His last notable composition was *Festival Polonaise* for Alexander II's coronation ball (1855). After the war he decided to study Bach and "the old church modes" with Dehn in Berlin, and in that city he died on Feb. 15, 1857.

Glinka may be fairly described as a dilettante of genius. His work, small in bulk, is the foundation of practically all later Russian music of any value. *Life for the Tsar*, Italianate as some of it is, showed how music could be written "in Russian"; *Ruslan* provided models, not only in its oriental and "fantastic" conventions (whole-tone scale, etc.) but also in lyrical melody and colourful, transparent harmony and orchestration, on which Balakirev, Borodin and Rimski-Korsakov formed their styles. Tchaikovsky, who preferred the earlier of the two operas, wrote that "the whole oak is in the acorn." Likewise the clear, brilliant scoring of the "Spanish overtures" provided the basis of Rimski-Korsakov's orchestral technique.

BIBLIOGRAPHY.—M. D. Calvocoressi, *Glinka* (1913); A. V. Ossovski (ed.), *M. I. Glinka: Issledovaniya i materialy* (1950) and *M. I. Glinka, Literaturnoe nasledie*, 2 vol. (1952–53); V. Protopopov *et al.*, *Pamyati Glinki (1857–1957): Issledovaniya i materialy* (1958); B. Dobrokhotov *et al.*, *M. I. Glinka: Sbornik Statei* (1958). (G. AB.)

GLIWICE (Ger. GLEIWITZ), a town of southern Poland, the district capital of the Katowice województwo (voivodship). Pop. (1961) 134,900. Gliwice forms part of the urban group and is one of the oldest towns of the Upper Silesian industrial region, and is a junction on the Wrocław (Breslau)-Cracow railway line. It has an inland port and dock installations on the Gliwice canal, which links the Silesian coal basin via the Oder river with the Baltic sea. The development of Gliwice as an industrial centre started at the end of the 18th century with iron casting and a foundry. Nearby deposits of coal suitable for coking facilitated the development of the coke and chemical industries, and there are a number of heavy industries and food factories. The town has a college of engineering (opened 1945) and two theatres. From 1312 Gliwice (chartered in 1276) was the capital of the Gliwice principality, which along with other Silesian principalities became a vassal of Bohemia, from which it passed to the kingdom of Prussia with most of Silesia. In 1742 it was incorporated in the kingdom of Prussia. After World War I and the partition of Silesia (1921) it remained German. About 30% of the town was destroyed in World War II, after which it returned to Poland. (K. M. WI.)

GLOBEFLOWER, any plant of the genus *Trollius* of the family Ranunculaceae (*q.v.*), of which there are about 15 species in northern regions. They take their name from the globelike shape of the flower. There are several North American and more Eurasian species, including the American globeflower (*T. laxus*), native to eastern North America, and the common European globeflower (*T. europaeus*). The latter is often cultivated, especially in several of its horticultural forms, one of which has orange flowers though most species are yellow. Also cultivated is the handsome *T. ledebouri* from Siberia, often two to three feet high. (N. TR.)

GLOCKENSPIEL, a percussion instrument of definite musical pitch consisting of steel bars of varying lengths. The glockenspiel was originally a set of graduated bells; later, steel bars, arranged chromatically in two rows on a frame, were substituted. The compass is from 2½ to 3 octaves; the music is written two octaves lower than the notes heard. The keys are struck with small hammers of wood or ebonite; occasionally metal hammers are used. A glockenspiel with a keyboard mechanism is used when chords are to be played, as, for example, in Mozart's *Magic Flute*. The glockenspiel is used with great effect in Handel's *Saul*; in "The Bell Song" from Delibes' *Lakmé*; in Tchaikovsky's *Nutcracker Suite*; in *Die Walküre* and *Die Meistersinger von Nürnberg* by Wagner; by Elgar in *The Dream of Gerontius*. A lyre-shaped glockenspiel is used in military bands. (J. BL.)

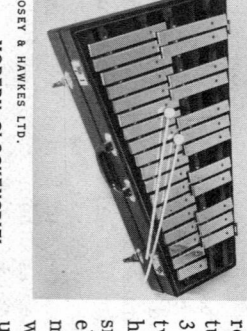

BOOSEY & HAWKES LTD.

MODERN GLOCKENSPIEL

GLOMMA (GLÅMA), a river in the eastern part of south Norway. Its sources are small lakes close to the Norwegian-Swedish frontier southeast of Trondheim, and streams from these drain into Lake Aursunden at 689 m. (2,260 ft.) above sea level. Below this lake the river is known as the Glomma. It flows southward through the Österdal valley to Kongsvinger where it turns westward for a few miles, then southwest into Lake Öyeren (103 m. or 338 ft.); it then continues southward to Sarpsborg and empties into the Skagerrak at Fredrikstad on the eastern side of Oslo fjord. Its total length is 365 mi. The biggest tributaries in Österdal are the Folla, Atna and Åsta from the west, the Rena and Flisa from the east, but its important tributary is the Vorma from the north, between Kongsvinger and Öyeren. The Vorma is the outlet of Lake Mjösa, fed by the river Lågen. The total catchment area of the Glomma is 16,236 sq.mi. The waterfalls of the river are low and where they are exploited for hydroelectric production several are usually dammed together to make a larger fall. Flumes (artificial channels) have been constructed as bypasses at falls and power plants. The available water power is about 700,000 kw.; more than 30 power plants have an aggregate installation of 410,000 kw. Flood disasters have often caused damage to houses and farmland along the river, especially in the flat valley north of Kongsvinger, but the banks have now been strengthened. Glomma is navigable for ships up to Sarpsborg. About 12,000,000 timber logs are floated yearly on the Glomma. The timber logs are floated yearly on the Glomma. (L. H. HG.)

GLORIA, in general a doxology or ascription of praise, specifically two ancient Latin hymns *Gloria in excelsis* and *Gloria Patri*. See DOXOLOGY.

GLORIOSA, a small genus of tuberous rooted plants of the lily family (Liliaceae; *q.v.*), natives of tropical Asia and Africa. They have slender stems that climb by tendrillike prolongations of the narrow generally lance-shaped leaves. The flowers, which are borne in the upper leaf-axils, are very handsome; the six, generally narrow, mostly red and yellow petals are bent back and stand erect, the six stamens projecting beyond them. They are grown as greenhouse plants or outdoors in summer and often called climbing-lily or glory-lily.

GLORY, in works of art, is a general term for any radiance or light appearing around the body of a holy person, such as a nimbus, halo, aureole, *mandorla* or *vesica piscis*. Its purpose is to represent spiritual character through the symbolism of light. The sun disk was used in ancient Egypt to symbolize a divine being's specific relation to the sun. In Hellenistic and Roman art the sun-god and emperors appear with a crown of rays. Because of its pagan origin, this form was avoided in early Christian art. By the 5th century, however, a disk-shaped form behind the head, called a nimbus or halo, was fully accepted. Originally reserved for Christ and the Virgin, the nimbus was soon used for the Aristae saints also. A cross within a round nimbus became identified with representations of Christ in the middle ages. The triangular nimbus symbolized the Trinity. For some time, in the 5th century, living persons of eminence were equipped with a square nimbus; the memory of this custom is preserved in the academic mortarboard.

The aureole consists of a large circular or oval (from which the Italian name *mandorla*, "almond") area representing illumination around the figure. Frequently a nimbus was added. The aureole appeared only toward the end of the Romanesque period, probably inspired by the light symbolism of the Apocalypse. Its greatest artistic realization was reached in the 16th century when the abstract shape of the *mandorla* had changed into a more naturalistic representation of a radiating light (*e.g.*, Grunewald, "Ascension," Colmar; Raphael, "Liberation of St. Peter," Vatican).

In its development from the middle ages to the baroque the nimbus underwent a fuller artistic evolution than the aureole. Originally it appeared as a disk behind the head of the holy person. In Florentine painting of the Renaissance the disk began to be shown in perspective, following the movements of the figure. Increasingly, the nimbus became a material object and lost its spiritual quality (*e.g.*, angel in F. Cossa's "Annunciation," Dresden).

Another form of the nimbus became popular in Netherlandish painting of the 15th century. It consisted of a representation of light rays emanating from the head of the holy person (*e.g.*, the Van Eyck altarpiece at Ghent). In this form the historic character of the nimbus as a symbolic light was recovered. A new idea was expressed by the German painters of the early 16th century who gave to the nimbus the character of a real light (*e.g.*, A. Dürer's engraving of "St. Jerome"). But it was only with Tintoretto in the middle of the 16th century that all these ideas were combined in one new form. The nimbus was now represented as a supernatural light emanating from the head of the holy person. This new interpretation was the standard form in the baroque period (*e.g.*, Rembrandt, "Christ at Emmaus," Louvre).

The nimbus as well as the aureole is also found in the Buddhist art of India. Their earliest date of appearance is the late 3rd century B.C. and it is likely that these ideas were originally brought to India by the Greek invaders.

See Joseph Wilpert, *Die römischen Mosaiken und Malereien der kirchlichen Bauten vom 4.–13. Jh.* (1917). (P. M. L.)

GLOSS AND GLOSSARY. The Greek word *glossa*, meaning originally a tongue, then a language or dialect, gradually came to denote any obsolete, foreign, provincial, technical or otherwise peculiar word or use of a word.

In late classical and medieval Latin, *glosa* was the vulgar and Romanic, *glossa* the learned form. The diminutive *glossula* occurs in Diomedes and elsewhere. The same meaning is borne by *glossarium*, which also occurs in the modern sense of "glossary," as do the words *glossa*, *glossae*, *glossulae*, *glossemata*, expressed in later times by *dictionarium*, *dictionarius*, *vocabularium*, *vocabularius* (*see* DICTIONARY). *Glossa* and *glossema* are synonyms, signifying (1) the word which requires explanation; or (2) such a word (called *lemma*) together with the interpretation (*interpretamentum*); or (3) the interpretation alone.

Early History.—The making of collections and explanations of such *glossai* was at a comparatively early date a well-recognized form of literary activity. Even in the 5th century B.C., among the many writings of Abdera was included a treatise entitled *Peri Homerou e orthoepeies kai glosseon*. It was not, however, until the Alexandrian period that the *glossographoi*, glossographers (writers of glosses), or glossators, became numerous.

Of many of these perhaps even the names have perished; but Athenaeus the grammarian (*c.* A.D. 250) alone alludes to no fewer than 35. Among the earliest was Philetas of Cos (d. *c.* 290 B.C.), the elegiac poet, who was the compiler of a lexicographical work entitled *Atakta* or *Glossai* (sometimes *Ataktoi glossai*). Next came his disciple Zenodotus of Ephesus (early 3rd century B.C.), the compiler of *Glossai Homerikai* (uncommon words in Homer); he was succeeded by his greater pupil, Aristophanes of Byzantium (*c.* 260–180 B.C.), whose great compilation, *Peri Lexeon* (still partially preserved in that of Pollux), is known to have included *Attikai lexeis*, *Lakonikai glossai*, and the like. From the school of Aristophanes issued more than one glossographer of name—Diodorus, Nicander of Colophon (*Glossai*, of which some 26 fragments survive) and Aristarchus (*c.* 210 B.C.), the famous critic, whose numerous labours included an arrangement of the Homeric vocabulary (*lexeis*) in the order of the books. Contemporary with the last named was Crates of Mallus, who, besides making several new contributions to Greek lexicography and dialectology, was the first to create at Rome a taste for similar investigations in connection with the Latin idioms. From his school proceeded Zenodotus of Mallus, the compiler of *Ethnikai lexeis* or *glossai*, a work said to have been designed chiefly to support the views of the school of Pergamum as to the allegorical interpretation of Homer.

Of later date were Didymus Chalcenterus (*c.* 63 B.C.–A.D. 10), who made collections of *lexeis tragodoumenai komikai*, etc.; Apollonius Sophista (*c.* 20 B.C.), whose Homeric *Lexicon* has come down to modern times; and Neoptolemus, known distinctively as *o glossographos*. In the beginning of the 1st century of the Christian era Apion, a grammarian and rhetorician at Rome during the reigns of Tiberius and Claudius, followed up the labours of Aristarchus and other predecessors with *glossai Homerikai*, and a treatise *Peri tes Rhomaikes dialektou*; Heliodorus, or Herodorus, was another almost contemporary glossographer; Erotian also, during the reign of Nero, prepared a special glossary for the writings of Hippocrates. To this period also Pamphilus, the author of the *Leimon*, from which Diogenianus and Julius Vestinus afterward drew so largely, most probably belonged. In the following century one of the most prominent workers in this department of literature was Aelius Herodianus, whose treatise *Peri monereus lexeos* has been edited in modern times, and whose *Epimerismoi* survives in an abridgment; also Pollux, Diogenianus (*Lexeis pantodape*), Julius Vestinus (*Epitome ton Pamphilou glosson*) and especially Phrynichus, who flourished toward the close of the 2nd century, and whose *Eclogae nominum et verborum Atticorum* has frequently been edited.

To the 4th century belong Ammonius of Alexandria (*c.* 389), who wrote *Peri homoion, kai diaphoron lexeon*, a dictionary of words used in senses different from those employed by older and approved writers; Hesychius, whose *Lexikon* has come down only in a 15th-century recension. From the 5th century date Cyril, the basis of *Synagoge lexeon chresimon*; Orus of Miletus (*Peri polysemanton lexeon*), and Orion of Egyptian Thebes who flourished in Alexandria, *c.* 425.

Compilations of Justinian.—To a special category of technical glossaries belong a large and important class of works relating to the law—compilations of Justinian. Although the emperor forbade under severe penalties all commentaries (*hypomnemata*) on his legislation, yet indexes (*indikes*) and references (*paratitla*), as well as translations (*hermeneiai kata poda*) and paraphrases (*hermeneiai eis platos*), were expressly permitted, and lavishly produced. Among the numerous compilers of alphabetically arranged *lexeis Rhomaikai* or *Lateinikai*, and *glossae nomikae*, Cyril and Philoxenus are particularly noted; but the authors of *paragraphai* or *semeioseis*, whether *exothen* or *esothen keimenai*, are too numerous to mention. A collection of these *paragraphai ton palaion*, combined with *neai paragraphai* on the revised code called *ta basilika*, was made about the middle of the 12th century by a disciple of Michael Hagiotheodorita. The collection of these glossaries is known as the *Glossa ordinaria ton basilikon*.

Latin.—In Italy, also, during the period of Byzantine ascendancy, and later, after the extinction of Byzantine sway in the West, various glossae (*glossae*) and scholia on the Justinian code and various legal treatises were produced. The series of legal glossators was closed by Accursius (1182-1260) with the compilation known as the *Glossa ordinaria* or *magistralis*, the authority of which soon became very great. For some account of the glossators on the canon law, see CANON LAW. (*See also* GLOSSATORS, LEGAL.)

Latin glossography, like Greek, had its origin chiefly in the practical wants of students and teachers, of whose names we only know a few. No doubt even in classical times collections of glosses (glossaries) were compiled, to which allusion seems to be made by Varro and Verrius-Festus. The *scriptores glossematorum* were distinguished from the learned glossographers like Aurelius Opilius, Servius Clodius, Aelius Stilo and L. Ateius Philologus, whose *liber glossematorum* Festus mentions.

Verrius Flaccus (who died under Tiberius), and his epitomists, Festus and Paulus, have preserved many treasures of early glossographers no longer extant. He copied Aelius Stilo, Aurelius Opilius, Ateius Philologus and others. *De verborum significatu*, the treatise *De obscuris Catonis*. He often made use of Varro and was also acquainted with later glossographers. Perhaps the *glossae asbestos* may be ascribed to him. Festus was used by Pseudo-Philoxenus (*see* below).

Bilingual Glossaries.—The bilingual (Gr.-Lat., Lat.-Gr.) glossaries also point to an early period, and were used by the grammarians (1) to explain the peculiarities (*idiomata*) of the Latin language by comparison with the Greek; and (2) for instruction in the two languages. The most important remains of bilingual glossaries are two well-known lexica; one (Latin-Greek), formerly attributed, but wrongly, to Philoxenus (consul A.D. 525), clearly consists of two closely allied glossaries (containing glosses to Latin authors, such as Horace, Cicero, Juvenal, Virgil, the Jurists, and excerpts from Festus), worked into one by some Greek grammarian, or a person who worked under Greek influence (his alphabet runs A, B, G, D, E, etc.); the other (Greek-Latin) is ascribed to Cyril (Stephanus says it was found at the end of some of his writings), and is considered to be a compilation of not later than the 6th century. Furthermore, the bilingual medico-botanic glossaries had their origin in old lists of plants, as Pseudo-Apuleius in the treatise *De herbarum virtutibus*, and Pseudo-Dioscorides; the glossary, entitled *Hermeneumata*, printed from the *Cod. Vatic. reg. Christ.* 1260, contains names of diseases. Somewhat similar are names of animals in Polemius Silvius.

Of Latin glossaries of the first five or six centuries of the Roman emperors few traces are left, if Verrius-Festus is excepted. Of this early period we know by name only Fulgentius and Placidus. All that is known of these tends to show that he lived in north Africa in the 6th century, from whence his glosses came to Spain, and were used by Isidore and the compiler of the *Liber glossarum* (*see* below). These glosses are known from (1) *Codices Romani* (15th and 16th centuries); (2) the *Liber glossarum*; (3) the *Cod. Paris. nov. acquis.* 1298 (11th century), a collection of glossaries, in which the Placidus-glosses are kept separate from the others. (Fabius Planciades) Fulgentius (c. A.D. 468-533) wrote *Expositio sermonum antiquorum* in 62 paragraphs, each containing a lemma (sometimes two or three) with an explanation giving quotations and names of authors. Next to him come the *glossae Nonianae*, which arose from the contents of the various paragraphs in Nonius Marcellus' work being written in the margin without the words of the text; these epitomized glosses were alphabetized and afterward copied for other collections. In a similar way arose the *glossae Eucherii* or *glossae spiritales secundum Eucherium episcopum* found in many manuscripts, which are an alphabetical extract from the *formulae spiritalis intelligentiae* of St. Eucherius, bishop of Lyons, c. 434-450. The so-called *Malberg glosses*, found in various texts of the *Lex Salica*, are not glosses in the ordinary sense of the word, but precious remains of the parent of the present literary Dutch, namely, the Low German dialect spoken by the Salian Franks who conquered Gaul from the Romans at the end of the 5th century. The antiquity and the philological importance of these glosses may be realized from the fact that the Latin translation of the *Lex Salica* probably dates from the early 6th century. (*See* J. Grimm's preface to J. Merkel's edition [1850],

and H. Kern's notes to J. H. Hessels's edition [1880] of the *Lex Salica*.)

The Middle Ages.—During the 6th, 7th and 8th centuries glossography developed in various ways; old glossaries were worked up into new forms, or amalgamated with more recent ones. It ceased, moreover, to be exclusively Latin-Latin, and interpretations in Germanic (Old High German, Anglo-Saxon) and Romanic dialects took the place of or were used side by side with earlier Latin ones. Among Celtic glosses the most important are Old Irish, and of these Bishop Cormac's and O'Davoren's have been edited by Whitley Stokes, the former also by Kuno Meyer. The origin and development of the extant late classic and medieval glossaries can be traced with certainty. While reading the manuscript texts of classical authors, the Bible or early Christian and profane writers, students and teachers, on meeting with any obscure or out-of-the-way words, which they considered difficult to remember or to require elucidation, wrote above them, or in the margins, interpretations or explanations in more easy or better-known words. The interpretations written above the line are called interlinear, those written in the margins of the manuscripts marginal glosses. Again, manuscripts of the Bible were often provided with interlinear literal translations.

Types of Glossaries.—1. From these glossed manuscripts and interlinear versions glossaries were compiled; that is, the obscure and difficult Latin words, together with the interpretations, were excerpted and collected in separate lists, in the order in which they appeared in the manuscripts, with the names of the authors or the titles of the books whence they were taken or placed at the head of each separate collection. In this arrangement each article by itself is called a gloss; when reference is made only to the word explained it is called a gloss, while the explanation is termed the *interpretamentum*. In most cases the form of the lemma was retained just as it stood in its source, and explained by a single word, so that lemmata appear in the accusative, dative and genitive, explained by words in the same cases; the forms of verbs were treated in the same way. Of this first stage in the making of glossaries, many traces are preserved in the late 8th century *Leyden Glossary*, where chapter iii contains words or glosses excerpted from the *Life of St. Martin* by Sulpicius Severus; ch. iv, v and xxxv glosses from Rufinus, and so forth.

2. By a second operation the glosses came to be arranged in alphabetical order according to the first letter of the lemma, but still retained in separate chapters. Of this second stage the *Leyden Glossary* contains traces also.

3. The third operation collected all the accessible glosses in alphabetical order, in the first instance according to the first letters of the lemmata. Here the names of the authors or the titles could no longer be preserved, and consequently the sources of the glosses became uncertain.

4. A fourth arrangement collected the glosses according to the first two letters of the lemmata, as in the *Corpus Glossary* and in the still earlier *Cod. Vat.* 3321 (Goetz, *Corp.* iv, I sqq.), where even many attempts were made to arrange them according to the first three letters of the alphabet. A peculiar arrangement is seen in the *Glossae affatim* (Goetz, *Corp.* iv, 471 sqq.), where all words are alphabetized, first according to the initial letter of the word and then further according to the first vowel in the word (a, e, i, o, u).

No date or period can be assigned to any of the above stages or arrangements. For instance, the first and second are both found in the *Leyden Glossary* (end of 8th century) whereas the *Corpus Glossary* (beginning of 8th century) represents already the fourth stage. For the purpose of identification titles have been given to the various nameless collections of glosses, derived partly from their first lemma, partly from other characteristics, as *glossae abstrusae*; *glossae abavus major and minor*; g. *affatim*; g. *ab absens*; g. *abactor*; g. *Abba Pater*; g. *a, a*; g. *Vergilianae*; g. *nominum*; g. *Sangallenses*.

A chief landmark in glossography is represented by the *Origines* (*Etymologiae*) of Isidore (d. 636), an encyclopaedia in which he, like Cassiodorus, mixed human and divine subjects together, and the etymological part of which (book x) became a great mine for later glossographers. His principal sources are Servius, the fathers of the church, and Donatus. Next comes the *Liber glossarum*, chiefly compiled from Isidore, but with all articles arranged alphabetically; its author lived in Spain c. A.D. 690–750; he has been called Ansileubus, but this name may be merely that of some owner of a copy of the book. Here come, in regard to time, some Latin glossaries already largely mixed with Germanic, more especially Anglo-Saxon interpretations: (1) the *Corpus Glossary* (eds. J. H. Hessels, W. M. Lindsay), of the beginning of the 8th century, in Corpus Christi college, Cambridge; (2) the *Leyden Glossary* (end of 8th century, ed. J. H. Hessels, Plac. Glogger), in Leyden manuscript Voss. Q° Lat. 69; (3) the *Epinal Glossary*, written in the beginning of the 9th century and published in facsimile by the London Philol. Society from the manuscript at Epinal; (4) the *Glossae Amplonianae*, i.e., three glossaries preserved in the Amplonian library at Erfurt, known as Erfurt[1], Erfurt[2], and Erfurt[3], which are arranged alphabetically according to the first or the first two letters of the lemmata.

The first great glossary or collection of various glosses and glossaries is that of Salomon, bishop of Constance, who died A.D. 919. An edition of it was printed c. 1475 at Augsburg as *Salemonis ecclesie Constantiensis episcopi glosse ex illustrissimis collecte auctoribus*. Its sources are the *Liber glossarum*, the glossary preserved in the 9th-century manuscript *Lat Monac.* 14429, and the *Abavus major Gloss*. The *Liber glossarum* has also been the chief source for the important (but not original) glossary of Papias, of A.D. 1053, who also wrote a grammar chiefly compiled from Priscian. It is also the source of (1) the *Abba Pater Glossary*, published by G. M. Thomas (*Sitz. Ber. Akad. Münch.*, 1868, ii, 369 sqq.); (2) the Greek glossary *Absida lucida*; and (3) the Lat.-Arab. glossary in the *Cod. Leid. Scal. Orient.* No. 231 (published by Seybold in *Semit. Studien*, Heft xv–xvii, 1900). The *Paulus-Glossary* is compiled from the second *Salomon-Glossary* (*abacti magistratus*), the *Abavus major* and the *Liber glossarum*, with a mixture of Hebraica. (Goetz enumerates 103 manuscripts of this treatise).

Osbern of Gloucester (c. 1123–1200) compiled the glossary entitled *Panormia* (ed. Angelo Mai as *Thesaurus novus Latinitatis*, from *Cod. Vatic. reg. Christ.* 1392), giving derivations, etymologies, testimonia collected from Paulus, Priscian, Plautus, Horace, Virgil, Ovid, Mart. Capella, Macrobius, Ambrose, Sidonius, Prudentius, Josephus, Jerome, etc. Osbern's material was also used by Hugucio, whose compendium was still more extensively used

The great work of Johannes de Janua, entitled *Summa quae vocatur catholicon*, dates from the year 1286, and mostly uses Hugucio and Papias; its classical quotations are limited, except from Horace; it quotes the Vulgate by preference; it excerpts Priscianus, Donatus, Isidore, the fathers of the church; it borrows many Hebrew glosses, especially from Jerome; it mentions the *Graecismus* of Eberhardus Bethuniensis, the works of Rabanus Maurus, the *Doctrinale* of Alexander de Villa Dei, and the *Aurora* of Petrus de Riga.

The gloss manuscripts of the 9th and 10th centuries are numerous, but a diminution becomes visible toward the 11th. A peculiar feature of the late middle ages are the medico-botanical glossaries based on earlier ones. The additions consisted in Arabic words with Latin explanations, while Greek, Latin, Hebrew and Arabic interchange with English, French, Italian and German forms. Glossaries of this kind are (1) the *Glossae alphita*; (2) *Sinonoma Bartholomei*, of the end of the 14th century, ed. J. L. G. Mowat; (3) the compilations of Simon de Janua (*Clavis sanationis*, end of 13th century), and of Matthaeus Silvaticus (*Pandectae medicinae*, 14th century).

There are many biblical glossaries, mostly mixed with glosses on other, even profane, subjects, as Hebrew and other biblical proper names, and explanations of the text of the Vulgate in general, and the prologues of Hieronymus. There is the *Glossae veteris ac novi testamenti* (beginning "Prologus graece latine praelocutio sive praefatio") in numerous manuscripts of the 9th to 14th centuries, mostly retaining the various books under separate headings. Special mention should be made of Guil. Brito, who lived about 1250, and compiled a *Summa* (beginning "difficiles studeo partes quas Biblia gestat pandere") which gave rise to the *Mammotrectus* of J. Marchesinus, about 1300, of which there are editions of 1470, etc. *See also* DICTIONARY.

Modern History.—The modern historical interest in glosses and glossaries began with J. Scaliger (1540–1609), who in his edition of Festus made great use of Ps.-Philoxenus, which enabled O. Müller, the later editor of Festus, to follow in his footsteps. Scaliger also planned the publication of a *Corpus glossarum*, and left behind a collection of glosses known as *glossae Isidori*. The study of glosses was greatly furthered through the publication, in 1573, of the bilingual glossaries by Henri Stephanus (Estienne). In 1600 Bonav. Vulcanius republished the same glossaries, adding (1) the *glossae Isidori*, which now appeared for the first time; (2) the *Onomasticon*; (3) *notae* and *castigationes*, derived from Scaliger. In 1606 Carolus and Petrus Labbaeus published, with the help of Scaliger, another collection of glossaries, republished, in 1679, by Du Cange, after which the 17th and 18th centuries produced no further glossaries, though glosses were constantly used or referred to by scholars at Leyden, where a rich collection of glossaries had been obtained by the acquisition of the Vossius library. In the 19th century came Osann's *Glossarii Latini specimen* (1826); the glossographical publications of Angelo Mai (*Classici auctores*, vol. iii, vi, vii, viii, 1831–36, containing Osbern's *Panormia*, Placidus and various glosses from Vatican manuscripts); Fr. Oehler's treatise (1847) on the *Codex Amplonianus* of Osbern, and his edition of the three Erfurt glossaries, so important for Anglo-Saxon philology; in 1854 G. F. Hildebrand's *Glossarium Latinum* (an extract from *Abavus minor*), preserved in a Cod. Paris. lat. 7690; in 1857, Thomas Wright's vol. of Anglo-Saxon glosses, which were republished with others in 1884 by R. Paul Wülcker under the title *Anglo-Saxon and Old English Vocabularies*; L. Diefenbach's supplement to Du Cange, entitled *Glossarium Latino-Germanicum mediae et infimae aetatis*; Ritschl's treatise (1870) on Placidus, which called forth an edition (1875) of Placidus by Deuerling; G. Loewe's *Prodomus Corporis Glossariorum Latinorum* (1876), and other treatises by him, published after his death by G. Goetz (1884); in 1885, H. Sweet, Latin-Anglo-Saxon glossaries in *Oldest English Texts*; in 1890, J. H. Hessels, apograph of the *Corpus Glossary*, 1906 the *Leyden Glossary*, and in 1900, Arthur S. Napier, *Old English Glosses*, collected chiefly from Aldhelm manuscripts. Goetz's own great *Corpus glossariorum Latinorum*, appeared in seven volumes between 1888 and 1923, the last two being separately entitled *Thesaurus glossarum emendatarum*, containing many emendations and corrections of earlier glossaries by the author and other scholars. In the 20th century appeared W. M. Lindsay's *Corpus Glossary* and *The Corpus, Epinal, Erfurt, and Leyden Glossaries*, both in 1921, and his *Palaeographia Latina*, in 1922. W. M. Lindsay, with the collaboration of J. Whatmough, J. F. Mountford, J. H. Thomson *et al.*, edited *Glossaria Latina* (four volumes) in 1926–1930 for the British Academy.

BIBLIOGRAPHY.—Among encyclopaedic articles the chief are J. Tolkien's article "Lexicographie" and G. Goetz's article "Lateinische Glossographie", in Pauly-Wissowa, *Real-Encyclopädie der classischen Altertumswissenschaft*. Comparable to Goetz's *Corpus* is the great collection of Steinmeyer and Sievers, *Die althochdeutschen Glossen*, 4 vol. (1879–98), containing a vast number of glosses culled from Bible manuscripts and manuscripts of classical Christian authors. See also many important articles in *Anglia*, *Englische Studien*, *Archiv f. latein. Lexicographie*, *Romania*, *Zeitschr. für deutsches Alterthum*, *Journal of English and Germanic Philology*, *American Journal of Philology*, *Classical Review*. On glossai see J. Whatmough, *Poetic, Scientific, and Other Forms of Discourse*, ch. 4 (1957); J. Whatmough, and J. H. Thomson, *Ancient Lore in Mediaeval Latin Glossaries* (1921) is an important guide to the problem of gloss derivation. Modern writers on dialects commonly extract relevant items, *e.g.*, F. Bechtel, *Die griechischen Dialekte*, 3 vol. (1921–24); J. Whatmough, *Dialects of Ancient Gaul* (1949–51).
(J. H. HES.; C. T. O.; J. WH.)

GLOSSATORS, LEGAL. The current methods of the glossators (*see* GLOSS AND GLOSSARY) were applied during the 11th century, particularly in Pavia and Ravenna, to the interpretation of Roman legal texts, but the age of the legal glossators really began with the revival of the study of Roman law at Bologna at the end of the century. Irnerius, originally a teacher of the free arts, was urged by the countess Matilda to study law in Rome. Later he returned to his native Bologna, and there became a teacher of law. The discovery of an almost complete manuscript of Justinian's *Digest* (or *Pandects*) at Pisa gave a strong impetus to the revived study of Roman law. One of the first tasks of the school of legal glossators which Irnerius founded was a reconstruction of the *Digest* by a comparison with other existing manuscripts.

Among the most distinguished successors of Irnerius were the "four doctors"—Bulgarus (q.v.), Martinus Gosia, Hugo de Porta Ravennate and Jacobus de Boragine—who lived in the time of Frederick Barbarossa; Placentinus, who introduced the writings and methods of the glossators to France; Vacarius (q.v.), who founded a school of law in Oxford; Joannes Bassianus, pupil of Bulgarus and master of Azo; Azo (q.v.), notable in England for the use made of his work in the writings of Bracton; and finally Azo's pupil Franciscus Accursius, the last of the glossators, for many years a professor at Bologna, who died in 1260.

The legal glossators were not content with mere interlineation and explanation of words in the texts. Their explanatory notes were also written in the margins and included references to parallel passages in other parts of Justinian's *Corpus Juris*—indeed, the usefulness of this aspect of their work for the study of Roman law still survives. Texts were analyzed and compared in order to discover how far they supported or supplemented each other, and attempts were made to reconcile contradictions. The glossators thus did the spadework for subsequent generations by sifting and co-ordinating the available legal material.

From this stage they proceeded to a deeper analysis by means of two principal methods. (1) Distinctions. This method, previously used in the Pavia school, consisted in the analysis of a general term or concept into divisions and subdivisions down to the most minute details of differentiation. (2) Summaries. The practice of making a summary of the contents of texts was common to all glossators. In the hands of the legal glossators these *summae* (nicknamed *brocardica*) became coherent statements of legal rules which, collected together in large compilations, paved the way for the legal textbooks of later centuries.

In the middle of the 13th century Accursius undertook the task of collecting and arranging the vast number of annotations made by his predecessors in one complete work. This compilation, supplemented by the annotations of Accursius himself, has the title of the *Glossa ordinaria* or *magistralis*, but is usually known as the Great Gloss or more simply as The Gloss. For nearly a century its authority was no less than that of the original Roman texts.

The glossators laid the foundation for the study of Roman law in Europe at a time when increasing commercial relations between individuals and between states were soon to necessitate an advanced legal system. Whether they were concerned with these trends or even with the current legal needs of their day is open to doubt. Their discussions tended to be academic and were carried to an extreme refinement of ingenuity. They regarded the Holy Roman empire as the successor of the old Roman empire and themselves as the successors of the jurists of Justinian's *Digest*. They were concerned with the scientific explanation of the texts before them, not with the earlier history of those texts; they looked neither forward nor backward. Yet the society in which they lived compelled their attention to the political implications of several of the rules which they found in the Roman texts. It is probable that they leaned toward the concept of a strong central governmental authority. It was the task of their successors, the postglossators (sometimes called commentators), to effect a closer liaison between the revived Roman law, the law of the Italian cities and the practical legal necessities of their day.

The influence of the glossators spread beyond Italy. Many students were attracted to the Bologna school, from which lawyers went out into the governments and courts of Europe. Their work affected both the processes and the substance of legal thinking for many centuries.
(Rl. P.)

GLOSSOP, an industrial town and municipal borough (1866) in the High Peak parliamentary division of Derbyshire, Eng., 14 mi. E.S.E. of Manchester. Pop. (1971 prelim.) 24,147. It is a centre of cotton manufacture in Derbyshire and has also woolen and paper mills, dye, print and bleaching works. It is situated near the northwestern boundary of Derbyshire, being built on the foothills which lead to Kinder Scout, the highest point of the Peak district (q.v.), and is surrounded on three sides by the Peak District National park. Although it is an industrial town, mostly stone built, its unique position as the natural gateway to the Peak makes it also a residential area. Glossop hall, formerly the seat of Lord Howard, lord of the manor, was acquired by the corporation and houses Kingsmoor mixed boarding school. On a hill near the town is Melandra castle, the site of a Roman fort guarding Longdendale and the way into the Peak district. To the north, in Longdendale, there are five reservoirs belonging to the water-supply system of Manchester.

GLOUCESTER, GILBERT DE CLARE, 6TH EARL OF (1243–1295), and 6th earl of Hertford, was born on Sept. 2, 1243, son of Richard, 5th earl, and of Maud de Lacy. He married in infancy Alice de Lusignan, niece of Henry III, and succeeded his father in July 1262 while still a minor. Resenting Henry's refusal of immediate seizin, he joined the rebel barons (1263) and decisively helped the victory of Simon de Montfort at Lewes (May 14, 1264), becoming one of the triumvirate which controlled the government. In Feb. 1265 he quarreled with Montfort, plotted the way to Edward's escape from Hereford in May and contributed decisively to Edward's victory at Evesham on Aug. 4, gaining hugely in the subsequent royalist scramble for the rebels' lands. Dissatisfied with Henry's treatment of disinherited rebels, Gloucester seized London (April 1267) and compelled Henry to implement the negotiated *Dictum de Kenilworth*. He did not join Edward's crusade (1270–73) but co-operated loyally with Edward's lieutenants when Henry died.

The greatest of marcher lords, Gloucester built Caerphilly, the first concentric castle in Wales, to guard Gwent and Glamorgan from Llywelyn's aggression (1268–71). While commanding Edward's forces in south Wales during David's sudden revolt in 1282, he was badly defeated at Llandeilo and was superseded; but he helped to suppress Rhys ap Maredudd's revolt in 1287. After divorcing Alice, he married Edward I's daughter, Joan of Acre (April 30, 1290), surrendering all his lands to Edward and receiving them back entailed to his and Joan's descendants. Defying Edward's recent prohibition of private warfare in the marches, Gilbert attacked Humphrey de Bohun, earl of Hereford (1290); Edward imprisoned and deprived both earls, restoring them immediately on payment of heavy fines. Gloucester suppressed a local Welsh rebellion in 1294–95. He died at Monmouth on Dec. 7, 1295.

BIBLIOGRAPHY.—F. M. Powicke, *Henry III and the Lord Edward*, 2 vol. (1947), *The Thirteenth Century, 1216–1307* (1953); T. E. Morris, *The Welsh Wars of Edward I* (1901). (R. F. T.)

GLOUCESTER, HUMPHREY, DUKE OF (1390–1447), the fourth son of Henry IV and Mary de Bohun (d. 1394), was born in 1390. He was created duke of Gloucester by his brother Henry V on May 16, 1414. In the invasion of France in 1415 he commanded the artillery at the siege of Harfleur; he showed rash courage at Agincourt, where he was wounded, and he owed his life to the king's valour. Humphrey served in the later campaigns in Normandy from 1417 until Jan. 1420, when he returned home. He held office as the king's lieutenant in England until Henry V's return in Feb. 1421, and again from May to Sept. 1422 during the king's last absence in France.

In accordance with Henry V's will, Gloucester claimed the regency of England on behalf of the infant Henry VI. In parliament in Dec. 1422 the office of lord protector was created, which, in the absence of John, duke of Bedford (see BEDFORD, EARLS AND DUKES OF), was held by Gloucester. His marriage, probably in 1423, with Jacoba (q.v.), countess of Holland and Hainault, had serious repercussions on Bedford's policy in France. This marriage was annulled in 1428 and Gloucester was then able to marry his mistress, Eleanor Cobham. Soon after returning to England from his invasion of Hainault in April 1425, he had a violent quarrel with his uncle, Henry Beaufort, bishop of Winchester and later cardinal, who, as chancellor, was the king's chief minister. Civil war was averted only by the hurried return from France of Bedford, who staged a formal reconciliation in the Leicester parliament (March 1426). Gloucester's lord protectorship was terminated by Henry VI's coronation on Nov. 6, 1429, but during the king's visit to France (April 1430–Feb. 1432) he acted as his representative in England. The death of Bedford on Sept. 14, 1435, made Gloucester heir to the throne, and he won popularity as a leader of the war party when Philip of Burgundy made a separate peace with the French, but his attack on Flanders in 1436 had little result. After cardinal Beaufort's influence was predominant; the ineffectiveness of Gloucester's protest against the release of the duc d'Orléans in 1440 shows that he was powerless. In 1441 his wife, Eleanor Cobham, was condemned for practising sorcery against the king and was imprisoned for life. The replacement of Beaufort by William de la Pole, earl of Suffolk, as the king's chief adviser in 1443 led eventually to Gloucester's own ruin. On arriving at Bury St. Edmunds to attend parliament on Feb. 18, 1447, he was arrested. He died on Feb. 23; the popular belief that he had been murdered was voiced in Jack Cade's rebellion in 1450.

Gloucester's political career was a failure; his ability was mediocre and he was ambitious, self-seeking and unscrupulous. He is best remembered as the first notable English patron of humanism. Among the Italian scholars sometime in his service were Pier Candido Decembrio, Leonardo Aretino, Antonio di Beccaria and Titus Livius, who was commissioned to write a life of Henry V. English men of letters befriended by Gloucester included John Whethamstead, abbot of St. Albans; Thomas Bekynton; John Capgrave the historian; John Lydgate; and Gilbert Kymer, who was the duke's physician. He presented a large part of his great collection of books to Oxford university and contributed toward the cost of building the room called Duke Humphrey's library. His books are said to have been dispersed at the Reformation and only 3 of about 270 volumes he gave still remain in the Bodleian library. His liberal patronage of scholars and learning and the unpopularity of his reputed murderers gave rise to the legend of "good Duke Humphrey."

BIBLIOGRAPHY.—K. H. Vickers, *Humphrey, Duke of Gloucester* (1907); J. S. Roskell, *The Commons in the Parliament of 1422* (1954); R. Weiss, *Humanism in England,* 2nd ed. (1957). For contemporary sources, *see* C. L. Kingsford, *English Historical Literature in the Fifteenth Century* (1913). (T. B. P.)

GLOUCESTER, ROBERT, EARL OF (c. 1090–1147), the main supporter of Matilda in the civil war with King Stephen, was a bastard son of Henry I of England. His father married him to Maud (Mabel), daughter and heiress of Robert FitzHamon, lord of Gloucester and Glamorgan, fiefs which included respectively the rich town of Bristol and the castle of Cardiff; in 1122 his great position was recognized by a grant of the earldom of Gloucester. Present at Henry I's death in Dec. 1135, he probably favoured the claim to the English throne of his half-sister Matilda, wife of Geoffrey, count of Anjou, in accordance with his father's wishes. But after Easter 1136 he made a cautious and conditional homage to Stephen, count of Boulogne. In 1137 he quarrelled with Stephen and came out openly as a leader of Matilda's party. He took her to England in Sept. 1139 and at the head of her forces won from Stephen most of western England and south Wales. The zenith of his career was reached in 1141. In February he captured Stephen at Lincoln and imprisoned him at Bristol, and in June he accompanied Matilda to Westminster for her coronation, which was prevented, however, by the hostility of the Londoners. In the fighting connected with the siege of Winchester that followed Matilda's retreat from London, Robert was captured, and after hard bargaining was exchanged for the king. He was the mainstay of the Angevin cause in England till his death on Oct. 31, 1147. Contemporary chroniclers agree in calling him able and sagacious, and William of Malmesbury (whose special patron he was) rightly stresses his disinterested loyalty. He was a benefactor of writers and founded the religious houses of St. James, Bristol (1136–37), where he was buried, and Margam, Glamorgan (1147). (G. W. S. B.)

GLOUCESTER, THOMAS OF WOODSTOCK, DUKE OF (1355–1397), a prominent opponent of his nephew Richard II of England, was born at Woodstock on Jan. 7, 1355, the seventh (but fifth surviving) son of Edward III. He married (before Aug. 1376) Eleanor (d. 1399), elder coheiress of Humphrey de Bohun (d. 1373), constable of England. Thomas acquired this office through his wife. He was created earl of Buckingham at the coronation of Richard II (July 1377), and earl of Essex (1380). He led an unsuccessful expedition to aid the duke of Brittany against the French (1380) and was responsible for crushing the last outbreak of violence in the peasants' revolt at Billericay (June 1381). He was created duke of Gloucester in 1385.

Gloucester and Thomas Arundel, then bishop of Ely, acted as emissaries from a discontented parliament to the king (Oct. 1386). They demanded the dismissal of the chancellor, Richard's favourite, Michael de la Pole, earl of Suffolk; it is probable that in an angry scene Gloucester threatened his nephew with deposition. Richard yielded and Gloucester and his ally, Richard FitzAlan, earl of Arundel, became members of a "great and continual council," set up to control affairs. A year later the king's position appeared stronger; Gloucester and Arundel, alarmed, disobeyed a summons to court and mustered forces at Harringay park, north London, afterward moving to Waltham Cross. There emissaries from the king effected a compromise; a parliament was to be summoned in Feb. 1388 for the trial of five of the king's friends. One of them, Robert de Vere, duke of Ireland, was defeated by Gloucester and his friends at Radcot bridge (Dec. 1387). When parliament met, Gloucester was the leading "appellant" (*i.e.,* accuser) of the king's friends and secured their conviction of treason. The appellants received £20,000 for saving the realm. They controlled policy for a year, after which a period of compromise began; during this time Gloucester was made lieutenant of Ireland (1392) and accompanied Richard there (1394–95).

The king may have heard rumours that Gloucester and Arundel were plotting against him early in 1397; Gloucester retired to Pleshey, Essex, where he had founded (1394) a college of chantry priests. He was arrested there by the king in person (July 11, 1397) and sent to Calais in the charge of the earl of Nottingham. When he was "appealed" in a parliament which met on Sept. 17, 1397, Nottingham answered that he was already dead. It is probable that Gloucester had been murdered at the Prince's inn, Calais, on Sept. 9, 1397, and this possibly by his nephew's orders. According to one of Nottingham's servants, John Hall, who was afterward executed for his share in the crime, Gloucester was suffocated "with a fetherbed."

BIBLIOGRAPHY.—J. Tait, "Did Richard II Murder the Duke of Gloucester?" *Owens College Historical Essays,* ed. by T. F. Tout and J. Tait (1902); R. L. Atkinson, A. E. Stamp, H. G. Wright, "Richard II and the Death of the Duke of Gloucester," *English Historical Review,* vol. xxxviii (1923) and xlvii (1932); M. McKisack, *The Fourteenth Century* (1959).

GLOUCESTER, a city, county and parliamentary borough, port, county town and cathedral city of Gloucestershire, Eng., 103 mi. W.N.W. of London by road. Pop. (1971 prelim.) 90,134. Gloucester lies on the river Severn between the Cotswolds, on the east, and the northern part of the Forest of Dean. The Gloucester and Berkeley or Gloucester and Sharpness ship canal, opened in 1827, runs 16 mi. S.W. to Sharpness docks in the Severn estuary.

The cathedral originated in the foundation of an abbey in 681, the present church being dedicated in 1100 and its first mitred abbot being appointed in 1381. At the Dissolution the abbey was disbanded and became the seat of a bishopric with the abbey church of St. Peter as its cathedral, rededicated to the Holy and Indivisible Trinity. Gloucester lay in the see of Worcester until 1541 when the separate see was constituted, with John Wakeman, last abbot of Tewkesbury, as first bishop. The diocese covers the greater part of Gloucestershire, with small parts of Wiltshire, Oxfordshire, Worcestershire, Herefordshire and Warwickshire. The cathedral consists of a Norman nucleus, with additions in every style of Gothic architecture, being especially rich in early Perpendicular work. It is 420 ft. long and 144 ft. broad and its beautiful 15th-century pinnacled tower, with an internal flying buttress, rises 225 ft. The nave is massive Norman with Early English roof; the aisles, chapter house and crypt (one of the four apsidal cathedral crypts in England) are Norman. The choir has Perpendicular tracery over Norman work and the splendid east window is the largest Perpendicular window in England. Between the apsidal chapels is a Perpendicular cross Lady chapel, and north of the nave are the cloisters with the first example of fan vaulting (1351-77). There are shrines of Osric, Edward II, Robert Curthose (eldest son of William the Conqueror), Bishop Warburton, Edward Jenner and others. The Festival of the Three Choirs is held annually in the cathedral (the first time being in 1724), and those of Worcester and Hereford in turn.

Gabled and timbered houses preserve the ancient aspect of the city and there are some Regency terraces. None of the old public buildings is left, but the New inn (early 15th century), an interesting half-timbered house with a galleried courtyard, was one of the original pilgrim hostels. The Bell inn (1650) was the birthplace of George Whitefield and Herbert Cardinal Vaughan. The Fleece hotel has a galleried courtyard (16th century) and a 12th-century vaulted cellar. Bishop Hooper's lodging (16th century) was opened as a folk museum in 1935. Of the churches St. Mary-de-Lode, with a Norman tower and chancel, is on the site of a Roman temple; St. Mary-de-Crypt is from the 11th century; St. Michael's was connected with the ancient abbey of St. Peter; and St. Nicholas' was originally the chapel of of the city wall. Near St. Mary-de-Crypt are remains of Greyfriars and Blackfriars priories and of the city wall. There are three endowed schools: the King's Cathedral school (1545); the Crypt grammar school, founded by Dame Joan Cooke (1539); and Sir Thomas Rich's school (1666). Robert Raikes held the first Sunday school in Gloucester in 1780.

Gloucester possesses factories for making railway rolling stock, aircraft and components, agricultural implements, insulating material, aluminum bungalows, furniture, matches, motion-picture cameras, etc., and has heavy and light engineering works, shipyards and many long-established timber mills. Its principal imports are timber, grain and petroleum products; its main exports are its own manufactured goods. It is also a market town.

The Severn fisheries for salmon and lampreys are important and in 1953 the city high sheriff revived the custom (begun in the reign of Henry I) of sending a lamprey pie to the sovereign. The tidal bore in the river attains its extreme height, 9 ft., just below the city, at Stonebench.

History.—Gloucester (Caer Glow, Gleawecastre) was the Roman municipality or *colonia* of Glevum, founded by Nerva, A.D. 96-98. Its situation and the foundation in 681 of the abbey of St. Peter by King Osric favoured the growth of the town. It became the capital of Mercia and before the Conquest was a borough with a royal residence and a mint. It has been granted numerous fairs and charters, the first by Henry II, and was incorporated by Richard III in 1483, being made a county in itself. The chartered port of Gloucester dates from 1580. James I raised Gloucester to city status in 1605. Its iron trade dates from before the Conquest, tanning was carried on before the reign of Richard III, bell-founding was introduced in the 14th and pinmaking in the 17th century, and the long-existing coal trade became important in the 12th to the 16th century. The sea-borne trade in grain and wine existed before the reign of Richard I.

The town formerly returned two members to parliament, but after 1885 returned one member.

See also references under "Gloucester" in the Index.

GLOUCESTER, a manufacturing, fishing and summer resort city of Essex county on Cape Ann in northeastern Massachusetts, U.S., was originally settled in 1623. During the 17th and 18th centuries, Gloucester flourished as a shipbuilding, maritime and fishing centre, in competition with nearby Salem and Newburyport. The first ship to be called a schooner is said to have been built in Gloucester about 1713. Along with manufacturing, fishing and a declining foreign commerce dominated Gloucester's economic life during the 19th century. After 1900 the economy was primarily industrial, with fish processing the leading industry. Secondary dependence was on fishing and on a large seasonal tourist and resort business, drawn to Cape Ann by historical associations, the scenic rocky coast and salt-water recreational facilities, and to the city by its picturesque water front, narrow streets and weathered colonial buildings. Of special interest are the reef of Norman's Woe on the east coast of Cape Ann where occurred the wreck of the "Hesperus," immortalized in Longfellow's famous poem; Hammond's castle; and the well-known bronze statue of a fisherman, a memorial to Gloucestermen lost at sea.

In the later 19th and early 20th centuries, immigrants from Portugal, Italy and a few from the Scandinavian countries settled in Gloucester, adding their traditions to its culture.

Incorporated as a town in 1642 and as a city in 1873, it adopted the council-manager form of government in 1949. For comparative population figures *see* table in MASSACHUSETTS: *Population.* Gloucester is described in many books including: Rudyard Kipling, *Captains Courageous*; James B. Connolly, *Gloucestermen* (1930); and Percy MacKaye, *Dogtown Common* (1921). Samuel Chamberlain's *Gloucester and Cape Ann* (1938) includes many photographs of the area.
(F. L. S.)

GLOUCESTER CITY, originally the seat of Old Gloucester county, became a part of Camden county, in southwestern New Jersey, U.S., when Camden county was detached in 1844. Gloucester city is on the Delaware river, opposite Philadelphia, Pa., and adjoins the city of Camden on its southern boundary.

The first settlement occurred in 1623, when Fort Nassau, the first Dutch outpost in the Delaware valley, was built near the mouth of Big Timber creek. In 1664 the English gained control and in 1677 a group of Irish Quakers occupied what the Indians called Arwamus. This was renamed Gloucester point after a place on the Severn river in England.

Prior to the American Revolution, Elizabeth Griscom, better known as Betsy Ross, eloped from Philadelphia to Gloucester City where she married John Ross at Hugg's tavern. For this she was "read out of meeting" by the Quakers in 1774. Hugg's tavern was razed in 1929 to make way for a county park.

Incorporated as a city in 1868, Gloucester City grew with the expansion of the nearby shipbuilding works started in 1899 in Camden. In the second half of the 20th century its industries included the manufacture of building materials and roofing, paperboard boxes, cork products, infants' dresses and chemicals. In 1957 it became the site of the New Jersey end of the Walt Whitman bridge over the Delaware. For comparative population figures *see* table in NEW JERSEY: *Population.* (H. F. Wi.)

GLOUCESTERSHIRE, a west-midland county in England, is divided into two unequal parts by the Severn and its estuary. The greatest length from northeast to southwest is 60 mi. (97 km.) and the greatest breadth 43 mi. (69 km.). Bristol, since 1373 a county in itself, is geographically (but not administratively) part of the county. The geographical area of Gloucestershire, including the county boroughs of Bristol and Gloucester, is 1,257.7 sq.mi. (3,257 sq.km.) of land and inland water.

Physical Features.—The county shows three distinct areas: the Cotswolds, the Severn valley and the Forest of Dean.

The Oolitic uplands of the Cotswolds (*q.v.*) on the eastern half extend from Meon hill in the north to Landsown, near Bath (Somerset), in the south. Their height averages about 700 ft. (213 m.), though Cleeve and some other points exceed 1,000 ft. (305 m.). They form an undulating tableland of about 300,000 ac., with parts considerably dissected with steep valleys, as near Stroud. The valleys of the Churn, Coln, Leach and Windrush, to the southeast, and those of the Cotswold villages, built of the native stone and in the native style. Where wooded the Cotswold escarpment is one of the country's most striking features.

Next comes the level Lias and Trias clay country of the valley of the Severn, lying between the foot of the Cotswold escarpment and the river's banks. In the north it forms the Vale of Evesham which merges into the fertile vales of Gloucester and Berkeley, when it later proceeds to widen out. The Severn enters the county near Tewkesbury and is joined by the Warwickshire Avon, dividing into two round Gloucester, and slowly expanding to form the Bristol channel. The tidal wave or "bore" may be seen to advantage near Gloucester. Nearly all the Severn's tributaries, such as the Swilgate, Chelt, Frome or Stroudwater and the Little Avon, enter on the left bank, the Leadon near Gloucester, and the Wye entering on the right bank. The Bristol Frome and the Boyd flow south to the Bristol Avon, which joins the Severn at Avon-

GLOUCESTERSHIRE

mouth, as the county boundary with Somerset, in the impressive Clifton gorge (see Avon).

The third county area is the hilly, elevated tract between the Severn and Wye, reaching to more than 800 ft. at Ruardean, being mainly occupied by the now restricted Forest of Dean with its oaks and poor peaty soil of the coal measures. It is bordered on Severnside by a strip of fertile farm land, and on the west by the limestone cliffs of the attractive Wye valley. (*See also* DEAN, FOREST OF.) Geologically, the strata have generally a descending order from east to west. On the extreme southeast, by Fairford and Cirencester, is an intrusion of Oxford Clay, succeeded by the Oolitic area of the Cotswolds, with outlying hills such as Bredon, Churchdown and Robinswood. The Oolite yields the building-stone which weathers to give the typical Cotswold grayish tint. Next come the Liassic lowlands of the vales of Evesham and Gloucester. To the Lias succeeds a narrow belt of New Red Sandstone, broken by the upper part of the Severn estuary. On the extreme southwest are Carboniferous rocks in the coal fields of the Bristol basin (between Bristol and Kingswood on the south and Tortworth on the north and the Forest of Dean, while associated with the latter is a limited area of the Devonians. Silurian rocks occur at Tortworth and May hill (969 ft.). In the north-west are the Archaean rocks of the south Malverns. In the Forest of Dean coal measures (there about 2,765 ft. thick) the strata form a basin between Mitcheldean, Coleford and Lydney. On the outside are rings of Carboniferous limestone (in which hematite occurs), Millstone Grit and Old Red Sandstone. The iron from the hematite was formerly worked locally.

Climate is temperate and the prevailing winds westerly and southerly. The rainfall varies throughout the county, averaging about 32 in. annually, April and May being apparently the driest months. The average annual mean temperature at sea level is roughly between 50° and 51° F. (10° and 10.56° C.).

In the sheltered Vale of Gloucester the soil is rich and this area is the chief seat of tillage, with the Cheltenham district having market gardening. The Forest of Dean is cold and much of it barren, but elsewhere there are woods and coppice. The higher parts of the Cotswolds, predominantly grassland, have an abundant and varied flora, particularly in the valleys and woods. Orchids and the fritillary abound, the latter by the river meadows in the east. The Newent area has extensive daffodil fields. Vineyards, important in medieval times, no longer occur.

Many typical British mammals are found (such as the fox, badger, stoat and weasel) and a few red squirrels and fallow deer inhabit Dean forest. There is a wide variety of bird life, with an important sanctuary at the Wildfowl trust near Slimbridge on the Severn, which is also a noted salmon-fishing river, the fish being netted between Tewkesbury and the estuary. The young of the eel (elvers) are taken in large quantities, being mostly eaten locally. The lamprey, formerly a royal delicacy, is no longer sought for food. The river Coln at Fairford and Bibury is well stocked with trout.

The National trust has taken over a number of historic and scenic sites, such as the Chedworth Roman villa, Hailes abbey (near Winchcombe) and Snowshill manor, together with Minchinhampton and Rodborough commons (580 and 242 ac.), Haresfield beacon and Standish wood (348 ac.). Hidcote Manor garden and other places. In 1939 the Forest of Dean became a National Forest park.

History and Antiquities.—Gloucestershire contains many relics of its past, being particularly rich in long barrows (*e.g.,* Belas Knap, above Winchcombe, Hetty Pegler's Tump, near Uley, and others at Nympsfield, Notgrove and elsewhere) together with numerous round barrows. The Cotswolds have the remains of many camps and settlements of the Iron Age, with an important Belgic site at Bagendon. The Roman occupation is reflected in its roads (such as the Fosse way and Ermine street), its villas and towns. One of the most remarkable villas is of the courtyard type at Woodchester, the extensive pavement (49 sq.ft.) being periodically uncovered. Many villas, formerly excavated, are no longer on view. The important Roman towns of Glevum (Gloucester) and Corinium (Cirencester) are constantly producing remains of the occupation. The Roman station at Lydney has a temple to the god Nodens. In Saxon times much of the district was peopled by the Hwicca tribe in the kingdom of Mercia, when the great Offa's dike was constructed, part passing through the county. About the year 1000 the old kingdom of Hwicce was divided, the southern part and the forest forming the county much as it is today, as is mentioned in the Anglo-Saxon Chronicle of A.D. 1016. The great castles of Berkeley, Bristol, St. Briavels and Gloucester were built during the Norman times of turmoil, and the county was the chief theatre of the wars in Stephen's reign. In Edward II's reign war again broke out in the shire, when the men of the county rose against the unpopular Despensers. At Tewkesbury in 1471 Queen Margaret was defeated in the Wars of the Roses. It was in Henry VIII's reign that the Gloucester diocese was created (1541) from those of Worcester and Hereford. In the Civil War of the 17th century the county was mainly on the side of parliament, and though Cirencester and Bristol fell to the king's forces, parliamentary Gloucester successfully withstood a siege in 1643.

Meanwhile the Forest of Dean was assuming an importance not only for its ironworks but also for its coal mining and timber production for shipping, in Stuart times and later. During the 14th century the wool trade of the Cotswolds was developing, and rearing sheep for wool replaced corn growing as the main agricultural pursuit. In the reign of Edward III Flemish weavers were introduced into the county and the manufacture of cloth was established. Stroud, with its good water supply, was an important centre for broadcloth. Bristol was prospering as a port and as a clothing district, the Canynges family there being of considerable influence in the 15th century. Several of the main trade centres of the Cotswolds were Cirencester, Northleach, Fairford, Chipping Campden, Tetbury and Winchcombe. The prosperity of the local merchants is shown in their financing the building and adorning of many of the Cotswold and Bristol churches, and the fine houses, market places, grammar schools and almshouses remain as monuments to the wealth of such men as William Grevel and Baptist Hicks (Viscount Campden) at Chipping Campden. The weavers and dyers enjoyed a fair prosperity until the late 18th century, when the industry began to decline, and the long-famous handloom weaving finished with the advent of mechanization, though Stroud still manufactures high-grade cloth. A single flock remains of the old Cotswold sheep or Cotswold "lions" as they were called. By the 1960s the wool towns had increased in popularity as vacation centres.

With the 18th-century fashion for spas, Cheltenham, Hotwells and Clifton attained great fame. In World War II Bristol, in particular, received damage from air attack, the cathedral also being damaged.

Many interesting examples of architecture remain to reflect the county's past. At Deerhurst church and elsewhere is Saxon work, with Norman work in Gloucester cathedral, Tewkesbury abbey and Bishop's Cleeve, many of the churches of this period having tympanum heads to the doorways. In Gloucester cathedral, Chipping Campden, Northleach and Winchcombe are examples of Perpendicular work. Fairford church has notable stained glass, and Kempley and Stoke Orchard have restored wall paintings. Monastic houses were numerous (the basis perhaps for the adage "as sure as God's in Gloucestershire"), with abbeys at Gloucester, Tewkesbury, Bristol and Cirencester, and important remains at Hailes, Flaxley and Kingswood. Many churches still have bells from the early foundries at Gloucester. The ancient local families, those of Guise, Ducie, Bathurst, Berkeley, Tracy and others, have all left their marks, and important houses such as that at Badminton, the home of the duke of Beaufort, still remain.

Population and Administration.—The total population, including the county boroughs of Bristol and Gloucester, was 1,069,-454 in 1971 (prelim. census report), an increase of 6.7% since 1961, partly due to a large influx of people during World War II with the evacuation of key industries from London. The chief centres of population are as follows: Bristol (1971 prelim.) 425,203; Gloucester 90,134; Cheltenham 69,734; Kingswood 30,269.

There are two county boroughs (Bristol and Gloucester) and two municipal boroughs (Cheltenham and Tewkesbury) together with 6 urban and 15 rural districts (298 constituent parishes). There are two courts of quarter sessions and 21 petty sessional divisions. The assizes (Oxford circuit) and quarter sessions are held in the Shire hall, Gloucester, the county's seat of administration. Bristol returns six members to parliament, Gloucester and Cheltenham one each, with one for each of the four county divisions (Cirencester and Tewkesbury, West Gloucestershire, Stroud, and South Gloucestershire). Ecclesiastically the county is in the province of Canterbury and mainly in Gloucester diocese, divided into the archdeaconries of Gloucester and Cheltenham, with parishes in and near Bristol in the Bristol diocese, established in 1897. There is a Roman Catholic diocese of Clifton.

Industries and Communications.—Agriculture remains the county's main industry. The Severn valley is the great milk and cheese area, the most popular herd being the British Friesian. Gloucester, the main market town, is also an artificial insemination centre. Gloucestershire gave its name to the Old Spots pig. There are also dairy herds on the Cotswolds, traditional sheep-farming land. Cotswold farms are generally large by English standards, 250–700 ac. and above, several estates having extensive and well-timbered parks. The hills are an important farming area with cornlands producing about 30 cwt. an acre, winter wheat and barley being the main crops. The county has only 32,000 ac. of rough grazing, as against 600,000 ac. of crops and grass. The Forest of Dean has about 10,000 ac. of rough common grazing, some unfenced. There is also mixed farm land, for milk production, with stock raising and sheep farms. The county has several large poultry farms. Apple and pear orchards (for cider and perry) are to be found in the Newent and Berkeley vale areas, with extensive plum orchards in the Huntley and Blaisdon area, and with fruit growing near Toddington. The farmers and horticulturalists join the neighbouring shires of Hereford and Worcester in the Three Counties show.

Gloucestershire had, by mid-20th century, increased in importance as a manufacturing county, though many of its traditional industries had practically disappeared. World War II brought about a great industrial expansion, particularly in the aircraft and ancillary industries (as at Brockworth near Gloucester, and Filton near Bristol). The university city of Bristol is the main industrial centre with its large port and docks at Avonmouth and is wide variety of manufactures such as engineering, tobacco, chocolate and paper. Gloucester, an inland port, is engaged primarily with engineering, timber, matches, railway carriages and the nylon industry. It is an important gas-manufacturing station. Cheltenham has industries connected with aircraft, clocks and brewing, and the Stroud, Nailsworth and Dursley area also has a wide variety of industries, such as plastics, engineering and scientific instruments. Paper is made near Winchcombe, and Tewkesbury has its flour mills and boat building. The nuclear power station at Berkeley and a large chemical works at Thornbury are modern developments. There are several deep coal mines in the Forest of Dean, forming part of the South-Western division of the National Coal board, with an annual output of about 500,000 tons. There are also some small mines licensed for private operation. The Freeminers have ancient rights for working local coal or iron, confirmed as an act of 1838. There are also wire and cable works, tin-plate works at Lydney and rubber factories and stone quarrying, but the tin-plate works was closed in 1957. North of Bristol the coal deposits are centred on Coalpit Heath, in two series, each about 2,000 ft. thick. The strontium ore, celestite, is found in "pockets" at Yate.

Two main regions of British railways serve the county. The Western region line runs from London and continues to south Wales via Gloucester, while the Midland region line from the midlands and the north passes to Bristol and the south, each having branch lines. A tunnel under the Severn also connects London direct with south Wales and Fishguard. The Severn is navigable throughout the county for small vessels but the Gloucester and Berkeley canal (completed in 1827) enables shipping up to 650 tons to reach Gloucester and the midlands. Another canal, the Thames and Severn, formerly of importance, was opened in 1789 and begins at Lechlade on the Thames and joins the Stroud-water canal to enter the Severn at Framilode. Part of the great Ross Spur motorway passes through the northwest of the county to join the midlands with south Wales. Gloucester and Cheltenham share a civil airport at Staverton.

BIBLIOGRAPHY.—Gordon E. Payne, *A Physical, Social and Economic Survey and Plan of Gloucestershire* (1946); *Gloucestershire County Handbook, 1959-1960*; J. C. Cox, *Gloucestershire*, 8th ed., rev. by H. Stratton Davis (1949); Cotteswold Naturalists Field Club, *Flora of Gloucestershire* (1948); Bristol and Gloucestershire Archaeological Society, *Transactions for 1876, etc.* (1876–); Lewis Wilshire, *The Vale of Berkeley* (1954); H. P. R. Finberg (ed.), *Gloucestershire Studies* (1957); David Verey, *Gloucestershire*, vol. i, *The Cotswolds*, vol. ii, *The Vale and the Forest of Dean*, "Buildings of England Series" (1970).

(B. C. F.)

GLOVERSVILLE, a city of Fulton county about 45 mi. N.W. of Albany, in eastern New York, U.S., forms with adjoining Johnstown a small metropolitan centre in the industrialized Mohawk valley. The cities are adjacent to the Adirondack State park; forest land covers over 60% of the county and there are many lakes and streams in the immediate vicinity. Small dairy farms are the principal form of agriculture.

Glovemaking and the tanning of leather, which remain the most important industries of the region, began in the colonial period. After 1800, wide-ranging peddlers from Gloversville exchanged tinware for deerskins with the settlers in the Mohawk valley. The greater supply of skins, the large amount of tannin available and the abundant water supply accelerated the expansion of the industries. By 1900 the region made 80% of the gloves manufactured in the United States. The factories were usually small and the workers often of English or German origin.

Located within ten miles of the New York State Thruway and the New York Central railroad, the New York State Barge canal, Gloversville became a wholesale and retail distribution centre. It was called Stump City until 1828. Incorporated as a village in 1851, it became a city in 1890. For comparative population figures of both Gloversville and Johnstown, *see table in* NEW YORK: *Population.*

(H. S. PR.)

GLOVES. Glovemaking is an ancient art, as attested by the well-formed linen gloves with a drawstring closing at the wrist found in the tomb of the young Egyptian king Tutankhamen. Greek and Roman literatures contain many allusions to gloves. In medieval Europe both fabric and leather gloves, often richly jeweled and embroidered, were worn by princes and prelates, and to the glove of the period there was attached not only a due economic, aesthetic and utilitarian value but a rich depth of symbolism as well. By the 14th century gloves were worn by the upper classes generally, particularly by men; however, it was not until the 16th century, when Catherine de Médicis, queen of France, set the fash-

A COTSWOLD SCENE DURING HARVEST TIME NEAR PAINSWICK VILLAGE, GLOUCESTERSHIRE

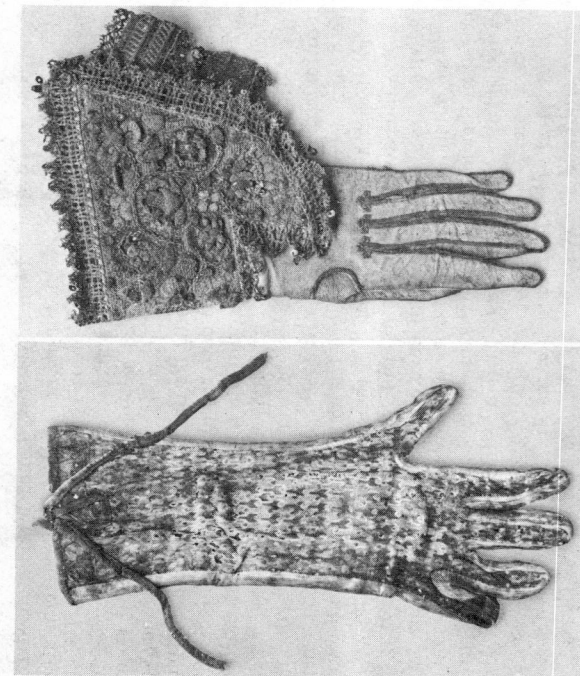

(LEFT) TAPESTRY WOVEN GLOVE WITH DRAWSTRING CLOSING AT THE WRIST BELONGING TO THE EGYPTIAN KING TUTANKHAMEN. IN THE CAIRO MUSEUM, EGYPT. (RIGHT) EMBROIDERED LEATHER GLOVE: ENGLISH, LATE 16TH CENTURY

ion, that they became a standard item of dress for women. Another influential figure was Queen Elizabeth I of England, who favoured rich, ornate gloves. During this era ladies' gloves of soft kidskin were introduced, and Grenoble, France, became the centre of kid glove manufacture. In 1834 a citizen of Grenoble, Xavier Jouvin, made an important contribution to the industry by inventing the cutting die that made possible a glove of precise fit; thereafter, gloves became more and more common.

Leather Gloves.—Although the kid glove retains its supremacy as the aristocrat among gloves, other skins, including those of young lambs (also called doeskin), capeskin, cabretta, pigskin, buckskin and reindeer, are utilized in modern glove manufacture. The skins are converted into leather by tanning (see LEATHER). Certain tanning processes produce glove leather that is washable. Various finishes are used. A smooth, bright finish, commonly called grain or glacé, is produced by buffing on plush-covered wheels. A suede or nap finish is produced by shaving or skiving off the top-grain or hair side of the skin, either by hand or by machine, and then buffing the leather with emery.

There are generally eight components of a leather glove: palm and back (one piece); thumb, three forks or fourchettes—slender pieces of leather that form the sides of the fingers—and three quirks, or diamond-shaped pieces, inserted at the bottom between the fingers. In cutting gloves, a single trank, or rectangular piece of leather the size of the glove, may be cut by hand to a desired pattern with shears, or a number of tranks may be cut simultaneously by a weighted, sharp, steel die. The glove is closed by stitching, the thumbs, quirks and fourchettes being set in and sewed with great care. Some sewing is done by hand but most is done by machines, which have been developed so that their stitching closely resembles that done by hand. The completed glove is dampened, tailored on an electrically heated metal hand of the exact size and shape of the glove and then buffed.

Fabric Gloves.—Unlike the fabric gloves of antiquity, which were made of woven material, modern fabric gloves are knit. Prior to World War II silk was a favoured material, but cotton and man-made fibres, such as rayon and nylon, have since become the staples of the glove industry.

Early fabrics were knit on tricot knitting machines equipped with needles resembling crochet hooks. The resulting fabric was not tightly knit, and two layers of material were bonded together with adhesive to furnish a duplex fabric of sufficient body. This led to the development of the simplex knitting machine that produces a single-knit but double-faced fabric of good body that has

the same appearance on each side—the so-called "double-woven" fabrics. The simplex machine uses two sets of spring needles set back to back with two guide bars that feed yarn to both sets of needles.

Glove fabrics are processed by scouring; i.e., treatment with soap and a mild alkali followed by a thorough rinsing and partial drying. They are then impregnated with a solution of caustic soda (sodium hydroxide) to produce maximum shrinkage. All traces of caustic soda must then be removed by an acid bath. The fabric is next immersed in a dye bath, rinsed and dried. The material may be given the appearance of suede leather by running it over rollers covered with glass cloth or emery.

The finished fabric is cut into glove-size squares, arranged face side to face side so that left and right hands may be cut together, and built up in layers through which a knife-sharp glove die is forced. Between-finger gores and thumbs are cut separately and are attached when the cutout glove is folded over and stitched together. An additional seaming imparts a tubular form to the fingers. As in the case of the leather glove, the fabric glove is tailored on an electrically heated metal hand.

Knit Gloves.—Machine-knit gloves, rivaling in colour, pattern interest and stitch variation those knit by hand, are made of wool, man-made fibres and heavy cotton yarns and can be produced with or without seams.

Seamless gloves may be knit in two ways: the cuff and palm body may be knit on a circular machine and then transferred to a flat fingering machine, or the entire glove may be fashioned on a flat machine. When two machines are used, the operator must exercise great care in transferring the loops of yarn, or stitches, of the palm body from the needles of the circular machine to those of the flat fingering machine.

Seamed, or wrought, gloves are produced as straight selvage pieces on a flat knitting machine. The glove is completed by folding the piece so that complementing parts fall together and then closing the glove by stitching.

Machines for knitting gloves are equipped with patterning devices that produce predetermined decorative designs in desired colours during the knitting process.

Other Gloves.—Many types of special protective gloves have been developed, such as the surgeon's gloves of very thin rubber and the much heavier ones used by electrical workers. Asbestos gloves protect against burns, as do gloves made of a heavy, twisted loop pile fabric similar to terry cloth. Thousands of tiny air cells in the fabric provide insulation against heat; the cushioning quality of the material also protects the hands against cuts and abrasions. Treating Canton flannel gloves with semifluid polyvinyl plastic produces a remarkably versatile plastic-coated work glove that is heat resistant, impermeable to most fluids and proof against acids, alkalies, industrial oils and greases and many chemical solvents. The hands of the X-ray technician may be shielded against radiation by gloves impregnated with lead.

See C. Cody Collins, Love of a Glove (1947); Justine Randers-Pehrson, The Surgeon's Glove (1960). (E. L. Y.)

GLOWWORM, a name loosely applied to crawling luminous insects emitting light either continuously or in prolonged glows rather than in brief flashes as do most fireflies. Principal types of glowworms are: (1) wingless adult females of certain lampyrid beetles (the European genus Lampyris [C, D] is the glowworm of literature); (2) larvae of lampyrid fireflies (A, B; common in the Americas) and of elaterid fireflies (tropical); (3) larvae and larviform adult females of certain beetles of the genera Phengodes (North America; E) and Phrixothrix (South America) and (4) larvae of certain gnats (e.g., the cave-dwelling Bolitophila of New Zealand and Platyura of the central Appalachians).

Glowworm photogenic organs vary widely in size, number location and structure, suggesting independent evolutionary origins of light-producing ability. In Phengodes the light is emitted by solitary giant cells; in Bolitophila by modified excretory organs; in Platyura by modified salivary glands; and in Phrixothrix, Lampyris and lampyrid larvae by organs similar to, but simpler than, the "lanterns" of flashing types of fireflies. The light is usually greenish, but the "railroad worm" (Phrixothrix) has a red head-

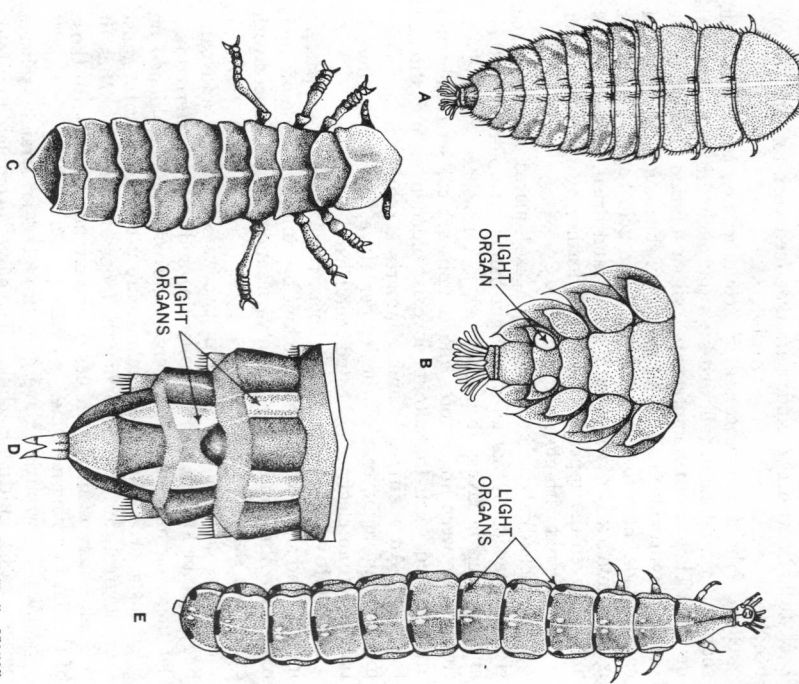

GLOWWORM LIGHT ORGANS. (A) DORSAL VIEW OF PHOTURIS PENNSYLVANICA LARVA; (B) VENTRAL VIEW OF ABDOMEN OF PHOTURIS LARVA; (C) DORSAL VIEW OF FEMALE LAMPYRIS NOCTILUCA; (D) VENTRAL VIEW OF ABDOMEN OF LAMPYRIS; (E) DORSAL VIEW OF PHENGODES FRONTALIS

light in addition. In *Lampyris*, *Phengodes* and *Phrixothrix* the flying male, which may itself be nonluminous, is attracted to the female's light; and in *Platyura* and *Bolitophila*, where the larvae spin sticky webs, food insects are attracted. In most glowworms, however, the function of the light is unknown.

Little also is known about glowworm life history and behaviour. Typically these live on or under the soil surface, feeding on snails and slugs, and larval development occupies two years. A few species are aquatic. See FIREFLY; BIOLUMINESCENCE.
(J. B. Bu.)

GLOXINIA, the common name for a showy tuberous rooted plant botanically classified as *Sinningia speciosa*, belonging to the family Gesneriaceae (*q.v.*) and a native of Brazil. Gloxinias are popular in the garden and as house plants. They grow eight to ten inches in height and produce large tubular flowers surrounded by attractive foliage of a soft, velvety texture. The blooms are characterized by their richness and variety of colouring, which ranges from shades of blue and purple through pink and crimson to white. After blooming, gloxinias need a rest period; the roots should be stored at about 45° F. (7° C.) till spring. The preferred method of propagation is by seed planted indoors in late winter, but choice varieties can be increased by cuttings. Gloxinias may be put outdoors in summer in moist, rich soil in a warm but shady location. *Gloxinia* is also the generic name for related plants of little horticultural interest. (R. T. V. T.; X.)

GLUBB, SIR JOHN BAGOT (GLUBB PASHA) (1897–), British commander of the Arab legion (Jordanian army)

GLOXINIA HYBRID (SINNINGIA SPECIOSA) IN OSA VARIETY

from 1939 to 1956, was born at Preston, Lancashire, on April 16, 1897, the son of Maj. Gen. Sir F. M. Glubb. He was educated at Cheltenham and the Royal Military academy, Woolwich. Glubb was first drawn to the Arabs when, after being thrice wounded in World War I, he went to Iraq as a lieutenant in the Royal Engineers. Working among the tribes there, he learned their language and customs, eventually resigning his British army commission in 1930. In 1930 he joined the Arab legion and used his skill with the tribes to put down border raiding between Transjordan and Saudi Arabia. His talent lay in transforming the hitherto lawless but naturally martial Bedouins into modern soldiers; they formed the elite of the legion when he assumed command in 1939. His devotion to the Arabs was coupled with a profound belief that their future lay with the west. He was thus a sensitive interpreter of King Abdullah's pro-British policies. As Arab nationalism developed after the Palestine war (1948), Glubb's influential position in Jordan aroused so much criticism that in 1956 King Husain, under great political pressure, dismissed him. On returning to England Glubb was knighted. His works include *The Story of the Arab Legion* (1948), *A Soldier With the Arabs* (1957), *Britain and the Arabs* (1959), *The Empire of the Arabs* and *The Great Arab Conquests* (1963), *The Course of Empire* (1965), *A Short History of the Arab Peoples* (1969), and *The Life and Times of Muhammad* (1970). (A. DE.)

GLUCINUM: see BERYLLIUM.

GLUCK, CHRISTOPH WILLIBALD (1714–1787), German composer and reformer of music drama during the second half of the 18th century, was born on July 2, 1714, at Erasbach, near Berching, in the Upper Palatinate. His paternal forebears, mostly foresters, came from the border territory between the Upper Palatinate and Bohemia; nothing is known of his ancestors on his mother's side. His father, Alexander Gluck (born Oct. 28, 1683), had come to Erasbach as ranger in 1711–12; the family then moved to Reichstadt near Böhmisch-Leipa in Bohemia. Between 1722 and 1727 they lived near Böhmisch-Kamnitz and after this, until 1736, in Eisenberg (near Komotau), where Alexander Gluck held the post of master forester to Prince Lobkowitz.

Christoph Willibald, whose father probably intended him to continue in the family employment of forestry, at an early age showed a strong inclination toward music. In order to escape from disagreements with his father, the young Gluck finally left home. Supporting himself by his music he made his way to Prague, where he played in several churches and presumably completed his musical studies, though probably not with the composer B. M. Černohorský, as has often been maintained. He went to Vienna in the winter of 1735–36. There he was discovered by a Lombard nobleman. A. M. Melzi, who took the young musician with him to Milan, where Gluck, apart from fulfilling his duties in the Melzi family chapel, spent four years studying composition with G. B. Sammartini, from whom he learned the new Italian style of instrumental music. Probably the six trio sonatas printed in London in 1746 were the fruits of his studies with Sammartini in Milan. They show Gluck fully conversant with the Italian setting *a tre*; occasionally there are somewhat buffoonesque effects after the style of Pergolesi. As to the sequence of the movements, Gluck follows no model: all six sonatas are like divertimentos and they consist of two movements with a minuet as conclusion. Besides the six "London" sonatas, Gluck probably composed further trio sonatas under Sammartini. The only other surviving ones (one in E major and one in F major) seem from their style, however, to have been written later (after 1750).

On Dec. 26, 1741, in the Teatro Ducal in Milan, Gluck earned his first great dramatic success with his first opera, *Artaserse*, to a libretto by P. Metastasio. Until 1745 there followed an annual succession of operas for this theatre: *Demofoonte* (1742), *Arsace* (in collaboration with G. B. Lampugnani) (1743), *Sofonisba* (1744) and *Ippolito* (1745). In addition Gluck wrote *Cleonice* (*Demetrio*) (1744) and *La finta schiava*, a pasticcio (1744), for Venice; *Il Tigrane* (1743) for Crema, and *Poro* (1744) for Turin. In these early works, of which mostly only fragments have survived, Gluck largely follows the existing operatic fashion, with Metastasio as librettist and J. A. Hasse as composer, though occasional intensely passionate outbursts and the beginning of characterization foreshadow the great dramatic composer he later was to become. In 1745 Gluck, who was now well known as an operatic composer, was invited to England at the instigation of Lord Middlesex, director of Italian opera at the Haymarket theatre, London, in order to appear in opposition to Handel. The plan failed as, owing to the political chaos caused by the Stuart rising, all theatres in London were closed before Gluck arrived in England. When the situation became calmer, theatrical activities recommenced with a performance of Gluck's opera *La Caduta de' giganti* on Jan. 18, 1746; the libretto was by F. Vanneschi glorifying the duke of Cumberland, who was considered to be the hero of the day. This work, as well as Gluck's second London opera, *Artamene*, produced on March 15, 1746, consisted largely of music from his own earlier works, lack of time having forced Gluck to this device. Neither opera met with success. On March 25, shortly after the production of *Artamene*, Handel and Gluck together gave a concert in the Haymarket theatre consisting of works by Gluck and an organ concerto by Handel, played by the composer. Gluck had won Handel's interest and the latter's much-quoted criticism of Gluck's contrapuntal ability (Handel said that Gluck "knows no more counterpoint than my cook") must not be taken too seriously. Gluck himself, according to the Irish singer Michael Kelly, tried for the rest of his life to emulate Handel, whom he described as the "divine master of our art."

After he left England (possibly in 1746) Gluck came into contact with the traveling opera companies of P. and A. Mingotti and after 1749 with G. B. Locatelli. On June 29, 1747, the Mingotti company performed Gluck's opera-serenade *La Nozze d'Ercole e d'Ebe* at Pillnitz castle, near Dresden, on the occasion of the double wedding between the electoral families of Bavaria and Saxony. By the beginning of 1748 at the latest, Gluck was back in Vienna, at work on Metastasio's *Semiramide riconosciuta*, with which, on May 14, 1748, the Burg theatre was inaugurated and which proved a brilliant success for the composer. At that time Gluck met his future wife, Marianne Pergin, the 16-year-old daughter of a rich merchant. In the same year, Gluck, as conductor of the Mingotti company, traveled via Hamburg to Copenhagen, where he composed the opera-serenade *La Contesa dei Numi* in celebration of the birth, on Jan. 29, 1749, of the heir to the Danish throne. The introduction, which leads directly into the first scene of the work, was probably inspired by the composer and theoretician J. A. Scheibe, who was at that time working in Copenhagen. During the following two winters Gluck was with the Locatelli company in Prague, where he wrote *Ezio* (1749–50) and *Issipile* (1751–52). On Sept. 15, 1750, Gluck was married to Marianne Pergin in the church of St. Ulrich in Vienna. Their marriage was a harmonious one though it remained childless. Later Gluck adopted his niece, Marianne. Before the young couple set up a permanent home in Vienna in the winter of 1752–53, Gluck took his wife to Naples for the summer of 1752, where he composed music for Metastasio's drama *La Clemenza di Tito* after having rejected the text of *Arsace*, which he had already once set to music.

In Vienna, Gluck soon found a patron in the imperial field marshal Prince Joseph of Saxe-Hildburghausen, who engaged him first as leader of his orchestra and later as *Kapellmeister*. Gluck gave successful performances of his symphonies and arias at weekly concerts at the prince's palace and made a particular impression with his opera-serenade *Le Cinesi*, which was performed at the end of Sept. 1754 in the presence of the emperor and empress at a magnificent celebration at Schlosshof castle. This success may well have contributed to the decision of Count Giacomo Durazzo, director of the court theatre, to entrust the provision of the "theatrical and academic music" for the imperial court to Gluck. In the spring of 1755 Gluck's opera-serenade *La Danza* was performed at the imperial castle of Laxenburg, and on Dec. 8 of the same year followed *L'Innocenza giustificata*, the libretto for which Count Durazzo had himself assembled from arias by Metastasio and recitatives of his own. The following year (1756) Vienna saw *Il Re pastore* and *Tetide*, while the first performance of the opera *Antigono* was given during a visit to Rome. In Rome Gluck

was created knight of the Golden Spur. After his return to Vienna, Gluck began to conquer new fields. Count Durazzo had ordered from Paris a number of French *vaudeville* comedies by C. S. Favart, among others, which he wished Gluck to set to music as E. R. Duni, P. A. Monsigny and F. A. Philidor were doing at the time. *Tircis et Doristée* (1756) may have been a first attempt at this genre. After 1758 Gluck proceeded more independently and composed for such works as *La Fausse esclave*, *L'Ile de Merlin* (1758), *La Cythère assiégée*, *Le Diable à quatre*, *L'Arbre enchanté* (1759), *L'Ivrogne corrigé* (1760) and *Le Cadi dupé* (1761), which contained, in addition to the overture, a steadily increasing number of *airs nouveaux* in place of the original *vaudevilles*. In *La Rencontre imprévue*, first performed in Vienna on Jan. 7, 1764, no *vaudeville* remains at all, with the result that the work is a perfect example of *opéra comique*. Gluck gave the scores of *Le Cadi dupé* and *La Rencontre imprévu* particular charm by using "oriental" instrumental effects. In many of the arias tuneful melody and programmatic writing foreshadow the later developments in Gluck's operatic style. This is especially noticeable in the first examples of complex scene development in *L'Ile de Merlin* and *L'Ivrogne corrigé*, written respectively four and two years before *Orfeo*.

In Feb. 1761 Raniero Calzabigi, a friend of G. Casanova, came to Vienna. In Paris he had become acquainted with and assimilated the ideas, partly directed against Metastasio, of such poets and literary men as D. Diderot, F. M. von Grimm, Rousseau and Voltaire. Calzabigi's libretto for *Orfeo ed Euridice*, conceived in this spirit, was enthusiastically greeted by Durazzo, who immediately put him in touch with Gluck. On Oct. 17, 1761, was given the first performance of their first work of collaboration, the dramatic ballet *Le Festin de pierre* (Don Juan). Gluck later composed the music for the dance dramas *Semiramide* (1765) to a scenario by Calzabigi and *L'Orfano della China* (1766). The choreography for these works was created by the Viennese ballet master G. Angiolini. Together with Calzabigi, Gluck also wrote the three Italian "reform operas," *Orfeo ed Euridice* (1762), *Alceste* (1767) and *Paride ed Elena* (1770).

Gluck himself, in his foreword to *Alceste*, has described his and Calzabigi's aims with the words *semplicità, verità e naturalezza* ("simplicity, truth and naturalness"). These demands primarily affected the libretto. In place of the involved plots in the manner of Metastasio there was to be a simple, true and natural action in the tradition of the classical drama; in place of the courtly conventions, there was to be the purely human element. The chorus, again on the classical pattern, began to have equal importance with the main characters of the action and participated directly in the dramatic events. The function of the music was, in Gluck's own words, *di servire alla Poesia per l'espressione, e per le situazioni della Favola, senza interromper l'Azione, o raffreddarla con degl' inutile superflui ornamenti* ("to serve poetry by means of expression and by following the situations of the story, without interrupting the action or stifling it with a useless superfluity of ornaments"). The *recitativo secco* was banished (except in *Alceste*); *ariosi*, chorus and mime were welded together with declamatory style and expressive orchestral writing to form scenes and groups of scenes as parts of a great work of architecture. As Gluck himself confessed, the impulse toward opera reform came from Calzabigi, but it must also be recognized that Calzabigi proceeded largely from the ideas put forward after 1750 by the Parisian poetic and literary circles mentioned above, while important new musical features (e.g., the complex scene development) were the contributions of Gluck's own genius.

Besides the three Italian "reform operas," which were not written as the result of a particular request, there appeared a series of commissioned works, partly after librettos by Metastasio: *Il Trionfo di Clelia* (Bologna, 1763), the second version of *Ezio* of 1750 (Vienna, 1763) and, after a short visit to Paris in the spring of 1764, *Il Parnaso confuso*, *Telemacco* and the dance drama *Semiramide*, all written for the second marriage of Joseph II in 1765. The opera-serenade *La Corona*, written in the same year, was not performed owing to court mourning for the death of the emperor Francis I. In Florence in 1767, Gluck gave performances of his festival opera *Il Prologo*, together with T. Traetta's *Ifigenia in Tauride*; *La Vestale*, the revised version of *L'Innozenca giustificata* of 1755, followed in Vienna in 1768; and, in Parma in 1769, he presented *Le Feste d'Apollo*. His plan, conceived shortly after this in 1771–72, was to set to music a dramatic text based on John Dryden's *Ode for St. Cecilia's Day*. It apparently came to nothing.

In the autumn of 1772 Gluck played his newly completed opera, *Iphigénie en Aulide* (text by the marquis Le Blanc du Roullet after Racine) for the English music historian Charles Burney, who was spending some time in Vienna. The Paris opera agreed to stage this work and, as Gluck had undertaken to provide six more similar operas, he went to Paris in the autumn of 1773. The performances of *Iphigénie* on April 19, 1774, and of the French version of *Orfeo* in the summer of the same year met with tremendous success. In Vienna, Gluck was appointed official court composer, but he soon took leave to return to Paris. Here the new version of *L'Arbre enchanté* in 1775 brought him little success, while the completely rewritten *Cythère assiégée* proved a failure. The French version of *Alceste*, which was produced during his third visit to Paris on April 23, 1776, also met with disapproval. Deeply distressed by this, as well as by the death of his beloved niece, Marianne, Gluck left Paris in May 1776, and returned to Vienna. In Paris Gluck left both friends and enemies, who began to form two opposing parties: his adherents, the Gluckists, under the leadership of Abbé Arnaud and J. B. Suard; his opponents, called Piccinists after N. Piccini who had been prevailed upon to come to Paris in the summer of 1776 to write opera in opposition, were led by J. F. de la Harpe and J. F. Marmontel. Even G. B. Martini in Bologna was drawn into the struggle, which reached its full fury in 1777. Gluck, in Vienna, had completed *Armide* (on the text by P. Quinault) but had destroyed his sketches for *Roland* (also by Quinault) on hearing that Piccini was setting the same text for Paris. At the end of May 1777, Gluck returned to Paris.

At the first performance of *Armide* on Sept. 23, the war of the theatres reached a climax, but soon after the performance of Piccini's *Roland* on Jan. 27, 1778, the struggle abated again. Gluck retired to Vienna and his last visit to Paris began at the end of 1778, when he took with him his two latest completed dramatic works, *Iphigénie en Tauride* and *Écho et Narcisse*. The performance of *Iphigénie* on May 18, 1779, brought him his greatest success in Paris, but *Écho* (which was first performed on Sept. 24, 1779) met with little appreciation. Gluck, who had suffered a stroke during the rehearsals of *Écho*, left Paris for the last time at the beginning of Oct. 1779.

Gluck's great French "reform operas" are more strongly governed by the principle of contrast than the Italian works; the declamatory style of the vocal line is more marked than in the Viennese operas and the power and orchestral colour are more intense. The works are constructed in shorter sections, which frequently follow each other without a break, and the spacious conception of the scenes is partly sacrificed in order to achieve a greater degree of dramatic and psychological flexibility.

Gluck spent the last eight years of his life in Vienna and in Perchtoldsdorf nearby, in the care of his wife, continuing to work tirelessly. His attention turned again to F. G. Klopstock's *Hermannsschlacht*, which had occupied him as early as 1770; he revised *Écho et Narcisse* and, together with the Viennese poet J. B. von Alxinger, produced a German version of *Iphigénie en Tauride*, first performed in Vienna on Oct. 23, 1781, on the occasion of the visit by the grand duke Paul Petrovich, later Tsar Paul I. At this time the paths of Gluck again crossed those of Mozart, as had already occurred once in Paris; they met on several occasions, but no close personal relationship developed between them. In 1781 Gluck suffered a second stroke, which partly paralyzed him, and his physical powers began to decline. Only a few years before his death he published his *Klopstock Odes*.

These odes, only seven of which survive, must have been written soon after 1770 and are the first examples of his mature style. Their simple melodic line and strict declamation give the first hint of the late Gluck (e.g., "Ich bin ein deutsches Mädchen"). A song such as "Die Sommernacht," on the other hand, is frankly romantic in mood. On Nov. 15, 1787, Gluck had a further stroke, from which he died. Two days later he was buried in the central cemetery in Vienna amid general mourning. The Requiem Mass included at a performance of Gluck's own *De Profundis*, conducted by A. Salieri.

A monumental edition of Gluck's French operas was begun in 1873 by F. Pelletan, B. Damcke, C. Saint-Saëns and J. Tiersot. Selected works were published by the Gluck society, founded shortly before World War I. A complete edition of Gluck's works was begun by Rudolf Gerber in 1951, and by 1967 eleven volumes had been published.

BIBLIOGRAPHY.—H. Abert (ed.), *Gluck Year Book*, 4 vol. (1913–18); M. Cooper, *Gluck* (1935); A. Einstein, *Gluck*, Eng. trans. by Eric Blom (1936); F. Gerber, *Ch. W. Gluck* (1950); R. Haas, *Gluck und Durazzo im Burgtheater* (1925); C. Hopkinson, *Bibliography of the Works of C. W. von Gluck* (1959); E. Newman, *Gluck and the Opera* (1895); A. Schmid, *Ch. W. Ritter von Gluck* (1854); S. Wortsmann, *Die deutsche Gluck-Literatur* (1914); A. Wotquenne, *Catalogue thématique des oeuvres de Ch. W. Gluck* (1904), with amendments and addenda by J. Liebeskind (1911). *See also* Gluck's letters, J. G. Prud'homme (ed.), *Journal of the International Music Society*, vol. xiii (1911–12); collected correspondence and papers, ed. by H. and E. H. Mueller von Asow, Eng. trans. by S. Thomson (1962).
(G. Cr.)

GLUCOSE: *see* Carbohydrates.

GLUCOSIDES: *see* Glycosides, Natural.

GLUE: *see* Adhesives.

GLUTATHIONE is a sulfur-containing substance found within almost all kinds of living cells. It can protect an animal against radiation damage to some extent, if large dosages are administered almost simultaneously with exposure to radiation. This protective action may be associated with the ready reaction of glutathione with the peroxides that are formed on irradiation of the tissues.

Liver and yeast are particularly rich in glutathione, which may reach a concentration in tissues as high as 0.1 or 0.2%. Because of the expense of its chemical synthesis, glutathione is generally obtained by isolation from natural sources. When purified, it is usually obtained as a white, amorphous solid, which is exceedingly soluble in water.

The physiological function of glutathione has been investigated extensively since the discovery of the compound in 1921 by Sir Frederick Gowland Hopkins of Cambridge university. Great interest has centred on the fact that glutathione can affect the activity of a variety of enzymes that are essential for the normal operation of any living cell. The activating effect of glutathione on enzymes is associated with the chemical action of the sulfur group. In glutathione, the sulfur normally is present in a reduced or sulfhydryl (-SH) form.

Enzymes also contain sulfhydryl groups, and often are inactivated by oxidation of these -SH groups to the disulfide (-SS-) form. Glutathione reacts with these -SS- groups to regenerate the -SH groups of the enzyme. The reaction involves a simultaneous conversion of the -SH groups of glutathione to the -SS- groups, which are in turn reconverted to the -SH form by the action of an enzyme known as glutathione reductase. Thus, by a cyclic chemical process, the glutathione operates as an agent controlling the activity of enzymes within the cell.

The chemical name of glutathione, γ-L-glutamyl-L-cysteinylglycine, indicates that it is made up of three amino acids, linked together as shown in the structural formula:

$$HOOC—C—CH_2—CH_2—C—N—C—C—N—CH_2—COOH$$

These odes, only seven of which survive, must have been written... The bonds between the amino acids are known as peptide bonds. Glutathione is structurally related to proteins, which, however, have a greater molecular size because they contain many more amino acids.

(B. V.)

See also ENZYMES; PROTEINS.

GLUTEN, a yellowish-gray powdery mixture of proteins, occurs in wheat and other cereal grains and is composed chiefly of gliadin and glutenin. Its presence in flour helps make the production of leavened, or raised, baked goods possible since its chainlike molecules form an elastic network that traps the carbon dioxide gas and expands with it. Besides its use in flour, gluten also is used in special high-protein breakfast foods and other cereal foods, in adhesives and as meal for cattle food. It also may be used in the manufacture of the meat flavour intensifier sodium glutamate (monosodium glutamate) and of some amino acids, such as glutamic acid.

Gluten occurs in nature in combination with carbohydrates, lipids and minerals. The carbohydrates consist mainly of starch, which functions as a filler and can be removed by prolonged washing with water, in which the gluten is insoluble.

The properties of gluten vary according to its source, since different proteins are present in different amounts in the different cereals and also in the different varieties of a cereal. The existence of variations is of prime importance since the baking qualities of flours, as is shown by the rheological behaviour of doughs prepared from different kinds of wheat flours. The dough can be soft and extensible or tough and elastic, or it can display these properties in varying degrees without approaching the extremes. The behaviour of the dough, in any case, reflects the gluten content of the particular flour. The highly variable qualities of gluten have become the object of intensive study in an effort to determine the chemical or biochemical causes of diversity in gluten characteristics.

(E. L. Y.)

GLYCAS, MICHAEL (fl. 12th century), the Byzantine author of a world chronicle, probably came from Corfu. He is called *grammaticus* in some manuscripts. Little is known of his life except that he was blinded by order of Manuel I in 1159 apparently for some kind of political offense. His *Biblos Chronike* ("World Chronicle"), from the Creation to the death of Alexius I (1118), was written for his son.

(J. M. Hy.)

GLYCERIDES: *see* OILS, FATS AND WAXES.

GLYCEROL (GLYCERIN), a trihydric alcohol, is a component of all animal and vegetable fats and oils. A sweet, colourless, odourless, sirupy liquid in its pure state, it was discovered by Karl Wilhelm Scheele in 1779 and named *ölsüss*. Michel Chevreul, in working on fats in 1813, studied the substance further and called it glycerin (Gr. *glycus*, "sweet"). Theophile Pelouze (1836), Pierre Berthelot and others identified it chemically; its structural formula, CH₂OH.CHOH.CH₂OH, was determined in 1855 by C. A. Wurtz. The name was changed later to glycerol since the *-ol* ending indicates it is an alcohol. Obtainable from fats and oils by saponification (*see* OILS, FATS AND WAXES), it also occurs widely in nature in combination with various acids in such substances as lecithin (eggs and various organs) and cephalin (brain, liver and other organs). It is customary to refer to the pure chemical product as glycerol, whereas the term glycerin denotes commercial grades with varying glycerol content.

Applications of Glycerin.—Applications fall into two distinct groups: (1) those arising from glycerin's physical properties: humectancy, viscosity, solvent power, nontoxicity, antifreeze properties and the like; (2) those arising from its three chemically reactive hydroxyl groups—used by nature in the structure of fats and oils (glycerides) and by industry for many derivatives. These range from explosive nitroglycerin (*q.v.*) to highly resistant resins. Alkyd resins based on glycerin enter a wide range of protective coatings. The "short-oil" type is used in baking enamels for automotive and other machine finishes. "Long-oil" glycerin alkyds are used in brushing enamels and exterior house paints. Other major markets include explosives, tobacco (as a humectant), cellophane (as a plasticizer), dentifrices, skin lotions, mouth washes, cough preparations, drug solvents, serums, vaccines and suppositories.

Growing application of mono- and di-glyceride emulsifiers—particularly in the food field—has led to increased use of glycerin in their manufacture. These derivatives act as softening agents in

baked goods, plasticizers in shortening and stabilizers in ice cream. Another group of glycerol esters, the acetoglycerides, are used as protective food coatings.

Glycerin is no longer used commercially as an automotive antifreeze; however, many specialized applications for the antifreeze properties of glycerol solutions have been developed. One of the most significant is its use as a protective medium for freezing red blood cells, sperm cells, eye corneas and other living tissue.

Physical Properties.—Pure glycerol has a molecular weight of 92.06. It has a specific gravity of 1.26557 at 15° C., an average specific heat of 0.6469 in the range from 16° C. to 179° C., a refractive index of 1.47399 at 20° C., a flash point of 177° C. and a melting point of 17.8° C. (although glycerin is seldom found in crystalline form). It boils at 290° C. with some decomposition at atmospheric pressure but is unchanged at diminished pressure (*e.g.*, 182° 20 mm. and 152.03° 5 mm.). It is miscible with water and alcohol in all proportions but less so with ether and with fixed and volatile oils.

Some of its more important physical characteristics are: (1) low vapour pressure and high boiling point, which make it nonvolatile at ordinary temperatures; (2) solubility and solvent properties that are comparable with those of water and the lower aliphatic alcohols; (3) high viscosity as an aid to lubrication; (4) low freezing point, which is valuable in antifreeze mixtures; and (5) hygroscopicity, which aids the retention of moisture and freshness in a wide variety of consumer products. Biologically, it has a food value comparable with that of carbohydrates and a sweetening value approaching that of sucrose.

Chemical Properties.—Glycerol, because of its three hydroxyl groups, reacts readily with many organic and inorganic compounds to form esters (alkyd resins, ester gums, nitroglycerin and the fatty acid esters), aliphatic and aromatic ethers, acetals, amines, halohydrins, tartrates, acetates and metallic glycerides. The more important derivatives are: (1) alkyd resins and ester gums, which are basic ingredients of many modern protective coatings; (2) nitroglycerin, which is used in the production of explosives; and (3) numerous further products that are used as solvents, emollients or emulsifiers in edibles, drugs and cosmetics.

The reaction of glycerol with tartaric acid and the formation of polyesters were studied by Jöns J. Berzelius in 1847, and later research on the glycerol-phthalic acid reactions laid the foundation of the present protective coating industry. Ascanio Sobrero (1846) noted the reaction of nitric acid with glycerol to form nitroglycerin, and Alfred B. Nobel (1868–75) converted this highly explosive material into safer and more convenient forms of use. Nitroglycerin is an important component of double-base powders and has been used extensively in rocket powder. (*See* EXPLOSIVES; *Dynamites*; CORDITE.)

As originally shown by Louis Pasteur (1858), glycerol is a natural product (about 3%) of the alcoholic fermentation of sugar by yeast and is therefore present in varying percentages in all wines and beers. Carl Neuberg (1912) and others showed that if the fermentation occurs in the presence of a salt, such as sodium sulfite, sugar can yield in excess of 30% of its weight in glycerol.

Manufacture.—About half of the world's supply of glycerin by 1966 was produced as a co-product in the saponification or hydrolysis of fats. World production of synthetic glycerin is increasing rapidly and by the mid-1970s probably will account for better than 75% of world production.

In the manufacture of soap by the kettle process, fats (of which about 10% of the weight is glycerol) are treated with alkali and yield (along with soap) a "spent lye" consisting of glycerol solution and salt. This spent lye is filtered and concentrated to "soap-lye crude," a grade of glycerin containing 80% glycerol.

More modern soapmaking starts with the production of fatty acids by hydrolysis. This reaction is carried out in a high-pressure splitting tower in which steam is caused to react continuously with the hot fat. Other fat-splitting methods, using autoclaves or using the Twitchell (catalyst) process, are also employed in fatty acid production. All produce a salt-free "sweet water," which upon evaporation yields a crude glycerin of 88% glycerol content known as "saponification crude." Fatty alcohols, in particular lauric alcohol and related types from coconut oil, have become increasingly important as intermediates for detergents. Production of fatty acids or esters for hydrogenation to alcohols and sodium-reduction methods of fatty alcohol production are secondary sources for crude glycerin.

There are basically four routes of glycerin synthesis: allyl chloride, acrolein, propylene oxide and simultaneous hydrogenation and hydrogenolysis of refined sugar. In the first method allyl chloride may be converted to glycerol by two routes. It may be treated with aqueous chlorine, and the resulting mixture of glycerol dichlorohydrins dehydrochlorinated to epichlorohydrin, which is then hydrolyzed to glycerol; or the allyl chloride may be hydrolyzed to allyl alcohol. When the latter method is used, the allyl alcohol is chlorohydrinated with aqueous chlorine solution to yield a mixture of monochlorohydrins, and these are hydrolyzed to glycerol in 90% yield based on allyl alcohol. The product from either of the above procedures is a dilute aqueous solution containing 5% or less glycerol. This crude glycerol is concentrated to about 80% in multiple effect evaporators and salt removed by centrifuging. Additional concentration of the product, followed by final desalting, yields 98% glycerol. Finally, coloured substances are removed by solvent extraction and the product refined by steam-vacuum distillation.

Acrolein-based glycerol manufacture proceeds by epoxidation and reduction, followed by hydration. The acrolein is epoxidized to glycidaldehyde by treating it with aqueous sodium hypochlorite solution or with hydrogen peroxide. If desired, glycidol can be obtained via any of the above routes. Alternatively, acrolein can be converted to allyl alcohol by reduction, and the allyl alcohol hydroxylated with aqueous hydrogen peroxide to yield glycerol in 80–90% yield based on allyl alcohol.

In the third route, propylene oxide-based glycerol can be produced by rearrangement of propylene oxide to allyl alcohol over trilithium phosphate catalyst at 200–250° C. From the allyl alcohol glycerol can then be obtained via any of the above routes. The fourth method of producing glycerin on a commercial scale (which accounts for about 10% of U.S. production) is by the simultaneous catalytic hydrogenation and hydrogenolysis of refined sugar. The reaction is carried out at temperatures of 190–230° C. at hydrogen pressures of about 2,000 p.s.i., in a continuous autoclave system. The reaction results in the production of several polyhydric alcohols and the glycerin is separated from the mixture by distillation, and then further purified by treatment with activated carbon, filtration and distillation.

Distillation in the presence of steam in vacuum stills is the primary means of purifying glycerin, with redistillation and bleaching to obtain the highest grades. Ion exchange processes, however, do provide alternative means of purification. All of the methods result in a grade of glycerin that meets, or exceeds, U.S.P. standards.

Commercial Grades.—Crude Glycerin.—This grade, in purities of 80% and 88%, although an important article of commerce, has little direct utility. A substantial tonnage moves from smaller plants and from foreign soapmakers to U.S. glycerin refiners to supplement their own production of crude glycerin.

Refined glycerin is sold by U.S. producers on individual product specifications that differ in minor respects from company to company. Glycerin for a particular field of use—say for cellophane or alkyd resins—may be designated as such by the producer in meeting special tests of the consuming industry.

Glycerol, U.S.P.—This clear, colourless product conforms to the specifications of the U.S. *Pharmacopoeia* (minimum specific gravity 1.249 at 25° C.), and is chemically pure except for about 4% of water. It is employed in drugs, foods, toilet goods, tobacco, food wraps, liners for bottle caps and wherever glycerol may be used for human consumption. Glycerol of the same quality, but sold at a higher concentration (minimum specific gravity 1.2595 at 25° C.), is also supplied. British standards for chemically pure glycerol (B.P.) are similar, except for specific gravity limits of 1.255 to 1.260 at 20° C.

High-Gravity Glycerin.—This is a commercial grade of glycerin conforming to Federal Specification O-G-491a, grade B, and commonly supplied at not less than 99% concentration (specific gravity 1.2595 at 25° C.). It is directed to glycerin's largest U.S. field of use, the manufacture of alkyd resins. Glycerin from propylene, referred to as synthetic glycerin, conforms to these specifications but is commonly supplied at 99.5% glycerol content.

Dynamite glycerin is comparable in concentration with high-gravity glycerin grades, but less emphasis is placed on minimum colour requirements. Yellow distilled is a refined grade meeting less critical standards of colour, with concentration not less than 96% glycerol.

See C. S. Miner and N. N. Dalton, *Glycerol* (1953); Glycerine Producers Association, *Glycerine Properties and Applications* (1957). (N. N. D.; E. S. Px.)

GLYCOLS, the generic name of a class of alcohols having two hydroxyl (—OH) groups on different carbon atoms. The glycols of lower molecular weight are colourless, oily liquids boiling at about 180° C. Several of the lower glycols are important commercially, but the glycols of high molecular weight have little or no commercial importance. Hundreds of them have been prepared for scientific studies. This is particularly true of the pinacols that are obtained by the reduction of ketones and undergo the pinacolone rearrangement.

Ethylene glycol, $HOCH_2CH_2OH$, is a colourless, oily liquid possessing a sweet taste and a mild odour. Its alternate names include ethylene glycol and 1,2-ethanediol.

Ethylene glycol and its derivatives are of commercial importance; both the glycol and its derivatives are generally obtained from ethylene oxide. Large quantities of ethylene glycol are used annually as antifreeze in automotive cooling systems. Its availability at low cost and its high antifreeze efficiency (low molecular weight coupled with the relatively high heat capacities and low viscosities in aqueous solution) admirably suit ethylene glycol for this service. Other important commercial uses are in the manufacture of man-made fibres, low-freezing explosives, industrial humectants and brake fluid.

Ethylene glycol boils at 197.2° C., freezes at —13° C., and is heavier than water; its specific gravity at 20° C. is 1.113 referred to water at the same temperature. Ethylene glycol and some of its derivatives are mildly toxic to warm-blooded animals and should not be used in food and pharmaceutical preparations. It is produced commercially from ethylene gas through the intermediate, ethylene oxide. The oldest process consists of treating ethylene with hypochlorous acid to produce ethylene chlorohydrin, $HOCH_2CH_2Cl$. The chlorohydrin is then converted to the glycol by the action of an alkali such as calcium hydroxide or sodium bicarbonate. Ethylene glycol can also be produced from formaldehyde, hydrogen and carbon monoxide. It is usually produced commercially, however, through ethylene oxide, which is obtained either by the oxidation of ethylene or by the dehydrochlorination of ethylene chlorohydrin. In all three processes, the glycol is obtained as dilute solutions and is recovered and purified by evaporation and distillation procedures.

Ethylene glycol exhibits many of the reactions common to primary alcohols (see ALCOHOL: *Nomenclature*). Careful oxidation yields glycolic acid. Heating the reaction mixture produces oxalic acid. With dehydrating agents, ethylene glycol yields acetaldehyde. Heat alone at 500° C. produces the same change. Halide acids react readily with one hydroxyl group to produce halohydrins. Alkali metals replace the alcoholic hydrogen atoms. With dicarboxylic acids, linear polyesters are obtained; the fibre Dacron (Terylene), for example, is such an ester with terephthalic acid (see PHTHALIC ANHYDRIDE AND PHTHALIC ACIDS: *Phthalic Acids*).

Commercial ethylene glycol condensation polymers (polyethylene glycols) have the general formula $HOCH_2CH_2(OCH_2CH_2)_nOH$. They are produced from ethylene oxide or by combining ethylene glycol with ethylene oxide, and range from liquids to waxlike solids.

The ethers of ethylene glycol are of considerable importance, particularly as organic solvents. They are made by the direct addition of ethylene oxide to the corresponding alcohol. Ethylene glycol monoethyl ether (2-ethoxyethanol), $C_2H_5OCH_2CH_2OH$, is produced by the action of ethylene oxide on ethyl alcohol. The corresponding ethers of diethylene glycol (i.e., dioxane) and other ethylene glycol condensation polymers are prepared in a similar manner.

Propylene glycol, also known as 1,2-propanediol, has the formula $CH_3CHOHCH_2OH$. Its properties and uses generally resemble those of ethylene glycol (its boiling point, for instance, is 189° C.) with the important exception that propylene glycol has a low order of toxicity. It is produced commercially through propylene oxide either by direct oxidation of propylene or from propylene chlorohydrin. Propylene glycol is used in antifreezes, resins, plasticizers, brake fluids, tobacco, food, pharmaceuticals, cosmetics and printing inks. Propylene condensation polymers are produced from propylene oxide or by combining propylene glycol with propylene oxide and range from liquids to waxlike solids. Ethers are produced by reacting propylene oxide with monohydric alcohols.

Hexylene glycol, 2-methyl-2,4-pentanediol, $(CH_3)_2C(OH)CH_2CH(OH)CH_3$, is obtained by the reduction of diacetone alcohol, which, in turn, is produced by the dimerization of acetone under the influence of alkalies. Hexylene glycol boils at 198.27° C. and is miscible with aliphatic and aromatic hydrocarbons, water, fatty acids and alcohols. It finds application in brake fluids, as an anti-agglomerate in the manufacture of portland cement and as a solvent for dyes and synthetic-based inks. It is used in the synthesis of the sulfolane that is used in liquid-vapour and liquid-liquid extraction processes of the petroleum industry.

GLYCONIC, a type of aeolo-choriambic colon (see PROSODY, CLASSICAL), employed in Greek and Latin lyric verse, consisting of aeolic base (⏑⏑) and —⏑⏑—; e.g.,

a) ⏑— montium domin(a) ut fores
b) ⏑— silvarumque virentium
c) ⏑⏑ Dianae sumus in fide

The base rarely takes the form —⏑, as in (c). In Horace it usually takes the form ——, as in (b) and in Catullus —⏑, as in (a). The catalectic version of the glyconic is the "pherecratean"; e.g.,

Lyric stanzas may be composed of three or four glyconics followed by a pherecratean; e.g., Aeschylus, *Agamemnon* 381–384, Catullus xxxiv and lxi. Horace combines glyconics and pherecrateans with pinacolone, $(CH_3)_3$-CCOCH₃, by dehydration with acid reagents. Some commercial interest was shown in this compound in Germany during World War I, for by catalytic dehydration it is possible to convert pinacolone to 2,3-dimethyl-1,3-butadiene (also called diisopropenyl), from which synthetic rubber can be made. (D. G. Z.; N. C. S.)

Pinacol, tetramethylethylene glycol, 2,3-dimethyl-2,3-butanediol, $(CH_3)_2C(OH)C(OH)(CH_3)_2$, is obtained from the bimolecular reduction of acetone by amalgamated magnesium. Its most important reaction is its rearrangement to pinacolone in his lyric stanzas; e.g., *Odes* I, iii, v, vi. A verse compounded of a glyconic and a pherecratean is called a "priapean"; e.g., Catullus xvii:

⏑— —⏑⏑— —⏑⏑—|| ⏑—⏑—
O Colonia quae cupis || ponte ludere longo.

(L. P. E.)

GLYCOSE: see SUGAR.
GLYCOSIDES, NATURAL. The term glycoside is applied to a large number of substances found mainly in plants. Formerly the names glucoside and aglucone were used, but these terms came to be restricted to those glycosides that contain only glucose as their sugar component. While the exact biological function of the plant glycosides is not established, it is probable that their formation provides the plant with a means of storing, in a harmless form, toxic and physiologically active materials which may be liberated by enzymes, in small quantities, when required.

Glycosides are solids, generally crystalline, and most have a bitter taste. Their solutions show the property of rotating the plane of polarized light, usually to the left. Under the influence of aqueous solutions of acids they can be split (hydrolyzed) by the elements of water (H-OH) into one or more sugars and a

nonsugar portion termed the aglycon. This change can also be effected by naturally occurring substances present in trace amounts in neighbouring cells. These substances are known as enzymes and are effective only for one glycoside or for a group of closely related glycosides. The aglycons are widely diversified in chemical structure but all contain a hydroxyl (OH) group through which they combine with the sugar. From the standpoint of chemical structure, a glycoside is a mixed acetal and shows all the properties of such a combination.

Most of the natural glycosides have been assigned names derived from the botanical names of their plant sources. Thus arbutin is a colourless, crystalline, bitter substance that was first extracted from the leaves of the small evergreen shrub *Arbutus uva-ursi;* later it was found in other plant sources, such as the leaves, bark and roots of many varieties of the common pear. Arbutin is hydrolyzed by acids or by the enzyme β-D-glucosidase present in the mixture of enzymes known as almond emulsin, extractable from the bitter almond. Arbutin thus can be split into the sugar D-glucose and the aglycon hydroquinone; its rational chemical name is therefore *para*-hydroxyphenyl-β-D-glucopyranoside.

The term "pyranoside" refers to the size of the internal cyclic acetal in the sugar moiety and "β-D" designates the spatial orientation of the "glycosidic carbon," marked with an asterisk in the following formula:

Arbutin

$C_6H_{12}O_6$ + HO— Hydroquinone (1,4-dihydroxybenzene)   D-Glucose

Glycosides are usually at least sparingly soluble in water and since only soluble substances are transportable in a plant by movements of sap, it is at least useful as a working hypothesis to assume that the plant converts into glycosides: (1) harmful or useless substances which must be transported to the barks, fruit rinds or seed coats, where they can do no harm and will eventually be shed; (2) necessary but harmful substances, which may be useful later; (3) decorative or attractive substances, such as floral pigments, formed in the leaves and transported at the proper season to the flowers or fruits. Experimental support for the theory that glycoside formation in the plant is a detoxication mechanism is provided by the finding that 2-chloroethanol (ClCH₂CH₂OH), a substance which breaks the dormancy of tubers, is converted by plant tissue to 2-chloroethyl-β-D-glucopyranoside. Such a detoxication mechanism also operates in animals. Thus, when hydroquinone is fed to a dog, the following substance appears in the urine:

Para-hydroxyphenyl-β-D-glucopyranosiduronic acid

Many glycosides of D-glucuronic acid with steroidal fragments are normally present in urine and the nature of these materials is modified by such biological conditions as pregnancy.

The plant glycosides exist in a bewildering variety both in regard to their sugar components and, especially, in the nature of their aglycons. To their presence in plants are ascribable the many uses of plant materials established by primitive peoples and exploited by modern civilization. The medicines, condiments and dyes from plant sources occur largely as glycosides. As their chemical nature has become established, most, but not all, of these substances have been replaced by synthetic products. This has been especially true of plant or vegetable dyes, but many condiments and some medicines are still derived from plant extracts. Arbutin, described above, is an example of a simple, colourless, phenolic glycoside, many varieties of which are found in plants. Arbutin is accompanied by methylarbutin, which contains hydroquinone monomethyl ether as its aglycon.

Glycosides of aliphatic alcohols are represented by the purgatives convolvulin and jalapin, whose sugars are in glycosidic combination with the hydroxyl groups of hydroxylated fatty acids and are thus related to the constituents of castor oil. The β-D-glucopyranoside of the terpene alcohol geraniol occurs in *Pelargonium odoratum*. Although most glycosides are characterized by their bitter taste, stevioside is one of remarkable sweetness. It is extractable from the leaves of *Stevia rebaudiana*, a wild shrub of the Compositae family, native to Paraguay. Stevioside contains three units of D-glucose, two of which are in combination with each other; its aglycon, steviol, is a diterpenoid.

The saponins are glycosides of aliphatic alcohols and are widely distributed in plants. They are characterized by their property of producing foams when shaken in aqueous solution. They are toxic to fish and were used as a fish poison by primitive peoples, since the fish so killed were not toxic to humans when eaten. The saponins yield a variety of sugars on hydrolysis; some yield D-glucuronic acid. Their aglycons are termed sapogenins and may be classified as either triterpenoid or steroid. Glycyrrhizin, the saponin of licorice (*Glycyrrhiza glabra*) root, contains a triterpenoid sapogenin, while sarsasaponin, from Mexican sarsaparilla root, contains the steroid sarsasapogenin. (See SAPONINS AND SAPOGENINS.)

Another large group of steroid glycosides that are not saponins are collectively known as the cardiac glycosides. These are powerful heart poisons but are useful heart stimulants in minute dosages. The primitive tribes of Africa employ extracts of the seeds of *Strophanthus* and of the wood and bark of the ouabaio as arrow poisons. Extracts of the bulbs of the squill have been utilized in medicine since ancient times, but better known in modern medicine are the extracts of *Digitalis* or common garden foxglove. The flower of the lily of the valley also yields such extracts. The cardiac glycosides from all of these divergent plant sources are related chemically. On hydrolysis they yield a large variety of unusual sugars but their physiological action lies in the aglycons which possess chemical structures related to those of the steroids.

A group known as the cyanogenetic glycosides is found in the kernels of peaches, cherries and plums and in other parts of a variety of plants. These are mainly glycosides of mandelonitrile ($C_6H_5.CH[OH].CN$). When hydrolyzed by enzymes or by acids they liberate poisonous hydrocyanic acid together with benzaldehyde and one or more sugars, chiefly D-glucose. To this group belongs amygdalin, one of the earliest investigated glycosides. The sugars of amygdalin are two molecules of D-glucose combined as the disaccharide gentiobiose.

Salicin is the active constituent of willow (*Salix*) bark and has long been used as a remedy against fever and in acute rheumatism. Its hydrolytic products are D-glucose and saligenin [salicyl alcohol, *ortho*-hydroxybenzyl alcohol, $C_6H_4(OH)(CH_2OH)$]. Phloridzin (phlorizin, phlorhizin), from the bark of the Rosaceae (apple, pear, cherry and plum tree), is the D-glucoside of a rather complicated phenolic aglycon. Its administration produces a type of diabetes in the dog and this circumstance has been utilized in studies of the disease.

The condiment mustard is prepared by grinding mustard seed with salt, spices and vinegar. A variety of mustard seeds are used, but all contain a glycoside in which a D-glucose entity is directly attached to a sulfur atom rather than to an oxygen atom.

Many of the vegetable dyes formerly so widely used were glycosides. One of the chief of these was madder (*Rubia tinctorum*), formerly grown commercially in the near east. The main glycoside of the madder root yields on hydrolysis the sugars D-glucose and D-xylose, present in disaccharide combination, and 1,2-dihydroxyanthraquinone, or alizarin. Alizarin is employed in the dye industry (certain metallic salts) to form lakes in a wide variety of colours. It was the first vegetable dye whose chemical structure was determined and as a result of this the natural product was replaced by a synthetic preparation of better quality. An interesting yellow dye, known as Indian yellow, is prepared in Bengal by feeding mango leaves to cattle and isolating the dye from the urine. It is a glycoside of D-glucuronic acid attached to a structure quite closely related to alizarin and known as 4,7-dihydroxyxanthone.

The wide variety of pigments present in flowers and fruits are largely mixtures of glycosides with carotenoids. Most of the blue colours and some of the red are glycosides (anthocyanins) of aglycons known as anthocyanidins, which are reduction products of hydroxylated phenyl-benzo-γ-pyrones. Glycosides of the latter constitute a large group of yellow pigments widely distributed in fruits, flowers, bark and other pigmented plant structures. A typical yellow glycoside is quercitrin, present in oak bark (see QUERCITRON BARK).

BIBLIOGRAPHY.—J. J. L. van Rijn (H. Dieterle), *Die Glykoside* (1931); G. Klein, *Handbuch der Pflanzenanalyse*, vol. iii, pt. 2 (1932); R. J. McIlroy, *The Plant Glycosides* (1951). (M. L. WM.)

G-MEN, or government men, a journalistic term for special agents of the United States department of justice, bureau of investigation. The phrase is supposed to have obtained currency after the capture of a notorious criminal, George ("Machine Gun") Kelly, in Sept. 1933. (See FEDERAL BUREAU OF INVESTIGATION.) By analogy, investigative agents of the U.S. department of the treasury became known as T-men.

GNAT, a common name for any of several species of small flies, particularly those that are annoying or that bite man. In North America the term is often applied to the black flies, biting midges and certain other small flies that hover about the eyes of man and other animals. In Britain the name usually refers to mosquitoes (see MOSQUITO) or less commonly to crane flies (family Tipulidae).

Black flies (family Simuliidae) include many species that are hump-backed between the bases of the wings and are therefore also known as buffalo gnats. Female black flies suck blood, and their bites can cause painful swelling. Several species attack livestock; severe infestations occasionally cause the death of a victim. Certain other black flies are pests of poultry and are locally known as turkey gnats. The tiny biting midges (family Ceratopogonidae), so small that they can easily crawl through an ordinary mosquito screen, are sometimes called gnats. Species of *Culicoides*

COURTESY OF A. E. CAMERON AND THE CANADIAN DEPT. OF AGRICULTURE

FEMALE BLACK FLY (SIMULIUM SIMILE)

especially are familiar pests along the seashore, in wet forests and near inland waters (see SAND FLY). Their bites carry no known disease but are extremely annoying. Some flies, several species of *Hippelates* (family Chloropidae), are a nuisance to man because they congregate near the eyes to feed on available exudate or merely swarm about the face; they are popularly known as eye gnats. Although they do not bite, they may carry the bacteria of pinkeye, an acute conjunctivitis.

Also known as gnats are several kinds of small, nonbiting flies such as the midges (family Chironomidae), some of which superficially resemble mosquitoes. In summer adult midges may emerge from streams or lakes, where the immature stages are spent, in such numbers that the air is filled with the hum of their wings and they may be attracted to lights by the thousands. Fungus gnats are common in forests, where they congregate in great numbers in darkened crannies, as beneath overhanging banks and in culverts (see FUNGUS GNAT). Certain small, dusky species, the larvae of which feed on fungi associated with potted plants, are often seen in houses. Winter gnats (family Trichoceridae) are slender, dark brown or gray flies resembling crane flies. They are occasionally seen on sunny days in late autumn, winter and spring. Small fruit flies, or vinegar flies, species of *Drosophila* (*q.v.*), are locally known as vinegar gnats.

See also FLY.

GNATCATCHER, the name given to birds of the American subfamily Polioptilinae (family Regulidae, kinglets). About 12 species are recognized. Gnatcatchers are small, slender, grayish and white birds with relatively long, slender tails. They build beautifully symmetrical compact nests of plant down and other

BY COURTESY OF L. H. WALKINSHAW

BLUE-GRAY GNATCATCHER (POLIOPTILA CAERULEA CAERULEA)

soft materials bound together with spider webs and covered with lichens. The nests occur at elevations of a few feet to as much as 70 ft. above the ground. Although the name gnatcatcher has come to be applied generally to these birds, they by no means are restricted in diet to, or even show any noticeable partiality for, these insects. They feed on all small insects, and occasionally have been known to seize others large enough to require tearing apart before they can swallow them. Stomach contents of these birds have revealed longicorn beetles, jointworm flies, caddis flies and other insects.

The best-known species is the blue-gray gnatcatcher (*Polioptila caerulea caerulea*) of the eastern United States, in which the male has a black forehead. The western gnatcatcher (*P. c. amoenissima*) breeds from California and Colorado south into Mexico. The plumbeous gnatcatcher (*P. melanura melanura*) breeds from southeastern California, southern Nevada and the Rio Grande valley southward; the black-tailed gnatcatcher (*P. m. californica*) occurs in the San Diego district of California. Other races and species occur in Central and South America, extending as far south as Argentina and Chile.

(G. F. Ss.; Hr. Fn.)

GNEISENAU, AUGUST WILHELM ANTON, GRAF NEIDHARDT VON (1760–1831), Prussian field marshal and one of the chief organizers of victory against Napoleon, was born at Schilda, near Torgau, on Oct. 27, 1760, of a noble but impoverished family of Upper Austria. His mother died when accompanying his father (a Saxon artillery officer) on service during the Seven Years' War. Brought up in poverty, he was eventually educated in Würzburg at the expense of his maternal grandfather. After short periods at Erfurt university and in an Austrian cavalry regiment, he was in Canada in 1782–83 as a lieutenant in an Ansbach unit hired by the British government.

In 1786 he obtained employment in the Prussian army, but remained on garrison duty in Silesia until 1806, when he fought at

Jena as a company commander. The successful defense of Kolberg against the French in 1807 laid the foundation for his advancement. When in 1808 King Frederick William III dismissed Stein and the reform party, Gneisenau relinquished his commission and went on secret missions to London and St. Petersburg to explore the possibilities of further resistance to Napoleon. At the beginning of 1813 he joined G. J. D. von Scharnhorst (*q.v.*), then chief of staff, as his "first general staff officer." In this capacity he was largely responsible for the plan of operations of the Prussian and Russian armies for the spring of 1813. After Scharnhorst had died of wounds at Prague (June 28, 1813), Gneisenau became chief of the general staff. The strategic plan of the battle of Leipzig and the winter campaign of the allies was mostly his work and in March 1814 he had the satisfaction of seeing allied troops enter Paris. (*See* NAPOLEONIC WARS.)

Gneisenau was a remarkable and unusual man in many ways. He saw clearly that the mercenary Prussian army had to be transferred into a citizens' army animated by liberal ideas and that a staff system of educated officers had to be substituted for control by the king. His sojourn in England had led him to hope that the Prussian monarchy and nobility might be remodeled on the British pattern. He combined to an unusual degree the qualities of a military thinker and a man of action.

On Napoleon's escape from Elba he became chief of staff to G. L. von Blücher (*q.v.*). It was largely his drive and organizing ability which brought about the countermarch of the Prussian army to attack the French flank at Waterloo on the evening of June 18, 1815.

In 1816 he resigned because his liberal convictions were in conflict with the government policy of reaction. It was not until 1825 —on the anniversary of Waterloo—that he was made a field marshal. In 1831, during the Polish revolution, he was appointed commander of the forces protecting Prussia's eastern frontier. He died of cholera at his headquarters at Posen on Aug. 23, 1831.

See H. Delbruck, *Leben des Feldmarschalls Gneisenau,* 2 vol., 4th ed. (1920); Walter Görlitz, *The German General Staff: Its History and Structure, 1657–1945,* Eng. ed. (1953).
(C. N. B.)

GNEISS, in geology a generic term signifying a large and varied series of rocks with a banded and usually foliated structure in which layers of minerals with a granular texture alternate with thin layers composed of lamellar or fibrous minerals, usually in parallel arrangement. The term originally was used by the miners of the Erzgebirge in Germany to designate the country rock in which the mineral veins occur. The word is of Slavonic origin meaning rotted, or decomposed, in allusion to the altered character of the country rock in the immediate vicinity of the ore veins.

The foliation of gneiss may be frequently interrupted and the ease of splitting of the rock is usually much less in evidence than in the case of schists (*q.v.*). Gneisses, however, may also be built up wholly of granular minerals, the gneissose structure being given by the alternation of bands of different mineral composition; *e.g.*, pyroxene gneiss.

As used in its widest sense, gneiss is a structural term rather than a name applied to rocks of a particular mineral composition or genesis. Thus gneisses may be of igneous or metamorphic origin, and have a great range of chemical composition. The minerals of the granular bands usually consist of quartz, feldspar (orthoclase, microcline, plagioclase) or both, and the lamellar or fibrous bands are usually composed of chlorite, mica (muscovite, biotite), graphite, amphibole, sillimanite, etc.

According to their origin, gneisses are subdivided broadly into four groups: (1) primary gneisses, (2) injection gneisses, (3) orthogneisses and (4) paragneisses.

Primary gneisses are plutonic igneous rocks possessing a banded structure, in which a parallel arrangement of the lamellar or fibrous minerals (if present) is evident. These rocks owe their structures to a flow movement in a magma in which crystallization has already progressed. Primary gneisses are often of granitic composition and build up great areas of Pre-Cambrian Archean formations. Much of the Lewisian gneiss of Scotland, the Laurentian gneiss of Canada and the igneous gneisses of other continental shields may be rocks of this character. The setting up of gneissic banding in a fluid magma by flow movement presupposes a magmatic heterogeneity which in nature arises either by imperfect differentiation or by the incorporation of foreign material within the magma.

In many Archean shields, the granite gneisses are characterized by containing numerous bands of rock, usually of the nature of amphibolites or hornblende schists, representing basic igneous rocks of earlier date incorporated in the magma during intrusion.

Migmatite gneisses (from the Greek *migma*, "a mixture") are mixed, composite or injection gneisses sometimes extensively developed in crystalline schist formations which have been invaded by granitic intrusions.

They develop both by mechanical injection of fluid between the folia of schists and by intimate soaking and metasomatism whereby new feldspar (orthoclase and plagioclase) arises in the body of the schist, conspicuously in the form of porphyroblasts, or large pseudoporphyritic crystals, but also in finer elements in the ground mass. In advanced stages, particularly where the schist is of argillaceous or clayey type, the resultant rocks may simulate primary granite gneisses with but vague remnants or "ghosts" of the original schist to tell the story of their origin.

The term orthogneiss refers strictly to igneous rocks in which a gneissic structure has been superimposed by metamorphism, but the name is used by some writers to include also primary gneisses. Criteria for the distinction of orthogneisses from primary gneisses are sometimes difficult to establish, and are chiefly provided in the textural and structural relations of the rocks. They may be evidenced by signs of crushing (cataclastic structure), relict textures, or where the whole rock has been totally recrystallized by the textural relations of the minerals. In primary gneisses the form development of the crystals is largely dependent on the order in which the minerals have crystallized from the magma, while in totally recrystallized orthogneisses the growth of the minerals has taken place in an essentially solid environment, and the form development is dependent on the crystallizing power of the several minerals, giving rise to crystalloblastic texture (*see* METAMORPHISM). Some of the best-known orthogneisses are those of the granulite districts of Saxony and the Austrian Waldviertel near Krems.

Many gneisses are undoubtedly sedimentary rocks brought to their present state by such agents of metamorphism as heat, movement, crushing and recrystallization. This may be demonstrated partly by their mode of occurrence; they accompany limestones, graphite schists, quartzites and other rocks whose sedimentary origin is never in doubt. In many cases bulk chemical composition is a certain clue to their origin, since they correspond in this particular to normal sediments and not to any known igneous rocks. Structural or textural criteria, such as bedding, evidence of original pebbly or clastic character, are not infrequently to be found. The chemical composition of paragneisses is reflected in their mineralogical constitution.

Gneisses derived from argillites may be rich in biotite, muscovite, cordierite, almandine garnet, staurolite, chloritoid, kyanite and sillimanite, some of which minerals are practically unknown in metamorphosed igneous rocks, while gneisses derived from limestones or dolomites carry such characteristic minerals as grossularite, idocrase, wollastonite, scapolite or forsterite. Some paragneisses are rich in feldspar and quartz and may show so close a resemblance to gneisses of igneous origin that by no single

These basic bands become injected along planes of bedding or foliation by the granitic material and ultimately in places become so intimately intermingled with the magma as to produce a gneiss of hybrid origin. Less advanced stages of this process where injection takes place along the foliation planes of inclusions or of the country rock adjacent give rise to injection gneisses.

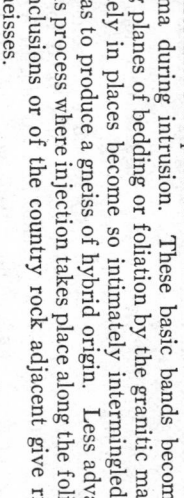

BIOTITE GNEISS

character, chemical or mineralogical, can their original nature be definitely established.

(C. E. T.)

GNEIST, RUDOLF VON (1816-1895), German jurist and political thinker who exercised a profound influence on the growth of German administrative law, was born in Berlin on Aug. 13, 1816, the son of a judge of the supreme tribunal. From 1833 to 1836 he studied law, especially Roman law under Karl Friedrich von Savigny, at Berlin university. In 1841 he became a judge, and from 1847 he sat in the high court in Berlin. Though he was no revolutionary, he soon had to resign because of his opposition to the reactionary policy of the Prussian government after 1848.

After resigning his judgeship, Gneist devoted himself to academic studies. Already in 1842 he had become a reader in Roman law at Berlin university. Gradually, however, he turned his attention from this subject and won a growing reputation with lectures on assizes, on public and oral proceedings, on English and French judicial organization and on Prussian, German and English constitutional and administrative law. Between 1850 and 1860, completely withdrawn from political affairs, he wrote his great work on English constitutional law.

Though he had remarkable success as a teacher, it was only in 1858 that he became a full professor in Berlin—a position that he was to hold until his death. In all his works, most of which even carried the words "English" or "self-government" in their titles, he drew upon English conditions past and present. His writings earned him a widespread reputation. For more than 20 years (from 1868) he was president of the German jurists' association; and he received honorary degrees from Edinburgh, Berlin (doctor of philosophy), Bologna and Rostock.

Gneist's political career began in 1845 with his election as a town councilor in Berlin. This gave him considerable experience in local politics, which was of great value to him for his later academic treatises on "self-government." He lost his seat because of his views on the reaction after 1848, but regained it in 1858.

He was also a member of the Prussian house of representatives from 1859 to 1893, of the *Reichstag* from 1867 to 1884 and of the Prussian state council from 1884. A liberal by conviction, he joined the moderate National Liberal party in 1866, though originally he had been inclined more to the Progressive party. Later he turned to a more conservative liberalism, under the influence of Lorenz von Stein (Stein's theory—developed about 1850—is based on the dualism of state and society). Bismarck frequently asked his advice. In the *Kulturkampf* period (1871-78) Gneist opposed the Jesuits and the demand for denominational schools. He took a strong interest in political matters without holding any extreme views. This position is particularly apparent in his writings. Though these do not always stand up to scholarly criticism, they reveal a powerful and practical political mind that could at the same time present clearly defined legal conceptions. These assets also explain Gneist's great popular success.

At the height of his success Gneist resumed his career as a judge. His untiring advocacy of an independent administrative jurisdiction was rewarded when, at the founding of the Prussian supreme administrative court in 1875, Gneist was invited to become a member of it. This court was then the highest of its kind in Germany, and Gneist exercised a decisive influence in the development of its jurisdiction. Gneist died in Berlin on July 22, 1895.

Gneist's main field of work was public law. Here he emphasized the idea of "self-government"; by this he understood the administration of public affairs by self-responsible, honorary officials appointed by the king from among the aristocracy and the middle classes, in contrast to an administration from above by professional civil servants or elected bodies. His model was the administration of the English counties by the justices of the peace whereas most other contemporary advocates of "self-government" inclined rather to the Franco-Belgian systems. Though Gneist's presentation of English conditions was not always accurate, since he sometimes saw them in the light of preconceived political notions, his writings nevertheless provided a basis on which the German middle classes came to participate widely in public administration. The greater part of the German administration remained, however, in the hands of the professional civil service, mainly because the needs of the modern state favoured the growth of specialization in this field, so that the term "self-government" is hardly any longer applied in the specific meaning used by Gneist.

The most pregnant of Gneist's ideas proved to be his demand for the establishment of independent administrative courts run by legal and administrative experts charged with the control of the administration. The German states one after another set up an independent administrative jurisdiction which was repeatedly extended. The opening of the federal administrative court in Berlin on June 8, 1953, and the promulgation of the federal code for administrative procedure on Jan. 21, 1960, completed the development which Gneist had initiated.

Gneist's writings include *Das heutige englische Verfassungsund Verwaltungsrecht*, 2 vol. (1857–60; later editions under different titles); *Englische Verfassungsgeschichte* (1882; Eng. trans., *History of the English Constitution*, 1886); *Verwaltung, Justiz, Rechtsweg: Staatsverwaltung und Selbstverwaltung nach englischen und deutschen Verhältnissen* (1869); *Das englische Parlament* (1886; Eng. trans., *English Parliament*, 1889).

BIBLIOGRAPHY.—O. von Gierke, *Rudolf von Gneist* (1896); E. Schiffer, *Rudolf von Gneist* (1929); E. Meister, *Kampf der Konservativen und Liberalen um die ... Gneistschen Verwaltungsreformen* (1929); H. Heffter, *Die deutsche Selbstverwaltung im 19. Jahrhundert* (1950).
(W. M.-F.)

GNIEZNO, a town of Poland, in the Poznan *województwo* (province), is a district capital and one of the two capitals of the Warsaw-Gniezno Roman Catholic archdiocese. Pop. (1960) 8,820. Situated on the Poznan-Torun railway in a region of many lakes, it is a trade centre and has industries processing local agricultural produce. Gniezno is rich in fine old buildings, among which the cathedral is outstanding. Its 12th-century Romanesque door, cast in bronze, showing episodes from the life of St. Adalbert (St. Wojciech), is one of the finest examples of early medieval Polish art. Gniezno was one of the oldest fortresses of the Polan tribe (8th century A.D.) and the first capital of the Piast state. Its importance increased greatly after the burial in the cathedral of the remains of St. Adalbert. In A.D. 1000 the town became the capital of the archdiocese (the first in Poland independent of the German) and the place of coronation of Polish kings. It obtained town rights in 1243. Gniezno came under Prussian rule (1793) and passed to Poland in 1919. During World War II the Germans established there one of the first forced-labour camps in Poland. The cathedral, damaged by incendiary bombs in 1945, was being restored after its original Gothic style in the 1960s.
(K. M. WI.)

GNOME AND GNOMIC POETRY. The Greek word *gnome* means moral aphorism or proverb. Short memorable sentences enshrining traditional wisdom are found in early Greek literature, both poetry and prose, from Homer and Hesiod onward. Their form may be either imperative, as in the famous command "know thyself," or indicative, as in the couplet by Theognis of Megara (6th century B.C.): "No mortal who misled a stranger or a suppliant, Polypaides, has gone unheeded by the immortal gods." (The tense of the last verb is the so-called gnomic aorist, English usage generally prefers the present tense; *e.g.,* "Too many cooks spoil the broth.") Such aphorisms were collected into anthologies, called *gnomologia*, and used in instructing the young. Aeschines, the 4th-century B.C. Athenian orator, remarks that as children we learn the gnomes of the poets so that as adults we may practise them. One of the best known *gnomologia* was compiled by Joannes Stobaeus in the 5th century A.D., and such collections remained popular in the middle ages.

Gnomes appear frequently in Old English epic and lyric poetry. In *Beowulf* they are often interjected into the narrative, drawing a moral from the hero's actions with such phrases as "Thus a man ought to act" and "Fate often aids a man not doomed to die, when his courage holds good" (the equivalent of the modern saying "God helps those who help themselves"). The main collections of Old English gnomes are to be found in the 10th-century *Exeter Book* (*q.v.*) and the Cotton Tiberius manuscript (early 11th century), clearly examples of early verse, abrupt and disconnected, yet picturesque and of great power.

See Pauly-Wissowa, *Real-Encyclopädie der classischen Altertumswissenschaft*, suppl. vol. 6, col. 74–90 (1935); B. C. Williams, *Gnomic Poetry in Anglo-Saxon* (1914).

GNOMON originally meant an instrument for allowing one to know the time. In its simple and primitive form it seems to have been a rod placed vertically on a plane surface, and later upon the surface of a hemisphere. The term was at one time substantially synonymous with vertical line. From this early use it came to represent a figure like a carpenter's square, but usually with equal arms. Seeking to relate number to geometric forms, the early Greek mathematicians imagined squares as built up of gnomons added to unity. For example, they saw that $1 + 3$, $1 + 3 + 5$, $1 + 3 + 5 + 7$, and so on, are squares, and that the odd numbers in a figure like this were related to the geometric gnomon. Such numbers were, therefore, themselves called gnomons. The early idea of a geometric gnomon was extended by Euclid (*q.v.*; c. 300 B.C.) to include a figure consisting of two parallelograms forming an L. Four or five centuries later Hero of Alexandria extended the term to mean that which, added to any number or figure, makes the whole similar to that to which it is added. This usage is also found in the writings of Theon of Smyrna (c. 125) in connection with figurate numbers (*q.v.*). For example, the pentagonal numbers are $1 + 4$, $1 + 4 + 7$, $1 + 4 + 7 + 10 \ldots$; and the gnomons in this case are $4, 7, 10 \ldots$; *i.e.*, they constitute an arithmetical series with a common difference of 3.

The sundial (*q.v.*), with a gnomon as a vertical needle, is said to have been introduced into Greece by Anaximander (*q.v.*; 575 B.C.).
(D. E. S.; X.)

GNOSTICISM, derived from the Greek word *gnostikos* (one who has *gnosis*, "knowledge"), is a term used by modern scholars to designate a religious movement of late antiquity, with which the Christian church came into contact. Gnosticism is not primarily or exclusively a Christian heresy but rather a religion in its own right, which is also known from pagan sources such as the *Corpus Hermeticum* and the *Oracula Chaldaica*, and from the oldest sources of Jewish mysticism, which can be traced back to the 1st and 2nd centuries A.D. Though it is not always easy to distinguish Gnosticism from Greek philosophy and the Christian religion, it has certain characteristics of its own which are alien to Greek or Christian tradition, such as the depreciation of the cosmos and the rejection of atonement. Historically most important is Christian Gnosticism, the systems of which can be proved to have existed in the 2nd century and which extended into Manichaeism (*q.v.*), a Gnostic world religion.

Origins.—In the Dead sea scrolls (*q.v.*) the knowledge of God and the opposition of light and darkness are strongly stressed. Their authors, probably the Essenes, may be considered as forerunners of Gnosticism, though no coherent Gnostic system can be proved to lie behind their conceptions. More important for Gnosticism are the early *Merkabah* mystics of Palestinian Judaism (*see* CABALA), who conceived their doctrine concerning the ascent through the heavens and the "measuring of the body of God" as an esoteric lore for the elect, a higher knowledge of things heavenly and divine. This current may have been stimulated by the magic and syncretism of the contemporary Hellenistic world, but it developed in the very midst of Judaism itself. It has been shown that both the terminology and the concepts of this Jewish mysticism survive in later Gnosticism. At its Jewish stage, however, Gnosticism remained monotheistic and preserved the distinction between man, even at the highest point he can reach, and the transcendent God.

The first Gnostic about whom something can be said with confidence is Simon Magus (*q.v.*), a Jewish heterodox teacher from Gitta in Samaria, who may have considered himself as the magical incorporation of the great power of God (Acts viii, 9–10). In his school a certain Helen was venerated as the image of Sophia, the "first idea of God," who generated the world and fell. This seems to be mainly a combination of a local cult of Helen with elements of Jewish wisdom and Greek philosophy. The fundamental conception that evil is due to a break within the Godhead is new and remained characteristic for all Gnostic schools. There is, however, no trustworthy evidence that Simon Magus distinguished between the creator and the highest God. His *gnosis* was still Jewish and monotheistic. This is Gnosticism in its earliest form. The same must be said about the gnosticizing circles which are alluded to in the later part of the New Testament, especially in the Epistle to the Colossians. Stress on "knowledge," cult of angels, ascetic or libertinistic tendencies, though perhaps already gnostic, did not yet imply dyotheism.

This dualistic phase was reached after the expansion of Gnosticism into the Hellenistic world and under the influence of Platonic philosophy (especially that of the *Timaeus*) from which the doctrine was borrowed that a lower demiurge was responsible for the creation of this world. This teaching is to be found in the *Apocryphon* of John (early 2nd century) and other documents of popular *gnosis* found near Naj' Hammadi in upper Egypt in the 1940s and in the *Pistis Sophia*, a 3rd-century Gnostic work in Coptic belonging to the same school. The learned *gnosis* of Valentinus, Basilides (*qq.v.*) and their schools presupposes this popular *gnosis* which, however, has been thoroughly Hellenized and Christianized and sometimes comes very near to the views of middle-Platonism (especially the teaching of Numenius).

Nature.—Gnosticism has its own conception of man, the world and God, expressed in various ways and based on a typical religious experience. The unconscious self of man (or some man) is consubstantial with the Godhead, but because of a tragic fall it is thrown into a foreign world which is completely alien to its real being. Through revelation from above man becomes conscious of his origin, essence and transcendent destiny. This revelation is often identified with the call of Jesus (not to be found in the Gospels, which the Gnostics regard as merely an exoteric allegory, but rather in a visionary experience or the initiation into a secret doctrine). So Gnostic revelation is to be distinguished both from philosophical enlightenment, because it cannot be acquired by the forces of reason, and from Christian revelation, because it is not rooted in history and transmitted by Scripture. It is rather the intuition of the mystery of the self. The world, produced from evil matter and possessed by evil demons, cannot be a creation of a good God; it is mostly conceived of as an illusion, or an abortion, dominated as it is by Yahweh, the Jewish demiurge, whose creation and history are deprecated. This world is therefore alien to God, who is for the Gnostics depth and silence, beyond any name or predicate, the absolute, the source of good spirits who form together the pleroma or realm of light. These conceptions are expressed in various myths, which have used material from many oriental and Greek religions, but serve to express a basic experience which is new, the discovery of the unconscious self or spirit in man which sleeps in him until awakened by the Saviour.

Gnosticism in the technical sense of the word should be distinguished from Encratism, which taught the rejection of marriage as well as the heavenly origin of the soul and "knowledge" but did not express this view in myth and knew of no split within the Godhead. It is misleading to quote (as is often done) the Odes of Solomon, the teaching of Tatian, the Gospel of Thomas or the Acts of Thomas, which are encratic, as witnesses of Gnostic doctrine. Encratism, which is deeply rooted in primitive Christianity and for a long time and in various countries remained a current within Christianity, was rather older than classical Gnosticism. It served as a starting point for the Gnostic speculations and made it possible for the Gnostics to link up their views with Christianity.

Influence.—Scholars differ in their assessment of Gnostic influence. Following R. Reitzenstein, R. Bultmann supposes that a pre-Christian Gnostic myth of the saved Saviour, of Iranian origin, had a considerable influence on St. Paul, on the author of the Gospel of John and on the Christology of the Synoptic Gospels. Neither the Valentinian "Gospel of Truth" nor the Dead sea scrolls contains such a myth and it remains uncertain that it existed at all before Manichaeism. The Mandaeans (*q.v.*), a Gnostic sect still existing in Iraq, may have developed out of a Jewish sect under the influence of Syrian Gnosticism in the 3rd century. It seems doubtful whether the nucleus of their teachings influenced primitive Christianity, though their writings contain many striking parallels to the Gospel of John. If Gnosticism is mainly a product of the 2nd century, it may preserve Christian elements which have been gnosticized and for the inexperienced eye appear to be Gnostic. So the influence of the learned *gnosis* of Valentinus, Basilides and others upon Christianity seems to have been mainly negative:

1. They considered Christ primarily as the exclusive revealer, but they denied the reality and necessity of atonement. Therefore they very often negated the humanity of Christ, which led to the so-called docetism (*q.v.*). Against this view the Fathers of the Church, especially Irenaeus, underlined the reality of the incarnation and stressed the importance of the work of Christ.

2. They denied the reality of the creation as the theatre of God's glory, and the place of fulfillment of his designs and of obedience to his commandments, thus rejecting the Old Testament. Against this the Fathers maintained the identity of Creator and Saviour and developed a theology of history.

3. They annulled the unity of the human race by dividing it into spiritual, psychic and material classes. This led the Fathers to extol free will and personal responsibility of each individual.

Thus the development of Christian doctrine was to a large extent a reaction against Gnosticism. Some Christians, however, especially Clement of Alexandria and Origen (*qq.v.*), tried to integrate Gnostic values into their own religion: Christ is the revealer of "true *gnosis*," pre-existent fall of the spirits, image of God in man, return of all to their spiritual origin. It was, however, more an atmosphere and a certain attitude than specific teachings that were adopted.

It is difficult to discern when and where the Gnostic movement was halted by the church. In Rome the Gnostics Valentinus and Cerdo as well as the semi-Gnostic Marcion (*q.v.*) were excommunicated as early as A.D. 150, but at the same time the Gnostics seem to have remained members of the church in Egypt. In the west the last remnants of Gnostic groups were dissolved in the 4th century only with the help of the state. In the Syrian east all sorts of Gnostic conventicles seem to have continued their existence and may even have influenced the Paulicians and so the Bogomils and Cathari (*qq.v.*) of the middle ages. Moreover, Gnostic Manichaeism spread in Asia as far as Turkistan and China. On the whole the history of extension and extinction of the Gnostic groups after the 4th century (with the exception of Manichaeism) remains largely unknown; therefore the relation of medieval Gnosticism (Catharism, Bogomilism, etc.) to ancient forms of *gnosis*, albeit probable, cannot be demonstrated with certainty.

After the opinions of the Gnostics had become known in the 16th century through the edition of the works of their opponents, the antiheretical Fathers, which contained large extracts from their teachings, and after the new appraisal of the heresies through the work of the German Protestant theologian Gottfried Arnold (in the late 17th century) and others, Gnostic ideas had a considerable influence upon such idealists as Goethe, Novalis and Hegel. The theosophical movement of the 20th century, with which Gnosticism has much in common, rightly claims the Gnostics as its spiritual ancestor (*see* THEOSOPHY). Jungian psychology, which owes not a little to this movement, can be of some help in interpreting Gnostic mythology and may help to show that behind it there is a religious experience of a certain type. Modern Gnosticism, however, is monistic, whereas ancient Gnosticism is basically dualistic.

For the semi-Gnostic Hermetic treatises, *see* HERMES TRISMEGISTOS. *See also* references under "Gnosticism" in the Index.

BIBLIOGRAPHY.—*Collections of Gnostic works:* W. Völker, *Quellen zur Geschichte der christlichen Gnosis* (1932); W. Till, *Pistis Sophia*, 2nd ed. (1954), *Apokryphon Johannis* (1955); M. Malinine, H. C. Puech and G. Quispel, *Evangelium Veritatis* (1955); Kendrick Grobel, *The Gospel of Truth* (1960); R. M. Grant, *Gnosticism* (1961). *General works:* H. Jonas, *Gnosis und spätantiker Geist*, 2 vol. (1933-54), *The Gnostic Religion* (1958); A. J. Festugière, *La Révélation d'Hermès Trismégiste*, 4 vol. (1944-54); H. C. Puech, *Le Mani-*

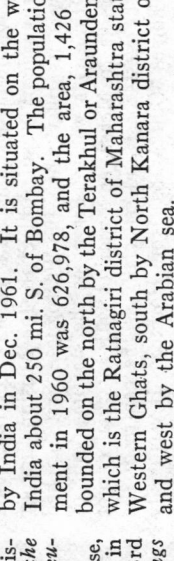

chéisme (1949); R. M. Wilson, *The Gnostic Problem* (1958); G. Quispel, *Gnosis als Weltreligion* (1951); R. Reitzenstein, *Das iranische Erlösungsmysterium* (1921); R. Bultmann in *Zeitschrift für die Neutestamentliche Wissenschaft*, vol. 24 (1925).

Naǧ' Hammadi: F. L. Cross, *The Jung Codex* (1955); J. Doresse, *Les Livres secrets des Gnostiques d'Égypte* (1958); H. C. Puech in E. Hennecke-W. Schneemelcher, *Neutestamentliche Apokryphen*, 3rd ed. (1959); W. C. van Unnik, *Newly Discovered Gnostic Writings* (1960).

Gnosticism and Judaism: G. Scholem, *Major Trends in Jewish Mysticism*, rev. ed. (1946), *Jewish Gnosticism, Merkabah Mysticism and Talmudic Tradition* (1960); R. M. Grant, *Gnosticism and Early Christianity* (1959). (G. Q.)

GNU (WILDEBEEST), the common name for two kinds of large African antelopes, about the size of a pony. The southern African form, the white-tailed gnu, or black wildebeest (*Connochaetes gnou*), is dark brown with long black tufts on the snout, chin, throat and chest, and long, flowing white tail. The horns, present in both sexes, grow forward and downward and then turn upward at their tips. Black wildebeest no longer exist as truly wild animals, but are preserved within fences on a number of southern African farms. The brindled gnu, or blue wildebeest (*C. taurinus*), is reasonably abundant over much of central and southeastern Africa, from northern Zululand to Kenya. It is silvery-gray with dark vertical bands on the sides, and has a black mane, tail and face, whitish cheeks and a tuft of dark hair on chin and throat, but no tuft on the face or chest. The shorter hairs of the tail are whitish. The horns spread sideways and turn up at the tips.

Both kinds of gnus stand higher at the withers than at the rump. Gnus live in herds, often of very large size, and graze on the grasses and low scrub of open plains. When disturbed they dash away to a short distance and then wheel round to gaze at whatever has frightened them. In flight they toss their heads, prance about and throw up their heels in a wild erratic manner ludicrous to the human onlooker. They do not move more than 20 or 30 mi. from water sources, which they visit every two or three days. A single young is born after a gestation of eight to nine months. After the birth of the calves, the bulls and cows move off in separate groups. *See also* ANTELOPE.
(L. H. M.)

GO (I-GO), a skilled maneuver game for two players, probably Japan's most popular board game, originated in China as *wei-ch'i*. An ancient Chinese encyclopaedia attributes its invention to Wu Ts'an; other sources credit it to the emperor Gio in 2356 B.C. It is also attributed to the emperors Yan and Shun. It was reportedly brought to Japan in A.D. 735 by Kibi Dajin. The Go institute was founded by the first national champion, Hon-inbō-Sansa; the earliest recorded game is dated A.D. 1253. Go is played on a square wooden board (*goban*) checkered by 19 vertical lines and 19 horizontal lines. It is played with 181 black and 180 white *go-ishi* or flat, round "stones." Each player in his turn places a stone on the intersection of two lines (a *me*) which constitutes one unit of territory. A stone or group of stones can be captured if it can be completely enclosed by the opponent, leaving no connected vacant point. The winner is the player who has conquered the largest territory by establishing a boundary made of his own stones. Go demands great skill, strategy and patience, and is capable of infinite variety; yet the rules and pieces are so simple that children can play. Special handicap rules allow players of unequal skill to play together. A Japanese Go association, founded in 1924, supervises tournaments, rules and players. Gobang was an English version.
(P. Fr.)

GOA, the name of the capital of former Portuguese India (Estado da India) and of the surrounding territory, which was more exactly described as Goa settlement, prior to its annexation by India in Dec. 1961. It is situated on the western coast of India about 250 mi. S. of Bombay. The population of the settlement in 1960 was 626,978, and the area, 1,426 sq.mi. Goa is bounded on the north by the Terakhul or Arunden river (beyond which is the Ratnagiri district of Maharashtra state), east by the Western Ghats, south by North Kanara district of Mysore state and west by the Arabian sea.

With Damão and Diu (*qq.v.*), Goa settlement formed a single administrative province ruled by a governor general, and a single ecclesiastical province subject to the archbishop of Goa, who is primate of the east and patriarch of the East Indies. There were legislative and executive councils which worked in collaboration with the governor. Goa settlement comprised the four districts conquered early in the 16th century (1510) and known as the Velhas Conquistas (Old Conquests); seven districts acquired later (Novas [New] Conquistas); and the island of Angediva or Anjidiv. The settlement, with a coast line of 62 mi., is hilly, especially in the Novas Conquistas, including a portion of the Western Ghats rising to nearly 4,000 ft. The two largest rivers are the Mandavi and the Juari, which together encircle the island of Goa (Ilhas), being connected on the landward side by a creek. The island is triangular, the apex (called the *cabo* or cape) being a rocky headland separating the harbour of Goa into two anchorages: Aguada at the mouth of the Mandavi on the north and Mormugão (Marmagão) at the mouth of Juari on the south. There are three cities in Goa: Old Goa, New Goa (Pangim) and Mormugão.

Old Goa is, for the most part, a city of ruins. The chief surviving buildings include the cathedral, founded by Affonso d'Albuquerque in 1511, rebuilt in 1623 and still used for public worship; the convent of St. Francis (1517), a converted mosque rebuilt in 1661 (with a portal of carved black stone), the only relic of Portuguese architecture in India dating from the first quarter of the 16th century; the chapel of St. Catherine (1551); the church of Bom Jesus (1594–1603) containing the shrine of St. Francis Xavier (*see* XAVIER, SAINT FRANCIS); and the 17th-century convents of St. Monica and St. Cajetan. The college of St. Paul is in ruins.

Pangim (Panjim or New Goa), originally a suburb of Old Goa, is built (like the parent city) on the left bank of the Mandavi estuary. Pop. (1950) 31,950. It is a modern port and contains the archbishop's palace, government house and barracks; it has a medical school, teachers' training college and several secondary and primary schools. Pangim became the residence of the viceroy in 1759 and the capital of Portuguese India in 1843.

Mormugão, with its modern breakwater and quay and sheltered by the promontory of Salsette, is the best port between Bombay and Kozhikode (Calicut). A railway connects it (south of the Juari estuary) with Castle Rock on the Western Ghats and so with the Southern railway (narrow or metre gauge). Goa exports coconuts, fruit, spices, manganese and iron ores, fish and salt, but its trade is small and its manufactures few. Rice is the staple product, with fruit, salt, coconuts and betel nut.

The population of the Velhas Conquistas is largely Christian and that of the Novas Conquistas, Hindu. The Christians generally speak Portuguese. The Hindus speak Konkani. Economic conditions in Goa caused emigration on a large scale, mainly to the eastern coast of Africa and to India. Large Goanese colonies have consequently been formed in Bombay, Mozambique, Natal, etc. Many Goanese are partly of Portuguese descent and bear Portuguese names as a result of intermarriage between early Portuguese settlers and the local inhabitants. They inherit the seafaring habits of their ancestors and many find employment as stewards, etc., in liners.

History.—The ancient Hindu city of Goa, of which hardly a fragment survives, was built at the southernmost point of the island and it was famous in early Hindu legend and history. In the *Puranas* and certain inscriptions its name appears as Gove, Govapuri, Gomant, etc. The medieval Arabian geographers knew it as Sindabur or Sandabur and the Portuguese as Goa Velha. It was ruled by the Kadamba dynasty from the 2nd century A.D. to 1312 and by Muslim invaders of the Deccan from 1312 to 1367. It was then annexed by the Hindu kingdom of Vijayanagar and later conquered by the Bahmani dynasty, who founded Old Goa in 1440.

W. SUSCHITZKY

BRINDLED GNU (CONNOCHAETES TAURINUS)

With the subdivision of the Bahmani kingdom after 1482, Goa passed into the power of Yusuf Adil Shah, the Muslim king of Bijapur, who was its ruler when the Portuguese first reached India. At this time Goa was important as the starting point of pilgrims from India to Mecca, as a market with no rival except Kozhikode on the west coast and especially as the centre of the import trade in horses (Gulf Arabs) from Hormuz. It was easily defensible by any power with command of the sea, and was attacked in March 1510 by the Portuguese under Albuquerque. The city surrendered without a struggle, and Albuquerque entered it in triumph.

Three months later Yusuf Adil Shah returned with 60,000 troops, forced the passage of the ford and blockaded the Portuguese in their ships from May to August, when the cessation of the monsoon enabled them to put to sea. In November Albuquerque returned with a larger force and, after overcoming a desperate resistance, recaptured the city, massacred all the Muslims and appointed a Hindu, Timoja, governor of Goa.

Goa was the first territorial possession of the Portuguese in Asia. Albuquerque and his successors left almost untouched the customs and constitutions of the 30 village communities on the island, only abolishing the rite of suttee (q.v.). A register of these customs (*Foral de usos e costumes*) was published in 1526.

Goa became the capital of the whole Portuguese empire in the east. It was granted the same civic privileges as Lisbon. In 1542 St. Francis Xavier mentions the architectural splendour of the city; but it reached the climax of its prosperity between 1575 and 1600. The appearance of the Dutch in Indian waters was followed by the gradual decline of Goa. In 1603 and 1639 the city was blockaded by Dutch fleets, though never captured, and in 1635 it was ravaged by an epidemic. In 1683 only the timely appearance of a Mogul army saved it from capture by Maratha raiders, and in 1739 the whole territory was attacked by the same enemies and only saved by the unexpected arrival of a new viceroy with a fleet.

The seat of the government was moved to Mormugão and in 1759 to Pangim. Cholera epidemics were one of the chief reasons for the migration of the inhabitants from Old Goa to New Goa. Between 1695 and 1775 the population of Old Goa dwindled from 20,000 to 1,600 and in 1835 it was inhabited by only a few priests, monks and nuns.

During the 19th century events of importance affecting the settlement were its temporary occupation by the British in 1809 as a result of Napoleon's invasion of Portugal; the governorship (1855–64) of Conde de Torres Novas, who inaugurated a great number of improvements, and the military revolts of the second half of the century. The most notable of these was the revolt of Sept. 3, 1895, which necessitated the dispatch of an expeditionary force from Portugal. The infante Affonso Henriques, duke of Oporto, accompanied this expedition and exercised governor's powers with the title of viceroy from March to May 1896.

After Indian claims on Goa in 1948 and 1949, Portugal came under increasing pressure to cede Goa, with its other possessions in the subcontinent, to India. A crisis was reached in 1955 when satyagrahis (nonviolent resisters) from India attempted to penetrate the territory of Goa. At first the satyagrahis were deported, but later when large numbers attempted to cross the borders the Portuguese authorities resorted to force and casualties were inflicted. This led to the severance of diplomatic relations between Portugal and India on Aug. 18, 1955. Tension between India and Portugal came to a head when on Dec. 18, 1961, Indian troops supported by naval and air forces invaded and occupied Goa, and the territory of Portuguese India was, by constitutional amendment incorporated into the Indian Union in 1962.

Christianity.—Some Dominican friars came out to Goa in 1510, but no large missionary enterprise was undertaken before the arrival of the Franciscans in 1517. A Franciscan friar, João de Albuquerque, came to Goa as its first bishop in 1538. In 1542 Francis Xavier took over the Franciscan college of Santa Fé for the training of native missionaries; this was renamed the College of St. Paul, and became the headquarters of all Jesuit missions in the east, where the Jesuits were commonly styled *Paulistas*. By a bull dated Feb. 4, 1557, Goa was made an archbishopric with jurisdiction over the sees of Malacca and Cochin, to which were added Macao (1575), Japan (1588), Angamale or Cranganore (1600), Meliapur (Mylapur; 1606), Peking and Nanking (1610), together with the bishopric of Mozambique, which included the entire coast of east Africa. In 1606 the archbishop received the title of primate of the east, and the king of Portugal was named patron of the Catholic missions in the east; his right of patronage was limited by the concordat of 1857 to Goa, Malacca, Macao and certain parts of British India. The Inquisition was introduced into Goa in 1560; five ecclesiastical councils, which dealt with matters of discipline, were held at Goa—in 1567, 1575, 1585, 1592 and 1606. By the concordat and missionary agreement with the Vatican (May 7, 1940), Goa recognized the lawful existence of the Catholic church and the exercise of its spiritual mission according to the canon law. The additional protocol signed on Sept. 25, 1953, made the archdiocese of Goa coincident with Portuguese India.

BIBLIOGRAPHY.—J. N. da Fonseca, *An Historical and Archaeological Sketch of Goa* (1878); the travels of Varthema (c. 1505), Linschoten (c. 1580), Pyrard (1608); J. Fryer, *A New Account of the East Indies and Persia* (1698); A. Hamilton, *A New Account of the East Indies* (1774); Silva Rego, *Documentos para a Historia do Patroado Português do Oriente*, 10 vol. (1947–54); Gonçalves Pereira, *India Portuguesa* (1954). (A. A. G. P.; L. D. S.; X.)

GOALPARA, a town and district in the Brahmaputra Valley of Assam, India. The town (pop. 1971 prelim, 16,703) stands on the left bank of the Brahmaputra, 75 mi. W of Gauhati, with which it is connected by road. It was the frontier outpost of the Muslim power, and has long been a great centre of river trade. It has a college affiliated to Gauhati University. The town declined in importance after the district headquarters were removed to Dhubri in 1879.

GOALPARA DISTRICT covers an area of 4,007 sq.mi. Pop. (1971 prelim.) 2,220,644. It is situated astride the Brahmaputra where the river bends southward from Assam into Bangladesh (formerly East Pakistan). Along the banks of the river grow clumps of cane

BERNARD MOOSBRUGGER FROM BLACK STAR

RELIGIOUS PROCESSION IN THE PORT OF MORMUGÃO, A CITY OF GOA. THE GOANESE HAVE BEEN MOSTLY CATHOLIC SINCE THE 16TH CENTURY, AND THE BAROQUE CHURCH IS IN THE STYLE OF PORTUGUESE CHURCHES OF THAT TIME

and reed; farther back stretch fields of rice cultivation, broken only by the fruit trees surrounding the villages; and in the background rise the forest-clad hills overtopped by the white peaks of the Himalayas. The Brahmaputra annually inundates vast tracts of country. Extensive forests yield valuable timber and there are about 900 sq.mi. of reserved forest where wild elephants, buffalo, boars, sambar, and deer abound. Rice forms the staple crop of the district but jute is important in the flood plain, and pulses, mustard, tobacco, sugar, and a little tea are also grown.

Dhubri (pop., 1961, 28,355), the administrative headquarters of the district, stands on the right bank of the Brahmaputra where that river takes its southward bend.

GOAT. Goats belong to the family of hollow-horned ruminants, or Bovidae (q.v.), and are members of the genus *Capra*, closely allied to the sheep. Domesticated goats are descended from the pasang (*Capra aegagrus*). Probably the east was its original home, the earliest records being Persian. *C. aegagrus* is probably represented in Europe by the Cretan and Cyclades races, now crossed with the common goat (*C. hircus*). For other wild goats *see* IBEX; MARKHOR; MOUNTAIN GOAT.

Products.—In China, Great Britain, Europe and North America the domestic goat is primarily a milk producer. By good management its limited breeding season and the consequent difficulty of maintaining a level supply of milk throughout the year can be largely overcome. For large-scale milk production, goats are inferior to cattle in the temperate zone but superior in the torrid or frigid zone.

The goat is especially adapted to small-scale production of milk for the family table. One or two goats will supply sufficient milk for a family throughout the year and can be maintained economically in small quarters where it would not be practical to keep a cow.

Goat's milk is pure white in colour and compares favourably with cow's milk in flavour and keeping qualities under sanitary conditions. It has certain characteristics differing from cow's milk which make it more easily digested by infants, invalids and persons allergic to cow's milk. The curds of goat's milk are much smaller, more flocculent and very soluble. The fat globules are smaller, finer, more easily assimilated and remain by nature in emulsion, so homogenization is unnecessary. These qualities explain why the goat has long been known in Europe as the "wet nurse" of infants. It has been estimated that the annual retail value of goat's milk sold in the United States is over $10,000,000. The retail price per quart varies from 40 to 55 cents. Large commercial dairies milk as many as 400 goats. Goat's milk is also used to make cheese. (For world production statistics *see* DAIRY INDUSTRY; MILK.)

The Angora and Cashmere goats produce wool or mohair (q.v.). (*See also* CASHMERE.) The flesh is edible, that from young kids being quite tender and more delicate in flavour than lamb, which it resembles. The goat has long been used as a source of milk, cheese, mohair and meat and its skin has been valued as a source of leather. (For world production and uses *see* LEATHER: *Major Types of Leather*.) Goats are also used to keep sheep spread out and on the move.

Distribution and Kinds.—There are many breeds of goat, which may be roughly grouped: the prick-eared, e.g., Swiss goats; the eastern or Nubian, with long drooping ears; and the wool goat, e.g., Angora. While it is usually easy to distinguish hair breeds from sheep, certain hair breeds of the latter are, to the layman, only distinguishable from goats by the direction of the tail, upward in goats, downward in sheep.

Of the Swiss goats, from which many of the best modern breeds are derived, the Toggenburg and Saanen are most important. The French breeds have much Swiss blood. In Germany the many varieties trace to Swiss breeds. There are many goats of Swiss type throughout Scandinavia and the Netherlands, where they are held in high esteem.

The Maltese goat probably contains eastern blood and is an important source of milk on the island of Malta. Many goats are found in Spain, northern Africa and Italy, among them the Murcian, Grenada and La Mancha.

Nubians are African goats, chiefly Egyptian. They are usually large, short-haired goats with large lop ears and Roman noses. They may be of any solid colour, parti-coloured or spotted. The goats in Israel and Syria have long hair and large lop ears. Black, with or without white, is the commonest colour. Most Indian varieties have lop ears, the best coming from the Jumna river area.

In Britain the native goat was small, with short legs, long hair, usually gray but of no fixed colour and with no definite markings. The widespread use of pedigree males, mostly of Swiss extraction, to improve the milk yield, resulted in the almost total disappearance of the native types.

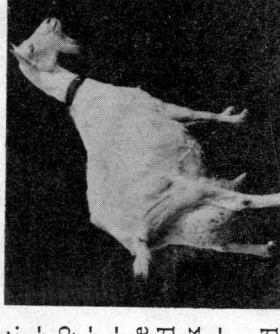
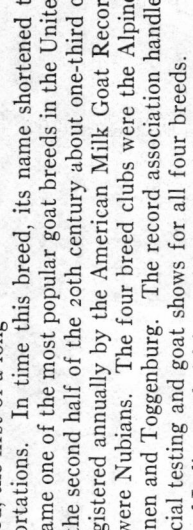

BY COURTESY OF MRS. CARL SANDBURG

SAANEN DOE

In 1896, a Jumna Pari (Indian) male goat (Sedgemere Chancellor) was imported by a British breeder. Since 1850 goats of Nubian and other lop-eared breeds had come to England in various ways. These eastern-type goats, variously described as Persian, Indian, Syrian, etc., and characterized by long pendulous ears and convex facial outline, won prizes at shows and found public favour. With the importation of Chancellor, serious breeders took up the project of developing an improved Nubian-type goat. Eventually the Anglo-Nubian name was adopted for this made breed and a section of the herdbook established for registering approved progeny.

Interest in this new breed spread to the United States and in 1910 three Anglo-Nubians were imported, the first of a long line of importations. In time this breed, its name shortened to Nubian, became one of the most popular goat breeds in the United States. In the second half of the 20th century about one-third of the goats registered annually by the American Milk Goat Record association were Nubians. The four breed clubs were the Alpine, Nubian, Saanen and Toggenburg. The record association handles registry, official testing and goat shows for all four breeds.

The goats of India, north Africa and Syria have been maintained since early times chiefly for their milk, and it is not surprising that Nubians have made fine milk records. In England a Nubian set a breed record with more than 4,250 lb. of milk in 365 days of lactation. This record compared favourably with a 305-day lactation record made in California by a Nubian which produced just under 4,660 lb. of milk and 193 lb. of butterfat.

In both England and the United States the Swiss breeds are considered, on the average, superior in quantity of milk produced, while the Nubians are known as leading in butterfat production. A Saanen goat in Great Britain produced more than 6,400 lb. of milk in 365 days of lactation, bearing out the reputation of the Saanen breed in its Swiss homeland and in the countries to which this breed has spread. In the U.S. a Saanen produced more than 4,900 lb. of milk and 180 lb. of butterfat; a Toggenburg produced more than 4,700 lb. of milk and 191 lb. of butterfat; and a French Alpine produced more than 4,600 lb. of milk and 130 lb. of butter-

COURTESY OF MRS. CARL SANDBURG

FOUR TOGGENBURG DOES

fat. The last three records are for 305 days of lactation.

Of the wool goats there are two main types: the Angora, or Mohair, and the Cashmere, or Shawl, goat. Angoras have been established in South Africa, Australia, the United States and Canada. About three-quarters of the mohair produced in the United States comes from Texas. The Angora is a poor milker. The soft, silky hair covers the whole body and most of the legs with close-matted ringlets. If not shorn in spring the fleece drops off naturally as summer approaches. There is an undergrowth of short hair. The average weight of fleece is about 2½ lb., though good specimens yield up to 12 lb. The Angora must have a dry climate and then stands cold well.

In the Cashmere, which is more like the common goat than the Angora, it is the undergrowth which is valuable. The longer the hair, the more abundant the fine undergrowth. These goats are rather small, with lop ears and twisted horns.

Husbandry.—Five dairy goats can be housed in a 10 ft. by 12 ft. shelter and will require less feed than one cow. They produce best on alfalfa or other leguminous hay as roughage, with a grain mixture coarsely ground of about 15% protein content. The subsistence ration for the dry doe is 1 lb. of grain daily. Milking goats are fed 1 lb. of grain daily, above the subsistence ration, for 3 lb. of milk produced. They should have free access to salt and water.

If they are kept dry, sufficiently exercised in fresh air and sunshine and intelligently fed, they are very hardy animals. If they are on pasture, or tethered, they should be moved frequently to fresh ground as a precaution against infestation by worms. They prefer browse to pasture, and goats that are stall-fed should have branches and leaves brought to them. They are relatively free from tuberculosis and goat's fever, or brucellosis (q.v.), in the

United States and Great Britain. The diseases and parasites that affect goats and sheep are discussed in the article SHEEP.

The normal lifespan of a goat is 8 to 12 years. They average two kids in a litter. Triplets are very common and quadruplets and quintuplets are occasionally dropped.

The female goat, variously called "Nanny" or "Doe," is ready for the male ("Billy" or "Buck") between September and February, during which time they come in heat every three weeks. The gestation period is 21–22 weeks. Goats are sexually mature at 6 months, but it is unwise to mate females before they are 15 months old, and a male should be used sparingly until 12 months old. See also references under "Goat" in the Index volume.

BIBLIOGRAPHY.—C. G. Potts and V. L. Simmons, "Milk Goats," Farmers Bulletin No. 920, U.S. Department of Agriculture (1955); W. L. TeWalt, Improved Milk Goats (1942); D. Mackenzie, Goat Husbandry (1957); British Goat Society Herd Books (annual); American Milk Goat Record Association Handbooks (annual); Dairy Goat Journal (monthly). (H. E. J.; M. L. F.; L. P. Sc.)

GOATSUCKER, a misleading common name for the nightjars, birds of the family Caprimulgidae. See NIGHTJAR.

W. SUSCHITZKY

COMMON GOAT (CAPRA HIRCUS)

GOBAT, CHARLES ALBERT (1843–1914), Swiss philanthropist and worker for international peace, awarded the Nobel peace prize in 1902 jointly with his compatriot Elie Ducommun, was born at Tramelan in the Bernese Jura, on May 21, 1843. After studying at Basel, Heidelberg and Paris, he took his degree in law and set up practice in Bern. Concurrently he lectured on French civil law at the Paris Sorbonne. On transferring his office to Delémont, he took an increasingly active part in local government and public administration. He was elected to the cantonal council in 1882, presided over the government board of Bern in 1886 and 1887, and in 1884 was elected to the national council. In 1890 he became a member of the Swiss federal council.

Gobat was president of the fourth conference of the Interparliamentary union held at Bern in 1892. In this capacity he helped to found its permanent bureau. Henceforth, for more than 20 years, the work of the bureau absorbed his time and his energy, and in 1906 Gobat succeeded Ducommun as director. He wrote several books on international affairs and on history, including Le Cauchemar de l'Europe (1911). He died at Bern on March 16, 1914.

(L. R. A.)

GOBAT, SAMUEL (1799–1879), second Anglican bishop in Jerusalem, was born at Crémines, Bern, Switz., on Jan. 26, 1799. Trained as a missionary in Basel, Paris and London, he was sent by the Church Missionary society overseas, chiefly to Ethiopia. He became widely known as a missionary and linguist.

The Jerusalem bishopric had been founded as a joint Anglo-Prussian venture in 1841, on the suggestion of Frederick William IV of Prussia, to protect Protestant Christians in the middle east and to combine a united Protestantism with the Orthodox Eastern Church to counteract Roman Catholic influence in Jerusalem. Efforts were to be made to convert Jews but not members of other Christian churches. Co-operation between Anglicans and Lutherans was uneasy, since Tractarians in England disliked working with a nonepiscopal body and German Protestants opposed any form of episcopate.

On the death in 1845 of Michael Alexander, first Anglican bishop, it became the turn of the Prussian crown to nominate a successor, and Frederick William chose Gobat, who was consecrated in 1846. He was allowed some latitude in applying the terms of his appointment in proselytizing, particularly from the Orthodox Church, which caused bitter controversy at a time of deteriorating political relations. From 1851 Gobat was aided by the Church Missionary society in establishing schools and in starting medical work among the Muslims. He died in Jerusalem, May 11, 1879. In 1886 the connection with the Lutheran Church ended and the reconstructed bishopric became fully Anglican.

See Samuel Gobat, His Life and Work, Eng. trans. by S. M. S. Clarke (1884). (J. D. Ta.)

GOBEL, JEAN BAPTISTE JOSEPH (1727–1794), archbishop of Paris and Hébertist, was born at Thann, Alsace, on Sept. 1, 1727. He became suffragan bishop of the French port of the diocese of Basel. As deputy to the estates-general of 1789 he took the oath of the civil constitution of the clergy, and in 1791 was consecrated archbishop of Paris. On Nov. 7, 1793, he came before the bar of the Convention and resigned his episcopal functions, proclaiming that he did so for love of the people, and through respect for their wishes. The followers of J. R. Hébert (q.v.), who were then pursuing their "worship of reason," claimed Gobel as one of themselves, and he was thus involved in the fate of the Hébertists, being condemned to death with P. G. Chaumette, Hébert and Anacharsis Cloots. He was guillotined on April 12, 1794.

See G. Gautherot, Gobel, évêque métropolitain constitutionnel de Paris (1911).

GOBELIN, the name of a family of dyers and clothmakers who probably came from Reims and in the middle of the 15th century established themselves in the Faubourg St. Marcel, Paris. The first head of the firm, named Jehan (d. 1476), discovered a scarlet dyestuff and spent so much on his establishment that it was named la folie Gobelin. In the third or fourth generation some of the family purchased titles of nobility. BALTHASAR GOBELIN

(d. c. 1617), who became successively treasurer general of artillery, treasurer extraordinary of war, councilor secretary of the king, chancellor of the exchequer, councilor of state and president of the chamber of accounts, in 1601 received from Henry IV the lands and lordship of Brie-Comte-Robert. The name of the Gobelins as dyers cannot be found later than the end of the 16th century. In 1601 the Gobelins lent their works to Henry IV, who set up there 200 workmen from Flanders, to make tapestries; in fact the Gobelin family had never produced any tapestry.

In 1662 the works in the Faubourg St. Marcel were purchased by Colbert on behalf of Louis XIV and transformed into a general upholstery manufactory, in which designs were executed under the superintendence of the royal painter, Charles le Brun (q.v.). The establishment, closed in 1694, was reopened in 1697 for the manufacture of tapestry, chiefly for royal use and presentation. The industry was suspended during the Revolution but revived by Napoleon; in 1826 the manufacture of carpets was added. See also TAPESTRY.

GOBI, one of the world's largest deserts, mostly in the Mongolian People's Republic and the Inner Mongolian Autonomous Region of China and covering parts of the province of Kansu and the Ningsia Chinese Muslim Autonomous Region. It occupies a vast arc of land in the Mongolian plateau, 300–600 mi. wide and over 1,000 mi. long, running southeast from the eastern borders of Chinese Turkistan and the Mongolian Altai, and then east and northeast to the Hsing-an (Khingan) mountains of Manchuria. The south slopes of the Khangai mountains in central Outer Mongolia (Mongolian People's Republic) bound it in the north and the plateau of Tibet and the Ho-lan Shan (Ala Shan) and Yin Shan ranges in the south.

The term Gobi desert often has not been well defined. At times it has been applied to all the desert and semidesert lands east of the Pamirs and north of the plateau of Tibet and the Great Wall. Properly, the Tarim (including Takla Makan; q.v.) and Dzungarian basins of Chinese Turkistan are separate from the Mongolian Gobi, as is the Ordos desert south of the Yin Shan. Gobi to the Mongol refers to the level, alkaline, often marshy and sometimes grassy bottoms of the broad, shallow basins which the Mongols call *tals.* Gobi is thus associated with basin structures believed to have been scoured out by the wind and is descriptive of terrain. By transference, the term Great Gobi or Gobi desert has come to be applied to the area here defined. Although the Gobi surface is a plateau with an altitude of about 3,000 ft. in the east and about 5,000 ft. in the west and south, the bounding mountains on all sides give it a basin character. In addition to the low swells separating the basins in the Gobi desert, its surface is interrupted occasionally by worn, flat-topped folded ranges and in the west by the complex uplifted fault blocks of the Altai which extends at diminishing altitude into the Gobi.

Sometimes in the plains the edges of the sedimentary strata are exposed to view, and these form the great fossil fields of Mongolia, indicating that a change has occurred from a past humid climate to the present desert state. Lakes such as the Ulan Nuur, Orog Nuur and Böön Tsagaan Nuur northwest of Dalan Dzadagad in Outer Mongolia are only a small fraction of the size that elevated strand lines show they once were. Several culture horizons have been distinguished in the Gobi area. Finds have been made of relics representing Eolithic, Upper Paleolithic, Azilian (Mesolithic), Neolithic and Metallic cultures.

The Chinese name Sha-mo (sand desert) often applied to the Gobi gives a misleading impression of its character, for only small sections of the Gobi comprise sandy or dune deserts. Much of it is of bare rock over which one can drive by car easily for long distances in any direction. Toward the north and southeast of the desolate centre, the precipitation gradually increases from 1 or 2 in. to 6 or 8 in. Scattered bunch grass appears, then the short grass steppe grazed by livestock watered from wells or at rare streams. Such streams entering the Gobi are seasonal in their flow. The largest in the eastern Gobi is the Kerulen (Hereleng) which flows out of the Henteyn Nuruu (Khentei mountains) and diminishes in volume to terminate in Hu-lun Chih (Hulun Nuur), but during floods may continue on to become a tributary of the upper Amur. Flowing into the Gobi from the Tibetan rimlands in the south and irrigating oases are the branching O-Chi-na Ho (Etsin Gol) and, farther west, the Su-lo Ho. Gobi rivers terminate in salt lakes or disappear in the sand. Trees are almost nonexistent, although xerophytic shrubs such as saxaul may be found as well as stunted willows and tamarisk near streams and wells. Although the water table is high and water often may be found within 20 ft. of the surface, the water may be brackish. In the Gobi Altai which rises to over 9,300 ft. and in other similarly high mountains, desert steppe grass covers the entire lower two-thirds of the slopes. Above this, there appears a mountain variant of feather grass.

The animal life of the Gobi includes the Djejran gazelle and the Dzeren antelope. Marmots or ground squirrels feed on grass seeds, and their holes are numerous in the steppelands. Sheep and goats are the most important domestic animals, constituting 57% of the total, followed by cattle (24%). Horses form only about 4% and with the cattle are concentrated in the moister southeast. About 15% are the two-humped camels that comprise the desert transport animals. In the southeast, Chinese farmers long have invaded the nomad grasslands. Under the Communist regime nomad and farmer alike were regimented. State directed collectives were organized both in Outer Mongolia and in the Inner Mongolian Autonomous Region for livestock breeding and, in the latter, for mechanized farming. The Chinese Communist collectives were changed to communes in 1958, the latter being similar in character to the former state farms.

Soviet-Mongol exploration located coal deposits at Tawan-Tolgoi and an oil field at Sayn Shanda on the Trans-Mongolian railroad. In the western Gobi, exploitation of the Yü-men oil field was expanded by the Chinese Communists in the late 1950s. The extension of the Kansu railroad to the oil field brought large population increases to the oasis towns in the southwest Gobi sections of the Kansu corridor. See also MONGOLIA. (H. J. Ws.)

GOBINEAU, JOSEPH ARTHUR, COMTE DE (1816–1882), French man of letters who in his career as a diplomat formed ideas on social and racial behaviour reflected in his ethnological, historical and imaginative writings, was born at Ville-d'Avray, near Paris, on July 14, 1816, of a Bordeaux family. Educated by private tutors and at a college in Switzerland, he developed an enthusiasm for languages, both European and oriental, and, after failing to enter the military academy at St. Cyr, settled in Paris, where he was received into the aristocratic circles of the Faubourg St. Germain. He wrote some *romans-feuilletons,* married (1845) and, in 1849, was appointed *chef de cabinet* by Alexis de Tocqueville during the latter's brief period as foreign minister. Subsequently he was first secretary to the French legation at Bern (1851), held posts at Hanover and at Frankfurt and, in 1855, was sent to Teheran, where he remained for four years. After a period in France he was sent back to Teheran as minister (1861), then to Athens (1864) and to Rio de Janeiro (1869). Absent without leave in 1870, he witnessed the Franco-German War and the Paris commune. His last diplomatic post was at Stockholm (1872). His liaison with the comtesse de La Tour (Marie Mathilde Ruinart), separating him from his wife and children, led to his retirement in 1877. Thenceforward he lived mainly in Italy. He died at Turin on Oct. 13, 1882.

Gobineau's reputation as a writer has passed through two phases. At first he was acclaimed as an ethnologist for his *Essai sur l'inégalité des races humaines,* 4 vol. (1853–55; partial Eng. trans., *The Moral and Intellectual Diversity of Races,* 1856, and *The Inequality of Human Races,* 1915). In the 1960s, however, he was chiefly respected for a novel, *Les Pléiades* (1874; Eng. trans., *The Pleiads,* 1928). The *Essai,* in brief, stated the racial superiority of the white race over others, and the group which he labeled "Aryans" as representing the summit of civilization. This theory was the germ of the *gobinisme* that spread through Germany, which Gobineau himself regarded as a distortion of his views. (See INTERRACIAL RELATIONS: *Racialist Thinking.*)

In the years that followed the appearance of this essay Gobineau had the liberating experience of Persia. He continued to be the gifted amateur, publishing such works as the *Traité des écritures*

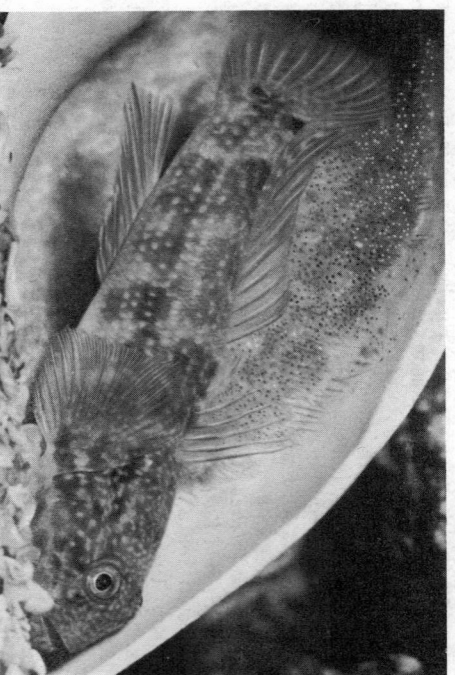

MALE FRILLFIN GOBY (BATHYGOBIUS SOPORATOR) GUARDING EGGS ATTACHED TO AN EMPTY BIVALVE SHELL

W. N. TAVOLGA

cunéiformes, 2 vol. (1864), and the *Histoire des Perses*, 2 vol. (1869). The formative influence on him, however, was *The Thousand and One Nights*, from which he took over the figure of the "king's son," using it as the central inspiration of *Les Pléiades*: "the book of an aristocrat," he wrote, "which opposes the conversation of exceptional beings to the confused clamour of the masses." The three young men, his heroes, are "king's sons"; they travel, they converse, they tell each other stories and they are happy. Apart from *Les Pléiades*, the best works of Gobineau's last years were *Souvenirs de voyage* (1872; Eng. trans., *The Crimson Handkerchief*, 1929), *The Nouvelles asiatiques* (1876; Eng. trans., *The Dancing Girl of Shamakha*, 1926, and *Tales of Asia*, 1947) and *La Renaissance* (1877; Eng. trans., 1913 and 1928), the latter a volume of dialogues in which, through such figures as Cesare Borgia and Michelangelo, Gobineau proclaimed his unchanging creed of individualism. There are critical editions of *Les Pléiades* and of *La Renaissance* by Jean Mistler (1946 and 1947).

GOBLET, RENÉ (1828-1905), French statesman, prominent in the crises of the 1880s and prime minister in 1886-87, was born at Aire-sur-la-Lys, Pas-de-Calais, on Sept. 26, 1828. He studied law and was elected deputy for the Somme. He was appointed undersecretary for justice under William Waddington (1879), minister of the interior under Charles de Freycinet (1882) and minister of education and cults first under Henri Brisson (1885) and again in Freycinet's third government (1886). He sat with the extreme left in the chamber, but was frequently in conflict with his political associates, including Léon Gambetta. On Dec. 16, 1886, Goblet formed a government in which he took over the portfolios of the interior and of cults. His appointment was defeated at the elections of 1889 by a Boulangist candidate, but sat on the extreme left in the senate from 1891 to 1893, becoming violently anticlerical and urging the suppression of the concordat. He was re-elected to the chamber as a Radical deputy for Paris in 1893, but failed to obtain a seat in 1898. Goblet died in Paris on Sept. 13, 1905.

See A. Dansette, *Le Boulangisme, 1886-1890* (1938); J. Chastenet, *La République des Républicains* (1954) and *La République triomphante* (1955).

GOBY, generally, any one of a numerous group—the Gobioidei —of largely marine and warm-water spiny-rayed fishes, characterized by having a few (usually six) flexible spines in the separate first dorsal fin; the pelvic fins are either set close together (in the family Eleotridae, known as "sleepers") or united into a suck-ing disc (in the Gobiidae, or gobies proper). Most of the several hundred known species range in length from one to four inches, but a few of the sleepers exceed one foot; some, like *Pandaka pygmaea* of the Philippines, are the smallest known vertebrates, only about one-half inch long. Male gobies guard encapsulated oval eggs, which are attached at one end by short adhesive threads, in a layer on discarded shells or in crevices. Most gobies are bottom dwellers; many, e.g., *Bathygobius* species, are limited to the edge of tropical shores.

Well-known species include: a ten-inch rock-pool inhabiting species of Europe, *Gobius capito*; the mudskippers (*Periophthalmus*), bulging-eyed little fishes that inhabit mud flats around the Indian ocean and the East Indian region, usually resting with the front parts out of water; the very hardy, burrow-inhabiting mudsucker, or long-jawed goby (*Gillichthys mirabilis*), the chief bait fish of southern California, with the upper jaw prolonged in the adult to beyond the gill opening; and a blind, pink species, *Typhlogobius californiensis*, which lives with a blind shrimp (a *Callianassa* species) in burrows under stones between tide marks along the shores of southern California. See also FISH: *Survey of the Bony Fishes: Perches and Perchlike Fishes.* (C. L. HS.)

GOD: see THEISM; RELIGION.

GOD, CHURCHES OF, a group of 20 or more pentecostal denominations that developed from the so-called Latter Rain revival early in the 20th century. They adhere to the ultraconservative or fundamentalist theology, including holiness as a work of grace subsequent to conversion or justification, and "speaking in other tongues as the Spirit gives utterance."

The revival began in the Great Smoky mountains in 1886 under the leadership of R. G. Spurling and his son, Baptists, and W. F. Bryant, a Methodist. It was taken over by A. J. Tomlinson, a colporteur, who convened an assembly in 1906 at Camp creek in Cherokee county, N.C. Two years later he established headquarters at Cleveland, Tenn., under the name of Church of God. He promoted the movement with vigour, and churches were established in various parts of the country.

Splits began to occur in 1917 when the Chattanooga congregation seceded and took the name of the Original Church of God. Other divisions followed and numerous independent groups were formed. The causes were not theological but were due to rivalries among local leaders and opposition to Tomlinson's absolute power as general overseer. He was virtually deposed in 1922.

On Tomlinson's death in 1943 disputes between his sons led to further schisms. Homer A. Tomlinson set up the Church of God, World Headquarters, at Queen's Village, N.Y., and his brother became head of the Cleveland group known as the Church of God Over Which M. A. Tomlinson Is General Overseer. Another Cleveland body is the Church of God (Cleveland, Tenn.), called the Elders' Church, from its form of government.

Among the sects growing out of the Tomlinson movement are the Mountain Assembly Church of God; Church of God, Incorporated; Church of Jesus; Bishop Poteat's Church of God; Bible Church of God; Jesus and Watch Mission; Churches of Our Lord Jesus Christ of the Apostolic Faith; Remnant Church of God; Apostolic Church of Jesus Christ; Non-Digressive Church of God; Justified Church of God; Holstein Church of God; Church of God of the Bible; Glorified Church of God; and several others. The Church of God (Anderson, Ind.) is not a pentecostal body and repudiates speaking in unknown tongues. The Church of God (Oregon, Ill.) is an Adventist body. *See also* PENTECOSTAL CHURCHES.

BIBLIOGRAPHY.—C. W. Conn, *Like a Mighty Army, Moves the Church of God, 1886-1955* (1955); E. T. Clark, *The Small Sects in America* (1957); H. A. Tomlinson (ed.), *Diary of A. J. Tomlinson*, 3 vol. (1949-55); F. S. Mead, *Handbook of Denominations in the United States*, 2nd rev. ed. (1961); *Yearbook of American Churches.* (E. T. CL.)

GODALMING, a municipal borough of Surrey, Eng., lies across the river Wey on the old London-Portsmouth road, 33 mi. (53 km.) S.W. of London. Pop. (1971 prelim.) 18,634. It is a residential town with an attractive shopping centre on busy High street. The church of SS. Peter and Paul is principally Early English and Perpendicular, built of local Bargate stone which is no longer quarried. A fine old group of almshouses, dating from 1622 is administered by the Carpenters' company. Westbrook house, home of Gen. James Edward Oglethorpe, founder of the colony of Georgia, is now the Meath Home for Incurables. The old town hall, built in 1814 on the site of market house, is now a local history museum. Public open spaces include the Phillips Memorial ground, with a cloister to the memory of Jack Phillips, wireless operator of S.S. "Titanic." Charterhouse school, 1 mi. N. of Godalming, was transferred from Charterhouse square, London, in 1872 and has 120 ac. of grounds with spacious buildings in the Gothic style. (*See also* CHARTERHOUSE.) Godalming's industries include woolen manufactures and light engineering.

Local excavations have revealed evidences of a former Romano-British settlement. Godalming (Godelminge) belonged to King Alfred and was a royal manor at the time of Domesday. It was granted to the see of Salisbury by Henry II but reverted to the crown in the reign of Henry VIII. In 1563 it was constituted a market town with powers to hold a market, annual fair and a court of piepowder or piepoudre (a summary court of record formerly held at fairs and markets to administer justice in transactions) in 1575. This charter was confirmed in 1620 and a new charter granted by Charles II in 1666. Extensions were made to the borough in 1892, 1928 and 1933. (S. C. D.)

GODARD, BENJAMIN LOUIS PAUL (1849–1895), French composer of operas, light piano pieces and songs, was born in Paris, Aug. 18, 1849. He was a child prodigy on the violin. He studied composition under Henri Réber and in his youth wrote symphonies, concertos, chamber music and piano pieces. His opera, *Pedro de Zalaméa* (1884), was produced at Antwerp, and his *Symphonie legendaire*, op. 100, was performed in Paris in 1886. His other operas include *Jocelyn* (1888), long known for its "Berceuse," and *La Vivandiere* (1895). Godard's music is slender and sentimental, showing at its best an affinity with Chopin and Schumann. He died of tuberculosis at Cannes, Jan. 10, 1895.
(E. Lr.)

See M. Clavie, *Benjamin Godard* (1905).

GODAVARI, a river of central India, flows across the northern Deccan from the Western Ghats to the Bay of Bengal. Its source is within 80 mi. of Bombay, near the Thal Ghat where the main railway from that city to the lower Ganges basin crosses the Ghats. Its general course is somewhat south of east. With its main southern tributary, the Manjra, it drains the larger part of the former state of Hyderabad, now partly in Maharashtra, partly in Andhra Pradesh. Near the 80th meridian it is joined by the Pranhita bringing from the north the drainage of the Mahadeo hills. Above this point the main river flows in a wide valley and frequently breaks up into several channels. At the Pranhita junction it leaves the lava plateau country and enters a trough of easily eroded rocks that extends to the sea. It is this feature which accounts for the wide break in the Eastern Ghats and the great depth of the coastal plain at the mouths of the Godavari and Krishna. Sixty miles from the sea it leaves the trough and breaks through the Ghats in a magnificent gorge only 200 yd. wide. The extensive delta is virtually continuous with that of the Krishna and is connected with that river by canal.

The upper river is almost dry during winter and spring and is almost useless for irrigation. The delta on the other hand is one of the richest rice-growing regions in India. The water is derived from the Godavari by an anicut—a low dam directing the stream flow into the head of the canal system. The Godavari is one of the rivers sacred to Hindus.
(T. Her.; L. D. S.)

GODAVARI, EAST AND WEST, two districts of Andhra Pradesh, India, which were formerly part of Madras, comprising three dissimilar natural regions: the Agency tract in the northwest, underdeveloped and infertile; the exceedingly rich and fertile delta of the Godavari along the coast which is the largest rice granary of south India; the intermediate upland taluks. The Godavari river, after which they are named, divides the districts. Forty miles from the sea, at Dowlaishwaram, is the famous anicut (dam) nearly 2½ mi. in length, constructed by Sir Arthur Cotton in 1890, which has made the delta a perennial rice field.

At the beginning of the 16th century this region was overrun by the Muslims. At the end of the struggle with the French in the Carnatic, Godavari with the Northern Circars was conquered by the British and finally in 1765 ceded to them, except for the small territory of Yanam (6 sq.mi.) which remained a French possession till 1954, when it was transferred to India. The districts were created in 1925 from the old Godavari and Krishna districts.

EAST GODAVARI district has an area of 4,181 sq.mi. and a population (1961) of 2,608,375. The present headquarters, Kakinada, lies on one of the mouths of the river, while Rajahmundry was the old capital. The port facilities at Kakinada are poor because of the heavy silting of the Godavari and ships must lie several miles offshore. There is an engineering college and a medical college. Rajahmundry has also an arts college, a government training college and two oriental colleges (one exclusively for women), all affiliated to Andhra university. At Samalkot, in the heart of the sugar-growing tract of the delta, is a large distillery and sugar refinery.

WEST GODAVARI district has an area of 2,980 sq.mi. and had a population (1961) of 1,978,257. The district was carved out of the Krishna district in 1925. Its capital is at Eluru, noted for its woolen carpets, the dyes and wool for which are produced locally. Both districts were once famous for the manufacture of fine cotton cloths, especially saris, at such centres as Peddapur in East Godavari and Palakollu.
(G. Kn.)

GODDARD, CALVIN HOOKER (1891–1955), U.S. army officer, military historian and criminologist who is chiefly remembered for his pioneering work in scientific crime detection and for his writings on the history of firearms, was born in Baltimore, Md., Oct. 30, 1891. He graduated from the Johns Hopkins university school of medicine in 1915, served with the U.S. army medical corps in World War I (becoming a major in 1918), with the ordnance department in World War II, and with the corps of military police in the Korean War. He was promoted to the rank of colonel in 1950. A lifelong interest in guns, combined with medical knowledge, qualified Goddard as an expert witness in many famous legal cases of the 1920s and led him in 1930 to organize a scientific crime detection laboratory in Chicago, Ill. He developed instruments and techniques for identifying the weapon from which a given bullet was fired. A talented writer, he contributed scores of articles to military and scientific publications. He died in Washington, D.C., on Feb. 22, 1955.
(H. C. T.)

GODDARD, RAYNER GODDARD, BARON, OF ALDBOURNE (1877–1971), lord chief justice of England whose work in controlling the crime wave that followed World War II was of outstanding social importance at that time. He was born in London on April 10, 1877, and educated at Marlborough college and at Trinity college, Oxford, where he graduated in 1898. After being called to the bar at the Inner Temple he became recorder of Poole in 1917 and took silk in 1923. From 1925 to 1928 he was recorder of Bath, and from 1928 to 1932 recorder of Plymouth, being raised to the bench as a judge of the high court (king's bench division) in 1932. At the bar his most important practice was in commercial cases, but his experience as recorder doubtless laid the foundation of his wide knowledge of the criminal law, with which the general public learned chiefly to associate his name. In 1938 Goddard became a lord justice of appeal and in 1944 a lord of appeal in ordinary, being also in that year created a life peer. The most distinguished part of his career, however, started when, in 1946, he was appointed lord chief justice. He found himself confronted with a wave of crime following the end of World War II, and, by a combination of a certain measure of severity with a scrupulous regard for legal proprieties, he was the inspiration of the judiciary and magistracy in bringing this situation under control. He retired in 1958. He died in London on May 29, 1971.
(W. T. Ws.)

GODDARD, ROBERT HUTCHINGS (1882–1945), the father of U.S. rocketry, was born Oct. 5, 1882, at Worcester, Mass. As a student at Worcester Polytechnic institute he began to speculate on means of reaching the fringes of outer space by the use of rockets. After taking his Ph.D. at Clark university in Worcester in 1911 he became a member of the Clark faculty and later attained the rank of full professor.

In 1919 the Smithsonian institution published Goddard's now

classic report entitled "A Method of Reaching Extreme Altitudes" and provided funds for his rocket research. During the 1920s he turned from solid to liquid propellants and in 1926 fired his first liquid fuel rocket. Supported by Clark university and the Guggenheim foundation, he continued his experiments with liquid fuel rockets and gyroscopic controls at a desert site near Roswell, N.M. He demonstrated that rockets operated in a vacuum better than in atmosphere and developed the theory of step rockets consisting of several stages as a means of reaching the moon. Progress was slow and few people recognized the potential importance of his work, and he was often derided as being "moon mad."

During World War II the U.S. navy employed Goddard to develop rocket motors and jet-assisted take-off (Jato) devices for aircraft and moved his laboratory to Annapolis, Md. He was engaged in this work at the time of his death on Aug. 10, 1945. His patents were, however, used by the Nazi government in its V-2 rocket program and later by the U.S. in its space-probe efforts. In 1960 the U.S. government paid the Guggenheim foundation $1,000,000 for infringing Goddard's patents, and in 1962 the National Aeronautics and Space administration (NASA) dedicated the Goddard Space Flight centre at Greenbelt, Md.

See Robert H. Goddard, *Rocket Development*, ed. by Esther C. Goddard and G. Edward Pendray (1948). (S. P. J.; X.)

GODDARD AND TOWNSEND, two families of cabinet-makers of Newport, R.I., during the 17th and 18th centuries. Both families were Quakers of English ancestry and they intermarried. In four generations, 20 Goddard and Townsend craftsmen are known, and the high point of their excellent productivity was reached during the early and mid-18th century. These cabinet-makers were especially noted for furniture in the Queen Anne and Chippendale styles, identified by an original type of shell carving, and a surface treatment called blocking. No exact European prototypes existed for their innovations. Many of the best-known pieces, high chests of drawers and secretary bookcases, generally executed in mahogany from the West Indies or South America, have well-documented histories.

Noted individual craftsmen were Christopher Townsend (1701–92) and his son John (1732–1809); Job Townsend (1699–1765) and his sons Job, Jr. (1726–78), and Edmund (1736–1811); and John Goddard (1724–85) and his son Townsend (1750–90).

See Wendell D. Garrett, "The Newport Cabinetmakers: a Corrected Check List," *Antiques*, 73:558–561 (June 1958). (J. T. Br.)

GODEFROY (GOTHOFREDUS), a French noble family which numbered among its members several distinguished jurists and historians. The family claimed descent from Symon Godefroy, who was born at Mons about 1320 and was lord of Sapigneulx near Berry-au-Bac, now in the *département* of Aisne.

DENIS GODEFROY (Dionysius Gothofredus; 1549–1622), jurist, son of Léon Godefroy, lord of Guignecourt, was born in Paris on Oct. 17, 1549, and died at Strasbourg on Sept. 7, 1622. He studied law in the Low Countries and in Germany, and embraced Calvinism. This change of faith led to his residence abroad, first at Geneva (1580–89), where he became professor of law, and then at Heidelberg (1600), where he was head of the faculty of law and was employed from time to time on diplomatic missions by the elector Palatine. His most important work was the *Corpus juris civilis* (Geneva and Lyons, 1583), which went through 20 editions, the most valuable of them being that printed by the Elzevirs at Amsterdam in 1663 and the Leipzig edition of 1740.

His eldest son, THÉODORE GODEFROY (1580–1649), was born at Geneva on July 17, 1580. He abjured Calvinism and was called to the bar in Paris. He became historiographer of France in 1617 and was employed from time to time on diplomatic missions. He was employed at the congress of Münster, where he remained after the signing of peace in 1648 as chargé d'affaires until his death on Oct. 5, 1649.

The second son of Denis, JACQUES GODEFROY (1587–1652), jurist, was born at Geneva on Sept. 13, 1587. He was educated in France but returned to Geneva, where he held various important public offices. He died on June 22, 1652. His edition of the *Codex Theodosianus* (4 vol. Lyons, 1665; 6 vol. Leipzig, 1736–45), on which he worked for 30 years, became a standard authority on the decadent period of the western empire. Jacques Godefroy was held to be the most learned jurist of his time. Among his numerous other works were several dealing with historical and political questions.

DENIS GODEFROY (1615–81), eldest son of Théodore, succeeded his father as historiographer of France.

GODFREY OF BOUILLON (GODEFROY DE BOUILLON) (c. 1060–1100), a leader in the first crusade, was the second son of Eustace II, count of Boulogne, by his marriage with Ida, daughter of Duke Godfrey II of Lower Lorraine. He was designated by Duke Godfrey as his successor; but the emperor Henry IV gave him only the mark of Antwerp, in which the lordship of Bouillon was included (1076). He fought for Henry, however, both on the Elster and in the siege of Rome, and he was invested in 1082 with the duchy of Lower Lorraine. His career as duke was not especially distinguished, but he seems to have been notably pious, and when the first crusade was preached, he soon joined the expedition at considerable personal sacrifice. He sold to the bishop of Verdun his rights and possessions in that county and pledged his county and castle of Bouillon to the bishop of Liège.

Godfrey began his march in Aug. 1096. Accompanied by his brothers Eustace and Baldwin (the future Baldwin I [q.v.] of Jerusalem), he led a body of perhaps 15,000 crusaders from the lands of the Meuse and the lower Rhine. He took the route through Hungary and the Balkans and arrived at Constantinople on Dec. 23, 1096. As the first of the crusading princes to arrive he had the difficult problem of reaching a satisfactory relationship with the emperor Alexius. Godfrey was at first unwilling to swear the oath of allegiance that the emperor required, but was prevailed upon to do so in April 1097. His example was followed by the other princes. From this time until the beginning of 1099 Godfrey appears as one of the minor princes, while men like Bohemund and Raymond, Baldwin and Tancred were determining the course of events.

In 1099 he came once more to the front. The mass of the crusaders were weary of the political factions that divided some of their leaders, and Godfrey, who was more of a pilgrim than a politician, became the natural representative of this feeling. He was thus able to play his part in prevailing upon the reluctant Raymond of Toulouse to march southward to Jerusalem, and he was prominent in the siege, his division being the first to enter when the city was captured. It was natural therefore that, when Raymond refused the offered dignity, Godfrey should be elected ruler of Jerusalem (July 22, 1099). He refused the title of king, assuming that of "advocate" of the Holy Sepulchre. The new dignity proved more onerous than honourable, and during his short reign of a year Godfrey had to combat the Arabs of Egypt and the opposition of Raymond and the patriarch Dagobert. He was successful in repelling the Egyptian attack at the battle of Ascalon (Aug. 1099), but he failed to acquire the town of Ascalon after the battle; the citizens would surrender only to Raymond, and Godfrey refused to accept these terms.

Left alone, at the end of the autumn, with an army of about 2,000 men, Godfrey was yet able, in the spring of 1100, probably with the aid of new pilgrims, to exact tribute from towns like Acre, Ascalon, Arsuf and Caesarea. But already at the end of 1099 Dagobert, archbishop of Pisa, had been substituted as patriarch for Arnulf (who had been acting as vicar) by the influence of Bohemund; and Dagobert, whose vassal Godfrey had at once piously acknowledged himself, seems to have forced him to an agreement in April 1100, by which he promised Jerusalem and Jaffa to the patriarch, in case he should acquire in their place Cairo or some other town, or should die without issue. Thus were the foundations of a theocracy laid in Jerusalem; and when Godfrey died (July 1100) he left the question to be decided, whether a theocracy or a monarchy should be the government of the Holy Land.

Because he had been the first ruler in Jerusalem, Godfrey was idolized in later saga. He was depicted as the leader of the crusades, the king of Jerusalem, the legislator who laid down the assizes of Jerusalem. He was none of these things. Bohemund was the principal leader of the crusade; Baldwin was the first king;

the assizes were the result of a gradual development. In reality he would seem to have been a quiet, pious, hard-fighting knight, who was chosen to rule in Jerusalem because he had no dangerous qualities and no obvious defects.

Godfrey was the principal hero of two French *chansons de geste* dealing with the crusade, the *Chanson d'Antioche* (ed. by P. Paris, 2 vol., 1848) and the *Chanson de Jérusalem* (ed. by C. Hippeau, 1868). In addition, the parentage and early exploits of Godfrey were made the subject of legend. His grandfather was said to be Helias, knight of the Swan, one of the brothers whose adventures are well known, though with some variation, in the familiar fairy tale of "The Seven Swans," almost identical with the Lohengrin (*q.v.*) legend. *See also* CRUSADES.

BIBLIOGRAPHY.—Godfrey is made the central figure of the first crusade in the history of that expedition by Albert of Aix, written *c.* 1130. For modern work *see* J. C. Andressohn, *The Ancestry and Life of Godfrey of Bouillon* (1947); S. Runciman, *History of the Crusades*, vol. i (1951); H. Pigeonneau, *Le Cycle de la croisade et de la famille de Bouillon* (1877); A. Hatem, *Les Poèmes épiques des croisades* (1932). Two later and interesting attempts to reassess Godfrey's character and achievement *see* H. Glaesener, "Godefroid de Bouillon était-il 'un médiocre,'" *Revue d'histoire ecclésiastique*, vol. xxxix (1943), and M. Lobet, *Godefroid de Bouillon: Essai de biographie antilégendaire* (1943)

GODFREY OF VITERBO (1125–*c.* 1200), chronicler, of Italian or German origin, spent probably some of his early years and his old age at Viterbo, where his family had property. He was educated at Bamberg, and after being chaplain to Conrad III he spent nearly 40 years as chaplain and notary in the service of Emperor Frederick I Barbarossa (*q.v.*), who employed him on many diplomatic missions. His most important historical work is the *Gesta Friderici I*, a panegyrical account, in verse, of Frederick Barbarossa's reign from 1155 to 1181. Although generally of scant value as a historical source, it contains accounts of events which Godfrey himself had witnessed. His *Speculum regum*, in verse, which he dedicated to Henry VI, is a mirror of princes in the form of historical narratives from the Deluge to Pepin III, in which he tries to trace a common Trojan origin for the Romans and Franks. He was best known for his universal history, in verse and prose, from the Creation to 1186, entitled first *Memoria seculorum* and in its final version, *Pantheon*. His authorship of the short *Gesta Heinrici VI*, in verse, is controversial.

BIBLIOGRAPHY.—Works ed. by G. Waitz in *Monumenta Germaniae historica, Scriptores*, vol. xxii (1872); *see also* W. Wattenbach, *Deutschlands Geschichtsquellen im Mittelalter . . .*, vol. ii, 6th ed. (1894); E. Schulz, "Die Entstehungsgeschichte der Werke Gotfrids von Viterbo," *Neues Archiv der Gesellschaft für ältere deutsche Geschichtskunde*, vol. 46 (1925).

GODFREY, SIR EDMUND BERRY (1621–1678), English magistrate, remembered chiefly for his part in the "popish plot," was born on Dec. 23, 1621, and was educated at Westminster school and Christ Church, Oxford. He entered Gray's Inn but soon abandoned law for commerce. He was later made a justice of the peace for the city of Westminster and was knighted in Sept. 1666 for his services during the Great Plague of London (1664–65).

In Sept. 1678, Titus Oates (*q.v.*) and two other men laid before him information which "revealed" a Roman Catholic plot to murder Charles II and put his brother James on the throne. Feeling ran high and Godfrey felt his life endangered but took no precautions. He failed to return home on Oct. 12; five days later his body was discovered in a ditch on Primrose hill, Hampstead. The evidence strongly suggested murder. Two months later Miles Prance made a confession in which he claimed to have been present when Godfrey was murdered by hirelings in the courtyard of Somerset house, London, while Roman Catholic priests looked on. On his evidence Robert Green, Lawrence Hill and Henry Berry were tried and hanged in 1679. Prance's later confession of perjury was too late to save them and the mystery of Godfrey's death remains unsolved.

GOD IN CHRIST, CHURCH OF, is the name of several small religious denominations in the United States.

The Church of God in Christ (Mennonite) is a branch of the movement founded by Menno Simons (*q.v.*). This branch arose in 1858–59 in Wayne county, O., under the leadership of John

Holderman, who, as a result of visions, felt called to preach, although he was not chosen by lot according to custom. He led about 20 followers from the Old Mennonite Church. This group regarded itself as the only true church. The tenets depart from conventional Mennonite theology and practice (*see* MENNONITES) only in refusing to accept interest on loans and laying on of hands following baptism.

The Church of God in Christ (Pentecostal) is a small pentecostal body related to the Churches of God (*see* GOD, CHURCHES OF) founded in the early 1930s with headquarters at Bluefield, W.Va. It grew out of the so-called Latter Rain revival led by A. J. Tomlinson and embraces the ultraconservative fundamentalist theology, holiness as a second work of grace subsequent to justification, and "speaking with other tongues as the Spirit gives utterance." (*See also* PENTECOSTAL CHURCHES.)

Another Church of God in Christ is a Negro pentecostal sect founded by C. H. Mason, who withdrew from the Baptist Church at Memphis, Tenn., in 1895 to become the "chief apostle" of a group emphasizing entire sanctification and speaking in "unknown tongues." The first congregation was formed in a cotton gin at Lexington, Miss. In 1921 a sect that had been formed in 1915 by J. H. Moore and his son at Enid, Okla., also under the name of Church of God in Christ, united with the Mason group but withdrew in 1925 in a dispute over a state charter and reorganized as the Free Church of God in Christ. Holiness, divine healing and speaking with tongues constitute its leading principles. A similar Negro holiness sect, the Free Christian Church of Christ, was formed by E. D. Brown, a Methodist, at Redemption, Ark., as a result of a disagreement over church finances.

BIBLIOGRAPHY.—E. T. Clark, *The Small Sects in America* (1949); F. S. Mead, *Handbook of Denominations in the United States* (1961); *Yearbook of American Churches*; for the pentecostal or Latter Rain movement *see* C. W. Conn, *Like a Mighty Army, Moves the Church of God, 1886–1955* (1956); Homer A. Tomlinson (ed.), *Diary of A. J. Tomlinson*, 3 vol. (1949). (E. T. CL.)

GODIVA (GODGIFU) (*fl. c.* 1040–1080), famous for her legendary ride through Coventry. With her husband Leofric (*q.v.*), earl of Mercia, she founded (1043) a monastery at Coventry and endowed it with half the land of Coventry and 24 lordships. Godiva appears several times in Domesday Book as one who held land in King Edward's time; but she must have been living after the Norman conquest since she is recorded as holding the village of Madeley, Staffordshire, "even after King William's accession."

The earliest extant source for the story of Lady Godiva's ride through Coventry is the *Chronica* (under the year 1057) of Roger of Wendover (d. 1236). He recounts that Godiva's ceaseless importunity in imploring her husband to reduce Coventry's heavy taxes led him in exasperation to declare that he would do so if she rode naked through the crowded market place. After ensuring that she had his permission, Godiva undertook the ride, accompanied by two soldiers, her hair covering all her body except her legs. On her return Leofric issued a charter freeing Coventry "from servitude." Other chronicles repeated the story with variations, the soldiers quickly disappearing from the accounts. Ranulf Higden (d. 1364) in his *Polychronicon*, and Henry Knighton (d. *c.* 1396) who followed him, put the ride early in the morning and say that Leofric freed the town from all tolls save those on horses. An *inquisitio* or inquiry made in the reign of Edward I shows that at that time no tolls were paid in Coventry except on horses. The *Chronicle at Large* of Richard Crafton (d. 1572) asserts that Godiva first required "the rulers of the city" to order all to remain indoors at the time fixed for the ride. She then galloped through the town, accompanied by her husband, escorts and her gentlewoman, so that the people heard the horses but did not see her. "Peeping Tom" did not join the legend until the 17th century; a manuscript in Coventry archives states that Godiva's horse neighed during her ride, whereupon a citizen let down his window and looked out. All other accounts seem to mention Tom's punishment; he was immediately struck either blind or dead. The Godiva procession, which from 1678 formed part of Coventry fair, has been held at intervals of seven or eight years ever since.

Many medieval chroniclers such as Florence of Worcester or Roger of Hoveden, who mention Leofric and Godiva with respect, do not refer to the ride and it does not feature in the chronicles of monasteries such as Ely or Evesham, of which Godiva was a benefactress. It has been suggested that the story really derived from the long continuation at Coventry of some pagan or semipagan fertility rite.

See F. B. Burbridge, *Old Coventry and Lady Godiva* (1952).

GODKIN, EDWIN LAWRENCE (1831–1902), Anglo-U.S. editor and founder of the *Nation*, was born in Moyne, County Wicklow, Ire., Oct. 2, 1831. After graduating in 1851 from Queen's college, Belfast, and studying law in London, he was special correspondent for the *London Daily News* in the Crimean War. After editorial work on the *Belfast Northern Whig*, he went to America late in 1856, writing letters descriptive of a southern tour for the *Nation*. He continued his connection with this journal while studying law in New York. He was admitted to the bar in 1858, and because of his impaired health he and his wife, Frances Elizabeth Foote, traveled in Europe 1860–62. At about this time Godkin was offered a partnership in the *New York Times* by its editor, Henry Jarvis Raymond; but although attracted by the offer, he in 1865 carried out a long-cherished dream by founding the *Nation*. This quickly became the foremost review in the country—as James Russell Lowell put it, because of the "ability, information and unflinching integrity," of the editor. Indeed, the periodical was so superior that Charles Dudley Warner, editor of the *Hartford Courant*, styled it the "weekly judgment day."

In 1881 Godkin sold the *Nation* to Henry Villard, owner of the *New York Evening Post*, of which paper the *Nation* became the weekly edition. Godkin himself became associate editor of the *Post*, succeeding Carl Schurz as editor in chief, 1883–99, and shaping the policy of that journal. Under his leadership the *Post* broke with the Republican party in the presidential campaign of 1884, when Godkin's opposition to Blaine did much to create the so-called Mugwump party (*see* MUGWUMP), and his organ became completely independent. He consistently advocated currency reform, the gold basis, a tariff for revenue only, and civil service reform, rendering the greatest aid to the last cause. His attacks on Tammany Hall were so frequent and so fearless that he was several times sued for libel because of biographical sketches of certain leaders in that organization, but the cases were dismissed. His opposition to "jingoism" and to imperialism was able and forcible.

Godkin retired from his editorial duties in 1899 and died in Greenway, Devonshire, Eng., May 21, 1902.

BIBLIOGRAPHY.—Rollo Ogden (ed.), *Life and Letters of Edwin Lawrence Godkin*, which has a list of Godkin's writings, 2 vol. (1907); accounts in W. G. Bleyer, *Main Currents in the History of American Journalism* (1927); O. G. Villard, *Some Newspapers and Newspapermen* (1926); Allan Nevins, *The Evening Post* (1922); and H. F. Pringle, "Godkin of the Post" in E. H. Ford and E. Emery (eds.), *Highlights in the History of the American Press* (1954).

GODOLPHIN, SIDNEY (1610–1643), English Royalist and poet, born at Godolphin hall, Cornwall, was baptized on Jan. 15, 1610. Educated at Exeter college, Oxford, he became intimate with Ben Jonson, Thomas Hobbes and other men of letters. He was a member of parliament for Helston from 1628. A staunch Royalist, he was one of the last to leave the house of commons when the king ordered his supporters to withdraw. He joined the Royalist forces under Sir Ralph Hopton and on Feb. 9, 1643, was killed in action at Chagford, Devonshire.

The earl of Clarendon pays a notable tribute to Godolphin in his *History* and Hobbes praises him in *Leviathan*. A few of his poems were published in the 17th century; of these the chief is *The Passion of Dido for Aeneas*, a translation from the *Aeneid*, apparently unfinished at his death and completed and published by Edmund Waller (1658). Other poems survived in manuscript collections. Godolphin's best lyrics have a fine strength and delicacy.

The first complete edition was by G. Saintsbury, in *Minor Poets of the Caroline Period*, 3 vol. (1905–21). *See also Poems*, ed. by W. Dighton (1931), with a biographical introduction.

GODOLPHIN, SIDNEY GODOLPHIN, EARL OF (1645–1712), English statesman and skilled financier, who remained almost continuously in office throughout the successive governments of 1679 to 1710. He was born at Godolphin hall, Cornwall, and christened on June 15, 1645, a cadet of an ancient Cornish family. In 1662 he became page of honour to the king, beginning a lifetime of court service and court politics. As page, he became intimate with John Churchill (later duke of Marlborough), his lifelong political ally, who was then page to the duke of York. During that period also he met his future wife, Margaret Blagge, a maid of honour to the duchess. Churchill and Godolphin remained in constant association, and the two families became linked by marriage and by their common kinsmen, the Boscawens and Lord Fitzharding. The Godolphins and Boscawens controlled several Cornish constituencies (Godolphin himself was returned for Helston, 1668–79, and St. Mawes, 1679–81) and by 1701 the whole Marlborough-Godolphin connection mustered 12 members of parliament.

The strength of Godolphin's and Churchill's position lay in the favour they enjoyed at court. After holding several court and diplomatic offices, Godolphin became a lord of the treasury on March 26, 1679, under the influence of Lord Sunderland. Godolphin now revealed his character as a court politician. He supported Sunderland's negotiations with William of Orange in 1679, and concessions to the exclusionists, but retained favour when Sunderland fell in 1681. In 1684, after the latter's return to power, Godolphin became secretary of state and then first lord of the treasury, and was created baron. He continued to serve at the treasury in various capacities under James II and almost continuously under William III till 1696. He was lord treasurer from 1700 to 1701 and from Anne's accession in 1702 until 1710. Godolphin's long service at the treasury during this generation exemplifies not only his own aptitude in making himself acceptable to successive courts but the premium put upon financial skill by the pressing difficulties of English government. Under his protection a corps of officials who embodied the fiscal expertise painfully acquired under Charles II survived in office for 20 years after the revolution of 1688 and did much to preserve the machinery of state from the worst effects of parliamentary faction. He was created earl of Godolphin in 1706.

Godolphin's adroitness was revealed just before the full in 1688. He served James II to the end and voted for a regency, but he immediately obtained office under William III, and while the king was abroad in 1695 and 1696 was one of the lords justices who managed the government. Godolphin nevertheless insured his prospects by contact with Jacobite agents and just before the publication of Sir John Fenwick's revelations in 1696 his differences with the Whig Junto came to a head and he resigned. In opposition Godolphin co-operated with Robert Harley (later earl of Oxford) and the New Country party to such good effect that he was taken back as head of the treasury in 1700 and Harley became speaker of the house of commons.

In Anne's reign Marlborough, Godolphin and Harley formed the core of the new ministry to the chagrin of Lord Rochester, the queen's uncle, and his High Tory allies. The party tactics of the latter, their pursuit of the Occasional Conformity bill, their attacks upon the Junto and William III's grants were extremely inconvenient to the government, and Godolphin persuaded the queen gradually to eject the Tories from those offices they possessed. By the election of 1705 the breach was complete, and for the next two years Godolphin sought to keep the Whig Junto from acting with the Tories in opposition by making the minimum of concessions. He secured valuable services from them in the negotiation of the union with Scotland (1706–07), but his efforts to dispose of ecclesiastical patronage in their favour led to a breach with Harley in 1708 and undermined his credit with the queen whose churchmanship Harley flattered. Godolphin moreover had suffered badly from the attacks of the Tory propagandists and looked for protection to the Whigs. To the Whigs Godolphin was also drawn by Marlborough's efforts in the field, by Godolphin's handling of finance and by Harley's parliamentary management. The latter was replaced in 1708 by the Whig Junto. Committed now to war to the end in Spain, Marlborough and Godolphin lost office with their new allies when Anne, prompted by Abigail Masham and Harley, encouraged by the unpopularity of the war and the prosecution of Henry Sacheverell (*q.v.*), dismissed the Whigs in 1710. Despite long personal friendship Anne dismissed Godolphin without an audience, and after his fall the fiscal administration became subject to a political spoils system. He died at St. Albans on Sept. 15, 1712.

In private life Godolphin was a confirmed gambler, and was among the first to improve English race horses by importing Barb and Arab sires, including his famous stallion, the Godolphin Arabian.

See H. Elliot, *The Life of Sidney, Earl of Godolphin* (1888); Sir Tresham Lever, *Godolphin, His Life and Times* (1952).

(W. R. WD.)

GODOY, MANUEL DE (1767–1851), duque de Alcudia and príncipe de la Paz, Spanish statesman whose power was supreme during the French revolutionary period. Born at Castuera (Badajoz) on May 12, 1767, of an old but impoverished family, he followed his brother to Madrid in 1784 and like him entered the royal bodyguard. Tall, broad-shouldered, and fair-complexioned, he was generally lethargic in manner, but could be active when necessary, and was often good company. He attracted the attention of Maria Luisa of Parma, wife of the infante Carlos, later King Charles IV, and was soon her lover, the weak infante not only acquiescing but becoming Godoy's lifelong patron, ready under his wife's domineering influence to believe that here was Spain's man of destiny. On Charles IV's succession (1788) Godoy was launched on a spectacular career, and by 1792 he was field marshal, first secretary of state, and duque de Alcudia. The conde de Aranda, his predecessor as secretary, had refused to face the startling new situation caused by the French Revolution; but when Louis XVI was guillotined (1793), Godoy was forced to act and for Godoy, and Gen. Antonio Ricardos occupied Arles-sur-Tech (Pyrénées-Orientales), but after Ricardos' death in March 1794 French armies invaded Catalonia and Gascony. Spain, now an ally of the British, helped them to hold Toulon until December 1793 when it was abandoned. Godoy came to terms with France at the Treaty of Basel (1795), for which he was created Prince of the Peace by the Spanish king, even though he had just signed away Santo Domingo.

So far Godoy had been more fortunate than wise; from now on he began to make mistakes which ended disastrously for himself and Spain. He sought closer friendship with France and bought it dearly at the Treaty of San Ildefonso (1796). Spain now put its fleet, its army, and later its forts at France's service, and soon, under Bonaparte's tightening grip, the country was at war with Britain. A year later the folly of such policy was seen when the British defeated the Spanish navy off Cape St. Vincent, a forewarning of what would happen at Trafalgar (1805), when Spain's sea power was utterly destroyed. At home enemies forced Godoy into eclipse (1798), but in 1801 he regained power, while his enemies joined the prince of Asturias, afterward king Ferdinand VII, and thus began the dissension between Godoy and Ferdinand leading to Ferdinand's rebellion against Charles IV, a nationalist protest against appeasement. Three events stand out during this last period of Godoy's power: the Escorial Proceedings which brought his quarrel with the Fernandistas into the open; the Treaty of Fontainebleau (1807), by which certainly Portugal and possibly eventually Spain itself were to be ceded to France in return for which Godoy was to gain valuable estates, while Charles was to be emperor of Spanish South America—in fact the culmination of Godoy's ambitions; and the Aranjuez rebellion (March 1808), when the result of these ambitions appeared in the loss of the Spanish throne by both father and son at Bayonne to Joseph Bonaparte. Caught by Spanish nationalist rebels after Aranjuez, Godoy escaped death through the intervention of the French cavalry leader Joachim Murat and was exiled with the ex-king and queen, remaining with them until Charles IV's death in Rome (1819). Thereafter he lived generally in France, dying in Paris on Oct. 4, 1851. Although Godoy's political influence on Spain was catastrophic, he held enlightened views and weakened the Inquisition, founded medical and veterinary schools, and reformed educational methods.

GODUNOV, BORIS FEDOROVICH (c. 1551–1605), tsar of Muscovy from 1598 to 1605, was the most famous member of the ancient Russian family of Saburov-Godunov, of Tatar origin, which migrated from the Golden Horde to Muscovy in the 14th century. Boris' career of service began at the court of Ivan IV the Terrible. In 1571 he strengthened his position by his marriage with Maria, the daughter of Ivan's favourite, G. L. Malyuta Skuratov. In 1580 the tsar chose Irina, the sister of Boris, to be the bride of the tsarevich Fedor, on which occasion Boris was promoted to the rank of boyar. On his deathbed, in 1584, Ivan appointed Boris one of the guardians of Fedor, his successor, who was of somewhat weak intellect. The reign of Fedor Ivanovich began with a minor rebellion in favour of the infant tsarevich Dimitri, the son of Ivan's seventh wife, Maria Fedorovna Nagoi. This resulted in the banishment of Dimitri, with his mother and her relations, to their appanage at Uglich. On the occasion of Fedor's coronation (May 31, 1584), Boris was given honours and riches, but he held only the second place in the regency during the lifetime of his co-guardian, Nikita Romanovich Yuriev; on the death of Yuriev, in 1585, Boris was left without any serious rival. A conspiracy against him by all the other great boyars and the metropolitan Dionisi, which sought to break Boris' power by divorcing the tsar from the childless Irina, ended in the banishment or tonsuring of the malcontents.

Henceforth Godunov was omnipotent. The direction of affairs passed entirely into his hands, and he corresponded with foreign princes as their equal. The English referred to him as the lord protector. His policy was generally pacific but always prudent. In 1595 he recovered from Sweden the towns lost during the reign of Ivan IV. Four years previously he had defeated a Tatar raid on Moscow, for which service he received the title of *sluga*, a dignity even higher than that of boyar. Toward Turkey he maintained an independent attitude, supporting an anti-Turkish faction in the Crimea and furnishing the Holy Roman emperor Rudolf II with subsidies in his war against the sultan. Godunov encouraged English merchants to trade with Russia by exempting them from tolls. He civilized the northeastern and southeastern borders of Muscovy by building numerous towns and fortresses to keep the Tatar tribes in order. Samara (Kuibyshev), Saratov and Tsaritsyn (Stalingrad) and a whole series of lesser towns owe their existence to him. He also recolonized Siberia, which had been slipping from the grasp of Muscovy, and formed scores of new settlements, including Tobolsk and other large centres. It was during his government that the Muscovite Church received its patriarchate, which placed it on an equality with other Eastern churches. It was Boris' internal policy to support the middle classes at the expense of the old nobility and the peasants; his *ukaz* (decree) forbidding the peasantry to transfer themselves from one landowner to another and thus binding them to the soil led to the institution of serfdom in its most grinding form. The sudden death of the tsarevich Dimitri at Uglich (May 15, 1591) has been attributed to Boris, but historians are not in agreement over this question.

On the death of the childless tsar Fedor (Jan. 7, 1598), a national assembly unanimously elected Boris tsar on Feb. 21. The Romanov family, who had been his chief rivals, were disgraced and banished. Boris was the first tsar to import foreign teachers on a great scale, the first to send young Russians abroad to be educated, the first to allow Lutheran churches to be built in Russia. He also felt the necessity of a Baltic seaboard and attempted to obtain Livonia by diplomatic means.

Boris was undoubtedly one of the greatest of the Muscovite tsars. The opposition with which he had to contend arose mainly because dynastically he was an upstart and tsar only by election. His great qualities, however, were overbalanced by an incurable suspiciousness. He encouraged informers and persecuted suspects on their unsupported statements. The Romanov family especially suffered severely from such denunciations. In 1603 a pretender appeared in Poland, claiming to be the tsarevich Dimitri (*see* DIMITRI, FALSE). With the support of King Sigismund of Poland, this pretender was leading a small army, reinforced by the Don Cossacks, into southwestern Russia when Boris died suddenly (April 23, new style; 13, old style, 1605), leaving one son who succeeded him for a few months as Fedor II and then was murdered by enemies of the Godunovs.

Boris Godunov's life was the subject of a drama by Pushkin, which in turn served as the basis of an opera, *Boris Godunov*, by the Russian composer Modest Mussorgsky.

See S. F. Platonov, *Boris Godounov, tsar de Russie* (1929).

(R. N. B.; N. An.)

GODWIN (GODWINE) (d. 1053), earl of Wessex and Kent from c. 1018 to 1053 and the most powerful Englishman in the reign of Edward the Confessor, was the son of one Wulfnoth and became a favourite with Canute, whom he accompanied to Denmark in 1019. He married Gytha, sister of Canute's brother-in-law, Ulf. On Canute's death he supported Hardicanute, but later joined Harold's party. He arrested the atheling Alfred when he came from Normandy in 1036, and was held responsible by Hardicanute for his murder, but bought his peace. He had great power in the early part of Edward's reign, securing an earldom, including Herefordshire, Gloucestershire, Oxfordshire, Berkshire and Somerset, for his son Sweyn in 1043, and East Anglia for Harold (afterward Harold II) in 1044, and in 1045 he married his daughter Edith to the king. He got Sweyn reinstated in 1050, although he had seduced an abbess and murdered his cousin, Beorn. In 1051, however, he defied the king by refusing to punish the men of Dover for their affray with Eustace of Boulogne, and with his sons he gathered forces, declaring their intention of avenging insults against the king and his people perpetrated by Normans in Herefordshire. Earl Leofric of Mercia and Earl Siward of Northumbria supported the king, and when Godwin and his sons refused to appear before the witan in London unless hostages were given them, they were outlawed and the queen sent to Wherwell abbey. Edward's favouring of foreigners caused a reaction in favour of Godwin. He had gone with his wife and his sons Sweyn, Tostig and Gyrth to Flanders; he returned with a fleet in June 1052 and won much support in Kent, Surrey and Sussex before returning to Flanders. Later he made contact with Harold, who with his brother Leofwine had gone to Ireland, and they went together in September to Southwark. Edward was unable to resist, and Godwin and his family were restored to their former possessions and offices. Godwin died on April 15, 1053. Later sources contain much legendary matter; there may have been a current vernacular saga.

BIBLIOGRAPHY.—*Anglo-Saxon Chronicle;* F. M. Stenton, *Anglo-Saxon England,* 2nd ed. (1947); C. E. Wright, *The Cultivation of Saga in Anglo-Saxon England* (1939).

(D. Wk.)

GODWIN, EDWARD WILLIAM (1833–1886), English architect, designer and writer, was mainly responsible for the Victorian Japanese vogue and was an important contributor to the "aesthetic" movement. Born in Bristol, he was articled in 1849 to the city surveyor there and in 1854 set up his own practice, specializing in ecclesiastical architecture in the west of England and in Ireland. In 1861 he won a competition for Northampton town hall and its decorations and furniture with a design in the personal French Gothic revival style of all his early work. In the following year he married and is said to have decorated his house in the Japanese manner, the first of its kind in the country. He moved to London in 1865 and designed Dromore castle and Glenbegh castle, both built in Ireland between 1867 and 1871. His later architectural work was on a smaller domestic scale and included houses for artists at Bedford Park (1875) and the White House (1877) in Chelsea for his friend James A. M. Whistler, whose paintings were often framed to Godwin's designs. From 1865 onward he designed furniture, textiles and wallpapers for commercial production and private clients. As a result of his association with Ellen Terry he had a great interest in all aspects of the theatre—an interest inherited by their son Edward Gordon Craig (*q.v.*)—and designed costumes and sets for many Shakespearean and other productions. He died in London on Oct. 6, 1886.

(E. M. As.)

GODWIN, FRANCIS (1562–1633), English bishop and historian, wrote the first story of a space voyage in English literature —*The Man in the Moone, or a Discourse of a Voyage Thither by Domingo Gonsales, The Speedy Messenger.* Born at Hannington, Northamptonshire, Godwin was a student of Christ Church, Oxford, when the Italian philosopher Giordano Bruno introduced his revolutionary scientific ideas to the university. He subsequently held two Somerset livings, and became subdean of Exeter (1587). Favourable royal notice of his two historical works led to his consecration as bishop of Llandaff (1601), and his translation to Hereford (1617).

In *A Catalogue of the Bishops of England* (1601), a competent historical compilation, Godwin's ironic intelligence was demonstrated in a series of thumbnail Theophrastan character studies. His *Rerum Anglicarum, Henrico VIII, Edwardo VI, et Maria regnantibus* (1616; Eng. trans, 1630) chronicled the Reformation in England with deft detachment and with justice to those with whom his Puritanism could not sympathize (Queen Mary was "a Lady, very godly, merciful, chast, and every way praiseworthy, if you regard not the errors of her Religion"). Godwin's *Nuncius Inanimatus* (1629) was a quasi-scientific work.

The Man in the Moone was probably begun c. 1603–06, completed c. 1629–30, and published in 1638; by 1768 at least 25 editions had appeared, in English, French, Dutch, and German. It was both an extension of utopian romance (influencing Swift and Cyrano de Bergerac) and a curious anticipation of modern science fiction. Godwin's complex tone ranges between an easy acceptance of the new scientific temper of Copernicus, Kepler, Galileo, and Gilbert, and an attractive credulity in the field of biology. On the one hand the debates Copernican theories of diurnal rotation, magnetic and gravitational force, and orbital motion; on the other he deploys analogies from the natural history of Pliny, the herbals, and the lapidaries. The power for Domingo's space flight is provided by harnessing the annual migration of geese to the moon. Arrived there, Domingo found a utopian kingdom with a language so subtle "so as if they will utter their mindes by tunes without wordes," and where, as on earth before the Fall, "food groweth everywhere without labour."

BIBLIOGRAPHY.—*The Man in the Moone and Nuncius Inanimatus,* ed. by G. McColley (1937); W. M. Merchant, "Bishop Francis Godwin, Historian and Novelist," *Journal of the Historical Society of the Church in Wales,* vol. v, no. 10 (1955).

(W. M. Me.)

GODWIN, MARY WOLLSTONECRAFT (1759–1797), English miscellaneous writer, a passionate advocate of woman's right to a place in society equal to that of man, was an influential figure in the radical group that included her husband William Godwin, Thomas Paine, Thomas Holcroft and William Blake. Of Irish extraction, she was born, probably at Hoxton, London, on April 27, 1759. Her father, Edward John Wollstonecraft, after dissipating the greater part of his patrimony, tried to earn a living by farming, but increasing difficulties forced the family to a wandering existence, from Hoxton to Edmonton, to Essex, to Beverley in Yorkshire, to Laugharne in Carmarthenshire and back to London. After Mrs. Wollstonecraft's death in 1780 and her husband's second marriage, the daughters, Mary, Everina and Eliza, tried to earn their own living. Mary at first lived with Fanny Blood, a girl of her own age whose father, like Wollstonecraft, was addicted to drink. Everina lived with her brother Edward, and Eliza married a Mr. Bishop. After this unhappy marriage had ended in a legal separation, the three sisters lived with Fanny Blood at Islington and at Newington Green, and opened a school which survived for two years. At Newington Green Mary was introduced to Dr. Johnson, who, Godwin says, "treated her with particular kindness and attention."

In 1785 Fanny Blood married Hugh Skeys, a merchant, and went with him to Lisbon where she died in childbed. Mary was deeply moved and wrote to Fanny's brother, George Blood, "I have lost all relish of pleasure, and life seems a burden almost too heavy to be endured." She left Newington Green and became governess in the family of Lord Kingsborough in Ireland—too successfully, for she was dismissed after a year on the grounds "that the children loved their governess better than their mother." She next undertook work for James Johnson the publisher, of St. Paul's churchyard, but left England because she wished to observe the Revolution in Paris in 1792, remaining there through the Terror and passing as the wife of Capt. Gilbert Imlay, an American. They had not been formally married but Imlay terms her in a legal document: "Mary Imlay, my best friend and wife." Two groups of letters, among the best of her writings, were written to Imlay in these years, during his absence in Le Havre for several months in 1793, and again in 1795, when she went on business to Norway on his behalf. Meanwhile, in the spring of 1794, Mary gave birth to a child at Le Havre, whom she named after her friend, Fanny Blood. But her relationship with Imlay was deteriorating; he left her for a period at Le Havre and on her return from Norway in 1795 he proposed to separate from her, offering her and her child an annuity which she refused. There was a brief reconciliation but their relationship finally broke down. She attempted to drown herself by leaping from Putney bridge but was rescued by watermen.

She had returned to London late in 1795 to work for Johnson and in 1796 met William Godwin. Their mutual admiration and respect became a profound affection and they lived together for several months, Godwin writing later that "ideas which he is now willing to denominate prejudices, made him by no means willing to conform to the ceremony of marriage." But for the sake of their future child Mary (who was to become the wife of Shelley) they were married at St. Pancras church on March 29, 1797, concealing the fact with some diffidence from their friends. The marriage was wholly happy. Godwin's description of his wife, "that smile of bewitching tenderness," has a tone remarkable in a man of his austerity, and there is an unmawkish but tender playfulness in their courteous determination to respect each other's way of life: Mary writes to him, "Did I not see you, friend Godwin, at the theatre last night? I thought I met a smile, but you went out without looking round. We expect you at half-past four." This time of happiness was brief. On Sept. 10, 1797, ten days after her daughter's birth, she died, and was buried in the churchyard of Old St. Pancras, but her remains were later removed by Sir Percy Shelley to the churchyard of St. Peter's, Bournemouth.

Many of Mary Wollstonecraft's social ideals have been realized and the modern critic is in a good position to re-assess significant parts of her writing other than the social. Even her early hackwork for Johnson's publishing house has its interest. Her translation of Johann Lavater's *Physiognomy* establishes an intellectual relationship with Henry Fuseli (*q.v.*), and her translation of Christian Salzmann's *Elements of Morality* was the first of her works to be illustrated by William Blake. Her warm and vivid letters (see *Letters Written During a Short Residence in Sweden, Norway and Denmark,* 1796; also *Bibliography*) may be considered in relation to the highly personal fiction, her first novel, *Mary* (1788), a tribute to her friend Fanny Blood, and the *Original Stories from Real Life* (1791), the 1796 edition of which was illustrated by Blake. Her early *Thoughts on the Education of Daughters* (1787), foreshadowing her mature work on woman's place in society, has an austerity arising from her own early experiences which is transformed in the radiant *Lessons for Little Fanny* addressed to her daughter.

Nor was her more intellectual handling of history and sociology untouched by experience. Her *Historical and Moral View of the Origin and Progress of the French Revolution,* of which only the first volume (1794) was completed, was based on her own observations, while personal loyalty to Thomas Paine prompted the *Vindication of the Rights of Men* in 1793. All these were focused in her *Vindication of the Rights of Woman* (1792), the highly charged individual radical group which centred upon the home of the publisher, Johnson, and which included Godwin, Paine, Thomas Holcroft and Blake (and, after 1793, William Wordsworth). There had been sporadic expression in England and France of unease at the social subjection of woman; this had intensified in the thinking of the *philosophes* and there is a striking concurrence between Mary Wollstonecraft's argument and the bill prepared by the marquis de Condorcet for the Convention of 1792, urging uniform education for men and women. In that year she wrote her *Vindication* in six weeks, and appeals in the opening pages to the social justice of the constitution established by the Convention. The core of the book, however, is not political but educational. Her central plea is for the illumination of woman's mind: "Tyrants and

sensualists are in the right when they endeavour to keep women in the dark, because the former only want slaves, and the latter a plaything." Her central theme was argued with a vigorous freedom of speech which caused deep offense: "Marriage will never be held sacred till women, by being brought up with men, are prepared to be their companions rather than their mistresses." But, as Godwin made more qualifications in the rigour of his argument than is popularly supposed, so Mary Wollstonecraft advocated no mechanical equality between the sexes: "Whatever tends to incapacitate the maternal character takes woman out of her sphere." This balance of intellectuality with ardour, of passionate advocacy with warmth of sympathy made her one of the permanently influential writers in her powerful group of friends.

BIBLIOGRAPHY.—Editions of her works include: *Posthumous Works,* 4 vol. (1798); *Original Stories,* ed. by E. V. Lucas (with Blake's illustrations, 1906); *Love Letters to Gilbert Imlay,* ed. by Roger Ingpen (1908). See E. R. Pennell, *Mary Wollstonecraft Godwin* (1898); E. R. Clough, *Mary Wollstonecraft and the Rights of Woman* (1898); De Routen, *Mary Wollstonecraft and the Beginnings of Female Emancipation* (1923); M. Linford, *Mary Wollstonecraft* (1924); R. M. Wardle, *Mary Wollstonecraft* (1951); and the bibliography for GODWIN, WILLIAM. (W. M. ME.)

GODWIN, WILLIAM (1756–1836), English writer and philosopher whose rationalistic and anarchical views influenced the work of the romantic poets, was born on March 3, 1756, at Wisbech, Cambridgeshire, the son of a Nonconformist minister. Both his parents were Calvinists and Godwin was educated for the dissenting ministry at Hoxton academy, by Andrew Kippis and Abraham Rees of the *Cyclopaedia,* and, more Calvinist than his teachers, became a Sandemanian, or follower of John Glas (*q.v.*), whom he describes as "a celebrated north-country apostle who, after Calvin had damned ninety-nine in a hundred of mankind, has contrived a scheme for damning ninety-nine in a hundred of the followers of Calvin." He became a minister at Ware, Stowmarket and Beaconsfield, and while at Stowmarket his friend, Joseph Fawcet, a republican, introduced him to the teachings of the French philosophers. He moved to London in 1782 and writing gradually replaced his ministerial calling. He published a *Life of Chatham* anonymously in 1783, a series of sermons, *Sketches of History,* in 1784, in which he pronounced that "God himself has no right to be a tyrant," and in 1785, introduced by Kippis, he began to write "Sketches of English History" for the *New Annual Register;* he also joined a club called the "Revolutionists" and associated with Lord Stanhope, Horne Tooke and Thomas Holcroft (*qq.v.*).

In 1796, after he had finished his most influential writings, he met Mary Wollstonecraft (*see* GODWIN, MARY WOLLSTONECRAFT), and married her in 1797, both suppressing their dislike of the sacrament of marriage for the sake of possible offspring. Their happy marriage was tragically brief, for she died on Sept. 10, a few days after the birth of her daughter Mary (who became the wife of Shelley). Godwin wrote: "I honoured her intellectual powers and the nobleness and generosity of her propensities; mere tenderness would not have been adequate to produce the happiness we experienced." He was left to fend for his infant daughter and his stepdaughter, Fanny Imlay, and in 1801 he married, most unsuitably, Mrs. Mary Jane Clairmont (whose daughter Jane, called Claire, became Lord Byron's mistress), who treated her stepchildren harshly. With Mrs. Godwin's co-operation he became a bookseller under the pseudonym of Edward Baldwin, publishing historical compilations and children's books, the most notable being Charles and Mary Lamb's *Tales from Shakespeare* (1807) and his own *Life of Chaucer* (1803). He was in constant financial difficulties and the business was wound up in 1825; meanwhile, in 1824, he had begun his *History of the Commonwealth of England from its Commencement to the Restoration of Charles II,* completed in 1828. In 1833 the government of Earl Grey made him yeoman usher of the exchequer, with a small stipend and apartments in New Palace yard, where he died on April 7, 1836.

In the nicely poised struggle between Edmund Burke and the radicals, Godwin, far more than Joseph Priestley, Thomas Paine, Sir James Mackintosh or Richard Price (*qq.v.*), was the thoroughgoing intellectual, denying tradition, sentiment, feeling or habit as forces motivating man's conduct. Truth and justice are thus left as the sole ideals for society, to be pursued without rancour and abjuring even the sanctions of legislation, with the ideal goal a benevolent anarchism. Godwin's writings are of a piece, whether arguing his political opinions in brief works of journalism or at length in *Political Justice*, or persuading readers to his social tenets through his novels. Indeed a passionate consistency marks both his personal relations and his career as a writer. The core of his work was *The Enquiry Concerning the Principles of Political Justice, and its Influences on General Virtue and Happiness* (1793). Rejecting all contemporary forms of government, and especially monarchy as "a species of government unavoidably corrupt," without belief in innate principles and declaring man to be the creature of his environment, Godwin necessarily assumed the perfectibility of mankind. But there were conditions. Since the governing facts of man's environment are fourfold—those which arise from his education, the government under which he lives, and the "prejudices" of both religion and social order—these are the conditions which must be controlled and modified in order to achieve his moral freedom. Since, moreover, man's will to perfectibility is directed by his opinions, processes of persuasion—though not of force—must be employed to motivate his conduct. These persuasive forces in Godwin's view are wholly intellectual, for he ignores all involuntary and emotive springs of human judgment and conduct. Though he advocates startling innovations in social theory (and rejects the "contract theory" prevailing in current political thought, especially in France), Godwin is not afraid of his apparently dangerous revolutionary arguments: "Excesses are never the offspring of speculative reason ... but of power endeavouring to stifle reason." Hence any censorship or repression is not only unnecessary but a denial of man's nature.

Important particular conclusions proceeded from the generalizations of *Political Justice*. Crime must be restrained if violent, but benevolence and not retribution must be society's attitude to the criminal. It has been assumed by writers influenced by Godwin that his works laid the foundations for the mutually contradictory doctrines of communism and anarchy. In fact their germ, though undeveloped, is to be found in two separate elements in his thinking. He advocated neither the abolition nor the "communalization" of property, but it was to be held, a sacred trust, at the disposal of him whose need was greatest. His most powerful personal belief was that "everything understood by the term co-operation is in some sense an evil," from which proceeded his most influential anarchic doctrines, and in particular his rejection of the contract of marriage between free individuals, whose sole bond should be mutual respect.

Godwin's creative writing is largely an imaginative realization of his social doctrines, but judgment of his novels has been distorted by preoccupation with their didactic aspects and the neglect of his earlier writings. In 1784 he published anonymously *Imogen: a Pastoral Romance*, purporting to be "originally composed in the Welch language" and from the pen of the "ingenious" Rice ap Thomas, who has probably "taken the Masque of Milton as a model." The novel, written with skill, extends the arcadian pastoral tradition into an 18th-century version of prelapsarian man; it may be regarded as the visionary foundation of Godwin's ideal commonwealth. After ten years of political writing he published *Caleb Williams, or Things as they are* in May 1794; it was written to demonstrate "that the spirit and character of the government intrudes itself into every rank of society," and the "necessity" by which every wrongdoing inexorably produces its chain of evil consequences. The clash of the innocent Caleb Williams, the brutal Tyrrel, and Falkland, obsessed with a false and self-regarding "chivalry," is vividly examined, and the novel conceals a just psychological realism beneath febrile and inflated language. *St. Leon* (1799) marks an important modification in Godwin's thinking. *Political Justice* had conceded that "there are occasions in which it may be necessary to supersede private judgment for the sake of public good"; by 1795, in *Considerations on Lord Grenville's and Mr. Pitt's Bills*, he was to state that "the greatest problem of political knowledge is how to preserve to mankind the advantages of freedom, together with an authority strong enough to control every daring violation of security and peace"; now, with his affec-

tion for Mary Wollstonecraft feelingly recollected in the character of Marguerite in *St. Leon*, the mature modification of his anarchism is completed in the preface, "the affections and charities of private life being everywhere in this publication a topic of the warmest eulogium, while in the *Enquiry Concerning Political Justice* they seemed to be treated with no degree of indulgence and favour." Godwin's ventures into drama were not more successful than those of the romantic poets, though John Kemble produced *Antonio* at the Drury Lane theatre in 1800 and George Colman had a modest success in 1796 with *The Iron Chest*, his adaptation of *Caleb Williams*.

Godwin's influence and reputation followed curious courses. In his own day, though his associations and writings were subversive and, as the 1795 preface to *Caleb Williams* records, "the humble novelist might be shown to be constructively a traitor," he was never seriously attacked, either for the original preface of 1794 or for his part in the treason trials of that year. Though he was the object of the romantic poets' satire, it was in the disarming character of "Mr. Higgins of St. Mary Axe," and Pitt thought the author of a three-guinea work of sedition scarcely merited prosecution. But his influence on the romantic poets was profound: William Wordsworth's *Guilt and Sorrow* is wholly Godwinian; Samuel Taylor Coleridge and Robert Southey pursued "Pantisocracy" under his inspiration; Shelley's poetry is an incandescent version of his theories. The radical parties in 19th-century Britain and Europe acknowledged his influence, while the years since World War II have seen a revival of interest in both his political and creative writings.

Godwin's chief works are: *The Enquiry Concerning Political Justice* (1793), edited by F. E. L. Priestly, three volumes (1946); *The Enquirer* (1797); *Memoirs of the Author of the Rights of Woman* (1798); *Faulkener, a Tragedy* (1807); *Essays on Sepulchres* (1809); *Lives of Edward and John Philips, the Nephews of Milton* (1815); *Mandeville, a Tale of the Times of Cromwell* (1817); *Of Population, an Answer to Malthus* (1820); *Cloudesley, a Tale* (1830); *Thoughts on Man* (1831); *Lives of the Necromancers* (1834); *Miscellaneous Essays* (1873).

BIBLIOGRAPHY.—C. Kegan Paul, *William Godwin, His Friends and Contemporaries*, 2 vol. (1876); Pierre Ramus, *William Godwin, der Theoretiker des kommunistischen Anarchismus* (1907); Raymond Gourg, *William Godwin* (1908); Lives by H. N. Brailsford, *Shelley, Godwin, and Their Circle* (1913); Lives by F. K. Brown (1926) and G. Woodcock (1946); D. Fleisher, *William Godwin, a Study in Liberalism* (1951); A. E. Rodway, *Godwin and the Age of Transition* (1952); R. Glynn Grylls, *Godwin and His World* (1953); D. H. Monro, *Godwin's Moral Philosophy* (1953); K. N. Cameron (ed.), *Shelley and His Circle* (Carl H. Pforzheimer library collection, 1961). Shorter studies include W. Hazlitt, "Godwin," in *The Spirit of the Age* (1825); Leslie Stephen, "Godwin and Shelley," in *Hours in a Library* (1892); W. M. Merchant, "Wordsworth's Godwinian Period," in *Comparative Literature Studies* (1942); J. W. Marken, "The Canon and Chronology of Godwin's Early Works," in *Modern Language Notes*, lxix (1954); P. N. Furbank, "Godwin's Novels," in *Essays in Criticism* (1955); Patrick Cruttwell, "On Caleb Williams," in *Hudson Review* (1958). (W. M. ME.)

GODWIN AUSTEN, MOUNT: *see* K2.

GODWIT, the name of four large (14–18 in.), long-billed species of wading birds comprising the genus *Limosa* of the family Scolopacidae. As a group they are virtually cosmopolitan, breeding in northern latitudes and migrating southward to winter in the tropics and southern temperate regions. Godwits frequent grassy plains, wet meadows, prairie sloughs and marshes. Their food consists of insects, crustaceans and similar animal matter. In spring, as with many shore birds, the males circle in the air and utter a special call or song. The nest, a shallow hollow in the ground, is lined with dry grass. The three or four eggs are deep olive to brownish, variously

MARBLED GODWIT (*LIMOSA FEDOA*)

HUGH M. HALLIDAY FROM NATIONAL AUDUBON SOCIETY

spotted, blotched or scrawled with dark brown.

The black-tailed godwit (*L. limosa*), one of the larger species, breeds across northern Eurasia and winters south to eastern Africa and Australia; it occurs in the new world only as an accidental visitant. The bar-tailed godwit (*L. lapponica*) has generally the same breeding and wintering ranges as the black-tailed godwit. The Hudsonian godwit (*L. haemastica*), a smaller bird with a slightly upturned bill, formerly bred abundantly in arctic America but is now much reduced in numbers; it winters on the coasts of South America. The marbled godwit (*L. fedoa*), largest of the American species, breeds on the prairies of Canada and winters south to Peru.

(E. R. Be.)

GOEBBELS, (PAUL) JOSEF (1897–1945), the leading propagandist of the German National Socialist party, was born at Rheydt (Rhineland) on Oct. 29, 1897, the son of a manual worker. Infantile paralysis left him with a permanent limp, and he was rejected for military service. He studied at Bonn and Heidelberg universities with financial aid from a Roman Catholic charity, received his doctorate from the Jewish historian of literature, Friedrich Gundolf (Gundelfinger), in 1921, and took up journalism. In 1925 he became secretary to the Nazi leader Gregor Strasser and editor of the Strasser brothers' journal. As the split between the Strassers and Hitler widened he transferred his allegiance to Hitler in Feb. 1926. Hitler made him *Gauleiter* (district party leader) of Berlin, where he showed his talent for agitation and propaganda, both in public meetings and in his own newspaper, *Der Angriff*. In 1928 he was elected to the *Reichstag*, and in November Hitler put him in charge of party propaganda, a post in which he contributed largely to the growing strength of the Nazi movement. Characteristically, he found a political martyr in Horst Wessel, a pimp killed in a brawl, but once a party member; and some doggerel verse that Wessel had written for *Der Angriff* was promoted as the party song. In 1932 Goebbels organized five successful campaigns (two for the presidency, one for state and two for *Reichstag* elections) and revitalized a dispirited party, which from 1930 to 1932 doubled its percentage of the votes cast —an achievement that Hitler owed to Goebbels more than to any other man.

Once in power, Hitler made Goebbels minister for public enlightenment and propaganda, and the full resources of the *Reich* became available to him for propaganda which he, lacking any moral code save that of a nihilist, organized without regard for truth or principle. He showed an immediate realization of the possibilities of the radio, the cinema and other newly developed means of mass communication and brought off several brilliant propaganda coups; for example, it was he who thought of bringing the *wagon-lit* of 1918 to Compiègne for the signing of the French armistice of 1940. His most vicious onslaughts, both in themselves and in the agitation that they stimulated, were against the Jews.

In Dec. 1931 Goebbels married Magda Quant, the divorced wife of a Jewish businessman. They had six children. He had affairs with a number of other women. The most serious of these was with the Czech actress Lyda Baarova, which appeared to be bringing Goebbels and his wife to the point of divorce when Hitler intervened and ordered him to break off the affair. While amassing an enormous wardrobe of well-made suits, Goebbels was renowned for the extreme frugality of his table. Neither this nor his malicious wit endeared him to his associates; and with those whose authority clashed with his, such as Göring and Ribbentrop, he was often on very bad terms.

During World War II Goebbels urged more radical measures to mobilize Germany's resources and a greater use of political possibilities, first in exploiting discontent in Russia, then in attempting a compromise peace when the war was going against Germany. But as the situation became more desperate he became tougher and more nihilistic. Still *Gauleiter* of Berlin, he stayed there throughout Allied bombing and continued to administer the government of the city under bombardment. He tried to keep up the fighting spirit of the people by stimulating fear of their fate if they surrendered, while advocating the denunciation of the Geneva convention and the shooting of captured Allied airmen. After the

abortive plot of July 20, 1944, against Hitler's life, Goebbels was given full powers for the "total" mobilization of manpower and resources. In April 1945 he urged Hitler to remain in Berlin, where he had been since January, never leaving the chancellery or its bunker; Goebbels was the only one of the original Nazi leaders to stay with Hitler to the end. In the bunker his cynical and destructive intelligence seemed absorbed by the mystical egotism of Hitler, whom he exalted further by comparing him to Frederick the Great and foretelling a fresh "miracle of the house of Brandenburg" after the death of Roosevelt. Hitler named him chancellor, and Goebbels added an appendix of his own to Hitler's testament —his last great act of propaganda. After Hitler's death Goebbels and Martin Bormann made an unsuccessful attempt to negotiate with the Russians. Goebbels then killed his family and himself (May 1, 1945).

His *Vom Kaiserhof zur Reichskanzlei* (1934) gives the official version of the Nazi's rise to power; his *Tagebücher 1942–43* (ed. by L. P. Lochner, 1948), although undoubtedly written with an eye to later publication, is an important source for the Nazi mentality in wartime conditions.

See H. Fraenkel and R. Manvell, *Dr. Goebbels: His Life and Death* (1960).

(W. Kp.)

GOEBEL, KARL (IMMANUEL EBERHARD) VON (1855–1932), a leading German botanist of the 19th century, author of a celebrated work on the organs of plants, was born in Billigheim, Baden, March 8, 1855. He studied under Wilhelm Hofmeister, Heinrich Anton de Bary and Julius von Sachs, receiving a doctorate in 1877. After holding teaching positions at various places, in 1891 he was appointed professor at Munich, where in 1909–14 he built the Botanical institute and garden in Nymphenburg. He was devoted to objective research rather than speculation, and to observation of living plants in all their great variety. He traveled extensively, in the Indies, South America, Australia, New Zealand and the United States. His crowning publication was the great *Organography of Plants* (1898–1901), of which three editions appeared in German and one in English. He died in Munich on Oct. 9, 1932, having retired as emeritus professor the year before.

(H. W. Rr.)

GOEBEN, AUGUST KARL VON (1816–1880), Prussian general of the wars of 1864, 1866 and 1870–71, was born at Hanover on Dec. 10, 1816. He saw service with the Carlist army in Spain, thereafter re-entered the Prussian army and in about 1848, when serving as a staff officer, met the elder Helmuth von Moltke (*q.v.*) with whom he formed a lasting friendship. In 1860 he served with Spanish troops in Morocco and was present at the battle of Tetuan. By 1863 he was a major general, and in the war against Denmark in 1864 he distinguished himself as brigade commander at Rackebüll and Sonderburg. In the Austrian war of 1866 he commanded a division and acquitted himself well in the campaign against the Bavarians round Würzburg in the Main valley.

In 1870 Goeben commanded the VIII (Rhineland) corps and was successful at the battles of Spicheren and Gravelotte (Aug. 6 and 18). On Jan. 8, 1871, he succeeded E. von Manteuffel in command of the 1st army and soon brought the war in northern France to a successful conclusion by the victory of St. Quentin (Jan. 18–19).

Goeben was an exceptionally able man who, given the opportunity, would almost certainly have risen to greater distinction. He died at Coblenz on Nov. 13, 1880, while in command of the VIII corps. He wrote *Vier Jahre in Spanien* (1841) and *Reise- und Lagerbriefe aus Spanien und vom spanischen Heere in Marokko* (1863).

(C. N. B.)

GOERDELER, KARL FRIEDRICH (1884–1945), German municipal administrator, the recognized leader of the German resistance movement against Hitler, was born at Schneidemühl (Pila in Poland) on July 31, 1884, the son of a civil servant. He studied law and economics and from 1911 was a member of the municipal administration at Solingen. During World War I he fought mainly on the Russian front, becoming in Feb. 1918 a member of the German military administration in Minsk. After the Armistice of Nov. 11, 1918, Captain Goerdeler was attached to the headquarters of the XVII army corps in Danzig where, in June 1919, he advised his commander, Gen. Otto von Below, that the destruction of restored Poland was the only way to keep the 1914 eastern frontier. In 1922 Goerdeler was appointed second burgomaster of Königsberg and on May 22, 1930, he became chief burgomaster of Leipzig. Twice, in 1931–32 and in 1934–35, he served as *Reichskommissar* for control of prices. His relations with the Nazi party, never cordial, worsened during 1936, and on March 31, 1937, he was forced to resign as chief burgomaster of Leipzig. Almost immediately he began conspiring against Hitler. As an admirer of Bismarckian tradition he was afraid of the consequences for the German people of Hitler's plans of conquest. In World War II, after the defeat at Stalingrad, some of the German military leaders joined him in planning a *coup d'état* and a negotiated peace, but even in the autumn of 1943 Goerdeler, the would-be chancellor, stated in a memorandum transmitted to the Allied governments that the future peace treaty should recognize the "1914 frontier" against Poland, France, Belgium and Denmark and that Germany should retain the Sudetenland and Austria (including the southern Tirol). The attempt of July 20, 1944, to assassinate Hitler failed. Goerdeler went into hiding but was arrested on Aug. 12 near Marienwerder (Kwidzyn in Poland), when he was visiting the grave of his parents. Sentenced to death on Sept. 8, he was hanged at the Plötzensee prison on Feb. 2, 1945.

See G. Ritter, *Carl Gördeler und die deutsche Widerstandsbewegung* (1955).

GOES, HUGO VAN DER (c. 1440–1482), the greatest Flemish painter of the second half of the 15th century, whose strange, melancholy genius found expression in religious works of profound but often disturbing spirituality. Early sources disagree about his birthplace (Ghent, Antwerp, Leiden, and Bruges are mentioned), and nothing is known of his life before 1467, when he was accepted as a master in the painters' guild in Ghent. From then until 1475 he received many commissions from the town of Ghent and provided decorations (heraldic shields, processional banners, etc.) for such occasions as the marriage of Charles the Bold in Bruges (1468) and the translation of the remains of Philip the Good to Dijon (1473). In 1474 he was elected dean of the guild, but the following year—when he was at the climax of his career—he decided to enter Roode Kloster, a priory near Brussels, as a lay brother. There he continued to paint, and received distinguished visitors; he even undertook journeys. In 1481 a tendency to acute depression culminated in a mental breakdown. He died in 1482 and was buried in the priory grounds. An account of the artist's last years at Roode Kloster, written by a monk, Gaspar Ofhuys (who apparently resented some of his privileges), has survived.

Hugo's masterpiece, and his only securely documented work, is the large triptych "The Adoration of the Shepherds" (in the Uffizi, Florence). It was commissioned by Tommaso Portinari, agent for the Medici in Bruges, who is portrayed with his family on the wings. The painting was sent to Florence c. 1475. One of the greatest of the early examples of northern realism, it yet subordinates this to spiritual content, uses still-life detail with symbolic intent, and shows unprecedented psychological insight in portraiture—even of children.

Hugo's earlier and more tentative style shows that he had studied the leading Netherlandish masters of the first half of the 15th century: a diptych in the Kunsthistorisches Museum, Vienna, betrays an awareness of the art of Jan van Eyck in the "Fall of

COPYRIGHT A.C.L. BRUSSELS

DETAIL FROM "DEATH OF THE VIRGIN" BY HUGO VAN DER GOES. IN THE MUSÉE COMMUNAL, BRUGES

Man," while the "Lamentation" is reminiscent of Rogier van der Weyden. A comparison between the large "Adoration of the Magi" and the curiously elongated panel "The Nativity" (both in the Staatliche Museen, Berlin) reveals the direction in which Hugo's late works were to evolve. The "Adoration" is spatially rational, compositionally tranquil, and harmonious in colour; the "Nativity" is disturbing even in its format—an emotionally charged supernatural drama on an uncomfortably low stage revealed by the drawing of curtains. It is this disturbing element, with its exploitation of space and colour for emotional potentiality rather than rational effect, that characterizes the later works. It appears in the panels (c. 1478–79) that were probably designed as organ shutters (on loan from Holyrood Palace to the National Gallery, Edinburgh): here the tragically conceived Trinity and the church scene with donor (Sir Edward Boncle or Bonkil) are by Hugo himself, whereas the portraits of James III of Scotland and his queen were probably painted by an assistant who must have accompanied the panels to Scotland. In the "Death of the Virgin" (Musée Communal, Bruges), executed not long before Hugo's death, colour is particularly disturbing, and poignancy is intensified by the controlled grief seen in the faces of the apostles, Hugo's art, with its affinities to Mannerism (see MANNERIST ART AND ARCHITECTURE), and even his tortured personality have found a particularly sympathetic response in the 20th century.

See J. Destrée, *H. v. d. Goes* (1914), the standard biography, E. Panofsky, *Early Netherlandish Painting* (1953) gives a critical survey of relevant bibliography (pp. 498–499).
(Ka. B. M.)

GOETHALS, GEORGE WASHINGTON (1858–1928), U.S. engineer and army officer known as the builder of the Panama canal, was born in Brooklyn, N.Y., June 29, 1858. He was graduated from the U.S. Military academy, West Point, in 1880. In the same year he was commissioned in the corps of engineers, U.S. army.

From 1880 to 1907 he obtained valuable training in canal, river and harbour construction work while on various assignments in connection with the civil works program of the army engineers. He also served as an instructor at West Point. In 1907 he was called to the White House by Pres. Theodore Roosevelt and told of his selection as chairman and chief engineer of the Isthmian Canal commission, succeeding John F. Stevens. In Jan. 1908 he was placed in complete charge of construction work and government in the Canal Zone by an executive order signed by President Roosevelt.

In 1914 the Panama canal was declared open to commercial traffic; Pres. Woodrow Wilson appointed Goethals the first governor of the canal, and the National Geographic society presented him with a special medal. In March 1915 he was promoted to major general and received the thanks of congress for distinguished service. He retired from the army at his own request in 1916 and in Jan. 1917 resigned as governor of the canal. He was recalled to active duty with the army in Dec. 1917, serving until March 1919. From 1919 to 1928 he was president of the engineering firm of George W. Goethals and company and served as adviser to the Port of New York authority. He died at his home in New York city on Jan. 21, 1928. In March 1954 a monument of heroic size was dedicated in Balboa, Canal Zone, as a memorial to Goethals.
(E. C. I.; X.)

GOETHE, JOHANN WOLFGANG VON (1749–1832), German writer, universally acknowledged to be one of the giants of world literature. The bulk and diversity of his output is in itself phenomenal. In the lyric vein he displays a unique variety of theme and style; in fiction he ranges from fairy tales which have proved a quarry for psychoanalysts through the poetic concentration of his shorter novels and *Novellen* to the "open," frankly symbolic form of *Wilhelm Meister*; in the theatre from historical, political or psychological plays in prose through the chiselled classicism of blank-verse drama to the vast modern mystery that is *Faust*. Besides all this he was the last European to attempt the many-sidedness of the great Renaissance personalities: critic, journalist, painter, theatre manager, statesman, educationalist, natural philosopher—his writings on science alone fill about 14 volumes. But in letters, diaries and conversations he has left a record of a way of living and creating which transcends such stock dualisms of western thought as conscious-unconscious, feeling-thought, thinking-doing, theory-practice, ideal-real, analysis-synthesis, reflection-spontaneity, form-life. He achieved in his 82 years a wisdom often termed Olympian, even inhuman; yet almost to the end he retained a willingness to let himself be shaken to his foundations by love or sorrow. He disciplined himself to a routine which might armour him against chaos; yet he never lost the power of producing magical short lyrics in which the mystery of living, loving and thinking was distilled into sheer transparency.

And at last there was granted him a gift, uncanny even to himself, of tapping at will the springs of creativity in order to complete the work he had carried with him for 60 years. When, a few months before his death, he sealed his *Faust*, he bequeathed it with ironic resignation to the critics of posterity to discover its imperfections. Its final couplet, "Das Ewig-Weibliche/Zieht uns hinan" ("Eternal Womanhead/ Leads us on high"), epitomizes his own feeling about the central polarity of human existence: woman was to him at once man's energizer and his civilizer, source of creative life and focus of the highest endeavours of both mind and spirit.

There was in Goethe a natural, if not always painless, swing between poles of existence often thought to be mutually exclusive, and an innate commitment to change and process. And in the last letter he ever wrote he rounded off what has sometimes been called his greatest work, his life, by setting the seal of his approval on this unitary-polar mode of human growth, describing the art of living as the intensification of inborn talents through a judicious surrender to the natural rhythm of opposing tendencies.

Early Life.—Born on Aug. 28, 1749, in Frankfurt am Main, Goethe came of middle-class stock, and never ceased to praise this *Bürgertum* as a breeding ground of the finest culture. His father, Johann Kaspar Goethe, was of north German extraction. A retired lawyer, he was able to lead a life of cultured leisure, traveled in Italy and amassed a well-stocked library and picture gallery in his handsomely furnished house *am grossen Hirschgraben*. His mother, Katharine Elisabeth Textor, daughter of a *Bürgermeister* of Frankfurt, opened up to her son valued connections with the patriciate of the free city—her very name bears witness to the humanistic influences which had induced a Renaissance ancestor to latinize the German *Weber*. Thus even in his heredity Goethe unites those opposing tendencies which have always prevailed in the German lands: the intellectual and moral rigour of the north and the easygoing artistic sensuousness of the south. Of eight children only Wolfgang, the first born, and a sister, Cornelia, survived.

In his autobiography, *Dichtung und Wahrheit* ("Poetry and Truth"), written from a vantage point which frankly seeks to read the meaning out of events, to discern life's pattern of unity in variety and continuity within change, Goethe has left an unforgettable picture of a happy childhood. Here are set out with acute psychological insight the emotional complexities of his bond with Cornelia, which found expression in numerous portrayals of the brother-sister relationship in his works; his passionate attachment to a barmaid Gretchen, which foreshadowed the rejection pattern of many of his loves; the broadening of outlook which came with French occupation during the Seven Years' War; the coronation of Joseph II in the Frankfurt *Römer*, with its indelible impressions of medieval pageantry; the fervent religiosity of Pietistic circles, which led him to declaim F. G. Klopstock's *Messias* as a kind of Lenten exercise, to write a prose epic on Joseph and a poem

THE GRANGER COLLECTION

GOETHE, PORTRAIT BY J. K. STIELER, 1828

on Christ's descent into hell. The French army had brought its own troupe of actors, and their performances intensified a passion for the stage first kindled in him by his grandmother's gift of a puppet theatre, and inspired a lifelong devotion to Racine. A love of things English was fostered by friendship with a young clothier from Leeds (Goethe's paternal grandfather was a fashionable tailor) with whom Cornelia, seeing herself as the heroine of a Richardsonian novel, fell hopelessly in love. Wolfgang's reaction was the inception of a novel in letters, a kind of linguistic exercise in which four brothers correspond in different languages.

In Oct. 1765 Goethe was sent to study law at his father's old university of Leipzig, though he himself would have preferred to read classics in the newly founded university at Göttingen where English influence prevailed. In Klein-Paris (as he calls it in *Faust*), by contrast, a world of elegance and fashion made the young provincial feel like a fish out of water. The frenchifying influence of J. C. Gottsched (*q.v.*) still dominated the theatre and provided a repertory of the best plays of contemporary Europe. But C. F. Gellert (*q.v.*), now in the heyday of his fame, presented the new "sensibility," of Edward Young, Laurence Sterne and Samuel Richardson. Goethe praised his lectures as "the foundation of German moral culture" and learned from them invaluable lessons in epistolary style (many of the passionately self-dramatizing letters of this period may be read as anticipatory exercises for *Werther*) and in social conduct. These were reinforced by the robust elegance and ironic sagacity of the works of C. M. Wieland (*q.v.*), brought to his notice by A. F. Oeser, friend and teacher of J. J. Winckelmann (*q.v.*) and director of an academy of painting. From Oeser he learned a love of Greek art and two things which stood him in good stead all his life: to use his eyes and to master the craft of whatever he undertook. A visit to Dresden, "the Florence of the north," as J. G. Herder called it, opened his eyes to the splendours of rococo architecture as well as classical statuary. Nor was music neglected: a new society, under the direction of J. A. Hiller (*q.v.*), provided splendid performances which eventually became world famous as the *Gewandhaus* concerts.

The literary harvest of Leipzig was a songbook in the prevailing anacreontic mode, ostensibly inspired by the daughter of the wine merchant at whose tavern he took his midday meal. But neither his 1766–67 poems *Das Buch Annette* (as he called her in rococo fashion) nor the *Neue Lieder* of 1769 made any pretense of real passion. Yet it was in connection with these literary trifles that he subsequently made his famous, and much abused, statement that all his works were "fragments of a great confession." It was of them too that he wrote what might have served critics as a corrective: "*Pour l'amour véritable, il ne faut pas qu'un poète en sente.*" The same pastoral note is struck in two plays in alexandrines, *Die Laune des Verliebten* and a more sombre farce, *Die Mitschuldigen*, which foreshadows the psychological preoccupations of later works. From then on rococo was one element in Goethe's repertoire to be drawn on as occasion demanded. It was to reappear in the setting of *Torquato Tasso* and *Die Wahlverwandtschaften*; he was to pay tribute to its charm in *Anakreons Grab* (1806) and amalgamate it with eastern influence in enchanting poems of the *Westöstlicher Divan* (1819).

Storm and Stress.—Goethe's stay in Leipzig was cut short by severe illness, and by the autumn of 1768 he was back home. A long convalescence fostered introspection and religious mysticism. He played with alchemy, astrology and occult philosophy, all of which have left their mark on *Faust*. On his recovery it was decided that he should pursue his legal studies in Strasbourg as a first stage on the way to Paris and the Grand Tour (never actually completed). His stay there proved a turning point for his whole life and work. In this German capital of a French province he experienced a reaction against the cosmopolitan atmosphere of Leipzig and under the impact of the great cathedral proclaimed his conversion to the Gothic "German" ideal. More decisive still was the influence of J. G. Herder (*q.v.*) who spent the winter of 1770–71 there undergoing treatment for his eyes. From him Goethe learned the role played by touch, the haptic sense, in the growth of the mind; a new view of the artist as a creator fashioning forms expressive of feeling; a new theory of poetry as the original and most vital language of man; the virtues of a new style, that of the *Volkslied* and the poetry of "primitive" peoples as enshrined in the Bible, Homer and Ossian (*see* MACPHERSON, JAMES). It is this new sense of felt immediacy, and of the plasticity of his linguistic medium, that informs the lyrics he wrote to Friederike Brion, the pastor's daughter of Sesenheim. They mark the beginning of a new epoch in the German lyric. Such poems as "Mailied" and "Willkommen und Abschied" are still the most popular, though not the greatest, of his *Lieder*. The latter, especially in its revised form of 1790, touchingly expresses the guilt he felt that this time he himself had the role of deserter and rejecter; and the whole idyl as recounted in *Dichtung und Wahrheit* reveals that cross-fertilization of life and literature which he increasingly saw as a potent factor in human development. For both Goldsmith's *Vicar of Wakefield* and Thomas Percy's ballads—to say nothing of Friederike's Alsatian costume—played their part in attracting him to this female embodiment of the new spirit of German poetry.

If, as Herder maintained, energy was one of the marks of poetry, it was clearly in the passions acted out on the stage that it could find its most vital expression. And where more vital than in the colossal figures of "Gothic Shakespeare"? In writing the *Geschichte Gottfriedens von Berlichingen mit der eisernen Hand dramatisiert* (1771) Goethe was deliberately vying with him. For the "History," the Shakespeare cult was launched and the *Sturm und Drang* (*see* GERMAN LITERATURE) was provided with its first major work of genius. The manifesto of the movement, heralded by Goethe's *Götz von Berlichingen*, a radically tautened version of this "History," had appeared after Goethe's enthusiastic *Rede zum Schäkespears Tag* (on the model of the Stratford festival two years before), ... return to Frankfurt in Aug. 1771. *Von deutscher Art und Kunst*, as it was called, contained a defense of German nationality by the historian J. M. Möser, two essays by Herder championing Ossian and Shakespeare, and a rhapsody on Gothic architecture by Goethe.

Though ostensibly in practice as a lawyer, the young poet now found himself caught up in a whirl of literary and social duties—helping to edit the *Frankfurter Gelehrte Anzeigen*, for instance—and it was to break loose from this that he left for Wetzlar, seat of the supreme court of the empire. But again literature won the day over law and an impassioned yet self-ironic ode in free verse, "Wandrers Sturmlied," is testimony both to a recently inspired admiration for Pindar and to a hesitant certainty that he himself may be destined for greatness. And in Wetzlar he experienced a new passion, this time for a girl safely out of reach from the start, Charlotte Buff. Her betrothed, Johann Christian Kestner, showed great understanding until, as it seemed to him, he found the affair exposed to public gaze in *Die Leiden des jungen Werthers* (*The Sorrows of Young Werther*; 1774).

But much besides the Wetzlar experience had gone into the making of this novel: Herder's scathing comments on his young pupil's lack of formal- and self-mastery; the recent indictment by G. E. Lessing (*q.v.*) of the Neoplatonic doctrine of artistic creation in *Emilia Galotti*, a passing attraction to the daughter of Sophie von La Roche, who probably endowed his heroine with her black eyes. And it was only when Kestner reported the suicide of a Wetzlar acquaintance who had killed himself out of hopeless love that all this was precipitated into a plot. If *Werther* took the world by storm it was because, in Thomas Carlyle's words, it gave expression to "the nameless unrest and longing discontent which was then agitating every bosom." But this first novel is no sentimental tear-jerker. Nor is disappointed love its real theme. It is rather what the 18th century called Enthusiasm: the fatal effects of a predilection for absolutes, whether in love, art, society or the realm of thought. The mind that conceived its symmetry, wove its intricate linguistic patterns and handled the subtle differentiation of hero and narrator was moved by a formal as well as a personal passion. Even the title has been trivialized in translation: *Sorrows* (instead of "Sufferings") obscures the allusion to the

Passio Christi, and individualizes what Goethe himself thought of as a "general confession," in a tradition going back to St. Augustine.

Besides *Werther* and *Götz*, the period 1771–75 saw the appearance of a number of magnificent hymns—lyrical or dramatic, according to whether the influence of Pindar or Shakespeare prevailed—"Cäsar," "Mahomets Gesang," "Der Ewige Jude," "Prometheus," "Sokrates," "Satyros," "Der Wanderer"; the inception of *Egmont* and *Faust* (this so-called *Urfaust*, or "original" Faust was discovered by a lucky chance in 1887); the completion of *Clavigo* (1774), a play of more "regular" form on a theme of Beaumarchais, and of *Stella* (1775), with its conciliatory ending of a *mariage à trois*, subsequently conventionalized into tragedy. Two operettas, *Erwin and Elmire* and *Claudine von Villa Bella*, reflect a return to the elegance of rococo inspired by his betrothal to Lili Schönemann, daughter of a rich banker, who moved in fashionable circles which were soon to prove unbearably restrictive to the young *Stürmer und Dränger*. From the conflicts of this love he took refuge, as so often, in nature, and in a poem written on the lake of Zurich, "Auf dem See," created the first of those many short lyrics in which language of radiant simplicity is made the vehicle of inexhaustible significance. With his departure for Weimar in Nov. 1775 the engagement was allowed to lapse.

Weimar.—Going to Weimar was the major turning point of Goethe's life. He went on a visit to the reigning duke, Charles Augustus. It remained his home—despite Napoleon's "*venez à Paris*"—until his death there on March 22, 1832. From now on mastery of life became his chief concern and *Wilhelm Meisters Lehrjahre* ("Wilhelm Meister's Years of Apprenticeship"), the title he eventually gave his next novel (1795–96), suggests the long apprenticeship such mastery involves. He served his own in the immemorable and ever increasing official duties the young duke heaped on his willing shoulders until, as indispensable minister of the little state, he was inspecting mines, superintending irrigation schemes and organizing the issue of uniforms to its tiny army.

He served his apprenticeship, too, in his passionate devotion to the wife of a court official, Charlotte von Stein (*q.v.*). For the first time he found himself in love with a woman who could also meet him on the intellectual plane. From the 1,500 or so letters he wrote her we can see her become the guiding principle of his life, teaching him the graces of society, dominating the details of his daily existence, engaging his imagination and desire, yet insisting on a relation governed by decorum and conventional virtue. She would be his sister and nothing more; and the sublimation she increasingly enforced on him, though irksome, could inspire the almost psychoanalytical probings of "Warum gabst du uns die tiefen Blicke?", the tortures of Orest and their assuagement by Iphigenie, the delicate one-act play, *Die Geschwister* ("Brother and Sister"; 1776), and such well-loved lyrics as "An den Mond," "Der Becher," "Jägers Abendlied," "Seefahrt" and the two exquisite "Wandrers Nachtlieder."

In these and other poems of this period—"Grenzen der Menschheit," "Gesang der Geister über den Wassern," "Das Göttliche," "Harzreise im Winter," "Ilmenau"—nature has ceased to be a mere reflection of man's moods and has become something existing in its own right, a setting for an idea, or a force indifferent, even hostile to him. This new "objectivity" is in tune with Goethe's growing scientific preoccupations. Yet such is his versatility that he could, when he chose, revert to the temper of "Der König in Thule" (written in 1774) and compose ballads such as "Erlkönig" or "Der Fischer," in which nature bears the projection of unconscious forces; while a number of *Singspiele* or musical plays betoken his readiness and ability to provide light entertainment for the court. *Der Triumph der Empfindsamkeit* ("The Triumph of Sensibility"; 1777/78) even satirizes the "sensibility" his own *Werther* had helped to foster.

Italy.—But neither the cares of state nor those of a frustrating love affair were conducive to the peace and leisure required to complete works of such magnitude as *Egmont*, *Faust*, *Tasso* and *Iphigenie* (a prose version of this last was sufficiently advanced to be put on before the court in 1779 with Goethe himself as Orest). And in Sept. 1786, in dramatic secrecy and with the haste of one pursued, he set out on his long-postponed Italian journey. This flight was at once a death and a rebirth. And it was in these terms that he wrote of it in his letters. He sought the renewal of himself, both as man and artist, and so deliberately cut himself off from his emotional, literary and cultural past, scoring the "Gothic follies" he had once acclaimed, rejecting Juliet's tomb in Verona in favour of the Greek steles in the museum, finding delight in Palladio's churches rather than in San Marco or the doge's palace, devoting barely three hours to Florence, and ignoring completely the medieval glories of Assisi for the sake of its temple of Minerva, feverishly bent on arriving in Rome, "capital of the ancient world," but seeing even that as a prelude to the classical grandeur in Sicily, "key to the whole," a prelude to the world of Homer which he recaptured in a glorious dramatic fragment, *Nausikaa* (1787). And just as he sought and found the *Urmensch*, or archetypal man, in the forms of Greek antiquity, so in these landscapes there came to his mind the extension of this idea to plants as well. In his literary work these pursuits led to the creation of beings who are individual manifestations, but of a clearly discernible type; to themes which are universal and timeless but treated in a highly differentiated way; to the measured cadences of verse which are yet vibrant with personal passion.

This new conception of form is apparent in the revision of the four plays he had taken with him to Italy. *Faust, Ein Fragment*, published in 1790, is quite clearly, by its excisions as well as its additions, a step in the direction of the stupendous cultural symbol the play would eventually become rather than any attempt to weld into dramatic unity the sharply individualized episodes of *Urfaust*. *Egmont*, though not actually cast into verse, is raised to the level of poetic drama not by virtue of its frequent iambic rhythms but by a thickening of the verbal texture, so that when music finally takes over it seems the inevitable culmination of a gradual convergence and sudden contraction of themes rather than the "*salto mortale* into the world of opera" Schiller was to dub it. By such means the personal and the political aspects of the problem become completely interfused—Egmont and his Klärchen, the most lovable characters Goethe ever created, are embodiments of an inner freedom which is a heightened form of the easygoing independence of the Netherlands people—and what had started as a dramatic portrayal of a daemonic individual is transformed into a tragedy of the very idea of freedom, of its fate in a world ruled not just by calculation or intrigue but by unpredictable conjunctures of persons and events.

In *Torquato Tasso* such linguistic density is carried to lengths only possible in verse. Goethe spoke of having expended a positively "unlawful care" on it. But this is not inappropriate to a play about a poet, an artist whose medium is the ordinary vehicle of communication between men. The tragic conflict here arises from misunderstandings about the various modes of language and the temperamental clashes are presented as concomitants of this rather than as the prime focus of interest (though there is enough psychology to justify Mme de Staël's description of Goethe as "le Racine de l'Allemagne"). Even the much-criticized slightness of the outward action has point in a study of the "poetical character" per se, a creature for whom "any little vexation grows in five minutes into a theme for Sophocles." By placing him in a society which, far from being indifferent or hostile, cherishes him and values his work, Goethe has thrown into sharpest relief the incurable "discrepancy" between poet and world and this rift is not healed by Tasso's discovery that even the extremes of anguish can be transmuted into imperishable verse.

But it was perhaps *Iphigenie auf Tauris* (1787) which benefited most from his encounter with classical antiquity. And yet Schiller was right in calling it "astonishingly modern and un-Greek." Like *Tasso*, it, too, treats of the problems of communication: of the unforeseeable power of words once they are released into the world; of the double face of language which conceals as much as it reveals; of truth, whose opposite is not just an outright lie but the withholding of self. But it treats, too, of man's power to free himself from his myths by recognizing them as projections of his own unconscious, of his power to break the chain of events which

seems to determine his present (symbolized in the monotonously regular crime sequence of the race of Tantalus) by a reorientation of outlook. The conciliatory ending, which Euripides contrived by a *dea ex machina*, here comes with the apparent suddenness of new insight: the words of the oracle are susceptible of a different interpretation. In its synthesis of Greek and Christian values, its elevation of the physical to the spiritual through the identification of Iphigenie with the divine sister, Diana, this play represents the highest achievement of 18th-century humanism.

The chief lyrical product of the Italian journey was the *Römische Elegien* (the "Roman Elegies"; written 1788–89, published 1793). In their plastic beauty and unabashed sensuality, their blending of erotic tenderness with an enhanced sense of our cultural heritage, these pagan, highly civilized poems are unique in any modern language. Had they been written in the metre of Byron's *Don Juan*, Goethe acknowledged, they might easily have been offensive; but the classical distichs lend them that veil of aesthetic distance which reveals even as it shrouds. The true begetter of these elegies was not some passing Roman amour but Christiane Vulpius, daughter of a humble official, whom Goethe had taken into heart and home soon after his return from Italy in April 1788. Christiane bore him several children but it was not until 1806, when life and property were threatened by the French invasion, that the nonconformist eventually conformed and in grateful recognition of its indissoluble bonds regularized their union in the eyes of society.

His first Italian journey finally brought home to Goethe that, for all his interest and talent, he was not destined to be a painter. Despite diligent practice with his artist friends in Rome, he was never able to master this medium to the point where it became expressive of his deepest feeling, and with rare exceptions his numerous drawings have no more than the charm of a sensitive amateur. But his abiding preoccupation with the visual arts left an indelible mark on his literary as well as his scientific work and gave added precision to his many critical and aesthetic essays. And it was on this first visit to Italy, too, that he finally reached the decision that he must shed his administrative duties and devote himself henceforth to his true vocation of literature and science.

The French Revolution.—A return visit to Italy in 1790 brought nothing but disappointment, and a restlessness aggravated by the revolutionary events in the outer world. The *Venetian Epigrams* of 1790 reflect something of this discontent. In 1792 Goethe accompanied his duke on the disastrous campaign into France, was present at the battle of Valmy and wrote up his experiences in two still very readable war books, *Die Kampagne in Frankreich 1792* and *Die Belagerung von Mainz*. His liberal-conservative attitudes found expression in *Reineke Fuchs* (a recasting of the Low-German satire), the *Unterhaltungen deutscher Ausgewanderten* and three plays, *Der Gross-Kophta, Die Aufgeregten* and *Der Bürgergeneral*, which, though artistically unsuccessful, are of interest in being among the few examples of political literature produced by German poets. But it was only as the French Revolution receded that he was able to transmute its overwhelming actuality into timeless poetry. It still forms the background of his Homeric treatment of the refugee problem, *Hermann und Dorothea* (1797). It fills the whole canvas of *Die Natürliche Tochter* ("The Natural Daughter"; 1804). Planned as a trilogy, but never completed, this was Goethe's final reckoning with the greatest event of his time. Beneath the coolness of its formal perfection there stirs a profound concern with revolutionary phenomena, with the role of death and destruction in the perpetuation of social and cultural, no less than of natural, forms of life.

Schiller and the Classical Ideal.—The human and spiritual isolation in which Goethe found himself on his return from Italy was unexpectedly relieved by the development of a friendship with Schiller. His acceptance of a formal invitation to contribute to a new journal, *Die Horen* (1795–97), called forth Schiller's now-famous letter of Aug. 23, 1794, in which, with marvelous insight, he summed up Goethe's whole existence. Here, it seemed to him, was the very embodiment of the naïve poet—but consciously naïve, moving from feeling to reflection, and then transforming reflection back into feeling, concepts of the mind back into percepts of the senses. It was this conscious assent to a mode of thinking different from Schiller's own more abstractive reflection which made possible their immensely fruitful partnership, and the four volumes of their daily correspondence offer not only an invaluable commentary on the ideals and achievements of the greatest period of German literature but astonishing insight into the processes of artistic creation. Some of the works Goethe produced during the next few years are embodiments of their classical ideal. *Hermann und Dorothea*, one of the best-loved, is his attempt to "produce a Greece from within." In it he claimed to have "separated the purely human from the dross." The characters are types—except for the hero and heroine they have no proper names, and even theirs are symbolic—and like those of the *Odyssey* they vindicate peace and home and the domestic virtues. Yet, as always in Goethe's works, these are shown as never secure for long, as constantly in need of being fostered by man's efforts to be human and humane. In the Helena act of *Faust, Part II* (which was written in 1800, published separately in 1827, and, with the rest of Part II, in 1832), he captured the Greek spirit so successfully that competent critics hold that if translated into Attic Greek it might well pass for a lost fragment of the Athenian stage.

A never completed epic, *Achilleis*, is his last attempt to "be a Greek after his own fashion." Other works of this period are in tune with Schiller's growing conviction that the only future for literature in a world which increasingly clamoured for the naturalistic and the tendentious lay in a hermetic closing of the poetic world by a frank introduction of symbolic devices. *Wilhelm Meisters Theatralische Sendung* ("Wilhelm Meister's Theatrical Mission"; a manuscript of this version turned up in 1910) is now widened to a vocation for life, a theme dear to the heart of Schiller, who had himself just completed a treatise on the aesthetic education of man (*Briefe über die ästhetische Erziehung des Menschen*; 1795), and wholly in tune with their joint conviction that art, though not the handmaid of either truth or morality, has nevertheless its own peculiar part to play in making better men and better citizens. Fictional realism is now blended with abstraction; characterization, however psychologically acute, subordinated to an over-all poetic significance; and the presence in a novel of contemporary society of such mysteriously compelling figures as the Harper and Mignon seems to justify Goethe's claim that his novel is *durchaus symbolisch* ("thoroughly symbolic").

It was Schiller, too, who turned his thoughts to the continuation of *Faust* and discerned the difficulties involved in reconciling this "barbarous composition" with their classical ideal, in blending the evident seriousness of its "idea" with that element of "play" which was the prerequisite of the art of the future. By his insistence on such problems he inspired the fictional framework of *Faust's* "Prelude on the Stage" no less than the philosophical framework of the "Prologue in Heaven." If in spite of such indications the world insisted on reading *Faust, Part I* (1808) as a love story which stamped its author as a romantic, it was because at this stage the almost unbearable pathos of the Gretchen tragedy had not yet found its place in the wider tragedy of western man.

Goethe and Schiller blamed the failure of the journals in which they strove to propagate their ideals of art and literature (Goethe's *Propyläen*, 1798-1800, was a quasi-successor to Schiller's *Horen*) on the indifference of an uncultivated public and vented their disappointment in *Xenien*, about 400 mordant distichs in the manner of Martial. A more positive reply to their detractors was a wonderful harvest of ballads. Goethe's own—"Der Schatzgräber," "Die Braut von Korinth," "Der Zauberlehrling"—differ from his earlier ones in that man rather than nature now holds sway. The "white" magic of reflection is consciously, even ironically, introduced. And in the ballad, with its blend of lyric, epic and dramatic elements, Goethe now discerned the *Urei*, or archetypal form, of poetry, by analogy with the *Urpflanze* he had discovered in the vegetable world.

Goethe's Relation to the Romantics.—With Schiller's death in 1805 Goethe felt he had lost "the half of his existence" and he wrote a magnificent tribute to his great friend in *Epilog zu Schillers Glocke*. His intellectual loneliness was eased in some measure by his relations to the new school of Romantics then flourishing in Jena. For they had much in common. Friedrich von Schlegel (*q.v.*) had begun his career with a book extolling Greek culture and gone on to praise the orient as the summit of romantic thought and poetry. His brother Wilhelm's absorption in form and metre was after Goethe's own heart and he could not be indifferent to their enthusiastic praise of *Wilhelm Meister* or to Novalis' description of him as "the vicegerent of poetry upon earth." In Bettina Brentano (daughter of his old love, Maximiliane von La Roche; *see* ARNIM, BETTINA VON) he found an ardent response to both his genius and his humanity, and her *Briefwechsel Goethes mit einem Kinde* (1835) remains one of the most delightful books in German literature, whatever doubts may be cast on its reliability. Though Goethe decried the Romantics as "forced talents," amateurishly oblivious of the virtues of form, though he deplored their catholicizing tendencies, their uncritical addiction to all things medieval, their attempts to blur the literary genres and confuse the boundaries between art and life, he yet remained open to many of their enthusiasms, even letting himself be moved to a renewed interest in Gothic architecture. And in *Die Wahlverwandtschaften* ("Elective Affinities"; 1809) he drew heavily for his thematic material upon their preoccupation with "the night-side of nature," with the animal, magnetic affinities which attract human beings to each other as elements are attracted in the chemical world.

But this novel offers no support at all for a superstitious surrender to forces natural or supernatural, for a subhuman abdication of moral responsibility; any more than it offers a plea for the free love advocated in Friedrich von Schlegel's *Lucinde*. Catastrophe follows inexorably upon the arbitrary interpretation of signs and portents; the heroine enters upon a path of renunciation which brings her near sainthood; marriage may be presented with ruthless realism as "a synthesis of impossibilities" but it remains nevertheless "the beginning and end of all civilization." The Romantics were here taught a lesson of social behaviour—and of artistic form. The narrative is conducted with a serene impartiality, and all the classical values of plasticity, restraint and symmetry are brought to bear on a subject which is sensational to the point of improbability.

By their translations—romanticism is translation, Clemens Brentano declared—the Romantics were opening up the literary treasures of the world, and *Weltliteratur* was to become one of Goethe's most treasured concepts. Its aim was, as he put it, to advance civilization by encouraging mutual understanding and respect—whether through translation or criticism (his own attempts to interpret Serbian poetry to the Germans is an excellent example of this latter) or through the blending of different literary traditions. Two great ballads, "Der Gott und die Bajadere" and "Paria," and two exquisite cycles, the late and lesser-known, *Chinesisch-Deutsche Jahres- und Tageszeiten* ("Chinese-German Hours and Seasons"; 1830), and the *West-Östlicher Divan* ("Divan of West and East"; 1819), are his own outstanding attempts to marry east with west. This latter is a book of love in all its aspects—tender, playful, sensuous, ironic, wise and wanton—all of it irradiated by that quality of *Geist*—of intellect, spirit, wit—which he discerned as "the predominant passion" of Persian poetry. His living muse this time, Marianne, the young wife of his friend von Willemer, was perhaps the most completely satisfying of all his loves, so attuned to him in spirit that she could even take a hand in the creation of some of these poems.

The Last Decade.—But the world vision of the aging poet did not only find expression in a silent communing with the past. In his last years Goethe found himself a world figure and little Weimar became a Mecca that drew a constant stream of pilgrims from both the old world and the new. Reports of his stiffness and reserve in the face of almost daily invasions are far outweighed by the testimony of those to whom he showed warmth, understanding, an insatiable curiosity about what was going on in the outside world and an abiding openness to the present and the future. This is nowhere more apparent than in *Wilhelm Meisters*

Wanderjahre (*Wilhelm Meister's Travels*, 1821–29), with its commitment to social and technological progress (what he would most like to see before he died, Goethe once said, was the completion of the Panama and Suez canals), to a type of education better adapted to modern specialization than the old *humaniora*, to a world no longer centred wholly in Europe—a major "complication" of his plot is a resettlement plan for emigrants in the land of the future ("Amerika, du hast es besser!"). *Wanderjahre* points the truth that mastery of life is not conferred at the end of the "apprentice years" and henceforth an inalienable possession, but a ceaseless wandering in which the goal turns out to be the way, and the way the goal.

At first sight the subtitle *Die Entsagenden* ("Renunciation") seems curiously at odds with such purposeful unrest. But renunciation for Goethe implies no passive resignation to the *status quo*. It is a growing acceptance of the limits imposed by life itself, limits arising from the nature of space and time, and from the conflict of interests and potentialities. The apparent formlessness of the novel reflects the duality of its title. It meanders, its narrative interspersed with tales, anecdotes, episodes and maxims, having but the loosest connection with the plot, but a formal, if often subterranean, connection with the poetic significance. These interpolations, like the increasingly symbolic characters, display the whole spectrum of human modes of renunciation. The "whole man" is here represented not by any single individual but by a constellation of many, and the informing principle is the spatial one of configuration rather than the temporal one of succession.

Faust (for an indication of the contents *see* GERMAN LITERATURE: *The Age of Goethe: Classicism*), too, is often decried as formless, though the climate of criticism is now more propitious to the discovery of its "law." The array of lyric, epic, dramatic, operatic and balletic elements, of almost every known metre, from doggerel through *terza rima* to six-foot trimeter, of styles ranging from Greek tragedy through medieval mystery, baroque allegory, Renaissance masque, *commedia dell' arte* and the "temerities of the English stage," to something akin to the modern revue, all suggest a deliberate attempt to make these various forms a vehicle of cultural comment rather than any failure to create a coherent form of his own. And the content with which Goethe invests his forms bears this out. He draws on an immense variety of cultural material—theological, mythological, philosophical, political, economic, scientific, aesthetic, musical, literary—for the more realistic Part I no less than for the more symbolic Part II (first published posthumously in 1832): if Faust's wooing of Helena in the "Classic-Romantic Phantasmagoria" (as the first publication of the scene in 1827 called it) is accomplished by teaching her the unfamiliar delights of rhymed verse, his seduction of Gretchen is firmly set in the long tradition of erotic mysticism going back to the "Mothers," timeless source of all forms of being, annuls the historical time sequence—but as a drama of the diverse potentialities which coexist in western civilization (*see* FAUST).

This Faust, unlike his creator, is the very type of western man, with two souls warring within his breast and a restlessly inquiring spirit. To the 19th century his ceaseless striving seemed a good thing in itself. To a generation shocked into doubts about progress and the value of action the disastrous consequences of his attempts to experience "the weal and woe of all mankind" (the *libido sciendi* of Marlowe's Faustus is here but briefly indulged and as swiftly transcended) loom larger than the quotable "message" of any of the speeches, and his ultimate "salvation" becomes correspondingly suspect. Yet the love that bears his mortal remains to "higher spheres" does not mitigate the ironic defeat of his highest mortal endeavour. If the seal of approval is set on a spirit which has eluded Mephisto's every effort to lull him into sloth, the evil into which it led him is not condoned. It needs the combined intercession of human wisdom and human suffering, human innocence and human experience, before compassionate verdict is passed on the erring and straying of this soul "in ferment." Indeed, none of Goethe's conciliatory endings, except that of *Iphigenie*, really removes the sting of tragedy. Critics have tended to excuse or deplore them by reference to his own *konziliante Natur* (his "conciliatory nature"). But at least as relevant is his preoccupation with the form of Greek trilogies and tetralogies, and his unorthodox interpretation of Aristotle's catharsis as an effect only likely to be produced in the spectator if there is a corresponding element of "reconciliation" in the structure of the play itself. The apotheosis of the hero, whether Faust's, Egmont's or Ottilie's in the *Wahlverwandtschaften*, is always set in a context reminiscent of a theophany and of the ritual origins of tragedy.

Nor can his interest in the cathartic effect of music be ignored. Unlike Novalis, for whom music was "the key to the universe," Goethe was profoundly aware of its dual nature and as suspicious as Plato of its orgiastic power. As in every art he looked for the taming of the dionysiac by the apolline, nowhere more movingly symbolized than by the taming of the lion through the piping of the little child in his *Novelle* of 1828, a theme he had already discussed with Schiller as far back as 1797. And increasingly he turned to music for assuagement of his own suffering. His *Trilogie der Leidenschaft* ("Trilogy of Passion"; 1823–27) is at once the lyrical precipitate of an old man's anguished love for a girl of 18 and a tribute to the cathartic effect of this "heavenly art" which restores to life even as it soothes. His *Zauberflöte, Zweiter Teil* is a tribute to his favourite Mozart's *Magic Flute*: Mozart would, he thought, have been the ideal composer for *Faust*. And one of the comforts of his later years was an intimate friendship with the composer K. F. Zelter, whose most brilliant pupil, the young Mendelssohn, afforded him hours of musical delight and deepened his musical understanding—though he never succeeded in reconciling him to the daemonic aspects of Beethoven's music.

Science and Philosophy.—By common consent *Faust* is one of the supreme, if as yet unclassified, achievements of literature. But there were moments when Goethe rated his scientific work higher than all his poetry. His predilection for his *Farbenlehre* ("Theory of Colour"; 1805–10) has something of the love of a parent for a problem child, and nothing is easier than for the physicist to pick holes in his systematic attempt to prove Newton wrong, or for the psychologist to find the cause of his stubbornness in his sense of mathematical inadequacy or in his neurotic attachment to the doctrine that light is one and indivisible and never to be explained by any theory of particles. On the other hand, the usefulness of the *Entoptische Farben* ("On Entoptic Images"), is generally acknowledged, while the Historical Section is something of a pioneer work in the writing of the history of science. His work in botany and biology is less controversial. His *Metamorphose der Pflanzen* ("Attempt to Explain the Metamorphosis of Plants"; 1790) is a model of presentation and the drawings in it are a botanist's delight. His main thesis, that all the parts of the plant are modifications of a type-leaf, has met with a measure of acceptance, though his categorical neglect of the root is regarded as an unscientific exclusion of a possible area of relevance. His hypothesis of a typeplant, by contrast, commands no interest among orthodox botanists today. His discovery in 1784, arrived at independently even if he was not the first to make it, of a recognizable *os intermaxillare* (the premaxilla of modern anatomists) in the human species was yet another result of his sustained quest for unity and continuity in nature and caused Darwin to hail him as a forerunner.

But what makes for the continuing interest of Goethe's science is not his discoveries: he could not always claim priority for them at the time nor was he in the least interested to do so. It is his insight into his methods of arriving at them. Few have been as aware of the mental processes involved in the study of natural phenomena; more alive to the hazards which beset the "scientist," at every level, from sheer observation to the construction of a theory; more conscious of the unwitting theorizing involved in even the simplest act of perception. And no one has argued more convincingly that the only way of coping with this inescapable involvement of the observer in the phenomena to be observed is to let "knowledge of self" develop with "knowledge of world." Such scrupulous awareness of his own mental operations was, of course, of paramount importance in morphology, the science Goethe founded and named. Morphology, as he understood it, was the systematic study of formation and transformation—whether of rocks, clouds, plants, animals or the cultural phenomena of human society—as these present themselves to sentient experience. He did not propose it as a substitute to the quantitative sciences, which break down forms as we know them and by converting them into mathematical terms ensure a measure of prediction and control. He was not, contrary to common belief, opposed to analysis—one of his favourite maxims was that analysis and synthesis must alternate as naturally as breathing in and breathing out—and his only objection to physics was its increasing tendency to claim monopoly of understanding. What he was aiming at was rather a humanizing supplement, an understanding of nature in all its qualitative manifestations, and one of his most impassioned pleas is for a concert of all the sciences, a co-operation of all types of method and mind.

This impulse, to find a scientific as well as an aesthetic corrective to the inevitably esoteric tendencies of specialization, is nowhere more apparent than in his two elegies on plant and animal metamorphosis in which he tries to present to imagination and feeling what has been understood by the mind. They eventually took their place in a cycle of philosophical poems entitled *Gott und Welt* ("God and World"). Though no orthodox believer, Goethe was by no means the pure pagan the 19th century liked to imagine. Spinoza's pantheism certainly struck a sympathetic chord, for the deist idea of a God who, having created the world, then left it to revolve, was repugnant to him. But he was and remained a grateful heir of the Christian tradition—*bibelfest*, rooted in the Bible—as his language constantly proclaims. And it was from this centre that he extended sympathetic understanding to all other religions, seeking their common ground without destroying their individual excellencies, seeing them as different manifestations of an Ur, or archetypal, religion and thus giving expression, in this field as elsewhere, to the essentially morphological temper of his mind. "Panentheism" has been proposed as a more exact term for his belief in a divinity at once immanent and transcendent, and he rebuked those who tried to confine him to one mode of thought by saying that as poet he was polytheist, as scientist pantheist, and that when, as a moral being, he had need of a personal God, "that too had been taken care of." This was one of the meanings he attached to the text: "In my father's house are many mansions."

Appraisal.—A day will come, Carlyle predicted in a letter to R. W. Emerson, when "you will find that this sunny-looking courtly Goethe held veiled in him a Prophetic sorrow deep as Dante's." And since World War II there have been many attempts to replace the image of the serene optimist by that of the tortured skeptic. The one is as inadequate as the other—as inadequate as T. S. Eliot's conclusion that he was sage rather than poet—though this is perhaps inevitable when a writer is such a master of his own medium that even his prose proves resistant to translation. Even his Werther knew that the realities of existence are rarely to be grasped by Either-Or. And the reality of Goethe himself certainly eludes any such attempt. If he was a skeptic, and he often was, he was a hopeful skeptic. He looked deep into the abyss; but he deliberately emphasized life and light. He lived life to the full at every level; but never to the detriment of the civilized virtues. He remained closely in touch with the richness and the adventure of life; but he shed on it the light of reflection without destroying the spontaneity of its processes. He was, as befits a son of the Enlightenment, wholly committed to the adventure of science; but he stood in awe and reverence before the mystery of the universe. Goethe nowhere formulated a system of thought. He was as impatient of the sterilities of logic chopping as of the inflations of metaphysics, though he acknowledged his indebtedness to many philosophers, including Kant. But here again he was not to be confined. Truth for him lay not in compromise but in the embracing of opposites. And this is expressed in the form of his *Gespräche* ("Conversations"), contain the sum of his wisdom. As with proverbs,

one can always find among them a twin which expresses the complementary opposite. And they have something of the banality of proverbs too. But it is, as André Gide observed, "*une banalité supérieure.*" What makes it "superior" is that the thought has been felt and lived and that the formulation betrays this. And for all his specialized talents there was a kind of "superior banality" about Goethe's life. If he himself felt it was "symbolic" and worth presenting as such in a series of autobiographical writings, it was not from arrogance but from a realization that he was an extraordinarily ordinary man in whom ordinary men might see themselves reflected. Not an ascetic, a mystic, a saint or a recluse, not a Don Juan or a poet's poet, but one who to the best of his ability had tried to achieve the highest form of *l'homme moyen sensuel*—which is perhaps what Napoleon sensed when after their meeting in Erfurt he uttered his famous "*Voilà un homme!*"

See also references under "Goethe, Johann Wolfgang von" in the Index.

BIBLIOGRAPHY.—*Works, Drawings, Correspondence, Conversations: Goethes Werke* (Vollständige Ausgabe letzter Hand), 40 vol. (1827–30); a continuation of this: *Nachgelassene Werke*, 20 vol. (1832–42); both also in a *Taschenausgabe*. The standard critical edition was published in Weimar at first under the auspices of the grand duchess Sophie (hence known as the *Weimarer Ausgabe* or *Sophienausgabe*), 133 vol., including the scientific works, diaries and letters (1887–1919); a new critical edition by the Deutsche Akademie der Wissenschaften zu Berlin is in progress (1952–). Of modern editions the most noteworthy are: the *Jubiläums-Ausgabe*, ed. by E. von der Hellen, 40 vol., plus an invaluable *Registerband*, with introductions and including selections from the scientific works, correspondence and conversations, with useful indexes (1902–12); the *Gedenkausgabe*, ed. by E. Beutler, 24 vol., including selections from the scientific works (1948–54) plus *Ergänzungsband I*: Hempel, 36 vol. (1868–79), and by C. Höfer and C. Noch, *Propyläen Ausgabe*, 49 vol., presenting the writings in chronological order (1909–32). There are innumerable Selected Works. *Goethes Amtliche Schriften*, ed. by W. Flach (1950; in progress). Goethe's drawings and sketches are being published in the *Corpus der Goethe-Zeichnungen*: vol. i, *Von den Anfängen bis zur italienischen Reise von 1786*, ed. by G. Femmel (1958); see also L. Münz, *Goethes Zeichnungen und Radierungen* (1950). *Goethes Gespräche*, ed. by W. von Biedermann, 10 vol., 2nd ed. (1909–11); J. P. Eckermann, *Gespräche mit Goethe, 1823–32*, 3 vol. (1836–48, many times reprinted). The only complete collection of Goethe's letters is in the *Weimarer Ausgabe* (see above); see also letters to Goethe ed. by R. K. Goldschmidt-Jentner, *Eine Welt schreibt an Goethe* (1937). His correspondence with particular individuals, German and foreign, is conveniently listed in the *Hamburger Ausgabe*, vol. 14 (see above); see also D. F. S. Scott, *Some English Correspondents of Goethe* (Matthew ["Monk"] Lewis, T. Holcroft, Sir Walter Scott, P. P. Gillies, Sir John Bowring, Lord Leveson-Gower, Sarah Austin, etc.; 1949).

Translations: There is still no uniform edition in English (but see J. Porchat, *Oeuvres Complètes*, 10 vol., 1860–63) though the chief works have been frequently translated and many of them are to be found in Bohn's Standard Library, 14 vol. (1846–90). For details *see* L. and E. Oswald, A. Dickson, *Goethe in England (and America)* in *Publications of the English Goethe Society*, 2 vol. (1909, 1951). Translations include: *Wilhelm Meister's Theatrical Mission* by G. A. Page (1913); *Wilhelm Meister* by Thomas Carlyle (1824; Everyman ed.); *Faust I and II* by A. G. Latham (1902–06; Everyman ed., 1908); other translations of *Faust I and II* by B. Taylor (1870–71; World's Classics, 1932); P. Wayne (Penguin ed., 1949); Louis MacNeice (1951); B. Jessup (1958). *Egmont* by Michael Hamburger in *The Classic Theatre*, II ed. by E. Bentley (1959); *Kindred by Choice (die Wahlverwandtschaften)* by H. M. Waidson (1961); *Werther* by B. Q. Morgan (1957); *Die Leiden des jungen Werther*, *Werther* by H. Steinhauer (1962); *Werther: the New Melusine, Novelle* by V. Lange (1949); *Novelle* by C. P. Middleton (1959); *The West-Eastern Divan* by Edward Dowden (1914). The *Briefwechsel* with Schiller and a collection of early and miscellaneous letters are in Bohn (see above); that with Carlyle, ed. by C. E. Norton and C. M. Sym (1957). *Conversations With Eckermann* by John Oxenford, 2 vol. (1850; vol. 6 of Bohn).

Biography and Criticism: The best introduction in English is still G. H. Lewes, *Life and Works of Goethe* (1855; 18th ed., 1903). Others available in English are by A. Bielschowsky, 3 vol. (1905–08); B. Croce (1923); G. Brandes, 2 vol. (1925); also E. Ludwig, *Goethe: the History of a Man*, 2 vol. (1928); H. W. Nevinson, *Goethe, Man and Poet* (1931); J. G. Robertson, *Life and Works of Goethe* (1932); L. Lewisohn, *Goethe: the Story of a Man* (1949); A. Schweitzer, *Goethe* (1949); K. Viëtor, *Goethe the Poet* (1949); E. Staiger, 3 vol. (1952–59); F. Gundolf (1916); H. Meyer (1951);

Günther Müller, 3rd ed. (1955). French works by J. M. Carré (1927); H. Lichtenberger, 2 vol. (1937–39); A. Fuchs (1946); E. Jaloux, 2nd ed. (1949); J. F. Angelloz (1949); C. du Bos (1949). Criticism in English includes B. Fairley, *Goethe as Revealed in His Poetry* (1932), *A Study of Goethe* (1947); Thomas Mann, *Three Essays* (Eng. trans. 1932); *Essays on Goethe*, ed. by W. Rose (1949); A. R. Hohlfeld, *Fifty Years With Goethe* (1953); E. M. Wilkinson and L. A. Willoughby, *Goethe: Poet and Thinker* (1962); R. Peacock, *Goethe's Major Plays* (1959).

On Faust: Urfaust and Fragment, ed. by R.-M. S. Heffner, H. Rehder and W. F. Twaddell (1954–55); H. G. Fiedler, *Textual Studies of Goethe's Faust* (1946). Further interpretations of *Faust* in English by F. M. Stawell and G. L. Dickinson (1928); R. D. Miller (1939); D. J. Enright (1949); B. Fairley, *Goethe's Faust* (1953); A. Gillies (1957); Stuart Atkins (1958); see also E. M. Butler, *The Fortunes of Faust* (1952); A. I. Frantz, *Half a Hundred Thralls to Faust* (1949).

Science, Philosophy, Aesthetics, etc.: Sir Charles Sherrington, *Goethe on Nature and on Science*, 2nd ed. (1949; unsympathetic); as corrective, Agnes Arber, *Goethe's Botany*, including trans. of *Die Metamorphose der Pflanzen* (1946) and *The Natural Philosophy of Plant Form* (1950); R. Michéa, *Les Travaux scientifiques de Goethe* (1943); R. D. Gray, *Goethe: the Alchemist* (1952); E. Heller, *The Disinherited Mind* (1952); C. G. Carus, *Goethe, dessen Bedeutung* (1863); O. Harnack, *Goethe in der Epoche seiner Vollendung*, 3rd ed. (1905); G. Simmel, *Goethe* (1913); A. Farinelli, *Goethe, Saggio* (1933); E. Spranger, *Goethes Weltanschauung* (1946); L. L. Whyte, *The Next Development in Man* (1944); K. J. Obenauer, *Goethe in seinem Verhältnis zur Religion* (1921); P. Demetz, *Goethes "Die Aufgeregten": Zur Frage der politischen Dichtung in Deutschland* (1952); K. Viëtor, *Goethe the Thinker* (1950); H. M. Wolff, *Goethes Weg zur Humanität* (1951); F. J. von Rintelen, *Der Rang des Geistes: Goethes Weltverständnis* (1955); P. Stöcklein, *Wege zum späten Goethe: Dichtung, Gedanke, Zeichnung*, 2nd ed. (1960); M. Jolles, *Goethes Kunstanschauung* (1957); H. J. Weigand, *Goethe: Wisdom and Experience*, selections in English (1949); Günther Müller, *Maximen und Reflexionen* (1943); Thomas Mann, *The Permanent Goethe* (1948); W. Leppmann, *The German Image of Goethe* (1961).

Weltliteratur: J. M. Carré, *Goethe en Angleterre* (1920); W. Rose, *From Goethe to Byron: the Development of "Weltschmerz" in German Literature* (1924); J. G. Robertson, *Goethe and Byron* (1925); Stuart Atkins, *The Testament of "Werther" in Poetry and Drama* (1949); F. Norman, *Henry Crabb Robinson and Goethe*, 2 vol. (1930–31), and J. B. Orrick, *Matthew Arnold and Goethe* (1928); both in *Publications of English Goethe Society*; F. Strich, *Goethe and World Literature* (1949); H. Trevelyan, *Goethe and the Greeks* (1941); a corrective to E. M. Butler, *The Tyranny of Greece Over Germany*, 1935); J. Boyd, *Goethe's Knowledge of English Literature* (1932); B. Barnes, *Goethe's Knowledge of French Literature* (1937); H. Oppel, *Das Shakespeare-Bild Goethes* (1949); A. Federmann, *Der junge Goethe und England* (1949).

Cultural Background: H. A. Korff, *Geist der Goethezeit*, 5 vol. (1923–58); E. Beutler, *Essays um Goethe*, 2 vol. (1941–47); *Goethe und seine Welt*, with 580 illustrations, ed. by E. Beutler, H. Wahl, A. Kippenberg (1932). A. Bergstraesser, *Goethe and the Greeks* (1949); W. H. Bruford, *Theatre, Drama and Audience in Goethe's Germany* (1950) and *Culture and Society in Classical Weimar, 1775–1806* (1962).

Bibliography: Only the researcher will consult the vast compilation in Goedeke's *Grundriss*, iv (1910–13), to be superseded by H. Pyritz, *Goethe-Bibliographie* (1955; in progress). Vol. xiv of the *Hamburger-Ausgabe* (1960) is adequate for most purposes. *The Goethe Handbuch*, ed. by A. Zastrau (1955; in progress), provides alphabetical references to all topics relating to Goethe. H. Kindermann, *Das Goethebild des XX. Jahrhunderts* (1952), is in effect a lively *catalogue raisonné* of European and American critical literature during the 20th century.

Goethe Societies: Wiener Goethe Verein, 1878; Weimarer Goethe Gesellschaft, 1885; English Goethe Society, 1886, with sister societies in the Commonwealth of Nations from 1949; Goethe Society of Maryland and the District of Columbia, 1932; Japanese Goethe Gesellschaft, 1932. All issue publications.
(E. M. Wr.)

GOETHITE, a very common iron mineral consisting of hydrated iron oxide, the principal component of rusted iron. Goethite is the stable iron mineral under the hydrous, oxidizing conditions near the earth's surface. It occurs as a direct precipitate (*e.g.*, in bogs), and as a weathering product of other iron minerals, sometimes making an important ore of iron, as in Alsace. In most deposits goethite is very fine-grained, occasionally as fibrous radiating masses. The name goethite was originally given, in honour of the poet and natural philosopher Johann Goethe, to a less common iron mineral (now known as lepidocrocite (*q.v.*). The composition of goethite is $FeOOH$, equivalent to the chemical formula α-$Fe_2O_3.H_2O$. The structure is based on a nearly close-packed arrangement of large oxygen or hydroxyl ions, with ferric ions between alternate layers. The packing gives a symmetry of structure and form that is pseudohexagonal (orthorhombic) and the weak interlayer bonding results in one perfect cleavage and in a tabular or prismatic external form. The colour is blackish brown in single crystals, ranging through all shades of brown and yellow as the size of crystals decreases. The hardness is 5 and specific gravity 4.2.
(W. T. HR.)

GOFFE (GOUGH), **WILLIAM** (d. *c.* 1679), English soldier and regicide active in the military affairs of the Commonwealth, was the son of Stephen Goffe, rector of Stanmer, Sussex. He was a captain in the New Model army in 1645 and took part in the Windsor prayer meeting of 1648 when the army decided to put King Charles I on trial. He was one of Charles's judges and signed the king's death warrant. Goffe commanded a regiment both at Dunbar and at Worcester, and he was one of the major generals in 1654. In 1654 also he became member of parliament for Yarmouth, and in 1656 for Hampshire, and then he sat in the upper house. He succeeded John Lambert as major general of the army in 1658. After Oliver Cromwell's death, Goffe supported Richard Cromwell as lord protector. Goffe was excepted from the royalist Act of Indemnity but escaped with his father-in-law, Edward Whalley, to New England. There they were befriended and lay in hiding until the hunt for them had died down. From 1664 onward they lived in Hadley, Mass. When in 1675 Indians attacked the place, Goffe is said to have rallied the inhabitants and to have driven off the raiders. This traditional story was incorporated by Sir Walter Scott in his *Peveril of the Peak.*
(S. R. Br.)

GOG, in the Bible, a hostile power that is to manifest itself in the world immediately before the end of things (Ezek. xxxviii *seq.*, Rev. xx). Magog, who is joined with Gog in the passage in Revelation, is the name of Gog's origin in this passage in Ezekiel. In Gen. x, 2 (and Ezek. xxxviii, 2) Magog appears to represent a locality in Armenia.

The legends attached to the gigantic effigies of Gog and Magog in Guildhall, London, are of unknown date. According to the *Recuyell des histoires de Troye*, Gog and Magog were the survivors of a race of giants descended from the 33 wicked daughters of Diocletian; after their brethren had been slain by Brut and his companions, Gog and Magog were brought to London (Troynovant) and compelled to officiate as porters at the gate of the royal palace. Effigies similar to the present have existed in London from the time of Henry V. The earlier ones, destroyed in the Great Fire, were replaced in 1708; these were burned in an air raid in 1940 and new figures were installed in 1953.

GOGH, VINCENT WILLEM VAN (1853–1890), the greatest and most revolutionary Dutch painter after Rembrandt, was born on March 30, 1853, the eldest of six children of a Protestant pastor, at Groot Zundert (Brabant). The artistic career of Vincent van Gogh was extremely short, lasting only ten years (1880–90); during the first part he was acquiring technical proficiency and confined himself almost entirely to drawings and water colours. His first productive period of oil painting begins in 1884. During the ensuing six years, he produced about 700 drawings and 800 oils, only one of which was sold during his lifetime. Vincent was always desperately poor, but he was sustained by faith in the urgency of what he had to communicate, and by a younger brother, Theo (1857–91), who believed implicitly in his genius and provided for him out of his own meagre earnings. The letters which Vincent wrote to Theo (from 1872 on) give a graphic account of his aims and beliefs, hopes and disappointments, of his fluctuating physical and mental state, of his pictorial methods and of his daily life. Van Gogh expressed himself so vividly and analyzed things so acutely that his *Collected Correspondence* ranks not merely as a great autobiographical record but as great literature. Vincent's working life can be roughly divided into two periods. The first (1873–85), during which he wrestled with temperamental difficulties and sought his true means of self-expression, was a period of repeated apprenticeships, failures and changes of direction. The second (1886–90) was a period of dedication, rapid development and fulfilment, until his progress was interrupted by a succession of mental crises (1889–90) ending in an at-

GOGH

tempted suicide on July 27, 1890, and his death two days later. Vincent's early years in his father's parsonage were happy, and he loved wandering in the countryside. At 16, he was apprenticed to the art dealers Goupil and Co., of which his uncle was a partner. Vincent began at their branch in The Hague, going later to London (1873–74) and Paris (1874–75). Daily contact with works of art aroused Van Gogh's artistic sensibility, and he soon formed a taste for Rembrandt, Hals, J. van Ruisdael, C. Troyon, Jules Dupré and J. Maris, although his preference was for Millet and Corot, whose influence was to last throughout his life. Vincent disliked art dealing; moreover, his approach to life darkened when his love was rejected by a London girl (1874), for his burning desire for human affection had been thwarted. From then on he became increasingly solitary. He became a language teacher and lay preacher (England), and later (1877) a bookseller in Dordrecht. Impelled by a longing to give himself to his fellow men, Vincent envisaged entering the ministry and took up theology, but abandoned this project for short-term training as an evangelist in Brussels (Aug. 1878). A conflict with authority ensued, for Vincent disputed the orthodox doctrinal approach, failed to get a nomination and after three months left to do missionary work among the mining population of the Borinage. There he experienced the first great spiritual crisis of his life (winter, 1879–80). He was sharing the life of the poor completely, but in an impassioned moment gave away all his worldly goods and was thereupon dismissed for too literal an interpretation of Christian teaching. Penniless and with his faith destroyed, he sank into despair, cut himself off from everyone and began seriously to draw, thereby discovering (Aug. 1880) his true vocation. Vincent decided that his mission from then on would be to bring consolation to humanity through art, and this realization of his creative powers restored his self-confidence. He immediately went to study drawing at the Brussels academy, then in April 1881 moved to his father's parsonage at Etten and began to work from nature.

Van Gogh worked hard and methodically but soon perceived the difficulty of self-training and sought the guidance of more experienced artists. In Jan. 1882 he settled at The Hague to work with Anton Mauve; he made visits to museums and had meetings with painters such as Van Rappard and G. Breitner. Vincent thus extended his technical knowledge and experimented (summer 1882) with oil paint. In Sept. 1883 the urge to be "alone with nature" and the peasants took him to Drenthe, a desolate part of northern Holland frequented by Mauve, Van Rappard and Max Liebermann, where he spent three months before returning home, which was now at Nuenen. Vincent remained at Nuenen from Dec. 1883 till Nov. 1885 and during these years his art grew bolder and more assured. He painted three types of subject—still life, landscape and figure—all interrelated by their reference to the peasants' daily life, to the hardships they endured and the countryside they cultivated. Emile Zola's *Germinal* had greatly impressed Van Gogh, and in many of his pictures, *e.g.*, "Weavers" and "The Potato Eaters," sociological criticism is implicit. Eventually Vincent felt too isolated in Nuenen.

His understanding of the possibilities of painting was evolving rapidly; through studying Hals he saw that academic "finish" destroys the freshness of a visual impression, while Veronese and Delacroix taught him that "colour expresses something by itself." This led to enthusiasm for Rubens' "simple means," of his direct notation, and of his ability to "express a mood . . . by a combination of colours" proved decisive. Simultaneously, Van Gogh "discovered" Japanese prints and began to use pure colours. His refusal to follow academic principles led to rows at the Antwerp academy, where he was enrolled, and after three months of hard work and near-starvation he left precipitately (early March 1886) to join Theo in Paris. There, still concerned with improving his drawing, Vincent worked for three months under F. Cormon, in whose studio he met Toulouse-Lautrec and Emile Bernard, who opened his eyes to the latest developments in French painting and subsequently introduced him to Paul Gauguin; at the same time, Theo showed him Impressionist paintings at Goupil's, and introduced him to Camille Pissarro, Georges Seurat and others of the group. By this time Vincent was ready for such revelations, and the changes which his painting underwent in Paris (1886–88) led to the expansion of his personal idiom. His palette at last became colourful in a series of "Flower Still Lifes" (summer 1886) executed under the influence of Adolphe Monticelli; thereafter his vision became less traditional and his tonalities lighter (first views of Montmartre) until (spring 1887) the Impressionist influence became paramount (more views of Paris). Later (summer 1887), in outdoor views of Montmartre, Suresnes, Asnières and Chatou, Vincent was painting in pure colours and using a broken brushwork which is at times pointillistic. Finally his post-Impressionist style crystallized (Dec. 1887–Feb. 1888) in some interpretations of prints by Hiroshige and in masterpieces such as "Portrait of Père Tanguy" and "Self-Portrait in Front of an Easel."

After two years, Van Gogh was tired of city life, physically exhausted, and longing, "to look at nature under a brighter sky," because he realized that the veiled light of the north obliged him to "respect tonal values," whereas his passion was for "the Japanese way of feeling and drawing" and for "a full effect of colour." He left Paris on Feb. 20, 1888, for Arles. In his pictures of the following 12 months—his first great period—Vincent strove to respect the external, visual aspect of a figure or a landscape, but found himself unable to suppress his own feelings about the subject. These found expression in vivid formal simplifications or exaggerations and an almost arbitrarily intense use of colour. Vincent's pictorial conception is thus partly expressionist and partly symbolist. His procedure was not scientific or calculated, however, but spontaneous and instinctive, for he worked with great speed and intensity, determined to capture an effect or a mood while it possessed him. His Arles subjects include blossoming fruit trees, views of the town and surroundings, self-portraits, portraits of Roulin the postman and his family and other friends, interiors and exteriors of his house, a series of sunflowers and a "starry night." Van Gogh knew that his approach to painting was revolutionary and individualistic, but he also knew that some tasks are beyond the power of isolated individuals to accomplish. In Paris he had hoped to form a separate Impressionist group with Gauguin, Toulouse-Lautrec, Bernard and Anquetin, whom he supposed to have similar aims. He rented and decorated "a yellow house" in Arles with the intention of persuading them to join him and found there a working community of "Impressionists of the South." Gauguin arrived on Oct. 20, 1888, and for two months they worked together; but while each influenced the other to some extent, their relations rapidly deteriorated because they had opposing ideas and were temperamentally incompatible. On Christmas Eve, 1888, Vincent broke under the strain and cut off part of his left ear. Gauguin left and Van Gogh was taken to a hospital; he returned to the "yellow house" a fortnight later and resumed painting: "Self-Portrait With a Bandaged Ear," still lifes, "La Berceuse." Within a month he was back in the hospital. At the end of April 1889, fearful of losing his "capacity for work," which he felt returning and regarded as a guarantee of sanity, he asked to be "temporarily shut up" in the asylum at St. Rémy de Provence in order not to be alone and to be under supervision. Vincent stayed there for 12 months, haunted by recurrent attacks, alternating between calm and despair and working intermittently ("Garden of the Asylum," "Cypresses," "Olive Trees," "Les Alpilles," portraits of doctors, interpretations of Rembrandt, Delacroix, Millet). The keynote of this phase (1889–90) is fear of losing touch with reality and a certain sadness. Confined for long periods to his cell or the asylum garden and having no choice of subjects, Van Gogh fought against having to work from memory; his inspiration depended on

"PORTRAIT OF ARMAND ROULIN" BY VINCENT VAN GOGH (IN THE MUSEUM FOLKWANG, ESSEN)

direct observation and he distrusted Gauguin's process of "abstraction." At St. Rémy Vincent toned down his violent colour contrasts of the previous summer and tried to be calmer; but as he repressed his excitement he involved himself more imaginatively in the drama of the elements and of natural growth and decay, developing a style based on dynamic forms and a vigorous use of line (line often equated with colour). The best of his St. Rémy pictures are thus bolder, more moving and more visionary than those of Arles.

Vincent himself brought this period to an end. Oppressed by homesickness—he painted souvenirs of Holland—and loneliness, he longed to see Theo and the north once more and arrived in Paris on May 16, 1890. Four days later he went to stay with Dr. Gachet, a friend of Pissarro and Paul Cézanne, at Auvers-sur-Oise. Back in a village community such as he had not known since Nuenen (1885), Van Gogh worked enthusiastically and his choice of subjects (fields of corn, the river valley, peasants' cottages, the church, the town hall) reflects his spiritual relief. A modification of his style follows; natural forms are less contorted, pale fresh tonalities, the brushwork is broader and more expressive, the vision of nature more lyrical. But this phase was short. Quarrels with Gachet, feelings of guilt at his inescapable dependence on Theo (now married and with a son) and inability to succeed, despair of ever overcoming his loneliness or of being cured, drove him to suicide (July 1890). Six months later Theo, too, was dead (Jan. 25, 1891).

The name of Van Gogh was virtually unknown when he took his life. He had exhibited a few canvases at the Salon des Indépendants (1888–90) and at Les XX in Brussels (1890), and both salons showed small commemorative groups of his work in 1891, but his first one-man shows were posthumous (1892). Only one article on him appeared during his lifetime (Albert Aurier in Mercure de France, Jan. 1890). His fame was made largely by other painters (E. Bernard, M. Denis) and dates from the early years of the 20th century; since then his reputation has never ceased to grow and he has exerted a powerful influence on the development of modern painting (Matisse, Derain, Vlaminck, the German Expressionists, Picasso), especially in the field of colour.

See also references under "Gogh, Vincent Willem Van" in the Index.

COLLECTION: THE MUSEUM OF MODERN ART, NEW YORK; ACQUIRED THROUGH THE LILLIE P. BLISS BEQUEST

"THE STARRY NIGHT" BY VINCENT VAN GOGH, 1889. IN THE MUSEUM OF MODERN ART

BIBLIOGRAPHY.—Verzamelde Brieven van V. van Gogh, 4 vol, ed. by V. W. van Gogh (1952–54; original texts of all existing letters); Complete Letters of Vincent van Gogh, 3 vol. (1958). See also J. B. de la Faille, Catalogue de l'Oeuvre de V. van Gogh, 4 vol. (1927), also Les Faux van Gogh (1930); W. Scherjon and J. de Gruyter, Van Gogh's Great Period (1937); C. M. Brooks, Jr., V. Van Gogh: a Bibliography (1942); W. Weisbach, V. van Gogh, 2 vol. (1949); J. Leymarie, Van Gogh (1951); D. Cooper, Drawings and Watercolours by V. van Gogh (1955); M. E. Tralbaut (ed.), Exhibition catalogue V. van Gogh (Oct. 1957); V. Van Gogh (1969). (Ds. Cr.)

GOGOL, NIKOLAI VASILEVICH (1809–1852), Russian humorist, short story writer, novelist and dramatist, author of the novel Mërtvye dushi ("Dead Souls"), was born in the Ukrainian township of Sorochinsk on March 31 (new style; 19, old style) 1809. The son of a small Ukrainian landowner, he received his education first at a preparatory school in Poltava and, from May 1821 to June 1828, at the Nezhin grammar school. At Nezhin he made a name for himself as a talented boy-actor and as a versatile contributor to the different school magazines, for which he wrote "an historical tale"; a "satire" on the inhabitants of Nezhin; a ballad, "Two Fishes"; "The Robbers," a tragedy in iambic pentameters; and an epic poem, on "Russia Under the Tartar Yoke"; none has been preserved. Already during his last years at school he decided to seek literary fame in St. Petersburg (Leningrad). He left for St. Petersburg in Dec. 1828, a few months after passing his final examinations, taking with him the manuscript of Hans Kuechelgarten, a long, sentimental narrative poem, which he published in 1829 at his own expense under the pseudonym of V. Alov. The poem ("the creative work of a young man of talent," as Gogol described it in his introduction) received hostile notices in two prominent St. Petersburg and Moscow periodicals, which hurt his pride so much that he collected all the copies of the poem from the bookshops and burned them. Having previously failed to obtain a job as an actor at the St. Petersburg state theatre and determined not to apply for a job in the civil service. in spite of the letters of recommendation he had brought from home, he made up his mind to emigrate to the United States, which he regarded as "the ideal land of happiness and productive labour." He embarked for Lübeck on the first stage of his journey, traveled as far as Sweden, then changed his mind and sailed back to St. Petersburg. "God has humbled my pride," he wrote to his mother on his return, "It is His sacred will."

Left without means, Gogol had to look for a job in the hated civil service. He obtained one in the department of public works, but stayed there for only three months, transferring to the department of the royal estates, where he remained from April 1830 to March 1831. He spent all his free time working feverishly at his Ukrainian tales, the first volume of which was published as Vechera na khutore bliz Dikanki ("Evenings on a Farm Near Dikanka") under the pseudonym of Rudy Panko ("Red-haired Panko") in Sept. 1831. The second volume followed in March 1832. These stories made him famous throughout Russia. They still remain the most imaginative and least dated works in Russian literature, for in re-creating the customs and popular beliefs of Ukrainian country folk, Gogol did not attempt to paint a true picture of their lives but mingled realism with fantasy. The remarkable feature of most of these stories—Sorochinskaya yarmarka ("The Sorochinsk Fair"), Vecher nakanune Ivana-Kupala ("St. John's Eve"), Maiskaya noch ("A May Night") and Propavshaya gramota ("The Lost Letter") in the first part, and Noch pered Rozhdestvom ("Christmas Eve") and Zakoldovannoye mesto ("The Bewitched Spot") in the second—is, as the critic Vissarion Belinski expressed it, "their quiet, good-natured humour, in which the author pretends to be a simpleton"; and indeed, Gogol's characteristic method of projecting his own personality into the story, superimposing his own emotional life upon it and conducting the narrative on the subjective and objective planes simultaneously can already be clearly detected in these stories. The first of the two other stories of the second volume of the Evenings, namely, "The Terrible Vengeance," deals with the universal theme of the conflict of good and evil, and in the second, "Ivan Fëdorovich Shponka and His Aunt," Gogol makes effective use of the insignificant details of the most ordinary situation in order, as he put it, "to extract the extraordinary from the ordinary."

Gogol had earlier published some articles and stories, including some chapters from an unfinished historical novel, in magazines. The editor of one of the magazines introduced him to the romantic poet Vasili Zhukovski who, in turn, introduced him to Aleksandr Pushkin in May 1831. It was Pushkin who gave Gogol the subject of his play *Revizor* (1836; *The Government Inspector*; also translated as *The Inspector General*) and his novel *Mërtvye dushi* (1st part, 1842; English translation, *Dead Souls*, 1922).

For the time being, however, Gogol showed an enthusiasm for education, history being the special subject of his choice. Having resigned from the civil service, he obtained a job at a St. Petersburg boarding school for the daughters of the nobility, which he held for several years. At the end of 1831 he began writing a history of the Ukraine and announced his intention of writing a history of the world, neither of which he ever published. He did succeed, however, in obtaining 'the post of reader of medieval history at St. Petersburg university in 1834, a post which he held for only one year. At the beginning of 1835 he published two volumes of articles and short stories, *Arabeski* ("Arabesques") and *Mirgorod*, and completed *The Government Inspector*. Besides the articles dealing with history, art and architecture, *Arabesques* included three of Gogol's St. Petersburg stories: *Portret* ("The Portrait"), *Nevski Prospekt* ("Nevsky Avenue") and *Zapiski sumasshedshago* ("The Diary of a Madman"), while *Mirgorod* included three of his most famous stories—*Starosvetskie pomeshchiki* ("The Old World Landowners"), as deeply moving a tale as any he ever wrote, *Kak possorilsya Ivan Ivanovich s Ivanom Nikiforovichem* ("The Story of the Quarrel of Ivan Ivanovich and Ivan Nikiforovich"), *Viy*, the last fantastic story Gogol wrote—as well as his historical novel *Taras Bulba*. Before leaving Russia for Italy in 1836 Gogol published two more stories—*Nos* (1835; "The Nose"), a bitingly satirical exposure of the stupidity of officialdom and the snobbery and self-complacency of the Russian upper classes, and *The Carriage* (1836), a satire on provincial life.

Gogol wrote his dramatic masterpiece *The Government Inspector* in less than two months, finishing it on Dec. 4, 1835. It was performed for the first time on April 19, 1836, in the presence of the emperor Nicholas I, who is said to have remarked: "Everyone has caught it, but I have caught it more than anyone." The play, however, was violently criticized by many influential people who interpreted it as an attack on the established order. Gogol wrote a defense of it in dialogue form, *Teatralny raze'zd* ("After the Play"), published in his collected works in 1842. He defended his play on the score that abuses by government officials could be rectified by exposing them on the stage, and, in reply to his critics who claimed that there was not a single honest character in the play, he claimed that there was one such character, namely laughter—for, he wrote, "even he who is not afraid of anything in the world is afraid of ridicule," an opinion which he was shrewd enough to modify by remarking a little earlier in *After the Play* that 'some of us who are ready to have a good laugh at a man's crooked nose, have not the courage to laugh at a man's crooked soul.' But as the play deals with those abuses due not to national and historical causes but deeply rooted in man's character, its significance as a work of art has been generally recognized and it is universally acknowledged to be one of the masterpieces of European drama.

Gogol's other plays include *Zhenit'ba* ("Marriage"), a comedy in two acts subtitled "An Utterly Incredible Affair," finished in 1835 and revised in the spring of 1836; *Igroki* ("The Gamblers"), a one-act comedy dealing with cardsharpers, written in 1832 and revised in 1842; four dramatic scenes, *Utro delovogo cheloveka* ("A Morning of a Business Man"), *Tyazhba* ("A Lawsuit"), *Lakeiskaya* ("The Servants' Hall") and *Otryvok* ("A Fragment"), the three last representing fragments of his first play *Vladimir tretiei stepeni* ("Vladimir Third Class"), written in 1831-32; and the first act and two scenes of the second act of a historical play, "Alfred the Great," the only artistic remnant of his studies of European medieval history, written in 1835, in which he portrays the English king as the ideal ruler who curbs the lust for power of his nobles and fosters the spread of learning.

The storm of criticism which *The Government Inspector* aroused confirmed Gogol's belief in the moral influence of art, but it also drove him out of Russia where he felt he could not find the necessary peace of mind to write *Dead Souls*. He left St. Petersburg by sea for Lübeck on June 18, 1836, and remained abroad for 12 years, returning to Russia only twice, in 1838-39 and in 1841-42, for a stay of eight months each time. He lived mostly in Rome, which left a deep impression on his mind, though the only artistic result of his stay there is the fragment of a novel of Roman life published in 1842 under the title *Rim* ("Rome"). Most of his time in Rome was occupied with the writing of the first part of *Dead Souls*, though by the end of 1841 he had also completed his famous story *Shinel* ("The Overcoat") and thoroughly revised *Taras Bulba* and *The Portrait*.

Gogol spent eight years, from 1834 to 1842, on the writing of the first part of *Dead Souls*, and ten years, from 1842 to 1852, on the second part. The third part, in which he planned to show the conversion of his hero Chichikov to a life of virtue, was never written. Gogol had never been in doubt about the sensation the publication of the first part of *Dead Souls* (in May 1842) would produce in Russia, but as his work on the second part proceeded, the theme of the novel took on more and more grandiose proportions in his mind. Writing to Zhukovski shortly after, Gogol declared that the first part of his novel was "quite insignificant" when compared to the other parts which were to follow it. "It reminds me," he declared, "of the steps of a palace of colossal dimensions hastily constructed by some provincial architect." But the difficulties of building such a palace of virtue, in which, as he wrote at the end of the first part, "the untold riches of the Russian soul" would bring about the spiritual regeneration of so consummate a crook as Chichikov, became apparent to Gogol as soon as he reached Rome in 1842. By the beginning of 1845 his attempt to write the second part had driven him into a state of nervous collapse and at the end of June he burned all he had written of it. He then attempted to achieve the same result of bringing about the lasting reconciliation of the hostile social and economic forces in Russia by a book published in 1847, *Vybrannye mesta iz perepiski s druzyami* ("Selected Passages From Correspondence With My Friends"). The *Selected Passages*, which consist of 32 articles, most of which are based on letters written to a small circle of his friends and in which he tried to justify serfdom and the reactionary policies of Nicholas I, were condemned even by Gogol's closest friends. One of them, Sergei Aksakov (*q.v.*), the author of *Semeinaya Khronika* ("A Family Chronicle"), wrote to Gogol in Jan. 1847 that he had been grossly mistaken and that, "while thinking of serving God and humanity," he had "insulted God and humanity." The most biting denunciation of the *Selected Passages*, however, came from Belinski who had been the first to hail Gogol as the greatest genius Russia had produced, but who now denounced him as "a preacher of the lash, an apostle of ignorance, a champion of obscurantism and a panegyrist of Tartar customs."

The failure of the *Selected Passages* made Gogol resume his work on the second part of *Dead Souls*, but not before he had gone on a pilgrimage to Jerusalem, where he arrived on Feb. 15, 1848, and where he hoped, as he expressed it in the prayer he had composed for the occasion, to obtain renewed strength to return to his work with zeal and courage for the benefit of his country. The pilgrimage, too, was a failure. "Never before," Gogol wrote, "have I been so little satisfied with the state of my heart as when I was in Jerusalem." The resumption of his work on the novel was laborious and painful. By the time he had finished the second part he had fallen completely under the influence of a religious fanatic, Father Matthew Konstantinovski, who demanded that he should destroy it and enter a monastery. After a tremendous inner conflict, Gogol carried out Father Matthew's demand and burned the completed second part of *Dead Souls* on the night of Feb. 24 (N.S.; 12, O.S.), 1852. He then took to his bed, refused all food and died in great pain on March 4 (N.S.; Feb. 21, O.S.), 1852.

What Gogol meant to the great Russian writers of the 19th century is perhaps best expressed in the tributes paid to him by Turgenev and Dostoevski. "Gogol," Turgenev wrote, "was more than a writer to us: he has revealed us to ourselves." To Dostoevski Gogol's significance lay in the fact that "he laughed all his life at himself and us and we all laughed with him and we laughed so long that the end we began to cry. . . ." "Gogol," Dostoevski continues, "put before us a whole gallery of money-grubbers, landsharpers and plunderers. All he had to do was to point a finger at them and at once a mark appeared branded on their foreheads which stayed there forever so that we never forgot who they were and, above all, what their names were." It was, indeed, Gogol's remarkable gallery of different types of the Russian ruling class that was finally instrumental in destroying the respect of the Russian people for their rulers. This Dostoevski clearly perceived when (in his *Diary of a Writer*) he stressed the revolutionary significance of *Dead Souls*. After describing Gogol's characters in his novel as "the most profound creations of the Russian genius," Dostoevski declared that they gave rise in the Russian mind "to the most turbulent ideas which one cannot help feeling it is impossible to solve now, if indeed ever." But the human types created by Gogol transcend their purely national character and are truly universal, for they reveal characteristics common to all mankind. In this sense they are, in fact, immortal. For portrait *see* RUSSIAN LITERATURE.

BIBLIOGRAPHY.—*Works*, trans. by Constance Garnett, 6 vol. (1922–28); *Collected Tales and Plays*, trans. by L. J. Kent (1965); D. Magarshack, *Tales of Good and Evil* (1949), includes trans. of *Taras Bulba*, *The Terrible Vengeance, Ivan Fyodorovich Shponka and His Aunt, The Portrait, Nevsky Avenue, The Overcoat* and *The Government Inspector. See also* J. Lavrin, *Gogol* (1926); D. Magarshack, *Gogol: a Life* (1957). (D. MK.)

GOGRA (GHAGHARA), a river of northern India, rises in Tibet near Lake Manasarowar, not far from the sources of the Brahmaputra and the Sutlej. It passes through Nepal as the Karnali and becomes the most important waterway in Uttar Pradesh. It joins the Ganges (Ganga) at Chapra after a course of 600 mi. Its tributary, the Rapti, is also commercially important. The Gogra is also called the Sarju, and in its lower course the Deoha. (L. D. S.)

GÖHRDE, a forest of Germany, in the *Land* of Lower Saxony, immediately west of the Elbe, between Wittenberg (in the German Democratic Republic) and Lüneburg (in the Federal Republic of Germany). It has an area of about 85 sq.mi. and is famous for its oaks, beeches and game preserves. The Hohenzollerns formerly had a hunting lodge within the forest. In an encounter there on Sept. 16, 1813, Napoleon's forces were defeated by the allies under the Russian general Wallmoden. The small village of Göhrde had 199 inhabitants in 1961.

GOIÂNIA, capital of Goiás state, Brazil, located on the *planalto central*, about 2,500 ft. above sea level. The city was planned in 1933 to replace the old, unhealthful state capital, Goiás, about 70 mi. N.W. Built along modern lines and situated on the Meia Ponte, a tributary of the Paranaíba river, it has wide avenues, new buildings and attractive parks. In 1937 the state government moved in and the official inauguration was held in 1942. Goiânia is connected by railway (via Leopoldo de Bulhões) to Anápolis (40 mi. N.E.) and to other parts of Brazil by airlines. It is an administrative centre, and is the seat of the state university, but is less important in the economic life than Anápolis. Its population has grown ([1960] 132,577; [1968 est.] 345,085) as people have been attracted to it from the rural areas. (P. E. J.)

GOIÁS, an inland state of Brazil, formerly spelled Goyaz and Goiaz, was selected in 1956 as the site of the federal district and capital of Brazil, Brasília (*q.v.*). The state of Goiás is bounded by the states of Maranhão on the north, Mato Grosso and Pará on the west, Maranhão, Bahia and Minas Gerais on the east, and Minas Gerais and Mato Grosso on the south. Its area is 247,912 sq.mi. Its population (1968 est.) was 2,745,711. The chief cities, in addition to Brasília, are Goiânia, the state capital since 1937, Goiás, the old state capital, Anápolis, Ipameri, and Catalão, all located in the southern part of the state.

Goiás lies wholly within the Brazilian highlands. In the south it occupies the larger part of the *planalto central*, or central plateau, the vast level surface of which stands between 2,500 and 3,000 ft. above sea level. A few rounded ridges stand higher than this, the highest being the Chapada dos Veadeiros (5,505 ft.). The *planalto central* forms the divide between three of Brazil's largest river systems: to the south Goiás is drained through the Paranaíba, a tributary of the Paraná; to the east it is drained by tributaries of the São Francisco; and the greater part of the state is drained northward through the Araguaia and the Tocantins. None of these rivers is navigable except for short distances. The southern

part of the state is covered with a woodland savanna known in Brazil as *campo cerrado*. To the north, where the Araguaia and Tocantins have eroded deep valleys, the land is covered with tropical rain forest, or selva. The whole area enjoys moderate temperatures, except in the deeper valleys which are warm enough to permit survival of malaria mosquitoes. The year is divided into a rainy season (October–March) and a dry season (April–September).

The first Portuguese exploration of this interior part of Brazil was carried on by expeditions from São Paulo in the 17th century. In a few places gold and diamonds were found in the stream gravels; one of the chief mining areas was in a tributary of the Araguaia and there the old colonial town of Goiás was located. In 1744 this large inland area, much of it still unknown by white men, was made a captaincy general, and in 1822 it became a province of the empire of Brazil. It became a state in 1889.

Outside the federal district the greater part of Goiás is still very thinly populated. Only a few isolated settlements are scattered throughout the northern two-thirds of the area. The chief concentration of settlement is in the southeast, across the border from Minas Gerais. Anápolis, reached by rail from Rio de Janeiro and São Paulo, is a rapidly growing frontier town, serving the new zone of pioneer settlement in an "island" of forest to the northwest, the Mato Grosso de Goiás. Farm settlement has also moved into smaller forested areas along the valleys of the southeast. The open campos, however, offer only poor pasturage, and their use for agriculture remains uncertain. The state produces quartz crystals, diamonds, titanium, nickel and chromium. (P. E. J.)

GOIDÀNICH, PIER GABRIELE (1868–1953), Italian linguist, whose main scholarly interest was in the Romance languages, Old Latin and Indo-European, was born on July 30, 1868, in Volosca (Istria). He obtained his doctorate at the University of Pisa, where he also was professor of the comparative history of the classical and neo-Latin languages from 1899 to 1906. He then was transferred to the University of Bologna, where he remained until his retirement.

A prolific writer, he was, in philosophy and methods, in continued disagreement with the neolinguistic school, created and guided by his compatriot Bartoli. Goidànich's arguments can be seen in his "Neolinguistica o linguistica senza aggettivo?" *Archivio glottologico italiano* (*AGI*), vol. 21, pp. 59–105 (1927), and "Il mio insegnamento di glottologia," *AGI*, vol. 30, pp. 1–51 (1938), the latter of which, written in the year of his retirement, is his scholarly testament. He was editor of the *AGI* from 1910 to 1926, and coeditor from 1926 to 1953 (until 1946 with his rival Bartoli). In this journal he published numerous articles. Goidànich died on Nov. 1, 1953, at Bologna. (E. PM.)

GOIDELIC DIALECTS: *see* CELTIC LANGUAGES.

GÓIS, DAMIÃO DE (1502–1574), among the most outstanding of Portuguese humanists, was born of a patrician family at Alenquer on Feb. 2, 1502. Under King John III he was employed abroad after 1523 on diplomatic and commercial missions, and he traveled widely in Europe. He knew many leading scholars intimately, was acquainted with Luther and Melanchthon and in 1532 became the pupil and friend of Erasmus. Góis took his degree at Padua in 1538. He married in Flanders and settled at Louvain, then the literary centre of the Low Countries, where he was living in 1542 when the French besieged the town. Taken prisoner, he was confined for nine months in France, but was rewarded later for his services by a grant of arms from Charles V. He returned to Portugal in 1545 and in 1548 was appointed chief keeper of the archives and royal chronicler. In 1558 he was commissioned to write a history of the reign of King Manuel, and the first part appeared in 1566.

Damião de Góis was a man of wide culture and genial manners, and a skilled musician. He wrote both Portuguese and Latin with classic strength and simplicity. His portrait, by Albrecht Dürer, shows an open, intelligent face, and the record of his life proves him to have been upright and fearless. But his historical work gave offense to the great families; a denunciation to the Inquisition in 1545 was taken up later, and in 1571 he was arrested. He was sentenced to a term of strict reclusion at the monastery of Batalha. Later he seems to have returned to Alenquer where he died suddenly on Jan. 30, 1574. For portrait see article PORTU-GUESE LITERATURE.

(E. P.; A. B.; N. J. L.)

BIBLIOGRAPHY.—Góis's Portuguese works include the *Crónica do felicíssimo rei Dom Emanuel*, 4 pt. (1566–67), also ed. by A. J. Lopes and J. M. Teixeira de Carvalho in 4 vol. (1926); *Crónica do príncipe Dom João* (1567), ed. by A. J. Gonçalves Guimarães (1905). Among his major Latin works are *Fides, religio, moresque Aethiopum* and *Deploratio Lappiae Gentis* (1540). Some of his Latin treatises are available in Portuguese translation in *Opúsculos históricos de Damião de Góis* (1945). See also G. J. C. Henriques, *Inéditos Goesianos*, 2 vol. (1896–98); J. de Vasconcelos, *Damião de Góis* (1897); F. M. de Sousa Viterbo, *Estudos sobre Damião de Góis* (1900).; M. Bataillon, "Le Cosmopolitisme de Damião de Góis," in *Études sur le Portugal au temps de l'humanisme* (1952); A. F. G. Bell, "Damião de Góis, a Portuguese Humanist," in *Hispanic Review* (1941). (N. J. L.)

GOJAM (GOJJAM) (q.v.), is a western province of Ethiopia south of Lake Tana (q.v.), is encircled east and south by the Blue Nile (Abbai). Pop. (1962 est.) 1,437,400. Area, 23,784 sq.mi. (61,600 sq.km.). The provincial capital is Debra Markos (pop. [1967] 21,536). In the east the Choke Mountains rise to 13,622 ft. (4,152 m.) in Mt. Birhan. The west slopes toward the Sudan plains with a peak at Mt. Belaya (about 10,500 ft. [3,200 m.]) and is drained by the Beles River and its tributaries. The Abbai Gorge (5,000 ft. below the level of the plateau) and the mountainous country have encouraged an independent spirit in Gojam. It was a powerful medieval kingdom and remains of important centres exist in the east. In western Gojam dwell Nilotic groups and an isolated group of Sidama (q.v.), the Shenasa, live on the northern bank of the Abbai. From Debra Markos the road to Addis Ababa is carried by a concrete bridge over the Abbai. North of Debra Markos the road extends to Bahr Dar on Lake Tana and thence along the eastern shore of the lake to Gondar. Bahr Dar (pop. [1967] 12,463) is a rapidly growing industrial centre. There is regular communication across the lake with Gorgora in Begemdir Province. Gojam is a rich agricultural region producing livestock, grain, oilseeds, and coffee. Its honey is used in making the national drink *tej*, which resembles mead.

(G. C. L.)

GOKALP, ZIYA (pseudonym of MEHMED ZIYA) (1875–1924), Turkish sociologist, writer and nationalist leader, was born in Diyarbakir. He entered the Istanbul Veterinary school in 1896 but his active membership in a secret revolutionary society led to imprisonment and then "exile" to his home town. After the Young Turk revolution (1908) Gokalp took part in a committee conference of the secret Society of Union and Progress in Salonika and, settling there, played an important part in the activities of the committee which later virtually ruled the country. His contributions to the literary periodical *Gench Kalemler* gave impetus to the campaign for language reform. When the Balkan War broke out he was appointed to the chair of sociology at Istanbul university, soon becoming the intellectual leader of the Nationalist movement. After the 1918 Armistice, he was exiled to Malta with a number of leading Turkish politicians. Freed after the Nationalist victory, he returned to Diyarbakir, publishing there the periodical *Küchük Mecmua*. Later he moved to Ankara, worked in the ministry of education and was elected member of parliament in 1923. He died in Istanbul on Oct. 25, 1924.

An ardent ideologist of Pan-Turanism, Gokalp greatly influenced the politicians and writers of his generation.

See Z. Fahri, *Ziya Gökalp, sa vie et sa sociologie* (1936); U. Heyd, *Foundations of Turkish Nationalism* (1950).

(F. I.)

GOKHALE, GOPAL KRISHNA (1866–1915), political leader of the moderate nationalists in India, was born on May 9, 1866, in Kotluk village, Ratnagiri district (Bombay state), of a Chitpavan Brahman family. After graduating from Elphinstone college, Bombay, in 1884, he became professor of history and political economy at Fergusson college, Poona. He resigned in 1902. For long an influential member of the Indian National Congress party, Gokhale advocated constitutional methods of agitation. He was a brilliant exponent of financial problems. He was also known for his scrupulous honesty. When in England in 1897 as a witness before the royal commission on Indian expenditure, he repeated allegations made to him against British soldiers employed on plague prevention in the Deccan. On returning to India, he found that these allegations were unsubstantiated, and therefore made a public and unqualified apology, which was much criticized by the extreme nationalists. In 1899 he became a member of the Bombay legislature, and in 1902 represented its nonofficial members in the central legislature. In 1905 he became president of the Congress party.

Gokhale was much concerned with social reform, and in 1905 founded the Servants of India society, whose members took vows of poverty and lifelong service to their country in a religious spirit. He opposed the ill-treatment of untouchables by caste Hindus, and on their behalf. In 1912 he was appointed a member of the Islington commission on the public services in India. He died at Poona on Feb. 19, 1915.

See T. V. Parvate, *Gopal Krishna Gokhale* (1959). (KE. A. B.)

GOLASECCA, one of a number of sites on the Somma plateau at the southern end of Lago Maggiore, Italy, where cremation cemeteries of the early Iron Age have been found. Each tomb contains a jar-shaped burial urn covered with an inverted bowl; the urn holds the ashes of the dead, together with a small accessory vase and weapons, *fibulae* and small objects of bronze, iron, amber or glass. The burial was almost always surrounded by a circle of unworked stones. The pottery found in the burials is of two styles, one hand-made and decorated with incised geometric patterns, the other generally wheel-made, slipped and patterned with darker clay and highly burnished, but the presence of both types in the same burials indicates that they are contemporary. The second type was exported to Este, though Atestine pottery is not found at Golasecca.

Swords of Hungarian and other northern types, and bronze ornaments identical with some found in Picenum, indicate other trade connections. The civilization, corresponding in date with the Arnoaldi period at Bologna (c. 650–500 B.C.), is closely connected with that of the Comacines, whose earliest graves, however, are earlier than the Golasecca group. The most famous Golasecca tomb, that of a warrior from Sesto Calende, is datable by a bronze *situla* of Certosa shape but of local manufacture to the end of the 6th century B.C.

Material from Golasecca is to be seen at Turin in the Palazzo dell'Accademia delle Scienze, and in the Sforza castle in Milan.

See also ARCHAEOLOGY: *The Iron Age in Europe*.

BIBLIOGRAPHY.—D. Randall-MacIver, *The Iron Age in Italy* (1927); F. von Duhn, *Italische Gräberkunde*, vol. i, pp. 130 ff. (1924); J. Whatmough, *The Foundations of Roman Italy*, ch. 5 (1937). (E. H. Rt.)

GOLCONDA, a fortress and ruined city of India, in the Deccan, lies 5 mi. W. of Hyderabad city. The fortress, on a granite hill, is more than 3 mi. in circumference with concentric curtain walls built of cyclopean masonry blocks; some palaces, mosques and other buildings remain. About 600 yd. to the northwest are the arcaded and domed Qutb Shahi tombs. Golconda has given its name in English literature to the diamonds which were found in the southeast of the Qutb Shahi dominions and cut at Golconda.

From 1518 to 1687 Golconda was the capital of a powerful Shi'a kingdom, one of the five Muslim sultanates established in the Deccan (q.v.) after the disintegration of the Bahmani kingdom. Its rulers, the Qutb Shahis, were overthrown by the Mogul emperor Aurangzeb in 1687, whereupon Golconda was annexed to the Mogul empire.

See Abdul Majeed Siddiqui, *History of Golcunda* (1956).

(J. B-P.)

GOLD is a dense, valuable, bright yellow, and lustrous metallic chemical element. Because of its appearance, unalterability, and occurrence in the native condition, it was one of the first metals to attract the attention of man. The history of gold is unequaled by that of any other metal because of its value in the minds of men from earliest times. Primitive people even thought that they had been blessed or cursed simply because they possessed gold nuggets or objects of art.

Gold is extremely inert and is considered to be virtually indestructible. It is usually found in a comparatively pure form in nature. Early civilizations placed great emphasis on the possession of this attractive and workable metal. Because of its durability, the beautiful and elaborate gold workmanship of Egyptian, Minoan, Assyrian, and Etruscan artisans can still be seen—sometimes in near perfect condition—several thousand years after being made. (See SILVER AND GOLD WORK.)

As the metamorphosis from the primitive marketplace to an increasingly complex economic system transpired, men learned that gold was the one material other men would accept in exchange for goods and services. Upon this fact was founded the system of using gold as the backing for modern world finances. (See GOLD RESERVES; GOLD STANDARD.)

No matter how much gold is extracted from the ground, man never seems to possess enough. The entire aim of the alchemists of the Middle Ages was to produce gold from base metals. Many of the advances in early chemistry were a direct result of their experiments. History abounds with tales of endeavours to obtain large quantities of gold and the power that goes with it. Each era includes stories of the frauds that were perpetrated and the hardships that were endured because of men's desire for gold.

Naturally occurring metallic, or native, gold usually has variable amounts of silver, copper, platinum, palladium, or certain other elements admixed with it. Purity of gold is reported as fineness, parts of gold per 1,000, or as percent of purity. Pure gold is called 24 carat, and alloys may be 12, 14, 16, 22, etc., carat, depending on the percentage of gold in the alloy; a 12-carat gold alloy is 50% gold.

40% gold, and sylvanite, $(Au,Ag)Te_2$, steel-gray in colour and containing up to 28% gold combined with some silver.

Gold is also found in the sea, but while the total amount is estimated at billions of tons, since the concentration of gold is only .000006 parts per 1,000,000 parts of water, it is not considered economically feasible to mine the sea for its precious metal.

OCCURRENCE

Historic Sources.—Alluvial deposits of native gold found in or along streams were the principal sources of the metal for the ancient civilizations of the Middle East. The washing of gold ores is depicted on Egyptian monuments of the 1st dynasty (2900 B.C.). The famous legend of the Golden Fleece was based on an expedition (about 1200 B.C.) to seize gold that was washed out of the river sands with the aid of sheepskins in the region later known as Armenia. Rich deposits were known in Lydia and the lands of the Aegean, and in Persia, India, China, and other lands.

During the Middle Ages the chief sources of the European supply of gold were the mines of Saxony and Austria, and Spain also produced some gold.

The era of gold production that followed the discovery of the Americas was in all probability the greatest the world had witnessed to that time. The exploitation of mines by slave labour and the looting of palaces, temples, and graves in Central and South America resulted in an influx of gold that unbalanced the economic structure of Europe and disturbed its political structure. From the discovery of America by Columbus in 1492 to 1600, more than 8,000,000 oz. of gold, or 35% of world production, came from South America. South American mines—especially in Colombia—continued in the 17th and 18th centuries to account for 61% and 80%, respectively, of world production; 48,000,000 oz. were mined between 1700 and 1800.

Russia became the leading producer in 1823, and for 14 years contributed the bulk of the world supply.

During the second great era of intensive production, the 25 years following 1850, more gold was produced in the world than in the 358 years immediately previous, chiefly because of discoveries in California and Australia. A third marked increase in world gold recovery was in the period from 1890–1915, when discoveries were made in Alaska, the Yukon, and on the Rand in Transvaal, S.Af. Beginning in the 1920s, gold production was increased by the development of gold fields in Canada. A big factor in the increase in the world supply was in introduction of the cyanide process (q.v.) for recovery of gold from low-grade ores and ores containing minute particle-size gold.

Throughout the years gold production increased until the average yearly production was about 40,000,000 oz., which was greater than production between 1493–1600 or 1600–1700. Since most mined gold goes through countinghouses and mints, a fairly ac-

THE BETTMANN ARCHIVE

KLONDIKE MINERS PANNING FOR GOLD. PHOTO, 1897

GEOLOGY

Gold is widely dispersed throughout the earth's crust. It exists in association with most copper and lead deposits, and although the quantity present is often extremely small, the gold is readily recovered as a by-product in the refining of these base metals.

Large masses of rock rich enough to be called ores are unusual. Those that do exist are usually quartz lodes or veins. They may also be deposits that originated from veins, such as river gravels and the gold-bearing quartz conglomerate beds (called "bankets" or "reefs") of the Witwatersrand system in the Transvaal and Orange Free State in South Africa. The origin of vein enrichment is not fully known, but it is believed that the gold was carried up from great depths with other minerals, at least partly in solution, and later precipitated (see ORE DEPOSITS). The mineral most commonly associated with gold, other than quartz, is pyrite, FeS_2, or "fool's gold," the yellow disulfide of iron. Other minerals commonly associated with gold deposits include chalcopyrite, $CuFeS_2$; arsenopyrite, $FeAsS$; sphalerite, ZnS; and stibnite, Sb_2S_3.

The gold mined during the great gold strikes of California, Colorado, and Alaska was removed by the placer method from alluvial deposits in which metallic gold occurred in the form of gold dust, larger grains, irregularly shaped masses, or occasional nuggets dispersed through the sand or caught in rock crevices. Through the action of weather and water, the gold-containing siliceous material eroded away, and the metallic gold concentrated in the beds of streams and rivers. The miners were able to separate the gold because it is approximately seven times as heavy as the material with which it is found, and it tends to accumulate as the surrounding material is washed away.

The other type of deposit in which gold is ordinarily found is called a lode or vein, and the mining of such deposits is called lode or vein mining. As in placer mines, the gold is generally in the free or native state, and rarely in chemical combination with other elements. The gold tellurides are an exception. Even the gold in pyrite is metallic, and consists of minute inclusions dispersed within the crystals or as a thin film along their cleavage planes. For the most part, the gold found in rock is invisible to the naked eye, although sometimes it does occur as grains or flakes large enough to be seen, and more rarely as specimen rock. Crystals, an inch or more across, have been found in alluvial deposits in California. "Boulders" of pure gold were found in the early days of the Australian gold rush of 1851. Gold tellurides are found principally in Western Australia and Colorado: the principal ores are calaverite, $AuTe_2$, a bronze-yellow telluride that contains

curate account of all gold mined since 1493 is recorded. **The Great Gold Strikes.**—The first major gold strike in North America occurred at Sutter's mill near the Sacramento River in California. In the winter of 1847–48, John Augustus Sutter (q.v.) was having a sawmill built. His contractor found gold, and soon the word was out. Sutter and the contractor, who had agreed to become partners, were soon besieged by thousands of trappers, miners, farmers, lawyers, preachers, sailors, soldiers, and school-teachers, who lived under conditions that only the promise of gold could make them endure. Although the average production in the California gold fields was barely half an ounce (15.6 g.) per man per day, some 2,500,000 oz. (77,760,000 g.) of gold passed through buyers' and dealers' hands in one 12-month period. (See CALIFORNIA: History: The Gold Rush.)

Approximately ten years later, stories were told that the Chero-kee Indians in the Arkansas River region of Colorado had struck gold. Thus began the second gold rush. "Pike's Peak or Bust" was the motto of those who hurriedly gathered their possessions and rushed to the newly opened fields. More often than not, it was "bust," for most of the claims made for the Pike's Peak region were untrue. However, hopes soared, and many endured the perils of starvation and Indian attack in order to become wealthy. Few did. (See also COLORADO.)

Bitter cold was the hallmark of the next big gold strike. The Klondike gold rush of 1898 has probably fired imaginations more than any other event in the annals of man's drive for gold, perhaps because so much had to be endured to extract the precious metal in an environment that fought the extraction at every turn. Yet, even with the worst that nature could summon, the prospectors extracted millions of dollars worth of gold from this previously almost barren land. (See KLONDIKE; DAWSON; YUKON TERRITORY.)

In Australia, the gold rush panic began in 1851. While the gold found in North America was usually in the form of dust or very fine grains, it was commonplace in Australia to find nuggets of gigantic size and value. The "Sierra Sands" nugget weighed 1,117 oz. (36,391 g.) or slightly over 93 lb. The "Lady Hotham" weighed 1,177 oz., and the "Welcome Stranger Nugget" weighed over 2,000 oz. The largest find in Australia at that time, the "Holtermann Nugget," weighed over 200 lb. (75 kg.). The Australian fields were indeed the answer to the dream of overnight wealth. Often, nuggets of substantial size were located only a few inches below the surface of the earth and were found quite by accident, as was the 200 lb. nugget. (See AUSTRALIA: History.)

It is interesting to note that in all the gold rushes described here the mining was done by individuals. These individuals, or perhaps groups of twos or threes, staked their claims, worked them, and derived the rewards. That was not the case in the greatest gold producing area the world has seen to date—the Witwatersrand area in the Republic of South Africa.

In 1886, a down-on-his-luck diamond digger from Kimberley named George Harrison discovered gold while working on the farm owned by the widow Oosthuizen. Within a month of the discovery, Harrison sold his claim for £10 and was never heard of again. By the end of the year the area had been proclaimed a gold field, with the village called Johannesburg (q.v.) as its centre, and many prospectors had moved in. The geology of the Rand (Witwatersrand) necessitated large machinery to extract the ore from the ground economically, and it very quickly became apparent that this was not a field for the small worker with his crude methods. Thus, the early arrival of the financiers from the Kimberley diamond mines heralded a period of great activity in buying and selling of claims and the consolidation of small companies into what became the great mining groups, able to mobilize capital and technical organizations to exploit the resources effectively.

The very early mines were confined to the rich outcrops from which the gold was recovered by simple washing procedures. In 1890 the first setback occurred when pyritic (sulfur-bearing) ore was encountered. At that time, these deposits could not be treated economically for their gold by the established methods. The experts felt the field was through, and a disastrous slump occurred.

However, within two years the rush was on again because by that time the cyanide process (q.v.) for extracting gold from the sulfide had been perfected, and exploration had proved that the deposits extended to great depths. During the South African (Boer) War (1899–1902) mining ceased in this area for the last time; two years later, it started again.

Since 1901, the story of South African gold mining operations has been one of continual growth and expansion. Industry high-lights include the discovery of the Far East Rand (where the reefs did not outcrop) in the early 1900s, and the introduction of geo-physical prospecting (q.v.) in 1930, which resulted in the dis-covery of the famous West Wits Line, otherwise known as the Far West Rand. More recent are the discovery of the Orange Free State goldfields in 1939 and the simultaneous opening of eleven major mines in that area after World War II. Since that time the Evander field, in the Witwatersrand geological system, has been opened some 70 mi. (113 km.) east of the East Rand.

Although the gold mines in South Africa are all in one geological system—the Witwatersrand system—historically and geographi-cally these operations are divided among seven goldfields. From east to west there are the Evander field, the East Rand, the Central Rand, the West Rand, the West Wits Line (or Far West Rand), the Klerksdorp field, and the Orange Free State field. Geographi-cally, the Witwatersrand, or "Rand," is the series of hills running from the East Rand, through the Central Rand, to the West Rand. The Evander field, the West Wits Line, Klerksdorp, and the Orange Free State field do not belong to the Rand proper, geographically, but are in different series of hills.

A striking contribution to the economy of gold mining in South Africa was the development of methods for the recovery of uranium from the tailings. This occurred shortly after World War II and resulted in providing a substantial amount of the world's uranium production.

MAJOR GOLD-PRODUCING COUNTRIES

Four countries produce a total of over 85% of the world's gold. Of the estimated 50,000,000 troy ounces produced annually, the Republic of South Africa leads with about 30,000,000; the U.S.S.R. is estimated to produce about 5,500,000; Canada, 4,000,000; and the United States 1,500,000.

Republic of South Africa.—More gold is mined annually from the Witwatersrand in the Republic of South Africa than from any other part of the world. The gold mine area, which is approxi-mately 300 mi. (480 km.) long, runs in a rough arc from east to west from Evander to Klerksdorp and then turns south across the Vaal River into the Orange Free State. The central portion, the Rand, is unique because of the form of its deposits. The gold-bearing ore is a gray pebble conglomerate containing gold that is, more often than not, so finely divided that it cannot be seen with the naked eye. Occasionally, the veins or reefs outcrop on the surface, but most of these visible ore deposits have been mined. The dip or angle of the reefs varies considerably, and, for the greater part, the ore-bearing horizons do not outcrop on the surface but lie at considerable depths, so that the mines in South Africa are now worked at levels of between 3,000 and 12,000 ft. (900 and 3,700 m.) below the surface.

Rand operations are mechanized to work deposits that contain gold varying from 2 pennyweights (dwt.) ($\frac{1}{10}$ oz., 1.56 g.) per ton in some of the older mines on the Central Witwatersrand, to 15.4 dwt. per ton at West Driefontein on the West Wits Line, to 21 dwt. per ton on Free State Geduld in the Orange Free State. The largest single producer in the 1960s was the West Driefontein mine with an annual output of about 2,000,000 oz.

Union of Soviet Socialist Republics.—Gold deposits in the Soviet Union are found in the Urals, Kazakhstan, the Transcau-casia, Central Asia (Uzbekistan and Kirgiz Republics), in Siberia (Transbaikal area, the basins of the Kolyma, Aldan, and Lena rivers), and the Far East (Chukotsky and Kamchatka peninsulas). Nearly 70% of all the gold mined in the Soviet Union comes from alluvial deposits. The mining operations are highly mecha-nized. The level of mechanization at the Yakutzoloto fields in Eastern Siberia is as high as 90%. Hundreds of dredges treat tens of millions of cubic metres of rock per year in the alluvial gold fields.

Canada.—Canada, in recent years, has accounted for about 10% of the world's gold. Its deposits are scattered throughout its entire land mass, although the major gold-producing areas are in British Columbia, Ontario (Porcupine and Kirkland Lake), northwestern Quebec, and the Northwest Territories.

Gold mining in Canada started after the California gold strike. The amount of gold mined per year increased until it reached its peak in 1941 when 5,340,000 oz. (166,090,000 g.) were produced. Since that time, gold mining in Canada has decreased, and in 1947, the government of Canada enacted the Emergency Mining Act which subsidized high-cost producers. This assistance has continued and has prolonged the operating lives of many of the gold-producing companies.

During the first decade of the 1900s, Canada's largest single producer of gold was discovered, the Hollinger Mine in Ontario. Some 270,000 oz. (8,398,000 g.) of gold per year are extracted from this property. Newer mines, such as the Giant Yellowknife in the Northwest Territories, took up the slack as the output of older mines like the Hollinger began to diminish.

United States.—The principal gold mining sections of the United States are South Dakota, Utah, Alaska, California, Arizona, Washington, Nevada, and Colorado. The output from Utah and Arizona is almost entirely a by-product from base-metal mining. The Homestake Mine at Lead, South Dakota, is a lode mine and the nation's leading gold producer. In the 1960s this mine annually treated almost 2,000,000 tons of ore to recover more than 600,000 oz. (18,662,000 g.) of gold, about 40% of the nation's output. Since 1877, this one mine has produced 27,333,000 oz. of gold, worth $956,655,000 at the $35-per-ounce figure. The Utah Copper Mine in Bingham, Utah, the second largest producer in the U.S., recovers gold as a by-product of copper mining. This one mine processes about 24,000,000 tons of ore per year for copper; and each ton contains about 14 cents worth of gold. Placer mine operations are concentrated primarily in Alaska and California; the gold is recovered chiefly by bucketline dredges.

Other Countries.—Gold is produced in lesser but nationally important quantities in many other countries including Australia, Mexico, Nicaragua, Colombia, Sweden, India, Korea, Japan, the Philippines, the Democratic Republic of the Congo, and Ghana.

MINING

Gold is recovered in one of three ways: (1) by placer mining of alluvial deposits, (2) by lode or vein mining, or (3) as a by-product of base-metal mining. Placer mining is the oldest method. Basically, it entails taking advantage of the high density of gold to separate it from the much lighter siliceous material with which it is found. Alluvial deposits, which are mined by placer methods, are the gold-bearing sands and gravel that have been deposited by rapidly moving streams and rivers where they widen or, for some other reason, lose speed. As the current slows, the sediment being carried downstream has an opportunity to settle.

Placer Mining.—Although the basic principles of placer min-

ing have not altered since early times, the methods have been improved considerably, chiefly in mechanical procedures. During the great American gold strikes of California, Colorado, and Alaska, placer mines were almost exclusively the source of gold, and the panning method was one technique utilized by the individual miners. In this method, the miner employed a pan or a batea (a pan or basin with radial corrugations) in which he placed a few handfuls of dirt and a large amount of water. Through circular motion of the pan, the siliceous material was washed over the side; the denser material remained in the centre of the pan. After many of these washings, only the gold and the other heavy minerals were left. At this point, if the gold particles were large enough, it was comparatively easy to separate them from other materials. If not, further concentration was needed.

The cradle or rocker was an improvement over the pan and the batea. The cradle resembled a child's cradle for which it was named, and it could process larger quantities of ore. Gravel was shoveled onto a perforated iron plate, and water was poured on. The finer material dropped onto the apron which distributed it across the riffles, which were pieces of wood or iron perpendicular to the bottom and sides of the cradle. During this time, the entire apparatus was rocked. As the material moved through the rocker, the gold was caught by the riffles. When enough gold was accumulated, the riffles were cleaned. Although the cradle or rocker is largely obsolete, the riffle remains and is still widely used in sluice boxes and corduroy tables. The name is applied to any strip, bar, or groove placed at right angles to the flowing stream to provide a protective spot where the gold can settle. The corduroy table consists of wide sloping plates with shallow sides which hold a coarse corduroy cloth. Periodically, the corduroy is removed and washed by hand in boxes partly filled with water to recover the gold-rich concentrates.

In California, thick beds of gravel on the hillsides were worked by hydraulic mining. Powerful jets of water at pressures of hundreds of pounds per square inch were passed through giant swivel-mounted nozzles to break down the gravel banks and wash the material through lines of sluices. Although great volumes of water and many miles of pipes and flumes were required, the cost of treatment was only a few cents per yard. Therefore poor ground could be treated at a profit. However, the millions of tons of tailings that were washed into the Yuba and Feather rivers had such an adverse effect on farming further down the valleys that an injunction was obtained against hydraulic miners in 1880, and the work thereafter was strictly limited.

In the early 1900s, dredging became the most important branch of placer mining and remains today as probably the most important single technique. The ladder dredge generally used the world over is similar to that employed for deepening harbours and rivers (*see* Dredges and Dredging). (*See also* Mining, Metal: *The Mining Cycle: Mucking.*) The gold-mining dredge originated in New Zealand and achieved its greatest popularity on the rivers there and in California. This method of placer mining is the major technique used in the U.S.S.R.

Paddock dredging, a later development in the western United States, enables all placer deposits to be treated even if they are not in or near a riverbed. The dredge floats in a pond that is continuously extended by the digging equipment at one end while simultaneously being filled by the waste or tailings at the other end. In this way, the dredge moves across the country taking its pond or reservoir with it. By piling more gravel around the reservoir and increasing the water level, the dredge can be made to work its way uphill. In 1910 there were 72 operating dredges in California. After World War II, however, only a few remained in operation.

Lode Mining.—Many of the practices used in the underground mining and exploration of gold lode or vein deposits are similar to those used for other metals. Tremendous tonnages of gold ore are treated throughout the world since most gold mines have an extremely low percentage of gold. For example, in the United States, the Homestake Mine processes three tons of ore for every ounce of gold it obtains. Ordinarily, a vertical shaft is sunk that allows the miner to get to the lode. The horizontal working levels

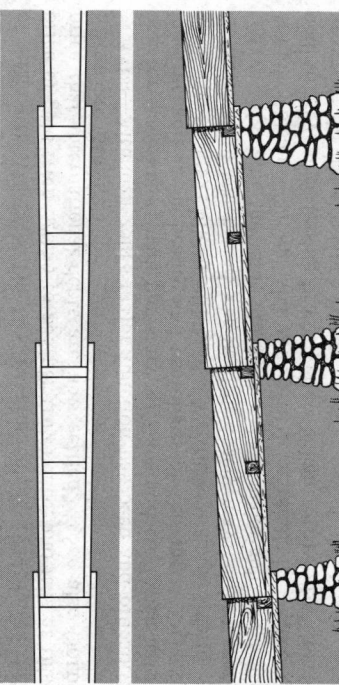

FIG. 1.—SLUICE BOXES. INCLINED WOODEN TROUGHS FOR SEPARATING GOLD FROM GRAVEL. SHOWING PLAN (TOP). GRAVEL CONTAINING GOLD, IS CARRIED DOWN THE SLUICE BY A STREAM OF WATER. THE GOLD SINKS TO THE BOTTOM AND LODGES BEHIND THE CROSSBARS

GOLD

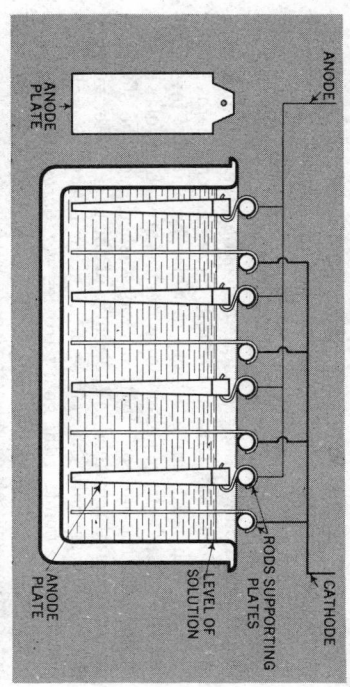

then follow the vein. In the case of the Homestake Mine, the working depth is 6,800 ft. below the surface. Since 1877, some 200 horizontal miles have been worked at this mine. (See also MINING, METAL.)

By-Product Recovery.—A large percentage of the gold recovered, particularly in the U.S. and Canada, is retrieved as a by-product in base-metal mining; that is, as a consequence of the mining of copper, lead, zinc, etc. Annual U.S. production of gold is approximately 1.5 million oz., of which about one-third is recovered as a by-product of base-metal operations. About 15% is recovered by placer mining and about 50% from the direct treatment of gold ore.

Not only is gold recovered as a consequence of base-metal mining operations, but other metals, notably silver and platinum, are recovered as by-products of gold ore processing. For example, silver is commonly associated to some degree with gold in nature, usually at the ratio of one part by weight of silver to four parts of gold. Platinum and other platinum-group metals are found in some gold ores. Uranium is recovered as a by-product or co-product of gold ores in several mines of the Witwatersrand system (principally in the West Rand, West Wits Line, Klerksdorp, and Orange Free State areas) in South Africa. It is a major source of revenue at some mines. Also from the Witwatersrand system, approximately five to seven thousand ounces of osmium, along with iridium, are recovered annually as by-products of gold mining.

Ore Reserves.—The world's total recoverable gold reserve is estimated at approximately 1,000,000,000 troy ounces (31,103,-000,000 grams). Of this, the gold resources in the fields of the Witwatersrand system in the Republic of South Africa are estimated at more than one half of the total, or 500,000,000 oz. The gold reserves in the Soviet Union, although not made public, are also believed to be very large. According to the Bureau of Mines, U.S. Department of the Interior, a preliminary estimate of domestic gold reserves, based on data compiled in a study of the nation's gold potential, shows a total of 20,000,000 oz. of gold, virtually all of which is recoverable under current economic and technologic conditions.

EXTRACTION AND REFINING

The ore obtained from vein or lode mining is very nearly all extraneous material. The gold is usually found as particles so small that most often they can be seen only under a microscope. Therefore highly economical extraction techniques must be used to separate the very small amount of gold from a very large amount of ore. Some of this separation has already been performed during placer mining since the product of this mining operation is a first-step concentrate. (See also ORE DRESSING.)

The gold in placer ores is usually separated from the siliceous material by amalgamation (q.v.) in which mercury and gold combine to form a gold amalgam which is readily separated from the ore. After the separation, the amalgam is processed by heating it to vapourize the mercury, the amalgam is condensed for reuse, leaving a crude bullion.

Ore recovered from vein mining ultimately goes through the same processing as that recovered from placer mines. However, because of the bulk and quantity of the ore, and the very low concentration of gold contained in it, the ore must first be crushed and reduced in size until the particles are approximately $\frac{1}{60}$ in. ($\frac{1}{1000}$ cm.) or finer. The product of the crushing mills (rod and ball) is then amalgamated in the same manner as the placer ore. Often mercury is added directly to the rod and ball mills, thereby saving an extra step. By this technique, approximately 70% of the gold in the ore is recovered.

The remaining gold is recovered by a cyanidation process in which the gold is dissolved by a very dilute solution of sodium or calcium cyanide to produce gold cyanide. The resulting gold-containing cyanide solutions are treated by adding a small amount of extremely fine zinc powder; they are then filtered. The zinc replaces the gold in the cyanide solution. The gold precipitates as a black powder, which is mixed with fluxes and smelted. The impurities form a slag leaving the gold behind as crude bullion. Amalgams from lode mining operations are treated in a similar fashion to that described for placer mining ores. (See also AMALGAMATION; CYANIDE PROCESS.)

The gold bullion recovered by these techniques is still impure and must be processed further. Two methods are in general use. The first is a chlorine process invented in 1869 in Australia. In this process, the gold is melted in clay pots, and a stream of chlorine gas is bubbled through it. The chlorine reacts chemically with the silver and most other impurities, but does not react with the gold until nearly all the silver is removed. The silver and other chlorides form a dross on the surface of the molten metal which is skimmed off. The silver is later recovered by electrolysis. Platinum, which is sometimes present, is not recovered by this process, and remains in the gold.

The other technique, used particularly by the United States Mint, is an electrolytic process introduced there in 1902. Partially refined gold is cast into thick plates that form the anodes (positive electrodes) in a porcelain cell filled with an electrolytic solution of gold chloride and hydrochloric acid. The cathodes (negative electrodes) are thin rolled plates of pure gold suspended in the cell alternately with the impure plates. A current is passed through the anode to the cathode through the liquid, thus dissolving the anodes and precipitating pure gold on the cathodes (see ELECTRO-METALLURGY). During the process, silver is converted into insoluble silver chloride and falls to the bottom of the cell. Other metals, including platinum, dissolve and remain in solution. The platinum is subsequently recovered and sometimes pays for the whole operation. See also METALLURGY.

USES

Monetary.—By far the largest single use for gold is as the backing for the world's currency. Approximately 60% of all the gold mined to date is held by governments and central banks for this purpose. The estimated world monetary gold reserve, excluding the Soviet Union and its satellites, is approximately $40,000,-000,000; about 40% of this reserve is held by the United States. The gold is used not only to back the paper currencies of the individual countries but also to settle trade differences between countries. It is accepted by all nations of the world as the means of settling their debts. The U.S. government, in 1934, raised the price of gold from $20.66 to $35 per troy ounce, and it is at this price that international debts are now settled. (See also GOLD STANDARD; MONEY.)

Arts.—Although gold's major function has been and probably will for sometime remain monetary, artisans and craftsmen have long recognized the beauty and usefulness of this metal. There are ancient edifices gilded with gold. Artistic remnants of various civilizations in which gold was used profusely may be seen even today. Many of the same attributes which make gold valuable as money also make it valuable as an artistic material: its inertness, malleability, and pleasing bright yellow colour. (See GOLD-BEATING; SILVER AND GOLD WORK.)

Industrial Uses.—The high electrical conductivity of gold (ordinarily spoken of as 71%, which means 71% of the International Annealed Copper Standard) accounts for the largest single industrial use for the metal. Where high reliability, corrosion resistance, and high electrical conductivity are needed in electrical and electronic circuits, gold is employed. It is generally used to plate contacts, terminals, printed circuits, and semiconductor systems. The reliability of gold is especially important in the critical areas of space apparatus and instrumentation. Space and defense programs call heavily upon another of gold's properties—its ability to reflect up to 98% of incident infrared radiation. U.S. satellites such as Discoverer 14, Ranger, Mariner, and others have utilized gold to reflect this radiation. Without the protection afforded by the thin gold layer (0.000025 to 0.000005 in. [0.000635 to 0.000127 mm.] thick), temperatures would rise above acceptable levels. Gold also is an efficient barrier to the high intensity solar radiation found in outer space. To filter out both the ultraviolet and infrared radiation, a gold layer was plated on the visor of Gemini 4 astronaut Edward H. White.

The vacuum of space requires special techniques to overcome its hostility. One special problem is that of lubrication. Since ordinary lubricants are sometimes subject to radiation deterioration or volatilization, hard gold alloys are used to coat bearings in space vehicles.

The chemical industry has put gold's corrosion resistance to good use in many applications. Equipment for handling sulfur-containing gases at high temperatures is gold plated to protect the structural materials from contamination and subsequent damage. Also, heavy electrodeposited platings of gold are used on copper and soft steels to provide seals for high-pressure reaction vessels.

Gold brazing and soldering alloys find a multitude of uses in areas where chemical inertness, good wetting action, and fairly high strengths are required. Examples are found in aircraft and spacecraft as well as in the more mundane use of making glass-to-metal seals in vacuum tubes. Gold is also used in windows. The metal is applied to plate glass to be used in the construction of large office buildings. In this particular application, gold film is used to reflect much of the sun's heat-producing (infrared) energy, thus lowering air conditioning requirements without unduly reducing the transmission of light. An added value is the beauty that the soft gold colour contributes.

Gold is also used in medical and dental applications. It has long been used to repair and replace decayed teeth. And there are other areas of medicine in which gold can be beneficial. As an example, radioactive colloidal gold (Au^{198}) is used to treat arthritis. New medical applications for gold may be found in its use for the treatment of certain types of punctures, skin ulcers, burns, and certain nerve-end operations.

ALLOYS

Gold can be combined with silver in all proportions, and the resulting alloys are soft, malleable, and ductile. The naturally occurring alloy containing about 20% silver was known to the ancients as electrum (see SILVER AND GOLD WORK; NUMISMATICS). The colour of alloys of gold gradually changes from yellow to white as the proportion of silver increases; over 70% silver results in alloys that are white. These gold-silver alloys are used to make trial plates, or standards of reference, with which the fineness of gold wares and coins is compared. The jewelry industry also uses these alloys extensively, especially an alloy called "green gold" (75% gold, 25% silver).

Copper hardens gold and forms alloys of reddish-yellow colour which have comparatively low melting points. Several of these are used as brazing alloys. The triple alloys of gold, silver, and copper are malleable and ductile. They possess a rich gold colour, and are often used for the production of gold wares. Hot nitric acid attacks all but the richer alloys of gold containing silver or copper or both. If the proportion of gold is less than 33%, practically all the silver and copper is dissolved.

Stress corrosion cracking occurs occasionally in service in the lower carat alloys (below 14). In general, the corrosive agent must dissolve the copper and silver. Mercury will cause highly stressed gold alloys to crack and this occurs most rapidly at about 50 atomic percent. However, as a general statement, most of the higher gold content alloys are extremely resistant to stress corro-

sion cracking even when heavily cold worked.

Some of the gold-palladium and gold-platinum alloys are ductile and are used in jewelry. A gold-platinum alloy was known in pre-Columbian Ecuador (see SILVER AND GOLD WORK: North and South America). Alloys containing 10-20% palladium are nearly white.

The gold-palladium-iron alloys, designed primarily for potentiometer wire, develop exceptionally high electrical resistivity when properly cold worked. The optimum alloy contains 49.5% gold, 40.5% palladium, and 10% iron. It develops a resistivity of 1,100 microohm-cm after annealing at 500° C (932° F) for 24 hours.

Plating Alloys.—Since gold at $35 an ounce is one of the more expensive engineering materials, it is often used in the form of a plating or thin film, particularly in the electronics industry, and gold alloys have been developed specifically to satisfy electronic requirements.

Prior to 1953, virtually all electroplated gold was deposited from a hot cyanide electrolyte. In 1953 a new solution was developed which contained a small amount of silver and had a deposited hardness of 115 DPH (diamond pyramid hardness) as opposed to the hardness of only 65 DPH of the then conventional deposit. Several subsequent electrolytes were based on this innovation including one that contained up to 4% antimony and deposited a bright coating. This was of particular interest to semiconductor engineers who desired to produce specific transistor performance characteristics. Later, an electrodeposit solution was developed in which mild organic acids were combined with alkali metal-gold salts at pH's of about 3.0 and above. This system is used to produce high purity (99.99%) gold electroforms as thick as 0.25 in. (0.635 cm.). The purity of this solution is also of importance for use in isotope preparation. Other acid gold deposits range in hardness from 85 DPH for 99.99% pure gold deposits to over 500 DPH for those alloyed with nickel, copper, etc. Cobalt and indium are also added to gold plating solutions to vary the characteristics of the deposit.

Comparatively new innovations in the gold plating industry are electrolytes from which can be deposited gold alloys with gold contents as low as 80%. An 80-20 gold-nickel alloy is produced by this technique. It has a hardness in excess of 500 DPH, and the deposited alloy has a melting point of 945° C which makes it valuable for use in brazing metals to be used in space. More recently, an electrolyte of neutral pH has been developed from which copper and other metals may be added to a deposit containing from 50% to 80% gold. A 75-25 gold-copper alloy of this type has a hardness that can be varied between 325 and 450 DPH through the use of a simple heat treatment. Its melting point of 899° C has led to its use as a brazing material in joining vacuum tube components.

PROPERTIES AND COMPOUNDS

The more important physical properties of gold are given in the accompanying table. Those properties that have made it especially valued, its colour and lustre, resistance to corrosion, mal-

Symbol	Au
Atomic number	79
Atomic weight	196.967
Isotopes (naturally occurring isotope in italics)	186, 188-196, *197*, 198-201, 203
Crystal system	face-centred cubic
Hardness, Mohs' scale	2.5-3.0
Melting point (° C)	1,063.0
Boiling point (° C)	2,970
Electrical resistivity at 20° C, microhm-cm.	2.44
Thermal conductivity at 20° C, cal/sec/sq.cm/cm/° C	0.74
Magnetic specific susceptibility, cgs units	-0.15×10^{-6}
Tensile strength (approx.), psi	19,000
Modulus of elasticity (approx.), psi	11.6×10^6
Specific heat at 20° C, cal/g	0.0306
Latent heat of fusion, cal/g	15.0
Latent heat of vaporization at bp, cal/g	446
Superconducting transition temp. (° K)	not superconducting above 0.006
Density at 20° C, g/cc vacuum-distilled	18.88
cast	19.3
Density in vicinity of melting pt, g/cc solid	18.474
from X-ray data	19.4
liquid	17.361
Coefficient of linear expansion, 18-100° C, per degree	14.3×10^{-6}

Some Physical Properties of Gold

leability and ductility, electrical conductivity, etc., have been discussed above in relation to its history and uses.

The general chemical properties of the element are best indicated by the position of gold in subgroup Ib of the periodic table (see PERIODIC LAW) along with copper and silver, and its place at the bottom of the electromotive force series (see BATTERY). Its characteristic valences are plus one (aurous compounds) and plus three (auric compounds.) Gold ions will receive electrons from any other metal to resume the metallic state, e.g., $3Pt + 2Au^{3+} \rightarrow 3Pt^{2+} \rightarrow 2Au$. Gold exhibits co-ordination numbers of 2 and 4, (see VALENCE: *Co-ordination Number*), which helps to explain its complex compounds. It is insoluble in nitric, hydrochloric, or sulfuric acids but is soluble in hot selenic or telluric acid. Aqua regia (q.v.) is the usual solvent for gold. The metal reacts according to the equation

$$Au + 5H^+ + 4Cl^- + NO_3^- \rightarrow HAuCl_4 + NO + 2H_2O$$

The product is chlorauric acid, the precursor of salts such as $NaAuCl_4.2H_2O$, which is used in toning photographic prints. Gold will also dissolve in aqueous solutions of alkaline sulfides and thiosulfates. Alkali cyanides, even in dilute solution, will slowly attack finely divided gold if oxygen is available. The reaction is

$$2Au + 4CN^- \tfrac{1}{2}O_2 + H_2O \rightarrow 2Au(CN)_2^- + 2OH^-$$

Oxides and Hydroxides.—Gold and oxygen do not combine directly under any conditions; therefore all oxides and hydroxides must be made by indirect methods. When aurous chloride, AuCl, is treated with dilute potassium hydroxide, KOH, a violet-black powder, AuOH or hydrated Au_2O, is formed. It is also possible that the Au_2O changes to a mixture of spongy gold and Au_2O_3. If the powder is heated to about 200° C, it loses water, giving a violet-brown product which at 250° C decomposes into gold and oxygen. The oxide and hydroxide have feebly basic properties and are capable of forming salts with halogen acids. When an excess of KOH is added to the violet-black powder obtained by treating AuCl with dilute KOH, the results are AuO_2 and gold metal.

Auric hydroxide, a brownish-black powder, is produced by precipitating a solution of auric chloride or of chlorauric acid, $HAuCl_4$, with a limited amount of caustic alkali. The hydroxide, on drying over phosphoric oxide, forms a brown powder of auryl hydroxide, AuO(OH). This powder can be dehydrated at 140° C to form the trioxide which, on further heating to 170° C, is said to lose oxygen and form the oxide, Au_2O_3. Higher temperatures decompose Au_2O_2 into oxygen and metal. Auric oxide is capable either of forming salts with the halogen acids or of acting as an acid anhydride by combining with strong bases to form aurates. Potassium aurate, $KAuO_2.3H_2O$, is a yellow crystalline compound; $Ba(AuO_2)_2$ is a yellow precipitate.

Halogen Compounds.—Cold fluorine does not attack gold, but at dull-red heat the reaction forms a yellowish deposit. The gold fluoride is completely hydrolyzed by water.

The chlorides of gold known with certainty are aurous chloride, AuCl, and auric chloride, $AuCl_3$; the identity of an intermediate chloride, Au_2Cl_4, is doubtful. AuCl is almost always formed by heating $AuCl_3$; the optimum temperature is about 175° C, and several days are required to complete the reaction. If a higher temperature is used, complete decomposition into gold and chlorine occurs. This decomposition of auric into aurous chloride takes place to some extent even in hot aqueous solutions.

Aurous chloride is a yellowish-white solid that is insoluble in cold water but undergoes slow decomposition into gold and soluble $AuCl_3$.

Auric chloride can be obtained either by heating chlorauric acid to 200° C in a stream of chlorine or by dissolving gold in chlorine water, preferably in darkness. It is obtained as a reddish-brown powder or as ruby-red crystals. While it slowly decomposes in light, it can be sublimed unchanged in a stream of chlorine.

Two bromides of gold are known: AuBr and AuBr₃, corresponding to the two chlorides. The auric bromide, $AuBr_3$, pre-pared by the action of bromine water on finely divided gold, forms dark brownish-red crystals and in its reactions resembles the corresponding chloride. The monobromide is obtained by heating the tribromide or $HAuBr_4$ to 105°-200° C. Auric bromide forms bromaurates, $MAuBr_4$, similar to the chloraurates. These procedures have been used in determining the atomic weight of gold.

On mixing aqueous solutions of potassium iodide and $AuCl_3$ or $HAuCl_4$, some auric iodide, AuI_3, is produced; but, being somewhat unstable, it decomposes to a large extent, forming aurous iodide, AuI, and free iodine. The latter reaction is complete on warming. Although unstable by itself, in combination with alkali and alkaline-earth iodides, auric iodide forms a stable series of complex iodoaurates. The potassium salt, $KAuI_4$, crystallizes in black, lustrous prisms. Iodine in aqueous or (preferably) aqueous-alcoholic solutions combines with metallic gold to produce aurous iodide, a white or lemon-yellow powder insoluble in water.

Other Compounds.—*Gold Cyanides.*—In the presence of air, gold dissolves in aqueous solutions of potassium or sodium cyanide to form potassium or sodium cyanaurite, $KAu(CN)_2$ or $NaAu(CN)_2$, and on precipitating this solution with dilute hydrochloric acid, aurous cyanide, AuCN, is deposited in insoluble, microscopic, hexagonal yellow plates. Auric cyanide, $Au(CN)_3$, has not been isolated with certainty but stable complex salts are known with alkali and other cyanides. Potassium cyanaurate, $KAu(CN)_4.3H_2O$, forms colourless efflorescent crystals. The silver salt, $AgAu(CN)_4$, is formed by precipitating a solution of $KAu(CN)_4$ with silver nitrate. From this salt, cyanauric acid, $HAu(CN)_4.3H_2O$, is obtained by removing the silver with hydrochloric acid and crystallizing the solution.

Auric nitrate and sulfate hydrolyze so extensively that auric oxide will dissolve only in concentrated solutions of nitric or sulfuric acid. The yellow metal will not combine directly with sulfur, but does so with tellurium to readily form $AuTe_2$.

Fulminating Gold.—When auric oxide or a gold solution is treated with concentrated ammonia, a black powder called fulminating gold, $2AuN.NH_3.3H_2O$, is formed. When dry it is a powerful explosive, since it can be detonated either by friction or by heating the compound to about 145° C, it should always be handled with great caution.

Purple of Cassius.—When a solution of auric chloride is precipitated with a solution of stannous chloride a reddish or purplish precipitate containing both metallic gold and tin hydroxide is produced. The composition of this precipitate is as variable as is its colour. Formation of the precipitate is a delicate test for gold. Purple of Cassius is used in the preparation of ruby glass.

ANALYSIS FOR GOLD

Gold will dissolve in sodium polysulfide to form sodium thioaurate, $NaAuS_2$, and is therefore classed with arsenic and antimony in a subgroup of Group II in qualitative analysis. As the solution of $NaAuS_2$ along with such compounds as Na_3AsS_4 is acidified with HCl, the gold precipitates as a sulfide (and some free Au) along with arsenic sulfide. The sulfides are rendered soluble with chlorine, and the addition of ammonium hydroxide, NH_4OH, would give a solution of NH_4AuCl_4 with $(NH_4)_3AsO_4$. From this solution oxalic acid will selectively precipitate spongy gold but not arsenic.

The usual qualitative test for gold ion free from interfering metals is the formation of red-purple colloidal gold by adding such reducing agents as ferrous sulfate, stannous chloride, or formaldehyde. Readily identifiable red crystals may be obtained by the use of gold ion plus cocaine hydrochloride.

The prospector or expert with a gold pan can estimate the value of a placer deposit by counting and evaluating the size of the gold specks remaining after panning a specific quantity of the deposit. Accurate determination of the gold content in rock is accomplished by a fire assay process which involves the melting of a weighed quantity of ground ore with fluxes to form a slag with the siliceous part of the rock (see further ASSAYING).

See also references under "Gold" in the Index.

BIBLIOGRAPHY.—A. F. Taggart, *Handbook of Mineral Dressing, Ores*...

and Industrial Minerals (1945); A. King (ed.), Gold Metallurgy on the Witwatersrand (1952); J. V. N. Dorr and F. L. Bosqui, Cyanidation and Concentration of Gold and Silver Ores, 2nd ed. (1950); J. W. Mellor, Comprehensive Treatise on Inorganic and Theoretical Chemistry, vol. iii (1923); National Research Council, International Critical Tables of Numerical Data of Physics, Chemistry and Technology, 7 vol., ed. by E. W. Washburn et al. (1926-33); R. E. Kirk and D. F. Othmer (eds.), Encyclopedia of Chemical Technology, vol. 7 (1951); N. V. Sidgwick, Chemical Elements and Their Compounds, vol. 1 (1950); Gmelin's Handbuch der anorganischen Chemie, 8th ed. (1954); E. M. Wise, Gold: Recovery, Properties, and Applications (1964); C. H. V. Sutherland, Gold: Its Beauty, Power, and Allure (1960); Garry Hoyt, Lust for Gold (1962); C. A. Hampel, Encyclopedia of Electrochemistry (1964); The Dines Newsletter, vol. ii, no. 95 (May 28, 1965); D. H. McLaughlin, The Many Uses of Gold (1961); J. V. Sherman, "New Sourdoughs," Barron's (June 21, 1965); J. Liston, "Digging for Gold Over One Mile Deep," Popular Science (Nov. 1964); U.S. Department of the Interior, Bureau of Mines, Mineral Facts and Problems, Bulletin 585 (1960), Minerals Yearbook (annually); T. Lyman (ed.), Metals Handbook, 8th ed., vol. i (1961); A. E. Focke and H. D. Roth, "Gold—The Many-Faceted Metal" Modern Chemicals (Nov.-Dec. 1965); H. E. McKinstry, Mining Geology (1948); W. H. Emmons, Gold Deposits of the World (1937)

For current figures on production see the Britannica Book of the Year.

(C. E. Wi.; H. D. R.)

GOLD AND SILVER WORK: see SILVER AND GOLD WORK.

GOLDBEATING, the reduction of fine gold to thin leaf by beating, is one of the most ancient arts. In the Odyssey, Homer made note of the anvil and hammer used in producing thin sheets of gold. Ancient Rome gleamed with decorations in gold leaf and Pliny the Elder noted that a small quantity of gold could be beaten into 750 leaves, each four digits square.

Gold becomes workable when alloyed with small amounts of silver and copper. Gold and the alloying metals are melted and poured into a small mold to form an ingot. When cool, an ingot 2 in. long, $1\frac{1}{8}$ in. wide, and $\frac{1}{8}$ in. thick is run through electrically driven rollers until it becomes a ribbon more than 20 ft. long, $1\frac{1}{8}$ in. wide, and $\frac{1}{1,000}$ in. thick. The ribbon is cut into about 200 squares, each $1\frac{1}{8} \times 1\frac{1}{8}$ in. The squares are then ready for the first beating process.

First, the squares are placed between sheets of vellum or heavy paper that form a cutch, or packet. The cutch is enclosed in a sheepskin and then beaten on the stone block with a hammer until the squares measure 4 in. on a side. Each square is carefully removed from the cutch with wooden pincers, placed on a leather cushion, and cut into four parts with a steel blade.

Next, the 2 × 2-in. squares are placed between skins made from the membranes of the large intestine of cattle. This pack of skins (a shoder) is beaten until the squares are again 4 × 4 in. Each leaf, after being lifted from the shoder and placed on a leather cushion, is divided into four equal parts. Too fragile to be touched by steel, the leaves are cut with a wagon, a tool that resembles a miniature sled with Malacca reed runners.

Finally, the squares (again, 2 × 2 in.) are placed between fine skins that comprise a package about 5 in. square, called a mold. This is beaten until the leaves approximate the dimensions of the mold. They have been reduced to a translucent thinness (about $\frac{1}{280,000}$ in.) and are so delicate that, when lifted to the leather cushion, they can be moved and straightened with a light breath. They are trimmed to about $3 \times 3\frac{3}{8}$ in. and are put up in book form between sheets of tissue paper that is dusted with powder; each book contains 25 gold leaves.

Gold leaf is used in gilding and is applied in executing ornamental designs, lettering and edgings on paper, wood, ceramics, glass, textiles, and metal. Gold leaf may also be reduced to powder. See also GILDING.

(E. L. Y.)

GOLDBERG, ARTHUR JOSEPH (1908–), lawyer, associate justice of the U.S. Supreme Court (1962-65), and U.S. representative to the United Nations (1965-68), was born in Chicago, Ill., on Aug. 8, 1908. He was the youngest of eight children of Joseph and Rebecca Goldberg, both Russian immigrants. He attended Chicago public schools, De Paul University, and Northwestern University Law School. After being admitted to the Illinois bar at the age of 20, he practised law in Chicago from 1929 to 1948. His work in the 1936 political campaign brought him into contact with many labour leaders; he won national attention as counsel for the Chicago Newspaper Guild during its 1938 strike. In 1948 he became general counsel for the Congress of Industrial Organizations (CIO) and the United Steelworkers of America, with headquarters in Washington, D.C. There he won a reputation as a skilful debater and a master of the art of conciliation and compromise. He was instrumental in effecting the merger of the American Federation of Labor (AFL) and the CIO (1955), and in expelling Communists and hoodlums from the labour movement. In 1961 President Kennedy appointed Goldberg as secretary of labour, and in that post his dynamic leadership and successful conciliation activities earned him wide and favourable attention.

In August 1962, when Justice Felix Frankfurter resigned from the Supreme Court because of ill health, President Kennedy named Goldberg as his successor. Justice Frankfurter had been the principal spokesman on the court for the position of judicial restraint, deference toward the political branches, and concern for states' rights. Goldberg's appointment shifted the court's balance toward more liberal and activist positions in several fields.

On July 20, 1965, President Johnson appointed Justice Goldberg as U.S. representative to the United Nations, succeeding Adlai E. Stevenson, who had died on July 14.

At the UN Goldberg led in resolving the financial crisis brought on by the failure of certain nations to pay their peace-keeping assessments, by announcing a shift in the U.S. position; he helped persuade domestic critics that ending the UN stalemate was more important than trying to apply penalties. In September 1965, as president of the Security Council, Goldberg was instrumental in bringing about negotiations that led to a cease-fire between India and Pakistan and in December 1965 he conferred with Pope Paul VI and with French President De Gaulle on the war in Vietnam. He resigned from his UN post on April 25, 1968, and became a partner in a New York law firm. In 1970, as the Democratic candidate for governor in New York, he lost to Nelson Rockefeller. Goldberg moved to Washington, D.C, in 1971, where he practised law.

(C. H. P.; X.)

GOLD COAST: see GHANA.

GOLDEN BULL, a term applied to documents whose political importance was emphasized by authentication with a golden seal (bulla), but chiefly used for the elaborate charter issued by the Holy Roman emperor Charles IV in 1356 to stabilize the German constitution. Its importance was twofold. First, it excluded the intervention of the papacy—for generations a main cause of dissension—in the election of the German ruler. Second, it acknowledged the position won by the princes, thus bringing to a close developments initiated in Frederick II's Privilegium in favorem principum ecclesiasticorum (1220) and Constitutio in favorem principum (1232). Earlier rulers had struggled to reassert the crown's authority; Charles IV frankly recognized that Germany was no longer a monarchy but a federation of principalities. By 1356 the tendency to consolidation of the principalities was irreversible; furthermore, if papal interference was to be excluded, the co-operation of the princes was essential. The Golden Bull undoubtedly contributed to a restoration of peace and order and established the constitutional framework for German political life down to the peace of Westphalia in 1648.

Returning to Germany in July 1355 after his coronation as emperor in Rome, Charles IV immediately summoned the princes to deliberations at Nürnberg, which resulted in the promulgation of the first 23 chapters of the Golden Bull on Jan. 10, 1356; the concluding 8 chapters were added after further negotiation with the princes in Metz on Dec. 25, 1356. Much of the lengthy document is taken up with electoral ceremonial, questions of precedence and other details that it was necessary to define to avoid controversy. The purpose was to place the election of the German ruler firmly in the hands of the seven electors and to ensure that the candidate elected by the majority should succeed without dispute. That the electoral college (see ELECTORS) consisted of three ecclesiastical and four lay princes had been established since 1273; but it was not always clear who these seven were. Therefore the Saxon vote was now attached to the Wittenberg (not the Lauenburg) branch of the Saxon dynasty; the vote was given to the count Palatine (not to the duke of Bavaria); and the special position of Bohemia, of which Charles himself was king, was expressly recognized. In addition Charles established succession by primogeniture, attached the electoral vote to the possession of certain lands, and decreed that these territories should never be divided. The candidate elected by the majority was regarded as unanimously elected and entitled to exercise his royal rights immediately. Thus the pope's claim to examine rival candidates and to approve the election was ignored. Furthermore, by instituting the duke of Saxony and the count Palatine as regents during the vacancy, the Golden Bull excluded the pope's claim to act as vicar.

These results were achieved only by concessions to the electoral princes, who were given sovereign rights, including tallage and coinage, in their principalities. Appeals by their subjects were severely curtailed; conspiracies against them incurred the penalties of treason. Moreover, the efforts of cities to ensure autonomous development were repressed, with serious and long-lasting consequences for the future of the German middle classes. In theory, these privileges were confined to the seven electors; in practice, the princes as a body quickly adopted them.

There is an edition of the text, with commentary, by K. Zeumer, *Die goldene Bulle Kaiser Karls IV* (1909).

See J. Bryce, *The Holy Roman Empire*, new ed. (1906, with reprints); G. Barraclough, *The Origins of Modern Germany* (1946). (G. Bн.)

GOLDEN CALF, a Hebrew object of worship mentioned specifically in the Old Testament in connection with Aaron (Ex. xxxii; *cf.* Ps. cvi, 19 ff.) and Jeroboam I (I Kings xii, 25–30). The making of such a calf (more correctly a bull) by Jeroboam is referred to throughout both books of Kings as the supreme act of apostasy, but Jeroboam's intention was to stabilize his kingdom by continuing an ancient Canaanite practice. He transferred to Yahweh the ancient mode of representing Baal by placing a calf in both the early shrines at Bethel and Dan. Bull worship (condemned in Hos. x. 5; xiii, 2) continued until the end of the northern kingdom, and Josephus describes a golden heifer at the northern shrine in the 1st century A.D. It is not certain whether Yahweh was represented as a bull himself, or as standing on a bull. There is a representation from Arslan-Tash in northern Syria of Hadad Baal standing on the back of a bull, and Ugaritic texts actually refer to him as a bull. Yahweh is probably described in the Old Testament as the "bull" of Israel (though English versions usually translate the term as "mighty one"; *e.g.*, Gen. xlix. 24; Ps. cxxxii, 2, 5; Isa. i, 24), but the practice of representing him thus was officially forbidden in the Deuteronomic reform (*cf.* II Kings xxiii, 15).

The account of Aaron's making a golden calf for the Israelites to worship during Moses' absence on Mt. Sinai (Ex. xxxii) seems originally to have been part of the cult story associated with the shrines of Bethel and Dan. The connection of Aaron with the making of the image, together with the sacred dance, feasting and licentious conduct (all indicating a fertility cult), may be regarded as original. But in its present form, modified by later exilic thought that was in opposition to the Aaronic priesthood, the event furnishes an occasion for the selection of the Levites.

See T. J. Meek, *Hebrew Origins*, rev. ed. (1950). (A. S. H.)

GOLDEN CLUB (*Orontium aquaticum*), a North American aquatic plant of the arum family (Araceae; *q.v.*), found in shallow ponds and less frequently in swamps from Massachusetts to Florida, chiefly near the coast. This handsome aroid, the only species of the genus, is sometimes transplanted in water gardens. It is a somewhat fleshy perennial, with thick oblong, ascending or floating leaves, five to ten inches long, and bearing in early spring a narrow but dense cluster (spike) of small bright yellow flowers, terminating a flattened stalk, six inches to two feet long, which rises above the water.

GOLDENEYE, a diving duck (*Bucephala* or *Glaucionetta*), breeding in far northern regions, from where it migrates south in winter. It nests in hollow trees and in burrows along banks of inland water. The adult male is mainly black above, with a round, white eye patch and white scapulars; the lower parts are white, the legs orange; in the female dark brown replaces black. An elaborate courtship, during which the drake may dive and bob up just in front of the female, occurs in the early spring. Goldeneyes are known also as whistlers, from their swift whistling flight.

The European goldeneye (*B. clangula clangula*) breeds across the northern half of Europe and Asia to the limit of trees; the American goldeneye (*B. c. americana*) is found in Canada and the plains border states; and the Barrow's goldeneye (*B. islandica*), which has a crescent-shaped instead of a round white spot in front of the eye, in the mountains from Alaska to Colorado, and in Labrador, Greenland and Iceland. They winter south to the Mediterranean and Burma, South Carolina and California, rarely to the Gulf of Mexico. (G. F. Ss.; X.)

GOLDEN FLEECE, in Greek mythology, the fleece of the ram on which Phrixus and Helle escaped. (*See* ARGONAUTS.) For knighthood of the Golden Fleece *see* KNIGHTHOOD, CHIVALRY AND ORDERS: *History: The Secular Orders of Medieval Christendom*.

GOLDEN GATE, a strait in California, U.S., connecting San Francisco bay with the Pacific ocean, and separating San Francisco from Marin county. The Gate is about three miles long and from one to two miles wide. Its channel is more than 300 ft. deep. In an earlier geologic period, the strait was the lower end of a river which poured fresh water into the Pacific, but subsidence of land in the region and a rise in the ocean level brought invasion by sea water and the formation of the present magnificent bay. The Gate may have been seen by Sir Francis Drake in 1579, but the effective discovery was made by Spanish explorers (1769–75). The name apparently originated with John C. Frémont and became popular during the gold rush period.

Although the strait is the ocean gateway to San Francisco and its harbour, it constituted a barrier to land travel in the area until the construction (1933–37) of the famous Golden Gate bridge at a cost of $35,000,000. A suspension bridge, with a central span of 4,200 ft. and towers that rise 746 ft. above the water, it was built by Joseph B. Strauss for a special bridge district consisting of six counties; it was financed by bonds secured by revenues from tolls and also by the general taxing powers of the San Francisco-Oakland Bay bridge. The latter, built by the state with federal aid at a cost of $77,000,000, consists of two suspension bridges over the west channel, a tunnel through Yerba Buena Island and a cantilever span over the east channel. Double-decked, it is over four miles long (over eight miles long counting approaches).

In 1939 San Francisco celebrated these great achievements in bridge building at its Golden Gate exposition on Treasure Island. *See also* San Francisco. (D. E. F.)

GOLDEN GLOW, a double-flowered cultivated variety (*Rudbeckia lacinata hortensis*) of a tall coneflower (*q.v.*), native to North America, widely grown in the United States, Canada and England as an ornamental plant. It is a showy summer bloomer, usually four feet to seven feet high, with smooth, much-branched stems, more or less divided leaves and numerous flowering heads 2½ to 3½ in. across, crowded with brilliant golden-yellow much-doubled ray flowers.

Originally derived from a weedy herb common from Quebec to Florida and westward, the cultivated golden glow has become ubiquitous in the garden. It has propensity to spread. To some gardeners the plant is a coarse, invasive perennial. (N. Tr.)

GOLDEN HORDE (Russian *Zolotaya Orda*), the Russian designation of the khanate of Kipchak, the westernmost Mongol empire, which from the middle of the 13th century to the end of the 15th remained a major political factor in eastern Europe and the middle east.

The ill-defined "western parts" of Chingis (Jenghiz or Genghis) Khan's empire formed the appanage of his oldest son, Juchi, who, however, predeceased his father (1227). Juchi's son Batu (*q.v.*), in a series of brilliant campaigns, expanded its frontiers to encompass most of European Russia, from the Urals to the Carpathians. It is difficult to know how far east and north into Siberia the lands of the Golden Horde extended. In the south the Black sea, the Caucasus, the northern shores of the Caspian and the frontier with the Il-khanid empire (in Persia) formed its approximate borders. Batu, who, though virtually independent, never ceased to recognize the suzerainty of the great khan, died in 1255.

Under the rule of Berke (1255–66), Batu's brother, the Golden Horde became more autonomous, an evolution partially caused by Berke's conversion to Islam, which made him a reluctant partner in the Mongol campaign against the caliphate and a natural ally of the Mamelukes of Egypt. The creation of such a north-south axis, via Constantinople, had incalculable consequences: it built a Muslim barrier between Europe and the pro-Christian Il-khans, opened Russia to Muslim influences, both cultural and commercial, and created an antagonism between the lands of Russia and Persia. Though Berke's immediate successors were not Muslims, the final conversion of the khan Uzbek (1312–42) confirmed Islamic preponderance within the Golden Horde. Mutual tolerance notwithstanding, the religious difference prevented the Turkish-speaking populations of the horde from amalgamating with the Christian Slavs. The purely Mongol elements had been quite insignificant even initially and were soon absorbed by the various Turkish contingents which constituted the bulk of the Mongol army. It was thus an Islamic, Turkish nation of cattle breeders that held the key position on the great traditional south-north trade routes and was to exert an overpowering influence on the destinies of the Slavs.

The Mongol invasion of Russia in 1237–40 did more than destroy a few cities; it brought to an abrupt end the promising evolution of Kievan Russia. Muscovite Russia, which was to emerge from the receding Mongol tide, was geographically, socially and culturally a different state, ruled from a capital more distant from the European centre of gravity than Kiev had been. Moreover, the Mongol presence, an alien element in the Slav world, greatly impeded the natural interactions of political forces and enabled Lithuania to gain control of a large part of western Russia. There resulted the split of the formerly united Russian nation into Russians proper (or Great Russians), Ukrainians and Belorussians.

The eyes of the khans of the Golden Horde were directed southward and eastward rather than toward Europe, and Mongol interest in the internal affairs of the Russian princes was small. The choice of Sarai Batu (1243), on the lower Volga, as their capital testifies to this orientation; and Sarai Berke, to which Uzbek transferred the capital, was still in the south, about 30 mi. E. of present-day Volgograd (formerly Stalingrad). This splendid town of about 600,000 inhabitants, with its beautiful mosques, water mains, centrally heated houses and public baths, its busy Egyptian and Syrian merchants and craftsmen, was a cross product of Muslim and central Asian civilizations.

To rule under the Mongols, Russian princes had to receive a patent (*yarlyk*) from the khan. This was usually granted to the local candidate, provided that he was likely to keep his people under control and be efficient in collecting the taxes. This task, originally performed by the Mongols themselves, was later left to the Russians. It was in their capacity as tax collectors that the khans most appreciated the Muscovite princes, who could thus consolidate their power. In the second half of the 14th century internecine wars much weakened the Golden Horde and led the Russian princes to refuse payment of taxes. The decisive blow, however, came from Timur (*q.v.*), who in 1395, in a campaign against his former protégé Tokhtamish, destroyed Sarai Berke. The Golden Horde split into three parts of which the Crimean khanate (see CRIMEA) survived till the end of the 18th century. *See also* KIPCHAK; MONGOL EMPIRES; RUSSIAN HISTORY.

BIBLIOGRAPHY.—Bertold Spuler, *Die Goldene Horde: die Mongolen in Russland, 1223–1502*, 2nd ed. (1965); G. Vernadsky, *The Mongols and Russia* (1953); B. D. Grekov and A. Y. Yakubovski, *Zolotaya Orda i ee padenie* ("The Golden Horde and Its Downfall," 1950). (Ds. Sr.)

GOLDEN MOLE, a burrowing molelike animal, species of which belong to the south African family Chrysochloridae, order Insectivora (*see* INSECTIVORE). They are named from the bright metallic bronze, green or violet lustre of their rich brown fur. Although resembling true moles (*q.v.*) in habits and to some extent in appearance, they differ in several anatomical features, among them being the possession of enormous claws on the two middle digits of the forelimbs.

GOLDEN-RAIN TREE, a Chinese tree, *Koelreuteria paniculata*, widely grown as an ornamental. It has leaves with 7–15 leaflets that are arranged alternately or in pairs along a central stalk and are toothed, lobed or divided into smaller leaflets. The yellow summer-blooming flowers, borne in clusters terminating the branches, produce three-angled, inflated, papery capsules about two inches long, containing three to six round, brown to black seeds.

The tree, which grows to 40 ft. tall and attains a trunk diameter of 2 ft., is easily raised from seed. It does well in ordinary soil, prefers full sun and is hardy as far north as northern Illinois. In some areas it is called "pride-of-India," a name properly belonging to *Melia azedarach*, the Chinaberry or China-tree. The golden-rain tree is a member of the soapberry family (Sapindaceae). (J. W. Tr.)

GOLDENROD, the popular name for plants of the genus *Solidago*, of the family Compositae (*q.v.*), comprising about 120 species, natives chiefly of North America, a few, however, occurring in the old world and in South America. They are erect perennial herbs, mostly from two to eight feet high, often unbranched or slightly branched, with undivided, toothed or entire, sessile or almost sessile leaves and very numerous small heads of brilliant yellow (rarely white) flowers arranged in conspicuous terminal or axillary clusters. Hybridization between closely related species occurs freely in nature, making species identification difficult.

JOHN H. GERARD

TALL GOLDENROD (SOLIDAGO ALTISSIMA)

The European goldenrod (*S. virgaurea*), the only British species, bearing a long cluster of showy flower heads, is found in woods and thickets. It is one of the best garden plants of the genus; many other species also are cultivated for ornament, especially *S. canadensis*, *S. cutleri* and the seaside goldenrod, *S. sempervirens*. The goldenrods are characteristic plants in eastern North America, where about 60 species occur. They are found almost everywhere—in woodlands, swamps, on mountains, in fields and along roadsides.

With the asters, whose bright colours they complement, the goldenrods form one of the chief floral glories of autumn from the Great Plains eastward to the Atlantic. While numerous handsome species occur in the Rocky mountain region and on the Pacific coast, they are less abundant and conspicuous than in the eastern states. Among the best-known eastern species are the early goldenrod (*S. juncea*), the late goldenrod (*S. gigantea*), the tall goldenrod (*S. altissima*), the Canada goldenrod (*S. canadensis*), the dwarf goldenrod (*S. nemoralis*), the wreath goldenrod (*S. caesia*), the pale goldenrod or silverrod (*S. bicolor*), the sweet goldenrod (*S. odora*) and the showy goldenrod (*S. speciosa*). Among the western species are *S. occidentalis*, found from the Rocky mountains westward; *S. californica*, the *oreja de liebre* ("rabbit's ear") of the Spanish Californians; and the coast goldenrod (*S. spathulata*) of central Californian shores. The copious pollen of most species is responsible for many cases of hay fever. (N. Tr.)

GOLDEN ROSE, an ornament made of wrought gold and set with gems, generally sapphires, which is blessed by the pope on the fourth Sunday in Lent (Laetare Sunday) and sent, as one of the highest honours he

PALAZZO PUBBLICO, SIENA

GOLDEN ROSE WITH FOUR PRINCIPAL BRANCHES. ROSES AND FOLIAGE IN GOLD, AND A HANGING BERYL. GIVEN TO CITY OF SIENA BY POPE PIUS II IN 1458; MADE BY SIMONE DI FIRENZE

can confer, to some distinguished individual, ecclesiastical body or religious community or, failing a worthy recipient, kept in the Vatican. Many of these historical examples of the goldsmith's art, being of great value, have been melted down. The origin of the custom is obscure, the first reliable accounts dating from the 11th century. Of more symbolic than material significance, the rose was usually sent, like the papal cap and sword, for political as well as religious reasons, together with an explanatory letter. Three were sent to Henry VIII of England, the first in 1510 by Julius II seeking support against Louis XII of France. In 1684 one was sent to the wife of John Sobieski, who aided Vienna against the Turks.

Princess Charlotte of Nassau, grand duchess of Luxembourg, was accorded the golden rose in 1956.

See Sir C. Young, *Ornaments and Gifts Consecrated by the Roman Pontiffs* (1864).

GOLDEN RULE, the name in English, at least since the mid-16th century, for the precept in Matt. 7:12 (Luke 6:31): "So whatever you wish that men would do to you, do so to them." The name implied that this rule of conduct excelled all other rules as gold was deemed to excel all other metals. It is a summary of the Christian's duty to his neighbour and states a fundamental ethical principle. In its negative form, "Do not do to others what you would not like done to yourselves," it occurs in the 2nd-century documents *Didache* and the *Apology of Aristides* and may well have formed part of an early catechism. In the Matthaean version Jesus himself says that it is "the law and the prophets," and it recalls the command to "love the stranger (sojourner)" as found in Tob. 4:15, and again in Hillel and Philo.

Beyond this, it appears in one form or another in Plato, Aristotle, Isocrates, and Seneca, to say nothing of the "reciprocity" principle enunciated by Confucius.

The negative form, repeated by Thomas Hobbes, is hardly a satisfactory principle of ethics, since it gives no incentive to active benevolence. Even the positive form might be said to require some limiting term such as "whatever *good* things you would like men to do to you," for a man might conceivably wish some evil to be done him, as for instance in a suicide pact. Still such criticism is misplaced: in the Gospels the principle is set forth as a general exhortation, not as a scientific definition.

Modern moralists recognize its importance, and Christian writers in particular emphasize it as a first principle. Charles Gore (*Philosophy of the Good Life*, 1930) regards it as an instruction in the practical carrying out of the second great commandment in the law (Lev. 19:18; Mark 12:31), "You shall love your neighbor as yourself." This love he explains as no mere sentimental feeling but as the set of the will issuing in action. William Temple (*Nature, Man and God*, 1934) maintains that if the ground of all the universe of our being is personal love we may penetrate to it and so find the power to will aright.

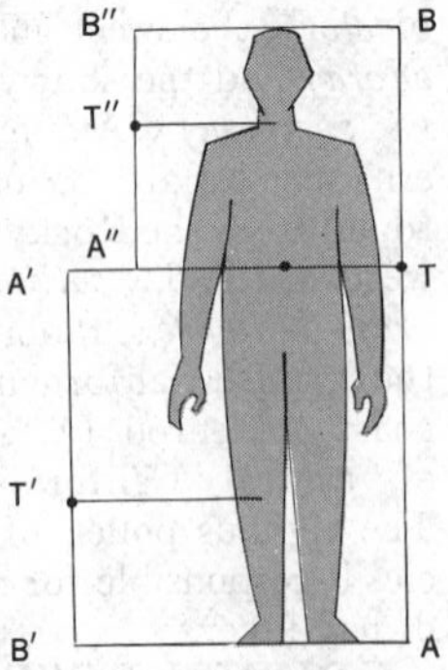

In the mid-20th century exponents of Situation Ethics claimed that the Golden Rule is not simply the dominant principle but the only principle essential to the living of the good life. It can, however, be easily shown that life would be immeasurably more brutish if such principles as truth, honour, and justice were left in abeyance.

It is a nice question whether, in a conflict of duties, the Golden Rule should override all other ethical principles. In a case of projected euthanasia, or of revealing to a patient the gravity of an illness, is what one would like to have done to oneself the best guide? (J. W. C. W.)

GOLDEN SECTION, or extreme and mean ratio, is the division of a length such that the smaller part is to the greater as the greater is to the whole. It is much used

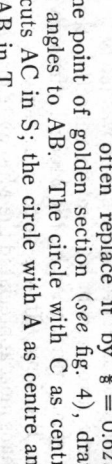

FIG. 1.—HEIGHT OF HUMAN BODY DIVIDED IN GOLDEN SECTION AT NAVEL, T; LOWER PORTION IS FURTHER DIVIDED AT KNEE, T', WHILE UPPER PORTION IS DIVIDED AT THE THROAT, T'

as a "key" or "proportion" in design, linking different parts numerically or geometrically. The main measurements of many buildings of antiquity and of the middle ages follow a key; those of the low as a key; those of the Parthenon on the Acropolis of Athens are governed by the golden section. Architects, sculptors and painters of all times have used keys. The Franco-Swiss architect Le Corbusier has developed a scale (the Modulor), based on the human body, whose height is taken as divided in golden section at the navel (fig. 1). The golden section is a frequent norm for modern industrial design; it is also much found in animals and plants. It is pleasing and harmonious to the human eye (for instance the "golden" rectangle whose sides are in the ratio of golden section,

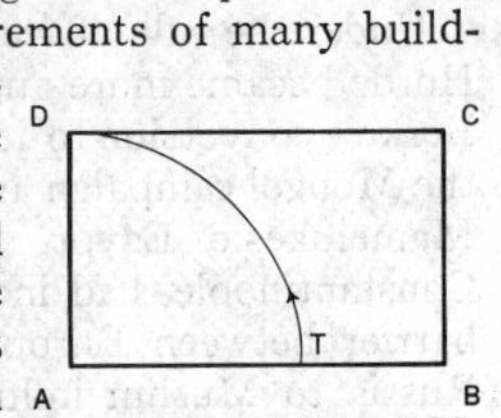

FIG. 2.—GOLDEN REC-TANGLE HAS SHORT AND LONG SIDES IN RATIO OF THE GOLDEN SECTION

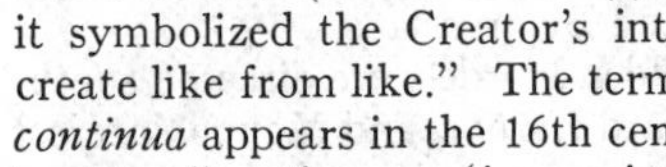

fig. 2).

The golden section was discovered by the Greeks about the middle of the 5th century B.C., probably from the regular pentagon: its diagonals form the pentagram, which contains 200 golden ratios. The pentagram goes back to Babylonian culture; the Pythagoreans used it as a sign of salvation.

FIG. 3.—RATIOS OF MAJOR AND MINOR SEGMENTS OF LINE DIVIDED IN THE GOLDEN SECTION (see TEXT)

The Greek term for the golden section is "the division of a line in extreme and mean proportion." The Italian mathematician Luca Pacioli called it *divina proportione* (divine proportion); the German Johannes Kepler (d. 1630) called it *sectio divina* (divine section), for to him it symbolized the Creator's intention, "to create like from like." The term *proportio continua* appears in the 16th century; probably by translation this became "continuous (*i.e.*, uninterrupted) division," in the 18th century. The term "golden section" first appears in 1830.

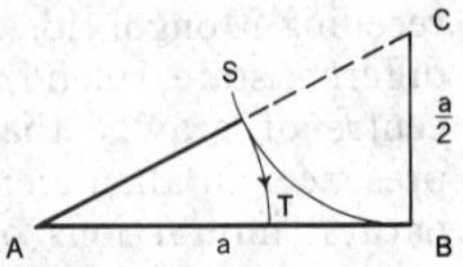

Fig. 3 shows a line AB = a, divided in golden section at T, with M the major and a − M = m the minor segment, and a/M = M/(a − M). This gives M/a = 0.618 . . . , the golden number, which is irrational (an unending decimal); architects and artists often replace it by $\frac{5}{8}$ = 0.625.

FIG. 4.—METHOD OF CONSTRUCTING POINT T OF GOLDEN SECTION OF LINE AB

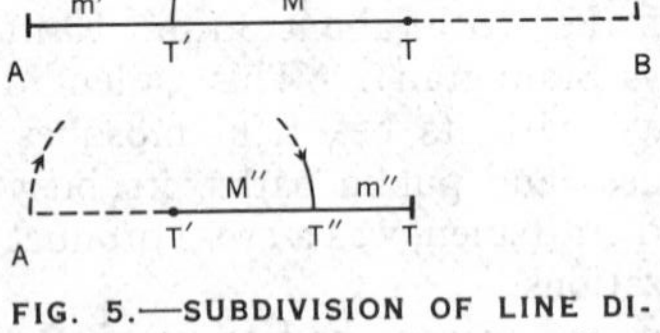

To construct T, the point of golden section of AB, draw BC = a/2 at right angles to AB. The circle with C as centre and a/2 as radius cuts AC in S; the circle with A as centre and AS as radius cuts AB in T.

FIG. 5.—SUBDIVISION OF LINE DIVIDED IN GOLDEN SECTION: T' IS POINT OF SECTION OF SEGMENT TT'

In art, the foremost property of the golden section is this (see fig. 5): cutting TA at T' so that TT' = TB, the line TA is now divided in golden section at T', with T'T' = M' its major segment. T'T' can be similarly divided at T'' with T'T'' = M'' its major segment, and so on. This leads to a series of decreasing lines cut in golden section without further construction, and to a series of increasing lines likewise cut (see fig. 6): extending BA to T₁ with T₁A = AT, the line BT₁ is cut in golden section at A. Setting a = 1, gives the ratios:

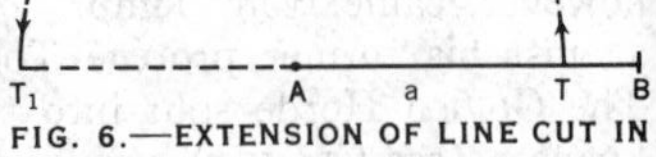

$$\cdots : 0.145 : 0.236 : 0.382 : 0.618 : 1 : 1.618 : 2.618 \cdots$$
$$\cdots : TT' : AT : AB : TB \cdots$$

FIG. 6.—EXTENSION OF LINE CUT IN GOLDEN SECTION: A BECOMES POINT OF SECTION OF SEGMENT BT₁

See P. H. Scholfield, *Theory of Proportion in Architecture* (1958). (K. ME.)

GOLDENWEISER, ALEXANDER (1880–1940), U.S. anthropologist whose interests embraced a broad spectrum of cultural problems, was born on Jan. 29, 1880, in Kiev, Russia, and went to the United States in 1900. He studied anthropology under Franz Boas at Columbia university, where he took his Ph.D. in 1910 and lectured in anthropology from 1910 to 1919. He subsequently taught at the Rand School of Social Science, the New School for Social Research, the University of Oregon and Reed college.

Goldenweiser did field research among the Iroquois and published the first American textbook in anthropology (*Early Civilization*, 1922; rev. ed., *Anthropology*, 1937). In *Totemism* (1910) he stressed the psychological factors common to different tribal cultures. In dealing with problems of diffusion v. independent invention of culture traits he introduced the principle of limited possibilities, showing that in many cases this principle explained similarities in a satisfactory manner. He pointed out that diffusion was not a mechanical process but depended partly on the receptivity of cultures to proffered traits. He was interested in primitive man's knowledge and in primitive science, theoretical and applied. He noted the tendency toward overelaboration of a trait or a complex, especially in art, which he called "involution." His analyses and interpretations of cultural problems ranged widely, encompassing intellectual movements in psychology and psychoanalysis. He died on July 6, 1940, in Portland, Ore.

For bibliography, *see* Wilson D. Wallis, "Alexander Goldenweiser," *American Anthropologist*, vol. 43, no. 2, pp. 252–253 (April–June 1941). (W. D. WA.)

GOLDFADEN, ABRAHAM (1840–1908), Hebrew and Yiddish poet and playwright, originator of Yiddish theatre and opera, was born in Old Constantine, Russia, on July 12, 1840. He published volumes of Hebrew and Yiddish poems prior to his graduation from a rabbinical seminary at Zhitomir in 1866. He then taught in Russia until migrating in 1875 to Poland, where he founded two Yiddish newspapers. After moving to Rumania, he organized at Jassy in 1876 what is generally recognized as the first Yiddish theatre. In 1878 he returned to Russia with his troupe, gaining considerable success until the prohibition of Yiddish plays in 1883.

After moving again to Poland, he revived his theatre in Warsaw under a German guise. In 1887 he migrated to New York city, where he established the first illustrated Yiddish periodical and worked with the Roumanian Opera House. He went to London in 1889 and reorganized the Yiddish theatre that had been founded there in 1888. In 1903 he settled in New York and opened a dramatic school. His best-known works are *Shulamit* (1880) and *Bar Kochba* (1882). Since many of his dramatic works are set to his own music, he is also considered to be the founder of Yiddish opera. He died in New York on Jan. 19, 1908. (O. G. B.)

GOLD FERN, a handsome American fern (*Pityrogramma triangularis*), native to the Pacific coast region from Alaska to Lower California, so called because the leaves (fronds) are coated beneath with a yellow powder. The dark-brown, glossy leafstalks (stipes), 6 in. to 12 in. high, rise from the rootstock in tufts, and bear triangular-shaped, somewhat leathery leaves, three to four inches long and broad, which are more or less deeply cut into rounded lobes.

A related tropical American species, *P. calomelanos*, popular in greenhouse cultivation, with whitish powder on the undersurface of the fronds, is called silver fern; but a variety with gold-coloured powder is called gold fern.

See also FERN.

GOLDFIELD, a mining ghost town in the desert in southwestern Nevada, U.S., is the seat of Esmeralda county. Rich gold ore was discovered there in 1902 and the ensuing rush resulted in a city with an estimated population of 40,000. The mining boom lasted from 1903 to 1918, although the production of the mines started dropping off at the end of 1910, when production of ore reached an all-time high valued at more than $11,000,000. The mines were the scene of a bitter labour struggle in 1907 and 1908, resulting from a conflict between the miners (organized as a branch of the Western Federation of Miners) and the operators. In December 1907 federal troops under Gen. Frederick Funston were stationed in the town, following an appeal to Pres. Theodore Roosevelt by the governor, John Sparks, and remained there until March 7, 1908. Following their withdrawal work was gradually resumed, on the operators' terms.

After 1918 Goldfield's population decreased rapidly to less than 200. The 200-room Goldfield hotel was closed, although it was reopened briefly during World War II to accommodate the servicemen stationed at nearby Tonopah air force station. In the second half of the 20th century tourists kept the few people still living in Goldfield in business. (D. W. Ds.)

GOLDFISH (*Carassius auratus*), a fish belonging to the carp family (Cyprinidae) and native to eastern Asia but introduced into many other parts of the world. Its many breeds have long been popular as aquarium and pond ornamentals. It is closely related to the crucian carp (*Carassius carassius*) of Europe and northern Asia; both species resemble the common carp (*Cyprinus carpio*) in having a long dorsal fin, but differ from it in having no barbels. Goldfish were first domesticated by the Chinese at least as early as the Sung dynasty (960–1279). They later were introduced into Japan about 1500, Europe around 1700 and into America around 1875.

In the natural state the colour is usually greenish-brown or gray, and the form of the body and ot the fins is similar to that of the common carp. However, this species is extremely plastic: individuals occur, for example, in which the brown or black pigment is absent or restricted to spots; some may be golden or all white, or white with silvery patches; and still others may be jet black. Numerous other abnormalities occur: the dorsal fin may be absent, the tail fin trilobed, the eyes may protrude excessively. Chinese aquariists, observing these variations, conceived the idea of selecting out such abnormal specimens and breeding them to develop strains having particularly desired qualities. As a result of centuries of careful experiments in China and Japan, more than 125 breeds of fancy goldfishes have been produced.

Goldfish are omnivorous, feeding on minute invertebrates, especially small crustaceans; insect larvae; worms; eggs of frogs; snails and fish; and a variety of aquatic plants. The growth of the young, as well as the form and colour of the adults, depends on proper feeding. The best food for all ages of goldfish is small crustaceans, and aquariists devote much care to cultivating these organisms. This diet may be supplemented with chopped mosquito larvae, small aquatic worms, pulverized yolks of hard-boiled eggs, scraped raw lean beef, cereal, etc.

Goldfish spawn for the first time when they are a year old and continue each year thereafter for six, seven or even more years. The spawning season occurs in the spring or summer, depending on the temperature. As the season approaches, the colours become brighter, the abdomen of the female enlarges (owing to

VEILTAIL GOLDFISH

TROPICAL FISH HOBBYIST MAGAZINE

enlargement of the ovaries) and the males often develop temporary minute excrescences, each about the size of a pinhead, on the gill covers and sometimes also on the back and the pectoral fins. Before spawning, the fish become extremely active, the males chasing the females, at first aimlessly but gradually more purposefully, back and forth across the aquarium, bumping their abdomens to facilitate the release of the eggs. The eggs then sink and adhere by means of their sticky surface to aquatic plants, on which they will hatch in eight or nine days (at 65° F.). In captivity goldfish have been known to live for 25 years; however, the average life span is usually much shorter.

Escaping from ornamental pools in parks and gardens, the goldfish has become naturalized in many ponds and streams of the eastern United States, notably in the Potomac river. In some localities it occurs in sufficient abundance to be marketed as a food fish. Upon resuming life under natural conditions, it reverts to its original greenish-brown colour and usually attains a length of 6 to 12 in. *See also* AQUARIUM.

See also H. R. Axelrod and W. Vorderwinkler, *Goldfish in Your Home* (1958); W. T. Innes, *Goldfish Varieties and Water Gardens* (1960). (L. A. WD.)

GOLDIE, SIR GEORGE DASHWOOD TAUBMAN (1846–1925), British colonial administrator and founder of the Royal Niger company, was born on May 20, 1846, at the Nunnery, Isle of Man, the youngest son of Lieut. Col. John Taubman Goldie-Taubman, speaker of the house of keys. Sir George resumed his paternal name, Goldie, by royal licence in 1887. He was educated at the Royal Military academy, Woolwich, and commissioned in the Royal Engineers in 1865, but resigned his commission in 1867. He traveled for several years in Africa, principally in Egypt and the Sudan, and first visited west Africa in 1877, when he conceived the idea of uniting the British trading firms on the lower Niger river, then in cutthroat competition, into a chartered company to govern the area for the crown.

Goldie had combined all British commercial interests on the Niger into a single United African company by 1879, but his application for a royal charter was refused in 1881 on the grounds that British influence was not paramount in the Niger area. The company bought out the only two competing French firms in 1884, thus enabling the British government to claim at the Berlin conference (1884–85) that British interests were supreme on the lower Niger. A British sphere of influence was recognized and Goldie's company received its charter in July 1886 and took the name of the Royal Niger company. Goldie became vice-governor of the company and was made governor in 1895 on the death of the first holder of that post, Lord Aberdare.

Under the charter the company was authorized to administer the country on the banks of the Niger and Benue rivers, together with the hinterland, and Goldie was largely responsible for the organization of the new government. He kept a close watch on its activities and in 1897 organized and accompanied a force of the company's troops against the slave-raiding states of Nupe and Ilorin. Goldie also initiated and took part in negotiations with the French and German governments which settled the boundaries of the British sphere of influence administered by the company. It was clear, however, that a chartered company was at a disadvantage in dealing with international questions and the charter was accordingly revoked, the British government taking direct control of the company's territories on Jan. 1, 1900. The ceded territories together with the small Niger Coast Protectorate (already under direct control of the government) were formed into the two protectorates of northern and southern Nigeria.

From the first, and throughout the period of the charter, Goldie guided the destinies of the company and took an active part in its administration, with a scrupulous respect for the rights of the African inhabitants. It was largely due to his inspiration, perseverance and administrative ability that northern Nigeria became later an orderly and prosperous British protectorate, and subsequently one of the regions of an independent Nigeria.

Goldie visited Rhodesia in 1903–04 to examine the question of self-government by the Rhodesians. In 1902–03 and in 1905–06 he was a member of royal commissions set up in connection with the South African War. From 1908 to 1919 he was an alderman of the London County council and chairman of its finance committee. He was a fellow of the Royal society and was president of the Royal Geographical society from 1905 to 1908. He was for two periods president of the National Defence association. Goldie was created knight commander of the order of St. Michael and St. George in 1887 and was made a privy councilor in 1898. He died in London on Aug. 20, 1925.

See Dorothy Wellesley, *Sir George Goldie* (1934); J. E. Flint, *Sir George Goldie* (1960). (A. C. Bs.)

GOLDMAN, EMMA (1869–1940), international anarchist, was born in Kovno, Lith., June 27, 1869. The daughter of a government theatre manager, she spent her early life in Königsberg and St. Petersburg. She emigrated to the United States in 1885 and worked in a clothing factory in Rochester, N.Y., where she attended meetings of German socialists. Later she worked in New Haven, Conn., where she met a group of Russian anarchists.

By 1889 Emma Goldman had espoused anarchism and had moved to New York city where she became associated with the Russian anarchist Alexander Berkman. In 1892 he was sentenced to a 22-year jail term for the attempted assassination of Henry C. Frick during the Homestead steel strike in Pittsburgh, Pa. Emma Goldman continued her activities as an anarchist lecturer despite one year in prison for inciting a riot in New York city in 1893. After Berkman's release in 1906 she resumed her association with him. They carried on anarchist activities until 1917 when they were arrested for obstructing the military draft and served two years in prison. They were deported to Russia in 1919. Although Emma Goldman had previously favoured the Soviet government, her stay in Russia disillusioned her. She went to England and later to Canada and Spain, meanwhile writing *My Disillusionment in Russia* and her autobiography, *Living My Life*. She died in Toronto, May 14, 1940, on a trip to Canada.

See Ishill, *Emma Goldman, a Challenging Rebel* (1957). (B. Mr.)

GOLDMARK, KARL (1830–1915), Hungarian composer of operas and violin music. The son of a poor Jewish cantor, he was born May 18, 1830, at Keszthely. He studied the violin in Vienna under Leopold Jansa and J. Böhm and elementary theory under G. Preyer. In composition he was self-taught. Following the success of his String Quartet, opus 8 (1860), he wrote the overture *Sakuntala* (1865) and his most successful opera, *Die Königin von Saba* (Vienna, 1875). During this period he was also known as a piano teacher and critic. Among his later operas are *Götz von Berlichingen* (Budapest, 1902) and *Ein Wintermärchen*, after Shakespeare's *A Winter's Tale* (Vienna, 1908). His work, showing the influence of Hungarian folk music and of Mendelssohn and Wagner, also includes two violin concertos, two symphonies, choral and chamber works. He died at Vienna, Jan. 2, 1915.

His nephew, RUBIN GOLDMARK (b. New York city, 1872; died there, 1936), a pupil of Dvorak, was the teacher of Aaron Copland, George Gershwin and other U.S. composers, and in 1924 was appointed head of the composition department of the Juilliard School of Music.

See L. Koch (ed.), *Karl Goldmark* (1930); E. T. Rice, *Address in Memory of Rubin Goldmark* (1936).

GOLDONI, CARLO (1707–1793), a prolific Italian dramatist and reformer of the traditional Italian comedy of his day, was born at Venice, on Feb. 25, 1707, the son of a doctor. In 1721 he ran away from school at Rimini with a company of players, and was later expelled (1725) from the Collegio Ghislieri, Pavia, for a satire against the ladies of the town. In 1731 Goldoni took a degree in law at Padua university, after which, as well as holding diplomatic appointments and engaging in various theatrical activities, he practised as a lawyer at Venice (1731–33) and Pisa (1744–48).

The desire to write for the stage was always strong in Goldoni, and in 1734, after making a false start with a lyric tragedy called *Amalasunta* (1732), he joined the Imer company at the San Samuele theatre, Venice. *Belisario*, a tragicomedy in verse, pleased the public, and there he also wrote a number of successful interludes (*La birba*) and scenarios (*Le trentadue disgrazie di Arlec-*

chino) for the *commedia dell'arte* (*q.v.*). However, his belief that comedy ought to "correct defects" made him feel that a radical reform was necessary in the Italian theatre. Wishing to create a comedy of character, he followed the example of Molière and sought to delineate the realities of social life in as natural a manner as possible. His first essays in this style were *Mòmolo cortesan* (1738) and *La donna di garbo* (1743), in which he suppressed improvisation by writing his parts in full and began to free the actors from the traditional practice of wearing masks on the stage. Other plays followed—some interesting for their subject, others for their characters—and in time Goldoni succeeded in replacing the improvised and frequently licentious farce typical of the comic theatre in Italy in his day with a new, yet essentially Italian, comedy of manners that was both moral in tone and a faithful "mirror of life" (*La vedova scaltra*, 1748; *Il cavaliere e la dama*, 1749; *La locandiera*, written 1752, first performed 1753).

Between 1748 and 1762 Goldoni worked as a professional playwright for the companies of Girolamo Medebac and the patrician Francesco Vendramin at the theatres of Sant'Angelo and San Luca (1753-62) in Venice. During this period he effected his dramatic reform. In one season alone (1750-51) he wrote 16 new plays, including *Il teatro comico*, *Pamela* and *La bottega del caffè*, embodying his theories. Throughout these years Goldoni's success was opposed by his rivals, Pietro Chiari and Carlo Gozzi, and in 1762 he left Venice for Paris, where he had been invited to direct the Comédie Italienne (1762-64). Goldoni subsequently taught Italian to the French royal princesses, and for the wedding of Louis XVI he wrote in French one of his best-known works, *Le Bourru bienfaisant* (1771). He also wrote his *Mémoires*, between 1783 and 1787, at Versailles. As a result of the Revolution Goldoni lost his pension and he died in poverty in Paris on Feb. 6?, 1793.

Goldoni wrote in both prose and verse, and in Italian, Venetian dialect and French. He composed librettos for the *opera buffa* and a wealth of occasional verse. His best plays are those in Venetian dialect, such as *I rusteghi* (1760), *La casa nova* (1760) and *Sior Todero brontolon* (1762), and especially the vivid "popular" comedies which mirror the elemental and passionate life of the poor (*Il campiello*, 1756; *Le baruffe chiozzotte*, 1762).

BIBLIOGRAPHY.—Goldoni's complete works were published in 44 vol. (1788-95 and 1827). Modern editions are the *Opere complete*, 39 vol. (1907-54), and *Tutte le opere*, ed. by G. Ortolani, 14 vol. (1935-56). *Opere*, ed. by F. Zampieri, is a good selection in one volume (1954). *Mémoires*, in French, Eng. trans. by John Black (1877). See also G. Ortolani, *Della vita e dell'arte di C. Goldoni* (1907); H. C. Chatfield-Taylor, *Goldoni* (1913); E. Rho, *La missione teatrale di Carlo Goldoni* (1936); M. Dazzi, *Carlo Goldoni e la sua poetica sociale* (1957). (D. M. WE.)

GOLD RESERVES. As distinguished from private hoards of gold held by individuals and nonfinancial institutions, gold reserves have been held from ancient times by kings, princes, governments and banks. The reserves have been accumulated by rulers and governments primarily to meet the costs of waging war, and in most epochs governmental policy has greatly emphasized the acquiring and holding of "treasure." Banks have accumulated gold reserves to redeem their promises to pay their depositors in gold.

During the 19th century banks supplanted governments as the principal holders of gold reserves. Commercial banks received deposits subject to repayment in gold on demand and issued notes (paper money) that were redeemable in gold on demand; hence each bank had to hold a reserve of gold coins to meet redemption demands. In the course of time, however, the preponderant portion of the gold reserves shifted to central banks. As the notes of commercial banks were wholly or largely replaced by notes of the central bank, the commercial banks needed little or no gold for note redemption. The commercial banks also came to depend upon the central bank for gold needed to meet the demands of their depositors.

In the 1930s many governments required their central banks to turn over to the national treasuries all or most of their gold holdings. Thus by the terms of the Gold Reserve act of 1934, the U.S. treasury took title to all gold coin, gold bullion and gold certificates held by the federal reserve banks, giving gold certificates of a new type and gold credits on its books in exchange. The U.S. treasury placed most of its gold reserve at Fort Knox, Ky. But not all governments "nationalized" gold, with the result that the status of gold reserves varies from country to country. In some countries monetary gold reserves are held exclusively by the national government; in others they are held largely by the central bank; and in still others they are held partly by the government and partly by the central bank.

Regardless of the holder, however, the use of gold reserves is now limited almost exclusively to the settlement of international transactions. *See also* GOLD STANDARD; MONEY. (R. P. KE.)

GOLDSBORO, a city in east-central North Carolina, U.S., and the seat of Wayne County, is 3 mi. N of the Neuse River, about 45 mi. SE of Raleigh. An early railway junction, Goldsboro was settled in 1838 and named after M. T. Goldsborough, a civil engineer for one of the railways.

Incorporated in 1847, Goldsboro soon became an important trading and shipping centre for the primarily agricultural North Carolina coastal plain. It has become one of the largest bright-leaf tobacco markets, and in recent years a number of industrial plants have located there. The city adopted the council-manager form of government in 1917.

In the campaign of 1865, near the end of the Civil War, the Union armies under William T. Sherman and John Schofield united there before the final advance to Durham.

A major state mental health complex, consisting of Cherry Hospital and O'Berry Center for Children, is located in Goldsboro and serves the eastern one-third of North Carolina. Also located there are the state Oddfellows Orphans' Home and Seymour Johnson Air Force Base.

Pop. (1960) 28,873, (1970) 26,810. For comparative population figures *see* table in NORTH CAROLINA: *Population*. (DA. ST.)

GOLDSBOROUGH, LOUIS MALESHERBES (1805-1877), U.S. naval officer, was born Feb. 18, 1805, in Washington, D.C. He was senior naval member of a commission that explored California and Oregon in 1849-50, and superintendent of the United States Naval academy, 1853-57. On Sept. 23, 1861, Goldsborough was placed in command of the Atlantic blockading squadron, and on its division later in the year retained command of the North Atlantic squadron, which controlled the Virginia and North Carolina coasts.

His fleet captured Roanoke Island in Feb. 1862 and destroyed Confederate vessels, for which he received the thanks of congress and was promoted to the rank of rear admiral, July 16, 1862. He asked to be relieved of command of the blockading squadron, Sept. 4, 1862, after a dispute over naval participation in the attack on Richmond, and served in Washington until the end of the war. He retired in 1873 and died Feb. 20, 1877. (J. B. HN.)

GOLDSCHMIDT, MEÏR ARON (1819-1887), Danish writer of Jewish descent whose intimate knowledge of the customs and psychology of orthodox Jews in Denmark forms the background of many of his novels and short stories. He was born Oct. 26, 1819, at Vordingborg, and, after going to school in Copenhagen, planned to study medicine but became a journalist instead. In 1840 he founded *Corsaren*, a satirical weekly expressing his radical, republican ideas. His own witty, and often politically ambiguous, contributions made it influential. A feud with Sören Kierkegaard caused him to give up the paper and go abroad in 1846. His first novel, *En Jöde* (1845; Eng. trans., *The Jew of Denmark*, 1852), described the gulf between the Jew and Danish society. It was followed by *Fortællinger* (1846). Returning in 1847, Goldschmidt abandoned radicalism and founded a new periodical, *Nord og Syd*, in which his novel *Hjemlös* (which he himself translated into English as *Homeless*, 1861) was serialized (1853-57). He visited England several times and thought of settling there but decided to remain a Danish writer. In the 1860s he was regarded as Denmark's most important novelist, but later his conservatism created a gulf with the new radical movement led by Georg Brandes. He died at Copenhagen, Aug. 15, 1887. Goldschmidt's finest descriptions of Jewish life are to be found in his short novels, included in collections, "Maser," "Levi og Ibald," *Avromche Nattergal* (1871) and "Mendel Herz," and in *Ravnen* (1867), one of the outstanding Danish novels of the 19th century, in which Jews are depicted with an unusual blend of sympathy and irony. Several works, notably "Erindringer fra min Onkels Hus" (in *Fortællinger*, 1846), describe life in a provincial town. *Hjemløs* and *Arvingen* (1865; Eng. trans., *The Heir*) are based on personal reminiscences. Goldschmidt is an exquisite stylist, especially in his short stories. His philosophy of retributive justice, or nemesis, underlies most of his novels, and also his memoirs, *Livserindringer og Resultater* (1877).

See H. Kyrre, *M. Goldschmidt*, 2 vol. (1919); E. Bredsdorff, *Corsaren* (1941). (E. L. Br.)

GOLDSCHMIDT, VICTOR (1853-1933), German crystallographer, was born in Mainz on Feb. 10, 1853. He studied in the mineral sciences at the Freiberg Mining academy and at Munich, Heidelberg and Vienna. His first major publication was *Index der Krystallformen*, three volumes appearing from 1886 to 1891—a catalogue of the known forms of crystals of all minerals. New tables of angles to meet his new needs were devised, calculated with vast outlay of energy and published in 1897 as *Krystallographische Winkeltabellen*. Next began the compilation and publication of all published figures of crystals of minerals. This *Atlas der Krystallformen* in nine volumes appeared from 1912 to 1923. His interest in number series appearing in crystal symbols expanded to a philosophic theory of number and harmony which led to an analysis of musical harmony, of colour and the development of the colour sense in man and finally to the spacing of the planets about the sun. He died in Salzburg on May 8, 1933. (C. Pe.)

GOLDSCHMIDT, VICTOR MORITZ (1888-1947), Norwegian mineralogist, petrologist and geochemist who not only laid the foundation of a new science of inorganic crystal chemistry but of the modern orientation and much of the impulse to its phenomenal development. Born in Zürich on Jan. 27, 1888, he moved to Christiania (Oslo) in 1900, became a pupil of W. C. Brögger (*q.v.*) and was appointed professor and director of the Mineralogical institute there in 1914. Until 1942 his interests and activities were to be associated with his chair, apart from a period of six years at Göttingen (1929-35). Goldschmidt's achievements in mineralogy and petrology rank in importance with those of his illustrious teacher and predecessor. They were sustained and succeeded by researches of brilliant distinction. Outstanding among his numerous memoirs were *Die Kontaktmetamorphose im Kristiania-Gebiete* (1911); *Die Injektionsmetamorphose im Stavanger Gebiete* (1921); *Geochemische Verteilungsgesetze der Elemente*, 8 vol. (1923-38) and his treatise *Geochemistry*, edited by A. Muir and published posthumously (1954). He became a foreign member of the Royal society in 1943 and died in Oslo on March 20, 1947. (C. E. T.)

GOLDSMID, the name of a family of Anglo-Jewish bankers, descendants of Aaron Goldsmid (d. 1782), a Dutch merchant who settled in England about 1763. Two sons, Benjamin (1753-1808) and Abraham (1756-1810), became important financial brokers in London during the Napoleonic war. A nephew, Sir Isaac Lyon Goldsmid, Bart. (1778-1859), was a successful financier, chiefly known for his efforts to obtain emancipation for Jews in England, and for founding University college in London. In 1841 he was made the first Jewish baronet. His son, Sir Francis Henry Goldsmid (1808-78), became the first Jewish barrister and was a member of parliament in 1860. A grandson of Benjamin, Goldsmid, Sir Frederick John Goldsmid (1818-1908), was director-general of the Indo-European telegraph and helped to settle boundary disputes between Persia and Afghanistan in 1872. (J. R. Lr.)

GOLDSMITH, OLIVER (c. 1730-1774), Anglo-Irish journalist, essayist, novelist, dramatist, and poet, remains one of the foremost names in English literature, which he enriched with such enduring works as *The Vicar of Wakefield*, *The Deserted Village*, and *She Stoops to Conquer*. He was a man irritable and envious, yet lovable and generous; in practical matters often a feckless fool, yet intuitively sane and wise; in talk often ridiculous, yet a writer of Irish liveliness, wit, and unfailing charm.

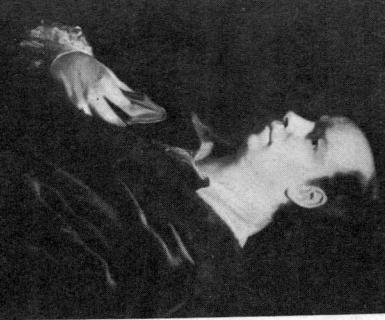

GOLDSMITH: PORTRAIT FROM THE STUDIO OF SIR JOSHUA REYNOLDS, c. 1770

His family, though needy, was less obscure than is sometimes supposed, and had included, on both sides, dignitaries of the church and members of parliament. He was the second son of the Rev. Charles Goldsmith (d. 1747), himself an impoverished younger son, a curate, and small farmer at Pallas in central Ireland, who soon after Oliver's birth there (Nov. 10, probably 1730 or 1731) moved to the adjacent hamlet of Lissoy, near Lough Ree. Kindly, humorous, improvident, Charles Goldsmith seems partly portrayed in *The Vicar of Wakefield*, and in the father of *The Man in Black*. Oliver himself, an ugly, undersized, pock-marked oaf of a boy, often baited, yet capable of sharp or gay retaliations, went to Trinity college, Dublin, in 1745 as a sizar. Often in scrapes with authority, especially with his brutal tutor, the Rev. Theaker Wilder, over shirked work, doused bailiffs or "idle women," he once even fled the university. Having finally graduated, he became, during 1750-52, mainly an indolent playboy at home. He tutored, but quarreled with the family; thought of the church, but was rejected; of the law in London, but lost his ship and his resolution at Cork; of America, but gambled away his good uncle Contarine's £50 in Dublin. Finally (1752-54) he managed to study medicine—without much effect—at Edinburgh and Leiden. Then ensued his famous Grand Tour—on foot, with a flute—through Flanders, France, Switzerland, Italy, and Tirol, till he landed early in 1756, still penniless, at Dover.

Now began a harsh struggle, as an apothecary's assistant, school usher, physician, and hack writer—reviewing, translating, and compiling. In 1758 he was foiled in a scheme for going out to work as a doctor on the Coromandel coast in India. It remains amazing that this young Irish vagabond, unknown, uncouth, unlearned, unreliable, was yet able within a few years to climb from his Grub street gutter to mix with 18th-century aristocrats and the intellectual élite of London. But Goldsmith had one quality, not possess—the gift of style; of being, even on paper, his real self. His rise began with the *Enquiry Into the State of Polite Learning* (1759), a slight work, far from learned, yet already characteristically alive. Soon he emerged as an essayist also, in *The Bee* and other periodicals; above all, in his *Chinese Letters*, collected as *The Citizen of the World* in 1762. The same year brought his *Life of Nash*. Already he was acquiring those distinguished and often helpful friends whom he alternately annoyed and amused, shocked and charmed—Thomas Percy, Dr. Johnson, Sir Joshua Reynolds, David Garrick, Edmund Burke, and James Boswell. The obscure drudge of 1759 became in 1764 one of the nine founder-members of The Club, that select body, including Reynolds, Johnson, and Burke, which met weekly for supper and talk at the Turk's Head in Soho. He could now live better, lodge better, dress better—indeed too well. But he still ran continually into debt, and was forced to undertake more hack work. English, Roman, and Grecian histories; biographies; verse anthologies; translations; works of popular science—the list of them appalls. At times he potboiled his genius to rags. Yet even in his potboiling he was often an excellent cook. And always there was amusing; he cut out the dull and dronish. Many of these makeshift compilations went on being reprinted far into the 19th century. But he was an ill steward of his true excellence. The wonder is that he found time and energy for his lasting works. For he came late to literature, at nearly 30; 15 years later, he was dead. Yet by 1762 he had established himself as an essayist with his *Citizen of the World* (which borrows Montesquieu's device of satirizing western society through oriental eyes, with less daring and wit, but more indulgence and humour"; by 1764 he had won a reputation as poet with *The Traveller*, embodying both his memories of tramping Europe and his political ideas; and in 1770 confirmed that reputation with the more famous *Deserted Village*, which contains some of his most charming portraits and landscapes, while denouncing, with less exaggeration than used to be thought, the evictions of the country poor at the whim of the well-to-do. In 1766 he revealed himself as a novelist with *The Vicar of Wakefield* (completed in 1762)—a book that still lives, however melodramatic its plot, by its style, its sharp, yet good-natured irony, and the characters of the shrewd, absurd, delightful Dr. Primrose and his family. In 1768 Goldsmith turned to the theatre with *The Good-Natur'd Man*; followed in 1773 by the much more effective *She Stoops to Conquer*. This (along with the more brilliant plays of Richard Sheridan) has outlived all other English comedies from the early 18th century to the late 19th, despite moments of rather farcical horseplay, by the humour and humanity of such characters as Kate Hardcastle and Tony Lumpkin. Thus in the seven years 1762–68 Goldsmith had successfully invaded four different, and difficult, fields of literature.

During his last decade he is made more vivid for us by the pen of Boswell, his jealous rival in the spellbound, though not always charmed, circle of Johnson—a Goldsmith snubbed, yet loved, by the Master; mocked now for his bloom-coloured coat, now for his brawl with Thomas Evans the bookseller (whose *London Packet* had lampooned his fondness for Mary Horneck, a girl 22 years his junior whom he had met through Reynolds, and of whose family he was an intimate friend); yet capable on occasion of matching his "little fishes" against Johnson's "whales." But, despite not inadequate earnings, Goldsmith's debts deepened to £2,000. Maybe his extravagance and finery, like his jealous touchiness, need sympathy rather than censure, as neurotic results of a humiliated childhood. Early in 1774 he was attacked by kidney trouble and rashly dosed himself with James's Powders. His physician, noting his rapid pulse, asked if his mind were at ease. "No, it is not," were Goldsmith's last words. Next morning he died (April 4, 1774).

For Sir John Hawkins, Goldsmith was "an idiot"; for Horace Walpole, an "inspired idiot", "a fool the more wearing for having some sense"; for Garrick, an angelic writer who yet "talked like poor Poll"; for Hester Thrale, disagreeable, with "impudence truly Irish." But often Goldsmith's Irish humour was misunderstood by the dull Saxon. Those who knew more of him, thought better. At the news of his death Burke wept, and Reynolds threw down his brushes for the day. Johnson's Latin epitaph seized on two essential qualities—Goldsmith's versatility, and his grace: "There was almost no branch of literature that he did not attempt; none that he attempted, and failed to adorn." Even Boswell missed "poor Goldsmith." Much more did the outcast creatures who wept on his stairs, and Mary Horneck who preserved through a long life a tress of hair from his coffin.

Literary Characteristics.—Goldsmith's deficiencies are obvious. He was unlearned. He forgot even what was in his own books. Often he was hasty, superficial, and perfunctory—a literary highwayman who lightheartedly pillaged the *Encyclopédie*, Marivaux, Montesquieu, d'Argens, and others. Yet he shows how those who really have originality cannot help being original; while those who have none, fuss about it in vain. And so, with all his frailties, Goldsmith remained, for Johnson "a very great man"; for Reynolds, "a man of genius"; for Byron, one of the very few poets who, like Pope, were "all good"; for Thackeray, "the most beloved of English writers"; for Macaulay, an author unsurpassed in the power of being "uniformly agreeable." By 1820 relic-hunting pilgrims had carried off from Lissoy, twig by twig, all that remained of Goldsmith's hawthorn; and in 1864, when it was a question of statues for Ireland's worthies on Dublin's College Green, though Swift, Berkeley, and Burke were his rivals, the first choice was Goldsmith. But one of the most telling tributes of all comes from the ripe wisdom of Goethe—"To Shakespeare, Sterne, and Goldsmith my debt has been limitless."

Whence springs this power of a man seemingly so simple to impress men not simple at all? Chiefly perhaps from the charm of personality that breathes through his style—his warmth of heart, his mischievous irony, his spontaneous interchange of gaiety and sadness. He was, as an actor—"natural, simple, affecting"; though both men, curiously, often failed to be so in company. Alcibiades in Plato's *Symposium* likens the ugly Socrates to the satyr Marsyas, whose simple fluting bewitched his hearers as no bravuras could. The ugly, fluting Goldsmith showed something of the same unaffected charm. Hence his hatred for all pretense and pretentiousness—for sophistry, pedantry, criticism; for sentimental comedy; for the sentiment of Sterne, the artificial epithets of Gray, the "disgusting solemnity" of blank verse. It is by their human personalities that his novel and his plays succeed, not by brilliance of plot, ideas, or language. So too even with his essays. Montesquieu's *Lettres persanes* are read for their ideas, paradoxes, and epigrams; but *The Citizen of the World* is read for figures like the Man in Black, or the soldier, porter, and prisoner who so solemnly and ludicrously extol British liberty by the window of a jail; or the snobbish Tibbses "connoisseuring" the poor widow out of her pleasure in wine and custard at Vauxhall. So too even in the poems. Here yet again it is the characters that are remembered rather than the landscapes—the village parson, the village schoolmaster, the sharp, yet not unkindly portraits of Garrick and Burke. Goldsmith's poetry, however, lives also by its own special music, mellowing the heroic couplet to an autumnal grace far unlike the drum-roll of Dryden, the rapier-clash of Pope, the granite of Johnson, the sea-shingle of Crabbe; till it recalls, at moments, the April sweetness of Chaucer.

"Sweet as the primrose peeps beneath the thorn."

"The hawthorn bush, with seats beneath the shade,
For talking age and whispering lovers made."

Such simple melody, so free from the "disgusting solemnity" of 18th-century blank verse, seems deeply characteristic of him who in his youth had piped to poor French peasants by the Loire, and whose indignation pitied the English or Irish rustics uprooted from their homes at the fiat of the great. His aristocratic century, with all its polish, was often coarse, crude, or cruel; Goldsmith helped to humanize its imagination, without growing sickly or mawkish. That is what Goethe saw and admired. Goldsmith left his readers neither harsher, nor bitterer, nor more barbarous, as even genius has sometimes done; he left them warmer in sympathy, saner, and more civilized. Other writers, no doubt, have done that even better; yet there remains, perhaps, nothing better that any writer can ever do.

BIBLIOGRAPHY.—*Works:* There is no complete edition of Goldsmith's works later than J. W. M. Gibbs (1884–86); but there are many of particular works. *See* especially *Poetical Works* (1906); *Poems and Plays* (1889; reprinted in Everyman's Library, 1910); *Citizen of the World*, 2 vol. (1891; 1900), all ed. by A. Dobson; *Vicar of Wakefield*, ed. by O. Doughty (1928); *New Essays*, ed. by R. S. Crane (1927); *Collected Letters*, ed. by K. C. Balderston (1928); *Selected Works*, ed. by R. Garnett (1950). *See also* I. A. Williams, *Seven XVIIIth Century Bibliographies* (1924).

Biography: Sir James Prior, 2 vol. (1837); Washington Irving (1844; 1850); J. Forster (1848; 1903); S. L. Gwynn (1935); W. Freeman (1951); R. M. Wardle (1957).

Criticism: W. M. Thackeray, *The English Humorists of the 18th Century* (1853); Lord Macaulay, article in the *Encyclopædia Britannica*, 8th ed. (included in *Miscellaneous Writings*, 1860); A. L. Sells, *Les Sources françaises de Goldsmith* (1924); Sir Joshua Reynolds, *Portraits*, ed. by F. W. Hilles (1952).
(F. L. Lu.)

GOLD STANDARD, a monetary system in which the standard unit is a fixed weight of gold or is kept at the value of a fixed weight of gold. It has two main variants: the internal gold standard and the international gold standard. In an internal gold standard system gold coins circulate as legal tender or paper money is freely convertible into gold by the monetary authorities at a fixed price. In the international gold standard system gold or a currency which is convertible into gold at a fixed price is used as a means of making international payments. The use of the internal gold standard implies that countries are all on an international gold standard, so long as free movement of gold is allowed, because in these circumstances it can be used for international payments. It is possible for an international gold standard to exist in the absence of any internal gold standard. Such a system was, in fact, reestablished after World War II. Gold coins no longer circulate in any major country and private citizens of most countries have no right to exchange their paper money for gold. On the other hand, gold continues to serve as an international means of settlement between the major central banks. The exchange values of most national currencies are fixed in terms of gold or in terms of currencies whose value is fixed in terms of gold. This implies that exchange rates between nearly all the major national currencies are normally held within very narrow limits of fluctuation.

History.—The gold standard was first put into operation in Great Britain in 1821. Prior to that time the principal world monetary metal had been silver. Gold had, for many centuries, been used intermittently for coinage in one or another country, but never as the single reference metal, or standard, to which all other forms of money were coordinated or adjusted. The adoption of gold monometallism in Great Britain in 1821 was not imitated by any important country for about 50 years. In the intervening period silver, or a bimetallic regime of gold and silver, was the prevailing standard outside the British Isles. (*See* BIMETALLISM.) But in the 1870s the monometallic gold standard was adopted by Germany, France, and the United States. Before the end of the century many other countries had followed the lead of the financially important nations. After the turn of the century only China, Mexico, and a few small countries continued to use silver as standard money.

The full internal and international gold standard of the pre-1914 world was operated in differing ways in different countries. In its most complete version there was free coinage, free melting, and free movement of gold. This meant that anyone had the right: (1) to tender gold in unlimited quantities to the monetary authorities and to receive therefor an equal weight of gold in the form of money; (2) to export or import gold coin or gold bullion at will; all without any substantial charges being imposed by the monetary authorities.

Fundamentally, the same position could be achieved where paper currency was used if the monetary authorities were willing: (1) to buy or sell gold in unlimited quantities at a fixed price in convertible paper money per unit weight of the metal; (2) to refrain from restricting the import or export of gold coin or bullion.

Even before World War I some countries used a variant of the gold standard that later became increasingly popular, namely, the gold-exchange standard. In this system, a substitute for the export and import of gold was set up. It consisted of an offer by the monetary authorities of one country to buy and sell the currency of other gold standard countries at a fixed price in the paper currency of the country making the offer. In effect, this provided, "internationally," the necessary two-way market for gold in the currency of the country concerned, but, since the cost of transfer of the metal from the foreign to the home country was negligible in relation to its value, the procedure did not impair the essentials of the gold standard. It was much cheaper to maintain a gold-exchange standard than to preserve the unqualified gold standard, and the gold-exchange standard was therefore popular in poorer areas, *e.g.*, the colonies of relatively rich nations.

The reign of the full gold standard system was short, lasting only from the 1870s to the outbreak of World War I. That war saw recourse to inconvertible paper money or to restrictions on gold export in nearly every country of the world.

After World War I it was generally accepted that both the internal and the international gold standards should be reestablished. By 1928 the task had been practically completed, although gold coins were no longer in general circulation in most countries and more extensive use was made of the gold-exchange standard. Almost as soon as the gold standard had been reestablished, it collapsed through the pressures resulting from the great depression. The first major collapse was that of the United Kingdom in 1931 when convertibility of sterling into gold at a fixed price was abandoned and the sterling exchange rate was al-

lowed to depreciate in terms of the currencies still on gold. In 1933 the U.S. dollar was also allowed to depreciate. A small group of continental European countries led by France continued the struggle to maintain convertibility at the old price until 1936. This gold bloc collapsed because the depreciation of sterling and the dollar meant that the exports of the gold-bloc countries were at a competitive disadvantage in world markets. By 1937 not a single country remained on the full gold standard.

The United States, however, set a new minimum dollar price for gold to be used for purchases and sales by foreign central banks. This action, known as "pegging" the price of gold, provided the basis for the restoration of an international gold standard after World War II. By the time the postwar international currency system was being planned there was general dissatisfaction with the fluctuating exchange rate system of the 1930s. The postwar system was one in which most exchange rates were pegged either to the dollar or to gold. On occasions, however, the pegged rates were altered; the new gold standard did not achieve the apparently immutable exchange rate pattern of the pre-1914 or interwar gold standards. The reestablishment of this international gold standard occurred in 1958 when the major Western European countries reestablished the free convertibility of their currencies into gold and dollars, for international payments. In 1971, however, the United States withdrew the free convertibility of dollars into gold. Except in France, there had been no restoration of an internal gold standard by the early 1970s.

Principles.—The virtues of the gold standard are twofold: (1) it limits the power of governments or banks to cause price inflation by excessive issue of paper currency; (2) it creates certainty in international trade by providing a fixed pattern of exchange rates. The limit to the power to inflate the currency is most obvious where there is full internal convertibility of paper currency into gold. People can then be expected to prefer to hold gold rather than paper; if the monetary authorities try to issue too much paper money they risk a loss of confidence in it. The international gold standard does not provide the same limits to inflation because it is consistent with a broadly uniform degree of inflation in all countries. The effective limit to the freedom of action of the authorities is that if they inflate too fast the goods of their country will price themselves out of world markets and balance of payments difficulties will follow.

There are three main disadvantages of the gold standard: (1) it may not allow sufficient flexibility in the supply of money; (2) it makes it difficult for a single country to isolate its economy from depression or inflation in the rest of the world; (3) the process of adjustment for a gold standard country facing a payments deficit can be lengthy and painful.

The inflexibility of the gold standard system arises because the supply of newly mined gold is not closely related to the growing needs of the world economy for a supply of money. In practice, the use of gold was increasingly supported and then supplemented internally by the use of paper money; if this had not happened, a serious shortage of money would have developed and economic progress would probably have been much slower. The shortage of gold for international use, which was serious in the late 1920s and again in the late 1950s, was partially alleviated by the international use of national currencies and by the development of international organizations such as the European Payments Union and the International Monetary Fund (*q.v.*; IMF).

The disadvantage of the gold standard to countries which wish to isolate themselves from depression or inflation in the rest of the world arises from the fact that the gold standard system does not permit exchange rate changes and is not compatible with substantial controls over international trade and payments.

The third disadvantage of the international gold standard—that the process of adjustment back to payments equilibrium can be lengthy and painful—has been demonstrated many times. The working of the gold standard helps to create monetary equilibrium but at the price of an increase in unemployment or a decline in the rate of economic expansion. Experience suggests that even if unemployment is heavy, wages and prices fall very slowly and full adjustment is painful and prolonged.

There are two main automatic consequences of a payments deficit that has resulted from a switch in world tastes away from the goods of a country. One is that the decline in exports or the loss of domestic markets to foreign producers means increased unemployment. The second is that the loss of international reserves resulting from the payments deficit induces a contraction in the domestic monetary circulation and so leads to a rise in interest rates. The traditional view, which was particularly strong in England, was that this credit contraction should be reinforced by deliberate central bank restrictive action.

The adjustment process described is unsatisfactory in that it tends to correct the payments difficulties of a deficit country at the price of substantial unemployment. This is not, however, the end of the adjustment. Supporters of the gold standard consider that this unemployment will cause wages and prices to decline, and so enable the goods of the deficit country to compete more successfully in world markets. Ultimately, the full adjustment process is supposed to lead back to a position of as high economic activity in the country that suffered from a deficit as in the rest of the world, but where its price level is lower than in the rest of the world.

These disadvantages led to criticism of the gold standard in the 1930s when the world pattern of exchange rates was flexible. By contrast, the disadvantages became obvious, and the IMF system was established after World War II to combine the advantages of the gold standard and the flexible rate system. It provided that exchange rates should normally be pegged but that the peg could be moved if a country found itself in "fundamental" payments disequilibrium. The early postwar years saw extensive reliance on controls and currency inconvertibility. When this period ended in 1958 the international currency system had come to rely less on exchange rate adjustment than was envisaged when the IMF was established, and the post-1958 system has been a close approximation to a second restoration of the international gold standard.

The dollar price of gold was unpegged in 1971–72, resulting in the revaluation of the principal world trading currencies. Although the use of gold as a monetary basis appeared to be declining, future currency stability on some other basis was hard to discern. In May 1972 the increase in gold price led to resumed consideration of gold as a monetary base.

See MONEY; CURRENCY; INTERNATIONAL PAYMENTS; see also references under "Gold Standard" in the Index.

BIBLIOGRAPHY.—W. Adams Brown, Jr., *The International Gold Standard Reinterpreted 1914–34* (1940); League of Nations, *International Currency Experience: Lessons of the Inter-War Period* (1944); John Maynard (Lord) Keynes, *The Economic Consequences of Mr. Churchill* (1925); R. G. Hawtrey, *The Gold Standard in Theory and Practice* (1948); R. Triffin, *Gold and the Dollar Crisis* (1960); I. Shannon, *The Economic Functions of Gold* (1963) *International Liquidity* (1964); G. Cassel, *The Downfall of the Gold Standard* (1966); National Industrial Conference Board, *Gold and World Monetary Problems* (1966). (A. C. L. D.; GA. S.)

GOLDWATER, BARRY MORRIS (1909–), U.S. senator from Arizona and Republican presidential candidate in 1964, was born in Phoenix, Ariz., on Jan. 1, 1909. He came of an old Arizona family, whose founder, Mike Goldwater, a Jewish merchant from Poland, had arrived in the state in 1862. Educated at Staunton Military Academy, in Virginia, he spent one year at the University of Arizona before beginning work at his family's department store in 1929.

He served as a ferry pilot in the Air Transport Command during World War II, and became a lieutenant colonel. Retaining his military interests after the war, he rose gradually to the rank of major general in the Air Force Reserve and participated in the formation of the Arizona Air National Guard.

President of Goldwater's, Inc., from 1937 to 1953, Goldwater did not take an active interest in politics until 1947. Two years later, he was elected to the Phoenix City Council. In 1952 he ran for the U.S. Senate against the incumbent, Sen. Ernest W. McFarland, Democratic majority leader of the Senate, and won by a narrow margin.

As a senator Goldwater was a thoroughgoing conservative, criticizing many aspects of the Eisenhower administration's foreign and domestic policies. Running for reelection in 1958 he again defeated McFarland—this time by a large majority.

During the administration of Pres. John F. Kennedy, Goldwater strongly attacked the Democrats, criticizing their foreign policy as feeble and charging them with the aspiration to create a quasi-socialist state. He opposed centralizing legislation, and upheld state and local powers.

In January 1964 Goldwater formally announced that he was a candidate for the Republican nomination for president. Of the seven primaries in which Goldwater allowed his name to be entered, he won five—those of Indiana, Illinois, Nebraska, Texas, and California. His victory in the California primary on June 2—though by a margin of little more than 1% over Gov. Nelson Rockefeller—virtually delivered to him the Republican nomination and symbolized the defeat of the "liberal" or "moderate" Republican faction. On July 15, in San Francisco, the Republican convention nominated Goldwater on the first ballot. His running mate, the vice-presidential nominee, was Congressman William E. Miller of New York State.

As the Republican nominee, Goldwater fought a determined campaign against Pres. Lyndon B. Johnson, under serious handicaps. The prosperity of the nation worked in Johnson's favour, and many Republican businessmen endorsed the Democratic ticket. Even more of a handicap was the charge that Goldwater was "extreme," particularly in foreign policy, and might rashly carry the country into war. The Goldwater-Miller ticket was decisively defeated in the election on Nov. 3, carrying only Arizona and five states of the deep south.

In January 1965 Goldwater resumed the syndicated newspaper column he had started in 1961 and in 1968 was again elected to represent Arizona in the U.S. Senate.

Among Goldwater's writings are *The Conscience of a Conservative* (1960), a statement of his political philosophy, and *Why Not Victory?* (1962), an exposition of his views on foreign policy. He also published several books and a number of magazine articles on the history and the topography of Arizona. (R. K.; X.)

GOLEM, in Jewish folklore, an image endowed with life. In the Bible (*i.e.*, Ps. cxxxix, 16) the word signifies an unformed substance and hence an unmarried woman may be called a golem. Medieval legends applied it to wooden images given life by the saints, and with the oppression of the Jews arose stories, such as that of Rabbi Low, of golems that protected their masters. Much golem literature has been written, good examples being Henry Illiowizi's "The Baal Shem and His Golem" in *In the Pale* (1897) and Gustav Meyrink's *Der Golem* (1916; Eng. trans. 1928).

GOLF, a game which originated in Scotland, is played by striking a small ball with various clubs from a teeing ground into a series of holes on a course. The player who holes his ball in the fewest strokes is the winner.

The game is discussed under the following main headings:

I. HISTORY

While golf as the game is known today originated in Scotland, the place and time are obscure. However, it was so popular in the 15th century that the 14th parliament of King James II of Scotland decreed in 1457 that "fute-ball and golfe be utterly cryed downe, and not to be used" because they interfered with the practice of archery, an essential element in the defense of the realm. This legislation provided the first written reference to the playing of golf. That the game was well established is further supported by the fact that two subsequent Scottish parliaments found it necessary to issue similar decrees—in 1471 and 1491—

in efforts to suppress the game, and it appears that none of the three was effective. The invention of gunpowder near the end of the 15th century may have contributed to ending the proscription by lessening the importance of archery. At any rate, James IV (1473–1513), whose third parliament had passed the last of the three decrees, developed into an avid golfer. His daughter Mary, queen of Scots (1542–87), played golf at St. Andrews and her son James VI of Scotland, later James I of England (1566–1625), played at Blackheath common, London. The earliest rounds of golf, however, apparently had been played on linksland on the eastern coast of Scotland.

1. Precursors of Golf and Related Games.

—The family tree of golf may go back to the Roman empire. The Romans played a game in the fields called *paganica* (from *paganus*, "countryman") in which a club and a ball stuffed with feathers were used. The Roman legions, as they advanced over Europe and into Britain, may have carried *paganica* with them. If so, that would account for the development of similar games in several European countries: cambuca (cambrel or cammock) in England, *jeu de mail* in France, *het kolven* in the Netherlands. All of these involved striking a ball across the countryside with a stick. Cambuca (a name also given to the club used in the game) was played in the 13th and 14th centuries and was described in a record of 1363, printed in Thomas Rymer's *Foedera*, as "the game of a crooked stick or curved club or playing mallet with which a small wooden ball is propelled forward." Coincidentally, cambuca was forbidden in 1363 in an order to the sheriffs of England, in order that man "shall in his sports use bows and arrows, pellets and bolts."

Het kolven, played in the Netherlands, provided some of the important terminology of the game (see *Glossary*, below) and some interesting references in art. The word golf stems from the Dutch *kolf*, which in turn is related to the German *Kolbe* and the Danish *kolbe*, meaning "club." The mound on which the Dutchman placed his ball was a *tuitje*, pronounced "toytee." The hole to which he directed his ball was a *put*. If anything was in his way, he said, *stuit mij*, pronounced "stytmy" ("it stops me"). There is, too, an old Dutch proverb: "You must play the ball as it lies." The earliest reference to *het kolven* is in an illuminated Book of Hours, done by Simon Bennink with the assistance of pupils in his studio at Bruges between 1500 and 1520, and now in the British museum. A miniature depicts three players on a green with a hole, each player with a club and ball and one of them attempting to hole out. From the same period, a sketch by David Vinck-Boons and other evidence reflects a similar game played on ice. The painting "Frost Scene" by A. van de Velde, dated 1668, portrays four "golfers" in competition, two Dutchmen in knickerbockers and two Scots in kilts.

2. Early British Golfers' Associations.

—It is generally conceded that the Royal Blackheath Golf club of London is the oldest existing golf club in the world, but its origin is as obscure as that of the game itself. James I, whose reign began in 1603, played golf on Blackheath common, and a society of golfers was formed at Blackheath in 1608. A group of golfers was flourishing there in 1766, for a silver club bears the inscription: "August 16, 1766, the gift of Mr. Henry Foote to the Honourable Company of Goffers at Blackheath." The Royal Burgess Golfing Society of Edinburgh claims to have been founded in 1735. The Company of Gentlemen Golfers, now the Honourable Company of Edinburgh Golfers, was formed in 1744 by a group that played over the five holes of the Leith links. The lord provost, the magistrates and the council of the city of Edinburgh presented to the company a silver club that was first played for in April 1745. The club subsequently transferred its activities to Musselburgh and finally to the Muirfield links, with which it has been associated in modern times.

The earliest known rules are the 13 recorded in the first minute book of the Honourable Company of Edinburgh Golfers. The first signer was John Rattray, who was captain in 1744, 1745 and 1751. The code, therefore, cannot be more recent than 1751 and more likely was entered in the minute book when the competition for the silver club was instituted, in 1745.

The Royal and Ancient Golf Club.—The Society of St. Andrews, now the Royal and Ancient Golf Club of St. Andrews, Scotland, was formed on May 14, 1754, by a group of 22 golfers who played there. The rules which the society adopted were almost identical with the Edinburgh Gentlemen Golfers' rules. An allusion to scholars' holes and soldiers' lines not constituting hazards indicates that the rules were copied from the Gentlemen Golfers' code when the St. Andrews golfers were playing at Leith, since there were both scholars' holes and soldiers' lines at Leith but no soldiers' lines at St. Andrews. These two clubs played major roles in the development of the game in Scotland. Eventually the Royal and Ancient Golf club (R. and A.) became, by common consent, the oracle on rules. In 1919 it accepted the management of the British open and amateur championships. The R. and A. thus became the governing body for men's golf in the British Isles and throughout most of the commonwealth. The Musselburgh Golf club offered a prize for a women's competition, Dec. 14, 1810, and a Ladies Golf club was formed at St. Andrews in 1872. The Ladies Golf union, which governs women's golf, was organized in 1893.

3. United States.

—Golf or something akin to it may have been played in the new world in the 17th and 18th centuries. The record of a court in Ft. Orange (now Albany, N.Y.) reveals that the sheriff there filed a complaint against three men who had been playing *het kolven* on the ice on a Sunday in 1657. The magistrates of Ft. Orange on Dec. 10, 1659, issued an ordinance to "forbid all persons to play 'het kolven' in the streets." While these documents are sometimes cited as evidence of the earliest playing of golf in the United States, the game does not seem to have been the linksland pastime handed down by the Scots. There seems little doubt, however, that the following advertisement, which appeared in James Rivington's *Gazette* in New York on April 21, 1779, referred to golf: "To the Golf Players: The season for this pleasant and healthy exercise now advancing, gentlemen may be furnished with excellent clubs and the veritable Caledonian balls by enquiring at the Printer's." However, there is no record of golf in New York during the subsequent century. The next evidence appears in the Carolinas. The *South Carolina and Georgia Almanac* of 1793 published, under the heading "Societies Established in Charleston," the following item: "Golf club formed 1786. Dr. Purcell—President. Edward Penman—Vice President. James Gardiner—Treasurer and Secretary." The *Charleston City Gazette and Daily Advertiser* of Sept. 18, 1788, reported: "There is lately erected that pleasing and genteel amusement, the kolf baan. Any person wishing to treat for the same at private sale will please apply to Mr. David Denoon in Charleston, or to the subscriber on the spot." Later notices dated 1791 and 1794 referred to the South Carolina Golf club, which celebrated an anniversary with a dinner on Harleston's green in the latter year. The *Georgia Gazette* of Sept. 22, 1796, announced the anniversary of the Savannah Golf club, and one Miss Eliza Johnston was invited to a "Golf Club ball" in Savannah on New Year's Eve, 1811, according to an invitation in the possession of her family.

JERRY COOKE

ARNOLD PALMER LINING UP A PUTT DURING THE 1960 BRITISH OPEN CHAMPIONSHIP. IN THE CENTRE BACKGROUND MAY BE SEEN THE CLUBHOUSE OF THE ROYAL AND ANCIENT GOLF CLUB OF ST. ANDREWS, SCOTLAND, FOUNDED IN 1754

Although these fragments constitute the earliest clear evidence of golf clubs in the United States, the clubs appear to have been primarily social organizations that did not survive the War of 1812.

The first permanent golf club in the western hemisphere was the Royal Montreal Golf club, established in 1873. In subsequent years golf was played experimentally at many places in the United States without taking permanent root until, in 1885, it was played in Foxburg, Pa. The Dorset Field club, in Dorset, Vt., claims to have been organized and to have laid out its course in 1886, and there is no reason to doubt the claim; however, the evidence is based entirely on personal recollection. The Foxburg Golf club has provided strong support for the claim that it was organized in 1887, is the oldest golf club in the United States. The course came into existence and has the oldest U.S. golf course. The course came into existence through the interest and generosity of Joseph Mickle Fox of Philadelphia, a summer resident of Foxburg who is believed to have been introduced to golf and to have acquired his first left-handed clubs and gutty balls while in Scotland in 1884.

Next oldest course, after Foxburg, may be that of the Middlesborough (Ky.) Golf club which apparently was founded in 1889 by English immigrants. The course is still in existence, but there is a question as to whether play has been continuous on it. The next oldest golf club organized in the U.S., after Foxburg, almost surely is the St. Andrew's Golf club of Yonkers, N.Y., named after the famous Scottish club and organized by John Reid and four friends on Nov. 14, 1888. This club played an outstanding role in the history of golf in the United States. The story of its founding bears similarities to the story of Foxburg's less-celebrated origin. Robert Lockhart, a Scot living in New York, shipped home some golf clubs and balls while on one of his annual trips to Scotland. On his return he tried them out on the banks of the Hudson river where 72nd street ends and later used them to introduce the game to his friends John Reid and John B. Upham in a pasture across from Reid's home in Yonkers on Feb. 22, 1888. Following the blizzard of March 1888 the men convened again, with other potential converts, in another pasture at the corner of Broadway and Shonnard avenue, Yonkers, laid out a course and played through the summer, and organized as a club in the fall. The club moved several times but has been permanently established at Hastings-on-Hudson, N.Y., since 1897.

The United States Golf Association.—One of St. Andrew's many notable contributions to the welfare of the game was its leadership in organizing the United States Golf association (U.S.G.A.). In 1894, after having completed its links in Yonkers, the club planned a tournament for the amateur championship of the United States, on Oct. 11–12–13, and invitations were sent to the various golf clubs throughout the country. The tournament was to be played according to the rules of the R. and A. and the prizes were diamond and gold, silver and bronze medals. At the same time the Newport (R.I.) Golf club decided to hold a championship in September, the prize to be a silver cup. As a result there were two U.S. championships in 1894. H. O. Tallmadge, secretary of the St. Andrew's club, suggested the formation of a national association to establish uniform rules and conduct tournaments; he was assisted by Laurence Curtis of The Country club of Brookline, Mass. On Dec. 22, 1894, the Amateur Golf Association of the United States was formed by representatives of five of the leading golf clubs of the country. The name was soon changed to the American Golf association and finally to the United States Golf association. The five founding clubs were the St. Andrew's Golf club, the Newport Golf club, the Shinnecock Hills Golf club, Southampton, N.Y., The Country club, Brookline, and the Chicago Golf club. The U.S.G.A., which grew to include more than 3,400 clubs and courses, is a voluntary association of golf clubs whose purpose is to promote and conserve the best interests and true spirit of the game as embodied in its traditions. To this end it adopts, enforces and interprets rules of amateur status and rules of the game; conducts nine national championships (open, amateur, women's amateur, women's open, amateur public links, junior amateur, girls' junior and senior amateur and women's senior); co-operates in sponsoring six international amateur team events (the Walker cup, Americas cup, Eisenhower trophy and senior men's for men; and the Curtis cup and the Espirito Santo trophy for women); finances turf-grass research and provides a turf-grass advisory service; maintains a golf museum and library in Golf house, its New York headquarters; and, in general, acts as a national authority.

The second oldest national organization in the United States is the Western Golf association. Founded in 1899 as a sectional organization to embrace the territory west of Buffalo, N.Y., it developed as a national authority on caddies and caddie welfare and sponsors the Evans Scholars foundation to assist deserving caddies in obtaining a college education.

Another prominent organization is the Professional Golfers Association of America (P.G.A.), organized by professional golfers at the instigation of R. Wanamaker in 1916 to promote interest in the game, elevate the standards of professional golf and advance the welfare of its members. This association has a membership of some 6,000 professional golfers. In addition to its P.G.A. championship, it shares in the conduct of an international professional match for the Ryder cup and co-sponsors a series of tournaments for professionals in a circuit that circles the United States throughout the year, with prizes for individual events ranging up to $250,-000.

4. 20th Century.—The most significant growth in golf in the 20th century occurred in senior organizations after 1905, when Horace L. Hotchkiss arranged the first seniors' tournament, for players 55 and older, at the Apawamis club, Rye, N.Y. Hotchkiss, who was more than 60 at the time, attempted to prove that golf was not a young man's game. The tournament was such a suc-

cess that within ten years the number of contestants had passed the 300 mark and it had become apparent that a senior organization was in order. The United States Seniors' Golf association was organized on Jan. 17, 1917, in New York, with a membership of 400, which within six months increased to 500 and subsequently to 1,000. The idea spread rapidly. While the United States seniors' tournament is the leading event of its kind, many other membership and invitation events of the same type developed to meet the demand—the American Seniors' Golf association, the Western Seniors' Golf association, the North and South senior tournament and others. There are at least 50 senior golfing organizations in the United States alone. Members of the United States Senior Women's Golf association play annually. In 1918 the governor general of Canada presented a trophy to be played for annually by the United States Seniors' Golf association and the newly formed Canadian Seniors' Golf association. Another match was initiated with the Senior Golfers' society of Great Britain.

Golf has achieved some popularity in at least 51 countries since that many are represented on the World Amateur Golf council. The World's Amateur Golf council was organized by officials of the U.S.G.A. and the R. and A. in 1958, and its first tournament, for the Eisenhower cup, was held that year at St. Andrews. The Australian team (Bruce Devlin, Robert Stevens, Doug Bachli and Peter Toogood) won the 18-hole play-off from the U.S. team (Charlie Coe, Billy Joe Patton, Frank Taylor and Bill Hyndman III). The biennial Americas cup tournament was organized by the U.S.G.A., the Royal Canadian Golf association and the Asociacion Mexicana de Golf in 1952. The amateur team match between the United States and Great Britain for the Walker cup has been held running biennially since 1922; the professional team match between the same two countries for the Ryder cup since 1927; and the women's amateur team match, also between the same countries, for the Curtis cup since 1932.

Golf has achieved its greatest popularity in the United States, where more than 10,000,000 men, women and children played at least ten times a year on more than 8,500 golf courses in the second half of the 20th century, according to a survey conducted by the National Golf foundation. The same source estimated that over 800,000 ac. were devoted to golf.

II. EQUIPMENT AND THE DEVELOPMENT OF THE GAME

A. THE FEATHER-BALL ERA

1. The Feather Ball.—Golf, like *paganica*, was originally played with a leather-covered ball stuffed with feathers, and the principles of the modern rules were developed in this era. The feather ball or feathery remained the standard for at least four centuries, until about 1848. The making of feather balls was a tedious task, and most ball makers could produce only about four "specials" (top-grade balls) a day. The best balls sold for up to five shillings apiece; in bulk, rarely less than £1 for a dozen. In the making, the leather was softened with alum and water and cut into four, three or two pieces. These were stitched together with waxed thread outside in and reversed when the stitching was nearly completed. A small hole was left for the insertion of boiled goose feathers. The ball maker held the leather cover in his hand, with a stuffing rod, a tapering piece of wrought iron 16 to 20 in. long and fitted with a wooden crosspiece to be braced against the ball maker's chest. When the stuffing iron failed, an awl was brought into play, and a volume of feathers which would fill the crown of a beaver hat eventually was inserted into the leather cover. The hole was then stitched up and the ball hammered hard and round and given three coats of paint. Feather balls were seldom exactly round. In wet weather they tended to become sodden and fly apart. They were easily cut on the seams and a player was fortunate if his ball endured through two rounds. Originally, there appear to have been ball makers in each golfing community, but in the middle of the 18th century the Gourlay family, of Leith and Musselburgh, became pre-eminent and a "Gourlay" was accepted as the best feather ball on the market. The patriarch of the family was Douglas Gourlay, at Leith, but it was his son, at Musselburgh, who brought the family name into greatest renown. Their principal competitor was Allan Robertson of St. Andrews, son of the noted player Davie Robertson. He turned out 2,456 feather balls in 1844 and was unalterably opposed to the introduction, shortly thereafter, of the gutta-percha ball. When he caught "Old Tom" Morris playing a gutta ball in 1852 they had words, and Morris left St. Andrews, not to return until after Robertson's death in 1858.

2. Early Clubs.—The full, free style known as the St. Andrews swing developed out of the feather-ball period. The clubs, at first rudimentary, tended toward the end of the period to be long, thin and graceful, and the feathery was swept from the ground with a full swing that also tended to be long and graceful. The shafts were whippy and the grips thick. The earliest known club maker was William Mayne of Edinburgh, who received a royal warrant as club maker and spear maker from James VI in 1603. A notebook of that period indicates the nomenclature of clubs Mayne must have made by noting payments for the repair of "play clubis," "donker clubis"; and an "irone club." While there are no known examples of these clubs, their rudimentary nature is known from the art of the times. Among the oldest known clubs is a set of six woods and two irons at Troon Golf club, Scotland; these were found in Hull, Eng., with a copy of a Yorkshire paper dated 1741. All six are shafted with ash. Only one wood and one iron have grips. The woods are weighted with lead and faced with bone, the lead extending from near the toe two-thirds of the way to the heel.

Club making advanced markedly in the last century of the featherball era, with the advent of the real artists—Simon Cossar of Leith; the successive generations of McEwans of Leith and Musselburgh; Hugh Philp and James Wilson of St. Andrews; White of St. Andrews. Cossar, Philip, Wilson and the McEwans were noted for their woods; Cossar, Wilson and White for irons. White is credited with giving Robertson and "Young Tom" Morris such refined irons that they were able to introduce a wide range of new strokes into the game. Douglas McEwan made his club heads from small cuts of hedge thorn that had been planted horizontally on sloping banks so that the stems grew at an angle at the root and created a natural bend for the neck. The shafts, spliced onto the heads, were made of split ash.

By the first half of the 19th century, clubs had come to be divided into four classes: drivers, spoons, irons and putters. Drivers were distinguished by their long, tapering, flexible shafts and their small raking heads. They comprised "play clubs," which had little loft and were designed for use over a safe ground only, and "grassed drivers," which had more loft and were designed to lift a ball from a heavy or downhill lie or over a hazard. Spoons

GOLFERS AND SPECTATORS SEARCHING THE ROUGH FOR A BALL, LOST DURING AN AMATEUR TOURNAMENT IN DEAUVILLE, FRANCE

were of four types: long spoons, middle spoons, short spoons and baffing or baffy spoons, the distinction being in the degree of loft. For a time there was also a fifth spoon, variously known as a cleek and a niblick, a well-lofted club with a small head designed to drive a ball out of a rut. There were three irons: driving irons, irons known as cleeks and having narrow lofted faces and long shafts, and bunker irons. Driving putters were used for approach work over unencumbered terrain and green putters, on putting greens. With these sets, players negotiated their feather balls over holes measuring 80 to 400 yd. In the era of the feather ball there were no championships, but four of the great players of the period returned the following card in a feather-ball match at St. Andrews in 1849:

Out

```
Willie and Jamie Dunn.............6 5 4 6 6 6 4 4 5—46
Allan Robertson and Tom Morris, Sr...6 5 6 5 5 5 5 4 4—45
```

In

```
Willie and Jamie Dunn.............5 3 5 6 5 5 6 6—46—92
Allan Robertson and Tom Morris, Sr...6 4 5 6 5 5 6 6—48—93
```

B. THE GUTTA-PERCHA ERA

1. The Gutta Ball.—Gutta-percha is the evaporated milky juice or latex produced by various trees. It is hard and non-brittle, becomes soft and impressible at the temperature of boiling water and retains its shape when cooled. It is not affected by water except at boiling temperature.

The first gutta-percha ball is believed to have been made in 1845 by the Rev. Robert A. Paterson from gutta-percha packing which had been used around a statue of Vishnu sent from India. The earliest such balls, produced under the name "Paterson's patent," were brown in colour and were handmade by rolling the gutta-percha on a flat board. They had smooth surfaces lined to simulate the seaming of a feather ball, and ducked quickly in flight until they had been marked and cut in play. They were not introduced into the game generally until 1848, when the makers had learned to apply effective permanent markings or indentations to the surface so that the balls would fly properly.

Gutta balls were far easier to make than featheries, since they consisted solely of the single lump of molded gutta-percha. The best-known balls were the hand-marked private brands of the club makers, such as the Auchterlonies, Old Tom Morris and Robert Forgan, and the bramble-marked and patent brands such as the Eureka, Melfort, White Melfort (of white gutta-percha), White Brand, Henley, O.K., Ocobo, Silvertown No. 4, A.1, Clan, Thornton, Park's Special and Agrippa. The Agrippa, with bramble marking, became a great favourite. The A.1 floated, but most guttas did not. The gutta remained the standard ball until 1901-02, when the rubber ball replaced it.

The introduction of the gutta ball occasioned one of the great rejuvenations in the history of the game. Its lower cost, longer life, improved flight, truer run on the greens and the fact that it did not fall apart in the rain attracted an enormous number of new players, and the feathery was quickly replaced. The influx of new players, in turn, forced the conversion of the old course at St. Andrews to a full 18 holes. Until the gutta ball was developed, golfers played out along what later became known as the left-hand course, until they reached the end hole. There they turned around and played in to the same holes. If two groups approached a green simultaneously, preference was given to those playing out. However, as golfers multiplied with the advent of the gutta ball, the links proved too narrow to accommodate them, and about 1857 they were widened sufficiently to turn the greens into double ones so that two holes could be cut in each one.

Calibre of play improved greatly with the advent of the gutta ball. Robertson, when finally won over to it, shattered all precedent by scoring a 79 at St. Andrews in 1858, and this record stood until Young Tom Morris made a 77 in 1869.

2. Clubs.—The gutta-percha ball was harder than the feather ball and put considerable strain on the slender clubs with which feather balls had been stroked. Thus wooden heads gradually became shorter and squatter in shape. Hard thorn was discarded for the softer apple, pear and beech in the heads, and leather insets appeared in the faces. Hickory, originally from Russia and later from Tennessee, replaced ash in the making of shafts. Iron clubs increased in number and variety and became vastly more refined. The superlative play of Young Tom Morris at St. Andrews (see *Outstanding Players,* below) is credited with popularizing the iron clubs he used so deftly. A full range of clubs at the zenith of the gutta-ball period consisted of seven woods—driver, bulger driver (a wood with a convex face), long spoon, brassie, middle spoon, short spoon and putter—and six irons—cleek, midiron, lofting iron, mashie, niblick and cleek putter. From these the golfer usually selected about eight. The range of clubs that Willie Park, Jr., had in winning the British open championships of 1887 and 1889 was bulger driver, straight-faced driver, spoon, brassie niblick, wooden putter, cleek, iron, mashie, iron niblick and Park's patent putter.

The increase in the number of clubs brought about another innovation in the early 1890s, the introduction of a simple sailcloth bag in which to carry them. Previously, the few clubs a player might need had been carried loose under the arm. The introduction of the gutta ball did not change the identity of the club makers, but required them to develop new designs and materials. Douglas McEwan lived until 1896 and bridged the periods of the feathery and the gutta. He was followed by his son Peter and by his four grandsons, who constituted the fifth generation of club-making McEwans. James Wilson, who had made clubs for the feather ball under Hugh Philp, set up shop at St. Andrews in 1852, and Philp then took in his nephew, Robert Forgan. Forgan and his son Thomas continued the business under their own name after Philp's death. R. Forgan was the first to appreciate the merit of hickory shafts and T. Forgan produced the bulger driver and the ebony putter. Old Tom Morris, the Andersons and the Auchterlonies were other noted club makers of St. Andrews, and there were Ben Sayers at North Berwick, Willie Park, Sr., at Musselburgh, the Simpsons at Carnoustie and many more.

In 1891 Willie Dunn, son of Willie of the famed Dunn twins of Scotland, arrived in the United States to lay out the course at Southampton, N.Y., for the Shinnecock Hills Golf club and remained to make clubs. Other Scottish professionals crossed the Atlantic in the 1890s and contributed to the establishment of U.S. club making. The trade itself was little changed. Wooden heads were cut out of a block, filed, spoke shaved, chiseled, gouged, leaded, boned, smoothed with glass paper, sometimes stained and treated with a hare's-foot dipped in a mixture of oil and varnish. Whereas the club heads used by Robertson were only $5/16$ in. deep, the depth gradually increased to 1 in. and, for a time, 2 in. Iron heads were hand forged from a bar of mild iron, heated, hammered, tempered, emery wheeled and polished, and the socket was pierced for the rivet and nicked. Hickory shafts were seasoned, then cut, filed, planed, scraped and glass-papered down to the required length, shape and degree of whippiness, which was the real art. Shafts for wooden heads were finished in a splice, glued onto the heads and whipped with tarred or waxed twine. Shafts for irons were finished with a prong to fit into the socket and holed for the iron cross rivet. Strips of untanned leather, shaped with a chisel, were nailed to the top of the shafts, wound on spirally over a cloth foundation, rolled tight between two polished boards and nailed at the bottom. Both ends of the grip were bound with twine and the whole grip was then varnished.

C. THE ERA OF THE RUBBER BALL

1. Development of the Ball.—The rubber ball was the invention of Coburn Haskell, a golfer of Cleveland, O., in association with Bertram G. Work of the B. F. Goodrich company. In 1898 Haskell adapted the art of winding rubber thread produced by Goodrich under tension on a solid rubber core to produce a ball far livelier than the gutta. The earliest covers were of black gutta-percha, lightly lined by hand. Paint tended to fill the indentations, causing the ball to duck in flight just as the first, smooth gutta balls had. Dave Foulis, a Chicago professional, put a rubber ball in an Agrippa mold and produced the bramble marking that was common to both the late gutta and early rubber balls. Haskell balls, placed on the market in 1899, became known as "bounding

GOLF

billies." It is estimated that they could be hit about 25 yd. farther than the gutta, just as the gutta was about 25 yd. longer than the feathery. The consensus at first, however, was that the distance gained did not offset the difficulty of controlling the lively ball on the green. Walter J. Travis of New York, considered the best putter of his day, resolved this debate by using a Haskell ball from an Agrippa mold in winning the U.S. amateur championship in Sept. 1901. Thereafter, the gutta became a relic of the past, and the game was again revolutionized and popularized as it had been with the advent of the gutta.

The day of the ball made by hand in the professional's shop was ending. A. G. Spalding & Bros., at Chicopee, Mass., a manufacturer of sporting goods, had undertaken production of gutta balls in 1898 and obtained a licence to produce its first rubber ball, the Spalding Wizard, in 1903. Soon thereafter the balata cover was developed for Spalding, and its improved adhering qualities made it an important innovation. Earliest experiments with the rubber ball concerned the core. It was determined that, for resilience, mobile cores were best, offering the least resistance to the distortion to the ball caused by club-head impact. Operating on this theory, the Kempshall Golf Ball company produced the Kempshall water core, in which a small sac of water was substituted for solid rubber. The competition to produce a ball that could be driven longer distances was under way. Manufacturers tried lead in solution in an effort to combine weight with a mobile core, but this proved potentially injurious to curious children and animals. Zinc oxide was substituted, but the pigment tended to settle and unbalance the ball. In the 1920s true solutions involving glue, glycerin and water were developed for the first-line balls.

More telling improvements were made in winding, the critical factor in the modern ball. Machines replaced men and were constantly improved. The object of the winding process is to obtain the greatest tension and closest possible approach to the breaking point of the rubber thread. The earliest thread was of wild rubber from the Amazon basin; development of plantation rubber led to greatly improved quality.

Ultimately, in the late 1960s a molded golf ball was introduced and proved highly resistant to cutting and marking.

Early rubber balls were made with the bramble and reverse-mesh markings of the gutta ball, but experiments led to improvements as they revealed the best relationship of both depth and area of indentation to the ball's total surface. William Taylor, in England, reversed the markings on his molds to produce the dimple, in contrast to the bramble, in 1908. The mesh, in contrast to the original reverse mesh, was a natural aftermath. Haskell balls at first were light and large, about 1.55 oz. in weight and 1.71 in. in diameter, and they floated. In the absence of regulations governing size or weight, manufacturers pursued one another's leads in the quest for the most efficient combination. Heavy solutions in the core increased the weight to about 1.72 oz. in the first decade. Then both size and diameter underwent a gradual reduction to 1.62 oz. and 1.63 in. about the time the Haskell patent expired in 1915. Expiration of this patent increased the competition, which had tended to make courses obsolete. Therefore, in 1920 the U.S.G.A. and the R. and A. agreed that after May 1, 1921, balls used in their championships must weigh not more than 1.62 oz. and measure not less than 1.62 in. and the two organizations would take such steps as were deemed necessary to limit the power of the ball. The ball actually was unchanged by this regulation; it continued to measure 1.63 in., .01 in. above the minimum. In 1923 the U.S.G.A. decided that the power should be reduced. A series of experiments under William C. Fownes, Jr., of Pittsburgh and Herbert Jaques, Jr., of Boston led to the introduction in the United States in 1930 of the so-called "balloon ball," weighing not more than 1.55 oz. and measuring not less than 1.68 in. in diameter. This ball, with no regulation of its velocity, became standard in the United States on Jan. 1, 1931, and was the first deviation from the British ball. It proved too light to hold on line in flight in a wind or on a green as it lost momentum, and it survived only one year. The slightly heavier ball, weighing not more than 1.620 oz. and measuring not less than 1.680 in., became standard in the U.S. on Jan. 1, 1932. The velocity of this ball was not regulated, how-

ever, until the U.S.G.A. completed a satisfactory testing machine in 1941. After Jan. 1, 1942, the U.S.G.A. required that the velocity of the ball be not greater than 250 ft. per second as measured on the association's machine under specified conditions. The ball used in Great Britain is slightly smaller.

2. Modern Clubs.—Golf was being overtaken by the industrial revolution when the rubber ball came into the game at the beginning of the 20th century. These two factors wrought major changes in the clubs and the methods by which they were produced as craftsmanship moved out of the individual professional's shop and into the factory. The harder rubber ball brought about the use of persimmon and, later, laminated club heads. Hard insets appeared in the faces. Increased demand led to the adaptation of shoe-last machine tools for the fashioning of wooden club heads. Sockets were bored in the club heads, and shafts were inserted rather than spliced. Drop forging completely replaced hand forging in the fashioning of iron clubs, and faces were deepened to accommodate the livelier ball and were machine lined to increase the spin on the ball in flight. Stainless steel replaced carbon steels. Seamless steel shafts took the place of hickory. Composition materials were developed as an alternative to leather in grips, and the grip foundations were molded in so many ways that they were regulated in 1947. Inventive minds created novel clubs, not only centre-shafted and aluminum putters and the sand wedge but also types that were such radical departures from the traditional form and make that they could not be approved by the U.S.G.A. or the R. and A. Modern club making in the United States began when Julian W. Curtiss of A. G. Spalding & Bros. purchased some clubs in London in 1892 for resale in his company's retail stores. Two years later, Spalding employed some Scottish club makers and began producing its own clubs. Hand modeling of woods and hand forging of irons did not long survive the demands of factory production. Within the first decade the Crawford, McGregor & Canby company in Dayton, O., a maker of shoe lasts, was turning out wooden heads; foundries were converting drop-forging processes to iron heads; and Allan Lard in Chicopee was experimenting with perforated steel rods for shafts. A. W. Knight of the General Electric company joined this inventive movement and produced an aluminum-headed putter with the shaft attached near the centre rather than at the heel. Travis used this "Schenectady" putter in winning the British amateur championship in 1904.

The importance of these developments was such that, in promulgating its revised code of rules in Sept. 1908, the R. and A. appended the notation that it would not sanction any substantial departure from the traditional and accepted form and make of golf clubs. This principle has been invoked many times in an effort to preserve the original form of the game. When Jock Hutchison won the British open in 1921 with deeply slotted faces on his pitching clubs, the R. and A. immediately banned such faces and the U.S.G.A. concurred with a regulation governing markings which became effective in 1924. After Horton Smith had so effectively used a sand wedge with a concave face designed by E. M. MacClain of Houston, Tex., the principle of concavity was

BURKE UZZEL, "LIFE." © TIME INC.

MOTORIZED GOLF CARTS ELIMINATE MUCH OF THE WALKING IN THE GAME

banned in 1931. However, Gene Sarazen developed a straight-faced sand wedge and used it so well in winning the British and U.S.G.A. opens in 1932 that he completed the revolution of bunker play. Experiments with steel shafts went through several phases. Lard's perforated steel rod was no substitute for hickory, and the locked-seam steel shaft proved not to be the answer either, although the U.S.G.A. approved such shafts in 1924. However, in 1924 the Union Hardware company of Torrington, Conn., drew a seamless shaft of high-carbon steel which could be heat-treated and tempered. Approved by the R. and A. in 1929, it substantially replaced hickory in the early 1930s. Later, shafts of fibre glass and of aluminum were introduced.

Improvement of the shaft was accompanied by the general introduction of numbered rather than named clubs, and by the merchandising of matched sets rather than individual clubs; clubs had become more numerous and more finely graduated than the names which had been applied to them and shafts could be manufactured to specifications for flexibility and point of flex. Whereas formerly a golfer seeking new clubs went through a rack of mashies until he found one that "felt right" and then tried to find other clubs of similar feel, he later bought a whole set manufactured to impart the same feel. The merchandising aspect of this development was, perhaps, something more than a happy coincidence for the manufacturers. In any case, the merchandising opportunities inherent in the numbered and matched sets were carried to an extreme, and in 1938 the U.S.G.A. limited the number of clubs a player might use in a round to 14. The R. and A. concurred in a similar edict the next year.

III. OUTSTANDING PLAYERS

1. Great Britain.—As golfing associations, or clubs, developed, there arose a group of professionals who made golf balls, fashioned and repaired clubs and gave lessons. Many of them were great players. The first of these was Allan Robertson (1815–58) of St. Andrews who, legend states, was never beaten in a stake (money) match played on even terms (that is, not giving his opponent a handicap). His apprentice was the man eventually known as Old Tom Morris (1821–1908), professional, greenkeeper and patriarch of St. Andrews. When Old Tom was 30, he moved to the Prestwick Golf club which offered a belt as a challenge trophy for an open championship in 1860. Willie Park, Sr., then 27 and one of the famous golfing brothers from Musselburgh, won it with a 36-hole score of 174; but Old Tom won in 1861, 1862, 1864 and 1867. His son, Young Tom Morris (1850–75), succeeded him and won for three successive years, retiring the prize belt. Young Tom won his first professional tournament at the age of 16. He was 18, 19 and 20 when he won his three successive open championships. In the absence of a prize, there was no championship in 1871, but a cup which has been in competition ever since was put up in 1872 by the Prestwick Golf club, the R. and A. and the Honourable Company of Edinburgh Golfers, and Young Tom won it to score a fourth successive victory. Shortly thereafter he died, at the age of 25.

The British amateur championship was not started until 1885 after the Royal Liverpool Golf club at Hoylake, Eng., had proposed a tournament "open to all amateur golfers." The tournament attracted nearly all the best amateurs of the time and the winner was Allan F. MacFie, but it was not immediately recognized as the championship. The following year, the Royal Liverpool suggested to the R. and A. that the tournament be established as the amateur championship, and 24 clubs joined together to purchase a trophy and manage the event. Among British players who won the amateur championship at least two times after 1900 were John Ball (1907, 1910 and 1912), H. H. Hilton (1911 and 1913), E. Holderness (1922 and 1924), C. Tolley (1920 and 1929), J. Carr of Ireland (1953, 1958 and 1960) and M. Bonallack (1961 and 1965).

The Ladies Golf union was formed rather late, in 1893, and the first British Women's championship was held that year, at St. Anne's, Eng., and won by Lady Margaret Scott, as were the next two championships.

One of the first outstanding woman golfers was Dorothy Campbell, who won the British women's championship in 1909 and 1911, was runner-up in 1908 and semifinalist in 1904, 1905 and 1906. She won the U.S. championship in 1909, 1910 and 1924 and the Canadian championship in 1910, 1911 and 1912. Twice married, she was Mrs. John V. Hurd, then Mrs. Edward Howe. She became a resident of the U.S. early in the century. She won more than 750 prizes in golf.

Another British woman, Joyce Wethered, won the women's open championship in 1922, 1924, 1925 and 1929, the English women's title five years in a row, 1920–24, and represented Britain in numerous international matches. In 1935 she toured the United States as a professional representing a London store, and competed most creditably against the best men and women golfers. She became Lady Heathcoat-Amory. Other British women's championship winners of note have included Enid Wilson, who won in 1931, 1932 and 1933; Mrs. Andrew Holm, in 1934 and 1938; Pamela Barton, in 1936, in which year she also won the U.S. championship, and 1939; Miss F. Stephens (Mrs. Roy Smith), in 1949 and 1954; and Mrs. G. Valentine, in 1955 and 1958.

At the end of the 19th century golf had taken hold in the United States and was soon played in almost every country in the world. Meanwhile England was producing great players. J. H. Taylor and H. Vardon, together with J. Braid, a Scotsman, won the open championship 16 times between 1894 and 1914. Vardon, the greatest player that the world had seen up to that time, won the title six times. These three supreme golfers were known as "the great triumvirate" and were primarily responsible for the formation of the Professional Golfers association in 1901. This body (which has about 2,000 members) is responsible for professional tournaments and for the biennial Ryder cup match (for professionals) when it is played in Great Britain.

2. United States.—The first official United States open, amateur and women's amateur championships were held in 1895, and the respective winners were Horace Rawlins, Charles B. Macdonald and Mrs. Charles S. Brown. An unofficial open, at match play, in 1894 was won by Willie Dunn.

After World War I the influence of the many Scottish golfers who had emigrated to the United States became evident. U.S. golfers (principally Walter Hagen and Robert T. [Bobby] Jones, Jr., who achieved the unparalleled performance of winning the open and amateur championships of Great Britain and the U.S. in the same year, 1930) monopolized the British open championship until T. H. Cotton won in 1934, a feat he repeated in 1937 and 1948.

By the early 1930s U.S. dominance of the international scene was growing. From 1933 until 1958 the only victories by British teams in the biennial matches against the United States were in 1938, when the amateurs won the Walker cup, in 1952 and 1956 (the match was tied in 1965), when the women won the Curtis cup, which they retained in 1958 with a tie, and in 1957, when the professionals won the Ryder cup.

Walter J. Travis was the first great U.S. golfer. He was born in Australia, but his golf was wholly learned in the United States. Of striking appearance, with jet black beard and impeccable garb, he was unpopular with fellow golfers because of his austere, taciturn demeanour. But he proved his ability as a golfer by winning the U.S. amateur in 1900, 1901 and 1903, by reaching the semifinals in five other years and by winning the qualifying medal in 1900, 1901, 1902, 1906, 1907 and 1908. He won the British amateur title the only year he entered this event—1904.

Jerome D. Travers learned his golf at Nassau Country club, Long Island, under the tutelage of Alec Smith, famous Scots professional who went to the U.S. in 1898. Travers was a player with indomitable courage, an ability to outgame an opponent at match play and nerve that rarely failed him in a crisis. He won the amateur championship in 1907, 1908, 1912 and 1913, and was finalist in 1914; he won the open title in 1915; and he won a long list of sectional championships.

Francis D. Ouimet became a national hero in 1913 when, unknown as a golfer except around Boston, he tied Vardon and Ted Ray, two of the best British professionals, at 304 strokes for 72 holes in the U.S. open, held at Brookline, and defeated them in a play-off, enabling the U.S. to retain the title. The following year

GOLF

Ouimet won the amateur, and he repeated 17 years later, in 1931. He was a semifinalist in 1923, 1924, 1926 and 1927; and was runner-up in 1920. He was a member of the United States team against Great Britain for the Walker cup from the first of these international matches in 1922 to 1949, serving as captain in 1932, 1934, 1936, 1938, 1947 and 1949.

Charles ("Chick") Evans, Jr., first showed promise as a golfer around Chicago in the period 1906-10. He was runner-up in the U.S. amateur of 1912 and the U.S. open of 1914, winning the western amateur title in both those years and also in 1909 and 1915. In 1916 he became the first golfer to win the U.S. amateur and open in the same year; his score of 286 in the open stood as the record low for 20 years, until Tony Manero scored 282 in the 1936 open. In 1942, at the age of 52, Evans fought his way against excellent competition to the final of the Chicago city championship, where he was defeated by a youthful opponent. Evans competed in 50 U.S.G.A. amateur championships and won 57 individual matches through 1962 but could not compete in 1963, at the age of 73, because of illness.

Bobby Jones is regarded as the greatest amateur golfer of modern times. His career was brilliant from his debut in national competition in the U.S. amateur of 1916 until his unparalleled performance in 1930 of winning all four of the world's most difficult titles—the British amateur, the British open, the U.S. amateur and open in the same year. This feat became known as Jones's "grand slam." During his golfing career Jones won the British open three times, the British amateur once, the U.S. open four times and the U.S. amateur five times. He played for the U.S. against Britain in the Walker cup team matches in 1922, 1924, 1926, 1928 and 1930.

W. Lawson Little, Jr., first appeared in national competition in the 1929 U.S. amateur, where he was defeated in the semifinal round by Francis Ouimet. In 1934 he won both the United States and British amateur titles and the following year repeated his victories in both events. Little turned professional in 1936, won the Canadian open that year and the U.S. open in 1940. Jack Nicklaus won the U.S.G.A. amateur twice, in 1959 and 1961, by the time he had reached the age of 21, but he turned professional later that same year and compiled an even more impressive record by winning the U.S. and British opens, the P.G.A. championship and the Masters.

Arnold Palmer, who first won the U.S.G.A. amateur, in 1954, and then turned professional, compiled another great modern record in winning the U.S. open, British open and the Masters.

Professional golfers contributed richly to the history of the game in the United States, and while it was well into the 20th century before there was a native-born champion among them, the over-all record of the pros was remarkable. No other country produced so many able players; Walter Hagen and Gene Sarazen were particularly outstanding.

U.P.I. COMPIX

BOBBY JONES IN A PRACTICE ROUND OF THE NATIONAL AMATEUR CHAMPIONSHIP AT PEBBLE BEACH, CALIFORNIA, IN 1929

U.P.I. COMPIX

A. D. (BOBBY) LOCKE, OF JOHANNESBURG, SOUTH AFRICA, DRIVING OFF THE FIFTH TEE IN THE 1947 PHILADELPHIA INQUIRER INVITATIONAL TOURNAMENT AT CEDARBROOK COUNTRY CLUB. HE WON THE $15,000 FIRST PRIZE WITH A 7-UNDER-PAR SCORE OF 277 FOR THE 72 HOLES

Walter Hagen first appeared on the national scene in the 1913 U.S. open at Brookline, where he gave an excellent account of himself, considering his competitive inexperience, and placed fourth against an expert field. The following year at Chicago he won the event. His golf, entirely self-taught, was unorthodox; he had no desire to copy the smoother swings of his fellow professionals. He scorned to practise by the hour, as was the practice of other pros. To Hagen, more than to any other golfer, goes the credit for breaking down the barriers between amateurs and professionals. Between 1914 and 1936 Hagen won the U.S. open twice, the British open four times (a feat matched after World War I only by A. D. Locke of South Africa and P. W. Thomson of Australia), the P.G.A. championship five times (including four in a row—1924, 1925, 1926, 1927), the Canadian, French and Belgian opens once each and at least 45 other events of lesser importance. In all he participated in not less than 200 open tournaments and was rarely out of the money. In addition, he played in about 1,500 exhibition matches in the U.S. and other countries, many of them for high fees or stakes. He is said to have earned around $1,000,000 during the 22 years he was rated as a top-flight golfer.

Gene Sarazen reached golfing fame in 1922 by winning the U.S. open at Chicago and proved he was a golfer of more than passing ability by adding the professional title that same year at Oakmont, Pa., and the following year came his way for ten years, but during this titles of importance came his way at Pelham, N.Y. No further period he was a constant competitive threat. In 1940 he tied Lawson Little for the U.S. open championship with a score of 287, but lost the play-off with 73 to Little's 70.

As Hagen, Sarazen and Tommy Armour passed their prime, other professionals carried on but it was not until the late 1930s that the so-called pro circuit, underwritten by civic and club organizations throughout the country, began putting up major prize money for the experts. Robert E. Harlow developed this circuit and was the first tournament manager of the P.G.A. Fred Corcoran succeeded him in 1937. That year, aggregate prize monies totaled $100,000; when Corcoran left the field in 1947, they totaled $650,-000. In the second half of the 20th century the P.G.A. circuit offered approximately $5,000,000 in prizes annually.

Other names in U.S. professional golf history include J. Barnes, who won the professional title in 1916 and 1919, L. Diegel, who won in 1928 and 1929, D. Shute, who won in 1936 and 1937, and R. Guldahl, who won the open title in 1937 and 1938. Byron Nelson, Ben Hogan and Sam Snead, after 1940, combined to win the major portion of prize monies. Following World War II Nelson retired from serious tournament participation. After winning the U.S. open and the P.G.A. title in 1948, Hogan, following his recovery from serious injuries suffered in an automobile accident, returned to the golfing circuit in 1950 and won the U.S. open in that year and in 1951 and 1953, the year he also won the British open (to duplicate the feats of only two other Americans, Bobby Jones and Gene Sarazen) and scored a record 14-under-par 274 to win the U.S. Masters.

The Masters tournament, an open, invitational event played each spring at Augusta, Ga., was originated in 1934. Hogan's record fell to 25-year-old Jack Nicklaus (1963 winner) in 1965 when he scored a 17-under-par 271, including one round of 64, tieing the record set by Lloyd Mangrum in 1940. He won by 9 strokes over four-time Masters champion Arnold Palmer (1958, 1960, 1962, 1964) and Gary Player of South Africa (winner in 1961); Jones called it "the greatest performance in golfing history."

In the United States from 1900 to 1930, four women golfers were outstanding. First of these was Margaret Curtis, who won the women's championship in 1907, 1911 and 1912. Alexa Stirling of Atlanta, Ga., won her first national title while quite young in 1916 and repeated in 1919 and 1920. She was runner-up in 1921 and 1923 and in 1925, as Mrs. W. G. Fraser. She also won the Canadian championship in 1920 and 1934.

Another great U.S. woman golfer is Mrs. Glenna Collett Vare, who won her first women's title in 1922 and repeated on five occasions—1925, 1928, 1929, 1930 and 1935. She made four attempts at the British championship but was turned back—on two occasions in the final round. Mrs. Vare's extended hold on women's golf was broken when Virginia Van Wie of Chicago replaced her as champion during the three seasons of 1932, 1933 and 1934. Miss Van Wie forfeited her title without contest in 1935, when Mrs. Vare regained the title by defeating Patty Berg. Betty Jameson won the title twice in a row, in 1939 and 1940. And Mrs. Vare won the women's U.S. senior championship.

The greatest names in women's golf after World War II included Mrs. Mildred ("Babe") Didrikson Zaharias, Patty Berg, Louise Suggs, Betsy Rawls and Mickey Wright, all of whom played professionally. Mrs. Zaharias, an Olympic winner in track and field in 1932, picked up a golf club that year at the invitation of Grantland Rice and from that time played the game with astounding success. She regained her amateur status long enough to win the British women's amateur title in 1947—the first American to do so. She turned pro again and embarked on a series of successful golf tours. The women follow a professional circuit similar to that of their male counterparts. From 1946, when the women started their own open championship, Mrs. Zaharias continued to be the leading woman player until her death in 1956.

Television enhanced the popularity of golf, such tournaments as the open, masters and several others being given network coverage on the final day. The first tournament of national import to be televised was the 1947 U.S. open, in St. Louis, and the televising of golf attained great popularity by the 1960s. For records of the major championships, see SPORTING RECORD.

IV. THE MODERN GAME
A. PLAYING THE COURSE

The game consists in playing the ball from a teeing ground into a hole by successive strokes in accordance with the rules. The stipulated round consists of 18 holes, and most golf courses have 18. Standard 18-hole courses measure from 6,500 to 7,000 yd.;

U.P.I. COMPIX

"BABE" DIDRIKSON ZAHARIAS WAS THE LEADING WOMAN GOLFER FROM THE LATE 1930S THROUGH THE EARLY 1950S

individual holes, from 100 to 600 yd. However, some courses have only nine holes and these are played twice in a stipulated round. The clubs are designed for the various positions in which the ball may come to rest and for the various distances to the hole. The objective is to hole the ball in the fewest strokes.

There are two distinct forms of play: match play and stroke (medal) play. In match play the player and his opponent are playing together and competing only against each other, while in stroke play each competitor is competing against every other player in the tournament. In match play, the game is played by holes and each hole is won by the player who holes his ball in the fewer strokes. If both players hole in the same number of strokes, it is halved. When a player has won one more hole than his opponents, he is said to be one up. The match is won by the player who is leading by a number of holes greater than the number of holes remaining to be played, as, for example, three up and two to play. In stroke play, the competitor who holes the stipulated round or rounds in the fewest total strokes is the winner. Amateur championships once were all at match play and professional and open championships at stroke play, over 72 holes. The U.S. amateur championship and some other amateur events have been changed to stroke play.

In both match and stroke play, players can compete as individuals or as partners. When two players compete as partners, each playing his own ball, the better ball on each hole is their score for that hole; this is a four-ball or best-ball match. Two players may compete as partners with two others, each pair playing alternate strokes on a single ball; this is a match foursome.

Players of varying abilities compete against each other by using handicaps. A handicap is the number of strokes a player receives to adjust his score to a common level. The better the player, the smaller his handicap, and the best players have handicaps of zero and are called scratch players. A scratch player whose average score is 70 can have an enjoyable match with a player whose average score is 80 by giving him a handicap of 10 strokes. Handicap golf is limited to amateur competitions, and championship tournaments are played without handicaps.

The starting place for each hole to be played is the teeing ground. The front is indicated by two markers, and the teeing ground is the rectangular space two club lengths in depth directly behind the line indicated by the markers. The player tees his ball anywhere within this space, usually setting it up on a small wooden or plastic peg, and strikes it toward the hole. The stroke from the teeing ground is called the drive.

The preferred line to the hole is generally a clear, mowed route called the fairway. The fairway is customarily bordered by longer grass called rough, and farther from the fairway there may be woods. At strategic places along the preferred line to the hole and

U.P.I. COMPIX

BEN HOGAN, DEFENDING CHAMPION IN THE U.S. OPEN GOLF CHAMPIONSHIP, TEES OFF AT OAKLAND HILLS (MICHIGAN) COUNTRY CLUB IN JUNE 1951

GOLF

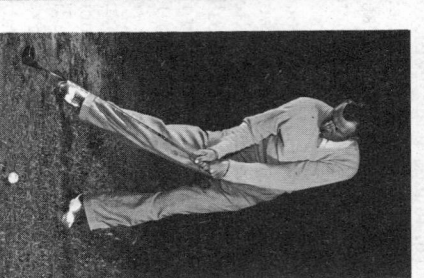

FRANK J. SCHERSCHEL

A WELL-EXECUTED TEE-SHOT

From upper left, the backswing, downswing, and follow-through of a smooth tee-shot

1. To initiate the backswing, the left hip is turned to the right. The shoulders, arms, hands, and club follow in one coordinated movement, with the club shaft kept in line with a straight (but not tense) left arm. The club head starts low and follows the body turn
2. Most of the player's weight has shifted onto his braced right leg, the left side is relaxed and the left heel has lifted slightly
3. At the top of the swing, the wrists are fully cocked and remain so until just before the ball is hit. There is a full body turn, essential for power. The club shaft is horizontal, with both hands well under the shaft. A full grip is maintained with the left hand.
4. The left hip starts the downswing. The left arm is straight without tenseness. As the body uncoils, it pulls the straight left arm down, and the wrists are still cocked.
5. The player's weight gradually shifts off the right foot. The left hip has turned well out of the way of the left arm. Wrists are uncocked to bring the club again into alignment with the left arm for a powerful blow.
6. As the club approaches impact, the wrists and legs have straightened. The right hand hits hard and the left hand grip must support it
7. The club head follows the line of flight until the wrists naturally begin to turn
8. Note that, until now, the head has been held steady to preserve balance, and the right elbow has been kept comfortably close to the right hip to give the swing compactness
9. At the finish, the body has turned to face the line of flight. The player balances on his left heel

guarding the putting green are obstacles called bunkers, depressions in the ground filled with sand (sand traps). Some bunkers require the player to skirt or cross streams or ponds. Both bunkers and bodies of water are termed "hazards."

The hole itself measures 4½ in. in diameter, is at least 4 in. deep and is set in an area of turf specially prepared and maintained and closely mowed for putting. When the player putts, he uses a straight-faced club and rolls the ball across the putting green toward and eventually into the hole. An expert player plays most holes in four strokes, a drive of 225 to 250 yd., a shot to the green and two putts. However, every course contains a few short holes on which the expert might be expected to drive onto the putting green and a few long holes on which the expert might require a drive and two more strokes to reach the putting green. On the former, he would be expected to make 3 and on the latter 5, since two putts on each green is the standard.

Every course in the United States has a par, which is defined as the score an expert would be expected to make, and many courses also have a bogey, which is defined as the score that a moderately good golfer would be expected to make. Both par and bogey are defined by the U.S.G.A. as errorless play without flukes and under ordinary weather conditions, allowing two strokes on the putting green. However, par is essentially a U.S. term that came into use in the early 1900s as a base for computing handicaps under the system devised by L. Calkins of Plainfield, N.J. Bogey is essentially a British term that came into use in England in 1891 and was derived from a mythical Colonel Bogey, who was described as uniformly steady but never overbrilliant. As the terms developed, bogey was sometimes, although not always, one stroke higher than par. Thus, colloquially in the United States, bogey often is used to indicate a score one stroke above par.

B. CLUBS

In the average good player's set there are either 3 or 4 wood clubs and 9 or 10 irons (no more than 14 clubs may be carried during a round). No two clubs in a set are the same. There are differences in length and suppleness of shaft, weight, size and shape of head, the angle at which the shaft ends and the head begins (the lie) and the angle of the face of the club from the vertical (the loft).

The various clubs are known both by number and by name. The names have come down from the early days of golf; the numbers are a U.S. innovation dating from the early 1920s, when matched sets came in and it was found more practical to indicate club gradations by consecutive numbering than to stamp the name on the club's sole. (See *Equipment and the Development of the Game,* above.)

1. Wood Clubs.—*Number One (Driver).*—Used from the tee for maximum distance; has a large head and a deep, almost vertical face. For the average player the driver is 42 to 43 in. long and weighs between 13 and 14 oz. and the face has an angle of loft of about 10°.

Number Two (Brassie).—So called because the sole of the club originally was covered with a brass plate. Used mostly for long shots from good fairway lies, the club has a slightly smaller and shallower face than a driver but with more loft.

Number Three (Spoon).—Shorter shaft and shallower face than driver or brassie, but face has considerably more loft. The club is used to play the ball from lies too poor for a brassie, and also for strokes when the use of a driver or brassie would send the ball beyond the green.

Number Four (Baffy).—Smaller head, shallower face and more loft than a spoon. It will hit a ball about as far as a number one iron.

Number Five.—A great favourite with players who have an aversion to iron clubs, it replaces the number three or four iron. It has a small and compact head.

2. Irons.—*Number One (Driving Iron or Cleek).*—A long shaft and an angle of loft of about 20°. Used for tee shots and full shots of 190 to 205 yd. from lies too "heavy" for a wood. A difficult club to use, it produces a long, low shot. Note: all distances here and below are calibrated for the medium-hitting player. The professionals get more distance.

Number Two (Midiron).—Slightly more loft, for shots from 180 to 190 yd.

Number Three (Mid Mashie).—For 170–180-yd. shots.
Number Four (Mashie Iron).—For 160–170-yd. shots.
Number Five (Mashie).—For shots between 150 and 160 yd. Ball pitches high and stops quickly after hitting the ground. This club is also used for pitch-and-run shots from 30 to 50 yd. off the green; the ball travels part of the way through the air, then rolls the rest of the way.

Number Six (Spade Mashie).—For shots between 140 and 150

yd. and also for playing the ball from high grass or difficult lies, when getting out is more important than distance.

Number Seven (Mashie Niblick).—Resembles the spade mashie, but has still more loft and head weight. Used for shots between 130 and 140 yd.; puts plenty of backspin on the ball.

Number Eight (Pitching Niblick).—Still more loft, for shots of from 120 to 130 yd.

Number Nine (Niblick).—Face has a loft of about 47° and the head is heavy, to carry it through long tough grass or heavy sand. A ball, properly hit, rises almost vertically and upon hitting the ground may jump backward as a result of the backspin this club imparts.

Number Ten (Wedge).—Face has a loft of more than 50°, but the club has a broad flange on the sole. There are two types of wedges—the sand wedge to use in bunkers and the pitching wedge for pitch shots.

The Putter.—A club with a short stiff shaft and a straight or nearly straight face, for rolling the ball on the green. There are many styles of putters.

C. THE GRIP

While a golf club may be gripped in various ways and satisfactory shots result, the so-called overlapping grip seems to be the most commonly used among expert players and the most frequently taught by golf instructors. Fig. 3 shows the progressive stages of the hands of a right-handed player in assuming this grip, which is used for all clubs except the putter. (For recommended putting grip, *see under Putting,* below.)

While the overlapping grip is almost universally used among golfers, the interlocking grip has its advocates. This grip differs from the overlapping in only one particular—the little finger of the right hand does not overlap the left forefinger, but instead fits down between the left fore- and middle fingers.

D. TYPES OF SHOTS

Descriptions are for right-handed players.

1. The Wood Shot.—With the wood clubs, the player assumes a generally square stance in relation to the intended line of flight. He should feel comfortable and well balanced. The club head is placed on the turf directly back of the ball, with the face at right angles to the flight line. Keeping his eye on the ball, the player starts the club back slowly along the ground until the extended arms naturally lift it. This action continues to the top of the swing, at which point the club shaft is approximately horizontal, with both wrists underneath it. The left arm is fairly straight but not rigid, with just enough elbow bend to permit freedom. The right elbow is kept close to the body. The backswing must be unhurried; a fast jerky backswing will destroy timing.

The downswing is started by a co-ordinated pull of the left hip, shoulder, arm and hand, slowly at first, then accelerated as the ball is neared. Care must be taken not to "hit" too soon; greatest acceleration should be achieved at the moment of impact with the ball. At impact the left arm and club shaft are in alignment and the club follows through along the line of flight until the arms naturally bring it up and around to the rear.

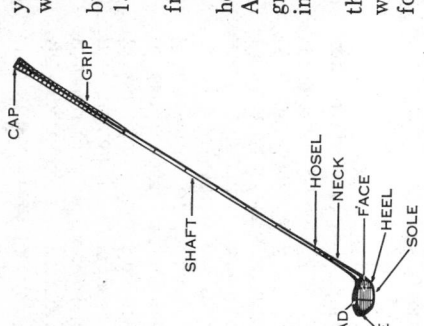

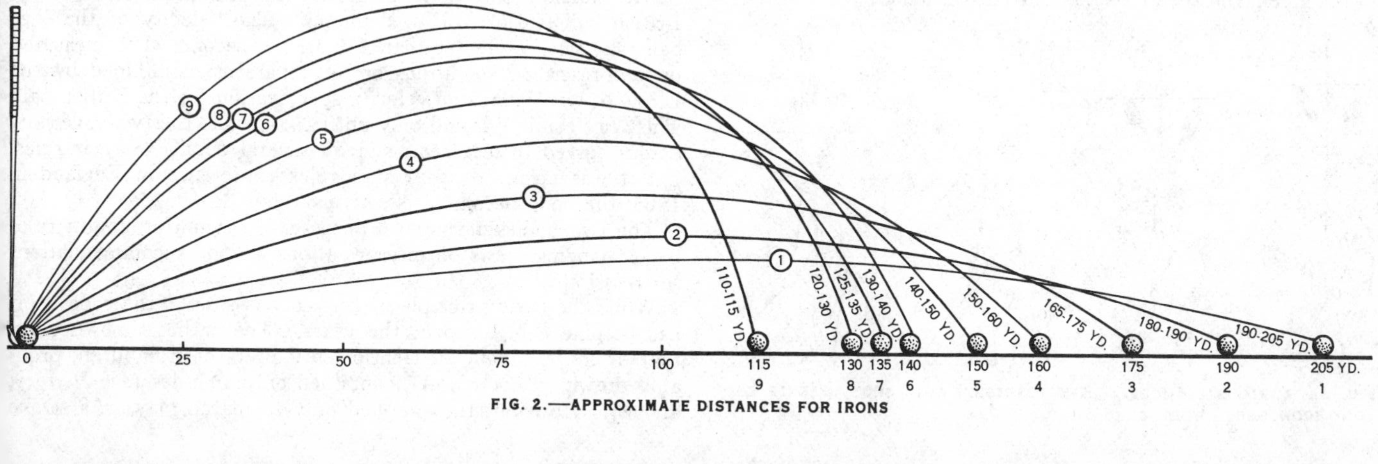

FIG. 1.—PARTS OF A GOLF CLUB

CAP
GRIP
SHAFT
HOSEL
NECK
FACE
HEEL
SOLE
HEAD
TOE

FIG. 2.—APPROXIMATE DISTANCES FOR IRONS

110-115 YD.
120-130 YD.
125-135 YD.
130-140 YD.
140-150 YD.
150-160 YD.
165-175 YD.
180-190 YD.
190-205 YD.

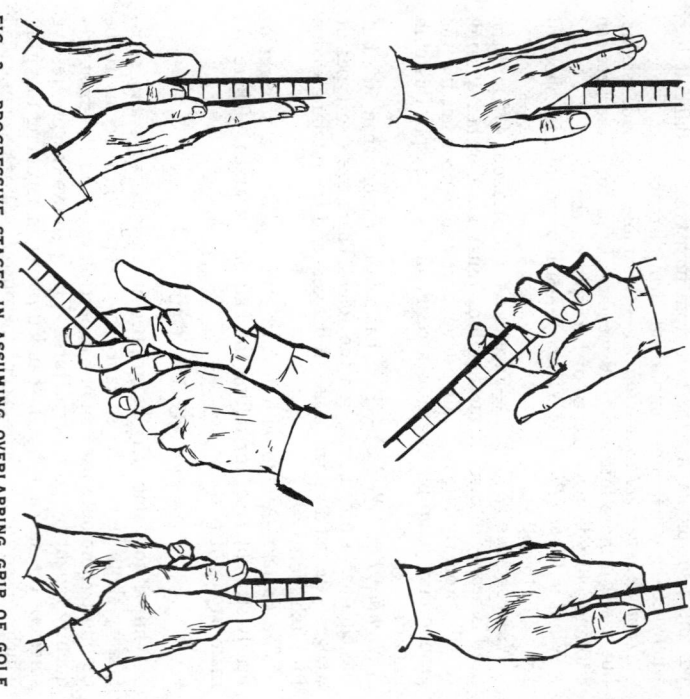

FIG. 3.—PROGRESSIVE STAGES IN ASSUMING OVERLAPPING GRIP OF GOLF CLUB

2. The Iron Shot.—The technique employed in hitting an iron shot is somewhat different from that used with the woods. Iron shots are hit more crisply and downward; the club head comes in contact with the ball and continues down and through, taking some turf (called a divot). This aids in control and imparts back-spin to the ball so that it rises readily and comes to rest without much roll—a desirable feature, since irons are rarely used for distance shots but rather for shots of medium to short length. It is easier for the golfer to gauge the travel of a quick-stopping ball.

Actually, contact with the ball and the turf must be almost simultaneous, since to hit the turf back of the ball will rob the shot of much of its power, while picking the ball clean will result in a flat shot and too much roll.

The stance for long irons is not greatly different from that employed with a wood, with the ball off the left heel, but as the iron selected for a shot becomes progressively shorter (that is, a shorter shaft and a face more laid back) the ball is played more and more toward the right foot. The swing is inclined to be more upright and, especially on the shorter shots, the backswing and follow-through are less full.

3. Approaching.—When the player has come within close range of the green, two methods of play are open to him—he may pitch the ball all the way up on backspin to stop his ball near the pin, or he may play a chip shot in which the ball flies part way through the air, as to the edge of the close-clipped surface of the green, and then rolls the remaining distance.

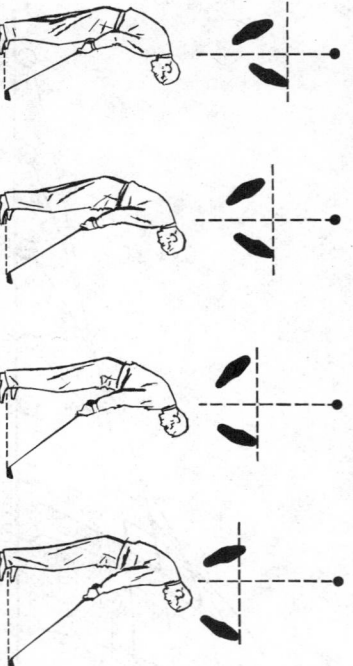

FIG. 4.—VARIOUS STANCES. LEFT TO RIGHT: CHIP SHOT, MASHIE SHOT LONG-IRON SHOT, WOOD-CLUB SHOT

4. Shots From Sand.—Even the expert player will rarely complete his round without having to play his ball from the loose sand in a bunker. For this he uses his sand wedge. An open stance is used—that is, the left foot is considerably withdrawn from the line to the cup. Care is taken to worm the feet well into the sand to ensure a firm footing through the stroke. The club is carried up more vertically than in other shots and then sent down at a spot behind the ball, follow-ing a path that cuts across the line to the hole.

This places a layer of sand between the ball and the club head; the ball thus is blasted from the sand without actually being touched with the club.

When the player's ball is in a bunker at a distance from the green and lies well perched on the sand, it is possible to play an ordinary iron shot and get considerable distance.

5. Putting.—The putt, once the ball is on the green, is the most delicate shot in golf. The player must hit the ball along a line that allows for very little margin of error, and with enough force to roll the ball to the hole but not too far beyond in case the hole is missed. And since most greens are not level but have numerous minor pitches and slopes great care must be taken to select the proper line, which may be far to one side or the other of the hole.

The grip for putting differs from the grip for other clubs. The hands are placed on the shaft so the palms are opposed and parallel to the putter blade. This is for the purpose of relieving all muscular strain in the wrists during the stroke. The player stands quite erect (see fig. 5) with his head directly over the ball and his feet close together and square to the line of putt. The ball is generally played off the left foot, in which case the player's weight is balanced rather more over the left leg than the right.

Knees are slightly bent to avoid tenseness. Hands are kept close to the body, with the left elbow moved out to point along the line of putt. Head and body are not allowed to move during the stroke. The putter is soled square across the line of putt, then brought back low along the ground. On the downstroke the putter still maintains its position square in the line of putt, hits the ball crisply in dead centre, then follows through straight toward the hole. Straddling the ball in the "croquet" stance was banned under R. and A. and U.S.G.A. rules, effective 1968.

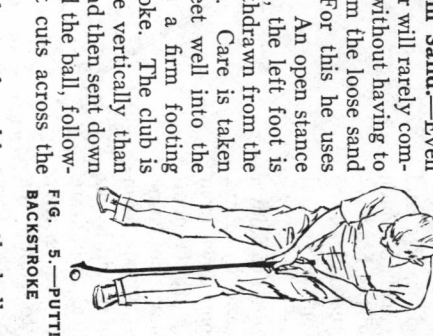

FIG. 5.—PUTTING STANCE AND BACKSTROKE

E. RULES OF GOLF

The rule-making golf organizations are the R. and A. and the U.S.G.A. As a result of a series of conferences in England and Scotland in 1951, the two bodies agreed on a uniform code of rules to govern play all over the world. The only difference is in the specifications for the ball. The minimum size for the United States ball is 1.680 in. in diameter; the minimum size for the British ball is 1.620 in. in diameter. The velocity of the U.S. ball may not be greater than 250 ft. per second when measured under prescribed conditions on an apparatus maintained by the U.S.G.A. but there is no velocity specification for the British ball.

This "uniformity" lasted only until 1959, when the two governing bodies agreed to disagree again on several details of their rules, but it was achieved again at a rules conference in England in 1966, the code becoming effective on Jan. 1, 1967.

The two bodies attempt to perpetuate the uniformity in rules by exchanging views on interpretations and on recommendations for revision.

While the basic principle of the rules is simple, the code itself has become complex over the years. The earliest known code, that of the Company of Gentlemen Golfers of Edinburgh, probably drawn up about 1745, contained only 13 rules (see History, above). However, they applied only to match play. As stroke play, foursomes, three-ball and four-ball play came into favour, additional rules had to be drawn. A rule that is fair for two opponents playing against each other might not work at all in stroke play, where each competitor is playing against the entire field. For example, if one ball strikes another on the putting green in singles match play, the owner of the ball struck may replace it or not as he chooses. No one except the two players involved has any interest in the incident. However, the owner of a ball so struck in stroke play must replace it, in fairness to all the other competitors in the field. Also, a rule that is satisfactory in individual play might be completely inadequate when two play as partners in either a match foursome or a four-ball match. There is an additional source of complexity in the fact that golf is played not on uniform fields or courts but on a wide variety of natural expanses.

The number of situations that can develop around a golf ball in play is almost limitless, and the rules makers have attempted over the years to cover as many as possible. Even so, it is impossible to cover all eventualities in rules, and both the U.S.G.A. and the R. and A. issue a series of interpretations each year.

The basic principle of the rules is to require that the ball be played from the teeing ground into the hole by successive strokes played from the club. The rules are designed to promote this objective and to prevent the game from becoming one of maneuver by hand. They have been summarized in the statement: "Play the ball as it lies and take the course as you find it." This means that, as a general rule, the ball is to be teed and not touched again with the hands until it is lifted from the hole. The player is expected to employ his own skill with his clubs to avoid rough, hazards and other difficulties and to play his ball without improving its lie in any way.

There are exceptions to this general rule that complicate the code. The rules, for example, provide means of proceeding when a player is physically unable to play his ball as it lies because he has lost it, hit it out of bounds where play is prohibited or into a water hazard where he cannot get at it. The means of proceeding in such cases involve a penalty of one stroke and playing another ball in a specified position. If, for example, a player's drive from the tee goes out of bounds, that stroke is counted as one, he adds a penalty stroke to his score and his next stroke is his third. The rules permit a player to take relief without penalty when his ball comes to rest in a temporary accumulation of water (as opposed to a permanent water hazard), in ground under repair, against a shed or in a paper bag or near any other artificial structure or substance foreign to the course. Thus the rules contain not only penalties for infractions or inability to proceed in normal fashion but also rights and privileges that a player may exercise in certain situations.

Additionally, of course, the rules define the various areas of the course, such as teeing ground, through the green, hazards and putting green, in each of which rules and procedures may differ. The rules also provide for orderly progress of play.

Golf is played on the honour system. A player is expected to count his own strokes even though he may miss the ball completely; to acknowledge the fact promptly if he violates a rule and incurs a penalty and to avoid interfering in any way with his opponent's or fellow competitors' play. When a referee accompanies players, his primary duty is to settle questions of fact and of golfing law. It is a basic requirement of good sportsmanship in golf to develop a working knowledge of the rules so that one will not through ignorance take advantage of another player, in either a tournament or an informal game. Few players or officials are able to answer all questions that may arise in the differing forms of play, and the experienced ones usually carry rules booklets for reference. The official rules for the United States may be obtained from the U.S.G.A.

F. RULES OF AMATEUR STATUS

Golfing rules of amateur status are most strict. The U.S.G.A. and the R. and A. both define an amateur as "one who plays the game solely as a non-remunerative or non-profit-making sport."

The rules prohibit an amateur from playing for a money prize, from accepting a prize readily convertible into money or exceeding a stipulated value and from receiving compensation for giving instruction. The rules also prohibit amateurs from accepting payments in any form, directly or indirectly, toward expenses incurred in connection with a golf competition, with a few specific exceptions under which the British are slightly more liberal. British amateurs may accept payments toward expenses incurred as members of an international team only. The U.S.G.A. also permits amateurs to accept payments toward expenses incurred as participants in its amateur public links championship and in competitions limited to members of educational institutions, industrial organizations and military services. Otherwise, amateur golfers are expected to adhere strictly to the classic ideal that amateurs play purely for pleasure and at their own expense.

Additional rules in both codes are designed to deter amateurs from commercializing in any way on their skills or reputations as golfers. However, professionals and amateurs may compete together at will and frequently do. Also, professionals in other sports may play as amateurs in golf provided they conduct themselves in accordance with the rules of amateur status. A golfer who has relinquished his amateur status but has not been a professional for more than five years may regain amateur status by applying to the governing body in his country and serving a probationary period of two years from the date of his last violation of the rules.

V. GLOSSARY

The following terms are used in printed accounts of golf matches and in books of instruction; also included are some vernacular expressions in common usage among players.

Ace.—A hole scored in one stroke.

Addressing the ball.—A player has "addressed the ball" when he has taken his stance by placing his feet in position for and preparatory to making a stroke and has also grounded his club (*see* Ground), except that in a hazard a player has addressed the ball when he has taken his stance preparatory to making a stroke.

All square.—An even score, neither side being a hole up.

Approach.—A stroke or shot to the putting green.

Apron.—The last few yards of fairway in front of the green.

Away.—The farthest from the hole.

Backspin.—Backward rotation of the ball, causing it to stop abruptly.

Bent grass.—A species of grass used for putting greens.

Best ball.—Match in which a single player competes against the best ball of two or more.

Birdie.—One stroke under par for a hole.

Bisque.—A handicap stroke or strokes to be taken when desired, with the provision that the player must announce his choice to use a bisque on any hole before teeing off for the next hole.

Blind.—An approach position from which the green cannot be seen.

Bogey.—A one-over-par score for a hole. Originally, the score a moderately good golfer would be expected to make on a hole.

Borrow.—In putting, to play to either side of the direct line from the ball to the hole to compensate for roll or slant in the green.

Bunker.—An area of bare ground, often a depression, usually covered with sand. (*See* Sand trap; Hazard.)

Bye holes.—Holes remaining after a match is finished, that is, after one side is more holes up than remain for play.

Caddie.—Person who carries a player's clubs.

Carry.—Distance from where a ball is hit to where it first strikes the ground.

Casual water.—Any temporary accumulation of water, as a puddle after rain.

Chip.—Short approach shot, on which the ball flies close to the ground.

Concede.—(*a*) To grant that an opponent will hole out a dead ball (*see* Dead) in one more stroke. (*b*) To grant that an opponent has won a hole before play has been completed.

Course.—The terrain over which the game is played; the whole area within which play is permitted. (*See also* Links.)

Cup.—The hole into which the ball is played, 4¼ in. in diameter and at least 4 in. deep. (*See also* Hole.)

Dead.—A ball is said to be "dead" when so near the hole that putting it in on the next stroke is a "dead" certainty; a ball is said to fall dead when it pitches with little or no run.

Default.—To concede a match to an opponent without playing against him; to fail to appear for a scheduled match.

Divot.—A piece of turf cut out by a club during a stroke, which should always be replaced before the player moves on.

Dog-leg.—A hole that bends sharply to left or right between tee and green.

Dormie.—A side is dormie when it is as many holes up as remain to be played.

Down.—In match play, a side is down when it has lost more holes than it has won.

Draw.—Controlled hook (see Hook).

Duffer.—An unskilful player; also, to hit the ball poorly.

Eagle.—Two strokes under par for a hole.

Face.—(a) Slope of a bunker. (b) Part of the club head that strikes the ball.

Fade.—Controlled slice (see Slice).

Fairway.—The closely cut turf intended for play between tee and green.

Flagstick.—Movable straight indicator, usually a lightweight pole with a numbered flag, placed in the hole to show its location; sometimes referred to as the pin.

Follow-through.—Continuation of the swing of the club after the ball has been struck.

"Fore!"—Warning cry by a player to any person in the way of his ball.

Forecaddie.—A person employed to indicate the position of balls on the course.

Four-ball match.—A match in which there are two players to a side, each side playing its better ball against the better ball of the other side.

Foursome.—A match in which there are two players to a side, each side playing one ball.

Gobble.—A boldly hit putt which finds the hole.

Green.—Putting green around a hole.

Gross.—A player's score before deducting any handicap.

Ground.—To sole or rest the club lightly on the ground, preparatory to striking the ball (see Addressing the Ball).

Ground under repair.—Any portion of the course under repair or maintenance. If a ball should land on ground under repair or if the ball may be lifted and dropped, without penalty, as near as possible to where it lay, but not nearer the hole.

Halved.—A hole is halved when each side has taken the same number of strokes.

Handicap.—The number of strokes a player receives to adjust his score to a common level, the generally accepted common level being scratch, or zero-handicap golf.

Hanging.—A hanging ball is one which lies on a downslope.

Hazard.—Any bunker or water hazard.

Heel.—(a) Part of the club head nearest the shaft. (b) To hit from this part and send the ball at right angles to the line of play.

Hole.—(a) The hole into which the ball is played (see Cup). (b) One of the 18 units, or holes, on a course, consisting of teeing ground, fairway, rough, hazards and putting green.

Hole-high.—A ball that lies even with the hole (cup) but to one side or the other.

Hole out.—Make the final stroke in playing the ball into the hole.

Honour.—The privilege of driving off, or playing from the teeing ground, first.

Hook.—To curve the ball widely to the left.

Hosel.—Socket on the club head into which the shaft is fitted.

Lateral water hazard.—A water hazard running approximately parallel to the line of play and so situated that it is impractical to keep the spot at which a ball crosses the hazard margin between the player and the hole.

Lie.—(a) The inclination of a club when held on the ground in the natural position for striking. (b) The situation of the ball.

Like.—Stroke which makes a player's score equal to his opponent's on a given hole.

Line.—The direction in which a player desires his ball to travel.

Links.—A golf course, especially a seaside course.

Loft.—(a) To elevate the ball. (b) Backward slant of the face of the club.

Long game.—The strokes where attaining distance is the more important factor.

Loose impediments.—Natural object not fixed or growing, as a stone, leaf or twig.

Marker.—(a) A scorer in stroke play appointed by a tournament committee to record a competitor's score. (b) A marker indicating the front edge of a teeing ground or the boundaries of a hole.

Match play.—Reckoning the score by holes won and lost.

Medal play.—Stroke play (see Stroke Play).

Mixed foursome.—Foursome in which a man and a woman play as partners.

Nassau.—A system of scoring under which one point is awarded for winning the first 9 holes, one for the second 9, and a third for the full 18.

Net.—Score after deducting handicap.

Observer.—Person appointed by a tournament committee to assist a referee in deciding questions of fact and to report to him any breach of a rule or local rule.

Obstruction.—Anything artificial that has been erected, placed or left on the course.

Odd.—Stroke that makes a player's score one more than his opponent's on a given hole.

Out of bounds.—Ground on which play is prohibited.

Outside agency.—Referee, observer, marker, forecaddie or other agency not a part of the match or, in stroke play, not a part of a player's side.

Par.—Theoretically perfect play, or the score an expert would be expected to make on a hole, calculated on the number of strokes required to reach the green plus two putts. Par is calculated on the basis of distance. Women's par for a course is slightly higher than par for men. U.S.G.A. standards for computing par are:

	Men's par	Women's par
Par 3	up to 250 yd.	up to 210 yd.
Par 4	251 to 470 yd.	211 to 400 yd.
Par 5	471 and over	401 to 575 yd.
Par 6		576 yd. and over

Penalty stroke.—A stroke added to the score of a side under certain rules.

Pin.—Rod or pole to which flag is attached (see Flagstick).

Pitch.—An approach on which the ball is lofted in a high arc (see Chip).

Pitch-and-run.—An approach on which a part of the desired distance is covered by the roll of the ball after it strikes the ground.

Pivot.—The turn of the body as a stroke is played.

Pull.—To hit the ball so that it will curve to the left.

Putt.—(a) To run a ball along the ground in an approach, instead of chipping or pitching it. (b) Distance a ball rolls after it lands.

Putting green.—All ground of the hole being played that is specially prepared for putting or is otherwise defined as such by the committee.

Referee.—Person appointed by the tournament committee to accompany players to decide questions of fact and rules of golf.

Rough.—Long grass bordering the fairway, also at times between tee and fairway; may include bushes, trees, etc.

Rub of the green.—Any deflection or stoppage of a ball by an outside agency; the ball is played as it lies, without penalty.

Run.—(a) To run a ball along the ground as it lies, without penalty.

Sand trap.—A bunker having a layer of sand (see Bunker).

Sclaf.—To hit the ground behind the ball, derived from a Scots term meaning "a slight blow."

Scratch player.—One who receives no handicap allowance.

Short game.—Approach shots and putts.

Single.—Match between two players.

Slice.—To curve the ball widely to the right.

Square.—When a match is even.

Stance.—Position of player's feet and body when addressing the ball.

Stroke.—Forward movement of the club with the intention of fairly striking at and moving the ball.

Stroke hole.—Hole on which a handicap stroke is given.

Stroke play.—Reckoning the score by total strokes, also known as medal play.

Tee.—An artificial peg or a pinch of sand on which the ball may be placed for the first stroke on each hole.

Teeing ground.—Starting place for the hole to be played, indicated by two marks on the ground; also called the tee.

Three-ball match.—Match in which three play against one another, each playing his own ball.

Threesome.—Match in which one player competes against two, who play alternate strokes with the same ball.

Through the green.—The whole area of the course except hazards and the teeing ground and putting green of the hole being played.

Up.—In match play, a side is up when it has won more holes than it has lost.

Water hazard.—Any sea, lake, pond, river, ditch, surface drainage ditch or other open water course regardless of whether or not it contains water, and anything of a similar nature (except casual water).

BIBLIOGRAPHY.—*History*: B. Darwin et al., *A History of Golf in Britain* (1952); Robert Browning, *A History of Golf; the Royal and Ancient Game* (1955); H. S. C. Everard, *A History of the Royal and Ancient Golf Club of St. Andrews From 1754-1900* (1907); W. E. Hughes, *Chronicles of Blackheath Golfers* (1897); H. B. Martin, *Fifty Years of American Golf* (1936); Horace Hutchinson, *Fifty Years of Golf* (1919); James Lindsay Stewart, *Golfiana Miscellanea* (1887); Game (1893); R. Clark (ed.); *Golf: a Royal and Ancient* Harry B. Wood, *Golfing Curios and the Like* (1911); Thomas S. Aitchison and George Lorimer, *Reminiscences of the Old Brunstsfield Links Golf Club* (1902); Andrew Lang, *St. Andrews* (1893); H. B. Martin and A.B. Halliday, *Saint Andrews Golf Club, 1888-1938* (1938); Charles Blair Macdonald, *Scotland's Gift, Golf* (1928); Robert Harris, *Sixty Years of Golf* (1953); Samuel L. Parrish, *Some Facts, Reflections and Personal Reminiscences Connected With the Introduction of the Game of Golf Into the United States, More Especially as Associated With the Formation of the Shinnecock Hills Golf Club* (1891); Frederic H. Curtiss and John Heard, *The Country Club, 1882-1932* (1932); P. Lawless Frank G. Menke, *The Encyclopedia of Sports* (1953);

(ed.), *The Golfer's Companion* (1937); Herbert Warren Wind, *The Story of American Golf* (1956); J. B. Salmond, *The Story of the R. & A.* (1956).

Golf Instruction: Alex J. Morrison, *A New Way to Better Golf* (1932); Richard D. Chapman and Ledyard Sands (eds.), *Golf as I Play It* (1940); Chick Evans, *Golf for Boys and Girls* (1954); Harry Gottlieb, *Golf for Southpaws* (1953); Patty Berg and Mark Cox, *Golf Illustrated* (1950); Robert T. Jones, Jr., and Harold E. Lowe, *Group Instruction in Golf* (1939); Tommy Armour, *How to Play Your Best Golf All of the Time* (1953); Sam Snead, *Natural Golf*, ed. by Tom Shehan (1953); Joe Novak, *Par Golf in 8 Steps* (1950); Ben Hogan, *Power Golf* (1948); Ernest Jones and Innis Brown, *Swinging Into Golf* (1946); Henry Cotton, *This Game of Golf* (1948); Byron Nelson, *Winning Golf* (1946).

See also The Golf Journal, formerly *USGA Journal and Turf Management*, published by the United States Golf Association. (J. P. Eh.)

GOLGI, CAMILLO (1843–1926), Italian physician and Nobel laureate noted for basic researches in neurology, was born in Cortona, July 9, 1843 (or, according to some sources, July 7, 1844). After taking his degree at Pavia in 1865 he became physician at the home for incurables in the village of Abbiategrasso. There, despite the primitive means of investigation available, he discovered his silver nitrate method of staining nerve cells and fibres—a method which gave the key to the finer structure of the nervous system.

In 1883 Golgi demonstrated in the central nervous system multipolar cells with many branching processes (Golgi cells) that establish connections with other nerve cells. This discovery led to W. von Waldeyer-Hartz's conception of the neuron as the unit of the nervous system and was fundamental for the development of modern neurology.

Apart from histological researches, Golgi was famous for his observations on malaria. He showed that the parasite of quartan fever differs from that of tertian, that malarial paroxysms are coincident with sporulation of the parasites and that the severity of a malarial attack depends on the number of parasites in the blood. He also made valuable observations on pellagra and on the causation of mental disease.

In 1906 Golgi, jointly with S. Ramón y Cajal (*q.v.*), was awarded the Nobel prize for physiology or medicine for his work on the structure of the nervous system. He died in Pavia on Jan. 21, 1926. (W. J. Br.)

GOLGOTHA (Aramaic "Skull") was the name of the spot where Christ was crucified (Matt. xxvii, 33; Mark xv, 22; John xix, 17), outside Jerusalem; otherwise called by the Latin name (also "skull"), Calvary (*q.v.*).

GOLIARD, a name applied to those wandering students (*vagantes*) and clerks in England, France and Germany, during the 12th and 13th centuries, who were better known for their rioting, gambling and intemperance than they were for their scholarship.

The derivation of the word is uncertain, but it was connected by them with a mythical "Bishop Golias," also called *archipoëta* and *primas*—especially in Germany—in whose name their satirical poems were mostly written. The jocular references to the rules of the "guild" of goliards should not be taken too seriously, though their aping of the "orders" of the church, especially their contrasting them with the mendicants, was denounced by church synods.

Their satires were almost uniformly directed against the church, attacking even the pope. In 1227 the Council of Trier forbade priests to permit the goliards to take part in chanting the service. In 1229 they played a conspicuous part in the disturbances at the University of Paris in connection with the intrigues of the papal legate.

During the century that followed they formed a subject for the deliberations of several church councils, notably in 1289, when it was ordered that "no clerks shall be jongleurs, goliards or buffoons," and in 1300 (at Cologne) when they were forbidden to preach or engage in the indulgence traffic. This legislation only became effective when the "privileges of clergy" were withdrawn from the goliards.

Along with their satires went many poems in praise of wine and riotous living. A remarkable collection of them, now at Munich, from the monastery at Benediktbeuern in Bavaria, was published by Schmeller (3rd ed., 1895) under the title *Carmina Burana*. Many of these, which form the main part of songbooks of German students today, were delicately translated by John Addington Symonds in a small volume, *Wine, Women and Song* (1884). The collection also includes the only known two surviving complete texts of medieval passion dramas—one with and one without music.

The word "goliard" itself outlived these turbulent bands which had given it birth, and passed over into French and English literature of the 14th century in the general meaning of jongleur or minstrel, quite apart from any clerical association. It is thus used in *Piers Plowman*, where, however, the *goliard* still rhymes in Latin, and in Chaucer.

BIBLIOGRAPHY.—O. Hubatsch, *Die lateinischen Vagantenlieder des Mittelalters* (1870); B. Spiegel, *Die Vaganten und ihr Orden* (1892); M. Haezner, *Goliardendichtung und die Satire im 13ten Jahrhundert in England* (1905); the article in *La Grande Encyclopédie*; Helen Waddell, *The Wandering Scholars* (1927); also K. Breul, *The Cambridge Songs* (1915).

GOLIATH, the name of the giant by slaying whom David achieved renown (I Sam. xvii). The Philistines had come up to make war against Saul, and this warrior came forth day by day to challenge to single combat. Only David ventured to respond, and armed with a sling and pebbles he overcame Goliath. The Philistines, seeing their champion killed, lost heart and were easily put to flight. The giant's arms were placed in the sanctuary, and it was his famous sword that David took with him in his flight from Saul (I Sam. xxi, 1–9). In another passage it is said that Goliath of Gath was slain by a certain Elhanan of Bethlehem in one of David's conflicts with the Philistines (II Sam. xxi, 18–22); the parallel I Chron. xx, 5 avoids the contradiction by reading "Elhanan . . . slew Lahmi the brother of Goliath." But this old popular story has probably preserved the more original tradition, and if Elhanan is the son of Dodo in the list of David's mighty men (II Sam. xxiii, 9, 24) the resemblance between the two names may have led to the transference.

GOLITSYN, BORIS ALEKSEEVICH (1654–1713), Russian statesman, Tsar Peter I's tutor and friend, came of a princely family claiming descent from Gediminas of Lithuania. Born on July 30 (new style; 20, old style), 1654, he became court chamberlain in 1676. In 1683, in spite of his association with the opposition party, the regent Sophia Alekseevna, discerning his abilities, appointed him head of the *Kazanski prikaz*, the government department concerned with the administration of the lower Volga region, a post he occupied (at any rate nominally) until the end of his life. In 1689 it was Golitsyn who directed the actions of the Naryshkin faction during its successful struggle for power with Sophia and her adherents and in 1690 Peter rewarded him with the dignity of boyar.

From then on he was associated with most of the tsar's major enterprises—the White sea expeditions of 1694–95, the Azov campaigns of 1695–96 and the shipbuilding operations at Voronezh in 1697. In 1697–98 he did not accompany Peter abroad but remained in Moscow as one of the triumvirs in charge. In 1698 he persuaded the other boyars of the need for stern measures against the seditious *streltsy* and, once order had been re-established, took part in the interrogation and execution of the guilty. After the Russian defeat at Narva in Nov. 1700 he rapidly recruited and trained the much-needed fresh regiments of dragoons. He ruled the province of the lower Volga delegated to him like a despot and the Astrakhan revolt of 1705 brought to light his venality, which had been ruining the population. He consequently lost Peter's confidence (though not his affection) and the authority over Astrakhan. Golitsyn died on Nov. 8 (N.S.; Oct. 28, O.S.), 1713, a few months after taking monastic vows.

See N. N. Golitsyn, *Rod knyazei Golitsynykh* (1892). (L. R. Lr.)

GOLITSYN, BORIS BORISOVICH, Prince (1862–1916), Russian physicist known for his work on methods of earthquake observations and on the construction of seismographs. Born on Feb. 18 (old style), 1862, in St. Petersburg, he was educated in the naval school and naval academy. In 1887 he left the active service for scientific studies and went to Strasbourg. In 1891 he was appointed *Privatdozent* at the University of Moscow and in 1893 professor of physics at Dorpat. The same year he was elected fellow of the Academy of Sciences in St. Petersburg and in 1908 a member of the academy. His early research was in spectroscopy.

His valuable book, *Lectures on Seismometry,* was published in 1912 and translated into German in 1914. He received the degree of doctor of science from the University of Manchester in 1910 and in 1911 he was elected president of the International Seismological association. In 1913 he was appointed director of the Central Physical (later Geophysical) observatory at St. Petersburg and achieved good results in the organization of meteorological service throughout Russia, especially during World War I. He died on May 4, 1916, in New Peterhof, near St. Petersburg.

(A. Foe.; X.)

GOLITSYN, DMITRI MIKHAILOVICH, PRINCE (1665–1737), Russian statesman, who tried to limit the powers of Empress Anna Ivanovna and paid dearly for his failure, was born on June 13 (new style; 3, old style), 1665. In 1697 he was sent to Italy to learn "military affairs," and in 1704 was appointed to the command of an auxiliary corps in Poland against Charles XII. From 1715 to 1719 he was governor general of Kiev. In 1719 he was made senator and from 1719 to 1722 he was also president of the Kamer-kollegia. Implicated in the disgrace of the vice-chancellor P. P. Shafirov, he was soon deprived of all his offices and dignities, which he recovered only through the mediation of the empress Catherine I. Golitsyn remained in the background till the fall of Prince A. D. Menshikov in 1727. During the last years of Peter II (1728–30) Golitsyn's high aristocratic theories had full play.

On the death of Peter, Golitsyn conceived the idea of limiting the autocracy by subordinating it to the authority of the supreme privy council, of which he was president. He drew up a form of constitution which the empress Anna Ivanovna was forced to sign at Mitau (Jelgava) before leaving for St. Petersburg. Anna lost no time in repudiating this constitution, and never forgave its authors. Golitsyn lived in retirement till 1736, when he was arrested on suspicion of being concerned in the conspiracy of his son-in-law Prince Constantine Cantemir. He was really being prosecuted for his antimonarchical sentiments. A court, largely composed of his antagonists, condemned him to death, but the empress commuted the sentence to lifelong imprisonment in Schlüsselburg and confiscation of all his estates. He died in prison on April 25 (N.S.; 14, O.S.), 1737, after three months of confinement.

GOLITSYN, VASILI VASILIEVICH, PRINCE (1643–1714), Russian statesman, in charge of foreign affairs in the years preceding the revolution of 1689. In 1676 Tsar Alexis promoted him boyar and appointed him to a military command in the Ukraine carrying with it wide political powers. In 1682, the last year of the reign of Fedor Alekseevich, Golitsyn played an important part in the deliberations of the commission for the reorganization of military service and on its behalf recommended the abolition of *mestnichestvo* or hereditary precedence. The regent, Sophia Alekseevna, made Golitsyn her principal minister and favourite. In 1682 she put him at the head of the *posolski prikaz* or foreign office; in 1684 she conferred upon him the rare distinction of keeper of the great seal and made him a *blizhni boyarin.* In the conduct of foreign affairs, his chief field of activity, Golitsyn resumed the negotiations with Poland broken off in 1684, and reached a compromise settlement embodied in a treaty of perpetual peace and alliance (1686). The abortive expeditions of 1687 and 1689 against the Crimean Tatars, both led by Golitsyn, followed. He would not commit Russia to the papal, German, Polish and Venetian war against Turkey but improved Russia's commercial relations with Sweden, Poland, England, Brandenburg, Saxony and the Netherlands. The treaty of Nerchinsk concluded with China in 1689 prevented the outbreak of a war that Russia could not have won. During the crisis of 1689 Golitsyn adopted a passive and temporizing attitude, but this did not save him from disgrace. Peter the Great stripped him of his rank and possessions and banished him to the far north for incompetence in the Cri-

mean expeditions and treasonable designs. He died at Kologory, near Pinega (Arkhangelsk province), on May 2 (new style; April 21, old style), 1714.

(L. R. Lr.)

GOLOVIN, FEDOR ALEKSEEVICH, COUNT (1650–1706), Russian statesman and diplomat, was a typical representative of the generation of courtiers who had backed Peter I the Great in his boyhood and later served him competently when he was tsar. In 1685 the regent Sophia Alekseevna promoted Golovin *okolnichi* (court official) and in the same year V. V. Golitsyn (q.v.) sent him to the Amur area to negotiate with China. The peace of Nerchinsk (1689) was the outcome of his mission, for which he was rewarded with the rank of boyar in 1690. In 1695 and 1696 he took part in the Azov campaigns and in 1697–98 in Peter's grand embassy to western Europe, ranking as second envoy and employed to secure trained men and technical supplies for Russia's growing navy.

In 1699 Golovin was put in charge of the new naval department with the rank of admiral general. In addition he was responsible for several *prikazy* ("offices") concerned with the administration of certain regions, and was director of ordnance and of the mint. As head of the foreign department he directed the negotiations that led to the conclusion in Constantinople of a peace treaty with Turkey in 1700, conducted the diplomatic preparations for the Northern War and, after its outbreak, took part with Peter or represented him in negotiations with Russia's ally King Augustus II of Poland. Golovin died on Aug. 13 (new style; 2, old style), 1706.

(L. R. Lr.)

GOLOVKIN, GAVRIIL IVANOVICH, COUNT (1660–1734), the first state chancellor of the Russian empire, belonged to a family connected with the tsaritsa Natalia Naryshkina, mother of the future emperor Peter the Great. Attached to Peter's court in his youth, Golovkin took good care of him during the regency of Sophia Alekseevna (1682–89). He accompanied Peter on his first tour of western Europe, and worked with him in the Dutch shipbuilding yards. Having been in charge of foreign affairs from 1706, he was appointed state chancellor on the battlefield of Poltava (1709). Already a count of the Holy Roman empire (from 1707), he was made a count of the Russian empire in 1710.

Under the empress Catherine I the chancellor became a member of the newly created supreme privy council and was also made the custodian of Catherine's will. This will left the imperial succession to Peter the Great's descendants, beginning with the young Peter II, one of whose guardians Golovkin was to be. On Peter II's death in 1730, however, Golovkin, having destroyed the will, declared himself in favour of giving the succession to the duchess of Courland, Anna (q.v.) Ivanovna, granddaughter of Peter the Great's father, Alexis. Under Anna he was a member of the first Russian cabinet, and his resolute support of imperial autocracy wrecked the proposed constitution whereby the Dolgorukis and Golitsyns sought to make Russia a limited monarchy. He was one of the richest and stingiest magnates of his time.

GOLOVNIN, VASILI MIKHAILOVICH (1776–1831), Russian naval officer, circumnavigator of the world, was born on April 8 (old style; 20, new style), 1776, in the province of Ryazan. He received his education at the Kronshtadt naval school and from 1801 to 1806 served as a volunteer in the English navy. In 1807 he was commissioned by the Russian government to survey the coasts of Kamchatka and of Russian America, including also the Kuril Islands.

Golovnin sailed round the Cape of Good Hope, and on Oct. 5, 1809, arrived in Kamchatka. In 1810, while attempting to survey the coast of the island of Kunashiri, he was seized by the Japanese, remaining prisoner until Oct. 13, 1813. Golovnin was presently appointed to the command of a voyage of circumnavigation. He started from St. Petersburg on Sept. 7, 1817, sailed round Cape Horn, and arrived in Kamchatka in the following May. He returned to Europe by way of the Cape of Good Hope, landing at St. Petersburg on Sept. 17, 1819.

He died on July 12, 1831. Golovnin's works include: *Journey to Kamchatka,* two volumes (1819); *Journey Round the World* in two volumes (1822); and *Narrative of My Captivity in Japan*

1811-1813, two volumes (1816). The last was translated into French, German and English (1824).

A complete edition of his works was published at St. Petersburg in five volumes in 1864, with maps and charts, and a biography of the author by N. Grech.

GOLSPIE, a town and parish in east Sutherlandshire, Scot., and the seat of the county administration, lies on the North Sea coast, 11 mi. NNE of Dornoch by main roads. There is a senior secondary school and a residential school (built 1902) with courses in commerce, agriculture, building, and engineering. The chief occupations include agriculture, sheep farming, building, and estate work. St. Andrew's Church stands on the site of the ancient chapel of St. Andrew the Apostle. Dunrobin Castle (1 mi. NE) dates from 1070 and was the Scottish seat of the countess of Sutherland. An obelisk indicates where former earls of Sutherland rallied their clans, and Ben Bhragie (1,384 ft.) is crowned by a statue of the 1st duke of Sutherland by Sir Francis Legatt Chantrey. There are an ancient cemetery, the ruins of two Pictish towers, and the remains of an ancient Caledonian stone circle. Golspie, with Rogart and Lairg, forms a Scottish district council (pop. [1971 prelim.] 3,185). (H. G. MacD.)

GOLTZ, COLMAR, BARON VON DER (1843–1916), Prussian soldier and military writer, was born at Bielkenfeld, East Prussia, on Aug. 12, 1843, and entered the Prussian infantry in 1861. In 1864 he entered the Berlin military academy, but was temporarily withdrawn in 1866 to serve in the Austrian war, in which he was wounded at Trautenau. He joined the topographical section of the general staff and at the beginning of the Franco-German War of 1870–71 was attached to the staff of Prince Frederick Charles. In 1871 Goltz was appointed professor at the military school at Potsdam, and the same year was placed in the historical section of the general staff.

In 1878 Goltz became lecturer in military history at the military academy at Berlin, where he remained for five years. He published, in 1883, *Rossbach und Jena* (new and rev. ed., *Von Rossbach bis Jena und Auerstädt*, 1906), *Das Volk in Waffen* (Eng. trans., *The Nation in Arms*), both of which quickly became military classics. In June 1883 his services were lent to Turkey to reorganize the military establishments of the country. He spent 12 years in this work, the result of which appeared in the Greco-Turkish War of 1897, and he was made a pasha and a *mushir* or field marshal. On his return to Germany in 1896 he became a lieutenant general. In 1900 he was made general of infantry, in 1908 colonel general and in 1911 field marshal. He retired in 1913.

In Aug. 1914 Goltz was appointed governor general of Belgium, then occupied by German forces. In November of the same year he was attached to the Turkish headquarters as aide-de-camp general to the sultan. He was placed in the chief command of the 1st Turkish army in Mesopotamia and succeeded in investing General Townshend's British forces at Kut-el-Amara in Dec. 1915. He died on April 19, 1916, at Baghdad; he was said to have been poisoned by the Young Turks.

Goltz's last work was *Kriegsgeschichte Deutschlands im 19ten Jahrhundert*, two volumes (1910-14).

GOLTZ, RÜDIGER, GRAF VON DER (1865–1946), German army officer who at the end of World War I tried to build a German-controlled *Baltikum* in Latvia, was born at Züllichau (Sulechow, Pol.) on Dec. 8, 1865, the son of a Prussian landlord. He was in command of an infantry division in France when, in March 1918, he was appointed commander in chief of a special division to be sent into Finland to help the Finnish national army against the Finnish-Russian Red army. His force landed at Hanko (Hangö) on April 3 and entered Helsinki ten days later. After the armistice of Nov. 1918, however, he and his division left Helsinki for Königsberg in East Prussia on Dec. 16; and in Jan. 1919 he was appointed by the German high command "governor" of Liepaja (Libau in Latvia) with orders to stop the Red army's advance toward East Prussia. He arrived at Liepaja on Feb. 3, assuming the command of the so-called VI reserve corps composed of a reserve guard division, a volunteer "iron" division, a locally recruited German *Landeswehr* and a Latvian battalion. With this force he advanced to the lower Dvina (Daugava) river and, on

May 22, took Riga, where he tried to set up a pro-German government; but on June 19–22 he was defeated near Cesis (Wenden) by an Estonian-Latvian army and had to evacuate Riga, to which a national Latvian government was then able to return. When Gen. Sir Hubert Gough, head of the Allied military mission to the Baltic countries, ordered him, on July 19, to take his force back to Germany, Goltz resisted for five months, using all sorts of stratagems, but finally, on Dec. 18, retreated to East Prussia.

Goltz described his Baltic adventures in *Meine Sending in Finnland und im Baltikum* (1920), which he later rewrote in a "Third Reich" spirit under the title *Als politischer General im Osten* (1936).

He died at Kinsegg in Bavaria on Nov. 4, 1946.

GOLTZIUS, HENDRIK (1558–1617), Dutch engraver, was born in 1558 at Mülebrecht, in the duchy of Jülich. After studying painting on glass for several years under his father, he learned the use of the burin and was employed by Philip Galle to engrave a set of prints of the history of Lucretia. Marriage with a rich widow at 21 enabled him to set up in independent business at Haarlem, where he spent the rest of his life, except for a tour in Germany and Italy in 1590. He died at Haarlem on Jan. 1, 1617.

Goltzius' portraits, mostly miniatures, are masterpieces of their kind, both on account of their exquisite finish and as fine studies of individual character. Of his larger heads, the life-size portrait of himself is probably the most striking example. Six scenes from the life of the Virgin are called his "masterpieces," from their being attempts to imitate the style of the old masters. In his command of the burin Goltzius is not surpassed even by Dürer; his eccentricities and extravagances are counterbalanced by the beauty and freedom of his execution. He began painting at the age of 42, but none of his works in this branch of art displays any special excellence.

GOLUCHOWSKI, the name of an ancient family of the Polish nobility, made counts by the Austrian empire after the partitions of Poland. Two members of this family played an important part in Austrian politics.

Count AGENOR GOLUCHOWSKI (1812–1875) was born at Skala, in eastern Galicia, on Feb. 8, 1812. He studied at Lwow university, served in the Galician *Statthalterei* under F. S. von Stadion and did excellent work on the Galician agrarian reform of 1847. He served three periods as governor of Galicia, 1849–59, 1866–68 and 1871–75. From Aug. 1859 to Dec. 1860 he was Austrian minister of the interior, during which period he secured for Galicia a degree of autonomy not enjoyed by any other Austrian crownland; and as governor of Galicia he secured the introduction of Polish as an official language. He was the principal author of the federalist "October diploma" of 1860 (*see* AUSTRIA, EMPIRE OF). An excellent administrator, Goluchowski transformed the policy of the Austrian Poles from romantic revolutionism to their eminently successful later policy of co-operation with the Austrian government in return for national concessions in Galicia. He died in Lwow on Aug. 3, 1875.

His son AGENOR GOLUCHOWSKI (1849–1921) was born at Skala on March 25, 1849, entered the Austro-Hungarian diplomatic service, served in Berlin, Paris and Bucharest (1887–93) and became Austro-Hungarian minister of foreign affairs in May 1895. The appointment caused surprise, but Goluchowski enjoyed the emperor Francis Joseph's personal confidence; his policy was peaceable and practical and generally conducted with an eye on economic necessities. In particular he showed a conciliatory spirit toward Russia, for which he was often blamed by more bellicose people. He was author of the Austro-Russian agreement of 1897, which temporarily ended the two powers' rivalry in the Balkans, and of the Mürzsteg program of 1903 for reforms in Macedonia. At the same time, he stood loyally by the German alliance. It was to Goluchowski that the German emperor William II addressed the famous telegram after the Algeciras conference, saying that he had proved a "brilliant second" and could rely on the imperial gratitude. As a Pole, Goluchowski was unpopular with the Magyars, who believed him to be inspiring Francis Joseph's opposition to the use of the Hungarian language in the army. He resigned office on Oct. 21, 1906. He died in Lwow on March 28, 1921.

GOMARUS, FRANCISCUS (original surname GOMMER) (1563–1641), Dutch theologian, representative of the most rigid Calvinist principles, was born at Bruges on Jan. 30, 1563. He studied at Strasbourg, Neustadt, Oxford and Cambridge and was pastor of a Reformed Dutch church in Frankfurt am Main from 1587 till 1593, when the congregation was dispersed by persecution. In 1594 he was appointed professor of theology at Leiden, where he became the leader of the opponents of Jacobus Arminius. He disputed with Arminius before the assembly of the estates of Holland in 1608, and was one of the five Gomarists who met five Arminians or Remonstrants in the same assembly of 1609. On the death of Arminius, Konrad Vorstius, who sympathized with his views, was appointed to succeed him and as a result Gomarus resigned his professorship in 1611. He became preacher at the Reformed church at Middelburg and taught theology and Hebrew in the newly founded *Illustre Schule*. Later he was professor at Saumur, then at Groningen. He took a leading part in the synod of Dort (1618) as an opponent of Arminianism (q.v.). He died at Groningen on Jan. 11, 1641.

Gomarus' works were collected and published in one volume folio, in Amsterdam, in 1645. *See also* DORT, SYNOD OF.
(R. A. F.)

GOMBERT, NICOLAS (c. 1500–c. 1556), one of the foremost Flemish composers of his generation. He traveled widely as singer and *magister puerorum* of the domestic chapel of the emperor Charles V, later holding positions with the cathedral chapters of Courtrai and Tournai. A follower, and possibly a pupil, of Josquin Després (q.v.), he wrote sacred music developing the imitative technique of Josquin but using a freer, less symmetrical design. Some of his *chansons* recall the naturalistic onomatopoeia of Clement Janequin. Of his works 10 Masses, 8 Magnificats, about 160 motets and about 60 *chansons* survive in printed and manuscript sources.

BIBLIOGRAPHY.—J. Schmidt-Görg, *Nicolas Gombert* (1938); *Nicolai Gombert, Opera Omnia*, ed. by J. Schmidt-Görg (1951 et seq.); G. Reese, *Music in the Renaissance* (1954); H. Eppstein, *Nicolas Gombert als Motettenkomponist* (1935).
(B. L. TR.)

GÖMBÖS, GYULA (1886–1936), Hungarian statesman who tried to remodel Hungary on dictatorial racialist lines in understanding with Italy and Germany, was born at Murga, near Tolna, on Dec. 26, 1886, of middle-class parentage. His mother spoke only German. He began his career as a professional officer and soon became conspicuous for his extreme anti-Habsburg views. In 1919 he organized a network of counterrevolutionary societies, some secret, others public. He was minister of defense in the *émigré* Szeged government, where he formed a close connection with Adm. Miklós Horthy (q.v.), the later regent. He organized the armed resistance shown to the king, Charles, when he attempted to recover his throne in 1921. Driven into opposition during István Bethlen's "era of consolidation," he led a small racialist party.

He was made minister of defense on Oct. 10, 1929 (when he arranged for his own promotion from captain to general); and on Sept. 30, 1932, he was carried into the premiership on the wave of "right radical" unrest then sweeping Hungary. His ambition was to remodel Hungary internally on dictatorial lines and to ally Hungary to Germany and Italy, but the opposition of conservative forces at home, and the antagonism between Italy and Germany over Austria, were too strong for him. When he died in Munich, still in office, of a liver complaint (Oct. 6, 1936), he had hardly realized a single point of his program: he had even been forced publicly to recant his anti-Semitic views. Yet his influence had been immense and did not cease with his death. The radicalization of Hungarian society and the definitive commitment of Hungary to a Fascist orientation in foreign policy were largely due to him.
(C. A. M.)

GOMEL, an *oblast* (established 1938) in the Belorussian Soviet Socialist Republic of the U.S.S.R., lies in the southeast of the republic, occupying the level plain of the middle Dnieper and its tributaries, Sozh, Berezina, and Pripyat. Much of the plain is swampy, especially in the west, while nearly all the remainder is in dense mixed forest of oak, pine, and hornbeam. Only in the east are there higher areas under the plow. Along the rivers are broad floodplain meadows, forming excellent hay land and pasture after the spring floods. Sands and sandy soils are widespread. The climate is modified continental, with an average temperature in January of 20° F (−6.67° C) and in July of 65° F (18.33° C). Rainfall is 22–26 in. a year. The population (1970 prelim.) was 1,534,000, of whom 616,000 were urban. The main agricultural products are flax, hemp, potatoes, and dairy produce. The timber industry is well developed and paper is made at Dobrush, furniture at Mozyr and Rechitsa. Gomel, on the Sozh, is the administrative centre.
(R. A. F.)

GOMEL, a town and administrative centre of Gomel Oblast in the Belorussian Soviet Socialist Republic of the U.S.S.R., stands on the Sozh, a tributary of the Dnieper, 174 mi. (280 km.) SE of Minsk. Pop. (1970 prelim.) 272,000. The first reference to the town dates from 1142. After a long period under Lithuania, it was acquired by Russia in 1772. Heavy damage was sustained in World War II when Soviet forces retook it from the Germans. Large-scale reconstruction was undertaken after the war. Most of the industry of the *oblast* is now concentrated there, with a wide range of timber industries, producing sawtimber, matches, veneer, and furniture. Rivercraft are built and repaired. Other manufactures include machine tools, agricultural machinery, peat-working equipment, superphosphate fertilizers, textiles, and footwear. Gomel is a major rail junction, with lines to Minsk, Brest, Chernigov, Bakhmach, and Bryansk.
(R. A. F.)

GOMER, in the Old Testament, the wife of the prophet Hosea. The first three chapters of the Book of Hosea are concerned with the marriage of Hosea and Gomer, a harlot, and the birth of their three children. See HOSEA, BOOK OF.

GOMERA, an island in the province of Santa Cruz de Tenerife, part of the Spanish archipelago of the Canary Islands (q.v.). Pop. (1960) 27,790. Area 146 sq.mi. It lies 20 mi. W.S.W. of Tenerife and is almost circular, measuring 15¾ mi. from north to south and 13 mi. from east to west. The coasts, especially on the west, are rugged and precipitous and the land rises to the flattish dome of Garajonay (4,879 ft.) in the centre of the island. There is a nearly continuous plant cover, consisting above 1,600 ft. of tree heather scrub with some evergreens, e.g., faya and Canarian holly, and in the lower areas composed mainly of succulent plants such as euphorbia and sempervivum, with thistles and brambles. Choughs are common birds and the scrub provides cover for partridges and other birds. The lower levels are semiarid but because of the plentiful supply of fresh water from springs, the valley bottoms are irrigated and bananas and date palms are grown. In the south, vines, figs, cereals and tomatoes are cultivated. There are no industries other than agriculture, some salting of tunny fish, and a little boatbuilding. The only roads are short and follow the lines of the larger valleys.

San Sebastián de la Gomera, on the east coast, the chief port and capital, has a sheltered roadstead and is backed by the steep cliffs of a wide ravine. It has a mole where the interisland steamers berth. Pop. (1960) 7,577 (mun.). It was the last stopping place of Christopher Columbus on his first transatlantic voyage in 1492, and the house where he stayed and the church he attended are tourist attractions.
(X.)

The Whistled Language of Gomera.—Many Gomerans possess the ability to talk by whistling, an art acquired from the Guanches (q.v.). Whistlers commonly insert two fingers into the mouth, using the same modifications in position of lips, tongue, etc., as in speech. In this manner they are able to produce greatly magnified birdlike sounds, which closely imitate the rhythm, tone and other intricacies of spoken Spanish; they thus overcome the difficulty of speaking from hilltop to hilltop without having to cross the *barrancos* or deep ravines that gash the mountain slopes. The most expert are found among the goatherds dwelling in the mountains around Chipude, where there is no other means of swift communication.

In the chronicle of the expedition of Jean de Bethencourt in 1402, an implausible legend of missing tongues is related, to account for the origin of the whistled language. A more scientific explanation is that it has been of slow development, perfected from necessity after generations of practice. René Verneau (1891) and Earnest A. Hooton (1925) and others who visited the archipelago for research state that whistling is not a code system but a true method of conveying thought.

In 1934 an official test was conducted by the island's government in order to authenticate the fact that conversations phrased in simple words could be carried on by this method. Separated beyond shouting distance, whistlers exchanged 13 unrehearsed messages, composed by a witness and dictated to them. All messages, as sent and as received, were recorded in writing. Upon subsequent comparison of notes, 11 messages proved to have been transmitted and understood exactly; 2 showed inconsequential discrepancies: the expression "piece of paper" had been substituted for the less familiar word "newspaper"; and the command, "pick up two stones," was performed by picking up only one.

A document certifying the particulars of the test was placed in the archives of the island; official copies are in the library of the University of Arizona (Tucson) and the Free Library of Philadelphia.

BIBLIOGRAPHY.—*Enciclopedia Universal Ilustrada Europeo-Americana* (1907-30); E. A. Hooton, *The Ancient Inhabitants of the Canary Islands*, Harvard African Studies, vol. 7 (1925); A. Samler Brown, *Madeira, the Canary Islands and the Azores*, 14th rev. ed. (1932); Annette Gest Very, "Talking by Whistling," *Natural History* (Oct. 1946); A. Gordon-Brown, *Madeira and the Canary Islands* (1959).
(A. G. V.; R. P. Be.)

GOMES, DIOGO (fl. 1440-1482), Portuguese explorer of the Gambia and discoverer of the Cape Verde Islands, was sent by Prince Henry the Navigator in about 1456 to explore the Guinea coast. Passing beyond the Rio Grande, he was swept back by currents and went far up the Gambia to the town of Cantor. There he made commercial treaties with the Negro chiefs and saw a flourishing trade in gold coming from the south. He had with him an interpreter called Jacob to facilitate communication with Prester John in Abyssinia. In 1460, on the second voyage, he joined with António da Noli and on their return landed in Santiago in the Cape Verde Islands. Their ships later separated and Noli was the first to report the discovery and is credited with it. Portuguese records of exploration from 1448 to 1470 are almost nonexistent, but Gomes dictated accounts of his voyages, and of other earlier exploratory voyages under Prince Henry, to Martin Behaim about 1484, when both lived in the Azores.

Behaim made notes in German, which were translated into Latin by Valentim Fernandes. They were found in a codex in the Royal library at Munich in 1847.

See G. Pereira, "Diogo Gomez," *Bol. Soc. Geogra. Lisbon*, series xvii no. 1, p. 267 ff. (1899); G. R. Crone, *The Voyages of Cadamosto*, Hakluyt Society, second series, no. lxxx, p. 91 ff. (1937). (A. Ds.)

GÓMEZ, JUAN VICENTE (c. 1857-1935), Venezuelan dictator, known as "the tyrant of the Andes," was a nearly full-blooded Indian. Of poor birth, he was raised in San Antonio, Táchira state, where he attained wealth and local influence before helping Cipriano Castro shoot his way into the presidency. He served as commander in chief of the army and vice-president, and when Castro went to Europe in 1908 for medical treatment, the faithless Gómez seized power and had himself named president. He completely dominated the country until his death in 1935. He silenced the provincial *caudillos* and the Catholic Church and kept the army contented by providing it with modern equipment. Gómez' friendly relations with his neighbours, the U.S., and the nations of western Europe, and large-scale material development, made possible by revenues from the rapidly expanding petroleum industry, served to draw attention away from a brutal dictatorship. Gómez combined an insatiable acquisitiveness for money and power with an abundant capacity for immorality. When he died Dec. 17, 1935, he was the "dean" of all Latin-American tyrants, with 27 years to his credit, still busily adding to his riches, and, as a bachelor, to a long list of illegitimate children. See VENEZUELA: *History*. (J. J. J.)

GÓMEZ, LAUREANO ELEUTERIO (1889-1965), Colombian politician. was born Feb. 20, 1889, in Bogotá. He obtained an engineering degree in 1909 from the National university and entered politics and journalism. Gómez held numerous high public offices and in 1932 became chief of the Conservative party, leading its fight against the Liberal party in congress from 1932 to 1943. He exploited Liberal factionalism to restore Conservative control of government in 1946 and his presidential administration (1950-53) was noted for economic development and intense rural political violence. Illness forced him to cease active presidential duties on Oct. 31, 1951, which he resumed on June 13, 1953, only to be immediately overthrown by Gen. Gustavo Rojas Pinilla, who seized the presidency.

In exile (1953-57) Gómez concluded agreements with Liberal chief Alberto Lleras Camargo establishing the national front which forced out Rojas on May 10, 1957. He died on July 13, 1965, in Bogotá. See COLOMBIA: *History*. (R. L. Ge.)

GÓMEZ DE AVELLANEDA, GERTRUDIS (1814-1873), Spanish lyrical poet and dramatist remembered chiefly for her poems, was born at Puerto Príncipe (now Camagüey), Cuba, on March 23, 1814, and moved in 1836 to Spain, where she published her first poems (1841) under the pseudonym of LA PEREGRINA ("The Pilgrim"). Her novels, such as *Sab* (1841) and *Guatimozín* (1846), are of no great importance. She obtained, however, a series of successes on the stage with *Munio Alfonso* (1844), a tragedy in the new romantic manner; with *Saúl* (1849), a biblical drama; and with *Baltasar* (1858). La Avellaneda had a grandiose tragical vision of life, a vigorous eloquence rooted in pietistic pessimism, and a dramatic gift effective in isolated acts or scenes, but she was deficient in constructive power and in intellectual force. Her lyrics, though instinct with melancholy beauty or the tenderness of resigned devotion, too often lack human passion and sympathy. She died on Feb. 1, 1873.

See E. B. Williams, *The Life and Dramatic Works of G. Gómez de Avellaneda* (1924); E. Cotarelo y Mori, *La Avellaneda y sus obras* (1930).

GÓMEZ FARÍAS, VALENTÍN (1781-1858), Mexican liberal leader, notable for his social reforms of 1833-34 that make him a precursor of Benito Juárez. Born in Guadalajara on Feb. 14, 1781, and trained as a physician, he first became prominent in politics in 1822. In 1833 he was elected vice-president in the administration of Antonio López de Santa Anna (*q.v.*). His energetic support of laws that were designed to prune the temporal powers of the church, reduce the influence of the army and the landowning gentry and reform the university, caused his exile to New Orleans in 1835. A zealous lifelong advocate of federal republican government, he admired the U.S., but this changed to distrust by the time of the Mexican War, during which he was again vice-president. Personally devout, he was nonetheless an anticlerical, an attitude that has made him a controversial figure in Mexican history. He died in Mexico City on July 5, 1858.

See Vicente Fuentes Díaz, *Gómez Farías, padre de la reforma* (1948). (C. A. Hn.)

GOMPERS, SAMUEL (1850-1924), for many years the most prominent U.S. labour leader, was born in London on Jan. 27, 1850, and emigrated in 1863 to New York, where he followed his father's trade of cigar making and became a naturalized citizen in 1872. As a labour leader, Gompers gained a world-wide reputation for conservatism. In a period when the U.S. was bitterly hostile to labour organizations, he evolved the principles of "voluntarism," which stressed that unions should exert coercion by economic actions, *i.e.*, strikes and boycotts. In 1886 Gompers led the national organization of cigar makers from the Knights of Labor to form the American Federation of Labor (A.F.L.), of which he was president from 1886 to 1924 (except for one year, 1895). He distrusted the influence of intellectual reformers, fearing any activity which would divert labour's energy from economic goals. To make unionism respectable as a bulwark against radicalism and irresponsible strikes, he encouraged binding, written trade agreements and advocated the primacy of national organizations over both local unions and international affiliations.

Gompers kept the A.F.L. politically neutral until pressed by employer tactics, including an open-shop drive, and by federal court injunctions which greatly weakened labour's economic weapons, the strike, picket line and boycott. The Democratic platform of 1908 included an anti-injunction plank; hence, Gompers supported Bryan's unsuccessful presidential candidacy. With the victory of Woodrow Wilson in 1912, the Clayton amendments to the Sherman Antitrust act (1914) and the Adamson act (1916) were passed and a cabinet post for labour was created (1913). Gompers hailed the Clayton amendments as labour's "Magna Carta," but the U.S. supreme court interpretation of the act vitiated this hope. He died at San Antonio, Tex., Dec. 13, 1924. (R. M. R.)

See J. R. Commons et al., *History of Labour in the United States* (1921); Samuel Gompers, *Seventy Years of Life and Labor* (1925).

GOMPERZ, THEODOR (1832-1912), German philosopher and classical scholar, was born at Brünn (Brno, Czech.) on March 29, 1832. He studied at Brünn and under Hermann Bonitz at Vienna. Professor of classical philology at Vienna from 1873 to 1901, he was elected a member of the Academy of Science in 1882. He received the D. Ph. *honoris causa* from Königsberg (Kaliningrad) and the D. Litt. from Dublin and from Cambridge and became correspondent for several learned societies. He died Aug. 29, 1912, at Baden-bei-Wien, Aus. His *Griechische Denker; eine Geschichte der antiken Philosophie* ("Greek Thinkers: a History of Ancient Philosophy"), 2 volumes (1893-1902; new ed., 3 volumes, 1922-24; Eng. trans., 4 volumes, 1901-12) is the work for which he is chiefly remembered.

GOMUŁKA, WŁADYSŁAW (1905-), Polish Communist, was brought to high office at the end of World War II, then fell a victim to Stalinist persecution, but emerged from the events of 1956 to exert his influence for more than a decade. He was born at Krosno, in southern Poland, on Feb. 6, 1905, and he began work as a plumber at the age of 14. In 1921 he organized a Socialist youth association, and in 1926 he joined the clandestine Communist Party of Poland. In 1932, after being shot in the leg in a skirmish with the police in Łódź, he was sentenced to four years' imprisonment for conspiracy; but in 1934 he was released. He then went to Moscow, to the Lenin Communist Higher School. On his return to Poland he was rearrested (1936).

In 1939, when the Germans invaded Poland, Gomułka escaped from prison at Sieradz and fled to Warsaw. After the fall of Warsaw he made his way to Soviet-occupied Lwów; but in June 1941 the Germans took Lwów also. Gomułka then started working as an underground Communist organizer. From July 1942 he was operating in Warsaw, under the name of "Comrade Wiesław." Elected to the Central Committee of the new Polish Workers' Party, he was made secretary-general of the party in November 1943; in July 1944 he moved to the Soviet-reoccupied part of Poland. On Dec. 31, 1944, Gomułka was appointed deputy premier in the provisional government formed under Soviet protection at Lublin. He kept this post in successive Polish cabinets till January 1949 and from November 1945 was also minister for the Recovered Territories. Meanwhile he remained secretary-general of the Polish Workers' Party till Bolesław Bierut succeeded him on Sept. 3, 1948. On Dec. 15, 1948, the Polish Workers' Party and the Polish Socialist Party were merged to form the Polish United Workers' Party (PZPR).

Accused by Stalin of nationalist deviation, Gomułka was dismissed from the government in January 1949 and expelled from the PZPR in November. On July 31, 1951, he was arrested. On April 21, 1955, two years after Stalin's death, he was released; but this became publicly known only after N. S. Khrushchev's denunciation of Stalinism (Feb. 25, 1956), and Bierut's death (March 12).

Gomułka was restored to membership of the PZPR on Aug. 4, 1956. He was co-opted to its Central Committee and to the Politburo on Oct. 19, when Khrushchev and other Soviet leaders were to arrive in Warsaw to settle matters. On Oct. 21 he was elected first secretary of the PZPR, a post he held until Dec. 20, 1970. He resigned, ostensibly for reasons of ill health, but it was generally believed that the rioting that ensued after the government imposed price increases was the primary cause. In the wake of his resignation, he was suspended from the party's Central Committee, and in May he resigned from the Council of State. He remained, however, a deputy in the Parliament. (K. Sm.; X.)

POLAND: *History*.

GONADS, DISORDERS OF: *see* REPRODUCTIVE SYSTEM.

GONÇALVES CRESPO, ANTÓNIO CÂNDIDO (1846-1883), Portuguese poet who introduced Parnassianism into Portuguese literature, was born in Rio de Janeiro, Braz., on March 11, 1846. He went to Portugal as a youth and studied at the University of Coimbra. He married the writer Maria Amália Vaz de Carvalho, who introduced him to Lisbon society and the literary *salons* of the capital. He was a member of parliament for a short time, and also editor of the *Jornal do Comércio* and a contributor to literary journals. He was a founder of the review *A Folha*, which stimulated Portuguese interest in French Parnassian poetry. Gonçalves Crespo produced only two volumes of verse: *Miniaturas* (1870) and *Nocturnos* (1882), both of which reveal the formal influence of Théophile Gautier, Leconte de Lisle and François Coppée. Though, as their titles suggest, many of his themes are romantic, he displays a greater precision, more careful observation and a finer sensibility than many of the romantics. Though he cannot be considered a great poet and several of his poems are only conventional *salon* art, he was a craftsman in verse who renewed and refreshed the poetic vocabulary of his day.
He died at Lisbon on June 11, 1883.

BIBLIOGRAPHY.—Prefaces by T. de Queirós and M. A. Vaz de Carvalho to the *Obras completas* (1897); Cândido de Figueiredo, *Figuras literárias* (1906); J. J. Cochofel, "Gonçalves Crespo" in *Perspectiva da Literatura Portuguesa do Século XIX*, vol. ii (1948). (N. J. L.)

GONÇALVES DIAS, ANTÓNIO (1823-1864), Brazilian poet, wrote the nostalgic "Song of Exile," probably the most memorized poem in the Portuguese language. Born near Caxias (Maranhão), he was educated at the University of Coimbra, Portugal. His collection of poems, *Primeiros Cantos* (1846), was enthusiastically praised by a distinguished Portuguese contemporary, Alexandro Herculano. The poet's immediate popularity was enhanced by *Segundos Cantos e Sextilhas de Frei Antão* (1848), and especially *Ultimos Cantos* (1851), which virtually closed the cycle of his lyrics.

In the final decade of his life he held various governmental posts, in which he surveyed the school system of northern Brazil, studied European educational institutions, did research on Brazilian historical sources in European archives and participated in a scientific expedition. The unfinished epic poem on the Indian tribe *Os Tambiras* (1857), an unsuccessful attempt at creating a "Brazilian Iliad," and the *Dicionário da Língua Tupi* (1858) reflect his preference for indigenous subjects. He went to Europe in 1862 and upon his return trip was drowned in a shipwreck within sight of the coast of his native state (Nov. 3, 1864).

Many of his poems were inspired by a series of fleeting romances which consoled, and afflicted, his insatiable heart. In this and other respects, including the excessive vehemence of several of his amorous complaints, he remained a typical romanticist; however, he often succeeded in attaining the utmost spontaneity, and a subtlety of expression in perfect consonance with the natural genius of his people. Modern critics tend to consider him the most representative poet of Brazil.

BIBLIOGRAPHY.—Manuel Bandeira's definitive edition of *Obras Poéticas*, 2 vol. (1944); Lúcia Miguel Pereira, *A Vida de Gonçalves Dias* (1943); Samuel Putnam, *Marvelous Journey*, pp. 111-114 (1948); Manuel Bandeira, *Gonçalves Dias* (1952). (A. M. R.)

GONCHAROV, IVAN ALEKSANDROVICH (1812-1891), a leading 19th-century Russian novelist. Born on June 18 (new style; June 6, old style), 1812, into a wealthy merchant family at Simbirsk (now Ulyanovsk), he graduated from Moscow university in 1834 and served for nearly 30 years as an official, first in the ministry of finance and afterward in the censorship. The only out-of-the-way event in his externally uneventful life was his voyage in 1852-55 as secretary of a Russian admiral; this was described in *Fregat Pallada* ("The Frigate Pallas," 1858).

His most notable achievement lies in his three novels, of which the first was *Obyknovennaya istoriya* (1847; Eng. trans., *A Common Story*, 1917). This immediately made his reputation when it was acclaimed by the influential critic Vissarion Belinski (q.v.). But it is a relatively immature work when compared with *Oblomov* (1859; Eng. trans., 1954), generally accepted as one of the half-dozen most important Russian novels. The hero, Oblomov, is perhaps the most famous single character in Russian literature and is a triumph of characterization, being an extreme portrait of laziness and ineffectiveness which has been taken by some as reflecting a typical Russian character trait. Contemporary Russian critics exaggerated the social criticism which they believed the novel to contain, especially as the information about the hero's early life could be interpreted as an attack on serfdom. Goncharov's third novel, *Obryv* (1869; Eng. trans., *The Precipice*, 1915), although a remarkable work, cannot stand comparison with *Oblomov*. In all three novels Goncharov is concerned to illuminate the clash of an easy-going dreamer with an opposed character who typifies businesslike efficiency. This seems to reflect a wish on Goncharov's part to bring himself to approve of such features of modernity as growing industrialization and technical efficiency, while his real sympathies are with the traditions of the old-world Russia in which he was himself brought up. Of Goncharov's minor writings the most influential was an essay on Aleksandr Griboedov's play *Gore ot uma* ("Woe From Wit"). He died in St. Petersburg on Sept. 27 (new style; 15 old style), 1891.

See J. Lavrin, *Goncharov* (1954); A. A. Mazon, *Un Maître du roman russe, Ivan Gontcharov* (1914). (R. F. Hr.)

GONCOURT, the name of two remarkable French writers of the 19th century who achieved distinction as art critics, historians, novelists and diarists, and of the academy and prize which the elder Goncourt founded. EDMOND LOUIS ANTOINE HUOT DE GONCOURT was born at Nancy, May 26, 1822, and died at Champrosay, July 16, 1896. JULES ALFRED HUOT DE GONCOURT, his brother, was born in Paris, Dec. 17, 1830, and died in Paris, June 20, 1870.

Left a modest fortune when their mother died in 1848, the Goncourts devoted the rest of their lives to art, history and literature. They were proud to the point of arrogance, glorying in their aristocratic breeding, their artistic tastes, and above all their neurotic sensibility, which they regarded as an essential quality of a modern writer: sickness, they asserted, "makes a man sensitive like a photographic plate," while Edmond told Emile Zola that "our entire work is built on nervous illness." They never married, ostensibly out of loyalty to their art, but probably because of unfortunate experiences with the opposite sex: Edmond may have been impotent, Jules certainly suffered and died from syphilis, and the novels of both brothers are profoundly misogynistic. And although very different in temperament—Edmond was ponderous, reserved and sentimental, Jules volatile, witty and ironic—they felt, thought and wrote in close unison, living harmoniously together for more than 20 years, and collaborating so successfully that it is impossible to attribute with certainty any particular passage in their writings to one brother.

As art critics their most notable achievement was *L'Art du dix-huitième siècle* (1859–75), a pioneer work now recognized as a classic, in which they rescued Antoine Watteau and other masters of 18th-century French art from the discredit into which they had fallen. They failed to show the same discernment when judging their contemporaries, placing A. G. Decamps above Delacroix and Paul Gavarni above Daumier, attributing too much importance to Japanese art, and remaining blind to the merits of the French Impressionists, despite the fact that they themselves were trying to achieve the same effects in literature.

Their historical studies—*Histoire de la Société française pendant la Révolution* (1854), *Portraits intimes du dix-huitième siècle* (1857–58), *La Femme au dix-huitième siècle* (1862), etc.—were inspired by a new and fruitful concept of history. Infected from early youth with a fanatical enthusiasm for *bibelots* or *objets d'art*, the Goncourts maintained that a historian could not fully understand a period of which no dress pattern or dinner menu had survived. Concentrating their attention on their favourite period, the 18th century, they used just such material as dress patterns and dinner menus to create pictures of the age which have both great charm and considerable value.

The same meticulous documentation and the same attention to the so-called trivialities of life went to the writing of the Goncourts' novels, which they described as "history which might have taken place." Again, just as they had studied many different classes of

18th-century society in their histories, so they covered a vast range of 19th-century milieux in their novels: the world of journalism and literature in *Charles Demailly* (1860), the hospital in *Soeur Philomène* (1861), upper middle-class society in *Renée Mauperin* (1864), the servant and shopkeeper milieux in *Germinie Lacerteux* (1864), the artistic world in *Manette Salomon* (1867), the Church in *Madame Gervaisais* (1869), and in the novels written by Edmond alone, the brothel in *La Fille Élisa* (1877), the circus in *Les Frères Zemganno* (1879), the theatre in *La Faustin* (1882), and court circles in *Chérie* (1884). By their frank presentation of upper and lower classes, and their wealth of impressive if not always accurate medical detail, these works point the way to the modern social novel: *Germinie Lacerteux* deserves particular mention in this respect as the first realistic French novel of working-class life and the book which inspired Zola's *L'Assommoir*. But with the exception of such short, compact works as *Soeur Philomène* and *La Fille Élisa*, the Goncourts' novels suffer from over-long expositions, excessive description, fragmentary chapters, and a self-consciously aristocratic and artistic attitude on the part of the authors.

The distinctive style employed by the Goncourts, their notorious *écriture artiste*, was specially devised to match the modernity of their subjects. They maintained that tortured syntax and a vast vocabulary teeming with neologisms and technical terms were necessary to render the moral and material complexities of modern life. Critics in the 20th century tend to dismiss the resultant style as mannered and obsolete, failing to realize that countless words and constructions introduced by the Goncourts have been so completely integrated into the French language that their origin is now forgotten. The *écriture artiste* has had greater success and wider influence than is generally acknowledged.

The Goncourts were never popular with either the public or their fellow writers, and they attributed this to an unkind fate and professional envy. Their first novel, *En 18 . . .*, was published the morning after the *coup d'état* of 1851 and went unnoticed. Their play *Henriette Maréchal*, produced at the Théâtre-Français in 1865, provoked political demonstrations and was rapidly taken off. Their admiring disciple Zola reaped a considerable fortune, established a world-wide reputation, and became the leader of the Naturalist movement in French literature, by copying their methods. Year by year they became more obsessed by the question of their reputation; in his last conversations before his death in 1870, Jules dwelt with morbid insistence on their claims to immortality, and the surviving brother did his best to ensure the survival of their name by all the means at his disposal. He opened a literary *salon* in the so-called *Grenier*, two rooms in his house at Auteuil, and in 1882 announced that he intended to leave his fortune to endow a literary academy. This academy was to consist of ten writers who would receive a stipend and award a prize of 5,000 fr. every year to the author of an outstanding work of literature. After prolonged litigation the Académie Goncourt was officially constituted in 1903, with J. K. Huysmans as its first president. The real monetary value of both stipend and prize is now small, but the academicians derive a certain prestige from their position, and the winner of a Prix Goncourt gains immense profit from the sale of his work.

In the last analysis, however, the Goncourts' best defense against the oblivion they dreaded has proved to be their *Journal*. Begun in Dec. 1851 and continued until July 1896, it was published in part by Edmond during his lifetime, the last of nine volumes appearing a few weeks before his death. By the terms of his will, the entire text might have been made public in 1916, but the Académie Goncourt, fearing a crop of libel actions, decided otherwise. Publication of the integral work began only in 1956, and ended three years later. Full of critical judgments, scabrous anecdotes, descriptive sketches, literary gossip and thumb-nail portraits, the complete *Journal* is at once a revealing autobiography and a monumental history of social and literary life in 19th-century Paris.

BIBLIOGRAPHY.—Pierre Sabatier, *L'Esthétique des Goncourt* (1920); Robert Ricatte, *La Création romanesque chez les Goncourt* (1953); André Billy, *Les Frères Goncourt* (1954); Robert Baldick, *The Goncourts* (1960).
(R. BA.)

GOND: *see* GONDWANA.

GONDA, a municipal town and district in the Fyzabad division of Uttar Pradesh, India. The town, 75 mi. E.N.E. of Lucknow, is a junction on the North-Eastern railway metre-gauge system between Lucknow and the Nepal frontier. Pop. (1961) 43,496.

GONDA DISTRICT (2,829 sq.mi.; pop. [1961] 2,073,237) is an alluvial plain extending from the Gogra river across the Nepal frontier. Part is subject to frequent floods. The main industries are the making of sugar and alcohol, and oilseed crushing. At Balrampur, 18 mi. N.E. of Gonda, is a college of Gorakhpur university. Ten miles northwest of Balrampur is Sahet Mahet (Set Mahet), the site of the ancient Sravasti. Sravasti was a monastic estate given to the itinerant Buddha by a princely disciple, and till the 4th century A.D. was a Buddhist centre and local capital. The modern name indicates Sahet, site of Buddhist monasteries now marked by mounds, and Mahet, a large ruined crescent-shaped fortress. Excavations have disclosed sites of ten temples and five stupas or relic domes.

(B. Sr.)

GONDAR, the capital of Begemdir province, Ethiopia, and a former capital of the country, stands at about 7,500 ft. elevation on a basaltic ridge from which streams flanking the town flow to Lake Tana, about 21 mi. S. Pop. (1970 est.) 35,331. It was a small village when chosen early in the 17th century by the negus Susenyos (Seged I) as his capital. His son Fasilidas (A'lem Seged, 1633–67) and later emperors built castles and palaces of which the ruins stand within a walled "imperial enclosure"; the most important are: the castle of Fasilidas, the palace of Iyasu the Great (1682–1706), the House of Song built by David III (Adbar Seged, 1716–21), and the palaces of Massih Seged (Bakaffa, 1721–30) and his wife Mentuab (regent, 1730–60). The style of the castles, ascribed to Portuguese influence, also has connections with earlier Ethiopian buildings and with palaces in the Hadhramaut cities near the original home of the Aksumites. Few remain of the 44 churches reputed to have existed in mid-18th century, but Gondar is still an important centre of the Ethiopian Coptic Church. On the Epiphany (observed on Jan. 19) a public baptismal ceremony, the Temqat (Timkat), is attended by many dignitaries at the Bath of Fasilidas. Most of the townsfolk are Christians, but Muslims and groups of Falashas dwell in the surrounding country. Cotton, cloth, ornaments of gold, silver, bone and ivory, copperware and leather-work are local products. The modern hospital has an attached college training medical staff for rural clinics.

The Scottish traveler James Bruce (q.v.) in 1770–71 lived at Gondar in the nearby castle of Koosquam and estimated the town's population at 10,000 families. During the period 1750–1890 Gondar suffered much from the civil wars then raging and was more than once sacked, notably by the dervishes under Abu Anga in 1887; however, after British pacification of the Sudan (1889), trade revived between Gondar and the Blue Nile regions. Following the Italian conquest and occupation of Ethiopia, Gondar fell in World War II to British, Sudanese and Ethiopian troops on Nov. 28, 1941, after a siege of several months.

(G. C. L.)

GONDOMAR, DIEGO SARMIENTO DE ACUÑA, CONDE DE (1567–1626), Spanish diplomatist, who achieved a great reputation in England for his craftiness, was a member of a prominent noble family in Galicia. His diplomatic fame rests largely on his two embassies to England (1613–18 and 1620–22). The chief objective of his first mission was to persuade the English government to abandon its alliance with France and the Protestant countries on the continent and to form an alliance with Spain. His courtly manners and keen intellect, as well as his wit, made a strong impression on James I, and his influence is described by Arthur Wilson (*The History of Great Britain*, 1653): "Gondomar had as free access to the King as any Courtier of them all (Buckingham excepted) and the King took delight to talk with him; for he was full of Conceits, and would speak false Latin a purpose in his merry fits to please the King; telling the King plainly, He [James] spoke Latin like a Pedant, but I speak it like a Gentleman." Gondomar's ascendancy over the king developed to such a degree that on some occasions he could practically dictate royal policies. Consequently, he became the object of much criticism. A Puritan minister, Thomas Scot, attacked him in a pamphlet, *Vox Populi* (1620); and the dramatist Thomas Middleton made him the hero-villain (the Black Knight) of his play *A Game at Chess* (1622), which was suppressed by order of the privy council. The English public generally detested him. At the height of his unpopularity, in 1622, he was recalled to Spain and there made a member of the council of state. Except for a mission to Vienna, his diplomatic career was over, and he died in 1626.

BIBLIOGRAPHY.—*Correspondencia oficial de Don Diego Sarmiento de Acuña, conde de Gondomar,* 4 vol. (1936–45); F. H. Lyon, *Gondomar* (1910); Garrett Mattingly, *Renaissance Diplomacy* (1955).

(R. C. Jo.)

GONDWANA, part of middle India inhabited by the Gonds, a group of aboriginal peoples exceeding 3,000,000 in number. The name Gond occurs first in the chronicles of Muslim historians of the 14th century, who also coined the term Gondwana for the hilly and then sparsely populated country extending from the Vindhya mountains in the north as far south and east as the lower Godavari river and the Eastern Ghats. This tract was then mainly inhabited by tribal populations, and powerful Gond dynasties wielded authority over extensive areas. The three most important Gond kingdoms were those of Garha, Deogarh and Chanda, and their rulers continued to hold power as tributaries of the Mogul emperors. In the 18th century they were conquered by the Marathas and the greater part of Gondwana was incorporated in the dominions of the Bhonsla raja of Nagpur, while some districts fell to the nizam of Hyderabad. Between 1818 and 1853 the greater part of the region passed to the British, but in some minor Chhattisgarh states the rule of Gond rajas continued until 1947. Chhattisgarh is now divided between the states of Madhya Pradesh, Maharashtra and Andhra Pradesh, but substantial groups of Gonds are also found in Orissa.

There is no cultural uniformity among the various branches of the Gond. Most advanced are the Raj Gonds, who had developed an elaborate feudal order. Local rajas, linked by ties of blood or marriage to the royal house (e.g., that of Chanda), exercised authority over groups of villages. The majority of Gonds speak various, and in part mutually unintelligible, dialects of Gondi, an unwritten Dravidian language. Other groups have lost their own language and speak Hindi, Marathi or Telugu in accordance with the language dominant in their respective habitat. All those still speaking Gondi describe themselves as Koitur.

A rich mythology validates a complex system of exogamous, patrilineal clans grouped into larger exogamous units deriving their solidarity from the cult of deities connected with the ancestors of the group. Hereditary bards, belonging to the Pardhan community, maintain the traditions of the clans through the medium of an extensive oral literature. Except for the fortified seats of rajas

GONDOPHARES (probably 1st century A.D.), an Indo-Parthian king, whose realm included Arachosia, Kabul and Gandhara, was first known from the apocryphal *Acts of Judas Thomas the Apostle.* It is said that St. Thomas visited the court of Gondophares where he was put in charge of the construction of a royal palace. He was imprisoned for spending the money entrusted to him on charitable purposes on the king's behalf. Meanwhile Gad, the king's brother, died, and the angels took him to heaven and showed him the palace which St. Thomas had built there by his good deeds. Gad was restored to life and both he and his brother were converted to Christianity. Some scholars recognize the name of Gondophares, through its Armenian form Gathaspar, in Gaspar, the first of the "three wise men," who came from the east to worship Christ at his nativity. Another apocryphal work, the *Evangelium Ioannis de obitu Mariae,* in the view of some scholars, supports the story of St. Thomas' visit to Gondophares.

The coins of Gondophares, bearing his Indian name Guduphara, depict Zeus, Pallas, Nike and the Indian deity Shiva. On the basis of the Takht-i-Bahi inscription (Peshawar district) Gondophares ruled for at least 26 years; most scholars believe from about A.D. 19 to 45.

BIBLIOGRAPHY.—*Cambridge History of India,* vol. i (1922); J. E. van Lohuizen-de Leeuw, *The Scythian Period* (1949); R. B. Whitehead, *Catalogue of the Coins in the Panjab Museum Lahore,* vol. i (1914); A. E. Medlycott, *India and the Apostle Thomas* (1905).

(A. K. N.)

settlements were formerly of little permanence, and cultivation, though practised with plows and oxen, involved frequent shifting of fields and clearing of new tracts of forest land. Legislation on land tenure during the British period has led to greater stability of holdings, which are now individually owned. Though often in contact with caste Hindus, the Raj Gonds continue to stand outside the Hindu caste system, acknowledging neither the superiority of Brahmans nor feeling bound by Hindu rules, such as the ban on cow-killing. The highlands of Bastar (q.v.) are the home of three important Gond tribes, i.e., the Murias, Bisonhorn Marias and Hill Marias. The latter, inhabiting the rugged Abujhmar hills, are the most primitive. Slash-and-burn cultivation on hill slopes is their traditional type of agriculture, and hoes and digging-sticks are still more widely used than plows. The villages are periodically moved, and the commonly owned land of each clan contains several village sites occupied over the years in rotation. Bisonhorn Marias, so called after their dance headdresses, live in less hilly country, and have more permanent fields cultivated with plows and bullocks. The same applies to the Murias known for their youth-dormitories (ghotul) in the framework of which the unmarried of both sexes lead a highly organized social life of their own, receive training in civic duties, and are free to have premarital sexual relations. The religion of all Gond tribes centres in the cult of clan and village deities, propitiated with animal sacrifices, including sacrifices of cows or bulls, and there is also extensive ancestor worship. There is a belief in the survival of two separate aspects of the human personality: the shade which goes to the land of ancestors and departed, and the soul-substance which returns to the supreme god Bhagwan and may be reincarnated in the family of the deceased. The erection of monuments of crude stone or carved wooden pillars in honour of departed kinsmen is customary among the Gonds of Bastar.

BIBLIOGRAPHY.—W. V. Grigson, *The Maria Gonds of Bastar* (1938); Verrier Elwin, *The Muria and their Ghotul* (1947); C. von Fürer-Haimendorf, *The Raj Gonds of Adilabad* (1948). (C. v. F.-H.)

GONDWANALAND. Continental masses—South America, Africa, peninsular India, Australia, Antarctica—now separated widely by the southern oceans share many striking features of geologic history and of the distribution of ancient and living organisms. The Austrian geologist Eduard Suess proposed accordingly in the early 1900s that these masses were, until early Mesozoic time, parts of a supercontinent, the intervening regions having foundered subsequently to abyssal oceanic depths. Suess named the supercontinent Gondwanaland, after the Upper Paleozoic and Mesozoic formations of the Gondwana region of central India, which display typical developments of some of the shared geologic features. In the 1920s the German meteorologist Alfred Wegener argued on geological and paleoclimatological grounds that the now scattered land masses instead are the far-traveled fragments of a smaller supercontinent, which in Late Paleozoic and Early Mesozoic time occupied middle and high southern latitudes, new ocean basins having formed behind the subsequently diverging land masses. Wegener redefined the name Gondwanaland to apply to this austral paleocontinent, and the name is now used in that context. A. L. du Toit of South Africa and many other geologists produced much additional evidence to support Wegener's general concept, while greatly modifying many details. Following long dispute, it is now widely recognized that the disruption of austral Gondwanaland is indeed required by concordant conclusions from the data of many independent fields.

The geologic unity of the Gondwanaland fragments is particularly apparent in the sequences of sedimentary rocks, mostly continental, of Late Carboniferous through Jurassic age present on each land mass: the Gondwana System of India; the Karroo System of southern Africa and Madagascar; the Beacon Sandstone of Antarctica; and similar strata in Brazil and southern South America, the Falkland Islands, and Australia and Tasmania. The sections typically begin with tillites and glaciofluvial sediments that record widespread and repeated continental glaciation. Ice largely covered the Gondwanaland subcontinents during the Late Carboniferous and earliest Permian, but glaciation began earlier in the Carboniferous in the South American-African sector, and ended later in the Early Permian in southeastern Australia and Tasmania. Rare intercalations in the basal Permian glacial sections of each subcontinent bear the distinctive cold-water marine-pelecypod *Eurydesma* fauna; the continental glaciers reached sea level even in regions now tropical and subtropical. Temperate-climate Permian deposits succeed the glacial sediments and record paleoclimatic gradients warming northward or northwestward in South America, Africa, India, and Australia. The Mesozoic was in general warmer in South America and Africa than in Australia and East Antarctica. Fossil floras and faunas are strikingly similar throughout the Gondwanaland terrane when assemblages of about the same age and paleoclimatic setting are compared, demonstrating easy biological migration between the now separate lands. Especially well known is the *Glossopteris-Gangamopteris* temperate land flora of the Permian, which varies little in generic content throughout the Gondwana lands; even at the specific level, there is great similarity between the Permian floras of India, now north-tropical, and of East Antarctica, now south-polar.

The climatology and biogeography of Late Carboniferous and Permian Gondwanaland cannot be accounted for by postulating continental geometry like that of the present but with the Earth's axis in a different position than it is now (the Gondwanaland fragments are scattered from high southern latitudes to the equator and beyond, no matter where an axis be conjectured on the present globe). Nor can global chilling be invoked to explain the widespread glaciation, for much of the rest of the Earth was at the same time tropical; when now tropical India was covered by ice, now polar Spitsbergen and northern Greenland were tropical. Only a clustering of the Gondwanaland pieces at high southern latitudes during Late Paleozoic time accounts with rational paleolatitudes for the distribution of paleoclimatic indicators and for the paleobiogeographic unity.

In the late 1950s and the 1960s, the method of determination of paleolatitude by remanent magnetic orientations in rocks was applied to suitable materials throughout the Gondwanaland fragments. These quantitative determinations confirmed the more general paleolatitudes inferred on paleoclimatic grounds. In ancient as in recent time, continental glacial deposits formed at high latitudes, temperate deposits in middle to high latitudes, and tropical materials at low latitudes.

The shapes of the continental slopes (the submerged boundaries between the continental plates and the deep ocean basins), the continuity and other characteristics of tectonic and lithologic provinces, paleoclimatic and paleomagnetic latitudes, and other parameters so constrain possible reconstructions of Gondwanaland that there is now little ambiguity regarding its gross geometry in Late Paleozoic and Mesozoic time.

The most thoroughly documented ties are those joining South America and Africa across the South Atlantic. When those continents are joined in the obvious manner suggested by their shapes, Precambrian and Middle Paleozoic orogenic belts now truncated by the ocean are found to continue without interruption across the join; stratigraphic, paleontologic, lithologic, chronologic, and other features are neatly matched. The continental ice sheets which in Late Carboniferous time flowed onto South America (in what is now a westward direction but was then more northerly) carried voluminous rock debris which can be matched to bedrock in southern Africa but which has no possible South American source. The striking similarities in stratigraphy and paleontology of Upper Paleozoic and Mesozoic sedimentary rocks continue upward to the middle of the Cretaceous, in which freshwater ostracod faunas are shared between the opposed continents. South America and Africa began to separate in the Middle Cretaceous, and the mammal fauna of South America evolved from the shared Cretaceous stock, isolated on its island continent until the building of the volcanic Panamanian land bridge in Late Tertiary time.

Fewer or less completely documented ties of similar nature link western India to East Africa and Madagascar, eastern India to western Australia, southern Australia to East Antarctica, and Antarctica to southern Africa. Some of the separations can be dated by geologic, paleontologic, and paleomagnetic means, and by the marine-magnetic data on ocean floor spreading: India separated from Madagascar and Africa late in the Cretaceous, drifted northward as an island continent during the Early Tertiary, and collided with mainland Asia in the middle Tertiary, forming the Himalayas in the closing gap. Australia and East Antarctica probably did not separate until very early Tertiary time, but the antiquity of the living and known fossil Australian mammals—marsupials and monotremes—indicates that those continents likely rifted from Africa and India well back in Jurassic time. A find as far back as Lower Triassic, however, in 1969 has established a link in the Antarctic, along with other fossil remains.

The history of Gondwanaland since the Early Carboniferous is now reasonably well understood, but there remains much uncertainty regarding its older evolution. Little can be said with confidence about the Precambrian configuration. The record is much better for the Early and Middle Paleozoic, when Gondwanaland apparently was internally coherent and moved as a whole relative to the Earth's axis. The Lower and Middle Paleozoic is in general characterized by high-latitude indicators on the African and South American side, and by warm-climate indicators on the Australian side. As Australia moved southward toward the pole during Middle and Late Paleozoic episodes of rapid motion, South America and Africa moved correspondingly toward the tropics on the other side. The supercontinent in effect moved beneath its waxing and waning polar ice sheet. As late as the Early Carboniferous, Gondwanaland was somehow joined at the Australian end to Eurasia, the missing pieces perhaps being represented by the disjunct continental fragments of the Tarim, Tibetan, and Chinese platforms of Asia. *See also* PERMIAN SYSTEM for a map of Late Paleozoic Gondwanaland.

BIBLIOGRAPHY.—J. C. Crowell and L. A. Frakes, "Late Paleozoic Glacial Facies and the Origin of the South Atlantic Ocean," *23rd Internat. Geol. Congress Report*, v. 13, p. 291-302 (1968); P. J. Darlington, Jr., *Biogeography of the Southern End of the World* (1965); A. L. du Toit, *Our Wandering Continents* (1937); J. Francheteau and J. G. Sclater, "Paleomagnetism of the Southern Continents and Plate Tectonics," *Earth and Planetary Science Letters*, v. 6, p. 93-106 (1969); E. P. Plumstead, "Fossil Floras of Antarctica," no. 9, *Scient. Rep. Transantarct. Exped. 1955-58* (1962). (W. Hn.)

GONFALONIER, a title of office in certain western European states in the middle ages, meaning banner-bearer (ultimately from Old High German *gundfano*, "war-banner"; Fr. *gonfanon*; It. *gonfalone*). The kings of France were gonfaloniers of St. Denis as successors of the counts of Vexin after the annexation of Vexin by Philip I in 1077. In Italy, gonfalonier was the title of civic magistrates. In Florence, after 1250, the military companies were under gonfaloniers, but as civic military service declined they functioned, after the 14th century, principally as a high communal magistracy. The honorary title of gonfalonier of the church (*vexillifer ecclesiae*) was conferred by the popes, from Boniface VIII (1294-1303) until the 17th century, on sovereigns and princes, sometimes on commanders of papal armies. (N. R.: X.)

GONG, a percussion instrument of oriental origin consisting of a circular metal plate, cast or hammered, with the outer edge turned down all around. It hangs in a frame and is struck with a heavy-ended beater covered with felt or leather. There are two types of orchestral gongs, each with its individual tone quality: the large, flat, Chinese gong (tam-tam) with a deep, dark tone of indefinite pitch; and the Burmese gong of heavy metal with a raised boss in the centre, which produces a bell-like note of definite pitch. Puccini uses a set of tuned gongs in *Turandot*. (J. Br.)

GÓNGORA Y ARGOTE, LUIS DE (1561-1627), Spanish poet, who brought to perfection the poetic style called, after him, Gongorism, was born on July 11, 1561, at Córdoba, where his father was the owner of a famous library. He studied at the University of Salamanca and was already known as a poet when Cervantes praised him in the *Galatea*. In 1585 he settled in Madrid, taking full orders and securing a court chaplaincy in 1617. In 1626 a stroke impaired his faculties and he returned to Córdoba, where he died, May 23, 1627.

Part of Góngora's work was, during his lifetime, the subject of the most furious controversy in Spanish literary history. His light verse—*romances, letrillas*, satires, songs for the guitar—was widely esteemed, but he was considered to have violated the principles of poetry and of language in his long poems *Polifemo* (1612) and *Soledades* (1613-17). In these he elaborated his style (known as *culteranismo*) by the introduction of numerous Latinisms of vocabulary and syntax, and by exceedingly complex imagery and mythological allusions. For three centuries his name was synonymous with obscurity and pedantry, but in the 20th century an astonishing revaluation of Góngora took place; he came to be considered one of Spain's greatest poets, and powerfully influenced the poetry of the generation of the 1920s. The *Polifemo* and *Soledades* are part pastoral, part epic; they appeal brilliantly to the senses in their descriptions of persons, nature and rustic scenes. An important collection of his letters survives.

BIBLIOGRAPHY.—*Obras completas* (1943); D. Alonso, *La lengua poética de Góngora* (1950) and *Estudios y ensayos gongorinos* (1955). (C. C. Sh.)

GONIOMETER, an instrument for measuring the angles of crystals; there are three kinds—the contact goniometer, the reflecting goniometer and the X-ray goniometer.

The Contact Goniometer.—This instrument consists of two metal rules pivoted together at the centre of a graduated semicircle (*see figure*). The instrument is placed with its plane perpendicular to an edge between two faces of the crystal to be measured, and the rules are brought into contact with the faces; this is best done by holding the crystal up against the light with the edge in the line of sight. The angle between the rules, as read on the graduated semicircle, then gives the angle between the two faces. The rules are slotted, so that they may be shortened and their tips applied to a crystal partly embedded in its matrix. The instrument illustrated is employed for the approximate measurement of large crystals.

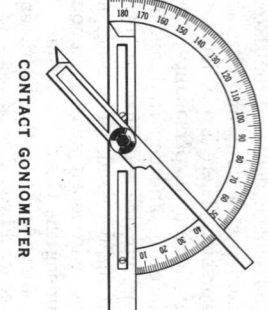

CONTACT GONIOMETER

The Reflecting Goniometer.—This is an instrument of far greater precision, and is always used for the accurate measurement of the angles when small crystals with smooth faces are available. Such faces reflect sharply defined images of a bright object. By turning the crystal about an axis parallel to the edge between two faces, the image reflected from a second face may be brought into the same position as that formerly occupied by the image reflected from the first face; the angle through which the crystal has been rotated, as determined by a graduated circle to which the crystal is fixed, is the angle between the normals to the two faces.

Several forms of instruments depending on this principle have been devised. The earliest type consisted of a vertical graduated circle reading degrees and minutes, which turned about a horizontal axis. A great improvement was effected by placing the graduated circle in a horizontal position. Many forms of the horizontal-circle goniometer have been constructed; they are provided with a telescope and collimator (*q.v.*), and in construction they are essentially the same as a spectrometer, with the addition of arrangements for adjusting and centring the crystal on a stage on the horizontal circle. Light from any convenient source is passed through the slit of the collimator and the image reflected from the crystal face is viewed in the telescope. The crystal holder can be adjusted to bring the image exactly on the cross wires of the telescope. The circle can then be rotated until the image from a second crystal face is brought on the cross wires of the telescope. The angle through which it has been turned is the angle between the two face normals.

However, with a horizontal-circle goniometer, it is necessary to mount and readjust the crystal for the measurement of each zone of faces (*i.e.*, each set of faces intersecting in parallel edges). Further, in certain cases, it is not possible to measure the angles between zones. These difficulties have been overcome by the use of a two-circle goniometer. The crystal is set up and adjusted with the axis of a prominent zone parallel to the axis of either the horizontal or the vertical circle. The positions of the faces are fixed by the simultaneous readings of the two circles.

Some disadvantages are overcome by adding still another graduated circle to the instrument, with its axis perpendicular to the axis of the vertical circle, thus forming a three-circle goniometer. With such an instrument measurements may be made in any zone or between any two faces without readjusting the crystal.

Goniometers have been devised for measuring crystals during their growth in the mother liquid and for cutting section plates and prisms from crystals (precious stones) accurately in any desired direction. An ordinary microscope fitted with cross wires and a rotating graduated stage serves the purpose of a goniometer for measuring the plane angles of a crystal face or section.

The Weissenberg X-ray Goniometer.—This is an instrument used in recording X-ray reflections from crystals. The crystal oscillates through about 200° around an edge, as a cylindrical camera is translated back and forth parallel to the crystal rotation axis. In M. J. Buerger's design the angle which the rotation axis makes with the X-ray beam is variable. *See also* Mineralogy: *Crystal Morphology.*

(L. J. S.; J. D. H. D.)

GONJA, the Hausa name for the Ngbanya chiefdom occupying the lower third of the Northern Region of Ghana, with the Ashanti (q.v.) to the south and Dagomba (q.v.) to the northeast. The people (74,000 in the 1960s) fall into three estates: rulers, Muslims and commoners. Most of the commoners claim to be autochthonous; they speak various Gur and Guang (one group of the Kwa) languages (see African Languages: *The Niger-Congo Family*). The rulers and Muslims, who speak a Guang language called Gbanyito, claim descent from Mande immigrants from the Niger bend, who settled south of the Black Volta in the early 17th century. Defeating the Dagomba, they gained control of their present territory, which includes Salaga—formerly an important entrepôt in trade with the north. In the 18th century eastern Gonja was subjugated by the Ashanti.

The paramount chief, the Yagbumwura, who resides at the administrative centre, Damongo, is selected in rotation from the chiefs of the five eligible divisions. The main occupation is mixed farming: yams, cassava, pearl millet, sorghum, maize (corn), with some cattle. *See also* Ghana: *The People.*

See M. Manoukian, "Tribes of the Northern Territories of the Gold Coast," *Ethnographic Survey of Africa: Western Africa* (1952).
(Jo. R. G.)

GONORRHEA, a venereal disease initiated by the microorganism *Neisseria gonorrhoeae,* occurring nearly always as the result of direct sexual contact and treatable in most cases by penicillin. *See* Venereal Diseases; *see also* references under "Gonorrhea," in the Index.

GONVILLE (Gonvile), **EDMUND** (d. 1351), founder of Gonville hall, now Gonville and Caius college, at Cambridge, Eng., is thought to have been the son of William de Gonvile and the brother of Sir Nicholas Gonvile. The foundation of Gonville hall at Cambridge was effected by a charter granted by Edward III in 1348. It was called, officially, the Hall of the Annunciation of the Blessed Virgin, but was usually known as Gunnell or Gonville hall. Its original site was in Free-school lane, where Corpus Christi college now stands. Gonville apparently wished it to be devoted to training for theological study, but after his death the foundation was completed by William Bateman, bishop of Norwich and founder of Trinity hall, on a different site and with considerably altered statutes.

See also Caius, John.

GONZAGA, an Italian princely house that ruled the town of Mantua between the 14th and the 18th centuries. Their origins are uncertain, but by the 12th century the Corradi family of Gonzaga were established as members of the feudal gentry owning estates near Mantua, to which during the 13th century they managed to add other extensive properties at Verona and Brescia, Cremona and Reggio, Ferrara and other places. They took their name from the village and castle of Gonzaga, situated midway between Mantua and Reggio, and it was in these two cities, especially Mantua, that they first achieved political importance. In Mantua they prospered by supporting and finally supplanting the Bonacolsi (q.v.), whom they overthrew with help from the Scaligeri in 1328.

Luigi Gonzaga (1268–1360) led the revolt of Aug. 16, 1328, against Rinaldo Bonacolsi and was then himself proclaimed hereditary captain general by the commune (Aug. 28). In the following year he was nominated imperial vicar by Louis IV the Bavarian. With imperial authority the Gonzaga also extended their control for a time over Cremona, Reggio and Asolo, but in 1371 they were compelled to sell and surrender Reggio to the Visconti, who during the later 14th century imposed on the reluctant Gonzaga a species of feudal hegemony. In spite of this the Gonzaga successfully consolidated their rule over Mantua, and their court became a centre of princely patronage.

Francesco I Gonzaga (1366–1407), ruler of Mantua from 1382, also acquired dominion over Legnago, Le Stiviere and other small places, many of which were subsequently granted out with other domains in appanage to members of the ruling family. From these collateral lordships, in particular the principalities of Bozzolo and Sabbioneta, many distinguished personalities in Gonzaga history were to come: for example Scipione Gonzaga (1542–93), of the line of Bozzolo, cardinal, patron of the arts and friend of Tasso. Francesco I was created marquis of Mantua in 1403, and this title was revived in 1433 for his son Gianfrancesco I (1395–1444). Under Gianfrancesco the first school inspired by humanistic principles was founded in 1423 in one of the family's villas near Mantua by Vittorino da Feltre. This school, which outlived Vittorino by many years, was attended not only by the Gonzaga children but by many pupils from outside, rich and poor, foreign and Italian, among them Federigo da Montefeltro. Artists also found their way to Mantua, notably Andrea Mantegna and Leon Battista Alberti, and during the 15th century the capital city and its dependencies were embellished and transformed.

This movement quickened under the influence of Isabella d'Este (1474–1539; *see* Este, House of), wife of the fourth marquis Francesco II Gonzaga (1466–1519), and during the reign of his successors, who raised the Mantuan lordship to the height of its prestige and power. In the dangerous and difficult politics that engaged northern Italy after the French invasion of 1494, the Gonzaga eventually sided with the emperor Charles V, a choice rewarded in 1530 when the marquis Federigo II Gonzaga (1500–40) was made duke of Mantua and granted the marquisate of Montferrat (Monferrato). Federigo's brother, Ferrante I (1507–57), who spent most of his long military career in the Habsburg service and administered the duchy of Milan for the emperor between 1546 and 1554, obtained the county of Guastalla (1539). Another brother, Ercole (1505–63), was the presiding cardinal at the Council of Trent from 1561 until his death. It was during the 16th century that the court of Mantua achieved its greatest brilliance. Palaces and villas were lavishly commissioned and splendidly adorned, among them the famous Palazzo del Te designed by Giulio Romano, and many artists as well as writers of distinction found employment or encouragement in Mantua: Baldassare Castiglione and Matteo Bandello, Boiardo and Ariosto, Berni and Bembo, Raphael, Leonardo, Titian and Monteverdi. But under Vincenzo I (1562–1612), whose reign began in 1587, extravagance began to get the better of good taste and sound economy. Revenue was increasingly squandered in licence and display, and by 1627, when the question of succession to the duchy of Mantua became a cause of conflict in Europe, the financial condition of the Gonzaga was desperate.

What made the Mantuan succession so critical a question was the union of Mantua with Montferrat and the strategic importance of both states to the rival powers of France and Austria. A conclusion sought in 1608 by marrying Francesco, Vincenzo's eldest son, to Margaret, daughter of Charles Emmanuel I of Savoy, was ineffective; Francesco died prematurely in 1612, leaving an infant girl, Maria, as his only issue, and while his brother Ferdinando (1587–1626) took control of Mantua, Charles Emmanuel tried to impose his claims on Montferrat by war (1613–18). Neither Ferdinando Gonzaga nor his brother and successor Vincenzo II (1594–1627) had any children, and long before Vincenzo died the problem of succession had been perplexing the courts of Europe.

Though their sister Eleonora (1598–1655) had been married to the emperor Ferdinand II in 1622, Ferdinando and Vincenzo II had wanted to leave their duchy to the French branch of the family—that is, to the house of Gonzague-Nevers, founded by Federigo II Gonzaga's son Ludovico (Louis; d. 1595), who had inherited titles and acquired conspicuous power in France. Consequently, in the War of the Mantuan Succession (1628-31), which broke out on Vincenzo's death and which may be regarded as a phase of the Thirty Years' War, France supported Ludovico's son Charles, duc de Nevers. This Charles's son Charles, duc de Rethel (d. 1630), coming duke as Charles I in 1631, though only after enemy troops and plague had together wasted the territory and town of Mantua, until then among the richest in Europe. His elder daughter Marie Louise de Gonzague (1612-67) was married successively to two kings of Poland, Wladyslaw IV and John Casimir; and her sister Anne (1616-84) was the princesse Palatine who played so subtle a role in the Fronde (see Fronde: *The War of the Princes' Imprisonment* [Jan. 1650-Feb. 1651]).

Charles I died in 1637. Of his profligate and feeble grandson and great-grandson Charles II (1629-65) and Ferdinand Charles (1650-1708), little need be said. Mantua remained involved in the conflicts of Habsburg and Bourbon, paying the penalty of war; and it was as unregretted victims of the War of the Spanish Succession that the Gonzaga ceased to rule. Austrian troops overran Mantua in 1707, and just before his death Ferdinand Charles, who had favoured the French, was declared guilty of treason to the empire and deprived of his duchy. Charles II's sister Eleonora (1628-87) had been married to the emperor Ferdinand III in 1651.

Bibliography.—C. D'Arco, *Studi intorno al municipio di Mantova*, 7 vol. (1871-74); A. Luzio, *I Corradi di Gonzaga* (1913); P. Torelli and A. Luzio, *L'archivio Gonzaga*, 2 vol. (1920-22); S. Brinton, *The Gonzaga* (1927). (P. J. J.)

GONZAGA, SAINT ALOYSIUS (1568-1591), one of the most venerated of modern saints and patron of Roman Catholic youth, was born at Castiglione in Lombardy on March 9, 1568, the eldest son of the marquis of Castiglione, cousin of Guglielmo Gonzaga, duke of Mantua. He was educated at the ducal courts of Florence and of Mantua and at the royal court of Madrid, where he was page to the heir of Philip II. In 1585, against the strongest opposition, he resigned his inheritance and entered the Society of Jesus at Rome. One of his spiritual directors was the renowned theologian St. Robert Bellarmine (*q.v.*). Shortly before ordination, while nursing plague victims, he caught the disease and died on June 21, 1591, at the age of 23.

Most characteristic of the virtues of Aloysius Gonzaga was his intense love of chastity. His practices of prayer, austerity, humility and charity were also heroic, while his all-absorbing love for God raised him to high mystical union. Yet his exalted holiness has much of human appeal, especially his strong and constant heroism and his generous enthusiasm for the Christian ideal. Aloysius' reputation suffered from pietistic biographers, but a truer estimation of him as a normal young man has been established by modern scholars, notably Cyril C. Martindale, S.J., and F. Schroeder, S.J. He was canonized in 1726 by Benedict XIII. Pius XI in 1926 renewed his designation as patron of Catholic youth (originally proclaimed in 1729), affirming that many of the newer canonized saints had been inspired by the example of St. Aloysius.

His feast day is June 21.

Bibliography.—*Acta Sanctorum*, vol. xxv, June 21, p. 726-1027 (1867); V. Cepari, S.J., *Life of St. Aloysius*, ed. by F. Schroeder, S.J., Eng. trans. by F. Goldie, S.J. (1891); Ludwig Koch, S.J. (ed.), *Jesuiten-Lexikon*, vol. xliii, xliv (1934); Cyril C. Martindale, S.J., *The Vocation of Saint Aloysius* (1937); Maurice Meschler, S.J., *Life of Saint Aloysius*, Eng. trans. (1911); *Letteri e scritti spirituali e annotati dal P. E. Rosa* (1926). (M. P. H.)

GONZAGA, TOMÁS ANTÓNIO (1744-1810?), the finest 18th-century Portuguese writer of love poetry. He was born in Oporto on Aug. 11, 1744, his father being a magistrate of Brazilian origin and his mother the daughter of a British merchant. In 1752 he went to Brazil where his father held juridical appointments, but he returned in 1763 to study law at Coimbra, where he graduated in 1768. In 1782 he returned to Brazil on being appointed judge in Vila Rica. Here he fell in love with the 16-year-old Maria Joaquina Doroteia de Seixas, the *Marília* of his lyrics, but on the eve of marriage to her in 1789 he was arrested on a charge, almost certainly false, of being an accessory to a separatist, anti-Portuguese conspiracy. After three years' imprisonment he was sentenced to exile for life in Mozambique. There in 1793 he married a rich heiress and for the rest of his life held important legal positions in the colony. He died there early in 1810.

His reputation as a poet rests on *Marília de Dirceu*, the first section of which appeared in 1792. This group of lyrics, written before his arrest, expresses the joy of love and the expectation of married happiness, while his second group of poems, which were written in prison and appeared in 1799, express yearning for his beloved and past happiness. Gonzaga borrowed his forms from Anacreon and Theocritus, but the matter, the natural, elegant style and the harmonious versification are his own. *Marília de Dirceu* became one of the most frequently reprinted volumes of poetry in the 19th century in Portugal and Brazil.

Gonzaga's complete works were published in 1942. See also M. Rodrigues Lapa, *Marília de Dirceu e mais poesias* (1937). (N. J. L.)

GONZÁLEZ, MANUEL (1833-1893), Mexican soldier and president, born in 1833 in Matamoros, Tamaulipas, became a general during the civil war of 1858-60 and president in 1880, at the virtual dictation of Porfirio Díaz. As president, González successfully defended Mexican rights in a boundary controversy with Guatemala and granted widespread railroad and mining concessions, but many have criticized his administration for corruption and waste. A land survey law favoured large holders and speculators, and an effort to rehabilitate the currency with new nickel coins brought disastrous inflation. In 1884 when González left the presidency, Mexico was nearly bankrupt. He died on May 8, 1893. (D. M. Pr.)

GONZÁLEZ DE CLAVIJO, RUY (d. 1412), Spanish diplomat and traveler, was born in Madrid and became chamberlain to King Henry III of Castile and León. On the return of his first embassy from the court of Timur, Henry dispatched another which included González and a Tatar adviser. They sailed from St. Mary Port, near Cádiz, on May 22, 1403, touched at Gaeta, Rhodes and Constantinople, went by the south coast of the Black sea to Trebizond, and proceeded inland by Erzurum, Tabriz, Teheran and Meshed to Samarkand, where they were favourably received by Timur. They returned successfully after great difficulties and reached Spain on March 1, 1406.

González de Clavijo died in Madrid on April 2, 1412. His narrative presents a unique account of Timur's court by a European observer.

Bibliography.—Two manuscripts of González de Clavijo's narrative are preserved in the Biblioteca Nacional, Madrid; his *Embajada a Tamor Lân* was edited by F. López Estrada (1943); English versions of *Embassy to Tamerlane* by Sir Clement Markham (1859) and by G. Le Strange (1928). (R. A. Sn.)

GONZALO de Córdoba (1453-1515), el Gran Capitán, Spanish military leader renowned for his exploits in southern Italy, was the second son of Pedro Fernández de Córdoba, intendant of Andalusia, and of Elvira de Herrera. He was sent to court at 13 and became page first to the pretender, Henry IV's half-brother Alfonso, and then to Alfonso's sister Isabella. Gonzalo distinguished himself in the fighting following Isabella's accession (1474) and played an increasingly important role in the war against the kingdom of Granada, displaying singular ingenuity in the capture of fortified places, adapting his methods to the age of gunpowder then beginning. He was one of the two commissioners to conduct the final negotiations with Boabdil for the surrender of Granada (1492). Gonzalo's successful association with the Catholic sovereigns and Isabella's confidence in him set him on the road to fame.

In 1495 the queen gave him command of an expedition in support of the Aragonese king of Naples against the French in Italy. Gonzalo quickly achieved success on behalf of his ally and at the request of Pope Alexander VI defeated a lingering French garrison in Ostia, for which he was given a Roman triumph and a Golden Rose (March 1497). In 1500 he was sent to Italy in command of a larger force, for co-operation with Louis XII of France against the Ottoman Turks, but also to be ready to counter French ambitions in regard to Naples. Together with the Venetians, he captured the strongly held island of Cephalonia. The immediate Turkish threat having been removed, a secret agreement was signed by the king of France and Ferdinand dividing the kingdom of Naples between them. The French disputed and overran the agreed lines of the division and by 1502 were engaged in a war with the Spaniards under Gonzalo in which he won the striking victories of Cerignola, Monte Cassino and the Garigliano. In this last battle he brought about the surrender of far larger and more heavily armed forces by an unexpected night attack on Dec. 27, 1503, across the flooded estuary by means of pontoons, during one of the severest winters known in Italy. It was typical of the military ingenuity of *el Gran Capitán* (as Gonzalo was by then known), who in his earlier campaign in Italy had used rapid marches by men picked for physical fitness to achieve surprise against an army adhering to the older medieval formalities of warfare.

Ferdinand recalled Gonzalo from the viceroyalty of Naples in 1507, though he was reluctantly obliged to name him for command again following a French threat after the battle of Ravenna (1512). Gonzalo died in Granada, of malaria contracted in Italy, on Dec. 1, 1515.

See G. de Gaury, *The Grand Captain* (1955).   (G. de G.)

GOOCH, SIR DANIEL, BART. (1816–1889), English mechanical engineer and railway pioneer, who was also responsible for laying the first successful transatlantic cables, was born at Bedlington, Northumberland, on Aug. 24, 1816. In 1837 he joined the Great Western Railway under M. I. Brunel, and as locomotive superintendent developed a new eight-wheeled class of locomotive. One of these, named "Lord of the Isles," was awarded a gold medal at the Great Exhibition of 1851. During 1865–66 Gooch, as a director of a telegraph construction company, superintended the laying of the first two transatlantic cables. In 1866 he was recalled to be chairman of the Great Western Railway and was created a baronet for his services. He supported Brunel as a champion of the broad gauge, but he failed to convince others; within a few years of his death at Clewer Park, near Windsor, on Oct. 15, 1889, the Great Western changed to standard gauge.

See *Diaries of Sir Daniel Gooch* (1892).   (T. M. S.)

GOOCH, GEORGE PEABODY (1873–1968), English historian, whose writings are mainly concerned with modern diplomatic history, was born in London on Oct. 21, 1873. He was educated at King's college, London, and Trinity college, Cambridge, and then studied in Berlin and Paris. He was Liberal member of parliament for Bath (1906–10) and for Reading in 1913. Gooch became a leading diplomatic historian and one of the earliest authorities on recent German history. He was joint editor of the *Cambridge History of British Foreign Policy* (1922–23) and *British Documents on the Origins of the War, 1898–1914* (1926–38). President of the Historical association (1922–25), he was later president of the National Peace council (1933–36). He died at his home near Beaconsfield, Eng., on Aug. 31, 1968.

His many writings include: *Germany and the French Revolution* (1920); *Franco-German Relations, 1871–1914* (1923); *English Democratic Ideas in the Seventeenth Century* (1927); *Courts and Cabinets* (1944); *Maria Theresa and other Studies* (1951) and *The Second Empire* (1960).

GOODE, GEORGE BROWN (1851–1896), U.S. zoologist under whose direction the collections at the National museum were entirely reorganized and recatalogued in a scientific manner and displayed with an educational aim in view, was born in New Albany, Ind., on Feb. 13, 1851. After graduating from Wesleyan university at Middletown, Conn., he spent a year at Harvard studying natural history under Louis Agassiz. In 1874 he became chief of the division of fisheries at the National museum, Washington, D.C., and in 1887 assistant secretary of the Smithsonian institution in charge of the National museum, which position he held until his death at Washington, on Sept. 6, 1896.

His ideas of museum administration and display influenced nearly every important museum of the period. They were also spread by the remarkable government exhibits prepared by Goode for the Centennial exhibition of 1876, the World's Columbian exposition of 1893, exhibitions at Berlin (1880), London (1883) and Madrid (1892–93) and many others. Goode wrote *American Fishes* (1888) and in 1896 published his most important scientific work, *Ocean Ichthyology.*

The *Annual Report* of the U.S. Nat. Museum for 1897 contains a bibliography of Goode's publications together with memoirs by S. P. Langley and others.

GOOD FRIDAY is the Friday in Holy Week (*i.e.,* two days before Easter day) on which the yearly commemoration of the crucifixion of Jesus Christ is kept. References are found in the 2nd century to fasting and penance on this day by Christians, who from very early times had observed every Friday as a fast day in memory of the crucifixion. The Roman missal prescribes a rite primitive in many of its elements and containing none of the medieval additions customary on other days of the year. The service was revised in 1956 to restore it to its proper function, *i.e.,* of prayer and scripture reading followed by the veneration of the cross and the communion of the people; it is held at 3 P.M., the traditional time of Christ's death on the cross. It resembles the rite of 4th-century Jerusalem described in the account written by Etheria (*see* CHURCH YEAR: *Jerusalem*). After two lessons from the Old Testament and the account of the crucifixion from St. John's Gospel there follows a series of collects for all conditions of men. This part of the service is a relic of the early Christian prayer service (synaxis) preceding the Eucharist. The cross is then unveiled and venerated by priest and people while the *Improperia* ("Reproaches") are chanted. The service concludes with communion of the congregation from hosts consecrated on the previous day. (*See* MAUNDY THURSDAY.) This communion of the people was in vogue between the 4th and 7th centuries but gradually fell into disuse. The rite used to be known, erroneously, as the Mass of the Presanctified, though it was not a celebration of the Eucharist but merely the communion of the officiating priest.

In the Orthodox Church, where Good Friday is known as Great Friday, the liturgy of the Presanctified is used. At vespers there is a solemn re-enactment of the burial procession of Christ, who is represented by the *epitaphion,* a piece of material bearing an image of the dead Saviour.

The Book of Common Prayer provides for a celebration of the Eucharist on Good Friday though in practice this is largely ignored and the chief service of the day is often that known as the Three Hours Devotion (12 noon to 3 P.M.), a series of sermons, hymns and prayers centred on the cross. In Lutheran churches it is customary to have a service of Holy Communion on Good Friday. Other Protestant churches generally hold services on Good Friday, sometimes followed by communion, and in many areas joint services take place as an expression of Christian unity. *See* also HOLY WEEK; LENT.

BIBLIOGRAPHY.—L. Eisenhofer, *The Liturgy of the Roman Rite* (1961); L. Duchesne, *Christian Worship,* 5th ed. (1931); H. Thurston, *Lent and Holy Week* (1904).   (L. C. S.)

GOOD-KING-HENRY (*Chenopodium bonus-henricus*), a rank-growing perennial herb of the family Chenopodiaceae, found in Great Britain and naturalized in North America. It is a smooth, dark green, little-branched plant, about 2 ft. high, with usually entire arrowhead-shaped leaves. The plant is sometimes cultivated as a potherb under the name mercury or all-good. *See* also CHENOPODIUM.

GOODRICH, SAMUEL GRISWOLD (1793–1860), U.S. publisher and author known under the pseudonym of "Peter Parley," was born at Ridgefield, Conn., Aug. 19, 1793. Largely self-educated, he became a bookseller and publisher at Hartford and later in Boston. There, beginning in 1828, he published for 15 years an illustrated annual, the *Token,* to which he was a frequent contributor both in prose and verse. The *Token* contained some of the earliest work of Nathaniel Hawthorne, N. P. Willis, Henry W. Longfellow and Lydia Maria Child. In 1841 he established *Merry's Museum,* which he continued to edit until 1854. In 1827 he began, under the name of "Peter Parley," his series of books for the young, which embraced geography, biography, history, science and miscellaneous tales. Of these he was the sole composer of comparatively few, but in his *Recollections of a Lifetime,* 2 volumes (1856)," he wrote that he was "the author and editor of about 170 volumes," of which about 7,000,000 copies had been sold, and gave a list both of the works of which he was the author or editor and of the spurious works published under his name.

Goodrich was chosen a member of the Massachusetts house of representatives in 1836, and, of the state senate in 1837, and in 1851–53 he was consul at Paris, where he remained until 1855. He died in New York May 9, 1860.

GOODRICH (Goodricke), **THOMAS** (d. 1554), bishop of Ely, one of the most zealous supporters of the Henrician Reformation, was the son of Edward Goodrich of East Kirkby, Lincolnshire, and was educated at Cambridge. Convocation consulted him about the legality of Henry VIII's marriage to Catherine of Aragon. He became royal chaplain about 1530 and was promoted under the patronage of Anne Boleyn and Thomas Cromwell to the bishopric of Ely in 1534. In 1537 he helped to draw up the *Institution of a Christian Man* (known as the *Bishop's Book*) and translated the Gospel of St. John for the Great Bible of 1539. Under both Henry VIII and Edward VI he was one of the commissioners for the reform of ecclesiastical laws. On the accession of Edward in 1547 he was made a privy councilor. He assisted in compiling the first Book of Common Prayer and in Nov. 1550 was appointed one of the commissioners for the trial of Bishop Stephen Gardiner. In Jan. 1551 he succeeded Richard Rich as chancellor and held this office during the nine days' reign of Lady Jane Grey; but he made his peace with Queen Mary by associating himself with the order sent to disarm Lady Jane's claim. He conformed to Roman Catholicism and, though deprived of the chancellorship, kept his bishopric until his death on May 10, 1554, at Somersham, Huntingdonshire.

See L. B. Smith, *Tudor Prelates and Politics 1536–1558* (1953); R. B. Pugh (ed.), *Victoria History of the County of Cambridge and the Isle of Ely* (1953).

GOOD SHEPHERD, SISTERS OF OUR LADY OF CHARITY OF THE (R.G.S.), a Roman Catholic order of religious founded at Angers, France, in 1833, as a descendant of an earlier order founded by St. John Eudes in 1641. The Good Shepherd sisters are concerned with the care of fallen women, conduct reformatories, homes for alcoholics, etc. The habit is a white tunic and scapular, with blue girdle and black veil. The mother house is at Angers. See WOMEN'S RELIGIOUS ORDERS.

GOODSIR, JOHN (1814–1867), Scottish anatomist who made important early studies of cell physiology and pathology, was born at Anstruther, Fife, on March 20, 1814. He was educated at St. Andrews and at Edinburgh. In 1838 he communicated to the British association a paper on the origin and development of the human teeth, and about the same time he was elected to the coterie called the "Universal Brotherhood of the Friends of Truth," which comprised artists, scholars, naturalists and others whose relationship became a potent influence in science. He worked at marine zoology but human anatomy, pathology and morphology formed his chief study.

In 1840 he moved to Edinburgh, where he was appointed conservator of the museum of the College of Surgeons. In his lectures in 1842–43 he insisted on the importance of the cell as a centre of nutrition and pointed out that an organism is subdivided into a number of departments. R. Virchow recognized his indebtedness to these discoveries by dedicating his *Cellularpathologie* to Goodsir, whom he described as "one of the earliest and most acute observers of cell-life." In 1843 Goodsir became curator in the University of Edinburgh. He died at Wardie near Edinburgh, on March 6, 1867.

GOODSPEED, EDGAR JOHNSON (1871–1962), U.S. New Testament scholar and translator, was born in Quincy, Ill., Oct. 23, 1871, and educated at Denison university, Granville, O. (A.B., 1890), Yale and The University of Chicago (Ph.D., 1898). After further study at Berlin and work on Greek papyri in Egypt, he joined the faculty of The University of Chicago in 1902, serving there until his retirement in 1937, as professor from 1914 and Ernest DeWitt Burton distinguished service professor from 1933. A pioneer in papyrology, Goodspeed collaborated with Grenfell and Hunt in publishing *The Tebtunis Papyri* (1907). This and other studies in Hellenistic Greek, such as his *Index Patristicus* (1907) and *Index Apologeticus* (1912), prepared him for his most famous work, *The New Testament: an American Translation* (1923). Goodspeed also translated into modern American idiom *The Apocrypha* (1938) and *The Apostolic Fathers* (1950), and edited New Testament manuscripts and texts of early Christian writers, including *Die ältesten Apologeten* (1914). His work as New Testament interpreter is marked by grammatical and historical rather than theological exegesis, an example being *The Meaning of Ephesians* (1933). *An Introduction to the New Testament* (1937), his major contribution to this field, considers the later books of the New Testament as profoundly influenced by the collection and publication of Paul's letters. He had previously dealt with the New Testament canon in *The Formation of the New Testament* (1926), in which he regards the New Testament as consisting of several successive collections. Other works are *A History of Early Christian Literature* (1942); *Paul* (1947); *A Life of Jesus* (1950); numerous books on the Bible designed for the general reader; essays; and one mystery story, *The Curse in the Colophon* (1935). Goodspeed died at Los Angeles, Calif., on Jan. 13, 1962.
(Sh. E. J.)

GOOD WILL, a title for an intangible asset occasionally shown in accounting reports. Good will is measured by the difference between the current market value of the entire firm and the sum of the net individual assets at current values. Good will is seldom recorded initially or increased unless ownership has changed and there is a bona fide cost to support the valuation.

At one time it used to be thought that the good will of a business consisted solely of the good will of its customers, and represented the reputation that the business had acquired in their minds as a result of fair dealing over a reasonably extended period of time. Modern thought recognizes that second only to the esteem of customers is the esteem of supplying houses and employees.

Enterprise value may be greater than the current value of total net assets because accountants traditionally do not treat all valuable relationships as individual assets. Thus, high worker morale, engineering efficiency, sales ability, shrewd management policies and favourable public relations influence enterprise value but are not recorded individually as assets. Good will becomes a composite or master valuation account for such values.

The buyer takes over individual assets at current values and is seldom interested in values recorded by previous owners. If location is important, land and leasehold values should reflect the fact; if patents and trade-marks are worth more than recorded amounts, they should be valued currently; if established connections and outlets are valuable, their purchase represents a legitimate organization and development asset. Where feasible it is preferable to separate specific sources of value from good will and thereby encourage clear-cut classification and rational amortization.

Prospective purchasers, trustees and estate administrators make their own estimates of enterprise value and tend to disregard any previously recorded good will. Such an approach is probably superior to that which asks the accountant to revalue good will periodically so that reported total assets will always represent his individual estimate of enterprise value.
(C. T. D.)

GOODWIN, THOMAS (1600–1680), an outstanding representative of English Puritanism, was born, like many Puritans, in East Anglia (Rollesby, Norfolk), on Oct. 5, 1600, was educated at Cambridge (Christ's college) and lived abroad (Arnhem, Holland) in the 1630s because of Archbishop William Laud's persecution. As the leading member of the "dissenting brethren" of the Westminster assembly in the 1640s, Goodwin embraced, like his friend John Cotton in Massachusetts, the Independent or Congregational form of church government as the middle way between the Puritan right and left—Presbyterianism and sectarianism. Together with John Owen and others, Goodwin drafted the Savoy declaration of faith for Congregationalism of 1658 (see CONFESSIONS OF FAITH, PROTESTANT). His own rejection of Arminianism and adherence to the covenant of grace closely paralleled the theological main stream of Puritanism, but he also possessed a mystical strain of apocalypticism that became prominent among some sectarians in the 1650s. Under the commonwealth and protectorate

Goodwin headed Magdalen college, Oxford, was a trier of heretical ministers and served as a court chaplain to Oliver Cromwell. At the latter's deathbed Goodwin reportedly reassured the lord protector of that conviction of salvation that was a distinguishing characteristic of Puritan saints. Goodwin died on Feb. 23, 1680. According to Anthony Wood, Goodwin and Owen were "the two Atlasses and Patriarchs of Independency."

His *Works* were published in 5 volumes in 1681–1704 and reprinted in 12 volumes in 1861–66. (L. F. Sr.)

GOODWIN, WILLIAM WATSON (1831–1912), U.S. classical scholar, author of important works in Greek grammar and philology, was born in Concord, Mass., on May 9, 1831. He graduated from Harvard in 1851, studied at Bonn, Berlin and Göttingen, receiving his Ph.D. degree from there in 1855; was tutor in Greek at Harvard in 1856–60 and Eliot professor of Greek thereafter until his retirement in 1901. In 1882–83 he was the first director of the American School of Classical Studies at Athens. Goodwin edited the *Panegyricus* of Isocrates (1864) and Demosthenes' *De Corona* (1901), and assisted in preparing the 7th edition of Liddell and Scott's *Greek English Lexicon*. He revised an English version by several writers of *Plutarch's Morals*, five volumes (1871), and published the Greek text with literal English version of Aeschylus' *Agamemnon* for the Harvard production of that play in June 1906. His most important work was *Syntax of the Moods and Tenses of the Greek Verb* (1860; enlarged edition 1890). Besides making accessible to American students the works of J. N. Madvig and P. Krüger, it presented original matter, including a "radical innovation in the classification of conditional sentences," notably the "distinction between particular and general suppositions." Both this and his *Greek Grammar* (1870) in later editions were largely dependent on the theories of B. L. Gildersleeve for additions and changes. He died in Cambridge, Mass., on June 16, 1912.

GOODWIN SANDS, a dangerous line of shoals at the entrance to the Strait of Dover from the North sea, about 6 mi. from the Kent coast of England, from which they are separated by the Downs (*q.v.*). The sands, which stretch for about ten miles, are partly exposed at low water. They present a major hazard to navigation and are frequently the scene of wrecks, in spite of lights and bell buoys. Attempts to erect a lighthouse have failed. Tradition finds in the Goodwins the remnant of an island called Lomea, which belonged to Earl Godwine (11th century) and was afterward submerged. Borings through the sand to the underlying chalk show this to be highly improbable. Four lightships mark the limits of the sands, and are in communication with the coastal lifeboat stations.

GOODYEAR, CHARLES (1800–1860), U.S. inventor, whose discovery of the process of "vulcanization" made possible the commercial use of rubber, was born at New Haven, Conn., Dec. 29, 1800, the son of Amasa Goodyear, an inventor (especially of farming implements) and a pioneer in the manufacture of hardware in the U.S. In 1821 Charles Goodyear entered into a partnership with his father at Naugatuck that continued till 1830. Already he was interested in an attempt to discover a method of treatment by which India rubber could be made into articles that would stand extremes of heat and cold. To the solution of this problem the next ten years of his life were devoted. For a time he seemed to have succeeded in treating a treatment of the rubber with nitric acid. In 1836 he secured a contract for the manufacture by this process of mailbags for the U.S. government, but the rubber fabric was useless at high temperatures. In 1837 he worked with Nathaniel Hayward (1808–65), who had been an employee of a rubber factory in Roxbury and had made experiments with sulfur mixed with rubber. Goodyear bought from Hayward the right to use this imperfect process. In 1839, by dropping on a hot stove some India rubber mixed with sulfur, he discovered accidentally the process for the vulcanization of rubber. In 1844 his first patent was granted. Numerous infringements had to be fought in the courts, the decisive victory coming in 1852. In the same year he went to England, where articles made under his patents had been displayed at the International exhibition of 1851, but he was unable to establish factories there. In France and England he lost his patent rights by technical legal

defects; in the United States his patents were infringed mercilessly, and he was cheated by some of his business associates. In France a company for the manufacture of vulcanized rubber by his process failed, and in Dec. 1855 Goodyear was arrested and imprisoned for debt in Paris. He died in New York city July 1, 1860, worn out by work, poverty and disappointment. He left his family heavily in debt, though his invention made millions for others. He wrote an account of his discovery entitled *Gum-Elastic and Its Varieties*, two volumes (1853–55).

See also B. K. Peirce, *Trials of an Inventor: Life and Discoveries of Charles Goodyear* (1866); A. C. Regli, *Rubber's Goodyear: the Story of a Man's Perseverance* (1941).

GOOKIN, DANIEL (1612–1687), American colonial magistrate, soldier and protector of the Indians, was born in Kent, Eng., in 1612. Gookin went to Virginia during his boyhood in the company of his father. His Puritan sympathies brought him to the colony of Massachusetts in 1644. There he became a militia captain, deputy to the colonial legislature, member of the governor's council and finally major general. In 1656 he was appointed superintendent of the Massachusetts Indians, an office he held until his death. Working closely with the clergyman John Eliot, Gookin protected the Indians against maltreatment by white settlers and for that reason suffered unpopularity during the Indian wars. He wrote three books, none of which was published during his lifetime: *Historical Collections of the Indians in Massachusetts*, published in 1792; *Historical Account of the Doings and Sufferings of the Christian Indians of New England*, published in 1836; and a history of New England that has never been found. He died March 19, 1687.

See F. W. Gookin, *Daniel Gookin, 1612–1687* (1912); S. E. Morison, *Builders of the Bay Colony* (1930). (B. K. B.)

GOOLE, a municipal borough (1933), market town and inland port in the Goole parliamentary division of the West Riding of Yorkshire, Eng., 27 mi. S.W. of Hull and 23 mi. S.E. of York. Pop. (1971 prelim.) 18,066. Situated on flat land at the confluence of the Ouse and the Don, which later becomes the Humber, Goole is the terminus of the canal system of the former Aire and Calder navigation, to which it owes its existence. The docks were formally opened in 1826, and now handle extensive coal shipments from the Yorkshire and east Midlands coalfields. The port, located about 47 mi. from the North sea, can accommodate vessels of up to 2,000 tons burden, and larger vessels on the spring tides; it has nine interconnected wet docks and a quay length of 3 mi. The principal imports are food and provisions, strawboards, wool and scrap; exports include iron and steel manufactures, coke, pitch and textiles. Regular services operate between Goole and north European and coastwise ports and the town is also a railway centre. Other industries are shipbuilding and repairing, engineering, flour milling and the making of fertilizers and clothing, and the town is surrounded by an extensive agricultural area of rich warp land. A special feature is the system of conveying coal on the canal from the collieries by trains of compartment boats ("Tom puddings"), and of hydraulic lifts for discharging them without further handling into the holds of seagoing vessels. The 750,000 gal. water-storage tower is one of the largest in the country. In the town are two public parks, gardens, a market hall and cattle market.

GOONA (GUNA), a town, *tehsil* and district of Madhya Pradesh, India. The town (pop. [1971 prelim.] 42,335) is 130 mi. S of Gwalior on the main Bombay-Agra Road and the Western Railway. Originally a small village 5 mi. N of Bajranggarh (the former district headquarters), it became a British cantonment in 1844 and has since become a trading centre.

GOONA DISTRICT (area 4,271 sq.mi.; pop. [1971 prelim.] 783,-541) formerly contained the seven feudatory lands of Scindia, the ruling house of Gwalior. On May 28, 1948, it became a district of Madhya Bharat and was merged in Madhya Pradesh on Nov. 1, 1956. The district is an elevated plateau about 1,800 ft. above sea level, drained toward the north by the Betwa, Sind, and Parbati rivers. The eastern and western regions are cultivated and well populated, while the central hilly tract covered by state forest provides timber and bamboos. The principal crops are wheat, barley, jowar, pulses, and fibres. (S. M. A.)

GOOSE, the common name for waterfowl of the family Anatidae in which the beak is roughly conical in shape, as compared with the more spatulate beak of the duck (q.v.). Most geese further differ from ducks in that the sexes are alike in plumage and form a strong and often lasting pair bond. The male (sometimes called "gander") participates in nesting and in rearing the young, often vigorously defending his mate and the nest. Like ducks, geese molt all of their flight feathers simultaneously, becoming temporarily flightless but in many species gaining stronger plumage for the subsequent migration. Migrating geese frequently travel in long lines, sometimes in the form of an open "V."

The most representative member of the subfamily is the graylag goose (*Anser anser*), from which the domestic goose has been derived. It breeds in suitable localities from Lapland to Spain and from Scotland to China. The nest is placed in heather or grass, and five or six eggs form a clutch. The genus *Anser* constitutes the "gray" geese and includes, besides the graylag, the bean goose (*A. fabalis*), the pink-footed goose (*A. f. brachyrhynchus*) and the white-fronted goose (*A. albifrons*), all breeding in the northern part of the old world and migrating south in winter. American members of the group are the white-fronted goose and, in the north, the snow goose (commonest is *Chen hyperborea*, the snow goose proper, white with black primaries) and the emperor goose (*Philacte canagica*) of the Aleutian Islands. The blue goose (*Chen caerulescens*), with a slate-coloured body and white head, breeds far north and winters along the Gulf Coast from Louisiana (the greatest number) sparingly to Veracruz, Mex.

The "black" geese include the barnacle goose (*Branta leucopsis*), breeding in Spitsbergen, northeast Greenland, and northwest Siberia, supposed of old to be produced from barnacles (Lepadidae); and the brant goose (*B. bernicla*), with a circumpolar breeding range. To this group also belongs the well-known Canada goose (*B. canadensis*) of North America. Other species occur in North America and Asia.

The Hawaiian goose, or nene (*B. sandvicensis*), found only in Hawaii, was on the verge of extinction in 1950, but has been restored by the breeding of captive birds, notably in England. The largest living goose is the Chinese goose (*Cygnopsis cygnoides*; sometimes given as *Anser cygnoides*), the original stock of the eastern domestic races. *Cnemiornis calcitrans* is a fossil goose from New Zealand, remarkable for its unusual kneecap and its loss of flight. The Egyptian and Orinoco geese (*Alopochen* and *Neochen* species) and, less clearly, the Abyssinian blue-winged goose (*Cyanochen cyanoptera*) possess tracheal and other anatomic characteristics setting them apart as sheldgeese, a group within the subfamily Anatinae. Other sheldgeese belong to the South American genus *Chloephaga*, which includes the kelp goose (*C. hybrida*) and the upland goose (*C. leucoptera*). The coscoroba (*Coscoroba coscoroba*), intermediate between geese and swans, is sometimes called the swan goose (a name often applied also to the Chinese goose).

Geese, like other game birds, are widely hunted; for a discussion of their place in sport, see HUNTING: *Shooting Small Game*; in game management, see GAME BIRDS. The domesticated breeds are raised, much more in Europe than in the U.S., for their flesh, eggs, and feathers. Locally in Western Europe geese are force-fed noodles or other foods to cause enlargement of the livers, from which organs the paste delicacy called pâté de foie gras is produced. See also POULTRY AND POULTRY FARMING.

See Jean Delacour, *The Waterfowl of the World*, vol. i (1954); F. H. Kortright, *The Ducks, Geese and Swans of North America* (1943).
(Hr. N.; X.)

GOOSEBERRY, a well-known fruit bush of the northern hemisphere, closely related to the currants and frequently placed

MASLOWSKI & GOODPASTER FROM NATIONAL AUDUBON SOCIETY
CANADA GOOSE (BRANTA CANADENSIS)

in the same genus, *Ribes*, of which there are about 150 species, mostly natives of western North America. If separated, the currants are *Ribes* and the gooseberries *Grossularia*. They belong to the family Saxifragaceae (q.v.). Currants are nonspiny and the flowers are borne in racemes, whereas gooseberries are spiny and produce their flowers singly or in twos and threes.

The gooseberry is far more important in Great Britain and northern Europe than in North America. In Europe it is made into preserves, and frequently eaten out of hand. In the U.S. most varieties are used as jellies, preserves and in pies. European gooseberries are derived from the species *Grossularia reclinata* (or *Ribes grossularia*), native in northern Africa and from Spain east to the Caucasus and north to Scandinavia. It was cultivated in English gardens as early as 1600. Hundreds of varieties are known and are classed as early, midseason or main-crop, and dessert kinds. May Duke is the chief early variety; Keepsake is also grown. Both mostly about East Grinsted in Sussex. Leveller is the principal variety and by special care berries one ounce each in weight are obtained. Dessert varieties are picked from July 1 to about Aug. 15 and are marketed ripe. Most gooseberries are interplanted in fruit orchards and spaced as follows: the early, 3 by 6 ft.; the late, 4 by 4 ft. Stable manure and potash are used as fertilizer. The bushes are propagated by cuttings taken in the fall and disbudded at the base to form a tree-shaped plant.

In America the European gooseberries are attacked by powdery mildew. Hybridizing the European varieties with American species produces resistant varieties. Poorman and Pixwell are the chief varieties in the United States and Fredonia, Clark, Poorman and Silvia are good in Canada. Pixwell fruit is medium sized, Clark is large. Poorman is large fruited, bright red. Glendale succeeds as far south as Maryland to Missouri. In Canada thornless varieties have been originated.

Powdery mildew, serious on European varieties, may be controlled with commercial lime-sulfur, 1½ gal. to 50 gal. of water. Anthracnose and leaf spot may defoliate the plants unless controlled by spraying with Bordeaux mixture. The chief insect of red currants and gooseberries, the "imported" currant worm, quickly strips the plants of leaves but is readily controlled by powdered hellebore. The gooseberry, as well as the currant, spreads the blister rust (q.v.) and is prohibited from certain areas where white pine is important. State regulations regarding the planting of gooseberries may be obtained from state authorities.
See also references under "Gooseberry" in the Index.
(G. M. D.)

GOOSSENS, a distinguished family of Belgian and English musicians.

EUGÈNE GOOSSENS (1845–1906), Belgian conductor, was born in Bruges, Feb. 25, 1845. He was admitted to the Brussels conservatory, where, from the age of 14, he studied the violin. In 1882, after several years' experience as an operatic conductor in Belgium, France, Italy and England, Goossens was made conductor of the Carl Rosa Opera company. He died in Liverpool on Dec. 30, 1906.

EUGÈNE GOOSSENS (1867–1958), son of the above, was also a conductor. He was born in Bordeaux, France, on Jan. 28, 1867, and was educated in Bruges, at the Brussels conservatory and at the Royal Academy of Music, London. He played the violin with the

J. HORACE McFARLAND
THE KEEPSAKE GOOSEBERRY (G. RECLINATA)

Carl Rosa Opera company and was a member of the orchestra of the Royal opera, became conductor of the Carl Rosa Opera company in 1899 and of the British National Opera company in 1926. He died in London, July 31, 1958.

SIR EUGENE GOOSSENS (1893–1962), English composer and conductor and son of the above, was born in London on May 26, 1893. He received his musical training at Bruges conservatory, the Liverpool College of Music and the Royal College of Music, London. In 1921, after several years of association with Sir Thomas Beecham, he formed an orchestra with which he gave a series of concerts which included a performance of one of his own works. He was conductor of the Rochester (N.Y.) Philharmonic orchestra from 1923 until 1931, when he became director of the Cincinnati (O.) Symphony orchestra. He remained in Cincinnati until 1946 and during this time was musical director of the biennial Cincinnati May festivals. In 1947 he became resident conductor of the Sydney (New South Wales, Austr.) Symphony orchestra and director of the New South Wales Conservatorium of Music. He was knighted in 1955. In 1956 he resigned his Australian positions.

In composition Goossens' output is considerable. Of particular interest is his chamber music, which includes: Suite for flute, violin and harp (1914); *Five Impressions of a Holiday* for piano, flute or violin and cello (1914); *Fantasy* for string quartet (1915); *Pastoral and Harlequinade* for flute, oboe and piano (1924); *Fantasy* for wind instruments (1924). He also wrote two operas, *Judith* (produced in 1929) and *Don Juan de Mañara* (1937), both with librettos by the English novelist Arnold Bennett; a ballet, *L'École en crinoline* (1921); two symphonies (first performed 1946); songs and music for piano, cello and violin. His book *Overture and Beginners* was published in 1951. He died at Hillingdon, Middlesex, on June 13, 1962.

LEON GOOSSENS (1897–   ), English oboist, brother of the above, was born in Liverpool on June 12, 1897. He was the first oboist of the Queen's Hall and Covent Garden opera orchestras and of the London Philharmonic orchestra after it was founded in 1932; he made a great reputation as a solo and chamber music performer. His two sisters, Marie (b. 1894) and Sidonie (b. 1899) Goossens, became well-known harpists.

GOPHER, a name applied to either of two related rodents and less commonly to a tortoise. The pocket gophers, rodents of the family Geomyidae, occur from Guatemala to southern Canada, excluding northeastern United States and eastern Canada. Present-day pocket gophers comprise 8 genera and 37 species, one of which contains numerous subspecies (races). They are 5 to 18 in. long, including the short, sparsely haired tail, have thickset bodies, a loosely attached skin, small eyes and ears, chisellike front teeth and long claws. A characteristic feature is the presence of large fur-lined cheek pouches (the "pockets") that open externally, not into the mouth. The different species vary from almost white to black, but the colour of an individual is nearly uniform. They live alone in extensive, rather shallow, underground burrows, marked by a series of rounded earth mounds. The food consists of the under-

ground parts of plants obtained as the animal tunnels along; occasionally the gopher ventures a foot or so from the burrow entrance above ground to collect succulent herbs, the stems of which are cut into short pieces and carried in the pouches to storage chambers.

Since pocket gophers do not hibernate, hoarding is a necessity. The several underground storage chambers are kept stocked with stems, roots and tubers to be eaten during winter. The nest itself, located close to the storage chambers, is lined with finely shredded vegetation. For most of the year gophers are solitary, tolerating company only in the spring when mating takes place. About four weeks after mating the young are born, from one to nine composing a litter. The female cares for the helpless, naked, blind young for about six weeks, at which time they begin to develop rapidly; in several more weeks they leave the mother's burrow to dig their own nests.

The chief genera in North America are *Thomomys*, the smooth-toothed pocket gophers, found widespread in western regions, and *Geomys*, the eastern pocket gophers.

Gopher is also loosely applied to any one of the hibernating ground squirrels (*see* SQUIRREL), or spermophiles (genus *Citellus* [*Spermophilus* of some authors]), especially to the 13-lined ground squirrel. Unlike the silent pocket gophers, these forms have calls varying from soft squeaks to shrill, penetrating whistles.

Because of their burrowing and feeding habits, both ground squirrels and pocket gophers often become nuisances, especially in lawns and golf greens; in some localities they are rather serious pests of economically important crops. However, these burrowing animals have, in the past, done much to condition the soil of the now fertile plains of western North America. Trapping, poisoning or fumigation of the burrows are successful methods of control. (*See also* RODENT.)

The tortoises to which the name gopher is applied in the southern U.S. are of the genus *Gopherus* (*see* TURTLE). (K. R. KN.)

GÖPPINGEN, a town of Germany which after partition of the nation following World War II was located in the *Land* (state) of Baden-Württemberg, Federal Republic of Germany. It lies on the Fils river 22 mi. E. of Stuttgart. Pop. (1961) 48,937. A rail junction and also well served by highways, Göppingen manufactures machinery, toys, textiles, leather, plastics, precision instruments, etc. Notable public buildings are the Late-Gothic Oberhofen church and the town castle (16th century). Göppingen was founded as town in the 12th century by the Hohenstaufen. It was devastated in the Thirty Years' War and in 1782, for the second time, was largely destroyed by fire. Its population was doubled after World War II by refugees from eastern Europe. (M. AK.)

GORAKHPUR, a city, district and division of Uttar Pradesh, India. The city, with a population (1961) of 180,255, lies 150 mi. N. of Varanasi (Benares) on the left bank of the Rapti, a northern tributary of the Gogra, below its confluence with the Rohin. Protective embankments have been constructed running parallel to the Rapti. The city is believed to have been founded in about A.D. 1400 around the Gorakhnath temple, when the stronghold of the Satasi Raja of the Srinet Rajputs was first established there. Akbar made Gorakhpur a strong Muslim garrison town and headquarters of one *sarkar* (division) of Oudh, and during Aurangzeb's rule the Jami Masjid adjoining the Urdu bazaar was built. British influence on the growth of the city began to be felt after the cession of the district to the East India company in 1801. The military function of the city did not cease and it continued to be the chief Gurkha recruiting centre.

The modern development of the town started with the introduction of the railway in 1885 and it is now the headquarters of the North-Eastern railway with a railway colony. In 1947 Gorakhpur became a regional centre of road transport. Gorakhpur university, which has a number of affiliated colleges located throughout the district, was founded in 1956. Industries include locomotive workshops, textile manufacture, particularly handloom cloth, engineering, papermaking and printing, and the manufacture of tobacco, chemicals, and dyes. About 45% of the population are employed in industry and commerce.

GORAKHPUR DISTRICT (area 2,439 sq.mi.; pop. [1961] 2,565,-

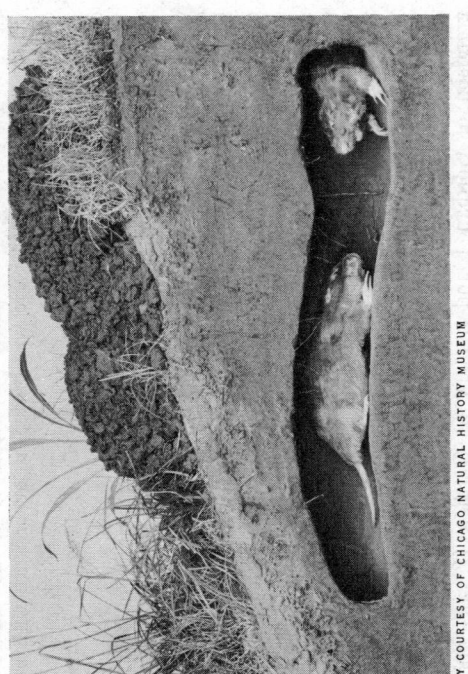

TYPICAL TUNNEL OF THE POCKET GOPHERS (GEOMYIDAE)

182) lies immediately south of the lower Himalayan slopes, in the northeastern corner of Uttar Pradesh. The monotony of the flat alluvial plain is broken by a few sand hills, representing former levees of the streams. The district is drained by the rivers Rapti, Ami and Gogra and is studded with lakes and marshes. Patches of reserved forests are found in the north. Because of the proximity of the Himalayas summer heat is reduced and the average annual rainfall exceeds 50 in. The high water table and fertile soils are conducive to agricultural prosperity but there are frequent and destructive floods. The chief crops are rice, barley, wheat and sugar cane. Several sugar mills have been established. Kasia, reputed scene of Buddha's death and cremation and a noted place of pilgrimage, is 34 mi. E. of Gorakhpur city.

GORAKHPUR DIVISION comprises the four districts of Gorakhpur, Deoria, Basti and Azamgarh and has an area of 9,612 sq.mi. The population (1961) was 9,975,370 with an average density of 1,038 per sq.mi.
(R. L. Sɪ.)

GORAL (*Naemorhedus goral*), a small Asiatic goatlike animal having slightly backward curving cylindrical horns and a coarse brownish-gray coat. It is a ruminant (cud chewer) related to the chamois (*q.v.*) and serow, but distinguished from them by peculiarities in skull form, by smaller size, shorter horns and the absence of face glands. Gorals range from the Himalayas to eastern Siberia. *See also* BOVIDAE.
(J. E. HL.; X.)

GORCHAKOV, a noble Russian family, descended from Mikhail Vsevolodovich, prince of Chernigov, who in 1246 was assassinated by the Mongols. PRINCE ANDREI IVANOVICH (1768–1855), general in the Russian army, took a conspicuous part in the final campaigns against Napoleon. ALEKSANDR IVANOVICH (1769–1825) served with distinction under his relative A. V. Suvorov in the Turkish wars and took part as a general officer in the Italian and Swiss operations of 1799 and in the war against Napoleon in Poland in 1806–07 (battle of Heilsberg). PETR DMITRIEVICH (1790–1868) served under M. F. Kamenski and M. I. Kutuzov in the campaign against Turkey, and afterward against France in 1813–14. In 1820 he suppressed an insurrection in the Caucasus, for which service he was raised to the rank of major general. In 1828–29 he fought under P. K. Wittgenstein against the Turks, won an action at Aidos and signed the treaty of peace at Adrianople. In 1839 he was made governor of Eastern Siberia, and in 1851 retired into private life. When the Crimean War broke out he offered his services to the emperor Nicholas, by whom he was appointed general of the VI army corps in the Crimea. He commanded the corps in the battles of Alma and Inkerman. He retired in 1855 and died at Moscow, on March 18, 1868.
See also GORCHAKOV, ALEKSANDR MIKHAILOVICH; GORCHAKOV, MIKHAIL DMITRIEVICH.

GORCHAKOV, ALEKSANDR MIKHAILOVICH, PRINCE (1798–1883), Russian statesman from an ancient Russian noble family, was born in St. Petersburg on July 15 (new style; 4, old style), 1798. He grew up in the European atmosphere of *salon* and court life in St. Petersburg. He began his diplomatic career in 1817, then gained valuable experience as member of Russian delegations at the congresses of Troppau, Laibach and Verona. From 1822 he served in embassies and legations in London, Rome, Berlin, Florence, Vienna, Stuttgart and again Vienna, where in 1854 he became ambassador. The slowness of his ascent of the diplomatic ladder was due largely to the hostility of the foreign minister, Count Nesselrode.

Gorchakov gained prominence from a special mission to Vienna during the Crimean War. Winning a reputation there as a stalwart defender of Russian interests and as an Austrophobe, he loomed as the natural successor to Nesselrode, discredited by the Crimean debacle. The emperor Alexander II appointed him foreign minister in April 1856. His able handling of diplomatic aspects of the Polish insurrection of 1863 and the elimination in Oct. 1870 of the galling Black sea clauses of the treaty of Paris brought him to the peak of his power and popularity. In 1866 he was made chancellor.

During the 1870s his prestige waned before the dynamism of Bismarckian Germany. Gorchakov in 1873 played an important part in the formation of the *Dreikaiserbund*, a loose, defensive alliance between Russia, Germany and Austria-Hungary. His cordial relations with Bismarck cooled, however, during the war scare of 1875 when he warned Germany against aggression toward France. During the Balkan crisis (1875–78); hampered by illness and age, his role in determining Russian policy diminished. Strongly opposed to the Panslav's agitation in Russia and to their cries for war with Turkey, he remained true to the *Dreikaiserbund* and to their cause of peace. When his diplomatic efforts failed to solve the crisis, he obtained Austrian neutrality by the Budapest convention of Jan. 1877 and counted on German support in case of trouble with Vienna. He persisted in his efforts to achieve a peaceful settlement in his efforts to achieve a peaceful settlement on the very eve of the Russo-Turkish War. (*See* EASTERN QUESTION.)

Gorchakov's waning influence was revealed clearly in 1878. Count N. P. Ignatiev disregarded Gorchakov's moderate instructions when he concluded the harsh treaty of San Stefano with prostrate Turkey. When the congress of Berlin (*q.v.*) was convened at the insistence of Great Britain and Austria-Hungary, Gorchakov was only the nominal head of the Russian delegation. Nevertheless, he shared the odium with Count P. A. Shuvalov for concessions made there to the western powers. He regarded the Berlin treaty as the darkest page in his official career. After serving as foreign minister for 26 years and as chancellor of the Russian empire for 16 years, he retired in 1882 and died in Baden-Baden on March 11 (N.S.; Feb. 27, O.S.), 1883.

Gorchakov is considered one of the greatest statesmen of tsarist Russia. Critics stress his vanity and jealousy, his unwillingness to train a successor or to retire to his easy chair. Some claim that most of his successes were planned by others. Gorchakov's diplomatic ability prior to 1878 is not seriously disputed, however. He stands as one of the important and able diplomats of 19th-century Europe.

See J. Klaczko, *Deux chanceliers: Le Prince Gortchakoff et le Prince de Bismarck* (1876).

GORCHAKOV, MIKHAIL DMITRIEVICH, PRINCE (1793–1861), Russian army officer, served in the campaigns in Persia in 1810 and in 1812–14 against France. During the Russo-Turkish War of 1828–29 he was present at the sieges of Silistra and Shumla. He was appointed a general officer in 1830, served in the campaign in Poland, was wounded at the battle of Grochow and distinguished himself at the taking of Warsaw. In 1846 he became chief of staff of the Russian army and adjutant general to the tsar. In 1853 Gorchakov led the forces which entered Moldavia. When Russia subsequently declared war against Turkey in 1854, he was appointed commander in chief of the troops that occupied Moldavia and Walachia and besieged Silistra. In 1855, at a critical time in the operations, he was appointed commander in chief of the Russian forces in the Crimea, replacing Prince Menshikov. Gorchakov's defense of Sevastopol, the northern part of which he continued to defend until peace was signed in Paris, was conducted with skill. In 1856 he was appointed governor general of Poland to succeed Prince Paskevich, which post he held until his death on May 30, 1861. He was buried, in accordance with his wish, at Sevastopol.
(D. MᴀᴄK.)

GORDIAN (GORDIANUS), the name of three successive Roman emperors in the 3rd century A.D.
(R. L. Gғ.)

GORDIAN I (Marcus Antonius Gordianus), emperor in March 238, an elderly senator of literary tastes to whom Philostratus (*q.v.*) dedicated his *Lives of the Sophists*, was proconsul of Africa early in 238, when a group of rebellious landowners resisted and killed the financial officers of the emperor Maximin. They proclaimed Gordian emperor, but three weeks later he killed himself after his son's death in battle (see *Gordian II*, below). In the meantime, however, the revolt he began ended with the defeat of Maximin (Gaius Julius Verus Maximinus, *q.v.*).

GORDIAN II (Marcus Antonius Gordianus), emperor 238, ruled for three weeks in Africa with his father Gordian I.

GORDIAN III (Marcus Antonius Gordianus), emperor 238–244, grandson of Gordian I and nephew of Gordian II, was born about 225. When his father and uncle were killed at the beginning of 238, the senate proclaimed Maximus and Balbinus (qq.v.) emperors; both the people and the guards in the city distrusted the senate's emperors, and insisted on making young Gordian *Caesar*, heir to the throne. After the defeat of Maximin, Balbinus and Maximus were killed by the guards in a riot and Gordian became sole emperor in August. The government was directed first by his mother and later by his father-in-law, the praetorian prefect Timesitheus, who enjoyed the confidence of the senate, and undertook a Persian campaign accompanied by Gordian in 242. In 243 Timesitheus was succeeded by the Arabian Philip, and in the spring of 244 young Gordian was murdered by his troops and succeeded by Philip. (JN. R. M.)

GORDIAN KNOT, a proverbial term for a problem solvable only by drastic action. In 333 B.C. Alexander the Great, on his march through Asia, was shown at Gordium in Phrygia the chariot of the ancient king, Gordias, with its yoke lashed to the pole by a knot of which the ends were hidden. It was to be untied only by the conqueror of Asia. In the popular account, probably invented as appropriate to an impetuous warrior, Alexander cut the knot through with his sword. But earlier versions make him find its ends, either by cutting into the knot or by drawing out the pole. (H. W. PA.)

GORDIUM (GORDION), capital of ancient Phrygia, the ruins of which lie at the junction of the Sangarius (Sakarya) and Tembris (Porsuk) rivers about 50 mi. W.S.W. of Ankara in the Ankara *il* of Turkey. On the Royal road between Ancyra (Ankara) and Dorylaeum (Eskisehir), the original settlement grew in importance because it lay at a river crossing on an important route from the plateau to the sea. According to the legend it took its name from Gordius, a Phrygian peasant called to the throne in obedience to an oracle of Zeus which commanded the elevation of the first person to ride up to the temple in a wagon. The king afterward dedicated his car to the god, and another oracle decreed that whoever succeeded in untying the knot of cornel bark made from the traces should conquer all Asia (*see* GORDIAN KNOT).

The Phrygian kingdom flourished under kings successively named Gordius and Midas, and reached its greatest power in the 8th century B.C. The king referred to in Assyrian records as Mita of Mushki was evidently a Midas contemporary with Sargon II of Assyria (722–705 B.C.). Early in the 7th century the Phrygian power was shattered by an incursion of the nomadic Cimmerians. Gordium was burned, Midas committed suicide, and the hegemony of Anatolia passed to the Lydians. Under the Persian empire Gordium was rebuilt as an important market and garrison town, and in 333 it was visited by Alexander the Great, following the Royal road in his campaign against Darius III. During this visit Alexander untied the knot (or cut it with his sword; accounts vary), and subsequently he went on to fulfill the oracle by his conquests. In the 3rd century B.C. Gordium fell to the Galatians, but it was abandoned in 189 B.C. at the approach of a Roman army under Manlius Vulso, and disappeared from history. In imperial times only a small village existed on the site.

Archaeology.—Excavation after 1950 has shown that the settlement goes back to the Early Bronze Age, perhaps the end of the 4th millennium B.C. A stratum belonging to Hittite times suggests that the route which was the reason for the city's importance was already in use. The Phrygian city of the 9th and 8th centuries, together with the tombs excavated in its cemeteries, has yielded much information about the material culture of the Phrygians, hitherto almost unknown. The city was fortified by high walls of masonry, pierced by a gateway planned and built in accordance with the best principles of military architecture of the time. Within lay a number of public buildings constructed of stone, wood and crude brick. These were mostly on the so-called Megaron plan with entrance through a vestibule to a large inner room, usually with a round hearth near its centre. The largest of these rooms measured about 60 by 50 ft., with galleries running along three of its sides. Another building contained a mosaic floor of natural pebbles laid in geometric designs of dark red, white and blue. The roofs, probably gabled, were of reeds covered by a layer of clay. All of these buildings had been burned in the Cimmerian raid and their rich contents—vessels of pottery and bronze, iron implements and wooden furniture carved in relief, inlaid with wood of contrasting colour or decorated with inset plaques of ivory carved in an individual Phrygian style—were fragmentary. Better-preserved specimens were found in the tombs. The wealthy Phrygians were buried in tomb chambers constructed of wood and covered by huge grave mounds (tumuli). The largest of these, originally about 200 ft. high, covered a burial that had been preserved intact, doubtless the tomb of a Phrygian king. The rich furnishings of the tomb included inlaid furniture and many bronze vessels, some of which showed Assyrian influence while others were of local manufacture. Four inscriptions indicate that the Phrygians were already familiar with alphabetical writing before the end of the 8th century.

BIBLIOGRAPHY.—Articles by R. S. Young in *Bulletin of the University Museum, Philadelphia*, "The Gordion Tomb," vol. i, no. 1 (1958), "Gordion: Phrygian Construction and Architecture," vol. ii, no. 2 (1960); in *American Journal of Archaeology*, articles in the form of reports for the years 1953, 1955–57 inclusive and 1959, vol. 59–62 and 64 (1955–58 and 1960); article by G. R. Edwards, "Gordion Campaign of 1958: Preliminary Report," in *American Journal of Archaeology*, vol. 63 (1959). (R. S. Yo.)

GORDON, the name of a Scottish family from Berwickshire with more than 157 main branches. A laird of Gordon fell in the battle of the Standard (1138). The families of the two sons ascribed to him, Richard Gordon of Gordon (d. 1171) and Adam Gordon of Huntly, were eventually united by marriage of their great-grandchildren Alicia and Sir Adam. A grandson of this marriage, Sir Adam (d. 1333), was justiciar of Scotland in 1310, and attached himself at the time of the battle of Bannockburn to Robert Bruce, who granted him (c. 1311–19) Strathbogie in Aberdeenshire, to which he gave the name of Huntly from the Berwickshire estate. Sir Adam had two sons; the younger son, William of Glen-kens in Galloway, was the ancestor of William I of Lochinvar, of which branch Sir John, 7th laird, was created (1633) viscount of Kenmure. Many Irish and Virginian Gordons are of this branch. The elder son, Adam, inherited the Gordon-Huntly estates. He had two grandsons, Sir John (d. 1394) and Sir Adam (d. 1402). Sir John had two illegitimate sons, Jock of Scurdargue, ancestor of Pitlurg and the earls of Aberdeen, and Tam o' Riven. From these most northern Gordon families derive. Sir Adam's daughter and heiress Elizabeth married Sir Alexander Seton, who with her was confirmed (1408) in the barony of Gordon-Huntly and in Strathbogie. Their son Alexander (d. 1470) was created earl of Huntly in 1445 (*see* HUNTLY, EARLS AND MARQUESSES OF). His son George (d. 1502), 2nd earl, took the name Gordon and perpetuated the chiefship. His heir male George (c. 1649–1716), 4th marquess, was created duke of Gordon in 1684.

Alexander (c. 1678–1728), 2nd duke, joined the 1715 Jacobite rising but was pardoned. Of his children Lord Lewis Gordon (d. 1754) was a celebrated Jacobite general, subject of the song "Oh Send Lewie Gordon Hame"; Cosmo George (c. 1720–52) succeeded as 3rd duke and is primarily remembered for the notoriety of his third son Lord George Gordon (q.v.; 1751–93). Alexander (1743–1827), 4th duke, was keeper of the Scottish great seal (1794–1827). The dukedom became extinct after George (1770–1836), 5th duke, who with his mother, "duchess Jean" (Maxwell), raised the 2nd Gordon Highlanders.

The marquesate of Huntly and chiefship of clan Gordon passed to the 5th duke's cousin and heir male, George (1761–1853), 5th earl of Aboyne. Lady Charlotte (1789–1842), sister and co-heiress of the 5th duke, married Charles, 4th duke of Richmond and Lennox, whose son took the name Gordon-Lennox. The dukedom of Gordon was (under protest) then revived in 1876 for Charles (1818–1903), 11th duke of Richmond and 6th duke of Gordon. Adam Gordon of Aboyne (d. 1537) became earl of Sutherland in right of his wife Elizabeth, countess of Sutherland, sister of the 9th earl. The turbulent Gordons of Gight, deriving from William (d. 1513), third son of the 2nd earl, were maternal ancestors of Lord Byron the poet.

Among many Gordon soldiers of fortune were Col. John, one of the murderers of Wallenstein, and Patrick of Auchleuchries (1635–99), who entered the service of Sweden (1651) and later supported Tsar Alexis of Russia. In 1688 he helped secure Peter the Great's ascendancy and crushed the Streltzi revolt. The Gordons fill a considerable place in Scottish ballads. "Baron o' Brackley," and "Edom (Adam) o' Gordon," describe incidents in the 16th-century feuds between Forbeses and Gordons; "Geordie" of the ballad "The Duke of Gordon's Daughter" is said to allude to the 4th earl of Huntly; "The Fire of Frendraught" to a feud (1630) between Crichton of Frendraught and Gordon of Rothiemay; the "Gallant Gordons Gay" figure in "Chevy Chase"; and Gordon of Earlston, a covenanter, in "Bothwell Bridge."

BIBLIOGRAPHY.—William Gordon, *History of the Ancient, Noble, and Illustrious House of Gordon,* 2 vol. (1726-27); Charles, 11th marquess of Huntly, *Records of Aboyne* (1894); *The House of Gordon,* ed. by J. M. Bulloch, 3 vol. (1903); and J. M. Bulloch, *The First Duke of Gordon* (1909). (T. I.)

GORDON, AARON DAVID (1856-1922), theoretician and spiritual mentor of the Zionist co-operative movement, was born at Troyanov in the Ukraine on June 9 or 10, 1856. He distinguished between two sources of knowledge: cognition and experience. Man's unique faculty for self-awareness elevates him above nature (experience) but simultaneously alienates him from the cosmos. Only by working the soil, the particular sphere which the cosmos has entrusted to man, can man once again participate in creation and reintegrate himself into the cosmos. Gordon's Zionism derived from this central idea. Jews, he believed, could overcome their alienation if they returned to the homeland from which they were exiled and worked its soil. He was particularly influenced by Nietzsche, Tolstoi, and Bergson. The personal example he set by migrating to Israel in 1904 and turning farmer inspired Israel's early pioneers. He helped found Deganiah, Israel's first collective community, where he died on Feb. 22, 1922. His Hebrew works fill five volumes, and his *Selected Essays* were published in English in 1938. (Ea. Sr.)

GORDON, ADAM LINDSAY (1833-1870), one of the first Australian poets to write in a distinctively Australian idiom, was born at Fayal in the Azores on Oct. 19, 1833, the son of a retired Indian officer who taught Hindustani at Cheltenham college. Gordon was educated in England at Cheltenham and Worcester Royal grammar school.

Gordon's youth was so wild and reckless that in 1853 his father sent him to South Australia, where he joined the mounted police. He then became a horsebreaker, but on his mother's death in 1861 inherited £7,000 and also obtained a seat in the house of assembly. He had the reputation of being the best nonprofessional steeplechase rider in the colony. In 1867 he moved to Victoria, set up a livery stable at Ballarat and published two volumes of poems, *Sea Spray and Smoke Drift* and *Ashtaroth.* In 1869 he settled at New Brighton near Melbourne, publishing a third volume of poetry, *Bush Ballads and Galloping Rhymes* (1870). It brought him more praise than money and, discouraged by his failure to make good his claim to property in Scotland and suffering from the effects of a bad fall from a horse, he committed suicide at New Brighton on June 24, 1870.

Gordon's poetry is chiefly English in inspiration but where it is local, it is vividly so. His nature lyrics contain his best poetry. His strong rhythms and simple homespun philosophy make his poetry memorable, and some of his lines have been adopted into the vocabulary of the average Australian.

BIBLIOGRAPHY.—Gordon's *Poems,* ed. by F. M. Robb, with biographical introduction (1912); *see also* J. Howlett Ross, *The Laureat of the Centaurs* (1888); E. Humphris and D. Sladen, *Adam Lindsay Gordon and His Friends in England and Australia* (1912); E. M. Humphris, *The Life of A. L. Gordon* (1933); E. Morris Miller, *Australian Literature From Its Beginnings to 1935* (1940). (C. M. H. C.)

GORDON, CHARLES GEORGE (1833-1885), British soldier, who first made his name as a commander of irregular troops in China and subsequently as governor general of the Sudan for the khedive of Egypt, became world-famous during his lifetime for his brilliant, singlehanded defense of Khartoum against the forces of the Mahdi. He was a deeply religious, if unorthodox, Christian and one of the last of the long line of English eccentrics. He was born on Jan. 28, 1833, at Woolwich, where his father, Gen. H. W. Gordon, royal artillery, was inspector of the carriage department. There he spent a lively childhood, the fourth son in a large and uproarious family. In 1848 he became an officer-cadet at Woolwich, where he was constantly involved in what he himself described as "fearful rows." He passed out as second lieutenant in the royal engineers in June 1852 and was posted in 1854 to Pembroke Dock, where he experienced his first conversion, under the influence of "a very religious captain of the 11th." Meanwhile the Crimean War had commenced and Gordon managed to get himself ordered on active service. He reached Balaklava on New Year's day, 1855, and in the trenches before Sevastopol speedily proved himself an exceptionally enterprising, intelligent and courageous subaltern. He spent nearly two and a half years, after the conclusion of the peace of Paris, with the international commission engaged in surveying the new frontiers between Russia and Turkey.

Service in China.—Gordon returned to England toward the end of 1858, was gazetted captain on April 1, 1859, and volunteered a few weeks later for active service in the desultory war with China which had just commenced. He was present at the occupation of Peking and the destruction and looting of the summer palace. In the spring of 1862 he contracted smallpox and wrote to his sister, "I am glad to say that this disease has brought me back to my Saviour." The British troops, under Gen. Charles Staveley, were sent in April 1863 to protect the European settlement in Shanghai from the T'ai Ping rebels, who had overrun the rich central provinces, capturing Nanking and scores of lesser cities, and were now threatening the European trading centre of Shanghai (*see* T'AI P'ING REBELLION). The leading citizens there had recently commissioned an American adventurer, F. T. Ward, to raise a defense force of 3,000-4,000 men—a mixture of ignorant peasants and the riffraff of Shanghai, officered by European adventurers and desperadoes and optimistically entitled "the Ever-Victorious army." Ward was killed in Sept. 1862. His successor, another American, was soon dismissed, and Gordon, now a brevet major, was appointed to the command in the spring of 1863.

In operations lasting about 18 months Gordon proved himself one of the greatest commanders of irregulars of all time. Not only did he turn his little army of ragamuffins into a disciplined and formidable fighting force but time and again he crushed an enemy vastly superior in numbers, who found that because of Gordon's use of armed steamboats and his rapid movements, the devious waterways, on which they had hitherto relied as an impregnable defense, actually ensured their defeat. His ascendancy over his own "rabble" was complete. Twice he quelled incipient mutinies singlehanded by sheer will power and personality. When his men hesitated to leave cover he would drag them into the open by the pigtail. And he himself would invariably be found at the point of greatest danger, unarmed save for a light cane, which became known to the superstitious soldiery as "Gordon's wand of victory." When the rebels had been crushed Gordon refused the munificent gifts of money offered him by the emperor, and since he had spent his pay, and more, on comforts for his troops, "left China as poor as I entered it."

Returning to England in Jan. 1865, Gordon stubbornly refused the invitations from ministers and generals which were showered on him and even tore up his Chinese diary lest it should one day contribute to the legend which threatened to take shape. He was however to be henceforth widely spoken of as "Chinese" Gordon. He was promoted brevet lieutenant colonel and made a companion of the Bath, the traditional reward of the government's less distinguished civil servants. By September he had been appointed royal engineer officer in command at Gravesend. There he devoted most of his spare time to philanthropic activities among the poor and particularly among the street urchins of Gravesend, many of whom he fed, clothed, taught and eventually placed in employment, often keeping in touch with them for the rest of their lives. He spent much time also on evangelism, printing and distributing tracts, which he would leave by the wayside on a country walk or even throw from a train to men working on the line. During these years, and indeed for the rest of his life, he studied the Bible daily, and from it deduced, unaided, the somewhat unorthodox creed on which henceforth he sought to found his every action. He never joined church or sect and was content to live by his own interpretation of the Bible, the whole of which he believed to be verbally inspired.

Governor of Equatoria.—Gordon left Gravesend in Sept. 1871, having been appointed by Gladstone's government to the vacant English membership of the Danubian commission with headquarters at Galatz (Galati, Rum.). Thanks to a chance meeting in Constantinople with Nubar Pasha, prime minister of Egypt, in 1873 he was offered the post of governor of Equatoria, which he accepted after much hesitation, insisting that the salary of his predecessor, Sir Samuel Baker, should be reduced for him from £10,000 to £2,000. Gordon's province stretched southward down the Nile from the Egyptian Sudan, with no fixed boundaries to the still uncharted south. In the Sudan the Egyptian administration was contemptible, in Equatoria it did not exist. The khedive's mudirs encouraged and profited by the slave trade, which it was Gordon's chief business to suppress and which flourished throughout Darfur and the Bahr el Ghazal. Gordon arrived in Cairo on Feb. 6, 1874, and frightened the normally procrastinating pashas into transacting business with such unusual rapidity that a fortnight later he set out, ahead of his staff, for Gondokoro, where he arrived after a journey of 25 days, during which he covered the 250 mi. from Sawakin to Berber on a camel at record speed. His prodigies of endurance on camelback soon became a legend in the desert. Gordon's two and a half years in Equatoria was a period of intense strain and incessant toil. Most of his staff died or were incapacitated by disease; that Gordon himself remained healthy and vigorous was probably due to his own confidence that he could not succumb rather than to the unconventional nostrums that he compounded from his own medicine chest. He succeeded in establishing a line of stations stretching to the frontier of Uganda, mapped the Nile and the great lakes and did much to suppress the slave trade, despite constant obstruction from the Egyptian governor of the Sudan, who had little desire to see the trade disappear.

Governor General of the Sudan.—Gordon returned to England on Christmas Eve, 1876, but after much hesitation, and at length after the toss of a coin, agreed to resume service with the khedive early in 1877, after stipulating that he should be appointed governor general of the Sudan, with the Equatorial provinces. He thus acquired sole responsibility for more than 1,000,000 sq.mi. inhabited by savage and hostile peoples among whom poverty, tribal warfare and the slave trade were endemic. "I go up alone," he wrote home, "with an infinite Almighty God to direct and guide me."

Gordon went first to the borders of Ethiopia, where he interviewed and temporarily pacified Walad-el-Michael, the rebellious lieutenant of King John; and thence to Khartoum, his capital, where he was ceremonially installed and during a stay of only 15 days decreed a series of sweeping administrative reforms. On May 19 he set out with 300 men for the province of Darfur, where 16,000 Egyptian troops were hemmed in by a large force of insurgents. He moved, as usual, at top speed and far in advance of his own little contingent. Characteristically, on reaching the neighbourhood of the rebels' army, he rode into their camp alone, save for an interpreter and a small escort, and so overawed the 3,000 warriors paraded there that half of them came over to join him and the rest retreated. After visiting the provinces of Berber and Dongola, he journeyed with an escort of only ten men through the mountains of the Ethiopian border for another interview with Walad-el-Michael, whom he succeeded in persuading to come to terms. In 1879 he once more pursued the slave traders in Darfur, and with the aid of his gallant subordinate, the Italian Romolo Gessi, the revolt was finally crushed. After an arduous and perilous journey to confer with King John he returned to Cairo in Jan. 1880, resigned his appointment and, after extracting an apology from Nubar Pasha for some disparaging remarks on a companion of the Bath by challenging him to a duel, returned to England.

China, South Africa and the Holy Land.—In May 1880 Gordon unaccountably accepted the post of private secretary to the viceroy designate of India, the marquess of Ripon, but resigned it soon after the viceregal party reached India. Two days after his resignation was announced, he accepted an invitation from Sir Robert Hart, inspector general of customs in Peking, to go to China. There he succeeded in dissuading, first, his old friend Li Hung Chang from rebelling against the central government and, subsequently, the central government from embarking on war with Russia. His interview with the grand council was characteristically unconventional and when the interpreter refused to translate his undiplomatic language Gordon snatched up a dictionary, placed his finger on the Chinese word for "idiocy" and thrust it under the startled eyes of each minister in succession. He was back in England in October. In December, when staying with the rector of Twywell in Northamptonshire, he experienced what may be called the final stage of his conversion, which led him for the first time to become a regular communicant. Thereafter his character became more gentle and the outbursts of fierce irritation began to disappear. He was in command of the royal engineers in Mauritius (April 1881–April 1882) and then accepted an invitation from the government of Cape colony, where he reorganized the colonial forces. He visited a rebellious Basuto chief and would have lost his life when a rival chieftain attacked his host's camp had it not been, once again, for what S. F. Oliver called the "mesmeric influence, quite inexplicable in scientific terms," which he exercised over primitive peoples. His memorandum on the Basuto became the basis of the eventual reconstruction of Basutoland as a protectorate.

Gordon returned to England in Nov. 1882; though pressed by King Leopold II of Belgium to assume command in the Belgian Congo, he felt called to a contemplative life rather than to further action and left England for the Holy Land on Dec. 28. He spent nearly a year studying the Bible and the topography of Palestine. On Jan. 1, 1884, he was in Brussels and had decided to resign his commission and accept King Leopold's invitation.

Final Mission to Khartoum.—Meanwhile, however, a disastrous situation had developed in the Sudan. An obscure fakir, having announced himself as the Mahdi, "the expected one," had declared a holy war and overrun the province of Kordofan. Gladstone's government, having reluctantly found itself compelled to crush Arabi Pasha's rebellion in Egypt, had become the solitary European power behind the khedive's throne. When the khedive's army, under Col. William Hicks, had been destroyed by the Mahdi's dervishes the British government was gradually forced, largely by public opinion, first to abandon its illusion that the Egyptian Sudan was no concern of Britain's and then to invite Gordon to step into the breach. Unfortunately, from the outset ministers were never wholly clear whether Gordon was being sent merely to report on the military situation or to undertake single-handed the immensely dangerous task of withdrawing the Egyptian garrisons from the Sudan. In Cairo, however, with the approval of Sir Evelyn Baring, the British agent, Gordon was appointed governor general by the khedive and instructed to evacuate the Sudan and establish an organized government there. The British government approved in due course, but, though they had explicitly instructed Gordon to "perform such other duties as may be communicated to you by Sir Evelyn Baring," ministers, and particularly Gladstone, were never afterward able wholly to rid themselves of the notion that a purely advisory mission had been dangerously and improperly expanded into executive action.

Gordon reached Khartoum on Feb. 18, 1884, and had succeeded in evacuating 2,000 women, children and sick and wounded before the Mahdi's forces closed in on the town. From that time the British government's refusal of all the urgent requests of the man whom it had dispatched singlehanded on the forlornest of forlorn hopes and its prolonged procrastination made disaster inevitable. As soon as he reached Khartoum Gordon asked that Zebehr, a former slave trader but possessing great influence as a descendant of the Abbasids, should be sent up to Khartoum. After long delay the government, wary of public opinion, finally declined on March 11 to sanction the appointment. It similarly refused Gordon's request that a small force should open the road from Sawakin to Berber, though this was supported by Baring and the military authorities in Cairo. The siege of Khartoum commenced on March 13 but it was not until August that, under the increasing pressure of public opinion, supported in private by the angry expostulations of the queen, the government agreed that some steps, still undefined, to relieve Gordon should be taken, and not until November that a relief force under Lord Wolseley set out from Wadi Halfa. It was doomed to failure, if only because the government which had authorized it six months too late never wholeheartedly desired or believed in it. The resistance of Khartoum until Jan. 26, 1885, is one of the remarkable achievements in military history, and was solely due to the skill, energy and indomitable spirit with which Gordon, without staff or confidants, inspired and dominated the feeble Egyptian garrison. After learning of two victories won by Lord Wolseley the Mahdi's troops had even been on the verge of raising the siege, but the further unaccountable delay of the relief force encouraged them to make a final assault at a gap in the ramparts caused by the falling of the Nile. The garrison was butchered, and Gordon with them. The relief force reached Khartoum three days too late.

Gordon was five feet nine inches tall, and slight and wiry. Every recorded description of him dwells upon his clear, blue eyes and their magical influence. The legend that he was a secret drinker, popularized by Lytton Strachey in his *Eminent Victorians*, was based upon the evidence, occasionally misquoted, of a discredited witness.

See Lord Elton, *General Gordon* (1954); B. M. Allen, *Gordon and the Sudan* (1931).
(Go. E.)

GORDON, CHARLES WILLIAM: *see* CONNOR, RALPH.

GORDON, LORD GEORGE (1751–1793), English demagogue, the instigator of the Gordon riots in 1780, was the third and youngest son of Cosmo George, duke of Gordon, and was born in London on Dec. 26, 1751. He was educated at Eton and entered the navy, rising to the rank of lieutenant in 1772; however, would not promise him a command, and he resigned his commission shortly before the beginning of the American Revolutionary War. The pocket borough of Ludgershall was bought for him in 1774 by Gen. Simon Fraser, whom he was opposing in Inverness-shire, in order to bribe him not to contest the county. He was considered flighty and of little importance.

In 1779 Gordon organized and made himself head of the Protestant associations formed to secure the repeal of the Catholic Relief act of 1778. He headed the mob which marched in procession from St. George's fields to the houses of parliament on June 2, 1780, in order to present the monster petition against the acts. A terrific riot ensued which continued several days, during which the city was virtually at the mercy of the mob. At first, indeed, they dispersed, after threatening to make a forcible entry into the house of commons. But they reassembled soon afterward and destroyed several Roman Catholic chapels, pillaged the homes of many Roman Catholics, set fire to Newgate prison and broke open all the others, attacked the Bank of England and several other public buildings, and continued the work of violence and conflagration until the interference of the military, by whom no fewer than 450 persons were killed and wounded before the riots were quelled.

For his share in instigating the riots Lord George was arrested on a charge of high treason; mainly through the skilful and eloquent defense of Thomas (afterward Lord) Erskine, he was acquitted on the ground that he had no treasonable intentions. His life was henceforth full of crackbrained schemes, political and financial. He was excommunicated by the archbishop of Canterbury in 1786 for refusing to bear witness in an ecclesiastical suit, and he was convicted in 1787 of libeling the queen of France, the French ambassador and the administration of justice in England. He was, however, permitted to withdraw from the court without bail and made his escape to the Netherlands; because of representations from the court of Versailles, however, he was commanded to quit that country and, returning to England, was arrested and sentenced in Jan. 1788 to five years' imprisonment in Newgate, where he lived at his ease, giving dinners and dances. As he could not obtain securities for his good behaviour on the termination of his term of imprisonment, he was not allowed to leave Newgate, and there he died on Nov. 1, 1793. He had become a convert to Judaism in 1786 and had undergone the initiatory rite.

GORDON, JOHN BROWN (1832–1904), Confederate army officer and political leader in Georgia during the Reconstruction, was a popular hero in the state. Born Feb. 6, 1832, in Upson county, Georgia, he attended the University of Georgia and later practised law in Atlanta. At the outbreak of the Civil War he joined the Confederate army as captain of volunteers and passed successfully through the grades to major general. He participated in several major battles and during the course of the war was wounded eight times.

At Appomattox he commanded one wing of Gen. Robert E. Lee's army with the instructions to cut through Gen. U. S. Grant's line. Gordon made the last charge and was taking the federal breastworks when news of his chief's surrender ended his action. Following the war he settled in Atlanta and was a member of the Democratic national conventions of 1868 and 1872. He served in the U.S. senate from 1873 to 1880, when he resigned, and again from 1891 to 1897. Gordon was also governor of Georgia (1886–90), and from 1890 commander in chief of the United Confederate Veterans. He wrote *Reminiscences of the Civil War* (1903).

Gordon died in Miami, Fla., Jan. 9, 1904.

GORDON, SIR JOHN WATSON (c. 1788–1864), Scottish portrait painter, who after Sir Henry Raeburn's death in 1823 succeeded to his practice, was born in Edinburgh, where he trained for four years under John Graham at the Trustees' academy. He began to paint historical subjects but turned to portraiture. He lacked Raeburn's brilliant colour and dramatic modeling, preferring in his later work clear gray tonalities.

Gordon exhibited at the Royal Academy from 1817 on; he became an academician in 1851. A member of the Royal Scottish Academy in 1829, he succeeded to its presidency in 1850 and was knighted. His sitters included Sir Walter Scott (1820), Sir Alexander Hope (1835, Linlithgow) and Thomas De Quincey (1845, National Portrait gallery, London).

He died in Edinburgh on June 1, 1864.
(D. L. Fr.)

GORDON, LEON (JUDAH LOEB BEN ASHER) (1830–1892), Hebrew poet and novelist, the leading poet of enlightenment (*Haskalah*), was born at Vilnius, Lithuania, on Dec. 7, 1830, and died at St. Petersburg on Sept. 16, 1892. Gordon's early historical poems and fables were later followed by powerful satires in verse aimed against the harsher aspects of rabbinic Judaism. His last poems reflect bitter disillusionment with the ideals of *Haskalah*. Although of limited poetic talent, Gordon's advocacy of social and religious reforms proved widely influential, and his skilful use of post-Biblical idiom increased the flexibility of modern Hebrew. His poems were collected in *Kol Kithbe Yehuda* (1883–84); his stories in *Kol Shire Yehuda* (1889).
(D. Pa.)

GORDON, PATRICK (1635–1699), Scottish soldier of fortune who became a Russian general, was born at Auchleuchries, Aberdeenshire, on March 31, 1635. In 1651, having arrived in Danzig to try his luck in Poland, he was helped by a fellow countryman to enter the Jesuit college at Braniewo (Braunsberg) but absconded in 1653. Between 1655 and 1660 he fought in the Polish-Swedish war, frequently changing sides. In 1661 he took service in the Russian army as a major and in 1662 was promoted colonel for crushing the Moscow riots against the debased copper coinage. In 1666 he visited England as envoy of the tsar but the result of his mission was not considered satisfactory and his career suffered a setback. As the Russian rulers' distrust of the west diminished, Gordon's position improved, especially as he had used the intervening years to acquire an expert knowledge of ballistics and fortification. His repeated attempts to prove unsuccessful. In 1678 his defense of Chigirin (Ukraine) against the Turks established his professional reputation. In 1686–87 he revisited England and returned to Russia as James II's envoy extraordinary. In the unsuccessful Crimean expeditions of 1687 and 1689 he was quartermaster general and gave strategic advice to the commander in chief, Prince V. V. Golitsyn. During the crisis of 1689 the support lent to Peter I by Gordon and his troops against Sophia Alekseevna proved decisive. Gordon, a full general since 1687 and rear admiral from

1694, became the young tsar's chief military counselor. In 1698 during Peter's absence he stifled an attempt by the rebellious *streltsy* to put Sophia back in power. It was Gordon who obtained Peter I's permission for the erection of a Roman Catholic church in Moscow. He died in Moscow on Dec. 9 (new style; Nov. 29, old style), 1699.

Gordon left a diary of his life in English which was translated into German and published in Russia by M. A. Obolenski and M. C. Posselt (*Tagebuch des Generals . . .* , 3 vol., 1849–53). *Passages From the Diary of General Patrick Gordon*, edited by J. Robertson, appeared in English in 1859.   (L. R. LR.)

GORE, CHARLES (1853–1932), English theologian, bishop and monastic founder, was a dominant figure in the Church of England for almost half a century. As the leading exponent of "liberal catholicism," which united traditional high churchmanship with biblical criticism and social radicalism, he not only contributed largely to the development of modern Anglicanism but also played an active part in English public life. Born at Wimbledon on Jan. 22, 1853, of distinguished Anglo-Irish ancestry, he was educated at Harrow and at Balliol college, Oxford. Elected fellow of Trinity college, Oxford, in 1875, he was ordained deacon in 1876 and priest in 1878. His influence on the church at large began with his work as vice-principal of the theological college at Cuddesdon (1880–83) and as first principal of Pusey house, Oxford (1884–93). After a short rural incumbency at Radley (1893–94), he spent seven years in a strenuous and effective ministry as canon of Westminster. From its foundation in 1892 until 1901, Gore was also senior (superior) of the Community of the Resurrection. Consecrated bishop of Worcester in 1902, he was translated to the new see of Birmingham in 1905 and to Oxford in 1911. In 1919 he resigned his see and settled in London, where he preached and wrote extensively, lectured at King's college and served London university as dean of the theological faculty (1924–28). He died in London on Jan. 17, 1932.

Throughout his life Gore consistently upheld the Anglo-Catholic view of the church. His first important writings, *The Ministry of the Christian Church* (1888; 4th ed., *The Church and the Ministry*, 1899), an apologia for episcopacy and apostolic succession, and *Roman Catholic Claims* (1888), were designed to vindicate the Catholic claims of the Church of England, and in later years Gore approached reunion conversations, alike with nonepiscopal churches and with Roman Catholics, from the same standpoint. He did not think, however, that the Tractarian message could simply be repeated without reformulation. Whereas the Oxford movement (*q.v.*) had confronted aggressive secularism with a blunt affirmation of the church's supernatural life and apostolic authority, Gore and his school believed that the time had come to correlate Christian theology with scientific and historical knowledge and to translate it into social action. This conviction found expression in *Lux Mundi: a Series of Studies in the Religion of the Incarnation* (1889), which Gore edited.

To conservative churchmen this manifesto seemed more a betrayal than a restatement of the Tractarian protest against "liberalism." Gore in particular gave offense, both in this and in his Bampton lectures on *The Incarnation of the Son of God* (1891), by his "kenotic" interpretation of Christ's human knowledge. His position was in fact somewhat ambiguous. On the one hand, a deep conservatism appeared in his unwavering adherence to the historic creeds and his insistence on their use as a test of clerical orthodoxy; biblical criticism might be welcomed, because biblical inerrancy was not an authoritative dogma, but credal statements, including assertions about miracles, demanded unqualified assent. Gore's philosophy, on the other hand, was open to attack from the side of traditional orthodoxy, since the idealistic assumptions underlying his treatment of divine immanence in nature and history were not so easily reconciled with classical Christian views of the supernatural as he supposed them to be. It is not surprising, therefore, that neither traditionalists nor liberals found his attempted synthesis of Christian faith and critical reason wholly satisfactory. Nevertheless, his place in the history of Christian thought is assured by his widespread influence as the champion of a reasoning faith.

for social reform. As *Christ and Society* (1928) indicates, his interest in industrial relations, housing, popular education, international peace and other social issues stemmed from his fundamental theological conviction of the unity of grace and nature in the divine purpose. From this premise he concluded that his pastoral office demanded the broadest concern for human welfare, as well as watchful care for the good order of the church.

The Reconstruction of Belief, three volumes (1921–24), contains the fullest statement of Gore's teaching. In addition to works already mentioned, *The Body of Christ* (1901) and *The Philosophy of the Good Life* (1930) are especially noteworthy.

The standard biography is G. L. Prestige, *The Life of Charles Gore* (1935); J. Carpenter's *Gore: a Study in Liberal Catholic Thought* (1960) is a reliable account of Gore's position.   (E. R. F.)

GORÉE, an island just south of Cape Verde, Republic of Senegal, and one of the earliest European settlements in west Africa, is a barren volcanic rock 3,117 ft. long and 1,115 ft. broad commanding the entrance to the roadstead of Dakar. Pop. (1958) 900. Area 88 ac. The fort of Saint Michel occupies the rocky eminence in the south; the low-lying part is mostly a town of narrow streets. There is a shortage of water and since the rise of Dakar the island, which has a healthier climate than the mainland, has had little importance except as a resort. Among the 18th-century buildings are the Maison des Esclaves and the historical museum.

Gorée was first occupied by the Portuguese, the navigator Diniz Diaz landing there in 1444. From 1595–1677 it was a port of call for the Dutch, who in 1617 bought it from the local chief and fortified it. They called it Goeree, after the island near the mouth of the Rhine, Neth. In 1663 it was captured by the British under Commodore Robert Holmes, but in the following year was retaken by Adm. M. A. de Ruyter, who established a trading post. In 1677 Adm. Comte Jean d'Estrées seized Gorée and razed the forts. Thereafter the French rebuilt the forts (Saint Michel and Saint François) and town, which became one of the chief centres of the slave trade. In their wars with France the British held Gorée during the periods 1758–63, 1779–83 and 1800–16. In 1779 it was ravaged by yellow fever, and from 1784 the governors preferred to live at Saint-Louis. The abolition of slavery in the French colonies (1791) put an end to the chief trade of the island. In 1859 it ceased to be a separate colony and was joined to Senegal, becoming a commune of Dakar in 1929.   (J. D.)

GORETTI, SAINT MARIA TERESA (1890–1902), a devout Italian girl who was murdered while resisting attempted rape. She was born at Corinaldo on Oct. 16, 1890, the eldest child of farm workers. Her father died shortly after the family had moved to Nettuno in 1900. While her mother worked in the fields, Maria looked after the house and younger children. On July 5, 1902, a youth of 20, Alessandro Serenelli, who lived in the same house, mortally wounded her with a stiletto when she resisted his attempt to ravish her. She died, after forgiving him, on July 6, which is kept as her feast day. She was canonized in 1950. After his release from prison, Serenelli received forgiveness from Maria's mother in 1947.

See J. Carr, *Blessed Maria Goretti* (1949); A. Gits, *A Modern Virgin Martyr* (1956).   (H. R. WN.)

GORGAN (GURGAN), formerly Asterabad, a town of the Mazanderan *ostan* (province), Iran, lies on a small tributary of the Qareh Su, 23 mi. from the Caspian sea and 185 mi. E.S.E. of Teheran, at the foot of a steep wooded spur of the Elburz mountains. The population (1964 est. 36,707) has greatly increased since 1900. Most of the houses are built of baked bricks, with tilted and tiled roofs because of the frequent rains. Occupying a commercially and strategically important position, the town dates back to remote antiquity. Its surroundings are dotted with mounds or *tappeh*, the remains of Neolithic and Bronze Age settlements. During the disorders in Persia in the 18th century, Asterabad was frequently ravaged but was reinforced by the Kajar dynasty. It was renamed Gorgan in the 1930s. The chief articles of trade are cotton, rice, wheat, salt, sesame oil, soap and carpets; trade was favourably affected by the trans-Iranian railway which ends at the nearby port of Bandar-e Shah.

The former province of Gorgan-Asterabad had long suffered from the inroads of the Turkoman tribes who occupied the plain north of the Qareh Su. In modern times this plain was settled by the tribesmen and turned into a flourishing granary. (H. Bo.)

GORGAS, WILLIAM CRAWFORD (1854–1920), U.S. army surgeon, who contributed greatly to the building of the Panama canal by introducing mosquito control to prevent yellow fever and malaria, was born at Mobile, Ala., on Oct. 3, 1854. He was educated at the University of the South, Sewanee, Tenn., and Bellevue hospital medical college, New York city, receiving his M.D. in 1879. In 1880 he entered the medical corps of the U.S. army. During the Spanish-American War he served as a major in the medical corps and was sent, after the Santiago expedition, to Havana, Cuba, where he was in charge of yellow fever patients. From 1898 to 1902 he was in charge of sanitation measures in Havana, and conducted many experiments on the transmission of yellow fever by the mosquito. Because of his success in eliminating yellow fever there he was made assistant surgeon general, U.S. army, with the rank of colonel in 1903.

In 1904 Gorgas was sent as chief sanitary officer to Panama, where two of the main obstacles to building the canal were yellow fever and malaria (*qq.v.*). In two years he eliminated yellow fever from the canal region. In 1907 he was appointed a member of the Isthmian Canal commission by Pres. Theodore Roosevelt and in 1908 was U.S. delegate to the first Pan-American medical congress. He was president of the American Medical association, 1908–09.

In 1914 Gorgas was made surgeon general, U.S. army, with the rank of brigadier general, becoming major general in 1915. In 1918 he was retired. He then became the permanent director of the yellow-fever work of the International Health board of the Rockefeller foundation. He went to Central America, and under his direction investigations of yellow fever were made in Guayaquil, Ecuador, and in Guatemala. In 1919 he accepted a contract mission by Peru to carry out a sanitary program in that country. He died in London, July 3, 1920, and was buried in the Arlington National cemetery, Arlington, Va.

In his honour were established the Gorgas Memorial Institute of Tropical and Preventive Medicine, Inc., Washington, D.C., and the Gorgas Memorial Laboratory of Tropical Research, Panama.

GORGES, SIR FERDINANDO (*c.* 1566–1647), military adventurer and founder of the colony of Maine, was born in Somerset, Eng., probably in 1566. Little is known of Gorges' early life except that he received a modest inheritance and acquired a good education. In 1589 he was in command of a small body of troops fighting for Henry IV of France and was knighted in 1591. He had a colourful military career during early manhood but his most memorable work was his persistent promotion of New England colonization.

From 1605 until his death, Gorges spent much energy and money attempting to organize and obtain royal sanction for schemes of settlement, although he never went to North America in person. In 1605 he was a member of the Plymouth (North Virginia) company and in 1620 he developed the Council for New England. To it was granted all land in North America between the 40th and 48th parallels of north latitude. Gorges' views that colonizing should be a royal endeavour and that colonies should be kept under rigid control was a constant threat to the Puritans of the Massachusetts Bay colony, who favoured greater freedom for themselves.

Gorges was the recipient of several grants of land during his lifetime but receipt of the charter for Maine in 1639 was the climax of his career. Although his agents set up a provincial government in Maine, the English Civil War and Gorges' advancing age prevented him from fulfilling his American plans. After his death Maine was absorbed by the colony of Massachusetts Bay. Gorges wrote two pamphlets, one called *Brief Relation . . .*, advertising the Council for New England and the other, *Brief Narration . . .*, publicizing his province of Maine.

See Richard Arthur Preston, *Gorges of Plymouth Fort* (1953); Henry Morrill Fuller, *Sir Ferdinando Gorges (1566–1647)* (1952). (B. K. B.)

GÖRGEY (GÖRGEI), **ARTHUR** (1818–1916), Hungarian army officer famous for his role during the revolution of 1848–49, was born at Toporcz (now in Czechoslovakia) on Jan. 30, 1818. As a young man he served in the Austrian army, but left it to study chemistry in Prague. When Hungary raised a national army in 1848 (*see* HUNGARY: *History*), he joined it and soon proved his worth. He commanded a corps in the attempt to relieve Vienna (Oct. 30, 1848) and on Nov. 1 was given command of the Hungarian forces on the upper Danube. When the Austrian armies invaded Hungary in December, Görgey, knowing his troops to be still raw, insisted on withdrawing and refused to defend Budapest. The consequent tension between him and Lajos Kossuth (*q.v.*) was heightened by his issuing, on Jan. 5, 1849, an order to his troops which read like a defiance of the authority of the committee of national defense; but his brilliant spring offensive drove the Austrians almost out of Hungary. After the declaration of independence on April 14 he agreed to couple his command with the post of minister of defense. It was no secret, however, that he disapproved of the dethronement of the Habsburgs; and the "peace party" hoped to persuade him to move his armies to the western frontier, proclaim himself military dictator and reach a settlement with Austria before the threatened Russian intervention could materialize. This he refused to do and continued to conduct operations with extraordinary skill and courage against increasing odds. On Aug. 11, when Hungary's situation had become clearly hopeless, Kossuth abdicated as "governor" in favour of Görgey, who capitulated to the Russian commander at Világos on Aug. 13, 1849.

The Russian emperor intervened personally to save Görgey from court-martial and death. He was interned in Klagenfurt until 1867, when he was allowed to return to Hungary. Thereafter he lived quietly at Visegrád until his death in Budapest on May 20, 1916. The ungenerous accusation of treason long maintained against Görgey by Kossuth and his supporters was utterly discredited by documents published in 1918. He indeed thought much of what the Hungarian extremists did to be both foolish and wrong, but sacrificed his feelings to what he regarded as the higher interest. He published a defense of his own work, *Mein Leben und Wirken in Ungarn, 1848–1849* (1852), and an anonymous paper entitled *Was verdanken wir der Revolution?* (1875).

See D. Kosáry, *A Görgey-kérdés és Története* (1936). (C. A. M.)

GORGIAS (*c.* 483–376 B.C.), Greek sophist and rhetorician who made important contributions to rhetorical theory and practice, was a native of Leontini in Sicily. In 427 he headed an embassy to ask for Athenian help against the Syracusans. He later came to reside permanently in Greece, where he became a professional teacher of rhetoric. He died at Larissa in Thessaly. Two surviving rhetorical exercises, the *Helen* and the *Palamedes*, are probably genuine, and there are fragments of speeches. In a lost work, *On Nature or on That Which Is Not*, which is summarized by Sextus Empiricus and in the pseudo-Aristotelian treatise *De Melisso, Xenophane, Gorgia*, he argued that there is no being; or that if there is being, it cannot be known; or that if there is being and it can be known, it cannot be communicated to others. He is a central figure in Plato's *Gorgias*, but Plato treats him as a rhetorician rather than as a philosopher. *See* also SOPHISTS.

BIBLIOGRAPHY.—For fragments and testimonia *see* H. Diels and W. Kranz, *Fragmente der Vorsokratiker*, vol. ii, 7th ed. (1954). For his philosophy *see* M. Untersteiner, *The Sophists*, Eng. trans., vol. i, ch. iv–ix (1954) (speculative). For Gorgias as a rhetorician *see* F. Blass, *Die attische Beredsamkeit*, vol. i (1887). (G. B. Kd.)

GORGON, a figure in Greek mythology. Homer speaks of a single Gorgon, whose head is represented in the *Iliad* as fixed in the centre of the aegis (breastplate) of Zeus. In the *Odyssey* the Gorgon is a monster of the underworld. Hesiod increases the number of Gorgons to three—Stheno (the mighty), Euryale (the far-springer) and Medusa (the queen)—and makes them the daughters of the sea-god Phorcys and of his sister-wife Ceto. Their home is in the extreme west; according to later authorities, in Libya. The Attic tradition, reproduced in Euripides, regarded the Gorgon as a monster produced by Gaea, the goddess Earth, to aid her sons against the gods, and slain by Athena.

The Gorgons are represented as winged female creatures; their hair consists of snakes; they are round-faced, flat-nosed, with large tongues lolling out and with large projecting teeth. Medusa was the only one of the three who was mortal, hence Perseus was able to kill her by cutting off her head. From the blood that spurted from her neck sprang Chrysaor and Pegasus, her two sons by Poseidon. The head, which had the power of turning all who looked upon it into stone, was given to Athena, or buried in the market place of Argos. Heracles is said to have obtained a lock of Medusa's hair from Athena and given it to Sterope, the daughter of King Cepheus, as a protection for the town of Tegea against attack.

The hideously grotesque original type of the Gorgoneion, as the Gorgon's head was called, was used generally as a protection against the evil eye. Later classical art showed Medusa as coldly beautiful; the realists of Hellenistic times gave her face an agonized expression. Various rationalistic accounts are given by late authors. More reasonable is the explanation of anthropologists that Medusa, whose virtue is really in her head, was originally a ritual mask. It also is possible that the staring or pursuing faces, common in nightmares, have a good deal to do with her.

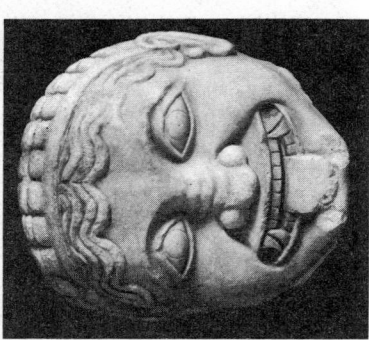

MARBLE HEAD OF GORGON; EARLY 6TH CENTURY B.C. IN THE ACROPOLIS MUSEUM, ATHENS

MANSELL-ALINARI

GORGONZOLA, a town in Milan province, Lombardy, Italy, lies 12 mi. (20 km.) E.N.E. of Milan. Pop. (1961) 9,046 (commune). Its most important industry is the making of the well-known gorgonzola cheese, which, soft when freshly made after being drained twice, is oven dried for 20 days and then pierced with copper needles to promote the internal formation of the characteristic greenish mold (*Penicillium roqueforti*). This cheese is also made in other parts of Lombardy and in Piedmont and Emilia. *See* CHEESE. (M.T.A.N.)

GORILLA, the common and generic name of the largest of the anthropoid (manlike) apes. There are two distinct species of the gorilla, in geographically separated areas: (1) the lowland gorilla (*G. gorilla*), inhabiting the rain forests of western Africa from the Cameroons to the Congo River; and (2) the mountain gorilla (*G. beringei*), confined to the mountainous eastern regions of the Congo-Uganda borderland, at altitudes of 10,000 ft. The former is short-haired, the latter long-haired; the two also differ in size and proportions, *G. beringei* having shorter arms and broader hands and feet. There are also minor differences in the shape of the skull.

Although related to the chimpanzee (*q.v.*), the gorilla differs from it in various ways: it is larger (an adult male gorilla may attain a weight of 450 lb. or more and a stature of 5½ ft.); it has large flaring nostrils and smaller ears; and it is less intensely black, its coat being more iron-gray, with a tendency to redden on the scalp (and sometimes elsewhere), and the adult developing a pale gray saddle over the loins. The gorilla normally stands on all four limbs, but the arms are used chiefly as crutches, the weight being carried on the flexed knuckles, not on the palms. It occasionally stands erect.

Much has been written about the strength and ferocity of the gorilla, but modern studies have shown them to be peaceable creatures unless unduly disturbed. Intruders may be faced by the male leader of a group, who may show aggressive tendencies in attempting to protect his dependents, but commonly this resolves itself into chest beating, vocalization, or short rushes toward the intruder, followed in most instances by a discreet withdrawal. Nevertheless, males can be dangerous, their method of attack being a strong blow with the hand. The voice is deep and resonant because of the presence of air sacs connected with the larynx and extending beneath the skin to the chest. Vocal utterances include a deep roar and a staccato bark.

Females care for their young up to about the third year, at which time the young (termed juveniles to about age six) begin to assert their independence, while still traveling and sleeping with the group. Black-backed males (six to ten years old) are free to move from group to group. The leader of a group is usually a silver-backed male (over ten years old), toward whom the members show an affectionate and loyal allegiance.

A typical day is spent feeding and resting. At dusk the leader generally initiates nest building, on the ground or in the lower branches of trees. The ground beds are crudely and hastily fashioned by bending and breaking leafy herbs to form a more or less oval mat; the tree platforms are more carefully constructed of heavier twigs and boughs. Sometime after sunrise, after 12 or more hours of sleep, the troop stirs and gradually resumes its unhurried foraging over a vaguely defined territory, only to construct new nests at dusk. Almost exclusively vegetarian, the gorilla eats fruit; roots and young shoots, especially wild celery combined with large quantities of roughage; bark; and fibrous material from young banana trees. Native plantations are sometimes raided.

Temperamentally the gorilla is more self-centred and introspective than the chimpanzee, lacking the latter's lively disposition and exhibiting less curiosity and adaptability. Consequently it is less suited to captivity. However, captive individuals studied experimentally have shown a capacity for problem solving and have clearly demonstrated the existence of insight, memory, and anticipation of experience.

A single young is born at varying times of the year, the gestation period being about 260 days. Gorilla births in captivity— still events of note—have become less rare since the first one, recorded in Columbus, Ohio, in 1956. Although little is known about their life expectancy, some gorillas may live for more than 25 years. *See also* PRIMATES; APE.

BIBLIOGRAPHY.—G. B. Schaller, *The Year of the Gorilla* (1964); W. K. Gregory (ed.), *Anatomy of the Gorilla* (1950); A. Moorehead, *No Room in the Ark* (1959); F. G. Merfield, *Gorillas Were My Neighbours* (1956); J. Wordsworth, *Gorilla Mountain* (1961); A. H. Schultz, "Some Distinguishing Characters of the Mountain Gorilla," *J. Mammal*, 15:51–59 (1934); R. M. Yerkes and A. W. Yerkes, *The Great Apes* (1929). (W.C.O.H.; X.)

GORING, GEORGE GORING, LORD (1608–1657), English soldier, who fought on the Royalist side during the Civil War, was the son of George Goring, earl of Norwich, and was born on July 14, 1608. He served in the Dutch army and was lamed at Breda in 1637. Returning to England in 1639, he was made governor of Portsmouth. Extravagant, ambitious, untrustworthy, and unprincipled, he changed sides twice during the struggle between king and Parliament. Goring abandoned Charles and took part in the "first army plot" of March 1641, which he promptly betrayed to Parliament. He joined Charles I again in Aug. 1642, lost Portsmouth to the Parliamentarians and shortly after went to Holland to obtain Royalist recruits from Englishmen serving with the Dutch. As general of the horse, Goring defeated Thomas Fairfax at Seacroft Moor in Yorkshire in March 1643, but in May he was made a prisoner by Fairfax at Wakefield. He became lieutenant general of the Royalist horse in Aug. 1644 and later had independent commands in the south and west, but there was much friction between him and other commanders, including Prince Rupert. Goring went to relieve Oxford (April 1645), was engaged in the operations around Taunton and on July 10 was defeated by Fairfax at Langport. He retired in Nov. 1645 and went to France. Later he commanded some English regiments in the Spanish service where he died in 1657. (S. R. Br.)

GÖRING, HERMANN (1893–1946), a military and economic leader and one of the most showy public figures of National Socialist Germany, was born at Rosenheim (Bavaria) on Jan. 12, 1893, the son of a colonial official. He became an army officer in 1914 and joined the air force when supposedly unfit for active service in World War I. In 1918 he commanded, with distinction, the Richthofen squadron and won the iron cross first class and the *Pour le Mérite*. After the war he worked for the Fokker Aircraft Works and for Svenska Lufttraffik in Sweden. He met Frau Karin von Kantzow (née Countess Fock), whom he married after her divorce, and went to live near Munich. There he saw Hitler at a public meeting and joined forces with him. Hitler immediately made him commander of the *Sturmabteilungen* (SA). In the Munich *Putsch* of November 1923 Göring was wounded and arrested but escaped to Austria. During a long recovery he became addicted to morphia, but he was cured after returning with his wife to Sweden. Back in Germany in 1927, he reestablished contact with Hitler, who had him elected to the *Reichstag* in 1928.

Göring used his contacts among industrialists and aristocrats to Hitler's advantage and arranged his first meeting with Hindenburg, on Oct. 16, 1931—the day before his wife Karin died in Sweden. After the Nazi success in the elections of July 1932, Göring became president of the *Reichstag*. When Hitler came to power he appointed Göring *Reichsminister* without portfolio, commissioner for air and Prussian prime minister and minister of the interior. Göring filled the Prussian administration and police with Nazi appointments before handing over the police to Himmler in 1934. He was also promoted general by Hindenburg. Göring's complicity in the burning of the *Reichstag* (Feb. 27, 1933) was assumed from his official position and from the existence of an underground tunnel from the *Reichstag* president's house to the became both *Reichsminister* for air and commander in chief of the air force (*Luftwaffe*) in 1935. By this time he could live in luxury. He took over a small palace in Berlin and, to the north, a hunting lodge, which he named Karinhall and where he built a mausoleum for the remains of his first wife. On April 10, 1935, he married the actress Emmy Sonnemann.

Göring supported Hitler's economic policy against the caution of Hjalmar Schacht, and Hitler put him in charge of a four-year plan (1936). He was thereafter economic dictator of Germany, with vast powers for the acquisition of property and the direction of industry. In 1937–41 he organized the state-owned industrial and mining enterprises under the name of Hermann-Göring-Werke. He backed Hitler against his generals and in 1938 "framed" Werner von Blomberg and Werner von Fritsch to bring about their dismissal. He took a leading part in the operation of the *Anschluss* with Austria but foresaw the dangers of an attack on Poland and made some furtive last-minute attempts to reach a compromise with England. He was appointed Hitler's successor on the outbreak of World War II and created *Reichsmarschall* in 1940. Göring's economic dictatorship was extended to the defeated countries and to Russia, and he used his power with unrestrained harshness. Meanwhile, however, the *Luftwaffe* had failed either to subjugate England or to defend Germany. Göring was discredited thereby; his health declined, he again became addicted to drugs, and began to lose all but formal authority. In April 1945, believing Hitler to have abandoned the direction of Germany, Göring assumed that the time had come for him to take over as deputy and volunteered to do so unless Hitler sent countermanding orders. Instead Hitler dismissed him from all offices and expelled him from the party (April 23), while Martin Bormann independently ordered his arrest. Captured by U.S. forces, he was brought to trial at Nürnberg. He was found guilty of all charges and sentenced to death. On Oct. 15, 1946, the evening before his execution, he took his own life with a phial of poison that he had kept hidden.

(W. Kr.)

GORIZIA (German, Görz; Serbo-Croatian, Gorica), a town of northeastern Italy, administrative centre of Gorizia Province in the Friuli-Venezia Giulia region, lies on the Isonzo 27 mi. (44 km.) NNW of Trieste by road. Pop. (1961) 43,656 (commune). It has a mild climate, being protected against the north winds by some high ground, which was the scene of fighting in World War I and stretches from the Colle del Castello to the banks of the Isonzo. It is crossed by the Corso Italia, an avenue of trees. The cathedral contains the treasures of the dissolved patriarchate of Aquiléia; the Gothic church of S. Spirito (18th century) has a 16th-century wooden crucifix; next to the church is the War Museum. The museum of the history of art is in the Baroque Attems Palace. In the Piazza della Vittoria there are the Palazzo della Prefettura, the church of S. Ignazio, and the Baroque fountain of Nettuno (Neptune). Agriculture and the manufacture of textiles and machinery form the main occupations. There are numerous brick kilns.

Gorizia is the ancient Gorica, dating from 1001. At an important road junction, it expanded under the rule of the counts of Pusteria. It then passed to the Habsburgs, and under them it became a noted cultural centre.

During World War I it suffered much damage. The Battle of Gorizia between Austrians and Italians took place in the vicinity (August 1916). By the *diktat* of Feb. 10, 1947, the border with Yugoslavia touches the town on the north, excluding from it the station of Montesanto. The adjoining Yugoslav town of Nova Gorica was developed after the border settlement.

GORIZIA PROVINCE (pop. [1961] 140,222; area, 183 sq.mi.) has 20 communes. Gradisca d'Isonzo still has portions of the wall planned by Leonardo da Vinci; at Redipuglia an immense war cemetery contains 100,000 dead of the 3rd army of whom more than half are unknown. Monfalcone has a famous naval dockyard, and rising above it is the Rocca di Teodorico; Grado has a popular bathing beach and also possesses a cathedral, fine mosaic pavements and Roman ruins.

(M. T. A. N.)

GORKI, MAKSIM (1868–1936), pen name of the Russian author Aleksei Maksimovich Peshkov whose plays, novels and memoirs of working-class life brought him an international reputation. He was born on March 28 (new style; 16, old style), 1868, at Nizhni Novgorod, since renamed Gorki in his honour, and his earliest years were spent in Astrakhan, where his father, a former upholsterer, became a shipping agent. When the boy was five his father died; Gorki returned to Nizhni Novgorod to live with his maternal grandparents, who brought him up after his mother remarried. The grandfather was a dyer whose business deteriorated and who treated Gorki harshly. It was from his grandmother that he received most of what little kindness he experienced as a child. The bitterness of these early experiences later led him to choose the word *gorki* ("bitter") as his pseudonym. Technically of lower middle-class origin, he lived in such poverty as a child and young man that he is often considered the greatest "proletarian" in Russian literature. This circumstance, coinciding with the rise of working-class movements all over the world, helped to give Gorki an immense literary reputation which his works only partly merit.

He knew the Russian working-class background intimately, for his grandfather afforded him only a few months of formal schooling, sending him out into the world to earn his living at the age of eight. His jobs included, among many others, work as assistant in a shoemaker's shop, as errand boy for an icon painter and as dishwasher on a Volga steamer, where the cook introduced him to reading—soon to become his main passion in life. Frequently beaten by his employers, nearly always hungry and ill-clothed, he got to know the seamy side of Russian life as few other Russian authors before or since. His late adolescence and early manhood were spent in Kazan, where he worked as a baker, docker and night watchman. It was here that he made his first contact with Russian revolutionary ideas, meeting representatives of the Populist movement, whose tendency to idealize the Russian peasant he came to reject. During this period, oppressed by the misery of his surroundings, he attempted suicide by shooting himself. Leaving Kazan at the age of 21, he became a tramp, doing odd jobs of all kinds during extensive wanderings through south Russia.

It was in Tbilisi (Tiflis) that Gorki began to publish stories in the provincial press, of which the first was *Makar Chudra* (1892), followed by a series of similar wild romantic legends and allegories which have now only a documentary interest. But with the publication of the story *Chelkash* (1895; first Eng. trans., 1902) in a leading St. Petersburg journal a success story began as spectacular as any other in the history of Russian literature. *Chelkash* itself remains one of his outstanding works and is the story of a colourful harbour thief in which elements of romanticism and realism are mingled. It began Gorki's celebrated Tramp period, during which he described the social dregs of Russia. He expressed sympathy and self-identification with the strength and determination of the individual hobo or criminal, thus tapping a vein which was new in Russian literature, for such characters had previously been described more from the outside. Also to the Tramp period belong *Malva* (1897), *Byvshyye lyudi* (1897; "Former People") and *Dvadtsat shest i odna* (1899; Eng. trans., *Twenty-Six Men and a Girl*, 1902). The latter, which describes the sweated labour conditions in a bakery, is often regarded as his best short story. So dramatic was the success of these works that Gorki's reputation quickly eclipsed even that of Chekhov and he began to be spoken of almost as an equal of Tolstoi.

With the turn of the century Gorki embarked on a series of plays and novels, all less excellent as works of art than his best earlier stories. The first novel, *Foma Gordeev* (1899), continues to illustrate his admiration for strength of body and will in the person of the masterful barge owner and rising capitalist Ignat Gordeev, who is contrasted with his relatively feeble and intellectual son Foma, a "seeker after the meaning of life," as are many of Gorki's other characters. From now on the rise of Russian capitalism became one of Gorki's main fictional interests. Other novels of the period are *Trode* (1900; "Three of Them"), *Ispoved* (1908; "A Confession"), *Gorodok Okurov* (1909; "Okurov City") and *Zhizn Matveya Kozhemyakina* (1910; "The Life of Matvey Kozhemyakin"). These are all to some extent failures because of Gorki's inability to sustain a powerful narrative such as he was well able to begin, and also because of a tendency to overload his work with irrelevant discussions about the meaning of life. *Mat* (1907; Eng. trans., *The Mother*, 1929) is probably the least successful of the novels, yet has considerable interest as Gorki's only long work devoted to the Russian revolutionary movement. Simultaneously Gorki was producing a series of plays—*Na dne* (1902; Eng. trans., *Lower Depths*, 1912), *Vassa Zheleznova* (1910), *Dachniki* (1905; "Summer Residents"), *Vragi* (1906; "The Enemies") and others. The most famous of these is *Lower Depths*, which still enjoys great success abroad and in Russia, putting on the stage the kind of doss-house character which Gorki had already described so extensively in narrative fiction.

Between 1899 and 1906 Gorki was living mainly in St. Petersburg (Leningrad), where he became a Marxist and joined the Russian Social Democrat party. His enormous earnings, which he largely gave to party funds, were for a time one of the party's main sources of income. In 1901 the Marxist review *Zhizn* ("Life") was suppressed for publishing a short revolutionary poem by Gorki, *Pesnya o burevestnike* ("Song of the Stormy Petrel"). Gorki was arrested but released shortly afterward and went to the Crimea, having now developed tuberculosis. In 1902 he was elected member of the Russian Academy of Sciences, but his election was soon withdrawn for political reasons, an event which led to the resignation of Chekhov and Korolenko from the academy. At about this time Gorki founded a publishing business called *Znanie* ("Knowledge"), which led to the emergence of a movement sometimes called the *Znanie* school of fiction. *Znanie* aimed to give a forum, in so far as censorship conditions permitted, to young writers with revolutionary proclivities whose work was "tendentious," a word which has commonly been used as a term of praise by Russian critics and readers. Gorki took a prominent part in the 1905 revolution and was arrested in the following year, being again quickly released, partly as the result of protests from abroad. He toured America in the company of his mistress, an event which led to his partial ostracism there and to a consequent reaction on his part against the United States expressed in stories about New York, *The City of the Yellow Devil* (1906).

On leaving Russia in 1906 Gorki spent seven years as a political exile, living mainly in his villa on Capri, which became an intellectual centre for politically disaffected Russians. Meanwhile, although his writings continued to enjoy the favour of ordinary Russian readers, he had lost much of his former popularity with the intelligentsia, for the literary fashion had veered against philosophising tramps and now that the first excitement had subsided the more cultured reader was becoming conscious of Gorki's

defects. Though still essentially in alliance with Lenin's movement, he was somewhat out of favour even there owing to his espousal of a religio-philosophical trend called *bogostroitelstvo* ("God-building"), preached in his novel *Confession* and regarded as a heresy by more orthodox Marxists. Politically Gorki was a nuisance to his fellow Marxists because of his insistence on remaining independent, but his great influence was a powerful asset which from their point of view outweighed such minor defects. During World War I he agreed with the Bolsheviks in opposing Russia's involvement in the struggle and after the October Revolution of 1917 he gave them his full support. During the years 1917 to 1921 he helped to alleviate the miseries which, in these years of war Communism, his fellow writers shared with the rest of the population. He was often able to see that they received payment if only for work such as translating.

It is to the decade ending in 1923 that the production of Gorki's greatest masterpiece belongs. This is the autobiographical trilogy *Detstvo* (1913–14; Eng. trans., *Childhood*, 1915), *V lyudyakh* (1915–16; Eng. trans., *In the World*, 1917) and *Moi universitety* (1923; Eng. trans., *My Universities*, 1924)—the last-named title being sardonic since Gorki's only university had been that of life, and his wish to study at Kazan university had been frustrated. This long work is one of the finest autobiographies in Russian. It deals only with the years of Gorki's childhood and early manhood and shows his strength as a now relatively extrovert writer who had to some extent turned his back on the excessive "philosophizing" of his early period. It reveals him as an acute observer of detail with a flair for describing people—his own family, his numerous employers and a panorama of minor but memorable figures who flit across his pages. In a way it is hardly the story of Gorki himself, for seldom was an autobiography more reticent (even his attempted suicide receives only a line or two). The book is permeated with a wonder at the mystery, cruelty and colour of life which, as it might seem, Gorki was now less earnestly eager to understand or interpret, being content to portray. But it does contain numerous messages, which now are usually left to be deduced by the reader rather than openly preached, notably protests against motiveless cruelty, continued emphasis on the importance of toughness and self-reliance ("I very early realized that a man is made by his resistance to the milieu which surrounds him") and musings on the value of hard work often couched in his characteristic rhetorical style, as where he speaks of the dockers' "drunken joy" in unloading a Volga barge, a joy "than which only the embraces of a woman are sweeter."

My Universities was finished in Italy, to which Gorki emigrated, being based on his villa in Sorrento in the period 1921–28, when he made excursions to Germany and elsewhere, but did not return to Russia. One of the reasons for his retirement was poor health, but a disillusionment with Russia in the first years after the Revolution seems to have played a part in his decision. In 1928 he yielded to pressures to return, and the lavish official celebration of his 60th birthday in Russia in that year was beyond anything he could have expected. In the following year he returned to Russia permanently and he lived there until his death in 1936. His return coincided with the establishment of Stalin's total ascendancy. In the atmosphere of the 1930s, so much harsher than that of the 1920s from which he had fled, Gorki was less able to intervene on behalf of persecuted fellow workers and became a prop of Stalinist political orthodoxy. He was now more than ever the undisputed leader of Soviet writers, and when the Soviet Writers' union was founded in 1932 he became its first president. At the same time he helped to found the literary method of Socialist Realism, henceforward the compulsory official technique which all Soviet writers were bound to follow.

Gorki remained active as a writer. Despite his close association with official Stalinist literary doctrine, almost all his fiction of the period is concerned with the period before the Revolution. In *Delo Artamonovykh* (1925; Eng. trans., *The Artamonov Business*, 1948), one of his best novels, he showed his continued interest in the rise and fall of pre-Revolutionary Russian capitalism. The immense and more ambitious *Zhizn Klima Samgina* (1927–36; "Life of Klim Samgin") is a tetralogy which attempts a portrait of the Russian intelligentsia between 1870 and 1924. There were more plays—*Yegor Bulychov* (1932); *Dostigaev i drugie* (1933; "Dostigaev and Others"; Eng. trans., *The Last Plays*, 1937)—but the most generally admired work to follow his autobiography is a volume of reminiscences of Russian writers (Eng. trans., *Reminiscences of Tolstoi, Chekhov and Andreev*, 1949). Here the memoir of Tolstoi is so lively and free from the hagiographical approach traditional in Russian studies of their leading authors that it has sometimes been acclaimed as Gorki's masterpiece. Almost equally impressive is Gorki's study of Chekhov. At the other end of the scale come some of his pamphlets devoted to topical events and problems, such as his *Belomorkanal* (1934; Eng. trans., *The White Sea Canal*, 1935), in which, as elsewhere, he sank to glorifying the most brutal aspects of Stalinism—in this case the construction of the canal by the forced labour of largely political prisoners.

Some mystery attaches to Gorki's death, which occurred suddenly in 1936 while he was under medical treatment. Whether his death was natural or not is unknown, but it came to figure in the trial of Bukharin and others in 1938, at which it was claimed that Gorki had been the victim of an anti-Soviet plot by the "Bloc of Rightists and Trotskyites." The former police chief, Yagoda, who was among the defendants, confessed to having ordered his death. Some western authorities have suggested that Gorki was done to death on Stalin's orders, having finally become sickened by the excesses of Stalinist Russia, but of this little evidence has been put forward, other than that it was characteristic of Stalin to frame others on the charge of accomplishing his own misdeeds.

After his death Gorki was canonized as the patron saint of Soviet letters, the formula "Gorki said . . ." often being used to clinch a literary argument. His reputation abroad has also remained high, but it is doubtful whether posterity will deal with him quite so kindly. His success was at least partly due, both in Russia and to a lesser extent abroad, to political accident. His style, though gradually improving through the years, retained its original defects of excessive striving for effect, of working on the reader's nerves by the piling up of emotive adjectives and by tending to overstate everything. Chekhov, his opposite in these matters, had given him good advice in the interesting correspondence which ensued when Gorki appealed to him for literary advice in the 1890s, but this advice was only partly effective. Among other defects, in addition to his weakness for philosophical digressions mentioned above, is his lack of any sense of humour and a certain coarseness of emotional grain. But his eye for physical detail, his talent for making his characters live and his unrivalled knowledge of the Russian "lower depths" are weighty items on the credit side. He was the only Soviet writer whose work embraced the pre-Revolutionary and post-Revolutionary period so exhaustively, and though he does not quite stand with Chekhov, Tolstoi and others in the front rank of Russian writers, he remains one of the biggest and most fascinating figures of his age. For portrait *see* article RUSSIAN LITERATURE.

See Alexander Kaun, *Maxim Gorky and his Russia* (1932); for a bibliography of recently translated works by Gorki, *see* Gleb Struve, *Soviet Russian Literature 1917-1950*, pp. 393-394 (1951).   (R. F. Hu.)

GORKY (GORKI), an *oblast* of the Russian Soviet Federated Socialist Republic, U.S.S.R., is situated in the Middle Volga Basin. It became an *oblast* in 1936. From 1954 to 1957 the southern part was separated as Arzamas Oblast, but later again became part of Gorky Oblast as a *rayon*. Gorky Oblast is bisected by the Volga; the northern half is a low plain, drained by the Vetluga and Kerzhenets, and is mostly in dense coniferous forest of spruce, pine, and fir, with some birch, while lower parts are often swampy; soils are poor podzols. The southern half is higher; rolling morainic hills, with deciduous trees, especially oak, as well as conifers, and open areas of forest-steppe; it has better gray forest soils and degraded black earths. The climate is markedly continental, with a January average temperature at Gorky of 12° F (−11° C) and a July average of 68° F (20° C). Rainfall is about 20 in. a year.

The area of the *oblast* is 28,880 sq.mi. (74,800 sq.km.). The population (1970 prelim.) was 3,683,000, of whom 2,378,000 (65%) were urban. Most lived in the huge conurbation of Gorky (1,170,000) and its satellite towns: Dzerzhinsk (221,000), Bor (1969 est. 51,000), Balakhna, and Pravdinsk. Others of note (1969 est. 62,000), among the 23 towns of the *oblast* are Kulebaki, and Shakhunya. All the area along the Volga and lower Oka is highly industrialized, but elsewhere there are only pockets of industry. Steel is made at Kulebaki and Vyksa, textiles and foodstuffs in Arzamas. In the forested areas timber working is developed on a large scale and Pravdinsk makes the newsprint for *Pravda*. At Gorodets, above Gorky, a large hydroelectric plant has been built on the Volga. The main agricultural area lies south of the Volga, where grains are dominant, occupying 65% of the cropped area, notably rye, oats, spring wheat, and buckwheat. Potatoes and flax are important and some maize (corn) is grown for fodder. Communications are excellent, with the navigable Volga and railway west to Moscow, railways east and northeast to the Urals and Kirov and south to Saransk, and the eastern highway from Moscow.   (R. A. F.)

GORKY (GORKI), formerly NIZHNY NOVGOROD, a town and the administrative centre of Gorky Oblast of the Russian Soviet Federated Socialist Republic, U.S.S.R., stands at the confluence of the Volga and Oka rivers, 260 mi. E of Moscow. Pop. (1970 prelim.) 1,170,000. The town was founded in 1221 by Yuri Vsevolodovich, prince of Vladimir, as Russian colonization advanced to the Volga, into the lands formerly occupied by the Mordvinians. Its strategic site on the great Volga route from the Baltic to Central Asia, with links via the navigable Oka to the "cradle" of Muscovy (the Vladimir-Moscow region) and via the Kama to the Urals and Siberia, ensured its importance. In 1392 the town was incorporated into the principality of Moscow and acted as a forward base against the Volga Tatars. From there Ivan III in 1469 and Ivan IV in 1552 launched their expeditions against the Tatars. (*See* IVAN.) The Russian conquest of the Volga in the mid-16th century brought increased trade to Nizhny Novgorod. In 1817 an annual fair was established there which became the largest and most important in Russia, attracting traders and goods from all over Europe and Asia. The fair continued down to the Revolution. Maksim Gorki was born there in 1868, and in 1932 the town was renamed in his honour.

The great volume of trade passing through the town led to the early utilization of serf labour in manufacturing and later of heavy industry, especially engineering. Gorky's industrial importance grew steadily, much stimulated in World Wars I and II by the occupation and destruction of plants in more westerly areas. Modern Gorky is one of the largest cities of the U.S.S.R. and the centre of a vast conurbation strung out along the Volga and lower Oka. The Gorky car factory makes the "Volga" medium car. The shipyards, established in 1849, build ships, hydroplanes, barges, oil tankers, floating cranes, and river icebreakers. Also made are diesel engines; machinery for the timber and papermaking industries, and a wide range of machine tools. Other products include textiles, footwear, plastics, furniture, tobacco, and foodstuffs. Bor, across the Volga, makes glass, especially safety glass for cars. Dzerzhinsk makes chemicals and fertilizers, Balakhna and Pravdinsk paper, and Bogorodsk leather goods and shoes. Kstovo has a major oil refinery. Power for the conurbation comes from two thermal electric plants in Gorky, the Balakhna peat-burning plant, and the Gorodets hydroelectric station on the Volga. Gorky has good communications by river, road, and rail. Railways connect it with Moscow and Kirov and with Arzamas on the Trans-Siberian Railway, and there are suburban lines to Pravdinsk, Pavlovo, and Bor. There is also an airport.

The city is the site of the N. I. Lobachevski State University (1918), and other higher educational establishments include institutes of agriculture, medicine, and engineering. There is a state art museum. The drama theatre, one of the oldest in Russia, was established in 1798. Historic buildings include the kremlin, which dates from the 14th century.   (R. A. F.)

GÖRLITZ, a town of Germany which after partition of the nation following World War II became a regional capital in the Bezirk (district) of Dresden, German Democratic Republic. Pop. (1964) 88,824. Görlitz is about 56 mi. ENE of Dresden and lies on both sides of the Neisse River. It is a frontier town, and after

1945, when the Neisse became the Polish-German boundary, that part of the town lying on the east bank of the river came under Polish administration and was named Zgorzelec. The town is a railway junction and the chief centre of Upper Lusatia, with many industries, the best known being the nationally owned vehicle-building works. There are also machinery, cloth, and wood factories, and a construction training school. Lignite is mined in the region. To the southwest is a lookout point, the Landeskrone, on a 1,400-ft. basalt peak. Historic buildings include the Late Gothic Peter Pauls Kirche, and remains of a 14th-century castle. Görlitz grew out of the Slav settlement Gorelic, first mentioned in the 11th century. It reached its economic peak in the Middle Ages when it was known for clothmaking craftsmanship. In 1635 the town became a part of Saxony and later, in 1815, of Prussia. (R. A. F.)

GORLOVKA, a town of Donetsk Oblast in the Ukrainian Soviet Socialist Republic, U.S.S.R., lies in the centre of the Donets Basin (Donbass) industrial area, 25 mi. (40 km.) N by E of Donetsk city (formerly Stalino). Pop. (1970 prelim.) 335,000. Gorlovka was founded as a mining settlement in 1867; it became a town in 1932 and is one of the largest coal-mining centres of the area. Its many pits include some of the deepest of this field. There is also a large engineering industry making coal-mining machinery and a chemical industry (nitrate fertilizers). A network of railways links Gorlovka to neighbouring towns. (R. A. F.)

GORNO-ALTAY AUTONOMOUS OBLAST (GORNO-ALTAYSKAYA AVTONOMNAYA OBLAST) forms the southeastern part of Altai Kray (q.v.), of the Russian Soviet Federated Socialist Republic, U.S.S.R., bordering on the Mongolian People's Republic. Created in 1922 as Oirot Autonomous Oblast and renamed in 1948, it covers an area of 35,753 sq.mi. (92,600 sq.km.). Almost all the oblast is mountainous (gorno) rising from low foothills in the north to the main ranges of the Altai Mountains in the south, culminating in Mt. Belukha (14,783 ft.). Relief is highly complex, consisting of a series of high plateaus and ranges, trending roughly northwest to southeast, very greatly dislocated by faulting and rifting to form deep valleys and broad depressions. The highest ranges are the Katunsky, the North and South Chuya, and the Chikhacheva, while the chief valleys are those of the Biya and the Chuya-Katun, the headstreams of the Ob. The mountains are densely forested with Siberian larch, spruce, Scotch and Siberian pine, and Siberian fir. Higher up the forests yield to alpine meadow, which in turn gives way to rock, snow, and ice. In the Altai are more than 800 glaciers. The summits above the snow line are known as belki. The valleys and basins have steppe vegetation, developed on chestnut and black earth soils, much of which is now under the plow. Boundaries of vegetation zones vary greatly in height, according to exposure, but are usually higher to the south. The climate is strongly continental, although relief causes considerable local variation. January temperatures average about −20° F (−28.9° C) but may be lower in sheltered hollows. Summers are cool, about 58°–60° F (14.4°–15.6° C) because of the height. Rainfall varies considerably, up to 50 in. or more on the western ranges and falling to 12 in. or less in the east and in the valleys.

According to the 1970 preliminary census the population was 168,000, of whom 24% were urban, living in the administrative centre of Gorno-Altaysk (34,000), formerly Oirot-Tura, and the urban district of Aktash (2,000). The Altaitsy people, sometimes known as Oirots, form about one-quarter of the population and Russians more than 70%. Along the upper Argut and Chuya are some Kazakh villages. The Altaitsy, of whom the 1959 census enumerated 45,000 in the Russian S.F.S.R., are a Turkic group of peoples, sometimes erroneously considered as Kalmyks. They form two groups, the northern, consisting of the Tulabari, Chelkantsy, and Kumandintsy, and the southern, the Altaitsy proper, the Telengity, Telesi, and Teleuti, although these tribal distinctions are fast disappearing. Formerly nomadic herdsmen, living in tents, the Altaitsy have now largely been settled and have taken up agriculture. Nevertheless stock rearing remains the basis of the economy and large numbers of cattle, for both meat and dairy produce, sheep for meat and wool, goats, horses, yaks, and reindeer are all kept (see also ALTAIC PEOPLES). The oblast is well supplied with natural pasture and haylands. The area under crops, on the fertile valley soils, has been considerably increased under the Virgin and Idle Lands Plan and is dominated by oats, followed by barley, winter rye, wheat, vegetables, and potatoes. Beekeeping is important, while the cones of the Siberian pine are collected for oil. Hunting is carried on, chiefly for squirrel, and silver-fox fur farming has been introduced. Timber cutting is mainly along the Biya, down which the logs are rafted. Many minerals have been located, including iron ore, coal, marble, asbestos, graphite, and cinnabar, but mining in the 1960s was confined to gold, mercury, and other precious metals. Manufacturing is limited to Gorno-Altaysk, with textile, furniture, and meat-packing industries. The town has a scientific research institute of Altai language, literature, and history. The village of Chemal is a health resort. The main axis of communication is the Chuya highway from the railhead of Bisk to Gorno-Altaysk and thence along the Katun and Chuya and over the Derbet-Daba pass into Mongolia. (R. A. F.)

GORNO-BADAKHSHAN AUTONOMOUS OBLAST (GORNO-BADAKHSHANSKAYA AVTONOMNAYA OBLAST) forms part of the Tadzhik Soviet Socialist Republic at the extreme southeast of the U.S.S.R. It borders on China (Sinkiang Uighur Autonomous Region) in the east and Afghanistan in the south and west. The capital is Khorog (q.v.). Before the Russian Revolution the western part of the oblast came under the khanate of Bukhara (q.v.), and the eastern was part of Russian Turkistan. The present oblast was created in 1925. It comprises the Pamir Uplands (see PAMIRS) including the Lenin (23,405 ft. [7,134 m.]) and Communism (formerly Stalin, 24,590 ft. [7,495 m.]) peaks, and is seismic. The climate is continental, with little precipitation and great daily and annual variations of temperature. The Pyandzh River, a headstream of the Amu Darya (Oxus), flows along the southern and western frontiers and its many tributaries intersect the oblast in the form of mountain torrents. Of the lakes, Kara-Kul is the largest in area and Sarez the deepest (approximately 1,657 ft. [505 m.]).

The economy of the oblast is conditioned by its inaccessibility and the difficulty of communications, which are confined to road and air transport. The main activity on the bleak, sparsely inhabited high plateau in the east is yak breeding. In the west, where up to 90% of the population lives, grain and fruit are grown where possible in the narrow valleys, the dryness of the climate making irrigation necessary. Small hydroelectric stations have been built for local needs, but the oblast's rich hydroelectric potential remained virtually unused in the early 1970s. The exploitation of gold, coal, mica, and rock-crystal deposits is hindered by the difficulties of the terrain. Near Khorog there is an important botanical garden and research centre. The population (98,000 in 1970 [prelim.], 86,000 of whom were rural) was over 80% Tajik (Tadzhik) with 11% Kirgiz and 5% Russian. The chief motor roads are those from Khorog to Osh and to Dushanbe. (G. E. WR.; A. SH.)

GÖRRES, (JOHANN) JOSEPH VON (1776–1848), the most variously gifted German Catholic writer of the 19th century, was born at Coblenz on Jan. 25, 1776. As a schoolboy he sympathized with the ideals of the French Revolution and in 1797 published a republican periodical, Das rote Blatt (later Rübezahl). An unsuccessful visit to Paris in 1799 as a political negotiator on behalf of the Rhenish provinces disillusioned him and for a time he withdrew from active politics. He married and taught natural science in Coblenz. A period lecturing at Heidelberg (1806–07) brought him into contact with the leaders of German romanticism, particularly Achim von Arnim and Clemens Brentano (qq.v.) with whom he edited the Zeitung für Einsiedler (later Trösteinsamkeit). His interest in German folk literature thoroughly awakened, he published in 1807 Die deutschen Volksbücher, a collection of late medieval narrative prose. His Mythengeschichte der asiatischen Welt (1810) expresses much of German romanticism's fascination by the orient.

Returning to Coblenz in 1808, he lived quietly until the national struggle against Napoleon led him to found the newspaper Rheinischer Merkur in 1814. Its fiery journalism caused Napoleon to refer to it bitterly as the fifth great power, but its equally ruthless criticism of the reactionary policies of the German states after Napoleon's fall led to its suppression in 1816. Görres's pamphlet *Teutschland und die Revolution* (1819) forced him to flee to Strasbourg, and there and in Switzerland he lived in poverty for several years. In 1824 he formally returned to the Roman Catholic Church, from which he had lapsed. In 1827, at the invitation of Ludwig I of Bavaria, he became professor of history at Munich, where a circle of liberal Catholic scholars gathered around him. Görres was the most vigorous Catholic spokesman in a number of controversies, but the main task of his later years was the writing of his monumental *Christliche Mystik* (4 vol., 1836–42). He died on Jan. 29, 1848, at Munich.

Enthusiasm, sincerity and abundant linguistic vitality made Görres a figure of commanding influence. The *Görres-Gesellschaft*, founded in 1876 to advance Catholic studies, testifies to the power of his name. It publishes a number of important periodicals and has institutes in Rome, Madrid and Jerusalem.

BIBLIOGRAPHY.—Görres's *Gesammelte Schriften* (political writings) appeared in 6 vol. (1854–60); letters (3 vol.) were added in 1858–74. In 1926 a critical edition, initially ed. by W. Schellberg, was begun under the auspices of the *Görres-Gesellschaft*; 16 vol. had been issued by 1960. *See also* J. Galland, *J. von Görres* (1876); J. N. Sepp, *Görres und seine Zeitgenossen* (1877); W. Schellberg, *J. von Görres* (1926); R. Saitschik, *J. Görres und die abendländische Kultur* (1953). (G. T. Hu.)

GORST, SIR JOHN ELDON (1835–1916), English statesman, a member of Lord Randolph Churchill's "fourth party," was born at Preston on May 24, 1835, and graduated third wrangler from St. John's college, Cambridge, in 1857. He was awarded a fellowship, but preferred to travel; he sailed for New Zealand in 1859, married a fellow passenger on the way and soon found himself entangled in Anglo-Maori relations and in danger of his life. Having had more than enough excitement, he brought his family back to England; long afterward he published an account of his antipodean adventures in *New Zealand Revisited: Recollections of the Days of My Youth* (1908.)

Gorst was called to the bar in 1865 and entered parliament in 1866 as member for Cambridge. He lost his seat in 1868, as did many other Conservatives, and Disraeli entrusted him with a thorough overhaul of the party's machinery. Gorst traveled all over England and Wales in five years of hard work that laid the foundation both of the Conservative victory in the general election of 1874 and of many later successes, for he established efficient local committees in every potential Conservative seat. In 1875 he reentered parliament himself in a by-election at Chatham and became a queen's counsel. No official notice was taken of his work for the party, and he made some mark as an independent debater before he joined, in the new parliament of 1880, Lord Randolph Churchill's "fourth party," whose only other members were Sir Henry Drummond-Wolff and Arthur Balfour. They were all keen debaters, who goaded Gladstone or the leader of the opposition with equal invective; they toyed, Gorst especially, with concepts of "Tory democracy," which they believed they inherited from Disraeli. Churchill's influence secured for Gorst the office of solicitor general and a knighthood in Lord Salisbury's short government of 1885–86. Gorst later held various minor offices—undersecretary for India, deputy chairman of commons' committees, financial secretary to the treasury and vice-president of the education committee—in turn, resigning the last of these in 1902. He was the unopposed member for Cambridge university from 1892 till he quarreled with his party and lost his seat to a tariff reformer in 1906. Gorst stood unsuccessfully as a Liberal at Preston in 1910. Gorst died in London on April 4, 1916, after a career that never quite matched his undoubted energy and abilities.

SIR JOHN ELDON GORST (1861–1911), his elder son, English colonial administrator notable for his work in Egypt, was born in Auckland, N.Z., on June 25, 1861. He graduated from Trinity college, Cambridge, in 1883, entered the foreign service and was soon posted to Cairo. He succeeded Alfred (afterward Lord) Milner in 1892 as undersecretary for finance; two years later he took up a newly created appointment as adviser to the Egyptian minister of the interior, and in 1898 he became financial adviser to the Egyptian government. His financial policies were unadventurous but sound. Under Lord Cromer's guidance, he helped to prepare the Egyptian details of the Anglo-French entente of 1904, and after a period (1904–07) as assistant undersecretary at the foreign office, he returned to Egypt in 1907 as successor to Lord Cromer. (*See* EGYPT: *History*.) He died in Wiltshire on July 12, 1911. He had been knighted in 1902.
(M. R. D. F.)

GORTER, HERMAN (1864–1927), outstanding Netherlands poet and a socialist politician, was born at Wormerveer, Nov. 26, 1864, the son of the journalist, Simon Gorter. He studied classical languages at Amsterdam and was connected with the avant-garde periodical *De Nieuwe Gids* (*see* DUTCH LITERATURE). In 1889 he published the lyrical nature epic *Mei*, in which the impermanence of sensuous beauty is expressed through a myth of the mortal May, and the blind god, Balder, between whom union is impossible. The theme of the first canto is joy in the beauty of the Dutch spring landscape, which is followed by a second theme—melancholy because beauty is fleeting. *Mei*, which represents a peak of poetic art in the Netherlands, was followed by the sensitive *Verzen* (1890) and poems inspired by Spinozism. After his conversion to socialism in 1896 Gorter found inspiration in its teaching. His political poetry is purely visionary: in a new community a new beauty will be established. His Marxism had an aesthetic basis. A Communist for a short time, he soon found himself in conflict with Lenin and during the last years of his life fought a lonely battle. Besides poetry Gorter wrote historical literary reviews and other Marxist essays. He died in Brussels on Sept. 15, 1927.

See Henriëtte Roland Holst, *Herman Gorter* (1933); J. de Kadt, *Herman Gorter, neen en ja* (1947). (Gn. W. Hs.)

GORTON, JOHN GREY (1911–), prime minister of Australia, 1968–71, was born in Melbourne, Austr., on Sept. 9, 1911. He was educated at Geelong Grammar School and Brasenose College, Oxford. In November 1940 he joined the Royal Australian Air Force and served as a fighter pilot in Britain, Singapore, Australia, and Papua. Severely wounded in action, he was discharged in 1944. Gorton was elected (1949) senator for Victoria. He represented Australia at several international conferences, was minister for the navy (1958–63), and became minister of works in 1963. At the time of the death of Harold Holt (prime minister, January 1966–December 1967) he was minister for education and science and leader of the government in the Senate. He was elected leader of the Liberal Party on Jan. 9, 1968, and was sworn in as prime minister the following day. While in power Gorton headed a coalition of the Liberal and Country parties. After failing to win a vote of confidence held by the Liberal Party on March 10, 1971, he resigned as prime minister and accepted the post of defense minister and was elected deputy leader of the Liberal Party. In August 1971 Gorton was dismissed as defense minister and subsequently resigned as deputy leader of the party.

GORTON, SAMUEL (1592–1677), colonial religious enthusiast and first settler of Warwick, R.I., was born in Gorton, Eng. He became a clothier in London before he migrated to Boston, Mass., in 1637. In Boston he immediately became involved in serious religious disputes and was banished from the community. He met similar opposition in Plymouth and later in Aquidneck (Newport) and Providence. Gorton inspired development of a small religious sect called Gortonites who contended that true believers shared God's perfection and that heaven and hell had little reality. When Gorton finally sought a haven at Shawomet, his purchase of land there was contested. Massachusetts intervened, finally trying him in Boston and banishing him. He went to England where he published an account of his grievances against Massachusetts. Returning to Boston in 1648 with an order for the land he claimed, Gorton returned to Shawomet, which he renamed Warwick, and remained there the rest of his life.

BIBLIOGRAPHY.—Nathaniel Morton, *New Englands Memoriall* (1669), ed. by Howard J. Hall, pp. 108–110 (1937); *Winthrop's Journal, 1630–1649*, ed. by J. Franklin Jameson, vol. ii. For Gorton's writings, see Peter Force, *Tracts*, vol. iv.

GORTYNA: *see* CRETE: *Archaeology*.

GÖRTZ, GEORG HEINRICH, FREIHERR VON (1668–1719), German-born statesman, attained prominence as the financial and diplomatic adviser to Charles XII (q.v.) of Sweden. His service of successive dukes of Holstein-Gottorp, who ruled over parts of Schleswig and Holstein, began in 1698. When the ducal lands were in danger of being incorporated in Denmark, Görtz secured their restitution (1713). But his overtures to Russia and Prussia, which envisaged the cession of Swedish possessions in the Baltic and the succession to the Swedish throne of Charles Frederick, duke of Holstein-Gottorp and nephew of the childless Charles XII, caused resentment in Sweden. Görtz, in a meeting with Charles after the king's return from Turkey (1714), convinced him of his good faith and henceforth was one of Charles's most energetic advisers, first in the realms of credit and finance, and later also of diplomacy. Görtz, however, was not the originator of many of the expedients which were used to raise money, though his fertile brain and his willingness to serve Charles XII's cause resulted in his taking over a great deal of the work involved in channeling Sweden's resources into the war effort. Though he had a fairly free hand in diplomatic negotiations with the Jacobites, the Prussians and the Russians, the king reserved for himself all decisions; and the negotiations of Görtz were only part of a large-scale diplomatic offensive which had other important if lesser-known helpers.

Görtz's imprisonment (Feb.–Aug. 1717) by the Dutch—at the request of George I of England because of Görtz's intrigues with the Jacobites—hardly interrupted the diplomatic offensive of Sweden. When Görtz was freed he completed that part of the plan which envisaged separate negotiations with Russia; from the opening of the Aaland Islands congress in Jan. 1718 Görtz's time was spent either at the congress or in travels to Stockholm and to Charles XII's headquarters to report progress and receive new instructions. In Dec. 1718 he was on his way for such a periodic report, not knowing of the death of the king, when he was arrested on the orders of Frederick of Hesse (afterward Frederick I of Sweden), who feared that Görtz might work for the candidature of Charles Frederick and against that of Hesse's wife, Ulrika Eleonora, the younger sister of Charles XII. The widespread desire among the Swedish administrators and officers to undo absolutism and to end the financial and administrative innovations of the late king, without openly besmirching Charles XII's reputation, found in Görtz the ideal scapegoat. He was accused of alienating the affections of the late king from his people, was sentenced to death and was executed in Stockholm on March 12, 1719, after a trial which both contemporaries and posterity have condemned as a judicial murder. His unselfish and loyal service to Charles XII is now generally admitted.
(R. M. HA.)

GÖRZ: see GORIZIA.

GORZÓW WIELKOPOLSKI (Ger. LANDSBERG AN DER WARTHE), a town in western Poland, Zielona Gora wojewodztwo (province), lies 120 km. (75 mi.) W.N.W. of Poznan. It is a district capital and the seat of a Roman Catholic bishopric. Pop. (1970 prelim.) 74,300. The town is situated on the lower Warta (Warthe) river at its confluence with the Klodawa. The town centre is on the right bank of the Warta, the industrial district on the left. It has a well-developed chemical industry (artificial textile factories) and timber and food industries.

As a frontier castle of Pomerania and Poznania (or Wielkopolska, Great Poland), Gorzow was conquered in the 13th century by the Brandenburgers, who founded a settlement there in 1257. Its German name derives from this period. Although it belonged to the New Mark (newly conquered lands beyond the Oder), the town was subordinate before the partitions to Polish overlords both ecclesiastical and temporal. During World War II more than half of the town was destroyed; it returned to Poland in 1945.
(T. K. W.)

GOSCHEN, GEORGE JOACHIM GOSCHEN, 1ST VISCOUNT (1831–1907), British economist and administrator, did useful work under both Liberal and Conservative governments in the last part of the 19th century. The son of William Henry Goeschen, a London banker of German origin, he was born in London on Aug. 10, 1831. He was educated in Saxony, at Rugby and at Oriel college, Oxford, where he was president of the union and took a first class in classics in 1853. He became prominent in the banking world early and was made a director of the Bank of England at

27. His Theory of the Foreign Exchanges (1861) was long famous. Goschen entered parliament in 1863 as Liberal member for the City of London, a seat he held till 1880, when he was elected for Ripon. He made his mark at once in the house of commons, became a junior minister in Nov. 1865 and sat in the cabinet as chancellor of the duchy of Lancaster for the first half of 1866. In Gladstone's great cabinet of 1868 Goschen was at first president of the poor law board, where he projected useful reforms, and then, from March 1871 to Feb. 1874, first lord of the admiralty. He and the French negotiated (1876) with the khedive in Cairo the decree that established the dual Anglo-French control of Egyptian bonds.

Goschen stoutly opposed Disraeli's policy in the eastern crisis in 1876–78. He did not join Gladstone's government in 1880 because he disapproved of the impending extension of the franchise, but he did accept the post of special ambassador to Constantinople and helped to settle various Balkan frontier questions in 1880–81. He refused Gladstone's successive offers of the viceroyalty of India, a secretaryship of state or the speakership. He found himself more and more at variance with extreme Liberals, and carried East Edinburgh in 1885 against a radical. When Gladstone declared for Irish Home Rule, Goschen opposed him vigorously. But he lost his Edinburgh seat in the election of July 1886 and only returned to the house of commons in Feb. 1887 for St. George's, Hanover square. When Lord Randolph Churchill resigned in Dec. 1886, Goschen took his place as chancellor of the exchequer ("I forgot Goschen," said Churchill) and operated a successful conversion of the national debt in 1888. He was in opposition from 1892 to 1895, and returned to the admiralty as first lord in Salisbury's coalition cabinet (1895–1902) where he supervised large expansions of the fleet. He retired with a viscounty in 1900, but kept up an interest in politics and economics; he was one of the weightiest free-trade Unionists in the tariff controversy of 1903–06. He became chancellor of Oxford university in 1903. He died at his home in Sussex on Feb. 7, 1907.

One of his brothers, SIR (WILLIAM) EDWARD GOSCHEN (1847–1924), was British ambassador in Berlin on the outbreak of war in 1914. His elder son, GEORGE JOACHIM (1866–1952), who succeeded him as 2nd viscount, was Conservative member of parliament for East Grinstead from 1895 to 1906 and governor of Madras, 1924–29.
(M. R. D. F.)

See A. R. D. Elliot, Life of Lord Goschen, 2 vol. (1911).

GOSFORTH, an urban district of Northumberland, Eng., adjoins Newcastle upon Tyne on its northern side. Pop. (1971 prelim.) 26,826. The Great North road almost halves the district and provides its main shopping street. Gosforth is a modern and almost entirely residential town for industrial and commercial Tyneside. St. Nicholas parish church was rebuilt on the present site in 1799. In the district, wholly or partly, are two golf courses, three rugby football fields and one cricket field. The Woolsington airport is about 4 mi. to the northwest. Gosforth house, built by James Paine in 1755–64, was restored in 1921 after being burned by suffragettes in 1914. It lies behind the Newcastle race course. (C. S. PE.)

GOSHAWK, literally goosehawk (Accipiter gentilis), one of the largest short-winged hawks, which has long been used in falconry. The genus Accipiter may be distinguished from Falco (the falcons) by the smooth edges of the beak, the short wings, and the long legs and toes. The sexes differ greatly in size, the male being about 20 in. long and the female up to 26 in. long. The goshawk feeds on small mammals, especially squirrels, and birds of all kinds, including game birds and

KARL H. MASLOWSKI
GOSHAWK (ACCIPITER GENTILIS), TRAINED FOR FALCONRY, TIED TO PERCH

domestic pigeons and poultry. In its many geographic races it ranges, usually in coniferous woodlands, across central and northern parts of Europe and Asia, south to Corsica, Sardinia, Albania and Iran. The races common in North America are the eastern goshawk (*A. g. atricapillus*), from northwestern Alaska to Michigan and Maine, south in the mountains to Pennsylvania, and the western goshawk (*A. g. striatulus*), from Alaska to California and New Mexico. *See also* FALCONRY; HAWK.

GOSHEN, an Old Testament place name of unknown meaning.

1. The region in Egypt in which Jacob and his sons were settled as shepherds (Gen. xlv, 10; xlvi, 1, etc.), praised as "the best of the land" (Gen. xlvii, 6), called also, anachronistically, "the land of Ramses" (Gen. xlvii, 11). It was spared by the plagues (ex. viii, 22, in Hebrew text verse 18; ix, 26). Apparently Goshen was situated on the eastern edge of the Nile delta, close to the desert, but, since no certain mention of Goshen occurs in Egyptian documents, the exact location is disputed, as is its extent (Judith 1, 9, 10 being hyperbolic).

2. One of the districts of southern Palestine conquered by Joshua (Josh. x, 41; xi, 16), probably so called after its main town Goshen (Gosom in the Septuagint), not yet identified, but according to its position in the list of Josh. xv, 51 to be found southwest of Hebron.
(L. H. Gr.)

GOSLAR, a town of Germany in the *Land* (state) of Lower Saxony, which after partition of the nation following World War II was included in the Federal Republic of Germany, lies on the Gose river at the northern foot of the wooded Harz mountains, 80 km. (49.7 mi.) S.E. of Hanover by road. Pop. (1961) 41,374.

Founded in 922 and with archives dating from 937, Goslar achieved importance under the emperor Otto I (912–973), when silver ore was discovered in the Rammelsberg. Parts of the old town walls remain and the 16th-century towers, particularly the Breites Tor (Broad Gate), Zwinger and Achtermann. There are interesting stone and half-timbered buildings of the 13th to the 16th centuries and, on the outskirts, new building estates. By the market place stands the town hall, originally a 12th-century building but rebuilt later and containing a homage chamber with unique decorations. The imperial palace was built about 1040 by the emperor Henry III whose tomb is in the St. Ulrich chapel; it was completely restored in the late 19th century. All that is left of the cathedral (consecrated 1050; demolished 1819) is a porch. The Neuwerkkirche (1186), the church of the Neuwerk monastery, is pure Romanesque; other monastery and parish churches are St. James's (12th century, rebuilt in the 15th) the Romano-Gothic Market church that contains more than 100 incunabula in its library, and the 12th-century Frankenberg church. There are guild-halls belonging to the bakers' and the cloth merchants' guilds, the latter (1494) is now the Kaiserworth hotel. The museum contains works of art from the former cathedral, the metal 11th-century "Crodo" altar being especially valuable.

Besides silver mining there are chemical and optical industries and lead works; office furniture and men's clothing are made.

In the 11th and 12th centuries there were frequent meetings of the *Reichstag* in Goslar and in the mid-13th century it became a member of the Hanseatic league. In 1320 the municipal law was codified and was later adopted by many other towns. In 1290 Goslar obtained an imperial provostship and thereby gained the freedom of the empire which it maintained until 1802 when it became Prussian. In 1807 it went to the kingdom of Westphalia, in 1814 to Prussia, in 1815 to the kingdom of Hanover and in 1866 it passed with this kingdom back to Prussia. In 1936 Hitler made it the headquarters of the Nazis' agricultural organization. It was undamaged in World War II and so received many refugees from other towns.
(K. G. Br.)

GOSLICKI, WAWRZYNIEC (1530–1607), Polish Roman Catholic bishop, diplomat and political writer, best known as author of *De optimo senatore*, published under his Latin name of Laurentius Grimalius (from Grzymala, the specific name of his family's coat of arms) Goslicius, was born in 1530 of country gentry near Plock. He was educated in Cracow (from 1556), Padua (from 1567), Bologna and Rome. In 1569 he joined the royal chancery and served two Polish kings, Sigismund II Augustus and Stephen Bathory. He was also successively appointed bishop of Kamieniec Podolski (1586), Chelm (1590), Przemysl (1591) and Poznan (1601). He was the only Roman Catholic bishop who in 1587 signed the compact of Warsaw granting equal rights to all citizens of Poland in matters of religion. He died on Oct. 31, 1607.

In 1568 Goslicki published in Venice his principal work, *De optimo senatore*, in which he revealed himself an essentially European political thinker and also a precursor of Catholic liberalism. On the basis of the Polish constitution he expounded a political theory of general interest. Opposing both absolute monarchy and popular supremacy he recommended that the senate should stand between the sovereign and the people, controlling the former and representing the latter. Goslicki was the earliest political theorist to advocate the right of revolt against tyranny. *De optimo senatore,* appeared in 1598 under the title *The Councellor Exactly Portraited;* although it was adapted to suit Elizabethan England, it was immediately banned, as was the second, shortened, edition, *A Commonwealth of Good Counsaile* (1607). Finally, in 1733, there appeared a more correct translation by William Oldisworth under the title *The Accomplished Senator.* There are reasons to believe that Polonius in Shakespeare's *Hamlet* expresses views based on those in *De optimo senatore.*

BIBLIOGRAPHY.—T. Filipowicz, "The Accomplished Senator," *Proceedings of the American Society of International Law* (April 1932); W. J. Stankiewicz, *The Accomplished Senator of Laurentius Goslicius* (1946); J. A. Teslar, "Shakespeare's Worthy Counsellor," *Sacrum Polonie Millenium,* vii (1960).
(K. Sм.)

GOSNOLD, BARTHOLOMEW (fl. 1572–1607), English navigator and explorer of North America. In 1602 he sailed the "Concord" from Falmouth to the Azores, then westward to what is now the state of Maine, thus establishing the shorter northern route over the customary one by way of the Canary Islands. He explored the coast southward, naming Cape Cod and Elizabeth Island (now Cuttyhunk). While on Cuttyhunk he sowed crops that sprang up nine inches in two weeks. He sailed home with furs and with so much sassafras (a supposed remedy for syphilis) that it depressed the market. His enthusiasm for America helped bring about the granting of royal charters for the London and Plymouth companies in 1606. The same year he sailed as commander of the first "Godspeed" (40 tons), one of the three vessels carrying the first permanent settlers to Virginia. He was also one of seven councilors appointed to govern the new colony. He supported John Smith in his efforts to make the unruly colonists orderly and industrious. He opposed settling at Jamestown because it was swampy and was among the many who died there from malaria (swamp fever), Aug. 22, 1607.

See John Smith's *The General Historie of Virginia* (Arber's edition, 1884 or 1910) which includes John Brereton's narrative of the 1602 voyage as well as Smith's account of Gosnold in Virginia; Bradford Smith, *Captain John Smith* (1953).
(B. Sм.)

GOSPELS, derived from the Anglo-Saxon *godspell,* "good tidings," which translates the Latin *evangelium* (from Greek *euaggelion*). It is commonly assumed that the term gospel denotes primarily a written account of Jesus' life. In fact, however, as the German poet-philosopher Johann Gottfried Herder remarked, Christianity did not start with the writing of gospels but with preaching, and Peter's first sermon at Pentecost was already the complete Christian gospel. Indeed, the word was used by the early Christian church in a quite distinct sense long before any written account of Jesus' life existed.

Earliest Christian Use of the Word.—It is quite certain that the term "evangel" (as well as the verb "to evangelize") was first employed in the Greek-speaking church rather than by Jesus and the Aramaic-speaking Christians of Palestine. In the Greek world, this term was widely used for "news" or "message" of any kind—profane or sacred, political or private. A pre-Christian occurrence of the word in connection with the emperor cult is found in the Priene inscription in praise of Augustus (9 B.C.) : "The birthday of the God was the beginning of the evangels due to him." In the Greek version of the Old Testament, the Septuagint, the noun is used three times, twice meaning "reward for good news." The verb occurs more frequently, but neither it nor its Hebrew equivalent is used in a technical sense. Only in a few passages (mainly from Deutero-Isaiah) does the word seem to have a special religious meaning, but the influence of these on the early Christian use of the word cannot be proved. Thus it seems to have been a profane word adopted by the Christians to denote the act of proclaiming the message as well as the message itself.

No emphasis can be placed on the etymological meaning "good" news. In certain New Testament passages (Luke iii, 18; Acts xiv, 15; Rev. x, 7 and xiv, 6) it does not mean good news at all but simply news, and it is elsewhere used as synonymous with other words denoting preaching, proclamation and word. It was used for the oral preaching of the early Christian missionaries (not for written documents), and this meaning continued in use through the 2nd century A.D. Already in the Pauline Epistles (excluding the Pastorals), the term gospel is used frequently (56 times), often in a technical Christian sense, without reference to any content. Whether or not this is an originally Pauline contribution (the noun and verb never occur in this sense in the Johannine literature, James, Jude or II Peter), it is certainly an inner Christian development, without any pagan or Jewish antecedents. The consciousness that there was only *one saving message, the gospel,* is uniquely Christian.

Gospel as a Name for Writings.—Paul also provides the first indication of how the term gospel developed into the designation for a written document. I Cor. xv, 1 ff. and Rom. i, 1 ff. speak of the gospel as an orally transmitted formula which describes the Christ-event, Jesus' death and resurrection. A more developed creedal formula is called gospel by Ignatius of Antioch (early 2nd century A.D.). Since our Gospels basically are expanded creedal formulations, gradually extended backward to include the narratives of Jesus' life, it is easy to see why such written accounts later were called Gospels. In the Gospel of Mark, however—apparently the first of these written accounts—the "gospel" is not yet identified with the written book but denotes the history of that revelation which is identical with Jesus' life, death and resurrection. Nevertheless, Mark's work is the potential beginning of a new use of the term, by which not only the oral preaching of the Christ-event, but also its written account could be called gospel. Such use was transferred to other writings, Matthew and Luke, which include the "remembered words of the Lord," as originally distinct from the oral gospel (cf. I Clem. xiii, 1-2; Acts xx, 35), within the Marcan framework. The earliest witness to this new use of the term is the heretic Marcion (early 2nd century A.D.), who described Luke's Gospel as "the Gospel" in contradistinction to "the Apostolicon" (a collection of Pauline epistles). A few years later Justin Martyr speaks of the "Memoirs of the Apostles" —a term derived from the "remembrance of the words of the Lord"—and in a few instances adds "which are called gospels." This is the first witness to the use of the plural. Since then the word gospel has come to be used for a great number of other unrelated accounts of Jesus' life and collections of his words, such as John's Gospel and numerous noncanonical writings.

The present article deals only with the four Gospels received by the church in general, and with the history of the tradition which led to their composition. For further information see BIBLE: *Canon of the New Testament;* MATTHEW, GOSPEL ACCORDING TO SAINT; MARK, GOSPEL ACCORDING TO SAINT; LUKE, GOSPEL ACCORDING TO SAINT; and JOHN, GOSPEL ACCORDING TO AND EPISTLES OF SAINT.

Formation of the Gospel Tradition.—Between Jesus' crucifixion and the first composition of a written gospel at least one generation elapsed. Older criticism tried to bridge this gap either by reference to the oral testimony of disciples and eyewitnesses, who were said to have written at least one or two of the Gospels (Matthew and John); or by the hypothetical reconstruction of primitive written sources of the canonical Gospels. Later New Testament criticism has attempted to discover the tradition behind the written accounts. So-called form criticism (M. Dibelius, R. Bultmann, V. Taylor, F. C. Grant and others) has opened up the possibility of reconstructing the history of the material incorporated in the Gospels. This is a history of transmitted oral traditions, which were primarily small, independent units (such as single stories or short sayings), and not of extended accounts, oral or written. By isolating these small units or forms, determining their original "life situation," evaluating the motives of alterations and recognizing editorial techniques used when such tradition became written gospel, it is possible to describe the preliterary history of the gospel formation.

The earliest church conceived of Jesus' words and works not as biography or objective history. From the very beginning the "life situation" of all the tradition about Jesus was the preaching and teaching of the church, in the course of which the transmitted stories and sayings served as a guide for the new life of the Christian people. The need of instructing new believers and of defending the faith, the expression of church life in worship and liturgy and the development of theology as a matter concerned with the saving event in the man Jesus of Nazareth were moving factors in the formation of the tradition. In this sense it was the church that created the gospel tradition.

The traditional material incorporated in the Gospels is basically of two kinds, each with numerous subclassifications: (1) narratives, including stories about the person of Jesus (birth stories, baptism, passion and resurrection), miracle stories (healings and wonders) and tales (such as the Emmaus road incident); and (2) sayings—prophetic and apocalyptic, proverbial, legal, ecclesiastical, Christological and parable. Often also single sayings were transmitted as the central features of little anecdotes, which Dibelius calls paradigms. With regard to form, almost all the above categories have parallels in Hellenistic oral folklore and late Jewish oral traditions. Thus, stories of Greek heroes and Hellenistic wondermen provided a pattern for the legends about Jesus, and the form of the sayings is clearly patterned after Old Testament prophecy, Jewish apocalyptic and wisdom speculation and rabbinic law. A peculiarly Christian "form" is found only in the narratives centred around the passion of Jesus and in the sayings about the theological significance of Jesus as "the one who has come." Just as this unique form is integral to the core of the gospel proclamation, so the literary form "gospel" is unique to Christianity, without precedent or parallel. To compare the Gospels with the Greek writing of history or biography would precisely miss their uniqueness, which is rooted in the fact that here the church preached the coming of the divine in a particular historical person—Jesus Christ.

The "Synoptic Problem."—The first three Gospels, Matthew, Mark and Luke, are known as Synoptic Gospels because they have such an agreement in structure, content and wording that they can easily be arranged in parallel columns so as to provide a synoptic view of their content (from Gr. *synopsis; syn,* "along with," *opsis,* "view"). By such an arrangement, the question of the kind of literary relationship that exists among these three Gospels is necessarily forced upon the observer. This question, called the Synoptic problem, has been elaborately studied in modern times.

The traditional solution explains the striking similarities on the basis of the priority of Matthew or of a supposed primitive Matthew in a Semitic language; this is sometimes identified with the so-called Gospel According to the Hebrews (see APOCRYPHA, NEW TESTAMENT). Mark is consequently seen as dependent on Matthew, Luke on both Matthew and Mark (and John on all three Synoptic Gospels).

Theologians of the rationalistic period were the first to challenge this long-accepted hypothesis: (1) J. J. Griesbach (in 1774—75) held that Mark used not only Matthew but also Luke (hypothesis of usage). (2) G. E. Lessing (in 1776 and 1778) and J. G. Eichhorn (in 1794) argued that all three Synoptics utilize a lost Aramaic gospel (primitive Gospel hypothesis). (3) J. G. Herder (in 1796–97) and J. C. L. Gieseler (in 1818) thought this primitive Gospel was transmitted orally (tradition hypothesis). (4) F. Schleiermacher (in 1832) assumed the existence of small written collections or fragments out of which the Evangelists composed their writings (fragments hypothesis).

All these attempted explanations have survived in one form or another, and though all of them certainly contain some truth, most Protestant and some Roman Catholic scholars hold that only one hypothesis explains the Synoptic problem satisfactorily: the so-called two-source hypothesis. The evidence given by K. Lachmann (in 1835), that Mark as the earliest Gospel must have been the source for both Matthew and Luke, was supplemented by the work of H. J. Holtzmann (1863), B. H. Streeter (1925) and many others, the two-source hypothesis has taken the following form, in which it is widely accepted among Protestant scholars:

1. Matthew and Luke used the Gospel of Mark, from which they drew most of their narrative material as well as the basic outline of the life of Jesus.
2. Matthew and Luke used a second source (Q), no longer extant, which contained for the most part only sayings.
3. Matthew and Luke each had one or more other sources for the material peculiar to their respective Gospels.

Mark.—The hypothesis may be stated as follows: Mark, either in its present form or in a slightly different earlier Greek form, was the first written Gospel and was a source for Matthew and Luke.

Of the 661 verses contained in the authentic text of Mark, more than 600 are reproduced or represented in Matthew and about 350 in Luke. Only 31 verses in Mark are wholly unrepresented in either Matthew or Luke. Furthermore, in the material common to all three Gospels, there is very seldom verbatim agreement of Matthew and Luke against Mark, although such agreement is common between Mark and Matthew or Mark and Luke or all three. Where Matthew and Luke agree against Mark, several explanations are possible: (1) secondary harmonization of the texts of Matthew and Luke; (2) Matthew and Luke in particular instances preferred a parallel tradition rather than Mark's wording; (3) possibly the present Mark is slightly different from the recension used by Matthew and Luke.

The following sections in Mark are represented in both Matthew and Luke according to the Marcan sequence, although Matthew and Luke often insert other material into this framework: Mark i, 1–15, 39; ii, 1–iii, 12; iv, 1–12; vi, 14–16, 30–44; viii, 29–ix, 8, 14–37; x, 13–30, 32–34, 46–52; xi, 1–11, 15–19, 27–33; xii, 1–27, 35–40; xiii, 1–20, 24–32; xiv–xv (almost completely). Many Marcan passages not contained in this list are entirely missing in Luke but are still to be found in Matthew, often in the Marcan order; thus, Matt. xiv, 1–xxviii, 10 completely follows Mark's order (Mark vi, 14–xvi, 8) throughout without any changes of position. On the other hand, the first part of Mark (i, 40–iii, 12 and iv, 1–v, 23) is almost entirely taken over in Luke (v, 12–vi, 19 and viii, 4–56), whereas Matthew often deviates here. These findings cannot be explained except on the supposition that the Greek Gospel of Mark was the direct source for Matthew and Luke.

It must be emphasized that since Matthew and Luke used the Greek Mark, they cannot be considered as translations from Aramaic prototypes, though, of course, non-Marcan materials in Matthew and Luke may well have a more direct Semitic background.

Q.—The postulation of a second common source of Matthew and Luke, the "Saying-Source," conventionally designated Q (from German *Quelle*, "source"), constitutes a more complicated problem. The sayings found in both Matthew and Luke but absent from Mark are the chief reason for this postulation. Many of these saying parallels show a great verbatim agreement; moreover, they are sometimes given in the same sequence, though usually this is not true on a large scale. Furthermore, a number of sayings are "doublets"; i.e., they are given twice in Matthew or Luke or both, once in a setting from the Marcan context and a second time according to Q. Examples of such doublets are: (1) Matt. xii, 12 (=Luke vi, 18) taken from Mark iv, 25; the same saying in Matt. xxv, 29 (=Luke xix, 26) without Marcan parallel (i.e., from Q). (2) Matt. xvi, 24 ff. (=Luke ix, 23 ff.) taken over within the Marcan context from Mark viii, 34 ff.; the same sayings in Matt. x, 38 ff. (=Luke xiv, 27; xvii, 33) from Q. These and other phenomena seem to justify the hypothesis that Q was one written document available to Matthew and Luke alike.

But other observations make such a conclusion less certain: within the Q material, Matthew and Luke show less agreement than they do in their reproduction of Mark. Especially the sequence and order of the Q material lacks consistency. For this reason attempts to reconstruct Q, though numerous, have remained entirely speculative, at least as far as the original order of sayings in Q is concerned. In addition, the extent of the Q-recension used by Matthew seems to have been different from that used by Luke. Thus, Q certainly was not such a clearly defined written document as was Mark. Nevertheless, some statements about Q can be made with relative confidence: (1) it was available to Matthew and Luke as a written source; (2) the language was certainly Greek, although most of the Q material contains distinct "translation Greek" with a strong Semitic flavour. Often such linguistic peculiarities are found in the Q material of both Matthew and Luke in parallel passages, thus indicating that these Q traditions must go back to one and the same translation of an Aramaic original, which might have already existed in a written form.

Attempts have been made to refer to this Aramaic Q a statement about Matthew made by Papias and quoted in Eusebius: "Matthew compiled the sayings in the Hebrew language, and every man translated them as he was able." Papias himself meant to speak of the Gospel of Matthew, but his statement in no way fits our Matthew, which is not a collection of sayings and which never existed in an original Aramaic form. Possibly Papias mistook a tradition about an Aramaic Q for a statement about Matthew. But even if Papias thus witnesses to a written Aramaic Q, it could not have contained all the present Q material. In many instances Matthew and Luke do contain parallel sayings that originated from different translations of the same Aramaic saying; on the other hand, a few Q sayings are Greek formulations without Semitic background.

Thus it may be concluded that Q represents the still flexible but at least partly written sayings tradition of the Greek-speaking church, which rested largely on similar Palestinian collections in Aramaic. Though Q reflects certain theological tendencies, mainly those of the first decades of the church in Palestine, it could not be called the work of an "author," and thus is not literature and certainly not a Gospel. Q may have taken written form before the middle of the 1st century and was translated into Greek probably before A.D. 70. The early Greek church, of course, as well as Paul himself, knew sayings of the Lord in the Greek language. But all attempts to prove a direct use of the Saying-Source Q in any other apostolic, postapostolic or 2nd-century literature have failed. After Matthew and Luke used it, Q apparently proved to be no longer of any value and quickly disappeared.

Other Sources.—The authors of Matthew and Luke also clearly depend upon other sources for most of the material peculiar to each of them. Most probably this is the case with the material in the great Lucan digression, or "travel narrative" (Luke ix, 51–xviii, 14), for which a special written source (containing among other traditions the most valuable "great parables") apparently was available to Luke. The infancy stories of Luke, and of Matthew as well, also go back to special traditions, whether written or oral. Finally, the resurrection narrative in Luke is not from Mark but has a tradition of its own. Scholars have tried to reconstruct a "proto-Lucan Gospel," but none of the suggestions is conclusive, although the existence of special literary sources available to Luke cannot be doubted. The character of the material peculiar to Matthew forbids even more the reconstruction of a special proto-Matthew. This material is largely nonliterary, having its origin and life situation mainly in the liturgy and the regulations of the church's life. All attempts to exploit the peculiarities of Matthew and Luke to establish a new hypothesis about the origin of and relationship among the Gospels have not shaken the two-source hypothesis but rather have served to supplement and confirm it.

The Fourth Gospel.—The Gospel According to St. John stands apart. Developments in higher criticism do not even favour dependence of John upon the Synoptic Gospels. Nevertheless, this Gospel is in some ways related to the Synoptic tradition. Its account of Jesus' passion and resurrection is parallel to and evidently more primitive than the source used by Mark. It employs a written narrative containing signs and miracles of Jesus, which again is very close to the tradition recorded in Mark but at the same time shows some rather primitive features. The Johannine tradition about the Baptist also goes back to the same root as the parallel Synoptic accounts and has preserved much valuable information now lost in the Synoptics. On the other hand, John's Gospel always presents the material with its own peculiar interpretation, adding discourses from traditions that have no parallels in the Synoptic Gospels, a feature that gives the Fourth Gospel an entirely different character. In appearance it is more theological, sometimes called more spiritual, yet John's Gospel was written with even more emphasis upon the historicity of the revelation than were the Synoptic Gospels. Thus John presents a mature interpretation of the gospel of revelation in the historic person Jesus of Nazareth, as seen consciously from the distance of a third-generation Christianity in the last decades of the 1st century.

Character of the Gospels.—The oral gospel was not preached in order to give historical or even biographical information; neither did the Gospel literature, as the final fruit of early-Christian preaching, come into existence in the interests of history in the modern scientific (objective) sense of that word. The tradition behind the Gospels was sustained at every stage for the sake of preaching and edification, with apologetic and theological motivation. The Gospels and the tradition behind them had a religious purpose. Nonetheless, there is some material of historical value in them. Not only do they attest the fact that Jesus was truly a historic person, but also they include several historical "blocks" that are not entirely dissolved by theological interpretation—the passion narrative, for example, and many of the sayings and parables (especially those that show Jesus' unique eschatological consciousness). Thus the venture of writing a "life of Jesus" remains a legitimate task for the historian.

But for understanding of the character of the Gospels it is important to recognize that even such historical data were handed down only as they served theological purposes and not for their own sake. This does not suggest that the essence of the Gospels is spiritual information or "eternal truth" as opposed to "history." Rather it is the announcement that revelation has come as the Jesus of history. The Gospels present this historical revelation in its true meaning; i.e., history in its real, theological dimension. History and theology, historical Jesus and risen Lord, are thus inseparably bound together in one story. See Jesus Christ; see also references under "Gospels" in the Index.

Bibliography.—Text: K. Aland, Synopsis Quattuor Evangeliorum (1964); Huck and Lietzmann, Synopse der drei ersten Evangelien, 10th ed. (1950), Eng. trans, Gospel Parallels (1949); E. D. Burton and E. J. Goodspeed, A Harmony of the Synoptic Gospels (Greek, 1920; English, 1917).

General: B. W. Bacon, The Beginnings of the Gospel Story (1909); F. W. Beare, The Earliest Records of Jesus (1962); M. Black, An Aramaic Approach to the Gospels and Acts, 2nd ed. (1954); F. C. Burkitt, The Gospel History and Its Transmission, 3rd ed. (1911); H. Guy, A Critical Introduction to the Gospels (1955); P. B. W. Stather Hunt, Primitive Gospel Sources (1951); X. Léon-Dufour, Concordance of the Synoptic Gospels (1956); R. H. Lightfoot, Locality and Doctrine in the Gospels (1938); C. G. Montefiore, The Synoptic Gospels, 2nd ed. (1927); E. F. Scott, The Purpose of the Gospels (1949), The Validity of the Gospel Record (1938); V. H. Stanton, The Gospels as Historical Documents (1903–09); D. E. Nineham (ed.), Studies in the Gospels, essays in memory of R. H. Lightfoot (1955); R. O. P. Taylor, The Groundwork of the Gospels (1946); C. C. Torrey, The Four Gospels, 2nd ed. (1947); A. Loisy, Les Evangiles Synoptiques (1907); K. L. Schmidt, Kanonische und apokryphe Evangelien und Apostelgeschichten (1944); J. Wellhausen, Einleitung in die drei ersten Evangelien, 2nd ed. (1911).

Synoptic Problem: W. E. Bundy, Jesus and the First Three Gospels (1955); W. R. Farmer, The Synoptic Problem (1964); F. C. Grant, The Gospels, Their Origin and Their Growth, 2nd ed. (1957); J. C. Hawkins, Horae Synopticae, 2nd ed. (1909); W. L. Knox, The Sources of the Synoptic Gospels (1933, 1957); W. Sanday (ed.), Oxford Studies in the Synoptic Problem (1911); P. Parker, The Gospel Before Mark (1953); B. H. Streeter, The Four Gospels: a Study of Origins, 8th ed. (1953); E. Hirsch, Frühgeschichte des Evangeliums, 2nd ed. (1951); H. J. Holtzmann, Die Synoptischen Evangelien (1863); Synoptische Studien, A. Wikenhauser zum 70. Geburtstag dargebracht (1953).

Form Criticism: M. Dibelius, From Tradition to Gospel (1934); B. S. Easton, The Gospel Before the Gospels (1928); F. C. Grant, The Earliest Gospel (1943); R. H. Lightfoot, History and Interpretation in the Gospels (1934); E. B. Redlich, Form Criticism, Its Value and Limitations, 2nd ed. (1948); H. Riesenfeld, The Gospel Tradition and Its Beginnings (1957); V. Taylor, The Formation of the Gospel Tradition (1953); R. Bultmann, Die Erforschung der synoptischen Evangelien, 2nd ed. (1930), Die Geschichte der synoptischen Tradition, 3rd ed. (1958); K. Grobel, Formgeschichte und synoptische Quellenanalyse (1937); K. L. Schmidt, Der Rahmen der Geschichte Jesu (1919). (H. H. Ko.)

GOSPORT, a municipal borough (1922) in the Gosport and Fareham parliamentary division of Hampshire, Eng., on a peninsula between the west side of Portsmouth Harbour and the Solent, 18 mi. SE of Southampton. Pop. (1971 prelim.) 75,947. Gosport, originally part of the manor of Alverstoke held by the bishops of Winchester, prospered during the 16th and 17th centuries because of the rising importance of the Royal Navy. Primarily a victualing station, it flourished during the Napoleonic Wars. Later it shared in the Navy's development of Portsmouth with which it is connected by steam and floating bridge ferries. It is now the site of many important naval establishments. Gosport was one of the main embarkation areas for the Allied invasion of France in 1944 and suffered considerable war damage. Reconstruction projects were undertaken. Parts of the old town north and south of the High Street were cleared and replaced with industrial and residential developments. Holy Trinity Church contains the organ, originally belonging to the duke of Chandos, on which Handel is said to have played. Industries include shipbuilding and sailmaking, the making of wallpaper and paint, radio and radar, tools, air components, pens, clothing, and light engineering.

GOSSAERT, JAN: see Mabuse, Jan.

GOSSE, SIR EDMUND (1849–1928), English man of letters, eminent for his valuable work in bringing foreign literature home to English readers, was born in London, Sept. 21, 1849, son of the religious zoologist P. H. Gosse. His early life, recounted in the best and most enduring of his many books, Father and Son (1907), followed a pattern common in his generation: a love-hate relationship with a puritan father, followed by escape into the exhilarating world of belles-lettres. Gosse, however, never became an aesthete or a bohemian; he kept to decorous beaten tracks: the British museum, the board of trade (where he was translator for nearly 30 years) and the house of lords (librarian, 1904–14).

Gosse was a prolific versifier, translator, literary historian, critic and journalist, and in his own time he was very influential. He had the misfortune, however, to be working just before the modern revolution in standards of scholarship and criticism, so that much of his output now appears amateurish. Moreover, most of his best books, such as his translations of Ibsen (Hedda Gabler, 1891; with W. Archer, The Master-Builder, 1893), his literary lives and editions (e.g., Thomas Gray, 1884; Donne, 1899; Sir T. Browne, 1905), his literary histories (18th Century Literature, 1889; Modern English Literature, 1897) and his critical essays (e.g., Critical Kit-Kats, 1896; French Profiles, 1905), though written with charm and gusto, have been outclassed by subsequent work in these fields. Nevertheless he deserves credit as a pioneer, particularly in the study of Scandinavian and French literature, and English literature of the 17th and 18th centuries. And his evident relish for literature, as a thing to be savoured and enjoyed, is something that modern critics too often lack. In Father and Son all Gosse's finest gifts—grace, irony, wit and tolerance—combine to form a minor classic of autobiography. Gosse was knighted in 1925 and died in London, May 16, 1928. (B. Wy.)

GOSSE, PHILIP HENRY (1810–1888), British naturalist and popularizer of zoological subjects, was born at Worcester on April 6, 1810. In 1827 he became a clerk in a seal-fishery office at Carbonear, Nfd., where he beguiled the tedium of his life by investigations into natural history. After an unsuccessful interlude of farming in Canada he traveled in the United States, taught for some time in Alabama and returned to England in 1839.

A visit to Jamaica in 1844 led to accounts of the birds of that island and to his A Naturalist's Sojourn in Jamaica (1851). For the rest of his life he devoted himself to the description of the animal life, mainly the invertebrates, of the British seas and fresh waters. The nature of the numerous successive popular or semi-popular volumes which Gosse himself illustrated is shown by specimen titles, such as A Naturalist's Rambles on the Devonshire Coast (1853); Evenings at the Microscope (1859); and A Year at the *Shore* (1865). Technical accounts of the minute rotifers (with C. T. Hudson) retain usefulness for reference.

Gosse's membership in the Plymouth Brethren involved him in the complete rejection of all ideas of evolution. Two years before the appearance of Darwin's *Origin of Species* Gosse expressed the nonevolutionary position in a unique book, *Omphalos* (1857). He was elected fellow of the Royal society in 1856. He died at St. Marychurch, Devon, on Aug. 23, 1888.

See Peter Stageman *et al.*, *Bibliography of the First Editions of Philip Henry Gosse, F.R.S.* (1955). (K.P.S.)

GÖTA CANAL is the artificial waterway (not now of value for through traffic) that crosses Sweden to connect Lake Vänern with the Baltic. It utilizes lakes for the greater part of its course, and provides inland navigation from Göteborg to Stockholm. The Göta river drains Lake Vänern and, with locks to surmount the falls at Trollhättan, is part of the navigation. The first section to be canalized (Trollhätte canal) was completed in 1800; it has six locks with a sill depth of 18 ft. and allows seagoing craft to pass from Göteborg to Karlstad and other ports on Lake Vänern. The Göta canal proper leads from Sjötorp to Viken on Lake Vättern and from Motala on the east of that lake to Mem on Slätbaken, an inlet of the Baltic, utilizing on the way the small lakes of Boren and Roxen. More than 20 locks raise it from Vänern (145 ft.) and across the water parting to Viken (292 ft.) and it descends by five locks to Roxen (109 ft.).

The navigation distance from Göteborg to Stockholm is about 360 mi. (about 50 mi. in the open Baltic). The voyage takes about 2½ days. The Göta canal has 47 mi. of artificial works and includes 58 locks. Unfortunately the canal, which was inspired by Count von Platen with the advice of Thomas Telford and opened in 1832, was built to what is now regarded as an inadequate cross section but it revived not only inland areas such as Motala but also the port of Söderköping. (A. C. OD.)

GOTAMA BUDDHA: see GAUTAMA BUDDHA.

GOTARZES (Godarz), name of two Parthian kings of Iran. GOTARZES I (reigned 91-87, perhaps even to 81/80 B.C.) appears first as "satrap of satraps" under Mithradates II in a Greek inscription at Bisitun. A name carved nearby, Gotarses Geopothros ("son of Gew"), may also represent him, though taken by E. E. Herzfeld for Gotarzes II. Subsequently Gotarzes and his queen Asibatum are known only from Babylonian tablets. Achieving royal rank in Babylonia while Mithradates still governed in Iran, he remained sole ruler at the latter's death.

GOTARZES II reigned from A.D. 44 to 51, after a prolonged struggle with Vardanes. Tacitus, as against Josephus, alleges a brief earlier reign by Gotarzes, not reliably confirmed by coins, in A.D. 39. Gotarzes had then slain his brother, Artabanus, when a second brother, Vardanes, surprised him by a breakneck two-day ride and expelled him to Hyrcania. Fear of the nobles reconciled the two for a time, then fighting was renewed and Vardanes' murder in A.D. 46 or 47 left Gotarzes unopposed. Later another rival, Meherdates, returning from exile at Rome, was defeated and captured near Karafto in Kurdistan. When Gotarzes perished in A.D. 51 by assassination or disease, another brother, Vologaeses I, was already issuing coins. Rare drachmas designate Gotarzes "titular" son of Artabanus II and bear his personal name, also found on tetradrachms dated A.D. 46-47, regnal year 3.

BIBLIOGRAPHY.—N. C. Debevoise, *Political History of Parthia* (1938); R. H. MacDowell, *Coins from Seleucia* (1935); E. T. Newell in A. U. Pope (ed.), *Survey of Persian Art*, vol. i, pp. 489 ff. (1938). (A. D. H. B.)

GÖTEBORG (GOTHENBURG), the second largest city of Sweden, its largest seaport, and capital of the *län* (county) of Göteborg och Bohus, is 240 mi. W. of Stockholm in the valley and on the heights of the Göta river estuary, the centre being 5 mi. above the river mouth in the Kattegat. Pop. (1970 prelim.) 485,785.

Göteborg was founded in 1619 by Gustavus II Adolphus (charter dated June 4, 1621), but earlier urban settlements had already existed on the site. A settlement of the same name had been founded in 1607 on the island of Hisingen, to the north, by Charles IX, but it had been destroyed by the Danes. A considerable number of the earliest inhabitants of the present town were foreigners, mainly Dutchmen, but also Englishmen, Scots, Belgians and Germans. As a result of this is still provided by the canals, built in the Dutch style, and by the planning of the city centre.

The city's prosperity was laid in the early 18th century by the founding of the Swedish East India company, and during Napoleon's continental blockade it became Europe's chief market for British goods. A second period of wealth started with the opening of the Göta canal (1832) and the setting up of a transoceanic service. The town was strongly fortified until 1807, and around the main wall a moat was dug, which still encircles the old part of the city. The forts called Skansen Lejonet ("the Lion") and Skansen Kronan ("the Crown") are other relics of the old fortifications. Part of the canal system has been filled in, and in its place are two important streets, Östra Hamngatan and Västra Hamngatan. The Gustav Adolfs Torg, the central square of the city, includes the town hall (1750), the exchange (meeting place of the city council and the town's administrative centre; 1849) and the law courts (1672, restored 1732, 1817) with an annex (an interesting example of modern Swedish architecture; 1935-37). Nearby, west of the Kristine church (1648, rebuilt 1780), stand the former office and warehouse buildings of the Swedish East India company (1750-62) and the house of its manager, Nicholas Sahlgren (1735); the company's premises house the Cultural History museum, and the house is occupied by the city finance department. In this part of the town also is the cathedral (1633, rebuilt 1815-25, restored 1956-57). Southward, Östra Hamngatan continues as Kungsportsavenyen, called "the Avenue," leading to Götaplatsen, round which stand the city theatre (1934), art gallery (1923), concert hall (1935) and municipal library (1967).

Outside the old moat and alongside it lies a continuous park area more than a mile long traversed by Nya Allén. At the junction of the Avenue with Nya Allén stands the city's opera house, Stora Teatern (1859). The city has universities, graduate schools (economics and business administration, social work and public administration) and a navigation school. Sahlgrens hospital (1782), with more than 2,300 beds, is the largest in Sweden. Museums include the Maritime museum and aquarium, the Natural History museum and the Röhss Museum of Art and Crafts. Among the larger parks are Slottsskogen, the botanical gardens and Trädgårdsföreningen (the Garden society).

Göteborg is Sweden's chief seaport, and approximately 12,000,000 tons of goods are discharged and loaded there each year. It has been a free port since 1921 and is used by more than 70 shipping lines. The harbour is rarely obstructed by ice. Fish catches are landed there and sent by rail to the rest of the continent. Göteborg is connected to the rest of Sweden by the Göta canal and by railway lines. Both internal and external air services use Torslanda airport, 7 mi. W. of the city. Principal exports are mineral oils, fruit and iron. Shipbuilding yards on Hisingen Island are among the largest in the world. There are also refineries, foodprocessing plants and factories that manufacture ball bearings, automobiles and textiles. (Lo. S.)

GÖTEBORG OCH BOHUS, a *län* (county), occupying the most westerly area of Sweden. It comprises the greatly indented coastal zone on the Skagerrak and Kattegat west of the Göta river but extends south and east to include Göteborg city. Area 1,986 sq.mi. Pop. (1960) 624,762. The district is more Norwegian than Swedish in character and has granite outcrops of value for quarrying, but it has poor soils and vegetation only suitable for sheep grazing. The indented coast, protected by numerous islands, has many fishing villages and at Lysekil boatbuilding and fish canning are carried on. The principal towns are Göteborg, Uddevalla and Marstrand. The tourist industry is important. (A. C. O.)

GOTHA, a town of Germany which after partition of the nation following World War II became a regional capital in the *Bezirk* (district) of Erfurt, German Democratic Republic. Pop. (1971 prelim.) 57,248. The town is 19 mi. (31 km.) W. of Erfurt on the northern edge of the Thuringian forest. A rail junction, it has food industries, machinery and vehicle building enterprises, as wel as the nationally owned Hermann Haack (formerly Justus Perthes), geographical-cartographical publishers. Justus Perthes also published the *Almanach de Gotha.* Electrical equipment, precision instruments, textiles, chemicals and musical instruments also are manufactured there.

The old inner town is encircled by suburbs and is dominated by the Friedenstein castle (17th century) on the Schlossberg. In the castle are extensive collections, including a picture gallery, a cabinet of engravings, a collection of antiquities and a section on local folk-lore and geography. Gotha's historical buildings include the 12th-century Margarethen-Kirche, the 11th-century town hall and a *Gymnasium* founded in the 16th century. In 1875 the congress that united the Eisenachers and the Lassalleans into the Socialist Labour Party of Germany was held in the town, adopting the Gotha program, sharply criticized by Karl Marx.

The chronicles mention Gotha for the first time in the 10th century; in old documents it is also called Gotegewe and later Gotaha. In 930 the settlement was fortified and surrounded with ramparts on orders of its then lord, the abbot of the Hersfeld cloister, about 50 mi. to the west. Gotha received its municipal charter in 1189. In 1247 it came under the control of the landgraves of Thuringia, and when that ruling line died out it became part of the electorate of Saxony. From 1640 to 1825 Gotha was the residence of the dukes of Saxony-Gotha and from 1826 to 1918 it was, along with Coburg, the residence of the dukes of Saxe-Coburg-Gotha.

GOTHENBURG, Sweden: *see* GÖTEBORG.

GOTHIC ART AND ARCHITECTURE. Gothic art and architecture are the visual expression of the energetic new civilization that first emerged in northwest Europe early in the 12th century and subsequently extended to all Europe, with local colourings. The intellectual values of this civilization and the disposition of its material wealth promoted the visual arts to an unusual degree. This article is divided into the following sections to cover the subject:

I. INTRODUCTION

The artists who invented and practised the style now called Gothic would not have understood the use of such a term. "Gothic" was first applied to the style, derogatorily, by Italian Renaissance writers. The interest of the early humanists in classical culture inspired Italian artists to employ classical forms. In 1419 Filippo Brunelleschi introduced the classical orders in Florence. According to his biographer, Antonio Manetti, Brunelleschi revived the good architecture of the Romans, which the Vandals, Goths, Lombards, and Huns had destroyed and replaced with their own inferior architecture. Filarete held that the barbarians in general, and the French and Germans in particular, were responsible for the bad architecture that thereafter was usually called *maniera tedesca* ("German style"). The so-called Pseudo-Raphael, in 1510, attributed the discovery of the pointed arch to the Germans, who, having no hatchets, bent together the branches of trees to form a roof. Later Giorgio Vasari narrowed down the list of culprits to the Goths who had sacked Rome in 410. The architecture then termed Gothic spanned the period from 410 to 1419 and its characteristic member was said to be the pointed arch. Christopher Wren (1632–1723), knowing that Muslims used pointed arches, evolved the theory that Gothic was of Saracenic origin.

In the 18th century the Byzantine and Carolingian styles were distinguished and historians found it useful to divide the long period that remained. François Blondel the Younger in 1771 divided architecture into two periods: *architecture gothique ancienne,* from the 6th to the 11th centuries; and *architecture gothique moderne* up to Francis I (1515). The term Romanesque was first applied to 11th- and 12th-century architecture by W. Gunn and C. de Gerville in 1819, and thereafter the word Gothic was confined to its present meaning. The style was praised, with certain reservations, by J. G. Soufflot in 1743 and M. A. Laugier in 1755 and 1765 in France. Goethe praised it unreservedly in his dithyramb on the facade of Strasbourg Cathedral (1773) and enthusiastic comments, somewhat better substantiated, by Romanticists followed. The 19th century saw the beginning of the serious study of the topography and history of the style. Scholars were aware that Gothic had nothing to do with the Goths. Some of them introduced new terms, *e.g., stile ogival, Germanischer Stil,* but the abusive name Gothic had become a term of honour. Ultimately it came to signify a neutral concept.

II. GOTHIC ARCHITECTURE

1. The Emergence of the Style.—So far as Gothic architecture is concerned, the desire to build splendid churches went hand in hand with technical invention. But the peculiar character of Gothic architecture was a necessity of the age, and there is a foreshadowing of the great unified architectural interiors of the Gothic cathedrals in non-architectural work, such as the paintings in the nave of Saint-Savin near Poitiers, where the painter has endowed the Romanesque barrel vault with a central band running from west to east like the Gothic ridge rib of later centuries and where narrative sequences compel one to look at the vault in a dynamic new way. Furthermore the Romanesque cathedral of Autun, with its remarkable display of historiated capitals illuminating the interior by means of vividly conceived histories of saints and patriarchs, also begins to move into the liberal world of Gothic ideas just as much as does Durham Cathedral with its precocious use of the pointed arch and rib vaults.

Proto-Gothic and Gothic architects favoured the pointed arch and the rib vault for aesthetic and technical reasons. Technically the ribs represented the final stage in the evolution of scaffolding. Originally scaffolds consisted of wooden barrel vaults crossing one another. In oblong bays, which were usually preferred, the resulting groins were doubly curved three-dimensional lines, in many cases distorted by the great weight of the stones supported by the scaffold. After various experiments, the method was radically changed. First, wooden arches were constructed for the diagonal groins, then from these arches the boards were laid for the severies (*i.e.,* the compartments of the vault). These ensured precise lines for the groins. To avoid distortions the wooden diagonal arches were replaced by arches of stone, called *ogives* by the 13th-century architect Villard de Honnecourt. While the attempt to solve certain problems of geometric construction, technique, and statics was important in the development of the rib, its real function was aesthetic, to furnish precise lines. The diagonal rib was not a continuation of a structural member of the wall; since these members were frontal their continuations could only be frontal transverse arches. Diagonal ribs, on the contrary, required diagonal supporting shafts. The statement that Gothic developed from the top down is valid, but it must be emphasized that the structural character of the ribs conformed to Norman stylistic use of strong articulation.

The rib was an aesthetic improvement suited to the structural character of a Romanesque building such as Durham Cathedral, where ribs were connected with groin vaults in the choir in 1093, the earliest examples in Europe. The diagonality of the rib, however, opposed the frontality of the capitals and plinths of the piers and still more it disturbed the spatial character of the architecture. All compartments of Romanesque churches were built as separate units combined according to the principle of addition. The space of a Romanesque groin vault looks like a single unit resting horizontally upon the space below. The rib, however, divides the space of the vault into interdependent parts. Each arch involves the imagination of the plane in which it lies. As a result the vault and the space beneath it become a unit divided by the planes of the diagonal ribs. This led the architects to turn the shafts in a diagonal direction. The chief reason for the transformation from the Romanesque into a new style was the principle of division and fusion of the bays, which governed the building in all its aspects. Thus, a building resulted which seemed to be a whole differentiated into parts like an organism, while in Romanesque buildings one form was added to another, producing a whole by addition, as in the formation of crystals. The process of transformation continued through more than four centuries. (See ARCH AND VAULT: *Gothic Principles of Construction*; ROMANESQUE ART AND ARCHITECTURE.)

2. Early Gothic Architecture.—In about 1137 Suger, abbot of Saint-Denis near Paris, began the reconstruction of his church by building two bays at the west of the old Carolingian nave and erecting the west facade. The architect was not yet able to solve all the problems presented by ribbed vaults. He set the springers of the ribs, even within the same bay, at different levels, but his design of the facade became the model for succeeding Gothic facades. The three portals form a continuous zone. The oculus window (circular) in the centre above the window of the upper story, although still small, concentrates the whole composition. The towers, originally two, continue with their buttresses those of the lower parts. The choir was built in 1140–44 by a second architect. Its central part had to be replaced in 1231, but the ambulatory and the second ambulatory, a continuous row of chapels, are still intact. There all difficulties in the construction of ribbed vaults were overcome by using pointed arches. The diagonal ribs are half circles, but are light and have round profiles. The capitals of the slender columns which separate and at the same time fuse the two ambulatories are chalice-shaped, at least in the lower parts, so that the force seems to rise through them without interruption. The advanced crocket capitals of the columns toward the chancel date from a restoration of about 1200. Suger was proud of his church which he speaks of as exhibiting "the beauty of length and breadth" and as "shining with wonderful and uninterrupted light." Contemporary with this first truly Gothic architecture was the choir of Sens, its interior elevation, arcade, triforium, and clerestory perhaps like the lost central part of Saint-Denis, except that Sens had alternating piers with sexpartite vaults. This vault form was repeated at Senlis and other churches.

The next main Early Gothic cathedrals of France were Noyon (after c. 1150), Laon (after c. 1160), and Paris (1163). Though all used the sexpartite vault, each has individual features. At Laon the arms of the transepts have strong extensions and flat endings. Notre-Dame at Paris has double aisles, the flat endings of its transept having been flush with the outer aisles before they were extended (c. 1250). A major problem at this time was how to form piers. In the main apse of Noyon the clustered shafts rise above the abaci of the column capitals; there, equal supports were required. In the nave the use, originally, of the sexpartite vault required the alternation of piers and columns. As seen from the west this variety gives the effect of richness, but lacks uniformity. The master of Laon, therefore, repeated in his choir and transepts the form of the supports used in the nave, after experimenting with the form at Noyon. A second master continued it in the apse, corresponding to the number of ribs columns around the main thick piers at the uneven places. It was logical to raise five shafts above the abaci at the uneven places and three at the even places, corresponding to the number of ribs springing from each in sexpartite vaults. This, however, was not consistent with the uniform row of columns in the arcades. Therefore the master of Notre-Dame in Paris mounted groups of three shafts above all round piers. In this he was progressive, but the master of Laon, retained the round form in the main apse, while the master of Laon, had already introduced the polygonal apse (in its original stage), the straight sides of the polygon being better

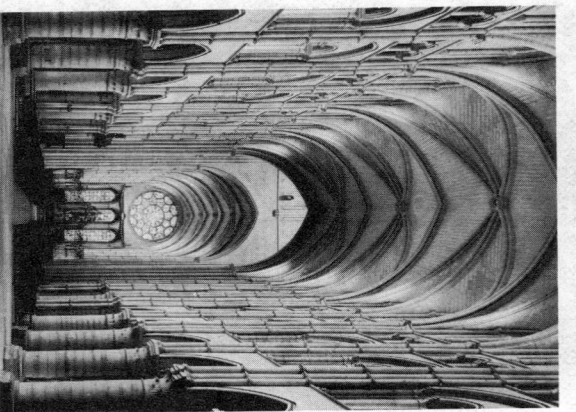

EARLY GOTHIC ARCHITECTURE

(TOP LEFT) ARCHIVES PHOTOGRAPHIQUES, (LEFT) JEAN ROUBIER, (ABOVE) MARBURG-ART REFERENCE BUREAU

(Top left) Interior of the south transept, Soissons Cathedral, France; c. 1177. (Left) Nave of Laon Cathedral, France; after c. 1160. (Above) West facade of Laon Cathedral, France; c. 1190

suited to the straight stained glass windows. The columns of Laon and Paris are short in relation to the whole height of the elevation but are nevertheless of ample girth in relation to their vigorously carved crocket capitals and give an impression of noble strength. The high wall above the main arcade is penetrated by great openings, allowing views of windows beyond. Perhaps the most beautiful monument of this Early Gothic development is the apsidal south transept of Soissons Cathedral, begun 1176, in which the elevation is composed of a screen of slender verticals and narrow lance-like arches, the wall surface as it were dissolving before the continuous band of windows.

Early Gothic produced a system for the church interior and slowly altered stylistically the exterior as well. This occurred automatically when windows and portals received pointed arches. Round arches lead the eye from one springing point over the crown to the other, emphasizing the horizontal diameter. Pointed arches lead the eye from both sides at the same time up to the crown, emphasizing the vertical axis. The Gothic profiles of windows and portals make the walls look thin. The exterior also has the effect of attracting rather than repelling the beholder,

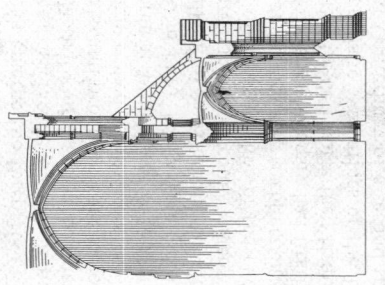
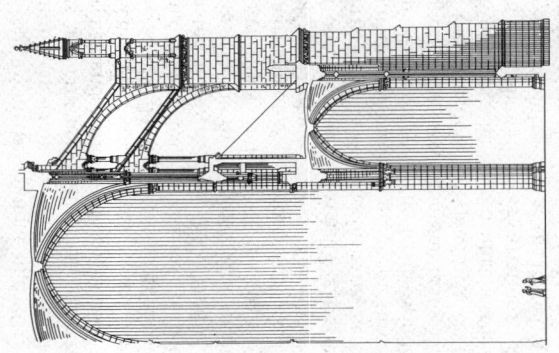
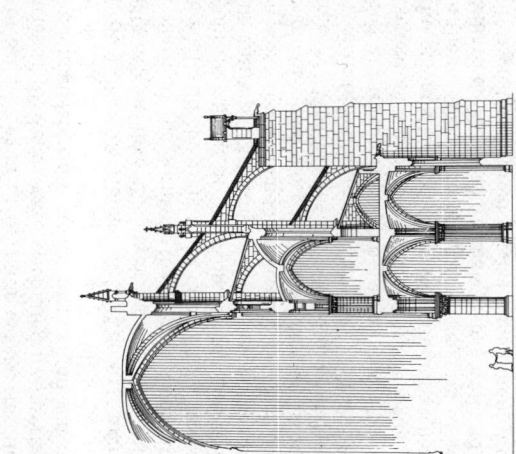

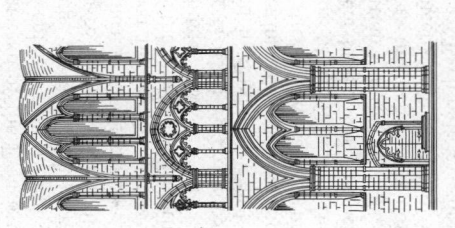
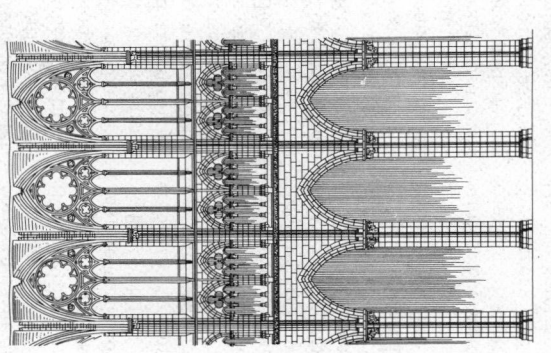

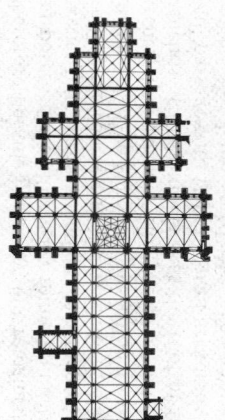
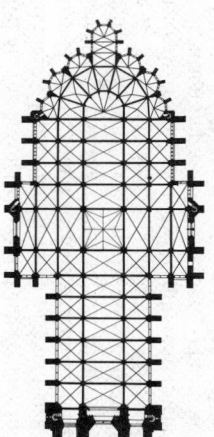
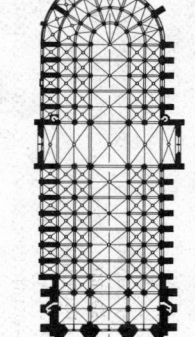

A

B

C

AFTER DEHIO AND BEZOLD

CROSS SECTION, ELEVATION, AND GROUND PLAN OF: (A) NOTRE DAME CATHEDRAL, PARIS, 1163; (B) AMIENS CATHEDRAL, FRANCE, 1220; (C) SALISBURY CATHEDRAL, ENGLAND, 1220

especially at the portals. This effect was greatly enhanced by the introduction of flying buttresses at the choirs and naves, in France first at Notre-Dame in Paris. The aesthetic impression given by these quarter-circle arches is that they counteract in an upward direction the thrust of the vault and roof. In reality they lead the thrust down to the buttresses at the walls of the aisles; but their chief stylistic function is to surround the clerestory with space which belongs to the building and to the limitless space beyond. The limits of the cathedral become fluid.

In the west front of Laon (c. 1190) a monumental example of Gothic relief was created by placing the main part of the façade with its wheel window in such a way that it stood out from the plane of the towers, and the three portals in turn stood out from the main wall. The arches of the three entrances are crowned with gables, thrust down so that they touch the arches and both spaces penetrate each other. Pinnacles rise between the gables, and simpler ones rise above the dwarf gallery of the second floor. The towers end in octagons with diagonally advancing tabernacles, from which emerge the foreparts of bulls. The master of Notre-Dame in Paris (façade c. 1208) maintained in contrast to the dynamic plasticity of Laon a balance between his verticals and horizontals, and produced a façade of truly classic harmony.

Although ribbed vaults were built in England after Durham, for example at Winchester in 1107 and in the crypt of Gloucester Cathedral in 1120, Early Gothic did not really emerge until 1174 when William of Sens rebuilt the choir of Canterbury Cathedral. The contemporary account given by a monk of Canterbury, Gervase, of the rebuilding of the choir gives a unique insight into the role of the designer-architect in the creation of the cathedral. William of Sens obviously had firsthand knowledge of the cathedrals of the Île-de-France then rising, notably Laon. He showed the wide artistic sympathies of the Early Gothic age. The introduction at Canterbury of a second transept was modeled after the great Romanesque Abbey of Cluny, and the coloured columns are supposed to have been patterned after a church at Valenciennes. Flying buttresses may have been used here for the first time at Canterbury. A specifically English form of Gothic began with St. Hugh's choir at Lincoln (1192). As early as about 1180, when the cathedral at Wells was begun, the English horizontal fusion of the bays was used instead of the French vertical fusion. The architect of Lincoln invented a new pattern of ribbed vaults with two bosses in each ridge rib and with extra ribs rising from the springing point to these bosses. These ribs were called tiercerons and lay on the surface of the severies. These vaults collapsed when the central tower fell in 1239 and were rebuilt in their original form. They were the forerunners of the star vaults in the nave of the same building.

3. High Gothic Architecture.—The system of flying buttresses used in Canterbury and Notre-Dame in Paris made the already existing galleries seem superfluous, at least from the standpoint of statics. The master who built the Cathedral of Chartres after the fire of 1194 omitted the galleries, heightened the aisles, and lengthened the upper windows downward, returning to a three-story elevation like that of Sens. The flying buttresses also made it possible to broaden the windows of the clerestory, designed as pairs of lancet windows each of nearly the same breadth as those in the aisles. Each pair was surmounted by an oculus which harmonized with the round wall arches of the quadripartite ribbed vaults. The alternating system of piers used with sexpartite vaults therefore became necessary, but remained hinted at, for aesthetic purposes, in the alternately round and octagonal piers. Each pier carries four shafts, round on the octagonal, octagonal on the round, muting the contrast in the form of the giant members. The shaft facing the nave supports five colonettes rising to the transverse arches, the diagonal ribs, and the wall arches. The triforium, which is at the same level as the roof of the aisles, is treated as a wall passage with rows of small arcades. This elevation improves on those of Laon and Paris. The entire building is simpler and more unified, and sets the standard for the new High Gothic phase of architecture.

The Cathedral of Bourges, built about 1200, has equal round piers. The vaults are sexpartite, like those of Notre-Dame in Paris, but higher and differently proportioned. The cross section with double aisles was also copied from Paris. The transept was omitted. Flying buttresses bridge both pairs of aisles in the upper part. Special flying buttresses for the lower aisles are evidence of this generation's enthusiasm for this specifically Gothic member. In the Cathedral of Rouen, begun after the fire in 1200, the shafts supporting the quadripartite vaults rise up to the vault with only a slight interruption at the springing line of the arcade. Galleries were planned, but, with Chartres in mind, were omitted. Their openings were kept, however, and in the aisles a group of thin colonettes was arranged on the level of the omitted vaults, a unique and attractive invention.

The Cathedral of Reims, begun 1210, continued the tradition of Chartres. The masters of Reims were celebrated by inscriptions and images inset in a huge labyrinth device, of the kind which survives on the floor of the nave of Chartres and which was drawn in his sketchbook by Villard de Honnecourt. The first architect of Reims, Jean d'Orbais, who set his stamp on the whole design of the cathedral, clarified the form of the piers. They are all round with single shafts in the four main directions. The abaci of all the shafts join the abacus of the main column and give the impression that the entire pier is turned $45°$, corresponding to the ribs. The ribs are pointed, the round arch having thus been driven from its last stronghold. The most important new detail was in the form of the tracery. At Chartres each clerestory window was a group of three separate units, one juxtaposed with the other. The Reims windows are transformed into a single unit, the outer contour being designed as a pointed arch, the whole being then divided by a central colonette supporting two pointed arches and an oculus between them. This form was to be the germ of countless variations. Villard de Honnecourt knew Reims well and took it as the model, with stylistically progressive attenuation of proportions, for his own Cathedral of Notre-Dame at Cambrai. He redrafted Reims to resemble Amiens in height and elegance. The master of the nave of Amiens, begun in 1220, attained an ultimate correctness in all the elements of his design—the piers, in their relation to the arcades and the shafts of the vault, the tracery in the triforium, and, by means of the common shafts, the fusion of the triforium and clerestory. The nave of Amiens (1220–36) has been praised as the culmination of the Gothic style.

The architect of the nave of Saint-Denis (1231) continued the trend of Amiens by more closely combining the triforium with the clerestory and by flattening the roof of the aisles, so that the triforium could be illuminated with glass. This reduced the elevation of the nave to only two stories, as had been done before, though in another way, in the festive choir of Le Mans (1218). Contemporary with Amiens was the Cathedral of Salisbury, begun in 1220, a classic representative of English horizontalism. The shafts of the vaults begin between the arches of the triforium. The flow of space is strengthened by the specifically English round form of all abaci. There is no French tracery; nor are there flying buttresses. The Sainte-Chapelle in Paris (1243–48), rising above an undercroft, has, like all chapels of the great cathedrals, only one story. The windows dissolve the walls completely. The building consists of structural groups of shafts, and the grill formed by the tracery and by the light passing through the stained glass. On the exterior, gables, which before were combined only with portals, crown the tracery windows. They overlap the eaves of the high roof and, with the accompanying pinnacles, weaken the horizontal line. The most progressive work of its generation was a church of small size, Saint-Urbain at Troyes (begun 1262). The choir has no ambulatory and a single chapel on each side parallel to the chancel. A triforium was not required because the roofs of the chapels are saddle roofs, but the apse received a pseudo-triforium as continuation of the chapel windows, which have different tracery patterns inside and out, both being visible together. The structural members are so reduced in breadth that they almost suggest metalwork. The capitals are omitted partly to produce a continuous upward flow, an innovation that appeared in the southern portal of Notre-Dame in Paris shortly before. This, with its flat pierced gables, stands at the opposite extreme of Gothic design from the vast deep portals of Laon and Chartres.

PLATE I

GOTHIC ART AND ARCHITECTURE

"Angel Blowing the Trumpet" from the Douce Apocalypse; c. 1260. In the Bodleian Library, Oxford, Eng. (Douce MS 180)

Silver gilt reliquary of SS. Lucian, Maximian, and Julian, from the Sainte-Chapelle, Paris; 13th century. In the Musée de Cluny, Paris

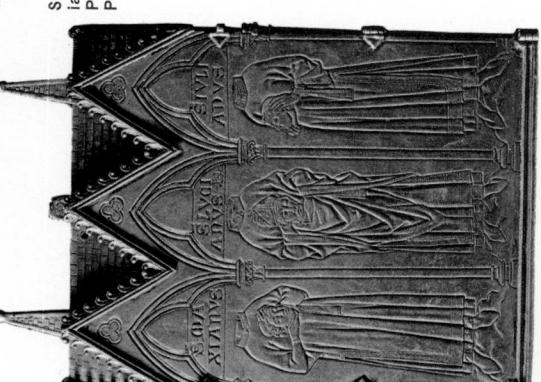

Pistoia Pulpit, by Giovanni Pisano; completed 1301. In the Church of S. Andrea, Pistoia, Italy

EARLY GOTHIC

Facade of the Cathedral of Siena, Italy; 1284–1377

Jesse Tree window, 12th century; west front of Chartres Cathedral, Chartres, France

GOTHIC ART AND ARCHITECTURE

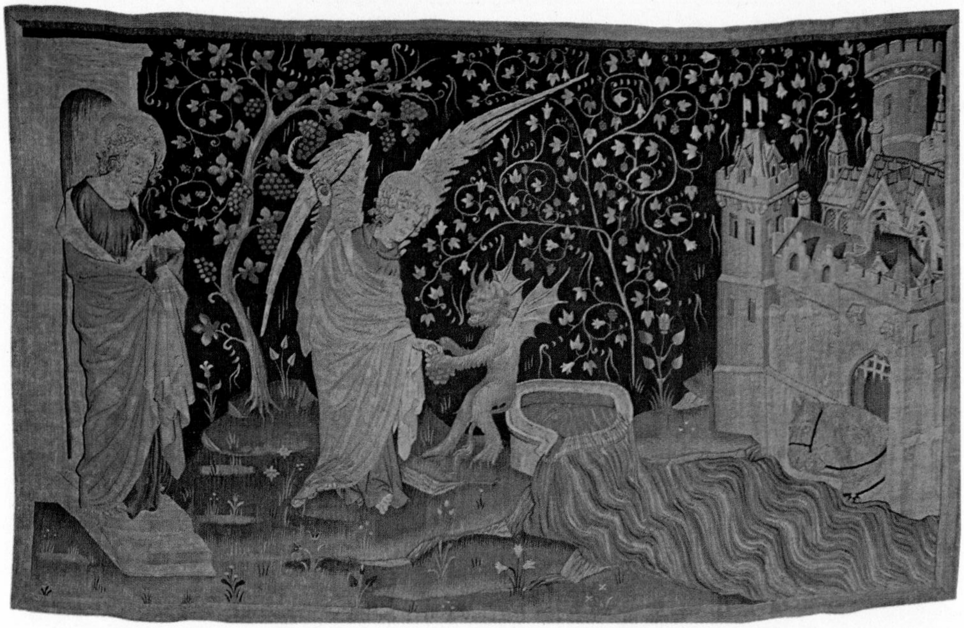

"Vintage Thrown into the Wine Press," illustrating Rev. 14:19, from the Angers Apocalypse, tapestry executed by Nicholas Bataille; begun 1377. In the Château of Angers, France

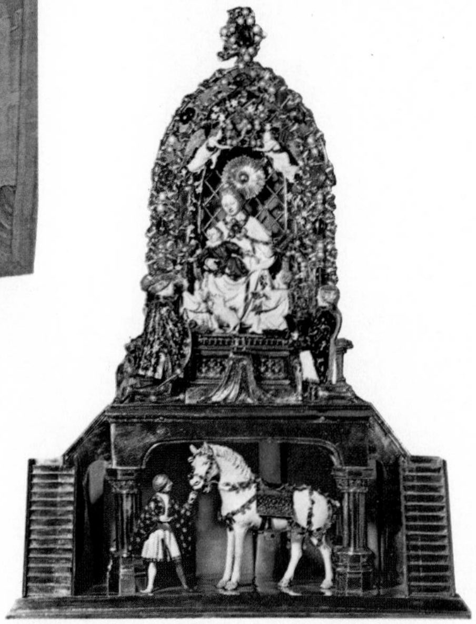

"Goldenes Rössel," French altar tabernacle; before 1404. In the Treasury of Altötting, Bavaria

LATE GOTHIC

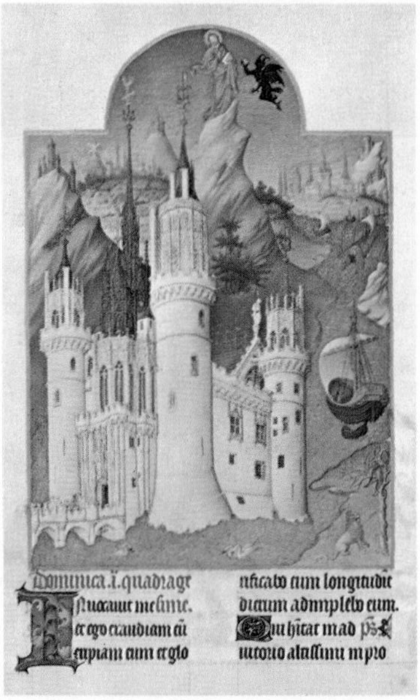

The Temptation of Christ from *Les Très Riches Heures du Jean, duc de Berry,* by Pol de Limburg and brothers; before 1416. In the Musée Condé, Chantilly, France

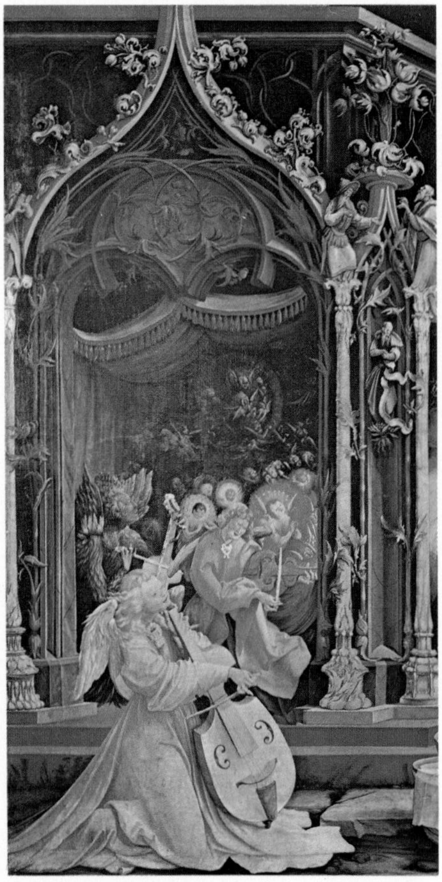

"The Concert of Angels" from the Isenheim Altarpiece, by Mathias Grünewald; completed by 1516. In the Unterlinden Museum, Colmar, France

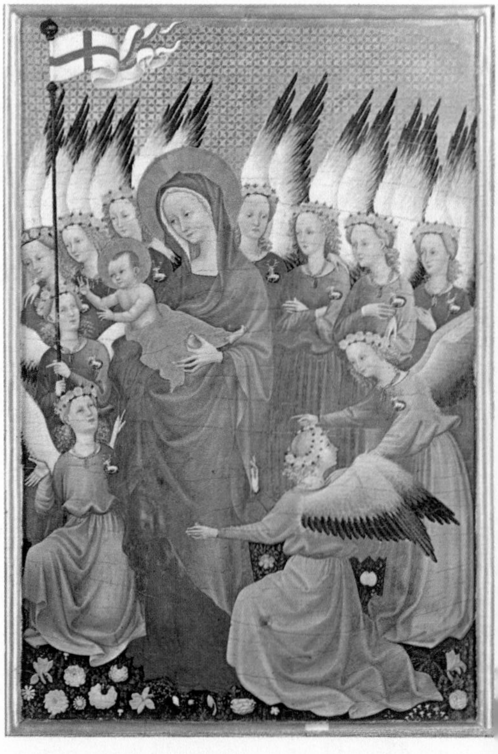

"The Virgin and Child with Angels," right leaf of the Wilton Diptych; *c.* 1395. In the National Gallery, London

GOTHIC ART AND ARCHITECTURE

The nave of Strasbourg Cathedral, begun about 1245, was based on that of Saint-Denis. Westminster Abbey, begun at the same time, was influenced by common features of French Gothic rather than a single model. Strasbourg and Cologne were works of Germans, Westminster the work of an Englishman, all of them able to continue the French tradition with deep understanding. The Angel Choir (1255) of Lincoln Cathedral has a big French tracery window at the straight east end, although otherwise the elevation of the chancel follows pure English tradition and the vaults with ridge ribs and tiercerons emphasize the horizontal unity of the space. Churches of the French High Gothic style elsewhere are Our Lady's Church at Trier (1227), the Church of St. Elizabeth at Marburg (1235), the Cathedral of Halberstadt, (1239), the Cathedral of Toledo, Spain (c. 1225), Ste. Gudule at Brussels (c. 1225), and the Cathedral of Utrecht (1254).

The design of the west front of Strasbourg Cathedral by Master Erwin, of 1277, shows the autonomy of tracery, as does the splendid composition of the *portail des libraires*, the entrance of the north transept of Rouen Cathedral of about 1280. In both cases the gable of the portal is perforated and grows up freely before the parapet, the row of tracery, and the tight pattern of the rose window. In Strasbourg the tracery is continuous, forming a grill before the facade. Although it seems unreasonable to perforate the roof of a tower with tracery, this did occur in the stylistic development. It is seen in Freiburg im Breisgau (1310), and again later in the design for the spires of Cologne, executed in 1848 after the original plans drawn during the Gothic period. The preponderance of tracery led also to such richly decorated works as the southern side of St. Catherine in Oppenheim, of 1317.

4. Gothic Tracery: Development of Curvilinear and Rectilinear Styles.—Tracery is one of the most striking details with which to evaluate the various phases of the Gothic style. The first form of tracery, already described, was followed by the forms of three and more lights with three or more circles. In the destroyed church of Saint-Nicaise at Reims, begun in 1231, cusps were introduced; these were small pointed members growing out of the profiles of the pointed arches. The transfer of tracery to the big round windows led Frenchmen to call this phase of 13th-century architecture the Rayonnant style. In the second half of the century the circles were replaced by rounded triangles, quadrangles, etc. (polygons consisting of three or more curved sides). This form appears for the first time in the small triangular windows of the undercroft in the Sainte-Chapelle and soon after in Westminster Abbey. Later it supplanted all circles in the traceries. The rounded polygon is a continuous series of pointed arches round a centre. In England big rose windows are exceptional—for example, in the eastern transept of Durham (1235)—and rectangular windows with pointed arches or groups of lancet windows are the rule. In Germany, too, long windows were sometimes preferred, for example in the facade of St. Elizabeth at Marburg, about 1275. In France the big oculus remained an almost indispensable means of achieving aesthetic balance in the composition. Yet it was in France that the slenderness of proportions became exaggerated. The limit was reached in the choir of Beauvais Cathedral (1247), which collapsed in 1284.

Meanwhile the style spread through Europe. The Cistercians, often said to have brought Gothic to all countries, were slow to accept it. Its rich detail was

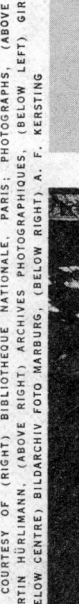

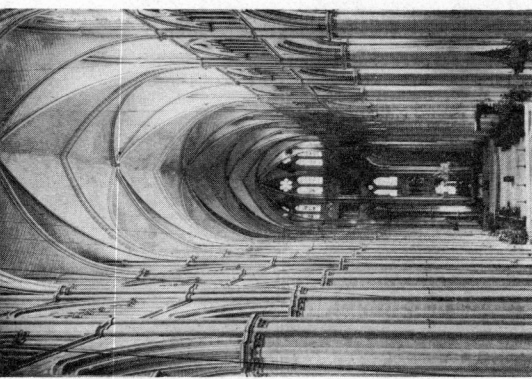

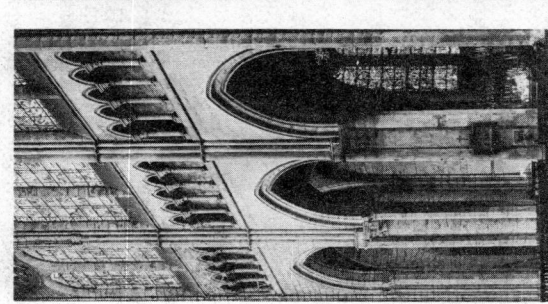

HIGH GOTHIC ARCHITECTURE

(Above left) Interior of Chartres Cathedral, France, showing three story elevation: main arcade, triforium, clerestory; after 1194. (Above right) Nave of the Cathedral of Bourges, France; begun c. 1200. (Right) Exterior and interior elevation of a bay of the Cathedral of Reims from an album by Villard de Honnecourt; c. 1235. In the Bibliothèque Nationale, Paris (Ms. 19093). (Below left) Interior of Sainte-Chapelle, Paris; 1243–48. (Below centre) South transept of Notre-Dame, Paris; mid-13th century. (Below right) Angel Choir, Lincoln Cathedral, England; late 13th century

antipathetic to their asceticism. They replaced the triforium with closed walls although the windows with their Gothic relief created the impression of thinness and gave the walls qualities of Gothic lightness. Italy was hesitant in adopting Gothic architectural forms. There, wall surfaces were used extensively for frescoes as at Assisi (1228) and at Sta. Croce in Florence (1294–95). The latter even had an open timber roof like many other churches of the mendicant orders.

In Amiens ribs received a sharp edge to emphasize their middle line. Later architects developed pear-shaped profiles for ribs, shafts, and mullions of tracery. These lines, consisting of a convex part continued by a concave one, were then used as ogee arches in traceries in places where the pointed arches of the lights continued directly into adjoining circles. They appeared first, perhaps, in Saint-Urbain at Troyes and not much later in the Cistercian Heiligenkreuz in Austria. In England the ogee arches isolated from tracery were used in the Eleanor crosses after 1292. They became the prevailing form of the Curvilinear style. The upper part of the ogee arch was bent forward to form the nodding arches. The most splendid example of this three-dimensionality is the row of niches in the Lady Chapel at Ely, after 1321. In traceries the concave-convex line could be substituted for all con-

cave figures of the High Gothic style. Such tracery is fully developed in the reredos of Beverley Minster, Yorkshire (1334), and in the big west window of York Minster (1338).

In the Curvilinear style soft "textile" lines replaced the rigid structural curves of the earlier style, and in tracery the emphasis was upon the creation of complete continuity. These modifications also affected the vaults. In the chancel of Exeter Cathedral (c. 1300), the diagonal ribs, together with the ridge rib and the tiercerons, though still suggesting structure, formed a continuous pattern without emphasis on the transverse arches marking the limits of the bays. There, however, the basic form was still the quadripartite vault; the cone of the fan vault had not yet appeared. An approach to the latter was the vault of the chapter house at Wells (c. 1300) where the ribs of different function have the same pro-

GOTHIC TRACERY

(Above) Part of the cloisters, Gloucester Cathedral, England; 1351. (Right) West facade of Strasbourg Cathedral, France; 1277. (Far right) Interior of Sta. Croce, Florence, Italy; 1294–95.

1300 and in the screen at Southwell Minster about 1325. The vault at Prague was the first real net vault on the Continent. Parler was also the first to use an even number of sides for the polygon of a choir, at Kuttenberg, in 1360. This meant that there was no longer a wall frontal to the axis, and that diagonality prevailed.

5. The Last Phase.—Later architects transferred the form of the hall to the choirs. The ambulatory and the chapels were then drawn into the unified flow of the entire space. An early work of this kind had been the choir of Holy Cross, Schwäbisch Gmünd, of 1351. A late one was that of St. Lorenz in Nürnberg, of 1445. Many of these churches, built on the one-story system, had extraordinarily elongated windows which also dominated the exterior, together with the enormous roofs covering both nave and aisles. In German territories magnificent towers and spires were built,

file and the central portion looks like a complete fan vault except that it rests on the central pier and is continued by severies to the walls. The vaults in the choirs of Wells (c. 1329), Tewkesbury (c. 1335), and Gloucester (after 1337), have the basic form of barrel vaults. Fragmentary ribs (liernes), rising like branches from diagonal ribs or from tiercerons, counteract the feeling of structure to give the impression of textile nets.

The Court School, in building St. Stephen's Chapel in the Palace of Westminster (begun 1292, burnt 1834), created the Rectilinear or Perpendicular style which, with its rigid vertical and horizontal lines, was the opposite of the Curvilinear or Decorated. Yet these grill-like patterns also were applied in such a way as to create continuity and the feeling of infinite expandability. The rows of vertical mullions climbing up the extrados of the pointed arch were not static anymore. The spandrels filled with these fragmentary forms were seemingly cut by the arch. The most impressive work in this style was the choir of Gloucester Cathedral, where the late Gothic decorative grill stands in front of the original Romanesque structure. In the transept the vertical lines are crossed by the oblique lines of enormous buttresses. In Gloucester true fan vaults were used in the cloister for the first time, in 1351. They consist of concave inverted cones. Halves of these cones rise on each side of the gallery. All the ribs are equal; the space between them is filled with Curvilinear tracery. The separation of bays is practically eliminated, and there is a continuous flow of space.

In Germany the Rectilinear form was little used, although a parallel can be seen in the west front of Strasbourg. In High Gothic times hall churches were preferred, and thereafter continued in almost exclusive use. The tendency toward spatial continuity altered the form of the piers, for example in the Wiesenkirche in Soest of 1331. The shafts were combined with the pier so that its core was scarcely recognizable, capitals were omitted, and the ribs continued the shafts with the same profile. The leading architect of Germany was Peter Parler (1330–90) who, at the age of 23, was called to Prague to continue the cathedral. He built complicated vaults with hanging bosses and ribs rising free through space. Parler seems to have been influenced by English Late Gothic, as free ribs were used at Bristol Cathedral about

CULMINATING FEATURES

(Left) Henry VII's Chapel, Westminster Abbey, London; 1502. (Above) South porch of Albi Cathedral, France; 1520—35. (Right) West facade of Saint-Maclou, Rouen, France; 1434—70. (Below) Entrance facade of House of Jacques Coeur, Bourges, France; 1430

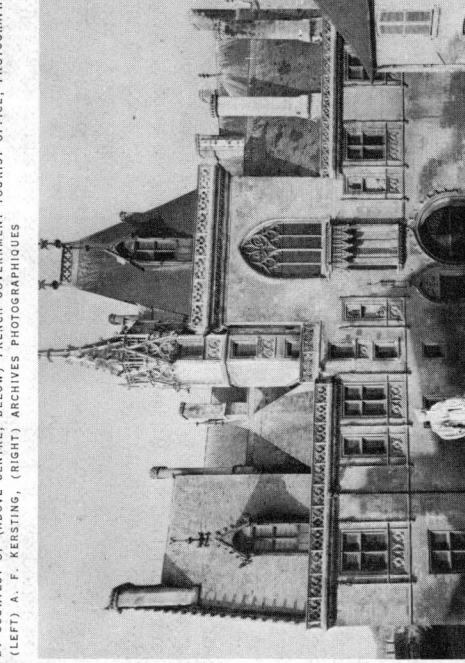

notably the towers of St. Stephen in Vienna (after 1359), and of Strasbourg Cathedral, whose octagon dates to 1400 and whose spire was finished in 1439. The tower at Vienna rises with continuously diminishing extension. The stories are not sharply separated and are pushed upward like the parts of a telescope. The Strasbourg spire dissolves in wreaths of small tabernacles containing staircases leading to the apex. In France the English Curvilinear style was adopted at Amiens in the chapel of Cardinal la Grange of 1373. The traditional verticalism applied to the tracery of the Curvilinear transformed its character into upward flaming forms, hence the name Flamboyant. It changed the rose windows into explosive patterns such as that of the Sainte-Chapelle in Paris of 1485. An impressive work in this style is the upper part of the facade of Rouen Cathedral of about 1490.

Some regional variations of Gothic are obviously dependent on the material available. Regions which have no stone suitable for building used brick and adapted Gothic forms to it, for example in northeast Germany, Bavaria, southern France, and the Netherlands. Specifically national talents are clearly evident in the Late Gothic churches of Spain and Portugal. The Cathedral of Gerona (1417), with its vault 73 ft. (22 m.) in width, is the widest in Gothic architecture. Many Spanish churches are notable for their extraordinary dimensions. Seville is the largest. Milan Cathedral (begun 1387) is another Late Gothic colossus.

Culminating features of the Gothic style were found in many countries in the years around 1500—the Laurentius portal at Strasbourg, Henry VII's Chapel at Westminster Abbey, with its hanging fan vaults, the totally perforated Flamboyant porch of Saint-Maclou at Rouen, and the south porch of Albi Cathedral, where the surface of the buttresses, fretted and spiked, seems to kindle into flame. This visual effect is actually achieved in the fantastic architecture painted in 1515 as the shrine of the Virgin in Mathias Grünewald's Isenheim Altar.

Insofar as the ribbed vault in all its stages, tracery, Gothic

"textile" pattern. This mixture of principles of structure and texture the composition of the palace Cà d'Oro in Venice, of 1421, is derived. The Palace of the Popes at Avignon, of 1334, shows closed walls and contains occasional Gothic details. Late Gothic style is felt strongly in the Flamboyant decoration of the Salle des Pas Perdus in the palace of Jean de Berry at Poitiers, of 1393, and in the picturesque private house of Jacques Coeur at Bourges, about 1430. The last phase may be represented by the Albrechtsburg in Meissen, of 1471, with its many varieties of Late Gothic vaults and its picturesque irregularity, the Vladislav hall in the palace in Prague (1493), and the Palais de Justice at Rouen, of about 1500, with its big rectangular windows which are nearly Renaissance in character, but with free tracery rising before the dormer windows.

profiles, etc., were used in secular buildings, such structures may be included in a survey of the Gothic style. The palace of the archbishop at Sens (1240) has big High Gothic windows, with tracery and buttresses adorned with tabernacles and crowned by pinnacles. In the facade of the Palazzo Vecchio in Florence (1299), on the other hand, although it too has Gothic windows, the heaviness of the closed walls prevails. The ducal palace at Venice shows in its two lower stories the Gothic dissolution of the wall by the arrangement of open galleries combined with Late Gothic tracery in the second floor, but the wall rising above is flat and adorned with a definitely

III. GOTHIC SCULPTURE

1. Early Gothic Sculpture and the Influence of Mosan Art.—The earliest Gothic sculptures were made by the goldsmiths and stone carvers attracted to the Île-de-France by the great new works being erected there in the second quarter of the 12th century. Experienced artists from many parts of Europe gathered at Saint-Denis: metalworkers from the Meuse valley (whose style is generally called Mosan), stone sculptors from northern Italy, and possibly also from southern and western France and Burgundy.

The public and processional entrances at the west end of the abbey church were decorated with doors of gilded bronze, those of the main central portal having reliefs of the Passion, Resurrection, and Ascension. The golden gleam of the metal symbolized for Abbot Suger the illumination of the dull dark human understanding by the Light of Christ. These doors have not survived, but we know of them from Suger's account of the abbey. The brightness of the bronze reliefs, and the colours of the painted stone sculpture around the doorways, and the shimmer of the stained glass windows to be seen inside the church were taken up by a mosaic placed at Suger's orders over the left door of the façade. The juxtaposition of a mosaic and three-dimensional sculpture, which Suger admits was unusual, suggests that the monumental portal design was influenced by contemporary Mosan metalwork where pictorial scenes in enamel inlay were combined with figures cast in the round.

The symbolic and didactic significance of the doors was extended by the stone sculptures. In the semicircular tympanum over the main doorway was represented the Last Judgment. Relief sculpture on the jambs, representing the wise and foolish virgins, emphasized the role of the portals as the gates through which the faithful Christian would pass to salvation. The most striking features of the portals, so far as the future development of Gothic stone sculpture was concerned, were, first, the column figures (large statues placed against the columns flanking the doorways, as it were supporting the capitals with their heads and repeating in human form the vertical accent of the architectural members); and, second, the rows of figures carved on the archivolts of the arches of the portals, which also follow and emphasize the main architectural forms and constitute a dimensional frame and a kind of protective nimbus around the iconographic centre of the composition, the Judgment tympanum. The conflation of architectural and sculptural elements—what can be called architectonic sculpture—differentiates, as far as form is concerned, Gothic art from the earlier Romanesque style. Early Gothic art is recognizable by its attempt to create an organic unit of the architecture and sculpture of the portals, by the emergence of a similar organic quality in the depiction of individual figures, a new restraint, sensibility, and realism in the definition of stance or movement, drapery, and the human face, and by the overall impression of a noble seriousness of mood.

The highly experimental portal designs of Saint-Denis made their impact first on the sculptured doorways erected at the west front of Chartres Cathedral about 1150. A sculptor previously employed at Saint-Denis evidently worked on the column figures of the right door at Chartres, the drapery tending to fall into firm linear patterns which in no way detract from the coherence and plasticity of the figures. The other column figures at Chartres, notably those of the central doorway, are extremely attenuated, a treatment which might be regarded as a mannered stylization typically Romanesque, were it not that the sculptor was consciously emphasizing the role of his statues as vertical accents in the whole architectural design. Besides, these slim motionless figures are endowed with an extraordinary inner vitality and provide a picture of a serene and ennobled humanity outside the range of Romanesque. The christological program of the portals has as its kernel, from the point of view of the historian of medieval civilization, the upper portion of the right tympanum where the Virgin is represented as the throne of wisdom supporting the Christ child and attended in the adjacent archivolts by great scholars of the past and by personifications of the subjects studied in the cathedral school at Chartres.

A number of slightly later Cathedral portals, for example at Bourges, Le Mans, and (much simplified) at Rochester in England, imitate slavishly the attenuation and the static rigid frontal pose of the column figures from the central portal of Chartres. But the tradition established at Saint-Denis of rather more mobile figures, stouter in build, and with more variation in the suspension and drag of their draperies, offered greater scope for future exploration and was, besides, supported and spread by the continuing mastery of the Mosan goldsmiths. As early as around 1110 Reiner of Huy made a brass baptismal font, still preserved at Liège, where the figures in the scenes from the ministry of St. John the Baptist are shown bending and turning, sometimes viewed from the back, and with fluid draperies revealing the bulk and motion of the body. Suger describes an enormous gold cross made for Saint-Denis in the 1140s (now lost) which is partially reflected in the small Mosan cross base from Saint-Bertin now in the museum at Saint-Omer. The corners are marked by the four Evangelists seated in various poses, one of them turning forcefully to look upward. Surviving from this period are a large number of small stalwart figures on portable altars, lecterns, and cross bases, representing the Evangelists, prophets, and personifications of the four elements symbolizing the physical environment of man. As early as c. 1125 a Romanesque sculptor at Moissac had used the motif of snakes descending from the breasts of a female figure as an image of the punishment of the lustful, and indeed rendered the naked human body and its festoon of serpents in such a way as to make it the epitome of the macabre. But the same motif was used by 12th-century Mosan artists in its venerable classical sense, handed down through Carolingian models, as signifying fecund Mother Earth giving nourishment to all her offspring. This positive and wholesome attitude is typical of Mosan artists, being revealed also in the systematic iconographic program to which they remained faithful throughout the 12th century, which emphasizes the logical concordance of the Old and New Testaments and the right service rendered to the Creator and Saviour by all natural things.

The vitality of Mosan figures and their form-defining draperies are reflected in the animated and decorative, but coherent sculptures erected on the portal of Senlis Cathedral about 1175. In disposition and relation of figures to the column, bases, and lintel, the Senlis sculptures are fundamentally indebted to Saint-Denis, but the column figures are not now the generalized company of Old Testament kings and queens, ancestors of Christ, but are specifically the patriarchs and priests who were recognized by the church as foreshadowing the redemptive death of Christ, and these figures, termed *Christophores*, bearing their prophetic victims, Abraham with Isaac, Aaron with the sacrificial lamb, anticipate the special mission of the Virgin who bore Christ in her own body. The lintel and tympanum celebrate the Virgin, patroness of so many Gothic cathedrals, showing her Dormition and Assumption. The basic meaning of the imagery is of course to acclaim the doctrine of the Incarnation, which gave splendour and validity to the created physical world and to human creativity in art as well as in government and in sacred and scientific learning.

2. Monumental Portal Sculpture and Increasing Realism.—In the second half of the 12th century the interest of architects in a rich variety of forms and an elevation at once monumental and open, after the manner of scaffolding, encouraged the development of deeply recessed doorways with powerful mobile figures accumulated round them, as at the cathedrals of Paris, Laon, and Sens, and also other schemes employing subtle groupings of figure sculptures. The period was one of outstanding inventiveness in stone sculpture both in the Île-de-France and in neighbouring territories. One of the most elegant and experimental monuments built in the late 12th century was a cloister erected at the church of Notre-Dame-en-Vaux at Châlons-sur-Marne where figures representing the wise and foolish virgins, Christian virtues in the form of armed watchful soldiers, kings, apostles, and patriarchs of the *Christophores* type were placed sometimes singly, sometimes in twos or threes against columns or clustered colonettes of varied design, crowned with capitals carved with long crisp fronds of acanthus, the whole marked by a radiant sensibility of style.

In the 12th century England too had its bronze-casters and stone sculptors but little of their work survives. The great bronze doors of Bury St. Edmunds Abbey, contemporary with those of Saint-Denis, are lost. They were made by Hugo, a professional sculptor and painter, whose extant illuminations mark him out as the most advanced artist in England around 1130-40. The patronage of the ambitious prelate Henry of Blois, bishop of Winchester, gave encouragement to the arts. Unfortunately no certain trace of has survived in southern English 12th-century stone sculpture of

menacing demon is about to enfold the patriarch in his ape-like arms. Below this is the equally tense and dramatic scene of the Judgment of Solomon. About the same time work was begun on the huge rood screen of Chartres, of which fragments are preserved in the crypt. The relief of the Nativity has a fine spacious composition, clear details, and remarkable tenderness of mood. On the south transept of Chartres three immense portals were erected c. 1210–20, celebrating the triumph of the Church. The column figures representing the apostles and members of the Christian hierarchy, the complex tympana reliefs and crowds of archivolt figures show the energy, confidence, and encyclopaedic range of early 13th-century sculpture.

The technical development in stone sculpture at this time was toward greater realism in pictorial detail, a strength and martial dignity of pose in individual figures, and a form-revealing drapery style using densely drawn small parallel pleats. The source of this style is still Mosan metalwork which, in the last quarter of the 12th century and first quarter of the 13th, achieved its supreme heights in the work of Nicholas of Verdun, who made among many other works the enamel plaques of the ambo (now a retable) at Klosterneuburg dated 1181, the reliquary of the Three Magi at Cologne about 1190, and the reliquary of the Virgin at Tournai dated 1205. The reliefs of the Tournai shrine tell the story of the Nativity. In the scene of the Visitation the Virgin and the aged Elizabeth are clothed from head to foot in flowing draperies which express the bulk, movement, and organic quality of the figures, and the faces are portrayed with subtle skill. The angels attendant on Christ seated in judgment at one end of the shrine have a stalwart casual stance and massive draperies recalling the public statuary of the antique world. The same proto-Renaissance style is found on a miniature scale but with no less essential grandeur and eloquence in the attendant figures grouped around the cross fashioned for the Latin emperor of Constantinople in 1206 by the Mosan goldsmith Gérard, another artist whose work anticipates that of the Île de France stone sculptors by many years.

The sculptors called in to help with the creation of the new Cathedral of Reims after 1210 had been trained in the Nicholas-Gérard style. At Reims is found the climax of this development, statuary of a grandeur and amplitude not seen in Europe since the decline of antique stone sculpture. The Apostles of the Judgment portal of about 1225 are big burly relaxed figures which fulfil the Gothic tenet of organic unity. The Last Judgment scene above contains naked figures rising from urns and classical sarcophagi, and a group of holy virgins seated frontally, the foreshortening of the limbs and the bulk of the bodies conveyed in a convincing manner. Perhaps the most memorable figures by the sculptors of the Reims classical workshop are the group of the Virgin and St. Elizabeth on the west front, which restate on a grand scale and with an authentic classicism of style and mood the humane and substantial figures in the equivalent scene on the Tournai shrine. The sketchbook of Villard de Honnecourt, the north French architect, contains many designs for statues whose inner coherence and flowing multiple-pleated draperies adhere firmly to the Reims tradition. But Villard's conception of sculpture was not shaped only by the impact of the Reims statuary, but by the older Mosan traditions which underlay Reims, since his sketchbook contains vari-

(LEFT) ARCHIVES PHOTOGRAPHIQUES, (RIGHT) GIRAUDON

MONUMENTAL PORTAL SCULPTURE

(Left) Apostles of the Judgment Portal, north transept, Reims Cathedral, France; c. 1225. (Right) Saints, south transept, Chartres Cathedral, France; c. 1210–20. Figure on left is St. Theodore; after 1224

the influence of the antique statues which, to the surprise of his contemporaries, Henry purchased in Rome and which he presumably conveyed back to his palace at Winchester. Antique carved gems, however, were a familiar feature of medieval reliquaries and other objects of metalwork, and inspired perhaps by these antique imagery appears in English metalwork in the second half of the 12th century, for example in a bronze and enamel ciborium crowned with statuettes of the centaur Cheiron and the child Achilles, and in a bronze group representing the first labour of Hercules where the gaunt outline of the naked wrestler and the prancing wiry lion is almost Etruscan in effect. The elegant ivory altar cross now in the Metropolitan Museum, New York, English work of the second half of the 12th century, has elaborate learned christological imagery of the kind being experimented with in France at the same time and characteristic of Early Gothic iconographic thinking. In monumental stone sculpture the most progressive works which have survived are column figures and fragments of archivolt sculpture once forming a giant portal or portals at the Abbey of St. Mary, York. These date to about 1200 and show the familiarity of north English sculptors with the style of Châlons and Sens, and also independent knowledge of the vivid physiognomy and powerful build of Mosan bronze figures. The York statues comprise a group of apostles and patriarchs and prophets of the *Christophores* type, holding symbols of the Passion. One figure, now headless, has drapery regularly scored by deep pleats, giving the whole figure coherence and dignity in a manner suggesting a free interpretation of antique models.

The most splendid of the great church portals of the *Christophores* kind was erected about 1210 at the north transept of Chartres. The patriarchs stand on either side of the central door of the transept, with the ancestral line of Christ, in the image of the Jesse Tree, carved in the archivolts, and the Dormition, Assumption, and Coronation of the Virgin on the lintel and tympanum above, this last scene represented with a noble dignity befitting the humanistic theme which it celebrates. The slightly later flanking portals show important developments in the handling of relief sculpture and in narrative and descriptive art. The most remarkable sculptures represent the sufferings of Job, who lies outstretched on the rough hummock of his dung heap and is quarreled over by the vigorously posed figures of his friends and his wife, while a great

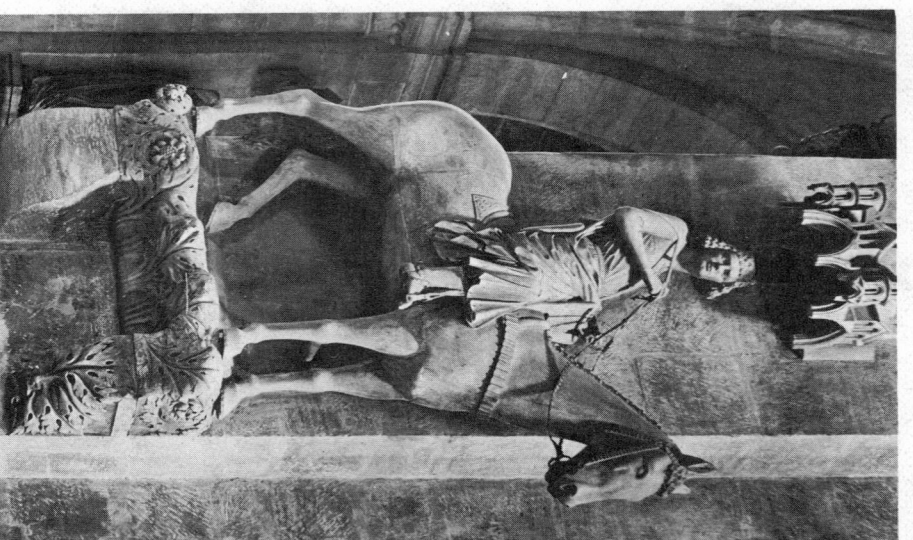

ous designs for metalwork which recall in precise detail extant Mosan pieces, notably his design for a lectern on a triangular base and topped by an eagle, where the statuettes of the sitting evangelists turn and twist exactly like their Mosan counterparts on the Saint-Bertin cross base. Villard's sketchbook further supplies independent witness to the interest which the artists of the High Gothic period felt in the art of antiquity.

3. Establishment of Naturalism.—The sculptors who in the 1230s moved from Reims to work on the decoration of Bamberg Cathedral carried with them this interest in classical models and this bold experimental approach to subject matter. The Virgin and St. Elizabeth in the Visitation group at Bamberg evolve naturally from the Tournai and Reims versions, but the harsh and masculine head of the aged Elizabeth comes nearest of all northern medieval sculptures to the combined realism and authority of Roman portrait busts and may be a copy of such an object, probably of a male portrait. The Bamberg workshop also investigated new themes for monumental sculpture, in the figure of an unknown king or emperor mounted on a horse, the first major equestrian statue outside Italy since the fall of Roman civilization, and in the full-scale naked figures of Adam and Eve placed as flanking statues on the Adam portal. Compared with the classical figures at Reims, the Bamberg statues are less grandiloquent, more personalized, more naturalistic, and draperies alter from the classical standards in one of two ways, either by becoming indented and hacked in a more ragged manner or by being tackled very plainly and realistically, falling vertically and clinging close to the body. Both the jagged and the simpler designs of drapery are found among the statues produced at Reims after the breakup of the classicizing workshop after about 1230. On the west front of Reims the second architect of the cathedral, Jean le Loup, promoted a sculptural style more linear, elegant, and intimate, using thin textures, draperies with big broken folds, thin sharp faces, and taller, slighter proportions. Some of these statues wear smiles, which pucker the cheeks and narrow the eyes. Such analysis of

transient expression, of pleasure and grief, also appears in the Last Judgment tympanum at Bamberg and in the grinning St. Stephen on the Adam portal. This new approach is most remarkably exemplified at Naumburg (about 1250) where the group of Christ on the cross attended by the anguished Virgin and St. John has an immediacy and human impact hitherto unparalleled. The head of Christ shows an almost Baroque emotionality and breadth of handling which contrasts with the naturalistic but still intensely restrained and stylized heads on the west front of Chartres of only 100 years before. Inside the rood screen, the enclosure of the west choir of Naumburg contains statues placed on brackets around the walls, singly or in pairs. These represent benefactors of the Cathedral of Naumburg. These men and women, warriors, widows, husbands and wives, heroes and villains, represented in contemporary dress, cheerfully smiling, cautiously watchful, or ready with sword and shield as if to fight old battles again, mark the climax of the post-classicizing phase of High Gothic sculpture, exhibiting a realism born of a confident acceptance of the visible world and a growing secular spirit.

The acceptance into art of the plethora of visual phenomena in nature is seen in the observation of foliage. By the fourth decade of the 13th century sculptured foliage shed its last formal pattern qualities and became botanically correct and vital. The cut twigs of vine and ivy, carved in the 1240s in the Sainte-Chapelle, when originally coloured and gilded, must have evoked to perfection the glint and rustle of leaves in sun and breeze. Characteristically at Naumburg, behind the donors and on the rood screen, the German sculptors celebrate the beauty of nature in the same way. Naturalistic foliage also began to appear in England in the 1240s in the royal works at Windsor and the new choir of Westminster Abbey, built as an act of devotion to St. Edward the Confessor by King Henry III. The refined tastes and sensibility of the court caused great advances in English sculpture. The psychological studies which have been noted in sculpture in France and Germany can be paralleled by small corbel

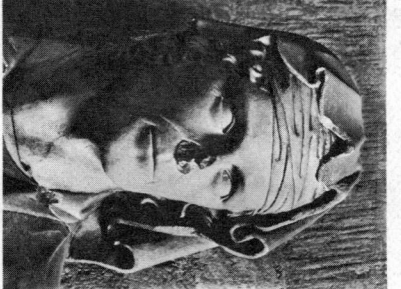

NATURALISM IN SCULPTURE

(Far left) Bamberg Horseman, possibly a king or emperor, Bamberg Cathedral; c. 1230–40. (Top left) Head of St. Elizabeth, Bamberg Cathedral. (Bottom left) Tomb effigies of the Earl and Countess of Menteith, Inchmahome Priory, Scotland; c. 1290. (Above) Adoration of the Magi, English ivory group; 13th century. In the National Museum, Copenhagen

heads in the tribune gallery at Westminster Abbey and by the beautiful little head of a sleeping youth from the royal palace at Clarendon, Wiltshire, which wears an ecstatic expression, as if the dreamer saw visions, and which in its technical finish and fineness has something almost of the touching frailty of a bird's egg. The best workmanship of the age was expended upon the great national shrines, that of St. Thomas of Canterbury, inaugurated in 1220, and that of St. Edward, inaugurated in 1269. A beautiful bronze lectern at St. Albans is said to have so impressed Henry III that he ordered a replica for the chapter house at Westminster. None of these monuments of High Gothic metalwork has survived. Nor are many English ivories of the 13th century still extant. Their appearance and temperamental quality may, however, be judged from the carving representing the Adoration of the Magi in the National Museum in Copenhagen. The design of the faces and figures is very close to English manuscripts like the Amesbury Psalter of about 1230. The naïveté, sweetness, and dignity of the queenly Virgin, the Christ child, and the three kings offering gifts make the Copenhagen ivory a key work in the definition of Gothic art. The tense and active posture of the human body, already noted in the first half of the 13th century in the remarkable effigy of a knight from a tomb at Dorchester, Oxfordshire, in which the figure, full of ferocious energy, has his legs thrown across one another and lifts one arm to draw his sword from its sheath. The finest collection of sculptures in England in the second half of the 13th century appears at Lincoln, where lordly and elegant figures, with crisp, sharp-pleated draperies, stand poised in niches and on corbels on the exterior of the Angel Choir, the English never having accepted, except momentarily at Rochester and York, the French idea of figures accumulated on the recessed sides of doorways. From the stylistic tradition of Lincoln stems one of the most intellectually and formally fascinating monuments of 13th-century sculpture in Britain: the tomb of Walter Stewart, earl of Menteith, and his wife Mary, of around 1290, in the ruined priory in the tiny island of Inchmahome in Perthshire. In a French illuminated manuscript of the *Roman de la Poire*, of about 1260, typical of the courtly Romance literature highly popular with aristocratic lay society, Tristan and Iseult are represented sitting side by side on a long throne-like bench, Tristan with his legs crossed, stretching out his right arm to embrace Iseult, while she places her left hand in his. Similar gestures appear in the Menteith tomb. The effigies, lying side by side, stretch out their long slender arms to one another, each with one hand tenderly placed upon the other's neck. The countess' robe falls in a series of sharply indented pleats with a strong sweep from breast to feet, like the Lincoln figures, and the earl has the tense turning pose of the Dorchester knight. Unconsciously reviving the imagery of the Etruscan sarcophagi from Vulci, these statues, weathered and mutilated but still beautiful, celebrate the devotion of the Christian husband and wife in terms of the high romances of the age, and splendidly evoke an open-hearted civilization free from the sophisticated pessimism of the 16th-century Renaissance voiced by Andrew Marvell's verse "To his Coy Mistress."

4. Italian Gothic Sculpture.—The reanimation of Italian sculpture by northern Gothic ideas began in the south, in Apulia, during the reign of the Hohenstaufen emperor Frederick II. A colossal bust of Frederick, found near Bari, shows him as an antique emperor crowned with a wreath and wearing a mantle caught up by a morse inscribed S.P.Q.R. The head has the harsh vigour and psychic energy of the Bamberg St. Elizabeth and belongs naturally to the German development already traced, though the antique references are given a peculiar emphasis and polemic urgency by the political pretensions of the emperor. The classicizing tendencies which have been noted in northern Gothic sculpture were an aspect of the maturing general outlook of medieval men, the overall affirmation of Christian and humane values; but even the most advanced classicizing statuary, that at Reims, retained as its natural context—and indeed as its artistic motivation—the monumental architecture of the cathedral. Italy now introduces a new note. The huge heads of antique deities from the Capua Gate exhibit an academic classicism and an interest in and appreciation of antiquity for its own sake which marks the beginning of Renaissance art in Italy. Niccolò Pisano (c. 1220–c. 1283), who was trained in Apulia, combines this academic classicism with northern Gothic influences in his Pisa Baptistery pulpit of 1259. Niccolò's reliefs have as their most obvious northern counterparts the relief panels on rood screens at Chartres, Bourges, and Naumburg. His drapery has large folds which speak of his familiarity with Gothic models of the 1250s as opposed to the 1220s, for example with manuscripts like the Basel Psalter. The powerful, long-bodied, broad-chested Christ in the allegorical Crucifixion in the Psalter is strikingly similar to Niccolò's. The male and female heads carved by Niccolò are close to heads of Jupiter or Livia on classical gems, but Niccolò may also owe something to the forceful head types drawn and cast by Nicholas of Verdun. The pulpit by Niccolò's son Giovanni Pisano (c. 1250–after 1314) at Pistoia uses pointed arches below the relief panels, the rapid rise and fall of these arches being part of the great thrust and dynamism

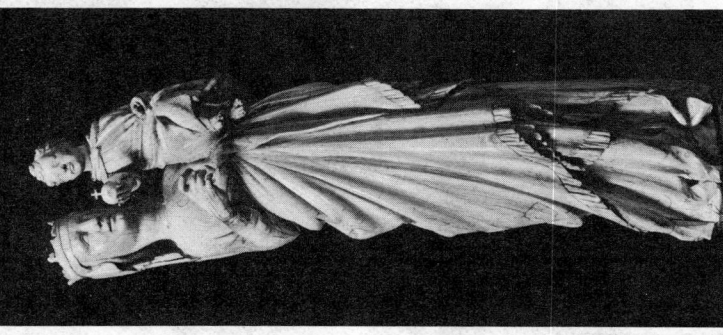

ALINARI

VIRGIN AND CHILD BY GIOVANNI PISANO, 1299. IN PISA CATHEDRAL, ITALY

with which he endows his sculptures. Storytelling of the kind developed at Chartres around 1220 no doubt influenced Giovanni and also pictorial design in northern illuminated books such as psalters and apocalypses, but Giovanni's reliefs are full of invention, motion, and psychological tension, and his individual figures have unusual vigour and bravura. His ivory Virgin in Pisa (1299) infuses characteristic energy into the mild and laconic northern Gothic standing Virgin type. No contemporary northern full-scale statues have the brooding intensity and vehemence of pose of Giovanni's prophets and sybils designed for the west front of Siena Cathedral, about 1290. At Siena and Florence cathedrals, and so far as the bronze free-standing figures are concerned, at Orvieto, sculpture is imposed on the big simple architectural designs rather as the Gothic sculptures were added to the unaccommodating architecture of Bamberg. At Orvieto, however, from 1310 to 1330, the huge flat walls between the portals were used for stone sculptured reliefs, a disposition of sculpture which went out of northern practice with the beginnings of Gothic sculpture, at Chartres. The Orvieto Genesis, Gospel, and Judgment reliefs develop yet further the rich pictorial detail launched by Giovanni Pisano at Pistoia and in his Pisa Cathedral pulpit. This increase in pictorial complexity and variety parallels in sculpture the beautiful inventions of Jean Pucelle in the Calendar and margins of his books of hours. The graceful narrative scenes at Orvieto foreshadow the bronze sculptures of Andrea Pisano and Lorenzo Ghiberti at the Baptistery of Florence, in which the door itself becomes again the area selected for sculptural display.

5. Later Northern Sculpture and Stylization.—Great sculptural programs continued to be initiated in the North. The dominating idea is an overall richness of effect. Portal statues like those on the west front of Strasbourg Cathedral participate in and merge into a play of surface patterns. Draperies take on an elegant rolling rhythm, and the underlying bulk of the figure seems to shrink back and dissolve within the deeply indented and swinging sheathes of the cloth. After 1300 foliage carving turns away from its encounter with scientific realism and favours a new buoyant formalized style of knobbed and streaming leaves, magnificently displayed in the triumphal arch in St. Elizabeth's Church

GOTHIC ART AND ARCHITECTURE

LATER NORTHERN SCULPTURE

(Above) Head of Edward II from his tomb effigy, Gloucester, Eng.; c. 1330. (Right) Wooden crucifix, Enebakk, Nor.; c. 1240. (Far right) Triumphal arch over rood screen, Church of St. Elizabeth, Marburg, Ger.; c. 1300

at Marburg and the Easter sepulchre or Percy tomb in Beverley Minster. Here foliage, figures, and undulating architectural forms are fused together to superb decorative effect, similar to that sought in English embroideries of the period. The riot of motifs encrusting the gables and cusps of the Beverley tomb is typical of the visual appetite of northern artists in the 14th century, an appetite which occasionally seems to outrun their capacity to construct a logical system of representation of man's physical environment. The use of model books, encouraging as it does a rich but incoherent visual content, is given full scope in the carved wooden seats in the great canopied stalls at Lincoln and Chester and rather later at New College, Oxford, which are admirable in craftsmanship and full of literary references and satiric and licentious humour. The same odd mixture of piquant detailed realism and overall fantasy was displayed in the luxurious royal gold plate of the period, nefs and cups, wine coolers, and private shrines and reliquaries: for example, Jean de Berry's reliquary of the Holy Thorn at the British Museum, London, where the dead rise from golden graves; and the *Goldenes Rössel* at Altötting, with its horse of gold, enameled white, awaiting its royal master who kneels like a single Magus to the Virgin in a bower of jeweled flowers. These are among the few survivors of a vast treasury of goldsmiths' work whose prestige and technical efficiency were famous throughout Europe. The skill of one northern goldsmith, Gusmin, all of whose work has vanished, is vouched for by the greatest Italian metalworker of the early Renaissance, Ghiberti.

Alongside this vein of joyous indulgence in the variety and beauty of nature and of the life of the times, there developed from the early 14th century onward a strain of melancholy vehemence in sculptures, both large and small, relating to the Passion of Christ, intended to attract and direct devotion. The Crucifixion had of course been a subject of highly important sculptures from the early Middle Ages and had been interpreted in many different ways. A wooden crucifix from Enebakk in Norway, of about 1240, combines elegance of line with delicacy and restraint of feeling. In the 14th century violence and tension is introduced into the subject, with deliberate and frequently exaggerated emphasis on Christ's agonies. The huge pinioned Christ from Friesach, of about 1300, is like a tortured Prometheus, while the sculptor of a crucifix at Coesfeld, of about 1340, has fallen back into purely Romanesque grotesquery and stylization. Sculptured groups on which might be concentrated the meditation of the devout were selected from the sequence of events leading to the Passion and Burial of Christ. The love and dependence of the faithful Christian on Christ is symbolized by the sensitive group of St. John leaning on Christ's breast, of about 1300, from the region of Lake Constance, while the pity and contrition of the Christian for the sufferings of Christ is summed up by the numerous statues of the Virgin holding her dead son on her knees—the Virgin and Child theme, as it were, hideously altered, of which a distinguished example is the drastic and painful Pietà Roettgen.

One notable reversal to older Gothic principles takes place from about the mid-14th century onward in tomb and memorial sculpture. About 1330 the face of the alabaster effigy of Edward II at Gloucester was carved as a beautiful idealized type, based on the model of the "sacred face" of Christ frequently depicted by illuminators in the 13th century, but given a picturesque and mannered treatment in the undulating locks of hair and the coiling beard. As a brilliant decorative motif this type of royal head long remained popular with the woodcarvers of cathedral stalls. But although drapery continued to be handled in a stylized and decorative way, realistic portraiture, already investigated in his imaginary likenesses by the master of Naumburg in the 13th century, appears again in Peter Parler's tomb effigies of the ancestors of the emperor Charles IV in the Cathedral of Prague, in Parler's busts in the clerestory representing men and women concerned in the building of the cathedral, and also in the tombs ordered by Charles V of France for himself and his family. The heads of the French kings carved by Jean de Liège and André Beauneveu are sharply individualized and seem shrewdly aware of the spectator. Standing figures of St. Louis and his queen, of about 1370, are conceived again with the naturalism and the eye for vitalizing details of pose and expression which marked the Naumburg experiment. The climax of this development comes with the work of Claus Sluter (c. 1350–1406) at Dijon, around 1390, in the statues of the duke and duchess of Burgundy presented by their patron saints to the Virgin and Child on the facade of the Chartreuse de Champmol. The Virgin is obviously related to the Visitation Virgin at Bamberg and the mourning Virgin at Naumburg, though more ample and swaying in pose, as befits the great theatrical tableau in which she participates.

In their realism, their heavy robes, their majestic presence, as well as their position in relation to the spectator, the kneeling donors at Champmol provide a cultural and stylistic parallel for the portraits of the donors in Masaccio's similarly illusionistic and dramatic Sta. Maria Novella fresco of the Trinity. Masaccio's monumental figures owe a debt to the example of Giotto 100 years earlier, and were in turn to appeal profoundly to Michelangelo, the giant of the High Renaissance, a hundred years later. In the same way Sluter's art is indebted to the most original and daring sculptures of the High Gothic period, while the massive bearded prophets in his *Puits de Moïse* ("Moses Well"), a vast stone monument iconographically akin to the Mosan typological parallels of the 12th century, provided inspiration for the painter Grünewald for the statuesque figure of St. Anthony in the Isenheim Altarpiece.

IV. GOTHIC PAINTING

1. French Early Gothic Pictorial Art.—From the early Middle Ages onward it is impossible to draw a sharp line of distinction between manuscript illumination and wall painting. These two branches of painting are mutually dependent, and as will be seen, they should not be isolated from such kindred arts as stained glass designing, enamel work, and figured textiles. The intimate connection of book illumination and large-scale murals is well illustrated by the most extensive surviving monument of medieval French wall painting, the picture cycles at Saint-Savin-sur-Gartempe near Poitiers, which, despite size and breadth of treatment were evidently copied from manuscript models belonging to the workshop or provided by the monastery. It may be assumed that this early 12th-century workshop consisted of lay and itinerant artists because similar paintings were executed in churches in Poitiers itself, suggesting a professional team able to serve various different clerical communities in turn. It may also be suspected that the workshop contained artists proficient in manuscript illumination, since two distinguished manuscripts are by or close to the hands of the wall painters of Saint-Savin, namely the splendid Sacramentary of Saint-Étienne at Limoges and the Life of St. Radegunda at Poitiers. This active efficient workshop was typical of the early 12th century, when many huge monastic churches were being completed and according to age-old tradition were not considered finished until they were decorated with histories and sacred images. Saint-Savin, where every wall surface including the vault bore pictures, carried this principle to an experimental extreme, integrating the whole interior by colour and the narrative flow of the imagery in a manner which is in a sense proto-Gothic; but even in churches such as Cluny in which the main visual effects were achieved by the grandeur and fastidiousness of the architectural design and its details, wall paintings were placed at certain focal points. The style of painting practised at Cluny and its outliers early in the 12th century is seen in the chapel at Berzé-la-Ville. Compared with the Western French paintings the Berzé paintings are much more elegant and metropolitan, already showing a knowledge of the Italo-Byzantine damp-fold style of drapery. A closely similar style, also using damp-fold drapery, is found in tinted drawings made in a group of Cistercian manuscripts in the early 12th century. The Cîteaux Legendary contains a page celebrating the Virgin as the Mother of God, surrounded by Old Testament types of her Virginity and enthroned on the Tree of Jesse, the theme from Isaiah which particularly appealed to 12th-century theologians and artists. This fine drawing, which had Greek antecedents, has a marked firmness and straightforwardness in its depiction of the human body. The work is contemporary with the font of Reiner of Huy and is similar in mood.

The early 12th century was a time of quickened international contacts. Sensitive and ambitious ecclesiastical patrons were able to encourage artists to fuse diverse traditions and to break out into new areas of invention and expression.

Since wall painting was regarded as a necessary adjunct to architecture, it was probably inevitable that Abbot Suger's first major act of patronage at Saint-Denis around 1130 was that he summoned "the best painters I could find from different regions, and reverently caused the walls to be repaired and becomingly painted with gold and precious colours." The painting of the old church had been, he says, in his mind since he was a child; that is, since before 1100. It is significant that this was only a makeshift, a last Romanesque endeavour before the great Gothic Age was launched by Suger with his new sculptured facade and his glorious choir. The nature of the choir of Saint-Denis—with its flowing interlocking spaces and the rapid visual liaison created between columns, rib vaults, and shafted window frames—reduced wall to the minimum and did away with the possibility of any extensive program of paintings. But animation of the interior by figures and colours was in fact given more importance than ever, endowed with a sort of magical force in the glittering and glowing stained glass windows which were a major feature of the Saint-Denis choir. The designs for the windows were probably provided by the Mosan metalworkers who produced the inlaid enamel scenes on the great cross, the medallion layout of the windows being

similar to that used in Mosan enamels and the figure style and iconography having marked resemblances. A window of the Passion at Châlons-sur-Marne, of about 1150, shows the clear stamp of Mosan imagery and style. The grandest window at Saint-Denis was the Jesse Tree window with its beautifully lucid representation of the flowering stem, the kingly ancestors, and Christ enthroned at the top surrounded by the great ring of doves signifying the gifts of the Holy Spirit. This brilliant depiction of the up-to-the-minute christological theme made an impact on artists all over Western Europe. It was immediately repeated in one of the lancets on the west front of Chartres, and in various modified forms appeared in England in the mid-12th century, in glass, manuscript illumination, and even—at Lincoln—in monumental sculpture. The glass at Saint-Denis is damaged and much restored, but Chartres possesses several Early Gothic windows—the big bold Gospel scenes in the west wall, depending on some illuminated Psalter, and the tall stately image of the crowned Virgin, robed in shimmering blue, known as Notre-Dame-de-la-Belle-Verrière.

2. English Early Gothic Pictorial Art.—The personality corresponding to Suger in 12th-century England was Henry of Blois, under whose patronage Winchester was a major centre of artistic activity, attracting artists from such places as Bury St. Edmunds and St. Albans. The palace of the Bishop of Winchester at Wolveseye was decorated with a cycle of Old and New Testament scenes which in the next century so much impressed King Henry III that he commissioned paintings on its model in his own palace at Windsor. The great Winchester Bible, worked on haphazardly by a large number of different artists, some still essentially Romanesque, exhibits in its later stages a marked change in feeling and style. The initial to Isaiah, for example, omits all the rhythms and decorative flamboyance of the earlier initial to Jeremiah and depicts God and Isaiah confronted as man to man, with a new severity and concentration of design. The grave gentle face of God parallels the beautiful sculptured heads of the figures on the west front of Chartres. Figures grow in bulk as they cease to writhe and gesticulate across the flat pages. In the unfinished initial to Psalm 109 the figures of God, Father, and Son, seated side by side, are depicted with a new realism and soberness of mood. This dignified and humane manner was no doubt magnificently displayed in the lost paintings in the king's presence chamber in the royal palace at Winchester of around 1180, which included material from the bestiary (q.v.), the popular book of animal lore. Two of the finest English manuscripts of around 1200 are bestiaries (Ashmolean, Oxford; Aberdeen University Library), containing slim prancing figures and posturing beasts set against the sheen of gold backgrounds. There is a new quickness and elegance of design here and a new taste for lively small-scale figures which becomes more marked as the 13th century proceeds. But monumentality, a grand-scale conception of the human figure with emphasis on its spatial thrust and bulk, is also an essential part of Gothic painting both in work of around 1200 and in several central works of the 13th century. The difference between the large- and small-scale figures is to some extent one of function rather than of style. Both monumental figure designs and small quickly moving crowded compositions are found among the windows made for the new choir of Canterbury Cathedral, begun by William of Sens after 1174. At Canterbury roundels showing seated prophets with scrolls recall in their movement and curved draperies Mosan figures on cross bases and portable altars. The most advanced continental and English metalwork no doubt helped to shape pictorial style. The case of Master Hugo of Bury St. Edmunds, a lay artist back in the 1130s who was both metalworker and illuminator may be recalled, and the case of the monk of St. Albans, Walter of Colchester (d. 1248), whom Matthew Paris praises as an incomparable painter and sculptor.

3. English Psalters and Their Influence.—Around 1200 English scriptoria were busy turning out large quantities of books, notably psalters furnished with prefatory bible pictures forming a sort of picture encyclopaedia of the history of the world from its creation to the coming of Christ and his Church. This kind of lavishly illustrated psalter was originally not geared specifically to secular taste; but it obviously had a great appeal to lay people,

who as the century moved on tended more and more to commission or purchase attractively illuminated books of devotion. The range or variety of the English bible cycles produced in the early 13th century, notably those designed by W. de Brailes, an artist whose name is known from his signature on several illuminations, suggests that professional artists had access to a very large pictorial archive such as might be provided by the ancient monastic libraries of England. The debt to the past is not merely in iconography. Stylistically work of the first half of the 12th century seems to have had an appeal, and even Anglo-Saxon works are evoked. De Brailes had a special flair for popular illustration. He depicts the unhappy history of the first human family with dramatic verve and a sort of gritty humour, offering a 13th-century parallel for the original and vivid carvings of Gislebertus of Autun, the great 12th-century sculptor.

English psalters with prefatory pictures became known abroad, for example the psalter now in Leiden University Library, which was made for Geoffrey, archbishop of York, an illegitimate son of Henry II, and which passed by gift or purchase at his death into French royal hands. King Louis IX (Saint Louis) learned to read in this psalter, as is known from a 14th-century note inscribed at the beginning of Psalm 1. This provides an example of a book handed down within the patron class—there are many such examples in French royal circles in the 14th century—influencing pictorial compositions and iconography over a long period of time. The export of the Leiden Psalter, among other books, accounts for the widespread appearance in continental art of some unusual English iconographic types. The influence of the English picture-book kind of psalter is exhibited in the Ingeborg Psalter (Chantilly, Musée Condé), illuminated about 1200 and owned by the queen of Philip Augustus of France. This manuscript has at the beginning Old and New Testament scenes and a series of pictures celebrating the Virgin, similar in subject matter to scenes painted by de Brailes. The style of the Ingeborg Psalter is related to the monumental painting style used in Canterbury around 1200, not probably through direct contacts but because of a common inheritance from Italo-Byzantine sources. The magnificent *contrapposto* pose of the prophets down the margins of the Ingeborg

Psalter Jesse Tree, and the trick of binding one arm close to the body under the mantle are paralleled exactly in 12th-century mosaics in the Palatine Chapel at Palermo, Sicily. Crumpled, heavy, and rather spiky drapery similar to the mosaics is used in the Old Testament scenes, along with thoroughly Byzantine iconography, despite the fact that the basic idea of the picture cycle as such is English. In the New Testament scenes a smoother style of drapery with running oval folds appears, closely allied to the style of Nicholas of Verdun. In the full-page picture of Pentecost the big figures are swathed in cascading drapery which by its drag and indentations conveys the bulk of the figures. Figures overlap one another and block out architectural members, suggesting, however tentatively, the existence of pictorial space. The architectural frames within which the figures gather become, tentatively, actual structures. The artist even attempted to depict location and furnishings by a sort of shorthand, similar to that employed in certain of the paintings of the history of St. Francis at Assisi, of the 1290s. Theophilus is redeemed by the Virgin before a draped altar seen from the side and under a lamp attached to the upright framing column and suspended from the framing arch. The gold background stands for depth, for space, not for restriction and spacelessness. The pleasure in mass and depth, exhibited here, stems from the same aesthetic taste that produced the great portals of Chartres and Reims.

The second Ingeborg Psalter style with its curved dense streams of oval pleats is found in a missal from Anchin and a north French psalter decorated with New Testament scenes in the Bibliothèque Nationale. In the form of majestic pen drawings the same style appears in the sketchbook of Villard de Honnecourt, which apart from architectural plans and elevations contains figure scenes and single figures, for example an enthroned Christ clothed in splendidly rippling draperies and the tall profile figure of one of the two mothers in the scene of the Judgment of Solomon, with delicate streaming folds covering her feet as in the latest sculptures on the north porch of Chartres. Villard provides a sort of minor bestiary with drawings of a snail, a lobster, a porcupine, and a remarkable array of lions, including one seen strictly from in front, staring and smiling, said by the artist to be drawn from the life, an early reference to the consideration of natural appearance by medieval artists, which heralds the naturalism of High and Late Gothic art.

4. Bible Illustration and Stained Glass at Chartres.—The same style of flowing folds, form-defining and unifying, is used in the vast historical and typological cycles of illustrations in the *Bible moralisée*, represented in volumes divided among libraries in Paris, Oxford, Toledo, Vienna, and New York. This great scholarly and pictorial undertaking executed in the reign of St. Louis owes in its iconography a debt to the English Psalter tradition but at the same time crystallized a new encyclopaedic model which in its turn influenced English 13th-century book illumination and sculpture. The sweep and motion of the compositions, together with the cohesive and fluent figure and drapery style, connects the *Bible moralisée* with the designs produced by the stained glass workshops set up in the early 13th century at Chartres. The symbolical Good Samaritan window in the nave of Chartres shares with the *Bible moralisée* its Genesis iconography, dynamic movement within the compositions, and medallion layout. Many Chartres windows have small-scale figures in quatrefoils and medallions, but there are also monumental figures—for example, in the clerestory lancets in the choir the Annunciation and Visita-

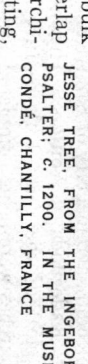

MUSICIANS GOING TO EARL RICHARD OF CORNWALL'S RECEPTION AT CREMONA, FROM THE "CHRONICA MAJORA" BY MATTHEW PARIS, 1245–59. IN CORPUS CHRISTI COLLEGE, CAMBRIDGE (MS. 16)

tion display a short, broad proportion of figure and streaming, deeply pleated folds similar to the earliest of the classical workshop sculptures at Reims. Similar monumentality is found in the lancets of the north and south transepts. In the windows below the Rose in the south transept, given by Queen Blanche about 1230, the forcefulness of the faces of the evangelists and prophets recalls the heroic heads drawn by Nicholas of Verdun in the enamel plaques on the Klosterneuburg Altar and on the Shrine of the Three Magi. The draperies in the evangelist-prophet windows have still some references to the oval pleat system, but folds are now flatter with straight edges, and the silhouette is sharply angular. This same change toward a sharper treatment of drapery, while retaining the sense of weight and breadth of the figures, is seen in the prefatory pictures of Queen Blanche and the young Louis IX and the scribes in the *Bible moralisée*.

A monumental style, classical in the dignity and presence of the figures but simpler and more naturalistic in the fall and gathering of drapery, is displayed in the series of bible pictures painted in Paris around 1250, the so-called Maciejowski Bible. Originally probably a psalter to end all psalters, this volume survives only as a bible picture-book, with Old Testament scenes featuring kings and knights and caparisoned horses, pavilioned encampments, siege engines and routs, linking the heroic warfare of God's chosen people in the time of Abraham or Joshua with the life of the 13th-century aristocracy, and in particular with St. Louis' crusading campaigns. The superlative decorative quality and vigour of these illuminations make it easy to imagine them inflated to the size of murals in the palaces of the French king. Scenes from the martyrdoms of saints, dating from this mid-13th-century monument of stylistic poise and strength, survive in the Sainte-Chapelle, and a similar graceful and refined yet strong style is found in the tinted drawings illustrating the history of the famous 7th-century goldsmith St. Eloi. A reliquary made around 1260 for the Sainte-Chapelle represents three martyrs in the same admirable drawing style as the scenes.

5. The Parisian Court Style and Its Influence on England. —After this noble and harmonious phase, the increasing metallic lightness of stonework which marks the Parisian Court Style in architecture sweeps the figurative arts away into an elegant and perhaps over-fastidious style in the Psalter of St. Louis in the Bibliothèque Nationale. Here tall, slender, tiny-headed figures move lithely against architectural elevations of brittle prettiness and flatness, delineated with fine, sharp details but no longer substantial and space-defining. The lyrical St. Louis Psalter style was applied with great effect to the illustration of romances, for example in the North French *Roman de la Poire*, in which Eros is represented like a seraph and the courtly lovers sit side by side on thrones after the pattern of the Coronation of the Virgin, and the *Lancelot*, where the exquisite protagonists are poised elegantly before wide schematic patterned backgrounds.

The court art of Paris made rapid impact in England, thanks to the family ties between the French and English royal houses. The favourite mode of illustration in England in the middle years of the 13th century was by pen drawings tinted with colour wash. This tradition of narrative illustration based on Old English precedents is exemplified by the art of Matthew Paris, the monk of St. Albans whose style offers an English parallel to that of Villard. At the same time there was growing up in other English centres a more elegant and mannered style, drawing its potency from the experience of the creation of the great Gothic cathedrals such as Salisbury, and in court circles from contacts with the Île-de-France. A Westminster manuscript of the *Life of St. Edward the Confessor* has touches of the new sharp-fold style and, a notable novelty, trees and shrubs sprouting naturalistic oak and vine leaves, following the realism of the carved capitals in the Sainte-Chapelle. The drawings in the *Life of St. Edward* may have some relation to wall paintings at Westminster. The records of royal expenditure in the reign of Henry III speak of splendid schemes of decoration executed throughout the reign by the express command of the king, in his many residences. The subjects chosen vary from the great moral theme of the Wheel of Fortune to sacred images of the Virgin and Child, from the "likeness of Winter"

ordered for the queen's chamber at Westminster to the colossal figures of triumphant Christian Virtues on the window splays of the king's huge Painted Chamber at Westminster. On the opposite wall of the Painted Chamber "all the warlike histories of the Old Testament" were portrayed. The range of the iconography and the sheer scale of the paintings as they can be reconstructed from the original commissions and from copies is most impressive. The history of Western mural painting is distorted by the wholesale destruction of these works. The sensibility and progressiveness of the royal paintings can be guessed from one remarkable survivor from the reign of Henry III, the retable in Westminster Abbey, a strikingly early example of panel painting in which the best-preserved figure, that of St. Peter, has the suave elegance of the figures in St. Louis' Psalter, but the painterly technique is difficult to parallel outside Italy and then only at a date rather later than 1260.

Close in style to the retable are the illustrations in the Douce Apocalypse, painted in brilliant colours but retaining the plain vellum backgrounds of the tinted drawing tradition. Dating to about 1260, the Douce Apocalypse is stylistically as advanced as anything in Europe at that date, having complex figure groups, ponderous stooping and turning figures, fine naturalistic foliage and lavish pictorial detail. The manuscript is an outstanding example of the English 13th-century taste for illustrated versions of the Book of Revelation. Several slightly varying cycles of Apocalypse illustrations were designed in England around the middle years of the 13th century and representatives of these cycles were exported and were carefully copied in France and the Netherlands in the 14th century.

6. German Gothic Painting.—Thanks to the influence of Mosan metalworkers, notably Nicholas of Verdun, on German centres such as Cologne, a classicizing style close to that of the Ingeborg Psalter was familiar in Germany early in the 13th century. The vigorous pictures in an evangeliary from Cologne contain figures clothed in incessantly scooped and streaming folds, for example the shrouded Christ in the Deposition scene and the sleeping Jesse in the Tree of Jesse page. Close to Villard's woman from the Judgment of Solomon are the allegorical figures portrayed in a manuscript of the visions of the mystic St. Hildegarde of Bingen, at Lucca. A modification of the flowing pleated drapery style, tending toward broader, sharper folds giving a jagged outline to the figures, occurs in a psalter of about the mid-13th century from the diocese of Basel, for example in the drawing of the Virgin seated on the throne of Solomon, guarded by lions, which recalls the grand composition of the contemporary wall painting of the same theme at Gurk Cathedral. In German 13th-century art humanistic subjects like the Virgin and Child were popular, and great interest was shown in dramatic psychological aspects of the biblical narratives. In the Basel Psalter Christ kneels before the cross which he is about to mount.

The addition of sentiment to the familiar scenes of Christian iconography is paralleled by the symbolic extension of these scenes, interpreting their spiritual meaning in concrete pictorial forms. In the Basel Psalter Christ is nailed to the cross by Virtues, heroic female figures like those in the Painted Chamber at Westminster. The Flagellation scene contains executioners wielding great scourges of matted twigs, dressed in up-to-date garb. The Resurrection shows soldiers with helmets or great cloth hats or hats strung on a long leather strap round the neck, details unequaled in their prosaic realism until Flemish panel painting of the 15th century. Together with the realism of the figures one finds naturalistic foliage on the trees in the Garden of Gethsemane and carved on the capital of the Flagellation column, paralleling the appearance of sharp naturalistic foliage on actual capitals at Naumburg. Naumburg is also brought to mind by a Mainz Cistercian breviary of about 1260 where Christ's ancestors are represented as couples seated on benches or standing, clad in fashionable modern dress, like the highly characterized pairs of donors in the Naumburg choir.

7. Gothic Painting in the Late 13th and Early 14th Centuries.—In Paris in the last quarter of the 13th century the principal illuminator was Honoré, whose work is close in style to Parisian ivories of the period, and also to the earlier Douce Apocalypse and Westminster Retable. In his Gospel Lectionary of the Sainte-Chapelle a sense of plasticity is displayed in the figures, their draperies and settings. The history of David page in the breviary paid for by King Philip the Fair in 1296 contains fine monumental groups of figures with thin-textured, subtly modeled draperies. Honoré's illustrations in the splendid *Somme le Roy* in the British Museum show a steady increase in the pictorial investigation of the natural world. The illuminated book as it developed in northwest Europe around 1300 is more elaborate and sensuously beautiful than anything in the whole previous history of illumination. A great tradition evolved in Northern France, the Netherlands and England, wherein not merely picture pages and initials were illuminated but the margins also were sumptuously enriched with foliage fronds and fantastic or realistic beasts and strutting groups of figures with thin-textured, subtly modeled draperies. The charm of this style, the sheen and undulation of the draperies, the voluminous figures, the great diapered backgrounds, the magnificent architectural frames, and the wealth of subsidiary details cascading into the margins, are excellently displayed in the psalter of Robert de Lisle, in the British Museum.

The Psalter of Johannes von Valkenburg (c. 1290) shows German succumbing to French influences. The emergence of an early mode of "international Gothic" results in many resemblances between English and German art, first through common allegiance to France and then through direct contacts. The picturesque large-scale figures in Abbess Cunegonde's Passionary of 1320 have an emotional power like that exhibited in the vigorous Holkham Bible, an English picture-book close to the springs of popular 14th-century religion. A painting of St. Michael and the dragon, a detached leaf from a Cologne manuscript, in which the meandering hemline of the huge patterned mantle reveals and conceals the coloured lining, has strong ties of style and mood with the de Lisle Psalter.

Panel paintings have survived from the early 14th century in both England and Germany. The same long-fingered, tense-faced, tall, mannered figures in soft clinging vesture occur among the saints on the retable from Thornham Parva in Suffolk and the paintings of the Gospel narrative added to the back of Nicholas of Verdun's retable at Klosterneuburg, in 1324-29. One of the ways in which English art made itself known on the Continent was in the form of the embroidered copes and other vestments, known as *opus anglicanum*, designed in the best illuminators' workshops and following the iconographic program favoured in psalters and books of hours: standing saints with their symbols, the Old and New Testaments, and the history of the life and death of the Virgin. These grand textiles, worked with marvellous technical proficiency in coloured silks and gold thread and often heavy with pearls, were avidly sought by continental patrons, notably the popes, and the figure compositions, for example those of a cope now at Bologna, full of a Giotto-like firmness of figure and Lorenzetti-like variety of detail, must have made a forceful impression on Italian artists and been one of the methods whereby northern Gothic art became known in Italy and blended with Italo-Byzantine and Early Christian traditions of centres like Rome.

8. Italian Gothic Painting and Its Widespread Influence.—Cimabue (1240?-after 1302?), Cavallini (c. 1250-c. 1330), Duccio (c. 1255-c. 1319), and Giotto (1266/67-1337) stand at the beginning of the Gothic phase of Italian painting. Giotto's frescoes of the history of the Virgin and Christ at Padua, so far as the presentation of physical bulk and the noble dignity of the figures are concerned, crown the classicizing tendencies apparent in the early 13th century in the North, in the Ingeborg Psalter and the sculptures at Reims. Giotto's Vices and Virtues at Padua descend from the Virtues at Westminster, of the 1260s, but his art has a new firsthand quality, a power of observation which endows with unprecedented conviction and verisimilitude the biblical and human scenes portrayed. Though exercised in a different context, Giotto's intelligence is similar to that of Dante. He thinks afresh about everything. Just as Dante's shadow, speaking of his solidity, of his being alive, startles the souls in Hell and Purgatory, so Giotto's figures and imagined scenes startled by their lifelike appearance generations of painters who followed him. The style of Siena in which similar visual values were expounded in a softer and more decorative manner formed a bridge between the new discoveries of *trecento* Italy and Northern traditions, all the easier to cross since accuracy of observation and an interest in the representation of space were independently developing in the North.

The Klosterneuburg panel of the Resurrection and "Noli me tangere" contains Italian motifs in the projecting corbeled architecture of the tomb, and in the dramatic pose of Christ and the Magdalen echoes Giotto's version of the subject at Padua. From the early 14th century Italian art began to make itself felt also in English painting, quite haphazardly at first, in occasional motifs and figure types and landscape schemes. In the East Anglian Gorleston Psalter Crucifix page, the cliff-edge platform on which the figures stand and the kneeling Magdalen clinging to the cross have obvious links with the work of Simone Martini. Simone himself was present at Avignon from 1340 and executed panel paintings and important wall paintings in the Cathedral of Notre-Dame-des-Doms, but Sienese influence—notably that of the "Maestà" of Duccio—had already been absorbed by the greatest French painter of the first half of the 14th century, Jean Pucelle, perhaps as a result of a visit to Italy in the 1320s. Pucelle's response to Italy does not consist of raw references stranded within the linear decorative language of the North but is exhibited in his advanced mastery of space, together with a deepening of feeling and greater variety of pose and setting, combined with a fresh, lyrical yet restrained treatment of the borders. Coincidences in composition between scenes from the life of St. Louis in the hours and wall paintings in the Sainte-Chapelle, now known only from 17th-century copies, suggest that here again an illuminator turned his skill to large mural paintings, employing the same visual formulas as in his miniatures. Pucelle's manuscripts and his workshop model book exercised a long-lived influence in French painting, extending even into the last quarter of the 13th century for Jean de Berry.

Other places in Europe apart from Avignon, Paris, and East Anglia were influenced by Italian *trecento* art. Catalonia produced paintings in a purely Italian style, for example the Retable of St. Mark from Barcelona by Arnau Bassa, of 1346. In Bohemia the emperor Charles IV, one of the outstanding art patrons of the Middle Ages, imported panels by the Italian Tommaso da Modena and brought together Italian, German, and French artists, to whom are due manuscripts like the *Liber Viaticus* made for Charles's chancellor, close to contemporary Italian illumination in the bright, light colours and ostentatious use of foreshortening, and also an array of paintings in the Castle of Karlštejn. The

Chapel of St. Catherine contains wall and panel paintings in a mixed German-Sienese manner, dating to the 1350s. A feature of the Karlštejn program was the splendidly crowned and vested full-length portraits of the emperor's ancestors and predecessors and the portraits of Charles himself adoring the Virgin and Child or his choice reliquary crosses. Remarkably precocious frescoes of the history of Christ, with deep crowded compositions, fluent lustrous draperies, substantial figures, and forceful characterization of heads, were painted about 1360 in the Emmaus Monastery at Prague. Master Theodoric, Charles's court painter, in 1365 decorated the Chapel of the Holy Cross at Karlštejn with a Crucifixion and a host of panel paintings of saints, huge-headed with rounded gleaming draperies, related ultimately to Sienese art but highly personal in their massive bulk and solemn air. On the vault are painted scenes from the Apocalypse. In their mystical quality and their almost abstract emphasis on simple solid forms, projecting and receding with smooth surfaces, they anticipated the expressive use of chiaroscuro and the weird smouldering intensity of the Wittingau Altar Passion scenes, about 1380, and the chunky forceful figures placed in a shrill hard light in the Grabower Altar of Master Bertram of Hamburg, of 1379-83.

9. **Later Gothic Art and Books of Hours.**—Marginalia as developed by Pucelle early in the 14th century were given extraordinary importance and coherence in the Bible of Jean de Sy of 1355, perhaps by Jean Bondol of Bruges, a magnificent monument of narrative art full of graceful invention. Bondol also designed the cartoons (1376-78) for the Apocalypse Tapestries at Angers, commissioned by Louis, duke of Anjou. These designs look back to models originating in England. The scene of the winepress of the wrath of God (Rev. 14.19), for example, corresponds exactly to the same scene in the English 13th-century Lambeth Apocalypse. The sympathy exhibited by Pucelle for the depth-finding and humanistic art of Italy was continued in the last quarter of the 14th century by the artists working in Paris, and for members of the French royal family in centres like Dijon and Bourges. The Parement of Narbonne, grisaille painting on silk representing scenes from the Passion, with taut, sharply conceived portraits of Charles V and his queen kneeling at prayer, has an impressive quality of barely restrained vehemence in its poses and expressions.

The hand of the Master of the Parement is seen also in *Les Très Belles Heures de Notre Dame* commissioned by Jean de Berry in the 1380s, where the powerful and rugged figures swathed in heavy flowing draperies have links with the Emmaus frescoes of the 1360s. In Jean de Berry's Psalter the painter-sculptor André Beauneveu depicts the 12 apostles and 12 prophets as massively draped figures poised on huge three-dimensional thrones. The grace and sweetness of Pucelle's manuscripts, absent in the more incisive draftsmanship of the Parement Master, reappears in the scenes representing the passion in Jean de Berry's *Petites Heures* (Paris, Bibl. Nat.), while the same tenderness and ease, but with a new imaginativeness and naturalism of handling, appears in the illustrations by Jacquemart de Hesdin in *Les Très Belles Heures de Jean de Berry* (Brussels, Bibl. Royale). Jacquemart's pages open into vaulted chambers or long winter landscapes with windmills and distant castles. In the variety of his figures and his mastery of tone and atmosphere a new level of pictorial realism, qualitatively as remarkable as that of Giotto, is achieved. The final peak of Jean de Berry's patronage is the sumptuously illuminated *Les Très Riches Heures* (Chantilly, Musée Condé) painted by Pol de Limburg and his brothers before 1416, in which a completely poised style of great verve and elegance is exhibited, superbly well informed about the best international standards in art. The famous Calendar pictures go far beyond Jacquemart in the realism and sensibility of their architectural portraiture and their changing seasonal landscapes. The richness of content, formal complexity, and spatial illusionism of these great manuscripts led inevitably, both from the patron's and the painter's points of view, to an expansion of panel painting. Close to Jacquemart in mood, though perhaps as late or later than *Les Très Riches Heures* is the Wilton Diptych in the National Gallery, London, showing Richard II of England presented by his patron saints to the Virgin and Child. The unknown painter of the Diptych had complete understanding of the true International Gothic visual language, combining an interest in pictorial space and physical presence with flowing surface patterns and brilliantly decorative texture and colour, making a convincing and concrete image of a dream world of touching youthfulness and beauty. The crowned portrait of King Richard in Westminster Abbey, a public picture, not intended like the Wilton Diptych for private devotional purposes, is the English equivalent to the royal portraits at Karlštejn, the palace of Richard's father-in-law. The highest delicacy of feeling combined with grandeur of composition appears in the circular panel in the Louvre by Jean Malouel, ingeniously conflating the imagery of the Trinity, the Man of Sorrows, and the Descent from the Cross.

The strong style of the Parement Master is recalled by the brilliantly coloured and fascinatingly picturesque altar wings (1394-99) that were painted by Melchior Broederlam of Ypres for the Chartreuse de Champmol. These panels prepare the way for the rise of Flemish painting in the 15th century, for the genius of Jan van Eyck and the Master of Flémalle. Their work moves out of the internationally practised Gothic style into a recognizably rational Renaissance style which, while still celebrating the marvels of the medieval faith, finally conquers the world of physical reality.

See also GOTHIC REVIVAL; ILLUMINATED MANUSCRIPTS; IVORY CARVING; METALWORK, DECORATIVE; RENAISSANCE ART AND ARCHITECTURE; ROMANESQUE ART AND ARCHITECTURE; STAINED GLASS; and TAPESTRY.

BIBLIOGRAPHY.—*General.*—*Europäische Kunst um 1400*, Catalogue of Council of Europe Exhibition, Vienna (1962) ; *L'Europe gothique XIIe–XIVe siècles*, Catalogue of Council of Europe Exhibition, Paris (1968) ; P. Frankl, *The Gothic: Literary Sources and Interpretation through Eight Centuries* (Eng. trans. 1960) ; H. Hahnloser, *Villard de Honnecourt* (1935) ; G. Henderson, *Gothic* (1967) ; H. Karlinger, *Die Kunst der Gotik* (1927) ; E. Mâle, *L'Art religieux du XIIIe siècle en France* (1902) ; M. Meiss, ed., *Studies in Western Art: Acts of the Twentieth International Congress of the History of Art*, I (1963) ; E. Panofsky, *Abbot Suger on the Abbey Church of Saint-Denis* (1946). *Architecture.*—J. Bony, "The Resistance to Chartres in Early Thirteenth-Century Architecture," *Journal of the British Archaeological Association*, XXI (1958) ; and "French Influences on the Origins of English Gothic Architecture," *Journal of the Warburg and Courtauld Institutes*, XII (1949) ; R. Branner, *Burgundian Gothic Architecture* (1961), *La Cathédrale de Bourges et sa place dans l'architecture gothique* (1962), *St. Louis and the Court Style in Gothic Architecture* (1965) ; J. Fitchen, *The Construction of Gothic Cathedrals* (1961) ; P. Frankl, *Gothic Architecture* (Eng. trans. 1963) ; M. Hastings, *St. Stephen's Chapel* (1955) ; E. Panofsky, *Gothic Architecture and Scholasticism* (1951) ; C. Seymour, *Notre-Dame of Noyon* (1939). *Sculpture.*—A. Andersson, *English Influence in Norwegian and Swedish Figuresculpture in Wood, 1220–70* (1949) ; Comte J. de Borgrave d'Altena, "L'Art mosan," *Bulletin des Musés royaux d'Art et d'Histoire* (1951) ; T. G. Frisch, "The Twelve Choir Statues of the Cathedral at Reims," *Art Bulletin*, 42 (1960) ; A. Katzenellenbogen, *The Sculptural Programs of Chartres Cathedral* (1959) ; R. Koechlin, *Les Ivoires gothiques français* (1924) ; E. Panofsky, *Die deutsche Plastik des elften bis dreizehnten Jahrhunderts* (1924) ; J. Pope-Hennessy, *Italian Gothic Sculpture* (1955) ; W. Sauerländer, "Sens and York," *Journal of the British Archaeological Association*, XXIII (1959). *Von Sens bis Strassburg* (1966) ; L. Stone, *Sculpture in Britain: the Middle Ages* (1955). *Painting.*—M. Aubert, *Le Vitrail en France* (1946) ; R. Branner, "The Painted Medallions in the Sainte-Chapelle in Paris," *Trans. Am. Phil. Soc.*, N.S. 58, part 2 (1968) ; F. Deuchler, *Der Ingeborgpsalter* (1967) ; L. Grodecki, "Les peintures du château de Karlstein et l'art français," *Bulletin monumental*, CXV (1957) ; G. Henderson, "Studies in English Manuscript Illumination," *Journal of the Warburg and Courtauld Institutes*, XXX (1967) and XXXI (1968) ; *Les Manuscrits à peintures en France du XIIIe au XVIe siècle*, Catalogue of Exhibition, Bibliothèque Nationale, Paris (1955) ; M. Meiss, *French Painting in the Time of Jean de Berry* (1967) ; K. Morand, *Jean Pucelle* (1962) ; O. Pächt, "A Giottesque Episode in English Mediaeval Art," *Journal of the Warburg and Courtauld Institutes*, VI (1943) ; H. Swarzenski, *Die lateinischen illuminierten Handschriften des XIII. Jahrhunderts am Rhein, Main, und Donau* (1937). (G. D. S. H.)

GOTHIC LANGUAGE, the earliest of the recorded Germanic languages (*q.v.*) and the only east Germanic language on which there is trustworthy information. Knowledge of it is derived primarily from the remains of a Bible translation. This is presumably the translation referred to by several early church historians, made for the Visigoths living along the lower Danube by a Visigothic bishop of the Arian church named Ulfilas (q.v.), who lived during the 4th century.

The surviving manuscripts are not originals but much later copies thought to have been written in northern Italy during the period of Ostrogothic rule (493–555). They include considerable portions of the New Testament, but only parts of Nehemiah from the Old Testament. Though most of them are palimpsests, a handsome exception is the famous *Codex Argenteus*, written in silver and gold letters on purple parchment and containing (in 187 leaves remaining from an original 330 or 336) portions of the four Gospels in the order Matthew, John, Luke, Mark. Closely related to these biblical manuscripts are 8 leaves containing fragments of a commentary (the *Skeireins*) on St. John's Gospel. Minor, nonbiblical texts include a fragment of a calendar, two deeds containing some Gothic sentences, and a 10th-century Salzburg manuscript which gives the Gothic alphabet, a few Gothic words with Latin transliteration, and some phonetic remarks with illustrative examples. The only other source of information about Gothic and dialects closely related to it are the Vandalic, Visigothic and, especially, Ostrogothic names which occur in Greek and Latin writings. About Gepidic, Rugian and Burgundian, all thought to have been similar to Gothic, little or nothing is known.

In the 4th and 5th centuries Gothic must have spread at least thinly over much of southern Europe. It disappeared, however, with surprising rapidity. There is no evidence for its survival in Italy after the fall of the Ostrogothic kingdom, and in Spain it is doubtful whether the Visigoths retained their language until the Arabic conquest. In the 9th century the German monk Walafrid Strabo mentioned Gothic as still being used in some churches near the lower Danube. After that time it seems to have survived only among the Goths of the Crimea, who were last mentioned in the 16th century, when the Flemish diplomat Augier Ghislain de Busbecq (q.v.), in Constantinople as ambassador from Ferdinand I of Austria, made a collection of words and phrases that show that their language was still in essentials a form of Gothic.

Alphabet.—The Gothic alphabet, said to have been created by Ulfilas, consisted of 27 symbols. Two of them functioned only as numbers, the remaining 25 as both numbers and letters. (One of these, x, was used only in transliterating Greek χ.) The shape, numerical value and ordering of the symbols show clearly that the alphabet was based primarily on that of the Latin alphabet.

Consonants.—The phonological structure reflected in the consonant symbols is fairly clear. (The Gothic letters are given here in the customary transliteration.) There seem to have been three voiceless stops *p t k*, three voiceless nonsibilant spirants *f þ h*, three stop-spirants (or stops) *b d g*, two sibilants *s z*, two nasals *m n*, two liquids *l r*, and two semivowels *w j*. The remaining consonant symbols, *q* and *ƕ*, may have represented separate phonemes /kʷ/ and /hʷ/ or simply the clusters /kw/ and /hw/. The nasal /n/ was presumably velar before *k, q, g*; in these positions it was usually written (as in Greek) with the letter *g* (or *gg*): *driggk* "drank," *briggan* "you two," *briggan* "to bring," though occasionally (as in Latin) with the letter *n*: *þank* "thanks," *inqis* "you two," *briggiþ* "bring ye."

Vowels.—The alphabet contained five simple vowel symbols: *i e a o u*, from which four compound symbols were also made: *ei ai au iu*; in addition, *w* was used in transliterating Greek *υ* and *οι* (both = [ü] in contemporary Greek). The phonological structure underlying these symbols is not entirely clear, and scholars have suggested three different solutions. (1) A literal interpretation assumes that each symbol (simple or compound) represented only one vowel or diphthong. The compound symbols *ei ai au* are assumed to stand for monophthongs (the corresponding *ε*, and *α*, of contemporary Greek stood for monophthongs), and Gothic *ai* and *au* were used to transliterate the Greek monophthongs written *ε* and *o*); the status of *iu* as monophthong or diphthong is considered uncertain. This interpretation gives a system of eight vowels /i ɪ ε a ɔ o u/, spelled *ei i e ai a au o u*, plus the uncertain *iu*; no contrast between short and long vowels is assumed, because none is indicated in the spelling. (2) An etymological interpretation assumes that short vowels and long vowels and diphthongs of Proto-

Germanic remained respectively short, long and diphthongal in biblical Gothic. This gives a system of five short vowels /i ε a ɔ u/, spelled *i ai a au u*; seven long vowels /i ē ɛ̄ ā ɔ̄ ō ū/, spelled *i ei ... ū/*, spelled *ei e ai a au o u*; and three diphthongs /ai au iu/, spelled *ai au iu*. This analysis assumes that Ulfilas' spelling system did not distinguish between short and long *a* and *u*, nor between short, long and diphthongal *ai* and *au*. (3) A mixed interpretation agrees with (1) in assuming that *ei ai au* always stood for monophthongs, but with (2) in assuming that the short/long contrast was maintained. This gives a system of five short vowels /i ε a ɔ u/, spelled *i ai a au u*; and seven long vowels /i ē ɛ̄ ā ɔ̄ ō ū/, spelled *ei e ai a au o u*; and one diphthong /iu/, spelled *iu*. This analysis assumes that Ulfilas' spelling system did not distinguish between short and long *a* and *u*.

History.—Gothic is of particular interest because it antedates by three to four centuries the earliest recorded stages of the other Germanic languages. (Only a few Norse runic inscriptions are older.) Accordingly, it possesses a number of archaic features which had been almost or entirely lost by the time the other languages began to appear: in its verbs a passive voice, a dual number and one type of past tense formed with reduplication; and in one noun class a special vocative case. At the same time, it also shows many changes from Proto-Germanic. In final unstressed syllables most long vowels have been shortened, and most short vowels lost; *erþō > airþa* "earth," *staunaz > stains* "stone." Among the consonants, final voiced spirants have been unvoiced: nom. *hlaibaz*, acc. *hlaiban > hlaifs, hlaif* "bread" (but dat. *hlaiba*); nom. *stadiz*, acc. *stadan > staþs, staþ* "place" (but dat. *stada*); nom. acc. *hatezan > hatis* "hate" (but dat. *hatiza*); and perhaps also nom. *dagaz*, acc. *dagan > dags, dag* (= [daxs dax]?) "day" (but dat. *daga* = [daga]?). Though an understanding of the vowels depends on the interpretation chosen (see *Vowels*, above), the following changes are clear. PGmc. **e* and **ē* have coalesced in the vowel spelled *e*: **baer-, *hēr > baer-, her* "here." PGmc. **a* and **e* give Gothic *i* in most environments, but *ai* before *r, h, ƕ*: **gebanan, *gibidi > giban, gibiþ* "to give," "he gives," but **beranan, *biridi > bairan, bairiþ* "to bear," "he bears," etc. Similarly, PGmc. **[u ~ o]* gives Gothic *u* in most environments, but *au* before *r, h, ƕ*: **hupin* (acc.), **jokan > hup, juk* "hip," "yoke"; but **wurtiz, *wordan > waurts, waurd* "root," "word"; etc.

BIBLIOGRAPHY.—*General survey:* James W. Marchand, "The Gothic Language," *Orbis*, vol. 7, pp. 492–515 (1958). *Text:* Wilhelm Streitberg, *Die gotische Bibel*, 3rd ed. (1950). *Grammars:* Joseph Wright, *Grammar of the Gothic Language*, 2nd ed. (1954); Fernand Mossé, *Manuel de la langue gotique*, 2nd ed. (1956); Wilhelm Braune, *Gotische Grammatik*, 16th ed. (1961); Wolfgang Krause, *Handbuch des Gotischen* (1953). *Dictionary and Concordance:* Ernst Schulze, *Gotisches Glossar* (1848); *Etymological Dictionary:* Sigmund Feist, *Vergleichendes Wörterbuch der gotischen Sprache*, 3rd ed. (1939). *Ostrogothic:* Ferdinand Wrede, *Über die Sprache der Ostgoten in Italien* (1891). *Vandalic:* Ferdinand Wrede, *Über die Sprache der Wandalen* (1886). *Bibliography:* Fernand Mossé, "Bibliographia Gotica," *Mediaeval Studies*, vol. 12, pp. 237–324 (1950), supplements in vol. 15, pp. 169–183 (1953), vol. 19, pp. 174–196 (1957). (W. G. MN.)

GOTHIC REVIVAL, a term first used in England in the mid-19th century to describe buildings being erected in the style of the Middle Ages. Its meaning has since been expanded to embrace the entire neo-Gothic movement. The date of its beginning is not easy to pinpoint. Throughout Europe, particularly in those countries north of the Alps where the Gothic tradition had been strong, a nostalgia for the past—affecting the arts in general—had continued into the post-medieval period. In the case of architecture, even when there was no particular liking for Gothic, conservatism and local building practices had conditioned its use as the style for churches and collegiate buildings. In its earliest phase Gothic Revival is not easily distinguished from Gothic Survival.

The Gothic Revival in the arts was sustained from the early 18th century by a critical and philosophical inquiry into what was meant by "truth to nature," and the place in poetry (in its widest sense) of inspiration, imagination, and "feeling." Poets and critics, conscious that an emphasis on reason and on classical models was inadequate as a form of expression for their emotional and sentimental hankerings, looked back to the Middle Ages—and, in England and Germany, to the remoter past of Germanic or Celtic mythology and legend. The word "Gothic" changed its meaning as a critical term: from being used to identify the poets of a former age with the historic Goths—regarded as a "rude and brutish" race—it came to mean a quality of grandeur and strength transcending rules (as when Pope, in 1725, compared Shakespeare to "an ancient majestic piece of Gothic architecture ... strong and solemn ..." despite irregularity of structure and "dark, odd and uncouth passages"). Later, what was "dark, odd and uncouth," itself became praiseworthy; Horace Walpole's "Gothic romance," *The Castle of Otranto* (1765), itself not wholly serious in intent, dwelt on the macabre, supernatural, and irrational, borrowing its "stage properties" from a romanticized idea of the Middle Ages.

Underlying and informing this critical-philosophic revival of the Gothic was the work of scholars, antiquarians, and historians. In England, for example, the editions of, and introductions to, the works of Chaucer, Spenser, and Milton that began to appear early in the 18th century reestablished a continuity with what the 18th century saw as "Gothic" (in this case medieval) poetic principle and practice. Similarly, the collection and editing of early manuscripts and records (both literary and historical) was a sign of revived interest in the past for itself, and of a wish to find in it a source of strength. In literature alone, much of this change of emphasis in the 18th century is often regarded as "pre-Romantic;" but although it is one of the complex interactions of forces from which the Romantic movement developed, it has its own place as an aspect of the wider aesthetic "Gothic Revival."

The first self-conscious imitation of Gothic architecture for reasons of nostalgia appeared in England in the early 18th century, when it was accompanied and invigorated by a liking for the Gothic mood. Poets in particular upheld the Gothic Revival in its first phase and were responsible to a large extent for the conditioning of taste and the acceptance of a style that had been vilified by leaders of fashion in Renaissance and post-Renaissance times.

Buildings erected at that time in the Gothic manner were for the most part frivolous and decorative garden ornaments, more Rococo in spirit than the Gothic they sought to imitate. But with the erection of Strawberry Hill by Horace Walpole and his committee of amateur advisers, a new and significant aspect of the revived style was given convincing form, and by the beginning of the 19th century picturesque planning and grouping provided the basis for experimentation in architecture. Gothic was especially suited to this aim. Scores of houses in the castellated style were built in England during the closing years of the 18th century.

With developing archaeological interest a new and more earnest turn was given to the movement—a turn that coincided with the religious revivals of the early 19th century, resulting in a spate of church building in the Gothic style. Only toward the middle of the century were the seriousness and moral purpose which underlay this movement formulated as a doctrine and presented to architects as a challenge to the intellect. A. W. N. Pugin, in England, was the first to codify the principles of the Gothic Revival. But there were other professionals of revolution; E. E. Viollet-le-Duc in France and John Ruskin in England were indeed far more persuasive and influential as exponents. They gave to the movement a moral and intellectual purpose. The second half of the 19th century saw the active and highly productive period of the Revival. By then the mere imitation of Gothic forms and details was its least important aspect; architects were intent to create original works of architecture based on an analysis of the principles underlying Gothic architecture and deeply infused with its spirit. The great buildings of the Gothic Revival all date from this period. Once a conviction in the intellectual honesty and moral rectitude of the Gothic Revival lapsed, the movement quickly degenerated into a simple stylistic revival.

The great achievement of the mature Gothic Revival was that it restored common sense to architecture. By the end of the 18th century the discipline imposed by the classical style had become so rigid and codified and so restrictive that all ease of organization and all convenience of planning was impossible. The height, the breadth, and the width of any room of pretension was determined by rules; even the size of the door and window openings was controlled by these rules. When it came to detail, the formulas of Neoclassicism were even more inhibiting. The height of a column and all related moldings were fixed by its diameter, and the application of details derived from Greek and Roman temples was so unsuited to the complexities even of early 19th-century planning that very few architects could handle the syntax; a crisis ensued every time a corner had to be turned or a junction effected. The Gothic Revival swept aside this difficulty. Henceforth all plans, all arrangements, all moldings even, could follow the apparently wayward pattern imposed by external limitations and, most important, by use. Rooms could be of the size and shape required, they could be set in relation one to another according to convenience, and openings could be placed exactly where they were needed. The particular and appropriate success of Alfred Waterhouse's vast and complex public buildings would have been impossible before the Gothic Revival.

The other great contribution that the Gothic Revival made to architecture was the encouragement of freedom and honesty of structural arrangement. Structural elements could be provided as and where they were needed. There was no need for dissimulation. French architects, and Viollet-le-Duc in particular, were the first to appreciate the applicability of the Gothic skeleton structure, with its light infilling, to a modern age, and the analogy was not lost on subsequent architects at a time when the steel frame was emerging as an important element of structural engineering. Functionalism and structural honesty as ideals in the modern architectural movement are a legacy of the Gothic Revival.

The Gothic Revival was, not surprisingly, felt with most force in those countries in which Gothic architecture itself was most in evidence—England, France, and Germany. Each conceived it as a national style, but each gave to it a strong and characteristic twist of its own.

ENGLAND

The Gothic Revival in England was largely conditioned by literary theory and practice. The so-called "Revolution of Taste" in the mid-18th century—marked by publication of Richard Hurd's *Letters on Chivalry and Romance* (1762) and Thomas Percy's *Reliques of Ancient English Poetry* (1765) had, of course, its antecedents. Even Pope—so often regarded as the supreme English votary of neoclassicism—in his Ovidian heroic epistle, *Eloisa to Abelard* (1717), showed what later came to be thought of as a "Gothic" sensibility and style. Thomas Gray, however, especially in his poems of the 1750s and later, and in his letters, was the first major poet to seek his inspiration in a "Gothic" past—not only medieval but Celtic and Icelandic. Thomas Warton—poet and critic, and author of *Observations on the Faerie Queen* (1754), the first worthwhile critical study of Spenser—acquired his interest in the Middle Ages from architecture, and in his work on medieval English cathedrals and churches connected the literary aspect of the Gothic Revival with the work begun by a group of antiquaries in the late 17th century, and continuing into the 18th. Antiquarianism also accounted for a continuing interest in the Middle Ages: Sir William Dugdale and Roger Dodsworth issued the first volume of the *Monasticon Anglicanum* in 1655; and Thomas Tanner published *Notitia Monastica* in 1695. In 1707 the Society of Antiquaries, abolished under James I, was reestablished, and one of its members, Browne Willis (1682–1760), was responsible for the rebuilding in 1724–30, by Edward Wing, of the church at Fenny Stratford, Buckinghamshire, in a simplified Gothic style. As a monument to Gothic survival rather than revival, for the Gothic tradition of building continued strong in England. Wren (1632–1723) and Hawksmoor (1661–1736) both worked at times in a Gothic style, but with no inherent sympathy for Gothic and with no conscious feeling of retrospection. Collegiate buildings in both Oxford and Cambridge were for the most part Gothic throughout the 17th and well into the 18th century, when the transition from a survival

GOTHIC REVIVAL

(Top left) Midland Hotel at St. Pancras Station, London, by Sir George Gilbert Scott, 1867–74. (Top right) Manchester Town Hall by Alfred Waterhouse, 1869–77. (Centre right) Fonthill Abbey, Wiltshire, by James Wyatt, 1796–1806, from John Rutter's "Delineations of Fonthill," 1823. (Bottom left) Strawberry Hill, Twickenham, built for Horace Walpole by William Robinson, Robert Adam and James Essex, 1748–77. (Bottom right) All Saints' Church, Margaret Street, London, by William Butterfield, 1849–52

to a revival phase took place, almost imperceptibly. Curiously enough, it was Hawksmoor's partner, Sir John Vanbrugh (1664–1726), England's great exponent of the Baroque spirit, who made the first successful attempt to evoke sensations of the medieval past. In 1717 he built a house for himself at Greenwich that was intended to conjure up a "castle air." It is a simple, robust, brick building that relies for its effect on slender proportion rather than detail. But it is an isolated work of its kind.

The Picturesque.—Only toward the end of the 18th century did "picturesque" take on a precise meaning, affecting the planning and the forms of English architecture, but from the late 17th cen-

tury onward isolated gardens and estates were laid out to take advantage of the irregularity of landscape to result in compositions which approximated to those to be seen in the paintings of such men as Claude Lorrain, Salvator Rosa, and Gaspard Poussin. Hence the denomination of the style as "picturesque." Sir Roger Pratt set out a nonaxial garden.

But it was rather William Kent (1684–1748), in response to the literary ideal of "naturalness" of such men as Temple, Addison, and Pope, who first fashioned the picturesque landscape that was to be made famous by Lancelot (Capability) Brown (1716–83) and introduced into it occasional buildings, often in a Gothic style, to serve as a focus of interest.

Kent first used the fanciful rococo Gothick that was to become characteristic of the 18th century in 1732, on a gateway in the Clock Tower at Hampton Court. He reconstructed the Tudor buildings of Esher Lodge some time between 1729 and 1739, introducing similar quatrefoil openings, and used them again in the early 1730s, in the "Temple of the Mill" at Rousham, Oxfordshire, where he laid out one of the first irregular gardens. The ornamental character of the Gothic Revival was thus established from the start, and it was popularized as such within a few years by Batty Langley (1696–1751), author of *Gothic Architecture Improved by Rules and Proportions* (1742). Pretensions to archaeological accuracy appear in two churches built in 1753, that at Shobdon, Herefordshire, and the charming, though now derelict, octagonal chapel at Hartwell, Buckinghamshire, by Henry Keene (1726–76). Keene was an ardent admirer of Gothic. He had begun Gothicizing Arbury Hall, Warwickshire, as early as 1750. It was, however, to the amateurs Sanderson Miller (1717–80) and Horace Walpole (q.v.; 1717–97) that the credit for a full-scale domestic Gothic Revival was due.

Miller, a Warwickshire squire, began about 1745 by inserting pointed arches in the south front of his Tudor house at Radway, Warwickshire. Later he put up a garden ornament in the form of a mock Gothic castle at nearby Edgehill, the idea of which became fashionable and made a reputation for him as a designer of Gothic extravaganzas. His most significant work was Lacock Abbey (1754–55), Wiltshire, whose symmetrical, flattened facade is thinly decorated with Gothic motifs. Walpole's Gothic, though apparently as lighthearted, was more serious. When in 1748 he decided to rebuild his house, Strawberry Hill, at Twickenham, Middlesex, he proposed to reflect faithfully in its architecture his tastes for topography, history, and heraldry. He formed a "Committee on Taste" to advise him on the design. Among the members were the amateur archaeologists Richard Bentley (1708–82) and John Chute (1701–76) of the Vyne, Hampshire, both of whom provided designs. The architect responsible for the execution of most of the work was William Robinson (c. 1720–75). During the early phase of building, alterations and interior decorations were made in a pretty, decorative style with a freedom unhampered by any serious archaeological study. Nor was there any real feeling for medieval composition in the massing of the elements. But in 1761, when a vast circular tower was added to the southwest corner of the house, Walpole gave evidence of a deliberate attempt to achieve an asymmetrical, picturesque composition. The west of the house was more freely grouped. Finally, in 1776, James Essex (1722–84), probably the most earnest Gothicist of the period, inserted the Beauclerc Tower between the west end and the round tower, making the whole the first and most determined example of a large-scale picturesque composition.

The fortuitous appearance and the deliberate irregularity of Strawberry Hill were exploited in many late 18th-century buildings. James Wyatt (1746–1813) built Lee Priory (1783–90), Kent, for Walpole's friend Thomas Barrett. His Sheffield Place and West Dean, both in Sussex, are similar. All three have somewhat more aspiration to archaeological accuracy than Strawberry Hill. But the extravagant nature of Wyatt's Gothic tastes is apparent in that most sensational of all Gothic Revival buildings, Fonthill Abbey (1796–1806), Wiltshire, designed in the first instance as a landscape feature for the arch-Romantic, William Beckford (1759–1844). The great central tower collapsed in 1807 and most of the building has today disappeared, but in John Rutter's *Delineations of Fonthill* (1823) one can still experience some of the grotesque spectacular quality of this building that made it, for a short time, notorious.

Although many classical architects, including Sir William Chambers and Robert Adam, applied Gothic details to the exterior of their country houses, they displayed no great interest in the style and always retained strict symmetry of composition. George Dance (1741–1825) used it more thoughtfully and originally in his occasional Gothic buildings—the facade of the Guildhall (1789), London, Coleorton House (1804–08), Leicestershire, Ashburnham Place (1813–17), Sussex, and the churches of St. Bartholomew-the-less (1789), London, and Micheldever (1808), Hampshire. William Porden (c. 1755–1822) though, was closest to Wyatt in such buildings as Eaton Hall (1804–12), Cheshire and his Gothic alterations to Taymouth Castle, Perthshire.

Walpole's innovation assumed real significance only toward the end of the century after the theory of the picturesque had evolved and publicized by Richard Payne Knight (1750–1824), author of *The Landscape, a Didactic Poem* (1794), and, later, the *Analytical Enquiry into the Principles of Taste* (1805), and by his friend Uvedale Price (1747–1829), who wrote an *Essay on the Picturesque* (1794). Already Knight had given architectural form to his ideas of rugged, irregular and apparently "natural" composition in Downton Castle, Herefordshire, near Ludlow, started in 1774 and completed in 1778. This was the first irregularly planned castellated building with a classical interior. It inspired a vast range of such buildings. John Nash (1752–1835) is the best-known and most proficient exponent of the style. Starting with his own house, East Cowes Castle, on the Isle of Wight, in about 1798, he exploited the deliberate irregularity of plan and silhouette afforded by the castellated or Gothic style; from Caerhays (1808), Cornwall, in the south, to Ravensworth Castle (1808), Durham, in the north Nash littered England with picturesque castles, houses, and ornamental cottages all of vaguely Gothic or Italianate inspiration.

Sir John Soane (1753–1837) attempted the Gothic style on at least three occasions—at Port Eliot (1804–06), Cornwall, at Ramsay Abbey (1804–06), Huntingdonshire, and for the library at Stowe (1805–07), Buckinghamshire—but like his master Dance, strongly influenced by the French neoclassical theorists, J. L. de Cordemoy and M. A. Laugier, he attempted to distill the effects of Gothic rather than to imitate the style. His suspended arches and his clustered ribs rising sheer from the floor and continuing round the vault are, ultimately, of Gothic inspiration.

The Influence of Antiquarianism.—The great change that occurred at the beginning of the 19th century, when the Gothic Revival moved from a phase of sentimental and picturesque attraction to one of greater archaeological exactitude, was determined largely by the research and publications of antiquarians. Foremost of these was John Carter (1748–1817), author of *Ancient Architecture of England* (1795 and 1807), in which Gothic details were more faithfully and accurately recorded than in any earlier publication. Thomas Rickman (1776–1841) designated the various styles of medieval architecture in *An Attempt to Discriminate the Styles of English Architecture* (1817), and the French refugee Augustus Charles Pugin (1762–1832), who was first employed by Nash, produced a series of meticulously measured details in *Specimens of Gothic* (1821–23). The great popularizer of Gothic archaeology was John Britton (1771–1857), who diffused a knowledge of the medieval buildings of Great Britain with two series of books, *The Architectural Antiquities of Great Britain* (1804–14) and *The Cathedral Antiquities of Great Britain* (1814–35).

For many years architecture lagged far behind scholarship. Buildings continued to be put up in an effete, decorative, and unconvincing Gothic style. Dozens of castellated houses were built during the first decades of the century. The first successes of Sir Robert Smirke (1780–1867), Lowther Castle (1806–10), Westmorland, and Eastnor Castle (c. 1810–15), Herefordshire, were in this style. The most spectacular was Windsor Castle, by James Wyatt's nephew, Sir Jeffry Wyatville (1766–1840), who began the remodeling in 1824. Gothic was also adapted for collegiate work. William Wilkins (1778–1839) built the screen and hall at King's College, Cambridge, between 1824 and 1827 and Rickman added New Court to St. John's College, Cambridge, between 1827 and 1831. But Gothic was to be most widely used, and even exploited, for church architecture; not because it was thought more appropriate than classical architecture but because it was cheaper.

Commissioners' Churches.—The Church Building Act of 1818 providing for the expenditure of £1,000,000 on churches brought Gothic to the fore as the ecclesiastical style. Rickman had already built St. George (1812–14), St. Michael-in-the-Hamlet (1814–15), and St. Philip (1816), all in Liverpool, in a thin Gothic style using cast iron; John Pinch (c. 1770–1827) had erected St. Mary (1814–20), Bathwick, Bath, in a more robust Gothic mode. But it was the commissioners' discovery that a Gothic church cost less than one with a stone portico that determined its widespread use. The first church to which the commissioners contributed, St. Luke's (1820–24), Chelsea, London by James Savage (1779–1852), was splendidly vaulted in Bath stone, but meanness and meagreness progressively controlled the design of their churches—in particular those by Rickman and Francis Goodwin (1784–1835). Of the 214 churches built for the commissioners, 174 were Gothic.

National Gothic.—Gothic was established as a national style when in 1836 the commissioners for the rebuilding of the Palace of Westminster (Houses of Parliament) accepted a Gothic design by Sir Charles Barry (1795–1860). This was to be the first public building of any consequence in the style. Barry had already experimented with Gothic in no less than nine churches—the best-known being St. Peter's (1824–26), Brighton—and had built King Edward's Grammar School (1833–37) in Birmingham in the Gothic style. His great and elaborate Palace of Westminster is not however a convincing essay in Gothic composition. The plan is formal, the facade to the river altogether symmetrical, and the detail repetitive. But it derives a picturesque effect from the placing and proportioning of its two towers, St. Stephen's (Big Ben) halfway along the north face, with the squatter Victoria tower in the west facade. In England it was not imitated—though in Budapest it was commemorated in Imre Steindl's Parliament House (1883–1902). Work at Westminster was completed slowly and was finished only after Barry's death. By then the Gothic Revival had been put on an altogether different footing, paradoxically, by the man who was responsible for all the Gothic details of both the King Edward's Grammar School and the Palace of Westminster, A. W. N. Pugin (1812–52), son of the author of *Specimens of Gothic.*

A. W. N. Pugin (*q.v.*) was a Catholic convert. He was intent to show that Gothic was an expression of the Catholic spirit and was thus the only form of architecture properly suited to its ritual. In his *Contrasts* of 1836 he also sought to show that architecture reflects the state of a society by which it is built. The society of the Middle Ages was good; therefore Gothic architecture was good. In *True Principles of Pointed or Christian Architecture* (1841) he first laid down firm principles for the Victorian Gothic Revival. Architecture, he held, should be honest in its expression. Every feature of a building should be essential to its proper functioning and construction, and every feature of this construction should be frankly expressed. Architecture was to be judged by the highest standards of morality. Such concepts are a part of Pugin's French heritage; they were common-place in 18th-century France (Sir Edward Hall alone in Great Britain had tried earlier to analyze the structural expressiveness of Gothic architecture), but Pugin's ideals came as a revelation to British architects and gave to the Gothic Revival a wholly new seriousness of purpose.

Most of the buildings in which Pugin attempted to give form to his ideas were built between 1837 and 1844. His first church of any consequence was St. Marie's (1838–39), Derby; his most influential were St. Wilfrid's (1839–42), Hulme, Manchester, and St. Oswald's (1840–42), Old Swan, Liverpool; but all three, like most of his other buildings and even his own favourite, St. Augustine's (1846–51), built near his house at Ramsgate, Kent, though solid and broadly-proportioned and far more convincingly imbued with the spirit of Gothic than earlier buildings, are not successful as works of architecture. Pugin was too much con-cerned with the minutiae of medieval detail. When incomplete in their detail and furnishing his churches are grim; fully and ex-pensively finished, as at St. Giles's (1841–46), Cheadle, Cheshire, they appear overexquisite.

The Ecclesiological Society.—Pugin's doctrines were taken up and upheld by the Anglican reformers, the Tractarians of Ox-ford and the Camdenians of Cambridge. The Ecclesiological So-ciety, into which the Camden Society was transformed in 1845, so successfully aroused the liturgical enthusiasm of the clergy that most architects employed by the Established Church in the years that followed were subject to the most doctrinaire of disciplines. Numerous architects were castigated by the critics of the *Ec-clesiologist*, though R. C. Carpenter (1812–55)—who in 1838 had applied neo-Tudor details to Lonsdale Square in Islington, London —was consistently upheld for the "correctness" of his work, as were those far more original and competent architects William Butterfield (1814–1900) and J. L. Pearson (1817–97). Pearson's masterpiece was St. Augustine's (1870–80), Kilburn Park Road, London.

William Butterfield.—Butterfield is remembered today chiefly for the polychromy of his collegiate work at Keble College (1868–76), Oxford, and Rugby School (1868–72), but he was re-sponsible for a range of simple, though no less rigorous and emphatic country parsonages and churches in Yorkshire, culmi-nating in the group at Baldersby St. James (1856), and those bold, ruthless, and highly idiosyncratic churches, St. Matthias's (1850–52), Stoke Newington, London; St. Alban's (1858–61), off Hol-born, also in London; St. Augustine's (1866), Penarth, near Cardiff, and All Saints' (1868–74), Babbacombe, Devon. Butter-field brought a new vigour to the Gothic Revival. The building which first gave evidence of his power and originality was All Saints', Margaret Street, London, designed in 1849 and largely completed by 1852. This church was sponsored by the Ecclesi-ological Society. But it is not its liturgical correctness that makes it so important to the history of the Gothic Revival. From the pavement to the top of the tower the church was built in bands of red and black brickwork. This set a fashion for "structural polychromy." Internally marbles and tiles were used to cover all surfaces in richer coloration. Butterfield became famous for his polychromy.

The Influence of Ruskin.—This taste for polychromatic dec-oration was initiated, encouraged, and sustained by the greatest apologist of the Gothic Revival, John Ruskin (*q.v.*; 1819–1900). In 1849 he published *The Seven Lamps of Architecture* in time to influence Butterfield at All Saints', Margaret Street. His *Stones of Venice* appeared between 1851 and 1853. Within a few years architects throughout England were adapting the details and colour combinations of Italian, especially Venetian Gothic, architecture for myriad clients who had been enraptured by Ruskin's mel-lifluous descriptions and high-sounding sanctions for a Gothic Revival. Like Pugin and the Camdenians he judged Gothic to be a style with a firm moral basis. He himself made only one notable attempt to direct the design of a Gothic building; in 1854 he secured the appointment of Sir Thomas Deane (1792–1871) and Benjamin Woodward (1815–61) as architects to the University Museum (1855–59), Oxford. The completed building, with col-umns and trusses of cast iron in the manner advocated by Viollet-le-Duc, was distasteful to Ruskin, as indeed were almost all the concrete results of his literary influence.

High Victorian Gothic.—By the middle of the 1850s Gothic had become the established mode for church architecture in Great Britain, though it was of course considered appropriate to many other types of architecture. In the prodigiously productive dec-ades that followed, the style was applied by a host of industrious and competent architects to many buildings that had no medieval precedents. The most active practitioners of Gothic were Sir George Gilbert Scott (1811–78) and George Edmund Street (1824–81). Both were busy restorers of medieval cathedrals and churches, but they found time to build a great number of new buildings in the Gothic style. Scott designed no less than 800. His first success was the Martyrs' Memorial (1841) in Oxford; others included the Albert Memorial (1862–72), Hyde Park, Lon-don, Glasgow University (1866–71), and the vast and picturesque Midland Hotel (1867–74) at St. Pancras Station, London. He firmly established the supremacy of England as arbiter in the Gothic Revival by winning a competition in 1844 for the Niko-laikirche (1844–63), Hamburg. Street, who was trained by Scott, designed about 260 original buildings, starting with a number of small churches and schools in Cornwall, an outcrop of churches in Oxfordshire, Buckinghamshire, and Berkshire, and another in Yorkshire. His churches vary in style, from the elaborate, decora-tive polychromy of St. James-the-Less (1858–61), Thorndike Street, London, through the more forcefully detailed style of St. Philip and St. James's (1860–62), Oxford, to the bare barn of St. George's (1861), Oakengates, Shropshire. His most famous and probably his noblest work was a secular building, the Law Courts, London, competed for in 1866, but not begun until 1874 and only completed after his death in 1882. His influence was exerted not only through his architecture but through his famous publication *Brick and Marble Architecture of the Middle Ages in Italy* (1855).

The other great secular work of the Gothic Revival, Manchester Town Hall, was won in competition in the same year as the Law Courts, 1866, and begun in 1869. The designer was Alfred Waterhouse (1830–1905), an architect almost as active as Street but one who was responsible for very few churches. Waterhouse demonstrated conclusively that because of its flexibility Gothic was not only suitable but was virtually the only revival style applicable to the design of the large and complex buildings re-quired by Victorian administration and institutions. He was a master planner. He first achieved fame as a result of a competi-tion for the Manchester Assize Court (1859–64); then followed the ingenious Town Hall (1869–77) and later Owens College (1870–98) there. For Oxford he designed Balliol College (1865–69); for Cambridge, the Union (1865–67), Gonville and Caius College, started in 1870, and buildings at Pembroke College (1871–72). His vast London buildings include the Natural History Mu-seum (1873–81), the Prudential Assurance (1879, 1899–1903), and University College Hospital (1897–1906).

Though Scott, Street, and Waterhouse dominated the mature phase of the Gothic Revival, they were not always responsible for the most interesting and experimental work of the period.

William Burges (1827–81) designed St. Finbar's Church of Ireland Cathedral in Cork (1863–76) in a curious 12th-century French style. In 1865 he started at Cardiff Castle, and ten years later at Castell Coch, to interpret medieval architecture with much merry and decorative freedom. His interiors in these buildings are a riot of decoration. He adopted the same style for his own house, Tower House, 9, Melbury Road, London (1875–80). His friend, E. W. Godwin (1833–86), on the other hand, was more restrained; he built two small and neat town halls in the Gothic style, one at Northampton (1861–64), the other at Congleton (1864–67), Cheshire. Other notable Gothicists were G. F. Bodley (1827–1907), who often employed William Morris (1834–96) and his associates, including Ford Madox Brown and Sir Edward Burne-Jones, to decorate his churches; and Philip Webb (1831–1915), who had himself been a pupil with William Morris in the office of Street and was to build for Morris the famous Red House (1859–60) at Bexley Heath near London. Little in this building is overtly Gothic—it is intended to evoke rather the solidity and sound craftsmanship of medieval architecture, an ideal that was to be taken up later by Richard Norman Shaw (1831–1912).

The Gothic Revival lingered on late in the 19th and survived even into the 20th century. J. L. Pearson designed Truro Cathedral in Cornwall in 1880, completed by his son F. L. Pearson (1864–1947), as was his last work, the Cathedral of Brisbane, Austr., designed in 1897 but begun after his death in 1901. Similarly Sir Giles Gilbert Scott (1880–1960), the grandson of Sir George Gilbert Scott, maintained the family tradition by designing a cathedral for Liverpool in 1903, in a Gothic style which was surprisingly firm; Sir Ninian Comper (1864–1960) continued to employ it right up to the time of his death. But by then it lacked lustre.

Dissemination of the Gothic Style.—Scott, Butterfield, and Carpenter all supplied designs for churches in the British Commonwealth, but their designs were often modified and slowly executed. Sir George Gilbert Scott's cathedral at Saint John's, Newfoundland, begun in 1846, was completed only 40 years later by his son, Gilbert Scott (1839–97). Butterfield's Anglican cathedral in Melbourne, Austr., St. Paul's, designed in 1847 and started in 1850, was finished only in 1934. The direct influence of the English leaders on Colonial Gothic was thus small, and numerous churches built in the British dominions during the second half of the 19th century were mostly in a meagre, uninspired Gothic mode. Occasionally, practised exponents of the style emigrated to the dominions: W. W. Wardell (1823–1900) emigrated to Melbourne in 1858, where he built the English, Scottish and Australian Bank, St. John Evangelist's at Toorak (1860–73), and St. Patrick's Catholic Cathedral (1860–1939); Thomas Fuller (1822–98) travelled to Canada where in partnership with Chilion Jones he designed the grandiose Gothic Parliament House, Ottawa, in 1859, built 1861–67 by F. W. Stent and by A. Laver (1839–98), another emigrant from England.

FRANCE

In France a taste for medieval legend survived into the 16th-century aristocratic circles and was nurtured not only by the works of Ariosto and Tasso but by books on heraldry and blazonry by humanist scholars. More remarkable as evidence of a conscious interest in the Middle Ages were the topographical studies and guidebooks published from the middle of the 16th century onward by such men as Gilles Corrozet (1510–68) and his successors, Jacques Dubreul, Germain Brice, and Claude Saugrain. Their works give evidence of a widespread and continuing popular response to Gothic building. Critical comment indicates, in particular, an interest in the lightness and skill of Gothic construction—qualities also appreciated by the Benedictines of the congregation of St. Maur, who devoted their energies from 1632 onward to historical research and laid the foundation upon which historical criticism in France still rests. But their compendious manuscripts were seldom set in type. *Les monuments de la monarchie française* (1729–33), by the greatest of these scholars, Bernard de Montfaucon (1655–1741), was abandoned after the printing of no more than the first of the proposed five sections.

Survival and Revival.—Though the Maurists undertook major, if sometimes eccentric, reconstructions of their medieval buildings and built many new ones in the Gothic style, there is little evidence that their self-conscious interest led to any form of revival. Gothic survival was ubiquitous. The Gothic tradition of building continued strong, especially in ecclesiastical circles, far into the 18th century.

The Wars of Religion, in the 16th century, served to consolidate, if they did not invigorate, the standards of Gothic taste and execution in France. Thousands of workmen were employed to restore and rebuild churches that had been destroyed by the Huguenots, and most new Catholic churches, in accordance with the clergy's need of a display of steadfast conservatism, were more or less medieval in style. All this was a case of Gothic survival, and only in the case of St. Pierre at Corbie, where in the first decade of the 18th century the Maurists set aside a design for a classical facade in favour of one in the Gothic manner, is a Revival spirit discernible. Similarly, Louis XIV's decision of 1707 (when Bernard de Montfaucon was his confessor) to replace Poitevin's classical design for the west front of Sainte-Croix at Orléans with one "dans l'ordre Gothique," might have been inspired by a spirit of retrospection rather than the conservatism that conditioned its rebuilding after destruction by the Huguenots. The foreman, Guillaume Hénault (who also prepared a design in 1718 for a Maurist chapel in Orléans—Classical inside, Gothic outside), drew up the new west front, but his design was replaced in 1739 by Jacques Gabriel's (1667–1742) magnificent, highly ornamented scheme, completed only in 1829, which first gave convincing expression to an evocative, sentimental feeling for Gothic. Sainte-Croix, however, is an isolated phenomenon of this kind of feeling for Gothic.

Interest in Gothic Structure.—French admirers of Gothic architecture regarded it primarily as a challenge to the intellect. Philibert Delorme (1505/10?–70) in the 16th century and François Derand (1591–1644) in the 17th century analyzed the construction of the Gothic vault. They were quick to appreciate it as a highly efficient and economical framework of columns and ribs, supporting infilling panels, and counterbalanced by buttresses and flying buttresses—as something, indeed, of a structural scaffold. It was this structural elegance that those early 18th-century enthusiasts of Gothic, Michel de Frémin and the Abbé J. L. de Cordemoy (1631–1713), sought to infuse into contemporary architecture. In the *Nouveau Traité de toute l'architecture* (1706) Cordemoy proposed that a new, honest, and economical architecture might be arrived at by abstracting the principles of Gothic construction and applying them in a perfectly regular classical way. There was no question of reviving the Gothic style; interest in Gothic was to be altogether transmuted into classical terms. Cordemoy's ideas were taken up somewhat tentatively by architects in Lorraine and the Franche-Comté during the early years of the century, but more spectacularly throughout

PARLIAMENT HOUSE, OTTAWA, BY THOMAS FULLER, CHILION JONES, F. W. STENT AND A. LAVER, 1861–67

France after their reappraisal by the Abbé M. A. Laugier (1713-69), in his *Essai sur l'architecture* (1753), and, in particular, in the church of Sainte-Geneviève (now known as the Panthéon) in Paris, designed in 1755 by J. G. Soufflot (1713-80). The building of this great church in a style confirming the Neoclassical ideal but on principles derived from Gothic architecture gave a wholly new impetus to the study of Gothic construction. French architects were imbued with a rational appreciation of Gothic wholly without parallel.

English Influence and the Picturesque.—The frivolous lighthearted "Gothick" of 18th-century England never took hold in France. Gray's, Young's, and Harvey's works were translated c. 1770, and in 1774 the authentic Gothic horror burst upon France with a translation of Horace Walpole's *The Castle of Otranto*. There was a native French vogue for troubadour literature, sustained both by scholars such as La Curne de Sainte-Palaye (1697-1781) and authors like the comte de Tressan (1705-83), but it was the intrusion of English ideas that prompted more authentic representations of the medieval world in stage settings and history paintings after 1772. Certainly, the Gothic taste in architecture was wholly conditioned by the introduction of the informal landscape garden.

In 1772 J. L. Goetz designed a row of shops in the Gothic style along the south side of Strasbourg cathedral, but they are the only example of their kind. Six years later L. Carmontelle designed a "moulin Gothique" for the Parc Monceau, Paris. Soon after Olivier and, later, P. Bernard (b. 1761) designed a number of Gothic conceits for M. Bostoky's estate outside Amiens. By 1781 when the prince de Ligne published his *Coup d'oeil sur Beloeil* there were a number of English gardens in France with mock-Gothic pavilions, and during the last two decades of the century many more were built. But, Sainte-Croix apart, the French made no attempt to imitate, let alone rival, the splendours of Strawberry Hill and Fonthill Abbey.

Revolution and Romanticism.—To the revolutionaries Gothic architecture seemed a symbol of the vested power of the aristocracy and the church. Many buildings were wantonly destroyed. Yet popular interest in the picturesque charms of Gothic architecture was sustained and even intensified during the closing years of the century by such men as A. L. Millin (1759-1818), author of *Antiquités nationales* (1790-96), and more especially by Alexandre Lenoir (1761-1839) who in 1795 turned the largest of the Paris depots for plundered works of art, the Petits-Augustins (now the École des Beaux Arts), into the Musée des Monuments Français. Here, by clever juxtaposition and subtle lighting, the Middle Ages seemed to be endowed with an aura of magic. By suggesting a relationship between a chivalric past and the actual forms of Gothic sculpture and architecture Lenoir coloured the imagination of a whole generation of Romantics. The great Romantic Chateaubriand (1768-1848) was fascinated by what he termed Lenoir's "Elysée." The celebrated chapter on Gothic

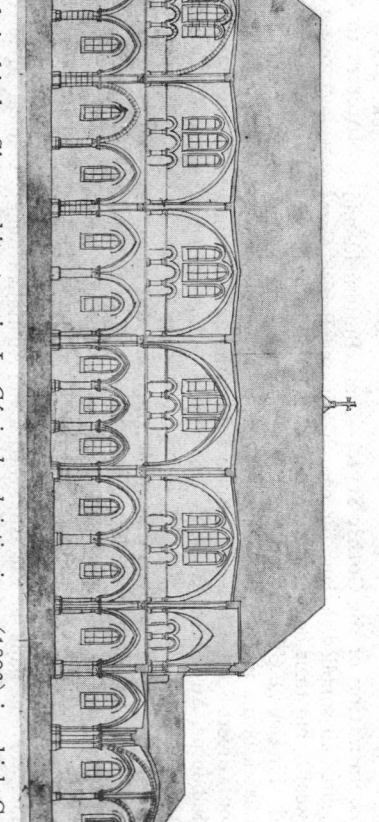

(Above) Church of St. Eugène, Paris, by L. A. Boileau, 1854. (Right) West front of cathedral of Sainte-Croix, Orléans, by J. J. Gabriel, 1739-1829. (Below) Church of Saint-Denis de l'Estrée, Saint-Denis, 1860-67, drawing by the architect E. E. Viollet-le-Duc

architecture in *Le Génie du christianisme* (1802) in which Gothic is not only taken as the symbol for the old French Catholic spirit but is traced beyond, through the forests of Gaul, to nature herself, was directly inspired by Lenoir's work. Inevitably, a Romantic Gothic image was popularized in the years that followed; playwrights, novelists, and painters were seduced by the charms of Gothic. Even antiquarians succumbed to the romantic myth, and from 1810 onward a spate of popular guidebooks and studies of Gothic architecture were published, the most conspicuous being the *Voyages pittoresques et romantiques dans l'ancienne France* by Baron Taylor, Nodier and de Cailleux, which was started in 1820 and continued for more than 50 years.

In spite of a few Gothic-inspired fantasies, and an archaeological interest in medieval architecture that found expression in the neo-Romanesque church of Saint-Paul (1835) at Nîmes by C. A. Questel (1807-88), architecture remained a virtually impregnable stronghold until after 1840, when a hard core of Gothic revivalists began to emerge. This was composed of consistent medievalists who were stirred primarily by archaeological preoccupations. Stimulated by the activity of English scholars in Normandy—especially the Rev. G. D. Whittington—Auguste Leprévost (1787-1854), C. A. de Gerville (1769-1853), and later Arcisse de Caumont (1801-73) patiently studied the medieval remains of that region and slowly forged the science of French Gothic archaeology. Caumont's *Essai sur l'architecture religieuse du Moyen Age* was printed in 1824, his *Cours d'antiquités monumentales* from 1830 to 1841. In 1834 he founded the Société Française d'Archéologie and began publication of that authoritative journal, the *Bulletin monumental*.

An equally important aspect of the Gothic Revival was inaugurated by Victor Hugo in 1831 when he published *Notre-Dame de Paris*, the explicit purpose of which was the glorification of Gothic as a national and catholic style of architecture. A. N. Didron (1806–67), future editor of the *Annales archéologiques*, was stirred by this book to pursue his scholarly, propagandist career, as was the comte de Montalembert (1810–70), who at once took up the cause of Gothic and identified it with the Catholic Revival. In 1839 he published *Du catholicisme et du vandalisme dans l'art*, a shallow but influential work which sprang from an over-hasty response to the teachings of the German "Nazarene" painter J. F. Overbeck (*q.v.*), whom he met in Rome, and A. W. N. Pugin, whom he met in England. But it was the Protestant statesman Guizot who first gave real impetus to those ideas for which Hugo and Montalembert fought. In 1830 he inaugurated the organizations that seven years later became the Commission des Monuments Historiques.

All the serious, acceptable architects of the Gothic Revival were amateur archaeologists and they acknowledged an archaeological standard of taste. They designed from the first in the 13th-century style, and nearly all had restored at least one Gothic building before they undertook to build anything new. The patronage of the Commission des Monuments Historiques and later of the Service des Édifices Diocésains (formed in 1848) for whom thousands of medieval buildings were restored and enlarged was thus of enormous importance in furthering the aims and the technical skill of the Gothic revivalists. The men who sustained the Gothic Revival were almost all taught by the commission's leading architects, J. B. A. Lassus (1807–57) and E. E. Viollet-le-Duc (1814–79). Lassus trained Viollet-le-Duc first on the restoration of Saint-Germain-l'Auxerrois (1838), then at the Sainte-Chapelle (1842), then at the Sainte-Chapelle (1842), then at the Sainte-Chapelle (1842).

Notre-Dame in Paris and to build a new sacristy in the Gothic style; this was regarded as an official sanction for the Gothic Revival. But although a picturesque revival of Gothic had already been initiated in the provinces, official sanction for a full-scale revival was not easily accorded. The members of the French Academy, faithful to Neoclassical ideals, were firmly against it.

In 1844 the north tower of the abbey church Saint-Denis, begun under Abbot Suger (*q.v.*) in 1135, was found to be in danger of collapse. All Gothic men were aghast. Didron tactlessly accused the Conseil des Bâtiments Civils, or Council of Civil Buildings, who were charged with the approval of all building plans in France, of irresponsibility. Its members, mainly academicians, retaliated by arbitrarily stopping the construction of three churches in the Gothic style that Didron had acclaimed in the *Annales archéologiques*. Didron launched a counteroffensive; he demanded a public inquiry into the restoration of Saint-Denis. Under threat of this inquiry which was powerfully supported by the prefect of the Seine, M. Rambuteau, the council was forced to approve the plans for Sainte-Clotilde in Paris by F. C. Gau (1790–1853), which they had held up for over four years. It became a *cause célèbre*. A furious pamphlet war followed from which the Gothic revivalists emerged triumphant, and in 1852 Didron estimated that 200 neo-Gothic churches had been built or were in the process of construction. But the victory was short-lived. Sainte-Clotilde, as completed by Gau and his successor T. Ballu (1817–85) in 1857, was an anomalous expression of revivalist ideals. Didron disliked it intensely, and the dispute caused many admirers of Gothic architecture to reflect seriously on the merits of a Gothic Revival.

Lassus went on to build Saint-Nicolas (1848) at Moulins, Saint-Pierre at Dijon (1852), and Saint-Jean-Baptiste de Belleville (1854) in Paris. Viollet-le-Duc constructed Saint-Gimer (1853–57) at Carcassonne, the church of Nouvelle Aude (1855) and Saint-Denis-de-l'Estrée (1860–67) at Saint-Denis; he restored the Château de Pierrefonds (1858–70) to a state of colourful medieval splendour for Louis Napoleon, and in his great *Dictionnaire raisonné de l'architecture française* (1854–68) and the *Dictionnaire raisonné du mobilier français* (1858–75), together

running into 16 volumes, he provided the vital visual and intellectual inspiration required to sustain the Gothic movement. But he was by no means a convinced revivalist. All but one of his secular works are in an uneasy Renaissance mode. He determined to think his way beyond the romantic attractions of the Gothic style. Pursuing the inquiries of the 18th-century theorists, he envisaged an architecture of the 19th century that would be based on the rational system of construction and composition that he saw to exist in Gothic but would in no way imitate its forms and details. Architecture, he thought, should be the clear expression in 19th-century materials of 19th-century structural and functional needs. He was unable to accept the challenge of his own ideas. Both he and his disciples—P. Abadie (1812–84), E. Boeswilwald (1815–96), E. L. Millet (1819–79), M. Ouradou (1822–84), A. de Baudot (1834–1915), E. Corroyer (1835–1904), F. Narjoux (1836–91), and E. Duthoit (1837–89)—continued to design buildings in a weak Gothic style. They confined their Gothic work almost exclusively to church design. There were many less thoughtful and determined men who put up imitations of Gothic architecture in the late 19th century, but the Gothic Revival was never a full-blooded affair. Some of the finest buildings designed after the medieval manner—Saint-Pierre-de Montrouge (1864–72) in Paris, by J. A. E. Vaudremer (1829–1914) is one—were isolated works by men who worked outside the orbit of the Gothic revivalists, men who had no qualms about the intellectual honesty of their chosen mode of expression.

GERMANY AND CENTRAL EUROPE

As in France, German interest in medieval legend, history, art, and architecture was sustained throughout the Renaissance period both by the general public and by scholars and antiquarians. Interest was focused, in particular, on the cathedrals of Strasbourg and Cologne, buildings that were to assume an almost symbolic significance in the history of the Gothic Revival. In his *Rerum Germanicarum Epitome* ("Epitome of Things German"; 1505), Jakob Wimpheling extolled Strasbourg Cathedral as the rarest and most excellent of buildings, and O. Schadaeus' guide to the cathedral *Summum Argentoratensium Templum* (1617) was the first illustrated guidebook ever devoted to a single medieval building and, in spite of its title, was written in German. Other 17th- and early 18th-century histories and guides—and there were many—give ample evidence of a respectful appreciation of Gothic, despite the jibes of fashionable leaders. Appreciation of Gothic was a traditional and emotional affair, far removed from the studied and analytical interest of the French. Not surprisingly, English Gothic sentiments permeated Germany with the mid-18th-century taste for things English. Edward Young's *Conjectures on Original Composition* (1759) enjoyed a vogue in Germany that it never aspired to in England. English attitudes and ideas were developed to provide the German Gothic Revival with its peculiarly impassioned character.

The *Sturm und Drang* movement of the late 18th century invested Gothic with extraordinary and unparalleled qualities; it seemed to such men as Herder, and under his inspiration to Goethe, to be of the most sublime and exalted inspiration; an expression at once of all nature, all things divine and infinite. Goethe's paean to the cathedral of Strasbourg—and to its builder Erwin von Steinbach—was a 16-page pamphlet *Von Deutscher Baukunst* (1772). This was an inspiration to all future revivalists. There Goethe epitomized Gothic as the expression of the German spirit. Gothic became a German architecture, and such it was to remain in the estimate of all Germans and even German scholars for 50 years and more. Goethe's passion for Gothic was not long sustained, but his enthusiasm was shared by other contemporaries, notably, Friedrich von Schlegel, who in his *Briefe auf Reise durch die Niederlaunde, Rheingegenden, die Schweitz, und einen Theil von Frankreich* ("Letters"; 1806) saw Gothic not only as an expression of the German spirit, but specifically of a German Catholic spirit. This belief he shared with the brothers Sulpiz (1783–1854) and Melchior (1786–1851) Boisserée, by whom he was largely inspired.

Sulpiz Boisserée was the most active and enthusiastic of early

GOTHIC REVIVAL

Gothic revivalists. His great preoccupation was the cathedral of Cologne, which he measured minutely, starting in 1808 but continuing up to the publication of *Ansichten, Risse und einzelne Theile des Doms von Köln*, issued between 1823 and 1831. The purpose of this study was the restoration and completion of the unfinished cathedral. He enlisted the moral support even of Goethe and the financial support of King Frederick William III, who in 1824 ordered the preservation of the fabric. This work of conservation was carried out by F. H. Ahlert (1788-1833), under the guidance of K. F. Schinkel (1781-1841), and after his death by the most gifted of Schinkel's pupils E. F. Zwirner (1802-61). The task of completion was started in 1842, at the command of King Frederick William IV, and was carried through after Zwirner's death by Richard Voigtel (1829-1902), who finished the work only in 1880. The building of the cathedral of Cologne was an expression of German nationalism and marked the beginning of the Gothic Revival proper in Germany.

Earlier expressions of the Gothic Revival in architecture were of a Rococo or picturesque nature and were much influenced by contemporary fashions in England. Between 1725 and 1728, Effner, gardener to the elector Maximilian Emmanuel of Bavaria, built the Gothic-inspired Magdalenenkapelle in the grounds of the Nymphenburg Palace in Munich. In 1755 Frederick the Great himself designed the Nauener Tor in Potsdam and in 1768 Prince Franz of Anhalt-Dessau laid out his park in the picturesque manner and scattered it in the years that followed with Gothic hermitages and ruins. Other 18th-century gardens were similarly embellished: the Neuer Garten in Potsdam, laid out in the 1780s for Frederick William II by Carl Gotthard Langhans or the more spectacular ruined Ritterburg (1793-98), in the park of the landgrave William IX of Hesse at Wilhelmshöhe. There were even odd or idiosyncratic interpretations of Gothic—the tower of the cathedral of Mainz (1767-74) by Franz Ignaz Neumann (1733-85) or the Laugier-inspired remodeling of the Nikolaikirche in Leipzig (1784-97) by Johann Carl Friedrich Dauthe (1749-1816). In the latter church, Gothic ribs were transformed into palm fronds. The first architect of any distinction to take an active interest

in Gothic was Karl Friedrich Schinkel (*q.v.*). He was inspired by Friedrich Gilly's engravings of the castle of Marienburg in East Prussia (1799) to paint between 1810 and 1815 a number of visionary studies of Gothic buildings in the manner of Caspar David Friedrich. He designed several stage sets in the Gothic style. His first serious architectural composition was a Gothic mausoleum designed in 1810 for Queen Louisa of Prussia. He did other equally romantic designs in Gothic, the most spectacular being that for a cathedral in the Leipziger Platz, Berlin. But none of his ambitious Gothic projects was executed. Those that were built are of little consequence—a war memorial on the Kreuzberg (1818-21), Berlin, chiefly remarkable for the fact that it is entirely of cast iron; the Werdersche church (1821-31), Berlin, in brick and terra-cotta; the enlargement of the Kolberg Town Hall, in Pomerania, begun in 1829, and the Schloss Babelsberg (1835-49), near Potsdam, which was intended as an essay in the English castellated style.

Other prominent Neoclassicists who experimented with Gothic were Friedrich von Gärtner (1792-1847), designer of the Ludwigskirche (1829-40), Berlin, and the Wittelsbach Palace (1843-50), and Gottfried Semper (1803-79), who provided the plans for the Cholera Fountain in Dresden (1843). But their handling of Gothic forms was stiff and awkward, as was that of most German architects of the period. The Mariahilfkirche (1831-42), outside Munich, by J. D. Ohlmüller (1791-1839); Heinrich Hübsch's churches at Freiburg (1829-38), Bulach (1834-37), and Rottenburg, and F. A. Stüler's Berlin churches—the Jacobikirche (1834); Alexis de Chateauneu's Petrikirche in Hamburg (1843); the whole series designed by K. A. Heideloff (1788-1865), beginning with the Catholic church (1845-47) in the Weststrasse, Leipzig, no less than Heinrich Strack's Petrikirche (1846-50) in Berlin, and F. A. Stüler's Berlin churches—the Jacobikirche (1844-45), Markuskirche (1848), and Bartholomäuskirche (1854-58)—were all adulterated and unconvincing essays in the style.

The first significant church of the Gothic Revival was the Votivkirche (1856-79) in Vienna by Heinrich von Ferstel (1828-83). Indeed Vienna was the centre of the most active and intriguing adaptions of Gothic. Friedrich von Schmidt (1825-

(ABOVE) "GOTHIC CATHEDRAL BY THE WATER." DETAIL FROM A PAINTING BY KARL FRIEDRICH SCHINKEL, C. 1823, IN THE NATIONAL GALLERY, BERLIN. (LEFT) VOTIVKIRCHE, VIENNA, BY HEINRICH VON FERSTEL, 1856-79

91), who had worked under Zwirner at Cologne, was the leading revivalist. He built no less than eight churches in Vienna, ranging in date from the Lazaristenkirche (1860-62) to the Severinkirche (1877-78); most of them are brick-vaulted hall churches, but the most ambitious, the Fünfhaus parish church (1868-75), is centrally planned. He was the architect also of the Academische Gymnasium on the Beethovenplatz (1863-66) and the Town Hall (1872-83).

Along the Rhine several great castles were restored and dramatized with spiky Gothic trimmings; in Dresden there was a minor outburst of revivalism, starting with two houses Am Elbberg, in a Venetian Gothic mode by an architect named Ehrhardt, and including the Kreuzschule (1864-65) and the Sophienkirche by C. F. Arnold (1823-90), and the Johanniskirche (1874-78) by G. L. Möckel (1838-1915), but these works cannot be said to have contributed much to the course of architectural history. The Gothic Revival in Germany was not a concerted movement and there is no specific term in German to describe it. One of

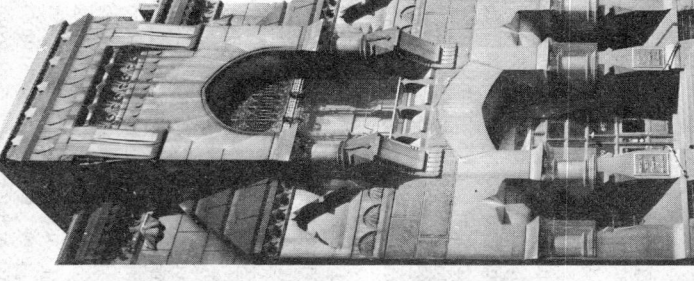

(Left) Trinity Church, New York, by Richard Upjohn, 1839–46. (Centre) Provident Life and Trust Company Bank, Philadelphia, by Frank Furness, 1879. (Top right) John J. Herrick House, Tarrytown, N.Y., by A. J. Davis, 1855. (Bottom right) Trinity College Dormitories, Hartford, Conn., by William Burges, 1874–82

the rare buildings that may be considered as characteristic of a specifically German revival and exuberantly Gothic is the Munich Town Hall (1867–74, enlarged 1899–1909), by G. J. von Hauberrisser (1841–1922).

ITALY

The Gothic Revival never really took hold in Italy. The Gothic café extravaganza, Il Pedrocchino (1837), next to the Neoclassical Pedrocchi café in Padua by Giuseppe Japelli (1783–1852), and Pelagio Palagi's pavilion, La Margheria (1834–39), at Racconigi are isolated examples. The revival was confined in the main to the completion of church facades, starting with that of the cathedral in Milan (1806–13) by Carlo Amati and Giuseppe Zanoia. It included B. C. Morandi's fanciful addition to the front of the cathedral at Biella (c. 1825), the facades of Sta. Croce (1857–63), Florence, by Nicola Matas (1798–1872), the cathedral in Florence (1867–87) by Emilio de Fabris (1808–83), and that in Naples (1876–1907) by Enrico Alvino (1809–72), Nicola Breglia, and Giuseppe Pisanti (1826–1913). Alvino, together with L. della Corte and G. Raimondi, was responsible also for the inaccurate completion of the facade of the cathedral in Amalfi.

UNITED STATES

The Gothic Revival in the United States was inevitably a stylistic import; it was not the outcome of deeply felt original sentiments of either a romantic or moral nature. At first it was regarded only as a facet of architectural historicism. Architects later adopted the aspirations and ideals of Pugin, the Camdenians, and even of Viollet-le-Duc, and attempted to use the Gothic style in conformity with the principles that they had laid down, but few were consistent (the Episcopalians alone adhered to the doctrines of the Ecclesiologists) and fewer still had sufficient firsthand knowledge of the style to interpret it with any conviction.

Drawings exist for Gothic garden pavilions for Jefferson's Monti-

cello, but the first recorded building in the Gothic style was Sedgeley, outside Philadelphia, erected in 1798 to the design of Benjamin H. Latrobe (1764–1820), who had been born and trained in England. The thin, etiolated Gothic of this house was repeated in other of his designs—an unexecuted project for Baltimore Cathedral (1805); the Bank of Philadelphia (1807–08); Christ Church (1808), Washington, and St. Paul's at Alexandria (1817), Virginia—but he was essentially a classicist. As, indeed, were other early practitioners of Gothic—William Strickland (1787–1854), who built the Masonic Hall (1809–11) and St. Stephen's (1822–23), both in Philadelphia, and Charles Bulfinch (1763–1844), architect of the Federal Street Church, Boston, completed in 1809.

The first Gothic Revival church of any consequence, St. Mary's Seminary in Baltimore (1807), was designed by a Frenchman, Maximilien Godefroy (c. 1760–1833). Others were built in the early decades of the 19th century—e.g., St. Luke's at Rochester, N.Y. (1824–26)—but not before the 1830s was a series of churches put up in and around Boston that gives evidence of a consistent Gothic Revival movement—Solomon Willard's Bowdoin Street Church (1830) and the First Methodist Episcopal Church in Temple Street, both in Boston, and St. Peter's (1833) and the First Unitarian Church (1836–37) in Salem, Mass., are examples. Most of these churches are constructed of granite; they are consequently plain and simple in detail. In sharp contrast are the light, timber churches with intricate and fanciful Gothic details put up at the same period, in particular by Bishop John Hopkins, author of an *Essay on Gothic Architecture* (1836).

The active, enterprising architect of the next phase of the Gothic Revival was Richard Upjohn (1802–78). In 1835 he built a somewhat thin and vitiated Gothic mansion, Oaklands, at Gardiner, Me. He achieved fame, however, as a builder of churches. St. John's (1836), Bangor, Me., was his first Gothic church; but it was Trinity Church (1839–46), New York, in a flat, harsh Gothic style that established his reputation. This was built for the Episcopalians and was rigidly "correct" in the ecclesiological sense. During the next 30 years he designed no less than 40 Gothic churches, mostly for the Episcopalians. Externally they appear as brittle, uninspired adaptions of English models, but in his internal work, and especially in such buildings as the First Parish Church (1845–46), Brunswick, Me., he showed himself to be an extraordinary and unparalleled manipulator of timber arcading and trussing. Equally important as exemplars of intrinsically American interpretations of the Gothic Revival theme are his churches entirely of timber—wooden framed and sheathed with vertical boarding and battening—such as St. Paul's at Brunswick, Me., of 1845 or St. Thomas's, Hamilton, N.Y., of 1847.

The timber tradition (or "carpenter's Gothic") was in no way limited to ecclesiastical work. Upjohn's *Rural Architecture* (1852) applied the same method of design to the construction of timber houses and cottages. Decorated with details deriving from Gothic sources this domestic architecture was, in sheer quantity, the chief expression of the Gothic Revival during the middle years of the century. Powerful support for the movement came also from A. J. Downing (1815–52), landscape gardener and architectural critic, who was a close friend of the architect A. J. Davis (*q.v.*; 1803–92). Davis designed the first plantation mansion in the Gothic style, Belmead (1845), in Powhatan County, Virginia, and more significantly, Ericstan (1855), the John J. Herrick house in Tarrytown, N.Y., which introduced castellated Gothic into the Hudson River valley. Downing leaned heavily on the theorists of the English Picturesque movement—his major work *A Treatise on the Theory and Practice of Landscape Gardening Adapted to North America* (1841) is, indeed, a paraphrase of their arguments—but in his pattern books *Cottage Residences* (1842) and *The Architecture of Country Houses* (1850) he provided an inherently American variant on the "Stick Style," with its use of board-and-batten finish to imitate half-timbering, that was soon diffused widely as the "Bracketed Cottage Style."

About 1860 the Gothic movement entered a new and determinedly serious phase. James Renwick (1818–95), who had designed the Smithsonian Institution in Washington in 1848 in a neo-Norman style, used continental models again in 1859 when building St. Patrick's Roman Catholic cathedral in New York. Most architects of the period, however, sought inspiration from England. They acclaimed the writings of Ruskin—though the complete American edition of his *Stones of Venice* only became available in 1860. The first building to give expression to his teachings was perhaps the Alumni Hall, Union College, Schenectady, N.Y., designed in 1856, begun 1858, built 1872–75, by E. T. Potter (1831–1904), a pupil of Upjohn. The banded and pointed arches of this building at once suggest the influence of Ruskin. More successful—and controversial—as an exponent of the Ruskinian aesthetic was Peter B. Wight (1838–1925), architect of the National Academy of Design, New York City (1863–65). There the Venetian Gothic mode came into its own. Wight and Potter—and later Potter's brother William Appleton (1842–1909)—were responsible for a number of collegiate and public buildings in this harsh, polychrome Gothic style, but it was William Robert Ware (1832–1915) and his partner Henry Van Brunt (1832–1903) who were to become its most fashionable exponents. In 1859 Ware built St. John's Chapel at the Episcopal Theological Seminary in Brattle Street, Cambridge, Mass.; six years later he and his partner started the First Church (Unitarian) in Boston, and in 1870 they began Memorial Hall at Harvard, a conspicuous if not altogether polished exemplar of the style. Other purveyors of "Collegiate Gothic" were Richard M. Hunt (1827–95) architect of the Yale Divinity School (1869) and Russell Sturgis (1838–1909), a partner of Wight, who designed the austere Farnam Hall (1869), at Yale University, the adjoining Durfee Hall (1871) and Battell Chapel (1876), and later Lawrence Hall (1885). John H. Sturgis (1834–88) and Charles Brigham (d. 1925), architects of the Museum of Fine Arts on Copley Square (1876) and the Church of the Advent (1878), both in Boston, attempted in their competition design of 1872 for the Connecticut State Capitol building in Hartford, to give to this tough, uneasy Gothic style something of monumental grandeur. Their design was reminiscent of that William Burges submitted in 1866 for the Royal Courts of Justice in London. The competition however was won by Richard M. Upjohn (1828–1905), son of the church builder, who provided a Gothic project that was equally grandiose if more equivocal in expression. It stands today as an exuberant reminder of 19th-century sensibilities. Within a few years Hartford was to possess an authentic Burges building, Trinity College. Only a small part of Burges' magnificent design of 1873 was executed. The work was superintended by the Hartford architect G. W. Keller (1842–1935).

The Gothic Revival survived into the 20th century, with R. A. Cram (*q.v.*; 1863–1942) as its most ardent exponent. Cram regarded Gothic as particularly suitable for educational establishments and his graduate college (1913) and chapel (1929) at Princeton University are among his finest achievements. Gothic elements are also responsible for the medieval towers aspect of many of the early skyscrapers. But the only architects of real originality to emerge from the late Gothic Revival movement were Frank Furness (1839–1912), well known for the vigorous handling of Gothic motifs on the Pennsylvania Academy of Fine Arts (1872–76) and a series of banks in Philadelphia—the most extraordinary of which was the Provident Institution on Chestnut Street (1879)—and that distinguished architect H. H. Richardson (1838–86) who used Gothic as a point of departure for the creation of a distinctive and altogether personal style, finer in many respects than anything produced by the European Gothic revivalists. He started his Gothic career with the Unity Church (1866–69), Springfield, Mass. During the following years he developed his robust, broadly proportioned style: a series of churches—Grace Episcopal Church, West Medford, Mass. (1867–68); Brattle Square Church, Springfield (1870–72), Boston and the North Congregational Church, Springfield (1872–73)—culminating in Trinity Church on Copley Square, Boston (1872–77). Overt Gothic influence is evident in most of his early works, but Gothic was to be superseded by Romanesque paradigms, to which he gave so strong an imprint of his own sense of style that they are rarely disquieting and in his late works, such as the Allegheny County Buildings and Jail in Pittsburgh (1884–88), are transformed into an architecture of splendour far removed from the stylistic conceit of revivalism.

BIBLIOGRAPHY.—*General:* H. R. Hitchcock, *Architecture, Nineteenth and Twentieth Centuries* (1958) gives further bibliography (pp. 463–472). *England:* C. L. Eastlake, *A History of the Gothic Revival* (1872); C. Hussey, *The Picturesque* (1927); Sir Kenneth Clark, *The Gothic Revival* (1928, revised and enlarged ed. 1950); Sir J. Summerson, *Architecture in Britain, 1530 to 1830* (1953, 4th ed. 1963); P. Ferriday (ed.), *Victorian Architecture* (1963). *France:* R. Lanson, *Le goût du Moyen Age en France au XVIIIe siècle* (1926); Paul Léon, *La vie des monuments français* (1951); L. Hautecoeur, *Histoire de l'architecture classique en France* (iv, 1952; v, 1953; vi, 1955; vii, 1957); R. D. Middleton, "The Abbé de Cordemoy and the Graeco-Gothic Ideal," *Journal of the Warburg and Courtauld Institutes* (xxv, 1962; xxvi, 1963). *Germany:* H. Schmitz, *Die Gotik im deutschen Kunst- und Geistesleben* (1921); W. D. Robson-Scott, *The Literary Background of the Gothic Revival in Germany* (1965). *Italy:* E. Lavagnino, *L'arte moderna Turin* (1961). *United States:* C. L. V. Meeks, *Italian Architecture 1750–1914* (1966); R. H. Newton, *Town and Davis: Architects* (1942); W. Campbell, "Frank Furness, an American Pioneer," *Architectural Review* (cx, 1951); R. B. Stein, *John Ruskin and Aesthetic Thought in America, 1840–1900* (1967). (R. D. M.)

GOTHS

GOTHS, a Germanic people described by Roman authors of the 1st century A.D. as living in the neighbourhood of the mouth of the Vistula river. According to their own legend, reported by the mid-6th-century Gothic historian Jordanes (*q.v.*), they had originated in southern Scandinavia and had crossed in three ships under their king Berig to the southern shore of the Baltic sea where they settled after defeating the Vandals and other Germanic peoples. Tacitus, whose knowledge of these distant regions is less reliable than his knowledge of the Germans living near the Roman frontier, states that the Goths at this time were distinguished by their round shields, their short swords and their obedience toward their kings. Jordanes goes on to report that they migrated from the Vistula region under Filimer, the fifth king after Berig, and after various adventures arrived on the north and northwestern coasts of the Black sea.

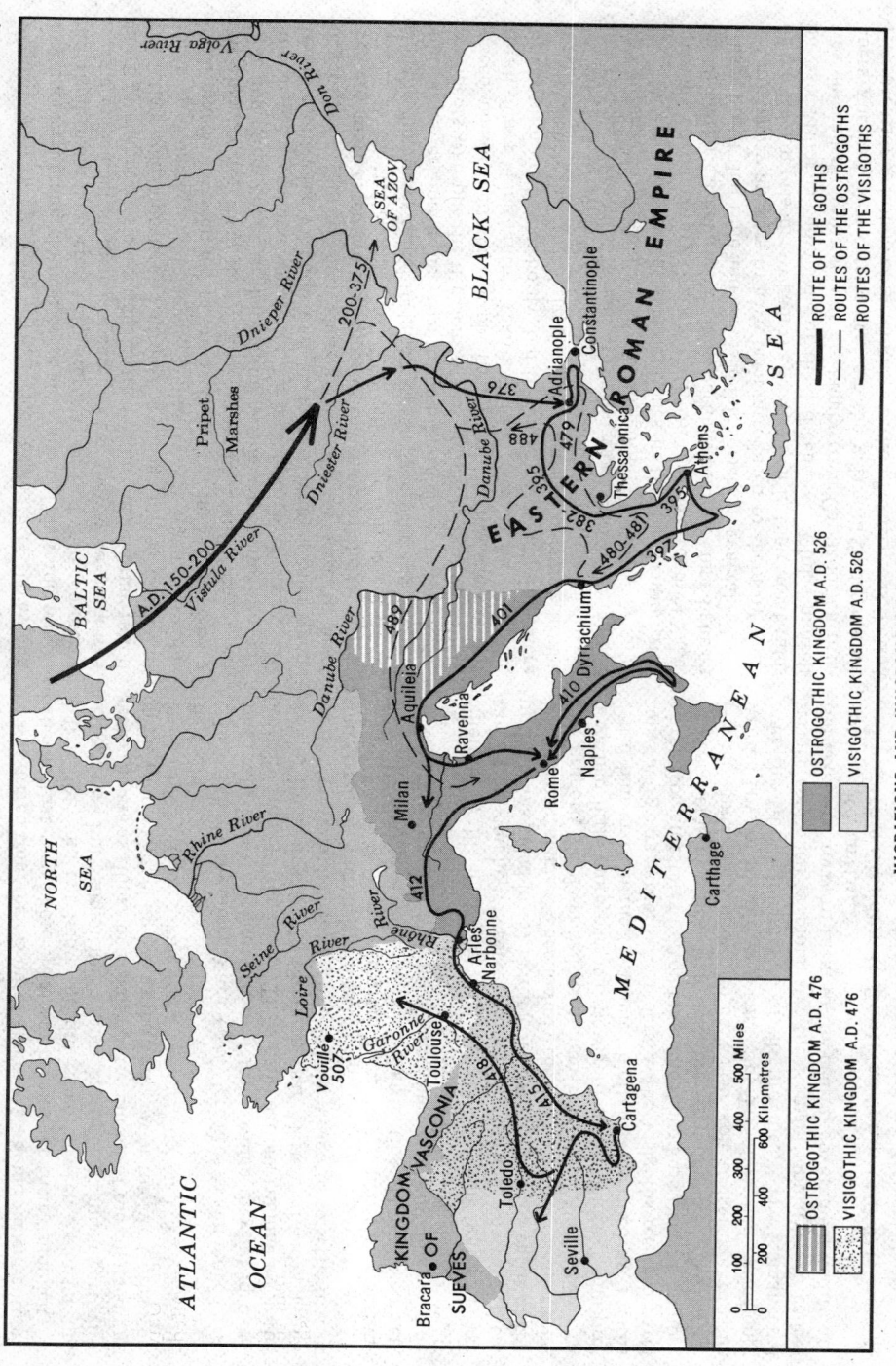

MIGRATIONS AND KINGDOMS OF THE GOTHS

ROUTE OF THE GOTHS
ROUTES OF THE OSTROGOTHS
ROUTES OF THE VISIGOTHS

OSTROGOTHIC KINGDOM A.D. 526
VISIGOTHIC KINGDOM A.D. 526

OSTROGOTHIC KINGDOM A.D. 476
VISIGOTHIC KINGDOM A.D. 476

This movement took place in the second half of the 2nd century A.D. and it may have been pressure from the Goths that drove other Germanic peoples to exert heavy pressure on the Danubian frontier of the Roman empire during the reign of Marcus Aurelius. Throughout the 3rd century Gothic raids on the Roman provinces in Asia Minor and the Balkan peninsula were numerous and in the reign of Aurelian (270–275) they obliged the Romans to evacuate the trans-Danubian province of Dacia, which some of the invaders then occupied. These Goths, living between the Danube and the Dniester rivers, became known as Visigoths and those in what is now the Ukraine as Ostrogoths. The latter name apparently means eastern Goths but *Visigothi* appears not to mean western Goths—they shrank from calling themselves by the name of the ill-omened west where the sun sinks and dies away—but rather the "valiant" or "gallant" people.

Ostrogoths.—The Ostrogoths built up a huge empire stretching from the Don (ancient Tanais) to the Dniester (ancient Tyras) rivers and from the Black sea to the Pripet marshes (southern Belorussia). A list of their subjects, given by Jordanes (*q.v.*), includes a number of peoples from the Germanic Heruli (*q.v.*) living on the Baltic coast east of the Vistula. But the value of this list is doubtful and most of the names in it cannot now be identified. Jordanes' list of the Ostrogothic kings is also of very dubious worth. The kingdom reached its highest point under King Ermanaric (*q.v.*), who is said to have committed suicide at an advanced age when the Huns attacked his people and subjugated them *c.* 370. Although many Ostrogothic graves have been excavated south and southeast of Kiev, regrettably little is known about their empire. In particular, it is not known how they managed to overrun so vast a kingdom and subdue so many nations of mounted archers so how they exploited their subjects. A spearhead found in 1858 at Kovel in the Ukraine is inscribed with the word *tilarids* or the like in runes, and although the point has been much debated the implication appears to be that the Ostrogoths were literate in

the 3rd century. Unlike the Germans of Tacitus' time, they used the potter's wheel almost universally; their trade with the Romans was highly developed.

After their subjugation by the Huns little is heard of the Ostrogoths for about 80 years, after which they reappear in Pannonia on the middle Danube as federates of the Romans. But a pocket of them remained behind in the Crimea when the bulk of the people moved to central Europe and these Crimean Ostrogoths preserved their identity throughout the middle ages. Indeed, Augier Ghislain de Busbecq, who arrived in Constantinople in 1554 as the ambassador of the emperor Ferdinand I, gives a list of Germanic words still used by them in the Crimea and these words are sometimes believed to be Gothic in its latest form.

After the collapse of the Hun empire (455) the Ostrogoths under Theodoric (*q.v.*) began to move again, first to Moesia (*c.* 475–488) and then to Italy. Theodoric became king of Italy in 493 and died in 526. For the events immediately following *see* AMALASUNTHA. Amalasuntha was succeeded by Theodahad on whom Justinian declared war in 535, the year after Belisarius had completed the overthrow of the Vandals in Africa. The war continued with varying fortunes under Theodahad, Witigis (536–540), Ildibad, Eraric (540–541), Totila (541–552) and Teias (552–554), who fell in the final battle of Mons Lactarius (Monte Lattari near Naples). The war, of which a detailed narrative survives by the contemporary historian Procopius, caused untold damage to Italy—at one stage it is said that Rome itself was left uninhabited—and the Ostrogoths thereafter had no national existence. They had been converted to Arian Christianity, it seems, soon after their escape from the domination of the Huns and in this heresy they persisted until their extinction. All extant Gothic texts were written in Italy before 554.

Visigoths (c. 275–376).—The Visigoths in Dacia during the 4th century were agriculturalists rather than pastoralists and their army was mainly composed of infantry rather than of cavalry. They normally used the potter's wheel and they traded very ex-

GOTHS

tensively with the Romans. Their chief export was slaves and they imported grain, clothing, wine and coins. This trade was so important that a number of Latin words associated with commerce became embedded in their language. That they were literate is shown by the inscription in runic characters on the gold ring found with other gold objects at Pietroasa, a village in the district of Buzău in Rumania. Moreover, Ulfilas (q.v.), whom Eusebius of Nicomedia consecrated as an Arian bishop in 341, devised a new alphabet for them in which he wrote his translation of the Bible and other works, so that writing was now used, for the first time in the Germanic world, for the propagation of ideas.

In the 4th century the Visigoths were led in wartime by a chief whom they called a "judge" and whose powers do not seem to have been any more extensive than those of the chiefs of the Germanic peoples in the 1st century A.D. The elders or optimates, as the Romans sometimes called them, appear to have been the decisive political power among the Visigoths and the chiefs were the executive agents who put the decisions of the optimates into operation. Indeed, one of their chiefs explicitly refused to allow the Romans to call him a "king" rather than a "judge," for, as he said, "the former term implies authority, but the latter wisdom." But there is no evidence that the Visigoths had a general assembly of the warriors like those of the Germanic peoples of the time of Caesar and Tacitus. The most famous of the judges was Athanaric (q.v.), who enforced a persecution of the Visigothic Christians in 369-372. A vivid account of some episodes in this persecution survives in a contemporary Greek narrative of the martyrdom of Saba, the Visigothic Catholic saint. This document throws some light on village life at that time and on Visigothic society in general.

Christianity appears to have been introduced to them by some of the Roman prisoners whom they carried off in their great raids on Asia Minor in the middle of the 3rd century. Ulfilas himself was descended on one side of his family from the village of Sadagolthina. His successor as bishop of the Goths, a certain Selenas, was the son of a Gothic father and a Phrygian mother. In the middle of the 4th century Christianity was represented among the Visigoths both by Catholics and Arians and monasticism was not unknown. But the Christians appear to have formed only a small minority of the population and their numbers may have fallen about 347 when a persecuting judge drove Ulfilas and others from the country. The Christians, it seems, were drawn mostly from the humbler strata of society, though whether they included many slaves is unknown. (The question of slavery among the Goths at this date is very obscure.) But they sent out missionaries to the Ostrogoths in the Ukraine and to the Gepidae in the mountains north of Transylvania, though apparently with little success. Christianity survived the persecution of Athanaric but the people as a whole were still pagan when the Huns fell upon them in 376 and drove them across the Danube into the Roman empire.

Visigoths as Federates (376-475).—The Visigoths were allowed to enter the empire but the exactions of Roman officials soon drove them to revolt and plunder the Balkan provinces, assisted by some Ostrogoths. On Aug. 9, 378, they utterly defeated the army of the emperor Valens on the plains outside Adrianople (see EDIRNE), killing the emperor himself. For four more years they continued to wander in search of somewhere to settle. In Oct. 382 Valens' successor, Theodosius I, settled them in Moesia as federates, giving them land there and imposing on them the duty of defending the frontier. They remained in Moesia until 395.

It appears to have been in this period that they became Arian Christians; at any rate, after 395 the Roman authors who refer to them speak of them as Christians and Arians and never as pagans. Why they became Arians rather than Catholics is a problem of the utmost difficulty. (For the traditional view of this matter see ULFILAS.) It cannot have been because Valens was an Arian for, as we have seen, they appear to have been still mainly pagan at the time of Valens' death, nor was Valens a person whose example they would have been likely to admire. It can hardly have been because Ulfilas was an Arian for Ulfilas died at latest in 383 when the conversion must still have been in a very early stage; moreover, Ulfilas is not known to have lived among them after he was driven from their country about 347. Some ancient authors believed that they chose Arianism because of their "simplicity"; that is, they did not know the difference between Arianism and orthodoxy. But "simplicity" cannot have played much part with such scholars as Ulfilas or Selenas or the author of the commentary on St. John's Gospel known as the *Skeireins* or the two Goths who wrote to St. Jerome asking for a commentary on 178 passages of the Psalms.

In 395 the Goths under Alaric (q.v.) left Moesia and moved first southward into Greece and then to Italy, which they invaded repeatedly from 401 onward. Their depredations culminated in the sack of Rome in 410. In the same year Alaric died and was succeeded by Ataulphus (q.v.), who led the Visigoths to settle first in southern Gaul, then in Spain (415).

In 418 they were recalled from Spain by the patrician Constantius, who later became emperor as Constantius III, and were settled by him as federates in the province of Aquitania Secunda, between the lower reaches of the Garonne and Loire rivers. Their chieftain Wallia died soon after the settlement in Aquitaine was carried out and he was succeeded by Theodoric I, who ruled them until he was killed in 451 fighting against Attila in the battle of the Catalaunian plains. Theodoric is the first Visigothic leader who can properly be described as a monarch; even Alaric seems to have had little more personal power than the "judges" who preceded him or even the Germanic chieftains described by Tacitus. As federates the Visigoths received parts of the Roman estates in Aquitaine and Theodoric issued a number of laws, some of which dealt with property relations. No earlier German chieftain is known to have been able to legislate, to issue written laws or to enforce them. But Theodoric had power only over the Germanic inhabitants of his province. The Roman civil service continued to administer the Roman population, to collect the taxes and forward them to the central government and to administer Roman law.

Visigothic Kingdom in Gaul and Spain (475-711).—While persistently trying to extend their territory, often at the empire's expense, the Visigoths continued to be federates until 475, when chieftain Euric declared himself an independent king. Euric also codified the laws issued by himself and his predecessors and fragments of his code, written in Latin, have survived. It was under him, too, that the Gallic kingdom, of which the capital was at Toulouse, reached its widest extent. It stretched from the Loire to the Pyrenees and to the lower reaches of the Rhône and it included the greater portion of Spain. Euric was himself a fervent Arian, though it is perhaps an exaggeration to say that he persecuted the Catholics of his kingdom. He was succeeded by his tolerant son Alaric II, who in 507 was defeated and killed by Clovis and the Franks at the decisive battle of Vouillé near Poitiers. Although some Catholic bishops in Alaric's realm had favoured a Frankish victory, there is no evidence that the bulk of the Roman population of the Visigothic kingdom did so; indeed, several Catholic Roman aristocrats fought against Clovis at Vouillé.

As a result of Vouillé the Visigoths lost all their possessions in Gaul apart from Septimania, a strip of land stretching along the coast from the Pyrenees to the Rhône with Narbonne as its capital, which the Franks were never able to wrest from them although they often tried to do so. Henceforth, until they were finally destroyed by the Muslims in 711, the Visigoths ruled Septimania and much of Spain, with Toledo as their capital. Northwestern Spain, however, was occupied by the independent kingdom of the Sueves (Suebi), of which the capital was Bracara (Braga), until the Visigothic king Leovigild overthrew it in 585 and incorporated it in his own dominions. Also, in 552 an Arian usurper called Athanagild invited the Byzantines to Spain and Justinian's armies occupied two regions of the peninsula, a larger one centred upon Cartagena in the southeast and a smaller one in Algarve in the southwest. Despite repeated Visigothic attacks the Byzantines held these territories until they were finally expelled by King Swinthila in 629. In Spain the Visigothic kings continued their legislation and Euric's code was several times revised, notably by Alaric II (see BREVIARY OF ALARIC) and Leovigild, until in or soon after 654 King Recceswinth abolished Roman law altogether;

thereafter Romans and Goths alike lived under Visigothic law. Leovigild abolished the ban on intermarriage between Roman and Goth, which had been a capital offense before his time, but the two peoples had not fully merged even at the time of the destruction of the kingdom. The Roman provinces of Spain were retained as administrative units and Roman governors continued to administer them, or at any rate the Roman population in them, until the end of the kingdom. But little is known about the Visigothic administration or about the armed forces.

The Arian kings were extraordinarily tolerant of Catholics and Jews. The Jews suffered few disabilities. The Catholics could build and repair churches and found monasteries in freedom. Their books seem to have circulated without hindrance and they held a considerable number of councils and synods. But Leovigild was forced to exile some Catholic dignitaries during the revolt of his Catholic son Hermenegild in 580–584. Leovigild's successor, however, his younger son Reccared (586–601), was himself converted and at the third Council of Toledo in 589 proclaimed Catholicism as the official religion of the kingdom. During the preceding years he had crushed several Arian revolts and after 589 little is heard of Arianism in Spain. The king immediately began the burning of Arian books and not a single Gothic text has survived in Spain. In the 7th century Latin literature flourished there to a greater degree than in contemporary France and Italy, its most distinguished representative being St. Isidore (q.v.) of Seville. But the entire century was a period of clerical terror and was disfigured throughout by a hideous persecution of the Spanish Jews. This oppressive state, rent by civil war and rebellion, was an easy prey to the Muslims, who invaded it from north Africa in 711 and overran it without difficulty. See SPAIN: History.

See GERMANIC LANGUAGES; GERMANIC PEOPLES; see also references under "Goths" in the Index volume.

BIBLIOGRAPHY.—On early Gothic history and the Gallic kingdom: L. Schmidt, Geschichte der deutschen Stämme: Die Ostgermanen (1934). On the Goths' relations with Rome: J. B. Bury, History of the Later Roman Empire (1923); E. Stein, Histoire du Bas-Empire (1949–60); and on the Crimean Ostrogoths, A. A. Vasiliev, The Goths in the Crimea (1936). There is no satisfactory English account of the Visigothic kingdom in Spain; see R. Menéndez Pidal, Historia de España, vol. iii (1940). For archaeological discoveries there: H. Zeiss, Die Grabfunde aus dem spanischen Westgotenreich (1934). On Gothic Christianity: C. A. A. Scott, Ulfilas: Apostle of the Goths (1885); H. E. Giesecke, Die Ostgermanen und der Arianismus (1939); and on the conversion of the Germans generally: K. D. Schmidt, Die Bekehrung der Germanen zum Christentum (1939). The Gothic text of the fragments of Ulfilas' Bible have been edited by W. Streitberg, Die gotische Bibel (1908–10). (E. A. T.)

GOTLAND, an island in the Baltic sea belonging to Sweden and lying between latitudes 57° and 58° N., 50 mi. E. of the Swedish mainland. It has a length of 77 mi. N.N.E. to S.S.W. and a maximum breadth of 31 mi. Area 1,167 sq.mi. Pop. (1950) 58,995; (1960) 53,358. With the islands of Fårö, Gotska Sandön, Lilla and Stora Karlsö it forms Gotland län (county).

The plateau of Gotland is formed of Silurian limestone which lacks surface drainage and presents karst (q.v.) terrain. The coast is characterized by limestone columns called raukar. In the areas with a clay cover bogs develop while conifers occur particularly on the steep cliffs of the west, but the poor growing conditions result in short trunks. Agriculture is based on grain cultivation, particularly barley and rye, sugar beet (about 70,000 tons a year for the local sugar beet factory) as well as market gardening and flower cultivation to serve the Stockholm market. Fårö is sandy, and used for sheep grazing. Some cement is manufactured and fishing is carried on. The capital and chief port is the ancient walled city of Visby (q.v.) on the west coast; Gotland is popular with tourists. The dialect of the island is distinctive.

(A. C. O'D.)

History.—Archaeological finds (especially hoards) indicate that even in the Bronze Age, Gotland traded extensively with other regions, including the southern and eastern shores of the Baltic. Finds from the Iron Age include more than 5,000 Roman silver coins of that period out of about 7,000 in all Scandinavia; the Roman trade route to the mouth of the Vistula river was clearly extended oversea to Gotland. Other trade routes, established in the Viking period between the Baltic lands and the Islamic and Byzantine empires, caused a stream of Arabic and Byzantine coins (mostly of the early 9th to mid-10th centuries) to flow northward; the peasant traders of Gotland brought home much of this currency. Thereafter came an influx of western European coins, especially German and Anglo-Saxon. These coin finds are evidence of the continued wealth and enterprise of the Gotlanders.

In about 900 Gotland belonged to Sweden, paying an annual tax to the Swedish king for protection, but was otherwise an independent peasant community. In 1285 King Magnus Ladulás additionally exacted the *ledungslame* (a Swedish internal tax) and in 1288 reasserted his authority, but without interfering with Gotland's autonomy.

The foundation of the commerce of the Gotland peasant traders was their trading house at Novgorod (q.v.) which they maintained throughout the middle ages and which made them the leading intermediaries in the exchange of goods between Russia and western Europe. That leadership attracted to Gotland the German merchants, who in mid-12th century had already obtained their own Baltic port at Lübeck. They came to Visby, whence the Gotlanders embarked each spring and autumn on trading ventures to Novgorod. The German settlers, whose coming greatly increased the community's prosperity, organized themselves as a guild and in 1225 were allowed to form a separate congregation at the German church of the Virgin Mary (the Mariendom). By mid-13th century Visby held two similar but separate communities, one German and the other local. Thereafter the Gotland peasant traders lost many of their old markets to German competition. The Gotlanders in Visby were forced to co-operate with the Germans, and the townsfolk and country dwellers were completely separated in 1288. Visby became a Hanseatic town (see HANSEATIC LEAGUE) and until mid-14th century most of the Novgorod trade passed through it. In the following years this trade began to follow other routes and the German Baltic trade swung more to Skåne in Sweden and to Norway, so that Gotland declined. Christianized in the 11th century, its medieval prosperity was reflected by its many fine churches (97 rural and 17 in Visby), most of which are still in use.

In the course of conflicts between Sweden and Denmark over the Skåne and Blekinge provinces, the Danish king Valdemar IV (q.v.) in 1361 conquered Gotland after defeating its peasant levies in a famous battle outside the walls of Visby. Excavation of the mass grave on the battlefield has yielded valuable knowledge of medieval military equipment. Although the conquest did not greatly alter conditions on the island, it sundered Gotland from Sweden for nearly 300 years.

In 1394 the *Vitaliebröder* (victual brotherhood), so named because they had once been charged by the Hanseatic merchants to take provisions to Stockholm, seized Gotland as a base for piracy. They were driven out in 1398 by the knights of the Teutonic Order, who held the island until 1408, when it passed to Eric of Pomerania (q.v.). After his dethronement in 1439 Eric settled in Gotland and made it once more a base for raids in the Baltic, until compelled to surrender it to the Danish king. Eric's castle, built to form part of the walls of Visby, became the seat of Danish noblemen who assumed rulership of the island.

Throughout the period of Danish rule in Gotland, the Swedish claim was never relinquished, and in 1524 Gustavus I Vasa unsuccessfully attempted a reconquest. Sweden formally ceded Gotland to Denmark as the peace of Stettin (1570) but regained it by the peace of Brömsebro in 1645. The countryside was impoverished, many farms were deserted and many churches in ruins, but under Swedish rule conditions steadily improved. In the wars with Denmark (1675–79) and Russia (1808–09) Gotland was temporarily occupied by foreign troops, and in 1855 during the Crimean War it was used as a base by British and French warships. Toward the end of the 19th century the strategic importance of the island caused it to be strongly fortified by Sweden. (H. U. Y.)

GOTŌ-RETTŌ, Japanese archipelago (literally, five-island chain) lying off the western coast of Kyushu, administered by Nagasaki prefecture. There are more than 100 islands (34 are inhabited) with a total area of 266 sq.mi. stretching about 62 mi. from northeast to southwest.

The five largest and most densely settled islands are Fukue,

Hisaka, Naru, Wakamatsu and Nakadōri, in south-north sequence. Largely created by volcanic activity, the islands have mountainous interiors. Intensive dry-land farming is practised on terraces and slopes, with irrigated rice restricted to a few slender coastal plains. Fishing is the main economic activity for large ports like Fukue (Fukue Island), Narao (Nakadōri Island) and many smaller ports. In the northern half of the archipelago, fishing leads agriculture in importance and the islands' economy focuses on Sasebo. However, fishing is secondary to agriculture in the southern half and regular ferry service ties the regional economy to Nagasaki.

(J. D. Ee.)

GOTTER, FRIEDRICH WILHELM (1746–1797), German dramatist and poet, in 1770 founder with H. C. Boie of the Göttingen *Musenalmanach*, was born at Gotha, Sept. 3, 1746. He studied law at Göttingen, became archivist in Gotha in 1766 and a year later secretary to the Gotha legation in Wetzlar. From 1771 he was a government official in Gotha, where he was a patron of the court theatre. He died at Gotha, March 18, 1797.

Gotter's plays, many of them rewritings of French pieces, are in the French classical tradition. Linguistically skilful, they were successful on the stage in spite of the anticlassical influence of the *Sturm und Drang* movement. Best-known are *Merope* (1774, after Voltaire), *Mariane* (1776, after J. F. de La Harpe) and *Die Geisterinsel* (1797), a play based on Shakespeare's *The Tempest* and praised by Goethe. Gotter also published poems (*Gedichte*, 2 vol., 1787–88). His *Literarischer Nachlass* came out in 1802.

(K. Ge.)

GOTTFRIED VON STRASSBURG (*fl.* 1210), one of the greatest medieval German poets. The dates of his birth and death are unknown, as are the circumstances of his life, and the only information about him consists of references to him in the work of other poets and inferences from his own work. The breadth of learning displayed in his epic *Tristan und Isolde* reveals that he must have enjoyed the fullest education offered by the cathedral and monastery schools of the middle ages, and this, together with the authoritative tone of his writing, indicates that, although not himself of noble birth, he spent his life in the society of the well-born. *Tristan* was probably written about 1210. Gottfried is thus a literary contemporary of Hartmann von Aue, Walther von der Vogelweide and Wolfram von Eschenbach.

The Celtic legend of Tristan (*q.v.*) and Iseult (Ger. Isolde) reached Germany through French sources. The first German version is that of Eilhart von Oberge (*c.* 1180), but Gottfried, although he probably knew Eilhart's poem, based his own work on the Anglo-Norman version of Thomas of Brittany (1160–70). The story centres in Tristan's journey to Ireland on behalf of his uncle, King Mark of Cornwall, to bring back Isolde as the king's bride. On the return voyage, Tristan and Isolde unwittingly drink a magic potion which makes them fall in love with each other. They seek to outwit Mark, but are eventually discovered, and Tristan flees to Brittany, where he marries another Isolde, "Isolde of the white hands." Here Gottfried's poem breaks off and the story is completed by Gottfried's continuators, Ulrich von Türheim and Heinrich von Freiberg. In the course of further adventures Tristan receives a wound from a poisoned spear, and only the first Isolde, who has since become Mark's wife, can heal him. She is summoned from Cornwall. Word is to be brought to the sick Tristan when the vessel returns: it is to mount a white sail if she is on board, a black sail if she is not. The ship is sighted, flying a white sail. Tristan's jealous wife, however, tells him that the sail is black, and when Isolde arrives, she finds Tristan dead. Overcome with grief, she joins her lover in death.

Gottfried's moral purpose, as he states it in the prologue to his poem, is to present to courtiers of fine feeling (*edelia herzen*, literally "noble hearts") an ideal of the love relationship. The core of this ideal, which derives from the romantic cult of woman in medieval courtly society, is that love (*minne*) ennobles through the suffering with which it is inseparably linked. This Gottfried enshrines in a story in which actions are motivated and justified, not by a standard ethic, but according to the fictional "rules of love" affected by court circles (*see* COURTLY LOVE.) Thus the love potion, from being the direct cause of the tragedy, has become (as already in Thomas's version) the mere outward symbol of a situation brought about by the inner nature of the relationship between the lovers—an adulterous relationship, yet approved by the "courts of love" by reason of its spontaneity, its exclusiveness and its completeness.

Although unfinished, Gottfried's is the finest of the medieval versions of the Tristan legend and one of the most perfect creations of the medieval courtly spirit, distinguished alike by the refinement and elevated tone of its content and by the elaborate skill of its poetic technique. Apart from *Tristan* Gottfried is known also to have written lyric poems, but only two *Sprüche* have survived which can with reasonable certainty be ascribed to him.

BIBLIOGRAPHY.—Gottfried's *Tristan* has been edited many times, notably by R. Bechstein, 4th ed. (1923). There is an Eng. trans. by A. T. Hatto (1960). *See* also Gottfried Weber, *Gottfrieds von Strassburg Tristan und die Krise des hochmittelalterlichen Weltbildes um 1200* (1953); G. Ehrismann, *Geschichte der deutschen Literatur bis zum Ausgang des Mittelalters* ii, 2, 1, pp. 297–336 (1954), both containing full bibliographies.

(Ro. J. T.)

GÖTTHELF, JEREMIAS: *see* BITZIUS, ALBERT.

GÖTTINGEN, a university town of Germany which after partition of the nation following World War II was located in the *Land* (state) of Lower Saxony, Federal Republic of Germany. Pop. (1961) 81,300, including about 9,000 students. Situated on the upper course of the Leine river, 67 mi. S. from Hanover, the town is surrounded by ramparts. The old streets are crooked and narrow with 15th–16th-century half-timbered houses and Gothic churches. Göttingen possesses a medieval town hall, in front of which stands the Goose Girl fountain. A marketing centre for southern Lower Saxony, it has developed important manufactures, chief among which are optical and scientific instruments. The town has excellent transportation facilities.

First mentioned as Gutingi in 953, Göttingen received municipal rights about 1210 and during the 14th century occupied an important place in the Hanseatic league. In 1531 it joined the Reformation movement, and suffered considerably in the Thirty Years' War. It had not yet overcome the results of that war when it was again brought into prominence by the establishment of the university, and a marked increase in its industrial and commercial prosperity took place.

The Georgia Augusta university, founded by George II of England (the elector George Augustus of Hanover) in 1734 and opened in 1737, soon became one of the most famous of European universities. Political disturbances, including the expulsion in 1837 of seven professors—*die Göttinger Sieben*, among whom were the brothers Grimm—for protesting against the revocation of the liberal Hanoverian constitution of 1833 reduced the prosperity of the university (*see* HANOVER). Strong mathematics and physics faculties led to its revival in the late 19th century. The main university building, in the classical style, is the Aula on the Wilhelmsplatz. The University library, containing well over 2,000,000 volumes and including valuable manuscripts and incunabula, is one of the richest collections in Germany. The university has faculties of theology, law and politics, medicine, philosophy, mathematics and natural science, forestry, agriculture and economics. Some historic university buildings, all institutes located at various places throughout the city, are (since 1964) being rebuilt in a modern style at a campus area of nearly 4 sq.mi. at the outskirts of Göttingen. The Max Planck society was transferred to Göttingen in 1945, and 8 of its 52 institutes are there. The Academy of Sciences (*Sozietät der Wissenschaften*), which collaborates closely with it, publishes the *Göttingische gelehrte Anzeigen*. In the town there are four museums and a congress hall.

(H. Mr.)

GOTTSCHALK (GOTTESCALC, GODESCALCHUS) OF ORBAIS (d. *c.* 867–870), German theologian and poet—while his verse is not unimportant, it is his theology, Augustinian in expression, that gives him renown—was born of noble Saxon parentage at the beginning of the 9th century. Dedicated a child oblate at the abbey of Fulda, he was dispensed from his obligations in 829 at the synod of Mainz, over the objection of his abbot, Rabanus Maurus. Forced to resume monastic life, he settled at Orbais in France. Irregularly ordained a priest at Reims between 835 and 840, Gottschalk was preaching in northern Italy in 840 (when Bishop Noting of Verona complained about his views on predestination) and in the Friuli area five or six years later. Either before or after 845–846, he exercised a ministry in the Balkans. At the synod of Mainz (848), he was censured for heresy by the new archbishop, Rabanus Maurus, who transferred him to the jurisdiction of Hincmar of Reims, metropolitan of the province in which Orbais was situated. Unable to secure Gottschalk's recantation (849), Hincmar deposed him from the priesthood and imprisoned him at the abbey of Hautvillers, where he later died unreconciled. In several treatises and in synods at Quiercy (853) and Thuzey (860), Hincmar espoused a predestination doctrine contrary to that of Gottschalk.

Gottschalk inclined toward a traducianist explanation (*see* CREATIONISM AND TRADUCIANISM) of the human soul's origin, defended the term *trina Deitas* in describing the Triune God, contended (against Paschasius Radbertus) that while the eucharistic and the resurrected Body of Christ are one, the first is *sumptibilis* and the latter *inconsumptibilis*. His position on divine predestination has been clarified by Dom Germain Morin's discovery (1930) at Bern of Gottschalk's own *De praedestinatione*, subsequently edited by Dom Cyrille Lambot. Gottschalk taught a double predestination, that of the elect to eternal glory and that of the reprobate to damnation, yet a damnation conditioned by God's foreknowledge of sin (*propter praescita ipsorum propria futura mala merita*). He held that the divine salvific will was limited and that Christ's redemption extended only to the elect. Though the synod of Valence (855) and the theologians Prudentius of Troyes, Florus of Lyons and Ratramnus of Corbie shared similar views, criticism of Hincmar of Reims was as much the occasion for this agreement as was sympathy for the monk of Orbais.

BIBLIOGRAPHY.—His verse may be found in *Monumenta Germaniae Historica, Poetae*, vol. iii, pp. 707–738; vol. iv, pp. 934–936; vol. vi, pp. 86–106; Cyrille Lambot, *Oeuvres théologiques et grammaticales de Godescalc d'Orbais* (1945), and "Lettre inédite de Godescalc d'Orbais," *Revue Bénédictine*, 68:41–51 (1958); G. Morin, "Gottschalk retrouvé," *Rev. Bén.*, 43:303–312 (1931); Klaus Vielhaber, *Gottschalk der Sachse* (1956); J. Jolivet, *Godescalc d'Orbais et la Trinité* (1958); *Lexikon für Theologie und Kirche*, 2nd ed., vol. iv, pp. 1144–45 (1960).
(H. G. J. B.)

GOTTSCHALL, RUDOLF VON (1823–1909), German writer, at first a liberal enthusiast, later an established conservative literary figure, was born at Breslau on Sept. 30, 1823, the son of a Prussian officer. As an undergraduate at Königsberg, Breslau, Leipzig and Berlin he embraced liberal doctrines, and his early poetry and plays (*Robespierre*, 1845; *Lord Byron in Italien*, 1847) were full of yearning for freedom. Later his sympathies swung toward conservatism and he settled down as a man of letters, attaining great influence through his novels, plays and criticism. For many years he edited the *Blätter für literarische Unterhaltung* (1865–88) and a monthly magazine, *Unsere Zeit*. He died at Leipzig on March 21, 1909. His main collections of poetry are *Lieder der Gegenwart* (1842), *Neue Gedichte* (1858) and *Späte Lieder* (1906). He wrote a comedy, *Pitt und Fox* (1854), and his novels include *Im Banne des schwarzen Adlers* (1876), *Verschollene Grössen* (1886) and *Moderne Streber* (1896). His *Die deutsche National-Literatur des . . . 19. Jahrhunderts* (1855) was later expanded and reached a seventh edition in 1901.

See his Dramatische Werke, 12 vol. (1884); C. Dietsch in *Alt Preussische Biographie*, I (1941).
(W. D. WI.)

GOTTSCHED, JOHANN CHRISTOPH (1700–1766), German literary theorist and critic who introduced French 18th-century classical standards of taste into German literature, especially drama, was born on Feb. 2, 1700, at Judithenkirch near Königsberg. He studied at Königsberg. In 1730 he was appointed professor of poetry at the University of Leipzig, and in 1734 became professor of logic and metaphysics there. His lectures, writings, editorship of several literary journals and work for dramatic reform, in which he collaborated with the actress Karoline Neuber (*q.v.*), led to the establishment of a so-called "Leipzig school" of acting and criticism. Gottsched died at Leipzig on Dec. 12, 1766.

Gottsched's most influential work was his *Versuch einer kritischen Dichtkunst für die Deutschen* (1730), the first German treatise on the art of poetry to apply the French classical standards of reason and good taste advocated by Nicolas Boileau. His aims to purify German as a literary language and to develop a classical German style were advanced by his *Ausführliche Redekunst* (1728) and *Grundlegung einer deutschen Sprachkunst* (1748). He wrote several plays on classical principles, of which *Der sterbende Cato* (1732), an adaptation of Joseph Addison's tragedy, is the most notable. His *Deutsche Schaubühne* (6 vol., 1740–45), containing mainly translations from the French, provided the German stage with a classical repertory to replace the improvisations and melodramas previously popular. He also prepared a bibliography of German drama, *Nötiger Vorrat zur Geschichte der deutschen dramatischen Dichtkunst* (1757–65). His influence decreased after 1740 when he came into conflict with the Swiss writers, J. J. Bodmer and J. J. Breitinger (*qq.v.*), who demanded that poetic imagination should not be hampered by artificial rules.

Gottsched's wife, LUISE ADELGUNDE VIKTORIE, née KULMUS (1713–62), helped her husband in his work of dramatic reform, and was the author of several popular comedies. She also translated French classical dramas, Addison's *Spectator* (9 vol. 1739–43), Pope's *Rape of the Lock* (1744) and other French and English works.

BIBLIOGRAPHY.—Gottsched's *Gesammelte Schriften* were edited by E. Reichel (1902–06). *See also* E. Wolff, *Gottscheds Stellung im deutschen Bildungsleben*, 2 vol. (1895–97); H. Lachmann, *Gottscheds Bedeutung für die Geschichte der deutschen Philologie* (1931); G. Schimansky, *Gottscheds deutsche Bildungsziele* (1939). Frau Gottsched, *Lustspiele*, R. Buchwald and A. Köster (eds.), 2 vol. (1908). *See* P. Schlenther, *Frau Gottsched und die bürgerliche Komödie* (1886).
(A. Gs.)

GOTTWALDOV (until 1948, ZLÍN), a city of Gottwaldov region, Czechoslovakia, lies on both banks of the Dřevnice river, a few miles above its confluence with the Morava. Pop. (1961) 59,751. Zlín was a 14th-century south-bank village that grew rapidly during the first Czechoslovak republic, the nucleus of its activity being the famous and old-established shoemaking enterprise of the Baťa family. After World War II, in which it suffered some damage, its manufacturing development was spectacular; leather and footwear industries continue important, producing one-third of all the footwear in Czechoslovakia, but rubber and timber industries are also significant. At nearby Otrokovice are Czechoslovakia's largest tanneries.
(H. G. S.)

GÖTZ, HERMANN (1840–1876), German composer known for his comic opera based on Shakespeare's *The Taming of the Shrew*, was born at Königsberg on Dec. 7, 1840. He went to Berlin in his youth where, between 1860 and 1862, he studied with Hans von Bülow and H. Ulrich. In 1863 he was appointed organist at Winterthur, Switz., and about this time formed a lasting friendship with Brahms. From 1870 he lived at Zürich, where he was music critic of the *Neue Zürcher Zeitung*. His opera *Der Widerspenstigen Zähmung* (*The Taming of the Shrew*) was produced at Mannheim on Oct. 11, 1874, and achieved immediate success for its spontaneous style and lighthearted characterization. A later opera, *Francesca da Rimini*, completed by Ernst Frank (Mannheim, 1877), was less successful. Götz also wrote chamber and choral works, an overture, a piano concerto and a symphony. He died at Hottingen, near Zürich, on Dec. 3, 1876.

See G. R. Kruse, *Hermann Goetz* (1920).

GÖTZ, JOHANN NIKOLAUS (1721–1781), German poet, one of the group known as the *Anakreontik*, was born at Worms on July 9, 1721. After studying theology at Halle he held various church offices. At Halle he met J. W. L. Gleim and J. P. Uz, and it was he who published (1746) the Anacreontic translations and pseudo-Anacreontics which gave the group their name. Afraid that his profession would cause scandal, he published his first collection, *Versuch eines Wormsers in Gedichten* (1745), anonymously. Of his poems "Die Mädcheninsel" is best known, probably because it was praised by Frederick the Great. He died at Winterburg, Baden, on Nov. 4, 1781.

See works in *Deutsche Literarische Denkmale des 18. und 19. Jahrhunderts*, vol. 42 (1893); letters ed. by C. Schüddekopf (1893).

GOUACHE, a type of opaque water colour, and, by extension, a picture painted in this medium. Water colour (French and German *aquarelle*) is the specific term for the transparent method (*see* WATER-COLOUR PAINTING); gouache is applied opaquely. Whites and pale tints are produced by the addition of white pigment, ordinarily zinc white (Chinese white). Gouache colours contain the same ingredients as water colours but are compounded with more vehicle and inert pigment. Artists sometimes combine gouache, water colour and pastel in the same picture. Water colour is like a stain in the paper, and the tiny pigment particles become enmeshed in its fibres; gouache colour lies on the surface, forming a continuous layer or coating. Tinted papers and smooth papers can be used instead of the special rough-finish, handmade papers which are indispensable in creating the sparkling, transparent water colour. Gouache paintings are characterized by a directly reflecting brilliance, different from that of water colour. The medium has its own kind of brushstrokes. When applied with bristle brushes it exhibits a slight but effective impasto quality; gouache paint is also capable of being worked out to smooth, flawless colour fields with sable brushes.

(RH. M.)

GOUDA, an old town of the Netherlands, in the province of South Holland, lies on the Gouwe at its confluence with the IJssel, 12½ mi. N.E. of Rotterdam by rail, 16 mi. E. of The Hague. Gouda, at the junction of primary east-west and north-south roads, and intersected by many canals, is called the "Heart of Holland." Pop. (1960) 41,937. The town was well known in the 17th and 18th centuries for the clay pipes it sent all over Europe. Modern industries include the manufacture of candles (an old Gouda product) and other stearine products, pottery factories and a flax and hemp spinning mill. The name Gouda, however, is best known in connection with the famous cheese that is marketed there. Some Gouda cheese is still made on the farms, some of it in the town's cheese factories, the largest of which is a co-operative.

In the centre of the Market, the largest market square in the Netherlands, is the Gothic town hall, founded in 1449 and restored in 1947-52. The Weighing House, built 1668, is adorned with reliefs in marble. The Grote Kerk (St. John's), rebuilt after a fire in 1552, is celebrated for its complete set of 64 stained-glass windows dating from 1556 to 1603; the best are from the hand of the brothers Dirck and Wouter Crabeth. The organ is a specially fine one and the concerts in the church attract thousands of visitors.

Gouda was chartered in 1272 and was a centre of the medieval cloth trade.

(K. F. O.)

GOUDIMEL, CLAUDE (*c.* 1514-1572), French composer noted for his settings of the metrical psalms, was born in Besançon. He worked there and also in Paris, Metz and in Lyons, where he died on Aug. 28, 1572, in the anti-Huguenot riots. Though he also wrote Latin church music and chansons, Goudimel is remembered for his vernacular psalm settings. The incomplete collection of 1551-56 presents an extended motetlike treatment of the text; the 1564 "cycle sets only the first verses, with the traditional tune usually in the treble. The 1565 book is written in the simplest note-against-note style; the tenor normally has the melody. It proved enormously popular and was widely adopted by the Reformed churches.

BIBLIOGRAPHY.—*Les pseaumes mis en rime* . . . (1565), facsimile edition ed. by P. Pidoux and K. Ameln (1935); "Les cent cinquante pseaumes de David," ed. by H. Expert, *Les Maîtres musiciens de la Renaissance française* vol. ii, iv and vi (1894-97); G. Reese, *Music in the Renaissance* (1954).

(B. L. TR.)

GOUDY, FREDERIC WILLIAM (1865-1947), U.S. printer and typographer who designed more than 100 type faces, was born March 8, 1865, in Bloomington, Ill. While working as an accountant in a bookstore in Chicago he became interested in typography and in 1905 established the Village press at nearby Park Ridge, Ill. He moved the shop to New York city in 1906 and to an old mill at Marlborough, N.Y., in 1908. His shop came to specialize in limited-edition book publishing using type of his own drawing. After 1913 he worked exclusively in type design, producing such faces as Goudy Old Style, Kennerley, Village and Forum. When his plant was destroyed by fire in 1939, about 75

of his original type designs were lost. He was author of *The Alphabet* (1918), *Elements of Lettering* (1921), *Typologia* (1940) and the autobiographical *Half-Century of Type Design and Typography, 1895-1945* (1946). He died at Marlborough on May 11, 1947.

(C. E. Mo.)

GOUGH, SIR HUBERT DE LA POER (1870-1963), British soldier, commander of the 5th army during World War I, was born in London on Aug. 12, 1870, and was educated at Eton and Sandhurst. He joined the 16th lancers in 1889, served in the Tirah expedition (1897) and in the South African War (1899-1902). He commanded the 3rd cavalry brigade in 1914 and opposed the use of force at the Curragh to compel Ulster to accept Home Rule. In France during World War I, Gough commanded a cavalry division in 1914, became commander of the 5th army on its formation (1916) and was prominent at the battle of the Somme (1916) and at the battle of Ypres (1917). His army met the main force of the German offensive (March 1918) and was compelled to withdraw with considerable loss under heavy pressure. Although his skilful handling of the battle led to the eventual stemming of the German advance, he was subjected to much criticism and the government insisted on his removal from the command. He retired in 1922 and the award of the knight grand cross of the Bath in 1937 was a token of amends for the harshness of his dismissal 19 years earlier. His writings include *The Fifth Army* (1931) and *Soldiering On* (1954). He was knighted in 1916. He died on March 18, 1963, in London.

(R. G. TH.)

GOUGH, HUGH GOUGH, VISCOUNT (1779-1869), Irish soldier, prominent in the Peninsular War and in India, was born at Woodsdown, Limerick, on Nov. 3, 1779. He entered the army in 1794, and took part in the occupation of the Cape of Good Hope in 1796 and in the West Indies campaigns of 1797-1800. An adjutant at 15, a major by purchase at 25, he commanded the 87th (Royal Irish fusiliers) regiment in the duke of Wellington's armies in Portugal and Spain. Severely wounded in the stubborn fighting at Talavera (1809), he yet led the 87th to resounding victory at Barrosa, capturing a French eagle, and was promoted lieutenant colonel with his commission antedated to Talavera. He took a leading part in the notable defense of Tarifa, at Vitoria captured the baton of Marshal Jean Baptiste Jourdan, and at Nivelle was again seriously wounded. For his peninsular services he was knighted in 1815 and awarded a pension.

Then, for almost 20 years, Gough was left on half pay, seeing action only against the peasantry of southern Ireland (1821-24). However, having risen to the rank of major general (1830), he was given command in Mysore in 1837. He led the expedition against China, the "Opium War," from 1840, and through two years of operations displayed strategic vision, tactical skill, much humanity and political wisdom. After the treaty of Nanking (Aug. 1842) he was created a baronet and in 1843 was appointed commander in chief in India. Gough defeated the Maratha army of Gwalior at Maharajpur in Dec. 1843, and defeated the Sikh army in 1845-46 (*see* SIKH WARS) at Mudki, Ferozeshah and Sobraon, forcing the Sikhs to sue for peace. He commanded again in the second Sikh War (1848-49), and after heavy engagements at Ramnagar and Chillianwalla, crushed the Sikhs decisively at the battle of Gujrat. In both Sikh Wars the British forces suffered unexpectedly heavy losses. For these the numbers, discipline and courage of the Sikhs were mainly responsible, but both Lord Hardinge and Lord Dalhousie blamed the tactics of Gough, while popular outcry after Chillianwala led to his supersedure by Sir Charles Napier.

Created a baron after the first Sikh War, Gough was raised to a viscounty after the second, and in 1862 was made field marshal. He died on March 2, 1869.

See R. S. Rait, *Life and Campaigns of Viscount Gough*, 2 vol. (1903); Sir W. Lee-Warner, *Life of the Marquis of Dalhousie*, 2 vol. (1904).

(J. B. HA.)

GOUIN, SIR LOMER (1861-1929), Canadian politician, was born at Grondines, Que., on March 19, 1861. Educated at Laval and McGill universities, he was called to the bar in 1884 and became queen's counsel in 1900. In 1897 he was elected as a Liberal to the Quebec legislature and from 1905 to 1920 was prime minister and attorney general of the province. Gouin opposed Henri Bourassa strenuously, but he supported Sir Wilfrid Laurier in 1917 and refused to join Sir Robert Laird Borden in a coalition government to implement conscription. In 1921 Montreal Conservatives supported Gouin rather than Arthur Meighen and they viewed Gouin (who became minister of justice in that year) as their special representative in the government of Mackenzie King. Gouin was a Canadian representative at the fourth assembly of the League of Nations and pressed for a definite interpretation of article 10 of the covenant, under which each member undertook to respect and protect the territorial integrity and existing political independence of all the others. He resigned his federal post in 1924 in the belief that King conceded too much to the low-tariff views of western Progressives. He died at Quebec on March 28, 1929.

(K. W. K. M.)

GOUJON, JEAN (c. 1510?–1568?), the greatest French sculptor of the mid-16th century. The first record of him documents his activity in 1540 as an architectural sculptor in Rouen. His earliest mature masterpiece was the superb relief decoration made in 1544–45 for the rood screen of the church of St. Germain l'Auxerrois, Paris, now in the Louvre, which also marked the beginning of his collaboration with the architect Pierre Lescot. The especially beautiful relief of the Deposition illustrates all of the characteristics of Goujon's personal variation of mid-16th-century mannerism, in which the highly subjective and rarefied ideals of beauty created by the artist's imagination were not compromised by reference to what was thought "imperfect Nature." These attenuated and hypersensitive human forms were skilfully coerced onto a plane in poses which are audaciously unlineal and suggest aesthetic movements as unreal as those of the ballet; the whole was then exquisitely embroidered with a linear play of nervous, finely divided draperies.

Goujon's masterpiece was the famous relief ornamentation of the later altered Fontaine des Innocents in Paris (1547–49), where the six extraordinarily narrow spaces between the pilasters are filled with elegantly elongated figures of nymphs. At about the same time Goujon must have made the less fine reliefs on the Hôtel Carnavalet, which were executed largely by assistants. Goujon's brilliant reliefs on the court façade of the Old Louvre (c. 1549–53) were irresponsibly recut by 19th-century restorers. The later ones in the attic above show how his late work was bolder in relief and freer from his early architectural restraint. The great hall inside contains Goujon's most ambitious sculpture, especially the famous gallery with caryatids carved in the round, but these too were falsified by restoration. Recent scholarship has refuted many traditional attributions to Goujon. His career after 1562 remains largely a mystery; some have thought that as a Protestant he fled Paris.

See Pierre du Colombier, Jean Goujon (1949); Anthony Blunt, Art and Architecture in France, 1500–1700 (1953).
(J. HM.)

GOULBURN, the principal city on the southern tablelands of New South Wales, Austr., lies 137¼ mi. S.W. of Sydney by rail. Pop. (1966) 20,849. Named after Henry Goulburn, a former undersecretary for the colonies, it was laid out in squares in 1833 with its principal thoroughfare, Auburn street, running north and south. Notable buildings are the courthouse (1887), Riverdale cottage (an example of early colonial architecture, c. 1847) and an Anglican and a Roman Catholic cathedral, founded in the 1870s. There are parks, technical colleges and state and denominational schools. Goulburn lies in a productive agricultural and pastoral district, and holds large stock and wool markets. It is on the main Sydney-Melbourne railway and road, with branch lines and roads to Canberra and other places.
(S. H. Hu.)

GOULD, AUGUSTUS ADDISON (1805–1866), U.S. zoologist who specialized in the study of mollusks, an expert on Massachusetts invertebrates, was born in New Ipswich, N.H., April 23, 1805, and graduated at Harvard in medicine in 1830. His reputation was world-wide; his writings fill many pages of the publications of the Boston Society of Natural History. He published with Louis Agassiz (q.v.) the Principles of Zoölogy (2nd ed., 1851); he edited the Terrestrial and Air-Breathing Mollusks (1851–55) of Amos Binney (1803–47). The two most important monuments to his scientific work are "Mollusca and Shells," vol. xii of United States Exploring Expedition . . . Under the Command of Charles Wilkes, U.S.N., published by the government (1852), and the Report on the Invertebrata of Massachusetts (1841). He died in Boston Sept. 15, 1866.

His other works include The Study of Botany in Connection With Medicine (1835); Description of Shells (1848); The Naturalists' Library (1849); Animal Life in the Ocean at Great Depths (1862); Otia Conchologica (1863); Search Out the Secrets of Nature (1885).

See National Academy of Science, Biographical Memoirs, vol. v, pp. 91–113, and Bibliography, pp. 106–113 (1905).

GOULD, BENJAMIN APTHORP (1824–1896), U.S. astronomer, best known for his work in connection with longitude determinations, was born at Boston, Mass., Sept. 27, 1824. He graduated from Harvard college in 1844, studied mathematics and astronomy under C. F. Gauss at Göttingen, and returned to the U.S. in 1848. He was in charge of the longitude department of the U.S. coast survey (1852–67); he developed and organized the service, was one of the first to determine longitudes by telegraphic means and employed the Atlantic cable in 1866 to establish longitude relations between Europe and America. The Astronomical Journal was founded by Gould in 1849; and its publication, suspended in 1861, was resumed by him in 1885. From 1855 to 1859 he was director of the Dudley observatory at Albany, N.Y., and in 1859 he published a discussion of the places and proper motions of circumpolar stars to be used as standards by the U.S. coast survey. Gould undertook (1868), on behalf of the Argentine republic, to organize a national observatory at Córdoba; he began to observe there, with four assistants, in 1870; and in 1874 he completed his Uranometria Argentina (published 1879). He then made a zone catalogue of 73,160 stars (1884) and a general catalogue (1885) compiled from meridian observations of 32,448 stars. He died in Cambridge, Mass., Nov. 26, 1896.

GOULD, JAY (JASON) (1836–1892), U.S. railroad executive and financier, was born in Roxbury, N.Y., May 27, 1836. Starting as a surveyor, he turned to railroad employment in 1863 when he was appointed manager of the Rensselaer and Saratoga railway. He also bought and reorganized the Rutland and Washington railway. In 1868 he was elected president of the Erie railway, which he and James Fisk controlled. A fraudulent stock sale in 1868–70 led to litigation and forced Gould out of the company. During his control of the Erie, he and Fisk admitted William Tweed, then state senator, to the directorate and in turn received favourable legislative support from the politician. Gould's speculation in gold resulted in the panic of "Black Friday" on Sept. 24, 1869, when the price of gold fell from 163½ to 133. Later Gould realized a large profit upon relinquishing his control of the Union Pacific railway. Beginning with investments in the Missouri Pacific railway he built up the "Gould system" of railways in the southwestern states. His later interests included the Western Union Telegraph company and elevated railways in New York city. He died on Dec. 2, 1892.

His eldest son, GEORGE JAY GOULD (1864–1923), was also prominent as owner and manager of railways. He became president of the Little Rock and Fort Smith railway (1888), the St. Louis, Iron Mountain and Southern railway (1893), the International and Great Northern railway (1893), the Missouri Pacific Railroad company (1893), the Texas and Pacific railway (1893) and the Manhattan Railway company (1888). He was also vice-president and director of the Western Union Telegraph company.

His eldest daughter, HELEN MILLER GOULD SHEPARD (1868–1938), became widely known as a philanthropist and for her gifts to U.S. army hospitals during the war with Spain.
(W. H. D.)

See Richard O'Connor, Gould's Millions (1962).

GOULETTE, LA, a town in Tunisia in the governorate of Tunis et Banlieue forming an outport of Tunis, is situated on the offshore bar of the Bahira lagoon, on a former channel (goulet) which has been widened into a basin at the entrance to a 6-mi. canal leading to Tunis. Pop. (1966) 31,830 (comm.). The old quarter, with its port, a palace and an old Hispano-Turkish fortress, lies inland of the new town along the beach. A residential and bathing resort for the inhabitants of Tunis, La Goulette imports coal and petroleum and exports phosphates and iron ore. It is also a fishing port and has a large electric power station.

(J.-J. Ds.)

GOUNOD, CHARLES FRANÇOIS (1818-1893), French composer whose fame chiefly rests upon his opera *Faust*, a model of 19th-century French operatic style, was born in Paris on June 18, 1818. His father, François Gounod, was a painter of some distinction; his mother, a woman of wide education, was a capable pianist and gave Gounod his early training in music. He was educated at the Lycée St. Louis where he remained until 1835. After taking his *baccalauréat* in philosophy he began to study music with Anton Reicha. On Reicha's death in 1836 Gounod entered the Paris conservatory, where he studied under Halévy and Lesueur, winning the Grand Prix de Rome in 1839 with the cantata *Fernand*. In Italy he devoted much of his attention to the study of Palestrina and was so deeply influenced by him that a mass in imitation of the style of the Italian master was among his earliest important compositions. On completing his course in Rome he proceeded to Vienna, where his Mass and Requiem, composed in Italy, were performed in 1842 and 1843 respectively. On leaving Vienna to return to Paris, he passed through Prague, Dresden and Berlin and spent four days in Leipzig with Mendelssohn, who arranged for Gounod to hear a performance of Mendelssohn's Scottish Symphony and took him to the Thomaskirche, where he gave him a recital of organ works by Bach.

On his return to Paris Gounod became organist and *maître de chapelle* at the church of the *Missions Étrangères* and for two years he was mainly occupied with the study of theology and the writing of religious music. In 1846 he attended a course at the seminary of St. Sulpice and it was expected that he would take orders. In 1847 he decided, however, against entering the priesthood and, abandoning his projected Requiem and *Te Deum*, turned his attention to composing for the operatic stage.

His first operas, *Sapho* on a libretto by Émile Augier (first performed in 1851) and *La Nonne sanglante* on a libretto by Eugène Scribe and Germain Delavigne based on M. G. Lewis' *Monk* (first performed 1854), together with his incidental music for F. Ponsard's tragedy *Ulysse* (first performed 1852), were very favourably reviewed by Berlioz, although in general their reception was not very enthusiastic. In his *Messe solennelle à Ste. Cécile* (1855) he attempted to blend the sacred with a more secular style of composition. An excursion into comic opera followed with *Le Médecin malgré lui* to a libretto by M. Carré and J. Barbier based on Molière's comedy. From 1852 Gounod worked on *Faust* on a libretto by Carré and Barbier based on Goethe's tragedy; its production on March 19, 1859, marked a new phase in the development of French opera. This work has continued to overshadow all his subsequent stage works, including the fairly successful *Mireille* (1864) and *Roméo and Juliette* (first performed 1867), as well as his later oratorios.

In 1852 Gounod had become conductor of the *Orphéon* choral society in Paris, for which he wrote a number of choral works, including two masses. From 1870 he spent five years in London, where he formed a choir to which he gave his name and with which he made a number of public appearances. Eventually this organization became the Royal Choral society.

In his later years Gounod devoted himself almost entirely to the writing of oratorios, many of which were first produced in England. He was made a grand officer of the Legion of Honour in 1888 and died at St. Cloud on Oct. 18, 1893.

Among other works he wrote *Gallia*, a lamentation for solo soprano, chorus and orchestra inspired by the French military catastrophe of 1870 and first performed at the Albert hall, London, at the opening of the international exhibition on May 1, 1871; the oratorios *La Rédemption* and *Mors et Vita*, first performed at the Birmingham festival in 1882 and 1885 respectively; 13 operas (one unfinished); music for plays, including *Les Deux Reines*, a drama by E. Legouvé, and *Jeanne d'Arc* by Barbier; a large output of church music; orchestral music; pianoforte solos; and songs. Gounod introduced an original sense of melody though it often deteriorated into sentimentality. He wrote well for the voice and he was a skilful orchestrator. His sacred music lacked fervour. His "Meditation" (Ave Maria) adapted from the first prelude of Bach's *Well-Tempered Clavier* illustrates his sentimental manner. Gounod wrote the following literary works: *Ascanio de C. Saint-Saëns* (1889); *Le Don Juan de Mozart*, Eng. trans. by W. Clark and J. T. Hutchinson (1895); *Mémoires d'un artiste*, Eng. trans. by A. E. Crocker (1896).

BIBLIOGRAPHY.—C. Bellaigue, *Gounod* (1910); M. A. de Bovet, *Ch. Gounod*, Eng. trans. (1891); J. C. Prod'homme and A. Dandelot, *Gounod: Sa vie et ses oeuvres*, 2 vol. (1911); P. Landormy, *Gounod* (1942), *Faust de Gounod* (1944).

(F. E. G.)

GOURAMI (*Osphromenus gourami*), a large, fresh-water food fish native to Asia, where it is widely cultured in ponds. Being omnivorous and tenacious of life, it often attains a length of 2 ft. and a weight of 12 to 14 lb. or more. It possesses an accessory respiratory organ above the gills, enabling it to live in warm, stagnant water and even for some time out of water. The flat oblong gourami is the largest member of the family Anabantidae, to which belong also many small aquarium fish called gourami— pearl gourami (*Trichogaster*), kissing gourami (*Helostoma*), etc. *See also* AQUARIUM; FISH.

GOURD, a name commonly used to designate the hard-shelled, ornamental fruits of two very different species, *Cucurbita pepo* var. *ovifera* and *Lagenaria siceraria*. These species are vigorous, trailing annual herbs of the gourd family, Cucurbitaceae (*q.v.*). Technically, botanists have broadened the term to include fruits of the wax gourd—*Benincasa hispida*; teasel gourd—*Cucumis dipsaceus*; sponge gourd—*Luffa cylindrica*; and snake gourd— *Trichosanthes anguina*.

Cucurbita pepo var. *ovifera*, the yellow-flowered gourd, includes the small ornamental gourds used for decorative purposes. Nest

JOHN H. GERARD

SPOON GOURD, A FORM OF CUCURBITA PEPO VAR. OVIFERA: (LEFT) PISTILLATE FLOWER WITH SMALL GOURD; (RIGHT) MATURE GOURD

Egg, Pear-shaped, Bicolor, Spoon and Ladle gourds are common forms of this species. *Lagenaria siceraria*, the white-flowered gourd, has extremely large fruits. Some may attain a length of three feet or more, and fruits with diameters of one and one-half feet are not uncommon. Typical varieties are the Bottle, Kettle, Hercules Club, Dipper and Sugar-trough gourds.

Both species have a long history of association with man, and neither has ever been found in the truly wild state. *C. pepo* var. *ovifera* is native to northern Mexico and the eastern United States. *L. siceraria* probably comes from tropical Africa, but evidence on this point is not decisive. Archaeological specimens of the latter species have been recovered in both hemispheres. Specimens found in an Egyptian tomb are dated at the time of the 5th dynasty (3500-3300 B.C.), and in Peru seeds, shells and some intact fruits have been recovered from a large midden at Huaca Prieta in strata dated at about 3000 B.C. For primitive peoples without either metalware or pottery, the *Lagenaria* gourds served many purposes. They were used for cutlery, utensils, scoops, ladles, containers of all sorts, fish-net floats, whistles and rattles. In modern times the immature fruits have been used to a limited extent for food, but their chief use is for ornamental purposes. They are frequently painted bright colours, then used as decoration. Many of the smaller gourds of *C. pepo* var. *ovifera* are naturally banded, striped or mottled in various shades of green and yellow, while the solid white ones may be painted to suit the decorator's taste. Others are warted, and some are prized for their bizarre shapes.

C. pepo var. *ovifera* has comparatively large triangular-shaped leaves that are often deeply lobed. Stems and leaves are covered with short bristles that give them a harsh touch. The flowers are large, showy, and orange-yellow in colour. They are of two kinds, male and female, both produced on the same plant. Usually the male flowers appear a week or more in advance of the female flowers and are located toward the extremities of the runners. *Lagenaria* has musky-scented, large, heart-shaped leaves, of soft, velvety texture. The beautiful snow-white flowers open in the evening and close late the following morning. Like *C. pepo*, each plant bears male and female flowers.

Identical methods of culture can be followed with both the yellow-flowered and white-flowered gourds. The seeds should be planted in the spring immediately after danger from frost has passed. They require a long growing season to mature a crop of fruits, and are killed with the first autumn frost. Well-drained mellow soils of good fertility are preferred. A warm, sunny location is best for maximum growth. Trellises, fences or walls for the vines to crawl over are excellent for obtaining clean, well-shaped fruits, of maximum colour, without blemishes or ground spots.   (T. W. W.)

GOURGAUD, GASPARD, Baron (1783–1852), French soldier who shared Napoleon's exile at St. Helena, was born at Versailles on Sept. 14, 1783. He served in the campaigns of 1803–05, at Saragossa, and in the Danubian campaign of 1809. He acted as ordnance officer to Napoleon throughout the Russian campaign of 1812, served in the campaign in Saxony, and saved the emperor's life at Brienne. Though one of the royal guards of Louis XVIII in 1814, he joined Napoleon in the Hundred Days (1815), was named general and aide-de-camp, and fought at Waterloo. On St. Helena Gourgaud tired of the life at Longwood and the friction with Montholon, and went to England, where he published his *Campagne de 1815*. He returned to the army in 1830, became a deputy to the legislative assembly in 1849, and died in Paris in 1852.

Gourgaud's works include: *La Campagne de 1815* (1818); *Napoléon et la Grande Armée en Russie: examen critique de l'ouvrage de M. le comte P. de Ségur* (1824); *Réfutation de la vie de Napoléon par Sir Walter Scott* (1827); *Mémoires pour servir à l'histoire de France sous Napoléon*, with Montholon (1822–23); and *Bourrienne et ses erreurs*, with Belliard *et al.*, two volumes (1830). His most important work is the *Journal inédit de Ste.-Hélène*, two volumes (1899; new ed, by Octave Aubry, 1944).
See B. Jackson, *Notes and Reminiscences of a Staff Officer* (1904).   (P. F. DE L.)

GOURMONT, REMY DE (1858–1915), French novelist, poet and playwright, was the most intelligent contemporary critic of Symbolism. His writings contributed largely to the spread of the aesthetic doctrines of the Symbolist movement (*see* SYMBOLISTS) in France, England and the United States. Born at Bazoches-en-Houlmes (Orne) on April 4, 1858, he became a law student at Caen and entered the Bibliothèque Nationale in 1881. He was dismissed in 1891 as a result of an allegedly unpatriotic article he had published in the *Mercure de France* of which he was a founder.

His 50 volumes are mainly collections of articles. They include: (1) the six volumes of *Epilogues* (1903–13) which comment on contemporary life; (2) the seven volumes of *Promenades littéraires* (1904–27) and the three volumes of *Promenades philosophiques* (1905–09) containing literary and philosophical essays; (3) books devoted to studies of style, language and aesthetics (*Le Latin mystique*, 1892; *Esthétique de la langue française*, 1899; *La Culture des idées*, 1900; *Le Chemin de velours* and *Le Problème du style*, 1902). His strength as a literary critic lies in his sure judgments of contemporaries and his insistence that criticism should be based on aesthetic principles alone. His range of interests links him with the 18th-century *philosophes* whose paradoxical skepticism he shared, although some of Gourmont's work is marred by a superficial cynicism. His novels (*Sixtine*, 1890; *Les Chevaux de Diomède*, 1897; *Le Songe d'une femme*, 1899; and *Un Cœur virginal*, 1907) are experiments which fail because the characters are intellectual symbols rather than human beings, but the later ones contain passages of intelligent and paradoxical dialogue. Gourmont is acknowledged to be an important formative influence on T. S. Eliot and Ezra Pound among others. He died in Paris, Sept. 27, 1915.

Jean de Gourmont (1877–1928), his brother, also contributed to the *Mercure de France*. He wrote some poems and a novel, *La Toison d'or* (1908).

BIBLIOGRAPHY.—M. Coulon, *L'Enseignement de R. de Gourmont* (1925); E. Bencze, *La Doctrine esthétique de R. de Gourmont* (1928); P. E. Jacob, *Remy de Gourmont* (1931); G. Rees, *Remy de Gourmont* (1940); K. D. Uitti, *La Passion littéraire de Remy de Gourmont* (1962).   (GA. R.)

GOUROCK, a small burgh and seaside resort of Renfrewshire, Scot., on the south bank of the Clyde, 25½ mi. W.N.W. of Glasgow. Pop. (1971 prelim.) 10,922. Gourock pier is the railhead for most of the Clyde passenger steamers, and Cardwell bay, at the eastern end of the town, is extensively used by Clyde yachtsmen. Tower hill (480 ft.) rises behind the town and divides it into three parts: Kempock (east), Ashton (west) and Midton (centre). A relic of pagan times is the tall gray stone, locally known as "Granny Kempock," formerly regarded as a talisman. Industries include yacht building and repairing and marine engineering. Gourock became a burgh of a barony in 1694.

GOUT is a disease associated with an inborn error of metabolism, manifest by acute attacks of distress in one or more of the joints of the extremities. It is one of the oldest diseases described in medical literature. Colchicine, the drug most useful in treatment, is one of the oldest in therapeutics (*see* COLCHICUM). Gout is not rare; the incidence is at least 5% of all significant problems in the field of systemic arthritis. There is a hereditary element in the causation, incidence in some families being very high. The male-female ratio is 20:1.

Some patients develop gout secondary to a chronic blood disease. It may appear initially in any decade of life, and between attacks the patient experiences no articular symptoms. Kidney stone, albumin in the urine and elevation of blood pressure are related phenomena.

Acute symptoms of gout develop suddenly and persist for days or weeks if proper treatment is not followed. Heat, redness, tenderness and pain of the affected joints are observed. The body temperature may rise several degrees. The concentration of uric acid in the blood is elevated. A number of factors—including acute infection, emotional upset, surgical operation, direct injury, overindulgence in food or alcohol or administration of certain drugs—may precipitate an acute attack. Precipitation of microscopic amounts of uric acid in the cartilage precedes the first attack. Uric acid deposits appear in the ear or under the skin about the joints many years later and only in a minority of patients.

Significant progress in the management of gout was a product of the mid-20th century. This resulted in a form of therapy more satisfactory than any available for other major types of joint disease. Full amounts of colchicine are used in the treatment of the acute attack. Following regression of acute symptoms, prophylaxis requires daily ingestion of colchicine as well as of an agent for eliminating uric acid from the body, the preferred drug in this group being probenecid. The prophylactic regimen should be maintained for several years, depending upon the severity of the affliction.

A high intake of water aids in the elimination of uric acid from the body. A normal balanced diet is recommended save for the avoidance of high purine foods; *i.e.*, liver, kidney and sweetbreads. Alcohol in moderation is permitted. A patient who adheres to the prophylactic regimen should lead a normal life, pursue normal activities and should suffer little or no distress from acute attacks.

A few patients die prematurely because of kidney disease, but longevity in gout is normal. Chronic deforming changes are not common.

(J. H. T.)

GOUTHIÈRE, PIERRE (1732–c. 1813), French metalworker, perhaps the most celebrated of his time, was baptized at Bar-sur-Aube on Jan. 19, 1732, the son of a saddler. He obtained his diploma as a master gilder at the same time as he married the widow of his former employer, Ceriset (1758). He executed a great quantity of metalwork, the best of which was superior to that of any of his rivals in that great period of French craftsmanship. He collaborated with the most eminent cabinetmakers and interior designers of his day. The severity of his design was felicitously counterbalanced by the grace and suppleness of the molding. He invented the process of dull gilding.

His personal reputation began in 1769 with the magnificent jewel chest for Dauphiness Marie Antoinette. From then onward he did work at Fontainebleau, supplied the duc d'Aumont in Paris, Madame du Barry at Louveciennes and the comte d'Artois at Bagatelle. Nevertheless he ran into financial difficulties and became bankrupt in 1788. The Revolution completed his downfall. He died in Paris in 1813 or 1814.

Gouthière's immense prestige is partly explained by the famous public sale in Paris in 1782 of the collection of the duc d'Aumont, in the course of which Louis XVI and Marie Antoinette acquired many columns and vases in porphyry or marble mounted by the famous metalworker. Pieces from the sale include a splendid red jasper bowl in the Wallace collection, London, and pieces at the Louvre, Paris.

See Jacques Robiquet, *Vie et oeuvre de Pierre Gouthière* (1921).

(S. Gr.)

GOUVION-SAINT-CYR, LAURENT DE (1764–1830), French marshal under Napoleon and minister of war under the Restoration, was born at Toul on April 13, 1764, of good family. An art student in Paris when the French Revolutionary Wars broke out, he joined the artists' battalion in 1792 and was soon on the staff of the army of the Rhine. In June 1794 a Jacobin *représentant en mission* made him general of division; and his firmness in the battles of 1795 before Mainz and Mannheim led to his being given a corps of 20,000 men in the army of the Rhin-et-Moselle under J. V. Moreau in Germany in 1796.

A sequence of corps commands showed Gouvion-Saint-Cyr's capacity: in 1798 in Rome, when he restored order in the mutinous army, in 1799 on the Rhine under J. B. Jourdan, before Genoa under Barthélemy Joubert and then on the Rhine again under Moreau. Each change, however, was marked by friction and resentment: and in the battles of Stockach and Novi (1799) his wing alone was unbroken gave rise to the charge, always exaggerated, that he could not be trusted to support his colleagues.

Gouvion-Saint-Cyr was not opposed to the rise of Napoleon Bonaparte, who made him a councilor of state (1800), employed him in Spain (1801), sent him to occupy Apulia (1803), appointed him a grand officer of the empire (1804) and created him count (1808). He had been superseded by André Masséna, however, for the conquest of Naples in 1806 and was not yet a marshal; and when the command in Catalonia, where he had been successful, was given to Marshal Augereau in 1809 he showed his resentment so flagrantly that he was exiled to his estate for a year.

In the Russian campaign of 1812 Gouvion-Saint-Cyr commanded the small Bavarian corps and marched on the left wing to the Dvina under Marshal Oudinot (who had been junior to him in the old army of the Rhine). Taking command of the corps after Oudinot was wounded, he defeated the Russian attack at Polotsk and was at last made a marshal on Aug. 27. In the second repulse of the Russians at Polotsk in October he was badly wounded. An attack of typhus in March 1813 ended what might have been his most important command—in eastern Germany under Eugène de Beauharnais. He had a new corps at the battle of Dresden (Aug. 1813) and in operations on the Bohemian frontier. For two months he was for the first time directly under Napoleon's command. They met and talked as two masters of war; but Napoleon left him behind at Dresden, where he remained during the crisis at Leipzig. His campaigns ended with his capitulation, with 33,000 men, at Dresden in Nov. 1813.

After the Restoration, Gouvion-Saint-Cyr's cool, impartial judgment made him a great minister of war, first in three critical months after Waterloo and again from Sept. 1817 to Nov. 1819 (after having been minister of marine from Feb. 1817). His reforms created a new army, 240,000 strong, and Napoleon's good officers were recalled to lead it. In his retirement he wrote the standard account of the campaigns of 1792–97, *Mémoires sur les campagnes des armées du Rhin . . .* (1829), in which his own role is, however, occasionally perhaps overstressed; and also *Mémoires* for the years 1797–1815, published posthumously (1831). Gouvion-Saint-Cyr died at Hyères on March 17, 1830. (I. D. E.)

GOVERNMENT is concerned specifically with that side of social life which is focused upon consent, control, power and authority. Wherever men attempt to work together through organization, government arises, for no organization can function without some pattern of rule which determines who is in ultimate charge. Government as a field of study is, therefore, inseparable from the study of man and society in all times and places.

The rich materials which modern critical history and anthropology have made available, if properly implemented by what psychology, sociology, economics, jurisprudence and the other social studies have to contribute to the analysis of the process of governing men, provide an unprecedented opportunity for developing a science of government.

DEFINITION AND CLASSIFICATION

Government, State and Nation.—Government has been defined in many different ways by a long list of philosophers and social scientists from Plato and Confucius to those of the present day. These definitions have frequently been cast in terms of the purpose of government.

The most commonly acknowledged end or purpose of government has been either justice or the public good. But there have always been conflicting views which, while admitting that justice or the public good ought to be the end of government, have insisted that it has rarely, if ever, actually achieved any such ideal. Conceiving of themselves as realists, such writers and students of government have alleged that the actual end of government appears to be some sort of self-satisfaction of those who do the governing, be this the acquisition of additional power, or glory, or riches or any combination of these and other desires of the human heart.

Looking back over the last 2,500 years of this debate, the detached observer is obliged to conclude that none of these views represents the whole truth, and that all of them contain some truth. As a result, there has been a tendency since the 19th century to discard ends as a key to defining government and a predisposition to concentrate on the process of government—how government works. This is known as the functional view. It might be summed up in the definition that a government is a group of human beings, large or small, who control the operations and the changes of an organization. The "revolution of nihilism," however, has taught the perils of ignoring the ends of government.

While it is usual to think of a nation or other large group when speaking of a government, and employing the expression *the government*, it is obvious that all other groups as well have some kind of government, whether they be families, business enterprises, trade unions, churches, universities or anything else. But in modern times these group governments are typically subordinated to *the* government; they operate within the framework of a legal system which owes its authority, if not its existence, to *the* government. This fact of being on top of all the other governments, which characterizes *the* government and is enforced by *the* government, is by no means as self-evident as one is inclined to assume. In other times and places other groups, such as churches, have had independent and sometimes superior authority. If the world community ever gets to the point of developing fully its own government, that government probably will be superior to the governments of nations.

When viewed as independent and legally self-sufficient organizations, modern nations are spoken of as states. The word state arose in Europe during the 16th and 17th centuries in the course of the very development which made the nation the focal point of power and authority. In fact, the concepts of state and nation are so intimately linked that the expression national state is really a pleonasm. It is important to distinguish the much broader phenomenon of government (defined above) from the concept of the state, although many writers, especially in Europe, continually confuse the two and speak of the theory of the state when they really mean the theory of government.

The concept of the state crystalized in the period of determined struggle of secular rulers against the medieval notions of independent power. These rulers needed a concept which might effectively challenge the church by investing the nation with a halo comparable to that possessed by the mystic body of the believers. Medieval writers had laboured to develop the idea of the visible and the invisible church. State and nation came to occupy a comparable position in the social philosophy of secular writers. It is no accident that the founders of the modern theory of the state—Niccolo Machiavelli, Jean Bodin, Thomas Hobbes—were all violently antiecclesiastical. The portions of their works in which they denounce the ecclesiastical authorities as "the kingdom of darknesse" (Hobbes) and the like are now rarely read, but they show that the concept of the state arose in the fight against the church. At the same time, it is interesting that Richard Hooker's great treatise on government is entitled *The Laws of Ecclesiastical Polity*; in defending the Elizabethan settlement, the judicious Hooker had to face the transfer of authority from church to state.

Classification of Governments.—Since the days of Plato and Aristotle, governments have been classified in a great many different ways. The Greek philosophers adopted a scheme of classification which was compounded of a strictly numerical criterion and a very general value judgment.

In doing this they undoubtedly built upon an older tradition of which some evidence survives, such as the famous discussion of the Persian king Darius, reported by Herodotus, and the work of the sophist Hippodamus of Miletus. Plato saw the several forms of *politeia*, or political order, as corruptions of the ideal order which he delineated in the *Republic*. It has often been overlooked that he addressed himself to the order in the polis (city) only; his classification is not supposed to cover the political systems of the barbarians, though broadly speaking he inclines, as most Greeks, to see these despots as analogues to the tyrant in the polis. *Tyrannos* was, of all the *politeias*, the worst and most corrupt, with the tyrant himself the most unhappy of men. It is the rule of one who is completely lacking in virtue. Its opposite is, relatively speaking, the best, the rule of one who is a man of virtue. The same distinction holds for the other four possible political orders: if a few virtuous men rule, the result is aristocracy; if a few unvirtuous ones, oligarchy; if many possessing some virtue, timocracy; if many without virtue, democracy. This classification which turns upon virtue (*arete*) in the rulers was eventually qualified by Plato in two directions. On the one hand, he recognized that for the virtue of rulers may be substituted a law of comprehensive scope, and on the other hand he came to feel that a mixture of the three numerical schemes (one, the few, the many) might be best. These ideas found comprehensive expression in his late works, especially *The Laws*.

Aristotle built upon this foundation, while introducing some significant changes. The discussion is not cast in terms of an ideal, but rather in those of a standard or model. This model is conceived in relation to the end (*telos*) of the polis: the happiness of its citizens. Happiness itself is comprehensively conceived, embracing as it does the largely contemplative life of the few philosophers, as well as the more mundane concerns of wealth, friends and family. Aristotle's model he calls *politeia* or political order as such. In Aristotle's terms there was a good and a bad rule of one, of a few and of many. These he called monarchy and tyranny, aristocracy and oligarchy, polity and democracy. His concept of the polity corresponds to the idea of a constitu-

tional democracy in the United States, whereas he uses the term democracy to denote a constitutionally unrestrained rule of the majority. Without retaining their precise Aristotelian meaning, these terms have become a part of the general political vocabulary of modern man. Yet other writers and thinkers have added many a differentiating concept to this group of six. Thus, the rule of the rich has been called a plutocracy, the rule of the priests theocracy, the rule of officials bureaucracy (*q.v.*). The last term is of modern origin. In the 16th and 17th centuries it was customary to divide governments into monarchical and republican, a usage which finds expression in the U.S. constitution when it provides that each state shall have a "republican form of government." The mid-20th century brought to the fore a classification into democratic and dictatorial or totalitarian governments, while other ideas such as socialism, liberalism and conservatism have also served as a basis of classification.

Perhaps the classification of most universal significance is that which is determined by the key aspect of the pattern of control: whether power is concentrated or divided. All more stable power is based on organization and the control of organization. Without common objectives there can be neither organization nor power. Power, therefore, always presupposes several human beings who are joined together in pursuing a common objective. "All human associations are established for some purpose," is the opening phrase of Aristotle's *Politics*. That would seem to preclude a genuine division of power. Yet actually objectives may be common because: (1) they are spontaneously shared; (2) they are mutually supplementary; or (3) though conflicting, they are outweighed by other considerations. If organization results in the third case, it is because those who want it get the others to co-operate by constraining or coercing them, and thus making them prefer the avoidance of the threatened penalty to whatever induced them to object.

In order to avoid a situation in which conflicting objectives predominate, power may be divided; different groups in the community may be entrusted with different tasks and charged with restraining other groups.

This theory of constitutionalism, which has been stated in many different forms (*see* CONSTITUTION and CONSTITUTIONAL LAW), affords a basis for classifying governments according to whether they are constitutional or not, or more exactly according to the extent to which they are constitutionalized. Force or constraint and consent are the two intertwined bases of power and control, with complete constraint and complete consent the unreal extremes between which most human organizations and their governments can be ranged. All power situations contain both force and consent, although in crude, everyday speech we often talk as if there were some governments which are completely based on consent and others completely on force. Actually, governments may be classified according to the degree of either force or consent involved in their operation.

Finally, there is found a species of informal classification which characterizes the government by naming the class or group which is in control. Plutocracy and theocracy are really part of this classification. But we often speak of undertakings such as military government, colonial government and feudal government. It is obvious that such a scheme of classification is indeterminate as long as it does not comprise all conceivable groups which might control. But sociologists using these terms have often failed to analyze adequately what they assumed; namely, that the particular group actually governed. On the whole, it is fair to state that too much has been made of the problem of mere classification.

In opposition to all such schemes of classification, there have been from time to time students of government who have set out to discover the common features of all schemes of government. The phrase "invisible government" has been coined to suggest that no matter what the outward form there always is an invisible government of the few, and that all governments are merely formal disguises for the rule of an elite or special class. Perhaps the most ambitious attempt along this line was made by the Italian Gaetano Mosca, who in his *The Ruling Class* maintained this view with much show of historical learning. Although further refined and generalized by Vilfredo Pareto in his general sociology with its theory of the elite, it is not a tenable view; the task of governing cannot be divorced from the wielding of legitimate authority, and the informal participation of diverse individuals does not constitute these as a class in the sense of Mosca, or an elite in Pareto's understanding.

COMPARATIVE GOVERNMENT

The comparative study of governments is an uncompleted task. Modern governments have been effectively compared and an overall theory based on experience has been presented by such writers as James Bryce, G. D. H. Cole, Herman Finer and Carl J. Friedrich. Such undertakings used to be limited to contemporary governments of western European origin. The much more extensive task of systematic comparison and evaluation of the process of government covering all cultures and groups is now being done. It will be well, however, to present some of this knowledge in general survey form in the following sections. We may conveniently use a historical plan and discuss the following major fields of experience: (1) primitive government, (2) large-scale (Asian) despotism, (3) Greco-Roman republicanism, (4) medieval (European) government, (5) modern western government.

HISTORICAL SURVEY

Primitive Government.

—The government of so-called primitive peoples displays a great variety of forms. Anthropologists have shown conclusively that all these people do possess governments, be they ever so rudimentary. Many of them combine religious and governmental functions, so that high priests are often kings and vice versa. Frequently kings are deified in that they are supposed to be endowed with supernatural powers and are regarded with awe. These views are reflected in a number of institutions of the Greek city-state, as well as of Rome. They are also recognizable in the institutions of imperial Japan. China and elsewhere. But it would be a mistake to assume that these primitive forms of government are necessarily despotic in their practical workings. As a matter of fact, few of them are. Even in warlike tribes where the king is often the military leader some species of consent pattern is worked. The characteristic feature which differentiates primitive government from the later forms is the lack of any kind of regularized or institutionalized administration. If writing is used at all, it is primitive, and the frequent lack of any considerable employment of currency prevents the development of accounting practices. Primitive government, in its most general connotation, may be described as a government incidental to tribal life and informally linked to its general patterns of behaviour and belief.

Asian Despotism.

—Throughout Asia there arose, in conjunction with the development of literacy, the general increase in culture and the forward march of technology, especially in warfare, a species of government which is passing only in modern times. These governments are usually spoken of as despotic, although this term is something of a misnomer, because they were quite limited in scope and, while extending over large land masses, they often included the greatest variety of governmental practice in local jurisdictions. These great systems seem really to have been slow extensions of primitive tribal governments, usually were based upon an underlying homogeneous group growing out of the conquering tribe, and on the whole showed a remarkable viability. They were invariably monarchical in structure, and the monarch was usually invested with divine attributes, if he was not actually deified. They were, it has been held by some, in no sense states, as the west has understood this term, and the trials and tribulations which China encountered in its efforts to grow into a modern state are in part attributed to the fact that the preceding pattern of government had not yet developed any such close-knit system of administration or of legislation as had been established by the monarchies of the west when they were overthrown by their several revolutions (see below). It was contended by others that these oriental despotisms were "states" in a particularly virulent sense. Karl Wittfogel, for instance, argued that these despotisms, especially Chinese despotism, represent a power system which

embodies total power in the sense of totalitarian dictatorship. He believed that this kind of government arose in response to the technical requirements of an agriculture which depended wholly upon irrigation. Hence he called these societies "hydraulic." The central piece of this form of government would then be a bureaucracy, described as monopolistic and characterized by "total terror, total submission and total loneliness." This elaborately argued contention has met with sharp criticism.

Whatever may be the eventual conclusion regarding the nature and value of this type of government, there can be little doubt that while it is ill-adapted to the modern world and a machine technology, it served the people reasonably well as long as they lived under a system of handicraft production, whether in industry or agriculture. As the remarkable state of culture in all its forms (literature, arts, music and religion) attests, these systems were fairly tolerant of, if not positively interested in, human creativity. An occasional outburst of violence such as that which occurred in China under Shih Huang Ti (246-210 B.C.) merely shows that this system of government is habitually ill-adapted to extreme governmental control. Its worst feature, in the long run, was unquestionably its tendency to fall to pieces when the court circles grew corrupt, lazy and indifferent. At such times these systems often plunged into anarchy and became exposed to sudden invasions by outsiders, especially barbarians of bellicose disposition. But these despotic systems lasted longer than any other known form of government to date, and were swept away only by the onrush of modern industrial civilization with its multiplicity of governmental tasks.

Greco-Roman Republicanism.

—When the city-states of the so-called classical world are considered, one is on more familiar ground. Not only have the great writers of antiquity, such as Aristotle, Thucydides and Polybius, left an explicit record of the government of these remarkable communities, but a vast amount of the most searching learning has gone into the critical examination of these records, a learning associated with names such as Numa D. Fustel de Coulanges and Theodor Mommsen, which combined a deep grasp of the problems of government with thorough historical scholarship.

The remarkable cultural flowering that occurred in Greece at the height of the power of the city of Athens cast a golden glow over these city-states. As later ages marveled at the Periclean age, they inclined toward idealizing its political institutions. Yet, from a modern viewpoint, it is all-important to remember that even the most democratic of these republics, such as Athens, rested upon a broad basis of slavery. The citizenry was, in other words, an upper class whose privileged position permitted it to participate in public affairs. The defense of slavery by both Plato and Aristotle, though often treated as a deplorable aberration, is really of central importance to their political philosophy. They believed in a superior race, and not in the "common man everywhere."

Upon the substratum of this slave population, the size of which has been variously estimated, the city-states were originally organized as monarchies under tribal kings. These were gradually superseded by military aristocracies, which in turn gave way to an aristocracy of wealth and to an ever widening body of citizens. The divergent rate of progress in different cities toward this kind of democracy eventually led to a situation in which most Greek cities were split into a democratic and an aristocratic faction, each epitomized by one leading city—Athens or Sparta. The conflict between the two types of government culminated in the disastrous and long-drawn-out struggle known as the Peloponnesian War (q.v.; 431-404 B.C.). While frequently represented as a fight between two ideologies, it was in fact as much a war between rival imperialisms, and it prepared the way for the final subjugation of all Greek cities by the kingdom of Macedon and later by Rome. The Greeks experimented extensively with federation as a solution to their problem of combining unity with independence of the cities, but the federations proved no match for enemies whose government rested upon the more solid basis of territorial control. (See GREECE: History.)

The Roman republic, which eventually achieved the overlordship of all Greek cities, in Sicily, in Asia Minor and in Greece proper, followed the tradition of the Greek cities at first, but soon grew beyond it by developing a solid territorial foundation. This foundation was provided by the conquest of the Italic cities and the subsequent settlement of Romans on the land, conferral of Roman citizenship upon the inhabitants, or both. Furthermore, Rome evolved a complex constitutional structure in which monarchical, aristocratic and democratic elements were skilfully blended. Perhaps the most extraordinary feature of this government was its dual executive, wielding the imperium, or power to command. After a time, two consuls replaced the monarch as the chief executives; they had practically identical functions, and could not act one without the other (see CONSUL). Finally, there was the praetor, who also shared the imperium. At the heart of the republic's government we find a legislative establishment, compounded of the fathers (patres) and the "people" (populus). Originally, the people were only the patricians, but after a long struggle the nobles had to allow the plebeians to share in the offices (magistratus) and to adopt decisions of their own (plebiscita). The military assembly (Comitia centuriata) and plebs decided what laws were wanted, expressing their preferences, but only upon proposals (rogationes) by the magistrates. The fathers, organized as the senate, were presumably only consulted, and their decisions took the form of a senatus consultum. But actually the senate became the dominant body in Rome to which both magistrates and people deferred. Thus the letters SPQR (Senatus Populusque Romanus, "the senate and the Roman people") were the magic symbols of Roman power, as well as of Roman subjection to law. Among the offices, the most important were the fiscal (quaestors) and the judicial ones, primarily a number of praetors holding juris-dictio. Among these last, the praetor peregrinus exerted a profound influence upon the development of Roman law, because he interpreted the Roman civil law for the many foreigners doing business in Rome. This body of law, known as the jus gentium, implemented the jus civile and came to form the hard core of the Corpus Juris Civilis as it was eventually codified by Justinian (6th century). There were other important officers, such as the censors and the tribunes of the people, who provided a further check to the consuls and other magistrates, and, finally, there was the dictator. This office, which superseded all others, came into being only in emergencies, and was strictly limited to six months. It eventually became the basis for the destruction of the republic. The subtle mixture of monarchical, aristocratic and democratic elements which has evoked the admiration of students of government ever since continued as an outward ritual long after the effective power had become completely concentrated in the hands of the Caesar imperator. (See ROMAN LAW.)

It was a common trait of all the republics of the ancient world that the city or polis combined in interlocking functions the task of government with the exercise of religion. Thus, the great temples, such as the Acropolis in Athens, were the centres of the city's life, and their architecture clearly reflects this function. While all the Greek cities acknowledged the common Olympus with its Zeus, Hera and the other gods and goddesses, each city had its own special god from whom the local gentry claimed to be descended. Citizenship was, therefore, invested with the religious halo of belonging to the cult community, and it is not surprising that to the Greeks the good life appeared inconceivable outside the polis. Patriotism, under such conditions, had a deeper foundation and a nobler appeal than within modern nations whose religious life and ideals transcend the nation and its government. Much confusion has resulted from the attempts of modern philosophers, from Machiavelli to Georg W. F. Hegel and the fascists, to apply Greek ideas concerning the polis to the modern nation-state.

This close tie between religion and politics caused the basic difficulty the Roman empire faced with the rise of Christianity. For the Christians refused to accept the deification of the emperor which had been evolved in response to problems which Roman rule in Asia had posed. Hence, the very best emperors, more especially Marcus Aurelius, were inclined to persecute the Christians most severely, because of their attachment to the religio-spiritual foundation of their empire. Even after the Christian faith had become the Roman state religion, under Constantine, the situation

of the Roman government was an equivocal one: a church as a radically autonomous corporate entity, unrelated to and not seen as the creation of the Roman government (state), was not accepted until much later. Pope Gelasius I (5th century), who is usually though incorrectly credited with stating the doctrine of the "two swords," first effectively argued this position. In the eastern part of the empire it never achieved ascendancy. But in the west, the dualism of church and government became accepted doctrine, and it is within this context that the heritage of Roman law was bequeathed to medieval Europe.

Medieval Government.—The medieval system of government was extraordinary in its rich diversity combined with a claim to resplendent unity. Centred in the unity of Christianity, the universal empire and the universal church both gloried in aspirations which they never succeeded in realizing. The doctrine of the two swords, the secular sword of worldly empire and the ecclesiastical sword of spiritual guidance toward salvation, rationalized the dominant fact of medieval government: a continuing struggle between temporal and ecclesiastical authorities to achieve supremacy. By the time the Holy Roman empire came essentially to be "of the German nation" (14th century), the emerging national monarchs, especially of England, Scotland, France and Spain, were much concerned with claiming for themselves the position of imperator and Caesar, and the curious competition for the imperial office between Francis I of France, Henry VIII of England and Charles V of Spain and Germany highlights how long this idea of universal empire persisted in spite of the obvious independence of the great kingdoms.

These kingdoms and principalities themselves underwent an interesting evolution in the course of which their governments became constitutionalized. The system of "government by estates" (Ständestaat), which was common throughout Europe (except in Italy) on the eve of the Reformation, provided a genuine division of power between the monarch, the aristocracy and the commoners. Its pattern is most familiar through the English system of a king in parliament, but it was actually more highly developed elsewhere. Tudor absolutism foreshadowed the breakdown of this type of government by skilfully manipulating the estates into a position of impotence.

But there was a third pattern of government to be found in the medieval world; namely, city republics. These republics were strongest in Italy, but they achieved a powerful position likewise in Germany and the Low Countries. Bruges and Antwerp, Lübeck and Cologne, Strasbourg and Augsburg, Venice, Milan and Florence—all these and many more were brilliant centres of an urban secular culture which grew up under the aegis of a republican scheme of government. These city republics underwent a governmental evolution resembling that of the cities of the ancient world until they were absorbed into the rising territorial states or became, like Milan and Florence, themselves such states. But since they were, unlike the cities of Greece, embedded in a broader pattern of government—the universal realm of emperor and pope—their preoccupation with commerce as contrasted with politics made them the precursors of the great trading nations of the present time.

Modern Government.—Modern government is not a clearly defined term, but it roughly includes three different types: monarchical absolutism, constitutionalism and totalitarianism.

Monarchical Absolutism.—Of these three forms of government, monarchical absolutism is pretty much a thing of the past, but it was the predominant form from the 16th to the end of the 18th centuries. Indeed, modern government owes one of its most distinguishing features, bureaucracy, primarily to these absolute monarchs. Using the term dispassionately to designate the body of public officials engaged in administering the government's business, we are justified in saying that this bureaucracy constitutes the core of modern government. Arising in England and in the papal administration in the 14th century, and subsequently in other realms, such as France, Spain, Austria, Prussia and the Netherlands, the bureaucracy rationalized administration by regularizing its operations, such as recordkeeping and correspondence, by differentiating its functions and by training its personnel. Without these achievements, modern government is unthinkable.

But modern government is likewise unthinkable without legislation; *i.e.*, a growing body of explicit, man-made rules by which the individual can live without fear of interfering with his neighbour. This point became clear in the 16th century, when the growing commerce and industry necessitated numerous alterations in existing law. While some, like Jean Bodin (*Six Livres de la ré-publique*, 1576), claimed this function of legislating for the monarch, others, especially in England, claimed it for the people or their representatives. To be sure, the term "people" had a rather restricted connotation, limited as it was to the more well-to-do in town and country, but it served as a harbinger of the coming democratization.

A third element in the evolution of modern government is the courts of law. The majesty attributed to the law was reflected in the social position of judges. Even such absolutists as Frederick the Great of Prussia found it expedient to recognize the importance of leaving a good deal of independence to the judges. While the principle that judges should be bound only by the law is actually an extension of the general principle of administration that demands objectivity, it acquired a distinct significance in Great Britain and the United States, and later in Europe, as a pillar of modern government.

Legislation by popular representatives and an independent judiciary were steps on the road toward constitutionalism. Both implied a division of power between the monarch, or crown, and others, and hence led away from the concentration of powers characteristic of monarchical absolutism. Either or both may find a place in an authoritarian pattern, such as those of Prussia and Austria after the Napoleonic Wars (1805–15), but their full development is not possible except after the establishment of genuine constitutionalism.

Modern Constitutionalism.—Constitutionalism in its broadest connotation may be defined as a government which is limited by a constitution. Such a constitution may be constructed in a great variety of ways. It may be built around a monarchy, or it may be a republican scheme; it may provide a unitary or a federal system; it may set up a parliamentary executive or some other kind; it may contain a bill of rights or it may not; but whatever the detailed arrangements, it will always seek to make sure that no one man, or group of men, is in a position to exercise legitimate power without some effective restraint placed upon him to relinquish it, share it or seek it periodically at the hands of the electorate. No matter how skilfully balanced, the ultimate sanction for the maintenance of any constitutionalism lies in the determination of the people to maintain it. This determination, which has been called constitutional morality and of which Jean Jacques Rousseau as a Swiss proudly spoke as the unwritten law "graven upon the hearts of the citizens," has in the last analysis decided the success or failure of constitutional government.

There used to be much concern over whether a constitution was rigid or flexible. Students comparing the situation in the United States and Great Britain, as for instance Bryce, were fond of dwelling upon this theme. More realistic analysis has disclosed this difference to be rather elusive. Rigid and flexible are ill-defined terms which hide rather than explain the real problems. The third French republic had a constitution which proved too easy as well as too difficult to change. It was not a question of general rigidity or flexibility, but rather that it was badly drawn. The U.S. constitution used to be classed as rigid, but it acquired and lost again a provision for prohibiting the sale of intoxicating liquor, such as has not been adopted in Great Britain.

Much more central and significant is the problem of federalism. A constitution which guarantees to a number of component units of government an independent jurisdiction is characterized thereby as a federal constitution. Extended controversies have raged over how to define a federal constitution. This formalistic battling over words has delayed a realistic study of the political nature of these federal schemes. Leaving the insoluble problem of who is the sovereign in a federal setup, we may say that federalism is a system of government that divides political power territorially under a constitution. Even the most effectively centralized government will grant some measure of decentralized authority to local bodies. In terms of objectives, federalism seeks to balance, under a constitution, partly general and common objectives, and partly particular and conflicting objectives when these objectives are distributed in space. Thus, the Swiss constitution leaves all educational matters to the cantons so that cantons with a French-speaking majority may differentiate themselves from the German-speaking majority in the country as a whole.

Federal patterns of government frequently owe their existence to a preceding federation or league of governments. It is, therefore, possible to analyze such governments pragmatically in terms of the institutions which are characteristic of such federations. The United States, Switzerland and Germany, as well as several dominions, are examples of this. Three characteristic federal institutions may be mentioned here: (1) a legislative assembly composed of representatives of the component units, be they called states, cantons or provinces, as if they were equals or near-equals; (2) an executive in which, or in the selection of which, the component local units participate; (3) a judicial body or bodies for the settlement of disputes between the component local units and the union government according to the charter or constitution. (*See* FEDERAL GOVERNMENT.)

Even more important than the question of federal government is that of parliamentary government. Is the executive dependent upon the support and confidence of the elected representative assembly or has he an independent position and a separate mandate from the people? England is the home of parliamentary government, and it is principally in England and the dominions that this system has worked well. The admirers of the system are generally inclined to credit it with the superior performance of British politics, but comparative analysis suggests at least two contravening considerations. First, it would seem that parliamentary government depends for its success upon unwritten conventions which in turn depend for their operation upon certain common beliefs and behaviour patterns found only in Britain and its dominions. Second, parliamentary government does not in actual operation correspond to the alleged theory. The supposed responsibility to the parliament is actually restricted to a few dominant issues, whereas many minor matters are decided by the party in power in accordance with considerations of expediency and tactics which may not be shared by the majority of the people or even of parliament. This may also be true of major issues.

In England, the system itself is a congeries of conventions which grew from small beginnings as the party system developed. There was an increasing tendency for the house of commons to be divided into a majority and a minority party, with the result that the majority party controlled the body and presented itself to the crown as the obvious basis of a solid government whose leader might reasonably be asked to head the government. The party leader would then naturally invite his leading associates to share the government with him, and hence Britain has always been inclined toward collective responsibility of the cabinet (*see* CABINET). However, the prime minister has become increasingly important, and general elections tend to focus attention upon him much as quadrennial elections do upon presidential candidates in the United States.

Such leading students of parliamentary government as Sir Ivor Jennings suggest that the term parliamentary government is not accurate, so far as the 20th-century British system is concerned, and that one should rather speak of cabinet government. The function of parliament seems to them to be rather that of a deliberative assembly in which various views concerning proposed policies of the government are subjected to analysis and criticism, while the actual government is carried on by a cabinet which is organized directly from the people. In support of this view one can point to the fact that since World War I no cabinet which had an actual majority in the house of commons has been overthrown by vote of parliament. Elections have been held either because the five-year term was nearly over or because the party in power deemed it strategic to do so.

In France a rather different system was constructed by men whose intention it had been to establish parliamentary government on the British model. Under the third and fourth republics the French parliament became paramount. It is important to know that this omnipotent parliament was not clearly divided into a majority party supporting the government and a minority party opposing it, but consisted of a great many groups, more or less related to a complex multiparty system. The great committees of parliament (unknown in England), and more especially its leading members, secured a considerable share in the governing functions, and in co-operation with the permanent high bureaucracy really ruled the country. This system, while giving excellent results in the sphere of administration, was characterized by stalling, when major decisions had to be taken, and finally collapsed when the Algerian problem. A different and more authoritative system which purported to be a blend of British and U.S. (presidential) elements was established in 1958.

The French kind of parliamentary system was adopted in Germany after World War I with disastrous consequences. To be sure, there the situation was complicated by other factors, including the aftermath of a lost war and federalism, but the parallel developments in Italy and elsewhere suggest that this system of government by parliament is not viable. It should be noted that its abandonment by Germany after World War II, and the substitution of a more stable form which is a skilful adaptation of the British model, gave good results, even though combined with federalism.

The Scandinavian countries, Belgium and the Netherlands also made a reasonable success of parliamentary government. Whether this fact is attributable to a basis of beliefs and traditions comparable to those that prevail in England, or to the presence of a monarchy with a settled willingness to accept constitutionalism, or to both, it is difficult to determine.

The nonparliamentary executive may be of two prevailing kinds. In the United States, the president is, for all practical purposes, elected directly by the people and is or becomes thereby the leader of his party. In all matters of general policy involving legislation or the spending of funds he must successfully manage his party in congress, both senate and house, or his hands are tied. Grave difficulties confront him if, as a result of a congressional election, the representative assembly becomes dominated by the opposition party, as happened to Woodrow Wilson in 1918, to Herbert Hoover in 1930, to Harry S. Truman in 1946 and to Dwight D. Eisenhower in 1956. However, the lack of party discipline sometimes makes it possible to carry on with the support of votes from the opposition as was done for many years in the state of New York where Democratic governors had to work with Republican legislatures. The nonparliamentary executive type of government of the presidential form has been vigorously attacked and critically contrasted with the parliamentary type by students of U.S. government, such as Woodrow Wilson (*Congressional Government*, 1885). Its failings are generally admitted, but it is doubtful that they are more serious than those of the parliamentary type.

The conciliar type of nonparliamentary executive is illustrated by Switzerland. Its stable and ably conducted democratic government is under a federal council composed of the heads of the various departments who choose a chairman as president of the republic for one year. The members of this council separate their administrative function clearly from their legislative tasks. When the legislature repudiates a proposed policy, the council does not resign, but either drops it or prepares another proposal. It is curious, indeed, that the Swiss system has not found more imitators, for it appears well adapted to the task of governing a small country on a republican basis. (*See* SWITZERLAND: *Government.*)

Totalitarian Dictatorship.—In spite of profound differences in general outlook and objective, as a pattern of government the totalitarian dictatorships have a great deal in common. They represent a distinct and ultramodern pattern of government. The totalitarian dictatorships all claim to be set up for the people and they all make a show of some sort of popular support, either through unfree sham elections, through plebiscites or through other forms of mass acclaim, customarily reinforced by denunciations of constitutional democratic regimes as capitalist and imperialist plutocracies. Yet these regimes are usually characterized by several of the following practices and institutions.

First, totalitarian dictatorship originates in a *coup d'état* through which an organized minority seizes power by armed force or constitutional fraud or both. Second, it continues because this minority, organized as a party, takes over complete ultimate control of the government, the leader of the party becoming, in effect, the monocratic head of the government. Third, it constitutes this controlling party as an aggressive elite which seeks to abolish all other pre-existing social and class differentiations and thus atomizes the electorate, dissolving even the family into often warring individuals. Fourth, it establishes as complete a control over all forms of expression, including science, religion and the arts, as possible, subordinating all persons engaged in these creative pursuits to rigid governmental supervision and control. Fifth, it institutes an elaborate governmental propaganda which continually swamps all subjects with news and opinions, with the end of securing their allegiance or at least acquiescence. Sixth, it develops a systematic reign of terror for the purpose of crushing all opposition by spying upon, summarily arresting and liquidating all enemies of the state, using summary procedures and arbitrary sentences, including long detention in concentration camps and every species of physical torture. Seventh, it establishes complete control over all economic activities for the purposes of integrating the economy and subordinating all enterprise to the ends of the government. Eighth, it invariably includes a vast military establishment among these purposes of government, on the ground that the defense of the state is of paramount importance.

This kind of government is sometimes identified with despotism, tyranny and absolutism. These identifications are misleading. Any careful comparison of the traits just delineated with the structure of government in those older autocracies will immediately disclose striking contrasts. Most important among these is the totalitarian mass party, fired by a faith in a total reconstruction of society—a kind of secular religion—which is completely lacking in past autocratic government. It is the actual autocrat in a totalitarian dictatorship, speaking through its leader or leaders who are bound to it by faith and ritual. These governments have shown themselves capable of accomplishing extraordinary feats. The industrialization of the U.S.S.R., the near-conquest of all of Europe by Hitlerite Germany, the revolutionary transformation of the ancient Chinese society, politically, socially, culturally and economically—these are outstanding examples of totalitarian governmental achievement. The stupendous sacrifices in human suffering involved in these undertakings seem amply justified in the eyes of the rulers and the ruling party by the achievements. The ominous appeal of totalitarianism in Asia and Africa results from these accomplishments. Since freedom in most of these formerly colonial peoples is at best a vague hope, whereas national independence and the standard of living are pressing, ever present realities, it appeared quite possible in the second half of the 20th century that totalitarian government would continue to spread.

So all-inclusive a system of governmental control was never before in the history of mankind developed by anyone. Even the extreme tyrannies of men such as Shih Huang Ti, Domitian and the *condottieri* of the Italian Renaissance lacked, because of technological inefficiencies, the asphyxiating effect of modern totalitarianism. The extraordinary effectiveness of modern weapons, such as tanks, airplanes and nuclear bombs, as well as their initial cost, render individual revolutionary effort hopeless at the outset. Consequently, not one of these totalitarian dictatorships has been overthrown from within. Only superior external force has brought on their downfall.

Local Government.—The ever increasing size and complexity of government on the national and international level in the second half of the 20th century revived interest in the local community, and the growth of great metropolitan centres further contributed to this concern. The importance of the local community in the functioning of constitutional government is generally recognized. Even the totalitarian systems, in attempts at administrative decentralization or communalization, manifested the abiding role of the local community. These tendencies were in part motivated by the fact that local communities have proved rather resistant to the pressures of totalitarian government. Politico-sociological analysis discovered a fruitful area of field studies in the more intimate life of local communities. The slogan of "grass roots democracy" testified to the trend.

But it is one thing to recognize the importance of the local community and another to organize it effectively for self-government in an age of mass industry. While local functions increased, along with other governmental trends, these functions were continually more in need of effective integration within larger governmental units. Britain's proud tradition of local self-government, for example, had to yield to the point where the local activities became largely centrally directed. Under these circumstances, a general tendency developed to make the selection of local personnel the focal point of local autonomy. But unless such personnel have policy issues on which to contend for acceptance, their autonomy will be precarious and party bureaucracy will be able to subject them to the party will.

There is no one pattern of local government that is clearly preferable to all the rest. Britain, France, Switzerland, Germany and other European countries each evolved one or more patterns of their own, in which mayors, clerks, councils and local officials were arranged in various ways. The United States too has a number of patterns. Noteworthy are the so-called city-manager type, the newest form, in which local government is assimilated to the operation of a business enterprise, and New England town-meeting government, the oldest form, where the whole community decides basic policy. (See CITY GOVERNMENT; LOCAL GOVERNMENT; UNITED STATES [OF AMERICA]: *Administration and Social Conditions: Local Government in the States.*)

Military Government.—The end of World War II brought in its train military occupations on an unprecedented scale. In Italy, Austria, Germany and Japan the victors had to assume governmental authority for a transition period. Such military government, defined as government by the military over occupied enemy populations, when conducted by constitutional democracies, is sometimes comparable with emergency government. Military government is in its nature authoritarian, but according to international law it is neither lawless nor despotic. In working for the military government endeavours to re-establish first of all government according to law (the "rule of law") as the necessary basis for free institutions. In the process of eliminating the totalitarian elements, it is often very severe and obliged to create new law retroactively. The lawless nature of the preceding totalitarian system makes this unavoidable. (See MILITARY GOVERNMENT.)

World Government.—The San Francisco charter, drafted and adopted in 1945, became the constitution of a confederation of nations, the United Nations. While originally hopes were high that this constitution might mean the start of a world government, the sharp conflicts which arose between the United States, Great Britain and their friends on one side, and the Soviet Union and its satellites on the other, made it abundantly clear that the United Nations was not going to operate as a functioning government but rather as a permanent gathering of the representatives of most of the governments of the world. Several important governments were, in the early 1960s, outside the UN. Because of the division of Germany between Communist and non-Communist regimes, agreement on UN membership for neither could be secured. Equally symbolic had been the situation of China. While the vast majority of Chinese, living under Communist rule, remained unrepresented, the Nationalist government on Formosa occupied a permanent seat on the UN Security Council. The People's Republic of China (Communist), however, was admitted to the UN on Oct. 25, 1971, and the Formosa government was expelled.

The organization of the United Nations consists of two general bodies for policy decisions: the General Assembly, in which each member state is represented by one vote, and which in the early 1970s had over 130 members; and the Security Council, composed of 5 permanent members—the U.S., the U.S.S.R., Great Britain, France and the People's Republic of China—and 6 nonpermanent members, elected by the assembly. The permanent members of the council have a veto on certain decisions, which protects their sovereignty (*q.v.*). These vetoes aroused a great deal of indignation and criticism, not only of the power principally exercising them, the U.S.S.R., but also of the Security Council as such. Its importance accordingly declined, but this decline also reflected the fact that the UN was in the process of becoming a world forum rather than a world government.

In spite of its weakness as an instrument of government, the UN must not be underestimated as a political instrument. A number of serious conflict situations were attenuated by means of its good offices, and the secretary-general at times took important initiatives. Furthermore, certain of its affiliated bodies, such as the European Economic commission (EEC) and the UN Educational, Scientific and Cultural organization (UNESCO), are accomplishing important tasks. Thus, while the UN was not an effective world government, it was developing a number of governmental functions. Both the United States and the U.S.S.R. looked upon it as an important factor in the world community and in cooperation with their allies and satellites sought to mold it to their purposes. Yet in the long run what is perhaps more significant, since these two superpowers would have readily at their disposal other means of international action, is the fact that the United Nations organization activates and gives a measure of real influence to small nations which when well represented often wield influence out of proportion to their position in the world of pure power politics.

The problems inherent in so loose an organization as the UN led to insistent demands for amending the charter. A great deal of labour went into these reform efforts, but nothing came of them because the very conditions which led to the complaint, such as the veto of the great powers, or the position of Formosa, also prevented any change. Given a radical change in international relations, and a sharp decline of world tensions, such plans might, however, take concrete shape. The UN, it was felt by its supporters, deserved to be maintained, if only to be in existence when such a day should arrive. Genuine world government did not seem feasible, though some world governmental functions were in operation. The danger existed that the prestige of the UN might decline to the point where it could no longer be maintained. Its greatest current problem is the lack of adequate funding, with many members in arrears and the U.S. bearing an excessive share. In view of the solid work that is being accomplished in special fields, and because of the value of a meeting ground of all nations for the discussion of the world's problems, the continued operation of the United Nations is generally believed assured.

See also references under "Government" in the Index.

BIBLIOGRAPHY.—Systematic consideration of comparative government has been a virtual monopoly of British and U.S. scholarship. See, however, Gunnar Heckscher, *The Study of Comparative Government and Politics* (1957). Of the many works in this field, the most complete are Herman Finer, *Theory and Practice of Modern Government*, rev. ed. (1949, 1951, etc.), and Carl J. Friedrich, *Constitutional Government and Democracy*, 4th ed. (1968).

Continental European studies of the same general problem usually adopt a more legalistic and juridical viewpoint. Among these works three are of outstanding merit: Jean P. H. E. Esmein, *Éléments de droit constitutionnel français et comparé*, 8th ed., rev. by H. Nezard (1927-28); Alessandro Passerin d'Entrèves, *La dottrina dello stato* (1962; Eng. trans. by A. Passerin d'Entrèves, *The Notion of the State*, 1967); Herbert Krüger, *Allgemeine Staatslehre* (1964). To these may be added Maurice Duverger, *Manuel de droit constitutionnel et de science politique* (many editions) and Georges Burdeau, *Traité de science politique* (1949-57).

Of the more theoretical analyses of modern government, see the abstract, systematic treatment in Harold Lasswell and Abraham Kaplan, *Power and Society* (1950); see also Karl Loewenstein, *Political Power and the Governmental Process* (1957); David Easton, *A Systems Analysis of Political Life* (1965). A. D. Lindsay's *The Modern Democratic State* (1947) is incomplete but valuable. For the totalitarian dictatorships see Sigmund Neumann, *Permanent Revolution* (1942), which constituted a useful beginning; also C. J. Friedrich and Z. Brzezinski, *Totalitarian Dictatorship and Autocracy*, 2nd ed. (1965); and Karl A. Wittfogel, *Oriental Despotism* (1957).

There are also certain broad sociological studies of society with a major focus on government interpreted as persistently oligarchic, especially Arthur F. Bentley, *The Process of Government* (1908); Max Weber, *The Theory of Social and Economic Organization*, Eng. trans. by A. M. Henderson and T. Parsons from *Wirtschaft und Gesellschaft*

(1947); G. Mosca, *The Ruling Class*, Eng. trans. by Hannah D. Kahn from *Elementi di scienza politica* (1939); and V. Pareto, *Mind and Society*, Eng. trans. by Andrew Bongiorno and Arthur Livingston from *Trattato di sociologia generale*, 4 vol. (1935). The studies by Bertrand de Jouvenel, *La Pouvoir* (1947) and *De la Souveraineté* (1955), deserve mention.

The works cited above contain ample bibliographical guides to the literature covering the more specialized areas of the broad subject considered in this article.

(C. J. Fʀ.)

GOVERNMENTAL ARCHITECTURE comprises those buildings whose function is to serve governmental purposes, such as town halls, capitols, courthouses, parliament buildings, post offices, customhouses and similar structures.

GENERAL HISTORY

The history of governmental building goes back to the dawn of human society and may be found as an adjunct of the temple, the royal residence or the communal dwelling, according as the governmental organization was theocratic, autocratic or communal. A theocratic autocracy existed where king was also priest; where primitive communism was surrounded by religious taboos, the theocratic and communal state overlapped. Thus, among some peoples, structures were at once temples and meeting houses and also served as council chambers.

Primitive developments of the communal idea were found among the American Indians; the council house of the Onandagas was such a structure, 80 ft. long and 17 ft. wide. Among the town-building Indians of the southwest, where the tie between religion and government was strong, round rooms called *kivas* or *estufas*, sometimes built underground, were used for secret rites and for council deliberations.

In such autocratic civilizations as that of Egypt, governmental functions were centred in the royal palace, which had halls of audience and courts where the king and his counselors met and where executive orders and judicial decisions were rendered. The great columned halls of the Persian palaces at Susa and Persepolis (6th and 5th centuries B.C.) and the palace of Solomon at Jerusalem, especially the "House of the Forest of Lebanon" (I Kings vii, 2) were built for official rather than residential use.

Greece.—In prehistoric Greece, a combination of the autocratic and democratic appeared, as in the courtyards, reception halls and throne room of the palace of Cnossus in Crete (c. 1800–1200 B.C.). On the mainland, the autocratic element prevailed, as portrayed by the residential palace of Tiryns (c. 1200 B.C.).

The growing complexity of governmental systems in the independent cities of Greece necessitated special governmental buildings. At first only subdivisions of an open place or agora, these later became well-articulated structures adjacent to the agora. The most important of these was the *bouleuterion*, or council hall, in which were located the legislative and executive functions. Nearby stood the *prytaneum*, or town hall, where the city hearth fire burned continuously; banquets were held and the commanding general had his residence. The courts, usually held in colonnades, or stoas, were occasionally convened in open areas reserved for them, such as the Areopagus (Ares' hill) in Athens. At Priene and Miletus in Asia Minor extensive remains of the *bouleuterion* exist which show a building nearly square with seats arising in stages on three sides. At Miletus the seats are curved like those in a Greek theatre. At Megalopolis a much larger hall (late 4th century B.C.), known as the Thersilion, was built for the meeting of a large governing council. This building, 220 ft. long by 172 ft. wide, had a roof supported on columns placed behind each other in radiating lines, thus affording the widest possible view of the centre of the hall where the speaker stood. At Olympia the *bouleuterion* was an even more complex structure, consisting of a square central hall with an apse-ended building on each side, divided by columns ranged down the centre.

There were two forms of *prytaneum*: (1) a circular primitive form, recalling the *tholos*, or early Greek beehive hut, and (2) a more developed sort in which the *megaron*, or hall, of the Mycenaean palace is recognizable. At Priene the resemblance to the typical Greek house was particularly strong; at Olympia the hearth fire was kept in a hall at the front with a large court at

the rear, smaller courts on each side and halls for banquets.

Rome.—The highly developed civic systems of the Roman empire were reflected in its mature types of governmental architecture. The group of governmental buildings surrounding the Roman Forum was, in fact, the earliest prototype of the modern national capitol. The buildings themselves, however, were merely developments of such structures found in smaller Roman cities, like Pompeii. There, one end of the forum was filled by three buildings sharing a common façade, the central being the *curia* (town council chamber) and those at the sides, the offices of the *duumvirs* and the *aediles*. The central building thus served the legislative function, and those at the sides, an executive function. All three were rectangular with apses at the end. On one side of this group was an enclosed court, thought to have been the *comitium*, or voting place, of the citizens. On the opposite side stood the basilica (*q.v.*). Thus, all the functions were housed in buildings designed for governmental purposes.

In Rome itself the details were different, and additional elements appeared, yet the basic idea was the same. The *curia* or senate house, whose walls still stand as the church of S. Adriano (rebuilt by Julius Caesar and Augustus after a fire and rebuilt again by Diocletian after the great fire of A.D. 283), was a rectangle 75 ft. wide and 85 ft. long, probably with columns dividing it into three aisles, and an apsidal tribune at the end. The senate house was situated at one end of this large building; at the other end was a smaller apsidal hall, originally the *secratarium senatus*, now the church of Sta. Martina. Between these were two other halls used as archives and executive offices. Stairs led to the second floor. The whole formed a richly decorated and magnificent building. Not far away on the slope of the Capitoline hill stood the national archive building known as the *tabularium*, built by Sulla, the massive masonry and monumental arcades of which still overlook the Forum. Across the Forum from the *curia* stood the Roman treasury, incorporated into the temple of Saturn. The judicial functions were carried on in various basilicae, especially the Basilica Aemilia and Basilica Iulia.

At the opposite end of the Forum stood the *regia*, the Roman equivalent of the Greek *prytaneum* and the ritual centre of Roman life and government. The official residence of the *Pontifex Maximus*, it was closely related to the *Atrium Vestae* and the temple of Vesta with the ever burning city fire.

Middle Ages.—The social pattern of the feudal system was not conducive to the development of governmental architecture. With the rise of the powerful municipalities of the 12th century, the reaction against feudalism throughout Europe found expression in the building of town halls. At first the town hall was merely a meeting place for the citizens, frequently only a belfry erected adjacent to a public square. By the middle of the 12th century styles in Italy and France became more defined.

In Italy the *palazzo pubblico* resembled the town houses of the wealthy, being built around a court and having high crenellated walls. Often it served as the official building, with meeting halls for governing bodies, and also as the residence of the commanding general. In Florence two separate buildings, the Palazzo Vecchio (1298) and the Bargello (mid-13th to mid-14th century), were used, the first as the town hall, the second as the residence of the chief magistrate and the prison. These, like most Italian town halls, have belfries attached. Other municipal halls were the Palazzo Pubblico at Siena (1293–1309) and the Palazzo della Ragione at Padua (1172–1219), whose upper hall, added in 1420, is 267 ft. long and 89 ft. wide, entirely free of interior supports. The *broletti* or town halls in many of the smaller cities are not less characteristic than the governmental palaces which have been cited.

The French town halls usually combined an arcaded market hall on the ground floor with the governmental halls above and a belfry nearby. The 12th-century town halls at St. Antonin, in almost perfect preservation, and at La Réole are typical of the period. As the power of the municipalities increased, the richness of the town halls did likewise, as demonstrated by those at St. Omer (14th century) and St. Quentin (16th century). Meanwhile the market hall was forced out and the entire building devoted to governmental purposes.

Between 1400 and 1600 the town hall received its greatest development in the powerful commercial cities of the north. In these a new influence was operative—that of the guildhall. The merchant guilds had become closely related to municipal government; in some cases the governing body of a city was called a guild. Thus the hall of the corporation of the City of London is known as the Guildhall. In some towns of the Low Countries, the town hall and the guildhall were combined, as at Ypres, Belg., where the town hall was known also as the cloth hall. This splendid building (1200–1304), a rectangle 50 ft. wide and 462 ft. long, had a cloth market on the ground floor and meeting halls, law courts, banquet rooms and municipal offices on the upper floor. The structure, rated one of the most monumental examples of secular Gothic in Europe, was rebuilt after being destroyed during World War I. Other commendable Flemish examples are those at Arras (completed in 1494, the belfry 1554), Louvain (1448–63), Brussels (1402–54) and Ghent (completed 1533). In Germany the most beautiful town halls are those at Lübeck (13th century), Tangermünde (1373–78) with remarkable brick Gothic detail, Brunswick (14th century) and Goslar (15th century).

Renaissance.—A broadly similar type of town hall design continued in use throughout the Renaissance period except in Italy. The prevailing taste in Italy led to the erection of smaller but more elegant single buildings such as the beautiful Palazzo del Consiglio at Verona (c. 1500, by Fra Giocondo), whose exquisite early Renaissance polychrome façade has been much admired, and the equally rich Municipio of Brescia (c. 1500). The Palazzo Senatorio (completed 1603), by Michelangelo, on the Capitoline hill in Rome is significant for its successful attempt to give the structure a form both dominant and monumental yet differing from the early Renaissance forms of north Italy.

Outside Italy, where the medieval tradition persisted, the Renaissance town halls simply applied classical details to such building types as had been developed before; e.g., the town hall of Bremen (15th century, reconstructed 1609) and the old city hall of Paris (destroyed in the civil war of 1871). In rebuilding the latter the old plan was merely enlarged and the old style preserved. The modern tradition of municipal building was modeled on the medieval town hall.

Another important type of governmental building that took form during the middle ages was the courthouse or *palais de justice*. Most medieval examples are of the Late Gothic period because only then had judicial processes become sufficiently divorced from royal, monastic or feudal domination to necessitate separate buildings. The earliest existing are the Maison de Pierre at Chartres and the Salle le Roi at Montdidier (both 14th century). By far the most famous is the lavish Palais de Justice at Rouen, begun before 1474 and completed before 1509. This magnificent building, built around three sides of a courtyard, contains, in addition to smaller courtrooms, two splendid halls and a beautiful chapel. It is in this use of large halls that originated the tradition for providing in every courthouse a great lobby where lawyers may confer with their clients.

No such development of national governmental buildings can be found during this period. What national unity existed was centred in the residence of the sovereign, and when national councils or legislative bodies finally arose they were housed either in a royal palace or in religious buildings. To this day the French senate sits in the Luxembourg palace. In England the king's council met wherever the monarch happened to be, and the English parliament convened at the nearest convenient spot to the royal palace at Westminster, which was the chapter house of Westminster abbey, until 1547 when parliament moved to St. Stephen's chapel within the palace itself. This remained the meeting place of the house of commons until 1834 when the palace was burned.

GOVERNMENT BUILDING TYPES

Expressions of the legislative, judicial and other functions of government in architectural terms has resulted in buildings of a monumental nature, frequently symmetrical, to impress and uphold the dignity of government.

Capitols and Legislative Buildings.—*The United States.*—A national capitol building, built solely for the housing of a national government, was first projected in the U.S. A competition for the design of the Capitol at Washington, D.C., was held in 1792 and was won by William Thornton. His carefully articulated plan provided large halls for the senate and house of representatives, separated by a central rotunda. Begun in 1793 and burned during the War of 1812, it was not completed in its original form until the 1830s. The earlier Capitol may be described as the work of Thornton, Étienne Sulpice Hallet, Benjamin Henry Latrobe and Charles Bulfinch, successively its architects. The old house of representatives became Statuary hall and the old senate was long used by the supreme court. By the 1850s the structure was considered inadequate and a wing was added at each end to accommodate the house and the senate. The original low dome was replaced by the commanding cast-iron dome which now crowns the rotunda and is generally regarded as one of the world's finest. These changes were completed in 1865 by Thomas U. Walter.

The domical legislative hall became almost a convention in the building of state capitols. Even such a proper Greek temple as Gideon Shryock's old capitol in Frankfort, Ky. (1828–29), is crowned by a dome and a lantern to light the circular rotunda. The gilded dome of the earlier Massachusetts statehouse, by Bulfinch (1798–1808), was a notable example. Connecticut's old statehouse, now the city hall at Hartford, also by Bulfinch (1792–96), received its cupola in 1822. The rotunda at Ohio's statehouse at Columbus (1838–59) is lantern-crowned, but the cupola is not domical. The work of several architects, it is one of the finest U.S. state capitols.

George B. Post, architect of the Wisconsin capitol at Madison (1904–14), was compelled by the nature of the site to adopt a cruciform plan with four equal wings radiating from the dome-crowned rotunda. Although some consider the plan somewhat compromised, the massing contributes to an enhancement of the dome. In his masterful Nebraska state capitol at Lincoln (completed 1932), Bertram G. Goodhue designed a vast rectangle, divided into four light courts and surmounted by a 400-ft. central tower which forms a monumental beacon, dominating the Nebraska landscape for miles. Of somewhat similar massing is the Louisiana state capitol at Baton Rouge (1930–32), by Weiss, Dreyfous and Seiferth. In several western states room for a capitol group is provided; e.g., the state capitol group at Olympia, Wash., where the buildings of architects Wilder and White may expand in response to the state's needs.

Europe.—The addition to the old Palais Bourbon (the building used by the *chambre des députés* in France), by Bernard Poyet (1807), of a 12-columned, pedimented front and the influence of the U.S. Capitol established the classical direction in modern legislative architecture for the next century. The *chambre des députés*, reconstructed (1822–23) by Jean de Joly, and the senate in the Luxembourg palace (1836–41) by Henri de Gisors, were ornamental developments of a classical amphitheatre plan. This plan, which had been used so successfully in the U.S. Capitol, had simplicity and directness and was widely copied in halls for bicameral legislative bodies.

The English Houses of Parliament on the Thames in London, designed by Sir Charles Barry (1840–60), form a unique group, both in style and plan. There, the house of lords and house of commons are only parts of a vast asymmetrical composition which includes members' dining rooms and libraries, the speaker's residence and all the apartments required by a lavish tradition. The picturesque details and ornament were the work of A. W. N. Pugin, a specialist in medieval design, who succeeded in harmonizing two soaring towers and the main horizontal mass of the structure with little reference to interior function. Governmental architecture at Ottawa and elsewhere in Canada was influenced by this precedent.

A somewhat baroque edifice was the Reichstag in Berlin, by Paul Wallot and Friedrich von Thiersch (1882–94; burned during World War II). The plan featured a great assembly hall approached through an arched entrance and a grand foyer. Distributed around two lateral light courts were lounges, refreshment rooms, library, writing rooms, committee rooms and consultation chambers. A single domical roof reflected the unicameral legislative body.

In the Budapest, Hung, parliament house by Imre von Steindl (1883–1902) a central dome and flanking pavilions were veneered with Gothic finery. The Austrian parliament house in Vienna, by Theophil von Hansen (1874–83), is as classic as Hungary's capitol is romantic and compares favourably with legislative buildings around the world.

International Organizations.—Buildings connected with the developing 20th-century idea of international control in certain spheres commenced with the Palais des Nations, Geneva, Switz., as a headquarters for the League of Nations. Designed as a combined project by four of the winners of an international competition, and based on an axial plan, it was completed in 1936, only shortly before the failure of the League.

After World War II and the formation of the United Nations, the headquarters for the new organization were built (in 1948–52) on a fine site fronting New York's East river, and designed by an international group of architects headed by Wallace K. Harrison. The 39-story, steel-framed rectangular slab of the secretariat building contrasts well with the lower conference and general assembly buildings, with their numerous council and committee rooms in addition to the main auditorium.

Another notable international building is the UNESCO headquarters in Paris, completed in 1959 and designed by Marcel Breuer, Pier Luigi Nervi and Bernard Zehrfuss.

City and Town Halls.—A modern town hall requires a chamber or hall for the town council meetings and offices for the mayor and councilmen and their secretaries, for the town clerk, and for the financial and administrative departments of the town government; e.g., the tax board, the chief of police, the building inspector. Town halls frequently contain rooms for receptions and banquets and also provide an auditorium for public gatherings.

France.—The most monumental example of the continental city hall is the Hôtel de Ville in Paris, rebuilt after the Commune by Ballu and Deperthes (1874–82). Following the original Francis I style on the exterior, it was decorated inside with all the elaborate detail then in vogue. Its great *salles des fêtes* and magnificent stairways make it one of the most gorgeous and effective official suites in the world. The precedent has affected French municipal building ever since. Later French city halls, showing a similar type of Renaissance classicism, lavish decoration and elaborate plan, include those at Neuilly-sur-Seine, by Dutocq and Simonet (1885); at Versailles, by Le Grand (1897); and at Tours, by Laloux (1905).

Great Britain.—In England the Gothic revival of the mid-19th century affected much municipal building. The town hall at Manchester, by Alfred Waterhouse (1868–77), with its picturesque outline and original detail, is typical of the best Gothic revival design. Later examples showed a greater simplicity of composition and freedom of style. That at Sheffield, by Mountford (1897), in a free early Renaissance style, is representative of the larger examples; that at Oxford, by H. T. Hare (1897), in modified Jacobean, is characteristic of the smaller. The growing complexity of city government has led to a type of building in which the council chamber and mayor's suite are subsidiary to the great amount of clerical space required. The London County Council hall, by Ralph Knott (1908–22), which best exemplifies this tendency, is a vast structure in the late English Renaissance style. Swedish influence is clearly seen in a few civic buildings of the 1930s, including Norwich city hall (1938) by C. H. James and Rowland Pierce.

Elsewhere in Europe.—In Germany the most interesting municipal buildings are those couched in modern forms. The somewhat bizarre *Stadthalle* at Hanover, by F. E. Scholer and Paul Bonatz (1913), contains a large circular hall which functions as a municipal auditorium. As restrained as the *Stadthalle* is fantastic is the town hall at Joensuu, Fin. (1913), by Eliel Saarinen. The city hall at Stockholm, Swed., by Ragnar Östberg (completed 1924), is a dignified structure surmounted by a graceful tower and skirted on the ground floor by a charming arcade. Inside it is enhanced by brilliant colour decorations; mosaics and other fine examples of Swedish craftsmanship. This design exerted considerable influence on subsequent European buildings, as did the more severely rectangular building of Hilversum, Neth, town hall by W. M. Dudok (1928–36).

A more recent town hall building at Rodovre, Den. (1954), is typical of several designs in this field by the architect Arne Jacobsen. In outline it is simple to the point of severity.

Canada.—The ambitious project for the city hall and town centre in Toronto, and the new city hall at Edmonton, Alta., by Dewar J. Stevenson and Stanley, are indicative of modern civic-building programs in many parts of Canada.

Ottawa city hall (1959) with its island site in the Rideau river and its parklike surroundings is a straightforward and effective building by Rother, J. Bland and C. E. Trudeau.

The United States.—Town and city halls in the United States reflect their regional environments. In the east, colonial types predominate; in the west, Spanish colonial and other sun-loving vernaculars are found, as in the Highland Park city hall in Dallas, Tex., by Lang and Witchell. The colonial town hall at Tewksbury, Mass., by Kilham and Hopkins, and the town hall at Peterborough, N.H., by Little and Russell, illustrate smaller examples in the east, while Bigelow and Wadsworth's town hall at Wheaton, Mass., typifies the larger ones.

Perhaps New York city shows the evolution of the U.S. city hall better than any other municipality. By 1802 the demand for an adequate city hall resulted in the erection of an exquisite structure, long outgrown but still in use, by architects Mangin and McComb (1803–12). The French precedent is sensed, particularly in its domed rotunda, the monumental staircase, council chamber, offices and reception rooms. When a larger building became necessary the solution was the New York municipal building, by McKim, Mead and White (1908–10), a skyscraper of 23 stories treated in a classical vein to offset the appearance of a commercial structure. The Oakland, Calif., city hall, by Palmer, Hornbostel and Jones (1908–13), has a 3-story classical base, from which a tower of 11 stories arises, crowned by a cornice. Above it stands a lantern of baroque design. Cities and counties sometimes unite to erect a city-county building, as in the case of Chicago and Cook county, Ill. (1907–11), Detroit and Wayne county, Mich., and Indianapolis and Marion county, Ind., the latter two being erected in the 1950s.

Occasionally the city hall is the key structure in a square or park. This is the case of Springfield, Mass., where two classical, colonnaded buildings flank a municipal clock tower by Pell and Corbett, architects (1908–13).

The huge city hall at San Francisco, Calif., by Bakewell and Brown (1913), rivals a state house in scale and magnificence. It is domical, with a central pavilion in the form of a classic temple, flanked by Doric colonnades on a high basement. The dome on a high drum is beautifully profiled and carries an ornate lantern. This structure is a part of the civic centre, where an auditorium, an opera house, the library and other structures are grouped together.

Perhaps the most successful U.S. solution for a metropolitan city hall is that at Los Angeles, Calif., by Austin, Parkinson and Martin, completed in 1928. For the first time, the two elements—the town hall and the municipal office building—were combined in the same structure and given an adequate architectural expression. This building is also a part of the civic centre.

Judicial Buildings.—The modern courthouse, in its essential elements, has remained almost as close to its traditional ancestry as has the modern court system. A monumental lobby, courtrooms and rooms for judges, lawyers and witnesses and the archives, all were found in the courthouse of the 15th century.

Europe.—The difference between the law courts of London, by George E. Street (completed in 1882), and the *palais de justice* in Rouen, built 400 years earlier, is principally one of detail. The *palais de justice* in Paris is typical of the 19th-century continental courthouse. It dates from various construction periods from the 13th century onward. Its present form is largely a result of rebuildings after the Commune. Two other elaborate courthouses illustrate European precedent: the *palazzo di giustizia* in Rome, by Calderini and Basile (1883–87), monumental in composition but somewhat marred by much meaningless, small-scaled ornament; and the rather more interesting *palais de justice* at Brussels, by Joseph Poelart (1866–83), which dominates the city from its hilltop site. The Peace palace at The Hague, Neth. (1907–13), by Cordonnier and Van der Steur, also belongs in this category. A fine neoclassical building of an earlier date, but owing little or nothing to Gothic precedent, is the Four Courts, Dublin, Ire., by James Gandon (1785).

The United States.—In the U.S. the courthouse received a definitive form. Such buildings go back to the somewhat medieval Talbot County courthouse in Maryland (1680–81), a brick structure with end chimney, a steep roof and dormers. The lovely brick Chowan County courthouse at Edenton, N.C. (1767), is full-blown Georgian. By 1724 the embryo of the present-day courthouse could be found in the courthouse at Chester, Va. As late as 1770 a log-cabin courthouse, 20 ft. wide by 24 ft. long with "two small sheds at each end, for jury rooms," was built in Botetourt county, Va. The annals of almost every county in the old Northwest Territory indicate that the early county buildings were of log construction, as were the prisons and jailers' houses. Benches, jury boxes and judges' stands in these rude centres of justice were of puncheon construction. The traditional elements have remained the same, the basic unit consisting of the courtroom proper, with space for the public, witnesses, jury box, judge's bench, counsel, clerks and the press; the judge's chambers; and the jury room.

Of southern origin were the square, brick courthouses of Ohio, Indiana, Illinois and as far west as Independence, Mo., during the 1830s. Until 1870 courthouses of two types were erected: (1) a square, two-story, brick building with a hip roof, crowned by a cupola, and (2) the typical Greek revival temple, with or without a cupola. The courtroom was generally on the second floor, with offices on the ground floor. The early state capitol buildings at Corydon, Ind. (1812), built as the courthouse of Harrison county, and at Chillicothe, O. (1800), were of similar design. Since the time of the Greek revival the classical style has been almost universally used for judicial architecture. Many trends in courthouse design culminated in the New York County courthouse (completed 1927), built by Guy Lowell. The original design called for a circular plan but for practical considerations it was changed to a hexagon, with a surmounting rotunda and six light courts providing excellent communication. The result is a structure at once functional, beautiful and interesting.

Post Offices.—Many European governments have relegated public services to existing structures, as in Rome where a former monastery was adapted to the postal service. Naples erected a new post office, by G. Vaccaro and G. Franzi (1932–36). Other imposing postal facilities are the general post office in London (1910), by Sir Henry Tanner. Far more interesting, however, is J. Crouwel's post office in Utrecht, Neth. (1918–24).

In the middle of the 19th century Robert Mills designed, among other governmental structures in Washington, D.C., an office building for the post office department that exhibited simple and straightforward planning. U.S. post offices present a good cross section of the architectural vicissitudes that have befallen the nation. Some achieve real distinction, others do not. Post offices in Peoria, Ill., Gary, Ind., and Miami, Fla., illustrate high standards of design. Many postal structures throughout the U.S. have been designed by government architects in Washington, but the post office in the national capital (1911–14) was designed by private architects, Graham, Burnham and company. The post offices of New York city were designed by McKim, Mead and White (1913), and those of Denver, Colo., by Tracy, Swartwout and Litchfield.

In Great Britain, buildings to house postal and telephone services are designed principally by staff architects of the ministry of works. The neo-Georgian style common in the interwar period gave way in the 1950s to a more functional and less monumental style.

Customhouses.—Although there are some fine early examples such as the Dogana, Venice (c. 1631), by Baldassare Longhena, and the small-scale customhouse, King's Lynn, Norfolk (1683), by Henry Bell, the 18th-century customhouse in Dublin, Ire., by James Gandon (1791) marks an important point in the development of this type of building. With dome, riverside arcading and portico, Gandon's building is a much-praised landmark.

The London customhouse, of which an earlier version was probably the work of Sir Christopher Wren, was designed by David Laing (1817) and partially rebuilt by Robert Smirke, having a handsome Ionic-columned river front to the Thames. At Liverpool another Greek Ionic order supported the portico of John Foster's customhouse (1828) which was destroyed by bombing in 1941. The early customhouse in New York city (later the U.S. subtreasury), by Town and Davis (1834–41), the customhouse in Boston, by Young and Rogers (1837–47), and the customs structures at Newburyport, Mass. (1835), and at New Bedford, Mass. (1836), both by Robert Mills, constituted milestones in U.S. customhouse design. All were of Greek revival extraction. The present Renaissance-style New York city customhouse (1899–1905) is the work of Cass Gilbert.

Administrative Buildings.—The need for administrative buildings increased with the scope of function generally performed by governments. Maximum office space being the prime requirement, the new buildings only too frequently have been dull and uninspired in conception. In some European capitals ministries have been housed in altered palaces, as in Paris and Vienna. In London, where they are assembled along Whitehall and Parliament street, the government offices make an impressive ensemble, although few of the individual buildings are distinguished, Sir Charles Barry's treasury (1846) being the most satisfactory façade. In Washington, D.C., which Pierre Charles L'Enfant laid out along classical lines, governmental architecture has closely followed classical precedent. Among the earlier classical examples were the post office, the patent office and the treasury building, all the work of Robert Mills. The Library of Congress, by Smithmeyer, Pelz and Casey (1886–97), the senate and house of representatives office buildings, by Carrère and Hastings (1906–09; additions 1933), the department of commerce, by York and Sawyer (1928–32), the national archives building, by John Russell Pope (1927–35), the supreme court building, by Cass Gilbert (1934), and the National Gallery of Art are illustrative of the classical trend. On the other hand, the Smithsonian institution, by James Renwick (1846–52), and the state, war and navy building, by A. D. Mullet (1871–88), interesting in their way, can scarcely be said to belong in this company. The Washington monument, by Henry Bacon (1912–22), and the Jefferson memorial, by John Russell Pope, accord well with the capital's classical pattern.

The erection of the Pentagon (q.v.) was something of a break with classical precedent, but structures erected thereafter, although contemporary in trend, harmonized with existing buildings. This was important, since something of a boom in governmental building, costing upward of $300,000,000, took place in mid-20th century. All U.S. governmental agencies employ private architects on major construction projects but several departments maintain an architectural staff for the purpose of maintenance, minor repairs and alterations.

Ministries or embassies in foreign capitals are accorded architectural treatment on a level with their high prestige value. For some of these, governments lease existing quarters; for others, special buildings are erected. The United States initiated an adventurous and extensive program of embassy buildings in the mid-1950s of which the most notable and controversial is Eero Saarinen's embassy building in Grosvenor square, London. Other U.S. embassy designs of considerable merit include those at Manila, Phil., by A. L. Aydelott and Associates, and at Oslo, Nor., by Saarinen.

In contrast, the heavy, neoclassical British embassy in Rio de Janeiro, completed in 1950 to the designs of R. R. Prentice, seems anachronistic.

U.S.S.R.—The sittings of the supreme soviet and various other conferences and functions of government take place within the buildings of the Kremlin, Moscow, principally in the Bolshoi Kremlyovsky palace (1838–49); other more recent administrative offices have been completed in the massive and ornamental style of Soviet building current in the middle and latter part of the 20th century.

In Russia, as in most Communist-dominated countries, the bulk of building work is in the hands of official architects and subject to direct government control.

Capital City Planning.—Development of a federal government, economic and social changes, or rapid expansion of an emergent nation may create a need, both for purposes of efficiency and prestige, for an entirely new capital city. An early example was Washington, D.C., with spacious axial planning centred on the capitol. In 1911 a competition for the design of the Australian city of Canberra was won by W. B. Griffin of Chicago, and the first of the buildings was opened in 1927. The building of New Delhi, India, from its inception in 1912 to the completion in 1930, marks a high level of architectural achievement. Sir Edwin Lutyens initiated the design and was responsible for the viceroy's house, probably his finest work. He was later joined by Sir Herbert Baker whose council chamber and secretariats flank the two-mile main axis.

When India became independent in 1947 and the state of Punjab was divided, the former capital went to Muslim Pakistan, leaving Hindu Punjab without a capital. It was decided to build a new capital city (Chandigarh), designed by world-renowned architects and planners. The design of the city was entrusted to the French architect Le Corbusier in association with the English architects Maxwell Fry and Jane Drew. A group of Indian architects and planners also worked on the project. The town was designed in self-contained sectors, each with its green belt and commercial facilities, and work at Chandigarh started in 1951. It is characterized by Le Corbusier's individual and unorthodox ideas. As well as the legislative assembly building and secretariat there is much residential development but perhaps the most outstanding structure is the supreme court, with concrete frame, brick partitions and a structural umbrella raised above the main frame and roof to counteract extreme weather conditions.

In 1957 President Kubitschek of Brazil broke ground for a new capital city, to be called Brasília, in remote, undeveloped, upland country in the state of Goiás; it replaced Rio de Janeiro as federal capital in 1960. Oscar Niemeyer designed the lakeside presidential palace and Brasília palace hotel which, with one or two other buildings, formed a "skeleton capital"; Lúcio Costa won the competition for the general city plan, conceived in the form of a bent bow and arrow, the arrow forming the 5-mi.-long Avenida Monumental, terminating in an impressive complex of executive, legislative and judicial buildings and cathedral.

See also articles on styles—BAROQUE AND POST-BAROQUE ART AND ARCHITECTURE; MODERN ARCHITECTURE; etc.—and such articles as ROMAN ARCHITECTURE. See also references under "Governmental Architecture" in the Index.

(T. F. H.; R. N.; E. C. D.)

GOVERNMENT CORPORATIONS are corporate bodies that are wholly or partly owned by the government and are utilized primarily for business-type functions or services. First widely employed during World War I to provide the operating and financial flexibility required by certain emergency programs involving construction and operation of merchant vessels, trading in commodities and comparable government activities, the government corporation later became a common form of organization for public enterprises in nearly all countries and at all levels of government. The incorporated agency became the instrument for carrying out major parts of the United States economic recovery program in the 1930s; for developing great river valleys of Afghanistan, India and the United States; for administering nationalized industries in Great Britain and other countries; for financing, constructing and operating superhighways in Pennsylvania, New York and other states; and for promoting the economic development of "underdeveloped" nations, particularly in Asia and Latin America.

The activities in which government corporations have been most widely employed—transportation, communications, manufacturing, mining, resource development, atomic energy, marketing, port development and management, utility services, various types of banking, credit and insurance functions—reflect the radical change in the economic role of the state during the 20th century. Older and more traditional public enterprises such as postal services; tobacco, match and salt monopolies; and, to some extent, telephone and telegraph services are rarely incorporated, and continued to be administered in the 20th century as government bureaus. This form of organization continued to exist when the main purpose of the enterprise was to supplement public revenues, as with the football pools in Norway and other government lotteries, or to control consumption, as with liquor monopolies in a number of U.S. states and Canadian provinces.

As defined by Pres. Franklin D. Roosevelt when he recommended establishment of the Tennessee Valley authority in 1933, the government corporation's purpose is to provide an agency "clothed with the power of government but possessed of the flexibility and initiative of private enterprise." Although the organization and powers of government corporations differ significantly, not only from country to country but also within a single country, most have the following attributes which distinguish them from public enterprises organized as normal government agencies: (1) legal personality separate and distinct from the government which enables the corporation to sue and be sued, enter into contracts and acquire property in its own name; (2) independent financing from revenues and treasury or public borrowing rather than from annual appropriations by the legislature; (3) freedom from many of the restrictive statutes applicable to government supply activities and general budget, accounting and audit laws and regulations; and, in most countries, (4) authority to hire and determine the compensation of employees without regard to civil service laws.

The special powers granted to corporations are designed to enable the government, when it is acting more as a business agent than a sovereign, to render service and discharge its obligations to purchasers of its goods and services as nearly as possible in the same manner as a private business.

Use has also been made of the corporate form of organization to avoid constitutional or statutory limitations on public borrowing. As separate legal entities, government corporations may be authorized to issue revenue bonds or other evidences of debt without creating general state obligations. The desire to find means of financing public improvements that would not conflict with constitutional debt limitations accounts in large measure for the great increase in the number of incorporated public authorities such as the Alabama Building corporation and the New York Thruway authority at the state and municipal level in the United States.

Corporations may be acquired or created by the government in several ways. The government has converted a number of corporations, originally established for private purposes, to public enterprises by obtaining control of some or all of the corporation's capital stock. The United States, for example, became the owner of the Panama Railroad company (merged with Panama Canal company, 1951) when it purchased the assets of the French Canal company in 1904. The Railroad company had been chartered as a private corporation by New York state in 1849. The Renault and Gnôme-Rhône motor companies were taken over by the French government and became government corporations because their private owners had collaborated with Germany during World War II.

Many government corporations have been organized as joint-stock companies under authority of general incorporation laws applicable to privately owned corporations. Except for the War Finance corporation, for instance, World War I corporations were chartered by the United States under general incorporation laws either of states or the District of Columbia. In 1945, however, congress prohibited this practice and required that existing state-chartered corporations such as the Commodity Credit corporation and the RFC mortgage company either be liquidated or reincorporated by federal law. Great Britain and Canada also came to regard the joint-stock company as not well suited to a public enterprise, but this view was not fully accepted elsewhere. Joint-stock companies were set up extensively in France, Italy, Belgium, Turkey and other countries favouring mixed enterprises whose stock is partially owned by private interests. The only examples of mixed enterprises in the United States are the federal intermediate credit banks, banks for co-operatives, and the Federal National Mortgage association. The first and second banks of the United States were also created on this pattern.

The trend continued toward organization of government-owned enterprises as public corporations with no capital stock. A public corporation is created by a special law defining its powers, duties and immunities and prescribing the form of management and its relationship to established departments and ministries. Great Britain pioneered in developing this type of agency with the Port of London authority (1908) and through it carried out the nationalization of the Bank of England and other basic industries. Examples of public corporations were the British Broadcasting corporation, British Overseas Airways corporation, Tennessee Valley authority (U.S.), St. Lawrence Seaway Development corporation (U.S.), St. Lawrence Seaway authority (Canada), Water Resources authority (Puerto Rico), Sumerbank (Turkey), National Insurance institute (Israel), Air-India International and Overseas Telecommunications commission (Australia). State trusts in the Soviet Union also acquired many of the characteristics of public corporations.

Enterprises jointly owned by central and state governments or by two states represent a special type of government corporation. The Damodar Valley corporation (1948), as an example, was set up by the government of India and the states of Bihar and West Bengal. New York and New Jersey created the Port of New York authority in 1921 by interstate compact to operate bridges, tunnels, airports, port and terminal facilities serving New York city and nearby communities.

With the rapid growth of government corporations, the issue of public accountability became important. To free corporations from red tape and partisan interference, existing controls to assure public accountability and responsiveness to direction by politically responsible officials were abandoned, but without providing adequate substitutes. Except in the United States, corporations generally were made independent of the government; policies, budgets, and accounts were not subject to review by the executive or legislature. Management was frequently vested in boards dominated by government departments and employee and consumer organizations. Enterprises partly owned by private interests have presented unique problems of public control. These factors led some to fear that corporations might become a fourth branch of government.

Great Britain, the U.S., Canada, and Turkey have taken steps to assure public accountability without unnecessary red tape. Great Britain and Canada have made public corporations subject to direction by the minister concerned with the corporation. While he does not interfere in day-to-day operations and cannot be questioned in Parliament about such matters, he often issues general directions. Ministers may also possess authority to veto or approve issuance of bonds, large capital outlays, pensions, and comparable corporate actions. In Great Britain, the house of commons has established a select committee on nationalized industries to which matters relating to control, administration and performance of nationalized industries are referred.

The U.S. in 1945 and Canada in 1951 recognized the need for developing special controls over government corporations by providing for a budget and audit "with due allowance given to the need for flexibility." Turkey provided for an annual review by the General Economic Commission and an annual audit inspection by the prime minister's High Control Board.

See also PUBLIC ENTERPRISE.

BIBLIOGRAPHY.—International Institute of Administrative Sciences, *Administrative Management of Public Enterprises* (1966); United Nations, *Report of Seminar on Organization and Administration of Public Enterprises* (1967), *Some Problems in the Organization and Administration of Public Enterprises in the Industrial Field*, detailed bibliography (1954); W. A. Robson (ed.), *Public Enterprise; Developments in Social Ownership and Control in Great Britain* (1937), (ed.), *Problems of Nationalized Industry* (1952); Ernest Davies, *National Enterprise; the Development of the Public Corporation* (1946); Sidney Goldberg and Harold Seidman, *The Government Corporation* (1953); *Elements of a Model Charter* (1953); Wolfgang Friedmann (ed.), *The Public Corporation: A Comparative Symposium* (1954); A. Hanson (ed.), *Public Enterprise* (1955). (Hd. Sx.)

GOVERNMENT DEPARTMENTS

GOVERNMENT DEPARTMENTS. The administration of the various governmental functions is entrusted to specialized agencies, often called departments, such as the Department of Commerce and the Department of Agriculture in the United States. Taken together, the departments are sometimes referred to as the departmental system and make up a large part of the executive branch. In contrast to the legislative and the judicial branches, the executive branch is the government's arm of action, the instrument for the performance of its continuing functions. Responsible operation of the departmental system requires not only executive control in each department but also direction and coordination by a chief executive.

This article is organized into sections and subsections according to the following outline:

I. PATTERNS OF ORGANIZATION

The governmental agencies which make up the departmental system in various countries frequently bear designations other than department. Illustrations of such designations are ministry, administration, service, authority, board, commission, and even foundation. In many instances the choice of the designation is based on the logic of a legislative or administrative intent, even though the intent may remain obscure to the citizenry. In other cases the designation has been the fruit of passing circumstance.

Government departments may be viewed from quite different angles. To the administrative official they represent the necessary machinery for the accomplishment of particular public purposes. To the politician they are power structures to be captured and held in the contest for control. To the ordinary citizen they may appear to be forbidding bastions of authority, indifferent to his own needs, but perhaps inexcusably subservient to various organized interest groups. To the rank and file of government employees who spend their days in its offices, the department may be an unrelenting taskmaster and an animating social centre.

In the sense of human beings who identify themselves with a department as its management or its personnel, one may speak of a departmental point of view or a departmental tradition. Usually the greatest influence on the formation of these characteristics has been exerted by the higher civil servants. But where the political leadership in the departments does not change frequently, the person at the top can impress himself strongly upon the institutional mind of his department. In the same way, however, institution on particular issues, so continuing struggles go on within each department among different specialized staff groups and between these and the agents of general control. Effective direction of a department requires considerable resources of personal ability as well as of technical knowledge and experience.

While differences of internal organization and of cultural development between countries have produced inevitable differences—superficial or profound—in their governmental machinery, it will be found under modern conditions that common political, social, and economic necessities tend to give the same functions to government departments in one country as they give in another, however diverse their theory of the proper arrangement and scope of governmental organs.

Organization Types.—It is less important to know that the number of departments and the allocation of jurisdictions among them differ (subject to frequent changes in the individual countries themselves) than it is to realize that the various countries follow different patterns of departmental organization. Thus, United States practice treats each department as one great administrative body, including headquarters and field agencies, all of these performing their duties under the name of the department. European tradition favours using different designations for headquarters (ministry, etc.) and field offices, and keeping the ministries small by several devices. One method is that of delegating ample discretionary powers to regional offices, called in Great Britain divisional; another is to transfer large-scale operations that must remain centralized to special agencies of a secondary, or subordinate, character. For instance, the collection of customs and internal revenues, as well as governmental minting, engraving, and printing, are functions performed in the United States within the Treasury Department, while in Great Britain these functions are separate institutions, without Cabinet rank, which in their political and financial decisions depend on the Treasury but constitute no part of it; in France they are entrusted to so-called directions générales under (dependent on) the Ministry of Finance, as is the administration of state-owned land and enterprises.

The policy of detaching operations from the ministries was systematically followed in the German *Reich*, where almost all operations that required a considerable number of employees were transferred to subordinate agencies, which in contrast with the ministries (*i.e.,* the ministries) were called Höhere Reichsbehörden, and worked each under the supervision of one of the ministries (*e.g.,* Statistisches Reichsamt under the Ministry of Economics, Patentamt under that of justice). Methodical use of this device kept the German ministries so small that at the end of the Weimar Republic (1932) two of them had fewer than 200 employees, most had fewer than 400, and the largest (Finance Ministry) had less than 1,000. This old tradition was resumed in the Federal Republic of Germany after World War II.

It is common practice in the major countries to place each department under the administrative responsibility of a single head. The apparent exceptions to this rule in Great Britain are nominal rather than actual in most of the cases, as with the Treasury and the Boards of Education and of Trade. Collegial boards have kept practical significance, however, for the Admiralty in Great Britain and for agencies with quasi-legislative or quasi-judicial functions, such as the U.S. Interstate Commerce Commission, the British Transport Commission, or the civil service commissions in both countries, for government corporations, for some policy-forming agencies in smaller states, and in local government units.

Next in line under the department head, Great Britain and Germany have developed the office of the permanent undersecretary (called secretary in some British, and after 1920 Staatssekretär in all German ministries), who constitutes a one-man channel that must not be bypassed in official contacts between the lower levels and the department head. The duties of U.S. undersecretaries are dependent upon the responsibilities assigned by the secretary. Some U.S. departments have an additional undersecretary assigned to a specific function, such as the undersecretary for monetary affairs in the Treasury. In French ministries—except that of foreign affairs, which has a secrétaire général—directeurs, each in charge of one division, are placed immediately under the minister. In Germany, such division heads, called Ministerialdirektoren, constitute the next lower level under the Staatssekretäre. Likewise, in Great Britain and the United States, assistant secretaries or similar officers are often given directive functions over large fields of work under the undersecretary. But this is not always so; especially in the United States, many assistant secretaries work independently of the undersecretary, reporting directly to the secretary. Parliamentary undersecretaries have often been appointed not only in Great Britain but also in France for political or specific functions but are unknown in the U.S. and in Germany.

The greatest difference in organization, however, prevails at the base of departmental headquarters. European practice favours systematic distribution of the entire work among a body of subject-matter aides, trained for ministerial service and for the consideration of overall viewpoints; they are called principals in Great Britain, chefs de bureau in France, and Referenten or Sachbearbeiter (in various grades, such as Ministerialrat—formerly Geheimer Regierungsrat—Oberregierungsrat, and Regierungsrat) in Germany. The functions of these aides are, of course, greatly affected by the detachment or nondetachment of operational services (*see above*). The more operational functions are transferred to subordinate agencies, the less the ministerial aides have to deal with operations and the more their work concentrates on planning, advice, initial steps in the execution of decisions made at headquarters, contacts with other departments, and contacts with subordinate field agencies or operating services. This is the usual situation of the Referenten in German ministries, of British principals, and of French chefs de bureau. On the other hand, the fact that operating services in the United States usually constitute part of the departments makes the U.S. bureau chiefs the heads of such operating services. In their respective fields they function also as the direct advisers of their superiors, with no permanent aides between them and the secretary's level. In criticizing this type of organization it has been said that the natural weight of the large operating services tends to impair the desirable balance within departmental headquarters and to make the overall organization heavy footed and lopsided.

In the Soviet Union, state ownership of all means of production greatly increased the operating functions of the government and, consequently, multiplied the number of departments, which has at times exceeded 50 on the national level. There are, for example, several separate departments for various branches of industry. A considerable part of the management of the national economy and of industrial operations is passed on to public trusts (government corporations) as well as to the individual republics; in the latter case, the individual republic appoints the department head in charge of the execution, who then has a dual responsibility—on the one hand to the all-union ministers, on the other to the government of the constituent republic.

See further sections on administrative and social conditions in articles on countries.

(A. Br.; F. M. M.; Wr. J. C.)

II. UNITED STATES

1. Types of Agencies.—The U.S. departments are the apparatus by means of which the government carries on its various functions other than those of a legislative or judicial character. This broadly inclusive meaning of the term is identical with the federal government's usage of the term agencies. In the period after World War II the total number of federal agencies remained at about 60. But only certain of these agencies were designated as departments.

Not all agencies of the government, in the first place, are part of the executive branch, in the sense of being under the president's control. Some are agencies of the legislative branch—for instance, the Library of Congress, with its legislative reference service as a pool of experts available to the committees of Congress and its individual members alike; the Government Printing Office, headed by the public printer; and the federal government's audit agency, the General Accounting Office under the comptroller general, who serves for an exceptionally long term of 15 years. A somewhat larger number of agencies are neither in the legislative branch nor under the president's orders, but are controlled or directed by individuals appointed by the president with the advice and consent of the Senate. These agencies are often spoken of as the independent regulatory commissions and boards, usually created by statute as bipartisan establishments and deliberately placed outside the reach of the president's legal power of command. Most of the principal agencies of the federal government having quasi-legislative and quasi-judicial functions are of this type, such as the Interstate Commerce Commission, the Federal Trade Commission, the Federal Power Commission, the Securities and Exchange Commission, and the National Labor Relations Board.

Within the executive branch, thus narrowly defined, there are further distinctions between agencies. One group is formed by the government corporations; for example, the Tennessee Valley Authority, the Export-Import Bank of the United States, and the Panama Canal Company. Another category is represented by the considerable number of agencies that are comparable in many respects to departments but lack this title. These agencies include the Atomic Energy Commission, the Veterans Administration, the National Science Foundation, the General Services Administration, and the Postal Service. Many are single headed, like the departments; others are directed by plural bodies, like the independent regulatory commissions and boards. Again, like the departments, most of these executive agencies perform functions that in some direct way affect the public or parts of it, as so-called line activities. A few executive agencies, however, have the task of attending to needs of management that exist throughout the executive branch—for instance, the Civil Service Commission for recruitment, classification, and other aspects of personnel administration, and the General Services Administration for office space, procurement of supplies, and disposition of records. The most important category of federal agencies is formed by the so-called executive departments, relatively few in number but collectively the backbone of the executive branch.

2. Number, Rank, and Size.—The 11 executive departments of the federal government, in order of their official rank, are these: State and, next, Treasury, both since 1789; Defense, established in 1949, with its three military departments, Army (created as War Department in 1789), Navy (1798), and Air Force (1947); Justice (1870), with antecedents reaching back much further; Interior (1849); Agriculture (1862); Commerce (1903); Labor (1913, previously joined with Commerce); Health, Education, and Welfare (1953), as an elevation of the former Federal Security Agency; Housing and Urban Development (1965); and Transportation (1966). The Post Office Department, created in 1872, was made an independent agency by legislation enacted in 1970.

The Executive Office of the President, a staff organization created in 1939 to assist him in the general direction and coordination of the departments as well as the other agencies of the executive branch, is not itself a department. It is a presidential establishment for purposes of program planning, analysis of problems and issues, review and formulation of proposals, and administrative control. The Executive Office of the President includes, among others, the White House Office, the Office of Management and Budget, the Council of Economic Advisers, the National Security Council, the Central Intelligence Agency, the Domestic Council, the Office of Economic Opportunity, the National Aeronautics and Space Council, and an Office of Emergency Preparedness. On the president's level, the concerns with particular functions that come forth from the departments and the other agencies of the executive branch are met by the counterpressure of a government-wide orientation. Such broader orientation is typical of the presidency, as the foremost organ for the expression of national points of view under the Constitution.

Between the Executive Office of the President, as a staff organization looking at matters across the board, and the departments of the executive branch, each absorbed in its own functions, there develops a creative tension. The outcome, ideally, is a constructive interchange, with a broadening effect upon decisions. Realistically, however, it is also possible that the result, in the individual case, is determined by political compromise.

Departmental strength is a product of many factors, one of which is size. By quantitative measurements, the departments, like the other agencies of the executive branch, show striking variations. The largest, by a wide margin, is the Department of Defense.

One measure of the growth of the departmental system is the increase in civilian and military personnel in the executive branch. The grand total rose steadily from less than 1,000 civilian employees and 1,300 military personnel during Washington's administration to more than 2,500,000 and some 3,000,000, respectively in the second half of the 20th century.

3. Common Characteristics.—Like the heads of almost all executive agencies, department heads are appointed by the president with the advice and consent of the Senate. Only department heads bear the distinctive title of secretary—as, for instance, secretary of labour. The title is not common to all, however. The top officer of the Department of Justice has the designation of attorney general, dating back to the beginnings of the republic.

Department heads have neither the right nor the duty of participation in the affairs of Congress, as is normally the case under parliamentary government. On the other hand, the principle of acceptability of the president's choices for his official team carries with it certain limitations to be observed in the exercise of his appointive power. For one thing, men with a passion for unpopular causes, a reputation for unorthodox opinions, or a lofty disdain for politicians do not make good material for presidential nominations, though such men may be pillars of wisdom and integrity. There is also the matter of geographic balance in picking candidates, besides other factors of political strategy which no president can ignore. But affiliation with the other party is no bar, for on occasion a bipartisan appearance is politically desirable.

As far as their relationship with Congress is concerned, department heads confine their role essentially to supplying information and advice, often as pleaders, mostly in testimony before congressional committees. In such testimony, as in other public statements, the members of the president's team are supposed to reflect his policies. But the interest they have in advancing their departmental programs may induce them to be more responsive to the legislative committee dealing with the department's affairs or to organized groups which regard themselves as the department's clientele than to the goals sought by the president. To be sure, in a formal sense, expressed by the Constitution, department heads are the subordinates of the president; he can fire them at will. Yet a disciplinary action so extreme is practical only on very rare occasions, when in the nature of all circumstances its application would not inflict serious damage upon the prestige of the president's administration. As a matter of fact department heads are able to move rather freely in a no-man's-land of political convenience, checked only by such factors as their loyalty to the president and their fear of the price of a full-scale conflict with him.

Only department heads and the U.S. representative to the United Nations are automatically members of the Cabinet (q.v.). The president, however, is free to request the regular attendance of other officials, such as the director of the Office of Management and Budget. The practical importance of the Cabinet and its efficiency in performance are roughly proportionate to the president's own intentions and working methods. For lack of a necessary constitutional function, the Cabinet operates as a meeting of presidential advisers, but the president does not withdraw behind the Cabinet. There is thus no collective responsibility of the Cabinet for the government's program, in the sense of British political doctrine.

Nevertheless, if only because of the implied exclusiveness, Cabinet rank is valued highly. Automatic Cabinet status also has certain small but conspicuous privileges. For example, by law only Cabinet members among the heads of executive agencies enjoy the privilege of being called for at their homes in the morning and driven back at the end of the day in their own official cars. On the other hand, Cabinet status does not imply willingness to sit in the Cabinet or to use the Cabinet for the making of decisions. When it comes to getting the Cabinet for the president's approval for a particular matter, a department head settles the business directly with the president or his staff assistant rather than propose it for the Cabinet agenda. It is then left for the president to make sure that the subject has the benefit of scrutiny by additional eyes before he commits himself.

Assurance that such scrutiny is provided as a normal procedure is perhaps most evident in the field of proposed legislation. Under arrangements made initially in 1921, the Bureau of the Budget (renamed the Office of Management and Budget in 1970) became the presidential clearinghouse for legislative proposals advanced by executive agencies. The test question in this matter is whether or not the individual proposal is in accord with the president's program. In furnishing clearance, the Office of Management and Budget not only is guided by decisions made by the president but also seeks the advice of all other agencies having an interest in the particular matter, thus helping to establish a common position within the executive branch. In addition, when agencies are asked by congressional committees to convey their views on pending bills, the same clearance procedure is applied. When any agency insists, it may send its views to the Congress when it differs from the views of other agencies or the Office of Management and Budget, but this is rare. But it must add the finding of the budget office concerning the relationship of the bill to the president's program. The same kind of consultation throughout the executive branch is obtained by the budget office before a proposed executive order is passed on to the president for his consideration and signature.

In basic internal organization, the departments show considerable similarities. The top nucleus is generally known as the secretary's office. Upon it converge the demands for decisions which rise constantly in the normal course of business from the next lower level—the great functional groupings made up of bureaus, offices, or divisions. These, in turn, are subdivided successively as need requires, down to the smallest working unit. It is natural to imagine the departments as a mighty cluster of central agencies. In actual fact, however, the headquarters organization of the departments at the nation's capital in Washington, D.C., is usually only the smallest part. More than nine-tenths of all federal employees are stationed in the field, mostly in the United States, but also on foreign soil, as in the case of the Foreign Service and various specialized missions.

Departmental direction is therefore in great part a matter of communication, as in all far-flung and large-scale organizations. No department can be much more than the reflection of its sense of purpose. Such sense of purpose does not exist apart from the men and women who arrive at a specified time in the morning and fill a dead building with their devotion to duty as well as their familiar routines. But solidarity and cohesion around aims to be accomplished develop more easily in the small working group than in a vast organization. Moreover, conflicts of purposes and interests between different components, specialization in the performance of particular functions, and the localized perspective of the personal workplace keep the individual parts of a departmental mandate from appreciating the importance of the departmental mandate as a whole. Thus the objectives of the department, however frequently emphasized from the top, may yet lack a strong appeal internally. They may remain distant and rather blurred images for the rank and file, preoccupied with what is closest to the individual desk. This tendency toward personal isolation, never completely overcome by even the most resourceful kind of coordination, may make the department as a unified whole a rather distant objective for all but those occupied with general management. The individual employee's allegiance may be limited, therefore, to the particular unit or sector in which he works, especially when the department is a multi-purpose one or is the outgrowth of many changes.

Withdrawal into the small-scale world of the individual working group—a world to be kept secure, agreeable, neat, and unmolested by bigger things outside—is a familiar trait of bureaucratic behaviour. It is a trait that should not be condemned rashly because, paradoxically, it also has a certain therapeutic value. It is an antidote to the growth of a bureaucracy so unified in an independent concept of mission as to rise above control by elective policy makers. The vast physical expansion of the executive branch of the federal government in the 20th century has often been lamented. It has been seen as a forerunner to what is predicted by some as the coming tyranny of the managers. But the habits of bureaucracy as they manifest themselves in the departmental operations of the federal government are all on the other side. In the United States, bureaucracy, in public administration, is a force of division; it is not a single body with its own sense of direction.

Lack of unity in the permanent officialdom is thus a natural condition, promoted by the absence of a recognized higher career service reaching up right below the department head and his political aides, like the British administrative class. On the other hand, the respect accorded the administrative class in England demonstrates that a higher career service, under the pervasive influence of its own ethics, can be a strong restraint upon the zest for power among its members. So indoctrinated, the civil service is able to guard itself against both excessive solidarity and bureaucratic self-aggrandizement. U.S. civil servants, under a weaker service spirit and larger departmental entities, are more inclined to put priority on that part of the departmental program for which they have individual responsibility, as contrasted with other parts. A strong-willed subordinate, convinced of the public benefits of his division's work, may feel free to concentrate on building up support for it. He may go out to reinforce his position by clandestine alliances with good friends in Congress and among the leaders of interest groups even though the head of his department may see things quite differently. Under auspices of a loosely organized party system, congressional-presidential government is characterized by a high degree of dispersal of power. Thus channels of command both within the departments and from the president downward can be obstructed by underlings with greater ease than one might expect at first thought.

All of this makes the job of managing a department a good deal harder than need be. Single-handed, of course, a department secretary would accomplish little. He must multiply himself, so to speak, by leaving part of the job to lieutenants in whom he can repose his full political as well as personal confidence. These are the undersecretary and the assistant secretaries, occasionally also a deputy secretary, as in the Defense Department. Like the secretary himself, they are among the political officers who are appointed by the president with the advice and consent of the Senate. In contrast with past practice, these selections are rarely mere patronage appointments. The reason is the increased public pressure upon the president—in the day of the service state—to make a satisfactory record in the conduct of his administration, as a matter of good politics.

Yet presidents face considerable difficulty in persuading well-qualified citizens to undertake this kind of public service and to stay in the post after having accepted. Businessmen in particular, but also labour leaders and members of the professions, often require vigorous prompting to make themselves available for an indefinite tour of duty in Washington, D.C. This is not merely a matter of personal and family finances but also the reflection of a political environment notorious for its frustrations and its lack of charity in public criticism. Recruitment of top-calibre men and women for high political positions, especially for the leadership of the executive departments, emerged as one of the unsolved problems of U.S. government.

In each department the number of presidentially appointed top officials is small, although the impetus they give the department is noticeable. To extend themselves sufficiently far, both outside and inside the department, they need special assistants, mostly brought in from other walks of life as policy advisers, contact men, or confidential assistants, whose appointments last usually only as long as the presidential tenure. The great bulk of the departmental personnel consists of permanent employees having regular civil-service status.

Although civil servants legally can be shifted around to suit the preference of an incoming departmental high command, no department is easily stripped of its established ways. Like other large-scale organizations, departments carry their burden of inertia, as they also display their share of initiative, persistence, and drive. Departmental management must seek to cope with these conflicting impulses in such a way as to meet desirable standards of performance. Actual performance, by and large, though showing variations within departments and from department to department, compares fully with the standards of private business.

In their day-by-day administration, almost all departments have come to place considerable reliance on groups of management specialists. Most of these are engaged in program planning, review of operations, budgeting, organization and methods work, personnel administration, accounting, and the like. In several departments, in 1950, all or most of these specialized elements of departmental management were combined under the new office of administrative assistant secretary, intended to be filled by career men.

4. Executive Reorganization.—Year upon year, new administrative activities are authorized by Congress, and established ones either change or disappear because of changing circumstances and policies. In their cumulative effects, these changes make it necessary to reexamine the organizational structure of the executive branch at frequent intervals. Good organization might rapidly deteriorate in time if additions, modifications, or eliminations of activities were allowed to happen without any thought of a general plan. Bad organization might fall into an intolerable state under such conditions.

Some rudimentary logic underneath the departmental system of the federal government can be discovered from the historical record of its growth. The dates, given earlier, of the beginnings of the executive departments supply a key. Finance, foreign affairs, and defense, together with justice and the postal service, were a natural grouping for an era when the federal government was mainly concerned with the administration of functions considered suitable for the common agency of an association of sovereign states.

Eventually, the diversified natural resources under federal control, including the public lands, called for recognition on the Cabinet level and brought forth the Department of the Interior. Then, with the full momentum of a development that led the republic from its agrarian start into the charged atmosphere of an industrial order, there followed the parade of clientele departments with nationwide responsibilities—one looking after the farmer, another serving the businessman, and the last acknowledging the interests of the worker. A further step was taken with the establishment of a full-fledged department underwriting important aspects of economic and social opportunity—the Department of Health, Education, and Welfare.

If that much underlying reason is conceded, it must not be concluded that the departmental system, as a product of history, ought to be left in peace. On the contrary, proposals for achieving a more rational structure of the executive branch have been made quite frequently. Many of these proposals rest on fairly abstract theories of what is variously assumed to be the essence of sound organization. The departments, however, are massive structures reinforced by precedent and tradition and cannot easily be changed. They are singularly unresponsive to the preachings of people stirred by a sense of organizational tidiness. Moreover, all the organized interests, economic and social, that have a stake in the departmental setup view with deep suspicion any marked departure from familiar arrangements. Each interest is fearful of coming out the loser.

But real gains may be attained even by some patient, piecemeal improving. That has been done rather persistently. Four new Cabinet rank departments were created in the period 1949–66: Defense; Health, Education, and Welfare; Housing and Urban Development; and Transportation. The usual procedure, applied on all levels of government in the United States, is to set up a formal inquiry into existing conditions, in the hope of bringing forth concrete recommendations with a fair chance of adoption. Inquiries of this type on the federal level include the President's Committee on Administrative Management with Louis Brownlow as chairman (reporting in 1937) and the (first) Commission on Organization of the Executive Branch headed by former president Herbert Hoover (reporting in 1949). Examples on the state level were the so-called "little Hoover commissions" set up on the federal model. It was not surprising that one of the first steps

taken by Dwight D. Eisenhower upon assuming office as president in 1953 was to add an official advisory committee on government organization, under the chairmanship of Nelson A. Rockefeller. In addition to this, shortly afterward a second Hoover Commission was created, whose purpose was to deal with the more explosive question of the proper scope of governmental functions. Its reports proved correspondingly more subjective and controversial.

These bodies, pursuing a broadly evolutionary approach, have done useful work. Cumulatively, they managed not only to get action on a whole series of proposals for desirable changes but also to shape a working doctrine of executive reorganization. The Brownlow committee, for instance, made history by breaking ground for the concept of the Executive Office of the President. Implicit in this concept was the idea that executive responsibility should be matched with sufficient authority and clearly centred in the top man, but its exercise should be bolstered by a balanced grouping of staff units bringing coordinating skill as well as specialized judgment to bear upon decisions. Another element in the working doctrine of executive reorganization, reaffirmed by the first Hoover Commission, was the demand that activities be fitted into patterns, each dominated by a basic governmental purpose. This criterion of departmentalization sounds simple but is much less simple in practical application. Still another point of doctrine is the general rule that both the number of departments and the total number of agencies of the executive branch ought to be held to a minimum; that, ideally, the lesser agencies ought to be brought into some defined relationship with one or another department, as the president's span of control is naturally limited; and that novel public functions, especially while still experimental or when undertaken for the duration of an emergency, might best be constituted as—possibly temporary—agencies rather than as new departments.

As in the federal government, so also in state and local governments, the desirable structure of the departmental system was linked with the concept of a fully responsible chief executive. The strengthening of the governor's position, on the one hand, and the gradual replacement of the weak-mayor type of municipal organization by the strong-mayor type or the council-manager plan, on the other, led to some consolidation of the executive branch. This included a reduction of the number of agencies practically accountable only to themselves. Both in local and in state government, however, various officials are frequently elected side by side with the chief executive, who therefore has no effective control over them.

Together with placing limitations on the number of departments and making each a repository of reasonably related functions, staff units have been built around the chief executive in state and local government. In addition, the concept of a department of administration gained some popularity, especially on the state level. This department is usually visualized as an agency combining responsibilities for budgetary planning, fiscal control, improvement of management and procedures, periodic inspection, and provision of central services, such as purchasing and car pools. Not surprisingly, in the states as well as the counties and municipalities, progress along the lines of executive reorganization has been slow. In state government, for example, it is not exceptional to encounter more than 30 departments and a total of more than 100 agencies, including many not subject to the governor's general direction.

With the president constitutionally the coequal partner of Congress in the performance of the tasks that have fallen to the federal government with the growth of an industrial society, it might be thought that he can do as he pleases in reorganizing the executive branch. This could be regarded as an obvious inference from his role as the responsible chief executive of the nation. But it is not widely assumed that such actually is the legal authority of the president. As a practical matter, it appears accepted that the president requires congressional authorization to reorganize the executive branch. Securing adequate authority for him is doubly important because evidence shows, as could perhaps be expected, that Congress, left to itself, is not a particularly good architect of executive structure.

Despite much urging from official and unofficial quarters before as well as after World War II, Congress failed to see compelling reasons for granting the president continuing authority to carry out reorganizations. Instead, taking its cue from the report of the Brownlow committee, Congress passed a succession of short-term reorganization acts (of 1939, 1945, and 1949, the last prolonged repeatedly by new legislation). Each of these acts laid down essentially the same procedure for setting in motion the wheels of organizational change, first written into law in the act of 1939. In briefest outline, the president would come forth with specific reorganization plans and transmit them to Congress. Congress then could express its disapproval of the individual plan. If no such disapproval had been voted, the plan would take effect after 60 days, having practically the force of law. Each reorganization act, as a limitation, extended a protective hand over certain agencies for various reasons. For disapproval, the acts of 1939 and 1945 required agreement by both the Senate and the House of Representatives, whereas under the act of 1949 objection on the part of either of the two chambers was sufficient if expressed by a majority of the total membership of that chamber. In the consideration of the Prolongation Act of 1953, a move in the committee stage to whittle down this majority requirement by substituting a simple majority was stopped in the nick of time. The Prolongation Act of 1957 eliminated the requirement that disapproval be expressed by a majority of the chamber's "authorized membership," thus greatly increasing the chance of congressional disapproval. The legislative veto, obviously, should operate only on the basis of substantial congressional sentiment against any particular reorganization plan.

Although in part because it was never employed in disregard of political realities, this novel procedure, on the whole, was notably successful. Instances of disapproval remained the distinct exception. On the side of accomplishments, reorganization plans provided the structure of the Executive Office of the President, one of the most important events in the modern administrative history of the federal government; strengthened the authority of top management on the departmental level; created the Department of Health, Education, and Welfare (1953), the Department of Housing and Urban Development (1965), and the Department of Transportation (1966). In 1967 the president recommended the creation of a Department of Business to combine the Department of Commerce and the Department of Labor, the latter having been a part of the former until 1913. This recommendation was not adopted by Congress. Other important agencies established were the U.S. Information Agency (1953) and the Equal Employment Opportunity Commission (1965). More often, reorganization plans were used to achieve a more satisfactory allocation of particular activities to existing agencies. It has also happened that Congress incorporated the substance of a reorganization plan into legislation.

A number of reorganization plans were aimed specifically at creating better conditions for effective management within the individual agencies. In the first place, in regard to plural bodies like the Federal Trade Commission an effort was made to build up the position of the chairman into a kind of administrative chief, without affecting the prerogative of the body as a whole to settle important business by vote. Secondly, in single-headed agencies it was sought to do away with impediments to the freedom of the man at the helm to organize his agency for greatest efficiency. This meant the elimination of statutory barriers, a difficult obstacle to overcome. The campaign in support of wider managerial leeway at the top level in the various agencies advanced a considerable distance but also suffered telling defeats in Congress.

A reorganization program of such scope calls for extensive analysis of what is wrong in the first place, careful determination as to what to tackle and what to leave untouched for the time being, and shrewd exploration of the strategy and tactics of how to formulate individual proposals and when to act. Some of these judgments are necessarily political. Many of them are technical, often involving very complex situations. Staff work for the president in the technical development of reorganization plans had been an assignment of the Bureau of the Budget's Office of Executive Management. The bureau itself was reorganized in 1970 and renamed the Office of Management and Budget.

Many proposals for reorganizing the federal executive agencies are introduced into Congress each year, such as those proposing a Cabinet Department of Education, a separate Department of Health, and a Department of Consumer Affairs.

Below is outlined the machinery for the conduct of the principal executive functions of the federal government.

5. Foreign Affairs.—The central figure in American foreign policy is the president; he holds the final authority and personally makes the most critical decisions concerning foreign affairs. The organization charged with the conduct of the nation's international affairs is the Department of State. Its head, the secretary of state, is the president's principal adviser in the formation of foreign policy and his principal agent for its coordination and implementation.

The exact role played by the secretary of state is shaped by the philosophies and personalities of the president and the secretary. The secretary of state, however, will normally assist the president on international problems by presenting to him all elements of the problem, alternative courses of action, and essential differences of opinions, and by giving his own views and recommendations. In a more formal vein, the secretary of state is a statutory member of the National Security Council, a body created in 1947 within the Executive Office of the President to assist the president in the clarification and resolution of the complex issues of national security. In 1947 the Policy Planning Council was created within the State Department to provide the secretary with the reflective analysis and creative proposals to suggest the future course of the nation's diplomacy.

To implement foreign-policy decisions and conduct normal diplomatic relations with governments abroad, the Department of State is organized into a Washington headquarters and nearly 300 embassies, legations, consular posts, and special missions located in more than 100 nations throughout the world. The U.S. ambassador to a foreign nation is the personal representative of the president and has full responsibility for the implementation of American foreign policy in the country of his assignment by all U.S. government personnel in that country. To handle the steady flow of nearly 2,000 daily messages exchanged with these foreign posts, the Washington offices of the department are organized into five regional bureaus, each one headed by an assistant secretary. These five regional bureaus represent Africa, Latin America, East Asia and the Pacific, Europe, and the Near East and South Asia. A separate bureau is organized to provide guidance and support for United States participation in international organizations such as the United Nations, and international conferences, of which there are some 600 annually. Other offices provide the secretary with expert advice on foreign economic matters, scientific and technological aspects of U.S. foreign policy, and with research and analysis on foreign intelligence.

Responsibility for the issuance of passports and visas, as well as for the protection and welfare of American citizens abroad, is vested in the Bureau of Security and Consular Affairs. Other bureaus within the department deal with public affairs, congressional relations, and education and cultural-exchange programs.

The secretary's authority to "direct, coordinate, and supervise the interdepartmental activities of the United States government overseas" (except for military activities) is derived from a presidential statement of March 4, 1966. This responsibility is discharged primarily through the undersecretary and the regional assistant secretaries of state. The head of each regional bureau acts as the executive chairman of the Interdepartmental Regional Group (IRG). This group consists of designated regional representatives from the Department of Defense, the Agency for International Development (AID), the Central Intelligence Agency (CIA), the Organization of the Joint Chiefs of Staff, the United States Information Agency (USIA), and the White House or National Security Council staff. Regional matters requiring more attention are brought before the Senior Interdepartmental Group (SIG). Under the chairmanship of the undersecretary of state, the SIG is composed of the directors of AID, USIA, and CIA, the chairman of the Joint Chiefs of Staff, the deputy secretary of defense, and the president's assistant for national security affairs.

Two important additions to the traditional means of carrying on U.S. foreign relations have come into being since World War II. A program of foreign aid to Europe, first proposed by Secretary of State Marshall in 1948, has evolved organizationally into a separate agency within the State Department. The Agency for International Development is responsible for administering non-military assistance to selected nations throughout the world. This assistance is divided into categories of loans, grants, investment surveys, and development-research activities. Since 1945, over $45,000,000,000 has been distributed in AID programs. (See also FOREIGN AID PROGRAMS.)

The second innovation, the Peace Corps, was proposed by President Kennedy in 1961. As an agency within the State Department, the Peace Corps arranges for the placement abroad of volunteer men and women of the United States to developing nations of the world. These volunteers help fill the developing nations' critical needs for skilled manpower and seek to promote a better understanding between the American people and the peoples served. (See also PEACE CORPS.)

6. Finance: Revenue and Debt.—In the United States, as in Great Britain, the Treasury has been a vital factor in the development and the operations of the entire national administrative system. In Britain, Treasury control means not only coordination of fiscal and economic policies but also central superintendence over the departments in the performance of such management functions as budgeting and personnel. In the United States, most managerial and many operational responsibilities originally developed in the Treasury Department. But as the government grew and matured, managerial responsibilities gravitated toward the presidency, the biggest shift being effected in 1939 by the transfer of the Bureau of the Budget from the Treasury to the Executive Office of the President. Operational responsibilities have been transferred to other departments; other agencies now include major responsibilities once residing in the Treasury.

The Treasury maintains two primary responsibilities. First, the secretary of the treasury serves as fiscal adviser to the president, along with the Council of Economic Advisers and the Office of Management and Budget. Second, the department administers most revenue collections, the manufacturing of coin and currency, and many law-enforcement activities.

The responsibility for federal fiscal policy involves the Treasury in three major areas. First, it is the secretary of the treasury and his experts who present to Congress, for the president, the tax proposals of the executive branch, and who in turn serve Congress as principal sources of technical information. The proposals of the executive branch in these as in all other matters are simply presidential recommendations. Congress is constitutionally free to modify or ignore the recommendations and to initiate its own legislation.

A second area revolves around the Treasury responsibility to finance federal deficits and to oversee, with other agencies, the nation's monetary, financial, and economic affairs. The department must minimize the cost of debt financing while supporting a money market capable of meeting public and private credit demands, of stimulating national economic growth, and of maintaining international monetary stability. Although Federal Reserve policy may directly affect rates of interest on Treasury financing, the Treasury has no legal authority over the Federal Reserve System. Nor has the Treasury direct control over many governmental lending programs, such as those providing building loans or agricultural credit. These and other activities beyond Treasury's control make Treasury's relationship with other agencies of crucial consequence to the economy. Treasury's regularized review of fiscal and economic affairs with the Office of Management and Budget and the Council of Economic Advisers has become known as the "Troika," and the "Quadriad" when it includes the Federal Reserve System, backbone of the country's private banking business and chief guardian of sound money conditions.

The third area of policy guidance deals with the balance of payments and other aspects of international monetary and financial affairs. The Treasury's Office of the Assistant Secretary for International Affairs collects and analyzes current information about the economic positions and policies of other nations having a bearing upon United States financial and monetary programs. The Treasury negotiates, with foreign governments, international monetary arrangements and other aspects of international finance. The secretary serves as chairman of the National Advisory Council on International Monetary and Financial Policies, in effect a Cabinet committee for purposes of coordinating United States participation in international financial and lending institutions.

In the Treasury Department the fiscal and the administrative assistant secretaries represent the growth of the career civil service to the highest level. The fiscal assistant secretary is in charge of the Fiscal Service, including supervision of the Bureau of Accounts, the Bureau of the Public Debt, and the Office of the Treasurer of the United States, which is essentially the banking facility for the federal government. The assistant secretary for administration supervises the department's work in general management matters.

The main divisions of work in the Treasury demonstrate how broad its operating functions remain. Its chief components in addition to the Fiscal Service are: the Bureau of the Mint, the Bureau of Engraving and Printing, the United States Savings Bonds Division, the Office of the Comptroller of the Currency (who supervises the so-called national banks), the Internal Revenue Service (which collects all federal taxes and has an extensive field service of its own), the Bureau of Customs (also responsible for physical protection of the president and certain other political leaders, and for suppression of counterfeiting and forgery of federal and foreign currencies and financial obligations).

7. Defense.—The mission of the Department of Defense is to provide, through its military strength, a solid foundation for the national policy of the United States. The forerunner of the Department of Defense, the National Military Establishment, was created by the National Security Act of 1947, and evolved from the experiences of World War II. While combat and service components of the Departments of the Army and the Navy fought together in various theatres of operation under unified direction of overseas commanders, the individual military departments reported separately to the president. The conflicting and competitive policies of these departments prevented a truly effective, coordinated, and unified military effort. To overcome this organizational deficiency, the National Military Establishment was created, and the Cabinet post of secretary of defense was established to provide overall policy and direction of the military departments without destroying their individual identities. Concurrently, the Air Force was created as a third military department on a coequal basis with the Departments of the Army and the Navy.

The original National Security Act of 1947 provided the secretary of defense with limited authority and staff to exercise control. However, subsequent amendments to the basic act in 1949, 1953, and 1958 have greatly strengthened the authority and ability of the secretary to direct defense policy. In the 1949 amendment, the Department of Defense as we know it today was established.

In 1970, the Department of Defense consisted of the secretary of defense, the deputy secretary of defense, the Armed Forces Policy Council, the director of defense research and engineering, eight assistant secretaries (administration, comptroller, health and environment, installations and logistics, international security affairs, manpower and reserve affairs, public affairs, and systems analysis), the special assistant to the secretary and deputy secretary of defense, the general counsel, three assistants to the secretary of defense (atomic energy, legislative affairs, and telecommunications), and the defense adviser for the U.S. mission to the North Atlantic Treaty Organization. These civilian officials represent the policy and resource-management staff of the secretary of defense.

The civilian secretaries of the military departments (Army, Navy, and Air Force) are responsible for the administration of their particular departments, and are responsible for training, equipping, and providing combat-ready forces to the combat commands.

The combat forces of the Army, Navy, Air Force, and Marine Corps are under unified and specified combat commands, organized on either a functional or a geographic basis. A unified command contains combat forces from more than one service, such as the Pacific Command, which is comprised of all Army, Navy, Air Force, and Marine Corps units in the Pacific area. A specified command is composed of units from a single service; for example, only Air Force units are contained in the Strategic Air Command (SAC). SAC is the only specified command in the Department of Defense.

The commanders of the unified and specified commands are responsible to the president and the secretary of defense. By secretarial delegation, the Joint Chiefs of Staff exercise operational direction over the unified and specified commands.

The Joint Chiefs of Staff are the principal military advisers to the president, the National Security Council, and the secretary of defense. The Joint Chiefs of Staff consist of the chairman, Joint Chiefs of Staff, who is the nation's highest-ranking military officer; the chief of staff, United States Army; the chief of naval operations; the chief of staff, U.S. Air Force; the commandant of the Marine Corps on matters concerning the Marine Corps. The chiefs are appointed by the president to four-year terms.

The Joint Chiefs of Staff are supported by the Joint Staff, which is limited by law to not more than 400 officers. This staff is organized along conventional military staff lines, and performs such functions as developing strategic concepts and war plans, reviewing the operating plans of the unified and specified commands, and establishing unified doctrine for operations. The Joint Staff also provides the Joint Chiefs of Staff with planning factors and requirements for the development of plans relating to the overall force structure. An assignment to the Joint Staff provides military officers a unique opportunity to work on coordinated plans and to develop an understanding of the integrated effort required under today's concept of joint operations.

Within the Department of Defense there are five defense agencies. These agencies were established to provide integrated and unified effort in support activities that generally cut across service lines. The defense agencies have consolidated functions that were previously fractionalized among the military services. The Defense Atomic Support Agency, Defense Intelligence Agency, and Defense Communications Agency report to the secretary of defense through the Joint Chiefs of Staff. The Defense Supply Agency and Defense Contract Audit Agency report directly to the secretary of defense.

As a top-level management tool, the Armed Forces Policy Council was established to advise the secretary of defense on broad policy matters. The council brings together the top civilian and military leaders so that all aspects of a problem can be exposed and alternative solutions explored. The secretary of defense is the chairman of the council; other members include the deputy secretary of defense, the secretaries of the military departments, the Joint Chiefs of Staff, and the director of Defense Research and Engineering.

Since the prime mission of the Defense Department is to provide military support for United States national policy, including U.S. foreign policy, close coordination with the Department of State is essential. The primary method of achieving this coordination is through the Senior Interdepartmental Group (SIG) and the Interdepartmental Regional Groups (IRGs). The defense representatives to the SIG are the deputy secretary of defense and the chairman, Joint Chiefs of Staff. The SIG is chaired by the undersecretary of state. The IRGs include lower-ranking civilian and military experts from the Department of Defense and the Department of State, with each IRG addressing a specific geographic area. The IRGs develop policy recommendations for the approval of the SIG. At the national level, the SIG operates in close coordination with the National Security Council.

The need for the military to consider implications of political, economic, and scientific factors in the development of military plans and military advice requires that senior military officers have a broad education in these disciplines. To this end, the military departments have established an extensive continuing-education system for their officers. Included in this educational system are joint-service schools such as the National War College, Armed Forces Staff College, and Industrial College of the Armed Forces, as well as individual service schools such as the Naval War College, Air University, and Army War College. These schools are conducted on a highly professional, graduate-school level to train future military leaders as broadly educated officers who understand the importance of political, economic, and scientific factors on military planning.

The Department of the Army, through its Corps of Engineers, also performs important civil functions in improving rivers, harbours, and waterways for navigation, in constructing flood-control and similar projects in various parts of the country, and in administering the laws governing navigable waters.

'8. Department of Justice.—In the American system of separated powers, justice is determined primarily in the courts of law. The principal mission of the Department of Justice is to represent the federal government before those courts. Other major functions of this department include: advising the president and other executive agencies on legal matters; administering the federal Bureau of Prisons, the Immigration and Naturalization Service, and the Community Relations Service; investigating violations of federal law; and coordinating federal law enforcement and federal assistance to state and local law enforcement.

The head of the department is the attorney general of the United States. Historically one of the earliest Cabinet positions, and traditionally less political than most Cabinet offices, the attorney general has evolved into a combination of prosecutor, counsellor, and administrator. He is assisted in these responsibilities by the deputy attorney general, who also coordinates the nearly 100 United States attorneys' offices, located in each federal judicial district, and undertakes preliminary screening of recommendations of candidates for federal judgeships, whose nomination by the president must also be confirmed by the Senate. The third principal official in the department is the solicitor-general, who, subject to rarely exercised review by the attorney general, determines which cases involving the federal government will be appealed, and briefs and argues all cases in which the federal government appears before the United States Supreme Court.

Although routine litigation is handled by the United States attorneys in the field, specialized areas are handled centrally by the seven litigating divisions. Of these, two divisions have broad policy authority to shape enforcement programs in specific areas.

The Antitrust Division is responsible for enforcing the broad mandates of the Sherman and Clayton acts to maintain a competitive economy. By selecting cases to be litigated, and marshalling arguments and evidence in those cases, this division, through the courts, has significantly influenced national economic policy.

A second major enforcement program is the responsibility of the Civil Rights Division. Formed in 1957, this division now administers the Civil Rights acts of 1957, 1960, 1964, 1965, and 1968 in the fields of discrimination in public facilities, public accommodations, voting, employment, and housing. Criminal matters are divided among the Criminal Division (concentrating on such matters as organized crime, criminal fraud, and political and election violations), Internal Security Division (espionage and subversive activities), and Tax Division (except liquor- and narcotics-tax offenses). The Tax Division also processes all civil federal tax matters before all federal courts other than the Tax Court of the United States. The remaining litigating divisions are the Civil Division, representing the United States in all otherwise unassigned civil matters, including most claims in the Court of Claims, and the Land and Natural Resources Division, which supervises condemnation of property on behalf of federal agencies, litigation involving federally owned land, and administration of Indian claims. The Office of Legal Counsel, not a litigating division, provides legal advice to the attorney general and to other agencies of the government.

A number of bureaus within the department are responsible

for investigation of federal criminal offenses. The Federal Bureau of Investigation (known widely as the FBI) is the largest single federal investigating agency. Operating parallel to but substantially independently from the rest of the department, this bureau maintains special-agent's offices in most major cities, as well as extensive laboratory and staff facilities in the capital. A second investigating bureau is the Bureau of Narcotics and Dangerous Drugs. Formed in 1968 out of two predecessor agencies (the Bureau of Narcotics in Treasury and the Bureau of Drug Abuse and Control in HEW), this bureau has primary responsibility for research, education, and enforcement in the narcotics and dangerous-drug fields. Another major addition to the department is the Law Enforcement Assistance Administration, responsible under the Omnibus Crime Control and Safe Streets Act of 1968. The federal Bureau of Prisons operates all federal penal facilities, and also provides technical assistance to state penitentiary systems.

9. Resources.—In this field the most important role is played by the Department of the Interior. The activities of this department centre upon the management, conservation, and development of the natural resources of the United States. The department also promotes the welfare of the inhabitants of the island possessions of the United States and of the Trust Territory of the Pacific Islands, in addition to exercising guardianship over U.S. Indians and promoting the interests of the natives of Alaska.

The principal division of work on the department's top level is in terms of fish and wildlife, mineral resources, public-land management, and water and power development. The technical review staff conducts studies of various programs and maintains liaison between the department and its field committees, which serve as organs of coordination in the main geographic areas.

The Interior Department is divided into these main elements: the Bureau of Indian Affairs, trustee of the lands belonging to the Indians and source of public services to them, as long as they are not yet absorbed into American life; the Bureau of Land Management, responsible also for the granting of grazing permits on the public range; the Bureau of Mines, which has as its tasks the conservation of mineral resources, the conduct of research in mining and utilization of mineral substances, and the promotion of safety in the mineral industries; the Bureau of Reclamation, in many respects a rival of the Army Corps of Engineers as the builder of public works to bring water to the lands of the west, including development of power; the Fish and Wildlife Service; the Bureau of Outdoor Recreation; the Geological Survey, a research bureau engaged in compiling and publishing information about the nation's mineral, water, and other resources; the National Park Service, with about 180 national parks, historic sites, and recreation areas; and the Bonneville, Alaska, Southwestern, and Southeastern Power administrations, which market electric power generated at federal reservoirs.

10. Agriculture.—The foremost mission of the Department of Agriculture is to promote the general interests of those who produce from the soil—"agriculture" being a collective term that includes enterprises organized as private corporations, owners of family farms, homesteaders, tenants, and sharecroppers. The mission of the department is not limited to farmers but is also directed to assisting rural communities, conserving and improving land, water, and timber, improving household management for families generally, and eliminating malnutrition.

Each USDA agency has its own primary functions. The Agricultural Stabilization and Conservation Service carries out price-support and production-adjustment programs. The Commodity Credit Corporation finances these programs. The Federal Crop Insurance Corporation insures crop-production costs against loss from weather, insects, and diseases. The Farmer Cooperative Service helps farmers help themselves through joint action. The Commodity Exchange Authority maintains fair trading practices and competitive pricing on designated commodity exchanges. The Foreign Agricultural Service expands exports through market-development activities, and the Foreign Economic Development Service provides training and instruction to improve agriculture in developing countries. The Farmers Home Administration extends credit to enable farmers to buy or improve their farms and finances farm and rural housing, recreational facilities, small rural business enterprises, and community water and sewer systems. The Rural Electrification Administration brings electric and telephone service to rural people. (The Farm Credit Administration is an independent agency not under the control of the USDA.)

The Soil Conservation Service provides technical and financial help to individuals and communities in conserving and improving land and water resources. The Forest Service manages the nation's 154 national forests and 19 national grasslands. The Agricultural Research Service and the Cooperative State Research Service, which works closely with state experiment stations and forestry institutions, carry out research on the production, marketing, and utilization of agricultural products as well as research on nutrition and the control and eradication of plant and animal diseases and pests. The Economic Research Service and the Statistical Reporting Service provide economic and statistical information on crops and livestock, prices and income, conservation, and rural development, foreign agriculture, and other data. The Extension Service, the education arm of the department, helps farmers, rural residents, and the general public apply research and technology to farm, home, and community development. The Consumer and Marketing Service grades and inspects agricultural commodities, provides marketing services, and promotes fair play in agricultural markets. The Food and Nutrition Service administers the food stamp program and other programs of food assistance to children and the needy.

11. Commerce.—The responsibilities of the federal government in the field of commerce, broadly defined, are widely scattered. The Commerce Department is essentially a service agency with almost no regulatory duties except export-import controls and strategic-materials stockpile management. Regulatory duties are exercised for the most part by such independent bodies as the Federal Trade Commission, which seeks to guard fair competition; the Securities and Exchange Commission, which polices the stock market; and the Interstate Commerce Commission, the Civil Aeronautics Board, the Federal Communications Commission, and the Federal Power Commission, with regulatory powers over surface transport, air transport, wire and radio communication, and hydroelectric power and natural gas.

The Department of Commerce deals with domestic and international commercial affairs. The first field is handled by the Office of Business Economics, devoted to long-range as well as short-run analyses of the national economy, which are made available in the form of the monthly *Survey of Current Business*; the Bureau of the Census; and the Economic Development Administration. The second field falls within the competence of the Bureau of International Commerce, which publishes *International Commerce*.

The department performs a number of basic national services. These are represented by the Bureau of the Census, as one of the federal government's major fact-finding and statistical agencies; the National Bureau of Standards, conducting for the government fundamental research and related technical activities in physics, mathematics, chemistry, and engineering; the Patent Office; and the Maritime Administration, concerned with aid to shipping. In 1970 the National Oceanic and Atmospheric Administration (NOAA) was created to conduct research on the atmosphere and marine resources. The Bureau of Commercial Fisheries, formerly in the Interior Department, was transferred to NOAA, which also oversees the Environmental Science Services Administration, the parent body of the Coast and Geodetic Survey and the National Weather Service.

Of considerable importance to the national economy are independent agencies, such as the Federal Home Loan Bank Board, the Federal Deposit Insurance Corporation, and the Atomic Energy Commission. The Small Business Administration, also independent, provides financial and other assistance to small business.

12. Labor.—The fundamental mandate of the Department of Labor is to foster the welfare of American wage earners, improve their working conditions, and advance their opportunities for profitable and rewarding employment.

The department's organizational structure takes into consideration new emphasis on the disadvantaged and the more traditional focus on the workingman. Primary responsibility for the training of the disadvantaged lies in the Manpower Administration.

Included in the Manpower Administration are the U.S. Training and Employment Service, which administers the major manpower training programs (the Neighborhood Youth Corps, the Work Incentive Program, On-the-Job Training) and oversees state employment service; the Unemployment Insurance Service, which reviews state unemployment-insurance operations; the Bureau of Apprenticeship and Training, which formulates standards for the training of skilled workers in industry; and the Job Corps for the training of disadvantaged youth.

A variety of services for American wage earners are provided by the Wage and Labor Standards Administration. The Bureau of Labor Standards promotes occupational health and safety, investigates potentially hazard-producing processes and machines, and develops recommended control standards. The Bureau of Employees' Compensation is charged with the administration of the accident-compensation program for federal employees and certain types of private employment subject to federal legislation. The Women's Bureau serves as a focal point for efforts to make more effective use of abilities and potentials of women in all aspects of society. The Wage and Hour and Public Contracts Division assures minimum rates of pay, in general, and protection of youthful workers against exploitation, in particular, and supervises the observation in government contracts of fair employment.

Concern with labour-management relations is centred in the Labor-Management Services Administration. The Office of Labor-Management and Welfare-Pension Reports requires the public disclosure of the financial affairs of labour organizations and regulates some of their internal procedures, particularly with respect to the election of union officers. The Office of Veterans' Reemployment Rights helps returning veterans obtain reemployment and related benefits with their former employers. The Office of Labor-Management Relations Services participates in particular dispute-problem situations.

Other bureaus include the Bureau of International Labor Affairs, charged with the responsibility for the participation of the United States in the International Labour Organisation, and the Bureau of Labor Statistics, the main repository within the federal government of information about employment, manpower, productivity, earnings, hours and wages, industrial relations, accidents, price trends, and costs, as well as standards of living. This information is made public in special bulletins and in the *Monthly Labor Review.*

Essential additional functions are carried out by such separate agencies as the National Labor Relations Board, concerned with protecting collective bargaining and eliminating unfair labour practices; the Federal Mediation and Conciliation Service; and the National Mediation Board, applicable to railway labour.

13. Health, Education, and Welfare.—The Department of Health, Education, and Welfare was established in 1953 as an elevation of the Federal Security Agency. Its total budget is the largest of all domestic departments. The department administers some 250 different programs, the oldest of which is the Public Health Service hospitals established in 1798. There are seven operating agencies in the department. The National Institutes of Health, the Health Services and Mental Health Administration (which includes the National Institute of Mental Health), the Food and Drug Administration, and the Environmental Health Service comprise the four operating units of the Public Health Service. Legislation in the 1960s greatly expanded the health activities of the department.

The Office of Education was for many years limited primarily to providing statistical information and technical advice along with some small programs of federal aid for limited categories of education. The enactment in the mid-1960s of federal legislation providing for major programs of federal aid to education changed the basic character of the office to an operating agency with extensive administrative functions and substantial funds for schools, colleges, and universities. The Social Security Administration, originally the Social Security Board, administers the social security program (old-age, survivors, and disability insurance) and the Medicare program. The social security program is the largest single insurance system in the world. The Social and Rehabilitation Service, established in 1967, includes the Community Services Administration, the Rehabilitation Services Administration, the Administration on Aging, the Assistance Payments Administration (which handles federal funds to the states for welfare), and the Medical Services Administration (which administers federal funds for Medicaid). The Office of Child Development reports to the Office of the secretary of HEW.

Financial aid is provided through the department to the American Printing House for the Blind, Louisville, Ky.; Gallaudet College for deaf students, Washington, D.C.; Howard University, Washington, D.C., founded in 1867 to provide higher education for Negroes; and St. Elizabeths Hospital, Washington, D.C., a government institution for the mentally ill. (Wr. J. C.)

14. Housing and Urban Development.—In 1965, upon the recommendation of President Johnson, Congress authorized the establishment of a new Cabinet Department of Housing and Urban Development. Robert C. Weaver (*q.v.*) was appointed the first head of the department and thus became the first Negro to sit in a president's Cabinet. The nucleus of the department was the Housing and Home Finance Agency, which Weaver had headed since 1961. It was a large, diffuse organization that had developed over the years and included such agencies as the Federal Housing Administration, Urban Renewal Administration, and Public Housing Administration. Assistant secretaries administer the department's programs in research and technology, housing production and mortgage credit, metropolitan planning and development, renewal and housing management, model cities, and equal opportunity. (F. M. M.; Wr. J. C.)

15. Transportation.—The Department of Transportation was established in 1966 with appointment of its first secretary, Alan Boyd, formerly undersecretary of commerce. A consolidation of 31 previously existing agencies and bureaus, the department was concerned with problems ranging from rush-hour traffic to supersonic air travel, and including auto safety. Among the organizations included in the new department were such independent agencies as the Federal Aviation Agency and the St. Lawrence Seaway Development Corporation, and the following from other departments: the Bureau of Public Roads and the Great Lakes Pilotage Administration (Commerce); the Coast Guard (Treasury); and the Alaska Railroad (Interior).

16. Postal Administration.—Although the Post Office Department managed the largest business in the world, until 1971 the basic management decisions of the department affecting rates, employee wages, facilities investment, and numerous operational guidelines were made by the Congress. In addition, postmasters were presidential appointees with life tenure, further reducing the management flexibility of the departmental top staff.

The six basic functional divisions that administered the department were the Bureau of Operations, responsible for the basic mail-processing and delivery activities including international transportation of mail; the Bureau of Planning and Marketing; the Bureau of Finance and Administration; the Bureau of Facilities; the Bureau of Personnel; and the Bureau of Research and Engineering. Within the office of the postmaster general a special assistant handled international postal affairs, and another special assistant was in charge of public information and educational programs. Finally, the Bureau of the Chief Postal Inspector combined auditing and police functions and was responsible for the security of the mails as well as for the prevention of their use in violation of federal law (fraud, espionage, obscenity, etc.).

The U.S. postal system continued to experience significant growth in mail volume without significant change in methods or mechanization from its earliest days. As a result of the deficits and dissatisfactions this promoted, considerable interest had been building to significantly change postal procedures and organization. The ultimate recommendation in this area came in June 1968, when a presidential commission appointed to study the postal service recommended that the department be removed from Cabinet status and transformed into an independent government corporation (similar to the Tennessee Valley Authority) to be administered by a presidentially appointed board. This was fully implemented by the passage of the Postal Reorganization Act, signed by the president on Aug. 12, 1970, which created the United States Postal Service, effective July 1, 1971. (*See* POSTAL SERVICES.)

(WR. J. C.)

III. GREAT BRITAIN

The executive powers of the central government in Britain are, by law or convention, vested in ministers who sit in Parliament. Each minister is individually answerable to Parliament for any exercise of the powers vested in him, whether action is taken by him personally or in his name by subordinates. Each minister has a retinue of officials who form a single establishment over which he presides personally. Some ministers in addition are responsible for other establishments which are separately organized and are often distinct legal entities, but which through constitutional evolution have come to work in ultimate subordination to a particular minister. All these official establishments are generally called government departments. Those over which ministers preside personally, and through which they perform their main executive duties, are often referred to collectively as ministries. Most of the others are charged with routine and relatively uncontroversial administrative tasks. The two groups comprise an immensely variegated collection of institutions, the range of whose functions and internal organization makes accurate brief generalization almost impossible. Three characteristics are common to all but a few, however: each is the entire responsibility of a minister, each is financed by direct grants from Parliament voted by an orthodox procedure, and each is staffed by members of a centrally recruited and integrated civil service.

All the ministries and a few of the other establishments can usefully be classified as major departments, and the rest as minor departments, but there is much room for argument as to exactly where the line between them should be drawn. Moreover, there is even doubt in some cases as to whether an institution is or is not a government department. There are a host of public authorities, variously entitled generically "nondepartmental bodies," "independent administrative authorities," "public corporations," etc., which are usually collegiate in form and in respect of which ministers have certain statutory powers. A few of them have certain characteristics—for instance in their financing and staffing—similar to those of unmistakable government departments, while a few of those institutions usually referred to as departments could not conceivably be regarded as government departments. In short, the very term government department cannot be precisely defined. In this context, the most that can be said safely is that after a Conservative government had taken office in 1970, there were about 15 major and some 50 minor government departments.

1. General Background, Nomenclature, and Status.—Contemporary Britain is used to the concept of a government department as a body of officials having its own continuous existence, its own traditions and philosophy, apart from the ministers who preside over it or are responsible for its actions for at most a few years at a time and often for much shorter periods. This does not imply that the minister is a mere cipher whose presence is nothing more than a necessary constitutional formality; indeed, while the strengths of ministers vary widely, the impact of ministers on a department will have at least the effect of lowering its status in relation to other departments, whereas a strong minister cannot only raise a department's relative status but can mold its stored traditions and procedures into a powerful and characteristic personal instrument which may bear the impress of his suzerainty for a generation. Nonetheless, his mastery is based on a delicate balance between his own personal and political authority on the one hand, and his officials' expertise and experience on the other.

This whole concept reflects complete acceptance of the modern system of responsible cabinet government, but that system only came to full maturity in the middle of the 19th century. The origins of the central departments go back centuries before that, to a time when the central government was contained in the personal household of the medieval king: when there was no question of responsibility to anyone except the king, no "constitutional" opposition, and, therefore, no distinction between a "political" executive and a "neutral" civil service.

The major departments have sprung from three main sources—from individual officers of household and state, from the Privy Council, and from Parliament. The first source had produced, early in the 17th century at least the embryo forms of the Lord Chancellor's Department; the Treasury; the Post Office, and the Ministry of Public Building and Works (the last two to cease existence as separate government departments in 1969 and 1970, respectively). It also produced the office of secretary of state, which was shared by two men of equal standing as early as 1540 and, while remaining a single office, has since been divided among as many as eight heads of departments simultaneously. The Board of Trade (set up in the 17th century but ceasing to be a ministry in 1970) and some of the scientific research organizations were in form committees of the Privy Council, while the Department of Education and Science and the Ministry of Agriculture, Fisheries, and Food derived from similar committees. The remaining ministries or their immediate forerunners were created by acts of Parliament in the 19th and 20th centuries. Until 1915 it was usually the practice of Parliament to establish in each case a board composed of some existing ministers plus a new minister, who was made president of the board. Since 1915 new ministerial offices have been set up by statute without any hint of collegiate authority. Thus, constitutions of departments because the British have indulged an indigenous weakness for retaining outward institutional forms after the realities have long ceased to correspond with them. Thus, the basic constitutional simplicity and uniformity of the system is by no means apparent from a list of contemporary ministers and departments. The straightforward "minister of . . ." and "ministry of . . ." is used for fewer than half the departmental chiefs and their major departments. The other ministries are the "offices" of secretaries of state or are "departments" under a secretary of state or a minister. The Treasury is answerable to the chancellor of the exchequer, and so on.

The variety of origins is reflected in the variety of titles and nomenclature.

It would be incorrect to declare that government departments form a hierarchy, if by this is implied the existence of a strict line of command running downward from one supreme department. Each minister must answer personally to Parliament for anything done in his name by his officials: he cannot escape responsibility by claiming that he was merely carrying out the instructions of a "senior" colleague, for the constitution does not recognize any inequality between ministers, and therefore cannot do so between their departments. But just as the prime minister has become more than the traditional "first among equals" in a ministerial context, so there is to some extent if not a hierarchy at any rate a degree of aristocracy among departments in Whitehall which perhaps has to be felt rather than explained. Some of the departments which are in the front rank are also among the most ancient, simply because they deal and have dealt for centuries with the most fundamental functions of government. But formal precedence derived from origins and nomenclature is no longer a safe guide to relative status. Tangible proofs of current political and administrative importance, rather than antiquity or title, are the hard main bases of such distinctions as exist. Thus, now that there are too many ministries for all their chiefs to be members of the Cabinet, those which are directly represented in the highest council of the state are inevitably lifted a little above their fellows. A department whose minister was unknown to the constitution

20 years ago but who now sits in the Cabinet may carry more weight, for the time being at any rate, than a department headed by a secretary of state and dating back to the 15th century.

Departments are shown in a proper perspective if they are grouped roughly according to their functional affinities, though there can be no absolute precision about what each major function of government comprises. In the following sections all the ministries are mentioned, but only a selection of the minor departments is included. Administrative organization exclusively concerned with Scotland and Wales is referred to briefly in a final paragraph. (See also SCOTLAND: *Administration and Social Conditions*.) Most of the text treats of departments which deal with the whole of the United Kingdom or with England and Wales as one unit. The first section deals with the overall control of the government machine and with the supervision of the economy; it has pride of place in a departmental context primarily because it includes the Treasury, whose position has been unique, and whose influence has extended far beyond normal financial boundaries.

2. The Treasury: Economic and Administrative Supervision.—The Treasury began in the 12th century as one part of the financial machinery of the kingdom which was concerned exclusively with the receipt and issue of money. At its head was the lord high treasurer, but his office was put "in commission" on several occasions in the late 17th century, and permanently in 1714. The lords commissioners of the Treasury are the formal heads of the department, but the first lord is now always prime minister, the junior lords are government whips in the House of Commons, and the effective ministerial chief is the second lord, or chancellor of the exchequer, who first appeared on the Treasury scene in the 13th century.

The modern Treasury is the nearest equivalent in Britain to a ministry of finance, but it does both more and less than the ministry of finance in other countries. The Treasury does not collect revenue; this is done mainly by two large departments also answerable to the chancellor of the exchequer—the Board of Inland Revenue and the Board of Customs and Excise. Moreover, much specialized financial work is carried on by such minor departments as the National Debt Office, the Paymaster General's Office, the Royal Mint, and the Public Works Loan Board, all ultimately responsible to the chancellor of the exchequer. The Treasury itself is a relatively small department, concerned primarily with the big aspects of fiscal policy, domestic and external, including the preparation of the annual budget.

But the function which gives the Treasury its peculiar prestige in British administration is its responsibility for controlling departmental expenditure. The control is not simply a straightforward exercise of crude authority. The Treasury does not have officers attached to other departments to watch over their spending, nor is it concerned with the audit of departmental accounts. Control is achieved rather through continuous and delicate negotiations between the Treasury and departments before the former gives its approval for proposed expenditure by the latter. In the last resort, Treasury control depends for its effectiveness on the strength of the chancellor of the exchequer in the Cabinet. As the chancellor is always a very senior minister, his political strength is usually considerable. In addition, the connection of the prime minister with the department (even if largely nominal), the high calibre of the Treasury staff, the conventional high status of the department, and the well-understood "rules of the game" in Whitehall have combined for a century to make the Treasury though not the master, at least more than the equal of the other departments. From the 1860s onward the control of expenditure gave the Treasury far-reaching powers over the structure, the pay, and the working conditions of the civil service. The permanent headship of the Treasury was formally recognized as the most important post in the home civil service in 1920. The department extended its influence into the sphere of organization and methods, and into the general arrangement of the whole central administration. In 1968, however, following the recommendation of the Fulton Committee's *Report on the Civil Service*, the government established a separate department under the prime minister's general direction to deal with civil-service affairs.

Since World War II there has been a continuous problem of how to allocate the new functions of overall control of the economy and the supreme direction of economic planning. For several years during and after the war a small central staff of economists and statisticians was attached to the Cabinet Office, which is mainly a nonpolicymaking secretariat whose origins go back to the secretariat of the Committee of Imperial Defence set up in 1904. The Cabinet Office, responsible to the prime minister, took its present form in 1916 and has grown considerably in recent years. By 1953 most of the economists and planning officers had been moved into the Treasury, with the task of coordinating the economic policies of other departments and of advising the chancellor of the exchequer on the making of national economic policy. In 1964, most of the medium- and long-term planning responsibilities were entrusted to a separate Department of Economic Affairs, till its responsibilities were devolved in the late 1960s and then re-subsumed in 1970 under the Department of the Environment. Thus at the beginning of the 1970s the Treasury itself was still responsible for fiscal and financial policy and for the control of public expenditure, with the Cabinet Office continuing and extending its coordinative role, strengthened further in 1970 by the extension of its powers of review of the policies of the various departments.

3. Public Order and Justice.—One of the most distinctive characteristics of British government, which marks it off from the other countries of Western Europe, is the relatively low degree of central executive control over local administration, particularly in the context of police power. There are over 100 police forces, and all save the Metropolitan Police, whose area covers greater London, are under local control. In British central administration the extent of local autonomy is also reflected in the lack of any departments which a continental European would readily recognize as ministries of the interior and of justice. Central powers relating to matters of justice and internal order are exercised in England and Wales by the Home Office and the Lord Chancellor's Departments.

The Home Office is the main department of the secretary of state for the Home Department (or home secretary) and took its present basic form in 1782. It was throughout most of the 19th century the natural choice for any new functions needing domestic administration, but as this sphere of government grew, various blocks of work were removed and became the nucleus of the business of new departments. The practice of turning first to the Home Office has remained, however, with the result that in addition to its major continuing functions, the department is responsible for exercising a miscellaneous group of powers to which no other department has a better claim. Its major continuing task is helping to ensure the maintenance of public order—a term which covers inspecting and giving advice to local police forces, the organization of the lower criminal courts, a general interest in the working of the criminal law, and the promotion of necessary amendments. It also deals with such matters as immigration and naturalization, civil defense, aliens, certain safety regulations, the care of children deprived of normal home life, election administration, control of dangerous drugs, inspection of local fire services, liquor licensing, etc. Prison administration was organized by a separate prison commission until 1963, when it became a direct responsibility of the Home Office. The Metropolitan Police is headed by a commissioner who is answerable to the home secretary.

In England and Wales the organization of the lower civil courts and all the superior courts, the appointment of minor judicial officers, and the duty of advising the crown on the appointment of judges of the Supreme Court are the principal administrative functions of the lord chancellor, whose small department has grown from the dimensions of a mere private office in the course of the 20th century. The lord chancellor is also answerable to Parliament for the work of the public trustee, the Land Registry, and the Public Record Office. Responsibility for the conduct of the most important crown prosecutions and for all government litigation rests in England and Wales with the attorney general and with the solicitor-general, who are served by a small professional staff that comprises the Law Officers' Departments. The attorney general also supervises the work of the director of public prosecutions.

4. External Affairs.—The earliest secretaries of state were primarily occupied with diplomatic duties, and from 1640 divided their interests geographically, one secretary taking the countries of northern Europe as his sphere of influence, the other dealing with southern Europe and with the relatively little domestic administrative business which came the way of the secretaries. In the 17th and 18th centuries, Scottish and colonial business were added, and a third secretary of state held office from 1707 to 1725, from 1741 to 1745, and between 1768 and 1782. In this last year the geographical division of interest was changed; the northern secretary became in effect the foreign secretary, and the southern secretary became responsible for home and colonial affairs. In 1801 a third secretary of state was appointed, this time for war and colonies, and in 1854 these two subjects each became the responsibility of a separate secretary. Meanwhile, since 1786, the British government had assumed certain responsibility for India, where the East India Company still held sway, and had appointed a board of commissioners for the affairs of India. Full governmental control followed in 1858, under a new secretary of state for India. For the next 70 years there were three "external" departments—the Foreign, Colonial, and India offices. After World War I, as a result of the development of self-government in some of the larger colonies—called dominions after 1907—the dominions branch of the Colonial Office was made into a separate Dominions Office in 1925, and a new office of secretary of state for dominion affairs was created. In 1937 a Burma Office was established, though it and the India Office remained the responsibility of a single minister. In just over two decades after the end of World War II, all but a tiny handful of the British colonial territories achieved independence, most of them choosing to become full members of the Commonwealth. This enormous change was reflected administratively in the disappearance of the India and Burma offices in 1947–48, and in the renaming of the Dominions Office as the Commonwealth Relations Office at the same time. The Colonial Office retained its separate status until 1966, when the remaining colonial responsibilities passed temporarily to the renamed Commonwealth Office. In 1968, the Commonwealth Office and the Foreign Office were put together as the Foreign and Commonwealth Office, whose officials (from previously separate corps) hold posts which are interchangeable with posts at missions overseas, and are known collectively as Her Majesty's Diplomatic Service. As the colonial responsibility declined, interest in and extension of aid to developing countries continued and developed. In 1961 the Department of Technical Cooperation was formed, and in 1964 was renamed Ministry of Overseas Development, which, in 1970, was planned to become a branch of the Foreign and Commonwealth Office.

5. Defense.—The evolution of two departments to deal comprehensively with the administration and control of the Navy and Army was slow and complicated. The Admiralty and War Office were, in short, the results of bringing together over a long period a large assortment of naval and military administrative authorities, and the Air Ministry, established in 1918 by removing the relevant sections of the two older departments and merging them, took the same constitutional form, which reflected a compromise between the special military need for operational flexibility and the insistence of Parliament on ultimate civil control. Each department was headed by a board or council comprising the highest service officers together with the minister as chairman, a junior minister, and the secretary, who was a civil servant.

The concept of a single, interservice strategy, of coordinated naval and military planning, was first given institutional recognition in the creation of the Committee of Imperial Defence and its secretariat in 1902–04. The value of this device was demonstrated by its being the basis in World Wars I and II of the War Cabinet Organization, and in 1946 the military secretariat was adapted and extended to form a Ministry of Defence. The minister of defense sat in the Cabinet, and his powers in general defense matters were steadily increased. In 1958 a Defence Board on the lines of the Board of Admiralty and the Army and Air councils was appointed, with the minister of defense as chairman.

The three service departments retained a direct responsibility for the detailed administration of the Navy, Army, and Air Force, but after 1946 their ministers were not members of the Cabinet. In 1964 the Admiralty, War Office, and Air Ministry were merged in a new unified Ministry of Defence, under a secretary of state, assisted by three ministers of state and three parliamentary undersecretaries. Each pair of these ministers was formally attached to one of the armed forces, but in 1967 the three ministers of state were replaced by two. One of the new ministers became responsible for the administration of the three services, while the other was made responsible for equipment. Henceforward the Navy, Army, and Air Force were represented in the government only by the three parliamentary undersecretaries.

The problem of allocating responsibility for the supply and equipment of the defense forces has a long history. The most ancient predecessor of modern departments in this context was the Board of Ordnance, set up in the 15th century and abolished in 1855 during the Crimean War, when the need to consolidate administrative authority in the Army and Air Office was the prevailing view. In World War I the task of supplying the Army was entrusted to a Ministry of Munitions, which was disbanded in 1921. The Ministry of Supply was established in 1939, and in 1946 took over the functions of a wartime Ministry of Aircraft Production. For some war and postwar years the Ministry of Supply had also civil responsibilities, especially in connection with the control of raw materials for industry, and under the Labour government of 1945–51 was charged with the general supervision of the iron-and-steel and heavy-engineering industries. After 1951, however, the department was relieved of much of its nonmilitary work, and concentrated on supplying the Army and Air Force with most of their stores, and the Navy mainly with aircraft. In 1959 the Ministry of Supply was abolished, and its functions returned to the three service ministries, except for the supply of aircraft and missiles, which was a major responsibility of a Ministry of Aviation between 1959 and 1967, and subsequently of the Ministry of Technology till the latter's abolition in 1970, when a separate Ministry of Aviation Supply was temporarily created.

6. Trade, Industry, Communications, Agriculture.—One of the features of contemporary British administration is the existence of recognized channels of contact between the state and every trade and industry, through which there is a two-way traffic—various degrees of control, advice, and assistance passing down from the government, and information and requests for help and cooperation passing upward from producers and traders. The responsibility for dealing with these economic units or groups is widely distributed among the major departments. Some trades and industries have special links with departments whose primary administrative interests are not economic—for example, the manufacturers of drugs and medical appliances look to the Department of Health and Social Security, while the construction industry turns to the Ministry of the Environment. But there are departments whose whole concern is either with one or more groups of producers and traders, or with a range of administrative matters of general concern to the commercial world.

The Post Office ceased in 1969 to be an orthodox government department and became, instead, a public corporation. As an organization, the office was the oldest government department. A master of the posts was appointed about 1512, and a general post office was established by Cromwell in 1657. It remained a self-contained unit whose enormous growth had encompassed not merely the postal service but also a near monopoly of telecommunications; it was, in addition, a savings bank, separated in 1969 as the Department for National Savings, and it still provided an ubiquitous "counter" service for various other departments on an agency basis. (See also POSTAL SERVICES.)

The Board of Trade was for long the main progenitor of departments dealing with economic matters. As a committee of the Privy Council, the board had an almost continuous existence since 1621, but its later constitution dates from 1786, and its formal duties laid down in an order in council of that year were "the consideration of all matters relating to trade and foreign plantations." Until the middle of the 19th century the board's role was mainly consultative and advisory, but thereafter it became, under the unequivocal leadership of its president, a powerful executive department exercising regulatory powers over commercial practice, shipping and railways, patents, fisheries, etc., while also developing further as the central department concerned with domestic industry and external trade.

The board's range of functions was greatest just before World War I. During that war, and frequently since, the board lost parts of its work to new departments, and from time to time has regained some of those responsibilities. The complex pattern of transfers and retransfers between the board and the departments which were mostly offshoots of it reflected the great increase in governmental functions relating to economic affairs and the changing pressures and emphases of political and economic conditions and government policies. The board had a general advisory, stimulative, and consultative role in relation to the whole world of manufacture and commerce; it was a regulatory department with many routine functions concerning companies, bankruptcy, patents, etc.; it was the central department which all trades and industries other than those allotted to other departments considered to be "their" channel of communication with the central government; and it was the central authority concerned with the operational aspects of shipping and civil aviation. In 1970 the board, together with the Ministry of Technology, was subsumed under the new Department of Trade and Industry.

The Department of Employment and Productivity (renamed Department of Employment in 1970) was the title bestowed in 1968 on the Ministry of Labour, first detached from the Board of Trade in 1917, and from 1939 to 1959 called the Ministry of Labour and National Service. It offers a wide range of services to employers and employees, mainly through a national network of employment exchanges, and is vitally involved in the distribution of manpower and with the maintenance of good relations between management and the trade unions. The Ministry of Transport (dating from 1919 and responsible for governmental functions concerning railways, roads, road transport, ports, and inland waterways) in 1970 became part of the new Department of the Environment. This big new department, like the Department of Trade and Industry, was set up to unify responsibilities that had previously been scattered, and it took over their functions from the Ministry of Housing and Local Government, the Ministry of Transport, and the Ministry of Public Buildings and Works, though separate ministers continued to be responsible for the departmental sections which these had now become, under the secretaries of state for trade and industry and for the environment, respectively. The Ministry of Power, whose origins are traceable to the subordinate Mines Department of the Board of Trade set up in 1920, is concerned primarily with fuel and power policy, with the publicly owned coal, gas, and electricity industries, and with private petroleum and natural-gas enterprises. In 1969 it came into the Ministry of Technology, itself part of the Department of Trade and Industry since 1970.

The need to stimulate the effective application by industry of the findings of the most modern research led to the creation of the Ministry of Technology in 1964. Within three years, the new department had become the sponsor of the engineering, shipbuilding, aircraft, and electronics industries, and it had inherited from the disbanded Ministry of Aviation that department's defense-supply responsibilities till in 1970 it became part of the new Department of Trade and Industry. At the same time a temporary Ministry of Aviation Supply was created to take care of its aerospace research interests.

Government did not become administratively interested in agriculture until 1883, when a Privy Council Committee was set up, which gave place six years later to a statutory Board of Agriculture with its own president. It had very limited functions and in 1903 was strengthened by acquiring responsibility for fisheries from the Board of Trade, thereupon taking the title of Board of Agriculture and Fisheries. After 1912 it was concerned only with agriculture in England and Wales, and it was never concerned with fisheries in Scotland. In 1919 the board became a ministry. During World Wars I and II, the department had no part in the administration of controls on the distribution of food, which was handled by a separate Ministry of Food. After 1945 the greatly expanded Ministry of Agriculture and Fisheries continued to administer an enormous range of subsidies, technical advisory services, and a variety of controls. In 1955, when the second Ministry of Food was abolished, most of its remaining functions were handed over to the Ministry of Agriculture and Fisheries, which has since been known as the Ministry of Agriculture, Fisheries, and Food. The department has within its purview domestic food production and marketing in England and Wales, all external procurement, and the internal distribution of foodstuffs.

7. Social Services.—For the early history of social service administration in Great Britain see POOR LAW and SOCIAL WELFARE. Between 1830 and 1930 the adaptation of the poor law and interest in public health brought about the evolution of two new administrative phenomena—a national structure of "all-purpose" elected local councils, and central departments to cooperate with and supervise those councils. Between World Wars I and II, the principal central department was the Ministry of Health, which was set up in 1919 to replace the Local Government Board of 1871. The Ministry of Health was not only responsible for the central supervision of poor-law work and public-health services, and for the general constitutional and financial aspects of the local government system, but was also involved in the supervision of most of the growing contributory insurance programs. Unemployment insurance, however, was administered first through the Board of Trade and then through the Ministry of Labour. Mass unemployment disorganized the plans so badly that a special body had to be formed in 1934—the Unemployment Assistance Board—to relieve the strain on both the unemployment-insurance program and on the local authorities who were providing public assistance.

The acceptance of the basic proposals of the Beveridge Report during World War II made it inevitable that the central administrative organization of the relevant social services, which had grown up piecemeal, should be much extended but at the same time be concentrated in fewer departments. The years from 1943 to 1951 saw not only the initiation of the National Health Service in 1948, but also three large departmental changes. In 1943, a separate Ministry of Town and Country Planning relieved the Ministry of Health of part of its general responsibility for environmental services. In 1944, a Ministry of National Insurance took over the programs of national insurance and industrial-injuries insurance, and later introduced a new service of family allowances. And in 1948 the old Unemployment Assistance Board, which had been renamed the Assistance Board in 1940, became the National Assistance Board and was made responsible for all necessary residual financial assistance, thus "nationalizing" public assistance and freeing the local authorities and the Ministry of Health of all their old poor-law functions. The burden on the Ministry of Health became very great, however, and in 1951 the department was divided. General local-government matters and environmental services such as housing, water supply, and sewerage were taken over by the Ministry of Town and Country Planning to form the Ministry of Housing and Local Government (briefly re-created as the Department of Local Government and Regional Planning in 1969 and since 1970 a part of the Department of the Environment)—the direct descendant of the Local Government Board of 1871-1919. The central administration of the National Health Service was left to the Ministry of Health.

After 1951 there were further extensions and amalgamations. In 1953 the Ministry of National Insurance was combined with the Ministry of Pensions—a department which dated from 1916 and had been charged with the care of war pensioners—to form the Ministry of Pensions and National Insurance. This department was renamed Ministry of Social Security in 1966, and the National Assistance Board became the Supplementary Benefits Commission, within the new ministry, at the same time. In 1968 the Ministries of Health and of Social Security were merged into a single Department of Health and Social Security under the control of a new secretary of state. (See also SOCIAL SECURITY.)

8. Education and Scientific Research.—The principal central authority is the Department of Education and Science, created in 1964 to bring together two hitherto separate strands of administrative development. Governmental concern for education began in the 1830s with a modest grant of public money for schools, and in 1839 a committee of the Privy Council was set up to take charge of the distribution of subsequent grants. A department appeared under the committee in 1856, and in 1899 both gave place to a Board of Education with its own president. In turn, this was converted into the Ministry of Education in 1944. This organization continues as part of the present department and oversees the school system, which is under the immediate control of local authorities. University education is supervised by the University Grants Committee, which came within the purview of the Treasury from its origin in 1919 until 1964, but is now within the departmental sphere of the secretary of state for education and science.

Scientific research sponsored by government has had a much shorter and more complicated institutional history. Defense research has always received the most attention and funds, and has always been—and remains—predominantly a responsibility of the military authorities. Civil science has become steadily more important during the 20th century, and some institutions were established before World War I, such as the National Physical Laboratory and the Development Commission, dating from 1900 and 1909, respectively. Between 1916 and 1965 there grew up four major research organizations—the Department of Scientific and Industrial Research (DSIR), the Medical Research Council, the Agricultural Research Council, and the Nature Conservancy. These were formally supervised by committees of the Privy Council but in fact had had considerable autonomy. After World War II there was increasing concern for research in technology, and among major innovations were the National Research Development Corporation (NRDC, 1949) and the Atomic Energy Authority (AEA, 1954). The Ministry of Technology functioned in 1964-70; meanwhile, in 1965 the Privy Council research committees were abolished. Much of the technological work of the old DSIR was transferred to the Ministry of Technology, along with responsibility for the NRDC and the AEA. The secretary of state for education and science was given the main role of supervising and encouraging civil science. He is advised by the Council for Scientific Policy; research is carried on by the Science Research Council, the Medical and Agricultural Research councils, the Natural Environment Research Council, and the Social Science Research Council.

9. Common Services.—Much work is done by departments for each other on an agency basis, and a number mainly provide services common to all or a large number of departments. The largest of these was the Department of the Environment in 1970. It became part of the Department of the Environment in 1970. It was the modern counterpart of the surveyor general of works, whose immediate predecessor was the Office of Works set up in 1851 and first converted into a ministry roughly its present form in 1940. Its main common-service task had been to provide accommodation, furnishings, heating, cleaning, etc., for departments, and to meet the very large demands of the defense departments for works services. In addition, it had certain responsibilities for parks and palaces, museums, and ancient monuments, and was responsible for the Building Research Station. No other common-service department is presided over by a minister personally; Her Majesty's Stationery Office, which provides stationery, printing services, and mechanical office equipment, is ultimately responsible to the chancellor of the exchequer. So, too, is the Treasury solicitor, whose department handles the legal work of departments without their own legal officers, and the Central Office of Information, which provides publicity material for other departments. Among minor departments largely if not always primarily concerned to provide common services are the Ordnance Survey, the Government Actuary, the Central Statistical Office, and the General Register Office.

10. Scotland and Wales.—Since the appointment of a secretary for Scotland in 1885, there has been a steady process of domestic devolution from Whitehall to Edinburgh. Scotland's minister—now a secretary of state—exercises his powers through four departments—Home and Health, Agriculture and Fisheries, Education, and Development. Much of the legal administration in Scotland is carried on through the lord advocate's department. In 1964 a Welsh Office was established, in Cardiff, under a secretary of state. His responsibilities include roads, housing, new towns, forestry, the organization of local government, and from 1970 child care functions and a share in the administration of the urban program of grants. He is also generally concerned with government policy for Wales, particularly in the context of economic and planning matters.

BIBLIOGRAPHY.—*United States:* U.S. National Archives and Records Service, *United States Government Organization Manual* (annual); President's Committee on Administrative Management, *Report with Studies* (1937); (first) Commission on Organization of the Executive Branch of the Government, *General Management of the Executive Branch* (1949); Schuyler C. Wallace, *Federal Departmentalization: a Critique of Theories of Organization* (1941); F. Morstein Marx (ed.), "The Departmental System," *Elements of Public Administration*, 2nd ed., ch. 9 (1959); Herbert Emmerich, *Essays on Federal Reorganization* (1950); Council of State Governments, *Reorganizing State Government: a Report on Administrative Management in the States and a Review of Recent Trends in Reorganization* (1950); Marver H. Bernstein, *The Job of the Federal Executive* (1958); B. D. Karl, *Executive Reorganization and Reform in the New Deal* (1963); William L. Cary, *Politics and the Regulatory Agencies* (1967)

Great Britain: W. R. Anson, *Law and Custom of the Constitution*, vol. ii, 4th ed. (1935); K. B. Smellie, *A Hundred Years of English Government*, 2nd ed. (1951); Royal Institute of Public Administration, *The Organization of British Central Government, 1914-1964*, ed. by D. N. Chester, written by F. M. G. Willson (1968); Sir James Marchant (ed.), "The Whitehall Series," of books on individual government departments, 12 vol. (1925-35); Sir Robert Fraser (ed.), "The New Whitehall Series," first 13 vol. (1954 et seq.); *Memoranda*, vol. i-iii, submitted to the Royal Commission on Scottish Affairs (HMSO, 1952-54); *Britain, an Official Handbook* (annual); *Annual Reports* of various departments (HMSO); *The Reorganization of Central Government*, Cmd. 4506 (Oct. 1970).
(F. M. G. W.; X.)

GOVERNOR, a common political title for the official head of a dependent or component unit in a larger constitutional structure. Governorships of one type have existed in the British, French, Dutch, and other empires; those of another type exist in the states of the United States, and in Brazil and Mexico. (For the first type, *see* GOVERNOR-GENERAL.)

In the state governments of the United States, the governorship derived from British origins but traced a separate course. The earliest state constitutions, through reaction against nonresponsible colonial executives, subordinated the executive branch to the legislative. In 11 states governors were elected by the legislatures, generally for short terms. Subsequent discontent with overpowerful legislatures, and the analogy of the strong presidency, created a counteraction to emancipate the governor from legislative dominance. In the mid-19th century, further constitutional changes in many states, conforming to the doctrines of Jacksonian democracy, necessitated a long ballot to fill the principal executive positions, the governorship included, by popular election. The governor, coordinate with the legislature, consequently lacked adequate authority over the officials elected with him. By 1900, as state governments assumed new functions, legislatures also proceeded to multiply the number of separate administrative agencies. These were largely exempt from control by the governor because they were too numerous to supervise and many were headed by boards. The governorship was structurally unfit for its growing burdens, leadership sometimes gravitated from constitutionally elected officials to a party "boss" beyond the people's reach.

A reform movement, gathering momentum before World War I, proposed to democratize the government by simplifying its machinery and throwing squarely upon a strengthened executive branch the responsibility of public service. Following World War II, renewed interest in the improvement of state government resulted in further recommendations and action. Among specific remedies suggested were the short ballot, reducing the number of elective officials; reorganization of administrative agencies by a reduction in their number and consolidation of their functions; the adoption of a more businesslike executive budget, prepared and proposed by the governor; an increased emphasis on state planning; and centralization of many administrative and finance management functions in departments of administration or finance. Governors increasingly emerged as leading figures in most state governments. By the early 1960s, they served for terms of four years in the great majority of the states. More truly than in the 19th century, they functioned as chief executives, wielding effective authority over most administrative agencies and shouldering political responsibility.

Simultaneously, governors with public appeal actively initiated legislative policy. When occupying the position of party leaders, they placed between the executive and legislative branches a political link belying the dogma of the separation of powers.

BIBLIOGRAPHY.—Leslie Lipson, *The American Governor From Figurehead to Leader* (1939); Coleman B. Ransone, Jr., *The Office of Governor in the United States* (1956); Joseph E. Kallenbach, *The American Chief Executive: The Presidency and the Governorship* (1966)

(D. M. M.; L. LIP.; P. L. I.)

GOVERNOR, an automatic device designed to regulate the speed of a steam or gasoline engine or other prime mover. In most governors this speed is measured with the aid of centrifugal flyweights. The flyweights are driven at a speed proportional to that of the prime mover. The centrifugal force of the flyweights is balanced, completely or in part, by the force of compression of a speeder spring. In the simplest governor the motion of the flyweights is mechanically transmitted through the output shaft of the governor to the throttle or some equivalent device that meters the rate at which energy is fed to the prime mover (fig. 1). The steady state speed of the prime mover is set by the position of the end of the speeder spring opposite to that at which the flyweight force is applied.

A governor is designed to keep the prime mover speed at its assigned value regardless of variations in the load and changes in ambient conditions.

Where precise control is required, or an appreciable amount of power must be drawn from the governor to move the energy metering mechanism, a hydraulic governor is generally employed. A hydraulic governor (fig. 2) has as one component a mechanical governor, called in this instance a ballhead, similar to that shown in fig. 1. The output of the ballhead is amplified by a pilot valve and servomotor. The servomotor is usually a cylinder containing a piston and the output shaft of the governor is connected to the piston.

The valve controls the flow of oil to the two sides of the piston in the cylinder. In the case of a gasoline engine, or a dual fuel oil and gas engine operating on gas, the governor output shaft is often attached to the throttle.

An aircraft propeller governor controls the speed of the engine driving the propeller by varying the pitch of the propeller and thus changing the engine load. A diesel engine is controlled by connecting the governor output shaft to the rack which meters the rate at which fuel is injected.

On a steam turbine the governor positions the steam valve or valves which control the steam flow to the turbine. Similarly, a governor for a hydraulic reaction turbine of the Francis type positions the gates which vary the rate of water flow to the turbine. For a Kaplan turbine the governor also varies the pitch of the propeller blades through an extra servomotor. Governors for Pelton impulse turbines vary the areas of the jets of water striking the turbine buckets. The areas are varied rapidly by cutting into the jets with blades, and at the same time varied slowly by positioning needles in valves from which the jets emerge.

The output shaft of a gas turbine governor is connected to the fuel valve of the turbine. Provision is normally made to bring a combustion chamber temperature measurement, obtained directly or through the use of a computer, to the governor so as to limit the maximum and minimum fuel rates and thus keep this temperature within design limits. Computation of the combustion chamber temperature is necessary for fast limiting, and is based on the laws of thermodynamics relating this temperature to other physical variables.

Governors on oil and gas pipeline turbine-compressor units actually control pressure in the line. With the aid of pneumatic components the governor speed setting is adjusted from a measurement of this pressure.

The speed of the compressor is increased or decreased so as to keep the pressure constant.

Hydraulic positive displacement pump-motor units are used to provide infinitely variable speed ratio drives. The governor is driven by the motor, while the governor output is connected to a "wobble plate" which adjusts the rate of fluid flow out of the pump to the motor.

The speed of the output shaft of a hydraulic torque converter is controlled by a double governor, one driven by the engine and the other by the convertor, with the governors in a series combination rather than parallel.

The simplest mechanical governor is of the proportional type. A governor is said to be proportional if its output mechanism takes a position in proportion to the prime mover speed. For a speed droop governor, or governor on droop, on an isolated prime mover, the steady state prime mover speed is a function of the load, decreasing when the load is increased, and increasing when the load is decreased.

The simplest type of mechanical governor is of the constant-speed isochronous type.

The simplest type of hydraulic governor is of the constant-speed isochronous type. Such a governor will continue to make a correction as long as the prime mover speed deviates from the set value. The standard aircraft propeller governor is of this type.

The simple isochronous governor is an integral or reset governor, in that the out-

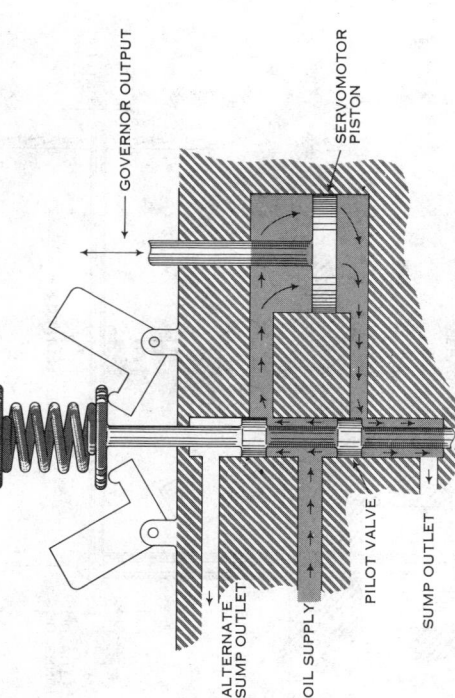

FIG. 2.—SCHEMATIC DRAWING OF SIMPLE ISOCHRONOUS HYDRAULIC GOVERNOR

GOVERNOR OUTPUT · SERVOMOTOR PISTON · ALTERNATE SUMP OUTLET · OIL SUPPLY · PILOT VALVE · SUMP OUTLET

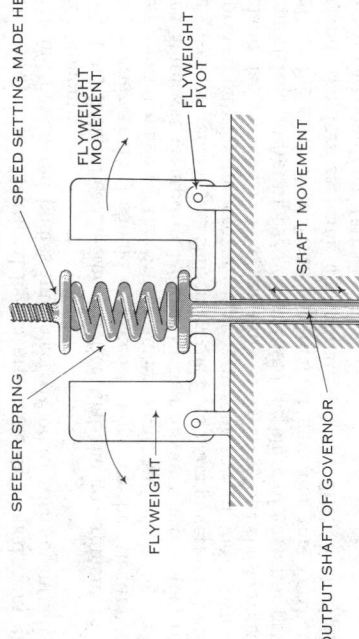

FIG. 1.—SCHEMATIC DRAWING OF SIMPLE MECHANICAL GOVERNOR

SPEED SETTING MADE HERE · FLYWEIGHT MOVEMENT · FLYWEIGHT PIVOT · SHAFT MOVEMENT · SPEEDER SPRING · FLYWEIGHT · OUTPUT SHAFT OF GOVERNOR

BY COURTESY OF MARQUETTE DIVISION, CURTISS-WRIGHT CORP.

FIG. 3.—CUTAWAY VIEW OF ISOCHRONOUS DASH-POT GOVERNOR

put is a mathematical integral of the input. Since such a governor will often indulge in "hunting," or self-oscillation about the preset value of speed, a governor with a dashpot (fig. 3) is often employed to yield both proportional and integral control.

The dashpot is a differentiating device whose output is the rate of change of the input.

The input to the dashpot is the servomotor piston position, while the output of the dashpot is a force applied to the ballhead of the governor in parallel with the speeder spring force. The addition of the dashpot to the governor makes the governor sensitive to engine acceleration as well as speed.

The amount of acceleration sensitivity increases with the time lag in the dashpot.

An inertial element in parallel with the flyweights is sometimes employed in place of the dashpot.

Any governor may be made into a speed droop governor (fig. 4) by the proper use of feedback from the output of the governor to the ballhead.

When two or more prime movers are operated in parallel, as when they drive alternators connected to the same electrical load, only one of the governors can be isochronous. The others must be on speed droop. Through adjustment of the amounts of feedback in the governors, arbitrary division of load between the units can be achieved.

The load on a prime mover may be measured directly to produce a load control governor whose output depends on this load as well as the speed of the prime mover.

The speed of a prime mover is sometimes measured by a pump instead of a ballhead, using the output pressure of the pump as a measure of speed.

Electrical governors are employed in various installations where the prime mover drives an electrical generator whose output is an indication of prime mover speed. They are also used where this speed is measured by a special generator, a common version of which has a gear varying the magnetic field at a pickup coil. In electrical governors an electrohydraulic transducer is employed to convert the electrical signal into useable power at the servomotor. Digital computer techniques may be used for discrete rather than continuous control.

The major hydraulic governor problems have been solved by the introduction of a "double" governor obtained by combining a simple hydraulic isochronous governor (fig. 2) with a droop governor (fig. 3) into one unit, employing a single ballhead and adding governor outputs hydraulically in a single servomotor. The problems solved are the independent adjustment of the governor parameters of gain, lead, and lag; the increase of the ranges of these parameters to those needed to match any engine and load; the avoidance of the influence of temperature variations due to oil viscosity; the elimination of floating pistons which may stick; and the ability to use a remote servomotor without mechanical feedback to the rest of the governor.

(R. O.)

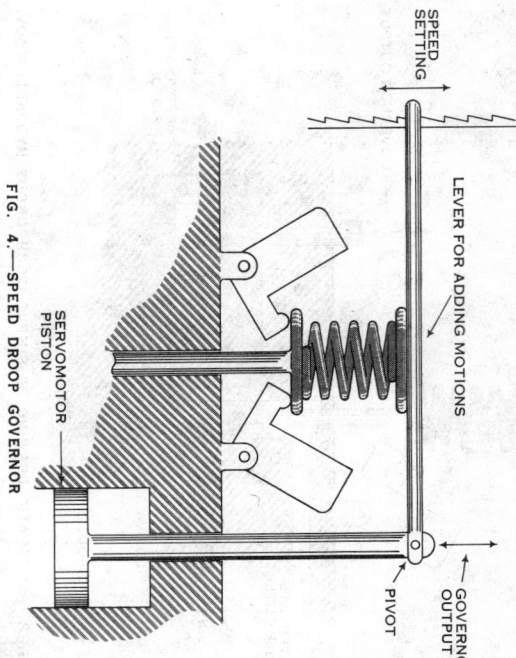

SPEED SETTING

LEVER FOR ADDING MOTIONS

SERVOMOTOR PISTON

GOVERNOR OUTPUT

PIVOT

FIG. 4.—SPEED DROOP GOVERNOR

GOVERNOR-GENERAL

GOVERNOR-GENERAL. The term governor-general indicates primarily that the officer holding the title is set over a number of officers holding that of governor or even lieutenant governor. An alternative term sometimes used is governor in chief; in British usage it still survives in the formal title of the governor of Jamaica, which is captain general and governor in chief. In this sense governor-general has occurred in the usage of most colonial powers.

In British constitutional practice the powers of a governor-general, like those of a governor (q.v.), must be derived either from the commission which he has received from the crown, or from some other statute either of imperial or local legislation, but in the case of dependent territories the title governor-general is now usually restricted to federations.

During the evolution of the British Empire into the Commonwealth of Nations, the status and function of the office of governor-general have undergone changes corresponding to the progress of territories toward self-government and independence. These changes have been of the same character as those in the status and functions of governor from the time of the earliest colonies to the 20th century, in which local legislatures have developed from official and nominated bodies into elected bodies with, eventually, full autonomy.

By 1890 it had become the practice that the government of a self-governing colony should be asked to approve the selection of the governor made by the British government, and when the Irish Free State was created in 1922, a further advance was made, for the governor-general was chosen by the Free State government and approved only by the crown. The representative of the crown in Ireland had previously held the rank of viceroy, but the Government of Ireland Act of 1920 constituted the office of governor-general for the Irish Free State and that of governor for Northern Ireland, the former being appropriate for the Irish Free State since it had dominion status.

In 1926, in the course of developing events in Canada, it was decided that the functions of the governor-general should be limited to representation of the crown, unless any dominion preferred that he should also perform any functions on behalf of the British government.

In 1930 the Imperial Conference declared that appointment of a governor-general should rest on the authority of the commonwealth nation concerned, and this development resulted in the appointment of their own citizens by some commonwealth countries. It concluded that the following statements flowed naturally from the governor-general's new position: the parties interested in the appointment are the crown and the dominion concerned; the constitutional practice that the crown acts on the advice of responsible ministers applies; the ministers who tender advice and are responsible for it are those in the dominion concerned; they tender formal advice after informal consultation with the crown; the channel of communications between the crown and any dominion government solely concerns the crown and such government.

In 1932 the Irish Free State asserted successfully its right to secure removal by the king of a governor-general who was *persona non grata*: this revealed the difference between the position of the governor-general and that of the crown, for it showed that the former held office only at the pleasure of the government of the day. In the exceptional constitutional position of the former Federation of Rhodesia and Nyasaland the position of governor-general was similar to that in an independent commonwealth country. In cases in which the constitution authorized him to use his discretion in exercising any power conferred on him, he could do so either contrary to ministerial advice or without it, though in practice he ought to have acted in accordance with such advice unless either the advice conflicted with instructions given by the crown or he considered he ought to reject it even at the risk of causing the ministers to resign.

In India, the evolution of the office of governor-general was slightly different. In accordance with the provisions of the Regulating Act of 1773 Warren Hastings became the first governor-general. When the rule of the East India Company came to an end and the Indian empire was created, Lord Canning, the first governor-general of the imperial government, received also the title of viceroy. The holder of the office was generally known by that title until the Indian Independence Act of 1947, which established the offices of governor-general for India and for Pakistan. The filling of these posts necessitated a departure from normal practice because there could be no ministers formally to advise the crown until a governor-general had been appointed and ministers had taken office. In these circumstances the leaders of the Congress Party and the Muslim League were consulted and their advice was formally tendered to the crown by the U.K. government. Much the same happened in the case of Ceylon in 1948 and Ghana in 1957. On commonwealth nations' becoming republics recognizing the crown as head of the commonwealth, the office of governor-general disappears and a president takes his place. In the case of Malaya, which became an independent nation in 1957 (and in 1963 merged with other states to form Malaysia) a new form of limited monarchy was devised. (W. H. Is.)

GOW, NIEL (1727–1807), Scottish violinist known for his publications of old Scottish melodies, was born at Strathbrand, Perthshire, on March 22, 1727. He taught himself the violin as a youth and became renowned as a player of Scottish dance music. Eighty-seven of his strathspey reels were published in six collections between 1784 and 1822. Some of these melodies were original, some traditional, some adaptations of traditional airs. He died at Inver, Perthshire, on March 1, 1807. Three of his sons, William, John and Andrew, contributed pieces to their father's collections. John and Andrew became publishers of music in London. Gow's fourth son, NATHANIEL (1763–1831), was equally well known as a violinist and composer of Scottish dances, and the tradition extended to Nathaniel Gow's son, NIEL the younger (c. 1795–1823), composer of "The Lament of Flora Macdonald" and other songs.

See H. G. Farmer, *History of Music in Scotland* (1947); J. Glen, *The Glen Collection of Scottish Dance Music*, 2 vol. (1891 and 1895).
(CS. CH.)

GOWER, JOHN (d. 1408), English poet and friend of Chaucer. Regarded as almost Chaucer's equal until the 16th century, he was later eclipsed by his younger contemporary. Gower retained his position in the history of English literature, however, being recognized as second only to Chaucer in his influence, especially on the makaris, or "Scottish Chaucerians," and on the courtly use of allegory; and as an outstanding representative of his age, not least in writing with ease in English, French, and Latin. In the 1950s and '60s, interest in him was revived by scholars, translators, and editors who demonstrated that he could still be read with pleasure, and that his English *Confessio amantis* in particular, in which he rivals Chaucer in ability to set a collection of skilfully narrated stories within an effective framework, has much to offer the modern reader.

Life.—The known facts about Gower's life are few. His family probably came from Yorkshire, but he owned manors in Norfolk, Suffolk, and Kent, while certain features of the language he uses suggest that he lived for the most part in southeastern England. In 1378 Chaucer, when leaving for Italy, gave power of attorney to Gower and to Richard Forester, a lawyer. Some years later Chaucer directed to "moral Gower" and "philosophical Strode" (Ralph Strode) his *Troilus and Criseyde*, begging them to correct it where necessary (*Troilus and Criseyde*, book v, ll. 1,855–59). In Gower's *Confessio amantis* (book viii, ll. 2,925 ff.) Venus similarly associates Gower with books of "moral vertu"; both references must be to his didactic works in French and Latin, and not to the *Confessio*, with which the epithet "moral" has become improperly associated.

In his *Miroir de l'omme* Gower says "*je ne suys pas clers . . . Ainz ai vestu la raye mance*": this suggests that though not a "clerk" (*i.e.*, not in orders), he wore the "rayed" gown of a serjeant-at-law, or court official. Other allusions and various documents indicate that he knew London and the legal profession well, and in the *Confessio* he professes acquaintance with Richard II (Prologue, ll. 39 ff.). An allegorical account of the Peasants' Revolt in his Latin *Vox clamantis* shows that he followed that rising with deep concern; another passage depicts, as if from firsthand knowledge, Richard's reconciliation with the London commune (1392). To Richard he originally dedicated the *Confessio*, but transferred the dedication to Henry of Lancaster, who in 1393 gave a collar to "an esquire John Gower." Gower was not an uncommon name but this gift may well have been the collar of SS shown on the poet's effigy. Five weeks after Henry of Lancaster's coronation as Henry IV (1399), he bestowed on Gower two pipes of wine a year for life, by way of reward for complimentary references in the *Cronica tripartita* (see below).

By 1398, and perhaps for some time earlier, Gower was living (as a layman) in the Priory of St. Mary Overy, Southwark. In that year Bishop Arundel of Winchester granted a licence for his marriage to a fellow parishioner, Agnes Groundolf, whom the poet was to eulogize in her epitaph as *uxor amans humilis* (his "loving, gentle wife"). She outlived him. In addressing a copy of *Vox clamantis* to Arundel, c. 1400, Gower describes himself as *senex et cecus* ("old and blind"); he was by then probably over 60. His will was proved on Oct. 24, 1408. He left bequests, including a large *martilogium* (calendar), to Southwark Priory (now Southwark Cathedral), and established a chantry. His elegant Gothic tomb, restored in the mid-1950s, may still be seen there; in the effigy the poet's head rests on the three volumes of his major works, in Latin, French, and English; and figures of Pity, Mercy, and Justice, his favourite virtues, are depicted praying for the repose of his soul.

Works: *The "Speculum meditantis" or "Miroir de l'omme."*—Of the three major works, the *Speculum meditantis* (long thought lost) survives only in one (incomplete) manuscript, identified in 1895 by G. C. Macaulay under the title *Miroir de l'omme*. It is written in French, in 12-line stanzas, comprising some 30,000 octosyllabics. Opening impressively enough with a description of the Devil's marriage to the Seven Daughters of Sin, and of their offspring, it next devotes equal space to the marriage of Reason and the Seven Virtues. But instead of the expected *psychomachia* (or confrontation, in the manner of the *Psychomachia* of Prudentius, *q.v.*) comes a searing examination of the sins of English society in the period just before the Peasants' Revolt of 1381; the comminatory tone makes for tedium, but it is relieved at the very end by a long hymn of praise to the Virgin.

The "Vox clamantis" and "In Praise of Peace."—The *Vox clamantis* (of which ten manuscripts are extant), consisting of 10,265 elegiacs, belongs in its revised form to a later period. It is essentially didactic and, as its biblical title—with its reference to the voice of one crying in the wilderness—suggests, homiletic in tone, being in part a further criticism of the three estates of society, in part a mirror for a prince. Gower's political doctrines are traditional but his feeling for the duties of king, clergy, and commons is deep. For phrasing he is greatly indebted to Ovid, and to the *Aurora* of the medieval Latin poet Petrus Riga, but the work is not mere pastiche: it is remarkable that a layman who apparently had no university education could at this period write Latin verse of such continuous fluency. To the latest form of the work he added a *Cronica tripartita*, in 1,062 leonine hexameters. Its three parts treat the reign of Richard under elaborate heraldic figures (the nobles who had opposed Richard being represented by their heraldic devices); the description of Richard's deposition and death is of some historical interest. Against its pro-Lancastrian sentiment should be set the cautionary note that sounds throughout the poem on *Peace* (c. 1399–1400), the 55 stanzas in English (an early example of rime royal, *q.v.*) in which he pleads urgently with the new king to avoid the horrors of war. Peace, national or personal, is indeed the poet's abiding theme.

Balades.—In the *Miroir* Gower says that as a young man he had written "*fols ditz d'amours*"; the 51 French *balades* that survive may represent what he later came to regard as these "foolish" love ditties. They are worthy of comparison with those of Machaut, Deschamps, and Froissart, who had made the *balade* the fashionable medium for love poetry. Those on St. Valentine's Day are particularly charming, and justify Puttenham's description (in his *Arte of English Poesie*, 1589) of Gower as a "Courtly Maker." Like the *Confessio amantis*, they reflect the refinement and elegance of the English court, for which most of his verse was intended. Of later date is a series of French *balades* described as a *Traitié pour essampler les amantz mariés.*

The "Confessio."—The eight books of the *Confessio amantis* are preceded by a Prologue in which we glimpse the poet meeting Richard II on the Thames. "As I bi bote cam rowende" [rowing]. The king bids him "boke [write] some newe thing," but the Prologue itself is devoted to another survey of the human condition. Novelty enters with the first book, where the poet announces that "the stile of my writinges Fro this day forth I thenke change." Forthwith he presents himself as a forlorn lover in May, complaining to Venus, who directs him to Genius, her priest. Save for the reentry of Venus at the end of book viii, and the coda, thereto, the remainder of the poem is cast in the form of Amans' confession of his sins against love to Genius, who instructs him through a diversity of exemplary tales, chiefly adapted from classical and medieval sources. It is the restrained narrative art of these stories that constitutes Gower's chief appeal today. They show some affinities with the Ovid of the *Metamorphoses*, and Gower shares Ovid's fascinated interest in the workings of "Kind," or Nature—an interest that produces a rare tenderness (as in the tale of the incestuous love of Canace and Machaire, book iii). He sees hapless lovers as "enchanted," and lingers over Pygmalion's plight:

> He keste hire colde lippes ofte
> And wissheth that thei weren softe
> And ofte he rouneth in hire ere,
> And ofte his arme now hier now there
> He leide, as he hir wolde embrace,
> And ever among he axeth grace,
> As thogh sche wiste what he mente.
>
> (Book iv, ll. 405–411.)

Formally, Genius and Amans derive from the *Roman de la Rose* (*q.v.*; in which also Genius is priest of Nature) but Gower's priest is both more *courtois* and more Christian, a preacher of *charité* (*caritas*) as much as of *amour*. There is no place in the poem for the adultery that Gower elsewhere stigmatizes as *gallicum peccatum* ("the French vice"). The best stories (*e.g.*, the tale of Florent, book i—an analogue of Chaucer's *Wife of Bath's Tale*) show characters in a state of moral tension. Amans himself is sympathetically yet realistically portrayed, not least when Venus reappears and with kindly humour dismisses him from her service, though not before sending greeting through him to "Chaucer, my poete." Thus Gower gracefully acknowledges the gift of *Troilus*, and we may well believe that each poet genuinely appreciated the distinctive gifts of the other.

The coda in which the poet points to that place, "where resteth love and alle pes" has been thought a failure, but, in fact, it represents a successful harmonization of all the earlier themes. The supposed digressions (*e.g.*, on pagan mythology in book v, where Gower, in effect, offers his modest counterpart to Boccaccio's *Genealogia deorum gentilium*) also fall into place on closer scrutiny.

The "softe pas" of Gower's twin octosyllabics has lulled too many modern readers into overlooking the originality of his construction, the rationale of his morality, and the wit and precision of his language. But in the 15th and 16th centuries he was commonly ranked with Chaucer: John Skelton thought "his matter . . . worth gold," and Ben Jonson referred to him with respect.

BIBLIOGRAPHY.—*Editions and Translations:* The only complete edition of Gower's works is by G. C. Macaulay, 4 vol. with introductions, etc. (1899–1902): vol. i contains the French works, vol. ii and iii the English (also issued separately by the Early English Text Society, E.S. lxxxi–ii, 1900–01), and vol. iv the Latin; with a Life. There are early editions of the *Confessio amantis* by William Caxton (1483) and by Thomas Berthelet (1532 and 1554). The *Cronica, In Praise of Peace*, and some of the minor Latin poems were printed in T. Wright, *Political Poems and Songs*, 2 vol., Rolls Series (1859–61). *In Praise of Peace* was included in early folio editions of Chaucer, and ed. by W. W. Skeat in his *Complete Works of Chaucer*, vol. vii (1897). A selection from the *Confessio amantis*, with excerpts from the other works, and bibliography, was ed. by J. A. W. Bennett as *Selections from the Confessio* in the Clarendon Medieval and Tudor Series (1968). There is a modern prose rendering of most of the *Confessio* by Terence Tiller (1963); and a translation, with notes, of the *Major Latin Works* by Eric W. Stockton (1962).

Criticism: C. S. Lewis, *The Allegory of Love* (1936; rev. ed. 1951); M. Wickert, *Studien zu John Gower* (1953); essays by J. A. W. Bennett and J. Lawlor in J. Lawlor (ed.), *Patterns of Love and Courtesy* (1966); Two chapters in Arthur B. Ferguson, *The Articulate Citizen and the English Renaissance* (1965), deal at length with Gower's political theory. Biographical data is fully presented in John H. Fisher, *John Gower, Moral Philosopher and Friend of Chaucer*, chap. 2 (1964).

(J. A. W. B.)

GOWER, a peninsula, and rural district in west Glamorgan, Wales. Present usage confines the name to that area southwest of a line from Loughor to Swansea and lying between Burry inlet on the north and the Bristol channel on the south. The name is derived from the Welsh province of Gwyr or Guhir which had a much greater extent northward between the rivers Loughor and Tawe.

The area is dominated by a plateau surface ranging in height between 150 ft. and 450 ft. surmounted by ridges rising above 600 ft. In the north a ridge (571 ft.) in Pennant Grit runs from Penclawydd to Town hill, Swansea, rising steadily from west to east and broken by a gap, followed by the railway, at Dunvant. Immediately to the south is a vale, drained by the river Clyne, along the outcrop of the Lower Coal series. Between this and the Devonian sandstone ridges of west Gower the main plateau surface rises to 414 ft. in Clyne common. The ridges of Cefn Bryn (610 ft.), Llanmadoc hill (609) and Rhossili down (633) form a horseshoe of high land reflecting the synclinal folding of the Paleozoic rocks of the south and west. The rivers of Gower are generally short and swift-flowing, being deeply cut below the plateau surface and providing valleys covered in deciduous woodland.

The coast of Gower is remarkable for its beauty. The south coast, in particular, from Mumbles head to Worms head has a series of inlets such as Langland, Caswell and Oxwich bays with fine cliff scenery developed in the various rock strata. Rhossili bay has a large area of sand dunes extending northward to Whiteford point. The north coast is less attractive and has coastal marshes as far as Loughor.

Gower has a long history of occupation by man. The skeleton found (1823) in Goat cave, Paviland (near Rhossili), and generally known as "The Red Lady of Paviland" (now believed to be male) is only one of the signs of Paleolithic occupation. The higher ground of the west has megaliths and tumuli of various ages. Hilltop camps were occupied during the Iron Age and later. The Roman period saw Loughor (Leucarum) as a minor settlement while a villa has been found near Oystermouth. The period between the Roman withdrawal and the Norman conquest saw the spread of Celtic Christianity into Gower with the establishment of several churches, *e.g.*, Bishopston, dedicated to St. Teilo. The coastal area, however, bears many signs of Scandinavian intrusion, mainly in the place names, *e.g.*, Burry Holms, in contrast to the Celtic interior. Shortly after A.D. 1100 Gower was conquered by Henry de Newburgh (or Beaumont), earl of Warwick, who set up a marcher lordship over much of the same area as the Celtic province of Gwyr. An important division was soon established between Gower Anglicana, southwest of a line from Llanrhidian to Clyne common, and Gower Wallicana to the north of this line. English Gower saw quite intense Norman settlement probably with the introduction of Flemish settlers moving from Pembrokeshire. The contrast between these two areas still persists in the place names and settlement patterns. By the Act of Union, 1536, Gower was incorporated with the county of Glamorgan although previously contacts had been dominantly with the west.

From the 16th century onward Gower has remained marginal to the development of the coal field, although some coal was mined in the north particularly in the 16th and 17th centuries. It is dominantly now an agricultural area with the emphasis on mixed and dairy farming. At Bishopston and Rhossili there are important areas of market gardening. This is only one sign of the influence of the large industrial population to the north. The villages of eastern Gower have many inhabitants who work in Swansea and travel daily. The other great influence on Gower, resulting from its scenery, is the tourist industry which has far more than a local appeal; the development of small holiday resorts has been accompanied by an increase in the areas of caravan (trailer) parks. In 1956 Gower peninsula was declared an area of outstanding beauty; certain coastal areas are also preserved under the National trust.

See L. D. Nicholl, *The Normans in Glamorganshire and Gower* (1936); E. G. Bowen (ed.), *Wales* (1957).   (E. M. Dr.)

GOWRIE, JOHN RUTHVEN, 3RD EARL OF (*c.* 1577–1600), Scottish conspirator, one of the principals in the mysterious "Gowrie conspiracy" of 1600, was the second son of William (*c.* 1541–84), 4th Lord Ruthven and 1st earl of Gowrie. He succeeded his elder brother, the 2nd earl, in 1588. From his father and grandfather he inherited a tradition of treason and intrigue and in his youth was involved in the schemes of Francis Stewart, earl of Bothwell.

After an excellent education at the university of Edinburgh, he went abroad to continue his studies at Padua. He seems to have been universally regarded as a young man of high character and a scholarly turn of mind. While abroad he earned the friendship of the reformer Theodore Beza and his return to Scotland in 1600 was welcomed by the party of the Presbyterian ministers. Shortly after his return he annoyed James VI by opposing in the convention of estates the king's proposals for taxation. On Aug. 5, 1600, he and his younger brother, Alexander Ruthven, were slain in mysterious circumstances at Gowrie house in Perth.

Certain facts are well established. As James was setting out from Falkland to hunt early on Aug. 5, he was accosted by Alexander Ruthven and after the hunt accompanied him to Gowrie house. Alexander sent two messengers and Gowrie concealed where they had come from and also the fact of James's expected arrival at Gowrie house. No preparations were made for the king's reception and the earl commenced dinner without waiting for him. James arrived with a small retinue and after dining accompanied Alexander upstairs. A false alarm was raised that the king had left and this was insistently supported by Gowrie against the statement of his own porter. James's retinue were preparing to leave when they saw the king struggling at a turret window and heard his cry for help. They thereupon forced an entrance to the turret and in ensuing struggles Gowrie and his brother were killed.

However, for certain crucial events, the only surviving witness was the king, supported in one instance by a single very dubious corroborator. James's story was that Alexander enticed him to Perth to examine an unknown man with a pot of gold whom he had found and secretly imprisoned. When the king and Alexander had gone up to the turret, Alexander locked the door, threatened James with a dagger, and after some argument there was a struggle. A third man who was present disobeyed Alexander and in fact assisted the king. This man mysteriously disappeared from the scene, only to re-emerge some days later and confirm the king's evidence.

In spite of an inquiry on an unprecedented scale, involving several hundred witnesses, the true explanation of the "Gowrie conspiracy" was a mystery at the time and will probably remain so. James's story was received with incredulity by the majority of his own contemporaries. Various explanations have been put forward, but that which represents the affair as a royal plot to kill the Ruthvens involves too many probabilities to be seriously considered. The suggestion that the affair arose from an unpremeditated brawl is more acceptable; but the weight of evidence is against it, in particular the concealment of James's impending arrival at Gowrie house and the very implausibility of the king's own story. The balance of probabilities strongly suggests that the Ruthvens miscarried in a plot to seize the king's person. Yet for such a plot no clear motive can be found in contemporary politics or in the careers and characters of the principal participants.

See W. F. Arbuckle, "The Gowrie Conspiracy," *Scottish Historical Review*, vol. xxxvi (1957).   (J. K. Ba.)

GOWRIE, a belt of fertile alluvial land in Perthshire and Angus, Scot. Occupying the northern shore of the Firth of Tay, the Carse of Gowrie extends east of Perth city to the confines of Dundee. It measures 15 mi. in length and its breadth from the river toward the Sidlaw hills varies from 2 to 4 mi. The soil is especially suitable for small fruit cultivation, particularly straw-

berries. The district is noteworthy for its castles and mansions, among which may be mentioned Megginch castle near Errol, dating from 1575; Kinnaird castle, erected in the 12th to 15th centuries and restored in the 1850s; Rossie priory, the seat of Lord Kinnaird; and the 15th-century Huntly castle.

GOYA Y LUCIENTES, FRANCISCO JOSÉ DE (1746–1828), Spanish painter and engraver, who, trained in the foreign traditions fashionable in 18th-century Spain, became one of the most characteristically Spanish artists of all times and a foremost European painter and engraver of the 19th century. He was born on March 30, 1746, at Fuendetodos, near Saragossa, and died in Bordeaux, France, on April 16, 1828. His enormous and varied production of paintings, drawings and engravings, relating to nearly every aspect of contemporary life, reflects the period of political and social upheavals in which he lived.

Goya began his studies in Saragossa under José Luzán, a local artist trained in Naples, and was later a pupil in Madrid of the court painter Francisco Bayeu, whose sister he married in 1773. He went to Italy to continue his

SELF-PORTRAIT BY GOYA

studies and was in Rome in 1771. In the same year he returned to Saragossa where he obtained his first important commission for frescoes in the cathedral, which he executed at intervals during the next ten years. These and other early religious paintings made in Saragossa are in the baroque-rococo style current in Spain and are influenced in particular by the great Venetian painter G. B. Tiepolo, who spent the last years of his life in Madrid (1762–70), where he was invited to paint ceilings in the royal palace.

Goya's career at court began in 1775, when he painted the first of a series of over 50 cartoons (mostly preserved in the Prado, Madrid) for the royal tapestry factory, Santa Barbara, on which he was engaged until 1792. These paintings of scenes of contemporary life, of aristocratic and popular pastimes, were begun under the direction of the German artist A. R. Mengs, the great exponent of neoclassicism who, after Tiepolo's death, had become undisputed art dictator at the Spanish court. In Goya's early cartoons the influence of Tiepolo's decorative style is modified by the teachings of Mengs, particularly his insistence on simplicity. The later cartoons reflect his growing independence of foreign traditions and the development of an individual style, which began to emerge through his study of the paintings of Velázquez in the royal collection, many of which he copied in etchings (*c.* 1778). Later in life he is said to have acknowledged three masters: Velázquez, Rembrandt and, above all, nature. Rembrandt's etchings were doubtless a source of inspiration for his later drawings and engravings, while the paintings of Velázquez directed him to the study of nature and taught him the language of realism.

In 1780 Goya was elected a member of the Royal Academy of San Fernando, Madrid, his admission piece being a "Crucifixion" (Prado), a conventional composition in the manner of Mengs but painted in the naturalistic style of Velázquez. "Crucifixion," which he doubtless knew. In 1785 he was appointed deputy director of painting at the academy and in the following year painter to the king, Charles III. To this decade belong his earliest known portraits, of court officials and members of the aristocracy, whom he represented in conventional 18th-century poses. The stiff elegance of the figures, in full-length portraits of society ladies as the "Marquesa de Pontejos" (National Gallery, Washington), and the fluent painting of their elaborate costumes also relates them to Velázquez' court portraits; and his representation of "Charles III as Huntsman" (of which several versions exist) is based directly on Velázquez' royal huntsmen.

GOYA Y LUCIENTES

The death of Charles III in 1788, a few months before the outbreak of the French Revolution, brought to an end the period of comparative prosperity and enlightenment in which Goya reached maturity. The rule of reaction and political and social corruption that followed, under the weak and stupid Charles IV and his clever, unscrupulous queen Maria Luisa Teresa, ended with the Napoleonic invasion of Spain. It was under the patronage of the new king, who raised him at once to the rank of court painter, that Goya became the most successful and fashionable artist in Spain; he was made director of the academy in 1795 (but resigned two years later for reasons of health) and first court painter in 1799.

Though he welcomed official honours and worldly success with undisguised enthusiasm, the record that he left is of his patrons and of the society in which he lived is ruthlessly penetrating. After a serious illness in 1792, which left him permanently deaf, his art began to take on a new character which gave free expression to the observations of his searching eye and critical mind and to his newly developed faculty of imagination. During his long convalescence he painted a series of small compositions which he described in a letter to the director of the academy (1794) as enabling him "to make observations for which there is no opportunity in commissioned works, in which fantasy and invention have no scope." He referred to the subjects as "popular diversions" but those that survive (Academy of San Fernando, Madrid) include a "Madhouse," a "Procession of Flagellants," a "Tribunal of the Inquisition," these unconventional themes being painted in a bold, sketchy technique and strong colours with an effect of exaggerated realism that borders on caricature. For his more purposeful and serious satires, however, he now began to use the more intimate mediums of drawing and engraving. In the "Caprichos," a series of 80 etchings published in 1799, he attacked political, social and religious abuses, adopting the popular imagery of caricature, which he enriched with highly original qualities of invention. His masterly use of the recently developed technique of aquatint gives them astonishing dramatic vitality and makes them a major achievement in the history of etching (q.v.). Despite the veiled language of designs, and captions and Goya's announcement that his themes were from the "extravagances and follies common to all society," they were probably recognized as references to well-known persons and were withdrawn from sale after a few days. However, a few months later Goya was made first court painter. Later he was apparently threatened by the Inquisition and in 1803 he presented the plates of the "Caprichos" to the king in return for a pension for his son.

While uncommissioned works gave full scope for "observations," "fantasy" and "invention," in his commissioned paintings Goya continued to use conventional formulas. His decoration of the church of San Antonio de la Florida, Madrid (1798), is still in the tradition of Tiepolo; but the bold, free execution and the expressive realism of the popular types used for religious and secular figures are unprecedented. In his numerous portraits of friends and officials a broader technique is combined with a new emphasis on characterization. The faces of his sitters reveal a lively discernment of personality which is sometimes appreciative,

particularly in his portraits of women, as that of "Doña Isabel Cobos de Porcel" (National Gallery, London.), but is often far from flattering as in his royal portraits. In the group of "Charles IV and His Family" (1800, Prado), which recalls the composition of Velázquez' "Meninas," Goya, despite his position as court painter, has portrayed the ugliness and vulgarity of the principal figures so vividly as to produce the effect of caricature.

In 1808 Goya was at the height of his official career when Charles IV and his son Ferdinand were forced to abdicate in quick succession, Napoleon's armies entered Spain and his brother Joseph was placed on the throne. Goya retained his position as court painter to the usurper; but in the course of the war he portrayed Spanish as well as French generals and in 1812 he painted an equestrian portrait of the "Duke of Wellington" (Apsley House, London). It was, however, in a series of etchings, "Los Desastres de la Guerra" (first published 1863), for which he made drawings during the war, that he recorded his personal reactions to the invasion and to the horrors and disastrous consequences of the war. The violent and tragic events, which he doubtless witnessed, are represented not with documentary realism but in dramatic compositions—in line and aquatint—with brutal details which create a vivid effect of authenticity.

On the restoration of Ferdinand VII in 1814, after the expulsion of the invaders, Goya was pardoned for having served the French king and reinstated as first court painter. The "Charge of the Mamelukes" and "Execution of the Defenders of Madrid" (Prado) were painted to commemorate the popular insurrection on May 2, 1808. Like the "Desastres" they are compositions of dramatic realism, and their monumental scale makes them even more moving. The impressionistic style in which they are painted foreshadowed and influenced later 19th-century French artists, particularly Manet, who was also inspired by the composition of the "Execution." In several portraits of Ferdinand VII, painted after his restoration, Goya evokes more forcefully than any description the personality of the cruel tyrant, whose oppressive rule drove most of his friends and eventually Goya himself into exile. He

"FAMILY OF CHARLES IV" BY FRANCISCO GOYA. IN MUSEO DEL PRADO, MADRID

painted few other official portraits but those of his friends and relations and his "Self-Portraits" (1815, Prado; Academy of San Fernando) are equally subjective. Some of his religious compositions of this period, the "Agony in the Garden" and "Communion of S. Joseph of Calasanz" (1819, 1820, Madrid), are more suggestive of sincere devotion than any of his earlier church paintings. The enigmatic "black paintings," with which he decorated the walls of his country house, the "Quinta del Sordo" (1819–23, now in the Prado) and the "Proverbios" or "Disparates," a series of etchings made at about the same time (though not published until 1864), are, on the other hand, nightmare visions in expressionist language, that seem to reflect cynicism, pessimism and despair.

In 1824, when the failure of an attempt to establish a liberal government had led to renewed persecution, Goya applied for permission to go to France for reasons of health. After visiting Paris he settled in voluntary exile in Bordeaux, where he remained, apart from a brief trip to Madrid, until his death. There, in spite of old age and infirmity, he continued to record his impressions of the world around him in paintings and drawings, and in the new technique of lithography, which he had begun to use in Spain. His last paintings include genre subjects and several portraits of friends in exile: "Muguiro" (Prado), "Moratín," "Pío de Molina" (private collections), which show the final development of his style toward a synthesis of form and character in terms of light and shade, without outline or detail and with a minimum of colour. If there is little evidence for the legends of Goya's rebellious character and violent actions, he was undoubtedly a revolutionary artist. He had no immediate followers, but his many original achievements, from the "Caprichos" to his late paintings, profoundly impressed later 19th-century French artists—Eugène Delacroix was one of his great admirers—who were the leaders of new European movements, from romanticism and realism to Impressionism; and his works continued to be admired and studied by the Expressionists and Surrealists in the 20th century.

BIBLIOGRAPHY.—L. Matheron, *Goya* (1858); A. L. Mayer, *Francisco de Goya* (1923; Eng. trans., 1924); F. Zapater y Gómez, *Goya, noticias biográficas* (1924); V. de Sambricio, *Tapices de Goya* (1946); F. D. Klingender, *Goya in the Democratic Tradition* (1948); F. J. Sánchez Cantón, *Vida y Obras de Goya* (1951; Eng. trans., 1964), *Museo del Prado, Los Dibujos de Goya* (1954), also *Goya and the Black Paintings* (Eng. trans., 1964); X. Desparmet Fitz-Gerald, *L'Oeuvre Peint de Goya* (1928–50); Tomás Harris, *Goya* (1964). (E. Hs.)

GOYAZ: *see* GOIAS.

GOYEN, JAN JOSEPHSZOON VAN (1596–1656), one of the most gifted of Dutch landscape painters, was born at Leiden on Jan. 13, 1596, learned painting under several masters at Leiden and Haarlem, and settled at The Hague about 1631. He was one of the first to emancipate himself from the tradition of minute painting of detail embodied in the works of Brueghel and Savery. Though he preserved the dun scale of tone peculiar to those painters, he studied atmospheric effects in black and white with considerable skill. His influence on Dutch art was marked. He died at The Hague on April 27, 1656.

Between 1610 and 1616 Goyen wandered from one school to another. In the latter year he joined Esaias van der Velde, and some of his earlier pictures show the influence of Esaias very perceptibly. The landscape is minute; details of branching and foliage are given, and the landscape serves as a stage for genre scenes. After 1625 these peculiarities gradually disappear. Atmospheric cool tints are the principal feature of Goyen's landscapes. His buildings, water and shipping sometimes have the strength, if not the colour, of Albert Cuyp.

Though he visited France once or twice, Goyen chiefly confined himself to the scenery of Holland. One of his largest pieces is a view of The Hague, executed in 1651 for the municipality and now in the town collection of that city. Most of his panels represent reaches of the Rhine, the Waal and the Maas. But he sometimes sketched the downs of Scheveningen, or the sea at the mouth of the Rhine and Scheldt; he liked to depict the inshore calm and rarely painted seas stirred by more than a cooling breeze. He painted winter scenes, with ice, skaters and sledges. More than 1,000 of Goyen's pictures are catalogued by Hofstede de Groot. They may be seen at museums in Boston, New York city (Metro-

politan Museum of Art), Detroit and Toledo, among others. The National gallery, London, has several of his works.

GOZLAN, LÉON (1803–1866), French novelist, dramatist and journalist with a biting wit, made his name under the July monarchy and in the early years of the second empire. He was born in Marseilles, 26 Fructidor year XI (Sept. 11, 1803). When his father, a Jewish shipowner, was ruined financially, Gozlan left school and worked on a cargo boat trading on the African coast, living for a time in Senegal. He later ran a boarding school in Marseilles and then worked in a bookshop in Paris, where, through the help of his fellow townsman, Joseph Méry (1798–1865), he entered journalism and contributed to *Le Corsaire*, *Le Figaro* and *L'Artiste*. His first novel was *Le Notaire de Chantilly* (1836). His friendship with Honoré de Balzac (*q.v.*), to whom he devoted two books which have often been reissued, *Balzac en pantoufles* (1856) and *Balzac chez lui* (1862), saved him from undeserved oblivion. He died in Paris, Sept. 14, 1866.

See H. Talvart and J. Place, *Bibliographie des auteurs modernes de langue française* (1941). (R. PT.)

GOZO (ancient GAULUS), an island of the Maltese group in the Mediterranean sea, lies 3¼ mi. N.W. of the nearest point of Malta, is 9 mi. in length and 4½ mi. in extreme breadth and has an area of 26 sq.mi. Pop. (1961 est.) 27,506. Its chief town, Victoria, formerly called Rabat (pop. [1961 est.] 6,491), stands near the middle of the island on one of a cluster of steep conical hills in a highly cultivated district. The prehistoric temple Ggantija is of the same type as Hagar Kim in Malta but larger. Gozo has been called the Scotland of Malta; it still possesses something of a separate and distinctive outlook and way of life. Gozo is held by some to be the legendary Ogygia where Calypso entertained Odysseus. (W. B. FR.)

GOZZI, CARLO, CONTE (1720–1806), Italian dramatist and a fanatical controversialist with a persecution mania, who spent his life in defending Italian culture against foreign influences, was born at Venice on Dec. 13, 1720. He joined the purist *Accademia dei Granelleschi* and in a satirical almanac called *La tartana degli influssi* (1757) directed his wit against the theatrical innovations of Pietro Chiari and Carlo Goldoni. Between 1761 and 1765 Gozzi produced ten grotesque *Fiabe* (*L'amore delle tre melarance*—the basis for Prokofiev's *The Love of Three Oranges, Turandot*—the basis of Puccini's opera, and *L'augellin belverde*, modern ed. by E. Masi, 1885) or dramatizations of popular and oriental tales, with which he sought to revitalize the dying *commedia dell'arte*. His other works include the *Marfisa bizzarra* (1761–68; modern ed. by C. Ortis, 1911)—a verse satire on 18th-century Venice—and the *Memorie inutili* (1797; modern ed. by D. Bulferetti, 1928; Eng. trans., 1890), an autobiography in which he described, vividly and with humour, his military experiences in Dalmatia (1741–44), his stormy relations with the actress Teodora Ricci and with Pier Antonio Gratarol, his rival in her affections, and his many literary polemics.

Gozzi died at Venice on April 4, 1806. His *Opere* were published in 8 vol. (1772–74) and in 14 vol. (1801–03).

See T. Mantovani, *Carlo Gozzi* (1926); G. Ziccardi, *Forme di vita e d'arte nel Settecento*, pp. 111–180 (1931). (D. M. WE.)

GOZZI, GASPARO, CONTE (1713–1786), Italian poet and essayist, elder brother of Carlo Gozzi (*q.v.*), was born at Venice Dec. 4, 1713. He published (1760–62) the *Gazzetta Veneta* (modern ed. by B. Romani, 2 vol. 1943), a chronicle of Venetian life, and the *Osservatore* (modern ed. by E. Spagni, 1914), both written in a pure Italian style. His other works include satirical verse *Sermoni* (1763), the *Difesa di Dante* (1758) against Saverio Bettinelli, which marks the beginning of the revival of interest in the *Divina Commedia* in Italy, and a program for educational reform. He died at Padua, Dec. 27, 1786. His *Opere* were edited by A. Dalmistro, 16 vol. (1818–20).

See M. A. Viglio, *Gasparo Gozzi* (1916); G. de Beauvillé, *Gasparo Gozzi, journaliste vénitien* (1937). (D. M. WE.)

GOZZOLI, BENOZZO (1420–1497), Italian painter, whose masterpiece is the fresco cycle in the chapel of the Palazzo Medici, Florence, was born in Florence in 1420. In 1444 he was engaged with Lorenzo and Vittorio Ghiberti on work on the third bronze door of the baptistry in Florence and in 1447 was active as an assistant of Fra Angelico in Rome, where his hand has been identified in a number of Angelico's frescoes in the chapel of Nicholas V in the Vatican. In 1447 he was engaged, as Angelico's principal assistant, on the fresco on the ceiling of the Cappella di S. Brizio in the cathedral at Orvieto, which he appears to have completed after Angelico's return to Rome (1448/49). In the second half of 1449 he was employed at Montefalco (near Foligno). From Montefalco, Gozzoli moved to Viterbo, where after 1453 he painted nine frescoes of scenes from the life of St. Rose of Viterbo (destroyed), and then to Perugia in connection with an altarpiece for Collegio Gerolominiano (signed, dated 1456; Galleria Nazionale dell' Umbria, Perugia).

In 1458 he was in Rome, and thereafter returned to Florence. Gozzoli's masterpiece, the frescoed chapel of the Palazzo Medici, dates from 1459/60. By 1463 he was at work at San Gimignano on a cycle of 17 scenes from the life of St. Augustine in the choir of S. Agostino (last scene signed and dated 1465) and in 1464 completed a fresco at S. Sebastian there.

Between 1469 and 1485 Gozzoli's attention was monopolized by his most extensive commission, for a series of 25 frescoes of Old Testament scenes for the walls of the Camposanto at Pisa. He is mentioned in Florence in 1497 and died at Pistoia on Oct. 4 of that same year. An exceptionally prolific artist, Gozzoli made extensive use of studio assistants and his work as a whole has a rather empty facility. His work at Orvieto is distinguished from Angelico's by its dry schematic forms. In the "Procession of the Magi" on the walls of the Palazzo Medici, on the other hand, he emerges as an artist of great decorative talent, with a pronounced gift for landscape and portraiture. The views of the Val d'Arno which form the background of these frescoes and the portraits of the Medici included contributed to their enduring popularity.

See R. van Marle, *The Development of the Italian Schools of Painting*, vol. xi (1929); B. Berenson, *The Drawings of The Florentine Painters*, 2nd ed. (1938). (J. W. P.-H.)

GRAAF, REGNIER DE (1641–1673), Dutch physician known for his studies on the pancreas and on the reproductive organs of mammals, was born July 30, 1641, at Schoonhoven. He was educated at Louvain, Utrecht, Leiden and Angers and for a short time practised medicine in Paris but returned to Delft in 1667 and remained there until his death, Aug. 17, 1673. Graaf was the discoverer of the ovarian follicles, which are still known as Graafian follicles.

GRABBE, CHRISTIAN DIETRICH (1801–1836), German dramatist whose plays, though uneven in quality, anticipate later work. He was born in Detmold on Dec. 11, 1801, studied law in Leipzig and became a solicitor as well as a military justiciary in his home town. Love affairs and his own inner restlessness drove him to abandon his profession in 1834, however, and after some months of poverty in Frankfurt am Main he went to Düsseldorf where the poet K. L. Immermann, who was working for the theatre there, tried to help him. But although Grabbe found publishers for his plays, dissipation drove him to an early death in Detmold on Sept. 12, 1836.

One of Grabbe's main themes is the shipwreck of the great on contemporary narrowness and obtuseness. In spite of his exaggerated dramatic pathos he achieved a mordant satire, and a sometimes laconic, sometimes episodic, succession of scenes and images which anticipates film technique as well as impressionism and expressionism. His plays are boldly experimental in form and rich in ideas but seldom meet the practical demands of the theatre.

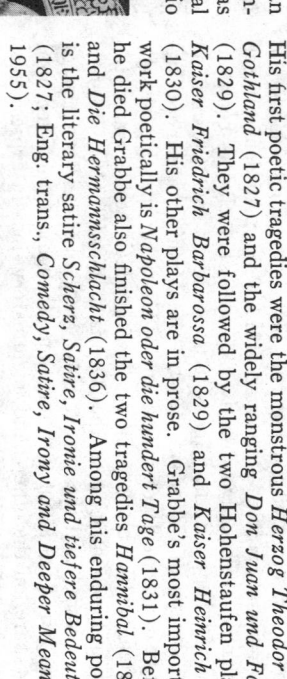

ALINARI

SELF-PORTRAIT DETAIL FROM "PROCESSION OF THE MAGI" BY BENOZZO GOZZOLI. IN THE PALAZZO MEDICI, FLORENCE

His first poetic tragedies were the monstrous *Herzog Theodor von Gothland* (1827) and the widely ranging *Don Juan und Faust* (1829). They were followed by the two Hohenstaufen plays, *Kaiser Friedrich Barbarossa* (1829) and *Kaiser Heinrich VI* (1830). His other plays are in prose. Grabbe's most important work poetically is *Napoleon oder die hundert Tage* (1831). Before he died Grabbe also finished the two tragedies *Hannibal* (1835) and *Die Hermannsschlacht* (1836). Among his enduring poems is the literary satire *Scherz, Satire, Ironie und tiefere Bedeutung* (1827; Eng. trans., *Comedy, Satire, Irony and Deeper Meaning*, 1955).

BIBLIOGRAPHY.—Works, ed. by O. Nieten, 6 vol. (1908) and B. von Wiese, 2 vol. (1943); A. Bergmann, "Literaturbericht über Grabbe," *Germanisch-Romanische Monatsschrift*, no. 22 (1934); F. J. Schneider, *C. D. Grabbe* (1934); B. von Wiese, *Die deutsche Tragödie von Lessing bis Hebbel*, ch. 18–20, 2nd ed. (1952); F. Martini, "Grabbe, Napoleon oder die hundert Tage," in *Das deutsche Drama vom Barock bis zur Gegenwart*, ed. by B. von Wiese, vol. ii (1958). (JM. M.)

GRABSKI, WLADYSLAW (1874–1938), Polish statesman who reorganized his country's monetary and financial system, was born at Borow, near Lowicz, on July 7, 1874. He studied history in Paris and economics in Halle, Ger. A Socialist in his youth, he later joined the National Democratic party and was elected a member of the Polish constituent *sejm* (q.v.), but soon left for Paris as third Polish delegate at the peace conference. Returning to Warsaw, he became minister of finance in Dec. 1919. From June 23 to July 24, 1920, he was prime minister. In this capacity he went to Spa, Belg., to ask the Allied supreme council for immediate aid to Poland in arms and munitions. He served again as minister of finance from Jan. to Sept. 1923. On Dec. 19, 1923, he became prime minister again. To stop inflation he created, on Feb. 1, 1924, a new Polish currency, the zloty (exchanged at 1,800,000 Polish marks for one zloty, the U.S. dollar being equivalent to 5.18 zlotys); and on April 28, 1924, he founded the Bank of Poland, whose capital was subscribed by the nation. In the summer of 1925, however, he had to face a new crisis. Germany declared a "tariff war" on Poland, and the Deutsche Bank sold massive quantities of zlotys on the money markets of Berlin and Vienna. The new Polish currency declined in July, losing almost 50% of its gold value. Criticized in the *sejm*, Grabski resigned on Nov. 14, 1925. After Piłsudski's *coup d'état* of May 1926, Grabski retired from active politics, becoming professor at the Warsaw Agricultural high school. He published his own account of his greatest achievement, *Dwa lata pracy u podstaw państwowości naszej* ("Two Years' Work at the Foundation of Our State"), in 1927 and a summary of his democratic political philosophy, *Idea Polski* ("Poland's Mission"), in 1935. Grabski died in Warsaw on March 1, 1938. (K. SM.)

GRACCHUS, GAIUS SEMPRONIUS (154–121 B.C.), Roman radical statesman, younger brother of Tiberius Gracchus (q.v.), possessed the integrity of his brother and was more acute and farsighted. Married to Licinia, daughter of P. Crassus Mucianus (see CRASSUS), he was a foundation member of the agrarian commission set up in 133; he was quaestor in 126, serving two years in Sardinia. He returned in 124, deflected vexatious attempts at prosecution and was elected tribune for 123 with an extensive and imaginative program of reform, largely aimed at attacking the powers of the senate. His most contentious and important proposal, which followed an attempt of M. Fulvius Flaccus as consul in 125, was to admit Latins to Roman citizenship and give Latin rights (q.v.) to Rome's Italian allies (*socii*). Gaius Gracchus was tribune in 123 and again in 122, immediate re-election to the tribunate having evidently been recently legalized. His proposal for the extension of the *civitas* belongs to 122. On the dating of his other measures the two main sources, Plutarch and Appian, disagree, and certainty is impossible.

He re-enacted his brother's agrarian law. Among his measures that were passed and were of basic importance in the whole remaining history of the Roman republic were a *lex de capite civium Romanorum*, enacting that only the people (in its assemblies) could establish capital courts; a carefully devised and economically sound *lex frumentaria*, guaranteeing every Roman householder domiciled in Rome a monthly grain ration at a modest price (the corn being shipped to Italy between harvest and winter and stored in huge new granaries at Rome); a *lex de provinciis consularibus*, which remained operative until 52, by which the consular provinces were to be named before the consuls were elected, so that the senate could no longer use the allocation of provinces as a means of coercing consuls of whose politics it disapproved; a law for the establishment of overseas colonies, the colony of Junonia on the site of Carthage being actually proposed by his colleague Gaius Rubrius; a *lex Acilia* (so called because it was formally moved by his colleague Manius Acilius Glabrio) *repetundarum*, much of the text of which survives, by which in the permanent court, established in 149 to try prosecutions for extortion, senators were replaced as jurymen by rich Romans who were not senators, a class of people known later as the equestrian order (see EQUITES); a *lex de provincia Asia*, by which (through public auctions held by the censors in Rome every five years) the collection of taxes in the rich new province of Asia was to be sold by the government to syndicates (*societates*) of rich businessmen (*publicani*), who were to organize the collection through their own paid staff in the province. Gracchus did not foresee that in Asia (and subsequently in other provinces) these last two measures, neither objectionable in itself, would in association encourage partnership in corrupt practice between the Roman administration and the tax-collecting agencies.

The farsighted proposal for the extension of the citizenship, whose enactment would have prevented the Social War (see RO-MAN HISTORY), was reserved for 122. Conservative opposition to the measure was already well organized; M. Livius Drusus (*q.v.*), another tribune for 122, was to steal Gracchus' support by outbidding him for popularity. Gracchus, who was further handicapped by having to go to Africa in connection with the foundation of Junonia, relied on two powerful supporters—M. Fulvius Flaccus, who, by the extraordinary act of holding the tribunate (in 122) after the consulship, showed his enthusiasm for a measure that was in origin largely his own, and the consul Gaius Fannius, whose friendship for Gracchus did not in the end influence him to support the measure, of which he disapproved.

Inauspicious reports came from Junonia; the citizenship bill was dropped, probably vetoed by Drusus; L. Opimius, an enemy, was elected consul for 121, and when in that year a tribune, Minucius, proposed to rescind the bills Gracchus had passed, rioting started. Gracchus and his supporters seized the Aventine hill; the senate for the first time in history proclaimed martial law, passing what was later called "the last decree" (*senatus consultum ultimum*) calling on the consuls to save the state. In the subsequent fighting both Gracchus and Flaccus were killed.

Gaius left no children, unless F. Münzer's suggestion is right that the infamous Sempronia who helped Catiline in 63, the wife of D. Junius Brutus, consul in 77, and mother of one of Caesar's murderers, was his daughter.

BIBLIOGRAPHY.—Ancient sources in A. H. J. Greenidge and A. M. Clay, *Sources for Roman History 133-70 B.C.*, 2nd ed. (1960); F. Münzer in Pauly-Wissowa, *Real-Encyclopädie der classischen Altertumswissenschaft*, ii A, 1375-1400 (1923); J. Carcopino, *Autour des Gracques* (1928); H. Last in *Cambridge Ancient History*, vol. ix, ch. 2 (1932); E. Badian, *Foreign Clientelae*, ch. 8 (1958); H. H. Scullard, *From the Gracchi to Nero* (1959). For the *lex Acilia*, C. G. Bruns, *Fontes iuris Romani antiqui*, 7th ed., pp. 55 ff. (1909). For Sempronia, F. Münzer, *Römische Adelsparteien und Adelsfamilien*, pp. 272 ff. (1920).
(J. P. V. D. B.)

GRACCHUS, TIBERIUS SEMPRONIUS (163-133 B.C.), whose agrarian reforms, together with the reforms of his younger brother Gaius Sempronius Gracchus (*q.v.*), raised constitutional issues of great importance in the history of the Roman republic (*see* ROMAN HISTORY: *The Fall of the Republic*). He and his brother were brought up by their mother Cornelia, assisted by the rhetorician Diophanes of Mytilene and the Stoic Blossius of Cumae. He served under his brother-in-law, the younger Scipio Africanus, in Africa during the last Punic War (147). Quaestor in 137, he served in the Numantine Wars in Spain, and saved the army by concluding an agreement with the enemy. This agree-

As tribune in 133, he was obsessed with the problem, which contemporary census figures reflect, of declining Roman manpower, from the particular point of view of recruitment for the legions. Much of Italy had been depopulated in the previous half-century through the absorption of independent small farms into the great ranches (*latifundia, saltus*), and Tiberius proposed to reclaim state land (*ager publicus*) occupied, often since several generations, by squatters (*possessores*; chiefly owners of the large estates), and to distribute it in small holdings, probably of 30 *iugera* (roughly 19 ac.) each; he aimed thus to improve and increase Roman stock by putting Romans back on the land. He hoped to soften opposition on the part of the *possessores* by allowing them to convert part of their existing holdings of *ager publicus* (500 to 1,000 *iugera*, according to the size of their families) into privately owned freehold. For the administration of the scheme a permanent board of three with, in all probability, a rotating chairmanship, was to be established. Romans alone were to be beneficiaries of the scheme, but as Latins and Italians were among the *possessores*, the scheme was bound to have repercussions on Roman relations with them.

A tribune, M. Octavius, having vetoed the proposal when it came before the *concilium plebis* ("assembly of the people"), Tiberius, in an altogether unconstitutional fashion, secured his deposition by vote of the plebs, and the bill was passed. The three commissioners elected were himself, his brother and his father-in-law, Appius Claudius Pulcher. The difficulties in establishing title were far more difficult and the practical issues more complicated than Tiberius had foreseen. When the senate tried to sabotage the bill by voting the commissioners no money for its implementation, Tiberius proposed that the wealth recently bequeathed to Rome by Attalus III of Pergamum be applied to this purpose. He then offered himself as a candidate for re-election to the tribunate for 132. While re-election without interval in the case of the curule magistracies was forbidden by law, the position concerning the tribunate was uncertain. The presiding tribune was undecided. Rioting started, Tiberius being at a disadvantage because his supporters, chiefly men living outside Rome, were working in the harvest fields and were not available. The consul P. Mucius Scaevola refused to intervene, and P. Scipio Nasica Serapio (consul in 138) assumed the responsibility of leading out a party of senators, in conflict with whom Tiberius was killed. The consuls of the following year, acting as a tribunal, tried and executed many of his supporters. Wisely, however, the work of the commission (on which Tiberius' place was taken by P. Licinius Crassus) was allowed to continue. That it was active down to 129, when Scipio Aemilianus secured a restriction of its powers, is evident from surviving boundary stones which record its adjudications. The problem of the inadequacy of recruits for the Roman legions, which Gracchus' land bill could never have solved, was solved in the event partly by Marius (*q.v.*) and partly by the enfranchisement of the Italians after the Social War of 90-89 B.C.

BIBLIOGRAPHY.—A. H. J. Greenidge and A. M. Clay (comp.), *Sources for Roman History, 133-70 B.C.*, 2nd ed. (1960); F. Münzer, "Ti. Sempronius Gracchus" (no. 54) in Pauly-Wissowa, *Real-Encyclopädie der classischen Altertumswissenschaft*, ii A, 1409-1426 (1923); F. Taeger, *Tiberius Gracchus* (1928); J. Carcopino, *Autour des Gracques* (1928); H. Last in *Cambridge Ancient History*, ix, ch. 1 and 2 (1932); E. Badian, *Foreign Clientelae* (1958), especially ch. 8; H. H. Scullard, *From the Gracchi to Nero* (1959).
(J. P. V. D. B.)

GRACE, WILLIAM GILBERT (1848-1915), greatest English cricketer of Victorian times, was born July 18, 1848, at Downend, Gloucestershire, and died at Eltham, London, Oct. 23, 1915. During his career he scored 54,896 runs (including 126 centuries) and took 2,876 wickets in first-class cricket, which he played from 1865 until 1908. He could still handle a bat much later: in his last match his not-out score was 69 for Eltham v. Grove Park on July 25, 1914, when he was 66. At 16 he went in first for Gentlemen v. Players at Lord's cricket ground, London, and on his last appearance for the Gentlemen at the Oval cricket ground, London, in 1906, he made 74 on his 58th birthday. In 84 matches for Gentlemen v. Players he amassed 6,000 runs and took 271 wickets. His prowess and achievement were comprehensive: in Aug. 1876 he scored, in consecutive innings, 344 out of 546 for

Marylebone Cricket club v. Kent; 177 out of 262 for Gloucestershire; and a not-out score of 318 for Gloucestershire v. Nottinghamshire; and a not-out score of 318 for Gloucestershire v. Yorkshire at Cheltenham. In 1880 he was on the team that played the first match against Australia in England.

The legend of "W. G." presents him as shaggy and ponderous with a huge yellow cap atop a swarthy head and face; the earliest extant photographs show him bearded like the pard. At 24 his weight was not more than 12 stone, 7 lb. (175 lb.). But in his heyday he was an athletic figure, a swift runner and able to throw a ball 100 yd. Grace evolved the first principles of modern batting, combining forward and back techniques; many of his performances were achieved on rough and untrustworthy wickets, such as are unknown to modern players. His personality, his inexhaustible energy and gusto and his physical power of dominance made him a national figure. He was Johnsonian in that cricket was his life and dictionary, though in his spare time he practised medicine. Of him, J. C. Shaw, famous and accurate bowler of the period, said "I puts the ball where I likes, but he puts it where he likes."

See CRICKET.

BIBLIOGRAPHY.—A. A. Thomson, Great Cricketer (1957); Lord Hawke, Lord Harris and Sir Home Gordon (eds.), Memorial Biography of Dr. W. G. Grace (1919); B. Darwin, W. G. Grace (1934); C. Bax, W. G. Grace (1952).

GRACE, in Christian theology, the gift of divine favour that grants salvation. The English term is the usual translation for that Greek charis, which occurs in the New Testament about 150 times (two-thirds of these in writings attributed to Paul). Although the word must sometimes be translated in other ways, the fundamental meaning in the New Testament and in subsequent theological usage is that contained in the Epistle to Titus (in the text used as the Epistle for Christmas day): "The grace of God has appeared for the salvation of all men." At the hands of Christian theologians almost from the beginning, the biblical concept of grace has undergone development and clarification, becoming the leitmotiv of Christian doctrine. Augustine, Thomas Aquinas, Martin Luther, Karl Barth—whatever else may divide these theologians, each of them would regard himself, and correctly, as a doctor gratiae, a teacher and expositor of divine grace. Because of its fundamental place in Christian teaching, grace is perhaps best understood in juxtaposition with the several other themes of theological thought that have played a prominent role in the history of the Christian doctrine of grace.

Nature and Grace.—According to Thomas Aquinas, "when a man is said to have the grace of God, there is signified something supernatural bestowed on man by God." Thus supernatural grace is part, in fact the foundation, of the supernatural order, which is to be distinguished from the natural order. At least since Irenaeus, Christian theologians have interpreted the story of creation to mean that in addition to his natural capacities Adam was endowed with a supernatural grace. When he fell into sin, he lost this grace, but his "nature" retained its integrity: man was still human even after the Fall. This Augustinian distinction between nature and grace was intended to avoid both the Manichaean heresy that man had lost his essential humanity through the Fall and the Pelagian heresy that man did not need the gift of grace to begin moving toward his restoration. Yet long after Augustine theologians continued to debate the extent of human capacity apart from grace—i.e., the relation of grace to free will—as well as the preparatory or prevenient function of grace before conversion and faith. Both these questions were prominent in the controversies of the Reformation, coming up also after the Reformation in Jansenism on the Roman Catholic side and in Arminianism on the Protestant side.

The Grace of Christ.—When the New Testament speaks of grace, it usually means the grace given in Christ. "The grace of our Lord Jesus Christ be with you": this closing greeting from the Epistle to the Romans has its counterpart at the beginning or the end of most of the Pauline Epistles. Although grace is identified with Jesus Christ, this does not mean that there is no grace before Jesus or apart from the history of Jesus. The grace of God sends Christ, and Christ brings the grace of God. Therefore a grace has appeared in the history of Israel and continues to appear in the history of men and of nations. Protestant theology refers to this as common grace; Roman Catholic theology also speaks of the uncovenanted graces of God. The connection between grace and Christ was, however, the occasion for a fundamental conflict between Roman Catholicism and the Reformers. John Calvin defined justification as "the acceptance with which God receives us into his favour [grace] . . . ," the remission of sins and the imputation of Christ's righteousness," which clothes the believer with a merit and a righteousness not his own. Thus grace was exclusively something in God. The Council of Trent, on the other hand, defined grace also as something infused by God into man; therefore it anathematized the teaching that "men are justified either by the sole imputation of the righteousness of Christ or by the sole remission of sins, to the exclusion of the grace and the charity which is infused into their hearts by the Holy Spirit and remains in them; or also that the grace by which we are justified is only the good will of God." (See also JUSTIFICATION.)

Grace and Merit.—The definition of grace as the free gift of divine favour excludes any notion of prior human merit; in the axiom of Augustine, "the grace of God would not be grace in any sense if it were not gratis in every sense." Christian orthodoxy has taught, therefore, that the initiative in the relationship of grace between God and man is always on the side of God. But once God has granted this "first grace," man does have a response to give and therefore a responsibility to assume for the continuance of the relationship. Although the ideas of grace and of merit are mutually exclusive, neither Augustine nor the Protestant defenders of the principle of "grace alone" could avoid the question of reward in the relationship of grace; in fact, some passages of the New Testament seem to use charis for "reward." The conflict over imputation noted earlier is reflected in differing interpretations of merit and reward: the Roman Catholic theology of grace stresses the "habitual" character of the life created by the gift of grace and therefore ascribes merit to the obedience of the law of God; classical Protestantism spoke of a co-operating grace after conversion as a way of including man's activity in the life of grace, but it avoided language that would suggest that man earns something by his obedience in grace. Of course, where the message of Protestantism has become primarily ethical, this emphasis upon grace has tended to diminish.

The Means of Grace.—As the gift of divine favour that grants salvation, grace is conferred through means. At the Council of Florence it was affirmed that the sacraments "contain grace and confer it upon those who receive them worthily." Luther went so far as to argue that "God gives no one his Spirit or grace except through or with the external word," by which he meant the preaching of the gospel and the administration of the sacraments. The Thirty-Nine Articles of the Anglican Church called the sacraments "sure certain witnesses and effectual signs of grace and God's good will toward us," by the which he doth work invisibly in us. But Reformed and "Free Church" Protestantism has not bound grace to the means of grace as closely as this. Thus the Westminster Confession warned that "the grace which is exhibited in or by the sacraments, rightly used, is not conferred by any power in them." Yet even those traditions and theologians who have insisted upon predestination and upon the freedom of God to grant grace when and where he pleases have also taught that the proper use of God, the sacraments and sometimes prayer and penitence—would tend to strengthen, though not to guarantee, the presence of grace. Conversely, the most sacramental of theologies have been obliged to assert that while the saving grace of God is bound to the means of grace, it is not bound by them.

The State of Grace.—Statistically speaking, the most common meaning of the term grace in Christian language is certainly that contained in the biblical greeting, repeated millions of times daily: "Hail Mary, full of grace!" The Greek participle, "you who have been 'graced,'" conveys the idea that Mary has been the object of divine grace, and it has been understood to mean that she is a channel of grace in a unique way. Over and above this, the

Testament and the Christian tradition have described the "graces" (charismata), some special and some more usual, conferred by the Holy Spirit; the Eastern Orthodox Confession of Peter Mogila refers to seven such charismata. Even one who has not received a special charisma, however, is said to be en chariti, in a state of grace, which is the condition of being liberated from sin and of possessing the gifts of the indwelling Holy Spirit. Where grace is closely tied to predestination, as in orthodox Calvinism, grace is said to be irresistible and the state of grace ultimately invincible. Better perhaps than any of the other connotations of the term, the idea of the state of grace unites the favour of God, the means by which this is conferred, the human response to God's favour and the divine response to this in turn. For all of these are properly called "grace," and taken together they summarize the meaning of Christian faith and life. See also references under "Grace" in the Index volume.

BIBLIOGRAPHY.—The Doctrine of Grace, a symposium edited by W. T. Whitley for the Committee on Faith and Order (1932); J. Van der Meersch, "Grace," Dictionnaire de théologie catholique, vol. vi, pp. 1554-1687; Gillis P. Wetter, Charis (1913); James Moffatt, Grace in the New Testament (1932); G. H. Joyce, The Catholic Doctrine of Grace (1950); Charles Journet, The Meaning of Grace (1960); Philip Watson, The Concept of Grace (1959); G. C. Berkouwer, The Triumph of Grace in the Theology of Karl Barth (1956). (J. J. Pn.)

GRACES, Greek goddesses of fertility. The name (cf. Venus) refers to the "pleasing" or "charming" appearance of a fertile field or garden. (Gr. Charites, Lat. Gratiae.) Their number varies; sometimes only one Charis is mentioned, but usually they are three: Aglaia (brightness), Euphrosyne (joyfulness) and Thalia (bloom). They are daughters of Zeus and Hera (or Eurynome, daughter of Oceanus), or of Helios and Aegle, a daughter of Zeus. At Sparta there were two Graces, Kleta and Phaenna; at Athens two, Auxo and Hegemone, associated with the goddess Aglauros in the oath taken by youths belonging to the military college of the ephebi. Frequently the Graces are taken as goddesses of charm or beauty in general and hence are associated with Aphrodite, Peitho, Hermes; the union of Hephaestus with Charis in the Iliad is probably a mere allegory (Craftsmanship weds Beauty). In works of art they were represented in early times draped, later as nude female figures.

GRACIÁN Y MORALES, BALTASAR (1601-1658), the most important 17th-century Spanish prose writer after Quevedo (q.v.), was baptized at Belmonte near Calayatud, Jan. 8, 1601, studied at Calatayud and Saragossa, became a Jesuit (1619) and later rector of the Jesuit college of Tarragona. His educational and literary theories, enunciated respectively in El discreto (1646; Eng. trans. The Compleat Gentleman, 2nd ed, 1730) and in his rhetorical treatise on the "conceited" style, Agudeza y arte de ingenio (definitive version, 1648), are exemplified in his masterpiece, the great philosophical novel El Criticón (1651-53-57; Eng. trans. The Critick, 1681), published pseudonymously in defiance of his superiors, whose disciplinary action precipitated his unsuccessful petition for release from the society. He died at Tarazona, Dec. 6, 1658. There are numerous modern editions and studies of his major works, which also include El héroe (1637; Eng. trans. The Hero, 1726) and El Oráculo manual (1647; Eng. trans. The Oracle, 1953); his influence on Schopenhauer was notable.

BIBLIOGRAPHY.—A. Coster, Baltasar Gracián (1913); A. F. G. Bell, Baltasar Gracián (1921); Obras completas, ed. by A. del Hoyo (1960). (F. S. R.)

GRACKLE, a name given to various birds of the family Icteridae in the new world, a group that includes blackbirds, orioles and troupials. The grackles include 12 species classified in 8 genera restricted to or best represented in the tropics. Most have uniform glossy black plumage, but the females of Quiscalus, Holoquiscalus and Cassidix are dingy gray or brownish, and certain tropical species are in part bright yellow or scarlet. Their habits vary, but most grackles are omnivorous and when in abundance may damage crops. They also destroy the eggs and young of other birds, and the rice grackles (Scaphidura oryzivora) of Central and South America customarily lay their eggs in the nests of other birds.

ALLAN D. CRUICKSHANK FROM NATIONAL AUDUBON SOCIETY

BOAT-TAILED GRACKLE (CASSIDIX MEXICANUS)

The best known grackle of the United States is the common or purple grackle (Quiscalus quiscula), which occurs in most of eastern North America. It is a beautiful bird, purplish or greenish black in colour with a long, graduated tail, and grows to a length of about 12 in.; several subspecies and intergrades are recognized, including the Florida purple grackle (Q. q. quiscula) and the typical purple grackle (Q. q. stonei). The bronzed grackle (Q. versicolor) is sometimes considered a subspecies of Q. quiscula. The boat-tailed grackle (Cassidix mexicanus), which ranges from Delaware and the Gulf Coast to Colombia, is much larger (16 in.) and has a more expansive, keellike tail. It is known locally as the crow blackbird, or jackdaw, the latter in reference to its imagined similarity to the common jackdaw (Corvus monedula) of Europe.

See also Bird. (E. R., Be.; X.)

GRADIENT WIND, a generalization of the geostrophic wind (q.v.) for flow along curved trajectories. Friction is disregarded, and the wind is assumed to be parallel to the isobars (lines of constant pressure). The gradient wind gives a better representation of the true wind than the geostrophic, particularly when the wind speed and trajectory curvature are large, as in the case of hurricanes and fast jet streams between 25,000 and 50,000 ft. elevation.

Whereas the geostrophic wind needs for its computation only the pressure distribution along a constant level surface or the slope distribution of a constant pressure surface, the gradient wind needs in addition the knowledge of trajectory curvature. In general this is not known; however in cases in which the wind speed is much greater than the speed of the flow patterns (a condition generally satisfied when the gradient wind is most useful), the curvature of the stream lines is a good approximation to the trajectory curvature. Further, streamline curvature above the friction layer is well represented by curvature of isobars or contour lines of isobaric surfaces (see Ekman Spiral). The figure illustrates the theory of gradient wind. Conditions in the northern hemisphere, i.e., where the Coriolis force acts to the right of the wind, are assumed (see Motion, Principles and Laws of). When the Coriolis force exceeds the pressure gradient force (see figure [A]) the air is continually deflected to the right, leading to anticyclonic (clockwise in the northern hemisphere) curvature of flow. This situation can be represented by a balance between the Coriolis force and the sum of pressure gradient and centrifugal forces. Then, the wind speed is larger than geostrophic. Since the centrifugal force depends on the square of the wind speed and the Coriolis force only on its first power, gradient equilibrium in the anticyclonic case is impossible for fast winds; hence anticyclones (high pressure centres) cannot become intense.

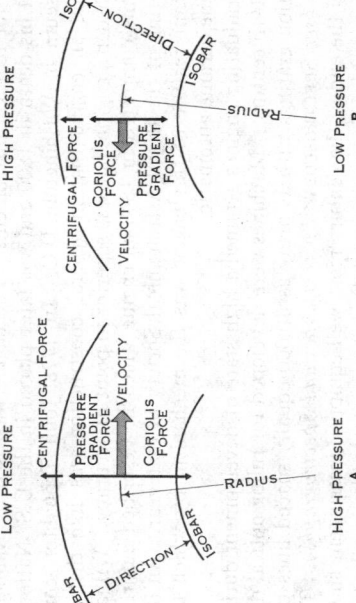

THE BALANCE OF FORCES FOR GRADIENT WINDS IN THE NORTHERN HEMISPHERE WITH (A) CLOCKWISE ROTATION AND (B) COUNTERCLOCKWISE ROTATION OF THE AIR

In the figure, B illustrates the case in which the pressure gradient force exceeds the Coriolis force so that the flow is curved in a counterclockwise sense (cyclonically). Here, the pressure gradient force balances the sum of Coriolis and centrifugal forces. Under these conditions, the wind is less than geostrophic; however, the speed of the wind is not limited, so that the strength of counterclockwise storms (cyclones) may be very large.

In the southern hemisphere, where the Coriolis force acts to the left of the wind, the term cyclonic refers to clockwise flow and anticyclonic to counterclockwise flow. The discussion of gradient wind above can be applied to the southern hemisphere, provided that the terms "cyclonic" and "anticyclonic" are used in this sense throughout. However, clockwise must be replaced by counterclockwise, and vice versa.

(H. A. P.)

GRADUATION AND CALIBRATION. Graduation is the process of dividing an interval into a number of smaller ones. Usually these divisions are of equal magnitude but occasionally they are related to each other according to some mathematical formula, as is the case for the distances between graduating marks on the dial of an alternating-current electric meter.

The word "graduation" is derived from the Latin *gradus*, "step," implying that graduation is performed by "stepping off" equal intervals in the larger interval to be divided.

Calibration is the process of measuring anything against a standard to determine the extent to which it meets specified requirements. The term is most frequently applied to the testing of measuring devices; e.g., electric meters, surveying tapes, speedometers, thermometers, etc. It applies equally well to the testing of precise machine articles, e.g., bearings, shafts, screw threads, etc., which must fit to close tolerances.

The word "calibration" is derived through the French *calibre* and Italian *calibro* from the Arabic *qâlib*, a "form" or "mold," in connection with gunnery, since the mold for the bullets had to conform to the bore or calibre of the gun.

The term is also used by some instrument manufacturers to describe the process of adjusting an instrument and its scale reading at the time of manufacture so that the indications of the instrument will be correct. They prefer the term "standardization" for subsequent processes of determining residual errors or errors which develop after the original adjustment. Graduation usually means the placing of the original marks on a scale or dial; and calibration, the determination of the correctness with which they were placed.

Development of modern technology owes much to the art of precise graduation, for without it parts would not work properly when fitted together. Prior to the 18th century all graduation was performed strictly as handwork. During the 18th century a number of dividing engines were developed. Henry Hindley, about 1739, constructed an engine for accurately cutting the teeth in clock gears and for dividing instruments. Jesse Ramsden, in 1766, made his first dividing engine which, although good enough for dividing the circle of the common surveying instruments, was not sufficiently accurate for nautical instruments used in the determination of position. In 1775 Ramsden completed his second and much improved engine; that one was capable of dividing circles for nautical instruments. The engine was used by Ramsden until his death in 1800 and was later placed in the U.S. National Museum in Washington, D.C. In 1778 John Troughton completed an engine that in general construction was like that of Ramsden's engine, but was superior in point of accuracy. William Simms completed in 1843 an engine which he described before a meeting of the Royal Astronomical Society in that year. An important feature of this engine was the mechanism by which the engine became automatic.

Graduating engines attained a high state of development during the 19th century. Machines were developed for ruling optical diffraction gratings with as many as 30,000 equally spaced lines per inch (*see* Spectroscopy: *Spectroscopes and Spectrographs*). Toward the end of the century most well-equipped instrument shops were capable of performing both linear and circular graduation with high accuracy since the facilities required for precise machining, gear cutting, etc., and precise graduation are similar.

Most precise graduation is accomplished by special engines designed for this purpose. Modern graduating engines are commercially available with guaranteed accuracies of 1 sec. of arc for circular graduation (better than 1 part per 1,000,000), and of .0001 in. for linear graduations. Special ruling engines for optical gratings have been developed in which the position of the ruling tool is electronically controlled and guided by means of photocells which are actuated by interference fringes, thus governing its position to within a fraction of the wave length of light.

Process of Graduation.—Original graduation can be performed in two ways. One involves bisecting the interval to be graduated with a beam compass, or similar instrument, and successively bisecting the intervals obtained until the desired fineness of division is attained. The other involves the use of a trial subinterval and stepping off intervals of the larger interval with a pair of dividers or a similar device. This process can be repeated until the desired accuracy of the divisions is attained. The former process can be employed if the total number of divisions desired is a power of 2; if not, the second process must be employed. Both may be used if the number of divisions is a multiple of a power of 2 and other numbers.

The precise commercial graduating engines incorporate automatic correcting mechanisms. Although the gears, racks and screws which position the graving tool in each engine are fashioned with great care, some residual errors remain. A system of levers operated by a correcting cam adjusts the position of the graving tool to correct for the errors of each engine. Another device used to improve accuracy employs multiple lead screws and multiple ways so that irregularities in any single part will be averaged out.

Calibration.—The concept of calibration involves measurement. In its broadest sense it includes comparison with a standard, which may result in acceptance or rejection of the article because it does not conform closely enough to the specifications set forth for it, issuance of a certificate or construction of a table or chart for it stating the extent to which it departs from the standard or adjustment of the article so that it conforms with the standard to within allowable errors. Underlying this must be a sound science of measurement and a statistical theory of errors.

Importance of Calibration.—The high technological development of modern life has resulted in increased importance for the process of calibration. In earlier times only the weights and measures used in commerce were subjected to any verification, and often even this was not done well or at all. Most manufactured articles consisted of parts that were individually made according to the pattern of the particular artisan. Parts of an article made by one person were not required to fit with parts made by another. With the development of quantity production, however, this procedure had to change. Large plants began to manufacture goods for commerce, and different parts of various articles were made by different individuals. After manufacture these parts were required to fit together, and this was possible only if they had been made to specified dimensions. Therefore, gauges had to be distributed in the various departments of each manufacturing plant to serve as standards by which the dimensions of each part were fixed. As these gauges were used continually they would change and therefore they required calibration by comparison with master gauges.

Calibration of measuring devices is also important in the exchange of scientific information. In order that one scientist be able to collate his work with another it is necessary that there be agreement between them on the sizes of units and that the measuring devices which each uses be calibrated by comparison with agreed upon standards.

International Standards.—The first great step toward realization of an international system of standards was taken by 17 nations when they signed a treaty on May 20, 1875, to establish an organization to improve and maintain the metric system of units. The metric system was brought into being by the French National Assembly through decisions made between 1791 and 1795. Its use in commercial transactions was made compulsory in that country on July 4, 1837, and by many other nations subsequently, and its commercial use was made permissive in the United States and the British empire. It is based on the metre as a unit of length and the kilogram as a unit of mass.

In order to carry out its mission, the organization set up by the treaty of 1875 had a number of prototype standards fabricated and distributed among the participating nations. They were standards of length, consisting of bars of platinum-iridium on which were engraved two parallel lines 1 m. apart, and standards of mass, consisting of platinum-iridium cylinders weighing 1 kg. each.

One of the prototype metre bars and one of the prototype mass standards were selected as the international standards and placed in the International Bureau of Weights and Measures at Sèvres, a suburb of Paris. The various national standards are frequently sent to the international bureau for calibration.

The standards of length and mass, together with a standard of time fixed by the motion of the earth, and a standard of temperature, fixed by the temperature at which water is in equilibrium with its vapor and ice, serve to fix the sizes of all other units of measurement in accordance with certain agreed upon definitions. The major standardizing laboratories of the world construct standards for other units such as the volt, the unit of electromotive force, and the ohm, the unit of electrical resistance. The standards so constructed are intercompared and a "best" value for each national standard is adopted by international agreement.

Because of this system the metric standards of all nations are kept on a uniform basis. Instruments calibrated in terms of the standards of one nation agree with those calibrated in standards of another to within the error of observation.

Prior to an international agreement in 1959 some differences existed between certain units used by the English-speaking countries. For example, one U.S. yard was approximately equal to 0.9144018 m. by its definition and the British yard was equal to 0.9143986 m. as given by comparison with the British standard yard. The U.S. and British pounds were 0.4535924277 kg. and 0.453592338 kg., respectively. Although these differences are trivial for most purposes, they become bothersome in precise calibration work. For this reason the directors of the national standardizing laboratories of the English-speaking countries agreed to adopt an international yard (0.9144 m., exactly) and an international pound (0.45359237 kg., exactly) and to use these equivalents in all calibrations from 1959 on unless otherwise required. This makes the international inch equal to 2.54 cm., exactly. However, for most international comparisons the metric system is used and scientific results are usually stated in metric units. Electric units are based on the metric system.

Accuracy of Calibration.—In order that required accuracy be achieved in the calibration of a device it is necessary that the accuracy of the standard with which it is compared be considerably greater, since some uncertainty is bound to be attached to any comparison. For example, the uncertainty in the length of a 50-m. surveying tape expressed in terms of the international prototype metre is bound to be considerably greater than the uncertainty in a national prototype metre; and a 1-lb. weight certified by a local sealer of weights and measures is subject to considerably more uncertainty than a national prototype kilogram.

To assure adequate precision of intercomparison a very high standard of accuracy is maintained in national standardizing laboratories. High-quality metre bars can be compared with each other with a probable error of 3 parts in 10^8. (The meaning of this is that in a large number of repeated intercomparisons 50% of the results will agree to within this range.) Masses of 1 kg. may be intercompared with a probable error of 4 parts in 10^9. Frequency and time standards may be compared with probable errors of a few parts in 10^{10}, using atomic standards of frequency introduced in the later 1950s, although these comparisons may not be referred to the defined standard of time—the tropical year 1900 at 12 hr. E.T. (*see* Time Measurement)—with equal accuracy. Some of the electric standards may be intercompared with probable errors smaller than 1 part of 10^6, although standards for the defined units themselves are not realized with this accuracy.

Lower accuracies are associated with the best practice in calibrating standards for some other quantities.

Where the magnitude of the quantities being measured differs appreciably from the defined standard, lower accuracies result. Thus 50-m. base-line tapes are calibrated with probable errors of 2 or 3 parts in 10^7 and end gauges of 1 in. with probable errors of 1 part in 10^6, at best.

Another illustration of the importance of accuracy in calibration of measuring devices is afforded by the application of quality control. Suppose a commodity such as sheet metal is required to be produced having a certain thickness with a tolerance of plus or minus 0.003 in. If the gauge used to test specimens of the material has an uncertainty in its calibration of plus or minus 0.001 in., any specimen which gauges more than 0.002 in. from the specification must be rejected because the gauge error plus the measured departure from specifications may add to more than 0.003 in. Obviously, many satisfactory specimens will be unnecessarily rejected if the unknown gauge error and the measured departure are opposite in sign. If the uncertainty of the gauge calibration is as small as 0.0001 in. the number of specimens unnecessarily rejected will be greatly reduced.

Laboratory Calibration.—Many laboratory instruments are, by nature, so variable in performance that frequent calibrations are required. This is also true for relatively stable equipment when results of the highest accuracy are required. Under such conditions calibrations of the instrument are conducted before and after each measurement, or as often as circumstances require. This calibration is performed by making measurements with the instrument on a standard sample similar to the unknown to be measured.

A few illustrations: In determining the composition of a gas of unknown composition with a mass spectrometer, a gas of similar but known composition is often tested by the spectrometer before and after the unknown. If a certain component of the known gas is found to be 1% lower in abundance than it is known to be, then the same component in the unknown gas will be estimated to be 1% higher then it was measured to be. Similarly when a chronometer is used in timing astronomical events such as eclipses, the chronometer is checked with radio time signals immediately before and after the event is observed. The checking of the chronometer constitutes a calibration of that instrument and a more correct timing of the event is obtained through the use of radio time signals as a standard than if complete reliance had been placed on the chronometer alone.

See also Weights and Measures; Metrology.

Bibliography.—*Graduation*: B. L. Page, "The Graduation of Precise Circles," *Surveying and Mapping*, 13:149–161 (1953); I. Pope, "Techniques for Ruling and Etching Precise Scales in Glass and Their Reproduction by Photo-Etching," U.S. National Bureau of Standards *Circular 565*; E. Leibhardt, "A Dividing Gear for a Ruling Engine," *J. Opt. Soc. Amer.*, 40:623–624 (Sept. 1950); J. Strong, "New Johns Hopkins Ruling Engine," *J. Opt. Soc. Amer.*, 41:3–15 (Jan. 1951); G. R. Harrison and J. E. Archer, "Interferometric Calibration of Precision Screws and Control of Ruling Engines," *J. Opt. Soc. Amer.*, 41:495–503 (Aug. 1951); E. Leibhardt, "Improved Method for Lapping a Dividing Gear for a Ruling Engine," *J. Opt. Soc. Amer.*, 42:447–460 (July 1952); A. G. Ingalls, "Ruling Engines," *Scientific American*, vol. 186, no. 6, pp. 45–54, 90–96 (June 1952).

Calibration: Sir R. T. Glazebrook (ed.), *A Dictionary of Applied Physics*, 5 vol. (1922–23), particularly vol. 3; *Collected Researches*, National Physical Laboratory (1905–35), replaced by *Abstracts of Papers*, National Physical Laboratory (1936–35); *Precision Measurement and Calibration*, U.S. National Bureau of Standards Handbook 77 (1961); Ulrich Stille, *Messen und Rechnen in der Physik* (1955).
(A. G. McN.; X.)

GRADUS (Gradus ad Parnassum, "a step to Parnassus"), a Latin (or Greek) dictionary, in which the quantities of the vowels of the words are marked. Synonyms, epithets and poetical expressions and extracts are also included under the more important headings, the whole being intended as an aid for students in Greek and Latin verse composition. The first Latin gradus was compiled in 1702 by the Jesuit Paul Aler (1656–1727), a famous schoolmaster. There is a Latin gradus by C. D. Yonge (1850); English-Latin by A. C. Ainger and H. G. Wintle (1890); Greek by J. Brasse (1828) and E. Maltby (1815), bishop of Durham.

GRADY, HENRY WOODFIN (1850-1889), U.S. journalist and orator, was born in Athens, Ga., May 24, 1850. He graduated from the University of Georgia in 1868 and took postgraduate work at the University of Virginia. A letter to the *Atlanta Constitution*, written while he was a student, evidenced his journalistic talents and led him into journalism. He became the editor of several small newspapers and then Georgia representative of the *New York Herald* before buying a quarter interest in the *Atlanta Constitution* in 1880. He was editor of that paper until his death. A capable journalist, he was also a talented orator. During the late 1880s he made a number of famous addresses, including one on "The New South," in Dec. 1886, that helped to pacify north-south animosities of the post-Civil War period. He died in Atlanta, Ga., Dec. 23, 1889.

GRÄFE, the name of a German family noted for its contributions to medicine and surgery.

KARL FERDINAND VON GRÄFE (1787-1840), surgeon, was born in Warsaw, Pol., on March 8, 1787, studied in Germany and became professor of surgery in Berlin. He was a pioneer in German plastic surgery and was responsible for significant surgical innovations, including technical improvements of blood transfusion, Caesarean section, rhinoplasties and repair of cleft palate. Gräfe has been called the father of modern plastic surgery. He died at Hanover on July 4, 1840.

ALBRECHT VON GRÄFE (1828-70), his son, considered the founder of modern ophthalmology and a pioneer in ophthalmic surgery, was born on May 22, 1828, at Berlin. He studied in Berlin, Vienna, Prague, Paris, London, Dublin and Edinburgh as an ophthalmic specialist and became one of the greatest eye surgeons of the century and an authority on diseases of the brain and nervous system. He was noted also as a great and revered teacher and as the founder, with F. C. Donders (*q.v.*), of the *Archiv für Ophthalmologie*, which contains most of his important publications. Albrecht von Gräfe is connected historically with the operation for cataract by linear extraction (1867-88). He is best known to medical students for the eye sign in exophthalmic goitre, which is named for him. Among his other contributions are iridectomy for glaucoma (1857), the establishment of sympathetic ophthalmia as

GRAF, URS (c. 1485-1527), Swiss draftsman, engraver and goldsmith, was born at Solothurn, the son of the goldsmith Hugo Graf, and probably studied under his father and then at Basel. His art is inspired by that of Dürer and of Baldung Grün. After a period of travel he settled in Basel in 1509. In 1514 he executed a reliquary of St. Bernard for the monastery of St. Urban. This, his chief work as a goldsmith, was sold by the city of Lucerne in 1850 and has since disappeared. Graf is best known for his drawings, executed in sure and bold linework. There are extant 100 woodcuts for which he made the drawings; a number of engravings, etchings and nielli, and some 200 drawings by his hand. The greater part of Graf's work is dated and signed by his monogram.

See bibliography and memoir by I. Abrahams in *Jewish Quarterly Review*, iv, pp. 165 ff. (1892).
(J. G. Ws.)

GRAETZ, HEINRICH (1817-1891), German-Jewish historian, author of a famous history of the Jews, was born at Xions, Posen, on Oct. 31, 1817. In his early youth he spent three years as the pupil of Rabbi S. R. Hirsch, the fighter for enlightened Jewish orthodoxy. He took his doctorate at Jena in 1845 and during his university years came under the influence of the Hegelian school of historiography, the method of which conditioned his early view of Jewish history. His 11-volume *Geschichte der Juden* (1853-76; abridged Eng. trans. 1891-92) remains even after a century the most picturesque account of Jewish history. Graetz also published exegetical works on several books of the Hebrew Bible and took an active part in the anti-Semitic controversy during the 1880s in Germany, during which he was attacked by Heinrich von Treitschke. He soon left the camp of enlightened orthodoxy and remained until the end of his life a follower of the moderately conservative middle-way party to which the famous rabbinic seminary at Breslau, where Graetz taught from 1854, belonged. From 1869 he was also honorary professor at Breslau university. He died in Munich on Sept. 7, 1891.
(H. J. SG.)

a clinical entity (1866), his demonstration that often blindness and visual defects connected with cerebral disorders are traceable to optic neuritis (1860) and the introduction of the use of Helmholtz' ophthalmoscope in diagnosis. He died in Berlin of tuberculosis at the age of 42, on July 20, 1870.
(I. H. L.)

GRAFFITO, from the Italian word meaning "scribbling" or "scratching," has been adopted by archaeologists as a general term for the casual writings, rude drawings and markings on ancient buildings, in distinction from the deliberate writings known as inscriptions. These graffiti, either scratched on stone or plaster by a sharp instrument or, more rarely, written in red chalk or black charcoal, are found in great abundance, *e.g.*, on the monuments of ancient Egypt. The subject matter of these scribblings by boys, street idlers and the casual passer-by includes scrawls, rude caricatures, election addresses and lines of poetry. Apparently private owners of property felt the nuisance of the defacement of their walls; at Rome near the Porta Portuensis was found an inscription begging persons not to scribble (*scariphare*) on the walls.

Graffiti are important as illustrating the forms and corruptions of the various alphabets used by the people, and may guide the archaeologist to the date of the building. But their chief value is twofold. First, they are important to the linguist for the information they furnish about the spoken language of the period and place and occasionally about other languages as well, as in the case of the ancient Greek mercenaries who scribbled their names, in the Cypriote dialect and syllabary, on an Egyp-

PONTIFICIA COMMISSIONE D'ARTE SACRA

GRAFFITI: (TOP) REFERS TO THE GROOM CONSTANTIUS, 4TH CENTURY, FROM THE CATACOMB OF DOMITILLA, ROME; (BOTTOM) DEPICTS A SEVEN-BRANCHED CANDLESTICK AND OTHER SYMBOLS FROM THE JEWISH CATACOMB OF VIGNA RONDANINI, 4TH CENTURY

tian sphinx, or the Greek "tourist" from Pamphylia who carved his name on the great pyramid at Giza. And second, graffiti are invaluable to the historian for the light they throw on the everyday life of the man in the street of the period, and for the intimate details of customs and institutions. The graffiti dealing with the gladiatorial shows at Pompeii are in this respect particularly noteworthy.

The most famous graffito is that generally accepted as representing a caricature of Christ upon the cross found on the walls of the Domus Gelotiana on the Palatine in Rome in 1857, and now preserved in the Kircherian museum of the Collegio Romano.

GRAFT HYBRIDS: see CHIMERA.

GRAFTING (IN PLANTS)

is the general term for the operation of placing a portion of one plant (bud or scion) into or on a stem, root or branch of another (stock) in such a way that a union will be formed and the partners will continue to grow. This term includes budding (bud grafting) and grafting proper (scion grafting and approach grafting or inarching). Budding and grafting proper differ only in the amount of plant material placed on the stock. In modern horticulture grafting is used for many reasons: to repair injured trees, to produce dwarf trees and shrubs, to avoid certain diseases, to retain varietal characteristics, to adapt varieties to adverse soil or climatic conditions, to ensure pollination, to produce multifruited or multiflowered plants and as the only method of propagation for some species.

Although grafting was known to the ancients, it was not fully understood by them. Many records existed before the birth of Christ calling attention to instances of grafts that occurred in nature. Pliny the elder, writing on the various kinds of natural grafting, called attention to combinations of cherry growing on willow, plane on laurel and laurel on cherry, which resulted from the germination of foreign seeds that were caught in a crack or hollow of an established tree. The subsequent independent growth of the seedling, upon hasty observation, might be construed as resulting from actual tissue union between the two plants. Many of these reports can be attributed to the observer's imagination, since plants having widespread genetic make-up are not generally compatible.

In theory any two plants that are closely related botanically and that have a continuous cambium can be grafted. Grafts between species are often successful, between genera occasionally so, between families nearly always failures. Within the genus closeness of botanical relationship is not an infallible guide as to probable success, but in the absence of recorded experience it is the best available. The ability of two plants to continue to grow or be compatible when joined together by the asexual practice of grafting is mediated by many complex physiological and environmental factors.

Compatibility or congeniality in grafting is of various degrees. Apple grafted on oak fails immediately; apple grafted on pear may grow well for one or two years but gradually weakens and dies. Some lilacs exist for a number of years on privet stocks but fail ultimately. The common apricot is, other things being equal, the best stock for apricot varieties, but in moist soils in cool regions apricot trees flourish better on certain plum stocks than on apricot. These differences in adaptability of closely related plants that can be successfully grafted permit a greater degree of adjustment to soil conditions than would ordinarily be possible.

The establishment of union between grafted components is effected through the formation of a loose growth of cells (callus) contributed by both elements. These cells fuse into a mass so continuous in compatible grafts that the precise location of the line of union is frequently impossible to determine. There is, however, no evidence of a fusion of individual cells. At the initial union the cells are usually isodiametric; in the secondary stage tissue differentiation begins. Just as in wound healing, union proceeds more rapidly if the wounded areas are protected against drying out, and in most forms of grafting rapid knitting is essential to maintenance of life in the scion.

The principles involved in grafting are based on the matching of scion and stock cambiums (meristematic tissue, the cells of which are undifferentiated and capable of frequent cell division). Cambial tissue in most woody trees and shrubs is an inconspicuous single cell layer covering the central core of wood and lying directly beneath the bark.

The success or failure of any grafting operation is based upon the compatibility of each plant part, closeness of fit and cambial contact. The union is initially held in place by pressure exerted by the stock, grafting tape or by rubber budding strips applied over the point of union.

The numerous operative procedures by which grafted plants are produced fall into two major groups known as budding and grafting. Though these terms are well understood in ordinary usage, definite separation between them is impossible in some cases. Perhaps the best differentiation between budding and grafting is that offered by Charles Baltet, who defined grafting as any method which employs as a scion a portion of a plant comprising the complete circumference, no matter how long it may be. This distinction considers only the mechanical operations involved with no reference to the manner in which union is established.

Budding (Bud Grafting).—As generally understood, budding is effected by raising or removing a segment of bark of the stock and inserting a segment of the scion, containing a bud, into the wound thus made. The piece inserted may be shield or patch shaped. In budding apple, pear, peach, orange, etc., the bark is lifted away from around an upright or inverted T-shaped incision (fig. 1[A]) and the bud is then inserted under the bark (fig. 1[B]) and tied securely in place with raffia or rubber budding strips (fig. 1[C]). In budding nut trees better results are usually obtained by removing a piece of bark, generally rectangular in shape, from the

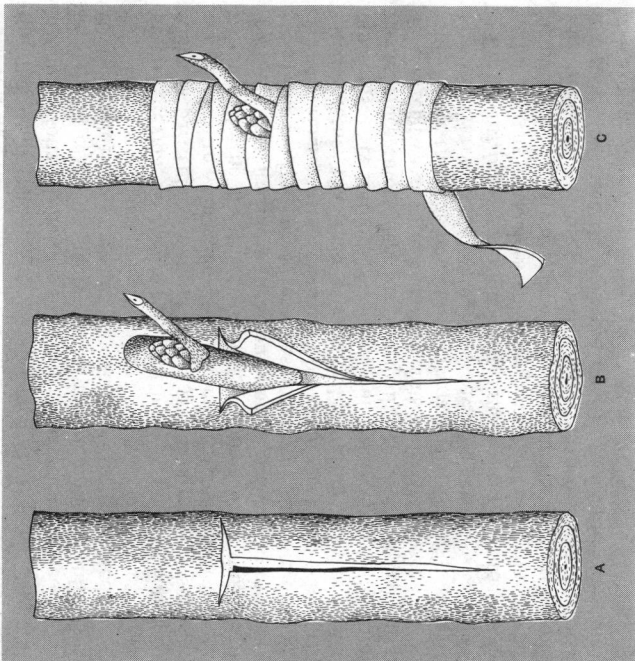

FIG. 1.—THE TECHNIQUE OF BUDDING, SHOWING (A) BARK OF STOCK OPENED FOR INSERTION OF BUD; (B) METHOD OF INSERTING BUD INTO INCISION; (C) STOCK WITH BUD TIED IN PLACE WITH A RUBBER BUDDING STRIP

stock and replacing it with a piece of bark carrying a bud from the tree whose reproduction is desired. In these cases tying and waxing are generally employed in order to ensure cambial contact and to protect the bud from desiccation and from disease organisms.

Ordinarily budding is practicable only during the period in which the bark slips freely on the stock. Most budding operations in nurseries in temperate zones are done from midsummer to late summer. The shield of the inserted bud usually unites with the stock within 14 days, but growth from the bud is not expected or desired until the following spring, when the stock is cut back close to the inserted bud to force its development.

In southern and Pacific coast states of the United States the long growing season permits June budding of peach and other stone fruits as early as stocks are workable; i.e., when the stock is pencil-size in diameter. Stone fruit seedlings growing from seed planted in early spring or the preceding fall are budded actually in May rather than in June in many nurseries. The top of the stock is broken over at once (to stimulate bud growth) but not removed until the bud has grown several inches; this procedure produces a budded tree ready for planting in the orchard in the autumn of the same propagating year in which the seed for the stock was sown.

Budding may also be employed in producing double-worked trees. A bud of the intermediate variety is first placed on the selected rootstock in the usual manner and forced. The following year the desired scion variety is budded on the intermediate; the whole process taking about three years.

Grafting Proper.—In one form or another, grafting proper is used on plants either in the growing or dormant stage. Deciduous fruit trees are grafted ordinarily with dormant scions and frequently when the stocks are also dormant. In many of them (e.g., apple) callus formation takes place at relatively low temperatures while the plant is dormant, thereby resulting in a graft which at planting time has an incipient union. This permits bench grafting, a process in which dormant scions are grafted on small roots or pieces of roots, also dormant, during winter by workmen indoors. The grafted plants are stored in moist sand, sawdust or peat moss until spring, when they are lined out in nursery rows. Dormant scions may be grafted onto growing trees throughout the growing season, but the growth of the scion and healing of the stub consequent upon late grafting are much inferior to those obtained from spring grafting.

In grafting plants having evergreen foliage, such as the orange, the leaf blades are removed from the scion in order to restrict moisture loss while the union is forming. Grafted conifers, however, are not defoliated, but are placed in a somewhat shaded location in a closed case. In many plants, including most conifers, root regeneration is so slow that they seldom can be grafted successfully bare rooted, and therefore the stocks must be well established in pots previous to the time of grafting. In grafting the mango, which is particularly difficult, small potted stocks are sometimes placed close to young shoots of the mother tree which may then be united to the stock by inarching or approach grafting (see below). In this procedure the scion remains attached to the mother tree, being cut free only after it has united with the potted stock.

The various types of operation by which stock and scion are so fitted together that they may unite by grafting number into the hundreds. Six methods, however, will satisfy almost all requirements, since choice depends principally on ease of execution and on the relative sizes of the stock and scion. When the stock is much larger than the scion the cleft graft (fig. 2[A, B]) or a bark (crown) graft (fig. 2[E]) is more advantageous.

Cleft Grafting.—The cleft graft, usable when the stock is dormant (i.e., its bark does not slip) involves sawing the stock at right angles to its stem, splitting the stem and then inserting scions with the bases cut approximately wedge shaped so that their cambial zones (between the bark and wood) lie alongside the cambial zones of the stock.

Bark (Crown) and Inlay Grafting.—These methods involve cutting off the stock, as with the cleft graft, and either inserting a wedge-shaped scion between bark and wood of the stock (true bark graft) or removing a portion of the bark into which is fitted exactly the scion from which half the circumference of the basal portion has been removed (inlay graft). The bark graft is practicable only when the bark of the stock separates readily from the wood. Since these grafts are usually made above the ground, all cut surfaces should be coated with one of the proprietary grafting compounds or with grafting wax, to protect against drying out. These grafts can be made on stems of any size, but satisfactory healing is rarely obtained without undue effort when the stubs exceed 2 in. in diameter.

Splice and Tongue Grafting.—The splice graft and its modified form, the tongue graft (fig. 2[C, D]), are suited to cases in which stock and scion are very nearly of the same diameter. A straight slanting cut is made, at a rather narrow angle, removes the top of the stock. A similar cut is made at the base of the scion. The two are joined so that the cambial zones match, after which they are tied securely

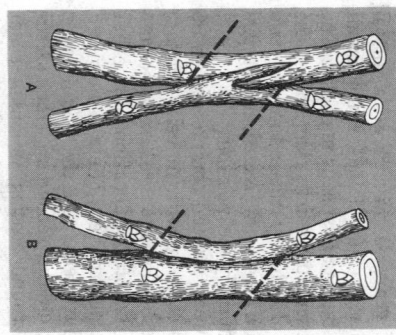

FIG. 3.—TYPES OF INARCHING: (A) FITTING TONGUES; (B) APPLYING EXPOSED SURFACES. SCION: (RIGHT) STOCK. DOTTED LINE SHOWS WHERE CUTS ARE MADE AFTER SCION AND STOCK GROW TOGETHER

in place. The tongue graft adds to the slanting cut a longitudinal split in the cut surfaces of stock and scion, in each case about one-third of the distance in toward the centre from the longest lip. These two pieces are then fitted together giving increased contact of the cambium zones; this method provides a fit that is less easily displaced than the simple splice graft. Both splice and tongue grafts made above ground are waxed or coated with grafting compound in order to prevent excessive drying from sun and exposure. Similarly, if these grafts are to stand below ground, it is common to wrap the graft union with cloth-backed grafting tape.

Side and Veneer Grafting.—With conifers and with some other plants one of the side grafts is generally employed. Into the stem of the stock, generally rather close to the soil line, a long diagonal downward cut, traversing about a third of the diameter, is made; into this is fitted the scion with its base trimmed to a wedge shape. If the base portion of the scion wood is removed and the scion, cut only on one side, is fitted against the exposed surface of the stock, the operation is known as veneer grafting. These two methods are suitable for use in cases where union of stock and scion are slow to take place.

Inarching.—This may be accomplished by making an upward diagonal incision in the scion and a similar downward incision in the stock, fitting together the two tongues thus created, tying in position and treating with a grafting compound (fig. 3[A]). It may also be effected by removing a small longitudinal piece of bark and wood from the scion and fit-

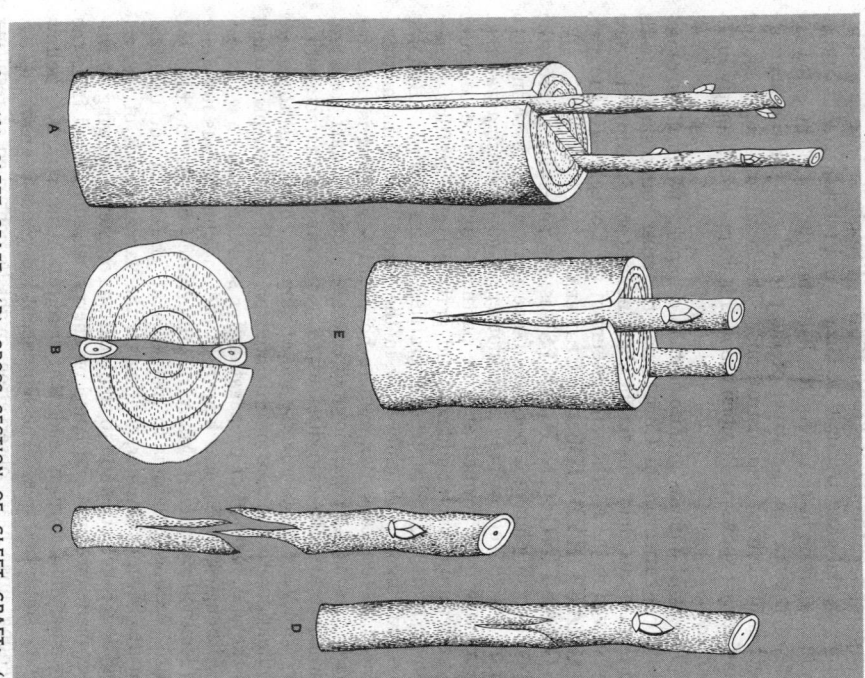

FIG. 2.—(A) CLEFT GRAFT; (B) CROSS SECTION OF CLEFT GRAFT; (C, D) TONGUE (WHIP) GRAFT; (E) BARK (CROWN) GRAFT

ting exactly the exposed portion of the scion into a slot on the stock from which the bark has been removed (fig. 3[B]). Both of these methods permit union of stock and scion to be established before either is severed.

Bridge Grafting.—Closely related to the above methods in the structure of the approaches made is bridge grafting, but its use is in tree repair rather than in propagation. Where a portion of the bark of a tree has been removed by an injury (severe frost or foraging animals), the wound may be bridged over by a number of long scions, whose ends eventually unite with the healthy tissue above and below the wound.

See also ARBORICULTURE; CHIMERA; HORTICULTURE AND GARDENING; PLANT PROPAGATION.

BIBLIOGRAPHY.—L. H. Bailey (ed.), *Standard Cyclopedia of Horticulture*, 3 vol. (1928; reissue 1954); R. J. Garner, *Grafter's Handbook*, 2nd ed. (1959); H. T. Hartmann and D. E. Kester, *Plant Propagation* (1959); J. P. Mahlstede and E. S. Haber, *Plant Propagation* (1957); Royal Horticultural Society, *Dictionary of Gardening*, 4 vol. and supplement, 2nd ed. by P. M. Synge (1956); J. S. Wells, *Plant Propagation Practices* (1955). (JN. P. M.)

GRAFTON, DUKES OF. The English dukes of Grafton are descended from HENRY FITZROY (1663–90), the second illegitimate son of Charles II by Barbara Villiers, duchess of Cleveland. After some initial hesitation he was officially recognized and became "the most popular and most able of the sons of Charles II." He was provided for by a marriage in 1672 to Isabella, daughter and heiress of Henry Bennet, earl of Arlington, and was created earl of Euston and duke of Grafton in 1675. At James II's coronation he was lord high constable. In the Monmouth rebellion he commanded the royal troops in Somerset, but in 1688, with John Churchill (afterward duke of Marlborough), he seceded to William of Orange, in whose service he died on Oct. 9, 1690, after receiving a wound at the storming of Cork.

AUGUSTUS HENRY FITZROY (1735–1811), 3rd duke, great-grandson of the 1st duke, was educated at Westminster school and at Peterhouse, Cambridge. He was secretary of state in 1765 under the marquess of Rockingham but retired the following year. Pitt (becoming earl of Chatham) formed a ministry in which Grafton was first lord of the treasury (1766). He led the ministry after Chatham's resignation in 1768. As a politician Grafton was diffident and ineffective. Political differences and the attacks of "Junius" led to his resignation in Jan. 1770. He was lord privy seal (1771–75) in Lord North's ministry but resigned since he was in favour of conciliatory action toward the American colonists. In later years he was a prominent Unitarian. AUGUSTUS (1821–1918), 7th duke, served as a general in the Crimean War and held court appointments under Queen Victoria, Edward VII and George V. CHARLES (1892–1970), 10th duke, succeeded to the title in 1936; at his death, HUGH DENIS CHARLES (1919–   ), 11th duke, succeeded to the title.

GRAFTON, RICHARD (c. 1513–1573), English chronicler and printer of the Great Bible (1539) and the first and second Book of Common Prayer, received the freedom of the Grocers' company in 1534 and was its warden, 1555–56. In conjunction with Edward Whitchurch he published a modified version of Miles Coverdale's English Bible, which was printed in Antwerp in 1537 and known as the Matthew Bible. In 1538 he went to Paris, where the revised Coverdale New Testament was reprinted "for Richard Grafton and Edward Whitchurch." They began printing the folio known as the Great Bible by special licence obtained from Francis I at Henry VIII's request but the work was suddenly stopped by the French government, the presses were seized and Grafton fled. His patron, Thomas Cromwell, bought the presses and type, and printing was completed in England; the book appeared in 1539. (For the significance of these translations *see* BIBLE, TRANSLATIONS OF.)

In 1544 Grafton and Whitchurch secured the exclusive right of printing church service books, and on Edward VI's accession Grafton was appointed king's printer. In this capacity he produced the *Book of Homilies* (1547), the Book of Common Prayer (1549 and 1552) and the *Acts of Parliament* (1552 and 1553). In 1553 he printed Lady Jane Grey's proclamation and signed himself the queen's printer. For this he was imprisoned for a short time by Mary; he seems thereafter to have retired from active business. His historical works include a continuation (1543) of John Hardyng's *Chronicle* from the beginning of the reign of Edward IV to Grafton's own times. After retiring from printing he published *An Abridgement of the Chronicles of England* (1562), *A Manuell of the Chronicles of Englande* (1565), *Chronicle at Large, and Meere Historye of the Affayres of England* (1568). Grafton was interested in London hospitals, being master of Bridewell, 1559–60, and of Christ's hospital, 1560.

He died in London in 1573 and was buried on May 14.

See J. A. Kingdon, *Incidents in the Lives of Thomas Poyntz and Richard Grafton* (1895) and *Richard Grafton, Citizen and Grocer of London* (1901).

GRAFTON, a city of Clarence county, New South Wales, Austr., lies on the Clarence river 42 mi. from its mouth and 434 mi. N.E. of Sydney by rail. The population of Grafton and South Grafton was (1966) 15,944. It became a municipality in 1859 and a city in 1861, and is the seat of an Anglican bishop. The river is navigable to the city for ships of moderate burden and for small vessels to a point 35 mi. beyond. The entrance to the river and the river channel has undergone artificial improvement for seagoing ships. Rail and air services link the city with Sydney and Brisbane. Primary industries include dairying and the production of sugar cane, maize, vegetables, timber, fruit and beef cattle. Secondary industries are the processing of timber, meat and dairy products, match manufacture and brewing. Grafton is a popular tourist resort.

GRAHAM, SIR JAMES ROBERT GEORGE, BART. (1792–1861), English statesman who played an important part as Sir Robert Peel's confidant and adviser, was born at Netherby, Cumberland, on June 1, 1792, and educated at Westminster and Christ Church, Oxford. Member for Hull and then for St. Ives from 1818 to 1820, Graham withdrew from politics to manage the family estates in Cumberland, gaining repute as an expert in agricultural economics and technique. Returning to parliament for Carlisle in 1826, he sat for Cumberland from 1827 until 1837, and from 1838 for Pembroke, Dorchester and Ripon, before representing Carlisle from 1852 until his death at Netherby, Oct. 25, 1861.

From the beginning an advanced Liberal, Graham became first lord of the admiralty under Lord Grey in 1830. He proved an efficient, economical administrator and was a member of the cabinet committee which drafted the first Reform bill. In office Graham's radicalism rapidly waned, and in 1834 he resigned with his friend Lord Stanley (later Lord Derby) over proposals to divert revenue from the Irish Church. While refusing to join Peel's first ministry, he abandoned the Whigs in 1835, and soon emerged as Peel's most valuable lieutenant in the commons, bitterly hostile to his old colleagues. Home secretary from 1841 to 1846, Graham's influence upon social and economic policy was considerable, notably over the corn laws; but, despite his talents, his record in his own office was neither popular nor successful since he was particularly disliked by protectionist Tories. After 1846 Graham readily accepted Peel's support for the Whigs, though refusing office several times. When the latter died in 1850, Graham became the leading Peelite in the commons and helped to promote the Aberdeen coalition of 1852 in which he returned to the admiralty. The performance of the navy in the Crimean War suggests that his insistence upon economy did not conduce to efficiency. Graham resigned soon after the formation of Palmerston's ministry in 1855 and ceased to play any prominent part in politics, though remaining active behind the scenes.

Industrious, well informed and authoritative, Graham never attained the success his ability merited. Pompous and repellent in manner, incapable of conciliation, he was unpopular in parliament, being regarded as both vindictive and unreliable. Nevertheless, he was highly esteemed by all leading politicians, and his importance lies in his standing as an adviser and consultant. Next to Peel, he was the main architect of the new conservatism, and acted as Peel's right-hand man in his most famous administration. Moreover, after 1850 the younger generation of Peelites, such as W. E. Gladstone and Sidney Herbert, looked mainly to Graham for guidance if not leadership; and his counsel tended toward collaboration with the Whigs and Radicals, out of which the later Liberal party was to develop, rather than Conservative reunion.

(A. F. T.)

GRAHAM, MARTHA (1895?–), U.S. dancer, choreographer and teacher, one of the most important and controversial exponents of modern dance, was born in Pittsburgh (the exact date of birth is not known). She was educated in California, and in 1916 began dance studies there under Ruth St. Denis and Ted Shawn. Following her debut with the Denishawn company two seasons later, she was given the leading role in Shawn's Aztec ballet *Xochitl* (1920). In 1923 Martha Graham left the Denishawn company to appear in the *Greenwich Village Follies*. She made her debut as a concert soloist in 1926, in New York city. She had already begun to formulate her personal technique, exploring uncharted worlds of movement in her search for the form of dance which would most clearly express inner emotion.

A theatrical artist of intense power and individuality, she has drawn her subjects from such diverse sources as the American Indian (*Primitive Mysteries, El Penitente*), American frontier life (*Appalachian Spring*), and Greek legend (*Cave of the Heart, Night Journey*). Vitally concerned with contemporary music, she has commissioned 'scores' from Aaron Copland, Norman Dello Joio, William Schuman and other distinguished American composers.

(LN. ME.)

GRAHAM (afterward CUNNINGHAME-GRAHAM), **ROBERT** (d. 1797?), Scottish poet famous for his lyric "If Doughty Deeds My Lady Please," was the son of Nicholas Graham of Gartmore and Lady Margaret Cunninghame. He started life as a planter in Jamaica, where he was for a time receiver-general. In 1784 he was elected rector of Glasgow university and from 1794 to 1796 was M.P. for Stirlingshire. Politically he is remembered as the mover of a bill of rights, in which the Reform bill of 1832 was foreshadowed, and as an ardent advocate of the ideals of the French Revolution; but it is for his lyrics that he has remained famous.

GRAHAM, THOMAS (1805–1869), British chemist often referred to as "the father of colloid chemistry," was born at Glasgow on Dec. 20, 1805. He was educated at Glasgow university, now the Royal Technical college, under Thomas Thomson and then at Edinburgh under Thomas Hope. His father, a wealthy businessman, wished him to become a clergyman and, when the boy persisted in his intention to become a chemist, withdrew his support. He then made his living by teaching and writing. He was professor of chemistry in the Anderson institution, Edinburgh (1830–37), then at University college, London (1837–55), and master of the mint (1855–69). He was a fellow of the Royal society (1836), and one of the founders of the London Chemical and Chemical society (1841) and president of the Cavendish society in 1846.

His first paper, published in 1825, dealt with the absorption of gases by liquids, and the first of his important memoirs on gaseous diffusion appeared in 1829. By measuring the rate at which gases diffuse through a plug of plaster of paris, Graham developed the law, known by his name, "that the diffusion rate of gases is inversely as the square root of their density." He further studied the flow of gases, through fine tubes, and by effusion through a minute hole in a platinum disk; he found that the relative rates of effusion of gases are, like their rates of diffusion, inversely proportional to the square roots of their densities.

His early work led him to examine the diffusion of one liquid into another, and as a result of the experiments he divided bodies into two classes—crystalloids, such as common salt, and colloids, of which gum arabic is a type—the former having high and the latter low diffusibility; this division has since been modified. He invented many of the terms used in colloid chemistry. Graham observed that in the passage through a parchment membrane these differences still held, and so was led to devise a method, "dialysis," for the separation of colloids from crystalloids. He also proved that the process of liquid diffusion causes partial decomposition of certain chemical compounds, the potassium sulfate, for instance, being separated from the aluminum sulfate in alum by the higher diffusibility of the former salt.

In 1833 Graham studied the three forms of phosphoric acid (ortho, meta and pyro). The differences among them were attributed to the fact that they contained different amounts of basic water, replaceable by metallic oxides, united with a given quantity of phosphoric anhydride. (See *Alembic Club Reprint,* No. 10, 1906.) From this work the important concept of polybasic acids developed. In 1835 he published the results of an examination of the properties of water of crystallization as a constituent of salts; definite compounds of salts and alcohol, analogous to hydrates, can be obtained, and these were called "alcoholates." In his final paper he described palladium hydride, the first known instance of a solid compound formed from a metal and a gas. He was led to assume the existence of a metal hydrogenium.

Graham died in London on Sept. 11, 1869.

BIBLIOGRAPHY.—Graham's *Elements of Chemistry,* first published in 1833, went through several editions, and also appeared in German, remodeled under J. Otto's direction. His *Chemical and Physical Researches* were collected by James Young and Angus Smith and printed "for presentation only" at Edinburgh in 1876, Smith contributing a valuable preface and analysis of its contents. See also T. E. Thorpe, *Essays in Historical Chemistry* (1923); A. W. Hofmann, *Zur Erinnerung an vorangegangene Freunde* (1888); E. Jordis, *Ostwald's Klassiker,* no. 179 (1911); W. Ramsay, *Essays, Biographical and Historical*; W. Odling in E. Farber's *Great Chemists* (1962).

(R. E. O.)

GRAHAM, WILLIAM FRANKLIN ("Billy") (1918–), U.S. evangelist, probably the world's best-known preacher in the mid-20th century, was born near Charlotte, N.C., on Nov. 7, 1918. Ordained minister in the Southern Baptist Church in 1939, he took a bachelor's degree at Wheaton (Ill.) college in 1943 and became minister of a church in Western Springs, Ill. Soon after, however, he turned to traveling evangelism. A fiery and magnetic preacher, he attracted increasingly large audiences all over the United States. In 1949 at Los Angeles, Calif., he preached to more than 350,000 persons during an eight-week revival, and this number later was often exceeded. His first tour outside the United States took place in 1954–55, when he visited Great Britain and continental Europe; 1,000,000 attended his revival in Glasgow. From that time on he traveled extensively throughout the world.

Following the tradition of businesslike evangelistic techniques originated by Dwight L. Moody (q.v.), Graham built up a large organization to help stage his "crusades" and to counsel and conduct follow-up work with the thousands who answered his call to "decide for Christ." Many religious leaders have expressed doubts as to the permanency or efficacy of the conversions that occur under the enthusiasm generated by mass evangelism and about its long-run benefit to the church. Graham's methods, however, were not divisive, and he received strong support from many Protestant churchmen.

Graham's published works include *Peace With God* (1953); *The Secret of Happiness* (1955; sermons on the Beatitudes); *My Answer* (1960; selections from his newspaper advice column); and *World Aflame* (1965).

See J. Pollock, *Billy Graham* (1966), an authorized biography; J. E. Kilgore, *Billy Graham, the Preacher* (1968).

GRAHAME, KENNETH (1859–1932), British essayist and storyteller, best known for his children's book *The Wind in the Willows,* was born on March 8, 1859, in Edinburgh, the son of an advocate. He lost his parents as a small child, was brought up (with his two brothers and one sister) by his grandmother in Berkshire, and educated at St. Edward's school, Oxford. Not being able to proceed to the university, for financial reasons, he entered the Bank of England of which he was secretary from 1898 to 1908. In 1893 *Pagan Papers,* a collection of his essays from W. E. Henley's *National Observer,* heralded the appearance of a new master of style; but *The Golden Age* (1895) and *Dream Days* (1898) revealed his special gifts. These two collections of essays and sketches captured the essence of childhood with at once a reality and a magic that was a new revelation. Although not themselves books for children, they have influenced the spirit of all subsequent children's literature.

Grahame's only other work (apart from the whimsical short story "The Headswoman" in *The Yellow Book*, Oct. 1894, published separately 1898) captured young as well as old: *The Wind in the Willows* (1908) is one of the few great children's classics, as ageless and dateless as *Alice*. It was dramatized successfully by A. A. Milne in 1929 as *Toad of Toad Hall*. Grahame wrote no more, beyond a handful of essays and prefaces. He had married in 1899. His only son died tragically at the age of 20, and he retired to Pangbourne by the Thames, dying in his sleep on July 6, 1932.

See P. R. Chalmers, *Kenneth Grahame: Life and Writings* (1933); Peter Green, *Kenneth Grahame: a Study of His Life, Work and Times* (1959).
(R. L. GR.)

GRAHAME-WHITE, CLAUDE (1879–1959), English aviator and engineer who pioneered in British aviation, was born on Aug. 21, 1879. He was educated at Bedford and studied engineering. He owned one of the first gasoline-driven motorcars in England, and worked at a motor engineering business in London until he became interested in aeronautics in 1909. In that year he gained an aviator's certificate of proficiency, being the first Englishman to do so. The following year he entered many flying races in Europe and in the United States, where he won the Gordon Bennett cup. He founded the first British flying school at Pau in France, in 1909. In 1910 he joined a company to run the Hendon aerodrome of London. At the outbreak of World War I in 1914, he was commissioned in the royal flying corps, but later was recalled to superintend the construction of government planes. He wrote many treatises on aircraft, dealing with its history, its technical development and its use in warfare, including: *The Aeroplane, Past, Present and Future* (1911); *The Aeroplane in War* (1912); *Flying, an Epitome and a Forecast* (1930).
Grahame-White died in Nice, France, Aug. 19, 1959.

GRAHAMSTOWN (GRAHAMSTAD), a cathedral city and an educational and legal centre in the Cape of Good Hope province, Republic of South Africa, lies in a broad, shallow valley near the source of the Kowie river, 84 mi. N.E. of Port Elizabeth by road (107 mi. by rail). Pop. (1960) 32,195 of whom 10,500 were Europeans. Grahamstown is notable for the simple dignity of its older buildings, of which streets and for the simple dignity of its older buildings, of which the chief is the Anglican cathedral of St. Michael and St. George, built in stages from 1824 to 1952. It incorporates part of the original church (1824–30) which served as a refuge for women and children during the Kaffir invasion of 1834–35. Other older buildings include St. Patrick's Roman Catholic procathedral, the Methodist Commemoration church, the Shaw hall, the Old Provost (originally a military prison) and the city hall. Rhodes university (1904) occupies extensive grounds on the western side of the town, adjoining the botanical gardens of about 100 ac. and the Albany museum (1855) which has fine specimens of local animal life and important historical collections. There are several important denominational schools and an Anglican training college for women teachers. The eastern division of the supreme court is located in Grahamstown, which is also the seat of an Anglican bishop.

The city is linked by the national road with Port Elizabeth and East London (105 mi. E.N.E.). It is named after Col. John Graham, who founded a frontier garrison post there following the Kaffir War of 1812. The British government assisted British settlers to establish themselves in the district in 1820, and Grahamstown soon became the chief centre of the eastern Cape colony, but was superseded by Port Elizabeth after that seaport was linked to the interior by railway.
(F. G. v. D. R.)

GRAHN, LUCILE (1819–1907), Danish ballerina and choreographer, was one of the most celebrated dancers of her time, noted for lightness and technical virtuosity. Especially memorable was her appearance with Marie Taglioni, Fanny Cerrito and Carlotta Grisi in Jules Perrot's famous *Pas de Quatre* at Her Majesty's theatre, London, in 1845. Born June 30, 1819, in Copenhagen, she studied under Auguste Bournonville, and in 1836 was the first to dance the title role in his version of *La Sylphide* at the Danish Royal theatre. A quarrel with Bournonville led to her virtual exile from Denmark after 1839, but she danced successfully throughout Europe and was choreographer at the Munich Opera, 1869–75. She died April 4, 1907, in Munich.
(LN. ME.)

GRAIL, THE HOLY, the famous object of quest for the knights of Arthurian romance (*see* ARTHURIAN LEGEND). Controversy has raged round the origin of this theme which has fired the imagination of writers all over western Europe. Some scholars, such as Jessie Weston in her well-known book, *From Ritual to Romance* (1920), have linked it with fertility rites, others would associate it with the Celtic hero Brân the Blessed, while still others trace it back to the Christian liturgy. The precise etymology of the word *graal* is still uncertain, but it was used in a number of regions of France to denote a wide-mouthed vessel. It appears in an early version of the *Roman d'Alexandre* (*see* ALEXANDER ROMANCES) and is described by Helinandus at the beginning of the 13th century as a *scutella lata et aliquantulum profunda* ("wide and somewhat shallow dish"). The first extant text to give it a special significance as a mysterious, holy vessel seems to be *Le Conte del Graal* or *Roman de Perceval*, written by Chrétien de Troyes (*q.v.*) between 1179 and 1191. Chrétien declares that he received the book for the story of the Grail from his patron Philippe d'Alsace. There may indeed have been a book, although medieval writers do sometimes invent written sources to give authority to their work, but there are no means of determining its contents or the extent of Chrétien's debt to it. Chrétien never finished this work, although there exist a number of continuations by other writers. As he used in his romances a technique of progressive revelation and deliberately withheld explanations in order to create suspense and an atmosphere of magic, many different theories have been put forward as to what he meant by the Grail.

Here briefly is the information which he himself gives us. The hero, Perceval de Galles, who has been brought up in deliberate isolation from the world by his widowed mother, has abruptly left home to be knighted at Arthur's court and is now in search of adventure. He has been given some instruction by an older knight, Gornemant, and has been warned not to ask too many questions. Although it has been prophesied that he will achieve great things, he is still very inexperienced and literal-minded and has no inkling of the real meaning of chivalry. He meets a lame man fishing on a river and is told to go to a castle for lodging. When he arrives he finds his host lying on a couch and sees a strange procession. First comes a squire bearing a bleeding lance, followed by two more, each carrying a ten-branched candlestick, then a damsel holding a *graal* which gives forth great light, and after her another damsel with a silver platter. While Perceval and his host eat at table, this procession passes before them several times. The young knight is curious, but he remembers his instructions and asks no questions. He goes to bed and wakes in the morning to find the castle deserted. He then meets a damsel who tells him that his host was the Fisher King who has been wounded by a spear thrust through both thighs. She reproaches Perceval for his silence; if he had asked about the Grail the king would have been healed. Later a hideous damsel tells Perceval that by his failure to ask the question ladies would be widowed, lands laid waste and many knights slain. Perceval sets forth on a search for the Grail but he has forgotten God and spends many years on fruitless adventures. Then one Good Friday he meets his hermit uncle who gives him an explanation of chivalry and then tells him that the Grail is very holy, that it contains the Host and that the Fisher King's father has been nourished from it for 12 years. Perceval has been unable to ask the necessary questions because of his sin. The rest of the romance is concerned with the adventures of Gawain (*q.v.*), who goes in quest of the bleeding lance which, he is told, will one day destroy the land of Logres. Perceval never returns to the Grail castle, although most scholars assume that if Chrétien had finished the romance, Perceval would have asked the question which healed the Fisher King, and Gawain would have achieved the adventure of the bleeding lance.

In Chrétien's poem, therefore, the Grail is given definitely Christian connections by the hermit, and Perceval's quest for it is linked with his gradual realization of the spiritual meaning of chivalry. Some scholars have indeed suggested a link between the ritual of the Eastern Church and the Grail procession, and have seen in the Grail the chalice or ciborium and in the lance the lance of Longinus. It is, however, difficult to fit into a rigidly theological interpretation of the theme some elements such as the destruction to be wrought by the lance and the association of the healing of a king wounded across the thighs with the restoration of a land laid waste. Indeed, much of the fascination of the Grail theme in Chrétien lies in this very combination of different; only half-explained elements and it is a characteristic example of his skill in giving a new and exciting form to a series of knightly adventures. A German poet, Wolfram von Eschenbach (q.v.), gives a deeper mystic meaning to the story in his *Parzival*, in which the Grail is a stone. (For other versions see PERCEVAL.) There is also a romance in German, *Diu Krône*, by Heinrich von dem Türlin (c. 1220), in which Gawain is the Grail hero.

The Grail is given a more exclusively Christian significance in the work of Robert de Boron at the end of the 12th century or early in the 13th. This author wrote an early history of the Grail, *Joseph d'Arimathie* or *Le Roman de l'estoire dou Graal*, in which, by linking it with a story to be found in the apocryphal Gospel of Nicodemus, he identifies it with the vessel of the Last Supper, entrusted to Joseph of Arimathea who also used it to catch blood from the body of Christ. Joseph and his brother-in-law Bron or Hebron, the Rich Fisher, set up a Grail table in memory of the Last Supper. At this table is an empty seat, reserved for the descendant of Bron: anyone else sits there at their peril. The Grail is to be brought to the west, to the *Vaus d'Avaron*, by Bron and his son Alain. Robert de Boron also wrote a *Merlin* of which only the beginning has survived in its original verse form (see also MERLIN). In the prose version the Grail is connected with the founding of the Round Table by Arthur's father Uther on the model of the Grail table and also containing a Perilous Seat. In two manuscripts the prose versions of Robert de Boron's *Joseph* and *Merlin* are followed by a quest known as the *Didot Perceval* in which Perceval achieves the adventure of the Perilous Seat. There is some difference of opinion among scholars as to whether or not this is a reworking of a quest by Robert de Boron.

There is another 13th-century Perceval quest, *Perlesvaus*, but in the Quest which was to have the widest influence and which has come down to English readers through Malory, the chief Grail hero is Galahad. This *Queste del Saint Graal* forms part of the prose *Lancelot*, often known as the Vulgate cycle. Although in this version the Grail theme is still given the outward trappings of romance, its real meaning has nothing to do with knightly adventure but is austerely theological. A. Pauphilet, in *Études sur la Queste del Saint Graal* (1921), was the first to point out the signs of strong Cistercian influence, and E. Gilson showed similarities between the Vulgate *Queste* and the mystical doctrines of St. Bernard (q.v.) of Clairvaux. He suggests that the Grail is the symbol of divine grace and that the theme of the romance is not the quest for salvation but for the divine vision, the mystical union with God which represents the supreme flowering of grace and for which chastity is essential. The three stages in achievement reached respectively by Lancelot, Perceval and Bohort, and Galahad, correspond with St. Bernard's different states by which man can rise toward perfection in the life of mysticism. Lancelot (q.v.), because of his sin with Guinevere, can only see the Grail in a dream, while asleep; Perceval (q.v.), chaste by the grace of God, and Bohort, with only one involuntary lapse from chastity, receive higher revelations in visions; Galahad, the virgin knight, whose genealogy is linked with that of Christ and whose very name can be a mystic appellation of Christ, is the only one to rise to the divine ecstasy, to look right inside the Grail and to behold those mysteries which cannot be perceived by human senses or described by a human tongue. Those knights, such as Gawain, who do not seek the help of a human mystery fail utterly. In the Vulgate cycle, by making Galahad Lancelot's son, the Grail Quest is linked with the story of Lancelot and Guinevere, and the chivalry inspired by earthly love is surpassed by that inspired by heavenly love. In the last branch of the cycle, the *Mort Artu*, the final disaster is linked with the withdrawal of the Grail, symbol of grace, from the kingdom of Logres.

The Grail theme has thus been given a deeply spiritual significance, has come to form the culminating point in Arthurian romance, and has proved fruitful as a literary theme. Scholarly speculations as to its origins have had their influence on works such as T. S. Eliot's *The Waste Land*.

BIBLIOGRAPHY.—*Early History of the Grail*: Robert de Boron, *Le Roman de l'estoire dou Graal* (*Joseph*), in the Classiques Français du Moyen Age (C.F.M.A.) (1927) / *Perceval Quest*: *Le Conte du Graal* or *Roman de Perceval*, ed. by W. Roach (1956); *The Continuations of the Old French 'Perceval' of Chrétien de Troyes* are all to be published (except that of Gerbert de Montreuil, ed. by M. Williams, C.F.M.A.; 1922) by W. Roach. The First Continuation appeared in 3 vol. (vol. i, 1949; vol. ii, 1950; vol. iii, part i, 1952; part ii, 1955). C. Potvin, *Perceval le Gallois*, 6 vol. (1866-71), gives all the continuations; Wolfram von Eschenbach, *Parzival*, ed. by A. Leitzmann (1947-50), Eng. trans. by J. L. Weston (1894) and major parts by M. F. Richey (1935); *Didot Perceval*, ed. by W. Roach (1941); *Le Haut Livre du Graal, Perlesvaus*, ed. by W. A. Nitze and T. Jenkins, 2 vol. (1932-37), Eng. trans. by Sebastian Evans, *The High History of the Grail* (Temple Classics, 1898; Everyman's Library, 1910). *Gawain Quest*: *Diu Krône*, ed. by G. H. F. Scholl (1852); Eng. trans. in J. L. Weston, *Sir Gawain at the Grail Castle* (1904). *Galahad Quest*: *La Queste del Saint Graal*, ed. by A. Pauphilet, C.F.M.A. (1923, 1949); *The Works of Thomas Malory*, vol. ii, ed. by E. Vinaver (1947). For critical discussion of Grail problems see *Colloques internationaux du Centre Nationale de la Recherche Scientifique*, no. iii, "Les Romans du Graal" (1956). (E. M. K.)

GRAIN, the dry fruit or caryopsis of cereals, and hence cereal plants generally. (See FRUIT; CEREALS.)

A grain is also the smallest unit of weight, both in Great Britain and the United States. Its origin is thought to be the weight of a grain of wheat. The troy grain $= \frac{1}{7000}$ of a pound, the avoirdupois grain $= \frac{1}{7000}$ of a pound; in diamond weighing the grain $= \frac{1}{4}$ of the carat $= .7925$ of the troy grain. (See WEIGHTS AND MEASURES.) The term also refers to the arrangement of fibres and other cells in wood. See WOOD; *see also* references under "Grain" in the Index.

GRAINGER, PERCY ALDRIDGE (originally GEORGE PERCY GRAINGER) (1882-1961), Australian-born pianist, conductor and composer, known for his pioneer work in folk music. Born at Melbourne, July 8, 1882, he studied there with Louis Pabst and in Germany with James Kwast and Ferruccio Busoni. He began his career as a pianist in 1900. In 1906 he became a friend of Grieg, under whose influence he helped to discover the wealth of English folk music. He settled in the United States in 1914 and was naturalized in 1919. In 1932 he was appointed head of the music department at Melbourne university. In 1935 he built the Grainger museum at Melbourne for the preservation "of all things bearing upon the musical life of Australia." He died at White Plains, N.Y., on Feb. 20, 1961. Grainger's works include the orchestral works *Molly on the Shore*, *Shepherd's Hey* and *Mock Morris*. In his chamber music, notably the two *Hill Songs*, for 23 and 24 solo instruments, he experimented with novel rhythmic and structural problems. He also perceived the possibilities of electronic music.

GRAIN PRODUCTION AND TRADE. True grains are the fruits of the grasses (q.v.), members of the botanical family Gramineae. They are characterized by monocotyledonous seed kernels, as contrasted to the pulses (peas, beans, etc.) and oilseeds (castor-oil seed, linseed, etc.), most of which are members of Leguminosae and have dicotyledonous seeds. These grains are grown primarily for their starch or calorie content. The pulses and oilseeds are cultivated largely for their protein and fat content. The cereal grains contain from 70% to 80% starch by weight, except for oats, barley, paddy rice, and millet, which, because of their fibrous hulls, have somewhat less.

This article deals with the principal uses of grain, including its importance in human diet, grain production and competition among grains for land, marketing arrangements and functions, and world trade. Additional information on production will be found in the *Agriculture* sections of articles on countries, states, and provinces, as ARGENTINA; MICHIGAN; SASKATCHEWAN. *See also* articles on specific grains: BARLEY; CORN; RICE; etc.

USES

Importance in Human Diets.—Since the dawn of civilization, the true grains have been fundamental to human life. No considerable densities of population can be sustained without either considerable production of grain within the area or access to imports. Hunting and pastoral production yield much less food per hectare

Root crops such as potatoes, yams, and cassava usually yield more calories than grain; however, these crops require more labour, are difficult to store and transport, and provide a less balanced diet.

The cereals are grown principally for their energy content, but they also provide a considerable share of the proteins needed in human and animal diets. The protein content of whole wheat is 11% to 13%, and that of ordinary white wheat flour about 10% to 12½%. Oatmeal has a slightly higher protein content; rice contains only 7%; corn (maize) 9%; millets 6½% to 12%; and sorghum, 10%. Relatively low-income countries heavily dependent on cereal diets balance their protein needs primarily with pulses, oilseeds, and fish. Relatively high-income countries, which consume a high proportion of animal products, get their protein from this source and use oilseed cake and meal to supplement the cereals and roughage fed to their animal populations.

Low-income countries with limited land and other resources are forced to consume a large share of their grain production directly for human food. A much greater population can subsist on a given level of agricultural resources by utilizing the primary cereal production directly instead of feeding it to livestock.

The world (excluding the Chinese mainland and the U.S.S.R.) obtains about half of its calorie intake from cereals, about one-fourth from other crops, and one-fourth from animal products. Before World War II almost 70% of the calorie intake in Africa, the Near East, and the Far East came from cereals, and China obtained an estimated 70% to 80% of its calorie intake from cereals. There is little information available on the U.S.S.R. However, after the death of Joseph Stalin in 1953, the government stated that animal numbers had changed little from Czarist times, indicating a heavy dependence on cereals and other crops to feed the growing population. The diets of the northern European countries, the United States, Canada, New Zealand, and Australia have the lowest proportion of cereals, ranging from one-fourth to one-third of the total calorie intake. (See also CEREALS.)

Declining Proportion of Cereals in Human Diets.—All regions except Latin America, Africa, and the Near East had a decline in total calorie intake after World War II as compared to the prewar period (down to about 2,350 from about 2,450 cal. per day, but still about 3,000 in Western Europe, North America, and Oceania). All regions except Oceania had a decrease in the percentage of calories supplied by cereals. Any considerable shift in human diets from cereals to animal products would have to be accompanied by large increases in the production of the feed grains (oats, barley, sorghums, corn) relative to that of the food grains (wheat, rye, rice). However, for a large proportion of the world's population, the primary problem is securing a higher level of calorie intake; improving the quality of diets is of secondary importance.

Industrial Uses.—In addition to their use as human food and animal feed, grains have long been the principal raw material for the brewing and distilling industries. Cereals are also used for industrial alcohol, starches, films, polymers, and other products. Although total utilization for these purposes is small, the production and consumption of alcoholic beverages made from grain has increased steadily in many countries.

regions. Rye is important only in Europe and the U.S.S.R. where the combination of infertile soils and a cool climate restricts the choice of crops. Barley, like wheat, is important in all regions. Oats production is confined to Europe, U.S.S.R., North America, and Oceania; the remaining regions are largely too hot or dry for it. Corn (maize) is produced in all regions of the world, but the major concentrations are in the Western Hemisphere countries (the United States, Mexico, Brazil, and Argentina) and in Africa (South Africa). The millets and sorghums are important crops in only

TABLE I.—*Area Used for Cereals as a Percent of Total Arable Land and Land Under Tree Crops**

Region	Total arable land and land under tree crops (in 000,000 ha.)	Used for cereal crops — Area in grain (in 000,000 ha.)	Used for cereal crops — Percent of total
Europe	152	71.2	46.8
U.S.S.R.	230	131.4	57.1
North America	227	79.9	35.2
Latin America	96	43.3	45.1
Near East	85	31.5	37.1
Far East†	372	265.6	71.3
Africa	260	51.1	19.7
Oceania	35	9.9	28.3
World total	1,457	683.9	46.9

*1964–65 crop year. †Includes estimated data for mainland China.
Source: Food and Agriculture Organization of the United Nations, *Production Yearbook*, 1965.

PRODUCTION

The importance of cereal production to human nutrition is indicated by the proportion of arable land devoted to it. Approximately half the estimated area of arable land, fallows, and orchards in the world is used for cereal production (Table I). In the Far East where there is heavy population pressure upon the land resources, approximately 70% of the land area is devoted to cereals. In other parts of the world where population pressures are not so great, the proportion devoted to cereals is smaller, amounting to only one-fifth in Africa. When allowance is made for the necessary fallow in dry areas, somewhat over half the world's arable land is devoted to cereal grains.

Regional Production Patterns.—The results of different combinations of environmental, consumer preference, and economic factors are shown in Table II. Wheat, because of wide adaptation and high favour with consumers, is an important grain in all

three regions: the Near East, Far East, and Africa. They are the best cereal crops for the extensive hot, dry areas in these regions. Rice production is geographically the most concentrated of any of the cereals. It is the dominant crop in the Far East. It is not a very important crop in any other region as a whole, but is important in individual countries; e.g., Brazil, Spain, Italy, and Egypt. The bulk of the crop is grown in the alluvial plains around the edge of the Asian land mass from India to China and in the Japanese, Philippine, and Indonesian islands off the coast of Asia.

Relative Importance and Requirements of the Individual Cereal Grains.—Farmers' and peasants' choices of the crop or crops grown depend on a number of environmental and economic considerations. The individual grains compete with each other and with other crops for land. Estimates of the proportion of cereal land occupied, the proportion of the total cereal crop accounted for by each cereal by region, and world totals (exclusive of mainland China) are given in Table II.

Wheat occupies the largest area, about 30% of that devoted to cereals, followed by rice (almost 20%), corn (16%), and millet and sorghum (about 15%). Barley occupies about 10%, oats and rye less than 5% each. Much of the U.S.S.R. is either too dry or too cold for rice or corn. Almost two-thirds of the U.S.S.R. cereal is devoted to wheat and rye. Only about 15% is in corn, millet and sorghum, and rice combined. The U.S.S.R.'s drive to produce more corn succeeded in increasing corn area from about 7.5% of

TABLE II.—*Relative Importance of the Principal Cereal Crops by Area and by Production, by Regions**

Region	Wheat	Rye	Barley	Oats	Corn	Millet and sorghum	Rice
	(% of total area in cereal crops)						
Europe	41.0	12.6	18.7	11.5	15.7	0.1	0.4
U.S.S.R.	51.7	12.8	16.5	4.3	11.8	2.7	0.2
North America	39.9	1.2	8.1	14.5	29.2	6.0	0.9
Latin America	20.5	1.8	3.2	2.0	55.4	4.1	12.7
Near East	56.8	2.2	21.9	1.2	6.3	7.9	3.4
Far East†	12.4	—	2.8	0.1	8.2	24.4	52.1
Africa	13.7	—	8.0	0.7	25.7	46.1	5.5
Oceania	73.7	—	9.1	14.1	1.0	2.0	—
World total	31.3	4.1	10.3	4.5	16.5	15.1	18.1
	(% of total cereal production)						
Europe	38.4	10.4	22.4	9.9	17.8	0.1	1.0
U.S.S.R.	51.0	9.3	19.6	3.8	13.5	2.4	0.3
North America	26.9	0.6	9.6	1.9	48.2	6.5	1.7
Latin America	25.9	1.2	2.9	1.7	50.2	3.6	14.3
Near East	49.5	2.0	17.9	0.1	10.5	8.0	10.4
Far East†	7.7	—	2.1	0.1	7.1	9.4	73.6
Africa	11.5	—	6.8	0.5	32.5	39.5	9.2
Oceania	79.8	3.0	9.0	9.7	1.5	1.5	1.5
World total	26.8	3.2	10.8	4.4	22.2	7.5	25.1

*1964–65 crop year. Total areas harvested and total production by regions shown in Table III. †Excludes mainland China.
Source: Food and Agriculture Organization of the United Nations, *Production Yearbook*, 1965.

the total in 1959–60 to almost 12% in 1964–65, corn in the U.S.S.R. considerably exceeded rye production in 1964–65, a reversal of the historic relationship. Rice and wheat accounted for about 25% each and corn for more than 20% of world cereal production in the second half of the 20th century.

In general, three factors determine the competitive position of the individual cereals within a region: (1) biological adaptation to the physical environment; (2) consumer preferences; and (3) economic considerations. (*See also* FARM MANAGEMENT.)

Biological Adaptation to Environment.—*Wheat.*—Wheat grows well under a wide variety of conditions in the temperate regions of the world. It grows best where the natural vegetation is grass, but also does well on many of the more fertile lands claimed from temperate forested areas. The greater part of the world's wheat is fall-sown winter wheat. It is relatively winter hardy; however, it will not thrive in many localities above latitude 55°–60° N or latitude 40° S. Wheat is damaged by high temperatures in the maturing stages; therefore, little wheat is grown (except in a few localities at higher altitudes) between latitude 30° N and 30° S, because temperatures warm up too rapidly in the spring.

Rye.—Rye is noted for its hardiness to cold, disease, and pests, and for its ability to perform more satisfactorily than wheat on poor, sandy soils. This combination of characteristics has relegated rye to the marginal land in the temperate climates.

Barley.—Barley grows where wheat and other temperate region cereals are adapted but is less winter hardy than wheat and rye. It usually competes with corn, oats, rye, and low-grade wheat as feed, although special types are grown in the United States and Europe for the malting industry for beer production.

Oats.—The oat is less winter hardy than wheat or barley but is more successful in wet climates. Like barley, it is used largely for animal feed.

Corn.—Corn (maize) requires a combination of warm, humid weather. Generally, nighttime temperatures must remain above 58° F (about 14° C), and annual precipitation should total 30 in. (about 76 cm.) or more with the bulk falling within the growing season.

Millets and Sorghums.—These are warm-weather crops more tolerant to drought than corn. Millet yields considerably less than sorghum, but will make a crop in a very short season under soil and climatic conditions too rigorous for sorghums.

Rice.—Unlike the other cereals, rice thrives in hot, humid weather on alluvial soils. The lowland varieties, which comprise the bulk of the crop, require waterflooding. Only the upland varieties important in some parts of China and a few other localities compete for land with other cereals.

Consumer Preferences.—Wheat is the preferred grain for human consumption in most of the Western world. It makes a white bread of light texture because of the elastic nature of the protein or gluten in the wheat flour. In the U.S.S.R. and Europe, rye bread is eaten where wheat yields are unsatisfactory, but rye makes a heavy, less satisfactory, dark bread. Wheat is gradually displacing rye as a bread grain as world real incomes rise.

Rice is the preferred food grain in the greater part of the Orient. Wheat and other grains are substituted where rice cannot be grown or is not available.

The remaining so-called coarse grains are more likely to be used for animal feed and compete on the basis of relative yields rather than consumer preference. Human populations ordinarily use these coarse grains for food only where the relative costs of producing wheat or rice are too high. Corn is used extensively in parts of Latin America and millets and sorghums in the relatively poorer and drier sections of Asia and Africa. (*See also* BREAD; FLOUR.)

Economic Considerations.—The returns from grain production are the result of yields, prices, and the costs of production. Thus, while the costs of producing the small grains (wheat, rye, barley, and oats) are not greatly different, wheat is so much favoured by consumers that it has a considerable price advantage over all the other temperate region grains.

Corn derives its competitive position by virtue of its very high yield relative to the other cereals and its consequent low cost per unit of production. This makes it the most competitive livestock feed in regions environmentally suited to corn production.

Rice has relatively high costs of production because of the labour involved, but its adaptation to hot, humid climates and favour with Oriental consumers make it the staple food crop in South and East Asia, including Japan, the Philippines, and Indonesia.

Area Harvested and Production.—An average of more than 680,000,000 ha. (1 ha. equals 2.471 acres) was devoted to cereals in the world by the 1960s (Table III). The largest increases in cereal area compared to pre-World War II were in Latin America, Africa, and Oceania; each increased by about 50%. The U.S.S.R. had more than regained its prewar level after a decline caused by World War II disruptions.

An average of over 1,000,000,000 metric tons of cereals were produced in the world in the 1960s. All regions shared in the gains, the largest increases being in Africa, Oceania, and Latin America.

The increased world production was the result of the increase in harvested area coupled with an increase in average yields as compared to the 1934–38 period. Increased yields in Europe and North America permitted these regions to increase production substantially in spite of decreased areas harvested. Extensive plans to increase grain production in the U.S.S.R. by adding to planted area and increasing average yields begun in the 1950s paid off in considerably increased production by the middle 1960s.

Competition Among Grains.—As noted above, the percentage of cereals in human diets appeared to be declining, particularly in the Western Hemisphere and Europe, with some tendency for replacement by animal products. Barley, corn, and sorghum production grew at a faster rate than wheat and rice, while world rye and oats production actually decreased. The same general trends also applied to the U.S.S.R. where the relative production of rye and oats decreased and strenuous efforts were under way to increase corn and other feed grain production.

While in some limited cases there may be substitution of corn for wheat or rice, resulting in a lower quality diet, the net effect of the rapidly rising production of feed grains should be an increase in the world animal numbers and a move to better quality diets. The increase in barley production was general over most of the world; however, a large share of the increase in corn and sorghums was concentrated in North America, which already had a high-quality diet. Africa, the U.S.S.R., and the Far East also shared in the corn and sorghum increase.

Until the second half of the 20th century, wheat had historically exceeded corn production because of its wide regional adaptability and high preference with consumers. The gradual increase in world real incomes and the slow replacement of cereal food by animal products in many areas permitted corn and sorghum production to expand faster than wheat after World War II. The gradual adoption of hybrid corn and sorghum varieties should

TABLE III.—*World Cereal Production by Regions**

Region	Area in cereals (in 000,000 ha.)				Production (in 000,000 metric tons)			
	1934-38	1948-52	1959-60	1964-65	1934-38	1948-52	1959-60	1964-65
Europe	79.7	73.2	73.8	71.2	118.0	110.4	147.0	159.2
U.S.S.R.†	107.0	92.5	115.6	131.4	79.5‡	86.5§	123.2	145.4
North America	99.3	103.9	98.6	79.9	108.5‡	169.1	207.5	191.6
Latin America	27.1	27.7	35.7	43.3	31.0	30.9	42.4	58.8
Near East	21.9	26.7	28.4	31.5	21.8	25.0	30.8	35.1
Far East‖	192.0	244.2	257.3	265.6	244.8	260.8	387.6	378.0
Africa	32.3	36.2	51.1	51.1	24.8	24.4	31.3	43.0
Oceania	6.3	6.3	7.4	5.2	5.2	7.8	13.4	13.4
World	565.6	610.7	659.0	683.9	627.8	713.9	977.5	1,021.5

*1964–65 crop year. †U.S.S.R. information for years before 1959–60 adapted from Commonwealth Economic Committee *Grain Crops* 1957. ‡1940. §1950–52. ‖Includes estimated data for mainland China, to the extent that estimates for individual grains include such data.
Sources: Food and Agricultural Organization of the United Nations, *Yearbooks of Food and Agricultural Statistics; Production Yearbooks* 1960 and 1965.

both increase yields and permit extension of the corn and sorghum growing area. These developments should permit corn and sorghum to continue their rapid growth in production and compete successfully with other cereals for a larger share of both land area and total cereal production.

Marketing.—The marketing system for grain consists of a chain of intermediary firms which value, transfer title, store, process, and transport the grain as it moves through the channels of trade from producers to consumers. The organization of the system varies somewhat among countries, but in general the first points of assembly are local country elevators which buy from producers. From local elevators part of the grain is shipped to processors, but most of it goes to large terminal or subterminal elevators for storage and distribution to domestic users or exporters (see GRANARY AND GRAIN ELEVATOR).

For discussion of economic factors see AGRICULTURAL ECONOMICS. See also COMMODITY MARKET; MARKET; and MARKETING.

WORLD TRADE

Most of the import supply of grain is utilized as human food, and only a relatively small proportion is used as animal feed and in industrial uses. The major food grains traded are wheat, rye, and rice. The major feed grains are barley, oats, corn, and sorghums and millets. The lower grades of wheat, a considerable proportion of rye, in addition to millfeeds (by-products of the milling industry), are also utilized as animal feeds and in industrial uses. Feed grains are also widely consumed as food in relatively low-income countries, but most feed-grain imports are used as animal feed.

The largest exporting countries have a high per capita consumption of animal food products, a declining per capita consumption of grain as food, seaports within their territorial boundaries, and, for the most part, relatively high per capita incomes. Grain used in the production of animal food products has a relatively low value use compared to its use as a human food. Because of the relatively stable consumption of grains as food in the major surplus areas, and its low value use as animal feed, the importing countries are able to outbid producers of animal food products for part of the grain supply in spite of generally higher transportation costs and, in many instances, lower per capita incomes. For many importing countries, imports supplement domestic production by serving as a source of grain with special characteristics, and by evening out swings in production. As a result many countries both export and import grain. Wheat in particular is imported by numerous countries. It is not produced in sufficient quantities in many countries and because it is used in many food products with wide consumer acceptance it has a worldwide market. For several countries (e.g., West Germany, United Kingdom, Japan, Brazil) imports are a major source of supply because domestic production is consistently well below their requirements.

On a per capita basis trade in grains stagnated in the period immediately following World War II. Smaller exports of the feed grains accounted for most of the decline. Total rice exports declined, but total wheat exports increased. The larger wheat exports went largely to Asian countries which substituted wheat for rice because of the smaller supply of rice available for importation.

World grain trade in the 1960s was characterized by the declining importance of Western Europe as a market for wheat and the increasing importance of the less developed nations of Asia as an export outlet. During the middle 1960s the United States exported large tonnages of cereal to the less developed countries, much of it on a concessional basis. The volume of world cereals trade about doubled between the mid-1950s and mid-1960s. Prospects for the future are dependent on increased demand for coarse grains in Western Europe and for wheat in the less developed countries of the world.

The chief institutional arrangements that affect the pattern of world trade include import and export controls in the form of tariffs, quotas, embargoes, currency convertibility restrictions, cartel agreements, and export and import subsidies. Other factors, such as production and marketing controls, production subsidies, subsidies for diversion to lower value uses, etc, also affect production and consumption and thereby the pattern of world trade. The International Wheat Agreement, first signed by participating countries in 1949 and periodically extended and modified, was designed to stabilize supplies and the price of wheat in international trade. Under this scheme signatory importing countries agreed to purchase a specified amount of wheat, usually about one-third of world trade, at a specified minimum price and the exporting countries agreed to supply this amount at a price of not more than the specified maximum price. The agreement had no provision for production controls, but United States domestic price supports and export subsidies stabilized the price of wheat in international trade (see also STABILIZATION AGREEMENTS, INTERNATIONAL).

See also FOOD SUPPLY OF THE WORLD.

BIBLIOGRAPHY.—J. S. Schonberg, *The Grain Trade—How It Works* (1956); N. Jasny, *Competition Among Grains* (1940); A. A. Hooker, *The International Grain Trade* (1939); Martin Abel and Anthony Rojko, *World Food Situation*, FAS Report No. 35, U.S. Dept. of Agriculture (1967). (E. R. BG.; C. P. SR.)

GRAM (GRAMME), the unit of mass in the metric system, equivalent to 15.4323564 gr. avoirdupois or to 0.2572 drachms (drams) or to 0.7716 scruples. This metric unit is very nearly equal (it was intended to be exactly equal) to the mass in a vacuum of one cubic centimetre of pure water at maximum density. The scientific definition of the gram, accepted by international convention, is that it be a mass of $\frac{1}{1,000}$ part of the mass of the international prototype kilogram, a platinum iridium alloy block carefully preserved at the International Bureau of Weights and Measures at Sèvres, France. The gram of force is defined as g dynes of force where g is the acceleration of gravity. It is the weight of a gram of mass and varies slightly from place to place on the earth as the factor g varies. See WEIGHTS AND MEASURES.

GRAM (CHICK-PEA; *Cicer arietinum*), a leguminous plant, called also garbanzo, Spanish pea, Egyptian pea, or Bengal gram, is cultivated as a pulse food chiefly in the south of Europe, Egypt, and western Asia as far as India and little grown in the U.S. It is an annual herb with zigzagging branches, and alternatively arranged pinnately compound leaves, with small, oval leaflets. The flowers are borne singly in the leaf axils on a stalk about half the length of the leaf and jointed and bent in the middle; the corolla is blue-purple. The inflated pod, one to one and one-half inches long, contains two roundish seeds. It was cultivated by the Greeks in Homer's time under the name *erebinthos*. Alphonse de Candolle in his *Origin of Cultivated Plants* suggests that the plant originally grew wild in the countries to the south of the Caucasus and to the north of Persia. In the east the seeds, which are very nutritious, are eaten raw or cooked in various ways, both ripe and unripe, and when roasted and ground serve the same purposes as ordinary flour. In Europe the seeds are used as an ingredient in soups.

GRAMINEAE: see GRASSES.

GRAMMAR. The word grammar is now understood in several senses, as the entry for it in a good modern dictionary will show. (See, for example, *grammar* in *Webster's Seventh New Collegiate Dictionary*.) None of these senses show much kinship to the original Greek *grammatikos*, "of letters." This article approaches grammar in the four principal modern senses of the word.

I. The Phenomena of Language with Which Grammatical Studies Attempt to Deal
II. The History of Grammar and of Grammar Books
III. The Systematic Description of Grammatical Phenomena
   1. Descriptive Grammar
   2. Structural Grammar
   3. Transformational-Generative Grammar
IV. The Use of Grammar Books to Prescribe Correctness

I. THE PHENOMENA OF LANGUAGE WITH WHICH GRAMMATICAL STUDIES ATTEMPT TO DEAL

That a language has system is apparent to even the most casual observer. That it has an extremely complex, subtle system is unconsciously perceived by infants, as is apparent from their gradual mastery first of the more obvious features of the system, finally by their control as children and adults of all features of the system. (Here the mastery of the language's sound system will not be used as an example, though gaining control of it requires attentive listening and precise muscular coordination, as is apparent to any adult learning to speak a foreign language. See PHONETICS.)

The young child's sentences show that he is aware, for example, that words fall into categories, such as nouns, verbs, and adjectives, and that for each of these categories there are signals to be added, and that for each of these categories there are signals to modify their meanings. But at first the child notices only the more common and regular signals and assumes that they are always applicable. He may construct such a sentence as *The baddest mans runned away*, which demonstrates that (1) *bad* belongs to a category (adjective), whose meaning can be modified by the signals *-er, -est* (comparison), as in *larger, largest*; (2) *man* belongs to another category (noun) whose meaning can be modified by the signal *-s* (plurality), as in *dogs*; (3) *run* belongs to a category (verb) whose meanings can be modified by the signal *-ed* (past time), as in *called*. Because most adjectives, nouns, and verbs can regularly be modified by the addition of *-er, -s,* and *-ed* respectively, the child assumes that all such words are treated in the same way. He soon discovers that the system of his language is slightly less regular than he assumed. But his "mistakes" show that his language learning is founded on a perception of system in his language.

The examples of system just given illustrate what in grammatical terminology is called inflection; the study of such forms is morphology. In addition to mastering the phonological (sound) system of his language and its morphological system, the child also gets control of its syntax (syntactical system), the patterns of arranging words in sense units (sentences). Again his "mistakes" show his early grasp of the main features of the system: *Me want supper*, where the more heavily stressed form *me* has made the stronger initial impression and temporarily functions as the first person form in both subject and object positions. Later he will learn that for certain pronouns (*I-me, he-him, she-her, we-us, they-them*) two forms are available, the first normally preceding the verb, the second normally following it. But for his first sentences he prefers the regularity of *it* and *you*, usable in either position.

It is customary, then, to consider the phenomena of language under the headings of phonology, morphology, and syntax, where patterns are apparent, and of lexicon or vocabulary, where much less system is readily discoverable. Because patterns are apparent in the sounds, the forms, and the sentences of a language, it is also customary to refer to the phonological, morphological, and syntactic structures of a language.

Though structure is used in a variety of senses, there is a strong implication of potential visibility about it: the structure of a church, of a plant, of the body, of an atom, of the solar system, etc. These are all things of which diagrams can be made, which, however complex, have a tangible reality that can be depicted and hence studied at leisure in detail because they are material things juxtaposed in space. Language structures, on the other hand, are basically acoustical phenomena, juxtaposed in time, which have meaning only to speakers of the language. When all speakers of the language are dead, the language and all its structures die with them. (Such "dead languages" as Latin and Greek are no exception. Those who read these languages have partially resuscitated their structures by means of the written record.) Because of this sequential characteristic of language it is impossible to represent its total structure graphically and difficult to describe it completely.

Nevertheless substantial portions of a language's structure are stored in a potential state in the minds of all native speakers of it, ready to be realized when the occasion requires. The structure whose extent can be most confidently measured is the phonological. The number of consonants, vowels, and diphthongs, of significant pitch levels and degrees of stress, pauses, and combinations of these, can usually be quite accurately counted; the total is normally well below a hundred—for English between 45 and 50, depending on the dialect and the method of the scholar doing the counting. This sharp limitation on the number of phonological units—called phonemes—can be readily verified by the layman who consults the pronunciation key of a good dictionary. He will find that the key seems to include almost his complete repertory of significant sounds. Those not represented in the key, he will be unlikely to miss—the intonation patterns, variations in pitch, stress, and timing, because for the most part they have no transcription in ordinary writing; and the number of significant ones is small.

The number of regular variations in grammatically significant English forms is very small: the noun has only two forms, the bare one (*cat*), and the *-s* one (*cats* or *cat's*—the apostrophe is a variant which exists only in writing and print). The adjective has three forms, the bare one (*large*), the comparative (*larger*), and the superlative (*largest*). And the verb has four forms, the bare one (*walk*), the third person singular present tense (*walks*), the past tense and past participle (*walked*), and the present participle (*walking*). The *-s* form of the noun and the *-ed* form of the verb each have three pronunciations determined by the immediately preceding sound.

The irregular forms are considerably more numerous, and their number cannot be so confidently counted. The number of frequently occurring irregular forms, though much larger than the regular forms, is limited: a few nouns and adjectives (*man, men; good, better, best*) and a good many verbs (*drink, sing, be*). The exact enumeration of irregular forms becomes next to impossible because of the great number of rare words in the total lexicon, particularly those from other languages. The commoner ones of these may have regular as well as irregular forms (*appendix, appendixes; appendices; gladiolus, gladioluses, gladioli; cherub, cherubs, cherubim*). The really rare ones sometimes have quite unexpected forms (*hetaira, hetairai; epiblastema, epiblastemata; halacha, halachoth*), and since the extent of the lexicon cannot be determined, neither can the number of the irregular forms. But to the ordinary user of the language, this fact is of little practical importance because the rare words are not in his vocabulary. His repertory of regular plus irregular grammatical forms is considerably larger than his repertory of phonemes but smaller than his total lexicon.

The repertory of syntactical patterns is the most difficult to arrive at—excepting, of course, the lexicon, which, as has already been mentioned, cannot be measured satisfactorily because it varies considerably with every individual and is constantly fluctuating.

Some obviously different patterns of word order are evident:

I can walk.	Can I walk?	He saw the man.	Did he see the man?
S v V	v S V	S v V O	v S v V O
The man gave the boy a ball.		A ball was given the boy by the man.	
S V IO O		S v V IO PO	

Using more or less traditional terms to describe the functions of the elements in these sentences, the symbols may be identified as follows: S = subject, v = auxiliary verb, V = main verb, O = object, IO = indirect object, PO = object of a preposition. Each of these elements instead of consisting of a single word or two may include a number of words which conform to established patterns. *The not very tall old man could have been going to start to work* has a subject phrase consisting of the first six words and a verb phrase consisting of the last eight. The order of the words in the verb phrase is an unalterable pattern; *old* and *tall* in the noun phrase might be interchanged, but otherwise the pattern is fixed.

These are a very few of the possible syntactic structures of English. The total number of such structures is undoubtedly large. A modern school of grammarians (transformational-generative; *see* LINGUISTICS) argues, however, that the very large number of these possible syntactic structures must be divided into two unequal groups: (1) a quite small number of primary patterns from which (2) the large number of secondary patterns can be derived. What is unarguable, however, is that all native speakers of English—as well as of other languages—have at their disposal a probably uncountable number of syntactic structures.

Inventories of the phonological, morphological, and syntactic structures, presented as systematically as the grammarian has found possible, have been attempted repeatedly for more than 2,000 years. The largest collections for English were made early in the 20th century by grammarians such as H. Poutsma and Otto Jespersen. Yet in the more than 3,700 pages of Jespersen's seven-volumes of *Modern English Grammar*, very few items would not be perfectly intelligible to a cultivated native speaker of English. Such a speaker has at least passive control of virtually all the structures Jespersen so assiduously collected and described.

In addition to the linguistic items in the three types of structure outlined above, every native speaker has a lexicon of many thousands of words. Few of these items have a perceptible systematic relationship to each other, but each one appears to have a correspondence to some part of the world of experience. *Dog, dish, heat, travel* presumably are verbal signs for some aspect of the real world (*see* SEMANTICS IN LINGUISTICS). And since our experience normally expands as we grow older, our vocabularies as adults are much larger than they were when we were children. An individual's lexicon probably grows as long as he lives, but since his experience always differs somewhat from his neighbour's, their vocabularies will be neither the same nor the same size. Inventory of lexicon is therefore much less possible than inventory of the three structures discussed earlier.

Another profound difference between the grammatical structures and inventory is the age at which each is learned and the completeness of the learning. Before a child starts to school he has normally gained full control of all the phonological devices of his language. He makes all the sounds as perfectly as does an adult speaker. Almost as much can be said for his control of the inflections. His difficulties with them are likely to be exclusively with the irregular forms of words he is only just being introduced to—*phenomenon, phenomena; radius, radii;* and so on. His skill in marshaling the great variety of syntactic structures may increase markedly as he grows older; but even at six he can usually understand any sentence he hears provided the vocabulary items in it are familiar to him.

The phenomena of language with which grammatical studies attempt to deal are then very numerous, highly complex, extremely subtle, and part of systematic structures which all native speakers of a language control almost perfectly by the time they are six years old. Yet because of the sequential nature of these structures, the fact that they must be apprehended as juxtapositions of sounds in time, the systematic description of them is far more difficult than is the description of phenomena which can be seen or touched. The difficulty is increased by the fact that a language exists only in its speakers, none of whom ever use it in exactly the same way; and that the relatively uniform practice of a culturally homogeneous group changes from one generation to the next. For example, the form *baddest*, used earlier in this section as an example of a child's naive faith in regularity, was, some hundreds of years ago, the normal superlative of *bad* in cultivated English.

II. THE HISTORY OF GRAMMAR AND OF GRAMMAR BOOKS

As has been pointed out, every member of a social group must very early become aware—unconsciously—that the language used by older members of his group has a structure and that he must master that structure if he is to participate in the activities of the group. Until he masters that structure he cannot talk or understand what those around him are saying and he must remain an outsider. This has necessarily been true ever since human beings have had speech.

But a conscious awareness of the existence of linguistic structure seems to have come very late in the history of language and in only two societies: that of Greece and that of India. (*See* GREEK LANGUAGE; INDIAN LANGUAGES.) The evidence of such awareness is to be found only in written records, and it may be that the evidence for other societies has perished. For Western culture, only the Greek tradition is really significant. That of India considerably antedates it, but since the Indian tradition did not become known in the West until the late 18th century and was limited in its influence to scholarly investigation, it will not be discussed here (*see* further SANSKRIT LANGUAGE).

For nearly 20 centuries the history of a conscious concern with the grammatical structure of language and of treatises on it is mainly the history of Greek grammar and Latin grammar derived from it. The impetus for this concern is not always clear from the surviving record, but the reasons for attempting to analyze language seem to have developed in this order: (1) Philosophers' concern with the nature of speech, well illustrated in Plato's *Cratylus*, where it is apparent from the dialogue that the arguments are not presented as novel but as well-established ideas deriving from pre-Socratic thinkers whose writings are now lost (compare SPEECH AND LANGUAGE). (2) Teachers' concern with the differences between an earlier and a later stage of a language and the resultant difficulties in understanding an earlier text. The Greek grammarians of Alexandria dealt with this problem in explicating the text of Homer and the other great writers of Greece. (3) Concern of teachers and others with the proper use of their native language. This attitude is evident not only in the writings of the grammarians themselves but in the attacks on them by authors such as Aulus Gellius and Sextus Empiricus. (4) The use of a systematic description of a foreign language to provide fundamental instruction in it for those who do not know it. This last concern with grammar, which most laymen today would perhaps consider its principal utility, did not develop until the Middle Ages when Latin had ceased to be anyone's native language and its position as the language of the Church required that the clergy know it. (5) The linguist's concern with the nature of language as a phenomenon in itself rather than as one aspect of philosophical inquiry. This concern is similar to (1), differing in its attempt to treat linguistics, hence grammar as a separate discipline. But the relationship with philosophy is not easily broken; both philosophers and linguists now find themselves dealing with related problems.

(1) The Greek philosophers dealt with grammar only tangentially. But in their discussions of language they attempted to classify linguistic phenomena into categories and thus provided the basis for such terms as noun, case, gender, verb, tense, etc.

(2) The oldest surviving Greek grammar is the *Techne* of Dionysius Thrax (1st century B.C.), probably the most influential single book in the Western world aside from the Bible, since all the traditional grammars of the West (and many of the Orient) derive from it. The accidents of survival of manuscripts make it impossible to determine how original Dionysius' analysis was. Other grammatical analyses were certainly more comprehensive and possibly more penetrating than his. Apollonius Dyscolus (2nd century A.D.) wrote an extended and systematic syntax of Greek, most of which is lost. But the popularity of Dionysius' little treatise was so great that even as late as the early 19th century it was still used in an English school as a beginner's text in Greek.

Dionysius' purpose is to describe the language of literature, that is, of what has been written; but whatever his original intention, his work soon became a manual of instruction in the Alexandrian schools and served as a foundation for the analysis, the reading, the explication, and, finally, the evaluation of a literary text. And in passing through the centuries the *Techne* became encumbered with a whole apparatus of commentaries.

The Roman grammarians added little to what they borrowed from the Greeks. In translating Greek grammars they were forced to recognize differences between the structure of their own language and the Greek, such as the absence of an article in Latin. And the first of the Latin grammarians, Varro (116–27 B.C.), perhaps because he was the first, perhaps because his interests extended into many subjects other than language, is the most original. Of his *De Lingua Latina* only books v through x, not complete, survive. His interest is encyclopaedic and historical, rather than analytic.

Roman culture developed in the shadow of Greek. It is always easier to imitate than to originate. And in view of the tremendous achievement of Greek culture, it is little wonder that the Romans should so regularly have attempted to adapt the Greek achievement to their own needs. The importance of this process with grammar lies in the pattern it established and in the fundamental difference between the original Greek grammatical description and the hundreds of derivative ones for other languages which it inspired. Greek grammar was based on an analysis of Greek; those who made it had no prior model; they probably knew no language other than their own, since few Greek speakers of the Hellenistic Age bothered with foreign languages. The grammar was therefore necessarily based on the facts of the Greek language. If the analysis was less penetrating than the philosophical analyses of the great age of Greek philosophy, the deficiency must be attributed to the gradual exhaustion of the Greek genius.

The Romans might have chosen to make an independent analysis of their own language. But they hardly had a chance to, for educated Romans had normally been taught Greek—not as we study a foreign language, from a grammar, but by an educated Greek slave

—and were virtually bilingual. So they studied Greek literature as Greek boys did, became acquainted with Greek grammar, and inevitably constructed a grammar for themselves on the Greek model. The same process has been repeated again and again in the West, though the model has become a Latin grammar derived from a Greek one. The point is made here to suggest what is probably a great handicap for any modern grammarian: he has always been educated through a grammar derived from Dionysius Thrax; therefore when he tries to construct a grammar of his own language or of the categories of Dionysius' grammar rather than those which may be peculiar to the language he is analyzing.

(3) Greek and Roman formal education of the Hellenistic Age put much emphasis on the study of earlier literature, and the study of grammar was a part of the preparation for the understanding of the literature. Since the grammars were based on the literature and the literature was written in an older state of the language, there would be discrepancies between the language of the grammars and the language of the students. Because the literature was great, the language in which it was written was presumably also great.

The grammar which described that language, it would be inferred, described what was good, and deviations from what was in the grammars would be considered less than good, inferior, or incorrect. So the grammars became a means of deciding what was correct or incorrect. The controversies were often acrimonious, as can be shown for Greek by Sextus Empiricus' *Against the Grammarians* and for Latin by passages in Aulus Gellius' *Attic Nights*.

Echoes of the philosophical origins of grammar appear in Julius Caesar's *De analogia*, which survives only in fragments. Caesar argued for the analogists, who demanded complete consistency in forms, though he also wanted no radical departure from established usage. Quintilian, though primarily a rhetorician, presents the classical argument for usage in his *Institutes* (I, vi, 1–45), and Horace makes the classical statement in his *Art of Poetry*: "Use is the judge, and law, and rule of speech" (line 72).

(4) The first systematic school instruction of a foreign language was undertaken by the Western Church at the beginning of the Middle Ages. Before that there had been many people who had learned one or more languages other than their native one, presumably from a native speaker of the language, either through casual contacts with the speaker, as must have been the case between the Greek traders of the Mediterranean basin and their non-Greek-speaking clients, or from a slave tutor, as was the case with the well-to-do educated Roman boy.

But the medieval Western Church had no native speakers to go to. Latin was dead as a first language, yet the Bible, the ritual, and the theological works which priests had to know were in Latin. Latin therefore had to be taught and Latin grammars became the textual basis of that instruction. The two which enjoyed the greatest popularity in the Middle Ages were that of Donatus (q.v.) written in the 4th century, and that of Priscian (q.v.) written a century or two later. The elements of the language were learned from Donatus; more advanced study was pursued in Priscian, whose work was more comprehensive and included, in books 17 and 18, a treatment of syntax derived from Apollonius Dyscolus. More than a thousand manuscripts of Priscian are extant, though they vary considerably in text because in the course of many copyings his work was altered and commentaries on it became part of the text, as was also the case with Donatus.

Beginning in the 12th century, the monopoly held by Donatus and Priscian was broken, though both continued to be used. Both writers had been pagans, and their grammars were based on the Latin of pagan Rome. And it was apparent to later medieval scholars that the Latin of Christian writers often differed from that of pagan writers. Also in the 12th century, Scholasticism, based on Aristotelian dialectic, came to dominate all branches of learning. The paganism of Donatus and Priscian robbed them of some of the authority the medieval scholar was so respectful toward, and the Scholastic dialectic introduced into grammar a demand for logic which the older grammarians, concerned only with description, had felt no need for. Dozens of new grammars were produced, one of the most important in verse, the *Doctrinale* (1199) of Alexander de Villa Dei, in 2,645 hexameter lines.

Renaissance scholars reacted against the medieval grammarians because of the very qualities which had caused the Scholastics to question Donatus and Priscian. The rebirth of interest in ancient Greek and Latin literature led them to reject Scholasticism and medieval Latin and to embrace the Latin of the pagan authors. Though the first of the Renaissance grammarians were Italian, e.g., Lorenzo Valla and Varinus, who published grammatical works in 1440 and 1470, 1475, and though better known scholars also wrote grammatical treatises, e.g., Erasmus (q.v.) about 1514, and Julius Caesar Scaliger (q.v.), the Italian-French philologist, in 1540, the most brilliant contributor to grammatical analysis from the 16th through 18th centuries was a Spaniard, Franciscus Sanctius Brocensis, in his *Minerva* (Salamanca, 1587).

By the beginning of the 17th century, grammars of the vernacular languages were starting to appear in considerable numbers. One of the most influential of these was written by two members of the Port Royal community, the philosopher Antoine Arnauld (1612–94) and the grammarian Claude Lancelot, and published in Paris in 1660. Approximately translated its long title reads: "Universal and logical grammar containing the foundations of the art of speech explained in a clear and natural manner; the reasons for what is common to all languages and the principal differences which exist among them; with numerous new comments on the French language."

Of English grammars, two appeared before 1600, one in English by William Bullokar, 1586, and one in Latin, perhaps by Paul Greaves, 1594. In the 17th century there were 34 more, and in the 18th century at least another 503. These totals include separate editions of a single title, some of which are numerous, though only in the 18th century. Ben Jonson's *English Grammar*, 1640, was republished only twice in the 17th century, but Robert Lowth's *A Short Introduction to English Grammar* (1762), reappeared at least 45 times before the end of the century, and that of Lindley Murray, *English Grammar* (1795), in its full and abridged forms made at least 16 appearances before 1801, when its popularity was only beginning; the 62nd edition of the full work appeared in London in 1864, the 133rd edition of the abridged version in the same year.

These grammars of English and of other vernacular languages were usually related to Latin grammars much as the Latin grammars of ancient times were related to Greek grammars, though fitting English into the framework of Latin was considerably more difficult than fitting Latin into the framework of Greek. Most of the English school grammars of the 19th and even the 20th centuries derive directly from the 18th-century Latinate ones. The most comprehensive is the immense *Grammar of English Grammars* (1851) of Gold Brown, an American, which is based, so the author asserts, on a study of over 500 earlier grammatical works, though he also asserts the superiority of his own.

(5) But in the 19th century the new discipline of linguistics (q.v.) began to produce grammars of many languages, grammars which departed radically from the medieval prescriptive approach. These new grammars attempted to describe systematically and comprehensively the language as it was and had been, though the traditional Latinate framework was still used. A few examples will suggest the variety: A comparative grammar, in German, of Sanskrit, Zend, Greek, Latin, Lithuanian, Gothic, and German, by Franz Bopp, 1833; a comparative grammar, in German, of the Indo-European languages, by Brugmann and Delbrück, 1886–1900; a grammar of the Romance languages, by F. Diez, 1836–44; a Germanic grammar by Jacob Grimm (of fairy-tale fame), 1819–37; a comparative grammar, in German, of the Slavic languages, by F. Miklosich, 1852–74; a French historical grammar, in French, by the Dane, K. Nyrop, 1899–1930; a grammar of Celtic languages, by J. K. Zeuss, 1853.

For English the more important ones, in some instances not completed until well into the 20th century, are: Eduard Maetzner, *Englische Grammatik* (3 vol., 1873–75); H. Poutsma, *A Grammar of Late Modern English* (4 vol., 1904–26); Otto Jespersen, *A Modern English Grammar on Historical Principles* (7 vol., 1909–49). As the number of volumes in each of these works suggests, they became increasingly comprehensive.

Though linguistic scholars had long recognized that the traditional nomenclature and organization of grammars was based on Greek and was therefore somewhat unsatisfactory for the description of other languages, not until well into the 20th century did grammars of English begin to appear that attempted a sharper break with the Latinate tradition by putting greater emphasis on analysis by grammatical structure than by word meaning. It was apparent to the new grammarians that such definitions as "a noun is the name of a person, place or thing" or "the subject of a sentence is the performer of the action" are rationalizations of what we have already become aware of in some other way. A favourite example is the opening stanza of Lewis Carroll's "The Jabberwocky." In "'Twas brillig, and the slithy toves/Did gyre and gimble in the wabe," we know that *toves* is a noun and the subject, though we have no notion of its meaning nor that it performs an action. The pioneer work was Charles Carpenter Fries's *The Structure of English: an Introduction to the Construction of English Sentences* (1952), though it had been to some extent anticipated by the same author's *American English Grammar* (1940). A much more elaborate treatment is Archibald A. Hill's *Introduction to Linguistic Structures: From Sound to Sentence in English* (1958), which, as the title suggests, makes phonological analysis an integral part of the description of grammatical structure, something that Fries had only touched on.

A recent approach called transformational-generative derives principally from two seminal works, Zellig S. Harris' "Co-occurrence and Transformation in Linguistic Structure," in *Language* (1957); and—considerably more influential—Noam Chomsky's *Syntactic Structures* (1957) and his *Aspects of the Theory of Syntax* (1965). A considerable number of school texts from elementary through college level soon appeared attempting to adapt the transformational-generative techniques to the classroom. An exposition of the approach, discussed below, is Emmon Bach's *An Introduction to Transformational Grammars* (1964).

III. THE SYSTEMATIC DESCRIPTION OF GRAMMATICAL PHENOMENA

"Today we find it hard to imagine a culture distinguished by great works of literary genius yet having neither a systematically formulated grammar nor an established grammatical terminology." Yet that was the situation in ancient Greece at the time of its greatest literary flowering, as the author of the article on grammar in the Pauly-Wissowa encyclopaedia of classical antiquity, *Realencyclopädie der Classischen Altertumswissenschaft* (1893–   ), felt it necessary to point out. For only during the first few centuries of more than 2,500 years of literate Western culture did such a situation exist. Yet during those few early centuries, Greece produced her greatest literary masterpieces—a rather dismaying fact for those who insist that good writing is impossible without a thorough conscious knowledge on the writer's part of the grammar of the language in which he writes.

Some grammatical terms do go back as far as the 5th century B.C. The ancestor of the word *grammar*, the Greek *grammatikos*, was probably used as early as that, but in the sense of learning one's letters. Aristotle (*Rhetoric*, bk. iii, ch. 5) says that Protagoras (c. 480–c. 410 B.C.) is reported to have classified nouns into masculine, feminine, and neuter genders. Plato in the *Cratylus* is the first to distinguish clearly between nouns and verbs, but on the basis of meaning, since his is a philosophical discussion, rather than on the basis of form, as the grammarians were later on to attempt to do. Aristotle puts the remaining words into one category, attempts a definition of the word, and suggests that verbs have tense. Much of this terminology is in the *Rhetoric*, which describes an art which is the counterpart of dialectic. That is why he is so little concerned with words other than nouns and verbs, since it seems to him that only these two really convey meaning.

The Stoics, though still primarily concerned with philosophical distinctions, added several terms for grammatical concepts because they needed them for their philosophical analysis. They subdivided Aristotle's third category into (1) articles and pronouns, and (2) prepositions and conjunctions. The Stoics also dealt in some detail with grammatical distinctions which are shown in Greek by changes in the forms of words: number, gender, case, voice, tense, and mood.

But all the grammatical analysis and terminology before Dionysius Thrax is imbedded in the philosophical writing it was intended to clarify and make more precise. In Dionysius for the first time a complete though very brief work is devoted exclusively to grammar, to an analysis of a language—Greek—for the sake of understanding its structure. His work is weakened, to be sure, by his preoccupation with language as recorded, with literature; so he starts with letters and syllables rather than with the living, spoken language, a practice which has been followed by thousands of writers of grammars ever since. Then come the definitions, many of which are still very familiar to us:

"A sentence is a combination of words, either in prose or verse, expressing a complete thought.

"A noun is a part of discourse having case endings, indicating a person or thing. . . .

"A verb is a part of discourse with endings to show tense, person, and number and indicating action or being acted upon. . . .

"A particle is a part of discourse having traits of both noun and verb. . . . [No longer considered a separate part of speech]

"An article is a part of discourse having case endings and being placed before . . . nouns. . . . [Modern English no longer has articles which show case.]

"A pronoun is a word indicative of definite persons and used in place of a noun. . . .

"A preposition is a part of discourse placed before other words in sentences. . . .

"A conjunction is a word conjoining or connecting thought in some order and filling a gap in the expression. . . ."

Though these definitions still rely on meaning to a considerable extent—"expressing a complete thought," "indicating action"—purely grammatical features are more important—"case endings," "placed before," "endings to show tense, person, and number." Dionysius does not, however, develop the grammatical significance of position of words in a sentence, and a detailed discussion of Greek syntax had to wait until the 2nd century A.D. in the work of Apollonius Dyscolus, which has had no comparable influence in the Western grammatical tradition.

The Roman grammarians added little of relevance to modern grammatical terminology. They systematized and expanded the work of their Greek predecessors and pointed out differences between Greek and Latin such as the existence of a case in Latin, the ablative, which does not occur in Greek. They did identify an additional word class, interjections, and Priscian puts greater emphasis on meaning in identifying parts of speech than Dionysius did, thus aggravating an already difficult problem in grammatical terminology (compare Fries, below).

This emphasis on meaning becomes of ever greater importance starting in the 12th century with the conquest of grammar by dialectic. The Scholastic grammarians were concerned with the *modi significandi*, what the word signifies or means and how what is meant is signified; by the 15th century, grammarians were therefore called *modistae*. These philosopher-grammarian-teachers no longer turned to the actual usage of the language as the basis for their grammatical rules but derived them from logic since they were convinced that language—at least Latin, the only language they studied—was a consciously devised artistic achievement and that its grammar therefore had universal applicability. Though they did not reconstruct Latin grammar on an a priori basis, they did have the schoolboy very much in mind and therefore dealt exhaustively with syntax, a matter that except for Priscian's books 17 and 18 had been largely ignored in the earlier school grammars. Their lasting contributions include the separation of *nomen* (noun) into the categories we now call adjective and noun, the introduction of the concepts of apposition and (for Latin) of ablative absolute; and the strictly syntactical utilization of subject- and predicate, up to then used as philosophical terms.

In the early modern period the grammarians of Latin turn again to the language of the Roman classics, making syntactical analyses of the classical language. One of the most penetrating of these was the *Minerva*; Sanctius devotes a third of that work to ellipsis, a grammatical concept which has been a godsend to grammarians ever since. (Ellipsis is the omission of words asserted to be understood, though not expressed: *whom* in "the man I saw," where a rule demands the inclusion of a relative pronoun.)

It should be apparent to anyone who has gone through 10 or 12 years of schooling in an English-speaking country that the impact of the Greco-Roman grammatical tradition has been lasting in its effect. All the grammatical terms in this section will have a familiar ring, though their exact meaning may not be by any means clear. Though all of them are in origin foreign words, they have been thoroughly naturalized and occur very commonly in ordinary writing and speech, though seldom with much precision of meaning.

A great deal of scholarly work has been done in grammatical analysis in the 19th and 20th centuries, both of English and of a great variety of other languages. But the direct impact of this work on the general public has been slight, though indirectly it has had some effect in improving the grammar books used in schools, principally at the college level. Because the scholarly work is often detailed, subtle, and complex, however, no more than an overview can be given here. It falls, roughly, into three, often closely related, categories: (1) descriptive grammar, (2) structural grammar, (3) transformational-generative grammar. The words preceding grammar in each label are by no means parallel, as will be apparent from the following discussions:

1. Descriptive Grammar.—The scholarly discipline called linguistics, though it has its roots in the 18th century and even earlier, is mainly a creation of the 19th century and was at first concerned with language relationships, particularly those of the Indo-European languages. Comparative linguistics rests heavily on comparative grammar. To make a confident comparison of the structures of two or more languages, reliable grammars of these languages must be available, grammars that are accurately descriptive. The languages to be compared (*see* the Bopp work above) included, in addition to Greek and Latin, Sanskrit, Persian (Zend), Lithuanian, Gothic, and German. For Greek and Latin, the Renaissance had produced descriptions based on a study of classical literature. For Sanskrit, Panini had provided an excellent description but according to a method very different from the Greco-Roman one. For Persian, Lithuanian, and Gothic, grammars had to be constructed from an examination of the texts. And for German and other living Indo-European languages it was soon realized that the existing grammars were more echoes of Latin grammatical features than complete descriptions of the languages themselves. So an important scholarly activity became the construction of accurately descriptive grammars of dead languages hitherto undescribed and of living languages misdescribed by the existing Latinate grammars. A further need for good descriptions of living languages was a pedagogical one. Notice that among the titles in Section II the major grammars of English and French are by scholars in small countries like Holland and Denmark where it is of critical importance for many people that they know such international languages as English, French, and German.

The scholars who produced these new grammars all had a solid foundation in Latin and Greek grammar. If their new grammars were to be used for comparisons with Greek and Latin, those comparisons would be easiest if the new grammars were cast, as far as possible, in the Greco-Latin framework. The scholars were aware that this was a hazardous procedure and attempted to guard against the risk.

A very few examples must suffice to illustrate the dangers. Dionysius' definition of a noun specifies that it has case endings. In Greek and Latin these case endings identify at least four cases, both singular and plural; fairly unambiguously: nominative, genitive, dative, and accusative. In English, however, inflection of the noun is limited to one ending, -s. Case function in Greek and Latin is usually signaled by a characteristic ending; in English it must be signaled in another way. *Dog* has the same form in each of these three sentences: *The dog is old, I see the dog, He gave the dog a bone.* Evidently the so-called nominative, accusative, and dative cases in English are signaled quite differently from the

way they are in Latin and Greek.

In Latin the active verb has six simple (single-word) tenses; these can be translated into English, and Latinate English grammars usually state that English has six tenses: present—*loves*, past—*loved*, future—*will love*, perfect—*has loved*, past perfect—*had loved*, future perfect—*will have loved*. The difficulties with these correspondences are, among others, that if tense implies a single word as in Latin, only two of the English constructions are tenses; and that the idea of the Latin form can often be expressed in English by more than one construction, the future, for example, not only by *will love*, but by *going to love, about to love*, even *loves*, as in *she loves me not today, she loves me tomorrow*.

The works of Sweet, Maetzner, Poutsma, and Jespersen, as well as many others, are representative of the descriptive grammarians of English working within the framework of the Greco-Roman grammatical tradition. If only because it is the oldest of the three approaches, it has so far been the most influential, particularly in the teaching of English as a foreign language.

2. Structural Grammar.—Many scholars, particularly in America, were dissatisfied with the results of the descriptive grammarians. They felt that there were inherent difficulties in trying to fit a language into a grammatical framework derived from the structure of another language; that such a procedure when applied to English might lead to the assumed existence of grammatical features in English which in fact are not present—like six tenses—and permit features to be ignored because they have no counterpart in the framework. They suspected, for example, that English phonology might have far more grammatical significance than even the elaborate treatments of it in a work such as Jespersen's suggested (vol. i, *Sounds and Spellings*, 455 pages); and that grammatical analysis based on a combination of formal features (forms of words, arrangement of words, phonological devices) and lexical meanings (senses of individual words) was insufficiently rigorous.

In their grammatical analysis, these grammarians attempted to disentangle what they considered the two essential and complementary kinds of linguistic signals in language, those giving grammatical meaning and those giving lexical meaning, the combination of the two giving total meaning. Dictionaries (lexicons) had provided exhaustive information on the meanings of individual words. The structural grammarians attempted to identify the grammatical meanings provided by the grammatical structure of the language. *You have seen him and Have you seen him?* can be analyzed from their printed forms as having the same grammatical meanings of statement and question. The words in both sentences are the same; the difference in grammatical meaning is signaled by the word order. But by an alteration of the intonation patterns of speech (pitch, stress, etc.) it is possible to make the statement *You have seen him* a question.

Fries's *The Structure of English: an Introduction to the Construction of English Sentences* (1952) is a systematic summary of the grammatical devices which can be satisfactorily demonstrated to a reader. George L. Trager and Henry Lee Smith, in *An Outline of English Structure* (1951) in a scant 86 pages, attempt an outline of all the grammatical devices available to a speaker of English. The extent of their departure from the scholarly descriptive traditional grammars can be suggested by the fact that neither book calls itself a grammar, though each one attempts to do what descriptive grammars had tried to do; Fries carefully avoids the terms noun, verb, adjective, and adverb, using instead Class 1, 2, 3, and 4; and Trager and Smith use an elaborate (and necessary) terminology in their subtle and penetrating description of grammatical devices.

3. Transformational-Generative Grammar.—An unabridged dictionary will have close to half a million entries, yet it does not include by any means the total vocabulary of the language. Part of that vocabulary—say 100,000 words as a minimum—can be arranged by a single speaker of the language into an enormous variety of sentences, many of which he has never heard or seen before, and some of which have never existed before. Yet these sentences are for the most part intelligible and acceptable to those who hear or read them. The transformational-generative grammarians attempt to explain this complexity as deriving from a few simple basic formulas, what they call kernels, consisting always of a noun phrase and a verb phrase; these kernels can be transformed into the great variety of sentences a language can produce; by the application of the appropriate rules it is possible to generate from the kernels all the sentences in a language.

This school of grammarians does not claim that their theory is particularly novel; for example, Chomsky believes that a child is endowed with a prepossession toward language learning, a capacity for recognizing linguistic universals—an attitude which is clearly reminiscent of the Port Royal grammarians (compare the title of the Port Royal grammar). What is new in their approach is the rigour with which they formulate the rules and the elaborate precision with which they symbolize the working out of the rules. They are also more concerned with discovering the rules by which all the acceptable sentences in a language can be generated than with offering a systematic description of the language as it is. Only a tiny example of the procedure and symbols can be given here.

One kernel sentence is of the type *The man opened a book*. This is first symbolized by S = Sentence. This sentence is then analyzed into its components, starting with the largest. S → NP + VP means that the sentence consists of or may be rewritten as noun phrase + verb phrase. Then each component is treated in the same way: NP → Det + N means that a noun phrase consists of determiner (article) + noun; VP → Tense + VT + Det + N means that the verb phrase consists of an auxiliary element of tense, *-ed*, applied to transitive verb + determiner + noun.

By the application of the transformation-passive rule (T-passive), from the sentence *The man opened a book* a new sentence may be generated. T-passive: NP_1 + Tense + VT + NP_2 ⟹ NP_2 + Tense + be + part + VT + (by + NP_1). This means that by applying the T-passive rule to the active sentence a passive sentence is generated consisting of the second noun phrase—the object—of the active sentence as subject, the tense auxiliary element of the verb of the active sentence—past—applied to *be*, giving *was*, the past participle of the transitive verb—*opened*—and *by* plus the first noun phrase—subject—of the active sentence, giving the transform *A book was opened by the man*. Listing all the operations symbolically in sequence we get:

S → NP + VP
NP → Det + N
VP → Tense + VT + Det + N
T-passive: NP_1 + Tense + VT + NP_2 ⟹ NP_2 + Tense + be + part + VT + (by + NP_1). The transform which has been generated by the transformation rule has a surface structure that differs from that of the kernel. But in understanding it the listener or reader subconsciously recognizes its original or deep structure.

The transformational-generative grammarians claim that their system of analysis is the most accurate and complete and that it has the advantages of formality, explicitness, completeness, and simplicity.

IV. THE USE OF GRAMMAR BOOKS TO PRESCRIBE CORRECTNESS

Grammar became an essential part of elementary instruction in the schools of Alexandria during the 1st century B.C. The Roman schools followed the lead of the Greek ones, using, however, a Latin grammar constructed on the Greek model. The primary purpose of grammatical instruction was an understanding of literary texts. There were proscriptions and prescriptions, but these were concerned mainly with the usages in the literary texts rather than with the oral practice of the schoolboys. The teaching affected only a tiny portion of the population, the very few who could afford a formal education, and probably had little influence on the pupils' use of their native language. The Greek or Roman aristocrat sent his son to school not for any vocational purpose but to give him the literary and rhetorical polish required by his social class.

There was a concern for propriety in language (compare Sextus Empiricus, Aulus Gellius, Julius Caesar, Quintilian, mentioned in Section II), but how important it was is hard to determine. When Latin came to be studied as a foreign language in the Middle Ages, correctness became of prime importance. Unless the writer or speaker conformed to the established usage of Latin, he would not be understood, nor could he expect to understand the Latin he read and heard unless he knew not only the meanings of the words but the significance of the cases, the tenses, the word order, which the Latin grammars attempted to explain. A control of what was in those grammars therefore became imperative if a man was to be literate, because in much of Europe the only reading matter was in Latin. A control of Latin grammar—or simply of grammar—became synonymous with literacy; the function of the elementary school was to teach it—hence grammar school. Those who could read had access to books on magic and therefore possessed a power denied to others—hence the special senses attached to some phonetic developments of grammar: Middle English *gramary*, *gramarye*, "magic," "enchantment"; Old French *gramare*, *grimaire*, "a book of conjuring"; Middle English *glamer*, Modern English *glamour*, "enchantment," "charm," "witchery."

The mastery of what was in a grammar book had become of great practical importance. It was no longer possible to acquire the language of learning from native speakers of it as Roman boys had learned Greek from their slave pedagogues. No one spoke Latin as a first language anymore. The normal authority for the proper use of a language—the native speaker of it—no longer existed for Latin. He was replaced by a new authority—the grammar book. And for about a thousand years this authority was nearly absolute in the world of scholarship; until about 1750, Latin was the language of instruction in all Western universities and the language in which nearly all learned works were written. Inevitably and unconsciously educated men acquired an enormous respect for Latin and for Latin grammar.

When the vernacular languages were at last accepted in the universities and as legitimate languages of scholarship, the older instructional pattern was transferred to them. If the correct use of Latin could be learned only in a (Latin) grammar school and from a Latin grammar, then the correct use of English would have to be learned in an English grammar school and from an English grammar. Though the absurdity of this analogy was apparent to some perceptive men—Sir Philip Sidney, *An Apologie for Poetry*, comments: ".. which I think was a peece of the Tower of Babilons curse, that a man should be put to schoole to learne his mothertongue"—most educators accepted it.

But there were no English grammars available, and it took a couple of centuries for an adequate supply to be produced. The figures in Section II show how the number of them increased from the late 16th century to the middle of the 19th. The method of their production was essentially that of the Romans, who attempted to fit Latin into the framework of Greek. It was harder, however, to fit English into the framework of Latin, and a quite different purpose underlay the adaptation. The Romans attempted to recreate in their own culture simulacra of what they admired in the culture of Greece. The writers of English grammars—though there are exceptions—had a strongly prescriptive and proscriptive purpose in addition to their desire to present a grammatical analysis of English. Their approach to grammar included two attitudes toward grammar which were quite unknown to the ancients: that a language could be correctly used only through a thorough grounding in a grammar book, and that a language was a logical system whose symmetrical structure is exhibited in a grammar book. Both these lessons had been inculcated by the Middle Ages, the first through hundreds of years of school experience, the second by the Scholastic philosopher-grammarians.

The English grammars were therefore imitations of Latin grammars in which English was made to conform as far as possible to the model of Latin. English was assumed to be inferior to Latin, especially where it departed furthest from Latin morphology and syntax. Because Latin was rich in inflected forms, the grammars attempted to preserve English forms which were disappearing. Thomas Gray originally entitled his elegy "Elegy Wrote in a Country Churchyard," but the grammarians corrected *wrote* to *written*. Because Latin does not put a preposition at the end of a sentence, the grammarians prohibited it in that position in English despite a thousand years of usage to the contrary. An irrelevant logic was applied to forms and constructions. Two negatives were disallowed by arguing that two negatives make a positive, though double negatives had been common among the best writers for centuries—Chaucer, for example.

Their effect has been enormous because a considerable part of the elementary and secondary instruction of all children has been based on them. It has been of at least three kinds: (1) The language habits of students have probably been altered to some extent; *ain't* is seldom heard from cultivated speakers, though a century ago it was common; the distinction *you were* (plural), *you was* (singular), strongly supported by Noah Webster, is no longer made by cultivated speakers. But many of the distinctions demanded by the grammars are ignored by nearly everybody outside the classroom; the *shall-will* distinction scarcely exists except in questions. (2) The vocabularies of most speakers of English have had a number of grammatical terms incorporated into them: sentence, noun, verb, tense, and so on, but the words are used vaguely and most speakers would be hard-pressed to give a precise definition of them; *grammar* itself, for example, has many different meanings, as can be seen from Lord Tolloller's use of it in Gilbert and Sullivan's *Iolanthe* when he sings to the shepherdess Phyllis: "But of birth and position I've plenty; I've grammar and spelling for two, and blood and behaviour for twenty." It may even be that a good many students get some notion of grammatical structure of the language, but if so it is an incomplete and distorted notion because of the bias of the grammars. (3) The most important effect of Latin-based English grammars is, however, the establishment of a conviction in most speakers of the language that in grammars there rests the final authority as to what is right and wrong in language, an authority for which there is little justification in most of the school grammars.

It should perhaps be added that the grammars from which foreign languages have for years been taught serve the same purpose that Latin grammars did in the Middle Ages, though they do their job a good deal better. At least the best of the most recent ones are based on sound descriptive studies of the languages they deal with, and the selected items they present are probably the most important for a beginner to master. An elementary grammar of French, German, or Spanish has a limited objective. It hopes to give the student a partial control of the language it presents. Therefore it should present only the more important grammatical features of the language, without going into minute details of variations and exceptions. It will necessarily be dogmatic and will inevitably falsify by oversimplifying the language. But since this is an inescapable part of its stated purpose—and should be so stated in the introduction—it cannot be condemned. If the student goes on to a more advanced study of the language, the more numerous and more complicated features of the grammar will be presented to him then.

New techniques in the teaching of modern foreign languages (aural-oral methods combined with a language laboratory) are supplanting such grammars, but they served their purpose moderately well, and many students got at least a fair working knowledge of the language through them. They are prescriptive and proscriptive, but a legitimate pedagogical device for students who are learning a language late and under very unnatural and unfavourable conditions and who cannot expect to really master it. The prescriptive grammars of English, on the other hand, are intended for students who already have a full unconscious control of the grammar of their language (discussed in Section I), and are, consequently, often confusing and superfluous.

BIBLIOGRAPHY.—H. Steinthal, *Geschichte der Sprachwissenschaft bei den Griechen und Römern*, 2 vol. (1890); G. Landgraf, *Historische Grammatik der lateinischen Sprache*, iii (1903); R. H. Robins, *Ancient and Mediaeval Grammatical Theory in Europe* (1951); Jean Collart, *Varron, Grammairien Latin* (1954); Henri-Irénée Marrou, *Histoire de l'éducation dans l'antiquité* (1948; Eng. trans., *A History of Education in Antiquity*, 1956); L. Kukenheim, *Esquisse historique de la linguistique française* (1962); Karl W. Dykema, "Where Our Grammar Came From," in Harold B. Allen, *Readings in Applied English Linguistics*, pp. 3–15 (1964); R. C. Alston, *English Grammars Written in English* (1965).

(K. W. Dy.)

GRAMMAR SCHOOL, in Great Britain, a secondary school (U.S. high school) that offers an academic course preparatory for university entrance and for the professions; it is differentiated from the technical and the modern school. In the United States, in direct contrast with the use of the term in Great Britain, grammar school designates a part of the elementary school system, the grades between kindergarten and junior high school or high school. It might be noted that British grammar school education begins at about age 11; U.S. secondary (high) school education begins at about age 14.

See ELEMENTARY EDUCATION; SECONDARY EDUCATION; EDUCATION, HISTORY OF.

GRAMME: *see* GRAM.

GRAMONT, ANTOINE AGENOR ALFRED, DUC DE (1819–1880), French statesman, who as foreign minister in 1870 played a decisive role in the events that led to the Franco-German War, was born at St. Germain-en-Laye on Aug. 14, 1819, the son of a legitimist who had been an *émigré* during the Revolution. He was educated at the École Polytechnique and commissioned in the artillery but resigned from it at once. Through the influence of his mother (the sister of the famous dandy Alfred, comte d'Orsay, who was a friend of the future emperor Napoleon III) he was appointed French minister at Kassel in 1851. Later he was minister at Stuttgart (1852) and at Turin (1853) and then ambassador in Rome (1857) and in Vienna (1861). As a diplomat he was a skilful as well as a dignified representative of his country but he did not entirely share Napoleon III's political views and was therefore not always taken into his confidence.

Gramont happened to be in Paris during a ministerial crisis in 1870 and largely by accident was chosen on May 15 to be foreign minister in Émile Ollivier's government simply as a stopgap, but he soon had a most important influence on its policy and its fate. Gramont had in 1866 advocated a military demonstration to obtain concessions from the newly aggrandized Prussia; since then he had advocated a French alliance with Austria, maintaining that Prussia had been pursuing a policy of deliberate trickery and deception toward France. When, therefore, the Hohenzollern candidature to the throne of Spain was discovered in July, he was most vigorous in resisting it as an extension of Prussian power and demanded its withdrawal in strong language. Above all it was he (with Napoleon's approval but probably without the cabinet's) who sent the fateful telegram on July 12 demanding that the king of Prussia should guarantee that the candidature would never be revived. This was rebuffed and the French government, feeling France to have been insulted, declared war. Gramont resigned with the rest of the ministry on Aug. 9. He took no further part in public life and died in Paris on Jan. 18, 1880.

Gramont has been strongly criticized for his conduct as foreign minister and for declaring war even though France was diplomatically isolated, but then he believed that only vigorous action would conciliate French public opinion. He published a defense of his conduct entitled *La France et la Prusse avant la guerre* (1872).

See C. de Grunwald, *Le Duc de Gramont* (1950).

(T. Ze.)

GRAMONT, PHILIBERT, COMTE DE (1621–1707), French courtier of Gascon origin, the hero of Anthony Hamilton's *Mémoires du comte de Gramont*, was the younger son of Antoine II de Gramont, viceroy of Navarre, whose mother, Diane d'Andouins, comtesse de Gramont called "la belle Corisande," had been a mistress of Henry IV of France. Philibert was educated for the church but preferred a secular career. Known at first as the chevalier de Gramont, he served in the French army at the siege of Trino in Piedmont under Thomas of Savoy (1643) and in Germany under his half brother the marshal Antoine III de Gramont and under the duc d'Enghien. When the latter became prince de Condé he gave Gramont a high post in his household. Gramont remained with Condé's faction during the Fronde until 1654, when he made his peace with the French government after Condé's withdrawal to the Spanish Netherlands. In 1662, however, he was exiled from France—some said for competing with Louis XIV for Mlle de la Mothe-Houdancourt's favours. Arriving in England in Jan. 1663, he found a congenial atmosphere at Charles II's court. There he paid such attentions to the beautiful Elizabeth Hamilton, his future biographer's sister, that her brothers made him marry her in Dec. 1663. Allowed to return to France in 1676, he made three visits to England (1670–71) in connection with the negotiations preceding and following the treaty of Dover. Between campaigns in the Dutch Wars of 1672–78 he was in England again in 1676; he conveyed Louis XIV's congratulations to James II on the birth of a son in 1688. In his old age he provided Anthony Hamilton (*q.v.*) with the material for the *Mémoires*. After an apoplectic stroke in 1706, he died in Paris in the night of Jan. 29–30, 1707.

Hamilton portrays his hero candidly but with such skill that Gramont's grand air imposes on the reader just as it did on his contemporaries. But the subject matched the artist. Hamilton calls him an inimitable character, an amazing compound of good and bad, in fact *"l'admiration de son siècle"* (the wonder of his age). Even Gramont's enemies agreed as to his wit, impudence and ebullience. He was the sort of man about whom stories gather. He scandalized those about his deathbed who were repeating the Lord's Prayer, by remarking that it was a beautiful prayer, who had written it? He would seem to be the original of the outburst that Gascon noblemen would never have deserted Christ as His disciples, common fishermen, did. The duc de Saint-Simon, who hated him and accuses him of cowardice, has left a living picture of this "vieux sacripant de cour et de monde" (old court and society blusterer) with the face of an old monkey and never-failing success with ladies and with kings, a man to whom "everything was permitted and who permitted himself everything."

BIBLIOGRAPHY.—For editions of the *Mémoires* see HAMILTON, ANTHONY. *See* further Saint-Simon, *Mémoires*, ed. by A. de Boislisle, vol. xiv, pp. 262, 470 (1899); Ruth Clark, *Anthony Hamilton ...* (1921); W. H. Lewis, *Assault on Olympus: the Rise of the House of Gramont Between 1604 and 1678* (1958). (W. G. ME.)

GRAMOPHONE: see PHONOGRAPH.

GRAMPIANS, THE, mountains forming a part of the Scottish Highlands. The name is applied by some geographers to the whole mountain mass lying between Glenmore and the great fault which runs from Stonehaven on the North sea to Dumbarton on the Clyde. This is now more frequently called the Central Highlands. Others limit its application to the southern edge of this mountain mass where it overlooks the Lowlands. The name originated in a misreading from Tacitus of Mons Graupius, the site (not ascertained) of the battle in which Agricola defeated the Picts in about A.D. 83–84. This was shown on Hector Boece's map of 1527 as Mons Grampius. On historical grounds the latter usage therefore would appear to be the more correct. This southern edge is the most striking relief feature in Scotland. From the Lowlands it presents the appearance of a continuous mountain range, stretching for more than 100 mi. without a break and including peaks reaching to more than 3,000 ft. (Ben Lomond 3,192, Ben Alder 3,757). It is not, however, the formidable barrier it appears for it is broken by deep, if narrow, passes such as the Pass of Leny, the Pass of Killiecrankie and the Spittal of Glenshee. The rocks are chiefly schists and gneisses which make up a mountain range in southwest central Victoria, Australia, is also called the Grampians.

GRAMPUS, a name formerly loosely applied to any of the dolphins and porpoises but now usually given to a large dolphin that is more generally known as the killer whale. See KILLER WHALE: WHALE.

GRAMSCI, ANTONIO (1891–1937), Italian political leader and intellectual, co-founder of the Italian Communist party, was born at Alès, near Cagliari (Sardinia), on Jan. 23, 1891. From 1911 he studied history and philosophy at the University of Turin, joining in 1913 the Italian Socialist party and soon becoming an eloquent spokesman of its left wing. On May 1, 1919, he started in Turin a weekly newspaper, *L'Ordine Nuovo*, which exercised a considerable influence on the Italian intelligentsia of the left.

At that time he was already a convinced Communist and, together with Palmiro Togliatti and others, broke away from the Socialist party at its Leghorn (Livorno) convention in Jan. 1921. He was a co-founder with Togliatti of the Italian Communist party which took one-third (58,783) of the Socialist party's membership. In 1924 Gramsci was elected to the chamber of deputies and became the leader of the 19-strong Communist group. On Nov. 8, 1926, on the eve of the party's banning, Gramsci was arrested and deported to the island of Ustica. In 1928 he was sentenced to 20 years' imprisonment. He was held in a Rome hospital on April 27, 1937, where he became ill. He died in the prison of Turi di Bari, Gramsci's writings, *Opere*, were published in nine volumes (1947–54), one of the volumes, *Lettere dal carcere*, going into seven editions.

See P. Togliatti, *Gramsci* (1949); L. Lombardo-Radice and G. Carbone, *Vita di Antonio Gramsci* (1951).

GRANADA, LUIS DE (*c.* 1504–1588), Spanish Dominican preacher and spiritual writer, who made important contributions to teaching on Christian perfection, was born of poor parents at Granada, where he entered the order in 1524. He became prior at Córdoba (1544) and Badajoz (1554) and provincial of Portugal (1556–60). He was spiritual adviser to Queen Catherine of Portugal. He died at Lisbon on Dec. 31, 1588.

Luis' principal works, important also as Spanish prose, are: *Libro de la oración y meditación* (1554), on methodical prayer, akin to the systems of Ignatius Loyola and García de Cisneros; *Guía de pecadores* ("Sinners' Guide," 1556), on practical Christian virtue (both proscribed by the Inquisition in 1559, when any vernacular devotional book was suspected of illuminism, but reinstated in 1564); *Memorial de la vida christiana* (1566) and *Adiciones* to it (1574), on prayer. Spiritual classics that have enjoyed lasting popularity, they were translated during his lifetime into Latin, French, Italian and English (by R. Hopkins, 1582), and were esteemed by St. Teresa of Ávila and St. Francis of Sales. Luis also published sermons, catechetical works, biographies and a translation of the *Imitation of Christ*. A critical edition of his works by J. Cuervo was published in 14 volumes (1906–08).

See biography by J. Cuervo (1895); E. A. Peers, *Studies in the Spanish Mystics*, vol. i, 2nd ed. (1951); M. H. Lavocat in A. Vacant, *Dictionnaire de théologie catholique* (1926), s.v. Louis. (S. BH.)

GRANADA, a department and city in Nicaragua, Central America. The department has an area of 372 sq.mi. and a population (1963) of 65,643. It is bounded on the north by the department of Managua, on the west by Masaya and Carazo, Rivas on the south and Lake Nicaragua on the east. It is crossed by the Pan-American highway and the Pacific railroad. The clustered islands on the lake near Granada called Las Isletas (the little islands) are famous for their beauty and are favourite excursion spots for the Granadinos.

Principal towns besides the capital city are Nandaime and Diriomo. Main products are cattle and hides, cacao, sugar, cotton, rice and coffee.

GRANADA, the city, capital of the department and terminus of the Pacific railroad from the port of Corinto, is 36 mi. S.E. of Managua, the national capital. Pop. (1963) 28,507. It lies at an altitude of 180 ft. above sea level near Mombacho volcano, on the northwest shores of Lake Nicaragua where steamers and launches connect it with the lake towns. Granada is remarkable for its churches, schools and institutions.

Granada is the seat of the bishop and as headquarters of the Conservative party has greatly influenced the political life of the country. The city is typically Spanish and is laid out on a rectangular gridiron style. The houses are mostly one story, but include many fine mansions of the old families; the churches are massive and some are ornate.

Granada was founded in 1524 by Francisco Hernández de Córdoba and early became the hub of the Conservative life and trade of the region. From earliest times it has been a keen political and trade rival of León (*q.v.*), farther north, the centre of the Liberal party and now a more prosperous and populous business rival of Granada. Managua (*q.v.*) was founded between the two older cities as a political compromise. Granada was raided by pirates from the Caribbean many times in the 17th century. William Walker (*q.v.*) the U.S. filibuster, made Granada the centre of his attacks and his headquarters; he sacked and burned the city in 1857. (M. F.-G.)

GRANADA, the capital of the province and formerly of the kingdom of Granada, in the region of Andalusia, southern Spain, lies on the Genil river 430 km. (267 mi.) S. of Madrid by road. Pop. (1960) 157,178 (mun.). Granada is well situated at 669 m. (2,195 ft.) above the sea, on the northwestern slope of the Sierra Nevada, overlooking the fertile lowlands known as the Vega de Granada on the west and overshadowed by the peaks of Veleta (3,392 m. or 11,128 ft.) and Cerro de Mulhacén (3,478 m. or 11,411 ft.) on the southeast. The southern limit of the city is the Genil river (the Roman Singilis and Moorish Shenil), a swift stream flowing westward from the Sierra Nevada, with a considerable volume of water in summer when the snows have thawed. Its tributary, the Darro (the Roman Salon and Moorish Hadarro), enters Granada on the east, flows for more than a mile from east to west and then turns sharply southward to join the main river, which is spanned by a bridge just above the point of confluence. The waters of the Darro are much reduced by irrigation works along its lower course, and within the city it has been canalized and partly covered with a roof.

Granada comprises three main sections, the Antequeruela, the Albaicín and Granada, properly so-called. The first section, founded by refugees from Antequera in 1410, consists of the districts enclosed by the Darro and a small area on its right, or western, bank. It is bounded on the east by the gardens and hill of the Alhambra (*q.v.*), the most celebrated of the monuments left by the Moors. The Albaicín (Moorish Rabad al Bayazin, "Falconers' Quarter") lies northwest of the Antequeruela and west of Granada, properly so-called; is north of the Antequeruela and west of the Albaicín. The origin of its name is obscure; it may have been derived from *granada*, a "pomegranate," in allusion to the abundance of pomegranate trees in the neighbourhood and the fruit appears on the city arms. The Moors, however, called Granada Karnattah (Gharnatha), or Karnattah al Yahud, and possibly the name is composed of the Arabic words *kurn*, "a hill," and *nattah*, "stranger"—the "city" or "hill of strangers."

Granada is the see of an archbishop. Its cathedral (Santa María de la Encarnación), begun in 1529 by Diego de Siloé, and finished only in 1703, is profusely ornamented with jasper and coloured marbles, and surmounted by a dome. The interior contains many paintings and sculptures by Alonso Cano (1601-67), the architect of the fine west façade, and other artists. In one of the numerous chapels, known as the Chapel Royal (Capilla Real), is the tomb of Ferdinand and Isabella, the first rulers of united Spain. The Cartuja, or Carthusian monastery, north of the city, was built in 1516 in memory of the great captain Gonzalo de Córdoba (1453-1515), whose tomb is in the convent of San Jerónimo. Nearby stands the University of Granada which received its charter in 1531 and is now housed in a former Jesuit college.

After the Alhambra (*q.v.*), and such adjacent buildings as the Generalife and Torres Bermejas, which are more fitly described in connection with it, the principal Moorish antiquities of Granada are the 13th-century villa known as the Cuarto Real de San Domingo, admirably preserved and surrounded by beautiful gardens; the Alcázar de Genil, built in the middle of the 14th century as a palace for the Moorish queens; and the Casa del Cabildo Antigua, a university of the same period founded by Yusuf I, converted into a warehouse in the 19th century. Granada has an active trade in the agricultural produce of the Vega, and manufactures liqueurs, soap, paper and coarse linen and woolen fabrics. Railways run to Madrid, Algeciras and Barcelona.

GRANADA PROVINCE has an area of 12,531 sq.km. (4,838 sq.mi) and a population (1960) of 769,408; the mean population density is 61 per sq.km. or 159 per square mile. It is a relatively rich province with wide contrasts in the types of land, varying from the arid mountain zones to the fertile valleys. Crops include wheat, maize (corn), beans, potatoes, beetroot, sugar cane, tobacco (the biggest producing area in Spain) and cotton. Cereals are the most widely grown crop. There are also large quantities of olive and fruit trees (oranges, lemons, figs, almonds and pomegranates) and a considerable number of vineyards. The chief natural regions are: Hoya de Baza (pastoral and cereal producing), Hoya de Guadix (beet growing), the Vega de Granada, Tierra de Loja, Sierra Nevada and Las Alpujarras.

The province contains the lead mines of the Sierra de Gador, which were the richest in the world during the 19th century. The Marquesado region is the second biggest producer of iron ore (after Bilbao). The principal industries are based on agriculture, for example, sugar refining. The Granada coast line forms part of the so-called Costa del Sol ("coast of the sun") and includes the towns of Motril, Salobreña and Almuñécar, which all have fine beaches. Other important towns are Guadix, Loja and Baza.

BIBLIOGRAPHY.—Juan Sermet, *La España del Sur* (1955); Juan Castellanos, *Historia del reino de Granada*, 2 vol. (1886); Angel Ganivet, *Granada la bella* (1905); Santiago Alcolea, *Guía artística de Granada* (1951). (M. B. F.)

GRANADA, KINGDOM OF, was founded early in the 13th century out of the remnants of Almoravid power in Spain (*see* ALMORAVIDS) by Abu Abdullah ibn Yusuf ibn Nasr al-Ahmar, who became king as Mohammed I (1232-73). The kingdom comprised, principally, the modern provinces of Granada, Málaga and Almería. In 1246 Mohammed I secured the recognition of Ferdinand III of Castile (his neighbour on all terrestrial frontiers) in return for a vassalage which, though often ignored, remained in force until the kingdom's disappearance.

Granada's history is one of internal crises, due to the existence of a powerful landowning nobility with which, from the first, the monarchy had to come to terms, and to wars with Castile. Successive kings of Granada sought political support and military aid from Morocco. Moroccan recruits came to form special groups—the *al-guzat al-magariba*—whose function was to defend the frontiers; they caused the kingdom to undergo an intense process of arabization, to cut itself off from all Castilian influences and to develop an absolute form of government based on military support. The central government's economic resources, greatly depleted by the independence of the military governors (*ru'is*), depended mainly on the silk industry and on external trade; the latter flourished because of the fortunate position of the chief port, Málaga, on the route from the Mediterranean to the Atlantic. Granada paid close attention to the Strait of Gibraltar; for a whole century its rulers made efforts to secure control of the straits, allying to this end at different times with both Morocco and Castile. In 1306 Mohammed III (1302-09), then in possession of Ceuta and Gibraltar, seemed to have succeeded, but a powerful coalition soon reduced him to the modest position of vassal of the king of Castile. After 1340, when the battle of Río Salado settled the question of the straits in Castile's favour, Granada adopted a policy of isolation, taking advantage of any propitious circumstances to strengthen its land frontiers. It was in this period that Yusuf I (1333-54) and Mohammed V (1354-59 and 1362-91) finished building the Alhambra (*q.v.*).

Civil strife in Castile during the second half of the 14th century enabled Mohammed V and Mohammed VII (1392-1408) to develop a counteroffensive against Algeciras and the cities on the Guadalquivir, but from 1407 Castile took up the idea of conquering the kingdom of Granada as the last stage of the Reconquest. The campaign was a large and costly undertaking, conducted intermittently throughout the 15th century. Granada meanwhile disintegrated as a result of the internal struggles between one particular family faction, the Ibn Sarraj (*see* ABENCERRAGES), and the landowning aristocracy. The Catholic kings took advantage of this disunity; the last king of Granada, Boabdil (*q.v.*; Abu Abd Allah Mohammed XI), who ruled from 1482 to 1492, was an instrument of Spanish policy against his father, Mulay Hasan (1466-82; Abu-l-Hasan Ali). Nevertheless, the final conquest of Granada was difficult and expensive; the capital was taken on Jan. 2, 1492.
(L. S. F.)

GRANADOS, ENRIQUE (1867-1916), Spanish pianist and composer, a leader of the late 19th-century nationalist school, was born at Lérida, Catalonia, July 27, 1867. He showed musical talent very early and made his debut as a pianist at the age of 16.

About 1883 he studied composition with Felipe Pedrell in Barcelona, supporting himself by playing in a café. In 1887 he went to Paris for two years, perfecting his piano technique with Charles de Bériot, Jr., and returning to Barcelona in 1889, where he shortly afterward reappeared at concerts and established himself as a player of the front rank: his 12 *Danzas españolas*, which he introduced to the public, aroused great interest and popularity. The first of his seven operas, *María del Carmen*, was successfully produced in Madrid in 1898. In 1900 he founded a classical concerts society (which proved short-lived) and his own piano school, in which he produced many distinguished players. He wrote extensively and fluently, in a somewhat diffuse post-Lisztian style, for the piano, his masterpiece being the two sets of *Goyescas*, imaginative and poetic reflections of Goya's paintings and tapestries. (His interest in the 18th century is also exemplified in the attractive *tonadillas*, songs written "en estilo antiguo.") The *Goyescas*, remarkable for their combination of elegance and passion, were composed in 1911–13 and then amplified into an opera that was accepted for Paris but, because of war conditions, received its *première* in New York city in 1916. It was on his way back from this performance that Granados was drowned when the "Sussex" was torpedoed on March 24, 1916, by a German submarine.

See G. Chase, *The Music of Spain* (1941).   (L. SA.)

GRANARY AND GRAIN ELEVATOR. Grain storage facilities range widely from simple provisions—in certain dry climates grain is sometimes stored in piles on the ground—to elaborate structures with equipment for mechanical filling and emptying, turning, blending, weighing, fumigating, drying or ventilating. Some buildings are for storing only a few bushels; others have capacity for several million bushels.

The character of a grain storage, as well as its size, depends upon the service required of it. On a livestock farm the granary usually has several separate bins for the various kinds of grain to be fed. Each bin may be filled or partly filled several times a year. Usually grain will not be stored for more than one season. The bins may be emptied a little at a time, and convenience of location for feeding and easy accessibility for removing grain are important.

On cash grain farms, from which most of the grain is sold, storage bins are for disposing of the grain at harvest time until it is sold later in the season. In this case ease of filling is most important. Larger grain storages on farms have built-in elevators but portable elevators or conveyers came to be used extensively. Country elevators, located in smaller towns, serve to collect grain from farmers and ship it to terminals. Little grain is held for long periods. They are equipped with scales and with conveying equipment for filling, emptying and blending. They frequently also have driers.

Terminal elevators are the grain storages located at ports and railroad centres. They collect grain from the producing areas and supply the processors and feed mixers and distributors in deficit areas. The terminal elevators have many separate bins and usually are of concrete construction. A typical bin may be 100 ft. deep and 20 ft. in diameter. Sloping floors are used so that the grain may drain out by gravity. Conveyer systems are installed so that grain may be moved into or out of the building or from any bin to any other.

In the United States during the 1930s the federal government entered into a program of grain price stabilization which resulted in government acquisition of large quantities of some grains to be held for relatively long periods. Other governments have taken more or less similar action. This results in the need for still another class of grain storage buildings where grain may be held for several years or at any rate for a longer period of time than had been the customary practice. Such storages are located on farms, on government-owned bin sites or at grain elevators where they are operated in conjunction with storage and merchandising functions of the elevators. (*See also* AGRICULTURAL ECONOMICS.)

In addition there are special storage facilities for segments of the grain industry. The storage of seed grains, for example, has special requirements. It is necessary in this case to avoid mixing of various lots since even a few kernels of the wrong variety may reduce the value of the lot.

Each kind of grain imposes its own requirements on storages and handling equipment. For example, rice is customarily harvested before it is dry enough to store; thus rice storages must have driers. Frequently rice is dried and stored in the same establishment where it is later milled.

Control of Moisture Content.—All grains contain water, even when they are what is called dry. A bushel of wheat as ordinarily handled or stored contains about three quarts of water. Control of moisture content is important in successful storage of grains. Molds develop and insects thrive in grain only if it has enough moisture for their needs. The safe limit of moisture is usually between 10% and 15%, depending on the kind of grain, the climate and the length of storage period. Since grains do not lose moisture readily when stored in bulk, it is important to accept for storage only grain that has been tested for moisture and found dry enough to keep.

One of the problems in storage of grains in large bins is the movement of moisture from one part of the bulk to another. This may occur even in grain that is initially dry enough for safe storage. The local increase in moisture results in caking or molding and favourable conditions for insect breeding. The causes of the increase in moisture at the upper surface came to be understood only relatively recently.

The temperature of the interior grain in a large bin changes much more slowly than the atmospheric temperature. By late summer or fall the grain reaches its maximum temperature. The top surface and outer layers cool as winter approaches, but the centre stays relatively warm. About 40% of the space in a full bin is occupied by the air between the kernels, so there is a column of warm air in the centre of the bin surrounded by colder air near the walls. Since the warm air at the centre is light, it moves upward through the grain, being replaced by the colder heavier air near the walls which moves downward. This movement is very slow, but it continues as long as the temperature difference persists, which may be for several months.

This continuous stream of warm air must pass through the grain at the top surface which, during the fall and winter, is cold. On coming in contact with the cold surface grain some of the moisture from the warm air is condensed or absorbed on the cold grain. The slow increase in grain moisture content at the surface continues for several months and may result in serious damage.

The damage from moisture migration usually is limited to the top foot or two, but it becomes a possible source of insect infestation. In elevators the grain can be turned, that is, moved from one bin to another.

If the grain is turned before serious increase in moisture has occurred, the surface grain will be mixed with the rest. At the same time the warm and cold grain will be mixed together so that convection air currents will be checked temporarily. Turning, however, affords only temporary relief. Repeated turning damages the grain by breaking kernels.

From the late 1940s onward mechanical ventilation was used to prevent damage from moisture migration in both elevators and storages of intermediate size when storing large quantities of grain for several years. A fan draws air downward through the grain during cooler months. This eventually cools the grain to near the atmospheric temperature, and at the same time the natural upward convection is reversed so that warm air cannot contact the cold grain at the surface.

See also CROP DRYING AND PROCESSING: *Grain Driers*; FARM BUILDINGS; FARM MACHINERY; PORT.
    (W. V. HL.)

GRANBY, JOHN MANNERS, MARQUESS OF (1721–1770), British soldier, whose contemporary fame and popularity are commemorated by the large number of English inns and public houses named after him, was born in 1721, the eldest son of the 3rd duke of Rutland. He was educated at Eton and at Trinity college, Cambridge, and elected member of parliament for Grantham in 1741. He received a commission as colonel of a regiment raised to assist in quelling the Highland revolt of 1745. This corps never got beyond Newcastle, but as a volunteer on the duke of Cumberland's staff Granby saw active service in the last stages of the insurrection. He was in the Flanders campaign of 1747, was promoted major general in 1755 and three years later was appointed colonel of the Royal Horse Guards (Blues). He had married the daughter of the duke of Somerset and in 1754 had begun his parliamentary connection with Cambridgeshire, for which county he sat until his death.

Dispatched to Germany in 1758 during the Seven Years' War, he was at the battle of Minden and succeeded to the command of the British contingent after Lord Sackville's disgrace. On July 31, 1760, Granby stormed Warburg at the head of the British cavalry, capturing 1,500 men and ten pieces of artillery. A year later (July 15, 1761) the British defended the heights of Vellinghausen with great bravery, and in the last campaign Granby's men bore the brunt of the fighting. Returning to England in 1763 the marquess found himself the popular hero of the war. He was appointed to the ordnance on July 1, 1763, and three years later he became commander in chief, in which position he was attacked by "Junius." He died in debt at Scarborough on Oct. 18, 1770, after resigning most of his honours and offices.

GRANBY, a city of Shefford county, Que., Can., 40 mi. E. of Montreal, on the North Yamaska river. Pop. (1961) 31,463, of which 91% are French speaking. Its position in respect to principal rail and highway routes combined with the availability of a large labour force and the markets of metropolitan Montreal has enabled it to emerge as an important commercial and industrial centre. It has five Roman Catholic and two Protestant churches, a school of arts and trades, a classical college and a hospital. Manufacturing is of prime importance, the principal products being textiles, clothing, blankets, plastic and rubber goods, maple products, furniture and wood by-products, tobacco and refrigerators. It has one of the largest and best-known zoos in Canada.

(W. F. Ss.)

GRAN CHACO, meaning hunting ground, is a region in the interior of South America encompassing territory in northern Argentina, eastern Bolivia, western Brazil and Paraguay. Extending from about latitude 20° to 29° S., it is a part of the Paraná-Paraguay plain, bordered north by the Chiquitos plateau, east by the Brazilian highland and west by the piedmont ranges of the Andes; it merges with the pampas on the south. Its total area is about 300,000 sq.mi. The Gran Chaco contains areas of subtropical scrub forest, great swamps, broad plains dotted with the fanleaf palm and regions of desert plants. The average elevation is about 450 ft. above sea level, and the surface is generally flat. The annual average precipitation is about 54 in., but on the drier western side the annual rainfall is about 20 in.; drought and flood conditions are common. The average summer temperature in the south is 72° F. (22.22° C.) and in the north 75° F. (23.89° C.). Both the physical conditions and the climate bear a resemblance to the region bordering the Gulf of Mexico in North America.

Assets of the Gran Chaco include the quebracho tree (a major source of tannin), cotton, cattle and petroleum. The economic development of the region has been retarded by the climate, the lack of transportation facilities and the prevalence of tropical pests, notably the locust. Although limited pioneer settlement by Europeans has occurred in the eastern Chaco, the inhabitants are still largely nomadic tribes of Indians.

The Chaco Boreal, so named in order to distinguish it from the Chaco (Austral) lands of Argentina, has been disputed territory, being claimed by Bolivia on the west border and Paraguay, on the east. (See BOLIVIA; PARAGUAY.) This region is triangular in shape, with the apex at Asunción, the capital of Paraguay, and its sides made up of the Paraguay and Pilcomayo rivers, which form natural boundaries. Paraguay gained most of the disputed area as a result of the Chaco War (q.v.) of 1932–35. See also CHACO.

(J. L. TR.)

GRAND ALLIANCE, WAR OF THE, sometimes called the WAR OF THE LEAGUE OF AUGSBURG, a war fought by England, Holland, the Holy Roman emperor, and a number of other allies against France between 1689 and 1697. The uncertainty over its name is reflected in a similar confusion about the war's aims, character, and results. The military commanders have been criticized for the ineffectiveness of their methods of making war. The reputation of the French generals has suffered by comparison with the great Condé and the maréchal de Turenne, who had disappeared from the scene in 1675, the one retired and the other killed; on the side of the Allies, William III's achievement as a soldier has been eclipsed by that of Marlborough. Sieges rather than battles marked the progress of the war, with results less striking to the modern eye. Yet the deadlock which characterized the war was not so much military as diplomatic, and it resulted from the uncertain outcome of the Spanish succession, on which the balance of power between Bourbon and Habsburg in Europe depended. So long as Charles II of Spain remained alive (against every reasonable expectation), any war must be but a preliminary skirmish in which the great powers sought to strengthen their bargaining position against the day when Charles should at last die. If, then, there was for the time nothing important to fight about, it is not surprising that the generals found it difficult to achieve anything by fighting.

But war could not easily be avoided, since in its absence the circumstances of the rival powers might alter drastically. Thus Louis XIV's ambitions depended upon the emperor Leopold I's being unable to unite the German princes against Louis and so upon Leopold's continued entanglement with the Turks on the eastern frontier. Louis dared not allow his adversary a lengthy interval of peace in which he might extricate himself from his difficulties. In a sense, then, Louis was throughout his reign the aggressor. In any event, his ambition for glory made him, as he himself was to admit later, always too ready to engage in war. Yet it was not to war, but to the spoils of the Spanish inheritance, that could be secured by diplomacy, that Louis could look for the establishment of French hegemony over Europe.

This was the real issue at stake in the last quarter of the 17th century, the balance of power between Bourbon and Habsburg monarchies, as it had been since Henry IV became king of France, and the outcome of this struggle depended more upon diplomacy than upon war. War was an adjunct to diplomacy, as important as, but no more important than, marriage alliances. So long as diplomacy was stultified by the uncertain issue of the Spanish succession, so long would the wars be devoid of lasting consequences whatever the brilliance of the military commanders. The War of the Grand Alliance might not be worth investigation were it not that the long-lasting diplomatic deadlock produced new factors in the situation, notably the accession of England as a European power of first importance, which were to prove decisive in the eventual settlement of the Spanish succession in the war of 1701–13.

Character of the War.—The character of war had altered much during the 17th century. Most obviously, the size of armies had increased. The increasing wealth at the disposal of European governments allowed them to maintain larger armies, and improvements followed in military administration and supply. The effectiveness of infantry had been much increased during the previous wars of the 17th century not only by better regimental organization and drilling but also by improvements in the musket, which were to culminate in the introduction of the flintlock, and the substitution of the bayonet for the pike. But infantry could move only slowly, and a large army presented a considerable supply problem. This could be solved only by living off the country which involved dispersal over a fairly wide area. Only by occupying fortified places could an army in such a situation feel safe. During the vital weeks of a campaigning season the component parts of an army might be combined for offensive action, and it was necessary to collect supplies in advance for such an operation. This need called for large army bases equally well fortified. So the capture or recapture of fortresses was frequently an indispensable prelude to more ambitious strategic operations.

Such operations were not impossible, though until the development of the tactical possibilities of cavalry and artillery had caught up with those of infantry they were difficult. They were especially difficult where geographical obstacles lay between an army and its objective; and France, since the acquisition of the Franche-Comté and the occupation of Lorraine in the earlier wars of Louis XIV, was surrounded by natural barriers save for the southeastern coastal route from Italy and the northeastern frontier between the Moselle and the sea. Sébastien Le Prestre de Vauban (q.v.), the great builder of fortresses, provided for the northeastern frontier what nature had omitted. Flanders has always provided a natural gateway from Germany into France and vice versa, and it was there that the fiercest fighting of the war was to take place. In the event, the combination of a complicated river network and an elaborate defensive system of fortresses proved too much for the military commanders in the time available to them. Such a result, however, was not inevitable, but arose as much from the near balance of the forces engaged as it did from the intractability of the natural and man-made obstacles.

One other aspect of the character of the war needs to be considered. Since wars avowedly concerned the personal ambitions of princes, the clothing of religious controversy having been discarded, the civilian population ceased at ordinary times to be concerned directly in the struggle and came more and more to assume that role of neutral onlookers which Frederick the Great was later to regard as proper to them. The war began with a devastation of the Palatinate as harsh as any similar operation of the Thirty Years' War; but this proved to be exceptional as larger supplies of money and better methods of credit finance came to enable army commanders to purchase their supplies instead of seizing them by force. The burden of war thus became a financial one, borne by the countries responsible for the fighting rather than those fought over.

The Spanish Succession.—The problem of the Spanish inheritance, including territories in the Netherlands, in Italy, and in the Americas as well as Spain itself, began with the accession in 1665 of the epileptic and partly insane Charles II. This monarch was the medical curiosity of his age because of the many diseases from which he suffered. The product of much intermarriage, he was the last representative of his house in the male line, and, being impotent, would not produce heirs. On his demise, therefore, the inheritance would have to be through a female line and this would involve the rival Bourbon and Habsburg dynasties. Louis XIV had married the elder daughter of Philip IV and Leopold I the younger daughter, and their fathers had similarly married daughters of Philip III. Whereas both the wives of the French kings had renounced their claims on the Spanish succession at the time of their marriages, Leopold's wife was named in the will of Philip IV as the direct line of succession. So far, however, no male heir had resulted from this line and the problem remained unsolved and full of danger, the more so since as early as 1662 Louis had suggested that his wife's renunciation, which was conditional, might have to be considered invalid.

The possibility of securing at least a part of the Spanish inheritance was never far removed from Louis's calculations. He used the period of nominal peace established by the Treaties of Nijmegen (q.v.; 1678–79) to extend French power in Alsace, Lorraine, and the Spanish Netherlands. His method was to set up special courts to investigate the extent of his rights in recently acquired territories and then to use force or the threat of force to implement their invariably favourable findings. In Alsace the terms of the Peace of Westphalia substituting French for imperial sovereignty had been especially, and deliberately, vague, but now the policy of *Réunions* transformed the area into a French province. The three great bishoprics of Metz, Toul, and Verdun were declared by Louis XIV's special courts to be French, and in 1680 only Strasbourg lay outside his control.

The new French policy caused consternation in Germany and elsewhere but resistance to it proved difficult to organize. Spain was in a state of almost hopeless decline while the United Netherlands were exhausted by the recent war. The emperor Leopold was well aware of the danger of France inheriting the Spanish Empire, particularly since the death of his first wife Margaret, through whom his family could make its best claim to the Spanish throne. Margaret had died in 1673 leaving only a daughter, Maria

Antonia, born in 1669 and now of marriageable age. He agreed to her otherwise not very desirable marriage to the elector Maximilian Emanuel of Bavaria, formerly an ally of France, on condition that she renounce all claims to the Spanish throne, thus in his opinion making the line of succession run through his own mother, Philip III's daughter. The candidate whom he had in mind for Spain was a second son of his own, the archduke Charles, born in 1685 (the year of his daughter Maria Antonia's marriage) to his third wife Eleonore of Palatinate-Neuburg.

Leopold was less concerned over the immediate danger from France in 1680 because of the renewed threat of a Turkish advance on Vienna. He therefore withdrew his garrison from Strasbourg and the city was occupied by French troops in 1681. Louis went on to claim and besiege Luxembourg. This provoked opposition from Spain, Holland, and England, and a general war seemed possible. However, when the Turks actually besieged Vienna, even Louis, who had actively encouraged the enterprise, was compelled to call off the siege of Luxembourg. Louis probably hoped that Vienna would fall and that he might himself become Holy Roman emperor and defender of Christendom, but in July 1683 John Sobieski relieved the city of Vienna. Louis continued to goad his enemies and when Spain succumbed and declared war he again besieged Luxembourg. This kind of intermittent war might have continued but for the suggestion of a 20-years truce which satisfied the needs of all parties. France could consolidate her recent gains and the other powers could attempt to recover their strength, all in the expectation that time would work in their favour. The Truce of Regensburg was signed in August 1684, leaving Louis in possession of Strasbourg, Luxembourg, and Oudenaarde.

Leopold had agreed to the Truce of Regensburg in order to concentrate upon an offensive against Turkey. He argued that if Hungary could be recovered and the hereditary lands of the Habsburgs freed from the continuous burden of defense against the Turks, then he would be strong enough to challenge Louis XIV without depending upon the assistance of the German princes. So the League of Augsburg concluded between himself, the kings of Sweden and of Spain (in their capacity of princes of the empire), the elector of Bavaria, the Ernestine house of Saxony, and the circle of Franconia on July 9 (new style; June 29, old style), 1686, was not an important part of his policy. This alliance has been represented as the forerunner of the Grand Alliance by some historians who have therefore given its name to the War of 1689–97. In fact it was quite ineffective, providing no machinery for combined military action; and the states which constituted the mainstay of the Grand Alliance were not parties to it.

Leopold during these years was concerned as much with Turkey as with Germany, and a much more important alliance than the League of Augsburg was that already concluded with the elector Frederick William of Brandenburg. Frederick William, who had previously aligned himself with France, sent a contingent to help Leopold on the Danube in January 1686 and entered into a secret understanding with him against France in March. Habsburg troops advanced across Hungary in 1686 and in 1687, and on Sept. 6 (N.S.), 1688, after the rejection of Turkish offers of peace in the previous year, Belgrade was taken. Turkey now prepared to make much more attractive offers of peace, and Louis XIV saw the control of the situation slipping from his grasp. He determined therefore on another military demonstration like those of 1681–84, hoping that this would keep the Turks fighting and restrain Germany from rushing into the Habsburg camp.

Cologne and the Palatinate.—Apart from the existence of the League of Augsburg and the emperor's refusal to perpetuate the Truce of Regensburg, two disputes furnished Louis with pretexts for military intervention. The more immediate of the two was concerned with the archbishopric-electorate of Cologne. The archbishop-elector Maximilian Henry had in January 1688 appointed Wilhelm Egon Cardinal von Fürstenberg to be his coadjutor; when Maximilian Henry died in the following June, Fürstenberg put himself forward as a candidate for his succession. Fürstenberg, however, had had all his life been a protégé of France, and his accession to Cologne was unacceptable both to the emperor and to the pope, who gave their support to the rival candidate Joseph Clement, brother of the elector of Bavaria and first cousin once removed of Maximilian Henry. Louis thereupon sent French troops to uphold Fürstenberg. This move alarmed the German Protestant princes, who took measures to secure the Dutch against the possibility of a French attack; and the emperor, with papal encouragement, persisted in his recognition of Joseph Clement.

The other controversy in which Louis now decided to assert his claim was about the succession to the Palatinate. Charles, the last elector Palatine of the Simmern line, had died without heirs in 1685 and had been succeeded by the head of the Zweibrücken line, Philip William of Neuburg, the emperor's father-in-law. It was possible, however, to claim that some part of the succession ought to have gone to the elector Charles's sister Elizabeth Charlotte (Liselotte), the second wife of Louis's brother Philip, duke of Orléans. Though the duchess of Orléans was herself disinclined to insist on this pretension, the fall of Belgrade determined Louis to enforce it. On Sept. 24 (N.S.), 1688, he issued a manifesto setting forth the French grievances. A French army under the command of the dauphin then advanced into the Palatinate.

It is very doubtful whether France intended its action to lead to a major war. But at this point other developments occurred which took the determination of events out of French hands. Both William III of Orange and Louis XIV had sought to intervene in English politics since the restoration of the Stuart king Charles II in 1660, to prevent hostile activity by the English on the continent. Since 1685 James II had lost the loyalty of nearly all of his subjects, and an important body of them looked to William of Orange, the husband of the heiress apparent Mary, as their only salvation from tyranny. William, for his part, was an inveterate opponent of Louis XIV and welcomed the prospect of securing England as an ally. The birth of a male heir to James in June 1688 brought matters to a state of crisis in England, and William agreed to land an army there. Louis XIV was well aware of this intended invasion when he sent his troops into the Palatinate and in fact welcomed it as ensuring the absence of William from the continent so long as the expected civil war lasted in England.

Louis underestimated the reaction of Europe to his invasion of the Palatinate. True, Turkey was no longer willing to make peace with the emperor on acceptable terms and William of Orange was successful in expelling James II from England, while the emperor's recent victories enabled him to contain the Turks below Belgrade without much affecting the strength of his forces in the west. Moreover, the other German princes had been aroused rather than cowed by the French show of military strength; and France was already committed also against the Dutch and against Spain when the Dutch and the emperor concluded the Treaty of Vienna on May 12 (N.S.), 1689, with the avowed aim of restoring the settlements of Westphalia (1648) and of the Pyrenees (1659). This treaty, to which England, Brandenburg, Hanover, Saxony, Bavaria, Savoy, and Spain adhered in the course of the following 18 months, was the kernel of the Grand Alliance. The French found themselves faced at once by two strong armies: by the Dutch and the north German forces in Flanders under the imperial and Bavarian troops on the Rhine. In these circumstances they were compelled to withdraw from the advanced positions occupied in 1688. Bonn and Mainz were evacuated on the Rhine, while in Flanders an English contingent under Marlborough assisted George Frederick, prince of Waldeck, in defeating the French at Walcourt on Aug. 25 (N.S.; 15, O.S.), 1689.

The English Succession and the War in Ireland.—At this juncture, Louis was saved in part from the consequences of his miscalculation by events in Ireland. Although expelled from England without difficulty, James II could still command support in Ireland, almost all of which was controlled by the Jacobite earl of Tyrconnell (Richard Talbot) with an army of 40,000 men of uncertain quality. Louis XIV was thus able to restore his original plan of involving William of Orange in a civil war in England by sending James II to Ireland with a small French force to renew the conflict there. He landed on March 22 (N.S.; 12, O.S.), 1689, at Kinsale and at once accompanied Tyrconnell to the north where

the Protestant population had declared in favour of William III and secured Enniskillen and Londonderry. The siege of Londonderry began on April 29 (N.S.; 19, O.S.), but without a siege train no assault could be mounted. An English relieving force for Londonderry, sent by sea under Col. Percy Kirke at the end of May, was needlessly dilatory, but the blockade was eventually broken by Capt. John Leake's ships on Aug. 7 and the siege raised on Aug. 9–10 (N.S.; July 28 and 30–31, O.S.). At the same time a detachment of the Jacobite army was defeated by local forces organized by Col. William Wolseley, whereupon the siege of Enniskillen was likewise abandoned. The Williamite forces proceeded to overrun the whole of Ulster, and when the duke of Schomberg, sent with an army by William at the insistence of his English advisers, landed at Bangor near Belfast in August, he was able to advance southward immediately. He reached Dundalk, but there was held up. His army was small, much of it insufficiently trained, and rapidly being reduced by sickness. He was therefore unwilling to risk battle and eventually repaired to winter quarters in the north.

William at last became convinced of the necessity of making a serious effort in Ireland and in June 1690 went there himself with a considerable army, including Dutch and other foreign troops. He advanced on Dublin with 40,000 men and came across James II entrenched behind the Boyne River with a slightly smaller force, including a French contingent landed under the comte (later duc) de Lauzun in March. James's army had some good cavalry, but it was the infantry which settled the day in favour of William on July 11 (N.S.; 1, O.S.), 1690. James fled once more to France, but his army made a good retreat, though abandoning all of Ireland save the west and southwest. William advanced in Ireland but failed to take Limerick, which was defended by Patrick Sarsfield, in August; and after the earl (later duke) of Marlborough had taken Cork in September and Kinsale in October, fighting ended for the year with the war not yet completely over.

In 1691 Godard van Ginkel commanded for William in Ireland and the marquis de Saint-Ruth for James. Their armies met at Aughrim on July 22 (N.S.; 12, O.S.), where Saint-Ruth, after appearing to have the battle won, was killed and his army defeated. Even now, though the town of Galway surrendered and Athlone was already lost, Sarsfield held out in Limerick until Oct. 13 (N.S.; 3, O.S.) when a treaty was signed which brought the Irish war to a close. The war in Ireland had lasted for more than two years, and its outcome must not be allowed to disguise the fact that Louis XIV had succeeded in keeping William of Orange and 40,000 of his troops absent from the continent for the important campaign of 1690. So far, indeed, William's inheritance of the English crown had proved a liability.

The Continental War.—The ambitious plans of the allies in 1690 for a triple invasion of France, from Flanders, from the Rhine, and from Savoy all ended in disappointment or disaster. The death of Charles V of Lorraine, who had been the leading figure in the south German opposition to France, on April 18 (N.S.), caused the Rhine offensive to die away early. In Flanders, with 40,000 allied troops away in Ireland, Waldeck's forces were outnumbered by those of the duc de Luxembourg; and while awaiting reinforcements preparatory to an advance upon Dinant, Waldeck was attacked and defeated at Fleurus (q.v.) on July 1 (N.S.). Great hopes, however, were still entertained by the allies of Savoy. The western frontiers of that country offered an easy route into Provence, and on the other side was the Spanish Milanese, giving easy access to the hereditary territories of the Habsburgs in Austria. This strategic position had compelled (or enabled) the dukes of Savoy to adopt a vacillating policy toward the Franco-Spanish conflicts of the 17th century. In 1689, though French garrisons in Pinerolo (Pignerol) and in Casale and the army under Nicolas Catinat on the Alpine frontier seemed to make France's influence over Savoy secure, the apparent strength of the Grand Alliance nevertheless caused the duke, Victor Amadeus II, to hesitate before committing himself to Louis XIV; and in 1690, when compelled by the French to choose, he joined the allied cause in the hope of securing Pinerolo and Casale. Catinat reacted at once and, advancing into Piedmont, defeated Victor Amadeus at Staffarda on Aug. 18 (N.S.), 1690. A further setback overtook the allies in October, when the Turks retook Belgrade and the hopes of a Turkish peace disappeared.

Nor did 1691 bring much comfort. William III commanded in person in Flanders but, operating from Brussels, failed to prevent Luxembourg from taking Mons (April 8 [N.S.]). Without the support of the Brandenburg troops occupied in defending Cleves against a French diversion, he was unable to command favourable circumstances in which he could bring Luxembourg to battle, and the remainder of his campaign that year in Flanders was taken up with ineffective maneuvering. After William's return to England in the autumn, Waldeck, while moving the army into winter quarters, was attacked and defeated by Luxembourg at Leuze (Sept. 20 [N.S.]). Meanwhile Catinat continued his progress into Piedmont, and the French army of Catalonia, under the duc de Noailles, took Urgel. Thus, for two years France had more than countered all the threats of the Grand Alliance; the command of interior lines and great resources of manpower and of wealth had made it possible to defy the rest of Europe. This fact, and not the technicalities of the laws of inheritance, was to constitute the Bourbons' real claim to the Spanish succession.

The strength of the Allied cause on the other hand lay in the addition of England to their ranks. Up to 1692, much of its war effort had had to be devoted to Ireland, but this period had witnessed the establishment of Allied naval control over the Channel. In 1689 the French Brest fleet under the marquis de Château-Renault was strong enough to convey French troops to Ireland. The battle which resulted when he was attacked by Adm. Arthur Herbert at Bantry Bay (May 11 [N.S.; 1, O.S.]) was claimed as a victory by both sides. The next year the French admiral, the comte de Tourville, was reinforced by the Toulon fleet and so enjoyed a numerical superiority over Herbert, now earl of Torrington. Torrington at first refused to risk an engagement, and when he did was defeated at the Battle of Beachy Head (q.v.; July 10 [N.S.; June 30, O.S.], 1690). He subsequently withdrew back to the Thames, claiming that by this strategy he could avoid a decisive defeat and so by keeping his "fleet in being" deter the French from attempting invasion. His phrase was long employed to describe this important strategic concept, but it is probable that the motive for Torrington's actions was less sophisticated.

However, the French did not follow up their success but spent the year of 1691 in making raids on shipping; and when in 1692 Tourville, acting upon orders from home, sought battle, he was heavily defeated by the English admirals Edward Russell and George Rooke at the Battle of La Hogue (q.v.; May 29–June 3 [N.S.; May 19–24, O.S.]. The French never again during the war sought a general engagement at sea, and to some extent a permanent decline in France's naval fortunes may be dated from the Battle of La Hogue.

The campaign of 1692 in Flanders was begun by a French army led by the king himself, assisted by Vauban and covered by Luxembourg, laying siege to Namur (May 25 [N.S.]). An unexpected period of heavy rain disrupted William's plans for relieving the city, and on June 5 (N.S.) the town surrendered; the last stronghold, however, held out until July 1 (N.S.). William then spent the rest of the summer endeavouring to bring Luxembourg to battle; he succeeded, but Luxembourg commanded a strong defensive position at Steenkerke. In another battle of infantry (Aug. 3 [N.S.; July 24, O.S.] a determined attack by the British forces won some ground, but William's dispositions had been faulty, the success was not followed up, and at length his army was compelled to withdraw. Luxembourg, however, though left in possession of the field, had been sufficiently troubled to make him choose not to pursue the enemy.

The year 1693 proved to be another disappointing one for the Allies. Louis XIV launched a series of disconnected offensives. Catinat once more defeated the duke of Savoy, at Marsaglia (Oct. 4 [N.S.]), the army of the Rhine captured Heidelberg, the army of Catalonia took Rosas, and Luxembourg threatened Liège. William sent 20,000 men to relieve Liège and stood the rest of his army at Neerwinden, near Landen, to cover this force. There

he was attacked by Luxembourg in superior force on July 29 (N.S.) and, despite an obstinate defense, was again defeated. The campaign in Flanders closed with the French capture of Charleroi (Oct. 11 [N.S.]), while in the east the year's record was capped by the Austrian failure to recapture Belgrade. This series of reverses for the Allies was accompanied by a serious naval setback when a convoy of 400 ships bound for Smyrna was attacked and dispersed by Tourville off Lagos on its way into the Mediterranean, and about 100 ships were lost (June 27–28 [N.S.; 17–18, O.S.]. The escorting warships, commanded by Rooke, were quite inadequate for their task, and the episode pointed out the desirability of taking more offensive and direct action against the French at sea.

By now, William had despaired of achieving anything dramatic in Flanders, and he turned instead to his fleet. The Allies had so far made little use of their victory at La Hogue, concentrating their naval strength instead on protecting their commerce and defending the Channel. The French remained masters in the Mediterranean, a fact which accounts for the disaster to the Smyrna convoy. This policy was changed in 1694 with the institution of combined military and naval operations against Brest and in the Mediterranean. The former operation proved a dreadful fiasco, when the troops were landed at Camaret Bay (June 8 [N.S.; May 29, O.S.]) under General Thomas Talmash (Tolemache), they found the French completely ready for them and they had to be withdrawn almost immediately. The operations in the Mediterranean were instituted by William himself against the advice of most of the cabinet and embraced a new strategic concept. Up to now, the French had enjoyed the advantage of interior lines of communication and had been able to switch their forces between Flanders, the Rhine, Italy, and Catalonia with comparative ease. Thus, on May 28 (N.S.), 1694, Noailles had crossed the Ter and captured Palamós, Gerona, Ostalrich, and Castel-Follit without any of the Allies other than the hard-pressed Spaniards being able to do anything to oppose him. William resolved upon employing the fleet to offset this advantage. Russell left for the Mediterranean in June 1694 and stayed on the Catalan coast until well into the autumn when he withdrew to winter and refit—not in England, but at Cádiz. Thus he was able to operate off Catalonia again early in the spring of 1695, and it was this almost continuous protection that saved Barcelona from a combined attack by Noailles and the Toulon fleet under Tourville. This experiment, which marks the beginning of the concept of a British Mediterranean fleet, was ended when Rooke, who had taken Russell's place in September 1695, was recalled in the spring of 1696 on the reappearance of a French fleet under Château-Renault at Brest which, it was feared, might be the prelude to an invasion of England. The results produced by the experiment while it lasted did, however, indicate that the sea power of the Allies might indeed prove to be the answer to the interior lines of communication enjoyed by France. Operations in Flanders in 1694 were confined to attacking towns. William was again unsuccessful, but he could claim at least to have stopped any further French advance. He was helped in this by the fact that the Allies were now, because of a further effort made by England, at last enjoying a superiority in numbers there.

The year 1695 saw the death of Luxembourg, whose replacement by the less able maréchal duc de Villeroy provided William with the opportunity of securing his one tangible success of the war. In command of superior forces, William besieged the town of Namur. Although Villeroy had been successful in operations along the Flanders coast, he failed to outmaneuver the allied forces, and Namur fell to the Allies after a two months' siege.

The Peace of Rijswijk.—By 1695 a number of reasons were inclining Louis XIV to investigate the possibilities of a general peace. His resources were stretched in maintaining armies upon four fronts; the value of the Turkish diversion had declined after the recapture of Belgrade, after which only desultory fighting occurred on that front; and William III became a less stubborn opponent as his continuous record of defeat and disappointment began to arouse serious opposition to his war policy in England. But the most important motive for peace lay in new developments in the contest for the Spanish succession. A son, Joseph Ferdinand, had been born to Maria Antonia and the elector of Bavaria on Oct. 28 (N.S.), 1692, and in the mind of the Spanish government it was in this boy alone that there lay any prospect of maintaining the Spanish dominions intact on the death of Charles II. Neither Louis XIV nor the emperor Leopold was prepared to acquiesce in such a settlement, and for both of them the support of other European powers was vital. In 1695 Louis found himself still engaged in war and without an ally. His rival had succeeded in engaging his allies in the Grand Alliance to support his claims to the Spanish inheritance. Both Holland and England did this willingly since they hoped for commercial advantages from what they believed would be a continuation of the lax Spanish dominion over the American possessions. Moreover, Louis's main support at the Spanish court, Marie Louise of Orléans, the queen consort, had died on Feb. 12 (N.S.), 1689, and her successor was Maria Anna of Neuburg, sister to the empress. Despite his military successes, Louis's diplomatic position was insecure. At this moment news came from Spain that Charles might really be dying at last. Louis began the task of making peace first with Savoy. Victor Amadeus had seen his troops twice defeated and was doubtful of the determination of some of his allies to continue the war. When, therefore, Louis offered surprising concessions, he agreed, as he had so often done before and was to do again, to change sides. The Treaty of Turin, concluded in June 1696 after negotiations conducted with the utmost secrecy, not only restored all that France had conquered in the course of the war but also ceded Pinerolo and Casale to Savoy. Savoy then turned round on its allies and insisted that all fighting cease in Italy. The emperor could do nothing but agree. The fighting in Flanders in 1696 brought William III no successes, and the too began secret negotiations in the winter. The emperor still stood out, but further French successes in 1697, the naval raid on Cartagena in May and the capture of Barcelona in August, convinced him, too. Official negotiations were conducted during the summer at Rijswijk near The Hague; and the Treaty of Rijswijk (see RIJSWIJK, TREATIES OF), which ended the war, was signed by the powers concerned between Sept. 20 and Oct. 30 (N.S.), 1697. Once again, France agreed to restore all its military conquests and, in addition, made commercial concessions to Holland. Louis XIV also recognized William III as king of England and promised not to give any aid to his enemies (including, by implication, James II).

At first sight, Louis appears to have surrendered all that he had won in the war, and a closer examination of the terms of the peace supports that view. In any future war France could, in the military circumstances of the time, make a considerable military impression upon its enemies only if it began the war already in possession of the vital fortresses which ringed its frontiers. Yet, almost without exception, all such towns as had been captured were given up in 1697. Even so, it is misleading to conclude simply that France had been worsted in the War of the Grand Alliance. There is some truth in the suggestion that Louis had misjudged the re- action of Europe to his ambitions and overplayed his hand. In particular he had underestimated William of Orange, unsuccessful though that statesman was in war; for it was the advent of En- gland into the affairs of the continent that both turned the balance of power against France and also, by involving the overseas world in the destinies of Europe, introduced forces which a predomi- nantly continental power such as France could not control. In this last fact lies perhaps the worst mistake of Louis: his abandoning of the scheme of colonial and maritime expansion that had been advocated by Colbert in favour of the purely European policy fol- lowed by the marquis de Louvois. But the decisive role that En- gland was to play lay still in the future.

So far as the War of the Grand Alliance is concerned, Louis XIV's ambitions had not been seriously disturbed. His main objective was the Spanish succession. He had begun the war by invading the Palatinate in 1688 in order to prevent the emperor from making peace with the Turks and uniting Germany against him. In this he had to some extent succeeded; his armies had succeeded also in preventing William from crowning his lifelong opposition to him with success. The war, in fact, was never more than an interlude in the diplomatic struggle for the Spanish suc- cession and the century-old conflict between Bourbon and Habs- burg. When the death of Charles II of Spain appeared imminent, Louis withdrew from the war without much difficulty. That to do so he surrendered most of his military gains was not important. They were insignificant beside the gains offered by the Spanish succession. The Austrian advance against the Turks was resumed in 1697 and resulted in the victory of Zenta (Sept. 11 [N.S.]) under the young Prince Eugene of Savoy. The Treaty of Karlo- witz followed in January 1699, whereby the sultan surrendered all of Hungary and Transylvania.

In Spain, the crisis of the succession followed almost immedi- ately upon the conclusion of peace, and it was the decision of Louis XIV, who was isolated and to a large extent ignored in the subsequent negotiations.

An appraisal of the significance of the War of the Grand Alliance must be related in the first place to its origins. Both Louis XIV and Leopold I sought predominance in Europe, the former through the medium of the Spanish inheritance, the latter in contesting Louis's claim by establishing his power in his hereditary territories. There is little doubt that on balance Louis was the more successful. Leopold had had some success in defeating the Turkish menace and in building up an effective resistance to France. But the real credit for building up that resistance belongs to William III. It was he who had engaged England in the war and he who had made the most effective military effort. What he lacked was military success, and that might be remedied in the future. So, in the final analysis, the definite but necessarily indecisive achievements of Louis XIV and the potential consequences of the work of William III must be set against one another.

BIBLIOGRAPHY.—For political aspects of the war see C. G. Picavet, *La Diplomatie française au temps de Louis XIV, 1661–1715* (1930); also R. Fester, *Die Augsburger Allianz von 1686* (1893).

For land operations see J. de Beaurain, *Histoire militaire de Flandre,* 2nd ed., 3 vol. (1776); C. Walton, *History of the British Standing Army, 1660–1700* (1894); C. von Clausewitz, *Hinterlassene Werke,* vol. ix (1862); E. Hardy de Perini, *Batailles françaises,* vol. v (1906); also J. W. Fortescue, *History of the British Army,* vol. i (1899).

For naval operations see J. Ehrman, *The Navy in the War of Wil- liam III* (1953); R. D. Merriman (ed.), *The Sergison Papers,* vol. 89 of the *Publications of the Navy Records Society* (1950); Sir J. Corbett, *England in the Mediterranean,* 2 vol. (1904); C. M. B. G. de La Ron- cière, *Histoire de la marine française,* vol. vi (1932); Sir Herbert Rich- mond, *The Navy as an Instrument of Policy* (1953); also W. L. Clowes, *The Royal Navy,* vol. ii (1898). For Anglo-Dutch policy see S. B. Baxter, *William III* (1966); Sir George Clark, *The Dutch Alliance and the War Against French Trade, 1688–1697* (1923); Sir Winston Churchill, *Marlborough,* vol. i (1933). (I. F. B.)

GRAND BANKS. A portion of the continental shelf in the Atlantic ocean extending about 350 mi. (563 km.) off the southeast coast of Newfoundland; noted as an international fishing ground, the Grand Banks include a number of separate banks, chief of which are Grand bank, St. Pierre bank and Green bank. Depths on these banks average 30 fathoms, but there are many places with depths reaching 100 fathoms. The vicinity of the Grand Banks is the meeting place of the cold Labrador current and the relatively warm Gulf stream. Air masses passing over these contrasting water bodies produce fog frequently. The min-

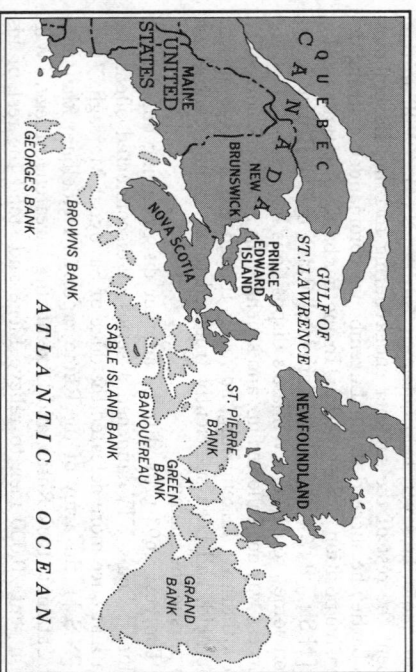

CHIEF FISHING AREAS OF THE GRAND BANKS

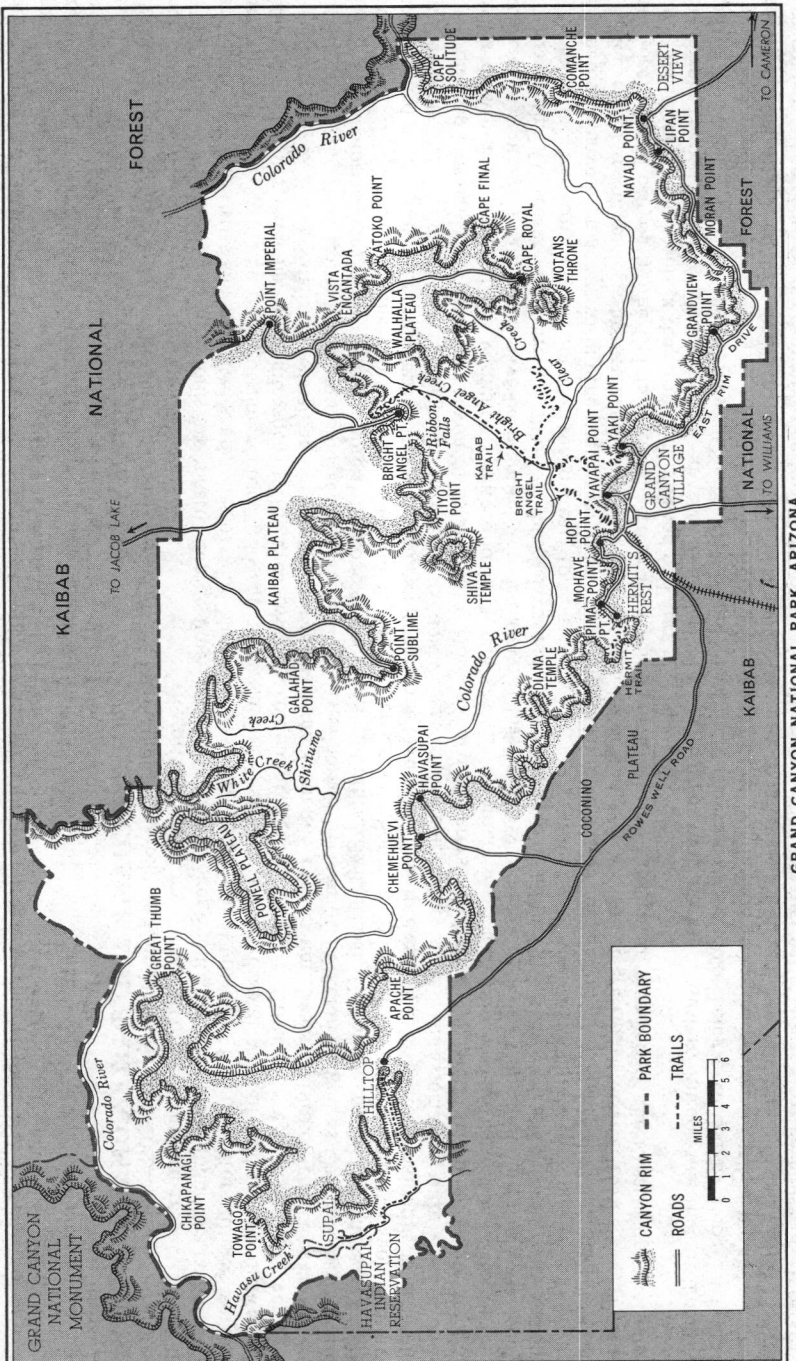

GRAND CANYON NATIONAL PARK, ARIZONA

CANYON RIM
PARK BOUNDARY
ROADS
TRAILS

MILES
0 1 2 3 4 5 6

gling of the cold and warm waters produces favourable conditions for plankton on which fish depend directly or indirectly for their food supply.

The fish of the Grand Banks have been looked upon as a great natural resource ever since John Cabot reported these riches more than four centuries ago. Among the species most plentiful are cod, haddock, rosefish, pollock, various flatfish, herring and mackerel. The trawler fleets of many nations, including Canada, the United States, the United Kingdom, Portugal, Spain and France, fish the Grand Banks. An international commission was organized in 1949 to study fish populations and to guard against depletion.

See also NEWFOUNDLAND. (C. N. F.)

GRAND CANARY (GRAN CANARIA) is an island in Las Palmas province forming part of the Spanish archipelago of the Canary Islands (*q.v.*). Pop. (1960) 400,837. Area 592 sq.mi. Grand Canary, the most fertile island of the group, is nearly circular in shape, with a diameter of 28 mi. and a coast line of 120 mi. The highest peak, Los Pechos, is 6,398 ft. Considerable tracts are covered with native pine. The hillsides are cut by many deep ravines, the northern slopes with their alpine climate and vegetation contrasting strongly with the arid southern side. Las Palmas (*q.v.*; pop. [1960] 193,862), the capital, has a large port. The chief occupations are agriculture, especially the cultivation of bananas and tomatoes and the production of tobacco, and the manufacture of embroidery, pottery and baskets. (R. P. BE.)

GRAND CANYON, an immense gorge cut by the Colorado river into the high plateaus of the northern part of Arizona. It is a broad, intricately sculptured chasm that contains between its outer walls a multitude of imposing peaks and buttes, of canyons within canyons and complex ramifying gulches and ravines. It ranges in width from 4 to 18 mi., its greatest depths lie more than a mile below its rim and it extends in a winding course from the head of Marble gorge, near the northern boundary of Arizona, to Grand Wash cliffs, near the Nevada line, a distance of about 280 mi. Its most impressively beautiful section, 56 mi. long, lies within Grand Canyon National park. Through it the river winds for 105 mi. In its general colour the canyon is a dull red but each strata or group of strata has a distinctive hue—pale buff and gray, delicate green and pink and, in its depths, chocolate-brown, slate-gray, violet and other sombre hues.

The impact of this scene was thus expressed by geologist F. E. Matthes: "The alpine mountain ranges of this country are equaled and exceeded in height, if not in spectacular beauty, by those of other lands, but though there are elsewhere deep canyons, some of even greater depth than the Grand Canyon of the Colorado, there is not one that can match its vastness, its majesty, its ornate sculpture, and its wealth of color. Whoever stands upon the brink of the Grand Canyon beholds a spectacle unrivaled on this earth."

History.—Discovery of Grand canyon is credited to members of the Coronado expedition of 1540. Two Spanish priests, Francisco Garcés and Silvestre Vélez de Escalante, rediscovered it in 1776. Beaver trappers examined it and members of government expeditions exploring the west looked it over. John Wesley Powell and companions descended the river in rowboats in 1869, and again in 1870 and published reports on the geography, geology and ethnology of the area. Prospectors in search of minerals explored its side canyons.

National Park.—Grand Canyon National park, containing 673,575 ac., was created in 1919. The north and south rims are connected by a paved road (217 mi.) and by a transcanyon trail (21 mi.). Scenic drives and trails lead to all important features. Campgrounds and a wide range of accommodations are available on both the north rim (8,200 ft.) and the south rim (7,000 ft.). There are more than 1,500,000 visitors annually. The famous mule ride into the canyon has increasing competition from the adventurous scenic rides down the river in motorboats or inflatable rafts. Pueblo and cliff-dweller ruins, with accompanying artifacts, are numerous, indicating prehistoric occupation, and living on reservations nearby are five Indian tribes.

Geology.—From the rock record of the canyon a large part of geologic history is revealed more clearly than in any other place in the world. Two stories are superlatively presented: (1) the building of the earth's crust featuring the kind, origin and age of exposed rocks; and (2) the cutting of the canyon, a story of erosion. Furthermore, all the processes of earth building are exemplified: submergence, deposition, uplift, folding and faulting and erosion. Extending from the river to Bryce canyon to the north, there is exposed a 23,000-ft. cross section of sedimentary rocks from old to recent in normal sequence. The "greatest single geological story" pertains to an unconformity where rocks of Algonkian, or Proterozoic (late Pre-Cambrian), age have been eroded away completely, leaving only a line, where third era rocks rest upon first era rocks, indicating a missing record of 500,-000,000 years of second era deposition.

The rock strata of the canyon's walls are mostly marine limestones, fresh-water shales and cemented sandstones of wind-blown origin (Paleozoic Age), the result of limey ooze, mud and sand laid down in water, later hardened into rock by the great weight of layers above. The crystalized, twisted and contorted unstratified rocks of the inner gorge are granite and schist (Archean or Early Pre-Cambrian Age) believed to be more than 4,000,000,000 years old. They constitute the roots of lofty mountains, their tops eroded away. Likewise, the superimposed Algonkian rocks are the roots of still another ancient mountain system planed down by prolonged erosion. Overlying the canyon rocks are butte remnants of Mesozoic age and the vermilion, white and pink cliff terraces of southern Utah, which have been entirely eroded away to the south. Of recent origin are the sheets of black lava and the volcanic cones covering portions of the plateau tops, some estimated to have been active within the past 1,000 years.

An event of recent geologic history has been the cutting of the mile-deep Grand canyon by the Colorado river, a river with volume, speed and cutting tools in the form of mud, sand and gravel. Sediments carried by the Colorado have been measured and reported to average 500,000 tons per day. Conditions favourable to vigorous erosion were brought about by the up-warping of the region, which steepened the river's path and allowed deep entrenchment. The depth of the canyon is due to the cutting of the river but its ten-mile width is explained by rain, wind, temperature and chemical erosion, helped by the rapid wear of soft rocks, all of which steadily widen it.

Amazingly, the canyon was cut by a reverse process for the river remained in place and cut as the land moved slowly upward against it. Only thus can be explained the canyon's east to west course across a south facing slope and the presence of plateaus which stand across the river's course without having deflected it. Minerals, mostly asbestos, copper, lead and some uranium, exist but not in sufficient quantity and availability for profitable mining.

In the sedimentary rocks plant and animal fossils are abundant, ranging from primitive algae in the lower strata to trees in the upper strata and from seashells and trilobites to the remains of dinosaurs (both bones and footprints), and camels, horses, ground sloths and elephants. These fossils give a picture of evolving life through the ages.

Biology.—There are great ranges in soil, temperature and elevation and of the five life zones, only that of tropical vegetation is absent. In the interior of the canyon vegetation is sparse and of desert type but on the plateaus grow forests of pine, fir, aspen and spruce. Animal life consists of about 100 varieties of birds, 60 mammals and 25 reptiles and amphibians. A half dozen kinds of fish live in the river and trout have been planted in tributary streams.

Plant and animal life on one rim differs somewhat from that on the other as shown in the Kaibab white-tailed squirrel of the north rim compared with the Abert gray-tailed squirrel of the south rim, which are regarded as varieties developing in a mutual isolation imposed by the barrier of the canyon.

Both the south rim (open year round) and the north rim (closed in winter) are accessible by automobile, railroad, bus and airplane.

See also COLORADO RIVER.

BIBLIOGRAPHY.—F. P. Farquhar, *The Books of the Colorado River and the Grand Canyon*, a selective bibliography (1953); E. Corle, *Listen, Bright Angel* (1946); W. F. Heald, E. D. McKee and H. S. Colton, *The Inverted Mountains*, ed. by R. Peattie (1948); H. E. Gregory, *Geology and Geography of the Zion Park Region, Utah and Arizona*, U.S. Geol. Survey Prof. Paper 220 (1950). The earlier literature on the Grand canyon includes a number of important works: see J. W. Powell, *Exploration of the Colorado River of the West and Its Tributaries* (1875); *Canyons of the Colorado* (1895); C. E. Dutton, *Tertiary History of the Grand Canyon District*, with atlas, U.S. Geol. Survey Monograph No. 2 (1882); F. E. Matthes, *The Grand Canyon of the Colorado River*, text on back of U.S. Geol. Survey Bright Angel Quadrangle Map (1906, 1927). (H. C. B.)

GRANDCHAMP AND TAIZÉ COMMUNITIES, two religious communities founded in the mid-20th century within the Reformed tradition in Switzerland and France respectively.

In the 1940s Roger Schutz, later the prior, founded a community of men at Taizé, a small village in Burgundy, for a life of worship and dedication in the traditional ways of celibacy, obedience and community of goods (see MONASTICISM). The first members came from the French and Swiss Reformed churches, and were later joined by men of Lutheran as well as Calvinist background from France, Switzerland, Germany, the Netherlands, Denmark and Spain. Some of the brothers are ordained and some are laymen who continue to exercise their professional skills in the context of the community's life. In association with Taizé, a community of sisters was founded at Grandchamp. One of the aims of the communities, which observe the same rule, is to further Christian unity, notably by work with the ecumenical movement.
See Roger Schutz, *This Day Belongs to God* (1961).
(A. MacD.)

GRAND DUKE, a title of sovereign princes ranking between kings and dukes (Italian *gran duca*; Ger. *Grossherzog*; French *grand duc*), and of certain members of the Russian imperial family.

The first grand duchy of western Europe was that of Tuscany (q.v.), the title grand duke being accorded by Pope Pius V to Cosimo de' Medici in 1569 and recognized, for Cosimo's son Francesco, by the Holy Roman emperor Maximilian II in 1575 (see MEDICI). This passed with Tuscany to the house of Habsburg-Lorraine in the 18th century.

The reorganization of Germany and of eastern Europe in the period of the Napoleonic Wars gave rise to new grand duchies: Berg for Joachim Murat, Baden for the former elector Charles Frederick, Hesse for the former landgrave Louis I of Hesse-Darmstadt and Würzburg for the dispossessed Ferdinand III of Tuscany, all in 1806; Warsaw (a duchy in 1807) for King Frederick Augustus I of Saxony in 1808; and Frankfurt for Karl Theodor von Dalberg in 1810. The congress of Vienna left the new title to Hesse and to Baden and in 1815 accorded it to the sovereigns of Saxe-Weimar-Eisenach, Mecklenburg-Schwerin, Mecklenburg-Strelitz, Luxembourg (which was then assigned to the king of the Netherlands), Oldenburg, Lower Rhine and Poznan (the last two for the king of Prussia). Fulda was ceded to the elector of Hesse as a grand duchy in 1816. After the overthrow of the republic of Cracow in 1846 the Austrian emperor Francis Joseph added grand duke of Cracowia to his titles.

The term grand duke is also commonly used to translate the Russian title *veliki knyaz*, literally "grand prince"; *i.e.*, a prince who had other princes subject to him. This title was used by the Kievan princes of the house of Rurik in their dealings with the Byzantine empire in the 10th century, by the rulers of Vladimir from the second half of the 12th century onward and occasionally by those of Muscovy, Tver, Ryazan, Nizhni Novgorod and Smolensk in the 14th-15th centuries. Eventually monopolized by the rulers of Muscovy, it was superseded by the title tsar for the sovereign from 1547. After Peter the Great's assumption of the title *imperator* (emperor), all descendants of the imperial house of Romanov bore the style *veliki knyaz* (or its feminine variants till 1886, when it was reserved for sons, daughters, brothers, sisters and grandsons of an emperor. The emperor himself was also grand duke of Smolensk, Lithuania, Volhynia, Podolia and Finland. Transylvania was erected into a grand principality (*Grossfürstentum*) by Maria Theresa as queen of Hungary in 1765.

GRANDEE (Spanish *Grande*), a title of honour borne by the highest class of the Spanish nobility. The title appears first to have been assumed during the late middle ages by certain of the *ricos hombres*, or powerful magnates of the realm, who had by then acquired vast influence and considerable privileges, including one—that of remaining covered in the royal presence—which later became characteristic of the dignity of grandee. The power of the magnates was so curtailed during the reigns of the Catholic kings and Philip I (Philip the Fair) that Charles I (the emperor Charles V) was able, by investing the title of grandee with a formal character (1520) and reserving to it those privileges which had formerly been exercised by the *ricos hombres* generally, to increase still further the authority of the crown.

Under Charles I the number of grandees was originally limited to 25. This figure was later increased and by the early 17th century the grandees of Spain had been divided into three classes: (1) those who spoke to the king and received his reply with their heads covered; (2) those who addressed him uncovered, but put on their hats to hear his answer; (3) those who awaited the permission of the king before covering themselves. All grandees were addressed by the king as "my cousin" (*mi primo*), whereas ordinary nobles were only qualified as "my kinsman" (*mi pariente*). The title of grandee, abolished under Joseph Bonaparte, was revived in 1834 when, by the *Estatuto real*, grandees were given precedence in the chamber of peers. The designation later, however, became purely titular, and implied neither privilege nor power.

GRAND FORKS, the second city in size in North Dakota, U.S., and seat of the county of the same name, stands at the confluence of the Red River of the North and the Red Lake River, 90 mi. S of the Canadian border in the northeastern corner of the state. The city is surrounded by prairies and is 350 mi. NW of Minneapolis, the nearest large U.S. city. It was the site of a North-West Fur Company post in 1801.

Permanent settlement began in 1871, and from 1873 to 1875 the Hudson's Bay Company operated a hotel and a retail store there. The town's future was assured when the Great Northern Railway arrived in 1880 and established headquarters for its large Dakota division. There was a flood of settlers, many Norwegian or Canadian, and, by 1910, 66% of its population were immigrants or the children of immigrants. Despite the decline in the state's population, Grand Forks almost doubled in size from 1940 to 1970. Pop. (1970) 39,008. For comparative population figures *see* table in NORTH DAKOTA: *Population.*

Primary dependence on retail merchandising and shipping of a large volume of spring wheat, potatoes, and sugar beets ended with World War I. A large state-owned flour mill and elevator and a beet-sugar refinery (in its twin city, East Grand Forks, Minn.) were opened. After World War II manufacturing firms grew in size and number until they employed one-tenth of the labour force, but more than 1,000 retail and wholesale establishments were the chief employers. Much growth was stimulated by construction of an Air Force base 15 mi. W. Rail transportation was supplemented by airlines using the municipal airport, an international port of entry.

In 1947 Grand Forks adopted the council-manager form of government, but reverted to the mayor-council type in 1964. The University of North Dakota, located in the city, is under state control and was established there by the Territorial Act of 1883. Its enrollment in the early 1970s was over 7,000.
(R. P. WI.; X.)

GRANDGENT, CHARLES HALL (1862–1939), U.S. philologist, an expert in phonetics and in the history of Romance languages, was born at Dorchester, Mass., on Nov. 14, 1862. He attended Roxbury Latin school and graduated from Harvard *summa cum laude* and head of his class in 1883. After three years' postgraduate study in Europe, he returned to Harvard as tutor in Romance languages (1886–89), then was director of modern language instruction in the Boston public school system for seven years. In 1886 he married Ethel Wright Cushing, who predeceased him by five years.

From 1896 he was professor of Romance languages and literatures at Harvard, becoming emeritus in 1932. He was acting dean of the faculty of arts and sciences in 1929, and exchange professor at Paris in 1915–16 and again in 1930–31. The University of Chicago (1916), Michigan (1922), Oberlin (1927) and Harvard (1923) conferred honorary doctorates on him.

Grandgent's scholarly publications included grammars of French and Italian, Old Provençal, Vulgar Latin, and a work called *From Latin to Italian,* all of them distinguished by a skilful and highly selective presentation. His lectures showed this same power of selection. He lectured for many years on Dante as well as on Romance linguistics and phonetics, and produced an edition of Dante (1917), in addition to *The Ladies of Dante's Lyrics* (1917), *The Power of Dante* (1918), and *Discourses on Dante* (1924). He was decorated by the governments of France and of Italy; and he was a corresponding member of the Accademia della Crusca. Grandgent's volumes of lighter essays give some idea of the man's humour and charm. He died on Sept. 11, 1939, at Cambridge, Mass.
(J. WH.)

GRANDI, ALESSANDRO (?–1630), Italian composer who was the first to use the word cantata in the modern sense. He was known to have been director of music to a religious confraternity in Ferrara in 1597. He remained in that city in various capacities until 1617, when he became a singer at St. Mark's in Venice. Three years later he became Monteverdi's assistant there, and it was during this period that he produced several remarkably fine books of songs called *Cantade et Arie,* published between 1620 and 1629. In these, he shows himself to be a pupil of Monteverdi and combines a gift for finding music to fit exactly the meaning of the words with one for attractive melody. His "cantatas" are the precursors of the ground bass songs of Henry Purcell, the voice varying the melody over a repeated bass. He also wrote religious songs in the same style, and these were known and copied by Heinrich Schütz (d. 1672).

In 1627 he left Venice to direct the music at the basilica of Sta. Maria Maggiore in Bergamo, where he died with his family during the plague of 1630.

See D. Arnold, "Alessandro Grandi, a disciple of Monteverdi," *The Musical Quarterly,* vol. xliii (1957).
(D. M. A.)

GRANDI, DINO, CONTE DI MORDANO (1895–   ), Italian Fascist statesman who in 1943 played a major role in bringing about the fall of Mussolini, was born at Mordano, near Imola, on June 4, 1895. His studies at the University of Bologna were interrupted by World War I, in which he served with distinction, attaining the rank of *alpini* captain. After the war, in 1919, he took a degree in law and joined the National Fascist party, soon becoming known nationally for his fiery eloquence and combativeness. In Oct. 1922, at the time of the "march on Rome," he was chief of staff to the quadrumvirate who led the operation. A member of the *direzione generale* of the Fascist party from 1921, he was in 1923 made lieutenant general of the *milizia*—a Fascist praetorian guard. In 1924 he joined the government as undersecretary of state of the interior, being transferred the following year to the ministry of foreign affairs. He served as Italian delegate to the council of the League of Nations and on Sept. 12, 1929, was appointed minister of foreign affairs. He retained this portfolio until July 20, 1932, when he was sent as ambassador to London. In March 1937 the king honoured him with the title of count. Recalled from London, he was appointed minister of justice on July 12, 1939. In Nov. 1939 he was elected president of the chamber of *fasci* and corporations. Opposed to Italy's participation in World War II, Grandi was dismissed from the government on Feb. 5, 1943, but remained a member of the Fascist *gran consiglio,* the party's supreme authority. It was at the meeting of this body that, on the night of July 24–25, 1943, Grandi attacked Mussolini and proposed a motion of no confidence in him—a motion passed 19 to 7. Soon afterward Grandi fled to Lisbon, and in Jan. 1944 a special Fascist tribunal sentenced him to death in absentia. In 1948 he moved to Brazil but later returned to Italy.
(R. P. WI.; X.)

GRAND ISLAND, a city and the seat of Hall county, in southeastern central Nebraska, U.S., on the Platte river, is 85 mi. W. of Lincoln and 140 mi. S.W. of Omaha. The town's name comes from the Grand Island in the Platte. The island was a landmark for early travelers and of importance to the Oregon, California and Mormon trails.

German settlers established Grand Island in 1857, about 50 mi. W. of the then westernmost community in the area. A major factor in Grand Island's development was its strategic location for transportation. The Union Pacific and Burlington railroads crossed there, developing a railroad centre, and it became later the major highway centre in central Nebraska. An important supply point for the surrounding agricultural area, Grand Island also became an irrigation centre as the Platte valley turned to irrigation early in the 20th century.

Industrial activity, largely based on agricultural production, includes sugar beet processing, meat packing and grain storage.

A veterans hospital and a soldiers and sailors home are among the federal institutions in Grand Island. The present town was laid out in 1866 when the Union Pacific reached the settlement; it was incorporated in 1873. Pop. (1970) 31,269. For comparative population figures *see* table in NEBRASKA: *Population.*
(W. D. A.)

GRAND JUNCTION, a city of western Colorado, U.S., elevation 4,600 ft., at the confluence of the Colorado and Gunnison rivers, from which its name derives, is the seat of Mesa county. Immediately following expulsion of the Ute Indians, white settlers rushed in and founded the town in 1881. It was incorporated in 1882, and in 1922 adopted the council-manager form of government.

It is the centre of an extensive irrigated region (fruit, truck gardening and general farming) and industrial and jobbing centre of a large area. In the 1950s it became the business, administrative and milling headquarters of a large uranium-producing area. The lake-jeweled Grand Mesa is 30 mi. E, said to be the world's largest flat-topped mountain, and a favourite scenic and recreational area. Colorado national monument, 8 mi. W., contains spectacular specimens of erosion, and is threaded by famed Rimrock drive.

For comparative population figures *see* table in COLORADO: *Population.*
(L. R. HA.)

GRANDMONTINES (GRAMMONTINES), a monastic order founded in 1077 at Muret near Limoges in France by St. Stephen of Muret (1046-1124), who, inspired by Italian examples of eremitical life, retired to the wilderness of Muret and, when joined by disciples, established a life similar to, and probably based upon, that of the Camaldolese (*q.v.*). After his death his followers moved a short distance to Grandmont, and their customs were written down in 1143 by the prior, Stephen of Lisiac. The Grandmontines embodied the eremitic, contemplative life pushed to its extreme; the monks were bound to rigid enclosure, absolute poverty and strict silence. The idea, as at Vallombrosa, of leaving all administration to lay brothers was also carried to its extreme. The latter abused their position and revolted, after which they were strictly subordinated to the monastic prior. The Grandmontines, who had three small houses in England, declined in fervour, were reformed in the 17th century, and disappeared finally during the French Revolution.
See M. Heimbucher, *Orden und Kongregationen* (1933-34).

GRAND PRAIRIE, a city of central Texas, U.S., between Dallas and Fort Worth. Industries include aircraft and boat manufacture. Settled at the close of the American Civil War, Grand Prairie was originally called Alexander Deckman in honour of its founder. Principally an agricultural town during its early years, Grand Prairie boomed after the establishment of an aircraft factory in 1940-41. Incorporated in 1909, it has a council-manager form of government.

For comparative population figures *see* table in TEXAS: *Population.*
(M. D. K.)

GRAND PRIX DE ROME, a group of scholarships to enable young French artists to study in Rome, later emulated by other countries' similar endowments; the *grands prix* were established in the 17th century and are still awarded in the 20th century. After the study of classical antiquity revived at the Renaissance promising artists were sent by their patrons to train in Rome. As part of his official patronage of the arts Louis XIV of France established an academy there for the same purpose; it was called the Académie de France, or Accademia di Francia. This move was prompted by Charles Le Brun (*q.v.*), who had previously been instrumental in founding the Académie Royale de Peinture et de Sculpture in Paris (1648), and the statutes (1666) decreed that the Grands Prix de Rome, which enabled artists to study at the Académie de France, were preferably to be awarded to prize-winning pupils from the older academy. Prizes were not awarded regularly for architecture until 1723. Most of the greatest French artists and architects of the period went to Rome as prize winners: among them the painters A. Coypel, J. H. Fragonard and J. L. David; the sculptors F. Girardon, Clodion and J. A. Houdon; and the architects G. M. Oppenordt and C. L. Clérisseau. The academy was closed during the French Revolution, from 1792 to 1801, and then reopened in its present building, the magnificent Villa Medici. In the 19th century prizes for engravers and musicians were created, when the most famous scholars included the painters J. A. D. Ingres, H. Flandrin and Albert Besnard; the sculptors P. J. David d'Angers and J. B. Carpeaux; the engraver Oscar Roty; the architect Tony Garnier; and the composers Hector Berlioz, C. F. Gounod, Georges Bizet and Claude Debussy.

In the second half of the 20th century annual competitions were still held for painters, sculptors, engravers, architects and musicians, the winner of the *grand prix* in each category being then entitled to spend several years at the Académie de France. Many other countries have also established academies. The American Academy in Rome (*q.v.*; Accademia Americana), founded in 1894, provides similar fellowships which are held for one year or more. Since 1912 the British School at Rome (Academia Britannica) has held annual competitions for one- or two-year scholarships in archaeology, painting, sculpture and (since 1919) engraving. Archaeology and history schools have been set up in Rome on the model of the art academies, among them the Istituto Archeologico Germanico (1829) and the French school (1873). The Accademia Polacco di Scienze e Lettere was founded in 1886 and the Istituto Svedese di Studi Classici in 1926.
See N. Pevsner, *Academies of Art, Past and Present* (1940).
(L. HR.)

GRAND RAPIDS, a city of Michigan, U.S., is in Kent County on the Grand River, 30 mi. from Lake Michigan and about 60 mi. WNW of Lansing. It was founded in 1826 by the Frenchman Louis Campau as a trading post where several important Ottawa Indian trails (now diagonal streets) converged at the rapids. It was incorporated as a village in 1838 and as a city in 1850. Ample waterpower generated in the 18-ft. fall of the river and the availability of valuable lumber from nearby pine and hardwood forests caused the establishment of many sawmills and woodworking industries.

Following the display of Grand Rapids furniture at the Philadelphia Centennial in 1876, the city gained a reputation as the furniture capital of America. Buyers the world over went to the furniture markets, first held in 1878. Diversification of industry began with the advent of World War I and the metal trades thereafter exceeded furniture in value and output. Nevertheless, Grand Rapids is the principal trading centre of western Michigan, including a large area devoted to fruit farming and truck gardening, and serves a population of 1,600,000. The city has a council-manager form of government, adopted in 1916. The city also maintained its supremacy in quality, style, and design. Other important products are business machines, carpet sweepers, aircraft instruments, auto parts and accessories, hardware, tools, machinery, baked goods, paper boxes, gypsum products, and refrigerator cabinets. More than 100 plants are engaged in the field of graphic arts. Grand Rapids is home, office, school, and church furniture produced by skilled craftsmen in more than 70 factories maintained its supremacy in quality, style, and design.

Higher education is provided by Calvin College, chartered in 1876 and affiliated with the Christian Reformed Church; Aquinas, a Roman Catholic coeducational college established in 1886; Grand Rapids Junior College (1914); a University of Michigan extension centre for western Michigan; and a Michigan State University centre for continuing education. Kendall School of Design offers courses in furniture and interior design and allied fields of art.

Cultural institutions include a municipal museum, the Public Museum (founded in 1854) devoted to natural history and ethnology and including historical and contemporary furniture exhibits; the public library containing the country's most important collection of books on furniture design and manufacture; an art gallery; a symphony; and a civic theatre.
(E. C. BE.)

Grand Rapids has about 50 parks, playgrounds, and park-school areas. Nearby are a number of Kent County parks, while 250 lakes and streams are within an hour's drive. Pop. (1970) city 197,649; standard metropolitan statistical area (Kent and Ottawa counties) 539,225. For comparative city population figures *see* table in MICHIGAN: *Population.* (F. L. D. M.)

GRAND RIVER, the name of several rivers in the central part of the United States.

Iowa-Missouri.—One of the more important branches of the Missouri river, the Grand rises in south-central Iowa near the city of Creston and flows almost due south into Missouri where it takes a southeasterly course, joining the Missouri near Brunswick in north-central Missouri. The only city of importance in the Grand's drainage basin is Chillicothe, Mo., which lies near the confluence of the Grand and the Thompson.

Michigan.—Commercially the most important river in west-central Michigan, the Grand rises near Jackson and flows almost due north to Lansing where it turns west to Spring Lake, which empties into Lake Michigan through a short channel near Grand Haven. Major cities on the Grand are Lansing and Grand Rapids. Navigation is possible as far as Grand Rapids, which owes its location to the development of water power from the river.

Missouri.—The Grand, sometimes known as the South Grand, rises in western Missouri about 30 mi. S. of Kansas City. It flows due east to join a west arm of the Lake of the Ozarks. (*See* NEOSHO.)

South Dakota.—Formed by the confluence of the North and South forks in Perkins county, S.D., the Grand flows eastward to join the Missouri near Mobridge, S.D. (R. R. D.)

GRAND TETON NATIONAL PARK, established in 1929, is located in the Jackson Hole region of northwestern Wyoming, U.S., near the Idaho line and about 25 mi. S. of Yellowstone National park. Comprising 310,350 ac., or 485 sq.mi., it includes most of the former Jackson Hole national monument. The snow-covered peaks of its spectacular Teton range, sculptured from the sheerest rock, rise to a maximum height of 7,000 feet above the valley of the Snake river—itself nearly the same distance above sea level. Formed by a series of titanic upthrusts, this gigantic fault block is traversed by great glaciers which have slowly crunched their way down the stream-cut canyons. Melting as they reached the bottom, they deposited their cargo of rock and debris into accumulations known as moraines. These are often forested with the sharp-pointed Engelmann spruce and pines so singularly straight and tall as to merit the designation of lodgepole.

These wooded deposits form the shores of frigid glacial lakes, which in varying size dot the region. Perhaps the most beautiful, and certainly the best known, is Jenny lake, but there are others with great individuality, such as Leigh, String, Bradley, etc., fed from roaring torrents, exemplified by the unforgettable Hidden falls. On the other hand, the largest body of water, Jackson lake, is formed by a dam across the Snake river. The streams in the park abound in fish, while herds of buffalo, elk and antelope roam at will. Throughout the summer season a succession of different varieties of wild flowers present ever changing tapestries, even beginning their bloom underneath the snow.

The highest peak, Grand Teton (13,766 ft.), is one of the most difficult to climb in the United States. (R. R. Mn.)

GRANDVILLE (professional name of JEAN IGNACE ISIDORE GÉRARD) (1803–1847), French caricaturist, whose works are characterized by a marvelous fertility of satirical humour, was born at Nancy on Sept. 13, 1803. He received his first instruction in drawing from his father, a painter of miniatures, and at the age of 21 went to Paris, where he soon afterward published a collection of lithographs entitled *Les Tribulations de la petite propriété.* He followed this by *Les Plaisirs de toutage* and *La Sibylle des salons*; his success was made with *Métamorphoses du jour* (1828), a series of 70 scenes in which individuals with the bodies of men and faces of animals played the human comedy. Grandville contributed drawings to many periodicals, including *La Caricature* and *Le Charivari*, and his political caricatures came to enjoy a general popularity. He illustrated several classic works of literature. He died on March 17, 1847.

GRANET, FRANÇOIS MARIUS (1775–1849), French painter and the only landscapist of his day to emerge from the neoclassical school, was born at Aix-en-Provence on Dec. 17, 1775. He was the pupil first of J. A. L. Constantin, a local landscape painter, and later, in Paris, of J. L. David. With a number of other artists —Ingres, Bartolini, Gros, Girodet—he lived and worked in the Capuchin convent in the Boulevard des Capucines. There he found the subjects which are most characteristic of his work—cloisters, cells and large quiet sunlit rooms, with mild historical compositions in the same tranquil settings. In 1802 Granet went to Rome where he stayed for 17 years. On his return to Paris in 1819 he exhibited in the Salon his "Choeur de l'Eglise des Capucins," which was so successful that 16 replicas were commissioned. His paintings and water colours influenced the evolution of Corot's style. In 1826 Louis Philippe made him curator of the pictures at Versailles. In 1848 he retired to Aix, where he died on Nov. 21 in the following year, leaving to his native town the greater part of his fortune and a collection of his works. (AA. B.)

GRANGE, THE, known officially as the National Grange, originally the National Grange of the Patrons of Husbandry, is a fraternal organization of farmers founded in Washington, D.C., in 1867 by Oliver Hudson Kelley and six associates. Growing slowly at first, the organization advanced rapidly during the agrarian discontent of the early 1870s, when its members, together with those of other groups, joined what was known as the "Granger" movement. Through political action centring in the middle west, an impetus was given to regulation of railways and grain elevators. Local and state Granges in the same region also sought to circumvent monopolies by extensive co-operative business enterprises. Their general failure, coupled with internal dissensions, caused a heavy decline in the membership between 1875 and 1880, though the organization retained a strong influence. In 1875 the first Grange was organized in Canada, but the order never attained a dominant place there. After 1880 the Grange gradually increased its membership, and its centres of strength in the second half of the 20th century were found in Ohio, New York and Pennsylvania in the east and Washington, California and Oregon in the west.

The following definition of the Grange was selected in 1938 as the prize-winning entry in its national contest: "The Grange is a great farm fraternity: building character; developing leadership; encouraging education; promoting community betterment; instilling an appreciation of high ideals; teaching through work and play the value of co-operation and service in the attainment of happiness." There are seven degrees in the Grange, and the names of these, as well as the ritual of the order, carry agricultural connotations. Membership is open to all members of farm families 14 years old or over. Local subordinate Granges are usually organized on a community basis and often adopt the community name. Many local Granges own their own meeting halls and carry on a variety of social, educational and recreational programs. State Granges carry out policies agreed upon by the local and county Granges. Each state Grange sends two delegates, a man and his wife, to the annual meetings of the National Grange. The delegates, the policy forming body, elect officers of the National Grange.

In the 1930s the National Grange supported the agricultural adjustment legislation. Its continued criticism of some features of it was an important factor in improvements in the parity formula and other price support legislation after World War II. One of its major interests became the improvement of the co-operative farm credit agencies and their removal from direct government control. Beginning in the 1940s the Grange began taking a more active part in national legislative issues than at any time since the 1870s. A distinctive feature of the Grange program in the second half of the 20th century was its advocacy of using a commodity-by-commodity approach in dealing with farm problems. It supported domestic parity programs for wheat and other important export crops. *See also* AGRICULTURAL ORGANIZATIONS; UNITED STATES (OF AMERICA): *History: Civil War and Reconstruction: The Grant Era.*

BIBLIOGRAPHY.—Charles M. Gardner, *Grange, Friend of the Farmer* (1949); David Edgar Lindstrom, *American Rural Life,* ed. by Herbert McNee Hamlin (1948); Walter W. Wilcox, *Social Responsibility in*

Farm Leadership (1956); U.S. Department of Agriculture *Yearbook*, "The Farmer in a Changing World," pp. 945–954, (1940).
(W. W. Wx.)

GRANGEMOUTH, a small burgh and seaport of Stirlingshire, Scot., on the southern shore of the Forth estuary and at the mouths of the Carron and its former right-hand tributary, the Grange Burn, 23 mi. W.N.W. of Edinburgh. Pop. (1971 prelim.) 24,572. Its history began in 1768 when digging was started for the Forth and Clyde canal, built by John Smeaton, which crosses the narrow "waist" of Scotland and enters the Clyde at Bowling. In 1777 the first foundation stone of Grangemouth was laid at the eastern end of the canal, which was opened in 1790. In 1843 the Old dock was opened and in 1859 the Junction dock was built to be followed by two wet timber basins for the Baltic trade. In Scotland Grangemouth is second in tonnage only to the port of Glasgow. Residential and industrial, it was early divided into two towns, an old and a new. Experiments in steam navigation were carried out on the canal in 1802 with the "Charlotte Dundas," which was built at Grangemouth. The chief industries are oil refining and the manufacture of its by-products, dyestuffs and other chemicals, timber importing and shipbuilding.

GRANITE, a word apparently already used in the Renaissance to designate granular rocks, taken over almost in this very broad sense by early geologists, but in petrography, that is, the systematic classification and description of rocks, nearly always used in a much more restricted sense as referring to coarse or medium grained rocks rich in quartz and feldspar. The restricted usage was not only common among the early scientific petrographers but was also favoured by their precursors, naturalists such as A. F. Cronstedt and J. G. Wallerius, for instance.

Even in this restricted sense granite is by far the most common plutonic rock known or suspected to be of magmatic origin. So abundant is it that in the various earth models proposed by geophysicists and geologists a shell of granite is supposed to underlie the immediately visible portions of the lithosphere.

Because of its use both for paving block and as a building stone, the quarrying of granite was at one time a major industrial activity. The widespread introduction of macadam and concrete for roads together with the cessation of building in the depression of the 1930s produced a paralysis which lasted until well after World War II. As the postwar building boom penetrated into the large cities the demand for structural stone and veneer led to a considerable revival of the industry. Except for tombstones, however, for which there is a continuing demand, the production of granite is geared to the fluctuating market for curbing in highway construction and veneer used in the facing of large industrial and commercial buildings. (*see also* QUARRYING.)

Composition and Occurrence.—Granite may occur in dikes or sills but more characteristically it forms irregular masses of extremely variable size. For the smaller of these—up to five miles or so in maximum dimension—a floor may sometimes be inferred on stratigraphic grounds but can rarely be proven beyond reasonable doubt. For the larger masses, known as batholiths, often hundreds or thousands of square miles in area, thicknesses cannot be estimated; such masses are often assumed to take their origin directly from the (hypothetical) underlying granite zone or shell of the lithosphere.

Intrusive rocks containing in excess of 40% (by volume) of quartz are virtually unknown. A lower limit to quartz content of granite is not so easily set, but rocks containing less than 20% of quartz are almost never named granite by those who describe them. Considerable evidence suggests that intrusive rocks of intermediate quartz content are less abundant than those rich in quartz (granite) or those in which quartz is scarce or lacking (gabbro).

The principal constituent of granite is feldspar (*q.v.*), both plagioclase and alkali-feldspar ordinarily being abundant. The relative abundance of the two kinds of feldspars has provided the basis for so many attempts at classification that even a brief review of the matter would turn this into an article about taxonomy rather than rocks. It is safe to say that in most rocks described as granite the ratio of dominant to subordinate feldspar is less than 2. In

this category fall most of the granites of the eastern, central, and southwestern United States, southwestern England (Cornwall, Devon), the Fennoscandian (Baltic shield) area, western and central France, Spain, etc. Indeed, examples are so numerous that it is difficult to select among them. Granites in which there is a great excess of plagioclase over alkali-feldspar are not at all rare, however, and in large regions of the western United States this is the common type; indeed, it is thought to be characteristic of the great series of batholiths stretching from Alaska and British Columbia southward through Idaho and California into Mexico. The least abundant granites appear to be those with a great excess of alkali-feldspar over plagioclase—the alkali granites. In the United States these are well known from Quincy and Cape Ann, Mass., Conway, N.H., Mt. Desert, Me. They occur in smaller bodies at numerous sites in rocks of the Christiania region of Norway, but their most extensive development is in northern Nigeria. Like most alkaline rocks, they have received attention out of all proportion to their abundance. In New England, for instance, a region relatively rich in alkali-granites, they probably account for no more than a few per cent of the known outcropping of granite.

The relative abundance of the different kinds of granite is a bothersome matter because the roots of many granite classifications go back to a time when the plagioclase series was either unknown or poorly known. If a granite was to consist primarily of feldspar and quartz it was thus necessarily what we now call an alkali-granite, and in most classifications these, by all odds the rarest members of the class, are still the "true" granites.

The minor essential minerals of granite may include muscovite, biotite, amphibole, pyroxene or, rarely, iron-olivine (fayalite). Usually no more than two or three of these are present. Amphibole or pyroxene-bearing granites never carry muscovite in significant amount. Biotite may occur in granite of any type and is usually present, though sometimes in very small amount. The sodic-amphiboles and pyroxenes (riebeckite, arfvedsonite, aegirine) are characteristic of the alkali-granites. When plagioclase is in great excess over alkali-feldspar the ferromagnesians usually include hornblende, and augite may be present as well; the principal, and sometimes the only, potash-bearing mineral in such rocks is biotite. If neither feldspar is in great excess of the other, neither amphibole nor pyroxene is likely to be an essential constituent; the dark minerals will then ordinarily be either or both biotite and muscovite. The maximum permissible dark mineral content varies from classification to classification, but rocks containing more than 20% (by volume) of dark minerals are rarely named granite, and in most granites the "colour index" is very much less than this. As with quartz, massive intrusives of intermediate colour index appear to be considerably less abundant than those either rich in heavy silicates (gabbro) or poor in them (granites).

Theories of Origins.—Controversy concerning the origin of granite has been alternately raging and simmering since the birth of scientific petrography, and there is as yet no general agreement on the subject; indeed, there are probably few areas of inquiry in which acknowledged specialists are in such unequivocal disagreement.

The principal contesting hypotheses may be classified as (1) magmatic or (2) transformist. The proponents of the former argue that granites are derived by intratelluric crystallization of a parent liquid or liquid-crystal mush (magma). The proponents of the latter argue that granites have formed without the intervention of magma, and sometimes even with no liquid at all, by the solid state metamorphism of pre-existing sedimentary rocks. A third group advances the metasomatic or hydrothermal hypothesis and regards granites as products of reaction between a dilute, largely aqueous fluid and previously consolidated sedimentary or metamorphic rocks. During the early 20th century the controversy was to a surprising extent regional or even national, the Scandinavians and French being devout metasomatists, the Germans and British equally devout magmatists. In the decade following World War I, however, a revival of transformism began almost simultaneously in France and Britain, and soon spread. By the middle of the century the controversy had lost all of its national and much of its scientific character. The theory of magmatic origin is perhaps strongest in the Soviet Union and the United States.

For further discussion of these hypotheses see GEOCHEMISTRY: *Geochemistry of the Lithosphere*; METAMORPHISM; METASOMATISM. See PETROLOGY; QUARRYING; see also references under "Granite" in the Index. (F. Cs.)

GRANITE CITY, an industrial city of Illinois, U.S., is located in Madison county on the Mississippi river, 10 mi. N.E. of St. Louis. The land on which Granite City stands was countryside until 1891, when Frederick G. and William F. Niedringhaus, St. Louis manufacturers, acquired a site for the expansion of their graniteware industry. From the Niedringhaus plant Granite City has grown to impinge on the borders of older communities and blend into the heavily industrialized area extending north from East St. Louis. More than a dozen railways help to feed Granite City's industries and distribute its manufactures. The production of steel, originally an auxiliary of the graniteware (enameled ironwear) industry, has assumed the premier place in the city's economic life. Graniteware, which gave the city its name, is no longer manufactured there. Granite City manufactures iron and steel, metal containers, railway equipment, chemicals and stoves. The city was founded in 1893 and incorporated in 1896. For comparative population figures see table in ILLINOIS: *Population.* (R. E. M.)

GRAN SASSO D'ITALIA ("Great Rock of Italy"), a mountain group of the Abruzzi region of Italy, containing the highest point (9,560 ft., or 2,914 m.) of the Apennines (*q.v.*), its peak Corno Grande, or Monte Corno. The summit is covered with snow for the greater part of the year, and there is a small glacier on the north slope of Corno Grande. The Alpine region beneath its summit is still the home of the wild boar, and here and there are dense woods of beech and pine. The group has other lofty peaks, among them the Pizzo d'Intermesole (2,646 m., 8,681 ft.), the Corno Piccolo (2,637 m., 8,651 ft.), the Pizzo Cefalone (2,532 m., 8,307 ft.) and the Monte della Portella (2,388 m., 7,835 ft.). The most convenient starting point for the ascent is Assergi, 16 km. (10 mi.) N.E. of Aquila, at the south foot of the Gran Sasso. (G. KH.)

GRANT, DUNCAN JAMES CORROWR (1885–   ), Scottish painter and decorative artist, whose style, particularly influenced by Paul Cézanne and modern French painting, is marked by bold brushwork and bright colours, was born at Rothiemurchus, Inverness-shire on Jan. 21, 1885. Educated at St. Paul's school, London, he afterward studied at Westminster School of Art and visited Paris, Italy, Greece and Tunisia. He worked with Roger Fry at the Omega workshops, London, in 1913, designing fabrics and furniture, besides executing some highly individual paintings such as "The Lemon Gatherers" (1910, Tate gallery, London) and "The Tight-Rope Walkers" (1918, Ralph Partridge). His later easel pieces were often less well composed than the three large decorative panels originally intended for R.M.S. "Queen Mary" (1935).

Grant also designed stage décor and lithographs, holding his first one-man show at the Carfax gallery in 1920. Grant became a member of the London Group in 1919.

See *Duncan Grant*, with introduction by Roger Fry, new ed. (1930); Raymond Mortimer, *Duncan Grant* (1944); Retrospective Exhibition Catalogue, Tate Gallery (1959). (D. L. FR.)

GRANT, SIR FRANCIS (1803–1878), Scottish portrait painter, whose portraits generally have a superficial brilliance suited to their subject, was born at Edinburgh on Jan. 18, 1803. Educated at Harrow, he gave up law for painting in 1827, and exhibited at the Royal Academy in 1834. At first a painter of animals and hunting scenes like "The Melton Hunt, going to draw the Ram's Head Cover" (1839), he turned to portraiture, chiefly of society sitters. He painted many of the celebrities of his day, including Scott, Macaulay, Disraeli, Palmerston and Russell, his brother Sir J. Hope Grant and his friend Sir Edwin Landseer. Grant's works were not of the highest artistic rank, a distinguished exception being "The Duke of Portland" (1853). Grant was elected a member of the Royal Academy in 1851, and became president and was knighted in 1856. He died at Melton Mowbray, Leicestershire, on Oct. 5, 1878. (D. L. FR.)

GRANT, ULYSSES S. (1822–1885), U.S. soldier and 18th president of the United States, was born at Point Pleasant, Clermont County, O., on April 27, 1822. He was descended from Matthew Grant, who sailed from Plymouth, Eng., to Dorchester, Mass., in 1630, and settled in Windsor, Conn., a few years later.

The Grant family remained in Connecticut until Noah Grant, Ulysses' grandfather, moved westward about 1790, settling in Ohio in 1799. His son, Jesse Root Grant, an enterprising tanner, married Hannah Simpson on June 24, 1821, at Point Pleasant, O., where their first child, whom they named Hiram Ulysses, was born the following year.

In autumn 1823, Jesse Grant moved his family to Georgetown, in adjoining Brown County, O., where five more children were born. Ulysses was educated through the local subscription schools, and one school year each at the Maysville Seminary at Maysville, Ky. (1836–37) and the Presbyterian Academy at

BY COURTESY OF THE LIBRARY OF CONGRESS

GRANT

Ripley, O. (1838–39). Later reminiscences of relatives, friends, and neighbours that portray Ulysses displaying qualities for which he became famous must be discounted; his boyhood appears normal for the time and place. Detesting the work around his father's tannery, Ulysses performed his share of chores on farmland owned by his father, developing considerable skill in handling horses.

Jesse Grant used his political connections to secure Ulysses an appointment to the United States Military Academy at West Point, N.Y., in 1839. Although Ulysses had no interest in military life, he accepted the appointment, realizing that the alternative was no further education. Before leaving home, Ulysses decided to reverse his original name from Hiram Ulysses to Ulysses Hiram. Through error, his appointment to West Point had been made in the name Ulysses S. Grant, perhaps because it was known that his mother's maiden name was Simpson, or because he was confused with his younger brother, Samuel Simpson. Through his cadet years he signed his personal correspondence "U. H. Grant," while Army officials continued to name him "U. S. Grant." After graduation, Grant began to use his Army name, maintaining, thereafter that the middle initial "does not stand for anything."

At West Point, Grant distinguished himself in horsemanship, showed considerable ability in mathematics, but lacked the incentive to compete for high class standing, graduating in 1843 ranked 21st in a class of 39. Upon graduation he was assigned as a brevet second lieutenant to the 4th U.S. Infantry, stationed at Jefferson Barracks, a few miles south of St. Louis, Mo. There he fell in love with Julia Boggs Dent (sister of his West Point roommate), who lived at the nearby estate of White Haven. When the 4th Infantry was ordered to Louisiana in May 1844, a move connected with the anticipated annexation of Texas, the transfer upset both Grant's romance and his hopes of assignment to West Point as assistant professor of mathematics. Before leaving, he gained Julia's assent to a secret engagement, later securing her parents' permission while on leave in April 1845.

In September 1845, the 4th Infantry sailed from New Orleans, La., to Corpus Christi on the Nueces River in Texas. Six months later Gen. Zachary Taylor marched his small army from the Nueces to the Rio Grande, across territory claimed by both the United States and Mexico, provoking clashes that led to war. Grant participated in Taylor's victories at Palo Alto, Resaca de la Palma, and Monterrey, showing particular gallantry at the last. Before the Battle of Buena Vista, Grant's regiment was transferred to Gen. Winfield Scott's army, which landed at Veracruz and advanced to Mexico City. Grant's assignments as regimental quartermaster and commissary, giving him detailed knowledge of army supply that proved invaluable later, were galling to the young officer who wanted action, even though he believed the war was unjust. His wish for action was gratified during the campaign against Mexico City, and his services during the battles of Molino del Rey (Sept. 8, 1847) and San Cosmé Garita (Sept. 13, 1847) brought him brevet commissions as first lieutenant and captain, though his permanent rank was first lieutenant.

Sailing from Mexico on July 16, 1848, Grant hurried to St. Louis, where he ended his four-year engagement to Julia Dent with their marriage on Aug. 22. During the next four years Grant was stationed at Sackets Harbor, N.Y.; Detroit, Mich.; and then Sackets Harbor again. On July 5, 1852, when the 4th Infantry sailed from New York for the Pacific coast, Grant left behind his wife and son, Frederick Dent Grant, born May 30, 1850. Another son, Ulysses S. Grant, Jr., was born July 22, 1852, and Grant was unwilling to risk his family on the dangerous crossing of the Isthmus of Panama.

Grant was assigned to duty at Ft. Vancouver, Oregon (later Washington) Territory, where he encountered inflated prices that forced him into unsuccessful business ventures to supplement his Army pay in order to reunite his family. Unhappy about the long separation from his family, Grant began to consider resigning. The final blow came when his promotion to captain on Aug. 5, 1853, brought orders assigning him to Ft. Humboldt, Calif., a dreary post with an unpleasant commanding officer. On April 11, 1854, he submitted his resignation from the Army. Allegations that he found consolation in drink during the unhappy years on the Pacific coast were never proved, yet affected his reputation nonetheless; whatever the truth of the matter, there were many reasons for his resignation, and it was submitted by his own choice. Furthermore, there is no reliable evidence that he drank to excess at any later time.

Grant settled on the Dent estate of White Haven, and began to farm 80 acres given to Julia by her father. Almost every farm in the neighbourhood had a name, often pretentious; Grant called his Hardscrabble, and the house, built largely by Grant alone, was made of logs. Two more children were born in Missouri; Ellen (Nellie) Grant on July 4, 1855, and Jesse Root Grant, Jr., on Feb. 6, 1858. Persistent ill-health (possibly malaria) and low crop prices following the Panic of 1857 defeated Grant's farming venture; a real estate partnership in St. Louis in 1859 was equally unsuccessful. In 1859 Grant's application for the post of St. Louis County engineer was rejected, with Grant receiving support only from the Democratic county commissioners. Earlier a Whig, Grant then gave his allegiance to the Democratic Party, where it remained until well into the Civil War. In May 1860, after many years of disappointment in Missouri, Grant took a post in a leather goods business, owned by his father and operated by his brothers, in Galena, Ill.

Civil War Service.—At the outbreak of the Civil War, Grant presided over a Galena war meeting called in response to President Lincoln's call for troops, then assisted in recruiting, equipping, and drilling the Jo Daviess Guards. He accompanied them to Springfield, where Gov. Richard Yates appointed him an aide and assigned him to duty in the state adjutant general's office, where his knowledge of military procedure proved valuable. He also served as mustering officer while awaiting a commission, though his letter of application to Washington was not even acknowledged. On June 15, 1861, Yates appointed him colonel of an unruly regiment (later named the 21st Illinois Volunteers), which had already driven an incompetent colonel into premature retirement. Assigned to northeastern Missouri, Grant was appointed brigadier general, before he had even engaged the enemy, through the influence of Elihu B. Washburne, U.S. congressman from Galena. Grant's new commission soon brought him command of the District of Southeast Missouri, headquartered at Cairo, Ill., from which he seized the vital position of Paducah, Ky., at the mouth of the Tennessee River, on Sept. 6. His first battle, at Belmont, Mo., Nov. 7, was inconclusive: intended as a diversionary attack, initial Union success was followed by the return of the Confederates in superior force, and Grant's men were lucky to scramble back on their transports with only slight losses.

In January 1862, dissatisfied with the use of his force for defensive and diversionary purposes, Grant asked Gen. Henry W. Halleck for permission to begin a campaign on the Tennessee River. As soon as Halleck assented, Grant moved in cooperation with a fleet of gunboats against Ft. Henry, which fell to the gunboat attack (Feb. 6) before the main body of troops arrived. Most of the defenders of Ft. Henry withdrew to far stronger Ft. Donelson, about 11 mi. away on the Cumberland River. Grant followed quickly, assaulted vigorously, and Ft. Donelson surrendered on Feb. 16 with about 15,000 troops. As the first major Union victory of the war, it was hailed with enthusiasm, and Grant's letter offering "no terms except an unconditional and immediate surrender" won acclaim.

Now a major general, Grant was removed from command for about a week when telegraphic failures led Halleck to assume that Grant refused to report. After his restoration to command, even greater trouble struck on April 6 when Confederates under generals Albert Sidney Johnston and P. G. T. Beauregard attacked his army unexpectedly at Shiloh Church, near Pittsburg Landing, Tenn. By the end of the day, Grant's men had been pushed back to the Tennessee River. The next day, however, aided by reinforcements brought by Gen. Don Carlos Buell, Grant drove the Confederates from the field. Outcry over the heavy Union losses (1,754 killed) hurt Grant's reputation, and Halleck took personal command of the army during a tedious advance to Corinth, Miss. Grant considered resigning while second in command, but was dissuaded by his close friend, Gen. William T. Sherman.

In July, Halleck was called to Washington as general in chief, putting Grant back in command. Successes by Gen. William S. Rosecrans, Grant's subordinate, at Iuka (Sept. 19) and Corinth (Oct. 3–4) strengthened the Union position so that before the end of the year Grant could begin his advance toward Vicksburg, the last major Confederate stronghold on the Mississippi River. The campaign opened with a series of frustrating failures: Grant's supply base at Holly Springs was captured, an assault by Sherman along Chickasaw Bayou was repulsed with heavy Union losses, and a series of attempts to get to Vicksburg via bayous and canals north and west of the city all failed. During this period Grant displayed the qualities of aggressiveness, resilience, independence, and determination, which led to final victory. On April 16, 1863, Adm. David D. Porter's fleet ran past the Vicksburg batteries so successfully that more transports followed a few days later. On April 30, Grant finally landed south of Vicksburg, then advanced rapidly on Port Gibson (May 1), Grand Gulf (May 3), and Raymond (May 12). Then, in a masterful move, Grant turned his back on Vicksburg to capture the state capital of Jackson, thus isolating Vicksburg. Union victories at Champion's Hill (May 16) and Big Black River (May 17) completed the encirclement of Vicksburg, which surrendered with a loss of about 30,000 men after a siege lasting until July 4. Port Hudson, La., the last Confederate post on the Mississippi, necessarily fell a few days later; Grant had cut the Confederacy in half.

Following his defeat at Chickamauga, Ga., Sept. 19–20, Rosecrans had retired to Chattanooga and allowed Gen. Braxton Bragg to besiege the city. On Oct. 17, Grant was given command of the Military Division of the Mississippi, including the departments of the Ohio, Cumberland, and Tennessee, with orders to relieve Chattanooga. After opening a precarious supply route, Grant fought the three-day Battle of Chattanooga, Nov. 23–25, driving Bragg from his strong defensive position on Orchard Knob, Lookout Mountain, and Missionary Ridge back into Georgia. With his western campaigns completed, Grant was appointed to the newly restored rank of lieutenant general in March 1864, and given command over all the armies of the United States. He showed tact as well as wisdom by leaving Halleck in the post of general in chief to serve as liaison with President Lincoln and Secretary of War Edwin M. Stanton, also assuring that administrative details would be competently managed. In another wise move, he left Gen. George Gordon Meade in command of the

Army of the Potomac while establishing his headquarters with it to coordinate its actions with those of other armies. His basic plan for the 1864 campaign was to immobilize Gen. Robert E. Lee near Richmond while Sherman led the western army through Georgia. Having cut the Confederacy in half through his Mississippi River campaign, he now proposed to bisect the eastern half.

The spring campaign of the Army of the Potomac began with heavy casualties in the Wilderness (May 5–7), at Spotsylvania (May 8–20), and Cold Harbor (June 1–3); but Grant persisted in his determination "to fight it out on this line if it takes all Summer," and by mid-June had pinned down Lee at Petersburg, only a few miles from Richmond, in a battle that gradually settled into a siege. While Grant held Lee at Petersburg, Sherman's army cut through Georgia and cavalry forces led by Gen. Philip H. Sheridan destroyed railroads and supplies in Virginia. On April 2, 1865, Lee was forced to abandon his Petersburg line, and the inevitable surrender followed on April 9 at Appomattox Court House.

That Grant's army vastly outnumbered Lee's at the close of the conflict should not obscure Grant's achievements; the Union had had numerical superiority in Virginia ever since the first Battle of Bull Run in July 1861, yet Grant was the first to make these numbers count. If the bloody, methodical advance of spring, 1864, was Grant's, so were the lightninglike lunges of the last stage of the Vicksburg campaign. If Grant seemed to reap inevitable victory in 1864–65, he had rebounded from defeat at Shiloh. Grant's success was due in large measure to an administrative ability that applied equally to supplies and subordinate commanders. Coming to the conflict with scant respect for the art of war, he exceeded other generals in his receptiveness to innovation, versatility, and capacity for growth.

After the Civil War.—After the war Grant transferred his headquarters to Washington and busied himself in the work of Reconstruction. When Pres. Andrew Johnson thought of bringing Lee to trial for treason, Grant reminded him of the surrender terms at Appomattox and fought as vigorously for Lee as he had once fought against him. In late 1865, Grant toured the South at Johnson's request, was greeted with surprising friendliness, and submitted a report recommending a lenient Reconstruction policy. On July 25, 1866, Congress established a new rank, general of the armies of the United States, to which Grant was immediately appointed. Shortly afterward, relations between Grant and Johnson began to disintegrate. Reluctantly accompanying Johnson on a trip to dedicate a monument to Stephen A. Douglas in Chicago, Grant quickly learned that Johnson viewed the "swing round the circle" as an opportunity to explain his political differences with the Republican Party to the people. Johnson's angry and undignified responses to hecklers cost him Grant's sympathy.

In July 1867 Johnson informed Grant that he intended to remove Stanton from the War Department in order to test the constitutionality of the Tenure of Office Act, passed by congressional Republicans, which required the assent of Congress to removals from office. On Aug. 12, Grant was ordered to serve as secretary of war *ad interim.* When Congress reconvened and insisted upon the reinstatement of Stanton, Grant resigned his secretaryship (Jan. 14, 1868), thus infuriating Johnson, who believed that Grant had promised to hold on to the office in order to provoke a court test of the constitutionality of the Tenure of Office Act. Johnson's angry charges against Grant brought an open break and strengthened Grant's Republican ties. As a result, the Republican National Convention at Chicago on May 21, 1868, nominated Grant for president almost without opposition. The last line of his letter of acceptance, "Let us have peace," became the Republican slogan. In the election, Grant emerged with a popular majority over his Democratic opponent, Horatio Seymour, former governor of New York, of only 306,000 in a total vote of 5,715,000, which illustrated the precarious nature of Republican ascendancy and the necessity of maintaining political control of the South.

Grant's Presidency (1869–77).—Grant entered the White House on March 4, 1869, at the age of 46, the youngest man elected president to that time and the most inexperienced in politics. He had voted only once before in a presidential election, casting his ballot for Democrat James Buchanan. In his inaugural address Grant declared: "The office has come to me unsought; I commence its duties untrammeled." In assembling his cabinet he showed the decisiveness and independence he had exhibited as a commander, with less fortunate results. He appointed A. T. Stewart as secretary of the treasury, discovered that his business interests made him ineligible, then appointed George S. Boutwell of Massachusetts to the post, although his state was already represented in the cabinet by Attorney General E. R. Hoar. Chief of Staff John A. Rawlins was appointed secretary of war even though he was a dying man because Grant wanted to honour a faithful friend. Elihu Washburne was given a two-week courtesy appointment as secretary of state to prepare him for a permanent appointment as minister to France. Washburne was followed in the State Department by the extremely able Hamilton Fish. Grant's appointments to office were uneven in quality but sometimes refreshing; nobody but Grant would have appointed a Seneca, Ely S. Parker, his former staff officer, as commissioner of Indian affairs.

On March 18 Grant signed his first law, one that pledged the government to redeem in gold the greenback currency issued during the Civil War, thus placing himself with the financial conservatives of the day. He appointed George William Curtis, an able reformer, to head the first Civil Service Commission established by Congress, and backed its recommendations, but abandoned the effort in view of congressional intransigence. He was more persistent when the Senate rejected a treaty of annexation with Santo Domingo. He believed that Santo Domingo offered a valuable naval base, opportunities for investment, and a possible solution to race problems. Although he forced Hoar out of his cabinet for opposing annexation and ultimately had his bitterest opponent, Sen. Charles Sumner, deposed as chairman of the Senate Foreign Relations Committee, he was unable to get the treaty through the Senate. A happier aspect of foreign policy was the negotiation of the Treaty of Washington, which provided for the settlement by international tribunal of American claims against England arising from the wartime activities of the British-built Confederate raider "Alabama."

On May 1, 1872, a Liberal Republican convention met at Cincinnati to denounce vindictive Reconstruction and corruption in government, which it called Grantism. Horace Greeley was chosen by the Liberal Republicans, and, later, by the Democrats. Greeley's earlier radicalism, lifelong opposition to the Democratic Party, high tariff views, and well-known eccentricity repelled many who opposed Grant. The Republican convention nominated Grant, who won reelection easily with a popular majority more than doubled.

During the campaign it was learned that Vice-Pres. Schuyler Colfax, vice-presidential nominee Henry Wilson, and a number of other prominent Republican politicians were involved in the Crédit Mobilier of America (*q.v.*), a shady corporation designed to siphon profits of the Union Pacific Railroad. More bad news followed. In 1875 Secretary of the Treasury Benjamin H. Bristow exposed the operations of a whisky ring that had the aid of high government officials in defrauding the government of tax revenues. When the evidence touched the president's private secretary, Orville E. Babcock, Grant regretted his earlier statement: "Let no guilty man escape." Grant blundered in accepting the resignation of Secretary of War William W. Belknap on the same day he was impeached on charges of accepting bribes from an Indian agent; Belknap escaped conviction since he was no longer a government official. Discouraged and sickened, Grant closed his second term by assuring Congress that "Failures have been errors of judgment, not of intent." These and other scandals have become the best-remembered feature of the Grant administration, obscuring more positive aspects. Grant's lenient Reconstruction policy did much to lessen sectional animosity. His veto of a bill to increase the amount of legal tender currency (April 22, 1874) diminished the currency crisis during the next quarter century. In his closing days in the White House he dealt so gracefully with the controversy caused when both Republican Rutherford B. Hayes and Democrat Samuel J. Tilden claimed election to the presidency that his role has been virtually forgotten.

Later Life; Grant as an Author.—After leaving the White House Grant started on a trip around the world. Everywhere he received great public attention and acclaim, some of it directed to him personally, some designed for the people he had represented for eight years. He returned to San Francisco in September 1879 to find the same thunderous welcome at home and the Stalwart faction of the Republican Party anxious to nominate him for a third term. Although he did nothing to encourage his political supporters, he received more than 300 votes in each of the 36 ballots of the 1880 convention, which finally nominated James A. Garfield, and would probably have been nominated if the two-term tradition had ever been broken before. In August 1881, Grant bought a house in New York City and began to take an interest in the investment firm of Grant and Ward, in which his son, Ulysses S. Grant, Jr., was a partner. He put his capital at the disposal of the firm and encouraged others to follow without being well-informed about the business. In May 1884 the firm collapsed. Ferdinand Ward was discovered to be a remarkable swindler who had impoverished the entire Grant family and had even clouded the general's reputation.

Already ailing, Grant found he had no money and owed substantial sums. To support his family Grant began to write reminiscences of his campaigns for the *Century Magazine*, and found this so engaging that he began to prepare his memoirs. In November, however, he began to feel the pain in his throat later diagnosed as cancer. Now the Grant of Shiloh and the Wilderness was roused once more. Despite excruciating pain, he signed a contract with his friend Mark Twain to publish the memoirs, and resolved grimly to complete them before he died. In June 1885, to avoid the summer heat, the Grant family moved to a cottage at Mount McGregor in the Adirondacks, and there he died, July 23, 1885. Amid considerable public mourning his body was buried in Riverside Park, New York City, where an elaborate tomb was dedicated in 1897.

Grant won his last great battle when he completed his memoirs shortly before his death. The two volumes, published separately in 1885 and 1886, enjoyed remarkable sales that brought at least $450,000 to the Grant family. *The Personal Memoirs of U.S. Grant* exhibit equanimity, candour, and a surprisingly good sense of humour. Written with modesty and restraint, they retain high rank among military autobiographies. They were Grant's last gift to the American people.

See also references under "Grant, Ulysses S.," in the Index.

BIBLIOGRAPHY.—An excellent brief biography is Bruce Catton, *Grant and the American Military Tradition* (1954). More detailed biography is available in Lloyd Lewis, *Captain Sam Grant* (1950); Bruce Catton, *Grant Moves South* (1960), *Grant Takes Command* (1969); and William B. Hesseltine, *Ulysses S. Grant, Politician* (1957). Analyses of Grant as a soldier include J. F. C. Fuller, *The Generalship of Ulysses S. Grant*, 2nd ed. (1968); T. Harry Williams, *Lincoln and His Generals* (1952) and *McClellan, Sherman and Grant* (1962); and Kenneth P. Williams, *Lincoln Finds a General* (vol. 3–5, 1952–59). *Personal Memoirs of U.S. Grant* (2 vol., 1885–86) are also available in a 1 vol. abridgment (1952). Grant's correspondence is in John Y. Simon (ed.), *The Papers of Ulysses S. Grant* (1967–). (J. Y. S.)

GRANTH, literally meaning, "the book," is the name given to the Sikh scripture. The fifth Sikh guru, Arjan, began the compilation of the Adi-Granth, or Granth Sahib, in A.D. 1603 and included his own hymns, those of his predecessors, gurus Nanak, Angad, Amardas and Ramdas (*see* SIKHISM), together with hymns of various early and medieval saints of different religions and castes. In 1705–06 the tenth and last guru, Gobind Singh, added the hymns of the ninth guru, Teg Bahadur, and enjoined that after him the Granth would take the place of the guru. Every hymn is set to music. The language is mostly Punjabi or Hindi, interspersed with Marathi, Persian, and Arabic words. Their theme is the union of the human soul with its Maker through annihilation of egoism; for perfection, the service of humanity and the adoption of the highest ethical standards are inculcated and the renunciation of worldly activity forbidden.

After the death of Guru Gobind Singh his hymns and other writings with those of his court poets were compiled into a book known as the Dasm-Granth.

See K. Singh, *Guru Shabad Ratnakar* (1930); T. Singh, J. Singh et al., *Selections from the Sacred Writings of the Sikhs* (1960). (B. J. Sr.)

GRANTHAM, a municipal borough in the Grantham parliamentary division of the Parts of Kesteven, Lincolnshire, Eng., on the Witham river, 25 mi. S.S.W. of Lincoln by road. Pop. (1970 est.) 26,660. It is an important junction on the main railway line from London to Scotland. Of Saxon origin, the town (Grandham) is mentioned in the Domesday survey as part of the royal demesne the manor having belonged to Edith, queen of Edward the Confessor. It remained a royal possession until the time of William III though often granted for a lifetime to such feudal families as the De Warennes, from whose checky shield the borough coat of arms is derived. The charter of incorporation was granted by Edward IV in 1463 and self-government of the town and soke was thereafter exercised through 13 "comburgesses," one of whom was annually elected alderman—the title retained by the town's chief citizen until the Municipal Corporations act of 1835. The town remained a parliamentary borough until 1918. The wool trade of the middle ages added to Grantham's prosperity. The parish church of St. Wulfram, mainly Early English and Decorated, is one of the finest medieval churches in England, the tower and spire (14th century) rising magnificently to a height of almost 280 ft. A small priest's room over the south porch houses a chained library which was presented to the church in 1598. Grantham was created a bishopric suffragan in the diocese of Lincoln in 1905. King's school, refounded early in the 16th century by Richard Foxe, bishop of Winchester, still uses the old school building and headmaster's house of about that period. The greatest of its pupils was Sir Isaac Newton, who was born at Woolsthorpe, a few miles south of Grantham. The Angel hotel is said to be where Richard III signed the death warrant of the duke of Buckingham in 1483. The 18th-century George hotel was praised in Charles Dickens' *Nicholas Nickleby* as one of the best inns in England. A market is held in Grantham's ancient market place on Saturdays. The chief industries are concerned with mechanical engineering including particularly oil engines and road rollers. A local firm invented the "caterpillar" track at the beginning of the 20th century, and it was so named by troops during a trial at Aldershot in 1908.

GRANTS, a town of Valencia county, N.M., U.S., 78 mi. W. of Albuquerque, is called the "uranium capital of the world" because of the extensive uranium mining and milling activities in the vicinity. The town dates from 1881 when the Grant brothers, contractors building the Atlantic and Pacific (later the Atchison, Topeka and Santa Fe) railroad, established a construction camp at what became known as Grants station. Originally a livestock shipping centre, Grants later was supported by lumber and vegetable growing industries. Uranium ore was first discovered near Grants in 1950 by Paddy Martinez, a Navaho Indian, and further exploration revealed that more than 70% of the world's known uranium reserves were located in the area. Pop. (1970) 8,768, a decrease of 14.7% from the 1960 figure. (For comparative population figures *see* table in New Mexico: *Population*.) (H. T. B.)

GRANULITE. To German, Scandinavian and most English and North American petrologists a granulite (from Lat. *granulum*, "a little grain") is a crystalline schist or gneiss which contains certain mineral assemblages characteristic of high pressure and fairly high temperature; *i.e.*, granulite facies. The typical minerals in granulites are anhydrous, such as pyroxene, garnet, cordierite, sillimanite and kyanite (cyanite), together with feldspars and quartz. The hydrous minerals biotite and hornblende are not abundant in granulite. Muscovite is never present in a true granulite. The typical granulite is a quartzofeldspathic rock with magnesium-rich garnet (pyrope) and sillimanite or kyanite: the Rutile is a common accessory. Certain basic gneisses with diopside or hypersthene and a characteristic brown hornblende are also called granulites; e.g., the norite granulite of Lapland in north Finland. The alkali feldspar in granulites is often a microperthitic orthoclase or a feldspar with a triclinicity intermediate between orthoclase (which is monoclinic) and microcline (which is distinctly triclinic). Mesoperthites, *i.e.*, perthites with about 50% albite and 50% orthoclase, are much more common in granulites (and charnockites) than in other kinds of deep-seated rocks.

Antiperthitic plagioclase, *i.e.*, plagioclase with exsolved blebs of potash feldspar, is typical for granulites, as well as rocks belonging to the charnockite kindred.

Granulites may be fine grained or coarse grained; the texture is a sugary mosaic of irregular grains fitted together.

Occurrence.—Granulites occur chiefly in the Pre-Cambrian basement complexes in various parts of the world, the areas in Saxony and Lapland perhaps being the best known. Such rocks have also been described from India, Ceylon, Madagascar, Norway, the United States, Canada, Greenland and Brazil. Granulites are intimately associated with rocks of charnockitic affinity in the field. Some granulites are actually identical to rocks of the charnockite (*q.v.*) family.

Origin.—Although some petrologists consider granulites to be of magmatic origin (P. Eskola in his study of the Lapland granulites), most students believe that they are metamorphic rocks recrystallized under the high P,T (pressure, temperature) conditions of granulite facies. *See* METAMORPHISM. (H. Rg.)

GRANULOMA INGUINALE, a chronic, mildly contagious venereal disease initiated by a microorganism called the Donovan body. It is treated successfully with antibiotics. *See* VENEREAL DISEASES.

GRANVELLE, ANTOINE PERRENOT DE (1517–1586), Franc-Comtois cardinal, a high-ranking member of the Spanish administration under Philip II, active in Brussels at the beginning of the Netherlands revolt, was born at Besançon, Aug. 20, 1517, the son of Nicolas Perrenot de Granvelle, chancellor of Emperor Charles V. Granvelle was educated at Padua and at Louvain, ordained priest and, in 1540, consecrated bishop of Arras; in 1560 he was made archbishop of Malines, and the next year a cardinal. Together with his brother Thomas Perrenot de Chantonay, Granvelle received thorough instruction in public affairs; he also derived from his father a high regard for the absolute, unrestricted authority of the monarch (as opposed to the ambitions of wealthy noblemen), which was to lead to a clash between him and the Netherlands aristocrats.

In 1560 Philip appointed Cardinal de Granvelle, who was not a foreigner to the Netherlands (to the intellectual atmosphere of which he was also tied through his interest in painting and poetry and his somewhat epicurean outlook), chief counselor to Margaret of Austria, regent in the Netherlands. His political principles and possibly also his class consciousness (as a member of the lesser nobility) contributed to a gradual estrangement between him and the leaders of the Netherlands magnates, William the Silent and the counts of Egmond and Horn. In his reports to Philip, Granvelle denied that any serious trouble was in the offing. The king himself was slow to discern the real character of the discontent and—owing perhaps to the influence of Margaret, who sided with the noblemen—regarded Granvelle's difficulties as a personal affair. On his order Granvelle left the Netherlands on March 12, 1564. Later Philip concluded that the Netherlands revolution would have never developed had he supported Granvelle. After serving for some time in Italy, where he prepared the victory at Lepanto, Granvelle was appointed to the Spanish council of state, becoming the only non-Spanish member of that body. There his principles, hardened by experience, certainly did not make Philip's attitude to the Netherlands less intransigent. Granvelle died in Madrid on Sept. 21, 1586. *See also* NETHERLANDS.

BIBLIOGRAPHY.—P. Geyl, *The Revolt of the Netherlands Against Spain, 1555–1609* (1932); William T. Walsh, *Philip II* (1937); C. V. Wedgwood, *William the Silent* (1944); Bernard H. M. Vlekke, *Evolution of the Dutch Nation* (1945); Bohdan Chudoba, *Spain and the Empire, 1519–1643* (1952). (B.CA.)

GRANVILLE, GRANVILLE GEORGE LEVESON-GOWER, 2ND EARL (1815–1891), English statesman, was foreign secretary in Gladstone's first and second administrations, and succeeded him as leader of the Liberal party for a time. He was the grandson of the 1st marques of Stafford (1721–1803). His father, the 1st earl (1773–1846), who married a daughter of the 5th duke of Devonshire, was, as Lord Granville Leveson-Gower, a member of parliament from 1795 to 1815, and a successful diplomat; he was a special ambassador to the tsar during 1804–07, and in 1824 his friend George Canning made him ambassador to Paris where he remained till 1841.

The 1st earl's eldest son was born in London on May 11, 1815, and educated at Eton and at Christ Church, Oxford. After a short spell as attaché to his father in Paris, he was elected Whig member of parliament for Morpeth in 1836 and 1837, and for Lichfield in 1841. He married in 1840 the widowed Lady Acton (d. 1860) heiress of the great Rhineland house of Dalberg. Granville held various minor offices under Lord John Russell from 1846, and promoted the great exhibition of 1851 with such success that he was admitted to the cabinet while paymaster general. He succeeded Lord Palmerston in Dec. 1851 as foreign secretary for the remaining three months of the government's life. He was president of the council (1852–54) and chancellor of the duchy of Lancaster (1854–55) in Lord Aberdeen's coalition; he returned to the former office under Palmerston in 1855, and also became leader of the Liberal peers in the house of lords, a post he retained, save for an interval during 1865–68, until his death. Borrowing his cousin's gold plate from Chatsworth, he went on a special embassy in 1856 to attend the coronation of the tsar. He was chancellor of the University of London, 1856–91, during which time he supported the admission of women.

Granville attempted, without success, to form a government in 1859. He resumed the presidency of the council under Palmerston and Russell from 1859 to 1866. This post brought him into further contact with Queen Victoria, whose favourite Liberal minister he was henceforward. His most important political services were rendered as intermediary between her and Gladstone. He was Gladstone's closest political friend from 1868, and served in three of his cabinets; he was secretary of state for the colonies in 1868–70 and in 1886, and for foreign affairs in 1870–74 and 1880–85.

Granville was an ideal negotiator, but as an initiator of policies Gladstone overshadowed him. The Franco-German War, which broke out a few days after Lord Clarendon's death, brought Granville to the foreign office, took both him and Gladstone by surprise and brought on the only serious difference between them. Granville got the cabinet to override Gladstone's wish to protest at the annexation of Alsace-Lorraine. Otherwise they worked in close, constant and harmonious co-operation; and Gladstone found that, as he once wrote to Granville, "it is impossible for any man to talk over a difficulty with you and not to find himself nearer to a solution at the end than he was at the beginning." In the winter of 1870–71 at the London conference Granville handled the Russian denunciation of the treaty of Paris with dexterity, and secured the point of form that future treaty denunciations would require in law the consent of all signatories; but he had to concede the point of substance, a Russian fleet in the Black sea. The only other significant negotiation of these years was the settlement of the "Alabama" arbitration (*q.v.*). Granville became the official leader of the whole Liberal party when Gladstone first retired, and protested more mildly at Conservative policy in the great eastern crisis of 1876–78. He was again asked to form a government in 1880, but at once gave way to Gladstone. During his last spell at the foreign office Bismarck, in effect, dictated much of British foreign policy, and Granville's own powers were clearly failing. He was one of the few Whig peers who stood by Gladstone in the Irish Home Rule crisis of 1886.

He died in London on March 31, 1891, and was succeeded by the 3rd earl (1872–1939), the son of his second marriage, in 1865, to Castalia Campbell of Islay, Argyll.

See his *Life* by Lord Edmund Fitzmaurice, 2 vol. (1905); *The Gladstone-Granville Political Correspondence, 1868–1876*, ed. by Agatha Ramm, 2 vol. (1952). (M. R. D. F.)

GRANVILLE, JOHN CARTERET, EARL (1690–1763), English statesman, best known as Lord Carteret, who was prominent in politics under the first Hanoverians, was born on April 22,

1690, the eldest son of George, 1st Lord Carteret, whom he succeeded in 1695. He was educated at Westminster school and Christ Church, Oxford, and acquired an abiding interest in languages and literature, being one of the few noblemen of his time to speak German fluently. He took his seat in the house of lords on May 25, 1711. Although most of his relations were Tory, he quickly showed his independent judgment by voting with the Whigs for the Hanoverian succession. He secured minor office in 1714, and his first important appointment came in 1719 when he was sent to Sweden as ambassador. This promotion was due to James Stanhope, to whom he had remained loyal in his quarrel with Robert Walpole and Lord Townshend. Carteret displayed considerable diplomatic skill and he played an important part in the long and arduous negotiations that brought an end to the Northern War in 1721. George I, as elector of Hanover, was personally and keenly interested in the affairs of northern Europe and he was impressed by Carteret's ability.

After his return from Sweden, Carteret was appointed ambassador to the congress of Cambrai but, before he could take up his appointment, the death of James Craggs, the younger, led to his promotion in 1721 as secretary of state for the southern department, an office which he held, without great distinction, until 1724. Carteret's promotion had been due to the earl of Sunderland, the rival of Walpole and Townshend, and after Sunderland's death in 1722, Walpole and Townshend steadily intrigued against Carteret by undermining George I's confidence in his judgment. Carteret placed too much reliance on his friend Sir Luke Schaub, the British ambassador at Paris, and he was too proud and too indolent to fight his enemies on their own terms.

Carteret lost his office in 1724 and was promoted, in order to get him removed from London and the court, to be lord lieutenant of Ireland in the place of the duke of Grafton. At this time the violent agitation in Ireland against Wood's halfpence, skilfully fanned by the virulent diatribes of Jonathan Swift in the *Draper's Letters*, made a new appointment essential. For the next six years Carteret remained in office, hoping to win back his secretaryship of state by compliance with the policy of Walpole and Townshend. This he failed to do, and from 1730 he entered into opposition to Walpole and became one of his most eloquent and prominent critics in the house of lords, attacking Walpole's policy toward Spain with particular violence. He succeeded, however, in retaining both the sympathy and liking of George II, who welcomed his appointment as secretary of state in 1742 after the fall of Walpole. Overconfident by reason of the king's support, Carteret pursued an energetic policy in support of the empress Maria Theresa but paid little attention to the intrigues of his colleagues or the violent denunciations of the opposition, who accused him of sacrificing the interests of Great Britain to those of Hanover. However, behind the scenes, Walpole was using all his influence to get rid of Carteret, whose arrogance and contempt left him without a supporter. His dismissal was forced on the reluctant king in 1744.

This marked the end of Carteret's effective career as a statesman, and he himself seems to have given up his ambition to direct British foreign policy. Although he became president of the council in 1751 and retained the office until he died, his influence either on policy or appointments was small. His major contribution to politics in his later life lay in the studied and ornate speeches with which he regaled the house of lords, where he was regarded as one of the most outstanding orators of his day. He was a man whose considerable gifts were vitiated by a lack of judgment that was the effect of a self-regarding and self-indulgent nature. He was both too arrogant, too indolent and too fond of a jibe to make an effective politician. Carteret, who had become Earl Granville in 1744, died in London on Jan. 2, 1763.

BIBLIOGRAPHY.—There is no adequate *Life* of Carteret. The best is by N. W. Baring Pemberton (1936). *See also* Basil Williams, *Carteret and Newcastle* (1943).
(J. H. Pr.)

GRANVILLE, a fortified seaport and bathing resort of northwestern France, in the *département* of Manche, at the mouth of the Bosq, 85 mi. S.W. of Cherbourg by rail. Pop. (1962) 9,439. The upper town stands on a promontory and is surrounded by ramparts; the lower town, with bathing beaches and promenade, and the harbour lie below it. The barracks and the church of Notre Dame are in the upper town. The port consists of a large tidal harbour and a floating basin and is the port of Normandy for British goods. Its principal exports are eggs, vegetables, fish, lard and butter, and it imports mainly coal, timber and raw materials. Granville is a centre for yachtsmen and tourists and for visitors to the Channel Islands. Deep-sea fishing is carried on, and industries include shipbuilding, the preserving of vegetables, metal founding and ropemaking, as well as the manufacture of chemical fertilizers, shoes and biscuits.

GRANVILLE-BARKER, HARLEY (1877–1946), British dramatist, producer and critic, who profoundly influenced the 20th-century theatre and the presentation of Shakespeare's plays, was born in London on Nov. 25, 1877. He began his stage training at 13, and at 15 Charles Hawtrey gave him a London part. He preferred work with William Poel's Elizabethan Stage society and Ben Greet's Shakespeare repertory company to a West End career, however, and in 1900 joined the experimental Stage society. In 1904 he undertook management of the Court theatre with J. E. Vedrenne and made theatrical history by introducing the public to Ibsen, Maeterlinck, Galsworthy, John Masefield, Gilbert Murray's translations from Greek, new plays by Shaw and many other works. His wife Lillah McCarthy played most of the leading roles. The Court became an authors' theatre, and among new plays produced there were several of his own: *The Voysey Inheritance* (1905), showing Shaw's influence; *Prunella* (1906), a charming fantasy written with Laurence Housman; *Waste* (1907); and *The Madras House* (1910).

Also revolutionary was his treatment of Shakespeare. Instead of traditional scenic décor and declamatory elocution, Barker successfully introduced, in the Savoy productions of *The Winter's Tale* and *Twelfth Night*, continuous action on an open stage and rapid, lightly stressed speech. He was active in promoting a national theatre and by 1914 had every prospect of a brilliant dramatic career.

After World War I, however, during which he served with the Red Cross, he found the mood of the postwar theatre alien and contented himself with work behind the scenes, as president of the British Drama league, for instance. He settled in Paris with his second wife, Helen, an American, collaborating with her in translating Spanish plays, and writing his five series of brilliant *Prefaces to Shakespeare* (1927–48), an important contribution to Shakespearean criticism, which threw fresh light on the plays by analyzing them from the standpoint of a practical playwright with firsthand stage experience.

In 1937 Barker became director of the British institute of the University of Paris. He fled to Spain in 1940 and then went to the United States, where he worked for British information services and lectured at Harvard university. He returned to Paris in 1946 and died there the same year, on Aug. 31.

See W. Bridge-Adams, *The Lost Leader* (1954); C. B. Purdom, *Harley Granville-Barker* (1955).
(W. A. Dn.)

GRAPE. The grape genus *Vitis*, of the family Vitaceae (*q.v.*), comprises about 60 species native to the north temperate zone, especially North America, among them the wine grape or grape of history, *V. vinifera*, and several others that produce juicy edible fruit. In addition to its importance as a fruit producer, the grape is also valued for its ornament and shade when grown on garden trellises and arbours; *V. coignetiae*, the glory vine, is prized for its brilliant red autumn foliage. Fossilized grape leaves, stem pieces and seeds unearthed from Miocene and Tertiary deposits in the northern hemisphere—the European continent, North America, England, Iceland—indicate the long existence and wide distribution of the "vine," as it was known to the ancients. Certain of the present species closely resemble the fossil forms.

History.—Old world grape culture (viticulture) dates far back. Seeds found in the remains of the Swiss lake dwellings of the Bronze Age and entombed with mummies in Egypt closely resemble seeds of the oldest and most extensively cultivated species of today. Viticulture's tradition is nearly as old as man; details for grape and wine production figured in the hieroglyphics of the 4th (2400 B.C.), 17th and 18th dynasties of Egypt. According to

GRAPE

GRAPE CLUSTERS, LEAVES AND VINE

J. HORACE MCFARLAND CO.

the Bible, Noah planted a vineyard. In Homer's time wine was a regular commodity among the Greeks. Pliny described 91 varieties of grapes, distinguished 50 kinds of wines and described vine-training methods.

Viticulture probably had its beginnings in the area around the Caspian sea, generally recognized as the place of origin of *V. vinifera*, the best-known grape. From there grape growing in the old world spread to parts of Asia Minor, then to Greece and from there to Sicily. The Phoenicians carried the grape into France about 600 B.C.; the Romans planted grapes in the Rhine valley not later than the 2nd century A.D.; and there is evidence that they introduced them into England. Coinciding with the westward spread of grape culture, grapes were moved into the orient by way of India. As new lands were colonized the grape was taken along, so that it is cultivated on all continents and islands where the climate is favourable.

For centuries, one species, *V. vinifera*, supplied all of the grapes grown by civilized man. It is the grape mentioned in the Bible, the grape of myths and poets, the grape that provides the wines and raisins of commerce and most of the world's table grapes. It is the old world grape, the European grape and, more recently in America, the California grape.

There was no real need for other species until eastern North America was colonized. But there *V. vinifera* was destroyed by an aphidlike insect called the grape phylloxera and by several diseases. Fortunately, North America had many native species of *Vitis* that had lived with these enemies and developed resistance. The colonists were then able to turn to the native *V. labrusca* and hybrids of it with vinifera and other American species, to create a new and different grape industry in that part of America. Varieties with a strong *V. labrusca* strain, the so-called slip skins, have a pronounced aromatic, or so-called foxy, flavour and are grouped as labruscan grapes.

In the southeastern part of the United States, varieties of *V. rotundifolia* are cultivated. These are the muscadine grapes. The berries are borne in very small clusters, mature irregularly and drop when ripe. In all but the most recently created self-fruiting varieties, the flowers are pistillate, making it necessary to interplant a limited number of male vines. These varieties are nevertheless important, since they and their fruit are very hardy under hot and humid conditions.

Europeans introduced American grapes when these became available. The early importations, in mid-18th century, were grown without mishap. However, in 1845 powdery mildew was discovered on grapes in a hothouse in England. Two years later it was observed in France, where in the space of ten years, until a control measure could be found, it reduced production 70%. Downy mildew and black rot, two other diseases of American origin, were identified in the south of France in 1878 and 1885, respectively.

While powdery mildew was ravaging the French vineyards additional American grapes resistant to it were imported, 1858–62, and with them phylloxera. Phylloxera took little more than two decades to destroy most of the vineyards of France, and in the early 1870s resistant rootstocks were sought out in America by French viticulturists. The magnitude of this effort is indicated by the fact that by 1890, 2,400,000 ac. of vineyard were again flourishing, this time on rootstocks of American species or hybrids. Among widely used rootstocks are selections of *V. rupestris, V. riparia* and *V. champinii*; hybrids of these, and *V. cinerea, V. Berlandieri, V. candicans, V. solonis* and *V. monticola*; or hybrids of vinifera varieties with certain American species.

The fight against phylloxera also involved attempts to develop resistant vines, by hybridizing *V. vinifera* varieties with American species. Resistance to both phylloxera and various diseases was sought. Because of their resistance to fungus diseases, some of these hybrids are grown extensively in parts of Europe and in the eastern U.S. They are grafted on phylloxera-resistant stocks.

Plant and Fruit Characteristics.—In North America the grape is a woody vine, climbing by means of tendrils (modified branches) and when untrained often reaching a length of 50 ft. or more. In arid regions it may form an almost erect shrub. The leaves are alternate, palmately lobed and always tooth-edged. Small greenish flowers, in clusters, precede the fruit, which varies in colour from almost black to green, red and amber. Botanically the fruit is a berry, more or less globular, within the juicy pulp of which lie the seeds. In many varieties the fruit is covered with a whitish powdery bloom. All grapes contain sugar (glucose and fructose) in varying quantities depending on the variety. Those having the most glucose are the most readily fermented.

Kinds of Grapes.—On the basis of parentage grapes may be grouped as vinifera (typified by *V. vinifera*), labruscan (typified by *V. labrusca*) and muscadine (typified by *V. rotundifolia*). In the course of time, however, hybridization and backcrossing became so extensive that parentage has been considerably mixed and, in some cases, almost obscured for many varieties.

On the basis of use, grapes are grouped as wine grapes, raisin grapes, table grapes, sweet juice grapes and canning grapes. The mature fruit of all varieties—about 8,000—will ferment into a kind of wine when crushed, and most of them can be dried or eaten fresh. But only a limited number of varieties produce standard or higher quality wines; three varieties account for most of the raisins of commerce; only 15 to 20 varieties are grown extensively as table grapes; a single variety yields the bulk of sweet juice produced in the U.S.; and only a few varieties are used for canning.

A wine grape may be defined as a variety known to be capable in some locality of producing an acceptable wine. Table (dry) wines require grapes of high acidity and moderate sugar content, while dessert (sweet) wines are the product of grapes that are high in sugar and moderately low in acidity. In addition, high quality wines—those of outstanding bouquet, flavour and general balance—require grapes that possess individuality. Examples of such grapes are the White Riesling, Semillon, Cabernet Sauvignon, Tinta Madeira and similar varieties when they are grown under favourable climatic conditions.

Raisin grapes are those varieties that produce an acceptable dried product: soft in texture, of little tendency to stickiness, pleasing in flavour, large or very small and seedless. Only the Thompson Seedless (Sultanina), Muscat (Alexandria) and Black Corinth varieties meet most of these requirements.

Grapes used fresh, either as food or for decoration, are called table grapes. They must be pleasing to the eye and to the palate. Large size, brilliant colour and unusual form are appreciated. When grapes must be shipped long distances to markets or stored for a considerable period, important qualities are firmness of pulp, toughness of skin, adherence to the stem (pedicel) and resistance of the stems to desiccation or browning. These qualities are possessed to a degree by the Tokay, Emperor, Cardinal, Red Malaga, Almeria and Ribier (Alphonse Lavallee), all of which are grown in California, South Africa, Australia, Chile, Argentina and elsewhere. The raisin grape Thompson Seedless is also, because of its seedlessness, a popular table grape in the U.S.

Sweet juice grapes are those varieties that produce a juice acceptable as a beverage when preserved by pasteurization, germproof filtration or freezing. The juice must retain the natural, fresh-grape flavour. In America, grape juice has generally been preserved by pasteurization. When vinifera varieties, including the strong-flavoured Muscats, are pasteurized by the usual methods they lose their fresh flavour and acquire an unpleasant, cooked taste. The taste of strong-flavoured American varieties, particularly the Concord, is less affected by pasteurization, which largely accounts for the general use of Concords for juice in the United States. In central Europe a sweet juice of renown is made of certain vinifera varieties. Preservation is effected by germproof filtration or storing under carbon dioxide pressure. Freezing is a valued technique in grape juice preservation.

Grapes are largely canned in combination with other fruits as fruit salad and fruit cocktail. Only seedless types are used. Grapes are also prepared as jams, jellies and conserves.

CULTURE AND HANDLING

Influence of Climate.—Vinifera grapes require long, dry, warm-to-hot summers and cool winters for their best development. Humid summers favour the development of diseases that attack the fruit, while severe winter conditions (0° F. [about −18° C.] or below) will destroy unprotected vines. Spring frosts occurring after the vines start growth will kill the shoots and clusters. Winter rains are needed for soil moisture; summer rains make disease control more difficult; rains during the ripening and harvest periods, if they are of considerable duration, may cause rotting of the fruit. Where raisins are produced by natural sun-drying, as in California, a month of clear, warm, rainless weather is essential after the grapes are mature.

Varieties possessing the characteristics of *V. labrusca* will withstand humid summers and cold winters better than will the true vinifera. They may in fact do better where summer rains of short duration are the rule. Varieties of *V. rotundifolia* thrive in the very warm, humid regions of the southeastern states of the U.S.

Just as climate broadly limits grape growing to the temperate zone, it further limits the highest development of individual varieties to specific localities within this zone. For example, the table grape Tokay fulfils itself only in a ten-square-mile area of central California—the warm, dry vineyards at Lodi. In certain areas of Europe individual climate is so subtly suited to the needs of the White Riesling, Pinot Noir, Cabernet Sauvignon and Chardonnay varieties that only highly localized areas produce some of the greatest table wines of the world.

Temperature is by far the most important climatic factor, affecting maturity date and palatability. Time of maturity is established by the total summation of heat, between full bloom and a given degree of maturity. Palatability, however, is influenced more by the summation of heat during the ripening period. Cool weather will mean higher acid content and a sour taste; hot weather will mean lower acid content and a sweet taste.

Vineyard Soils.—Grapes are adapted to a wide range of soils. Although growers often express a preference for certain soil types, surveys of soils used successfully in grape production in many different localities show a great variety of types, ranging from blow sands to clay loams, from shallow to very deep soils, from highly calcareous to noncalcareous soils and from very low to high fertility.

Extremes are not generally desirable, however, and poor drainage or excess salts are to be avoided. The highest tonnages are produced on the deeper and more fertile soils. They are especially preferred for raisins and common wine grapes.

Establishing the Vineyard.—Commercial grape varieties are propagated with cuttings, segments of canes or grafts. These are usually grown for one year in a nursery to develop roots. The use of clean soil permits the use of cuttings of fruiting varieties, but the presence of either phylloxera or nematodes (roundworms) requires the use of grafts or rootstocks. The grafts consist of a segment of a stem of a fruiting variety placed on a rootstock cutting. Both grafts and rooted rootstock cuttings are employed. The latter are field budded to the desired fruiting variety in late summer after being planted in the vineyard. The union of grafted or budded vines must be above the soil, to prevent the production of scion roots.

Planting distances may vary widely. In European and most other countries the planting distances range from 3 to 4 ft. in either direction; in California, where cultivation is largely mechanized, the widest vine spacing, 6 by 12 ft. and 8 by 12 ft., is generally employed.

Training is necessary to develop a vine of desirable form. It is accomplished by pruning the young vine and then tying it and its growth to a support. Two vine forms are generally used; headed vines and cordon vines. In the headed vine there is a straight, vertical trunk or stem of desired height, with arms radiating out from its top to form the head. The most widely used cordon is the bilateral, in which the trunk rises vertically to the desired height, where it is divided into two branches extending horizontally in opposite directions along the row. Arms rise from the horizontal parts of the divided trunk. Headed vines are common for wine and raisin grapes and some table varieties. The bilateral cordon is useful for large-clustered grapes. These are the common commercial systems, but minor variations occur in some producing areas, and in addition the vine can be readily trained to walls, pergolas and arbours.

Stakes are standard supports for all head-trained and spur-pruned vines, while trellises are usual for vines that are cordon-trained and spur-pruned or head-trained and cane-pruned. The stakes used in California are usually 2 by 2 in. split redwood. The trellis most generally used has two wires, placed 34 and 48 in. from the ground, while a flat or sloping top trellis with two or three additional wires is widely used for table grapes.

Pruning.—Pruning is the most important single vineyard operation. With wine and raisin varieties, it is usually the sole means of regulating the crop, largely determining not only the quality of the fruit but also the quality of the wood for the next year. At the annual pruning, from 90% to 95% or more of the year's growth is removed, leaving the spurs or fruit canes, or both. Spurs may be used on varieties whose basal buds (near the point of origin of the canes) are fruitful; and fruit canes are necessary when the variety produces such small clusters that many are required for a full crop.

Growth and Flowering.—Grapevines have climbing stems, which late in the spring start a rapid growth that reaches a peak in early summer, then slowing, with little further shoot elongation after the fruit begins to ripen. The leaves continue to function until the end of the season.

The leaves, tendrils, flowers and lateral shoots arise from the nodes. The flowers are borne in a cluster. The primordium of the flower cluster is formed during the year preceding its bloom, differentiation into a fruitful bud beginning with the accumulation of carbohydrates in the shoots soon after their growth slows down, in early summer. By leaf fall, the cluster primordia have developed into initial points for individual flowers. Thus, the number of flowers and the shape of the clusters are determined in the year prior to that in which the fruit is produced. The formation of the flower parts (calyx, corolla, stamen and pistil) follows leafing out in spring, requiring six to eight weeks, depending on weather and variety, before the complete flower has developed to the point of blooming.

Set of the Berries.—In normal setting (development) of the fruit, pollination is followed by fertilization, and this in turn by seed development. But normal fruit setting may fail in a number of varieties, either partially or nearly completely. As a result these varieties typically show a wide variation in berry size and shape. Four definite types of fruiting or fruit setting occur among varieties. Although all these types are found in many varieties, the proportion of types within an individual variety is relatively constant. The commonest type of setting is that in which normal seed development occurs. Each carpel of the ovary has one, two or more seeds, and the berries are relatively uniform in size and shape. According to variety, they are round, oval or fusiform (tapering at ends). Some varieties of this type are not perfect in set and produce at most only one or two seeds to a berry. With much elongated berries, the presence of a single or two adjacent seeds may cause the berries to be falciform (gherkinlike) in shape.

In a second type most of the seeds produced are empty. Empty seeds result from embryo abortion after the seed is well advanced in its development. Some varieties produce less than 3% of viable seeds. The berries of such varieties are nonuniform in both size and shape.

Two other types of setting produce seedless fruit. In one, fertilization takes place, but early abortion prevents seed development (stenospermocarpy), producing a fruit setting common to a number of important varieties, such as Thompson Seedless. In the other seedless type, fruit setting is by stimulative parthenocarpy (see FRUIT). Here the berries are very small and round, with no trace of seeds. Seedlessness and small size, however, have made the Black Corinth (representative of this type) of commercial importance. It supplies the dried currants of commerce.

Thinning Table Grapes.—Three methods of thinning have been developed as an aid in correcting fruit setting in certain table grapes, for not all varieties set equally well. Some set clusters that are too compact; the clusters of others are well filled; those of others are loose to the point of being straggly; and still others set shot berries (of parthenocarpic origin) along with the normal berries. Berry thinning will improve quality when an overabundance of berries makes the clusters too compact, or overlarge clusters interfere with proper colouring and maturing. In California, berry thinning consists in cutting the rachis (flower-bearing stalk) to leave only the desired number of berries; in other areas individual berries are removed. Thinning soon after fruit set gives a marked increase in the size of seeded berries. Thinning flower clusters soon after they emerge is another method. It improves the carbohydrate nutrition of the flowers retained, giving a better set of normal berries. Flower-cluster thinning is useful on varieties that have loose or straggly clusters or tend to set shot berries with standard pruning methods.

A third method, cluster thinning, involves removal of entire clusters soon after the berries have set. By leaving enough fruiting wood at pruning to produce a full crop in poor years and then reducing the overload by cluster thinning in good years, larger crops of high-quality fruit can be produced every year. Cluster thinning improves the nutrition of the fruit that is retained, enhancing seeded berry size and colour.

Girdling.—This operation (also called ringing) involves the removal of a complete ring of bark, $\frac{3}{16}$ to $\frac{1}{4}$ in. wide, from the trunk or from a cane below the fruit that is to be influenced. The girdle prevents downward movement of carbohydrates (through the phloem) improving the nutrition of the fruit. For best results the girdle must be open to be effective. During bloom it increases the set of seedless berries; during the period of rapid growth of seedless berries it increases berry size; during the early ripening period of seeded varieties it may accelerate colouring and ripening. These effects of girdling in seedless grape varieties can be produced by spraying with the proper concentration of plant growth regulators, such as 4-chlorophenoxyacetic acid and gibberellin.

Cultivation and Irrigation.—In areas of rainless summers and where periods of drought are a common occurrence, weeds are destroyed to prevent their robbing the vines of soil moisture. A winter cover crop or growth of native plants is usually encouraged. On rolling soils and hillsides it is of great value in checking erosion. The winter cover is destroyed at the end of the rainy season or at the spring cleanup. Cultivation is repeated only often enough to destroy, or prevent weed growth. This conserves soil moisture only by eliminating weeds and not by virtue of loosening or pulverizing the soil.

In irrigated vineyards the matter of weed competition is of less importance. Such vineyards are usually cleaned up in spring and kept free of weeds during the period of rapid vine growth. When ample soil moisture is available weed growth after midsummer is controlled only to prevent undue interference with the various vineyard operations.

Vinifera grapes do best in dry, warm-to-hot summers. Irrigation is required where the rainfall is insufficient or the soil too shallow to store sufficient water to meet the moisture requirements of the vine. The soil must be wetted as deep as the roots penetrate during the late fall, winter or early spring. After growth starts, irrigation is not needed until the vines have almost exhausted the available water in the soil area containing most of the roots. Irrigation should be repeated as often as this point is reached. The amount and frequency of the applications of water are determined by the texture and depth of the soil, climatic conditions and type of grapes grown.

Harvesting.—A grape is ripe when it has reached the stage best suited for the use to which it is to be put. The containers in which table grapes are moved to market and the methods of packing the fruit in the containers vary greatly from country to country. The least amount of handling that is consistent with thorough trimming and efficient packing is imperative. The sooner the grapes are cooled after picking, the better will be their quality when they reach the market. When grapes are to be shipped long distances or held in storage (at 31° F. [about 0° C.]) for prolonged periods, it is advisable to treat them with sulfur dioxide. In shipment, the sulfur dioxide is applied by displacing the air of the standard refrigerator car with sulfur dioxide diluted with air to a concentration of approximately 1.5% by volume. Grapes in cold storage are treated at given intervals by releasing .2% sulfur dioxide into the air as it enters the storage room. A sizable proportion of the crop is made into raisins (see RAISIN).

PESTS AND DISEASES

Pests.—The grapevine and its fruit are seriously attacked by a number of insects and diseases. In California and other arid regions there are fewer pests. The principal insects attacking the vine are the grape phylloxera (*Phylloxera vitifoliae*) and the root knot nematode (*Meloidogyne javanica*). They are combated by using resistant rootstocks. The grape leafhopper (*Erythroneura elegantula*) is controlled with DDT or other modern insecticides; the western grape root worm (*Adoxus obscurus*) and the grape leaf folder (*Desmia funeralis*) are controlled with Sevin, endrin or cryolite; and the spider mites (*Tetranychus pacifus* and *Tetranychus wilmetti*) can be controlled by some of the new organic phosphate miticides, either as dusts or sprays. In more humid regions there are in addition the berry moths (*Polychrosis botrana* and *Clysia ambiguella*) and various beetles and caterpillars. They may be controlled with DDT, arsenicals, toxaphene or Sevin.

Diseases.—Diseases affecting the grape under arid conditions are powdery mildew (*Uncinula necator*), prevented by dusting sulfur on all green parts of the vine; and black measles, caused by *Fomes igniarius*, which can be controlled by sodium arsenite spray while the vines are dormant. Under humid conditions the grape is attacked by black rot (*Guignardia bidwelli*), anthracnose (*Gloeosporium ampelophagum*) and downy mildew (*Plasmopara viticola*), which are controlled with Bordeaux sprays or organic fungicides; *Cryptosporella viticola*, which is controlled with sodium arsenite or captan; and numerous minor diseases.

A number of viruses infect the vine. Fanleaf (infectious degeneration), Yellow Mosaic, Pierce's disease and leaf roll do extensive damage in many grape areas. There is no cure. Much can be done to prevent spread by the careful selection of buds and cuttings. Selection of vines for cuttings is most effective when the vines are observed in late spring and again when the crop is almost mature. An important project in the University of California's college of agriculture, at Davis, is the production of virus-free planting stock of grapes.

PRODUCTION

Acreage devoted to cultivation of grapes averaged more than 3,350,000 in the late 1960s in France, Italy and Spain; more than 1,000,000 in Turkey and the U.S.S.R.; and more than 500,000 in Algeria, Argentina, Greece, Hungary, Portugal, Rumania, Yugoslavia and the U.S. Countries with more than 100,000 ac. of vines include Afghanistan, Australia, Brazil, Bulgaria, Chile, Germany, Iran, Morocco, Syria and South Africa.

The larger areas of grape production in eastern North America border on the Great Lakes around Ontario, Can., and in the U.S. in New York, Pennsylvania, Ohio and Michigan. Districts of less importance are in Missouri, Arkansas, Iowa and Washington, with scattered plantings in almost every other state. The Concord is the variety most extensively grown.

California, with the principal grape-growing state of the U.S., produces about 3% of the wines of the world, and leads all countries in the production of table grapes (20%) and raisins (40%).

See RAISIN; WINE; FRUIT; FRUIT FARMING; HORTICULTURE AND GARDENING; and references under "Grape" in the Index.

BIBLIOGRAPHY.—U. P. Hedrick, *The Grapes of New York* (1908); Karl Müller, *Weinbaulexikon* (1930); P. Viala and V. Vermorel, *Traité général de viticulture amᴘelographie* (1909); M. B. Hoffman, "Grape Production in New York," *New York Agricultural Experiment Station Bulletin 375* (1937); "Growing Grapes in Washington," *Washington Agricultural Experiment Station Extension Bulletin 271* (1951); "Grape Growing in Kansas," *Kansas Agricultural Experiment Station Circular 248* (1949); C. A. Magoon and E. Snyder, "Grapes for Different Regions," *U.S. Department of Agriculture Farmers' Bulletin 1936* (1943); L. M. Smith and E. M. Stafford, "Grape Pests in California," *California Agricultural Experiment Station Extension Circular 445* (1955); A. L. Quaintance and C. L. Shear, "Insects and Fungus Enemies of the Grape," *U.S. Department of Agriculture Farmers' Bulletin 1220* (1926); A. J. Winkler, *General Viticulture* (1962).
(A. J. W.; X.)

GRAPEFRUIT (*Citrus paradisi*), also known as pomelo, a tree and its citrus fruit, belonging to the family Rutaceae. It is probably an offshoot of the pummelo or shaddock (*q.v.*). Certainly the grapefruit and pummelo are closely related, and some students consider it probable that the grapefruit originated from the pummelo as a mutation.

History.—In 1814 John Lunan in his *Hortus Jamaicensis* mentioned that there was a small variety of the shaddock resembling the grape in flavour. The place of origin of the grapefruit is not certain, but it probably originated in Jamaica, for, in spite of careful search, it has not been found native in southeastern Asia or in the East Indian archipelago, where the pummelo is widely grown, or in any other region where any other *Citrus* species is native. As a fruit for home consumption, grapefruit became well established in the islands of the West Indies before its culture spread to the mainland.

Plant and Fruit Characteristics.—The grapefruit tree grows to be as large and vigorous as an orange tree; a mature tree may be from 15 to 20 ft. high. The foliage is very dense, leaves dark shiny green, larger than those of sweet orange but smaller than those of the pummelo, nearly glabrous, with petioles broadly winged. Flowers are large, white, borne singly, or in clusters in the axils of the leaves; petals are similar to those of sweet orange but usually larger. The fruit, which is lemon-yellow when ripe, ranges from four to six inches in diameter and averages twice as large as a medium-sized orange, the size depending upon the variety and upon cultural conditions; the pulp is usually of a light yellowish colour, somewhat intermediate between that of the orange and that of the lemon, tender and usually very full of juice, with a distinctive mildly acid, very pleasing flavour. Several varieties, originated by bud mutations, have pink or red pulp of varying intensity of colour; some of these varieties have a slightly pinkish cheek overlying the normal yellow colour of the peel.

The total soluble solids of the juice (principally sugars) increases during fruit growth and development and at maturity usually varies from 8% to 12% (fresh-weight basis). The concentration of the total acidity of the juice gradually decreases during fruit growth and, at maturity, the fruit may contain from 1% to 1.4% total acids (fresh-weight basis). The grapefruit is richer as a source of vitamin C than most of the fruits and vegetables normally consumed by man; it is exceeded only by the orange and the lemon. The vitamin C content of grapefruit juice depends upon the variety, soil fertility and the season of the year when the fruit is picked; it may average from 39 to 47 mg. per 100 grams. Early in the season of maturity, the vitamin C content is higher than it is later.

Varieties.—At least 23 varieties of grapefruit with normal-coloured pulp and 4 varieties with pink or reddish pulp have been propagated in the United States. Most of the fruit produced in the U.S. is of either the Marsh (seedless) or Duncan (seedy), yellowish-pulp varieties. The Ruby and Webb are the principal varieties having red pulp; the actual quality of these varieties is comparable to that of the normal-coloured varieties, and they have become increasingly popular in the fresh-fruit market because of their attractive appearance, for use at banquets and other social functions.

The grapefruit hybridizes readily with other species of *Citrus*. The tangelo, an intrageneric hybrid, is the result of a cross between the mandarin orange (some varieties of which are known as tangerines) and the grapefruit (also known as pomelo). One of the most promising of these hybrids, the Sampson tangelo, was produced in 1897, in Florida, by W. T. Swingle, an investigator employed at the time by the United States department of agriculture. This fruit has considerable merit as a juice fruit and as a source of seed for rootstock purposes.

Culture and Handling.—Grapefruit trees thrive and produce the best quality fruit on sandy but relatively fertile soils. Supplementary fertilization is necessary in practically all the producing areas in the U.S.

In addition to the usual nitrogen, phosphorus and potassium, the fertilizers or sprays should contain supplementary nutrients, or microelements in the form of copper, manganese, zinc, iron and boron. In Florida the area of greatest grapefruit production is on the light sandy soils which require additional micronutrients applied as a fertilizer to the soil or as a spray to the foliage. The trees come into bearing early and may be expected to produce commercially profitable crops by the fourth to sixth year after being planted in the orchard. Mature trees may produce remarkably large crops—1,300 to 1,500 lb. of fruit per tree. Culture and pest-control problems of grapefruit are comparable to those of other citrus crops (*see* LEMON and ORANGE).

By the early 1960s about 90% of world production was in the United States, concentrated in Florida, Texas, Arizona and California. Grapefruit has become popular as a breakfast fruit in various parts of the world and production has expanded to other citrus-growing countries, notably Israel, Jordan, South Africa and Brazil.

Production and Use.—The rapid expansion of grapefruit acreage in the U.S. caused serious problems in the sale and distribution of the fruit. Fresh fruit from Florida and Texas is not available throughout the entire year. The season of shipment is primarily from late fall to early spring, with the peak of the marketing season in midwinter. To avoid an overproduction at one period, and a shortage of grapefruit at another, the preservation of the fruit by canning and freezing developed into important industries. The two products which have taken most of the fruit off the fresh-fruit market are the juice and the prepared segments. The latter product is very frequently used as a basis for salad making. The segments may be packed in sugar syrup. More than half of the crop produced in the United States is marketed in canned or frozen form. This makes grapefruit available to the general public the year round and is an important service to both the consumer and the producer of this popular fruit. The processing of grapefruit juice is comparable to that of orange juice. It is sometimes advisable to add cane or beet sugar to grapefruit juice as it is canned. The yield of grapefruit juice under factory conditions will approximate 70 to 90 gal. per 2,000 lb. of fruit.

See also FRUIT FARMING.

BIBLIOGRAPHY.—W. T. Swingle, "The Botany of Citrus and Its Wild Relatives of the Orange Subfamily (Family Rutaceae, Subfamily Aurantioideae)," *The Citrus Industry*, vol. i, ch. iv (1943); T. R. Robinson, "Grapefruit and Pummelo," *Econ. Bot.*, 6:228 (1953).
(L. D. B.; W. B. Sr.)

GRAPE HYACINTH, the name given to any species of *Muscari*, a genus of the lily family (Liliaceae, *q.v.*), comprising about 50 species, natives chiefly of the Mediterranean region and southwest Asia. They are small bulbous plants with narrow fleshy basal leaves and small usually blue urn-shaped or globose flowers, nodding or pendulous, in a more or less dense cluster terminating a single flowering stalk.

The common grape hyacinth (*M. botryoides*), called also grape-flower, babies'-breath and bluebell, widely cultivated in gardens, is

GRAPE HYACINTH (MUSCARI BOTRY-OIDES)

native to southern Europe and western Asia and has run wild in meadows and thickets in the eastern United States. It has narrow erect leaves about as long as the flower stalk, which latter usually grows from 4 in. to 12 in. high, bearing at the top many globose blue, or in some varieties white, or pink, faintly scented flowers, about $\frac{1}{8}$ in. long, crowded in a cluster.

The starch grape hyacinth (*M. racemosum*), native to Europe and found in sandy fields in England and Scotland, has become naturalized in the eastern United States. It grows about a foot high and bears numerous blue flowers. About a dozen other species are cultivated, notably the musk hyacinth (*M. moschatum*), the tassel hyacinth (*M. comosum*) and the beautiful feather hyacinth (*M. comosum monstrosum*). The latter two produce mostly sterile flowers. All make sheets of colour when naturalized en masse in the lawn.

The bulbs should be planted in early autumn about three inches deep and three inches apart in rich light soil. (N. Tr.; X.)

GRAPE SUGAR: see CARBOHYDRATES: *Monosaccharides:* D-*Glucose.*

GRAPH. A graph is a pictorial representation of a functional relationship. Whenever one variable is functionally related to another (that is, they vary together in some definite way), then the relationship may be geometrically realized in the form of a graph. Generally the easiest graphs to prepare are those involving two variables, each of which ranges over a segment of a line; thus $y = f(x)$, where $a \leq x \leq b$ and y is a real number. In a common example, y (the dependent variable) might represent sales of a cough medicine, and x (the independent variable) could represent the months of the year. A simple graph of the relationship covering a period of five years would probably show that sales rise during the colder months.

As the number of independent or dependent variables increases, the problem of graphing becomes more difficult and special techniques must be adopted to make a geometric display at all possible. If, for example, both x and y are complex numbers then a direct geometric representation would require a four-dimensional geometry. Techniques for geometric representation in such cases are an important topic in the theory of functions of a complex variable (*see* FUNCTION; ANALYSIS: *Functions*).

The advantage in producing a graph of a given function represented by an analytic expression (a formula of some kind, or a table of values) lies in helping people understand the consequences of a formula or column of many-digit numbers. Interest is usually focused on such basic geometric properties of the function as the zeros (roots) of the function, *i.e.,* places where $f(x) = 0$; the poles of the function, *i.e.,* where $1/f(x) = 0$; the maxima and minima of the function (fig. 1); and so on (*see* CRITICAL POINTS; STATISTICS).

Co-ordinate Systems.—Consider first a rectangular Cartesian co-ordinate system and a graph in such a system (*see* ANALYTIC GEOMETRY). Draw a horizontal straight line and at any convenient point on it erect a vertical line. The intersection point is called the origin and all measurements are referred to it. Lay off along each line the unit of measure appropriate to the corre-sponding variable, the independent real variable x being usually laid off along the horizontal line that is then called the x-axis; the vertical line becomes the y-axis. Now to each value x in the interval $a \leq x \leq b$ associate the geometric point at a distance x from the origin on the x-axis. Measure directly above the point x, just plotted, the distance $y = f(x)$ and mark this point; this is the point (x,y) on the curve being plotted. After a sufficient number of points have been plotted a smooth curve can be drawn connecting these points. This is the desired graph; it is the locus of points satisfying the functional relationship.

Note that the only choices available in setting up a rectangular system are the choices of the scales along the x- and y- axes. It is usual to choose them equal to each other and in multiples of a fixed unit, but this is not necessary. In fact, a very important type of graph is obtained when the distance laid off on one or the other axis is not the x or y variable itself but some function of that variable; a frequent choice for this function is the logarithm (*see* LOGARITHMS). Consider a type of one-dimensional graph or scale where the distances y for a number of different values, say $x_1, x_2,$ ... are laid off on a line from a given origin. The corresponding points $y_1 = f(x_1)$, $y_2 = f(x_2)$, ... may be relabeled as $x_1, x_2,$ ... as is done, *e.g.,* on the face of a slide rule where the function f is the logarithm to the base 10.

If there is a logarithmic scale on the y-axis and a uniform scale on the x-axis, the graph is semilogarithmic; with logarithms plotted on both axes, the graph is logarithmic. A semilogarithmic graph is most convenient for a function of the form $y = 10^x$ since such a graph is a straight line in this co-ordinate system; similarly a logarithmic graph yields a straight line for a function of the form $y = x^a$ (*see* fig. 2). In general semilogarithmic graphs are made if a small absolute error in one variable results in a small relative error in the other one; logarithmic graphs are desirable if a small relative error in one variable results in a small relative error in one.

In the polar co-ordinate system (fig. 3) a fixed point 0 and a fixed horizontal line A emanating from it are given. To locate a point (r,ϕ) in this system, a new line is drawn through 0 making the angle ϕ with line A and the distance r is measured along the new line.

These co-ordinate systems are two-dimensional. The rectangular Cartesian systems generalize to three dimensions when a z-axis is added. The polar co-ordinate systems have two possible generalizations; one is to spherical co-ordinates with two independent angular co-ordinates and a radial one; the other is to cylindrical co-ordinates with one angular co-ordinate and a radial one (both in a plane) and one rectangular co-ordinate perpendicular to the plane.

Graphic Solutions: Implicit Functions.—Graphs can be used in visualizing mathematical functions and in quickly obtaining estimates for solutions of functional equations (*see* NOMOGRAPHY). For example, suppose the solution is sought for two linear equations in two unknowns. Each equation can be graphed as a straight line and the geometric or graphic statement of the problem is to find the intersection point of the two lines. Similarly if the solutions are sought of the system $f(x) = 0$, $g(x) = 0$, graphs are made of $y = f(x)$ and $y = g(x)$ and these curves are inspected for simultaneous zeros (roots). To find the values of x for which $f(x) = g(x)$ the curves $y = f(x)$, $y = g(x)$ are graphed

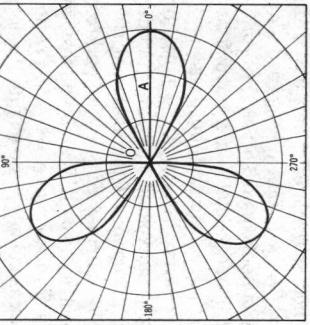

FIG. 1.—SOME GEOMETRIC PROPERTIES OF A FUNCTION. THE FUNCTION $y = f(x)$ HAS ROOTS AT x_1 AND x_4, RELATIVE MINIMA AT x_2 AND x_6, A RELATIVE MAXIMUM AT x_3 AND A POLE AT x_5

FIG. 2.—THE GRAPH OF $y = 49x^{1.61}$ IN LOGARITHMIC CO-ORDINATES

FIG. 3.—THE GRAPH OF $r = \cos 3\phi$ IN POLAR CO-ORDINATES

and their intersections noted as in fig. 4.

In the 1960s, with a large variety of computing instruments (*see* COMPUTER) available to the applied mathematician, the importance of graphic methods has diminished. In principle, however, many of the most important numerical techniques may be used graphically, and in fact arose from graphic methods. To illustrate, consider the method of false position. Draw the graph of $y = f(x)$ near a zero of f and choose two approximants x_1 and x_2 to the zero x_0 of f. Join by a straight line the two points $\{x_1, y_1 = f(x_1)\}$, $\{x_2, y_2 = f(x_2)\}$. Designate the point where this line crosses the x-axis as x_3. Naturally, x_3 is a better approximation to x_0 than either x_1 or x_2. Then, in general, choose two approximants x_1 and x_2 to the zero x_0 of f. A related method is the Newton-Raphson procedure: given now an approximation x_1 to x_0, construct at the point (x_1,y_1) the tangent line to the graph $y = f(x)$ and designate the point where this crosses the x-axis by x_2. This is an iterative method for approximating the true root x_0 as closely as desired, and converges much faster than the method of false position.

Graphic Solutions: Differential Equations.—To solve a differential equation of the form $f(x,y,y') = 0$, where $y' = dy/dx$ a very good preliminary orientation with regard to the over-all shapes of the curves and some of the more basic properties of the solutions is available through simple graphic means. For example, consider the family of curves $f(x,y,a) = 0$, where a is an arbitrary parameter; these curves are called isoclinals. In general for each a there is a curve in this family and at each point of such a curve the solution of the differential equation has slope a. If the general shape of the solution of the differential equation is wanted, start at a point on an isoclinal determined by a particular a and draw a very short line in the direction a; it meets a nearby isoclinal determined by a neighbouring value a' to a. There proceed in the direction a'; and so on. The curve so drawn is a locus of points satisfying $f(x,y,y') = 0$ and hence is a solution. In this way the family of isoclinals as well as the integral curves or solutions can be mapped out in the x,y-plane.

It is occasionally convenient also to graph the points where the integral curves have maxima and minima; this locus is given by the equation $f(x,y,0) = 0$, i.e., $y' = 0$.

These techniques are useful for preliminary first orientation but are generally not good enough for detailed study of a particular solution. In this event good graphic techniques are also available. Suppose the solution of $y' = f(x,y)$ through x_0,y_0 is sought. First draw the line through that point with slope $y_0' = f(x_0,y_0)$. This line determines at $x_1 = x_0 + \Delta x$ a new point (x_1,y_1) on the curve. At this point recalculate the slope $y_1' = f(x_1,y_1)$ and proceed as before. In case this method is too crude it may be refined as follows. The curve just obtained can be used to graph a curve for y' as a function of x. Using a planimeter or some other means, this can be integrated and a new approximation can be found to the solution. This can be repeated, and increasingly accurate approximations obtained.

For fuller discussions of the use of graphic methods in mathematical analysis and in the communication of empirical data *see* P. H. Hill, *Problems in Graphical Analysis* (1959); C. F. Schmid, *Handbook of Graphic Presentation* (1954).

(H. H. GE.)

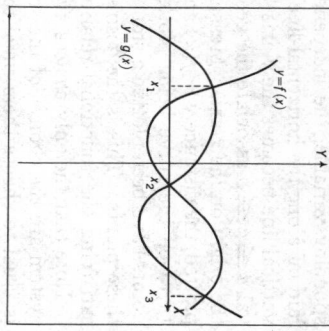

FIG. 4.—INTERSECTIONS OF TWO FUNCTIONS: $f(x) = g(x)$ AT x_1, x_2 AND x_3

GRAPHITE, a mineral consisting of the element carbon, crystallizing in the hexagonal system, in contrast to the same element crystallizing in the cubic system as diamond. Usually such dimorphous pairs are rather similar in their physical properties, but not so in this case. Graphite is black, opaque and very soft (hardness = 1); diamond may be colourless and transparent, and is the hardest naturally occurring substance known. Graphite is a good conductor of electricity; diamond is a poor conductor. The specific gravity of graphite is 2.2, and for diamond, 3.5. Diamond has a perfect octahedral cleavage, while graphite has basal cleavage. Graphite crystals are rare, and only occasionally are six-sided plates found. The plates or cleavage flakes are flexible but not elastic. Graphite has a greasy feel and rubs off on anything it touches, leaving a black mark, thus the name from the Greek verb *graphein*, "to write." The lustre is bright metallic, black lead, bears a striking resemblance in many physical properties to molybdenite (q.v.), consisting of molybdenum disulfide, which also has a greasy feel and is soft enough to write on paper.

Although differing so markedly from diamond in physical properties, graphite has a closely related structure. In both minerals each carbon atom is bonded to four adjacent carbon atoms. In diamond these four strong bonds are arranged tetrahedrally, giving great strength in three dimensions. In graphite, three equal bonds lie nearly in the horizontal plane, while the fourth is weaker and is in a vertical position. Thus while there is good bonding in two dimensions, it is lacking in the third, and allows easy separation into thin sheets.

Graphite occurs mainly in the older crystalline rocks, gneiss, schist, quartzite and marble; sometimes in granite and pegmatites; and is found as isolated scales embedded in these rocks, or as large masses or vein fillings. It has also been observed as a product of contact metamorphism in carbonaceous clay slates near their contact with granite, and where igneous rocks have been intruded into beds of coal; in these cases the mineral has clearly been derived from organic matter. The graphite found in granite and in veins in gneiss, as well as that contained in meteoric irons, cannot have had such an origin. As an artificial product, graphite is well known as scales in gray pig iron, and in the graphitic powder, or "kish," that forms in iron furnaces; it is also produced artificially on a large scale in electric furnaces. The graphite veins in the older crystalline rocks are probably akin to metalliferous veins and the material derived from deep-seated sources. The decomposition of metallic carbides and the reduction of hydrocarbon vapours have been suggested as possible modes of origin. Graphite veins often reach a thickness of several feet, and sometimes possess a columnar structure perpendicular to the enclosing walls. These are found in the crystalline limestones and other Laurentian rocks of New York and Canada, in the gneisses of the Austrian Alps and of Ceylon. Important occurrences in addition to the Austrian Alps (West Germany, Austria) and Ceylon include the island of Madagascar, Mexico, Norway, Republic of Korea and the U.S.S.R. (the western Siberian platform).

(L. S. RL.)

Natural Graphite Production.—Most natural graphite, both flake and amorphous, is recovered from shallow open-pit mines by stripping the overburden, and removing the graphite-bearing rock with power shovels and trucks. In Ceylon, Mexico and North Korea, however, where the graphite veins are folded or dip steeply, underground mining is required. Because of the nature of its occurrence, graphite must be subject to a refining process. The character of the graphite in a particular deposit and its intended use determine the extent of refining. Flake graphite is processed by wet and dry grinding to remove the larger impurities, and flotation removes the remaining impurities. The flotation product is filtered, dried and passed over an air table to obtain a uniform product. Amorphous graphite is processed by grinding and air separation except in Ceylon, where there is a preliminary hand sorting at the mine and later grading by combined manual and machine methods. Refined natural graphite contains at best 90% to 98% carbon, with the major part containing 90% to 94% carbon. The original dis-

Manufactured Graphite Production.—The

BENJAMIN M. SHAUB

SPECIMEN OF NATURAL GRAPHITE FROM CEYLON, A MAJOR PRODUCER

covery that graphite could be manufactured was made by Edward G. Acheson (q.v.) while experimenting with the effect of high temperatures on carborundum or silicon carbide (q.v.). It was found that carborundum decomposed at about 7,500° F. (4,107 C.), the silicon being vaporized and the carbon being left behind in the graphitic form. In 1896 Acheson was granted a patent for the manufacture of graphite, and commercial production began in 1897. Petroleum coke, anthracite culm (hard coal dust) or mixtures of carbon, quartz, sand and sawdust were used as late as 1918 to produce manufactured graphite. Since 1918, however, petroleum coke, which consists of small imperfect crystals of graphite surrounded by organic compounds, has been almost the only raw material utilized. After heating until all the volatile material has been driven off the remaining product, graphite, with a carbon content of 99% to 99.5% or better, is cooled, pulverized and graded to uniform sizes.

Uses.—The value of graphite to industry is based upon suitable application of one or more of its inherent qualities, such as unctuousness, or plastic qualities; refractoriness, or ability to withstand high temperatures; conductivity of heat and electricity; inertness to a large range of reagents; and miscibility with other materials and liquids. The most important uses of natural graphite are in lubricants, crucibles, foundry facings, shoe and stove polishes, brake linings, pencils, packings, steelmaking, batteries and carbon brushes.

Manufactured graphite competes with natural graphite in some uses, among which are lubricants, foundry facings, pencils, polishes, batteries and carbon brushes.

Only manufactured graphite of a purity of better than 99.5% is suitable for use as a reactor moderator, for which it is used more extensively than any other material, and as structural material in atomic energy plants. Other major uses are in electrodes, electrolytic cells, bushings, disks, electrical contacts and furnace linings.

See ATOMIC ENERGY: *Achievement of a Chain Reaction;* CARBON; FURNACE, ELECTRIC; PENCIL; *see* also references under "Graphite" in the Index volume.

BIBLIOGRAPHY.—E. G. Acheson, "Graphite Its Formation and Manufacture," *Jour. Franklin Inst.,* pp. 475-486 (1899); J. F. Fletcher and W. A. Snyder, "Use of Graphite in the Atomic Energy Program," *Bull. Am. Ceram. Soc.,* vol. 36, no. 3, pp. 101-104 (March 1957); C. L. Mantell, *Industrial Carbon* (1946); G. R. Gwinn, "Graphite for the Manufacture of Crucibles," *Min. Tech.* (July 1945, trans. 1947); "Graphite," *Industrial Minerals and Rocks,* pp. 415-435 (1949); W. C. Kalb (ed.), *Carbon, Graphite and Metal Graphite Brushes* (1946); Speer Carbon Co., *Black Magic, The Story of Manufactured Carbon* (1949); H. Spatzek and G. Frank, "Austrian Graphite Miners Use New Chemical and Flotation Methods," *Mining World,* vol. 18, no. 6, pp. 56-59 (June 1956). (G. R. G.)

GRAPHOLOGY: see HANDWRITING.

GRAPHOLITE, a class, Graptozoa or Graptolithina, of extinct colonial marine animals of uncertain relationship. They are preserved most commonly on bedding planes of black shale as flattened, leaflike, twiglike or weblike films of carbon that resemble pencil marks—the name is from the Greek meaning "written stone." Their remains are restricted to the lower half of the Paleozoic era with greatest abundance in the Ordovician and Silurian periods during the interval from about 500,000,000 to 350,000,000 years ago.

Uncrushed examples showing fine details of structure, *e.g.,* impressions of muscle attachment are occasionally found in limestone and flint, and may be recovered by acid dissolution of the rock matrix surrounding the remarkably resistant chitinous skeletal material.

Many groups of graptolites show marked evolutionary changes in time, and many species are diagnostic of restricted time units. They therefore are important as indicators of geologic age. Four successive graptolite faunas are recognized over the world, each in characteristic stages of evolutionary development. From older to younger, these are: Anisograptid, Dichograptid, Diplograptid and Monograptid faunas. The first three occur in the Ordovician, the last in the Silurian. They are further subdivided by O. M. B. Bulman into nine chronological subfaunas and many zones of local extent.

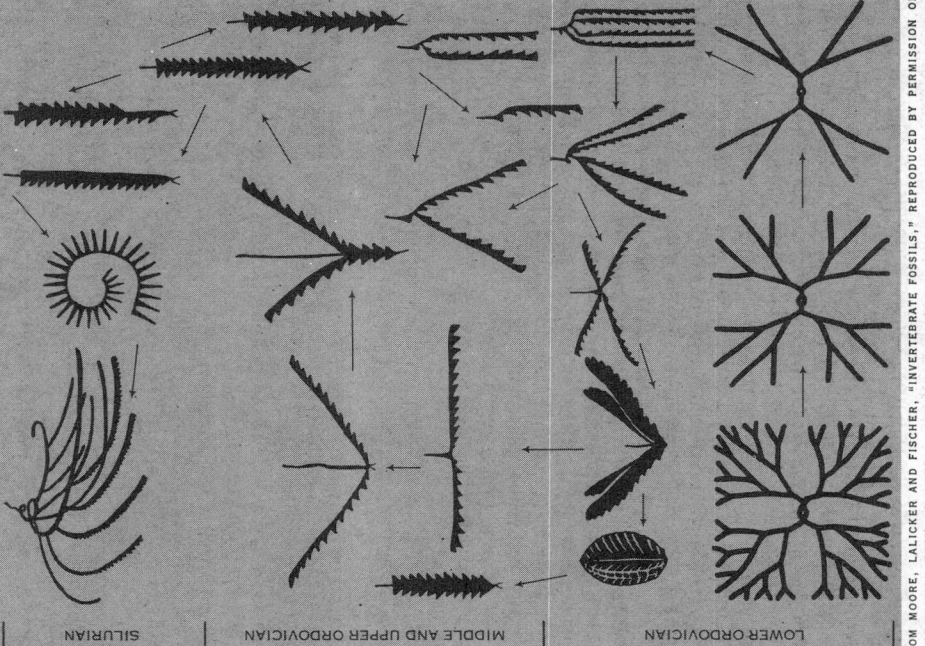

SILURIAN

MIDDLE AND UPPER ORDOVICIAN

LOWER ORDOVICIAN

FROM MOORE, LALICKER AND FISCHER, "INVERTEBRATE FOSSILS," REPRODUCED BY PERMISSION OF MCGRAW-HILL BOOK CO., INC.

EVOLUTIONARY TRENDS OF GRAPTOLITE COLONIES DURING THE ORDOVICIAN AND SILURIAN PERIODS SHOWING CHANGES IN NUMBER AND POSITION OF BRANCHES

The growth habit and form, deduced from preserved specimens, indicate that the first individual of a graptolite colony was the conical sicula, which was attached to the sea bottom by a flexible stalk or was suspended by a chitinous thread (the nema) to a floating object. One or more series of successive cuplike buds (thecae) comprised the branches (stipes), whose growth direction is characteristic of particular genera and species. One or both edges of each stipe may be saw-toothed.

Evolution of graptolites was characterized by persistent tendencies or trends that affected independent groups (*see* figure). These tendencies include progressive reduction in the number of stipes from many to one during the Ordovician; gradual changes in the direction of stipe growth from downward (pendent) to upward along the nema (scandent); and elaboration of the apertures of the thecae.

Most of the primitive graptolites, the tiny bushlike Dendroidea, with thickened stems and expanded attachment bases, apparently were attached to the sea floor. Their weblike remains usually are associated with the fossils of bottom-dwelling organisms of shallow waters and are restricted in geographic distribution; but *Dictyonema flabelliforme,* one of the most advanced and most widely distributed species of the group, probably lived suspended from floating objects which carried it throughout the world.

It is believed that the more advanced graptolites of the order Graptoloidea also were attached to floating seaweeds, the decomposition of which supplied carbonaceous material to the fine-grained black shales in which graptolites are so characteristically found.

The biological affinities of the graptolites are in doubt. The chitinous exoskeleton reflects little of the original anatomy, leaving as evidence only the form and mode of colony development. Graptolites have been considered members of such divergent groups as sponges, corals, plants, bryozoans, cephalopods, coelenterates and pterobranches; however, only the last two groups deserve serious consideration as possible graptolite relatives.

The comprehensive work of R. Kozlowski in 1948 pointed to discovery of supposed nematothecae (cups bearing nematocysts or stinging cells) in Cambrian graptolites, tended to regard them as specialized coelenterates.

BIBLIOGRAPHY.—Birger Bohlin, "The Affinities of the Graptolites," Bull. geol. Instr. Univ. Uppsala, vol. 34 (1950); O. M. B. Bulman, "Graptolithina," pt. v, Treatise on Invertebrate Paleontology (1955) and "The Sequence of Graptolite Faunas," Palaeontology, vol. 1 (1958); R. R. Shrock and W. H. Twenhofel, Principles of Invertebrate Paleontology (1953). (N. D. N.)

GRASMERE, a village and lake of Westmorland, Eng., is in the heart of the Lake district (q.v.). Pop. (1951) 1,043. The village lies near the head of the lake, 13 mi. S.S.E. of Keswick and 4 mi. N.W. of Ambleside. The valley is very beautiful and almost encircled by mountains. To the north the road to Keswick climbs the Dunmail Raise pass, and to the southeast the road to Ambleside follows the Rothay river which flows into Grasmere. On the south is Loughrigg fell and on the west Silver How, beyond which is Easdale, a subsidiary valley. The village still preserves some of its picturesque appearance, though developed as a tourist centre, and the neighbourhood has become residential since William Wordsworth and his sister Dorothy settled at Dove cottage in 1799. There Wordsworth brought his wife and they remained in the district the rest of their lives. The cottage (later the home of Thomas de Quincey) and the adjacent Wordsworth museum are open on weekdays. St. Oswald's church is architecturally curious, but unassuming. In the churchyard are the graves of the Wordsworth family and of Hartley Coleridge, son of S. T. Coleridge. The Rushbearing, an ancient custom, is observed annually on the Saturday nearest St. Oswald's day, Aug. 5, and Grasmere sports, an athletics meeting with a local flavour, is held on the third Thursday after August bank holiday.

The lake of Grasmere is oval in shape, being about 1 mi. long and ½ mi. broad, with an island in the middle. (B. L. T.)

GRASSE, capital of an arrondissement in the département of Alpes-Maritimes (till 1860 in that of Var), France, 12½ mi. N.N.W. of Cannes by rail. Pop. (1962) 25,161. Grasse is built in an amphitheatre at a height of 1,066 ft., on a south slope facing the Mediterranean. It possesses a mild climate and is well supplied with water. The town is particularly celebrated for its perfumes, and the distilling of essences is its chief industrial activity. For this purpose roses and other flowers and oranges are cultivated abundantly in the neighbourhood. The town also manufactures wax, soap and olive oil. There are a subprefecture and a tribunal of commerce.

From 1244 to 1790 Grasse was an episcopal see; thereafter it was included in the diocese of Fréjus till 1860, when the region was annexed to the newly formed département of Alpes-Maritimes. The town has a 12th-century cathedral, now a simple parish church, and an ancient tower of uncertain date near the 13th-century town hall (formerly the bishop's palace). The library contains the muniments of the abbey of Lérins, on the island of St. Honorat opposite Cannes. The town has a Fragonard museum (Fragonard was born there), and in the chapel of the old hospital are three pictures by Rubens.

GRASSE, FRANÇOIS JOSEPH PAUL, MARQUIS DE GRASSE-TILLY, COMTE DE (1722–1788), French naval commander who engaged British forces during the American Revolutionary War, was born at Bar (Alpes Maritimes). In 1734 he took service on the galleys of the order of Malta, and in 1740 entered the French service. Shortly after France and the United States joined forces in the Revolutionary War, he was dispatched to America as commander of a squadron.

In 1779–80 De Grasse fought the English off the West Indies. In 1781 he was promoted to the rank of admiral and was successful in defeating Adm. Samuel Hood and in taking Tobago. When Washington and Rochambeau determined to march to Virginia to join forces with Lafayette's army against Cornwallis, Washington requested the co-operation of De Grasse's fleet. De Grasse therefore sailed from the Indies to the Chesapeake river, where he was joined by a fleet under Count de Barras. A British force under Adm. Thomas Graves attempted to prevent this juncture by engaging De Grasse's fleet when it arrived at the Chesapeake but was unsuccessful. French naval supremacy in the waters off Yorktown was instrumental in the success of the siege of that city.

After Cornwallis' surrender, De Grasse returned to the West Indies, where he captured the island of St. Kitts in Jan. 1782. In April, however, he was defeated by Admiral Rodney and taken prisoner. On his return to France, he published a Mémoire justificatif and was acquitted by a court-martial in 1784. He died in Paris, Jan. 11, 1788.

GRASSES. Of all the groups of flowering plants (angiosperms; q.v.) none is of greater importance to man, or more widespread, than the grasses. Although only those plants that belong to the large family Gramineae (or Poaceae) may properly be called grasses, the term grass is commonly used for many other plants, of widely different families, that superficially resemble true grasses in their foliage; e.g., knotgrass (Polygonaceae), cotton grass (Cyperaceae), rib grass (Plantaginaceae), blue-eyed grass (Iridaceae), yellow-eyed grass (Xyridaceae), star grass (Amaryllidaceae), bear grass (Liliaceae) and eelgrass (Potamogetonaceae). The grass tree of Australia, a desert plant allied to the lilies and rushes, has a tall, unbranched, soft-woody, palmlike trunk which bears a crown of long, narrow, grasslike leaves and stalked heads of small densely crowded flowers. In agriculture the word "grass" has an extended significance in that it may include the various forage plants, especially the legumes.

Grasses were recognized as a natural group long before there was a science of botany or a system of classification. Common lawn, pasture and meadow grasses such as bluegrass, bent grass, timothy and fescue are the best known, and the wild prairie grasses and such weeds as crab grass and quack grass also are familiar. The grains or cereals, such as wheat, rice, oats, barley and corn (maize), are also true grasses, as are sugar cane, sorghum and millet, and even the giant woody-stemmed bamboos.

Geographic Distribution.—The Gramineae are the world's most universally distributed flowering plants. R. Pool estimated in 1948 that perhaps 30% of the land vegetation of the globe is dominated by grasses, or at least may be classified as potential grassland. Probably the best-known and most extensive of these areas are the steppes of Asia and the prairies and plains of North America. Other regions in which grasses are dominant, although sometimes mixed with scattered trees, are to be found in South America, Africa and Australia. In number of species the Gramineae are far exceeded by the Compositae, Orchidaceae and Leguminosae, but with respect to numbers of individuals, grasses hold undisputed first place. Numerous species, moreover, have such wide ranges that the proportion of grasses to other families in the various floras of the world is much higher than the number of species would indicate.

Species of grasses are most numerous in the savannas of the tropics, but the number of individuals is greatest in temperate and cold regions of the world. As the colder latitudes are approached, grasses become relatively more numerous, and in arctic and antarctic regions they comprise about one-fourth of all the species. They reach the limits of vegetation, except for some lichens and algae, in the polar regions and on mountaintops. Indeed, on all the great mountain systems of the world, grasses are the dominant plants above timber line. They are dominant also in arid regions, as well as on sand dunes, in salt marshes and in other places where conditions for plant life are exceedingly severe. Grasses are essentially plants of the open and are rarely seen in dense forests. A few broad-leaved species grow on the forest floor in the tropics, and in temperate regions, also, there are a few woodland grasses.

Some species of grasses are almost cosmopolitan, such as the common reed, Phragmites communis. A number of others are found throughout the warm regions of the earth; e.g., Hackelochloa gramularis, *Eleusine indica, Cynodon dactylon* and such weeds as *Echinochloa* and *Setaria*. In contrast to these wide-ranging grasses are the relatively few genera with extremely limited distribution. Examples of such endemics are *Anomochloa* of Brazil, *Opizia* of Mexico and *Buergersiochloa* of New Guinea.

STRUCTURE

Grasses, even when not in flower, may be recognized and readily distinguished from members of other plant families by the following structural features. The stems are jointed, hollow as in wheat or oats, or pithy as in maize, sugar cane and sorghum. The leaves are alternate in two ranks, and consist of two parts, the sheath and the blade. The sheath surrounds the stem like a tube but is usually open along one side, and the blade is more or less divergent. At the junction of the sheath and blade there is usually a small membranous organ (sometimes represented only by hairs, or missing) known as the ligule. Members of the closely related sedge family are often confused with grasses, but for the most part they have solid triangular stems on which the leaves are borne in three ranks. The leaf sheath, moreover, is always closed and the ligule is lacking.

Root.—In grasses the roots are fibrous and are often much branched and widely spreading. These, in combination with underground and creeping aerial stems, serve to anchor the plants firmly in the soil. Roots of many grasses are extensive, and in some species the roots of a single plant, if dug up and placed end to end, would total a length of several miles. These extensive root systems enable grasses to hold the soil in position against the forces of water and wind, thus rendering them of great value in the prevention of erosion and floods and in the reclamation of devastated areas.

The cord grasses (species of *Spartina*) are important soil builders, and many square miles of salt marshes have been reclaimed as a result of their presence. One species, *S. townsendi*, has been planted extensively along the coast of the Netherlands, where it is adding to the usable land area at a spectacular rate.

Stem.—In perennial grasses underground stems or rootstocks (rhizomes) are often well developed; they may be long and creeping as in quack grass (*Agropyron*) and marram or beach grass (*Ammophila*). That rhizomes are stems and not roots is evident from the fact that they have distinct joints (nodes) and sheathing scales (leaves), features that are lacking in roots. Rhizomes are always solid and the internal structure is that of the usual monocotyledonous stem.

Some grasses produce, instead of rhizomes, extensive horizontal stems that creep along the surface of the soil (stolons). An example of a stoloniferous species is buffalo grass (*Buchloë*) of the North American plains.

Both rhizomes and stolons, being stems, give off branches from their nodes, and adventitious roots are also formed. Thus each node is potentially capable of giving rise to a new plant. Grasses possessing these structures, and especially rhizomes, are able to form dense sod, and for this reason bluegrass (*Poa pratensis*) and bent grass (*Agrostis*) are valuable for lawns and golf greens. In the formation of rhizomes and stolons, which are really branches from the main shoot, these break directly through the sheath in the axil of which they originate. In other cases, the branches grow upward inside the sheath, which is ultimately pulled away from the parent culm. This latter mode of growth is seen in the tillering of cereals, and results in a tufted plant with many erect branches from the lower nodes of the young stem. It is also the manner of growth of the bunch grasses so common in arid grasslands.

The upright stems (culms) of grasses are usually cylindrical (rarely flattened) and conspicuously jointed. The nodes are always solid, whereas the internodes (fig. 1) are commonly hollow but occasionally solid as in maize and sugar cane. At the base of each internode there is an actively growing (meristematic) region in which the cells continue to divide for a considerable period, and this causes the stem to elongate. When the culms are forced into a horizontal position, because of the action of rain, wind, animals or other agents, they tend to rise again by bending at the nodes. This is accomplished by the action of a growth hormone (auxin), which, under the influence of gravity, tends to accumulate on the lower side of the stem, causing increased multiplication and enlargement of the cells. Auxin is present even when the culm is erect, but it is evenly distributed around the stem with the result that growth is uniform and no bending occurs.

The exterior of the culm, which is more or less concealed by the leaf sheaths, is usually smooth and often highly polished, the epidermal cells containing an amount of silica sufficient to leave, after burning, a distinct skeleton. A white siliceous material (tabasheer), found in the joints of several bamboos, was once thought to have medicinal properties. In some grasses a few of the lower nodes become swollen and subglobular, these functioning as storage organs.

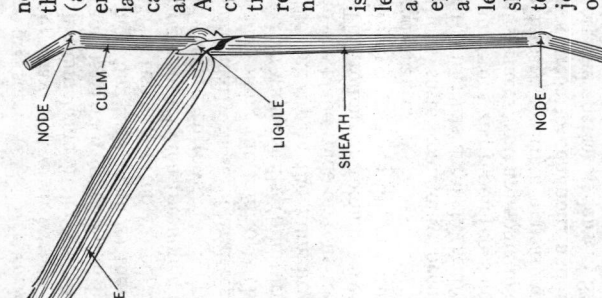

NODE

CULM

LIGULE

BLADE

SHEATH

NODE

FIG. 1.—INTERNODE OF A GRASS CULM WITH ITS LEAF (BLADE AND SHEATH)

Examples of such bulbous grasses are timothy (*Phleum*) and tall oat grass (*Arrhenatherum*).

Although many grasses produce only simple culms, branching from the upper nodes is not uncommon. Branches originate in the axils of sheaths and at the point of origin there is produced, on the side next to the parent culm, a characteristic two-keeled organ (prophyllum), which is the first leaf of the branch. Many tropical grasses are much branched, particularly the bamboos. *Dinochloa*, a Malaysian genus, is scandent and climbs over trees as much as 100 ft. in height.

Among grasses other than bamboos, *Olyra* and *Lasiacis* are also woody climbers, and their culms and branches often attain a length of many feet.

Grass culms grow with great rapidity. In bamboos a height of 25 ft. may be attained in a single month, and some species have been known to grow 2 or 3 ft. in a period of 24 hours.

Leaves.—These are borne singly at each node and are two-ranked, the leaf at each succeeding node being turned 180° from that immediately below. The leaf consists of two distinct portions, the sheath and the blade. The sheath encircles the stem and may be shorter or longer than the internode. It forms a firm protection for the internode, and particularly for the younger basal portion (growing zone or meristem), which remains delicate and fragile for a considerable period. As a rule the sheath is split down its entire length, but in a few grasses (species of *Poa, Bromus,* etc.) the margins are united. Occasionally the sheaths are much dilated, and in *Hygroryza*, a Malaysian aquatic, they actually serve as floats. At the summit of the sheath, at its junction with the blade, there is usually a small membranous appendage (sometimes an inch or more in length) called the ligule. In some species this organ is represented only by a tuft of hairs, while in others it is lacking altogether. In certain grasses (species of *Muhlenbergia* and others) in addition to the ligule there is a green, erect, tongue-like process extending upward from each margin of the sheath.

The blade is borne at the summit of the sheath and diverges from the culm at a more or less acute angle. In some cases there are produced, one on either side at the base of the blade, small outgrowths which tend to clasp the culm. These appendages, known as auricles, are most frequently seen among members of the tribe Hordeae. The usual form of the blade is familiar—sessile, more or less ribbon-shaped, tapering to a point and entire at the edge. In a few grasses, such as *Pharus, Pariana, Zeugites* and bamboos, there is a short petiole between the sheath and the blade. In most bamboos, moreover, the blade is articulated with the sheath, from which it is deciduous. Although most grasses have narrow linear leaves, there are some (e.g., *Streptochaeta, Olyra, Pharus*) in which the blade may be two inches or more wide and not more than twice this dimension in length. In all grass leaves, however, the venation is strictly parallel, although in a number with broad blades (including the bamboos) there are connecting cross veins as well. The tissue is often raised above the veins, forming longitudinal ridges, usually on the upper face; the stomata are in lines in the intervening furrows.

The blades of many grasses, particularly those of arid regions, are capable of rolling up or folding along the midrib. This is accomplished by means of large thin-walled cells (bulliform or motor cells) situated between the veins. As the humidity decreases, these cells lose water and the blade folds or rolls toward the leaf margin. This rolling or folding serves to protect the plant against excessive drying, since the majority of the stomata occur on the protected surface.

Epidermal appendages of various sorts commonly occur on blades and sheaths. Frequently the leaf has a rough (scabrous) texture, due to the presence of numerous sharp-pointed siliceous spicules. These may occur on all surfaces, and are sometimes of sufficient size and frequency to impart a serrate appearance to the leaf margin. Epidermal hairs are also common, and these may be weak or stiff, long or short and sparse or dense. Sometimes the base of the hair is enlarged and bulbous. Examples of extreme hairiness are found in the common velvet grass (*Holcus lanatus*) and *Alopecurus lanatus* of Asia Minor.

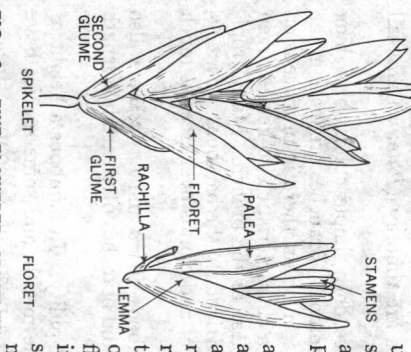

FIG. 2.—FIVE-FLOWERED SPIKELET OF FESTUCA AND A PARTIALLY OPENED FLORET

(Labels: SECOND GLUME, FIRST GLUME, SPIKELET, RACHILLA, FLORET, PALEA, LEMMA, STAMENS, FLORET)

Inflorescence.—In grasses the unit of the inflorescence is the spikelet and not a single flower as in the case of many other plants.

Spikelets, discussed below, almost never occur singly on a plant, but a number of them are aggregated to form an inflorescence. Familiar grass inflorescences are the tassel of maize, the head of wheat and the panicle of oats. The simplest type of inflorescence is the spike, as seen in wheat or rye, in which the spikelets are sessile along the main axis. A raceme differs from a spike in that the spikelets are pedicelled. Simple racemes are rare in grasses, an example being semaphore grass (*Pleuropogon*).

The commonest type of inflorescence found among grasses is the panicle, characterized by having pedicelled spikelets borne on a branching axis. Strictly defined, a panicle is a compound raceme, but in the Gramineae the term is applied to any branching inflorescence, even though some of the spikelets in the group may be quite sessile.

Panicles may be open and diffuse, as in bluegrass, or much contracted and spikelike, as in timothy. Sometimes the panicle branches are directed to one side, as in orchard grass or cockfoot (*Dactylis*) and dog's tail (*Cynosurus*). Spikes or racemes also may be asymmetrical, with spikelets borne on one side of the axis only, as in crab grass (*Digitaria*), cord grass (*Spartina*), and grama (*Bouteloua*).

The spikelet, as the name suggests, is itself a miniature inflorescence—a spike (fig. 2, 3). A generalized spikelet consists of a short axis (rachilla) bearing, in two-ranked arrangement, a series of modified leaves (bracts), some of which produce flowers in their axils. The two lowermost bracts, which are empty, are called glumes. These are not borne at precisely the same level, but one glume (lower or first glume) is slightly below the other (upper or second glume). The bracts above the glumes are designated lemmas (formerly called flowering glumes). Facing each lemma and partially enclosed by it, is a second bract (palea), which bears the enclosed flower. The lemma and palea with the enclosed flower are termed the floret (fig. 2). The lemma bears an odd number of nerves or veins (1, 3, 5, 7, etc.), and the palea is two-nerved and

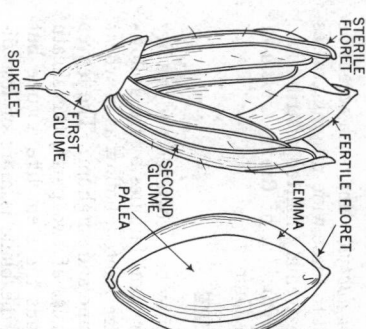

FIG. 3.—SPIKELET OF PANICUM AND DETAIL OF FERTILE FLORET

(Labels: STERILE FLORET, FERTILE FLORET, FIRST GLUME, SECOND GLUME, PALEA, LEMMA)

somewhat flattened on the back, which is next to the rachilla.

The flower in grasses is much reduced, consisting typically of a single pistil bearing two feathery stigmas, and three stamens. At the base of the pistil there are two small scales (lodicules), which are thought to represent the perianth. At flowering time (anthesis) the lodicules become much swollen, and this causes the lemma and palea to separate, exposing the stamens and stigmas (fig. 4). In the flowers of some bamboos there are three lodicules, six stamens and three stigmas.

Such flowers are considered to resemble most closely the ancestral type. In the flowers of some other grasses (e.g., *Oryza* and *Ehrharta*) six stamens also are found occasionally, and three lodicules rarely occur in flowers of genera other than bamboos (e.g., *Stipa*). Infrequently in the flowers of some bamboos and in those of *Pariana* and *Luziola* (which are unisexual), more than six stamens occur; up to 100 have been counted.

When the typical flower of Gramineae is compared with that of the general monocotyledonous type, as represented by Liliaceae, it is found to differ in the following ways: (1) the outer perianth whorl (sepals) is missing entirely; (2) the inner whorl (petals) has one member missing, the remaining two being represented by lodicules; (3) the inner whorl of stamens is lacking; (4) one stigma is no longer present, and only one carpel of the ovary is functional. As indicated above, however, each of the usually missing organs can be found normally, or as an occasional development, in some genera.

The flowers of grasses are so reduced and exhibit such uniformity in their structure that they are of minor importance in classification. The spikelets, on the other hand, show great variability, and their modifications and arrangements are very useful in identification and in suggesting relationships. Glumes are almost universally present, although occasionally one (e.g., *Leersia, Reimarochloa*) or even both (e.g., *Lolium, Paspalum*) may be wanting. Usually they are similar in shape and texture, but the first is often smaller and with fewer nerves. Sometimes the midnerve is extended as a bristle (awn), and the glumes may be reduced entirely to bristles as in some species of *Elymus*. Among members of the tribe Andropogoneae, the first glume is usually indurate, sometimes strongly so, and may be sculptured (*Hackelochloa*). In the more primitive grasses, lemmas are similar to the glumes, but many modifications occur. In certain genera (*Panicum, Phalaris, Olyra*) the lemma is hard and shining, whereas the glumes are very thin and transparent. The firm lemmas of *Stipa* and *Aristida* have a sharppointed base (callus), which is formed where the lemmas break away obliquely from the rachilla. Awns are very common on lemmas, and these may be straight or bent one or more times. When they are bent (geniculate) the basal segment is often twisted. In addition to the median awn, there may be additional ones formed by the extension of the lateral nerves (e.g., *Pappophorum*). The palea, which

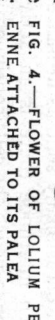

FIG. 4.—FLOWER OF LOLIUM PERENNE ATTACHED TO ITS PALEA

(Labels: STIGMA, ANTHER, FILAMENT, PALEA, OVARY, LODICULE, STAMEN)

is considered to be homologous with the prophyllum, is two-nerved and usually two-keeled, although the two nerves may be so close together that they appear as one (*Cinna*). The keels may be broadly winged (*Distichlis*) or bearded (*Triplasis*). Occasionally the palea is much reduced or completely lacking, as in some species of *Agrostis*. Ordinarily the palea falls from the plant attached to its lemma, but in numerous species of *Eragrostis* it persists upon the rachilla after the lemma has fallen.

The number of florets per spikelet varies from one (Agrostideae) to nearly 60 in some species of *Eragrostis*. In grasses that have their spikelets composed of several florets, these are usually similar in size and shape, but those toward the summit may be somewhat smaller, sterile or may lack paleas. Occasionally reduced or sterile florets occur at the base of the spikelet just above the glumes (*Uniola*). Sterile florets also occur below the fertile one in some apparently one-flowered spikelets. Thus in the Phalarideae a pair of staminate or neuter florets subtend the single perfect one. Spikelets of the Paniceae and Andropogoneae also have one functional floret, and below this is a sterile one, which may be reduced to the lemma. Spikelets may be strongly flattened either from the side or from the back, or plump and even circular in cross section. In outline, too, they exhibit a wide range of variation, from those of *Eragrostis* or *Distichlis*, often narrow in proportion to their length and with the margins nearly parallel, to those of *Paspalum*, which are sometimes almost circular. Another important characteristic of spikelets is the manner in which they break apart, thus freeing the seed from the parent plant. In some cases (e.g., *Panicum*) the spikelet falls as a unit; in certain other cases, such as the Festuceae, the rachilla breaks up above the glumes and between the florets, each of the latter falling separately and with an internode of the rachilla attached.

True involucres, consisting of subtending bracts, are rare in the Gramineae, although involucrelike structures do occur, being formed in various ways. In *Setaria*, *Pennisetum*, etc., the one or more whorls of simple or feathery bristles that occur below the spikelet represent abortive branches of the inflorescence. In *Cenchrus* these become fused and more or less indurated, forming a sort of bur that encloses the spikelets. In Job's-tears (*Coix*) the hard and shining beadlike structure is a much-modified bract or leaf sheath.

FLOWERING, GERMINATION AND DISPERSAL

Flowering.—Most grasses are chasmogamous—*i.e.*, their florets open to expose the stamens and pistil—but some are cleistogamous, the pollination taking place within the closed spikelets. There are a few species (e.g., *Amphicarpum* and *Chloris chloridea*), moreover, that in addition to the usual inflorescence bear cleistogamous spikelets on special underground stems; still others (e.g., *Danthonia*) produce them within the lower sheaths. Cross-pollination is effected by wind, and the pollen is very light and with a perfectly smooth surface.

Most annual grasses are self-fertile, but many perennials and some annuals are self-sterile, being unable to set seed without cross-pollination. These latter species usually have large anthers, which become fully exserted from the floret. The self-fertile annuals, in contrast, often have very small anthers, which may protrude from the open floret slightly, if at all.

The process of flowering in a typical grass proceeds somewhat as follows: The first noticeable sign is that the inflorescence becomes much more open, the branches spreading from the axis. This is accomplished by means of the swelling of a pad of spongy tissue (pulvinus) located in the axil of each branch. When this has occurred, and if conditions are favourable, the lodicules become greatly swollen and exert sufficient pressure at the base of the floret to force the lemma and palea apart. The filaments of the stamens next elongate rapidly, pushing the anthers from the floret, where they hang in the air. At the same time the feathery stigmas spread and project laterally, one on each side of the open floret. The anthers next split longitudinally, releasing the pollen, which is scattered by the slightest breeze. At the completion of flowering, the lodicules lose their turgidity and the floret gradually closes.

A few species of grasses are dioecious, the spikelets of an individual plant bearing either stamens or pistils but not both. Others are monoecious, unisexual flowers occurring on the same plant, in which case entire spikelets may be either staminate or pistillate, or some of the florets within the same spikelet may bear only stamens, others only pistils. A somewhat comparable condition (polygamy), in which both perfect and unisexual flowers occur on one individual and often within the same spikelet, is also common among grasses, especially among members of the Paniceae and Andropogoneae. When unisexual flowers of both sexes, or unisexual flowers along with perfect ones, occur on the same plant, it is usual for these to bloom at slightly different times, thus promoting cross-pollination. Even when the flowers are all perfect, often the stamens shed their pollen either before or after the stigmas are mature, and this also decreases the possibility of self-fertilization.

Fruit and Seed.—The fruit, which develops from the ovary of the pistil, is usually small, ovoid or rounded, and furrowed along one side. It is entirely occupied by the single seed, from which it is not to be distinguished, the thin wall (pericarp) of the fruit being completely united with the covering (testa) of the seed. This characteristic fruit is properly termed a caryopsis (fig. 5), although it is often referred to as a grain. This latter term, however, is less precise, since it is often applied to fruits of a quite different nature, such as those of buckwheat, and to seeds of some species of *Amaranthus*.

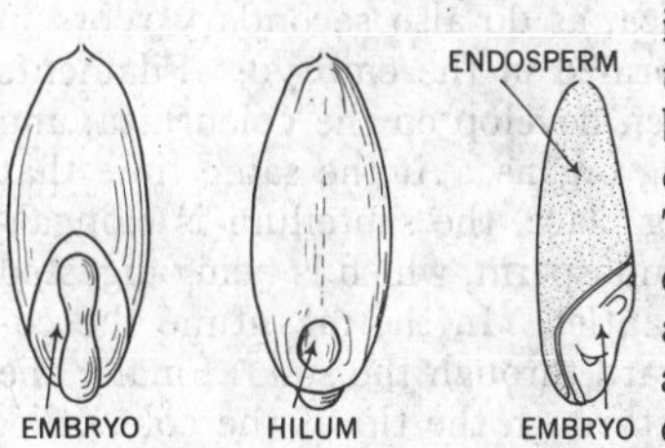

ENDOSPERM HILUM EMBRYO HILUM EMBRYO

FIG. 5.—CARYOPSIS OF DIGITARIA SANGUINALIS IN FRONT AND BACK VIEWS, AND IN LONGITUDINAL SECTION

Although the caryopsis is of almost universal occurrence among grasses, other types of fruits rarely occur. In *Sporobolus*, *Eleusine* and some other genera, the fruit is a utricle, the pericarp being quite free from the seed. Among the Bambuseae, the pericarp is sometimes hard, forming a nut; in others it is thick and fleshy, forming a berry that is often as large as an apple. In *Melocanna*, one of the bamboos, the berry is edible, somewhat pear-shaped and may attain a length of three or four inches. The small seed germinates within the fruit, the shoots often attaining a length of six inches or more before the fruit falls from the parent plant.

Ordinarily the pericarp and testa are thin and the outline of the embryo is clearly visible. It occupies a position at the base of the caryopsis on the side facing the lemma. Often the embryo is small, but in some cases (e.g., *Echinochloa* and *Spartina*) it is nearly as long as the seed. Opposite the embryo, on the other side, is a more or less evident dot or line (the hilum) that marks the point of attachment of the ovule to the ovary wall. The space inside the seed coat that is not occupied by the embryo is filled with endosperm, starchy material that, when the seed germinates, serves to nourish the developing plantlet. The outermost layer of endosperm (the aleurone) consists of regular cells filled with small protein granules. The remainder is made up of large polygonal cells containing numerous starch granules in a matrix of protein.

The structure of the embryo (fig. 6) and its position within the seed are unique and quite different from the Cyperaceae or other monocotyledons. On the

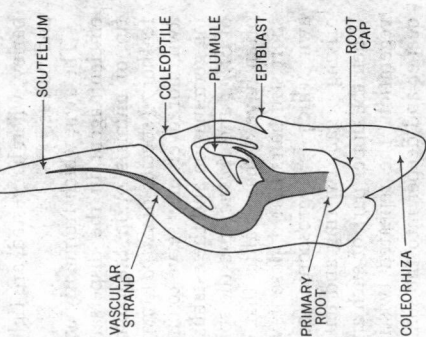

SCUTELLUM COLEOPTILE PLUMULE EPIBLAST ROOT CAP VASCULAR STRAND PRIMARY ROOT COLEORHIZA

FIG. 6.—EMBRYO OF BECKMANNIA, SHOWING THE VARIOUS PARTS

side next to the endosperm is the single seed leaf (cotyledon) or scutellum. This platelike organ bears, on the surface in contact with the endosperm, an epithelial layer containing enzymes that aid in the digestion of the starchy issue during germination. On the side opposite the scutellum, and inserted at about the same level, there may be a small organ (epiblast), which some authors have considered to be a reduced second cotyledon. In some grasses the epiblast is large and conspicuous, in others it is small, and in many it is altogether lacking.

The primary root is enclosed in a sheath (coleorhiza). The epicotyl or plumule is enclosed in a sheath (coleoptile) that typically has two vascular bundles, one on either side. Vascular tissue extends from the root into the shoot, with a side branch to the scutellum. Although there has been a certain amount of disagreement with respect to the homologies of the parts of the grass embryo, it has come to be generally agreed that the scutellum is the cotyledon and that the coleoptile represents the first true leaf of the plant.

Germination.—When a seed germinates, the coleorhiza expands, lengthens and ruptures the pericarp. The coleoptile, with its enclosed epicotyl, next appears. Soon afterward the primary root breaks through the coleorhiza, as do also secondary roots in those cases in which they are formed in the embryo. Filaments closely resembling root hairs often develop on the coleorhiza, and these probably serve as absorbing organs. At the same time that these external changes are taking place, the scutellum is elongating and pushing deeper into the endosperm, which is being digested slowly to feed the developing plantlet. In the meantime the coleoptile is pushing vertically upward through the soil. Finally the first true leaf appears, emerging through the tip of the coleoptile. The primary root persists for only a short time, the function of absorption being assumed by adventitious roots that arise from the nodes at the base of the primary shoot.

Dispersal and Migration.—In grasses the seed rarely falls free, and among wild species even the grain seldom separates from the parent plant devoid of its lemma and palea. Often whole spikelets serve as propagable shoots, and these may have parts of the inflorescence attached to them. In some cases short spikes fall from the parent plant; in others the axis of the inflorescence breaks up at the joints, each spikelet falling attached to an internode of the rachis. In grasses with several-flowered spikelets, the rachilla usually breaks apart between the florets, each of these falling with a short rachilla joint attached. The persistent lemma and palea, and other parts when present, serve to decrease the specific gravity, and the grain is thus more readily carried by the wind. Lemmas and paleas may also afford a certain amount of protection in that they prevent excessive drying or too rapid wetting of the embryo.

Among cultivated cereals there has been a conscious selection for those in which the grains fall free from their enveloping scales, as this greatly facilitates their harvest. In some cases, however, the combination of easily separating caryopses and high yield has not been achieved, and such grains as oats and barley, when harvested, are tightly enclosed between their lemmas and paleas.

The awn, which frequently occurs on the lemma, is often a very efficient agent in the dispersal of fruits. It may catch in the fur of animals or in the plumage of birds, or, when long and feathery (species of *Stipa*), may act as a sort of parachute. The awn, moreover, may serve to bury the fruit in the soil, thus hastening germination and the establishment of a new plant. The florets of *Stipa* and *Avena*, and the spikelets of *Heteropogon* and others, often have a sharp callus that easily penetrates the soil and also short stiff hairs that oppose its withdrawal. The bent and twisted awn, which is hygroscopic (sensitive to moisture), serves as a driving organ, twisting and untwisting with changes in humidity. When the upper part of such an awn is caught in the ground or in vegetation, the repeated twisting causes the fruit to be driven deeper and deeper into the soil. (Grass fruits of this type sometimes cause injury to sheep when they catch in the wool and burrow through the skin.)

A very efficient means of seed dispersal is seen in those grasses in which the large open panicles break off at maturity and are blown long distances by the wind, scattering their fruits as they go. Examples of such grasses are *Eragrostis spectabilis* and *Panicum capillare*.

Vivipary, or the germination of seeds within the fruit upon the parent plant, was mentioned above as occurring in *Melocanna*. The condition has also been observed in some other grasses. The conversion of the spikelet, above the glumes, into a leafy shoot (proliferation) is often confused with vivipary. Proliferated spikelets are occasionally found among many genera of grasses, and these are often the result of particular environmental conditions. In some grasses, however, this peculiarity is genetically determined; there are races known in which it occurs regardless of the conditions of the environment.

At one time it was believed that proliferated spikelets were of considerable importance in reproduction, but it has been found that under natural conditions these seldom grow into new plants.

CLASSIFICATION

In early attempts at a scientific classification of plants a group of Gramina was recognized, and this, though bounded by nothing more definite than habit and general appearance, contained the Gramineae of modern botanists. The early systematists, however, often included also in the group the Cyperaceae (sedge family), Juncaceae (rush family) and some other monocotyledonous plants with inconspicuous flowers. The sexual system of classification developed by Linnaeus (1753), which was based on the numbers of stamens and pistils, served to separate the true grasses more distinctly; most of them fell under the order Digynia of his class Triandria, whereas the allied plants, with few exceptions, were distributed under other classes and orders.

There are about 500 genera and perhaps 5,000 species of grasses known, and each year more are discovered and described. Although it is relatively easy to recognize members of the family, their great complexity, as well as the extreme reduction and uniformity of the flowers, renders classification very difficult. Since the flowers themselves offer few clues as to relationships, reliance must be placed upon other characters; hence the classification of grasses has been built up largely from a study of vegetative structures, especially glumes, lemmas and paleas (all more or less modified leaves).

The difficulty of classification is further increased by the realization that much parallel evolution has occurred, with the result that superficial similarity does not necessarily indicate close phyletic relationship. A classification system on which all botanists can agree has not been formulated.

Grasses may be separated rather readily into two great groups or subfamilies. Robert Brown (1814) was apparently the first author to record the observation that in some grasses (Panicoideae) there is a tendency for aborted flowers to be borne at the base of the spikelet, whereas in others (Festucoideae) aborted or rudimentary flowers occur above the fertile ones. It was pointed out later by George Bentham (1882) that in the Panicoideae the spikelet usually breaks away below the glumes, thus falling as a unit, whereas in the Festucoideae the spikelets break above the glumes and between the florets, these falling individually. Further, in the Panicoideae the spikelets are flattened from the back (dorsally), whereas in the Festucoideae the compression is from the sides (laterally), and the glumes and lemmas are often somewhat keeled. Not only are these groups recognizable on morphological grounds, but they have been found to differ also with respect to chromosome size and number, leaf epidermis and anatomy, embryo and seedling and in some other characters.

In his monograph on the Gramineae, E. Haeckel (1887) further divided the family into 13 tribes. This system, often with some slight modifications, has been used widely throughout the world and is probably the best-known classification of the grasses. The principal change made in Haeckel's system was to reverse the order of the tribes. The classification outlined below, a modified Haeckel system, is essentially that used in A. S. Hitchcock's *Manual* of Grasses of the United States, the standard work on the family for America. The first nine tribes are treated as members of the subfamily Festucoideae, while the remaining four fall under the Panicoideae.

SUBFAMILY FESTUCOIDEAE

Bambuseae.—This is the group of bamboos (by some given subfamily rank as the Bambusoideae), usually tall grasses with woody stems. The blades are often broad and articulated to the sheath, to which they are attached by a short petiole. The spikelets bear from two to several florets which are usually awnless, and these are arranged in panicles, racemes, fascicles or compact heads. The tribe numbers about 60 genera, most of which are tropical; one genus, *Arundinaria*, is native to the United States. In those parts of the world where bamboos are abundant, they are of great economic importance.. The woody culms are used in all kinds of construction, for vessels, and water pipes, and also furnish fibre from which an excellent quality of paper is manufactured. Bamboo shoots are an article of food in the orient, and the grains are also eaten, especially in time of famine. (See BAMBOO.)

Festuceae.—In this tribe, the fescues, the spikelets are also two- to several-flowered and are borne in open, contracted or spikelike panicles, or sometimes in racemes. The glumes are usually shorter than the lowest floret. The lemmas are awnless or awned, the awn straight or zigzag and borne on the tip or from between the teeth of a minutely forked apex. When mature, the spikelets break above the glumes and between the florets. As circumscribed here, the tribe includes about 125 genera, most of which are characteristic of temperate or cool regions. Many common meadow grasses belong in this tribe, such as bluegrass, fescue (*qq.v.*), brome grass and orchard grass or cocksfoot.

Hordeae.—Spikelets in members of the Hordeae, the barley tribe, are often similar to those of the Festuceae (sometimes they are reduced to one flower), but the inflorescence is always a symmetrical spike, the spikelets borne on both sides of the rachis, which may be continuous or break apart at the joints when mature. Often the glumes are reduced to bristles or awns, or one may be as long as the spikelet, more or less obscuring the florets within. This tribe comprises only about 25 genera, but although small it is very important economically. Some of the most valuable cereals, wheat, barley and rye (*qq.v.*), are members of the Hordeae.

Aveneae.—As in the preceding tribes, the oat tribe, the spike-group, the oat tribe, are also two- to several-flowered. They are borne in open or contracted panicles or occasionally in racemes. The glumes are longer than the lowest floret, and may be as long as the spikelet, more or less obscuring the florets within. The lemmas are usually awned from the back (dorsally), the awn commonly bent and twisted. The rachilla and callus of the florets are often hairy, and frequently the inflorescence has a shiny or silvery appearance. There are about 45 genera in this tribe, among them velvet grass (*Holcus*), tall oat grass (*Arrhenatherum*) and the cultivated oat (see OATS).

Agrostideae.—This tribe, comprising the bents, is somewhat unnatural, containing a number of unrelated genera. The characters which these share in common and which delimit the tribe are one-flowered spikelets borne in open, contracted or spikelike panicles. The inflorescence is never a true spike or a one-sided raceme. The lemma may be awnless or awned, and the awn may be straight or bent and twisted, and borne either terminally or dorsally. The floret usually disarticulates above the glumes, falling free from them, but in some cases the spikelet falls as a unit.

The Agrostideae comprises about 65 genera, most of which are found in temperate and cool regions. Bent grass, marram grass (*qq.v.*), timothy and muhly (*Muhlenbergia*) are members of this tribe.

Phalarideae.—In this, the canary grass tribe, the spikelets have one perfect terminal floret; below this are two others that are staminate or neuter, sometimes reduced to small scales. The inflorescence is an open or contracted panicle. As treated by Hackel and many subsequent authors, the tribe consists of six genera, among them sweet grass (*Hierochloë*) and canary grass (*Phalaris*).

Chlorideae.—The form of the inflorescence is the most characteristic feature among members of the Chlorideae, the grama tribe. The spikelets may be one- or several-flowered, awned or awnless, sessile or pedicellate, but they are always borne in two rows on one side of a continuous rachis. These spikes or racemes may be solitary, digitate or arranged as branches of an elongated axis. In some cases only the lowest floret of the spikelet is fertile, the others being sterile and often much reduced or rudimentary. There are perhaps 40 genera in this tribe, most of them inhabiting warm regions. Included are such important forage grasses as buffalo grass (*Buchloë*) and the grama grass (*Bouteloua*) of the southwestern United States and northern Mexico.

Zoysieae.—As in the preceding tribe, the form of the inflorescence is of prime importance in delimiting this group, the tobosa grass tribe. The spikelets are usually one-flowered, sessile or subsessile in short spikes of two to five (single in *Zoysia*), each spike falling entire from the continuous rachis. All the spikelets may be perfect, or perfect and staminate ones may occur together in the same inflorescence. Often three are found together, the central one being perfect while the two laterals are staminate. This tribe comprises about 17 genera of tropical distribution, particularly in dry regions and on seashores. *Hilaria*, the short grass of the Texas plains, is a member of the tribe, as is also *Zoysia*, the genus from which the tribal name is derived.

Oryzeae.—In this, the rice tribe, the spikelets, which are borne in open panicles, are one-flowered and perfect or unisexual. The glumes are occasionally well developed, but usually they are small or may be completely lacking. The stamens are often six in number. As defined by Hackel, the tribe includes about 16 genera, but some of these are of doubtful affinities. The best-known member, cultivated rice (*q.v.*), is one of the most important food plants in the world.

SUBFAMILY PANICOIDEAE

Melinideae.—Members of this group have well-developed glumes and two-flowered spikelets. The upper floret is perfect, the lower being staminate or neuter and often represented only by a lemma. There are seven or eight genera in this tribe, all occurring in tropical regions. Most are unimportant, but *Thysanolaena*, a native of Asia, is often a troublesome weed. *Melinis*, with a single species, found in both South America and Africa, is prized for forage and is sometimes cultivated.

Paniceae.—The spikelets in the Paniceae, the panicum tribe, are distinctive, being dorsally compressed and two-flowered, although appearing one-flowered until examined carefully. The glumes are membranous in texture, the first often shorter than the second. Occasionally the first glume is completely lacking. The upper floret is perfect, the lemma and palea indurated or firmer than the glumes, often hard and shiny. The lower floret is staminate or neuter, sometimes reduced to the lemma, this of the same texture as the glumes. Awns occasionally occur on the glumes or on the lower lemma, but almost never on the fertile one, and when present on this latter organ, the awn is usually short.

The Paniceae comprises 80 or more genera, most of them found in tropical and warm regions. Many are troublesome weeds, such as crab grass, foxtail grass (*qq.v.*) and witch grass (*Panicum capillare*). A few are grown for the grains—*e.g.*, millets (*Panicum miliaceum* and *Setaria italica*)—and some are used for forage. (See also MILLET; PANICUM.)

Andropogoneae.—The spikelets of the Andropogoneae, the sorghum tribe, are also two-flowered, with the upper floret perfect and the lower staminate or neuter. The glumes, however, are firmer than the lemmas, and the latter are commonly awned, the awn often well developed, bent and twisted. The spikelets usually occur in pairs on the inflorescence axis or its branches, the usual arrangement being that one of the pair is sessile and fertile, while the other is pedicellate and staminate or neuter. Rarely the upper spikelet is wanting. The axis usually disarticulates at the joints, and the pair of spikelets fall attached to a short internode. This tribe comprises 50 or more genera, most of which are tropical. Some are important forage grasses, and the group also includes sugar (q.v.) cane (*Saccharum*), sorghum (q.v.) and oil grasses (*Cymbopogon*), this latter group furnishing citral, an essential oil used in perfumes.

Maydeae.—In this group (also called Tripsaceae), the Indian corn tribe, the plants are monoecious, the spikelets being unisexual. The staminate spikelets are borne in pairs, or occasionally in threes. The pistillate spikelets are more or less embedded in a thickened axis or enclosed within a thickened sheath. The glumes and lemmas are awnless. This small tribe of seven genera is closely allied to the Andropogoneae, the chief distinction being that in the Maydeae the staminate and pistillate spikelets are borne in different inflorescences or in different parts of the same inflorescence. Corn (q.v.; Indian corn or maize [*Zea mays*] is a member of this tribe, as is also Job's-tears (*Coix lacryma-jobi*).

Other Classifications.—The classification outlined above, although quite unnatural in many respects, is perhaps the most satisfactory available. Other systems have been suggested, the most notable, perhaps, being that of C. Hubbard (1934), in which 27 tribes were recognized, many of which previously had been designated as subtribes. In several respects this system is more natural than Haeckel's, although it is somewhat less satisfactory for the nonspecialist because of the large number of tribes, often based on minor characters.

R. Pilger presented in 1954 an even more detailed system, in which he recognized 9 subfamilies and 35 tribes. Although he indicated that it was based on the latest information from all disciplines, his system is far from natural in many respects and, because of the large number of subfamilies and tribes, is unwieldy and difficult to use.

Even though a natural classification for the Gramineae acceptable to all botanists has not been worked out, data bearing on the subject are accumulating as the result of researches along various lines. Perhaps the most useful information has come from the study of the epidermis of the leaf and its anatomy, the structure of the embryo, and chromosome size and number, although root-hair development, starch-grain structure and other studies also prove helpful in some cases. Using the newer techniques, the subfamily Panicoideae, as classically treated, proves to be quite natural, but this is not true of the other subfamily, Festucoideae. The tribes Chlorideae and Zoysieae, for example, are misplaced in the Festucoideae, even though this is not evident from a study of the gross external features alone. These are the only complete tribes for which a shift to the other subfamily is indicated. Among several of the other tribes, however, there are genera which prove to be unrelated to the majority with which they have been associated. This is especially true with respect to the tribes Festuceae and Agrostideae, in which numerous genera have been found to have panicoid affinities, even though most of the genera are festucoid.

See GRASSLAND; *see* also references under "Grasses" in the Index.

BIBLIOGRAPHY.—E. Hackel, *The True Grasses*, trans. by F. L. Scribner and E. A. Southworth (1890); H. M. Ward, *Grasses* (1901); J. W. Bews, *The World's Grasses* (1929); Agnes Arber, *The Gramineae* (1934); Alma Moore, *The Grasses* (1960); Agnes Chase, *First Book of Grasses*, 3rd ed. (1959); R. J. Pool, *Marching With the Grasses* (1948); U.S. Department of Agriculture, "Grass," *1948 Yearbook of Agriculture* (1948); A. S. Hitchcock, *Manual of the Grasses of the United States*, U.S. Department of Agriculture, Misc. Publ. no. 200, 2nd ed. rev. by Agnes Chase (1950); C. E. Hubbard, *Grasses* (1954); G. L. Stebbins, "Cytogenetics and Evolution of the Grass Family," *Amer. J. Bot.*, 43:890–905 (1956); J. R. Reeder, "The Embryo in Grass Systematics," *Amer. J. Bot.*, 44:756–768 (1957); M. E. Francis, *The Book of Grasses* (1920). (J. R. Rr.; X.)

GRASSHOPPER, any of the leaping insects belonging to the orthopterous families Acrididae (formerly Locustidae) and Tettigoniidae that, in the northern hemisphere, are so common in fields and along roadsides in midsummer and early autumn. Grasshoppers are virtually cosmopolitan; they are found in a variety of habitats—mountains, deserts, marshes, temperate forests and meadows—but occur in greatest numbers in lowland tropical forests, semiarid regions and grasslands. About 10,000 species are known, of which almost 600 occur in the United States and Canada, and only a few in Britain. Many species are varying shades of green, olive or brown; some are garishly marked with yellows and reds. They are almost entirely herbivorous, with many species being restricted to certain plants, but most feeding on any suitable vegetation. Only a few species assume economic importance as crop pests. In certain parts of the world grasshoppers are eaten as food, dried, jellied or ground into a meal.

The femora of the hind legs are greatly enlarged, well adapted for leaping. Males, and infrequently females, often make a buzzing sound (stridulation) by rubbing the toothlike ridge on the inside of the hind femora against the raised vein on the outside of the closed front wings. A cracking sound (crepitation) produced during flight is made by a few species. In most species auditory organs are present at the base of the abdomen.

Some grasshoppers possess remarkable adaptations; the South American *Marellia remipes*, for example, lives most of its life on the floating vegetation, actively swimming and ovipositing on the underwater surfaces of aquatic plants. Most species are large enough to be conspicuous, while some are among the insect giants. The largest species are more than 4½ in. long (*Tropidacris latreillei*, South America).

The Acrididae are the common short-horned grasshoppers, which include the inoffensive nonmigratory sorts and the often destructive swarming and migratory locusts (*see* LOCUST). They are characterized by short, usually heavy antennae, a robust four-valved ovipositor and three-segmented tarsi (end parts of the legs). The acridids usually lay their eggs in the soil in packets or pods of about 100 or more eggs being enclosed in a hardened secretion. In temperate regions only one to a few broods are produced each year. The eggs hatch after a resting period (diapause), which is usually broken by the advent of seasonal rains. The newly hatched young (nymphs), miniature replicas of the adults, pass through a series of molts, finally metamorphosing directly to the adult stage.

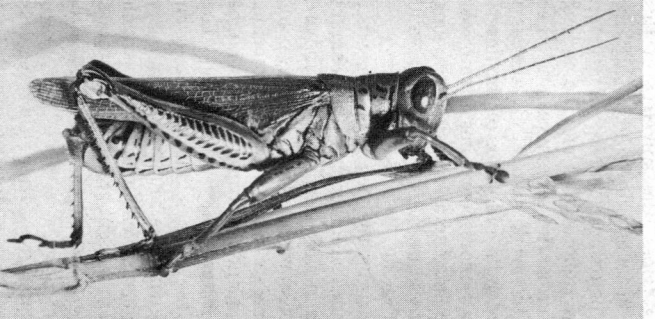

J. M. CONRADER

FIG. 2.—DIFFERENTIAL GRASSHOPPER (MELANOPLUS DIFFERENTIALIS), A DESTRUCTIVE SHORT-HORNED GRASSHOPPER COMMON TO THE WESTERN U.S.

One of the larger acridid genera, in species and numbers, is *Melanoplus*, which includes the commonest grasshoppers in North America. The lubber grasshopper (*Brachystola magna*) is a common large acridid of the southwestern and western U.S. Except for a few species, acridids are seldom present in sufficient numbers to cause serious damage. Populations are controlled in nature partly by several predators (birds, frogs, snakes and the larvae of certain flies).

The Tettigoniidae comprise the long-horned grasshoppers and the katydids (*see* KATYDID). These forms are characterized by long, filamentous antennae, swordlike ovipositor and fou...

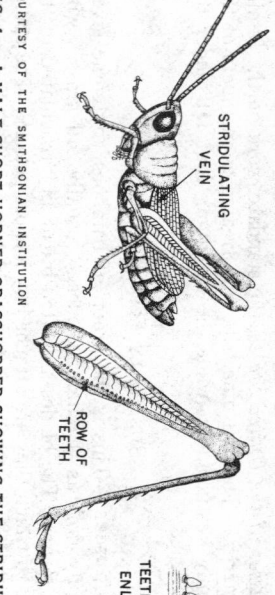

COURTESY OF THE SMITHSONIAN INSTITUTION

FIG. 1.—A MALE SHORT-HORNED GRASSHOPPER SHOWING THE STRIDULATOR APPARATUS (AFTER ALLARD). SOMEWHAT ENLARGED

STRIDULATING VEIN

ROW OF TEETH

TEETH MORE ENLARGED

segmented tarsi. Those most often encountered are the meadow grasshoppers (*Orchelimum, Conocephalus* and other genera) and cone-headed grasshoppers (*Neoconocephalus,* etc.), which usually inhabit low vegetation, frequently in marshy areas and sometimes in great numbers. Their heads are cone-shaped between the eyes. Some terrestrial species are wingless or short-winged.

Grouse or pygmy locusts (family Tetrigidae) are sometimes called pygmy grasshoppers (*see* GROUSE LOCUST).

See ORTHOPTERA.

(H. J. G.)

GRASSLAND may be considered as any area devoted to the production of forage grasses, legumes, or combinations of grasses and legumes with other herbage plants, used for grazing, hay, grass silage, or green feeding. Green feeding, soiling, zero pasture, green chop, and other terms are used to describe the process of harvesting and feeding green pasture crops mechanically, instead of grazing directly by livestock.

Grassland agriculture is as old as the domestication of animals (*c.* 10,000 B.C.). Dairying in Europe based upon feed from grassland was, under way by 4000 B.C. In some areas dairying has changed little since its beginning between 4000 B.C. and 2000 B.C., nor has the culture of grassland which supplies the feed for livestock, including the improvement of the forage plants themselves.

This article deals with the role of grassland in agriculture, the various kinds of grassland and their improvement and uses and the improvement of forage grasses and legumes. For specific information about the occurrence and agricultural uses of grassland, the reader is referred to the articles on individual countries, *e.g.,* ARGENTINA; AUSTRALIA, COMMONWEALTH OF, and especially to the sections of those articles dealing with physical geography and agriculture. Botanical characteristics are discussed in the article GRASSES and there are separate articles appearing under the common names of the more important species of grasses and legumes. *See also* AGRICULTURE; RANGE (IN AGRICULTURE).

IMPORTANCE OF GRASSLAND

Grassland produces the world's most extensively grown crop. Its acreage exceeds the combined acreage of wheat, corn (maize), cotton, oats, barley, rye, soybeans, sugar beets, rice, flax, peanuts, potatoes, and tobacco. In terms of the livestock feed supply, grassland furnishes over half of the total in many countries and as much as 85 to 90% of the total in others.

Grassland and the grass crop dominate the nonforested agricultural land area of every continent. Over 200 major grass and legume species and thousands of species of limited distribution adapted to various soil and climatic conditions are grown on the world's grassland. One or several of the many kinds of grasses and legumes grow in each of the numerous grassland habitats from the tropics to the permafrost of the Arctic region, and from regions of high rainfall (over 100 in. a year) to semiarid regions that receive less than 10 in. of precipitation a year. Annual grassland production varies from a few pounds to tons per acre, depending on climate, soil productivity, and crop management.

Livestock feed for domesticated animals is the major contribution of grassland, but not its only one. In certain situations the soil and water conserving attributes may be more important than the feed produced, since a grass or grass-legume cover retards water runoff, increases the rate of infiltration into the soil, and reduces or prevents soil erosion by wind or water. As a rotation crop, well managed grassland restores productivity that is lost by growing cultivated crops (*see* ROTATION OF CROPS).

Grassland also supplies the major portion of the feed for many kinds of game animals and especially big game. More specialized uses of grassland are to maintain highway shoulders, separation strips and embankments; to provide a suitable surface of pleasing appearance for recreational areas, such as golf courses, playing fields, parks and lawns; and to provide protective cover on roadways of limited use, fire lanes, waterways, airstrips, around buildings, and on other normally turfed areas.

KINDS OF GRASSLAND

Sown or Seeded Grassland.—This is the largest and by far the most productive supplier of nutritious forage; it includes tame

pasture, tame hay, meadow, rotation hay or pasture, temporary pasture, and annual forage crops. Generally these are found in areas of moderate to heavy rainfall on land once occupied by natural forest. Soils in these areas are well supplied with moisture during much of the year, with some leaching occurring due to the percolation of excess water. They are the grasslands that support the intensive, highly developed livestock industry in New Zealand, western Europe, the United Kingdom, humid regions of North America, and other parts of the world. Smaller acreages of sown grassland have been established on submerged areas reclaimed from the sea, and on irrigated deserts. During most of the growing season, and when properly managed, herbage from these grasslands constitutes an adequate diet for sheep and cattle. Dairy cattle produce nearly as much milk when their entire ration comes from well managed pastures as they produce with any other feed or combination of feeds. Beef cattle make optimum growth and may be fattened satisfactorily on forage alone. Sheep seldom receive anything but feed from grassland whether kept on sown or natural grassland. Horses that have access to ample amounts of good quality hay or pasturage may receive no other feed except during periods of heavy work. Swine and poultry obtain less, but often an important fraction, of their rations from grassland (*see also* FEEDS, ANIMAL).

Annual yields, on a dry forage basis, of 12,000 lb. to the acre are not uncommon from sown pastures or meadows. This amount of high quality forage is sufficient to meet the feed requirement of one high producing dairy cow for one year. Alfalfa (*Medicago sativa*) yields of 20,000 lb. or more are not uncommon in warm, irrigated regions, and can be attained with proper management on productive soils in the temperate zone. Tropical and subtropical grasses have given yields of dry matter in excess of 40,000 lb. to the acre. These high yields more closely approach the maximum potentials than the average yields of sown meadows and pastures, but can be realized over substantial areas with good management.

Sown grassland may be used as a temporary crop grown in rotation with other cultivated crops or it may be nearly permanent. Within these extremes will be found pastures and hay fields ranging from a few months to several years of age. The permanence and productivity of sown grassland depend upon intended use as well as management, soil, and climatic factors. These, in turn, usually determine the life span of a permanent pasture. Stands of productive forage varieties may be maintained for two to four years in rotation with small grain and other cultivated crops. On productive cropland or irrigated land, the grass crop may be grown only one year out of ten or more (*see* ROTATION OF CROPS).

Hilly land too steep to plow without serious danger of erosion is seldom cropped and should remain in grass most of the time, if farmed at all. Such areas may be seeded, limed, and fertilized with aircraft adapted for such uses. Thus treated, and properly grazed, hill land not suitable for the production of other crops becomes an efficient producer of livestock feed.

Species of the following grasses and legumes are those often used to establish sown grasslands:

Grasses

Bermuda grass (*Cynodon*)	Millets and bristle grasses
Bluegrasses (*Poa*)	(*Setaria*)
Bluestems (*Andropogon*)	Molasses grass (*Melinis*)
Brome grasses (annual and	Needle grass (*Stipa*)
perennial) (*Bromus*)	Oat grasses (*Arrhenatherum*)
Buffalo grass (*Buchloë*)	Pangola grass (*Digitaria*)
Canary grasses (*Phalaris*)	Para grass, guinea, switch grass,
Carpet grass (*Axonopus*)	blue panic grass, etc. (*Panicum*)
Cocksfoot, orchard grass	Redtop (*Agrostis*)
(*Dactylis*)	Rhodes grass (*Chloris*)
Dallis, Bahia, etc. (*Paspalum*)	Rye grass (*Lolium*)
Dropseeds (*Sporobolus*)	Smilo and rice grass (*Oryzopsis*)
Fescue grasses (*Festuca*)	Sudan, Johnson, etc. (*Sorghum*)
Grama grasses (*Bouteloua*)	Timothy (*Phleum*)
Kikuyu, napier grass, buffel grass,	Veldt grass (*Ehrharta*)
etc. (*Pennisetum*)	Wheat grasses (*Agropyron*)
Love grasses (*Eragrostis*)	Wild rye (*Elymus*)
Meadow foxtail (*Alopecurus*)	

Legumes

Bird's-foot trefoil (*Lotus*)	Chick-pea (*Cicer*)
Bur clover, alfalfa, etc.	Clover (*Trifolium*)
(*Medicago*)	Crotalaria (*Crotalaria*)

Fenugreek (*Trigonella*)
Hyacinth bean (*Dolichos*)
Kaimi and Spanish clover (*Desmodium*)
Koa haole (*Leucaena*)
Kudzu (*Pueraria*)
Lespedeza (*Lespedeza*)
Lupines (*Lupinus*)
Milk vetch (*Astragalus*)
Pigeon pea (*Cajanus*)
Sainfoin (*Onobrychis*)
Soybean (*Glycine*)
Sweet clover (*Melilotus*)
Vetch (*Vicia*)

Natural Grassland.—This group embraces a wide array of types ranging from desert grass-shrub combinations to the tall grass prairie. Unlike the sown grasslands that occupy areas cleared of forest vegetation, natural grasslands are themselves the end product of natural forces that favoured grass and other plant growth more than that of trees. Fire has been an important factor in preventing the invasion of some grasslands by undesirable woody species. Controlled burning remains a valuable management practice on certain temperate and tropical grasslands. On the other hand, frequent fires may weaken perennial grasses and open stands to invasion by annual weeds. Natural grasslands in semiarid and arid regions are subject to severe damage from plowing, and from the effects of overstocking, either alone or in combination with prolonged drought.

Natural grasslands generally occupy those areas between the climatic extremes of humid woodlands and dry desert shrub. The transition belts, therefore, between typical grass prairie and either of these extremes contain more or less tree growth on the one hand, or desert shrub on the other. Soil moisture, rather than total rainfall, usually determines the extent of natural grassland. If the upper layers of soil are moist during part of the year, but the deeper layers remain dry, tree growth cannot compete with grass. The savannas of the tropics annually receive substantial total rainfall, but a long dry period each year, combined with high temperatures and evaporation, prevents the development of forests.

Temperature or soil moisture may limit the effective growing season in natural grasslands to a few weeks of the year. Thus, tender grass feed of high nutritive quality is available for relatively short periods compared with the season of lush growth in sown grasslands. However, the absence of a long season of green forage growth is supplemented by naturally cured, leafy forage of acceptable feed value for several weeks after growth has stopped, particularly in arid regions. Those species found in arid regions tend to exceed those of the wet tropics in feed value after maturity. Associated browse plants, including some species of sagebrush, also reinforce the feed supply of natural grasslands in semiarid regions, especially between growing seasons. In addition to carbohydrate and protein, some of them supply exceptionally high quantities of vitamin A. The productivity of natural grassland varies widely but averages much less than that of sown grassland. Forage production may range from a few pounds to several hundred pounds to the acre.

GRASSLAND IMPROVEMENT

Before 1930 little research had been conducted on grassland improvement, compared with work on crops such as wheat, cotton, rice, maize, and many others. Because perennial grasses and legumes grow on land that is too steep or too rough and rocky for cultivated crops, there has been considerable reluctance in accepting them as species that can respond effectively to improved management practices. This unfortunate situation has often prevailed when perennial forages were included in rotations on tillable land. Thus it is not surprising that the profit from many grass crops falls below their potential. Moreover, a profitable return from the grass crop (since three-fourths or more of it is harvested by grazing) is as dependent upon proper utilization by livestock as it is upon the successful growing of the crop. Wise animal husbandry, therefore, is an essential ingredient of successful and profitable grassland agriculture.

Grassland improvement research must take into account the end use of the crop. Higher feed value, better seasonal distribution of production, or greater palatability are often more important objectives than higher forage yields, per se, since the final measure of profit from grassland is milk, beef, mutton, or other products from forage-consuming animals. Increased use of applied fertilizers, especially nitrogen, phosphorus, calcium, magnesium, potassium and sometimes molybdenum, cobalt, and other trace elements, has improved both yield and quality of humid area grasslands. Conservation and the return of animal manures are essential unless heavy applications of chemical fertilizers are made. With few exceptions, larger applications of fertilizer nutrients on sown grasslands have been profitable. Forage yields in humid areas are doubled or tripled by good soil fertility practices alone.

It is axiomatic that well managed natural and seeded grasslands are basic to a successful and profitable livestock industry. Although true on a worldwide basis, important changes have occurred in the United States. The availability of feed grains and rising labour costs have contributed to the increase in drylot milk and meat production characterized by highly automated feeding systems. In California where average milk production is just over 10,000 lb. per cow, dairy cows are seldom on pasture. They are fed high levels of concentrates and depend heavily on stored feeds such as hay. However, comparable levels of production can be obtained from grasslands, as shown in the Netherlands where average milk production is about 10,000 lb. per cow. These cows are always on pasture and no concentrates are fed during the grazing season.

In intensive livestock production systems, grasslands will continue to provide feeder stock for fattening as well as replacement heifers for dairy herds maintained in drylots. The role of grasslands in the United States and in many other countries will be affected by human population pressure, and the emphasis on growing grain crops for direct human consumption. Under these cir-

Reseeding is sometimes essential to obtain the maximum output from grassland. Natural grassland that has deteriorated from misuse may require reseeding after the destruction of brush and weeds. Sown grassland may require occasional cultivation or plowing and reseeding to reestablish a good legume-grass balance for maximum production of nutritious forage. Also, as superior varieties of forage grasses and legumes are developed, reseeding is required to utilize them promptly. Top seeding without any land preparation is possible, but successful establishment of grassland by this method is exceptional. Immediate seeding in the ash following burns is, perhaps, the most noteworthy exception.

Improvement by proper grazing management is difficult to achieve. Yet this is the principal method of economically maintaining and improving the natural grassland of subhumid and semiarid regions around the world. The vegetative cover is usually sparse, yet surface protection is essential to increase water intake and to reduce erosion by wind and water. To provide adequate cover with living or dead vegetation, as much as 50% of the grass growth should remain on the land. Continuous overgrazing reduces the vigour of the grass, invites encroachment of weeds and brush, and brings on general deterioration. These grassland areas are often too extensive in size and too low in yield to justify large-scale, costly renovation treatments that may be profitable in humid grasslands. Improvement may be accomplished by (1) reseeding selected sites of higher yield potential; (2) construction of water-spreading systems that divert runoff and aid in the more uniform infiltration of water; and (3) adjusted grazing practices that allow natural reseeding and the accumulation of desirable vegetative cover. In the United States several native and introduced grasses have been used to seed depleted ranges and abandoned cropland. Weeping love grass in combination with low rates of nitrogen fertilizer has tripled the carrying capacity in portions of the southern Great Plains. Brush control operations in south Texas have been followed with successful seedings of buffel grass and blue panic grass in combination with native grasses. Crested and intermediate wheat grass are valuable sources of early spring pasture in the northern plains and intermountain regions, before natural grasslands are ready to graze. Fertilizers may be profitable on some natural grasslands. In northern portions of the Great Plains region the carrying capacity of grasslands has been doubled with low rates of applied nitrogen. Beef production per acre on some natural grasslands in Uruguay and Argentina has increased twofold with an application of phosphate. With all improvement practices, success depends upon proper grazing management.

cumstances stored and processed forages must assume greater importance in intensive feeding systems. Similarly, world needs for animal protein will encourage greater effort to increase the yield of animal products from seeded pasture and natural grasslands. Forages do not compete directly with cereal grains for they can be grown during off seasons on tillable land and on land unsuited for grain production.

UTILIZATION OF GRASSLAND

Pasturage, hay, grass silage, and haylage are derived from grassland, in that order of importance. Because the grazing animal is the most economical harvester for most grassland conditions, three-fourths or more of the world's grass crop is grazed off. However, grazing is not always available throughout the year, or the feed value of the crop available for grazing during part of the year is so low that other high quality forage is essential. Such forage is provided by hay or grass silage harvested when the grass or grass-legume combination is at a nutritious stage of growth.

Pasturage.—Good management practices and forage crop sequences that provide high quality pasture during most of the growing season can minimize the need for other feeds. The value of legumes in grassland agriculture is best realized in this connection. As a supplier of nitrogen to the associated grass, as well as to itself, the nitrogen-fixing legume helps maintain a satisfactory protein level in the legume-grass mixture during much of the growing season. Also, for reasons not fully understood, the animal performance on grass-legume pastures is often superior to that on grass alone, even on grass nitrogen fertilized to maintain the same protein level. Although the higher content of phosphorus and calcium in legumes is sometimes beneficial, properly fertilized grass supplies most animal requirements for these minerals. The high digestible energy content of lush growing clover or growth regulating substances in some legumes may partially explain this phenomenon.

To provide such pasturage, no other group of legumes has been utilized as extensively as several species of *Trifolium*. Grass-legume combinations that include these species comprise some of the best grazing lands in the world. Rye grass and white clover, Ladino clover and orchard grass (cocksfoot), and crimson clover and rye grass are examples. Where adapted, these pasture combinations produce large yields of top quality forage that satisfies the needs of high producing grazing animals. At the same time, these grass-legume associations thrive under properly managed continuous or rotational grazing systems (*see* also LEGUMINOSAE).

To supplement permanent pastures, temporary grazing, including feeding on root crops, is provided. Crops for temporary grazing are planned to be at their peaks of production during periods of low production from the permanent pasture. Such annuals as sorghum-Sudan grass hybrids, pearl millet, and lupine may be planted especially for this purpose. Winter grazing may be provided by reseeding crimson clover in a sequence of Bermuda grass and crimson clover. The same field produces Bermuda grass abundantly throughout the warm and hot periods of the year after the crimson clover has matured and died. Winter grains also are used for grazing, either for brief periods in advance of heading to permit the harvest of a grain crop later, or for grazing off completely.

On natural grasslands in many areas, plant growth is permitted to cure "on the stump" for grazing during periods when there is no growth. Often such feed is supplemented with a protein concentrate, such as cottonseed cake or soybean oil meal. Considerable grazing may be obtained also from adjacent grain stubble or recently planted winter grains if the natural grassland borders cropped areas. Over vast areas, however, the green and cured forage alone, which may or may not include browse plants, comprises the feed supply. When concentrates or high quality preserved forage (hay or silage) are not available to balance low-grade roughages, the grazing animals lose weight, may fail to produce offspring, or even die of starvation. Nevertheless, many flocks and herds go through this seasonal cycle and make phenomenal gains when the season of good pasturage returns.

Hay.—Hay is feed produced by dehydrating green forage to a moisture content of 15% or less. The same grasses and legumes grown for pasture may be used for hay although certain legumes, particularly alfalfa (lucerne), and some erect growing grasses, are better suited for hay production than for pasturing. The protein content of grasses and legumes decreases and fibre and lignified tissue increases as growing plants advance in maturity. These changes are associated with a decline in digestible dry matter and crude protein, and a reduction in intake when hay is fed to milking cows. The highest quality hay is produced when the crop is cut well in advance of maturity. The protein content at this time may be 20% or higher. To obtain maximum hay yields from a meadow on a sustained basis, including the maximum protein, the crop must be permitted to advance in maturity beyond the point of optimum feed quality. The most satisfactory compromise is to cut the crop for hay during the early bloom stage while the protein content (dry basis) is 14 to 18%. (Young legume growth may contain over 30% protein and mature grass less than 4% on a dry basis.)

For good hay, the crop must be cut at the proper stage of maturity, handled so as to retain the leaves, and cured to prevent spoilage or discoloration. Under field conditions, during periods of rainy weather, losses may exceed 50%. To avoid such losses, hay may be mow cured in the barn with forced air either heated or not heated. The cost of special machinery and equipment for this purpose has limited this procedure. Or, the hay may be placed in small piles or stacks in the field until it is dry enough for storage in large stacks or in the barn. Properly cured hay with 20% or less moisture may be stored for months without danger of spoilage. Most of the hay harvested in the United States (up to 84%) is baled. Hay conditioners, machines that either crimp or crush the freshly mowed crop, have helped to reduce the time interval from mowing to storage, and the danger of excessive weather damage. It has been found that properly conditioned hay with a moisture content of approximately 25% can be baled without danger of spoilage. Improvements in current field wafering and pelleting machines could bring further change to accepted hay-making practices. (*See* CROP DRYING AND PROCESSING.)

Silage.—Where weather conditions preclude the possibility of making high quality hay, making silage has become important as a forage preservation measure. Compared with corn silage, grass silage is low in total energy, but in other respects it is equal to or better than corn silage, when properly made. Grass-legume combinations can be made into good silage easier than protein-rich legumes alone. The green material should be chopped fine enough to assure good packing and the exclusion of air from the mass of chopped material, whether placed in a tower silo, stack, trench, or pit. The crop should be cut at the same or slightly earlier stage of maturity as is required to make high quality hay. A high-moisture content in the ensiled material facilitates compaction and the exclusion of air. However, excess moisture (above 70%) seeps away and carries valuable nutrients with it. Excess moisture in the silo may also interfere with the fermentation processes that produce the best quality silage. Since freshly harvested forage contains from 75 to 80% moisture, it is difficult to adjust the moisture content of the forage precisely throughout the ensiling period. It is good practice to fill the bottom half or two-thirds of the silo with forage with 68 to 70% moisture content, and the remainder with material with excess moisture. The heavy wet material on top helps to pack the entire mass and seals the exposed top surface better than drier material.

Airtight covers properly installed practically eliminate the danger of loss due to spoilage. Though it is possible to make and preserve silage in a trench, pit, or stack, losses may approach or exceed 50% unless precautions are taken to protect all exposed surfaces from air. Lightweight covers have been developed for this purpose. Good silage has a clean, acid odour and taste, no mold or sliminess, and a pH (acidity) of 3.5 to 4.5. (*See* also ENSILAGE.)

Haylage.—Haylage is forage dried more than conventional silage but less than hay. If properly handled it possesses the potential benefit of high feeding value and lower storage losses than silage. Forage is dried to about 50% moisture and stored in a gastight silo. Haylage losses may not exceed 5% while direct cut silage losses may range from 20 to 25%. Airtight storage is a prerequisite to successful production, and the lack or expense of such storage may limit haylage production.

Green Feeding.—In addition to pasture, hay, silage, and haylage, the grass crop may be cut and fed fresh. This practice of green feeding (soiling) is not new, but has been revived for a number of reasons. Some of these reasons are associated with special problems, such as the inaccessibility to adequate pasturage of large, commercial dairy herds or cattle feeding establishments. Other reasons include: (1) reduction of the danger of bloat that may occur when grazing animals are given unlimited access to pasture legumes; (2) unsuitability of the herbage species for grazing, but adaptability to mechanical harvest at regular intervals; (3) higher net feed recovery per unit area; and (4) higher net financial returns from the enterprise. The latter two reasons are not generally valid. They depend upon several conditions and alternatives such as topography and soil-moisture conditions, cost of machinery, labour, and fencing, and the skill of the operator in managing grazing animals. Though green feeding is practised with justification and profit under some conditions, its disadvantages have limited its use (see also Feeds, Animal).

BREEDING AND IMPROVEMENT OF FORAGE GRASSES AND LEGUMES

New plant introduction has made a remarkable contribution to the development of forage resources throughout the world. This is especially true in the Americas where many valuable grasses and legumes are native to Africa, Asia, and Europe. In the humid portions of North America none of the major cultivated species is a native species. Introduced grasses and legumes are likewise of great importance in New Zealand, Australia, and in parts of South America. The collection and introduction of grasses and legumes remains an important source of material for plant breeding research, for direct use as forages and for use in soil conservation plantings.

Plant breeders have made significant contributions in developing superior grass and legume varieties. However, research has been limited to a comparatively small number of species, and much of it is of recent origin. Little forage breeding work was conducted prior to the mid-1930s. Lack of emphasis on forage breeding as well as unsatisfactory progress in some improvement programs can be attributed to one or several of the technical problems peculiar to the grasses and legumes. These include: (1) most forage crops are cross-pollinated; (2) controlled hybridization is difficult because of small floral organs; (3) many forages exhibit varying degrees of self-sterility which limit inbreeding; (4) most important species are polyploids (with high chromosome numbers) with complex inheritance patterns; (5) selections and progenies of perennial forages must be tested for longer periods than annual crops to determine their merits; (6) population size is reduced by the cost of establishing and maintaining perennials in breeding nurseries; and (7) evaluation procedures for species that will be utilized by livestock are not clear-cut.

Research involving specialists in genetics, breeding, entomology, pathology, nematology, physiology, forage management, and animal nutrition has become an essential element in well organized forage improvement programs. Major objectives include tolerance to environmental hazards; resistance to diseases, insects, and nematodes; and higher yields of quality forage.

Rapid progress can be made in identifying plants or field collections that are more vigorous or better adapted in a specified environment. These ecotypes (strains developed by natural selection) may be named and multiplied for use in forage plantings. "Akaroa" orchard grass from New Zealand, "Trailway" side-oats grama and "Champ" big bluestem from the United States, are just three examples of ecotypic testing, have been used to select varieties that represent an advance in at least one significant characteristic. Late maturity was achieved in developing "S143" orchard grass (United Kingdom), "Pennlate" orchard grass (U.S.), "Essex" timothy (U.S.); bacterial wilt resistance was the principal advantage of "Ranger" alfalfa (U.S.); "Kenland" red clover (U.S.) possessed southern anthracnose resistance; and "Piper" Sudan grass (U.S.) was characterized by a reduction in prussic acid potential. Although these varieties and others represent solid advances, it has become increasingly apparent that multiple objectives must be attained in forage improvement. Alfalfa provides a good example, for the continued prominence of this crop depends on the availability of new varieties with resistance or tolerance to a wide range of plant pests. Typical varieties include "Dawson" (U.S.) with resistance to pea aphids, spotted alfalfa aphids, and bacterial wilt, and "Washoe" (U.S.) that is resistant to the same pests plus stem nematodes. The need for broad spectrum resistance has stimulated the development of plant populations that possess a very broad genetic base. These populations provide both public and private plant breeders with source material from which they can develop varieties to meet the needs of specific areas or regions.

Crosses among grasses, because of the relative ease with which certain species can be hybridized, has intrigued plant breeders as a rapid approach to the development of superior grasses. In the past, failure to appreciate the complexity of the problem has led to very disappointing results. Typical of recent investigations are well planned studies in the United States, the United Kingdom, the Netherlands, and West Germany to transfer the nutritive value and palatability of rye grass to persistent but less nutritious tall fescue. Infertility problems in wide crosses can be circumvented when it is practical to increase the sterile or near sterile hybrid vegetatively. This approach has been used to plant productive Bermuda grass hybrids. Thus the Bermuda grass variety "Coastal" has been established vegetatively on several million acres in the southern United States.

Chromosome numbers have been doubled with colchicine (to produce artificial autopolyploids) to facilitate hybridization and to produce new varieties. Considerable emphasis has been devoted to this breeding technique in Sweden and in other European countries. As a result, polyploid varieties of rye grass, red clover, alsike clover, and white clover have gained a degree of prominence.

The discovery of cytoplasmic male-sterility in sorghum has enabled plant breeders to develop hybrid forage types, and to produce sorghum-Sudan grass hybrids for grazing, silage, and green feed. Cytoplasmic male-sterility has also been found in pearl millet, and efforts are being made to find usable sources of male-sterility in perennial species. In Bahia grass, good combining self-sterile clones have been planted vegetatively for the production of hybrid seed. Research on the nature of apomictic reproduction (asexual seed produced without fertilization) in the grasses has been very rewarding. "Higgins" buffel grass (U.S.), a productive, fertile, true breeding apomictic variety, was developed by crossing a sexual aberrant type to a vigorous, low seed yielding apomictic strain.

Research on the composition of forage crops offers much promise in improving the quality of new varieties. It has been demonstrated that alfalfa varieties differ in saponin content, and that selection for low saponin content is feasible. Saponins are biologically active constituents that could affect the quality of dehydrated forages. Foliar diseases have been found associated with the amount of estrogen in forages. Alfalfa varieties and selections resistant to foliar diseases are low in coumestrol, the principal estrogen in this species. In one test the coumestrol content of diseased alfalfa samples averaged 49 parts per million (ppm) while the healthy control averaged 1.0 ppm. Differences have been found within forages in digestibility, protein and carotene content, and in levels of toxic or semitoxic substances that may affect animal performance. Fistulated steers have been used to measure the digestibility of selected plants. "Coastcross 1" Bermuda grass selected by this technique equals the "Coastal" variety in yield but is 11 to 12% more digestible. In a feeding trial, steers gained up to 30% more on "Coastcross 1" than on "Coastal." Improving the quality and yield potential of forage grasses and legumes is attainable, and highly essential if these crops are to retain a prominent place in production of animal products.

Bibliography.—American Association for the Advancement of Science, *Grasslands* (1959); W. Davies, *The Grass Crop*, 2nd ed. (1961); J. R. Harlan, *Theory and Dynamics of Grassland Agriculture* (1956);

H. D. Hughes et al., *Forages*, 2nd ed. (1962); R. W. Ingham et al., *Grass Silage and Dairying* (1949); D. Meredith (ed.), *Grasses and Pastures of South Africa* (1956); E. H. McIlvain and D. A. Savage, *Advances in Agronomy*, vol. vi, pp. 1-61 (1954); *Proceedings, Ninth International Grassland Congress*, Brazil (1965); *Proceedings, Tenth International Grassland Congress*, Finland (1966); *Proceedings, International Symposium on Plant Introduction*, Honduras (1966); *Proceedings, Second National Grassland Conference*, University of Tennessee (1965); U.S. Department of Agriculture, "Grass," *1948 Yearbook of Agriculture* (1948).
(D.F.Bd.; A.A.H.)

GRASSMANN, HERMANN GÜNTHER (1809–1877), German mathematician chiefly remembered for his major work, *Die Ausdehnungslehre* or calculus of extension, was born at Stettin (now Szczecin, Pol.) on April 15, 1809, where he taught until his death on Sept. 26, 1877. In *Die Ausdehnungslehre* (1844) he developed the idea, due to Leibniz, of an algebra in which symbols representing geometric entities (points, lines, planes . . .) are manipulated according to certain rules. In suitable circumstances this calculus proves far more powerful than earlier methods of co-ordinate geometry. To Grassmann is due also the notion of representing subspaces of a given space (*e.g.*, the lines in three-dimensional space) by co-ordinates; this leads to a mapping by points of an algebraic manifold, called the Grassmannian.

Somewhat similar ideas were propounded independently and contemporaneously by W. R. Hamilton in his quaternion theory; indeed Grassmann, Hamilton (and also G. Boole) were the pioneers in the field of modern algebra. Although Grassmann's methods were only slowly adopted, because of his obscure exposition, they eventually inspired the continental school of vector analysts. Later, through the work of E. Cartan, they have shown their utility in the study of differential forms, with its important applications to analysis and geometry.

For an introduction to Grassmann's work *see* H. G. Forder, *The Calculus of Extension* (1941). (L. R.)

GRASS-OF-PARNASSUS, any herbaceous plant of the genus *Parnassia* (family Saxifragaceae; *q.v.*), found in damp places throughout the north temperate zone. They are occasionally cultivated in bog gardens.

The white regular flower is rendered attractive by a circlet of scales, opposite the petals, each of which bears a fringe of delicate filaments ending in a yellow knob. These glisten in the sunshine and look like a drop of honey. Nectar is secreted at the base of each of the scales.

There are 40 to 45 species of *Parnassia*, of which the commonest is *P. palustris*. About 13 other species occur in North America, mostly in the northern United States and Canada.
(N. Tr.; X.)

GRATIAN (FLAVIUS GRATIANUS) (359–383), Roman emperor from 367 to 383, was born at Sirmium in Pannonia in 359, the son of Valentinian I (*q.v.*). On Aug. 24, 367, he was proclaimed *Augustus* by his father, now emperor, at Samarobriva (Amiens). His education was entrusted to the poet Ausonius. In 374 he married the 12-year-old Constantia, posthumous daughter of Constantius II. When Valentinian died on Nov. 17, 375, Gratian was appointed sole ruler of the west at Augusta Treverorum (Trier), but on Nov. 22 his four-year-old half brother Valentinian II was proclaimed emperor by the troops at Aquincum (near Budapest) without the knowledge of Gratian, who, however, recognized him as a colleague. Under Ausonius' influence Gratian tried to make his rule mild and popular. Most of his reign was spent in Gaul repelling the barbarians who lived across the Rhine; and Gratian, engaged with these, was unable to reach his uncle Valens, emperor of the east, in time to take part in the disastrous battle of Adrianople in 378. On Jan. 19, 379, he appointed Theodosius (*q.v.*) to rule as emperor of the east, and thereafter devoted himself to the defense of the west, though he occasionally visited Italy. (He had been in Rome in 376.)

Late in his reign the bishop Ambrose (St. Ambrose) gained great influence over him, and he omitted the words *pontifex maximus* from his title, the first emperor to do so, and ordered the statue of Victory to be removed from the senate house in Rome. An embassy of the senators, led by Q. Aurelius Symmachus, failed to persuade him to rescind his instructions on this matter. In 383 his wife died childless and was buried in Constantinople on Sept. 12. In the same year, while in the province of Raetia, preparing to repel the Alamanni, he heard that Magnus Maximus (*see* MAXIMUS) had been proclaimed emperor by the troops in Britain and had crossed over into Gaul. Gratian hurried as far as Paris to meet the usurper; but his troops, jealous of the favour he showed to some Alani mercenaries, deserted him. With a few companions he set out to escape beyond the Alps, but was treacherously murdered in Lugdunum (Lyons) on Aug. 25, 383, by Count Andragathius. Gratian was a likable person, interested in literature and a fluent speaker, but neither very effective nor very efficient. His great interest was hunting, a sport that sometimes interfered with his attention to his duties. He was an earnest Catholic and took many steps against the pagans. The historian Ammianus Marcellinus, a shrewd judge of character, felt that Gratian would have been comparable to the best of the emperors had not his associates brought out his weaknesses.

See A. Piganiol, *L'empire chrétien: 325–395* (1947); E. Stein, *Histoire du Bas-Empire*, vol. i (1960). (E. A. T.)

GRATIAN (GRATIANUS, MAGISTER GRATIANUS) (fl. c. 1140) has been called the father of the science of canon law because his writing and teaching initiated a new branch of learning in the 12th century, the study of church law as a discipline distinct from theology. By confusing him with later personalities, bibliographers have sometimes given his name wrongly as Johannes Gratianus or Franciscus Gratianus. Very little is known about Gratian's life. He was born, presumably in the late 11th century, in central Italy somewhere between Orvieto and Chiusi, perhaps at the hamlet of Carraria-Ficulle. Professed as a monk in the Camaldolese congregation of the Benedictine order, he became lecturer (*magister*) at the monastery of SS. Felix and Nabor in Bologna, the city which just then began to acquire fame as centre of the revived study of Roman law and a new civil jurisprudence. There he completed, in or shortly after 1140, his *Concordia discordantium canonum*, a collection of nearly 3,800 texts touching upon all fields of church discipline, which he presented in the framework of a treatise designed to resolve into harmony (*concordia*) all the contradictions and inconsistencies existing in the millenary tradition of rules accumulated from divers sources (*discordantes canones*). Gratian is once mentioned in 1143 as consultant to a papal judge, and there is evidence that he was dead before 1159.

Later generations of chroniclers tacked several legends onto this meagre record of his life, pretending that he was a half brother of the celebrated theologian Peter Lombard, or that he became a bishop or even a cardinal. Actually his person is entirely effaced by his work. Although by no means the first systematic compilation of canon law, it proved to be the right book at the right time because of its completeness and because of its superior method in combining the juristic with the scholastic approach. For the former, Gratian was indebted to the Bolognese doctors of civil law; for the latter, some directives had already been given by earlier canonists—*e.g.*, Ivo of Chartres—but a more direct influence came from the trends of contemporary theology in France.

The *Concordia discordantium canonum*, soon to be cited for short as *Decreta* or *Decretum Gratiani*, became the basic text on which the masters of canon law lectured and commented in the schools, first at Bologna, soon also at Paris, Oxford and other centres of learning. What is more, without ever receiving formal approbation, it was used as a book of authorities for the "old" law in the practice of the papal Curia. Even after much of its content had become obsolete by later papal legislation, it remained the first part of the traditional corpus of canon law of the Roman Catholic Church until the codification of 1917. *See also* CANON LAW.

GRASS-OF-PARNASSUS (PARNASSIA)

RUTHERFORD PLATT

BIBLIOGRAPHY.—Stephan Kuttner, "The Father of the Science of Canon Law," *Jurist*, vol. i, pp. 1-18 (1941); Alphonse Van Hove, *Prolegomena* (*Commentarium Lovaniense in Codicem iuris canonici*, vol. i, book 1, 2nd ed., pp. 338-348, with full bibliography (1945); *Studia Gratiana*, ed. by Giuseppe Forchielli and Alfons M. Stickler, 12 vol. (1953-67); J. Rambaud-Buhot, *New Catholic Encyclopedia*, vol. vi (1967). (S. G. K.)

GRATTAN, HENRY (1746-1820), Irish statesman devoted to achieving independence for Ireland, was born in Dublin on July 3, 1746. His father, James Grattan, was for years recorder of Dublin, and his mother was daughter of Thomas Marlay who became chief justice. At Trinity college, Dublin, Henry Grattan acquired a devotion to the classics and was inspired by the great orators. Called to the Irish bar in 1772, he made no serious effort to practise, but continued his pursuit of eloquence on the model of the greatest contemporary and classical masters. He was at first drawn strongly to life in England, but he was given a seat in the Irish parliament by Lord Charlemont, and was soon involved in the campaign of Henry Flood (*q.v.*) for national independence and the agitation for free trade. Flood at this time had forfeited his popular leadership by accepting government office and Grattan, with his brilliant eloquence, quickly became the leading spokesman of the nationalist agitation, which aimed at liberating the Irish parliament from its subservience to the English privy council.

Repeal of Poynings' Act.—Grattan formally demanded in April 1780 the repeal of Poynings' act, which had made all Irish legislation subject to approval by the English parliament. The Irish agitation gained impetus quickly under the impact of the American Revolution and it was soon connected with the new demand for relaxation of the anti-Catholic laws. In the absence of adequate defensive forces against possible French invasion, the Irish volunteers came into being as a spontaneous military organization. The Catholics were still forbidden to carry arms but the more influential of them co-operated generously. In this new situation Grattan's inspired speeches and patriotism made him the recognized champion of Irish independence and reform. At a mass meeting of the Ulster volunteers at Dungannon in Feb. 1782, resolutions were passed demanding both legislative independence and a relaxation of the penal laws. Grattan's earlier attempts to achieve these reforms in parliament had all been defeated, but on April 16 he moved for the third time his Declaration of Rights and it was carried unanimously in both houses. The English parliament soon yielded and Grattan, as a sign of national gratitude, was voted a grant of £50,000 to buy an estate. With this he later bought Moyanna, near Stradbally in Queen's county.

Grattan's sense of his own contribution to winning Irish independence was expressed in his famous assertion: "I am now to address a free people.... I found Ireland on her knees, I watched over her with a paternal solicitude. I have traced her progress from injuries to arms, and from arms to liberty.... Ireland is now a nation; in that new character I hail her, and bowing in her august presence I say *Esto Perpetua*." However, the English government only conceded a repeal of Poynings' law. It created two independent legislatures but retained one overriding executive under the control of Westminster. The result was "an ingenious blend of native oligarchy with a despotism controlled by an alien democracy, a system well calculated to bring out the worst qualities inherent both in absolute and in popular government" (A. E. Zimmern, *Henry Grattan*, 1902). Grattan himself was to protest bitterly in 1791 that "the Irish government in its perverted state, is composed of responsible officers who are not resident and resident officers who are not responsible."

Political Conflicts.—Absorbed in legal and political conflicts which were often remote from reality, Grattan was blind to the actual predominance of English control and to the close restrictions upon the composition of the Irish parliament, with its majority of pocket-borough representatives. The Catholics, though they formed the mass of the people, could not even vote in political elections. He urged their right to vote but at first scarcely contemplated their admission to parliament. Grattan's immediate problem after the concession of legislative independence in 1782 was the personal rivalry of Henry Flood, who now accused Grattan of accepting less than the "simple repeal" which would have sig-

nified a formal surrender of English authority in Ireland. He had, moreover, encouraged a total disbanding of the Irish volunteers, while Flood demanded their revival. His prestige fell heavily during the bitter controversy with Flood about "simple repeal." But it revived quickly when Grattan brought forward the contentious proposal for commuting tithes, which were levied chiefly upon a Catholic population of peasants, to provide endowments for an alien Protestant church.

In the surge of popular excitement and infusion of democratic ideas which followed the French Revolution, Grattan regained his lost popularity as a champion of free institutions and was in 1790 elected for Dublin city. He supported Sir Hercules Langrishe's Catholic relief bill in 1792, which had been largely inspired by Edmund Burke. When Lord Fitzwilliam was appointed in 1794 as the new Irish viceroy pledged to introduce wide reforms and measures for Catholic relief, Grattan renewed his efforts but was overwhelmed by the diehard reaction in Dublin castle, which obtained Fitzwilliam's recall in Feb. 1795.

A new phase of stern repression and military violence followed, and Grattan protested repeatedly with impassioned speeches. Yielding to the combined discouragements of ill-health and political defeat, he retired from parliament in May 1797, after issuing a rousing "Letter to the Citizens of Dublin." Military repression became more ruthless and widespread while the United Irishmen's society pursued their preparations for a rebellion; plans which were believed to be secret but were betrayed in all directions by informers and paid government spies.

Union, 1801.—Grattan, suffering from acute physical disability, had retired to England, and he was there during the rebellion of 1798. Immediately after its suppression William Pitt set in motion his plans for bringing about a legislative union of the Irish and English parliaments. Grattan became the foremost leader of resistance to that policy. He had an intense belief in the sacred cause of Irish national independence, even though it meant in practice the continuance of oligarchic government by the Protestant and landowning ascendancy. His agitation for parliamentary reform and for Catholic relief had made him appear as an ally of the United Irishmen, whose aims were avowedly Jacobin and republican. He was now formally expelled from the Irish privy council, and even from the Dublin merchants' guild. But Pitt's undisguised efforts to bribe a majority of the Irish parliament into voting its own extinction revived Grattan's former prestige. He rose nobly to the demands made upon him. He had no seat in parliament, but was enabled to buy a pocket borough in Wicklow on Jan. 15, 1800, in time to take an active part in the house of commons during its last session. Though he was still in his early 50s he was too weak to stand and was allowed to address the house seated. The debates were prolonged until May 26 when Grattan delivered his final oration against the impending union, declaring that "I will remain anchored here with fidelity to the fortunes of my country, faithful to her freedom, faithful to her fall."

For some years after the union of 1801, Grattan remained outside parliament, but in 1805 he was elected to the English house of commons as member for Malton. C. J. Fox and Lord Grenville regarded him as a useful ally, but he refused their invitation to accept office in 1806, as he had previously refused in 1782 and 1795. Henceforward he devoted himself almost entirely to the fight for Catholic emancipation, subject to safeguards which he thought necessary to protect the Protestant establishment. His efforts were hampered by the rise of a bolder and more confident Catholic agitation in Ireland, led by the young barrister Daniel O'Connell (*q.v.*), who refused to accept any proposal for a government veto upon the choice of Catholic bishops. Grattan had readily accepted the veto proposals in the belief that the Catholic Church in the United Kingdom must be subject to some political control. His bill for Catholic relief in 1813, which contained the veto provisions, was narrowly defeated in the house of commons. He defied his doctors by undertaking the long journey to London in May 1820 for a last debate on Catholic rights. He was too ill to fulfill his purpose and he died in London, on June 6, 1820. On his deathbed he commanded his son to commemorate his words "I die with a love of liberty in my heart and this declaration in favour of my country in my hands." He was buried in Westminster abbey, close to the tombs of Pitt and Fox.

Grattan's principal gifts were as a public orator of superb and compelling eloquence who could arouse both popular enthusiasm and devoted service. His personal integrity and pure patriotism were never in question. But he lacked the ability to master complicated questions and he had no aptitude for dealing with the rapidly changing conditions of his age.

BIBLIOGRAPHY.—*Memoirs and Speeches of Henry Grattan*, 5 vol., ed. by his son Henry Grattan (1839–46); W. E. H. Lecky, *Leaders of Public Opinion in Ireland* (1912); A. E. Zimmern, *Henry Grattan* (1902); Stephen Gwynn, *Henry Grattan and His Times* (1939).
(D. G.)

GRAUBÜNDEN (Fr. GRISONS; It. GRIGIONI; Romansh GRISHUN), most easterly of the Swiss cantons and the largest, though relatively sparsely populated. Pop. (1960) 147,458, giving a density of 53.7 per square mile. Its area is 2,745 sq.mi., of which more than a half is classed as productive (forests covering about one-fifth of the total), but it has 138.6 sq.mi. of glaciers, ranking in this respect next after the Valais and before Bern. The whole canton is mountainous. The principal glacier groups comprise those of the Tödi (11,876 ft.) to the north; the Medels (10,-531 ft.) to the southwest; the Adula group to the southwest, including the Rheinwaldhorn (11,161 ft.); the Bernina (13,284 ft.), to the southeast, the most extensive of the Albula, and Piz Kesch (11,214 ft.) to the east; and the Silvretta group including Piz Linard (11,191 ft.) to the northeast.

The principal valleys are those of the upper Rhine and of the Inn (or Engadine, *q.v.*). The main sources of the Rhine are in the canton. The valley of the Vorder Rhein is called the Bündner Oberland, that of the Mittel Rhein the Val Medel and that of the Hinter Rhein, in different parts of its course, the Rheinwald, the Schams valley and the Domleschg valley. The upper valley of the Julia is named the Oberhalbstein. Other streams join the Ticino and so the Po, the Adda and the Adige. The inner valleys are the highest in central Europe; among the loftiest villages is Juf, 6,998 ft. (the highest permanently inhabited village in the Alps), at the head of the Avers valley.

Below Chur, near Malans, good wine is produced, while in the Val Mesocco, maize (corn) and chestnuts flourish. Forests and the mountain pasturages are the chief source of wealth. There are many mineral springs. The climate, except on the southern slope of the Alps, is Alpine but seldom severe. Many tourists visit the valleys, spas and resorts in the canton, which include Arosa, Davos, St. Moritz, Pontresina, Flims, Klosters, Lenzerheide, Scuol-Tarasp-Vulpera, Celerina, Samedan, Sils (Segl) and Zuoz. Railways and roads link up Graubünden with all countries of Europe. From Landquart and Chur the Rhaetian railway runs over the Bernina pass to connect with the Italian railways and over the Oberalp pass to the Gotthard railway and the canton of Valais. The many Alpine passes and valley highways enable the motorist to explore the region. Federal postal motor coaches link up all the side valleys.

The German-speaking part of the population live mainly around Chur, Arosa and Davos, the Italian-speaking in the Val Mesocco, Val Bregaglia and the valley of Poschiavo. The characteristic tongue of Graubünden is a survival of an ancient Romance language which has a fairly important literature, and is still widely spoken. It is distinguished by two dialects: Romansh, which prevails in the Bündner Oberland and in the Hinter Rhein valley, and Ladin, which survives in the Engadine and in the neighbouring valleys of Bergün, Oberhalbstein and Münster. There are, however, in these regions German-speaking people, mostly as a result of immigration from the upper Valais in the 13th century. Much of the population is engaged in catering for tourists, but there is a considerable trade with Italy, particularly in the wines of the Valtellina. Some lead and silver mines were formerly worked, but are now abandoned.

The canton is divided into 14 administrative districts and includes 224 communes. It sends members to the federal *Ständerat* and to the federal *Nationalrat*. The cantonal constitution has created a legislature (*Grossrat*—no numbers fixed by the consti-

tution) elected by universal suffrage. The "obligatory referendum" obtains in the case of all laws and important matters of expenditure and revisions of the constitution. Chur (*q.v.*) is the cantonal capital.

History.—The greater part (excluding the three Italian-speaking valleys) of the modern canton of Graubünden formed the southern part of the province of Rhaetia (Raetia [*q.v.*]; probably the aboriginal inhabitants, the Rhaeti, were Celts rather than, as was formerly believed, Etruscans), set up by the Romans after their conquest of the region in 15 B.C. The Romanized inhabitants were to a certain extent Teutonized under the Ostrogoths (A.D. 493–537) and under the Franks (from 537 on). Governors called *Praesides* are mentioned in the 7th and 8th centuries, while members of the same family occupied the episcopal see of Coire (Chur) which was first mentioned in 452.

About 806 Charlemagne made this region into a county, but in 831 the bishop procured for his dominions exemption ("immunity") from the jurisdiction of the counts. Before 887 the see was transferred from the Italian province of Milan to the German province of Mainz (Mayence). The bishop became a prince of the empire in 1170 and later allied himself with the rising power (in the region) of the Habsburgs. This led in 1367 to the foundation of the *Gotteshausbund* (League of God's House), chiefly in order to stem his rising power. In 1395 the abbot of Disentis, the men of the Lugnetz valley and the great feudal lords of Räzuns and Sax, joined in 1399 by the counts of Werdenberg, formed another league, called the *Oberbund* (comprising the highlands in the Vorder Rhein valley) or the *Grauer Bund* (Gray league), the word gray deriving from the homespun gray cloth which was worn by the men and which has given rise to the name of Grisons (French *gris*, Romansh *grisch*) or Graubünden (the Gray leagues) for the whole canton. The view that the name derives from the league of counts (*graven* or *grafen*) cannot be maintained. In 1436, the third Rhaetian league was founded by the former subjects of the count of Toggenburg, whose dynasty then became extinct; they included the inhabitants of the Prätigau, Davos, Maienfeld, the Schanfigg valley, Churwalden and the lordship of Belfort (*i.e.*, the region round Alvaneu), and formed ten bailiwicks, whence the name of the league—*Zehngerichtenbund* (League of Ten Courts). In 1450 *Zehngerichtenbund* concluded an alliance with the *Gotteshausbund* and in 1471 with the *Oberbund*; but of the so-called triple perpetual alliance at Vazerol, near Tiefencastel, there exists no authentic evidence in the oldest chronicles, though diets were held there. In 1496 the possessions of the extinct counts of Toggenburg passed to the elder Habsburgs, the head of whom, Maximilian, was already emperor-elect, and desired to maintain the rights of his family there and in the Lower Engadine. Hence in 1497 the *Oberbund* and in 1498 the *Gotteshausbund* became allies of the Swiss confederation.

War broke out in 1499, but was ended by the great Swiss victory (May 22, 1499) at the battle of the Calven gorge (above Malles) which, added to another Swiss victory at Dornach (near Basel), compelled the emperor to recognize the *practical* independence of the Swiss and their allies of the empire. In 1526, by the articles of Ilanz, the last remaining traces of the temporal jurisdiction of the bishop of Coire was abolished. In 1512 the three leagues had conquered from Milan the rich and fertile Valtellina, with Bormio and Chiavenna, and held these districts as subject lands until in 1797 they were annexed to the Cisalpine republic. After the emperor had formally recognized, by the treaty of Westphalia (1648), the independence of the Swiss confederation, the rights of the Habsburgs in the Prätigau and the Lower Engadine were bought up (1649 and 1652). In 1803, after a brief inclusion in the Helvetic republic, the district entered the reconstituted Swiss confederation as the 18th canton of the Graubünden or the Grisons. *See also* ENGADINE; JENATSCH, GEORG; VALTELLINA.

BIBLIOGRAPHY.—"Codex diplomaticus Raetiae" (1848–69) from *Archiv. der Gesch. der Republik Graubünden*, ed. by C. von Mohr, and continuation by C. Jecklin, *Urkunden zur Verfassungsgesch. Graubündens* (1883); *Bündnergeschichte*, 3 vol., by various authors (1900–02); S. Andrea, *Das Bergell, Wandergn. u. Gesch.* (1901); G. Theobald, *Naturbilder aus den rhätischen Alpen*, 4th ed. (1920); F. Pieth, *Bündnergeschichte* (1945).
(P. Ju.)

GRAUN, KARL HEINRICH (c. 1704–1759), German composer known for his sacred music, was born at Wahrenbrück, Saxony, in 1703 or 1704. He was a chorister in his youth at Dresden. At an early age he composed a number of sacred cantatas and other pieces for the church service. He completed his studies under J. C. Schmidt (1664–1728) and profited much from the Italian operas performed at Dresden under Antonio Lotti. In 1725 Graun made his debut as a tenor in opera at Brunswick in a work by G. C. Schürmann, but, not being satisfied with the arias assigned to him, he rewrote them and, in consequence, was commissioned to compose a whole opera for the next season. This work, with five other operas and two settings of the Passion, belong to his Brunswick period. In 1735 the crown prince of Prussia, later Frederick the Great, engaged Graun at Rheinsberg, where he composed a number of cantatas. On Frederick's accession to the throne in 1740, he sent Graun to Italy to engage singers for a new opera company to be established in Berlin. On his return to Berlin he was appointed *Kapellmeister* and composed about 30 operas to Italian words. Graun's Passion cantata, *Der Tod Jesu* (1755), long held a place in Germany similar to that enjoyed by Handel's *Messiah* in England, being regularly performed in Holy Week for a century and a half after its composer's death. The *Te Deum* written in 1757 to celebrate the Prussian victory at Prague was also a favourite work with German audiences. He died at Berlin on Aug. 8, 1759.

As a composer Graun was a leading exponent of the "Berlin school," which also included C. P. E. Bach, Graun's elder brother Johann Gottlieb, J. J. Quantz and Frederick the Great himself. The Berlin school was one of the first groups to show the rising preclassic style; one of the chief charms of the music is the fascinating combination of old and new melodic and formal concepts.

JOHANN GOTTLIEB GRAUN (c. 1703–71), elder brother of the preceding, was a violinist and orchestral leader, known for his chamber music and symphonies. He entered the service of Frederick the Great at about the same time as his brother and was conductor at Berlin and Potsdam from 1740 onward.

See A. Yorke Long, *Music at Court* (1954).
(Cs. Ch.)

GRAU SAN MARTÍN, RAMÓN (1887–1969), Cuban political leader, writer and physician, was born Sept. 13, 1887, in Pinar del Río into a wealthy family. He took a University of Havana medical degree in 1908, and also studied medicine in Europe. He became professor of physiology at the University of Havana in 1921 and for the next 27 years divided his time between politics, medical practice and teaching. A political progressive, he was jailed in 1931, participated in the overthrow of the dictator Gerardo Machado (Aug. 1933), and became provisional president (Sept. 10, 1933–Jan. 14, 1934) after Fulgencio Batista's sergeants' revolt. Grau San Martín broke with Batista, established the Auténtico party, went into exile (1935–38), and in 1940 led his party to successful control of the constitutional convention. He lost the presidential election of 1940 to Batista, but was elected to the presidency in 1944. He initiated social reforms and, on completing his term in 1948, retired from politics. His administration was characterized by internal dissension and social unrest, but he was credited with strict adherence to democratic principles. He wrote a dozen books on politics, more on medicine, and contributed regularly to medical and scientific journals. He died in Havana July 28, 1969.
(C. C. Cv.)

GRAVE: *see* CEMETERY; FUNERARY RITES AND CUSTOMS.

GRAVEL, an aggregate of more or less rounded rock fragments coarser than sand, technically more than two millimetres in diameter. Gravel beds in some places contain accumulations of heavy minerals, such as metallic ores, as cassiterite, a major source of tin, or native metals in nugget form. A notable example of the latter is the extensive auriferous gravel of Tertiary age in California, goal of much hydraulic mining. Gravels are also widely used building materials (*see* CONCRETE.).

The rounding of gravel results from abrasion in the course of stream transport or milling by the sea. Gravel deposits accumulate in parts of stream channels or on beaches where the water action is too rapid to permit sand to remain. Because of changing conditions, gravel formations are generally more limited and more variable in coarseness, thickness and configuration than are sand or clay deposits. Persistent accumulation of gravel or pebble beds may take place along an inner breaker zone, on a beach otherwise sandy. Cobble and pebble beaches (shingle beaches) often take their origin from the points of rocky cliffs.

In many regions there are marine gravels wholly resembling those of the seashore, at levels tens of hundreds of feet above tide level. Such gravel terraces (or raised beaches) may extend great distances and indicate that the sea at one time stood relatively higher. River gravels occur mostly in the middle and upper parts of streams where the currents are most active. Ancient terraces of gravel are found at levels much above those of the present rivers. They mark a former greater activity of streams or are evidence of uplift of the land or lowering of the sea, whereby the rivers have been able to cut their beds to a lower level. The Lafayette and related terrace gravel formations of the Atlantic and Gulf coastal plains of North America are products of both fluvial and marine action.

Fragments in gravels range from pebble to boulder size. Prolonged weathering and extended transport by long rivers on continental masses result in more complete rounding and selection as to size and physically and chemically durable rock materials. Gravels on smaller land masses, and where siliceous rocks are missing, are less well selected and less recognizable as definite rock formations. Conglomerates (*q.v.*) are cemented gravels. *See also* ALLUVIUM; BEACH; SEDIMENTARY ROCKS.
(C. K. WE.)

GRAVENHAGE, 'S: *see* HAGUE, THE.

GRAVES, ROBERT RANKE (1895–), English poet, novelist, essayist and scholar, one of the most gifted and versatile English men of letters of his time, was born at Wimbledon on July 26, 1895, the son of A. P. Graves, the Irish song writer, and a descendant of Von Ranke, the great German historian. Graves's work in verse and prose combines scholarship with a lyrical and narrative gift that has a direct and wide appeal.

Graves served during World War I with the Royal Welsh Fusiliers and his autobiography, *Good-Bye to All That* (1929, revised edition 1957), is a classic among modern war memoirs in its blunt, unadorned grimness. After the war was over he went to Oxford university and was allowed to quality for his degree by writing a thesis on modern poetry. His critical writings, always lively, have shown a growing intolerance of the work of a number of his contemporaries. He began before 1914 as a typical "Georgian" poet, but his war experiences and the difficulties of his personal life gave his later poetry a much deeper and more painful note, though Graves remained a traditionalist, rather than a modernist, in form. His sometimes almost unbearably sad love poems are among the most poignant in modern English and he has also considered his prose work—apart from *The White Goddess* (1947), a book which bases poetic inspiration on sexual love and dread—as of minor importance compared to his poetry. Of his numerous historical novels, at once deeply scholarly and boldly speculative, perhaps the best is *I, Claudius* (1934). His writings on the Christian religion, particularly *King Jesus* (1946), occasioned much discussion among scholars and critics. He published his *Collected Poems* in 1959. From 1961 until 1966 Graves was professor of poetry at Oxford university. With Omar Ali-Shah, he published a translation of the *Rubaiyat* of Omar Khayyam (1967).

BIBLIOGRAPHY.—Martin Seymour-Smith, *Robert Graves* (1956); G. S. Fraser, *Vision and Rhetoric* (1959); J. M. Cohen, *Robert Graves* (1960); D. Day, *Swifter Than Reason: the Poetry and Criticism of Robert Graves* (1963); F. H. Higginson, *A Bibliography of the Works of Robert Graves* (1966).
(G. S. F.; X.)

GRAVESEND, a municipal borough and river port in the Gravesend parliamentary division of Kent, Eng., on the right bank of the Thames, 22 mi. ESE of London. Pop. (1971 prelim.) 54,-044. At Swanscombe, about 2 mi. W., fragments of the skull of Swanscombe man dating from the Great Interglacial Age were found during quarrying (1935–55). Nearby was situated the Roman settlement of Vagniacae. Gravesend is mentioned in Domesday Book as Gravesham, possessing a landing place, or hithe, on the river. Although the town was originally concerned with agriculture, Richard II granted sole ferry rights for conveying passengers to London. Arising out of these ferry rights, for more than four centuries many illustrious persons were received in the borough on their way to and from the capital. The borough was incorporated in 1562, the present charter dating from 1632. Pocahontas (q.v.), the American Indian princess, died at Gravesend in 1617, and was buried in St. George's church, since 1953 known as St. George's Chapel of Unity (Pocahontas memorial with two windows presented by the Society of Colonial Dames in Virginia). Leonard Calvert (second son of Lord Baltimore and first governor of Maryland) set sail from Gravesend in 1633.

For a variety of reasons, not least of them the ferry rights, the town for centuries has been closely associated with administrative duties in relation to shipping on London's river. From the 16th century onward it became increasingly active in the handling of Britain's expanding maritime trade. Gravesend is now the centre for customs, the Port of London Health authority and the Trinity House pilots. There is a passenger and vehicle ferry across the Thames to Tilbury.

The town's prosperity increased greatly during the first half of the 19th century when, as a result of the coming of the steamboat, Gravesend became well known as a health resort and watering place. This period saw rapid growth, the building of the Town pier and the Royal Terrace pier, and the purchasing and layout of many parks and public gardens. There followed a process of transition to its present state as a modern industrial, commercial and maritime centre. Jetties of paper mills, cement factories, engineering works, tire and rubber works, printing works, shipbuilding and repair slipways flank the river frontage opposite Tilbury docks. Gravesend is the shopping, commercial, educational and entertainment centre for a prosperous industrial belt stretching along several miles of the south bank of the Thames. To the south and east on rising ground lie the residential areas of the town, which are bounded by agricultural land.

GRAVIES: *see* Food Preparation: *Stuffings and Gravies.*
GRAVING DOCK: *see* Dock.
GRAVITATION. The study of gravitation is the physical science concerned with the attraction of bodies for one another. This article is divided into the following four main sections covering the principal aspects of gravitation:

    I. Introduction
   II. Measurements of Gravitational Force
  III. Measurements of the Acceleration Due to Gravity
        A. Absolute Measurement of Gravity
        B. Relative Measurements of Gravity: Pendulum Measurements
        C. Relative Measurements of Gravity: Gravity Meters
   IV. Theories of Gravitation

I. INTRODUCTION

The traditional tale of Sir Isaac Newton and the falling apple is of significance for its stress upon the fact that bodies tend to fall toward the earth. They fall because they have weight, and the cause of their weight is the attraction that exists between the matter of which they are formed and the matter that comprises the earth.

This attraction is an all-pervading force that depends only upon the masses of the bodies and upon their distance apart. The earth therefore exerts an attraction on the moon just as it does on an apple. The demonstration that these two particular attractions follow the same mathematical law was the main contribution made by Newton to the study of heavenly bodies. The idea of interaction among members of the solar system and even of all separate masses was not new. Ptolemy (fl. 2nd century A.D.), whose formulation of the elaborate scheme of cycles and epicycles used by Hipparchus for planetary and solar orbits in a geocentric system was accepted until the time of Copernicus (1473–1543), appears to have visualized some force that held bodies down to the surface of the earth and also maintained the entity of the universe. The revolution in astronomy begun by Copernicus and continued by J. Kepler with the help of the first well-recorded and accurate details of planetary motion by Tycho Brahe laid the foundations for the Newtonian generalizations that were to follow. Although Kepler was more intent upon unraveling the underlying mathematical harmony of the universe (*see* Cosmology) than upon a

search for empirical rules he did, in fact, with his three laws, summarize the experimental observations in a form which made them available for more advanced mathematical deductions.

Galileo's researches had shown that no continual exertion of force was needed to maintain a body in motion; and, as a corollary to this, that some force must be present to cause the planets and their satellites to keep to their orbits instead of flying off at a tangent. Some of Newton's contemporaries, including B. Hooke and C. Huygens, realized that Kepler's third law (that the squares of the periodic times that the planets take to describe their orbits round the sun are proportional to the cubes of their respective distances from the sun) implied a force which decreased inversely as the square of the distance. Newton's speculations about the cause of the fall of bodies led him to connect the behaviour of the apple with the deviation of the moon from a straight-line course. Bodies on the earth, whether deep down in mines or more distantly removed from its surface on mountaintops, always tended to move downward, and it appeared plausible that the force causing this was inherently connected with the earth and that there was no reason why it should not continue with an inverse square relation out into space.

The moon is about 240,000 mi. from the earth, *i.e*, 60 times the distance of bodies at the earth's surface from its centre. Therefore, assuming the inverse square law, the force exerted by the earth at the moon should be only 1/3,600 of that which it exerts at its own surface. The fall of a body toward the earth in one second should therefore be 3,600 times the distance that the moon is deviated from a straight-line path in space in the same time. Astronomical measurements show that in one second the moon must be pulled back into its circular orbit by 0.0044 ft. A body at the earth's surface should, therefore, fall 0.0044 × 3,600, *i.e.*, about 16 ft. per second, which is the value observed. One underlying inference from this calculation is that the earth's sphere behaves as if all of its mass were concentrated at its centre. Although in extraterrestrial calculations the sun and the planets can be regarded as massive points, the earth is by no means small compared with the distance between itself and an apple. Newton was for a long time held up by this difficulty, but at last showed that the gravitational force exerted by a sphere on external bodies was the same as would obtain if the whole mass were considered as acting at the central point. Therefore the calculation comparing the moon with the apple was valid, and the connection between gravitational effects at the surface of the earth and the forces controlling the motion of the planets was successfully demonstrated to be due to a single unknown cause.

The law of gravitation of classical mechanics deduced by Newton may be stated thus: mutual action exists between each particle of matter and every other such that each particle is attracted to every other with a force varying as the product of the masses of the particles and inversely as the square of the distance between them. This law is formulated as:

$$F = G\,\frac{M_1 M_2}{d^n} \qquad (1)$$

were F is the force between the two particles of mass M_1 and M_2, d is the distance between them and G is a constant for all kinds of matter and is called the gravitational constant. This constant has the dimensions $L^3 M^{-1} T^{-2}$ (L is length, M is mass and T is time), and a numerical value depending on the units used. The application of this law to the solar system not only rationalized all of Kepler's laws but enabled all the intricate movements of the planets and their satellites to be deduced in such a manner as to agree with observations. The law also showed the reason for the motion of the sea that results in the tides (*q.v.*). Kepler had thought that the tides were due to the moon, but had confused his ideas about this with his astrological beliefs. By calculating the attraction of both sun and moon on the waters of the earth Newton laid the foundation of modern tidal theory, including the amplifying effect of narrow channels on the height of tides. The gravitational attraction of the sun and moon affect the earth's crust, raising earth tides which show themselves as small movements of the apparently solid surface. Measurement of these movements provides information about the elasticity of the material comprising the earth.

For bodies at the earth's surface, the universal law of gravitation provides the basis for Galileo's observation that any body is attracted by a force proportional to its mass. The force F acting on a body of mass M_1 is its weight W, and is due to the whole attraction of the earth's mass M_2 acting as if concentrated at its centre. Therefore, $F = W = GM_1M_2/r^2$, where r is the radius of the earth. But the force per unit mass is W/M_1, which is equal to GM_2/r^2. The force acting on the body M_1 may also be considered as defined by Newton's second law of motion; i.e., $W = M_1a$ where a is the acceleration that would be caused by the attraction of the earth if the body were allowed to fall freely. Thus the force at the body is exactly the same as if it were being accelerated at a rate $a = W/M_1$, and when the attraction of the earth is expressed as a force per unit mass, it is exactly equivalent to an acceleration. Therefore the expression $g = GM_2/r^2$ (where g is the acceleration due to gravity) is important and much used in discussing the behaviour of bodies on the earth. This is the reason why Henry Cavendish's famous laboratory experiment was popularly known as weighing the earth.

Although the astronomical observations that helped Newton to formulate his general law of gravitation are sufficient to give the most accurate confirmation of the part of the law pertaining to distance, the relative accelerations of different satellites toward the same primary body only allow the calculation of the ratio of the masses of the different bodies. For example, the acceleration of a planet toward the sun and of a satellite toward the planet may be obtained from observations made on the orbits of satellite and planet. Thus, the acceleration of satellite toward planet is $G \times P/$(distance of satellite)^2, and the acceleration of planet toward sun is $G \times S/$(distance of planet)^2; where P and S are the masses of planet and sun respectively. By division G is eliminated to give the ratio P/S. Astronomy, in fact, gives the product $G \times$ mass but not the separate values of G or mass. In view of its fundamental importance, the experimental determination of the gravitational constant G assumed great significance for physicists immediately Newton's law was formulated.

The value of G is very small (6.7×10^{-8} c.g.s. units), as is evidenced by the fact that objects do not attract each other enough to move noticeably toward each other. Two large cannon balls placed one inch apart, for example, would show a mutual gravitational pull of about 0.1 dyne. It is not surprising that Newton discarded any idea of measuring such small forces with the experimental facilities at his disposal and turned to the larger attractions provided by the earth itself. Newton knew that gravitational forces were small because the product $G \times M$ was given by the measured acceleration due to gravity; and limits to M, the mass of the earth, were set by common sense. It is perhaps more in line with the historical development of the subject of gravitation to write the mass of earth in terms of the mean density Δ of the material forming the earth. Then

$$g = \frac{GM}{r^2} = \frac{G}{r^2}\left(\frac{4}{3}\pi r^3\Delta\right) = \frac{4}{3}\pi r(G\Delta) \quad (2)$$

so that

$$G\Delta = \frac{3g}{4\pi r} \quad (3)$$

Newton made a very good guess at Δ, using the following reasoning: "But that our globe of earth is of greater density than it would be if the whole consisted of water only, I thus make out. If the whole consisted of water only, whatever was of less density than water, because of its less specific gravity, would emerge and float above. And upon this account, if a globe of terrestrial matter, covered on all sides with water, was less dense than water, it would emerge somewhere; and the subsiding water falling back, would be gathered to the opposite side. And such is the condition of our earth, which, in great measure, is covered with seas. The earth, if it was not for its greater density, would emerge from the seas, and according to its degree of levity, would be raised more or less above their surface, the water and the seas flowing backwards to the opposite side. By the same argument, the spots of the sun which float upon the lucid matter thereof, are lighter than that matter. And however the Planets have been form'd while they were yet in fluid masses, all the heavier matter subsided to the centre. Since, therefore, the common matter of our earth on the surface thereof, is about twice as heavy as water, and a little lower, in mines is found about three or four, or even five times more heavy; it is probable that the quantity of the whole matter of the earth may be five or six times greater than if it consisted all of water, especially since I have before shewed that the earth is about four times more dense than Jupiter." (Principia, book iii, prop. 10; vol. ii, p. 230 of the edition of 1729.)

The mean density of the earth, determined by a variety of methods, is about 5.5; so that Newton's estimate is remarkably accurate. Although gravitational forces are small, the difficulties of measuring them in the laboratory have been overcome by using the great sensitivities of the torsion balance and the common balance to record the attraction between small suspended masses and larger fixed masses. In the field, a natural mass such as a mountain or a section of the earth's crust is selected. The mass of the attracting body is calculated from topographical and rock sampling surveys, and the force that the natural mass exerts on a small known mass can be used to calculate G directly. However, the experiments were usually so arranged that the attraction was compared with that of the whole earth for the small mass. This gives the mass of the earth in terms of the mass of, e.g., a selected mountain; hence Δ can be determined and G can be calculated. In one class of experiments, the sideways pull of a mountain on a plumb bob is compared with the downward pull of the whole earth. The quantity that is measured is the deflection of the supporting line of the plumb bob from the vertical as determined by observations on stars in a place remote from the effect of the mountain. The attractions may also be compared by observing their effects on the period of a pendulum of fixed length. Great accuracy can be achieved by timing a large number of pendulum swings.

Many attempts were made, after the discovery of the law of gravitation, to determine any modifications needed to take account of changes in external conditions. The behaviour of electric and magnetic fields is influenced by the media through which they operate; but there is no sign of any similar modification to the gravitational field by the interposition of any substance between two mutually attracting bodies. There is, for example, no evidence that the side of the earth more distant from the sun is shielded from the effect of the sun's pull by the side nearer to the sun; and the general conclusion from everything that can be observed is that a mass in Australia acts on a mass in London precisely as if the earth were not interposed between the two. The attraction of the earth, which gives weight to bodies on its surface, is not altered by temperature or by chemical reaction except insofar as any escape of energy occurs; and in general the attraction between bodies bears no relation to the physical or chemical conditions of the acting masses or to the intervening medium.

Some of the thoughts of early workers on gravitational effects were directed toward the possibility of changes in gravitation which might be caused by relative motion of masses or by a finite speed of travel of the gravitational influence. The rapid motion of the heavenly bodies might conceivably result in some change in either the direction or the amount of their attraction toward each other at each moment; but such was found not to be the case even with the most rapidly moving bodies of the solar system. If the action of gravitation were not absolutely instantaneous the force would not be exactly in the line adjoining two bodies but would be affected by the motion of the line during that time required for the influence to pass from the one body to the other. Then again, there were doubts as to whether the Newtonian law would hold at all distances. All experiments and observations were, however, consistent with the law, from the short distances employed in laboratory experiments to the long ranges used in interplanetary calculations. The possibility was recognized that some types of matter might behave differently from others, or that some form of anisotropy could exist, such as is observed in the optical or electrical properties of crystals, but none of the investigations that were carried out succeeded in showing that gravitation is related to anything other than the masses of the attracting and attracted bodies and their distance apart. However, all these old generalizations should be viewed in the light of more modern theories of gravitation.

Before the time of Einstein, the study of gravitation had borne no relation to other parts of physics for, despite all practical and theoretical endeavours, no nongravitational influence on gravitation had been detected. Einstein, however, in the general theory of relativity, accounted for gravitation in terms of a wider description of the world as a whole. (See RELATIVITY: *General Theory of Relativity*.) This theory was in itself an extraordinary intellectual achievement and, on the practical side, it enabled him to explain a minute discrepancy in the behaviour of the planet Mercury and to predict two new effects of gravitation on light, *i.e.*, the deflection of light rays by the attraction of heavy bodies such as the sun, and the decrease of frequency of light emitted from heavy bodies. The latter, however, is deduced from more elementary ideas than that of general relativity. Einstein himself and other workers endeavoured to construct yet more general theories to include electromagnetic and other forces as well as gravitation. Other theoretical descriptions of gravitation alone also appeared but did not command the same wide assent as general relativity, while the problem of applying the ideas of quantum mechanics to gravitation remained unsolved in the early 1960s. Thus, although the practical calculation of gravitational effects can be carried out with extremely high accuracy over an enormous range of conditions, the relation of gravitation to other departments of physics remained in many respects still an enigma.

The more practical aspects of gravitation are concerned with the special case of the attraction of everyday objects by the earth. The force of gravity must be taken into account not only to ensure the accuracy of survey and navigation but also to facilitate theoretical discussions on the shape of the earth. Abnormal attractions of a plumb bob cause errors in the determination of distances from star sights. The plotting and possible use of the tracks of artificial satellites for measuring terrestrial distances add interest to these determinations, and the way in which the satellites move under the gravitational attraction of the earth enables the extent of polar flattening of the earth to be found very accurately. Artificial satellites have two uses in the study of the shape of the earth. In the first place they provide points of observation that are more clearly defined than are heavenly bodies, so that greater accuracy in measuring angular separations between different points on the earth's surface is attained. Secondly, since the artificial satellites are nearer the earth than natural orbiting bodies, the perturbations of their orbits are more sensitive to the attractive forces exerted by the earth.

The measurement of local values of the acceleration due to gravity has achieved great importance in determining the subsurface geology of the earth as an aid in finding oil and minerals. It is interesting to note that the first patented gravity meter was designed by Sir William Siemens in 1876 for use at sea, because "it would be possible for a captain to find the depth of water without a plumb-line." Unfortunately the isostatic balance that is operative over the oceans makes it impossible for the instrument to perform this function, but gravity measurements at sea may be useful for latitude determinations from submerged craft, and are certainly needed to calculate the true shape of the earth.

It is the value of g, the acceleration due to the gravitational attraction of the earth on bodies at its surface, rather than that of G, the gravitational constant, that is of most practical interest. The International Association of Geodesy, formed in 1863, ensures the uniformity of measurements over all parts of the earth. The observations of g consist mainly of comparisons with the accepted standard which was established in 1906 as the value at Potsdam, Ger., but the need for a more accurate absolute standard encouraged fresh determinations employing methods inherently more exact than the old pendulum measurements.

II. MEASUREMENTS OF GRAVITATIONAL FORCE

Practical determinations of G have been made since Pierre Bouguer's experiments in 1740, and an excellent account of this early work may be found in J. H. Poynting, Sir J. J. Thomson and G. W. Todd, *Properties of Matter*, ch. iii (1947). The experiments fall naturally into two classes. In the one, the attraction for a small mass of a topographical feature, such as a mountain, is compared with the attraction of the whole earth for the mass. In the other, an artificial mass is constructed in the laboratory and the force of attraction between it and a known small mass is measured. Although the use of topographical features provides a large value of one of the attracting masses in the relation $F = GM_1M_2/r^2$, the forces are still small because the distances are necessarily greater than in laboratory experiments, the terrestrial determinations of G (or Δ) require painstaking observations and their accuracy is limited by the uncertainty of the mass determination of the particular feature chosen.

Comparison of the Earth's Pull With That of a Natural Mass.—*Bouguer's Experiments.*—The earliest experiments made by Bouguer are recorded in his *Figure de la Terre* (1749). They were of two kinds. In the first he determined the length of the seconds pendulum and thus g at different elevations. At Quito, Peru (now Ecuador), which may be regarded as on a tableland with an elevation of about 9,400 ft., and again on the Isle of Inca at sea level, he determined g with pendulum apparatus. From the known difference in elevation of the two points of observation the measured value at sea level was projected to the elevation of the plateau by the inverse r^2 law, assuming that only free air occupied the intervening space. Actually his observed value of g at the elevated station was 1/6,983 greater than this calculated value, which difference he immediately assigned to the attraction of the 9,400 ft. of plateau material actually underlying the elevated station. Thus the experiment indicated that the attraction of the whole earth was 6,983 times that of the plateau. Since the attraction of the plateau could be calculated on the assumption that it was effectively an infinite slab of known thickness, Bouguer concluded that the density of the earth was 4.7 times that of the plateau. This result is obviously much too large.

In the second type of experiment he attempted to measure the horizontal pull of a 20,000-ft. mountain by suitable observations on the deflection of a plumb line. Because of experimental difficulties his results were inaccurate, but the importance of the experiment lies in its indication of the possibilities of the method.

Maskelyne's Experiment.—In 1774 Nevil Maskelyne (*Phil. Trans.*, p. 495, 1775) repeated the plumb line deflection measurements at the mountain of Schiehallion in Perthshire, Scot. The mountain was chosen for its steeply sloping north and south flanks; the deflections of a plumb bob to north and south of the mountain were observed by taking star transits (*see* TRANSIT CIRCLE) and were compared with the latitude difference of the two observing stations as calculated from a survey on the ground.

Airy's Experiment.—A modification of Bouguer's experiment was carried out by Sir G. B. Airy (*Phil. Trans.*, p. 297, 1856) in 1854 at Harton mine near South Shields, Eng. This consisted in comparing gravity at the top and bottom of a mine by the swings of the same pendulum and thus finding the ratio of the pull of the intervening strata to the pull of the whole earth. If the earth is assumed to be made up of homogeneous concentric shells, the ratio of the two gravity movements may be written down in terms of G, the depth of the mine, the radius of the earth and the density of the outer shell that includes the mine. Stations were chosen in the same vertical, one near the head of the shaft and the other 1,250 ft. below in an abandoned working. The pull of the 1,250-ft. outer shell of the earth's crust was only 1/14,000 of the attraction of the whole earth. The volume of the shell was 1/5,500 of the inner sphere of the earth below the bottom of the mine shaft so that, assuming the density of the shell to be 2.5, the density of the

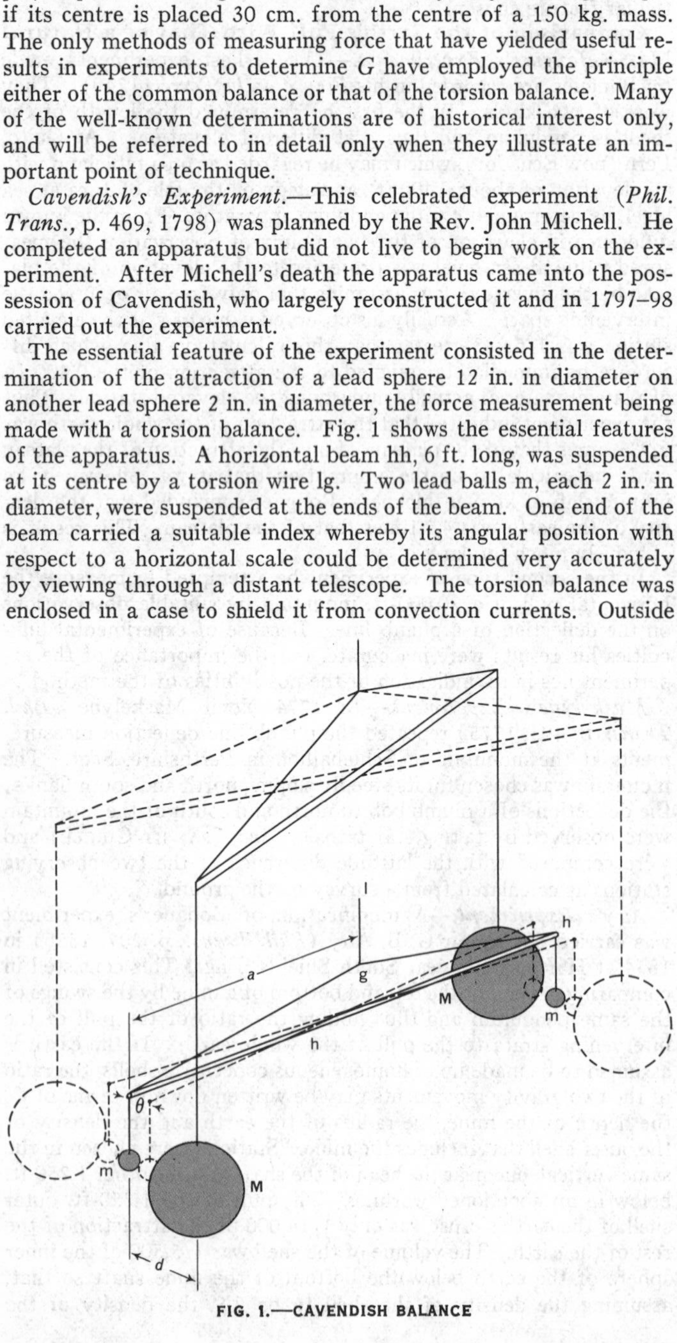

FIG. 1.—CAVENDISH BALANCE

earth was found to be $(14,000/5,500) \times 2.5 = 6.4$.

R. von Sterneck's Experiment.—Sterneck repeated the mine experiment in 1882–83 at the Adalbert shaft near Freiberg, Ger. However, although natural masses have the advantage of large size, so that forces are produced which can be compared with the attraction of the earth, they have the fatal defect that their density cannot be exactly determined. Even when a solid mountain block is selected, the extent of the root of this block and its relation to surrounding and underlying rock strata is uncertain; so that terrestrial observations are really more useful in studying the crust of the earth than in determining the fundamental gravitational constant. It is possible, with the aid of gravity meters, to improve on the techniques used in the old experiments of the Airy type, but the errors inherent in determining the mass of the attracting natural body will always be present. For this reason the accepted values of G are based on delicate experiments made in the laboratory.

Laboratory Methods of Determining G.—The forces between masses which can be accurately constructed and which can be handled in precision measurements are very small. For example, a sphere of 20 kg. mass is attracted by only 0.25 mg. weight if its centre is placed 30 cm. from the centre of a 150 kg. mass. The only methods of measuring force that have yielded useful results in experiments to determine G have employed the principle either of the common balance or that of the torsion balance. Many of the well-known determinations are of historical interest only, and will be referred to in detail only when they illustrate an important point of technique.

Cavendish's Experiment.—This celebrated experiment (*Phil. Trans.*, p. 469, 1798) was planned by the Rev. John Michell. He completed an apparatus but did not live to begin work on the experiment. After Michell's death the apparatus came into the possession of Cavendish, who largely reconstructed it and in 1797–98 carried out the experiment.

The essential feature of the experiment consisted in the determination of the attraction of a lead sphere 12 in. in diameter on another lead sphere 2 in. in diameter, the force measurement being made with a torsion balance. Fig. 1 shows the essential features of the apparatus. A horizontal beam hh, 6 ft. long, was suspended at its centre by a torsion wire lg. Two lead balls m, each 2 in. in diameter, were suspended at the ends of the beam. One end of the beam carried a suitable index whereby its angular position with respect to a horizontal scale could be determined very accurately by viewing through a distant telescope. The torsion balance was enclosed in a case to shield it from convection currents. Outside

the case, two 12 in. diameter lead spheres M were hung from an arm that could be turned on a vertical axis colinear with the suspension lg of the torsion balance.

Suppose that first the spheres are so placed that one is a distance d in front of the left-hand ball and the other is the same distance behind the right-hand ball. The gravitational attraction of the two sphere-ball pairs will be additive in tending to turn the torsion balance counterclockwise as viewed from above. If the big spheres are then moved around so as to be on the opposite sides of their adjacent small balls, the torque on the torsion arm will be reversed and it will turn clockwise. The angle 2θ between the two rest positions of the balance arm is four times as great as the deflection that would result from the approach of one sphere to one ball. (The cross-attraction of the right sphere on the left ball and the left sphere on the right ball has been neglected.)

By operating the torsion balance as a torsion pendulum and determining its period, or by other means, the torsion constant of the suspension may be determined. Thus the force acting at lever arm length a to produce the observed deflection 2θ may be calculated, and with the mass-values of M and m, and distance d known, equation (1) in principle gives directly the value of the gravitational constant G.

Cavendish performed his experiment in an outbuilding in his garden at Clapham common, London. He took great precautions to avoid inequalities of air temperature and consequent air currents by "... (placing) the apparatus in a room which should remain constantly shut, and to observe the motion of the arm from without by means of a telescope." Allowances were made for the attraction of the torsion bar that held the small masses and for currents by "... (placing) the apparatus in a room which should remain constantly shut, and to observe the motion of the arm from without by means of a telescope." Allowances were made for the attraction of the torsion bar that held the small masses and for that Cavendish's experimental work was of magnificent quality, and one of the few criticisms was that the time of vibration might have been more accurately determined. The mean value from 29 separate determinations of the density of the earth is given by Poynting (*The Mean Density of the Earth*, 1894) as $\Delta = 5.448 \pm$

0.033. However, the distribution of the 29 results shown by Poynting ranges from 4.8 to 5.8 and a realistic standard error would appear to be several times that quoted. One of the peculiar facts about measurements of G or Δ is the tendency to quote results to the third decimal place, when the scatter of the individual readings for one person's experiment and the divergences between one method of measuring G and another suggest that the accuracy of even the second decimal figure is in doubt. However, the work of Cavendish was undoubtedly very accurate for a pioneer experiment; in fact, it was not really improved upon until nearly a century later.

F. Reich (1838, 1852) and F. Baily (1841–42) made minor modifications to Cavendish's method but do not seem to have improved upon the original experiment. C. V. Boys concluded (published 1895) that smaller dimensions of the apparatus would reduce temperature variations and resultant air disturbances and therefore constructed a torsion balance with a beam only 2.4 cm. long. Boys was the first to make very fine quartz fibres, and he achieved the necessary sensitivity by using one of these fibres as the torsion wire. A notable feature of the work of the Jesuit K. Braun (published 1896) consisted in exhausting the chamber which surrounded the torsion balance, so that disturbances due to air currents were reduced to a minimum. Braun measured the time of vibration of the torsion system in position near to and removed from the attracting masses rather than the deflection of the beam.

Eötvös measured the periods of vibration of a torsion balance when the balance beam was in line with and when it was perpendicular to the line joining the centres of two fixed lead pillars, publishing his results in 1896.

P. von Jolly, between 1878 and 1881, measured the increase in weight of a 5 kg. mass caused by a lead sphere about 1 m. in diameter. The attraction of the lead sphere on the second pan of the balance was made negligible by arranging a vertical separation of 21 m. between the scale pans. A similar experiment was carried out, between 1884 and 1898, by F. Richarz and O. Krigar-Menzel. However, the best of the common balance experiments are due to Poynting.

Poynting's Experiment.—In 1878, Poynting published an account (*Phil. Trans.*, vol. 182, A, p. 565, 1891) of a preliminary experiment of the type of Jolly's but on a smaller scale with a view to demonstrating that the common balance could be adapted to gravitational measurements. He gave an account of the full experiment carried out with a large balance and with much greater care. The balance had a 4 ft. beam. The scale pans were removed and from the two arms were hung lead spheres, each weighing about 20 kg. at a level about 120 cm. below the beam. The balance was supported in a case above a horizontal turntable, the axis of which was vertically below the central knife-edge of the balance. On this turntable was mounted the attracting mass, a lead sphere weighing 150 kg. The centre of the large sphere was 30 cm. below the level of the centres of the hanging weights. The turntable could be rotated between stops so that the attracting mass was first directly below one of the hanging weights and then directly below the other. It was found necessary to add a second balancing mass to the turntable at twice the radius of the large balancing mass in order to eliminate a spurious tilting of the balance support due to the shifting weight of the turntable.

The balance beam was equipped with a special mirror arrangement which magnified the tilt of the beam about 150 times. About 5 m. from this mirror was a telescope and scale for observing the tilt of the mirror. The experiment indicated that in moving the attracting mass from under one weight to a position under the opposite weight the balance beam changed deflection a little more than 1 second of arc—equivalent to a change in weight of about 0.4 mg.

Heyl's Experiment.—After a careful review of the work of Boys and Braun, Paul R. Heyl concluded (*U.S. Bureau of Standards Journal of Research*, vol. 5, p. 1243, 1930) that increased precision in the determination of G could hardly be expected of the direct deflection method, whereas, as stated by Braun, the possibilities of the time-of-swing method had not been fully utilized. In his repetition of the Cavendish experiment, Heyl therefore decided to use only the general pattern of Braun's but with a considerable increase in the attracting masses.

The torsion pendulum consisted of two small spheres, 50 gm. each, hung from the ends of a very light separator rod about 20 cm. long which in turn was supported from its ends by truss wires attached to a fine tungsten filament about 1 m. long which comprised the torsion suspension. A small mirror attached at the point of suspension in conjunction with a telescope and scale 3.5 m. distant permitted observations of the angular motion of the moving system. A motion of one minute of arc of the moving system was exhibited as a shift of about 2 mm. of the scale in the field of the telescope. The timing of the torsion pendulum was accomplished by manually recording transits of the pendulum on a chronograph which also carried seconds signals derived from a Riefler clock rated daily against naval observatory signals.

The attracting masses were two 66 kg. steel cylinders mounted with axes vertical and suspended from a rotatable support such that the line forming their mass centres could be made coincident with the line of centres of the masses on the torsion pendulum or at right angles thereto (as in Eötvös' experiment). In the former position the gravitational forces add to the restoring force of the torsion wire and the period of the pendulum is a minimum. With the large masses at right angles to the axis of the pendulum the period is at a maximum. Particularly in the near position the attracting masses produce a nonuniform gravitational field and the pendulum oscillations are not strictly sinusoidal (nonisochronous), a detail which must be considered in timing the pendulum. According to Heyl the time of swing in the near position was usually about 1,754 sec. and in the far position about 2,081 sec., and each could be measured to about 0.1 sec. The difference, 327 sec., formed the critical quantity of the whole measurement

and was presumed accurate to about 1 part in 3,300.

Precautions were taken that all mass and length measurements were well within the tolerance required to assure that such quantities could not introduce errors in the derived value of G within about 1/10,000. The use of steel cylinders rather than the usual lead spheres was intended to ensure accuracy of measurement, uniform density and permanency of measured values at the cost of some inconvenience and mathematical labour.

Heyl used gold, platinum and glass balls as masses on the moving system, but not with the idea of obtaining any different value of G due to difference in material. The original gold balls were found to absorb mercury from the trap used in the evacuating system, and in five months their weights (49.10679 gm.) increased by 0.1379 gm. To avoid this difficulty the platinum balls were coated thinly with lacquer. The glass balls were made of high-quality optical glass ground truly spherical. This material was selected because it would permit visual examination to ensure perfect homogeneity of the mass.

The moving system was housed in an airtight container exhausted to a pressure of about 2 mm. of mercury to decrease the damping and minimize convection disturbances. The lower portion of the housing containing the beam system was of soft iron material to shield the pendulum magnetically, because the massive steel cylinders, when moved from one to another of the two observation positions, altered the earth's magnetic field. While the small masses used on the beam were not of ferromagnetic material, they were either paramagnetic or diamagnetic, and the resultant magnetic effect would be appreciable. The effectiveness of the magnetic shielding was tested by artificial magnetic fields before gravitational observations were made.

In order to start the pendulum swinging for an observation, bottles of mercury were moved manually in resonance with the gravitationally induced swings of the pendulum until the desired amplitude of oscillation had been attained. Thereafter these masses were removed from the vicinity and because of the low damping, adequate amplitude remained for the duration of the observation.

The results obtained by Heyl are shown in Table I, those using

TABLE I.—*Heyl's Results*

Gold	Platinum	Glass
$G = 6.683 \times 10^{-8}$	6.661×10^{-8}	6.678×10^{-8}
6.681	6.661	6.671
6.676	6.667	6.675
6.678	6.667	6.672
6.679	6.664	6.674
6.672		
Mean, $G = 6.678 \times 10^{-8}$	6.664×10^{-8}	6.674×10^{-8}
Average departure .003	.002	.002

the gold balls having been corrected for an assumed steady rate of absorption of mercury.

Heyl preferred to weight the results with the platinum and glass results and gives as a final value $G = 6.670 \times 10^{-8} \pm 0.005$.

Heyl and Peter Chrzanowski Experiment.—In view of the unexplainable inconsistencies in the several experiments of Heyl's 1930 work, it was repeated with various improvements, in particular photographic recording, and a change in the position of the large attracting masses (*Jour. of Research, Nat'l. Bur. of Stds.*, vol. 29, RP 1480, p. 1, July 1942).

In the 1930 experiments the 66 kg. steel cylinders were arranged with their axes vertical. In the later work the axes of these cylinders were laid horizontally. This simplified the measurement of distances and also eliminated some difficulties with slight departures from isochronism caused by the nonuniform field encountered by the pendulum when swinging with appreciable amplitude. In all other respects the general arrangement of the apparatus was the same as in the 1930 experiments. The balls used on the torsion pendulum were of platinum and weighed about 87 gm. each. The suspensions used were of two kinds: ordinary commercial hard-drawn tungsten lamp filament, 0.0012 in. diameter of 288 gm. tensile strength, and a specially straight-drawn and annealed filament of 0.0014 in. diameter and 284 gm. tensile strength. As will be evidenced in the results, the hard-drawn filament was superior for this work. This may be explained by the statement taken from the paper, "The times of swing with the annealed filament were about 1,880 and 1,640 seconds in the 'far' and 'near' positions respectively, with a difference of 240 seconds. With the hard-drawn filament (smaller diameter), the times of swing were increased to 2,920 and 2,200 seconds, with a difference of 720 seconds. This threefold increase in sensitivity with the hard-drawn filament apparently overbalanced any slight advantage of stability on the part of the annealed filament."

By a suitable lens system the image of the time-standard, after reflection from the mirror on the torsion pendulum, was focused on a photographic plate. As the pendulum swung, an image was recorded on the plate every 5 sec. The distance from the mirror to the plate was 490 cm. and a deflection of 1° at the mirror corresponded to a distance of 17 cm. at the plate. The sharpness of the lines recorded was such that 3 lines per millimetre could be resolved by a low-power microscope.

The results of the observations are shown in Table II. These

TABLE II.—*Results With Quartz Oscillator Time Standard*

Hard-drawn filament	Annealed filament
$G = 6.6639 \times 10^{-8}$	$G = 6.6670 \times 10^{-8}$
6.6756	6.6667
6.6769	6.6703
6.6762	6.6707
6.6751	6.6680
Mean, $G = 6.6755 \times 10^{-8}$	$G = 6.6685 \times 10^{-8}$

data indicate that the results for the hard-drawn filament give a precision twice that obtained with the annealed filament. Weighting the results in proportion, the weighted mean is $G = 6.673 \pm 0.0031 \times 10^{-8}$ and in view of the average departure from the mean appearing in the third decimal place, the final result is $G = 6.673 \pm 0.003 \times 10^{-8}$ (cm.^{3} gm.$^{-1}$ sec.$^{-2}$). The final result in the 1930 experiments was $G = 6.670 \pm 0.005 \times 10^{-8}$ (cm.^{3} gm.$^{-1}$ sec.^{3}). The authors conclude with the statement that "a carefully planned and executed attempt to increase the precision of the 1930 results has met with but slight success. The conclusion may be drawn that the limit of the possibilities of the torsion balance has been reached."

Zahradnicek's Resonance Method.—In 1932 J. Zahradnicek introduced (*Phys. Zeits.*, vol. 34, p. 126, 1933) an ingenious modification of the torsion balance method, by constructing an apparatus in which two torsion systems were arranged coaxially. The outer or primary balance was a U-shaped beam supported by a steel suspension wire, and carrying heavy lead weights. The inner secondary balance was smaller and lighter. The rest positions of the two balances were adjusted to be in the same vertical plane, so that each balance when displaced and released executed damped harmonic oscillations about the same zero.

The gravitational forces provided a coupling between the two oscillating systems, and the experiment comprised the adjustment of the period of the large primary balance to give resonance; that is, when the amplitude of the secondary compared with the primary was a maximum. The amplitude and the logarithmic decrement of the secondary were determined by observing a number of turning points photographically, and G was calculated by combining these results with measurable dimensions of the apparatus, such as the moment of inertia of the secondary balance and its period in the absence of the primary. The theory involves the computation of coupled oscillations, but the method appears to be capable of accurate results. Zahradnicek obtained $G = 6.659 \pm .02 \times 10^{-8}$.

Summary of Experimental Determinations of the Gravitational Constant G.—The results for G or Δ obtained by the various methods since Newton's time are shown in Table III. The last three observations, together with those of Braun and

Boys, are probably the most reliable. It is troublesome that the values obtained fall into two groups which differ by more than would be expected from the significant figures quoted by Boys and Braun and from the average departures from the mean given by Heyl. Heyl noted that the 1942 results with the hard-drawn filament differed from those with the annealed filament by an amount greater than could be accounted for by the separate departures from the mean. However, it is difficult to see where any systematic error could have occurred in Heyl's experiments, and the best value of G to adopt is probably the weighted mean of his 1930 and 1942 experiments. This is $G = 6.672 \times 10^{-8}$ (cm.^{3} gm.$^{-1}$ sec.$^{-2}$). The mean of the five best determinations (Boys, Braun, Zahradnicek, Heyl 1930, Heyl 1942) is 6.664×10^{-8}, with a root-mean-square error of ± 0.007. This value is probably accurate to better than 1 part in 500.

Experiments on the Qualities of Gravitation.—While theoretical considerations show that the gravitational constant G is independent of the nature of material composing the mass, experiments have been made to test the universal applicability of the constant. Eötvös and others working with the torsion balance showed that when the nature of the attracting masses was varied over a wide range of substances, it was independent of the nature of the masses within the experimental error of $10^{-9} G$. The same work showed G to be independent of the chemical combination of the elements in the masses. Various experiments have investigated the effect of anisotropic bodies, i.e., the value of G remains independent of the direction of the crystallographic axes to within $10^{-9} G$, the limit of experimental error. Herman Shaw showed that within experimental error, any variation in G with temperature must be less than $2 \times 10^{-6} G$ per degree centigrade. Q. Majorana collaborated with others to investigate the effect of shielding layers of different media and obtained negative results. Thus in one case 5 cm. of lead interposed between the attractive masses produced no change exceeding $2 \times 10^{-11} G$. Accordingly, G may be considered a universal constant independent of the state or nature of the mass body (not to be confused with the relativistic change of mass with velocity).

III. MEASUREMENTS OF THE ACCELERATION DUE TO GRAVITY

Introduction.—The attraction of the earth for bodies at its surface is the manifestation of gravitation that interests most persons. It is this attraction which causes bodies to have weight, and which makes them accelerate toward the earth when they have no support. This acceleration is derived directly from Newton's law of gravitation, which gives the force on a mass m at the earth's surface as $F = GMm/r^2$, where M and r are the mass and radius of the earth. A force on a body of mass m causes an acceleration g equal to F/m, so that $g = GM/r^2$. The force to which a body at an arbitrary place on the earth's surface is subject is the resultant of the forces due to rotation and to gravitational attraction. These cannot be separated experimentally, and observations of "gravity" refer always to this resultant. The value of gravity at some arbitrary place is due to the local distribution of matter as well as to the over-all constitution of the earth, and so itself has no general interest. If, however, this value is known in terms of the fundamental units of length and time, the force on a known

TABLE III.—*Historical Determinations of G*

Name	Date	G	Δ	Method
Newton	1670	6.6×10^{-8}	5.5	Estimate
Bouguer	1749	—	c.10	Attraction of plateau
Maskelyne	1775	—	4.5	Attraction of mountain
Airy	1856	6.565	6.565	Coal mine
Cavendish	1798	6.754	5.448	Torsion (deflection)
Reich	1838	6.61	5.58	Torsion (deflection)
Baily	1842	6.475	5.675	Torsion (deflection)
Boys	1895	6.658	5.5270	Torsion (deflection)
Braun	1896	6.6579	5.5275	Torsion (deflection)
Burgess	1901	6.64	5.55	Torsion (oscillation)
Eötvös	1896	6.65	5.53	Torsion (deflection)
Jolly	1881	6.465	5.692	Common balance
Poynting	1891	6.698	5.493	Common balance
Richarz	1898	6.685	5.505	Common balance
Heyl	1930	6.670±0.005	5.517	Torsion (oscillation)
Heyl	1930	6.659±0.02	5.52	Torsion (resonance)
Zahradnicek	1932	6.659±0.02	5.58	Torsion (resonance)
Heyl	1942	6.673±0.003	5.52	Torsion (oscillation)

mass subject to it provides a convenient and very accurate unit of force in terms of the fundamental units. Thus, in the absolute determination of the ampere by the current balance, the force between two coils carrying current is balanced against the gravitational force on a known mass, while in the determination of the gyromagnetic ratio of the proton, the force exerted on a coil carrying a current in a magnetic field is balanced against a similar gravitational force. For these and similar applications the acceleration due to gravity at the site should be known to 1 or 2 parts in 100,000, but, in the calculation of the pressure exerted by a column of mercury in a barometer, an accuracy of about 1 p.p.m. (part per million) is desirable, in order to correct for departures of local gravity from a standard value of 980.665 cm./sec.^{2} This very high accuracy was needed for work in progress in 1960 for the improvement of the precision with which the international temperature scale could be reproduced, for one of the main limitations was the accuracy of the measurement of the pressure at which water boils in the apparatus used to establish the $100°$ C. point. If this temperature is to be established to $10^{-4}°$ C., the pressure should be known to 3 p.p.m.

The absolute value of gravity also enters into determinations of the size of the earth. If ω is the moon's angular velocity and d its distance, then the acceleration which it owes to the earth's attraction is $\omega^2 d$; by the inverse square law, the value of gravity at the earth's surface, radius r, is $\omega^2 d(d^2/r^2)$. ω is known very precisely, d is equal to $r/\pi_{☾}$ where $\pi_{☾}$ is the moon's parallax, and so g is equal to $\omega^2 r/\pi_{☾}^3$ from which r can be found in principle and compared with survey determinations. Uncertainties in $\pi_{☾}$ are of the order of 1 in 10^4, i.e., of the same order as uncertainties in survey measurements of r, so that a very exact value of g is not required in this calculation. Now, however, that the moon's distance can be measured to about 1 in 300,000 by radar methods, a value of g accurate to 1 p.p.m. would be valuable. In geophysics, unit acceleration has been named the "gal" (after Galileo); 1 gal = 1 cm./sec./sec., or, 1 milligal (mgal.) = 0.001 gal = 0.001 cm./ sec./sec., representing about $1 \times 10^{-6}\,g$.

The absolute value of gravity is of no direct interest for gravity measurements used in geodesy or in geophysical investigations. In all geodetic work, the variations of gravity over the surface of the earth enter as the ratios of differences of gravity, ∂g, to the value at some convenient reference point. Not only are the uncertainties in measured values of ∂g far greater than 1 p.p.m., but the uncertainty in g does not even enter the measured values because all methods of measuring differences of gravity in fact measure ratios $\partial g/g$. Thus, with invariable pendulums, the periods at two places are compared and the result is expressed as the ratio $\partial g/g = T_2^2/T_1^2 - 1$. Gravity meters also measure the difference as ratio. The one way in which the absolute measurement of gravity may help in geodesy is by providing a check on relative measurements. At present all measurements depend ultimately on rather few pendulum observations made at great intervals of latitude, gravity meters being calibrated by comparison with these observations. The differences of gravity involved are about 3,000 mgal. and the pendulum errors appear to be about 0.3 mgal. but there is evidence that errors of a few milligals may occur; in particular there are discrepancies of this order in the observations between the sites of the absolute gravity stations at Ottawa, Can., Washington, D.C., and Teddington, Eng. An absolute method that could be used at different sites would provide a valuable check on relative observations with pendulums.

An absolute determination of gravity requires many months of careful planning and experiment. Variations in gravity over the surface of the earth can therefore be studied more easily and quickly by taking relative measurements in which the total time needed is little more than the time of travel. Detailed knowledge of these variations is required in several fields, but mainly in geodesy and geophysics. In geodesy (q.v.) gravity measurements are used to study the detailed shape of the earth (the geoid), and the deflections of the vertical. In geophysical applications, attempts are made to relate values of gravity at the surface of the earth to mass distributions or density variations below ground. On a regional scale these studies may relate to the strength and nature of the earth's crust, whereas detailed local surveys are used to study shallow geological structure, as in the search for mineral and oil deposits.

A. ABSOLUTE MEASUREMENT OF GRAVITY

Methods that have been used for the measurement of the acceleration due to gravity in terms of the fundamental units of length and time must now be considered. (See METROLOGY; FRACTION: *Other Types of Fractions*.)

Until World War II, the direct observation of a freely falling body was not a practical method of making such measurement, because the time involved for any reasonable distance is quite short (a few seconds) and could not be measured with adequate precision. All measurements, therefore, used the pendulum in some form or other, and all the most accurate have used the reversible pendulum. The principles of this method, and the results obtained with it, will be discussed first; afterward other types of pendulum will be considered. The technical developments in time measurement stimulated by radar during World War II made it possible to time the free motion of a body under gravity with necessary precision; a number of such experiments have been carried out or planned and are described below.

The theoretical computation of the behaviour of any physical system is necessarily made with a rather idealized model, and in absolute determination of physical quantities it is most important to see that the parameters of the model correspond to the quantities actually measured on the physical system. It is also essential to eliminate all forces other than that to be measured very precise.

The Reversible Pendulum.—By a reversible pendulum is meant a body which may be suspended as a pendulum from two separate points of itself such that the periods of oscillation about these points are the same. The centre of mass of the body then lies in the line joining the centres of oscillation, and the distance h between these centres is equal to the length of the simple pendulum having the same period T, so that $g = 4\pi^2 h/T$. The definition of the parameters h and T for such a pendulum can be made very precise.

Flat, polished planes are attached to the pendulum, so that the centres of oscillation lie in them and the pendulum is supported with one or more of these planes resting on an accurately lapped knife-edge bearing. Then, apart from a small allowance for elastic deformation, the length h is equal to the separation of the planes (which are necessarily parallel). Since h is defined by two flat polished planes, it may be determined, for example, by optical interference, with very high precision. Thus, h is well defined both in principle and as a matter of practical metrology. The period T is also well defined and may be measured with great accuracy by permitting the pendulum to swing for a long time.

There is a small addition to the classical theory. E. Rieckmann pointed out that when gravity increases linearly downward, the value measured with the reversible pendulum is that at a distance h below the point of support.

It is the nongravitational forces that give rise to the greatest errors with the reversible pendulum. Of these, magnetic and electric forces can be avoided by suitable choice of materials. Air surrounding the pendulum has three effects (the buoyancy pressures reduce the restoring force, the air carried with the pendulum increases the inertia and the motion is damped by viscous losses) but all may be avoided by swinging the pendulum at an air pressure of 0.1 millibar or less.

The effects of elastic yielding and other movements of the support, and of the elastic bending of the pendulum, discussed below, can be determined sufficiently accurately, and the largest uncertainties are those due to the effects of the knife-edge support. The problems associated with the knife-edge can be stated but the behaviour of the knife-edge is not at all well understood.

The effect of an elastic support is that the point of support is displaced a distance $y = -k\theta$, where k is a constant depending on the moment of the pendulum and the rigidity of the support, and θ is the amplitude of the oscillation.

In the usual notation, $k/h = q$, and the change of period T is $\frac{1}{2}qT^2$; q is best found dynamically. If two pendulums of equal period and inertia are set up on the same support and one is left at rest and the other made to oscillate with amplitude θ_1, the amplitude of the one initially at rest is θ_2 after time t, and $\frac{1}{2}qT = \theta_2/\theta_1 \times T^2/\pi^t$; q will be different for the two positions of a reversible pendulum.

If the support is in irregular motion (due to microseisms, for instance) the period changes in a random manner with standard deviation $\sigma(T)$ given by $T^{-1}\sigma(T) = (2n)^{-\frac{1}{2}}/\theta_o \times \sigma(v)/g$, where $\sigma(v)$ is the standard deviation of the ground motion, n is the number of oscillations and θ_o is the amplitude.

In past work, n has been very large (10,000), so that the effect of ground motion has been unimportant, but now that T can be measured sufficiently accurately with relatively few oscillations, care should be taken not to reduce n too far lest the ground motion effects become significant.

Ground motion and sway can be eliminated by swinging two pendulums together with a phase difference of π, when the mean period of the two is unaffected by these errors. In portable apparatus for relative measurements it is very important to use two pendulums but, in absolute measurements, although it might be convenient, it does not seem so fundamentally necessary, since the support may be made very stiff and the experiments may be continued for long enough to make the effect of microseisms negligible.

The elastic bending of the pendulum both alters the inertia of the system and applies couples to the support. Suppose that, when the pendulum is held at the knife-edge as a horizontal cantilever, the displacement perpendicular to the axis is $K(x)$ where x is the distance measured along the axis. $K(x)$ can be found from the elementary theory of a bent beam (of variable section and stiffness, in general).
A. R. Curtis (report, 1951) showed that

$$g = g_{obs}\left(1 + \frac{1}{mk^2}\int xK(x)\rho dx - \frac{1}{mh}\int K(x)\rho dx\right) \quad (4)$$

where k is the radius of gyration, h is the distance of the centre of gravity from the centre of oscillation, ρ is the line density and m is the mass of pendulum. H. Jeffreys (report, 1949) showed, by a very general method, that g_{obs}, the observed value of gravity, is always less than the true value.

Corrections for all the foregoing effects may be determined with high precision; the effects of forces at the knife-edge support, on the other hand, are not properly understood. Experiments with "knife-edges" of very large radius (e.g., 1 cm.), have given results that agree with theoretical calculations based on elastic deformation of the cylinder and plane, but extrapolation to radii of the order of 10–100 mμ does not agree with observation. More consistent experimental results are obtained with lapped as compared with ground edges, and it is evident that some of the discrepancies between theory and observation must be due to minute geometrical imperfections. It is probable that the effects of knife-edge forces do not exceed a few parts in a million in the best experiments, but there is so far no independent evidence of this.

The reversible pendulum was first used by H. Kater, for whom it is commonly named (1818), but his absolute measurements did not include the effects of the air and of bending of the pendulum. The experiments performed by F. Kühnen and P. Fürtwangler at Potsdam, published in 1906, were the first in which proper corrections were made for such effects, and their results superseded all previous ones and were taken as the basis for the international gravity formula that is still adopted. Values of gravity consistent with the Kühnen-Fürtwangler absolute value are referred to as being in the Potsdam system.

Heyl and G. S. Cook (published 1936), working at the national bureau of standards (NBS), Washington, used reversible pendulums of fused silica in the form of simple tubes. The planes were fixed to the pendulums and the distance between them was measured by normal line standard comparator methods. The periods were obtained from visual observations of coincidences with a Shortt clock, the swings lasting for about 5 hr. Sway was measured interferometrically, but the results appear rather inconclusive. The pendulums were swung in air at a pressure of about 50 micro-

bars and the results were extrapolated linearly to zero pressure; as the density of the pendulum is about 1 g./cm.^{3}, it would have been safer to work at a lower pressure. Some radioactive sand was placed in the pendulum case to prevent electrostatic charges from accumulating.

Jeffreys re-examined the results of Heyl and Cook, applying certain small corrections that they ignored, and obtained the following revised value: g(NBS) = 980,081.6 mgal., with a standard deviation of 1.2 mgal. computed from the variability between different knife-plane combinations.

J. S. Clark in his determination made at the National Physical laboratory (NPL), Teddington (report, 1939), paid particular attention to the rigidity of his pendulum (for which the elasticity correction was 1.0×10^{-6} as compared with values of from 1.8 to 3.5×10^{-6} for the determination of Heyl and Cook), and to the finish of the knives and planes, which were lapped, and in these respects his results appear superior to those of Heyl and Cook. The planes were fixed to the pendulums and the distance between them was measured interferometrically, so that all the advantages of the arrangement were realized. The pendulum was made of nonferrous Y-alloy and had a coefficient of linear thermal expansion of about 22×10^{-6}° C., so that there is a slight uncertainty about the length owing to the fact that the temperature of the pendulum cannot be measured during actual swings. The swings were timed by a precise mechanical chronograph against a quartz-crystal oscillator, using mechanical contacts on the pendulum that were brought into action at the beginning and end of the swings. There is clearly a possibility that the first few nominally free vibrations after the mechanical contact was disconnected were in fact slightly perturbed. The pendulum was swung in air at a pressure of never more than 7 microbars. Jeffreys recalculated the elasticity correction, which Clark had applied with the wrong sign, and gave g(NPL) = 981,183.2 mgal., with a standard deviation of 0.6 mgal. based on the residuals.

The difference of gravity between NPL and NBS according to these measurements is 1,101.6 mgal., while a discussion of the direct measurements of the difference by relative methods gives 1,097.9 mgal.

The value of gravity at the NPL in the Potsdam system is 981,196.0 mgal. at the mean height of Clark's pendulum, and his value is thus 12.8 mgal. less than the Potsdam value.

A new reversible pendulum determination, published in 1956, was made in Leningrad at the All-Union Scientific Research Institute of Metrology (VNIIM) by P. N. Agaletskii and K. N. Egorov. They used three fused silica pendulums each of mass 4.6 kg. and of lengths 40, 60 and 75 cm., and obtained the value of 981,919.0 mgal. compared with the value on the Potsdam system of 981,930.8 mgal., a difference of 11.8 mgal., which is very close to the discrepancy found by Clark.

R. Schroeter's pendulum experiment at Potsdam involved the swinging of two pendulums together with a phase difference of 180° as in relative pendulum measurements (see below) in order to eliminate the effects of microseisms and of the movement of the support.

The Long Pendulum.—The purpose of the long pendulum is to obtain a system as close as possible to the ideal simple pendulum. A spherical bob is suspended by a wire so long and fine that the elastic energy stored in bending the wire is very small compared with the total energy of the system. A. A. Ivanov, working at the VNIIM in Leningrad, used pendulums 20 m. and 30 m. long; his work showed the possibilities of the method, but since he worked at atmospheric pressure, his allowance for the effects of the surrounding air is probably inaccurate (results published 1936).

T. J. Kukkamäki of the Finnish Geodetic institute was preparing in 1959 a new determination in which he proposed to work in vacuum. The length of the pendulum could be changed from 100 m. to 200 m., the difference being measured optically by the Väisälä interference comparator.

The Free Motion of a Body Under Gravity.—All the experiments so far completed in which the free motion of a body is timed, have involved releasing the body from rest and timing it as it falls freely. Let the times at which it passes points with heights x_1, x_2 and x_3 be t_1, t_2 and t_3 respectively. These are related by three equations such as $x = ut + \frac{1}{2}gt^2$, ignoring the change of gravity with height. The value of gravity is then given by

$$\frac{2(X_1T_2 - X_2T_1)}{T_1T_2(T_1 - T_2)} \qquad (5)$$

where $X_1 = x_1 - x_2$; $X_2 = x_2 - x_3$; $T_1 = t_1 - t_2$; and $T_2 = t_2 - t_3$. Since the origins of time and distance are essentially arbitrary, it is the differences X and T that are actually measured.

Examination of the formula for g shows that even in the most favourable conditions the relative error in g will be at best three or four times the relative errors in time and distance measurements. This is the first of the three limitations of the simple fall method, and it cannot be overcome by observing more intervals. The second limitation is that the time intervals are defined by events occurring at different speeds. For instance, in one arrangement of the experiment a graduated scale falls in front of a camera and is illuminated by very short flashes of light. The images formed in the camera become more and more spread out as the speed of the scale increases; the intervals X have thus to be measured between a sharp image at one end and a diffuse one at the other, so that possibilities of systematic error arise. The third limitation is that the resistance of air around the bar directly affects the acceleration. If the distance between the body and the container is less than the mean free path of the molecules the calculation of the resistance becomes very simple; e.g., the resistance to a rod after it has fallen through 1 m. in air at a pressure of 1 microbar is 7×10^{-6} of the gravitational force. The rod should therefore fall in air at a pressure of less than 0.1 microbar.

The three limitations of the simple fall experiment are overcome if the body is projected upward and timed during its upward and downward flight. Suppose it to be timed as it passes across two planes separated by a height H, and let the time between its passage upward across the lower plane and its passage downward across the same plane be T_1, while the corresponding interval for the upper plane is T_2. Then $g = 8H/(T_1^2 - T_2^2)$. The relative error in g is therefore the best that can be achieved for given relative errors in length and time (this is also true for pendulum experiments). Since the speeds of the body upward and downward across a particular plane are equal, the time intervals are defined by events of equal sharpness and, accordingly, ambiguities of interpretation or differential time delays in apparatus will not introduce systematic errors. The effect of air resistance in the rise-and-fall experiment is also far less important than in the simple fall experiment, for it may be shown that a resistance proportional to velocity has no first-order effect on the apparent value of gravity. The rise-and-fall type of experiment is therefore more attractive than the simple fall type.

By 1960, however, only free fall experiments had been completed. Two of these were performed at the VNIIM in Leningrad. In the one due to Agaletskii, described in 1956, a graduated scale was allowed to fall freely in a box which itself fell almost freely in air. The motion of the scale in the box was recorded photographically, while that of the box was recorded magnetically on a steel wire stretched vertically. Since the velocity of the scale relative to that of the box was quite small, the aerodynamic forces on the scale were unimportant.

A. I. Martsinyak described in 1956 a second determination in which a silica rod about 1 m. long fell in air at a pressure of 0.2 mm. of mercury. The rod was coated with a photographic emulsion and as it fell was illuminated by images of two very narrow slits placed in front of discharge tubes controlled from a quartz-crystal oscillator. Thus a series of photographic images, formed at accurately known times, appeared on the bar. The scatter of the results in both these experiments was quite large (± 20 mgal.), and the results differ appreciably from that of the pendulum determination at the same place.

A. Thulin published in 1958 the results of an experiment at the Bureau international des Poids et Mesures at Sèvres, France, on the lines of preliminary work described in 1952 by C. Volet. An accurately graduated platinum-iridium scale 1 m. long fell in front of a camera and was illuminated by carefully controlled flashes of light lasting for less than 1μ sec. His result was 980,927.7 mgal. with an estimated uncertainty of 1 mgal. H. Preston-Thomas completed a similar experiment at the National Research council, Ottawa, Can. In both these experiments, the bar fell in air at a pressure appreciably less than 1 microbar. J. Faller, at Princeton university, made a determination with a falling component of an optical interferometer.

Experiments employing the rise-and-fall method were completed at the National Physical laboratory, Teddington, by A. H. Cook, and at the Bureau international des Poids et Mesures, Sèvres, by A. Sakuma. The excellent agreement between the results of Cook and Sakuma demonstrates the advantages of the rise-and-fall method.

TABLE IV.—Absolute Measurements of Gravity

Site	Date	Method	Value of g at observed site mgal.	Potsdam system g mgal.	Difference from Potsdam system mgal.
Geodetic institute, Potsdam, Ger.	1906	Reversible pendulum			
National bureau of standards, Washington, D.C.	1936	Reversible pendulum	980,081.6	980,098.4	−16.8
National Physical laboratory, Teddington, Eng.	1939	Reversible pendulum	981,183.2	981,196.0	−12.8
All-Union Scientific Research Inst. of Metrology, Leningrad, U.S.S.R.	1956	Reversible pendulum	981,919.0	981,930.8	−11.8
		Falling bar	981,921.5		−9.3
		Falling bar	981,923.0		−7.8
Bureau international des Poids et Mesures, Sèvres, France	1958	Falling scale	980,927.7	980,940.8	−13.1

The results of various absolute determinations of gravity are summarized in Table IV.

B. RELATIVE MEASUREMENTS OF GRAVITY:
PENDULUM MEASUREMENTS

Pendulum measurements of differences of gravity (strictly of the ratios of one value to another) have been carried on since the time of Newton, when it was noticed that the rate of a pendulum clock varied with latitude, a fact which was interpreted in terms of the spheroidal figure of the earth. Kater (1818) made the first reliable series of relative observations in the British Isles; some of these are correct to one or two milligals.

Few accurate measurements were made after this until the Dutch geodesist F. A. Vening-Meinesz (Observations de pendule dans les Pays Bas, 1913–1921, 1923) introduced the technique of using two pendulums swinging together in opposite phase. Extensive programs of accurate pendulum observations have been completed since 1945, using improved modern techniques. Pendulums, however, are not used for detailed survey but to provide the framework within which details may be interpolated by means of gravity meters.

In relative measurements the ratio of two values of gravity is determined by means of the equation $g_1/g_2 = T_2^2/T_1^2$ which holds for the periods of oscillation of a pendulum of constant length. The period is usually about 1 sec. and should be timed to about 1 part in 10^8. The usual procedure is to compare the frequency (1 cycle per second) with that of a standard quartz-crystal-controlled oscillator (100 kc./sec.), either photographically or photo-electrically, using beams of light reflected from mirrors on the pendulums. The frequency of the standard oscillator is checked by radio transmission which now can be received almost everywhere over the earth.

All accurate work is done with two pendulums swinging in opposite phase. The total force exerted by the two pendulums on the support is then zero, and the periods are not perturbed by the reaction of the support. Thus a more portable apparatus can be used than would be possible if the supports were stiff enough to make the reaction on a single pendulum sufficiently small, while the separate measurement of the sway effect, which would consume valuable time in field work, need not be made. Furthermore, in the two-pendulum method, the perturbations due to ground motion are eliminated, to first order, from the mean of the period of the two pendulums.

It is more important in relative measurements that perturbing forces should be constant rather than that they should be measurable. Thus it is not necessary to work at a pressure where the rate of change of period with pressure is not too great. With metal pendulums a pressure of about 20 mm. of mercury is convenient. Similarly, the pendulums should always be swung with the same amplitudes, so that the correction for the change of period with amplitude does not vary much.

Pendulums should be made of a material with a small coefficient of thermal expansion, since it is difficult to measure the temperature of an isolated body in a partially evacuated enclosure. Invar ($q.v.$, an alloy), which is satisfactory from this point of view, is ferromagnetic, so that arrangements have to be made to annul the earth's magnetic field and to demagnetize the pendulums. Invar is also rather unstable. Fused silica has an even lower temperature coefficient than invar and is nonmagnetic; on the other hand it has sometimes given trouble through electrostatic charging, while, because of its low density, the change of period with air pressure is four times as great for fused silica as for invar. Molybdenum is used in an Italian apparatus described by C. Mazzon in 1957.

The main difficulty with relative measurements is the fact that the observer is ignorant of the behaviour of the knife-edge support. All extended series of pendulum observations show erratic changes of the equivalent lengths of the pendulums both with invar and with fused silica, and often the changes of the pendulums within the same group are correlated. The standard deviations of most good observations lie between 0.2 and 0.5 mgal.

Following Vening-Meinesz' pioneer work, the Cambridge two-pendulum apparatus was designed by Sir Gerald Lenox-Conyngham, and has subsequently been used extensively in Europe, Africa and the Americas. It employs invar pendulums and the earth's vertical magnetic field is annulled with a system of Helmholtz coils.

The Gulf apparatus has pendulums of fused silica. The box in which the pendulum swings is maintained at a constant temperature by a thermostat and contains some radioactive sand to eliminate electrostatic charges. The apparatus has been used in North and South America, Europe, Africa and elsewhere; the results obtained with it and with the Cambridge apparatus agree well at many common stations. With these two sets of apparatus, observations have been made along two lines of stations running from north to south through the Americas and from Europe to south Africa, so that bases are provided for accurate measurements with gravity meters in these regions.

C. RELATIVE MEASUREMENTS OF GRAVITY: GRAVITY METERS

By common usage the term gravity meter (or, occasionally and undesirably, gravimeter) can be applied to any instrument, except normal pendulum equipment, used for the measurement of small differences in gravity. The idea of using a direct-reading gravity meter rather than the pendulum is old, but the early aim was primarily to provide a gravity-measuring device sufficiently sensitive to record temporal variations in g, rather than to invent a portable instrument for use in the field.

The practical applications of gravity meters require an instrument capable of detecting differences in g of 0.1 mgal, or less, and since such differences are always superposed on a total g of about 980,000 mgal, the instruments must have sensitivities of at least 1/10,000,000 g. That is, a simple gravity meter comprising a spring with a mass at the lower end and having an initial elongation of about 10 cm. would exhibit a change in gravity of 1 mgal as a change in elongation amounting to 1×10^{-6} cm. or about 1/50 the wave length of visible light. This example suffices to illustrate the magnitude of the sensitivity requirements. Nevertheless, since about 1935, more than 20 satisfactory types

of gravity meter have been produced for land use. Many of these are light, easy to transport and of high accuracy, some measuring to 100th part of a milligal.

Classification of Gravity Meters.—Gravity meters exhibit wide variation in design. A primary classification may be made into (1) static or balance gravity meters, in which measurements are made with a system in equilibrium; and (2) dynamic gravity meters, which depend on measurements of changes in frequency of a moving system. Some writers have recognized a third class of gas-pressure gravity meters, but these can be considered as a special form of the balance type. Dynamic gravity meters, sometimes regarded as a modified form of pendulum equipment, are rather specialized and very few in number.

Practically all the instruments in current field use are of the balance type, and the term gravity meter usually refers to this type unless specifically stated otherwise. Balance gravity meters may be separated into two broad classes: the unastatized or stable type, and the astatized or unstable type. Some writers use the terms static and astatic to distinguish these two classes, but this terminology leads to confusion in view of the primary classification made above. Instruments in the former class contain a main elastic element which exerts a restoring force opposed to the effect of gravity. Instruments in the latter class contain an additional element which, when balance is disturbed, provides an auxiliary force in the same direction as gravity and of magnitude almost equal, but opposite in sign, to the restoring force exerted by the main elastic element. The two classes are illustrated in fig. 2.

At (A) is shown schematically the simple unastatized system. The displacement diagram shows the constant downward force due to the weight mg and the upward restoring force CS of the spring, proportional to displacement. Obviously the equilibrium displacement of the spring will be at the intersection of the two force curves and the sensitivity of the system will increase as the angle β decreases, a result which, because of the linearity of the curve CS, can be accomplished only by increasing the length and the equilibrium elongation of the spring if the spring loading is to be held within tolerable limits. This provides a direct-deflection instrument with a linear scale over any range of gravity, and a calibration constant which is a function only of the spring constant and the suspended mass regardless of any operational adjustments.

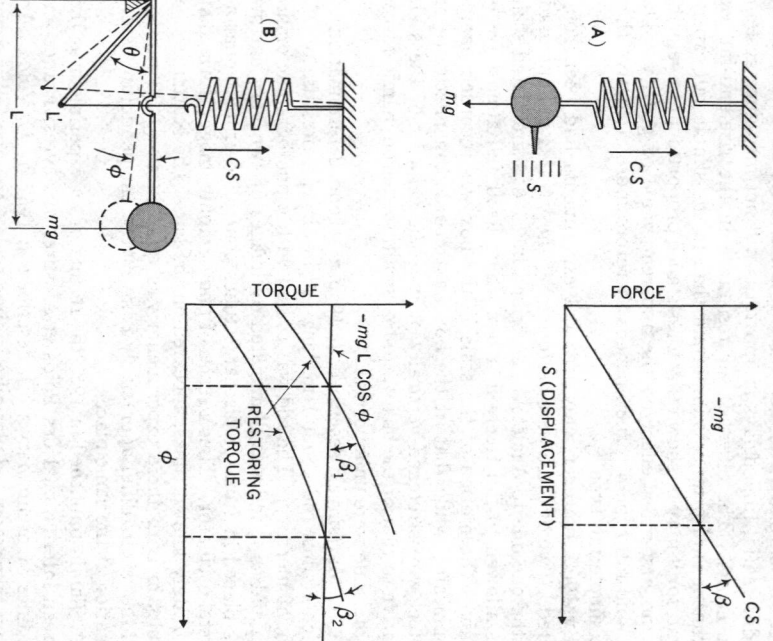

FIG. 2.—PRINCIPLE OF UNASTATIZED (A) AND ASTATIZED (B) GRAVITY METERS

Such an instrument must be provided with a high order of mechanical, optical or electrical magnification to permit accurate measurement of the small deflections due to the small changes in gravity to be detected.

On the other hand, fig. 2 (B) illustrates the principle of astatization and the resulting torque-displacement characteristics. Here the moving system comprises an arm hinged at one end and carrying a weight mg at the other end. With the spring attached to the weight arm, the system would have characteristics similar to those of the unastatized system (A). But the spring is attached to a lever arm L' at an angle θ with respect to the weight arm L and if the angle θ is quite large the spring restoring-torque curve becomes strongly nonlinear. A similar effect results if the spring is attached to the weight arm L but its upper support is moved to the left so that its force is applied at an angle θ to the moving arm. Now, by adjustment of the system such as a change in the angle θ, the restoring-torque curve may be made to have any desired characteristic intersecting the gravitational deflecting-torque curve with angles β_1, β_2, or even vanishingly small angles. Thus angle β may be made arbitrarily small and the sensitivity arbitrarily great, up to the point of instability when $\beta = 0$. By devices equivalent to fig. 2 (B) it is possible to simulate the behaviour of extremely long springs and thereby attain very high sensitivities. However, it is evident that with each change in adjustment the sensitivity and hence the scale value of such an instrument will be changed. Moreover, even for a fixed adjustment, if the astatization is pronounced the nonlinear feature precludes a strictly linear scale. This practically dictates the design of a null rather than a direct-deflection instrument. Thus in astatized types a very fine auxiliary spring with linear restoring-torque characteristics is used to bring the moving system back to a fixed zero, this auxiliary spring having a linear scale calibrated to read gravity changes. Since the range of such an auxiliary scale may be limited, special provision must then be made to cover wide ranges.

Numerous embodiments of the astatizing principle are represented in a wide variety of gravity meter designs, a few of which have been developed into commercially successful instruments. It is of interest to note that some of these are basically vertical seismographs, since the sensitivity problems are identical, the gravity meter requiring high sensitivity to the steady acceleration g, while a vertical seismograph must record the periodic motional accelerations associated with seismic waves. It is pertinent to consider the relation between the sensitivity of a gravity meter and its period.

As already mentioned, the elongation S of a spring supporting a weight mg is $S = mg/c$ where c is the spring constant or restoring force per unit elongation. The period T of the same system vibrating in simple harmonic motion is $T = 2\pi\sqrt{m/c}$. From these two equations $S = gT^2/4\pi^2$, and the elongation δS due to a change in gravity δg is $\delta S = \delta g T^2/4\pi^2$. Thus for a simple unastatized gravity meter the sensitivity is proportional to the square of the period.

The same considerations apply to the astatized type except that in all such instruments the geometry of the system permits adjustment of the effective spring constant to arbitrarily small values so that the period and sensitivity are correspondingly increased. Consider, for example, the elemental spring balance previously mentioned, having an initial displacement of 10 cm. and a sensitivity of 1×10^{-6} cm. per 10^{-7} g. The period of the system in fig. 2(A) would be approximately 0.63 sec. Now, to obtain a 100-fold increase in sensitivity the astatizing device of fig. 2(B) may be adjusted to a period of 6.3 sec., assuming the rotational moment of inertia of the beam system to be negligible. With such an adjustment the instrument simulates the performance of an elemental balance having an initial equilibrium elongation of the spring of about 1,000 cm. and yet the actual elongation need not exceed a few centimetres. Evidently the magnification required in an astatized system decreases with the degree of astatization, and the practical limits are determined by the attainable stability of the adjustments. Astatized devices represent a very attractive design from the viewpoint of attaining adequate sensitivity for portable instruments.

Attention is again called to the fact that the gravity meter and the seismograph are both acceleration-sensitive devices and moreover the sensitivity criterion of both instruments is a long period. Since g represents a steady-state vertical acceleration while seismographic disturbances are periodically varying accelerations having strong vertical components, it is necessary to incorporate a very-low-frequency filter between the moving system and the indicating mechanism of a sensitive gravity meter. In most devices this is wholly impractical and in any type the best that has been done is the elimination of high-frequency microseismic disturbances with some suppression of the long-period (10–20 sec.) earthquake waves. Thus no gravity meter has yet been designed that permits operation during earthquake disturbances, and for this reason field operations may be effectively shut down for periods of many hours during which these transient accelerations far exceed the required reading accuracy. In this connection it is of interest to record that during periods of outstanding earthquake activity the gravity meter may be utilized for studying the earth's behaviour. Following the Chilean earthquake of May 22, 1960, remarkable confirmation of the periods of free oscillation of the earth as a whole was obtained on analyzing the daily charts taken from a sensitive recording gravity meter operated in Los Angeles, Calif.

General Considerations Affecting Gravity Meter Design. —Any instrumental system sensitive to minute changes in gravity is liable to be displaced by small forces which may arise internally from imperfect elastic behaviour of the materials used or from external causes such as varying temperature and pressure or shocks experienced during transport.

Most gravity meters, when kept at a fixed point, show a time-variation of scale reading which is called the drift. Occasionally, abrupt changes (jumps or tares) occur, which may exceed the small gravity differences being measured. Field surveys must therefore be planned in such a way that the drift can be allowed for, and the reproducible accuracy of a gravity meter depends in large part on its drift being small and, preferably, being linear with time.

These and other aspects of field use lead to general considerations on the following matters:

Creep and Hysteresis.—The elastic material must be stable so that creep rates and hysteresis effects are small. The excellent mechanical properties of fused quartz make this suitable either in the form of helical springs or as torsion fibres, though its thermal coefficient of elasticity is relatively high. Many instruments use metal springs, and certain nickel-chromium-iron alloys have excellent properties when properly cold-drawn or rolled and heat-treated, but their magnetic properties must be examined. In some cases creep may be reduced by proper adjustment of loading.

Clamping.—Hysteresis and other mechanical effects can be reduced if clamping is designed so that the displacement is substantially constant. In many gravity meters this means holding the weight to within a few ten thousandths of an inch. Some modern light quartz systems omit clamping altogether.

Temperature Effects.—With many gravity meter spring materials and systems a variation of only 0.002° C. is enough to cause a deflection corresponding to about 0.02 mgal. Various methods adopted to avoid such effects include use of low-temperature coefficient materials, compensation by means of bimetallic strips and maintenance of constant temperature by electrical thermostats or ice baths. Frequently these three methods are employed in conjunction. Some recent quartz systems use compensation only, but are housed in a sealed chamber surrounded by a Dewar flask. Thermostatically controlled meters often have an instrument chamber surrounded by two heating chambers, the inner heating chamber being maintained about 1° C. above the outer, and both being maintained several degrees above the external temperature. Thus the temperature within the instrument chamber is stabilized, as also is the temperature gradient through the chamber walls. Such controls may keep short-period temperature fluctuations to within 0.001° C.

Pressure Effects.—As well as the effects of changed steady pressures, the influence of rapid small changes in pressure should be eliminated. These changes arise in field use with fast transport where large elevation changes occur, and may produce abrupt changes of reading which die away slowly as the internal pressure stabilizes. This is known as the adiabatic effect. Many instruments have a barometric compensator in the form of a hollow drum on the moving system to correct for changes in air buoyancy, and many are sealed to the atmosphere. Some combat the adiabatic effect in both these ways.

Level Sensitivity.—The level sensitivity must be adequate for the required accuracy of the gravity meter. Bubbles in the level should be mounted so that their adjustment and relation to the moving system are not easily disturbed, and yet be convenient for simple readjustment if required.

Magnetic Effects.—Gravity base stations are often conveniently placed in or near buildings and it is therefore desirable to eliminate magnetic effects caused by ferromagnetic materials in the system. Some meters incorporate magnetic screening either of the spring alone or of the entire instrument.

Measuring Micrometers.—In many instruments the auxiliary reading spring is operated by a measuring micrometer which must be of high accuracy and carefully mounted. Irregularities in the micrometer screw may give rise to isolated errors in the gravity measurements. Eccentricity in the reading dial may introduce a periodic error which varies throughout the gravity range.

Damping.—All vibrational modes of the moving system should be as nearly aperiodic as possible, consistent with sensitivity. Air damping is commonly used and electromagnetic damping is practical, but all traces of ferromagnetic material must be eliminated from moving components. Care must be taken to avoid minute unidirectional damping forces induced by periodic motions.

Container.—For a field instrument the outside container must facilitate convenient handling and comfortable operation, and be able to withstand transport shocks. Many modern instruments illustrate the advantages that result when the outer container and ancillary apparatus, such as tripods and shockproof carriers, are treated as an integral part of the design.

Stable or Unastatized Gravity Meters.—One of the earliest descriptions (1932) of a stable spring instrument designed for commercial geophysical exploration is that by K. Hartley. Though little used, and now obsolete, this instrument is of historical interest as the first null-recording meter. Later, A. Hoyt (published 1941) used a ribbon helical spring and measured changes in gravity by observing the rotation of a suspended mass with a high-magnification optical system. The direction of creep could be controlled by adjusting the mass, so that the drift could be made very small. Furthermore, the large difference in period of the vertical and rotational oscillations of the spring made an excellent filter for cutting out seismic disturbances.

In the gas-pressure gravity meter of H. Haalck, described in 1933, a sealed volume of gas is the elastic medium, a mercury column being kept in equilibrium by the gas pressure. Temperature control is of great importance, and the instrument was kept in ice when used for measurements in a ship on rivers in Germany. Though its sensitivity is low, probably 3 mgal. at best, it is of interest for its unusual design and for its potentialities for measurement at sea.

In the Boliden gravity meter, described in 1938, changes of gravity produce vertical displacements of a spring-supported plate. These displacements cause changes of capacity within a condenser, that are measured electrically by an ultramicrometer device, using a null method.

The Nørgaard gravity meter (report, 1941) consists of a nearly horizontal quartz pendulum supported at one end by a horizontal torsion thread which is fixed to a quartz frame; it thus resembles the early quartz gravity balance of Threlfall and Pollock, described in 1900. The pendulum carries a platinum ring and a small concave mirror. An identical mirror is fixed to a rigid arm extending from the quartz frame. Measurements of the angular separation between the two tilt positions of the frame for an angular coincidence are translated into changes of g. The quartz system is immersed in fluid to reduce temperature effects and to protect the apparatus against shocks. No thermostat is carried. The instrument's wide range without need for resetting makes it suitable for long-range measurements. During 1957 meters of a similar type were used for experiments on surface ships in the U.S.S.R. The Soviet instrument was presumably a development of the GAE-2 gravity meter (1955).

In the Graf-Askania gravity meter described in 1938, a beam carrying a mass at one end is supported at the other end by two horizontally suspended metal helical springs which keep the beam almost horizontal. Displacements of the beam are restored by a sensitive tension spring attached close to the mass. The angular rotation of the horizontal helical springs is observed through a photoelectric device. Temperature compensation is provided, using a second pair of springs mounted within the main springs. A thermostat is also fitted and there is a compensator for barometric changes. The instrument has a direct measuring range of about 800 mgal. which can be reset, using an auxiliary spring, to give a total range of about 4,000 mgal. Attached to the mass is a small cage with a movable ball. Displacement of the ball between two fixed positions gives a standard deflection for checks of scale constancy.

Unstable or Astatized Gravity Meters.—The earliest gravity meters, such as that of M. Perrot (1862), were designed to record temporal variations of g, and high sensitivity requirements led to the early use of astatized instruments.

R. Tomaschek and W. Schaffernicht (report, 1932), following A. Schmidt (report, 1900) and others in using a trifilar suspension, developed a gravity meter with a sensitivity of about 0.001 mgal. This was apparently the first gravity meter using a nickel-chrome-iron alloy for its spring. Though extremely sensitive, the instrument was designed for observatory use, and bifilar and trifilar suspensions have not been adopted for the construction of portable meters. A bifilar instrument described by H. Brown in 1939 apparently had little field use.

Some unstable gravity meters have been designed which use a horizontal torsion fibre or spring as restoring member; *e.g.,* the instrument by G. Ising, described in 1937, for which close temperature control by ice bath was required. In the gravity meter designed by L. M. Mott-Smith (report, 1937), a horizontal quartz fibre carries at its mid-point a light quartz spring which provides the astatizing force. The entire system is very small, but it is housed in a sealed container mounted in a bulky liquid thermostat. No clamping is required in view of the lightness of the system and the high degree of air damping.

S. v. Thyssen (description, 1939) used a quartz beam supported on a knife-edge, while the Truman or Humble gravity meter (described in 1937) is based on a system of two opposed vertical springs and a hinged lever.

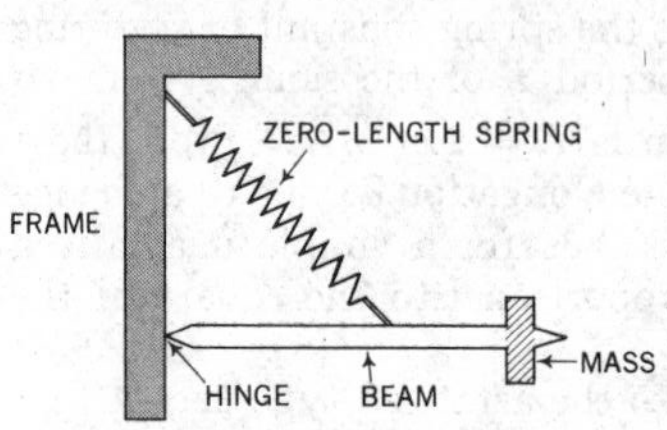

The similarity between a sensitive gravity meter and a long-period seismograph has already been mentioned, and it is therefore not surprising that the successful design of L. J. B. LaCoste's seismograph (fig. 3), described in 1934, should be used as a basis for many gravity meters.

FIG. 3.—PRINCIPLE OF THE LACOSTE SEISMOGRAPH

FRAME — HINGE — BEAM — ZERO-LENGTH SPRING — MASS

As gravity changes, the beam moves and the moment exerted by the inclined spring varies in the same sense as the moment due to gravity, thus providing the astatization desired. The beam can be restored to the null position by the action of an additional fine reading spring, by varying the point at which the mainspring is attached or through a system of levers. Another important innovation in the LaCoste instrument was the "zero-length spring," in which the extension of the spring due to the weight of the beam in the null-position is balanced by an opposing tension set into the spring during manufacture, so that the changes in the length of the spring will be directly proportional to the changes in gravity causing them. This is the only astatized system in which the deflection is symmetrical about the equilibrium position, and this property facilitates the averaging of readings under disturbed conditions.

Meters employing these two principles include the LaCoste-Romberg, Frost, Heiland, Magnolia, North-American and Western gravity meters, and most metal-spring gravity meters in operation are of this general type. Their direct-measuring range is usually about 100 mgal. but they can be reset over a range of about 5,500 mgal. for all latitudes. Those especially designed for long-range work have a greatly extended continuous range; the LaCoste-Romberg geodetic meter has a world-wide range without needing to be reset. In some meters the beam is air-damped through its rectangular construction, its movement being confined within a rectangular damping box. Barometric compensation is provided, though some instruments are also sealed. Instruments usually have a double-thermostat system and must operate at constant temperature. Fig. 4 gives a slightly more detailed impression of the internal construction of the Western gravity meter. Outer heating chambers are not shown, nor is the optical system. A cross hair fixed to the beam is viewed through a microscope.

Most metal-spring gravity meters are extremely sensitive to changes in temperature. In consequence, the necessary thermostats, insulated housings and storage batteries increase the size and total weight of the equipment. A typical instrument may be 16 in. high with a 13 in. diameter, weigh more than 30 lb. and require a heavy tripod weighing about 12 lb. The appearance in 1948 of small temperature-compensated gravity meters without storage batteries established a remarkable advance in portability. In 1959 instruments of this type were the Atlas, Worden and World-Wide gravity meters.

The Worden gravity meter has about a 5 in. diameter, is 12 in. high and weighs less than 6 lb. Ancillary tripod and carrying case weigh only an additional 8 lb. The moving system itself is barely 3 in. high, and since it is very light (the mass-element weighs only 5 mg.) no clamping is necessary. Except for a small temperature compensator, the entire system is made of fused quartz. It is mounted in the lower part of a Dewar flask, sealed in a partial vacuum (c. 5 mm. of mercury).

The spring system of this meter is illustrated in fig. 5. Any change in the gravitational pull on the mass causes the hinged beam to rotate, moving the pointer from the null position. The length of the mainspring is also altered, and the pointer can be brought back to zero by adjusting the tension in the fine spring. Linkage between mainspring and fine spring is made through a nonlinear spring comprising two arms of different thermal expansions to provide temperature compensation. The mainspring itself is a zero-length spring; in other respects this part of the system is very similar to that shown in fig. 2(B). It is possible to tilt the frame through a small angle, thereby modifying the inclination of the mainspring and altering the astatization. In this way the amount of movement of the pointer for a small change in gravity can be adjusted. The quartz elastic system is so constructed that its response to gravity is proportional to the cosine of the angle of tilt, which allows the scale constancy to be checked by tilting.

On many Worden gravity meters the fine dial has a range of about 80 mgal. and the coarse spring is used as a reset mechanism. On other meters the coarse spring has a special reading dial for use over the world gravity range. Because of its wide range, strict linearity of the coarse dial is important and this depends largely on the micrometer screw. To check the performance of this screw it is normal practice to relate reading changes of the coarse dial to corresponding changes of the fine dial at different gravity levels.

Dynamic Gravity Meters.—In the Holweck-Lejay "inverted pendulum" described in 1930, the mass, a quartz cylinder 6 cm. long and of 4 mm. diameter, is supported along its axis from below by an elinvar spring a few centimetres long and about 0.025 mm. thick. The lower end of the spring is fixed to a rigid base. When the mass is displaced sideways the restoring force of the spring opposes the effect of gravity. In consequence the period of the system is considerably longer than that of a normal pendulum of the same dimensions. It can be made more portable than the normal equipment and its timing requirements are less stringent.

A dynamic gravity meter constructed by R. L. G. Gilbert and described in 1949 depends for its operation on the change of frequency of the natural vibration of a vertical wire stretched by a weight. For an ideal wire the fundamental frequency is given by

$$\frac{1}{2l}\sqrt{\frac{Mg}{m}},$$

where l is the length of the wire, m its mass per unit length and M the suspended mass. In the practical instrument the wire is replaced by a beryllium copper strip about 5 cm. long. This hangs vertically between the poles of a permanent magnet and acts as a resonant element in an oscillator circuit. The output frequency is compared with a crystal frequency standard. The wire vibrates at about 1,000 cycles per second and its phase can be measured to about 0.1 cycle. Since the frequency is affected by air pressure and temperature the apparatus is evacuated and placed in a thermostat. The instrument possesses integrating properties, useful for measurement of gravity at sea. Comparison tests against a Vening-Meinesz pendulum apparatus, carried out in H.M. submarine "Talent," suggested a probable error of 1.5 mgal. A further application of very special interest was made in 1952, using a prototype designed for lowering down boreholes. This incorporated several refinements, such as a compensating device to eliminate the effect of creep in the vibrating wire and a gimbal system for automatic leveling. Observations were made at depths down to 1,226 ft. in an oil well near Eakring, Nottinghamshire; the accuracy obtained was approximately 0.7 mgal. (report, 1952). A Soviet instrument operating on the same principle was developed and underwent trials in the Caspian sea during 1956 (report, 1959).

Calibration of Gravity Meters.—Observations made with a gravity meter give data in scale divisions which must then be converted into milligals. The conversion factor is called the calibration factor, and its accurate determination is very important, particularly where the gravity interval is large. The theoretical calibration factor may be calculated from the dimensions of some instruments, but this has not proved satisfactory in practice. Ob-

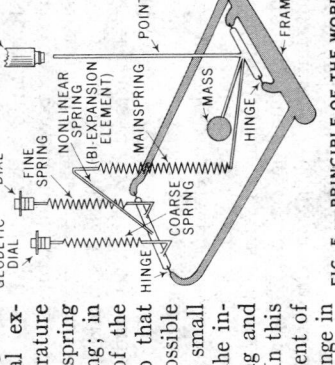

FIG. 5.—PRINCIPLE OF THE WORDEN GRAVITY METER

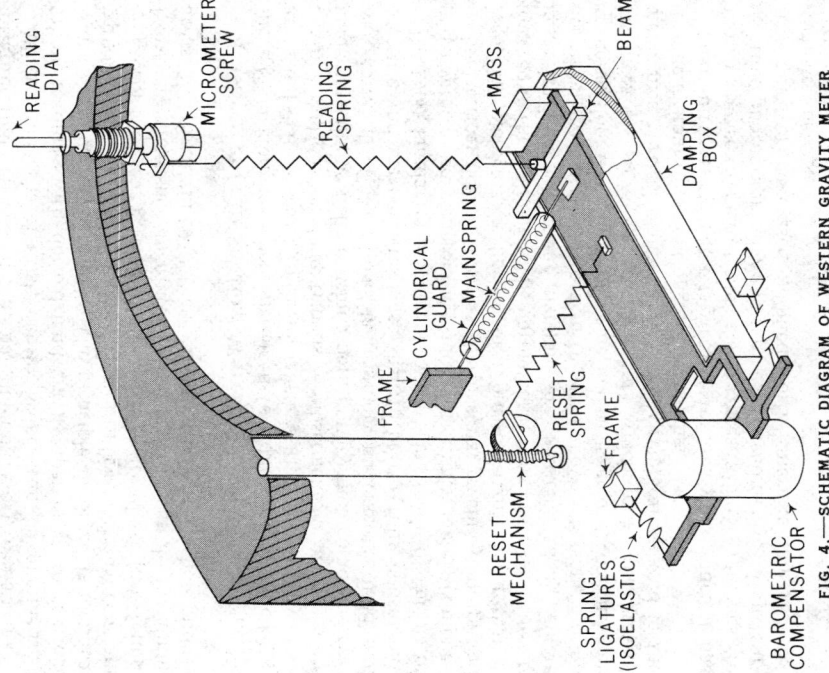

FIG. 4.—SCHEMATIC DIAGRAM OF WESTERN GRAVITY METER

servations of the effect of placing a known mass on the moving system lead to better results, though the technique requires great precision. Several manufacturers tilt the meter through a measured angle at a place where the value of gravity is approximately known. The direct method is to take a series of instrumental readings at places of known gravity, and it is now generally accepted that the only really satisfactory way to calibrate a gravity meter for use over a large range of gravity is to compare its readings with pendulum observations at a series of points covering the whole gravity range. A series of pendulum stations has been established through Europe, Africa and the Americas in order to provide suitable calibration points. In Britain, pendulum stations at Southampton, Teddington, Cambridge, York, Newcastle, Edinburgh and Aberdeen provide satisfactory control for internal measurements (report, 1953). After calibration, gravity meters can be used most effectively as a means of interpolation between the pendulum stations which form periodic checks on constancy of calibration.

Corrections to Measurements.—Any measured value of gravity at the surface of the earth is the resultant of such component factors as (1) the gravitational attraction of the earth as a whole; (2) centrifugal force caused by the earth's rotation; (3) elevation; (4) unbalanced attractions caused by surface topography; (5) tidal variations; and (6) unbalanced attractions caused by irregularities in underground density distributions.

Most geophysical surveys aim at evaluating (6) in order to interpret the geological structure, and it is therefore necessary to make proper allowance for the other factors.

The first two factors imply a variation of gravity with latitude that can be calculated on the assumption that the earth has a shape approaching that of the international (*see* GEODESY) reference ellipsoid of whose equatorial radius is 6,356,909 m. and which has a polar flattening of $\frac{1}{297}$. The sea-level value of gravity $g\gamma$ at any latitude ϕ is given as $g\gamma = 978.049(1 + 0.0052884 \sin^2 \phi - 0.0000059 \sin^2 2\phi)$. This is the 1930 international gravity formula. In this formula the constant 978.049 is a statistically deduced value for the sea-level value of gravity at the equator, and is based on values at a large number of scattered stations referred to the international base at Potsdam. This formula remains internationally agreed for geodetic and geophysical purposes, though in 1953 the World Meteorological organization adopted a formula more consistent with modern absolute measurements which gives values about 13 mgal. lower.

The decrease in gravity with elevation, due to increased distance from the centre of the earth, can be calculated from the gravity formula and the radius of the earth. It amounts to −0.3086 mgal./m. or −0.09406 mgal./ft. This factor, however, assumes that material of zero density occupies the space between the point of observation and sea level, and it is therefore termed the free-air correction factor. In practice, the mass of rock material which occupies this space must be considered. Where the topography is reasonably flat this is usually calculated by assuming an infinite slab of thickness h, the height of the station, and an appropriate density σ, as +0.04185 σh mgal./m. or +0.01276 σh mgal./ft. This is commonly called the Bouguer correction factor.

Terrain or topographic corrections can also be applied to allow for the attractions due to surface relief, as described by S. Hammer in 1939. Densities of surface rocks must be known.

Tidal effects are small periodic variations of gravity that arise mainly from the attractions of the sun and moon. Their amplitude is usually much lower than 0.3 mgal. for a time of 6 hours. The amount can be calculated and allowed for, though in many surveys field procedure combines tidal effect with instrumental drift.

In defining anomalies, the observed gravity g_o is compared with the theoretical value $g\gamma$ for the latitude of the station. The difference is then corrected for the elevation of the station h, using the free-air correction factor F, with or without the Bouguer correction factor B. The topographic correction T is also applied, giving: free-air anomaly $= g_o - g\gamma + Fh + T$, and Bouguer anomaly $= g_o - g\gamma + (F - B)h + T$. Bouguer anomalies are those most commonly used in exploration surveys. In geodetic work, free-air anomalies or isostatic anomalies in which a further correction for crustal material has been applied, are those generally adopted.

Measurements Underground.—Measurements of gravity at known depths below ground can provide information about rock densities and about the vertical gradient of gravity which is important in some interpretation methods. In a normal land survey rock densities are used both in reducing observations to a datum level and in subsequent interpretation. Density values can be derived from laboratory measurements on borehole samples, but it is difficult to ensure representative sampling and it is uncertain whether the values will accurately reflect conditions *in situ* where rocks may be modified by compression or by water content. Values suitable for surface reductions can sometimes be found by making closely spaced observations over a local topographic feature and selecting a density value to give the minimum correlation between height and anomaly. The densities for deeper strata cannot be obtained in this way, yet they need to be more accurately known since interpretation depends on the small differences between strata.

Where mine shafts exist, density values can be obtained by taking readings with normal land gravity meters at the surface and at various levels below. The principle involved is identical with that used in Airy's determination of the gravitational constant G, except that G is given and the mean density of strata is found. However, since such measurements are only possible in mining areas, N. J. Smith in 1950 discussed the need for a borehole gravity meter.

Measurements in Shallow Water.—In several areas gravity surveys on land have been extended to explore adjacent coastal areas and shallow seas. In the initial stages this was done by making observations on long tripods. Subsequently, surveys were made with diving bells in which both gravity meter and observer were lowered. Conventional land gravity meters were used, and pressure and magnetic responses had to be carefully considered.

By 1960, similar measurements were being made by means of underwater gravity meters in which the gravity meter, equipped with electrical devices such as thermostats, leveling motors and recording elements, is housed in a pressure-tight casing that is lowered to the sea floor. The normal measuring processes of leveling, releasing, reading and clamping are then effected by remote operation from a control box in the ship above. Seismic motion of the sea floor is often troublesome, and has been overcome in some instances by servo-operated elevators which move the gravity meter in a vertical plane. Integration circuits are placed in the reading system for smoothing and averaging.

The Gulf gravity meter is suitable for this work, since it has a low response to microseismic disturbances, while its readings are recorded photographically and can be averaged easily. Many surveys, however, have used modified North-American and LaCoste-Romberg meters.

Underwater surveys have been made in depths of about 500 ft., though few measurements are made deeper than 300 ft., which is the maximum depth reached during a geodetic survey of the North sea. The instruments described above enable gravity measurements to be made almost as accurately underwater as on land, but elevations may be one or two feet in error. They give satisfactory anomaly values and can be used in areas too shallow for submarine measurements.

Measurements at Sea.—For a complete study of earth curvatures, geodesists require free-air anomalies (or isostatic anomalies) over the whole surface of the earth. Since the oceans cover nearly three-quarters of the globe, it is of outstanding importance that measurements be taken at sea. Unfortunately, such work is beset with great difficulties owing to the disturbing accelerations encountered (discussed by B. C. Browne, 1937).

After the use of the three-pendulum apparatus on land, Vening-Meinesz further developed it for use at sea in a submarine, publishing his results in 1924. When an instrument in the earth's gravitational field is also subject to accelerations x, y and z along orthogonal co-ordinate directions fixed with respect to the earth, z being taken vertically, the magnitude of the total resultant acceleration that the instrument experiences is $[(g + \ddot{z})^2 + \ddot{x}^2 + \ddot{y}^2]^{\frac{1}{2}}$, or approximately $g[1 + \ddot{z}/g + (\ddot{x}^2 + \ddot{y}^2)/2g^2]$.

On a ship at sea, the accelerations x, y and z are periodic with zero mean, and the average total acceleration taken over many periods of the wave motion is $g[1 + (\langle\ddot{x}^2\rangle + \langle\ddot{y}^2\rangle)/2g^2]$, the symbols $\langle\ \rangle$ denoting time averages. However, this is not the mean value of gravity as given by pendulum observations, because the observed quantities are the mean values of the periods which are proportional to $g^{-\frac{1}{2}}$ and, provided that the periods of the wave motion are long compared with the pendulum periods, the apparent value of gravity is $\langle\ddot{z}^2\rangle/4g$ less than that measured by a linear instrument. Thus it is necessary to measure the three components of the wave accelerations with accelerometers of suitable periods, in order to correct the apparent value of gravity. Since the amplitudes of wave motion are greatly decreased at about 100 ft. below the sea surface, the corrections may be kept to about 10 mgal. by working in a submarine. With pendulum apparatus it is in fact essential to do this.

The three pendulums of the Vening-Meinesz apparatus swing about parallel axes in a common plane, and the outer ones are set swinging in opposite phase while the centre one is initially at rest and gains velocity as a result of the motion of the ship. The differences of angular position between the inner pendulum and each of the outer ones are recorded photographically, together with time marks from a quartz-crystal-controlled standard-frequency oscillator; the differences behave like the amplitudes of fictitious pendulums from which the first-order effects of the motion of the ship have been removed. The pendulums are not swung in a sealed case and the atmospheric pressure, temperature and humidity must be measured very carefully.

If the ship has an east-west component of velocity v, its radial acceleration will be $(r\omega \sin\theta + v)^2$, where r is the radius and ω the angular velocity of the earth, and θ is the colatitude. The measured value of gravity is therefore too small by $2\omega v \sin\theta$; this is known as the Eötvös correction and amounts to 7.5 mgal. per knot at the equator. (The need for the correction was first pointed out by G. G. de Coriolis about 1840.) The uncertainty of this correction, which is due to the difficulty of determining the velocity v for a ship far from land, is in fact the largest source of error in gravity measurements at sea. Next in importance come uncertainties in position affecting the comparison of observed gravity with that to be expected on an ideal spheroid, while observational errors, despite some occasional erratic results, seem to be least serious.

The earliest attempts to measure gravity at sea were made on surface ships in 1903 by O. Hecker, using a barometric method. Later, barometric instruments were used experimentally by W. G. Duffield, H. Haalck and G. Nørgaard (report, 1938), but use of the Vening-Meinesz pendulum apparatus in submerged submarines remained the standard technique. In 1949 the dynamic gravity meter of R. L. Gilbert was tested in a submarine.

During 1954-55 a modified version of the Graf-Askania meter, known as the Graf sea gravity meter, had preliminary trials on surface ships. In 1956 more extensive trials, conducted on board the U.S. submarine "Becuna" at submerged depths between 200 and 250 ft. during a cruise in the western Mediterranean sea, the eastern Atlantic ocean and the English channel, included comparisons with a Vening-Meinesz pendulum apparatus (report, 1957). The beam of the sea gravity meter is heavily damped, and suitable filaments prevent movement in the horizontal plane. The apparatus is suspended in gimbals adjusted to counteract the effect of horizontal accelerations, and has a modified reading system whereby the amplified photocell output is fed to a pen recorder. After the tension springs of the gravity meter have been adjusted until the recording pen stays on the record, the chart is run for from 15 to 25 min., and the record integrated with time, in order to obtain the apparent average value of gravity. In 1956, under smooth sea conditions, the record showed an amplitude of about 150 mgal. with a period of about 3 sec., apparently due to imperfect depth keeping, but the difference between the gravity meter and the Vening-Meinesz apparatus was only 1.2 mgal.

A modified version of the LaCoste-Romberg land gravity meter has also been used. The sensing element is a null-reading device using a spring of linear response over several thousand milligals.

Through photoelectric cells, deflections of the beam are indicated both directly on a beam-position micrammeter and also, in an integrated form, on a timing indicator. The sensing element is mounted in a gimbal system employing a servomechanism, and, since it closely follows the apparent vertical, the first- and second-order corrections of Browne may be applied. The first-order correction is determined independently, by means of a special depth recorder in which a strain-gauge pressure element gives depth to within ±10 cm. Its output is recorded on a fast-moving time recorder from which the value of the vertical velocity at the beginning and end of an observation can be derived to within 1 cm./sec. For the second-order horizontal-acceleration correction, apparent deflections of two long-period pendulums in the meter are fed into a circuit that computes the correction and applies it, through a differential, to provide a corrected gravity reading which is recorded in digital form. Readings are averaged each 30 min. The gravity meter showed mean differences of +1.1 mgal. and a root-mean-square difference of 3.3 mgal., from measurements obtained with pendulums (described, 1958). Tests with a stabilized platform indicate that the gravity meter can be used on a surface vessel. Other experiments in the U.S.S.R. and Japan have been reported briefly (1958). While by 1960 the Vening-Meinesz pendulum apparatus remained the accepted standard for measurements of gravity at sea, it was foreseen that the development of gravity meters for use on surface ships might soon make possible a vast improvement in the survey of the oceans. The main difficulties to be overcome, described in 1960 by Hamson, were alignment errors and cross-coupling effects which arose if accelerations due to the ship's motions were correlated with periods involved in the instrument suspension so as to produce a constant deflecting couple on the beam system. Phases between rolling and pitching in relation to size of ship and length of swell required further study, but preliminary considerations suggested that satisfactory operation was most feasible on a large tanker (report, 1960).

Measurements in the Air.—Since 1946 many geophysical instruments have been adapted for use in aircraft. Air-borne methods have many advantages, and from time to time the possibility of conducting gravity surveys from the air was considered. The problems involved are the same as those found with measurement in surface ships, but the greater velocities and accelerations encountered make their correction an even more formidable task. Nevertheless, an accuracy of 10 mgal., possibly sufficient to give a preliminary broad indication of the existence of large-scale regional anomalies in new areas, was reported in 1960 in air-borne tests using a modified form of LaCoste-Romberg sea gravity meter. It was suggested in a discussion in 1957 that surveys of the vertical gradient of gravity might be easier to perform, but instrumental details were not given.

Gravity Gradients.—Accurate methods for the measurement of the gradient and curvature components of the gravitational field were developed by Eötvös in about 1887, prior to his determination of the gravitational constant G. His instrument is a modification of the earlier Cavendish torsion balance and consists of a light horizontal beam, about 40 cm. long, suspended at its centre by a fine torsion wire. One end of the beam carries a mass of about 25 gm. and from the other end an equal mass hangs at the end of a wire about 55 cm. long. From observations of the rotation of the main torsion fibre, the gradient and curvature components of the earth's gravitational field at the centre of the system can be determined. The instrument is very sensitive: the horizontal gradient can be measured to about 1×10^{-6} mgal./cm.

A developed form of this torsion balance was the first gravitational instrument to be used for petroleum exploration and had widespread use from about 1923 until about 1936. Thereafter, it was almost entirely replaced by gravity meters, which are more easily portable, quicker to read and less influenced by local irregularities of terrain. (For further account, see L. L. Nettleton, *Geophysical Prospecting for Oil*, pp. 63-99, 1940.)

Temporal Variations of Gravity.—The existence of small, periodic variations of gravity due to the attractions of the sun and moon has been known for many years. The resultant amplitudes can be computed on the assumption of a rigid earth, but these will not reflect the natural state of things, because the earth is not rigid but yields to these forces in an elastic manner. The ratio of the gravity variation for a yielding earth to that for a rigid earth depends on the gravimetric factor, $\delta = 1 - 3k/2 + h$, where h and k are Love numbers (see TIDE: *Bodily Tides*). Determination of this factor is of interest for obtaining information about the rigidity of the earth. In practice such gravity measurements are combined with simultaneous observations of deviations of the vertical by horizontal pendulums or tiltmeters. Combined analysis then allows evaluation of the effective Love numbers.

Observations have shown that at any location δ may be affected by ocean tides, by tectonic influences or by meteorological effects which may cause irregular loading of the crust. Such effects, described in 1954, have been measured in Great Britain. Instrumental defects may be troublesome, since irregular instrument drifts, and pressure response in particular, may be difficult to identify. Separation of the various individual factors requires elaborate methods of harmonic analysis which must be applied to a set of continuous observations taken over a prolonged period, usually not less than 31 days. Effects due to maritime loading and tectonic influences are best studied from simultaneous observations taken at contrasting locations, for example, near to the coast and inland, and on both sides of major geological features. Simultaneous observations at 26 stations throughout the world during May 1949 yielded a value of 1.22 for δ (record, 1953). A fuller program was conducted during the International Geophysical year (1957–58), and preliminary analysis gave a value of 1.19.

Many standard land gravity meters have been fitted with photographic recorders for use in this work. In a modification of the LaCoste-Romberg meter described in 1957, the amplification of the measuring system of the land instrument is increased, and operates through a servomechanism, combined with an automatically recording photoelectric system. The meter is sealed against barometric effects and a special thermostat stabilizes temperature to 0.001° C. Simultaneous measurements with two such instruments agree to about 1 microgal.

An interesting use of continuous observations with a gravity meter may be mentioned. Sea tides at Shackleton base, occupied during the Transantarctic expedition, could not be measured by normal methods. A Worden gravity meter was fixed in the ice and readings taken at hourly intervals for eight weeks. Analysis of the readings showed that the sea tide varied from less than 2 ft. at neap tides to more than 11 ft. at spring tides (report, 1958).

Results and Current Activity.—Gravity surveys are conducted either on a regional scale, where the anomalies are usually related to areas of abnormal tectonic activity in the earth's crust, or on a local scale, when the anomalies can be related to density contrasts at relatively shallow depth.

The earliest observations related to the equilibrium of major mountain systems. Bouguer in the Andes, and Airy and J. H. Pratt in the Himalayas noted that the mountain ranges produce much less disturbance than might be expected from a calculation of their mass. The observations on the Himalayas led to the concept of isostasy (see GEODESY: *Isostasy*), which is the idea that extensive loads at the surface are balanced by the penetration of a low-density "root" into the denser substratum below the crust. Elaboration of these ideas led to the use of isostatic anomalies, in which correction for this penetration has been applied. Similar observations have been made on other young mountain ranges; i.e., the Rockies, the Pyrenees and the Alps. These all show strongly negative Bouguer anomalies amounting to a few hundred milligals, but much weaker isostatic anomalies. This is taken to indicate a regional compensation of the surface loading. However, for some older mountain ranges, such as the Appalachians, the Bouguer anomalies are weaker and the isostatic anomalies stronger, possibly owing to surface erosion.

In other areas, such as Fennoscandia (the geological area of Finland, Sweden, Norway and Denmark) and parts of Canada, negative isostatic anomalies are interpreted as meaning that these areas have been depressed, owing to heavy ice-loading in recent geological time, and have not yet recovered. Careful topographic surveys around the Gulf of Bothnia show, for example, that this area is rising by approximately one centimetre per year. Several important gravity features have been located by measurements at sea. In the Indonesian archipelago, narrow belts of very strong negative anomalies (−200 mgal.) follow an arc which lies just inside the deep ocean trenches. Inner arcs are associated with regions of strong seismic and volcanic activity. All these phenomena indicate that mountain-building forces are still active. A similar belt of negative anomalies with like tectonic associations exists around the Caribbean sea. Strong anomalies are also found over the great rift valleys.

Local surveys are conducted in very great detail, and intense activity in the search for petroleum must account for hundreds of thousands of gravity stations in many parts of the world. There has been much international co-operation in gravity measurements for geodetic purposes since 1948, the main object being the establishment of a single world system, and many intercontinental links have been made by means of air transport. When the international network is complete it will be possible to co-ordinate the results of many local exploration surveys for geodetic use.

In the late 1950s a new method of examining the earth's gravitational field became possible through observations on artificial satellites. It is of interest that analyses made so far emphasize the need for a revision of the spherical harmonic analysis of the surface gravity data to include all new information and to assess the causes of minor disagreement (report, 1958). Methods based on the analysis of surface gravity data are subject to uncertainties because there remain considerable areas where the gravity anomalies are not known and where more data are required. These are mainly the oceanic areas together with the polar icecaps and other remote places. Though many expeditions since World War II such as the Transantarctic expedition, have carried portable gravity meters, it is rarely possible to obtain surface heights that are sufficiently accurate for geodetic use. Long periods away from base reduce the reliability of the gravity measurements themselves, though interpolated gravity observations between seismic locations are valuable in assessing variations in thickness of the ice. It is unlikely that accurate heights will ever be readily available in such places. By the early 1970s, the main hope of an early increase in gravity data for primary geodetic use appeared to lie in the rapid expansion of satellite information.

IV. THEORIES OF GRAVITATION

The term "theory of gravitation" may mean one of two different things. In the first place, it may refer to the mathematical development of the consequences of the fundamental law of gravitational attraction. This law is the inverse square law of attraction and over the years there has been built up an extensive and detailed body of mathematical results giving rules for calculating the forces between bodies of all manner of forms. In this sense, the theory of gravitation is a calculating machine. The second sense in which this term is used is a much deeper one. Here an attempt is made to see how the fundamental laws of gravitation themselves may be related to other aspects of physics and stress is laid not so much upon practical calculations as upon understanding the significance of gravitation.

The "calculating machine" theory can be dealt with quite briefly. According to Newton the force F between masses m_1 and m_2 of very small dimensions acts in the line r joining them and is given by $F = -Gm_1m_2/|r|^3$. If now a quantity ϕ_1 be selected equal to $-Gm_1/r$, it is seen that the force on m_2 due to the attraction of m_1 is $-m_2\partial\phi/\partial r$ in the direction of m_1. ϕ is called the potential of mass m_1. The potential of a continuous body is merely the sum of the potentials of its elements

$$\phi = -G \int \rho d\tau/r \tag{6}$$

where ρ is the density and τ an element of volume.

All the problems of calculation on the basis of the inverse square law are thus equivalent to dealing with the properties of the potential. Now it may be shown that the potential satisfies Laplace's equation ($\nabla^2\phi = 0$) in empty space, and Poisson's equation ($\nabla^2\phi = 4\pi G\rho$) in matter. ∇^2 is the Laplacian operator in these differential equations, and has the form

$$\frac{\partial^2}{\partial x^2} + \frac{\partial^2}{\partial y^2} + \frac{\partial^2}{\partial z^2} \qquad (7)$$

in Cartesian co-ordinates.

All practical problems of gravitation are accordingly problems of the solution of the equations of Laplace or Poisson. Although the inverse square law is no longer to be considered rigorously true, yet its practical consequences are so very nearly correct that in all but a few special circumstances the great body of potential theory and celestial mechanics (q.v.) developed during the 19th century is still entirely valid in practice.

Although Newton himself deliberately refrained from speculating on the cause of gravitation and although the inverse square law is independent of any other aspect of physics; nonetheless it is interesting to analyze it a little more closely as an introduction to modern ideas on gravitation. The equations of Laplace and Poisson are equivalent to a theorem of C. F. Gauss relating the total flux of force (the word flux is derived from an analogy with the flow of water) across a surface, $\rightarrow \int \mathbf{gds}$, with the mass enclosed by the surface

$$\int \mathbf{gds} = 4\pi G \int_T \rho d\tau \qquad (8)$$

where g is the gravitational acceleration, ds is an element of surface and the integrations extend over the surface S enclosing the volume T.

If, instead of the inverse square law, Gauss's theorem be taken as a starting point (in electrostatics it is easier to prove Gauss's theorem experimentally than the inverse square law), it can be seen that this is more general than the inverse square law, for the latter only follows for a particular geometry, i.e., that in which the surface area of a sphere is proportional to the square of the radius. In this case, by symmetry, g is constant on the surface of a sphere and since S is proportional to r^2, g is inversely proportional to r^2. Thus it is seen that the law of force depends on the geometrical relations of the description of space utilized; and if a non-Euclidean geometry (see RIEMANNIAN GEOMETRY; SPACE-TIME) had to be used for this description there would not necessarily be an inverse square law.

The second point concerning this law is that the forces are derived from a scalar potential because there are no transverse forces. Electromagnetic forces, on the other hand, may be derived from a vector potential. Thirdly, gravitational forces in Newtonian theory do not depend on the velocities of the bodies. Fourthly, the effects of bodies add up as simple sums—the potential of two bodies is the sum of their separate potentials and not, for instance, their product. It will be shown that current ideas about gravitational forces differ significantly in some of these respects.

Although throughout the 19th century various theories and modifications of the inverse square law had been proposed, it is probably true that at the time when Einstein published his general theory of relativity the experimental evidence for the inverse square law, based on its application to problems of celestial mechanics, was more firm than ever. There was, in fact, only one discrepancy—the rate at which the perihelion of the orbit of Mercury rotated was about 42" per century greater than could be accounted for by inverse square law calculations. Einstein's object, however, was to try to understand the significance of gravitation and he approached the problem as a development of his theory of special relativity.

The first idea behind this theory is the principle of equivalence. According to this, it is not possible to distinguish between the effect of a uniform acceleration and the action of a gravitational force. This principle depends experimentally on the work of Eötvös, who showed that the inertial mass of a body, which determines its acceleration under a given force, is exactly equivalent to its gravitational mass, which determines the gravitational forces on it. The second idea is that the principles of special relativity can be applied locally even though a gravitational field is present. The third idea is that the path of a free particle in space and time is determined by geometrical properties of space and that these properties are themselves determined by the masses of bodies present. Thus Einstein deduced the properties of gravitation from more general ideas about the physical world.

Einstein's gravitational equations are far more complicated than the inverse square law, and although they coincide with it very closely in practical consequences, they predict three additional phenomena. First, the perihelion of Mercury should show a faster rate of rotation than that calculated from Newtonian theory; and the rate the equations predict agrees very closely with observation. Secondly, light should be deflected by the gravitational field of the sun. The experimental proof of this is very difficult, involving measurements of the apparent positions of stars during and after solar eclipses; but, although the scatter of results was great, each experimental observation made had a probable error large enough to embrace Einstein's theoretical value. Thirdly, the frequency of light emitted from heavy bodies should be slightly reduced. Until 1960 the experimental evidence for this was poor, but in that year experiments with an extraordinarily sharp γ-ray emitted by an isotope of iron confirmed it to within a few per cent. However, this "red shift" (see MÖSSBAUER EFFECT) follows from more general ideas than that of general relativity, depending only on the conservation of energy and on the effective mass of a photon of energy E being E/c^2 (a consequence of special relativity).

Thus, although the experimental tests of general relativity were not fully conclusive, Einstein's theory remained the only one to command general assent.

See also references under "Gravitation" in the Index volume.

BIBLIOGRAPHY.—L. L. Nettleton, Geophysical Prospecting for Oil (1940); P. R. Heyl, J. Res. Nat. Bur. Stand., vol. 29, p. 1 (1942); E. A. Milne, Kinematical Relativity (1948); A. Einstein, The Meaning of Relativity (1951); C. Møller, The Theory of Relativity (1952); Sir E. T. Whittaker, History of the Theories of Aether and Electricity (1953); papers from the Chapel Hill conference on gravitation, Rev. Mod. Phys., vol. 29, no. 3 (1957); W. A. Heiskanen and F. A. Vening-Meinesz, The Earth and Its Gravity Field (1958); H. Bondi, "Relativity," Rep. Progr. Phys., vol. 22, p. 97 (1959); V. Fock, Theory of Space, Time and Gravitation (1959); M. B. Dobrin, Introduction to Geophysical Prospecting (1960)

(T. F. G.; Wl. Bu.; Al. H. Co.; H. Sh.; R. D. W.)

GRAVURE, one of the major processes in commercial printing, is used to produce a wide range of printed materials, including newspaper supplements (e.g., book-review sections, feature magazines), catalogues, illustrated magazines, illustrated books, advertising literature, calendars, greeting cards and wallpaper and patterns in textiles, linoleum and oilcloth. It is also employed for printing labels and wrappers on aluminum foil, glassine, cellophane, vinyl and similar materials.

Gravure is an intaglio process, so-called because the design to be printed is etched or engraved below the surface of the plate. At the start of the gravure printing process, the plate is covered with ink and the surface is then wiped clean. When paper is pressed against the inked plate, the paper penetrates the sunken parts slightly and draws out the ink. Examples of intaglio printing produced by traditional hand methods (i.e., in which plates are inked by hand and printed on a hand-operated press) are etchings, engravings and aquatints. Hand methods are still used in some countries in printing postage stamps, paper money, bonds and other securities. Modern photomechanical applications are rotary photogravure, or rotogravure, which is used in the bulk of gravure printing; sheet-fed gravure, a slower method employed when high-standard reproductions are desired; and the original and now almost-extinct photogravure method, which is slowest of all but produces the finest results.

Rotogravure is a high-speed process that can print (from a roll of paper) the equivalent of 25,000 sheets per hour in one colour or 16,000 sheets per hour in four colours, with each sheet being about 44 by 70 in. or larger. The process is financially practical only on runs of 100,000 or more impressions. Sheet-fed gravure, in which sheets of paper are fed to the press mechanically and slower presses are used, is best for runs of 10,000 to 100,000. For press runs of less than 10,000 copies, the letterpress method usually is most economical (see PRINTING).

All copy (the material reproduced, or printed) in photomechanical gravure printing is photographed through a halftone screen;

other printing processes employ screens only for reproducing photographs and other copy with tonal gradations. Type matter, therefore, is slightly hazier in gravure than in other processes but is quite readable.

History.—In 1826 Joseph Nicéphore Niépce of France first used the action of light to make a plate for the printing press. He coated a pewter plate with a solution of Judean pitch (asphalt) and over this comparatively light-sensitive surface placed an engraved portrait of Georges Cardinal d'Amboise that he had previously made translucent by oiling. After the surface was given a long exposure to light to harden the asphalt, the soft lines were dissolved and the plate was etched and printed. (*See* PHOTOGRAPHY: *The Beginnings of Photography*.)

The basic principle of photogravure, and of almost all other photomechanical processes as well, was contributed by an Englishman, William Henry Fox Talbot. In 1852 he patented the first practical application of a phenomenon noted by Mungo Ponton in 1839 and Edmond Becquerel in 1840—that gelatin, when sensitized with a dichromate salt, hardens when exposed to light. The earliest form of the Talbot process involved coating a steel plate with gelatin and dichromate of potash, exposing it under a positive, washing away the unhardened gelatin and etching with platinous dichloride. In a later version of the process, Talbot coated the plate first with powdered resin to provide a stronger ink-holding grain, heated it to make it adhere and etched with ferric chloride.

Paul Pretsch of Vienna in 1853 bathed the exposed gelatin in cold water, causing the soft parts of the gelatin to swell. An electrotype could be made directly from this relief, or from a gutta-percha mold. Pretsch patented his process in England in 1854 and set up the first commercial firm for photomechanical printing.

Karl Klic (Klietsch) of Bohemia was instrumental in making photogravure a practical commercial process. In 1878 he exposed a positive transparency over carbon tissue, a film made of coloured gelatin sensitized with potassium dichromate and backed by a sheet of paper. (Carbon tissue film had been invented in 1864 by Sir Joseph Wilson Swan of England.) The film was pressed down on a copper plate coated with an even layer of resin or asphalt powder. The carbon tissue was developed in water; this method of development made the softest gelatin swell and removed the paper backing. The plate was etched with ferric chloride in successive baths of varying strengths. Klic's process produced sure and predictable results and became the preferred method for later workers.

Klic, working with Samuel Fawcett of Lancaster, Eng., also developed and introduced the method of rotogravure printing now in general use. In 1895 Klic formed the first rotogravure firm, the Rembrandt Intaglio Printing company, in Lancaster. The principle of the rotogravure press, however, was already known. Thomas Bell of England in 1783 had suggested using a doctor blade to remove ink from the surface of the plate. The most important early improvements in the design of rotogravure presses were made after 1904 by Edouard Mertens in Germany. (*See* PRINTING PRESS.)

Rotogravure Plates.—Procedures for making hand photogravure plates by the Klic method have already been described.

In rotogravure, separate negatives of type matter, other line copy and continuous-tone copy are assembled and positioned according to a prepared layout. After the negatives are retouched, a continuous-tone positive is made and also retouched to ensure opacity where desired. A sheet of carbon tissue is next exposed under a gravure screen. This screen is a film or sheet of glass on which fine transparent lines cross at right angles to form opaque squares. A screen with 150 lines per inch (called a 150-line screen) therefore has 22,500 squares per square inch. The lines of the screen allow the light to penetrate to the film and harden the gelatin. The square "islands" remain soft. Gravure plates are usually made with 150-line or 175-line screens.

The continuous-tone positive is placed in contact with the carbon tissue and exposed under an arc light. The soft squares are hardened in proportion to the amount of light that penetrates the varying grays of the positive. The carbon tissue is squeegeed (pressed with a rubber roller) to a cylinder that has been previously coated with copper by electrolytic action. The squares are etched to varying depths depending upon the degree to which they were hardened. The crossing lines of the screen, which are entirely hardened, are not etched at all. In this way, pits or wells of different depths are etched into the copper. For very long press runs the cylinder can be plated with nickel or chromium. (*See* ELECTROTYPING.)

Rotogravure Printing.—In rotogravure printing, the cylinder usually is arranged so that during its rotary movement it passes through a trough filled with a thin solution of fast-drying ink. On some presses the ink is applied to the cylinder by other methods; *e.g.*, spraying. A thin steel blade (the doctor) moves across the cylinder with a slight oscillating action and removes the ink from the surface but not from the wells beneath. The plate cylinder then comes in contact with the paper, which travels around an impression cylinder, and the paper draws the ink out of the wells in the plate. After being printed, the paper shows through thin deposits of translucent ink, thus creating pale grays; heavier ink deposits from the more deeply etched wells appear correspondingly opaque. Thus a full range of tonal values can be printed. Since some ink is carried on the surface of the plate cylinder, particularly in the darker areas, the marks of the screen are almost entirely obliterated. In colour printing, a separate cylinder is prepared for each colour. (*See* PRINTING.)

Other Methods.—The Dultgen halftone intaglio process is widely used in colour work. Two positives are made from the continuous-tone copy, one through the conventional letterpress halftone screen and the other without a screen. For four-colour printing eight positives are made, two for each colour. The screened positive, which breaks up the image into soft dots on the carbon tissue, is exposed first, followed by the unscreened positive, which hardens the dots to varying degrees. When etched, the dots are therefore of different sizes and also of different depths. This method thus uses two methods for controlling tonal values.

Other methods in general use are the Henderson process, which prepares plates rapidly; the Huebner method, which dispenses with the use of carbon tissue; and Intaprint, which produces intaglio dots without depth gradations.

BIBLIOGRAPHY.—Herbert Denison, *A Treatise on Photogravure* (1894), a clear exposition of the Talbot-Klic hand method; H. M. Cartwright, *Photogravure*, 2nd ed. (1939), the most thorough work on the subject; H. M. Cartwright and Robert MacKay, *Photogravure* (1956), a survey of European and American methods; J. S. Mertle and Gordon Monsen, *Photomechanics and Printing*, sec., "Photointaglio Procedures," pp. 325-354 (1957). (J. KA.)

GRAY, ASA (1810-1888), U.S. botanist whose *Manual of Botany*, after more than a century, remains the outstanding book in its field, was born at Sauquoit, N.Y., on Nov. 18, 1810. From James Hadley, professor of chemistry and materia medica at Fairfield academy, Herkimer county, N.Y., he obtained his first instruction in science. In the spring of 1827 he first began to collect and identify plants. His formal education, such as it was, ended in Feb. 1831, when he graduated in medicine from the Fairfield Medical school. In 1836 his first botanical textbook appeared under the title *Elements of Botany*, followed in 1842 by *Botanical Text-Book for Colleges, Schools and Private Students*, which developed into his *Structural Botany* (1879). He published later *First Lessons in Botany and Vegetable Physiology* (1857); *How Plants Grow* (1858); *Field, Forest and Garden Botany* (1869); and *How Plants Behave* (1872). These books served the purpose of developing popular interest in botanical studies. His most important work, however, was his *Manual of the Botany of the Northern United States*, within its geographical limits an indispensable book for the student of American botany, the first edition of which appeared in 1848.

Throughout his life Gray was a diligent writer of book reviews on natural history, and his reviews themselves often became treatises of literary and scientific value. The greater part of Gray's strictly scientific labour was devoted to a *Flora of North America*, the plan of which originated with his early teacher and associate, John Torrey of New York. Volume two of Torrey and Gray's *Flora* was completed in 1843; but for 40 years thereafter Gray gave up a large part of his time to the preparation of his *Synoptical Flora* (1878).

Gray's labours in the then new field of discovery and systematization of North American flora placed him at the head of U.S. botanists and on a level with the most famous botanists of the world. In 1856–57 he published *Statistics of the Flora of the Northern United States.* This paper was followed in 1859 by a memoir on the botany of Japan and its relations to that of North America, which Sir J. D. Hooker, English botanical explorer, called "in point of originality and far-reaching results its author's *magnum opus*."

From 1855 to 1875 Gray was both a critic and exponent of the Darwinian principles, having been for years in correspondence with Darwin. Though his religious views were those of the evangelical bodies in the Protestant Church, he openly avowed his belief that the present species were not special creations, but rather were derived from previously existing species.

In 1842 Gray accepted the Fisher professorship of natural history in Harvard university. He brought together by widespread exchanges a herbarium (later named the Gray herbarium), which became the largest and most valuable in America, and a library where there had been none and arranged the small garden already existing. Thereafter, the development of these botanical resources was part of his regular labours. His scientific life was mainly spent in the herbarium and garden in Cambridge, Mass.; but his labours there were relieved by numerous journeys to different parts of the United States and to Europe, all of which contributed to his work on the *Synoptical Flora.* He received from learned societies at home and abroad abundant evidence of their profound respect for his attainments and services. In 1872 he was elected president of the American Association for the Advancement of Science, and he was an original member of the National Academy of Sciences. He died in Cambridge, Mass., on Jan. 30, 1888.

His *Letters* (1893) were edited by his wife; and his *Scientific Papers* (1888) by C. S. Sargent. Also see *Gray's Manual of Botany,* 8th (centennial) edition—illustrated—largely rewritten and expanded by Merritt Lyndon Fernald, *et al.* (1950). (C. W. E.; X.)

GRAY, ELISHA (1835–1901), U.S. inventor, contestant with Alexander Graham Bell in a famous legal battle over the invention of the telephone, was born in Barnesville, Belmont county, O., on Aug. 2, 1835. Gray worked in a machine shop, reading in physical science at the same time, and for five years (1857–62) studied in Oberlin (O.) college, where he was professor of dynamic electricity from 1880 to 1901. On the same day (Feb. 14, 1876) that Alexander Graham Bell filed an application for a patent for a telephone Gray applied for a caveat announcing his intention of filing a claim for a patent for the same invention.

When Bell first transmitted the sound of the human voice over a wire ("Mr. Watson, come here; I want you") on March 10, 1876, he used a liquid transmitter of the microphone type previously developed by Gray and unlike any described in Bell's patent applications to that date and an electromagnetic-metal diaphragm receiver of the kind contrived and publicly used by Gray several months earlier. In the legal cases in which the Gray and Bell claims to have invented the telephone came into direct conflict, it seems to have been established that Bell had first transmitted the sound of the human voice by electric currents in a wire, but evidence seems to show that the transmission took place by means of mechanisms developed by Gray. (*See also* TELEPHONE.)

Gray died suddenly at Newtonville, Mass., on Jan. 21, 1901. His later years had been spent in further electrical experiments.

See the article on Elisha Gray in the *Dictionary of American Biography* and, especially, Lloyd W. Taylor, "The Untold Story of the Telephone," *Amer. Phys. Teach.,* 5:243–251 (Dec. 1937). (F. G. T.; R. S. FR.)

GRAY, SIR JAMES (1891–   ), British zoologist, outstanding for his work on the mechanism of cellular and animal movement, was born in London, Oct. 14, 1891. He was educated at Merchant Taylor's school and at King's college, Cambridge, where he was elected fellow in 1914. During World War I he served in the infantry. Returning to Cambridge in 1919, he gradually established one of the major schools of biological research in Britain. He became professor of zoology in 1937. For his own contributions to knowledge he received the royal medal of the Royal society.

He played a leading part in changing the main objective of 20th-century zoological research from evolutionary comparative anatomy to the functional analysis of living cells and living animals, particularly through his long and successful editorship of the *Journal of Experimental Biology.* Beginning research as a cytologist, his work was first particularly concerned with the mechanics of various kinds of cellular movements, and he is the author of a standard work on experimental cytology. Later he extended this application of mechanical principles to the analysis of animal movement in general. He has published numerous works, both specialist and popular, on movement of living systems of every size, from the spermatozoon to fish, whales, snakes and a great variety of terrestrial animals; and he has shown the interest and importance of the application of engineering principles to such biological problems. Among his publications are *Ciliary Movement* (1928), *Experimental Cytology* (1931) and *How Animals Move* (1953). (C. F. A. P.)

GRAY, JOHN DE (d. 1214), bishop of Norwich, Eng., a close supporter of King John, whose service he entered before his accession (1199), was rapidly promoted in the church until he became bishop of Norwich in Sept. 1200. By attempting in 1205 to make him archbishop of Canterbury King John started his long quarrel with Pope Innocent III, who quashed the election in favour of Stephen Langton. In 1209 De Gray was sent to Ireland to replace the baronial justiciar. There he extended the English frontier northward and westward, fighting campaigns on the Shannon and in Fermanagh but being defeated in 1212 by Art O'Maelsechlainn. He also carried out the reforms initiated by King John whereby the laws and customs of England were introduced into Ireland and a new coinage was struck.

On De Gray's return to England in 1213 he brought 500 knights to Barham Downs, near Canterbury, for the muster assembled against the expected invasion of Philip II of France. He also acted for the king on embassies to the French king (c. Dec. 1203) and the emperor Otto IV (July 1213). After the king's reconciliation with Innocent in 1213 De Gray, with others of the king's chief advisers, was excluded from the general pardon and made to go to Rome; there he so greatly impressed Innocent that he was recommended for the bishopric of Durham, but he died on his homeward journey at St. Jean d'Audely in Poitou on Oct. 18, 1214. He is buried in Norwich cathedral. (M. DK.)

GRAY, LOUIS HERBERT (1875–1955), U.S. linguist and orientalist, whose work combined traditional and modern approaches with an insistence on thorough mastery of the languages investigated, was born in Newark, N.J., April 10, 1875. After studying at Princeton and Columbia (Ph.D. 1900), he devoted most of his life to teaching and research, except for a brief span at the Peace commission (Paris, 1919–20). He taught at Princeton, Nebraska and Columbia, retiring from Columbia as professor emeritus of comparative linguistics in 1944. His competence also included Celtic, Germanic, Armenian, Georgian and Semitic; he was expert in hagiography and church history. Besides numerous articles he published some ten books, including *Indo-Iranian Phonology* (1902), *Introduction to Semitic Comparative Linguistics* (1934) and *Foundations of Language* (1939). He died in New York city on Aug. 18, 1955.

GRAY, PATRICK GRAY, 6TH BARON (c. 1559–1612), Scottish politician, known as "the master of Gray" until he succeeded as Lord Gray in 1609, whose intrigues were for some years of importance in Anglo-Scottish diplomacy. He was educated at St. Andrews university, St. Andrews, Scot. Although brought up a Protestant, he later became a Roman Catholic but his religious beliefs probably did not affect the course of his intrigues. He was employed by James VI in 1584 to negotiate an alliance with Elizabeth I of England. In the course of these negotiations he successfully plotted the fall of the Scottish chancellor, the earl of Arran (his personal enemy at court), and the restoration of a Protestant government in Scotland. The alliance (1586) between the two Protestant states was immediately tested by the English condemnation of Mary Stuart. Gray was sent by James to England to protest but performed his mission, possibly with the approval of James, in such a way as to make his protest merely formal. The indignation caused in Scotland by Mary's execution led to Gray's fall from power and, although he retained the king's favour, he was banished for a time and never regained a position of political influence before his death in 1612. His undoubted diplomatic ability was linked with such a complete lack of honesty that at one stage he was willing to act simultaneously on behalf of James, Mary and Elizabeth.

(T. I. R.)

GRAY, ROBERT (1809–1872), first Anglican bishop of Cape Town and metropolitan of South Africa, was born at Bishopwearmouth, Durham, Eng., on Oct. 3, 1809, the son of Robert Gray, bishop of Bristol. After attending University college, Oxford, he was ordained in 1833. In 1847 he was consecrated bishop of Cape Town, which had previously depended on the bishop of Calcutta, India. With very little help from England, he had to deal with inefficiency, hostility and neglect. In 1853, upon the establishment of the suffragan dioceses of Grahamstown and Natal, he was appointed metropolitan of South Africa. In that capacity he pronounced the deposition of Bishop J. W. Colenso (*q.v.*) for heresy, but his right of jurisdiction was questioned and the judicial committee of the privy council later reversed the judgment. Gray reorganized the South African church, dividing the original huge diocese of Cape Town into five bishoprics. He died at Cape Town on Sept. 1, 1872.

See H. L. Farrer, *Life of Robert Gray, Bishop of Capetown*, 2nd ed. (1883); A. Brooke, *Robert Gray, First Bishop of Cape Town* (1947).

(G. Hu.)

GRAY, THOMAS (1716–1771), English poet, whose *Elegy Written in a Country Churchyard* is one of the best-known English poems for its eloquent expression of universal feelings, was the son of Philip Gray, a prosperous scrivener in the City of London, by his wife Dorothy Antrobus. Born at their house in Cornhill on Dec. 26, 1716, he was a delicate boy, the only one of a large family who survived his infancy. He had a troubled childhood because of his father's harsh and at times violent treatment of his mother, who was obliged to run a milliner's shop in order to pay for their son's education. This situation, however, had eased considerably before Philip Gray's death in 1741.

Thomas was sent to Eton in 1725, and was extremely happy there. His closest friends were Horace Walpole, a son of Sir Robert Walpole, the prime minister, and Richard West, whose father was a distinguished lawyer. The influence of Eton, with its beauty and its ancient traditions, remained with him throughout life. In 1734 he became a scholar at Peterhouse, Cambridge, and left without taking a degree in 1738. His habits, as at Eton, were studious and reflective, and he began to write Latin verse of considerable merit. Apart from a few translations, he had not yet composed any English poetry.

Early in 1739 he set out with Walpole on a prolonged grand tour. They spent the remainder of that year in France, and crossed the Alps in November. The whole of 1740 was passed in Italy, with a long sojourn in Rome and shorter excursions to Naples and elsewhere. The spring months were spent with Horace Mann, the British minister at Florence. They returned to Florence from Rome in August, and remained there until April 1741, when they set out for Venice. On the way there a violent quarrel took place at Reggio; the two friends parted in anger, and were not reconciled until 1745. Gray spent a few weeks in Venice, and returned to England alone. On his way he stayed at the monastery of the Grande Chartreuse which had deeply impressed him on a brief visit earlier, and wrote there the beautiful alcaic stanzas beginning *O Tu, severi Religio loci*.

Throughout his years abroad Gray had continued his studies, and had acquired an intimate knowledge of classical and modern art. But at the age of 25 he had not prepared himself for any sort of career. He spent the first few months after his return to England at Stoke Poges in Buckinghamshire, where his mother and her sisters had retired to live after Philip Gray's death. He then took up residence as a fellow commoner at his old college of Peterhouse, in order to read for the degree of bachelor of laws, with a not very serious intention of an eventual career at the bar.

The spring and summer of 1742—the interval between his return from abroad and his establishment at Cambridge—witnessed a remarkable spell of creative activity. The sights and sounds of the Buckinghamshire countryside inspired him to write the "Ode on the Spring." Almost immediately after this he received news of the death of Richard West, to whom he had drawn closer since his estrangement from Walpole, and who was indeed his only intimate friend. His sorrow and loneliness found expression in the poems which now followed in close succession—the *Ode on a Distant Prospect of Eton College*, the "Hymn to Adversity," and the "Sonnet on the Death of Richard West." He also added to the ambitious philosophical poem *De Principiis Cogitandi*, which had been begun at Florence, some lines of remarkable intensity of feeling and beauty of expression. This passage was the culmination and the close of his Latin writing.

These poems hold an important place in Gray's exceptionally small output of verse. The "Ode on the Spring" and the Eton ode, in particular revealed his ease and felicity of expression, his evocative power which he possessed in so singular a degree. On the other hand not even his own century could wholly applaud the abstractions and personifications which abound in the Eton ode and the "Hymn to Adversity." The former poem was published in 1747; and it appeared again in Robert Dodsley's *Miscellany* of 1748, together with the "Ode on the Spring" and the graceful trifle about the cat drowned in a bowl of goldfish. They met with little attention, and there was no awareness that a new poet had arrived on a scene lately impoverished by the death of Pope.

Perhaps in 1742, perhaps at a later date, Gray embarked on a long meditative elegy. Opinions will continue to differ about the progress and the several stages of this poem's composition; but it was completed in its final form, and sent to Walpole, in the summer of 1750. In order to forestall its publication in a piratical magazine, which had chanced to obtain a copy, the *Elegy Written in a Country Churchyard* was hastily printed in the following year. Its success was instantaneous and overwhelming. It remains the most celebrated poem of its century, the most frequently quoted, the most loved perhaps of all English poems, the best loved by the ordinary man. Tennyson, a century later, spoke of its "divine truisms that make us weep." The voice of Johnson, a critic not usually disposed to be cordial toward Gray, summed up the contemporary reaction: "it abounds with images which find a mirrour in every mind, and with sentiments to which every bosom returns an echo."

Among the admirers of the *Elegy* were the Dowager Viscountess Cobham, the *grande dame* of Stoke Poges, and her young relation and companion Miss Henrietta Jane Speed. They introduced themselves to Gray, and he celebrated their first meeting in a poem entitled "A Long Story," a gay and fanciful example of the humorous vein in which he too seldom indulged. An attachment developed between him and Miss Speed, and at one time there were rumours that they intended to marry. But Gray was a man whose emotions had been deflected into the channels of friendship. A marriage between them would have been incongruous and almost certainly unsuccessful; and in any case the lady soon found a more appropriate husband elsewhere. Another outcome of the success of the *Elegy* was the publication in 1753 of the first collected edition of Gray's poems, in a handsome volume with remarkable illustrations by Walpole's friend Richard Bentley.

Through these years Gray had been living quietly at Peterhouse, reading, studying, taking short summer tours about England, cultivating his modest circle of friends and writing his admirable letters.

He took no part in university or college business, but simply resided in college as a gentleman of leisure. Nor did his new-found celebrity make the smallest difference to his habits. In 1756 he migrated from Peterhouse across the street to Pembroke hall, in consequence of a practical joke attempted by some undergraduates, who had become aware of his timidity about fire and the precautions he had taken in the event of an alarm. At Pembroke he continued, in a more friendly and congenial atmosphere, his accustomed way of life for the remainder of his days.

The popularity of the *Elegy* seems not wholly to have pleased him. Always distrustful of the popular voice, he chose for his next important poems the motto "vocal to the intelligent alone" from an ode of Pindar. The poems themselves were odes in the strict Pindaric form; and he intended that they should form the crown of his achievement. In "The Progress of Poesy" he set himself to glorify, with every adornment of rhetoric and eloquence, the poet's high calling. In "The Bard" he depicted a traditional episode during the final conquest of Wales. An ancient seer curses the invading forces and foretells the doom of the English monarchs who are to come, until a Welsh dynasty in the persons of the Tudor sovereigns ruled over the whole land of Britain. During the composition of this ode Gray was seized with an unwonted fervour of inspiration, so that, as he said later, "I felt myself the Bard."

The odes were published together in 1757, in a slender volume which was the first production of Walpole's private press at Strawberry Hill. They met with a mixed reception, and were widely criticized for their obscurity. Unquestionably they are difficult poems, and were still more difficult without the aid of the footnotes which Gray refused to provide in the original edition. They are full of metaphor and veiled allusion, rhapsody and incantation. And yet certain passages have an authentic note of mystery and romance, a foreshadowing of Coleridge and Keats. By contrast, melodies almost Wordsworthian in their pure simplicity were sounded in a poem of this time which Gray left unfinished, and to which his editor, W. Mason, in an edition published in 1775, gave the title of "Ode on the Pleasure Arising From Vicissitude."

The reception of the two Pindaric odes brought deep disappointment to Gray, and thereafter he virtually ceased to write poetry. He buried himself even more completely in private study, and especially in English antiquities and in natural history. He greatly admired the productions which that dubious figure James Macpherson published as The Poems of Ossian, and made investigations of his own into the Celtic and Scandinavian past. He had long contemplated a history of English poetry, and made some translations from Welsh and Icelandic originals for incorporation into this work. "The Descent of Odin," "The Fatal Sisters," "The Triumphs of Owen" and the rest have their place in the history of the romantic revival in England and indeed in Europe. His only other writings during this stretch of years were occasional verses in a satirical vein. Most of these were destroyed after his death; but two pieces, a political squib entitled "The Candidate" and the sombre and impressive lines on Lord Holland's villa on the North Foreland, have fortunately survived.

In 1768 the professorship of modern history was bestowed upon Gray by the duke of Grafton, the newly appointed chancellor of the university. He treated this office as a sinecure, although he had at first intended to deliver lectures and was much disturbed in conscience by his failure to do so. He expressed his gratitude to the duke by writing an ode to be set to music and sung at the ceremony of his installation. This Installation Ode (published in 1769) contained some noble passages, and was indeed a return to the grand manner which he had seemed to abandon after the failure of his Pindarics 12 years before.

During the last decade of his life Gray's summer tours sometimes took him further afield than had previously been his custom. He visited Scotland in 1765, and the English lakes in 1767 and 1769, describing the landscapes through which he passed in some of his finest letters. Late in 1769 he made the acquaintance of a young Swiss nobleman, Charles Victor de Bonstetten, and conceived for him a romantic devotion, the most profound emotional experience of his life. De Bonstetten only remained a few months in England, and Gray's letters after his departure reveal how intensely he felt their separation. His health, which was never robust, and about which he displayed a solicitude almost amounting to hypochondria, had been declining for some years; and he died in his rooms at Pembroke, after a sudden illness which was probably an acute form of uremia, on July 30, 1771. He was buried in the churchyard of Stoke Poges.

As a poet Gray was admired and influential out of all proportion to his modest output of verse. He was unquestionably the dominant poetic figure of the middle decades of the 18th century, and a precursor of the romantic revival which was soon to come. He was also one of the supreme letter writers in English literature. A man of studious instincts, of a retiring and somewhat melancholy temperament, he nevertheless set his mark upon his age; and in one poem, the Elegy Written in a Country Churchyard, he made a lasting contribution to the English heritage.

BIBLIOGRAPHY.—Editions: The last collection published in Gray's lifetime and supervised by him, Poems by Mr. Gray (1768), forms the basis of The Poetical Works of Gray, ed. with those of William Collins, for the "Oxford Standard Authors Series" by A. Lane Poole (1917; rev. ed. by L. Whibley, 1937), which also includes the text approved by Gray of poems not included in the 1768 edition. The Poems were also ed. by L. Whibley for the "World's Classics" (1939). The Correspondence of Thomas Gray was ed. by P. Toynbee and L. Whibley, 3 vol. (1935). Biographical and Critical Studies: The authorized biography, by W. Mason, Memoirs of the Life and Writings of Mr. Gray (1775), was prefixed to his edition of the Poems. A life by Sir Edmund Gosse appeared in the "English Men of Letters Series" (1882). D. C. Tovey, Gray and His Friends: Letters and Relics (1890) includes additional material. The standard modern life is R. W. Ketton-Cremer, Thomas Gray (1955). See also R. Martin, Chronologie de la vie et de l'oeuvre de Thomas Gray (1931), Essai sur Thomas Gray (1934); W. Powell Jones, Thomas Gray, Scholar (1937); Lord David Cecil, Two Quiet Lives (1948); C. S. Northup, A Bibliography of Thomas Gray (1917), continued by H. W. Starr, 1917–51 (1953), which includes works on Gray as well as by him.
(R. W. K.-C.)

GRAY (GREY), WALTER DE (d. 1255), archbishop of York from 1215 to 1255, was educated at Oxford and rose to high ecclesiastical office through service to King John. He was primarily an administrator both in secular and ecclesiastical affairs and his enemies attacked his alleged lack of scholarship. He became chancellor of England (1205), where he remained during the interdict (1208–13). He was elected bishop of Lichfield under royal pressure (1210), but the election was quashed. After John had made his peace with the church, Walter was elected bishop of Worcester (1214) with the support of the king and papal legate, and resigned the chancellorship. In 1215 John advanced him as a candidate for the see of York against the wishes of the chapter, but Pope Innocent III settled the subsequent appeal in favour of Walter, who had journeyed to Rome and who paid him a large service. On his return to England Walter attested the 1217 reissue of Magna Carta and the Charter of the Forest. He played a considerable part in restoring law and order to the north after the baronial revolt. He was sent on diplomatic errands to France (1226) and was appointed governor of the kingdom during Henry III's absence in Poitou (1242–43).

Walter was energetic in enforcing in his province the decrees of the fourth Lateran council, which he had attended. He visited monasteries, leaving injunctions at Selby, Newstead and St. Oswald's, Gloucester. He accelerated the establishment of vicarages, drew up provincial constitutions (1250) and encouraged new building at Southwell, Beverley, Worcester and Ripon. At York minster he built the south transept, where he was buried. He was among the first English prelates to keep records of his acts; his registers have survived. He continued, unsuccessfully, York's long quarrel with Canterbury, asserting the right to have his cross carried erect in the southern province, and claiming precedence (1237) as senior archbishop over Edmund of Canterbury. He died at Fulham on May 1, 1255.

See M. Gibbs and J. Lang, Bishops and Reform, 1215–1272 (1934); J. Raine (ed.), The Register, or Rolls, of Walter Gray, Lord Archbishop of York (1872).
(J. C. Ho.)

GRAYLING, a troutlike gamefish of the genus Thymallus, often placed in the family Salmonidae. It is a handsome silvery-purple fish, reaching a length of about 18 in., distinguished by rather large scales; unusually large eyes; a small mouth with feeble teeth; and a long dorsal fin, with 20 to 24 rays. Several species are known from the cold, clear streams of Eurasia and northern North America. Pollution of streams in North America has, however, reduced the numbers of this excellent food fish.

GRAYWACKE (GREYWACKE). The term graywacke, derived from German grauwacke for gray stone, was apparently first applied to certain Devonian and Lower Carboniferous rocks in the Harz mountains. Graywacke is a clastic rock, a microbreccia made up of fragments of pre-existing rocks, characterized by its dark-gray colour and toughness. Most graywackes consist mainly of angular quartz and rock particles, together with some feldspar and mica, set in a finer-grained matrix of shredlike chlorite and sericite. The rock fragments usually include slate, siltstone, phyllite, chert and a little felsitic material. Authigenic, that is, crystallized after deposition, carbonate and pyrite are common.

Graywackes occur in thin layers several inches to several feet thick, interbedded with shales or slates with which they form thick sequences. These are the "gray flags" or "grits" of the older petrographic literature. Associated rocks commonly include interbedded ellipsoidal greenstones, tuffs and thin-bedded cherts.

Graywackes may resemble basic tuffs, but differ in their high quartz content and lack of volcanic glass. Although commonly feldspar-rich, graywackes differ from arkose (q.v.) sandstones in their dark colour, which results from the fine-grained chloritic matrix. Graywacke has been erroneously defined as the basic equivalent of an arkose, perhaps because of its superficial resemblance to wacke, the partially weathered residue from basalts and related rocks. Related to graywacke is subgraywacke (low-rank graywacke), which differs in its better-rounded constituents and in its precipitated mineral cement.

Graywackes are probably of marine origin, perhaps deposited by turbidity currents in relatively deep water. This hypothesis explains the associated radiolarian cherts—supposedly of deep-water origin—and the lack of ripple marks, cross-bedding and benthonic (bottom-living) fossils, which characterize normal shallow-water sands, and the deposition of coarse debris concurrently with fine mud (of the matrix) as well as the graded structure seen in many graywackes.
(F. J. P.: X.)

GRAZ, the second largest city of Austria and capital of the *Bundesland* (federal state) of Styria (Steiermark), is situated on both banks of the Mur river about 180 km. (112 mi.) S.W. of Vienna by road. Pop. (1971) 249,211. Bounded on the north by the wooded Styrian Alps, Graz occupies a fine position at the opening of the Mur valley into the wide fertile plain of the Grazer Feld. An outlier of the Styrian Alps, the Schlossberg (1,552 ft.), dominates the town; a stronghold from pre-Roman times, it was laid out with parks from 1839. On the south slope stands the clock tower (90 ft. high, completed 1561); the belfry (115 ft., 1588) at the top of the Schlossberg contains the four-ton Liesl bell. The river flows to the west of the Schlossberg and the town park lies to the east.

The chief buildings of interest are in the old part of the town and include: the 16th-century Renaissance *Landhaus*; the 15th- to 17th-century armoury or arsenal, with a unique historical collection of armour and weapons; the 19th-century town hall in German Renaissance style; and the 15th-century castle, now used as government offices. The 15th-century cathedral of St. Aegidius is the most important ecclesiastical building. It is mainly in late Gothic, though later decorations and modifications in baroque have altered the original purity of style. The interior is remarkable for its costly stained-glass windows, shrines and paintings. The baroque mausoleum church (1614–1638) is nearby and the Mariahilf church (early 17th century) contains an image, "Our Lady of Succour," credited as miraculous.

Graz has many educational establishments headed by the university, founded in 1586 by the Austrian archduke Charles. Others include a technical high school, a commercial academy and trade school, teacher-training establishments and opera and music schools. There are an opera house, two theatres and an open-air theatre on the Schlossberg; an art gallery, the New gallery and the Künstlerhaus are used for art exhibitions.

Graz is on the main railway from Vienna to Maribor and Ljubljana, Yugos., and Trieste, and is also connected with Szombathely, Hung. The airport is at Thalerhof, 6 mi. S. of Graz. There is an active trade in cereals, fruit and wine from the nearby hilly country. Iron- and steelworks, precision and optical instrument factories, brewing, milling, leather, paper and cloth production, printing and lithography and railway workshops are the principal industrial activities. The tourist trade is also vital to the economy of Graz.

There was probably a fortress on Schlossberg in the 9th century. The name of Graz first occurs in a document of 1115 and it received town rights about 1240. It had been the centre of Styria for many years when it became the residence of the Leopoldine Habsburgs in 1379.

Protestantism established itself there about 1530 and flourished until oppressive measures by the archduke Charles restored the authority of Rome. The German astronomer Johannes Kepler (1571–1630) worked in the city. During the Napoleonic Wars Graz was held by the French in 1797 and in 1805. The town developed rapidly in the 19th century and received many privileges through the interest of the archduke John. It received its constitution as a city in 1850. In 1938 several communities were incorporated in greater Graz, with a consequent increase in the city's population.
(W. Se.; Fr. P.)

GRAZIANI, RODOLFO, MARCHESE DI NEGHELLI (1882–1955), Italian soldier and administrator, notable for his service in Libya and East Africa, was born at Filettino, near Frosinone. It., on Aug. 11, 1882. Before World War I he served in the army in Eritrea and later in Libya. In 1919 he was in command in Macedonia; he then served in Tripolitania until 1927. Graziani commanded the Italian forces in Libya in 1930–34. During this time he pacified the country, but in so doing became notorious for his harsh treatment of the people. Graziani was governor of Italian Somaliland (1935–36), viceroy of Ethiopia (1936–37) and honorary governor of Italian East Africa.

In 1939 Graziani commanded the Italian forces in Libya, and the following year advanced slowly against the British as far as Sidi Barrani. In 1941 his forces were heavily defeated by General Archibald Wavell and he resigned his post. After the Italia...

THE CLOCK TOWER (COMPLETED 1561) ON SOUTHERN SLOPE OF THE SCHLOSSBERG, GRAZ, AUSTRIA

BY COURTESY OF THE AUSTRIAN STATE TOURIST DEPARTMENT

armistice in 1943 he took the side of the Germans and became defense minister in the Italian Republican government. In 1945 he surrendered to the U.S. forces, which imprisoned him until 1946, when he was handed over to the Italian government for trial. He was kept in Rome and in the spring of 1950 sentenced to 19 years' imprisonment. In August of the same year, however, he was released and later became president of the neo-Fascist Italian Socialist movement. He died at Rome on Jan. 11, 1955.

(E. B. Bn.)

GRAZZINI, ANTON FRANCESCO (1503–1584), Italian writer who played an active part in the literary and linguistic controversies of his day. Born in Florence, March 22, 1503, he became an apothecary. He was a founder of the Accademia degli Umidi, in which he was known as Il Lasca.

In his numerous burlesque verses (mod. ed. *Le rime burlesche*, 1882), written in the manner of Francesco Berni, he strongly opposed humanism and Petrarchism, and in the discussions on the development of an Italian literary language he defended the Tuscan tradition. His own language is lively, at times approaching dialect, both in his comedies (*Gelosia, Spiritata, Strega, Pinzochera, Sibilla, Parentadi, Arzigogolo*, written 1540–50; mod. ed., by G. Grazzini, 1953), and in his *Cene* (mod. ed., by C. Verzone, 1890), a collection of 22 stories which, in the manner of Boccaccio, are told by a party of young people during a carnival. Although theoretically he maintained that modern comedies should not follow classical patterns, his own plays showed no originality of inspiration. Grazzini died in Florence, Feb. 18, 1584.

(G. A.)

GREASEWOOD, a name given to North American weedy shrubs of the genus *Sarcobatus* of the goosefoot family (Chenopodiaceae). Black greasewood (*S. vermiculatus*) is a characteristic plant of strongly alkaline and saline soils in the desert plains of the west. It is a much-branched, somewhat spiny shrub, 2 ft. to 10 ft. high, with small, fleshy, toothless and stalkless leaves. The creosote bush (*q.v.*), certain species of saltbush and various other plants are also called greasewood.

GREAT AUK (GAREFOWL), an extinct large flightless sea bird (*Pinguinus impennis*). Slightly smaller than a tame goose, it resembled its much smaller relative the razor-billed auk (*Alca torda*) in appearance, but a large patch of white occupied nearly all the space between the bill and the eye, while the bill itself bore eight or more transverse grooves. The body of the great auk was 30 in. long, the wings, used in swimming under water, being less than 6 in. long. It bred at St. Kilda, the Faeroe Islands, Iceland and Funk Island off Newfoundland. Fishermen used both the bird and its eggs for food. Enormous numbers were captured, the birds often being driven up a plank and slaughtered on their way into the hold of a vessel. The last specimens were taken in June 1844 at Funk Island; later reports are discounted. The bird's extinction is one of the sorriest chapters in man's heedless exploitation of nature. About 80 great auks and a like number of their eggs are preserved in museums. *See also* AUK.

GREAT AUSTRALIAN BIGHT, a wide indentation on the southern coast of Australia, extends, by the International Hydrographic bureau's definition, from the southwest of Western Australia to Tasmania; usually, however, the name is confined to the northern portion, from Cape Pasley and the Recherche archipelago to Eyre peninsula in South Australia. The head of the bight abuts on the arid Nullarbor plain and is bounded by a remarkably even and continuous line of cliffs 200–250 ft. high. West of Eucla (near the Western Australia–South Australia boundary) the old cliff line is bordered by a coastal sand plain. The shores

of the bight, first explored by Pieter Nuyts in 1627, are barren and forbidding, and E. J. Eyre, who made the first land journey along the coast in 1840, nearly died of thirst. The coast was surveyed by Matthew Flinders, the English explorer, in 1802. East of Ceduna and the Nuyts archipelago, Eyre peninsula is well enough watered for wheat farming and sheep raising. To the west of this peninsula lie the Investigator Islands. The bight, lying in winter in the full track of the westerly winds, has in Australia much the same reputation for storms and rough seas as the Bay of Biscay has in Europe.

(O. H. K. S.)

GREAT AWAKENING: *see* REVIVALISM.

GREAT BARRIER REEF: *see* BARRIER REEF.

GREAT BASIN, THE, named by John C. Frémont, who crossed the area in 1843 and 1845 and described its physical features, is a unique natural basin-and-range region in the western United States. It occupies the western third of Utah and the entire state of Nevada and on its margins spills over into eastern California and southern Oregon and Idaho. The 189,000 sq.mi. of the area resembles an inverted triangle with its 300-mi. base extending across northern Utah and Nevada and tapering on either side to the Mojave desert of California. The boundaries are rather sharply defined by the Wasatch mountains and Colorado plateau on the east and the Sierra Nevada on the west. To the north the Great Basin merges with the Columbia plateau, and the Mojave desert marks a rather indefinite southern border.

The topography, climate and drainage of the area set it apart from other natural regions of the United States. The Great Basin is divided about equally between rugged mountains and broad basins. The important mountain ranges are oriented north-south; they are commonly from 50 to 75 mi. in length and from 6 to 15 mi. in width. The mountains rise from 3,000 to 5,000 ft. above the surrounding valley floors. They have been referred to as fault-block mountains and their steeper faces are regarded as fault scarps. Between the ranges are the broad alluvial-filled basins. The elevation of these basins above sea level varies from 6,000 ft. in central Nevada to about 4,000 ft. on the east and west margins and 3,000 ft. on the south.

The climatic controls of the Great Basin tend to produce aridity. The high Sierras block the rain-bearing winds from the west. The annual rainfall averages about 10 to 12 in. in the basins, decreasing to 4 to 6 in. in the south. The limited summer rain comes in the form of torrential storms that cut arroyos and develop mud-rock flows; winter precipitation is generally in the form of snow. Summers are hot and winters cold, except in the south, where latitude and lower elevation combine to produce a mild winter.

The name "Great Basin" suggests the third natural feature of the region, namely, interior drainage. It is not, however, one large basin, but a composite of many separate basins. Interior drainage is, in part, an expression of the dry climate of the area. The balance between evaporation and precipitation is a delicate one; lakes fluctuate greatly and some of them occasionally become dry. The water in many of them, notably Great Salt lake, is brackish or salty. Klamath, Pyramid, Carson and Utah lakes are all fresh water.

The vegetation of the Great Basin is an expression of the climate, soil and topography. Salt grass and greasewood grow on the alkaline soils of the valley bottoms; cottonwood trees edge the few streams that cross the lowlands; sagebrush, scrub oak and juniper appear on the better-drained slopes. In the southern part of the basin subtropical desert plants and species of cactus and other thorny growth are common. At the higher elevations forests of pine and spruce appear.

The valleys along the eastern edge of the region were occupied by the Mormons in 1847 and Salt Lake City has become the metropolis of that area. In a similar manner many of the valleys on the western edge were developed with Reno as the major centre of activity. The primary economic activities of the Great Basin are copper and iron mining, irrigated agriculture and livestock production and, more recently, manufacturing.

See also UNITED STATES (OF AMERICA): *Physiography.*

BIBLIOGRAPHY.—Early reports on the Great Basin include: John C.

BY COURTESY OF THE AMERICAN MUSEUM OF NATURAL HISTORY

GREAT AUK OR GAREFOWL (PINGUINUS IMPENNIS)

(Dn. A.)

Frémont, (2nd) *Report of the Exploring Party to the Rocky Mountains* (1845); Clarence King *et al.*, *Report of the Geological Exploration of the Fortieth Parallel* (1870–80); G. K. Gilbert, "Lake Bonneville," U.S. Geol. Survey, *Monograph I* (1890); I. C. Russell, "Lake Lahontan," U.S. Geol. Survey, *Monograph XI* (1885). For general reference see N. M. Fenneman, *Physiography of Western United States* (1931); W. W. Atwood, *The Physiographic Provinces of North America* (1940).
(H. B. HA.)

GREAT BEAR LAKE, in Mackenzie district, Northwest Territories, is the largest body of fresh water entirely in Canada; 390 ft. above the sea, with depths that exceed 1,300 ft., it is 237 mi. long and 12,275 sq.mi. in area. From the northeast, reading clockwise, the five main inlets are Dease, McTavish, McVicar, Keith and Smith Arms. The eastern third lies in the Canadian Shield, the western two-thirds in the Interior Plains. Western and southern shores are well-wooded, eastern and northern less so.

The outlet is by 70-mi.-long Great Bear river (used with a portage road as a freight route) to the Mackenzie river. The lake freezes over in winter and much ice may be present in mid-July. Radioactive ores, principally pitchblende, were mined from 1933 near the company town of Port Radium at the eastern end of McTavish Arm; during World War II production went to the U.S. Manhattan atomic bomb project. Twenty-five years of nearly continuous mining exhausted the reserves.

The settlement of Fort Franklin is at the western extremity of Keith Arm.
(J. R. M.)

GREAT BEND, a city of central Kansas, U.S., on the Arkansas river, and the seat of Barton county, was on the old Santa Fe trail, which passed through the courthouse square. The city was founded about 1870 and incorporated in 1871. East of the city are the ruins of Fort Zarah (established 1864), from which soldiers escorted wagon trains through the dangerous stretch beyond.

Great Bend became a shipping point for wheat, livestock and other agricultural products, and there are grain elevators and flour mills. For comparative population figures *see* table in KANSAS: *Population*.

GREAT BRITAIN AND NORTHERN IRELAND, UNITED KINGDOM OF, the official title of the political unity of England, Scotland, Wales, and Northern Ireland. The effective union of the principality of Wales with England dates from 1301 when Edward I's son was created prince of Wales, although Wales was not enfranchised until the reign of Henry VIII. The name Great Britain was used in 1604, after James VI of Scotland had succeeded to the English throne, and it was formally adopted in 1707 at the date of the union of the Parliaments of England and Scotland. Ireland was similarly joined to Great Britain by the Act of Union in 1801, and the official title then became the United Kingdom of Great Britain and Ireland. In 1922, 26 Irish counties were severed from the United Kingdom as the Irish Free State (later Eire; since 1949 the Republic of Ireland), and from then onward the title of the United Kingdom of Great Britain and Northern Ireland was frequently used in official documents to designate those parts of the British Isles that were represented in the Imperial Parliament, meeting at Westminster.

On May 13, 1927, under the Royal and Parliamentary Titles Act of that year, it was proclaimed that in the royal style "Great Britain, Ireland and . . ." should henceforth be used instead of "the United Kingdom of Great Britain and Ireland." By the same act of Parliament it was enacted that "Parliament shall hereafter be known as and styled the Parliament of the United Kingdom of Great Britain and Northern Ireland."

Finally, on May 29, 1953, under the Royal Titles Act, a proclamation was issued by which the queen adopted the title of "Elizabeth the Second, by the Grace of God, of the United Kingdom of Great Britain and Northern Ireland and of her other Realms and Territories Queen, Head of the Commonwealth, Defender of the Faith." The form of title is varied for those independent Commonwealth member nations which owe allegiance to the crown, to suit the particular circumstances of each.

Although there is a single Parliament at Westminster for the whole of Great Britain and Northern Ireland, the original constituent kingdoms retain autonomy in different degrees. A secretary of state for Scotland was appointed in 1885 and separate departments in Edinburgh now deal with home and health, agriculture and fisheries, education, and development. Scotland also has its own separate legal system. From 1964 the secretary of state for Wales and the Welsh Office provided an increased amount of specialized treatment in matters affecting Wales. By the Government of Ireland Act, 1920, it was provided that Northern Ireland would continue to be represented at Westminster but that it should also have its own parliament (Stormont) for home affairs. In 1972 Westminster suspended Stormont and temporarily imposed direct rule.

This article deals with those subjects which concern the United Kingdom as a whole and is arranged as follows:

I. Population
II. Constitution and Government
   1. Crown
   2. Judiciary
   3. Executive
   4. Legislature
   5. Liberty of the Subject
   6. Established Churches
III. Defense
   A. Army
   B. Navy
   C. Air Force
   D. Civil Defense
IV. The Economy
   A. Production
      1. Agriculture
      2. Forestry
      3. Fisheries
      4. Mining
      5. Industrial Production
      6. Public Utilities
   B. Trade and Finance
      1. Overseas Trade
      2. The Department of Trade and Industry
      3. Currency and Banking
      4. National Finance
      5. Taxation
   C. Transport and Communications
      1. Inland Transport Prior to 1939
      2. Inland Transport in World War II
      3. Inland Transport After World War II
      4. Shipping
      5. Air Transport
      6. Northern Ireland
      7. The Post Office
      8. Broadcasting

For those subjects that essentially concern each country separately (e.g., geography, geology, people, administration, and social conditions) the articles ENGLAND; SCOTLAND; WALES; IRELAND; and IRELAND, NORTHERN should be consulted. See also BRITAIN; COMMONWEALTH OF NATIONS; ENGLISH HISTORY; LOCAL GOVERNMENT; LABOUR (TRADE) UNION.
(SN. G.; D. MT.)

I. POPULATION

During the first half of the 20th century the effect of the decline in the birthrate and in the average size of completed family was more than counterbalanced by the increased expectation of life. The population continued to increase but at a slower rate than in the 19th century. The growth rate in the early 1970s was about 0.5% per annum.

Toward the end of World War II there was a sharp increase in the number of births and, though the high postwar figures were not maintained, the birthrate remained significantly higher than prewar. The estimated population of the United Kingdom was 55,711,000 by mid-1970. Assuming that the annual number of births will increase gradually from 917,000 between mid-1970 and mid-1971 to 1,020,000 by the end of the 20th century, that death rates continue the past trend of decline over the projected period, and an outward migration balance of 30,000 a year until 2001, the population is expected to increase to 58,885,000 by 1981 and 66,488,000 by 2001. The proportion of the total under 15 years of age decreased from 32.5% in 1901 to 24% in 1961; the proportion aged 65 and over rose from 4.7% in 1901 to 8% in 1970. On the foregoing population projection the proportions in these two age groups are expected to be 24.8% and 12.3%, respectively, in 2001. The United Kingdom as a whole suffered a net loss of popu-

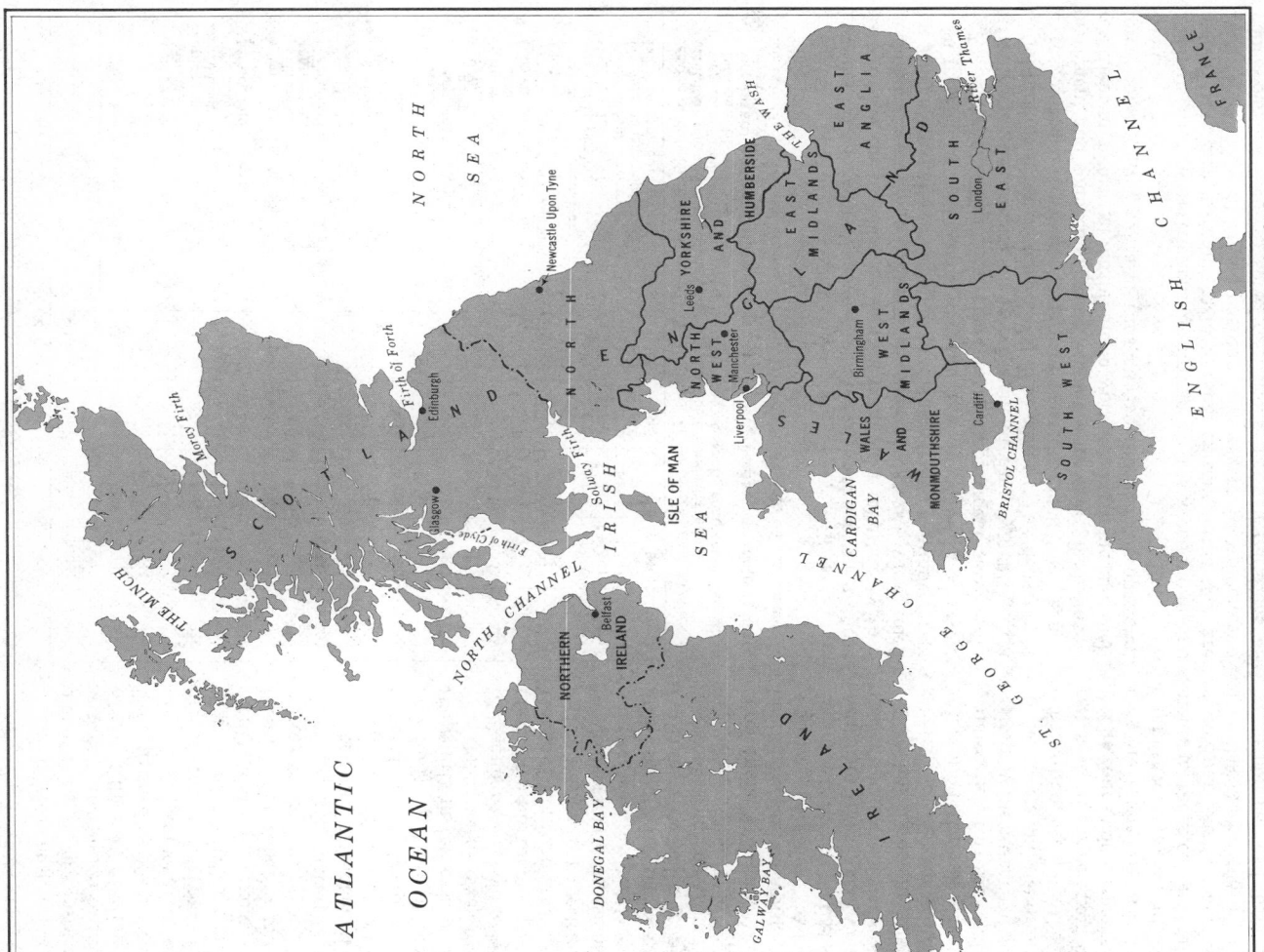

STANDARD POPULATION REGIONS OF ENGLAND, WALES, AND SCOTLAND

lation through migration during each intercensal period between 1901 and 1931, but between 1931 and 1951 there was a net gain of 465,000. The net gain to England and Wales was 758,000, but Scotland lost 220,000 and Northern Ireland 73,000. Scotland and Northern Ireland have consistently lost through migration during the 20th century, although their populations have continued to grow. Since 1951 there have been smaller net gains of population through migration in the U.K. as a whole. These were 12,000 between 1951–61, and 74,000 between 1961–66. Within both these overall gains is a pattern as between 1931 and 1951 of net inflows of persons into England and Wales (390,000 between 1951–61 and 311,000 between 1961–66), partly offset by net outflows from Scotland (282,000, 1951–61; 199,000, 1961–66) and from Northern Ireland (93,000, 1951–61; 38,000, 1961–66).

Between 1911 and 1961 population increased in all regions but by greatly varying proportions. For the U.K. as a whole the rise was 25%, for England 29%, for Wales 9%, for Scotland 6%, and for Northern Ireland 14%. Within England the increases varied from 13% in the North West region and 16% in the North to 38% in the South East and 45% in the East and West Midlands, respectively. The high rates of increase in the southern and eastern regions are explained partly by the growth in the number of persons working in Greater London and partly by the growth of places like Southampton, Portsmouth, and Oxford. The development of the automobile industry explains much of the growth of the Midlands. The decline in coal mining and other heavy industry and the increasing importance of light industries less dependent on raw-material sources attracted population southward and led to a relative decline of the regions to the north and west. The preliminary census for 1971 showed an overall population increase since 1961 in the United Kingdom as a whole of 5%, an increase in England and Wales of 5%, in Scotland of 1%, and in Northern Ireland of 7%. The pattern within England still showed the smallest growth in the North and North West regions (1% and 2%, respectively) but the largest increases appeared in East Anglia and the South West regions (13% and 10%, respectively).

The six main conurbations of England and Wales—Greater London, West Midlands, West Yorkshire, South East Lancashire, Merseyside, and Tyneside—occupy about 4% of the total area. In 1961 they contained 37% of the population, about the same as in 1871; by 1971 only 33% lived there. The Scottish conurbation of Central Clydeside (just over 1% of the country) contains 35% of the population. These conurbations contain many of the oldest and most important industrial and commercial centres, but they also include newer residential districts and are remarkably self-contained. Only a small amount of daily movement from residence to workplace occurs across their borders. See also the sections on *Population* in the articles ENGLAND; IRELAND, NORTHERN; SCOTLAND.

(W. BK.; N. CU.; M. J. A.)

Manpower.—The minimum working age in Britain is 15 years. By 1970 the total working population, which included some 73% of those between 15 and 65, was about 25,000,000. About 93% of British men in the working age group were in or seeking gainful employment. The corresponding figure for British women was about 50%. In addition to those of normal working age probably over 1,000,000 older men and women remained at work. Almost one-third of the female labour force was under 25 years of age.

Distribution of Manpower.—Also by 1970 about 38% of those in civil employment were engaged in mining and manufacture. Over half of the manufacturing employees were in the metals, engineering, and chemical industries. Only about 1½% of those in civil employment were engaged in agriculture and fisheries.

Unemployment.—After World War II the unemployment rate was generally much lower than during the prewar period and it was particularly low in the south and Midlands of England. The rate,

TABLE I.—*Distribution of Manpower in the United Kingdom**
(in 000)

Item	June 1961	June 1963	June 1965	June 1967	June 1970‡
Total working population	25,344	25,719	26,049	25,986	25,638
Males	16,754	16,942	16,996	16,853	16,416
Females	8,590	8,777	9,053	9,133	9,221
Armed Forces	474	427	423	417	372
Registered unemployed	287	497	299	503	555
Employers and self-employed	1,760	1,735	1,706	1,760	1,819
Distribution of employees:					
Manufacturing:					
Agriculture, forestry, and fishing	604	566	497	443	380
Mining and quarrying	736	686	629	555	418
Food, drink, and tobacco	830	833	839	852	891
Chemicals and allied industries	532	514	518	518	538
Metal manufacture	633	591	632	591	592
Engineering and electrical goods	2,142	2,148	2,287	2,348	2,283
Shipbuilding and marine engineering	263	224	219	208	199
Vehicles	898	874	870	824	842
Metal goods	560	549	591	569	640
Textiles	893	828	819	752	716
Leather, leather goods, fur	64	63	61	57	54
Clothing and footwear	595	568	558	524	501
Bricks, pottery, glass, cement, etc.	348	341	353	353	341
Timber, furniture, etc.	291	285	301	306	300
Paper, printing, and publishing	619	627	639	640	655
Other manufacturing	307	309	335	337	359
Construction†	1,517	1,582	1,700	1,591	1,367
Gas, electricity, and water	387	404	419	432	501
Transport and communication	1,731	1,711	1,655	1,629	1,591
Distributive trades	2,861	2,965	3,023	2,857	2,706
Financial, professional, and scientific services	2,661	2,874	3,108	3,339	3,851
Catering, hotels, etc.	569	584	622	591	577
Miscellaneous services	1,444	1,519	1,604	1,562	1,268
National government service†	532	559	566	587	573
Local government service†	765	815	772	840	858

*Because of different bases of calculation, the totals of employees in employment for 1963 and 1961 differ from the sum of the estimates for the industry groups.
†Owing to reclassification, figures up to 1963 are not strictly comparable with those from 1964 onward.
‡Owing to further reclassification, figures on an industry basis are not strictly comparable with earlier years.
Figures in the above table include Northern Ireland. Statistics in the text do not.
Source: *Annual Abstract of Statistics*, HMSO (1971).

however, was consistently higher than the national average in those parts of the country heavily dependent on older industries with a declining labour force. These "development areas," were aided by selective assistance to industry. Nonetheless, a minor recession resulted in the unemployment of over 1,000,000 by 1972.

Employment.—The main government employment services in Britain operate through the Department of Employment with a nationwide network of some 1,000 local offices. The department is responsible for a wide variety of activities, including general placement and counseling, youth employment work, disablement, resettlement, industrial rehabilitation, vocational training, and sheltered employment. It also runs an experimental Occupational Guidance Service.

There are few restrictions in Britain on the freedom of the employer to hire his adult male workers on any terms that are acceptable to them. (The position with regard to women and young persons involves some restrictions on such questions as hours of work, and it is illegal to employ women and young persons in certain jobs, such as underground mining.) Legislation, however, has provided the general work force with a measure of protection in employment.

This legislation includes the Terms and Conditions of Employment Act, 1959, whereby machinery was established to ensure the observance by the individual employer of terms agreed for his industry as a whole through collective bargaining. The Contracts of Employment Act, 1963, requires employers to give their workers a written contract embodying main conditions of service and establishes the right to a minimum period of notice. The Redundancy Payments Act, 1965, gives employees with a minimum of two years' service the right to compensation as the result of losing their jobs through redundancy.

More generally, employers not only have a common law responsibility for their work people but also are forced to maintain certain standards in respect to safety, health, and welfare by various legislative acts. These standards are enforced by official inspection. Voluntary action is, of course, also important and many employers provide standards well above the minimum required.

See also EMPLOYMENT AGENCY; LABOUR (TRADE) UNION; WORKMEN'S COMPENSATION.

(JE. D.; M. J. A.)

II. CONSTITUTION AND GOVERNMENT

The British constitution is partly unwritten and wholly flexible. There is no basic constitutional document, comparable with the written Constitution of the United States, since the main sources of the British constitution are: (1) legislative enactments of Parliament, such as Magna Carta (*q.v.*); (2) decisions of the courts of law; (3) conventions of the constitution, such as the conduct of the crown, Parliament, and the Cabinet in cases for which there is no formal law (*e.g.*, resignation of office by the government); and (4) literary sources such as the textbooks of political theorists like Albert Venn Dicey (*q.v.*). Since Parliament, comprising the monarch, the House of Lords, and the House of Commons acting in concert, is sovereign, it has unlimited legal power, and acts of Parliament, if complete and perfect, must be obeyed by all, though the right to test in the courts the legality of various applications of that power cannot be denied to the citizen. The action of one house of Parliament was successfully challenged in the courts in the case of *Bowles v. the Bank of England*, 1913. The collection of taxes by authority of resolutions of the House of Commons was held to be illegal since the resolutions had not yet been given the force of law by embodiment in an act to which the House of Lords and the king had given their formal assent.

The theory that the legislative authority of Parliament extends to all overseas possessions of the crown has long been modified in the case of the self-governing nations within the Commonwealth of Nations. By the Statute of Westminster, 1931, the British Parliament virtually renounced all its former powers over the dominions such as Canada, Australia, and New Zealand. Since then, acts of the U.K. Parliament have conferred independence upon India, Pakistan, Malaysia, Ceylon, Ghana, Nigeria, Sierra Leone, Tanzania, Cyprus, Uganda, Kenya, Jamaica, Trinidad and Tobago, and others. All (excepting Pakistan) owe allegiance to the crown or accept the sovereign as the head of the Commonwealth in which they remain independent but associate member (*see* COMMONWEALTH OF NATIONS).

The liberty of the subject under this flexible constitution is secured by the rule of law, based on the essential constitutional assumption that all governmental powers rest on law. Dicey claimed that this essential aspect of the constitution was characterized by the absence of arbitrary power, the subjection of official to the courts and the ordinary common law, and the fact that the constitution, being not the source but the consequence of individual rights, itself formed part of the ordinary law of the land.

The four main elements in the constitution are the legislature, the executive, the judiciary, and the two established churches, of England and of Scotland. The government, in the most general sense, comprises the first three, with many functions overlapping, since there is no separation of powers. The classic example of these overlapping functions is furnished by the office of lord chancellor (not tenable by a Roman Catholic). Its holder presides over the House of Lords as speaker in his capacity as member of the legislature. He also presides in a judicial capacity over the Supreme Court when the House of Lords meets as such. In addition he is a minister of Cabinet rank.

1. Crown.—The crown unites all four main elements in the constitution. The legislature is comprised of the crown, the Lords spiritual and temporal, and the Commons. The crown is head of the judiciary, and justice is administered in the sovereign's name. Supreme executive power is vested in the sovereign and many executive acts are also performed in the sovereign's name. Moreover, in 1534 the Act of Supremacy declared that the king was "the only supreme head on earth of the Church of England." This is the ultimate statutory authority for the appointment of the bishops by the sovereign on the advice of the prime minister (who need not be a member of the Church of England).

This interlocking of the organs of central government is a result of their common origin in the curia regis of the Norman kings, a body which performed all the functions of government without differentiating between them. It was the king's court meeting to do the king's business, and the same is true of all the descendants to which in course of time, with the multiplication and elaboration of business, it gave birth, although the sovereign has long since ceased to attend in person, save on formal occasions at his Privy Council and in his High Court of Parliament. The crown is now held in hereditary succession as limited and defined in the Act of Settlement of 1701 and as modified by His Majesty's Declaration of Abdication Act, 1936. This legislation amended the Act of Settlement of 1701 by excluding Edward VIII (who became the duke of Windsor) and his descendants from succession to the throne and provided that the Royal Marriages Act of 1772 should not apply to him. The influence of the monarch is quite small. However, he (or she) is kept fully informed of public policy and events and the royal consent must be formally obtained to all legislative measures.

2. Judiciary.—In Anglo-Saxon times the earliest forms of customary law were administered in three sets of courts: (1) national, those of the hundred and of the shire; (2) private, those of the lords of manors; and (3) municipal, those of the chartered boroughs. After the Conquest the local courts were slowly superseded by central courts and judges whose power emanated from the king, and the infinite varieties of customary law thus gave place to or were welded into one common law. This process was achieved mainly by extension of the use of royal writs; by introducing and extending the use of the jury (at first employed only where royal interests were concerned); by the institution and regulative influence of itinerant justices, who provided the necessary link between central and local government; and by the evolution from the curia regis of the three courts of common law at Westminster: Common Pleas, King's Bench, and Exchequer. But, since the common law developed slowly and procedure lagged behind the needs of a progressive society, the curia was still called upon to mitigate and to supplement, and there grew up, in spite of the jealousy of common lawyers, a body of equity rules alongside the common law; the administration of the two was finally fused by the Supreme Court of Judicature Act, 1873. As a result of this and subsequent supplementary acts, all the existing superior courts were consolidated into one supreme court of judicature consisting of two primary divisions: the High Court of Justice, with the subdivisions Chancery, King's Bench (from 1952, Queen's Bench), and Probate, Divorce, and Admiralty; and the Court of Appeal from the decisions of the judges of each of these divisions. The House of Lords became the final court of appeal from all the courts (other than ecclesiastical) of the United Kingdom, though there could be no such appeal unless either the Court of Appeal or the House of Lords itself gave leave, and that the jurisdiction of the House could be exercised only by peers judicially qualified. The judicial personnel of the House of Lords, together with such other members of the Privy Council as hold or have held "high judicial office" as defined by the Appellate Jurisdiction Acts, 1876 and 1887 (mainly Commonwealth judges), constitute the judicial committee of the Privy Council, which is the final court of appeal in certain cases from other parts of the Commonwealth and from the ecclesiastical courts of the United Kingdom. (*See* Court: *England;* Privy Council; English Law; Scots Law; Common Law; Judiciary and Court Officers.)

3. Executive.—The curia regis, composed of the tenants in chief, royal officials, and anyone else whom the king chose to summon, expanded or contracted according to the nature of its work. Daily routine would be left mainly to officials; the more serious occasions the larger the attendance of tenants in chief; and on occasions of greatest importance the officials formed a numerically insignificant technical element in a large feudal assembly. The terms employed to distinguish the larger and smaller gatherings achieved in time a certain significance until at last the larger assembly developed into the Great Council and the Parliament, the smaller into the King's Council. The latter, in spite of baronial machinations, had become, by the time of Henry VII, the instrument of the crown, and was used by the Tudors as the medium of prerogative government. But the stupendous labour involved in the Tudor conception of conciliar government necessitated further subdivision and specialization, and the King's Council and its functions were split up and divided among the Privy Council, the courts of Star Chamber, of requests, and of high commission. At the Restoration, however, of all the offspring of the King's Council, there survived only the Privy Council, with nothing left of its former legislative authority, meeting to transact mainly formal business.

The Cabinet.—This evolved in the 17th century from a committee of the Privy Council as the effective national executive, and was composed of an inner ring of confidential advisers of the crown. The king at first presided, but, when George I for lack of English ceased to attend, his place was taken by a minister, usually the first lord of the Treasury, who in time became known as the prime minister. The latter, normally the head of the party commanding a majority in the House of Commons, is appointed by the sovereign, with whose consent he in turn appoints the rest of the ministry and decides, though his choice is in practice narrowly restricted, which of them shall be members of the Cabinet (usually about 20 strong). All ministers are normally members of one or other house of Parliament and they are individually and collectively responsible to the crown, prime minister, and Parliament. (*See* Cabinet; Prime Minister.)

Ministerial Government.—As well as his Cabinet, the prime minister chooses about 25 ministers not in the Cabinet and about 50 junior ministers. Most Cabinet ministers head government departments, but not all, for certain nominal offices such as that of lord privy seal leave time for special tasks or planning; and some departments are led by a minister not in the Cabinet. This political leadership is very real. A minister is not necessarily an expert himself, and is subject to many pressures from outside and within; he must weigh the legislative proposals which he instructs his experts in the civil service to prepare, and, once convinced of their validity, argue for priority in the legislative program and defend them in Parliament. He may also have statutory obligations to submit reports and accounts to Parliament, or to make rules subject to parliamentary scrutiny (*see* Administrative Law). He must answer questions in Parliament conscious that the full glare of publicity will be directed upon any hint of weakness. In addition to his permanent officials, a minister may have the aid of junior ministers, who will share his tasks but lack many of his responsibilities, and of a parliamentary private secretary (unpaid as such) who, in return for the experience gained, will act as his eyes and ears in Parliament. An increase in the number of ministers, a change of style and title, a change in salary, or a transfer of functions requires an amendment to, or an order made under, an act of Parliament. There is no official public list of ministers, but a semiofficial list appearing in each bound volume of Hansard's official report of parliamentary debates, is in practice checked by the Cabinet Office. The size of the Cabinet, the number of ministers who are privy councilors, and the order in which their names are listed rest on nothing stronger than convention and the will of the prime minister. (*See* Civil Service: *United Kingdom;* Government Departments; Ministry, Government.)

4. Legislature.—Parliament was originally a periodic public assembly of the curia regis at its fullest expansion. It was therefore competent to perform all functions of government. But the one mainly stressed was the judicial function, for law declaring precedes lawmaking. Any subject might present a petition, and Parliament acted as a clearinghouse for such petitions, referring the suitor to the appropriate court and reserving for its own consideration in full assembly only such cases as were particularly difficult, protracted, or important. In the 13th century, however, the practice of summoning occasionally and experimentally delegates, sometimes from the shires, sometimes from the boroughs, and sometimes from both simultaneously, was instituted for certain purposes. One of these was the granting of money. To the demand for money the Commons replied with a demand for the granting of the petitions they had brought with them. Consideration of these common petitions came to occupy so much of Parliament's time that it was obliged more and more to leave the private petitions to be dealt with by Council or Chancery after Parliament had broken up. In other words, it was abandoning the righting of individual wrongs, a judicial function, in favour of the righting of the wrongs of the nation, a legislative function. It was Henry VIII, more than anyone, who helped Parliament to climb by precedents toward a sovereignty which it finally wrested from his successors at the Revolution Settlement of 1688.

House of Lords.—In the Parliament chamber sat originally the king, his counselors, and his greater tenants in chief, lay and spiritual. But the sovereign is now present only on rare and formal occasions, and with the growth of the doctrine of the peerage the presence of commoners became anomalous, so that counselors who were neither peers nor bishops preferred, unless incapacitated by tenure of judicial office, to seek election to the Commons. Membership in the House of Lords on Aug. 1, 1968, comprised 736 hereditary peers by succession, 122 hereditary peers of first creation, 155 life peers (of either sex) under the Life Peerages Act, 1958, 23 law lords, 2 archbishops, and 24 bishops: a total of 1,062. The government's comprehensive proposals for House of Lords reform were presented to Parliament in November 1968. These new proposals, if enacted, would have given a two-tier scheme of voting peers with a right to speak and vote, and nonvoting peers with a right to speak. Future membership would be by creation only (nonhereditary). Voting peers, initially about 230 with the government having a small majority over opposition parties, would be paid to play a full part in the work of the House and would be subject to an age of retirement. However, in April 1969, the prime minister announced the government's intention "not to proceed further at this time" with the Parliament (No. 2) Bill, which embodied these reforms. (*See also* PEERAGE.)

House of Commons.—The greatest power of state vested in the legislature is the power to impose taxes and to vote money to, or withhold it from, the various public departments and services. The exercise of this power is the right of the House of Commons alone, making that House the chief authority in the state. By a convention of the constitution not established till the 20th century, the prime minister is always a member of the House of Commons, instead of, as formerly, a member of either house. By thus directly submitting himself (and most of his senior ministers) to the daily criticism of that House, he further enhances its authority as compared with that of the House of Lords.

Steps which led, over the course of centuries, to the financial ascendancy of the Commons began in the second half of the 13th century, when counties and boroughs first received the royal writs of summons to send to Westminster representative knights and burgesses with full power to commit their constituent electors to the payment of taxes. The members of the Commons so summoned took the opportunity to raise grievances, and by one of the earliest and strongest conventions of the constitution they established the principle of "grievances before supply."

In 1340 a statute recognized that no tax should be levied without parliamentary consent, but parliamentary control of taxation was not yet complete. The crown's taxes on imports were held by Tudor lawyers not to be taxes on English subjects, and it was held that exports could be taxed in view of the royal prerogative to regulate trade. The last attempt of the crown to evade parliamentary control by devices in this manner was that of Charles I during the 11 years of absolute monarchy supported by revenue from "ship money." The Parliament of 1640 declared the collection of tonnage and poundage without the consent of Parliament to be illegal, and since the Restoration parliamentary control of taxation has never been challenged. Concurrently, the Commons was establishing its supremacy over the Lords in matters of finance by claiming the sole right of initiating taxation. In 1395 the Commons established the right to be the sole body to initiate measures proposing taxation when it refused to proceed with a number of Lords bills which sought to impose taxes.

The House of Commons consisted in 1969 of 630 members, 295 of them representing county divisions and the remainder borough (i.e., urban) constituencies. Those disqualified for membership include minors, undischarged bankrupts, clergymen of the Churches of England, Scotland, or Ireland, or of the Roman Catholic Church; civil servants, judges, and other categories excluded by the House of Commons Disqualification Act, 1957. Provision was first made in 1911 for salaries of £400 a year for all members of the Commons, and this has since been raised by steps to a salary of £3,250 a year (including £1,250 for "exceptionally heavy expenses"). Peers receive only traveling and expense allowances.

Franchise.—The extension of the franchise by stages culminating in universal suffrage made the House of Commons representative of practically all adults in the kingdom except the individuals who compose the House of Lords.

The knights of the shire from 1429 to 1832 were elected in the county courts by the 40-shilling freeholders. But in the boroughs no such uniformity prevailed, and, as time went by, the franchise tended to become more and more restricted. For in early days popular indifference was content to leave the duty of nominating representatives to the authorities, who thus in time developed a prescriptive monopoly, and charters of incorporation, issued later on, when representation had come to be regarded as a privilege, usually conferred (or were interpreted as conferring) the exclusive right of election on the governing body. In the course of centuries many boroughs returning members to Parliament had decayed and some had actually ceased to exist, while many large and flourishing towns remained unrepresented; and the franchise, as a result of corruption, was no longer a political privilege so much as an extremely marketable property. It was the agitation of the American colonies and the disasters resulting from George III's attempt at personal government that at last aroused public interest. The Reform Act of 1832 marked the first stage in the process, continued by the acts of 1867, 1884, 1885, and 1918, of extending the franchise to all adult males and reshaping constituencies into fairly equal electoral districts. The acts of 1918 and 1928 finally placed women on the same footing as men. The franchise laws were consolidated by the Representation of the People Act, 1948; while in 1969 Parliament approved the reduction of the minimum voting age from 21 to 18 years. (*See* ELECTORAL SYSTEMS; PARLIAMENT.)

Political Parties.—These gradually evolved inside and outside Parliament for the effective promotion of some common cause. Two manifestly separate alignments in the state can be traced back at least to the Civil War and perhaps to the Reformation. Sometimes these have been largely based upon identity of religion, class, or locality and sometimes upon those temperamental instincts to conserve or innovate which seem to distinguish men. Thus, Cavaliers and Roundheads have been succeeded by Tories and Whigs; Conservatives (later Unionists) and Liberals; Conservatives and Labour; with minor parties and groups such as Radicals, Communists, Scottish or Welsh Nationalists, appearing from time to time. The Nationalists were particularly prominent in the late 1960s, especially in Scotland. (*See* WHIG AND TORY; CONSERVATIVE PARTY [BRITISH]; LABOUR PARTY [BRITISH]; LIBERAL PARTY [BRITISH]; SCOTTISH NATIONAL PARTY; PLAID CYMRU.)

5. Liberty of the Subject.—The freedom of the individual, apart from the protection afforded by the franchise, is secured indirectly by the strict maintenance of the principle that no man can be imprisoned except under some legal authority, and by the provision of adequate legal means for the enforcement of this principle. The most important of such means is the writ of habeas corpus, which enables the judiciary to review the actions of the executive, while the jury system protects the subject from judicial abuses; and the Bill of Rights reinforced by the Mutiny Act (called after 1881 the Army Act) removes the threat to liberty inherent in the existence of a standing army. The right of the citizen to say or write anything which a jury think it amount to the right to freedom of the press are secured by the law of libel and freedom of discussion to liberty expedient should be said or written. The right of air views and grievances by petition, public meeting, and association is also assured. The Race Relations Act of 1965, which established as an offense the writing or speaking of words intended to stir up racial hatred against a "section of the public in Great Britain distinguished by colour, race, or ethnic or national origins," was seen by some as an infringement of these rights, but adequate safeguards were written into the act to prevent frivolous application. The citizen was further protected by the appointment in 1967 of a parliamentary commissioner, or ombudsman, to investigate grievances concerning the actions of the executive.

During time of war or national emergency the common good has necessitated drastic limitation on individual freedom. The Defence of the Realm Acts (D.O.R.A.), 1914–15, abridged the common law rights of the subject in many directions. Action under the Emergency Powers Act, 1920, permanent successor to this wartime measure, was made subject to parliamentary scrutiny. The act was brought into operation for a coal strike in 1921, for a general strike in 1926, and for subsequent similar emergencies.

On the eve of World War II Parliament passed the Emergency Powers (Defence) Act, 1939, which authorized the making of defense regulations by order in council. Some of the regulations created criminal offenses (such as looting and sabotage), while others gave blank powers to be filled in by ministerial orders. Further wartime limitations upon individual freedom gave complete governmental control over persons and property.

6. Established Churches.—Constitutionally, the Church of England enjoys the paramount position among religious bodies in England. (*See* ENGLAND, CHURCH OF; ENGLAND: *Religion*.) The Act of Settlement, 1701, requires the sovereign to be a member of the Church of England, and he takes an oath of adherence to the faith of that church on accession to the throne. The clergy of the Church of England conduct the coronation and all other religious functions of the state. Since 1539 the state has had the power to alter the doctrine and articles of belief of the church by means of legislation, and the Book of Common Prayer imposed in Edward VI's reign by the Act of Uniformity, 1549, is the basis of that in modern use. (In 1928 an attempt by the authorities of the church to obtain a revised prayer book did not secure the necessary parliamentary approval.) The Church of England Assembly (Powers) Act, 1919, delegated to the newly constituted assembly of the church, subject always to the control of Parliament, powers of legislation affecting the affairs of the church. The Church of England has, however, retained much of its medieval structure, forms, and titles. England is still divided into the medieval archbishoprics of Canterbury and York, and both archbishops sit with the Judicial Committee of the Privy Council when it is constituted the final court of appeal in all ecclesiastical causes. In the late 1960s, there were 43 bishops, but only 26 (viz., the two archbishops, the bishops of London, Winchester, and Durham, and 21 other diocesans in order of seniority, excluding the bishop of Sodor and Man) had seats in the House of Lords.

The established Church of Scotland is Presbyterian in constitution. Church government is by a hierarchy of courts rather than of persons. Each church is controlled by the Kirk Session, above which stand the Court of Presbytery, the Court of Synod, and finally the General Assembly. The assembly is presided over by a moderator (chosen annually by the assembly) during his term of office, next after the lord chancellor of Great Britain. The sovereign is represented by a lord high commissioner. (*See also* PRESBYTERIANISM; SCOTLAND, CHURCH OF.)

The Church of Ireland was legally disestablished in 1871. (*See* IRELAND: *History*.) The Church in Wales was disestablished by the Welsh Church Act in 1914.

Religious liberty, of which the first landmark is the Toleration Act of 1689, was gradually attained by the repeal, one after another, of the many statutes penalizing persons not of the Anglican persuasion. There is no longer any restriction on freedom of worship in Great Britain.

For local government *see* LOCAL GOVERNMENT and the appropriate sections in ENGLAND; IRELAND, NORTHERN; SCOTLAND.

(SN. G.; D. MT.)

III. DEFENSE

Although commitments outside Europe were greatly reduced after mid-20th century, Britain still has a number of defense responsibilities overseas. Treaties bind the U.K. to support the North Atlantic Treaty Organization (NATO) and the Southeast Asia Treaty Organization (SEATO) with sea, land, and air forces, and the Central Treaty Organization (CENTO) with its air striking force. In addition the U.K. retains certain global defense re-

sponsibilities within the Commonwealth of Nations, to allies and to friendly states such as some Persian Gulf sheikhdoms. This multiplicity of problems may involve British forces in operations in any climate or terrain, against an enemy armed with nuclear weapons or against primitive guerrillas.

Hence a compromise policy is necessary both strategically and for the design and pattern of equipment, which as far as practicable is standardized within NATO. Similarity of procedure is also sought, especially within the Commonwealth and in NATO. The larger Commonwealth countries have staff colleges between which officers are interchangeable. NATO has a defense college where a uniform system of staff work is taught. Similarity of signal procedure within NATO has also been achieved. It is, therefore, a primary condition of British defense policy and strategy that it should be flexible and based on great mobility. The airborne strategic reserves in the United Kingdom are ready to fly to any part of the world at short notice. British military policy, however, from 1967 aimed at withdrawing as many forces as possible from east of Suez and concentrating their deployment in Europe in support of the NATO alliance.

Such diverse conditions demand a complex system of higher direction, and this system entered an evolutionary phase in 1963, when the government decided to carry out drastic measures toward the unification of the three fighting services. In the following year a unified Ministry of Defence was created under a secretary of state, assisted by three ministers of state. The Defence Council, under the chairmanship of the secretary of state, is the command and administrative body for defense. It deals with general defense policy.

The management of the individual services, the Army, Navy, and Air Force, was vested in the Army, Admiralty, and Air Force boards of the Defence Council, which was also under the nominal chairmanship of the secretary of state, although his place was usually taken by the appropriate minister of state.

Day-to-day interservice matters of a purely military nature were dealt with by the Chief of Staffs Committee, presided over by the chief of the defense staff with the first sea lord, chief of the imperial general staff, and chief of air staff. A small operation staff was always at immediate readiness to man the war room in the Ministry of Defence on a joint service basis.

In 1967 the civil organization of the Ministry of Defence was changed. The three ministers of state (one for each service) were replaced by three parliamentary undersecretaries of state in charge of each of the three service departments. Two new ministerial posts were created: a minister of defense for administration and logistics, and a minister of defense for equipment, both having responsibilities covering all three services. Consequent on these changes the Army's chief of the imperial general staff lost his imperial status and became known as the chief of the general staff.

The Ministry of Defence, which had initially been an advisory and coordinating body, from 1964 became an executive ministry controlling all the armed forces of the U.K.

Between February 1967 and July 1968 the government published four statements on defense in the form of White Papers. Their main purpose was to explain the policy of withdrawing the bulk of Britain's forces from east of Suez and concentrating them in Europe and to give details concerning the reductions in strengths consequent on this policy. Further details concerning these matters are given in the statements on each service which follow.

See also INTELLIGENCE, MILITARY, POLITICAL, AND INDUSTRIAL.

A. ARMY

Origins.—Before the Norman Conquest the English land forces, whether for defense or for maintaining order, comprised all freemen able to bear arms. For such training as they had and for inspection of their arms the sheriffs were responsible. But the county levy or fyrd was not intended for anything but home defense, and Canute and his successors maintained, in addition, a body of household troops (*huscarles*; *i.e.*, housecarls) which formed the core of resistance to the Norman invaders at the Battle of Hastings.

After 1066 the Norman kings introduced into England the established continental system of warfare in which the decisive arm was the mailed horseman or knight. The actual combatant, needed, in the field, a team of auxiliaries: squire, page, groom, spare horse, and pack animal, with the services at hand of the shoesmith and armourer. Mounted troops needed the support, in addition, of infantry and artisans for sentry duty, bridging, and siege warfare.

The British contingents which served in the crusades and the armies which successive kings of England led in continental wars were organized and equipped in the approved fashion of the day. There evolved, however, on the Scottish and Welsh borders, a type of frontier warfare in which light infantry played an increasing part and in which the knight tended to become a mere mounted officer. Just as elsewhere in Europe the cavalryman's ascendancy came to be limited by the crossbow and, later, the pike and halberd, so in Britain he was dismounted by the longbow. This weapon, developed in the Welsh wars of Edward I, differed from previous bows in being made from imported Spanish yew, in being six feet long, and in shooting a yard-long shaft. In the hands of a strong man, trained in its use from boyhood it was accurate at 200 yd. (180 m.).

The great period of the English archer extends from Crécy (1346) to Agincourt (1415) and on into Tudor times. For an astonishingly long period a divided France was dominated by a relatively small army of English mercenaries. They were mainly archers, riding while on the march, dismounting to fight, and being led by officers of great experience. It was the proved efficacy of the longbow which, perhaps as much as anything, retarded the adoption in Britain of the firearm.

Serious large-scale warfare did not begin in Tudor times until the later years of Elizabeth I's reign. The national forces raised in 1588 to resist a Spanish invasion threat included many officers with experience gained in the Netherlands, but the county levies were of doubtful quality and the main army was deficient in firepower and cavalry. The Elizabethan Army made its chief task the conquest of Ireland, which would otherwise have become a Spanish base.

The Foundation of the Modern Army Under Cromwell.—The outbreak of the Civil War in 1640 found no regular military forces in existence on either side, except for an English garrison in Ireland. Charles I had intervened in the Thirty Years' War to the extent of raising an army of 10,000 men, and it was a part of this force which he afterward billeted—a normal wartime practice—on householders. He tried to finance his army by forced loans and exacted the loans by the threat of billeting troops on those who failed to pay.

These were among the matters set forth in the Petition of Right, and, in undertaking as he did to abandon these practices, Charles surrendered, in effect, his chance of maintaining an army at all. The immediate cause of the Civil War lay in Charles's effort to raise an army against the Scots, which he was unable to do without the sanction of Parliament.

The soldier most feared in the earlier phases of the war was Prince Rupert, the king's nephew, a foreign military expert. As a cavalry leader he found himself at the head of units whose disadvantage in equipment was outweighed by their excellent horses and fearless men. The parliamentarians' reply to the royalist superiority in mounted action was the New Model Army, first paraded in Windsor Park on Feb. 15, 1645. Symbolic of its national basis of recruitment was the scarlet uniform chosen for all its infantry, superseding the county uniforms and remaining in use for 300 years. The strength of the New Model Army lay in its cavalry, which was particularly well paid, armed, equipped, horsed, and disciplined, and the final parliamentarian success was mainly attributable to Oliver Cromwell, who outmatched Prince Rupert as a trainer and cavalry leader.

Cromwell's achievement was primarily one of discipline. He accepted the royalist innovation of charging with the sword but reduced the pace to a trot in order to maintain formation. What he thus lost in impetus he more than recovered in control and simultaneous impact. His units reformed knee to knee after initial success and could wheel, advance, or withdraw as ordered by trumpet signal. The effectiveness of these tactics was shown not only against the royalists, whose discipline remained weak, but against continental soldiers to whom this technique was a novelty. The professional discipline and nonlocal character of the New Model Army made it a strong basis for Cromwell's dictatorship as protector, but the unpopularity of his military rule was to exercise a profound influence on later British history. The idea of a standing army was associated with political tyranny, and Charles II, on his restoration in 1660, felt bound to disband the Army (80,000 strong) as almost his first and most popular act. To this general dispersal there was one significant exception. The Restoration had been mainly brought about by one of Cromwell's generals, George Monck (later 1st duke of Albemarle), and his own infantry regiment, now the Coldstream Guards, was retained. Efforts to find employment for the troops which became, and remain, the Life Guards and Horse Guards, together with another infantry regiment which became the Grenadier Guards.

Charles II's unpopular successor, James II, needed all the military support he could find. He used the duke of Monmouth's rebellion, which was crushed very largely by the queen's regiment ("Kirke's Lambs," so called from their badge), as pretext for raising further units, including the Royal Fusiliers, and so finally brought his forces up to a total of 20,000. With this army, encamped at Hounslow, he hoped to overawe London, and he proposed, moreover, to disband the "constitutional" force, the militia. But any dreams he may have had of establishing his monarchy on a military basis were abruptly ended in the Revolution of 1688.

Development in the 18th Century.—The accession of William III brought Great Britain into a continental war, affording scope both to the cavalry of the Cromwellian tradition and to the infantry regiments, which soon numbered 28. In 1690 Parliament voted the maintenance of 62,000 men, thus sanctioning the Whig policy of intervention in Europe. The British Army first established its name during the period 1688–1713.

The duke of Marlborough (see MARLBOROUGH, JOHN CHURCHILL, 1st duke of) was perhaps the greatest of English soldiers. Inheriting the regiments which had fought under William III in Belgium at Steenkerque, Neerwinden, and Namur, he made a European reputation for himself and for them. British infantry was famous for its steadiness, and the cavalry regiments distinguished themselves in the march across Germany in 1704 and in the battle which followed at Blenheim.

After the Peace of Utrecht (1713–14) the Army was reduced to 8,000 men in Great Britain and 11,000 overseas, the garrisons then including those at Gibraltar and Minorca as well as those in the colonies. The troops immediately needed on service, however, were those stationed in Scotland. These, after the accession of George I, had to suppress the rising of 1715. The 18th century was a period of relatively small standing armies, rigidly disciplined and trained. In the British Army the grant of a commission, and subsequent promotion, was normally by purchase. For the lower ranks discipline was strict and often savagely enforced, partly because the tactics of the period demanded a rigid obedience and partly because recruitment was mainly from the lowest classes of the community.

In the War of the Austrian Succession (1740–48) British troops took part in continental campaigns, fighting at Dettingen in 1743 under the personal leadership of George II, the last king so to accompany his army. In the midst of these campaigns, in 1745, troops were hurriedly summoned to meet the danger of a Jacobite invasion based on the Scottish Highlands. The defeat of the clans led to the final pacification of the Highlands and this led in turn to the subsequent raising of the Highland regiments, a plan to divert warlike instincts into a more useful channel.

The Seven Years' War (1756–63) led to the raising of new regiments on an establishment which, in 1761, reached the number of 67,776. To the Royal Artillery was now added the Horse Artillery, used for close cooperation with the cavalry and copied from the army of Frederick the Great of Prussia, England's chief ally during the war. Fully maintaining the British fighting reputation (e.g., at Minden, Ger., in 1759), the British Army of this period gained greater success in colonial warfare and combined operations. Gen.

James Wolfe's capture of Quebec showed the possibilities inherent in cooperation between Navy and Army, provided that the commanders could agree, as they sometimes failed to do. Afterward, however, in the American Revolution, it was painfully shown that the British Army as then organized was quite insufficient to guard the extensive empire without a superiority, both general and local, at sea.

The Army which had numbered 90,734 during the American Revolution was placed on a peace footing in 1783 and had been further reduced to 17,013 when war broke out in 1793. It was, in fact, being reduced in that year to 13,701, of which many were stationed overseas. With the French Revolution the character and scale of continental warfare had abruptly changed, small professional armies being replaced by conscript armies of vastly greater numbers, fighting not for adjustments of frontiers but for something approaching mutual destruction. The British Regular Army shared the fate of other similar forces at the outset of the war (1793–94) and withdrew to the British Isles.

Thereafter the augmented land forces were destined for several years to operate mainly in the West and East Indies. The destruction of the French colonial empire was largely completed, and British overseas territory was widened at the expense of the Netherlands as well as of France.

Great Britain itself, meanwhile, was repeatedly threatened with invasion, either from Ireland (as in 1798) or directly across the Channel (as in 1803 and 1805). These threats came to nothing because of British naval superiority but led nevertheless to great efforts of military preparation. Besides the raising of new regiments, the multiplication of battalions in the existing regiments and the embodiment of the militia, there was the volunteer movement which apparently originated in the mid-18th century. This was revived during 1793–94, the Dover Volunteers being among the first units to be formed. The Volunteers reached a peak number of 380,000 and were later transformed into the local militia in 1808. These various associations, raised, uniformed, armed, and equipped by voluntary effort, made a creditable appearance on parade but were never tested in battle.

The duke of York, whose reputation even as a commander in the field has been underrated, became commander in chief in 1798 and made it his business to introduce a new and uniform system of infantry training. This was based on the work of Sir David Dundas, who published the *Principles of Military Movements, Chiefly Applicable to Infantry* in 1788. This in turn became the basis for the official *Rules and Regulations* of 1792. When the duke was out of office, moreover, during 1809–11, it was Dundas who took his place. Copying the French model, battalions were grouped in brigades and brigades in divisions, with artillery attached and formation headquarters developed. In the green-uniformed Rifle Brigade there was introduced a skirmishing technique, with use of ground and open formation. During 1803–06 some line regiments learned something of the same art in the training camp at Shorncliffe under Sir John Moore, but they adhered nevertheless to the scarlet and to close formation in battle.

The 19th Century and Reform.—It was a newly trained army which took the field in Portugal in 1809, soon proving itself up to the standard of the French in everything but numbers. In leadership the choice might seem to lie between generals who had been defeated during 1775–83, generals whose experience was of combined operations and raids, and generals with no war experience at all. But Britain had another army in India, and it was from this that there now came Sir Arthur Wellesley, the victor of Assaye, with a reputation already made. The command in Portugal fell to him soon after the death of Moore at Corunna (La Coruña), Spain, and it was he who raised the British military reputation to the height it had reached under Henry V, under Cromwell, and under Marlborough. The Iberian Peninsula was the grave of the French legend of invincibility. In successive battles Wellesley (later duke of Wellington) gained an ascendancy over his opponents, and when the war ended for a time in 1814 he was leading his veterans into France (*see* PENINSULAR WAR). As the most uniformly successful of the allied generals he led the mixed army which defeated Napoleon Bonaparte at Waterloo, and by 1815 British military prestige was perhaps at its highest (*see* WATERLOO CAMPAIGN). The Army in 1812 comprised 245,996, of which a fair proportion were serving or had served overseas. During the peace which lasted, almost without interruption, until 1854, military stagnation was all but complete. The Army, fixed at a fairly high figure (71,790) in 1822, with the duke of York still commander in chief until 1827, rested on the legend of Waterloo. The duke of Wellington (commander in chief, 1842–52) was no reformer, and the Army owed much to the prince consort, who joined with the duke in preventing dueling among the officers. More important than this reform was the general superseding during this period of the flintlock smooth-bore musket by the rifle and percussion cap.

The Army which was sent to the Crimea in 1854 was led by veterans of the Peninsular War but was without recent experience of warfare. The problems presented by the campaign were new in that the lines of supply were exceptionally long. The Army was an agglomeration of battalions, individually of fine quality but unused to working together, without trained staff, administrative departments, or army organization of any kind. The lesson of the winter before Sevastopol was dearly bought, but was not thrown away (*see* CRIMEAN WAR).

From that time several war ministers and one commander in chief laboured perseveringly at the thankless and difficult task of reforming army organization. Foremost in the work was Sidney Herbert (later Baron Herbert of Lea), the soldier's friend, who fell a sacrifice to his labours (1861) but not before he had done much for the Army. The whole system of administration was revised. Improvements were made in every branch. The system of clothing the soldiers was altered, the contracts being taken from the colonels of regiments, who received a money allowance instead, and the clothing supplied from government factories. The pay, food, and general condition of the soldier were improved. His ordinary education and the military education of the officer were taken in hand. The Indian Mutiny of 1857, followed by the transference of the government of India, led to important changes. The East India Company's white troops were amalgamated with the Queen's Army, and the whole was reorganized.

The Franco-Prussian War had a marked influence on British military thinking. The year 1870 is, therefore, of prime importance in the history of the regular forces, and the ensuing period of reform is connected indissolubly with the name of Edward Cardwell (later Viscount Cardwell), secretary of state for war, 1868–74. In the matter of organization the result of his labours was seen in the perfectly arranged expedition to Ashanti (1874). As for recruiting, the introduction of short service and reserve enlistment together with many rearrangements of pay, etc., helped to treble the number annually enlisted as well as to build up a reserve which in the South African War yielded 80,000 men to maintain the strength of the Army in the field. The localization of the Army, subsequently completed by the territorial system of 1882, was commenced under Cardwell's regime, and a measure which encountered much powerful opposition at the time, the abolition of the purchase of commissions, was also effected by him (1871). In 1881 came an important change in the infantry of the line, which was entirely remodeled in two-battalion regiments bearing territorial titles. This measure (the "linked battalion" system) aroused great opposition. It was dictated chiefly by the necessity of maintaining the Indian and colonial garrisons at full strength and was begun during Cardwell's tenure of office, the principle being that each regiment should have one battalion at home and one abroad, the latter being fed by the former, which in its turn drew upon the reserve to complete it for war. On these general lines the Army progressed up to 1899, when the severe trials of the South African War hastened new schemes of reform, leading up to Richard (later Viscount) Haldane's "territorial" scheme (1908), which put the organization of the forces in the United Kingdom on a new basis.

Cardwell had left office before one of his most important reforms had been completed: organizing the forces in the United Kingdom in larger formations so that they could be employed as a field army. One of the first steps taken by Haldane was to advocate clear thinking in connection with army problems, and he developed the general staff, initiated by his predecessor, Arnold Forster, to undertake this important but previously neglected branch of military preparation. Within a few months, three principles had been laid down, and officially accepted to govern the military defense of the empire. The first of these was the essential need for a navy strong enough to ensure the safety of troops crossing the seas. The second principle was that of local provisions for military defense in all parts of the empire, to the utmost extent to which such provision could be furnished. The third was that of mutual support in times of emergency.

The Haldane reforms provided for the organization of the regular troops in the United Kingdom in six infantry divisions, one cavalry division and line-of-communication troops, as an "expeditionary force" (composed entirely of regulars) available for overseas service either as reinforcements for the small garrisons of different parts of the empire in the event of internal or external menace, or, if need be, as a field army capable of fulfilling treaty obligations. Furthermore, the need for strong drafts of men to keep units in the field in a protracted campaign was realized. The militia was called upon to provide drafts of trained men in time of war for the expeditionary force, and its name was changed to the "Special Reserve" of the Regular Army.

A further point that was realized was that, whether the British Isles were or were not subject to the menace of invasion, they could not be left denuded of troops. Manpower lay to hand in the force of Yeomanry and volunteers who, from patriotic motives, had volunteered to take part in the military defense of the United Kingdom in grave emergencies and to spend such time as they could spare from their civil vocations in undergoing training for the purpose. In face of opposition and criticism similar to that faced by Cardwell, Haldane, with the loyal cooperation of the units concerned, used this material to establish the territorial force, renamed "territorial army," in 1921, of which the first units appeared under arms in April 1908. The act which established this force provided that either the units or the individuals serving therein might volunteer for overseas service in grave emergencies. The extent to which this appeal met with response during the years 1914–18 belongs to the story of World War I (see WORLD WARS).

World War I.—With the outbreak of war in August 1914 the bulk of the Regular Army in the United Kingdom went to France, where it was later joined by most of the troops from overseas garrisons who were relieved by territorials. By December 1914, 2,413 officers and 66,805 men in the territorials were serving abroad. By April 1917 these numbers had risen respectively to 17,859 and 487,237. Up to the close of 1915, the voluntary direct enlistments in wartime into the territorial force numbered 725,842. Apart from individuals who volunteered for the Regular Army, the Yeomanry provided one complete division for overseas service, the territorial force of all arms 24 divisions.

Thirty "New Army" divisions were also raised on a plan instituted by Lord Kitchener to supplement the 11 "regular" divisions employed overseas. The need for more troops compelled Parliament to pass a conscription measure in March 1916, drafting men between the ages of 18 and 40, though soldiers were not to be sent out of the United Kingdom until their 19th birthday. The maximum age was later raised to 45 and, in 1918, to 50, while, because of the imminent peril, youths of 18 were also sent to fight in France. In December 1918 the British Field Army comprised 4 mounted (cyclist) and 4 infantry divisions, of which all except one were serving outside the United Kingdom. With a total establishment of 256,798, the British Regular Army began World War I with an actual peace strength of 247,432, an army reserve of 145,347, and "special reserve" of 63,933. The territorial force, with an establishment of 316,094, numbered 268,777, including 766 members of the Officers' Training Corps, also established by Haldane, with an establishment fixed at 1,110. Between the outbreak of war and conclusion of the Armistice, England provided 4,006,158, Scotland 557,618, Wales and Monmouthshire 272,924, and Ireland 134,202 men for the British Army, a total of nearly 5,000,000 for the United Kingdom. The total permanent wastage in British (Isles) military personnel up to January 1919 amounted to 1,892,100, including 500,000 killed or dead of wounds or other causes overseas, and about 37,000 in the United Kingdom. Roughly speaking, the number of British troops serving in various expeditionary forces at the time of the Armistice in November 1918 may be put at about 2,100,000, with 1,380,000 in the United Kingdom (excluding about 250,000 volunteers), 94,000 in India, and 11,200 as garrisons of defended ports. The total was about 3,600,000.

It was the policy of the British government for several years following World War I to maintain military forces of minimum strength. Year by year, however, hope for enduring peace in Europe gradually waned.

The Eve of World War II.—*Recruitment and Service.*—Until the measure of compulsion introduced in May 1939, all peacetime recruiting for the British Army had been on a voluntary basis. For the Regular Army, engagements were for long service (normally seven years with the colours and five on the reserve, with the option of extending colour service in most cases). Short periods of enlistment (one to four years) were also possible for all arms. Men enlisting on a normal engagement for general service were between the ages of 18 and 25. For the Territorial Army, enlistment for all arms was from 18 to 38 years of age, the term of service being four years.

Organization and Strength.—The peacetime composition of the Regular Army in the United Kingdom was 5 infantry divisions (14 brigades), the nucleus of an armoured division, and 2 antiaircraft brigades. The Territorial Army was composed of 12 infantry divisions (36 brigades), 5 antiaircraft divisions (22 brigades), 1 tank brigade, and 3 cavalry brigades. The Officers' Training Corps provided students at schools (junior division) and universities (senior division) with elementary military training to provide a potential reserve of young officers to meet a national emergency. Early in 1939 Parliament sanctioned the doubling of the Territorial Army, and in May of that year the United Kingdom, for the first time in its history, introduced peacetime conscription, the Military Training Act requiring all youths of 20–21 years of age to undergo a special course of training for six months.

Higher Command.—The government of the British Army was vested in the crown, command being placed in the hands of the Army Council. The Army Council, of which the secretary of state for war was president, included the chief of the imperial general staff, adjutant general, quartermaster general, master general of the ordnance, and financial secretary. Excepting when in training camps or on actual military service, the Territorial Army was administered by county associations.

Military Education.—Principal military educational establishments were the Royal Military Academy, Woolwich (for artillery, engineer, and signal corps cadets); the Royal Military College, Sandhurst (for cadets of cavalry, infantry, and other arms); the Senior Officers' School, Sheerness (for senior regimental officers); and the Staff College, Camberley (for the staff). The Imperial Defence College in London was for senior officers of the Army, Navy, and Air Force, and selected civil servants.

The Army of World War II.—On Sept. 3, 1939, the day the United Kingdom declared war against Germany, the Military Training Act of the previous May was superseded by the National Service (Armed Forces) Act, which extended the liability for military service to all men between 18 and 41 years of age. At the outbreak of war, too, the Territorial Army, the strength of which had been doubled in the spring of 1939, was merged with the Regular Army. With the increased demand for men in the armed forces in 1941, and, in order to provide a pool of partially trained youths, the war office recognized the army cadets and also the junior and senior training corps, which had carried on the work performed prior to hostilities by the Officers' Training Corps.

Composition.—The infantry, main bulk of the Army, was affected in its work by mechanization. While troop-carrying companies of the Royal Army Service Corps (RASC) transported most of the men, headquarter, company, and platoon trucks carried ammunition, tools, heavier weapons, and packs. In rifle battalions, carrier platoons were provided with small-tracked, armoured vehicles for light Bren machine guns, Tommy guns, antitank rifles, and two- and three-inch mortars. Machine gun battalions, entirely motorized, were equipped with medium machine guns, and reconnaissance battalions rode in light cars, carriers, motorcycle combinations, and motorcycles. The Tank Corps of World War I was succeeded by the Royal Tank Regiment, and this, in 1939, was united with mechanized cavalry and Yeomanry units to constitute the Royal Armoured Corps (RAC).

With the exception of muleborne mountain and pack artillery and heavy guns on railway mountings, all artillery in World War II was mechanized. The Royal Engineers consisted of a field (or combat) branch working with the divisions and corps; line-of-communication troops providing construction, electrical and mechanical services, and the like; and transportation services. Companies were also trained in bomb disposal and in the location of antitank mine fields. The Royal Corps of Signals, formed in 1920, operated wire and wireless telegraph and telephone services and also maintained communication by motorcycle dispatch riders and pigeons. The RASC, the supply and transport branch of the Army, brought up foodstuffs by land or water, moved the infantry, carried the heavy stores of the engineers, and drove the vehicles of the Royal Army Medical Corps and the Army Dental Corps.

The Queen Mary's Army Auxiliary Corps of World War I was the pattern for the Auxiliary Territorial Service (ATS), which was organized in 1938 and became the largest of the women's services. It was granted full military status on April 10, 1941, pay being roughly two-thirds that for male soldiers of equivalent ranks. Following passage of the National Service Act, 1941, single women between 20 and 30 were drafted into the ATS (which became the Women's Royal Army Corps in 1949). Besides working as cooks, clerks, telephonists, and drivers of army vehicles, the women were employed in radio location and almost every duty with antiaircraft batteries except actual operation of the guns.

The Local Defense Volunteers were organized in May 1940 to supplement field troops, and in November were incorporated in the Army as the Home Guard. Enrollment became compulsory in March 1942 for all men from 17 to 65 in civil defense regions. Fully equipped, men served a maximum of 48 hours every four weeks, receiving subsistence allowances while on duty but no pay. Their primary role was defense, to delay the enemy until regular formations moved to the attack.

At the outbreak of war the regulars, with their reserves, and including British components of the Indian Army, numbered about 400,000, and a like number were in the territorials.

Preparation.—The expeditionary force which went to France under General the Viscount Gort in 1939 comprised the I Corps under Lieut. Gen. Sir John Dill and the II Corps under Lieut. Gen. Alan Brooke (later Viscount Alanbrooke). Initially it totaled 5 divisions, but by May 1940, when active operations began, it had increased to 13 including one armoured division in the process of arriving from the U.K. This force showed the extent to which the United Kingdom had thrown away the lead in tank design which had been gained by the end of World War I. In the intervening years the Army had suffered through lack of funds, which had resulted in obsolescent equipment and unrealistic training. It was as much through luck as through judgment that the bulk of the troops were rescued from Dunkerque when French resistance collapsed. Although most of the British heavy equipment had been lost in the evacuation, the events of 1940 were a blessing in disguise. Instead of becoming involved in another continental war of the 1914-18 pattern, with casualties on a scale which the United Kingdom could certainly not have survived, the British Army was given the opportunity (as in 1794) to withdraw to the British Isles, reequip and reclothe itself, retrain its units, and revise its ideas. As the threat of invasion relaxed, the Army began to prepare for its future battles. With Sir Alan Brooke as commander in chief, home forces, the Army trained for mobile rather than static warfare. Tactical doctrine was revised in terms of armoured divisions and paratroops, individuals and units were trained in battle schools, and the offensive spirit was re-created by the example of the commando units which raided the coasts of occupied France. (*See also* WORLD WARS: *World War II.*)

The Army After World War II.—With the end of hostilities in 1945 it became clear that certain peacetime changes in Army organization would be necessary. In the infantry it was decided to retain the well-tried regimental system. Operational organization —as in the war—was based on the armoured division and the infantry division. It was, however, apparent that for a long time the bulk of the Regular Army would be stationed overseas: in Germany, Austria, the Middle East, and the Far East. This necessitated the abandonment of the Cardwell system (*see above*) by which units were linked in pairs, one stationed at home and one overseas, which had served so well in the past. The manpower situation was, however, considerably relieved by the withdrawal of all British troops from India, consequent on the granting of independence in August 1947 and the partition of the Indian subcontinent into the states of India and Pakistan. Conscription, first introduced in peacetime in May 1939, was continued, the period being for two years (except for a short time when it was 18 months) with the Regular Army and three and a half years part-time service with the Territorial Army or Army Emergency Reserve. For the time being the need for a reserve for the Regular Army was met by the class Z reserve, consisting of fit men of certain age groups who had served during World War II. The Territorial Army provided most of the units of antiaircraft command. Its field force units consisted of armoured and infantry divisions, and one airborne division, organized on prewar lines; but with modern equipment and drawing most of their officers and men from national servicemen who had completed their two-year period of full-time service. The system for the supply of regular officers was changed to the extent that all potential officers had to serve in the ranks, but their training as cadets remained the same. In 1952 the Home Guard was reconstituted, on a full establishment in vulnerable areas and on a cadre basis in areas of less importance. The main weakness was that, because of heavy overseas commitments, there was never an adequate strategic reserve of regular troops in the United Kingdom. By 1952, however, the Territorial Army had been built up to strength by the influx of national servicemen.

By the end of 1954 circumstances had arisen which had made a change in organization desirable in both the Regular and Territorial armies. These changes were necessary as a result of new weapons —nuclear weapons in particular—and changing political conditions overseas, which made essential some redeployment of the Regular Army. The main changes, which began in 1954, were as follows:
1. New scientific inventions had made existing antiaircraft defense obsolete. In 1955 antiaircraft command was abolished and the antiaircraft defense of the United Kingdom became the responsibility of the Royal Air Force. Nearly all the existing antiaircraft units—mostly territorial—were either disbanded or converted to other roles.
2. The Anglo-Egyptian agreement of 1954, by which all British troops were to be withdrawn from Egypt within 20 months, resulted in the redeployment in 1955 of army units which had been stationed in the Suez Canal Zone. A little more than one division was brought home to form the nucleus of a strategic reserve which had been lacking for so long.
3. In December 1955 a reorganization and modification in role of the Territorial Army was announced. Two infantry divisions were put on a "higher" establishment with the role of reinforcing the regular NATO division in the event of war. The remainder were placed on a "lower" establishment, the armoured divisions being converted to infantry and the airborne division being disbanded, except for one parachute brigade which was retained. The necessity for a Home Guard in war continued to be accepted, but the force was reduced to a cadre establishment.
4. In 1955 there was also a change in the conditions of national service. The two-year period of full-time service was retained, but the age of call up (previously 18) was to be increased gradually to 19 (by March 1958). There was also a considerable reduction in a man's statutory liability during his three and a half years part-time service. The latter was acceptable in view of the changed organization and role of the Territorial Army.

The call up ended in 1960 and the last national serviceman had left the colours by the end of 1962. Thereafter all Army personnel were long-service regulars enlisted on a voluntary basis. This major reorganization resulted in the amalgamation of several famous units of the Royal Armoured Corps and regiments of infantry and the disbandment of many units of other arms. Infantry regiments of the line were grouped into brigades for recruiting and some administrative purposes.

In July 1960 the government announced its policy for reorganizing the Territorial Army. The peacetime strength was reduced to about 123,000 and the number of major units from 266 to 195. A Territorial Army reserve brought the force up to a war strength of about 190,000 on mobilization. Its roles were concerned with home defense (including civil defense) and the support of the Regular Army overseas in an emergency.

The women's element of the Army consists of Queen Alexandra's Royal Army Nursing Corps (QARANC) and the Women's Royal Army Corps (WRAC). The duties of the QARANC are to provide the nursing staff in Army hospitals all over the world. The WRAC performs a variety of duties, but mostly clerical work at the War Office and at headquarters at home and abroad.

There are two cadet forces: the Combined Cadet Force (CCF) and the Army Cadet Force (ACF). Both are under general control of the Army. The CCF comprises contingents in schools and the ACF, formations of boys from given areas.

On Dec. 15, 1965, the government issued a White Paper *Reorganisation of the Army Reserves* (Cmnd. 2855), the main feature of which was the virtual abolition of the Territorial Army. The reconstituted force consisted of 73,000 officers and men, comprising "the volunteers" (a reserve to reinforce the Regular Army in an emergency) and "the territorials" (for home defense).

The next few years were to see more drastic cuts and changes in Army organization, particularly in the infantry, consequent on the policy decision made in 1967 to withdraw the bulk of Britain's forces from east of Suez and make the major defense effort in Europe in support of the NATO alliance. Details of the new policy were contained in the *Supplementary Statement on Defence Policy 1967* (Cmnd. 3357) published in July. Reductions of three Armoured Corps regiments, four Royal Artillery regiments, two Royal Engineers field squadrons, and eight infantry battalions were announced.

By January 1968 the last Army unit had left Aden and the South Arabian hinterland. The target year for the completion of the Army's redeployment was 1971, with the proviso that an Army garrison would remain in Hong Kong indefinitely.

The *Statement on the Defence Estimates* published in February 1968 (Cmnd. 3540) announced that future civil defense preparations would be on a care-and-maintenance basis.

The *Supplementary Statement on Defence Policy 1968* (Cmnd. 3701) published in July made still further reductions in Army strengths, either by disbanding or amalgamating units; the reduction in major units being six infantry battalions, one armoured regiment, and one artillery regiment. In 1969 it was announced that the infantry would be reorganized on a divisional basis for recruiting and other domestic matters—the six divisions to be known as Guards, Scottish, Queens, Kings, Prince of Wales's, and Light. Officers and men would join a particular division and could be posted to any unit in it, but as far as possible would remain with the unit of their choice.

The *Statement on the Defence Estimates* of February 1971 (Cmnd. 4592) gave notice of an increase in the authorized strength of the Territorial and Army Volunteer Reserve (T & AVR) by 10,000, to a total of 57,700. An additional T & AVR armoured car regiment was formed in 1971 as a reserve unit to support the British Army of the Rhine.

In 1970 a non-regular regiment—the Ulster Defence Regiment—was formed with the prime role of security in Northern Ireland.

In February 1972 changes in the U.K. command structure were announced. On April 1, Headquarters United Kingdom Land Forces was formed and all Army units came under its command. At the same time H.Q. Southern Command and Army Strategic Command were formed and H.Q. Western and Northern commands were to be abolished before the end of 1972.

On April 1, 1972, the approximate male strength of the Regular Army was 18,000 officers and 152,800 other ranks, plus 5,600 women, and about 8,200 men enlisted overseas.

Further aspects are discussed in ARMY; ARTILLERY; TANK.

(C. N. P.; C. N. B.)

B. Navy

Origins.—Alfred the Great was the first Englishman known to have given real thought to sea power. It is true that he won all his major victories over the invading Danes on land and it is now accepted that the destruction of the Danish fleet off Swanage, Dorset, in 878 was mostly, if not entirely, due to storm rather than force of English arms; nevertheless, he built warships—large for that time—and organized seaborne defense. By command of the Narrow Seas he held what he had won. Alfred is the father of British sea power, if not of the Royal Navy.

Norman and Plantagenet.—Alfred's Saxon successors allowed this strength to decay, content that naval activity should be defensive, local, and temporary. They reaped the bitter harvest in Duke William's unopposed passage and landing in 1066.

Subsequently, as long as the land on both sides of the Channel owed allegiance—at least nominally—to the same crown, there was some justification for this parsimonious policy. The Cinque Ports, a close-knit group in the southeastern corner of the kingdom, provided all that was needed for the discouragement of piracy and the occasional transit of armies.

John's loss of Normandy, however, renewed the threat posed by a hostile neighbour across the Channel. About this time the English, who still held Gascony, started to extend their trade to Spain and Portugal; which, in turn, necessitated their using the bigger, oceangoing, true sailing ship instead of the old, single-masted, oared vessel used for the short sea passage. These big new ships could be quickly and cheaply converted for military use merely by the addition of fighting tops on the masts and "castles" at each end. Sea warfare was still a matter of hand-to-hand fighting, with the ships regarded as no more than a means of bringing the soldiers to within striking distance. In such encounters sheer height was a great advantage; this the tops and castles provided.

In the great sea fight off Sluis, Flanders, in 1340, between the English under Edward III and the French under Nicolas Béhuchet, the latter decided to receive the attack at anchor, thus allowing Edward to concentrate at will. The English achieved a complete, though costly, victory. Edward rounded off the day by hanging his opponent, who thus paid the penalty of failing to appreciate that tactics also applied at sea.

The Big Gun.—The great improvement in gunmaking that occurred early in the 16th century, which led to their being mounted within the hull and fired through ports cut in the ship's side, brought about a fundamental change in naval warfare. First, the ship itself became the weapon and was no longer the transport of armed men; the object became to destroy or capture the enemy ships—by means of gunfire, though possibly aided by boarding. Second, the ship had to be built as a fighting ship. The age of the temporarily converted merchantman was past.

If Henry VIII did not personally invent the big-gun ship, he was certainly the first sovereign to recognize its tremendous fighting potential and, with the treasure amassed by his pinchpenny father, he built himself a splendid fleet of such vessels. The "Henri Grace à Dieu" and its sister ships enabled him to laugh at the threats of pope and kings alike.

Henry also laid down the organization to run these first of all "capital ships." The medieval office of admiral was raised to high admiral and, under the sharp eye of the sovereign, given wide responsibility for jurisdiction, administration, and command. A Navy Board looked after the Navy's material needs.

The Elizabethan Age.—Inevitably, once the danger was past (in this case Henry's quarrel with the pope), the strength of the fleet was allowed to decline, a process in no way discouraged by Mary's husband, Philip of Spain. When Elizabeth I came to the throne, however, queen and people alike quickly grasped the true value of sea power; not only to wage war but also to trade. In reality the two were inseparable, for trade with the West Indies (and later with the East) meant breaking by force the monopolies granted to Spain and Portugal, respectively, by Pope Alexander VI.

For 30 years, by the exercise of her unique diplomatic skill and by arming her sea venturers with letters of marque that gave a precarious legality to their depradations, Elizabeth avoided open war with Spain. Characteristically, she finally threw down the gauntlet only by inference—though this was clear enough—when in 1580 she dubbed Sir Francis Drake on board the "Golden Hind," fresh from his circumnavigation during which he had pillaged the Spaniards far and wide.

Even then it was five years before Philip could bring himself to declare war and another three before, straining the resources of his continental empire, he dispatched his "Invincible Armada" (1588) against the islanders. Its utter defeat, initiated by Drake and his fellow sea fighters, accelerated by the Spaniards' panic at the approach of fireships when they anchored off Calais and completed by the elements on the coasts of Scotland and Ireland, taught Philip the folly of sending soldiers to sea to fight seamen. It taught the English a lesson, too, of which they took good heed in the next four centuries: that their first and strongest line of defense lay on the sea. For all their valour, they realized that things would have gone ill for them had the duke of Parma and his veterans made that short but vital crossing. (See ARMADA.)

Ship Money.—James I wanted peace with Spain at any price. He got it by the simple expedient of stopping fighting. He also refused any further letters of marque, thus turning privateers into pirates. Within a few years the recently victorious English had not only been swept from the high seas but also had even lost control of their own territorial waters and estuaries.

Charles I saw the danger but went the wrong way about putting it right. His exaction of ship money—without the sanction of Parliament and from the whole country rather than, as always before, only from the coastal shires—was logically sound but legally invalid and politically disastrous.

He did use that money to build warships and they did help to turn the tide. Notwithstanding, this benefit was lost to sight in the greater conflict and, when the Civil War broke out, the fleet went over in a body to Parliament—and, by holding the ring against foreign interference, played a decisive part.

Oliver Cromwell and his friends understood the part that a strong fleet could play in their new expansionist policy. They built one—over 200 ships—and with it the "Generals at Sea" showed that they could win battles there too.

The Dutch Wars.—The enemy now was Holland and the prize no less than the maritime trade of the western world. In the dogged Netherlanders the English found their match. For a quarter of a century the contest raged. Every battle was a stand-up fight, with honours evenly divided, and it is debatable which side actually won the sea war.

The Dutch Wars, however, gave excellent schooling to what did not always lead to happy results in actual operations. In 1691 the *Fighting Instructions* were issued, to become a decade later the *Permanent Fighting Instructions*. In particular, these enforced the maintenance of the line of battle under all circumstances, but "general chase" and admirals infringed them literally at risk of their lives. In any case, the signaling system of the times provided no means of conveying any other orders. The result was predictable: not one victory in a stand-up fight between the battles of Cape Barfleur (1692) and The Saints (1782). There were, it is true, some bright flashes: Sir Edward Hawke's pursuit of the French into Quiberon Bay (1759), Adm. Edward Boscawen off Lagos in the same year, George Rodney's "Moonlight Battle" off Cape St. Vincent (1780), but all three were technically "chases."

The Golden Age of Sail.—At last, in 1783 the *Permanent Fighting Instructions* were laid to rest, their place being taken by far more flexible directives and, perhaps even more important, accompanied by Richard Kempenfelt's (and later Sir Home Popham's) signaling systems that gave effect to this new liberty.

When, in 1793, Britain was again at war with France, the Royal Navy had learned the lessons of the previous century and in Earl Howe, John Jervis (earl of St. Vincent), Viscount Duncan and, above all, in Lord Nelson had the men to win battles—frequently to the point of annihilation. As happened so often, the hour found the man. In each of his three great victories—at the Nile (1798), Copenhagen (1801), and Trafalgar (1805)—Nelson not only achieved military success but also a vital strategic purpose.

A Century of Peace and Change.—The instruments of sea warfare had altered little since the days of the Armada. In the century of almost unbroken maritime peace after the Napoleonic Wars they were to do so beyond all recognition: sail to steam; 32-pounder, smooth-bore muzzle-loaders to 15-in., breech-loading rifles; wooden hulls to iron and then to steel.

The Admiralty was understandably reluctant to cast aside what had served the country so well. Besides, the early steamers broke down; their paddles were not only highly vulnerable but also got in the way of the broadside batteries. For years the lords of the Admiralty clung to the old, familiar masts and sails; but in 1836 the screw propeller was patented and, nine years later, fitted to the steam sloop "Rattler," and sent out to its famous tug-of-war with the "Alecto," a paddler. It won with ease. The excuses of vulnerability and interference were thus removed. Off the Crimea steam proved its worth in war.

The Admiralty lords tried to compromise and in 1869 launched the "Captain": an iron-hulled, armoured, turret ship—fully rigged. It capsized. Even ten years later the "Inflexible" was rigged as a brig. By then, however, the battle was all but over. In 1873 the "Devastation" was completed: iron-hulled, armoured, with revolving turrets and not a single sail—the first modern battleship.

Although the gun was to continue to reign supreme for another 50 years—at all events in actions between major warships—around the end of the 19th century other weapons and methods of delivery were beginning to threaten its monopoly and to call for fundamental reappraisal, especially in the Royal Navy.

Britain, as the owner of by far the largest fleet of orthodox battleships, did not look with favour on the torpedo or torpedo boats whose business was to attack large ships at night. The answer was the torpedo-boat destroyer, starting in 1893 with the "Havock," followed by John Thornycroft's "Daring," and quickly growing in size, speed, and armament as its effectiveness became apparent and the inventions of the watertube boiler and steam turbine made high speed compatible with light weight.

Nor did the idea of the submarine appeal to the Royal Navy, seeing it (rightly) as an effective weapon for the weaker naval power and an excellent means of delivering the torpedo unseen by day as well as night. The first British submarine was ordered in 1901, 15 years after the French.

The Fisher Reforms.—At the turn of the century the Royal Navy was still immensely powerful—on paper—but many, inside the service and elsewhere, expressed misgivings about its fighting ability, untested for 80 years. Chief among the critics was Adm. Sir John Fisher. As first sea lord and with the backing of his political chief, Lord Selborne, he revolutionized the Navy's ships, training, and tactics.

Fisher foresaw that the new Navy would be highly technical, so when he brought the naval cadets ashore to the new Royal Naval College at Dartmouth he made sure that their instruction, while still broad, took note of this. He also insisted on more realism in training, with gunnery practices at ranges likely in war. He is, however, best remembered for his introduction of the all-big-gun battleship.

The "Dreadnought" mounted ten 12-in. guns. Its steam turbines drove it at 21 knots. Its commissioning in 1906 made every other battleship in the world obsolete—including the remainder of the British fleet. To meet the growing threat from Germany, further "dreadnoughts" followed in quick succession: 9 mounting 12-in. guns, 12 mounting 13.5-in., and 10 with 15-in., the last completed in the first two years of World War I.

A by-product of the dreadnought was the battle cruiser; of about the same size and gun armament as the battleship but faster and more lightly armoured. This hybrid type, about which controversy has flourished ever since, can be seen as the ultimate development of the armoured cruiser, itself the successor of the Nelsonian frigate but with less clearly defined or understood function. Thus, the two battle cruisers "Invincible" and "Inflexible," dispatched in a hurry in November 1914 to avenge the loss of the armoured cruisers "Good Hope" and "Monmouth" at Coronel, fully justified themselves when they outran and outgunned Adm. Graf von Spee's squadron off the Falkland Islands (Dec. 8, 1914). On the other hand, at Jutland they showed that they were quite unable to stand up to heavy gunfire.

The true descendant of the frigate, the scout relying on speed to avoid action with heavy ships, was the 6-in.-gun light cruiser that was first put in service in 1913.

World War I.—The Navy's task, as throughout its history, was to destroy the enemy battle fleet and then to protect shipping against raiders or corsairs. The Germans avoided battle at unfavourable odds by keeping their fleet in harbour. On the one occasion on which they were strategically trapped and forced to fight at Jutland (May 31, 1916), they escaped annihilation only by superior tactics. Although the High Seas Fleet never again risked such an encounter, its mere presence "in being" tied up a huge Grand Fleet for the rest of the war.

Meanwhile the Germans used the newest type of corsair, the submarine. The likelihood of its use, which was contrary to the rules of the Hague Convention, had been discounted. The age-old lesson of how to combat the *guerre de course* (trade warfare)—by convoy—was thought to be too difficult in the age of steam. Further, it was hoped that the corsairs could be defeated by search and patrol along shipping routes.

The result was catastrophic. The German U-boats, armed with torpedo and gun, exacted an ever increasing toll of merchant shipping, at little loss to themselves. In February 1917 Germany announced unrestricted submarine warfare. The effect was immediate. In April 1917 nearly 1,000,000 gross tons of British, Allied and neutral shipping were destroyed. Faced with Britain's greatest wartime crisis, the Admiralty, under strong political pressure, adopted the convoy system. It was immediately effective. The loss rate dropped sharply; more U-boats were destroyed. Nevertheless, at the end of the war the Navy realized that the submarine was still a most formidable weapon and much thought was given to the problem of trade protection.

The only amphibious operation of World War I was the assault on the Gallipoli Peninsula in 1915. Admirable in strategic concept, its disastrous outcome can be variously ascribed to uncoordinated direction, poor communication in the vital assault stage, total unsuitability of the craft used to put the troops ashore against modern determined opposition, but, above all, to the gratuitous sacrifice of surprise by allowing a two-month delay between the first naval bombardment and the landings. Gallipoli cast a shadow over all amphibious enterprises, until World War II showed that, given the right material, plans and tactics, this most complicated of maritime operations could not only succeed but at surprisingly small cost. (See WORLD WARS.)

The Years of the Treaties.—The end of the war found Britain with by far the largest active fleet (including 42 capital ships), the United States embarking on a vast building program, and Japan, which had used the war to consolidate its position in the Far East, eager to join the first rank of naval powers.

An arms race between the late allies was avoided by the Washington Treaty of 1922, which limited the capital-ship navies of Britain, the U.S., and Japan to a 5:5:3 ratio, with individual ships of not more than 35,000 tons "standard displacement" (*i.e.*, without fuel, water, or ammunition). Aircraft carriers were limited to 27,000 tons each and in the same ratio of total tonnages. Cruisers and other craft were limited in individual tonnage (10,000 tons) and gun size (8 in.), but not in numbers. The London Naval Treaty (1930) extended the numerical limits to cruisers and submarines.

Germany, which by the Versailles Treaty had been forbidden to build any ship larger than 10,000 tons and no submarines at all, was naturally not a signatory, but in 1935 it concluded the Anglo-German Naval Treaty. This recognized Germany's right to have a fleet 35% the size of that of Britain. Germany rightly judged that it was now tacitly freed from all restrictions. The German "Z" plan would by 1942 have produced a formidable fleet of 13 battleships, 4 aircraft carriers, a large number of cruisers and destroyers, and some 250 U-boats. Hitler's involvement, therefore, came too soon for his Navy. Nevertheless, by 1939 Germany was able to deploy powerful commerce raiders on the high seas. Most significantly, however, it had only 56 U-boats.

Maritime Air.—The interwar years were chiefly remarkable for the development of military air power, afloat as well as ashore. In World War I, although most of the Royal Naval Air Service's operational flying had been done from shore, either escorting coastal convoys or in direct support of the Army in France, it had also developed the carrier. This meant that the new Fleet Air Arm could now form an integral part of the fleet at sea.

Unfortunately, the period was marred by two separate, but connected, internecine wars: first, between the protagonists of air power as a war winner on its own, who claimed that warships—and especially battleships—were therefore obsolete; second, and in practical terms far more serious, the long wrangle between the Royal Air Force and the Royal Navy for control of the Fleet Air Arm, which was only finally resolved in 1937 when the Navy was given complete control of all ship-borne aircraft. By then time was running out, but the Navy had at least had control of its carrier-building and it entered World War II with seven carriers in commission and five more building. The previous divided control, however, left a legacy of "naval" aircraft that were slow, ill-armed, and short-ranged.

World War II.—Although the purpose of the Royal Navy, as ever, was to maintain command of the sea, the forces ranged against it and hence the weapons needed had radically changed. Despite the major German surface ships posing a threat by their mere presence, the likelihood of fleet action, on the pattern of Jutland, was remote. On the other hand, the possibility of encountering enemy U-boats or aircraft was ever present.

Early in the conflict the U-boats evolved highly effective wolf-pack tactics, which enabled them all too often to swamp the escort force by sheer weight of numbers. The availability of the French ports as U-boat bases could also be contrasted with the British lack of bases or any facilities in Eire.

Top priority was given to all kinds of antisubmarine material, except the vital air protection for convoys. Escorts were strengthened by the mass production of small "Flower"-class corvettes; radar, extensively introduced in 1941 and steadily improved thereafter, did much to remove the U-boats' previous nighttime advantage. In 1943 it at last became possible to give regular air surveillance to the entire Western Ocean convoy route and to give close air escort to all threatened convoys. Escort carriers became available to accompany convoys throughout or to bring support in danger areas. Liberator aircraft, hitherto all assigned to Bomber Command, were released and converted into Very-Long-Range (VLR) escorts. The "black gap" in mid-Atlantic was at last closed and the U-boats, forced to remain submerged, at least by day, were tactically immobilized.

Maritime operations in the Mediterranean, while working to the same concept, were totally different in detail and individual purpose. The Allied aim was to destroy the Axis forces in North Africa. The Navy played its part in attacking enemy convoys and protecting Allied shipping. The fortunes of land and sea were closely interlocked as the North African campaign exemplified.

Not until command of the seas around Europe was finally won was the Royal Navy able to return to the Pacific. There it contributed a carrier Task Force, integrated into the larger U.S. Pacific Fleet, to take part in the unique Pacific naval air war that primarily brought about the defeat of Japan.

Nearer home, once the Atlantic lifeline was secure—or at any rate holding—the prime maritime object became the landing on continental Europe. Although the bulk of the special ships and smaller craft came from across the Atlantic, British shipyards played their part and the Royal Navy produced many of the original ideas, testing them in grueling exercises and in raids such as that on Dieppe. Finally, Royal Naval crews manned a large part of the vast fleet which in June 1944 put the armies ashore in Normandy and finally laid the ghost of Gallipoli to rest.

The Immediate Postwar Period.—Despite the enormous losses suffered in six years of continuous warfare, the Royal Navy in 1945 was second in size only to that of the United States and, in addition, was the world leader in many aspects of maritime operations, especially antisubmarine. It now faced the task of adapting itself to the financial, material, and manpower restrictions of peacetime, of assimilating the lessons of the war, and of determining its own role within the national policy.

Many factors argued in favour of immediate and fundamental reappraisal; some even maintained that the atom bomb had made all other weapons obsolete, while others, more cogently, pointed to the rapidly changing international situation (in particular to the breakup of the uneasy wartime alliance with the U.S.S.R.), the rapid rundown of empire, and the increasing pace of technological advance. The Admiralty faced the dilemma of virtually scrapping and starting afresh with a small but modern fleet or of keeping available still-valuable ships to ensure defense in a highly unpredictable situation.

The latter was deemed the safest course. A large Reserve Fleet was maintained, some of which was at a high degree of readiness. Of those ships on order, most were immediately canceled and the majority of the few completed were placed in reserve.

The cost in men and maintenance effort was high. The Royal Dockyards, in addition to this work, were also called on to modernize a number of small ships and several large ones, on the principle that, although weapons and possibly radar, communications and operations rooms might be out of date, there was plenty of life in the basic hulls. In the case of the carriers, this "gut and renew" policy made for considerable economy and was continued throughout the next two decades. Operationally the rebuilt ships were as good as new in all essentials.

Within a few months of the end of the war a phased release of Royal Naval Reserve and Royal Naval Volunteer Reserve officers and ratings was in operation, on the equitable principle of "first in, first out." The lessons of World War I clearly had been taken to heart. In particular, the number of officer recruits accepted during the war for regular long-service commissions had been held to the prewar figure, with the result that there was no repetition of the "Geddes axe" (see GEDDES, SIR ERIC CAMPBELL) of the early 1920s.

The Navy's most urgent postwar operational task was to play a leading part in sweeping mine-free channels through the busy shallow waters around northwestern Europe. This was made doubly hazardous by the complication of modern firing mechanisms and by the fact that large numbers of mines had been laid from aircraft in "areas" rather than "fields." Within a few months narrow coastal routes were established, then progressively widened, being promulgated in the North Europe and Mediterranean Routing Instructions (NEMEDRI). It is greatly to the credit of the minesweeping forces of all maritime nations that these gave complete protection, although even in the 1970s unfrequented parts of the southern North Sea could not be guaranteed "mine-free."

The Korean War and Other Operations.—The Royal Navy was strongly represented off Korea (1950–53) in the first war fought from the start under the flag of the United Nations. With an average of an aircraft carrier, a cruiser, and half a dozen destroyers or frigates continuously in the actual fighting zone, the Navy, together with warships from Australia, Canada, and New Zealand, was in the main responsible for the west coast, while the U.S. Navy operated off the east.

Sea power played a large part in the Korean War. It brought troops to the rescue of the overrun South Koreans. It made possible the amphibious counterstroke at Inchon, whereas it completely denied the coastal waters to the enemy. In particular, carrier-borne aircraft once again demonstrated their versatility by giving close support to the UN army, as well as striking strategic targets. The Fleet Air Arm pilots, although flying the slower piston-engined aircraft, proved more than a match for any MiG fighters they met over the battlefield.

Judged by World War II standards, the effort was small and the seaborne opposition nonexistent, but the Navy learned many useful lessons, especially in carrier operations. There was also much valuable experience in afloat support, thus further integrating the Royal Fleet Auxiliary Service with the fighting ships. The war also gave a fillip to naval building: work was resumed on the four "Centaur"-class carriers and an ambitious program of small minesweeper replacement got under way.

In the other major naval operation, the assault on the Suez Canal zone in 1956, the Navy successfully lifted the force from Malta, supported the parachute drop at Port Said by the first-ever opposed helicopter-borne landing, and also gave gunfire and close air support.

The operation, however, did reveal the unsuitability of the World War II landing ships, owing to their slow speed which sacrificed surprise. Postwar experience was showing the great value of being able to deploy an amphibious force of about brigade-group strength. To achieve this the light fleet carriers "Albion" and "Bulwark" were converted to carry both helicopters and landing craft. They were followed by the purpose-built assault ships "Fearless" and "Intrepid" and six logistic landing ships, all able to handle helicopters.

On other occasions since 1945, the Royal Navy has produced forces when needed. For example, the unexpected Iraqi threat to oil-producing Kuwait in July 1961 produced, on the spot and within days, a force that included three carriers with full support. The pattern was repeated in the Rhodesian crisis of November 1965. Within days of the decision to deploy forces, the "Eagle" had crossed the Indian Ocean from Singapore and was ready to operate. Later, under the UN resolution of April 9, 1966, the Royal Navy was charged to ensure that no oil reached Rhodesia by sea through the Portugese East African port of Beira.

Two examples of naval assistance to maintain or restore order were the quelling of political riots in British Guiana in 1962 and the rapid response to a request from the government of Kenya to put down a mutiny in 1964. In the Indonesian confrontation of 1963–66 the Navy not only gave support by means of small craft up the numerous rivers, larger ships offshore, and Fleet Air Arm helicopter detachments based in the jungle, but also let it be seen that these were backed by powerful forces, including a carrier with nuclear capability.

The Navy has continued to bring relief to those struck by natural disaster: to the victims of the Sicilian earthquake in January 1968; and, on a far larger scale, in the aftermath of the Bay of Bengal cyclone of November 1970. Once again, in this latter, the Royal Navy was first on the scene in strength. The relief force was organized, loaded, and made the 1,500-mi. passage from Singapore in six days. Over 2,000 tons of food and medical stores were landed.

Postwar Development.—The carrier-borne aircraft emerged from the war as the Fleet's prime means of strike, reconnaissance, and air defense. Design and operation continued to develop. Jet aircraft first flew from a British carrier (December 1945), an undertaking soon rendered comparatively safe and simple by the three British inventions of the angled deck, mirror landing-sight, and steam catapult.

The Royal Navy also led the way in the new concept of the Operations Room as the command position in action. Here, all relevant data can be processed (in many ships by computer) and presented to the command in a clear and up-to-the-second picture on which decisions can be made. This is especially useful in aircraft carriers, whose "three-dimensional radar," feeding into the Action Data Automation (ADA), makes possible the effective control of high-speed aircraft in action.

At the same time, much research and development were devoted to guided missiles for defense against both surface and air attack. By 1960 a surface-to-air missile (SAM), later modified to be of some use against surface targets as well, was ready to be mounted on board the eight 5,500-ton guided-missile "destroyers," the first of which was launched that year.

Inevitably this led to conflicting views on the relative merits of the manned aircraft and the missile. This meant that the Navy did not present a united front in the larger battle on the very existence of the carrier force.

The Demise of the Aircraft Carrier.—The 1964 amalgamation of the three service ministries into a single Ministry of Defence, with a central organization to decide policy and three service departments to carry it out, brought the carrier battle to a climax. The Navy lost. *The Defence Review,* which accompanied the defense estimates for 1966–67, stated unequivocally that the new carrier (CVA 01, construction of which had been approved in 1964) would not be built and that the carrier force, then of five ships, would cease to exist in the late 1970s, its role being taken over by land-based aircraft.

With the later decision to withdraw from east of Suez by the end of 1971 the phasing-out of the carriers was readjusted accordingly. A change of government brought temporary reprieve for one carrier, but it was clear that by the mid-1970s even this single ship would be gone and British fixed-wing, carrier-borne air power, as at present understood, would be dead.

On the other hand, great emphasis has been placed on shipborne helicopters, especially in the antisubmarine role, where they combine speed, surprise, and invulnerability to counter-attack. The possibilities of seaborne vertical/short take-off and landing (V/STOL) were also being investigated. A "through-deck cruiser" (TDC), able to operate such aircraft, was being designed, though primarily as a means of operating large antisubmarine helicopters and as a command-and-control ship, to take the place of the defunct fleet carrier.

Personnel.—The Navy needs intelligent and skilful officers and men to operate and maintain its modern ships. For both it has had to compete with the other professions and industry.

On the officer side this challenge has been met by broadening the basis of entry, which until 1948 had remained virtually unchanged since the introduction of the Selborne Scheme in 1903—apart from the addition of the public-school entry in the early 1920s. The "Murray Scheme," started in 1960 after some not very happy experiments over the previous decade, provides a wide choice of age of entry and type of commission. Besides the basic 18-year-old cadetships, there are university cadetships, graduate entries, long or short service, with entry ages of 17 to 25, and as high as 40 for those already qualified.

The greatest problem on the rating side lies in retaining valuable trained men at the end of their first engagements, when their skills would command high salaries ashore. The Navy meets this by means of job interest, good working and living conditions, removal of unnecessary petty regulations, security of employment—all of which raise morale and encourage the *esprit de corps* essential to a fighting service.

It is probable, however, that the decision on whether to stay or go is a joint husband-and-wife affair. In recent years the Navy has made giant strides in providing married quarters, in cutting down periods of separation, and in the general welfare of families. All the same, the re-engagement rate—vital to a volunteer force—remains a problem.

NATO and Nuclear Deterrence.—British maritime strategy for the foreseeable future is largely bound up with that of the North Atlantic Treaty Organization (NATO), founded in 1949. The present "NATO Area," however, is bounded in the Atlantic by the Tropic of Cancer, which raises the question of the extent of cooperation between NATO members when their interests are threatened elsewhere; as, for instance, in the Indian Ocean. Proponents of the case for the "NATO world-wide" school have stated that NATO interests include the protection of shipping at sea everywhere. In the early 1970s, too, all but a handful of small warships were only "declared to NATO" in peacetime, in the meanwhile operating entirely under national direction. There was, however, a new trend in NATO thinking toward wider deployment and greater integration.

In 1969 the Royal Navy took over responsibility for nuclear deterrence from the Royal Air Force, with four Polaris-armed submarines—the submarines themselves and the nuclear warheads being provided by British and the missiles being provided by the United States under the Nassau Agreement of 1963.

The value of this small force, compared with the 41 such craft possessed by the United States, was the subject of much debate. Being immune from attack, their "second-strike capability" was assured, but whether this, in turn, was sufficient to deter a nuclear attack on Britain was a political question. The Navy's job was to be able to deliver. This it was prepared to do.

Despite the fact that deterrent forces, on both sides, use the oceans of the world to give themselves security and both tactical and strategic mobility, they are not (as such) instruments of sea power in its age-old, but still valid, meaning of ensuring the use of the sea by oneself while denying such use to the enemy.

The Future.—Conventional warships are still needed, but these, owing to the complexities of modern weapons systems, cost a great deal of money, to be obtained in competition with many other claims, especially from the nation's social services. *The Defence Review* set an annual target of "£2,000,000,000 at 1964 prices" for the total defense bill and this policy, or, at all events, the principle behind it, has since been accepted by both major parties. This, in turn, has dictated military commitment and hence government policy.

Irrespective of whether this logic of defense should be accepted, it would be totally unrealistic to hope to provide a maritime force able to give anything approaching world-wide protection to British interests which, despite the loss of empire, are still widespread. On the other hand, many other like-minded nations have similar and parallel interests to protect. There is therefore reason to hope that, whereas the Royal Navy cannot do the job alone, some practical solution can be found through NATO or, within that alliance, by very much closer coordination, perhaps leading to integration, of the maritime forces of the enlarged European Economic Community.

(J. M. PA.)

C. AIR FORCE

Military aviation in the United Kingdom dates from 1878, when a series of experiments with balloons was carried out at Woolwich Arsenal. On April 1, 1911, an air battalion of the Royal Engineers was formed, consisting of one balloon and one airplane company, with headquarters at South Farnborough, Hampshire, where the balloon factory was located. Meanwhile, in February 1911, the Admiralty had allowed four naval officers to take a course of flying instruction on airplanes at the Royal Aero Club ground at Eastchurch, Kent, and in December of that year, the first naval flying school was formed there. On May 13, 1912, a combined Royal Flying Corps (RFC) was formed with naval and military wings and a Central Flying School at Upavon on Salisbury Plain. The specialized aviation requirements of the Navy made it appear, however, that separate organization was desirable and on July 1, 1914, the naval wing of the RFC became the Royal Naval Air Service, (RNAS), the military wing retaining the title Royal Flying Corps. Meanwhile, the balloon factory had been renamed the Royal Aircraft Factory and undertook the design and manufacture of airframes and engines. A series of aircraft with the general designation "BE" (Blériot Experimental) resulted and did excellent service in the earlier stages of World War I. A number of private British designers also entered the field and most of the aircraft in use in the British and Empire Air Services in the latter half of the war were the product of British factories.

World War I.—On the outbreak of World War I the RFC, possessing a total of 179 airplanes and 1,244 officers and men, sent an aircraft park and four squadrons to France on Aug. 13, 1914. Aircraft were used for reconnaissance and spotting for artillery by means of air-to-ground wireless telegraphy. Soon, however, specialized types were produced for fighting, bombing, reconnaissance, and aerial photography, while speeds increased from 60 to 150 mph and engine power from 70 to more than 400 hp before the end of the war.

The growth and versatility of the air forces had demonstrated that air power had a separate and essential role to play in modern warfare, independent of, but in closest cooperation with, the older services. Practical recognition of this fact was given, shortly before the end of the war, by the creation of the Royal Air Force. On April 1, 1918, the RNAS and RFC were absorbed into the RAF, which took its place beside the Navy and Army as a separate service with its own ministry under a secretary of state for air. The RAF carried out its first independent operations during the closing months of the war in a series of strategic bombardments of targets in France and Germany by a specialized force of heavy bombers.

The strength of the RAF in November 1918 was nearly 291,000 officers and airmen. It possessed 200 operational squadrons and nearly the same number of training squadrons, a total of 22,647 aircraft.

Between World Wars I and II.—The peacetime pattern for the RAF provided for a total of 33 squadrons, of which 12 would be based in the United Kingdom and 21 overseas. Since the prospect of another European war was regarded as remote, the squadrons at home served as a strategic reserve for overseas reinforcement and as service training units for personnel prior to their posting to squadrons abroad. The preponderance in numbers of the overseas squadrons resulted largely from the system evolved by the air staff and adopted by the government of making use of air power as an economical method of maintaining order in undeveloped countries. During the 15 years from 1920 onward, relatively small air forces repeatedly crushed incipient disorder and maintained peace in Somaliland, in the Aden protectorate, and on the northwest frontier of India. In Iraq, between 1920 and 1932, the RAF exercised military control of the country with a force of eight squadrons of aircraft and two or three companies of armoured cars.

To train permanent officers for the flying branch of the service, a cadet college was established at Cranwell, Lincolnshire, in 1920. The RAF staff college was opened in 1922 at Andover, Hampshire. The need for trained mechanics, possessed of the various skills peculiar to a military aviation service, was met by the School of Technical Training at Halton, Buckinghamshire, where boys of 15½ were received as apprentices for a three-year course in their chosen trade. In order to ensure a constant supply of pilots and to build up a reserve, a short-service commission scheme was introduced in 1919. Young men were commissioned for four years (subsequently increased to six), of which the first year was spent in training, followed by service in active squadrons. At the conclusion of their engagement they passed to the reserve of air force officers for a further period of four years. Some years later, a medium-service scheme, with ten years' regular service followed by a period in the reserve, was introduced as an alternative. In 1925 an organization known as the Auxiliary Air Force was formed. Its members gave part-time service, undergoing flying and technical training at weekends and during holiday periods. By the outbreak of World War II this force possessed a number of highly trained fighter squadrons, which did such good service throughout the war that the prefix "royal" was added to its title at the end of hostilities.

By 1923 the prospects of permanent peace in Europe appeared less certain and a substantial increase in air defense expenditure was decided upon. The first steps toward implementing this decision were taken in 1925, when a new command, the Air Defense of Great Britain, was set up, with a proposed ultimate strength of 52 squadrons of fighters and bombers stationed in the United Kingdom. There were, however, delays in the buildup of the force and eight years later, when Adolf Hitler attained power in Germany, the RAF possessed only 87 squadrons, regular and auxiliary, at home and overseas. With the rapid deterioration of the international outlook in Europe, expansion was greatly increased and accelerated. From 1936 onward, the aircraft industry received powerful financial aid from the government to enable additional factories to be built to increase production, while many automobile firms turned their works over to the construction of complete aircraft or their components. To provide the crews to man the additional aircraft, the RAF Volunteer Reserve and the Civil Air Guard were formed to give flying training at civilian schools and flying clubs, while the university air squadrons, the first of which had been formed soon after World War I to teach undergraduates to fly and to encourage them to join the RAF as regular officers,

greatly expanded their activities. The Auxiliary Air Force, meanwhile, formed captive balloon units to provide protective barrages for heavily populated areas and specially vulnerable points. A part-time Observer Corps (later the Royal Observer Corps) had been formed some years earlier to give warning of impending attack by enemy aircraft and was now considerably expanded.

The Women's Auxiliary Air Force (WAAF), a re-creation of the Women's Royal Air Force (WRAF) of World War I, came into being as a separate service in June 1939, out of the (women's) Auxiliary Territorial Service, an army-sponsored organization which had been formed a year earlier and had recruited special air force companies. (In 1949 the WAAF became the WRAF once more.) Finally, though this did not occur until 1941, the Air Training Corps (ATC) replaced the air defense cadet units and the school air cadet corps of the immediate prewar years. In it boys received some preliminary air force training with a view to their eventual entry into the RAF.

World War II.—At the outbreak of war on Sept. 3, 1939, the first-line strength of the RAF in the United Kingdom was about 2,000 aircraft. These were grouped as follows: Fighter Command, concerned with home defense, with a small component detached to the expeditionary force in France until that country was overrun in June 1940; Bomber Command, for offensive action in Europe; and Coastal Command, for the protection of maritime routes, under the operational direction of the Navy. There were also Balloon, Maintenance, Reserve, and Training commands. Army Co-operation Command was created in 1940 and Ferry Command (subsequently expanded into Transport Command) in 1941. In the meantime great air forces were built up as requisite in North Africa, Italy, Burma, France, and elsewhere.

By the time the war ended, the strength of the RAF was 963,000, with 153,000 women in the WAAF. (For the part played by the RAF in the conflict in Europe see WORLD WARS: *World War II.*)

In order to provide the number of aircrew required to man the rapidly expanding front line strength, and to make good the heavy casualties suffered, training programs were undertaken in many parts of the Commonwealth early in the war. Canada, Australia, and New Zealand combined to operate the empire air training program, under which each of them recruited and trained pilots, navigators, and radio operators for service with the RAF. In addition, since the United Kingdom was the main base for operations against the Axis forces and was itself under constant threat of air attack, flying training became virtually impossible there and great numbers of aircrew pupils were sent to Canada, South Africa, and Southern Rhodesia to receive their training at schools specially established for the purpose. From June 1941 (six months before the United States entered the war) until the end of hostilities, British aircrew were also trained at civilian-operated schools in the United States.

In the course of the war, techniques were developed for landing individuals or bodies of troops behind the enemy lines, by means of parachute or glider. The RAF cooperated with the Army in the training and transport of parachutists and in towing troop-carrying gliders, whose soldier-pilots flew and landed them in the selected area when cast off by the towing aircraft.

Transport aircraft were widely used in campaigns all over the East to convey vast quantities of food, ammunition, and even vehicles and guns, and isolated bodies of troops in jungle and other difficult country were supplied for protracted periods entirely by parachute. It was mainly by means of the airlift that the Burma campaign was carried to a successful conclusion.

One other innovation was the formation of the RAF regiment for the protection of aerodromes against enemy attack. Armed with light antiaircraft weapons as well as with the ordinary infantry armament, they were trained on commando lines. They normally served under the orders of the local air force commander, but were so organized that they could fit smoothly into the army command structure in face of a widespread enemy threat.

Development After World War II.—When the wartime forces were demobilized in 1945 the total strength of the RAF was reduced to about 150,000. The subsequent deterioration in the international outlook led to a fresh expansion in 1951. By 1956 the total strength was up to 257,000, but by the early 1960s it had again retracted to about 150,000 (including 6,000 women in the WRAF), the majority of whom were stationed in the U.K., or in Europe, as part of the NATO forces.

The RAF regiment remained after the war as a regular arm of the service, organized in rifle and light antiaircraft squadrons. The WRAF became a regular service in 1949.

The changes initiated in 1963 and put into effect in 1964 provided for the Air Force to be administered by the Air Force Board of the Defence Council (see introduction to *Defense*, above). This is under the chairmanship of the secretary of state for defense.

There are nine other members of the Air Force Board: the parliamentary undersecretary of state for the Royal Air Force, the permanent undersecretary of state (Equipment), the chief scientist (Royal Air Force) and the deputy undersecretary of state (Air), who are civilians; and the chief of the air staff, the vice-chief of the air staff, the air member for personnel, and the air member for supply and organization, who are serving officers.

The organization of commands is as follows: Strike Command, comprising one bomber, one fighter, one maritime, and one signals group; Air Support Command with one transport group; Training Command with three groups; and Maintenance Command.

Overseas there are the Near East Air Force with headquarters in Cyprus; the Far East Air Force with headquarters at Singapore; Air Forces, Gulf, with headquarters at Bahrain; the 2nd Tactical Air Force in Germany; and a number of RAF elements forming part of NATO forces throughout Europe and the Mediterranean.

The service is organized in five main branches: general duties (aircrew and ground), engineer, supply, secretarial, and RAF regiment, with a number of ancillary branches such as medical, education, airfield construction, marine, chaplains, legal, provost, and catering. For many of these branches, other than general duties and RAF regiment, women serving in the WRAF are eligible. The Princess Mary's Royal Air Force Nursing Service provides nursing staff for RAF hospitals at home and abroad.

The Royal Auxiliary Air Force was retained as a flying force up to 1956, but the fighter squadrons were then disbanded for reasons of economy. The force continued as an integral part of the defensive structure, however, with special responsibilities in fighter command, where fighter control and radar reporting units of the Auxiliary Air Force played an important role in the early warning system. Both men and women were recruited for these duties.

The Royal Observer Corps also was perpetuated as a part of the strike command defensive network. Besides reporting low-flying enemy aircraft, the corps also has the responsibility of registering and reporting the amount of radiation resulting from explosion of nuclear weapons in time of war. The corps consists of part-time civilian volunteers of both sexes, with a few full-time officers.

The Volunteer Reserve (RAFVR) and the Air Training Corps (ATC) continued on a peacetime basis, administered by Training Command. The latter was open to boys between 14½ and 17¾ years of age interested in aviation and was organized in squadrons, which were either independent formations in a town or district or attached to a school as a cadet unit. In addition to normal ground training, there was a widespread gliding organization.

Recruitment and Training.—Entry to the commissioned ranks of the RAF and WRAF in all branches is through one of two avenues, the general list and the supplementary list. Broadly speaking, general-list officers have the assurance of a pensionable service career up to the age of 55 (with the option of retiring on pension after 16 years' service if desired, while supplementary-list officers enter for a pensionable career after the minimum qualifying period of 16 years (or at age 38), or alternatively for shorter periods with a gratuity on passing to the reserve. General-list officers enter either as cadets through the RAF college, Cranwell, or direct from universities or other professional institutions. Supplementary-list officers enter direct by selection subject to certain educational qualifications. A certain number of scholarships are available for schoolboys of 15½ and over to prepare them for entry to the cadet college. Flying training is carried out entirely on jet aircraft at flying schools in the United Kingdom, after which the officer proceeds to an operational conversion unit before being posted to a squadron. Though direct enlistment is the main source of manpower for the noncommissioned ranks, the need for highly skilled mechanics and tradesmen in the 22 different trade groups is supplied largely by apprentice or boy entrant training schools. Normally boys enter between the ages of 15 and 17, receive between 18 months and 3 years' training, and then engage for 12 years' service from the age of 18, with the possibility of serving up to the age of 55 if desired. Direct-entry airmen serve on similar terms, and airwomen in the WRAF, who are eligible for training in 18 of the RAF trade groups, serve normally for 3–6 years' regular service and may also continue for pension up to the age of 55.

Equipment.—Though most of World War II was fought in the air with aircraft powered by piston engines, the last year of hostilities witnessed the entry on both sides of the newly developed jet engine, which by the early 1960s had almost entirely ousted the piston engine in the RAF.

The great increase in speed and climb conferred by jet engines pointed to their value in fighters and it was in this field that reequipment first took place, the early Meteors and Vampires leading on to the Vulcans, Lightnings, and the V/STOL (vertical/short take-off and landing) Hawker Harriers of the mid-1960s. The bomber force was built up as the strategic deterrent and by 1966 its main armament consisted of Victor B.Mk 2 and Vulcan B.Mk 2 medium bombers, of which a number were armed with the Blue Steel air-to-surface nuclear standoff missiles. The reequipment of the bomber force led to fierce controversy over the respective merits of the British TSR 2 and the U.S. swing-wing F-111A; the government decided on the latter, but its order was later withdrawn for economic reasons and no major reequipment then took place.

The strategic transport force consisted of Britannias, Belfast long-range freighters, and VC-10 troop transports, each of the last-named capable of carrying 150 men or a number of armoured vehicles. At the same time, increasing use was made of helicopters, especially for tactical support of the Army.

The Air Defense Organization under the RAF includes the ballistic missile early warning system. The U.S.-British station at Fylingdales, Yorkshire, completed in 1963, was designed in conjunction with warning stations in Alaska and Greenland to give at least four minutes' warning of the approach of a missile. Reports from the warning stations were arranged to pass simultaneously to headquarters in the U.S., Canada, the U.K., and mainland Europe. The system was to be supplemented by the U.S. Midas space-satellite system, in conjunction with which a station in the U.K. was built at Kirkbride, Cumberland.

Further aspects are discussed in AIR POWER.

(D. CR.)

D. CIVIL DEFENSE

During World War II a large complex organization of trained civil defense services was built up. This was closed down completely after the end of hostilities in 1945. In 1948, because of international tension, it was decided to establish a civil defense organization as part of the system of national defense.

Under the Civil Defence Act, 1948, and the Civil Defence (Northern Ireland) Act, 1950, civil defense powers are exercised by several ministers. Civil Defence functions are discharged by local authorities and certain nationalized undertakings. The home secretary is responsible for coordinating the civil defense planning of all the civil agencies of government. In Scotland and Northern Ireland civil defense planning is the responsibility of the secretary of state for Scotland and of the minister of home affairs, respectively.

After the advent of the hydrogen bomb in 1954 increasing emphasis was placed on measures to maintain a framework of administration and essential supplies and services on which survival would depend after a nuclear attack. For operational purposes England is divided into nine regions and each of these, and Wales, would be under the direction of a regional commissioner in time of war. Each region is organized in a chain of control through regional and subregional controls established by central government and controls set up by local authorities. There is no regional organization in Scotland or Northern Ireland, but for operational purposes Scotland is divided into three zones. The purpose of the wartime control system is initially to direct life-saving operations and subsequently to marshal and coordinate essential supplies and services for the continued survival of the community. The police, ambulance, and fire services are all trained in civil defense.

Civil defense services are based on the operational plans of local and other public authorities for the smooth transition of their peacetime services to a war footing. In the event of a deteriorating international situation that seemed likely to lead to general war, the resources of local and central government would be devoted to placing the country on a war footing and to the issue of necessary public advice as to the measures families should take for protection. In this task the local authorities would be assisted by various voluntary organizations, such as the ambulance associations, the Red Cross, and the Women's Royal Voluntary Service. The Warning and Monitoring Organisation, of which the Royal Observer Corps forms a part, provides warnings of air attack and of radioactive fallout.

See also AIR POWER; CIVIL DEFENSE.   (J. B. Ho.)

IV. THE ECONOMY
A. PRODUCTION

The various aspects of production are also discussed in *The Economy* sections of ENGLAND; SCOTLAND; WALES; IRELAND, NORTHERN.

1. Agriculture.—The numbers engaged in agriculture in the United Kingdom have steadily decreased, but it still remains one of the important industries. Between 1871 and 1931 the population censuses showed a decrease in agricultural workers in Great Britain from about 1,500,000 to 1,170,000. The total of regular and temporary workers employed on agricultural holdings in the United Kingdom had decreased from 882,000 in 1951 to 345,000 by 1970. The industry employed about 12% of the total labour force in 1871; by 1970 it employed less than 2%.

The area devoted to agriculture in 1970 amounted to 47,347,000 ac. (19,161,000 ha.; more than 80%) of a total land area of 59,536,000 ac. (24,094,000 ha.). Of this, rough grazing accounted for about 16,600,000 ac. (6,718,000 ha.). In Scotland, where much of the land is mountainous, rough grazing forms about three-quarters of the agricultural land; in Northern Ireland, one-quarter; and in England and Wales, one-sixth. The division of the cultivated area between arable land and permanent pasture varies. In England and Wales about 55% is arable, in Scotland, more than 70%, and in Northern Ireland, 40%. (*See* Table II.)

The entry of cheap grain supplies from the newly opened areas of America and Australia caused a gradual reduction in the arable acreage from about 1870. Livestock became relatively more profitable and by the mid-1930s permanent grass had encroached on about 5,000,000 ac. (2,000,000 ha.); in addition, more than 1,000,000 ac. (405,000 ha.) returned to rough grazing. Such changes were much less marked in some parts of the country; in Scotland they were slight, probably because arable land, if left in grass for many years, reverts to rough grazing. The contraction in arable land was least in the eastern counties of England, where rainfall is light and good permanent pasture difficult to maintain.

Between 1939 and 1944 the proportion of arable land rose from 27 to 40%, or roughly what it had been in 1870. This arose from the emphasis placed on grain production during World War II in an endeavour to save shipping space. Thereafter, although government policy continued to encourage arable farming, the arable acreage declined from its wartime peak.

Crops.—The competition of overseas supplies had its main effect on the wheat and barley crops. During the 50 years following 1870 the acreage under wheat was about halved while that under barley was reduced by more than one-third; but the acreage under oats increased slightly. The greater relative fall in price was undoubtedly the main reason for the large reduction in wheat acreage. The bulk of the oats is used on the farms for animal feeding and is in consequence less even than that of wheat and barley, which tend to be heavily concentrated in the eastern counties of England.

In the early 1930s arable farming in the United Kingdom reached its lowest ebb. The wheat acreage was little more than one-third of what it had been in 1870; the acreage under barley had been halved and during the next few years was to shrink further.

The transition from peace to war resulted in a sharp increase in crop acreages. During the war years the acreage of wheat more than doubled; that of barley increased by 70% and of oats by 50%. The year 1943 marked the highest wheat acreage of the 20th century; thereafter it tended toward the prewar level. But barley acreage continued to expand up to 1966 and in 1970 was still six times as great as in 1939 and over twice the average for 1871-75. As with wheat, the stimulus given to oats production by wartime shortages and postwar restrictions on imports gradually weakened and the average declined continuously until 1966, thereafter increasing again.

Unlike the grain crops, the area in potatoes increased after 1870 to meet the demands of the rapidly growing population. The expansion was particularly great in eastern England, where between 1880 and 1930 acreage trebled. In Lancashire, Cheshire, and eastern Scotland there was little change, while in Northern Ireland the potato acreage was slightly reduced. During World War II the potato acreage doubled, as compared with 1938, but after the 1950s the trend was downward, the acreage falling from 829,000 in 1960 to 669,000 by 1970.

The acreage of mangolds (beets) was maintained until 1925 because of the value of this crop as cattle food. But turnips and swedes (rutabagas), which are expensive to grow and more liable to weather and pest damage, became less popular and by the 1960s occupied less than one-quarter of the area used in 1870; even during wartime the expansion was slight. During World War II the area in vegetables almost doubled, as compared with 1938. Thereafter it declined somewhat. (*See* Table III.)

When averaged over periods of years, crop yields show fairly steady progress since they were first estimated in 1885. After 1940 increases were particularly rapid because of the use of improved strains of seed and soil nutrients. Average annual yields per acre during the late 1960s were: wheat 31.4 cwt., sugar beet 17.4 tons, and lucerne (alfalfa) 39.1 cwt.

Livestock.—The movement away from arable farming, which was the main feature of British agriculture between 1870 and World War II, was accompanied by a growth in the importance of

TABLE III.—*Acreage of Certain Crops and Bare Fallow in United Kingdom*
(in 000 ac.)

Crop	Average 1941-45	Average 1949-58	Average 1959-63	Average 1963-66	Average 1967-70
Wheat	2,748	2,184	2,021	2,227	2,319
Barley	1,795	2,231	3,792	5,318	5,866
Oats	3,835	2,721	1,711	1,085	958
Potatoes	1,326	994	771	739	671
Turnips	832	569	423	339	267
Mangolds	288	212	114	66	29
Sugar beet*	408	423	429	442	461
Clover and rotation grasses*	4,327	5,345	6,888†	6,629	5,811
Bare fallow*	263	291	253	213	271

*Great Britain only. †Not strictly comparable with previous years.

TABLE II.—*Land Use, 1938, 1966, and 1970*
(in 000 ac.)

Land and year	England and Wales	Scotland	Northern Ireland	Total
Arable land				
1938	8,878	2,983	1,096	12,957
1966	14,130	3,389	965	18,484
1970	...	...	...	17,788
Permanent pasture				
1938	15,833	1,577	1,388	18,798
1966	10,195	921	1,083	12,199
1970	...	...	...	12,217
Rough grazing				
1938	5,615	10,448	526	16,589
1966	4,794	12,243	681	17,718
1970	...	...	...	16,629*

*Not strictly comparable with earlier years because of exclusion of about 1,000,000 ac. of small holdings in Scotland.

livestock, particularly cattle. The number of pigs remained fairly constant, while the number of sheep on the whole declined.

In the period 1871–75 to 1921–25 the total number of cattle increased by nearly one-fifth, to 7,743,000. The decontrol of veal prices before those of other meats at the end of World War I resulted in a sudden fall in numbers in 1920–21, but, thereafter, the trend was steadily upward. By 1939 there were about one-third more than in 1921. Until the early 1920s, the increase of cattle remained low in relation to the expansion in population; there-after, it was more rapid. The quantity of meat imported, which had risen rapidly prior to 1921, remained fairly steady till 1939. Increased imports of butter and (to a smaller extent) of cheese and manufactured milk supplemented home production.

During and after World War II the number of cattle continued to increase, reaching 9,629,000 in 1946 and 10,668,000 in 1955 and over 12,000,000 by the late 1960s. Imports of beef and butter were greatly reduced during the rationing period and have not recovered their prewar level; but cheese imports rose during the war and only after 1955 returned to their prewar figure. Liquid milk sold off farms increased by over 60% in the period 1940–60, compared with a rise of less than one-fifth in the number of cows in milk, indicating an increased yield of about 40%. During the 1960s output was stabilized at about 2,500,000,000 gallons, of which just over 60% was for liquid consumption, the remainder being made into butter, cheese, condensed milk, and other products.

The number of sheep, though fluctuating, declined after about 1870. Liver fluke and unfavourable weather in the first part of the period caused a sharp fall from 29,000,000 in 1871–75 to 25,-500,000 in 1881–85. This was partially recovered, but the general downward trend continued and was greatly accentuated during World War I and the years immediately following. Between 1933 and 1939 the sheep population rose to about 27,000,000, but the next ten years saw a sharp contraction and it was not till 1959 that the prewar total was restored. The expansion that occurred be-tween 1945 and 1966 is explained largely by the subsidies paid for hill farming.

Because of the speed at which they can be bred, pigs are subject to much more rapid fluctuations in number than cattle or sheep. Despite this, the average for quinquennial periods remained fairly constant at between about 2,500,000 and 3,000,000 until World War II. Feeding difficulties then led to a sharp decline to less than half the prewar total, but from 1948 the trend was upward. The number exceeded 6,000,000 by 1954, and continued to fluctuate around this figure, reaching a peak 8,088,000 in 1970. The system of guaranteed prices since the war has been largely responsible for the considerable expansion in pig rearing.

The number of poultry on farms in the United Kingdom con-tinues to increase. Between 1908 (the earliest date for which figures are available) and 1938 the number increased by about 85%, to 74,000,000. During the war a considerable reduction took place, but after 1945 the number began to rise and after a slight pause in the mid-1960s reached 143,430,000 in 1970.

Value of Agricultural Output.—The estimated value of produce sold off farms or consumed in farm households was estimated at £300,000,000 for the crop year 1937–38. Over 70% of this rep-resented livestock and livestock products, the rest being fairly evenly divided between farm crops and vegetables and other items. By the end of the 1960s the value of gross output had risen to over £2,250,000,000 annually, livestock products slightly losing in pro-portion to the total and farm crops gaining in relation to other items. The bulk of the sevenfold change in the value of gross out-put value was, of course, due to increased prices; when valued at constant prices the increase amounted to about 100%. As the value of the material imported from abroad or supplied by other industries increased to about seven times the prewar figure, the in-crease in the value of net output of agriculture at constant prices since 1937–38 was also about 100%. Farm incomes, that is, the profit income accruing to farmers, which was £56,000,000 in 1937-38, had, by the end of the 1960s, shown a tenfold increase, to about £550,000,000.

Agricultural Holdings.—The number of agricultural holdings in the United Kingdom in 1970 was 335,000, of which 172,638 were of less than 50 ac. (20 ha.), but those in Northern Ireland include rough grazing while those in Great Britain do not. These figures do not, however, indicate the number of farms, because a farm may contain more than one holding. Despite their deficiencies, the statistics indicate a fairly steady reduction in the number of hold-ings, especially in those under 20 ac. (8 ha.), between 1895 and 1938. The number of holdings exceeding 300 ac. (120 ha.) has tended to increase, but for some years after World War II there was also an increase in the number of holdings under 5 ac. (2 ha.).

Capital Invested and Mechanization.—The capital invested in agriculture in England and Wales was in 1931 estimated at £925,-000,000, of which £645,000,000 was the value of the land and build-ings and the rest working capital. In 1950 the total for Great Britain was put at £1,748,000,000 (tenants' capital in the form of crops, livestock, and machinery £1,280,000,000 and tenant-right valuation £100,000,000). The high degree of mechanization of modern agriculture, yielding an increased output by a greatly re-duced labour force, represents considerable investment in farm machinery. The number of tractors in use in Great Britain in-creased from about 200,000 at the end of World War II to over 500,000 in 1970, combine harvesters from 3,500 to 66,000, and pick-up balers from 1,900 to 105,000. During the ten years end-ing 1964 the number of grain and grass driers increased sixfold from 5,100 to 33,000; by 1970 the number had grown to 63,000. Most farms have milking machines with mechanical means of han-dling milk. Over three-quarters of the farms have electricity.

The Government's Role.—The shortage of shipping space during World War II and of foreign exchange immediately afterward forced the U.K. to aim at greater self-sufficiency in food produc-tion. Farmers were encouraged by grants and subsidies to reclaim land and revitalize it with lime and fertilizers, while labour short-age led to extensive mechanization. Most agricultural produce was purchased by the Ministry of Food at prices above those paid by consumers, the difference being made good by subsidies.

The Agricultural Act of 1947 embodied much of wartime experi-ence. It required the government to provide guaranteed prices and assured markets for the main products embracing about 70% of total output by value. The annual review of prices published after consultation with the National Farmers' Union and the set-ting of production targets for individual commodities were contin-ued. The act also provided measures to encourage efficient farm-ing, empowered the minister to dispossess offenders, and sought to ensure good husbandry by revising the relationship between land-lord and tenant. It provided for administration through the county agricultural executive committees, joint bodies representa-tive of the Ministry of Agriculture and the farmers. In 1948 the system was extended to Scotland; that part of the 1947 act relating to guaranteed prices applied also to Northern Ireland.

The Ministry of Food remained the chief purchaser of agricul-tural produce, but from 1953 onward it gradually relaxed its con-trol. Production targets were abandoned, grain was returned to private trade in 1953, and livestock and milk products were re-turned in 1954. The marketing boards for potatoes, milk, pigs, and bacon were revived and new boards were introduced for eggs, wool, and tomatoes and cucumbers. The removal of controls made it essential to devise a method of assisting home agriculture while maintaining an open market. This was done by introducing a sys-tem of deficiency payments to bring up the price of home produce sold in competition with imports to the guaranteed level.

Broadly, the marketing boards channel farm output through recognized merchants and are responsible for passing the Ex-chequer payments to producers. In some cases (hops, potatoes) production quotas may be fixed, but, in general, there is no restric-tion on quantity. The marketing of grain and fatstock is in private hands and about one-fifth of all meat is sold through the Fatstock Marketing Corporation, a producer-owned concern. Deficiency payments are made only on wheat sold off the farm, whereas for barley and oats payments are on an acreage basis, whether the grain is sold or used on the farm.

During the early 1950s the main emphasis in British agriculture was on output but toward the close of the decade official policy was redirected to ensure that production would be more economic and adapted to the needs of the market. Marketing boards and other institutions strove to encourage expansion in home consumption through publicity and research into more efficient methods.

Other financial assistance given to farmers includes grants and subsidies to improve hill and marginal land and to increase their production. The size of Exchequer assistance to agriculture declined during the first half of the 1960s, standing at £340,000,000 by 1971. Over two-thirds of this figure is comprised of deficiency payments.

Agricultural wages have been regulated on a county basis since 1924 in England and 1937 in Scotland. Agricultural wages acts were passed covering England and Wales in 1948 and Scotland in 1949. These provided for agricultural wages boards representing farmers and workers, together with independent members. Orders made by the boards specify minimum rates of wages and appropriate hours of labour; they also provide for holidays with pay and may specify the benefits in kind that may be reckoned as payment.

The principal source of credit for the agricultural industry is the joint stock banks, which made advances to farmers of about £500,000,000 in 1970. In addition several specialized agencies lend for longer periods. The chief of these are the Agricultural Mortgage Corporation formed by the Bank of England and the principal joint stock banks, the Scottish Agricultural Securities Corporation and the Agricultural Loans Fund in Northern Ireland. The Exchequer operates schemes for the provision of credit to small holders. (See also AGRICULTURE: The United Kingdom.)

2. Forestry.—Over 4,500,000 ac. (1,821,000 ha.), almost 8%, of the total land area of the United Kingdom is devoted to forest. Of this total more than 3,000,000 ac. (1,200,000 ha.) are directly under the control of the forestry commission. Production of wood in the U.K. is insufficient for industrial requirements. There are large imports of wood and wood products, but the bulk of imports are in the form of processed wood.

TABLE IV.—Home Production and Imports of Round Wood, 1965

(000 cu.yd.)

Item	Home productions	Imports
Industrial wood		
Saw logs, veneer logs, and logs for sleepers	2,486	602
Pulp wood, and pit props	1,253	1,363
Other	3	123
Fuel wood	513	122
Total	4,255	2,210

3. Fisheries.—The sea-fishing industry of the United Kingdom is among the most important in the world. The principal kinds of fish caught are herring, cod, haddock, plaice, sole, and hake, classed as wet fish, and shellfish, including crabs, lobsters, oysters, and shrimps. By 1970 the annual consumption of fresh fish was about 16 lb. per head of population and had been declining slowly. The principal grounds frequented by British fishermen are the North Sea, Icelandic waters, and those of the Faeroe Islands, the south and west of Ireland, the west of Scotland, the Barents Sea, the Irish Sea, and the English Channel.

The number of fishing vessels steadily decreased from more than 17,000 in 1913 to under 6,000 in 1970, but the decline in landings by the latter date had been reversed.

The industry's activities were greatly restricted during World War II and Fleetwood, Lancashire, temporarily became the most important fishing port. Landings in England and Wales in 1941 were reduced to one-sixth and in Scotland to less than half of their prewar level and did not fully recover until after the war. In Northern Ireland, on the other hand, landings increased throughout the war period. The postwar restrictions on meat supplies greatly encouraged the industry and landings and consumption continued to rise; but after 1950 a decline set in and by 1963 the landed weight (about 16,000,000 cwt.) was hardly more than three-quarters of the 1938 total. There was some recovery, however, and by 1970 the landed weight was 19,000,000 cwt. (about 90% of the 1938 total). The rising proportion of foreign-caught fish on the British market led to enactments in 1944, 1945, and 1948 designed to assist the herring, inshore, and whitefish industries with grants for equipment and motorboats to replace steam and sail.

About one-third of the total British fish catch consists of cod and codling; haddock made up between one-sixth and one-fifth, followed by whiting, coalfish (saithe), and plaice. About 10% of the total landings are herring and these form the principal item in Britain's fish export trade. In 1966 herrings amounted to about one-sixth of the total export of 30,000 tons. Most of the canned herring are exported, while the bulk of the canned fish consumed (principally salmon and sardines) is imported. (See Table V.)

Research sponsored by the government includes the study of the movements, habits, and feeding of fish, both inshore and out at sea, by fishery vessels; and research on hydrography, in the method of capture of fish, the breeding and cleansing of shellfish, etc. An important technical device used for locating shoals is the echo sounder. The principal ports for the distant waters fleet are Hull, Grimsby, and Fleetwood. (See also FISHERIES: United Kingdom.)

TABLE V.—Quantities and Value of Fish Landed in United Kingdom, 1938 and 1966*

Landings	1938		1966	
	Weight (000 cwt.)	Value (£000)	Weight (000 cwt.)	Value (£000)
British caught:				
England and Wales	15,533	12,233	17,928	39,214
Scotland	5,381	3,827	...	18,767
Northern Ireland	70	42	...	...
Total wet fish	20,984	16,102	17,928	57,981
Shellfish	...	504	640	3,482†
Imports of fresh and frozen fish	1,683	2,454	2,420	32,200

*Excluding salmon and trout.   †Excluding Northern Ireland.

4. Mining.—Coal.—By 1970 coal was still the most important source of power in the United Kingdom, though very closely followed by petroleum. The reserves available are thought to be sufficient for several centuries at the current rate of exploitation. Production by 1800 was still small—about 10,000,000 tons annually—but the development of the steam engine and of the iron and steel industries greatly increased demand. By 1913 production had reached 287,000,000 tons.

The coalfields of England lie mainly north and west of a line joining the Wash and the Bristol Channel, but there are small fields outside this area. The principal Welsh mining area is in the south and in Scotland in the rift valley separating the Highlands from the Southern Uplands.

The British coalmining industry reached its peak of prosperity in the decade preceding World War I. To obtain rapid exploitation of coal measures, landowners were induced to grant concessions freely over limited areas. In 1913 there were 3,270 mines at work, output per man shift was higher than in any other European coalfields except those of Upper Silesia, and 73,000,000 tons were exported, mainly to Europe.

During World War I the mines were under government control. The report of a committee set up in 1919 to consider the future of coalmining indicated a cleavage of opinion on nationalization. Government regulation of wages and hours of work ceased in 1921 and a subsequent stoppage of work lasting three months gained for the miners pay increases, a minimum wage, and the hope of shorter hours. This was made possible by a government subsidy of £10,000,000 to the mine owners. A prolonged stoppage from May to November 1926 exhausted both sides; the miners were forced to accept longer hours and wages were settled on a district basis.

It was not till the postwar boom ended that the true situation of the British coal industry became apparent. Exports that had been greatly reduced during World War I rose to a peak of 79,000,000 tons in 1923, but, thereafter, a long-period decline was probably accelerated by the interruption of supplies in 1926. Continental European producers were seriously competing in the export markets, methods of production were being improved, and output per man shift was gradually outstripping the British figure. To strengthen the industry through amalgamation and reorganization the Mining Industry Act of 1926 was passed and was further strengthened by the Coal Mines Act of 1930. Neither successfully overcame the owners' opposition to amalgamation, but the 1930 act helped to maintain coal prices until 1938. The number of mines in operation gradually decreased to about 1,950 by the beginning of World War II. This was partly due to the closing of a number of worked-out mines but mainly to amalgamations.

Nevertheless it was clear the amalgamation was not proceeding fast enough. The Coal Act of 1938 vested all unworked coal in Great Britain in a coal commission which was empowered to acquire it from the owners for £66,450,000 compensation for loss of royalties and to administer the leases held by the mining companies. The commission also received wide powers to enforce reorganization and amalgamation subject to the approval of the Railways and Canals Commission Court. Transfer of ownership of the coal deposits took place in 1942, but, because of the war, plans for the reorganization of the industry had to be set aside.

The committee that reported in January 1945 rejected nationalization and set out certain principles governing production, reasonable profits, and the workers' well-being. It recommended the establishment of a central coal board with powers of compulsory amalgamation when efficiency demanded it and the voluntary method failed; it also recommended the creation of an export organization to prevent price cutting. The report of the Technical Advisory Committee (the Reid Report) contrasted the rate of growth in output per manshift in Britain with that abroad, stressed the need for increased mechanization, and emphasized the economies obtainable from the more intensive exploitation of limited areas and by the integration of mines to form technically optimum units. The Nationalization Act was passed under the postwar Labour government, the National Coal Board was constituted in July 1946, and the industry taken over on Jan. 1, 1947. There were in 1964, 576 main collieries grouped into 41 areas that were basic units for commercial management. These areas were divided into nine divisions, each under the control of a divisional board that supervised and coordinated the work of the areas, formulated divisional policy, and was answerable to the National Coal Board.

TABLE VI.—*Coal Output*

Decennial average or year	Production (in tons)	Average number of persons employed*
1873-82	138,000,000	482,000
1883-92	170,000,000	552,000
1893-1902	203,000,000	713,000
1903-12	254,000,000	936,000
1913-22	241,000,000	1,068,000
1923-32	233,000,000	982,000
1933-42	221,000,000	754,000
1945	183,000,000†	709,000
1950	216,000,000	697,000
1955	208,000,000	699,000
1966	175,000,000	427,000
1970	142,000,000	287,000

*Prior to 1922 clerks and salaried persons (numbering 24,000 in 1922) are included; the numbers on colliery books exceed the numbers employed by 4,000. From the beginning of 1960 the figures of employment refer only to mines operated by the National Coal Board. Licensed mines employing 6,000 in 1959 are excluded.
†Production for years after 1943 includes opencast coal.

The capital investment program for the postwar coal industry as set out in 1950 envisaged an annual demand approaching 250,000,000 tons in 1965. This was revised, however, and more modest forecasts were made. In the years immediately following World War II the demand for coal for industrial, domestic, and export purposes was greater than the industry could meet. Consumption and shipments reached a peak of 230,000,000 tons in 1954 but thereafter declined to an annual average of 152,000,000 in 1968-70. The switch by industry to oil fuel in the 1950s was rapid; fluctuating coal exports averaged 5,700,000 tons in the early 1960s but declined sharply to reach 1,850,000 tons in 1967, from which they recovered to 3,300,000 tons in 1970. Output per manshift increased, but the labour force declined. A five-week national strike of miners in 1972 resulted in substantial pay rises. (See also COAL AND COAL MINING.)

Iron Ore.—Production varies considerably. In 1913 it was nearly 16,000,000 tons, but during the decade 1924-33 the annual average was little more than three-fifths of that amount. Thereafter output rose, reaching a peak of 18,000,000 tons in 1943. By 1970 total production had declined to 11,800,000 tons. About half the iron ore used by the British iron and steel industry is home produced, but the average iron content is about 28%, compared with 57% for imported ore. Most British iron ore is produced in England, the main areas being in Yorkshire, Lincolnshire, Northamptonshire, Cumberland, and Staffordshire.

Tin.—Cornwall is the main source of tin in the U.K., but its output supplies only a small proportion of national requirements, amounting by the late 1960s to only about 1,500 metric tons annually.

Zinc.—Zinc concentrates produced in the United Kingdom decreased from 1912 onward, but during World War II a temporary increase in output reached a peak of 16,000 tons in 1944. By the 1960s home production had once more shrunk to a negligible amount. It was formerly mined chiefly in North Wales, the North of England, the Isle of Man, and the county of Dumfries.

China Clay.—This mineral is extensively mined in Cornwall and is used in the pottery, papermaking, textile, and chemical industries. Output, which was 777,000 tons in 1913, shrank to 178,000 tons in 1943 but thereafter gradually expanded and by 1970 was over 3,000,000 tons. Almost 70% of this output was exported.

Fluorspar.—Fluorspar is mined in Derbyshire and is of importance in metallurgy. Annual production has been rising steadily since 1962 to reach 189,000 tons, about five times that of 1938.

Fuel Oil.—Indigenous production of crude petroleum furnishes only a small part of U.K. requirements. In 1918 the government began investigations and in 1919 a small well was drilled at Hardstoft, Nottinghamshire. There was considerable development during and after World War II; oil was found in Derbyshire, Nottinghamshire, Staffordshire, Yorkshire, Cumberland, Lancashire, Shropshire, and in Scotland, and in 1959 a new field was discovered at Gainsborough, Lincolnshire. Output reached 113,000 tons in 1943 but thereafter declined to 44,000 tons in 1948; and subsequently there was a steady increase, reaching a peak in 1964 (127,000 tons) followed by a considerable drop in production to around 80,000 tons per annum since 1965.

Oil shale abounds in Dorset, Somerset, Norfolk, Lincolnshire, and Yorkshire, but the Scottish deposits in Midlothian, Linlithgow, and Lanark are commercially the most important. Shale-oil production increased from 125,000 tons in 1938 to 199,000 tons in 1942 but declined, until by 1963 production was negligible.

5. Industrial Production.—The broad changes in the structure of manufacturing industries are indicated by data relating to manpower and production. The value of net output as given by the censuses of production indicates the contributions of the individual industries to the total national income.

The total number engaged in manufacturing rose from 6,800,000 in 1939 to about 8,900,000 by the end of the 1960s. The volume of production increased by nearly 70% since 1950. All the groups except textiles, clothing, leather, and wood and cork manufacture showed increased employment in the 1950s. The cloth... the 19th and early 20th centuries, lost ground, all their main sectors showing decreased employment in increasing production with a smaller labour force. The textile industries, which were so important in ... Workers in the textile trades formed 15% of all those in manufacturing in 1939; by the end of the 1960s this had shrunk to about 8%. Net output of textiles formed nearly 20% of the total value attributable to manufacturing in 1935; by 1970 it had declined to 7%, largely as a result of reduced exports in the face of foreign competition.

After World War II the decline in the textile and clothing industries was more than compensated by the increased employment in engineering and allied industries. The aggregate contribution of the latter group to the total manufacturing income increased from 28% in 1935 to more than 40% in the late 1960s. Between 1948 and 1970 the number of employees in the textile and clothing group fell by over 30% to 1,271,000, whereas the number in the engineering and allied industry increased by nearly 40% to 2,482,000. The increase was particularly marked in machine tools, electrical machinery, and wireless apparatus.

Vehicle manufacture and repair increased their labour force by over 20% after the war. Both the automobile and aircraft industries increased their labour force by over 40%, but the increase was partially offset by the lower level of employment in the manufacture and repair of locomotives and railway rolling...

GREAT BRITAIN AND NORTHERN IRELAND

TABLE VII.—*Iron and Steel Production*
(in 000 tons)

Product	1913	1938	1941	1946	1951	1961	1970
Pig iron							
Hematite	3,605	1,484	906	1,121	1,333	1,137	937
Foundry	3,802	1,229	1,082	1,135	1,417	1,196	699
Forge	2,530	151	101	66	70		
Basic		3,763	5,182	5,228	6,675	12,256	15,589
Direct castings	324	130	120	150	172	158	168
Ferroalloys			1				
Total	10,261	6,761	7,392	7,701	9,669	14,747	17,393
Steel							
Converter							
Acid	1,049	164	98	210	241	254	279
Basic	552	431	696	724	862	1,694	8,958
Open-Hearth							
Acid	3,811	1,720	1,808	1,229	1,259	611	160
Basic	2,252	7,743	8,945	9,900	12,277	17,773	13,004
Electric						1,648	4,893
Ingots	…	160	411	345	575		
Castings	…	63	161	134	245		537
All other ingots and castings	117	117	193	153	179	106	38
Total	7,664	10,398	12,312	12,695	15,638	22,086	27,869

stock. The volume of production in the vehicle industry more than doubled from 1948 and in 1970 it employed almost 10% of all persons engaged in manufacturing.

Net output of the chemical and allied trades showed a slight increase from 7% of the total in 1935. Between 1948 and 1970 manpower rose by more than 25% and production by well over 200%. The expansion in oil refining and other sections of the trade which have a high ratio of capital to labour was responsible for the rapid increase in production; the devaluation of the pound sterling in 1967 also had a beneficial effect on the industry by stimulating export growth. The proportion of total manpower engaged in the food, drink, and tobacco group of industries was the same in 1950 as in 1939, and it increased slightly through the 1960s. The processing of agricultural products and the manufacture of chocolate and sugar confectionery and soft drinks were the main expanding sections in the early part of the 1960s and canned foods in the latter part. Baking and brewing employed fewer than ten years earlier. The changes in this group of industries reflected something of the effects of higher income levels on consumption.

Iron and Steel.—The iron and steel industry can be divided into the production of pig iron, of crude steel, and of finished steel products. The U.K. production of pig iron in 1970 was 17,393,000 tons, compared with 9,633,000 tons in 1950 and an average 4,729,000 tons in 1930–34. More than half of the metal produced comes from ores imported chiefly from Sweden, Canada, northwestern Africa, Venezuela, and Spain. Of the home-produced ores about 95% originate in the East Midlands ore fields; a small amount of hematite is produced in Cumberland and Glamorgan.

British crude-steel production grew from a level of 5,261,000 tons in 1929 to 16,293,000 tons in 1950 and 27,869,000 tons by 1970. Of the latter some 33% was produced in Bessemer converters (only 6% in 1929), some 47% in open-hearth furnaces, and 19% in electric furnaces. About 79% of the total output was basic steel (as distinct from acid steel produced from hematite). The growth in the importance of the basic process, which can use ores high in phosphorus, can be judged from the increase in the proportion of basic steel in the total from 21% in 1900 to 67% in 1929. The raw materials from which crude steel is produced are pig iron and scrap; in 1970 scrap constituted 58% by weight of the steel produced.

The British steel industry developed round the available supplies of suitable coking coal and nonphosphoric ores (ores high in phosphorus could not be used in steel production until the introduction of the Thomas-Gilchrist basic process in the 1870s); and by mid-19th century the industry was concentrated in South Wales, Scotland, and the West Midlands. Increasing dependence on imported ores caused some shift toward coastal districts, particularly in South Wales. In the third quarter of the 19th century production on the northeast coast, based on Durham coal and Cleveland ores, moved into preeminence; the development of the industry in Lincolnshire dates from the same period. Changes in the sources of domestic ore affected the siting of blast furnaces after 1913 and pig-iron production in the East Midlands expanded at the expense of some older areas; but the older production centres proved remarkably tenacious. There was not much change in the relative importance of the main producing areas after 1929, but the East Midlands output of crude steel has continued to grow slowly at the expense of northeast-coast and Scottish production.

The outbreak of World War II found the British iron and steel industry repairing the injuries of the depression. More than £50,000,000 had been spent on modernization in the years immediately before the war and steelmaking capacity had increased by about 2,000,000 tons. During the war steel production (about 12,750,000 tons annually) averaged barely 1,000,000 tons more than during immediate prewar years, but new steels (especially alloys) were developed. Plants suffered heavy wear and tear.

In 1946 the British Iron and Steel Federation presented to the Ministry of Supply a plan for reconstruction aimed at increasing the annual capacity by 2,000,000 tons over a period of between five and seven years and at the same time reequipping more than one-quarter of the existing capacity. By 1949 the output of steel had reached 15,500,000 tons; but the demand rose much more rapidly than had been anticipated and in 1952 a second development plan envisaged a steel capacity of 20,500,000 tons by 1957–58. Further increases in capacity took place during the 1960s, but the fall in demand resulted in considerable spare capacity with output only rising by just over 5,000,000 tons during the decade.

The industry has been subject to substantial government control since the depression of the early 1930s. In 1932 the British Iron and Steel Federation was formed to foster reorganization and to confer with the Import Duties Advisory Committee on prices, costs, and development plans. The Labour government came to power in 1945 with the declared intention of nationalizing the industry, and, pending that, supervision was implemented through the Iron and Steel Board appointed by the minister of supply. In 1949 a large part of the industry was nationalized. The Iron and Steel Corporation was formed to take over by purchase of shares the major producers of iron and steel goods. In 1951, with the return of a Conservative government, steps were taken to denationalize the industry, and in 1955 the Iron and Steel Holding and Realization Agency was set up to arrange for the orderly sale of shares acquired by the corporation. The behaviour of the industry, however, was not left completely to free play of market forces, for at the same date a new Iron and Steel Board was set up to fix home prices and to regulate capital development.

Between 1946 and 1963 about £1,350,000,000 were spent on capital development in the steel industry. New techniques included the use of sinter in pig-iron production and oxygen blast in steelmaking, and the development of continuous rolling mills for producing sheet strip. During the same period the average size of plant increased, as the plants built in the postwar years have a much larger capacity than the old ones. As a result there were substantial increases in labour productivity and output per manyear was about 70% higher in 1970 than in 1937. These developments greatly reduced costs and U.K. steel prices were considerably lower than in many other steel-producing countries.

The election of a Labour government in 1964 was followed by the renationalization of the industry. On July 28, 1967, the Iron and Steel Act transferred to the British Steel Corporation the ownership of 13 major steel-producing companies, with a total turnover of over £1,000,000,000 and a labour force of 250,000 people. As a result the corporation became responsible for over 90% of the United Kingdom's production of crude steel.

Engineering.—Before World War II the industry specialized in high-quality goods of distinctive design and the United Kingdom was the chief exporter of steam engines, railway equipment, textile machinery, and heavy electrical machinery. In the production of the lighter products more susceptible to mass-production techniques (automobiles, machine tools, and light electrical equipment) the U.K. was overshadowed by the U.S. and Germany. In 1937 the U.K. ranked third after the U.S. and Germany as an exporter of engineering products mainly because the demand for the traditional specialties had not kept pace with that for the newer, mass-produced products.

During World War II the industry expanded rapidly to meet the needs of the war economy, and although there was a small contraction in 1946 the upward trend was soon resumed and in 1948 employment was one-third greater than in 1939. The main problem in the postwar years was to switch from the production of munitions to civilian goods; demand was kept at a high level by the need of industry to replace capital equipment. When the more urgent claims of reconstruction were satisfied, demand was sustained by the growth of new industries and industrial techniques at home and by the growth in the demand for capital goods abroad, particularly in developing countries. Between 1949 and 1970 the volume of engineering goods produced rose by 116% compared with a rise of just under 100% for industrial production as a whole.

Shipbuilding.—During the 1950s and early 1960s the average number engaged in shipbuilding and ship repairing in the U.K. fluctuated between 220,000 and 240,000, while annual output (in vessels of all classes) was between 1,200,000 and 1,500,000 gross tons. By 1970, however, the number employed in shipbuilding had declined below 200,000.

In 1913 the output of British shipyards constituted 58% of the world total, but with the depression in the early 1930s the industry went into a decline that lasted almost until World War II. The reduction in shipbuilding in the 1930s was accentuated by a substantial shrinkage in the volume of international trade. World tonnage launched fell from 2,889,000 tons in 1930 to 479,000 tons in 1933. British launchings fell from 1,500,000 tons in 1930 to 131,000 tons in 1933, when unemployment in the shipyards constituted 63% of the insured labour force. The decline of shipbuilding in the United Kingdom was far more severe than elsewhere and between 1931 and 1939 the output of British yards constituted only 30% of the world total.

In 1946 British output had recovered to 53% of the world total. About 4,000,000 tons of British merchant shipping had been destroyed during the war and there also ensued an intense demand from foreign owners whose fleets had been likewise reduced. Between 1945 and 1950 output amounted to 6,082,000 tons, of which about one-third was for foreign owners. By 1950 the employees in shipbuilding and ship repairing numbered 233,000, with a further 84,000 in marine engineering. This was higher than in the period preceding World War I and shows how the industry had in the postwar period made up the ground lost between the wars.

By 1950, however, the British mercantile marine exceeded its prewar size and world tonnage also was greater than in 1939. Moreover, in two of the United Kingdom's main competitors in shipbuilding, Germany and Japan, output was reviving. The outbreak of the Korean War in 1950 postponed the difficulties facing the industry, the ensuing steep rise in freight rates causing owners to place large orders for both dry-cargo ships and tankers. World tonnage launched increased from 5,096,000 tons in 1952 to reach a peak of 9,270,000 tons in 1958. The output of foreign yards, however, was growing faster than that of British yards and by 1958 the British proportion of world tonnage launched had fallen to 15%. By 1958 the considerable surplus of world shipbuilding capacity became obvious. With the decline in freight rates that followed came a substantial diminution in orders placed. There was increasing competition from foreign shipyards; by 1960 British output had fallen to 1,320,000 tons and further declined to 1,250,000 tons by 1970. The main shipbuilding areas are Clydeside, Tyneside, Merseyside, and Belfast (*see also* SHIPPING).

Motor Vehicles.—By the end of the 1960s the number of persons engaged in the manufacture and assembly of motor vehicles was under 490,000 (compared with 431,000 in 1961); this included those employed in producing parts and accessories. A further 20,-000 were engaged in the production of motor and pedal cycles (34,000 in 1961). The service trades related to the industry employed more than 400,000 (372,000 in 1961) persons at gas (petrol) stations, garages, and other distributive outlets.

The British automobile industry developed slowly before World War I, mainly because it concentrated on a quality product for a restricted market. In consequence the number of British automobiles produced in 1912 was only about 5% of the U.S. output. In the interwar years the British industry expanded more rapidly as firms adapted U.S. methods to the production of cheap light cars. Home sales were stimulated by tariff protection over most

of this period and in 1929 only about 5% of British demand wa[s] met by imports. Mainly because of the more rapid recovery from the depression, the British industry moved ahead relative to the U.S. industry during the 1930s and the ratio of British to U.S. output rose to 18% in 1938.

After World War II the industry enjoyed a further period o[f] rapid expansion. In 1959 its output was more than three time[s] that of 1937, the best prewar year. This was partly due to considerable success in the export markets; between 1948 and 1950 for example, when home sales were limited by administrative action, about 70% of the passenger automobiles produced were exported. The Commonwealth countries again provided a major outlet for motor vehicles in the immediate postwar years but the share of automobiles exported to the Commonwealth fell by about 20% during the 1960s. Sales to the U.S. and Europe (particularly Western Europe) expanded rapidly in the 1960s and by 1970 the U.S. accounted for 18% of export sales and Europe for over 40%.

About 90% of the British output of automobiles and tractors and a smaller proportion of commercial vehicles, is produced by four large manufacturers, the British Leyland Motor Corporation, Rootes, Ford, and Vauxhall. The last three are members of American groups. The rest of the automobile output is produced by a number of smaller manufacturers concentrating mainly on high-quality products. Account must also be taken of the numerous firms producing components, ranging from the large-scale producers of tires and electrical equipment to small factories making specialized parts. About 60% of the factory value of British cars is accounted for by components produced by outside suppliers.

Production in 1913 of motor vehicles of all types was 34,000. Passenger automobile production rose from 71,000 in 1923 to 379,-000 in 1937; in 1948 it was 335,000 and reached a peak of 1,868,-000 in 1964. Production of trucks, buses, and coaches was 24,000 in 1923, 114,000 in 1937, 177,000 in 1948, and 458,000 in 1970. Agricultural tractor production increased from 18,000 in 1937 to 114,000 in 1948; it reached 229,000 in 1963 and then fell to a rate of about 170,000 per annum in the late 1960s. Motorcycle production, 80,000 in 1923, was 131,000 in 1948 but declined steadily in the 1960s to under 100,000, having reached a peak of nearly 250,-000 in 1959.

Aircraft Industry.—World War I gave a tremendous impetus to the production of aircraft in the United Kingdom and the industry expanded steadily between the wars. The production of military aircraft was steadily increased from 1938 onward and the rate of growth of the industry rose sharply after 1940. Production doubled between the beginning of 1940 and the end of 1942.

After the war the industry had to concentrate its efforts on the development and production of civil aircraft. The constant tendency for the end products to become larger and more complex made it very expensive to develop new types to meet competition from abroad. The decline in the demand for military aircraft in the mid-1950s led the government to encourage a regrouping of the industry and production was concentrated mainly in the hands of two large airframe constructors, two aeroengine firms, and one helicopter concern. The government also assists in developing, proving, and producing aircraft and may participate in proceeds from the sale. By the early 1960s total output had changed little, but employment, having reached a peak of just over 300,000 in 1961, fell steadily to under 230,000 in 1970.

Exports are the key to the industry's problems for it is often not possible to cover costs from home sales. The value of sales abroad of new and used aircraft engines and parts increased from £102,-200,000 in 1956 to £151,400,000 in 1958. There was a sharp fall during the early 1960s, and in 1964 output sales fell to £102,000,-000. The years 1965 and 1966 saw a dramatic turnabout when the value of exports rose to £151,000,000 and £217,000,000, respectively. At the end of the decade sales were running at a level just under £250,000,000 annually, with hopes of substantial sales of the Anglo-French Concorde, built at a cost approaching £900,000,000. A blow to the industry was the bankruptcy in 1972 of Rolls-Royce, the bastion of British aerospace technology, caused by mounting losses in the development of the RB.211 engine for the U.S. Lockheed TriStar airbus.

Textiles.—From the end of the 18th century until World War I Great Britain was preeminent in the world cotton industry. In the last quarter of the 19th century over half of the world's spindles were in Lancashire, and Great Britain still held a leading position in 1913 with 39% of the world's spindles.

With the outbreak of war in 1914 the expansion of the industry ceased and output never again reached the prewar levels. The causes of this decline were twofold: increased competition abroad and insufficient adaptability within the industry at home. Countries such as India and China, which were formerly customers, became themselves producers and the rapid expansion of the Japanese cotton industry introduced the severest competition. In 1937 the quantity of British piece goods exported was less than one-third of the average prevailing before World War I, and although home demand for cotton goods increased slightly the British share of the world's cotton spindles had fallen to 26% by 1938.

During World War II the cotton industry contracted sharply; by 1945 the numbers employed had fallen to 209,000, or little more than half of those in 1938. Postwar demand was buoyant and the main problem was the shortage of labour. Production remained well below prewar levels and in 1949 sales of yarn and cloth abroad were little more than half those of 1937. The boom in textiles broke in 1951 and was followed by a steady deterioration in the competitive position of the British industry in international markets. Domestic production increased substantially in those countries that had been the traditional markets for cotton exports so that in 1960 only 11% of the world's production of cotton cloth entered international trade, compared with about 20% during the interwar period. At the same time there was a recovery of production in the major exporting countries and by 1960 the United Kingdom's share of world cotton trade had fallen to 7%, compared with more than 26% prewar. In 1970 cotton cloth production in the U.K. was less than one-fifth of that in 1937; exports had fallen to less than one-tenth of the 1937 level.

Nearly 400 plants went out of operation between 1955 and 1958. In 1958 imports of cotton cloth from overseas exceeded U.K. exports for the first time for two centuries and at the end of 1959 employment fell below 200,000 for the first time since the middle of the 19th century. Government efforts to aid the industry took two forms: the negotiation with Commonwealth cotton producers of a voluntary limitation on exports to the U.K.; and, under the Cotton Industry Act, 1959, arrangements for the elimination of surplus capacity through a plan financed partly from public funds and partly by a levy on existing producers. By the end of the 1960s the number of spindles in place in the industry had been reduced to under 8,000,000 mule equivalents and the number of looms to 68,000.

The wool textile industry followed roughly the same course after 1918, though its decline was far less serious. The woolen and worsted industries contracted sharply during World War II and sales abroad virtually ceased. In the postwar years the industry faced a substantial problem in rebuilding the labour force from the very low level of 126,000 in 1944, but unlike the cotton industry it was able to meet this difficulty. In the absence of many competitors from world markets the British wool industry expanded its overseas sales rapidly and by 1950 exports had reached the prewar level. The textile slump of 1951-52 brought an end to this period of exceptional growth and prosperity but the industry recovered rapidly. Although the 1950 figures were not again reached, the industry was able to compete successfully in international markets and the United Kingdom retained its position as the chief supplier of woolen and worsted goods. With the reconstruction of continental industries some competition in the home market came from cheap European woolens, but these constituted only a very small percentage of the British consumption.

Although the viscose rayon industry was developed in the U.K. at the beginning of the 20th century and British producers had a leading position before World War I, the rapid development of manufacture in the U.S., Japan, Germany, and Italy was such that by 1939 British production accounted for only 10% of world output of continuous-filament yarn and only 5% of staple-fibre output. The industry grew rapidly after World War II and by 1960 the production of yarns of all types was more than three times as large as in 1939. Among cellulosic fibres growth was particularly fast in the production of staple, used in the cotton, woolen and worsted, flax, and jute industries; but the most marked feature of the 1950s was the growth in the production of the noncellulosic fibres such as nylon, Terylene (Dacron), and the polyacrylonitrile fibres, Acrilan and Courtelle. In 1950 production of noncellulosic fibres was about 9,000,000 lb., or 2% of man-made fibre output; by 1961 production was 148,000,000 lb., or 35% of total output. As in most countries, the production of man-made fibres in the U.K. was concentrated in the hands of a few firms.

Chemical and Allied Industries.—The gross output of chemical manufactures increased from £762,000,000 in 1948 to more than £4,000,000,000 in the late 1960s. The average numbers employed rose from 486,000 in 1951 and averaged about 525,000 in the 1960s. These figures relate to activities ranging from the production of basic organic and inorganic chemicals and the refining of mineral oil to the preparation of pharmaceuticals and cosmetics. They seriously underestimate the growth in the importance of chemical techniques in the economy, however, for they ignore industries that use chemical processes in the production of some other products, for example, the synthetic-textiles industry.

The rapid growth of the industry dates from World War I. In 1914 British factories were equipped for the manufacture of explosives only on a small scale, and the industry had to be expanded rapidly with government assistance. The position regarding dyestuffs was even worse because over 80% of world output came from Germany and only 2% from the U.K. To stimulate the industry the German patents were revoked and by 1917 the essential national requirements were being met. After the war the strategic importance of the industry was fully realized and protection from foreign competition was given under the Dyestuff (Import Regulation) Act, which came into force in 1921 and prohibited imports except under licence. Though Germany recaptured the greater part of the export market British output of dyestuffs in 1937 was 31,633 tons, as against German output of 63,000 tons.

World War II brought a further rapid expansion and after 1950 production in the trade increased faster than in any other industrial group, the production index for 1970 being some 170% higher than the average for 1950 (compared with an increase of about 75% in all manufacturing industries over the same period). The industry embraces a wide range of activities. The production of general chemicals mounted with the increasing use of chemical processes in industry and agriculture; for example, the production of sulfuric acid increased from 1,660,000 tons in 1949 to 3,299,000 tons in 1970. But by far the most spectacular increase was in the production of plastics and synthetic resins. The production of thermoplastic resins, for example, increased from 65,000 tons in 1951 to 1,093,000 tons in 1970. Plastics probably accounted for less than 12% of gross output in 1966. The more traditional sections of the trade did not enjoy such rapid expansion. The production of dyestuffs and colours declined by 18% between 1951 and 1970, probably as a result of the depressed conditions of the textile trades. The production of soap declined by 150,000 tons over the same period, but this was more than offset by an increase of over 400,000 tons in the production of synthetic detergents.

About 300 firms in the U.K. employing more than 500,000 are engaged in the production of chemicals and allied products. The industry is characterized by a few large firms producing a wide range of products. The impetus toward large-scale operation derives largely from the necessity for very large research expendi-

TABLE VIII.—*Production and Employment in the Cotton Industry*

Output	1912	1924	1937	1951	1970
Output of singles yarn (000,000 lb.)	1,963	1,395	1,375	1,078	519
Output of cloth (000,000 linear yd. cotton)	8,050	5,978	3,640	2,202	686
Rayon and mixtures	...	48	482	759	530
Spindles running on singles yarn. (000,000)	55	57	39	28	4
Looms running (000)	786	633	419	312	68
Employment (000)	622	499	360	322	153

tures. While only the biggest firms can afford such expenditure there is an opposing tendency for the activities of a firm to become increasingly diversified as its research departments discover new products or techniques. By far the most important firm in the industry is Imperial Chemical Industries, which accounts for about 40% of the net output, if mineral-oil refining and coke ovens and by-products are excluded from the total.

6. Public Utilities.—*Gas.*—The British gas industry was nationalized in 1948 when 1,037 undertakings were taken over and compensation paid in the form of fixed interest stock redeemable at par in 1990–95. For administration the country is divided into 12 regions, each controlled by a board responsible for production and distribution. Coordination is achieved through the Gas Council which forms the link between the Department of Trade and Industry and the area boards. Consultative councils on which consumer interests are represented maintain liaison between the public and the area boards.

Gas consumption, after a pause in the late 1950s, increased during the 1960s, standing at over three times the 1945 level in 1970. Employment figures were slightly under 130,000. In the 1950s there was a considerable increase in output from coke ovens, refineries, and other sources. Discovery of natural gas under the North Sea resulted in plans for a much larger proportion of home sales to be supplied from this cheaper rather than traditional source.

Electricity.—The British electricity industry was nationalized on April 1, 1948, when about 540 local undertakings were taken over. The system covers Great Britain and is under the general control of the British Electricity Authority, which is responsible for the production and sale of electricity to the area boards. The 14 electricity boards are, like the authority, statutory bodies and are responsible for distribution; their areas correspond approximately with those of the generating divisions.

Prior to nationalization, coordination was the responsibility of the Central Electricity Board, a body set up under the Electricity (Supply) Act of 1926 to nationalize the industry. By 1939 the

TABLE IX.—*Electricity Production*

Item	1935	1948	1959	1963	1970
Installed capacity* (Mw.)	8,065	13,184	30,015	39,298	60,538
Electricity generated (GWh)	18,862	48,036	106,128	156,868	228,899
Methods of generation (GWh)					
Steam plant	18,053	46,562	103,819	153,620	223,714
Water power	625	1,345	2,175	3,074	4,981
Other	184	129	134	174	204
Fuel used (000 tons)					
Coal	12,236	28,715	45,985	67,211	76,047
Coke and coke breeze	175	420	1,149	675	122
Oil	24	73	4,245	5,118	12,387

*Great Britain.

regional supply systems had been linked by high-tension lines into a national grid and a large measure of concentration of generating capacity and of uniformity in frequencies and voltages had been attained, achieving considerable economies.

In 1970 the production of electricity was nearly nine times the level recorded in 1938. Almost half the sales are to factories and other industrial premises and over one-third to domestic and farm premises. Between 1938 and 1970 domestic consumption had increased almost fifteenfold. The generating capacity in the same period increased a little more than sixfold but plant utilization improved, the load factor increasing from 36.7% to about 52%.

About 2% of the total is generated from water power. The output of the hydroelectric schemes rose from 988,000 GWh. in 1938 to 4,981,000 GWh. by the end of the 1960s. The bulk of this is generated in the Highlands of Scotland under the control of the North of Scotland Hydro-Electric Board which was set up in 1943. Sales of electricity by 1972 were well over the £1,000,000,000 mark, while annual investment in plant and machinery was about one-half of this total.

Nuclear Energy.—Responsibility for the peaceful use of nuclear power in the U.K. was taken over in 1945 by the Ministry of Supply and an atomic energy research establishment was set up at Harwell, Berkshire. The Atomic Energy Bill empowering the government to control the use and development became law on Nov. 6, 1946. By the Atomic Energy Act of 1954, responsibility was transferred to the U.K. Atomic Energy Authority under the lord president of the council; in 1959 ministerial responsibility passed to the lord privy seal and the minister for science.

The 1955 program for nuclear-power generation provided for plants with a total capacity of 1,800 Mw. by 1965, but in 1956 a fall in the price of uranium and concern about supplies of conventional fuels aroused by the Suez conflict caused an increase in the planned capacity to 5,000 Mw. Generation of electricity by nuclear power commenced in 1962 when production was 944,000 GWh. Production increased rapidly in the next few years and in 1970 supplied nearly 10% of the total electricity generated.

Water Supplies.—Water resources in most of Scotland, Wales, and Northern Ireland are abundant. Ministerial responsibility covers the national water policy and there is a statutory central advisory committee for England and Wales. The supply of wholesome piped water is an obligation placed on local authorities by the Public Health and Water Acts. Local authorities either operate their own waterworks or (in England and Wales) may ensure that other bodies do so.

The largest water authority, the Metropolitan Water Board, supplies over 400,000,000 gal. daily to 540 sq.mi. of London and surrounding counties. Piped water reaches about 98% of the population of England and Wales and is provided in all Scottish and Northern Irish towns. Domestic supplies are charged for by a water rate based on the value of the house.

Many smaller undertakings may depend chiefly on rivers (as do London and Chester); on the English lakes (Manchester); on the Welsh lakes (Liverpool); on the Scottish lochs (Glasgow); or on artificial reservoirs (Bristol).

(M. J. A.)

B. TRADE AND FINANCE

1. Overseas Trade.—The aggregate value of imports and exports rose from £89,000,000 in 1826 to £632,000,000 in 1876 and toward the end of this period exports were increasing at an average rate of about 8% annually. However, the rate of growth diminished and at the beginning of the 20th century exports were growing at less than 1% annually. This decline was partly due to a reduction in world trade in manufactures but (more significantly) the British position was permanently affected by the industrialization of new countries. The U.K. share of world exports of manufactures fell from 38% in 1876–80 to 27% in 1911–13.

Because of the early development of industry British exporters succeeded in capturing a very large proportion of world manufacturing trade, but much of this was in the products typical of the period, i.e., consumer goods and especially textiles. In 1827–29 more than three-quarters of British manufactured exports were textiles and even by the end of the century textiles still accounted for more than half of the total. With the development of new manufacturing countries there was a shift in the composition of international demand and producer goods and the more complex forms of consumer goods became more important in total trade. To some extent the British economy adjusted itself to this shift and the proportion of producer goods to the total of manufactured exports grew from less than 10% in 1827–29 to more than one-third in 1911–13. But the adjustment was not fast enough, for the rapidly growing manufacturing countries (particularly Germany and the U.S.) were concentrating much more on the production of producer goods, and the largest proportion of British exports was in those commodities expanding least in world trade.

In spite of the weakness of British exports after 1876, however, imports continued to increase, not only absolutely but as a proportion of national income. The money value of imports more than doubled between 1870 and 1913 and the ratio of retained imports to national income grew from 21% in 1870–76 to 28% in 1911–13. The annual average trade gap (excess of imports over exports) rose from £174,000,000 for the years 1875–79 to £244,000,000 for 1910–13. This gap was filled by so-called invisible exports that increased sufficiently not only to fill the trade gap but also to leave available a large surplus to finance capital exports. These invisible exports consist of the earnings of shipping, insurance, and financial services, and income from tourism and overseas investment.

World War I accelerated the adverse forces at work. Countries cut off from their sources of supply were forced to develop their own manufacturing industries and services, so that when the war ended many of the traditional markets for British exports were closed. Moreover, in order to finance the war the United Kingdom had to realize overseas assets and income from abroad was correspondingly reduced. In spite of this, invisible earnings in the early 1920s still sufficed to offset the adverse balance of trade and to leave a small surplus for foreign investment. The annual average value of exports rose from £474,000,000 in 1910–13 to £865,000,000 for 1920–24. Although there was a continued decline in the value of some important export commodities (textiles, coal, ships, iron and steel), in a world starved of manufactured products and in the absence of German competition, the value of almost every other class of British exports increased.

In 1925 the United Kingdom returned to the gold standard with sterling at prewar parity. This had the effect of raising prices relative to those of competitors and placed British exporters at a disadvantage in world markets. The world slump aggravated the situation, and in 1931 the adverse balance of payments on current account exceeded £100,000,000. Exports fell by £387,000,000 between 1929 and 1931, but with the sharp reduction in the prices of primary products the value of imports fell by £359,000,000 over the same period even though their volume was virtually unchanged; thus the trade gap increased by only £28,000,000. The main reason for the adverse balance was the large fall in invisible exports. With the catastrophic fall in world trade after the onset of depression, the demand for shipping and other services was sharply curtailed and British earnings from invisible exports fell by £180,000,000 between 1929 and 1931.

The United Kingdom abandoned the gold standard in 1931 and soon afterward imposed moderate tariffs in an attempt to protect the home market. The immediate effect was a fall in imports; the volume of imports retained for home consumption fell by about 10% between 1931 and 1932. At the same time the fall in export prices stimulated British sales abroad, and mainly by reducing the adverse balance of commodity trade the deficit in the balance of payments was eliminated by 1933, although it reappeared in 1936, 1937, and 1938. In 1933, however, the U.S. also left the gold standard, and in 1936 the French franc was devalued. These changes removed the temporary advantages enjoyed by British exporters and the British proportion of total world trade again declined after 1933. It had been 10.75% in 1929, had fallen to 9.36% in 1931, and with the temporary advantage of devaluation had risen to 10.37% in 1933. By 1937 it had fallen again to 9.8%.

In 1932 representatives from the British Commonwealth met at Ottawa and agreed to extend to each other preferential rates of duty on imports (see IMPERIAL PREFERENCE). The effect of Commonwealth preference was to increase trade within the Commonwealth at the expense of trade between it and foreign countries. Thus the proportion of U.K. exports to Commonwealth countries to total exports grew from 39% in 1930 to 50% in 1938. The proportion of United Kingdom imports from Commonwealth countries to total imports grew from 25% in 1930 to 40% in 1938. But the gains in protected markets were not sufficient to offset the losses elsewhere and the British share of total world trade declined steadily after 1933.

The outbreak of war in 1939 greatly increased the problem of earning enough by exports to pay for imports, which, of course, included munitions of war. The difficulty did not lie in finding markets—the elimination of German exports and general shortages made it certain that anything exported would be readily bought—but in getting the necessary raw materials and labour. Imports too were reduced, partly because of a shortage of money and partly because of a shortage of shipping. Between 1938 and 1945 the volume of imports of all kinds fell by nearly 40%.

The operation of the war economy opened a huge gap in the balance of payments on current account, a gap that the United Kingdom could fill only by running down its capital. Between 1938 and 1945 the value of overseas assets was reduced from £3,545,000,000 to £2,417,000,000. Over the same period debts to the extent of £3,052,000,000 were accumulated in the form of sterling balances. The result was that by the end of the war the money value of British net income from overseas investments had been halved. Moreover, because of conditions in countries producing primary products, the prices of imports had risen more rapidly than the prices of exports, so that the terms of trade had moved against the U.K.; by 1947 the relative average price of imports in terms of exports was some 15% higher than in the prewar decade; by 1951 it was over 40% higher. It was therefore obvious that exports had to be increased and in the years following the war every effort was made to stimulate sales abroad. In 1944 the annual value of exports was less than one-third of that in 1938 but by 1951 it had been raised to 180% of the 1938 level.

The distribution of British overseas trade was profoundly affected by the war. In 1945 the world could be divided into five main areas: (1) the dollar area, a source of vital imports but too nearly self-sufficient to be an easy market for exports; (2) the rest of the Western Hemisphere, less important, but relatively untouched by war; (3) the countries of Western Europe, trying to build up their war-damaged economies by cooperative action and with United States aid; (4) other nonsterling countries; and (5) the sterling area. Of these the dollar area in 1938 took about 10% of British exports and furnished about 22% of imports; in 1947 the corresponding figures were 9% and 35%. This increased dependence upon the U.S. caused a recurring problem of the postwar years, the dollar shortage. Efforts were made to reduce the dependence and by the early 1950s the balance of trade with the dollar area was more satisfactory. The percentages for (2) underwent no great change but those of (3) and (5) showed a greater orientation of British trade toward Western Europe and the Commonwealth at the expense of (4), the other nonsterling countries.

Trends From the 1950s.—During the 1950s the British balance of payments on current account was in deficit in only two of the ten years, 1951 and 1955. Over the same period the balance of trade was in surplus only in 1956 and 1958.

Between 1952 and 1959 imports of goods rose by almost a third in volume, while exports rose by under a quarter (in value terms, the rises were 18% and 32% respectively). The rate of growth (by volume) of imports overtook that of exports somewhere in the mid-1950s, the growth of both being about 20% between 1952 and 1956. This was to a large extent due to the gradual removal of import controls inherited from earlier periods.

Manufactured goods were the dominant category in the growth of imports; the volume of finished and semimanufactured goods brought into the country increased by 50% between 1952 and 1959, while prices fell by about 3%. Payments abroad for fuels, which over the period were, on average, about half the size of the bill for manufactured goods, rose by 38% (in volume the rise was nearly 75%). Apart from a large rise of 12% between 1952 and 1953 the volume of food, drink, and tobacco imports rose at a more or less steady rate of about 3% a year. Imports of basic materials rose by only 10% in volume in the 1950s, though the cycle of industrial output caused fluctuations.

While the share of manufactured goods in total imports rose very strongly in the 1950s, the share of manufactures in total exports of goods remained very steady, at about 80%. There were some sharp declines in the exports of certain textiles, but these declines were more than compensated for by large increases in the export of machinery, vehicles, and aircraft. The number of new motor cars exported declined steadily from 1950 to 1953 from

TABLE X.—*Balance of Payments*
(£000,000)

Item	1913	1929	1938	1950	1958	1967	1970
Imports (f.o.b.)†	706	1107	835	2312	3377	5674	7882
Exports (f.o.b.)†	651	848	533	2261	3406	5122	7885
Visible balance	−55	−259	−302	−51	+29	−522	+3
Invisible balance	+292	+362	+232	+358	+315	+254	+576
Current balance	+237	+103	−70	+307	+344	−298	+559

Source: *U.K. Balance of Payments*, HMSO (1971).
†Including from 1964 a net adjustment for under-recording.

343,300 to 270,800, but by 1959 the number had increased to 569,000. The value of aircraft and aircraft parts increased from £28,700,000 in 1950 to £85,000,000 in 1959.

By the 1960s a deterioration in the balance of payments became apparent. The trade account remained in deficit from 1960 to 1967, while the current account as a whole was in surplus only in 1961, 1962, 1963, and 1966, there being large deficits in 1960, 1964, and 1967 (£255,000,000, £376,000,000, and £298,000,000, respectively).

Between 1960 and 1967 imports again increased by just under a third and exports by under a quarter in volume. The continuing discrepancy between the growth rates of imports and exports was sufficient to push the current account into serious deficit. This was in spite of a fairly steady favourable movement in the terms of trade. The volume of manufactured imports continued to rise fast—by 68% between 1960 and 1967—but prices rose too, and the increase in value was over 85%. The volume of imported fuels increased by 72%, but fuel prices were falling and payments abroad on this account rose by only 52%. Although exports continued to rise at an average rate of 3% per annum, Britain's share of world trade suffered a serious decline.

The situation was one in which it became more and more clear that at the parity of £1 = $2.80, Britain was becoming increasingly uncompetitive. Government policy, in defense of the parity, involved rather frequent resort to deflation, substantial use being made of lines of credit from international monetary organizations and overseas central banks to stem the short-term difficulties.

The large deficit in 1964 prompted the government to introduce a temporary import surcharge on certain manufactured goods. The surcharge was levied at 15% from October 1964 to April 1965, when it was reduced to 10%, and was removed at the end of November 1966; it had the effect of keeping down the rate of expansion of imports, and helped to bring the current account near to balance in 1966. The growth of imports was also slowed by deflationary measures brought in during July of that year.

The year 1967 saw a change in government policy. The Middle East war caused the closure of the Suez Canal in June; and between September and November, dockers in London and Liverpool were on strike. Both these factors affected exports to a far greater extent than imports. The fear of disastrous trade account figures precipitated enormous speculation against the pound. The government was unable to combat all these adverse factors, and on Nov. 18 devalued the pound by 14.3% (from £1 = $2.80 to £1 = $2.40). Large standby credits were made available by international monetary organizations to prevent further speculation against the pound; and the government introduced stiff deflationary measures, to ensure that devaluation would result eventually in the balance of payments swinging into a large surplus.

Large cuts in government spending were announced in January 1968, followed by a harsh budget in March, but the first results of devaluation were disappointing. Despite a 25% increase in exports in sterling terms for the second and third quarters of the year, the 1968 deficit was almost as large as that for 1967. The difficulty lay in the continuing high level of imports with large increases in some sectors. Consumer spending remained high and with the European monetary crisis in November the government imposed further deflationary measures. At the same time, the government imposed a temporary import deposits scheme.

The 1969 budget imposed further deflationary measures—though not so severe as those of the previous year—while, by the second half of the year, it became clear that the long-awaited response of goods exports to devaluation was coming through. (The response of the invisible balance had been more immediate.) The volume of total exports of goods and services increased by a further 9% in 1969—12% by value. The level of imports remained very high, however, despite the reduction of domestic demand pressures. Nevertheless, visible trade was in small surplus in 1970 for the first time since 1958, and as the 1971 recession developed the current surplus increased still further, to over £900,000,000, accompanied by a very sharp rise in unemployment.

Postwar Tariff Policy.—The United Kingdom's postwar trade policy was considerably influenced by commitments to international organizations designed to liberalize international trade. British membership of the International Trade Organization dated from 1948 and although Commonwealth preference was specifically excluded from the General Agreement on Tariffs and Trade (GATT) the U.K. observed the reductions in tariffs and restrictions on trade negotiated by the signatories to GATT. As a member of the Organization for European Economic Cooperation (or OEEC; *see* ORGANIZATION FOR ECONOMIC COOPERATION AND DEVELOPMENT) the U.K. also participated in the reciprocal removal of trade barriers in Europe during the 1950s.

After the Messina Conference in 1955 the United Kingdom took a leading part in the attempt to set up a free trade area embracing those European countries that were members of OEEC, but negotiations broke down and in 1957 the Rome Treaty established the European Economic Community (EEC). In 1959 the European Free Trade Area (EFTA) was established consisting of Austria, Denmark, Norway, Portugal, Sweden, Switzerland, and the United Kingdom. The EFTA convention required the U.K. to eliminate tariffs and quantitative restrictions on imports from EFTA countries by Jan. 1, 1970, but left the U.K. free to determine its trade relations with other countries. The U.K. was also a party to the Kennedy Round agreement on the reduction of trade barriers and most of the provisions of this agreement had been implemented by 1972. Although the U.K. failed in its applications for membership of the EEC in 1963 and 1967, the 1970–71 negotiations were successful, ultimately necessitating the elimination of tariffs on imports from EEC countries and the imposition of common EEC tariff on imports from other countries. (*See also* EUROPEAN UNITY; INTERNATIONAL TRADE ASSOCIATIONS AND CONGRESSES; TARIFF.)

2. The Department of Trade and Industry.

—The activities of the Department of Trade and Industry, the government department concerned with the general overseeing of the industry and trade of the United Kingdom, can be divided into three main sectors. First, it is concerned with the administration of the law relating to patents, trademarks, companies, insurance, and bankruptcy. For example, it administers the Companies Act, 1948, supervising the work of the registrars of companies in London and Edinburgh. Second, the department engages in a wide range of diverse functions relating to domestic industry and trade; legislation in 1960 and 1963 gave it considerable power to influence the regional distribution of industry. It supervises the work of the Monopolies Commission and the registrar of restrictive trade practices; and it carries on a variety of other activities ranging from the operation of the jute control to cooperation with the British Productivity Council. Finally, the department is concerned with overseas trade. It negotiates trade and commercial relations with foreign countries; it provides information and advice to exporters; it organizes British participation in trade fairs and exhibitions. The department is also responsible for the work of the Export Credits Guarantee Department, which provides credit insurance for British exporters.

(W. Bk.; N. Cu.; M. J. A.)

3. Currency and Banking.

—*The Pound Sterling.*—The monetary unit of the United Kingdom is the pound sterling, and its origins go back to Anglo-Saxon times when a pound (Tower) weight of silver was coined into 240 pennies. From the 14th to the 18th century gold and silver both circulated, their relative prices at the mint being changed to meet changes in their market values. During the 18th century, however, silver was consistently undervalued at the mint and largely disappeared from circulation; the gold guinea (21s.) became the main coin.

After a period of inconvertible bank notes from 1797 to 1821, the currency was again based upon gold with the sovereign (20s.) and half-sovereign as the principal coins. The silver and copper coinage was reduced to token money. From the 14th to the 18th century gold and silver were coined into 240 pennies. The smallest denomination was £5. In 1833 Bank of England notes were made legal tender. In 1844 (1845 for Scotland) the note issues of all other banks were limited in amount, and further restrictions eventually caused the English banks to cease issuing notes altogether.

The Bank of England was allowed to issue a fixed amount (known as the fiduciary issue) against government securities, and all further issues had to be covered pound for pound by gold or silver. Legally, silver could amount to one-fifth of the bank's total bullion stock, but in fact the bank held very little. An important consequence of this system was that the total supply of legal-tender money (gold and Bank of England notes) varied with, and only with, the inflow or outflow of gold resulting from changes in the balance of international payments.

During World War I gold coin was largely displaced by currency notes issued, in virtually unlimited amounts, by the Treasury through the Bank of England. Gold never circulated again, but the essence of the old system was restored by limiting the amount of currency notes (1919), making notes convertible into gold bullion at the old price (1925), and turning over the currency note issue to the Bank of England (1928). In 1931, however, the gold standard was again suspended and since then bank notes have not been convertible into gold.

In 1939 the Bank of England's gold stock was transferred to the exchange equalization account and, from then on, the whole note issue was backed by government securities. Formally, the amount of the issue was still fixed by Parliament, and the Currency and Banknotes Act of 1954 set a limit of £1,575,000,000. The Treasury was, however, given authority to sanction variations and by the early 1970s levels approaching £4,000,000,000 had been reached.

The currency was put on a decimalized basis in February 1971. The pound was retained as the main unit but became divisible into 100 new pennies. The changeover required the introduction of new coinage but note supply arrangements did not have to be altered.

After the suspension of the gold standard in 1931, the pound remained convertible into other currencies but at fluctuating rates. During World War II its international value was pegged on the basis of a dollar rate of $4.03, with all exchange traffic strictly controlled. This situation continued during the initial postwar phase, an attempt to return to formal convertibility with U.S. backing in 1947 collapsing within a few weeks. After the payments problem had been eased by a devaluation of the pound to $2.80 in 1949, the authorities gradually relaxed exchange controls, formal convertibility into all other currencies for current account purposes being finally restored at the end of 1958.

Thereafter the use of sterling as an international currency greatly increased. The British payments position remained basically weak, however, and after a series of crises during which controls on capital movements—which had never been wholly withdrawn—were tightened up, there was a new devaluation to $2.40 late in 1967. Thereafter the payments position moved into substantial surplus and, with reserves advancing to record levels, the pound developed considerable strength. During the international currency crisis that followed the U.S. decision in August 1971 to suspend all convertibility of the dollar, sterling was put on a floating basis. Under an interim international monetary reform agreement concluded four months later, it was given a new parity increasing its U.S. dollar value by 8¼%. But it was floated again in June 1972 after a capital flight from London had seriously eroded U.K. reserves. (*See also* MONETARY UNIT; STERLING AREA.)

Commercial Banking.—The Bank of England (*q.v.*) was founded in 1694 and shortly afterward was granted a monopoly of joint stock banking. Other banks were restricted to a maximum of six partners; but the discovery of new banking techniques, including the check system of deposit banking, encouraged their development and many hundreds of small private banks were formed during the succeeding century. The system was shown, however, to be unsound by the excesses of many of them and in 1826 and 1833 new laws ended the Bank of England's monopoly.

Many other joint stock banks subsequently came gradually to dominate the commercial banking field, absorbing many of the private banks in the process. Toward the close of the 19th century they themselves began to amalgamate to form much larger units. Shortly after World War I the point was reached at which the great bulk of the country's commercial banking business was concentrated in the hands of the "Big Five" London clearing banks,

and the authorities then called a halt until the late 1960s when the two smallest were allowed to amalgamate. In Scotland, commercial banking development was based from an early stage on a relatively modest number of substantial joint stock banks. But some of these combined in the mid-20th century to form larger units, while others became closely associated with London clearing banks.

Other Banks.—Many of the merchant banks that came into being in the earlier phases of banking development survived the rapid growth of competition from joint stock banks in the 19th century, mainly owing to their ability to offer more specialized services. Their development was greatly slowed down, however, until after World War II when changes in economic and financial conditions provided them with opportunities for rapid expansion; and by the late 1960s their share of U.K. banking was much larger than it had been earlier in the century. The same period produced a considerable upsurge in the activity of British overseas banks and accepting houses and the U.K. branches of foreign banks, hinging on London's emergence as the centre of the rapidly developing Euro-currency traffic.

The business of the merchant banks, accepting houses, British overseas banks, and foreign banks operating in London has, broadly speaking, much more of an international character than that of the commercial banks. The deposits of all institutions in these categories exceeded £30,000,000,000 by the early 1970s, of which more than half represented overseas funds. Some 60% of this was employed in advances and most of the remainder in cash, bills, and other liquid assets.

Another group of institutions that began to play a part of key importance in the British banking system in the 19th century were the discount houses. By providing a market for call money, for bills of exchange, and short-dated government securities, they help the major banks to deal with day-to-day variation in their resources. Some changes were made in 1971 in the arrangements under which they influence the money market, notably by their participation in the weekly tender for Treasury bills. This role remains important and continues to ensure them privileged access to the Bank of England as "lender of last resort" for adjusting their daily positions.

The Development of Central Banking.—At an early stage in its life the Bank of England established itself as banker to the government. Its emergence as banker to other bankers was slower to get under way but was greatly speeded up after the termination of its commercial banking monopoly in 1833 and the strengthening of its structure under the act of 1844.

Subsequently it also began gradually to assume such other central banking functions as custodian of official exchange reserves and controller of domestic banking activity. In the earlier stages a central feature of the techniques employed to execute these new tasks was the manipulation of bank rate to influence the behaviour of interest rates and the use of open market operations to keep the supply-demand relationship for money in the country at large in harmony with the national interest. After usury law restrictions on bank rate were removed in 1833, it was varied in accordance with the requirements of the external payments situation, being raised when the bank was losing gold and lowered when it was gaining it at an unduly fast pace. Because the size of the reserve had a direct bearing on the volume of domestic credit, these variations significantly affected the home economy.

The system was largely suspended at the outbreak of World War I; but it was later decided to reinstate it, and, after the way had been cleared by a vigorous deflationary exercise, there was a full return to gold standard working in 1926. The crisis precipitated by the restoration of the prewar sterling-gold parity, however, led to its suspension again in 1931.

The adoption of a floating rate system ended the traditional close connection between the balance of payments and the domestic money supply, and, since it was decided that advantage should be taken of this to make money cheap as a means of alleviating unemployment, bank rate was reduced to 2% and kept there. After a brief increase on the outbreak of World War II the rate was restored to 2% to help wartime financing and, after peace returned, for assisting rehabilitation. The Bank of England, which had been nationalized in 1946, had little more to do than ensure that supply and demand for credit were broadly kept in balance at interest rate levels corresponding to the current bank rate.

This phase ended in 1951 when it was decided to make more use of traditional credit controls in combating inflation. Initially, bank rate rose slowly, but the movement became more pronounced during the series of sterling crises that characterized the late 1950s and 1960s, levels of 7 to 8% being maintained for considerable periods. More use was also made of traditional methods of influencing the money supply through pressure on the credit base. These were only partially successful, and after the early 1960s the bank made considerable use of a new liquidity control weapon—its right to call on the commercial banks for special deposits as well as loans ceiling directives.

In view, however, of the malfunctioning of this system and the rapid growth of overseas bank and "parallel banking" institutions largely beyond its reach, a comprehensive mechanism was introduced in 1971. The new arrangements, treating all banks and comparable institutions alike for credit control purposes, were designed to make official policy felt primarily through the manipulation of interest rates and its impact on the banks' assets, preferences and reserve positions and thence on the total supply of money; consequently, the loans ceiling procedure was discontinued.

With slight variations, each institution is required to maintain a minimum ratio of $12\frac{1}{2}\%$ of "eligible reserve assets" to "eligible liabilities" and, in addition, to place a stipulated proportion of its funds in special deposits with the Bank of England on the same uniform basis when called on to do so. "Eligible assets" comprise cash, Treasury bills, or other paper that the Bank of England will turn into cash. "Eligible liabilities" comprise short-term sterling deposits and sterling certificates of deposit.

Rather more than half of the resources of the commercial banks come from non-interest-bearing current account balances used for check and credit transfers—the means whereby most money transmission, other than for wages and retail trade, is arranged. The remainder consists largely of time deposits, earning interest but subject to seven-days' notice of withdrawal or other limitations. In 1971, the "cartel" establishing a uniform maximum rate for such money was abolished.

Since the 1971 reform greatly reduced the proportion of resources the banks needed to hold in liquid form, they were required to devote the surplus to buying £750,000,000 government stock. This raised the proportion of assets employed in this form to 17%. (It had previously dropped to 10%, having averaged 50% during the first decade after World War II.)

Some 50-60% of the banks' funds are employed in advances. These are usually made on the overdraft principle, interest being paid only on the amount of the loan actually in use and at rates fluctuating in line with Bank Rate. From the late 1950s on, however, the banks engaged in fixed-term lending at predetermined rates for personal customers and business borrowers requiring finance not repayable on demand, as overdrafts normally are. (*See also* BANKING.)

4. National Finance.—*Origins of the Modern System.*—Many important features of the British system of national finance date from the struggles between crown and Parliament during the 17th century. The Bill of Rights (1689) finally established that the crown could levy only such taxes as had been granted by Parliament, and at about the same time it became usual for Parliament to "appropriate" money for specific purposes. The distinction was also introduced between the civil list (*q.v.*), which included the salaries of judges and other officers of state and (until 1820) the personal expenditure of the sovereign, and the supply services. Revenue for the civil list was granted to the sovereign for life but that for supply services was voted only from year to year. Thus, by the beginning of the 18th century, Parliament had to be called every year, and it had achieved a double measure of financial control through supply votes and through appropriation.

During the 18th century the main sources of revenue were taxes on land and houses and a great variety of customs and excise duties. These taxes covered peacetime expenditure but failed to meet the growing cost of wars, and so there arose a permanent national debt. Sovereigns had often borrowed for short periods in the past, but the permanent debt dates from the issue of £1,000,000 of life annuities in 1692. Two years later a group of merchants lent £1,200,000 in return for a charter of incorporation as the Bank of England. By 1715 the debt had reached £54,000,000, and it grew to £138,000,000 in 1763 and £249,000,000 in 1781. Several attempts were made to reduce the debt by means of sinking funds, and in 1785 William Pitt the younger appointed a body of commissioners for the reduction of the national debt, who were to receive £1,000,000 a year for the purchase of government bonds. The 18th century also brought a number of administrative changes including: the emergence of the chancellor of the Exchequer as the minister responsible for finance; the amalgamation of a number of government bond issues into a single issue of consolidated bank annuities (generally known as "consols"); a similar fusion of the many separate revenue accounts to form the consolidated fund; and the appointment of commissioners to audit the public accounts.

The wars of 1793-1815 were on a far larger scale than any previous conflicts. Government expenditure rose from less than £20,000,000 to more than £100,000,000 a year and, by the end of the war, probably amounted to between one-quarter and one-third of the national income. In the early years only a small part of this rise in spending was met by additional taxation, but Pitt introduced an income tax and this, together with heavier indirect taxation, raised revenue to £83,000,000 by 1814-15. The financial laxity of the early years had, however, started an inflation which persisted until the end of the war, when the general level of prices had roughly doubled. The rise in prices was sustained by an increased issue of paper money following the suspension of gold payments by the Bank of England in 1797. The relationship between this and the rise in prices was the subject of a famous controversy. It was generally agreed, however, that excessive government borrowing from the Bank of England had been a cause both of the suspension and the rise of prices and, in 1819, an act was passed forbidding the bank to lend to the government for more than three months at a time without the authority of Parliament. The war made necessary very large borrowing at high rates of interest. By the end of the war the debt had grown to £846,000,000, involving an annual charge of £32,000,000. In relation to national income, the debt was about as great as, and the annual charge much greater than, that left by World War II.

The 19th Century.—The fall in prices after 1815 raised the real value of the national debt and reduced the yield of taxes, and the budgetary position was aggravated when Parliament insisted on repealing the unpopular income tax in 1816. Gradually, however, the growing wealth of the country made itself felt and the difficulties of the chancellor diminished. Although government expenditure rose from about £50,000,000 a year in the 1840s to an average of £180,000,000 during 1911-13, national income was growing even faster. The rise in government spending in the late 19th century was largely due to defense, which took £77,000,000 out of a total budget of £197,000,000 in the fiscal year 1913-14. Debt services, at £25,000,000, cost less than in 1815, but new forms of spending in the social services included compulsory elementary education, old-age pensions (1908), employment exchanges (1909), and the beginnings of health and unemployment insurance (1911). The share of the central government in the cost of these services was more than £32,000,000 in 1913-14.

By the Corn Law of 1815 import duties were reimposed on grain, though here the motive was mainly protective; however, disciples of Adam Smith were waging a campaign for free trade and were steadily gaining influence. Duties were reduced and simplified in the budgets of 1842 and 1845; the Corn Laws were repealed in 1846; and the movement to free trade was continued and virtually completed in the budgets of 1853 and 1860, for which W. E. Gladstone was responsible as chancellor of the Exchequer. To make up for the loss of revenue on import duties, Sir Robert Peel reimposed the income tax in 1842. This was intended to be temporary, but the tax was never again removed, though it was reduced to only 2d. in the pound in 1874. Toward the end of the century, rising expenditure made it necessary to seek additional revenue, and public opinion was coming to favour the

(C. G. T.)

use of taxation as a means of reducing extreme inequalities of income. Estate duties, graduated according to the value of property left at death, were introduced in 1894. The standard rate of income tax was raised, with reduced rates for earned income (1907) and concessions for dependents, and in 1909 David Lloyd George introduced the supertax on incomes of more than £5,000 a year. This budget was rejected by the House of Lords but was passed in 1910. The Parliament Act of 1911 deprived the Lords of the power to reject a money bill. By 1920 the limit above which surtax was payable had been reduced to £2,000, but it reverted to £5,000 for earned incomes in 1963.

Throughout the 19th century governments tried to provide a surplus of revenue over current expenditure which could be used to repay debt and, in spite of new borrowing during the Crimean War and the South African War, the debt had been reduced to just under £650,000,000 by 1914. Interest charges were also reduced by several conversions, the most important being that of G. J. Goschen in 1888, which created 2¾% consols (consolidated annuities). Another development, minor at first but very important for the future, was the Treasury bill. These bills were first issued in 1878 and were modeled on the commercial bills of exchange that the London discount market specialized in discounting.

The Finance of World War I.—World War I raised government spending from less than £200,000,000 a year to a peak of nearly £2,700,000,000 during 1917–18. This included expenditure abroad and loans to Allies, but government purchases of British goods and services amounted to nearly half the national income. Income tax was raised until the standard rate reached 6s. in the pound (1918) with a further 4s. 6d. of supertax on the highest incomes, and big increases in duties on alcohol, tobacco, tea, and sugar. The only important new source of revenue was an excess-profits tax imposed on all profits above a standard rate. This tax created many anomalies but succeeded in bringing into the Exchequer a considerable part of the windfall gains generated by wartime inflation.

The yield of taxation was very far from keeping up with the growth of government spending. Between two-thirds and three-quarters of total expenditure was met by borrowing, and the debt had risen to £6,142,000,000 by March 31, 1919. Three long-term loans were raised between November 1914 and February 1917 on terms increasingly unfavourable to the government. Subscribers to earlier issues were given rights of conversion into later ones, and so nearly all this borrowing became concentrated in the 5% war loan of 1917, which raised £998,000,000 in cash and £1,130,000,000 in conversions. These loans were very costly and also created difficulty in the money market, when such huge sums had to be transferred in a short time. For the rest of the war, therefore, the government relied on the sale of medium-term bonds "on tap," i.e., available at a fixed price in any amount and at any time, a system that had been used for Treasury bills since 1915. Other features of wartime borrowing were the large volume of Treasury bills and of "ways and means" advances, and the effort to stimulate small savings. Small savers were encouraged to make deposits with the post office and trustee savings banks, and a special security, the war savings certificate, was created for their convenience.

The scale of wartime borrowing was far greater than could have been met out of the normal savings of the public, and was bound to lead to inflation. As in the Napoleonic Wars, rising prices were sustained by an unlimited issue of paper money, though this time the notes were, technically, issued by the Treasury and not by the Bank of England. Although inflation was moderated by administrative controls, prices roughly doubled during the war.

The United Kingdom made large loans to its Allies and undertook the financing both of its own and many Allied purchases in neutral countries. Until March 31, 1919, £1,741,000,000 was lent, mainly to France, Italy, and Russia. Britain, in turn, had to raise money in the United States and neutral countries. More than £500,000,000 of British-owned securities were sold in the United States and loans were also raised in the New York market. After the United States entered the war (April 1917) these needs were met by intergovernment transactions, and £841,000,000 of the United Kingdom's £1,365,000,000 external debt at March 31, 1919, was a direct liability to the United States government.

The Interwar Period.—National finance after World War I differed in several ways from its prewar pattern. In the 19th century government expenditure had been about one-twelfth of the national income; between 1919 and 1939 it was about one-fifth. Before World War I the national debt formed only about 5% of all private property; wartime borrowing raised it to about 25%. Moreover, the debt was held to a much greater extent by banks and other financial institutions in the City of London, so that debt management became very closely linked with monetary policy.

The higher level of government expenditure was caused partly by debt charges but also by developments in the social services. Unemployment insurance was greatly extended in 1920, and in 1926 a contributory old-age and widows' pension scheme was introduced. These services were financed by contributions from employers, employees, and the state. The heavy unemployment that occurred in 1921 and again after 1929, however, made the insurance fund insolvent, and the government had to make good the deficit in addition to its normal contribution. In 1934 the fund was again put on a sound basis by limiting the duration of claims to insurance benefits, and an Unemployment Assistance Board was created to provide for those who had exhausted their insurance rights. This was entirely financed by the government. Expenditure on education also rose and, in the financial years 1935–36 to 1937–38, these services cost an average of £264,800,000 out of a total annual budget of £887,900,000.

The excess-profits tax was repealed after World War I and the duties on tea, coffee, cocoa, and sugar were much reduced. Income tax never fell below 4s. in the pound, though changes in allowances gave further relief to lower incomes. Supertax (now known as surtax) was reduced at the lower and raised at the higher end of the scale. Estate duties and the taxes on alcohol and tobacco continued, with slight variations, at above their wartime level, and a new tax on hydrocarbon oils became an important source of revenue with the growing demand for gasoline. The other main tax change was the abandonment of free trade in 1931, when a general tariff was imposed on manufactured and semimanufactured goods. The tariff was intended for the protection of home industry rather than the raising of revenue, but it yielded £35,000,000 in 1938–39.

At the end of the war the national debt included more than £1,500,000,000 of Treasury bills and ways and means advances. A main object of debt management was to reduce these short-term liabilities (known as the floating debt) and especially to free the government from the need to raise short-term loans from the Bank of England. At first the policy, known as funding, had little success, for rising interest rates made it difficult to sell bonds. After the middle of 1921, however, interest rates began to fall, and in the next few years several medium- and long-term bond issues were made. The abandonment of the gold standard in 1931 was followed by a further fall in interest rates. High rates were no longer needed to protect the gold reserve, and the severe economic depression called for very low rates to stimulate industry and trade. Bank rate was reduced to 2% in June 1932 and remained there (apart from a brief period at the beginning of World War II) until November 1951. The first result of this cheap money policy was the conversion of the huge 5% war loan to a 3½% basis. By this time the funding program had been pressed so far as actually to create a scarcity of short-term assets in the London money market and the yield on Treasury bills fell to only about ¼%. These changes reduced the annual charge on the debt from £350,000,000 in 1920 to only £212,000,000 in 1934, but there was little net repayment of capital, and the nominal value of the internal debt was £7,247,000,000 on March 31, 1939.

The main item in the external debt was the loan from the U.S. government. By 1923 this amounted, together with accrued interest, to nearly $4,000,000,000. To set against it, the United Kingdom had nearly double this amount in loans to dominions and Allies and its share of German reparations. In 1923 an agreement was made for the repayment of the U.S. loan, with interest, over a period of 62 years by annual installments of $162,000,000 for the first ten years and $184,000,000 thereafter. The international economic crisis led to a one-year moratorium (the Hoover Moratorium) in June 1931. Germany did not resume reparations payments, and the United Kingdom, unable to collect from its debtors, made token payments on the U.S. loan until December 1933 and then ceased. (*See* WAR DEBT.)

Another result of the 1931 crisis was the setting up of the exchange equalization account. The account, which is managed by the Bank of England as agent for the Treasury, was intended to preserve some degree of stability in the foreign exchange market after the abandonment of the gold standard. In 1939, the whole national gold reserve was transferred to the account.

The Finance of World War II.—World War II made even larger demands on resources than World War I. Government expenditure rose from £927,000,000 in 1938–39 to £6,179,000,000 in 1944–45. During the war government spending took up about half the national product, a proportion only reached at the peak of World War I. Production was increased by absorbing the unemployed and by the work of married women and others not normally in paid employment, but it was also necessary to make big cuts in consumption and new investment, and to postpone repairs and replacements of all but the most essential capital equipment.

The use of real resources was governed by administrative controls including the rationing of consumer goods, the allocation of materials, the conscription and direction of labour, state purchase of many imports and regulation of others, control over borrowing, and the fixing of maximum prices. In these circumstances financial policy had two functions: to keep down private spending power so as to reduce the temptation to evade administrative controls, and to facilitate borrowing by the government.

In both these respects policy was much influenced by the work of J. M. (later Lord) Keynes. It was largely due to Keynes that the first official estimates of national income were published in 1941 and used by the chancellor of the Exchequer to calculate the 'inflationary gap." In wartime, with the government virtually the only borrower, the gap can be regarded as the difference between government borrowing and the savings that would be voluntarily forthcoming out of the current level of income. The presence of a positive gap therefore means that the government is creating additional purchasing power and that total spending, public and private combined, exceeds the current value of the goods coming onto the market, thus exerting a strong upward pressure on prices and undermining the system of controls.

For this reason the government imposed drastic increases in taxation. By 1941 income tax had been raised to 10s. in the pound, with a further 9s. 6d. in surtax on the highest incomes. Allowances were reduced and the rise in prices and wages brought many more people into the tax-paying range. Collection was simplified by the adoption of the "pay-as-you-earn" system in 1940. The excess-profits tax was reimposed, and raised to 100% in 1940, and there were heavy increases in the duties on alcohol, tobacco, and entertainment. The only important new tax, which remained a feature of postwar finance, was the purchase tax imposed on a wide range of luxury and semiluxury goods. Part of the increased income tax payments resulting from the 1941 budget and part of the excess-profits tax were credited to the taxpayers as "postwar credits," a form of compulsory saving that had been advocated by Keynes. Another aspect of war finance was the paying (from 1941) of subsidies on food in order to stabilize the cost of living, in return for which the trade-union leaders promised to moderate demands for wage increases.

The cornerstone of government borrowing policy was the continuance of cheap money. The fiduciary note issue of the Bank of England was raised whenever necessary, so that once again the country had a virtually unlimited supply of paper money. The Bank of England, in turn, provided the banks and the money market with unlimited liquid assets by being always willing to buy Treasury bills at a fixed rate, and the yield on bills was thus stabilized at 1%. The Treasury also borrowed directly from the banks by means of a new security, the Treasury deposit receipt. There was no repetition of the World War I attempt to market large blocks of long-term bonds. Instead, a number of short- and medium-term issues were offered on tap. There were three issues of 3% savings bonds with lives of 24–30 years, which realized £2,779,000,000, and six issues of 2½% national war bonds with

lives of 6–10 years, which brought in £3,400,000,000. The appeal to small savers was even more successful than in World War I. Besides savings bank deposits and savings certificates, the small saver was offered a defense bond, and these three media raised no less than £3,908,000,000. The total internal debt had grown to £23,-372,000,000 by March 31, 1946.

The finance of overseas purchases was again a major problem, with the supply of U.S. dollars as its focal point. Despite the requisitioning and sale of British-owned investment, reserves were virtually exhausted by the time the U.S. Congress sanctioned the arrangement known as lend-lease in 1941. The U.S. government was enabled to provide supplies without immediate payment, ultimate settlement to take the form of any benefit, direct or indirect, that the president might consider satisfactory. When the United States entered the war, the British government reciprocated by providing certain supplies and services for U.S. forces. Heavy expenditure was also incurred in other areas, particularly India and the Middle East, and was met partly by the sale or repayment of British-owned securities and partly by the accumulation in the hands of creditor countries of short-term credits (sterling balances) in London. The total loss of overseas assets and creation of new overseas liabilities between September 1939 and June 1945 was £4,198,000,000.

(E. V. MN.)

Postwar Financial Problems.—The damage inflicted by World War I on the immense financial strength the U.K. had developed in the 19th century was carried much further by World War II. Attempts to achieve rehabilitation made such slow progress in face of the rapid rise in government expenditure, inflation, and balance-of-payments deficits that the situation remained difficult during most of the ensuing quarter of a century, the pound twice over, although the second cut in the pound eventually produced—in 1949 and 1967—to secure relief. Moreover, although the second cut in the pound eventually produced a large surplus in the balance of payments, economic management continued to present considerable problems owing to the difficulty experienced in turning the improvement to account for promoting economic advancement, which had been at a slower pace in Britain through the 1945–70 period than in other industrialized countries. The four main issues of government concern were the budget, external payments, debt management, and the creation of an environment conducive to faster economic growth.

Defense spending fell sharply between the end of World War II and 1950. Thereafter it rose steadily, partly because of the fall in the value of money but also because it became more expensive to keep armed forces abroad after the independence of former colonial territories. The sterling crisis of 1964, however, led to a big effort to hold down all defense outlays and this was subsequently assisted by the decision to scale down drastically Britain's defense commitments overseas. Thus, in constant money terms, defense allocations in the early 1970s were a little below those of ten years earlier.

In the external-payments field the British authorities were confronted with a major financial problem when the wartime lend-lease arrangement with the U.S. was ended in September 1945. During the war, income from foreign investments, shipping, and other invisible exports had been severely eroded and the merchandise export trade greatly reduced. Late in 1945 Britain agreed to pay the U.S. $650,000,000 for supplies shipped after the war, while the U.S. made available a loan of $3,750,000,000 bearing interest at 2% and repayable over 50 years.

Most of the money received, however, was used up in 1947 in an attempt, in accordance with the terms of the U.S. loan, to reestablish the pound on a fully convertible basis. Thereafter, the inadequacy of the U.K.'s external reserve, and its consequent vulnerability to external capital flows, became a major problem, especially as the excessive buoyancy of imports brought the current account of the balance of payments into serious deficit every few years. Both in 1949 and 1967 the British authorities failed to contain exchange-market pressures generated by the resultant run on the pound and were obliged to devalue.

The problem presented by the country's vulnerability to movement of capital was accentuated by the fact that Britain's short-term indebtedness to foreign countries in respect of the sterling balances held in London had been increased very considerably by British wartime spending abroad. At the end of 1945 these liabilities totaled £3,660,000,000. Later the ownership of the balances changed materially, but the total remained virtually static until the early 1960s. Thereafter, another large increase took place, owing in part to the official policy of encouraging the use of London as an international financial centre, in part to the tendency for the balance-of-payments deficit to be financed by running up sterling debts, and in part to the growth of the practice of borrowing money from foreign central banks to reinforce the U.K. reserves. In the early 1970s British indebtedness abroad on sterling balances account was of the order of £7,000,000,000, of which about half was in respect of the official reserves of sterling-area countries.

Heavy borrowing to finance military spending produced another large increase in the national debt during World War II and this continued to rise fairly rapidly until the late 1960s owing to government borrowing to finance the nationalization of public utilities, the extensive development programs of the nationalized industries, and other public sector capital spending. Thereafter, the movement slowed down, due in part to the increasing inflow of money to the Exchequer arising from the repayment of earlier public-sector loans and in part to government endeavours to achieve an overall balance in the budget accounts. Even so, the total debt was about £33,000,000,000 by the early 1970s.

The constant necessity to raise new money to refinance maturing parts of the debt greatly complicated the task of implementing government monetary policy, especially after the London market became more exposed to international capital market influences in the 1960s, debt management considerations being apt to conflict with the requirements of broad economic policy. After much controversy it was decided in the early 1970s that much less importance should be attached in the formulation of interest rates policy to management implications for debt financing.

Local Government Finance.—Local authority financial activities were greatly curtailed by the nationalization after World War II of many of their public utility and trading services. In 1947 poor relief was transferred to the National Assistance Board, a central government institution (since 1966 incorporated in the Ministry of Social Security). The most important activities remaining in the hands of local authorities were education, housing, highways, police, fire brigades, and certain public-health functions.

In 1967 about one-quarter of local authority expenditure was met by revenue from properties owned by them, the remainder in roughly equal proportions by central government grants and rates charged on the rental value of land and buildings in their areas. Most local authorities were heavily involved in housing development during the postwar period, and the raising of the money required for this and similar purposes caused them considerable financial difficulty after the late 1950s, when they ceased to be entitled to borrow from the government-operated Public Works Loan Board. They subsequently became heavy borrowers on mortgage loans and also developed an extensive money market business. After the early 1960s, however, such activities became increasingly subject to central government control owing to the frictions they generated in the money market, while local authorities were also given wider access to central government funds.

Changes in Financial Policy.—The period following World War I greatly affected the part played by national finance in Britain's economy. Until that time the sole aim of the budget was to ensure that government spending on defense and debt charges was fully covered with some margin for debt redemption. The intention was that the taxes levied for this purpose should interfere as little as possible with the functioning of the free market economy. Such official economic management as there was made use primarily of monetary instruments like bank rate.

Arguments favouring the use of the national financial machinery in general and the budget in particular as a deliberate instrument of policy, as advocated by Keynes, had achieved a certain popularity in the 1930s, and they came to be generally accepted after 1945. It then became official practice to use the budget both for influencing the economic climate—for example, to damp down

business activity when it was tending to rise to an inflationary level —and to diminish the disparities between rich and poor. In consequence, whereas in the 19th century the budget covered only about one-twelfth of the national income, by the late 1960s it was absorbing about one-third. By that time, however, the process had reached a point at which it was thought to be inhibiting economic growth, and the first steps to arrest it were taken.

When the Labour government took over in 1964, it established a Department of Economic Affairs with the intention of adapting the economic management machinery in order to promote economic growth. However, recurring balance-of-payments trouble hindered the reorientation, and in the late 1960s overall control of economic policy still appeared to reside in the hands of the Treasury, with the new department taking a secondary role. The Conservative government elected in 1970 being committed to allowing "market forces" to play a bigger role, the Ministry was disbanded as part of a general reconstruction of the economic administration machinery, which also produced a Department of Trade and Industry and a Ministry for the Environment.

The vulnerability of the pound to external capital movements resulted in the country's international-banker functions coming under close scrutiny during the 1960s. From 1964 on, official policy was directed at reducing the use of London as a source of long-term capital for overseas development. Steps also were taken to reduce the country's vulnerability to payments pressures on account of the sterling balances problem; but official policy continued to encourage the development of London as an international market for financial traffic denominated in other currencies.

(C. G. T.)

5. Taxation.—Taxes in the U.K. fall into three major groups: taxes upon income, upon capital, and upon expenditure (indirect taxation). Various government departments administer the taxation system, those principally concerned being the Board of Inland Revenue, which collects the taxes upon income and capital and the stamp duties, and the Board of Customs and Excise, which collects the most important taxes upon expenditure.

Taxes Upon Income.—Income tax is levied at a standard rate of assessment, according to five different schedules depending upon the source of income. The tax is graduated by means of various allowances for family and other responsibilities, and earned income is taxed less heavily than other income, as earned-income relief is allowable. Income tax is deducted at source wherever possible, and most employees pay their income tax on a Pay-as-you-earn (PAYE) system, by which employers deduct the payments before paying salaries or other earnings.

Surtax is an additional graduated tax payable upon personal incomes which, after certain allowable deductions have been made, exceed £2,000 from all sources. The broad effect of these allowances is that surtax is generally not payable on earned income under £5,000. Income tax and surtax are assessed and collected separately, but basically they form part of a single scale.

Corporation tax, a single company tax upon profits, was introduced under the Finance Act, 1965, and replaced a dual system of income tax and profits tax. It is calculated essentially in accordance with income tax principles.

Taxes Upon Capital.—Estate duty is chargeable on the value of property (whether legally settled or not) that passes, or is deemed to pass, at death. The capital gains tax, introduced in 1965, relates to capital gains resulting from the disposal of assets after April 5, 1965. The short-term capital gains tax was abolished in 1971, after which tax on all capital gains became 30%.

Taxes on Expenditure.—These fall into the following groups: customs duties on imported goods, excise duties on home-produced goods and services, and purchase tax applicable to a wide range of home-produced and imported goods. Articles subject to customs and excise duties are usually free of purchase tax. Customs duties may aim at providing some measure of protection for home and Commonwealth products (a situation that will be affected by British entry into the EEC) or at raising revenue. There are revenue duties on tobacco, alcoholic drinks, hydrocarbon oils, betting, matches, and mechanical lighters. Other taxes on expenditure include the selective employment tax introduced in the budget of

May 1966, stamp duties, motor-vehicle duties, and licenses for various purposes, including television, motor vehicles, and dogs. The Conservative government elected in 1970 proposed to abolish completely purchase and selective employment taxes, substituting a single value-added tax. To reduce administrative costs an imputation tax and self-assessment by taxpayers, on French and U.S. models, respectively, also were proposed.

Rates.—Rates are taxes payable to the local authority and are based on the rateable value of real estate. The Rating Act, 1966, provided for rate rebates in certain cases where the applicant's income fell below certain limits. *See also* TAXATION.

(JE. D.; GA. S.)

C. TRANSPORT AND COMMUNICATIONS

1. Inland Transport Prior to 1939.—*Roads.*—Responsibility for roads for a long time had rested in the local parishes and there were few well-maintained national main arterials. In the heyday of the stagecoach demand for improved roads led to the formation of a number of privately financed turnpike trusts empowered to impose tolls on road users. With the coming of the railways in the 19th century their revenues were eroded and the roads reverted to a sorry state. Under the Local Government Act, 1888, responsibility for roads was vested in the local authorities, and not until the advent of the motorcar during the first decade of the 20th century was the construction and maintenance of a national road network considered as a central government responsibility. To finance the roads in 1909 the chancellor of the Exchequer, Lloyd George, imposed vehicle and fuel taxes. The Road Improvement Funds Act, 1909, set up a Road Board for the same purpose and new system of motor taxation was introduced and the Road Fund reconstituted. Subsequently much of its revenue was diverted from road expenditure to the Exchequer and financing of roads ceased to be by motor taxation through the Road Fund and was by direct Exchequer grant. The 170,000-mi. (274,000-km.) road network was classified into main trunk arterials designated Class I (24,000 mi. [39,000 km.]) and secondary roads Class II (15,000 mi. [24,140 km.]). By the Trunk Roads Act, 1936, the network was reclassified as trunk roads (4,456 mi. [7,171 km.]), Class I (23,089 mi. [37,157 km.]), Class II (17,634 mi. [28,861 km.]), and unclassified roads. The first became the direct responsibility of the Ministry of Transport, including their financing, and the remainder the responsibility of the local authorities. Financing of roads was by direct grant.

Railways.—The Stockton and Darlington Railway (38 mi. [61 km.] long), opened in 1825, was the first passenger-carrying public railway to use steam locomotives. The first important passenger railway, the Manchester and Liverpool, was opened in 1830. By 1838, when the link between Lancashire and London was completed, there were 89 railway companies and 500 mi. (805 km.) of track.

During the railway booms of 1836-37 and 1845-47 the companies proliferated. Fierce competition resulted in the first amalgamations. In the late 19th century, legislation was introduced to control the increasing potential monopoly of the railways. Great technical advances included the Severn Tunnel, the Forth Bridge, the development of electric traction, and the opening of the London Underground Railway. By 1913, 23,718 mi. (38,170 km.) of track had been constructed.

The government took control of the railways when war broke out in 1914. Claims for compensation were finally settled at £60,000,000. Under the act of 1919, which established the Ministry of Transport, the minister directed the railways pending more permanent controls. The act of 1894 had placed railway rates under the supervision of the Railway and Canal Commission established in 1886. A departmental committee of 1911 had counseled a "regulated extension of cooperation between railways rather than a revival of competition"; but the Railways Act of 1921 attempted to combine the benefits of amalgamation into large units with a detailed regulation of the railway's monopoly power.

Under the act the 120 companies were merged into four groups—Southern; Great Western; London, Midland, and Scottish; and London and North Eastern—so constituted as to include within each group both profitable and unremunerative lines. Supervision of charges was entrusted to a Railway Rates Tribunal.

Road-Rail Competition.—The railway amalgamations did not realize the far-reaching economies expected, and the new groups failed to earn the standard revenues laid down. This was partly because the general depression diminished staple traffic such as coal, but chiefly because of the rise of motor transport. This industry of small, highly competitive units, extremely flexible in operation, basing its charges on the costs of carriage, then confronted railway companies. The latter had been compelled for the most part to charge on the value of goods and were committed to extensive cross-subsidization of profitable and unprofitable traffic; they also were open to publication of charges, to public obligations, and, with a commercial outlook and staff, conditioned to operate in a framework of controlled monopoly. Motor transport made easy conquests of railway business, chiefly in the more valuable commodities. Competition from road-passenger transport was equally fierce. The Road Traffic Act of 1930 established a licensing system to control public-service vehicles and services, including routes, frequency, and fares.

A major step toward regulating road-rail competition followed. In 1932 the Salter Conference on road and rail transport recommended a licensing system and a registration duty for all goods vehicles. In 1933 the Road and Rail Traffic Act authorized area commissioners to grant three different types of licence: "A" for public carriers for hire, "B" for others, and "C" for traders carrying their own goods only. The last were issued on demand; applicants for "A" and "B" licences had to satisfy the commissioners that suitable transport facilities were not already available. For new or additional tonnage, applicants had to gather support from traders at a public hearing where witnesses could be examined by the railways or other objectors.

The railways were thus afforded some protection by restraining entry into road transport (which they themselves had been enabled to enter in 1928). Licensing, however, failed to prevent rapid growth of road-transport capacity and did not alter its competitive advantages. The railways were unable markedly to improve their financial position. By 1938, when railways carried 66,000,000 tons of general merchandise, minerals, and livestock in 1,200,000 freight cars, road vehicles numbered 500,000. The railways launched in 1938 a "Square Deal" campaign that sought relief from public control over charging and many of their public obligations; World War II forestalled any government action.

In 1933, the underground railways of London, already mainly controlled by the London Underground Group, were placed under the London Passenger Transport Board, together with all public road-passenger facilities (except taxis) in the London Transport Area.

Canals.—With the construction of the Bridgewater Canal to carry coal from Worsley to Manchester, opened to navigation in 1761, a period of intense canal construction began. A network of inland waterways was established that served the Industrial Revolution and contributed to Britain's prosperity in the 18th and 19th centuries. By linking the Mersey to the Trent the Grand Trunk Canal established a cross-England route, opened up the Midlands, and provided water transport for exports to Europe. The linking of the Thames to the Bristol Channel followed. This established Birmingham as the centre of a canal system that connected London, the Bristol Channel, the Mersey and the Humber, and stimulated its growth and prosperity. The Caledonian Canal across Scotland joining a chain of lakes was built between 1803 and 1822. The canals, however, had serious handicaps: goods were transported in narrow dumb barges, drawn mostly by horse along towpaths, and these had to be manually handled through the numerous locks and tunnels. Transport was excessively slow and the volume carried per unit was small. The railways, with greater carrying power and higher speed, inevitably encroached on the canals, bought out many of the canal companies cheaply, and closed down the larger part of the network—the canal era came to an end. The only major canal subsequently built was the 36-mi. (58 km.)-long Manchester Ship Canal opened to oceangoing vessels in the Mersey estuary in 1894. Following government control in World War I an official inquiry advised amalgamations and eight companies were merged into the Grand Union Canal linking London and the Midlands. By 1938 traffics had declined to 11,000,000 tons a year, around which figure they remained up to the 1970s.

Coastal Shipping.—Coastal trade expanded until 1913, when (excluding trade with Ireland) ships totaling 22,300,000 tons sailed from ports. Coasters successfully competed with railways for bulky cargoes such as coal and other minerals and bricks. During World War I coasters lost two-thirds of their prewar traffic. Afterward, further losses of heavy freight dependent on general industrial activity were limited by new locations of power industries, while the expansion in certain cargoes (notably oil) enabled coasters to regain their prewar tonnage by 1937. In 1936 tonnage carried was 38,000,000, of which 24,000,000 was still coal.

2. Inland Transport in World War II.—Railways and coastal shipping were taken under full government control at the outbreak and the more important canals in 1942; in 1943, 14,000 vehicles engaged in long-distance haulage came under direct government operation in the Road Transport Organization, while a further 20,000 vehicles were hired by the Ministry of Transport. The activity of buses and most of the 400,000 freight vehicles was regulated by allocations of fuel; some canal operations were subsidized; railway rates and (in part) road charges were regulated. The railways carried much of the increasing wartime traffic. By 1944 the number of freight vehicles in operation had declined by about 59,000, but freight traffic on the railways rose from 16,000,000 ton-miles in 1938 to 22,000,000 in 1945; passenger-miles from 1,237,000,000 to 1,373,000,000.

This expansion was achieved partly by restricting maintenance and the renewal of capital equipment; investment was confined to developments directly aiding wartime traffic. After 1945 many years were required to make good the depredations of track, rolling stock, and locomotives. Thus, although the railways were, by the end of the war, enjoying a greater share of traffic than for many years, their ability to consolidate their advantage was already limited. Road transport found shortages of materials and labour less hampering and could be made good more quickly.

3. Inland Transport after World War II.—Under the Transport Act, 1947, the postwar Labour government nationalized the railways, commercial long-distance road haulage, canals, and some docks and harbours. Responsibility was vested in the British Transport Commission (BTC), a public corporation, with the obligation to secure a "properly integrated system of public transport" and to pay its way taking one year with another. Management of the different nationalized modes was vested in executives appointed by the minister responsible. From the outset the BTC was handicapped by statutory obligations inconsistent with financial viability and by the exclusion from control of "C" licences, which greatly increased in number and encroached on rail traffic. Integration of the different transport modes, however, had made little progress when the Conservative government came to power in 1951 and changed policy.

The Transport Act, 1953, reversed the policy of integration by ownership and management. It provided for a large measure of denationalization of long-distance road haulage; relaxed the licensing system for goods vehicles to facilitate entry into commercial road haulage, and gave the BTC freedom to fix its charges subject to approval of a maximum by the Transport Tribunal. Subsequently the BTC's managerial structure was changed with the abolition of its executives, except London Transport, and the establishment of railway area boards. Restriction on their freedom to increase charges or close unremunerative services combined with increased road competition led to financial difficulties.

Denationalization of road haulage had proved difficult and disposal of vehicles was ended with the Transport (Disposal of Road Haulage Property) Act, 1956. Only 19,200 vehicles had been sold out of 29,200 offered and the nationalized British Road Services remained to operate some 15,000 vehicles. Meanwhile, goods vehicles increased in number and by 1956 some 1,120,000 vehicles were carrying 52% of all freight traffic. The position of the railways continued to worsen and the BTC, having made surpluses up to 1954, reported rising deficits, which by 1961 totaled £122,000,000, of which 65% represented service of capital. Reconstruction both of nationalized transport and its finances followed with abolition of the BTC, establishment of a British Railways Board (BRB), a Docks Board, an Inland Waterways Authority, and a Transport Holding Company to manage the residue of the BTC, including the British Road Services. Accumulated revenue losses of £400,000,000 were written off, £800,000,000 carried to a suspence account and £400,000,000 of interest-bearing capital retained. Under the Transport Act, 1962, certain restrictions on the railways were removed, including common-carrier obligations, and they became free to fix their charges. The minister's control over capital expenditure remained and some of his powers were strengthened. Meanwhile, a railway modernization plan launched in 1955 was carried out with diesel and electric traction replacing steam, signaling modernized, and freight services streamlined.

Following his appointment as chairman of BRB, Richard Beeching (later Lord Beeching) proposed reduction by stages of the railway network from 17,800 to about 8,000 route miles by closing unremunerative lines. Establishment of a liner train network of containerized services with special equipment and terminals also was planned. Later, following the return of a Labour government in 1964, a reassessment of the network resulted in a total of 11,000 route miles being retained to provide a network of main trunk services and the retention of lines required for economic or social purposes, to be subsidized out of public funds. The financial difficulties of the railways continued and the nationalized transport industry again was restructured under the Transport Act, 1968. By reducing the BRB's commencing capital debt to £300,000,000, authorizing grants for unremunerative services, infrastructure, and the cost of surplus track and other purposes, and by consolidating certain of the railway and road freight services in the National Freight Corporation (NFC), it was hoped to make the railways viable.

To the NFC were transferred the nationalized road haulage and majority interests in joint road/rail companies formed to operate the freight liner services and the railways freight sundries traffic and collection and delivery services. The NFC was made responsible for providing an integrated road and rail goods service with the railways, carrying those traffics it could as efficiently and economically as road. Further to restrict competiton from road traffic and aid the railways, a system of quantity licensing was to be introduced for long-distance road haulage, including those carrying on own account, the "C" licensees. A qualitative licensing system for management was provided for, to ensure the efficient operation of road haulage. The act also set up a National Bus Company (NBC) and a Scottish Transport Authority, to which were transferred the nationalized bus passenger undertakings, which between them, with the purchase of virtually all those remaining under private enterprise, had a practical monopoly of the major bus and coach services in the country. The NBC initially owned about 20,000 buses and became responsible for the basic network of services outside the main municipalities. The Scottish Transport Authority took over 5,000 buses and had a near monopoly of all road passenger services in Scotland. To coordinate all forms of passenger transport the act provided for Public Transport Authorities (PTA) to be established in the conurbations and major cities with most of their members appointed by the local authorities and others by the Minister of Transport. To them were to be transferred the municipal undertakings, and agreements had to be made with the NBC and BRB for services required from those bodies. Initially four PTAs were established in the conurbations of Greater Manchester, Merseyside, West Midlands, and Tyneside. The authorities were responsible for broad policy, and Public Transport Executives were appointed to operate the services. The authorities had power to precept on the rates to meet losses and maintain unremunerative services and the government could also make grants to them. On Jan. 1, 1970, London Transport with its monopoly of bus and underground railways was transferred to the Greater London Council and a London Transport Executive appointed to operate it. Its country bus and coach services were transferred to the NBC.

The Transport Act, 1968, had not been fully implemented with the change of government in 1970. The incoming Conservative government once again reversed certain aspects of the transport policy of its predecessor. Quantity licensing of long-distance road haulage ceased and in 1971 the licensing system that had been in force since 1936 was abolished and road haulage operators were free from applying to the Traffic Commissioners for "A," "B" or "C" licences and were enabled to operate as many vehicles on any routes they chose. "C" licencees previously confined to carry their own goods only were now permitted to carry for hire and reward on a parity with other operators. Qualitative licensing, however, was proceeded with. The existing PTAs were to be transferred to new local authorities. Initially some subsidies for uneconomic railway services were curtailed but later reinstated and infrastructure grants extended for rail and road passenger transport. It was proposed to dispose of some sections of the nationalized transport sector, mainly ancillary services. British Rail, having achieved surpluses in 1969 and 1970, had a deficit for 1971 and anticipated one for 1972, most of which the government would have to meet.

Meanwhile modernization progressed on British Railways, and by 1968 steam had been entirely replaced by high-powered diesel and electric traction. Electrification of the Southern Region system was completed and that of the main Euston to Manchester and Liverpool line, with its extension from Crewe to Glasgow authorized in 1971, as were north London commuter services from Moorgate/Kings Cross to Hertford and Hitchin. With its Intercity services linking the major cities, British Rail was operating the largest number of high-speed trains running up to 100 mph anywhere. Freight liner trains were serving the main industrial centres and ports. Modernization was paying off by the 1970s. The Intercity services increased their passenger carryings considerably, but economic conditions held back freight traffic and the liner train carryings were slow to develop. In the early 1970s technological advances being developed by British Rail included the Advanced Passenger Train (APT), with a potential speed on existing tracks and signalling of 125 mph, and tracked air-cushion vehicles. Modernization of urban transport was progressing with London Transport's fully automated Victoria Line coming into operation in March 1969 and extension of the Piccadilly underground line to London's Heathrow Airport and construction of the Fleet line authorized in 1971. In principle the construction of a rail tunnel under the English Channel linking England and France had been approved.

Roads.—Two measures paved the way for an improved national road network. A further 3,685 mi. [5,930 km.] of main roads were transferred to the Ministry of Transport under the Trunk Roads Act, 1946, and the Special Roads Act, 1949, enabled construction of motorways, but because of economic conditions the first motorway was not opened until 1958. Early in 1972, 1,000 mi. (1,609 km.) of motorways were under construction, with 1,839 mi. (2,959 km.) more planned.

Roads expenditure generally did not get underway until the 1960s and for economic reasons the program was periodically curtailed. In 1967 new procedures were established; both a firm program and a continuing preparation pool for trunk roads were to be built up, the latter to £1,350,000,000 for England by April 1971. A preparation pool was later established for "principal" roads also. In March 1969 the announced strategy for future trunk-road development in England was a total network of 2,000 mi. (3,218 km.) of high-class routes, costing £2,250,000,000, spread over 10 to 15 years. In May 1970 the proposals were revised and provided expenditure of £2,000,000,000 on the primary network over 15 to 20 years. By the 1970s, 90% of person-miles and 59% of all freight-ton-miles moved were on the roads.

Under the proposed reorganization of local government the 1,195 highway authorities for England, Wales, and Scotland were to be superseded by new county councils that would have responsibility for roads except trunk roads, which remained with the Ministry of Transport, and residential roads, for which District councils would be responsible.

4. Shipping.—Between 1870 and 1913 the British merchant fleet doubled in tonnage and, by substituting steam for sail, trebled its carrying ability. About 45% of world tonnage was British-owned, and British ships carried more than one-third of trade between foreign countries. During World War I more than one-third of British tonnage was lost and in the postwar period British owners faced pent-up demands; a sharp boom was followed by the 1921 slump. By 1939 the British Commonwealth proportion of the total mechanically propelled merchant shipping fleets was 30.9%, with a gross tonnage of 21,001,925; by 1970 the total British Commonwealth tonnage at some 36,000,000 gross was still the largest fleet in the world, although its share of world tonnage was only about 16%.

The chief features of postwar development in the British cargo-carrying merchant fleet included expansion in size and number of oil tankers, and of specialized bulk-cargo carriers, all-container, and roll-on/roll-off ships. The number of passenger ships declined with the increased competition from air services, and although Cunard replaced the Queen Mary and Queen Elizabeth I with the Queen Elizabeth II it ceased to run a regular year-round service across the North Atlantic in 1971. The Peninsular and Oriental Steam Navigation Company ceased to operate regular passenger services to the Far East in 1969 and to India in 1970; but many liners were diverted to holiday cruising. Consequent on these changes in both the composition of fleets and of services, the U.K. merchant fleet by the early 1970s was made up of 12,000,000 tons gross of oil tankers and whaling factory ships, 8,000,000 tons of passenger and cargo liners, and about 3,000,000 tons of tramp shipping. Container ships totaled 34 of 376,000 tons gross. The remainder comprised coastal and short sea shipping.

Many of the well-known British shipping companies were founded in the earliest days of steam navigation and some of them had even longer continuous histories. One of the largest shipping groups in the world is centred on the Peninsular and Oriental Steam Navigation Company, which in 1970 owned 240 vessels totaling 3,600,000 gross tons. The group also includes the Orient Line passenger services to Australia, New Zealand, and the Pacific Coast of North America and the refrigerated cargo-liner services to Australia and New Zealand, operated by ships of the New Zealand Shipping Company. It includes the Nourse Line, trading between the West Indies and India; the British India Steam Navigation Company, trading between Britain and India and East Africa, as well as to Australia and in the Indian Ocean; the Hain Steamship Company, engaged in worldwide dry-cargo tramping; and the General Steam Navigation Company, with a network of liner services ranging from the Mediterranean to the Baltic Sea. It also participates in the Oversea Containers consortium formed to operate container services between the United Kingdom and Australia.

The Cunard Line, apart from the Queen Elizabeth II irregular passenger service, operates cargo services on the North Atlantic routes and in 1970 owned a registered gross tonnage of over 600,000 tons. Cunard is also a constituent of the International Atlantic Container Consortium, which was operating both container and roll-on/roll-off ships between three U.S. ports, five ports on the West European continent, and two in the United Kingdom.

Of the Cunard affiliates, the Port Line sends refrigerated liners to Australia and New Zealand, and the Brocklebank Line sails to the Indian Ocean from Britain and the U.S. The Union-Castle Line operates passenger and cargo services to South and East Africa and in 1956 merged with the Clan Line, with its worldwide network of cargo-liner services, to form the British Commonwealth Shipping Company. The Furness Withy group owned in 1970 over 1,000,000 gross tons of shipping and controlled the Royal Mail Lines, operating passenger and refrigerated cargo-liner services to South America and cargo-liner services to the Caribbean and the Pacific Coast of North America, while their subsidiary, the Pacific Steam Navigation Company, operates passenger and cargo services o the west coast of South America; another member of the group, he Shaw Saville Line operates passenger and cargo services to Australia and New Zealand and its Ocean Steamship Company uns services to the Far East and Australia. Container services re operated by Manchester Liners to Canada and the U.S. tramp shipping companies tend to be larger in number and smaller in ize. Large tanker fleets are operated by major oil companies nd by a large number of independently owned and operated tramp anker companies. Of the 2,000,000,000 tons of freight moved annually in the U.K., about 5% was carried by coastal shipping n the early 1970s by a fleet of 310 ships of about 470,000 dwt. Of total carryings 14,000,000 tons represented the coasting coal rade.

Hovercraft.—The first regular hovercraft services began operating in 1967 and in August 1968 British Railways, with a 160-ton craft carrying passengers and cars, inaugurated a 30-minute cross-channel service between Dover and Boulogne, France. In 1972, during the peak holiday season, a total of 20 flights were operating on three cross-channel routes daily, as well as frequent daily services on two routes between the south of England and the Isle of Wight.

5. Air Transport.—Airlines were pioneered from 1919 onward by Britain and services between Britain, Europe, and the Commonwealth were developed after 1927 to increase the links with the empire. A government subsidy was paid from 1924 to 1935 to previously received grants-in-aid. By 1938 the empire airmail program embraced South and East Africa, India, Malaya, Australia, and Hong Kong. The principal expansion was in the European services, for which Imperial Airways received a decreasing subsidy in the 1930s. In 1936 the Air Ministry encouraged the independent British Airways, an amalgamation of three companies serving principally northwestern Europe. In 1939, Imperial Airways and British Airways were nationalized, becoming the British Overseas Airways Corporation (BOAC). In 1938 the government set up a licensing authority to control entry into domestic routes. Two additional public corporations were set up under the Civil Aviation Act, 1946: British European Airways (BEA) and British South American Airways (BSAA). Spheres of responsibility were divided between the three corporations with virtual monopoly for each of the British operators. BOAC took routes between the U.K. and other Commonwealth countries, the U.S., and the Far East; BEA took those between the U.K. and the continent of Europe and U.K. internal routes; and BSAA took routes between the U.K. and South America. In 1959 BSAA was merged with BOAC, which took over its South American services. In their early years all three corporations received large government subsidies, but these ceased for BOAC in 1951 and for BEA in 1955. The 1946 act also set up an Air Transport Advisory Council, the duties of which included consideration of representations regarding adequacy of facilities provided by the corporations and their charges. After a Conservative government took over in 1952 encouragement was given to independent operators and the Advisory Council assigned responsibility for deciding on applications for their operation. In exercising this new licensing function the ATAC's policy was to grant short-term licences to independents where the corporations' services were inadequate and to limit the frequency and quality of services where licences were granted on competitive routes. The rights of the independents to operate services were enhanced further by the Civil Aviation (Licensing) Act, 1960.

With the return of a Labour government in 1964 their operations again were restricted. Guidelines issued to the ATAC provided that in future only one British airline be licensed to operate on an international route and the independents cease operations in competition with BEA's domestic restricted routes. Restrictions on inclusive tours were relaxed for both the corporations and the independents. This change of policy enabled the corporations to convert deficits into surpluses and before 1970 BOAC had wiped out its accumulated deficit and had begun to build up reserves. Subsequently the fortunes of the corporation fluctuated, especially during exchange restrictions that curtailed travel, but over the years the traffics of both passenger and freight increased considerably. The near-monopoly of the corporations again was eroded following acceptance of the recommendations of the Edwards Committee (appointed by the Labour government) that a major "second force" airline be set up. It was proposed that the new private-enterprise airline be formed by merging the major independents and having allotted to it certain of the scheduled services of the corporations. In a White Paper, Labour accepted this recommendation except for the hiving off of any of the corporations' services; but before action was taken a Conservative government was elected. The two major independents, British United Airways and Caledonian Airways, merged into Caledonian-BUA to become the second force airline and were assigned a number of scheduled routes previously operated exclusively by the corporations, who vainly opposed the move. A British Airways Board (BAB) was appointed in 1971 to oversee the activities of the two corporations. Throughout, the public corporations conflicted with successive governments concerning purchase of aircraft, the appropriate minister exercising his directional powers on occasion. BEA, however, was the world's first airline to introduce both the British-built turboprop aircraft and BOAC the British-built Comet jet, which made the first scheduled North Atlantic jet flight. By 1970 BOAC was operating jumbo jets on many services and was planning the purchase of the Anglo-French supersonic Concorde. The BAB was assigned the task of decision making on future aircraft procurement by the corporations.

6. Northern Ireland.—By the early 1970s there were 14,109 mi. (22,706 km.) of public roads in Northern Ireland. The Ministry of Development was directly responsible for the trunk-road system and bore the entire cost of road maintenance and reconstruction. An extensive system of motorways also was planned, including an urban motorway system in Belfast. About 50 mi. (80 km.) were in use by the end of 1971. The Ministry of Development administered the Road Fund, from which grants were paid to the local authorities that were responsible for the other roads.

Gross expenditure on all roads by the early 1970s exceeded £18,000,000 annually. Gross capital expenditure planned for 1969–73 was about £75,000,000, compared with about £58,000,000 in the five-year period to 1968.

The reorganization of public transport in Northern Ireland was completed in 1968. Under the Transport Act (Northern Ireland), 1967, the Ulster Transport Authority was wound up and its assets and liabilities taken over by a new Northern Ireland Transport Holding Company. Northern Ireland Carriers Ltd. was formed jointly by the authority and the holding company to operate the road-freight services.

In February 1965 certain passenger and freight services on the railways were withdrawn and under the 1967 act responsibility for operating rail services on the remaining 200 mi. (322 km.) of track was transferred from the authority to the Northern Ireland Railways Co. Ltd., a subsidiary of the new holding company. The 1967 act provided for a licensing system for road-passenger operators to provide services in certain areas. Ulsterbus Ltd., a subsidiary of the holding company, took over the road-passenger services operated by the Ulster Transport Authority, which in the past had provided all public-road passenger services in Northern Ireland apart from Belfast city services. A number of privately owned bus undertakings operated services in certain areas.

See also the sections on *Transport and Communications* in the articles ENGLAND; IRELAND, NORTHERN; SCOTLAND; WALES; and the articles RAILWAY; ROADS AND HIGHWAYS; SHIPPING; TRANSPORTATION; WATER TRANSPORT, INLAND. (E. A. J. D.)

7. The Post Office.—A regular system for the carrying of mail within the United Kingdom by public posts was first introduced by royal proclamation of Charles I in 1635. Cromwell confirmed the state monopoly of letter mails by act of Parliament in 1657 and appointed the first "Postmaster General of England and Comptroller of the Post Office." Charles II, annulling all of Cromwell's acts, passed a similar statute in 1660, known as the charter of the Post Office. The Telegraph Act of 1868 authorized the postmaster general to take over the private inland telegraph services, and thereafter the Post Office began to develop cable telegraph services with the European mainland.

In 1912 it acquired all the assets of the National Telephone Company. By the 1960s it operated all inland telephone services, except those in Hull (Yorkshire) and the Channel Islands, which were operated locally under licence. The Post Office is also the operator in Great Britain of all international telecommunications services, including the transatlantic telephone cables to Canada and the U.S. The Post Office was also the U.K. instrument for the first Anglo-Canadian-U.S. transatlantic telephone cable. Subscriber Trunk Dialing (STD) within the U.K. was introduced at Bristol in 1958. By 1972 STD facilities were available to 8,940,000 subscribers on 3,670 exchanges and over 99% of all subscribers were connected to automatic telephone exchanges. Telex was operated by the Post Office from 1932. The first all-electronic public telephone exchange in Britain and the first of its kind in the world was opened on an experimental basis in 1962 at Highgate Wood, London. The first production electronic exchange in the world was brought into service at Ambergate, Derbyshire, in 1966.

The Post Office also provides services for the remittance of money and handles a wide variety of agency business for government departments, including the enforcement of broadcast receiving licensing for the Ministry of Posts and Telecommunications.

The National Giro, the current account banking service of the Post Office, opened in October 1968. All account records are kept in one place, the National Giro Centre at Bootle, Lancashire, where one of the largest complexes of modern computers and data processing equipment in Europe is used to process customers' instructions, keep accounts up-to-date, and produce daily statements. Anyone over the age of 15 can open an account with an initial deposit of £1. Paying someone by check costs 6p. Transfers between accounts, deposits, standing orders, cash withdrawals and stationery are free for customers who have their pay credited directly to their accounts. Otherwise it costs 8p to cash a check and 10p a pack for stationery and standing orders; transfers are free except for a 5p surcharge for debit transactions when the balance in the account is below £30. Payments into accounts by non-account holders cost 10p.

Organization.—In August 1966 the government announced its decision to transfer responsibility for the postal, telecommunications, and remittance services of the Post Office to a new corporation. From October 1, 1969, the office of postmaster general was abolished and responsibility for running the postal, telecommunications, and related services was transferred to the new public corporation known as the Post Office, which broadly corresponded to the public corporations that run the railways, the gas industry, and other nationalized public undertakings.

A new Ministry of Posts and Telecommunications was established, with responsibilities for (1) the functions of the former postmaster general in relation to frequency control and broadcasting, and (2) general oversight of the Post Office. A separate Department for National Savings (a government department responsible to Treasury ministers) was set up to administer the former Post Office savings service.

Responsibility for running the Post Office rests with the Board in its corporate capacity. Below Board level, apart from a small central headquarters, the Post Office is split into functional businesses responsible for running the postal, telecommunications, data processing, Giro, and remittance services, respectively. In the case of the two larger businesses (posts and telecommunications) there are separate headquarters, under a managing director, responsible for policy and oversight of operations. The country is divided into nine postal and nine telecommunications regions and one combined directorate for Northern Ireland. Each is controlled by a director or chairman who has wide devolved powers over expenditure, recruitment and personnel promotion. Postal regions are divided into head postmasters' areas and telecommunications regions into telephone areas.

The Data Processing Service has a London headquarters and six computer centres—three in London and one each in Derby, Portsmouth, and Edinburgh. It is organized into a Post Office Data Processing Service, providing a full range of services for the Post Office; and a National Data Processing Service, providing consultancy, training, and processing services for customers.

Finances.—From 1685 Post Office revenue formed part of the hereditary revenues of the crown and as such was at the personal disposal of the monarch. In 1711 part of the proceeds became payable to the Exchequer, and in 1760 the process was completed when, on the accession of George III, the hereditary revenues were surrendered to the state in return for a fixed "civil list." Post Office revenue was then paid into the Exchequer, net of expenses, until 1854 and thereafter as a gross sum, the expenses being drawn out again under parliamentary votes. This arrangement lasted until 1961, with a modification from 1956 which effectively permitted the Post Office to retain part of its profits after making a fixed annual contribution to the Exchequer. Legislation passed in 1961, in recognition of the commercial character of the Post Office, severed its finances from the Exchequer and transferred them to a fund under the management of the postmaster general. The Post Office Act, 1969, transferred to the new Post Office most of the assets and liabilities of the old. The Post Office has a statutory duty to "secure that its revenues are not less than sufficient to meet all charges properly chargeable to revenue account, taking one year with another." This general formula is based on that used in the acts setting up other nationalized industries. In practice the Post Office's financial policies are influenced by the financial targets agreed with the government. Separate targets are set for the postal and telecommunications businesses and the Data Processing Service. The postal target is expressed in terms of a percentage on expenditure, and the others in terms of a percentage return on net assets. With regard to capital investment, the Post Office is required to act in accordance with a general program settled from time to time with the approval of the minister of Posts and Telecommunications. As with other nationalized industries, nearly all the money borrowed by the Post Office for capital investment is loaned by the government; the Post Office has no power to issue stock or shares.

Overseas Telecommunications.—The first successful submarine telegraph cable was laid across the English Channel between Dover and Calais in 1850, and the laying of the first successful transatlantic cable, between the British Isles and Newfoundland, was completed in 1866. In 1922, when the Eastern and Associated Telegraph Companies, which then controlled a major part of the world's cable system, celebrated its jubilee, the total mileage of cable in the world was 325,000 (523,000 km.) and the capital invested in this one group alone amounted to £25,000,000, with a total for all companies of about £50,000,000.

In 1909 the Post Office took over from Lloyd's and Marconi's the ship-shore radiotelegraph services and from 1910 began to develop radiotelegraph services to Commonwealth and foreign countries. For several years before and after World War I there was severe competition between the cable and wireless companies. In 1924 the Marconi Wireless Telegraph Company secured a contract from the Post Office to provide beam wireless telegraphy stations for communication with Canada, Australia, India, and South Africa. A radiotelephone service was opened with New York in 1927 and was later extended to many other countries. In 1929 the "beam" radiotelegraph services, together with the Eastern Telegraph and associated overseas cable services, Marconi Wireless Telegraph Company, and the Pacific Cable Board, were amalgamated in Imperial and International Communications Limited (renamed in 1934 Cable and Wireless Ltd.), to operate most of the extra-European telegraph communications. On Jan. 1, 1947, the shares of Cable and Wireless Ltd. were transferred to the Treasury and in 1950 the governments of the Commonwealth countries took over the telecommunications assets, staff, and services in their respective territories—the company's assets in the U.K. being transferred to the Post Office. Cable and Wireless Ltd. continued to operate as a company owning 155,000 nautical miles of cable network, a fleet of cable ships, and all the cable and radio branches overseas, except those taken over by the Commonwealth countries. Telephoning between Great Britain and the rest of the world was developed exclusively by the Post Office, and telephone service is available to most places abroad and to ships at sea. In 1952 the operation of all international telecommunications services was made the responsibility of a Post Office External Telecommunication Executive.

During the immediate post-World War II period the Post Office laid several repeatered telephone cables under the North Sea, linking Great Britain with mainland Europe, and additional cables were laid for subsequent growth. In 1959 the first microwave radio system between Great Britain and France was brought into service and this also enabled television transmissions to be exchanged. In 1956 the Post Office, in conjunction with its counterparts in the U.S. and Canada, opened the first transatlantic telephone cable, repeatered every 44 mi. (71 km.). Traffic increased considerably after the opening of this cable and in 1961 Cable and Wireless Ltd. and the Canadian Overseas Telecommunication Corporation opened another telephone cable (known as CANTAT) linking the two countries. This was constructed of a new light-weight type of deep-sea cable designed by the Post Office. A third transatlantic telephone cable was laid in 1963 between Britain and the U.S.

Telephone operators in London can dial directly to subscribers in most countries in Europe and many countries in other parts of the world; a similar system exists in respect to direct access to subscribers on most automatic exchanges in the U.K. for operators in other countries. Subscriber-to-subscriber dialing between the U.K. and Europe was first introduced in 1963 with International Subscriber Dialling (ISD) from London to Paris; by 1971 the service was available to most subscribers in eight European countries, with further extensions in preparation. In 1968 the facility in the U.K. was extended to include subscribers in Birmingham, Edinburgh, Glasgow, Liverpool, and Manchester. The first ISD service beyond Europe from the U.K. was introduced in 1970 to New York City; in 1971 this was extended to cover the whole U.S. mainland. Subscribers in a number of European countries and in New York City have the ISD facility to dial directly to most subscribers in the U.K. Pictures, drawings, and diagrams can be transmitted to most overseas countries by telegraph carried by cable or radio. The Telex service enables business customers to communicate with customers abroad by means of teleprinters. Over 90% of calls are completed fully automatically.

The Post Office operates 12 coast radio stations for communication with ships at sea, for correspondence, weather, and distress services, and the "medico" services through which medical attention or advice can be obtained in case of illness or injury aboard. The Post Office took part in experiments carried out with the U.S. earthbound communications satellites (starting with Telstar, launched in July 1962) from the Post Office satellite communication ground station at Goonhilly Downs, Cornwall, with the U.S. provided by means of communication satellites. (T. DA.)

8. **Broadcasting.**—Broadcasting in the United Kingdom functions under powers conferred on the minister of Posts and Telecommunications by the Wireless Telegraphy Acts, consolidated in the act of 1949. There were two authorities: the British Broadcasting Corporation (BBC), established by royal charter in 1927, taking over the assets of the British Broadcasting Company, founded in 1922; and, until 1972, the Independent Television Authority (ITA), established by the Television Act of 1954. In a 1971 White Paper the government announced its intention of setting up a network of up to 60 local commercial radio stations as well as commercial television stations throughout the United Kingdom to be under the control of the Independent Broadcasting Authority (IBA), which would replace the ITA. The IBA came into existence on July 12, 1972.

In the United Kingdom, all users of television receivers must buy annual licences from the Post Office. A combined television and radio licence costs £7, with an additional £5 for colour television. The licence fee for radio only was abolished in 1971. By the early 1970s there were over 18,000,000 licences. Almost the whole of the BBC's income is derived from licence fees and is used mainly to pay for programs, studios, and transmitters. Programs broadcast under the auspices of the IBA are paid for by the sale of advertising time. The IBA appoints the program companies, owns and operates the transmitting stations, and is itself financed by annual rents paid by the companies.

In order to carry on its business of broadcasting as broadly stated under its royal charter, the BBC must acquire a licence from the minister of Posts and Communications. Subject to requirements laid down in the charter and in the Licence and Agreement, the BBC enjoys complete independence in its broadcasting. Responsibility for programs is borne by the Board of Governors, who are 12 in number and are appointed by the sovereign as trustees for the national interest. In Scotland and Wales responsibility is shared with the Broadcasting Councils for those countries. The BBC may not advertise or broadcast sponsored programs. It is required to refrain from broadcasting any opinion of its own on current affairs and matters of public policy and to be impartial in its treatment of controversy.

The BBC, which introduced the first regular television service in the world in 1936 and the first colour service in Europe in 1967, runs two television channels, BBC-1 and BBC-2. Program schedules are planned jointly to offer viewers a positive alternative. BBC-1 has been available for several years to over 99% of the population of the United Kingdom on the 405-line standard system, while BBC-2 was within reach of 87% of the population on the 625-line service on UHF by 1972. Both services transmit almost entirely in colour, using the PAL system.

In radio, the BBC operates four national networks. Radio 1 provides a service of "pop" music, while Radio 2 (which shares some programs with it) concentrates mainly on middle-of-the-road popular and light music. Radio 3 is the serious-music channel, but it also broadcasts intellectually demanding, spoken-word programs: drama, poetry, talks, and discussions. Radio 4 includes a large number of news and current affairs programs, documentaries, school broadcasts, and a wide range of entertainment. Stereophonic broadcasts on Radio 3 and are available for an average of more than 50 hours a week. In addition, the BBC broadcasts on both radio and television programs in support of Open University courses by means of which students working at home can qualify for a degree. The BBC also operates 20 local radio stations at major population centres throughout England.

The BBC's External Services broadcast to the world in English and 39 other languages for a total of more than 700 hours a week. Through relays, rebroadcasts, records, and tapes, many of the programs are distributed to other broadcasting organizations. External Services programs are financed by a grant-in-aid from the Treasury voted annually by Parliament. The government prescribes only the languages in which the External Services broadcast and the length of time each language is on the air.

The ITA, which consisted of 11 members appointed by the minister of Posts and Telecommunications, had 15 companies under contract, serving 14 regions. London was served by two companies, one broadcasting on weekdays and the other at weekends. A common news service was provided by Independent Television News Ltd. The Independent Television Companies Association assisted the companies in dealing with trade unions, sporting organizations, and other bodies, and generally ensured that the companies were in line on public issues connected with television broadcasting policy.

The BBC and IBA are active members of the European Broadcasting Union. Together, the members and the EBU take joint action in news-gathering. In this way each member television service acquires essential material at a shared cost. The EBU also organizes other international exchanges of television programs via the Eurovision network. The BBC, a founder member of the Commonwealth Broadcasting Conference, also cooperates with and gives considerable aid to Commonwealth broadcasting organizations. (Br. P.)

BIBLIOGRAPHY.—*General Works:* Current developments and statistics are summarized annually in *Britannica Book of the Year* in its main article on Great Britain, also under appropriate subject headings. *Britain: an Official Handbook* published annually by the Central

Office of Information is one of the best comprehensive reference books on the United Kingdom and contains a select bibliography.

Constitution and Government: Walter Bagehot, *The English Constitution* (1867) with an introduction by Richard Crossman (1963); Sir William R. Anson, *The Law and Custom of the Constitution,* 2 vol., new ed. (1922 and 1935); S. Gordon, *Our Parliament,* 6th ed. (1964); Sir David L. Keir, *The Constitutional History of Modern Britain since 1485,* 7th ed. (1964); A. V. Dicey, *Introduction to the Study of the Law of the Constitution,* 10th ed. (1961); E. C. S. Wade and G. G. Phillips, *Constitutional Law,* 7th ed. (1965); A. H. Birch, *Representative and Responsible Government: an Essay on the British Constitution* (1964); J. Harvey and L. Bather, *The British Constitution,* 2nd ed. (1968).

(D. Mr.)

Defense: Army: Sir John Fortescue, *History of the British Army,* 13 vol. (1899–1930); Sir Charles Firth, *Cromwell's Army* (1902); E. W. Sheppard, *A Short History of the British Army* (1950); Peter Young, *The British Army* (1967); *Brassey's Annual* (annual in October); *The Army Quarterly and Defence Journal* (quarterly); *Journal of the Royal United Services Institute* (quarterly); *Statement on Defence* (HMSO, annually).

Navy: Publications of the Navy Records Society (1894 *et seq.*); L. Laird Clowes, *The Royal Navy,* 7 vol. (1897–1903); J. S. Corbett, *The Successors of Drake* (1900), *The Campaign of Trafalgar* (1910), *Sir Francis Drake* (1890); Adm. Lord Jellicoe, *The Grand Fleet, 1914–1916* (1919), *The Crisis of the Naval War* (1920); J. S. Corbett and Sir H. J. Newbolt, *Official History of the Great War: Naval Operations,* 5 vol. (1923–38); G. A. R. Callender, *The Naval Side of British History* (1924); W. M. James, *The British Navy in Adversity* (1926); Alastair Mars, *Unbroken: The Story of a Submarine* (1953); C. E. T. Warren and J. Benson, *Above Us the Waves* (1953); with title *Midget Raiders* (1954); Capt. S. W. Roskill, *The Navy at War, 1939–45* (1960); Dudley Pope, *Flag 4: the Battle of Coastal Forces in the Mediterranean* (1954); P. K. Kemp, *Fleet Air Arm* (1954); Adm. Sir F. Dreyer, *The Sea Heritage* (1955); D. A. Rayner, *Escort* (1955); J. K. Laughton, *Nelson* (1900); C. Oman, *Nelson* (1946); Sir G. Callender, *Sea Kings of Britain,* 3rd ed., 3 vol. (1939); Adm. of the Fleet Lord Fisher, *Records* (1919), *Memories* (1919); G. Rawson, *Earl Beatty, Admiral of the Fleet* (1930); *Jane's Fighting Ships* (annual); *Brassey's Naval Annuals* (1886 *et seq.*); Arthur J. Marder, *The Anatomy of British Sea Power, 1880–1905* (1961); Michael Lewis, *The Navy in Transition, 1814–1864: a Social History* (1965); Philip Goodhart, *Fifty Ships that Saved the World; the Foundation of the Anglo-American Alliance* (1965).

(C. N. P.)

Air Force: Sir Walter Raleigh and H. A. Jones, *The Official History of the War in the Air,* 6 vol. (1922–37); A. O. Pollard, *The Royal Air Force* (1934); C. G. Grey, *A History of the Air Ministry* (1940); Lord Tedder, *Air Power in War* (1948); D. Richards and H. St. G. Saunders, *Royal Air Force 1939–45,* 3 vol. (1953–54); Gerald Bowman, *War in the Air* (1956); C. H. Gibbs-Smith, *The Aeroplane: an Historical Survey* (1960); Sir Charles Webster and N. Frankland, *The Strategic Air Offensive Against Germany, 1939–1945,* 4 vol. (1961); *Jane's All the World's Aircraft* (annual).

(D. Cr.)

The Economy: Annual Report of the Forestry Commissioners; UN Food and Agriculture Organization, *Yearbook of Forest Products Statistics; Annual Abstract of Statistics;* Electricity Council: *Report and Accounts* (annually); Gas Council: *Report and Accounts* (annually); *Reports on the Census of Production* (periodically); John Ashton and S. J. Rogers (eds.), *Economic Change and Agricultural* (1967); *Report on Overseas Trade* (monthly); *Accounts Relating to Trade and Navigation of the United Kingdom* (monthly); *Agriculture* (monthly); *Labour Gazette* (monthly); *Board of Trade Journal* (weekly); G. C. Allen, *British Industries and Their Organisation,* 4th ed. (1959); Duncan Burn (ed.), *The Structure of British Industry* (1958); "Iron and Steel," annual statistics for the U.K.; *Report of the Committee on the Working of the Monetary System* (1959); R. S. Sayers, *Modern Banking,* 5th ed. (1960), *Financial Policy, 1939–45* (1956); Henry Brandon, *In the Red: the Struggle for Sterling, 1964–1966* (1966); Glyn Jones and Michael Barnes, *Britain on Borrowed Time* (1967); Barbara Marlow, *Charting the British Economy* (1968); London and Cambridge Economic Service, *The British Economy: Key Statistics 1900–* (annual); Walford Johnson *et al., A Short Economic and Social History of Twentieth-Century Britain* (1967); Phyllis Deane and W. A. Cole, *British Economic Growth, 1688–1959: Trends and Structure,* 2nd ed. (1967); E. V. Morgan, *Studies in British Financial Policy, 1914–1925* (1952); annual White Paper *National Income and Expenditure; Finance Accounts Civil Estimates;* Central Office of Information Reference Pamphlet, *The British System of Taxation* (1960); Edwin A. Pratt, *A History of Inland Transport and Communication in England* (1912); C. B. Andrews, *The Railway Age* (1937); R. S. Pilcher, *Road Passenger Transport* (1937); L. T. C. Rolt, *The Inland Waterways of England* (1950); E. C. R. Hadfield, *British Canals* (revised 1969); R. H. Thornton, *British Shipping,* 2nd ed. (1959); J. Copeland, *Roads and their Traffic 1750–1850* (1968); P. Duff, *British Ships and Shipping* (1968); H. Perkin, *The Age of the Railway* (1970); W. Plowden, *The Motor Car and Politics 1896–1970* (1971); *The Reorganisation of the Post Office,* Cmd. 3233 (HMSO, 1967); British Broadcasting Corporation, *Local Radio in the Public's Interest: the BBC's Plan* (1966); David Attenborough, *BBC-2 a Lecture in The Corporation* (1966).

(W. Bk.; N. Cu.; E. V. Mn.; Je. D.; M. E. Be.; M. J. A.)

GREAT CHAIN OF BEING

GREAT CHAIN OF BEING, a conception of the structure of the universe that had a pervasive influence in western thought in Neoplatonism during the Renaissance and the early modern period, particularly in the 17th and early 18th centuries. The term denotes three general features of the universe: plenitude, continuity and gradation. The principle of plenitude states that the universe is "full," exhibiting the maximal diversity of kinds of existences; everything possible (*i.e.,* not self-contradictory) is actual. The principle of continuity asserts that the universe is composed of an infinite series of forms, each of which shares with its neighbour at least one attribute. According to the principle of linear gradation, this series ranges in hierarchical order from the barest type of existence to the *ens perfectissimum,* or God.

The idea of the chain of being was first systematized by the Neoplatonist Plotinus, though the component concepts were derived from Plato and Aristotle. Plato's "idea of the good" in the *Republic,* eternal, immutable, ineffable, perfect, the universal object of desire, is fused with the demiurge of the *Timaeus,* who constructed the world of becoming because "he was good, and in one that is good no envy . . . he desired that everything should be so far as possible like himself." Aristotle introduced a definition of the continuum and pointed out various graded scales of existence. Thus, in the words of Plotinus: "The one is perfect because it seeks for nothing, and possesses nothing, and has need of nothing; and being perfect, it overflows, and thus its superabundance produces an Other." "Whenever anything reaches its own perfection, we see that it cannot endure to remain in itself, but generates and produces some other thing. . . . How then should the most perfect being and the first good remain shut up in itself, as though it were jealous or impotent—itself the potency of all things. . . . Something must therefore be begotten of it" (*Enneads,* v, 2, 1; and v, 4, 1). This generation of the many from the one must continue until all possible varieties of being in the descending series are realized. "The world is a sort of life stretched out to an immense span, in which each of the parts has its own place in the series, all of them different and the whole continuous, and that which precedes never wholly absorbed in that which comes after" (*Enneads,* v, 2, 2).

The scale of being served Plotinus and numerous later writers as an explanation of the existence of evil in the privative sense of lack of some good. It also offered an argument for optimism: since all beings other than the *ens perfectissimum* are to some degree imperfect or evil, and since the goodness of the universe as a whole consists in its fullness, the best possible world will be one which contains the greatest possible variety of beings and consequently all possible evils.

The concept of the chain of being was unorthodox for scholastic theology because it was thought to conflict with the freedom of will of the deity. However, it had been clearly enunciated by Abelard in the 12th century. During the Renaissance and more especially in the 17th and early 18th centuries, it was almost universally accepted. A. O. Lovejoy points out that next to the word "nature," "the Great Chain of Being" was the sacred phrase of the 18th century. In Pope's *Essay on Man* (Epistle i, 1732) it is expressed most clearly. He speaks of the best possible systems (which infinite Wisdom must form)

Where all must full or not coherent be,
And all that rises, rise in due degree;

(45–46)

And later:

Vast chain of being! which from God began,
Natures aethereal, human, angel, man,
Beast, bird, fish, insect, what no eye can see,
No glass can reach; from Infinite to thee,
From thee to nothing.—On superior pow'rs
Were we to press, inferior might on ours;
Or in the full creation leave a void,
Where, one step broken, the great scale's destroyed:
From Nature's chain whatever link you strike,
Tenth, or ten thousandth, breaks the chain alike.

(237–246)

The principle of plenitude was really a disguised version of the principle of sufficient reason, fundamental to the systems of Leibniz and Spinoza. This principle required some reason for the existence of every entity; namely its roots in the eternal order, in the necessities belonging to essences and their relations. Thus seen, the principle of plenitude asserts that the universe is completely rational and intelligible.

The main 18th-century critics of these ideas were Voltaire and Samuel Johnson, who conclusively refuted the whole theory of "the scale of being," though their criticisms failed to gain proper recognition at the time. Nevertheless, it became increasingly apparent that the objects of our sensible experience do not constitute an unbroken continuum of forms. The principles of plenitude and continuity could, therefore, be saved only if it were assumed that the forms became actual in the course of a long period of time. The chain of being had to be seen as growing in time and so became a sort of cosmic evolutionism. Already Leibniz had spoken of "a cumulative increase of the beauty and universal perfection of the works of God, a perpetual and unrestricted progress of the universe as a whole."

See A. O. Lovejoy, *The Great Chain of Being* (1936).
(B. R. MA.)

GREAT CIRCLE, any circle on the surface of a sphere that marks the intersection of the sphere with a plane through its centre. Specifically, on the earth's surface each meridian of longitude is one-half of a great circle, but the Equator is the only parallel of latitude that is a great circle. Airplanes and ships follow a great-circle course whenever practical, because the arc of a great circle is the shortest distance between any two points on the surface of a sphere.

GREAT DANE, a working dog developed at least 400 years ago in Germany, where it was used for boar hunting. The Great Dane is typically a swift, alert dog noted for courage, friendliness, and dependability. It has a massive, square-jawed head and body lines that give it an elegant appearance. Its short coat is black, golden brown, brindle, blue gray, or white with black patches. The tallest of the working breeds, the Great Dane stands 28–32 in. high and weighs 120–150 lb. Its name was derived from one of its French names, Grand Danois ("big Danish"), though there is no known reason to associate Denmark with the history or origin of the breed.

GREAT DIONYSIA (City Dionysia), an ancient dramatic festival in which tragedy, comedy, and satyric drama originated, was held in Athens in March in honour of Dionysus, the god of wine. Tragedy of some form, probably chiefly the chanting of choral lyrics, was introduced when the tyrant Peisistratus refounded the festival (534–531 B.C.), but the earliest tragedy that survives, Aeschylus' the *Supplices* (Gr. *Hiketides*, "Suppliant Women"), dates from 463 B.C.

The festivals were attended by all Athenian citizens and visitors from throughout Greece. In the tragic competition, each of three tragic poets wrote, produced, and probably acted in three tragedies on a single theme. Each also presented a satyr play, which treated some heroic subject in burlesque fashion. Judges, chosen by lot, awarded a prize to the best poet. In comedy, introduced in 486, five poets competed for the prize, each with one play. The satyr play was always the work of a tragic poet, but the same poet never wrote both tragedies and comedies. In 440 comedy was also introduced into the Lenaea, the minor festival of Dionysus held in January, and tragedy was added ten years later.

GREAT DIVIDING RANGE, Australia: *see* EASTERN HIGHLANDS.

GREAT FALLS, the second largest city of Montana, U.S., is 93 mi. NE of Helena in central Montana, at an altitude of 3,330 ft., on the Missouri River, 12 mi. above the falls of the Missouri (93 ft. high) from which it derives its name; it is the seat of Cascade County.

The region is noted as a great wheat-growing and grazing area, although Great Falls is primarily an industrial city serving a large area as the manufacturing, commercial, financial, and jobbing centre. The main industries include a copper and zinc refinery, which also fabricates copper and aluminum wire, power plants, and flour mills. The municipal airport and the Malmstrom Air Force Base gained importance as stations on the polar route to Europe and through Alaska to the Orient.

In 1805 Lewis and Clark observed the nearby Giant Springs, one of the largest in the world, with a daily flow of 388,800,000 gal. of water, at a temperature of 52° F the year around. The city was founded in 1883 by Paris Gibson of Minneapolis, Minn., and incorporated in 1888. Gibson planned the wide tree-lined streets and a fine system of parks which were linked later by many boulevards. The Charles M. Russell Memorial Studio and museum is a favourite cultural attraction.

The population of Great Falls increased from 29,928 in 1940 to 39,214 in 1950, and by 1970 had reached 60,091. The Great Falls standard metropolitan statistical area (Cascade County) had, at its establishment in 1960, a population of 73,418. By 1970 it had reached 81,804. For comparative population figures of the city *see* table in MONTANA: *Population.*

The College of Great Falls, a Roman Catholic school, was established in 1932. The State School for the Deaf and Blind and a rehabilitation centre for crippled children, which serves the state, also are in Great Falls. A civic centre building contains a large auditorium, exhibit and recreational facilities in addition to city offices.
(M. G. BU.)

GREATHEAD, JAMES HENRY (1844–1896), British civil engineer, was born at Grahamstown, S.Af., on Aug. 6, 1844. He went to England in 1859 and during 1864–67 studied with P. W. Barlow. Barlow patented a tunneling shield—an iron ring forced forward by hydraulic jacks against the last erected lining ring of cast-iron segments, while men worked on the earth face ahead—and proposed a subway under the Thames near the Tower to exemplify his method. Greathead contracted for the work, which was completed in 1869. The Greathead shield, as it came to be called, was later used to bore the City and South London and the Waterloo and City railways under his direction, and on all the other railway tubes that were bored in the London clay after his death. Apart from his tunnels, Greathead was engaged on numerous railway works and took out a number of patents. He died at Streatham, London, on Oct. 21, 1896.

See memoir in *Proc. Inst. Civil Engineers,* vol. cxxvii (1897).
(S. B. HN.; X.)

GREAT LAKES, THE. The Great Lakes and their connecting waterways of the United States and Canada form the largest group of lakes in the world. The Great Lakes proper are Lakes Superior, Michigan, Huron, Erie and Ontario extending roughly from west to east. Their combined area is 95,170 sq.mi., and they drain a land area of 295,200 sq.mi. The lakes are connected to form a single drainage system which discharges down the St. Lawrence river. This system constitutes a waterway that extends nearly halfway across the North American continent. The distance by water from Duluth, Minn., at the head of Lake Superior, to the open Atlantic ocean is 2,340 mi.

Exploration.—Jacques Cartier ascended the St. Lawrence river as far as Montreal in 1535. Samuel de Champlain, founder of Quebec, traveled up the Ottawa river and explored the Georgian bay area of Lake Huron in 1615. Champlain and Étienne Brulé discovered Lake Ontario later in 1615, and it is probable that Brulé saw Lake Superior in 1622. Jean Nicolet traversed the North channel of Lake Huron and visited Lake Michigan and Green bay in 1634. Pierre Radisson and Médard des Groseilliers traveled extensively on Lake Superior in 1659.

The first white man known to have seen Lake Erie was Louis Jolliet, who returned from the Lake Superior country by way of the St. Clair river, Lake St. Clair, the Detroit river and Lake Erie in 1669. Lake Erie was the last of the Great Lakes to be discovered, partly because the powerful Iroquois Indians, who were unfriendly toward the French and their Indian allies, controlled the two lower lakes, and partly because the system of the Ottawa and Mattawa rivers leading to the upper lakes was a route more suitable to canoe travel than were the open waters of Lakes Ontario and Erie and the impassable Niagara river with its gorge and falls. By 1671 France had claimed all of the territory of the

GREAT LAKES

St. Lawrence river-Great Lakes region. The explorations of Jolliet and Father Jacques Marquette in 1673-74 added much to knowledge of the region about Lake Michigan. The first sailing vessel, the "Griffin," built under the direction of René Robert Cavelier de la Salle, traversed Lakes Erie, Huron and Michigan in 1679, but was lost on the return voyage.

France dominated an extensive fur trade for nearly a century, but the entire French territory embracing the Great Lakes was ceded to England in 1763, at the close of the French and Indian War. After the Revolutionary War a treaty in 1783 fixed a boundary between Canada and the United States in the Great Lakes region. That boundary was contested but not appreciably altered by the War of 1812. During that war the most extensive but generally indecisive conflict occurred on Lake Ontario. The battle of Lake Erie, in which a U.S. fleet under Commodore Oliver H. Perry was victorious, secured U.S. claims to the northwestern part of the region.

Physiography.—The lakes, which lie between latitude 41° 22′ and 49° 00′ N. and longitude 76° 04′ and 92° 06′ W., occupy elongated, somewhat crescentic basins, the long axes of which are oriented in several directions. Lake Superior, the most northerly and westerly of the group, extends from west to east for 383 mi. and is 160 mi. from north to south; Lake Michigan extends from north to south for 321 mi. and is 118 mi. from east to west; Lake Huron extends from northwest to southeast for 247 mi. and is 101 mi. from east to west; Lake Erie extends from east to west for 241 mi. and is 57 mi. from north to south; and Lake Ontario extends from east to west for 193 mi. and is 53 mi. from north to south.

The combined shore lines of the five lakes are 7,870 mi. long and enclose a water surface of 95,170 sq.mi. Of this, 60,960 sq.mi. are in the United States and 34,210 sq.mi. are in Canada. The drainage basin, including the lake surfaces, is 295,200 sq.mi. Mean annual precipitation in the region ranges from 29 in. at Lake Superior to 34 in. at Lakes Erie and Ontario.

The levels of all of the Great Lakes fluctuate seasonally, reaching their lowest stages in late winter and their highest stages in late summer. The usual range between the winter and summer mean levels, in any one year, has been between one and two feet. In the 106 years from 1860 to 1965 the differences between the lowest and the highest monthly mean stages of the whole period have been between 4.0 and 6.6 ft. in the various lakes. Short-period changes in level, caused by storms, generally do not exceed two feet, but a maximum change in lake level of ten feet has occurred within a few hours.

The water of the lakes is fresh. The water temperature in all of the lakes, below a depth of about 100 ft., remains close to 39° F. (3.89° C.) throughout the year. Surface water temperatures range from 32° F. (0° C.) in winter to 60° or 70° F. (15.66° or 21.11° C.) in summer. There are no appreciable lunar tides in the lakes, and surface currents generally are slight. Waves reach dangerous size, particularly during autumn and winter storms. Shore erosion, caused by storms occurring during years of high-water stages, has destroyed valuable lake-front lands.

Lake Superior, at the head of the system, stands at an average altitude of 600 ft. above mean sea level and is 1,333 ft. deep. It is the largest of the Great Lakes, with a surface area of 31,820 sq.mi., and it contains over half of the water of the entire system. The largest tributary is the Nipigon river, entering from the north, which drains Lake Nipigon, a body of water with a surface area of 1,870 sq.mi. The St. Marys river is the outlet of Lake Superior, connecting Whitefish bay with Lake Huron 63 mi. to the southeast. The mean annual discharge of the St. Marys river is 73,300 cu.ft. per second. (See SUPERIOR, LAKE.)

Lakes Michigan and Huron, which are connected by the Straits of Mackinac, are similar in many respects. They are at the same level, 579 ft. above mean sea level, and have about the same surface area. Lake Michigan, which lies entirely within the United States, covers 22,400 sq.mi.; Lake Huron covers 23,000 sq.mi. The greatest depth of Lake Michigan is 923 ft.; the greatest depth

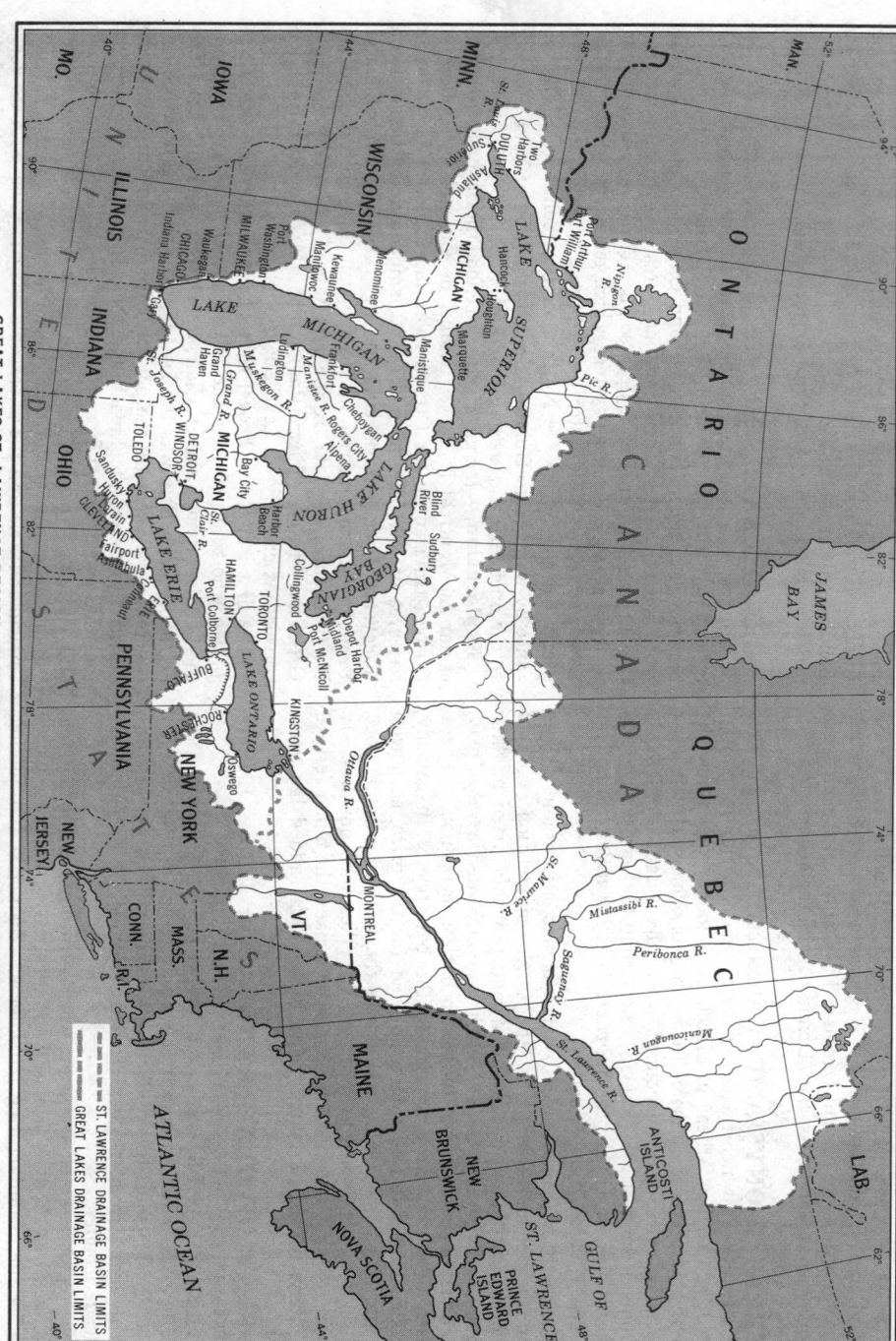

of Lake Huron, 750 ft. Lake Michigan includes Green bay, a large embayment lying on its western side. Lake Huron includes Georgian bay and the North channel, which lie on the northeastern and northern sides of the main lake. (*See* GEORGIAN BAY; HURON, LAKE; MACKINAC, STRAITS OF; MICHIGAN, LAKE.)

From the southern end of Lake Huron, the St. Clair river flows directly south for about 27 mi. into Lake St. Clair, which, at an altitude of 573 ft., is 6 ft. lower than Lake Huron. Lake St. Clair, which is 26 mi. from north to south and 24 mi. from east to west, has a surface area of 490 sq.mi. and a maximum natural depth of about 21 ft. An improved channel in the lake bottom connects the mouth of the St. Clair river with the head of the Detroit river. Lake St. Clair is connected with Lake Erie 31 mi. to the southwest through the Detroit river. The mean annual discharge of the Detroit river is 177,500 cu.ft. per second. (*See* SAINT CLAIR RIVER; SAINT CLAIR, LAKE.)

Lake Erie, which is 570 ft. in average altitude, has a surface area of 9,930 sq.mi. Because its maximum depth is only 210 ft., it is the only one of the Great Lakes whose bottom does not extend below sea level. With an average depth of only 58 ft., the lake has a water volume of 109 cu.mi., a little more than one-thirtieth of Lake Superior's volume. (*See* ERIE, LAKE.)

From the northeastern end of Lake Erie, the Niagara river flows about 28 mi. in a northerly direction. It descends 60 ft. to the brink of Niagara falls, drops 167 ft. in the falls and descends nearly 100 ft. farther in the course of the Niagara gorge. After leaving the gorge, the river traverses a plain for a distance of 7 mi. and enters Lake Ontario. The mean annual discharge of the river is 195,800 cu.ft. per second. (*See* NIAGARA RIVER AND FALLS.)

Ontario, the most easterly of the Great Lakes, has an average surface altitude of 245 ft. above sea level. The maximum recorded depth, 802 ft., is 557 ft. below sea level. With a surface area of 7,600 sq.mi., Lake Ontario is the smallest of the Great Lakes in area but it ranks third in maximum depth and its volume far exceeds that of Lake Erie. (*See* ONTARIO, LAKE.)

The St. Lawrence river leaves Lake Ontario at its northeastern end and flows 265 mi. to tidewater (sea level) at Trois Rivières (Three Rivers), Que.; from there to Quebec the distance is 77 mi., and from Quebec to the open Atlantic ocean the distance is about 750 mi. The mean annual discharge of the upper St. Lawrence river is 233,900 cu.ft. per second. The principal tributary to the St. Lawrence is the Ottawa river. (*See* SAINT LAWRENCE RIVER; SAINT LAWRENCE SEAWAY.)

Geology.—Lake Superior lies almost entirely within the Canadian shield, an area of very old (Pre-Cambrian) rocks which generally are hard and dense. The lake basin occupies a structurally downwarped and downfaulted basin which was filled with weaker rocks and then reopened in later geologic time by erosion. The other four Great Lakes lie in a younger (Paleozoic) rock province, mainly consisting of limestones, dolomites, shales and sandstones that have been consolidated but otherwise not strongly altered or deformed.

The lake basins are situated mainly in the outcrop belts of weak shale formations. The most striking bedrock feature in the region of the four lower lakes is the Niagaran Dolomite cuesta or ridge, which forms the western shore of Lake Michigan, the Door peninsula, separating Green bay from Lake Michigan, and the northern shore of Lake Michigan; it extends eastward, forming the islands which separate Lake Huron from the North channel and Georgian bay, curves southeastward to form the Saugeen peninsula between Lake Huron and southern Georgian bay, and, farther southeast, swings eastward south of Lake Ontario, where it forms the escarpment over which the Niagara river drops at Niagara falls. The region, in general, is a lowland of gently rolling hills and ridges separated by plains, swamps and lakes.

There is ample evidence that the Great Lakes did not exist before the Pleistocene (glacial) epoch. The deep lake basins were once broad valleys of trunk streams and their many tributaries, eroded generally in the belts of weaker rock. Several advances of the great continental ice sheets covered the region and further deepened many of the preglacial valleys. When the margin of the last major glacier retreated northward into the lake basins, only about 18,000 years ago, the first known lakes were formed. These were narrow ice-margin lakes that spilled southward over the divides and drained down the Wabash, Ohio, Illinois, Wisconsin and Mississippi rivers.

As the ice margin retreated the lakes expanded and coalesced; some of them then drained through new, lower outlets. Re-advances of the ice margin caused several modifications of the glacial lakes, including temporary return of their outflow to the older southern outlets. Further retreat of the ice reopened northern outlets and permitted further enlargement of the lakes. As the ice disappeared from the region, the land, which had been depressed under the weight of the ice, rose slowly and this caused further shifting of outlet channels. Uplift of the land in the northern parts of the region is still in progress, amounting to more than a foot per 100 years. (*See* PLEISTOCENE EPOCH.)

While bedrock formations constitute the framework of the Great Lakes region and form some of the higher lands, the rocks generally are covered by unconsolidated deposits left by the Pleistocene glaciers. These deposits include gravel, sand and clay of commercial value, and many of the rich soils of this agriculturally important region were formed on some of these deposits. The principal mineral resources which provide the basis for steel production in the region are iron ore in the Lake Superior district and from Labrador-Quebec, coal in Pennsylvania, Ohio and Illinois and limestone suitable for flux, quarried mainly on the shore of Lake Huron near Rogers City, Mich. Limestones and shales, produced in many areas, are the raw materials for the manufacture of cement. Other valuable mineral products of the region are copper from the Keweenaw peninsula of Lake Superior; nickel, cobalt and uranium from the district north of Lake Huron; and salt from New York, Pennsylvania, eastern Ohio and Michigan.

Commerce.—Because of the position of the Great Lakes deep in the North American continent and on the boundary between the United States and Canada, their utilization is of great importance. Towns and cities line the shore, no small part of whose growth and importance is directly associated with the abundant supply of fresh water available to them. Two of the five cities of the United States with populations of 1,000,000 or more, Chicago and Detroit, and the two largest cities of Canada, Toronto and Montreal, are on the Great Lakes and the St. Lawrence river.

Since the international boundary follows the long axes of four of the five Great Lakes, a boundary waters treaty was signed in 1909 which guaranteed the Great Lakes to be free and open to inhabitants of both countries on equal terms and established the principles concerning the use of boundary waters. An international commission of three members from Canada and three from the United States was established, and it is a source of great pride in international relations that there are neither fortifications nor warships along the Great Lakes boundary.

Transportation.—The Great Lakes and their connecting waterways constitute the most important system of inland water transportation in the world. Because of their situation in the interior of a continent which is a producer of heavy commodities, the Great Lakes provide the transportation system for enormous quantities of bulk freight hauled at a rate considerably lower than for other comparable inland systems.

The iron mines of Minnesota, Wisconsin and the upper peninsula of Michigan, and those of Quebec and Labrador, furnish enormous amounts of bulk freight which move to the iron and steel centres at the southern end of Lake Michigan, in the Detroit area, on and south of Lake Erie and on Lake Ontario. Coal from the Appalachian fields southeast of the lakes is an important return commodity from Lake Erie. Wheat and other grains from the United States and Canada west of Lake Superior move down the lakes to the cities on the southern and eastern shores and through the seaway overseas. Stone moves to the iron and steel mills and pulpwood and petroleum to the commercial and industrial centres.

Lake Michigan, the only lake to interrupt east-west railway and highway traffic, has a well-developed year-around railroad car, automobile and passenger ferry traffic. Eastbound, the railroad cars are loaded with iron and steel goods, wines and liquors and flour, grain, sawmill and fabricated paper products. Westward, the cars are loaded with coal, building cement, rock, newsprint and steel ingots, blooms, billets, slabs, sheets and bars. (*See* also WATER TRANSPORT, INLAND.)

Carriers.—Since most of the traffic on the Great Lakes consists of heavy, bulky, nonperishable commodities, special boats were designed to carry maximum loads under the specific conditions of the lakes, especially the length and depth of the locks in the canals. The characteristic lake bulk carrier is long and narrow, with machinery both forward and aft, and it has a cargo capacity up to 45,000 tons.

Special port facilities have been developed to accommodate the bulk carriers. At the ore docks on Lake Superior and on the St. Lawrence boats are loaded in a matter of minutes, and special unloaders at the receiving docks on the lakes remove the cargo in a few hours.

Overseas Trade.—Chicago, Toronto, Detroit, Cleveland, Milwaukee, Green Bay, Duluth-Superior and Fort William-Port Arthur are leading ports engaged in overseas trade. In dollar value the principal exports are machinery and machine parts, edible animal oils and fats, hides and skins, motor vehicles and vehicle parts, chemicals and tobacco; the principal imports are alcoholic beverages, steel-mill products, electrical and other machinery, motor vehicles, glass and glass products, wood pulp and tools.

Navigation Improvements.—The relatively regular shore lines of the Great Lakes limited the number of harbours. Private interests as well as the governments of the United States and Canada built docks and harbours, dredged channels, dug canals, installed locks and otherwise improved the lakes for navigation. Most of the major lake ports developed at the mouths of the short rivers which flow into the Great Lakes. These ports usually had an inner harbour on the dredged portion of the river and an outer harbour protected by extensive breakwaters constructed of piling, rock and concrete. Coast guard stations and storm warnings, as well as radio communication, radar and ship-to-shore telephone, protect traffic over the entire Great Lakes area.

Although there are about 200 harbours of all types, the important ones are the commercial and industrial cities of the southern Great Lakes and the ore and grain ports of Lake Superior.

Connecting Waterways.—Of critical significance to Great Lakes traffic are the connecting waterways, especially those in which there is a notable change in level from lake to lake. At Sault Ste. Marie (the "Soo"), passage around the rapids of the St. Marys river, between Lakes Superior and Huron is provided by canals and locks constructed on both the U.S. and Canadian sides of the river. Lake Michigan, which is connected with Lake Huron by the broad and deep natural channel of the Straits of Mackinac, is also connected with the Illinois and Mississippi rivers by the Chicago Sanitary and Ship canal, which has a minimum depth of nine feet (*see* MICHIGAN, LAKE).

In the St. Clair river-Lake St. Clair-Detroit river system, connecting Lakes Huron and Erie, improved channels provide a minimum depth of 27 ft. for both downbound and upbound vessels. (*See* SAINT CLAIR RIVER; SAINT CLAIR, LAKE.) The Welland Ship canal, extending about 27 mi. from Port Colborne, Ont., on Lake Erie to Port Weller, Ont. on Lake Ontario, provides for transit of vessels between the two lakes. The minimum depth in the canal is 27 ft. (*see* WELLAND SHIP CANAL). A system of canals operated by the state of New York, with federal support, provides free waterway communication between Lake Erie and the Hudson river. Branches of the system connect with Lake Ontario and Lake Champlain.

From Lake Ontario to the Gulf of St. Lawrence, the St. Lawrence river consists of three segments. The first extends to the mouth of the Ottawa river, a distance of 175 mi., and includes the Thousand Islands, shoals and rapids. The middle segment extends from the mouth of the Ottawa river 95 mi. to the estuary, and the broad estuary is the third segment. Through navigation in the St. Lawrence river is provided by the St. Lawrence seaway development, which was completed in 1959, with a minimum depth of 27 ft. (*see* SAINT LAWRENCE SEAWAY). The canals and channels connecting Lakes Ontario, Erie, Huron and Superior, which had been maintained for several years with a minimum depth of 21 ft. for upbound traffic and 25 ft. for downbound traffic, were dredged to 27 ft. following the opening of the seaway.

Timber Resources.—Magnificent stands of timber, principally pine, once covered the upper lakes region, but the virgin forests were destroyed by exploitative cutting between 1870 and 1910. Timber growth is considered the best use for much of the land, and nearly half of the forested area is held in federal and state forests.

Fisheries.—Commercial fishing for lake trout, whitefish, perch, suckers and chub, once an important industry on the lakes, declined seriously after about 1945. The decline was coincident with an invasion of the sea lamprey (eel). Control of the lamprey was sufficiently successful by 1965 to warrant restocking the lakes with lake trout and introducing salmon, and by the late 1960s these fish were increasing appreciably. Alewives, originally an ocean fish, had increased to such an extent by the late 1960s as to constitute a nuisance, especially in Lake Michigan; large numbers of dead alewives were washed onto shore, making many beaches virtually unusable. It was hoped that the lake trout and salmon would control the alewives (*see* also FISH; *Fish Culture*).

Pollution.—The use of the lakes for domestic and industrial water supply and for recreational purposes was adversely affected by pollution in some areas. The discharge of sewage, either untreated or inadequately treated, into tributary streams as well as directly into the lakes was a principal cause of pollution in the more densely populated parts of the region. Various organic and inorganic industrial wastes also were important factors in some areas. Lake Erie, because of its relatively shallow depth and small volume and because of the concentration of population and industrial plants in its watershed, was most heavily polluted. A program of remedial measures, including removal of settleable solids, oxidation of organic matter and reduction of pathogenic bacteria, which was required by law, resulted in a slight decrease in pollution in years of high or normal rainfall. Southern Lake Michigan and some other areas were polluted to a lesser extent, but increasingly effective programs of pollution abatement were needed. In an effort to combat and control pollution, the U.S. government established in 1965 the Federal Water Pollution Control administration, which was to work with state and local governments; the Great Lakes were major targets of the new program.

Tourism.—Recreation has developed as an industry of major importance in the region. Cool pleasant summers and numerous lakes in a wilderness setting have attracted tourists and sportsmen. Thousands of vacation cottages have been built along the shores of the Great Lakes and around inland lakes in the region. Vacationists make use of public campgrounds and tourist cabins in the summer; thousands of hunters visit the region during the autumn hunting seasons, and the cold snowy winters attract increasing numbers of winter sports enthusiasts.

For further information on the Great Lakes region, *see* articles on the various states and provinces bordering the lakes; *see* also references under "Great Lakes, The," in the Index.

BIBLIOGRAPHY.—Canadian Hydrographic Service, *Great Lakes Pilot* and charts (annually); U.S. Army Corps of Engineers, *Great Lakes Pilot* and charts (annually); U.S. Army Corps of Engineers, *Commercial Statistics of Water-Borne Commerce of the United States,* part 3 (annually); John H. Garland (ed.), *The North American Midwest* (1955); Harlan Hatcher, *The Great Lakes* (1944); Jack L. Hough, *Geology of the Great Lakes* (1958); W. Havighurst, *Great Lakes Reader* (1966). (J. L. Hн.)

GREAT MOTHER OF THE GODS, the ancient oriental-Greek-Roman deity commonly known as Cybele in Greek and Latin literature from the time of Pindar. She was also known under many other names, some of which were derived from famous places of worship; *e.g.,* Dindymene from Mt. Dindymus in Galatia.

Cybele is her favourite name in ancient and modern literature, while Great Mother of the Gods, or Great Idaean Mother of the Gods (*Mater Deum Magna, Mater Deum Magna Idaea*), the most frequently recurring epigraphical title, was her ordinary official designation.

The legends agree in locating the rise of the worship of the Great Mother in Asia Minor, in the region of loosely defined geographical limits which comprised the Phrygian empire of prehistoric times and was more extensive than the Roman province of Phrygia. Her best-known early seats of worship were Mt. Ida and Mt. Sipylus and the cities of Cyzicus, Sardis and Pessinus; the last-named city, in Galatia near the borders of Roman Phrygia, finally becoming the strongest centre of the Great Mother cult. But the existence of numerous very similar non-Phrygian deities indicates that she was merely the Phrygian form of the nature deity of all Asia Minor. From Asia Minor the cult of the Great Mother spread first to Greek territory. It found its way into Thrace at an early date, was known in Boeotia by Pindar in the 6th century B.C., and entered Attica near the beginning of the 4th century. At Piraeus, where it probably arrived by way of the Aegean islands, the cult existed privately in a fully developed state (that is, accompanied by the worship of Attis; q.v.) at the beginning of the 4th century, and publicly two centuries later. The Greeks always saw in the Great Mother a resemblance to their own Rhea and finally identified the two completely, though the Asiatic peculiarities of the cult were never universally popular with them. In her less Asiatic aspect (i.e., without Attis) she was sometimes identified with Gaea and Demeter. It was in this phase that she was worshipped in the Metroon at Athens.

In 204 B.C., in obedience to the Sibylline prophecy that said that whenever an enemy from abroad should make war on Italy he could be expelled and conquered if the Idaean Mother were brought to Rome from Pessinus, the cult of the Great Mother, together with her sacred symbol, a small stone reputed to have fallen from the heavens, was transferred to Rome and established in a temple on the Palatine. Her identification by the Romans with Maia, Ops, Rhea, Tellus and Ceres contributed to the establishment of her worship on a firm footing. By the end of the republic it had attained prominence, and under the empire it became one of the three most important cults in the Roman world, the other two being those of Mithra and Isis. Epigraphic and numismatic evidence prove it to have penetrated from Rome to the remotest provinces. During the brief revival of paganism under Eugenius in A.D. 394 occurred the last appearance of the cult in history. Besides the temple on the Palatine, there also existed minor shrines of the Great Mother in and near Rome.

In all her aspects, Roman, Greek and oriental, the Great Mother was characterized by essentially the same qualities. Most prominent among them was her universal motherhood. She was the great parent of gods and men as well as of the lower orders of creation. Especial emphasis was placed upon her maternity over wild nature. She was called the Mountain Mother; her sanctuaries were almost invariably upon mountains and frequently in caves; lions were her faithful companions. Her especial affinity with wild nature was manifested by the orgiastic character of her worship. Her mythical attendants, the Corybantes, were wild, half-demonic beings (see CORYBANT). Her priests, the Galli, were eunuchs attired in female garb, with long hair fragrant with ointment. Together with priestesses, they celebrated her rites with wild music and dancing until their frenzied excitement found its culmination in self-scourging, self-laceration or exhaustion. Self-emasculation sometimes accompanied this delirium of worship on the part of candidates for the priesthood.

Though her cult sometimes existed by itself, in its fully developed state the worship of the Great Mother was accompanied by that of Attis. The cult of Attis never existed independently. There is no positive evidence to prove the existence of the cult publicly in this phase in Greece before the 2nd century B.C. nor in Rome before the empire, though it may have existed in private. The philosophers of the late Roman empire interpreted the Attis legend as symbolizing the relations of Mother Earth to her children the fruits. In this interpretation they were not far wrong, for Cybele and all her kind are embodiments of the earth's fertility.

At Rome the immediate direction of the cult of the Great Mother devolved upon the high priest or Archigallus, called by the name of Attis, and upon a high priestess, Sacerdos Maxima. Its support was derived, at least in part, from a popular contribution, the stips. Besides other priests, priestesses and minor officials, such as musicians, curator, etc., there were certain colleges connected with the administration of the cult, called cannophori ("reed bearers") and dendrophori ("branch bearers"). The supervisory body of the quindecimvirs watched over this as over all other authorized foreign cults. Roman citizens were at first forbidden to take part in its ceremonies, and the ban was not removed until the time of the empire.

The main public event in the worship of the Great Mother was the annual festival, which took place originally on April 4 and was followed next day by the Megalesia, games instituted in her honour on the introduction of the cult. Under the empire, from Claudius on, the Megalesia lasted from April 4 to 10. Later a new annual cycle of festivals was instituted, extending from March 15 to 27, in the following order:

1. March 15, the sacrifice of a six-year-old bull, the high priest, a priestess and the cannophori officiating, the last named carrying reeds in procession in commemoration of the exposure of the infant Attis on the reedy banks of the stream Gallus in Phrygia.

2. March 22, the bearing in procession of the sacred pine, emblem of Attis' self-mutilation, death and immortality, to the temple on the Palatine, the symbol of the Mother's cave, by the dendrophori, a guild of workmen who made the Mother one of their patrons.

3. March 24, the "day of blood," a day of mourning, fasting and abstinence, especially sexual, commemorating the sorrow of the Mother for Attis. The frenzied dance and self-laceration of the priests and the self-mutilation of neophytes were special features of the day. The taurobolium (ceremony in which worshipers were baptized with the blood of a sacrificed bull) was often performed on this day.

4. March 25, all mourning was put off, and good cheer reigned in token of the return of the sun and spring, which was symbolized by the renewal of Attis' life.

5. March 26, a day of rest and quiet.

6. March 27, the crowning day of the cycle. The silver statue of the goddess, with the sacred stone, the acus, set in its head, was borne in gorgeous procession and bathed in the Almo, a tributary of the Tiber; the remainder of the day was given up to rejoicing and entertainment, especially dramatic representation of the legend of the deities.

The Great Mother is especially prominent in the art of the empire. No work of the first class, however, was inspired by her. She appears usually with mural crown and veil, well draped, seated on a throne and accompanied by two lions. Other attributes which often appear are the patera, tympanum, cymbals, sceptre, garlands and fruits. Attis and his attributes, the pine, Phrygian cap, pedum, syrinx and torch, also appear. In literature the Mother is often mentioned, but no surviving work of importance, with the exception of a poem by Catullus, is attributable to her inspiration. Her importance in the history of religion, however, is very great; for her cult, like the other mystic worships, was at once a rival to Christianity and a steppingstone to it. See also ROMAN RELIGION; Oriental.

BIBLIOGRAPHY.—Grant Showerman, "The Great Mother of the Gods," Bulletin of the University of Wisconsin, no. 43, "Philology and

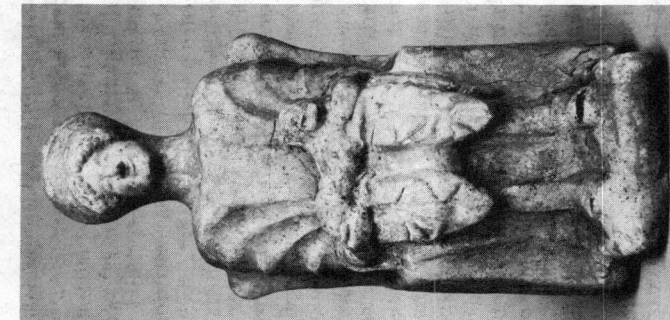

BY COURTESY OF THE BRITISH MUSEUM

TERRA-COTTA CYBELE EXCAVATED AT CAMIRUS, RHODES; EARLY 5TH CENTURY B.C.

Literature Series," vol. i, no. 3 (1901); Hugo Hepding, *Attis, seine Mythen und sein Kult* (1903); H. Graillot, *Le Culte de Cybèle dans l'empire romain* (1912).

GREAT PLAINS. A major flattish land-form area in North America extending from the Mackenzie river lowlands in northern Canada to the Rio Grande in the Big Bend section of Texas. The Great Plains lie directly east of the Rocky mountains and, in New Mexico, of the Basin and Range province. In general, they are about 375 mi. wide and slope gently to the east, where they merge with the central lowlands and the coastal plains.

The eastern border of the Great Plains is readily discernible in only a few places. In Texas the Balcones escarpment, west of Austin, rising to heights of 300 to 1,000 ft., provides a clear break between the Great Plains (there also referred to as High Plains and Edward's plateau) and the coastal plains. A somewhat more subdued escarpment is found in the Coteau du Missouri in North Dakota. Between these two escarpments the eastern border is usually associated with either the 1,500- or the 2,000-ft. contour line. In the U.S. these lines lie close to the 97th to 100th meridians, which are also frequently mentioned as border lines.

Below the mountain front on the west the Great Plains have an elevation of 5,000 to 6,000 ft. All major rivers have west-east axes and an average gradient of about ten feet per mile. Prominent streams are the North and South Saskatchewan, Milk, Missouri, Yellowstone, Powder, Little Missouri, Cheyenne, White, Niobrara, Platte, Republican, Kansas, Cimarron, Arkansas, Canadian, Red, Brazos and Colorado rivers.

Much of the plains area consists of gently tilted shale, limestone and sandstone discontinuously mantled by glacial deposits (in the north), loess and alluvial deposits. Although the plains are generally pictured as flat to rolling, conspicuous land forms characterize some of their parts. Among these are the Black hills of South Dakota and Wyoming, the badlands of South Dakota, the sand hills of Nebraska and a series of mountain outliers in Montana and elsewhere. Locally, cuestas, hogbacks, breaks and mesas are sculptured in the sedimentary bedrocks.

Because of limited precipitation, about 10 to 20 in. a year, grass is the prevailing natural vegetation. In central Alberta and Saskatchewan the limited but effective moisture also supports broadleaf and mixed coniferous forests. Moderate precipitation has meant limited leaching and the soils are usually of superior productivity when supplied with moisture.

Population in the plains area is relatively sparse. It is supported largely by grazing of livestock, dry farming of wheat and the production of sorghums and cotton. Farming under irrigation is expanding. Parts of the plains are well endowed with coal and lignite, petroleum and natural gas.

BIBLIOGRAPHY.—Nevin M. Fenneman, *Physiography of Western United States* (1931); Carl F. Kraenzel, *Great Plains in Transition* (1955); Walter P. Webb, *Great Plains* (1959); Mari Sandoz, *Love Song to the Plains* (1961); Waldo R. Wedel, *Prehistoric Man on the Great Plains* (1961); Eugene Fodor (ed.), *Rockies and Plains* (1966). (W. M. KN.)

GREAT RIFT VALLEY, a part of the most extensive rift on the earth's surface, extending over 50 degrees of latitude from the Jordan valley in southwest Asia to the Shiré tributary of the Zambezi in east Africa. In Africa it is marked by a line of narrow, deep and steep-sided lakes, including Rudolf, Magadi, Natron and Nyasa, by associated volcanic outpourings such as Mounts Kilimanjaro (19,340 ft.) and Kenya (17,058 ft.), and in places by steep edges like the Mau and Kikuyu escarpments. A western branch of the Rift valley, extending in a great arc from the northern end of Lake Nyasa, is occupied by Lakes Tanganyika, Kivu, Edward and Albert.

See also Physical Geography in AFRICA; KENYA; TANZANIA, UNITED REPUBLIC OF. (R. W. SL.)

GREAT SALT LAKE, in northwestern Utah, U.S., a large body of shallow, briny water, is the most extensive lake of its kind in the Western Hemisphere and the largest remnant of a Pleistocene lake that overspread the eastern part of the Great Basin (*see* UTAH). About 83 mi. (134 km.) long and 51 mi. (82 km.) wide, the lake has varied in area, from 2,400 sq.mi. (6,216 sq.km.) at high level in 1873 (4,211.6 ft. [1,283.7 m.] above mean sea level) to 950 sq.mi. (2,460 sq.km.) at low level in 1963 (4,191.35 ft. [1,277.52 m.]). The maximum depth is about 35 ft. (11 m.).

Salts held in solution are principally sodium chloride and sodium sulfate, but include various magnesium salts, potash, lithium, bromine, and borax. The lake is estimated to contain about 6,000,000,000 tons of salt, and about a million tons wash into it each year; the dissolved solids have ranged from about 15% in the 1870s to 28% in the 1960s.

Few things can live in this saturated salt solution (maintained by evaporation in the face of continued inflow from the Bear, Weber, and Jordan rivers), primarily algae, a few flagellates, protozoans and invertebrates, a small brine shrimp, and two brine flies.

Stansbury, Antelope, and Fremont islands, connected with the mainland when the lake is low, have been used for grazing purposes. Smaller islands serve as nesting sites for white pelicans, great blue herons, cormorants, terns, and gulls. A federal migratory bird refuge was established in 1928 in Bear River Bay.

Fathers Silvestre Vélez de Escalante and Francisco Domínguez were told of the lake in 1776, though they did not see it; and for many decades it was reflected on maps of America as a half-legendary body of water, usually named Timpanogos or Buenaventura. The lake seemingly was discovered independently in 1824–25 by two trappers, Étienne Provost and James Bridger, and by 1826 other fur hunters had circumnavigated it. John C. Frémont's formal explorations in 1843 and 1845 were followed by Howard Stansbury's detailed survey in 1850. The Lucin Cutoff (30 mi. [48 km.] of railway trestlework and fill), constructed across the lake in 1902–03 by the Southern Pacific Railroad, was replaced in 1957–60 by a rock causeway. This structure has had the effect of creating two lakes, the brinier to the north.

Popular beaches and resorts have long served visitors to the southeastern shores, and recreational development of Antelope Island was undertaken by the state in 1967. Salt-reduction plants have existed since 1850, but large-scale industrial exploitation waited upon the 1966 federal cession of 600,000 ac. of shoreline lands, which gave rise to new chemical industries.

See James E. Talmage, *The Great Salt Lake, Present and Past* (1900); Dale L. Morgan, *The Great Salt Lake* (1947). (D. L. M.)

GREAT SLAVE LAKE (ATHAPUSCOW), in Mackenzie district, Northwest Territories, Can., between latitude 60° 50′ and 63° 10′ N. and longitude 108° 50′ and 117° W. and 512 ft. above the sea, is about 298 mi. long, 62 mi. wide and 10,980 sq.mi. in area; it drains by the Mackenzie river into the Arctic ocean. The English explorer Samuel Hearne discovered the lake in 1771. The water is very clear and deep. The shore is indented by large bays, often with rocky slopes that form rugged cliffs fronting East Arm. The western shores are well wooded; the northern and eastern shores are largely barren. The navigation season is from about mid-June to mid-October, the lake freezing over in winter. Gold is produced in the Yellowknife and Rae areas. An inland fishing industry (whitefish, trout) was established in 1945 with packing plants at Gros Cap and Hay River. (J. R. M.)

GREAT SMOKY MOUNTAINS. In western North Carolina and eastern Tennessee, U.S., between Asheville and Knoxville, the Great Smoky mountains are the western segment of the high crystalline Appalachians and blend into the Blue Ridge escarpment on the east. The blue smoky haze that covers the region gave the mountains their name.

Originally the domain of the Cherokees, the Smoky mountains were explored in the mid-19th century by the geologists Thomas L. Clingman and Arnold Guyot. The highest segment of the mountains is occupied by the Great Smoky Mountains National park (*q.v.*), which extends 54 mi. between the Little Tennessee river on the southwest and the Pigeon river on the northeast, and is approximately 20 mi. wide. Highest peaks in the park area are Clingmans Dome (6,642 ft.), Mt. Guyot (6,621 ft.), Mt. Chapman (6,430 ft.), Mt. Collins (6,188 ft.), Mt. LeConte (6,593 ft.) and Mt. Kephart (6,150 ft.). The mountains are covered by forests, about 40% of which is virgin growth. There is an abundance of rhododendron, mountain laurel, wild flowers and animal life. Gatlinburg, Tenn., serves as park headquarters and offers a wide range

VALLEY IN THE GREAT SMOKY MOUNTAINS WHICH LIE BETWEEN ASHEVILLE, N.C., IN THE EAST AND KNOXVILLE, TENN., IN THE WEST IN EASTERN TENNESSEE AND WESTERN NORTH CAROLINA

of accommodations and services for tourists. A transmountain highway runs from Gatlinburg through Newfound Gap (5,048 ft.) to Cherokee, N.C., which is the site of a Cherokee Indian reservation. (M. C. P.)

GREAT SMOKY MOUNTAINS NATIONAL PARK, in eastern Tennessee and western North Carolina, was established for full development in 1934 to preserve the last remaining sizable area of southern primeval hardwood forest in the United States. The park, 516,626 ac. in extent, contains some of the highest mountains east of the Mississippi river, with Clingmans Dome (6,642 ft.) the tallest in the park.

Summits and ridges are crowned with a forest of red spruce except where open areas—balds—occur. Some of these are grown with rhododendrons (*R. catawbiense*), which display large purple-pink blooms in the early summer. The forests on lower slopes, traversed by rushing streams, are composed of such trees as hemlocks, silver bell, black cherry, buckeye, yellow birch and tulip tree, the latter sometimes attaining trunk diameters of six feet and larger. Understory trees on lower slopes and in the valleys are flowering dogwood, redbud and serviceberry; dense stands of mountain laurel, several species of brilliant-flowered azalea and the white-blossomed rhododendron (*R. maximum*) form almost impenetrable thickets. Wild flowers of many kinds are abundant in the spring and summer.

A few of the park's more important species of wildlife are black bears, white-tailed deer, foxes, bobcats, raccoons, ruffed grouse, turkeys and many colourful songbirds and insectivorous birds, the latter occurring in greatest numbers while migrating northward in spring.

During pioneer times, many families settled in the sheltered coves and valleys of the area, and a number of their picturesque, primitive farmhouses, barns and a mill are preserved in the park. Cades Cove contains such an exhibit, and there are a number of families remain and continue to farm in harmony with certain National Park service regulations. (Dx. B.)

GREAT TREK is the name given to a migration of the Boers from British jurisdiction in south Africa (see SOUTH AFRICA, REPUBLIC OF: *History*). About 12,000 *voortrekkers* and their families left Cape Colony between 1835 and 1843. Most of them settled in Natal, but when it was annexed by Great Britain in 1843 many moved across the Orange river and founded the Orange Free State (see ORANGE FREE STATE: *History*) and the Transvaal (see TRANSVAAL: *History*). Both of these later became Boer republics.

GREAT WALL OF CHINA, a defensive fortification extending about 1,500 mi. from the Gulf of Chihli of the Yellow sea to the gates of central Asia, is the greatest building enterprise ever undertaken by man. Walled frontiers between kingdoms in China date from at least the 4th century B.C., developing from the siege warfare of a people who lived in walled cities. In the 3rd century B.C. the "first emperor of Ch'in"—Ch'in Shih Huang Ti—after uniting China, linked up some already existing walls and built new sections to create the Great Wall, defending China from the Hsiung-nu or Huns on the north. It was built of earth and stone, and its eastern sections were faced with bricks. The Great Wall was frequently modified in later centuries. The sections built in the 15th and 16th centuries—which took in less territory than the "original" Great Wall—were about 30 ft. high and wide enough on top for a column of troops. Towers about 40 ft. high were built at intervals of 200 yd. Not all the outlying walls in Mongolia have been fully traced, mapped and identified as to date. *See also* CHINESE ARCHITECTURE. (O. L.)

GREBE, an aquatic diving bird of the family Podicipedidae, order Podicipediformes, containing several genera including *Podiceps* and *Aechmophorus*. The grebes are generally considered to be among the most primitive living families of birds. As a rule they are weak though fairly rapid fliers. Grebes are distinguished by the rudimentary tail, legs placed far back on the body, flattened shank and elongated toes furnished with broad lobes of skin in lieu of webs, bodily characteristics of adaptive importance to these divers. Although grebes are excellent swimmers, found on coastal and inland waters throughout the world, they are almost helpless on land and take to wing reluctantly. All species have short and close plumage, usually some shade of brownish gray above, often marked with red, and glossy white below.

Most species develop special nuptial adornments in the spring in both sexes, in the form of crests or tufts, and very remarkable mutual courtship ceremonies have been described (see COURTSHIP, ANIMAL). In some species, as the great crested grebes (*Podiceps cristatus*), this involves the partners facing each other, standing practically erect on the surface of the water, bowing, then dropping to a more horizontal position, and occasionally skittering over the water as if they were walking on the surface.

The nest, usually built among tangled vegetation in shallow waters, consists of a mass of water weeds in a shallow tray on which the chalky white eggs are laid. The parent covers the eggs before leaving the nest, so that the moist covering, besides screening the eggs from view, provides warmth as a result of its decay. The downy youth, striped black, white and brown, are often carried about on the parent's back, and if danger threatens, the adult tucks the young under its wings and dives with them.

Of the five European species, *P. ruficollis* is the well-known little grebe or dabchick (*q.v.*), with a wide range over the old world. The great crested grebe (*Podiceps cristatus*) is also a wide-ranging species. The subarctic red-necked grebe (*P. grisegena*) inhabits Europe and America, as does the horned or Slavonian grebe (*P. auritus*). Various other species inhabit North America, among which may be mentioned the western grebe

SLAVONIAN GREBE (PODICEPS AURITUS)

(*Aechmophorus occidentalis*), with a long slender neck and black and white plumage, and the pied-billed grebe (*Podilymbus podiceps*), the best-known grebe in America.

Several more are found in South America, of which the most remarkable is the flightless *Centropelma micropterum* of Lake Titicaca. The common-eared grebe (*Podiceps nigricollis*) breeds over Africa, Europe, northern Asia and western parts of Canada and the United States; four other species of *Podiceps* occur from Peru to the Falklands and Straits of Magellan. The Mexican grebe (*Podiceps dominicus*) of tropical South and Central America is a small bird reaching the West Indies and southern Texas; four other species occur in Australia, New Zealand, Malaya and Madagascar. *Podilymbus gigas* is confined to Lake Atitlan, Guatemala, while *A. major* ranges from Peru and northern Brazil to the Straits of Magellan.
(G. F. Ss.; Hr. Fn.)

GREBEL, CONRAD (1498?-1526), Swiss religious leader, the chief founder of Swiss-south German Anabaptism, was born in Zürich, the son of Junker Jakob Grebel of a prominent patrician family. He received a good humanist education at the universities of Basel, Vienna and Paris, but completed no degree. Returning to Zürich in 1520, he soon became an ardent supporter and associate of Huldreich Zwingli (*q.v.*) in the Swiss Reformation, only to break with him in late 1524 on the issue of the establishment of a free church, separated from the state.

In association with Felix Manz and Georg Blaurock, Grebel started such a church on Jan. 21, 1525, by performing the first adult baptism in modern history. The group was immediately plunged into persecution, and Grebel lived a harried life until his death of the plague in 1526 in Maienfeld, Grisons canton. He was imprisoned twice in Zürich for a total of at least six months. He left no writings other than letters, 69 of which are preserved in Sankt Gallen. Grebel's major emphases were on the voluntary believers' church, Christian discipleship and holy living, and an ethic of love which included rejection of all warfare. *See also* ANABAPTISTS.

See H. S. Bender, *Conrad Grebel ca. 1498-1526, The Founder of the Swiss Brethren, sometimes called Anabaptists* (1950). (Hn. S. B.)

GRECHANINOV, ALEKSANDR TIKHONOVICH (1864-1956), Russian composer notable for his religious music and music for children, was born in Moscow on Oct. 25, 1864. From 1881 to 1890 he studied the piano with V. I. Safonov and composition with S. I. Taneev and A. S. Arenski at the Moscow conservatory; from 1890 to 1893 he worked at composition and orchestration at St. Petersburg with Rimski-Korsakov. He soon became known by his songs, his first string quartet (1893) and the first of his five symphonies (1894). His opera *Dobrinya Nikitich* was produced in Moscow in 1903. (The later *Soeur Beatrice* was produced in 1912 but had to be withdrawn at once on religious grounds.) He composed in all media, producing a great quantity of piano music, songs and choruses, but his music lacks any strong personal stamp. His church music brought him an imperial pension, though his later religious music (from 1912 onward) introduces instruments and cannot be used in the Orthodox liturgy. With the 1917 Revolution he lost his pension and, after several visits to the west, he settled in Paris in 1925. There he published an autobiography. In 1940 he fled to New York, where he died—a U.S. citizen—on Jan. 3, 1956.

See A. Grechaninov, *My Life*, trans. by Nicolas Slonimsky (1952). (G. Ab.)

GRECO, EL (1541-1614), properly called DOMENIKOS THEOTOKOPOULOS, one of the greatest and most individual masters of Spanish painting, was born in Crete and trained in Italy. He spent the second half of his life in Spain and is known as a Spanish painter. In Italy he was called Il Greco, in Spain Domenico Greco or El Griego, but he is now generally referred to as El Greco. Nothing is known of his early life in Crete, then under Venetian domination, but there is reason to believe that he remained there until 1566 and that he received his first schooling in the Byzantine style of icon painting. The small signed triptych (Galleria Estense, Modena, Italy), one of his earliest known works, is dependent on Byzantine as well as Venetian models and there are traces of Byzantine influence in some of his later paintings. It is not known when El Greco left Crete for Italy, but it can be assumed that he was in Venice studying under the aged Titian some time before 1570, when he moved to Rome; for there can be no doubt that he is the artist recommended by the miniature painter Giulio Clovio in a letter of 1570 to Cardinal Alessandro Farnese: "There has arrived in Rome a young man from Candia, a pupil of Titian, who seems to my judgment to have a rare gift for painting...." There is a signed portrait of Clovio by El Greco (Naples Museum); he introduced this portrait together with those of Titian, Michelangelo, and Raphael, three of the masters to whom he was indebted, in one of his paintings of the "Purification of the Temple" (Minneapolis, Minn.). These and other works executed in Italy are mainly Venetian in style and colour but show a variety of sources. He was influenced by Tintoretto, Paolo Veronese, and Jacopo Bassano as well as Titian; in Rome he borrowed from Raphael and Michelangelo and was also affected by the prevailing Mannerist styles.

It is not known why or when El Greco left Italy for Spain; when questioned later in Toledo he refused to reply. Mancini, writing a few years after his death, relates that when it was proposed to repaint some of the nude figures in Michelangelo's "Last Judgment," El Greco's announcement that if the whole painting were demolished he could replace it with one that would be "decorous and seemly and no worse as a work of art" caused such indignation that he was obliged to leave Rome and retire to Spain. It is, however, probable that he went there with the prospect or hope of employment by Philip II in the decoration of his new palace monastery of the Escorial.

He was first recorded in Spain in August 1577, the date of his contract for altarpieces in S. Domingo el Antiguo, Toledo; there is evidence that he had already been in Madrid. He seems to have painted before he went to Toledo. The "Adoration of the Name of Jesus" (Escorial; model in the National Gallery, London), traditionally called the "Dream of Philip II," has been identified as an allegory of the Holy League, with portraits of Philip II, the pope, and the doge of Venice; and though on a much larger scale, this painting is not far removed in style from his later Italian paintings. The "St. Maurice and the Theban Legion" (Escorial) was commissioned in 1580 for the church of the Escorial, but was rejected for the altar for which it was painted because it did not please the king.

El Greco appears to have made no further attempt to obtain royal patronage and settled for the rest of his life in Toledo. He was extremely active as a religious artist, whose paintings were much sought by churches and convents. He also painted a number of portraits of church dignitaries and other distinguished persons; his few landscapes and genre compositions and one surviving mythological representation are among the first examples of these subjects in Spanish painting. In Spain he worked as an architect and sculptor as well as a painter and designed the frames and sculptures for some of his painted altarpieces. No building by him is recorded and few sculptures have survived.

It was only after his move to Spain that El Greco developed that highly individual style for which he is famous. While most of his paintings produced in Italy have later been attributed to Tintoretto, Veronese, and other Italian artists, his Spanish paintings have never been ascribed to anyone else. Though the transformation of his Italian sources was a gradual process, his early works in Toledo were already distinctive in character. In the "Espolio," which he painted for the cathedral soon after his arrival (1577-79), the elimination of space and dramatic concentration on the figures create a new, highly emotional effect. This painting involved him in a lawsuit concerning the price, in which he was ordered to correct certain "improprieties" in his treatment of the subject, though this was never done.

The "Burial of Count Orgaz," executed in 1586 for the church of S. Tomé, his first entirely independent work, established his fame in Toledo and is still his most celebrated painting. Here all the elements of his Spanish style appear in a composition for which there is no Italian iconographic precedent. The subject is the legend of a local Toledan nobleman of the 14th century who was rewarded for his pious deeds by the miraculous appearance of SS. Stephen and Augustine to carry his body to burial, in the presence of all the noblemen of the city. The miracle itself is represented in the lower half of the picture in comparatively realistic terms. The frieze of noblemen which forms the background to the burial, the saints and other attendants, have the appearance of individual though stylized portraits, their faces expressing various emotions from contemplation to rapture. Above, the scene in heaven, to which the count's soul is borne by an angel, is in an entirely different language. The elongated figures with floating draperies, grouped in exaggerated postures amid fantastic clouds, the violently contrasting colours and dramatic lighting emphasize the visionary character of the spiritual world. Later El Greco was to adopt this language for his representations of holy persons on earth as well as in heaven.

His portraiture shows a gradual development from the formal likenesses of his Italian period to an increasingly subjective interpretation. In a number of simple busts and half-length figures (many in the Prado, Madrid), the facial expressions give vivid impressions of personality and temperament. This effect is in no way diminished by increasing disregard for natural form and conventional modeling. On the contrary, in his late portraits of Cardinal Fernando Niño de Guevara (c. 1600, Metropolitan Museum, New York) and Fray Hortensio Félix Paravicino (c. 1606, Boston)—seated figures in the Renaissance tradition—he achieves his most remarkable effects of likeness with hardly any indication of the structure of the bodies and with a free impressionistic technique that eliminates detailed description.

For his devotional subjects El Greco created types that he hardly ever varied, but his interpretation changed with the development of his style. Thus, several examples of the "Purification of the Temple" (e.g., National Gallery, London), based on his Italian compositions of the subject, illustrate the transition from narrative description to symbolical interpretation. His representations of saints, St. Francis in meditation and ecstasy, the repentant St. Peter, St. Mary Magdalene, and St. Jerome—like the "Purification," themes of special doctrinal importance to the

Counter-Reformation Church—become transformed into visionary figures. Rocks, caves, or clouds provide mysterious settings and the exaggeration of postures, gestures, and facial expressions accentuates the spiritual meaning of the image. The number of replicas of these subjects that exist from his own hand and from his studio shows that they must have enjoyed great popularity. The painter Francisco Pacheco, who represented the orthodoxy of his time in matters of decorum and aesthetics, proclaimed El Greco to be the best painter of St. Francis of his age.

Among the major accomplishments of his late years was the decoration of the Capilla Mayor of the Hospital de la Caridad at Illescas, dedicated to a miraculous image of the Virgin, for which he designed the altars and probably executed the sculptures as well as the paintings (1603–04, no longer intact). The co-ordination of architecture, sculpture, and painting and the unity of subject matter in a composition intended to be seen from a single viewpoint foreshadow principles of Baroque design. In his last paintings, the complete harmony of form and content creates an emotional impact hardly surpassed by later Baroque artists. The distorted bodies in twisted, strained attitudes, seen against the spectral background of Toledo, give direct expression to the physical and mental torment of "Laocoön" (National Gallery, Washington, D.C.). The long attenuated figures, whose upward swirling movement is directed by the arbitrary and dramatic lighting, create an impression of a miraculous apparition of the "Assumption of the Virgin" (S. Vicente, Toledo); and the "Opening of the Fifth Seal" (Zumaya, Sp.), in similarly unrealistic language, powerfully evokes the mystic spirit of the ecstatic figure of St. John and of his apocalyptic vision.

The extraordinary originality of El Greco's Spanish style made his paintings a subject of dispute from the beginning. He failed to satisfy the conventional taste of Philip II, whose court painters were mediocre and moderate followers of Italian Mannerism. Yet he won considerable renown in Toledo both as an artist and as a remarkable if strange personality. At the same time he was involved in several lawsuits concerning the orthodoxy of his paintings and the prices that he demanded. The conventional Pacheco, who visited him in Toledo a few

years before his death, described him as "singular in everything as he was in his painting." Shocked by El Greco's opinions on art, particularly his statement that "Michelangelo was a good man who did not know how to paint," Pacheco had to admit that El Greco could not be excluded from the ranks of the great artists. Since his death various legends have been invoked to explain the so-called extravagance of El Greco's style, including a popular local legend that he was mad; in modern times attempts have even been made to prove that he suffered from astigmatism. But his extravagance had its roots in his Greek origin and Italian training, and his development from a minor Greco-Italian painter into one of the greatest artists that Spain has ever known must be attributed to the impact on him of his new environment. The exotic atmosphere of Toledo, a centre of intellectual and religious life, must have been particularly congenial to his own eccentric personality, and his "View of Toledo" (Metropolitan Museum, New York) in his late "visionary" style hardly exaggerates the

"LAOCOÖN" BY EL GRECO, c. 1610–14. IN THE SAMUEL H. KRESS COLLECTION, NATIONAL GALLERY OF ART, WASHINGTON, D.C.

extraordinary appearance of the city. His isolation there from the artistic activities at the court and from modern trends in Italy must also have contributed to his highly original formal development, and the lack of new models as well as Byzantine traditionalism would account for his frequent repetitions of compositions, figures, and rhetorical gestures. Above all, however, El Greco's zeal in his adopted country and they are particularly close in spirit and expression to the writings of the great Spanish mystics like St. John of the Cross, who was in Toledo when El Greco settled there.

El Greco had a few pupils and assistants, but his style was too personal to be communicated to followers and he remained an isolated figure. Until the end of the 19th century his paintings were practically unknown outside Spain. Since then they have provided a stimulus to many modern painters and El Greco is recognized as one of the world's great artists.

BIBLIOGRAPHY.—Manuel B. Cossío, *El Greco* (1908); A. L. Mayer, *El Greco* (1926); J. Camón Aznar, *Dominico Greco* (1950).; Halldor Soehner, "Der Stand der Greco-Forschung," *Zeitschrift für Kunstgeschichte*, xix, pp. 47–75 (1956); Harold E. Wethey, *El Greco and His School* (1962).   (E. Hs.)

GRECO-PERSIAN WARS, waged intermittently for a hundred years (c. 546–c. 448 B.C.), were due to the clash between Persian imperialism and Greek independence. The contestants were extremely unequal, but the Persians did not apply their strength consistently, and once their large-scale attack failed they made little attempt to maintain their foothold in Europe. The Greek states were puny in comparison. Yet a number of them combined so well and fought so skilfully that they not only defeated the Persian attempt at conquest in 480–479 but also extracted from Persia a treaty of nonaggression, known as the peace of Callias, about 448. Greek success was of cardinal importance. Independent states survived in Europe to inspire the cultural and political development of Greece and Rome long after the Persian empire fell to the Macedonians and Greeks.

Expansion of the Persian Empire (559–500 B.C.).—Within thirty years Cyrus and Cambyses created an empire that extended from the Indus valley to the Aegean sea and from the Caucasus to Arabia (see PERSIAN HISTORY). After the Persians defeated Croesus of Lydia about 546 the small Greek states on the Asiatic coast were reduced piecemeal, and Sparta, the strongest state on the Greek mainland, did nothing more than lodge diplomatic protests. Darius, who reigned from 522 to 486, consolidated and extended the Persian empire. From his capital, far inland at Susa, the royal roads led to about 20 provinces, called satrapies, which were governed by satraps possessing full military and civil powers. The conquered peoples owed tribute and military service to the king. So long as they fulfilled their obligations they were generously treated, being permitted to practise their own religion and manage their internal affairs, but disobedience was harshly punished by massacre or deportation. The imperial army consisted of the Median and Persian cavalry, archers and spearmen and of the best troops of the subject peoples; the navy was drawn from the Greek states of Asia Minor and from Phoenicia, Cyprus and Egypt. Supreme authority in war and peace was vested in the Persian monarch, whose absolute powers were tempered only by the custom of consulting his Persian officials. Darius was described as "the great king, king of kings, king of the countries possessing all kinds of peoples, king of this great earth far and wide." As the viceregent of the Persian god, Ahura Mazda, Darius laid claim to world rule.

In 514 Darius prepared to conquer Europe. Having made a reconnaissance by sea of Greece and Scythia, he decided to attack Scythia first, and instructed a Samian engineer to build a pontoon bridge across the Bosporus. The imperial army overran eastern Thrace, crossed the Danube, where the navy (consisting mainly of Greek contingents) had made a pontoon bridge, and advanced far into what is now the Ukraine, probably in 513. The Scythians retreated until Darius outran his lines of supply and then harassed his forces when he turned back. The Greek commanders in the Persian navy, although asked by the Scythians to cut the bridge over the Danube, remained loyal to Darius, but some Greek states bordering the Bosporus and the Hellespont rose in rebellion at the news of his discomfiture. These operations convinced Darius that a strong bridgehead in Europe was necessary. His generals punished the Greek rebels, established in southern Thrace a satrapy that cut off the Scythians from their Spartan allies and received the submission of the king of Macedonia. Meanwhile the Persian navy reduced Lemnos and Imbros (Imroz), and a Persian force was ready in 500 to attack Naxos, the strongest island in the Cyclades. This expedition was probably intended to pave the way for an invasion of Greece.

Ionian Revolt (499–493 B.C.).—Discontent in the Greek states of Asia Minor was caused as much by the Persian policy of supporting tyrants as by demands in tribute and service. It was exploited by two unscrupulous tyrants. Histiaeus, tyrant of Miletus, had been detained at Susa; his son-in-law Aristagoras, ruling at Miletus as his deputy, had promoted the Persian expedition to Naxos. In 499, when the expedition proved unsuccessful, Histiaeus and Aristagoras in their fear of Persia planned to raise the Greek states of Asia Minor in revolt. Aristagoras proclaimed a constitutional government at Miletus, and the tyrants were expelled from the other states. During the winter Aristagoras sailed to Greece in search of support. The Spartans, realizing their limitations as a land power, refused to send troops, but the Athenians promised 20 triremes and the Eretrians 5 triremes. When these ships arrived in 498 the Ionians started operations by capturing and burning most of Sardis, the capital of the satrapy—a spectacular success that brought out in support of the revolt the Greek states of the Bosporus and Hellespont, the Carians and the Greek cities of Cyprus. At this stage the Athenians withdrew their ships and the Eretrians probably followed their example.

The rebels had little chance of defeating the three Persian army groups that were deployed in 497, and everything depended on an offensive by sea in order to secure Cyprus and confine the Phoenician fleet to the southern Mediterranean. The Persians were quick to see the importance of Cyprus. One army group landed in the north of the island with a Phoenician fleet in support and attacked Salamis by land and sea. Here the Ionians defeated the Phoenician fleet, but the Cyprian Greeks were routed by the Persian army. The last Greek stronghold in the island capitulated in 496. Meanwhile two army groups regained control of the Bosporus and Hellespont, while two army groups regained control of the Bosporus and Hellespont, were delayed through a defeat at the hands of the Carians in 496 and mounted the final campaign in 495. While the Persian army held the coast near Miletus, a large fleet, recruited from Egypt, Phoenicia and Cyprus, advanced to harbours controlled by the army and engaged the Ionian fleet of 353 triremes near the island of Lade off Miletus. The Chian squadron fought with distinction, but the contingents of Samos and Lesbos fled at the outset. The Persian victory at sea was decisive. Miletus fell in 494, and the revolt was stamped out in 493.

The Ionian revolt was of great value to the Greek cause: it postponed the Persian attack on Greece until the Greek mainland states were capable of united action; it weakened Persian confidence and taught the Greeks some valuable lessons. Individually, the Greeks had outfought the Persians on land and sea, and resistance therefore did not seem hopeless; however, the need of close co-operation and strong leadership in the future was obvious. The Ionians had indeed created a council of deputies drawn from the individual states and had entrusted to it the direction of strategy, but they had failed to include in the council the Greeks of the Bosporus, Hellespont and Cyprus, and they had not appointed a commander in chief of the allied forces until the eve of the battle of Lade, when it was already too late.

Persian Attack on Eretria and Athens (490 B.C.).—Darius punished the ringleaders in Asia by execution or deportation, but he made a liberal settlement with the states. Democratic governments were permitted, a moderate rate of tribute was imposed and the states had to submit their disputes to arbitration. This was politic, since Darius hoped to use the Ionian fleet against Greece. In Europe his son-in-law Mardonius extended Persian rule to the borders of Macedonia, and his envoys visited the free Greek states to ask for "earth and water," the tokens of submission to Persia.

In 491 Eretria and Athens knew that an attack by sea was impending.

Before the Ionian revolt Sparta and Athens had been at war. The Persian threat brought them closer together. In 491 the Spartans tried to prevent their ally Aegina from joining Persia, and in 490 Athens attacked Aegina (the chronology is disputed; see AEGINA for a different view). These actions ensured its neutrality. Athenian policy toward Persia had vacillated before and during the Ionian revolt, but the will to resist was now strengthened by the Persian support of the exiled tyrant Hippias and by the advice of Miltiades, previously a ruler in the Chersonese, who had returned home with knowledge of Persian tactics. Even so, Sparta and Athens had no plans for united action when the Persian force, perhaps comprising about 25,000 fighting men, sailed across the Aegean, landed on Euboea and captured Carystus and Eretria. In Sept. 490 the Persian army landed unopposed on the plain of Marathon in northeast Attica, whence the lines of supply with Euboea and the east were easy and secure. The speed and the initiative of the Persians found Athens still isolated.

The Athenian army was at Athens, prepared to repel any landing in its vicinity; and the small fleet was ready to attack any Persian convoy heading for Aegina. When news came from Marathon, the assembly sent a runner to inform Sparta and decided on the proposal of Miltiades to send the heavy-armed hoplite army to the foothills above Marathon. The decision was wise; for the alternative, to stay and defend Athens, would have cut Athens off from Sparta by land and sea and exposed the city to blockade. At Marathon, however, the polemarch Callimachus and the ten generals (of whom each held operational command for one day, according to Herodotus; but see STRATEGUS) had to choose between attack and delay. Miltiades' advice prevailed: to attack as soon as opportunity offered. First the Athenians advanced their position to within a mile of the enemy by felling trees and making obstacles against the dreaded Persian cavalry. Then the opportunity came. Before dawn some Ionian deserters reported: "The cavalry are away." Miltiades, who chanced to hold the operational command, attacked at dawn. With a thin centre and strengthened wings the line of about 10,000 Athenians and 1,000 Plataeans charged the enemy infantry before the cavalry could return. The Greek wings defeated the Persians and wheeled inward to attack the Persian centre, which had driven the Greek centre back. The longer spear and heavier armour of the bronze-clad Greek infantryman prevailed over the Persian with his short spear, wicker shield and padded clothing. The rout was complete. According to Herodotus the Greeks lost 192 men, the Persians 6,400. The majority escaped to the fleet, which sailed at once, hoping to surprise Athens, but the Athenians—by a forced march—arrived that evening to defend the city. The Persians then departed. Next day a Spartan force, which had been delayed by religious observances at Sparta, reached Athens and went on to view the battlefield. (See also MARATHON, BATTLE OF.)

Expedition of Xerxes (480–479 B.C.).—The Persian failure was followed by a full-scale invasion. It was delayed by a revolt in Egypt and the death of Darius until 480, when Xerxes crossed the Hellespont in late spring with a vast army and a large fleet. The advance was slow and the fleet had to provision the army. The Greeks therefore had ample time to make preparations. The problem of uniting those states, about 30 in number, that had the will to resist Persia was solved by Sparta, which held a congress of delegates and formed a general alliance. The states agreed to stop all wars among themselves and conferred the command by land and sea on Sparta. The congress met regularly, each state having one vote, and decisions by the majority were binding on all members. It possessed recruiting, diplomatic and judicial powers. In the field the commander in chief, nominated by Sparta, consulted the commanders of the national contingents but made his own decision. Thus the Greek congress was a highly centralized and efficient organization for allied action. Its chief strength on land lay in the Spartans and their allies; at sea it lay in the Athenians, ably led by Themistocles, who had increased the fleet to 200 ships. It lay with Sparta to choose the time and place for applying the relatively small but excellent forces of the Greek congress.

The first decision, to hold the narrow Vale of Tempe between Macedonia and Thessaly, was abandoned when it was realized that the position could easily be turned. The Greeks then occupied the still narrower pass of Thermopylae with 6,000 or 7,000 hoplites and stationed 271 triremes at Artemisium in northern Euboea. The positions were linked by communication between the Spartan commanders, King Leonidas at Thermopylae and Eurybiades at Artemisium, who intended to halt and damage the Persian forces. Meanwhile Xerxes was advancing slowly. He made no use of separate columns, and his fleet suffered heavy losses in a storm when it was convoying supply ships along the coast. It was already August when Xerxes began the operations, which extended over three days.

On the first day he sent a detachment of 200 ships, unseen by the Greeks, to sail round Euboea and close the narrows of the Euboic channel, and he also attacked with his best infantry at Thermopylae, where the Greeks inflicted heavy casualties. During the afternoon the Greek fleet, having learned about the Persian detachment from a deserter, engaged the main Persian fleet with some success. The Greeks intended to sail south that night and destroy the detachment next day, but a tremendous storm kept the Greeks at Artemisium and wrecked the 200 Persian ships off south Euboea. On the second day news of the Persian disaster was brought up by a reinforcing squadron of 53 Athenian ships. Xerxes attacked again with no success at Thermopylae, and the Greeks sank some Cilician vessels off Artemisium. That evening a Greek traitor, Ephialtes, offered to guide the Persians along a mountain path and turn the position at Thermopylae. The Persian picked infantry called "Immortals" were entrusted to him. At dawn on the third day they began to descend toward the plain behind the Greek position. Leonidas retained the troops of Sparta, Thespiae and Thebes and sent the remainder south. He then advanced. He and his men fought to the death, except the Thebans, who surrendered. Meanwhile the Persian fleet attacked at noon. Both sides suffered heavy losses and the Greeks realized that they could only succeed in narrower waters. That evening, when the fall of Thermopylae was known, the Greek fleet withdrew down the Euboic channel and took station in the narrow strait of Salamis.

In September Xerxes, joined by many Greeks north of Attica, burned Athens. The city was almost deserted, for the Athenians on the advice of Themistocles had entrusted themselves to "the wooden wall" of their ships in accordance with a Delphic oracle. The Greek congress decided to fortify the isthmus and keep the fleet forward at Salamis. This decision caused dissension among the ship captains. Many wished to retire to the Argolic gulf. Themistocles clinched the matter by informing Xerxes of their desire; for Xerxes, who saw the end of the campaigning season close at hand, sent 200 ships that night to cut the Greek line of retreat and posted the main fleet of 1,207 ships off the eastern exit of the straits of Salamis. During the night the Greeks learned of his dispositions and intentions. At dawn they moved northward, feigning a retreat, drew the main fleet into the strait and then returned to engage at close quarters. A detachment under the Corinthian Adeimantus sailed to meet the 200 Persian ships. The 310 remaining Greek ships, stoutly built for ramming, had room to maneuver against the congested stream of Persian ships which, designed for boarding tactics, proved less handy under oar and fell foul of one another. The result was a complete triumph for Greek seamanship. The Persians fled in confusion. Soon afterward their fleet, superior still in numbers but not in morale, set sail for Asia.

That winter, while Xerxes departed to Asia, a large army wintered in Thessaly under the command of Mardonius. By skilful diplomacy he drew the Greeks forward in summer 479 to the northern foothills of Mt. Cithaeron near Plataea, where difficulties of supply forced the Greek army of 110,000 men to withdraw during the night. The withdrawal was disorderly and dawn found the army scattered. Mardonius at once attacked a group of 11,500 Spartan and Tegean hoplites who had halted on hilly ground. Their commander, Pausanias, undismayed by the swarms of Persian infantry, led his men downhill in close formation, charged at the double and overwhelmed the enemy. When the Athenians came up after defeating the Thebans, the Greeks stormed the camp and the survivors of the Persian army fled. Meanwhile the Greek fleet had passed to the offensive at Mycale on the Asiatic coast opposite Samos. The Persians refused battle, beached their ships and joined a large supporting army, but the Spartan king Leotychides landed his men farther north and attacked with complete success. The victories of Plataea and Mycale ended the Persian invasion.

Greek Offensive (478–448 B.C.).—The Greek triumph was due to Spartan leadership, Athenian loyalty and Greek fighting power. The Spartans, however, had no desire to campaign in Asia, whereas the Athenians were ready to deploy their fleet in support of the Ionians. Hence arose the Delian league (q.v.), formed by Athens as executive leader and by many Greek states on the islands and Asiatic coast, to defend Greek liberty and exact retribution from Persia. A series of successful operations culminated c. 466 in victory at the Eurymedon river in Pamphylia, where an allied force of 300 ships defeated a Persian army and navy. In 460 the Athenians and their allies supported Egypt in a successful revolt. But the Persian army returned to the attack; Egypt made a separate peace, and the Greeks, overconfident in their sea power, were trapped on the Nile and annihilated in 454. By this time the Athenians were at war with Sparta, but a truce on the Greek mainland enabled them to launch successful attacks on Cyprus in 450–449. A treaty of peace was concluded, probably in 448, by the Athenians and their allies and Artaxerxes I of Persia that recognized the liberty of the Greek states in Europe and Asia and kept the Persian fleet out of the Aegean. See GREECE: History.

BIBLIOGRAPHY.—Aeschylus, Persae; Herodotus, History; Ctesias, Persica; M. N. Tod, Greek Historical Inscriptions, vol. 1, part 2, 2nd ed. (1946); G. B. Grundy, The Great Persian War (1901); G. B. Gray, M. Cary and J. A. R. Munro in Cambridge Ancient History, vol. iv, ch. 1, 7–10 (1926); J. B. Bury, A History of Greece, 3rd ed. revised by R. Meiggs (1951); N. G. L. Hammond, A History of Greece, book iii (1959), and articles in Historia, iv, pp. 385 ff. (1956) and Journal of Hellenic Studies, lxxvi, pp. 32 ff. (1956). (N. G. L. H.)

GRECO-TURKISH WAR (1897). In the last quarter of the 19th century there was deep dissatisfaction in Greece. Between 1832 and 1881 Greece received no increase of territory, except for the transfer to it by Great Britain of the Ionian Islands on March 29, 1864. On May 24, 1881, as a result of the provisions of the treaty of Berlin (1878), a conference in Constantinople awarded Greece a new frontier from the southern slopes of Mt. Olympus in the east to the Arachtos river in the west, which gave it possession of the Thessalian plain and a small part of Epirus. The Greeks watched with growing concern the unification of Bulgaria in 1885 (see EASTERN QUESTION), while opinion was inflamed by conditions in Crete, where the Turks were in theory required to rule in accordance with the organic statute of 1868. In 1889 disturbances broke out in Crete, and the question of union with Greece was raised; from this time onward there was a state of endemic hostility in the island between the Muslims and the Greeks. In the years 1882–95 the Greek statesman Kharilaos Trikoupis used his influence to restrain Greek opinion, but following his resignation from the post of prime minister in 1895 chauvinistic tendencies got the upper hand, especially under the influence of the new prime minister, Theodoros Diliyiannis (q.v.).

On May 24, 1896, disturbances again broke out in Crete. Coinciding with the Armenian troubles in Turkey, they seemed to present Greece with the opportunity of annexing the island, since the insurgents were demanding a union. On Feb. 4, 1897, Greek troops under Col. Timoleon Vassos actually landed on the island to assist the rebels. Excitement in Greece was not reduced when the great powers intervened to isolate the Cretan revolt, landing marines at Canea and, on March 18, imposing a blockade upon Greece to prevent assistance being sent from the mainland to the island. The policy of the great powers was to support an autonomous Cretan regime but to prevent union with Greece. Thwarted of an opportunity of assisting their compatriots in Crete, the Greeks began to demand an attack upon the Turkish forces in the north. At the beginning of April 1897 Greek irregulars began to make their appearance in Macedonia, and on April 17 the Greek regular army under the command of the crown prince Constantine attacked the Turks. The Turks, however, had been undergoing reorganization under the guidance of Gen. Colmar von der Goltz and other German instructors since 1883 and proved more than a match for the Greeks. The Turkish commander, Edhem Pasha, counterattacked in Thessaly and took Larissa on April 27. On May 9 the Greek government submitted to the great powers by withdrawing its troops from Crete, and on May 20 an armistice was concluded with the Turks in the mainland. Under the terms of the peace settlement of Dec. 4, 1897, Greece was obliged to pay to Turkey an indemnity of £T4,-000,000, accept an international finance commission at Athens and submit to a minor northern frontier rectification in Turkey's interest.

The result, therefore, was one of humiliation for Greece and loss of prestige for the crown prince Constantine and his wife, Sophia, the sister of William II of Germany, who had professed good will toward Greece but whose instructors were loaned to the Turkish army. In Crete, however, after many stormy troubles—including an attack upon the British troops garrisoning Canea—the Turks withdrew on Nov. 14, 1898, and the Greeks accepted an autonomous regime under Prince George of Greece as high commissioner and the sultan as suzerain. Greece, however, found it impossible to resume an active foreign policy before 1911–12 in view of the Austro-Russian accord of 1897 to "put the Balkans on ice" and the German cultivation of Turkey. (R. F. LE.)

GRECO-TURKISH WAR (1921–22). The origin of the Greco-Turkish War of 1921-22 was the treaty of Sèvres (Aug. 10, 1920), by which among other provisions the Allied powers awarded to Greece eastern Thrace up to the Catalca (Chatalja) line and including Gallipoli, together with the district of Smyrna (Izmir). The situation was complicated by the fact that the Greek elections of Nov. 14, 1920, which followed the death of King Alexander, returned a royalist majority and led to the withdrawal of Eleutherios Venizelos from politics. On Dec. 20, King Alexander's father, King Constantine, who had been forced to vacate his throne by the Allies on June 12, 1917, on account of his pro-German policy, was restored as the result of a plebiscite. His advent to power brought about some disorganization in the Greek army on account of the dismissal of Venizelist officers; the Greek commanders in Turkey, Gen. Anastasios Papoulas and his successor, Gen. Georgios Hadjanestis, owed their positions to their political allegiance rather than to their military capacity. In Jan. 1921 a poorly equipped Greek army started an offensive into Anatolia and took the two railway junctions of Afyon (Afyonkarahisar) and Eskisehir, but was forced to withdraw in April as a result of a Turkish victory.

In July 1921 the Greeks resumed their offensive in order to forestall a Turkish attack. Afyon and Eskisehir were retaken and the Greek advance pressed forward in the direction of Ankara, but it was severely checked by Kemal in September on the Sakarya river, from which the Greeks were obliged to withdraw.

Great Britain and France, meanwhile, showed little unity of policy. The British prime minister, David Lloyd George, favoured the Greeks, but he was greatly hampered by the danger of repercussions in Muslim countries where British interests could be affected if too great a measure of support were given to the Greeks. On Oct. 20, 1921, France gave up the intention of occupying Cilicia, retaining only the sanjak of Alexandretta (Iskenderun). France, moreover, undertook to supply Turkey with arms. Such sympathy as France had for Greece was weakened when in Jan. 1922 Aristide Briand's government fell and was succeeded by that of Raymond Poincaré.

The Paris inter-Allied conference recommended on March 24, 1922, an armistice between the two parties, but the Turks under Kemal demanded the total evacuation of Anatolia. On Aug. 26,

1922, the Turks achieved a great victory at Afyon which compelled the Greek army to withdraw in disorder. On Sept. 9, 1922, the Turkish army recaptured Smyrna, where a large part of the Greek population was massacred. The Kemalist army was then free to march to the Bosporus, where the French authorities refused to offer resistance to their entry into Istanbul and the British authorities were compelled to follow the French example. The armistice of Mudanya, concluded on Oct. 11, 1922, admitted Turkish troops into Istanbul and made provision for renewed peace discussions at Lausanne between Turkey and the Allies.

The results of the campaign were important for Greece. A body of officers on the island of Chios, led by Col. Nikolaos Plastiras, demanded that Constantine abdicate. Ironically Constantine, forced to abdicate in 1917 under Allied pressure, was now compelled to give way to his son, George II, for having undertaken action with the encouragement of the Allies. On Nov. 28, 1922, the responsible Greek ministers were sentenced to death and executed. For Turkey the campaign ended more happily. After protracted negotiations the treaty of Lausanne was signed on July 24, 1923. Greece had to give up eastern Thrace and accept the Maritsa (Evros) river as its eastern frontier, while Turkey obtained Imbros and Tenedos. To some extent future causes of Greco-Turkish friction were removed by the transference of Greek and Turkish minorities to their respective homelands. The sultanate having been abolished on Nov. 1, 1922, Kemal's regime began with the prestige of a great military victory.

BIBLIOGRAPHY.—H. N. Howard, *The Partition of Turkey: a Diplomatic History, 1913–1923* (1931); A. A. Pallis, *Greece's Anatolian Venture—and After* (1937); Thomas Jones, *Lloyd George* (1951); E. S. Forster, *A Short History of Modern Greece, 1821–1956*, 3rd ed. (1958).
(R. F. LE.)

GREECE (Greek HELLAS; modern Greek ELLÁS or ELLÁDHOS [Kingdom of Greece]), a country of southern Europe, comprises the southern peninsula of the Balkans, the northern foreshore of the Aegean as far east as the Maritsa (Evros) river, and, except for Imroz Adası (Imbros Island) and Bozca Ada (Tenedos), all the main islands of the Aegean, including Crete and the Dodecanese. The name Greece (Latin *Graecia*) derives from *Graeci*, originally the Latin name of a Boeotian tribe (*Graioi*) which settled in Italy in the 8th century B.C. but later applied there to the Hellenic people as a whole. The capital is Athens (*q.v.*).

This article contains the following sections and subsections:

I. PHYSICAL GEOGRAPHY

1. Geology.—Structurally, Greece forms part of the system of folded mountains, thrown up in the Tertiary period, that crosses the old world from the western Mediterranean to Indonesia. In the Balkans these fold ranges consist mainly of sedimentary limestones which were crushed against a resistant central nucleus of hard crystalline rocks, the Rhodope massif (Rodhópi Óri), detached fragments of which are seen in the coastlands of Macedonia and Thrace.

The backbone range of central Greece is that of Pindus, which preserves the general north-northwest to south-southeast trend of the Dinaric ranges of Yugoslavia, of which it forms a projection. The Pindus mountains (Píndhos Óros) have a hard core of granites and serpentines, flanked with Cretaceous limestones. From them diverges eastward, in broad arcs, a series of ranges that form the various promontories of the east coast, and whose lines can be followed out into the several archipelagos of the Aegean. South of the Gulf of Corinth (Korinthiakós Kólpos), the general Dinaric grain of the Pindus can be traced again in the promontories of the southern Peloponnese, but beyond there these folds make a broad curve, the undrowned fragments of which can be seen in Crete (Kríti) and Rhodes (Ródhos).

After the folding of the mountains, which began in the late Cretaceous period and continued into the Miocene, the topography was vastly modified by rifting and subsidence, processes that still continue on a minor scale and result in earth tremors like those that caused havoc in the Ionian Islands (Iónioi Nísoi) in 1953. This fracture and collapse had various results. In the first place, the rivers of Greece often follow rift valleys, as in the case of the Vardar (Axiós) and Struma (Strimón). Second, deep enclosed depressions were formed, which were occupied by lakes. Throughout the Pliocene period these gradually filled with sediment to form wide flat plains, like those of Lárisa and Trikkala, often imperfectly drained through a single narrow outlet. Third, the main outline of the coasts was shaped at this time. Where the cleavage ran parallel to the general trend of the mountains, the resulting coast was straight and harbourless, as in Ilía (Elís). Where, however, the rifting ran across the grain of the folded ranges, long sheltered bays, like the gulfs of Corinth and Aegina (Aíyina) were the result. Last, the origin of the Aegean sea and its islands must be attributed to the fall of a whole major section of the fold mountains, between the eastern shore of the Greek mainland and the west coast of Asia Minor. In the Aegean the depth of the subsidence was greater in the south than in the north. Much of the sea between Lennos (Límnos) and Thrace is less than 1,200 ft. (366 m.) deep; off the Northern Sporades the sea is at most 5,000 ft. (1,524 m.) deep; even between the Cyclades and Crete maximum depths of about 8,000 ft. (2,438 m.) are recorded. The present sea level of the Aegean, therefore, stands approximately halfway between the deepest part of the sea bed and the highest crests on the mainland. South of Crete, the Aegean "platform" ends abruptly and the sea bed falls to depths of 20,000 ft. (6,096 m.) or more. A counter effect of the earth fracture of the Tertiary period was the volcanic eruption that produced the now extinct craters of Pátmos, Nísiros and Mílos (Melos), and that which is still from time to time active on Thíra or Thera (Santorin). On the mainland occasional deposits of tuff and lava, as at the cone of Méthana, as well as hot springs like those of Loutráki and Kíthnos (Thermiá), are further signs of volcanism. Finally, many details of the coast have been modified by silting, even since classical times, especially in the deltas of Thessaly (Thessalía).

The peculiar beauty of Greece is found not in the grandeur of its mountains and rivers, but rather in the infinite variety of its scenery and in the intimate juxtaposition of harsh white limestone crags, piedmont terraces with deep-green orchards of olives and figs, dusty plains of sparse, thorny pasture and limpid sea of cerulean blue.

2. Climate.—Summer is hot and dry almost everywhere in Greece, and the mean July temperature at sea level is usually very close to 27° C. (80° F.). The extreme heat is tempered to a small extent in the immediate vicinity of the coast, where a sea breeze blows in every afternoon. Temperatures are lower also in the higher mountains of northern Greece which, because of their elevation, enjoy an appreciable rainfall in summer and autumn. Elsewhere, the summer drought is unbroken, and the etesian winds, becoming steadily warmer in their movement southward, parch the earth over which they pass. These winds, which belong to the same system as the trades, are gentle, regular and reliable, and summer is the traditional sailing season in the Aegean.

With the break of the rains in late September, conditions change immediately. In winter the belt of eastward-moving cyclonic storms shifts southward to include Greece and the other Mediterranean lands. The winds at sea become squally and turbulent, changing direction as each cyclone passes by, and they may make sailing conditions as hazardous as those described in the account of the shipwreck of St. Paul (Acts xxvii). In Macedonia the north wind from the heavy, cold air mass of the central Balkans blows with particular force when it is drawn down the valleys of the Vardar and Struma into one of the cyclones over the Aegean. At one such time a thermometer reading as low as −10° C. (14° F.) was recorded at Salonika (Thessaloníki), and the nearby gulf had a thin coating of ice. This cold north wind, known as the bora, has its counterpart in the *shilok* or warm wind from the south, which on the west coast in the intermediate seasons may quickly warm the local atmosphere to as much as 6.7° C. (44.1° F.). The difference in temperature between northern and southern Greece is much greater in winter than in summer, for while Athens has a mean January temperature of 8° C. (46.4° F.), the corresponding figure at Salonika is 4.8° C. (40.6° F.). The west coast, where most of the winter winds blow onshore, has the mildest winters; at Corfu the mean temperature for the month of January is 10.2° C. (50.4° F.).

The rainfall varies markedly. The driest parts are the plains of the east, especially those of Thessaly with an annual total of usually less than 15 in. (38.1 cm.). Athens has an average annual fall of 15.4 in. (39.1 cm.), falling mostly between October and March. Salonika, where the summer drought is less extreme, has an annual average of 21.5 in. (54.6 cm.). The west coast is the wettest part, for there the winter cyclones strike the mountains squarely after collecting moisture in their passage over the Ionian sea; Corfu has an average annual rainfall of 50.4 in. (128 cm.). The winter rains, being of cyclonic origin, fall in downpours, often divided by long periods of clear days. Much of this torrential rain is lost by immediate seepage and runoff.

3. Drainage.—Since the rainfall of Greece is very unevenly distributed throughout the year, the regime of its rivers is extremely seasonal and, even in the winter, is irregular, rising with each cyclonic storm. In addition, the river beds are very uneven, as is usual in youthful and little-eroded mountain country; there is a clear contrast between the precipitous upper stretches of streams like the Aliákmon (Haliacmon) and their lower courses that meander over old alluvium-filled lake basins or deltaic swamps. For all these reasons, the rivers of Greece are of little value for navigation and they are also difficult to control for irrigation. The most copious and perennial are the Vardar and Struma, which have large catchment basins in the central Balkans, but whose lower sections alone lie in Greece. The other chief rivers that enter the Aegean from Greece are the Néstos (Bulg. Mesta), the Aliákmon, the Piniós (Salanvrías) and the Sperkhiós; the Evrótas of Lakonía (Laconia) is the largest stream of the Peloponnese, and Akarnanía (Acarnania) and Ipiros (Epirus) are drained principally by the Akhelóös (Achelous), the Arakhthos (Arta) and the Kalamás (Thíamis).

An individual feature of the drainage of the limestone districts is the katabothra or "swallow holes." These are enclosed depressions, formed by subsidence or solution, where the drainage sometimes disappears underground and, when the inflow is exceptionally heavy, accumulates to form a temporary surface lake.

4. Geographical Regions.—*The Peloponnese.*—This southern peninsula (modern Greek Pelopónnisos), formerly called Morea, was joined naturally to central Greece by a four-mile-wide (6.4 km.) isthmus, which is cut by the Corinth canal linking the gulfs of Corinth and Aegina. The most fertile part is the coastal plain of Pliocene marls and conglomerates in the north and west, the districts of Akhaïa (Achaea) and Ilía where the bulk of the Greek currant crop is grown. The two great alluvial depressions of Lakonía and Messinía are oases of fertility on either side of the dry, barren limestone wilderness of Taïyetos Óros (7,887 ft. [2,404 m.]) one of the least populated parts of Greece. But even in these lowlands the cultivated area is only that which has access to springs or irrigation water from the mountain slopes. Beyond this lies, according to the season, malarial swamp or dusty plain, a type of scenery that occurs throughout all the central part of the third great alluvial lowland of the Peloponnesian peninsula, that of Argolis.

The limestone plateau of Arkadhía (Arcadia), in the heart of the Peloponnese, is one of the most inaccessible parts of all Greece. The open hills carry a mean pasture, but among them lie occasional tectonic basins that contain some of the best cultivated land of the peninsula. Some, like the basin of Megalópolis, drain outward, in this case to the Alfiós (Alpheus). Others, like the plain of Tripolis, are true katabothra.

The east coast of the Peloponnese is deeply indented and has numerous small natural harbours. The coast of Ilía, on the other hand, was formed by a straight fault and has been further smoothed by the deposition of strand flats, through longshore silting. Katákolon is the only good harbour there. Sheltered by the island of Sfaktiría (Sphacteria), Navarino bay (Órmos Navarínou) in Messinia is one of the best natural harbours in Greece.

Central Greece.—The central range of Pindus throws off four spurs to the east. The most northerly of these, the Kamvoúnia Óri—which some geologists regard not as a fold range but as fragments of the old crust block—runs parallel to the straight faulted coast from Salonika to the Gulf of Vólos. It is a discontinuous chain, whose trend can be traced through Olympus (Ólimbos, 9,570 ft. [2,917 m.]), Óssa and Pelion (Pílion) out into the islands of the Northern Sporades. Between this range and the next, that of Óthris, whose line is continued in the Kandhílion Óros of northern Euboea (Évvoia), lie the three plains of Almirós, Tríkkala, and Lárisa, each marking the site of a lake basin of Tertiary times, since filled in with detritus. These last two plains are both drained by the Piniós, which leaves each through a constricted gorge, the lower one being the famous Vale of Tempe (Témbi) embowered within the forests of Óssa and Olympus.

Passing southward, the third range to leave the Pindus is that of Oíti or Oeta (7,060 ft. [2,152 m.]), which is continuous with the Óthris

PLATE I

GREECE

JOHN G. ROSS—PHOTO RESEARCHERS, INC.

Children playing on lower slope of Mt. Parnassus, traditional home of Apollo

RICHARD MEEK BY COURTESY OF "LIFE" MAGAZINE, © TIME INC.

Greek Orthodox wedding. Linked wreaths, blessed by priest, are placed on couple's heads by bridegroom's godfather

JOSEPH NETTIS

Siphnos, a town on Siphnos Island in the Cyclades. The buildings are made of whitewashed stone

PLATE II

GREECE

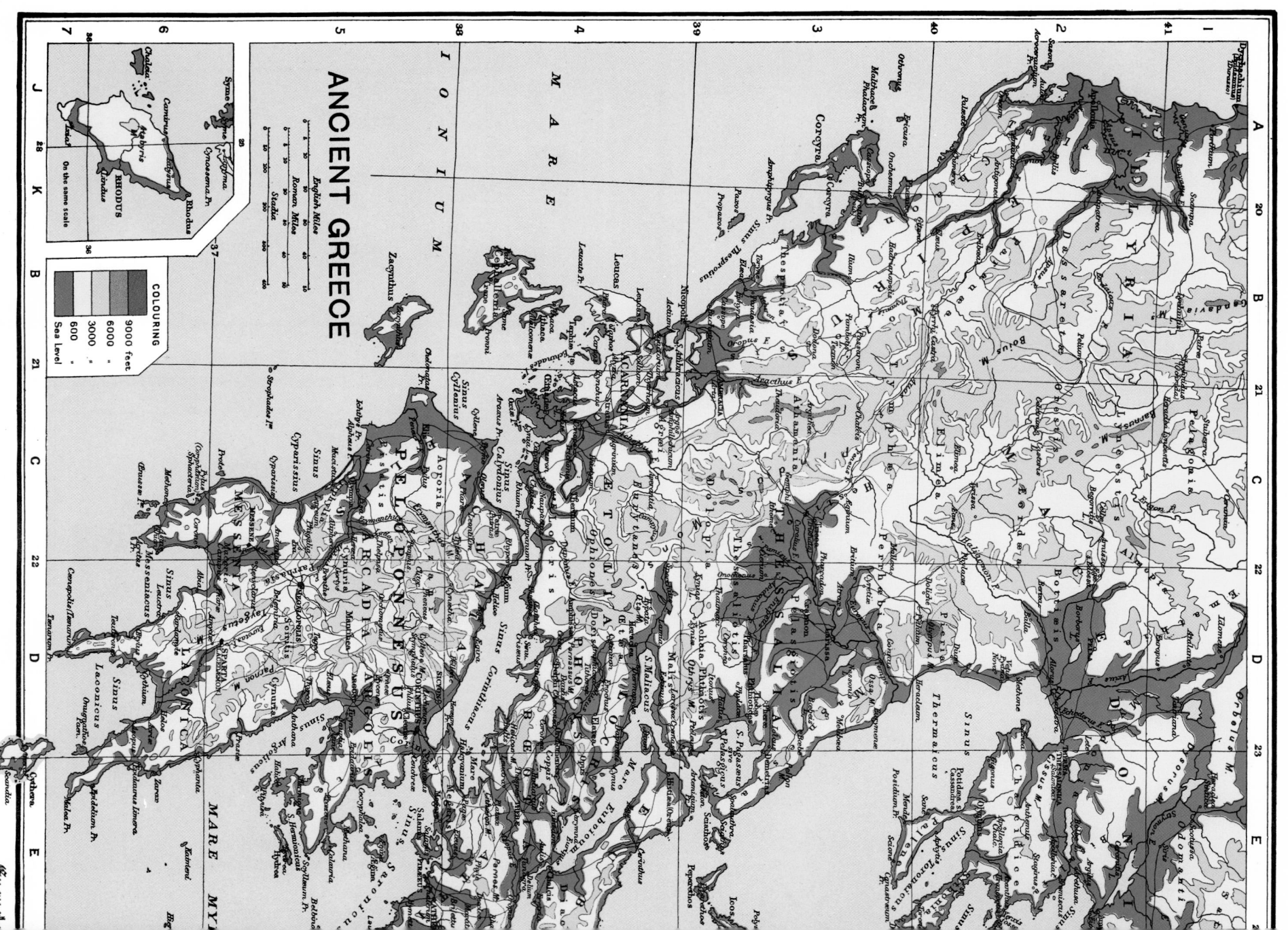

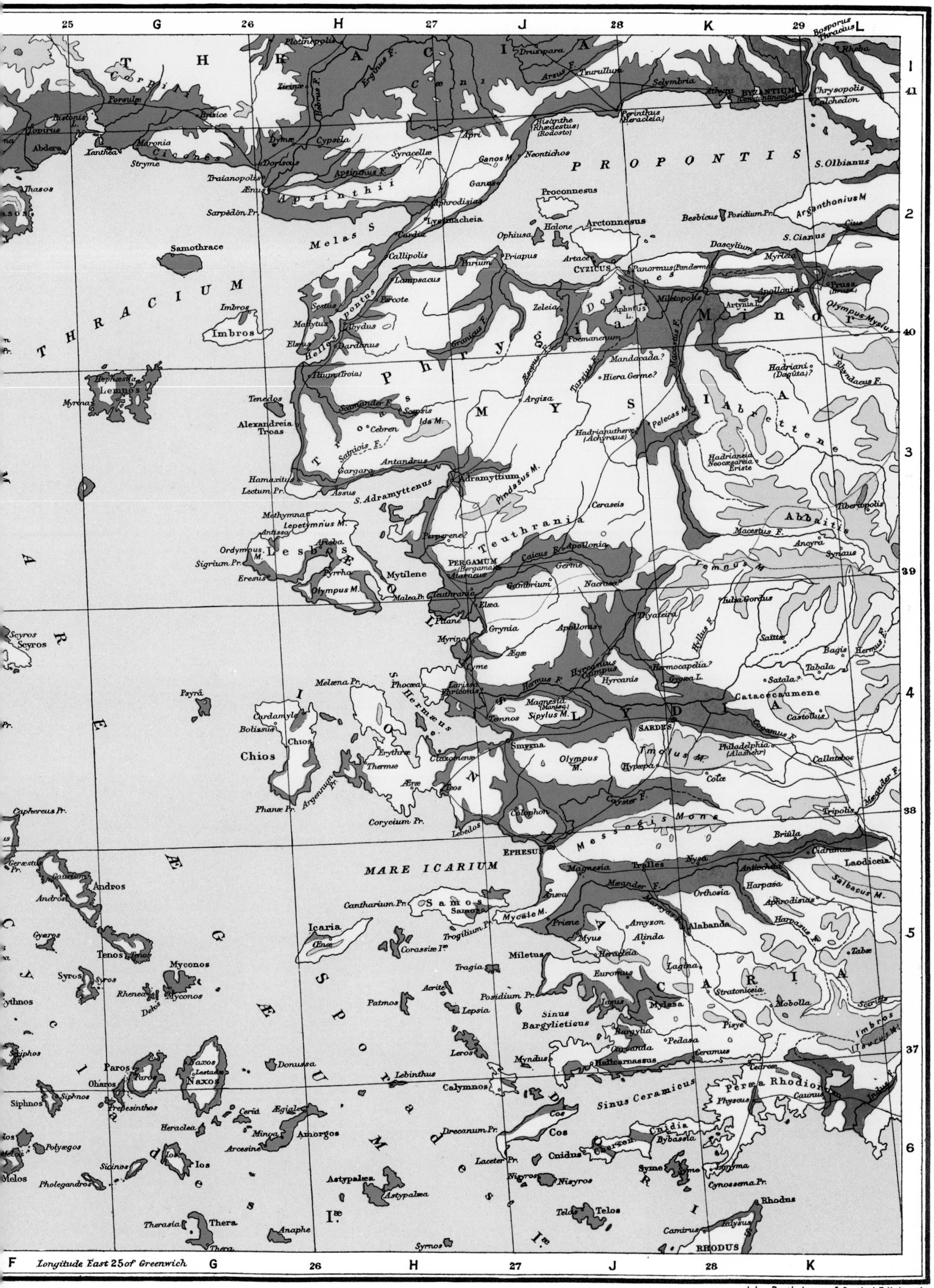

PLATE III

GREECE

John Bartholomew & Son, Ltd. Edinburgh

Longitude East 25 of Greenwich

PROPONTIS

MARE ICARIUM

RHODUS

THRACIUM

Imbros

Lesbos

Chios

Icaria

Samos

Patmos

Cos

SPORADES

Samothrace

Lemnos

Tenedos

SARDES

EPHESUS

PERGAMUM

Smyrna

Miletus

Mylene

Tralles

Magnesia

Olympus M.

Sipylus M.

Ida M.

Teuthrania

Phrygia

Mysia

Troas

Lydia

Caria

Aeolis

Ionia

Abrettene

Troia

Andros

Tenos

Syros

Paros

Naxos

Ios

Amorgos

Astypalea

Thera

Anaphe

Cyclades

Rhodes

Camirus

Lindus

Ialysus

GREECE

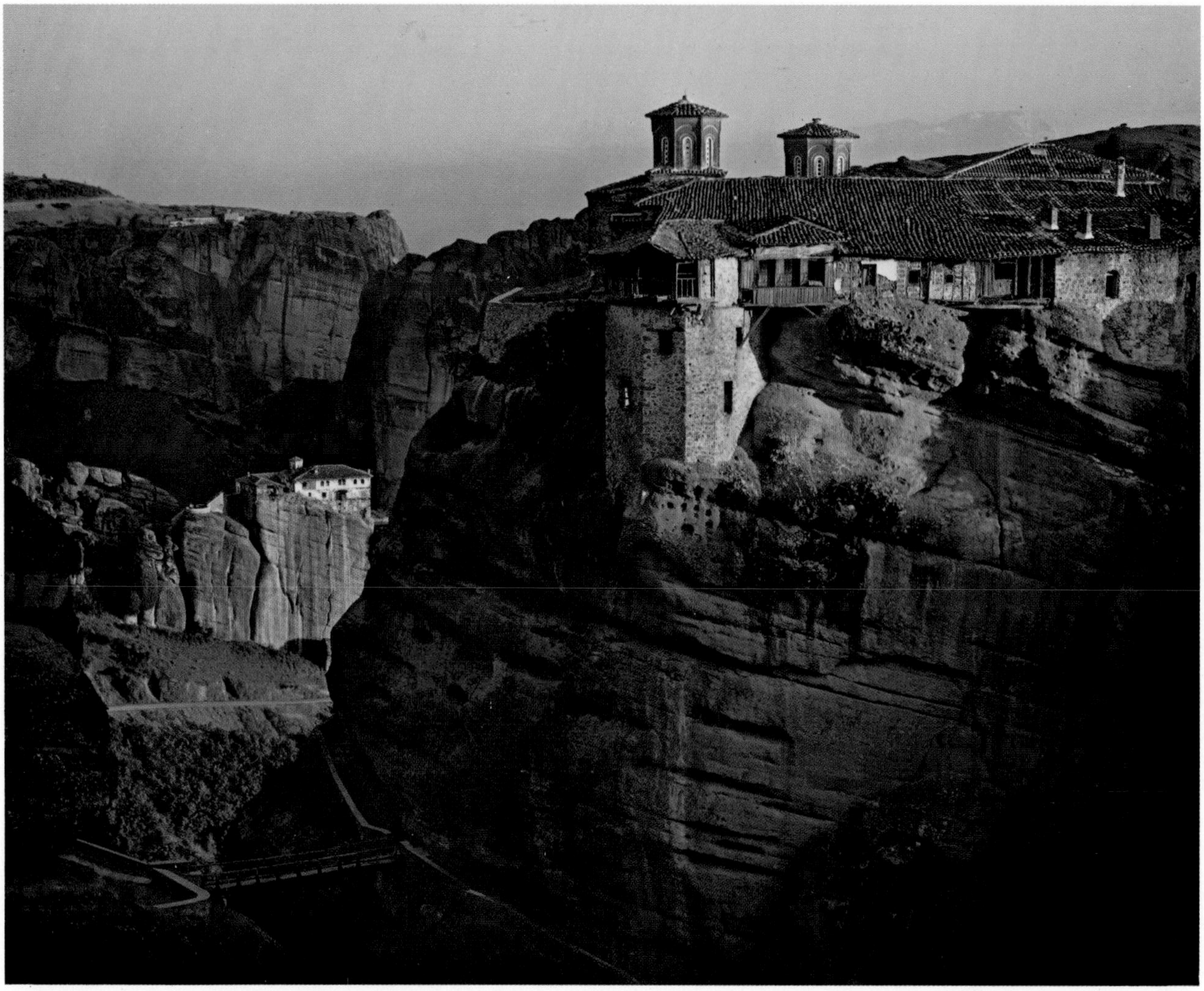

GEORGE HUNTER—PUBLIX

Barlaam or All Saints Monastery at Meteora in Thessaly. Massive rock formations are the result of erosion by a prehistoric sea

GEORGE HUNTER—PUBLIX

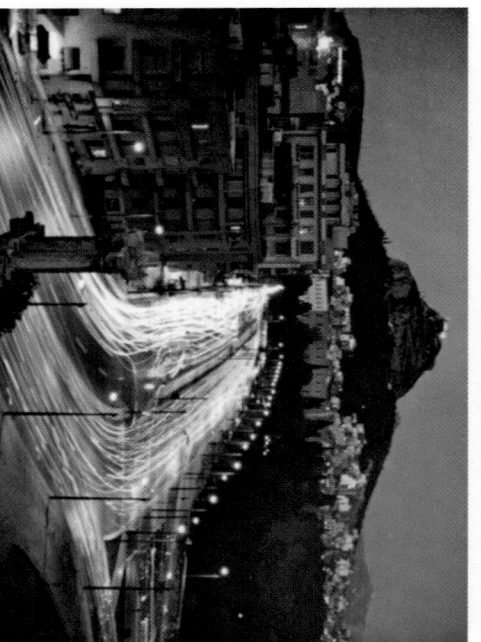

Athens at night. Mt. Lycabettus is in the background

GEORGE HOLTON—PHOTO RESEARCHERS, INC

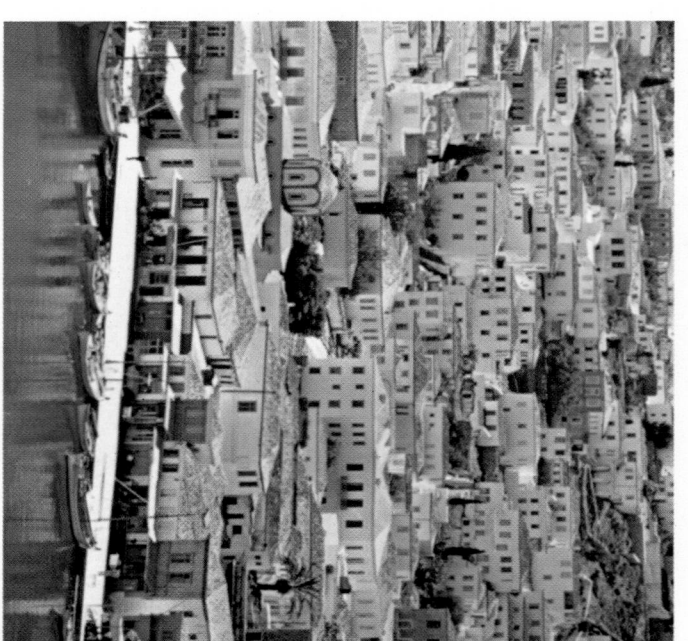

The waterfront at Hydra on the island of the same name, an important sponge fishing centre in the Aegean Sea

range, encloses the alluvium-filled tectonic trough drained by the Sperkhiós river. The pass of Thermopylae (Thermopílai) lies between the eastern tip of the Oíti range and the sea.

The fourth and most southerly of these subsidiary chains is that linking Parnassus (Parnassós, 8,061 ft. [2,457 m.]), Helicon (Elikón), Kithairón, Párnis and Hymettus (Imittós). Between this range and that of Oeta lie the lowlands of Phocis (Fokis) and Boeotia (Voiotía) drained by the Cephisus (Kifisós) and Asopós rivers. These plains, being exposed to the north, have a more continental and extreme climate than Attica, and the olive does not thrive. But due to careful drainage, the lowland above Thivai (Thebes) has always been good wheat country, and since 1893, when the seasonally fluctuating Lake Kopaïs was drained by a canal, much extra fertile farmland has been reclaimed in the plain of Phocis.

The depressions of Attica (Attikí) are among the least fertile basins of central Greece; summers are excessively hot, winter rainfall small and precarious. Athens, however, in the plain of the Attic Kifissós (Sarandapótamos), has the advantage of a central position, access to harbours in the Gulf of Aegina and the command of rich and varied resources of timber, pasture, and olive- and vine-growing country, the lead and zinc mines of Lávrion (Laurium) and the marble quarries of Pendelikón (Pendéli).

Western Greece and the Ionian Islands.—The southern extremity of the Pindus about Gióna (8,235 ft. [2,510 m.]) divides Attica and Phocis on the east from Acarnania and Aetolia (Aitólia) on the west; just as the northern Pindus on the region of Smólikas (8,651 ft. [2,637 m.]) separates Thessaly from Epirus. The regions to the west of the main watershed have far fewer fertile basins than those to the east.

Epirus consists of four parallel limestone ranges, separated by narrow valleys of softer sandstones from which the rivers escape through constricted gorges, like that of the Akhéron (Mavropótamos) at Soúli. The most extensive fertile plain is the basin of inland drainage at Ioánnina (Janina) in the mountains, whence a difficult road leads down the Árakhthos valley to the sea. Eastern Aetolia has some eroded Pliocene strata which make fair agricultural country, but the limestone heights of Acarnania and western Aetolia near the Gulf of Arta are very barren. (*See also* AETOLIA; ARTA.)

The main difference between the lands on either side of the Pindus, however, is climatic. On the western side, Epirus in particular is well-watered and snow lies on its higher mountains until mid-June. Unlike the rest of Greece, but in common with the central Balkans, the Epirote interior enjoys an appreciable rainfall in late summer and early autumn, and the olive, which thrives only where there is summer drought, is not found more than about 25 mi. (40 km.) inland from the west coast.

Like the mainland opposite, the Ionian Islands consist of heights of Cretaceous limestone and depressions of softer Pliocene strata, particularly of sandstone. Corfu (Kérkira) is fortunate in that, except for the limestone block of Pandokrátor in the north, it is composed entirely of these fertile Pliocene deposits and also enjoys a high rainfall. The southern islands are much drier. Cephalonia (Kefallinía) and Ithaca (Itháki) are almost entirely limestone and have a very broken relief. Leukas (Levkás) and Zákinthos (Zante) have steep cliffs to the west but more gentle slopes leading to the eastern coastal plains.

Macedonia and Thrace.—The faults or lines of breakage between the mountain blocks of the coastlands of northern Greece mostly trend northwest and southeast and give their direction, for example, to the lower Vardar, Struma and Néstos; but there are other series of faults, like those that run east and west to form lakes Korónia (Langadhá) and Vólvi (Besikíon), which separate the peninsula of Khalkidhikí (Chalcidice) from the rest of Thessaly.

Between the crystalline massifs were left deep lake basins that became encumbered with detritus in the Tertiary and Quaternary periods. Subsequent drainage and erosion have left a series of terraces, but malarial swamps in the lowest parts of these plains show that drainage is still not complete. These marshes are particularly extensive wherever the main stream leaves the basin through a constricted exit, as in the plain of Sérrai on the lower Struma, and in that of Dráma, on a tributary. The largest swamps of all, however, are in the coastal flats that are being built forward into the Gulf of Salonika by the combined deltas of the Vardar and the Aliákmon.

The three promontories of Khalkidhíkí were islands in the Tertiary period, as is shown by the Pliocene deposits at their roots. These Tertiary deposits also overlie much of the limestone of the Kassándra promontory, the lowest of the three. Those of Sithoniá (Lóngos) and Áthos (Aktí) consist largely of wooded hills of schistose rocks, though there is a steep block of limestone at the tip of Aktí. (*See* ÁTHOS, MOUNT.)

In western Macedonia, beyond the forested hills of Vérmion, lie the high enclosed lake basins of Tertiary deposits of Vegorrítis and of Kastoriá on the upper Aliákmon. Both these vales are dry and barren, by contrast with the higher valleys of Epirus on the other side of the Pindus watershed.

The Aegean Islands.—The islands of the Thracian sea are all Greek, except İmroz Adası and Bozca Ada (Tenedos) which are Turkish. Thásos is an ancient mineraliferous massif, like those of the Thracian mainland. Samothrace (Samothráki) is of volcanic origin; its coasts are smooth and harbourless, in contrast to Lemnos (Límnos) with the large strategic anchorage of Moúdhros.

Lesbos (Lésvos), Chios (Khíos) and Sámos are detached fragments, respectively, of the Troad (Troas), the Erythráean peninsula (Karaburun) and Mt. Messogís (Mykale, or Samsun Daği) on the mainland of Asia Minor. All are favoured with a mild and temperate climate and palms can be grown in sheltered corners of Chios. But the land surface in all three is rocky, the only extensive areas of fertile soil being in the southern part of Chios, which consists of limestones of relatively recent formation. In Lesbos, Mytilene (Mitilíni), originally an island colony, is the first port, but the deep Kólpos Kallonís is the finest natural harbour. The port of Chios is on the east side of the island of that name, lying opposite the small Turkish harbour town of Çeşmeköırfezi, on the mainland.

The Northern Sporades (the "scattered islands") continue the structural trend of Olympus, Óssa and Pelion and, like the mainland range, consist largely of crystalline rocks. (*See* SPORADES.)

Euboea, though a single island, includes projections of two of the mainland ranges, those of Óthris and Oíti, and its rocks range from the fertile Eocene sands and clays of the north through the barren limestone ranges of the centre to the ancient Primary crystalline formations of its southeastern extremity.

The Cyclades (or "the islands in a circle") were anciently considered to be disposed in a circle about Delos (Dhílos). They are the extreme summits of drowned mountains, in which two main ranges can be followed. The first leads from Euboea through Ándros, Tínos (Tênos), Míkonos, Ikaría and Sámos to the Mykale promontory of Asia Minor. The second may be traced from Cape Soúnion (Sunium) through Kéa (Kéos), Kíthnos, Sérifos, Sífnos, Kímolos and Amorgós as far as Levítha. Between these two main ranges are Páros and Náxos, which consist of very ancient metamorphic rocks, yielding marble of the one and emery of the other. Syros (Síros or Síra) and Delos lie slightly south of the main northern arc of islands.

The Dodecanese.—This group includes islands of varied geological structure. Kálimnos, Sími and Khálki consist almost entirely of hard gray limestone, which weathers into very poor, thin soil. In Léros, by contrast, fertile Tertiary marls overlie much of the limestone. The southern half of Pátmos is the collapsed western rim of an extinct volcano, consisting of purple porphyry, and Nísiros is a complete volcanic cone whose lavas have weathered into a very rich soil. Rhodes is the largest of the 12 islands. Its core of hard rocks rises more than 4,000 ft. (1,219 m.) above sea level and captures considerable rainfall, while the lower slopes are constructed of weathered marls and sandstones which make good farmland. The remaining islands of the 12 are Cos or Kos, Astipálaia (Astypalaea), Kárpathos, Tilos and Kásos. (*See further* DODECANESE.)

Crete.—This island is an extension of the arc of the Dinaric fold mountains, which have here been eroded, invaded by the sea in Tertiary times and later raised again. The landscape is mountainous, most of the island's area of flat land being concentrated in the central plain of Mesará.

In the extreme west the schistose rocks have weathered into rounded slopes, but the limestone heights of the Levka Ori ("white mountains") and Idhi (Ida; 8,058 ft. [2,456 m.]) have a more precipitous outline. The north coast, with its alluvial bays, is very different from the south coast, which falls to the sea in steep faulted cliffs. (See CRETE.)

(WM. C. B.)

5. Vegetation.—The vegetation in the southern and central regions is of Mediterranean type which, to the north and on the higher slopes of the mountains, merges into a central European type. The main plant cover is deciduous and evergreen forest and brushwood or scrub. More than half the land is under scrub and four distinct types of scrub communities can be recognized: maquis, found largely in the Peloponnese; pseudomaquis, in Macedonia and the north; phrygana on the hills of Attica, the Ionian Islands and the Cyclades; and shiblyak at higher altitudes. The chief plants of the maquis are Spanish broom, strawberry tree, oleander, bay, evergreen or holm oak, olive, myrtle, juniper, Judas tree, Aleppo pine and smoke tree. The tree heath is common except on limestone. Plants of the pseudomaquis include oaks, box, terebinth, juniper, jasmine and cherry laurel. Phrygana consists of scattered bushes, often thorny with gray-green leaves and a resinous aromatic sap, such as spiny burnet, Cretan thyme, marjoram, rockrose, lavender and broom. Shiblyak is composed mainly of Christ's thorn, sumac, smoke tree and barberry. On the very small area above the tree limit juniper and olive daphne are the chief woody plants.

In the lowlands the flora is of Mediterranean type consisting of trees, evergreen shrubs and herbaceous plants. In spring, and to some extent in autumn, the stony ground in the south and on the islands bears brilliant patches of grape hyacinth, star of Bethlehem, asphodel, crocus, fritillary, narcissus, iris, tulip and gladiolus; with annuals, such as anemones and poppies, succeeded in summer by composites, labiates and other hardier plants.

On the higher slopes bloom pinks, mullein, cyclamen, thyme and *Centaurea*; among the rocks are found bellflowers, saxifrages, violas, *Potentilla*, stonecrops, yarrows, *Draba*, etc. The stony river courses bear planes, poplars, willows, chastetrees, oleanders and terebinths. Aleppo and stone pines are especially characteristic of the southern and western coastal plains.

In the southern and central highlands, and at lower altitudes in the north, deciduous trees (oak and chestnut in particular) grow on the middle slopes with an undergrowth of sumac, Judas tree, European hop hornbeam, wild pear and bay. Above are coniferous forests dominated by the Grecian fir with little undergrowth except in the clearings where it is mostly of juniper, hawthorn and small-leaved lime. The clearings and ravines are bright in the spring and summer with crocuses, irises, tulips, fritillaries, asphodels, gentians, etc.

Above 650 ft. (198 m.) grow mostly forest and scrub. The woods are of the Mediterranean evergreen type on the lower slopes, mixed deciduous above and coniferous higher still. The Pindus ranges carry oaks and chestnuts and, above them, firs and pines; on Óthris are extensive oak woods; in Attica many of the Aleppo pine forests have been cut down; the higher slopes in the Peloponnese bear Greek fir and black pine; beech grows on the higher slopes in the north and chestnut in southern Macedonia and on the middle slopes of Olympus, Óssa and Pelion. Black pine forms the high forest of Olympus and is common on siliceous soils from about 2,000 to 4,500 ft. (600–1,375 m.).

(W. B. T.)

6. Animal Life.—In the middle regions of Greece (especially in the forested zones) the fauna is characteristic of central Europe and includes the wolf, wild boar and lynx (all rarely); the wildcat, marten, brown bear and roe deer. The chamois is a scarce example of alpine fauna. Mediterranean forms dominate the western and southern coastlines and reach farther inland in the valley regions, particularly that of the Vardar river. Among them are subtropical elements adapted to heat and drought. The Mediterranean mammals include the jackal, wild goat (bezoar) and porcupine. The birds include pelicans, storks, herons, many kinds of perching birds; and the great spotted cuckoo. Numerous birds from northern and central Europe migrate to Greece for the winter.

The region is rich in reptiles, with several kinds of fresh-water and terrestrial turtles, lizards (including geckos) and snakes (including some poisonous kinds). The numerous insect species include *Anopheles* mosquitoes, vectors of malaria, and the sandfly that transmits sandfly or pappataci fever. Sheep and goats are the most important domestic animals, with donkeys for riding and transport. *See also* BALKAN PENINSULA: *Geography.* (AN. LU.)

II. ARCHAEOLOGY

The visible and excavable remains of Greece are the country's greatest treasures. Roman governors and emperors both robbed the land of its works of art and added new monuments to the old towns and sanctuaries. With the revival of classical scholarship in the Renaissance, Greece, then under Muslim rule, was again visited by westerners. But soon the unabashed search for works of art was replaced by a genuine interest in what close study of the remains could contribute to the country's great history. In the 19th century began the series of scientific excavations that are carried on still. Particular attention has been paid to the restoration of ancient sites and equipping of museums. Visitors to them from overseas have become an important source of revenue to the state, and the occasion for important new roads and other facilities that have often brought prosperity to remote parts of the country.

1. Sites and Excavations.—The main bodies engaged in the excavation and study of Greek antiquities are the Greek State Archaeological service and the Greek Archaeological society, together with the various foreign schools established in Athens. Their activities may be summarized as follows:

Greek.—The Archaeological service shoulders the responsibility for the excavation of sites threatened with destruction by new building, museums, restoration and occasional excavations, while the Archaeological society conducts independent excavations. The most important Greek excavations have been on the Athenian Acropolis, at Sunium, Eleusis, the Amphiareion near Oropus, Thebes, Epidaurus, Sicyon, Mycenae (after Heinrich Schliemann; q.v.), Brauron and Pylos, as well as a host of minor sites. Publication of finds has rarely been able to keep pace with new excavations.

British.—The British school at Athens took over the responsibility for the great site at Knossós in Crete from Sir Arthur Evans, and also conducted major excavations of the prehistoric sites on Melos (at Philacopi) and at Mycenae. The main classical sites have been Sparta and Perachóra (near Corinth); and, since World War II, Chios (at Emporio) and Smyrna (Turk. Izmir).

French.—In Crete the French school excavated the Minoan palace at Mállia and minor sites of the archaic period. Its main sites have been the sanctuaries at Tegéa (Teyéa), Delphi (Dhelfoí) and Delos (Dhílos); and later at Argos and on the island of Thásos.

German.—Olympia is the most important of the sites excavated by German scholars. In Athens they have worked on the Theatre of Dionysus and Dipylon cemetery; in Thera on the early town; in Aegina and Sámos on the town and sanctuary sites. Since 1931 the school has concentrated its efforts upon the Agora in Athens. The most important recent excavations have been undertaken on the prehistoric sites of Pylos (Pílos) and Lerna, and the classical sanctuaries of Samothrace and Isthmia (near Corinth).

American.—The site of Corinth has occupied the American School of Classical Studies at Athens since its early days. At the Argive Heraeum an early excavation of the classical sanctuary was followed by one of the nearby prehistoric site (Prosymna) and other important prehistoric sites in Boeotia and the Peloponnese. Since 1931 the school has concentrated its efforts upon the Agora

Italian.—The Italian school excavated the Minoan palaces at Phaistos and Ayia Triada in Crete, prehistoric and classical sites on Lemnos, and various sites in the Dodecanese between the World Wars, while the islands were occupied by Italy.

Other Countries.—Excavations in Greece have also been undertaken by groups from Austria (Elis), the Netherlands (Argos), Denmark (Rhodes), Czechoslovakia (Samothrace), Sweden (prehistoric sites in the Argolis [Argolid]).

Progress After World War II.—Work has continued on several of the great sites (Athens, Sámos, Knossós, Mycenae, Olympia) as well as a few others of major importance (Pylos, Lerna, Brauron). The volume of excavation increases annually, but there has also been an awakened interest in topographical studies and the application of archaeological findings to historical problems. The new techniques of aerophotography and underwater exploration have also been practised in Greece, but the most spectacular finds from shipwrecks so far have been by chance.

2. Antiquities and Museums.—A great many of the Greek objects to be seen in European and American collections have in fact been found in Italy, in Greek or native tombs. But there were a number of important purchases by scholars and travelers in Greece itself in the years before the foundation of the Greek kingdom and its new antiquity laws. The most notable of these are the Arundel marbles, mostly now in Oxford; the Elgin marbles from Athens and the sculptures from Bassae, in London; the sculptures from the temple of Aphaea in Aegina, in Munich; pieces from Athens, Sámos, Olympia and Samothrace (the "Victory"), in the Louvre in Paris; and various pieces in Berlin, Vienna, Rome, New York, etc. Since the passing of laws that forbade the export of antiquities all finds have been confined to Greece and are the property of the state. The main collections are in the National museum in Athens, but there are other important museums in which the finest local finds are kept, as at Delphi, Delos, Olympia, Corinth, Salonika, Thebes, Vólos, Nauplia (Návplion), Eleusis, Sparta, Aegina, Rhodes, Iráklion (Crete) and the smaller museums in Athens in the Agora, the Ceramicus and on the Acropolis. The tendency now is for all the finds from an excavation to be kept in a museum on or near the site, provided that it is readily accessible to the ordinary traveler.

The Greek antiquities in foreign museums can be roughly divided into three classes: Greek objects that had been exported in antiquity and since discovered in native or Greek colonial sites, as in Italy and Sicily; objects made by Greeks living overseas in colonies or in Egypt under the Ptolemies; objects from Greece that left the country before the new antiquity laws were passed or—illegally—since then. Most of the collections mentioned in the following brief survey are composed of objects of the first two classes.

Italy.—The national museums of Rome, Naples, Palermo and Syracuse and the Vatican museums house the main finds from the Greek sites in Italy and Sicily. The museums of Florence (there is also sculpture in the Uffizi gallery), Orvieto, Tarquinia and the Villa Giulia museum in Rome are more especially for the finds in Etruria. Important provincial museums with local finds or older collections are in Turin, Venice (sculpture in the Doge's palace), Bologna, Ferrara (the finds from Spina), Taranto, Reggio di Calabria and Paestum. The larger sculpture galleries are filled mainly with works of the Roman period, albeit copying Greek originals. There are small collections of Cretan (Minoan) antiquities in Florence and Rome (Pigorini museum).

Germany.—In Berlin major collections are in the state museums; the Pergamum museum, whose contents were taken to the U.S.S.R. after World War II but have been returned; the Prehistoric museum, which held Schliemann's collections from Troy and Mycenae, which are said to have been lost in World War II. In Munich are the Glyptothek (with the Aegina sculptures) and Museum antiker Kleinkunst. There are many other important collections, generally in university towns, of which the following may be mentioned: Bonn, Karlsruhe, Kassel, Frankfurt am Main, Göttingen, Greifswald, Hamburg, Heidelberg, Leipzig, Tübingen and Würzburg. The fine collection at Dresden was destroyed in World War II.

France.—In Paris the Louvre is the greatest of the national collections and has a number of original sculptures from Greece; there are minor antiquities in the Petit Palais and the Cabinet des Médailles (Bibliothèque Nationale). Marseilles, Ensérume and Montpellier have some local Greek finds. Of the other collections the most important are in Lyons, Boulogne, Compiègne, Châtillon sur Seine (the Vix treasure); Laon and Sèvres (Musée Céramique).

Great Britain.—The British museum in London (the Elgin marbles); the Ashmolean museum in Oxford (Arthur Evans' Cretan collection) and the Fitzwilliam museum in Cambridge are the main collections. There are some smaller collections in university towns, notably Reading, Manchester and Edinburgh. There are still a number of important private collections, including country house sculpture galleries.

North America.—Most of the collections in the United States have been built up since 1900 from individual purchases. The largest are in the Boston Museum of Fine Arts, Boston, Mass., and the Metropolitan museum, New York. Other important collections are in Baltimore, Md. (Walters Art gallery); Philadelphia, Pa., Berkeley, Calif., Cambridge, Mass. (Fogg museum) and at Princeton, N.J. In Canada there is the Royal Ontario museum in Toronto; in Cuba there is a large private collection.

U.S.S.R.—The great collection in the Hermitage museum, Leningrad, includes finds from the Greek colonies on the Black sea; there are smaller collections in Moscow (Pushkin museum), Kiev and Odessa.

In addition to those mentioned above, other collections are listed below.

Switzerland.—The Historisches Museum and Kunstmuseum in Basel, the Musée d'Art et d'Histoire in Geneva, the Historisches Museum in Bern and a number of very rich private collections. Since World War II Switzerland has become the international centre for the sale of classical antiquities.

Belgium.—Musées Royaux d'Art et d'Histoire, Brussels.

The Netherlands.—Amsterdam University museum, the Rijksmuseum van Oudheden in Leiden and smaller collections in The Hague.

Spain.—The archaeological museums in Madrid and Barcelona and Museo del Prado in Madrid for sculpture.

Denmark.—The National museum, the Ny Carlsberg Glyptothek (sculpture gallery) and the Thorvaldsen's museum.

Austria.—The Kunsthistorisches and University museums in Vienna.

Cyprus.—The Nicosia museum.

Turkey.—The state museums in Istanbul and Izmir for finds in former Greek Asia Minor.

Czechoslovakia.—The National museum, Prague.

Poland.—The National museum in Warsaw and collections in Goluchow and Cracow.

Rumania.—Museums in Bucharest and Constanţa for finds from the Greek colonies on the Black sea.

Bulgaria.—The National museum in Sofia.

Australasia.—There are good small collections in Australia (Nicholson museum, Sydney) and in New Zealand (Otago museum, Dunedin).

Africa.—The museums in Cairo and Alexandria, especially for finds of the Ptolemaic period. The Cyrene (Shahhat) museum houses local finds.

The main subjects of Greek art and archaeology are discussed under AEGEAN CIVILIZATION; GREEK ARCHITECTURE; GREEK ART; POTTERY AND PORCELAIN; NUMISMATICS; INSCRIPTIONS; the main sites are described in separate articles on cities (*e.g.,* ATHENS; SPARTA; OLYMPIA) and islands (*e.g.,* CRETE; AEGINA). For an outline of the history of excavation in Greece, a discussion of the subject matter and the role of classical archaeology see ARCHAEOLOGY: *Classical Archaeology.* Recent excavations are summarized annually under ARCHAEOLOGY in the *Britannica Book of the Year.*   (J. Bo.)

III. HISTORY

The finer arts and crafts of civilized man, invented in Mesopotamia and in Egypt, were adopted and developed first in Europe by the Minoans of Crete and by the Mycenaeans of Greece during the Bronze Age. The civilizations of these peoples attained a high level before each in turn was overwhelmed. A dark age ensued in Europe. But memories of Bronze Age civilization survived in the rich saga and in the epic poems of which some were finally attached to the names of Homer and Hesiod. These memories, played an important part in the Greek renaissance of the 9th century B.C. But a new political, intellectual and social spirit came to birth with the city-state. This spirit was carried to the European shores of the Mediterranean sea and of the Black sea by Greek colonists from the 8th century B.C. onward and to Asia as far as the Indus valley by Greeks and Macedonians in the 4th century B.C. Even when Rome replaced Macedonia as the leading imperial power and later fell in turn to barbarian invasions in the 5th century A.D., the Greek civilization which had been a unifying factor in the Greco-Macedonian and the Greco-Roman world lived on for 1,000 years in the empire of the Byzantines while again there was a dark age in western Europe. It was enlightened by that rediscovery of the Greek outlook vital to the Renaissance that heralded the end of the middle ages and laid the foundations of modern western civilization. Thus Greek history has a wide scope, essentially universal and not parochial in interest.

It is the keystone of the arch that united east and west, it cast a bridge over two dark ages and has given continuity to man's development in Europe from the Bronze Age to modern times. It is essentially universal and not parochial in interest.

A. THE BRONZE AGE

1. The Minoan Civilization.—The civilization of Ur in Mesopotamia was already mature when the first waves of settlers came by sea from Asia to Greece not later than 3000 B.C. They occupied Cyprus, Crete, some of the Cyclades and the eastern areas of the Greek peninsula, which are warmer and drier than the western. When they arrived, they were familiar with agriculture and seafaring as well as with pastoral life. They were still in the Neolithic stage, for their tools were made of stone and obsidian, a vitreous lava found mainly on the island of Melos. At the beginning of the Bronze Age in Greece, c. 2600 B.C. (some scholars subdivide the Bronze Age into a Copper Age and a Bronze Age proper, and date its beginning earlier, c. 2900 B.C.), these sparse settlements were reinforced by further waves of settlers, conversant with the use of copper, who probably came from Asia and were similar in race to their predecessors. They were a comparatively peaceful and unwarlike people, for they lived in unfortified villages or hamlets and had more tools than weapons. They developed local variations of culture, but had in common the use or worship of stumpy statuettes which represented a female deity.

In the Neolithic period Knossós in Crete was an important centre. It controlled the main routes within the island, its port at Amnisus faced the Aegean sea, and its houses soon became considerable in size, with a main room in the centre and a cluster of smaller rooms round it. When the Cretans were reinforced by new settlers at the beginning of the Bronze Age, the skeletons which have been discovered in their two-roomed tombs show them to have had long, narrow skulls and to have been short men and women who averaged just over and under five feet respectively. Quite a different people appeared c. 2300 B.C. at Phaestus (Phaistos) in the plain south of Knossós; they were soon absorbed or eliminated, but they left their memorial in the huge circular buildings where they laid the bones of their dead. Apart from this short-lived intrusion the Bronze Age inhabitants of Crete developed their own culture continuously down to 1450 B.C.

After 2000 B.C. political power was wielded by dynasts at Knossós, Phaestus and Mallia and finally became concentrated in the hands of the ruler of Knossós. The central figure of Cretan religion was a female deity, represented in human form, clothed in Cretan dress and attended by priestesses and animal-headed humans. Her cult was associated particularly with sacred trees and with the snake, bull and dove. The furniture of ritual included a three-legged altar, a double ax and twin horns of consecration. There is a temple-tomb near the palace at Knossós which suggests that the dead rulers received worship as deities, whereas the graves of the commoners are too humble to have been the object of any cult. The Cretans were gifted in painting, gem cutting, metalworking and architecture. Their frescoes reveal a fresh joy in the beauty of the natural world and a love of dancing, boxing and a sport in which boys and girls somersaulted over the backs of charging bulls. Their well-built houses were of masonry usually bonded with tim-

ber, and the towns were often laid out on terraced slopes with paved streets and tiers of houses. The great palace at Knossós was a fine example of monumental architecture with spacious state rooms and numerous storerooms, where the wealth of the realm was hoarded.

Although the palaces and the towns were unfortified and peaceful scenes predominated in the frescoes, the Cretans made excellent daggers, spearheads and rapiers first of copper and then of bronze, and the roads that linked the countryside to the palaces were protected by guard posts. The great wealth of the palaces and the widespread prosperity in the island were due to the profits of trade, protected or exploited by Cretan naval vessels in which a prolonged keel beam served as a ram. In the 16th century B.C. Cretan colonies were planted on Cythera, Calymnos (Kálimnos) and Rhodes, a chain of islands controlling the southern Aegean, and at Miletus on the coast of Asia Minor. Articles of Cretan origin were exported to Egypt, Syria, Asia Minor, the Cyclades and Greece and, farther westward, to the islands of Lipara (Lipari) and Ischia off the western coast of Italy. The 15th century B.C. brought the greatest prosperity to Crete. Metals, textiles, manufactured goods and natural products were traded between the continents. Egypt, Syria and Troy grew rich as centres of exchange on the mainland. Crete controlled the sea routes toward southern Europe and the west, which were beginning to emerge from barbarism.

The art of pictographic writing had been practised for centuries in the east before it was adopted about the end of the 3rd millennium by Crete. Soon after 1700 B.C. the Cretans invented a linear script with signs for syllables and for numerals on the decimal system. This script has not yet been deciphered. As the people and culture of Crete owed their origins and developments predominantly to the east, it is probable that the Cretan language belonged to an Asian group distinct from the Indo-European group. Philologists see survivals of this Asiatic group in place-names ending in -ssos and -inthos, which are commonest in Crete and Asia Minor. Some aspects of Cretan culture, such as the palaces of the dynasts, the worship of deified rulers, the female deity, animal-headed humans and the predominance of peaceful pursuits, are also found in contemporary civilizations of the east; but so many features are peculiar to Crete that the first great civilization on European soil should be regarded as an independent entity. The ancient name of the island and of its people is unknown. Some have identified the island with "Keftu," whence envoys came to Egypt in the first half of the 15th century B.C. Others have accepted the names which were recorded centuries later by Homer: "Crete, where the race of Minos is" (Odyssey, xvii, 523) and its great city "Knossós where Minos ruled, holding converse with great Zeus every ninth year" (Odyssey, xix, 178). Following Homer, scholars speak of "Minoan" civilization, and attribute the legends of the Minotaur, Theseus and Ariadne to the great age of Crete.

After 1450 B.C., when Knossós had a monopoly of political power in the island and developed a distinct culture of its own in which there are signs of a more militaristic spirit, a new linear script is found at Knossós and also on the mainland of Greece. This script, unlike the earlier Minoan script, has been deciphered and it is widely accepted that the language it expresses is Greek. At least in the period 1450–1400 B.C., therefore, the rulers of Knossós would have spoken Greek and presumably were Greeks who had come from the mainland. They called the place "Ko-no-so" in their new script, which may be called the "Mycenaean" script after the name of Mycenae, which was the chief centre of Greek culture on the mainland. The intrusion of the Greeks marked the beginning of the end of Cretan ascendancy. About 1400 B.C. Knossós was sacked, and other leading cities of Crete were destroyed within a few decades of that date. The sackers of Knossós are unknown, but their action opened the way to peoples from the north who were pressing toward the riches of Crete and the near east.

2. The Mycenaean Civilization.—The early settlers in some of the Cyclades and in the warmer parts of the Greek mainland were reinforced c. 2600 B.C. by further settlers from Asia and developed their own distinctive cultures. The seafaring peoples of the Cyclades made little models of their ships in lead. They produced beautiful pottery and exported marble vases and figurines. They grew prosperous by carrying the trade of Minoan Crete, whose influence was particularly strong at Melos. Toward the end of the Bronze Age they engaged in raids on Egypt, where they were described, with others, as "the peoples of the sea." Centuries later the Greeks called them Carians, Leleges and Phoenicians—peoples whose affinities were with the coasts of Asia whence the settlers of the early Bronze Age had come (Herodotus, i, 171; Thucydides, i, 8); the most common later name for them, however, was Pelasgians. By virtue of their geographical position they acted throughout the Bronze Age as intermediaries between the Greek mainland and Troy, Asia Minor and Crete. On the mainland the Bronze Age settlers were interested primarily in agriculture. Their largest settlements were made in the plains of eastern Greece south of Mt. Othrys (Óthris), but they spread gradually into the western areas. The flat-roofed, rectangular houses of their unfortified villages were built close together and contained reserves of grain stored in large jars. By the beginning of the 2nd millennium the eastern areas had developed separate cultures north and south of the Isthmus of Corinth. Of these, the northern areas traded principally with Troy and with northwestern Asia Minor, the southern area (the eastern Peloponnese) with the Cyclades. Although both areas produced fine pottery, the eastern Peloponnese was more advanced in the arts. At Lerna, for instance, a large house was built on a complex plan suitable for a royal residence, and a stone statuette of exquisite workmanship was found in its debris. It is clear from this and other statuettes that religion was centred on a female deity. If they had been left in peace, the inhabitants of central and southern Greece might have continued to develop a civilization which was similar in many ways to those of the Cyclades and Crete, but in the years after 1900 B.C. they became the victims of aggression.

The districts of northern Greece that lie beyond Mt. Othrys were not occupied by the settlers who came from Asia at the beginning of the Bronze Age, c. 2600 B.C. The earlier wave of settlers remained in undisturbed possession of Thessaly and continued in the Neolithic stage of civilization until c. 2200 B.C. Their isolation may have been partly an effect of the climate. The Thessalian climate is intermediate between the warm Mediterranean climate of the south and the cold continental climate of upper Macedonia. Nor did the Neolithic people of Thessaly penetrate northward in the direction of Macedonia except at Sérvia (in a low-lying bend of the Haliacmon river), where they founded a small settlement. This settlement was destroyed c. 2500 B.C. by a much cruder people who were evidently nomadic hunters, the first of many groups who soon spread into central Macedonia and Chalcidice and some time later forced their way into Thessaly and occupied the sites of Dimini and Sesklo. These newcomers were quite unlike the earlier settlers of Greece. Their pottery was roughly made and incised with spiral decorations. They wielded stone battle-axes and they fortified their villages at Dimini and Sesklo with a ringwall. When they adopted a settled life, they built long narrow houses with pitched roofs, entry porches and sometimes apsidal ends, which were suitable for a cold damp climate. Archaeologists have called this type of house a megaron, after the Greek word for a long hall. Although the archaeological evidence in northwestern Greece is scanty, it suggests that groups of these newcomers entered Epirus and gradually moved down the western side of Greece as nomad hunters and shepherds. At Sérvia and at some sites in Thessaly, where they settled among the earlier inhabitants, their worship of the masculine aspect of life is indicated by the use of phallic emblems and male statuettes.

The ultimate origin of these newcomers is uncertain. Their way of life and the climate of the areas in which they settled suggest that they had come through the Balkans, and this suggestion is supported by the appearance of similar houses of an early megaron type in areas near Troy at the time of the first settlement there (c. 2600–2400 B.C.). The most probable hypothesis is that the settlers of Macedonia and of Troy were Indo-European—perhaps the first Indo-Europeans to reach the vicinity of the Mediterranean sea (see INDO-EUROPEAN). Another branch, ancestor to the

Illyrians, probably reached the Adriatic sea in the same period.

Newcomers disturbed the peace of the Greek peninsula during the middle Bronze Age (c. 1900–1600 B.C.) by irruption and infiltration. They may have entered from the western side of Greece. Early examples of megaron houses have been found at Eutresis in Boeotia, at Lerna and Tiryns in Argolis, at Korakou near Lechaeum in Corinthia and at Thermum (Thérmon) and Olympia in western Greece. Although they lowered the standard of civilization at first, they brought with them (or coincided with the arrival of) the potter's wheel, on which a fine pottery called Minyan ware, imitating metal shapes, was made; and they introduced the horse, bones of which have been found in Macedonia in contexts dating to c. 2100 B.C. Similar phenomena occurred at Troy, where new settlers founded the sixth city (c. 1900–1300 B.C.), made Minyan pottery and introduced the horse into Asia Minor (see TROY).

It is generally agreed that the newcomers of the middle Bronze Age were the first Greek-speaking peoples to reach central Greece and the Peloponnese. Their antecedents are a matter of dispute, but it is probable that they were descended from the Neolithic settlers of Macedonia, of whom a part occupied Dimini and Sesklo in Thessaly. Centuries later Hesiod gave a localized genealogy of the founders of the Greek race that supports this probability. He declared that Thessaly was ruled by Deucalion's descendants, "Hellen the war-loving king and his sons Dorus, Xuthus and Aeolus, delighting in horses," and that their cousins "Magnes and Macedon, delighting in horses, lived in the area of Olympus and Pieria." The Greek or "Hellenic" race was divided by dialect into three main groups in Hesiod's time—Ionians, Aeolians and Dorians—of which the ancestors were held to be Ion (son of Xuthus), Aeolus and Dorus. The division certainly existed early in the Bronze Age, and it may have begun in Macedonia, Epirus and adjacent areas in the period 2500–1900 B.C., because the Ionians and Aeolians entered central and southern Greece during the Bronze Age but the Dorians in general after the Bronze Age (see IONIANS; DORIANS).

When conditions became less troubled in the peninsula, the fusion of the Greeks and their predecessors produced a much more vigorous and artistic civilization than that of the early Bronze Age. This civilization, called Mycenaean, because it was first found by excavators at Mycenae in Argolis, lasted with fluctuating fortunes from c. 1650 to c. 1125 B.C. Rule was exercised by dynasties of kings who accumulated wealth on their citadels. At Mycenae the dynasties (Shaft Grave I, Shaft Grave II, Tholos Tomb I, Tholos Tomb II) are numbered by the excavators in accordance with their styles of burial, which were practised at other capitals of the time; and the objects buried with the first two dynasties show that they were Greek. The rulers of the first Shaft Grave dynasty (c. 1650–1600 B.C.) were buried with their weapons and with jewelry of gold, silver, electrum and ivory in tombs at the foot of deep vertical shafts, which were then filled up and marked by upright stone stelai engraved with scenes of war and hunting. The second group of shaft graves (c. 1600–1500 B.C.) was richer still in weapons, jewelry (including amber) and cups of precious metal; horse-drawn chariots were represented on the stelai; and remains were found of a boar's-tusk helmet (i.e., a leather cap on which slivers of tusk were sewn for greater protection). Death masks of gold and electrum show that the rulers wore moustaches, and the skeletons are those of a race of men between 5 ft. 6 in. and 6 ft. tall. The first group of tholos (beehive) tombs (c. 1500–1400 B.C.) and the second group (c. 1400–1300 B.C.) are examples of skilful architecture. A large circular tomb was excavated in a hillside and roofed over with a great dome (tholos) of conical shape, constructed of masonry blocks carefully wedged and counterweighted, and the whole was then covered with earth and a waterproof layer of clay. The tomb was entered by a walled passage which led to a massive doorway set in the side of the tholos. In the so-called Tomb of Atreus, built c. 1330 B.C., the dome is 40 ft. high. The period of the tholos tombs was even more prosperous than its predecessors, but it was followed by a gradual decline during which the rock-cut chamber tomb was in vogue.

At first the more advanced art of Minoan Crete inspired the Greek peoples, who soon traded direct with Crete and became the rulers of Knossós c. 1450 B.C. The Mycenaean script, designed to express the Greek language by syllabic signs, was probably invented at Knossós in the 15th century B.C. and taken to the mainland (see MINOAN LINEAR SCRIPTS). Greek settlements were planted in Rhodes c. 1450 B.C., and Greek traders and exports appeared beside those of Crete at Miletus, in Syria, in Egypt and in the west at Lipara. When Knossós and other cities of Crete were sacked c. 1400 B.C., the Greeks of the mainland replaced them as the leading naval power in the southern Aegean. They planted settlements in Crete, Cyprus and Cilicia and had trading stations at Ugarit and Poseidium (Al Mina) in Syria. Mycenaean pottery, which combined Minoan taste in decoration with greater technical skill and formal design, was exported in large quantities to Syria, Palestine and Egypt. Trade relations were also close with Troy, and Thessaly and lower Macedonia were influenced by Mycenaean culture as they offered ports of call on the sea route to Troy. The relative fewness of Mycenaean imports suggests that the Cyclades (apart from Melos, Thêra and Delos) probably preserved a hostile independence. Greeks also settled in the west at Acragas and Syracuse in Sicily and at Oria (Uria) and Taras (Tarentum) in southern Italy. Thus the Greeks became to an even greater extent than the Minoans of Crete the intermediaries of seaborne trade between Europe and Asia, and a general uniformity of Mycenaean culture prevailed by 1300 B.C. throughout the Ionian Islands (except Corcyra [Corfu]), the Greek peninsula (except Epirus and upper Macedonia) and the islands of the southern Aegean.

After 1300 B.C. Greek trade with Sicily, Troy, Syria and Egypt began to decline. Mycenaean culture lost its uniformity and developed local peculiarities. On the mainland men expected war and violence. Immense fortifications were built to enclose the citadels at Mycenae, Tiryns, Athens and elsewhere, and the slashing sword took the place of the rapier sword. The great palaces, built round a central megaron (of which the finest examples have been excavated at Mycenae, Tiryns and Pylos), were still wealthy, but their subjects in the open suburbs were exposed to attack and arson and declined in prosperity. As conditions worsened, the Greeks turned to piratical raids on Egypt, Cyprus and Caria and finally attacked and destroyed the fortified city of Troy c. 1200 B.C. The Trojan War opened the door to disaster. Barbarians broke into Asia Minor, overthrew the Hittite empire and set in motion a series of great raids by land and sea which destroyed the prosperity of the states in the eastern Mediterranean and brought the great civilizations of the Bronze Age to an end.

Present knowledge of Greek history in the Bronze Age is due mainly to archaeology, which constantly provides new evidence and new problems of interpretation. But there are also two kinds of literary evidence: Greek epic poetry composed from traditional sources before or after 800 B.C.; and contemporary Bronze Age texts in Greece, Asia and Egypt. The literary qualities of the Iliad and of the Odyssey are described elsewhere (see HOMER). This article is concerned with the extent to which they represent accurately the setting of the tenth year of the Trojan War and its aftermath. The Iliad (ii. 816-875) gives a "catalogue" of Troy's allies. As they were overwhelmed after the fall of Troy, the source of the catalogue, if historical, was composed in the Bronze Age; otherwise its contents would be fictitious and incorrect. In fact, the names of many allies in the catalogue occur in Bronze Age texts, both Hittite and Egyptian, and this is true also of Troy and its inhabitants (Greek Troía = Hittite Taroisha; Dardanoi = Egyptian Dardenui; Ilios = Egyptian Iliuna). The catalogue of Greek allies (Iliad ii, 485-768) draws a map of political power in Greece and in the islands that was no longer existing after the Bronze Age but has been fully borne out by excavation. The Greeks as a whole were called Akhaioi (Achaeans) and Danaoi in the Iliad; and these names in the forms Akaiwasha and Danauna or Denyen occur in Egyptian documents of the Bronze Age but were not in vogue later in Greece. The Odyssey too describes a political situation in western Greece which disappeared at the end of the Bronze Age, and its stories of piracy and raids are typical of the great raids on Egypt in 1192 and 1187 B.C., which were recorded in Egyptian documents. The paraphernalia of daily life described in both poems—bronze weapons, boar's-tusk helmets, equipment, drinking cups, furniture, metal inlay, etc.—are paralleled by Bronze Age objects and not by those of a later period. The very language of the poems contains dialectal forms which probably derive from a time when Arcadian and Aeolic dialects of Greek were widely spoken, that is, in the late Bronze Age. These and other considerations lead us to believe that not only the Iliad and the Odyssey but also the great body of saga on which Hesiod and other poets drew were derived in subject matter from the poetry and beliefs of the late Bronze Age. Archaeology has produced parallels for such survival from other parts of the Bronze Age world; for the Babylonian Epic of Gilgamesh persisted in Mesopotamia for more than 2,000 years, and some traditions recorded in the Hebrew book of Genesis are found to rest upon historical facts of the Bronze Age.

Contemporary Greek records in the Mycenaean script (the decipherment was still imperfect in the middle of the 20th century A.D.) prove that Greek was the language of the rulers of the palaces at Knossós and on the mainland c. 1450 B.C. and later; that some at least of the Olympian gods named by Homer were worshipped in Bronze Age Greece; and that some parts of Homer's picture of a feudal society are true to the conditions of the late Bronze Age. The script is mainly scratched on clay tablets, which served as inventory labels for stores, and the tablets have only survived when baked in a great conflagration. Fuller knowledge of this great period of history must depend on further archaeological discoveries and on a progressive decipherment of the scripts. See also AEGEAN CIVILIZATION; CRETE; and ARCHAEOLOGY: Classical Archaeology.

B. THE DARK AGE AND THE GREEK RENAISSANCE

1. The Migrations.

The collapse of Bronze Age civilization was followed by migrations that affected the Mediterranean world and lowered the standard of life for several centuries. Invading bands who probably came from the Danube valley destroyed the settlements in central Macedonia, and the impact of this assault started a great movement of peoples from upper Macedonia and Epirus, areas remote from Mycenaean civilization. According to legend it was led by a clan, the Heraclidae, who claimed descent from Heracles and called themselves Achaeans. Their chief followers were Dorians, speaking a broad dialect of Greek, who were brigaded in three tribes, Hylleis, Dymanes and Pamphyloi. Many other tribes were associated with them; they too spoke dialects of Greek, grouped by scholars under the title "Northwest Greek." The first invasions in the second half of the 12th century were sufficiently well organized to break down the resistance of the strongest Mycenaean powers. Thessaloi, led by Heraclidae, forced their way from southern Epirus into southwestern Thessaly, displacing Boiotoi who invaded Boeotia (then called Cadmeis). Dorians, led by Heraclidae, migrated from Doris between the Pindus range and Mt. Parnassus, crossed the Gulf of Corinth and broke into the Peloponnese; peoples who spoke the Northwest Greek dialect crossed the western end of the gulf and invaded the western Peloponnese. Once they had overcome resistance, other migrants followed in their wake. Thereafter, as Thucydides wrote (i, 2, 1), "migrations were of frequent occurrence, the several tribes readily abandoning their homes under the pressure of superior numbers." For when they had pillaged the Mycenaean cities and burned the palaces, the migrating hordes broke up into groups that roamed far and wide and did not accept the unfamiliar conditions of settled life.

Chaos and turmoil continued for two centuries in the Greek peninsula. Only Arcadia, in the mountainous centre of the Peloponnese, and Attica, lying on a peninsula off the main lines of invasion, succeeded in maintaining their independence. Elsewhere the earlier inhabitants were made subject to the invaders or driven out as refugees. In pursuit of loot, Dorian bands crossed the sea, occupied the southernmost islands of the Aegean and established themselves on the southern part of western Asia Minor. Aeolic-speaking refugees from Thessaly and central Greece ended their wanderings by settling in the northern part of Asia Minor hence called Aeolis and on the islands of Tenedos (Bozca Ada) and Lesbos (Lésvos). Ionic-speaking refugees fled first to mountainous Achaea and then to Attica, which the Dorians failed to enter by attack from the south. The last of the great migrations from Greece began *c.* 1000 B.C. when the Athenians launched the so-called Ionian migration, and ended *c.* 900 B.C. with the occupation of the Cyclades, the central sector of western Asia Minor and the adjacent islands. Meanwhile these and other migrating bands in Asia and Europe had enlarged the area of chaos to include Italy, Sicily and North Africa.

Excavation has exposed the poverty of the dark age in Greece. Men lived in scattered hamlets of hovels, having few material possessions and waging war against one another with the iron weapons that marked the transition from the Bronze Age to the Iron Age. Attica was an exception for a time. Formed into a unified state, according to tradition, by Theseus in the late Bronze Age, the people of Attica preserved their Mycenaean traditions as well as their political independence. The city of Athens was strengthened too by the influx of refugees, capable and courageous men, who led the Ionian migration overseas and spread the use of the fine protogeometric pottery which had been evolved in Attica. But, when the migration was finished, the general paralysis of communications on the mainland and in the Aegean affected Athens too, and the city became impoverished by isolation. Conditions were no less difficult overseas in the islands and on the coast of Asia Minor, where the Greeks had established themselves in isolated pockets on narrow coastal strips of land and had to fight for existence against the native peoples and against one another.

2. The 9th and 8th Centuries B.C.—An oasis of civilization in the near east survived the dark age. Its centre was Phoenicia, in Palestine, Syria and Cyprus, where kingdoms such as Solomon's Israel flourished. The Phoenicians maintained their skill as sea-farers, traders and artists; they planted Carthage and other colonies in the western Mediterranean; they developed the Phoenician alphabet, in which a separate sign or letter stood-not for a syllable but for a consonantal or vowel sound; and they produced finely worked ivories and embroidered textiles. In the 9th century contacts were renewed by Phoenicia and Cyprus with the southern islands of the Aegean, the eastern Peloponnese and Athens. Phoenician ivories were imported and Phoenician letters were adapted to express the Greek language. Several Greek alphabets were in existence by 800 B.C., and social intercourse gradually increased among the small communities of the mainland. Another legacy of the Bronze Age was epic poetry orally transmitted by those who still lived in such conditions as prevailed during the breakdown of the late Bronze Age. The strongest school of epic poetry was in Ionia, the traditional birthplace of Homer, whose lifetime was put in the second half of the 9th century by Herodotus (ii, 53). Of the works ascribed in antiquity to Homer the *Iliad* is the oldest; some scholars agree with Herodotus' date and others place the poem in the 8th century. The *Odyssey* is clearly later and was probably composed by a different author; even so, it should be dated before 750 B.C., to a time when the western Mediterranean was still unexplored by the Greeks. These great poems and many others, now lost to us, soon became known to the mainland and revealed the religious beliefs, personal ideals and material glories of the Mycenaean world to a population that was slowly emerging from the darkness of the Dorian invasion and its aftermath.

The renaissance of the Greek spirit in the 9th and 8th centuries was a gradual process, and it took place in conditions far different from those of the Bronze Age. Religion played a prominent part. Centres famous in Mycenaean times revived: Apollo again received worship at Delphi from the mainlanders, and Apollo's shrine at Delos attracted the Ionians of the islands. Religious leagues of a regional character, called amphictyonies (*see* AMPHICTYONY), were formed: the northern tribes worshiped at Anthela, the Boeotians at Coronea, some states near the Saronic gulf (Gulf of Aegina) at Calauria and the Ionians of Asia Minor at the Panionium on the peninsula of Mycale. Poetic competitions and athletic games were held at such religious festivals, and Olympic games were instituted in honour of Zeus at Olympia, in the western Peloponnese. Temples were built between 850 and 750 B.C. at Sparta, Perachora and at Dreros in Crete; and continuity in religion and in architecture was preserved from Mycenaean times at Thermum in Aetolia, where a Mycenaean megaron was superseded by a 10th-

or 9th-century temple of megaron type with an apsidal peristyle and this in turn by a classical temple.

A school of religious epic poetry grew up in central Greece. Its leading poet, Hesiod, whom Herodotus regarded as a contemporary of Homer, incorporated many Bronze Age legends in his *Works and Days* but added a strong sense of moral purpose which was characteristic of the mainland in his own day. The *Theogony*, which was composed considerably later, drew upon Bronze Age traditions and set the Greek pantheon in order.

The political traditions of the Mycenaean world were preserved on the mainland in Attica, where all the citizens belonged to four Ionian tribes and paid a rather loose allegiance to a central government, headed at first by a king and then by magistrates. The refugees from the mainland organized their small states on similar lines when they settled on the islands and the coast of Asia Minor. As the defensible centre in each case was a citadel or polis, these states were called *poleis* or city-states. The Dorians, however, developed a different kind of state in Crete and in Laconia. At the time of the conquest the Dorians reduced the local inhabitants to serfdom and generally did not marry outside their own circle. During the dark age the Dorian masters split up into small villages (*komai*), which tended to fight with one another and were themselves split by family and tribal feuds (for each district contained members of the three Dorian tribes). Under such conditions the Dorians might well be overthrown by their serfs. The Dorians of Crete put an end to the internal feuds in their villages by instituting a system of state education. Boys were taken from their homes at an early age and trained together until they entered rival troops at the age of 17; if they qualified after two years of rigorous discipline, they were admitted to a men's club or mess (*andreion*) and thereby received the full franchise. Members of a mess fed together and fought side by side during their active life. The troops and messes were maintained by the state, and the members were trained exclusively to serve the state in politics and war; for they formed the "warrior class" in contrast to the "land-working class" of serfs.

Kingship, which was appropriate to large tribal groups, declined in Crete during the dark age, and the villages elected ten executive magistrates to hold office for a year and to supervise the system of state education. A council, which had consisted of heads of clans in the tribal state, was now recruited from former magistrates to form a council of 30 elders, who held office for life. The assembly of citizens elected the magistrates and the elders but had little voice in policy, unless the council was divided in its views.

In Crete there were more than 100 states with such institutions, which agreed never to liberate the serfs in the frequent wars that they waged against one another. As Crete was geographically self-contained, the energies of their centralized city-states were absorbed within the island, but it proved otherwise on the mainland when the Spartans adopted similar institutions. In the plain of the Eurotas five Dorian villages combined politically to form the united state of Sparta and to impose much the same system of state education. Under the reform associated with the name of Lycurgus, those who were elected to the messes became full citizens, or Spartiates, at the age of 30 and were called "equals," those who failed to graduate in the state system became "inferiors" with lesser rights. The agricultural land was divided into equal lots, allocated to Spartiate families and worked by state-owned serfs, called helots. Kingship in the form of two royal houses had survived in Laconia, the two kings claiming suzerainty over all Lacedaemonians (inhabitants of Laconia). In the constitution of the new state the two kings were the military and religious heads, but they had equal powers in the council with 28 elders (*gerousia*), who were elected from equals of 60 or more years of age and held office for life. Five magistrates, called ephors (*see* EPHOR), who supervised the state education and the messes, were elected from the equals and held office for a year; at first they had little importance in the constitution. The assembly of Spartiates elected the elders and the ephors by acclamation, voted on proposals submitted by the council (for it could not initiate proposals itself) and passed decisions that were binding. The Dorian tribal system was replaced for military and political purposes by five new tribes, each containing the residents of one of the five constituent villages at the time of the reform and thereafter their descendants.

The Spartan state was the first example on the mainland of the famous definition of Aristotle (*Politics*, 1252ᵇ 28): "the partner-ship of several villages is the full-grown polis, which already pos-sesses the dimensions of virtually complete self-sufficiency." Its formation was dated by Thucydides (i, 18, 1) toward the end of the 9th century, and it rapidly showed its superiority over its neighbours. (The date and to some extent the character of the reform associated with the name of Lycurgus are much disputed; for the view given here see *Journal of Hellenic Studies*, lxx, pp. 42-64 [1950]; for different views and dates as late as the 6th cen-tury see DORIANS; LYCURGUS.) The warrior class of Sparta en-forced the king's suzerainty by reducing all Lacedaemonians to dependent status: the Perioeci ("people of the vicinity"), as they were called, henceforth obeyed the dictates of Sparta and served in the army, retaining only limited powers of internal self-govern-ment. The Lacedaemonian army then annexed Messenia after 20 years of war (c. 740-720 B.C.); the best land was allocated to Spartiates and worked by Messenian serfs, and the hill people be-came Perioeci. Two other Dorian states grew, as did Sparta, out of constituent villages in the 8th century, namely Corinth and Mégara. They conducted an indecisive war with one another for control of the Corinthian isthmus.

3. Colonizing Movement and Its Effects.—The pioneers of Greek colonization were the Ionians of Asia Minor. When life became more peaceful, they soon felt the pinch of overpopulation; for they held only a small foothold on the coast and could not overcome the vigorous peoples of the interior. Led by the Mile-sians, they sailed into the Black sea and planted their first colonies on its coasts in the first half of the 8th century. The Ionians of Chalcis and Eretria in Euboea opened up the west by planting colonies on the island of Aenaria or Pithecusa (Ischia) in the bay of Naples and at Cumae on the mainland opposite in the middle years of the 8th century. They were the first also to colonize Sicily. The Ionians of the islands were among the early colonists on the northern coast of the Aegean and on the island of Thásos. Al-though the Dorian states of the mainland came later, they founded the strongest colonies; e.g., Syracuse, Corcyra, Apollonia Illyrica, Ambracia, Leukas and Potidaea founded by Corinth; Byzantium and Chalcedon founded by Mégara; Taras (Tarentum) founded by Sparta; and Cyrene founded by Théra. The spate of colonization continued until c. 550 B.C., by which date hundreds of colonies were planted on the northern Mediterranean coast and islands from Spain to the Hellespont (except in the inner Adriatic), on all shores of the Black sea and on the African coast between Egypt and Carthage. The limits to the areas of colonization were set by the rival sea powers Etruria, Phoenicia and Egypt.

The Greek colony was a small independent unit, a replica and not a servant of its founder's original city; it was a polis in its own right, an *apoikia* or "settlement far from home." Thus the great variety of city-state institutions, alphabets, calendars, festivals and so on was perpetuated overseas in innumerable small states. Because the colonists aimed to establish a self-sufficient commu-nity, they went out in search of fertile land; but they chose sites in most cases that were suitably placed for trade. They were able to establish themselves at the expense of less civilized and less well-organized peoples by virtue of intelligence and fighting power; for they came usually in longboats of 50 oars, seized and fortified a small island or strong point and used their superiority of weapons and defensive armour to win good land. The Greeks adopted little from the natives of the sites that they colonized. Their colonies were rather outposts of a Greek civilization which was racially and culturally exclusive, but from them spread those hellenizing influences that transformed Europe during the Greek and Roman periods.

The Greek states of the homeland sent out their colonists for a variety of reasons. Sometimes they wished to rid themselves of surplus population or political malcontents, but they usually had their own positive interests in mind. The earliest colonies were planted to tap the trade in metals; and others were set up in areas rich in wheat, tunny fish or animal products. The colonies could thus trade with the homeland and particularly with the founding city. The commercial character of Greek colonization was so marked that the agricultural states of the homeland (the central Greek states, including Attica and the bulk of the Peloponnese) sent out no colonies, whereas the leading commercial states, such as Miletus, Chalcis, Eretria and Corinth, founded the largest num-ber of flourishing colonies.

As the colonies were planted Greek trade increased steadily. The traffic by sea, ranging from the Black sea shores below the Caucasus range to Spain, had its centre of exchange at the Isthmus of Corinth. The merchantmen, being unable to tack against the wind, sailed along the coasts and islands, taking advantage of the onshore and offshore winds rather than venturing across the open seas. The Corinthians, about 600 B.C., constructed a slideway (*díolkos*) for hauling vessels and cargoes across the four-mile span of the isthmus; Corinthian shipwrights invented the 50-oared long-boat; and the strategic position of its colonies, combined with its own wealth and naval power, gave the city of Corinth a strong hold on the western trade. The expansion of Greek trade within the colonial areas coincided with a period of close relations with Syria, Phoenicia and Egypt. The traffic which began in the 9th century revolutionized Greek ceramic art in 750-700 B.C., when the formal but austere dignity of geometric painting gave way to the orien-talizing style of polychrome painting and imaginative decoration. The new style was developed first in Crete, Corinth and Laconia and later in Athens and Ionia, but it spread rapidly throughout the Greek world, the potters of Corinth holding the lead until 550 B.C. Greek traders were active in the eastern Mediterranean, where stations were established at Naukratis in the Nile delta and at Poseidium near the mouth of the Orontes in Syria. Greek troops were employed as mercenaries by the kings of the east.

The Tyrannies.—Prosperity brought political troubles in its train. The traditional loyalties of the tribal state with its con-stituents—tribe (*phyle*), brotherhood (*phratry*) and clan (*genos*)—were centred in the racial units and were based upon the agricul-tural landowning system. The claims of birth were now upset by the claims of wealth. The first effects were seen among the aristo-cratic leaders, whose solidarity of interest was disrupted. At Corinth, where the Bacchiadae were the ruling clan, Cypselus, the son of a Bacchiad woman, seized power and set up a "tyranny" (unconstitutional rule) which was maintained by him and his de-scendants from c. 657 to c. 582 B.C. His example was followed at Sicyon, where tyranny lasted for a century, and at Mégara, where it was short-lived. The tyrants were not social revolutionaries but self-seeking aristocrats, who increased their own revenues by keep-ing the citizens at work and promoted the trade and prestige of their states with remarkable success. When they fell they left a legacy of political bitterness, from which oligarchy emerged once more triumphant. In these Dorian states the existence of the serf class also acted as a brake against social revolution. In the Ionian states, where all men were citizens, the tyrants at Ephesus and at Miletus, for example, overthrew the aristocratic order but failed to establish a stable government; and on their fall a period of faction ensued between oligarchs and democrats.

Solon.—The troubles that attended sudden prosperity were sometimes solved by "law-givers" or arbitrators. The most fa-mous of these, Solon of Athens, was appointed in 594 B.C., at a time when the wealthy were entitled under the laws of debt (1) to tie bankrupt debtors to the land and exact one-sixth of the produce and (2) to sell off a second category of debtors as slaves. The ex-planation of these two categories of debtors is disputed: the first probably comprised members of Athenian clans, who were pro-hibited by law from alienating land owned by the clan; the second was probably composed of *orgeones* (that is to say, members of guilds), who were Athenians originally by naturalization and not by blood and owned alienable goods. Solon liberated both cate-gories, forbade the tying or selling of bankrupts and made new laws of debt. He then carried a constitutional reform to safeguard the poor from oppression. He instituted a people's court of appeal in the Heliaea; there anyone could initiate a case, and the appeal from the ruling of a magistrate or the verdict of a phratry or clan court was judged by a panel drawn by lot from all citizens, however poor. He divided the people into four classes according to income and ruled that candidates for state offices should belong to this or that class; he thus eliminated the aristocratic principle of birth, which had hitherto been important in candidature for office. He left the constitution much as he found it (annual magistrates elected by the people; the council of the Areopagus, the members of which were elected for life from the former magistrates; and an assembly; see ECCLESIA), but he also nominated 400 members to serve for ten years on a new council or boule, which was to act as a steering committee for the assembly. Solon was a true arbitrator: he gave to each section of the state those powers which he considered it fit to wield. He enunciated for all citizens freedom of the person, equality before the law and a say in election and government, but he left the mass of real power in the hands of the Areopagus council and the wealthy class in the state, which was in the main the aristocracy of birth. He also took an important step to widen the economic basis of a country which was mainly agricultural and had stood aside from the colonizing movement: he invited craftsmen from other states to settle in Athens and to receive the franchise. He also adapted either the currency or the standard of weights and measures to facilitate trade within the commercial orbit of Corinth.

Currency and Coinage.—At some time (the exact date is disputed) during the expansion of the Greek states, 750–550 B.C., commercial exchange was lubricated by the adoption of currency from Lydia in Asia Minor, where a lump of electrum (a natural alloy of gold and silver, in which the proportion of gold is variable) was guaranteed at a definite price by the king of Lydia and stamped with his emblem of state, a lion's head (*see* NUMISMATICS). Most of the Greek states which engaged in commerce were coining in silver by the mid-6th century at latest, and the circulation of fractional currency in place of barter made it possible to accumulate mobile wealth more rapidly. Credit, usury and banking soon followed, and the foundations were laid of an active capitalism that has distinguished Europe from the east for many centuries.

C. CONFLICT BETWEEN GREECE AND PERSIA

1. The Persian Advance and the Growth of Sparta and Athens.—The expansion of the Greek states was favoured by external circumstances. No great power overshadowed the Mediterranean area in the period 750–550 B.C. The civilized states of Asia Minor, Syria, Egypt, Carthage and Etruria were less aggressive and less capable than the Greeks, and no really great wars broke out between the Greek states themselves (the conflict that involved the largest belligerent coalitions was the Lelantine War [*q.v.*] between Chalcis and Eretria and their several allies in the late 8th century). The situation changed when Cyrus the Great incorporated Lydia in the Persian empire c. 546 B.C.; and his successors reduced every state from the Mediterranean coast of Asia to the Indus valley and Egypt also. In 514–513 Darius I led the forces of the Persian empire across the Bosporus into Europe, marched north against the Scythians beyond the Danube and withdrew discomfited; but he retained control of the northern Aegean coast, conquered some Greek islands off Asia Minor and the Hellespont and received the submission of the king of Macedonia. In 500 the Persians were preparing to advance into the Aegean, where they were invited to intervene at Náxos in the Cyclades.

The Peloponnesian League.—The Greek states of the mainland took no steps to help the Greeks of the Asian coast and the islands when they were overrun by Persia. The Spartan government uttered diplomatic threats, but remained, no less than the others, immersed in its own affairs. By 546 B.C. Sparta had become the strongest power in Greece: a Messenian revolt (c. 640–620) had been put down; the rival military power of Argos had been defeated; and a military coalition known as the Peloponnesian league or, more accurately, the Spartan alliance, had been formed. As leader of a coalition Sparta had many attractions to offer, including a stable constitution, a superb standing army and a sound agricultural economy—(having banned the introduction of coinage, the Spartans had very little commercial interest, and they had no hunger for land). The Spartans' record moreover was good, in that they had deposed tyrants in some states and supported conservative government in general. Any state that joined the military coalition contracted a defensive alliance with Sparta, agreed to serve under Spartan command in time of war and undertook to provide help against the helots; and the contracting state received in exchange the protection of the leading military state against any aggressor. Having initiated this policy c. 550 B.C., Sparta brought almost all the Peloponnesian states, apart from Argos, into this coalition before 510.

Pisistratus and the Pisistratids.—Athens grew in power under a tyranny. When Solon retired there was a long period of party strife which ended in the final seizure of power by Pisistratus c. 546 B.C. He and his sons ruled Athens until 510 with a firm and consistent policy that brought the prosperity envisaged by Solon. Athenian pottery outstripped Corinthian and established a longlasting supremacy for black-figure and red-figure wares (*see* POTTERY AND PORCELAIN). Under Pisistratus Athens became one of the leading centres of commercial exchange, had very close relations with the Ionians, planted settlers on the Thracian Chersonese, on Lemnos and Imbros and held Sigeum in the Troad, thus securing some grip on the approaches to the Hellespont. After Pisistratus died in 528/527, the advance of Persia weakened the Athenian position. Two friendly tyrants, Polycrates of Sámos and Lygdamis of Náxos, fell from power, and Darius annexed the Chersonese and threatened Lemnos and Imbros. Athens moreover became embroiled in 519 with Boeotia, where a league of city-states had grown up under the leadership of Thebes and was trying to force Plataea into membership. When Athens made an alliance with Plataea, Thebes and Athens came to blows, and Athens was victorious. This success caused alarm to the other Greek states. In 514 Hipparchus, one of Pisistratus' sons, was assassinated by two Athenians, Harmodius and Aristogiton. In 510 Sparta, aided by Athenian exiles, used force to expel from Athens the leader of the Pisistratids, Hippias, who fled to Persia. Athens was then enrolled in the Peloponnesian league, which included Boeotia and other states in central Greece.

Cleisthenes.—Liberation did not bring peace to Athens. The aristocrats who had been ousted from authority or banished by the tyrants now struggled with one another for power. But the common people and especially the town dwellers, to whom the tyrants had brought prosperity, were a new factor in the situation; for they had gained some political experience in working the constitution and the laws of Solon under the tyrants, who kept the real control in their own strong hands. A returned exile, the aristocrat Cleisthenes of the Alcmaeonid clan, who was losing the struggle against his peers, espoused the cause of the commons. His rivals called in a Spartan garrison to occupy the acropolis in 508/507 B.C. The Athenians rose in disgust, forced the garrison (commanded by a Spartan king, Cleomenes I) to withdraw from Attica and authorized Cleisthenes to set up a constitution.

Cleisthenes' aim was to cut away the political power of the clans (*gene*) which made the rivalry of the aristocrats so dangerous and to give the members of guilds (*orgeones*) a part in the administration of the state. He therefore made residence instead of race the basis of the electoral system and replaced the four racial tribes with ten new tribes of residents in demes (about 170 areas similar in size to small parishes). As he wanted the new tribes to cut across both the local influence of the clans that owned big estates and the sectional interest of the town as opposed to the country, he constructed each new tribe out of demes usually not contiguous one with another and drawn in equal proportion from town, coast and inland. Having broken the racial principle (as the Spartans had done in their reform), Cleisthenes made tribal membership hereditary after 507 B.C. Each new tribe provided a military contingent; elected a general (*strategos*) and lesser officials annually; and for a council of state provided 50 members annually, selected by lot from candidates elected by its own demes in proportion to the population of each deme. The new council or boule of 500 members, inheriting the powers of Solon's council of 400, prepared all business for the assembly, carried out routine administration and was divided by tribe into ten committees of which there was always one, elected by lot, in permanent session for a tenth part of the year. Although Cleisthenes ensured the electoral and political rights of the commons, he left the constitution in the hands of the experienced class. The council of the Areopagus, as guardian of the constitution and the laws, had the right to veto a decree of the assembly and tried cases of treason. The chief magistrates (the nine archons) were still elected by the people en masse from members of the two richest classes (but see BOULE), and the 500 councilors had to be members of the top three classes, who had passed a scrutiny (*dokimasia*) by the outgoing council. There were thus sufficient checks on the assembly's sovereignty to make the constitution a balanced one, "admirably adapted to promote unanimity and preserve the state" (Plutarch, *Life of Pericles*, 3).

Athens and the Peloponnesian League, 506–500.—The constitution was soon tested. In 506 B.C. the Spartans advanced to Eleusis with their Peloponnesian allies, while Boeotian and Chalcidian armies invaded northern Attica at two points. The Athenians concentrated their army at Eleusis. But the Corinthians, who disapproved of an attack on Athens, left the Peloponnesian ranks, and this precipitated a quarrel between the two Spartan kings, who had equal powers of command. A deadlock resulted, and the whole Peloponnesian army went home. The Athenians then trounced the forces of Boeotia and Chalcis separately, annexed the best land of Chalcis and planted 4,000 Athenian settlers on it. Aegina then made an alliance with Boeotia and sent a strong fleet to ravage the coast of Attica. The Athenians approached Persia for help but when they were ordered to accept Hippias as tyrant broke off negotiations. Meanwhile Sparta was dealing with the problems raised by the fiasco of the recent invasion of Attica. A law was enacted whereby the two Spartan kings were forbidden to serve together, except in Laconia. Next, anxious to deprive Persia of a gambit for entering Greece, the Spartans brought Hippias over from Asia and promised to restore him as tyrant. They then asked their allies to send delegates to a conference at Sparta and explained their plan; but the Corinthian delegate protested, the others followed suit and Sparta acquiesced in the decision.

This conference not only saved Athens but also crystallized the organization of the Peloponnesian league. Thereafter, whenever a defensive alliance with Sparta was invoked, Sparta convened the delegates of the allies and explained the position. The delegates then voted, each state having one vote, whether the body of allies was to go to war; the decision of the majority, being binding on the minority, was reported to Sparta, which voted separately in the state's own assembly. If the two equal bodies—the congress of allies and the Spartan state—concurred, a common policy was adopted; otherwise no action was taken by the Peloponnesian league as a whole. This was a realistic procedure, which recognized that the agreement of Sparta was indispensable to the league.

2. **Ionian Revolt.**—The Greek states of the mainland thus were far from united in 500 B.C. when Persia accepted an invitation to intervene at Naxos. A member of the Persian royal house and a Greek called Aristagoras, who had been appointed tyrant of Miletus by Persia, tried to take Naxos by surprise in 499 and failed. Afraid of Persian resentment at this failure, Aristagoras made plans to raise the Ionian states in revolt. He resigned his tyranny at Miletus and persuaded the other states to depose their pro-Persian tyrants. Then he applied to Sparta for help. Sparta was already committed to enmity with Persia, but saw that the Spartan army, which counted 10,000 men at full strength, could do little or nothing to hold the narrow coastal fringe of Asia Minor against the vast resources of Persia. Sparta therefore refused. Aristagoras, however, went on to Athens, and the Athenian assembly gave him a squadron of 20 ships, thus earning the gratitude of the Ionians and the hostility of Persia. The only other help was five ships sent by Eretria.

The Ionian states that had deposed their tyrants decided in 498 to fight for their independence against Persia. It was a remarkably courageous decision; for the resources of Persia were vast and individually the Ionian states were puny by comparison. At first they held the initiative, for the Persians had to muster the fleets of their subjects in Cyprus, Phoenicia and Egypt. But the Ionians started by marching inland, where they burned Sardis but failed to capture the citadel. The Greek cities of the Bosporus and of the Hellespont rose in sympathy, thereby cutting off the Persian forces in Europe and opening the way for supplies from the northern coast of the Black sea. Most of the Carians, who were good soldiers, joined the revolt. Finally the Greek states in Cyprus attacked the Phoenicians in the island. Instead of coordinating their allies and sailing to Cyprus, the Ionians allowed Persia to take the initiative in 497. At this stage the Athenians sailed home. Two Persian army groups operated in Asia Minor, and a third was transported by the Phoenician fleet to Cyprus, where the Ionians brought them to battle on land and at sea. Although the Ionians were victorious at sea, the Persians kept the initiative by land and recovered the whole of Cyprus in 496 B.C. In Asia Minor one Persian army group reduced some Greek states in the area of the Hellespont, but the other group was finally annihilated by the Carians late in 496. During the winter of 496–495 the Ionian states sent deputies to a conference at the Panionium to make an agreed plan. They decided to raise no army but manned 353 ships, each contingent serving under its own captain. When the captains entrusted the command of the fleet to one of their number, the seamen mutinied. In midsummer of 495 a naval battle was fought at Lade, in which some Ionian squadrons fought well but others fled without engaging. The Persian fleet was decisively victorious, and by the summer of 493 the last of the rebels was reduced. (The chronology is disputed; for this account see *Historia*, iv, pp. 385 ff., 1955).

The Ionian revolt was not in vain. It showed the Greeks of the homeland that resistance to Persia was not hopeless and that coordinated policy, unified command and sea power were of the first importance. The Persians, too, learned a lesson. When they had meted out punishments, they permitted democratic government in the Ionian states, ordered them to keep the peace with one another and demanded tribute in accordance with a just assessment. This politic settlement was successful. The Ionians stayed quiet, while the Persians re-established their authority in Europe as far as Macedonia in 492 and raised forces in 491 to punish Athens and Eretria.

The policy of Athens had fluctuated during the revolt. When it ended in failure, the Athenians began to fortify their naval base at the Piraeus on the advice of Themistocles, who advocated resistance to Persia; and they sought a *rapprochement* with Sparta. In 491 Persian agents visited the Greek states and demanded earth and water, the tokens of submission. Several states medized (i.e., joined the Medes and Persians). One of them, Aegina, was still at war with Athens. At the request of Athens, Sparta compelled Aegina to revoke this submission to Persia in 491, but Aegina attacked Athens in the following year and was only held in check by Athens with the aid of Corinth. (The chronology is disputed; for this account see *Historia*, iv, pp. 406 ff., 1955; see AEGINA for another view.) Nevertheless, Athens could now count on the help of Sparta.

3. **The Persian Wars in Greece.**—A strong Persian expeditionary force sailed across the Aegean in 490 B.C. All the islands in its path submitted except Euboea, where Carystus and Eretria resisted but were quickly reduced. The Persian commanders, taking the advice of Hippias, landed unopposed at Marathon; supplies were ferried over from Euboea, and the plain was suitable for their cavalry, which was far superior to any Greek cavalry. When the Athenians learned of the landing, they sent a runner, Philippides (or Pheidippides), to inform Sparta (he reached Sparta, 140 mi. away, on the next day) and met in assembly to discuss strategy. On the proposal of Miltiades, who was general of a tribal contingent, they sent their heavy infantry to Marathon.

Marathon.—There the Athenian commander, Callimachus, pitched his camp on the foothills, where the Persian cavalry could not deliver an attack, and watched the Persian infantry drawn up along the shore. For a few days neither side moved. The Athenians numbered about 10,000 men and were reinforced by 1,000 Plataeans. The Spartans promised to send an army after the festival of Apollo, but that would not be for a week or more.

Miltiades had had considerable experience of Persian warfare. As ruler of the Thracian Chersonese, he had seen the army of Darius in 513 and followed the events of the Ionian revolt from close quarters. He therefore appreciated the fighting qualities of both sides at Marathón. The Greek heavy infantryman, the hoplite, wore defensive armour of bronze (helmet, breastplate and greaves), whereas the Persian infantryman wore a bonnet, a padded or scale-clad tunic and close-fitting trousers. The Greek weapons were a bronze shield, a six-foot spear and a sword, whereas the Persian had a wicker shield, a shorter spear and a sword. Miltiades knew that despite inferior numbers the Greek infantry would have a chance of defeating the Persian infantry at close quarters. Infantry tactics were similar on both sides; for the men fought in a solid line, several ranks deep. The Greeks, however, were more experienced: hoplite warfare (see HOPLITE) had been practised since 700 B.C., and the Athenians and Plataeans were seasoned soldiers. The Persians were a picked but composite force with far less tradition of infantry fighting. Miltiades, therefore, advised his fellow generals to attack as soon as opportunity offered. The votes of the ten generals were equally divided, and the casting vote lay with Callimachus, a civil magistrate (polemarch). He sided with Miltiades. Even so, each general had one day of operational command in turn (according to Herodotus; but see STRATEGUS). Those who had sided with Miltiades gave him their days, and it so happened that Miltiades commanded on the day of the attack. The circumstances that made the attack possible are not explained by Herodotus, the historian of the Persian Wars, and the following account is a reconstruction that is controversial. (See also MARATHON, BATTLE OF.)

While the armies waited, Miltiades advanced his position into the plain by felling trees and making stockades at night, until he was only a little more than a mile from the Persian infantry lines. The large force of Persian cavalry, perhaps 5,000 strong, maneuvered in the plain by day but needed water and pasture at night; these were best found at that time of year (September) in the springs and marshes at the far end of the Marathón plain. One night near dawn some Ionians serving with the Persians came to the stockades and said, "The cavalry are away." Miltiades drew up his men, strengthening the wings and thinning out the centre of the line, hurried across the plain in the dawn and charged the Persians at the double. Bitter fighting ensued. The Athenian centre was pushed back, but the weight and superior armour of the wings prevailed and both wings then turned inward and attacked the Persian centre from both sides. Once the melee of the infantry battle had started, the Persian cavalry could not intervene effectively, and the Greeks drove the enemy down to the sea, where their fleet took them off.

As the Persian fleet stood out toward Euboea, the Athenians on the battlefield saw flashes from a shield inland. The flashes were evidently a signal; for the fleet changed course and headed for Athens. Suspecting that the supporters of Hippias intended to surrender the city, the Athenians managed by a forced march to reach Athens just before the fleet entered the bay of Phalerum (Órmos Falírou). A landing was now impossible. The Persian fleet sailed for Asia. Next day the Spartan vanguard arrived and marched to Marathón to study the arms and tactics of the Persians. The Athenian dead, 192 in number, were buried where most of them had fallen. The burial mound still marks the spot. The Persians had lost 6,400 men and much of their prestige.

Preparations for War, 490–480.—Darius was now determined to invade Greece in force. But a revolt by Egypt, Darius' death in 486 B.C. and the reduction of Egypt by Xerxes, his successor, delayed the offensive until 480. Although the Greek states had ample warning, most of them made no preparations until the last moment. Athens showed more foresight. Miltiades led a fleet of 70 ships into the Aegean to secure the Cyclades against Persia. He was wounded in an unsuccessful attack on Páros and was later condemned on a charge of misconducting the operation. He died of his wound soon afterward. The offensive was then abandoned, but the Athenians made political preparations for the future. The aristocratic leaders, who were related to Hippias, and perhaps also other leaders favoured appeasement or collusion. Even the advocates of resistance differed in their strategy, because some trusted in their victorious army and others in their comparatively inexperienced small army and navy. The decision lay with the assembly from meeting to meeting, but there was a grave danger that the mood and therefore the policy of the assembly might fluctuate if it were to be exposed to the oratory of rival leaders. It was essential to make a lasting choice in good time. The means were found in ostracism (q.v.)—a procedure that may have been devised by Cleisthenes but was used now for the first time. If the assembly decided without debate to hold an ostracism, each citizen scratched the name of the man he wished to expel on a piece of pottery (ostrakon) and returned it at a later meeting. If the pieces of pottery exceeded 6,000, the man whose name headed the poll was banished for ten years but retained his property and citizenship. Between 488 and 482 ostracism was used frequently (thousands of ostraka have been found in the excavation of the Agora in Athens). Victims were Pisistratid and Alcmaeonid leaders and finally Xanthippus, connected by marriage with Cleisthenes, and Aristides, a colleague of Miltiades at Marathón. By this effective method the assembly selected Themistocles, the advocate of a naval strategy, as its leader for the war against Persia and authorized him in 483–482 to devote an unexpected yield from the state-owned silver mines to the building of warships ostensibly for the war with Aegina which was still going on. In 480 the victims of ostracism were recalled. The fleet then stood at 200 vessels and Themistocles was in charge.

Another problem at Athens was the machinery of command in the field. The preliminaries at Marathón had made this obvious. In 487 the assembly deprived the polemarch of his military functions and changed the procedure for appointing the nine chief magistrates. The demes now elected 500 candidates, of whom nine were selected by lot, scrutinized by the council and appointed. The ten generals were the only officials still appointed by direct election. They became the most important figures in Athens at a time when a war for survival was imminent. (See STRATEGUS.)

Effective resistance depended less on Athens than on Sparta. Whereas Athens was hemmed in by enemies (Thebes and Aegina), Sparta led a powerful military coalition and had shown prowess by inflicting a severe defeat on Argos at Sepea c. 495 B.C. When Xerxes sent envoys to ask all Greek states except Athens and Sparta for earth and water, Sparta held a Greek congress late in 481, at which delegates of about 30 states agreed to enter into alliance against Persia and to terminate all wars with one another. Argos, Crete and Syracuse were invited to join the alliance. Their refusal was reported when the delegates met in the spring of 480 at the Isthmus of Corinth. The problem of co-ordinating 30 states was solved by the statesmanship of the Spartans and their allies, who formed the bulk of the coalition. Each state, Sparta included, cast a single vote at a congress of delegates and agreed to obey a majority decision. The congress entrusted the command by land and sea to Sparta, decided the general lines of allied strategy, raised and allocated men and money, conducted diplomatic negotiations and threatened medizing states and persons. The member states of the congress entitled themselves "the Greeks" (Hellenes). Thus for purposes of defense a Greek league came into existence and evolved an efficient machinery of allied co-operation.

Artemisium and Thermopylae.—In the spring of 480 B.C. Xerxes entered Europe with a vast army, supported by a large fleet. His chief problems were supply and transport. He had laid some dumps in advance but depended mainly on the fleet, which was therefore tied to the army. The means of transport in a country without roads were pack horse and oxcart. Indeed the army advanced at so sluggish a rate that Xerxes brought the Greeks to battle on land only once in 480, and that was on ground chosen by them. The congress of the Greek league wanted to inflict a defeat on the Persian fleet, which would halt Xerxes' advance. They therefore posted the Greek fleet at Artemisium (Artemísion) in northern Euboea and a holding force of 6,000 or 7,000 hoplites at the pass of Thermopylae (Thermopílai) on the mainland farther down the Euboic channel. The fleets fought indecisively on three successive days. The Greeks had sufficient success to encourage them in view of their inferior numbers, but their base on the island became unsafe when the Persian army turned the position at Thermopylae. There the hoplites proved far superior in hand-to-hand combat, and the Spartan king Leonidas and his 300 Spartiates showed the spirit of free men by fighting to the death.

Salamis.—The congress of the Greek league chose the island of Salamis, off the Bay of Eleusis, as its next naval base and fortified the neck of the Isthmus of Corinth. Central Greece was left defenseless. Thebes joined the Persian forces, as Thessaly had already done, but the Athenians took to their ships on the advice of Themistocles, abandoned Athens to fire and pillage and let the council of the Areopagus represent the state during the emergency, while the people were dispersed as refugees. The political decision of the Greek congress was unpopular from the outset with some of the captains who had to put it into effect. The Greek fleet of 380 warships was faced by a Persian fleet which had replaced its heavy losses in storms off Thessaly and Euboea and now mustered about 1,400 ships (for the numbers of ships involved, as well as for other controversial matters connected with the battle of Salamis, *see* the full discussion in the *Journal of Hellenic Studies,* lxxvi, pp. 32 ff., 1956). When the Persian fleet conducted a reconnaissance off the eastern exit of the Straits of Salamis, the division of opinion flared up on the council of captains over which the Spartan commander, Eurybiades, presided. Many captains wished to withdraw their national contingents and defend their homes in the Peloponnese, for they were afraid of being bottled up and annihilated in the Straits of Salamis and the Bay of Eleusis. The decision lay with Eurybiades, but Themistocles did not wish the future of the Greek navy to hang on the Spartan's judgment. He sent a message that evening to Xerxes, saying the Greeks were divided and about to disperse and that he, Themistocles, was friendly to the Persian cause. The advisers of Xerxes, remembering the Greek dissensions at the battle of Lade, thought the message credible, and Xerxes acted upon it. He sent 200 ships that night to close the western exit from the Bay of Eleusis, off Mégara, landed picked troops secretly on an island at the eastern end of the straits and kept the main fleet under oar all night, patrolling the open water outside the eastern exit. Meanwhile the Greek captains wrangled into the small hours, until Aristides brought a report that the western exit was being closed by the enemy. Withdrawal was now impossible. The Greek command made its plans, aided by the captain of a ship from Ténos who deserted and gave details of the Persian dispositions.

The Greeks were experienced in naval warfare. Their ships were vessels of a uniform type, the trireme, driven in battle by about 170 oars and designed for ramming. They were more stoutly built and therefore lower and slower than the Phoenician galleys, which were designed for boarding tactics and carried more marines. The first problem for the Greek command was to offset their smaller numbers by drawing the Persian fleet into the straits. As dawn broke, the Greeks embarked at their bases halfway up the straits and rowed off northward out of sight. The Persian fleet, seeing them disappear, thought they were in flight and rowed into the straits. Then the Greeks returned in battle order to the narrowest part of the waters, maneuvered under oar to create favourable circumstances for ramming and went into the attack at the crucial moment. The Phoenician squadron, in the van, suffered heavy losses, and the leading files were driven back onto those that were still advancing. Then the Greek ships, encircling the Persian ships capsized and the sea was covered with wreckage and corpses (Aeschylus, *Persae,* lines 417–421). As a west wind rose, the Persians hoisted sail and fled to Phalerum, having lost the pick of their fleet. Next day Xerxes, who had watched the battle from the mainland, did not renew the engagement; for although his fleet was still far superior in number, he saw no hope of prizing the Greek fleet out of its strong position.

Plataea and Mycale.—The Greek victory at Salamis halted the Persian advance in September, the end of the campaigning season. Xerxes himself returned to Asia with his fleet and part of his huge army, but his general Mardonius wintered in central Greece with a formidable army. Despite Athenian, Plataean and Megarian pressure, the Greek congress at first kept its army at the Isthmus of Corinth and its fleet at Aegina to conduct a co-ordinated defense, if necessary; but it passed to the offensive on both land and sea in late summer, 479 B.C. Mardonius, having tried in vain to detach the Athenians from the Greek cause by diplomacy and then by ravaging Attica, withdrew his army of perhaps 150,000 men as the Greeks advanced. He chose his ground in the Boeotian plain below Plataea. There the Persian cavalry dominated the plain and the Greeks stayed on the foothills, where they soon ran short of supplies and water; for nearly 40,000 hoplites and 70,000 light-armed troops were dependent on pack horses traversing Mt. Cithaeron (Kithairón). One night in August the Spartan regent Pausanias ordered a general withdrawal, which was disrupted by the obstinacy of a Spartan officer who stayed at his post. Dawn found the Greek units scattered. Mardonius advanced at once, concentrating his best infantry against 10,000 hoplites of Sparta and 1,500 hoplites of Tegéa, who were isolated from the main Greek army.

Pausanias kept his troops in hand until he judged the moment ripe. Then he led his Spartans and Tegeans downhill at the charge. They overwhelmed the Persians with their superior weight, longer weapons and disciplined array, killed Mardonius and pursued the fugitives to their stockaded camp so closely that the cavalry could not intervene. The Greek centre was driven back from the plain; but the Athenians, 8,000 strong under Aristides, defeated the Thebans, joined Pausanias and stormed the camp. By nightfall the bulk of the Persian army was destroyed. Meanwhile the Greek fleet, commanded by the Spartan king Leotychides, drove the Persian fleet to the Asian mainland at Mycale. Leotychides landed his sailors and marines farther up the coast, destroyed the Persian fleet and inflicted very heavy casualties on a supporting army. The Ionians and Aeolians at once rose in revolt. The Persian invasion thus met with final disaster.

4. The Greek Offensive.—As Persia had vast resources, Xerxes was likely to attack again. The best method of hindering him was to punish the medizing states, to cut the communications between Europe and Asia and to keep the Phoenician fleet out of the Aegean. Late in 478 B.C. this was almost achieved; for Thebes had been punished and Thessaly invaded, and the navy under Pausanias had captured most of Cyprus and occupied Byzantium. But the revolt of the Ionians and Aeolians raised a difficult problem. Sparta and the other Peloponnesians still thought (as in 498) that Ionia could not be defended and therefore advised the Ionians and Aeolians to leave Asia. Athens, however, appreciating the nature of sea power, believed that Ionia could be protected and could help to protect the Aegean from the Phoenician fleet. The divergence of opinion between Sparta and Athens was also based on self-interest. Having lost a considerable proportion of their best troops at Thermopylae and Plataea, the Spartans wished to husband their manpower for the suppression of the helots and the strengthening of the Peloponnesian league. The chief asset of Athens was the fleet; for Attica was ruined, and the walls of Athens were being rebuilt against the wishes of Sparta. If Athens could win command of the Ionians of the islands and of Asia Minor, a mass of power comparable to that of the Spartan alliance would be created. Athens then played a skilful hand. In 478, after the victory at Mycale, the Athenian squadron under Xanthippus joined the Ionians in capturing Sestos in the Hellespont. In 478, when the Ionians offered the command of the Greek navy to the Athenian captain, Aristides. Athens accepted and Sparta acquiesced. They had combined to defeat Persia in the past and were both under oath to maintain the principles of the Greek league.

The Delian League.—An offensive and defensive alliance was contracted by Athens with each of a number of Ionian states separately in the winter of 478–477; these Ionian states did not necessarily make alliances with one another. Athens (with a fleet of 200 triremes) was thus the centre and leader of the coalition, but undertook to respect the autonomy of the other members. The allies met regularly on Delos Island in a synod, where each state had one vote and a majority vote was binding; the Athenian state took its own decisions separately. If the synod and Athens agreed, a joint policy was formed by the coalition, which was known in Greek as "Athens and the allies" and goes now under the loose title of the Delian league or confederacy of Delos. It resembled the Peloponnesian league closely, except that the alliance was offensive. The allies accorded to Athens the command at sea, a half-share of any booty and important executive powers; e.g., Athens decided which states should contribute money and which states ships and assessed the amount in each case. Athenian officials kept the accounts of the allied fund, which was placed in the temple of Apollo and Artemis at Delos, and Athenian commanders had disciplinary powers over the troops that each state had to supply in addition to money or ships. The coalition won a series of successes against the Persians in Europe and Asia, which culminated in an attack on a Persian army and a navy of 350 ships mustering at the Eurymedon (Kopru) river in Pamphylia c. 466 B.C. Under the command of Cimon the Athenian fleet of 200 ships, carrying about 5,000 hoplites, and the allied squadrons, amounting to 100 ships and carrying parties of marines and archers, sank 200 enemy vessels, forced a landing and defeated the Persian army. The policy of Athens was triumphantly vindicated.

Cimon and Sparta.—During these years Athens had to watch its relations with Sparta. Themistocles, who had deceived Sparta while the walls of Athens were being rebuilt, and Aristides and Xanthippus, who brought the Delian league into being, were in favour of democracy and hostile to Sparta, but the people put their trust in Cimon, a friend of Sparta, and in the council of the Areopagus, which had proved its excellence during the year of emergency. Themistocles was ostracized and then banished; he died in the pay of Persia. The Areopagus maintained friendly relations with Sparta. Athens was also careful to have the allies' agreement on matters of external policy and was probably supported by a majority vote of the Delian synod in forcing Carystus to join the coalition and in compelling Náxos, which had seceded, to rejoin on less favourable terms. But Cimon's victory of the Eurymedon created a new situation, because the allies were now safe from Persian attack and the last Persians in Europe were about to be expelled. In 465 B.C. Athens demanded from Thásos a share in certain possessions on the Thracian coast. As this demand infringed their autonomy, the Thasians seceded from the Delian league. Athens attacked Thásos, which was reduced by 462 B.C. and forced to rejoin the league as a dependent state: the Thasians were compelled to surrender their fleet, dismantle their walls, give up their mainland possessions and, thenceforward, contribute money to the allied fund.

The policy of Athens alarmed the Spartans, who secretly promised help to Thásos. But a terrible earthquake in 464 killed many Spartiates, and the helots rose in revolt. Sparta obtained help from its allies, including Athens, but in 462-461, while the Athenian army was in Messenia, the democratic leaders, Ephialtes and Pericles, carried a reform at Athens that ended the ascendancy of the Areopagus and installed a democratic constitution. Sparta dismissed the Athenian army with ill-concealed mistrust. In 461 the Athenian assembly ostracized Cimon and entered into alliance with Árgos and Thessaly, the medizing states, which were the enemies of Sparta on the mainland. The period of co-operation between Sparta and Athens, which had led Greece to success against Persia, was now at an end (*see also* GRECO-PERSIAN WARS; DELIAN LEAGUE).

5. Greek Civilization During Persian Wars.—Greek beliefs, as expressed by Homer and Hesiod, had much in common with the Bronze Age. The physical universe, for instance, was held to be a sphere, the upper half airy and light and the lower dank and dark, with the earth a flat disk floating midway between the two halves on the waters of the "underworld" and rimmed all around by the great river of Ocean. Matter was original, at first chaotic and confused but then of its own volition orderly and arranged. The gods were secondary in time, resident some in the heavens, some in the underworld, but unable to change the conditions of material existence. Men, created by the gods, were subject not only to the material world but also to the caprice of gods who

were at odds among themselves. These beliefs formed the background of the Babylonian epics (especially the *Epic of Gilgamesh*) and of early Egyptian religion, but they led to a state of fatalistic despair and superstitious terror, in which men became subservient to the magical incantations of an authoritative priesthood. The Greeks, however, retained a faith in man's free will, moral purpose and independent judgment: the legendary hero Achilles chooses to fight because he has his own standards of conduct and accepts the prospect of an early death. Likewise, they attributed the same qualities to the superhuman beings of their mythology: Prometheus chooses to give fire to man and accepts eternal suffering. But the consequences of such acts of free will do not lie solely within man's or god's control: they are subject to the immutable laws of physical life—heredity, disease, death and so forth. When Orestes murders his mother to avenge her assassination of his father, no man or god can prevent the onset of insanity.

Faith in free will, in moral purpose and in independent judgment had important political consequences. The Greeks despised the oriental subjects of the Persian monarchy. They defended the free city-state to the death. Solon told the Athenians that they were individually responsible for the internal relations of their society and that Athena, the goddess of their state, would be their guardian in the external fortunes of international and material life. Therefore he laid down a plan for social justice which the Athenians might implement of their own free will but which he would not enforce by seizing power. The colonizing movement and the wars against Persia and Carthage (*see* SICILY) made the Greek states more conscious of their common heritage and strengthened their belief in the benignity and power of their gods, over whom Zeus presided. Religious faith was strong; Olympia, Delphi and Delos became international centres that influenced the far-flung world of small city-states. Pindar expressed the orthodox piety, moral principles and personal ideals of the Greek world at the time of the struggle with Persia and Carthage. Aeschylus, who fought in the Persian Wars, saw Zeus as the governor of the nations who regulated the consequences of man's free will in accordance with his divine justice. He wrestled with the problem of God's relations with the physical laws of matter—with death, disaster and insanity. In his last trilogy, the *Oresteia* (458 B.C.), he brought the gods of light and the gods of darkness into harmonious agreement to use the immutable laws of physical life for the advancement and well-being of the human race.

The remarkable achievements of the city-state were due to a solidarity of feeling among the citizens, which sprang from the qualities that we associate with family life. Religion played a very important part in it. The gods of the state presided over the festivals of tribe, brotherhood and clan and required the full loyalty of all their members. The citizens expressed their gratitude in temples and in statues of the gods, and the plays of Aeschylus were enacted at a religious festival in honour of Dionysus. The common sense of obligation which united so many states in resistance to Persia was strengthened by the religious sanctions of the Panhellenic oath taken at the Isthmus of Corinth and Plataea. Yet this solidarity was beginning to split by 461 B.C. Sparta and Athens were on the verge of a war that might divide the Greek world. There were outbreaks of party strife within individual states, where the conflict of rich and poor weakened the traditional loyalties of tribe and clan. A new philosophy of life was growing up in the more sophisticated society of Ionia, where the individual man advanced the claims of individualism and denied the divine right of moral and religious restraints in society. The very independence of the Greek spirit was in danger of losing its sense of purpose and undermining its own achievements.

D. THE GREAT WARS IN GREECE

1. First Peloponnesian War, 460–445.—In Athens, after the political power of the Areopagus was overthrown, the council of 500 and the assembly controlled all legislation and enacted all decrees of state without let or hindrance. The constitution became a full democracy, a direct government by the majority of the people (*demokratia*). The council prepared the agenda for the assembly, directed the magistrates and heard charges of treason.

The people's courts gave a final decision, except in such matters of religious observance as were left to the Areopagus. The assembly had an unrestricted competence, except that any proposal which conflicted with the established laws could be impugned by any citizen and held up until a people's court gave a ruling. The limits set on candidature for office by Solon and Cleisthenes were swept away in 457 B.C., so that the poorest citizen became eligible for all magistracies, except those that carried religious or financial responsibilities. The ordinary man was directly involved in all aspects of political life to an extent unthinkable in a modern European state, and the majority had a deep devotion and enduring loyalty to the tenets of the revolution.

Democracy at Athens was confident and aggressive from the outset. The people engaged in war on two fronts in 460 B.C., endeavouring to break up the Peloponnesian league and to detach Egypt from the Persian empire. As Sparta was weakened by the helots' revolt and the Egyptians fought well against Persia, Athenian energy and courage achieved remarkable success in the first years of the so-called First Peloponnesian War. The navies of Athens and the confederates defeated the Peloponnesian navies, captured Aegina (457) and controlled the Gulf of Corinth from bases set up at Naupactus (Návpaktos) and Pegae. At the same time they protected the long lines of communication to Egypt and maintained an expeditionary force, which held the Persian garrison of Egypt under siege. Even when the Spartans operated in Boeotia, the Athenians and their allies, who included Thessaly, Argos and Mégara on the mainland, raised an army of 14,000 hoplites and held the enemy to an indecisive battle at Tanágra, in 457. In the same year Athenian forces overran Boeotia and took civilian hostages from Phocis and Opuntian Locris. Athens established, or favoured the establishment of, democratic governments in these mainland states, in the hope that they would remain loyal. The city of Athens itself was made almost impregnable—so long as Athenian sea power lasted—by long walls of thick masonry linking it to the Piraeus.

The Rise of Pericles.—The tide of Athenian success turned when Persia invaded Egypt with huge forces and made a separate peace with the majority of the Egyptians. Confident in their sea power, Athens and the allies continued to operate on the Nile, until the Persians diverted its waters, captured the fleet and annihilated a relieving squadron probably in 454. The sea power of the Delian league was suddenly crippled. The confederate states, already disgruntled by Athens' self-seeking policy, resented their losses in Egypt, and many of them in the southeastern Aegean rebelled from the confederacy. At this time the leading statesmen in Athens were Pericles, author of the democratic reform and enemy of Sparta, and Cimon, victor of the battle of the Eurymedon and friend of Sparta, who had been recalled from ostracism. Their policies were diametrically opposed except in regard to Persia. The people wisely used Cimon to negotiate a truce with Sparta for five years (451-446) and appointed him to command a fleet of 200 ships, which won several decisive victories over the Persians in the eastern Mediterranean in 450 and 449. Cimon, however, died during the campaign. For other purposes the people put their trust in Pericles. His policy was to complete a process that had already begun, the conversion of the confederacy into an empire and the application of democratic principles at Athens.

In the winter of 454-453 B.C. the fund of the confederacy was transferred from Delos to Athens. The vast sum of 8,000 talents, accumulated mainly from booty, passed technically into the keeping of Athens but effectively into the possession of the Athenians, who appointed Pericles to supervise the moneys. Then, while the Persian fleet was being held in Cyprus and Cilicia, the rebels in the Aegean were quickly reduced; for, having been ordered in the past to contribute money instead of ships, they had no fleets. They were given harsh treatment. Athens installed a garrison, set up a "democratic" council appointed in the first instance by Athenian commissioners (*episkopoi*) and exacted an oath of loyalty from each councilor and sometimes from each citizen, which ensured that anyone violating his oath could be summarily executed. Athenian cleruchies were also planted to picket the confederacy. (A cleruchy [*q.v.*] was a settlement in which each settler had an allocation or *kleros* of land and retained his Athenian citizenship.) Before 478 B.C. cleruchies had already been established on Lemnos, Imroz, the Thracian Chersonese, at Sigeum and Salamis; and soon afterward Scyros (Skíros) had been conquered and a cleruchy placed there. Now, between 450 and 446, the Athenians made their imperial purpose clear. They confiscated the best land of some of the "confederates" (*e.g.*, Andros and Náxos) and gave it to cleruchs, who acted as a deterrent against revolt and provided bases for naval operations. In addition Athens made the use of Athenian currency, weights and measures obligatory for all confederates.

On seizing the fund of the confederacy Athens became rich overnight and so could afford a more extravagant democracy. Pericles instituted state pay for those who rendered political and other services. Jurors, councilors, officials and troops—according to Aristotle 20,000 men in all—were soon in receipt of modest payments. Pericles asserted that the poorest citizen should thus be enabled to serve the democracy. His rivals accused him of political jobbery; for they believed he was buying votes with stolen money. In 451 B.C., on the proposal of Pericles, Athenian citizenship was restricted to those who were of Athenian parentage on both sides. Thus Athens became racially exclusive, at the expense mainly of the confederates. By closing the citizenship during the very process of empire building the Athenians showed themselves less wise than the Romans were later to be. While the truce held with Sparta, Athens made peace with Persia, probably in 448 B.C. The treaty, known as the peace of Callias, marked the successful conclusion of the Greek war against Persia. Under its terms the freedom of the Greeks in Asia was recognized, and the contracting parties—the Athenians and their allies and "the Great King"—agreed not to intervene in one another's territory and waters. Athens tried to represent this treaty as a Panhellenic triumph and invited all states that had been in the ambit of the Persian invasion to attend a conference at Athens, to restore the temples burned by Persia and to plan a general peace through-out the Greek world. Yet the offer of peace talks came strangely from the aggressors in the First Peloponnesian War, who were busily converting the Delian league into an empire for themselves. When the Spartans and their allies made no response, the other invitations were canceled.

Pericles had at least extricated his country from war on two fronts. After 448 B.C. the Athenians could concentrate their efforts against Sparta. On the surface they were strong. They had complete control of Aegean resources, as well as great wealth and an unrivaled fleet; they had Mégara, Boeotia and Locris in subjection. Phocis as an ally and Achaea, Naupactus and Troezen on their side; and they had alliances with Leontini in Sicily and with Rhegium in southern Italy. Only goodwill was lacking. Puppet governments euphemistically called "democracies," Athenian garrison troops and Athenian monopoly of policy deceived no one who had experienced them. Early in 446, when the truce was about to expire, refugees from Boeotia, Locris and Euboea defeated Athenian troops in Boeotia and forced Athens to evacuate that country. Then the states in Euboea revolted. As soon as Pericles crossed into Euboea with an army, Mégara revolted. The Peloponnesian league's army was already on the road to Attica, while the Boeotians and the Peloponnesians combined their forces near Eleusis. Then, at the very moment when the superior strength of Sparta was about to be applied, the Spartan king in the field, Pleistoanax, withdrew his army and went home. He was fined on a charge of having taken bribes from Pericles. Meanwhile Pericles reduced the whole of Euboea in a rapid campaign. In the winter of 446-445 a treaty of peace "for 30 years" was concluded between Athens on the one side and the Spartans and their allies on the other.

The terms of the Thirty Years' treaty recognized the Athenian empire and the Peloponnesian league. Sparta left Aegina and Naupactus under Athenian control, and Athens abandoned Achaea, Troezen and Mégara to the Peloponnesian league. The beneficiaries of the treaty were the two coalitions, and the prospects of its duration rested on the balance of power between them. Therefore Argos, as a strong military power, was to be kept neutral; but any other state could join either group at any time and enjoy the terms of the Thirty Years' treaty. It was a statesmanlike attempt to secure a lasting peace. There were provisions for the freedom of the seas and for arbitration in case of disputes. Peace and prosperity reigned for 15 years thereafter throughout the eastern Mediterranean. Yet these were years of preparation for war; for the peace between Sparta and Athens rested not on goodwill but on a balance of power that was becoming more and more precarious. The Spartans indeed, having no capital for new enterprises, had little hope of expansion and were content to husband their military strength within the bastion of the Peloponnese and to maintain the freedom of the western seas across which corn and goods were imported. Athens, on the other hand, had the capital and the spirit to expand; and Sparta felt that Athens was only waiting for a suitable opportunity to return to the attack.

2. Periclean Democracy and Imperialism, 445–431.—In the years of peace Athens decided future policy. The choice was between Cimon's successor, Thucydides, son of Melesias (not the historian), and Pericles. Thucydides stood for a qualified democracy, for co-operation with Sparta and for alliances with the Aegean Greeks; Pericles stood for a full democracy, for enmity with Sparta and for imperialism in the Aegean. Thucydides was ostracized in 443 B.C. Those who shared his views lay dormant until the revolution of 411.

The full democracy had such faith in Pericles that it acknowledged him to be the first citizen in the state, elected him annually as senior general and made him responsible for the great reserve fund on the acropolis. He owed his position to financial honesty, intellectual vision and force of character, not to any cabal or party. Indeed the politics of the democracy knew no party organization. He made the city of Athens beautiful by building the Parthenon and the Propylaea on the acropolis from public funds. He brought prosperity to the citizens by increasing sea-borne trade, by annexing land for cleruchs and by granting pay for service at home and in the empire. He claimed that the democracy was a model to all men. It gave to its citizens equality and freedom in speech, in law, in politics and in education; it provided full employment, good economic conditions and also humane treatment for resident aliens and slaves; and it combined these blessings with a constitution under which the individual citizen was directly involved in forming policy and in managing all aspects of administration. The Periclean democracy engendered an ardent loyalty in which idealistic principles and material interest frequently coincided.

Pericles consolidated the empire. Civilian hostages were deported from unruly subject states to Athens. Cleruchies were planted, for instance, at Chalcis and at Histiaea in Euboea and colonies of Athenians and their subjects at Amphipolis in Thrace and on the coasts of the Black sea. Between 445 and 431 there was only one incident that threatened the stability of the empire. Ordered to accept Athenian arbitration in a dispute with Miletus, the Samians stood on their rights as voluntary members of the "alliance"; for they still had their own fleet. Pericles then occupied Sámos and administered the usual punishment: a "democracy" supervised by a garrison and commissioners, the surrender of civilian hostages and a fine for disobedience. The Samians revolted, hoping for help from Persia and Sparta; but their hopes proved vain, and they capitulated after a lengthy siege in 439. Athens made them surrender their fleet, demolish their fortifications, give hostages and pay the cost of the war (1,276 talents) in installments over a number of years. The only state which revolted in sympathy, Byzantium, capitulated after the fall of Sámos. The empire was securely held. But, as Pericles said later, it was held under a tyrannical rule which Athens could not remit without danger (Thucydides, ii, 63).

Sparta and Persia were prepared to tolerate the Athenian empire as long as their own interests were not affected. But domination of the Aegean sea and the Black sea had not satisfied Athenian ambitions or apprehensions. Athens gained a strategic base in the northwest by helping Acarnania to defeat Ambracia, a colony of Corinth, and then contracting a close alliance with Acarnania and Amphilochia (c. 437 B.C.). The appearance of an Athenian fleet in the western sea alarmed the Peloponnesians and especially Corinth. But Corinth was not deterred on that account from quarreling with Corcyra, originally a Corinthian colony and now a considerable naval power. Sparta tried in vain to persuade Corinth and Corcyra to accept arbitration. They went to war in 435. The Corcyraean fleet of 120 triremes was victorious; but Corinth and some friendly states, many of which were members of the Peloponnesian league, mustered a fleet of 150 triremes in 433. At this stage Corcyra asked Athens for an alliance. The issue for the Athenians was clear: if they wished to preserve the general peace under the Thirty Years' treaty, they would refuse to help Corcyra; if they wanted to fish in troubled waters, they would grant an alliance at the risk of endangering the general peace. The assembly hesitated. On the first day of debate the majority was against an alliance, but on the second day it voted an alliance on the advice of Pericles. Corcyra seemed a prize worth having: the accession of its fleet would alter the balance of naval power decisively, and the Corcyraeans controlled the coasting route from the west to the Peloponnese. The Athenians combined audacity with cleverness. They granted Corcyra a defensive alliance, which was not a breach of the Thirty Years' treaty, and sent only ten ships, hoping perhaps that the prestige of Athens would halt Corinth and that the smallness of the force would not frighten the Peloponnesians as a whole. When the 10 ships were already on the way to Corcyra, they sent 20 more; they may have learned that Corinth was about to attack and hoped that the 30 Athenian ships would by their superior seamanship give the Corcyraean fleet an advantage. But the Athenian commanders were given orders to engage only if the Corinthians were about to force a landing on the island of Corcyra.

In Sept. 433 B.C. the Corinthians and their allies defeated the Corcyraeans in the southern channel, but broke off the action when the ten Athenian ships engaged to prevent a landing. The Corinthian fleet returned to the attack in the evening; but the fortuitous appearance of the other 20 Athenian ships from the south at this crucial moment caused the Corinthian fleet to withdraw and sail homeward. Athens then had bases on Corcyra, in Acarnania and at Naupactus and the assistance of the battered Corcyraean navy and, in the winter of 433–432, began to put pressure on Corinth and on Mégara as an ally of Corinth. Potidaea, an old Corinthian colony in Chalcidice, was ordered to break off relations with Corinth and to dismantle its sea walls. Economic sanctions were imposed against Mégara, whose commerce was excluded from all ports of the Athenian empire. Potidaea revolted, and the Corinthians and their Peloponnesian friends placed "volunteers" in the city before it was invested by Athens. Sparta, reluctant to engage in war against a naval power or to terminate the Thirty Years' treaty without legitimate grounds, was playing a waiting game; but Corinth, Mégara and other states made a *démarche* to Sparta, claiming that Athens' aggression had violated the treaty and invoking the defensive alliance on which the Peloponnesian league was based. The Spartan assembly then held a debate. The decision was taken by a large majority that Athens had violated the treaty. The Spartans reported this decision to the congress of allies which met and concurred. Thus the two organs of the Peloponnesian league decided to go to war unless Athens was prepared to retract. Abortive negotiations ensued. Then Sparta delivered an ultimatum: peace would continue only if Athens recognized the independence of the Greek states. Pericles spoke in the decisive debate at Athens. He advocated war and the assembly supported him. Their decision was that Athens would accept an offer of arbitration but not any ultimatum from Sparta. Negotiations ceased in the winter of 432, and Thebes, a member of the Peloponnesian league, committed the first act of war by delivering a treacherous attack on Plataea, an ally of Athens, in the following spring. The contemporary historian Thucydides saw the fundamental cause of this war in the growing power of Athens together with the growing apprehension of Sparta. He appreciated at the outset that it would be a great war, because it was likely to end in the destruction of one party or the other.

3. Great Peloponnesian War, 431–404.—The course of the war is described elsewhere (*see* PELOPONNESIAN WAR). In the Archidamian War (431–421) each side began with superior strength on its own element, and ten years of fighting increased the margin of superiority. Yet neither side could apply its superiority with decisive effect. Sparta could not force Athens to battle, or breach the impregnable walls; and the Peloponnesians, unable to campaign far afield or for long periods because they lived on their own agricultural produce, failed to exploit the advantage that the Spartan commander Brasidas gained in Chalcidice by raising Athens' subjects in revolt. The Athenians held the seas with their navy, but their warships could not impose a complete blockade on Peloponnesian merchantmen; and their sea-borne raids, effective though they were, did not serve as a prelude to an invasion of the Peloponnese. All this, according to Thucydides, was foreseen by Pericles, who expected a long war of attrition and thought that Athens would prove more buoyant than Sparta. On the whole he was correct. The Athenians lost more than one-third of their manpower in the plague and in action, and they spent more of the financial reserve than they had expected; but in 421, when the peace of Nicias (so named after the general who guided Athenian policy) was made, they had complete control of almost the whole empire, a great navy and the means of recouping their finances rapidly. Sparta suffered less loss of life than Athens, but was shaken internally by the revolts of the helots; and the allies, especially Mégara and Corinth, were impoverished and embittered. Sparta's control of the Peloponnesian league was very shaky in 421, and Argos seemed after a generation of neutrality to be a strong rival in military and political matters. The peace terms of 421 included the restoration of all places (except Plataea, Nisaea and some Corinthian possessions in the northwest) and of all prisoners captured in the war and an undertaking to submit to arbitration all disputes between the Athenians and their allies on the one hand and the Spartans and their allies on the other.

Pericles had originally gone to war in order to break the Peloponnesian league, the basis of Sparta's power in international affairs. The peace of Nicias provided a great opportunity for doing so by diplomacy, operating from strength. But Pericles had died in 429 and Athens was disunited. A worthy successor might have united Athens, created a block round Athens and Argos and used the Athenian army to lead a coalition against an isolated Sparta. Alcibiades tried but failed. The failure was the fault not so much of one man as of the Athenians collectively. They did not make a decisive choice between Alcibiades and Nicias, and their indecision lost them the chance of winning the peace. When war broke out again, the same indecision brought the Sicilian expedition to disaster (415–413) and crippled Athens' recovery later. On the other hand the Spartans kept their unity and their power of decision. The victory over Argos and Athens at Mantinea in 418, the re-formation of the Peloponnesian league and the winning of the war at sea by Persian money and Peloponnesian manpower were due to Sparta's tenacity and leadership. The hard necessities of war broke the political front at Athens, ruined the state's finances and brought the navy and the empire to an end in 404 B.C. They also strained the strength and warped the judgment of Sparta and undermined the loyalty of the Peloponnesian allies. Moreover the naval position in which the Spartans found themselves at the end of the war was one that they could not afford to maintain. The Greek states from the Aegean area to Sicily were torn and weakened by war and dissension. Persia and Carthage were the gainers. Without striking a blow they extended their field of political influence, while the Greeks were wearing one another down.

4. Greek Civilization, 458–404.—As fear of Persia receded, the city-state became the centre of existence. Whereas Aeschylus (525–456) had studied the relations between God and man in human history, Sophocles (c. 496–406) was concerned with relations between man and the city-state, in which God's purpose for man was revealed: the ideal qualities of the characters Oedipus and Antigone in his tragedies were seen in relation to their obligations to the state. Devotion to the state reached its highest level at Athens in the period between the wars, when prosperity and confidence reigned. The Parthenon and Propylaea were built by a people who felt an undivided affection for the city and for the goddess of the city, the maiden Athena. The principles of the democracy were expressed in an ideal form by Pericles, whose vision captured the imagination of his contemporaries and inspired the leading writers of the period—Sophocles, Thucydides and Aristophanes—even on occasions when they criticized the real Athens of the Peloponnesian War. It was an age of great intellectual and emotional power. Men carried principles to their logical conclusion in architecture, sculpture, drama and politics. At the same time they respected "the unwritten laws" of moral and religious restraint which gave a true balance and proportion to their art and to society. Athena and the gods of the family were not abstractions but demanded of their worshipers the highest standards in loyalty and nobility. The Periclean period at Athens was the acme of the Greek city-state. The light of the Greek genius was focused with brilliant intensity on the life of the polis— but only for a short time, for the lens was soon starred by disaster.

The Peloponnesian War broke the strands of traditional religion in Athens. The centres of family worship were lost when the Peloponnesians ravaged the countryside and refugees poured into the city. The horrors of the plague, the disaster at Syracuse and the final shock of utter defeat broke men's faith in the favour of the gods. The state was split by revolution. Citizens killed one another in civil war, and party loyalties took precedence over patriotism. Alcibiades was typical of many young Athenians whose intellectual ability was devoid of any religious scruple or moral principle, and their conflict with the older generation who remembered the days of Pericles is vividly portrayed in the comedies of Aristophanes.

The effects of the war on Athenian society were heightened by the teaching of the sophists (q.v.), who came from other parts of the Greek world and spread new ideas in the crowded city. Their lectures were stimulating and exciting. They covered the whole range of human thought with remarkable versatility and originality. Although individual sophists laid new foundations for philosophy and conduct, the general trend of their teaching was rationalist in method and agnostic in conclusion. Traditional religion in their view was the child of convention, and natural law indicated that might is right and that the individual pursues his own interest. Speculation in physics seemed to support this view, for Democritus reduced the operations of the universe to an interaction of atoms that were governed by some impersonal "necessity" or natural law, if not by random "chance." Medicine, too, emancipated itself from religion. "This disease," wrote Hippocrates of epilepsy (the so-called "sacred disease"), "is no more sacred than other diseases. . . . Its origin is in heredity . . ., and its cause lies in the brain, as is the case with all the most serious diseases."

The divine right of the city-state was severely shaken not only in Athens but throughout the Greek world, of which Athens was the cultural capital. The centre of interest was shifting toward the individual. Euripides portrayed the transition in his plays. They show the tragic consequences for the individual of war, tradition and conventional religion. His *Hecuba, Medea, Orestes* and *Hippolytus* are psychological studies of the individual woman or man who is not confined within the limits of the city-state. His dramas, therefore, have a modern quality. Aristophanes represented both sides of the conflict. He made fun of the die-hard traditionalists and challenged Athens' right to empire and men's justification of war; but he also pilloried the sophists and those who accepted the worst side of their teaching. He denounced the self-seeking individualists and the psychologists who rated human desires above moral restraint. In the end he gave his allegiance to his ideal picture of Athens and to the service of the city as it was despite its faults. Socrates was the only Athenian among the sophists. He questioned the assumptions of his pupils in all matters of religion, ethics and belief and professed to know only that he knew nothing. This stage of his teaching created many agnostics, who lost their traditional bearings and found refuge in individualism. But Socrates carried others forward to a new belief in the ultimate verities of goodness, truth and understanding; and his own life of humility in the service of philosophy inspired them to follow his example. When Athens had fallen, Socrates was put on trial "for not worshiping the gods whom the state worships, for introducing religious innovations and for corrupting the young men." He was found guilty of the charge. When he was sentenced to death, he refused to ask for mitigation of sentence. He died because city-state tradition was strong, but his martyrdom proclaimed the individual's right to free thought and belief. Thus a rift was opening between political life and personal philosophy, which Plato later described so simply: "A man who really fights for what is right must lead a private, not a public, life, if he hopes to survive, even for a short time" (*Apology*, 32a).

E. THE CITY STATES, 404–354: INDEPENDENCE OR COMBINATION?

The Spartans and their allies had fought for the independence of the Greek states. When they won, it was expected that several hundred independent states would emerge from the dismembered Athenian empire. But independence was not necessarily the panacea for international troubles. Its effect was seen in Sicily, where victory over Athens in 413 B.C. had left the Greek states free to engage in party strife and to fight against one another and the resulting chaos was exploited by the Carthaginians, who had added most of the Greek states to their empire by 404. The states of Greece and the Aegean area were already torn by civil strife and harboured strong animosities toward one another; and the Persians were more dangerous neighbours than they had been since the battle of the Eurymedon. It was clear to a few political thinkers, such as Isocrates, that Greek civilization could be preserved not by the untrammeled independence but by the co-operation and combination of the Greek states. On the other hand the politicians and the electorates were concerned primarily with the narrower issue of their own survival and expansion, often at the expense of neighbouring Greek states, and they were reluctant to enter any combination that limited their own freedom of action. Many wars were waged in the 4th century B.C. to decide whether independence (*autonomia*) or co-operation (*symmachia*) in various forms should be the guiding principle of Greek international affairs.

1. Sparta and the Movements for Independence, 404–371. —During the last stage of the Peloponnesian War the Spartans were liberating the small states in the Aegean. They naturally supported pro-Spartan parties, which were oligarchical rather than democratic in outlook; and Spartan troops were left to assist their parties in maintaining power. The Spartans moreover were winning the naval war on Persian subsidies and had agreed in return to surrender the Greek states of Asia Minor to Persia; and they saw that they would be able to break this agreement safely only if the small states of the Aegean were kept firmly in the Spartan bloc. Nor was their position easy on the Greek mainland. The wartime allies of Sparta, who were members of the Peloponnesian league, naturally felt alarmed for their own liberties when they saw the policy of Sparta in the Aegean.

The first reaction came at Athens. The oligarchs were particularly ruthless in killing and exiling their enemies (for instance, the men who had overthrown the oligarchy of "the 400" set up by the revolution of 411), and they soon had to call in a Spartan garrison. The leaders of the exiles obtained help from disgruntled members of the Peloponnesian league (especially Thebes, Mégara and Elis), established themselves in a frontier fortress on Mt. Parnes, and went on to capture the Piraeus, where the democratic element was strongest. They defeated the oligarchic forces and the Spartan garrison troops in a pitched battle at Munychia

(Munichia) in May 403 and made preparations to attack the walls of Athens. Late in the summer Sparta intervened. There were by then three factions in Attica: the extreme oligarchs held Eleusis, the moderate party was defending Athens from the Piraeus. The arrival of a Peloponnesian army ended the fighting and Sparta made a new settlement: Attica was split into two states, one centred on Eleusis and the other on Athens. The Spartans counted on the animosity between oligarchs and democrats to keep the states separate, but the democratic tradition of Athens soon asserted itself. In 401 Athens swallowed Eleusis, and Attica was unified under a democratic regime, which had the good sense to carry out all its formal obligations to Sparta.

Cyrus the Younger and Agesilaus.—Meanwhile there was a similar reaction to Spartan policy in the Aegean. Sparta broadened the basis of the oligarchical governments in the Aegean states, but insisted that they should follow Sparta in foreign policy and pay tribute to maintain a Spartan navy. The issue with Persia was still undecided, because Cyrus, the Persian viceroy in Asia Minor, was friendly with Sparta and did not take over the Greek states. In the spring of 401 B.C. Cyrus mustered a large army of local peoples and hired 13,000 Greek mercenaries, told Sparta of his plan to seize the Persian throne from his brother, Artaxerxes II Mnemon, and asked for Spartan aid. The Spartans in the past had always refused to commit themselves to war against Persia in Asia Minor, but now decided to give naval support to Cyrus and thereby accepted the risk of war with Persia. It was a bold decision, because Sparta's control of the Aegean states and of the Greek mainland was far from strong. Cyrus was defeated and killed at Cunaxa in Mesopotamia, and Sparta made an alliance with Egypt (which was in revolt) and sent out an expeditionary force in 400 B.C. to defend the liberty of the Greek states in Asia Minor. The adventures of the Greek mercenaries whom Cyrus had engaged gave Sparta some encouragement; for they proved themselves far superior to Persian infantry in battle and in skirmishing and they fought their way from Mesopotamia to the Black sea (the retreat is the subject of Xenophon's *Anabasis*). Sparta held the initiative for five years. The Spartan infantry raided far and wide inland and collected much booty, but it failed to capture strongholds and was harassed by the Persian cavalry. The navy was at first under separate command and operated independently. Then, in 396, the Spartan king Agesilaus II went out with reinforcements and was given command of the army and navy. Agesilaus, however, raided inland and did not emulate the strategy of Cimon, who had shown that it was essential to hold the southern corner of Asia Minor and to defeat or contain the Phoenician fleet.

The Corinthian War and the King's Peace.—The Greek states had little sympathy for Sparta in the war against Persia. Even those in Asia Minor which had supported the naval operations of Athens in the 5th century were alienated by Sparta's method of conscripting and requisitioning and by the use of mercenary soldiers, freed helots and Peloponnesian troops whose chief interest seemed to be booty. The islanders disliked the oligarchical governments which Sparta supported and lacked confidence in the Spartan admirals. The mainland states in Greece were more afraid of Sparta than of Persia. For the Spartans had also abused their position in the Peloponnesian league by launching attacks on Elis in 400 and 399 and by treating the country as Sparta had treated Thásos in 462.

When Agesilaus went out in 396, Corinth, Thebes and Athens sent no contingents, and it was known that Athenians were entering Persian service in the fleet which an Athenian naval officer, Conon, was commanding. In the summer of 395 the Boeotian league broke away from the Peloponnesian league, attacked Phocis in contravention of Sparta's orders and made an alliance with Athens. At this time a Persian agent toured the dissentient states of the mainland and gave subsidies to anti-Spartan leaders at Thebes, Corinth and Argos. The first attack by Sparta on Boeotia failed. Corinth, Argos and many of the states of central Greece joined the insurgents in 394, and Sparta recalled Agesilaus and his expeditionary force from Asia, because major operations on two fronts were impossible. The Persian navy then launched its offensive, defeated the Spartan navy decisively at Cnidus in Aug. 394 and sailed into the Aegean sea, expelling pro-Spartan oligarchs and tyrants from the islands.

This war of independence, called the Corinthian War, was inconclusive on land. The insurgent states failed to evolve a centralized system of command, and the Spartan army defeated all its rivals. Agesilaus fought his way from central Greece through Boeotia and brought his army into the Peloponnese. A stalemate ensued with heavy fighting at the isthmus, where Corinth and Argos held a strong defensive position. At first these two states formed a union under which each had had reciprocal rights in the other's territory; later Argos annexed Corinth. The decision in the war lay with the Persians. At first, in 393, they let Conon help Athens to rebuild the long walls (which had been demolished under the peace terms of 404) and to form a small fleet, but after 390 their attitude changed as the Athenians tried to regain some of their Aegean empire and to assist Cyprus, then in revolt from Persia. Sparta held on to the Hellespont and even attacked the Persians and the small Athenian fleet with some success. Persia's support was then switched to Sparta, and Athens was soon blockaded by a Spartan fleet operating from Aegina (387). In 386 all Greek states finally accepted the terms of a peace that was guaranteed by Sparta and Persia and called either the peace of Antalcidas (from the name of the Spartan negotiator) or the King's peace. The Greek states in Asia Minor, Clazomenae and Cyprus were to be subject to Persia, and all other Greek states were to enjoy independence, except Lemnos, Imbros and Scyros which were to be Athenian possessions. Persia undertook to attack any Greek state that refused to accept the peace "by land and sea, with ships and money."

Confident in the support of Persia, the Spartans interpreted "independence" in their own interest. They broke up every example of combination to which they could apply force. The Boeotian league was dissolved, so that each state there should be "independent," and Corinth was separated from Argos. Mantinea was forcibly split up into five "independent" villages in 384 B.C. The strong Chalcidian league was dissolved by Sparta in 379 after three years of fighting. The Spartans also interpreted independence in the sphere of internal government in each state as the rule of an oligarchic regime. They captured Thebes by treachery and replaced the democrats with pro-Spartan oligarchs; and they forced Phlius to capitulate after a long siege and gave the oligarchs a free hand. Sparta pursued a policy of "divide and rule" under the empty mask of independence. The members of the Peloponnesian league were controlled by intimidation; Sparta's own subjects were held down by oligarchic governments and by garrisons where they were needed; and Persia, Macedonia and Dionysius I, tyrant of Syracuse, were Sparta's allies. Those who suffered under this rule learned the truth of the Spartan saying: "We cheat boys with dice and men with oaths." But the basis of Spartan power was dangerously small. The Spartiates were a very small minority in the Spartan state itself, and the oligarchic parties in other states were a minority in each state. Sparta relied ultimately on the force of arms wielded by several thousand men in order to hold down most of the Greek states.

The War of Independence, 379-371: Leuctra.—The fight for independence began in 379 B.C. Seven exiles returned to Thebes at night and led a successful revolt. Sparta promptly isolated the area of trouble, but a Spartan officer made a foolish and unsuccessful attack on Athens, which caused such indignation that Athens made an alliance with Thebes. Two years of fighting ensued, and then the allies captured the passes over Mt. Cithaeron and kept the Spartan army out of Boeotia. Sparta then took the offensive by sea against Athens, which was building up a naval coalition. The Spartans suffered a series of defeats, but fought on at sea until a split developed between Athens and Thebes. At this stage Persia appeared again on the diplomatic scene. The representatives of Persia, Sparta and Athens, together with those of their allies, agreed to make peace on the principle of "independence," under which garrisons were to be withdrawn and general disarmament was to be carried out. The Spartans took the oath on behalf of their own city and its "allies," but the delegates of

Athens and those of the allies of Athens, including Thebes, took the oath individually. The Theban delegates then asked to be recognized as acting for the Boeotian league, but Sparta refused to permit this. Thebes withdrew from the peace. The Spartan army entered Boeotia before the Thebans could muster their allies in Boeotia and forced a decisive battle at Leuctra. The Thebans were outnumbered, but they had a general of genius in Epaminondas, who appreciated the importance of striking at the enemy's strongest point. He therefore massed his men 50 deep against the Spartan right wing, where the Spartan king Cleombrotus and the Spartiate troops were stationed, and charged at the double. The massed Thebans killed 400 Spartiates and routed all the rest of the enemy before the Theban centre and right wing came into action. The military reputation on which Sparta's supremacy had been founded was broken irretrievably, and the Spartan empire was destined to collapse rapidly and completely.

The Second Athenian Confederacy and the Boeotian League.—During the war of independence from 379 to 371, Athens and Thebes developed new and important ideas in the field of combined action by a number of states. The Athenians published the charter of a confederacy in March 377. In this, they undertook to respect the independence of any ally that entered the confederacy under a defensive alliance: specifically, they promised not to exact tribute, not to introduce a garrison, not to meddle with internal government and not to revive any territorial claims against an ally. The constitution of the new confederacy resembled that of the Delian league. Each allied state cast one vote at the congress of allies, and a majority decision was binding on them all; the Athenian state, however, stood outside the congress as a separate entity and took its own decision on any matter of mutual interest. If both bodies reached the same decision, the confederacy as a whole acted upon it. In such an event the Athenians were entrusted with full executive command and disciplinary powers in the field; but an ally could seek redress through the congress of allies sitting as a deliberative or judicial body. The allies also controlled their own treasury, recruited by contributions from members on an assessment by the congress, and the Athenians made grants in money and ships from the state treasury. The Athenians who broke the charter of the confederacy. Thus machinery was created whereby a group of states could combine in a common policy of defense and each state had precise safeguards for its own independence. In 376 Athens defeated Sparta in a naval battle off Naxos, and in the next few years the confederacy attracted about 70 states that revolted from Spartan rule in the Aegean and the Ionian seas. The Athenians set them a fine example by taxing their own resources heavily and providing the bulk of the fleet.

Thebes had always been the leading spirit of the Boeotian league. The numerous states of Boeotia had been grouped in the past into 11 wards, each of which had returned 60 councilors to form a strong central government, sitting at Thebes, and had contributed its quota of money, troops and generals (boeotarchs). Thus the federal state of Boeotia had adopted a system of proportional representation. But the Thebans of 379 B.C. regarded indirect government as oligarchical. When they liberated the states of Boeotia from Spartan rule, they created a democratic assembly of Boeotians, meeting at Thebes, in which policy was determined by direct vote. The executive officials—councilors, magistrates, army commanders, etc.—were elected by the wards, now reduced in number from 11 to 7. Thebes and its dependencies, which together formed three of the seven wards, played a predominant part in the league and supplied the ablest boeotarchs and the best hoplites in the war of liberation. The Boeotian league was particularly well designed for small states in an agricultural area of limited extent, and its success in overthrowing Sparta led many other states to emulate its constitution.

The second Athenian confederacy and the Boeotian league, as associations of free states, contrasted themselves with the imperial systems of Sparta and of Syracuse under Dionysius I. The pressure of Carthage on Sicily had created a situation in which Dionysius had succeeded in establishing himself as tyrant or dictator at Syracuse in 405, and his subsequent achievements made a great impression on the Greek world. He enlarged Syracuse far beyond the normal size of a city-state by destroying other states and deporting their population into his territory, and he amassed great armaments by ruthless confiscation of capital resources and by hiring mercenary troops in large numbers. His cosmopolitan forces conquered those Greek states of Sicily that lay outside the Carthaginian zone and also many Greek states in southern Italy, and he planted colonies on the Adriatic coasts and islands. Syracuse became the capital of an empire which was bound to the will of Dionysius and enjoyed commercial supremacy in the Greek west. In 371, when the Spartans were defeated at Leuctra, the tyrant was at the height of his power. Men admired his success but did not reckon the cost in terms of political morale and human degradation. The example of Dionysius may well have inspired Jason of Pherae in Thessaly. Jason had made himself tyrant of his own city-state and, by the end of 373, had forced the other Thessalian states to obey the commands which he issued as "ruler of Thessaly" or *tagos*—a title that had been in abeyance for many generations. In 371 Jason had the finest cavalry force and the largest mercenary army in Greece and was drawing substantial revenues from the peoples of Thessaly. These examples of the forced association of states into a powerful voluntary and the group aroused interest and alarm. They were studied by Isocrates, who preferred the voluntary association (as he argued in his *Panegyricus*) but believed that some sort of forced association might be better than internecine wars between individual states.

2. The Attrition of the Leading Powers, 371–355.—Although Athens and Thebes proclaimed similar principles, they were separated by a dislike born of many frontier disputes and two great wars. More recently, Athens had seized Oropus, a frontier post, and Thebes had destroyed Plataea and subjugated Thespiae. Therefore when the Thebans asked their Athenian ally for help after the battle of Leuctra, Athens made no answer but invited all Greek states to a conference. Athens' proposal was that the Greek states should ally themselves individually with the second Athenian confederacy as a whole and maintain the terms of the peace of 371 with the backing of Persia. This proposal was accepted by almost all the Greek states. But the diplomatic triumph of Athens did not arrest the revolt of the Peloponnesian states from the rule of Sparta. Democrats seized power in many states. Those in Mantinea and Tegéa founded an Arcadian league in the spring of 370 and invited the Boeotian league to assist it in the autumn. Meanwhile Thebes had been watching Jason, who had come south to help Thebes immediately after the battle of Leuctra but had taken the opportunity to seize Thermopylae on his return and to strengthen his net of alliances. Fortunately for Thebes, Jason was assassinated in the summer of 370. The Boeotian league then formed a strong coalition of central Greek states which included Euboea and Acarnania, hitherto members of the Athenian confederacy. The forces of this coalition, led by two boeotarchs, Epaminondas and Pelopidas, and those of their allies, the Arcadian league, Elis and Argos, ravaged the whole of Laconia and liquidated the Peloponnesian league forever. In the course of his two Peloponnesian campaigns, the chronology of which is disputed, Messene was fortified as the capital of the liberated Messenians and Megalopolis was built as the federal capital of Arcadia. These successes alarmed the Athenians. They took the radical step of making an alliance with Sparta and later with Sparta's ally Dionysius of Syracuse. They tried in vain to halt the progress of Boeotia by defending the isthmus, where Corinth and other states that were afraid of Argos sided with Sparta and Athens.

The Boeotian Ascendancy, to 362.—Boeotia was the leading land power for a decade. This state's democratic federalism was widely imitated. Leagues with sovereign assemblies and federal magistrates on a cantonal basis were formed in Thessaly and Aetolia (c. 367), as well as in Arcadia; and other federal states—Phocis, Acarnania and Achaea—were brought into alliance with Boeotia. Epaminondas advocated a liberal attitude toward the federal states and accepted the oligarchic governments of the member states of the Achaean league in 366 b.c, but the Boeotian assembly replaced them with democratic governments and installed garrisons to keep them in office. Pelopidas extended Boeotia's influence in the north, intervening successfully against Athenian interests in Thessaly and Macedonia. When Athens and Sparta sent envoys to Persia for help (367), Pelopidas won the favour of Artaxerxes II and tried to impose a "King's peace" on the Greek states in 366. The terms were "independence" for all states, and the Athenians were ordered to withdraw their fleet from the Aegean sea.

The confidence of the Athenians had been shaken by Boeotia's victories, and they knew that their confederates disliked the alliance with Sparta and Dionysius. There was now the further danger that Boeotia and Persia might launch a naval offensive. The Athenians therefore began in 366 to convert the confederacy into an empire. They captured Samos off Asia Minor, Sestos and Crithote in the Chersonese, Pydna and Methone in Macedonia and Potidaea, Torone and other cities in Chalcidice. They did not admit these cities to the confederacy but occupied most of them with cleruchies and used them as naval bases. They also made a treacherous and unsuccessful attack on Corinth and allied themselves with Alexander, tyrant of Pherae, in Thessaly and with Arcadia in the Peloponnese. The Boeotians pressed their advantage, defeated Alexander at Cynoscephalae (Pelopidas was killed) and then launched a naval offensive, probably in 363, under the command of Epaminondas. His fleet of 100 triremes sailed unchallenged to the Bosporus, where Byzantium and other members of the Athenian confederacy joined him in attacking Athenian corn ships sailing for the Piraeus. But continuous warfare from 378 had exhausted the finances of Boeotia, and Epaminondas returned home without exploiting his success. Affairs in the Peloponnese demanded his attention. The Arcadian league had broken away from the Boeotian coalition, attacked Elis, seized Olympia and appropriated the funds of the temple of Zeus. This act of sacrilege split the Arcadian league, and a Boeotian force became involved in a fracas between Tegéa and Mantinea. Epaminondas invaded the Peloponnese in 362 with forces drawn from Boeotia, Thessaly, Euboea, Locris and Aeniania. He was joined at Tegéa by troops from Argos, Sicyon, Messenia and part of Arcadia. The decisive battle took place near Mantinea, where the armies of Mantinea, Sparta, Athens, Elis and Achaea held a defensive position. Epaminondas outmaneuvered his opponents, overwhelmed the Mantineans and Spartans and was mortally wounded at a critical moment in the battle. The Boeotians and their allies halted. Soon afterward peace was concluded on the *status quo.*

The League of States.—The Greek states were exhausted by war after war and by the vicissitudes of party strife. In the winter of 362–361 all mainland states except Sparta formed a league. They promised to maintain a general peace among themselves, to settle disputes by negotiation and to protect members of the league against aggression by "a general alliance," that is, by collective security. Their aims for all member states were strength, prosperity and peace. They probably set up a federal congress, a court of justice and a central treasury; and they passed a resolution as "the Greeks" in which they refused to join a group of satraps who were in revolt from Persia. The attempt to form a league of Greek states was short-lived, because the leading states continued to form military coalitions among the members. The Athenians made alliances with Arcadia, Achaea, Elis, Phlius and the Thessalian league, and Boeotia sent troops into Arcadia in 361. The Athenians moreover pursued their imperialistic policy by punishing those "confederates" who had joined Epaminondas in 363 and by undertaking operations of war in Euboea, Thessaly, Macedonia, Corcyra, Thrace and the Hellespont.

The Social War and the Sacred War to 354.—Athens was strained to the utmost in 357, when Mausolus, satrap of Caria, supported the revolt of Chios, Rhodes, Cos and Byzantium from the confederacy. In the Social War (*i.e,* "War of the Allies"), as it is called, the Athenian fleet was defeated in 356, and threats by Persia caused the Athenians to make a peace in 355 (the motion was proposed by Eubulus; *see below*), under which the independence of the rebels was recognized. Meanwhile a so-called Sacred War had broken out in central Greece: provoked by menaces from Boeotia against Phocis, the Phocians under the leadership of Philomelus confiscated the treasure of the temple of

Apollo at Delphi, hired thousands of mercenary soldiers and defeated the citizen levies of Boeotia, Locris and Thessaly early in 354. The collapse of the great powers on the mainland was almost complete. Xenophon wrote with justice that after the battle of Mantinea "even greater confusion and indecision" descended upon the Greek states. In the west, too, there was anarchy and chaos. The empire of Dionysius I collapsed when exiles returned to attack his son and successor Dionysius II and drove him off to Italy. The leader of the liberators, Dion, was murdered in 354 B.C., and civil war raged in Syracuse.

3. Political and Economic Troubles.—Although the first half of the 4th century B.C. was racked by war, it was a period of widespread prosperity. Trade flowed in increasing volume from the outer parts of the Greek world—Spain and Massilia, the Adriatic coasts, Thrace and the Crimea, the eastern Mediterranean and Cyrenaica. At the same time Carthage and Persia accumulated large capital reserves. Athens was the leader of Greek commerce, but was rivalled in the 4th century by many states which engaged in sea-borne trade and acquired capital resources. Culture, too, was widely diffused. The Attic dialect and alphabet, Attic commercial law and Attic town planning were becoming characteristic of many parts of the Greek world. Any considerable city had its theatre, civic centre and gymnasium, whether in Sicily, Italy, Greece, Asia or Cyrenaica. Trade in books was beginning, and Greek manners were spreading into the hinterlands of the continents. Banking, marine insurance, commercial treaties, mortgaging and so on were fully developed. Isocrates spoke of a "Greek" culture and it was based on a prosperity that was expanding in spite of the spasms of war.

Prosperity made the states feel more constricted than ever by the narrow confines of their territories. They fought with their neighbours, to defend or extend their lands—Sparta with Arcadia, Arcadia with Elis, Corinth with Argos, Athens with Boeotia— and they fought to secure the seaways along which their exports and imports traveled. The distribution of wealth within the states was an even more potent cause of war. Capital accumulated rapidly in the hands of the wealthy, the gap between rich and poor tended to increase apace, unless a revolution led to a redistribution of property. In a moderate democracy the poorer classes, which usually were in the majority, viewed the rich with suspicion and laid on them many "liturgies" or voluntary offices that were costly to discharge. A dividing line existed too between those who had some capital and those who had none, the *aporoi*. As Aristotle pointed out, the granting of doles to the poor at Athens, for instance, was a palliative and not a solution; he advocated the making of capital grants that would raise a poor man above the line and start him in some business (*Politics*, 1320a 35), but few states had the resources and none the will to do so. The antagonism between rich and poor was reflected in the swing from oligarchy to democracy, which was given additional impetus by the imperialistic or "liberating" powers who exploited the internal situation in another state for their own advantage. It was made more dangerous in some states by the presence of large slave or serf populations and of foreign mercenary soldiers, as well as by the proximity of aggressive neighbours. The situation in Sicily as described in a Platonic letter is an extreme case: "There is never any end. What seems to be an end always links on to a new beginning. The circle of strife is likely to destroy both factions utterly, the faction of tyranny and the faction of democracy, and the Greek language will almost die out in Sicily as it becomes a province of Carthage or of Italy."

The stresses and strains which beset the city-state from within and from without weakened the solidarity and loyalty of the citizen body and favoured the growth of individualism. Life was becoming more specialized. Lawyers, financiers, philosophers, merchants and farmers, for instance, concentrated their energies on one pursuit and played less part in public life than they had done in the 5th century. War was often conducted by mercenary soldiers and mercenary rowers; leading generals of city-states, such as Chabrias, Iphicrates and even Agesilaus, hired themselves out to serve the rulers of Persia, Cyprus or Egypt. Finance was becoming more and more the sinews of war, and citizen levies diminished in importance and to some extent in quality. Corporate religion began to decline. Great temples were still built, but more attention was given to secular and civic buildings. Tragedy lost its religious inspiration and followed the lead given by Euripides toward psychological drama. Political comedy was changing gradually into a comedy of social manners, where chance placed individuals in ridiculous situations, and prose developed at the expense of poetry. Sculpture lost something of its idealism and gained in sensual beauty, in sentiment and in realistic portraiture. Philosophy was concerned with the soul or mind of man rather than with his conduct in the state. When Plato envisaged the ideal city, he appreciated that the philosopher would be reluctant to become a ruler.

Although the Greek world was troubled by so many rapid changes, it remained immensely vigorous in action and fertile in ideas. Greece was unrivalled in commercial capitalism, in the understanding of agriculture and of finance and in the skilful practice of the art of war. The greatest philosophies and the noblest prose of antiquity were created in this period, and sculpture and painting reached a high level of perfection. Greek thought was still conditioned by the defects of contemporary politics with remarkable insight. They believed that a more enlightened education and the intelligence that it would produce might reform the city-state from within, and they both gave a picture of an ideal city-state in which the effects of capitalism would be controlled by the authority of state laws. But each state was envisaged as a separate entity and divorced, as far as possible, from contacts with its neighbours. Isocrates had a more practical outlook. He also believed in the value of education, but he saw that interdependence was more important than independence in the crowded world of the city-states. Practical politicians and the electorates behind them devised many forms of association which met some of the new needs of interdependence: complete merging of city-states by force or by agreement, the growth of federal systems with a common citizenship (*sympoliteia*) or with an exchange of citizenships (*isopoliteia*); sharing of monetary or commercial advantages; organization for the formation of a league of states. But at the same time each city-state pursued an independent policy and often an imperialistic policy, as soon as it had reaped the temporary advantages of membership in an association. The liberal principles of the second Athenian confederacy and the Boeotian league did not withstand the temptations of success. The Greek world was exhausted and leaderless in 354 B.C., when a new power was growing in the north.

F. MACEDONIAN PERIOD

Macedonia was inhabited in the 4th century B.C. by peoples of Greek, Illyrian and Thracian stock. The Macedonians proper held the coastal plain at the head of the Thermaic gulf and had more Greek blood than their neighbours of upper Macedonia. Their royal house claimed descent from Heracles, son of Zeus, and the kings were recognized as Greek by the presidents of the Olympic games early in the 5th century. They claimed suzerainty over the cantons of upper Macedonia which had their own royal houses, but they were seldom able to exercise an effective suzerainty. Kingship in Macedonia, like that of the heroic age in the Homeric poems, was hereditary within one family and constitutional. The king owned all land and conducted all affairs of state in war and peace at his own discretion. He chose his own "companions" from the nobles of the land to advise him and serve with him in battle. They had a personal "kinship" with the king which enhanced his claim on their loyalty. The Macedonian people elected the king, tried cases of treason in which the king was a litigant and had power to depose him by their vote. They derived their land and citizenship from the king and owed him personal service, taxes and dues. They had no substratum of serfs or slaves, and as free men they consorted on easy terms with the king and his companions. The feudal institutions of Macedonia proper and of upper Macedonia were unlike those of the city-state and were regarded as barbaric by the Greeks.

As Greek manners spread inland, they were canalized by the royal house. Greek culture was adopted by the court and Macedonia traded with the sea powers of the Aegean, but the march of Greek political ideas that led to the growth of city-states in Thessaly was successfully resisted by the Macedonian kings.

1. Rise and Triumph of Macedonia.—Although Macedonia proper and the cantons of upper Macedonia were not closely united c. 360 B.C., they had a common interest in contending with their aggressive neighbours in Illyria, Paeonia and Thrace and with the Greeks who attacked them from Chalcidice or Thessaly or from the Aegean sea. In 359 the Illyrians killed the king, Perdiccas III, and 4,000 Macedonians in battle and annexed the western part of upper Macedonia. Athens, then still very powerful, Paeonia and Thrace were ready to invade and divide the country. The infant son of Perdiccas was elected king; and Philip, a brother of Perdiccas, was appointed regent. Having lived as a hostage at Thebes in the period of Epaminondas and Pelopidas, Philip at the age of 22 had a thorough knowledge of Greek warfare and diplomacy as well as of the methods of the Balkan peoples. He bribed his enemies in Paeonia and Thrace to keep the peace and concentrated his troops against a pretender, Argaeus, who landed with the support of 3,000 mercenary soldiers, sent by Athens, late in 359. Philip defeated the pretender. He let the mercenaries go free and made peace with Athens, which was then at war with the revived Chalcidian league and desired to capture Amphipolis. In 358 he subjugated the Paeonians, defeated the Illyrians decisively and won the support of Illyria's southern neighbour, Epirus, where he married Olympias, daughter of the Molossian king. These remarkable successes led the Macedonians to elect him king as Philip II. He now exercised effective suzerainty over upper Macedonia and began to incorporate the leaders of the cantonal royal houses into the ranks of his companions.

Philip's Alliance with the Chalcidian League.—The chief threat to Macedonia came from the Greek states. Fortunately for Philip, the Chalcidian league, in which the principal state was Olynthus, was at war with Athens over Amphipolis, an independent state supported by the league. In the spring of 357 B.C., Philip boldly laid siege to Amphipolis. When Athens was asked by Amphipolis to send a garrison to its aid, Philip made a secret pact to give Amphipolis to Athens, if Athens gave him Pydna, a city on the Macedonian coast that was an ally of Athens. The Athenian bases at Potidaea and Torone in Chalcidice kept the Chalcidian league occupied, while Philip prosecuted the siege and captured Amphipolis. He pronounced Amphipolis independent, attacked and took Pydna and negotiated with the Chalcidian league for a defensive alliance; for Athens was now engaged in the Social War (see above), and the Chalcidian league became the strongest power in the northwestern area of the Aegean. The alliance was consummated with the cession of a rich territory called Anthemus north of Chalcidice to the league; and Philip captured Potidaea and gave it to the league as well. As both powers were at war with Athens, they agreed under the terms of their alliance not to treat separately with the common enemy. But Philip was anxious not to embitter Athens and therefore let the Athenians depart from Potidaea without ransom. In 356 he advanced eastward from Amphipolis to help Crenides, a Thasian settlement, against the Thracians. Crenides received Macedonian settlers and gave Philip access to the gold and silver mines of Mt. Pangaeus (Pangaíon), from which he later derived a revenue of 1,000 talents a year. Athens organized a coalition of the kings of western Thrace, Paeonia and Illyria. Philip attacked them one by one. In Aug. 356 the Illyrians were defeated, Philip's horse won a race at the Olympic games, and Olympias gave birth to his first son, Alexander.

Philip advanced his power along the Thracian coast and captured the last Athenian base on Macedonian territory, Methone, in 354. But his main task in these years was to consolidate and develop his kingdom. He absorbed the royal houses of upper Macedonia into his entourage and chose young nobles to act as royal pages. He increased the prosperity of Macedonia by a trade pact with the Chalcidian league and by building roads and found-

ing colonies in the interior. Pélla, the capital, was a thriving inland port; and Crenides, renamed Philippi, brought him gold and silver from which he minted coins on the Thracian and Attic standards (see NUMISMATICS). The Macedonian cavalry, headed by the Companions, was the traditional arm of the country, and Philip raised the Macedonian infantrymen or "foot Companions" to a high pitch of efficiency by regular training. As he advanced his frontiers he annexed some territories and created new Macedonian citizens—some of them of Greek extraction—by granting them land in his enlarged realm. He was forming a national territorial state, capable of expanding its territory and citizenship in a way unknown to the Greek city-state. At the same time he represented himself to the city-states as an upholder of Greek ideas. He placed the heads of Heracles and of Zeus on his coins. He set up a copy of the treaty with the Chalcidian league at Delphi. He entered Thessaly to help the free states against the tyrant Lycophron of Pherae and he captured Pagasae for them in 354 before Athens was able to come to its relief. When the opportunity came to intervene in the Sacred War (see above), he was careful to represent himself as the champion of Apollo.

Onomarchus and Philip in Thessaly.—In central Greece Boeotia defeated the Phocians under Philomelus in the latter part of the year 354 B.C., but a new Phocian leader, Onomarchus, rallied his countrymen, hired more mercenaries and made alliances with the tyrants in Thessaly against the free states, which invoked Philip's aid. Onomarchus defeated Philip and his Thessalian allies twice in 353 and then turned to inflict heavy losses on Boeotia, which was the natural but probably not the formal ally of Philip. Onomarchus now ruled from Mt. Olympus to the Corinthian gulf, and was the ally of Athens, Sparta, Corinth, Mégara, Achaea and other states. Nevertheless Philip attacked him in Thessaly in 352, defeated his army of 500 cavalry and 20,000 infantry and inflicted almost 10,000 casualties; Onomarchus himself was killed; the remainder escaped to an Athenian fleet that lay offshore in support. This resounding victory caused the tyrants to capitulate. Philip allowed them to withdraw, reorganized the Thessalian league to include all Thessalian cities and accepted election as its president with command of its forces and some claim on its revenues. In the summer of 352 he led the Macedonian and Thessalian forces to Thermopylae, but he found the pass defended by the Phocians and their Athenian, Spartan and Achaean allies. He withdrew at once and switched his attack to Thrace. In 351 his eastern frontier was at the Hebrus (Maritsa) river, and he was on good terms with Byzantium and with Cardia, enemies of Athens.

Eubulus and Demosthenes in Athens.—During these years there had been considerable fighting in the Peloponnese and unrest among the island states in the Aegean. Athens had recovered steadily from the effects of defeat in the Social War. Its policy now was to refuse invitations to join in adventures in the Peloponnese or to intervene in party struggles in the Aegean. The democracy had become more extreme after 404, the council losing many of its powers to the assembly and to the people's courts and the orators gaining greater influence in the assembly. The process was checked in 354 when a conservative, Eubulus (in 355, at the time of the Social War, he had advocated peace), was elected chief commissioner of the theoric fund (money reserved for the relief of the poor) for four years and the commissioners were authorized to control general expenditure. During his tenure a law was passed whereby surplus revenue went into the theoric fund and could be diverted into the military fund only by a decision of the assembly. As the poor commanded a majority, they now had a financial interest in preserving the peace so as not to divert money from the theoric fund and were less ready to engage in adventurous wars than in the past. But Eubulus and the assembly were not pacifist: they sent expeditionary forces to counter Philip at Methone, Pagasae and Thermopylae; and they acquired the Chersonese and sent cleruchs to Sestos in 353–352. The chief opponent of Eubulus was Demosthenes, a brilliant orator, who advocated an adventurous policy in the Peloponnese, Rhodes and Thrace but did not denounce Philip as the chief enemy of Athens until he delivered the speech known as the First Philippic, probably in 350 B.C. (for different dating see DEMOSTHENES).

The Fall of Olynthus.—Chalcidice was the key to any offensive against Macedonia. Eubulus negotiated unsuccessfully with the Chalcidian league late in 352 B.C., and Philip forced the issue in 349 by asking the league as his ally to surrender two pretenders to his throne. The Chalcidians refused and treated separately with Athens, which was a breach of their alliance with Macedonia. Athens granted an alliance and sent 2,000 mercenaries and 38 triremes. Philip remained inactive until the sailing season ended. Then he took a number of Chalcidian cities by storm or negotia-tion and started a rising against the pro-Athenian governments in Euboea in Jan. 348. As Euboea lay on the sea route to Chalcidice, Athenian forces were sent there rather than to Chalcidice; but these forces suffered such reverses that Athens recognized the independence of Euboea and paid a large sum to ransom prisoners in July. Meanwhile Philip reduced all Chalcidice except Olynthus, to which Athens had sent a further force of 4,000 mercenaries and 18 triremes. A third force of 2,300 citizen troops and 18 triremes was held up by northerly winds. It arrived to find Olynthus in Philip's hands. Philip razed the city to the ground and incor-porated Chalcidice in his realm.

The End of the Sacred War.—Before the Athenians had re-covered from the shock of defeat in Euboea and in Chalcidice, Philip offered peace and alliance. Athens was in a weak position, because Phocis was now failing in the Sacred War, and Thessaly, Boeotia and Euboea formed a strong group. Even Demosthenes, who had criticized Eubulus and denounced Philip in the Olynthiac speeches, supported negotiations with Philip as a necessary step in extricating Athens from the Sacred War. An interruption oc-curred in the winter of 347–346, when Sparta and Athens tried to seize Thermopylae, but the plan miscarried. Peace and alliance were concluded between Macedonia and Athens in July 346 (the peace of Philocrates); but opinion in the Athenian assembly was divided, Eubulus and Aeschines proposing to implement the al-liance and Demosthenes trying to prevent its implementation. Philip and his allies, with the exception of the Athenians who re-fused to send a contingent, invaded Phocis and received the capitu-lation of the Phocians. The Amphictyonic council, guided by Philip, made a settlement that was merciful by Greek standards: the Phocians were disarmed, their towns were split into villages and they had to pay an indemnity to Apollo. The two votes of Phocis on the council were transferred to Philip, and he was elected presi-dent for the Pythian games in Sept. 346. Athens refused at first to acknowledge Philip's position. But the Amphictyonic council demanded an apology, and Athens apologized after a debate in which Aeschines was shouted down and Demosthenes emphasized Athens' isolation and the need to avoid a rupture with Philip and his allies.

Demosthenes' Policy of Resistance.—Between 346 and 340 Philip increased his control of the Balkan area by a series of cam-paigns and negotiations. He controlled Illyria as far north as Scodra (the modern Shkodër or Scutari in Albania,) Epirus, Thes-saly through the Thessalian league (of which he was elected presi-dent for life) and Paeonia and Thrace through vassal kings. His alliances reached as far as the Getae on the lower Danube, the Greek cities on the Black sea and the lesser states in the Pelopon-nese. The Aetolian league allied itself with him c. 343. The king-dom of Macedonia was becoming unified by economic prosperity and military success, and the subject peoples in the Balkan area were secured by military colonies, economic development and the prestige of the king himself. The very strength of Macedonia forced the Athenians to decide between Aeschines and Demos-thenes in the assembly and in the people's courts. They chose the policy of Demosthenes and won the alliance of other states which were apprehensive of Macedonia: Corcyra, Ambracia, Leukas (Levkas), Corinth, Achaea, Messenia, Byzantium, Abydos, Chios, Rhodes and Euboea, which sent delegates to a conference at Athens in March 340 B.C. and agreed in principle to participate in a war against Philip. Demosthenes was crowned for his services to the state.

Philip had hoped to win the Greek states by diplomacy. But the triumph of Demosthenes ended those hopes, and there was now a danger that Athens would find an ally in Persia, which had put down a series of revolts and held the Asian side of the Bosporus. Philip laid siege to Perinthus in the summer of 340 B.C. and then to Byzantium, as these cities had refused to implement their alliance with him; and he sent a letter of complaint to Athens that rescinded the treaty of alliance with Macedonia. Help was sent to Perinthus and Byzantium by Persia and Athens, which con-tracted a campaign as far as the mouth of the Danube. In 339 his friends on the Amphictyonic council offered Philip the com-mand of their forces in a new Sacred War against the Locrians of Amphissa. Philip accepted. When his Macedonian and Thessalian forces reached Cytinium in Doris, he sent envoys to ask the Boeo-tian league to join him in accordance with the alliance. Demos-thenes led Athenian envoys to Thebes and offered a favourable alliance to the Boeotian league, under which Athens would pay two-thirds of the expenses of war and serve under Boeotia's com-mand in the field. The assembly of the Boeotian league voted for alliance with Athens and denounced the existing alliance with Philip. The allies occupied strong defensive positions. They re-fused all overtures for peace that Philip made, and it was clear that Philip could overcome their opposition only by force.

Philip's Victory at Chaeronea, 338 B.C.—The Macedonian army was an unknown quantity to the citizen levies of Boeotia and Athens; for it had fought on Greek soil only in Thessaly and then against the mercenary troops of Onomarchus. The Macedonian cavalry was far superior to that of the allies: the heavy cavalry, wearing protective armour and equipped with shield, sword and lance, operated in wedge-shaped formations for close fighting; the light cavalry, armed like Greek cavalry with javelin and sword, was designed for skirmishing. The infantry carried a pike (*sarissa*) twice as long as the Greek hoplite's spear, fought in less close order and were more flexible in maneuver, and the phalanx or line of bat-tle was supported by units of specialized light infantry. In the summer of 338 B.C. Philip broke through the allies' position north of Amphissa, which was held by 10,000 mercenary troops. He offered in vain to negotiate with the citizen forces of Boeotia and Athens. A decisive battle was fought at Chaeronea between about 35,000 Greek hoplites and about 30,000 Macedonian infantry. Philip, commanding the right wing of the phalanx, made a bold maneuver of withdrawal that drew the Athenians opposite him out of their position. As the Greek line moved to its left to main-tain contact, a gap opened near the right wing, into which the young prince Alexander charged at the head of the companion cavalry. At the same time Philip delivered his attack. Both wings of the allied army were destroyed or captured; the centre broke and fled. Philip did not launch his cavalry in pursuit, as he had done with deadly effect in other battles. Boeotia capitulated and was treated as a treacherous ally; the league was disbanded and oligarchic government was installed at Thebes, where a Macedonian garrison occupied the acropolis. The Athenians accepted terms, under which they lost what had been left of the second Athenian confederacy, but kept Lemnos, Imbros, Scyros, Delos and Samos and entered into alliance with Macedonia. Philip entered the Peloponnese and was honoured by every state except Sparta, which proudly refused him entry but could not prevent his marching to Gythium in southern Laconia. The military might of Macedonia was triumphantly demonstrated with a minimum of bloodshed.

2. Greece Under Philip and Alexander.—The enemies of Philip had always claimed that he would follow the path of Greek imperialism and destroy or enslave the city-states that he con-quered. Isocrates, who was now 98 years old, wrote a letter to Philip in which he once again urged him to end the period of mad imperialism, to bring the Greek states into an association of good-will and to declare war on Persia. Nor was this an old man's fantasy. Isocrates had seen the ceaseless wars for hegemony in Greece and the consequences of social unrest, and he had ob-served Philip's ability to win the support of Thessaly and his enlightened generosity in victory. Demosthenes, on the other hand, found that generosity inexplicable. He distrusted Philip and Macedonia at the moment and for the future, because he was the advocate of untrammeled independence for his city-state, Athens.

Philip chose the way of co-operation. At his suggestion the Greek states of the mainland (except Sparta), together with many island states, formed a Greek league, which was ratified in 337 B.C. at Corinth and is also called the League of Corinth. The states undertook to keep the peace among themselves and to use military sanctions against any aggressor; to respect the constitution and liberty of one another and to unite in suppressing piracy and brigandage; and to refrain each in its own state from any executions or revolutionary procedures that were contrary to the existing laws. Each state elected a number of delegates, proportionate to its military and naval strength, who sat on the federal organ of government, "the council of the Greeks." All states were bound by the council's decisions, which were taken on a majority vote and covered all matters of federal government, including issues of foreign policy. At its first meeting the council entered into an offensive and defensive alliance for all time with "Philip and his descendants," decided to conduct a war against Persia and elected Philip to be commander of its armed forces and chairman of the council during the war, citing him as "a benefactor of Greece." The council then approved the presence of Macedonian garrisons in Thebes, Chalcis, Ambracia and Corinth and called up contingents for the war against Persia.

The settlement of Greece was certainly statesmanlike. It went much further than the league of 362 B.C. had gone to arrest the endemic troubles of the Greek states; and war with Persia would provide an outlet for their energies and surplus populations. Alliance with Macedonia did not amount to incorporation in a Macedonian empire. Philip avoided that step. It is uncertain whether he acted as a Greek with an interest in Greek affairs, as an enlightened statesman who wanted a strong union of powers against Persia, or as a hypocrite who preferred to dominate by appearing to unite his potential enemies in a Greek league. In any event the league held firm until Philip was assassinated in 336 B.C. It then elected his son and successor, Alexander III, to command its forces. A federal system was completed c. 336 in Sicily, where Timoleon had defeated the Carthaginians and established a moderate form of government in the Greek states.

The conquest of Persia by Alexander the Great and the army of the Greek league is described elsewhere (see ALEXANDER III, THE GREAT). This account is concerned with events in Greece. Before the expedition set out, the Thebans rose in revolt, in 336 B.C. and again in 335. Alexander pardoned the first offense and gave them an opportunity to retract from the second revolt. But the Thebans remained obstinate. Alexander then stormed the city with his own troops and with those of the Boeotian states that were hostile to Thebes. The punishment of the rebels was referred to the council of the Greek league, which condemned the population to slavery and allotted its lands to neighbouring states. Alexander executed the sentence. He could and should have prevented the council from passing such a sentence; for the liquidation of Thebes was interpreted as an act of Macedonian imperialism. He showed generosity toward Athens and other states that had helped to instigate the revolts of Thebes and also toward Demosthenes and other statesmen who had received subsidies from Persia, but the confidence that Philip had hoped to create between Macedonia and Greece was destroyed almost irretrievably.

In the opening years of the campaign against Persia (334 B.C. onward) Alexander respected the position of the Greek league. Island states were enrolled as members of the league, and a check was imposed on party strife and on revolutionary procedure. On the other hand the Greek states in Asia Minor were probably treated as part of Alexander's kingdom; for each was given a treaty by Alexander, and Greek and barbarian alike were governed by his regulations. As long as the Persian fleet stayed at sea, Sparta acted openly as the enemy of Macedonia, and Athens not only instituted conscription for young men but also intrigued with Persia. When the Persian fleet was disbanded, Sparta used Persian money to hire a large mercenary army, raised Elis, Achaea and part of Arcadia in revolt and invited Athens to join in the fight for independence. But Athens refused. The coalition, with 2,000 cavalry and 20,000 infantry, defeated one Macedonian army and attacked Megalópolis but was broken up in the autumn of 331 by Antipater, Alexander's deputy in Macedonia, who reinforced his army with contingents from the Greek league. The fate of Sparta and the rebellious states was entrusted by the council of the Greek league to Alexander. He forced Sparta to enter the league and made the rebels pay an indemnity to Megalópolis.

During the rest of Alexander's lifetime the Greek states made no move. The central issue in their party politics was the attitude to be taken toward him. In 330 B.C. Demosthenes won his case in Athens with his speech "On the Crown" in defense of Ctesiphon, whom Aeschines was prosecuting for having proposed that a crown should be given to Demosthenes after the battle of Chaeronea; and Aeschines left the country. A steady stream of exiles flowed from the Greek states to Asia, until Alexander decreed in 324, probably with the agreement of the Greek league, that all exiles should be reinstated. The states even granted Alexander "godlike honours" at his own request—some with gratitude and some with mockery. Greek envoys, wearing crowns in his honour, waited upon him at Babylon just before he died in 323 B.C., at the age of 32.

3. Macedonia and the Greek States, 323-224.—The conquests of Alexander in Asia brought great prosperity to the eastern Mediterranean. The accumulation of capital reserves enabled Athens to equip a large fleet and to improve the city's defenses, and other states on the mainland of Greece benefited from the years of peace. The wealthy class in most states favoured good relations with Macedonia. The democratic leaders were afraid of a *coup d'état* by the wealthy and resented the restrictions on foreign policy that had been imposed by the League of Corinth. As long as Alexander lived and conquered, they complied reluctantly with his wishes. But the news of his death and of the quarrels between his generals gave the democratic leaders some hope of throwing off the alliance with Macedonia. Large forces of Greek mercenaries were under arms: 8,000 men, commanded by an Athenian, Leosthenes, were at Taenarum in Laconia and 23,000 men were marching homeward from the east. The Athenian people decided to go to war. They engaged Leosthenes and his mercenaries and formed an alliance with the Aetolian league, but most of the Greek states—especially those that had reason to fear Athenian ambitions—opposed this policy or at least refused to co-operate. The allies began the Greek War, as they called it (it is alternatively called the Lamian War), with an army of about 30,000 men. They seized Thermopylae in Oct. 323 B.C. and blockaded a Macedonian army under Antipater in Lamia throughout the winter. Meanwhile an Athenian fleet of 170 ships sailed to the Hellespont but gained no allies. In 322 three Macedonian armies were operating in Thessaly and two Macedonian fleets held the northern Aegean. Superior numbers enabled Antipater to defeat and split the Greek allies. Athens surrendered unconditionally in Sept. 322. A year later the Aetolian league accepted moderate terms from Antipater, who was anxious to settle affairs and to intervene in Asia.

The lessons of the Greek War were clear. Athens was unable to unite the Greek states because of their mistrust and the forces of Athens and Aetolia alone were far inferior to the massive armies of the Macedonians. Antipater abandoned the policy of co-operation. Treating Athens as a traitor, he exacted an indemnity for the war, placed a garrison in Munychia to control the Piraeus and Athens and disfranchised the poorer class, so as to leave only 9,000 citizens as the electorate for an oligarchic government. The assembly passed sentence of death on the democratic leaders who had instigated the war. Demosthenes committed suicide. Antipater set up pro-Macedonian oligarchies in the Peloponnesian states and installed a Corinthian, Dinarchus (perhaps the speech writer of the same name; *q.v.*), to act as Macedonian governor of the Peloponnese. The freedom of Athens and of the Peloponnesian states was at an end. They were now subject to a Macedonian protectorate, which dictated their form of government and made them keep the peace.

From 320 to 275 B.C. the states of the mainland were involved in the wars of the Diadochi ("successors") of Alexander, who fought for power and ended by dividing the Macedonian empire into a number of fairly stable monarchies (see HELLENISTIC AGE). During these troubled years the Greek states were important to the rival kings and generals because they were able to provide troops and taxes. The policy of co-operation was applied for the last time in 303 by Demetrius I (Poliorcetes), who revived the League of Corinth and treated the Greek states as allies. Otherwise the Macedonians kept control, whatever their protestations may have been, by setting up puppet governments and imposing garrisons. In Athens, for instance, Antipater's son Cassander in 317 placed Demetrius Phalereus at the head of an oligarchic government under the protection of a Macedonian garrison; and this situation lasted till 307. The council of the Areopagus received many of its traditional powers, the rich were freed from the liturgies (public duties) imposed by the democracy and a strong control was set on all legislation; but behind this façade Demetrius Phalereus was a tyrant who ruled with Macedonian support. The successful revolt, in 280, was joined by Elis and by some states in Arcadia and Achaea but not by rivals of Sparta in the Peloponnese. But the very success of this revolt made Sparta's allies suspicious and uneasy and they fell away when Sparta attacked the Aetolian league and suffered heavy losses. In 275 the Antigonid dynasty was finally established on the Macedonian throne.

Between 275 and 224 the strength of Macedonia in Europe was weakened by the attacks of Pyrrhus of Epirus (d. 272) and by the intrigues of Ptolemy II Philadelphus of Egypt and other Hellenistic monarchs. The Greek states obtained a greater measure of independence. The most vigorous peoples were those of the hill country who developed as a league of cantons with a democratic assembly on the model of the Boeotian league since 367 at latest, and had been organized as a league of cantons with a democratic assembly, and in driving off the formidable Celtic invasion of 279. Now it expanded its territory by incorporating other states, which retained their own citizenship but assumed Aetolian citizenship under an act of sympolity, and it granted an exchange of citizenship with more distant states under an act of isopolity. The Aetolian assembly, which met twice a year, decided on policy and elected for the year a general who presided over the assembly and commanded its armed forces; and routine administration was carried out by a council, of which the members were elected by the cantons in numbers proportionate to their military strength. The general and his advisers, acting as a committee, were entrusted with wide powers, because the assembly met not so rarely; and a man could be re-elected to the generalship only after an interval of some years, lest he become too powerful and autocratic. By 224 the Aetolian league, having defeated its rival, the Boeotian league, included within its sympolity the core of central Greece from coast to coast and counted among its close allies by isopolity such states as Cephallenia and Chios. Just as the democratic city-states of the previous century had been, the Aetolian league was aggressive and warlike.

The Achaean league had been disbanded in the period of Macedonian domination. It formed again on a democratic basis c. 280 B.C., with an assembly of citizens over 30 years of age and a representative council of deputies. From c. 200 B.C. the assembly's powers declined. It met jointly with the council at irregular intervals to decide major issues. The predominance of the council made the policy of the Achaean league less adventurous than that of the Aetolian, and the member states had a greater degree of independence, rarely exchanging their citizenship by an act of isopolity. The number of annual generals of the league was reduced from two to one in 255. Then the general acted as president of the assembly and commander of its forces and shared with a small committee of officials the exercise of a strong executive authority; and the same man could be elected general in alternate years. This feature in the league's democratic constitution enabled Aratus of Sicyon to hold office every other year and gain a strong position of leadership. Aratus had a fanatical hatred of the tyrants whom the Macedonians supported, and he drove them out of city after city until by 228 the Achaean league comprised almost all states in the Peloponnese except Elis, Messenia and Sparta.

The greatest city-states of the past led a rising against Macedonia in 267 or 266 B.C. This was the Chremonidean War (so named after the Athenian leader), in which Athens and Sparta, in alliance with Ptolemy II Philadelphus of Egypt, proclaimed themselves champions of the liberty of the Greek states. But few of the states joined them. The Athenians fought gallantly, but were starved into surrender by the superior forces of Macedonia in 262; after this, they preserved their freedom by a policy of neutrality.

The Spartans lost their allies and remained a second-rate power, without Macedonian intervention, until 227 B.C., when they saw themselves threatened by the expanding Achaean league. Sparta indeed had been crippled, ever since the battle of Leuctra, by the small number of Spartiates, or full citizens, who owned sufficient land to pay their contributions to the messes. In 227, however, a Spartan king, Cleomenes III, changed the situation by revolutionary methods; he abolished debts and confiscated all land, which he redistributed in lots to increase the citizen body (see CLEOMENES). Having thus enlarged his army and announcing a program of social revolution, Cleomenes attacked the Achaean league and detached so many of its member states that its general, Aratus, called on Antigonus Doson, king of Macedonia, for help in 224.

4. The Coming of the Romans.—Between 224 and 205 B.C. the rulers of Macedonia struggled to regain a dominant position in Greece. As the price of help to Aratus, Antigonus Doson took over Corinth and founded another Greek league. This was similar to Philip II's League of Corinth and included the leagues of Thessaly, Phocis, Boeotia, Euboea, Epirus, Acarnania and Achaea. As the elected commander of the league's forces, Antigonus cornered and defeated the Spartans at Sellasia in 222, entered Sparta and cancelled the measures of Cleomenes. When Antigonus died, in 221, Philip V succeeded to the throne of Macedonia. He helped the members of the new Greek league against the Aetolian league, Elis and Sparta in another so-called Social War (220–217), which was indecisive. At the peace conference the Aetolian delegate spoke of "the cloud rising in the west," namely Rome, which had gained control of a part of the Illyrian coast and Corcyra in 229 and sent envoys to the Isthmian games at Corinth's invitation in 228. When the outbreak of the Second Punic War was followed by a series of Roman defeats, Philip allied himself with Carthage (215) and tried in vain to oust Rome from the Illyrian coast. Rome raised Philip's Greek enemies—the Aetolian league, Elis, Sparta and Messenia—against him in 212 or 211; fighting ended in Greece in 205 without any clear gain for either side.

The period from 205 to 146 was marked by the advance of Rome. Some Greek states called upon Rome for help, as they had called upon Persia and Macedonia, but they learned to their cost that the Romans had neither gratitude nor scruple where their desire for power was involved. The Romans' first step was to defeat Philip V at Cynoscephalae (197) and to confine him to Macedonia; they were helped in this by the Aetolian and Achaean leagues, Athens, Rhodes and Pergamum. It was then the Romans, not the Macedonians, who proclaimed that the Greek states were to be independent. They used Greek and Roman troops to enforce the transfer of Argos from Sparta to the Achaean league. Also, Rome gave the Aetolian league less territory than it claimed. The Roman army left Greek soil in 194, but the Aetolian league countered by inviting the Seleucid king Antiochus III into Greece. Antiochus came, in 192, but the Romans and Philip V of Macedonia drove him out and reduced the Aetolian league to impotence. The Romans then defeated Antiochus at Magnesia, on the other side of the Aegean, in winter 190/189, deprived him of Asia Minor west of the Taurus mountains and announced the freedom of the Greek cities there in 188.

Meanwhile Rome's ally, the Achaean league led by Philopoemen, was extending its territory; Sparta, which had been brought into the league in 192, tried to secede; but Philopoemen was able to enforce the annexation of the state in 188, after a number of leading citizens had been massacred. A few years of uneasy peace were marked by complaints which the Greek states made to Rome against one another and against Macedonia. Then, in 171, the Romans ordered Perseus, the successor of Philip V of Macedonia, to disband his forces. Perseus refused and Rome attacked. The Greek states played little part in the war. They watched the almost complete annihilation of the Macedonian army in the battle of

Pydna in 168 and the dismemberment into four republics of the kingdom that had towered over them for two centuries. The Greeks too were given a taste of Roman methods: in Epirus, where sympathy with Macedonia had been shown in two wars, the Roman army destroyed 70 towns and deported 150,000 men as slaves; although the Achaean league had declared for Rome, 1,000 leading citizens were deported to Italy; and Aetolia was weakened by Roman troops which helped the pro-Roman party in a civil strife. Even so, the authority of Rome was flouted. Then, in 148 a Roman army annexed Macedonia as a province; and in 146 another army defeated the forces of the Achaean league—Boeotia, Euboea, Phocis and Locris. This time the consul L. Mummius made an example of Corinth: the men were massacred, the women and children were enslaved and the city was razed. Rome ordered the disbanding of all leagues and the replacement of democracy by oligarchy in a number of states and announced that any breach of the Roman regulations would be punished by death. Thus the liberties of the Greek states were finally and completely abrogated. *See* MACEDONIA, KINGDOM OF; for the social, economic and cultural pattern of the Macedonian period *see* also HELLENISTIC AGE.

G. AUTHORITIES FOR ANCIENT GREEK HISTORY

Modern knowledge of the Bronze Age is derived from archaeological excavation (*see* AEGEAN CIVILIZATION) and from the poems attributed to Homer (*q.v.*). For the period of the Greek renaissance from the 9th century onward we rely on archaeology and on the remains of epic (*see* HESIOD), lyric and elegiac poetry. Political and military history begins with the works of Herodotus and Thucydides (*qq.v.*), who painted some of the background of the great wars which they described so brilliantly. Contemporary inscriptions and coinage have survived from the 6th century B.C. onward in increasing quantity; they check the accuracy of ancient historians and supplement their accounts in an infinity of ways. For the 4th century the contemporary history of Xenophon (*q.v.*) is filled out by the fragments of Ephorus and Theopompus, who were themselves the ultimate source of later works composed under the Roman empire—the *Lives* of Plutarch (*q.v.*) and the *Library* of Diodorus Siculus (*q.v.*). The whole body of classical literature, architecture and art provides the rich background against which the historical data are marshaled, and understanding of Greek politics owes most to the 4th-century orators and philosophers—Isocrates and Demosthenes, Plato and Aristotle.

For the Hellenistic period the scholar draws on a mass of contemporary inscriptions, coins and material remains, but with the outstanding exception of Polybius (*q.v.*) the works of contemporary historians have survived only in fragments. The career of Alexander has been preserved for us by a Roman governor of the 2nd century A.D., Arrian (*q.v.*), whose account rests on sources contemporary with Alexander and is supplemented by Diodorus Siculus and by Quintus Curtius Rufus. Our information about the Greek mainland from 323 to 146 B.C. is drawn mainly from Diodorus Siculus, Polybius, Plutarch's *Lives* and Livy; and an insight into social manners is afforded by the comedies of Menander (*q.v.*).

See also separate articles on subjects of special interest, for example, GREEK ARCHITECTURE; GREEK ART; GREEK LAW; GREEK LITERATURE; GAMES, CLASSICAL; and GREEK RELIGION; also articles on individual states, *e.g.*, ATHENS; SPARTA; CORINTH.

Contributions of the ancient Greeks in various fields are covered in detail in key articles such as PHILOSOPHY, HISTORY OF; LOGIC, HISTORY OF; SCIENCE, HISTORY OF. (N. G. L. H.)

H. POSTCLASSICAL HISTORY

1. Greece Under the Roman Republic.—After the collapse of the Achaean league the Roman senate appointed a commission to reorganize Greece as a dependency of Rome. Corinth, the chief centre of resistance, was destroyed; the national and cantonal federations were dissolved, commercial intercourse between cities was restricted, and the government was transferred from the democracies to the propertied classes, whose interests were bound up with Roman supremacy. Some favoured states such as Athens and Sparta retained their rights as *civitates liberae*, the other cities continued to enjoy local self-government but probably were subjected to payment of tribute. General powers of supervision were entrusted to the governor of Macedonia. The internal disorder that remained over from the previous political revolutions was checked by the historian Polybius, whom the senate deputed to mediate between the litigants.

Greece was seriously disturbed during the First Mithradatic War (88–85 B.C.). Many of its cities sided with Mithradates, whose success in detaching the Greeks from Rome is to be explained partly by the way in which his agents incited the imperialistic ambitions of cities such as Athens, partly by his promises of support to the democratic parties. The result of the war was disastrous to Greece. Apart from the confiscations and exactions by which the Roman general L. Cornelius Sulla punished the disloyal communities, the extensive and protracted campaigns left central Greece in a ruinous condition.

During the last decades of the Roman republic oppressive exactions by officials were not unknown. Still greater was the suffering produced by the rapacity of Roman traders and capitalists. Sicyon had to sell its most cherished art treasures in order to satisfy its creditors. A further hindrance to Greek prosperity was the diversion of trade which followed upon the establishment of direct communication between Italy and the near east. The coastal districts and islands suffered considerably from swarms of pirates who freely plundered the chief trading places and sanctuaries; *e.g.*, Delos in 69 B.C. This evil came to an end with the suppression of piracy in the Mediterranean by Pompey (67 B.C.), who settled some of his captives on the desolated coast of Achaea.

In the conflict between Julius Caesar and Pompey the Greeks provided the latter with a part of his excellent fleet. In 48 B.C. the decisive campaign was fought on Greek soil, and the resources of the land were severely taxed by the requisitions of both armies. Though Caesar treated the country quite leniently after his victory at Pharsalus, the Greeks supported the cause of Brutus after Caesar's assassination; but they were too weak to render much service. They subsequently passed into the hands of Marcus Antonius, who imposed further exactions to defray the cost of his wars. The levies and requisitions which Antonius made in 31 B.C. for his campaign against Octavian (the future Augustus) exhausted the country so completely that, after the battle of Actium, Octavian had to take prompt measures to avert a general famine. The depopulation that resulted from the civil wars was partly remedied by the settlement of colonists at Corinth and Patrae by Julius Caesar and Octavian; on the other hand, the foundation of Nicopolis Actia by the latter merely had the effect of transferring the people from the country to the city.

2. Roman Imperial Rule; Augustus to Diocletian.—In his reorganization of the provinces of the Roman empire Augustus incorporated Thessaly with Macedonia and converted the rest of Greece into the province of Achaea under the control of a senatorial proconsul resident at Corinth. Several states, including Athens and Sparta, retained their rights as free cities. The provincials were encouraged to send delegates to a synod at Argos to consider the general interests of the country and to uphold national sentiment. The Delphic amphictyony was revived and extended so as to represent in a similar fashion northern and central Greece.

Economic conditions did not greatly improve under the empire. Although new industries sprang up to meet the needs of Roman luxury, and Greek marble, textiles and table delicacies were in demand, the only cities that regained a flourishing trade were the partly Italian communities of Corinth and Patrae. Commerce languished in general, and the soil was mainly abandoned to pasturage. Such wealth as remained was amassed in the hands of a few great landowners and capitalists; the middle class continued to dwindle, and many persons became dependent on doles and largesses.

Seeing no future before them, the European Greeks were content to dwell in contemplation amid the glories of the past; and national pride was fostered by the undisguised respect with which the leading Romans treated Hellenic culture. To perpetuate this culture, the Greeks continued to set great store by classical education, and in Athens they possessed one of the chief universities in the Roman empire. At the same time the Greeks had so far lost their warlike qualities that they supplied scarcely any recruits to the army; and they retained too much local patriotism to crowd into the official careers of senators or imperial servants. Although in the 1st century A.D. the astute Greek man of affairs and the *Graeculus esuriens* ("hungry little Greek") of Juvenal abounded in Rome, both these types were mainly derived from the less pure-blooded population beyond the Aegean. The influx of Greek rhetoricians and professors into Italy during the 2nd and 3rd centuries A.D. was balanced by the large number of tourists who came to Greece.

In A.D. 15 the Greeks petitioned Tiberius to transfer the administration to an imperial legate. This new arrangement was sanctioned, but lasted only till A.D. 44, when Claudius restored the province to the senate. The years 66 and 67 were marked by the long visit of the emperor Nero, who wanted to display his artistic accomplishments at the various festivals: in return for the flattering reception accorded to him he bestowed freedom and exemption from tribute upon the country (this favour was speedily revoked by the emperor Vespasian). Important material benefits were conferred by Hadrian, who made a lengthy visit to Greece: besides erecting public works in many cities, he relieved Achaea of arrears of tribute and exempted it from various imposts; and he fostered national sentiment by establishing a new Panhellenic congress at Athens.

In the 3rd century Greece again experienced danger from foreign invasions. Already in 170 the Costoboci from beyond the Danube had penetrated into central Greece and sacked Eleusis before being broken up by the local militia. In 253 a Gothic army unsuccessfully besieged Thessalonica. In 267 the province was overrun by Gothic bands in collusion with a Herulian navy; these captured Athens and advanced as far south as Sparta; but a new landing in the north was defeated by the emperor Gallienus, and the victories of the emperor Claudius II in 269 put an end to the immediate danger.

(W. M.; X.)

I. BYZANTINE HISTORY

1. Early Byzantine Period.—After the reorganization of the empire by Diocletian at the end of the 3rd century, Achaea occupied a prominent position in the diocese of Moesia. Under Constantine the Great, Macedonia was a diocese of the prefecture of Illyricum and was subdivided into the eparchies of Thessaly, Achaea (including some of the Ionian and Aegean Islands), Epirus Vetus (including Corfu and Ithaca) and Crete while the other Greek islands formed an eparchy of the diocese of Asia. A complex hierarchy of imperial officials was introduced and the system of taxation elaborated so as to yield a steady revenue. The levying of the land tax was imposed upon the *dekaprotoi* ("ten leading men") who, like the Latin *decuriones*, were entrusted henceforth with the administration in most cities. The tendency to reduce all constitutions to the Roman municipal pattern became prevalent.

Although the elevation of Constantinople to the rank of capital in 330 was prejudicial to Greece, which felt the competition of the new centre of culture and learning and had to part with numerous works of art to embellish it, the general level of prosperity in the 4th century was rising. Commercial stagnation was checked by a renewed expansion of trade consequent upon the diversion of the trade routes to the east from Egypt to the Euxine (Black) and Aegean seas. Agriculture remained depressed, and many small proprietors were reduced to serfdom; but the fiscal interests of the government called for the good treatment of this class, whose growth at the expense of the slaves was a step in the gradual equalization of the entire population under the central despotism. This prosperity received a sharp setback in a series of unusually severe earthquakes in 375.

The emperors of the 4th century attempted to stamp out by edict the old pagan religion, but, except for the decree of Theodosius I by which the Olympic games were interdicted (394), these measures had no great effect and indeed were not rigorously enforced. Paganism was long to survive in Greece—particularly in the Laconian mountains. The sure footing gained by the Christian Church in Greece in the course of the 4th century was strengthened by the judicious manner in which the clergy, unsupported by official patronage and often out of sympathy with the Arian emperors, identified itself with the interests of the people.

The schools of Athens in the 4th century still retained much of their prestige, and the Cappadocian fathers, for instance Basil of Caesarea, went there for their classical studies. In the 6th century Justinian forbade pagans to teach philosophy in Athens; and there appears to be no evidence that this work was taken over in Athens by Christian scholars, who seem at this time to have been attracted to the more flourishing schools of Gaza and Alexandria. But even if the schools of Athens declined in the early middle ages, there is ample evidence that the Byzantines prized their Hellenic tradition. Although they called themselves *Rhomaioi* ("Romans") and were proud of their Christian orthodoxy, they never forgot their ancient Greek culture. Greece itself, however, was for a long time an obscure and neglected province, with no interests beyond its church and its commercial operations, and its culture declined rapidly.

Barbarian invasions, meanwhile, continued. The incursion of the Visigoths under Alaric (395-396) was accompanied by a systematic devastation that crippled Greece for decades (the arrears of taxation that resulted were remitted by the emperor Theodosius II in 428). Vandal pirates raided the country in 466 and in 475. The Ostrogoths under Theodoric were in Thessaly in 482. The Huns reached the Isthmus of Corinth in their invasion of 540 and Thermopylae in that of 558. The early part of the 7th century saw Greece invaded by hordes of Avars and Slavs; and numbers of Slavs settled in parts of Greece (though the country was never completely slavicized as J. P. Fallmerayer maintained).

2. From the Isaurians to the Angeli, 717-1204.—The emperors of the Isaurian dynasty in the 8th century continued the reorganization of the provinces into themes (administrative divisions) that appears to have been initiated by the 7th-century Heraclian emperors and subsequently extended to the rest of the empire. By the end of the 10th century Greece was divided among the themes of Hellas, the Peloponnese, Nicopolis, Dyrrachium, Cephalonia and Thessalonica, with the maritime themes of Sámos and of the Aegean sea. (Crete had its own governor, but from the early part of the 9th century to 961 it was in Muslim hands.) During the iconoclast controversy that raged intermittently from 726 to 843 Greece showed itself to be a strong supporter of the traditional use of icons—notably in 727 and in 823, when revolts broke out.

After the final renunciation of iconoclasm by the imperial government (843) and the establishment of the strong Macedonian dynasty (867), the Greek themes shared in the prosperity of the rest of the empire and had a flourishing economic life—particularly through the silk industry centred in Corinth and Thebes. In spite of imperial restrictions, the landed magnates (e.g., the Sgouri of Nauplia and the Cantacuzini of Messenia) built up large family estates in Greece as elsewhere. Northern Greece was open to attack from the Bulgars late in the 9th and early in the 10th centuries, but by 1018 the Bulgarian empire had been conquered by the Byzantines. Thessaly was occupied by nomad Vlachs at the end of the 11th century and became known as Great Walachia. Greece was also attacked from time to time by the ambitious Normans of southern Italy. Robert Guiscard took Durazzo (Dyrrachium) in 1082, whence his army advanced into Thessaly before it was driven out by Alexius I Comnenus. During 1147-48 the army of Roger II of Sicily sacked Thebes and Corinth and took back to Palermo some of the Byzantine silk weavers from these flourishing centres of the industry.

3. Late Byzantine Period.—With the crusaders' conquest of Constantinople in 1204 (see CRUSADES) and the subsequent establishment of a Latin empire, Greece was split between Latin conquerors and Byzantine aspirants to the imperial throne. In the north the Greek ruler Michael Ducas Angelus Comnenus set up an independent kingdom consisting of Epirus, Aetolia and Acarnania; the Epirotes for a time enlarged their territory and hoped to regain Constantinople. But when Constantinople fell to the rulers of Nicaea, Epirote territory and authority dwindled, and by 1340 what remained had either become part of the restored Byzantine empire or fallen to the Angevins of Naples or to the Palaeologi or fallen to the Angevins of the 15th century, after which this territory was conquered by the Ottoman Turks. Thessalonica, Thessaly, central and southern Greece and the islands were divided among the Latin conquerors after the Fourth Crusade, and a number of feudal principalities were set up. In the north the kingdom of Thessalonica was granted to Boniface of Montferrat, but it soon fell, first to Theodore, despot of Epirus, who took the title of emperor in 1223, then to the Byzantine emperor of Nicaea, John III Vatatzes, in 1246. After changing hands several times in the 14th and early 15th centuries Thessalonica was captured by the Turks in 1430.

The duchy of Athens (Attica and Boeotia) was granted as a fief by Boniface of Montferrat to the Burgundian Otto de La Roche, whose family kept it until 1308. It fell to the Almogávares (q.v.) in 1311. These Almogávares, otherwise known as the Grand Catalan company, had entered Byzantine service as mercenaries on the conclusion of peace between the French and the Aragonese in Sicily (1302). They soon quarreled with the Byzantines, however, and moved southward. Walter of Brienne, who had become duke of Athens on the extinction of the house of La Roche, engaged their services next, but quarreled with them in turn, whereupon they defeated him in battle. Settling on his lands, they set up their own form of government in the duchies of Athens and Neopatras, with Aragonese princes from Sicily as their dukes. This Catalan–Aragonese domination lasted until 1388, when it gave way to the Florentine lord of Corinth, Nerio Acciajuoli, who in 1391 acknowledged Amadeo of Savoy as prince of Achaia (Achaea or Akhaïa) and called himself "lord of Corinth and the duchy of Athens and Neopatras." The duchy of Athens was ruled by the Acciajuoli family (apart from a period of Venetian domination, 1395–1402) until it was conquered by the Ottomans in 1456–58.

The most flourishing Frankish principality in Greece was that of Achaia, or the Morea (the Peloponnese), under the Villehardouin family. It was originally a fief of Boniface of Montferrat and was granted to William of Champlitte, whom in 1205 Pope Innocent III called "prince of the whole province of Achaia"; but by 1209 it was held direct from the Latin emperor by Geoffroy de Villehardouin with the title of prince. The Frankish rulers found the Byzantine system of granting land in *pronoia* (*i.e.*, to the care of someone) not dissimilar from their own grants in fee and came to terms with the natives, who were allowed to hold their lands in return for military service to the conquerors. Toward the end of the 13th century the splendid Frankish civilization of the Morea began to deteriorate. William of Villehardouin, prince of Achaia, had already been decisively defeated by Michael VIII (Palaeologus) at the battle of Pelagonia (1259) and been forced after three years' captivity, to cede the Moreot strongholds of Mistra, Old Maina and Monemvasia (1262). The Palaeologi subsequently regained much more of the territory, which was reorganized in the 14th century as the Byzantine theme of the Peloponnese and governed by despots. usually members of the imperial family, with their centre at Mistra (still famous for its buildings and frescoes, the last flowering of Byzantine civilization). In 1381, however, another band of mercenaries, the Navarrese company, took possession of a considerable area in the name of Jacques de Baux, a claimant to the Frankish principality; and from 1383, when Jacques died, the Navarrese themselves ruled there till 1430, when they were overthrown by the Palaeologi. In the 15th century, however, there were renewed Turkish attacks, which the new Byzantine fortification, the Hexamilion across the Isthmus of Corinth, failed to stem, and Thomas and Demetrius Palaeologi were finally conquered by the sultan Mohammed II in 1458–60.

Venice long retained its Greek conquests. The partition of 1204 and subsequent acquisitions had given it a number of scattered possessions of strategic and economic value, ruled directly or by nominees or by special arrangement. The more important of these were: the Ionian Islands; Modon or Methóni (1206), Coron or Koróni (1206), Argos (1388), Nauplia or Návplion (1388) and Monemvasia (1464) in the Morea (Peloponnese); Crete (1204); and interests in the island of Euboea (shared with the Veronese family Dalle Carceri), as well as in numerous other islands and in the duchy of the archipelago. This last was organized under the leadership of the Venetian Marco Sanudo, who captured Náxos as early as 1204–05. By 1207 more than two dozen islands were held either by him or as fiefs from him, and henceforth the Latin archipelago was dominated by Venetian families such as the Sanudi and the Ghisi, the Barozzi and the Crispi. Venice held Nauplia and Monemvasia until 1540, Crete until 1669 (two strongholds there till 1715) and the Ionian Islands until 1797.

The Frankish conquest brought the establishment of a Latin ecclesiastical hierarchy, though the native Greek priests were left undisturbed and the higher Byzantine clerics continued to exist side by side with the Latins, though they often resided in Constantinople. It vigorously stimulated economic and cultural life in Greece and, on the whole, was accepted by the indigenous majority. It also evoked a revival of Hellenic patriotism among Greek leaders and thinkers in the Byzantine despotate of the Peloponnese. In particular, the humanist Georgius Gemistus Pletho put forward utopian plans for the new constitution based on Plato's republic, but such attempts to revive Greek political life could not stave off the Ottoman conquest.   (J. M. Hy.)

J. MODERN HISTORY

1. Greece Under the Turks, 1453–1821.

Turkish rule over Greece (*Tourkokratia*) is conventionally dated from 1453, when Constantinople was captured by the sultan Mohammed II and the last Byzantine emperor, Constantine XI, fell with his capital. In fact this date is no more than a symbol and a convenient average, for the greater part of the territory of the empire was already in the hands of the Ottoman Turks, and some parts of the remainder were to be outside Ottoman control for generations and even centuries longer.

At Trebizond (Trabzon), on the Black sea, a so-called Greek empire survived till 1461; on the mainland, the despotate of Epirus outlived Constantinople in independence for a generation; and many of the islands fell to the Ottomans only in the following centuries—Rhodes in 1522, Cyprus in 1571, Crete in 1669 and Ténos in 1715. The Ionian Islands almost entirely escaped Turkish occupation. But even those parts of Greek territory that escaped or delayed Turkish occupation were scarcely ever independent. The alternative was generally subjugation to the power of Venice, which proved generally more unpopular than that of the sultan. After Venice gained control of the Peloponnese by the peace of Karlowitz (1699), the Turks were able to recover it within 20 years with the ready acquiescence of the Greek population.

The comparative popularity of Turkish rule during the first centuries of the occupation was due to a number of contributory causes. In the first place, the rule of the early sultans was able and strong; at least it kept at bay the predatory powers of the west, collectively known to the Greeks as Franks, who had shown, by diverting the Fourth Crusade to Constantinople in 1203, that their fellow feeling for Christendom was barely skin-deep. In the second place, the doctrinal schism of Christendom had reached a degree of bitterness in the 15th century sufficient to make Muslims actually more welcome to Orthodox Greeks than the Catholics of Rome; and there were those who held that the fall of Constantinople was no more than the just due of the emperor and of the patriarch who had accepted reunion with Rome, on humiliating terms, at the Council of Florence in 1439. Mohammed II therefore astutely appointed Gennadius, the surviving leader of the party that had opposed reunion with Rome, to be patriarch under his rule, with full confirmation of his rights over the Orthodox community in return for their political obedience; and such tolerance toward Christians, who were, like the Ottomans, "people of the book," was in perfect accord with Muslim principle.

In the third place, Ottoman rule was not initially oppressive in its incidence on the subject communities, at least in the golden age of the empire (whose apogee is generally identified with the reign of Suleiman the Magnificent, in the middle of the 16th century). The Greeks in particular enjoyed freedom in two important spheres, apart from the practice of their religion, and these were interconnected, both in preserving the continuity of their national consciousness and in leading eventually to the struggle for independence.

One of these was freedom of trade, an occupation which the Turks thought inferior to the profession of arms and which enabled the Greek mercantile class to build up simultaneously contacts abroad, wealth, a tradition of independence and a merchant fleet which could be readily converted to warlike purposes. The second great freedom was that of education in the Greek language, which went hand in hand with the freedom of the church.

Next among the reasons why the Greeks acquiesced so readily for so many generations in the Turkish occupation was the nature of the Ottoman political system; but since it was this also which led ultimately to the struggle for independence, it is the least simple element in the story. The system was based on the traditions of the Turkish tribes' nomadic past, adapted to more settled conditions, but the system never fully assimilated the conception of fixed geographical frontiers or that of the nation-state. The one constant factor was the centralization of all power in the hands of the sultan, from whom alone all rights emanated. His empire was divided for administrative purposes into provinces under governors of his own nomination, of which Greece was distributed among six; but all the land remained the property of the sultan, who could dispose of it as he wished in fiefs allotted to Turkish settlers (usually loyal military adherents), or permit his non-Muslim subjects to live on it on payment of a land tax. There grew up piecemeal exceptions to the system, however. Some important garrison towns were subordinated directly to Constantinople instead of to the provincial governor; some areas achieved a special status (Chios, for instance, becoming a private appanage of the empress-mother of the sultan); and other areas, because of their inaccessibility, were left virtually to their own devices (e.g., parts of Crete and of the Pindus mountains and some of the smaller islands). A varying measure of local autonomy in the administration of justice was also tolerated, especially in the Peloponnese.

At the height of its power, Ottoman rule was not inhumanly oppressive. Its defect was that it was arbitrary and unpredictable, being too dependent on the character of individuals, especially on that of the sultan. The Greeks' principal obligations were to pay the capitation tax (kharaj), which simply entitled them to remain alive in the sultan's dominions, the land tax, the tax on commerce and occasional special levies according to their circumstances and way of life; and to contribute male children (about one out of five on average) to the sultan's private service, to be brought up as janizaries (q.v.). The last was a cruel practice (though not always to the worldly disadvantage of the Greek children, who might rise through it to great heights), and it was abolished before the end of the 17th century. The taxes, however, were not in themselves exorbitant by modern standards. The vice of the system was that the Greeks received no rights—not even the elementary rights of justice and security—in return. The result was, on the one hand, that they turned increasingly to the leaders of their own communities (especially to the priests and to the leaders of their own communities, known as *prokritoi* or primates); and, on the other, that in many areas lawlessness became endemic, in the form of the *klephtai* (brigands) and the scarcely more law-abiding *armatoloi* (men at arms or gendarmes) whom the Turkish government indiscriminately licensed to put down the brigands. Finally, the Greeks had one other course open to them in the ramshackle system which Ottoman administration became when the days of the great sultans were over; this was to penetrate and to usurp the system themselves, by climbing the rungs of power which the corps of janizaries and other opportunities opened to them. By the 18th century they had done this so successfully that four of the great offices of state (dragoman of the Porte, dragoman of the fleet and voivode or governor of each of the two Transdanubian provinces, Moldavia and Walachia) had become virtually Greek preserves. The Greeks who infiltrated the administration system in this way formed a distinct colony in Constantinople, known as the Phanariotes (from the Phanar, the quarter in which they lived).

All these factors contributed in different ways to the state of affairs that eventually made the liberation of Greece possible. But they took long to work in this direction, partly because the contributory factors were to some extent contradictory in their operation. There was little common sentiment between the sophisticated Phanariotes of Constantinople and the priests and peasants of central Greece or the brigands in the mountains.

Such manifestations of opposition to Turkish rule as occurred up to the 18th century were as spasmodic and unpurposeful as Turkish oppression. Greek uprisings were generally in response to deliberate and unscrupulous provocation by external powers in the course of great wars fought for no interest of the Greeks, and the latter were then generally the victims of both sides. At the naval battle of Lepanto in 1571, for instance, between the Turks and the forces of Don John of Austria, Greek islanders were by force of circumstances serving in both fleets; and mainland Greeks who rose in revolt at the instigation of Don John were simply put down without mercy by the Turks. In the following century the invasion of the Peloponnese by the Venetian general Francesco Morosini (whose guns were responsible for the destruction of the Parthenon at Athens in 1687) aroused not a spark of enthusiasm among the Greeks; and the return of the Turks to the Peloponnese in the following generation was accepted as the lesser evil.

It was not until the intervention of the Russians in the 18th century that a serious revolt was promoted on Greek territory; and again the motives were unconnected with any real demand for national independence. Meanwhile, the influential Greeks of Constantinople were in effect pursuing quite a different policy of their own, which was not to disrupt the Ottoman empire but to take it over as a going concern.

The Rising of 1770 and the Beginnings of Nationalism.—The rising in the Peloponnese in 1770 is virtually the beginning of modern Greek history. It was precipitated by the empress Catherine the Great of Russia as a diversion in one of the recurrent Russo-Turkish wars; but for the first time it struck a spontaneous response from the Greeks (especially the Peloponnesians) and thus came near to success.

The Russian claim to interfere in Greek affairs rested ostensibly on the possession of a common religion, which the tsars regarded themselves as entitled to protect, and on the inheritance of the Byzantine tradition as a result of the 15th-century marriage between the niece of the last emperor of Constantinople and the grand prince Ivan III of Muscovy, the first Russian ruler to call himself tsar. In practice, the real motive lay in the advantage that a Russian liberation (which meant annexation) of Greece would give the tsars over the Ottoman rulers, by opening a backdoor to Constantinople.

The Greeks, however, welcomed the approaches of the tsar's agents for reasons of their own. In the Peloponnese society was relatively advanced and ripe for self-rule and, being relatively well populated, that area suffered more than most from the land hunger which resulted from the rule that no land could pass from Turkish into Greek possession. The conjunction of a politically conscious and aggrieved upper class with a landless and therefore lawless lower class led naturally to a revolutionary mood.

The revolt of 1770, prepared and incited by Russian agents, took the Turks by surprise and was at first successful. But Russian help was late and inadequate (having to come by sea round Europe and through the Mediterranean); and, with the help of a blood-thirsty army of Albanians, the Turks eventually suppressed the rising in the Peloponnese, the only area in which it reached serious proportions. The Russians quickly abandoned the Greeks in order to pursue the war with Turkey elsewhere and brought it to a relatively successful conclusion in the treaty of Kuchuk Kainarji (1774). An ambiguous clause in this treaty gave the Russians a right "to make representations" on behalf of the sultan's Christian subjects at Constantinople; and this provided the excuse for all future Russian interventions in Greek affairs.

After about nine years of barbarous repression by the Albanian forces of the sultan, the Peloponnesians recovered a normal level of existence and prosperity. But when Catherine the Great tried again in 1786 to provoke a similar rising against the Turks, the Peloponnesians had naturally learned their lesson too well to respond. The only response came from elsewhere. The inhabitants of Suli (Souli), Epirus, then in southern Albania, rose against the sultan and were savagely suppressed by the provincial governor, Ali Pasha, from his capital at Janina (Ioannina). The Russians again abandoned their allies, but this time the consequences were more pregnant for the future. Ali Pasha's appetite was whetted by success, and within the next 30 years he proceeded to carve out for himself a large semi-independent slice of the sultan's empire. This remarkable figure unwittingly played a large part in making possible the Greek revolution of 1821. (*See* ALI [The Lion of Janina]).

Between the risings of 1770 and of 1821 history underwent a great change which decisively shifted the balance in favour of the Greeks. The American and French Revolutions, the rise and fall of Napoleon, the conflict of the great powers in the near east, the outbreak of nationalist revolutions as far away as South America and as near as Serbia, the weakness of the Ottoman empire as revealed by the virtual secession of Ali Pasha, the incitements of European liberals and poets, not only foreign (such as Lord Byron) but also native (such as Rhigas Pheraios), and the awakening of a national consciousness by native scholars (such as Adamantios Korais) as well as by merchants, politicians and priests all contributed to the outburst of 1821. The one factor that played relatively little part in bringing about the revolution was immediate Turkish oppression. It was rather the enfeeblement and relaxation of tyranny that fed the appetite for liberty, as it was the apparently imminent dissolution of the Ottoman empire that offered the opportunity of escape.

But the positive motives at work among the Greeks were dangerously confused. The aspirations of the different classes and regions were unreconciled. The Greek aristocrats of Constantinople, of the Transdanubian provinces and of the tsar's court had little in common with the peasants, priests and brigands of central Greece or with the wealthy merchant families of the islands; and no reconciliation had been attempted, or was possible, between those who looked to Russia, to England, to France or even elsewhere for patrons of Greek independence. The result was much confusion in the years of war (1821–29).

All the great powers had a more or less definite interest in Greek affairs by 1821. In Russia there were considerable Greek colonies, including that at Odessa which in 1814 founded the Philikí Etaireía (Friendly company) with the express object of promoting a Greek revolution; and there were also highly placed Greek officials, including the emperor's foreign secretary I. A. Kapodístrias (q.v.) and his aide-de-camp Prince Alexandros Ypsilantis. The Austrian empire was hoping to encroach eastward and southward as the Ottoman empire disintegrated and was seeking to play the same role in the northern Balkans that Russia sought to play in Greece. England and France alternated in intrigue throughout the near east during the Napoleonic Wars, wooing Ali Pasha, the sultan and the dissident Greek leaders with arms, money and promises by turns. The fate of the Ionian Islands was typical of the whole complex of forces at work. They were taken by the Russians (1799), by the Turks (1800), by the French again (1807) and by the British (1814) in the space of 20 years; and one of their dependencies, the mainland port of Parga, was even ceded to Ali Pasha by the British in 1817. From all such maneuvers of power politics, the Greeks were simply the sufferers; but experience was teaching them how to take advantage of these rivalries. The Ionian Islands, under British control, were a haven where armed irregulars from the mainland could take refuge under pressure. Russia provided a base from which the Philikí Etaireía could mature its plans, as well as a school of statecraft where Greeks could learn their political trade. Vienna was another haven of refuge and intrigue for Greek émigrés. The French were still reckoned the greatest soldiers of Europe even after Waterloo; and the fall of Napoleon released many military adventurers from whom the Greeks (as well as the Turks and Egyptians) could learn the art of war. Added to this was the newborn European liberal prejudice in favour of freedom, which provided the Greeks with money, arms, propaganda and philhellenes to fight at their side. Only the opportunity of revolt was needed, and this was finally provided by the open rebellion of Ali Pasha against the sultan Mahmud II in 1820. While the Turks were preoccupied with this dangerous threat, the Greeks in their turn rose in March 1821.

(For the events of the ensuing seven years *see* GREEK INDEPENDENCE, WAR OF; NAVARINO, BATTLE OF.)

2. First Phase of Independence, 1829–64.—Although the battle of Navarino (Oct. 20, 1827) made the independence of Greece a certainty, another two years passed before the fighting ended and nearly five before the new state took shape. Among the great powers, Navarino was not the end of a war but in effect the beginning of a new one. The sultan proclaimed a holy war (jihad) in Dec. 1827, and Russia declared war on Turkey on April 26, 1828. France and Great Britain, who had striven for six years to avert this climax, reluctantly withdrew their ambassadors from Constantinople. It was not until the Russian armies had almost reached Constantinople that, by the treaty of Adrianople (Sept. 14, 1829), the sultan formally accepted the independence of Greece as prescribed by the treaty of London (July 6, 1827), which the battle of Navarino had been fought to enforce. From this date all the great powers and other contestants finally resigned themselves to the two complementary facts that Greek independence could not be reversed and that it did not entail the general dissolution of the Ottoman empire. Europe settled down with a new equilibrium of the near east.

Neither the boundaries nor the constitution of the new Greek state were yet settled, however. During the Russo-Turkish War of 1828–29 desultory fighting continued on the Greek mainland, almost neglected by the preoccupied powers, and even the army of Ibrahim Pasha remained at large in the Peloponnese until a French expeditionary force was sent there in 1828 to ensure its withdrawal. While the conference of London debated at its leisure what should be the limits of the new state (varying from a minimum area, the Peloponnese alone, to a maximum area bounded on the north by the Árta-Vólos line), the Greeks set about enlarging their territory well beyond both the minimum and the maximum and lobbying to secure the addition of important islands such as Sámos and Crete. They were helped by the military skill of British free lances, such as Sir Richard Church and Frank Abney Hastings (qq.v.), as well as by the sympathetic connivance of French regulars, to install themselves well to the north of the Gulf and Isthmus of Corinth on both the western and eastern flanks of the Greek mainland during 1828–29, though they could not recover strongly held fortresses such as Athens. Foreign-born Greek leaders, such as Alexandros Mavrokordatos and Dimitrios Ypsilantis, also now played a notable part in consolidating Greek expansion, as well as popularizing Greek ambitions in terms familiar to the European courts; and, above all, Kapodístrias, who had been elected provisional president of Greece by the third national assembly (April 1827) and arrived to assume office in Jan. 1828, and who conducted Greece's foreign affairs with the utmost skill and devotion.

Kapodístrias and His Successors.—In his personal aspirations Kapodístrias was less successful. He had a clear but autocratic idea of the way to run his new country, a strong, centralized government with the last traces of local self-government suppressed; and without actually suggesting that his position should be made permanent, he clearly regarded himself as irreplaceable. Meanwhile the great powers, represented by the conference of London, cautiously sought a more conventional settlement.

At the time of Navarino, they still had in mind a ruler of Greece who would remain the sultan's vassal. The treaty of Adrianople, by confirming Greece's unqualified independence, made this impossible, and on Feb. 3, 1830, the throne of Greece was offered to Prince Leopold of Saxe-Coburg (the future king of the Belgians, uncle of the future Queen Victoria), who at first accepted. Kapodístrias, however, subtly hinted to him that the terms of the offer were inadequate to ensure Greece's viability, and he withdrew his acceptance. Kapodístrias continued his presidency while another candidate was sought, and he grew steadily more unpopular, not with the ordinary people, who benefited by his firm rule, but with the "primate" families (such as Koundouriotis of Idhra [Hydra] and Mavromikhalis of Maina) who had expected to inherit the Turkish feudal system under their own mastership, with the liberal-minded constitutionalists (led by Mavrokordatos, who refused to take office under the president) and with most of the irregular leaders of the war (except Theodoros Kolokotronis, who loyally supported Kapodístrias and became his licensed tax gatherer, on characteristically unorthodox principles). To the natural dissen-

GREECE

sions of the Greeks were added the intrigues of the three official residents, Russian, British and French, who were appointed to look after their countries' interests in Greece from 1828.

The end of Kapodistrias' unequal struggle with confusion came on Oct. 9, 1831, when he was assassinated at Nauplia (the first capital of Greece) by two members of the Mavromikhalis clan. He was succeeded by a triumvirate consisting of his brother Avgoustinos with two of the wartime leaders, Ioannis Kolettis and Kolokotronis; but anarchy soon supervened. Avgoustinos fled the country in April 1832, and Kolettis and Kolokotronis each tried to establish a government of his own (the former supported by Mavrokordatos, and each supported by a private army of irregulars). The chaos was mitigated only by the continued presence of a reduced French force to keep order in the Peloponnese, until at last the conference of London reached its final decision, which was embodied in a convention signed on May 11, 1832 (but dated May 7, because the British government had meanwhile fallen in the crisis of the Reform bill). By this convention Greece was established as an independent kingdom, under the protection of Great Britain, France and Russia, with its northern boundary along the Arta-Vólos line, and including some of the Aegean Islands (but not Crete or Sámos, for which Kapodistrias had fought in vain). Louis I of Bavaria, who was also a party to the convention, accepted the Greek throne on behalf of his 17-year-old son Otto who arrived at Nauplia on Feb. 6, 1833, and endeared himself by at once adopting the Greek national costume and the Greek spelling of his name, Othon. He was accompanied by three Bavarian advisers, as well as by a garrison of Bavarian troops to replace the French; and for the next ten years the government of Greece was virtually a Bavarian monopoly.

Otho.—The accession of King Otho (as he is usually called in English), backed by a generous loan from the protecting powers, was looked upon as the beginning of a new golden age for Greece. There were certainly agreeable episodes to record in the immediately following years: the transfer of the capital from Nauplia to Athens (1834); Otho's coming of age (1835) and marriage to Amalia of Oldenburg (1836); the foundation of the University of Athens (1837); and the establishment of diplomatic relations with Turkey (1839). But they were no more than episodes, and the political background was more ominous.

There were constant disorders in different parts of the kingdom, chiefly the result of discontentment of the wartime leaders who had been set aside in favour of Otho's new Bavarian administrators. There were major outbreaks of brigandage on the mainland in 1834-36 and again in 1839, and in the latter year conscription was first instituted.

There was a revolt in Crete in 1841, a year after the island had been restored from the Egyptian province of Mohammed Ali to the direct rule of the sultan Abdul-Mejid; and although this was juridically no business of the new Greek kingdom, it was one of the many incidents that reminded the Greeks that only a small part of their racial and religious kinship was under independent rule.

Above all, there was resentment of the alien and untactful rule of the Bavarian clique led by Graf Josef Ludwig von Armansperg, who was in effect absolute ruler of Greece from 1834 to 1837, though his title was changed from "president of the regency" to "archchancellor" when Otho came of age. It was not until Dec. 20, 1837, that a Greek, Konstantinos Zographos, was first appointed as the king's chief minister, and even thereafter the Bavarians continued to hold the ministry of war and to penetrate the administration effectively at many levels.

Resentment came to a head in 1843. On the night of Sept. 14–15 the royal palace was surrounded by a rebel force led by veterans of the War of Independence, whose chief demands were the removal of the Bavarians and the establishment of a constitution. It was a typically Greek revolution, conducted almost without bloodshed, with almost no bitterness (except against the Bavarians) and with a strong streak of conservatism and personal affection for the king. As soon as Otho had given way he became a national hero and the occasion a national holiday. A national assembly was convened (attended significantly by representatives from the unliberated areas of Thessaly, Macedonia and Epirus) which drew up a constitution providing for a lower house (*vouli*) and a senate (*yerousia*). This constitution, to which the king took his oath on March 16, 1844, remained in force for 20 years.

There followed a period of domestic quiescence, marred only by disagreeable episodes in Greece's foreign relations. With Great Britain there were a number of points of friction which did little credit to the protecting power. The British government was entitled to claim, as it vigorously did, the payment of interest on the international loan in 1847, as well as compensation for losses arbitrarily inflicted on British subjects (including the philhellene historian George Finlay and the Gibraltar Jew Don Pacifico); but

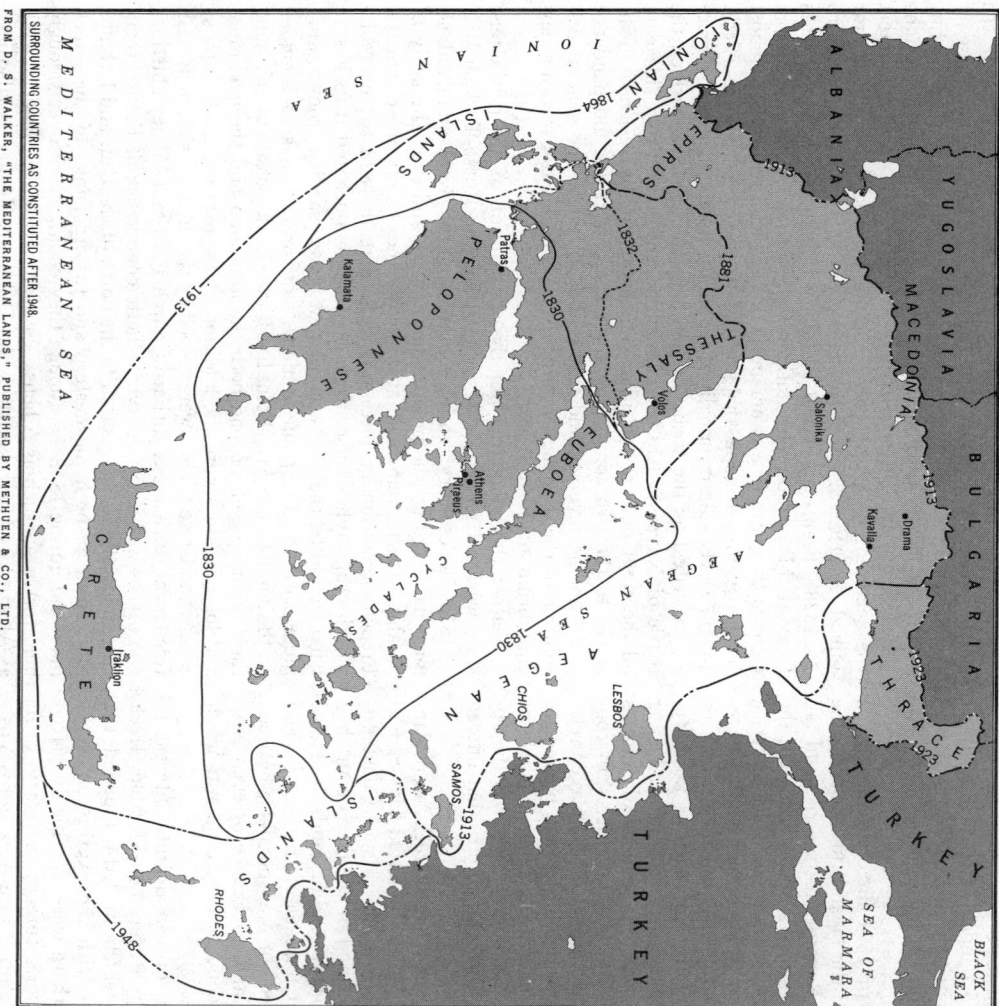

MEDITERRANEAN SEA

SURROUNDING COUNTRIES AS CONSTITUTED AFTER 1948.

FROM D. S. WALKER, "THE MEDITERRANEAN LANDS," PUBLISHED BY METHUEN & CO., LTD.

EXPANSION OF GREEK STATES, 1830–1948

hardly to enforce the claims, as Lord Palmerston insisted on doing in Jan. 1850, by ordering the Mediterranean fleet to blockade Piraeus and openly hinting an intention to annex two minor islets alleged to have formed part of the Ionian Islands. Palmerston's undignified conduct nearly brought down the government in which he was foreign secretary; he narrowly averted a vote of censure by one of the most celebrated speeches of his career. The British claims were reduced and met, but Otho came out of the episode with greatly enhanced prestige for his courageous refusal to be bullied. Unfortunately this success led him into a more foolhardy act of defiance four years later and to a passionate devotion to the cause of Greek irredentism known as the "Great Idea" (*Megali Idea*).

In the Crimean War the British and French sided with Turkey against Russia. Imprudently, but for obvious reasons, the Greeks sided with Russia, and Otho took the lead with strong popular support in an attempt to enlarge Greece's territory. There had been no major breach of the peace between Greece and Turkey for 25 years, though brigandage and frontier incidents had led to a brief rupture of diplomatic relations in 1847. Now the Greeks seriously set about trying to conquer Thessaly and Epirus. In Jan. 1854 they entered Epirus and defeated the Turks at Péta; in Thessaly they had little success. The Turks sent an ultimatum to Greece in March and began to expel Greeks from Smyrna and Constantinople in reprisal. In May British and French troops were landed at Piraeus to enforce Greek neutrality, and the occupation lasted until 1857. Greece's frontiers thus remained unchanged and its appetite unappeased. Otho, too, as the leader of Greek irredentism and the victim of the great powers' disciplinary action, reached the height of his popularity.

At the same time Greece's relations with Great Britain were exacerbated by the question of the Ionian Islands, which had been left under British protection by the treaty of Nov. 5, 1815. The national feeling of the Greek inhabitants of the islands had reached a dangerous intensity, which produced a serious rising on Cephalonia in 1849. Their future now became fortuitously connected with the unhappy end of Otho's reign. Otho misused his popularity to behave autocratically at home, while distracting his subjects with the prospects of fresh acquisitions of territory abroad. Despite a succession of patriotic Greek prime ministers, including several heroes of the War of Independence (Alexandros Mavrokordatos, Ioannis Kolettis, Kitsos Tzavelas, Georgios Koundouriotis, Konstantinos Kanaris), the king never fully accepted the role of a constitutional monarch. Opposition to him grew, first breaking out in a mutiny in the garrison of Nauplia on Feb. 13, 1862.

This was suppressed, but by October trouble was again brewing. While Otho and Queen Amalia were on a tour of the Peloponnese, the revolt began in Aetolia-Acarnania on Oct. 19 and spread to Athens on Oct. 22. Otho arrived back in his naval frigate on the following day to find a provisional government in power under Dimitrios Voulgaris, which had proclaimed his deposition and also its intention to maintain the monarchy. Otho never set foot in his capital again. The protecting powers recognized that the Greeks were acting within their rights in deposing their monarch and set about the search for a successor. More than a year passed before the right man was chosen.

It was at this point that the future of the Ionian Islands became bound up with the question of the Greek monarchy. For nearly half a century the British government had argued that its protectorate over the islands was essential to its security in the Mediterranean, though they had played no strategic role in events since the Napoleonic Wars. As recently as May 7, 1861, the chancellor of the exchequer, W. E. Gladstone (who had served briefly in the islands as lord high commissioner extraordinary in 1858–59) had stated that "it would be nothing less than a crime against the safety of Europe" to cede the islands to Greece. Yet exactly 18 months later, on Dec. 8, 1862, the British cabinet decided to renounce the protectorate in favour of Greece, and by the end of the year the decision was widely known to have been taken. (It has even been contended that the prime minister, Lord Palmerston, had personally reached this decision before the fall of Otho, that he offered the islands to Otho on condition that he would refrain from all provocation of Turkey, but that Otho refused.) In Greece the widespread knowledge of this new intention contributed to a characteristic revulsion of feeling in favour of Great Britain, which startlingly expressed itself in a plebiscite on the succession conducted in Dec. 1862. Out of 244,202 votes, 230,016 were given to Queen Victoria's second son, Prince Alfred, whom the British government had already officially declared ineligible, as being a member of the ruling family of one of the three protecting powers.

Various candidates of other powers were similarly ruled out. Finally the search ended with the choice of the 17-year-old William, second son of the heir to the throne of Denmark. On June 5, 1863, representatives of the three powers and Denmark signed a protocol in London recognizing his election (which the Greek assembly had enthusiastically carried on March 30) to the vacant throne, on the explicit understanding that the Ionian Islands would be ceded to Greece.

The treaty of cession was signed in London on Nov. 14, 1863, by representatives of Great Britain, France, Austria, Prussia and Russia (the powers that had established the protectorate) and confirmed by a further treaty between Greece and the three protecting powers (Great Britain, France and Russia) on March 29, 1864. The new king, who took the title "George I of the Hellenes" (his predecessor had been "king of Hellas"), had arrived in Athens on Oct. 30, 1863, and the British evacuation of the Ionian Islands was completed by the following June.

3. The New Monarchy, 1863–1924.—The half century of King George I's reign (1863–1913) was an era in itself in modern Greek history, an era in which Greece grew to the status of a power in its own right (even if still a minor one) instead of a semidependent ward of other powers (though the "protectorate" of Great Britain, France and Russia nominally lasted till 1919). The period was notable for the most considerable (but not the last) increases of Greek territory. Thessaly, most of Greek-inhabited Epirus and Macedonia, Crete and the majority of the Aegean Islands (except the Dodecanese) were added to the kingdom of the Hellenes. These advances were not achieved without setbacks, which were chiefly due to political instability at home; and the seeds were sown of troubles that were to bedevil the future—notably those of the constitutional dispute between supporters and opponents of the monarchy and those of mutual hostility between Greece and other successor states of the Ottoman empire (chiefly Bulgaria and Albania), which previously had either not existed or been separated from Greece by the surviving extension of Turkey in Europe. Nevertheless, it was also in this period that Greece produced its first two statesmen of recognized European eminence: Kharilaos Trikoupis (1832–96) and Eleutherios Venizelos (1864–1936). These two men differed from their numerous rivals not in the fervour of their support for Greece's expansionist claims, which were the main political issue of the period, but in the wisdom with which they recognized that the country needed sound administration in support of them.

On his accession, the new king inherited a legacy of political confusion bordering on anarchy and even violence. A succession of ministries came and went during his first year. But a clean break with the past came with the inauguration of the new constitution, to which he took his oath in Nov. 1864. It was highly democratic. It abolished the senate, replacing it with a council of state appointed by the crown (abolished in its turn a year later); it established elective local government; and it defined the position of the king, which was in effect that of a passive instrument of the will of the people.

This system came to be described, by an inversion of the usual term, as a "monarchical democracy" (*vasilevomeni dimokratia*); and there is a happy irony in the phrase, since *dimokratia* is also the Greek for "republic." King George I operated this constitution conscientiously and successfully for 47 years, until it was revised in 1911. He was also luckier than his predecessor in not being accompanied by a foreign garrison; and although he had Danish advisers in his train, the most unpopular of them, Count Wilhelm Carl Sponneck, left Athens in 1865. Greece was at last truly free—free to become great.

The Cretan Rising, 1866.—Though relative tranquillity was restored at home, the new reign's troubles abroad began soon. In 1866 the Cretans rose in revolt against Turkish rule, which in its decline had become truly oppressive. The sultan, Abdul-Aziz, sought not only to suppress the revolt but to transfer Crete back to Egyptian rule. A self-constituted Cretan assembly retorted by proclaiming its union with Greece, and although the king and government could not afford the risk of accepting the decision, many volunteers went from the mainland to support the islanders in arms.

The Cretans appealed to the great powers, of whom Great Britain alone was opposed to the solution of a plebiscite. In particular, European opinion was stirred by the heroic end of the monastery of Arkadi, whose abbot blew it up with the garrison and its attackers together rather than surrender alive. Though the revolt was crushed, the intervention of the powers obliged the sultan to grant administrative reforms, which were embodied in the organic statute of 1868.

The Cretan problem, which was to be coextensive with George I's reign, was thus shelved again. The sultan took his revenge on the Greeks two years later by creating in 1870 the Bulgarian exarchate, a separate ecclesiastical organization for Bulgaria, independent of the Greek Orthodox patriarchate which had been for so many centuries the unifying force of the Ottoman empire's Christian subjects.

The Russo-Turkish War, 1877–78.—The second crisis of the new reign was precipitated by the Russo-Turkish War of 1877–78. As in the Crimean War, many Greeks saw in it an opportunity to acquire Thessaly, if not Epirus and Crete as well. But a coalition government, in which Trikoupis was foreign secretary, held them in restraint, in the expectation that the great powers would sympathetically consider Greek claims at the peace settlement. The government fell, and Russian victories swept aside these restraints. The government fell, and its successor was only withheld from armed intervention by British mediation and by the collapse of Turkish resistance in Jan. 1878. In the treaty of San Stefano (March 3, 1878) between Russia and Turkey, Greece's territorial claims were ignored in the interests of creating "Greater Bulgaria" as a Russian satellite, with access to the Mediterranean through the Aegean sea and practically the whole of Macedonia incorporated in it.

The other powers refused to accept this settlement, which was upset by the congress of Berlin (June 1878); but still Greece received no satisfaction, beyond an injunction to the sultan Abdul-Hamid II to reach an agreement with King George for the modification of their common frontier. The fulfillment of this injunction was dragged out until 1881, when a conference at Constantinople finally defined a new frontier between Greece and Turkey from the southern slopes of Mt. Olympus in the east to the Arakhthos river in the west, giving Greece the greater part of Thessaly and a small corner of Epirus. It was in 1878, after the rejection of the treaty of San Stefano, that Great Britain secured the right to occupy Cyprus, in return for a guarantee given to Turkey that its Asiatic provinces should be untouched. (*See* Eastern Question.)

Trikoupis.—Between the next great foreign crisis in 1896, the domestic scene in Greece was dominated by Trikoupis. He became prime minister early in the '80s and remained in power, with brief intervals, until his resignation in Jan. 1895. During this period great advances were made in Greece's domestic administration. Roads and railways were extended, the merchant navy was expanded, brigandage was virtually suppressed and the financial administration was put on a sound basis which attracted the confidence of foreign investors. But this progress was subject to abrupt setbacks whenever Trikoupis' chief rival, Theodoros Dilliyiannis, a crafty but hotheaded parliamentarian, succeeded in replacing him.

One such occasion was shortly before the crisis provoked in Sept. 1885 by the Bulgarian annexation of Eastern Rumelia. Public opinion in Greece demanded compensating gains at Turkish expense, and Dilliyiannis mobilized. A brief war broke out between Bulgaria and Serbia, but the great powers intervened before Greece could begin hostilities against Turkey, and by a naval blockade Great Britain compelled the Greek government to demobilize in May 1886. Dilliyiannis' government fell, and Trikoupis returned to power. He dealt competently with the financial setback caused by Dilliyiannis' militant policy and retained the confidence of the king and people for nearly seven years. Even after Trikoupis' party had been defeated in a general election in 1890 (largely for having adopted a pacific policy in one of the recurrent Cretan crises in 1889), the king reappointed him prime minister in 1892, after dismissing Dilliyiannis for incompetence. This was the boldest constitutional step of George I's reign.

Crete and Macedonia, 1896–1912.—It was after Trikoupis' death (in April 1896), when Dilliyiannis was again prime minister, that the next major crisis in Greece's foreign affairs occurred, again over Crete. The chronic bitterness between Cretans and Turks broke out in violence and bloodshed at Canea (Khaniá), the administrative capital, in May 1896.

This time it was Dilliyiannis' turn to exercise restraint and to accept Turkish promises of reform. But these were not carried out, and the deteriorating situation culminated in a further outbreak of violence in Feb. 1897. Dilliyiannis announced that Greece could no longer remain indifferent and sent an armed force to annex the island. Thereupon Great Britain, France, Russia, Italy, Germany and Austria proclaimed an international protectorate and landed troops. The intervention of the great powers exasperated Greek public opinion, to the point of demanding war on Turkey; and in March 1897, while the expedition to Crete was still indecisive, the crown prince Constantine put himself at the head of the Greek forces in Thessaly in readiness for war. Hostilities were at first limited to skirmishing by irregular bands; but Turkey declared war on April 17, and Greece was defeated in a brief campaign (*see* Greco-Turkish War, 1897). Peace was signed on Dec. 4, 1897. Greece naturally had to withdraw from Crete, which remained under the occupation and protection of the great powers, and minor modifications were made to the northern frontier in Turkey's interest, but the indemnity originally demanded was reduced from £T10,000,000 to £T4,000,000. The prestige of the royal family suffered, until a characteristic reaction set in after an attempt to assassinate the king in Feb. 1898.

The repulse of Greek claims to Crete and Macedonia was looked upon as no more than temporary, and the two territories largely occupied political attention in Greece for the next 15 years, until the chance of a settlement came. In Crete the disturbances of 1896–97 represented a slight immediate advance for the Greek cause. The protecting powers (reduced to four by the withdrawal of Germany and Austria) proclaimed the administrative autonomy of the island; and after a further outbreak of violence in Sept. 1898 (in which the British vice-consul at Iráklion and a number of British soldiers were killed) they insisted that all Turkish troops should leave the island and invited the king's second son, George, to become high commissioner under the suzerainty of the sultan. Prince George arrived in Crete in Dec. 1898, for a term of three years prolonged till 1906. His tenure was marred and, finally, terminated by a dispute with a group of Cretan politicians, led by Venizelos, who seceded in March 1905 to set up a "provisional government" of the island at Thérisson.

Prince George was replaced in 1906 by Alexandros Zaïmis, a former prime minister and one of the most respected statesmen of modern Greece, under whose auspices Venizelos became the leading figure in the Cretan administration. Tranquillity and order were so effectively restored that in July 1908 the great powers felt justified in beginning the withdrawal of their forces.

At almost the same date, an event took place at the other end of the Greek world which upset the powers' calculations. This was the Young Turks' revolution, which set up the Committee of Union and Progress at Salonika, the principal town in Macedonia. Having compelled the sultan Abdul-Hamid to restore the lapsed constitution of Turkey, the committee then deposed him in 1909 and ruled the Ottoman empire in the name of his successor Mohammed V; but toward the end of the 19th century a state of undeclared civil war between Greek, Bulgarian and Turkish irregulars had prevailed in Macedonia, somewhat like the situation in southern

Greece before the War of Independence. The Young Turks' revolution worked a widespread transformation in the whole Balkan scene. It brought together Greeks, Bulgars and Serbs in the common interest of frustrating the "Ottomanization" of Macedonia; it provoked the Cretans yet again to declare the union of Crete with Greece in Oct. 1908 and to send a delegation (including Venizelos) to Athens to give effect to their decision; and it led to the formation in the Greek army of the Military league (May 1909) in imitation of the Committee of Union and Progress. Although the Greek government pursued the correct course of disowning the Cretan proclamation of union, the Military league succeeded in forcing many of its wishes on the king, including the dismissal of his sons from military and naval commands and the summoning of Venizelos to Athens in Jan. 1910.

From March 1910, when the Military league dissolved itself on the completion of its task, Greece moved swiftly to the climax of the Balkan Wars. A national assembly was elected in August, at Venizelos' instigation, to revise the constitution, but when it proved unamenable, Venizelos, having become prime minister for the first time on Oct. 18, dissolved the assembly and held a second election in December. From this election, which gave him a large majority, dated his extraordinary ascendancy over the Greek political scene.

His revised constitution was promulgated in June 1911; his peace was made with the royal family; the election of a chamber of deputies under the constitution of 1911 gave Venizelos a majority of five to one in March 1912; and he was ready to set about the creation of the Balkan league, which was to destroy the Ottoman empire in Europe. Still, however, he would not admit the Cretan representatives to the new chamber until he was ready and strong enough to face the consequences.

The Balkan Wars, 1912–13.—In the spring of 1912 Bulgaria concluded treaties with Serbia and Greece; Serbia and Greece had no conflicting interests and no formal alliance. In October the three governments presented joint demands to Turkey for reforms in Macedonia, which were unacceptable. Turkey declared war on Bulgaria and Serbia on Oct. 17. Venizelos admitted the Cretan representatives to the chamber and declared war on Turkey on Oct. 18. The First Balkan War (*see* BALKAN WARS) lasted seven months, interrupted by an armistice (December–January) for peace negotiations in London, in which Greece participated without accepting the armistice. The war was a success for the Balkan allies, particularly for Greece, whose armies captured Salonika, Préveza, Párga and Janina, besides the acquisition of Crete, Sámos and other islands. Constantine, who redeemed his reputation as a commander, succeeded to the throne on March 18, 1913, when King George I was assassinated.

Salonika was the point of friction between the allies, of whom the Bulgars at least also hoped to acquire it. Even before the defeat of the Turks was complete, Greece and Serbia began to negotiate a treaty of alliance against the danger of attack on either by their ally, Bulgaria. The First Balkan War was terminated on May 30, 1913, by the treaty of London, which abolished the Turkish empire in Europe. It ceded Macedonia to the Balkan league as a whole and left the disposition of the Aegean Islands to the powers. Two days later, the Greco-Serbian alliance was concluded; and within a month the Second Balkan War had begun with a Bulgarian attack on the two allies.

The Second Balkan War, in which Rumania joined Greece and Serbia, ended in a defeat of the Bulgars and a considerable recovery of lost ground by the Turks. It was terminated by the peace of Bucharest on Aug. 10, 1913. Bulgaria retained a small part of Macedonia and, at Dédéagatch (Alexandroúpolis), an outlet to the Aegean sea in western Thrace.

The fate of other areas liberated from Turkish rule by the upheaval of the two Balkan Wars was still not completely settled even when World War I broke out a year later. For instance, the Greeks continued to claim northern Epirus, part of the newly created state of Albania; the Turks refused to withdraw from several of the Aegean Islands; and the Italians remained in the Dodecanese, which they had occupied on an ostensibly temporary basis in 1912. Relations between Greece and

Turkey remained bad, and the Balkans seemed to be again on the brink of another convulsion when the outbreak of World War I in Aug. 1914 merged their parochial problems in the great upheaval of Europe.

World War I and Asia Minor.—World War I opened up a bitter difference between the king and Venizelos that lasted beyond their lifetimes and divided Greeks for a generation into royalists and republicans. The cause was that the two men disagreed on the likely course of the war and consequently on the interpretation to be put on the Greco-Serbian treaty in the event of Bulgaria's joining the Central Powers in hostilities against Serbia. Constantine was more uncertain of the outcome and therefore preferred neutrality, with a sympathy toward the Central Powers. The general staff, especially the chief of staff, Col. Ioannis Metaxas, supported the king with their military judgment. Though the crisis was not reached until Sept. 1915, when Bulgaria mobilized to attack Serbia, the two attitudes were clear from the start, when on Aug. 7, 1914, the king assured the German emperor William II (whose sister Sophia he had married) that he, though officially neutral, was on Germany's side in sympathy; and two weeks later Venizelos gave the entente to understand that his sympathies were wholly with them and that Greece would enter the war on their side if Turkey did so against them. Turkey in fact entered the war against the entente in Nov. 1914.

At this juncture the king's will prevailed, supported as he was by his chief of staff, and he was able both to keep Greece neutral and to retain Venizelos as his prime minister. The struggle between Venizelos and the general staff came to a head in March 1915, when the king dismissed his prime minister rather than accept the resignation of Metaxas. In Venizelos' place the king nominated Dimitrios Gounaris, who unfortunately chose to represent Venizelos as motivated by spite against the royal family. Gounaris retained power even after a general election in June but in the interval there had occurred the decisive events of Bulgaria's mobilization to attack Serbia, Greece's countermobilization and the arrival at Salonika of Allied forces on Venizelos' invitation. To restore the situation the king appointed Zaimis prime minister, with instructions to repudiate Greece's obligations under the Greco-Serbian treaty on the grounds that they applied only to "a war between one of the allied states and a single other power," not to a general European war. Even Great Britain's offer to cede Cyprus to Greece did not sway the new government, and it was soon withdrawn. Greece remained neutral; the king dissolved the chamber; and the Liberals abstained from the elections of Dec. 1915 in protest.

Neither Venizelos nor the Allies took further drastic measures against the king's government until after the surrender of Fort Rupel, on the Bulgarian frontier, to the Germans and Bulgars in May 1916. There then followed a series of increasingly strong Anglo-French ultimatums and, in September, Venizelos' secession from Athens to Crete, whence he proceeded to Salonika to set up a rival government. Although the Allies' terms were met by King Constantine's successive governments on paper, they grew steadily stiffer (especially after Dec. 1, 1916, when Allied troops landing at Piraeus were fired on by the king's troops as they approached Athens); and they culminated on June 11, 1917, in a demand that Constantine should leave the country, which he did the next day. His second son Alexander succeeded him (the crown prince George being both unwilling and unacceptable to the Allies). On June 26 Venizelos returned to Athens from Salonika as prime minister, and on June 29 Greece declared war on the Central Powers. Greek troops were not in action on the Macedonian front until May 1918, but they played a distinguished part in the final offensive in September and contributed an army corps to the French expedition into the Ukraine in December. Venizelos' subsequent triumph at the conference of Paris was the climax of his achievement.

As early as Jan. 1915 the entente had tried to tempt Greece into the war with the promise of territorial gains in Anatolia.

Venizelos exacted fulfilment of this promise, and the Allied supreme council in Paris authorized the landing of Greek troops at Smyrna in May 1919. This was the beginning of disaster both for Venizelos and for Greece. He himself stayed away from Athens too long for his own good, achieving diplomatic triumphs; securing, for instance, the treaties of Neuilly and Sèvres, terminating the war with Bulgaria and with Turkey, respectively; the agreement with the Italian foreign minister T. Tittoni (July 1919) on the terms of cession of the Dodecanese (q.v.) to Greece; an extension of the Greek area of occupation in Turkey (July 1919).; and, not least, the admiration of all the Allied representatives. But within two years the greater part of this edifice had collapsed. In Sept. 1920, on returning to Athens, Venizelos dissolved the chamber; in October King Alexander died; in November Venizelos was defeated at the polls; on Dec. 20 Constantine was restored to his throne on the crest of a wave of emotion; and in the following year the occupation of Smyrna developed into a catastrophic war with Turkey led by Mustafa Kemal Atatürk. The Greeks, ill-advised or imperfectly restrained by western politicians, launched in Jan. 1921 a general offensive in Anatolia, which was defeated and then, in July, obstinately renewed. By September they were in full retreat. (See GRECO-TURKISH WAR 1921–22.)

In October the prime minister, Gounaris, appealed to the British to intervene, while at the same time the French entered into an accord with Mustafa Kemal. The British government, being itself disunited on policy in the near east, was unable to rally its allies to a common policy, and by 1922 Greece's position was desperate. In Aug. 1922 the Turks launched a final offensive, which drove the Greeks out of Anatolia in September. The remnants of the Greek army rallied on the island of Chios under Gen. Nikolaos Plastiras, who put himself at the head of an antiroyalist revolution. Constantine, blamed for the disaster, left the throne to the crown prince George (Sept. 27), and six of his principal ministers and generals (including Gounaris) were court-martialed and (on Nov. 28, 1922) shot under Plastiras' orders. There followed one of the most erratic and unhappy periods in modern Greek history. The war with Turkey was liquidated by the treaty of Lausanne (July 24, 1923), which superseded the unratified treaty of Sèvres. An agreement for the compulsory exchange of Muslim and Orthodox populations between Greece and Turkey under the supervision of the League of Nations, following the similar Greco-Bulgarian agreement of 1919 (which, however, was on a voluntary basis), left Greece with a more homogeneous population, but also with nearly 1,500,000 refugees to assimilate. The country's troubles were aggravated by an incident on the Greco-Albanian frontier in Aug. 1923, which led to an Italian bombardment of Corfu and to the imposition of a heavy indemnity by the League of Nations, and by an abortive military rising in Macedonia in October, the promotion of which was attributed to the retired chief of staff, General Metaxas, and other royalist officers.

4. The Republic, 1924-35.—The new republic made an uneasy start, marred by friction with all its neighbours to the north and also with the powers. The British minister had actually been withdrawn after the execution of the six royalist leaders. Little more than a year after the republic's proclamation, and before it had a constitution, power was seized on June 26, 1925, by Gen. Theodoros Pangalos, one of the few soldiers who had been successful in the recent war with Turkey; on Jan. 3, 1926, he assumed dictatorial powers. Koundouriotis resigned and was re-

General Plastiras' revolutionary committee accordingly asked the young king, George II, to leave the country (which he did on Dec. 19, 1923) while the future of the monarchy was decided. Anxious to restore constitutional government, the committee held elections on Dec. 16, which were won by the Liberals. The committee then resigned, in Jan. 1924, and after a brief tenure of office by Venizelos (who resigned in February) a republic was proclaimed on March 25 and confirmed by a plebiscite on April 13. Adm. Pavlos Koundouriotis, scion of a family famous in the War of Independence and a hero of the First Balkan War, became president.

placed by the dictator after a travestied election. Pangalos was an eccentric though not a brutal ruler but his methods were dangerous and had virtually precipitated a war with Bulgaria in Oct. 1925, which only the intervention of the League of Nations forestalled. He held power only until Aug. 22, 1926, when he was deposed by another military coup d'état, led by Gen. Georgios Kondylis with the support of Col. Napoleon Zervas at the head of a force called the Republican guard. Kondylis hastened to restore normal government. He dissolved the Republican guard with some bloodshed in September; he restored Koundouriotis to the presidency; he organized elections in November; and after a coalition government had taken office under Zaimis, he retired from the scene. With some reconstructions, the same government held office until May 1928, and in the meantime a new constitution was promulgated on June 3, 1927. The government's fall was precipitated by the return of Venizelos, after several years' absence abroad, in March 1928. He became prime minister on July 3, dissolved the chamber a week later and won a large majority at the general election in August.

Venizelos held office for nearly four years, during which time he was largely successful in restoring normal relations with all Greece's Balkan neighbours. In Oct. 1928 an agreement was signed with Yugoslavia (which had denounced the Greco-Serbian alliance of 1913 in Nov. 1924) to negotiate all outstanding differences; in November a convention was signed with Albania; and in the same month a Greek minister was sent to Sofia for the first time since the war. There followed negotiations with Bulgaria on compensation for the property of exchanged populations in Jan. 1929; a treaty of friendship with Yugoslavia in March 1929; treaties of conciliation and arbitration with Hungary and with Austria in 1930; and a settlement of outstanding differences with Turkey in June 1930. At the end of Oct. 1930 Venizelos paid an official visit to Ankara. Meanwhile the League of Nations' Refugee Settlement commission had wound up its work at the end of 1930. The republic (of which Zaimis had been elected president in Dec. 1929) had begun to appear stable and accepted. But beneath the surface there were hostile currents.

A financial crisis in 1932 weakened Venizelos' position. In May his government fell over two measures which showed that the constitutional quarrel was not dead. One was to change the electoral system to that of proportional representation, the other to restrict the freedom of the press, which the royalists, under the leader of the Popular party, Panayiotis Tsaldaris, were alleged to be abusing. After two short-lived governments (the second again under Venizelos), a dissolution and a general election followed in September, under proportional representation.

The result was to elect many small groups (including the Communists) with no clear majority for any party. Tsaldaris formed a precarious coalition which fell in Jan. 1933. Another general election in March 1933 (by majority voting) enabled Tsaldaris to form a stable government, and it was this government which crowned Venizelos' work by signing a Balkan defense agreement with Rumania, Turkey and Yugoslavia on Feb. 9, 1934. (See BALKAN ENTENTE.) But by the following year a state of near deadlock had been reached between the two principal parties, Tsaldaris' Populists and Venizelos' Liberals; the latter controlled the senate and the former controlled the chamber. A battle was fought before the two agreed on the re-election of Zaimis as president in April 1934. The real issue was becoming increasingly plain: the Populists' intention to restore the monarchy.

5. The Monarchy Restored.—In March 1935 an abortive coup d'état was staged with the object of putting Venizelos in power and frustrating the royalists. Its failure was the end of Venizelos' career and made the restoration of King George II certain. Kondylis, who put down the rising, was made deputy premier; after a general election in June, he took part in a coalition government of the right wing under Tsaldaris. After internal disputes about the method whereby the monarchy was to be restored, Kondylis became first prime minister and then regent and organized a plebiscite on Nov. 3, which approved the restoration of the monarchy; King George was back in Athens by the end of the month. The constitution of 1911 was restored in place of that of 1927.

But the settlement was still uneasy. At a general election in Jan. 1936 victory rested almost evenly between a Liberal and Republican group led by Themistoklis Sophoulis in succession to Venizelos and a right-wing coalition of the parties of Tsaldaris and Kondylis and a tiny group led by Metaxas, the former chief of staff. Between these two coalitions the balance was held by 15 Communists. A succession of deaths left Metaxas the only possible prime minister, and on Aug. 4, 1936, he made himself dictator, with the king's consent, in order to forestall a Communist *coup d'état* under cover of a general strike, fixed for the following day. Metaxas' blow to the constitution and, especially, the king's acquiescence in it reopened bitter feelings between royalists and republicans, but probably saved Greece from anarchy.

World War II.—"The Fourth of August," as Metaxas' regime was called, produced administrative efficiency, a sound currency, and adequate defenses, at the expense of the parliamentary system. It was hostile to the Communists but otherwise not unpopular. Metaxas had been expected by many to side with Germany and Italy in the world struggle already developing. In fact he sought first to strengthen the Balkan entente inherited from Venizelos, which was extended by a nonaggression treaty with Bulgaria in July 1938. He accepted a British guarantee of Greece in April 1939, after Italy's annexation of Albania, but remained neutral on the outbreak of World War II. On Oct. 28, 1940, however, the Italians forced Greece into the war by invading the country from Albania.

The Greek army, under Alexandros Papagos (*q.v.*), drove back the invaders and had occupied about a quarter of Albania before the Germans also attacked Greece (via Bulgaria and Yugoslavia in April 1941). Greece was then rapidly overrun; and a small British force, which had arrived in March 1941 in fulfillment of the guarantee of 1939, was driven off the mainland by the end of April and off Crete a month later.

By this time Metaxas had died (Jan. 29), his successor had committed suicide, and King George II and his new government (under Emmanuel Tsouderos) had gone into exile.

The occupation of Greece lasted to Oct. 1944. It was marked by appalling suffering and great heroism. The Germans found successive dupes to make prime minister, but few others like them among the people. Resistance began with passive non-co-operation, developed into sabotage and the formation of guerrilla bands in 1941–42, and culminated on Nov. 25, 1942, with the destruction of the Gorgopotamos railway viaduct by a force of Greek guerrillas and British parachutists. This was the only occasion on which the two principal anti-German guerrilla forces, the Communist-controlled E.A.M.-E.L.A.S. (National Liberation Front and National Popular Liberation army) and Col. Napoleon Zervas' E.D.E.S. (Greek Democratic National army), co-operated in action. At other times they frequently fought each other, though not without undertaking independent actions against the common enemy, while the harbour they provided enabled the Allied liaison troops with them to carry out many activities that impeded the war effort of the Axis.

In a series of conflicts lasting from Sept. 1943 (immediately after the surrender of Italy to the Allies) to the summer of 1944, E.A.M.-E.L.A.S. eliminated all its political and guerrilla rivals except Zervas and set up a provisional government in the Greek mountains that by implication disowned both the king and his government in exile. A mutiny in sympathy occurred among the Greek troops in Egypt in April 1944 (when Tsouderos resigned); but after this had been suppressed and a precarious peace had been restored among the guerrillas, the two rival governments were brought together in a coalition under Georgios Papandreou, a former Venizelist Liberal. Accompanied by a small British force, his government returned to Athens as the Germans withdrew from Greece in October, but it disintegrated a few weeks later when the Communist members of the coalition refused to disband their guerrilla force. A bitter civil war broke out in Athens on Dec. 3, which the British military forces intervened to suppress with great difficulty, after E.A.M.-E.L.A.S. had overrun virtually all Greece except Athens and Salonika.

The Communist Rebellion.—The Communists accepted defeat and the disbandment of their forces at the conference of Varkiza in Feb. 1945. A period of political reconstruction followed, under the regency of the archbishop of Athens, Damaskinos, the king having agreed not to return to Greece pending a plebiscite on the monarchy. Many governments succeeded each other before an election was held in March 1946. The Communists abstained, and a royalist majority was returned. A plebiscite followed in September and restored George II. He died on April 1, 1947, and was succeeded by his brother Paul.

During 1946, a full-scale guerrilla war was reopened by the Communists, who had gone underground. The commitment of defending Greece became too much for Great Britain, and it was taken on by the U.S. government, with the announcement of the Truman doctrine (*see* TRUMAN, HARRY S.) on March 12, 1947. Massive help from the U.S. came just in time, for by the end of 1947 large areas were in Communist hands again, and on Dec. 24 the Communist leader Markos Vafades proclaimed a provisional government in the northern mountains.

Reconstruction and Recovery.—The rebellion did not end until 1949, after the defection of Yugoslavia from the Soviet bloc had closed a stretch of Greece's northern frontier to the rebels. On Oct. 16, 1949, the Greek Communist broadcasting station announced the end of open hostilities. Reconstruction was put in hand largely with U.S. funds and under U.S. guidance, but the continual change of governments inhibited progress. The election of March 1950 resulted in an unstable coalition of the Liberals and the left centre under Plastiras, and after frequent reshuffling of cabinets, another election was held in Sept. 1951.

A few weeks earlier a new phenomenon had entered the political field. Papagos, who had led the Greek army against the Italians in 1940 and against the Communist rebels in 1949, resigned as commander in chief and formed a new political group, the Greek Rally (Ellinikos Synagermos). It won the largest number of votes, but not enough to enable Papagos to govern alone, and he refused to enter a coalition. The result was another year of unstable government until on Nov. 16, 1952, another election was held, this time under the system of weighted proportional representation. The Rally obtained 239 seats out of 300, so that at last Greece was able to dispense with a coalition government. Papagos became prime minister and set about accelerating reconstruction. By the end of 1955, though still in need of U.S. assistance and in spite of a disastrous earthquake in 1953, Greece was well advanced in its recovery.

The Greeks could now assume a more considerable role in world affairs. The Dodecanese, ceded to Greece by Italy under the peace treaty of Feb. 1947, were formally annexed in 1948. Greece entered the Council of Europe in 1949 and the North Atlantic Treaty organization in 1951. A Greek contingent took part in the Korean War (1950–53). On Aug. 9, 1954, at Bled, Yugos., Greece signed a treaty of alliance with its ancient enemy Turkey and with Communist Yugoslavia.

The death of Papagos on Oct. 4, 1955, deprived Greece of its outstanding personality. However, Konstantinos Karamanlis, who as minister of public works had won wide popularity, formed a new government and ensured for the country some continuance of political stability. His position was confirmed at the election held on Feb. 19, 1956, when women voted for the first time. The National Radical union (Ethniki Rizospastiki Enosis [E.R.E.]), a new party, won 165 seats in the chamber of deputies, the opposition being divided into seven different groups, including the crypto-Communist.

In March 1958 a political crisis arose through the resignation of 2 ministers and 13 deputies from the E.R.E. because they disapproved of the government's intention to introduce a new electoral law that would favour the larger parties. Karamanlis thereupon resigned. In the subsequent general election, held on May 11, 1958, he was again returned, with 172 seats, but the Union of the Democratic Left (E.D.A.), which had received the support of the outlawed Communist party, obtained 79 seats. It was clear that Communist competition was by no means a thing of the past, but Karamanlis' position was strong enough to enable him to proceed with the development of Greece's economic resources.

When Karamanlis took over, one serious point of friction remained—the sovereignty of the British colony of Cyprus (*q.v.*). The campaign of Cypriot Greeks for union with Greece had been adopted by Papagos' government in 1954. The Greek claim soon spoiled harmony with Turkey, which thought that in the event of a British withdrawal the island should return to Turkey. Finally, by the Zürich agreement of Feb. 1959, Greece and Turkey in effect agreed to Cypriot independence.

A new general election, held on Oct. 29, 1961, was won for the third time by Karamanlis' E.R.E., which obtained 176 seats.

Throughout 1962 Georgios Papandreou's Centre union conducted a campaign against the government, disputing the validity of the last election. Papandreou also attacked King Paul, imputing interference by the crown in the government. Karamanlis resigned on June 11, 1963. A caretaker government supervised the election of Nov. 3, at which the Centre union obtained 140 seats, the E.R.E. 128, and the Progressive party 2 and the E.D.A. 30. Papandreou formed a new government but, failing to gain a vote of confidence, resigned. A new election (Feb. 16, 1964) gave him a clear majority (173 seats), and he returned to power. Paul I died on March 6, 1964, and his son Constantine succeeded.

On July 15, 1965, Constantine dismissed Papandreou from office for aiding penetration of the army by the left-wing organization Aspida, allegedly headed by his civilian son, Andreas Papandreou. After withholding confidence from two successive governments, the chamber on Sept. 25, 1965, finally approved one formed by Stephanos Stephanopoulos, the candidate of 45 dissidents from the Centre union; with the votes of 99 deputies of the E.R.E. and 8 Progressives, it held a majority of 4.

As regards Aspida, 28 officers were indicted in Oct. 1966; but while their trial was in progress, Panayotis Kanellopoulos, leader of the E.R.E., withdrew support from the government, and Stephanopoulos resigned on Dec. 21. The king promptly asked Ioannis Paraskevopoulos, a banker, to form a caretaker government with a view to holding an election in May 1967. Paraskevopoulos, however, had to resign office on March 30, and a government under Kanellopoulos was formed on April 3. He dissolved parliament on April 14, but on April 21, before elections could be held, a military *coup d'état* overthrew his government and transferred power to a group of army officers, acting in the king's name, but without the king's knowledge. A new cabinet was installed with Konstantinos Kollias, chief prosecutor of the supreme court, as prime minister on the king's insistence, but with three military men, Lieut.-Gen. Gregorios Spandidakis, Brig. Stylianos Patakos and Col. Georgios Papadopoulos, in key posts.

The government arrested large numbers of politicians, including Georgios and Andreas Papandreou, and eventually Kanellopoulos, as well as many alleged Communists. Though establishing a strict censorship and governing unconstitutionally, they announced in May 1967 that a new constitution would be drafted and submitted for a referendum. Meanwhile Andreas Papandreou was tried and sentenced in August to nine years' imprisonment for attempting to overthrow the regime. In the autumn there were several purges of the armed forces, the civil service and academics, and in December trial by jury was abolished.

On Dec. 13 the king broadcast from Lárisa an appeal to the forces and the people to overthrow the junta. The appeal failed, and the king and his family fled to Rome, where he stated that he had not opposed the coup because to do so would have caused bloodshed, and that he had hoped by remaining in Greece to persuade those in power to restore democracy; his only condition for returning was that there should be a timetable for the re-establishment of democracy. The government immediately appointed Gen. Georgios Zoitakis regent, and Papadopoulos and Patakos took over as prime minister and deputy prime minister, respectively, relinquishing military rank. An amnesty was proclaimed on Dec. 23 for all political prisoners, but only a few hundred were released, though they included Andreas Papandreou. Georgios, his father, had been released shortly before, though later he was put under house arrest; he died in 1968. The draft of the new constitution (July 1968) abolished the re-maining prerogatives of the king and provided for a unicameral parliament of 150 deputies (300 in the previous constitution) elected by secret ballot, with obligatory voting. The new constitution was approved on Sept. 29, 1968, by a national referendum. The number of registered voters was 6,508,894, but, though the voting was compulsory, only 4,633,602 voted "yes," but, though the new constitution King Constantine could return to his throne only after the first parliamentary election, unless the government decided to recall him at an earlier date. The regime stated, however, that a general election would be held only after the "revolution of April 21" had proved successful in reforming "Greek mentality."

In Jan. 1968 the Consultative assembly of the Council of Europe resolved that Greece should be expelled from membership if by 1969 there had been no return to parliamentary democracy. In Dec. 1969 Greece withdrew from the Council of Europe.

Opposition to the regime was organized from abroad, one of its creators being Andreas Papandreou. In July and Aug. 1971 the regime deprived many prominent expatriates of their Greek nationality for "engaging in anti-national activities abroad," including Papandreou, Georgios Plytas, former mayor of Athens, Helen Vlachos, publisher of the newspaper *Kathimerini*, and Melina Mercouri, an actress.

In Aug. 1971 the U.S. House of Representatives voted an amendment to the U.S. foreign aid bill suspending all aid to Greece until the restoration of constitutional rule in that country. The U.S. government reassured Athens, however, that a special escape clause permitted continuation of grants of military aid as before and that it would continue because that was in the interest of U.S. security.

On March 21, 1972, Zoitakis was dismissed and Papadopoulos took over as regent. It was believed that this move heralded the end of the monarchy.

(C. M. We.; B. S.-E.; X.)

IV. MODERN GREECE

A. THE PEOPLE

1. Racial Types.—The more primitive races that invaded Greece during the Dark Ages were subsequently always absorbed by the predominant Hellenic stock, with its higher civilization. This was the case with the Slavs who settled in various parts of Greece, as far south as the Peloponnese, during the 6th and later centuries A.D. Only the numerous Slav place names recall that these parts were once inhabited by Slavs. The Albanians, who also settled in large numbers in Greece during the 14th century, have retained their language but not their national identity.

The Vlachs (*q.v.*), a race of nomad shepherds who speak a Latin dialect intermixed with Greek, are of disputed origin; but their idiom, which is akin to Rumanian, indicates that they must have come from the lands included in modern Rumania. First mentioned by a Byzantine source as being in Macedonia *c.* 976, they are also found in Thessaly and Epirus.

In Macedonia, which supported a hotchpotch of races under Turkish rule, the Turkish and Bulgarian elements have disappeared since 1923, when the Greco-Turkish and Greco-Bulgarian exchanges of populations led to their replacement by Greek refugees and immigrants from Turkey and Bulgaria. Apart from a few Slav-speaking elements in the districts adjoining the Yugoslav frontier (Flórina, Kastoriá, and Pélla *nomoi*), Greek Macedonia is a linguistically and racially homogeneous area.

In Greek Thrace, however, there remains a considerable Muslim population that was exempted from compulsory exchange by a provision of the Lausanne Convention of 1923. It consists of two racially distinct elements: the Turks and the Pomaks. The Turks are descendants of immigrants settled there by the Ottoman conquerors in the 14th century. The Pomaks claim descent from the Thracian inhabitants of pre-Christian times. They became Muslims at the Ottoman conquest but speak a Slav dialect akin to Bulgarian, which they probably adopted when Thrace formed part of the medieval Bulgarian Empire.

2. Languages.—According to the 1961 census, 8,160,553 (97.2% of the population) spoke modern Greek as their mother tongue. The remaining 2.8% was composed of the following lan-

Area and Population of Regions and Departments

Regions and Departments (nomoi)	Capitals	Area* in sq. mi.	Population (1961 census)	Density per sq. mi.
Aegean Islands		3,506	477,476	136.2
Dhodhekánisos (Dodecanese)	Ródhos (Rhodes)	1,051	123,021	117.1
Khíos (Chios)	Khíos	334	62,223	186.3
Kikládhes (Cyclades)	Ermoúpolis (Hermoupolis)	995	99,959	100.5
Lésvos (Lesbos)	Mitilíni (Mytilene)	824	140,251	170.2
Sámos	Vathí	302	52,022	172.3
Central Greece and Euboea		9,508	2,823,658	297.0
Aitolía kai Akarnanía (Aetolia and Acarnania)	Mesolóngion (Missolonghi)	2,082	237,738	114.2
Attikí (Attica)	Athínai (Athens)	1,458	2,057,974	1,411.5
Evritanía (Eurytania)	Karpenísion	775	39,716	51.2
Évvoia (Euboea)	Khalkís (Chalcis)	1,492	166,097	111.3
Fokís (Phocis)	Ámfissa (Amphissa)	806	47,842	59.4
Fthiótis (Phthiotis)	Lamía	1,670	160,035	95.8
Voiotía (Boeotia)	Levádhia (Lebadea)	1,225	114,256	93.3
Crete		3,218	483,258	150.2
Iráklion (Herakleion)	Iráklion	1,025	208,374	203.3
Khaniá (Canea)	Khaniá	925	131,061	141.7
Lasíthi (Lasethi)	Áyios Nikólaos (Hagios Nikolaos)	698	73,880	105.8
Rethímni (Rethymne)	Réthimnon (Rethymnon)	570	69,943	122.7
Epirus		3,511	352,604	100.4
Árta	Árta	610	82,630	135.5
Ioánnina (Janina)	Ioánnina (Janina)	1,900	155,326	81.8
Préveza	Préveza	423	62,523	147.8
Thesprotía	Igoumenítsa (Egoumenitsa)	578	52,125	90.2
Ionian Islands		873	212,573	243.5
Kefallinía (Cephalonia)	Argostólion	300	46,314	154.4
Kérkira (Corfu)	Kérkira (Corfu)	249	101,770	408.7
Levkás (Leukas)	Levkás	169	28,980	171.5
Zákinthos (Zante)	Zákinthos	155	35,509	229.1
Macedonia		13,109	1,890,654	144.2
Áyion Óros (Mount Athos)†	Karyaí (Karyai)	129	2,687	20.8
Dráma	Dráma	1,353	121,006	89.4
Flórina (Phlorina)	Flórina	718	67,356	93.8
Imathía (Hemathia)	Véroia (Verroia)	664	114,515	172.5
Kastoriá	Kastoriá	646	47,487	73.5
Kaválla (Cavalla)	Kaválla	797	140,751	176.6
Khalkidhikí (Chalcidice)	Polýyiros (Polygyros)	1,158	79,849	69.0
Kilkís	Kilkís	1,012	102,812	101.6
Kozáni (Kozane)	Kozáni	2,197	190,835	86.9
Pélla	Édhessa (Edessa)	958	133,224	139.1
Piería	Kateríni (Katerine)	593	97,697	164.8
Sérrai (Serres)	Sérrai	1,532	248,041	161.9
Thessaloníki (Salonika)	Thessaloníki	1,352	544,394	402.7
Peloponnese		8,132	1,096,390	134.8
Akhaḯa (Achaea)	Pátrai (Patras)	1,210	239,206	197.7
Argolís	Návplion (Nauplia)	818	90,145	110.2
Arkadhía (Arcadia)	Trípolis (Tripolitsa)	1,664	135,042	81.2
Ilía (Elis)	Pírgos (Pyrgos)	1,036	188,861	182.3
Korinthía (Corinthia)	Kórinthos (Corinth)	885	112,505	127.1
Lakonía (Laconia)	Spárti (Sparta)	1,388	118,661	85.5
Messinía (Messenia)	Kalámai (Kalamata)	1,131	211,970	187.4
Thessaly		5,395	695,385	128.9
Kardhítsa (Karditsa)	Kardhítsa	977	152,543	156.1
Lárisa (Larissa)	Lárisa	2,137	237,776	111.3
Magnisía (Magnesia)	Vólos	994	162,285	163.3
Tríkkala	Tríkkala	1,287	142,781	110.9
Thrace		3,295	356,555	108.2
Évros (Hevros)	Alexandroúpolis	1,619	157,760	97.4
Rodhópi (Rhodope)	Komotiní (Komotine)	984	109,201	111.0
Xánthi (Xanthe)	Xánthi	692	89,594	129.5

*1958 resurveyed area; 1 sq. mi. = 2.59 sq. km. †Autonomous monastic administration.

guage groups: Turkish 179,895 (2.3%), of whom 92,219 belonged to the Muslim minority in western Thrace and the Dodecanese while 87,676 were Turkish-speaking Greeks from Asia Minor; Macedonian Slav (mostly in western Macedonia) 41,017; Vlach (spoken by the Koutsovlachs) 39,855; Albanian (spoken in parts of Attica, Argolis, and the islands) 22,736; Pomak (spoken by the Muslims of the Rhodope Mountains) 18,671; and smaller groups, mostly refugees, speaking Armenian or Russian. The Albanian- and Vlach-speaking populations are mainly bilingual. There are two forms of modern Greek: one (*Katharevousa*) is used in official documents, parliament, the courts and press; the other (demotic) is the language of everyday speech and literature. The liturgy of the Orthodox Church is *Katharevousa* (see GREEK LANGUAGE).

3. Customs and Religion.

Many distinctive customs of the Greek people, especially those of a religious character, survive from early Christian times and are associated with the various Christian festivals. Anthropologists have found elements of pre-Christian origin, especially in Macedonia and Thrace, where there are traces of the worship of Dionysus and other pagan deities.

The Orthodox Eastern Church is the established church in Greece, 97.9% of the population belonging to it (1951 census). The Orthodox Church of Greece is autocephalous, but is dogmatically united with all the other Orthodox churches. (*See* GREECE, ORTHODOX CHURCH OF.) It is governed by the Holy Synod of 12 members under the presidency of the archbishop of Athens and All Greece. Major decisions are taken by the Episcopal Assembly, consisting of all the members of the hierarchy, which meets annually in October or when convoked. There are 66 dioceses, of which 33 in the "New Countries" annexed after the Balkan Wars of 1912–13 (Macedonia, Epirus, the Aegean Islands, and Thrace) remain nominally subject to the ecumenical patriarch of Constantinople, though administratively their metropolitans participate in the Holy Synod and Episcopal Assembly in Athens. The churches of Crete (seven dioceses) and the Dodecanese (four dioceses) are not subject to the Church of Greece but to the Ecumenical Patriarchate. The Church of Crete, although not autocephalous, enjoys limited autonomy and is governed by a local synod presided over by the metropolitan of Crete, whose seat is at Iráklion. The four dioceses of the Dodecanese (Rhodes, Cos, Léros, and Kárpathos) have no corporate existence, each metropolitan being subject direct to the Ecumenical Patriarchate. Religious toleration and freedom of worship are guaranteed under the constitution, but proselytism is punishable by law.

Islam embraced 1.5% of the population (1951 census). The Muslim minority, which was concentrated chiefly in western Thrace, with a few thousands in the Dodecanese (Rhodes and Cos), consisted mainly of Turks (92,219) and Pomaks (18,671). The Muslims have their own communal councils presided over by the muftis of Komotiní and Rhodes respectively. The 28,430 Roman Catholics dwelled mostly in Athens and the islands formerly under Venetian rule. Their church, whose status is guaranteed under the London Protocol (1830), has a number of bishoprics (chiefly in the Aegean and Ionian Islands) and two archbishoprics (Corfu and Athens), and the archbishopric of Athens, dating only from 1875, is not officially recognized by the government. The Armenians (8,990), most of whom settled in Greece as refugees in 1922, belong mostly to the Gregorian Rite of the Eastern Church. In 1951 there survived 6,325 Jews out of about 80,000 who a decade earlier constituted the Jewish communities of Salonika and other towns. Most of them were deported to Poland and annihilated during the German occupation of Greece (1941–44).

4. Population.

At the first census taken in 1828 after the War of Independence, Greece had a population of less than 800,000 and an area of little more than 18,000 sq.mi. (46,620 sq.km.). By 1870 the population had approximately doubled, and its density, on an area of 19,381 sq.mi. (50,197 km.), was about 75 persons per square mile (32 per sq.mi.). The acquisition in 1881 of Thessaly and Árta increased the population to more than 2,000,000, and by 1907 Greece had 2,631,952 persons living in an area of 24,399 sq.mi. (63,193 km.). Greek successes in the Balkan Wars added Macedonia, Epirus, Crete, and the eastern Aegean Islands, and after World War I western and eastern Thrace were ceded by Turkey; by these additions the population had by 1920 increased to 5,531,474 and the area to 58,237 sq.mi. (150,833 sq.km.). A further increase to 6,204,684 by 1928 largely reflected the influx of refugees and immigrants from Russia, Bulgaria, and Turkey in the years 1918–24, but the area had been reduced to 50,147 sq.mi. (129,880 sq.km.) by the retrocession of eastern Thrace, Imbros (Imroz), and Tenedos (Bozca Ada) to Turkey in 1923. Between 1940 and 1951 the population increased by only 4%, reflecting the losses and privations suffered in World War II and in the Communist rebellion of 1947–49.

In the 1950s the increase in population amounted to 9.5%, and by 1961 the population of 8,388,553 occupied an area of 50,944 sq.mi. (131,944 sq.km.), which had been extended in 1948 through the cession of the Dodecanese by Italy. This corresponded to an average population density of 165 persons per square mile (63.58 per sq.km.). By mid-20th century the average death rate was 19.98 per 1,000 and the average birth rate was 7.1 per 1,000. The distribution of population by geographical areas (1961 census) was 6,973,506 (83%) on the mainland, the remainder in the islands. On the mainland, central Greece (including Euboea [Évvoia]) had 2,823,658 inhabitants and Macedonia 1,887,650.

The Peloponnese had a population of 1,096,390, or about 13% of the total. Epirus and Thrace had respectively 352,604 and 356,555 inhabitants, or about 4% apiece of the total. Of the island groups, Crete held 483,258 persons, or nearly 6% of the total population, the Aegean Islands, including the Cyclades and Dodecanese, 477,476, and the Ionian Islands 212,573.

The population of the municipal district of the capital, Athens, was 627,564 at the 1961 census, but Greater Athens, which includes the suburbs as well as its port of Piraeus (Piraiévs), had a total population of 1,852,709. Other large towns are Salonika with 378,444 inhabitants in the area of Greater Salonika, Patras (Pátrai) with 95,364, Vólos (Greater) with 67,424, Iráklion (Herakleion, formerly Candia) in Crete with 63,458, Lárisa (Larissa) with 55,391, Kaválla with 44,517, Sérrai (Serres) with 40,063, Khaniá (Canea) in Crete with 38,467, Kalámai (Kalamata) with 38,211, Ioánnina (Janina) with 34,997, Dráma with 32,195, and Corfu

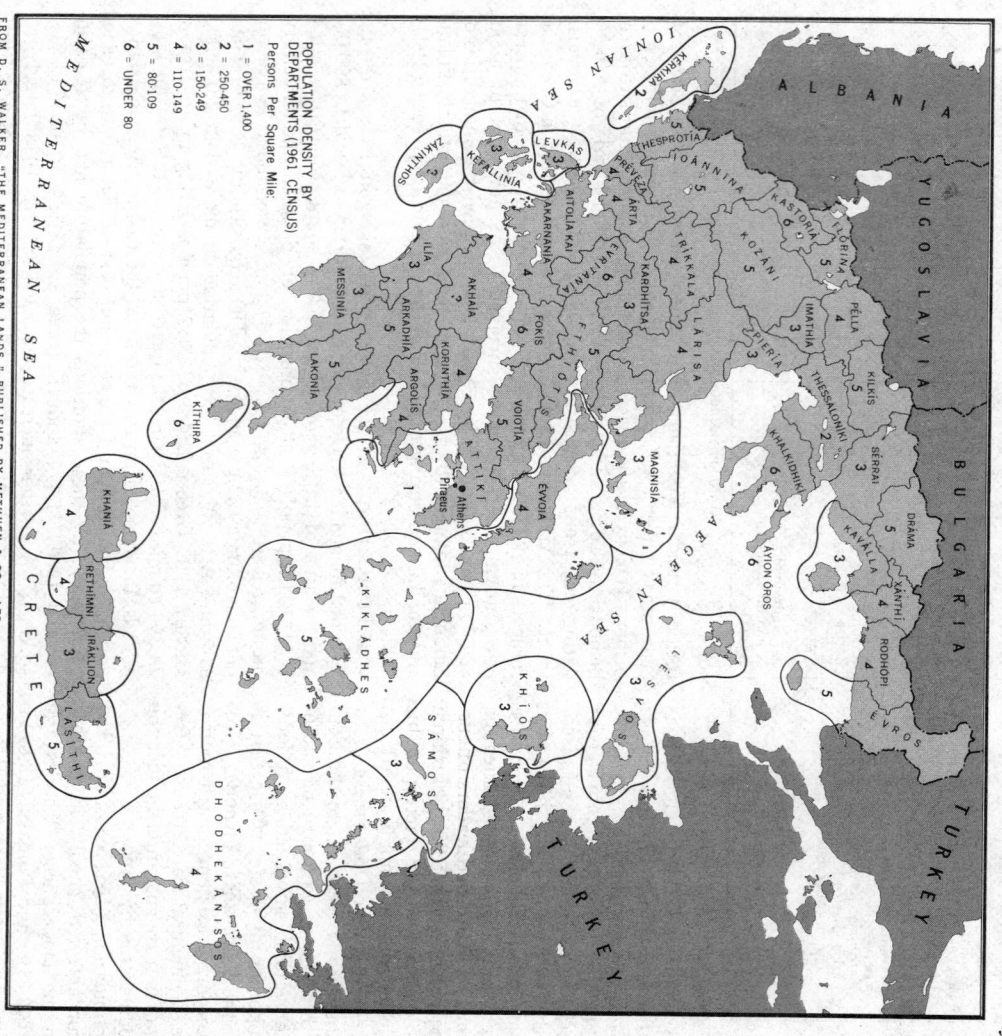

POPULATION DENSITY BY DEPARTMENTS (1961 CENSUS)
Persons Per Square Mile:
1 = OVER 1,400
2 = 250-450
3 = 150-249
4 = 110-149
5 = 80-109
6 = UNDER 80

FROM D. S. WALKER, "THE MEDITERRANEAN LANDS," PUBLISHED BY METHUEN & CO., LTD.
POPULATION DENSITY OF GREECE BY DEPARTMENTS (WITH THE EXCEPTION OF KÍTHIRA WHICH IS ADMINISTRA-
TIVELY PART OF ATTIKÍ)

GREECE

(Kérkira) with 26,991. In 1961, 43% of the population was classified as urban and 57% as rural.

B. ADMINISTRATION AND SOCIAL CONDITIONS

1. Constitution.—Greece is a constitutional monarchy governed under the constitution of 1968, which is a revised version of the 1911 constitution. The last revision (1967–68) was formulated by a special committee of prominent lawyers and constitutional law professors and specialists, headed by the former president of the Council of State, appointed by the revolutionary government after the army takeover of April 21, 1967. Apart from the opening articles defining the position of the established church, its principal provisions are those prescribing equality before the law, habeas corpus, immunity from arbitrary arrest, freedom of assembly and of association, and compulsory and free state primary education. It defines the authority of the crown, whereby the king appoints and dismisses the prime minister, and on his recommendation the members of the government, is head of the armed forces, and has the right to dissolve Parliament (but must simultaneously order the holding of elections within 45 days and the reconvening of Parliament within 80 days). The constitution further prescribes that the crown is hereditary and vested in the dynasty of King George I; the male offspring of the reigning sovereign have priority of succession, followed by the female. The heir to the throne must belong to the established church; in the king's absence abroad the crown prince or during his minority by a three-member regency.

Other articles relate to the form of government, the prerogatives and procedure of Parliament, and ministerial responsibility. It is laid down that ministers may be impeached by the Chamber.

The constitution provides that the Council of State (Symvoúlion Epikrateías) is the supreme court in matters of administrative law, with powers to examine the legality of ministerial decrees and to decide appeals on the validity of private citizens against the validity of ministerial or other official acts. Other articles provide for the permanence of civil servants, the election by universal suffrage of municipal and communal councils, and the liability of able-bodied male Greek citizens for military service. There are constitutional guarantees for foreign capital invested in Greece.

2. Government.—The Chamber of Deputies, a unicameral body, meets in Athens and is elected every five years. There is universal suffrage, women over 21 having been given the vote in May 1952. Voting is obligatory and secret. The electoral system is not prescribed by the constitution, but is regulated by statute and since the 1930s has been often changed, varying between majority and proportional representation systems. There are 150 deputies elected from 55 constituencies.

The civil service consists of permanent officials, irremovable except by a disciplinary court of senior civil servants, and temporary officials, removable by the minister. There are permanent directors-general for foreign affairs and a number of other departments; others have secretaries-general, who are temporary officials and change with the government. The secretary-general is the senior official after the minister, some of whose authority is delegated to him.

Local Government.—The Greek administrative system is largely modeled on that of the French, the country being divided into 50 *nomoi*, or departments, as shown in the table. There is a minister of northern Greece (Macedonia and Thrace) who is a member of the Cabinet, with headquarters at Salonika. Athens, with its suburbs and Piraeus, is divided into 22 municipal districts with their own mayors. The peninsula of Áyion Óros (Mount Athos) in Chalcidice forms a self-governing monastic community but has a civil governor, appointed by the government, who is responsible for public order outside the monasteries.

Municipal government, with elected mayors and urban and rural councils, was established in Greece in mid-19th century and is part of the constitution. Local authorities may levy certain taxation subject to the approval of the Ministry of the Interior, but the general expenses of the provincial services are defrayed by the national budget. Municipal and communal elections are held every four years.

3. Political Parties.—Since the introduction of parliamentary government in 1844, the plethora of political parties has been one of the main causes of Greek political instability. During the 19th century parties were named after their leaders—Tricoupists, Deliyannists, Theotokists, etc. After 1910, when Eleutherios Venizelos founded the Liberal Party, representing a genuine reform movement, the other parties likewise adopted progressive labels such as Populist, Radical, Progressive, and Agrarian, but their number did not diminish. Proportional representation, introduced under the republic (1924–36), favoured the existence of small parties and coalition governments.

With the withdrawal of Venizelos from the political scene in 1924 the Liberal Party broke up into a number of splinter parties; this condition continued after his death in 1936 and persisted into the 1960s.

In 1950, however, Marshal Alexandros Papagos founded the National Rally, which absorbed all the other right-wing parties and brought to Greece a period of stable government. On the marshal's death in 1955, he was succeeded by Konstantinos Karamanlis, who renamed the party the National Radical Union (Ethniki Rizospastiki Enosis). It was returned to power in the elections of 1956, 1958, and 1961. Parties of the centre include the Centre Union, which gained a clear majority in the 1964 election under Georgios Papandreou, and the Progressive Party (Komma Proodeftikon) of Spyros Markezinis.

At the extreme left is Enosis Dimokratikis Aristeras or E.D.A. (Union of the Democratic Left), under Ioannis Passalidis, into which other left-wing groups have merged. It gained 21 seats at the 1964 election and is virtually identical with the Greek Communist Party, which was proscribed in 1946 after it had fomented an armed rebellion against the state. The outlawed leaders of the Communist Party thereafter took refuge behind the "iron curtain" but maintained their organization with headquarters in one of the Communist states of Eastern Europe.

4. Living Conditions.—Wages in Greece are low by reason of chronic rural underemployment and because the low agricultural income compels many young peasants to seek employment in the towns and swell the ranks of unskilled labour. The minimum daily wage for male urban unskilled workers in the early 1960s was 52 drachmas (dr. 52) rising to dr. 80 in the building industry; skilled labour rates varied from dr. 80 to 150 (dr. 30 = U.S. $1; dr. 72 = U.K. £1). Minimum rates are fixed by the Ministry of Labour. Wage increases are fixed by collective agreements arrived at between employers and workers' representatives.

Housing in Greece is the business not of the local authorities but of the state. The Housing Department is part of the Ministry of Public Works and Ministry of Labour and is responsible for building houses for certain categories of citizens such as the victims of earthquakes and those whose villages were destroyed during the occupation of 1941–44 and the Communist insurrection of 1946–49.

Health.—In the early 1960s there were more than 1,000 hospitals and sanatoriums with bed facilities for about 49,000 patients. Incidence of typhoid has declined since sanitary conditions in hundreds of villages have been improved with U.S. aid.

5. Social Security.—Greece ratified and implemented the Washington Convention on the 8-hour day and the 40-hour week; the right to annual paid holidays was established in 1945. Engagements, dismissals, and industrial health and safety are regulated by legislation. Social insurance (old-age pensions, illness, and accidents) were established in 1930, and numerous mutual benefit institutions were established by the various trades and professions. In 1930 the government established an independent social-insurance fund (Idryma Koinonikon Asfaliseon, or I.K.A.). This fund, with which other funds have become affiliated, is financed by contributions from employers and workers. It provides relief in cases of sickness and accident, as well as old-age pensions. There is no general unemployment benefit, although certain categories of seasonal workers (*e.g.*, tobacco workers) draw benefit in the off season. Contributions vary; the worker insured with I.K.A. pays 1% of his emoluments to cover sickness benefit and another 1% toward his pension; the employer contributes 5% and 3% respectively. In 1962 the government extended social insurance to farmers and agricultural workers.

The Greek trade-union movement numbers more than 2,000 different unions, with a total membership of about 250,000. After World War II the Greek General Confederation of Labour (founded 1918) was reconstituted and affiliated to the International Confederation of Free Trade Unions.

6. Justice and Police.—The constitution provides for the independence of the judiciary and lays down that "justice is administered by judges appointed by the King according to the law." Judges of the higher courts are appointed for life, and others are irremovable unless convicted of a criminal offense. The supreme court is the Areopagus, which consists of two divisions, civil and criminal. There are 11 courts of appeal which can hear both civil and criminal cases, and 58 courts of first instance, with a criminal court at the seat of each. There are also 350 local courts under justices of the peace, who are paid members of the judiciary, and 47 magistrates' courts. Each court (with the exception of the last two categories) has its district attorney or public prosecutor. Procedure follows the French model; *i.e.*, the investigating magistrate examines the evidence and interrogates witnesses and, if he decides that there is a prima-facie case, refers it to the public prosecutor, who decides whether a charge shall be brought. If so, the case is heard in open court, the public prosecutor representing the crown and the accused being represented by counsel.

There are two bodies of police, the town police (*Astynomía póleon*) and the gendarmery (*chorophylakí*). Both are administered by the Ministry of the Interior and were reorganized by a British mission after World War II.

7. Education.—In October 1964 the Papandreou government passed a new education act that introduced radical changes into the system. Education was made compulsory until the age of 15 to cover both primary school (6 years) and part of gymnasium, or secondary school (3 years). After the gymnasium, a new type of school called the Lykeion (3 years) was added, but attendance at this was not compulsory. University entrance examinations were abolished, and pupils finishing the Lykeion and wishing to enter a university or a school of higher education had to pass an examination set by a special board that granted an "academic certificate." Education at all stages—elementary, secondary, and higher—is free, all fees of any kind being abolished. The teaching of Latin in secondary schools was also prohibited by the act. The most revolutionary change of all was the optional use of demotic (vernacular) as the vehicle of teaching in all schools from the lowest to the highest. The Education Act of October 1964 was practically abolished by "Law of Necessity," no. 129, published in September 1967, and the previous educational regime has been reestablished.

In the mid-1960s there were about 10,800 public or private primary schools, including about 500 night schools and more than 1,500 kindergartens, attended by about 50,000 pupils and staffed by about 22,000 teachers. There are also commercial and technical secondary schools. Public and private secondary schools together number about 900, with more than 310,000 pupils and about 9,000 teachers. For higher studies there are universities at Athens (National and Capodistrian University, founded in 1837) and at Salonika (the Aristotelian University, founded in 1925). In 1965 it was decided to establish four new universities, at Ioánnina, Kérkira, Pátras, and Iráklion. Athens also has a number of higher schools with university status: the Polytechnic (founded in 1836), the Higher School of Political Sciences, the College of Agriculture, the Higher School of Commerce and Economic Sciences, the School for Advanced Industrial Studies, founded in 1938 to provide higher professional education for executives. Athens also has schools of fine arts, music, drama, economics, and commerce. In the mid-1960s there were 14 teacher-training colleges with an enrollment of about 3,000.

The minister in charge of the prime minister's department is responsible for the upkeep of ancient monuments, for museums, and for supervising excavations, whether conducted by Greek or foreign archaeologists. The Ministry of Education has a Department of Arts responsible for music and the graphic arts; a Department of Letters responsible for theatres, motion pictures, libraries, and public records; and an Ecclesiastical Department.

8. Defense.—The Greek armed forces consist of an Army, Navy, and Air Force recruited on the basis of compulsory military service for all male citizens aged 21, for a period of two years. There is also a Home (National) Guard recruited from reservists for local security duties in frontier districts.

The Army consists of 1 armoured and 11 infantry divisions, with about 120,000 officers and men. The Navy, with one cruiser and a number of destroyers, frigates, submarines, and minor war vessels, totals more than 100 ships. The fleet is organized in two squadrons based on Salamís and Soúda (Soudhas) Bay, Crete, and with a training section at Skaramangá; it has about 19,000 officers and men. The Air Force, with approximately 23,000 officers and men, has about 300 operational aircraft; all 10 fighter squadrons are assigned to the 28th Allied Tactical Air Force. Defense, which absorbs about 30% of the Greek budget, is based strategically on membership of the North Atlantic Treaty Organization (q.v.), which Greece joined in 1952. The Ministries of War, Marine, and Military Aviation were in 1950 combined into a Ministry of National Defense.

C. THE ECONOMY

The Greek economy is basically agricultural, although some progress has been made in industrial development. A five-year development plan was announced in 1965 covering all sectors of the economy and including plans for raising the efficiency of agriculture, for encouraging private enterprise in industry, for improving communication, and for encouraging tourism.

1. Production.—*Agriculture.*—Although only about 25% of the land is cultivable (15% is forest or woodland and the remainder barren or rocky), more than half the population is directly engaged in agricultural activities. Greece is, however, far from self supporting in food; about one-half of the wheat and one-quarter of the other cereals consumed are homegrown.

The pressure on the land, already severe, was increased by the influx of refugees after the Greco-Turkish War of 1920-22, though the agrarian reform of 1924 expropriated large estates for settlement by the refugees. After 1952 a further redistribution effected by the revised constitution, all estates exceeding 65 ac. (26 ha.) being expropriated as small holdings for landless peasants. The average holding amounts to only about 1.5 ac. (0.6 ha.) to each peasant, and tends to decrease. The problems of such small-scale farming (finance, marketing, machinery) have been largely solved by the spread of agricultural cooperatives, which numbered approximately 8,000,000 in the late 1960s. At that time the government was pressing ahead with a plan to increase agricultural output by consolidating holdings, expanding irrigation, introducing new high-yielding varieties of crops, improving pastures, conserving soil, and above all by encouraging the application of artificial nitrogenous and phosphoric fertilizers.

(A. A. PA.; C. RO.)

Forestry.—The Greek forests were severely depleted in World War II by cutting for fuel, but reforestation programs and the prohibition of grazing in forest reserves restored the cover over 19% of the total surface of the country. Much of this is low scrub, however, and Greece produces only about one-third of its requirements of timber and wood products. It is hoped to increase steadily this proportion. Some turpentine and mastic (resin gum from the small evergreen shrub *Pistacia lentiscus*, chiefly from Chíos) are produced.

Fisheries.—After World War II the Greek fishing fleet was modernized, and distribution was reorganized with the aid of refrigeration, packing, and canning plants. In the late 1960s fisheries contributed about 1% of the gross national income and provided employment for about 50,000. There was at that time a marked move from local waters to banks off North Africa and in the Atlantic. Catches increased from about 35,000 metric tons in 1948 to an annual average of about 100,000 metric tons in the late 1960s. Sponge fishing, mainly from Kalamáta, yields about 100 tons annually, most of which is exported.

Mining.—The mining of metals in Greece is of great antiquity, the lead and zinc deposits at Laurium in Attica having reputedly been worked since the 5th century B.C. Not all the minerals are fully exploited. The mining industry suffered very severely from World War II and the succeeding civil strife; output in 1948 was only about one-eighth of that in 1939. But reequipment and rehabilitation of the mines with U.S. economic aid more than restored output in the 1950s. Mining employs more than 20,000 workers.

The scarcity of arable land has encouraged the cultivation of luxury crops, such as tobacco and currants, that bring relatively high prices in the export market. Tobacco, with an average annual crop of about 130,000 metric tons in the late 1960s, normally accounts for about 40% of the total value of Greek exports. The total area devoted to tobacco growing exceeds 340,000 ac. (140,000 ha.) and is mainly in Macedonia, Thrace, and the Agrinion district of central Greece. In 1967, 115,000 metric tons were exported, chiefly to the Federal Republic of Germany and to Eastern Europe. Currants and sultanas, with average annual crops of 80,000 and 70,000 metric tons respectively, are grown chiefly in the northern Peloponnese, particularly south and east of Patras and around Corinth (from which the word currant derives; *i.e.*, "raisins of Corauntz"). Other viticulture is conducted in most parts of Greece, including Crete and the Aegean and Ionian Islands; the average annual yield is 150,000 tons of grapes and about 3,500,000 hectolitres (hl.) (more than 92,000,000 U.S. gal.) of wine, little of which is exported.

The chief areas for wheat are Thessaly, Macedonia, and Thrace. The average annual crop in the late 1960s was 2,000,000 metric tons, but the yield per acre is among the lowest in Europe. Corn (maize) and barley, with average annual crops of 280,000 metric tons apiece, are grown mainly in Epirus. Olives, grown on 500,000 ha. of land in the low-lying coastal areas and in the islands (especially Corfu), are also an important product.

Greece is the third largest producer in the world of olive oil, with an average annual output of 150,000 metric tons, but little is exported. Rice production has expanded greatly since World War II; the average annual crop exceeds 110,000 metric tons. Cotton, grown around Sérrai and in Thessaly and Thrace, yields about 300,000 metric tons of cottonseed annually. Potatoes are widely grown and the average yield in the late 1960s was 600,000 metric tons annually.

Livestock.—The German and Italian occupation of 1941-44 and the Communist rebellion of 1946-49 played havoc with Greek livestock, but by the late 1960s the animal population exceeded the prewar figure, with approximately 1,125,000 cattle, 9,000,000 sheep, 4,500,000 goats, 600,000 pigs, 475,000 donkeys, 325,000 horses, and 220,000 mules. However, Greece remains backward in livestock production, dairying, and poultry keeping. Substantial imports of meat and livestock products (largely from Yugoslavia) and of eggs are necessary, and Greek production of hides and skins (which involves serious wastage because of primitive methods and lack of refrigeration) meets less than half the requirements of the tanning industry.

Deposits of iron ore, in Chalcidice and the islands of Seriphos (Sérifos), Kithnos, Siphnos (Sifnos) and Skyros (Skiros), by the late 1960s yielded more than 150,000 metric tons (iron content) annually. Bauxite output, from Eleusis and mines in the Mt. Parnassus area, was about 1,050,000 metric tons annually and was exported largely to the U.K. for cement manufacture. Pyrites, mined in Chalcidice and at Ermióni in the Peloponnese, yielded concentrates averaging 125,000 metric tons (sulfur content) annually. Other minerals worked are magnesite (about 150,000 metric tons annually), zinc (90,000 metric tons), lead, manganese, chrome, nickel, and salt. High-grade emery (about 7,500 metric tons) is produced from deposits in Naxos, but the demand was reduced by the increased use of synthetic abrasives.

Greek deficiencies in sources of fuel led in the 1960s to the large-scale exploitation of the lignite deposits that exist in several areas; by the late 1960s annual output was about 4,000,000 metric tons. The search for petroleum achieved only moderate success, oil being found near the Turkish frontier in Thrace and, more promisingly, in 1963 at Klésoura in west-central Greece.

Power.—The cost of energy in Greece is relatively high, mainly due to the expense of importing fuel oil. The only significant indigenous sources of power are lignite and hydroelectric stations. Thermal-power stations such as those at Ptolemais in Macedonia and Aliviérion in Euboea depend on lignite fuel. The two largest hydroelectric stations are at Kremastá (546 mw. installed capacity) and Kastrákion (240 mw.). By the mid-1960s annual production of electricity exceeded 3,700,000,000 kw-hr., of which about one-third was generated by hydroelectric plants. There are plans for constructing a more efficient power grid by eliminating the less efficient thermal stations and using more local lignite instead of imported oil.

Industries.—Lacking large reserves of power and suitable raw materials in quantity, except cotton, Greece is not well equipped for industrialization. After a period of expansion in the 1920s and 1930s, consequent to the influx of skilled labour from Asia Minor, there was recession in World War II. By the late 1960s, however, industry was employing about 500,000 workers. There was at that time a change in government policy from general decentralization of industry to encouraging concentration in industrial zones and parks with good facilities, notably in Athens, Salonika, Patras, Vólos, Kaválla, and Iráklion, and along the adjacent coastal strips.

The main industry is textile production, chiefly cotton spinning and weaving; in the early 1960s about 26,000 metric tons of cotton yarn and 120,000,000 m. of woven cotton fabrics were produced annually. The chemical industry, mainly at Piraeus, produces annually about 120,000 metric tons of sulfuric acid and 210,000 metric tons of superphosphates. On the other side of Athens, at Asprópirgos is an oil refinery with an annual capacity of about 1,400,000 metric tons of petroleum products. An integrated iron and steel works with an initial annual production of 300,000 tons was opened near Eleusis in 1963. The first Greek-built ocean-going vessel was launched in 1960 from the new shipyards at Skaramangá, near Piraeus. Industries of some importance are cement production (annual output in the early 1960s about 1,800,000 metric tons), cigarette manufacture (about 10,000,000,000 annually), and food processing.

Tourism.—Greece has the natural attractions of scenery, climate, and famous sites but is deficient in the roads and hotel amenities required by modern tourism. Great improvements were effected after 1949 by the National Tourist Organization, including improvements or additions to hotels and the roads leading to classical sites, and the organization of drama festivals, coach tours, and cruises. By the mid-1960s foreign tourists exceeded 800,000 annually, and the tourist industry earned the equivalent of more than $100,000,000 annually, or about one-third of the total value of Greek exports. With an average annual increase in tourist traffic of 20%, Greece anticipated more than 2,000,000 visitors by 1970.

2. Trade and Finance.—Before World War II an adverse balance of trade was a regular feature of the Greek economy, only about 60% of imports being paid for by exports. The national financial stability was dependent on invisible receipts from the earnings of Greek shipping and the remittances of emigrants. After the war, the visible trade gap widened considerably, and although the deficit was reduced by the devaluation of the drachma in 1953, U.S. economic aid continued to be an important prop to the Greek economy.

By the late 1960s the total volume of trade had increased by more than 200% as compared with the 1930s. This change reflected the rise in population, the general advance in prosperity, and the expansion of investments. Imports of foodstuffs (notably wheat) had decreased considerably by reason of the expansion of Greek agriculture. Coal and coke imports were also substantially smaller, though there was an increase in petroleum imports. Even so, the value of visible exports was still only about 33% of that of imports.

The direction of trade in the 1960s was marked by Greece's associate membership in the European Economic Community in 1961. The Federal Republic of Germany was the best customer and largest supplier, taking about 20% of the exports and providing about the same proportion of Greek imports. The United States and the United Kingdom remained significant importers and exporters; members of the Soviet bloc were customers of growing importance.

Banking and Currency.—The Bank of Greece is the centre of the credit system; it is the issuing bank, and holds the reserves of gold and foreign exchanges and the national accounts. It was established in 1928, taking over the note-issuing privileges of the National Bank of Greece, which remains the chief commercial bank. The other leading commercial banks were founded mostly with British capital or participation. A Post Office Savings Organization exists for the benefit of small depositors.

The new issue of currency put into circulation on May 1, 1954, consisted of drachma notes and coins and lepta coins (100 lepta = dr. 1) based on a value of dr. 30 = U.S. $1 (dr. 84 = £1 U.K.; since 1967, dr. 72 = £1 U.K.).

National Finance.—An extreme inflation in 1943–44 deprived most of the Greek people of their drachma savings. Many continued to hoard British gold sovereigns, which had been in common use in Greece before World War II and remained for long afterward the basis for most unofficial cash deals. The inflation culminated in a "stabilization" of the drachma at the rate of dr. 1 = dr. 50,000,000,000 (old) in November 1944. Confidence in the currency did not begin to return until the announcement in 1947 of U.S. economic aid, and an exchange rate of dr. 42,000 = £1 was established in 1949. In 1953 a further devaluation was made lowering the rate to dr. 84,000 = £1 (dr. 30,000 = $1), and in the currency issue of 1954, dr. 1,000 became equal to one drachma of the new issue.

Greece partially defaulted on the interest payments on its foreign debt in 1932 and suspended payment altogether in 1941, but interest payments on foreign loans contracted since World War II have been honoured. The history of Greek finance since 1948 is almost wholly one of U.S. aid, which enabled Greece to accumulate holdings of gold and foreign exchange amounting in the late 1960s to $371,000,000.

The budget, which covers the calendar year, normally consists of an ordinary budget for current expenditure and receipts, and an investment budget financed chiefly from foreign loans, internal borrowings, and grants from the ordinary budget. The principal sources of ordinary-budget income are indirect taxation, which represents about 70% of the whole and is obtained mainly from import duties, export charges, consumption and turnover taxes, and transaction taxes; direct taxation, derived from personal income tax, profit tax, and taxes on industrial production; and receipts from national monopolies, fees, and the like. The main heads of expenditure under the investment budget are electric-power development (irrigation, reclamation, mechanization, loans); development of mines, industries, and fisheries; improvement of communications, housing, and municipal projects; and the construction of schools and hospitals.

3. Transport and Communications.—*Roads.*—There are in Greece about 2,700 mi. (4,350 km.) of roads in the main national and provincial networks. The main national road runs from Athens to Salonika through Thebes, Lamía, Lárisa, and Kozáni. From Salonika there are roads westward to Flórina, northward through Évzonoi into Yugoslavia, and eastward to Kaválla, Komotiní, and across the Maritsa River into Turkey. The other principal roads are Athens-Corinth-Patras-Pyrgos; Corinth-Árgos-Trípolis-Sparta-Kalamáta; and Patras-Agrínion-Ioánnina. The main exit from Athens to the west and north follows a four-lane highway to Daphne, and a wide highway southeastward from Athens follows the Attic coast to Ákra (Cape) Soúnion. Vehicular ferries run between Patras and Brindisi, Italy, and between Igoumenítsa and Corfu, whose good roads are a relic of British rule. Rhodes is also well routed. A motorable road runs in Crete between Khaniá and Iráklion. In the late 1960s special attention was being paid to improving road links between the east and west coasts, as part of a general plan to open a gateway to Western Europe.

Railways.—The main Greek railway, of standard gauge, runs to Piraeus-Athens-Lárisa-Salonika. From Salonika run three lines: (1) westward to Flórina and Bitola (formerly Monastir), Yugos., with a branch to Kozáni; (2) northward through Idhoméni to Belgrade, Yugos.; (3) eastward through Sérrai, Dráma, and Alexandroúpolis to Svilengrad, Bulg., running through Turkish territory to serve Edirne and connecting at Píthion with the line to Istanbul. A metre-gauge railway from Piraeus runs through Athens and Corinth and around the Peloponnese; Thessaly is served by a line running inland from Vólos; and a metre-gauge railway through Mesolóngion serves Aetolia. There is also a standard-gauge railway from Piraeus to Athens and Kifisía. In the late 1960s the railways of Greece were being extensively modernized with special attention to coordination with road transport, doubling tracks, and standardizing gauges.

Shipping.—The modern Greeks have assumed a leading position as sea carriers, and their economy has benefited considerably thereby. The Greek merchant fleet increased from 335 ships (494,000 gross register tons) in 1920 to 1,750 ships (nearly 8,000,-000 tons) in the late 1960s. Special priority was then being given to the improvement of the ports of Patras and Préveza, the "western gate" to Europe. Piraeus, the main port, was continuing to expand, as were Kaválla, Vólos, and Iráklion, which serve the planned new industrial zones. In addition to ships registered under the Greek flag, a large tonnage of Greek-owned vessels is registered under Panamanian, U.S., Liberian, and British flags. The Greeks are active in sea-borne oil transport, with a tanker fleet of about 70 ships in the 1960s.

Air Transport.—In 1951 a law was passed forming Greek National Airlines as the sole domestic operator. This airline was uneconomic, and in 1957 its services and assets were taken over by Olympic Airways, a company with a majority Greek holding. In the late 1960s, the government, in collaboration with Olympic Airways, was sponsoring a long-term plan for improving air-transport facilities, particularly with an eye to developing tourist traffic. The new Athens Airport terminal was being completed; facilities were improved at Salonika, Rhodes, Kérkira, and Iráklion; the airstrips at Alexandroúpolis and Cos were extended; and a new airport was completed on Chios.

Telecommunications.—A government-controlled utility company operates the telephones and telegraphs and in 1957 took over the installations (except the cables to Malta and to Alexandria, Egy.) of the British-owned Cable and Wireless Ltd., which since 1866 had managed the Greek telegraph systems. The domestic telephone system includes most of the islands, which are connected to it by radio links. There were about 500,000 telephones in the late 1960s.

Radio broadcasting is conducted by the Hellenic National Broadcasting Institute, a government-owned corporation; many of the programs are sponsored commercially, but an evening "third" program consists of unsponsored music and cultural material. A television network was planned for the late 1960s, Greece being the only remaining country in Europe without one.

See also references under "Greece" in the Index.

(Wm. C. B.)

BIBLIOGRAPHY.—*General works*: R. Liddell, *Aegean Greece* (1954); R. Viollet, *Greece in Photographs* (1955); J. P. Kinross, *Portrait of Greece* (1956); K Kerényi, *Greece in Colour* (1958); H. Miller, *The Colossus of Maroussi*, rev. ed. (1958); P. L. Fermor, *Mani: Travels in the Southern Peloponnese* (1958); R. Tor, *Getting to Know Greece*, (1959); E. Whelpton and B. C. Whelpton, *Greece and the Islands* (1961); H. D. H. Miller, *Greek Horizons* (1961); A. Philippson, *Das Mittelmeergebiet*, 4th ed. (1922), *Das Klima Griechenlands* ( ); H. D. H. Miller, *Greek Horizons* (1961); A. Philippson, *Die griechischen Landschaften*, 3 vol. (1950-52); Sir J. L. Myres, *Geographical History in Greek Lands*, 3 vol. (1953); W. B. Turrill, *The Plant-Life of the Balkan Peninsula* (1929); A. J. B. Wace and M. S Thompson, *The Nomads of the Balkans* (1914).

Archaeology:—*General works*: The results of research in Greek archaeology and excavations are published in monographs or series devoted to individual sites, and in a number of periodicals. Of these the most important are: Greek: *Archaiologike Ephemeris*, *Archaiologikon Deltion*; *Ergon tes Archaiologikes Etaireias*; *Kretika Chronika*. Austrian: *Jahreshefte of the Austrian Archaeological Institute*. French: *Bulletin de correspondance hellénique*. German: *Jahrbuch of the German Archaeological Institute (with Archäologischer Anzeiger)*, *Mitteilungen of the schools in Rome and Athens*. British: *Journal of Hellenic Studies, Archaeological Reports*; *Annual of the British School at Athens*. Italian: *Annuario of the Italian School in Athens*. American: *Hesperia, American Journal of Archaeology*.

*The periodicals marked with an asterisk contain annual accounts of new work in Greece.

History: Classical Greece: G. Grote, *History of Greece*, new ed. 10 vol. (1888), reprinted in 12 vol. (1906); G. Busolt, *Griechische Geschichte*, 2nd ed. (1893-1904); E. Meyer, *Geschichte des Altertums* (1884-1902); J. B. Bury, *A History of Greece to the Death of Alexander the Great*, 3rd ed. rev. by R. Meiggs (1951); K. J. Beloch, *Griechische Geschichte*, 2nd ed. (1912-27); *The Cambridge Ancient History*, vol. i-viii (1924-30), rev. ed. by I. E. S. Edwards, C. J. Gadd and N. G. L. Hammond (1961 et seq.); M. Rostovtzeff, *A History of the Ancient World*, vol. i, 2nd ed. (1930); G. Glotz and R. Cohen, *Histoire grecque*, vol. i-iv (1925-38), part of *L'Histoire générale*, ed. by G. Glotz; H. Bengtson, *Griechische Geschichte* (with full bibliography) (1950); N. G. L. Hammond, *A History of Greece to 322 B.C.* (1959); L. Whibley (ed.), *Companion to Greek Studies* (1951).

Inscriptions and coins: M. N. Tod, *Selection of Greek Historical Inscriptions*, vol. i-ii, 2nd ed. (1946-48); B. V. Head et al., *Historia numorum*, 2nd ed. (1911).

Postclassical and Byzantine Greece: R. von Scala, *Das Griechentum seit Alexander dem Grossen* (1919); G. Finlay, *History of Greece, From Its Conquest by the Romans to A.D. 1864*, ed. by H. F. Tozer (1877); A. Bon, *Le Péloponnèse byzantin jusqu'en 1204* (1951); W. Miller, *The Latins in the Levant: a History of Frankish Greece, 1204-1566* (1908); J. Longnon, *Essays on the Latin Orient* (1922); R. Grousset, *L'Empire du Levant* (1946); J. Longnon, *L'Empire latin de Constantinople et la principauté de Morée* (1949); K. M. Setton, *Catalan Domination of Athens, 1311-1388* (1948); D. A. Zakythinos, *Le Despotat grec*, 2 vol., new ed. (1953); D. M. Nicol, *The Despotate of Epiros* (1957); *The Cambridge Ancient History*, vol. ix-xii (1932-39).

Modern Greece: For the period from the fall of Constantinople to the War of Independence the principal studies are in Greek. See however W. Miller, *The Turkish Restoration in Greece, 1718-1797* (1921). For 19th and 20th centuries see J. N. Mavrogordato, *Modern Greece: a Chronicle and a Survey, 1800-1931* (1931); W. Miller, *A History of the Greek People (1821-1921)* (1923), *The Ottoman Empire and Its Successors, 1801-1927*, new ed. (1936); E. S. Forster, *A Short History of Modern Greece, 1821-1956*, 3rd ed. (1958). On special aspects see E. Driault and M. Lhéritier, *Histoire diplomatique de la Grèce de 1821 à nos jours*, 5 vol. (1925-26); A. J. Toynbee, *The Western Question in Greece and Turkey*, 2nd ed. (1922); D. J. Cassavetti, *Hellas and the Balkan Wars* (1914); A. A. Pallis, *Greece's Anatolian Venture—and After* (1937); *Greek Miscellany* (1964); E. G. Mears, *Greece To-day* (1929); B. Sweet-Escott, *Greece: a Political and Economic Survey, 1939-1953* (1954); A. Papagos, *The Battle of Greece*, Eng. trans. (1949); C. M. Woodhouse, *Apple of Discord* (1948), *The Story of Modern Greece* (1968); F. A. Voight, *The Greek Sedition* (1949); Sir R. W. A. Leeper, *When Greek Meets Greek* (1950); E. C. W. Myers, *Greek Entanglement* (1955).

The Economy: A. D. Sissmanides, *Greek Tobacco* (1944); H.M.S.O., *Overseas Economic Surveys: Greece* (1956); *Greece: Economic Conditions, 1959* (1960); W. H. McNeill, *Greece: American Aid in Action, 1947-56* (1957); C. A. Munkman, *American Aid to Greece* (1958); General Statistical Service of Greece, *Statistical Yearbook of Greece*; Center of Planning and Economic Research (Athens), *Draft of the Five-Year Economic Development Plan for Greece, 1966-1970* (1965); Current history and statistics are summarized annually in *Britannica Book of the Year*.

GREECE, ORTHODOX CHURCH OF, the established church of Greece and one of the most important autocephalous branches of the Orthodox Eastern Church (q.v.). During the Byzantine empire and the subsequent occupation of the country by the Turks, the church in Greece was under the administration of the ecumenical patriarch of Constantinople. After the War of Independence (1821–28) Ioannis Kapodistrias, governor of the new state, opened negotiations with the patriarch for the independence of the Greek church but the final decision was taken during the minority of the new king of Greece, Otto I, a Bavarian Roman Catholic, through his Protestant regent G. L. Maurer who, fearing that the Turkish government might still be able to influence Greek politics through the ecumenical patriarchate, declared the Greek church autocephalous in 1833. The church received a constitution modeled on the German Protestant system and was placed under strict state control with a royal procurator attending all its synods. The ecumenical patriarch recognized the independence of the Greek church in 1850. Its constitution, amended in 1852, has remained unaltered except for two years when the church was free from state control (1923–25).

The supreme authority of the church is vested in the synod of all the bishops under the presidency of the archbishop of Athens and all Greece. A second synod, under the same presidency, consists of 12 bishops, each serving for one year only. The former deals with general church questions, the latter with details of administration. A bishop is appointed to his see by the smaller synod, which elects him from a list prepared by the larger synod and approved by the minister of education. After being consecrated by the smaller synod, he is responsible to both synods for the administration of his diocese. Bishops and the parish priests in larger towns are generally theological graduates of the universities of Athens or Salonika. Priests in smaller towns have usually studied theology for two years at higher seminaries after leaving high school, while village priests have normally received two years' ecclesiastical training without attending high school. Bishops are paid by a church fund and priests by the state. Many lay theological graduates, both men and women, become teachers of religion, which is taught compulsorily in the state schools. In every parish there is a women's welfare committee that cares for the needy, and deaconesses assist parish priests in social work. The Apostolike Diakonia (the official organization of the inner mission of the church) publishes religious, theological and liturgical books as well as church periodicals such as *Ecclesia, Theologia* and *Phone Kyriou*. It also runs the Sunday schools. There are several religious or church organizations of which the largest, Zoï ("Life"), is of a pietistic character. Within Greece itself the chief centres of monasticism are Mt. Athos and Patmos but few young men now feel drawn to this vocation. Nunneries are more flourishing. The church has been a member of the World Council of Churches from the beginning and has friendly relations with the Anglican, Old Catholic and eastern Monophysite Churches. (H. S. AL.)

GREEK ARCHAEOLOGY: see ARCHAEOLOGY; GREECE: *Archaeology;* ATHENS; AEGEAN CIVILIZATION; CRETE.

GREEK ARCHITECTURE, in this article, refers to the architecture of Greece from approximately 1100 B.C. to A.D. 300. The historic periods, conventionally known as Greek, during and after the dark ages of invasions, displaced populations and colonization, through the Greco-Roman period, will be covered here. The earliest prehistoric phase of Greek civilization in the later part of the Aegean period continued the earlier non-Greek phase and therefore will not be discussed (*see* PRE-HELLENIC ARCHITECTURE). Furthermore, only the historical evolution of Greek architecture as a whole will be traced; for the analysis of the orders *see* ORDER.

To the Greeks fell the role of inventing the grammar of conventional forms on which all subsequent European architecture was based. The materials at their disposal, wood and stone as well as mud, induced them to adopt a post-and-lintel system, as in Egypt, instead of massive walls and vaults, as in Mesopotamia. However, for molding their supports they chose conventional rather than naturalistic forms, therein resembling their Aegean predecessors; particularly Greek was the patient genius with which they perfected every element, rarely deviating from the forward path to invent new forms or new solutions of old problems. This conservative adherence to older types led to such masterpieces as the Parthenon

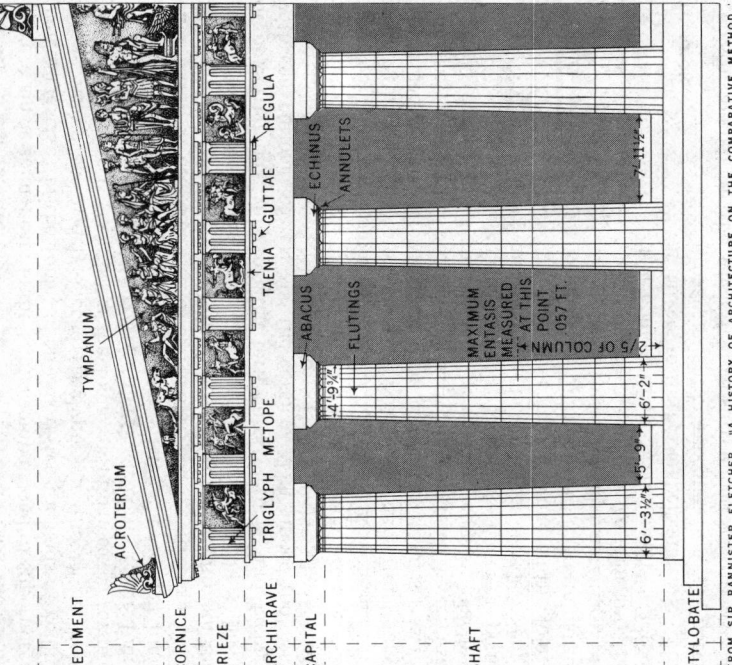

PEDIMENT
TYMPANUM
ACROTERIUM
CORNICE
FRIEZE
ARCHITRAVE
CAPITAL
SHAFT
STYLOBATE
ABACUS
ECHINUS
ANNULETS
FLUTINGS
TRIGLYPH
METOPE
TAENIA
GUTTAE
REGULA
MAXIMUM ENTASIS MEASURED AT THIS POINT .057 FT.
2/5 OF COLUMN
4'-9½"
6'-3¾"
5'-9"
6'-2"
7'-11½"

FROM SIR BANNISTER FLETCHER, "A HISTORY OF ARCHITECTURE ON THE COMPARATIVE METHOD." THE ATHLONE PRESS OF THE UNIVERSITY OF LONDON

FIG. 1.—NOMENCLATURE OF THE ORDER IN GREEK ARCHITECTURE, AS EXEMPLIFIED IN THE PARTHENON

(*q.v.*) and Erechtheum (*q.v.*).

Primitive Period (1100–600 B.C.).—While Greek domestic architecture began with the Dorian invasion, monumental religious architecture first appeared in the 9th century. Mere open areas with altars (Aegina, Sparta, Ephesus) no longer sufficed when gods were represented in large images, requiring special temples. The houses of men furnished the patterns: from the circular nomadic hut developed the horseshoe or apsidal plan (Eretria, Gonnoi), the oblong plan with curved walls (Thermon) and eventually the normal straight-sided oblong, the axis running east and west and the entrance always at one end. A porch (pronaos) might be added in front, a sanctuary (adytum) at the rear, repeating the Mycenaean megaron plan. Walls were of mud brick resting on stone socles, their free ends (antae and door jambs) encased in wooden sheathing. Simultaneously the roof developed from the nomadic thatched beehive, through the long ogival mud-brick vault (thatched in a model from Perachora), to the sloping hipped roof with wooden rafters, supported by girders resting on the side walls, and so, eventually, to gables.

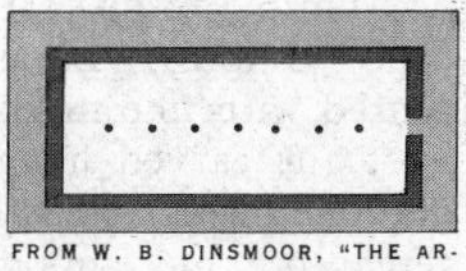

In wider temples these cross girders had to be reinforced by columns placed in single file along the main axis (Selinus, Prinias, Locri, Sparta, Neandria, Samos). Thus came into Greek architecture the characteristic post-and-lintel system. At first mere wooden posts, these internal supports were gradually molded, on opposite sides of the Aegean sea, into two different types, proto-Doric and proto-Ionic. The former, with its circular molded capital and square abacus, was copied in wood from such surviving Aegean works as the Lion gate at Mycenae. The proto-Ionic type, originated as an elongated capital, early transformed into stone; slender unfluted shafts (sometimes with special bases) were capped by garlands of drooping leaves from which sprang vertical volutes (Lesbos, Neandria, Larisa).

In an open pronaos, a central column repeated the axial colonnade (Locri, Prinias); next, because central columns obscured the cult image, the axis was opened by using two internal colonnades and so two columns *in antis* on the front. Thus the column first

FROM W. B. DINSMOOR, "THE ARCHITECTURE OF ANCIENT GREECE" (BATSFORD)

FIG. 2.—TEMPLE AT NEANDRIA

appeared on the exterior and introduced a new problem, the creation of an entablature. The transverse girder formed the architrave, a single solid beam in the Doric, compounded of superposed planks (fasciae) in the Ionic; upon this rested the ends of ceiling beams, heavy and widely spaced (triglyphs) in the Doric, light and closely spaced (dentils) in the Ionic. Mutular eaves formed by overhanging rafters characterized the Doric cornice; the Ionic was merely hollowed to shed rain water. The light wooden Ionic entablature is best known through imitations in native rock-cut tombs of Asia Minor; the Doric forms are revealed through the survival of terra cottas which protected the bulky timbers, black or blue triglyphs, gaily painted terra-cotta metopes and facings with conventional patterns on the cornice. The hipped roof was still retained in the earlier temple of Hera on the Silaris (near Paestum). The ridge of the hipped roof was soon prolonged to the front, forming a gable (pediment), the rear end sometimes remaining hipped (Thermon, model at Sparta). The gutter (sima) which had hitherto crowned the cornice on all four sides was retained even under the pediment in the western colonies (Syracuse, Geloan treasury at Olympia); but the mutules, equally anachronistic symbols of rafters under a pediment, remained even on the façade. Semicircular terra-cotta tiles covered the joints between the concave pantiles, terminating at the eaves in semicircular antefixes.

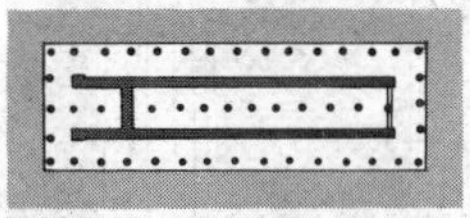

FROM W. B. DINSMOOR, "THE ARCHITECTURE OF ANCIENT GREECE" (BATSFORD)

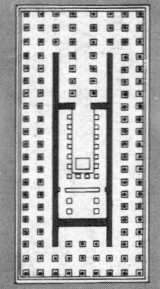

FIG. 3.—TEMPLE AT THERMON

The emergence of the column and the development of the orders inspired Dorian architects to further embellishments. The pronaos might be repeated in a rear porch (opisthodomus), or the whole temple surrounded by a peristyle. From the five lines of the flank walls and the axial and flank colonnades resulted pentastyle façades (Thermon); two internal colonnades required hexastyle façades (Heraeum at Olympia); the flanks were long in proportion, with 15 or 16 columns.

Archaic Period (600–500 B.C.).—The newly rich western colonies transformed the peripteral temple into limestone; the Ionian east soon followed with the greater splendour of marble. But the motherland of Greece remained conservative; during eight centuries the wooden columns of the Olympian Heraeum were gradually replaced in stone; as late as 513 B.C. marble was limited to one ostentatious temple façade (Delphi). Limestone, however, was coated with fine marble stucco; sandstone was often used in the west for carved members; terra-cotta cornice revetments were gradually eliminated and the terra-cotta gutters and even roof tiles replaced in more important temples by stone or marble.

FROM W. B. DINSMOOR, "THE ARCHITECTURE OF ANCIENT GREECE" (BATSFORD)

FIG. 4.—TEMPLE AT RHAMNUS

A few primitive types of plans survived, either apsidal (Delphi, Athens, Corinth, Olympia) or with axial colonnades (Olympia, Delos, Paestum, Metapontum). The simple diastyle *in-antis* plan long prevailed in Greece; the "hundred-foot" temple on the Athenian Acropolis was apparently tristyle *in antis* at both ends. But the most favoured temple plan was the hexastyle peripteral, sometimes (in Sicily) with the façade doubled for greater magnificence. The opisthodomus (rear porch) was customary in Greece, the closed adytum (secret chamber) in the west; the interior of the cella might have two rows of columns (in Greece) or none at all (in Sicily). The east outdid the west by doubling the colonnade on all sides, giving the octastyle dipteral plan (Ephesus, Samos, Magnesia), imitated also at Athens (Olympieum); at Corcyra and Selinus ("GT") the inner lines of columns were omitted, becoming pseudodipteral; at Acragas (Olympieum), while retaining the same vast total dimensions as at Selinus, the number of columns was reduced and the scale thereby so enlarged that the intervals were filled with walls, becoming pseudoperipteral. Colossal dimensions, with stylobates up to 180 by 365 ft., column diameters up to $13\frac{1}{4}$ ft. (Acragas), column spacings up to $28\frac{3}{4}$ ft. (Ephesus), gave opportunities for lavish display. The entrance was usually to the east (orientation) but in Asia Minor sometimes to the west.

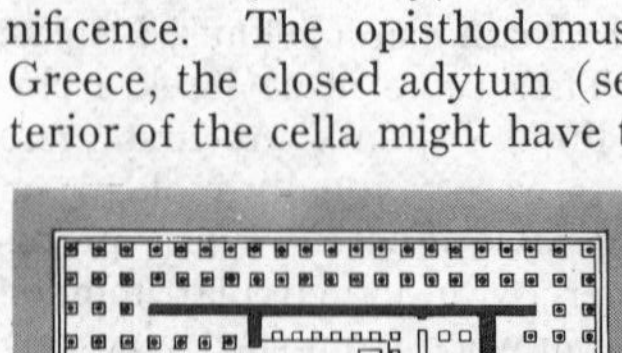

FROM W. B. DINSMOOR, "THE ARCHITECTURE OF ANCIENT GREECE" (BATSFORD)

FIG. 5.—TEMPLE AT EPHESUS (RESTORED)

The geographical cleavage between the styles continued. The western temples at Syracuse, Selinus, Acragas, Paestum, Pompeii, Tarentum, Metapontum and Corcyra, and those in Greece at Athens, Delphi, Eretria and Corinth, all were Doric. In the east, Naucratis, Ephesus, Samos, Naxos, Paros, Chios, Miletus and Magnesia furnish important landmarks of the archaic Ionic development. The Doric temple invaded the east, at Assos, suffering the intrusion of the Ionic frieze; reciprocally the Ionic temple penetrated the west, at Locri and Hipponium.

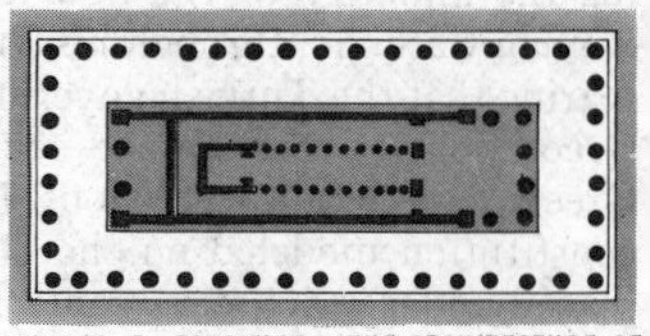

FROM W. B. DINSMOOR, "THE ARCHITECTURE OF ANCIENT GREECE" (BATSFORD)

FIG. 6.—TEMPLE "GT" AT SELINUS

In the Doric order the sudden change of material and timidity as to the strength of stone caused violent changes. Not only were column shafts often constructed as monoliths but proportions were at first extremely heavy, with intervals so close that the spreading capitals were nearly contiguous. With growing confidence, larger columns were eventually raised to 5 or even $5\frac{5}{8}$ diameters, with intervals up to $1\frac{2}{3}$ diameters. Spacings and diameters were often enlarged on the façades in Greece; uniform diameters but different spacings characterize most of the western peristyles. Triglyphs at first appeared only above columns, leaving horizontal oblong metopes between; interpolated triglyphs next reduced the metopes to vertical oblongs, which gradually approached squareness, the half mutules above the narrow metopes then becoming of full width. Relief sculpture succeeded painting in the metopes and pediments, changing in the latter to free statues; human and animal forms replaced the semicircular acroteria, and the antefixes changed from semicircles to prismatic forms, surmounted by palmettes.

The Ionic column, carrying a lighter entablature and longer habituated to stone, was more slender from the very beginning (about 8 diameters), with greater intervals ($1\frac{1}{2}$ to $2\frac{1}{3}$ diameters); particularly noteworthy were the enormous intervals at the centres of the façades. Though the entablature was friezeless, broad bands of relief sculpture were inserted wherever possible, as on the sima at Ephesus. But in Greece a new type of Ionic entablature was created to vie with Doric proportions; the fasciae of the architrave were suppressed, the dentils omitted and a high frieze inserted between architrave and cornice (Ionic treasuries at Delphi).

FROM W. B. DINSMOOR, "THE ARCHITECTURE OF ANCIENT GREECE" (BATSFORD)

FIG. 7.—OLYMPIEUM AT ACRAGAS

Both orders were awkward at the corners of peristyles. In the Doric, the difficulty lay in reconciling triglyph and column spacings, while bringing a triglyph out to the corner of the entablature; in the west it was met by widening the angle triglyph and the adjacent metope, in Greece by contracting the end columnar interval; finally, metope expansion was combined with column contraction. In the Ionic, the bracket capital seemed incapable of turning the corner, until at Ephesus was devised an awkward L-shaped capital with an angle volute.

Other forms displaying the versatility of the archaic designers were the hybrid Doric-Ionic capitals of Amyclae, the bell capitals of Delphi and the use of human figures as supports, both male (atlantes of Acragas) and female (caryatids of Delphi). Other types of buildings yielded new opportunities—simple templelike treasuries (Olympia, Delphi), the square hypostyle hall (telesterion) at Eleusis, the archaic circular tholos at Delphi, the apsidal senate house at Olympia, altars as at Miletus and Delphi, the throne at Amyclae and elaborate fountains of the tyrants (Athens, Megara, Corinth, Samos). In minor works like votive columns and grave monuments migratory architects mingled styles.

PLATE I

GREEK ARCHITECTURE

DORIC TEMPLES

Paestum, the so-called temple of Poseidon (c. 460 B.C.), one of the best preserved of Greek temples, seen from the southeast. Its heavy transitional proportions are relieved by numerous flutes

Athens, Hephaesteum (c. 450–440 B.C.), also called the Theseum; another well-preserved temple. It is surrounded by 34 columns and is 104 ft. in length

Delphi, hall of the Athenians, showing in the background columns of the temple of Apollo (4th century B.C.), re-erected in their original positions

A view of the south passage of the so-called temple of Concord (5th century B.C.) at Acragas (Akragas; mod. Agrigento, Sicily)

Olympia, temple of Zeus (5th century B.C.); Libon of Elis, architect. East front (restored), showing heavy proportions, as at Paestum, the effect being relieved by pediment sculpture (the shields are Roman additions). Overthrown by earthquakes, little now exists above the platform level

BY COURTESY OF (BOTTOM LEFT) B. T. BATSFORD FROM DINSMOOR, "THE ARCHITECTURE OF ANCIENT GREECE"; PHOTOGRAPHS, (ALL OTHERS) HIRMER—PUBLIX

PLATE VI

GREEK ARCHITECTURE

GREEK THEATRES

Theatre at Epidaurus (c. 340 B.C.); Polyclitus the Younger, architect. View showing the circular orchestra, 66½ ft. in diameter, with the foundation for the central altar, the surrounding auditorium, occupying three-fifths of the circumference, and the left entrance to the orchestra. The scene building, of which only the foundations remain, is of later construction

Theatre of Dionysus at Athens, on the south slope of the Acropolis, dating from the beginning of the 5th century B.C. View showing the circular orchestra and the marble thrones (on right) forming the lowest tier and the ordinary lime-stone seats rising behind

PHOTOGRAPHS, (TOP) EWING GALLOWAY, (CENTRE, BOTTOM) ALINARI

Theatre at Taormina, Sicily (4th century B.C.). View of the stage and its adjacent buildings, with Mt Etna and the rugged outlines of the coast in the background

Transitional Period (500–450 B.C.).—The grammar of forms and the types of buildings having been largely determined, the next step was that of refinement. The problem was all the more concentrated because the political subjection of the east to Persia now restricted architectural initiative to the Doric style of Greece and the west, which received fresh impetus from victories over Persia and Carthage. And in particular at Athens discovery of copious marble quarries contributed to the refinement of design.

Freedom was now abandoned in favour of strict canonization, resulting almost in monotony. Hexastyle peripteral Doric temples became universal: in Greece at Sunium, Athens (the unfinished older Parthenon), Aegina and Olympia; in the west at Syracuse, Himera, Gela, Caulonia, Acragas, Croton and Paestum. Work was continued on the never-finished colossi at Selinus and Acragas, with distinct changes of details. In the west, columns tended to be of uniform diameter and (except at Himera and Paestum) uniformly spaced on front and flank, apart from the contracted end intervals; and there appeared an innovation, double contraction at the corners. But in Greece some emphasis of the front, either with heavier columns or with wider spacing, was still prevalent; or the corner columns alone might be enlarged. The west adopted the opisthodomus of Greece, sometimes in addition to the adytum; but cella colonnades appeared in the west only at Paestum, apart from the huge octastyle at Selinus. Such internal colonnades were two (at Selinus three) stories in height, separated by architraves and carrying only ceiling and roof; the few known galleries (Aegina, Olympia) were later insertions; and stone staircases (Selinus, Himera, Paestum) ascended merely to storerooms above the ceilings. In this period the Ionic temple first appeared in Greece (Sunium), with the peristyle strangely confined to one front and one flank, and with the typical mainland form of entablature without fasciae or dentils. A larger but unfinished Ionic temple was begun at Delos.

Among other types of buildings, additional treasuries at Olympia, the reconstructed oblong telesterion at Eleusis and the similar Cnidian lesche (clubhouse) at Delphi, the old Propylon of the Athenian Acropolis, the colonnade of the Athenians at Delphi, the royal and painted stoas and the tholos at Athens, the Athenian theatre orchestra with wooden scene buildings and the imitation of the oriental gridiron city plan at Miletus, all paved the way for the masterpieces of the following period.

The Culmination at Athens (450–400 B.C.).—The middle period of the evolution centred at Athens, which signed peace with Persia in 449 B.C., and in the absence of military requirements was free to use the wealth of the Athenian confederacy in rebuilding the temples ruined by the Persians. Under the personal initiative of Pericles, and in the hands of architects like Ictinus, Callicrates and Mnesicles, and the sculptors Phidias and Callimachus, Greek architecture reached its zenith.

The Doric style of Greece naturally retained the leading place, and was employed not only in hexastyle temples at Bassae, Rhamnus, Sunium and Athens (Hephaesteum and temple of Ares) but also in the octastyle Parthenon on the Acropolis; besides these erected by Athenian architects, hexastyles are found near Argos (Heraeum), at Acragas (temple of Concord), Segesta and Delos (the last prostyle). Most of those structures were comparatively small, owing their effect to perfection of design and execution, and, in the case of those in Attica, to the beauty of marble and more slender proportions. Only Bassae retained the older system with heavier columns on the main façade and reduced spacing on both flanks; elsewhere uniformity prevailed, except at the corners. Cella colonnades were omitted except in the works of Ictinus, also in the Hephaesteum and at the Argive Heraeum; Ictinus obtained a new effect by returning

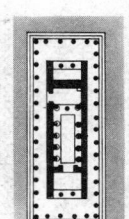

FROM BORRMANN, "GESCHICHTE DER BAUKUNST" (ALFRED KRÖNER VERLAG)

FIG. 8.—TEMPLE AT BASSAE

the colonnade across the back, at Bassae separating adytum from cella (the lateral columns being engaged to the flank walls), in the Parthenon forming an ambulatory around the statue. The false gallery with two stories of Doric columns appeared for the last times in the Parthenon, Hephaesteum and Argive Heraeum; a single Ionic order was preferred at Bassae (with three Corinthian capitals across the rear) and in the rear chamber of the Parthenon. The coalescence of the styles was marked by the inclusion of other Ionic elements, moldings and continuous friezes (Parthenon, Hephaesteum, Sunium). Sculptured reliefs in friezes and metopes, pediments filled with statues and crowned by great floral acroteria: these and the fine moldings and the marble ceilings enhanced by colour and gilding, broad masses of colour on triglyphs and in shadowed cornice soffits, further relieved the Doric simplicity.

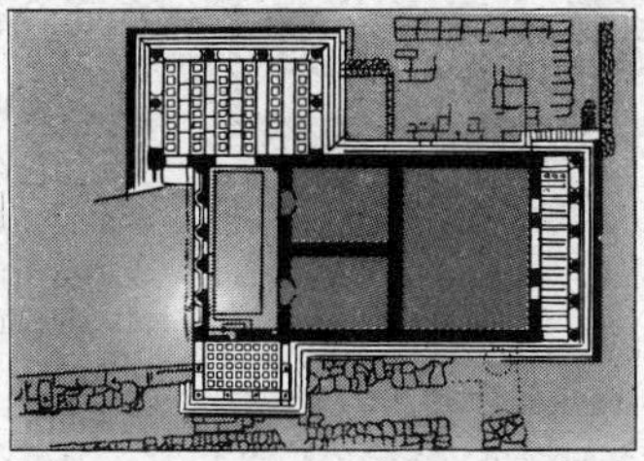

The Ionic style was also employed independently in three non-peripteral temples at Athens (on the Ilissus river, the Nike temple and Erechtheum on the Acropolis); its foothold in Greece was now assured. The amphiprostyle tetrastyle plan was preferred, though in the Erechtheum (q.v.) the rising ground at the east so elevated the stylobate that in the final plan six columns were required in the width; and the tetrastyle portico originally planned for the west end was revolved to the north flank to respect the sacred olive tree, balanced by the miniature caryatid portico on the south, and replaced on the west by a sham portico of engaged columns, producing an irregular T-shaped plan. Rampant antefixes above the sima of the Erechtheum, and its elaborately carved moldings, exceptional in the 5th century, foreshadowed the elaboration of the following period.

Another symptom of change was the creation of a third style, the Corinthian, first appearing inside the temple at Bassae. Like the Ionic capitals in the same colonnade, the Corinthian capitals represent an attempt to invent a form symmetrical on all sides, the bell capitals of Delphi being further elaborated with acanthus leaves, scrolls and palmettes.

Among buildings other than temples, the Propylaea (q.v.) at Athens take first rank in brilliance of conception. A cruciform plan 224 ft. in length (about equal to the Parthenon) would have formed a frontispiece across the west end of the Acropolis, with wings projecting westward to enframe the ascent; by war and priestly conservatism the design was curtailed until it resembled a lopsided T, only 154 ft. in length. The central building, with its Doric hexastyles and pediments dominating the north and south arms and west wings (without columns except on the return faces of the wings), formed the entrance, the central intercolumniation widened 6 ft. to allow the passage of festal processions, and the five doorways graded in width like the intercolumniations, with heights varying in proportion. The west ceiling was supported by six Ionic columns in immediate juxtaposition with the Doric. Hardly less notable were the redesigned telesterion at Eleusis, a great square at first with seven rows each of seven columns within, then with four rows of five (these two projects never completed), and finally with six rows each of seven, and the odeum at Athens with internal columns arranged in nine rows of nine; both had clerestory lanterns above the roofs. Corresponding advances in city planning were the importation of the gridiron system to Greece (Piraeus) and the west (Thurii).

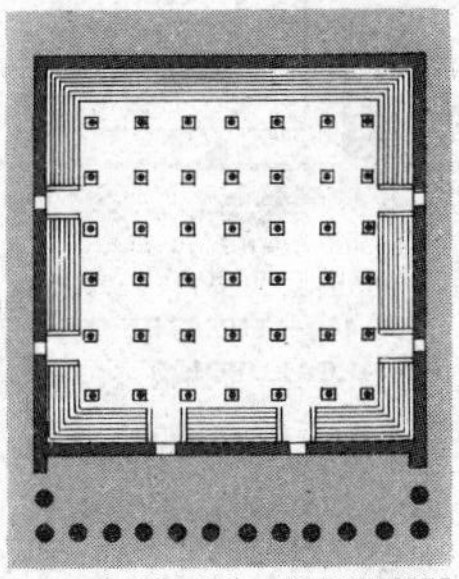

In these buildings, beauty of proportion was enhanced by "optical refinements," almost a speciality of the culmination. The curve of the platform, rising $\frac{3}{4}$ to $4\frac{3}{8}$ in. in a circular arc with a radius as great as $3\frac{1}{2}$ mi., gave vitality and corrected any sagging illusion in the colonnade. The entasis or swelling outline of the column shaft, preventing any sensation of concavity, attained its maximum ($\frac{1}{4}$ to $\frac{3}{4}$ in.) at half of the height, though in earlier and later periods it was much more pronounced. The inward inclination of the column axes (from $\frac{3}{8}$ to $3\frac{3}{8}$ in.) gave a pyramidal illusion of greater stability, the axes of the flank colonnades of the

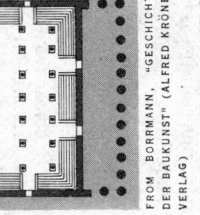

FROM BORRMANN, "GESCHICHTE DER BAUKUNST" (ALFRED KRÖNER VERLAG)

FIG. 10.—TELESTERION AT ELEUSIS

FIG. 9.—ERECHTHEUM, DRAWN BY GORHAM P. STEVENS

Parthenon meeting more than a mile above the pavement; walls, antae and other supposedly vertical surfaces might show similar inclinations. And the manner in which the various members were adjusted to each other, preserving these delicate relations and yet keeping the joints invisible, represents a triumph of calculation and stonecutting.

Fourth Century (400-300 B.C.).—The displacement of the political centre from Athens successively to Sparta, Thebes, Macedonia and Asia Minor was accompanied by unmistakable evidence of a decline from aesthetic perfection. The service of the gods began to be subordinated to that of men, and from the temple attention was diverted to a great variety of structures corresponding to the varied requirements of a more complex civilization. Even in religious architecture the striving for diversity and innovation is manifest in the increase of excessive ornament.

In Greece the Doric style was still preferred for temples, but, incapable of further perfection, was now modified. Hexastyle plans (Delphi, Epidaurus, Tegea, Nemea, Stratos, Ptoon and Olympia) were often shortened by omitting the opisthodomus; temples at Delphi and Epidaurus were hexastyle prostyle. Columns were more slender ($5\frac{5}{8}$ to $6\frac{3}{4}$ diameters) and entablatures correspondingly lower (one-quarter of the column height), the reduction occurring in architrave and cornice while the frieze remained high to preserve the squareness of metopes. The enrichment of the sima by carved rinceaus and rampant antefixes was counterbalanced by the loss of such delicacies as the hyperbolic echinus profile. Following the example of Bassae, Corinthian internal columns were employed at Tegea, Stratos and Nemea, Ionic at Epidaurus; an inner row of Ionic columns lined a Doric façade at Delphi.

More important was the Ionic Renaissance in Asia Minor. Not only hexastyle plans as at Priene but colossal octastyles again became the fashion, at Ephesus repeating the archaic plan, at Sardis omitting the inner flank colonnades and becoming semipseudo-dipteral. Even the decastyle plan with 120 external columns appeared at Didyma near Miletus, with the cella unroofed (hypaethral). Column proportions continued to be slender, though because of the enormous dimensions the intervals were contracted; some façades (Sardis, Ephesus) show, however, enormous central spacings. Such abnormal embellishments as sculptured pedestals, bases, drums and capitals were confined to the larger temples. The entablature always lacks the frieze (except at Didyma where the work was protracted into Roman times). Only in Greece (tholos at Olympia) or in nonreligious and hence less conservative Asiatic structures, executed with collaborators from Greece (mausoleum at Halicarnassus), did the frieze penetrate the entablature, now always in combination with dentils.

Important buildings other than temples were erected in both styles. In the Doric, treasuries at Delphi, choragic monuments at Athens, tholoi at Delphi and Epidaurus, the huge dodecastyle façade of the telesterion at Eleusis and the analogous assembly hall (Thersilion) at Megalopolis, porticoes up to 550 ft. in length as at Corinth, the arsenal of 430 ft. at the Piraeus, the Lion tomb at Cnidus (another Doric intrusion in the east), all testify to the vitality of the style. The tholos was reproduced in the Ionic style at Olympia; monumental Ionic tombs in Asia Minor, the Nereid monument at Xanthus (a temple raised on a lofty pedestal) and the mausoleum at Halicarnassus (with a pyramid in turn elevated above a peristyle of 36 columns, attaining a height of 136 ft.), have remained unsurpassed in their field. The Corinthian capital was developed as a secondary feature inside temples at Tegea, Nemea, Stratos and Didyma, inside tholoi at Delphi, Epidaurus and Olympia; but not until 334 B.C. was the style used independently and externally in a choragic monument at Athens, with an entablature devised by combining Attic frieze with Asiatic dentils.

A few noncolumnar designs require special mention. The Attic tomb stele with its ever deepening frame of miniature antae and entablature, or with an elaborate floral acroterion, became extinct as the century ended. But the theatre, now provided with a stone auditorium encircling more than half of the orchestra (Athens, Epidaurus, Eretria), its one-storied scene building (also in stone) containing several great openings and flanked by projecting pavilions (parascenia) and sometimes faced by removable wooden proscenium porticoes, was yet in its infancy. The stadium, either round-ended or rectangular, repeated the theatre form. The market place (agora) became, if not strictly rectangular, at least more formal; and the newly founded or rebuilt cities of the period followed the gridiron plan.

Hellenistic Period (300-100 B.C.).—The even balance between east and west which had characterized the preceding century was overthrown by the transference of the political centres to the oriental kingdoms of Alexander's successors, resulting in the domination of the oriental elements in Greek architecture. The Doric style, now on the downward path, appeared chiefly in small temples, either *in antis* (Selinus, Acragas, Taormina) or prostyle (Pergamum, Lycosura, Samothrace, Gortyna, Oropos); belated peripteral hexastyles occurred at Troy, Pergamum, Cos, Delos and Lebadea—the last symbolic, the abandoned plan of an eastern monarch (174 B.C.). A proposal to erect a Doric temple of Dionysus was actually countermanded in favour of the Ionic style; architects frankly wrote that "sacred buildings ought not to be constructed of the Doric order" because of the difficulty of spacing triglyphs and columns. The few who adhered to the style sought new methods of appeal: engaged columns, lighter proportions with slender columns and thin entablatures requiring the interpolation of extra triglyphs; columns with Ionic fluting or even bases. Wall surfaces were modeled, with emphasized joints and belt courses. The cella might even have an internal apse (Lebadea, Samothrace), or projecting aisles at the sides (Lusoi).

The Ionic style, now the successor rather than rival of the Doric, is best exemplified in three beautiful pseudodipteral octastyles (Messa, Sminthéum, Magnesia); less successful are smaller examples at Teos, Magnesia and Pergamum. Bases changed from the Asiatic to the Attic form, with plinths; capitals contracted in length; the rising echinus eliminated the downward droop of the cushion, and rinceaus filled the cushion and baluster. The entablature included the Attic frieze, and the dentils became small and meaningless, being used as decoration even in the raking cornice. These forms, and this moment of the Ionic supremacy, are reflected in the volume wherein Vitruvius interpreted Greek architecture to the Romans, using the Ionic as the typical order.

Now, however, the Ionic supremacy began to be threatened by the Corinthian style, best exemplified at Diocaesarea and in the dipteral octastyle Olympieum at Athens (174 B.C.). Its merits were most obvious in peristyles, the capital being symmetrical on all sides and the entablature unhampered by triglyphs; but its popularity extended even to distyle porches (Messene).

Even more important than temples were other types of buildings. Monumental sacrificial altars rose at Syracuse (74 by 653 ft.), Pergamum (the "Seat of Satan,"

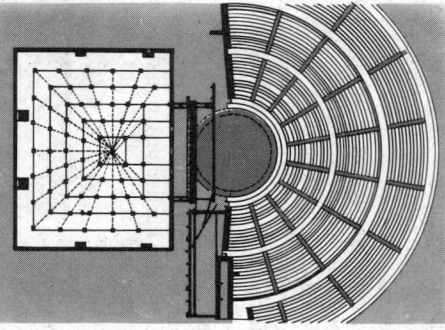

FIG. 11.—THEATRE AND THERSILION AT MEGALOPOLIS
FROM BORRMANN, "GESCHICHTE DER BAUKUNST" (ALFRED KRÖNER VERLAG)

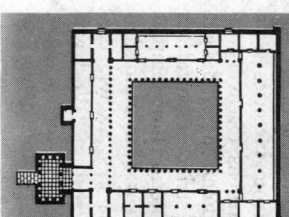

FIG. 12.—GYMNASIUM AT EPIDAURUS
FROM BORRMANN, "GESCHICHTE DER BAUKUNST" (ALFRED KRÖNER VERLAG)

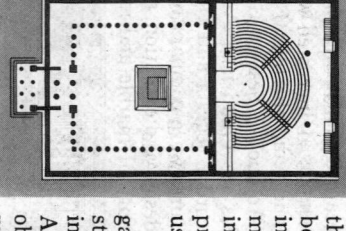

FROM BORRMANN, "GESCHICHTE DER BAUKUNST" (ALFRED KRÖNER VERLAG)
FIG. 13.—BOULEUTERION AT MILETUS

112 by 120 ft.), Priene and Magnesia. Doric porticoes surrounding the temple precincts (Ephesus, Priene, Magnesia); vast stoas built by Hellenistic kings for the cities of Asia (Pergamum, Assos, Priene) and Greece (Delos, Delphi, Athens, Megalopolis, Olympia), or, with slight modifications, used as market halls (Aegae, Alinda, Assos) and libraries (Pergamum); monumental propylaea (Samothrace, Delos, Lindos, Epidaurus, Olympia and Selinus); the tholos at Samothrace; the hypostyle hall at Delos; and gymnasiums (Epidaurus, Priene): all repeated earlier forms with slight variation. The long "Hall of the Bulls" at Delos surmounted at one end by a tower, the soaring lighthouse of 400 ft. at Alexandria and small senate houses with semicircular or rectangular auditoriums imitated from the theatre (Miletus, Priene) were innovations. The theatre itself received a colonnaded stone proscenium before the scene building, of which the great openings were elevated to an upper story (Oropos, Epidaurus, Priene, Ephesus). Commemorative monuments were more lofty, high pedestals (Delphi, Athens) or pairs of columns supporting entablatures (Delphi), forerunners of the Roman triumphal arch. Private houses changed from the megaron type to the peristyle court (Priene, Delos), and in their likeness were designed great hotels with central courts (Epidaurus, Olympia). The market place became a formally enclosed rectangle (Magnesia) rather than a picturesque group of colonnades and public buildings. The roads outside the city gates were lined with an ever increasing variety of sepulchral monuments, including the mausoleum type (Acragas, Mylasa) and tumuli with vaulted chambers (Pergamum).

The conquest of the orient had brought Greece into contact with the arch and vault, now freely used in supporting great masses over openings, as in city gates, retaining walls, corridors, staircases and sepulchral chambers. Sloping or intersecting barrel vaults were not uncommon. The post-and-lintel system was by no means supplanted, but the vaulting system of the orient was being perfected, ready for the Romans to assimilate with their Etruscan traditions. (See ROMAN ARCHITECTURE.)

Greco-Roman Period (100 B.C.–A.D. 300).—Many of the buildings erected in Greek lands during the Roman domination were still characteristically Greek. Doric was used in propylaea at Athens and Eleusis and in temples at Eleusis and Kourno. Greek Ionic appears in the circular temple on the Athenian Acropolis, in a propylon at Priene and particularly in a series of octastyle pseudodipteral temples in Asia Minor (Aezani, Ancyra, Aphrodisias). A hybrid Corinthian style with mixed Doric-Ionic entablatures occurs at Eleusis and Paestum. A simple type of Corinthian capital was used in the clock tower ("Tower of the Winds") at Athens. But the developed Corinthian orders of temples at Sagalassus, Euromus, Cnidus and Pergamum are hardly to be differentiated from those of imperial Rome.

Even though the decorative orders might be those of Rome, some buildings were still distinctive in type. Side by side with true Roman theatres, with wide, low stages and semicircular orchestras (Aspendus), were erected theatres of a compromise type, with equally wide but lofty stages and three-quarter circular orchestras (Termessus); both types had lofty scene buildings incrusted with columns, sometimes connecting with colonnades at the top of the auditorium. The stadium likewise remained characteristically Greek, with further elaboration, such as semicircles at both ends and colonnades at the top.

However, the basilicas, baths, triumphal arches and other forms which flourished everywhere in Greece and Asia Minor at this epoch can with more propriety be considered as part of the purely Roman development.

See ARCHITECTURE; BYZANTINE ART AND ARCHITECTURE; CAPITAL; GREEK ART; TEMPLE ARCHITECTURE; see also references under "Greek Architecture" in the Index.

BIBLIOGRAPHY.—General: Fowler and Wheeler, Handbook of Greek Archaeology (1909); A. Marquand, Greek Architecture (1909); J. Durm, Die Baukunst der Griechen, 3rd ed. (1910); F. Benoit, L'Architecture, Antiquité (1911); H. L. Warren, The Foundations of Classic Architecture (1919); D. S. Robertson, Handbook of Greek and Roman Architecture, 2nd ed. (1943); W. B. Dinsmoor, Architecture of Ancient Greece, 3rd ed. (1950); A. W. Lawrence, Greek Architecture (1957). Special: Stuart and Revett, The Antiquities of Athens, 5 vol. (1762–1830); Dilettanti Society, The Antiquities of Ionia, 5 vol. (1797–1915); A. Blouet, Expédition scientifique de Morée, 3 vol. (1831–38); L. Fenger, Dorische Polychromie (1886); F. C. Penrose, The Principles of Athenian Architecture, 2nd ed. (1888); Curtius and Adler, Olympia, Die Ergebnisse der Ausgrabungen, ii (1892–96); Dörpfeld and Reisch, Das griechische Theater (1896); Koldewey and Puchstein, Die griechischen Tempel in Unteritalien und Sicilien (1899); H. d'Espouy, Fragments d'architecture antique, 2 vol. (1896–1905) and Monuments antiques, i (1906); F. H. Bacon, Investigations at Assos (1902–21); W. H. Goodyear, Greek Refinements (1912); Stevens and Paton, The Erechtheum (1927).
(W. B. D.)

GREEK ART. After an introductory discussion of some general aspects of the study of Greek art, this article describes its development from about 900 to about 25 B.C.

I. INTRODUCTION

Greek art no doubt owed much indirectly to the Minoan-Mycenaean civilization (now known in its later stages to have been Greek), which disintegrated at the end of the 2nd millennium B.C., partly under the impact of a series of invasions from the Balkans. The period covered by the present article, however, begins about 900 B.C. with the kaleidoscopic rearrangement of invaders and earlier inhabitants into a new pattern, which was followed by a steady artistic development—continuing without interruption down to the conquest of Greece by Rome in 146 B.C. Even this diverted rather than interrupted the flow, and Greek artists continued to be predominant under the Roman empire and beyond that into the Byzantine. But after Greece had become a Roman province, Greek art fell increasingly under the patronage of Romans and was devoted either to expressing Roman ideals or to reproducing older works of art. It is therefore reasonable to regard the later years of the 1st century B.C., when the Roman empire was forming, as the later limit of the period.

1. Modern Classification.—Within this period it is convenient to distinguish five stages of development. Their names are modern and arbitrary, the divisions between them are not equally sharp and do not apply equally to all parts of the Greek world, but they serve as a general guide to successive trends.

The first is the geometric age (so-called from the rectilinear character of its art) from about 900 to about 800 B.C., when Greece was self-contained and contact with the outside world was rare.

The second, an orientalizing period, for about a century and a half from 800 B.C., is one of contact with the east, a contact which had been broken by the upheavals at the end of the 2nd millennium.

The third period, the archaic, from about 650 to about 480 B.C., is characterized by the gradual absorption of oriental elements and the rise and development of archaic Greek art.

The fourth period, from about 480 to about 330 B.C., is known as the classical; its beginning is marked by the rise of the sculptors Myron, Phidias and Polyclitus and the painter Polygnotus and its end by the work of Scopas, Praxiteles and Lysippus. (The word "classical," which originally meant simply "first-class," can also be used either in a narrower sense than this to denote only the Phidian age, i.e., 50 years in the middle of the 5th century B.C., or in a broader sense to cover the whole of post-Mycenaean Greek art from geometric to late Roman.)

The fifth period is the Hellenistic, from about 330 B.C., when the conquests of Alexander the Great opened new areas to the Greeks and the division of his kingdom among his Greek successors after his death in 323 diffused Greek art over the greater part of the known world, down to the late 1st century B.C. Hellenistic symbolism and Hellenistic technical skill continued as living traditions under the Romans; their products are treated under ROMAN ART.

2. Scope and Materials.—Greek art expressed itself not only in sculptures and wall paintings commissioned for the great religious centres, especially Olympia and Delphi, but also in the humblest articles of everyday use. Among the Greeks themselves the highest prestige was attached to the cult images in temples and to the dedications in the form of statues or paintings set up to commemorate victories in war or athletics. The paintings on vases, now the main evidence for the development of Greek draftsmanship and of inestimable value today, are hardly mentioned by an-

cient writers and, although they were in great demand, were evidently not considered important works of art.

Statues were of limestone, marble, bronze, gold and terra cotta and wood. After the archaic period the use of limestone was rare, as was the use of terra cotta for statues of large size. Full-size statues of gold and ivory were rare at all times because of their cost; statues with gilded wooden bodies and marble extremities were sometimes made instead. For statuettes, ivory and amber, limestone, marble, wood, gold, silver, bronze and terra cotta were used; of these terra cotta was by far the most common, bronze and marble less so, and the rest rare. Extremely valuable because they can often be dated with accuracy are the sculptures used for the decoration of buildings. These commonly consisted of acroteria, i.e., figures on the tops or ends of gables; of figures in the low triangular field of the pediment under the gable (both of these are usually almost in the round); of sculptured panels (metopes) of the Doric frieze, which are usually in high or very high relief; and of the continuous Ionic frieze, which is usually in low relief.

Coins, and engraved gems used as signets, which produce an impression in relief, are also to be considered as relief sculpture; in these mediums, at certain periods and in certain places, Greek artists produced works which have never been excelled.

3. Destruction of Works of Art.—Of the many thousands of statues produced during the period in which Greek art flourished, not more than a few dozen survive, and those mostly mutilated. Knowledge of the history of Greek sculpture depends partly on these and partly on the architectural sculptures—both of high importance, since they are original. Much can also be learned about the general development of sculptural style from the small bronzes, often of very high quality, and from the terra cottas. Of the small bronzes many, and of the terra cottas very many, have survived, but they were made by independent artists and did not copy contemporary statues closely. The great bulk of evidence comes from copies made by Greeks, for Roman patrons, of originals now destroyed. Ancient methods of copying were not so perfect mechanically as are those used today, but these ancient copies were carved by craftsmen of great technical skill, working in a tradition which had not been interrupted since classical times. Although they apparently reproduce the main measurements of the originals with precision, they naturally vary in quality, and it is sometimes not easy to decide—the original having been destroyed—how accurate in style the copy is; thus, although they are an indispensable source of information, they should not be accepted uncritically. In accordance with Roman taste, the copies are usually of the classical rather than the archaic period; this is fortunate, since proportionately more archaic originals have survived.

With paintings the case is different. The materials of sculpture, mainly bronze and marble, are durable, and were it not that bronze has intrinsic value and that marble when burned produces lime, many more statues might have been preserved. But paintings on wall plaster, on wood, and even on marble panels, are essentially perishable, and all the great ancient paintings have in fact perished. Contemporary vase paintings—so long as vase painting continued—often depicted the same subjects and sometimes faintly reflected the style and composition of some of them, but they were in no sense accurate or even intended copies; while wall paintings of the Roman period, for instance those from Pompeii, vary so much one from another in their treatment of any one subject that it is hazardous to conjecture which version is likely to be closest to the earlier Greek painting on which they may be based. With the exception of the mosaic, found in Pompeii, of a painting of Alexander and the king of Persia in battle—evidently a direct copy of a painting of the 4th century B.C.—there is nothing in painting to correspond to the straightforward copies of Greek statues that were evidently so abundant under the Roman empire.

4. Ancient Writers on Art.—The second source of knowledge of the lost Greek statues and paintings is description and comment by ancient writers. There were contemporary Greek treatises on individual masterpieces and on the history of art in general, the most famous of the first kind being the so-called "Canon"

("standard") by Polyclitus (q.v.), written to explain his theory of proportions in sculpture, which he embodied in a statue bearing the same name.

These earlier treatises are lost, but Pliny the elder (q.v.), the Roman writer, included in his *Natural History* brief accounts of Greek sculpture, painting and metalwork, and he knew some of these earlier writings or summaries of them. Pliny's *Natural History* is an encyclopaedia compiled uncritically from many sources; its contents are sometimes obscure and even contradictory, but in default of anything better they are of great importance.

Of very different character is the work of Pausanias (q.v.), a Greek born in Lydia in the early 2nd century A.D. He wrote a *Description of Greece* in ten books, the fruit of his own travels in the country for about 14 years up to A.D. 176. It is a comprehensive guidebook by an industrious but unimaginative traveler, whose artistic judgment is of negligible value and whose chief preferences are for religious buildings and dedications rather than secular and for earlier works of art rather than later. Since his account is almost all at firsthand and since he had access to inscriptions and records (e.g., the priestly records at Olympia) that have since perished, the value of his work is evident.

Other ancient writers refer to or discuss works of art, and of these the satirist Lucian (q.v.), of the mid-2nd century A.D., is the most important; he had a sculptor's training and wrote with understanding, but the bulk of his writing was not concerned with art. Among the others Quintilian (q.v.), the Roman writer on the art of rhetoric, shows good sense on the rare occasions when he draws analogies from the plastic arts.

II. THE GEOMETRIC AGE (c. 900–c. 800 B.C.)

In the 9th century B.C. Greece was settling down again after upheavals and migrations both into and out of the mainland, the details of which are by no means clear. It seems that invaders from the north brought with them the germs of a style that developed into the Greek geometric.

Greek geometric art was distinguished by its angularity. One of its most striking products was its fine pottery, with patterns painted in a lustrous black slip, the secret of which had been handed down from Mycenaean times through a phase known as protogeometric. Even these handsome pots, many of them several feet high (the larger ones were often used as monuments on graves), have an angularity of outline which accords well with the rectilinear character of the decoration upon them. The surface is completely covered with a network of fine patterns in which meander (key pattern), checker, triangle, herringbone and swastika are prominent. The decoration at first was abstract, but geometrized, being given angular silhouettes and set symmetrically, usually in a strip around the vase. Finally human beings appeared, either in strips around the vase or in panels. They are in silhouette, the head a blob (sometimes with a projection for the nose), the upper part of the body a triangle with apex downward, the legs reduced to their simplest taper forms, the arms mere sticks. As the style developed the silhouette of the head was enlivened by projections for beard, hair or crest of a helmet and lighted up by a space being left within it, in which a dot indicates the eye. The human beings are in action, often (since the vase had a funerary purpose) at a funeral in which a procession of chariots takes part and the dead man is shown laid out on the bier with women beside it, their hands to their heads in the attitude of mourning. Battles on land and sea are also shown; the warriors usually consist of the silhouette of a large figure-of-eight shield, head with helmet crest projecting above, legs below, and a couple of spears, or a sword at the waist; in the sea battles, ships break up and bodies float in the water among fishes.

In addition to the pottery, the geometric age produced some terra cottas and many small bronzes. The bronzes tended to be flat at first but became more solid and less angular as casting direct from wax models superseded cutting from bronze plates. Birds and other animals, especially horses, were popular and often admirably done; men, because of their less memorable shape, were not so successful; in the later stages of geometric art groups of

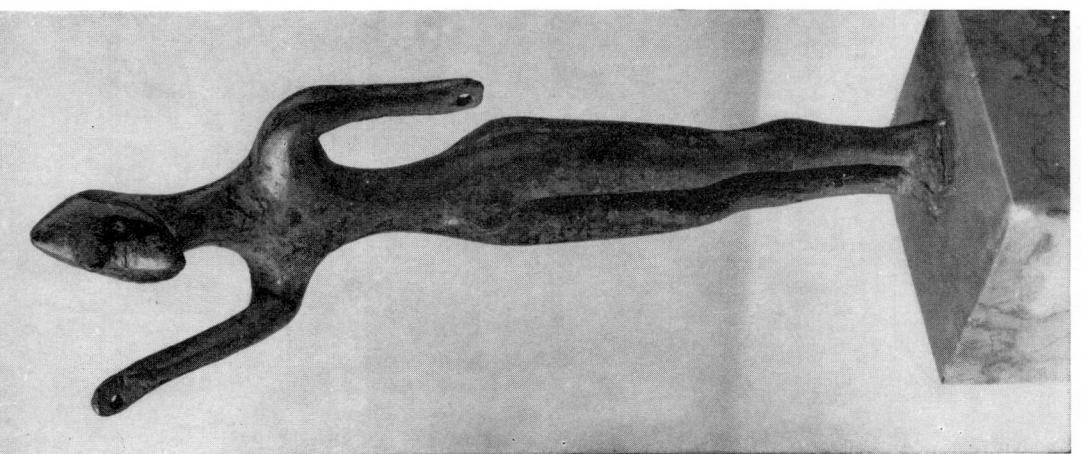

Bronze statuette of a warrior; 8th century B.C. From Olympia. The Louvre

Argive vase showing Odysseus blinding Polyphemus; about 700 B.C. From Argos

Bronze statuette dedicated to Apollo; about 675 B.C. Museum of Fine Arts, Boston

Head of a griffin, once the ornament of a caldron; about 650 B.C. Olympia Museum

Funeral procession and lions on Athenian vase; about 700 B.C. Antikensammlungen, Munich

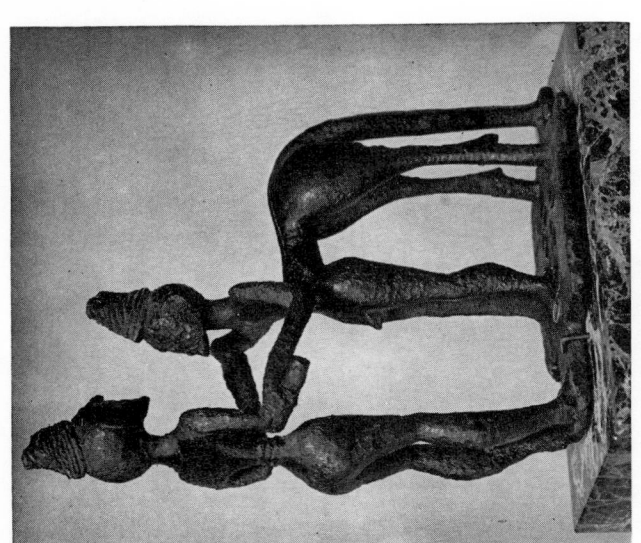

Bronze miniature group, man and centaur; 8th century B.C. Metropolitan Museum of Art

Geometric vase showing the mourning of the dead and a funeral procession; Athenian, 8th century B.C.

PLATE I

GREEK ART

GREEK SCULPTURE AND POTTERY: 8TH–7TH CENTURIES B.C.

BY COURTESY OF (TOP LEFT) THE METROPOLITAN MUSEUM OF ART, GIFT OF J. PIERPONT MORGAN, 1917, (TOP CENTRE) MUSEUM OF FINE ARTS, BOSTON, (BOTTOM CENTRE) ANTIKENSAMMLUNGEN, MUNICH; PHOTOGRAPHS, (TOP RIGHT) ARCHIVES PHOTOGRAPHIQUES, (CENTRE LEFT) D. A. I. ATHEN, (BOTTOM RIGHT) ÉCOLE FRANÇAISE D'ATHÈNES, (BOTTOM LEFT) MAX HIRMER

NOTE: THE PHOTOGRAPHS ON THIS PAGE AND THE FOLLOWING PAGES WERE SELECTED AND ASSEMBLED BY "ENCYCLOPÆDIA BRITANNICA," WITH THE ASSISTANCE OF THE VARIOUS MUSEUMS AND OTHER INSTITUTIONS ACKNOWLEDGED IN THE CREDIT LINES

PLATE II

FREE-STANDING SCULPTURE: ARCHAIC PERIOD

PHOTOGRAPHS, (TOP LEFT AND RIGHT, BOTTOM RIGHT) MANSELL-ALINARI, (BOTTOM LEFT) D. A. I. ATHEN, (BOTTOM CENTRE) ARCHIVES PHOTOGRAPHIQUES

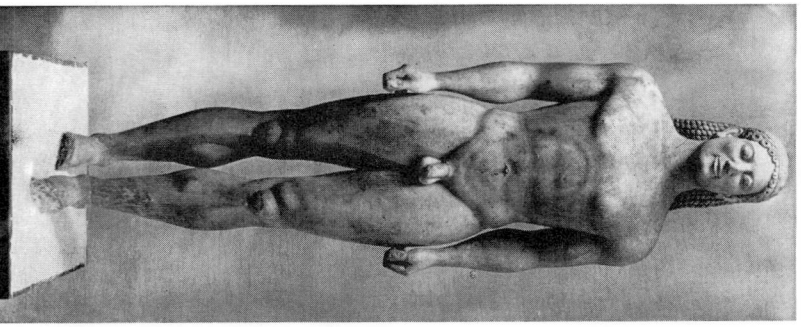

Kouros: grave statue of Kroisos; about 530 B.C. Found at Anavysos. National Museum, Athens

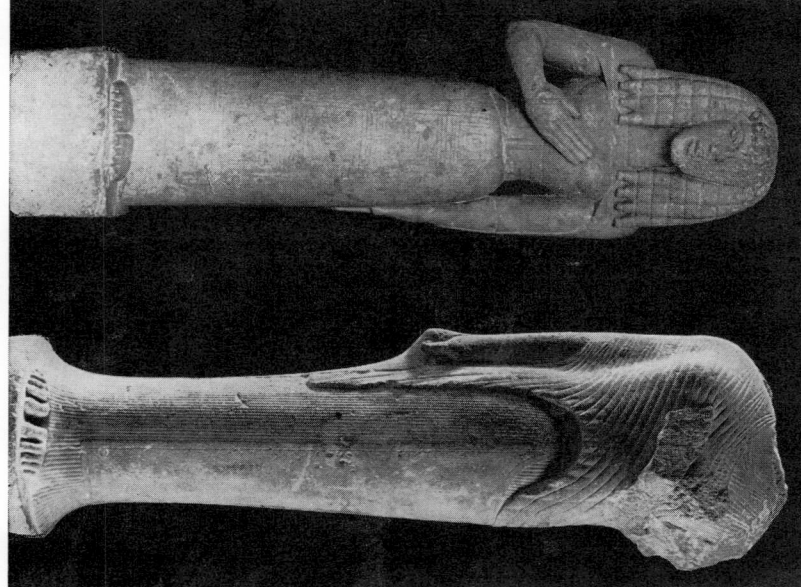

Left, the "Lady of Auxerre," Cretan statuette of limestone in the Daedalic style; about 625 B.C. *Right,* statue of a woman dedicated by Cheramyes to Hera; about 575 B.C. The Louvre

Kore carved by Antenor and dedicated by the potter Nearchos; about 520 B.C. Acropolis, Athens

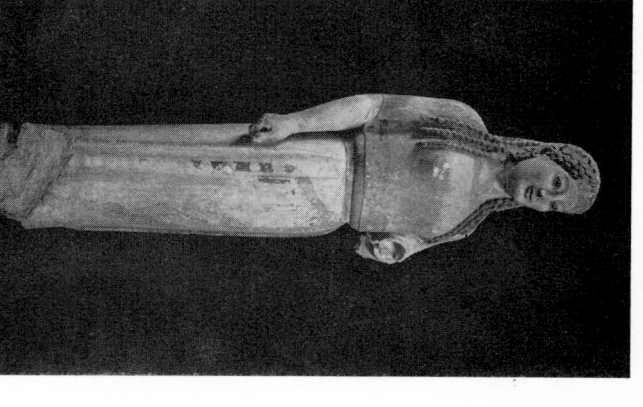

The so-called "Peplos *kore*"; about 540 B.C. Acropolis, Athens

Kore dedicated by Euthydicus; about 480 B.C. Acropolis, Athens

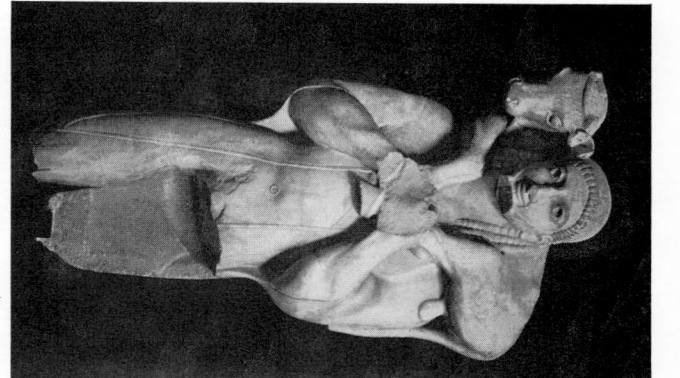

The "Moschophoros" (calf carrier); about 575 B.C. Acropolis, Athens

PLATE III

GREEK ART

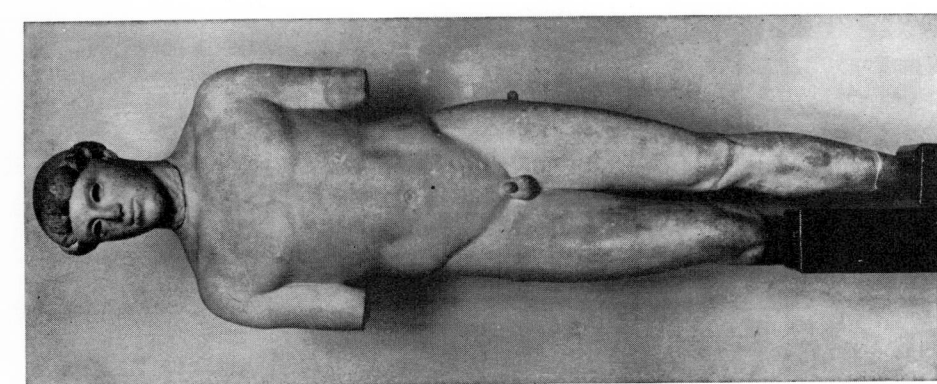

The "Critian boy"; about 480 B.C. Acropolis, Athens

The "Discobolus" (discus thrower), Roman copy of a bronze by Myron of about 450 B.C. Terme Museum, Rome

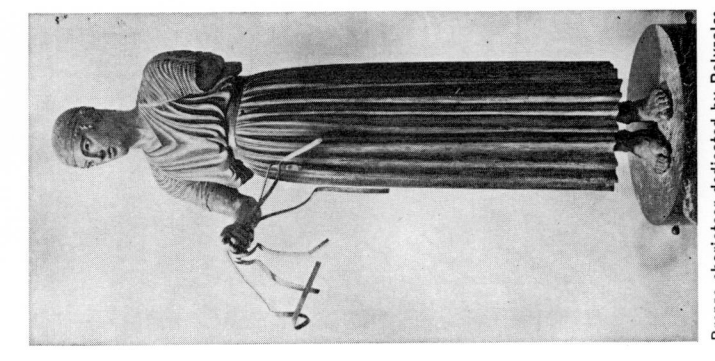

"Choiseul-Gouffier Apollo," Roman copy of a Greek bronze of about 460 B.C. British Museum

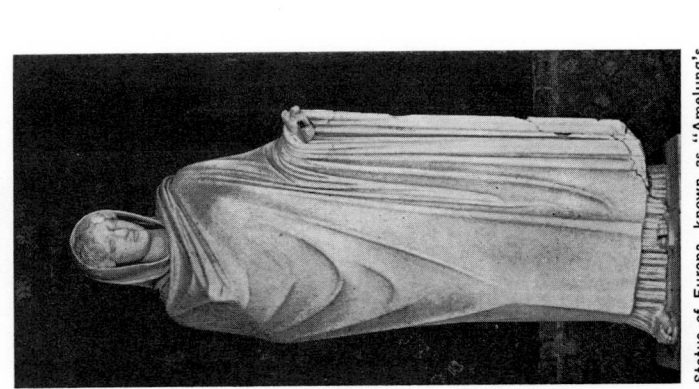

Statue of Europa, known as "Amelung's goddess," Roman copy of a Greek bronze of about 470 B.C. From Baiae

Bronze charioteer dedicated by Polyzalos of Gela; about 470 B.C. Delphi Museum

Bronze Zeus; about 450 B.C. Found near Cape Artemisium. National Museum, Athens

GREEK SCULPTURE: EARLY CLASSICAL PERIOD

PLATE IV

Hermes with the child Dionysus by Praxiteles; about 350 B.C. or slightly later. Olympia Museum

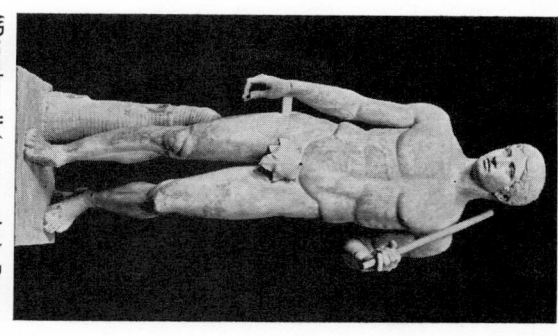

"Doryphoros" (spear carrier), Roman copy of a Greek bronze by Polyclitus; about 450–440 B.C. Naples

Aphrodite from Cyrene, Roman copy from a Greek statue of about 350 B.C. Terme Museum, Rome

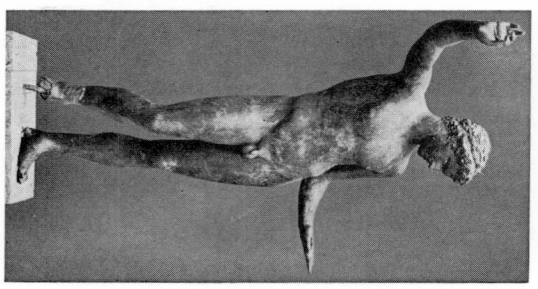

Bronze statue, thought to be by Praxiteles or one of his pupils; c. 330 B.C. From near Marathon. National Museum, Athens

Caryatid from the south porch of the Erechtheum, Athens; about 420 B.C. British Museum

Eirene (Peace) carrying Plutus (Wealth), Roman copy of a bronze by Cephisodotus; c. 370 B.C. From the Areopagus, Athens. Antikensammlungen, Munich

CLASSICAL GREEK SCULPTURE: 5TH–4TH CENTURIES B.C.

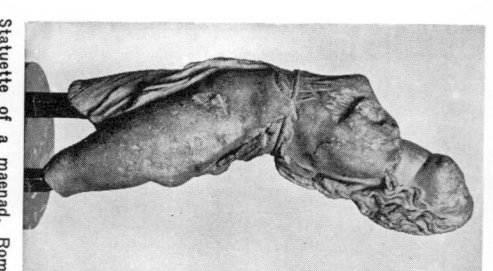

Statuette of a maenad, Roman copy of a Greek statue, possibly the "Maenad" by Scopas; about 350 B.C. Staatliche Kunstsammlungen, Dresden

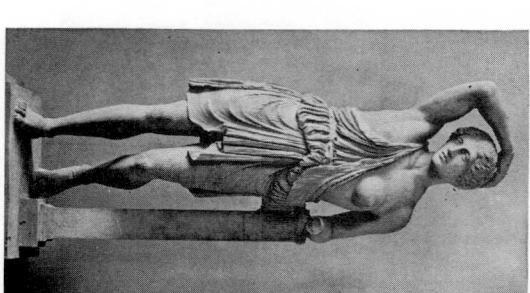

Marble statue of a wounded Amazon, Roman copy of Greek bronze, c. 440 B.C., possibly by Cresilas. Metropolitan Museum of Art

PLATE V

GREEK ART

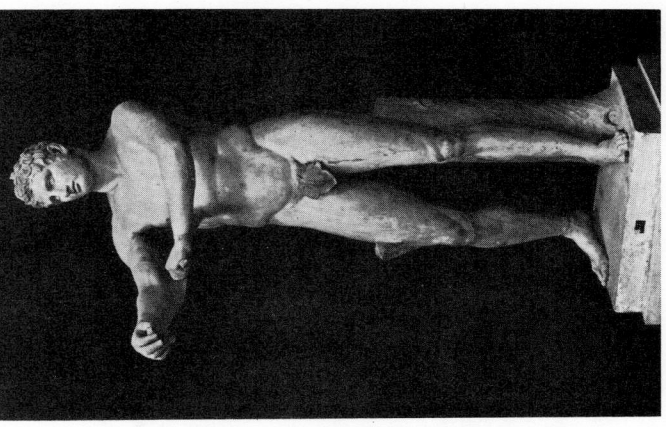

Gaul killing himself and his wife to avoid capture, Roman copy from a Greek original of about 250 B.C. Terme Museum, Rome

"Apoxyomenos" (athlete scraping himself), Roman copy of a bronze by Lysippus or his pupil Daippus; about 320 B.C. Vatican, Rome

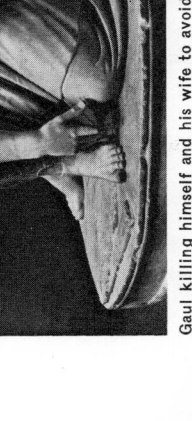

"Victory," from Samothrace; about 200 B.C. The Louvre

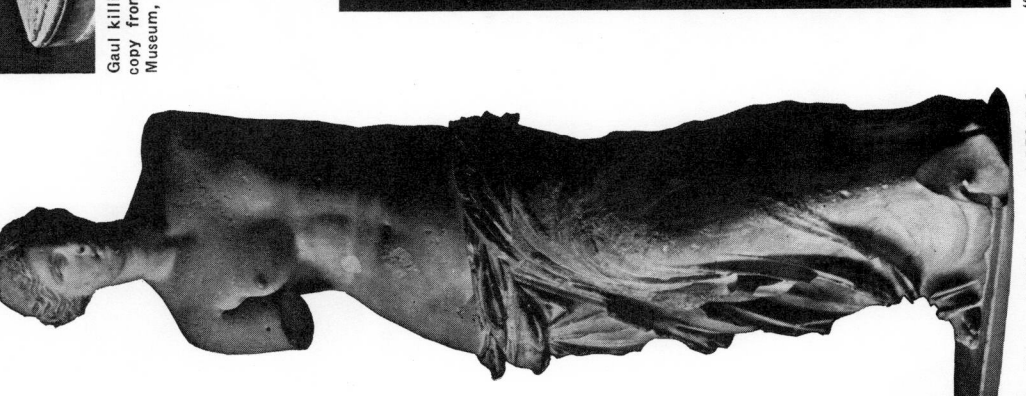

Aphrodite (the "Venus de Milo"); about 150 B.C. From Melos. The Louvre

Laocoon and his sons, by Agesander, Polydorus and Athenodorus of Rhodes; about 150 or 50 B.C. Vatican, Rome

Boxer resting, by Apollonius, son of Nestor; about 150 B.C. Terme Museum, Rome

The athlete Agias of Pharsalus, Thessaly, contemporary marble copy of a lost bronze by Lysippus; about 340 B.C. Delphi Museum

CLASSICAL AND HELLENISTIC SCULPTURE: 4TH–2ND CENTURIES B.C.

PLATE VI

GREEK ART

GREEK ARCHITECTURAL SCULPTURE: 7TH–5TH CENTURIES B.C.

Heracles and the apples of the Hesperides, metope from temple of Zeus, Olympia; about 460 B.C.

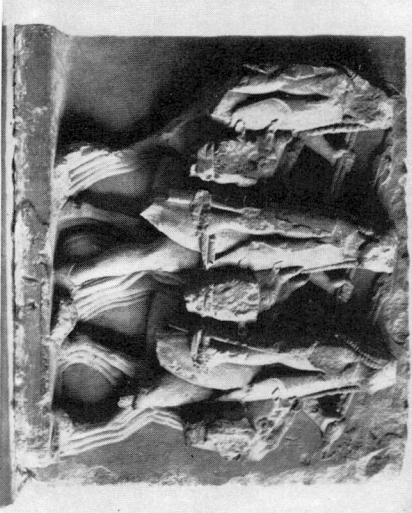

The Dioscuri cattle raiding, metope from the Sicyonian colonnade; about 575 B.C. Delphi Museum

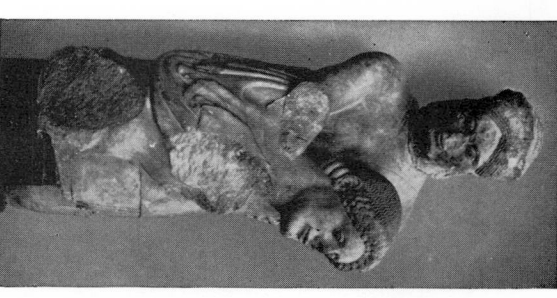

Theseus carrying off Antiope, fragment from west pediment of temple of Apollo, Eretria; about 510 B.C. Chalcis Museum

Apollo, fragment from west pediment of temple of Zeus, Olympia; about 460 B.C.

Gigantomachy, part of the frieze of treasury of the Siphnians; about 525 B.C. Delphi Museum

Seer, fragment from east pediment of temple of Zeus, Olympia; about 460 B.C.

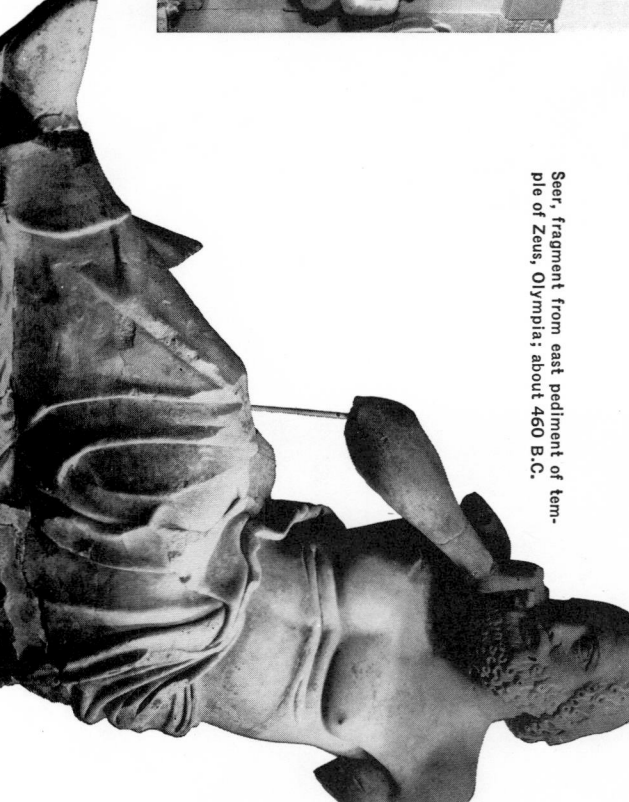

Gorgon from west pediment of temple of Artemis, Kerkyra (Corfu); about 600 B.C.

PLATE VII

GREEK ART

Female figures from east pediment of the Parthenon; about 430 B.C. The British Museum

Victory tightening her sandal, part of parapet of temple of Athena Nike, the Acropolis, Athens; about 410 B.C.

Resurrection of Alcestis or Persephone, column-drum from temple of Artemis, Ephesus; about 340 B.C. The British Museum

Lapith and centaur, metope from the Parthenon; about 445 B.C. The British Museum

Riders in the Panathenaic procession, part of west frieze of the Parthenon; about 440 B.C. The British Museum

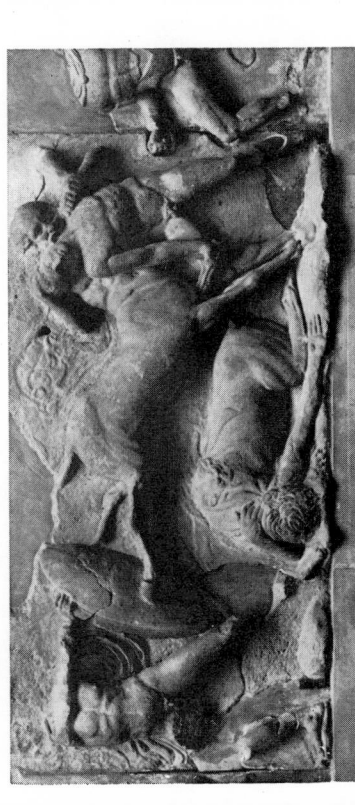

Lapiths fighting centaurs, part of frieze of temple of Apollo, Bassae near Phigalia; about 420 B.C. The British Museum

GREEK ARCHITECTURAL SCULPTURE: 5TH–4TH CENTURIES B.C.

PLATE VIII

GREEK ART

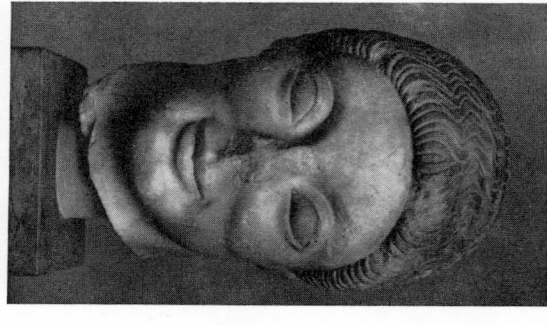

The "Rayet head"; about 520 B.C. Copenhagen

Head in the style of Scopas from the temple of Athena Alea, Tegea; c. 350 B.C. National Museum, Athens

Goddess; about 200 B.C. From Pergamon. Staatliche Museen, Berlin

Marble head of a young girl; about 300 B.C. From Chios. Museum of Fine Arts, Boston

Demosthenes, Roman copy from a bronze by Polyeuktos; about 280 B.C. Ashmolean Museum, Oxford

"Rampin horseman," dedicated on the Acropolis, Athens; about 560 B.C. The Louvre

Dying man, from the east pediment, Aegina; about 490 B.C. Antikensammlungen, Munich

Head of a youth, from a statue dedicated in the Dipylon cemetery; about 600 B.C. National Museum, Athens

GREEK PORTRAIT SCULPTURE: 7TH–2ND CENTURIES B.C.

Hygieia (Health), Roman copy from a Greek work of about 370 B.C. Museum, Rome

Poet, Roman copy of a Greek work of about 150 B.C. Naples

Heracles ("Aberdeen head"), style of Praxiteles; c. 340 B.C. British Museum

PLATE IX

GREEK ART

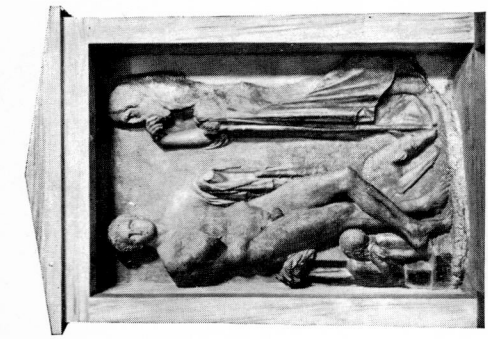

Gravestone showing father and son; about 320 B.C. From near the Ilissus. National Museum, Athens

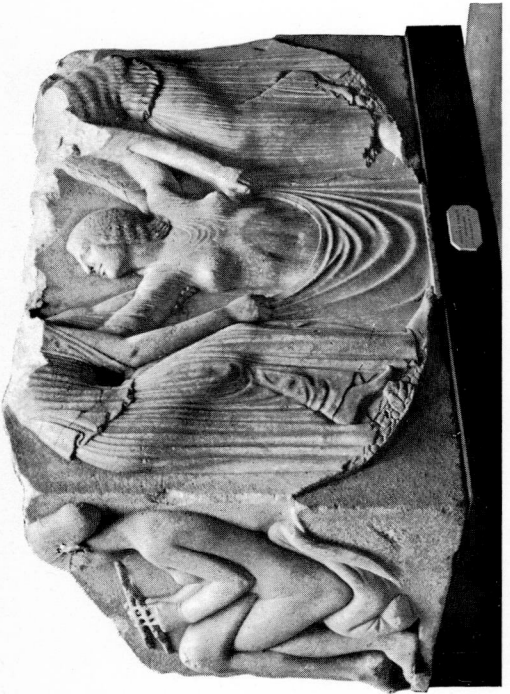

The "Ludovisi throne," perhaps the birth of Aphrodite; about 460 B.C. Terme Museum, Rome

Gravestone showing farewell of mother and daughter; about 350 B.C. National Museum, Athens

Battle of the Greeks and the Amazons, part of the frieze of the tomb of Mausolus at Halicarnassus; about 350 B.C. The British Museum

Gravestone of Dexileos; 393 B.C. Kerameikos Museum, Athens

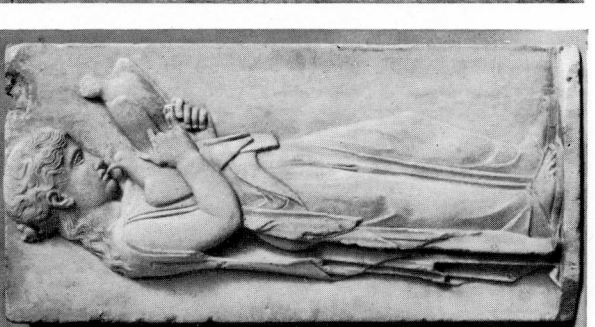

Girl with doves, marble tombstone from Paros; about 450 B.C. Metropolitan Museum of Art, New York

Athena mourning; about 470 B.C. Acropolis, Athens

Gravestone of Hegeso; about 400 B.C. National Museum, Athens

RELIEF SCULPTURE: 5TH–4TH CENTURIES B.C.

PLATE X

GREEK ART

GREEK PAINTING:
7TH–5TH CENTURIES B.C.

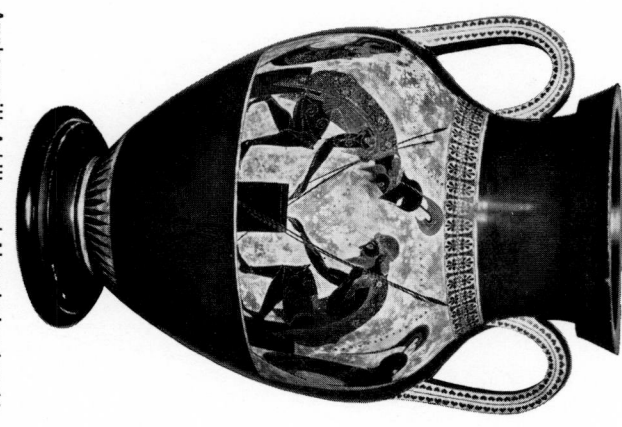

Quadriga and warriors on black-figured amphora;
about 530 B.C. The Metropolitan Museum of Art

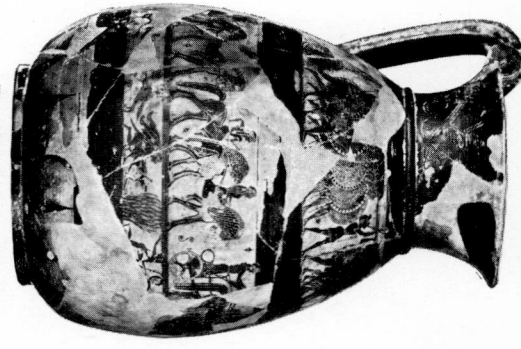

The "Chigi vase" with battle procession and hunting scenes; Proto-Corinthian, about 640 B.C. Villa
Giulia Museum, Rome

Rhodian plate with fight between Menelaus
and Hector; about 650 B.C. British Museum

Amphora with Achilles and Ajax playing draughts,
painted by Exekias; about 540 B.C. The Vatican

Red-figured mixing bowl showing the killing of
the Niobids; about 460 B.C. The Louvre

Girl playing double flute on red-figured
lecythus; about 480 B.C. The Metropolitan Museum of Art

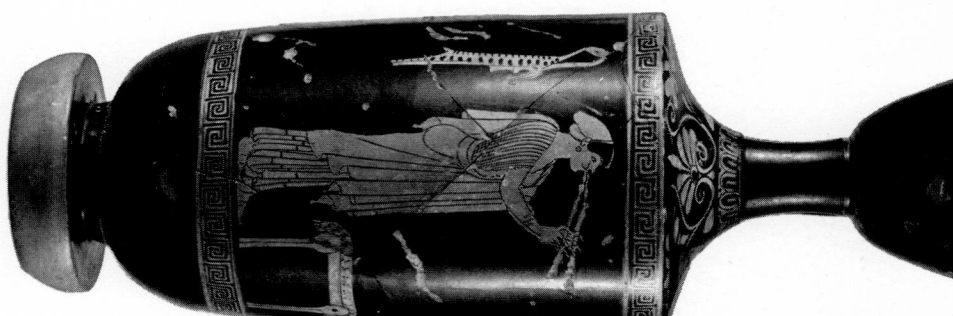

GREEK ART   835

some complexity were attempted—a doe with her fawn, a man fighting (or greeting) a centaur, even a lion hunt complete with dogs.

Geometric art was fairly widespread. Its main centre may have been Athens, since numerous pots of high quality were made there. Boeotia produced coarser pieces, often with lively scenes, and also a series of large safety pins with catchplates on which figures of animals or men were engraved. There are excellent bronzes from the Peloponnese. Particularly fine, though sparing of figure decoration, is the geometric pottery of Corinth; the decorative scheme commonly consists only of a series of parallel lines running around the pot, perhaps with a row of sharply pointed rays at the foot, but the fineness of the lines, the thinness of the clay and the neatness of the shapes gives proto-Corinthian geometric pottery, as it is called, a special charm.

III. THE ORIENTALIZING PERIOD (c. 800—c. 650 B.C.)

Greece in the geometric age was isolated from the neighbouring countries, partly because its inhabitants were largely newcomers and partly because the seas were dangerous except to ships of war. Toward the end of the 8th century, however, cultural links between Greece and its eastern neighbours, broken with the collapse of Mycenaean civilization at the end of the Bronze Age, began to be forged again.

There are likely to have been three kinds of contact with the east. The first was the importing of oriental objects, especially from Phoenicia and northern Syria, which may have come to Greece either direct or by way of Cyprus; that some at least came in Phoenician ships seems likely from the fact that similar imports were made at the same time into Italy. The second was the direct contact between the Greek cities and trading posts that had been established, mainly on the western coast of Asia Minor, with the peoples inland; the Greeks in Asia Minor were mostly of Ionian stock and consisted, at least in part, of those who had been driven out of mainland Greece by the pressure of immigration from the north. The third kind of link may have been the settling on Greek soil of oriental craftsmen.

Oriental imports were large in number but small in size. They consisted chiefly of small bowls or larger circular plaques of silver or bronze (embossed, inlaid or chased with bands of animals or figure scenes), of ivories, of textiles, and of scarabs and statuettes of men and animals in faïence. The style is not pure or original but usually an imitation—often a mixture—of Egyptian, Assyrian or Hittite; the subjects too are taken from these three sources and are sometimes mingled inconsequentially, although occasionally they tell a connected story. The surviving specimens of this orientalizing art are not necessarily a true sample, since objects in more precious materials (such as gold and silver) have probably suffered a high rate of destruction, while textiles have totally disappeared. Nevertheless, their general character is clear and—despite their degraded style—so is the effect of their richness and expert craftsmanship on the unsophisticated Greek.

The evidence for that effect is to be found mainly in the objects which, because of their lack of intrinsic value and their virtual indestructibility, have survived in the greatest numbers—namely, the decorated clay vases. It is in fact these that provide a steady and continuous index to the development of style from the geometric age down to the end of the 5th century and even, though less consistently, through the 4th. Oriental motifs found their way onto all makes of Greek vases. Curvilinear patterns, sometimes of wild exuberance, oust or jostle the older rectilinear ones; new subjects appeared, especially monsters, e.g., sphinx, siren, griffin, gorgon, chimera; exotic animals such as the lion became more popular. In the human figures the old silhouette was occasionally replaced by figures drawn in outline, and this technique existed alongside that of silhouette almost to the end of Greek vase painting. Silhouette itself was invigorated by a new device, that of indicating the details of figures by lines scratched into the surface of the clay before it was fired; this incision, as it is called, was probably imitated from chased work in bronze, and although the incised line has less flexibility than the painted line it possesses a brisk clean quality of its own.

The overwhelming force of the oriental impact and the completeness with which some workshops were dominated by imported models make it easy to overlook the fact that the more creative among the Greeks were using the new material not for blind imitation but for inspiration, and although it was to be two centuries or more before oriental subjects were eliminated, the style in which these subjects were rendered quickly became Greek; even abstract patterns copied from oriental models were soon given a Greek flavour. Nor were all the subjects oriental; as early as geometric times distinctively Greek myths appeared and continued—even at the climax of the orientalizing phase; if the total number of surviving objects had been larger it might have been possible to see how uninterrupted their sequence was. By the beginning of the 7th century there was already emerging in several centres a style that could no longer be called orientalizing except in accessories; in its boldness and grandeur here or its austere precision there it foreshadowed not only archaic but also classical Greek art.

IV. THE GREEK ARCHAIC PERIOD (c. 650—c. 480 B.C.)

The beginning of the archaic period is fixed approximately by the renewal of direct contact with Egypt and by its consequence, the first making of large stone and marble sculpture by the Greeks. Ancient writers state that the Greeks learned the art from the Egyptians, and the earliest Greek sculptures bear this out, for they have certain Egyptian characteristics. The Egyptians planned their statues and reliefs by a system of measurements, and the Greeks at first followed a similar system, although it is clear that they soon abandoned it and worked more freely. Even this freedom might seem limited to a modern mind, for Greek sculptors throughout the archaic and classical periods confined themselves to a comparatively small number of sculptural types and devoted themselves to perfecting these rather than to inventing new forms.

The Greeks were fortunate in possessing what the Egyptians lacked, a plentiful supply of white marble suitable for sculpture. The first quarries to be used to any great extent were in the Cyclades, especially Naxos and Paros. Naxos produced a faintly grayish marble with large crystals; Paros in its best quarries a white one, with smaller crystals, which came to be considered the finest material for sculpture. About the middle of the 6th century a marble of even smaller grain was discovered on the Athenian mountain Pentelikon, and from then onward it was used increasingly, especially in Athens. A soft limestone, poros (porinos lithos), was also quarried, mainly near the Piraeus, and was used in Athens, chiefly for architectural sculptures, until the late 6th century. Other Greek states not so fortunately placed, especially the colonies in Sicily and southern Italy, had to be content with local limestone or with imported marble which, owing to the difficulties of transport, must always have been costly.

The second major material of Greek sculpture, bronze, had both drawbacks and advantages in comparison with marble. The laborious processes of extraction and manufacture and its use for other purposes, especially armour, made it expensive; a statue in solid bronze would be impossibly costly, but until the perfecting of the lost-wax process, it was difficult to cast large bronzes hollow, and the alternative process of hammering flat sheets into sculptural shapes and assembling them on to a wooden core was clumsy and artistically unsatisfactory. On the other hand, bronze was not so difficult to transport as marble, since it was handled in small ingots which could be assembled piecemeal, and it was more durable. Moreover its colour did not need renewal.

All Greek marble sculpture was coloured, though few traces have survived. In archaic times the scheme was primarily decorative—the hair, for example, often being bright red or blue; men's flesh was brown, women's white; clothing was either coloured all over or picked out with patterns and borders reproducing woven or embroidered work; some details were gilded. As time went on the tendency was to make the colouring more naturalistic. The evidence seems to show that even the flesh surfaces were covered with a coating of colour; however, this was sufficiently thin to show the texture of the marble. The medium used may have been egg tempera or wax that was applied under heat. Bronze statues relied for their effect on the colour of the material, aided by the plating and inlaying of details in gold, silver or copper.

1. Archaic Freestanding Sculpture.—There is some doubt as to which of the Greeks were the first to become sculptors. One tradition names Daedalus, a Cretan, as the first; the name means "a skilled craftsman," and the 7th-century Daedalus may have been symbolic—as legendary as the miraculous artist of the same name in Homer. But Dipoenus and Scyllis, said to have been his pupils and, "the first eminent sculptors in marble," were not legendary, for wooden sculptures by them were seen by Pausanias in the 2nd century A.D. in the Peloponnese. They were said to have migrated to the Peloponnese about the 50th Olympiad (580 B.C.), and this would date their teacher, whatever his name, in the second half of the 7th century.

Daedalic Art.—Daedalus may be legendary, but the name is as useful now as it was to the ancients, and modern writers have agreed to apply the term Daedalic to a distinctive group of works of the second half of the 7th century, consisting chiefly of small terra cottas commonly though not exclusively found in the Dorian centres of Crete, Corinth, Laconia and Rhodes. The best-preserved statue of the style (or rather statuette, for it is less than 3 ft. high) is of limestone. It is now in the Louvre, Paris, but is known as the "Lady of Auxerre," because, although probably made in Crete, it was at one time in the museum of Auxerre. A life-size marble female figure of the same style was dedicated in Delos by a woman called Nicandre but is not so well preserved. As one of the earliest specimens of Greek sculpture, the "Lady of Auxerre" deserves careful study. The hair, being divided both horizontally and vertically into a rigid pattern, has the appearance of a wig, and it is indeed based on the wigs represented on Egyptian statues; the face is triangular in design, with the low forehead framed at the top by a row of spiral curls; the position of the arms—one close to the side, the other raised with the hand across the breast—is also imitated from Egyptian models. Un-Egyptian are the dress, which is held by a broad belt at the waist and reaches the ground, where the toes project neatly in front, and the details of form everywhere, especially perhaps the expression of the face. In short, everything but the basic sculptural composition is Greek, and even here the statue is more square in section than an Egyptian statue of the time. The kind of Daedalic male figure corresponding to this is a small bronze from Delphi, which, because of its material, is freer in its movement and indicates less clearly than the "Lady of Auxerre" or the large marble statues of the next generation the essential qualities of this style.

The Kouros Type.—Dipoenus and Scyllis were said to have trained pupils in the Peloponnese, and this is corroborated by the discovery of a pair of statues signed by a Peloponnesian sculptor—Agamedes or Polymedes of Argos—the style of which is evidently derived, at the distance of a generation or so, from the Daedalic. The dedication was made at Delphi by a priestess of Hera at Argos; the statues are of her sons, who, when the oxen failed to come from the field in time, dragged the cart in which she had to attend the festival, and died. The two statues are identical and well exemplify the male sculptural type now called for convenience *kouros* (youth) but used to represent a god (especially Apollo), an athletic victor, a dead man on his grave or otherwise, as occasion demanded, for more than a century, almost to the end of the archaic period. It is naked, with the left leg advanced and the arms stretched down the sides, as in Egyptian statues (on which the general composition is based); the weight is evenly distributed on both legs; shoulders and hips are level; the head looks straight to the front; and a plumb line dropped from midway between the eyes would exactly bisect both head and torso. The *kouros* type was adopted in all the schools of sculpture in archaic Greece—though perhaps more popular west of the Aegean than east—the only variation being the occasional bending of an arm so that the hand might hold an object. The proportions differ in different schools; some were more interested in the surface forms of the body, others in the underlying structure; some in one detail, others in another; throughout the 6th century more and more anatomical knowledge—gained not by dissection but from external observation—was gradually embodied in this basic sculptural conception, without modifying it fundamentally, and, on the unproved but not improbable assumption that the growth of this knowledge took place at about the same speed everywhere, it is now customary to date such statues by the amount of it they display.

The *kouros* type, though the favourite, was not the only type of male statue; men bringing offerings from their flocks, fighting men in their armour, horsemen with or on their horses—common subjects among small bronzes—are also found in large sculpture. The best-known and the best that has survived of the first subject is the "Moschophoros" (calf carrier) from the Acropolis at Athens, where the X-shaped interlocking of the man's arms and the calf's legs add to the strength and compactness of the composition.

The Kore Type.—The history of the other main type of archaic statue, the standing draped female (now conventionally called *kore*, "young woman"), is more complex, partly because of the various kinds of clothing that served as models. The "Lady of Auxerre" is a very early type of the Cretan school; of the eastern Greek school there is nothing quite so early, but eastern Greek statues of the first half of the 6th century suggest that they imitated Assyrian or Hittite models. A key piece here is the statue dedicated to Hera on Samos by Cheramyes, the composition of which is markedly different from the "Lady of Auxerre" (which has four facets, front, back and two sides, of which the front is by far the most important). The former is basically cylindrical rather than rectangular and therefore more easily suggests the third dimension and invites an all-round view. This indeed is a characteristic difference between eastern and western Greek in both sculpture and drawing, the eastern being more interested in flowing continuous line or surface, the western in precise and linear detail. Athenian art tends to have the merits of both—not by chance, for the Athenians were partly of Ionian stock—and though lacking neither creative capacity nor the discipline of the Ionian mainland, possessed, in addition to a native largeness of conception and design, a sensitiveness which enabled them to appreciate, adopt and transmute the creations of others.

It is thus fortunate that so much evidence comes from Athens, where in 480 and 479 the Persians sacked the Acropolis and threw down the numerous statues which had been dedicated there for a century or more. When the Athenians returned to their desolate city they collected the bulk of these shattered dedications and used them as filling material in making up the inequalities of the rocky platform of the Acropolis. Any piece of sculpture so buried must have been carved before 480, and this is obviously a valuable criterion for the development of archaic style, which about the time of the Persian invasion was undergoing a profound change; hence the adoption of 480 as the date at which the classical period may be considered to begin.

The statues found in the debris of the Persian sack of the Acropolis consist of pure native products; of statues imported from other Greek centres or made by sculptors emigrating from those centres; and of works made by Athenians that imitate those imported types and occasionally reflect something of their style. The dress they are shown wearing is usually one of two kinds, the Attic, or the Ionian, which became fashionable in Athens in the second half of the 6th century. The Attic peplos (like the Dorian peplos) was a large rectangular piece of heavy material which, when pinned on the shoulders and girt at the waist, produced broad surfaces and simple folds; the so-called "Peplos kore" of about 540 is a delightful example of the simple, subtle treatment to which it lends itself. The Ionian dress, consisting of a

GREEK ART

thin and voluminous garment with buttoned sleeves, with or without a separate cloak, not only produced a number of small complex folds but could be arranged in various ways. Many archaic sculptors had a liking for elaborate details, and the Ionian dress gave them ample opportunity to indulge it.

A Samian statue not much later than that dedicated by Cheramyes—in a group on Samos, the so-called "Geneleos group," from a sculptor's signature that appears on it—introduces a motif that was to become extremely popular among archaic sculptors; the figure grasps the drapery below the waist and draws it to one side, thus setting up a complex of diagonal folds which radiate from the hand; the cloak over the upper part of the body produces a series of rather deeper, vertical folds, but its upper edge is usually diagonal. The whole scheme is full of interest. What an Athenian sculptor makes of it can be seen in the *kore* carved by Antenor (the base signed by him almost certainly belongs to the statue), where the massive shoulders and the strong vertical folds both of the cloak and of the chiton (tunic) where it hangs down from the hand give it a grandeur and monumentality that is sometimes lost in the superficial brilliance of the more sophisticated *korai*.

The contribution of Ionian sculptors can best be gauged by a series also found on the Acropolis but closely related to a series found in the Ionian centre, Delos. There is a deliberate and successful attempt in the statue to treat body and drapery as separate entities instead of as a single mass; the drapery hangs in such heavy folds that it almost seems to weigh the body down. The ability to suggest the weight of drapery was present early in Ionia; *e.g.*, in the "Geneleos group," mentioned above, where the principal dedicator, a woman, is shown reclining, as if at a meal.

This pose, though not uncommon in small bronzes, is extremely rare in archaic sculpture. The seated pose, which offers special difficulties to the sculptor, is also rare, except in a series of statues arranged (as in some Egyptian sanctuaries) to form an avenue beside a sacred way from the harbour to the temple at Didyma near Miletus.

2. Archaic Architectural Sculpture.—In archaic architectural sculptures, of which a long series has survived although many

are fragmentary, the sculptor had to wrestle with the difficulties of composing designs that would fit the square or oblong panel of the Doric metope, the narrow band of the Ionic frieze and—most awkward of all—the low triangle of the pediment. Of early 6th-century Dorian sculpture the pediments of the temple of Artemis at Kerkyra (Corfu) and the metopes of the Sicyonian colonnade at Delphi—both of limestone—are excellent examples. The Sicyonian metopes display the Dorian simplicity and vigour in their broad flat planes and strong rhythm.

The better-preserved of the Corfu pediments has a large flying figure of Medusa in the centre flanked by panthers (she is in origin an earth-goddess and therefore mistress of the beasts) ; on a much smaller scale is the completely unconnected subject in the corners, a battle of gods and giants. One of the major problems of pedimental composition is not only to fit the figures physically into the rapidly narrowing field but also to unite them in a single subject with the central figure or figures, which must almost inevitably be of a larger scale because of the much greater height of the central space. In the Corfu pediment and in the so-called "Bluebeard"—another limestone pediment of about mid-6th century from the Acropolis at Athens—no attempt is made to reconcile either subjects or scale. Even in the archaic temple at Delphi, which was rebuilt with a marble facade about 525, the corners were filled (as was the centre of the "Bluebeard" pediment) with irrelevant groups of a subject borrowed from the orient, lions pulling down other animals.

Three late archaic pediments, all of marble, solved the problem : one (very fragmentary) of a temple of about 510 on the Acropolis at Athens filled the whole pediment with a gigantomachy (the war of the giants against the gods) ; a second, also very fragmentary, from Eretria, set the goddess Athena in the centre, with Theseus, her protégé, lifting the Amazon Antiope into his chariot. Chariots were later to be used successfully at Olympia and on the Parthenon, the horses with their large size and length of body being useful space fillers; however, in the pediments of the temple at Aegina (one carved just before 490, the other soon after) the problem was solved without the introduction of chariots or horses. In each of the pediments the goddess Athena holds

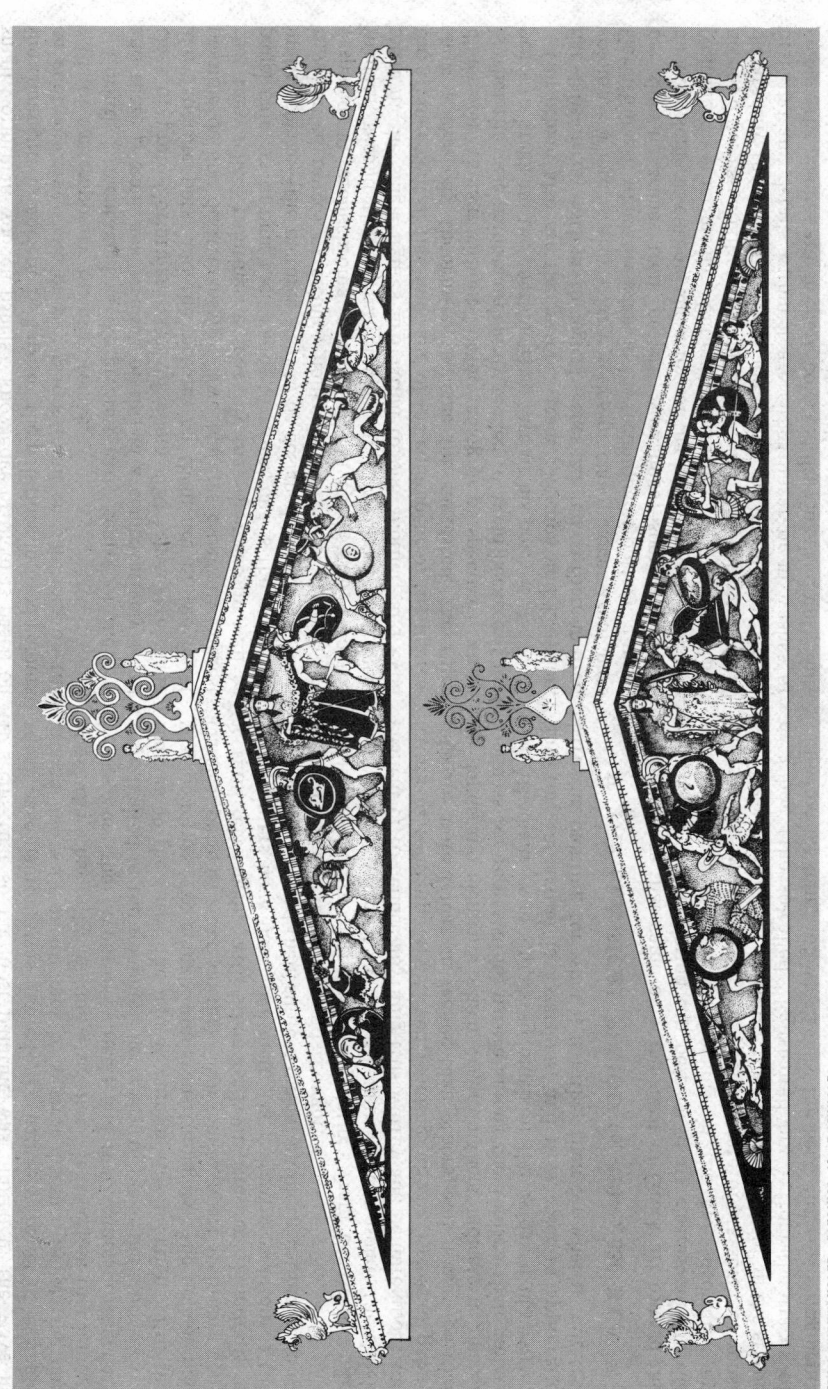

FROM FURTWÄNGLER, "AEGINA" (A. BUCHHOLZ)

FIG. 1.—EAST AND WEST PEDIMENTS OF THE TEMPLE AT AEGINA AS RESTORED BY FURTWÄNGLER

the centre—a deity can reasonably be on a larger scale than human beings without causing any uneasiness—but the rest of each pediment is filled with fighters, all on the same scale, all engaged in the same battle and filling the narrowing field by the postures of stooping, kneeling, crouching and lying, which occur naturally in such circumstances.

The best surviving example of archaic Ionian architectural sculpture is the frieze which decorated the four sides of the Siphnian treasury at Delphi (about 525). The scenes are skilfully designed—by emphasis on the overlapping of figures when the action is crowded and by suggesting the space and air round them when it is not—to minimize the feeling of constriction into two dimensions which is inevitable in a long, narrow, continuous composition.

It is characteristic of the archaic sculptor in both statues and reliefs that he failed to treat every part of the figure consistently. For instance, he may have modeled the shoulders and chest with depth and understanding but treated the diaphragm superficially and without interest. Moreover, his natural tendency was to create repetitive patterns; he devised, for example, a formula for the fringe of hair over the forehead but failed to link it organically with the independent pattern he had invented for the hair on the top of the head, or that again with the hair at the back. In relief sculpture or painting, the half-unconscious desire to present every feature in its most easily recognizable aspect led him to combine a profile head with a torso seen frontally and legs striding to one side. This lack of naturalistic articulation does not necessarily detract from the sculptural effect, although it is apt to become disquieting the more closely the general appearance of the statue approaches that of a living human being. The repetition of a small number of types year after year made for the continuance of these inconsistencies, for they became conventions. Where a sculptor was forced to render—and therefore to observe directly—a new subject, he often attained an astonishing degree of realism; an outstanding example is the head of a dying man from one of the pediments of Aegina.

3. Painting of the Archaic Period.—Since all the remains of archaic wall painting and panel painting have perished (except two small Corinthian wooden panels), knowledge of them is based on the comments of ancient authors, on the paintings in fired colours on contemporary vases or clay plaques, and on paintings on the walls of contemporary Etruscan tombs.

Corinth is mentioned as the greatest early centre of the art, and there is some confirmation of this in a comparatively small class of proto-Corinthian vases of about 650; these are small and exquisite pots, and the pictures on them are of the finest possible outline draftsmanship. Two features especially suggest that they reflect paintings, or possibly that they are by wall or panel painters turning their hands to vases: one is the polychromatic scheme—the pictures seem to be designed in a range (even if a limited range) of colours, unlike ordinary vases, which are designed in monochrome and then enlivened with coloured touches; second, the general composition, as well as the arrangement of the single figures in relation to one another, and even the arrangement of the limbs and of the equipment of the figures, show a carefully thought-out scheme for suggesting the third dimension (though without foreshortening or perspective), which is what the vase painter ordinarily tended to avoid because it appears to break up the continuous surface of his pot.

Corinthian also are the metopes from Thermon and Calydon, flat slabs of clay with mythological scenes painted on them in fired colours. There is also a large series of clay plaques from near Corinth itself, which are again in the technique of pottery, a number showing scenes from potters' workshops; some are in silhouette, some in outline, and a few of the latter may be based on paintings in other media. But even when they are in outline they do not differ essentially from silhouettes, since the outlines are not dictated by the forms drawn inside them; the outline was drawn first and any details within it are either linear or in washes of colour; the plaques are, in short, coloured drawings and not paintings. Athenian clay plaques of the 6th century, sometimes votive, were also in decoration of small buildings, sometimes votive, were also in

Archaic artists had been interested mainly in the outward ap-

vase technique, were made by vase painters and had no closer connection with any art of panel painting or wall painting in another medium than had the contemporary vases; the silhouette style is dominant.

Like the vase paintings, however, they display certain features that seem to have been invented in a major art; these are attempts to suggest recession in space, not by true foreshortening but by placing the elements one behind the other in such a pattern as to make their relative positions intelligible. The most obvious example is the four-horse chariot, which is often shown frontally at rest, but sometimes also in a three-quarter position at speed. There are also certain scenes and subjects that occur again and again on vases in such a form as to suggest that they all go back to a common original, and that perhaps a wall painting or panel painting.

Pliny says that Cimon of Cleonae invented *katagrapha*, which he translates as *obliquae imagines*, and this can hardly mean anything but foreshortenings. Unfortunately Cimon's date is uncertain, but toward the end of the 6th century there was a growing interest among Athenian vase painters—and since Athens was dominant in the art any judgments must be based on that city's products—in foreshortening. The change from black-figure technique (the figures in black silhouette with inner markings scratched through the black before firing) to red-figure (figures reserved from the red surface of the vase and surrounded with a black background, the inner markings made by lines of black or diluted black) had begun about 530. Red-figure, although still a silhouette technique, was a more flexible medium than black-figure and was thus capable of following any advances toward the rendering of depth which might be made in wall or panel painting. The attempts at foreshortening made in vase painting toward the end of the century may be so inspired but may be independent experiments. There is no sign anywhere of a general system of perspective or of a realization that such a system could be devised; simply a tendency to turn the body exactly toward or three-quarters toward, or even three-quarters away from, the spectator, instead of in profile; the use of foreshortenings within the individual figure; or the carefully represented overlapping of one figure on another. It seems that so far most painting was limited in the ways in which vase painting was limited; the figures were set on a single ground line with no attempt to suggest distance by placing one above the other or by making it smaller. It is certain that human beings were the favourite subjects and that landscape elements were limited to the minimum necessary to make the story clear; that, as on the vases, the figures were mostly in action. But the vase paintings, exceedingly numerous throughout the archaic and classical periods, stand on their own merits, apart from any conjectural relationship with other kinds of painting. Hundreds of vase painters have been identified: their drawing is often of the highest quality, and their subject matter an inexhaustible mine of information on Greek life and thought.

Although many of the archaic paintings from Etruscan tombs have a strongly Greek flavour, it is impossible to isolate the Greek element or to deduce anything trustworthy and definite about the nature of contemporary Greek painting. Some Etruscan paintings are more Ionian in feeling than others, and it may be that the landscape elements which occur in them indicate a greater fondness for representing nature among the Ionians than among the Athenians, who supply so much of the evidence otherwise; however, conjecture is hazardous, and it is wiser to appreciate Etruscan painting for what it is rather than for what it imitates.

V. THE CLASSICAL PERIOD (c. 480–c. 330 B.C.)

The change that came over the spirit of Greek art toward the end of the archaic period can be seen at its clearest among the statues of the Acropolis, especially in the *kore* dedicated by Euthydicus, which (from the perfect state of its surface) must have been carved shortly before the Persian sack, and in the statue of a boy (the so-called "Fair-haired boy," from the traces of yellow on his hair), of which only the head and small fragments have survived.

pearance of the finished statue. They aimed at producing a pleasing dedication—generalized man—not, primarily, a close imitation of a human being. Portraiture, in the sense of the portrayal of the facial or bodily peculiarities of a single person, did not exist. They thought of man in action—this is seen especially in reliefs and vase paintings—presenting a brave and even a gay appearance to the world; of his deeds rather than his thoughts. In the late archaic, as seen in the *kore* of Euthydicus, this gay extrovert mood changed suddenly to an introspective one; the archaic smile (which had long been fading) gave place to a solemn, almost sombre expression. The centre of interest had shifted inward, to the mind. The *kore* of Euthydicus and the "Fair-haired boy," are possibly the work of a single sculptor of strong personality. The change from archaic to classical was not exactly the same everywhere, although its general direction was the same. With the change of mood came a change in the attitude of the sculptor toward the type of statue he had inherited. The main composition and the arrangement of the dress are the same as in many statues of the preceding 50 years; he used the convention but modified it to show his new understanding of the solidity and organic structure of the body.

1. Early Classical Statues.—The statue of the "Fair-haired boy," embodied some of the changes resulting from a study of the effect of the uneven distribution of weight on the positions of the bones and the muscles, a study which was the death of the *kouros* type; however, it is so fragmentary that these changes are more easily demonstrated in a slightly later statue of different style, also from the Acropolis. This is known as the "Critian boy" because its style is similar to that of the bronze group (known only from copies) of the tyrannicides Harmodius and Aristogiton, by Critius and Nesiotes, set up in Athens in 478. The "Critian boy" might be said to have the same subject as a *kouros*, but it is an entirely different sculptural conception, and the realization that the old *kouros* design would not accommodate the new knowledge of the effects of stance, and its consequent abandonment, made possible a far more harmonious interrelation of parts than had been accomplished before; the torso was now organically connected with the legs and the whole body was satisfactorily articulated. The *kouros* was symmetrical about a central vertical axis; the head was frontal; shoulders, hips and buttocks were level; and the weight was evenly distributed on the two feet. In the "Critian boy" the weight of the body is mainly on one leg, the left; the other, thus freed, is set slightly forward, and the effect of this posture is shown in the raising of the left hip and buttock; the head is turned toward the free leg, and the resultant changes in the shoulders and chest are tentatively suggested. This stance is fully worked out in a slightly later statue of which many copies have survived, the best preserved being the "Choiseul-Gouffier Apollo," in the British museum, London.

The favourite female statue of the early classical period is the "peplos figure," so-called because it wears the Doric peplos; many small bronzes of the kind have survived, but no large ones, and it is necessary to depend on copies of these made in Roman times. The heavy Doric peplos tended to fall in simple folds, and this suited the early classical sculptor's mood, for these broad folds can be made to explain the main forms and the stance of the figure and to emphasize its solidity. In the upper part of the body the breasts create the two main folds which alone break the rectangular surface of the overfall, and in the lower part the series of strong vertical folds over the supporting leg serve to stress its function, while the free leg breaks the vertical mass sufficiently to show that it is free.

In the statue of Europa (known as "Amelung's goddess"), where the Ionic dress is represented, the chiton with its elaborate folds is almost hidden except round the feet, where it provides a strong vertical base; while the system of folds formed by the cloak, in which the whole figure is swathed, expresses clearly, but in the broadest possible fashion, the main shapes of the body and the stance.

The long, full dress of the charioteer, girdled high and gathered inside with cords on the shoulders to prevent it from flying in the wind, offered an entirely different set of forms to the sculptor;

the bronze in Delphi (about 470), which showed the victor standing in his four-horse chariot after the race, is the one surviving original statue of this subject. The long, fluted folds below the girdle are rendered with a considerable degree of naturalism; those above it are even more closely studied, as if from a posed model, while the feet and the one surviving hand almost look like casts from life. The face is more generalized, and the hair above the ribbon of victory recalls the archaic in its symmetrical patterning and its lack of depth; it hardly modifies the shape of the skull and shows far less plastic sense than the rest of the statue.

Although the preference of the early classical sculptor was for quiet poses, the action figure—popular with the archaic artist in small bronzes, reliefs and paintings, less popular in large free sculpture because of technical difficulties—did not die out. Indeed, with the improvement in bronze casting, the early classical sculptor was capable of producing bronze statues of heroic size in violent action; it is characteristic of the period and of a more intellectual approach to artistic problems that the moments chosen for representation, even in action figures, are those of equilibrium.

The bronze Zeus found in the sea off Cape Artemisium, an original of about 460, is shown not launching, but about to launch, a thunderbolt; his right arm, drawn back to its full extent, is momentarily still, and the spectator's mind does not uneasily wait for the finish, as it would if the final movement were already begun.

Myron.—A similar moment was chosen by Myron in his statue of a victorious athlete of about the same date, the "Discobolus," where the discus thrower is at the top of his swing. Although his work is known only from copies, Myron's is a personality that can be grasped. Apart from this revolutionary but completely satisfying "Discobolus," which almost succeeds in harmonizing the anatomy of a frontal torso and legs in profile, he made a statue of a runner Ladas at the moment of the finish; no copies are known, but the subject shows that Myron realized the freedom bronze gives the sculptor. His young Athena with the satyr Marsyas, who is about to pick up the flutes which the goddess has laid aside—a bronze group set up in Athens—and his Heracles, one of three colossal bronze figures on Samos forming a group of the hero being brought by Athena to Zeus after the completion of his labours, are known from copies in marble. No emotion is shown, and the violent action of the "Discobolus" finds no expression in the face, but there is a deep understanding of the essential character of the subject, especially as expressed in the body—the tense effort of the athlete in the prime of manhood, the almost girlish but still godlike Athena, the hero who has endured and accomplished much.

Phidias.—Phidias (*q.v.*), a slightly younger contemporary of Myron, was renowned in antiquity for his statues of gods. His colossal bronze Athena standing in the open on the Acropolis at Athens could be seen from the sea by travelers as they approached the harbour and must have been as well known as is the Statue of Liberty in New York; it was erected about 456, having been made from spoils captured from the Persians about 20 years before. Equally famous were his two statues of gold and ivory more than 30 ft. high, "Athena Parthenos" in the Parthenon at Athens (finished by 438) and Zeus, seated, in the temple at Olympia (before 432; *see* OLYMPIA: *The Remains*). Of "Athena Parthenos" there are copies on a small scale that give some idea of its general appearance. Of the Zeus—said to have deepened the religious concept of the deity—there are only miniature copies on coins, although some of the clay molds for the golden drapery, with other refuse from the making of the statue, have been found in the workshop of Phidias at Olympia. Even more highly esteemed on account of its beauty was the bronze statue of Athena by Phidias, called "Athena Lemnia" because it was dedicated on the Acropolis by Athenians setting out to found a colony on Lemnos in 450. Two marble copies have been recognized in Dresden, but a marble head of the same type in Bologna is more perfectly preserved and is of the finest workmanship.

2. Early Classical Architectural Sculpture.—*Olympia.*—Architectural sculpture of the early classical period is represented by the metopes and pediments of the temple of Zeus at Olympia,

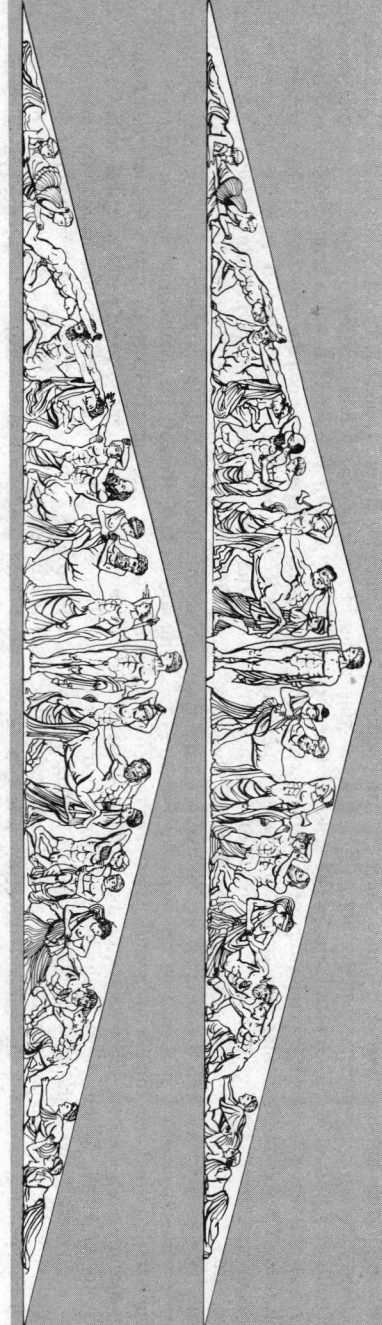

FIG. 2.—TWO CONJECTURAL RESTORATIONS OF THE WESTERN PEDIMENT OF THE GREAT TEMPLE OF ZEUS AT OLYMPIA

carved in the decade or so before 457. According to Pausanias the east pediment was by Paeonius (*q.v.*) of Mende, the west by Alcamenes (*q.v.*), an islander who worked much at Athens, but there is some reason to think he may have been misinformed. When allowance is made for the number and size of the sculptures and for the fact that many sculptors must have been employed, the style is remarkably homogeneous. It has some slight affinity with sculpture from the Aegean islands and may be a product of some island school, or of a school of sculptors from northern Greece, but so little is known about what was going on outside Athens at this time that it may equally well be Peloponnesian: the gravity and sincerity of the style agree with what is known of the Peloponnesian temperament.

A further difficulty is that the designers and executants were not necessarily from the same places; the system used in translating small-scale designs or models into figures over life-size in marble, and how much latitude was given to the craftsmen during the process, are not known.

The 12 metopes of the temple show the 12 labours of Heracles, who is often assisted by Athena; she stands by him when he is overcome by weariness after his first labour; she accepts the Stymphalian birds from him as a token of his achievement; she directs the cleaning of the Augean stables; and, finally, as daughter of Zeus, god of the sky, she raises the burden of the heavens from the shoulders of Heracles, who has been bearing it while Atlas fetched him the golden apples of the Hesperides. The east pediment shows the moments before the chariot race of Pelops and Oenomaus, an apparently calm scene but in reality not only tense—as the start of any race is, even when death is not the certain outcome—but also fraught with tragedy, for the fraud employed by Pelops to evade the savage conditions laid down by Oenomaus for those who sought his daughter in marriage was the beginning of the curse on the ancestors of Agamemnon, which pervades so much of Greek drama. The design of verticals formed by the five standing figures of the main group, Zeus being on a larger scale in the centre, and of horizontals formed by the horses, contrasts with that of the west pediment, the fight of Lapithae and centaurs at the wedding feast of Pirithous, where an undulat-

ing design of struggling men, women and monsters is dominated by the single upright figure of Apollo in the centre.

The sculptures of Olympia are a perfect example of the early classical spirit in their power, in their restraint and in their choice of subject, which prefers to show the time before or after an action, to suggest the motives or consequences of it, rather than to display only the action itself.

Selinus.—Almost contemporary with Olympia are the metopes of the Heraeum at Selinus, a Greek colony in western Sicily, which are of local limestone with the women's heads and extremities in marble imported from Paros in the Aegean; rather more of archaic convention survives in externals, but the spirit is already classical.

The "Ludovisi Throne."—The so-called "Ludovisi throne" (perhaps the end of a long altar), another contemporary work, may also be from a western colony—in southern Italy rather than in Sicily—though its sculptor may have had his first training in the Aegean. Despite much discussion, the subjects are still uncertain. The central scene seems to be the birth of a goddess—Aphrodite from the sea or Persephone from the earth—while on the side panels (which may have been cut down when re-used in Roman times) the naked girl and the cloaked woman burning incense perhaps symbolize her virginity and marriage. But although the meaning is obscure the sculpture is moving because of its intense sincerity; the delicacy of the sensitive detail is an inheritance from the archaic, but it lacks nothing of strength in design, and it is suffused with strong religious feeling. These architectural sculptures belong to the second quarter of the 5th century. From the third quarter come those of the Parthenon.

The Parthenon.—This formed a major part of Pericles' great building projects, known to have been supervised by Phidias, the leading sculptor of his time; it is therefore reasonable to suppose that the style of Phidias is to be seen in the sculptures of the Parthenon. He is likely to have decided the general plan of the sculpture and to have designed much of it; however, within a consistent general scheme there are clear divergences of style such as might arise from the employment of craftsmen of different ages, different ability and different antecedents. Phidias

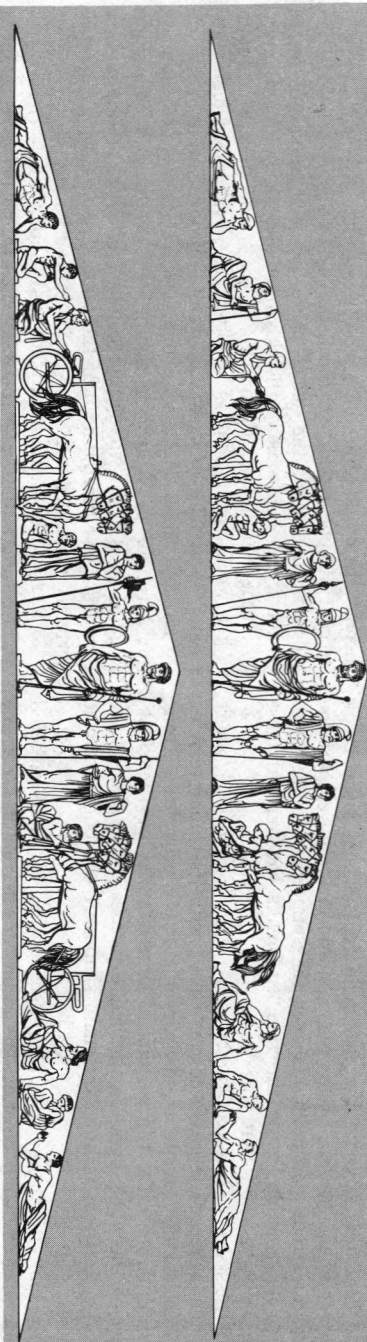

FIG. 3.—TWO CONJECTURAL RESTORATIONS OF THE EASTERN PEDIMENT OF THE GREAT TEMPLE OF ZEUS AT OLYMPIA

is known to have had an able pupil Agoracritus (*q.v.*), whose masterpiece was the statue of Nemesis at Rhamnus. On a project so vast he may well have employed another eminent sculptor (ancient records differ on whether he was a rival or pupil), Alcamenes, and there may have been others. In addition to the natural diversity of a number of talented craftsmen working under orders, more radical differences due to the creative talents of master sculptors given a fairly free free hand should be expected.

The sculptures of the Parthenon were begun soon after the middle of the 5th century. The metopes, because of the structure of the building, must have been set in position first, and most of those that have survived do in fact look earlier than the rest of the sculpture; they were probably carved between 447 and 440. The frieze (an Ionic feature, although the temple was Doric) would normally be next, in the years after 440, and that is what the building accounts, which have partly survived, seem to show. The subject of the frieze, the Panathenaic procession, is a single one and occupies all four external sides of the building within the colonnade. On the west, and rather less markedly on the east, the design is composed in such a way as not to overrun seriously the joints of the slabs, from which it would appear that these were carved or partly carved on the ground and finished in position on the building; whereas on the north and south, the crowded composition ignores the joints, suggesting that it was carved in place. The pedimental figures (probably about 438–432), being almost in the round, could be carved on the ground and hoisted into position afterward; their perfect finish at the back shows that this was done.

The 92 metopes of the Doric frieze, which surmounts the whole of the external colonnade, were in exceedingly high relief (in many places about 12 in.). On the east they depicted the battle of the gods and giants, appropriate here because, on the frieze just behind, the gods are shown assembled; on the west was the battle of Greeks and Amazons, symbolizing the victory of civilization over foreign barbarians; and on the north and south, somewhat strangely mingled with each other, scenes from the legend of Troy and from the battle of Lapithae and centaurs. The metopes of centaurs and Lapithae from the south side are the best preserved, and although much ingenuity is exercised to give variety to the composition and some are brilliantly successful, the subject was one which was beginning to lose interest; others are dull and even incompetent.

Pausanias in his account of the Acropolis at Athens ignores both metopes and frieze and mentions only the pediments in a couple of sentences. On the east, he says, the subject is the birth of Athena, on the west the contest of Athena and Poseidon for the land of Athens. According to legend, Athena was born fully armed from the head of Zeus, and archaic vase painters show a tiny doll-like figure emerging from the top of his skull. The designer of the east pediment of the Parthenon showed the moment after the birth, Zeus seated and Athena, already grown to full size, moving away (though destroyed in the 5th century A.D. the design is preserved in small reliefs). In the west pediment Athena and Poseidon had just produced the two gifts with which they sought the favour of the people of Athens (Athena the olive, Poseidon a salt spring symbolizing the sea) and were starting back from these portents, thus forming a V-shaped composition.

The practical advantage of both these designs is evident. By introducing two deities each slightly off centre instead of one exactly in the centre, the sculptor could make them less gigantic, thus not only easing the transition to the inevitably smaller figures farther away from it but also avoiding excessive flattening of

the central figure to bring it within the width of the pediment floor. The figures in the pediments of the Parthenon, as compared with those of earlier pediments, move more freely within their architectural frame. Even at Olympia the figures, for all their movement, are set for the most part facing the front or in profile one way or the other, with only tentative movements toward three-quarter positions. In the Parthenon there is a rhythmic movement, at one moment toward, at another away from the centre, and half toward or half away, with a preponderating balance inward; some of the figures are themselves subject to this rhythm, running, sitting or lying outward but with the head turning or half turning toward the centre. Their fragmentary condition forbids a detailed analysis of this subtle counterplay, but the drawings made not long before the building was destroyed by an explosion in 1687 indicate its general lines. (*See* PARTHENON.)

The Generation After Phidias.—This freedom of movement is part of a process which seems inevitable in the uninterrupted and comparatively limited conditions under which Greek sculpture developed. Although its strong stylistic tradition saved the artist from making mere reproductions of nature his aim, without an underlying design based (whether consciously or unconsciously) on geometrical proportions, increasing knowledge of the way the body worked and of the intricate forms and movements of drapery, combined with increasing technical skill and a marble capable of being given the most delicate details, did tempt him in the later 5th century to the rendering of effects that have little permanent sculptural value. The design no less than the execution of the pedimental figures of the Parthenon is masterly; yet in the more elaborate of them there is a hint that while something has been gained since Olympia, something has been lost, and that the style of Phidias has been copied and debased. In Athens, between the completion of the Parthenon and the end of the 5th century, there were sculptors who carried the refinement of this style to excess and exploited to the full the specious effect of clinging and tossing drapery, producing such hothouse masterpieces as the reliefs on the parapet round the bastion of Athena Nike at the southwestern corner of the Acropolis. There were also those who, in the earlier sculptures (the so-called caryatids) of the Erechtheum (*q.v.*)—begun 421 or possibly 431, interrupted by war and completed about 407—preserved the old grandeur, although the surface modeling had become more detailed.

The design of the caryatids, supporting figures of the south porch, may have been by Alcamenes, for they are close in the main lines of their composition—and even in some details—to a statue set up near the Erechtheum and recorded by Pausanias as having been dedicated by Alcamenes—though not necessarily the sculptor; it represented Procne, daughter of Pandion, a legendary king of Athens, who suffered barbarous treatment from her husband Tereus king of Thrace and in revenge killed her son Itys. The statue, perhaps dedicated after some incident in the Thracian campaigns of the 420s, has been found on the Acropolis; the head is fragmentary, the body fairly well preserved and in a distinctive style.

The Erechtheum is important in the history of Greek sculpture because some of the detailed building accounts have survived, and they give an indication of the way in which the production of the sculptures was organized. The friezes consist of figures about 20 in. tall, in very high relief, almost in the round; however, they were carved separately, with the backs flat, and were then fastened to a background of black Eleusinian limestone. The background of a frieze was always coloured, so that the final appearance would not be far different from normal, and the method was economical because it did not demand large blocks of expensive white marble which errors of carving on the sculptural face might spoil completely. What the craftsmen were given in the way of clay models or drawings to work from is not known, but it is known that they were paid 60 drachmas for the carving of each figure (irrespective of whether the craftsman was citizen, resident alien or slave), with a proportionate scale for smaller elements in the design. (The relative value of money is hard to estimate, but calculated on purchasing power the drachma would have been worth at that time nearly $3, or between 15s. and 20s.)

The frieze is in exceedingly low relief, never more than about 2¼ in. high, but the draftsmanship is such that the figures do not lack solidity. The design succeeds in suggesting the incidents in a long procession, the varying speed and character of the different elements in it and a sense of free movement, though any emphasis on the depth of space behind the figures is avoided. It was awkwardly placed and visible only at a steep angle from far below, so that the subtleties of execution must have been largely lost, although the greater depth of relief at the top of the frieze did something to counteract the steepness of the line of vision.

The disasters and casualties of the Peloponnesian War, together with the plague, the Sicilian expedition and the political turmoil of the end of the century, may have contributed to the feverish quality of some of the work of this time; they certainly decimated and dispersed the great concourse of highly skilled sculptors and craftsmen who had been assembled to give substance to the ideals of Periclean Athens.

3. Classical Sculpture Outside Athens.—The achievements of Athens have been stressed because, in addition to its high native achievement, its wealth and ambitious artistic program made it a magnet for artists from outside the city. Nevertheless, important sculpture was being made elsewhere in Greece during this period.

The School of Argos, and Polyclitus.—The other great centre in mainland Greece at this time was Argos. Ageladas (q.v.) of Argos was reputed to have been the teacher of both Myron and Phidias in the first quarter of the 5th century. His third pupil was said to have been Polyclitus the elder, and Polyclitus, though apparently a little younger than the other two, was certainly the leading sculptor of the Argive school about the middle of the century.

Although late in life (c. 420) Polyclitus made a colossal Hera of gold and ivory for her temple at Argos, he was known chiefly for his bronze statues of athletes, and especially for his "Doryphoros" (spear carrier), c. 450–440, which probably had more influence on Greek sculpture than any other. The "Doryphoros" was a statue embodying a theory of proportions, and also bore the title of the "Canon." Numerous marble copies have survived, and they agree so well with one another that it is fairly certain they reproduce the main design, although they necessarily fail to reproduce the minute finish for which Polyclitus was renowned. It was a thoroughly Greek idea to concentrate on a single comparatively limited problem, the representation in art of the naked male figure, and to work out exhaustively the effect of a one-legged stance on the other parts of the body. The "Doryphoros" is thickset and the head is large in proportion to the height; the muscular development is strong and general, as is appropriate in an all-round athlete. Although the proportions cannot now be recovered, the composition tells something of Polyclitus' method. There is a simple correspondence of function in the limbs; left arm and right leg are at work; right arm and left leg are free. In addition, the planes alternate through the body from head to foot; the plane of the head is turned to its right, of the torso to the left, of the thighs to the right and of the lower legs to the left. It was a criticism of Polyclitus in antiquity that his statues were rather square and made to one pattern; both these points have substance, and a theory of proportions is bound to entail a certain degree of monotony.

Statues of Amazons at Ephesus.—Tradition said that four sculptors—Polyclitus, Phidias, Cresilas (q.v.) and Phradmon—competed in making statues of an Amazon for the temple of Artemis at Ephesus, whose foundation was associated with the Amazons. These sculptors were contemporaries, and such a competition would have been possible about 440, though the story adds the unlikely sequel that the winner was decided by the sculptors' own votes and was adjudged to be Polyclitus, since each competitor, after putting himself first, put Polyclitus second. Nothing is known of the style of Phradmon, but three statues of Amazons have survived in marble copies; their style is that of the third quarter of the 5th century, and they have enough in common to suggest that they are part of a simultaneous dedication.

The type with the best claim to be Polyclitan is called the Capitoline because one of the more complete copies is in the Capitoline museum in Rome. This Amazon is twice wounded—above and below the right breast. The wounds are made the main motive of the statue, for the Amazon is drawing away her dress from them with her left hand, supporting herself with a spear held in her right. The Amazon ascribed to Cresilas (from the resemblance of its style to that of a head of Pericles whom Cresilas is known to have portrayed) is also wounded near the breast, but beyond a hint of weariness in the inclination of the head and the resting of the left elbow on a pillar, the wound is not made the motive of the statue. The third Amazon, that ascribed to Phidias, is unwounded. She carried a spear with which she was about to vault onto her horse, a feat mentioned by Xenophon in his treatise on horsemanship, but the horse was apparently not represented, and some writers believe that this Amazon is to be imagined as wounded in the leg and supporting herself on her spear, which would supply a motive for the drawing up of the dress from the left thigh.

Paeonius' "Victory."—There were other sculptors working in other parts of Greece and her colonies; some of their names are known from signatures on the bases of statues long destroyed or from references by ancient authors, but usually copies of their works cannot be identified. From Mende in Thrace, however, came a sculptor who was something of an innovator, and what was apparently his masterpiece has partly survived; this was the marble statue of Victory, by Paeonius, set up on a column 30 ft. high at Olympia, to commemorate a victory by the Messenians and Naupactians. The inscription mentions simply "the enemy," and Pausanias was told by the guides at Olympia that the victory was that at Sphacteria over the Spartans, their names being omitted because the dedicators feared to provoke them. Sphacteria was fought in 425, and the date fits the style of the statue.

It was an old subject, but it is here treated in a new spirit and with complete command of the material; the goddess appears to be floating down, this illusion being assisted by the way in which the drapery seems pressed against the body by the wind, by the cloak billowing behind and by the eagle beneath the feet, which provides the main support for the whole figure but contrives to suggest that it is unsupported.

The Peloponnese.—There is some architectural sculpture of the later 5th century from the Peloponnese. The metopes from the Heraeum at Argos, which housed the gold-and-ivory Hera of Polyclitus, are in a style derived from the contemporary Athenian, with its mannerisms of clinging and swirling drapery. One head, possibly from a pediment, has also been found; it is strongly Athenian in inspiration, but empty of feeling.

The sculptures from Bassae, near Phigalia (q.v.), are in another category; the very fragmentary metopes were in the overrefined sub-Phidian style, but the frieze, preserved almost complete, is without close parallel. The temple was of abnormal plan, since its long axis ran north and south instead of east and west; inside it was divided into two, the smaller room containing the cult-statue, which faced east through a door in the long eastern side of the building. Above the architrave of the larger room ran the frieze, sculptured in high relief. Its subjects were the battles of Greeks with Amazons and Lapithae with centaurs, arranged in such a way that the division between the subjects came a little way along each long side. The style here is not Athenian, although the designer evidently knew of the achievements of Athenian artists. The figures are stocky, with large heads; the action is extremely vigorous. The sculpture looks as if the carvers were provided with drawings, which they translated into marble according to their ability, for there is some unevenness of execution, the detail varies in fineness and the foreshortenings are managed with more skill in some places than in others. The designer may have been a Peloponnesian or a Greek from one of the colonies in southern Italy, and certain features, especially the momentary nature of some of the effects, make one suspect that he was primarily a painter rather than a sculptor.

4. The 4th Century.—The years around 400 seem to have been a time of quiescence in Greek sculpture, with the Attic school still subsisting on the Phidian legacy and the Argive on the Polyclitan. In free sculpture Athens seems to have produced nothing particularly worthy of note, but in reliefs there are the forerunners of that long series of grave reliefs which continued throughout the 4th century and which are an index not only to sculptural style but to thoughts and beliefs.

The pupils (probably nephews) of Polyclitus, Polyclitus the younger and Naucydes, still working mainly in bronze, kept up a respectable level of attainment. Polyclitus the younger, who, like other Greek sculptors, was also an architect, is known chiefly for his theatre at Epidaurus. Naucydes made a discobolus, of the type (known from several marble copies) where the athlete is about to take up his stand for the throw, holding the discus in his left hand and calculating his distance. Another statue, evidently by a different sculptor, is the bronze athlete found at Ephesus (perhaps an original), who is scraping himself free of oil and dust with a strigil. These are both in the Polyclitan tradition, but the sculptors were experimenting with subsidiary modeling, and instead of stressing only the main structure of bone and muscle, as Polyclitus did, they were attempting to suggest the appearance of the living surface, so that the statues must have looked more like flesh and blood and less like bronze. In the hair they introduced more movement and more plastic depth; instead of arranging the locks in a symmetrical pattern they swept them to one side or the other and made them stand up more freely from the surface of the skull.

The Athenian school was quiescent but not dormant; it was soon to produce a sculptor second in fame only to Phidias, one who has profoundly influenced the whole subsequent course of sculpture. This was Praxiteles (q.v.), whose life can be reconstructed with a fair degree of probability.

His father or uncle was Cephisodotus, whose own achievements were by no means negligible and who evidently contributed much to the formation of the new style. The best-known work of Cephisodotus was a bronze set up on the Areopagus at Athens, a statue of Eirene (Peace) carrying the child Plutus (Wealth). The cult of Eirene (a by-form of Demeter the earth-goddess) came to the fore after the defeat of the Spartans in 375 and the "Peace of Callias" in 371, and the statue was probably commissioned about that time. It appears on Roman coins of Athens, and there are copies in marble. Cephisodotus had reacted against the overdelicate style of his immediate predecessors and had turned for his inspiration to the period of just a century before his own time, studying the "peplos figures" of the early classical period. The composition is, however, broader in extent than the early classical figures, an effect attained by the right arm being held out to the side and supported on a long sceptre, by the child on the crook of the other arm and by the cloak hanging from the shoulders. In addition to breadth the figure conveys an exceptional feeling of weight and solidity, to which the firmly planted feet, the massive forms of the body, the voluminous drapery and the deepness of its folds all contribute. There is something new also in the poise of the head and in the face; the head is both turned and inclined more than hitherto, and the face has a sweetness of expression that does not conflict with the broad and simple modeling of its main features. Cephisodotus or a closely related contemporary made a marble statue of Hygieia (Health) for the Acropolis at Athens; a fragment of the head has been found, and there are many Roman copies. The head has a similar sweetness of expression and pure, simple, classical lines; the different dress—Ionic instead of Doric—is treated with a similar feeling for volume. These statues, carefully planned with an eye deliberately turned on the past, may be regarded as the first examples of conscious monumentality and academic classicism. Cephisodotus also made a statue of Hermes carrying the child Dionysus, which, although little reproduced by ancient copyists, is important as the forerunner of Praxiteles' statue of the same subject.

Praxiteles.—The earliest statues by Praxiteles himself look earlier in date than either Eirene or Hygieia; certainly they are less mature. The boy-satyr pouring wine, which enjoyed immense popularity, seems an unexciting work based closely on Polyclitan models, though with rather freer movement; the young Artemis (known from a copy in Dresden) is clearly influenced by Cephisodotus. But even in these there are signs of an original and less academic, if immature, personality. Praxiteles worked in both marble and bronze and was equally famous in each medium. The original models, or even full-sized prototypes, of his various creations may have been kept in his studio, and copies in marble and bronze, or versions slightly modified to suit the material, may have been made and sold after the original commission had been completed. The existence of some such system is implied by a story (which though ancient may be a later invention) of how the mistress of Praxiteles discovered which of his works he valued most by telling him that his studio was on fire and noting which he was most anxious about.

The so-called "Sauroctonus," a boy Apollo threatening a lizard with an arrow (a symbol of the killing of the dragon by Apollo at Delphi), was among the early though not the earliest bronzes, perhaps about 360. Instead of resting one elbow on a support the boy leans forward and rests his forearm against the tall tree stump up which the lizard runs; this allows a sweeping S-shaped curve to be imparted to the body, and it also permits greater projection and greater recession, the whole figure being tilted forward. It is customary to praise the plastic sense of the Greeks, but in fact their genius lay in suggesting rather than in representing the third dimension—not in their three-dimensional composition, but in the clarity and subtlety of their silhouette contours. This is shown by the fact that not until well on in the 4th century did sculptors seriously consider making statues intended to be seen from more than one viewpoint. This is not to say that they were malformed or unfinished; they were simply not intended for all-round views; like Greek architecture, which is four-sided, they offered at most a limited number of facets and not a three-dimensional continuum. Characteristically, the Greeks were content to set themselves a limited problem and seek a perfect solution; the test of its success is the imprint that was set on the whole of subsequent European sculpture and much of its painting. In the "Sauroctonus" the free leg is drawn right back and placed slightly behind the supporting leg; in a rather later marble by Praxiteles, the resting satyr, where the elbow rests on a tree stump and the whole body leans over to one side, the free leg is drawn even farther back and its foot placed well behind the other; moreover it is foreshortened in such a way that it looks deformed when seen from the side—proof that only a frontal viewpoint was intended.

The marble statue of Hermes, found at Olympia in the position described by Pausanias, is another leaning figure obviously by a sculptor who knew the Eirene and the Hermes of Cephisodotus, both of which have a similar motif. The Hermes of Praxiteles is however freer in its movement; the torso has a stronger but more flowing curve, and the arm (originally holding a bunch of grapes) is higher. There has been much discussion whether the statue from Olympia is by Praxiteles, as Pausanias says, or whether, on technical grounds, it is a later copy made to replace an original (perhaps a bronze) when that was taken elsewhere. The skeptics have some difficulty in agreeing on the date when the alleged copy was made, whether in Hellenistic or Roman times, and the difficulty arises partly because so few Greek originals have survived and partly because the conception, composition and style are clearly Praxitelean, and the statue, if not the original, differs from the original only in its finish (admittedly no slight matter, but not of primary importance for the present purpose). It may be that the statue at Olympia was a contemporary marble version of a bronze, modified (for instance by the addition of the tree stump) to suit the different material.

Very close to the Hermes in both style and execution are the head acquired by Lord Aberdeen in Greece in the early 19th century—perhaps a young Heracles—now in the British museum, and the head of Aphrodite at Petworth, Sussex, Eng. If these are not originals and yet are by the same hand, it is necessary to accept the curious hypothesis that three works by Praxiteles have survived in copies, all by the same copyist.

The most famous of the works by Praxiteles was the marble Aphrodite made for the people of Cnidus. The goddess was shown naked, laying aside her drapery on a water vessel that stood on a pedestal; these three elements formed the support necessary in marble. It was a bold innovation to show the goddess naked; the inspiration was said to have been Phryne, Praxiteles' mistress, when as an initiate at the Eleusinian mysteries she went down to the sea for ritual purification. Many copies have survived, mostly fragmentary, and although they make the main composition certain enough, none succeeds in giving any idea of the quality of the original. Possibly no casting of the Cnidian statue was allowed because of the delicate surface and colour, and copyists had to rely on statuettes modeled freehand. Where the ultimate effect depended on the play of light on an elaborately and subtly modeled surface—and this subtlety of the surface of the flesh was evidently one of the great achievements of Praxiteles—a full-sized cast would be essential if the effect was to be reproduced by the copyist.

A late work by Praxiteles or a pupil (about 330) is the bronze boy from the sea near Marathon. This is more concerned with all-round views than hitherto, a development paralleled, as will be seen, in the contemporary Argive-Sicyonian school. It is composed as a spiral advancing round an axis; although the figure appears to be leaning against a support it is in fact standing free and holding objects in both hands, possibly ribbons for use in a religious ceremony or as tokens of athletic victory. The faces of Praxiteles' statues are suffused with gentle feeling; they look less like gods and more like human beings than statues of the mid-5th century, but they do not display much emotion.

Scopas, Bryaxis, Leochares and Timotheus.—A great contemporary of Praxiteles, Scopas (q.v.), probably a Parian, was of a different bent. The literary tradition and the scanty remains testify to the emotional force of his sculpture. He was the architect of the new temple of Athena Alea at Tegea, the old one having been burned down in 395; reconstruction seems to have begun about 360. The fragments from the two pediments of this temple are in a new and distinctive style: the limbs are short and heavy; the heads are square and massive; the faces are broad; the eyes are set deep and in shadow, with the brows closely overhanging them; and the intensity of the gaze, expressing the strain of battle, is strengthened by the shape of the eye itself, which is small, short and round—a marked contrast to those of Praxiteles, which are long and narrow, and are formed in such a way that the centre portions of the lids tend to catch the light and give them a sunny appearance. That this is the style of Scopas is only an inference, but it is supported by the ancient notices of two other works, his group of sea creatures and his "Maenad" (bacchante). Direct copies from figures of the sea group are few and doubtful, the strongest claimant being a Nereid (mermaid) from Ostia; there are some heads of Tritons which may derive from it indirectly, and all have a wild, emotional expression that agrees well with the fragments from Tegea. A statuette of a maenad in Dresden is of much the same style in the strongly formed body, the taut pose and the tense gaze; it may be a copy—the only one—of the "Maenad" of Scopas. There had been plenty of action in Greek sculpture, especially in its reliefs, almost from the beginning, but it took nearly three centuries to break the monumental calm on the faces of the actors.

Scopas was one of the four sculptors (the other three being Bryaxis, q.v., Timotheus and Leochares, q.v.) invited to collaborate in the building of the tomb of Mausolus of Caria, nominally a provincial governor in the Persian empire but in reality an almost independent prince. Mausolus died in 353, and the building of his tomb at Halicarnassus, perhaps planned before his death, was undertaken by his devoted wife Artemisia. She herself died two years later, before it was finished, but the assembled artists under the architects Satyrus and Pythius carried it to completion. It eventually became one of the "seven wonders" of the world, partly because of its unusual form and partly from its rich decoration and exquisite finish. It was not a large building, though very large for a Greek tomb, and consisted of a high base on which rested a colonnade of 36 columns arranged in an oblong—either single, giving 9 on each façade and 11 on each side (counting the corner columns twice), or double, giving 6 on the façades and 7 on the sides. This colonnade supported a marble pyramid capped by a four-horse chariot.

The sculptural remains consist of the fragments of several portrait statues about ten feet high, two of which may possibly have stood in the chariot on top of the building. The best-preserved, which may be Mausolus himself, is a close if idealized study of a forceful personality, interesting as being a sympathetic portrait of a non-Greek by a Greek. There were also a number of rather smaller statues, but they are very fragmentary. The finest piece is the barrel of a horse with the lower part of its rider, and this, despite extreme mutilation, is masterly; the colossal horses from the chariot on the summit (said by Pliny to be the work of "Pythis," perhaps Pythius the architect) are by comparison commonplace, as are the numerous decorative lions.

There were also three friezes—centauromachy, Amazonomachy and chariot racing—that may have been set on or in the building or around its base. Little of the battle of Lapithae and centaurs has survived, and that is of poor quality. The chariot frieze is in very small fragments but of excellent style. Of the frieze of Greeks and Amazons about 90 ft. is preserved, which may be about a third of the original total, but since most of the slabs were built into the castle at Bodrum by the knights of St. John in the 15th century they have been severely mutilated. When C. T. Newton (q.v.) excavated the site of the Mausoleum in 1856 he found, in addition to the remains of free sculpture, three well-preserved slabs of this frieze; they are of exquisite finish and seem to be in Athenian style. Although the figures are in violent action, killing and being killed, the faces are perfectly calm and show no trace of the violent emotion associated with the style of Scopas, to whom they have sometimes been attributed. Other slabs show even wilder movement, but in all of them the figures are spaced out along the background with little overlapping. They are in very high relief, and, although the general movement is complicated, and limbs and drapery are often boldly foreshortened to suggest projection or recession from the main plane.

Numerous but unconvincing attempts have been made to ascribe the relief sculptures to the various sculptors, in view of Pliny's statement that Scopas was responsible for decorating the east side of the building, Bryaxis the north, Timotheus the south and Leochares the west. Differences both of design and of execution are apparent, and doubtless if all the sculptures had been preserved these would be less difficult to determine and evaluate, but it will probably never be known how much of the actual carving was done by the master sculptors themselves and how much by assistants. The evidence for the style of Scopas has been set out above.

Bryaxis was the sculptor of a famous statue in Alexandria of Sarapis, a Greek deity introduced into Egypt by Ptolemy I. Many copies of a statue of Sarapis have survived and are believed to go back to this statue; they display some resemblance of style to the statue of Mausolus.

A seated statue of Demeter from Cnidus, in the British museum, and a head of Alexander the Great, in Athens, may be by Leochares and should form the criterion for any work of his on the Mausoleum.

The style of Timotheus can be inferred from the sculptures of the temple of Asclepius at Epidaurus, although he was only one of several sculptors employed. This is usually dated c. 375 from the character of the building inscription; remains of two small pediments and two sets of acroteria (roof adornments) have survived, the figures being about half life-size. Like the Erechtheum, the temple is important in giving a glimpse of how the sculptural decoration of a building was organized. Each pediment cost just over 3,000 drachmas, and each figure used as an acroterium just over 700 drachmas. The sculptures are homogeneous in style and derive their inspiration from Athenian sculpture of the late

5th century, with their thin, sometimes calligraphic drapery, which almost ceases to exist where it touches the body. Three new features, however, distinguish them from Athenian sculpture: first, the faces have a sweet expression analogous to those of contemporary Athenian Cephisodotus, but with a touch of delicate wistfulness unlike his monumental serenity; second, some of the acroteria are Nereids, and their drapery is not only thin and clinging but damp, hanging limply where it is not stirred by the wind; third, and more lasting in its consequences, there is a careful study of heavy drapery, of the complicated folds which it produces when piled or looped up, and of the way in which cavernous folds can be used to provide a background of deep shadow against which the contours of the limbs stand out clearly. These are slight indications of the gradual change that was coming over Greek art and of the studiously sought-out effects which took the place of the majestic, seemingly simple and inevitable forms of 5th century sculpture.

The Artemision at Ephesus.—Rather later than the Mausoleum of Halicarnassus, and very different in character, are a series of reliefs from the temple of Artemis at Ephesus (q.v.). The archaic temple was destroyed by fire in 356; the new one, still unfinished in 333, repeated an unusual feature from it, namely the sculptured bottom drums of a number of its Ionic columns. Parts of both earlier and later sets were found in excavation, including a fairly complete specimen of the later, carved with the resurrection of Persephone or Alcestis. The movement is quiet and restrained, although, since several of the figures face the spectator, there is necessarily some foreshortening. The types are derived from statues of various periods—Hermes from a statue of Hermes by Polyclitus, Demeter from the statue of Eirene by Cephisodotus and Alcestis or Persephone from an Athenian type of the 5th century; the personification of Death, a softly modeled youth with large wings, may be an original creation. The general effect of a gentle melancholy is impressive, but the reliance on older types is symptomatic of a certain exhaustion of ideas.

Lysippus.—In the Peloponnese, a dominant new personality had arisen in Lysippus (q.v.) of Sicyon, an artist so prolific that there can be no doubt he must have had a number of assistants engaged in translating his basic ideas into bronze. Ancient authors describe the features of his style, and their description is borne out by the works—mostly copies—that can be attributed to him. He was said to have made the head smaller in proportion to the body and the body itself more lithe, thus increasing the appearance of height; as compared with the "Doryphoros" of Polyclitus, which the ancient critics may have had in mind, this is certainly true. His artistic ideals were summarized in his remark, of which only an ambiguous Latin version remains, that the earlier sculptors represented men as they were, but that he himself represented them as they appeared to be. Although many statues are probably copies after Lysippus, the evidence for his style rests primarily on two, the statue of the athlete Agias at Delphi and the statue in the Vatican of an athlete scraping himself with a strigil ("Apoxyomenos").

Lysippus himself worked only in bronze, and the statue of Agias is in marble, but it is almost certainly a contemporary copy, not highly finished, of a bronze signed by Lysippus in the hometown of Agias, Pharsalus in Thessaly. It was part of a family group set up by one Daochus a few years after 340, representing himself and his ancestors. Agias had died about 100 years before; the statue is therefore not a portrait from life, although it looks like one. The faulty modern restoration of the ankles has the effect of lessening the apparent height of the figure, which is tall and lithe though strongly built, while the head is small in proportion to the body. What distinguishes it even more sharply from the "Doryphoros" of Polyclitus is the alertness of the pose and the tenseness of the muscles, as if the man would at any moment spring into action, and although there is no spectacular breaking-through of the frontal plane of the composition, the head has a sharp turn, the gaze is directed into the distance and all the implied movement is away from the centre of the statue.

The "Apoxyomenos" of the Vatican is attributed to Lysippus because Pliny mentions his having made a well-known statue with this (not uncommon) subject. The existing statue is a copy made in Roman times from a bronze; the original was, from the style, a work of the later years of the 4th century, and it may possibly have been by Lysippus, or perhaps by a pupil, Daippus, who also treated the subject. If allowance is made for a few years' interval, the style agrees tolerably well with that of the statue of Agias, although the face is rounder, the features more generalized and the expression less intense. The statue has however the same alertness as Agias, appears ready to spring aside at any moment and—a significant innovation—it boldly breaks through the frontal plane, with its right arm stretched out to the front and its left arm crossing and masking the body; the complete freedom of movement in space and the all-round view would be more evident if the marble supports of leg and arm had not been added by the copyist.

The natural corollary of the interest in the accidental and in the expression of mood and emotion by 4th-century sculptors is portraiture. Portraits, or statues bearing the names of individuals, had been made for many years, but they were idealized portraits, in the sense that they showed the man not as an individual but as an embodiment of those qualities in which his excellence lay; even in the 4th century there was no sudden attempt to reproduce only the features of the man exactly as he was. There was, however, an introduction of such idiosyncrasies of feature as would make a statue recognizable as one particular person, and the Greeks tended to think not only of the face but of how the character was expressed in stature, posture and gesture.

5. Grave Reliefs and Votive Reliefs.—Before concluding the history of marble sculpture in the classical period, some account should be given of grave reliefs and votive reliefs. These were not confined to Athens, but, partly because of the inexhaustible supply of marble close at hand, they were produced in far greater numbers there than elsewhere, especially in the 4th century, and many have survived. The grave relief has a history going back into archaic times, when with its one—occasionally more than one—figure on a tall, narrow panel, it acted as an alternative or substitute for a statue; it was made in Athens, Naxos, Paros and elsewhere. This type of gravestone survived into the 5th century, but the finest examples then were from the Cyclades; the girl with her doves, now in New York, is from Paros. The reason for this is that at Athens there must have been some law which forbade their manufacture, for there is a gap of half a century until about 430, when they began again. The shape was still a panel, with a person, sometimes standing, sometimes seated, and usually engaged in the occupations of everyday life—a woman spinning, a man with the implements of his trade, a girl with her doll. Gradually it became more common to introduce other figures; the best-known example of the late 5th century is the gravestone of Hegeso, where the dead woman is handling a necklace from a casket that has been brought to her by a young girl. Gravestones in medium relief like this, and also in low relief, continue (they are often in the form of a large sepulchral vase of marble with reliefs on its surface), but in general the relief becomes higher as the 4th century goes on, until, late in the century, the figures—often two, sometimes three, sometimes even more—are almost statues in the round, set within an architectural frame consisting of a low gable supported on two pilasters, which may symbolize the house or the tomb. The increasing size and cost of these monuments led to their prohibition by a law of Demetrius Phalereus, then governor of Athens, about 317, when they cease abruptly.

At first sight the meaning of the grave reliefs seems obvious: the dead persons are shown as they were in life and as they would be remembered by the living. But it is possible that they were thought of as performing these everyday actions for the last time: the girl may be kissing her doves good-by, the woman may be putting away her jewels forever; the obvious scenes of farewell support this view. Alternatively, the dead may be thought of as continuing in the underworld a life similar to that which they lived on earth. A further problem is that, where two or three persons are shown, it is sometimes difficult to decide which is the dead.

The inscriptions normally consist only of a name; when two people appear and only one is named, then presumably the other is the survivor, but when there is a more elaborate inscription, it does not always seem to fit the scene. For instance, a woman is shown embracing a child, but only she and her husband and father (who do not appear) are mentioned in the inscription; she must, then, be depicted as the typical wife and mother, and the reliefs must have been considered as memorials of the family, commemorating both the living and the dead and their relationship.

Nowhere perhaps is the Greek preference for the ideal as against the accidental seen more clearly than here, for, although names are given, the heads are never portraits; the scenes of family life and the scenes of parting, becoming more emotional, in accordance with the general trend of art, as the 4th century progresses, are of universal application.

The heroizing of the dead was of remote antiquity; in Laconia in the archaic period a series of reliefs were carved in which a man and a woman were shown seated, the man holding a large wine cup; they are approached by people of a much smaller size, who bring offerings. The presence of a snake indicates a connection with the underworld; these are heroized ancestors being revered by their descendants. Another kind of hero relief, which originated outside Attica in early classical times but became extremely popular in the 4th century and the Hellenistic period, forms a link between the grave reliefs and the votive reliefs shortly to be described. This is the so-called "sepulchral banquet." On it a man and woman are shown at a meal, with a boy serving wine for a drink offering; in the background there is sometimes a horse, the symbol of a hero; or the man may wear a certain kind of cylindrical headdress associated with the underworld. This is evidently a ritual meal (perhaps imaginary and symbolic but perhaps sometimes actually taken by the survivors at the tomb) which indicates a belief in the continuation of life beyond the grave and in a continuing link between the dead and the surviving members of his family.

In classical times votive reliefs (reliefs offered to the gods), usually in commemoration of favours received, are mostly in the form of a long panel of marble (with a simple architectural surround suggesting rather than depicting a sanctuary) in low relief; the general effect, when the colour existed, must have been that of a small panel picture. At one end of the scene the deity is shown in profile facing inward and is approached by a worshiper or worshipers on a smaller scale. In Athens, where they are most plentiful, the majority of votive reliefs come from the late 5th and the 4th century and are sometimes of fine quality. They are valuable in showing the forms in which various deities were personified and, like the grave reliefs, because of their numbers and the period they cover, in acting as a guide to developments of style. More valuable still from this point of view are the reliefs that it was customary to carve at the top of the marble slabs on which treaties were inscribed, showing the deities of the two states which were parties to the treaty. Although they are not major works of art they can often be exactly dated and thus form a criterion for the style and sculptural types of a particular period; other undated reliefs can be grouped with them and a connected sequence thus obtained.

6. Painting of the Classical Period.—In the classical period it is possible to date some of the great painters and to gain some idea of their attainments. Ancient authors, especially Pliny, recorded names of the most famous, sometimes with a few remarks (difficult to interpret) on what each added to the art, sometimes with a number of trivial anecdotes; Pausanias described some of the wall paintings in detail. The contemporary vases, too, certainly reflect some of the advances made in major painting; but it is a reflection only, darkened by the different and more limited technique, by the curved and curtailed surfaces that the vases offer for pictures and by the vase painter's freedom to depart from his model when he wished. The nature of the main changes is clear. In composition the figures were set on different levels to suggest partly inequalities of ground, partly greater distance, although there is no diminution of their size; some indications of natural features were given, though kept to a minimum; the third dimension was indicated by a number of new and carefully studied foreshortenings of limbs and of inanimate objects such as armour; new poses involving difficult foreshortenings were invented; there was overlapping of one figure on another, and parts of the figures were hidden by the terrain. As for choice of subject, though battle scenes continued to be popular, the time before or after any event was often taken: the time of doubt and indecision or of reaction and despair.

In the second quarter of the 5th century, the period of the sculptures of Olympia, the chief names are those of Micon and Polygnotus (q.v.). Micon was an Athenian, and Pausanias mentions the subject and whereabouts of his pictures in Athens (Amazonomachy, centauromachy, the legend of Theseus and the Argonauts). One of his details gave rise to a proverb "Easier than Butes," meaning something very easily done—Micon had represented the hero Butes by his helmet and one eye, the rest doubtless being hidden by a rock or a rise in the ground (figures eclipsed in this way occur on vases of the time).

Far more famous was Polygnotus, a Thasian, who later became an Athenian. He twice chose as his subject the sack of Troy, once in the Stoa Poikile (painted colonnade) at Athens, once in the Lesche (clubroom) of the Cnidians at Delphi. Of this last painting and of the pendant picture in the same room, Odysseus summoning the soul of Tiresias in Hades, Pausanias gives a detailed account. When Delphi was excavated, a small discoloured patch of a plastered wall was found; this is all that remains of the original work, not of Polygnotus only, but of all the Greek wall painters. From Pausanias' description the general appearance of the pictures can be envisaged. There were numerous figures at different levels and in balanced design, but not closely related to one another in the action, since various episodes were taking place simultaneously. He stresses also the expression of emotions (in these two pictures mostly of fear, sorrow and misery) in the faces, but chiefly in the attitudes and gestures. Two examples may be given from the picture of Hades, of the allusiveness that was a feature of much Greek painting and sculpture: first, the demon Eurynomos "who eats the flesh of corpses. His colour is between blue and black, like that of the flies that settle on meat; he is showing his teeth and is sitting on a vulture's skin." Second, the hunter Actaeon, who had come upon Artemis bathing and had been torn to pieces by his own hounds; one version of the story said that he had disguised himself in a deerskin; another that he had been transformed by the goddess into a deer. Polygnotus showed "Actaeon with his mother; they hold a fawn in their hands and are seated on a deerskin; a hunting-dog is stretched at their side as a token of Actaeon's life and the manner of his death."

Two other statements about Polygnotus have some value, one on the style, the other on the content of his pictures. He was said to have opened the mouth and shown the teeth, to have varied the stiff archaism of the features and to have been the first to represent transparent drapery. This, by comparison with sculpture, describes correctly, if superficially, the change from archaic to early classical. Secondly (according to Aristotle, who speaks as if this was generally agreed), he imparted *ethos*—noble character—to his figures, making them seem "better than ourselves" (unlike his successor Dionysius of Colophon, who made them like ourselves, or the 4th-century painter Pausias, who made them worse); this judgment too can be understood by looking at early classical sculpture and at certain of the vases which reflect Polygnotan style. Polygnotus, and many later painters also, used only four colours—white, black, red and yellow and their mixtures—and he may have employed a limited amount of shading to indicate roundness or hollows in flesh and drapery, since contemporary vases use it, though very sparingly.

Of the next generation one of the leading painters was Panaenus, the brother of Phidias, who in his picture of Marathon was said to have painted the leaders of both sides as portraits (*iconicos*), though it is uncertain what degree of likeness this implies. In the last quarter of the 5th century came two painters who were clearly on the threshold of modern European drawing and painting: Parrhasius of Ephesus and Apollodorus of Athens.

Pliny, in a passage difficult to translate with precision but essential for an understanding of the advance being made at the time, explained the achievement of Parrhasius as subtlety of outline. He produced an outline "which expressed the contours of the figure. For the bounding-line should appear to recede, and its edge should imply the existence of the parts behind, and thus display even what it conceals."

Apollodorus on the other hand was called "the shadow-painter." Pliny says that he was "the first to express appearance (*species*), and to bring the brush to its rightful glory." Plutarch is more explicit: "Apollodorus was the first man to discover the gradation and change of colour in shadows." Among the vases, the finest of the lecythi (cylindrical oil vases often dedicated on graves), with outline drawings on a white ground, may give some indication of the achievement of Parrhasius; otherwise the vases fail us. The medium is incapable of giving any idea of the kind of advance made by Apollodorus; perhaps partly because wall painting and panel painting had so far outstripped it and skilled painters were abandoning the craft, there was a steep decline in the general quality of vase painting in Athens, although in the western colonies there were still painters of merit. For a short period in the middle of the 4th century the art revived, and the group of Athenian vases known as Kerch vases give some indication of the advances made in draftsmanship by major painters, but only in a general way.

Zeuxis (*q.v.*) of Heraclea (probably the Heraclea in the gulf of Taranto in southern Italy) was considered to have exploited the discoveries made by Apollodorus, his slightly older contemporary, and similar discoveries are ascribed to him, as for instance, "the relationship of lights and shadows." The story is told that for his painting of Helen for the city of Acragas he chose the five most comely models he could find among the virgins of the city in order to select their best features for incorporation in his single figure—a story which gives a clue to the aesthetic theory of the period.

VI. THE HELLENISTIC PERIOD (c. 330–c. 30 B.C.)

1. Hellenistic Sculpture.—After the 4th century the styles of individual masters are not so clearly discernible. Schools of sculpture were less static; skill in the art was widespread, and sculptors moved freely; there were rich commissions in many places, especially the east.

The School of Lysippus.—Lysippus' school at Sicyon still flourished. His brother Lysistratus invented a process for taking plaster molds of the human face from life, and he worked over wax casts from these molds for conversion into bronze—a clear indication of the way men's minds were running and, in a period when demand was brisk, obviously a time-saving process. There was a growing realism in Hellenistic portraiture; nevertheless it is difficult to find in Greek art before the 1st century B.C. any portrait which approaches the frank imitation of every individual feature such as is commonly found in Roman republican portraiture; even in later Hellenistic art there is always a tendency to idealism, to seek the typical rather than the accidental and to interpret and modify the features in such a way as to conform with the artist's concept of character.

A pupil of Lysippus, Eutychides (*q.v.*) of Sicyon, made a statue of the Tyche (*i.e.*, the Fortune, the essential personality) of the city of Antioch, which was founded in 300. This is the prototype of countless personifications of cities, provinces and countries in Greek, Roman and all later European art. The love of personification arose very early in Greece, but it increased greatly in the 5th and subsequent centuries in both sculpture and painting; every kind of abstract quality was personified, as well as places, mountains, rivers and other natural features. This was a substitute for exact representation; it was more explicit; and its popularity and convenience may well have delayed the development of naturalistic landscape painting. The city of Antioch was personified by Eutychides as a heavily draped woman sitting in a complicated pose on a rock, at the foot of which was the river-god Orontes as a youth swimming. It is a poetic approach, an attempt to express in sculpture the qualities of landscape, and

to contrast the stability of the rock and the city founded on it with the fluidity of the river at its base. Not only is the composition of the figure such as to emphasize the third dimension, but every fold in the carefully studied, voluminous drapery is designed either to enhance its solidity or to bind it to the rock. The differing textures and thickness of two kinds of cloth are shown; sculptors of the 3rd century were interested in any new variation that could be devised in drapery and were soon experimenting with the effect of an exceedingly thin, almost transparent cloak worn over a thicker dress, the folds of which showed through.

Another pupil of Lysippus, Chares, of Lindos in Rhodes, made a bronze colossus representing Apollo as god of the sun for the city of Rhodes. This was over 100 ft. high, and Philo of Byzantium, a later Hellenistic writer on mechanics, describes how it was cast piece by piece in position. Despite heavy reinforcement inside with stone and iron, it was overthrown by an earthquake 56 years later.

Alexandria.—Alexandria in Egypt, one of the numerous cities of the time which took their name from their founder, Alexander the Great, quickly became a vast trading and manufacturing centre. It was also the greatest ancient centre of learning and research, and the dissection undertaken there placed at the service of artists a knowledge of human anatomy that they had not so far possessed; whether for good or ill, this knowledge was soon displayed in Hellenistic art. Alexandria was also an art centre, but shortage of marble was one of the reasons it did not develop an important school of sculpture; a peculiarity of technique, so-called *morbidezza*, in which the planes of subsidiary modeling melt into one another without any sharp demarcation, is characteristic of much Hellenistic sculpture from Egypt, but, although common there, it is found in other places as well. Alexandrian artists seem to have been masters of the grotesque, and their caricatures of age and deformity are excellent; but again, this ability is not confined to Egypt. The lost original of the Aphrodite from Cyrene, copy of Roman date from a Greek work, has sometimes been claimed for Hellenistic Alexandria, but it may have been the product of a 4th-century school with an ideal of female beauty different from the Praxitelean.

Pergamene Sculpture.—Perhaps the most homogeneous group of Hellenistic sculpture was that of Pergamum; certainly it is the most easily distinguishable, partly because the evidence is abundant. Pergamum was a wealthy kingdom in Asia Minor, near the site of Troy, which for half a century was in danger from the Celts ("Gauls") who had swept down from the north and had invaded the mainland of Greece as well as Asia Minor, crossing the Hellespont in 278. This eastern band was defeated by Attalus I of Pergamum in 241, and the war ended some ten years later when they were confined to an area in central Asia Minor (Galatia). It is likely that the series of over-life-size statues, of which the "Dying Gaul" of the Capitoline museum in Rome is the most famous, reproduce a dedication made to commemorate the victory. Unlike the war memorials of the 5th and 4th centuries, which symbolized battles by depicting legendary conflicts with Amazons or centaurs, in the dedication of Attalus the real opponents are shown, and, although they had been a deadly menace to the Greeks of Asia Minor, the sculptors have rendered with sympathy both the physical type of these proud, ruthless invaders and their behaviour in defeat. The group in the Terme museum in Rome of the Gaul killing himself to avoid capture, after having stabbed his wife, is also copied from this dedication, and there are other fine fragments. The sculptors are apt to display too obviously their knowledge of anatomy, but in general the treatment is remarkably restrained. A dedication of smaller bronze statues of Gauls, Greeks, Amazons, Persians and giants set up in Athens, probably about 200 when Attalus I visited the city, is more exaggerated in both the modeling and the expression of the faces, and in spite of their ingenuity the poses tend to be theatrical and empty. More theatrical still is the external frieze of the great altar erected some time in the next 50 years by Eumenes II at Pergamum itself; it consists of several hundred feet of the highest possible relief, showing with astonishing technical skill and a wealth of mythological allusion the battle of the gods and giants. The internal frieze is of a peaceful subject in a less sensational style. It is interesting in its resemblance to a painting in the disposition of the figures, which are smaller in relation to the height of the frieze and are set at different levels, and in the introduction of elements of landscape.

Rhodian and Other Schools of Sculpture.—A strong case has been made for dating Laocoon and his sons—a famous group in the Vatican (by three Rhodian artists)—to the 2nd century, instead of to the generally accepted date in the second half of the 1st century B.C.; certainly its style and spirit have much in common with the Pergamene altar.

About the same date another Rhodian sculptor may have made the "Victory"—memorial to a sea battle—found on Samothrace, where excavations have shown that the whole monument of the victorious goddess alighting on the prow of the victorious flagship was placed in a partly natural, but partly artificial landscape setting, so that the ship appeared to be afloat.

Other schools of sculpture, or other individual sculptors of the time, were more academic and relied more closely on older masterpieces; a conspicuous example is the statue of Aphrodite (the "Venus de Milo"), found on Melos but carved by a sculptor of Antioch on the Maeander; he borrowed the general composition of a 4th-century statue in Corinth but altered the position of the arms, changed the action and modernized the drapery.

About this time, just after the middle of the 2nd century, Greece became a Roman province and the sack of Corinth by the Roman general Lucius Mummius flooded Rome with masterpieces of Greek sculpture and painting. By their increasing activity in politics but also of the art of eastern Greece; the last king of Pergamum bequeathed his kingdom to Rome, and a few years later, in 130, it became the Roman province of Asia.

Finally, the name of Pasiteles is significant for the understanding of the growing Roman taste for Greek art and the means by which it was satisfied. Pasiteles was a native of Neapolis (Naples), the Greek colony in southern Italy, who was established in Rome about the middle of the 1st century B.C. He was both metalworker and sculptor, wrote a long book on famous earlier works of art and seems to have reproduced many of them by perfecting methods of copying, especially by molding and by the use of the pointing machine; he has even been claimed as the inventor of this device, without which the thousands of copies from Greek original statues which were known to the romanized world could never have been produced.

2. Hellenistic Painting.—There is no significant aesthetic division between the painting of the mid-4th century and that of the early Hellenistic period, although there was some change of circumstances. Painters now worked more for persons and less for cities, came from many parts of the Greek world and accepted commissions in places widely separated; this was due to the political situation, to the power and wealth of Alexander's successors and of other princes and the corresponding decline in the power of the city-states, to the wider spread of Greek culture following Alexander's conquests and to the ease of travel.

Among a number of painters who are now little more than names, two of the late 4th century stand out, Protogenes and Apelles (*qq.v.*). Both wrote books on painting, and many anecdotes are preserved of their rivalry. Protogenes was a perfectionist and, from the anecdotes, aimed at complete illusion, attempting to conceal all traces of the artifice by which it had been achieved. Apelles was interested in the painting of light, for one of his pictures was of Alexander the Great with the thunderbolt, in which he darkened the figure of Alexander in order to enhance the apparent brightness of the thunderbolt; he also painted lightning. On the technical side he invented a glaze which was supposed to have had the effect both of making the colours more brilliant and of harmonizing them. His Aphrodite rising from the sea, painted for the city of Cos, was as famous as the Cnidian Aphrodite of Praxiteles, and his elaborate allegory of Calumny is known to the modern world through Botticelli's version of it based on a detailed description by Lucian.

Perhaps the most trustworthy single piece of evidence for the history of ancient wall painting is a mosaic discovered in the House of the Faun at Pompeii. The exact date of the mosaic itself is doubtful and of no great importance; what is important is that it reproduces a painting of the last years of the 4th century, almost certainly the battle between Alexander and Darius III, painted by Philoxenus of Eretria for Cassander the Macedonian, son of Antipater. Large patches are missing, and naturally every detail and fails altogether to reproduce some of the more subtle effects; nevertheless it is of unique value. It shows the dramatic concentration of the extremely complicated but carefully balanced composition—no longer episodic but centred on the personal encounter of Alexander and Darius, which summed up the victory of Greece over Asia. It shows the use which a leading painter of this time could make of elaborate foreshortenings, of turning movements in space, of specious effects like the reflection in the polished shield, and of the pattern of spears, signifying the ordered and disordered movement, deepening the perspective and implying the presence of troops which it would have been confusing to show. The Greek use of symbol and token is seen in this feature and also in the sample of abandoned equipment in the foreground, which does not aim at being a realistic presentation of the debris of battle. Much has been written about this mosaic, and it is certainly worth prolonged study.

In general, Hellenistic painters seem to have exploited without, perhaps, adding much to the achievements of their predecessors. Still life and genre began to appear as independent subjects, and the influence of the stage and of scene painting, strong in the 4th century, became stronger still. One important innovation was made, though its date and origin are uncertain: in the paintings of the adventures of Odysseus on the walls of a room in a house on the Esquiline hill in Rome, the human figures are on a far smaller scale in relation to the landscape than is customary before. It is true they have their names inscribed against them and that localities are personified in human form; furthermore, the painting is a continuous panorama, divided into episodes simply by a pretended architectural frame of painted pilasters; nevertheless the treatment of the landscape foreshadows that in European painting of the 15th century and after. The house on the Esquiline was of the 1st century B.C. and after. The paintings probably copy an earlier, Hellenistic original.

In complete antithesis to this is the picture of Arcadia in a scene of Heracles finding his son Telephus, a fairly direct copy of Roman art from a Hellenistic original of the 2nd century B.C. Arcadia is personified as a goddess of superhuman scale, accompanied by Pan; both wear wreaths, but otherwise natural objects are kept to the minimum of a few fruits. Different again both in spirit and in artistic presentation are the scenes of initiation from the Villa Item in Pompeii, perhaps freely copied from a 2nd-century Hellenistic original; the human figures are isolated-like statues against a monotone background, which is diversified by painted architectural elements; and some of them are borrowed (as in the column drum of the Ephesian Artemision) from types invented in sculpture.

Both in painting and in sculpture, taste tended to veer between the sensational and the academic, and, as may be seen from the two friezes of the altar of Pergamum, contrasting moods could exist together. There was, in short, no longer the steady, almost uniform development of the 5th, and even of the 4th century, but a variety in some ways not dissimilar from that of modern Europe. *See* Bronze and Brass Work; Byzantine Art and Architecture; Gem; Greek Architecture; Mosaic; Numismatics; Order; Pottery and Porcelain; and references under "Greek Art" in the Index.

BIBLIOGRAPHY.—I. *General*: G. M. A. Richter, *A Handbook of Greek Art*, 4th ed., rev., with extensive bibliography (1965); J. Boardman *et al.*, *The Art and Architecture of Ancient Greece* (1967). For literary sources see J. Overbeck, *Die antiken Schriftquellen*, with passages in ancient writers, not translated (1868); K. Jex-Blake and E. Sellers, *The Elder Pliny's Chapters on the History of Art* (1896); Sir James G. Frazer, *Pausanias' Description of Greece*, translation and commentary (1898); Pausanias, *Description of Greece,* with Eng. trans. by W. H. S. Jones and R. E. Wycherley (1935). *II. Greek Sculpture:* C. Picard, *Manuel d'archéologie grecque: La sculpture,* vol. i–v, a detailed history, with copious references (1935–66); G. M. A. Richter, *The Sculpture and Sculptors of the Greeks,* the most useful general work in English, new ed. (1950); R. Lullies and M. Hirmer, *Greek Sculpture* (1957). For signatures of sculptors see J. Marcadé, *Recueil des signatures de sculpteurs grecs,* vol. i, ii (1953–57). For special periods and subjects see G. M. A. Richter, *The Portraits of the Greeks* (1965); W. Lamb, *Greek and Roman Bronzes* (1929); H. K. Süsserott, *Griechische Plastik des 4. Jahrhunderts vor Christus* (1938); G. M. A. and I. A. Richter, *Kouroi* (1942); *Korai: Archaic Marble Maidens* (1968); H. G. G. Payne and G. M. Young, *Archaic Marble Sculpture from the Acropolis,* 2nd ed. (1950); G. Becatti, *Problemi fidiaci* (1951); M. Bieber, *The Sculpture of the Hellenistic Age* (1961); S. Adam, *The Technique of Greek Sculpture* (1967). For architectural sculptures see G. Rodenwaldt, *Korkyra,* vol. ii (1939); A. Furtwängler et al., *Aegina* (1906); B. Ashmole, N. Yalouris, and A. Frantz, *Olympia: the Sculptures of the Temple of Zeus* (1967); P. E. Corbett, *The Sculpture of the Parthenon* (1959); F. Brommer, *Die Skulpturen der Parthenon-Giebel* (1963); *Die Metopen des Parthenon* (1967); J. M. Paton (ed.), *The Erechtheum,* 2 vol. (1927). For tomb reliefs see A. Conze, *Die attischen Grabreliefs,* 4 vol. (1890–1922); G. M. A. Richter, *Archaic Attic Gravestones* (1944); K. Friis Johansen, *The Attic Grave-Reliefs of the Classical Period* (1951).

Many of the most important studies of Greek art are to be found in three kinds of publications, of which the following are examples:

(i) Reports of Excavations: G. Treu and A. Furtwängler, *Olympia,* iii, "Die Bildwerke" (1894–97) and iv, "Die Bronzen" (1890); T. Homolle et al., *Fouilles de Delphes* (1902 et seq.); H. A. Thompson et al., *The Athenian Agora,* vol. i, *Portrait Sculpture* (1953) and vol. xi, *Archaic and Archaistic Sculpture* (1965), by E. B. Harrison.

(ii) Catalogues of Museums: Athens: H. Schrader, E. Langlotz, and W. H. Schuchhardt, *Die archaischen Marmorbildwerke der Akropolis,* 2 vol. (1939). *Berlin:* C. Blümel, *Katalog der Sammlung antiker Skulpturen. Boston:* L. D. Caskey, *Catalogue of Greek and Roman Sculpture* (1925). *Copenhagen:* F. Poulsen, *Ancient Sculpture in the Ny Carlsberg Glyptotek,* rev. ed. (1951). *Cyrene:* E. Paribeni, *Catalogo delle sculture di Cirene* (1959). *London:* F. N. Pryce, *Catalogue of Sculpture,* vol. i, pt. i, "Prehellenic and Early Greek" (1928). *New York:* G. M. A. Richter, *Catalogue of Greek Sculptures in the Metropolitan Museum of Art* (1954). *Rome:* W. Amelung and G. Lippold, *Die Skulpturen der Vaticanischen Museen,* i–iii (1903, 1908, 1936); W. Helbig, *Führer durch die öffentlichen Sammlungen klassischer Altertümer in Rom,* 2 vol., rev. ed. by H. Speier et al. (1963–66); D. Mustilli, *Museo Mussolini* (1939); E. Paribeni, *Museo Nazionale Romano: Sculture Greche* (1953).

(iii) Periodicals: Journal of Hellenic Studies; Annual of the British School at Athens; American Journal of Archaeology; Hesperia; Acta Archaeologica (Copenhagen); *Bulletin de Correspondance hellénique; Revue archéologique; Jahrbuch des Deutschen Archäologischen Instituts; Mitteilungen des Deutschen Archäologischen Instituts; Jahreshefte des Österreichischen Archäologischen Instituts in Wien; Notizie degli Scavi di Antichità; Monumenti Antichi; Annuario della R. Scuola Archeologica italiana di Atene.*

III. Greek Architecture: D. S. Robertson, *A Handbook of Greek and Roman Architecture,* rev. ed. (1945); W. B. Dinsmoor, *The Architecture of Ancient Greece* (1950); A. W. Lawrence, *Greek Architecture* (1957); H. Berve, G. Gruben, and M. Hirmer, *Greek Temples, Theatres, and Shrines* (1963); R. Martin, *Manuel d'architecture grecque* (materials and technique) (1965).

IV. Greek Painting: M. H. Swindler, *Ancient Painting* (1929); E. Pfuhl, *Masterpieces of Greek Drawing and Painting,* Eng. trans., new ed. (1955); J. White, *Perspective in Ancient Drawing and Painting* (1956); M. Robertson, *Greek Painting* (1959). For vase painting see A. Furtwängler and C. Reichhold, *Griechische Vasenmalerei* (1900–32); Union Académique Internationale, *Corpus Vasorum Antiquorum,* for collections of ancient vases in various countries (1922 et seq.); E. Pfuhl, *Malerei und Zeichnung der Griechen,* vol. i–iii (1923; edition of vol. iii by C. Schefold entitled *Tausend Jahre griechische Malerei,* 1940); P. Jacobsthal, *Ornamente griechischer Vasen* (1927); Sir J. D. Beazley, *Attic White Lekythoi* (1938), *The Development of Attic Black-Figure* (1951), *A List of the Published Writings of J. D. Beazley* (1951), *Attic Black-Figure Vase-Painters* (1956), *Attic Red-Figure Vase-Painters* (1963); A. Lane, *Greek Pottery* (1948); G. M. A. Richter, *Attic Red-Figured Vases: a Survey,* rev. ed. (1958); R. M. Cook, *Greek Painted Pottery* (1960); M. Hirmer and P. E. Arias, *A History of 1000 Years of Greek Vase Painting* (1962); A. D. Trendall, *The Red-Figured Vases of Lucania, Campania, and Sicily* (1967).

V. Greek Terra Cottas: F. Winter, *Die Typen der figürlichen Terrakotten* (1903); R. A. Higgins, *Greek Terracottas* (1967); S. Mollard-Besques, *Catalogue raisonné des figurines et reliefs en terre-cuite grecs, étrusques et romains au Musée National du Louvre,* vol. i (1954). *VI. Coins and Gems:* C. M. Kraay and M. Hirmer, *Greek Coins* (1966); G. M. A. Richter, *The Engraved Gems of the Greeks and Etruscans* (1968).

(B. As.)

GREEK FIRE, the name applied generally to inflammable compositions used in warfare during ancient times and the middle ages, particularly to that first employed by the Byzantine Greeks at the siege of Constantinople in A.D. 673. The employment of incendiary materials in war is of very early origin; many ancient writers mention the use of flaming arrows, fire pots and such substances as pitch, naphtha, sulfur and charcoal. In later centuries saltpetre and turpentine made their appearance and the resulting inflammable mixtures were known to the crusaders as Greek fire or wild fire. But Greek fire, properly so called, was apparently of a somewhat different character.

It is said that in the reign of Constantine Pogonatus (A.D. 668–685) an architect named Callinicus, who had fled from Heliopolis in Syria to Constantinople, prepared liquid fire that could be thrown out in pots or projected like water from tubes, usually called siphons, mounted in the prow of a ship. The Greeks first employed this secret weapon when the Saracen ships approached Constantinople in the year 673, setting them afire and thus saving the city from attack.

The art of compounding this mixture, which was also referred to as sea fire, was a jealously guarded secret at Constantinople and on several later occasions proved of great advantage to the city. Its nature has remained a secret ever since. Some writers have supposed that the novelty introduced by Callinicus was saltpetre, but this view involves the difficulty that saltpetre was apparently not known until the 13th century and, in any event, would probably not have given the results that have been attributed to Greek fire.

A British army officer, Lieut. Col. H. W. L. Hime, after a close examination of the available evidence early in the 20th century, concluded that the secret ingredient of Greek fire was quicklime, which is well known to give off heat when mixed with water. Other writers have suggested that the essential ingredient of Greek fire was phosphide of calcium, but it seems unlikely that this substance was known in the middle ages. The most recent research by J. R. Partington concludes that Greek fire was a distilled petroleum fraction with other ingredients but not containing saltpetre.

Whatever it was, the mixture apparently took fire spontaneously when wetted, could not be put out with water, and was usually projected toward the enemy from tubes. A revival of the idea, greatly transformed in character by modern chemistry, was seen in the flame throwers (q.v.) that appeared in 20th-century warfare.

BIBLIOGRAPHY.—H. W. L. Hime, *Gunpowder and Ammunition, Their Origin and Progress* (1904); J. R. Partington, *A History of Greek Fire and Gunpowder* (1960); Edward A. Dieckmann, "Sunday Punch Weapon" in *Proceedings of the U.S. Naval Institute,* vol. 82, no. 10, p. 1088 (1956).

(H. C. T.)

GREEK INDEPENDENCE, WAR OF, the name given to the rebellion of the sultan's Greek subjects against Ottoman rule, a struggle which ended in the establishment of an independent kingdom of Greece. This rebellion originated in the activities of the Philiki Etaireia ("friendly band"), a patriotic conspiracy founded in Odessa in 1814. By that time the desire for some form of independence was common among Greeks of all classes, whose Hellenism, or sense of Greek nationality, had long been fostered by the Orthodox Church, by the survival of the Greek language and by the administrative arrangements of the Ottoman empire. Their economic progress and the impact of western revolutionary ideas intensified their Hellenism. Some dreamed of reviving the Byzantine empire; some merely thought in terms of succeeding to local Turkish rulers; and others aspired to establish a constitutional state. This last idea was canvassed (but without success) at the congress of Vienna, it being hoped that the Ionian Islands would be united to the mainland to form a Greek state. Nevertheless, the Etairists made at first little progress. They were, however, astute enough to seek a leader of rank. Although the Russian minister, Count I. A. Kapodistrias, refused the honour, they prevailed, in 1820, on Prince Alexandros Ypsilantis (q.v.) to take the leadership. A member of the Russian service, he had the emperor's approval, having assured him that he had no intention of taking action without adequate military preparations. Since Ypsilantis had the blessing of Russia, the

Etaireia expanded rapidly, and the leading Greeks (clergy, chieftains and wealthy landowners, known as "primates"), although fearful that they might lose their privileged position in the empire, joined the conspiracy lest it should succeed without them.

Outbreak of the Insurrection.—Ypsilantis hoped to train a select Greek force, which, in the Danubian principalities, would raise the native Rumanian population against the Turks. It was here that they might lose their privileged position in the empire. But before Ypsilantis' military preparations had made much progress, the Etairists in the Morea, believing that they were betrayed and in danger, appealed to him to act at once and he, with the consolation that the Turks were engaged against Ali Pasha in Albania, crossed the Pruth with small forces on March 6, 1821, only to be defeated, disavowed by Russia and deserted by the native population. On or about March 25, the traditional date of Greek independence, there were sporadic risings in the Morea (Peloponnese) followed by rebellions in Roumeli (Greece north of the isthmus of Corinth) and on several islands. The Muslims, greatly outnumbered, perished in thousands, but the Greek bands were too disorganized to reduce the stronger (chiefly maritime) fortresses or to occupy the passes of the Makrinoros in the northwest or of Thermopylae in the northeast. Hence the Turks, besides taking reprisals (they massacred Greeks in Asia Minor and on April 22 hanged the patriarch Gregorios in Constantinople), were able to attempt the reconquest of Greece.

Between 1822 and 1824 the Turks embarked on three campaigns. On each occasion they planned to send out fleets to supply and reinforce the Turkish garrisons in the maritime fortresses and to dispatch land forces through the Makrinoros and Thermopylae with orders to advance southward through the broken coastal plains and then to force the defiles of the isthmus of Corinth. But they were constantly harried by light Greek naval forces from the islands of Ydra, Spetzai and Psara, which used fire ships to great advantage. On land, the Greek forces, though disorganized, by making good use of the terrain sometimes inflicted heavy losses on their enemies. In 1822 the Greeks of western Roumeli held strong Turkish (chiefly Albanian) forces under Omer Vrioni at Missolonghi; and although the Muslims sacked Chios, admirals A. V. Miaoulis and Konstantinos Kanaris drove the Turkish fleet back to the Dardanelles. That same year the chieftains Theodoros Kolokotronis and "Niketas the Turkeater." In 1823 the Turkish military effort, because of disorders in Constantinople, was considerably less and somewhat belated; and the Muslims suffered defeats at sea by Miaoulis, in the passes of Helikon and Parnassus by the chieftain Odysseus Androutsos, and at Karpenisi in western Greece. Once again the Turkish forces were driven from Missolonghi. In 1824, although the Turks took the islands of Kassos and Psara, they were defeated in sea battles off Samos and failed, because of the insubordination of the Muslim Albanians, to achieve much in western Roumeli.

All this time the Greek military operations depended largely on the exertions of local chieftains and primates, who led bands augmented by the peasantry. But these bands, which lacked funds and supplies, were dispersed for long periods at a stretch, while the Greek ships were often engaged in piracy.

Civil Disorders in Greece.—This chaos in Greek military operations reflected the political scene. Repeated attempts to set working a central administration were frustrated by local leaders. On Jan. 1, 1822, a national assembly at Epidaurus proclaimed a constitution, which, drafted by Alexandros Mavrokordatos and Theodoros Negris, set up a central government consisting of a legislature and an executive committee of five, assisted by eight ministers. But this same constitution recognized the autonomy of existing regional authorities—the assembly of Missolonghi in western Greece, the *areopagus* of Salona in eastern Greece, and the Peloponnesian senate, a nonelected body in the Morea. These local assemblies were merely party gatherings and, even within these, there were fierce rivalries. When in Dec. 1822 a second national assembly was about to meet at Nauplia, Kolokotronis refused to give up the town, while his ally Petros Mavromikhalis (Petro Bey) drove the legislative committee out of Argos. In eastern Greece the chieftain Odysseus defied the government and even collaborated with the Turks. By the autumn of 1823 a civil war was raging, and no sooner had differences been composed than a second civil war broke out in 1824. On this occasion Kolokotronis was defeated by Roumeliot troops under Ioannis Koletis, who went to the aid of Georgios Kountouriotis, the president of the central government. For his misdemeanors, Kolokotronis was imprisoned on Ydra.

The Threat From Mohammed Ali.—Kountouriotis and his associate, Mavrokordatos, saw the necessity of raising loans and of organizing national and even regular forces. In Dec. 1823 the Greek government raised in London a loan which produced £315,000 in cash. The money was chiefly used to compose feuds and to fight the Moreots under Kolokotronis. When, therefore, in the winter of 1824–25 a new threat developed—the sultan had called upon his vassal, Mohammed Ali of Egypt, for help—the Greeks were short of funds and ill-prepared. Nevertheless, Mavrokordatos and Kountouriotis hastily assembled Roumeliot troops, a small corps of European Philhellenes, and naval squadrons to defend the Morea against the Egyptians who, having first gained a foothold on Crete, had made a base at Modon. But despite brilliant exploits at sea and on land the Greek forces were defeated, and the Roumeliots returned home to defend western Greece, where an invasion by the Albanians was expected. The Egyptians, under Mohammed's son, Ibrahim Pasha, captured New Navarino and soon advanced into the Morea, destroying crops and dwellings. In June 1825 Ibrahim threatened Nauplia, the seat of government, but Dimitrios Ypsilantis again came to the rescue and, assisted by Ioannis Makriyiannes and by a band of Philhellenes, forced him to retreat. For the rest of the year, and throughout 1826, the Greeks, though sorely pressed, defended their homeland from the mountains. True, in April 1826, Missolonghi, long besieged, fell to Ibrahim and in August the town, but not the acropolis, of Athens surrendered to Turkish forces. But so effective was the skirmishing of the Moreots (Kolokotronis had been released to lead them) and so successful the campaigns of the Roumeliot Georgios Karaiskakis in western Greece, that the Greeks held their own until the action of the British, French and Russian fleets in the bay of Navarino on Oct. 20, 1827, changed the whole military situation. (*See* NAVARINO, BATTLE OF.)

Diplomacy and the Greek Question.—The intervention of these three powers had been long delayed. At the outset of the war, France, England and Austria had proclaimed a policy of neutrality and the Russian emperor Alexander I had been reluctant to act without the approval of the European concert. The Greek attempt to secure the intervention of the powers at the congress of Verona (*q.v.*) in 1822 on the basis of a monarchy for Greece had completely failed. In Jan. 1824 the emperor, who hoped for assistance from the European concert in settling the Greek question, circulated a memorandum as a basis for a conference to be held at St. Petersburg. He proposed that in Greece there should be established three principalities, enjoying autonomy, but under Turkish suzerainty. These proposals pleased neither the powers, who feared Russian predominance in the Levant, nor the Greeks, who wanted complete independence.

Already the Greeks, ever since Russia had failed them, had begun to place their hopes in France and England. But in their efforts to deal with the powers, they were again divided. The Kapodistrian party (it was not pro-Russian) hoped to set up as president Kapodistrias who, since 1822, had been out of favour with the emperor and on leave of absence from the Russian foreign office. The French party planned to place Louis, duc de Nemours, son of the duc d'Orléans, upon the throne of Greece. Finally, there was an English party which had taken form when Lord Byron went to Greece in 1824. After Byron's death, the party tended to disappear but later in 1824 it was revived by Lord Guilford and by Greeks antagonistic to the Kapodistrians and Orleanists. In 1825, on his release from prison, Kolokotronis was won over to the English interest, as in a sense was Mavrokordatos, though he would have preferred the more subtle policy of stimulating the rivalries of France and England and of winning over Russia and Austria to a solution of the Greek question by the European concert. But circumstances favoured those who placed their hopes exclusively in England and their cause daily found new adherents. George Canning's recognition of Greek belligerent rights in March 1823, his refusal to take part in the conference of St. Petersburg, the raising of a second Greek loan in London, the possibility of obtaining the services in Greece of British naval and military commanders, the failure of the duc d'Orléans to give a definite undertaking to accept the throne for his son or to promise material support, the presence of French officers within the Egyptian forces—all led to the triumph of the pro-English Greeks, who in the summer of 1825, when all seemed lost, appealed to Canning to send them a king and make Greece a British protectorate.

Canning's Policy in Greece.—Although Canning favoured Greek independence he was unable to take unilateral action; but, having by his general policy dissolved the conservative alliance of monarchs, he was able, through Princess Lieven, wife of the Russian ambassador in England, to work for a settlement in the first instance with Russia. The resulting Anglo-Russian protocol of April 4, 1826 (which was the basis of the treaty of July 6, 1827, between France, Great Britain and Russia), was the cornerstone of Greek independence. Greece was to be established as an autonomous though tributary state under Turkish suzerainty. A secret article of the treaty stated that if the Turks and Greeks refused to accept an armistice the powers would then prevent collisions. Somewhat ambiguous instructions were then sent to the Levant and these, as interpreted by Admiral Sir Edward Codrington and others, led to the untoward event of Navarino (Oct. 20, 1827), when 60 out of 89 Turkish-Egyptian vessels were destroyed. By that time Canning had died: his successor, the duke of Wellington, refused to act with Russia, which on April 26, 1828, declared war on Turkey, citing the protocol of 1826. The protocol had stipulated that if the two powers in concert failed to solve the Greek question, then either of them might act separately.

Cochrane and Church.—The destruction of the Ottoman naval power at Navarino had allowed the Greeks to seize the initiative. In March 1827 Lord Cochrane (see DUNDONALD, THOMAS COCHRANE, 10th earl of) had at last arrived in Greece, but the contractors of the second London loan had failed to provide him with the promised steamships, from which wonders were expected. Gen. Sir Richard Church (q.v.) had also arrived, with a few officers, but without funds. Greece was at that time again on the verge of civil war, there being two assemblies and two governments. Church composed the feuds and the two assemblies united at Troezene in April 1827. This unity was essentially an alliance of the English and Kapodistrian parties. Church and Cochrane were appointed as military and naval commanders respectively, and Kapodistrias as president of Greece. On the sea Cochrane achieved very little of note. Church failed to relieve the acropolis of Athens, which the Turks were besieging, and witnessed its fall on June 5, 1827; but he kept some forces in the field and even before the battle of Navarino was about to make an assault on western Greece. Greatly disappointed that the battle was not followed by a settlement by the powers, at the end of Nov. 1827 he crossed the gulf of Corinth with his "thousand" to Dragomestre on the coast northwest of Missolonghi. In his attempt to encourage the chieftains of western Roumeli to revive the struggle, he was at first supported by Kapodistrias, who, arriving in Greece in Jan. 1828, wished to establish a claim for the inclusion of Roumeli in the confines of Greece.

The Greek Frontier.—Three allied representatives meeting at Poros (July–Dec. 1828) consulted Kapodistrias about the desirable Greek frontiers and did not greatly disappoint him in recommending the Arta-Volos frontier and the inclusion of Euboea and

Samos, though not Crete. But this frontier Wellington would accept only as a basis for negotiation and not as a settlement to be imposed; he also stipulated that Church's army be withdrawn from Roumeli (protocol of March 22, 1829). Kapodistrias was ready to order Church to withdraw, knowing full well that Church would refuse to do so. What he would have preferred was that a French army acting for Europe should occupy Roumeli, but until it came (and there was no certainty that it would) Church must remain where he was.

All this time Kapodistrias had realized that the frontier might depend on the choice of a sovereign, and, hoping to appease Wellington, had proposed Leopold of Saxe-Coburg (the future Leopold I, king of the Belgians), who had long wanted the Greek throne. On Feb. 3, 1830, the powers nominated Leopold but at the same time adopted the much less favourable Aspropotamos-Zeitouni frontier, excluding Crete and also Samos. Kapodistrias now encouraged Leopold to negotiate for the more northerly frontier and also for better conditions generally. Indeed Leopold showed much skill and tenacity in obtaining concessions. It is a legend that by exaggerating difficulties Kapodistrias intentionally drove Leopold into withdrawing his candidature. Leopold's resignation was a tactical move which failed: his resignation was accepted, whereas he had hoped he would be asked to remain and that he would ultimately get all he wanted, including the Arta-Volos frontier. That frontier had already been occupied when in May 1829 Church and his chieftains, after a long and arduous campaign, finally occupied the Makrinoros, thereby cutting the supply line to the Turkish outposts stretching southward to Missolonghi. Meanwhile, Dimitrios Ypsilantis, though unable to capture Athens, which remained in Turkish hands until 1832, occupied eastern Roumeli well beyond the northern boundary of Attica.

The Settlement.—After Leopold's resignation there was much confusion in Greece. Kapodistrias had made many enemies and on Oct. 9, 1831, he was assassinated by Konstantinos and Georgios Mavromikhalis. In Feb. 1832 the powers—having accepted, on Sept. 26, 1831, the Arta-Volos frontier—offered the crown to the young Otho of Bavaria and by their treaty with Bavaria (May 7, 1832) established Greece as a protectorate administered by Bavaria on behalf of the powers. By the treaty of Constantinople (July 1832) the Turks recognized Greek independence, renouncing all claims to suzerainty. But the settlement contained conflicting principles. Implicitly the Greeks were given constituent rights; implicitly Otho (who arrived on Feb. 6, 1833, with a regency to act for him) was given absolute power; and implicitly the protecting powers had rights of intervention. These contradictions were to become apparent in the early history of the Greek kingdom.

BIBLIOGRAPHY.—E. Driault and M. Lhéritier, *Histoire diplomatique de la Grèce*, 5 vol. (1925–26); C. W. Crawley, *The Question of Greek Independence: a Study of British Policy in the Near East 1821–33* (1930); C. M. Woodhouse, *The Greek War of Independence* (1952); D. Dakin, *British and American Philhellenes During the War of Greek Independence* (1955); N. Botzaris, *Visions balkaniques dans la préparation de la Révolution grecque, 1789–1821* (1962). For works in Greek, see the bibliographical material published in the *Journal of Modern History* by W. Miller, vol. ii and ix (1930–37), and by S. H. Weber, vol. xxii (1950).
(D. DN.)

GREEK LANGUAGE, one of the Indo-European family of languages. The modern language is the latest development of ancient Greek, of which the Attic dialect, out of many, became predominant. From Attic developed the Koine, or common dialect, which spread over Alexander's empire and throughout the Hellenistic world. The same tongue was used in the Byzantine empire and became the literary language of modern Greece, but the spoken tongue developed on different lines.

The name Greek was taken from that of an insignificant community (*Graioi*) with whom the Romans came in contact in Italy at Cumae, and was then extended to all other Greek-speaking cities. During the middle ages the Greeks called their language Romaic (and themselves Romans), the capital of the Roman empire having been transferred to Constantinople. They have, however, usually called themselves Hellenes and their language Hellenic.

This language is split into many dialects, classified as Attic, Ionic, Aeolic, Doric, Arcadian and Cyprian (see *Varieties of*

Dialect, below). The decipherment of Linear B (see MINOAN LINEAR SCRIPTS) has led to the hypothesis that the dialects are the result of the subdivision of an old form of Greek (now often called Mycenaean) that took place in Greece itself after c. 1500 B.C., and not, as used to be thought, of varieties of Greek laid down as separate strata. Difference of dialect may be illustrated by comparing a brief Aeolic text and its Attic version:

Στάλλα 'πι Σθενείαι ἔμμι τῶ Νικιάῖο,
Σθῆλη ἐπὶ Σθενείᾳ εἰμὶ τοῦ Νικίου τοῦ Γαυκῶ,

that is, "I am the memorial stone to Stheneias, son of Gaucos" but in the Aeolic, quite literally "to the Gaucian Nician Stheneias." This example also shows the uses of inflexion in Greek, which is highly inflected.

Morphology and Syntax.—The inflexions of Greek are of characteristically Indo-European type, with the usual categories of number, case, person, tense and aspect, mood, voice. The closest equivalents are found in Sanskrit, and it has been supposed that Indo-Iranian and Greek inflexions together justified a reconstruction of Indo-European. It would be truer to say that either throws light upon the other. The way in which the dative τῷ Νικιάῖο (of a patronymic adjective, Attic τῷ Νικιάῳ) in apposition to Σθενείᾳ (in normal Attic a genitive of the father's name τοῦ Νικίου is used), and then the genitive patronymic τὸ Γαυκῶ (in apposition to the genitive meaning contained in the dative patronymic, where normal Attic uses an independent genitive of the grandfather's name τοῦ Γαυκοῦ) is a nice illustration of the flexibility of Greek in matters of form and usage as compared with Latin or Old English and of the contrast between inflexion in Greek, but prepositions combined with order in modern English.

The same point may be made of the verbal system; e.g., μειδιάσας ἔφη means "he said with a smile," not "having smiled" (tense), for the aorist participle is concerned here with aspect (kind, not time of action) and therefore marks contemporary, not prior, time. Certain verbs (λανθάνω and two others) invariably have this construction. Again, the perfect "tense," of Greek marks in present time a completed event in τέθνηκε "he is dead," the present "tense" continuing action as in ἀποθνῄσκει "he is (an unconscionable long time a-)dying" (or "he is fading away like snow in the thaw"), and the ἀπο- of the present (with η not η, σκ not κ) is in contrast with the τε- of the perfect form.

Different styles have still others. The formulaic features of epic reveal its oral composition, the complete Iliad for instance being the growth of centuries and the work of many singers, perhaps perfected in the end by a single poet but certainly not an original composition of his. In the historians Herodotus and Thucydides the degree of compactness in the structure of the sentence, a grammatical matter, well matches the difference in the concept of history—Herodotus is a teller of stories, Thucydides tries to be more critical.

Again, the historians quote long speeches (how far authentic and how far fictitious is disputed), an orator like Demosthenes will quote the exact (if brief) testimony of a witness indirectly, and for indirect speech (oratio obliqua) new syntactic usages were devised, less rigorous than in Latin and more expressive of varieties of meaning, thanks to the existence of an optative as well as a subjunctive mood. Greek has a middle (or "boomerang") voice as well as a passive (which grew largely out of the middle forms). English "the fired a gun" (active), "the gun fired" (middle), "the gun was fired" (passive); and "the gun himself" (middle or reflexive) (i.e., "he was washed," passive) will illustrate the point of meaning. As to from λούω is active, λούομαι both middle and passive. The aorist passive is not derived from a middle but is either an old intransitive (ἐμάνη "he was mad") or an independent extension (ἐδόθη "it was given") of a form -θης (second person singular only; cf. Sans. adithas, middle). In fact, such aorist passives are conspicuously rare (and late) in epic.

Vocabulary.—The vocabulary of Greek is marked by a large number of compounds, the power of forming which has remained free and vigorous through the whole period of Greek. This is partly a matter of morphology (form), but it is much more a matter of expression (meaning). Aristophanes, for example, makes Euripides speak of Aeschylus in these words (Frogs 837-839):

ἀνθρωποῦν ἀγριοποιὸν, αὐθαδόστομον,
ἔχοντ' ἀχάλινον ἀκρατὲς ἀπύλωτον στόμα,
ἀπεριλάλητον, κομποφακελορρήμονα,

("A savage-creating stubborn-pulling fellow, unfettered, uncontrolled-of-speech, unperiphrastic, bombastiloquent," trans. B. B. Rogers). Thus Greek has a very large vocabulary. The Greeks, furthermore, developed science, logic, philosophy and mathematics in a way unparalleled until modern times in western Europe and its expansions overseas. Hence there was created a large scientific, logical, philosophical and mathematical vocabulary which is still in use; new demands in new sciences, or new developments in old sciences (e.g., electronics, microscopy or biology), are met by borrowing Greek words or by using Greek models for inventing new ones based on Greek.

(J. WH.)

The tongues of ancient and modern Greece differ so much that it

Name	Sign	Conventional transliteration	Name	Sign	Conventional transliteration
Alpha	A α	A	Nu	N ν	N
Beta	B β	B	Xi	Ξ ξ	X
Gamma	Γ γ	G	Omicron	O o	short O
Delta	Δ δ	D	Pi	Π π	P
Epsilon	Ε ε (short E)	E	Rho	P ρ	R (Rh initially)
Digamma	Ϝ	(lost)*	Sigma	Σ(C) σ or ς	S
Zeta	Z ζ	Z	Tau	T τ	T
Eta	Η η (long E)	long E	Upsilon	Υ υ	Y or U
Theta	Θ θ	TH	Phi	Φ φ	PH
Iota	Ι ι	I	Chi	Χ χ	CH
Kappa	Κ κ	C or K	Psi	Ψ ψ	PS
Lambda	Λ λ	L	Omega	Ω ω	long O
Mu	Μ μ	M			

*The digamma Ϝ disappeared early from the Greek alphabet. See the article F.

is necessary to deal with them in separate sections. The alphabet of both is shown in the table.

ANCIENT

Greek was spoken in one or other of its forms in the Balkan peninsula, on the west coast of Asia Minor, in south Italy and Sicily, and in the islands of the Ionian and Aegean seas. By the 4th century B.C. the political supremacy of Athens and the greatness of Attic literature had caused the Attic dialect to become the basis of a lingua franca for all Greeks, which in the long run superseded the other dialects. The conquests of Alexander the Great caused Greek, in the form of this lingua franca or Koine, to become the speech of the whole near east (Asia Minor, Syria, Mesopotamia, Egypt). Under the Romans these regions continued to use Greek, and in modern times Bulgarians, Russians and Serbians use a modified form of the Greek alphabet.

Authenticity of Texts.—The oldest documents, of the 15th century B.C., are clay tablets from the mainland of Greece (Pylos, Mycenae) and the island of Crete. They are inventories, written in a peculiar syllabary—not in the Greek alphabet—and were first deciphered in 1951. Later texts in alphabetic script have survived, some in the originals, others in copies. The originals are: (1) inscriptions, decrees, treaties, temple inventories, and dedications, engraved on stone and found in Greece and all over the near east; the earliest date from the 8th century B.C. and they become numerous in the 5th and later centuries; (2) documents (letters, contracts, petitions and accounts) written on papyrus between the late 4th century B.C. and the 8th century A.D., and preserved by the dry sands of Egypt, from which the excavations, mainly of the end of the 19th and beginning of the 20th century, have brought them to light in large numbers (see PAPYROLOGY). Papyri have not been recovered from other parts of the Greek-speaking world (except at Herculaneum, where they were buried by the eruption of Vesuvius in A.D. 79); but legal documents written on vellum in the 2nd and 1st centuries B.C. have been found at As Salhiyah (the ancient Doura-Europus in Mesopotamia), and at Avroman (Parthia).

The copies, on which almost all our knowledge of Greek literary works is based, are written at first on papyrus and later on vellum or paper. For long the oldest known Greek manuscripts were those containing the Greek Bible, written on vellum and dating from the 4th and 5th centuries, and the texts of other Greek works rested on vellum (later paper) manuscripts which were (in general) not older than the 9th and 10th centuries. These remain the broadest basis of present knowledge, but other excavations have brought to light papyrus manuscripts, some mere scraps, others very substantial rolls or books, of Homer and other classical texts, a few of them written in the 3rd, 2nd and 1st centuries B.C., and many of them in the earliest centuries of the Christian era. In a number of cases papyrus copies of works that had perished have been recovered, no copies in medieval manuscripts having survived (see GREEK LITERATURE).

Important accessions to knowledge of the language, its pronunciation, spelling and vocabulary, have resulted from the recovery of so many well-authenticated texts. So long as the medieval copies were the only source of knowledge it was impossible to have much confidence in the spelling that they offered, and certain variations which they exhibited, *e.g.*, the variation between ει and ι (τειμή-τιμή; ἀποτείσαι-ἀποτίσαι, etc.), presented a little-understood problem. Moreover, the grammatical treatises of Herodian (2nd century), Choeroboscus (6th century) and others show that these problems presented themselves already in the early centuries of the Christian era; these grammarians drew up lists of words recommending particular spellings in doubtful cases. It remained doubtful, however, how far the grammarians could be regarded as knowing the truth or as providing a trustworthy criterion for the correction of the manuscripts.

The inscriptions and papyri often provide evidence that settles once and for all a disputed question of spelling, for they date from a time when certain phonemes which later became identical were still distinct from one another. For instance the Greek of the 3rd century B.C. possessed the long diphthongs αι ηι ωι (the spelling ᾳ ῃ ῳ is not older than the 12th century). From the end of the 2nd century B.C. they were written α η ω without the iota. The uniformity with which this happens, and the appearance of the iota in the wrong place (spellings like ἄνωι for ἄνω are frequent), shows that the iota, which must have been pronounced in the 3rd century B.C., had ceased to be pronounced in the 1st century B.C. and was sometimes added in writing by persons who thought (rightly or wrongly) that they knew the older spelling. At least one erroneous restoration of iota has been perpetuated. Where medieval manuscripts (even the most accurate of them) and late inscriptions give ῥαθυμεῖν, the papyri of the 3rd century B.C. have ῥαθυμεῖν (without iota). Unlike ῥᾴδιος, the word can never have been pronounced with an iota. Many of the inscriptions and still more of the papyri were written by persons of little education, whose spelling tended to be phonetic; their very errors throw light on the pronunciation. One instance must suffice: the word ἑαυτοῦ in inscriptions and papyri of the 1st century B.C. is often written ἑατοῦ, whereas αὑτοῦ is not written ἀτοῦ. The reason is that ἑαυτοῦ was pronounced at first ἑαυτοῦ (being derived by contraction from ἑὸ αὑτοῦ like the Ionic ἑωυτοῦ which has a different contraction), later ἑατοῦ. By the study of such spelling variations the chief changes in the pronunciation of Greek can be dated with considerable accuracy. Many of the changes which mark the passage from ancient to modern Greek took place in the three or four centuries pre-ceding and the three or four centuries following the Christian era. The language of the period (2nd century) in which Herodian spoke and wrote was already so different from Attic that his spelling rules must be assumed to be based not on observation of contemporary pronunciation (it was in fact the divergence between this and the traditional spelling which made spelling rules a necessity) but on antiquarian research, and in this field the modern investigator has the advantage over him.

Nature of the Tradition of the Accents.—Greek texts, whether on stone, papyrus, vellum or paper, are usually written without spaces between the words, and the continuous use of breathings and accents is found only in medieval manuscripts from the 9th century onward. Inscriptions (with rare exceptions) and nonliterary papyri are entirely without breathings and accents. The same is often true of literary papyri, but these are sometimes more or less sporadically marked with breathings and accents, especially in epic, dramatic or lyric texts. The accentuated literary papyri are in the main not older than the opening centuries of the Christian era. On the other hand, the features of pronunciation of which breathings and accents are the written signs are more ancient than the use of the signs. From numerous references in Greek authors, and especially from Apollonius Dyscolus and his son Herodian, who wrote in the 2nd century A.D., many details have been learned regarding the accentuation of Greek, which was a variation of pitch; the syllable marked with the acute accent was high-pitched, the others, those which in the printed books are marked with the grave accent or with no mark at all, were spoken on the low pitch, while circumflexed syllables were spoken on a descending pitch, the first part of the syllable being higher than the second. Such is the most probable inference from the statements of grammarians and certain other evidence (*e.g.*, the marks found in accented papyri and the scanty remains of Greek music), though several points are still disputed.

The general accuracy, and at the same time the great antiquity, of the traditional accentuation of Greek in modern printed editions may be proved by means of a comparison between it and the accentuation of Vedic Sanskrit; the two exhibit a number of striking coincidences which point to an unbroken oral tradition in both cases from the hypothetical parent "Indo-European." In 1876 Karl Verner demonstrated that certain consonant changes in Germanic could be explained if the position of the accent thus observed in Greek and Sanskrit were admitted to have existed at one time in Germanic also. The antiquity of the distinction between the acute and the circumflex has been demonstrated by a comparison with the accentuation of modern Lithuanian, which has a corresponding distinction.

The breathings and accentual marks found in the text of a classical author, such as Plato, cannot have been copied, even at many removes, from his autograph: Plato did not write more than the bare series of letters forming the words. It is clear, however, that he pronounced an *h* or a high pitch even when he did not put it down in writing, and that those who, in transmitting his text, inserted the breathings and accentual marks (in the main Byzantine scholars of the 9th century) were guided by contemporary living speech (the position of the accent is in general the same in modern Greek) and by antiquarian knowledge to a very large measure of success.

Varieties of Early Greek.—The language of the inscriptions from the 7th to the 4th century B.C. presents varieties of two kinds, varieties of alphabet and spelling and varieties of dialect.

Varieties of Alphabet and Spelling.—The Greek alphabet is an adaptation of the Semitic alphabet and differs according to locality and date. One of these differences throws light on the language; viz., the varying mode of representing ε and ο sounds.

The contraction of ε+ε (ἐ+ἐ) must obviously have resulted, to begin with, in a long ē, and similarly the contraction of ο+ο must have given ō. Hence ει in the 4th-century Attic (and later Greek) form ἐπεστάτει (from ἐπεστάτε-ε) must have been pronounced from the beginning not as a diphthong but as a long ē, and similarly the ου of μισθοῦμεν (from μισθόομεν) must have been from the first pronounced ō, not as a diphthong ου. In the oldest inscriptions these sounds are in fact written ε and o (εϝεσττατε, μισθοϝεν). When ει and ου are thus demonstrably monophthongs, they are called "spurious diphthongs."

In the local Attic and many other alphabets there was no vowel symbol η (H), and no ω (Ω). In such alphabets E had to represent three sounds; viz., ε (as in φέρω), ē (as in ἐϝεσττατε) and the other kind of ē which was written η when that letter was introduced (ανεθηκε, later ανεθηκε). Similarly ο had to represent ο (in φερομεν), ō (in μισθοϝεν) and the other ō which was later written ω (δορον later δωρον).

But ει and ου are not always spurious diphthongs. In εἰμι ("I shall go") the ει is, in origin at least, a diphthong (Lith. einū, "I go," Lat. eo from ei-o through ēī(y)-o, ī-twr from eī-twr; Gr. ἴμεν shows the ī-element bereft of the ε). In ἐλήλουθα the υ is the same as in ἤλυθον, so that ου is here in origin a genuine diphthong. In early inscriptions, ει and ου are in certain words fixed and not capable of alternating with ε and ο. Thus ἐπέ, δοκεῖ (from δοκέ-ει), πρεσβεία, πειθομενος, are constant spellings, ἐπεί ("when"), εἰ, ἀτέλεια, οὐκ, οὐθένος, ἔπε (Dat. of ἔπος), of course without accents even in an inscription (W. Dittenberger, Sylloge³ 64), which has only ε and ο in place of the later ō.

Thus the early inscriptions sometimes yield information attainable in no other way; e.g., that οὐκ, οὗτος, ἔπε and φέρες φέρει have genuine diphthongs.

The spurious diphthongs sometimes owe their origin to what is known as "compensatory lengthening." Just as the long ā in πᾶς arises from a lengthening of the ă in *πανς (from *παντς, cf. gen. παντ-ός) to compensate for the loss of the ν, so the nominative *τιθεντ-ς became *τιθεντς and then τιθείς, which is written τιθες on the older inscriptions, τιθείς in later Attic, and τιθής in some other dialects. (An asterisk denotes that the word has been reconstructed.)

At the end of the 5th century B.C. the local Ionic alphabet, which possessed the vowel signs η and ω in addition to ε and ο, began to supersede the other Greek alphabets. It was officially adopted at Athens in place of the Attic alphabet in 403 B.C., and by the end of the 4th century it was in general use throughout Greece.

The ē and ō which resulted from contraction and compensatory lengthening were not everywhere written in the same way in the 4th century B.C. In some dialects, not τελεῖτε, τιθείς, διδούς, but τελῆτε, τιθῆς, διδὸς are found. Within the Doric area both spellings are found (e.g., in some places ἦμεν, in others εἶμεν, from esmen, infinitive of the verb "to be"). The difference, as between the dialects, is in most cases one of pronunciation, not spelling; in some dialects, however, a difference of both writing and of pronunciation (quality of vowel) occurs, in others only a difference of writing.

The distinction between genuine and spurious diphthongs shows itself even after general adoption of the Ionic alphabet in the case of contractions with a preceding vowel; e.g., ὁράεις ὁράε, become ὁρᾶς ὁρᾷ, which has the genuine ει, become ὁρᾶς ὁρᾷ (ὁρᾷς ὁρᾷ in medieval manuscripts), but ὁράομεν, which has the spurious ει, becomes ὁρᾶν. Similarly in οὐκ ὁμῶς τιμῆς ἔσει (Iliad ix, 605), τιμῆς is the contracted form of τιμάεις, which has the spurious ει ("eddy-") from -ϝευτ-ς; cf. gen. -ευτ-ος, Sans. -vant-). In Il. vii, 13, where the manuscripts have κουϝανος ὄρϝῦ' ἀελλῆς, P. Buttmann's conjecture, that the last word is a contraction of ἀελλῆεες "eddy-ing," involves only a change of accent (τὸ ἀελλῆς): it would be a mistake to write, as he proposed, ἀελλῆς.

The study of the ancient Greek language is based on written documents, and the textual critic seeks to restore and interpret the actual letters of the autograph in cases where this autograph is not extant.

The medieval manuscripts offer texts written in the Ionic alphabet, and in a spelling which, at its most accurate, is that of the 3rd century B.C. but which more often shows signs of the passing of the centuries between that date and the 9th and 10th centuries A.D. The spelling of the 3rd century B.C. is clearly not appropriate to authors of the 5th century B.C. (especially the beginning of it) or earlier; in the case of Homer the composition of the poems was earlier than the knowledge of writing in Greece.

Many of the great Athenians (Sophocles, Euripides, Aristophanes, Thucydides) wrote in the second half of the 5th century. They may well have used the Ionic alphabet, which inscriptions prove to have been used at Athens some decades before 403 B.C. Aeschylus, who wrote in the first half of the 5th century, is more likely to have used the Attic alphabet, employed in fragments of the earlier lyrics which are painted on Attic vases of the 6th and 5th centuries. The old spellings may well have survived longest in the case of the oldest books (Homer, Hesiod, Theognis, Alcman, etc.).

The study of the Homeric poems from this point of view has led to tangible results. In the older alphabets of Greece, ε and ο, as already mentioned, can stand for ē and ō ("spurious" ει and ου), and a single consonant is written where the later practice is to write it double (ἀλογλωσσος = ἀλλογλωσσους). Both features are to be seen in τειχιοσσης (= Τειχιουσσης) in a Milesian inscription of the 6th century B.C. In the line καιροσεων δ' ὀθονεων ἀπολειβεται ὑγρον ἔλαιον (Odyssey vii, 107), καιροσεων is the archaic spelling of καιροσσεων, a word which was so rare that the rhapsodes of the 6th century did not understand what it meant ἐξελύθη, the unaugmented form corresponding to the augmented ἐξελύθη, because it resembled the aorist passive of ἐκλύω meant ἐξελύθη, because the metre demanded a long vowel in the last place, it became ἐξελύθη.

The two instances just given (ἔγρετο, ἐξελύθη) show a Homer that was written in an alphabet that possessed no H but used E instead.

Certain other indications point to a time when the poems existed only in oral transmission and had not yet been written down. R. Bentley showed that many irregularities in the metre vanished when once it was admitted that at the time of the composition of the poems the language possessed the sound ϝ (written ϝ in dialect inscriptions), but nowhere written in the manuscripts of Homer). J. Whatmough has called attention to remainders of the Indo-European laryngeals which account for other metrical irregularities.

The traces of digamma (ϝ) consist of lengthenings of a preceding vowel (e.g., ὅπα καλὸς is really καλϝός—this form occurs in a Boeotian inscription of the 7th century B.C.), and of cases of hiatus (e.g., ὅπα ἀρνῶν Il. iv, 435—the dialect inscriptions have ϝαρήν (ϝαρνός). Apparent irregularities are due to the fact that early composers spoke the ϝ sound and others, of later date, did not. As for the laryngeal (Ḥ), it survives in lengthening before μ- (not from older μ̄), and in hiatus before words which had Ḥ- initially.

The reciters found στεομεν in their written texts of Il. xi, 348. The reciters found στεομεν in their written texts of Il. xv, 297, and lengthened the ε to ē (which they wrote ει, as has been shown), because, as the living form was στέομεν, it did not occur to them that στεομεν was the old way of writing στήομεν. The

In Il. xxiv, 154, ὅς ἄξει is defective both metrically and in point of sense; the parallel ὅς σ' ἄξει (line 183) shows that the poet meant in 154 ὅς ϝῆ' ἄξει, where ϝῆε is the older form of the Attic ἐ (Doric ϝε and Pamphylian ϝhε are found in inscriptions). Such cases (there are several of them) bring out clearly the reality of the sound, ϝ in Homer. In a number of other respects the spelling which is found in the manuscripts of Homer can be shown to be unoriginal. The first person plur. subj. of ἔστην is written στεομεν (Il. xv, 297), instead of στήομεν as the analysis requires (the root is στα, cf. Lat. stāre, which gives Ionic στη-, and the sign of the subjunctive in unthematic verbs is a short -ο or -ε). The later Ionic form στέωμεν (which arose by a regular change of -ηο- to -εω-; cf. βασιλῆος: βασιλέως) occurs in Il. xi, 348.

group -ηο- thus came to be written -εο- in many other words as well.

The word εἰνάτερες was believed by Herodian to be the plural of εἰνάτηρ. Inscriptions have proved however that the nominative sing. was εἰνάτηρ, and εἰνάτερες is the result of vocalic lengthening in which εἰ- represents the time of uttering an old γ-consonant initially. Here again, the lengthening of ε is expressed by the spurious diphthong, the introduction of which into the text can hardly be much older than the 4th century B.C. Other examples of εἰ and οὐ resulting from genuine old consonants (laryngeal) are εἰν ἀγορῇ, οὐλόμενος, Οὐλύμποιο and many others. The numerous forms of which ὁρόωντες, ὁράασθαι are specimens, in which the older ἄο, ἄε seem to have become οω and αα, have no parallel in dialect inscriptions. The poets (whether in writing or in oral composition) must have used the forms ὁράοντες, ὁράεσθαι. In the course of the transmission the later contracted forms ὁράοντες, ὁρᾶσθαι tended to be substituted, but the metre compelled the reciters to "pull out" the contracted forms into ὁρόωντες and ὁράασθαι, by prefixing in each case to the long vowel (which resulted from the contraction) its short form (ο, α). Forms, such as ναιετάει, which did not survive (there was no ναιετῶ in later Greek), were not exposed to this modernizing tendency and were left untouched. (See also HOMER: Language.)

Varieties of Dialect.—Distinct from differences of alphabet and spelling are differences between the spoken forms of the language in different places; i.e., differences of dialect. Knowledge of the dialects is derived mainly from inscriptions of the 6th, 5th, 4th and 3rd centuries B.C.; from the time of the Athenian supremacy the Attic dialect began to supersede the others, so that many documents show a mixture of non-Attic and Attic elements. In later centuries there were revivals of the use of dialects in inscriptions, but their artificial character is proved by the presence in them of forms which earlier inscriptions show to have been long obsolete, e.g., ραψάμυδος (=ραψῳδὸς) in a late Boeotian inscription, whereas earlier Boeotian inscriptions indicate that ϝ between vowels had long been lost. The literary documents written in dialect are often of larger compass than the inscriptions, and therefore in some ways more instructive, especially for the vocabulary; but the variations in the manuscript tradition (e.g., which of Hipponax, Hippocrates and Herodotus) constitute a difficulty which only the inscriptions can help overcome. The inscriptions have in fact enabled greater certainty in picking among the variants, as well as the detection (for instance) of the fact that the consistent absence of the so-called ν ἐφελκυστικόν from the manuscripts of Herodotus is not a feature of the Ionic dialect but is the result of unintelligent editing by some unknown ancient critic; the Ionic inscriptions have this ν in even greater profusion than the Attic (Ion. ἐποίεεν where Att. has ἐποίει).

The main dialect divisions are: (1) Ionic, of which Attic is a subdialect; (2) Aeolic; (3) Arcadian and Cyprian; (4) Doric. In the 6th and 5th centuries B.C. the local distribution was as follows: Ionic was spoken in the central part of the coast of Asia Minor, in many of the Aegean islands, in Euboea and the Chalcidian peninsula and (in its Attic form) in Attica. Aeolic is the collective name of the dialects spoken in the northern part of the Asiatic coast (Aeolis) including Lesbos, and (with a Doric admixture) in Thessaly and Boeotia. Arcadian and Cyprian are named from the places in which they were spoken; the recognition of their close resemblance in spite of the great distance between them was one of the surprises which resulted from the discovery of Arcadian and Cyprian inscriptions and of the deciphering of the Cyprian syllabary in the '70s and '80s of the 19th century. Lastly, Doric in many varieties was spoken in the Peloponnese (except Arcadia), in northwest Greece (Locris, Phocis, Epirus), in the more southerly Aegean islands, especially Thera, Crete, Cos, Rhodes, and on the neighbouring part of the Asiatic coast.

Colonists took with them the dialect of the mother city; Ionic was spoken in several Milesian settlements on the Black sea coast, and Doric in Syracuse and other Doric foundations in Sicily and south Italy.

Such, in outline, is the geographical distribution of the Greek dialects at the earliest time they are known. For an earlier period the main evidence is that of the Greek historians (especially Herodotus and Thucydides). From them may be learned that there was in early times a migration from Epirus into the Aeolic land of Thessaly, which drove before it another migration from Thessaly into Boeotia. At the time of the Trojan War, according to Thucydides, the later Boeotians were not yet in Boeotia. Herodotus, Strabo and Pausanias tell of the former presence of Ionians in Cynuria and on the shores of the Saronic gulf. The resemblance between the land-enclosed Arcadian dialect and the distant Cyprian is less surprising in light of the fact that Arcadian was at one time spoken as far south as the promontory of Taenarum. This is proved by the name of the festival to Poseidon which was celebrated there; viz., Ποhοίδαια. The dialect of Taenarum in historical times was Laconian (Doric), in which σ between vowels had become h. Accordingly Ποhοίδαια is the Laconized form of Ποσοίδαια, and an Arcadian inscription proves that Ποσοιδᾶν was the Arcadian name of the god. It may be inferred that Arcadian was once spoken throughout the Peloponnese and perhaps over a still wider area, before it was overwhelmed and shut in by the Dorian migration.

Greek and the Other Indo-European Languages.—The dialects show considerable differences from one another in respect of sounds, inflexions, syntax and vocabulary, and the comparison of the dialects with one another often throws light on the past, enabling a reconstruction of an earlier condition of the Greek language. In this reconstruction use is made at the same time of a comparison with the other Indo-European languages. In what follows an attempt will be made to indicate briefly some of the more important sound changes to which Greek owes its differences from the other languages.

Of the consonants which the parent speech had, Greek has lost H and intervocalic y and s; H survives only in Linear B, vocalized as e (e.g., ἔενσι "they are," older *Hesenti, Hittite ašanzi); Sans. tráyas "three," and Gr. (Cretan) τρέες are both descended from Indo-Eur. tréyes; Sans. tras-ati "trembles" and Gr. τρέ-ω come from tres-. At the beginning of a word both y and s became h: ὅς (rel. pron.) corresponds to Sans. yas (Indo-Eur. yos), and the article ὁ to Sans. sa (Indo-Eur. so). Sometimes y became ζ (Sans. yugâm, Gr. ζυγόν); but this ζ may also contain the old laryngeal, which also appears in aspirates, e.g., πλάθανον but πλάτος, and in original Indo-Eur. long vowels (by contraction). The earliest records of many dialects show a complete loss of the sound w (e.g., ὅϊς [ὄΐς] from Indo-Eur. owis, cf. Lat. ouis); but other dialects retain this sound (which is written ϝ [digamma]) e.g., ὄϝις (accus. plur.) is found in an Argive inscription of the 5th century B.C.

The loss of these four sounds often left two vowels standing next to one another in a word; this was at first tolerated but later led to contraction into a single vowel. These contractions occurred in the main after the composition of the Homeric poems, and the method of contraction differs in different dialects; hence, forms like ναιετάει in Homer, and the contrast between (e.g.) Att. τιμῶ, τιμᾷ and Dor. τιμῶ, τιμῇ or between Att. φιλῶ and Ion. φιλέω.

In combination with liquids and nasals, y, s and w often caused a lengthening of the preceding vowel before disappearing; ἔτεινα (pronounce ἔτένα) arose from ἔ-τεν-σ-α, τείνω (pron. τένω) from τεν-γω, Ion. ξεῖνος (pron. ξένος) from ξένϝος (πρόξεϝνος occurs in an inscription). Here, too, the dialects diverge; the details are too complex to be enumerated here.

A y following a guttural, dental or labial stop combined with it into a single sound: φυλακ-γω became φυλάσσω, μεθ-γος (cf. Lat. medius, Sans. madhyas) became μέσσος or μέσος, μεγ-γων became μέζων (Ion.), χαλεπ-γω became χαλέπτω.

A nasal before σ (which generally arose, as in μέσος, from a dental +y, sometimes from a dental +s) disappeared in most dialects (e.g., Att. πᾶσα from πάνσα, τιθεῖσα from τιθένσα), leaving behind it a lengthened vowel (Arc. πάνσα). Some dialects, however, retained the -νσ- combination (Arc. πάνσα). The vocalization or loss of H took place mainly in Indo-European itself.

When the numerous long vowels which arose from contraction

and from compensatory lengthening are left out of account, the remainder of the Greek vowels are found to be, in the main, survivals from the parent speech: e.g., μάτηρ (Dor. etc.), Lat. *māter*; δῶρον, Lat. *dō-num*, (F)ίς, Lat. *vīs*; μῦς, Lat. *mūs*; πλῆ-το, Lat. *plē-nus*; ἄγω, Lat. *ago*; δ(F)ίς, Lat. *onis*; φέρω, Lat. *fero*; sometimes when most of the languages agree in ŏ (πατήρ, *pater*, etc.) Sans. has ĭ (*pitar-*); in such cases the parent form is believed to have had an indistinct vowel like the first *o* in *potato*.

Indo-European *t, p, d, b* have survived unchanged in Greek (some instances will be found among the words already quoted). Sanskrit has the sounds *dh, bh*; these go back to Indo-Eur. *dH, bH*, which have yielded Gr. θ, φ (pronounced like *t, p*, in the Irish pronunciation of English); e.g., φέρω, Sans. *bhar-*, Lat. *fero*, Gr. φέρω, Sans. *dadhāmi*, Lith. *dĕ-ti* (infin. "to lay"), Gr. τίθημι.

The Indo-European gutturals are of two kinds, technically called palatals and labiovelars.

The palatals appear in Greek as κ, γ, χ, in Latin as *c, g, h*, and as gutturals in Celtic and Germanic: e.g., κίων, Lat. *hiems*. In the eastern group of Indo-European languages (Indo-Iranian, Armenian, Slavonic and Baltic languages) they appear as sibilants: e.g., Sans. *śvā* (stem *śun*) "dog," *himás* "frost, snow," Lith. *šun* "dog," Gr. Slav. *zima* "winter."

The labiovelars were sounds of the *qu* or *kw* type. They survive more or less clearly in Latin *quis*, *u-n-guit*. In some languages they drop the *u* or *w* element, and become *k, g* and *gh* (so in Sanskrit). Sometimes they appear as *p, b*; e.g., Oscan *pis* corresponding to Latin *quis*, Old Irish *ben* "woman" corresponding to English *queen*. In the Greek dialects they tend to appear before *a* and *o* vowels as labials (π, β, φ): e.g., ποινή, πων, καῖνα "punishment," Lith. *káina* "price" (all from Indo-Eur. *kwoinā*); -βόρος, Lat.-*vorus*, Sans.- *garás* "swallowing"; φόνος, Sans. *ghanás* (from Indo-Eur. *gwhonos*). Before *e* and *i* vowels they tend to appear as dentals: e.g., τίνω, τέσσα (from *kwet-, kwei-*; forms of the same root as in ποινή), τις, Lat. *quis*, θείνω, Sans. *hanti* "he kills," Hittite *kwenzi* "he kills" (Indo-Eur. *gwhen-ti*, from the same root as φόνος, ἔπεφνε, πέφαται). In Aeolic the labials appear even before *e*-vowels: e.g., πήλοι "far," Att. τῆλε; Boeot. πέτταρες, Att. τέτταρες, Dor. τέτορες (cf. Lat. *quatuor*). Occasionally a labiovelar develops into a Greek guttural, often owing to the neighbourhood of *u*: e.g., βου-κόλος with the same ending as αἰ(γ)-πόλος, cf. Lat. *colo, in-quil-inus*; κύκλος, Lith. *káklas* "neck," Eng. *wheel*; γυνή, Boeot. βανά, Eng. *queen*. The pronoun τις appears in Thessalian as κις; for πότερος, πῶς Herodotus has κότερος, κῶς.

The Greek πατρᾱ́σι (dat. pl. of πατήρ) corresponds very closely (even in respect of the accent) to the Sanskrit locative *pitṛ́su*. In this, as in many Sanskrit words, *ṛ* functions as a vowel. This "sonant" *ṛ*, as it is called, is descended from the same sound in the parent speech. In the other languages the result is *ṛ* preceded or followed by a short vowel: Greek ρα or ᾰρ, Lat. *or*, Lith. *ir*, Ger. *ur*, etc. The variation in the quality of the vowel is a sign that it has been separately developed in each language. The same phenomenon is observed in the case of *l, m* and *n*. Sonant *m*, for example, is observed in the word for 100, Indo-Eur. *ṃtom*, which *centum*, Lith. *śimtas*, Ger. *hund*; Greek ἑ-κατόν, and Sanskrit *śatám* indicate that sonant *m* became *a* in these languages. The same *ā* from *m* or *n* (to use the technical notation of these sounds) is found in πόδ-α from ποδ-ṃ (which has the same ending as the *o*-stem ἔργο-ν [from -*o-m*], Lat. *illu-m*), and in γεγράφαται (from γεγράφ-ṇται) which has the same ending as λέυ-νται.

The Aeolic dialect has ρο and not ρα in place of the sonant; e.g., στρότος and not στρατός from *strtos*. (R. McK.; J. Wh.)

KOINE AND BYZANTINE

Koine (κοινὴ διάλεκτος, "common dialect") is the name given to the fairly uniform Hellenistic Greek spoken approximately from the time of Alexander the Great to that of Justinian (late 4th century B.C. to middle 6th century A.D.), not only in Greece, Macedonia and the Greek islands and colonies but in large areas of Asia and Africa which had come under the sway of Greeks or Hellenized rulers. Although Greece had forfeited its political significance, Greek became even for many foreign or bilingual populations an international language of business, diplomacy and culture. The Koine as a spoken dialect can be reconstructed from a wealth of inscriptions and papyri. A literary Koine, often overlaid by sedulous imitations of classical models, can be recovered through careful textual analysis of such authors as Polybius or Diodorus; considerably more influence of the spoken language is apparent in the Greek of the Septuagint (*c.* 3rd–2nd century B.C.) and of the New Testament (1st century A.D.).

It is generally agreed that the basis of the Koine was the Attic dialect, distinguished above all others by the past political and literary prominence of Athens. The older Greek dialects other than Attic were already dying out in any case. Ionic contributed some few forms to the Koine like -σσ- for -ττ- in such words as γλῶσσα "tongue" and θάλασσα "sea." Furthermore, the polyglot populations of Alexander's empire and its successors modified to some extent the Greek they used in accordance with the speech habits of their own languages. It was in Asia Minor, for example, that the combination -*nt*- was pronounced -*nd*- (e.g., πέντε "five" became *pende*), as in modern Greek. Many foreign words were admitted, particularly from Latin or Hebrew, as Roman civilization and Christianity impinged on Hellenism. The rigorous influence of the schools and the rise of a purist movement, so-called Atticism, in the 1st century A.D. discouraged deviations from the classical norm in literary usage. Not so, however, in spoken Koine. As early as the 3rd century B.C. significant errors in spelling, indicative of an altered pronunciation, begin to occur in texts written by uneducated persons: ει for ι, ο for ω, ε for αι (see below, *Modern; Phonology*).

What makes the spoken Koine of particular interest to linguists is its gradual incorporation of many changes which were eventually passed on to Byzantine and modern Greek, such as the loss of musical accent and the simplification of paradigms through progressive loss of, e.g., the dative case, the infinitive, or the optative mood. Strict Atticists, like the grammarian Phrynichus (2nd century A.D.), drew up lists of reprehensible words and forms drawn from contemporary colloquial speech. It is a particularly apposite demonstration of Koine usage when terms castigated by Phrynichus have been transmitted to Byzantine and modern Greek.

Byzantine is the name given to the Greek used in the eastern Roman, or Byzantine, empire, which fell to the Turks in 1453. The official language of Byzantium and the vast domain which it controlled was as far as possible an imitation of classical Attic models. The spoken language, much divergent and tending in the direction of modern Greek, can be reconstructed from such authors as the Hellenized Syrian chronicler John Malalas (6th century), the hagiographer Leontius of Neapolis (7th century) and the emperor Constantine VII Porphyrogenitus (10th century).

MODERN

The beginning of modern Greek, or Romaic, may be conveniently dated from the capture of Constantinople (Istanbul) by the Turks in 1453. In addition to the Greek-speakers of Greece and the Greek islands, there are still Greek communities in Turkey. Many Greeks are concentrated in southern Albania, the U.S.S.R., Egypt and Rumania and in various sites in North and South America and also southern Italy. Since modern Greek has evolved via medieval Greek from the ancient ones, with the possible exception of Tsakonian, which retains features of ancient Laconian. The dialects differ greatly. They may be classified as western or eastern according to their loss or retention of final ν, but this is only partly satisfactory.

A striking feature of Greek ever since the medieval period has been the use of two sharply differentiated idioms for speaking and writing (διγλωσσία), and the resultant conflict between proponents of the two. The spoken language, called "demotic" (δημοτική), is the medium of everyday conversation and in recent years has been generally favoured for literary use. The written or "purifying" language (καθαρεύουσα), much closer to ancient Greek, is the official tongue of the Greek state. It is spoken only on formal occasions (e.g., in the Greek Orthodox liturgy, in the Greek parliament or in academic lectures), but is used almost exclusively for all official and most scientific writing and by most newspapers. The two varieties of Greek share the same phonetic system but differ in inflexion, syntax and vocabulary.

Phonology.—The melodic accent of ancient Greek has been replaced in the modern language by a stress accent like that of English, and the ancient quantitative distinctions of the vowels have been lost. Accented vowels, except when final, are slightly lengthened and are pronounced with a higher pitch. Retention of the ancient breathings in writing conceals the fact that aspiration has been lost: ἁλάτι "salt," is pronounced aláti. Similarly, while the ancient rules for accent are mostly maintained in the written language, the use of the acute, grave or circumflex accent is only an orthographic distinction. The spoken language shows much shifting of the ancient accent and a marked tendency to retain the stress on the same syllable throughout a paradigm: ἕτοιμος "ready," forms a feminine ἑτοίμη in contrast to written ἑτοίμη.

Greek has a five-vowel system with three back vowels (a, o, u) and two front (i, e), spelled in various ways: a for a; o, ω for o; ου for u; η, ι, υ, ει, οι for i; ε, αι for e. The combinations ευ, αυ are pronounced ev, av, or ef, af according to whether the following consonant is voiced or voiceless. The consonant system of ancient Greek has been considerably altered; the voiced stops have become voiced spirants and the voiceless aspirates voiceless spirants. Thus β and δ are pronounced like Eng. v and th in the; γ before a back vowel is the voiced counterpart of German ch in ach, while before a front vowel it is like Eng. y; θ is like Eng. th in think, φ like Eng. f, χ before a back vowel like Ger. ch in ach. The sounds b, d, g initially are rendered by the spellings μπ, ντ and γκ, but internally these combinations usually have the value of mb, nd, ng. A final n combines with an initial p, t or k to form the combinations mb, nd, ng, although this is not indicated in writing: τὸν πατέρα, tombatéra; τὸν τόπο, tondópo; τὴν κόρη, tingóri. These phenomena are evidence of "close juncture"; i.e., the running of words closely together. The spoken language shows a number of phonetic developments not always registered in the spelling: e.g., πτωχός "poor" becomes φτωχός; νύμφη "bride" becomes νύφη.

Grammar.—Both the spoken and written tongues have lost the dual number and the optative and infinitive moods; the dative case has virtually disappeared except for set phrases (e.g., δόξα σοι ὁ Θεός "Thank God!") and is replaced by the genitive or by the preposition σε (εἰς) plus accusative. In the spoken language the genitive plural of nouns is often replaced by ἀπό plus the accusative (note that all prepositions of popular origin govern the accusative).

Declension.—While the written language largely maintains the ancient declensions, the spoken language has simplified and modified them. The definite article has feminine plural οἱ (like the masculine) in the nominative and τίς in the accusative. Masculines of the ancient third declension have yielded a new inflexion in -ας, genitive -α (ὁ πατέρας "father," genitive τοῦ πατέρα); feminines of the ancient third declension have acquired a nominative in -α, genitive -ας (ἡ ἐλπίδα "hope," genitive τῆς ἐλπίδας). A new plural formation with syllabic supplement has been generalized in such a paradigm as ὁ ψωμάς "baker," plural οἱ ψωμάδες. The latter form also shows the -es ending of the ancient third declension, the use of which has been considerably extended to include many nominative and accusative plurals: οἱ μέρες "the days," (the written language, like ancient Greek, has αἱ ἡμέραι); τοὺς πατέρες (accusative) "the fathers" (instead of τοὺς πατέρας).

Adjectives.—In popular usage the accent of adjectives remains fixed throughout the paradigm: πλούσιος "rich," has genitive πλουσίου. While some of the ancient comparatives survive (μικρότερος "smaller"), a new comparative formation with πιό (from ancient πλέον) plus the positive (πιό μεγάλος "larger") is very common. The superlative is formed by putting the definite article before either of these comparatives (ὁ μικρότερος, "the smallest," ὁ πιό μεγάλος "the largest"). "Than" in a comparison is commonly indicated by the use of the genitive case or by ἀπό with the accusative: εἶμαι μικρότερος ἀπ' τον Πέτρο "I am smaller than Peter."

Numerals.—There are many new forms in common use: ἔξι "6," ὀχτώ "8," τράντα "30," σαράντα "40," πενῆντα "50," ἐξῆντα "60." The form δύο "2" is used by itself or for emphasis, but δυό when another word follows; ἑκατό "100" is used by itself or with a following noun, but changes to ἑκατόν when another numeral follows. Some expressions with numerals of special interest are: τρεῖς φορές "three times"; πέντε τοῖς ἑκατό "5%"; στὶς δέκα καὶ τέταρτο "at 10:15"; μισῆ ὥρα "half-hour"; πάρε τὴ δική βρίου τοῦ χίλια ἐννιακόσια πενῆντα "on Dec. 20, 1950."

Pronouns.—The emphatic forms of the first and second person are: (ἐ)μένα, (ἐ)σένα; plural (ἐ)μᾶς, (ἐ)σᾶς. The genitive plural of the third person for all genders is commonly τούς. In peasant speech there exists an indeclinable periphrastic pronominal expression of polite address: τοῦ λόγου σου "you." A new possessive pronoun is ὁ (ἡ)δικός: θέλεις μὰ πέννα; πάρε τὴ δική μου "Do you want a pen? Take mine." ἴδιος is used after a noun or pronoun to mean "self" (ἐγώ ὁ ἴδιος "I myself"), and before a substantive to mean "same" (ὁ ἴδιος ἄνθρωπος "the same man"). A new and common relative pronoun is formed from the adverb ποῦ "where": ἡ γυναῖκα ποῦ εἴδατε "the woman whom you saw." The interrogative adjective and pronoun "who," "which" is commonly ποιός: ποιός ἦρθε; (";," is the Greek sign of interrogation) "Who came?" ποιὸ βυβλίο θέλεις; "Which book do you want?" Invariable τί is used for "what," or "what sort of": τί (λογῆς) βυβλίο θέλεις; "What sort of book do you want?" (Note also τί ὥρα εἶναι; "What time is it?") Some indefinites function also in negative sentences with a different meaning: κανένας (written form κανείς), "some one" or "no one" (ἦρθε κανένας; "Did anyone come?" but κανένας δὲν ἦρθε "Nobody came"); so also τίποτε (τίποτα) means both "something" and "nothing." Other pronominal expressions are ὁ καθένας "each one"; κάτι (τι) "something"; ὁ κύριος τάδε "Mr. So-and-So"; κάποιο παιδί "a certain child."

Conjugation.—Modern Greek, like the Slavonic languages, constantly expresses the category of aspect as well as that of time in the verbal system. Each verb has two contrasting stems, an imperfective for continuous or repeated action and a perfective for momentary or single action. Thus γράφε μου συχνά "write me often" uses the imperfective stem; γράψε μου αὔριο "write me tomorrow" uses the perfective stem. This distinction is particularly important in the imperative, the future and the subjunctive (see H.-J. Seiler, L'Aspect et le temps dans le verbe néogrec, 1952). The ancient infinitive has been replaced by the subjunctive, a trait common to other Balkan languages; thus, θέλω νὰ εἶμαι "I wish to be" (νά as sign of the subjunctive is from ancient ἵνα). The imperative also is frequently replaced by the subjunctive: νὰ (ἂς) γράφουμε (γράψουμε) "let us write" (ἂς is for ἄφες "leave," "let"). The future tense is formed by prefixing the particle θά (for θέλω νά "I wish that") to the present or aorist subjunctive; as indicated above, the difference is one of aspect. When θά is added to an imperfect tense it forms a conditional: θά ἔχανα, "I should lose." Several new analytical forms, analogous to the composite perfect system of the Romance languages, are chiefly used in writing: ἔχω δέσει "I have bound," ἔχω δεθεῖ (or δεθῆ) "I have been bound" (δέσε, δεθεῖ are invariable here). The aorist passive in the spoken language differs from the ancient paradigm continued in the written language: χάθηκε "it was (has been) lost." A new invariable present active participle in -οντας is largely confined to the written style: γράφοντας "(in) writing."

Vocabulary.—In addition to the grammatical differences between spoken and written style noted above, examples of the many differences of vocabulary may be given (written form first): ἡ ἐπιστολή—τὸ γράμμα "letter"; ὁ οἶνος—τὸ κρασί "wine"; ἡ χείρ—τὸ χέρι "hand"; ἡ ῥίς—ἡ μύτη "nose." The following is an identical passage in both styles for comparison. (Spoken): Ἔνας χωροφύλακας σκοτώθηκε, καθὼς μάθαινε, μὲ μιὰ τουφεκιά.

(Written): Χωροφύλαξ τις ἐφονεύθη, καθ' ἃ πληροφορούμαι, διὰ δῆλου. ("A gendarme, I am told, was shot and killed.")

The vocabulary of the ancient language naturally remains the basis of modern Greek, with a far heavier concentration of ancient words, or neologisms modeled on ancient words, in the written style. In many cases (e.g., in medical and other technical terms), the ancient word is the only one available for writing or speaking: ἀπεργία "strike"; Λαθρεμβάτης "stowaway"; συνταγματάρχης "colonel"; ὑλισμός "materialism"; χρημα-τοκιβώτιον "safe"; περίστροφον "revolver"; διανοούμενος "in-tellectual"; ἐρασιτέχνης "amateur"; στρατόπεδον συγκεντρώσεως "concentration camp"; ῥιζοσπάστης "radical"; ποδόσφαιρον "football." In some cases the elements of a foreign word have been translated into Greek equivalents (translation loan): γραφειοκρατία reproduces French *bureaucratie,* "bureaucracy."

Foreign words which have penetrated the language in large numbers faithfully reflect the influence of various powers which have held sway in postclassical Greece or which have exerted cultural influence there, from the foundation of the eastern Roman empire (A.D. 325) through the Crusades to the Venetian and Turkish conquests. Examples:

Latin.—ἀκκουμπῶ "lean"; κάμαρα "room"; κελλί "cell"; κουκούδια "hood"; λουκάνικο "sausage"; μαντήλ "handkerchief"; πόρτα "door"; σοῦβλα "spit"; σπίτι "house"; ταβέρνα "tavern."

Slavonic.—βερβερίτσα "squirrel"; ῥούχα "clothes"; σανός "hay"; σβάρνα "harrow." There were relatively few borrowings, but these include some place names like Ἀράχοβα.

Rumanian (Vlach).—μιτουμποῦλι "bud"; σαρμανίτσα "crib." The few borrowed terms mostly refer to pastoral life.

Albanian.—πλιάτσικο "booty"; φλογέρα "rustic pipe." The very few borrowings include some place names like Σούλι.

Turkish.—γιαούρτι "yoghurt"; κάικι "caïque"; καρπούζι, "melon"; κέφι "good humor"; μανάβης "greengrocer"; μεζές "snack"; μενεξές "violet"; μπαρούτι "gunpowder"; παπούτσι "shoe"; σουργάς "pocket knife"; τεμπέλης "lazy"; τσάι "pocket." Many of the Turkish borrowings present in very large numbers during the occupation have become obsolete or have been replaced by native words.

Italian.—κάλτσα "sock"; καπετάνιος "captain"; κουμπάρος "best man"; πατάτα "potato"; πιάτο "plate"; τενόρος "tenor"; φουρτούνα "tempest." Many Romance borrowings have to do with maritime terminology.

See also references under "Greek Language" in the Index.

(G. M. M.)

BIBLIOGRAPHY.—*Ancient:* The fullest reference work (it is not al-ways up to date) is R. Kühner's *Ausführliche Grammatik der grie-chischen Sprache,* 3rd ed. by F. Blass and B. Gerth (1890-1904). For historical grammar of Greek see E. Schwyzer, *Griechische Gram-matik,* 3 vol. (1934-53); the best works for details of the spelling of Greek inscriptions and papyri are K. Meisterhans, *Grammatik der attischen Inschriften,* 3rd ed. by E. Schwyzer (1900); W. Crönert, *Memoria Graeca Herculanensis* (1903) (compares the Herculaneum papyri with the other papyri, inscriptions and mss.); E. Mayser, *Grammatik der griechischen Papyri aus der Ptolemäerzeit* (esp. vol. 1, 1906; vol. 2 [1926] contains the syntax); H. St. J. Thackeray, *Grammar of New Testament Greek,* rev. by W. F. Howard (1919-29); F. Blass, *Grammatik des Neutestamentlichen Griechisch,* 5th ed. by A. Debrunner (1921). On pronunciation, E. H. Sturtevant, *Pronunci-ation of Greek and Latin* (1940). The language of Homer is treated in P. Chantraine, *Grammaire homérique,* 2 vol. (1942-53); J. Wacker-nagel, *Sprachliche Untersuchungen zu Homer* (1916); K. Meister, *Die Homerische Kunstsprache* (1921). The dialects are treated by A. Thumb, *Handbuch der griechischen Dialekte* (1909), rev. in 2 vol. by E. Kieckers (1932); C. D. Buck, *Greek Dialects* (grammar, texts, vocabulary, rev. ed. 1955) and by F. Bechtel, *Die griechischen Dialekte* (grammar only). A conven-ient collection of dialect inscriptions is E. Schwyzer, *Dialectorum graecarum exempla epigraphica potiora* (1923), with index. The rela-tion of Greek to other Indo-Eur. languages is studied in K. Brugmann and B. Delbrück's large *Grundriss der vergleichenden Grammatik der Indogermanischen Sprachen,* 2nd ed. (1897-1916); more briefly in A. Meillet, *Introduction à l'étude comparative des langues indo-européennes* (1908) and later eds. On the laryngeals, J. Whatmough, *Poetic, Scientific and other Forms of Discourse,* ch. 3 (1957). Lexi-cons: *The Thesaurus Linguae Graecae* of H. Stephanus (Henri Etienne), first published in 1572, was greatly enlarged by K. B. Hase and the brothers W. and L. Dindorf (1831-65) and remains valuable, but does not cover the inscriptions and papyri. The vocabulary of the nonliterary papyri is covered by F. Preisigke, *Wörterbuch der griechischen Papyrusurkunden,* which was rapidly published at Berlin in 1924 and the following years. The papyri and inscriptions are in-cluded in the 9th ed. of Liddell and Scott's *Greek-English Lexicon* (1925-40). The New Testament vocabulary is treated in J. H. Moul-ton and G. Milligan's *Vocabulary of the Greek Testament Illustrated From the Papyri and Other Non-Literary Sources* (1914-29). Ety-mological dictionaries: E. Boisacq, *Dictionnaire étymologique de la langue grecque* (1916); H. Frisk, *Gr. Etym. Wtb.,* in progress (1954-). For the numerous special lexicons, H. and B. Riesenfeld, *Reper-torium lexicographicum Graecum* (1954).

Koine and Byzantine Greek: A. Debrunner, *Geschichte der griechischen Sprache,* vol. 2 (1954) (for a good short account of Koine and By-zantine Greek); A. N. Jannaris, *An Historical Greek Grammar* (1897); K. Dieterich, *Untersuchungen zur Geschichte der griechischen Sprache von der hellenistischen Zeit bis zum 10. Jahrhundert,* vol. 1, *Byzan-tisches Archiv* (1898); S. B. Psaltes, *Grammatik der byzantinischen Chroniken* (1913); G. Böhlig, *Untersuchungen zum rhetorischen Sprachgebrauch der Byzantiner* (1956); R. M. Dawkins, "The Greek Language in the Byzantine Period," in N. H. Baynes and H. St. L. B. Moss, *Byzantium* (1948); P. S. Costas, *An Outline of the History of the Greek Language* (1936); C. Ducange, *Glossarium ad scriptores mediae et infimae Graecitatis* (1688); E. A. Sophocles, *Greek Lexicon of the Roman and Byzantine Period* (1870); G. W. H. Lampe (ed.), *A Patristic Greek Lexicon* (1961-).

Modern: D. Dimitrakos, Μέγα λεξικὸν τῆς ἑλληνικῆς γλώσσης, 9 vol (1933-50); N. P. Andriotis, Ἐτυμολογικὸ λεξικὸ τῆς κοινῆς νεοελληνικῆς (1951); M. Triandafyllidis *et al.,* Νεοελληνικὴ γραμματικὴ τῆς δημοτικῆς (1941); A. A. Tzartzanos, Νεοελληνικὴ σύνταξις (τῆς κοινῆς δημοτικῆς), 2 vol. (1946-53); I. Kykkotis, *English-Greek and Greek-English Dictionary,* 2nd ed. (1947); R. Dawkins, *Modern Greek in Asia Minor* (1916); H. Pernot, *Grammaire du grec moderne, langue parlée,* 5th ed. (1930); H. R. Kahane and R. Ward, *Spoken Greek,* 2 vol. (1945-46); J. T. Pring, *Grammar of Modern Greek on a Phonetic Basis* (1950); *A Phrase Book of Modern Greek with Pronunciation* (1956); J. W. Fay, *Spoken Modern Greek* (1953); D. C. Swanson, *Vocabulary of Modern Spoken Greek* (1957); A. Mirambel, *La Langue grecque moderne* (1959).

GREEK LAW.

Greek law and legal thought have a history of more than 3,000 years and constitute a still-living tradition. A brief introduction into this Greek legal tradition may be facilitated by distinguishing five great periods roughly corresponding with landmarks in the political and national history of Hellenism. These are: an ancient Greek period, up to the time Greece became a Roman province; a Hellenistic period, up to the foundation of the Byzantine empire; a Byzantine period, up to the fall of Constanti-nople; a post-Byzantine period, up to the Greek revolution of 1821 (the War of Greek Independence); and a modern period, from 1821 on. The present article is restricted primarily to a discussion of substantive law and legal institutions; for early Greek specula-tion on the nature of law, see JURISPRUDENCE; PLATO; ARISTOTLE; NATURAL LAW.

(A. N. Y.)

ANCIENT GREEK LAW

The basis for the development of Greek law was laid by the rise in Greece of city-states (*poleis*). Primitively, all Greeks were tribal, or, to use their own term, ethnic. But between 1200 and 800 B.C., among those of them who had entered the area of the Aegean civilization, tribes were replaced by city-states. Of Greek tribal law little need be said. Its source was twofold. For the most part it issued from kindred groups—families and brother-hoods (*phratries*)—in which event it was also enforced by such groups. But it likewise sprang from the tribal government of kings, elders and assemblies; and tribal, and even intertribal, pres-sure operated to produce or maintain a general sameness in the rules and regulations of the lesser groups. Tribal law, and the law of the early city-states as well, consisted of customary rules preserved by popular memory. So long as they were thus in-tangible they could be changed only unconsciously by the slow processes of social growth. Thus, they seemed unchangeable. Nor did the gods withhold their hands after they had laid down the fundamental ordinances. From Zeus there came to every king, so Homer tells us, the dooms (*themistes*) according to which he settled disputes (*Iliad,* ix, 99).

Tribal justice had as its mainspring self-help. Its course may be illustrated in cases of homicide. Fear of vengeance at the hands of the kindred of the slain man drove his slayer, whether guilty or innocent, to seek exile, sanctuary or the protection of his blood brothers. But to avoid the feuds to which acts of violence and reprisals gave rise, recourse was had to commutation, and if this proved inefficacious, to arbitration. The oldest Greek trial of which we have record was one arising out of a dispute between a slayer and avenger as to the receipt or nonreceipt of blood money. The hearing was held publicly, in the place of assembly, and was attended by partisans of both contestants, who were restrained by public officers (heralds). The "daysman" (*istor*) or arbiter was supported by the elders. They sat on "polished stones in the sacred circle," and in their midst lay two pieces of gold to be awarded either to the disputant who made good his contention or to the elder who declared most righteously the rule of law (*dike*) governing the case (*Il.*, xviii, 497–508).

The scope of self-help was wider than the scope of kinsmen-help. The adulterer, no less than the homicide, could be dealt with directly by the party aggrieved; but since unmitigated self-help was socially suicidal, even if he were caught in the very act he might be ransomed if a bondsman went surety for him (*Odyssey*, viii, 344–599). Where death or violence were not its normal accompaniments the practice of affirming rights solely by self-help lasted longer. Until a late date a creditor might seize the person of his debtor for nonfulfillment of contract. Long after the rights of talion and "distress" had been subordinated to state law they continued to be legitimate remedies of international law.

The *Iliad* and *Odyssey* of Homer are the sole contemporary sources for early Greek law. They reflect its condition in the period of transition from the tribe to the city-state. Between Homer and the 7th century revolutionary changes in constitutional law occurred. They had comparatively little effect on the rules applicable within the family sphere; but the autonomy of the kinsmen groups in pursuing private vengeance was radically affected by the rise of an attitude toward homicide that lifted murder out of the category of ordinary acts of violence; the slayer was thought to pollute the entire community. So the state could no longer remain neutral.

The defects of unwritten laws were not so much their vagueness as their failure to cover new situations. They might coerce facts and outlaw novelties, like those of the ancient Spartans and the modern Albanians. But where new situations developed in spite of them, a frontier region of uncertainty arose in which the magistrates were unguided and unrestrained. Such was the characteristic aspect of justice in the "iron age" in which Hesiod wrote (700 B.C.). An obvious remedy was to separate the determining of law from the passing on facts and to leave one function only to magistrates. The function Rome left them was the one Athens took from them. In *c.* 683 B.C. it created a body of six "determiners of customs" (*thesmothetai; cf.* the Persian *databara*), to whom, it may be assumed, the chief magistrates (archon [q.v.], polemarch, king) were bound to refer for an authoritative definition of the "law" that bore on disputes brought before them.

In the 7th century the Greek city-states began putting their laws into writing. The method used was to entrust the task of determining all the laws and issuing them in the form of a code to a single individual described as a "law-determiner" (*nomothetes*). The early codes have all perished except for a few isolated passages, so that direct knowledge of them is slight. But it may be said that laws were, on the one hand, instructions issued for the guidance of boards and officials in the performance of their public duties, and, on the other hand, rules of general application containing prohibitions with their attendant penalties, and specifications as to what should be done in certain contemplated acts or situations. Since the rules were linked up for enforcement with definite organs of government, the entire code was arranged under the heads of the competent public authorities.

Greek law codes were accordingly a blend of public law, including the forms to be observed by priests in public worship, and private law. A precondition for their publication was the spread of literacy. Since they were demanded because of the inadequacy of traditions, they naturally appeared first in the colonies and in progressive states. The earliest *nomothetes* is said to have been Zaleucus of Locri in Magna Graecia. Charondas of Catana was, perhaps a younger contemporary. Other famous lawgivers were Draco of Athens (*c.* 621 B.C.), Pittacus of Mytilene and Philolaus of Thebes. The historical reality of Lycurgus (*q.v.*) of Sparta, Theseus of Attica, and even Minos of Knossus has been sustained by some recent writers, and the divinity of Zaleucus, Charondas and even Draco has been affirmed by others; unwisely in both instances.

Since each city-state had its own law, it is apparent that strictly there was no such thing as Greek law but only hundreds of local codes. And indeed in the sense in which England developed a common law and France "received" another, there was no possibility for a common law to arise in Greece, unless it be in the area of the short-lived Athenian empire (477–405 B.C.). The common law which Greece possessed was simply the law that was common to all its numerous codes. This need not have been inconsiderable. The law given by Zaleucus to Locri was adopted by Sybaris; that given by Charondas to Catana was shared by the other Chalcidian cities in Sicily and Italy, and what is even more remarkable, it was not only drawn on by Thurii but also used in Mazaca in Cappadocia. Nonetheless, cases of migratory codes were exceptional. The unity of Greek law, such as it was, depended rather upon the possession by all Greeks of a common stock of legal principles. This was partly an inheritance from a distant past. The rules governing marriage, right of succession (*anchisteia*), the disposition of heiresses, adoption—family life in general—were everywhere similar because they were derived from ancient Hellenic ideas. But it was also the outcome of reciprocal borrowing. Commerce in Greece was at all times international in part and largely in the hands of metics. The ideas of commercial right and wrong were established in the international ports and on the high seas by a kind of mental and moral barter. They were brought to greater precision by the negotiation of commercial treaties (*symbola*); and finally they became so consolidated that Demosthenes (xxxv, 45) could affirm that the laws governing commercial cases "were everywhere identical."

Between the 7th and 4th centuries codes tended to converge. The movement of law had to conform to the general movement in Greece, which was toward greater and greater uniformity. But there was an inevitable relation between laws and the character of states; and since for a long time noble or class-states, which had existed generally at the time laws were first codified, persisted in certain parts of Greece, the convergence was at first on two types of law rather than on one—an aristocratic and a democratic type. The former is well illustrated in the laws of Gortyna in Crete.

In their present form these laws consist of earlier and later portions, the latter a supplement made at *c.* 450 B.C. In this collection, especially in its earlier portions, the rules of a class-state predominated. A magistrate, unassisted by jurors, judged cases, and there was a special judge for the privileged class. The right to make a will was not recognized. Women inherited as well as men. The penalties for offenses varied with personal status. For private seizure of an alleged wrongdoer in advance of trial a fine of 10 staters was imposed if he was a freeman, one of 5 if he was a slave. Rape of a freeman or -woman was penalized by 100 staters, rape of an *apetairos* (a freeman who did not belong to a political society) by 10, and of a serf by 5; but if the violator was a slave the penalty was doubled. The number of witnesses required to prove an allegation varied similarly; five, for example, to convict a freeman, three to convict an *apetairos*, one to convict a serf. In the event of conflict the law defined which witnesses "were nearer," that is, should prevail.

The other type of code emphasized by contrast what the Greeks called *isonomia*. This meant, in terms of public law, the admission of all freeborn native adult males to equal share in the assemblies in which sovereign action was taken, and, in terms of private law, the canceling of all class distinctions. Athens is the classic example of this type, and the influence, power and policy of Athens helped greatly to spread throughout Greece the principles of law for which it itself stood. Historically there was a connection between political and legal equality, and in Athens both were realized finally on a basis of self-government in 507 B.C., after the expulsion of the Peisistratids. But they were not inseparable. In Boeotia, for example, a way was found to reserve participation on equal terms in the sovereign assemblies to citizens of the middle and upper classes without giving them any rights under private law which all freeborn native adults did not also have. Those owning a certain amount of property simply became "councilors"; and councilors alone were organized for the transaction of public business. For a brief time after the fall of the Four Hundred in 411 B.C. Athens itself adopted this form of *isonomia*. There the experiment failed politically and was not repeated.

Growth of Law in Athens.—In the centre of Greek law, as we know it, stands the law of Athens. It was first codified by Draco (*q.v.*). The thought then uppermost in the minds of the Athenians was to fix, once for all, existing customs. Stability, presumed for the law while it was unwritten, was naturally presumed for the written law also. But owing, as it seemed, to the rapacity of the rich and the extravagant hopes of the poor, the situation became so acute within a generation that Solon (*q.v.*), archon for the year 594 B.C., on being given the full power of the state to reconcile the warring factions, took the extreme step of issuing a new code of laws. The only part of Draco's code which he retained unchanged was the law of homicide. The constitutional provisions, including those regulating judicial procedure, were profoundly altered, notably by a rule, pregnant with history, authorizing appeal from judicial decisions of magistrates to a popular assembly organized as a court (*heliaia*). All freeborn adult males native in Attica were given the public-law rights of *isonomia*—membership on equal terms in the assembly and *heliaia*. For classes based on property. These new classes based on birth were recognized in the distribution of public offices and services. Whether they were also recognized in the assessment of legal penalties is uncertain; the spirit of the Solonian constitution was hostile to their maintenance. It struck at the roots of privilege by including wrongs done to citizens individually in the category of wrongs done to the state. In all cases (excepting homicide) which involved more than business settlements, Solon established the right of any citizen whatsoever to appear as public prosecutor.

Solon regarded lawmaking as an abnormal function of government and bound the Athenians by oath not to resort to it again for 100 years. This attitude toward it persisted under the Peisistratids, who preserved Solon's laws while administering them to serve their own ends. Cleisthenes (*q.v.*), too, was an extraconstitutional lawmaker. But at some point, not precisely determinable, between the time of Cleisthenes and the downfall of the Four Hundred in 411 B.C., the method of legislating through suspension of the constitution in favour of an autocratic *nomothetes* was abandoned for the more democratic method of vesting the lawgiving power in a board of *nomothetai*; and it was according to the more modern method that the regime of the Five Thousand was inaugurated in Aug. 411 B.C. and the democratic laws re-enacted on the overthrow of the Thirty and the Ten in 403 B.C. On the latter occasion it proved necessary both to make a general revision of the laws and to issue a new code. The legislative work was entrusted to a corps of 1,000 representatives taken from the demes, half by lot and half by popular vote (the *nomothetai*). This body issued the laws, old and new, in the form of drafts (*syggraphai*) and gave them to a 'commission of "publishers" (*anagrapheis*) for editing. This body had them cut on stone slabs in the King's Porch, where also the old code had been inscribed.

Thus far legislation was an occasional and not a regular function of government. But this view of it was now abandoned. Athens had henceforth a process by which the laws might be changed annually. It was initiated at the first meeting each year of the assembly. Votes were then taken on the laws, section by section, to determine whether or not they seemed adequate; first on the laws concerning the councils; secondly, on those classified as general (*koinoi*); thirdly, on those relating to the other magistrates. For the defense of laws judged inadequate five attorneys were elected; and during the succeeding three weeks anyone who chose might bring forward substitutes for laws under indictment and have them posted on the state bulletin boards. Then, at its third meeting, the assembly ordered *nomothetai* to be chosen. The *nomothetai*—on one occasion 1,001 in number (Dem., xxiv, 27)—were selected from the jurors (dicasts) impaneled for the year. Their proceedings, too, were in the form of a

trial with pleas by the proponents of changes and counterpleas by the attorneys for the defendant laws. But since their presiding officers consisted of the identical type of presidency used in the assembly, they also resembled the sovereign political body. Their decisions, too, were reached as in an assembly and not in a court —by open vote. Unlike a decree, a law could be enacted only after due notice had been given and the public interests had been defended by counsel. It emanated from a body carefully selected to ensure the representation of every section of the population, not, like a decree, from the group of citizens who chanced to be present at a particular meeting of the assembly. The *nomothetai* were dicasts; but they rendered a political, not a judicial, verdict. Hence, unlike the action of a court, it was subject to suspension, like the action of the assembly, if indicted for illegality, and became definitely binding only when reaffirmed by a regular tribunal.

The code was a thing of many complex interrelations. An alteration at one point might produce unsuspected trouble at others. The officials who had most to do with law enforcement were the *thesmothetai*. It was therefore made incumbent upon them to examine the code carefully in the course of their administration, and, if they found in it obsolete articles not so designated, or articles which contradicted or duplicated one another, to put on the bulletin boards the editorial revisions they deemed necessary. For the validation of these clerical corrections an ordinary meeting of the assembly was competent, but it was held constructively to take by lack of legal authority, the assembly passed votes requiring the chairmen and president who should preside at the first session of *nomothetai* to present for consideration the additions to the laws it desired. This may have led to an overweakening of constitutional law (Dem., xx, 89 ff.); but so long as this was fused with private law there was no alternative. The magistrates' courts, being incompetent to render judicial decisions except in trifles, were incapable of developing a body of judge-made law comparable to the Roman *jus honorarium*. Neither could law in Athens be court-made, since every verdict of the dicasts was independent of every other verdict.

Until the age of Pericles, the Athenians entrusted the function of acting as "guardian of the laws" to the Areopagus (*q.v.*). Then they did away with it as being derogatory to popular sovereignty. Yet the laws had to be safeguarded, not perhaps against the demos itself—for like the king the demos could do no wrong—but against individuals in council and assembly who should mislead it. The remedy applied was to hold all makers of motions at meetings of these bodies liable to public actions for illegality (*graphai paranomon*), thus placing the protection of the laws in the large category of public interests for the vindication of which each and every citizen in good standing might assume the role of state prosecutor. The test of illegality was whether the motion sought to accomplish something prohibited by the laws. There was, however, nothing illegal in persuading the assembly to use decrees (*psephismata*) to fill gaps in the laws; and in the 5th century, when legislation was still a quasi-revolutionary activity, this course was frequently followed. It was by means of decrees primarily that law was built up for the empire. The constitution of the council itself was extended by decree. New magistracies were created in this way. Decrees were therefore often indistinguishable from laws in subject matter, and since the courts were required to take account of them both, they might have precisely the same force as laws. Yet there was a fundamental difference between the two. A decree could be abrogated by a new decree without ceremony, whereas a law stood until annulled by further legislation. The revisions of 411–410 and 403 B.C. must have conferred the superior status of laws on many rules which previously had rested on decrees alone; and thenceforth the Athenians lessened the need for decrees to trespass on the province of laws by providing for annual legislation. Naturally they made the proposers of new laws liable to the same form of public action as the proposers of new decrees. And indeed they went even farther than this; they made them liable to public prosecution if the laws originated by them were found within a

resembled a court.

year to be inexpedient. After the twelve months had expired, laws, like decrees, alone were indictable, not their authors.

Official transcripts of the laws were ordered to be made on stone tablets in 410-404 B.C.; and to this measure we owe the preservation, though in a very fragmentary condition, of Draco's law on involuntary homicide, Cleisthenes' law on the Council of the Five Hundred, and a law of uncertain date governing grants of maintenance in the public hall or Prytaneum. On the occasion of the revision made in 403 B.C. a new text was issued in the Ionic alphabet then officially adopted. The new laws passed during the following 80 years were attached to the code in the form of the minutes of the sessions of *nomothetai* in which they originated, and like the laws of Rome they were regularly cited by the names of their proposers. A small number of these *novellae* have come into our possession textually, three in inscriptions. Most of the laws that have reached us, whether in whole or in part or in paraphrase, were entered by ancient grammarians at points where they seemed to be called for in the speeches of the Attic orators. These and others, culled from lexicographers and scholiasts and elsewhere, are collected in Telfy's *Corpus Juris Attici* (1868). The descriptive portion of Aristotle's *Constitution of Athens* (secs. 42-70), composed between 329 and 322 B.C., was based directly on the code of that epoch. Though it is confined to an exposition of public law and has survived without its final portions, it is by far the most extensive extant abstract of the Athenian laws. (*See* CONSTITUTION OF ATHENS.)

So far as can be judged from the specimens preserved, the laws of Athens were drafted in simple language. Some ancient phrases survived in their older portions. In style they resembled the laws of the Twelve Tables rather than the matured legislation of republican Rome. No attempt was made in them to define parties or objects by the use of synonymous terms and to then adhere rigorously to such definitions, a defect that opened the way to subterfuge in litigation (Lysias, x, 15) but that was less troublesome in the equitable processes of the dicastic courts than it would have been in courts guided by strict law. The laws dealt with concrete situations that had arisen in actual experience. Hence they were adequate because of their number and detail rather than because they embodied principles capable of wide application. The distinctions between the hundred and more actions open to suitors were drawn with acuteness, if not with oversubtlety. The rules of procedure were "at times casual and incomplete [set practice being taken for granted], at times minutely specific." Penalties for "criminal" offenses were remarkable for their severity—a reflex doubtless of the passion and intensity of Athenian political life; they included death (with atrocious cruelty in the case of common malefactors); fines that were often confiscatory; total or partial disfranchisement; and detention, but not imprisonment. The code was thought not to measure up to the standards of contemporary jurisprudence; but when it was refashioned by Demetrius of Phalerum to give effect to the Peripatetic theory of society (317 B.C.), the Athenians would have none of it. On the expulsion of the unpopular *nomothetes*—his office was an anachronism, no less than many of his laws—they revived the "laws of Solon," revised them to suit the altered circumstances and republished them (307-304).

Judicial System of Athens in the 4th Century.—Except for (1) a special group of public actions, itself divisible into subgroups, suits fell into two general categories: (2) *dikai*, or private suits, and (3) *graphai*, or public suits.

1. The special actions may be thought of as a residuum of the means in use before Solon for dealing with crimes against the state. The small fines (*epibolai*) imposable by administrative officials upon citizens who disputed their authority represented another such residuum. Their common characteristic is that the council and assembly or the magistrates were competent to punish, if they chose, without observing the regular forms of judicial procedure. The most striking example of executive justice is *apagoge* (with its variants *endeixis* and *hyphegesis*), the arrest and detention of malefactors (*kakourgoi*; e.g., thieves) caught in the act or of persons (exiles, state debtors and the like) caught exercising rights of which they had been legally deprived. If the prisoners admitted guilt, the "eleven" were authorized to inflict summarily the penal-

ties prescribed, ordinarily death; otherwise, they, or exceptionally the *thesmothetai*, had to conduct the case as a public action.

By far the most important of these special forms was impeachment (*eisaggelia*). Typically it may be described as the process designed to cover acts that may be loosely defined as treason. The offenses were at first left indeterminate, but eventually a law was elaborated including among them, specifically, treason and conspiracy to commit treason; betrayal of a city, ship, army or fleet; unauthorized traffic with an enemy, residence in his country or service in his army; the acceptance by a public man of bribes as a consideration for misleading the demos. From actions of this type many celebrated cases arose, notably the trial of the eight generals who commanded in the battle of Arginusae. The denunciation might be presented to either the council or the assembly and accepted or rejected by them. If accepted, the defendant was arrested, and if the matter was grave he was kept in prison pending trial. The council drew up the definite proposal for action, in the one instance on its own initiative, in the other at the request of the assembly. If the penalty deemed sufficient was a fine of 500 drachmas or less, the council was fully competent to impose it. Otherwise it transmitted its proposal, through the agency of the *thesmothetai*, to the assembly, which had to decide either to try the case itself, which it did by the process used in enacting a decree, or, as was more usual, to hand it over to a dicastery. The penalty was ordinarily death with confiscation of property. The dead bodies of traitors were cast beyond the boundaries of Attica. "Presentment" (*probole*) was somewhat similar to impeachment. Actions regarding contraband (*phasis*) and wrongful possession of public property (*apographe*) were also special in that those who prosecuted them paid court fees, as in civil suits, but received half or three-fourths of the penalty. This was the prime source of sycophancy (the trade of informing).

2. *Dikai.*—The characteristic feature of *dikai* was that the right to bring them rested upon the possession by the plaintiff of a private interest. But they fall into two altogether different classes: (a) actions for homicide, and (b) civil suits.

a. Because of its antiquity the law of homicide contained a relic of the primitive practice of self-help. It placed the obligation of seeking redress for homicide upon the kinsmen of the slain man—upon his father, brothers and sons as prosecutors, and upon his cousins, sons of cousins, male relatives by marriage and blood brothers (*phratores*) as co-prosecutors. A man belonging to the inner group alone had the right to bring action; or, more probably, his was the prior right, since in cases where it was permissible to arrange a settlement (*aidesis*), even the blood brothers were competent to act if none of the nearer relatives existed. Draco had recognized the essential difference between willful murder and other kinds of homicide; but it was a distinction that did not permit any discrimination in the religious ritual of the occasion; the king-archon presided and voted at all trials, the courts sat in holy places in the open air, and pending trial the accused was excluded from the agora and all shrines and religious ceremonies, but not imprisoned. When the offense charged was willful murder, or wounding or poisoning or arson with intent to kill, and the victim was an Athenian, the Areopagus as a whole formed the court; it sat on Ares' hill, and the penalty, when life was taken, was death, otherwise exile. Other kinds of homicide were regarded as of lesser seriousness, and a board of judges called ephetai—originally a commission, perhaps, of 51 Areopagites, later a panel of dicasts—constituted the tribunal. The place in which the trial was held varied with the nature of the defense. To the Palladium belonged cases of involuntary homicide and instigation thereto, the penalty being temporary exile; also suits for killing noncitizens—slaves, metics and foreigners. To the Delphinium belonged cases of justifiable killing, and to the Phreatto, accusations against citizens already in exile. The defendant pleaded from a boat anchored off the shore so as not to pollute the country by setting foot on it. In the Prytaneum the king-archon had the *phylobasileis*, instead of the Areopagus or the ephetai, associated with him as judges, and to it belonged trials which were purely ceremonial in character—where the "doer" was unknown or an animal or, as in the obsolete English law of "deodands," something inanimate. The objects found guilty were cast beyond the frontiers.

b. Civil suits could be brought only by the parties interested or their legal representatives. Their entry was governed by the general principle of Athenian law that magistrates should accept cases arising in the sphere of their own administration; but the principle was inapplicable to magistrates whose duties were mainly or wholly judicial. Of these the *thesmothetai* were comparatively unimportant in civil suits. The other two—the Introducers and the Forty—received civil suits only. The competence of the Introducers and the Forty was limited to suits which by reason of their special urgency had to be brought to trial within a month of the filing of the complaint (*dikai emmenoi*); but not all such suits came to them. Those that they received were actions arising from nonrestitution of dowry, from loans that were in the nature of an accommodation—where the rate of interest was low (12% or less) or the security poor—from transactions with business associates, partners or bankers, and from trierarchies. They also received actions for assault. For each pair of phylae (the largest political subdivisions) there was one Introducer.

Of the Forty, four acted for each phyle. If the object of litigation was worth 10 drachmas or less, they settled it with full authority. Otherwise they referred it to a public arbitrator (*diaitetes*), whose business was first of all to reconcile the parties. Failing in this he heard the case. If his decision was accepted by both parties, it was final. But if the loser chose to appeal from it, the arbitrator sealed up in caskets all the papers submitted at the hearing, those of each litigant separately, and referred the case back to the section of the Forty from which it came. This had then to take it to a public court, where the usual course was followed.

It was characteristic of civil suits that the winner himself had to obtain the rights awarded; but if he encountered resistance he could bring a suit of ejectment. The feature of this class of actions that calls for special notice was the provision for compulsory arbitration. It applied to all civil suits that came before the Forty, either directly, or indirectly from other magistrates. Excepting the monthly suits, which would not brook delay, most disputes about property, sales, leases, contracts, debts, etc., implicating either citizens (officeholders and nonofficeholders alike) or metics and other privileged aliens had to be submitted to arbitration. The task of arbitrating was reserved exclusively to the last class of citizens on the roll of those liable for military service; in other words, the Athenians in their 60th year. The appointment of the arbitrator for each case was made by lot, and the arbitrator on whom the lot fell could not decline to serve, unless he were holding office or absent from the country, without incurring the penalty of disfranchisement, to which he was also liable, on complaint to the whole body of arbitrators, if he abused his position. The state had more confidence in the average capacity of its sexagenarians than it had in their public spirit and integrity. But what of the litigants? That they would respect the findings of an obviously incompetent arbitrator, however unbiased he might be, was not to be expected. The essence of the system was "that in a large number of disputes the constitution did not compel two quiet citizens to face the ordeal of a trial in court, but provided a cheap and simple and reasonable means of getting justice" (W. Wyse).

3. *Graphai.*—The judicial vindication of a public interest was the object of these suits. They could be entered by any citizen in good standing. He might be himself the aggrieved party, but in that event, even if the award was pecuniary, it fell to the state, which in all cases exacted the penalty. As in private suits, the magistrates were confined to a passive role: before taking action they had to wait till private individuals filed complaints with them. The principle that executive competence determined judicial competence also prevailed.

Accordingly, the generals and the other army officers were alone competent to receive suits for infractions of military duty. To the archon and the polemarch came suits (private or public as the case demanded) concerning matters of family—the rights of widows, orphans, minors and heiresses, the management and division of family property, the appointment of guardians or patrons, etc.; to the archon, if they involved citizens; to the polemarch, if they involved metics and other privileged aliens. The king-archon received suits concerning religious matters—impiety, hereditary priesthoods, the share of families (*gene*) and priests in sacrificial offerings and the like. Since over 100 species of suits are known, divided about equally between *dikai* and *graphai*, it is impossible here to give a complete classification of suits and magistrates. But the role of the *thesmothetai* calls for special comment. The six men constituting this board had duties to perform in connection both with making and administering the law which make it almost unintelligible that they should have been elected by lot (after 487 B.C.) and changed every year. They acted as intermediaries of the council and the assembly in cases which went to the courts from either of these bodies; and they were alone competent to receive indictments of decrees and laws and their authors, as well as of officials who presided at sessions of the deliberative and legislative assemblies. They also received actions against the generals. Besides offenses against the state, many offenses against society were within their competence—theft, adultery, bribery and corruption of officials, councilors, and dicasts; usurpation of rights of citizenship, sycophancy, falsification or suppression of records, etc. Their civil suits were incidental.

The correct entry of suits required no small acquaintance with law on the part of average citizens, but so did the entire judicial system. The magistrates who accepted entries, with unimportant exceptions, were always new to their office and possessed neither more nor less legal training than litigants. All litigants had to be their own attorneys. The state depended wholly upon private initiative to set the judicial processes in motion. What was every-body's business proved to be the business of a low rather than a high type of citizen; so that the community was harassed by blackmailing and sycophants. Suits were as thick in Athens as leaves in Vallombrosa. Instead of employing fisticuffs or dueling or lawyers, the Athenians went to law. It has been said that they were a nation of lawyers; but it has been also said that they were a nation without lawyers. And both statements are true.

The duty of assessing the evidence and rendering the verdict devolved upon tribunals on which sat jurors (Areopagites, ephetai, dicasts) ranging in number from 201 to 2,500 and exceptionally to 6,000. The Areopagus was a fixed body of about 220 members made up of ex-archons, and cases of willful murder came to it automatically. Seeing that the archons were elected by lot with regard to local distribution, the Areopagites were simply typical Athenians; but they entered the tribunal fresh from an exceptional experience with the whole judicial system, and as the years passed they acquired a close knowledge of the law and physiognomy of murder. Hence their judgments were greatly respected.

The king-archon was the only magistrate for whom the tribunal was fixed in advance. The rest had to apply to the *thesmothetai*, who assigned panels of dicasts to them by lot, 201 or 401 for ordinary civil cases, 501 or 1,001 for ordinary public cases. The *thesmothetai* determined on which one of the days fixed by them for sessions each magistrate should have his case tried and in which courthouse the trial should be held. The selection of the panel of dicasts for each courthouse was made on the day of the trial by a most intricate process of lot (Aristotle, *Constitution of Athens*, secs. 63 ff.). Its objects were fivefold; to ensure (1) that each individual in each of the ten sections into which the *heliaia* was divided should have a like chance to serve; (2) that every panel, containing, as it must, a like number of dicasts from each phyle, should reproduce in miniature the whole people for which constructively it was to act; (3) that no one whatsoever should know in advance of the entrance of the dicasts into the courthouse who was to judge any particular case; (4) that no one should impersonate the dicasts selected; (5) that dicasts who failed to turn up in the courthouse should not receive their daily stipend of 3 obols. The Athenians desired every panel to speak with the voice of all Athens, uninfluenced by bribery, intimidation or collusion. And they got their wish.

The sorting of the evidence was made at a preliminary hearing (*anakrisis*). There the elements of the proof and disproof were assembled—the statements under oath of the parties, the deposition of witnesses, laws, decrees, contracts and the like. The testimony of slaves was admissible only when elicited by torture; that of women and minors was admissible only in murder cases, and that of the parties to the suit was not admissible at all. Hearsay evidence was excluded. The cross-examination of witnesses was not permitted. Till 403 B.C. the pleadings were oral, but written pleadings, found necessary in cases appealed under the system of public arbitration, were adopted generally early in the 4th century. There were permissible ways of barring suits by contesting their admissibility. A civil suit might be dropped at any time. The prosecutor, however, had to proceed with a public suit once it was instituted or pay a fine of 1,000 drachmas and forfeit the right to bring further actions, and he incurred the same penalty if he failed to secure one-fifth of the dicasts' votes. Court fees were collected in civil suits. Public suits more than paid for themselves by fines and confiscations. There were careful rules to govern default.

The presidency of the tribunal belonged either to the *thesmothetai* or, ordinarily, to the magistrate who was connected with the suit in its earlier stages. The president had to see that the trial followed the course laid down by law, and since his legal training was no greater than that of the litigants and dicasts he had no claim or right to intervene further. Also, since precedents had no legal standing, no one was needed to assess their bearing. The dicasts were in fact under oath to disregard them and to make decisions solely on the evidence and arguments presented, giving effect to laws and decrees where these sufficed, otherwise to their own sense of right. The proceedings in court consisted essentially of arguments addressed to the dicasts by the plaintiff and the defendant personally and by friends (not paid professional advocates) who appeared to support either party with their reputation and court experience. At the proper places the statements and depositions contained in the dossier of the preliminary hearing were read by the clerk of the court and acknowledged under oath by the litigants and the witnesses. The law authorized actions to compel the appearance of witnesses and the production by third parties of relevant documents, which also were read by the clerk. A time, greater in public than in private suits, was set for the entire argument. Half of it was given to each party, and the water clock, by which it was apportioned, was stopped during the reading.

Once the arguments were concluded the dicasts voted, without discussion, either to acquit or to condemn. The utmost care was taken to preserve secrecy and honesty in the balloting. If the vote was against the defendant, but the bare decision did not suffice to dispose of the case, an argument upon the penalty ensued, at the end of which the dicasts balloted to decide whose estimate, the winner's or the loser's, should be accepted. The court was powerless to substitute an estimate of its own, but a compromise could be reached if the litigants chose to meet each other halfway in their estimates. An appeal from the verdict was possible only in cases of nonculpable default or on the ground of perjury, and in the latter case only if notice to contest the verdict on this score were given before the dicasts voted. There is no dossier of a single trial that has been preserved and the opposing arguments have seldom been found.

The courts were a political as well as a judicial body. They were there to give the *coup de grâce* to discredited politicians; they were the heirs of ostracism. In private cases the speeches were often such as might be addressed to modern juries, and there is little reason to impugn the verdicts. The vicious tendencies of the judicial system are obvious: the contamination of justice by politics; the weakening of responsibility through its diffusion among so many jurors; the rendering of unlike decisions in like cases. But the correctives were also present: the unexampled familiarity of common men with law and legal practice; and their unique experience in taking collective action in large bodies. History contains no other instance of justice so thoroughly organized to accord with the principles of radical democracy. The Athenians were so situated that they did not feel the need either of delegating their government to picked representatives or of entrusting their justice to experts specialized in law. The Romans enshrined their justice in their great system and profession of the law and, thus safeguarded in their private rights, left their government to autocrats.

(W. S. Fe.; X.)

See also BOULE; ECCLESIA.

HELLENISTIC, BYZANTINE AND POST-BYZANTINE PERIODS

Hellenistic Period (146 B.C.–A.D. 565).—By the end of the 1st century B.C. all Greek *poleis* had become part of the Roman empire. For centuries, Roman law and Greek law lived and grew side by side. The principle of "personality" of the law was a fundamental precept of Roman law; Greek law thus governed the relations of the subject Greek population while Roman law applied to the legal relations of Roman citizens. In the year 212, however, the celebrated *Constitutio Antoniniana* of Emperor Caracalla granted Roman citizenship to practically all inhabitants of the vast empire, and thus, theoretically, Roman law became applicable to relations among "citizens" of Greek extraction.

The following centuries witnessed a struggle between native Greek law and imperial Roman law; and though Roman law finally prevailed and was able to displace Greek law in the official administration of justice, the victory was not achieved without compromise. The strict and inflexible Roman law had by that time been deeply influenced by Greek philosophical and legal thought and had become a Roman-Greek law, a virtual *Jus Greco-Romanum.* The Justinian legislation of the 6th century that concluded this development was predominantly the product of the Hellenic eastern provinces of the empire and largely reflected the work of the law schools of Constantinople and Beirut.

Byzantine Period (565–1453).—In spite of Justinian's prohibition of scientific elaboration on his monumental legislation, Greek translations (*indices* and *paratitla*), which were permitted, offered an opportunity for comment and scientific treatment and contributed to a further Hellenization of early Byzantine law. Moreover, the *Novellae* of Justinian, written mostly in Greek, those of his successors, written entirely in Greek, and the iconoclastic legislation of the Isaurian dynasty in the 8th century, were rooted in an unofficial Greek law which continued to live as custom. Direct connection with Greek legal tradition was particularly apparent in the Ecloga (A.D. 740) of Emperor Leo III and in three collections titled *Soldier's, Farmer's* and *Sea Law,* attributed to the same emperor. The Isaurian legislation, though later repealed as heretic, continued to influence all further Byzantine legislation.

The same trend—a return to Greek sources—is apparent in the legislative efforts of the Macedonian dynasty (9th and 10th centuries). The *Procheiros Nomos* and the *Epanagoge* of Basil I, while designed to substitute for the repealed Isaurian legislation, in effect preserved its very substance. Finally, the *Basilica* of Leo the Wise, the most important Byzantine recodification of the Justinian legislation, as well as the *Eparchikon Biblion,* dealing with guilds and associations, and several *Novellae* of the same emperor and of his successors resulted in a complete Hellenization of the law.

The foundation of the new law school of Constantinople by Constantine IX in 1045 gave new impetus to legal studies. In the following centuries several collections of considerable legal significance appeared, such as the *Epitome Legum, Ecloga Privata, Synopsis Basilikorum, Peira* (a collection of judicial precedents) and several *Canones, Nomocanones* and *Syntagmata,* dealing with the canon law of the Greek Orthodox Church. The *Hexabiblos* of Harmenopoulos, compiled by a local judge in Thessalonica in 1345, was one of the last Byzantine collections. Byzantine law, representing a fusion of Roman tradition, Christian ethics and Greek legal thought, exercised a deep influence on the legal systems of most eastern European and Balkan countries. (*See also* BYZANTINE EMPIRE: *Government: Legislation.*)

Post-Byzantine Period (1453–1821).—The fall of Constantinople in 1453, the dissolution of the Byzantine empire and the subjugation of the Greek people by the Turks mark the beginning of a fourth period in the history of Greek law. In spite of the Turkish conquest, Byzantine law did not become extinct but continued to regulate private relations among the Greeks. And, perhaps as a unique phenomenon in legal history, the law of a subjugated people not only was retained in force but also was allowed to expand and to become the subject of further elaboration. Several reasons may account for this development, among which the religious character of Turkish law and a wide measure of self-government accorded by the sultans to their Christian subjects seem to be of primary significance.

The religious character of Turkish law limited its application to controversies among Muslim subjects; and the Turkish judge (*khadi*), who was originally entrusted with the administration of justice among all subjects, was supposed to apply personal Christian law in controversies among Christians. Thus Byzantine law was formally kept in force. Further, the Turkish sultans granted a number of privileges to the subjugated Christian population and a large measure of self-government, which was exercised by elected or appointed local authorities and by the church. The patriarch of Constantinople was accorded the status of head of a nation, and gradually the patriarchate and the several *metropoleis* in the provinces became administrative and cultural centres of Hellenism. Because of growing nationalistic tendencies and because of the practices of the Turkish judges, who were naturally inclined to extend the application of Turkish law even to controversies among Christians, Greeks would go to local authorities and to the church for settlement of their disputes rather than to the *khadi*. In the course of the centuries, the jurisdiction of the local authorities and of the church, which was originally in the nature of arbitration, became clearly judicial and was extended from the fields of family law and succession to those of obligations and criminal law. It was in this way that an incipient system of courts emerged with the local authorities in the lower level, bishop's courts in the *metropoleis* functioning as courts of appeal, and the patriarch's synod in Constantinople acting as the court of last resort.

Local authorities and ecclesiastical courts applied Byzantine law, as it had been epitomized in several synoptical collections, such as the *Hexabiblos* of Harmenopoulos, which was most frequently used. At the same time, several local customs had emerged that were given the force of law by the courts and that in some instances, as in the islands of the Aegean sea, were codified. Though of a local character, these customs were not contrary to the general principles of Byzantine law and in most instances represented an adaptation of ancient law to the changed social and economic conditions. By local custom and through scientific elaboration, new institutions emerged which brought the Byzantine law into line with western European developments. Thus, direct agency became possible and contractual transactions were freed of most formal requirements; and the law of partnership and other associations, as well as the law of banking and exchange, became modernized.

Apart from collections of local customs and some synodical circulars regulating questions of family law and succession, the written sources of Greek law during the post-Byzantine period are scanty. Of extraordinary significance in this regard are the codes of the Danube principalities that were governed by Greek envoys of the sultan. All such codes were written in the Greek language and reproduced Byzantine law par excellence. Among them the constitution of Alexander Ypsilantis (1780), the code of Wallachia of John Caratzas (1818), and the *Syntagma* of Michael Photinopoulos (1765), a summary of *Basilica* in modern Greek, are among the first codifications in western Europe.

MODERN GREEK LAW

Constitutional History.—The Greek revolution of 1821 marks the beginning of a new era in the history of Greek law. The first revolutionary assembly adopted in Epidaurus (Jan. 1, 1822) a liberal and democratic constitution modeled on the French Declaration of the Rights of Man. A second constitution (Astros, 1823), established a powerful parliament, and a third constitution (Troizena, 1827), while still in principle liberal and democratic, vested all executive functions in a single man, the governor, Ioannes Kapodistrias. Kapodistrias, a native of the Ionian Islands and a former minister of the Russian tsar, dissolved the parliament and governed Greece with the assistance of an appointed consultative senate until his assassination in 1831. His death threw Greece into anarchy and chaos, and order was re-established only with the arrival of young King Otho (1833). Greece was governed for a while by a regency council, and then, after Otho's majority, by the king himself as an absolute monarch. A successful revolution in 1844 compelled the king to grant a constitution along the lines of the French charter of 1830, which made Greece a constitutional monarchy. Another revolution in 1862 overthrew Otho, and two years later a new democratic constitution was proclaimed by King George I. This constitution recognized the sovereignty of the people and vested all legislative authority in the parliament and the king. For the first time, universal male suffrage by secret ballot was guaranteed. As a result of a bloodless and peaceful revolution, the 1864 constitution was revised in 1911. During and following World War I, the revised constitution was suspended a number of times and finally was replaced in 1927 by a democratic constitution which abolished kingship. The monarchy, however, was restored in 1935 and the 1911 constitution was reintroduced. Following World War II, a new constitutional revision was undertaken which resulted in the adoption of the 1952 constitution. A successful coup d'état staged by the military on April 21, 1967, resulted in the suspension of most provisions of the 1952 constitution. A new constitution, prepared by a committee of experts, was endorsed in a referendum by more than 90% of the voters on Sept. 29, 1968.

Codification of Civil Law.—Recognizing an interrupted legal tradition, the first two revolutionary constitutions designated "the laws of our ever-memorable Byzantine Emperors" as a source of Greek civil law. In the 1827 constitution, however, a wish was expressed that all future codes should be based on French models. The influence of French doctrine and legislation in Greece may actually be traced to the years preceding the revolution, at a time when parts of the French commercial code of 1804 had been translated into Greek and were in use among Greek merchants, and to a Greek criminal code of 1823 based on that of France. In spite of the constitutional wish the adoption of French models was considered, did not become a Greek civil code. Governor Kapodistrias, clearly disregarding the constitutional directive, designated the Byzantine laws as the source of Greek civil law and in 1830 announced his plan for collecting and classifying them in an orderly fashion. This work was never accomplished.

Under King Otho four major codes, based on French and Bavarian models, were drafted by the Bavarian lawyer G. L. Maurer, a member of the regency council. Of these, the two dealing with the organization of justice and civil procedure, as amended by subsequent acts, remained in force in the second half of the 20th century. The other two, the penal code and the code of criminal procedure, were replaced by modern codes in 1951. Maurer, however, did not draft a civil code. An adherent of the historical school of jurisprudence, he believed that native institutions and ideas of law should prevail at least with regard to civil law and, accordingly, started collecting local customs and current interpretations of Byzantine laws that were regarded as manifesting the spirit of the people. This project was interrupted by his dismissal from the regency council in 1835.

Subsequently, a royal decree of 1835 declared that "the civil laws of the Byzantine emperors contained in the *Hexabiblos* of Harmenopoulos shall remain in force till the promulgation of the civil code whose drafting we have already ordered" and that "customs, sanctioned by long and uninterrupted use or by judicial decision, shall have the force of law wherever they prevail." This decree became the cornerstone in the edifice of civil law in Greece and profoundly influenced the path of the law during the next hundred years. Perhaps because of inadequacies in Harmenopoulos' compilation, the scarcity of copies of the *Hexabiblos*, and the increasing elaboration of Roman law by the Pandectists in Germany, the Greek courts adopted a broad interpretation of the decree. Thus the entire Byzantine legislation from Justinian's time up to the dissolution of the empire, contained not only in the *Hexabiblos* but in any collection, was reintroduced in modern Greece. For this purpose the work of the German Pandectists was not only useful but almost necessary. And Greek legal thought, which had been oriented almost exclusively toward France, became increasingly oriented toward Germany. Indeed, by the end of the century the redaction of the German civil code seemed to set a pattern for future codification. But at the same time the Greek jurists developed a more critical attitude and proceeded to new legislative efforts by evaluating achievements in western continental countries.

In accord with the decree of 1835 a committee was appointed to draft a new civil code. Although the final objective of the committee was not realized, its preparatory work resulted in important legislation in the field of civil law, including a comprehensive statute entitled "Civil Law" in 1856. This contained a variety of provisions, including rules on conflict of laws, rules pertaining to the validity and nonretroactivity of the law, and regulations involving registration of births, marriages and deaths. A draft civil code of 1874, based on French, Italian and Saxon models, was not adopted, partly because of constitutional difficulties.

In the meanwhile, Greek legislation had been introduced in 1866 into the Ionian Islands; later, in 1882, into the newly acquired provinces of Thessaly and Epirus; and, in 1914, into the islands of the Aegean, Crete and Macedonia. However, special provision was made regarding the Ionian civil code (1841), the civil code of Samos (1899), the civil code of Crete (1904) and the code of civil procedure of Crete (1880), which were allowed to remain in force. This situation gave rise to a conflict of local laws and increased the urge for a new civil code that would apply throughout the state.

After another attempt at codification failed in 1922, a new five-member committee was appointed to the task in 1930. This committee published a series of drafts in 1937, and in the following year G. Balis of Athens university was appointed to co-ordinate these. His project was successful and resulted in the passage of the civil code of 1940. The backbone of this code was Byzantine law, the national Greek tradition dressed in modern clothes. Far from being a revolutionary codification, it reproduced to a large extent law that was already in force, developed by judicial decisions and scientific elaboration. The comparative method was also widely used, and an attempt was made to modernize and systematize the law by employing legislative techniques tested in other modern continental codes.

The 1940 code was scheduled to become effective July 1, 1941. At that time, however, Greece had been overrun by the Axis forces. After the liberation of the country a new committee was appointed to make a final revision of the code, and a revised version was put into effect in 1945. Subsequently, this revision was repealed and the original 1940 code given the force of law retroactively from Feb. 23, 1946. By the introductory law of the code all local codes and customs were abrogated. The civil code, along with other legislation, was introduced in the Dodecanese Islands after their annexation in 1948.

POSITIVE LAW

Constitutional Law.—The 1952 revised constitution, although proclaiming the Greek Orthodox Church as the official church of the state, guarantees freedom of religion in accordance with well-settled constitutional tradition. Nonrecognition of titles of nobility and equality before the law for all citizens are fundamental precepts. The constitution further guarantees freedom of the press and of speech, freedom of association, the inviolability of private quarters, and forbids expropriation without prior compensation.

The regime is termed a "crowned democracy," and it is specified that all powers derive from the nation. The exercise of the legislative power is entrusted to the parliament and the king, the executive functions are vested in the king (although to be exercised by a responsible cabinet), and the administration of justice is committed to independent courts of law.

In spite of the silence of the constitution on the subject, the courts are expected, as in the past, to test the constitutionality of acts of parliament and to refuse to apply legislation conflicting with principles announced in the constitution. Unconstitutional and illegal administrative acts are subject to annulment by the council of state, a supreme administrative court modeled on the French *conseil d'état.* The performance of this court has greatly contributed to the establishment of the "rule of law" in the country.

Most provisions of the 1952 constitution guaranteeing individual and political freedom as well as the representative form of government were suspended after April 21, 1967, following a coup d'état by the military. The revolutionary government appointed a committee of experts to prepare a new constitution. The new constitution was endorsed in a referendum held on Sept. 29, 1968.

Civil Law.—The civil code of 1940, its introductory law and a number of supplementary specialized statutes constitute a coherent and interrelated system of legal rules known as modern Greek civil law. The code chiefly contains provisions of private substantive law, including rules on conflict of laws; rules of commercial law, civil procedure and public law are excluded. Following the traditional classification of the Pandectists, the 2,035 articles of the code are arranged in five "books." These are: (1) general principles; (2) law of obligations; (3) law of property; (4) family law; and (5) law of succession.

General Principles (art. 1–286).—These, as the term denotes, include provisions of a general character bearing upon the entire field of civil law which, in the absence of other specific legislation, may apply by analogy to all relations of private law. The first title deals with the source of law, its nonretroactivity and the notion of public policy; the next contains rules on conflict of laws; the following two titles regulate problems connected with natural and juristic personality—its creation, incidents and termination—and provide broad protection by establishing a "right of personality," and a principle of compensation for "moral" damage.

Title v deals with the fundamental concept of "juristic act," which rests on the idea that "will" and "consent" form the basis of legal transactions. Thus, defects of consent because of minority, limited mental capacity, fraud, threat and mistake may prevent the valid consummation of legal transactions, but without affecting the right of the innocent party to adequate compensation. In general, there is an attempt to balance social interests with individual claims of justice. In contrast to Roman law, the code develops a general theory of representative agency; it also contains provisions governing requisite formalities for certain instruments, establishes the categories of void and voidable acts, and confers upon the judge the power to determine cases in accord with equitable considerations. Reference to "justice," "equity," and "good morals" is thus frequent. Finally, the last title regulates the exercise of rights. Art. 281 creates a broad concept of abuse of right; *i.e.,* the exercise of a right manifestly in excess of limits prescribed by good faith and good morals and contrary to the social and economic purpose for which the right is accorded. The remaining articles concern self-defense, self-help and necessity.

Law of Obligations (art. 287–946).—"Freedom of contracting," "good faith" and "favour to the debtor" are fundamental precepts in the law of obligations. Since formation of contracts is dealt with in the general principles, the law of obligations regulates primarily problems connected with the performance and nonperformance of contractual and other obligations. In principle, any culpable violation of the debtor's obligation leads to his liability. Thus emerges a comprehensive concept of nonperformance based on fault, though technically the code distinguishes only delay and impossibility of performance. In the absence of agreement, place, time and method of performance are determined by well-defined rules. All validly concluded obligations are enforceable by action for damages or for specific performance at the discretion of the court. There are a number of specifically regulated contractual transactions (nominate contracts) such as donation, sale of goods, lease, loan, contract for work, brokerage, mandate and deposit. As to the sale of goods, the code distinguishes between contracts to sell and transfer of ownership as such. The seller may claim the purchase price and the buyer the delivery of the goods. In contrast to Roman law, the seller must transfer full ownership and not merely vacant possession.

Liability for civil wrongs rests in principle on fault, namely, negligence and intentional misconduct. Instances of liability without fault (strict liability) or semistrict liability (reversal of the burden of proof) are scarce and confined to a limited number of legal relations. The code announces a general tort principle: whoever causes damage to another through his fault, acting contrary to law or intentionally contrary to good morals, is liable to repair it. Certain torts, such as libel and slander, seduction, damage caused by animals and inanimate objects, and vicarious liability, are specifically regulated.

Law of Property (art. 947–1345).—Possession and ownership are clearly distinguishable concepts in the code. Possession is given a much larger measure of protection than in Roman law. Ownership, on the other hand, though an exclusive right, is not elevated to the status of an absolute; thus, clearly defined neighbourhood rights are established, expropriation, in the interest of the public or under due compensation is possible, and acts performed above or under the soil may not be enjoined if not harmful to the owner's interest. Further, in contrast to Roman law, horizontal division of immovables and separate ownership of flats is legally possible.

The methods of acquiring property by occupation, acquisitive prescription, accession, confusion and specification are systematically prescribed in accord with well-established notions of Roman law. With regard to contractual acquisition of property, actual delivery of movables, a notarized instrument and registration of real estate transactions are indispensable formalities. Ownership of movables may be acquired in good faith from nonowners, provided the goods were not lost or stolen. The latter requirement does not apply to money and negotiable instruments. Finally, there are provisions with regard to real rights, namely: servitudes, pledge, and real mortgages (*hypotheca*).

Family Law (art. 1346–1709).—This section regulates betrothal, marriage, relations of parents and children, adoption and legitimation, tutorship and custody.

Religious ceremony is essential for the validity of marriage. Greek citizens of the eastern Orthodox faith must be married by a Greek Orthodox priest, regardless of the place of marriage. The code establishes several impediments, both relative and absolute, in accord with current moral and religious beliefs; a defective marriage may be totally nonexistent, voidable or void. The personal relations of the spouses are based on the principle of equality. The husband is head of the family, while the internal administration of the household is the wife's responsibility. Mutual obligations for alimony and maintenance during marriage, due to predominantly moral considerations, are classified under personal relations; the husband's obligation is a primary one, while that of the wife is secondary and supplemental. Individual property rights of the spouses are not affected by marriage in the absence of prenuptial agreement. Such agreements are enforceable if concluded in accord with requisite formalities safeguarding the interests of the future family. The dowry system is given specific consideration: the wife remains owner of immovables given as dowry, while the husband has their administration and usufruct. Alienation of such immovables is allowed only under exceptional circumstances and always by judicial determination. Divorce is not favoured and is granted only on specifically enumerated grounds. Separation from bed and board has not been institutionalized.

Law of Succession (art. 1710–2035).—Basic institutions in this field are testamentary succession, intestacy and forced heirship. Freedom of testation, though a fundamental principle, is limited by the right of parents, spouse and descendants to a forced share and by the prohibition of certain *fideicommissa* (bequests which the donor asks the recipient to transfer to another). Wills may be either holographic, publicly declared or secret (*i.e.*, deposited for safekeeping with a notary). If executed in emergency, most of the cumbersome formalities can be dispensed with. Contracts with regard to future succession are unenforceable, and probate of oral wills is excluded. In contrast to Roman law, institution of an heir is no longer necessary for valid testamentary succession. In case of intestacy, which is frequent in Greece, there is a clearly defined order of succession by relatives and the surviving spouse. Property devolves to collateral relatives only up to the fourth degree, and inheritance by a nearer class excludes the rights of a more distant class of relatives. The code finally contains provisions with regard to disinheritance for cause, liability of the universal heir, appointment of executors, certificates of inheritance and the heir's action to recover property belonging to the estate. In contrast to Anglo-American practice, property vests upon the death of the testator in the heir, and thus the need for estate administration is minimized.

Commercial Law.—The French *Code de Commerce* of 1804, already in use among Greek merchants before the 1821 revolution, was officially adopted in postrevolutionary Greece. However, subsequent legislation has left only a small number of its original articles intact. The entire third part, dealing with bankruptcy, was replaced in 1878 by legislation inspired by Belgian and Italian sources; special statutes were substituted for obsolete provisions regulating business associations and stock exchange transactions; and in 1958 the second part, dealing with maritime law, was replaced by a new maritime code. In addition, a number of modern statutes were enacted to regulate fair trade practices, unfair competition, trade-marks, copyrights and bills of exchange.

In general, the commercial code regulates the professional activities of merchants (subjective criterion) and a number of enumerated commercial transactions and enterprises (objective criterion). Corporations are subject to commercial law without regard to their purpose or scope of activities. Several forms of business associations are possible, such as partnership, limited partnership and the stock corporation. Insurance business may be transacted only by corporations generally subject to strict state control.

Civil Procedure.—This branch of law is governed by the 1834 code of civil procedure, as amended by a series of modern statutes. The code provides for oral argument of all civil cases (which actually occurs only in a limited number of proceedings), and rests on the idea that the judge, sitting without a jury, is an impartial arbiter (adversary system). There are magistrate's courts (justices of the peace), courts of first instance, courts of appeals and a supreme court called Areopagus in memory of the past. Courts of appeals review both findings of fact and conclusions of law, while the supreme court is limited in its review to issues of law.

The competency of the courts is determined according to the subject matter of the dispute, and their local jurisdiction depends primarily on the domicile of the defendant. In addition, local jurisdiction may be based on the location of immovables, the place of conclusion or performance of a contract, the place of injury in case of torts, the place where an attachment is executed, and on jurisdictional agreements. While lack of competency may prove fatal for a plaintiff's action, lack of local jurisdiction is curable by transfer, and if incorrectly exercised the court's decision is not void but only subject to appeal. In accord with the civil code of 1940, the international jurisdiction of the Greek courts consists of the total of existing local and special competencies. Exceptions, expanding or limiting the scope of this jurisdiction, have been established by the courts on grounds of public policy.

When the money involved in a controversy exceeds a certain amount, written evidence is necessary. Exception is made with regard to commercial debts and in cases where production of documentary evidence is impossible or extremely difficult. The evidence, in any case, is evaluated freely by the judge.

Judgments are ordinarily executed by seizure of property and judicial sale. Foreign judgments may be executed in Greece in accord with exequatur proceedings. In practice, a re-examination of the foreign court's international jurisdiction and of all relevant facts precedes the issuance of such an order.

A new code of civil procedure, a product of the comparative method and of much scientific elaboration, acquired the force of law on Sept. 15, 1968. While retaining the fundamental precepts of the old procedural system, the new code is expected to simplify and expedite the administration of civil justice, to clarify a number of obscurities in the law and to modernize the courts.

Criminal Law and Procedure.—The penal code and the code of criminal procedure of 1834 were replaced in 1951 by two modern codes which are a product of a century-long local experience combined with contemporary criminal doctrine.

The new penal code is based, like the old one, on the principle *nulla poena sine lege* ("no punishment without law"). Offenses are classified, according to their gravity, as crimes, delicts or misdemeanours. Capital punishment is reserved only for extreme cases, including high treason and murder accompanied by aggravating circumstances. The code applies in principle to all offenses committed in Greece (principle of territoriality), crimes and delicts committed by Greeks abroad if punishable according to the law of the country involved (principle of personality), and to a number of crimes without regard to the nationality of the offender or the place of the offense (principle of universality). The new code of criminal procedure is based on the principle of publicity of information. The jury system is preserved only with regard to certain grave offenses; in the great majority of cases trial is conducted by a single judge or a panel of judges sitting without a jury. Criminal courts are not distinguishable from civil courts, and the same judge may perform both functions.

The new legislation provides for special treatment of juvenile delinquents and persons in need of psychiatric and medical assistance. An over-all effort for the rehabilitation of the nonprofessional criminal is apparent. Because of the predominantly agricultural nature of the Greek economy, the establishment and operation of agricultural penitentiaries for farmers is of great significance. Further, the judge is given much freedom in the determination of penalty, and, depending on good conduct during confinement, release on parole may be granted.

Social Legislation.—The 1909 peaceful revolution opened an era of legislative effort directed at the protection of the working class. Democratic institutions were strengthened, local government was improved, independence of justice was achieved and, by direct social legislation, the foundations of a modern labour law were laid. Special laws prescribe the employer's duty to provide a healthful place to work, regulate the employee's pay during annual vacation and define benefits to be received in case of illness. A landmark was the law of 1920 concerning termination of the employment contract and establishing the employee's right to compensation depending on the time of service. Other statutes regulate labour arbitration, collective bargaining, social security and workmen's compensation. Most differences arising out of labour relations are subject to a special accelerated procedure.

Private International Law.—Art. 4–33 of the civil code contain the rules of private international law. All these rules are bilateral; *i.e.*, they do not simply delimit the area of application of Greek law but refer to the "applicable system of law," which may be that of Greece or of any other country. Application of two different legal systems in the same case is avoided by singling out a predominant contact. Nationality rather than domicile determines capacity, personal relations, family relations and succession; domicile is important only with regard to stateless persons. The national law of the husband prevails in relations between spouses, and the national law of the father among parents and children. With regard to contracts, the parties are given full autonomy to select the applicable law, and in absence of express agreement the "proper law" of the contract governs. In all cases, application of foreign law may be excluded on grounds of public policy.

A new nationality code was passed in 1955 to regulate acquisition and termination of Greek citizenship. Citizenship is acquired by those born to Greek parents or to stateless parents in Greece, by naturalization, marriage, legitimation, judicial recognition and by service in the armed forces. Greek women married to foreigners do not lose their Greek citizenship except where they acquire the citizenship of their husband, and Greek nationality may be retained even in the latter case by a formal declaration before marriage. Greek nationality is lost by naturalization abroad by permission of the Greek government or by governmental action directed against those engaged abroad in activities inconsistent with their status as Greek citizens.

Aliens enjoy the private rights of citizens and are entitled to equal protection under the law. Some professions are reserved for citizens only, such as the practice of medicine and law.

Public International Law.—Customary public international law is an integral part of the law of the land, according to an 1856 decision of the Areopagus. Treaties, in order to have the force of law in Greece, must be promulgated by parliamentary act in accord with constitutional requirements. Greece is a member of many international organizations and specialized agencies and has participated in several international conventions. Treaties and domestic Greek laws based on international conventions for the unification of private law regulate, uniformly with other countries, transport by land, air and sea, protect certain commercial and industrial interests, and in general promote international intercourse and communication. Bilateral treaties of commerce and naviga-

tion, establishment and consular jurisdiction secure friendly relations with most other countries. *See also* GREECE: *Administration and Social Conditions.*

BIBLIOGRAPHY.—*General:* G. M. Calhoun and G. Delamere, *A Working Bibliography of Greek Law* (1927). *History:* L. Mitteis, *Reichsrecht und Volksrecht* (1891); R. Dareste, B. Haussouillier and T. Reinach, *Recueil des inscriptions juridiques Grecques* (1891–1904); K. E. Zachariae von Lingenthal, *Geschichte des griechisch-römischen Rechts,* 3rd ed. (1892; repr. 1955); L. Beauchet, *Histoire du droit privé de la République Athénienne,* 4 vol. (1897); J. H. Lipsius, *Das Attische Recht und Rechtsverfahren* (1905–15); P. Vinogradoff, *Outlines of Historical Jurisprudence,* vol. 2 (1922); E. Weiss, *Griechisches Privatrecht* (1923; repr. 1965); R. J. Bonner, *Lawyers and Litigants in Ancient Athens* (1927); G. M. Calhoun, *The Growth of Criminal Law in Ancient Greece* (1927); *Introduction to Greek Legal Science* (1944); U. E. Paoli, *Studi di Diritto Attico* (1930; repr. 1950); R. J. Bonner and G. Smith, *The Administration of Justice from Homer to Aristotle,* 2 vol. (1930–38); A. H. M. Jones, *The Greek City from Alexander to Justinian* (1940); A. Verdross, *Grundlinien der antiken Rechts- und Staatsphilosophie,* 2nd ed. (1948); P. Zepos, *Greek Law* (1949); E. Wolf, *Griechisches Rechtsdenken,* 3 vol. (1950–54); J. W. Jones, *The Law and Legal Theory of the Greeks* (1956); N. Pantazopoulos, *Historical Introduction into the Sources of Greek Law,* 2nd ed. (1958) (in Greek).

Modern Law (in Greek): G. Balis, *System of Civil Law,* 5 vol. (several editions since 1948); I. Spyropoulos, *Public International Law,* 4th ed. (1954); P. Zepos, *Law of Obligations,* 2 vol., 2nd ed. (1955–65); A. Toussis, *Labor Law* (1957); A. Litzeropoulos, *Law of Succession,* 2nd ed. (1958); G. Rammos, *Civil Procedure,* 5th ed. (1961–62); H. Kyriakopoulos, *Administrative Law,* 3 vol., 4th ed. (1961–64); D. Karanicas, *Penal Law,* 3 vol., 2nd ed. (1962–64); K. Karavas, *Commercial Law,* 2 vol., 2nd ed. (1962–65); I. Zessiades, *Criminal Procedure,* 2 vol., 2nd ed. (1964–65); G. Roilos, *Family Law,* 3rd ed. (1965–66); G. Maridakis, *Private International Law* (1967); and, in English, A. A. Ehrenzweig, C. Fragistas and A. N. Viannopoulos, *American-Greek Private International Law* (1957). (A. N. Y.)

GREEK LITERATURE has a continuous history extending from the 1st millennium B.C. to the present day. From the beginning its writers were Greeks living not only in Greece proper but also in Asia Minor, the Aegean islands and Magna Graecia (Sicily and southern Italy); later, after the conquests of Alexander the Great, as Greek became the common language of the eastern Mediterranean lands and then of the Byzantine empire, Greek literature was produced over a much wider area and also by those whose mother tongue was not Greek. Even before the Turkish conquest (1453) the area had begun to shrink again, and now it is chiefly confined to the territory of the kingdom of Greece.

The main divisions of this article are as follows:

I. Ancient (to the 4th Century A.D.)
  A. Classical Poetry
    1. The Epic Tradition
    2. Lyric Poetry
    3. Tragedy
    4. Comedy
  B. Early and Attic Prose
    1. History
    2. Rhetoric and Oratory
    3. Philosophy
  C. Hellenistic and Greco-Roman Periods
    1. Poetry
    2. Prose
      History
      Criticism
      Science and Topography
      Judaeo-Christian Writings
      Plutarch
      Second Sophistic Movement
      Philosophy
      The Novel
II. Byzantine (4th Century A.D.–1453)
    1. Characteristics
    2. Theology
    3. Hagiography
    4. Religious Poetry
    5. History
    6. Geography
    7. Philosophy
    8. Rhetoric
    9. Scholarship
    10. Military Science
    11. Law
    12. Secular Poetry
    13. Vernacular Literature
III. Modern (After 1453)
    1. Language

I. ANCIENT (TO THE 4TH CENTURY A.D.)

Of the literature of ancient Greece only a relatively small proportion survives. Yet it remains important, not only because much of it is of supreme quality but also because until the mid-19th century the greater part of the literature of the western world was produced by men who were familiar with the Greek tradition, either directly or through the medium of Latin, who were conscious that the forms they used were mostly of Greek invention and who took for granted in their readers some familiarity with classical literature.

A. CLASSICAL POETRY

Two things are likely to appear strange to anyone unfamiliar with Greek literature. First, Greek poetry was intended to be sung or recited publicly, not to be read in private; the audience might be a large part of the population of a city, as for a play, or a small private party, but poetry before the Hellenistic period (beginning c. 300 B.C.) was part of social activity. Secondly, the subject of Greek poetry was myth, that is to say the great mass of traditional material which was one of the peculiar riches of the Greek spirit; this was part legend, sometimes based on the dim memory of historical events like the fall of Troy or Thebes, part folk tale, part primitive religious speculation (see GREEK RELIGION). The myths of the Greeks, unlike those of most peoples, were not closely associated for the most part with religious ritual. Accordingly, although they told of gods and of half-divine, heroic men, and often suggest the forms under which the gods were visualized, they had no particular authority and could be varied and developed as the poet wished. Indeed in the early stages Greek thought advanced largely by the half-conscious refashioning of the myths to give expression to new conceptions. The poet enjoyed the immense advantage of using material familiar to his audience, who would be sensitive to every new emphasis or fresh interpretation of the ideal of heroic life which the myth contained.

1. The Epic Tradition.—At the beginning of Greek literature stand the two great epics, the *Iliad* and the *Odyssey* (see HOMER), in their existing form not earlier than the 8th century but with roots reaching far into the Mycenaean age (see AEGEAN CIVILIZATION), perhaps to 1500 B.C. The *Iliad* is the tragic story of the wrath of Achilles, the splendid hero, son of a goddess and richly endowed with all the qualities that make men admirable, who destroys himself by his own love of honour. Being slighted by Agamemnon, the Greek leader, he refuses to take any further part in the war against Troy; when the Greeks are hard pressed and Agamemnon offers amends, he persists in his refusal; the plight of the Greeks worsens and Achilles is so far moved by pity that he sends his friend Patroclus in his own armour to their aid; Patroclus saves the Greeks but is killed himself; Achilles in a frenzy of grief returns to the war and kills Hector, the slayer of Patroclus, and outrages his dead body. Finally he brings himself to restore the body to Priam, Hector's father, and the poem ends in reconciliation. Achilles' end is outside the poem, but right from the beginning the brilliant hero is shadowed by the knowledge of early death. With his readiness to sacrifice all to honour, Achilles embodies the Greek heroic ideal, and the contrast between his superb qualities and his short and troubled life reflects the sense of tragedy which was always a part of the sad wisdom of the Greeks, though in Homer, more than in later literature, the vitality is such that it is easy to forget the strain of melancholy. Whereas the *Iliad* is tragedy, as tragedy, the *Odyssey* is tragicomedy. It is an enriched version of the old folk tale of the wanderer's return and of his triumph over those who were usurping his rights and persecuting his wife at home. Odysseus too represents a Greek ideal. Though by no means inadequate in battle, he works mainly by craft and guile; only so can he defeat the superior strength of the Cyclops and the superior numbers of the suitors who have taken possession of his palace. During his ten-year journey home from Troy he loses first his fleet, then his own ship and crew, and back in Ithaca he moves disguised as a beggar in his own palace. Through all these hazards it is by mental superiority that he survives and prevails.

Both poems are based on plots which grip the reader, and the story is told in language which is simple and direct, yet full of natural eloquence and nobility. In the course of previous generations the epic storytellers had fashioned a linguistic instrument of extraordinary beauty and flexibility, even though, since it resembled no language ever spoken by Greeks, it was highly artificial. The *Iliad* and the *Odyssey*, though the oldest European poetry, are by no means primitive. They mark the fulfillment rather than the beginning of the literary form to which they belong. Whether or not the poems in their present form were composed with the aid of writing, they are in essence and in origin oral poetry. Nameless poets over a period of centuries had recited, or rather performed, the traditional stories, developing and modifying them in the process. Comparison with oral poetry as it has survived elsewhere suggests that the poet did not learn by heart a traditional work but was free to re-create his poems within a given framework with fresh detail. The conventional epic style was sufficiently rich in phrase and formula for it to be possible for a professional bard to perform the difficult feat of improvisation in a strict metre for comparatively long periods. If this is how the Homeric poems developed, it need cause no surprise that the world they reflect is full of so-called inconsistencies; weapons belong to both the Bronze and Iron Ages; objects like those found in Mycenaean excavations jostle others from the geometric period five centuries later; the fabulous wealth of Egyptian Thebes in the 15th century B.C. is referred to along with the activities of Phoenician traders in the 9th. But certain mysteries remain. What was the date of the great poet or poets who gave structure and shape to the two epics which survive? What was the social function of poems which take several days to recite? By what process and at what stage did these poems come to be recorded in writing? These are among the Homeric questions of today.

In the ancient world the *Iliad* and *Odyssey* stood in a class apart among epic poems. Of these there were a large number known later as the epic cycle, sometimes referred to as the work of Homer, sometimes associated with various shadowy figures of whom the latest in time was Eugammon of Cyrene (c. 600). They covered the whole story of the wars of Thebes and Troy as well as other famous myths. A number of shorter poems in epic style, the Homeric Hymns, include three addressed to Demeter, Apollo and Aphrodite which are of considerable beauty.

Didactic poetry was not regarded by the Greeks as a form distinct from epic, since it used the same metre and the same composite dialect. Yet Hesiod belongs to an altogether different world from Homer. He lived in Boeotia about 800 B.C. In his *Works and Days*, under pretense of advising his idle brother Perses, he describes the ways of peasant life and incidentally gives an unforgettable description of the dreary Boeotian plain afflicted by heat, cold and the oppression of a "gift-devouring" aristocracy. He believed passionately what is rarely hinted at in Homer, that Zeus cares about right and wrong and that Justice is his daughter. His other surviving poem, the *Theogony*, tells of the generations of the gods and attempts in mythical terms to supply a cosmogony and to reduce to a coherent system the mass of legends about the gods and their parentage. Near eastern influence is clearly to be seen, especially in some of the cruder speculation about the origin of the universe. Similar attempts at systematization were made by the Hesiodic school of poets, writers of "catalogues" which were often attributed to Hesiod himself. They tried to reduce to order the stories of gods and heroes and of the many aristocratic families who claimed descent from them.

By the end of the 6th century the epic tradition was a spent force until its revival in the Hellenistic period, and the few composers of epic narrative left little but their names. One of the last of them was Panyassis, the uncle of Herodotus, who wrote an epic on Heracles.

2. Lyric Poetry.—Hesiod, unlike Homer, tells us something of himself, and the same is true of the lyric poets, who were responsible for most of the poetry written in Greece between the decline of epic and the rise of drama. Except for Pindar and Bacchylides at the end of the period, only fragments of the works of these poets survive, but like Homer they show no signs of immaturity. There had always been lyric poetry in Greece, and in Homer there are occasional references to vintage songs, funeral dirges and the like. All the great events of life as well as many occupations had their proper songs, and here too the way was open to advance from the anonymous to the individual poet.

The word "lyric" is inadequate for describing the various categories of poetry which the Greeks distinguished. On the one hand, lyrics in the narrow sense, poems sung by individuals or chorus to lyre or sometimes to the flute, were called melic; elegiacs, in which the epic hexameter alternated with a shorter line, the pentameter, were traditionally associated with lamentation and a flute accompaniment, but they were used for many kinds of poem, often with a more personal tone than was appropriate to the hexameter, and were spoken as well as sung. Iambics were the verse form of the lampoon and usually of an abusive or satyrical character. Like the trochaic verse, which was used in much the same way, iambics were not normally sung. While the melic poets confined themselves for the most part to the numerous varieties of their own medium, iambics, elegiacs and trochaics were often written by the same poet, so that the main division comes between melic and non-melic writers. (See PROSODY, CLASSICAL.)

If Archilochus, from the Aegean island of Paros, was really writing as early as 700 B.C., he was the first of the post-epic poets, but there is some reason for dating him 50 years later. The not very numerous fragments suggest a trenchant personality to which he gave uninhibited expression. They reflect the turbulent life of an embittered adventurer and soldier of fortune, son of an aristocratic father and a slave mother. Scorn both of men and convention is the emotion which seems uppermost, and the story that he hounded to his death Lycambes, who had withdrawn his daughter from a promised marriage, is, true or not, a fair tribute to Archilochus' powers of invective. Though much of his poetry was unedifying, he was regarded throughout antiquity as a major poet.

Somewhat younger than Archilochus, Simonides or Semonides of Amorgos is represented by a long and rather laboured fragment in which women are compared to animals, and nearly a century later the iambics of Hipponax of Ephesus showed something of the savagery of Archilochus without his genius, but his vivid pictures of low life were much imitated by writers of the Hellenistic age.

Like the iambic writers, the elegiac poets came mostly from the islands and the Ionian regions of Asia Minor. Callinus of Ephesus, a little after 700, called on his countrymen to defend their city against the barbarians, but a more characteristic use of the elegiac was made by Mimnermus of the neighbouring city of Colophon, who sang in tuneful but low-spirited verse of the sweetness of love and the horrors of old age; since he exchanged verses on the latter theme with the Athenian Solon (b. c. 638 B.C.), he must have lived well into the 6th century. On the mainland of Greece Tyrtaeus roused the spirit of the Spartans in their desperate struggle with the Messenian rebels in the years after 650. His martial poems were among the few that Spartans were encouraged to be familiar with; today they are perhaps valued more for their historical than for their literary interest. The same is to some extent true of the poems in elegiac, iambic and trochaic metres by Solon. He was no professional poet, but at a time when books did not exist a poem was the best medium for propaganda, and he used verse to rouse the Athenians for the reconquest of Salamis c. 600 B.C., to express his views about the source of their political troubles and, after he had carried out his great reforms, to explain and to defend them, as well as to assert his faith that in the long run the gods see that justice prevails. Xenophanes (b. c. 560), rather in the same way, used his poems, both elegiac and hexameter, to propagate his revo-

lutionary religious and ethical ideas. The collection of elegiacs which has come down under the name of Theognis seems to be composed of poems of various dates suitable for use at drinking parties. Many of them are from the hand of Theognis himself (c. 580–530?). Some give uninhibited expression to his hatred of the lower-class rulers who had ousted the aristocracy of Megara; others are love poems, sometimes passionately reproachful, to the boy Cyrnus; others again are gnomic, neat statements of the commonplaces of Greek wisdom and morality (see GNOME AND GNOMIC POETRY).

About the beginning of the 6th century a new kind of poetry made its appearance in the island of Lesbos off the coast of Asia Minor. It was composed in the local Aeolic dialect by members of the turbulent and faction-ridden aristocracy. Alcaeus (b. c. 620) and Sappho, a few years younger, both spent part of their lives in exile. Alcaeus, absorbed in political feuds and in civil war, expresses with striking directness searing hate and blind exultation. With the same directness and infinite grace, Sappho, who seems to have enjoyed a freedom unknown to the women of mainland Greece, tells of her loves and, hardly less frequently, of her hates. Of the milieu in which she moved and of her relations with the girls who are named in her poems much has been guessed but nothing can be regarded as known. The remains of their successor in personal lyric, the Ionian Anacreon of Teos, a generation later, suggests a more convivial amorousness. His reputation has suffered from the ascription to him of a number of feeble poems of late date, the *Anacreontea* (see ANACREONTICS).

The Greeks did not themselves distinguish choral lyric as a separate category, but it was associated with the Dorian parts of the Greek mainland and the settlements in Sicily and south Italy as opposed to the poetry for solo performance of the Ionian coast and the Aegean islands, and for this reason it was composed in a dialect with a Doric flavour even when, as often, the poets were themselves of Ionian birth.

Choral lyric, quite apart from the music, of which little is known except that both lyre and flute had their appropriate uses, was highly complicated in structure. It did not use traditional lines or stanzas, but the metre was formed afresh for each poem and never used again in exactly the same form, though the metrical units from which the stanzas, or strophes, were built up were drawn from a common stock. The strophes, either single or in systems of three, were repeated through the poem, and in many cases their form was related to the accompanying dance. This elaborate art form with its need for a trained choir and skilled musicians was connected mainly with the cult of the gods or, as in the case of Pindar, the celebration of the victors in the great Hellenic games.

The earliest poet of choral lyrics of whose work anything survives was Alcman, whose choirs performed in Sparta in the late 7th century before the Spartans put aside the graces of life. His original home may have been Lydian Sardis. In the next century Stesichorus worked in Sicily, an area to which Homeric poems may not yet have penetrated, and his lyric versions of the great myths mark an important stage in the development of these stories. Simonides of Ceos in Ionia, whose long life extended far into the 5th century, was among the most versatile of Greek poets. He traveled far and wide in Greece, celebrating in Thessaly, in Athens and in Sicily the princely houses whose patronage he enjoyed. He was famed for his pathos, which is admirably revealed in his lines describing Danaë set adrift with her child on the open sea. But today he is best known by his elegiac epitaphs, especially those on the Greeks who fell in the struggle against Persia, the epitome of the grace,-restraint and sincerity to be found in the greatest Greek art.

But the supreme poet of choral lyric was Pindar from Thebes in Boeotia, a part of the Greek world otherwise undistinguished in the annals of poetry except for Hesiod and for Pindar's contemporary, if contemporary she was, the lyric poetess Corinna. Pindar (c. 520–440), though he composed many varieties of choral lyric, is known mainly by his epinician odes, poems in honour of the victors at the great games held at Olympia, Delphi, the isthmus of Corinth and Nemea. They were usually performed as part of the festivities which greeted the triumphant athlete on his return to his city.

Among Pindar's patrons were many of the most aristocratic houses of Greece, but they were patrons whom Pindar, intensely conscious of his own divine gift of inspiration, treated as equals. In honouring athletes in the hour of glory, when they were exalted almost to the level of the heroes of old from whom they claimed descent, Pindar felt he was making no unworthy use of his gift. Even in Pindar's day the athletic ideal was growing obsolete and it is hard to recapture in imagination, but the glowing magnificence of his tributes and the splendid passages of lyric narrative embedded in them still represent one of the extremes of poetic grandeur.

The last of the lyric poets was Bacchylides (b. c. 510), a nephew of Simonides, whose work, though often exquisite, is empty. The myth was losing its significance and becoming merely ornamental, and Bacchylides' treatment of it is a foretaste of the antiquarian prettiness of Hellenistic poetry.

3. Tragedy.—Before the 5th century Athens was celebrated rather for the visual arts than for poetry. But under the patronage of the tyrants, poets gathered at Athens and poetry had its part in the festivals with which the tyrants tried to popularize their rule. The decisive moment was when, in or about 534 B.C., tragedy became an official part of the spring festival of the Dionysia. Tragedy is generally believed to have developed from the dithyramb, the choral cult song of Dionysus (see DRAMA: *Greek Drama: Origins*). Arion of Lesbos, who worked at Corinth c. 600, was the first to write serious poetry in this medium. Lasus of Hermione, the teacher of Pindar, produced dithyrambs at Athens; and Thespis (6th century B.C.) possibly combining with them something of the Attic ritual of Dionysus of Eleutherae, invented tragedy by introducing an actor who conversed with the leader of the chorus and gave its songs a quasi-dramatic point of reference; but nothing approaching true drama was possible until Aeschylus (525?-456), the creator of the tragedy, introduced a second actor. However, his drama is still centred in the chorus, to whom, rather than to each other, his actors direct themselves.

It was customary at the tragic contests at the Dionysia for each of the three competing poets to produce three tragedies and a satyr play, the last being of a burlesque character with a chorus of satyrs who were part men, part horse or goat. Aeschylus, unlike later poets, usually made of his three tragedies a dramatic whole, treating a single story which might extend over a considerable period of time. His main concern was not dramatic structure and the portrayal of character but rather the presentation of human action in relation to the overriding purpose of the gods, though at times the accumulation of tension through long passages of lyric leads to scenes of tremendous emotional force. And the un-Greek opulence of his language and his richness of metaphor make him to most modern readers the most obviously exciting of Greek poets after Homer.

The successor of Aeschylus was Sophocles (495?-406), who abandoned for the most part the practice of writing in trilogies, reduced the importance of the chorus and introduced a third actor. The myth as the expression of an aristocratic and heroic ideal remained for him a satisfying theme and his heroes are still the heroes of Homer somewhat modified by contact with the standards of 5th-century Athens. But whereas Aeschylus tried to make more intelligible the workings of the divine purpose in its effects on man's life, Sophocles was readier to accept the gods as given and to reveal the values of life as it can be lived within the traditional framework of moral standards. He believed that in the fullness of time the wicked are punished, but not that all human suffering is punishment for wickedness. His earliest surviving plays, the *Ajax* and the *Antigone*, are the closest to Aeschylus both in stiffness of movement and in the awareness that the divine will is being fulfilled. Thereafter the actors become more detached from the background, and Sophocles' supreme skill in control of dramatic movement and his mastery of speech are devoted to the presentation of the decisive, usually tragic, hours in the lives of men and women at once "heroic" and human, such as Oedipus.

Euripides (c. 485-407), the last of the three great tragic poets, was only about ten years younger than Sophocles, but he belonged to a different world. When he came to manhood the Sophistic movement was in full swing (see SOPHISTS). Traditional beliefs were scrutinized in the light of what claimed, not always unjustifiably, to be reason, and this was a test to which much of Greek religion was highly vulnerable. The whole structure of society and its values was called in question. It is rarely possible to tell precisely what a dramatist thinks, but this movement of largely destructive criticism was clearly not uncongenial to Euripides, as it was to Sophocles. But as a dramatic poet Euripides found himself in an unfortunate position. He was bound to draw his material from myths, which for him had to a great extent lost their meaning. He strained and twisted them to make room for contemporary problems which were his real interest, and the divine presuppositions of the myth are accepted or rejected from moment to moment as the plot requires. In consequence, many of his plays suffer from a certain internal disharmony. On the other hand, his sensibilities and his moments of psychological insight bring him far closer than most Greek writers to modern taste. There are studies, wonderfully sympathetic, of wholly unsympathetic actions in the *Medea* and *Hippolytus*, a vivid presentation of the beauty and horror of religious ecstasy in the *Bacchae*, in the *Electra* a *reductio ad absurdum* of the values of a myth that justifies matricide, in the *Helen* and *Iphigeneia in Tauris* melodrama with a faint flavour of romance.

4. Comedy.—Like tragedy, comedy arose from a ritual in honour of Dionysus, a riotous ritual full of abuse and obscenity which was inspired not only by high spirits but by hopes of averting the attentions of evil demons and of encouraging fertility (see DRAMA: *Greek Drama: Origins*). The parabasis, the part of the play in which the chorus broke off the action and commented in their own persons on characters and events of the day, was probably a direct descendant of such revels. The dramatic element may have been derived from the secular Dorian comedy without chorus which is said to have arisen at Megara and was developed at Syracuse by Epicharmus (c. 530-c. 440). Hardly anything survives of his farces or of the mimes, short scenes of everyday life, of which Sophron of Syracuse was the most celebrated writer. At Athens comedy did not become an official part of the celebrations of Dionysus till 50 years later than tragedy, and the early years of its growth are correspondingly more obscure. The earliest comic poet of whom it is possible to form an impression was Cratinus. About 50 years later Aristophanes and Eupolis, who together with Cratinus make up the great trio of comic poets, refined somewhat the wild robustness of the older poet. But even so, for boldness of fantasy, for merciless invective, for unabashed indecency and, in the earlier plays, for freedom of political criticism, there is nothing like the Old Comedy of Aristophanes, whose work alone has survived. Cleon the politician, Socrates the philosopher, Euripides the poet are alike the victims of his masterly unfairness, the first in *The Knights*, the second in *The Clouds*, the third in the *Thesmophoriazusae* and *The Frogs*, while in *The Birds* the Athenian democracy itself is held up to a kindlier ridicule. As the war situation grew grimmer, direct political criticism became more dangerous and may have been the subject of legal restrictions. Aristophanes survived the fall of Athens in 404, but the Old Comedy had no place in the revived democracy. Except for short episodes the two plays of his of 4th-century date which have come down lack the sparkle and the poetic brilliance of his best work.

The gradual change from Old to Middle Comedy took place in the early years of the 4th century; the *Ecclesiazusae* and *Plutus* of Aristophanes belong to the transition. Of Middle Comedy no fully developed specimen has survived. It seems to have been distinguished by the disappearance of the chorus and of outspoken political criticism and by the growth of social satire and of parody; Antiphanes and Alexis were the two most distinguished writers. Some plays appear to have had intricate plots treated in a comparatively realistic spirit, and it was these which led on to the New Comedy of Diphilus, Philemon, and, most important, Menander, one of the most admired poets in the ancient world. The transition took place around 320. One complete play, the *Dyscolos*, and appreciable fragments of four others, out of Menander's 105 plays are extant on papyrus. New Comedy, as ancient critics were aware, was derived in part from Euripidean tragedy; its characteristic plot was a translation into terms of city life of the story of the maiden wronged by a god who bears her child in secret, exposes it and recognizes it years after by means of the trinkets she had put in its cradle. The god becomes a young man about town, the child a courtesan with whom a young man about town, when she is revealed as the daughter of free parents. However great the delicacy of the language and the subtlety of the portrayal of the recurring types, it is hard to believe that such essentially barren themes of amiable virtue and petty vice could ever again arouse an enthusiasm such as possessed the ancient world for several centuries after Menander's death.

B. EARLY AND ATTIC PROSE

By the end of the 7th century the first written codes of law were appearing and knowledge of reading and writing was becoming more widespread. This encouraged the development of a prose literature. When writing replaced verse as an aid to memory, it was natural that the poetry of the Hesiodic school, dealing with the origin of the world and with the ordering of the generations of gods and heroes, should continue in prose form and supply the beginnings both for philosophy and history. There is no positive evidence that fables associated with the name of Aesop and traditional stories like those that appear in Herodotus' history were written down in the course of the 6th century. No prose writer is known earlier than Pherecydes (c. 550 B.C.) of Syros, who wrote about the beginnings of the world, but the earliest extant author among many otherwise unknown names is Hecataeus of Miletus, who played the part of elder statesman at the time of the Ionian revolt (499-494); he wrote both about the mythical past and about the geography of the Mediterranean and surrounding lands.

Prose came late to Athens. The oldest extant piece of Attic prose is an antidemocratic essay on the constitution of Athens (preserved as a result of a false attribution to Xenophon), the sole example of a considerable pamphlet literature. It was probably written c. 430 B.C., just after the outbreak of the Peloponnesian War, and it is an example of effective rather than elegant expression. But since Athens had risen after the Persian Wars to be the capital of a great confederacy, distinguished foreigners had been frequent visitors or residents, among them Anaxagoras from Clazomenae near Ephesus, author of one of the earliest philosophic essays in prose, and sophists like Protagoras who contributed both to originating the study of language and to developing the theory of its use as a means of persuasion through rhetoric. All these, as well as the medical writers of the Hippocratean corpus, used the traditional language of prose, Ionic.

1. History.—By far the most important of the writers of history was Herodotus, who was born at Halicarnassus and, after travels which took him as far as the First cataract on the Nile, Babylonia and southern Russia, spent some time in Athens in the years after 450 before settling in the Athenian colony of Thurii in south Italy. The theme of his history, written in large part for Athenian readers, is the clash between Europe and Asia culminating in the Persian War, but it is likely that he began by writing an account of the countries on the fringe of the Greek world in the manner of Hecataeus of Miletus, and that the idea of writing history, a thing which so far existed only in the form of local, largely mythical, chronicles, occurred to him as his work progressed. The account of the war itself, which occupies roughly the second half of the work, must have been composed by means of laborious inquiry from those whose memories were long enough to recall events which happened when Herodotus was a child or earlier. The whole history, though in places badly put together, is magnificent in its compass and unified by the consciousness of an overriding power which keeps the balance of the universe even and humbles the ambition of those who aspire too high. Though his notion of historical causation is rather naïve—the impulse which leads men to action is usually simple and purely personal, most often the desire to avenge a wrong—he has served mankind better as the faithful recorder of what he saw and what he was told than he could ever have done had he subordinated his narrative to more sophisticated notions. The style is equable, conversational, yet capable of quiet solemnity, rarely self-conscious or artificial, and the earlier books in particular abound in enchanting digressions.

Of prose writers who were Herodotus' contemporaries the most important was Hellanicus of Lesbos, who wrote, among a large number of historical works and works on mythology, the first *Atthis*, a chronicle of the local legends and traditions of Attica.

Thucydides (c. 460–c. 400) was perhaps the first person to apply a first-class mind to a prolonged examination of the nature of political power and the factors by which policies of states are determined. At the outbreak of the Peloponnesian War (431–404) he recognized its momentousness and decided to record its history. As a member of the board of generals he acquired inside knowledge of the way policy is shaped. After his failure to save Amphipolis in 424 he spent 20 years in exile, which he used as an opportunity for getting at the truth from both sides. The result is a history of the war narrowly military and political, but of the most penetrating quality. It was Thucydides' belief not that history repeats itself but that the forces which go to make history are unchanging: the judgment and insight of statesmen and their necessary limitations, the psychological pressures of success and failure exerted both on peoples and individuals and the incalculable element of chance. His own interpretation of the workings of these forces are given mainly in the numerous speeches, often in balancing pairs, in which he reveals the essentials of the situation as it presented itself to the leading participants at decisive moments in the war. Scholars have found some difficulty in believing that these speeches reproduce as much of the substance of what was actually said as Thucydides appears to claim. And though the war is described throughout with an appearance of utter detachment, the author reveals much about his own ideals in his admiration for the sagacity of Themistocles and the authority of Pericles, who represents the spirit of that Athens which the war destroyed, and in his detestation of Cleon's demagogic opportunism.

The Greek of Thucydides, especially in the speeches, is of great difficulty. As he wrote he was forging the instrument to express the most complicated thought yet conveyed in writing. Though harsh and austere in the opinion of Greek critics, he was not uninfluenced by contemporary fashion, but he owes less to the euphuism of Gorgias (*see below*) than is often supposed. In using the new methods of grouping ideas in a balanced and antithetical pattern he sometimes failed to fit his subject matter to the pattern which he imposed upon it; this, together with an occasional overconcentration of thought, is the main source of the obscurity which has troubled ancient as well as modern readers.

Just as Thucydides had linked his work by means of a digression in his first book to the point at which Herodotus had stopped, so Xenophon (c. 430–c. 354) began his *Hellenica* where Thucydides' unfinished history breaks off in 411, as did Theopompus and Cratippus after him. He carried it down to the end of the war and later wrote a continuation down to 362. His work is superficial by comparison with that of Thucydides, but he writes with authority of military affairs and accordingly appears at his best in the *Anabasis*, an account of his participation in the enterprise of the Greek mercenary army with which the Persian prince Cyrus tried to expel his brother from the throne, and of the adventurous march of the Greeks after the murder of their leaders by the Persians, from near Babylon to the Black sea coast. Xenophon also wrote three books, *Memorabilia, Symposium* and *Apologia*, in praise of Socrates, whom he seems to have admired rather than to have understood. His other major work, the *Cyropaedia*, was a piece of acknowledged fiction, perhaps the first of its kind, an imaginary account of the education of the great Cyrus, the founder of the Persian empire. He wrote also a number of short essays of which those on hunting and horsemanship are the best. His personality is engaging, but his moralizing is rather prosy, and the survival of a possibly disproportionate bulk of his work is due to the high esteem in which his style was held in antiquity.

No other historical writing of the 4th century has survived except for a substantial papyrus fragment containing a record of events of the years 396-395. The two leading historians who are known to have covered this period are Ephorus (c. 405-330) of Cyme in Asia Minor who wrote the first universal history of Greece beginning in the heroic age with the coming of the Dorians

c. 1000 B.C. and continuing to his own time, a highly influential work much used as a source by later writers; and Theopompus of Chios. Both were closer in spirit to Xenophon than to Thucydides, lavish with moral judgments and rhetorical embellishment. They mark the beginning of the decline of history toward the position of a mere province of rhetoric, the composition of a narrative which will at once edify and divert a reader, so that it was possible, four centuries later, for Dionysius of Halicarnassus to censure Thucydides for choosing a historical subject so little to the credit of his countrymen as the Peloponnesian War.

More scientific work was done by the successors of Hellanicus in the field of regional histories, especially of Attica. Androtion and Cleidemus in the 4th century and Philochorus continuing into the 3rd century did valuable work in an unpretentious way, basing their conclusions to a considerable extent on the study of the Athenian archives. In the west Philistus (c. 430–c. 360) of Syracuse, himself a man of action, wrote a history of Sicily which was highly esteemed. The same cannot be said of Ctesias who at the court of Artaxerxes II (404–358) and wrote histories of Persia and India which were a byword for mendacity.

2. Rhetoric and Oratory.—In few societies has the power of fluent and persuasive speech been more highly valued than it was in Greece, and even in Homer there are speeches which are pieces of finished rhetoric. But it was the rise of democratic forms of government that provided the great incentive to study and instruction in the arts of persuasion, which were equally necessary for political debate in the assembly and for attack and defense in the law courts. Litigants were not represented by advocates and the only professional help available to the private individual was that of the speech writer, who could use his skill and knowledge to provide a speech to be learned and delivered before the jury (see RHETORIC).

The formal study of rhetoric seems to have originated in the democracy of Syracuse c. 460 B.C. with Corax and with his pupils Tisias and Gorgias (d. 376 B.C.); they also gave instruction in Athens. Corax is reputed to have been the first to write a *techne* or handbook on the art of rhetoric dealing with such topics as arguments from probability and the parts into which speeches should be divided; soon a number of such works were in circulation. Most of the Sophists had pretensions as teachers of the art of speaking, especially Protagoras with his doctrine that on each subject there is a stronger and a weaker (not a better and a worse) argument and that by art the weaker can be made to prevail, and Prodicus (c. 465–after 399 B.C.) of Ceos with his studies in the use of words.

Antiphon (c. 480–411), the first professional speech writer, was an opponent of democracy and influential behind the scenes politically. Three speeches of his have been preserved, all dealing with homicide cases, and three "tetralogies," sets of two pairs of speeches containing the arguments to be used on both sides in imaginary cases of homicide. Their authenticity has been doubted, but they are undoubtedly early, and they are of great interest because of the primitive ideas concerning bloodguilt and the duty of vengeance which they contain. The style of Antiphon is bare and closely knit and the structure sometimes rather crudely antithetical; he was little influenced by the technical advances of the late 5th century. Gorgias from Sicily, who paid a memorable visit to Athens in 427, introduced an elaborate balance and symmetry emphasized by rhyme and assonance by which the Athenians were for a short time much attracted; and Thrasymachus of Chalcedon, best known for his appearance in Plato's *Republic*, made a more solid contribution to the evolution of a periodic and rhythmical style.

Andocides (c. 440–c. 390) was involved in the scandal of the profanation of the Eleusinian mysteries in 415 (*see* ALCIBIADES) and spent much of his life in exile. His three speeches contain vivid narrative, but as an orator he was admittedly amateurish. Of the earlier generation of orators the most important was Lysias (c. 455–c. 380), who lived at Athens for many years as a resident alien and supported himself by writing speeches when he lost his wealth and all but his life in the troubled times which followed the fall of the city. Of all the Attic orators he is the one most likely to be read with pleasure today. His simple, lucid style has obvious charm, though those who preferred him to Plato carried their devotion to Attic purity rather far. His speeches, some of them written for litigants of humble station, show dexterous adaptation to the character of the speaker, though the most interesting of all is his own attack on Eratosthenes, one of the "Thirty Tyrants" imposed on Athens by the Spartans in 404 B.C., which contains a brilliant account of their reign of terror.

The 12 extant speeches of Isaeus, who was active in the first half of the 4th century B.C., all deal with testamentary cases, and are of interest mainly for the light they throw on Athenian law. But Isocrates, who was influential in Athens for half a century before his death at the age of 98 in 338, exerted an influence out of proportion to his talents. He perfected a periodic prose style which through the medium of Latin was widely accepted as a pattern, and he helped to give to rhetoric its predominance in the educational system of the ancient world. Because of the weakness of his voice and the diffidence of his temperament he did not himself speak in public, but after a short career as a writer of forensic speeches he set up a school of rhetoric and political science at Athens which was attended by many of the most distinguished figures of the period. His own writings were in the form of speeches, but were never intended to be delivered. He was the first master of the long periodic sentence in which the clauses are so grouped and subordinated to the sense of the whole that the reader is never in danger of losing the thread of the argument. This was a great achievement, but Isocrates had insufficient vigour and technical finesse to avoid monotony. He avoided the exuberant excess of his master Gorgias while retaining much of his balance and symmetry. He shows some insight into the political troubles of the Greek world with its endless bickerings between cities incapable of co-operation, and he dreamed of unity expressing itself in common action against Persia under the leadership of Athens or, when that became impossible, of Macedon. But he thought and wrote in generalities and drew his examples from bogus history; he may have done something to prepare Greek opinion for what was to come, but his appeal was to the emotions. Never has a political pamphleteer been so utterly devoid of incisiveness, and this defect in his mind was reflected in his style.

The greatest of the orators was by general consent Demosthenes (384/3–322), supreme in vehemence and power though lacking in some of the more delicate shades of rhetorical skill. In his case a number of deliberative speeches have survived, the actual words —or something very like them—spoken before the assembly, in addition to forensic speeches of which many are of a political character. He made efforts to rouse the Athenians to an awareness of the growing menace of Macedon, and in the series of three great speeches culminating in *On the Crown* his bitter feud with the opposing orator Aeschines lives again, the more vividly because the speeches which he answers are the only three of Aeschines that survive.

After Demosthenes, oratory faded together with the political setting to which it owed its pre-eminence. Of Hyperides (c. 390–322), an able all-round speaker, a good deal has been recovered on papyrus; of the statesman and financier Lycurgus (c. 396–325) a single speech survives, and of the undistinguished Dinarchus (c. 361–c. 290), probably three.

3. Philosophy.—Philosophic prose, the greatest literary achievement of the 4th century, derives from Socrates (who himself wrote nothing) and his characteristic method of teaching by question and answer, which leads naturally to the dialogue. Socratic dialogues were first composed by Alexamenus of Teos and the dialogue form was used also by Antisthenes, both disciples of Socrates. But by far the greatest of these writers was Plato (428/7–348/7), who came of a distinguished Athenian family. Shortly after Socrates' death in 399 he wrote some dialogues, mostly short, which probably owed a good deal to the prose mimes of Sophron of Syracuse; to this group of works belongs the *Apology*, an idealized version of Socrates' defense at his trial, and probably two profounder dialogues, *Protagoras* and *Gorgias*. In the decade after 385 he wrote the series of brilliant works, *Phaedo*,

Phaedrus, Symposium, culminating in the *Republic.* His *Socrates* is the most carefully drawn character in Greek literature. The personal touches, the mannerisms and turns of phrase which are here used with wonderful effect. Subsequent dialogues became more austerely philosophical; Socrates tends increasingly to be a mere spokesman for Plato's thought, and in the last of his works, the *Laws,* he is replaced by a colourless "stranger".

Plato's style is a thing of matchless beauty, though ancient critics, who were apt to entangle themselves in the rules they had invented, found it too poetical. All human experience is within its range; it fits itself to every nuance of a developing argument, rises to the heights of earnest eloquence in discourse on man's destiny, and reflects with equal faithfulness the wit and gaiety of a drinking party and the grandeur of Socrates in the condemned cell.

Plato's pupil Aristotle (384–322) was admired in antiquity for his style, but those of his works which have survived are all of the "esoteric" sort, intended for use in connection with his philosophical and scientific school, the Lyceum. They are without literary grace and approximate at times to lecture notes, the only exception being the *Constitution of Athens.* His works on literary subjects, the *Rhetoric* and, above all, the *Poetics,* had an immense effect on literary theory in the centuries after the Renaissance, which was not less potent because they were generally misunderstood. But in the ancient world Aristotelian doctrine was known mainly through the works of his successor Theophrastus (371/0–288/7), which are lost except for two books on plants and the famous collection of 30 *Characters,* sketches of human types much imitated by English writers of the 17th century.

With Theophrastus Attic prose dies out until the artificial revival in the 2nd century A.D. In the meantime a vast amount of prose was written, much of it of a very technical nature, but with few literary pretensions. Rhetoric, become a mere literary exercise in a world in which rhetoric was divorced from political influence, developed an ornate and flowery manner associated with the Asian school of Hegesias of Magnesia (fl. *c.* 300 B.C.).

C. HELLENISTIC AND GRECO-ROMAN PERIODS

Alexander the Great's conquest of Asia between 334 and 323 transformed Greek life. Macedonians and Greeks composed the new governing class over the whole of the eastern Mediterranean and much of the continent beyond, and Greek became the language of administration, a new composite dialect based to some extent on Attic and spoken with little variation over wide areas, the so-called koine or common language. At the same time the cities of Greece and Asia Minor, even when they preserved their independence, lost most of their significance. The city ceased to be the universal frame within which the life of the people was conducted. More than ever before the individual was becoming aware of his isolation and seeking consolation and satisfaction outside corporate society. Henceforward the impulse to artistic creation and its reward came from the individual patron and not from a city, and the poet's audience, except at Athens, where comedy was still a living form during the first third of the 3rd century, consisted of a body of highly cultivated readers scattered over the Greek world. The things which appealed to this audience were finished workmanship and wealth of learned allusion. Their self-consciousness led them to appreciate psychological subtlety, above all in the treatment of love, and since many lived in the great cities whose growth was a feature of the period they began to develop the townsman's sensibility to values which are taken for granted when all human life is within reach of the country. Nature began to take a new place in poetry.

An event of great importance for the development of the new tendencies was the founding of the Museum, the shrine of the Muses, at Alexandria, the most famous of Alexander's new cities. Ptolemy I, Alexander's general, to whom fell the kingdom of Egypt when the empire was divided up in the civil wars which followed Alexander's death, was inspired by Demetrius Phalereus, both a man of action and a member of the Peripatetic school of philosophers founded by Aristotle, to establish this institution with its enormous library and facilities for pursuing the life of scholarship. The chief librarian was a sort of regius professor and sometimes a poet, as well as tutor of the heir apparent. The task of accumulating and preserving knowledge was for the first time properly endowed; the Sophists had begun it, Aristotle, who attached more importance than did most philosophers to knowledge for its own sake, had continued it, his Peripatetic followers developed this rather than the philosophic side of their master's activity, and finally the scholars of Alexandria pursued with zeal numerous branches of research. To them are owed not only the texts of ancient authors but a great deal of the learning required for their elucidation. More often than not the scholars were the poets of the Hellenistic age, and their scholarship influenced their poetry more perhaps than their poetry their scholarship.

The Hellenistic period lasted from the establishment of the kingdoms into which Alexander's empire was resolved to the end of the 1st century B.C., when Roman supremacy had been extended over the near east and a new Greco-Roman culture began to develop. For the next three centuries, until Constantinople became the capital of the later Roman or Byzantine empire, Greek writers were conscious of belonging to a world of which Rome was the centre, even though by a convention rarely disregarded they ignored the existence of Latin literature.

1. Poetry.—The creative period of Hellenism was practically contained within the span of the 3rd century. To this period belong the outstanding poets, Theocritus, Callimachus and Apollonius of Rhodes, to whom ancient critics would have added Aratus. Theocritus (c. 310–250), born at Syracuse, was associated with Philetas of Cos, earliest of Hellenistic poets, and enjoyed the patronage of Ptolemy II at Alexandria. He was essentially a writer of mimes, short dramatic scenes of everyday life, and he is best known as the inventor of bucolic mime or pastoral poetry, in which he presented with varying degrees of realism scenes from the lives of shepherds and goatherds in Sicily and southern Italy; whether he adopted the device of later pastoral poetry and presented in the guise of rustics persons from higher walks of life is uncertain. He also dramatized with brilliant realism scenes from middle-class life, and in his second idyll Simaetha, who deserted her, by incantations to recover the love of the man who has deserted her, touches the fringe of tragedy. He used also another Hellenistic form, the epyllion, which is the modern name for the short scene of heroic narrative poetry in which heroic stature is often reduced by playful realism and delicate psychology. It may seem strange that one who touches so rarely on serious things should rank so high among poets, but in his hands the hexameter attained a lyric purity and sweetness unrivaled elsewhere, and in it he expressed the awakening delight in the charms of nature. His followers in bucolic were Moschus and Bion; not all the few poems ascribed to them are genuine and some are as late as the 1st century B.C.

Callimachus (fl. *c.* 260 B.C.) was a scholar as well as a poet, and his great catalogue of the Alexandrian library was of enduring importance. His most famous work, of which substantial fragments survive, was the *Aitia,* an elegiac poem describing the origins of various rites and customs; it was heavy with learning but diversified by passages of entertaining narrative. His six hymns show immense poetic expertise; solemnity, playful charm, downright humour, antiquarian sentiment—everything is there except religious feeling, which the obsolete gods of Olympus could no longer be expected to awaken unless used symbolically, as by the Stoic Cleanthes in his *Hymn to Zeus.*

Callimachus also wrote epigrams, and fragments survive of *Iambi,* a revival in milder terms of Hipponax. The form was used by a number of writers of the 3rd century, many of them under the influence of Cynic philosophy, to denounce the vanities of the world; their work, sometimes in mixed prose and verse, had connections with both satire and the popular sermon. Bion the Borysthenite, Menippus of Gadara, Cercidas and Phoenix of Colophon, the last two represented by appreciable fragments, were the chief writers in this field in the 3rd century B.C.

Callimachus seems to have advanced a poetic theory strongly hostile to the full-scale epic and favouring the high intensity possible only in shorter works. His epyllion *Hecale*, telling the story of Theseus and the boar of Marathon, was something of a manifesto in opposition to Apollonius of Rhodes (b. c. 295 B.C.), scholar, tutor to Ptolemy III and author of the only extant classical Greek epic apart from the *Iliad* and the *Odyssey*. Apollonius' epic on the voyage of the Argonauts is so full of local legend, connected with the places touched at by the voyagers, that the coherence of the poem is lost, but Medea's wild passion for Jason is marked by a new sort of romantic awareness of which there are only hints in Euripides and which is fully realized in the Dido episode of Virgil's *Aeneid*. Though Callimachus is usually counted the immediate victor in the controversy with Apollonius, who nonetheless achieved the office of head librarian, epics continued to be written in large numbers; Rhianus (275-195) wrote an epic on the war between Sparta and Messenia.

The desire to combine learning with poetry led to the revival of didactic verse, a form which had lost its *raison d'être* when prose came into general use. The *Phainomena* of Aratus (c. 315-c. 240), a work which enjoyed a strange celebrity and was several times translated into Latin, is a versification of a treatise on the stars by Eudoxus of Cnidus (c. 400-c.347); its appeal, not obvious to the modern reader, must have lain in the skill with which an intractable theme was handled in verse. Chance has preserved the poems of Nicander (probably 2nd century B.C.) on the unlikely subjects of cures for bites and antidotes to poisons. An even more repulsive example of versified erudition is the *Alexandra* attributed to Lycophron (fl. c. 285 B.C.), a riddling prophecy of 1,500 iambics spoken by Cassandra.

The mimes of Herodas (3rd century B.C.), short realistic sketches of low life in iambic verse, have affinities both with the nonpastoral mimes of Theocritus and with the satire of the 6th-century Hipponax. They perhaps give a hint as to the character of the literature of popular entertainment, now lost except for a few scraps such as the moving complaint of a deserted maiden, the *Fragmentum Grenfellianum* (c. 2nd century B.C.). Much of the theatrical entertainment of the early empire consisted of mimes, though the pantomime in which the dancer expressed himself entirely by gesture was even more popular.

After the middle of the 3rd century poetic activity largely died away, though the great period of scholarship at Alexandria and at Pergamum was still to come. A few names of poets are known only because of their influence on Latin writers: Euphorion (b. c. 275 B.C.) of Chalcis and Parthenius (fl. 1st century B.C.), the teacher of Virgil. Thereafter Greek poetry practically ceases apart from a sporadic revival in the 4th century A.D. There is one exception; epigrams, usually in elegiac couplets, a form which goes back at least to Archilochus, continued to be written far into the Byzantine period. They have survived mainly in the two great compilations, the Planudean and Palatine Anthologies (*see* ANTHOLOGY), based on several earlier collections of which the first of importance was the *Garland* of the Syrian poet Meleager of Gadara, made c. 100 B.C. This diminutive form was well suited to the exquisiteness of Hellenistic technique, and many of these little poems are of special interest because they seem to provide an outlet for the purely personal emotion so rarely expressed by Greek poets. Apart from poets otherwise known the chief epigrammatists were Asclepiades (fl. 270 B.C.), Leonidas (3rd century B.C.) of Tarentum and Philodemus (d. 40 B.C.).

2. **Prose.**—Of the great mass of Hellenistic and later prose, historical, scholarly and scientific, almost all has perished, unconsciously condemned to destruction by the readers and schoolmasters of the later Roman and Byzantine empires. What they selected for reading was copied from papyrus onto parchment and had some chance of survival till the age of printing; the rest was left to crumble away and only relatively few scraps on papyrus have been rescued from the rubbish heaps of Egypt. In a world addicted to rhetoric and indifferent to science, the businesslike but rarely elegant prose of the koine aroused no interest.

History.—Among historians Polybius (c. 200-c. 118), the most outstanding, has survived in a fragmentary condition. Himself a leader of the Achaean league, then for many years a hostage in Italy where he won the friendship of Roman Hellenists, he was in a good position to appreciate the great historical phenomenon of the time, the rise of Rome. He wrote mainly of events of which he had direct experience, often with great insight; his work, in 40 books of which 5 are extant, covered the period from 264 to 146. The surviving books of the universal history of Diodorus Siculus (1st century B.C.) are important to historians for the information derived from better writers which they contain. Considerable excerpts remain of the immense work of Nicolaus of Damascus (1st century B.C.), who was secretary to Herod and tutor to the children of Antony and Cleopatra, but they contain as much fable as history. The most considerable of lost historians was Timaeus (c. 350-c. 250), whose history of the Greeks in the west down to 264 provided Polybius with his starting point. Later historians were Dionysius of Halicarnassus (fl. c. 20 B.C.), the literary critic, about half of whose *Roman Antiquities* are extant, Appian of Alexandria, who lived at Rome at the time of Hadrian and wrote on Rome and its conquests, and Arrian (c. 96-c. 180 A.D.) from Bithynia, who is the most valuable source for the life of Alexander the Great.

Criticism.—The modest treatise *On Style* by an unknown Demetrius, sometimes identified with Demetrius Phalereus, is a piece of work in the Peripatetic tradition, perhaps as late as the 1st century A.D. It is generally believed that the treatise *On the Sublime* was written c. A.D. 40 by an otherwise unknown author (usually known as Longinus). Alone among ancient critics he does justice to creative literature as "the echo of a great soul," and he is exceptional for a Greek in that he mentions both Cicero and the Book of Genesis. On a lower plane Dionysius of Halicarnassus discussed with great subtlety the stylistic techniques of various writers. The so-called *Bibliotheca* of Apollodorus, long attributed to Apollodorus of Athens (c. 180 B.C.) but probably belonging to the Greco-Roman period, is a handy compendium of mythology, and in a sense a work of learning. The rest of the vast literary learning of the age is lost except for the little that was preserved by later commentators and a few papyrus fragments like Satyrus' chapters on Euripides.

Science and Geography.—Scientific work such as the astronomy and geography of Eratosthenes (c. 276-c. 192) of Alexandria, also a poet of some distinction, is known mainly from later summaries, but considerable quantities of the mathematicians, especially of Euclid (fl. 300 B.C.) and of Archimedes (c. 287-212), have been preserved.

The great medical writer Galen (c. 130-c. 200) was physician to both Marcus Aurelius and Commodus; an enormous volume of his work has survived. The medical writings of his contemporary Sextus Empiricus are lost, but his philosophical writings are an important source for the history of Greek philosophy. The survey of the Mediterranean by Strabo in the time of Augustus preserves much valuable information and so, in a more limited field, does the description of Greece by Pausanias, which is rich in local legend and useful to the archaeologist for its account of the monuments and works of art to be seen in the later part of the 2nd century A.D. The Greek achievement in astronomy and geography was summed up in the work of Ptolemy of Alexandria in the 2nd century A.D.

Judaeo-Christian Writings.—Prose of a different kind has come down from the eastern end of the Mediterranean. Greek became the language of the large settlement of Jews at Alexandria; Hebrew and Aramaic were forgotten by many, and the Septuagint, the Greek version of the Old Testament for Greek-speaking Jews, was completed by about the end of the 2nd century. Most of the Apocrypha is extant in Greek, and much of it was originally composed in that language. A surprising work, fragments of which are preserved in Eusebius of Caesarea, is the *Exagoge* of Ezekiel, a play in more or less Euripidean iambics on the exodus of the Jews from Egypt. In Alexandria the change from Macedonian to Roman rule made little difference. Philo in the early years of the Roman empire commented on the Jewish scriptures in the light of Greek thought. Josephus (c. 37-c. 98) fought on both sides in Roman-Jewish wars and wrote important works on Jewish history. The New Testament was written in popular Greek (koine), though in some parts the influence of Aramaic is to be suspected. Clement of Rome and Ignatius of Antioch were the most famous of the Apostolic Fathers. Justin Martyr (c. 100-c. 165) was the first in the line of Christian apologists which culminated in Clement of Alexandria (c. 150-c. 215) and Origen (c. 185-c. 254).

Plutarch.—The *Parallel Lives* of famous Greeks and Romans by Plutarch (c. 45-c. 120) of Chaeronea in Boeotia was for centuries one of the formative books for educated Europeans. Great figures from an idealized past are presented for the edification of the lesser men of his own day, and the anecdotes with which the *Lives* abound are of various degrees of credibility. They belong to biography rather than to history, though they are an important source for historians. A number of shorter works on a wide variety of subjects have come down under the title of *Moralia.* Plutarch's rambling curiosity and uncritical piety show the intellectual tide of Greece as being well on the ebb.

Second Sophistic Movement.—There was much concern over a question which had been argued ever since the days when Athens had ceased to be a free city: to what extent was Attic prose a norm which writers and especially orators were bound to follow? Those who preferred the more full-blooded Asiatic style could claim that they were escaping from an unprofitable bondage to the past, but hardly anything is left to show its quality. Many prose writers, notably Dionysius, had given their language an Attic flavour, but it was not until near the end of the 1st century A.D. that, with the movement which is flattered by the name of the Second Sophistic, the task of reviving a dead dialect was pursued with full vigour. These writers were orators in the sense that they gave displays of their virtuosity in a society which was still greedy for the spoken word and they published their speeches to be read in a wider circle; some of them also wrote essays and dialogues. Dio Chrysostom (c. 40-after 114) of Prusa in Bithynia exemplified in exile under Domitian the virtues of Stoic and Cynic philosophy, and was too intent on his message to be a mere stylist. His experiences as a wanderer in remote provinces gave his speeches an extraneous interest, but they have also many of the qualities of the sermon. A more thoroughgoing Atticist was Aelius Aristides (c. 117-189), a writer of undeniable brilliance, interesting mainly for his account of his prolonged search for an escape from illhealth. But the only writer of real consequence from this period was Lucian (c. 125-after 180) of Samosata in Syria. His works are mainly slight and satirical, but his gift of humour, even though it is repetitive, cannot be denied. His talent was for revealing the ridiculous side of things, and in an increasingly credulous world of astrologers, charlatans and miracle mongers he found much to ridicule, but an undue proportion of his effort was devoted to making easy fun of the moribund deities of Olympus. Yet he is the last Greek to show confidence in the validity of human reason as a test of the possible and the credible. The defect of this quality can be illustrated from the fascinating *Life of Apollonius of Tyana*, philosopher and mystic, by Philostratus (c. 170-c. 245 A.D.), who also wrote the *Lives of the Sophists.* A more valuable though less accomplished work is the *Lives and Opinions of Famous Philosophers* by an otherwise unknown Diogenes Laërtius probably of the 3rd century A.D. Other examples of learned miscellanies, often frivolous and always undiscriminating, are the compilations of Aelian and of Athenaeus, both of the same period as Philostratus.

Philosophy.—Philosophical activity in the early empire was almost confined to moralizings based on Stoicism. Epictetus (b. c. A.D. 50) has had a wide appeal to the serious-minded of all periods, and he influenced especially the philosophic emperor Marcus Aurelius (121-180), whose *Meditations* have taken their place beside works of Christian devotion. Many of Plutarch's *Moralia* are Platonic with vaguely mystical tendencies, but Plotinus (205-270) is the last major thinker in the classical world. He gave a new direction to Platonic and Pythagorean mysticism expressed in a style usually obscure but rising at times to real grandeur (*see* NEOPLATONISM).

The Novel.—The latest creation of the Greek genius was the novel, or erotic romance. It now seems likely that the first developments were as early as the 1st century B.C., and the origins reach back to such plays of love triumphant as the lost *Andromeda* of Euripides and the New Comedy, to Xenophon's daydreams about the education of Cyrus and to the largely fictitious narratives which were one extreme of what passed for history from the 3rd century B.C. onward. Of these last the best-known examples are the Alexander Romances, a wildly distorted and embroidered version of the exploits of Alexander the Great which supplied some of the favourite reading of the middle ages. Erotic elegy and epigram may have contributed something and so may the lost "Milesian Tales" of Aristides of Miletus (c. 100 B.C.), though these last appear to have depended on a pornographic interest which is almost completely absent from the Greek romances. Of the Ninus romance (dealing with the love of Ninus, founder of Nineveh), which was probably of the 1st century B.C., only fragments survive, but full-length works survive by Chariton (2nd century A.D.), Heliodorus (3rd century A.D.), Xenophon (2nd or 3rd century A.D.) of Ephesus and Achilles Tatius (2nd century A.D.); all deal with true lovers separated by innumerable obstacles of human wickedness and natural catastrophe and finally united. *Daphnis and Chloe* by Longus (between 2nd and 3rd century A.D.) stands apart from the others because of its pastoral rather than quasi-historical setting. The works of Dictys Cretensis and Dares Phrygius belong to the same period. They claim to give a pre-Homeric account of the Trojan War. The Greek originals are almost wholly lost, but the Latin version was for the middle ages the main source for the story of Troy.   (D. W. Ls.)

II. BYZANTINE (4TH CENTURY A.D.-1453)

1. Characteristics.—By Byzantine literature is meant the literature written in Greek during the so-called Byzantine period (c. 300-1453). After Byzantine art it is the most genuine and direct expression of Byzantine civilization—that is to say, of that self-contained medieval Christian culture of which the Byzantine empire was the vehicle. If it is to be rightly judged it is of no use either to apply to it the standards of value of modern literary criticism, or to bring to it a mind attuned by the classics to an overrating of Greek antiquity. Instead, an attempt must be made to understand the particular religious, political and social worlds from which it derives.

Byzantine literature was a constituent part of a civilization whose character was determined by the centralized structure of politics in the Byzantine empire, particularly by court life in Constantinople (Byzantium). Byzantine culture was the direct and organic continuation of Greco-Roman culture in Christian dress. In the 3rd century A.D. the spiritual foundations of literature and art were a mixture of religious and philosophical tendencies—a union of Neoplatonic emanation doctrine, Gnosis, heliolatry, emperor cult and magic. To this Christianity, strengthened and organized by three centuries of persecution, brought a new note which in the course of a further three centuries succeeded in becoming the dominant in all literary activity in the empire. This came about after Constantine the Great christianized Augustus' idea of a Roman world empire and made the Christian church the guardian of the Greco-Roman cultural tradition. It came about in the tough fight against the ancient powers of civilization—against paganism, Neoplatonism, Gnosticism and against the Christian heresies; and in the course of that fight there flowed from these into the new Christian orthodoxy an abundance of ideas and beliefs. In the process Constantinople, the "New Rome" on the Bosporus, raised by Constantine to be the new capital, drew all the significant powers of the empire to itself, allowing the old cities of learning and literature—Rome, Alexandria, Antioch, Athens—gradually to decay. Byzantine literature thus acquired a metropolitan, court and exclusively aristocratic character. This development explains many of its peculiarities, for instance the number and the solemnity of the laudatory speeches to the emperor and his family and the preponderance of poems on the emperor's glorious deeds, which become intelligible in view of the unique position which the Byzantine emperor held as Christ's substitute on earth; the praise won from his subjects is therefore paid primarily to Christ himself.

In the light of the same development Byzantine conservatism in the use of outward literary forms, particularly language, becomes understandable. This language had to preserve the forms of the speech of the New Testament and the Fathers and, on the other hand, those of the Attic models from the great literary past. For it was the pride of the Byzantines that God had given mankind his revelation (beyond which no advance in human knowledge seemed possible) in the Greek tongue; and that the classical poetry and most varied sorts of literature, was also clothed in this language; and that in addition the "Attic" language was up to that time the speech of the cultured in all the schools of the known world. Thus they would not permit this language to display in literature the leveling and simplifying influences which it suffered in daily use in the mouths of the people. This Byzantine pride in being the chosen people of the New Covenant and the heir of an unsurpassable spiritual culture is also the basic explanation of the principle of excluding all fertilization and invigoration by the ideas and literature of other nations. While the language of daily life developed according to its own intrinsic laws into modern Greek (a process practically completed by the middle of the 15th century), in the literary field Byzantium clung to speech forms artificially frozen at the Hellenistic Greek stage, falling into what was at times misunderstood Atticism. Mimesis (imitation of the ancients) became the principle behind all literary forms and scarcely allowed the genuine note of feeling and passion, springing straight from the heart, to appear in poetry or preaching. The undue value placed on form soon began to smother the sense for originality of content and invention; virtuosity in the mastery of verse technique or of the rules of rhetoric became an end in itself, so that metrical forms were even used, for example, in astronomical or legal treatises. On the other hand the consciousness of being in sole possession of the treasures of knowledge inherited from the ancients led to an overrating of erudition—hence the pedantic, obtrusively didactic form of many Byzantine writers or the gloss mania of philologists like John Tzetzes (d. 1185), who thought it necessary to annotate the copious literary conceits of his own letters.

In addition there is the all-pervading Byzantine rationalism, which forms a curious polarity to the religious tendency toward mysticism and which at times assumes that the secrets of nature and of the divine are to be stormed by a naïve prosiness. Further, there is the deeply rooted individualism, still to be seen in the Greek people, which caused a peculiar tension with regard to the confining bonds of ecclesiastical and political orthodoxy. These contrasts explain the discords which are to be felt in much Byzantine literature: the direct juxtaposition of devout Christian faith and an occasional flippant atheism; the lack of humour and the pleasure in malicious ridicule which appears from time to time; the tendency toward a bigoted asceticism shot through by fear of eternal retribution. All this explains why love lyrics form a very small part of early Byzantine literature and inner experience takes refuge in religious lyrics, though these are sometimes magnificent of their type.

The failings of Byzantine literature stem, therefore, largely from the religious and political tendencies of the time, though the psychological make-up of the Byzantine world also plays a part. The failings are balanced by certain merits. Thus, belief in the divine vocation of the Christian "Roman empire of the Greek nation" meant that Byzantine historical writing preserved the best traditions of the Roman *historia* right through the centuries until the end of the empire with only short interruptions, and accompanied Byzantine history to the end with a long series of highly finished accounts of events; it was the 12th century before western Europe had anything comparable to set beside this achievement. In these works Byzantine rationalism provides to a large extent not only a good descriptive survey of the fate of the empire but in addition information about the many neighbouring European and non-European peoples against whom the empire had perpetually to assert itself; in many cases Byzantine historical writing provides the only available information about the period. Then, the traditionalism of the Byzantines, their ambition to match the ancient models, saved for posterity the best of ancient Greek literature,

which served them as a pattern; even so, much was allowed to perish on the principle enunciated by the emperor Constantine VII Porphyrogenitus (d. 959) in the preface to his great series of excerpts: that it is better for mankind to possess a careful selection of a whole literature than an endless abundance of inferior work. As a result of the Byzantine tendency toward pedantry, many early scholia (explanatory notes) were preserved and added to by such Byzantine scholars as Eustathius of Thessalonica (d. 1194) or Maximus Planudes (early 14th century); without these scholia, begun by the Alexandrine scholars of the 4th century B.C., many passages in ancient literature would remain obscure. The comparative purity in which the ancient texts have come down to us is also largely due to the pedantry of Byzantine scholars. An especially important result of the speculative propensity of the Byzantines was the shaping of early Christian theology by the philosophically trained Fathers of the Church, particularly by the 4th-century Basil of Caesarea, Gregory of Nazianzus, Gregory of Nyssa; Christianity, at a critical stage in its history, was thus equipped to win its way against the philosophically supported religions and ideologies (Gnosticism, Neoplatonism) and to become the religion also of the educated and the upper classes. Further, one result of Byzantine melancholia was the mysticism embodied in its purest form in the Pseudo-Dionysius the Areopagite. This was important not only for theologians in the Christian east, such as Symeon the New Theologian (d. 1022) and Nicholas Cabasilas (14th century); after the 9th century it became influential in the west also and may be viewed as the root of one of the basic ideals of piety in European spiritual history. The rich garland of ecclesiastical Byzantine poetry, at once deeply felt and varied in form, sprang from the same piety, which penetrated all sections of life.

The Byzantine achievement in the sphere of popular poetry perhaps appeals most to modern taste. It is composed in the language of the people, that is to say in the language evolved from the idiom of daily life, and in the also popular pentadecasyllabic (15-foot) metre. The higher officials and clerics, the class which dominated literary criticism, did not therefore regard this folk poetry as "literature" at all and it consequently survived only in relatively late manuscripts (15th-17th century; *i.e.*, partly from the post-Byzantine period). Besides the extensive, imaginative epic of Digenes Akritas, whose origins go back to the 10th century, this poetry, filled with the spirit of the common people, includes a quantity of fairy tale and historical material clothed in epic form; the animal fables particularly show an overflowing power of invention and great epic talent.

In spite of the unquestioned superiority of Byzantine literature over western literature of the same period, which was written in Latin, and in spite of the admiration which the west entertained for Byzantine culture, the effect of the one on the other was comparatively small. On the one hand, the Byzantines, as has been mentioned, excluded on principle western literary forms and, up to the 12th century, western material and subjects; in the west, on the other hand, the Germanic conquests made a break in cultural tradition which meant that the knowledge of Greek was soon lost. Jerome and Rufinus translated a relatively small amount into Latin in the 4th and 5th centuries, but even Augustine could scarcely read the Greek authors in the original. The important influence of the 5th–6th century Pseudo-Dionysius the Areopagite was only transmitted to the west after his work had been translated into Latin in the 9th century by Abbot Hildwin of St. Denis and by Duns Scotus Erigena. A Latin translation of the *Pege gnoseos* ("Fountain of Knowledge") by John of Damascus also exercised a certain influence on Thomas Aquinas (d. 1274); on the other hand, it was not until *c.* 1400 that parts of Aquinas' writings were known in the Byzantine world and then they had no noticeable effect. Give and take in the realm of popular literature is more frequent and more noticeable, being an accompaniment of the contact of the lower classes through the crusades, especially in the 12th century; saga and story, much of which had come to Byzantium from the middle east, was at that time freely exchanged. In general, however, literary contact between the Byzantine empire and its western neighbours suffered from the mistrust which was increased by religious schism and the political rivalries aroused by the crusades.

Even in Egypt and Asia Minor, both of which were centres of theological literature in the 4th and 5th centuries, the influence of Greek literature could not withstand the revival of the vernacular (Coptic, Syriac), and after the provinces were conquered by the Arabs (641) it was completely lost.

On the other hand, Byzantine literature exercised a relatively strong influence on the peoples of eastern Europe, especially on the Slavs. There, to Bulgaria, to Serbia and, after Prince Vladimir's conversion to Christianity (c. 988), to Russia, Byzantine missionaries brought not only the Bible and liturgical texts but also the sermons of their best preachers and the "chronicles" (history books; see below) which were saturated with the spirit of Byzantine theocracy; and through their tenure of the most important missionary bishoprics they saw to it that the education and political and ecclesiastical life of the newly won converts remained Byzantine. It was by these means that Byzantine literature acquired its most important and, for world history, its most significant success.

2. Theology.—The great period of Greek theological literature, in the 4th and early 5th centuries, was largely the product of two factors: the establishment of Christianity as a permitted and then as the official religion of the state, and the stimulus afforded by heretical teachers such as Arius, Apollinaris, Nestorius and Eutyches (see also ARIANISM; MONOPHYSITES). The main theologians of the 4th–5th centuries were Athanasius (c. 295–373), the chief opponent of Arius and creator of the pattern for Byzantine hagiography in his life of St. Anthony of Egypt; Eusebius (c. 260–c. 340), who wrote the first ecclesiastical history as well as apologetic and antiheretical works and biblical commentaries; the three Cappadocian Fathers, Basil of Caesarea (St. Basil the Great; c. 330–379), who organized eastern monasticism, his brother Gregory of Nyssa (c. 330–c. 395), and their friend Gregory of Nazianzus (c. 329–c. 389), known as Gregory the Theologian, who was also a poet; John Chrysostom (c. 347–407), bishop of Constantinople, the great preacher; Cyril (376–444) of Alexandria, untiring opponent of Nestorius, who represented the Alexandrian school; Theodoret (c. 386–c. 457) of Cyrrhus, who represented the school of Antioch.

After the middle of the 5th century theological literature was largely concerned with combating heresy. Leontius of Byzantium (d. c. 545), the first to introduce Aristotelian definitions into theology, wrote against Monophysites as did Anastasius of Sinai (d. c. 700) and Maximus the Confessor, the 7th-century mystic. Iconoclasm was opposed by John of Damascus whose *Pege gnoseos* was the first comprehensive exposition of Christian dogma, and who was one of the chief composers of the kanons (see *Religious Poetry,* below). The works of Theodore Studites (759–826), who also attacked iconoclasm, include kanons and homilies which give much information about monastic life. The great bibliographer Photius (d. 895), patriarch of Constantinople, was the first to crystallize the differences between the Latin and the Eastern churches into rigid formulas. The emperor Leo VI the Wise (c. 866–911) wrote liturgical poems and homilies for a number of festivals. In the early 12th century Euthymius Zigabenus compiled his *Panoplia dogmatica,* an armoury of theology against all heresies.

At this time (11th to 12th century) there arose a tendency to introduce a kind of dialectic into theology in place of the accumulated citations from the Fathers, which had hitherto been the cherished and the only recognized method of supporting a dogmatic thesis. But, instead of developing into something like western scholasticism, this tendency, represented by Michael Psellus, John Italus (both 11th century) and Eustratius of Nicaea (d. c. 1120), soon fell under the reproach of heresy and disappeared. Anti-Latin writings increased in number; their authors include the emperor Theodore II Lascaris (1222–58); Gregory Palamas and Nilus Cabasilas (both 14th century). In the last century of the empire theological writing was almost wholly concerned with the Latin question and with hesychasm, the doctrine of the uncreated light on Mt. Tabor, of which Gregory Palamas was the defender.

3. Hagiography.—The literature consisting of the acts of the martyrs and the lives of the saints forms an independent group which is comparatively unaffected by theological issues. Its main interest centres in the personalities of the martyrs and saints themselves. Apart from Athanasius' life of St. Anthony, Palladius' Lausiac history (5th century), Cyril of Scythopolis' lives of St. Saba and six other Palestinian abbots (6th century) and the life of John the Merciful, bishop of Alexandria, by Leontius of Neapolis in Cyprus (7th century), the authors are mostly anonymous. Most of the acts of the martyrs date from the great persecutions before the Byzantine period; together with the later lives of the saints, they were revised in the 10th century by Simeon Metaphrastes on the rhetorical and linguistic principles of his own day. His new collection, in several volumes, largely superseded the older original texts (see also HAGIOLOGY; BOLLANDISTS). From the popular lives of the saints, which for the reading public of the Byzantine empire formed the chief substitute for modern belles-lettres, it is easy to trace the transition to the religious novel, of which the best-known example is the story of Barlaam and Josaphat.

4. Religious Poetry.—The oldest surviving religious poetry was composed in the ancient Greek metres and was for use in private devotions, not public services; belonging to this group are the so-called "maiden's song" in the *Symposium* of Methodius of Philippi (not "of Olympus" as he is mistakenly called; c. 311) and the religious poems of Gregory of Nazianzus (written between 381 and 389; the few poems extant under his name which are not in ancient metres are not by him). The heretic Apollinaris of Laodicea (4th century) turned the Psalms into hexameters, perhaps with the intention of evading the emperor Julian's interdict on Christian education. Synesius of Cyrene, bishop of Ptolemais (early 5th century), who was also the valiant defender of his city against its barbarian attackers, showed himself in the Christian hymns which he composed in classical metres to be saturated with the Neoplatonic spirit; the poems are a Christian counterpart to the pagan hymns of his contemporary Proclus.

More important than this private religious poetry are the Byzantine liturgical hymns. From comparatively modest beginnings the need for congregational hymns developed under the influence of the propagandist success which the Gnostics and above all the heretic Arius (d. c. 335) had with their religious poetry set to folk music. The model for the poetical development may well have been the Syrian church hymns. The earliest evidence which has been preserved, short poems (tropes) clinging closely to the language of the Scriptures, dates from the end of the 5th century. The verses are arranged in lines all with the same number of syllables, the accent (which here regulates the rhythm) coinciding with the emphasis. The principle behind ancient Greek prosody of regulating the rhythm by long and short syllables ceased to function; from about the 2nd century A.D. all syllables became the same length in Greek, so that accent took over the function of regulating rhythm. On this principle there grew up from the 5th–6th century the kontakion of several strophes, each having the same refrain, preceded by a strophe of irregular rhythmical form (the kukulion). The most prolific and successful writer of kontakia was the Syrian Romanos (6th century); besides the 85 kontakia which have survived under his name he probably wrote the famous *Akathistos* hymn to the Virgin Mary. The dramatic construction of some of the kontakia shows that this literary form was a substitute to the Byzantines for the religious and secular drama which they did not possess.

In the 7th century church poetry entered upon a new stage, characterized by an increase in artistic finish and a falling-off in poetical vigour, with the composition of the kanon, a poem built up out of eight or nine lyrics, all differently constructed. Andrew of Crete (c. 650–720) is regarded as the inventor of this new class of song. The most celebrated writers of kanons are John of Damascus and Cosmas of Jerusalem (both first half of the 8th century). Later, the composition of kanons was more particularly cultivated in the monastery of Studiu in Constantinople by its abbot, Theodore Studites, and others.

5. History.—Byzantine historical accounts fall into two groups:

historical works, describing a period of history in which the authors had lived and moved or one which only immediately preceded their own times, and chronicles, briefly recapitulating the history of the world. This second class has no exact counterpart in ancient literature. (See HISTORY: *Historiography*.)

Byzantine histories of contemporary events do not differ substantially in nature from ancient historical works, except in their Christian colouring. Yet even this is often very faint and blurred because of the close adherence to ancient methods. Apart from this, neither a new style nor a new critical method nor any radically new views appreciably altered the main character of Byzantine historiography.

The outstripping of the Latin west by the Greek east, which after the close of the 4th century was a self-evident fact, is reflected in historiography also. After Constantine the Great (d. 337), the history of the empire, although its Latin character was maintained until the 6th century, was mostly written by Greeks; e.g., Eunapius (d. c. 347), Olympiodorus (5th century), Priscus, Malchus (c. 490) and Zosimus, the last pagan historian (c. 500), all of whom, with the exception of Zosimus, are preserved only in fragments.

To this period also belong the 5th-century continuations of Eusebius' ecclesiastical history made by Gelasius of Caesarea (d. c. 394), by Philip of Side (fl. early 5th century) and by Philostorgius (d. c. 439), who shows Arian sympathies. These survive only in fragments and extracts. A complete church history for the years 305-439 was written by the lawyer Socrates (fl. early 5th century); the work of Sozomen (d. 443) provides a source partly independent of Socrates. Historiography received a great impulse in the 6th century. Procopius and Agathias described the stirring and eventful times of Justinian I; and Theophanes of Byzantium, Menander Protector, John of Epiphaneia, of whose works only fragments survive, and Theophylact Simocattes described the second half of the 6th century. The last independent ecclesiastical historian, Evagrius Scholasticus, who wrote the history of the church from 431 to 593, lived in the latter part of the 6th century. After his time there was little historical writing, beyond the compilation of a few chronicles, until a fresh impetus was provided by the revival of classical studies in the 10th century.

Several historical works are associated with the name of the emperor Constantine VII Porphyrogenitus (10th century). To his learned circle belonged also Joseph Genesius, who at the emperor's instance compiled the history of the period from 813 to 886. The priest John Cameniata wrote an eyewitness account of the taking of Thessalonica by the Cretan corsairs in 904, which is interesting from the point of view of historical and ethnographical science. Leo Diaconus left a graphic account of the period 959-975 which covered the wars of the Byzantines with the Arabs in Crete and with the Bulgarians. A continuation of this was undertaken by the philosopher Michael Psellus in work covering the period from 976 to 1077, a valuable supplement to which (describing the period from 1034 to 1079) was supplied by the jurist Michael Attaliates. The history of the empire during the first four crusades was written by Nicephorus Bryennius, his wife Anna Comnena and John Cinnamus; an exhaustive work by Nicetas Choniates (d. c. 1215) is authoritative for the history of the fourth crusade. The unhappy conditions and decay of the empire under the Palaeologi (13th-15th centuries) are described in a similar lofty style, though with a still closer following of classical models. The events which took place between the taking of Constantinople by the Latins and the restoration of Byzantine rule (1203-61) are recounted by George Acropolites, who emphasized his own share in them. The history of the succeeding period was written by George Pachymeres (d. c. 1310), Nicephorus Gregoras and the emperor John VI Cantacuzenus. Lastly, the death struggle between the Byzantine empire and the rising power of the Ottoman Turks was narrated by three historians, all differing in culture and in style, Laonicus Chalcocondyles, Ducas and George Sphrantzes. With them may be classed a fourth (though he lived outside the Byzantine period), Critobulus, a highborn Greek of Imbros, who wrote, in the style of the age of Pericles, the history of the times of the sultan Mohammed II (1451-67).

The essential importance of the Byzantine chronicles consists in the fact that they in part replace older lost works, and thus fill up many gaps (e.g., for the period from about 600 to 800, of which few records remain). They lay no claim to literary merit, but are often interesting from the linguistic point of view. The authors of the chronicles were mostly monks, which explains the strong clerical and popular tendency of these works. And it is due to these two qualities that the chronicles obtained a circulation abroad, both in the west and also among the peoples christianized from Byzantium, e.g., the Slavs, and in all of them sowed the seeds of an indigenous historical literature. Thus the chronicles, despite their jejune style and uncritical treatment of material, were of far greater importance for the general culture of the middle ages than the erudite contemporary histories designed only for the highly educated circles in Byzantium. The oldest extant Byzantine chronicle of universal history is that of John Malalas (6th century), which is also the purest type of this class of literature. In the 7th century the Paschal Chronicle (*Chronicon Paschale*) was completed. About the end of the 8th or the beginning of the 9th century George the Syncellus compiled a concise chronicle, which began with the creation and was continued down to the year A.D. 284. At the request of the author the continuation of this work was undertaken by Theophanes Confessor, who brought down the account from 284 to his own times (813).

Besides Theophanes there is for the years (813) history of the patriarch Nicephorus (d. c. 829) which was largely drawn from the same sources. Theophanes' chronicle was also extended to cover the period 813-886 by the so-called *Theophanes Continuatus* commissioned by Constantine VII Porphyrogenitus; this consists of five biographies of the emperors reigning during the period, Constantine VII Porphyrogenitus, who commissioned the work, himself contributing the life of his grandfather Basil. A further continuation for the period 886-961 was made by Theodorus Daphnopates. George the Monk compiled an influential chronicle of the world's history (from Adam until the year 842, the end of the Iconoclast movement) far more theological and monastic in character than the work of Theophanes. Among later chroniclers John Scylitzes stands out conspicuously. His work (covering the period from 811 to 1057), as regards the range of its subject matter, is something between a universal and a contemporary history. In the 11th century George Cedrinus embodied the whole of Scylitzes' work, almost unaltered, in his universal chronicle. In the 12th century the general increase in literary production was also reflected in the number of chronicles produced. From this period dates, for instance, the most distinguished and learned work of this class, the great universal chronicle of John Zonaras. Lastly, in the 12th century, Constantine Manasses wrote a universal chronicle in "political" verse (*see* below).

6. Geography.—Two works dealing with geography and topography deserve mention, the 6th-century *Topographia Christiana* of Cosmas Indicopleustes, which contains important information as to Byzantine trade, and the 10th-century history and description of Constantinople entitled *Patria*. Besides these there were handbooks of navigation, guides for pilgrims and catalogues of provinces, cities, metropolitan sees and bishoprics.

7. Philosophy.—Ancient Greek philosophy under the empire sent forth two new shoots—Neopythagoreanism and Neoplatonism. It was the latter with which moribund paganism essayed to stem the advancing tide of Christianity. The last great exponent of this philosophy was Proclus (410-485) in Athens. The dissolution, by order of Justinian I, of the school of philosophy at Athens in 529 was a fatal blow to this nebulous system, which had long outlived the conditions that made it a living force. Nevertheless, it had contributed many ideas to the world of early Christian thought, and contributed essentially to its philosophical framework. In the succeeding period philosophical activity was of two main kinds: on the one hand, the old philosophy, e.g., that of Aristotle, was employed to systematize Christian doctrine; on the other, the old works were furnished with copious commentaries and paraphrases. Leontius of Byzantium introduced Aristotelian definitions into Christology; but the real founder of medieval ecclesiastical philosophy was John of Damascus. As a result, however, of his having early attained to canonical authority, the independent progress of ecclesiastical philosophy was arrested; and to this it is due that in this respect the later Byzantine period is far poorer than the corresponding era in the west. In the 11th century there was a revival of philosophical studies, mainly because of Michael Psellus, who again laid more emphasis on Platonic ideas, as against Aristotelian, and John Italus, who attempted in vain to introduce into Byzantium a philosophy free from the tutelage of theology. The attempt of Gemistus Pletho, about the middle of the 15th century, to introduce, in conjunction with plans for a political restoration, the old pagan religion and the old Platonism also came to nothing.

Ethics was represented in Byzantium by the numerous "mirrors for princes"; in these the prince was exhorted to all the virtues, the prototype being that by the deacon Agapetus (6th century).

8. Rhetoric.—Ancient rhetoric was cultivated in the Byzantine period with greater ardour than scientific philosophy, being regarded as an indispensable aid to education. Among the almost tedious rhetorical productions of the time are to be found a few interesting pieces, such as the short dialogue entitled *Philopatris*, in the style of Lucian, which gives a remarkable picture of the times of Nicephorus Phocas (10th century). Lucian's *Nekyomantia* was also the prototype for the satirical *Mazaris' Journey to Hades* (composed c. 1414–15). An important branch of rhetoric for the Byzantines was the public speech, usually a state speech addressed to the emperor on feast days, particularly at Epiphany. In this field considerable fame was won by the pagan Libanius (d. 393), head of a school of rhetoric at Antioch, who numbered among his pupils John Chrysostom and Basil (afterward bishop of Caesarea) and whose thought profoundly influenced the emperor Julian. Of his writings there survive imperial eulogies, funeral speeches and more than 1,500 declamations and letters. Rhetorically elaborate letters were also considered by the Byzantines as a considerable artistic achievement; collections of them were made so as to preserve them for posterity. There are collected letters also of Photius, Psellus, Eustathius and Michael Choniates, archbishop of Athens, and many other important figures of Byzantine literature. The great number of treatises written on rhetoric also shows the high regard of the Byzantines for this literary form.

9. Scholarship.—Byzantium was dominated to an extravagant extent by the rules of what in modern times is termed classical scholarship. The numerous works which belong to this category, such as grammars, dictionaries, encyclopaedias, commentaries on ancient authors, extracts from ancient literature and metrical and musical treatises, are of little general interest, although of great value for special branches of literary study, *e.g.*, for tracing the influences through which surviving ancient works have passed, as well as for their interpretation and emendation; for information about ancient authors now lost; for the history of education; and for the underlying principles of intellectual life in Byzantium. The most important monument of Byzantine scholarship is perhaps the *Bibliotheca* or *Myriobiblon* of the patriarch Photius, which consists of 280 essays summarizing all he had read. Much literature now lost is thus preserved in epitome. Rather more than a century later appeared the *Suda Lexicon* (sometimes erroneously attributed to "Suidas"), an encyclopaedia including valuable biographical information on classical and Byzantine authors. Eustathius (d. c. 1194), archbishop of Thessalonica, was a commentator on classical texts; various scholia on the *Iliad* and the *Odyssey* and fragments of other lost writings survive in his works.

10. Military Science.—The Byzantines had shown an interest in military science since the time of Arrian (d. c. 180), who wrote an account of the campaigns of Alexander the Great. The *Strategikon*, a book attributed to the emperor Maurice (582–602), shows the changes made in Byzantine tactics in order to meet the attacks of contemporary invaders, the Avars, Persians and Turks. This treatise was several times brought up to date under the names, among others, of the emperors Leo VI and Constantine VII. The emperor Nicephorus Phocas (d. 969) is credited with an original manual on guerrilla warfare.

11. Law.—The emperors Leo VI the Wise and Constantine VII Porphyrogenitus issued the *Basilica*, the Greek translation of the emperor Justinian I's *Institutes* and *Digest*, which had been published in Latin; they were newly arranged and enlarged by the addition of the imperial constitutions of Justinian's *Codex* and its *Novels*, which had been in Greek from the first. The *Peira* is one of the collections of high court judgments which the chief justice Eustathius (11th century) caused to be compiled. The canon law was an important contribution of the Byzantines to jurisprudence.

12. Secular Poetry.—The metre of secular poetry is, for the most part, either the Byzantine regular 12-syllable verse which took the place of the ancient trimeter or the 15-syllable ("political") verse; more rarely the heroic and Anacreontic measures.

Epic popular poetry, in the ancient sense, begins only with the vernacular Greek literature (*see below*); but among the literary works of the period there are several which can be compared with the epics of the Alexandrian age. Nonnus (fl. c. 400) wrote, while still a pagan, an epic on the triumphal progress of the god Dionysus to India, and, as a Christian, a lengthy versification of St. John's Gospel. Paulus Silentiarius (6th century) wrote in perfectly correct Nonnian hexameters a description (*Ekphrasis*) of Hagia Sophia, built by Justinian I; the Church of the Apostles, also a splendid erection of Justinian I, had to wait until 940 to find a less gifted poet in Constantine of Rhodes. The historic epic was still carefully preserved by the Byzantines. In the 7th century George the Pisidian described in several iambic poems the wars of the emperor Heraclius. Later the deacon Theodosius (10th century) immortalized in extravagant language the capture of Crete by the emperor Nicephorus Phocas.

In the 12th-century revival of culture under the Commeni several long poems were composed in imitation of the ancient Greek romances. Two of these are written in the duodecasyllable metre: the story of Rodanthe and Dosicles by Theodore Prodromus, and an imitation of it, the story of Drosilla and Charicles by Nicetas Eugenianus; one in political verse, the love story of Aristander and Callithea by Constantine Manasses, which has only been preserved in fragments; and one in prose, the story of Hysmine and Hysminias by Eustathius Macrembolites. These Byzantine romances are of interest chiefly by way of contrast to the romances in the vernacular produced in the 13th and 14th centuries.

The detached and ascetic point of view which dominated the whole Byzantine period was fatal to the development of secular lyrical poetry. A few poems by John Geometres and Christopher (11th century) of Mytilene and others, in which personal experiences are recorded with some show of feeling, may be placed in this category. The dominant form for all subjective poetry was the epigram, which was employed in all its variations from playful trifles to long elegiac and narrative poems. George the Pisidian treated the most diverse themes epigrammatically. In the 9th century Theodore Studites immortalized monastic life in a series of epigrams. The same century produced the only Byzantine poetess, Casia, who wrote several epigrammatic productions and church hymns. Epigrammatic poetry reached its highest development in the 10th and 11th centuries, in the productions of John Geometres, Christopher of Mytilene and John Mauropus. Less happy are Theodore Prodromus (12th century) and Manuel Philes (14th century). From the beginning of the 10th century also dates the most valuable collection of ancient and of Byzantine epigrammatic poems, the *Anthologia Palatina* (see ANTHOLOGY).

The didactic poem was a much loved form among the Byzantines; this predilection was in line with their tendency, noted above, to instruct their fellow men rather intrusively and to display the fullness of their own knowledge. John Tzetzes wrote metrical commentaries on Homer, Hesiod, Pindar, Aeschylus, Euripides and Aristophanes. Constantine Manasses also composed a verse chronicle of the world of this kind.

Dramatic poetry, in the strict sense of the term, was as completely lacking among the Byzantine Greeks as was the condition necessary for its existence, namely, public performance. Apart from some moralizing allegorical dialogues (by Theodore Prodromus, Manuel Philes and others), the only work of the Byzantine period which resembles a drama, at least in external form is the *Christos paschon*. This cento on the passion, erroneously included among the works of Gregory of Nazianzus but written probably in the 12th century, is largely composed of lines taken from ancient playwrights, e.g., Aeschylus, Euripides and Lycophron; it was certainly not written for dramatic production.

13. Vernacular Literature.—The vernacular literature stands alone, both in form and in content. It shows remarkable originality of conception and probably also entirely new and typically medieval matter. While in the courtly literature prose is preeminent, in the vernacular literature poetry both in quantity and quality takes the first place. Though a few preliminary attempts were known (proverbs, acclamations addressed by the people to the emperor, etc.), longer Greek vernacular works were written down only from the 12th century onward; at first poems, most of which were cast in political verse. Toward the close of the 15th century rhyme came into use. The subjects treated in this vernacular poetry are exceedingly diverse. In Constantinople a mixture of the learned and the popular language was first used in poems of admonition, praise and supplication. To this oldest class (12th century) of vernacular works belongs the *Spaneas*, an admonitory poem in imitation of the letter of Pseudo-Isocrates addressed to Demonicus; a supplicatory poem composed in prison by the chronicler Michael Glycas; and several begging poems of Theodore Prodromus (Ptochoprodromus). In the succeeding period romances written in the artificial classical language, e.g., *Callimachus and Chrysorrhoe*, *Belthandros and Chrysantza*, *Lybistrus and Rhodamne*, also romances in verse after the western pattern such as *Phlorios and Platziaphlora* (the old French story of *Flore et Blanchefleur*), *Imberius and Margarona* and *Apollonius of Tyre*. The well-known stories from the *Physiologus* (see BESTIARY) about animals, plants and stones were put into political verse in this period, and other animal tales in political verse were also popular: *Paidiologus* (a book of birds), a history of animals, both satirical in intent, and a version of Reynard the Fox which relates the adventures of an ass, a wolf and a fox. Other satirical poems are the *Sachlikis*, which originated in 15th-century Crete, and its imitation by Markus Depharanas, also Cretan in origin. There are also several legendary and historical poems in which famous heroes and historical events are celebrated; for instance, poems on the exploits of Belisarius (Justinian I's general), the fall of Constantinople (1453), the taking of Athens (1458), the devastating campaign of Timur, the Chronicle of the Morea (the history of the Frankish government of the Peloponnese, 1204–92), the battle of Varna (1444) and the plague in Rhodes in 1498. The chief of these is the great heroic epic of Digenes Akritas, preserved in several versions, the oldest of which, a linguistic mixture of popular and literary language, dates from the 10th century. There is no doubt, however, that this epic originated among the people and was spread by folk singers before it was written down; large parts of it can still be recited by aged and illiterate people. Digenes Akritas represents the bold frontier warrior (*akrites*) on the Euphrates frontier in the 8th–10th centuries. The conversion of the emir indeed betrays Byzantine piety, and there are numerous oriental touches. But the emir's son, Digenes Akritas, in his feeling for nature and strong family affections has much in common with the Greek palikar of the klephtic ballads (see below). In these respects the poem may be regarded as the forerunner of such works as the great Cretan national romance, the *Erotokritos* (see below) and as forecasting much that is best in modern Greek popular poetry.

(K. K.; F. Dö.)

III. MODERN (AFTER 1453)

1. Language.—After the capture of Constantinople by the Turks in 1453, the destruction of Greek national life and the almost complete effacement of Byzantine civilization naturally involved a more or less complete cessation of Greek literary production in the subjected regions. Learned Greeks found refuge away from their native land; they spoke the languages of foreign peoples and, when they wrote books, they often used the languages of those peoples, though most of them also wrote in Greek.

It is, however, a mistake to regard 1453 as a sharp dividing line between Byzantine and modern Greek literature. As shown above, the germs of modern Greek popular poetry can be detected as early as the 10th century in the epic cycle of Digenes Akritas, and still more in the Greek verse romances of the 13th and 14th centuries. More directly a result of the conquest by the Franks is the chronicle of Leontios Makhairas, which deals with Cyprus in the 15th century. Here again the Greek vernacular language is employed. Italian influence had a predominating share in the production of the flourishing Cretan literature of the 16th and 17th centuries described below. The literary debt of modern Greece to the crusaders should not be overlooked. Among other things, they were responsible for the introduction of rhyming verse.

Modern Greece has inherited two literary styles—the consciously classical, known as the *katharevousa*, and the really living popular, known as the *demotiki*. Both have been greatly promoted by the invigorating influence of Italian and French literature. In the progress of these two literary streams the demotic of the 1880s reached a turning point when a group of young and gifted writers, the most important of whom was Kostis Palamas (1859–1943), founded the so-called "new school of Athens." This school was a reaction against the dead and conventional classical language and the flabby exuberance of the Greek romantics. In 1888 Ioannes Psycharis (1854–1929) became the leader of the movement with the publication of his famous book *To taxidi mou* (ostensibly a series of traveling impressions, but really intended to awaken the linguistic conscience of the Greeks). The battle flared up, and a number of distinguished critics, scholars and writers joined the struggle, which broadened into a reaction against the dead weight of the whole classical tradition, and advocated a return of Greek art and literature to contemporary life. This was greatly helped by the study of modern Greek folklore, then promoted by Nikolaos Politis (1852–1942), and by the researches of Konstantinos Paparrhigopoulos (1815–91) into medieval and modern Greek history. The battle ended with the decisive victory of the popular language, the *demotiki*, for all writings of an imaginative character. Even in works of science and in official documents its influence became increasingly felt.

The classical language was unsuited for the production of a really living drama. Hence, although numerous plays were written in the 19th century both in verse and in prose, only two names of older dramatists need be mentioned, Dimetrios Vernardakis (1834–1907) and Spyridon Vasiliadis (1844–74). The employment of the demotic and the choice of themes relating to contemporary life gave plays fresh vitality and did much toward the foundation of a national drama. G. Xenopoulos was the inaugurator of this. Together with him mention should be made of I. Kambysis (1872–1902), S. Melas (1883–1965), T. Moraitinis (1875–), N. Laskaris (1868–1945), P. Horn (1881–1941), D. Bogris (1890–), T. Synadinos, A. Terzakis (1906–) and G. Theotokas. A number of distinguished Greek poets like K. Palamas, A. Sikelianos and N. Kazantzakis have also written for the theatre, but their plays are more notable for their lyrical than for their dramatic qualities.

It is convenient to treat poetry and prose in two different sections, since few writers have distinguished themselves in both.

2. Poetry.—From the fall of Constantinople till the War of Greek Independence (1821–29) the most arresting poetry appeared in the Greek lands occupied by the Franks. The beginnings of modern Greek lyric poetry can be traced to Rhodes and Cyprus, then under the rule of the Knights Templar and the Lusignans.

Cretan Literature.—It was in Crete, however, that the most vigorous and remarkable literature flourished in the 16th and 17th centuries, when the island was under Venetian occupation; this was brought to a premature close by the Turkish capture of Candia in 1669. The progress made in versification can be traced from the unpolished, rhymed 15-syllable political lines of Georgios Choumis in his paraphrase of Genesis and Exodus, written early in the 16th century, to the finished handling of the same metre by Vikentios Kornaros in his great romantic poem *Erotokritos*, which probably dates from the middle of the 17th century and describes the trials and sorrows of two lovers, Erotokritos and Aretousa, whose love story is finally crowned with a happy ending. Though based on a French work, *Paris et Vienne*, which Kornaros probably knew through an Italian version, the *Erotokritos* has many purely Greek and local Cretan elements and can be fairly called "the national poem of Crete". In connection with this should be mentioned an interesting series of Cretan dramas. The best known, though not the best, of these is the *Erophili* of Georgios Chortatzis, inspired by G. B. Giraldi's *Orbecche* and written c. 1600. It describes the tragic history of the love of Panaretos, adopted at an early age into the court of King Philogonos of Egypt, for the princess Erophili, which results in the violent death of all three principal characters. These Cretan plays also include comedies, such as the *Stathis* and *Fortounatos* (17th century) which, though in the main borrowed from Italian and ultimately going back to Plautine and Terentian comedy, are interesting for the introduction of local characters and colouring. But the real gems of the Cretan drama are the pastoral comedy *Gyparis* and the mystery play *Thysia tou Abraam*, on the sacrifice of Abraham, also based on an Italian model, the *Isach* (1586) by L. Groto. Both are anonymous, though Kornaros has been supposed by some modern scholars to be the author of the mystery play. The *Gyparis* dates from c. 1600 and describes in a masterly and humorous manner the conversion to love of two shepherdesses, who had previously scorned it. In many respects it is extraordinarily modern. The *Thysia tou Abraam*, though in form a mystery play, is really a highly sympathetic study of family life. It is said to have been printed as early as 1535, but this may well be a mistake for 1635. Crete possesses an interesting series of popular songs, and in connection with these a charming pastoral poem, *I oraia voskopoula*. It is usually coupled with the name of Nikolaos Drymitinos, who published the version he selected in 1627. The language of this attractive Cretan literature has naturally incorporated a good many Venetian words, but its general character is that of a vigorous native tongue with a number of peculiar Cretan forms and idioms. Had Crete not been captured by the Turks in 1660, the course of the whole of modern Greek literature would probably have been quite different.

Folk Songs and Klephtic Ballads.—In those parts of the Greek world under Turkish domination, the only noteworthy poetry is to be found in the folk songs and the klephtic ballads (the klepht was an armed Greek living as a free man and an outlaw). The roots and subject of many of these go back to the Byzantine era and one, the *Chelidonisma*, has even been traced as far back as Greek antiquity. Greek folk songs fall into three main divisions: (1) The historical folk songs, treating of historical events as they caught the imagination of the people. The Akritic ballads, as sung in Asia Minor, the Aegean islands and Cyprus, the laments on the fall of Constantinople and certain klephtic ballads are among the most notable of this group. (2) The songs of everyday life, i.e., love songs, lullabies, marriage songs, working songs, dirges and carols. Here strong family feeling predominates. Death is personified in the form of Charos who struggles with his victim, is sometimes worsted, but as a rule triumphs in the conflict. (3) The *paralogis*, short narratives of a swift epic character, often almost summaries of folk traditions or folk tales. Some of the most beautiful and vivid verse written in Greek is to be found in the folk songs and the klephtic ballads. Most of the latter date from the 18th century and are excellent examples of an entirely spontaneous poetry composed in popular language and in the 15-syllable verse, rhymed and unrhymed. They are pervaded with the spirit of the forests and the mountains and, like so much of Greek popular poetry, personify trees, rocks and rivers. Even the mountains sing the prowess of the klephts, bewail their death and comfort the disconsolate wife or mother. Klephtic ballads have been a source of constant inspiration and rejuvenation to modern Greek poetry.

The Phanariotes.—The 18th century witnessed, side by side with the folk songs, the development of a different type of literature in the urban and cultivated society of the Phanariotes (the Greeks who gathered round the ecumenical patriarch in Constantinople). This can be seen as an endeavour to continue the classical Byzantine tradition and to link it with the great literatures of the west, notably that of France. Until the 1830s very little poetry of any value was produced from this source. But mention should be made of Kaisarios Dapontis (1714–74), whose long works of a moralizing and religious character, especially *Kathreptis ton gynaikon* ("Mirror of Ladies") and *Kipos Chariton* ("The Garden of Graces"), were praised and imitated by his contemporaries; of Rhigas (1757–98), whose patriotic poetry enjoyed widespread popularity; and also of Athanasios Christopoulos (1772–1849) and Ioannis Vilaras (1771–1823), in whose writings the influence of the Anacreontics and the 18th-century French drawing-room bucolics can be clearly seen. Vilaras is of particular interest, because the application to his verse of the extreme linguistic ideas expressed in his book *Romeiki glossa* led him to link personal lyric poetry with the folk-song tradition.

The Greek Romantics.—The liberation of Greece from the Turks (1828) made the capital of the new kingdom the centre of all Greek political and intellectual life. The Phanariotes moved first to Nauplia and then to Athens, mingling with the Greeks who came from the west to their newly freed country, and with the leading families that had fought and distinguished themselves during the War of Independence. In this mixed and unsettled society the romantic school of Athens flourished; its founder and leading spirit was Alexandros Soutsos (1803–63). He studied in Paris, where he came under the influence of the French romantics, but his exuberant and patriotic writings never succeeded in capturing the spirit of his models. As a satirist, however, he is often terse and vigorous. The influence he exercised upon Greek poetry was felt for many years. The other main representatives of the earlier days of the romantic school of Athens, his brother Panagiotis Soutsos (1806–68), Alexandros Rizos Rangavis (1809–92), Georgios Zalokostas (1805–58), Theodoros Orphanidis (1817–86), Elias Tantalidis (1818–76) and Ioannis Karasoutsas (1824–73), though their poetry varies in quality and character, are all slaves of a boundless romanticism, use mainly the *katharevousa* as their language and are painstakingly patriotic. Among them Rangavis is perhaps the most striking figure. A man of extraordinary fertility of mind, he achieved considerable charm in the classical style. His works include odes, hymns, ballads, narrative poems, tragedies and comedies and several prose works. Achilles Paraschos (1838–95) is the leading figure in the last period of the school. Alfred de Musset, Victor Hugo and Lord Byron were his idols, but the rhetorical profuseness and mock-heroic patriotism of his verses prevent him from ever rising to their level, though a spark of true poetry is often evident. His brother Georgios Paraschos (1822–86) and his contemporaries Angelos Vlachos (1838–1920), Alexandros Vyzantios (1841–98), Dimitrios Paparrigopoulos (1843–73) and Georgios Vizyinos (1849–96) were all overshadowed by his reputation, in spite of the greater sincerity and more delicate technique evident in many of their writings.

The School of the Ionian Islands.—Another school of poetry, parallel to the romantics of Athens, flourished in the Ionian islands, which were under British rule till 1864. Its founder and greatest representative was Dionysios Solomos (1798–1857), a native of Zante. Like others of the Ionian aristocracy of his day he was practically bilingual, and, having received his education in Italy, wrote his first poems in Italian. He soon, however, developed a preference for Greek. His early works in Greek were short lyrics, but the War of Independence stirred him to more ambitious projects. As the years passed, his philosophic approach to art and life deepened and expressed itself in verses of great delicacy and balance, unsurpassed in modern Greek. From the hymn of liberty (the first stanzas of which became the Greek national anthem) to *Hoi eleutheroi poliorkimenoi* ("Free Besieged"), which sings of the heroic resistance and sally at Missolonghi, the development of a highly spiritual nature can be traced. Unfortunately most of his mature work is known only from fragments, since his temperamental instability seems to have prevented him from finishing any of his major works. In the struggle that continued from Byzantine days between the *katharevousa* and the *demotiki* as the language of literature, Solomos marks a turning point. For, by choosing the latter, he pointed the way which Greek poetry was to follow after the demotic movement of the 1880s. Moreover, he introduced a number of western metrical forms (the sestina, the ottava rima, the *terza rima*, etc.), thus freeing Greek poetry from the monotony of the 15-syllable political verse mainly in use previously. Of the other poets of the Ionian school, Georgios Tertsetis (1800–74), Ioulios Typaldos (1814–83), Gerasimos Markoras (1826–1911) and Lorenzos Mavilis (1860–1912) must be mentioned, but undoubtedly Andreas Kalvos (1792–1869) and Aristotelis Valaoritis (1824–79) are the most distinguished. Kalvos drew his inspiration from the Greek classics and indulged in an austere and moralizing poetry and in a classicizing form of language, without exercising any notable influence on subsequent literature. Valaoritis, on the other hand, though deeply romantic and often too grandiloquent, was greatly admired by his contemporaries and is one of the authors who influenced Kostis Palamas in adopting the spoken tongue as the language of poetry. Thus Valaoritis became the link that connects the Ionian school with the new school of Athens.

The New School of Athens.—The feeling that Greek poetry, by employing the stilted *katharevousa* and by indulging in the weaker side of the romantic movement, was heading for utter sterility stirred a group of young poets to form about 1880 the new school of Athens. They aspired to become Greek Parnassians, masters of a restrained and objective art, but at the same time drawing their inspiration from contemporary Greece and using the living idiom. The central figure of this new school was Kostis Palamas (1859–1943), a man of versatile talent and wide reading. His many important poetic works portray modern Greek life, the continuity of Greek history and the social and spiritual convulsions of the late 19th and early 20th centuries. The long philosophic poem *Dodecalogos tou Gyftou*, perhaps his greatest achievement, shows the gypsy musician, symbol of freedom and art, gradually deepening into the patriot, the Greek and, finally, into the "Hellene," citizen and teacher of the world. His powerful epico-lyric work *I flogera tou Vasilia* and his collection of lyrics have established his reputation throughout the western world, and his influence upon all subsequent Greek literature has been profound. In poetry his distinguished contemporaries Georgios Drosinis (1859–1952), Ioannis Polemis (1862–1922) and Kostas Krystallis (1868–94), as well as his immediate successors Ioannis Gryparis (1871–1942), Kostas Chatzopoulos (1871–1920), Miltiadis Malakasis (1870–1943), Lambros Porfyras (1879–1932), Sotiris Skipis (1881–1951) and Z. Papandoniou (1877–1940), all acknowledged their debt to the leader of the school. It is the poets of this school who have explored the expressive and metrical possibilities of the spoken idiom and who introduced symbolism and free verse into Greek poetry, which has greatly enriched and enlivened it in the course of the 20th century. Of the women writers of the new school of Athens, Myrtiotissa (Theoni Dracopoulos; b. 1883), Aimilia S. Dafni (Aimilia T. Zoïopoulos; 1887–1941) and Maria Polydouri (1905–30) are noteworthy for the elegance and passion of their verses.

After Palamas, the most important figure in modern Greek poetry is undoubtedly Angelos Sikelianos. His vigorous verse has its roots in the new school of Athens, but his thought followed a different and often more obscure course. Greek nature and history are seen in the light of a Dionysiac mysticism. His rich incisive diction brings landscape and human form in clear-cut relief before the eyes.

The one great Greek poet who remained untouched by the influence of Palamas and the new school of Athens was Konstantinos Kavafes (Cavafy). An Alexandrian both by birth and by spiritual inclination, his main theme was the tragic glory of Hellenistic Greece and its decadence. But in his work historical memories and personal experiences were inextricably blended. In no other Greek poet is the tragedy of life so sensually expressed or sensuality felt more tragically, although the tragic outlook is relieved by exquisitely lyrical and often ironical passages. His writings, because of their reflection of modern tendencies in western culture, have been universally acknowledged.

Of the many other poets who wrote in Greece after the end of World War I, four only can be mentioned here: Kostas Karyotakis (1897–1928), whose pessimistic and often sarcastic poems are most arresting; George Seferis (1900–71), a genuine Symbolist, who records with true poetic touch the fate of modern man; the Surrealist Odysseus Elytis (1911–), whose lines are full of light and colour of the Aegean Islands; and Nikos Kazantzakis, better known as a novelist, who is also the author of a formidable "epic" poem *Odyssey*. Its hero, a modern Odysseus, wandering in the world of thought, seems to be haunted by the idea of nihilism. The size and style of the work are overwhelming, but there are long passages of great beauty and a use of language of extreme wealth and vigour.

Modern Greek poetry is mainly lyrical, and little satirical and hardly any dramatic verse of merit has been written. The satire of Andreas Laskaratos (1811–1901) and Georgios Souris (1853–1919)—who created a peculiar form of political satire in his weekly paper *Romios*—must be recorded, but it has lost much of its flavour. The chief poets who emerged after World War II, mainly Symbolists, Surrealists, or "poets of the absurd," were Georgios Themelis, Miltos Sachtouris, Zoï Karelli, Dimitrios Papaditsas, Takis Sinopoulos and Takis Varvitsiotis.

3. Prose.—After the fall of Constantinople Greek scholars helped to spread the knowledge of Greek to the west and stimulated the study of ancient philosophy. Encouragement was given to Greek culture in the 16th and 17th centuries by the Ecumenical Patriarchate of Constantinople, by the founding of schools in Constantinople, Bucharest and Jassy (Rumania) and by the printing of works in Greek by the hospodars (rulers) of Walachia. In the 18th century this educational work was continued and modern Greece owes a debt of gratitude to the Greek clergy, to the great Phanariote families of Constantinople and also to wealthy Greek merchants, who fostered schools and issued educational works in Greek from the printing presses of Venice, Trieste and Vienna. This work had an important influence in preparing the Greeks for their emancipation from Turkey. Most of the literature of this period was theological, but a good many books of an educational character were also produced. Representative names are those of the ecclesiastics Elias Meniatis (1669–1714) from Cephalonia, who lived and wrote in Venice; and Nikephoros Theotokis (1736–1800) and Eugenios Vulgaris (1716–1806), both natives of Corfu, who wrote in the literary language in defense of Greek Orthodoxy, but also produced works of mathematics, physics, geography, archaeology and philosophy in addition to translations. These men may seem to lack originality and their language may be on the whole artificial, but their work was of inestimable value to the Greek people in the dark conditions surrounding them at the time. The greatest name, however, among the forerunners of the Greek revival is that of Adamantios Korais (1748–1833) who, though he spent most of his life in Paris, exercised an enormous influence on his Greek contemporaries, partly by his unwearying issue of editions of classical Greek authors accompanied by stirring patriotic introductions, and partly by his efforts to reform the written language by assimilating the literary tongue with the living idiom of modern Greece.

From the Liberation to 1888.—In the first decades that followed the liberation of Greece, prose was confined mainly to journalism and scholarship. The few writers of creative literature turned to the west for their models and were attracted first by Sir Walter Scott, whose reputation was paramount on the continent at the time, and later by Alexandre Dumas the Elder, some of whose works were translated into modern Greek by Ioannis Skylitsis (1819–90). This accounts for the popularity in Greece of the historical novel between the years 1821 and 1888. Its most distinguished representatives, all of whom used a more or less austere *katharevousa*, were Alexandros Rizos Rangavis, Emmanouil Rhoidis (1835–1904), Spyridon Zambelios (1813–81) and Dimitrios Vikelas (1835–1908). Three novels call for special mention: Rangavis' *Authentis tou Moreos* ("Lord of the Morea"), dealing with the Frankish occupation of the Morea, Rhoidis' vivid historical-satirical novel about Pope Joan (1865) and Vikelas' *Loukis Laras* (1879), an attractive romance dealing with the massacre of Chios in 1822. In addition, the short story in the *katharevousa* was cultivated in this and the subsequent period by a number of writers, perhaps the most important of whom are Georgios Vizyinos (1848–94) and Ioannis Kondylakis (1861–1920).

The same period witnessed the development of a remarkable classical style by certain distinguished scholars. Two works of major importance stand out: the history of the Greek revolution by Spyridon Trikoupis (1788–1873) and the history of the Greek nation by Konstantinos Paparrigopoulos (1815–91), both of which are not only based on independent research and scholarly accuracy but also are written in a balanced and flowing style. Alongside them may be mentioned the writers of memoirs of the Greek War of Independence, and especially Gen. Ioannis Makryiannis (1797–1864), who writes in a vivid and personal demotic idiom and shows a keen perspicacity and objectivity.

The 20th Century.—With the publication in 1888 of *To taxidi mou* by Ioannis Psycharis (1854–1929) and the development of the demotic movement, modern Greek prose underwent a momentous change. For the outcome of the resulting long and bitter linguistic and literary battle was complete victory for the use of the vernacular not only in poetry but also in all prose works of an imaginative character. The writers of that period, helped by the researches in modern Greek folklore of Nikolaos Politis (1852–1921), turned to their "living roots" for inspiration, finding them in the life of the Greek village. Greece in the 1880s was still mainly inhabited by agricultural and seafaring communities, and had no large towns, with the possible exception of Athens. So the character of this new prose, which turned to the Greek countryside for inspiration, became preponderantly "pastoral," and this tendency continued till the turn of the century, when a more developed urban life made itself felt. A forerunner of the pastoral trend can be found in Pavlos Kalligas (1814–96), the distinguished jurist, whose novel *Thanos Vlekas* (1855) described in an austere *katharevousa* the unsettled conditions of the Greek countryside in the days following the liberation of Greece. But the novel found no successors till after the 1880s when Alexandros Papadiamantis (1851–1911) and Andreas Karkavitsas (1866–1923) distinguished themselves with their tales of villagers and fisherfolk. Papadiamantis, a native of Skiathos, is undoubtedly the greatest modern Greek short-story writer. In a personal and slightly archaic idiom he examined the psychology of the simple island people and described some moving incidents in their lives. His short novel *Fonissa*, one of the outstanding books in modern Greek literature, deals with an old woman of Skiathos who suffered so much herself and saw her daughters and all the women of the island so full of misery that she decided to kill all baby girls she could lay her hands on. The short stories of Karkavitsas, though different in texture, are of an almost equal emotional power. But his greatest achievement is his realistic novel *Zitianos* ("The Beggar"). Another important contemporary work is the biographical novel of Konstantinos Theotokis (1872–1923), *Zoï kai thanatos tou Karabela*, notable for its forceful realism and psychological insight. The "pastoral" short story also flourished in the hands of G. Drosinis (1859–1952), A. Eftaliotis (1849–1924), J. Vlachogiannis (1867–1945), C. Christovasilis (1861–1937), A. Travlandonis (1867–1943), D. Tangopoulos (1860–1926) and Z. Papandoniou (1877–1940).

The great social and economic changes that Greece underwent at the end of the 19th century soon found reflection in its literature. The expanding middle classes and the ensuing development of city life fostered the development of an "urban" literature hitherto unknown. This was also aided by Greek translations of French novels on big-city life, notably those by Émile Zola. Thus the urban novel was introduced into Greek literature by two writers of very different background and genius: first by Psycharis, whose cosmopolitan background was most appropriate for the development of such a literary genre, and second by Gregorios Xenopoulos (1867–1951), the gifted and prolific writer from Zante. The novels of Psycharis (the most successful of which is *To Oneiro tou Yianniri*, 1897) undoubtedly exercised a great influence upon contemporary Greek writers, but they are faulty in

construction, the heroes never come to life and the deep egotism of the author makes them difficult to enjoy. Xenopoulos, on the other hand, who had to earn a living out of his writing, serialized many of his works in Athenian newspapers, and so too often had to pander to the taste of his readers. His two best sellers were *Foteini Sandri* (*O kokkinos Vrachos*) and *Stella Violanti*. Psycharis and Xenopoulos were followed in their urban writings by Konstantinos Christomanos (1867–1911; the friend and secretary of the empress Elizabeth of Austria-Hungary) whose *Kerenia koukla* is full of delicacy and true feeling. At the same time Kostas Chatzopoulos (1871–1920) gave Greek literature its one Symbolist novel before 1920, *Fthinoporo* ("Autumn", 1917).

The end of World War I saw a group of young writers such as D. Voutieridis, Petros Pikros, Thrasos Kastanakis, Nikos Nikolaidis and Photis Kondoglou, who paved the way for the prose writers of the 1930s, when prose in the vernacular achieved maturity and novels of real significance appeared for the first time in Greek. Only a few of many important writers can be mentioned here. The first was Stratis Myrivilis, who took the literary scene by storm with his book *Zoï en tapho*, composed of a series of war impressions from the Macedonian front in the form of letters from a dead friend of the author to a girl in Lesbos. Myrivilis writes in a lively and robust demotic, in which dialectal and lyrical elements abound. His second and more mature novel, *Daskala me ta chrysa matia*, connected with the Asia Minor campaign which ended in the Greek defeat of 1922, was followed by many shorter stories of power and originality. His long novel *Panagia gorgona* (1955) treats of the life of a group of Greek refuggees from Asia Minor in a small village of Lesbos and concludes what modern Greek literary criticism calls the "war trilogy" of Myrivilis. Like Myrivilis, Elias Venezis (1904–) made his appearance with a striking book on his life as a prisoner of the Turks in 1922–23, called *Noumero 31328*. Of his important publications that followed, the most significant was his long novel *Aiolia*, full of childhood memories. The style of Venezis is less arresting than that of Myrivilis, and his mood on the whole more nostalgic, but clarity, beauty and humanity abound in his writings. One of the most gifted authors of the 1930s was Kosmas Politis (P. Taveloudis; 1888–), who in his *Eroica* (1938), a book on the actions and reactions of a gang of children, as well as in his later novels *Lemonodasos* and *Gyri*, proved himself a master of the long narrative. His psychological analysis of his heroes and his descriptions of natural beauty rank high in modern Greek literature. Georgios Theotokas' long novel *Argo* (1936), and his many other writings—essays, short stories, travel books, plays—show him to be a writer of ability and versatility and one of the best writers of a flowing and simple demotic. Other authors include A. Petsalis, A. Terzakis, P. Prevelakis, M. Karagatsis, T. Stavrou and Kleareti-Dipla Malamou.

After World War II the prewar generation remained the models for younger writers of both poetry and prose. Their continuing influence was exemplified in the achievement of Nikos Kazantzakis (1885–1957), who at an advanced age and after a long literary career—lyric and epic poetry, travel books, dramas, philosophical and critical essays—turned to the novel and achieved international recognition. His novels show outstanding creative powers and a full mastery of his medium. In spite of certain crudities, Kazantzakis is one of the great masters of Greek demotic prose, whose wealth and vigour he deeply explored.

Real literary merit was in many instances achieved by the *Chronografema*, a column in certain Athens newspapers treating of some daily event in a humorous or lyrical manner. In the hands of writers like P. Nirvanas (Petros Apostolides; 1886–1937) or S. Melas (1883–1965) it transcended the boundaries of journalism. The younger generation of writers which emerged from World War II and the ravages of the civil war of the 1940s had found its own voice by the 1960s. Vasilis Vassilikos, Rodis Provelengios, Nikos Kazdaglis, and Kostas Tachtsis should be singled out for their use of prose as well as for their imaginative powers. Renos Apostolidis and Spyros Plaskovitis are mainly notable as short story writers.

See also GREEK LANGUAGE, articles on individual authors, and references under "Greek Literature" in the Index.

BIBLIOGRAPHY.—Ancient: General Studies: The fullest account to the end of the 5th century B.C. is W. Schmid and O. Stählin, Geschichte der griechischen Literatur, 5 vol. (1929–48); A. Lesky, Geschichte der griechischen Literatur (1957), covers the whole subject. Gilbert Murray, Ancient Greek Literature (1897), is still inspiring. See also H. J. Rose, A Handbook of Greek Literature, 4th ed. (1950), and M. Hadas, A History of Greek Literature (1950). For detailed information on authors and topics see Pauly-Wissowa, Real-Encyclopädie der classischen Altertumswissenschaft (1893 et seq.), contains chapters on development in many departments of the subject with valuable bibliographies. For bibliography to date see J. Marouzeau, L'Année philologique, published annually. Special Studies: A. Koerte, Hellenistic Poetry (1929); U. von Wilamowitz-Moellendorff, Hellenistische Dichtung, 2 vol. (1924); C. M. Bowra, Greek Lyric Poetry From Alcman to Simonides (1936), The Early Greek Elegists (1938); E. Rohde, Der griechische Roman, 3rd ed. (1914). See also bibliographies to relevant sections of DRAMA and to the articles on individual authors. (D. W. Ls.)

Byzantine: General Studies: K. Krumbacher, Geschichte der byzantinischen Literatur, 2nd ed. (1897); K. Dieterich, Geschichte der byzantinischen und neugriechischen Literatur, 2nd ed. (1909); J. M. Marshall, "Byzantine Literature" in N. H. Baynes and H. St. L. B. Moss, Byzantium (1948); for the period 100–530 see W. von Christ, Geschichte der griechischen Literatur, part 2, vol. 2, 6th ed. (1909). For periodicals specializing in Byzantine studies see Byzantinische Zeitschrift (1892 et seq.) giving current bibliography; Byzantion (1924 et seq.); Byzantinoslavica (1919 et seq.); Ἐπετηρὶς ἑταιρείας Βυζαντινῶν σπουδῶν (1924 et seq.); Orientalia Christiana periodica (1935 et seq.); Dumbarton Oaks Papers (1940 et seq.); Studi bizantini e neoellenici (1924 et seq.); Zbornik radova vizantološki Institut (1952 et seq.). Anthologies: W. Christ and M. Paranikas, Anthologia Graeca carminum christianorum (1871); R. Cantarella, Poeti bizantini, 2 vol. (1948); G. Soyter, Byzantinische Dichtung (1938); C. A. Trypanis, Medieval and Modern Greek Poetry (1951); D. A. Zakythinos, Βυζαντινὰ κείμενα (1951); E. Kriaras, Βυζαντινὰ ἱπποτικὰ μυθιστορήματα (1955); G. T. Zoras, Βυζαντινὴ ποίησις (1956); the last two publications contain most of the vernacular poems mentioned; the remainder are edited as follows: Achilleis, ed. by B. Haag (1919); Lybistrus and Rhodamne, ed. by J. A. Lambert (1936); history of the donkey, wolf and fox, ed. by L. Alexiu in Κρητικὰ Χρονικά, vol. 9 (1955); Dephrasmos, ed. by S. Karaiskakis in Λαογραφία, vol. 11 (1934); Song of Belisarius, ed. by L. Cantarella in Studi bizantini e neoellenici, vol. 4 (1935); M. Pichard, Le roman de Callimaque et de Chrysorrhoe (1958); G. T. Zoras, Ἱστορία πτωχολέοντος (1959); S. Krawczynski, Ὁ πουλολόγος (1960); chronicle of the Morea, ed. by P. P. Kalonaros (1940); battle of Varna, ed. by G. Moravcsik (1935). Special Studies: H. G. Beck, Kirche und theologische Literatur im byzantinischen Reich (1959); B. Altaner, Patrology (1960); B. Tatakis, La Philosophie byzantine (1949); F. Dölger, Die byzantinische Dichtung in der Reinsprache, 2nd ed. (1961); E. Colonna, Gli storici bizantini dal IV al XV secolo (1957); G. Moravcsik, Byzantinoturcica, 2nd ed., 2 vol. (1958). For the influence of Byzantine literature see P. Courcelle, Les Lettres grecques en occident de Macrobe à Cassiodore, 2nd ed. (1948); A. Siegmund, Die Überlieferung der griechischen christlichen Literatur in der lateinischen Kirche bis zum 12. Jahrhundert (1949); F. Dölger, "Byzanz und das Abendland vor den Kreuzzügen," Relazioni del x congresso internazionale di scienze storiche, vol. 3, pp. 67–112 (1955). (K. K.; F. Dö.)

Modern: General Studies: K. N. Sathas, Νεοελληνικὴ φιλολογία, Βιογραφίαι ἐν τοῖς γράμμασι διαλαμψάντων Ἑλλήνων (1868); D. C. Hesseling, Geschiedenis der nieugriekse letterkunde (1921); French trans., Histoire de la littérature grecque moderne (1924); K. T. Demaras, Ἱστορία τῆς νεοελληνικῆς λογοτεχνίας (1952); S. Baud-Bovy, Poésie de la Grèce moderne (1946); A. Mirambel, La Littérature grecque moderne (1953); B. Knös, L'histoire de la littérature néogrecque (1962). For lists of Greek books in the 15th to 17th centuries see E. Legrand, Bibliographie Hellénique (1885–1928). For more recent publications see Collection de l'Institut français d'Athènes, Bulletin analytique de bibliographie hellénique (1946 et seq.). Special Studies: H. Pernot, Études de littérature grecque moderne (two series, 1916, 1918). A. Sachinis, Ἀναζητήσεις νεοελληνικῆς πεζογραφίας (1945); Πεζογραφία τῆς κατοχῆς (1948); Συγχρόνη πεζογραφία μας (1951); Τὸ ἱστορικὸ μυθιστόρημα (1957); C. A. Trypanis, Medieval and Modern Greek Poetry (1951); S. Hammer, Neograeca (1920); P. Sherrard, Modern Greek Poetry (1951); S. Hammer, The Marble Threshing Floor (1956); E. Keeley, and P. Sherrard, Six Poets of Modern Greece (1960). Cretan Literature: S. A. Xanthoudidis' edition of Kornaros Erotokritos (1915) is epoch making; see also his edition of Foscolo's Fortounatos (1922). For Cretan plays see K. N. Sathas, Κρητικὸ θέατρο (1897); J. Mavrogordato, "The Greek Drama in Crete," Journal of Hellenistic Studies, vol. 48 (1928); G. Megas, Θυσία τοῦ Ἀβραάμ (1943); F. H. Marshall and J. Mavrogordato, Three Cretan Plays (1929); F. H. Marshall, Klephtic Ballads and Folk Songs: E. Legrand, Chansons populaires grecques (1874); A. Passow, Popularia carmina Graeciae recentioris (1860); N. G. Politis, Ἐκλογαὶ ἀπὸ τὰ τραγούδια τοῦ ἑλληνικοῦ λαοῦ (1932); G. M. Apostolakis, Τὰ δημοτικὰ τραγούδια (1929); H. Pernot, Chansons populaires des XVe et XVIe siècles (1931). (CE. A. T.)

GREEK MUSIC

GREEK MUSIC (ANCIENT)

GREEK MUSIC (ANCIENT). The literature of Greco-Latin antiquity and the Church Fathers, the plastic and graphic representations and the findings of archaeology indicate an ancient Greek musical culture extending over more than 2,000 years.

History.—Heroic Age (c. 2000–c. 1100 B.C.).—The first Greek-speaking European peoples reached Greece about 2000 B.C., doubtless bringing their folk music with them. Greece thenceforth gradually came under the Minoan (Cretan) influence, with its Aegean and Egyptian elements, and about 1550 this influence promoted the first distinctively Greek culture, the Mycenaean. Greece early obtained from the Mediterranean area both instruments and musical and dance forms. Mycenaean remains include fragments of a lyre of Cretan type, while a smaller lyre (Phoenician type) and a bronze trumpet indicate Asiatic influence. Musical life was characterized by a strong ritual element.

Dark Age (c. 1100–c. 850 B.C.).—The Mycenaean and Minoan cultures declined with the invasion of the Dorians from Asia Minor, and myths indicate extensive new foreign influences. The legend in which the Greek Apollo flays the Phrygian Marsyas recalls the Greek preference for the lyre, the instrument of the Apollo cult, above the aulos or reed pipe, an instrument associated with the wine-god Dionysus. The precedence of lyre over pipe would seem to foreshadow the supremacy of reason in the artistic life of classical times. The Asiatic influence was nonetheless substantial. Tradition says the Phrygian Olympus (c. 900 B.C.) introduced the dactylic metre, the enharmonic genus, the aulos and melody patterns called nomos (pl. nomoi).

Early Classical Period (c. 850–c. 600 B.C.).—From Homer's time, Greek music was closely based on poetry. Poet-musicians, the professional bards of noble families, chanted epics in recitative style, accompanying themselves on the cithara (lyre). The nomos on a prescribed melody pattern gave rise to solo (non-recitative) vocal compositions that were cyclic in form without strophic repetitions, had a prescribed number of movements and were accompanied by the reed pipe or the lyre. There was also a purely instrumental nomos for the reed pipe, with descriptive associations. The dithyramb was originally a strophic melody sung by Dionysus worshipers. It developed into a choral genre c. 600 B.C., when it was sung and danced to the reed pipe by a circular chorus of 50 men and boys. Hymns and dances were also performed chorally in other cults, and at weddings and funerals, and were sometimes accompanied by the bardic lyre. Music also figured in the competitive festivals: the Olympia from 776 B.C. and later the Delphic Pythia, the Spartan Carnea and the Panathenia. From the 7th century, after the Homeric epics were committed to writing, poets turned to more popular themes sung to a smaller lyre called lyra, whence modern "lyric" poetry derives its name; others wrote for choral performance. Important among lyric poet-musicians were Archilochus of Paros (fl. 716–676 B.C.), Tyrtaeus (fl. till 668), Alcaeus (fl. from 611), Sappho (fl. c. 600) and Anacreon (550–465).

Classical Period (c. 600–c. 400 B.C.).—Greek culture now created the classical drama, developed certain basic attitudes to music and reached its zenith in Athens. The plays were essentially musicodramatic works written by poet-musicians, but descended from the cult rituals. Tragoedia (tragedy) means literally "goat song," after the ritual of the Dionysian dithyramb, while comedy kept the latter's ritual trappings (masks, etc.). The drama was at first mainly choral, though the chorus also gave a semicircular dance (orchesis) on that part of the stage called orchestra. The single actor was earlier the leader of the dithyrambic dance choir. A second actor was introduced by Aeschylus (525?–456) and a third by Sophocles (495?–406). The spoken dialogue alternated with solo songs (with lyre) or choruses (unaccompanied, or with

Music, with the other arts, was regarded as inspired by the nine Muses. The Greek word *mousike* had two meanings: first, it meant the culture of the intellectual faculties, which, with *gymnastike*, or bodily culture, provided a liberal education; and second—a meaning more comparable with the modern one—it signified the poetic text, its melody and the accompanying dance. The morally uplifting influence of music was taught by the school of Pythagoras (c. 585–c. 479), which thought it possible, by means of sensual harmony, to re-establish the primary intellectual harmony of the soul; *i.e.*, the harmony inhabiting the heavens before animating human bodies. Hence the doctrines of the harmony of the spheres, the *ethos* or characteristic influence of the various musical modes and the efficacy of numbers.

Late Antiquity (c. 400 B.C. to the Fall of the Roman Empire in the West, A.D. 476).—The 4th century B.C. saw the emergence of Greek science and the first formulations of music theory. The most practical approach was that of Aristoxenus (fl. late 4th century B.C.), while Euclid (c. 300) expounded Pythagorean theory and Plato (427–347) wrote on important musical themes. Theory received further serious attention only from the 1st century A.D., the most important work being that of Ptolemy, the neo-Pythagorean mathematician and astronomer (2nd century A.D.). Before the first theory was written, however, music and poetry had begun to diverge, and the styles of Aristophanes (c. 450–c. 388 B.C.), Miletus (fl. c. 400) and Philoxenus (430–380) show a progressively popular trend, after which drama rapidly degenerated into pantomime.

The only surviving examples of Greek music belong to this late period, and it is little indeed compared with survivals from other arts. Of about 20 possible fragments, written variously in a "vocal" and an "instrumental" notation, two remain unauthenticated and three or more are probably Byzantine reconstructions (*see* BYZANTINE MUSIC). Of the remainder, three are important: the two Delphic hymns to Apollo, carved on marble at Delphi (late 2nd century B.C.), and the epitaph of Seikelos for his wife, chiseled on a tomb at Tralles (Aidin), Turk. (1st century B.C. or later). The rest, in papyri, are to be seen in Cairo, Berlin, Oslo, Michigan and Oxford; the oldest fragment of all, a few choral lines from Euripides' *Orestes* (408 B.C.), is in the Rainer papyrus in Vienna (3rd–2nd century B.C.).

Forms and Principles of Composition.—The fragmentary relics hardly allow structural analysis, though certain fundamental principles of construction are known: poetic metre, verbal contour and musical time.

The units of poetic metre (feet comprising short and long syllables) fell into three main groups, exemplified by the *dactyl* – ◡◡; *iamb* ◡ – (cf. *trochee* – ◡); and *paeon* – ◡◡◡. The equivalent musical units comprised short and long notes: *duple* ♩ ♪, 2/4; *triple* ♩. ♪ (or ♩ ♪), 3/8; and *multiple* ♩. ♩, 5/8, as found respectively in the "hymn to Helios," "hymn to the muse" and "first Delphic hymn."

Declaimed poetry also had verbal contours—inherent tonal elements represented by the three speech accents: *acute* (rising), *grave* (falling) and *circumflex* (rising followed by falling, or level) —which *melopoeia*, the Greek art of melody making, aimed to enhance.

The two principles, poetic metre and tonic accent, are seen in combination in the "hymn to Helios," with its strictly anapaestic metre and 12 out of 16 acute accents matched by a rising melodic contour.

Further, Greek poetry, conceived without any dynamic stress of its own, could hardly escape the influence of the accompanying instruments and dance, which, by their very nature, required strong and weak beats, or musical time. Thus the noisy *thesis* (downbeat) of the choral dance leader's foot clapper was inevitably followed by a silent *arsis* (lifting).

Moreover, in postclassical times music already imposed its own formal patterns on poetic structure: the four metrically different lines of the "epitaph of Seikelos" are equally adjusted to a melody in 12/8 time. According to Dionysius of Halicarnassus, the *Orestes* of Euripides went still further toward purely musical form: its melody did not rise and fall with the speech

accents; it was identical in two rhythmically paired strophes. The Greek arts, whether plastic or dramatic, favoured linear form, hence rhythm took precedence over elements of colour. In music the latter were no doubt represented by occasional decorative two-note chords plucked on the lyre, by a drone on one of the *aulos* pipes accompanying the melody on the other, and by the accompaniment of a vocal melody in heterophonic variation. But the single line of melody remained paramount, and its intervals were classified in Greek music theory.

Theory.—The Greeks referred their music to the intervals of an octave (diapason), fifth and fourth, and they knew all the intervals of western music and more besides. The interval of a fourth was the practical unit of their tonal space; when divided into four notes it was known as a tetrachord. Of these notes the outer two were fixed, the inner two movable; and the position of the latter determined one of three *genera* whose intervals (reading downward) were: tone, tone, *leimma* (Latin, *limma*: "remainder" of the interval of a fourth after the subtraction of two tones) in the *diatonic*, as in the "epitaph of Seikilos"; minor third, semitone, semitone in the *chromatic*; and ditone, quarter tone, quarter tone in the *enharmonic*, as in the *Orestes* fragment. Finer intervals were classified in subgenera called *chroai* ("shades").

Three primary (diatonic) modes correspond to the three possible (descending) orders in which the intervals of the tetrachord run: Dorian (tone, tone, leimma), Phrygian (TLT) and Lydian (LTT). Such structures occur respectively in the "second Delphic hymn," "epitaph of Seikelos" and an instrumental piece from J. F. Bellerman's *Anonymous* (of late date). Two tetrachords joined together formed a *harmonia* (octave scale), and in the diatonic genus the seven such scales in use (with notes reading downward, and as on the white keys of the piano but allowing for differences in tuning) were as follows: a to A, Hypodorian (Aeolian); g to G, Hypophrygian (Ionian); f to F, Hypolydian; e to E, Dorian; d to D, Phrygian; c to C, Lydian; and b to B, an Hyperdorian. These *harmoniai* are called "modes" today, but they were only the scaffolding for the true modes (*tropos*, pl. *tropoi*) or melodic styles or contours (perhaps comparable with the Indian *raga* [*see* INDIAN MUSIC] and Arabic *maqam*), each with its particular *ethos*, or characteristic effect. A five-note scale was also early introduced into Greece from Asia. It is found as late as the "second Delphic hymn."

To embrace all the notes of the seven *harmoniai* in each of their three *genera* within the compass of a single octave, the Greeks had a theoretical scale of 21 sounds ("greater perfect system"); the seven *harmoniai* they related to each other in a continuous two-octave scale (*disdiapason*); for modulation they used an 11-note series ("lesser perfect system"); and to bring any scale within the limited compass (that of the Dorian *harmonia*) of the lyre, they had a transposing system.

The surviving musical fragments well illustrate certain aspects of classical theory and yet show differences that suggest only a frail link with the music of classical times. To what extent the theory represents musical practice at any one period may be legitimately questioned, for the theorists often disagree among themselves, with considerable confusion in terminology.

Instruments.—Ancient Greece appears never to have had a developed instrumental art. The role of its few instruments—all derived from non-Greek sources—was the accompaniment of poetry and the dance.

Strings.—The all-important national lyre existed in preclassical forms: *phorminx*, *citharis*, *chelys*, and in classical forms: *cithara* (professional), *lyra* (lyric poets, amateurs), *barbiton*. The harp was played by women: *magadis* (large), *pectis* (smaller), *psalterion* (later).

Wind.—The reed pipe (*aulos*), usually double and next in importance after the lyre, played *nomoi* and accompanied dithyramb and drama. The *syrinx* (shepherd's panpipe) was played to the flocks, and the *salpinx* (straight metal trumpet) had a military function. The *hydraulis* (water organ, Alexandria, 3rd century B.C.) became more popular in Rome.

Percussion Instruments.—These were introduced with the Dionysus and Cybele cults: *tympanon*, hand-beaten frame drum

(Mediterranean); *crotala*, hand clappers; *croupala*, foot clappers; and *cymbala*, cymbals.

Heritage.—Though nothing remains of ancient Greek musical practice and few instruments survive, the influence of classical theory was wide and lasting. The Greek empire carried it to Egypt and the Asiatic coasts, and possibly as far as India. In early Christian times the Gnostics used the Greek scale in their incantations, and Byzantium adopted the Greek modes (*see* BYZANTINE MUSIC). The Romans acknowledged Greek musical leadership and transmitted Greek theory to Europe through Boethius (c. 480–524 A.D.), and the early church drew upon its modes. But Islam is the principal heir to Greek theory through the Persians, Arabs and Turks, whose writings further influenced Europe from the 9th century. Thus Greek music, itself the heir to so much that of at least three more. *See also* AULOS; LYRE; MUSIC IN ANCIENT CIVILIZATIONS.

BIBLIOGRAPHY.—K. von Jan, *Musici scriptores graeci* (1895; *Supplementum*, 1899); H. Macan, *Aristoxenus* (1902); Émile Martin, *Trois documents de musique grecque* (1953); T. Reinach, *La musique grecque* (1926); C. Sachs, *The Rise of Music in the Ancient World* (1943).
(P. C.-Ho.)

GREEK RELIGION. The religion of the ancient Greeks is no longer absurdly abused nor foolishly idealized and can be seen clearly for what it was. It contained savage and barbarous elements as well as elements of civilization, although the savagery and barbarism are still sometimes exaggerated. It was creedless, developing without any authoritative writing like the Bible or the Koran, and without any inflexible tradition to hamper or to guide it. It varied from age to age, from place to place and probably also from class to class; being now more backward, now more advanced, but always retaining certain characteristics. It was, first, an anthropomorphic polytheism, the worship of a number (not very large) of gods, thought of as human in form and largely human in mind. These gods were neither passionless nor without faults. But as the history of this worship covers some 2,000 years, it can be seen that ideas, even popular ideas, on these matters were somewhat variable. The gods were normally, though not always, clear-cut figures, made concrete by poetry and art and surrounded by a large mythology. This, however, was not a body of dogma; the worshiper might believe, disbelieve or alter it to his taste.

The Greek religion was for the most part (but *see* MYSTERY) completely free from otherworldliness. It was a religion of every-day life, which sought for temporal blessings such as good crops, deliverance from enemies, health, or peace within the community. In historical times at least it was in its most conspicuous form an affair of the state, although family cult never ceased to exist, and individual religion developed strikingly as the importance of the Greek city-states declined from the 4th century B.C. onward.

Origins.—The people who in historical times called themselves Hellenes (Greeks) came to Greece from an unknown district, perhaps by way of Asia Minor. They brought with them only one deity whose name and native origin are certain, namely Zeus. It is likely that they also had a corn-goddess, whether or not they already called her Demeter, and she may by then have had a daughter, Kore ("the maiden"). The Greeks probably had additional names of deities such as Pluton ("the rich one"), who may well have been the deity of the earth's wealth, *i.e.*, of its crops. Only later, perhaps, was he identified with Hades, the god of the dead, an older form of whose name is Aides, perhaps meaning "the unseen." In any case Hades is not a god of the living, who therefore do not worship him. The dead likewise are no longer in charge of the gods worshiped on earth, and presumably do not worship them. Similarly, the name Helios (Halios, Eëlios) refers not only to the visible sun but also to the sun-god. He had no cult in Greece proper, however, nor had Selene, the moon; gods of the heavens are no concern of people who move on the earth. Zeus is a deity of the weather-sky, that is, of meteorological phenomena such as rain and snow. No other god or goddess of any importance has a name demonstrably Greek. Kronos' name is certainly unHellenic; Apollo's yields no convincing Greek etymology. Athena is a pre-Hellenic goddess, adopted by the incoming Greeks in Mycenaean times as the protectress of their chieftains' castles. Artemis, or Artamis, has a name possibly connected with *artamos*. This word, however, means "slaughterer" or "butcher," whereas Artemis is a huntress, a helper in childbirth and on occasion the sender of sudden and painless death to women. The name Hera, if Greek, is the feminine form of *hēros*, a nobleman or gentleman; it thus means "lady"—a title, not a proper name. The name of Hermes (Hermeias) may be etymologically connected with *hérma*, stone or rubble; he may have begun as the power haunting cairns put up to mark holy spots or to delimit paths, but this is uncertain. Persephone (her name has several forms) assuredly is not of Greek origin. Hecate comes from Caria, Hephaestus from the volcanic regions of Asia Minor, and Dionysus is a later arrival of Thracian or Thraco-Phrygian origin. There remain only a few minor powers. The Muses (Mousai) are supposed to derive their name from hypothetical Montiai, meaning "prompters" or "reminders." Pan (Pa-on, "feeder") is the little god of Arcadian goatherds. There are also the Nymphs ("nymph" means marriageable young woman or bride) and their like. It is not known when the cult of any of these powers began.

Some of the gods composing the classical pantheon were taken from the cults existing in the regions invaded by the Greeks. This occurred through the characteristic Greek power of adapting and naturalizing foreign influences, and there was little or no realization of the different origins of the gods. The great civilization of Minoan Crete had an elaborate religion, an outstanding feature of which was the worship of goddesses. Clear traces are to be found also of gods who are born, grow to maturity and die, probably every year, with the growth and decay of the seasonal vegetation. Both those elements influenced Greek cult and myth. In Greece proper are to be found deities with names that are not Greek and that show the characteristic suffixes (found also in place-names, etc.) of the pre-Greek language. Examples are *-nth-*, as in Hyakinthos, *-na-*, as in Athena, and *-ss-*, as in Phersephassa (Persephone). Also in Greece are fairly clear traces of an ancient cult of one or more goddesses. There is an ingenious modern theory that one of these, probably an earth goddess, was named or nicknamed "Da" (a word occurring in classical Greek as an ejaculation). It is contended that this syllable blended with Greek elements to compose two or three divine names, as in Demeter or Damater, "mother Da," and Posei-da-on, "husband of Da." For Poseidon was not originally a sea-god, nor were his earliest worshipers acquainted with the sea. He was a deity of the waters which fertilize the soil, and also, for some obscure reason, a god of horses.

It has been said that these deities are usually anthropomorphic. However, there are traces, probably very early, of their having taken bestial shape. Hera is *boōpis* in Homer; the word probably meant, to the poet, that she had large, cowlike eyes. It could, however, mean "cow-faced," and it is relevant that Hera's priestess Io is said to have been changed into a heifer either by the goddess or by Zeus. Athena is *glaukōpis*, a word used by Homer and other writers to mean "gray-eyed" or "bright-eyed"; but the bird with which Athena is associated, a kind of owl, is called *glaux*, and the epithet may originally have meant "owl-faced," while Zeus and Dionysus appeared under various animal guises. The latter commonly manifested himself as a serpent or a bull; a hymn sung in his honour at Elis actually calls him "noble bull." But such cases as these are comparatively rare and abnormal. In any event they have nothing to do with totemism, a wholly non-European phenomenon, but are examples of theriolatry, which is found in many parts of the world (*see* H. J. Rose, *Primitive Culture in Greece*, p. 47 ff.).

Growing knowledge of the near east gradually reveals the extent to which the early Greeks were influenced by the cults and beliefs of the great oriental civilizations bordering their district. It is justifiable to say, at least, that some Greek myths were related to certain myths current among these peoples, for example, the Hittites. Egyptian and other foreign influences probably entered

Greece by way of Crete, but details are still lacking with regard to this and other aspects of the early history of the eastern Mediterranean. The place of origin of the worship of Apollo, for instance, is still unknown, although it is certain that he had connections with Asia (*see* W. K. C. Guthrie, *The Greeks and Their Gods*, p. 74 ff.). A popular and sometimes locally important cult was that of the heroes, literally gentleman; *i.e.*, powerful and worshipful ghosts of real or imaginary men (sometimes women, *heroinai*), the most famous being Heracles. Minor and half-forgotten ("faded") gods were often confused with these beings. (*See* L. R. Farnell, *Greek Hero-Cults*.)

Development.—At some time earlier than the earliest evidence, that is, than the Homeric poems, the Greeks had combined most of their deities into one divine clan, the head or "house-father" of which was Zeus. Zeus was represented as the begetter of most of the younger deities, and as being himself the son of Kronos and the husband and brother of Hera. His position is that of a chieftain of the heroic age among his relatives and vassals. But this does not mean that he was the chief god in the cult of every community. At Athens, for instance, his festivals, which had increased in number to include some that were not his originally, were dwarfed in importance by those of Athena. Greek worship throughout the Archaic and Classical periods was essentially communal, although nothing prevented an individual from approaching any deity he chose on his own behalf. Every family had its observances, including the worship of the hearth-goddess Hestia, who scarcely achieved the status of a personal deity but always maintained close relations with the sacred fire from which she came. The larger groups, whether supposedly of kin, like the phratries or clans, or merely local, like the demes (townships) into which Attica was divided, had also their own worship; but the most important and impressive rites were naturally those conducted by the state. The nearest approach to a common governing religious body was the oracle of Apollo at Delphi; and even that, though it lent its sanction to innovations on occasion, was often content to tell inquirers that they would be well advised to "worship according to ancestral custom." The oracle had neither a recognized orthodoxy to enforce, nor a disciplined and obedient clergy to support it in any state that might prove recalcitrant. If Apollo were directly and materially concerned, strong measures might indeed be taken. The four "sacred" wars were all fought, nominally at least, in consequence of violation of the god's rights to certain territories; but this was hardly more than vindication of the divine proprietor's lawful claims. In general Delphi confined itself to giving advice. The inquirer, if he rejected this, did so at his own risk, and numerous tales pointed the moral that his consequent peril was real; but the effectiveness of such warnings depended on the degree of respect in which the oracle was held.

Under such a system, the nature of the cults and their distance from savagery varied greatly. In Arcadia and similar backward districts the simple people might perform archaic or grotesque ritual around a shapeless block of stone or a plank of wood, called perhaps only by some such laudatory epithet as "the good god." In a centre of culture, such as Athens, however, the holy places would be marked by stately and beautiful temples, each the dwelling of a deity represented, perhaps, by an ancient cult-statue, but probably also by a masterpiece of sculpture.

The ritual would be orderly and elaborate, comprising hymns, prayers and sacrifices. The hymns were often written by celebrated poets and musicians, although prayer does not seem often to have taken the form of long and invariable liturgical texts. Sacrifice might involve the killing of many beasts before the temple and a general feast on their meat. Normally there would be a procession for the carrying of sacred objects and the leading of victims for sacrifice.

It is evident that the reactions of those present would vary from simple trust that the time-honoured ritual would win the favour of the deity to deep reflection upon the nature of the power addressed, or of divinity itself. From the latter point of view, different deities were very variously adaptable to the growing interest in ethical and theological speculation. After Zeus himself, Apollo, whose title Phoebus, "pure one," represented his concern with purifica-

tions, was thought to be sympathetic to a developed and enlightened morality; anecdotes and alleged oracles were current in support of this idea. Artemis, originally in all probability a mother-goddess, developed into a sort of personification of chastity; Athena became wisdom in person. On the other hand, many minor deities such as Pan, the Nymphs, or Hermes showed no moral development, at least in normal Greek thought. The unpopular Ares, too, remained simply a god of violent death and destruction, usually from war, but sometimes from other causes such as plague. The forms of worship were, as usual, conservative, and retained some features obviously dating from early days and comparatively low stages of culture; but even they tended to shed characteristics that advancing morality regarded as objectionable. The practice of human sacrifice, for instance, is attested by numerous legends, by an occasional ritual simulacrum of manslaughter and by the substitution, certain in some cases, merely probable in others, of an animal victim for one originally human. The actual rite was very occasionally revived in historical times; but the idea of human sacrifice became so repugnant to general sentiment that it was practically abandoned from about the 6th century B.C.

The general attitude of the Greek toward his gods was respectful but not servile. Like many Europeans, he would on occasion jest with the objects of his worship. The "Homeric" hymn to Hermes bears witness to this trait, with its humorous tales of Hermes' early rogueries. So does the comic appearance of Dionysus, Heracles and other popular deities on the Attic stage, as in the *Frogs* of Aristophanes.

Personal Religion.—The very fact that the great public cults were managed by city-states gave them a certain artificiality. They were in many cases originally connected with the operations of farming, and therefore belonged to those times of the year at which these operations took place. But the festivals were regulated by the state calendar and this by no means always corresponded with the real seasons. Thus, for example, a ceremony connected with plowing might be held when no farmer was actually plowing his fields. Country dwellers, no doubt, found some compensation for this defect in the worship of their little local powers such as the Nymphs; but, even so, the greatest and most conspicuous forms of worship must have seemed somewhat detached from real life.

In addition to this feeling there was a growing idea that the destiny of the individual was of importance, at least to him, and that the state cults existed rather for the benefit of the community. Hence the immense popularity, from about the end of the 5th century B.C., of the cult of Asclepius, whose powers were exerted on behalf of individuals seeking cure for their diseases rather than to avert some public calamity as was the office, for example, of Apollo. There were also the movements such as Orphism (*see* ORPHEUS), which made eschatological speculations regarding the individual, and the philosophic schools, not least that of Platonism, with their ideas on ethics, the government of the universe and the destiny of the soul. Ethics were not divorced from the conventional worships, but those involved no moral code that might direct conduct in detail. All these tendencies toward regard for the individual were reinforced in Hellenistic times by the passing of the old city-states as important political units. This rendered the ordinary man much more helpless in public affairs than his ancestors had been. The geocentric theory of the universe, too, imperfect though it was, made the earth an insignificantly small place, while astrology, which was generally believed in, represented man as the victim of mechanical and irresistible fate. It is no wonder that in early Hellenistic days the cult of Tyche (Chance, Fortune) was widespread both in public and in private, and that later any system promising relief to man's helplessness was sure of adherents. Broadly speaking, such systems were of two kinds, both depending on knowledge, or *gnosis*, alleged to be supernatural and revealed (though Gnosticism, as such, is the name given to a Christian heresy). The first kind of system was the mystery religion. Mysteries were usually, though not always, of oriental origin, and claimed to secure for their initiates the favour of a particular deity, Isis or Mithra for example, who would care for their well-being, especially after death. Such patrons, being gods, were, according to the generally received theory, exempt from the centripetal influence of the stars, being above and beyond them, and thus beyond the reach of fate. The second system was the higher form of magic, "theurgy," which actually constrained the deities to help their clients. The lower forms of magic were also very popular. These aimed at compelling minor powers, notably the *biaiōthanatoi* (ghosts of violently and prematurely deceased persons), to help the sorcerer in the desired way, for example, by revealing the future to him, by winning for him the favours of influential persons, by tormenting his enemies or by laming the horses he had bet against. One of the reasons for the ultimate triumph of Christianity over the more respectable of its rivals was the fact that, being unencumbered by fantastic myth and ritual of uncivilized origin, it dealt with the eschatological and other spiritual needs of the time in a more rational manner than did its rivals. What was left of Greek rationality contributed a logical and coherent theology to the new religion. The most stubborn opposition to Christianity came from the simple and unreflective worship of the countryside which had behind it the force of ancestral custom. Compromises were numerous; for example, the cult of Asclepius was replaced by that of miracle-working saints, and the small shrines of the little rustic deities by those of Christian origin, it dealt with the eschatological and other spiritual needs of the time. Indeed, traces of the old worship are still found in popular customs in Greece and other countries.

See also articles on individual deities and references under "Greek Religion" in the Index volume.

BIBLIOGRAPHY.—*General:* L. R. Farnell, *Cults of the Greek States,* 5 vol. (1896–1909). Shorter accounts, besides the encyclopaedias and classical dictionaries: L. R. Farnell, *Outline History of Greek Religion* (1920), with good bibliography; M. P. Nilsson, *Greek Popular Religion* (1940), *A History of Greek Religion,* 2nd ed. (1949), *Greek Piety* (1948); H. J. Rose, *Ancient Greek Religion* (1948). *Survivals:* H. J. Rose, *Primitive Culture in Greece* (1925). *Crete:* M. P. Nilsson, *Minoan-Mycenaean Religion and its Survivals in Greek Religion,* 2nd ed. (1950). *Delphi:* H. W. Parke and D. E. W. Wormell, *The Delphic Oracle,* 2 vol. (1956). *Developments:* L. R. Farnell, *The Higher Aspects of the Greeks,* 2nd ed. (1912); C. H. Moore, *The Religious Thought of the Greeks,* 2nd ed. (1925). *Later Stages:* A. J. Festugière, *La Révélation d'Hermès Trismégiste,* 4 vol. (1944–54). *Brief Account:* G. G. A. Murray, *Five Stages of Greek Religion,* ch. 4, 5 (1925).
(H. J. R.)

GREELEY, HORACE (1811–1872), U.S. newspaper editor and political leader, was born near Amherst, N.H., Feb. 3, 1811. He was the eldest of the five children of Zaccheus Greeley, a poor farmer. Horace had an irregular schooling, but his precocity and an interest in printing became evident at an early age. In 1826 he entered the office of the *Northern Spectator* in East Poultney, Vt., where he remained for five years as an apprentice. Then, after visiting his parents, who had moved to Erie county in Pennsylvania, he went to New York to seek his fortune. He was then 20 years old. His New England background had given him a conditioning in religious piety, moral fervour and political conservatism. This last, together with the difficulties his family experienced in the depression of 1819–22, made him an ardent supporter of Henry Clay's protective tariff policies.

After a year and a half as a journeyman printer in New York, Greeley and an associate set up a small printing establishment. In 1834 Greeley became senior editor of a new literary magazine, the *New Yorker.* In 1836 he married Mary Youngs Cheney, a strong-minded schoolteacher. The *New Yorker* struggled along, never out of debt, through the depression that followed the panic of 1837. Gradually its editor's interest centred on political journalism.

Ardently patriotic, humanitarian in sentiment, but distrustful of radical solutions for the ills of society and disdainful of Jacksonian democracy, Greeley became a liberal Whig. His views, expressed in the *New Yorker,* caught the eye of New York state's Whig political boss, Thurlow Weed, who employed him to issue a campaign weekly, the *Jeffersonian,* in 1838, and a similar weekly, the *Log Cabin,* in the presidential campaign of 1840. These publications substantially aided the Whig cause in New York state, and marked the beginning of Greeley's political partnership with Weed and William H. Seward, governor of New York. Greeley's success with the *Jeffersonian* and the *Log Cabin* en-couraged him to a more ambitious newspaper venture. On April 10, 1841, he started the *New York Tribune,* a daily Whig paper dedicated to reform, economic progress and the elevation of the masses. The *Tribune* set a high standard among the papers of its day in news gathering, intellectual interest and moral fervour. It found a good clientele in New York city and a tremendous circulation as a weekly in the hinterland. Its editorial columns became a potent political influence.

For several years Greeley worked closely with Weed and Seward in liberalizing the Whig party in New York state and in exerting an influence upon Whig national politics. He helped make Seward governor in 1838 and played a part in elevating him to the U.S. senate in the winter of 1848–49. He aided Weed in battling for the antirenters, who opposed the perpetual leases that dated back to the colonial period, and against the conservative Whigs. But differences between Greeley and the other members of the triumvirate were always cropping up. They found him obstinate, mercurial and lacking in political sense, this last being especially evident when he was a member of the U.S. house of representatives for a few months in 1848–49. In his turn, he chafed over the political realism that led Weed to champion Gen. Zachary Taylor's nomination for president in 1848, and became increasingly bitter over the failure of his partners to support him for high public office. In 1854 he was determined to take an independent course in politics and dissolved the partnership.

The *Tribune* had taken an antislavery stand in the 1840s, but became violent in its opposition to slavery in the next decade. Greeley was dubious about the Compromise of 1850 (*q.v.*), especially its fugitive slave law, but he blew hot and cold on the measure as a whole. The Kansas-Nebraska act of 1854 provoked his bitterest moral condemnation. He took a prominent part in organizing the Republican party in 1854–55, and supported its nominee, John C. Frémont, for president in 1856. He and his paper were now anathema among the slaveholders. He was publicly caned by Congressman Albert Rust of Arkansas in 1856 and threatened with violence if he ever entered the south. He constantly fed the rising antislavery excitement in the north, bitterly attacking the Dred Scott decision of 1857, the slave trade and southern manners and morals.

Greeley helped defeat Seward for the Republican presidential nomination in 1860. This started a feud with Weed that went on for years. The *Tribune's* editor preferred the conservative Edward Bates of Missouri as a presidential candidate, and had no enthusiasm for Lincoln. He did, however, support the latter in the campaign of 1860.

As secession materialized after Lincoln's election, Greeley's position became obscure. He urged letting "the erring sisters depart in peace," apparently believing that absence of coercion would gain time and best guarantee the maintenance of the Union. His opposition to any compromise with slavery extension remained firm, but his dread of war was obvious.

Greeley pursued an erratic course during the Civil War. He early became convinced that, for military, social and economic reasons, the abolition of slavery was essential, and joined the radicals in urging emancipation. But he also wanted the war brought to a speedy end, and was greatly distressed by Union defeats and the mounting cost of the struggle in lives and treasure. This distress, together with his continued lack of confidence in Lincoln, produced fitful moods of defeatism. At times he was ready to restore the "Union as it was," never more so than in the summer of 1864 when he became involved in sterile peace negotiations with Confederate commissioners in Canada. Greeley opposed Lincoln's renomination in 1864, but as the end of the war came clearly in sight his spirits rose. He looked forward hopefully to the reconstruction of a nation entirely free.

Greeley's motto for reconstruction of the Union was "Universal Amnesty and Impartial Suffrage." This drew fire, for different reasons, both from the radical Republicans and the supporters of Pres. Andrew Johnson. Popular opinion in the North turned against Greeley when he signed the bail bond of Jefferson Davis. This ruined the theretofore large sale of his history of the Civil War, *The American Conflict.*

Greeley's interest in politics and political preferment remained keen after the war was over. Zealous for a large measure of Negro equality, he supported the 14th and 15th amendments and urged the impeachment of President Johnson. Repeatedly he sought state and national office, but was never elected. He supported Grant's campaign for the presidency in 1868, though without enthusiasm. He finally became convinced that Grant's attempt to maintain radical reconstruction in the south was a failure. He was also irritated by the administration's refusal to cut military expenditures and resume the redemption of paper money with gold or silver coin, and felt that Grant was thwarting his ambitions in New York state. Greeley broke away from the Republican party, joined the dissenters known as the Liberal Republicans, and accepted nomination for the presidency by them and by the Democrats in 1872.

In the dreary campaign of 1872 Greeley was so mercilessly attacked that, as he said, he scarcely knew whether he was running for the presidency or the penitentiary. Overwhelmed by the strain of the campaign, exhausted by his vigil at the bedside of his dying wife, harried by his debts and by the decline of his influence in the *Tribune* office, Greeley sank into a deep depression and died Nov. 29, 1872.

Horace Greeley was a strange mixture of liberalism and conservatism. A liberal nationalist, he believed in the inevitability of human progress and in America's leadership in the movement toward human freedom. He was for years an advocate of Fourierism (*see* FOURIER, [FRANÇOIS MARIE] CHARLES]) and in the 1840s spent time and money in attempts to establish Utopian socialist communities. He urged a variety of educational reforms, and was an unrelenting foe of liquor, tobacco, gambling, prostitution and capital punishment. Personally generous, he also advocated using the power of government to promote the general welfare. He urged free common-school education and championed producers' co-operatives. He was always sympathetic with European struggles against despotism. On the other hand, his basic tendencies were conservative. He did not trust the wisdom of the proletariat, and had only scorn for such radical reformers as Frances Wright and Robert Dale Owen. Fourierism appealed to him because it was a reform that promised all things to all men, rich and poor alike. His sympathies inclined more toward capital than toward labour, and he opposed woman suffrage.

Greeley was quick-tempered, and his judgment was often faulty. His desire for public office amounted to an obsession. But he was warmhearted, and his patience with his eccentric wife was exemplary. His clarity of utterance and the fervour of his convictions combined to produce some of the finest editorials in the history of American journalism. He was one of the great moral leaders of the United States and the greatest newspaper editor of his time.

BIBLIOGRAPHY.—Harlan H. Horner, *Lincoln and Greeley* (1953); James L. Stoddard, *Horace Greeley, Printer, Editor, Crusader* (1946); James S. Trietsch, *The Printer and the Prince* (1955); Glyndon G. Van Deusen, *Horace Greeley, Nineteenth Century Crusader* (1953)
(G. G. V. D.)

GREELEY, a city and the seat of Weld County, in northern Colorado, U.S., 53 mi. NE of Denver, at an elevation of 4,637 ft., is the trading centre of an irrigated agricultural region. Production includes sugar beets and livestock, and food processing and canning are the principal industries. The city is the seat of the University of Northern Colorado, founded as the State Normal School (1889) and known as Colorado State College until 1970.

Greeley was founded in 1870 as a cooperative agricultural colony by Nathan C. Meeker (1817–79), agricultural editor of the *New York Tribune*, with the active support of Horace Greeley, after whom it was named. Organized as a joint stock company in New York, the Union Colony purchased land, recruited colonists, and transported them to the new settlement. The town was organized in 1871 and incorporated as a city in 1885. In 1951 the city adopted the council-manager form of government. Pop. (1970) 38,902. For comparative population figures *see* table in COLORADO: *Population*. (L. R. HA.)

GREELY, ADOLPHUS WASHINGTON (1844–1935), U.S. soldier, scientist and arctic explorer, was born at Newburyport, Mass., on March 27, 1844. Enlisting as a volunteer in the Federal army he fought throughout the Civil War, rising from private to the rank of brevet major. After the war he joined the regular army as a lieutenant in the signal service becoming, in 1887, chief signal officer with the rank of brigadier general. During the first polar year, 1882–83, he commanded the United States station in Lady Franklin bay, the most northerly station for meteorological and magnetic observations. His party consisted of 24 officers and men of the U.S. army, and the station, Fort Conger, was built in latitude 81° 44′ N. In addition to scientific observations, sledging parties reached latitude 83° 24′ N. and explored the interior of Ellesmere Island, discovering Lake Hazen and reaching the west coast at Greely fjord. The relief ships failed to reach Fort Conger in 1882 and 1883 so the station was abandoned according to plan in Aug. 1883 and the party moved south, reaching Cape Sabine on Oct. 15. Shelters were improvised and the party faced a winter of 250 days before help could be expected, with rations for only 40 days. When the rescue party reached them on June 22, 1884, there were only seven survivors. Greely returned to army duties and pursued a distinguished career in Alaska, the Philippine Islands and elsewhere. He died on Oct. 20, 1935.

Greely published works on meteorological, electrical and geographical subjects. His main works were *Three Years of Arctic Service* (1886); *American Weather* (1888); *Handbook of Polar Discoveries*, 3rd ed. (1925); *Handbook of Alaska* (1909); *Reminiscences of Adventure and Service* (1927); and *The Polar Regions in the Twentieth Century* (1929). (L. M. Fs.)

GREEN, CHARLES (1785–1870), the most famous of Victorian balloonists, was born in London on Jan. 31, 1785. After leaving school, Green joined his father as a fruiterer, but left to take up ballooning as a profession, his first ascent being in 1821; between that date and 1852 he made over 500 ascents. On his first ascent, he introduced coal gas for ballooning as a cheaper substitute for hydrogen, a practice thereafter followed by most aeronauts. His most outstanding achievement was the voyage in 1836 from Vauxhall gardens, London, across Europe to Weilburg in Nassau, Ger. Taking Monck Mason and Robert Hollond (who paid for it), Green completed this journey of about 480 mi. nonstop in 18 hours, a long-distance balloon record for trips out of England not beaten until 1907. Green also planned, but never attempted, an Atlantic crossing. The small working model of his proposed balloon, flown in 1840, incorporated the first mechanically driven propeller ever to power an aircraft. He died in London on March 26, 1870. (C. H. G.-S.)

GREEN, DUFF (1791–1875), U.S. political journalist, member of Pres. Andrew Jackson's inner circle of advisers and diplomatic agent, was born in Woodford county, Ky., Aug. 15, 1791. After education at a local academy he taught school, studied medicine and served in the War of 1812. He then became a U.S. government surveyor and mail contractor in Missouri. He studied law in his spare time, entered politics and served in the Missouri constitutional convention of 1819 and later in both houses of the state legislature. In 1823 he purchased the *St. Louis Enquirer* which, under his editorship, supported Andrew Jackson for president the following year.

In 1826 Green moved to Washington, D.C., where he established and edited the *United States Telegraph* as the chief journalistic organ of the Jacksonian Democrats. After Jackson's election as president in 1828 Green was appointed printer to congress and became a member of Jackson's inner circle, the so-called "kitchen cabinet." He exerted considerable influence on the policies of the Jackson administration until he broke with the president in 1831 to support John C. Calhoun. In 1837 and 1838 he edited *The Reformer*, a free trade and state rights paper in Baltimore, Md., and in 1840, as editor of *The Pilot*, he supported the Whig candidates, William Henry Harrison and John Tyler. When Tyler became president after Harrison's death in April 1841 he appointed Green as his unofficial representative to England where Green was warmly received by the English free traders. His articles in English papers on banking and currency, American business and international improvements, the Anti-Corn Law league and English interests in Texas were widely read.

Green returned home in 1844 and founded and edited *The Re-*

public, a New York paper that advocated free trade, the building of roads and other internal improvements, civil service and postal reform, and the acquisition of Oregon, Texas and California. Later the same year President Tyler appointed Green as U.S. consul to Galveston, Tex. Green also went to Mexico and reported that that country would not surrender any territory to the United States. His letters concerning English antislavery activities in Texas helped precipitate the movement for the annexation of Texas that led in 1846 to war between the United States and Mexico.

Green had, meanwhile become interested in several business enterprises, including coal and iron mines, canals, railroads and telegraph lines. He built a portion of the East Tennessee and Georgia railroad, acquired extensive ironworks in Tennessee and organized several railroads in Georgia. He formulated plans for financing railroad construction through government mail contracts, bonds and land grants. He secured charters for a Southern Pacific railroad and organized the Pennsylvania Fiscal agency, chartered by Pennsylvania in 1859, for constructing the road, but the secession crisis brought the work to a full stop. Though an opponent of secession, Green threw in his lot with the Confederacy and ran his ironworks at Jonesboro, Tenn., under contract with the Confederate government.

Green spent his last years writing books and pamphlets on finance, currency and other economic issues, and in trying unsuccessfully to recover his interests in the Pennsylvania Fiscal agency. The Pennsylvania legislature in 1864 had converted it into the Crédit Mobilier of America (*q.v.*), which built the Union Pacific railroad. Green died at his home in Dalton, Ga., on June 10, 1875.

See Fletcher M. Green, "Duff Green, Militant Journalist of the Old School," *Am. Hist. Rev.*, vol. lii, pp. 247-264 (1947). (F. M. G.)

GREEN, GEORGE (1793-1841), English mathematician, who made contributions to mathematical physics, was born on July 14, 1793, at Sneinton, near Nottingham. He went into his father's business as a miller and his mathematics were practically self-taught. It was probably for this reason that Green used unusual methods of his own in solving the physical problems in which he was interested. In 1828 he published by subscription, at Nottingham, his *Essay on the Application of Mathematical Analysis to the Theory of Electricity and Magnetism*. In this memoir he generalized and extended S. D. Poisson's electric and magnetic investigations. He introduced the term "potential," and used what is now known as Green's theorem to investigate its properties in the case of magnetic and electric fields. This memoir was practically unknown until Lord Kelvin had it reprinted in 1846; it was followed in 1832 and 1833 by papers on the laws of equilibrium of fluids, on attractions in n-dimensional space and on the motion of a fluid agitated by vibrations of a solid ellipsoid. At the age of 40 he went to Cambridge where he was fourth wrangler in 1837. He was elected to a fellowship at Caius college in 1839, but poor health compelled him to return to Sneinton, where he died on March 31, 1841.

His collected papers, *The Mathematical Papers of the Late George Green*, were edited by N. M. Ferrers (1871).

GREEN, HENRIETTA HOWLAND (1835-1916), known as Hetty, U.S. financier, was born in New Bedford, Mass., Nov. 21, 1835. A fortune had been acquired by her family from shipping and trading interests. Her father, Edward Mott Robinson, and her aunt, Sylvia Ann Howland, both died in 1865 and by their wills she received an estate valued at $10,000,000. Her shrewd personal management of her holdings and keen financial ability increased the size of her fortune and for a long period she was reputedly the richest woman in the United States. When she died July 2, 1916, at New York city, her son and daughter received from her an estate exceeding $100,000,000 in value. (H. J. Sg.)

GREEN, JOHN RICHARD (1837-1883), English historian, the author of a popular social history of England. He was born at Oxford, Dec. 12, 1837, and educated at Magdalen College school and Jesus college. He took orders on leaving Oxford and in 1865 became the incumbent of St. Philip's, Stepney. His health, however, could not withstand the demands made upon it by this task and when offered the librarianship at Lambeth in 1869, he accepted. He held this post until shortly before he renounced orders in the autumn of 1877. Meanwhile Green had begun to write; between 1867 and 1874 he was a frequent contributor to the *Saturday Review* and from 1869 he was engaged on his *Short History of the English People* (1874), which was an immediate success, requiring five reprints during 1875, and later expanded into a four-volume work (1877-80). Green was constantly a victim of ill-health and he died at Mentone, March 7, 1883. He had married, in 1877, Alice Stopford, herself a historian, who was president of the Historical association, 1915-18, and was nominated to the Irish senate in 1922.

Green's reputation as a serious historian has suffered from the very popularity of his *Short History*. This work, which gave a liberal interpretation to the course of English history, and was deliberately written in a vivid and colourful prose style, possessed the inevitable defects of any attempt to compress the history of a nation into a single volume, and does not reveal Green as the careful and scientific historian that he was. In fact, his later books, *The Making of England* (1882) and *The Conquest of England* (1883), were valuable contributions to historical knowledge and through his friendship with W. Stubbs and E. A. Freeman he shares an interesting place in the development of English historiography.

GREEN, MATTHEW (1696-1737), English poet and author of *The Spleen* (1737; mod. ed. 1936), a gently satirical verse epistle describing "How I do myself demean, In stormy world to live serene." Little is known of him except that he was born and died in London, was a clerk in the customhouse and wrote occasional verse for the entertainment of his friends. *The Spleen* charms by its sincerity, ease and neatness of expression, in particular its apt use of literary allusion, the precision of its metaphors and the skillful handling of the octosyllabic couplet. Addressed to one of his friends, it was printed with a preface by another, and other minor poems were added in later editions. *The Grotto*, Green's only other considerable poem, was privately printed in 1733, and reprinted in *The Spleen and Other Poems*, ed. by R. K. Wood (1925), and in Hugh l'Anson Fausset's *Minor Poets of the 18th Century* (1930).

GREEN, THOMAS HILL (1836-1882), English philosopher, the typical English representative of what was in his time called Neo-Kantianism or Neo-Hegelianism, was born on April 7, 1836, at the rectory of Birkin, Yorkshire. He was educated at Rugby and at Balliol college, Oxford, of which he was, in 1860, elected fellow. His life thenceforth was devoted to teaching in the university; from 1878 until his death (at Oxford on March 26, 1882) he was White's professor of moral philosophy. His lectures form the substance of his two most important works; viz., the *Prolegomena to Ethics* and the *Lectures on the Principles of Political Obligation*, published posthumously.

English philosophical thought in the third quarter of the 19th century was dominated by the naturalism of Herbert Spencer and by the sensationalism of J. S. Mill. Green reacted unfavourably to both, holding that the former precludes a satisfactory account of human action and the latter a satisfactory account of human knowledge. His metaphysics begins by raising again the question of man's relation to nature. To ask "What is man?" is, he argued, to ask "What is experience?" for experience means that of which I am conscious. The facts of consciousness, which alone we are justified in asserting to exist, are valid evidence for whatever is logically involved in them. Now the chief characteristic of man is *self*-consciousness. The simplest mental act, the act of sense perception, is never merely a change, physical or psychical, but the consciousness of a change and of a distinction between the self and the object. Knowledge consists, in its simplest equally with its most complex constituents, of the work of the mind. To know is to relate. The assumption of John Locke and David Hume that the work of the mind is arbitrary because not "given to" man is unjustified by the results of exact science, with the distinction universally recognized, which such science draws between truth and falsehood, between the real and "mere ideas." This (obviously valid) distinction logically involves the consequence that the object of knowledge is an intelligible ideal reality, a system of thought relations. The existence of this ideal whole presupposes a "principle which renders all relations possible and is itself determined by none of them"; an eternal self-consciousness which knows in whole what we know in part. To God the world *is*, to man the world *becomes*.

The business of moral philosophy, according to Green, is to apply to the sphere of social life the results of the metaphysician's investigation into man's nature. The presupposition of ethics is the spiritual nature of man. Self-reflection reveals human capacity, human function, with, consequently, human responsibility. It brings out certain potentialities in the realization of which man's true good must consist. The idea of some "end" or "good," which man presents to himself as desirable for the realization of his true self, constitutes motive; and the determination to realize the self in some definite way constitutes an "act of will," which is neither arbitrary nor externally determined. The identification of the self with such a motive is a self-determination, which is at once both rational and free. Freedom is not a supposed ability to do anything but the power to identify one's self with that true good which reason reveals as *one's* true good. This good consists in the realization of personal character; hence the final good—that is, the moral ideal, as a whole—can be realized only in some society of persons who, while retaining their individuality, find this perfection attainable only when their separate individualities are integrated as part of a social whole. Society is as necessary to form persons as persons are to constitute society.

There is a natural transition from these ideas to Green's political philosophy. Moral goodness cannot be limited to the cultivation of self-regarding virtues, but consists in the attempt to realize in practice that moral ideal which self-analysis has revealed to us as *our* ideal. From this arises the ground of political obligation: the institutions of political or civic life are the concrete embodiment of our moral ideas and are valuable according as they develop the moral character of individual citizens. It is obvious that the final moral ideal is not realized in actually existing civic institutions; but the same analysis which demonstrates this deficiency points the direction for a true development. Hence arises the conception of rights and duties which ought to be maintained by law, as opposed to those actually maintained, with the further consequence that it may become occasionally a moral duty to rebel against the state in the interest of the state itself; that is, in order better to subserve that function which constitutes the *raison d'être* of the state. The state does not consist in any definite concrete organization formed once for all. It represents a "general will" which is a desire for a common good. Its basis is not an external coercive authority but the spiritual recognition, by the citizens, of that which constitutes their true nature. "Will, not force, is the basis of the state."

Green's teaching was, directly or indirectly, the most potent philosophical influence in England during the later part of the 19th century; the critical side of his work was especially effective. His constructive doctrines, however, though widely accepted at the time of publication, were presently judged not merely to contain unresolved difficulties but also to be altogether too imprecise in formulation and argument to warrant serious consideration. By 1950 Green's purely philosophical impact was negligible. He retained, however, a considerable reputation in the field of politics, both because of the effects of his own activities in public life, which helped to bring the English universities into closer touch with practical affairs, and because of his efforts to reformulate the doctrines of political liberalism in a way which laid less stress on the negative rights of the individual and more on positive action by the state. His address on "Liberal Legislation and Freedom of Contract" (1881; *Works*, vol. iii) gives early expression to some of the main ideas which underlay the setting up of the 20th-century "welfare state."

Apart from the introduction to his edition of Hume (1874), Green's main works were all published posthumously: *Prolegomena to Ethics* (1883) was followed by the collected *Works*, 3 vol. (1885–88), vol. iii containing an extensive memoir by R. L. Nettleship.

BIBLIOGRAPHY.—H. Sidgwick, *Lectures on the Ethics of T. H. Green* (1902); J. H. Muirhead, *The Service of the State: Four Lectures on the Political Teaching of T. H. Green* (1908); J. MacCunn, *Six Radical Thinkers* (1910); W. D. Lamont, *Introduction to Green's Moral Philosophy* (1934); H. A. Prichard, *Moral Obligation* (1949); J. Pucelle, *L'Idéalisme en Angleterre* (1955). (W. H. W.; X.)

GREEN, VALENTINE (1739–1813), British engraver, was born at Halesowen. He became a pupil of a line engraver at Worcester, and in 1765 he migrated to London and began work as a mezzotint engraver. He became a member of the Incorporated Society of Artists in 1767, and an associate engraver of the Royal Academy in 1775. During his career he produced about 400 plates after portraits by Sir Joshua Reynolds and other British artists, and by many old masters. He was one of the first to apply mezzotint to the translation of pictorial compositions and portraits.

GREEN, WILLIAM (1873–1952), U.S. labour leader, for many years president of the American Federation of Labor, was born March 3, 1873, at Coshocton, O. He was educated in public schools and began as a young man to interest himself in labouring conditions in Ohio coal mines. From 1900 to 1906 he was a sub-district president of the United Mine Workers of America, and from 1912 to 1924 international secretary-treasurer of that union.

In 1913 he was appointed a member of the executive council of the American Federation of Labor. He was elected president of the A.F. of L. on Dec. 19, 1924, and was thereafter re-elected for many successive terms. After the formation of the Committee for Industrial Organization (later the Congress of Industrial Organizations) in 1935, he fought a bitter duel with John L. Lewis for leadership of U.S. labour. Later the C.I.O. broke away from the A.F. of L., not to be reunited with it until three years after Green's death, which took place on Nov. 21, 1952, at Coshocton, O.

GREENAWAY, KATE (1846–1901), English artist and book illustrator, known for her very original and charming children's books, was born in London March 17, 1846. She began to exhibit drawings in 1868, and her first published illustrations appeared in such magazines as *Little Folks*. In 1879 she produced her first successful book, *Under the Window*.

Then followed *The Birthday Book, Mother Goose, Little Ann,* and other books for children, which had an enormous success and became very highly valued. "Toy-books" though they were, these little works created a revolution in book illustration; they were praised by John Ruskin (*Art of England* and *Fors Clavigera*), by Ernest Chesneau and Arsène Alexandre in France, by Richard Muther in Germany, and by leading art critics throughout the world. In 1890 Miss Greenaway was elected a member of the Royal Institute of Painters in Water Colours, and in 1891, 1894 and 1898 she exhibited water-colour drawings, including illustrations for her books, at the gallery of the Fine Art society (by which a representative selection was exhibited in 1902). Miss Greenaway's use of the quaint costume of the beginning of the 19th century lent humour to her fancy and so captivated the public taste that it has been said that "Kate Greenaway dressed the children of two continents." From 1883 to 1897, with a break only in 1896, she issued a series of *Kate Greenaway's Almanacs*. Although she illustrated *The Pied Piper of Hamelin* and other works, the artist preferred to provide her own text. She had great charm of character, but was extremely shy of public notice. She died at Hampstead, London, on Nov. 6, 1901.

See M. H. Spielmann and G. S. Layard, *Life of Kate Greenaway* (1905).

GREENBACK PARTY, a minor U.S. political party that flourished during the period 1874 to 1884 following the hard times brought on by the panic of 1873. Initially called the Independent National party, it gave prime emphasis to the idea, expressed in its first platform (1876), that "United States notes, issued directly by the Government and convertible on demand into U.S. obligations (bonds) bearing a rate of interest not exceeding one cent a day on each $100, and exchangeable for U.S. notes at par, will afford the best circulating medium ever devised." Peter Cooper (*q.v.*), its presidential candidate in 1876, received 81,740 popular votes. Two years later the party merged with various labour groups and changed its name to the Greenback Labor party, winning in the congressional election of 1878 more than 1,000,000 votes and electing 14 congressmen. With the prospect of becoming a major party, the Greenbackers in 1880 broadened their appeal and adopted a platform calling, in addition to their money reform, for the abolition of an 8-hour day, an end to the "importation of Chinese serfs," the regulation of interstate commerce, the adoption of a graduated income tax, unrestricted suffrage, the curbing of congressional committees and the regulation of "gigantic land, money and railway corporations." Despite this strategy, however, it received only 308,578 votes for its presidential candidate James B. Weaver and elected only eight congressmen. Four years later the Greenbackers and the Anti-Monopolists joined in the short-lived People's party and supported Benjamin F. Butler, who won only 175,370 votes. The Greenback Labor party then disintegrated. Many of its supporters later joined the Populist party.

From a broader perspective the Greenback party reflects, on a smaller scale, the same concern over "honest money" that marked Jacksonian democracy in the 1830s and the Bryan campaign in 1896.

(J. A. V.)

GREENBACKS, a popular designation for a form of paper money in the United States, so named from the green colour used on the notes. Greenbacks, or U.S. treasury notes, were first issued in 1862 under authority of the act of Feb. 25, 1862. By this and two later acts of congress the secretary of the treasury was empowered to issue $450,000,000 in noninterest-bearing notes. U.S. notes were also known as "legal tenders" although they were not legal tender for all purposes. In 1870 the U.S. Supreme Court ruled in *Hepburn* v. *Griswold* that Congress had no constitutional authority to make greenbacks legal tender for contracts entered into before the act was passed. This was reversed in the Legal Tender cases (*Knox* v. *Lee* and *Parker* v. *Davis*) of 1871.

The issues of greenbacks provided substantial revenue for the national government during the American Civil War, although they rapidly depreciated. The value of the notes in terms of gold declined to an average of 39 cents during July and August 1864, and remained at less than 90 cents until 1876. As the secretary of the treasury gradually accumulated a redemption fund in gold, their value rose in terms of gold. By 1879 greenbacks were made redeemable in gold. The quantity then outstanding amounted to approximately $347,000,000, and since that time the amount outstanding has remained at this figure with minor fluctuations. United States notes were made receivable in payments of customs duties on June 17, 1930, and became full legal tender under the act of May 12, 1933, as amended by public resolution no. 10 of June 5, 1933.

(A. Kp.)

GREEN BAY, a city and the seat of Brown County, in northeastern Wisconsin, U.S., where the Fox River empties into Green Bay, an inlet of Lake Michigan, is 112 mi. NW of Milwaukee. The first European in the area was Jean Nicolet, who arrived from Canada in 1634. Nicolas Perrot began to trade on the site of De Pere in 1668, and Claude Allouez, a Jesuit, founded a mission there in 1669; from that time on white men probably always lived in the vicinity. The French built a fort at the mouth of the river in 1717, and this spot became the heart of a small French-Canadian community that handled furs from a large area until after the War of 1812. Its most distinguished figure was a famous 18th-century Indian fighter, Charles de Langlade. The fur trade finally expired about 1845. (*See* WISCONSIN: *History.*)

An American community began when the U.S. Army built Ft. Howard in 1816 within the present limits of Green Bay. The first village plat was laid out in 1829, and Wisconsin's earliest newspaper, the *Green Bay Intelligencer,* appeared in 1833. Later, Brown County came to have large numbers of Germans, Belgians, and Dutch. In the period from 1890 to 1910, the population increased from 9,069 to 25,236. It more than doubled by 1950 and in 1970 it was 87,809. The standard metropolitan statistical area (Brown County), pop. (1970) 158,244, includes the city of De Pere, 5 mi. S, and the towns of Preble (parts of which were annexed in 1941 and 1943) and Allouez. (For comparative population figures *see* table in WISCONSIN: *Population.*)

In the second half of the 20th century Green Bay had the largest wholesale distributing business in the state after Milwaukee and Madison. Its harbour receives more than 3,000,000 tons of waterborne shipping a year. Its factories produce cheese, beet sugar, wood pulp and paper products; lumber, furniture, and machinery. In 1968 a rich deposit of manganese, considered recoverable, was discovered on the floor of the bay. From 1919 the city supported a professional football team, the Green Bay Packers.

At West De Pere the Roman Catholic Premonstratensian order founded St. Norbert's College in 1898. A liberal arts college, it became coeducational in 1952.

(W. F. Ry.)

GREENE, GRAHAM (1904–　　), English novelist, short-story writer, playwright, and essayist, whose outstanding literary gifts are most typically displayed in a highly original genre of naturalistic fiction with religious themes, was born at Berkhamsted, Hertfordshire, on Oct. 2, 1904. He was educated at Berkhamsted School, of which his father was headmaster, and at Balliol College, Oxford. He first earned his living as a journalist, reviewer, and film critic, and attracted attention as a novelist with *The Man Within* (1929), *The Name of Action* (1930), and *Rumour at Nightfall* (1931). These works, competent but derivative, tried to synthesize the Buchan or Stevenson story of action with contemporary introspective techniques. Thereafter, Greene divided his work into two categories: serious "novels" and lighter "entertainments." The entertainments *Stamboul Train* (1932) and *A Gun for Sale* (1936), with their crisp dialogue and fast scene changes, show the influence of the cinema, and became successful motion-pictures. The novels *It's a Battlefield* (1934) and *England Made Me* (1935) are subtler and more ambitious, influenced by the Joycean interior monologue and concerned with moral dilemmas. Although Greene became a Roman Catholic in 1926, he did not allow the preoccupations of his faith to play a central part in his fiction until *Brighton Rock* (1938), a realistic serious story about gangster violence that presents the good-and-evil of the theologians as a system distinct from the right-and-wrong of the secular moralists and, by a logic not acceptable to all readers, makes moral right inferior to evil as traditionally presented by Christian doctrine and teaching. *The Power and the Glory* (1940), *The Heart of the Matter* (1948), and *The End of the Affair* (1951) pursue this paradox further, and seem to argue that, in a fallen world, true sanctity can be found only in the exceptional individual whose awareness of his own sinfulness drives him to despair and even to suicide. Greene's Catholicism is revealed as unorthodox: he appears to subscribe to the Jansenist doctrine of man's inability to do good and reliance on Divine Grace alone. The novel *The Quiet American* (1955) and the entertainment *Our Man in Havana* (1958) look at the postwar world of political intrigue, espionage, and the struggle for world power between the United States and the U.S.S.R., and do not favour what is seen as the U.S. tendency to equate "good" with material progress. *A Burnt-Out Case* (1961) returns with a kind of relief to man's "fallen" condition as exemplified in a Congo leper colony; *In Search of a Character,* Greene's notes on the genesis of this novel, was published in the same year. Delineation of man's fallen state became even starker in *The Comedians* (1966), set in Haiti, in which Communism and Christianity are forced to a rapprochement: neither has "stood aside, like an established society, and been indifferent." In sharp contrast is *Travels With My Aunt* (1969), a comic novel in which Greene parodies his own style through a series of incidents involving international smuggling.

Greene's dramatic gifts are best seen in *The Living Room* (1953) and *The Potting Shed* (1957); in both, the themes of sin and grace are given traditional dramaturgical expression. *The Complaisant Lover* (1959), a brilliant comedy, was well received; but *Carving a Statue* (1964), returning somewhat heavy-handedly to theological subject matter, was neither an artistic nor a commercial success. Greene has published short stories in *Twenty-one Stories* (1954), *A Sense of Reality* (1963), and *May We Borrow Your Husband? And other Comedies of the Sexual Life* (1967); and has written several children's tales, the scripts of the successful films *The Fallen Idol* (1948) and *The Third Man* (1949; publ. 1950), as well as those for *Our Man in Havana* (1960) and *The Comedians* (1967), and travel books—*Journey Without Maps* (1936) and *The Lawless Roads* (1939). Critical and contemplative essays are collected in *The Lost Childhood* (1951). His autobiography, *A Sort of Life*, was published in 1971.

BIBLIOGRAPHY.—K. Allott and M. Faris, *The Art of Graham Greene* (1951); D. Pryce-Jones, *Graham Greene* (1963); R. O. Evans (ed.), *Graham Greene* (1963); P. Stratford, *Faith and Fiction* (1964); J. Atkins, *Graham Greene* (1957; 2nd enlarged ed., 1966); D. Lodge, *Graham Greene* (1966); M. Turnell, *Graham Greene* (1967); J. D. Vann, *Graham Greene: a Checklist of Criticism* (1970). (AN. BU.; X.)

GREENE, NATHANAEL (1742–1786), American Revolutionary War general, was born at Potowomut, Warwick township, R.I., Aug. 7, 1742. He settled in Coventry, R.I., in 1770 to manage a branch of his father's iron foundry. He served several terms in the colonial legislature, sympathized strongly with the Whigs and was elected commander of the little Rhode Island army organized in 1775. The continental congress made him a brigadier general in 1775 and a major general in 1776.

Greene served with Washington in the siege of Boston (1775–76) and in the fighting in and around New York city in 1776. At the time of the British capture of Ft. Washington, on the Hudson river, with its large garrison and extremely important stores in Nov. 1776, Greene was in command of the post and has been blamed for failure to evacuate it when Gen. Sir William Howe's approach was known. But the evidence clearly establishes the fact that Washington was responsible for the disastrous decision to remain. Greene was with Washington on the ensuing retreat across New Jersey, commanded the reserve at Brandywine and took part in the battle of Germantown.

At the request of Washington, on March 2, 1778, he accepted the office of quartermaster general (succeeding Thomas Mifflin) and succeeded with it as well as anyone could under the circumstances, meanwhile continuing from time to time to command troops in the field. In August he resigned the office of quartermaster general after a struggle with congress over the interference in army administration by the treasury board. On Oct. 4 he succeeded Gen. Horatio Gates as commander in chief of the southern army and took command at Charlotte, N.C., on Dec. 2. The army was weak and badly equipped and was opposed by a superior force under Cornwallis. Greene decided to divide his own troops, thus forcing the division of the British as well. This strategy led to Gen. Daniel Morgan's victory at Cowpens, S.C., Jan. 17, 1781, and to the battle at Guilford Courthouse, N.C., March 15, in which, after having weakened the British troops by continued movements, Greene was defeated indeed but only at such cost to the victor that three days after the battle Cornwallis abandoned his plan to conquer North Carolina, withdrew to Wilmington and then northeastward to Yorktown, Va. Thus left free to take the offensive, Greene turned swiftly to the reconquest of the inner country of South Carolina. This, in spite of a reverse sustained at Lord Rawdon's hands at Hobkirk's hill (April 25), he achieved by the end of June, the British retiring to the coast. Greene then gave his forces a six weeks' rest and on Sept. 8, with 2,600 men, engaged the British under Lieut. Col. James Stuart at Eutaw springs; the battle so weakened the British that they withdrew to Charleston, where Greene held them during the remaining months of the war.

Greene proved himself one of the ablest of Washington's lieutenants, both in service under Washington and in independent command. But his reputation as to character stands less high. The charges that clouded his later life of having been in secret partnership with John Banks, army contractor for Greene in the south, were not proved. There is, nevertheless, ample evidence of his having had, while he was quartermaster general, a secret partner-

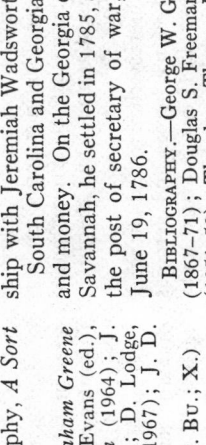
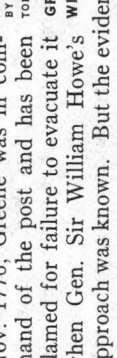
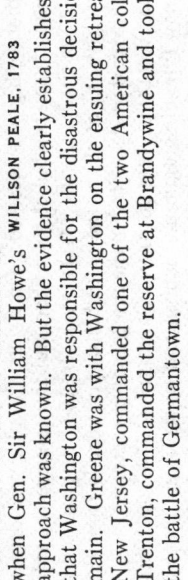

BY COURTESY OF INDEPENDENCE NATIONAL HISTORICAL PARK, PHILADELPHIA

GREENE, PORTRAIT BY CHARLES WILLSON PEALE, 1783

ship with Jeremiah Wadsworth, commissary general of purchases. South Carolina and Georgia voted Greene liberal grants of lands and money. On the Georgia estate Mulberry Grove, 14 mi. above Savannah, he settled in 1785, after twice refusing (1781 and 1784) the post of secretary of war, and there he died of sunstroke on June 19, 1786.

BIBLIOGRAPHY.—George W. Greene, *Life of Nathanael Greene*, 3 vol. (1867–71); Douglas S. Freeman, *George Washington*, vol. 3, 4 and 5 (1951–52); Theodore Thayer, *Nathanael Greene* (1960). (B. KN.)

GREENE, ROBERT (1558?–1592), was one of the most popular English prose writers of the later 16th century, Shakespeare's most successful predecessor in romantic comedy, evidently the first writer in England who succeeded, at least for a short time, in deriving a livelihood from his dramatic and prose works, and one of the earliest English autobiographers.

Greene was probably born at Norwich, Norfolk, where he was baptized on July 11, 1558. He matriculated at St. John's college, Cambridge, on Nov. 26, 1575, as a sizar (which shows that his parents were not wealthy), received the B.A. degree in 1578, and became M.A. in 1583 from Clare hall, where he wrote the prefatory epistle to the second part of *Mamillia*. He had evidently begun already to frequent London literary circles, since the first part of *Mamillia* was entered in the Stationers' Register on Oct. 3, 1580. In 1588 Oxford conferred a degree on him and thereafter Greene somewhat ostentatiously referred to himself on title pages as "Academiae Utriusque Magister in Artibus." About 1585 or 1586 he married, and had at least one child, but he soon deserted his wife and went to London. With his "jolly long red peake" he swaggered in bohemian society and, according to his own lurid accounts of his behaviour, became an intimate of cutpurses, rascals and prostitutes. Early in Aug. 1592, he tells us, he dined with his friend Thomas Nashe on pickled herring and Rhenish wine, and a month later, on Sept. 3, forsaken by his "quondam acquaintance," he died in London, attended only by a shoemaker and his wife and by his mistress, the sister of a rogue named Cutting Ball and the mother of Fortunatus Greene. On the day before his death he wrote to his "Sweet Wife," asking her to pay the bearer £10: "But for him I had perished in the streetes. Forget and forgive my wronges done unto thee, and Almighty God have mercie on my soule. Farewell till we meet in heaven, for on earth thou shalt never see me more."

Works.—Despite his early death Greene was a prolific writer and composed over 35 works between 1580 and 1592. Nashe observed that "In a night and a day would he have yarkt up a Pamphlet as well as in seaven yeare." Though his facility apparently amazed (and distressed) his contemporaries, it was a prerequisite for a man who expected to obtain an income from publication. Stationers paid small fees for manuscripts, and authors, in the absence of copyright laws, had no control over their books after they were published, profits from subsequent printings accruing to the publishers. A professional author like Greene had to write rapidly and to supply material attractive to the public. Hence, like most popular writers, Greene slavishly followed literary fashions. In his early prose writings he aped John Lyly's *Euphues*, modifying the excesses of the affected style but retaining Lyly's moral platitudes. In the later 1580s, he fashioned prose pastorals after Sir Philip Sidney's *Arcadia*; unrequited lovers penned interminable letters in balanced prose and pretended to dissect the subject of passion, though their comments have an amazingly unreal quality. Structurally these works resembled static operas; instead of conversations there were long speeches or letters (arias), there was little interaction between characters and no psychological reason for their conduct, and charming lyrics, not always organically related to the action, appeared unexpectedly, and give him a reputation also as a poet of metrical inventiveness and verbal felicity. Read aloud, as no doubt they were intended to be read, these pastoral romances were effective; like most Elizabethans, Greene had studied the precepts of classical and Tudor rhetoricians, and he and his audience both delighted in the traditional patterns and figures of speech characteristic of well-designed orations. Of these tales the most readable are *Tullie's Love* (1589), a nonhistorical account of Cicero's love for a woman of the upper class; *Menaphon* (1589), an implausible story of shepherds and shepherdesses, mistaken identities and complications which were suddenly resolved so that everything ended merrily; and *Pandosto* (1588), his finest romance and the direct source of Shakespeare's *A Winter's Tale*.

About 1590, probably because the literary climate had changed, Greene determined to abandon his lovesick heroes and heroines and to compose serious didactic works. In *Greene's Vision*, published after his death but written in 1590, he stated that Chaucer was no longer his guide, but the moral John Gower. Beginning with *Greene's Never Too Late* (1590), he related prodigal son stories, in which a youth invariably flouted the advice of his father, strutted off to sow his wild oats and then returned penitent and humble. Francesco, in *Francisco's Fortunes* (1590), abandoned his wife, succumbed to the lures of the strumpet Infida, who spurned him when he needed money, and eventually fell in with a company of actors who persuaded him to compose plays. That in these works Greene drew on his own experience is evident from two tracts printed posthumously in 1592, *Greenes Groatsworth of Wit, Bought With a Million of Repentance* and *The Repentance of Robert Greene, Maister of Artes*. The former purported to relate the story of Roberto, whose experiences were typical of Greene's other young profligates, but in the middle of his tale Greene suddenly dropped the disguise, "Heere (Gentlemen) breake I off Robertoes speach; whose life in most parts agreeing with mine." Hence the guilt of his characters and their terrors as to their prospects of salvation were his own. For Greene, particularly in his *Repentance*, blackened himself as the worst of sinners and set himself forth as an example to English youth, and particularly to his former acquaintances, Christopher Marlowe, Thomas Nashe and George Peele, who, he averred in *Groatsworth*, were destroying themselves through their immorality and jeopardizing their souls because of their atheism. These autobiographical pamphlets are perhaps Greene's most effective works, for, unlike his fiction, the story of "Robin Greene," who publicly affected bohemianism but inwardly was tormented by an uneasy conscience, is a moving study in pathos.

In the last year of his life Greene wrote a series of exposés of the Elizabethan underworld, beginning with *A Notable Discovery of Coosnage* (1591), in which he portrayed the deceptions of cony-catchers and petty thieves. Though he asserted that he was serving a lofty patriotic function in rooting out these criminals, most of his material was not original, and the author, despite his protestations, was clearly more intent upon entertaining his readers than in reforming evil. The most successful and amusing of these tracts was *A disputation between a he conycatcher and a she conycatcher* (1592), a discussion between a male and a female thief over their respective merits in duplicity. Another noteworthy pamphlet was *A quip for an upstart Courtier* (1592), which succinctly outlined abuses in approximately 60 Elizabethan trades and professions, and which contained the celebrated attack on Gabriel Harvey and his brothers, John and Richard, probably inserted just before publication at the instigation of Nashe, who was to continue the feud with the Harveys for the next four years. In answering Greene's attack in *Foure letters and certaine sonnets* (1592), Gabriel Harvey, with accuracy but with repellent malice, supplied many details about Greene's death. The *Groatsworth of Wit* also aroused controversy, for not only did Greene urge repentance upon his three friends but also assailed "an upstart Crow, beautified with our feathers, that with his *Tygers hart wrapt in a Players hyde*, supposes he is as well able to bombast out a blanke verse as the best of you; and being an absolute *Johannes fac totum*, is in his owne conceit the onely Shake-scene in a countery." This first reference in print to Shakespeare has evoked considerable discussion: earlier critics believed that Greene accused Shakespeare of plagiarism in *I Henry VI*, in which the italicized quotation appears; scholars were later of the opinion that the passage was a criticism of Shakespeare the actor, who, like many other players, rewrote the dramatist's words.

Greene's theatrical career presents numerous problems; the canon is disputed, the dates of the plays are conjectural, and his role as collaborator is a subject of much inconclusive discus-sion. One of his earliest plays appears to be *The Comicall Historie of Alphonsus King of Aragon* (written c. 1588, publ. 1599), a weak imitation of Marlowe's mighty line. *The Historie of Orlando Furioso* (written c. 1591, publ. 1594) was an adaptation of Ariosto's poem. *A Looking Glasse for London and Englande* (written c. 1590, publ. 1594), written jointly with Thomas Lodge, was a dramatic jeremiad to Englishmen, reminiscent of Lodge's *Alarum against Usurers* (1584) and Greene's own prodigal-son stories. *The Honorable Historie of frier Bacon, and frier Bongay* (written c. 1591, publ. 1594), though an attempt to vie with Marlowe's *Dr. Faustus*, was the first successful romantic comedy in English; here Greene for the first time realized his comic talent in drama. In *The Scottish Historie of James the fourth* (written c. 1590–91; publ. 1598), probably his last play, he used a tale by Giambattista Giraldi (*q.v.*; Cinzio, or Cinthio), but drew on fairy lore for Oberon (*q.v.*) and Bohan, and delineated almost Wordsworthian English maidens in Dorothea and Ida. It was a worthy forerunner of *As You Like It* and *A Midsummer Night's Dream*. As Marlowe anticipated the tragedies of Shakespeare, so in a lesser way Greene furnished a model in dramatic comedy and romance for the greatest genius of the age.

BIBLIOGRAPHY.—Greene's plays and poems were edited by Alexander Dyce, 2 vol. (1831) and by J. C. Collins, 2 vol. (1905). His complete writings were edited for the Huth Library by A. B. Grosart, 15 vol. (1881–86). The critical studies, J. C. Jordan, *Robert Greene* (1915) and René Pruvost, *Greene et ses romans* (1938), both contain bibliographies.
(E. H. MR.)

GREENER, WILLIAM (1806–1869), English gunmaker and inventor, was born at Felling near Newcastle upon Tyne in 1806 and began business in Newcastle in 1829. In 1844 he moved to Birmingham. His most important invention, the first expansive rifle bullet, consisted of an oval ball with a flat end with a cavity in which a metal plug was inserted. On firing, the plug was driven forward and caused the bullet to expand and thus engage the rifle grooves. (*See* SMALL ARMS, MILITARY.) In 1843 he patented a process with W. E. Stait for the manufacture of pencils from the hard graphite carbon deposited in the interior of gas retorts.

His son WILLIAM WELLINGTON GREENER (1834–1921) invented a new type of shotgun mechanism and wrote several books, including *The Gun and Its Development* (1881).

GREENHEART (BEBEERU), names given to a valuable South American timber tree, *Ocotea* (or *Nectandra*) *rodioei*, of the laurel family (Lauraceae). It is a large tree, native to the Guianas. The bark and the fruits of the tree contain bebeerine, formerly used as an antipyretic. Greenheart wood is of a dark green colour, sapwood and heartwood being distinguished only with difficulty. The heartwood is one of the most durable of all timbers, and its value is greatly enhanced by its resistance to decay and by its proof against the ravages of insects and many marine borers, which latter rapidly destroy piles and other submerged structures of most other kinds of wood.

Greenheart wood is one of the strongest and densest of all woods. It is used, chiefly in Europe, for piles and wharves and in bridges and ships; its excessive weight makes it unfit for other purposes.

GREENHOUSE, as generally understood, is an enclosed glass structure of variable size, shape and complexity in which plants are grown. In England it is sometimes called glasshouse. The simplest greenhouse provides protection only from the extremes of hot and cold, while the greenhouse of the advanced amateur and the commercial grower tends to provide the superior plant environment necessary for the production of fruit, vegetables or flowers of market value. A style of greenhouse often seen in parks and large estates is the conservatory; it is more ornamental than functional in design and houses exhibitions and specimen plants usually displayed in a naturalistic manner.

Location and Structure.—The first step in planning a greenhouse is choosing the proper location. The choice depends upon slope of land, which should be level, and upon convenience to other work areas. The placement of the greenhouse on the lot in relation to the sun is vital. In a properly situated greenhouse the sun follows a uniform path over the plants. Best growing results are obtained when the light is even and shadowless. All trees, buildings and anything else of any height should be kept away from the adjacent area. A year-round source of water for plant care is essential. In some areas it is possible to use lakes or streams; in others well water is the only source. The water must be chemically acceptable to the plants being grown. A water sample should be taken and a complete analysis made.

The next consideration is the style of greenhouse structure. The commercial grower uses either the span-type house or a modification called the ridge-and-furrow house. Most commonly used is the span house, in which the sides of the roof are of equal length and both side walls of equal height. The centre or the ridge of the house is generally 15 to 20 ft. high, and the rafters slope down to the sides about 8 ft. above the ground. The ridge-and-furrow house is nothing more than two or more span houses joined at the side wall. This saves money, as there are fewer walls and the heating costs are consequently less than for individual span houses totaling the same growing area.

The wood, if any, used in construction must be able to stand high moisture and humidity; some suitable woods are redwood, cedar and cypress. All nails, screws, pipe and other metal parts should be zinc-coated or made of aluminum or some other rust-resistant metal. The choice of glass is important, as roughly 85% of the average greenhouse is glass. In some areas, because of strong winds, hailstorms or heavy snowfall, it is necessary to use double-weight rather than single-weight glass. Fibreglass and plastics are sometimes used in place of glass.

Benches or growing areas for the plants must be provided within the greenhouse. These are usually made of wood with two- or three-foot-wide walks, usually running the length of the greenhouse, between them. Most nurserymen, amateur or professional, try to keep the walk area to a minimum. In bench building, a level growing surface with drainage for excess water must be provided.

The heating system can be either steam or hot water, the choice most often depending on the size of the growing area. Since boilers for steam heat are expensive, the small grower uses the less expensive (initial cost) hot-water system. The pipes carrying steam or hot water are distributed through the house. The amount of piping needed to give an even growing temperature varies according to the climatic conditions.

The last important factor in a greenhouse is ventilation. Openings are usually near the peak of the roof—controlled by mechanical arms for easier opening and closing—or automatically operated by electricity according to temperature fluctuations.

Plant Subjects.—The choice of plants to be grown depends on the type of greenhouse maintained. Three main kinds of greenhouse may be recognized: cool, warm and tropical. A few plants suited to each are listed below (only night temperatures, in degrees Fahrenheit, are given; day temperatures are permitted to rise 5°–10° on dull days, 10°–15° on sunny days).

Cool Greenhouse (45°–50°; fairly humid): cinerarias, cyclamens, carnations, fuchsias and a variety of bulbous plants including tulips, hyacinths and narcissus.

Warm Greenhouse (50°–55°; moderately humid): begonias, gloxinias, African violets, chrysanthemums, roses, Boston ferns, coleuses and, under drier conditions, cacti and succulents.

Tropical Greenhouse or Hothouse (60°–70°; very humid): caladiums, philodendrons, palms, poinsettias, codiaeums (crotons), bougainvilleas and passionflowers.

See FLOWER: *Commercial Flower Growing*; HOUSE PLANTS; *see* also HORTICULTURE AND GARDENING. (W. G. MC.; X.)

GREENLAND (GRØNLAND), the world's largest island, which forms part of the Danish kingdom, lies mostly within the Arctic circle. Its area is 840,000 sq.mi.; 708,069 sq.mi. are ice covered. It is situated between latitudes 59° 46′ N. (Cape Farewell) and 83° 39′ N. (Cape Morris Jesup) and longitudes 11° 39′ W. and 73° 08′ W. The extreme length of Greenland is about 1,650 mi. while its extreme breadth, at about 70° N, is nearly 800 mi. In the extreme north it is separated only by a 25-mi.-wide strait from Ellesmere Island in the Canadian arctic archipelago; a suboceanic ridge with soundings not exceeding 600 ft. connects it with North America. Greenland thus is situated on the American continental shelf. Another ridge joins northeast Greenland and Spitsbergen, and the Faeroe-Icelandic ridge unites Greenland with Iceland

(across Denmark strait), the Faeroes and Scotland; both these ridges have soundings of about 2,000 ft. *See* also DENMARK.

PHYSICAL GEOGRAPHY

Geology.—The whole of Greenland is similar to, and probably part of, the Laurentian shield of Canada. It is a mountainous plateau in which Pre-Cambrian rocks predominate but in the northern half of the island there are considerable areas of younger rocks. The Pre-Cambrian formations are mostly of granite and gneiss and are characterized by metamorphosed sedimentary and volcanic rocks. In the north and northeast there can be traced the continuation of the Caledonian foldings of Europe and Spitsbergen. These caused the high mountains of Peary Land and their westward continuation into Ellesmere Island, and are associated with an overthrust in the Franz Josef fjord area on the east. Vertical faults, younger than Ordovician, occur in the north and, probably connected with them, there are *solfataras* which are truncated cones or vents of volcanoes without lava. The rocks underlying the *solfataras* are limestones containing Cambrian trilobites. Volcanic activity and much faulting took place in east Greenland at the close of the Paleozoic period. In the Caledonian fold zone of the east a trough of Devonian rock was formed in which Old Red Sandstone and conglomerates were deposited. There are extensive Mesozoic sediments in the northeast. At about 70° N. on the east coast the lowest Mesozoic beds are Lower Triassic sandstones and shales, while later Triassic beds occur farther south on the same coast. Jurassic beds are found only on the east between Jameson Land and Danmark harbour. Cretaceous beds occur on both east and west but chiefly on the west where coal is found in the Cretaceous sandstones of the eastern edges of Disko Island and the borders of Nûgssuaq peninsula. The abundant fossils in those rocks give clear indication of a warm, temperate climate persisting until Tertiary times. Tertiary lavas, either surface flows or intrusive sills, are associated on both sides with rocks of that age and cover them in places. The sedimentary Tertiaries are chiefly sandstones on the west and Disko Island, Nûgssuaq and Svartenhuk peninsulas on the west and coast are the chief Tertiary basalt areas. The aftereffect of the volcanic activity in Tertiary times can be seen in warm springs in the Scoresby sound area in the east (temperature 140° F. [60° C.]), in the Julianehaab district in the south (104° F. [40° C.]) and in Disko Island (35.6° to 64.4° F. [2° to 18° C.]). Numerous raised beaches and terraces, containing shells of marine mollusca, etc., occur along the whole coast of Greenland and indicate that this large island has been raised, or the sea has sunk, in postglacial times. Their maximum elevation is about 600 ft. During recent times Greenland has been sinking. Through exact measuring it was stated that the sinking of the land in proportion to the surface of the sea amounts to 0.4 in. a year at Godhavn. The sinking and rising of the land have made it possible to define several phases of climate in postglacial times: high arctic,

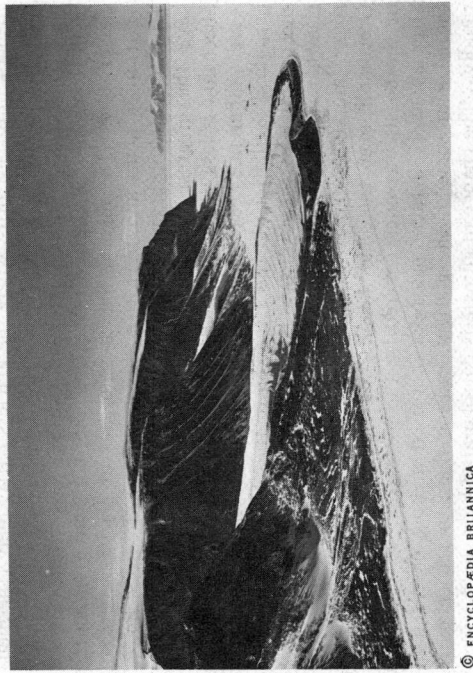

© ENCYCLOPÆDIA BRITANNICA

INGLEFIELD GULF AT KANAK, 80 MI. N OF THULE

arctic, high arctic, cold temperate, arctic.

Minerals.—The only known commercial source of natural cryolite is at Ivigtut and has been mined by a Danish company since 1865. Iron of meteoric as well as terrestrial origin is found on Disko Island and from it the Eskimos got iron for their weapons. From Cape York R. E. Peary, in 1897, brought to New York city the largest nodule of meteoric origin ever found, weighing 90 tons. Graphite is abundant, particularly near Upernavik, and has occasionally been mined. Coal of poor quality is found in the district around Disko bay and is mined for Greenland's own use. Steatite or soapstone has long been used by the natives for making lamps and vessels. Copper has been observed at several places but mining will not pay. Lead deposits found by L. Koch in the Mestervig area on the east coast were mined in the 1950s, the ore being exported by ship during the brief summer. Work in the mine ceased in 1965.

Natural Regions.—Greenland is divided into two natural regions: the ice sheet, which covers more than four-fifths of the country, and the coastal regions where the mountains rise out of the ice.

The Ice Sheet.—The interior of Greenland is covered by an enormous sheet of ice, burying all valleys and mountains far below its surface. Much of the rock floor on which the ice lies is at or slightly below sea level. The ice is contained by the mountain ranges, which form much of the Greenland coast. Its area is 708,069 sq.mi. and it is by far the greatest glacier of the northern hemisphere. Occasionally there emerge lofty isolated rocks known as nunataks (*see* NUNATAK). The ice sheet rises in the interior to a little above 10,000 ft. west of Scoresby sound on the east coast (maximum thickness 6,700 ft.; average 5,000 ft.) and descends gradually toward the coasts or the bottom of the fjords. The biggest glacier, the Humboldt glacier, more than 62 mi. wide, terminates in the Kane basin on the north coast, rising to a height of 328 ft. A transverse section of the surface of the ice sheet from the west to the east coast would show a regular curve, approaching an ellipse but with greater elevation toward the east. The smaller southerly dome reaches 9,200 ft.

In the interior the surface of the ice is composed of loose, dry snow which never melts but is transformed to ice by the pressure of the ever increasing snow masses, which also carry the ice outward to the borders. Some of the snow is carried off the ice by the outward-blowing winds and is piled up in the valleys and on the ice-bare rims of the coasts. Near its margin the ice sheet is broken up by numerous crevasses, some of them being 100–150 ft. deep. The steep ice walls at the edge show a striation called the blue bands. They are strata of compact, bright and bluish ice when the glacier moved forward and froze the air-free ice.

The ice sheet of Greenland must be considered as a viscous mass which by the vertical pressure in its interior is pressed outward and slowly flows toward the coasts. There the ice converges into the valleys and moves with increasing velocity, in the form of glaciers, into the fjords, where the glaciers partly melt (the melting water running as glacier rivers into the sea) and partly break off as icebergs. Since A. Helland (1875), several expeditions from Denmark, Britain, France and the U.S. have measured glacier flow. The highest known velocities of glaciers averaged 97 ft. in 24 hours and, over a shorter period, 100 ft. in 24 hours. The Rink, Jakobshavn and Upernavik glaciers on the west coast have the greatest velocities. Those on the east are slower. Sheet flow is less than 1 in. per day. There is, however, probably a great difference between summer and winter. There seem to be periodical oscillations in the extension of the glaciers and the ice sheet similar to those observed on the glaciers of the Alps and elsewhere. Numerous glacial marks, such as polished striated rocks, moraines, erratic blocks, etc., prove that the whole of Greenland, even the small islands and skerries (isolated rocks) of the coast, was once covered by the ice sheet. In the years after about 1930 there has been increased melting observed at the edge of some of the glaciers, causing them to recede more rapidly. The change in climate is corroborated by a slight warming of the North Atlantic and a small increase in temperatures in countries of northwestern Europe. (*See also* GLACIER.)

Coastal Regions.—The coasts of Greenland are deeply indented with fjords; the coasts of Melville bay and around Northeast Foreland are to some degree exceptions. The complete coast line of Greenland is estimated at about 25,000 mi. Numerous small islands lie off the coasts. The largest is Disko (3,200 sq.mi.), off the west, at 70° N.

In some parts the ice sheet extends down to the outer coast; elsewhere its margin is situated farther inland and the bare coastland is deeply intersected by fjords extending far into the interior, where they are blocked by enormous glaciers which discharge icebergs into them. The west coast is the most intersected, the largest fjords being Tasermiut, Godthaabfjord, Arfersiorfik, Umanakfjord, Karratsfjord, Southern and Northern Stromfjord; the last of these has a length of 116 mi. The largest systems of fjords, however, are found on the east coast, where the Scoresby sound system has a length of about 185 mi. and a breadth of about 125 mi. Franz Josef fjord with its branch, King Oscar fjord, forms a system of fjords on a similarly huge scale. These fjords are very deep and soundings indicate that they continue as deep submarine valleys on the coastal shelf. The fjords are drowned valleys caused by erosion and not by tectonic action.

For 500 mi. down the east coast runs a belt of high mountains, exceeding 7,000 ft. in height; Mt. Gunnbjorn in 69° N. measures 12,139 ft. and is the highest mountain in Greenland. Along the west coast the mountains are not generally quite so high, though even there peaks of 5,000 and 6,000 ft. are not uncommon.

Climate.—Greenland lies north of the 10° isotherm and thus has a polar climate. The weather is uncertain and changes suddenly from bright sunshine to dense fog or heavy falls of snow and icy winds. The July mean at Ivigtut is 49.8° F. (9.9° C.) and at Thule 40.5° F. (4.7° C.). The January means are 18.5° F. and −21.0° F. (−7.5° C. and −29.5° C.). A branch of the Gulf stream flows north on the east side of Davis strait and accounts for relatively high temperatures in southwest Greenland. On the east coast temperatures are lower than on the west, for the polar current washes the coast. On the coasts, particularly the southwest, frost is rare in June, July and August and the summer warmth is appreciable. Rainfall, which is mainly in summer, is heavy in the southwest but light elsewhere. Snow may fall in any month of the year. The Alfred Wegener expedition (1930–31) measured temperature in the lofty interior temperatures are always low. The February mean −52.9° F. (−47.2° C.) and July mean 12.8° F. (−10.7° C.). The minimum temperature in the winter was −85° F. (−65° C.), which occurred several times; the maximum temperature in the summer was 26.6° F. (−3° C.). French expeditions in the 1950s observed similar values. Radiation from the snow surface is largely responsible for the low temperatures. A thin layer of cold air lies almost permanently over the surface and mollifies the invading depressions, or low-pressure systems, but these cross the ice sheet, particularly from west to east. Cold winds glide outward from the inland ice and, heated by compression and blowing down valleys, sometimes give rise to warm, relatively dry, foehn winds. Precipitation decreases from 40 in. per year in the south to 8 in. per year in the north.

(H. Ln.; H. Lr.)

Vegetation and Animal Life.—Of the approximately 400 species of vascular plants found in Greenland more than 300 probably came from North America. About 50 of the rest may have been introduced by the early Norsemen and a few are survivals from the maximum glaciation. As the whole country lies north of the tree line there are no forests, but in the southwest, where the vegetation is less arctic and more abundant, there are groups of willows and birches up to 10 ft. in height. The dwarf arctic birch (*Betula nana*) reaches its northern limit in Greenland and the mountain ash (*Sorbus americana*) has much the same distribution. The alder (*Alnus crispa*) replaces the birch inland, forming scrub more than 3 ft. high in some places. The climax communities are probably heath consisting of *Vaccinium uliginosum, Cassiope tetragona, Empetrum nigrum,* andromeda, dwarf willows, mosses and other plants. A steppe vegetation, dominated generally by

THE HARBOUR AT JAKOBSHAVN, A FISHING VILLAGE AND ONE OF GREENLAND'S LARGER TOWNS, FOUNDED 1741, ON THE WEST COAST IN DISKO BAY

Carex supina, is found on some level areas, while on the hillsides moss campion, saxifrages, *Pyrola grandiflora*, *Dryas integrifolia*, Iceland poppy and many other alpines grow among the lichen-covered rocks. Among the boulders on the beaches *Oxyria*, willow herb and *Cerastium* are found and in the marshy places *Alchemilla*, cotton grass, sedges and equisetums are common.

At Umanak (70° 40′ N.) broccoli and radishes grow well; turnips, lettuce and chervil sometimes succeed but parsley cannot be raised. At Jakobshavn (69° 12′ N.), only about 15 mi. from the ice sheet, gardening succeeds well. In the Julianehaab district in the south flowering plants such as aster, nemophila and mignonette are cultivated.

The land mammals of Greenland consist of the musk ox, lemming and ermine in the north and east; reindeer, reintroduced from Scandinavia after being hunted almost to extinction; polar wolf and polar bear; and the arctic fox and arctic hare along most of the coast. The sea mammals—whales and seals—were formerly the chief food of the inhabitants. The six species of seal include *Phoca foetida* and *P. greenlandica*, which are the two commonest, and the walrus. Of the 60 species of birds breeding in Greenland, half are resident throughout the year and half are summer visitors. Of the visitors 60% come from North America. Sea birds are very numerous and the northeast of the island is one of the few breeding places of the barnacle goose and the pink-foot goose. Among birds of prey are the white-tailed eagle, the Greenland falcon and the snowy owl, while the commonest land birds are the ptarmigan, snow bunting and raven. Sea trout and salmon are found in the streams and small lakes of the south. The invertebrates include crustacea, insects, mollusca, annelids and arachnids. In the west mosquitoes are pests.

HISTORY

The history of Greenland is bound up with the history of arctic exploration (*see* ARCTIC, THE). Since the 10th century men have not only settled on the coast but have visited and explored the island in the course of their journeys into the polar regions.

DISCOVERY AND EXPLORATION

Exploration of the Coasts.—In the beginning of the 10th century the Norwegian Gunnbjorn Ulfsson (son of Ulf Kraka) is reported to have found islands to the west of Iceland. In 982 Eric the Red sailed from Iceland to find Gunnbjorn's land and spent three years on Greenland's southwestern coasts. On his return in 985 he called the land Greenland in order to make people more willing to go there and in 986 started again with 25 ships, of which 14 reached Greenland, where a colony was founded on the southwest coast. Communication between the Norse settlements and Norway was broken off in the 15th century, however. In the following century Danish and Norwegian expeditions tried in vain to re-establish the communication and the rediscovery of Greenland was made by the English navigator Martin Frobisher, who landed on the west coast of Greenland in 1578.

Other explorers, including Gaspar Corte-Real, had meanwhile seen it and the work of John Davis (1586–88), Henry Hudson (1610) and William Baffin (1616) afforded further knowledge of the west coast. The east coast was sighted by Hudson in about 73° 30′ N. in 1607 and in 1617 by the Dutchman Joris Carolus in about 66° N. During the 17th century the coasts were probably visited by many whalers who finished the rediscovery of the country's outline.

Exploration was impossible without bases on the coast and was not started until 1721, when the Danish-Norwegian missionary Hans Egede founded a settlement near Godthaab on the west coast. Egede studied the nature and the people, traveling northward and southward from Godthaab, and in 1752 Peder Olsen Walloe reached a point in 61° N. on the east coast.

In the 19th century scientific exploration was accelerated. The southern west coast was mainly explored by Danes from the Danish settlements there but in the northern region of the west coast English and American explorers were leading. John Ross (1818) found the polar Eskimos at Cape York; E. A. Inglefield (1852) sailed into Smith sound; E. K. Kane (1853–55) worked northward through Smith sound into Kane basin; and C. F. Hall (1871) explored Kennedy strait and Robeson channels to the north of Kane basin. The first to give more accurate information of the east coast was the Scottish whaler W. Scoresby (1822) who made the first fairly trustworthy map of the coast between 69° and 75° N. Captains E. Sabine and D. Clavering visited this coast in 1823 and met the only Eskimo ever seen in this part of Greenland. The German K. Koldeway expedition reached 77° N. (Cape Bismarck) in 1870 and the duke of Orleans penetrated to about 78° 16′ N. in 1905. The rest of the northern east coast was explored by the Danish L. Mylius-Erichsen–J. P. Koch expedition (1906–08), which discovered Northeast Foreland, the easternmost point. E. Mikkelsen (1909–12) mapped those regions. The southern part of the east coast was first explored by the Dane W. A. Graah (1829–30), and other Danes G. Holm and T. V. Garde (1883–85) and C. Ryder (1891–92) mapped respectively the coast from Cape Farewell to 65° 16′ N. and the Scoresby sound. The Dane G. Amdrup (1899–1900) explored the still unknown coast between Angmagssalik and 69° 10′ N. and the Swede A. G. Nathorst (1899) discovered the large King Oscar fjord.

Toward the close of the 19th century several explorers visited north Greenland, including L. A. Beaumont of the Nares expedition (1876), J. B. Lockwood of the Greely expedition (1882) and R. E. Peary on several journeys (1892, 1895 and 1901). The Danish exploration of north Greenland began in 1910 with the foundation of the station of Thule in North Star bay (in 76° 32′ N.) by K. Rasmussen. It was the base of five Danish expeditions under Rasmussen and L. Koch.

In 1924–34 expeditions under Rasmussen, Koch and Mikkelsen continued researches on the east coast, which was also explored by the English-Danish expedition under A. Courtauld and E. Munck (1935–36) and by E. Knuth's expedition in 1938–39. After World War II Koch and Knuth continued their work on the east coast. Great areas were mapped from airplanes.

Exploration of the Icecap.—Exploration of the great icecap, or inland ice, which covers the whole of the interior of Greenland, was attempted in the 18th century, but failed, and so did E. Whymper's and R. Brown's attempt in 1867. Jens Jensen reached, in 1878, the Jensen nunataks (5,512 ft. above the sea) about 45 mi. from the western margin in 62° 50′ N. A. E. Nordenskiöld penetrated, in 1883, about 80 mi. inland in 68° 20′ N. and two Lapps of his expedition went still farther on skis to about 43° W. , at an elevation of 6,600 ft. Peary and C. Maigaard reached, in 1886, about 100 mi. inland, a height of 7,500 ft. in 69° 30′ N. The Norwegian Fridtjof Nansen, with five companions, in 1888, made the first complete crossing of the inland ice, working from east to west, about 64° 25′ N., and reached a height of 8,922 ft. Peary and E. Astrup, in 1892, crossed the northern part of the inland ice between 78° and 82° N. and determined the northern termination of the ice covering. Mylius-Erichsen crossed the northeastern corner of the inland ice in 1907 and E. Mikkelsen in 1910. In 1912 K. Rasmussen and P. Freuchen crossed from Inglefield gulf to Danmarkfjord and back and verified that Peary Land is an integral part of Greenland and not, as previously supposed, separated by a strait. In 1913 the Swiss A. de Quervain crossed the inland ice from Disko bay to Angmagssalik and J. P. Koch and A. Wegener crossed from Louise Land on the northeast coast to Upernavik on the west coast. The first crossings of the inland ice by airplane were made in 1931 by the German W. von Gronau from Scoresby sound to Godthaab and by the American Parker Cramer from Holsteinborg to Angmagssalik.

The development of modern air traffic and the fact that Greenland weather is of fundamental importance for predicting conditions on the North Atlantic and in western Europe have meant that since about 1930 weather observations were an important reason for Greenland explorations. In 1930-31 a British expedition under H. G. Watkins made weather observations high on the inland ice 40 mi. N. of the Arctic circle; at the same time a German expedition under A. Wegener wintered 300 mi. farther north. In 1933 a University of Michigan and an airline group went up still farther. During World War II Allied military weather stations were at work and after the war there were weather stations from the south to the far north.

F. Johnstrup first advocated the foundation of a permanent geological survey of Greenland in 1944. Seven years later, in 1951, Gronlands Geologiske Undersogelse became a permanent institution and since then exploration has been centred on geology, structure, movement of the inland ice and hydrography. Both Danish and foreign expeditions have undertaken this work. (H. Ln.)

COLONIZATION AND POLITICAL DEVELOPMENT

Early Settlement.—After discovering Greenland sometime between 980 and 982, Eric the Red settled just north of the present Julianehaab. Soon two colonies had been formed, Eystribygð in the present district of Julianehaab, and Vestribygð, farther north, in the present district of Godthaab. At the height of their prosperity the colonists numbered about 3,000 on 280 farms. Numerous ruins indicate the location of these colonies. Somewhat later the colonists met the Eskimos farther north in the neighbourhood of Disko bay, where the Norsemen went to catch seals, walrus, etc. The Eskimos were probably migrating south at that time. Christianity was introduced by Leif (Leifr) Ericsson about 1000 and in 1126 Greenland got its own bishop, who lived at Garðar on Igalikofjord.

Greenland was a republic until 1261, when the colonists swore allegiance to the king of Norway, who in return charged himself with supplying them with commodities. In the 14th century deterioration in Greenland's climate made it difficult to breed cattle, the colonists' main livelihood. Moreover, the monopolistic trading policy, forced on the kings by the Hanseatic merchants, caused grave trouble to the Greenlanders' trade, and in consequence the colonists diminished in number and in the 15th century the settlement became extinct. The last vessel from Greenland returned to Norway in 1410 but vessels in the Icelandic fish trade may have visited Greenland until about 1500. Excavations in the Norse burial grounds show 15th-century European influence in the style and texture of the clothes; there is no indication of absorption into the Eskimo groups or of destruction by Eskimo onslaught. Skeletons which show malformation suggest extermination by excessive intermarriage and adverse conditions of life. (B. S. Be.)

Recolonization.—Norway had been united with Denmark in 1380-81 and in the 16th and 17th centuries the Danish kings several times planned to resume communication with Greenland. The recolonization of Greenland was begun in 1721 with the voyage of the missionary Hans Egede to Godthaab. He thought that he would find descendants of the Norsemen but he found only Eskimos. He was deeply disappointed but stayed and started medical and missionary work among them. It was his idea that the eco-nomic activities of the colony were to be entirely subordinated to his missionary work. This, however, proved impossible and a few years later the Danish state had to come to his assistance. Later the Greenland trade was assigned to private interests but in 1774 it was again taken over by the state and was carried on as a government monopoly until 1951, when Greenland was opened to private Danish enterprise, the government-owned Royal Greenland Trading company still continuing its activities. During the period of the government monopoly Denmark aimed to aid the Greenlanders in cultural respects so as to enable them gradually to establish contact with the outside world without becoming subject to exploitation. Consequently Greenland was shut off from free contact with the outside world and all resources were reserved for the Greenlanders who were to sell their surplus production in return for goods required for maintaining and further developing their standard of life.

Establishment of Danish Sovereignty.—At the dissolution of the union between Norway and Denmark in 1814 Greenland was retained by Denmark. Until 1916 Denmark's sovereignty extended only over the west coast between Cape Farewell and 74° 30′ N. and the one trading station of Angmagssalik on the east coast, founded in 1894. In 1916, however, the United States declared that it had no objection to the extension of Denmark's political and economical interests to the whole of Greenland. Similar declarations were made by other countries, including Great Britain, and in 1921 Danish sovereignty was extended to embrace the whole island, which led to a dispute with Norway regarding hunting and sealing rights in the uncolonized areas of the east coast. In 1931 some Norwegian hunters, on their own initiative, occupied the east coast between 71° N. and 75° N. in the name of the Norwegian king and after some hesitation the Norwegian government recognized the occupation. Denmark at once summoned Norway into the International Court of Justice at The Hague and in 1933 the occupation was found invalid, the premises stating that Danish sovereignty extended over both the colonized and the uncolonized areas of Greenland. In 1924 a colony had been founded on Scoresby sound on the east coast and the privately founded colony of Thule in the far north was taken over by the government in 1937.

On April 9, 1941, a year after the German occupation of Denmark, Henrik Kauffmann, Danish minister to the U.S., signed an agreement which made Greenland a temporary protectorate of the United States. Danish sovereignty was recognized and the arrangement was to last only for the war emergency; the United States obtained the right to build bases for aircraft and radio and weather stations and to "do any and all things necessary" to hold these positions. New York displaced Copenhagen as the key point for export and import arrangements but local Danish officials and the existing Danish government system continued almost unaltered. After World War II the communication between Greenland and Denmark was fully resumed but U.S. forces remained in some bases. On April 27, 1951, however, an agreement was signed in Copenhagen between Denmark and the United States for the joint defense of Greenland, concluded within the framework of the North Atlantic Treaty organization (NATO) and replacing the provisional agreement of April 9, 1941. In the areas under U.S. command the United States would enjoy certain rights of use without impairing Danish sovereignty; all defense areas could be used by the ships, aircraft or armed forces of other NATO countries; U.S. forces in Greenland would respect Danish laws and administration concerning the indigenous population. In accordance with this agreement the United States, in 1951, started the establishment of the great air and radar base at Thule. In 1947 a special committee of Greenlanders and Danes was set up to examine measures to modernize Greenland's political, social and economic life in accordance with the Greenlanders' desires and the necessity of bringing their way of life to conformity with the new epoch which had come to Greenland as a consequence of modern air strategy and air communications. The examinations resulted in the abolition of the monopoly of the Royal Greenland Trading company in 1951 and of the colonial status of Greenland in 1953, when Greenland became an integral part of the kingdom of Denmark. In the following years housing and health services were improved and harbour and canning facilities increased the possibilities of the fishing trade. In 1959 a new committee was set up to prepare further progress.

POPULATION AND THE PEOPLE

Probably in the 8th century Eskimos immigrated to Greenland from the Canadian archipelago and then moved southward along the west coast during the Norse settlement and reached the east coast around Cape Farewell, the route by the north coast being almost impassable because of the lack of hunting grounds.

From the 15th century, when the Norse colonists became extinct, until the beginning of the Danish colonization in 1721, the Eskimos were the only inhabitants of Greenland. Greenland was a closed territory until 1951 and therefore Danish immigration was small, the only Danes being officials and a few private citizens. In 1951 Greenland was opened to Danish subjects, and some Faeroese and a number of craftsmen, engineers and miners lived there temporarily. At the same time several thousand U.S. citizens lived at the Thule air base but without contact with the inhabitants of Greenland.

The Eskimos are called Greenlanders. Most of them have some Danish blood; only in the far north does the pure Eskimo (q.v.) exist. Both the Danish and the Eskimo languages are spoken. All Greenlanders are Christians of the Lutheran denomination. For ecclesiastical purposes Greenland comes within the province of the bishop of Copenhagen.

The first census in Greenland was held in 1805, when the population totaled 6,046. In the next 100 years this figure doubled. In 1950 the population was 23,642 and in 1958 it had reached 30,621, of which 28,171 were Greenlanders. Pop. (1960) 33,140. This rapid growth of population after 1950 had two causes: first, the high average birth rate remained constant, 41.9 between 1945 and 1949 and 46.1 in 1957, but the average mortality rate declined rapidly, 25.5 in the period 1945–49 and 11.2 in 1957; second, immigration after 1951 increased the number of persons not born in Greenland from 1,061 in 1950 to 2,278 in 1957. (The personnel of the Thule base is not included in the total population.) Most of the inhabitants live on the west coast, the largest towns being Godthaab (3,322), Julianehaab (1,741), Egedesminde (1,817), Holsteinborg (1,714), Sukkertoppen (1,636), Jakobshavn (1,393) and Vajgat (1,260). Other towns had less than 1,000 inhabitants. Since World War II the trend has been to move from the villages to the towns because the towns offer better facilities for fishing, and seal hunting—the main livelihood of the villages—has lost its importance. On the east coast the northernmost settlement in the Franz Josef fjord was abandoned in the 19th century and there are now only two settlements, Angmagssalik (pop. [1960] 612) and Scoresbysund (247), which comprise the mining district of Mestersvig. The population in northern Greenland, including the settlement near Thule, is 560.

ADMINISTRATION AND SOCIAL CONDITIONS

The people of Greenland enjoy equal political rights with all other Danish nationals. Greenland is represented in the Danish parliament by two members elected by all Danish subjects of 21 or more years of age—both Greenlanders and Danes living in Greenland.

The administration comes under the ministry of Greenland in Copenhagen, represented in Greenland by a governor (landshovdingen). For administrative purposes Greenland is divided into three areas, the western, eastern and northern. Eastern and northern Greenland are under the direct administration of the Greenland minister's department but the Greenland council (landsraadet), with the governor as president, and the Greenland local councils, perform the administrative work in western Greenland. All government bills containing provisions applying solely to Greenland must, before submission to the Danish parliament, be placed before the Greenland council. The right to vote at elections of councilors both to the Greenland council and to local councils is given to all who have the right to vote at parliamentary elections.

Import duties provide funds for the work assigned to the Greenland council and the local councils.

The growing concentration of the population in towns has improved the standard of living. Wooden houses have replaced the old-fashioned turf and snow cabins; water supply has been improved; some of the bigger towns have electricity; wages have increased and employment is good, more and more people—both men and women—working in the fishing and canning industries.

Greenland has a free health service paid for by the Danish government and run mainly by doctors and nurses trained in Denmark. The commonest disease was tuberculosis but a crusade launched against it in 1953 has greatly reduced the number of cases.

There is an old-age pension plan for those over 55 who are no longer capable of supporting themselves and their families and programs for the care of children and for public relief. These are paid for and administered by the Greenlanders themselves.

All settlements have schools, financed by the Danish government—primary, postprimary, commercial schools and a training college. Most of the teachers are natives.

There is no indigenous Greenland defense system. The Danish navy and air force patrol Greenland waters.

Greenland has 16 court districts. In these districts administration of justice is exercised by lay judges. From the 16 court districts there is possibility of appeal to Gronlands landsret (the appeal court of Greenland) formed by a judge, a graduate of the faculty of law of the University of Copenhagen and two lay judges. In some cases, especially trials of serious crimes, the appeal court of Greenland serves as court of first instance with appeal to the high court of Copenhagen and from there to the supreme court of Denmark. The penalty clauses are slowly being transformed from the old primitive pattern to those of modern Denmark. Imprisonment is still used in a few cases.

THE ECONOMY

Historically, the main trade of Greenland was hunting, especially seal hunting. After World War I seal hunting was, however, greatly reduced, partly because of the change in climate and partly because of overintensive hunting. The change in climate at the same time created suitable conditions for fishing, particularly for cod, which became the main trade of Greenland. This change in the structure of Greenland's trades from hunting and domestic economy to fishing with a view to exports and the consequent introduction of a monetary economy has more and more gathered the people into places where there are good harbours, repair shops, facilities for the purchase of goods and opportunities for the sale of fish and for work in fish stores and canneries. After 1950 this development was accelerated by the Danish government's measures such as the financing of new canning and freezing plants, the construction of piers for ocean going vessels and the improvement of the power and fresh-water supplies. The most important fishery product is cod, followed in order by wolf fish, halibut, shark- and cod-liver oil, shrimps and salted salmon. There are several canneries and deep-freezing plants and about 80 fishery stations where cod is salted or dried. The fishing fleet numbers between 500 and 1,000 motorboats.

Although fishing has become the main industry, hunting is still important. Leading products are feather and eider down, walrus hides, sealskins, blue fox, white fox and bearskins and sharkskins. Nearly half the population are dependent on fishing and hunting.

Only a few stretches of land on the southwestern coast can be utilized for sheep farming and other animal husbandry of secondary importance. Grass is grown and dried for winter feed. The stock of sheep in the 1960s was about 20,000; there were also a few head of meat cattle and some poultry. In 1952, 300 tame reindeer were transported from Norway to Greenland to start reindeer husbandry; by 1960 they numbered about 2,000. There are about 150 horses on the entire island and more than 10,000 sled dogs.

Mining operations are carried on at Qutdligssat (coal) and Ivigtut (cryolite—the only commercially significant natural deposit in the world). The annual output of the coal quarry by the 1960s was about 30,000 metric tons. At the cryolite quarry 17,000 metric tons were produced, two-thirds of which went to Denmark and the rest to the United States. A Dano-Swedish-Canadian company was set up in 1952 to mine the lead and zinc deposits discovered in east Greenland. Annual production amounted to about 10,000 metric tons for each.

In 1951 the government trading monopoly, administered in Copenhagen by a government board, was abolished and so was the previous price policy. Formerly, several goods (for instance, certain foodstuffs and implements) were sold to the Greenland population at prices lower than the actual cost prices whereas the prices paid to the Greenlanders for their products in periods of boom were somewhat lower than prices in the open world market. After 1951 the price level was adjusted to the world-market level. To counteract the detrimental effect of a drop in prices of Greenland products, a Greenland Price Equalization fund was established. A Greenland Trade Loan fund was also established to promote Greenland trade and industry and increase exports by loans or subsidies to individuals or companies. Ships of all nations were allowed to call at Greenland.

The rapid building up of industry after 1951 caused an excess of imports over exports. The main groups of imported goods are machinery, transportation equipment and processed metals, amounting to 25% of the total. Fuel, lubricants, etc., amount to 11% of the imports. Fishing and hunting products amount to 44% and mining products to 52% of the exports, about 45% of which go to Denmark and 25% to the United States; lesser amounts go to the German Federal Republic, Greece, Spain and Italy. About 90% of all imports are from Denmark.

In 1960 the first nuclear reactors went into operation at Camp Century, the U.S. scientific base 140 mi. inland from Thule. It supplies the Thule base with heat, light and water.

Communications.—Greenland has regular connections by ship to Copenhagen. A leading airline's polar route to Los Angeles has an intermediate landing at Søndre Strømfjord. Inland traffic is by ship or motorboat and to some degree by dog sleds. Airplanes are used but there are no regular inland air routes. Mail is carried by the Danish government postal service. There is radiotelephonic and radiotelephonic connection to Denmark and a Greenland radio station in Godthaab.

See also references under "Greenland" in the Index.

(H. LN.)

BIBLIOGRAPHY.—*General Works:* Danish Commission for the Direction of the Geological and Geographical Investigations in Greenland, *Meddelelser om Grønland*, 158 vol., containing many papers in English and German as well as in Danish and Greenland Eskimo (1879–); *Greenland Reports*, Expeditions Polaires Françaises (1948–); Kaj Birket-Smith, *Grønlandsbogen*, 2 vol. (1950); Ebbe Munck, *Det nye Grønland*, with Danish and English text (1952); Danish Prime Minister's Department, *Report on Greenland*, annual (1949–); *Annual Report of the Landsraad* (1954–).

Physical Features: Curt Teichert, *Geology of Greenland* (1939); Borge Fristrup, "Greenland Ice Cap," *Geografisk Tidsskrift* (1959); 62 (1921); Finn Salomonsen, *The Birds of Greenland* (1950–51).

Vegetation and Animal Life: Meddelelser om Grønland, vol. 60 and 62 (1921); Finn Salomonsen, *The Birds of Greenland* (1950–51).

Exploration and Scientific Research: Meddelelser om Grønland; F. Nansen, *The First Crossing of Greenland*, 2 vol. (1890); Curt Wegener, *Wissenschaftliche Ergebnisse der deutschen Grönland-Expedition Alfred Wegeners* (1933); Peter Freuchen, *Arctic Adventure* (1935).

History: Poul Norlund, *De gamle Nordbobygder ved Verdens Ende*, 2nd ed. (1936; trans. by W. E. Calvert, *Viking Settlers in Greenland and Their Descendants During Five Hundred Years*, 1936); Finn Gadd, *Grønlands Historie, 1500–1945* (1946); C. W. Schultz-Lorentzen, *Greenland*, vol. 2, *The Intellectual Culture of the Greenlanders* (1942); Kaj Birket-Smith, *The Eskimos* (1959); V. Stefansson, *Greenland* (1942).

Current history and statistics are summarized annually in the *Britannica Book of the Year.*

GREENLEAF, SIMON (1783–1853), U.S. legal educator, whose principal work, a *Treatise on the Law of Evidence* (3 vol., 1842–53), became a classic, was born at Newburyport, Mass., Dec. 5, 1783. He was educated at the Latin school there, read law with Ezekiel Whitman, and was admitted to the bar in 1806. The first reporter of the supreme court of Maine (1820), he was appointed Royall professor at the Harvard law school in 1833, succeeding Joseph Story (*q.v.*) as Dane professor of law and head of the school in 1846. The 16th edition of his *Treatise* (vol. 1) was prepared by John Henry Wigmore, who was thus led to his own monumental work in evidence.

Greenleaf, a noted practising lawyer, also wrote *A Collection of Cases Overruled, Denied, Doubted or Limited in Their Application* (1821) and *Examination of the Testimony of the Four Evangelists* (1846). He drafted the original constitution of the Independent Republic of Liberia. He died on Oct. 6, 1853, in Cambridge, Mass.

(A. L. LN.)

GREEN MOUNTAINS, a part of the Appalachian mountain system, North America, include the highest mountains and most rugged topography in Vermont, the "Green Mountain state." Geologically the folded and metamorphosed rocks of this area extend from central western Connecticut through western Massachusetts and Vermont and on into Canada (*see* APPALACHIAN MOUNTAINS). The name usually is applied to the group of mountains in Vermont that slope gently to the watersheds of the Connecticut valley to the east and rise abruptly above the Lake Champlain-Hudson river region to the west. The mountains are more subdued to the south. The range varies in width from a few miles to 30 mi. with a crestline above 2,000 ft., 32 summits over 3,000 ft. and the following peaks rising above 4,000 ft.: Mt. Mansfield (4,393 ft.), Killington peak (4,241 ft.), Jay peak (3,861 ft.).

The Green mountains contain the largest number of well-developed and well-equipped ski facilities in New England. Stowe, Pico, Killington, Mad River, Okema and Snow Valley are famous and popular resorts. The "Long trail," a part of the Appalachian Mountain club's "Maine to Georgia trail," transverses the range and hikers look down on famous slate, marble and granite quarries. Locations of east-west transportation routes in Vermont are controlled by the passes in the mountains. The Green mountains, except for the upper portions of the four highest peaks, are wooded with spruce, maple, beech and birch. Sawmills, small woodworking plants and paper mills turn the forest resources into useful products.

(A. S. CN.)

GREENOCK, a large parliamentary burgh and seaport, Renfrewshire, Scotland, on the south shore of the Firth of Clyde, 23 mi. W.N.W. of Glasgow by road or rail, 21 mi. by the river and firth. Pop. (1971 prelim.) 69,004. The town has a water frontage of nearly 4 mi. and rises gradually to the hills behind, in which are situated, about 2 mi. distant, Loch Thom and Gryfe reservoir, sources of the town's water supply. The older streets and buildings are on the comparatively level tract beside the firth. At the west end a fine esplanade extends from Princes pier to Fort Matilda, on the boundary between Greenock and Gourock. Shipyards stretch to Port Glasgow, 3 mi. E. At Greenock is the well-known anchorage, "the Tail of the Bank."

Public buildings include the municipal buildings; the McLean museum containing paintings by Sir James Guthrie, a native of Greenock, and other artists; the customhouse on the old steamboat quay; the sheriff courthouse; and the Watt institution founded in 1837 by a son of the famous engineer James Watt, who was born in Greenock in 1736. The Watt institution houses the Watt scientific library and the Greenock library. The Watt Memorial School of Engineering, Navigation, Radio and Radar stands on the site of the inventor's birthplace. The old North Kirk (1591), with its pre-Raphaelite windows, was moved to Seafield to make way for extension of the shipyards. A large cemetery in the southwestern district contains the tomb of Burns's "Highland Mary," removed in 1920 from the North Kirk graveyard. Parks and open spaces include Wellington park, Well park in the heart of the town, Whin hill and Lady Alice and Lady Octavia parks.

Greenock is under a town council consisting of 27 members including provost, bailies and councilors. There is a resident sheriff-substitute. It is a parliamentary burgh, represented by one member.

The staple industries are shipbuilding, engineering, sugar refining (1765), worsted and woolen manufacturing and production of aluminum ware.

Many warships and passenger liners have been constructed in the Greenock yards. Other industries include the manufacture of marine and other types of engines; the making of sailcloth, ropes, casks and barrels; and tin printing. Ships and machinery are the chief exports and sugar the chief import. The first harbour (finished in 1710) has been periodically improved and there are seven tidal harbours, Garvel graving dock and other dry docks, and the James Watt dock, the entrances to which are closed by caissons to keep in 30 ft. of water at low tide. The quay walls are more than 3 mi. in length.

In the early 17th century Greenock was a fishing village of one row of thatched cottages. In 1635 it was erected by Charles I into a burgh of barony under a charter granted to John Shaw, the government being administered by a baron-bailie, or magistrate, appointed by the superior. Its commercial prosperity received great impetus from the treaty of Union (1707), under which trade with America and the West Indies rapidly developed. The American Revolution suspended progress for a brief period, but a revival began in 1783 and within seven years shipping trebled. Meanwhile Sir John Shaw by charter (dated 1741 and 1751) had empowered the householders to elect a council of nine members, which proved to be the most liberal constitution of any Scots burgh prior to the Reform act of 1832, when Greenock was raised to the status of a parliamentary burgh with the right to return one member to parliament.

The town was a Free French naval base during World War II and was considerably damaged by air action. On Lyle road above the town a granite cross of Lorraine and anchor commemorates the French sailors who lost their lives in the battle of the Atlantic.

GREENOUGH, HORATIO (1805–1852), U.S. sculptor, critic and author, was born in Boston, Mass., on Sept. 6, 1805. As a youth he was encouraged to study art by his family and by the painter Washington Allston. In 1824, on graduating from Harvard, he went to Italy for two years of study, and after returning to Boston he went again to Italy in 1829 to remain there until his final return to the U.S. in 1851. His principal works as a sculptor are both in Washington, D.C.: the statue of George Washington, designed to be placed in the rotunda of the U.S. Capitol (now in the Smithsonian institution), and the group called "The Rescue," placed at the east entrance of the Capitol. Greenough was the first American to receive an important commission for sculpture from the U.S. government and the first American sculptor of his time to go to Italy to study sculpture.

Greenough's principal importance today rests almost entirely upon his few brief essays on art because in them he outlined the basic ideas of the theory of functionalism which has had so much influence, especially on modern architecture. These essays were originally printed in 1852 in Greenough's book, *Travels, Observations and Experiences of a Yankee Stonecutter.* In 1947 they were reprinted with the title *Form and Function.* Greenough died in Somerville, Mass., on Dec. 18, 1852.

His younger brother, RICHARD SALTONSTALL GREENOUGH (1819–1904), was also a sculptor. His most famous work is the statue of Benjamin Franklin in Boston.

See Charles R. Metzger, *Emerson and Greenough* (1954); Albert T. E. Gardner, *Yankee Stonecutters* (1945). (A. T. G.)

GREEN RIVER, the name of several U.S. rivers.

The GREEN RIVER, rising in the Wind River range of west-central Wyoming, flows southward until forced to detour around the bulk of the Uinta range into northwestern Colorado. There the Green enters Flaming gorge on the northern flank of the Uintas and continues into the Canyon of Ladore where it cuts through ancient red quartzites in the eastern edge of the Uinta uplift before it receives the Yampa in Pat's Hole (Echo park), Colorado. Leaving the Uintas at Split Mountain gorge in Dinosaur National monument, Utah, the Green continues southward through deep canyons cut into the Colorado plateau. It enters the Colorado river south of Moab, Utah, at Deadhorse Point.

Because of the youthful nature of the narrow, steep-walled canyons, there are only limited areas of extensive flood plains that can be developed through irrigation along the river itself. Within the 45,000 sq.mi. (116,550 sq.km.) drainage basin of the Green, however, more than 500,000 ac. (202,350 ha.) were under irrigation before the completion of the dam across the Flaming Gorge canyon. The Green supplies about 45% of the total water of the Colorado at the confluence of the two rivers, flowing about 4,793,000 ac.ft. per year, but is navigable only by special shallow-draft river boats and then only at high water.

The GREEN RIVER, which rises near Kings Mountain in central Kentucky, flows for 360 mi. (579 km.) generally westward through a well-defined gorge, then northwestward to the Ohio, which it enters just above Evansville, Ind. It receives the waters of Echo river, which flows underground through Mammoth cave, and drains numerous other underground caverns. Deepening of the channel of the Green to nine feet, dams and locks below Mining City dam allow small river boats to navigate a total of 200 mi. (322 km.) of the lower course through the western coal fields.

The GREEN RIVER, which rises in Lee county in north-central Illinois, enters Rock river east of Moline. Much of its broad, flat valley is swampy or artificially drained. Silted and sluggish, it is avoided by the Illinois-Mississippi barge canal, which parallels it for about 15 mi. (24 km.).

There are also two smaller Green rivers, one rising in the Cascade range of Washington and the other in the Green mountains of Vermont.
(C. N. C.)

GREENSAND. A geological term having a double significance. Among the sedimentary rocks it is used to indicate a sand or sandstone with abundant grains of glauconite (q.v.). Greensand is mined in Maryland and New Jersey. It is used primarily as a water softening agent and has some use as a soil conditioner and as a source of potassium. Stratigraphically the name is used for several subdivisions of the Cretaceous system in England.

GREENSBORO, a city in the heart of the Piedmont region in north central North Carolina, U.S., is 78 mi. (125 km.) NW of Raleigh. Established in 1808 as the seat of Guilford County, it was named for Gen. Nathanael Greene, commander of American Revolutionary forces at the Battle of Guilford Courthouse, fought in March 1781 near the city. The battle is commemorated there by a national military park.

Greensboro figured importantly in the American Civil War, for in this town the decision to end the conflict was made (1865), here the peace terms were proposed (agreed upon at James Bennitt's house near Durham's Station), the disposition of Confederate arms was arranged, and paroles were distributed to Confederate soldiers. Greensboro was at that time the temporary capital of the Confederacy and the temporary capital of North Carolina.

The early settlers of Greensboro included Scotch-Irish Presbyterians, German Calvinists and Lutherans, and English Quakers. The population, which increased from 3,317 in 1890 to 10,035 by 1900, was 19,861 in 1920, 53,569 in 1930, 119,574 in 1960, and 144,076 in 1970. The 1970 population of the Greensboro–Winston-Salem–High Point standard metropolitan statistical area was 603,895.

Greensboro was chartered as a city in 1870 and in 1921 adopted a council-manager form of government.

The city is a large wholesale distributing point, a leading agricultural trading post, an important insurance centre, and an industrial community with more than 300 active manufacturing plants, making more than 160 different products.

Institutions of higher education in Greensboro include the Agricultural and Technical College of North Carolina (est. 1891), a coeducational land-grant college which in 1967 became the North Carolina Agricultural and Technical State University; Bennett College, a liberal arts school for women, founded in 1873 as a coeducational school below college level and reorganized in 1926 as a women's college; Greensboro College, chartered in 1838 as a liberal arts women's college, opened in 1846 and coeducational since 1956; Guilford College, a coeducational liberal arts institution, chartered in 1834 and opened in 1837 as the New Garden Boarding School, and in 1889 renamed Guilford College; John Wesley College, founded in 1932 as the interdenominational People's Bible College, since 1958 the John Wesley College for Christian Education; and the University of North Carolina at Greensboro, chartered in 1891 and opened in 1892 as a liberal arts college for women, after several name changes became a branch of the consolidated University of North Carolina in 1932 and coeducational in 1963.

Greensboro was the home of Dolley Payne Todd Madison (1768–1849), the wife of James Madison, fourth president of the U.S., who as a child lived in what is now the city of Greensboro; of William Sidney Porter (O. Henry; 1862–1910), a native of the Greensboro area, where he lived during his first 20 years; and of Edward R. Murrow (1908–65), radio and television broadcaster, also a native of the Greensboro community who spent his childhood in the vicinity.

(E. S. Ar.)

GREENSBURG, a city of southwestern Pennsylvania, U.S., and the seat of Westmoreland County since 1785, 27 mi. (43 km.) SE of Pittsburgh, was named for the American Revolutionary War general Nathanael Greene. It is within an area abounding in natural gas and bituminous coal; its inhabitants are employed largely in industries producing coke, brick, automobile tires, plumbers' supplies, and steam fittings. The first court to convene west of the Alleghenies opened in the nearby village of Hannastown in 1773. When a Seneca Indian raid destroyed that village the county government was moved to Greensburg. Within three miles of the route taken by the army of General Forbes in its march to Ft. Duquesne in 1758 and on the Pennsylvania state road opened in 1784, the city from its earliest years was near Pennsylvania's major east-west transportation arteries. In 1852 the railroad reached the city. It was incorporated as a borough in 1799 and became a city in 1928.

Pop. (1970) 15,870. For comparative population figures see table in PENNSYLVANIA: *Population.*

(J. K. B.)

GREENSTONE, in geology, a term used by many of the earlier writers to indicate fine-grained dark-coloured and often considerably decomposed and altered basic igneous rocks, either intrusive or extrusive. It is still—like "felsite" (*q.v.*)—a useful word in descriptive field geology, since it indicates the appearance and general character of the rock but does not imply anything definite as to its exact nature and composition, which may be determined later by laboratory methods. For discussion of the latter, see PETROLOGY: *Methods of Investigation.*

GREENVILLE, largest city in the delta of the Yazoo and Mississippi rivers, in western Mississippi, U.S., is the most important port on the east side of the Mississippi river between Memphis, Tenn., and Vicksburg, Miss. (95 mi. S.). There is a $6,000,000 bridge across the Mississippi at Greenville. Old Greenville, an extinct town formerly south of the present city, became the seat of Washington county in 1827. Part of the old settlement caved into the river and the remainder of the town was burned by Federal troops during the American Civil War. During Reconstruction the new town was established at its present site, which was formerly Blantonia plantation; thereafter it was the county seat.

The original incorporation of the town occurred in 1870; its charter as a city dates from 1886.

Greenville is surrounded by rich agricultural delta land which produces the bulk of the world's long staple cotton. Diversification brought substantial production of corn, oats, rice, soybeans and alfalfa, and there are herds of beef cattle and hogs. Principal manufacturing industries include agricultural chemicals, rugs, woodworking and metal products.

Like the entire delta area along the Mississippi river, the city is protected by huge levees. In 1927 a break in the levee north of Washington county inundated a 7,500-sq.mi. area around Greenville, producing one of the most devastating floods ever to hit the delta. Federal flood-control projects have prevented the recurrence of such floods. The *Greenville Delta Democrat-Times* was established in 1888; its editor Hodding Carter won a Pulitzer prize in 1946.

Pop. (1970) 39,648. For comparative population figures see table in MISSISSIPPI: *Population.*

GREENVILLE, a city and seat of Greenville county in northwestern South Carolina, U.S., is on the Reedy river, about 100 mi. S.W. of Charlotte, N.C. First settled in the 1760s, the county of Greenville was created in 1786 with its seat at the village of Pleasantburg, a name soon changed to Greenville and so incorporated in 1831. Located in the foothills of the Blue Ridge mountains, Greenville prior to 1860 was a summer resort for many low-country planters. As western terminus of the Greenville and Columbia railroad it served as commercial centre for the piedmont and for entry into the nearby Appalachian mountains. Greenville provided strong opposition to nullification in 1832 and secession in 1860. Notable among unionists was Benjamin F. Perry, Greenville editor and later governor. After the Civil War, water power of the Reedy river was utilized to develop manufacturing that became the chief economic activity of the area.

The population of the city was 8,607 in 1890 and 11,860 in 1900. It almost doubled by 1920 (23,127) and increased from 29,154 in 1930 to 66,188 in 1960; in 1970 it was 61,208. (For comparative population figures see table in SOUTH CAROLINA: *Population.*) The population of the standard metropolitan statistical area (Greenville and Pickens counties) was 299,502 in 1970. Chartered as a city in 1868, Greenville established council-manager government in 1951.

The city leads the state in retail sales volume and in manufacturing. Textile mills dominate industry although there has been considerable growth in the chemical industry, food distribution, metal industries and industrial suppliers.

Greenville is the home of Furman university, opened in 1827 as a theological school at Edgefield and moved to Greenville in 1851 (Baptist, coeducational, about 1,300 students), and Bob Jones university, established in 1927 (nondenominational coeducational school emphasizing Bible study, about 2,000 students). There is a state park on Paris mountain 4½ mi. from the city at an elevation of 2,054 ft.

(L. P. J.)

GREENWICH, one of the 32 London boroughs constituting Greater London, Eng., lies on the south bank of the Thames, bounded east by Bexley, south by Bromley, and west by Lewisham. This inner London borough was established on April 1, 1965, under the London Government Act 1963 (see LONDON) by the amalgamation of the former metropolitan boroughs of Greenwich and Woolwich, excluding a small area north of the river. Area 19 sq.mi. (49 sq.km.). Pop. (1971 prelim.) 216,441. It comprises three parliamentary constituencies and includes the districts of Charlton, Eltham, New Eltham, Plumstead, Kidbrooke, and part of Blackheath.

The Roman Watling Street ran east and west on a ridge across the borough from the wooded summit of Shooters Hill, to the breezy common of Blackheath, and thence to Canterbury and Dover. There are about 1,750 ac. (708 ha.) of open spaces. On the southern slope, modern residential districts have grown up around the earlier settlements of Eltham, Blackheath, and Kidbrooke; to the north, older buildings, mostly 19th-century, cover the slopes which lead down to the industrial riverside area. Foot tunnels at Greenwich and Woolwich, the Blackwall Tunnel, and the Woolwich Free Ferry link the borough with Newham and Tower Hamlets on the north bank of the Thames. The borough is served by the Southern Region of British Rail.

Greenwich and Woolwich were mentioned respectively in a document of 918 as Gronewic and Uuluuich and they appear as Grenviz and Hulviz in the Domesday Book.

The parish church of Greenwich is dedicated to St. Alphege, archbishop of Canterbury, who was martyred there by Danes in 1012. The present building, designed by Nicholas Hawksmoor, dates from 1718; the tower was completed by John James, a local architect. Its interior (the work of Sir James Thornhill and Grinling Gibbons) was badly burned during World War II and was restored under the direction of Sir Albert Richardson. Gen. James Wolfe (d. 1759), the victor of Quebec, and Thomas Tallis (d. 1585), the Tudor composer and organist, are buried in the church where the keyboard of Tallis' organ is also preserved. The most notable buildings in Greenwich are situated in and around Greenwich Park (196.5 ac. [80.5 ha.]), which slopes steeply northward to the river, and where four of England's greatest architects, Sir Christopher Wren, Sir John Vanbrugh, and Inigo Jones contributed to a remarkable architectural grouping. The park was enclosed in 1433 by Humphrey, duke of Gloucester, and was later occupied by the Royal

Observatory. Subsequently, a house named Placentia was built along the riverbank, and this was enlarged and converted by the Tudor monarchs into a royal palace. It became a favourite residence of Henry VIII, who was born there, and who added a banqueting hall, armoury, and tiltyard; it was where he married Catherine of Aragon, Anne Boleyn, and Anne of Cleves, where his daughters Mary and Elizabeth were born, and where Edward VI died. The palace fell into disrepair during the Commonwealth, and Charles II commissioned John Webb to design a new one, of which only the present King Charles block was built. In 1694 as a thank offering for the naval victory of La Hogue, William and Mary instructed Wren to complete it as a naval hospital, patterned on the Chelsea Hospital for soldiers. Wren accordingly designed the largest twin-domed baroque edifice in England to accommodate 2,700 pensioners and Vanbrugh and Hawksmoor supervised its construction. The building which was opened in 1705 included the Painted Hall, so named for the frescoes completed by Thornhill in 1726, and the chapel that was redecorated (after the fire of 1779) by James ("Athenian") Stuart and William Newton in 1789. In 1873 the hospital was closed and the building became the home of the Royal Naval College. The Queen's House was designed by Inigo Jones and was the first Palladian building in Britain; it was commissioned by James I for Anne of Denmark, and was completed in 1637 for Queen Henrietta Maria, consort of Charles I. After being used as the residence of the ranger (keeper) of Greenwich Park, the Queen's House was in 1806 converted into a naval school and two wings joined by colonnades to the original building were added. In 1937 the school vacated the buildings which were reopened as the National Maritime Museum. In many American colonial charters, such as that of Virginia, tenure of land from the crown was granted "as of the manor of East Greenwich." Although the astronomical work of the Royal Observatory was transferred to Herstmonceux (q.v.) by 1958, the prime meridian mark from which all countries have reckoned longitude since 1884 is still to be seen. The observatory with its celebrated Octagon Room was founded in 1675 and designed by Wren; it is now known as Flamsteed House, after Sir John Flamsteed, the first astronomer royal, and was opened as an astronomical museum in 1960. The terra-cotta building, a Victorian extension to the observatory, was opened as a planetarium in 1965.

Woolwich, like Greenwich, rose to prominence during the Tudor period with the establishment of a dockyard and naval station. There was a shipbuilding industry in the reign of Henry VII; ships were later built for Drake and Raleigh, and the building of the "Great Harry" (1,000 tons) in 1514 marked an epoch in ship construction. Woolwich remained the navy's chief dockyard until the invention of the ironclad; the dockyard closed in 1869 and has since been used as a war department store. The Royal Arsenal was so named in 1805, but there had been a royal gun-carriage workshop on Woolwich Warren since 1683 where guns were first cast in 1716. The foundry, attributed to Vanbrugh, survives, but the greater part of the site is destined for development as a housing estate. The Royal Regiment of Artillery had its headquarters at Woolwich Warren from its formation in 1716 until 1775 when it moved to Woolwich Common. The Royal Military Academy, founded in 1741 in the Warren, was moved to Woolwich Common in 1806 and amalgamated with the Royal Military Academy at Sandhurst (q.v.) in 1947. The Rotunda Museum, presented by the Prince Regent, contains arms and ship models.

Other notable buildings include the 15th-century great hall of Eltham Palace, now part of Eltham Hall, the headquarters of the Army Institute of Education; Morden College (c. 1695), originally an almshouse for "decayed Turkey merchants" and attributed to Wren; Charlton House (1607-12), one of the best preserved Jacobean buildings in London; the Ranger's House (c. 1750), originally the home of Lord Chesterfield; and the Tudor Barn at Well Hall, Eltham. The clipper ship "The Cutty Sark" is in dry dock near Greenwich pier where it is preserved as a memorial to the merchant navy in the days of sail. (D. R. L.)

GREENWICH, a town (township) of southwestern Connecticut, U.S., and a prosperous suburb of New York city which is 28 mi. S.W., has been called the gateway to New England. Founded on Long Island sound in 1640 by the New Haven colony agents Robert Feaks and Capt. Daniel Patrick, who purchased land from four sachems for 25 English coats, it soon came under Dutch rule and finally, in 1650, under Connecticut's jurisdiction. During the American Revolution British troops under Gen. William Tryon overran Greenwich and looted freely. In organizing the town's defense Gen. Israel Putnam narrowly escaped capture by galloping down a precipice. After the war the little port town resumed its steady growth, reaching 3,790 in 1820, 6,522 in 1860, over 12,000 in 1900 and 40,835 in 1950; the population was 59,755 in 1970. For comparative population figures see table in CONNECTICUT: Population.

Greenwich capitalized upon its convenient location for commuters to New York city and is noted for its woods and hills rising gently from six miles of attractive coast line. Industries include the manufacture of marine engines, electrical generators, pumps, boats and sails, industrial felt, precision instruments, small castings, machine tools and magazine printing. Under strict zoning since 1927, the town has fine residential areas and high-ranking public and private schools. There are two large public libraries and a museum. Many authors and artists reside in the town. Public recreational facilities include three municipal beaches, over 400 ac. of parks, 300 mi. of bridle paths and a nature preserve. In 1933 the town adopted a representative town-meeting system of government. (A. E. V. D.)

GREENWOOD, ARTHUR (1880-1954), British political leader who throughout the 1930s was one of the most powerful figures in the Labour party and gave a clear lead toward resistance to Nazi aggression, was born in Leeds on Feb. 8, 1880. He was educated at elementary and secondary schools and at the university there. He was head of the economics and law department at Huddersfield technical college and later a lecturer in economics at Leeds university. During World War I he was a civil servant in the ministry of reconstruction. Entering parliament as Labour member for Nelson and Colne in 1922, he was parliamentary secretary to the minister of health in the first Labour government (1924) and was minister of health (1929-31) with a seat in the cabinet in the second.

Greenwood was defeated at Nelson and Colne in 1931. He returned to parliament in 1932 as member for Wakefield, but during his absence C. R. (afterward Earl) Attlee had become deputy leader of the Labour party, a post which otherwise would probably have been Greenwood's. When Attlee was elected leader in 1935 Greenwood stood unsuccessfully against him but subsequently accepted the deputy leadership. This post became of particular importance at the outbreak of World War II, when Attlee was ill. Greenwood spoke with great force in favour of unhesitating British intervention, and the general support he received in the house of commons had a considerable effect upon the Chamberlain government. L. S. Amery, a notable Conservative member, greeted his speech with the celebrated injunction: "Speak for England."

When the Churchill coalition was formed in 1940 Greenwood became minister without portfolio and a member of the war cabinet of five. He was mainly in charge of postwar reconstruction, but his ministerial work was not wholly successful and he was dropped from the government in Feb. 1942. For the remainder of the war he fulfilled the nominal functions of leader of the opposition but in fact gave general support to the government. After Labour's election victory of 1945 Greenwood again took nondepartmental office, this time as lord privy seal, with certain powers of supervision over social service questions. He continued in office until the autumn of 1947 (as paymaster general for the last few months) and was then retired. He remained in parliament until his death in London on June 9, 1954.

Greenwood was a man of considerable political talents and wide popularity. But a certain lack of precision and application in his later life meant that his promise was greater than his fulfillment. (R. J.)

GREENWOOD, FREDERICK (1830-1909), English journalist and man of letters, who achieved fame by his editorship of the Pall Mall Gazette, was born in London on March 25, 1830.

In 1862, when Thackeray resigned the editorship of the *Cornhill*, Greenwood became joint editor with G. H. Lewis and later sole editor. Using George Canning's *Anti-Jacobin* (published 1797) and the *Saturday Review* of 1864 as models he conceived the idea of an evening newspaper that was "to bring into daily journalism the full measure of thought and culture which was then found only in the reviews" and to use this in the Conservative interest. He obtained the financial support of George Smith and the *Pall Mall Gazette* was launched in 1865. Within a few years its influence both on politics and journalistic style was immense; no minister, Gladstone truly said, had ever had a more zealous, more able and more effective supporter for his policy than the *Pall Mall Gazette*. It was on his suggestion that Beaconsfield purchased in 1875 the Suez canal shares of the Khedive Ismail, which the government had not known were for sale and likely to be bought by France until informed by Greenwood. Characteristically he neither sought to obtain journalistic advantage from his prior knowledge of the purchase nor looked for any public acknowledgment.

When in 1880 the *Pall Mall* changed owners and supported the Liberals, Greenwood resigned and founded, with the financial backing of Henry Hucks Gibbs (later Lord Aldenham), the *St. James's Gazette*. This he made as influential as the *Pall Mall* until his resignation in 1888. The *Anti-Jacobin*, which he started in 1891, was not a success. He remained, however, an influential contributor to the press and a friend of the most eminent political figures of his day until his death at Sydenham on Dec. 14, 1909.

(E. F. Ws.)

GREENWOOD, JOHN (d. 1593), English Puritan and leader of the London Separatists, was educated at Corpus Christi college, Cambridge, and ordained priest. In Oct. 1587 he was arrested for Puritan activities, imprisoned in the Clink, Southwark, and in May 1588 committed to the Fleet prison. During this period he wrote *An Answer to George Gifford's Pretended Defence of Read Prayers* (1590), and, in conjunction with his fellow prisoner Henry Barrow (*q.v.*), tracts denying the scriptural authority of the English church and repudiating royal supremacy. He was at large again in Sept. 1592, when he was elected "teacher" of the Separatist church (*see* BROWNE, ROBERT). In Dec. 1592 Greenwood was again arrested; and in March 1593 was tried, together with Barrow, and condemned to death on a charge of "devising and circulating seditious books." After two respites, one at the foot of the gallows, he was hanged at Tyburn, London, on April 6, 1593.

BIBLIOGRAPHY.—H. M. Dexter, *The Congregationalism of the Last Three Hundred Years* (1880); C. Burrage, *The Early English Dissenters* (1912); M. M. Knappen, *Tudor Puritanism* (1939).

(G. Hu.)

GREENWOOD, in northwest Mississippi, U.S., 100 mi. N. of Jackson and 134 mi. S. of Memphis, Tenn., is the largest city between those two points and is the seat of Leflore county. In 1834 John Williams traveled up the Yazoo river and settled close to the junction of the Tallahatchie and Yalobusha rivers. That place soon became an important shipping point for cotton on its way down the Yazoo and the Mississippi rivers to New Orleans. Williams' Landing was incorporated as a city in 1844 under the name of the last great Choctaw chieftain, Greenwood Leflore, who was a wealthy cotton planter and slaveholder. Greenwood is a Mississippi delta community where Negroes and whites live in approximately equal numbers. Pop. (1970) 22,400. (For comparative population figures *see* table in MISSISSIPPI: *Population*.) Primarily a trading centre, Greenwood is the home of diverse industries and it has grain elevators with a total storage capacity of over 1,000,000 bu.

(E. H. Hs.)

GREETING CARD, an illustrated message that expresses, either seriously or humorously, affection, good will, gratitude, sympathy or other sentiments. Greeting cards are usually sent by mail in observance of a special day or event and can be divided into two general classifications, seasonal and everyday. Seasonal cards include those for Christmas, New Year's day, St. Valentine's day, St. Patrick's day, Easter, Mother's day, Father's day, graduation, Halloween and Thanksgiving day. Everyday cards include those commemorating birthdays, anniversaries, births or religious occasions, and cards of condolence, congratulations or friendship, as well as get-well cards, gift cards, *bon voyage* cards and thank-you cards.

The exchange of greeting cards in the United States is on a scale far beyond that in any other country although all English-speaking countries practise the custom to some degree and its popularity is growing in European and South American countries. In the latter 1950s nearly 300 greeting-card publishers in the U.S. annually produced about 5,000,000,000 cards having a wholesale value of about $275,000,000—a sixfold increase in volume in two decades. Approximately half of the total were Christmas cards; one-fourth were cards for other seasonal occasions; and one-fourth for everyday occasions. About $150,000,000 was expended annually for postage stamps on greeting cards.

Greeting cards are usually of stiff paper or cardboard but some are made of cloth, leather, Celluloid, vellum, metal and even wood, clay, cork or other materials. Size is determined by common usage, the availability of suitable envelopes, ease of mailing and the system of grading according to price and quality. Extreme exceptions are an inscribed grain of rice presented in 1929 as a Christmas greeting to the prince of Wales and a Christmas card sent to Pres. Calvin Coolidge in 1924 that was 21 × 33 in. The imprinted messages on cards may vary in length from a brief word or two to 100 words or more in prose or verse.

The exchange of illustrated greetings among friends dates from ancient times. In Egypt the new year was celebrated by the exchange of symbolic presents, such as scent bottles and scarabs inscribed *au ab nab* ("all good luck"). The Romans exchanged *strenae*, originally branches of laurel or olive, frequently coated with gold leaf. Symbols of seasonal good will, such as a Roman lamp impressed with the figure of Victory surrounded by *strenae*, were inscribed *Anno novo faustum felix tibi sit* ("May the new year be happy and lucky for you"). The acknowledgment of the new year with exchanges of good will continued in Europe through the early days of Christianity. In the 15th century master wood engravers produced inscribed prints which had the same intent as the modern Christmas and New Year's cards. One of these, by Master E. S., shows the Christ child with halo before a cross and holding a scroll on which appears *Ein guot selig ior* ("A good and happy year"). During the 18th and early 19th centuries copper-plate engravers were producing prints and calendars for the new year, and greetings by organizations, merchants and tradesmen were common.

The valentine is also regarded as a forerunner of the greeting card. Its history is related to pre-Christian Rome when boys drew the names of girls from a love urn on the feast of the Lupercalia, Feb. 15. The custom was introduced to England by the Romans and continued through the church. In order to adapt the practice to Christianity the church transferred it to the feast of St. Valentine (*q.v.*).

The paper valentine with inscribed sentiment dates from the 16th century and the first printed valentine may have been the frontispiece of *A Valentine Writer*, a book of verses that offered assistance to the inarticulate and was issued as early as 1669. By 1800 hand-painted copperplates by such artists as Francesco Bartolozzi were in demand. These were followed by woodcuts and lithographs, all in quarto size, some further embellished with an embossed frame. With the introduction of penny postage and the use of lace paper, delicately ornamented, became popular. In the U.S. crude woodcut valentines were produced by Robert H. Elton and Thomas W. Strong of New York but gave way to the lace-paper delicacies imported from England. The less expensive creations of Esther Howland of Worcester, Mass, first appeared in 1850.

Recognized as the first Christmas card is one designed in England by J. C. Horsley in 1843 for his friend Sir Henry Cole. An edition of 1,000 copies was placed on sale at Felix Summerly's Home Treasury office in London. It was printed by lithography on stiff cardboard, 5⅛ × 3¼ in, in dark sepia and hand coloured. The design shows a family party in progress, beneath which is the greeting, "A Merry Christmas and a Happy New Year to You." Inside panels, formed by a rustic trellis, are representations of Christmas charity. A similar card was designed by W. M. Egley and produced as an etching in 1848. While this card is more elaborate its design suggests a relationship to the Cole-Horsley card. The same may be said of a U.S. Christmas card of the same period designed by R. H. Pease of Albany, N.Y., which bore the inscription, "Pease's Great Variety Store in the Temple of Fancy." Sentiment cards (approximately 3 × 1½ in.) were also exchanged and collected in the U.S. from 1830 to the Civil War period and many have survived, among them an "expanding heart" Christmas present or greeting card in purse form dating from about 1850, which may be one of the first U.S. Christmas cards.

Greeting-card production in commercial quantities started in 1860, the first offerings being valentines with applied Christmas ornaments and verses. These were followed by embossed or lithographed letter sheets and envelopes in multiple colours with matching cards. The latter were actually visiting cards with holiday sentiments, similar to the sentiment cards so popular earlier in the U.S. Visiting cards, which date in Europe from the 16th century, had long been used also to carry messages of affection, respect or condolence. A card with its corner bent gave the comforting assurance of personal interest. Early commercial greeting cards bore illuminations copied from manuscripts in the British museum. There were also small cards with embossed frames, similar to the visiting cards but bearing illustrations of robins and children. These were issued in sets of six and were collected and mounted in albums or scrapbooks. The cards also appeared in booklet form, attached to make a strip.

The colourful printed card ran a parallel course with the lace-paper valentine. One of the English publishers, Marcus Ward & Co., employed Kate Greenaway as a designer. Her productions, in sets of from two to six, were used for more than one occasion, the same designs being frequently used for Christmas, New Year's day, St. Valentine's day, birthday and everyday. Some of the designs appeared as book illustrations and others were used in annual four-subject calendars.

Louis Prang of Boston is called the "father of the American Christmas card." He started with sets of album cards (flora, birds, animals, etc.) and continued with Civil War scenes by Winslow Homer. He also printed advertising and visiting cards with floral designs and in 1875 added seasonal greetings. These were an immediate success. Prang cards were among the best in the market and were much admired abroad. He instituted design competitions in 1880, a practice continued later in England by Raphael Tuck and in the U.S. with Hallmark Cards Art awards. Prang's business flourished until 1895 when a decline of greeting-card production in England and the U.S. resulted from overwhelming competition from European printers whose product was so inexpensive that it could not be ignored. Cards were delivered in blank form and sentiments were applied by local printers, the same design being used for several purposes. From 1900 to World War I the greeting-card business was practically a German monopoly.

The U.S.-made greeting card reasserted itself about 1910 and was given enormous impetus by World War I with its resultant increase in transiency, a situation that was repeated during World War II. In the intervening years the custom of exchanging cards on both seasonal and everyday occasions became firmly established in the United States. U.S. greeting-card manufacturers also assumed world leadership during this period and brought many innovations to the design and manufacture of cards in the realm of novelties, animation, three-dimensional effects and visual and sound effects.

In the period after World War II, a new type of humorous greeting, usually called "studio" or "contemporary" cards, was popularized. The cards are distinguished mainly by the line drawings in modern art style with which they are illustrated and a brittle, ludicrous type of humour. Although humour from the beginning has gone hand in hand with sentiment as a greeting-card theme, studio cards constitute the most important single development in the field in recent times. They are thought to have originated in Greenwich Village art studios but their distribution spread through retail outlets in all parts of the U.S. and even abroad. While it is estimated that 80% of all greeting cards were formerly sent by women, the advent of the studio card has drawn an increasing number of men to the practice of exchanging cards.

Traditional greeting cards retained their lead in popularity, however, and serious sentiments continued to outsell the humorous. A shopper engaged in the selection of a greeting card at the stationery counter of a retail store may have as many as 1,000 different cards from which to choose. Foreign-language cards are produced for both domestic use and for export in a dozen languages. Fine art from both old masters and contemporary artists is reproduced on Christmas cards in increasing volume, and both original art and written sentiments are frequently commissioned by U.S. manufacturers from well-known artists and writers.

See also VISITING CARD.

BIBLIOGRAPHY.—Gleeson White, Christmas Cards and Their Chief Designers (1894); E. D. Chase, The Romance of Greeting Cards (1956); Ruth Webb Lee, A History of Valentines (1952); G. Buday, Fifty The History of the Christmas Card (1954); C. S. Brigham, Fifty Years of Collecting Americana (1958); W. E. Henry and H. L. Warner, "Art and Cultural Symbolism: a Psychological Study of Greeting Cards." (C. G. A. M.)

GRÉGOIRE, HENRI (1750–1831), French bishop of the Constitutional Church, remarkable for his efforts to reconcile his ecclesiastical principles and his loyalty to the Revolution and for his courage in maintaining both in turn against changing regimes, was born at Vého in Lorraine on Dec. 4, 1750. As curé of Emberménil, he won academic recognition for his Éloge de la poésie (1773) and for his Essai sur la régénération politique, physique et morale des Juifs (1788) and was elected to the estates-general of 1789 as deputy for the clergy of Nancy. Hostile alike to aristocratic privilege and to racial prejudice, he worked for the union of the clergy with the third estate and collaborated with the Société des Amis des Noirs for the abolition of Negro slavery. After expressing his objections to certain errors in the Civil Constitution of the Clergy (enacted in July 1790), he took the oath that it imposed and became Constitutional bishop of Loir-et-Cher (the diocese of Blois).

As a deputy in the Convention, Grégoire in Sept. 1792 proposed the abolition of the monarchy and in November demanded Louis XVI's trial, but he was on a mission in Savoy during the trial itself. Though he caused the mention of a death sentence to be suppressed in the letter that he and his colleagues sent to Paris, he was later unjustly blamed as a regicide.

During the Terror and, especially, during the campaign against Christianity, Grégoire showed conspicuous courage. He professed his belief before the Convention when J. B. Gobel, bishop of the Seine, abjured his faith (Nov. 1793); he continued to wear clerical dress; and, as a member of the committee of public instruction, he tried to save monastery libraries and religious works of art. After the Thermidorian reaction (July 1794) and the institution of the Directory (Nov. 1795), Grégoire, who became a member of the council of the 500, continued to interest himself in education, helping to found the Conservatoire des Arts et Métiers and the Institut (of which he was later a member).

Grégoire's speech to the Convention on Dec. 21, 1794, was chiefly instrumental in securing the restoration of freedom of worship. The reorganization of the Constitutional Church was guided by him, and he was the moving spirit of the councils of Aug. 1797 and June 1801. Since the coup d'état of Brumaire (Nov. 1799), however, he had opposed Napoleon Bonaparte, and his election to the senate in 1801 was regarded as a protest against the consular regime and against the concordat with Rome. He resigned his bishopric in Oct. 1801 (as the concordat removed Constitutional bishops from their sees) and traveled in England, Holland and Germany to test prospects of church reunion. He published a Histoire des sectes religieuses depuis le commencement du siècle dernier ... in 1810. Having voted in the senate against the proclamation of the empire in 1804, he proposed the deposition of Napoleon in 1814.

Under the Restoration, Grégoire stood firmly by his views. He was expelled from the Institut, and his election as a deputy for Isère in 1819 was annulled. His writings of this period include an

Essai historique sur les libertés de l'église gallicane (1818) and *De l'influence du Christianisme sur la condition des femmes* (1821). On his deathbed he refused to retract his opinions despite the exhortations of the archbishop of Paris (Hyacinthe Louis de Quélen); and so, when he died, on May 20, 1831, he was refused Christian burial until Louis Philippe ordered it to take place in the church of the Abbaye-aux-Bois. Partisans of the Revolution staged a demonstration at his funeral.

BIBLIOGRAPHY.—H. Carnot (ed.), *Mémoires de Grégoire* (1837); L. Maggiolo, *La Vie et oeuvres de l'abbé Grégoire* (1884); A. Gazier, *Etudes sur l'histoire religieuse de la Révolution française* (1887); R. Grunebaum Ballin, *L'Abbé Grégoire et les Juifs* (1931) and *Henri Grégoire, l'ami des hommes de toutes les couleurs* (1948).
(J. LE.)

GREGORAS, NICEPHORUS (c. 1290-1360), Byzantine scholar and statesman, was born at Heraclea in Pontus. He early settled in Constantinople in the household of his patron and teacher Theodore Metochites. He won the favour of Andronicus II, but was in disfavour for a short time when Andronicus was deposed by his grandson Andronicus III. On the elder Andronicus' death (1332) Nicephorus was again used in diplomatic missions and was appointed to treat with papal legates for the reunion of the Greek and Latin churches (1333). His reputation as a scholar stood high, and he publicly disputed with the Calabrian monk Barlaam. His opposition to the teaching of the hesychasts (*see* HESYCHASM), which was supported by Gregorius Palamas and by the emperor John VI Cantacuzenus, and recognized at the synod of 1351, brought him imprisonment in the monastery of the Chora in Constantinople. He was freed in 1355 by John V Palaeologus after John VI's abdication.

BIBLIOGRAPHY.—The *History*, ed. by L. Schopen, vol. 1-2 (1829-30) and I. Bekker, vol. 3 (1855) in the Bonn corpus; and in J. P. Migne, *Patrologia Graeca*, vol. 148-149 (1865), together with some minor works. Book 37 (36) of the *History*, ed. by V. Parisot, *Notices et extraits*, 17, part 2 (1851). A selection of the letters edited by R. Guilland, with French translation in the "Budé Series" (1927). *See also* G. Moravcsik, *Byzantinoturcica*, vol. 1, 2nd ed., pp. 450-453 (1958); G. Ostrogorski, *History of the Byzantine State*, p. 415 ff. (1956); R. Guilland, *Essai sur Nicéphore Grégoras* (1926).
(J. M. HY.)

GREGORIAN CALENDAR or NEW STYLE CALENDAR, the calendar substituted in March 1582 by Pope Gregory XIII for the ancient church calendar, which was founded on two erroneous suppositions, namely, that the year contains 365¼ days and that 235 lunations are exactly equal to 19 solar years. The Gregorian calendar was introduced into Spain, Portugal and part of Italy the same day as at Rome; France and Germany followed and it was subsequently adopted in almost all Christian countries. For the computation of the Gregorian calendar *see* CALENDAR.

GREGORIAN MUSIC: *see* PLAINSONG.

GREGOROVIUS, FERDINAND (1821-1891), German historical writer, best remembered for his history of Rome, was born at Niedenburg, Jan. 19, 1821. His work is the fruit of the fascination which Italy (his home during 1852-74) exerted upon him. His *Geschichte der Stadt Rom im Mittelalter* (8 vol., 1859-72; Eng. trans., 1894-1900) is inaccurate in places and has been superseded, but retains value for its colour and vitality. He wrote a companion *Geschichte der Stadt Athen im Mittelalter* (2 vol., 1889) and planned a book on Jerusalem. Other works include *Wanderjahre in Italien* (5 vol., 1856-77) and *Lucrezia Borgia* (1874). He died in Munich, May 1, 1891.
See J. Hönig, *Ferdinand Gregorovius*, 2nd ed. (1944).

GREGORY, SAINT, THE ILLUMINATOR (c. 260-330), the "Apostle of Armenia," the greatest though not the first missionary to his nation, and organizer of its distinctive national Christian tradition. Under his influence King Tiridates, formerly a persecutor, accepted Christianity and proclaimed Armenia a Christian nation about 303. Later legends confuse rather than clarify Gregory's reputation; they make him a Parthian noble, long imprisoned for the faith in a well by Tiridates, and connect him with an exiled Roman virgin, later martyr, Ripsime, and the (later) ecclesiastical centre of Armenia at Echmiadzin. Gregory's church was in communion with the Greek Church through a special connection with the see of Caesarea, where he was consecrated to the episcopate, and it used Greek or Syriac, not yet Armenian, as its ecclesiastical language. But it possessed strong distinctive features, including a custom of hereditary succession in the episcopate which lasted for some time. Gregory's successor as catholicos (primate) was his son Aristakes, who took part in the Council of Nicaea in 325, and brought the Nicene creed to Armenia. Gregory is said to have died as a hermit some years later. His feast day is Sept. 30. *See also* ARMENIAN CHURCH.

BIBLIOGRAPHY.—A good account and discussion of sources may be found in Bardenhewer, *Geschichte der altkirchlichen Literatur*, vol. v, pp. 182-185 (1932). *See also* Butler-Thurston, *Lives of the Saints*; H. Gelzer, *Die Anfänge der armenischen Kirche* (1895); M. Ormanian, *The Church of Armenia*, ch. 3-4, 2nd rev. ed. (1955). (E. R. HY.)

GREGORY, SAINT, OF NAZIANZUS (c. 329-388), called *theologos* (the Theologian), one of the four great doctors of the east (the others being Basil the Great, John Chrysostom and Athanasius the Great; *q.v.*) and one of the three so-called Cappadocian Fathers (the others being Basil and Gregory of Nyssa; *q.v.*), one of the greatest of the champions of orthodoxy against Arianism, was born near Nazianzus in Cappadocia (Asia Minor) where his father, also named Gregory, had recently become bishop. At Caesarea and Athens he was a fellow student of Basil, who persuaded Gregory to join him in his monastic retreat in Pontus. About 361 Gregory hesitantly accepted ordination, as assistant to his father, and soon became a well-known preacher. He helped to secure Basil's election as bishop of Caesarea; to support Basil he was unwillingly made bishop of the unimportant town of Sasima but never took possession of his see. He administered the church of Nazianzus for a while after his father's death in 374, then withdrew to Seleucia in Isauria. After the death of the Arian emperor Valens in 378 (followed shortly by the death of Basil), Gregory was called to reorganize the orthodox church at Constantinople. There he achieved the distinction as pastor, teacher and controversialist that has won him the title of *theologos*, although a rival (Maximus the Cynic) was set up against him under the patronage of the bishop of Alexandria. On the arrival of the orthodox emperor Theodosius in 380 Gregory took over the great Church of the Hagia Sophia. The council that met at Constantinople in 381 to settle disputes in the Eastern Church (later recognized as the second ecumenical council) accepted him as bishop of Constantinople and supported the developed Nicene doctrine he had championed (*see* COUNCIL: *First Council of Constantinople* [381]). Weary of personal attacks he resigned his see before the end of the year and left the capital after a moving farewell discourse. For the rest of his life he lived at Nazianzus, whose church he again administered during a vacancy, or on his nearby estate of Arianzus. His festival is celebrated in the east on May 9.

The interest of Gregory's somewhat romantic career should not obscure his importance as a formulator of orthodox thought, especially in the *Five Theological Orations* delivered at Constantinople, and his letters defending the full humanity of Christ against the Apollinarian heresy. His works include many sermons (commonly called orations), letters and verse compositions, among them a long autobiographical poem.

Gregory's works (*editio princeps*, 1550) are printed in J. P. Migne, *Patrologia Graeca*, vol. xxxv-xxxviii, from the Benedictine ed., 2 vol. (1778-1840); *Five Theological Orations*, ed. by A. J. Mason (1899); selections are translated in *Nicene and Post-Nicene Fathers*, ser. ii, vol. vii (1894); theological orations and letters on Apollinarianism in *Library of Christian Classics*, vol. iii (1954).

BIBLIOGRAPHY.—See J. H. Newman's classical sketch in *The Church of the Fathers* (1840), reprinted in *Essays and Sketches*, vol. iii (1948), and Carl Ullman's still useful *Gregorius von Nazianz* (1825; 2nd ed.

1867; Eng. trans. 1851); Dorothy Brooke, *Pilgrims Were They All*, ch. iv (1943); H. Pinault, *Le Platonisme de Saint Grégoire de Nazianze* (1925); Paul Gallay, *La Vie de Saint Grégoire de Nazianze* (1943).
(E. R. Hy.)

GREGORY, SAINT, OF NYSSA (c. 330?–c. 395?), philosophic theologian and one of the Cappadocian Fathers (the others being his elder brother Basil the Great and Gregory of Nazianzus; qq.v.), was one of the acutest intellects of the 4th century and exercised deep influence upon the mystical tradition of the Eastern churches. He owed much intellectually and spiritually to his brother Basil and to his elder sister Macrina, superior of a nunnery on the family estate by the Iris river in Cappadocia. He was expected by his family to enter the ministry of the church, but was unsuited by temperament, and, despite his sympathy with the monastic ideals of Basil and Macrina, he married (it seems) one Theosebia and became for a time a rhetorician. But in 371 Basil made him bishop of the insignificant town of Nyssa. This was done much against Gregory's will, but under the emperor Valens the church policy of the government was Arian, and Basil, as metropolitan of Caesarea, wished to build up an orthodox front in his province. As bishop, however, Gregory acted so unwisely that Basil had to rebuke him sternly for embarrassing indiscretions. Pressure from the government led to Gregory's exile in 376; he returned after Valens' death in 378. Meanwhile, his writings were making him famous. With difficulty he declined an invitation to become bishop of the important city of Sebaste in 380. He was at the Council of Constantinople (381) and was nominated by Theodosius I as a norm of orthodoxy and touchstone of communion for the churches of Pontus. Little is known of the last years of his life except for his occasional visits to Constantinople to deliver funerary panegyrics for ladies of the imperial family or to attend a council there in 394. His feast day is Jan. 10 in the Orthodox Church and March 9 in the west.

Gregory's chief writings are the "catechetical oration" (a sketch of the pattern of Christian doctrine), four treatises vindicating Basil against the attacks of the radical Arian Eunomius, tracts against Apollinaris and the Macedonians (heretics who denied the Godhead of the Holy Spirit), a book on the creation of man, a dialogue on the soul and the resurrection, the life of Moses (describing the mystical ascent of the soul), a commentary on the Song of Songs, various exegetical sermons on biblical passages including the Lord's Prayer, and a few letters, of which the second, attacking the abuses of pilgrimages, is of special interest. A group of ascetical writings includes works on perfection, on the celibate ideal, and an attractive panegyric on his sister Macrina.

Among the Cappadocian Fathers Gregory in some degree stands apart. He had neither Basil's wisdom as a statesman nor Gregory of Nazianzus' eloquence as a preacher and orator (though he delivered the usual discourses at funerals, church festivals and annual commemorations of martyrs). As a thinker, however, he surpassed both. With them he shared the acknowledgment of the ascetic ideal and a broad theological position upholding Nicene orthodoxy against Eunomius and the "Pneumatomachi" who, while recognizing the divine Sonship of Christ, would not admit that the Holy Spirit was also consubstantial and coeternal in the Godhead. Gregory worked out in detail the technical distinction between *ousia* and *hypostasis*, where *ousia* signifies the Godhead which Father, Son and Holy Spirit share and *hypostasis* signifies the individuality of each "Person." He spoke (with Basil) of the Father as the source of the Godhead of Son and Holy Spirit, of the Son as begotten of, and of the Spirit as proceeding from, the Father. This, however, is the sole distinction within the Godhead. Tritheism he carefully disowns in a tract addressed to a certain Ablabius, "That there are not three Gods": the attributes and operations of all the Persons are identical. Gregory avoids implying that the divine essence is only generically identical in the three Persons; while denying that Father, Son and Holy Spirit are adjectives, he also affirms that they are less than fully substantial.

Though doctrines of the Trinity and of the person of Christ were thrust into the centre of his thinking by contemporary church debates, the subject that most interested him on the philosophical side was the doctrine of man. Gregory is deeply indebted to Plotinus and to Origen. But the biblical and philosophical traditions are in tension. He differentiates his doctrine of the soul from the Neoplatonist view, denying pre-existence and inherent immortality; the soul receives immortality by grace. Yet he also takes the creation of man in God's image to mean that man essentially belongs to the eternal world and is akin to God. It is his nature to seek for union with the source of his being. The soul's task is to know itself and perceive the archetypal beauty reflected within as in a mirror. Sin results from weakness of the creaturely will. By deliverance from the passions and the realm of sense perception, the soul can rise to the invisible world and enter even "the darkness where God dwells," there to enjoy the beatific vision which is not static but a ceaseless and unending advance.

The tension between biblical and Platonic streams in Gregory's thought is evident in his tract, modeled on the *Phaedo* of Plato, where he puts into the mouth of the dying Macrina a discourse on the soul and the resurrection. After valiant efforts to stave off the radically spiritualizing doctrine of Origen, Gregory ends by capitulating to a view virtually indistinguishable from it. He shared with Origen a universalist belief in the final salvation for all, though expressing himself tentatively and cautiously, holding that in this mysterious subject churchmen were free to speculate.

BIBLIOGRAPHY.—A critical edition by W. Jaeger and others is in progress (1952 et seq.). J. Gretser's text (1638), reprinted in J. P. Migne, *Patrologia Graeca*, vol. xliv–xlvi (1858), is unreliable. The best edition of the catechetical oration (with notes) is by J. H. Srawley (1903; 2nd ed., 1958) and of the life of Moses by J. Daniélou in *Sources chrétiennes* with French trans., 2nd ed. (1955). Select writings in English translation by W. Moore and H. A. Wilson in *Nicene and Post-Nicene Fathers*, 2nd series, vol. v (1893). English translation of the life of Macrina by W. K. L. Clarke (1916), of the treatises on the Lord's Prayer and the Beatitudes by H. C. Graef (1954), in *Ancient Christian Writers*, no. 18. See also H. F. Cherniss, *The Platonism of Gregory of Nyssa* (1930); H. Urs von Balthasar, *Présence et pensée* (1942); J. Daniélou, *Platonisme et théologie mystique*, 2nd ed. (1953); W. Völker, *Gregor von Nyssa als Mystiker* (1955).

(Hy. C.)

GREGORY, SAINT, OF TOURS (c. 540–594), Gallo-Roman bishop, historian of the Franks, whose works provide the major source for knowledge of 6th-century France, also played a notable part in some of the events he records. Gregory was born at Arverna (now Clermont-Ferrand) and was baptized Georgius Florentius; he changed his name on entering the church. He came from an influential senatorial family which numbered among its members many bishops, including all but five incumbents of the see of Tours, to which Gregory was appointed in 573.

Gregory's task as bishop was immense. He had to administer one of the most important dioceses in Western Europe—controlling and disciplining the often unruly and insubordinate clergy and religious (he quelled a riot in a convent) and struggling to inculcate Christian principles into a people accustomed to the violence of the blood feud—and to defend Catholicism against the Arianism of the neighbouring Visigoths. He had to keep order in Tours, which the fame of St. Martin had made a popular centre of pilgrimage; rebuild his cathedral church, destroyed by fire shortly before he became bishop; and uphold the church's right of giving sanctuary, even against a king's vengeance. He had to protect the church's treasure and property from the rapacity of secular officials such as Leudast, the notorious count of Tours. He also had certain secular judicial functions to perform, and was often occupied on the king's business. As a result of the frequent partitions of territory between the Merovingian rulers, Tours, during Gregory's 21-year episcopate, fell in turn under the control of no fewer than four kings. The most difficult and dangerous of these was Chilperic (q.v.) I, described by Gregory as the Nero and Herod of his time. Against Chilperic and all whom he considered guilty of wrongdoing, Gregory stood up courageously. He died at Tours in 594. His feast day is Nov. 17.

Gregory himself tells us that he wrote ten books of history, seven of miracles, one on the lives of the Fathers, a commentary on the Psalms, and a treatise on the offices of the church. His *Historia Francorum*, conceived in the tradition of Augustine and

Orosius, sought to demonstrate the spread of true Christianity through the conquests of Catholic kings, by the labours of missionaries and martyrs, and by the steadfast witness of the church against heresy. The fact that he dated the conversion of Clovis (q.v.), in effect the hero of the *Historia*, almost ten years earlier than modern scholars think likely, enabled him to regard that king's conquests as the achievements of a Catholic sovereign.

Gregory wrote in the barbaric Latin of his period, and his style was closer to that of the Vulgate than to that of the classical authors, of whom he had read little. Historians have regretted that he gives no descriptions of personal appearance, of buildings, clothing, or daily activities. But his narrative style, especially his dialogue, conveys personality more vividly than do many carefully descriptive accounts. His works also provide an unconscious but clearly drawn self-portrait, in which he emerges as a man of conviction and steadfast courage. Kindly and simple, perhaps garrulous and slightly fussy, impatient of heretics, and imbued with an unfailing belief in the miraculous, Gregory was nevertheless, according to his lights, a real and effective champion of the Catholic faith.

BIBLIOGRAPHY.—The complete edition of Gregory's works is that of W. Arndt and B. Krusch, *Gregorii Turonensis opera*, 2 vol. (1884–85); the *Historia Francorum* has also been edited by B. Krusch and W. Levison, 2 vol. (1937–51); Eng. trans. with introduction by O. M. Dalton (1927). See also J. M. Wallace-Hadrill, *The Long-Haired Kings* (1962).
(S. Mu.)

GREGORY, the name of 16 popes and 1 antipope.

ST. GREGORY I THE GREAT (c. 540–604), pope from 590 to 604, the last of the four great Fathers and doctors of the Western Church, was born in Rome of a patrician family, probably the famous gens Anicia. In 573 he appears to have been holding the imperial office of prefect of the city, the most important civil office of Rome. Feeling drawn to the monastic life, he resigned this high position, allocated his vast estates to the endowment of seven new monasteries and became a Benedictine (probably) monk in the famous abbey of St. Andrew on the Clivus Scauri in Rome, which he had previously founded. In 578 he became one of the seven deacons (*regionarii*) of Rome and the following year he was dispatched by Pope Pelagius II as *apocrisiarius* (resident ambassador) to the imperial court in Constantinople. During this period he commenced his *Moralia in Iob*, a monumental commentary on Job for St. Leander of Seville, which he finished a few years later in Rome. After several years at the Byzantine court he returned to the monastery of St. Andrew, where he was abbot for about five years. But when Pelagius II died in 590, the Roman clergy and people unanimously chose Gregory as his successor. Despite his vigorous attempts to escape the burdens of this high office, he was consecrated on Sept. 3, 590.

When Gregory ascended the papal throne, the western world was undergoing a great cultural and political transformation. Old Rome was already fading and the new barbarian kingdoms of Europe were in process of formation. Italy was being ravished by the Lombards and the old imperial exarchate of Ravenna was helpless to provide security in the face of this new fury. In the person of Gregory the papacy was forced by the wretched circumstances of the times to assume the responsibility for the temporal welfare of the Italian people, which the emperor had formerly assumed. By firmness of character and shrewdness of diplomacy, Gregory succeeded in stemming the advance of the Lombards and restoring some peace and security in Italy (598). The vast holdings of the church, which reached from Tuscany to Sicily, he organized into a unit that helped to stabilize Italian life and that formed the patrimony of St. Peter, the foundation of the papal states. In every sphere of religious and political life, Gregory stood for the supremacy of the Roman see in dignity, prestige and authority, without, however, detracting from the temporal office of the emperor or the spiritual function of the episcopacy. He is the first pope to use officially the title "servant of the servants of God." His care for the inner life of the church is seen in his great concern for the proper formation of bishops and priests, for the cultivation and expansion of Benedictine monasticism, for the correction and development of the liturgy and for the extension of the church's activity into missionary fields. Perhaps the greatest act of his pontificate was the foundation of the Anglo-Saxon mission which, under the leadership of Augustine, Benedictine monk of St. Andrew's in Rome, later of Canterbury, successfully undertook the conversion of England to Catholicism. Gregory died on March 12, 604, and was canonized by popular acclaim. His feast is celebrated on the anniversary of his death.

Gregory's reputation as a doctor of the church rests not so much on creative genius as on his didactic method. Much of his originality is the product of the psychological insight he brought to his treatment of the spiritual life. In addition to voluminous correspondence (854 letters) he wrote the *Moralia* in 25 books, dialogues on the lives of the saints of Italy, homilies on Ezekiel and the Gospels, and the *Liber regulae pastoralis*, a treatise on the apostolic work and spiritual life of a Catholic bishop that was to the medieval episcopacy what Benedict's rule was to medieval monasticism. Gregory was also active in the liturgical reform of the Roman rite, though the extent of his share in the composition of the Gregorian sacramentary has not yet been fully established. His works are built solidly on the patristic tradition, especially St. Augustine. His mastery of the spiritual sense (allegorical, moral and anagogic) of Scripture is manifested in his *Moralia* which, as a textbook for moral theology and biblical exegesis, exercised a profound influence on the intellectual and spiritual life of the subsequent centuries. His contributions to theology, exegesis, asceticism and liturgy, his rehabilitation and development of the patrimony of St. Peter, his lofty conception of the role of the papacy in the western world make him a veritable founder of the middle ages.

ST. GREGORY II (669–731), pope from 715 to 731, succeeded Constantine in May 715. He greatly encouraged the Christianizing of Germany by St. Boniface, whom he consecrated bishop in 722. Though a staunch adherent of the eastern empire, he vigorously and successfully opposed the emperor Leo III the Isaurian in the iconoclastic controversy (q.v.). Leo tried to rid himself of Gregory by violence but the pope, supported by the people of Rome and by the Lombards, died peacefully on Feb. 11, 731. His feast is Feb. 13.

ST. GREGORY III (d. 741), pope from 731 to 741, succeeded Gregory II. He condemned the iconoclasts at a Roman council in 731 and, as Gregory II had done, encouraged the Christianizing of Germany. He conferred the pallium on St. Boniface and was the first pope to appeal to the Franks for aid against the Lombards. He died in 741 and his feast is Nov. 28.

GREGORY IV (d. 844), pope from 827 to 844, succeeded Valentinus. He is chiefly remembered for his mediation in the struggle between Lothair and Louis the Pious. His support of Lothair against Louis and his presence in Lothair's camp resulted in the desertion of the emperor on the Field of Lies in 833. He promulgated the observance of the Feast of All Saints. Gregory IV died on Jan. 25, 844.

GREGORY V (Bruno of Carinthia) (d. 999), pope from 996 to 999, received nomination to the papacy from Otto III. Until the Council of Pavia (997) he was opposed by the antipope John XVI. His most memorable acts were the coronation of Otto III and his successful opposition to the technically incestuous marriage of the French king Robert II to Bertha (see ROBERT II). Gregory died in 999.

GREGORY VI (Giovanni Graziano, or John Gratian) (d. 1048), pope from 1045 to 1046, was esteemed by his contemporaries as a man of learning and probity. On May 5, 1045, he bought the pontificate from the unworthy Benedict IX (see BENEDICT) in order to save the papacy from scandal. At the Council of Sutri, held by Henry III in 1046, he was accused of simony. He abdicated on Dec. 20, 1046, and retired to Germany with Hildebrand (later Gregory VII). He died in 1048.

ST. GREGORY VII (Hildebrand) (c. 1025–1085), pope from 1073 to 1085, was not only one of the greatest but also one of the most successful reformers of the church in the middle ages. Soon after his death the principle for which he had stood became paramount in the thought and life of western Christian society for at least 200 years. This principle was that of the primacy of the spiritual before the temporal, or, more concretely, of the ecclesiastical be-
(R. E. McN.)

fore the political order. The great church reform of the second half of the 11th century, in which from c. 1060 to his death Gregory was the leading protagonist, was directed against the preponderance of familial and proprietary, of dynastic and political interests over the spiritual tasks of the church, against a situation which was in part a heritage of ancient theocratic ideas of rulership and in part a result of the more recent influence of feudalism. The reform had as its first aim the restoration of a truly religious clergy. This could be brought about only by the elimination of lay intervention in clerical elections and in the conferring of ecclesiastical offices; the latter type of intervention was lay investiture, a practice which has given the entire conflict between the reformers and their opponents in the late 11th and early 12th centuries the name "investiture struggle" (see INVESTITURE CONTROVERSY). Gregory, more clearly than any of his contemporaries, recognized that reform could be achieved only if papal primacy in the church became more of a reality than it had been for a long time; he therefore greatly extended the range of papal intervention in the affairs of all churches within the universal church, of which the Roman Church was the mother and head. To make papal leadership more effective, he also considerably increased the role of papal legates in the various countries of Europe. Gregory VII's pontificate thus was decisive for the growing centralization of the government of the church through and in the papal office. This holds true not only for church-state relations but even more so for the inner life of the church. So, for instance, it was through Gregory VII that the so-called Mozarabic liturgy of Spain began to conform to the Roman liturgy.

Ever since Gregory's own time he has been accused of the desire to dominate the church and even the world. Together with Innocent III, Innocent IV and Boniface VIII, he is one of the popes who in the minds of many has become a symbol of the alleged hierocratic ambitions of the medieval papacy. However, modern studies and re-evaluations carried out by scholars of many nations, especially after World War II, show Gregory VII in a different light. It has come to be widely admitted that his motives were religious and not political; further, it seems that he was striving for a minimal rather than a maximal solution of the problem of the church's existence in the world. Following his masters among the Fathers of the Church, St. Augustine and St. Gregory the Great, and as deeply conscious as they of the imperfections of all terrestrial life, he did not intend to force the world into an impossible condition of spiritual perfection but rather sought to guarantee the preservation of the church's sacerdotal essence, the corruption of which he felt to be the greatest danger for Christianity.

Early Career.—Hildebrand was born probably about 1025 in Tuscany of a nonnoble father named Bonizo; he was educated in the monastery of St. Mary's on the Aventine, in Rome. His first historically important action was his participation in the German exile of Pope Gregory VI (see above). Perhaps Hildebrand did not believe the accusation of simony; at any rate he thought the deposition unlawful. It was probably on his return journey after Gregory VI's death that he became a monk, perhaps in the famous Burgundian reform centre of Cluny. Back in Rome he was ordained subdeacon by the first pope of the church reform movement, Leo IX, c. 1049, and was made administrator of the great abbey of St. Paul's Outside the Walls. He became increasingly prominent in the reform movement during the three pontificates which preceded his own and was made archdeacon of the Roman Church in 1059 by Alexander II. He carried out several important legations: in 1054 to France, where he took part in the Council of Tours which pronounced the first condemnation of the eucharistic heresy of Berengar of Tours (q.v.), a condemnation which Gregory was forced to repeat personally in 1079; in 1058 to Germany, where he obtained confirmation of the election of Stephen IX (X); in 1059 to Milan, where he seems to have favoured the antifeudal religious and revolutionary Pataria movement; and probably also to south Italy, where in that year the rule of the Normans was recognized by the papacy in return for Norman feudal allegiance. The establishment of feudal suzerainty over Norman south Italy was one of the most important political connections ever entered upon by the papacy. As pope, too, Gregory tried to link princes and kings to the papacy by feudal and quasi-feudal ties, hoping thus to win their special obedience in such matters as church reform and crusade and their military and financial support. Hildebrand also played an important role in the Roman synod of 1059. He may have shared with Cardinal Humbert of Silva Candida the responsibility for the first clear prohibition of lay investiture, pronounced by the same Roman synod, in which he also won Nicholas II's approval for his attempt to oblige the Roman secular clergy to a life in common without individual property, an attempt symptomatic of the general trend toward clerical reform.

Pontificate.—Hildebrand was elected pope on April 22, 1073. The first two years of his pontificate were taken up not only with further steps toward the reform of the church, including a general prohibition of lay investiture enacted by the Roman lenten synod of 1075, but also with plans for the liberation of the Holy Land and other parts of eastern Christendom recently subjected to Seljuk invasion. Gregory hoped to lead a projected crusade personally and to crown this enterprise by the reunion of western and eastern Christians divided by the schism of 1054. In both undertakings he hoped for the co-operation of the young German king and prospective emperor Henry IV (q.v.), whose temporary submissiveness, however, was motivated then and later by political considerations. This became evident as soon as Henry had mastered his internal difficulties in Germany. Not only in the longstanding quarrel over the archbishopric of Milan but also with regard to several other Italian and German bishoprics he flouted Gregory's recent prohibition of lay investiture. Henry thus made it clear that he would not sacrifice rights in the ecclesiastical field, acquired by his predecessors over several centuries, to the pope's avowed purpose of setting aside such rights on behalf of laws of the church. It must indeed be admitted that the Gregorian program posited a very grave problem to the Christian kingdoms, and especially to Germany and the Holy Roman empire, where the whole structure of government had become largely dependent on the political, economic and moral support of the bishops and abbots, who were at the same time holders of vast feudal principalities. The king-emperor therefore wanted to keep a decisive voice in their election and the right to invest them with the insignia of their ecclesiastical offices, since the office and the appertaining material possessions were still generally considered as indivisible. True, Gregory had written Henry IV that he would be willing to apply the decree prohibiting lay investiture less strictly "wherever the honour of the eternal king and the salvation of souls were not at stake." But it was easy to see that he did not give up any principle and also that for the king to enter sincerely upon the pope's intention would have required much understanding and good will, in which Henry was singularly lacking. Thus the first great struggle between church and state in the medieval west broke out. It was to overshadow the whole pontificate of Gregory VII, who was forced to give up the plan of the crusade and to make concessions elsewhere—for instance, in England, where William the Conqueror, though sympathetic to the reform of the English church under Archbishop Lanfranc of Canterbury, strongly objected to the Gregorian program of centralization of the universal church under papal leadership.

The struggle with the Holy Roman empire began with Henry IV's convocation of an assembly at Worms in Jan. 1076. There, supported by the majority of the German episcopate and by some secular princes, he made a rash attempt to depose the pope by a letter, on the grounds that he was trying to upset the entire order of the Holy Roman empire and allegedly had threatened to deprive the king of his crown (actually Gregory had intimated the possibility of excommunication). This letter, read by Henry's envoys at the Roman lenten synod of 1076, caused a storm of indignation and was answered by the pope in the form of a public prayer addressed to St. Peter, in the course of which he forbade Henry the rule of his kingdoms of Germany and Italy and excommunicated him. It soon became evident that the pope's position was stronger than the king's. Not a few of the bishops who had been converted to the views of Gregory. The Gregorian party among the German bishops, together with three German dukes and other non-clerical opponents of the king, forced Henry to desist from government and to seek the pope's pardon. As an afterthought, Gregory was asked to judge the king's case personally at Augsburg, Ger.; it was also declared that Henry would automatically lose his throne if his excommunication lasted more than a year.

In this desperate situation Henry succeeded in dividing his enemies by his famous winter crossing of the Alps and his humiliation before Gregory, whom he intercepted on his way to Germany at Canossa in north Italy. Henry's crossing of Mont Cenis in one of the severest winters recorded in the middle ages was extremely hazardous and arduous. When he arrived at Canossa he was faced with the even harder task of obtaining absolution from the pope. Gregory hesitated to absolve and even to receive the king, who nevertheless on three successive days came to the castle and stood before the gate in the garb and attitude of a penitent. Gregory finally was induced to greater mildness by the persistent efforts of several mediators, and no doubt above all by his own priestly conscience, which obliged him to give the seeker of sacramental forgiveness every benefit of doubt, whatever well-founded suspicion of his sincerity he might have. Nevertheless these suspicions were so strong that the pope as a condition of reconciliation demanded and received an oath that Henry would not prevent Gregory's meeting with the German princes and would accept the pope's judgment or advice in his dispute with the latter. Perhaps because a number of the ecclesiastical princes had been won for the cause of church reform, Gregory hoped in this way to safeguard Henry's obedience or at least to make him amenable to papal wishes concerning the investiture problem and the whole complex ecclesiastical-political relationship.

Things were to turn out differently. Neither Gregorians nor anti-Gregorians could be sure of the results of Gregory's arbitership, and therefore neither side really desired the planned synod of Augsburg under the pope's presidency. The princes opposing Henry elected the duke of Swabia, Rudolph, as king to rule in his stead. The next few years were years of civil war in Germany, and it is in no way surprising under the circumstances that, unlike Rudolph, Henry IV never complied with Gregory's demands for church reform. The pope, however, blamed him above all for having frustrated, in spite of his oath, papal or legatine arbitration in Germany. On the basis of this accusation he deposed and excommunicated Henry for the second time during the Roman lenten synod of 1080, in which he also recognized Rudolph as king of Germany and repeated and generalized the prohibition of lay investiture. Not unnaturally this second condemnation was less effective than the first. Henry presided over a well-attended anti-Gregorian council at Brixen, which declared Gregory VII deposed and in his place elected Archbishop Guibert of Ravenna, the antipope Clement III (see CLEMENT). Above all, however, Henry's cause was improved by Rudolph's death in battle, which occurred in the same year. He soon had enough power to carry the war to Italy and Rome, putting Gregory on the defensive. Henry besieged Rome for three years before he was able to enter the city in 1084, to see his antipope consecrated and to be crowned by him as emperor. Even then, Gregory held out in the unconquerable castle of Saint Angelo long enough to be rescued by his south Italian Norman vassal Robert Guiscard, whose superior army caused the emperor to withdraw and to return to Germany. Robert's Norman and Saracen troops, however, carried out one of the worst devastations of Rome ever perpetrated, and it seems that the Romans placed the blame on the pope; at any rate he accompanied the Normans southward. His last encyclical letter from Salerno shows that he believed as strongly as ever in the justice of his cause. Gregory died at Salerno on May 25, 1085, uttering the famous words, "I have loved justice and hated iniquity, therefore I die in exile."

It can hardly be denied that in the single-minded pursuit of a great and a good cause, Gregory VII at times lost sight of reality. This must be noted especially with regard to some of his interpretations of historical precedents, for instance, on the occasions of Henry IV's excommunication and suspension or deposition as king. The same single-mindedness stood not only behind the frequent warlike utterances of the pope, on which many modern historians have remarked, but also behind the far-reaching identification of his own certainties with God's providential plan which, for instance, after Henry IV's second condemnation, made him prophesy that the king would be dead within a year, a prophecy so strangely contradicted by the death of the papally supported antiking Rudolph. But such flaws must be seen as the concomitants of heroic strength and courage in the defense of the spiritual freedom of the church and indirectly of mankind against domination by material power, however hallowed and consecrated.

Gregory VII was beatified by Pope Paul V and his feast was extended to the whole church in 1728; it is celebrated on May 25.

Writings.—Early in his pontificate Gregory VII had set down his program in the 27 short sentences of the so-called *Dictatus papae*, one of the personal dictations of the pope included in his authentic *Register* (still surviving in the Vatican archives and edited by E. Caspar in *Monumenta Germaniae historica: Epistolae selectae*, vol. ii [1920–23]), which is made up of copies of his letters. The sentences of the *Dictatus papae* were not a universally binding proclamation but almost certainly chapter headings for a planned collection of canon law. On the whole, they constitute forceful formulations and in part novel applications of doctrines concerning papal authority which had been stated explicitly or implicitly by the early church (though Gregory's source was in part the pseudo-Isidorian collections [see DECRETALS, FALSE] which he, like all his contemporaries, believed genuine). Several of the sentences, however, are without precedent, as, for instance, the claim to depose emperors and the claim to absolve the subjects of unjust rulers of their oath of loyalty, and some were not received by the *communis opinio* of the church. Gregory's charters were edited by L. Santifaller in *Quellen und Forschungen zum Urkunden- und Kanzleiwesen Papst Gregors VII*, part i (Studi e Testi, cxc [1957]).

(G. B. L.)

GREGORY VIII (Alberto de Morra) (d. 1187), pope from Oct. 21 to Dec. 17, 1187, of a noble family of Benevento, a Cistercian, was elected to succeed Urban III. He took immediate measures to restore Jerusalem to the Christians. He died at Pisa, in an effort to reconcile the rival seaports of Pisa and Genoa in order to expedite shipments to the Holy Land.

GREGORY VIII (Maurice Bourdin) (d. c. 1137), antipope from 1118 to 1121, a Benedictine. While archbishop of Braga he had been suspended by Paschal II in 1114 but later regained the papal favour. Sent to confer with the emperor Henry V concerning the investiture controversy, Bourdin defected to the cause of the emperor, who proclaimed him pope on the death of Paschal II. He was excommunicated by Gelasius II (1118) and by Calixtus II (1119) and died in exile.

(R. P. N.)

GREGORY IX (Ugolino of Segni) (d. 1241), pope from 1227 to 1241, was born in Anagni perhaps between 1160 and 1170. He was elected on March 19, 1227, to succeed Honorius III.

During the pontificate of Gregory IX the final life-and-death struggle between the papacy and the Hohenstaufen empire under its greatest ruler, Frederick II (q.v.), began. The main reason for this struggle was the pope's recognition of the very real danger to the papal states which resulted from Frederick's resolve to unite all of Italy under imperial domination. But this alone hardly suffices to explain Gregory's unrelenting determination to destroy the sort of imperial power which Frederick represented. There existed a deeper and more general conflict of character and outlook between this pope and this emperor. While to Frederick the Rome of Augustus was much more important than the Rome of the apostles, and the culture of the Muslims more congenial than that of the Christian schools, Gregory's fierce political energy as well as his legal and dogmatic concerns were motivated by ardent and fanatical zeal for the preservation of the mystical essence of Christianity. The same pope who in 1234 promulgated the great collection of papal law known as the decretals of Gregory IX or *Liber extra* (see CANON LAW), an answer as it were to Frederick II's classically inspired Constitutions of Melfi or *Liber Augustalis*, had also been the friend and protector of St. Francis of Assisi and above all of St. Dominic and his rising order. Again, the same pope who so greatly furthered the new learning by firmly establishing the University of Paris as an independent corporation (1231) and by taking the initiative in the adaptation of Aristotelian philosophy to the Christian faith, also instituted the papal Inquisition (*q.v.*) and, paradoxically enough, incorporated the antiheretical legislation of Frederick II, including burning at the stake, in his own laws.

When Ugolino was still cardinal bishop of Ostia (created 1206), Frederick II had taken the cross from his hands as a symbol of his crusading vow; but engaged first in the consolidation of the kingdom of Sicily and then in attempts to tighten imperial rule in Italy, he had postponed the crusade for many years. Finally, even the mild Honorius III, who had deviated from the policy of Innocent III in granting Frederick permission to keep the Holy Roman empire and Sicily united during his lifetime, declared that the emperor would become subject to excommunication if he did not set out on the crusade by Aug. 1227. Frederick actually did sail from Brindisi on Aug. 9, 1227, but almost immediately had to turn back because of an epidemic which had broken out in his fleet and by which he too had been afflicted. Gregory IX, who had succeeded Honorius in that year, let the law take its course and excommunicated Frederick. While in the so-called sixth crusade of 1228–29 (*see* CRUSADES) the excommunicated emperor gained great but ephemeral success in the Holy Land, Gregory recruited the first properly papal army to invade the kingdom of Sicily; it was easily beaten by the returning Frederick, who nevertheless found it advisable to accede to Gregory's demands with regard to the liberty of the church in Sicily and the territorial integrity of the papal states; on this basis the peace of Ceprano or San Germano of 1230 was concluded and Frederick was reconciled with the church. But a lasting understanding between pope and emperor was impossible because the latter would not give up effective government in Italy and the former had every reason to expect that Rome and the papal states would not be excepted from it.

By 1239 relations between Gregory and Frederick had deteriorated to such an extent that the pope again decided for an open break and excommunicated the emperor for the second time. Both sides invoked European opinion in high-flown manifestoes which are among the most impressive documents of medieval Latin and of medieval political and ecclesiological thought. Gregory IX here appears as a continuator of St. Bernard of Clairvaux and Innocent III, but lays great stress also on the forged Donation of Constantine (*q.v.*), then generally believed to be genuine, as a foundation of papal power. Gregory convoked a general council of the church for Easter 1241 to judge the emperor. The council could not take place during his lifetime, however, since Pisan ships carrying imperial troops attacked and defeated the Genoese ships which were meant to transport over a hundred prelates to Rome; they then became the emperor's prisoners. Shortly after this disaster, which was retrieved only under Innocent IV (*q.v.*), Gregory IX died, on Aug. 22, 1241.

The *Registers* of Gregory IX were edited in three volumes by L. Auvray (Bibliothèque des Écoles Françaises d'Athènes et de Rome, series ii), 1896–1910.

BLESSED GREGORY X (Teobaldo Visconti) (d. 1276), pope from 1271 to 1276, was born at Piacenza in Lombardy, probably around 1210. He studied in Paris and helped bring about the peace of Paris between Louis IX of France and Henry III of England (1259). In the late '60s he took the cross and in 1270 joined the future English king Edward I at Acre. There he was notified of his election as pope, which had taken place on Sept. 1, 1271, at Viterbo, having been brought about by a compromise after a vacancy of almost three years following the death of Clement IV. This long vacancy was due chiefly to the antagonism in the College of Cardinals between adherents and opponents of the king of Sicily, Charles I of Anjou (*q.v.*). Gregory was consecrated and crowned in Rome on March 27, 1272.

When Gregory X left the Holy Land he referred in his parting sermon to Ps. cxxxvi (cxxxvii), 5: "If I forget you, O Jerusalem, let my right hand wither!" His whole pontificate was indeed largely governed by his efforts to pave the way for a new crusade which would save and restore the Christian kingdom of Jerusalem. Gregory skilfully used the Byzantine emperor Michael VIII's justified fear of Charles of Anjou to induce him to consent to a reunion between the Greek and Roman churches, with recognition

of papal primacy, a reunion which was carried into effect at the 2nd general council of Lyons, the 14th general council of the church, in 1274; but the union never obtained the general allegiance of the Greek clergy and people and was to be repudiated by Michael's successor. While not breaking with Charles of Anjou, Gregory tried to neutralize his influence by recognizing the election of Rudolph I of Hapsburg as German king and prospective emperor. At the Council of Lyons he also issued the constitution *Ubi periculum*, which for the first time officially regulated the conclave at papal elections. Gregory X died at Arezzo on Jan. 10, 1276.

The *Registers* of Gregory X and John XXI were edited in two volumes by J. Guiraud and L. Cadier (Bibliothèque des Écoles Françaises d'Athènes et de Rome, series ii), 1892–1906.
(G. B. L.)

GREGORY XI (Pierre Roger de Beaufort) (1329–1378), pope from 1370 to 1378, last of the legitimate Avignon popes and the last French pope, was born in the diocese of Limoges in 1329 and was created cardinal in 1348 by his uncle Clement VI. Although not yet a priest he was unanimously elected pope at Avignon on Dec. 30, 1370. As pontiff he laboured for peace between England and France, but without success. Despite the opposition of France and of many of the cardinals, he listened to St. Catherine of Siena (*q.v.*) and returned to Rome on Jan. 17, 1377, a step of great importance in the history of the papacy. His months in Italy were marked by stress and strife. Gregory XI died on March 26, 1378.

GREGORY XII (Angelo Correr) (c. 1325–1417), pope from 1406 to 1415, last pope of the Roman obedience during the Great Western schism, was born of an old Venetian family at Venice c. 1325. He was created cardinal by Innocent VII in 1405 and elected pope by the Roman cardinals on Nov. 30, 1406. He clung to the papal dignity against Benedict XIII (*see* BENEDICT), the Avignon claimant, and protested against his deposition by the Council of Pisa (1409). Gregory, however, freely resigned, on July 4, 1415, after sanctioning the Council of Constance. He died as cardinal bishop of Porto on Oct. 18, 1417. (*See also* CONSTANCE, COUNCIL OF.)

GREGORY XIII (Ugo Buoncompagni) (1502–1585), pope from 1572 to 1585, was born on June 7, 1502, at Bologna in the papal states. Created cardinal in 1565, he was elected pope on May 13, 1572. Gregory promoted the Catholic reform and the Counter-Reformation energetically by executing the decrees of the Council of Trent. He founded numerous colleges and seminaries for the education of candidates for the priesthood and put them, for the most part, under the direction of the Jesuits. With the aid of distinguished astronomers, he corrected the errors of the Julian calendar and introduced in its place the one named for him (*see* CALENDAR). He was the second founder of the Roman college which took the name of Gregorian university. As ruler of the papal states, Gregory was less successful. He is also often blamed for his attitude toward the massacre of St. Bartholomew's day (*see* SAINT BARTHOLOMEW'S DAY, MASSACRE OF) and for his support of the Irish rebels against Elizabeth I. He died April 10, 1585.

GREGORY XIV (Niccolò Sfondrato) (1535–1591), pope from 1590 to 1591, was born at Cremona on Feb. 11, 1535. Created cardinal in 1583, he was elected pope on Dec. 5, 1590, and continued the policies of his immediate predecessors. He died on Oct. 15, 1591.

GREGORY XV (Alessandro Ludovisi) (1554–1623), pope from 1621 to 1623, was born on Jan. 9, 1554, at Bologna in the papal states. He was created cardinal in 1616 and elected pope on Feb. 9, 1621. Gregory made use of his young but capable nephew Cardinal Ludovico Ludovisi in the conduct of affairs, with the result that Catholic interests were greatly advanced. Gregory introduced the secret ballot in the election of the popes. He canonized Ignatius of Loyola, Francis Xavier, Philip Neri and Teresa of Avila. He established the first permanent board of control of Catholic foreign missions, the Roman Congregation of Propaganda. Gregory XV died on July 8, 1623.
(E. A. R.)

GREGORY XVI (Bartolomeo Alberto Cappellari) (1765–1846), pope from 1831 to 1846, was born at Belluno on Sept. 18, 1765, and entered the order of the Camaldolese. In 1799 he published *Il trionfo della santa sede contro gli assalti dei novatori*. Shortly after the restoration of Pius VII in 1814 he became vicar-general of the Camaldolese and in 1825 he was made a cardinal. A good monk and a good priest, who did much during his pontificate for the reform of the religious orders and priesthood and the development of missions, Gregory was less happy in handling the political relations of the church. Confronted almost as soon as he was crowned by a revolt in his own states, which he suppressed with the aid of the Austrians, he took his stand on the alliance of throne and altar even when a Roman Catholic people, the Poles, rose in revolt against the intolerable oppression of the tsars. He ignored the advice of the powers that he should introduce reforms into the administration of the papal states and refused his support to the liberal program of the ardent Breton priest Félicité de Lamennais (q.v.). He died in Rome on June 1, 1846.

See also PAPACY.

(E. E. Y. H.)

BIBLIOGRAPHY.—Gregory I: H. Davis, St. Gregory the Great: Pastoral Care in Ancient Christian Writers, vol. 11 (1950); Morals on the Book of Job in Library of the Fathers, 4 vol. (1844-50); J. Schnürer, The Church and Culture in the Middle Ages, 1:350-814 (1956); F. H. Dudden, Gregory the Great: His Place in History and Thought, 2 vol. (1905); P. Batiffol, Saint Gregory the Great (1929); E. Spearing, The Patrimony of the Roman Church in the Time of Gregory the Great (1918).

Gregory VII: Earlier work on Gregory is superseded by A. Fliche, La Réforme grégorienne, 3 vol. (1924-37); by La Réforme grégorienne et la reconquête Chrétienne (1940), vol. viii of A. Fliche and V. Martin (eds.), Histoire de l'église; by H. X. Arquillière, Saint Grégoire VII (1934); and by the monographs edited by G. B. Borino, Studi gregoriani, 6 vol. (1947-61). See also J. Whitney, Hildebrandine Essays (1932); G. Tellenbach, Church, State and Christian Society at the Time of the Investiture Contest, Eng. trans. by R. F. Bennett (1940); C. Erdmann, Die Entstehung des Kreuzzugsgedankens (1935; reprint 1955).

Gregory IX: A. Fliche and V. Martin, Histoire de l'église, vol. x (1950); P. Brezzi, in Storia di Roma, vol. x (1947); F. X. Seppelt, Geschichte der Päpste, vol. iii (1956); with bibliography; H. K. Mann, The Lives of the Popes in the Middle Ages, vol. xiii (1925); E. Kantorowicz, Kaiser Friedrich der Zweite (1927) and supplementary vol. (1931), Eng. trans. by E. O. Lorimer, Frederick II (1931). For the decretals of Gregory IX see A. G. Cicognani, Canon Law, 2nd ed. (1935).

Gregory X: A. Fliche and V. Martin, Histoire de l'église, vol. x (1929); J. Haller, Das Papsttum, 2nd ed. (1953); F. X. Seppelt, Geschichte der Päpste, vol. iii (1956), with bibliography; D. J. Geanakoplos, Emperor Michael Palaeologus and the West, 1258-1282 (1959).

Gregory XVI: E. Vercesi, I papi del sec. XIX, vol. ii (1936).

(E. E. Y. H.)

GREGORY, ISABELLA AUGUSTA, LADY (1852-1932), Irish writer and playwright, who, by her translations of Irish legends, her peasant comedies and fantasies based on folklore, and her work for the Abbey theatre (q.v.), played a considerable part in the Irish literary renaissance. She was born on March 5, 1852, at Roxborough, County Galway. In 1880 she married a neighbouring landowner and member of parliament, Sir William Gregory; her literary career did not begin until after his death (1892). In 1898 she met W. B. Yeats; she became his lifelong friend and patron, and played a part in the foundation of the Irish Literary theatre (1899). She became a director of the Abbey theatre in 1904. Lady Gregory wrote or translated nearly 40 plays. Seven Short Plays (1909), her first dramatic works, are among her best, vivid in dialogue and characterization. The longer comedies, The Image and Damer's Gold, were published in 1910 and 1913; and her strange realistic fantasies The Golden Apple and The Dragon, in 1916 and 1920. She also arranged and made continuous narratives out of the various versions of Irish sagas, translating them into an Anglo-Irish peasant dialect known as "Kiltartan" from a village on her estate, Coole park, County Galway. These were published as Cuchulain of Muirthemne (1902) and Gods and Fighting Men (1904). They were probably the most successful English versions of Irish epic and have great liveliness and actuality. She died on May 22, 1932, at Coole.

BIBLIOGRAPHY.—Lennox Robinson (ed.), Lady Gregory's Journals, 1916-1930 (1946); W. B. Yeats, Autobiographies (1946); George Moore, Hail and Farewell (1911-14).

(À. Cr.)

GREGORY, JAMES (1638-1675), Scottish mathematician and astronomer, famous in his day as inventor of the Gregorian reflecting telescope, was educated at the grammar school of Aberdeen and at Marischal college of that city. In 1663 he published his treatise Optica promota, in which he described his great invention. About 1665 he went to the University of Padua, where he studied for some years, and in 1667 published Vera circuli et hyperbolae quadratura, in which he discussed infinite convergent series for the areas of the circle and hyperbola. In 1668 he published also at Padua Geometriae pars universalis, in which he gave a series of rules for the rectification of curves and the mensuration of their solids of revolution. He was professor of mathematics successively at the universities of St. Andrews (1669-74) and Edinburgh (1674-75). James Gregory: Tercentenary Memorial Volume (ed. by H. W. Turnbull; 1939) contains Gregory's letters and posthumous manuscript and shows that he had anticipated several mathematical discoveries in number theory and differential calculus; e.g., Taylor's expansion.

Gregory died at Edinburgh in Oct. 1675.

(O. Oe.)

GREGORY THAUMATURGUS, SAINT (c. 213-c. 270), Greek church father, was born of noble pagan parents at Neocaesarea in Pontus (modern Niksar, Turk.). He studied law, but at Caesarea met Origen (q.v.) and became his convert (A.D. 233). He was consecrated bishop of his native town about 240 and, in spite of the Decian persecution, converted nearly the whole city during his office of 30 years. He was active at the first synod of Antioch (264-265), which condemned the heresies of Paul of Samosata (q.v.). His feast day is Nov. 17. His later fame was due to the stories of miracles which grew up around his missionary labours, hence the surname Thaumaturgus ("wonder-worker").

Gregory's works, which include the Panegyricus in Origenem, Metaphrasis in Ecclesiasten, Epistola canonica and Expositio fidei, throw light on the personality and method of Origen, on the organization of the church in Pontus and on Gregory's Trinitarian doctrine, approaching the Nicene type.

Editions of his works were published by G. Voss (1604) and others, and are reprinted in J. P. Migne, Patrologia Graeca, vol. x. See O. Bardenhewer, Geschichte der altkirchlichen Literatur, vol. ii, pp. 315-332 (1914), for full bibliography; also Schaff-Herzog, Encyclopedia of Religious Knowledge.

(E. R. Hy.)

GREIFSWALD, a town of Germany which after partition of the nation following World War II became a regional capital in the Bezirk (district) of Rostock, German Democratic Republic. Pop. (1964) 47,424. The town is about 56 mi. E. of Rostock and 2½ mi. W. of the Greifswalder Bodden, a bay of the Baltic sea, on the navigable Ryck river. A rail junction, Greifswald manufactures principally textiles and foodstuffs. The town was founded about 1240 by Dutch traders and received its municipal charter ten years later. In 1278 it became a member of the Hanseatic league. After the peace of Westphalia (1648) it came into Swedish possession and in 1815 passed to Prussia. The University of Greifswald (1456), renamed for the German patriotic writer Ernst Moritz Arndt, has faculties of mathematics and natural science, philosophy, theology and medicine. There are also an agricultural college, a medical college and an engineering school.

(E. Y. H.)

GREISEN, a modification of granite found in the tin districts of Cornwall and Saxony, consisting essentially of quartz and white mica, and characterized by the absence of feldspar and biotite. In the hand specimen the rock has a silvery glittering appearance from the abundance of lamellar, or layered, crystals of muscovite, but many greisens have much of the appearance of a paler granite. The commonest accessory minerals are tourmaline, topaz, apatite, fluorspar and iron oxides; a little feldspar more or less altered may also be present and a brown mica which is biotite or lithionite. The tourmaline in section is brown, green, blue or colourless, and often forms mostly large plates with imperfect crystalline outlines. The white mica quartz is rich in fluid enclosures. Apatite and topaz are both colourless and of irregular form.

Greisen occurs typically in belts or veins intersecting granite. At their outer edges they pass gradually into the granite. The transition between the two rocks is perfectly gradual, a fact which shows that the greisen has been produced by alteration of the granite. Vapours or fluids rising through the fissure have been the agents which effected the transmutation. They must have contained fluorine, boron and probably also lithium, for topaz, mica and tourmaline, the new minerals of the granite, contain these elements.

The alumina for these minerals is supplied by the biotite and feldspar of the granite, but it is noteworthy that albite is not replaced by the soda white mica, paragonite. The change is pneumatolytic, induced by the vapours set free by the granite magma when it cools. Probably the rock was at a relatively high temperature at the time.

A similar type of alteration, the development of white mica, quartz and tourmaline, is found sometimes in sedimentary rocks around granite masses.

Greisen is closely connected with schorl rock both in its mineralogical composition and in its mode of origin (see SCHORL). The latter is a pneumatolytic product consisting of quartz and tourmaline, and often contains white mica, thus passing by all stages into greisen. Both of these rocks frequently carry small percentages of tin oxide (cassiterite) and may be worked as ores of tin, and the central filling of the fissure often contains much wolframite, the chief ore of tungsten, as in Cornwall, Saxony, Tasmania and other centres of tin mining.

(J. S. F.; X.)

GREIZ, a town of Germany which after partition of the nation following World War II became a regional capital in the *Bezirk* (district) of Gera in the German Democratic Republic. Pop. (1964) 39,424. The town is in the narrow wooded valley of the Weisse Elster about 19 mi. WSW of Zwickau. The old town is on the right bank and the new town on the left bank of the river. There are worsted spinning mills, engineering and paper plants as well as a textile training school. Greiz is dominated by the Oberen Schloss (castle) on the left bank. The town was first mentioned in the 13th century, and it was the residence of the princes of Reuss, senior line, until 1918. It has a large park.

GRENADA, the southernmost of the Windward Islands in the West Indies, lies about 90 mi. (145 km.) N of Trinidad in the eastern Caribbean. Oval in shape, it has an area of 120 sq.mi. (311 sq.km.), including the island dependency, Carriacou (area, 13 sq.mi. [34 sq.km.]).

Relief and Geology.—The island is of volcanic origin with raised limestone beaches in the extreme north. A broken mountain range (highest point Mt. Saint Catherine, 2,756 ft. [840 m.]) crosses the island from north to south. Spurs separating steep-sided valleys reach toward the coast. In the centre of the mountain range at 1,740 ft. (530 m.) is Grand Etang, a circular lake 36 ac. (15 ha.) in extent, occupying the crater of an extinct volcano. Lake Antoine, another crater lake, lies on the northeastern plain almost at sea level. The island is watered by several streams and torrents which are longest on the eastern slopes. There are numerous freshwater springs, as well as hot chalybeate (ironbearing) sulfurous springs. The southern coast is much indented by bays.

Climate and Vegetation.—Grenada has a tropical maritime climate, with an equable temperature that varies with altitude and averages 82° F (27.7° C) in the lowlands. In the dry season extending from January to May occasional showers occur. Rainfall varies considerably in the rainy season with averages of 60 in. (1,524 mm.) in the coastal districts and of 150 to 200 in. (3,810 to 5,080 mm.) in the mountainous interior. Hurricanes occasionally occur. A wide variety of tropical fruits, flowering shrubs, and ferns grow on the island, and about 10,000 ac. (4,050 ha.), chiefly in the hilly interior, are wooded.

History.—Grenada was discovered in 1498 by Christopher Columbus, who named it Concepción. Neither the Spanish nor the British, to whom it was granted in 1627, settled on the island. The governor of Martinique, Dizel du Parquet, purchased it in 1650, and the French afterward exterminated the Caribs with ruthlessness. In 1665 Grenada came into the hands of the French West India Company, and in 1674 passed to the French crown. Cocoa, coffee, and cotton were introduced in 1714. During the wars between Great Britain and France, Grenada capitulated to the British forces in 1762, and was formally ceded the next year by the Treaty of Paris. The French recaptured the island in 1779,

but it was restored to Great Britain by the Treaty of Versailles in 1783. During 1795–96 there was a rebellion against the British rule, instigated and assisted by the French, but it was quelled by Sir Ralph Abercromby. After the slaves were emancipated in 1838 Grenada, with cocoa supplanting sugar as its staple, did not experience the depression that overtook the sugar-growing West Indian islands in the 19th century. The headquarters of the government of the British Windward Islands from 1885, Grenada joined the West Indies Federation (*q.v.*) in 1958. After the federation was dissolved in 1962 Grenada joined with the remaining territories in the Windward Islands, Barbados, and the Leeward Islands, in an attempt to form a new federation. On March 3, 1967, it assumed a status of association with the U.K.

Population.—The total population, estimated in 1969 at 104,188, is made up for the most part of inhabitants of African and mixed descent, although there is a small European community and a number of Indians. The capital, St. George's, had an estimated population of 8,644. Catholics predominate although there is a substantial Anglican minority. English is generally spoken but a French *patois* survives among the older peasantry.

The Economy.—The island is predominantly agricultural; more than half the labour force works on the land. Rich volcanic soil favours cocoa, nutmegs, bananas, mace, and limes. The territory has few manufacturing industries but efforts were being made to increase the tourist trade in the late 1960s. The landlocked harbour of St. George's is visited by several shipping lines, and there is an airfield at Pearls. Small coastal towns afford anchorage for fishing and trading vessels. The island has about 566 mi. (911 km.) of good roads. Grenada currency is based on the Trinidad and Tobago dollar (TT$4.80 = £1 sterling = U.S. $2.40).

See *A Year Book of the Commonwealth,* HMSO (annually).

(RD. T.; D. L. N.)

GRENADES, small explosive or chemical missiles used for attacking enemy troops, vehicles or fortified positions at close range. When designed to be thrown by hand they are called hand grenades, and when adapted for launching from a rifle or carbine, rifle grenades (*see below*). The term was also applied originally to any explosive shell fired from a gun. Most varieties of hand grenades are cheap and easy to manufacture and can be used effectively by troops with little training. Despite the steady 20th-century trend toward highly complicated instruments of war, the lowly grenade maintained its position as a valuable infantry weapon.

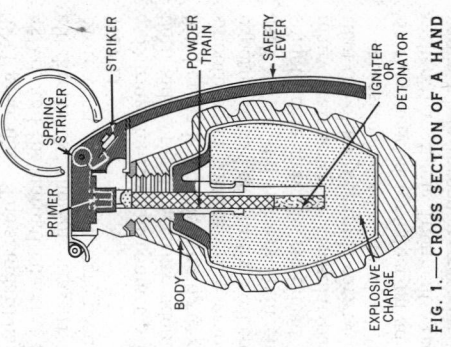

FIG. 1.—CROSS SECTION OF A HAND GRENADE (FRAGMENTATION TYPE) SHOWING PRINCIPAL PARTS

"Grenade" probably derived from the French word for pomegranate because of the resemblance to that fruit of early grenade shapes. In later years grenades were nicknamed "pineapples" because of the bulbous shape and rough exterior of the World War I models (*see fig.* 1), though they were in fact more nearly the size of a lemon. The rough exterior of the cast-iron grenade used during the first half of the 20th century was intended to make the case break into fragments about the size of a half lump of sugar when the explosive charge was detonated, but it did not always have that effect. Over the years grenades of many different shapes and sizes appeared, some spherical, others egg-shaped, still others cylindrical. One flat type with a handle resembled a hairbrush, and another was built like a wooden potato masher. Although there are historical references to grenades weighing as much as 6 lb., most have been much lighter, usually about 1½ lb.

Grenades probably came into use as early as the 15th century and were found to be particularly effective when exploded among troops in the ditch of a fortress during an assault. So important did grenades become in European armies of the 17th century that soldiers specially selected for strength and courage were trained as grenadiers (q.v.). But, after about 1750, grenades were virtually abandoned as the range and accuracy of firearms increased, lessening the opportunities for close combat. They did not come back into use on an important scale until the siege of Port Arthur during the Russo-Japanese War (1904-05).

Hand Grenades.—In the trench warfare of World War I (1914-18) both sides found hand grenades and rifle grenades effective in attacking enemy positions. The German army was well supplied with grenades of many shapes and sizes at the start of the war and took the Allies by surprise with its grenade attacks. After resorting to makeshifts such as the "jam pot," a tin can filled with an explosive and scraps of iron, the British army developed and used large quantities of the Mills grenade, often called the Mills bomb, both for hand and rifle launching. It was shaped like a pineapple, and its fuze was activated by a spring-driven lever fitted close to the outside of the grenade. Before throwing the grenade, the soldier removed a safety pin, meanwhile holding the lever in place with a firm grip until the grenade left his hand. The delay train of the fuze was usually set for four or five seconds, long enough for the missile to reach its target but not so long as to permit the enemy to pick it up and throw it back again. Contact grenades that exploded when they struck their target were also employed but proved less safe and effective than those with time fuzes.

During World War II a wide variety of hand grenades appeared, including many improvised forms such as the "Molotov cocktail," a gasoline-filled bottle with a lighted wick in its top. It was often thrown at tanks to set them on fire. The standard fragmentation or defensive grenade of the U.S. army at the start of World War II was similar to the Mills grenade. It consisted of a serrated cast-iron body holding about 2 oz. of blank powder, the whole weighing 22 oz. Blank powder of the kind used to load small arms blank cartridges had been adopted in the mid-1920s because TNT shattered the case into fragments that were considered too small to be effective. But blank-powder grenades proved unsatisfactory in combat and were replaced in 1943 by TNT grenades. The standard hand grenade could be thrown about 35 yd. and the normal effective range of fragments was 10 yd. in all directions, though stray fragments might fly much farther. More than 50,000,000 were produced for the U.S. army in World War II.

During the Korean conflict, when grenades were freely used by both sides, the U.S. army adopted a new type of fragmentation hand grenade, smaller and lighter than the earlier model and with a smooth outer surface. The grooved body was abandoned because experience had shown that, when filled with a high explosive such as TNT, it did not result in effective fragmentation. The new smooth-case grenade contained a powerful explosive, threw out many fragments in a regular pattern and was far more effective than the older pineapple variety.

Offensive grenades are of a different type and of less importance. As they depend for effect on an explosive blast over a small area rather than flying fragments, troops using them continue to advance while throwing grenades before them. The blast effect is naturally greatest in a confined area such as a trench or pillbox. The body of the offensive grenade has usually been cylindrical in shape, like a huge firecracker, and made of pressed paper with sheet metal end pieces. Larger than the fragmentation grenade, it contains 6 or 7 oz. of TNT but still weighs less than 1 lb. in all. It has sometimes been employed as a demolition device or fitted with a special fuze and concealed to form a booby trap to blast an unwary soldier who happened to move the object it was attached to.

Chemical Grenades.—Smoke grenades, similar in construction to offensive grenades, are used to lay down a local smoke screen to hide troop movements or for other tactical purposes. (See SMOKE: IN WARFARE.) For signaling to planes or to ground troops, smoke grenades come in a variety of colours. Illuminating grenades, as their name implies, put forth a short burst of light that may reveal the enemy's position at night, while other types of incendiary grenades contain a mixture for starting fires, while other types of chemical grenades contain tear gas or other chemical agents. (See CHEMICAL WARFARE.) Tear gas grenades are used by police to disperse mobs or to force fugitives to come out into the open.

Rifle Grenades.—There are in the Tower armouries specimens of flintlock muskets used for grenade projection as early as the 17th century, but they were apparently not very successful. When grenades were revived in the early 1900s, efforts were made to project them from rifles and thus increase their range. The commonest practice was to attach to the hand grenade a metal rod that fitted tightly into the muzzle of the rifle and was ejected by firing a blank cartridge. Improved grenade launchers that could be fitted to the muzzles of standard rifles came into use during World War II. They permitted firing grenades without damage to the rifle, resulted in more accurate fire and launched the standard hand grenade to a distance of 100 to 200 yd., filling the gap between the ranges of hand grenades and small mortars.

Grenades designed specifically for rifle launching generally have long, streamlined bodies, with fins at the rear to stabilize their flight (see fig. 2). One of the most important new types in World War II was the antitank rifle grenade designed for close, point-blank fire at armoured vehicles. It contained a special armour-piercing explosive known as a "shaped charge." With such a grenade a foot soldier could knock out a tank if he got close enough for a good shot. It was as an outgrowth of early efforts to devise an antitank rifle grenade that the bazooka rocket was developed. See also BAZOOKA.

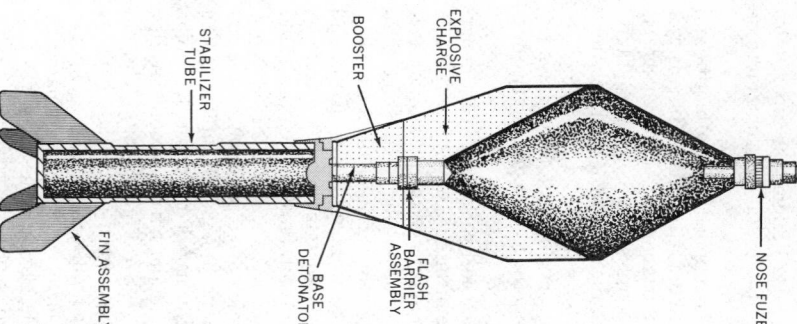

FIG. 2.—CROSS SECTION OF U.S. ANTITANK RIFLE GRENADE

GRENADIER.

The military employment of grenades (q.v.) necessitated the recruitment of men of exceptional physique to hurl them, but at the outset such troops were not organized in special units. The mid-17th century witnessed the formation within the battalion of special companies of powerfully built men to serve as grenadiers; they wore a mitre-shaped headdress of cloth or fur, this being more appropriate to the action of throwing the grenade than was the contemporary broad-brimmed hat. Grenadiers were more particularly employed in siege and trench warfare, and were armed with a heavy hatchet with which to cleave their way through barricades and other obstructions. After the gradual decline in the employment of the grenade in the 18th century, grenadiers were retained as storm troops, proudly taking the right of the battalion line on parade. Despite the depressive effect on the morale of the remainder of their units, the grenadiers from several line regiments—like the light companies—were frequently formed into special service battalions; this process was eventually rationalized by Napoleon, who recruited whole formations of these exponents of a specialized type of fighting. In the British army the brigading of grenadier and light companies as special task forces remained common practice until about 1858. The gradual adoption throughout Europe of the four-company battalion progressively encouraged the recruitment of separate grenadier formations, but their duties had come to differ little from those of the ordinary regi-

BIBLIOGRAPHY.—Maj. Gen. Thomas J. Hayes, Elements of Ordnance (1938); Maj. Theodore C. Ohart, Elements of Ammunition (1946); Charles J. Ffoulkes, Arms and Armament (1945); J. B. Sweet (ed.), Essentials of Military Training (1956). (H.C.T.)

ments of the line. Horse grenadiers made a fugitive appearance in both the British and the Belgian forces. In World War I battalion subunits were trained in both the throwing of hand grenades and the firing of rifle grenades.

In later years, the grenadier disappeared as a special type of infantryman, for nearly all ground combat troops were trained to use grenades.

(R. C. H.)

GRENADINE ISLANDS, a chain of about 600 islets in the Windward Islands, West Indies, stretch for 60 mi. (97 km.) from northeast to southwest between St. Vincent and Grenada (qq.v.). Some are a few square miles in area, others are mere rocky hummocks. For purposes of administration they are divided between St. Vincent and Grenada. The St. Vincent group (Bequia, Canouan, Mayreau, Mustique, Union Island, and associated islets) had a population of 5,068 in 1960.

Because of lack of water these islands are only slightly cultivated. Admiralty Bay on the west side of Bequia is a safe and commodious harbour.

Carriacou Island, the largest of the Grenadines with an area of 13 sq.mi. (37 sq.km.) is, with its associated islets, administered by Grenada. A ridge of hills rising to an altitude of 980 ft. (299 m.) crosses the island from northeast to southwest. On the west coast there are two good harbours: Hillsborough Bay on which the chief town, Hillsborough, stands and Tyrell Bay, farther south. Resorts and home sites are being developed on the islands of Bequia, Palm Island (formerly Prune Island), Petit St. Vincent, Union, and Young's Island. Airstrips, hotels, and yachting marinas have been constructed.

See *A Year Book of the Commonwealth*, HMSO (annually).

(Ro. T.; D. L. N.)

GRENFELL, GEORGE (1849–1906), English Baptist missionary and explorer of the Congo, was born at Sancreed, near Penzance, on Aug. 21, 1849, and educated in Birmingham. In 1874 he was sent by the Baptist Missionary society to the Cameroons with Alfred Saker and in Jan. 1878 joined T. J. Comber on the lower Congo. His mission stations on the Cameroons and Congo rivers helped to undo the evil effects of slave trading upon the tribes there. He made six voyages of exploration up the Congo, 1884–87, and drew up an independent survey as far as the equator at longitude 18° E. From 1900 to 1902 he explored the Aruwimi tributary of the Congo as far as Mawambi. Grenfell died at Basoko on the Congo, July 1, 1906.

His work increased the knowledge of Congo geography, anthropology and zoology, and he received the Royal Geographical society's gold medal in 1887.

See H. H. Johnston, *George Grenfell and the Congo* (1908) ; G. Hawker, *Life of George Grenfell* (1909).

GRENFELL, SIR WILFRED THOMASON (1865–1940), British medical missionary, was born on Feb. 28, 1865, at Parkgate, Cheshire. He was educated at Marlborough college and studied medicine at London hospital, qualifying in 1888. He spent one term, in 1887, at Oxford and was given their first honorary M.D. degree in 1907. A deep impression was made on him in 1885 by the visit to London of D. L. Moody, the American evangelist.

In 1888 he joined the Royal National Mission to Deep Sea Fishermen, fitted out the first hospital ship for the North sea fisheries and for several years cruised with it as a medical missionary. He was chosen by the mission in 1891 to start a pioneer service to the fishermen of the Labrador coast of Newfoundland and left England on June 12, 1892. In his first two months Grenfell treated 900 patients, the beginnings of an immense work of relief along the Labrador coast. In 1899 he was presented with the hospital ship "Strathcona."

His devotion to the welfare of the fishermen, his dauntless journeys by dog sled and his adventures in the icy Labrador seas, coupled with dwindling financial means, caught the imagination of generous friends in Canada, the U.S. and Britain. His hospital and children's home at St. Anthony's became the base of the Labrador work of the International Grenfell association, of which Grenfell was superintendent. Through Grenfell's work the needs of the fishing communities of Labrador for schools, institutes and

general welfare were also more adequately met by the government. He was created knight commander of the Order of St. Michael and St. George in 1927 and retired to Charlotte, Vt., in 1935. He died there on Oct. 9, 1940.

His books include his autobiography, *A Labrador Doctor* (1920), which was revised and republished as *Forty Years for Labrador* (1932).

See T. Lennox Kerr, *Wilfred Grenfell: His Life and Work* (1959) ; R. G. Martin, *Knight of the Snows* (1966). (C. N.)

GRENOBLE, the ancient capital of Dauphiné, a former province of southeastern France, and prefecture of the *département* of Isère, 75 mi. S.E. from Lyons by rail. Pop. (1962) 155,677. Grenoble was one of the most strongly fortified cities in Europe. Built at a height of 702 ft., the greater and newer part of the town rises on the left bank of the Isère and has wide thoroughfares and modern buildings. The original town (small in extent) was built on the right bank of the Isère at the southern foot of Mont Rachais. The main industry is the production of turbines and electrical machinery for hydroelectric power plants. The making of kid gloves, once most important, has declined, though it is still of significance. Other articles produced are cement, liqueurs, linen and leather goods.

Grenoble is the seat of a bishopric founded in the 4th century. It was formerly a suffragan of Vienne and is now in the ecclesiastical province of Lyons. The most remarkable building is the late 15th-century Palais de Justice, on the site of the old palace of the *parlement* of Dauphiné. Opposite is the church of St. André (13th century), formerly the chapel of the dauphins of Viennois, containing the tomb of Bayard. The cathedral church of Notre Dame dates in part from the 11th century. The church of St. Laurent, the oldest in the city (11th century), has a crypt dating from Merovingian times. The town library has a rich collection of manuscripts (among which are nearly all of Stendhal's autograph works) and printed books, which in part belonged till 1793 to the monastery of the Grande Chartreuse, near Grenoble (see CHARTREUSE, LA GRANDE). There is an art gallery, well known for its modern paintings, a Stendhal museum and a natural history museum. The university, which was founded in 1339, has faculties of law, sciences, letters and a school of medicine, and several other institutes and colleges are affiliated with it. The town also has a polytechnical institute, a school of electronic engineering and, since 1959, a centre of nuclear research. Stendhal was born at Grenoble in 1783.

Grenoble occupies the site of Cularo, a village of the Allobroges, fortified by Diocletian and Maximian at the end of the 3rd century. Its present name is a corruption of Gratianopolis, in honour of Gratian (4th century). After passing under the power of the Burgundians (c. 440) and the Franks (532) it became part of the kingdom of that kingdom a long struggle for supremacy ensued between the bishops of the city and the counts of Albon, the latter winning in the 11th century, taking the title of dauphins of Viennois in the 13th century. In 1349 Grenoble was ceded with the rest of Dauphiné to France (see also DAUPHINÉ). In 1562 it was sacked by the Protestants, but in 1572 the firmness of its governor saved it from a repetition of the massacre of St. Bartholomew's day. In 1590 the duc de Lesdiguières took the town in the name of Henry IV and constructed its fortifications, quays, etc. In 1788 the attempt of the king to weaken the power of the *parlement* of Grenoble roused the people to arms, and the "day of the tiles" (June 7, 1788) is memorable for the defeat of the royal forces. In 1790, on the formation of the *département* of Isère, Grenoble became its capital. The town received Napoleon eagerly on his return from Elba in 1815. Grenoble was formerly much subject to floods, especially from the Drac. One of the worst took place in 1219, while that of 1778 was known as the *déluge de la Saint Crépin*.

(M. Pт.)

GRENVILLE, GEORGE (1712–1770), English statesman, whose policy of taxing the American colonies, initiated by his Revenue act of 1764 and the Stamp act of 1765, started the immediate train of events leading to the American Revolution. He was the second son of Richard Grenville and Hester Temple, and younger brother of Earl Temple (see TEMPLE, RICHARD GRENVILLE-TEMPLE, 1st Earl), and was born on Oct. 14, 1712. He was educated at Eton and at Christ Church, Oxford, and trained for the bar. He entered parliament in 1741 as member for Buckingham—one of the "cousinhood" of Grenvilles, Temples and Pitts in opposition to Sir Robert Walpole. He became lord of the admiralty in the Pelham administration in 1744 and a lord of the treasury in 1747. He was appointed treasurer of the navy under the duke of Newcastle in 1754, but he was dismissed the following year, along with William Pitt, for attacking Newcastle's foreign policy. He was reappointed in 1756 under Pitt and the duke of Devonshire and resigned in April 1757 when Pitt and Lord Temple were dismissed. Resuming the same post in the war ministry of Pitt and Newcastle (1757–61), he improved the administration of the department. When Pitt and Temple resigned in 1761, Grenville remained in office. Lord Bute brought him forward in 1762 as leader of the house and secretary of state; but disapproving of the terms of peace which Bute's government had concluded with France and Spain, he declined to defend them in parliament and so, in the autumn, exchanged offices with the first lord of the admiralty. Bute recommended Grenville to George III in April 1763 to be his successor as premier and head of the treasury.

Grenville's ministry (1763–65) was unhappy and disastrous. His relationship with the king was one of constant friction, owing to George III's habit of continual consultation with Bute. This situation the responsible ministers soon felt to be intolerable, especially when Bute, in Aug. 1763, attempted to reconstruct the government with Pitt at its head. Apart from American taxation, other notable incidents during the Grenville administration included the prosecution of John Wilkes for seditious libel and the clumsy handling of the Regency act of 1765, which finally alienated the king and led immediately to the fall of the ministry.

Grenville was an able parliamentarian and financial administrator, but he was entirely lacking in finesse and statecraft. In active opposition after 1765, he castigated politicians opposed to the taxation of the American colonies, and his irresponsible speeches in parliament helped to bring about the passage of Townshend's Revenue act of 1767 and the consequent renewal of tension between Britain and the colonies. He died in London on Nov. 13, 1770.

BIBLIOGRAPHY.—Primary sources are *The Grenville Papers*, ed. with notes by W. J. Smith, 4 vol. (1852–53); Horace Walpole, *Memoirs of the Last Ten Years of the Reign of George II*, 3 vol. (1847); ed. by G. F. R. Barker, 4 vol. (1894). *See also Letters From George III to Lord Bute, 1756–1766*, ed. by R. Sedgwick (1939); E. S. and H. M. Morgan, *The Stamp Act Crisis: Prologue to Revolution* (1953); and J. Brooke, *The Chatham Administration, 1766–68* (1956). (I. R. C.)

GRENVILLE, SIR RICHARD (1542–1591), English naval commander, who took part in a celebrated action against the Spanish fleet, was born of an old Cornish family in June 1542. He fought with the imperial army against the Turks in Hungary (1566–68). Next he took part in suppressing a rising in Munster (1568–69). Then, between 1573 and 1575, he and his friends were busied with a project which, according to A. L. Rowse, "was the first to put into shape the idea of an English empire in the southern seas." They prepared an expedition to discover Terra Australis—the great continent that was believed to stretch diagonally across the southern Pacific—and to locate the western Pacific, end of the northwest passage. The voyage was not made, for the government was unwilling to endanger good relations with Spain, newly restored by the 1573–74 agreements. However, Grenville's twin purposes were to figure prominently in the original avowed aims of Sir Francis Drake's great voyage of 1577–80. For the next ten years, and again in 1587–88, Grenville was chiefly occupied in local affairs and in organizing the military defense of western England. However, he commanded for his cousin, Sir Walter Raleigh, the fleet of seven vessels carrying colonists in 1585 to Roanoke Island in the present North Carolina, and captured a Spanish vessel on his way back. He carried provisions to Roanoke in 1586, and, finding the colony deserted, left a few men to maintain possession. After the defeat of the Armada, he went again to Ireland, where he had a considerable interest in the plantation of Munster.

When Lord Thomas Howard was sent to intercept the homewardbound treasure fleet of Spain in 1591, Grenville was sent with him as second-in-command on board the "Revenge," a ship of 500 tons which had been commanded by Drake against the Armada. At the end of August Howard, with 13 ships and 2 or 3 ships of 500 tons at anchor to the north of Flores in the Azores. On Aug. 31 he received news that a Spanish fleet of 53 vessels was bearing up to meet the treasure ships. Being hopelessly outmatched, Howard gave orders to weigh anchor and stand out to sea. But, for some reason, the "Revenge" was delayed, and cut off from her consorts by the Spaniards. Grenville, though he could perhaps have escaped to the westward, resolved to try to break through the Spanish line. His ship was becalmed under the lee of a huge galleon, and after a hand-to-hand fight lasting 15 hours against 15 Spanish ships and a force of 5,000 men, the "Revenge" with her 190 men was captured. Grenville was carried on board the Spanish flagship and died a few days later. His exploit is commemorated in Tennyson's poem "The Revenge."

See A. L. Rowse, *Sir Richard Grenville of the Revenge* (1949).
(R. B. WM.)

GRENVILLE, WILLIAM WYNDHAM GRENVILLE, BARON (1759–1834), English statesman, youngest son of the prime minister George Grenville, was born on Oct. 25, 1759, and educated at Eton and Christ Church, Oxford. He entered the house of commons in Feb. 1782 for the family borough of Buckingham and became secretary to his brother, Earl Temple, lord lieutenant of Ireland, in the following September. He went out of office when the coalition ministry was formed in 1783, but became paymaster general of the forces in his cousin William Pitt's ministry at the end of 1783, and vice-president of the committee of trade in 1786. Grenville was sent on a special mission to France in 1787 to discuss questions relating to Holland. Elected speaker of the house of commons in Jan. 1789, he was appointed home secretary in June. Two years later he became president of the board of control. In Nov. 1790 he was created Baron Grenville and became leader of the house of lords. Transferred to the foreign office in 1791, he retained his post at the board of control until 1793. Grenville resigned with Pitt in 1801 on the question of Catholic emancipation, and, in strong opposition to the Addington ministry, he gradually separated himself from Pitt, who until 1804 supported Addington (afterward Lord Sidmouth).

When Pitt resumed the premiership in May 1804 Grenville refused to join him unless his ally Charles James Fox was also given office, but the king's veto stood in the way and Grenville remained in opposition until Jan. 1806 when, on Pitt's death, he formed a coalition ministry of Addington's followers, Foxites and his own friends. Its foreign policy was unsuccessful; it failed, among other things, to make peace with France. The ministry was weakened by the death of Fox (Sept. 1806) but achieved one glorious triumph in 1807, the abolition of the slave trade. Its advocacy of a Catholic Relief bill caused the king to dismiss it in March 1807, Grenville refusing to pledge himself never again to trouble the king on this subject. His refusal kept him out of office in 1809 and again in 1812. Until 1817, when he supported the government's measures to put down radicalism, he generally voted with the Whigs in opposition. A paralytic stroke ended his active political career in 1823. He died at Dropmore on Jan. 12, 1834.

See, for his correspondence, *Dropmore MSS*, 10 vol., Historical Manuscripts Commission (1892–1927); *Later Correspondence of George III*, ed. by A. Aspinall, vol. i and ii (1962–63). (A. Ar.)

GRESHAM, SIR THOMAS (1519?–1579), English merchant, royal factor and founder of the Royal Exchange. In his youth he attended Caius college, Cambridge, and was apprenticed to his wealthy uncle, Sir John Gresham. From 1551 to 1574 Sir Thomas resided part of the time in Antwerp, where he engaged in business as a private merchant banker and represented the English government as royal factor, or financial agent of the crown. The duties of this office involved the negotiation of new loans, the renewal or repayment of matured loans, the purchase and occasionally the shipment of specie to England.

with or without a licence of the king of Spain who also ruled the Low Countries. Gresham was consistently successful in public and private ventures even if his methods were sometimes high-handed or questionable.

The principle that "bad money drives good money out of circulation" has come to be called "Gresham's law." Actually this principle was never formulated by Gresham but was falsely attributed to him in 1857 by Henry D. MacLeod who misread a passage dealing with an entirely different problem: the fall of the exchange rate of the English pound as a result of Henry VIII's debasement. The principle known as "Gresham's law" was well known by 1550 and had been stated among others by Nicolaus Copernicus (1473–1543) in his essay on coinage. In England an obscure author, Humphrey Holt, in 1551 bewailed the fact that the heavier coins were being exported leaving only the baser sort in circulation and that the flood of debased coins had caused a general rise in prices "to the decay of all things." Gresham in 1559 was baffled because, contrary to his so-called law, base testoons of different fineness were all circulating at the same value. The explanation is simply that the worst testoons issued by Edward VI had not been issued in excessive amounts. The real contribution Gresham made to economics was not his alleged law but his proposal to create an equalization fund or "bank" to support the exchange rate of the pound sterling. Although this scheme was perfectly sound, it was rejected by Queen Elizabeth I because she could not spare the £10,000 necessary to carry it into effect. The idea was apparently lost, only to be revived nearly four centuries later as a result of the monetary disturbances which followed in the wake of World War I and the depression of the early 1930s.

In order to provide a convenient meeting place for the bankers (exchange dealers) in London, Gresham built the Royal Exchange (1566–68), which at first was called the "Bourse" and received its present name by royal proclamation in 1571. He also endowed Gresham college and created seven lectureships in the liberal arts. When he died in London on Nov. 21, 1579, he was reputed to be the richest commoner in England.

BIBLIOGRAPHY.—J. M. Burgon, *Life and Times of Sir Thomas Gresham*, 2 vol. (1839); F. R. Salter, *Sir Thomas Gresham* (1925); Raymond de Roover, *Gresham on Foreign Exchange* (1949).
(D. DD.; R. DE R.)

GRESHAM, WALTER QUINTIN (1832–1895), U.S. statesman and jurist, was born near Lanesville, Ind., March 17, 1832. He spent two years at Corydon seminary in Indiana and one year at Indiana university, after which he studied law and was admitted to practice in 1854. He campaigned for John C. Frémont in the presidential election of 1856 and won a seat for himself in the state legislature in 1860. He organized a company of volunteers in 1861 and rose to command a division under Gen. W. T. Sherman. In July 1864 he suffered a wound in the knee that left him lame for the rest of his life. He was breveted a major general of volunteers in 1865.

Following the war Gresham began to practise law in New Albany, Ind. After being defeated in 1866 and again in 1868 as a Republican candidate for congress, he was appointed judge of the federal district court for Indiana by President Grant in 1869. His modesty and integrity won the confidence and respect of a host of friends, regardless of parties. He became postmaster general and, for a month, secretary of the treasury under President Arthur. On Oct. 28, 1884, he was again appointed to the federal judiciary as a circuit court judge at Chicago.

At the Republican convention of 1884 he was considered as a possible candidate for president, though his name was not put in nomination. As Illinois' "favourite son" candidate at the convention of 1888 he was a strong contender, receiving 114 votes on the first ballot. But he drifted away from the party chiefly because of his opposition to high tariffs. Populist leaders, who liked his independence on the bench, sought to nominate him at the Omaha convention (1892) but Gresham declined. Instead he supported the Democratic candidate, Grover Cleveland, who appointed him secretary of state, March 7, 1893, a position he held until his death, May 28, 1895.

See Matilda Gresham, *Life of Walter Quintin Gresham, 1832–1895*, 2 vol. (1919).
(H. F. TR.)

GRESSET, JEAN BAPTISTE LOUIS (1709–1777), French poet and dramatist whose narrative poem *Ver-Vert* (1734), describing with wit tinged with malice the adventures of a parrot, decorously brought up in one convent, when he visits another, was an immediate and lasting success. Born at Amiens, Aug. 29, 1709, Gresset was brought up by Jesuits and, a brilliant pupil, was encouraged to enter the society in 1726. He studied at Paris and taught in a number of Jesuit schools, but was meanwhile writing light occasional verse. In 1734 he published *Ver-Vert*, which made him famous, and followed it by *Le Carême impromptu* and *Le Lutrin vivant*. Returning to Paris in 1735 for a year's study of theology, he wrote there *La Chartreuse* and *Les Ombres*: these lively accounts of life in a Jesuit college, precise and pointed in detail, led first to his banishment to the provinces and then to his expulsion from the order: he had not yet taken his final vows and the anticlerical tendency of his poetry was rather the result of natural frivolity and a keen eye for absurdity exercised in the only world he knew than of deliberate impiety. He returned to Paris and was warmly received, being granted an official pension. In 1740 he wrote *Edouard III*, the first French tragedy in which a murder was enacted on the stage. Other plays were the verse comedies *Sidnei* (1745) and his dramatic masterpiece, *Le Méchant* (1747), a witty exposé of *salon* life, instantly successful and highly praised for its pithy dialogue. He was admitted to the Académie Française in 1748 and caused some stir by his criticisms of nonresident bishops in his address there. In 1749 he retired to Amiens, where he was offered official employment at the Académie, and where he married. He came to regret his literary career and, although he continued to write, in 1759 he renounced his work for the theatre in a *Lettre sur la comédie*. He died at Amiens, June 16, 1777. His poem *Le Parrain magnifique*, written in 1758, remained unpublished until 1810.

See J. Wogue, *J. B. L. Gresset* (1894).

GRESSMANN, HUGO (1877–1927), German Old Testament scholar who was a prominent advocate of the religio-historical approach, was born in Mölln, Lauenberg, on March 21, 1877. After attending the University of Göttingen he was *Privatdozent* at Kiel (1902–06), where he wrote his first important book, *Der Ursprung der israelitisch-jüdischen Eschatologie* (1905), influenced by the methods of Hermann Gunkel's form criticism and by the *Religionsgeschichtliche Schule*, which applied to the Bible lessons learned from the history of comparative religion. In this work and in his posthumously published *Der Messias* (1929) Gressmann advanced the new theory that eschatology was not a late phenomenon in Israel but pre-exilic, and its popular form can be traced in many Old Testament passages. His works show the insights into the history and geography of Palestine gained by his association with the Deutsches Evangelisches Institut für Altertumswissenschaft in Jerusalem, which he visited in 1906 before going as professor to Berlin in 1907. After *Altorientalische Texte und Bilder* (1909; 2nd ed., 1926–27) he wrote *Die älteste Geschichtsschreibung und Prophetie Israels* (1910; 2nd ed., 1921) and *Die Anfänge Israels* (1914; 2nd ed., 1922), both forming volumes of Gunkel's *Schriften des Alten Testaments*. Gressmann's other important works were *Moses und seine Zeit* (1913) and *Die Lade Jahves* (1920). He died in Chicago, Ill., while on a lecture tour, April 6, 1927.

See *Zeitschrift für die Alttestamentliche Wissenschaft*, vol. 5, pp. 1–xxiv (1927) for memoirs of Gressmann and vol. 69, pp. 211–228 (1957) for a list of his works.
(A. S. K.)

GRETNA GREEN, a village in Gretna district council, Dumfriesshire, Scot., 9½ mi. N.W. of Carlisle and 23½ mi. E.S.E. of Dumfries by road, and ¾ mi. from the Sark river, there the dividing line between England and Scotland. The railway station at Gretna is on the English side. Pop. of Gretna village (1961) 3,051. It has long been famous as the goal of eloping couples seeking hasty marriage. Until 1754, the date of Lord Hardwicke's reform act, such marriages had commonly been performed in the Fleet prison in London by clergymen imprisoned for debt, but after that date runaways were obliged to cross the border, as it formerly sufficed under Scots law for couples merely to declare their wish to marry before witnesses. At Gretna Green the ceremony was usually performed by the blacksmith, although any person might officiate, and the tollhouse, the inn or (after 1826) Gretna hall were the scenes of many such weddings. As many as 200 couples were married at the tollhouse in a year. In 1856 the law required one of the contracting parties to reside in Scotland for 21 days before marrying, and after the Marriage (Scotland) act, 1939, these irregular marriages were declared illegal after July 1, 1940. During World War I a temporary manufacturing township for the provision of cordite was created on a tract of land about 10 mi. long and from 1 to 2 mi. wide, with Gretna Green in its centre. This land was sold in 1924. About 3 mi. N.E. is the site of the battle of Solway Moss, where in 1542 the English defeated the Scots under James V.

GREUZE, JEAN BAPTISTE (1725-1805), French genre and portrait painter, was born at Tournus, in Burgundy, on Aug. 21, 1725, of a poor family. His precocious desire to paint and draw was not well received, but his father was eventually persuaded to send him as a pupil to Charles Grandon, a portrait painter in Lyons. Grandon's talent was limited and the greatest service he performed for Greuze was to give him access to his collection of Dutch and Flemish engravings and to take him with him to Paris in the early 1750s. There Greuze enrolled at the academy and was befriended by the painter J. Sylvestre and the sculptor J. Pigalle. Greuze first exhibited at the Salon of 1755 and won an immediate success with his crowded and uplifting work "Un père de famille expliquant la Bible à ses enfants" (Dresden). Although Greuze's attention at this period was fixed on a simpler and more traditional type of genre painting in which the influence of 17th-century Dutch masters is clearly apparent (e.g., "L'Écolier endormi," Montpellier), the congratulations he received for this faintly bogus morality turned his head and established the lines of his future career.

In Sept. 1755 he left for Italy; he lived there for two years, one of the few artists of the 18th century to remain impervious to the almost fatal attraction of Italian painting. In 1759 he became acquainted with Diderot who encouraged his inclination toward melodramatic genre, and throughout the 1760s Greuze reached ever new heights of popular acclaim with "L'Accordée de Village" (1761, Louvre), "La Mort du Paralytique" (1763, Leningrad) and the drawings "Le Fils Ingrat" and "Le Fils Puni" (1765, Lille).

These were undoubtedly fertile years, for Greuze was also painting portraits whose worth has not declined, and a certain number of those allegories of girls lamenting the loss of their sparrows with which his name is indissolubly linked. Stimulated by his success to a mood of almost hysterical pride which antagonized all those with whom he came into contact, Greuze in 1769 presented a dreary classical piece entitled "Sévère et Caracalla" (Louvre) which was to entitle him to be admitted to the Academy as a history painter. This claim was rejected, and in the storm of resentment which followed, Greuze resigned from the Academy and for the next 30 years exhibited his works to the public in his own studio.

Throughout the 1770s Greuze was kept busy painting moralities of an increasingly minatory nature ("Le Fils Puni," 1778, Louvre; "La Mauvaise Belle-Mère," 1781) and was visited by many foreign dignitaries, notably the grand duke Paul Petrovich of Russia who commissioned from him a number of works. But his income was precarious, and by 1785, when he was reduced to painting bloated studies of girls, his once considerable talent was exhausted. He died in the Louvre on March 4, 1805, in great poverty.

Greuze abused his very real gifts in an attempt to give the public what it wanted. His large genre pictures, which are badly painted, were rapturously received by a public whose tastes had been formed by the novels of Samuel Richardson and Jean Jacques Rousseau. He is today remembered for his studies of girls in a state of calculated disarray; his fine portraits, his magnificent drawings are neglected. He had few pupils but many imitators and in his own lifetime was partially ruined by the vogue for sentimental genre painting which he himself had inaugurated.

Bibliography.—Mme De Valori, Greuze, ou l'Accordée de Village (1813); C. Mauclair, J. B. Greuze, sa vie, son oeuvre, son époque (1905); Jean Martin, Catalogue raisonné de l'oeuvre de J. B. Greuze (1908). (Aa. B.)

GREVILLE, CHARLES CAVENDISH FULKE (1794-1865), whose diary remains the outstanding source for the history of British politics in the first half of the 19th century, was a distant cousin of Lord Warwick and, through his mother, the grandson of the 3rd duke of Portland (q.v.), who was twice prime minister. Greville was born on April 2, 1794. Through his grandfather, Greville was appointed to the reversion to the secretaryship of Jamaica when he was seven, a sinecure which was abolished in his lifetime, though he was recompensed with the emoluments until his death. When he was ten he was given the reversion to the clerkship of the privy council. He was educated at Eton and at Christ Church, Oxford, but he left without a degree in 1814 to work as private secretary to the secretary for war, Lord Bathurst. He became clerk of the privy council when he was 27, and he discharged the duties of this office for nearly 40 years. This work brought him into close touch with the royal family and the leading public men of the time, and gave him a clear insight into public affairs, though he regretted that his work precluded him from taking part in politics.

Starting somewhat spasmodically when he left Oxford, but with increasing regularity after 1818, Greville kept a diary recording all important political events, embellished with an extremely shrewd (though not always eulogistic) commentary on individuals. He wrote his diary at the time of the events he described, read it through regularly in afterlife, but did not materially vary what he had originally written. The last entry was made in Nov. 1860 "with a full consciousness of the smallness of the interest or value" of the diary, a view not shared by posterity.

Another occupation of Greville's—his guidance of the policy of the Times of London—emerges from the official history of that journal published between 1935 and 1952. His advice and suggestions were courted by successive editors; sometimes contributions from him were published over the pseudonym "C"; he also wrote obituaries of a few very eminent men. He published several pamphlets, those on the corn laws (1846) and the precedence of Prince Albert (1840) meeting with considerable success.

Greville was a well-known personality on the turf. As a young man he managed the racing stables of George IV's brother, the duke of York. Later he raced in partnership with Lord George Bentinck and then with the duke of Portland. He once won the St. Leger, and he was unlucky not to win the Derby in 1845. Greville often laments in his diary the time he wasted in racing. He sold his horses in 1855. He was known as "Punch" and, behind his back, because of a rather sombre manner, as the "Gruncher." He never married.

At intervals between 1874 and 1887, his successor at the privy council, Henry Reeve, published the diary with many excisions and a certain softening of the text. It was widely enjoyed, though the publication was generally thought premature. In 1927 P. W. Wilson published further selections from the diary, using the copy made by Reeve. This copy is now in the Bodleian library at Oxford; the original manuscript is in the British museum. In 1938 a verbatim edition was published, edited by Lytton Strachey and Roger Fulford. (R. T. B. F.)

GRÉVIN, JACQUES (1538-1570), French poet and dramatist whose plays introduced classical forms into French drama, and also the author of medical treatises on antimony and poisons. He was born at Clermont-en-Beauvaisis in 1538 and became a doctor of medicine of Paris university. A friend and disciple of Ronsard and Du Bellay, he wrote love sonnets, La Gélodacrye (1560), and to Nicole Estienne, satirical sonnets, L'Olimpe (1560), and was an innovator in drama, claiming to follow the precepts of Aristotle and Horace. His comedies imitate the regular form of Plautus and Terence but have a contemporary subject and Parisian setting. Their tone is licentious. La Trésorière was performed at the Collège de Beauvais in 1559. Les Esbahis, and his regular tragedy, César (based on Plutarch and on Muret's Latin tragedy), were also performed there and published in his Théâtre (1561). After the Conspiracy of Amboise (1560), Grévin, being a Protestant, fled to England, where he was received in audience by Charles Elizabeth I. He soon returned to France but later went to Antwerp. He finally took refuge with the duchess of Savoy (Margaret of France), who made him her physician and counselor.

He died at her court in Turin on Nov. 5, 1570.

See Grévin's *Théâtre complet et poésies choisies*, ed. by L. Pinvert (1922); L. Pinvert, *Jacques Grévin* (1899). (M. G. M.)

GRÉVY, (FRANÇOIS PAUL) JULES (1807–1891), French statesman, third president of the third republic, was born at Mont-sous-Vaudrey (Jura) on Aug. 15, 1807. A lawyer by profession and a strong republican, he was deputy for Jura to the constituent assembly of 1848. Foreseeing the election of Louis Bonaparte as president of the republic, he proposed to vest the executive power in a prime minister responsible to the assembly. After the *coup d'état* of Dec. 2, 1851, he spent a short period in prison and then resumed practice as a lawyer. He returned to politics in 1868 when he was elected to the *corps législatif* as a member for Jura. He served as president of the national assembly from Feb. 1871 to April 1873, became president of the chamber of deputies in 1876 and finally, on the resignation of Marshal de MacMahon, was elected president of the republic on Jan. 30, 1879.

Faithful to his conviction, Grévy interpreted his constitutional powers in a restrictive sense. Nevertheless he did what he could to keep Léon Gambetta, whose exuberance he detested, out of power. He also kept a close watch over the conduct of foreign policy, often showing great wisdom, as during the affair of April 1887, when the Germans arrested the French official Guillaume Schnaebelé.

Grévy had been re-elected president of the republic on Dec. 28, 1885, but his second term of office was cut short by the scandal over the traffic in decorations of the Legion of Honour carried on by his son-in-law, Daniel Wilson. Grévy was not directly implicated, but did not fully appreciate his situation and was obliged to resign (Dec. 2, 1887). He died at Mont-sous-Vaudrey on Sept. 9, 1891. His *Discours politiques et judiciaires* appeared in two volumes in 1888.

See A. Barbou, *Jules Grévy* (1879); A. Dansette, *Histoire des présidents de la République* (1953). (Ab. D.)

GREW, NEHEMIAH (1641–1712), English plant anatomist and physiologist who shares with M. Malpighi the credit for laying the foundations of the science of plant anatomy, was baptized at Mancetter, Warwickshire, on Sept. 26, 1641. He graduated from Pembroke hall, Cambridge, in 1661, and took his M.D. at Leiden in 1671. He first practised medicine at Coventry, but soon moved to London. In 1672 he published his *Anatomy of Vegetables Begun*, which Malpighi had translated into Latin, and in 1673 his *Idea of a Phytological History*. Grew was elected a fellow of the Royal society in 1671, and in 1681, at the society's request, published *A Catalogue and Description of the Natural and Artificial Rarities . . . Preserved at Gresham College*. To this was appended *The Comparative Anatomy of Stomachs and Guts Begun*, being several lectures read before the Royal society in the year 1676. This last is said to be one of the most remarkable studies of the 17th century, and seems to involve the first use of the term "comparative," so favoured since that time. In 1682 Grew's famous *Anatomy of Plants* appeared. In this work, Grew was the first to point out that stamens are male organs; though he himself attributed the discovery to Sir Thomas Millington.

Grew died in London on March 25, 1712.

GREY, CHARLES GREY, 2ND EARL (1764–1845), English statesman, closely associated with the passing of the great Reform bill in 1832, was the eldest surviving son of Gen. Sir Charles Grey, afterward 1st Earl Grey, and was born at Fallodon, near Alnwick, on March 13, 1764. General Grey (1729–1807), who was a younger son of the house of Grey of Howick, had already begun a career of active service which, like the political career of his son, covered nearly half a century. In 1801 he was rewarded by Henry Addington with a peerage, as Baron Grey of Howick, being created in 1806 Earl Grey and Viscount Howick.

Young Grey was returned for Northumberland in 1786 and came forward as a vigorous assailant of the government of William Pitt. He was hailed by the opposition, and associated with Charles James Fox, Edmund Burke and Richard Brinsley Sheridan as a manager in the Warren Hastings impeachment. Grey became the trusted lieutenant of Fox, whom he was destined to succeed in the leadership of the party. As time went on, some differences arose between the two men on the conduct of the war, but there was never any open breach, and their personal relations remained those of close friendship. Grey was a pioneer of parliamentary reform. He joined in founding the Society of Friends of the People for promoting the reform of the franchise, he presented their petition to parliament, and in 1793 he moved the reference of this petition to a parliamentary committee. Fox did nothing to discourage this activity, but he did not support it. At a later date Grey passed some rather bitter criticism on the society, but at the time he had no doubts on the opportuneness of the agitation. Pitt suppressed the movement with a strong hand. In 1797 Grey again introduced proposals for parliamentary reform and, when these were rejected, promoted the foolish Secession. Since the parliament did not properly represent the nation and refused to reform itself, the opposition announced its intention of "seceding," or systematically absenting itself from parliament. This movement was originated by Grey, Lord Lauderdale and the duke of Bedford. Pitt easily defeated the secession maneuver, and Grey himself reappeared to protest against the Act of Union with Ireland, moved by his interest in Irish affairs.

When Pitt died in Jan. 1806 the "ministry of all the talents" was formed under Lord Grenville, with Fox as foreign secretary and Grey (from April 1806 to Nov. 1807 styled Viscount Howick) as first lord of the admiralty. On Fox's death, in the following September, Grey became foreign secretary and leader of the house of commons. When the cabinet proposed to concede a portion of the Catholic claims, the king demanded of it an undertaking never to propose similar measures again. This was refused, and the Grenville-Grey cabinet retired in March 1807. In the same year Grey's father died, and Grey went to the upper house. Opposition united Grey and Grenville for a time, but the parties finally split on foreign policy. When Napoleon returned from Elba in 1815, Grenville followed the traditions of Pitt and supported the ministry in at once renewing hostilities. Grey followed those of Fox and maintained the right of France to choose its own governors and the impossibility of checking the reaction in the emperor's favour. Grenville and Grey gradually drifted apart. Grey was in a small minority in opposing the suspension of the Habeas Corpus act in 1817, and the part which he took in 1820 in opposing the bill for Queen Caroline's divorce, though it won for him the respect of the nation, sealed the exclusion of himself and his few friends from office during the king's life. When in 1827 Grey came forth to denounce the ministry of George Canning, he declared that he stood alone in the political world. He scarcely exaggerated, for most of the Whigs followed the marquess of Lansdowne and supported Canning's and Lord Goderich's governments.

In 1827 Grey seemed to stand forth the solitary and powerless relic of an extinct party. In 1830 that party was restored to its old numbers and activity, supreme in parliament, popular in the nation, and with Lord Grey at its head. The duke of Wellington's foolish declaration against parliamentary reform (Nov. 2, 1830) suddenly deprived him of the confidence of the country, and a coalition of the Whigs and Canningites became inevitable. Grey was sent for by William IV on Nov. 16, 1830, and formed a coalition cabinet, pledged to reform. The question of the place to be offered to the indispensable Lord Brougham (q.v.) nearly wrecked his cabinet making, but the king in the end consented to Brougham's taking the lord chancellorship. Grey then appointed a committee of four to study the question and prepare a moderate measure of reform. Grey himself was an old-fashioned Whig and, when he took office, did not foresee how far he would go in reform. But now, faced with a formidable agitation, he saved the country from revolution by driving through a bold measure. In his view a reform sweeping enough to give general satisfaction would restore the aristocracy's popularity and ensure its continued pre-eminence. He called the bill "the most aristocratic measure that ever was proposed in parliament."

The second reading (March 23, 1831) of the first Reform bill was carried in the commons by a majority of one. An opposition amendment was also carried, however, and on April 22 parliament was dissolved. The second reading of a new bill was carried in the new parliament (July 7) by a majority of 136. When the bill had at length passed the commons after months of debate, it was Grey's task to introduce it to the lords. It was rejected (Oct. 8) by a majority of 41. Grey had the prudence and courage to remain in office, with the intention of introducing a third Reform bill in the next session. The second reading of the third bill in the commons was passed in December by a majority of 162. On April 9, 1832, Grey moved the second reading in the lords. A sufficient number of the opposition temporized, and the second reading was allowed to pass by a majority of nine. The intention was to mutilate the bill in committee. On May 7 Lord Lyndhurst secured a motion to postpone certain clauses by a majority of 35 against the government. Grey now reluctantly asked the king to give authority for the creation of peers to swamp the opposition. He greatly disliked demanding a creation; indeed but for his reluctance the demand would probably have been made months earlier; there was now no alternative. But William IV, at first favourable to reform, was alienated by the violent state of opinion. He rejected the proposal of his ministers and accepted their resignation on May 9, 1832. The duke of Wellington undertook the hopeless task, in which Sir Robert Peel declined to join, of constructing a ministry that would pass a restricted or sham Reform bill. After a week of the profoundest agitation throughout the country, the king, beaten and mortified, was forced to send for Grey and Brougham. He now angrily and reluctantly yielded to give certain clauses by a majority of 35 against the government. Grey now reluctantly asked the king to give authority for the creation of peers to swamp the opposition. The threat was sufficient, the necessary number of peers abstained, and the bill became law.

Grey took but little part in directing the legislation of the reformed parliament. Never anxious for power, he had executed the arduous task of 1831-32 rather as a matter of duty than of inclination, and he found an opportunity of retiring over the renewal of the Irish "coercion" bill. It became clear in the discussion on the bill that Lord Althorp, the leader of the house of commons, was privately opposed to retaining certain clauses which it was his duty to push through the house. Lord Althorp resigned, and Grey, who was now 70, resigned also (July 8, 1834). He was succeeded as premier by Lord Melbourne, who persuaded Lord Althorp to return to his post and to proceed with the bill in its milder form.

During most of his remaining years Grey continued to live in retirement at Howick, where he died on July 17, 1845.

BIBLIOGRAPHY.—C. Grey, Some Account of the Life and Opinions of Charles, 2nd Earl Grey (1861); Correspondence of Earl Grey and William IV . . . Nov. 1830 to June 1832, 2 vol. (1867); Correspondence of Princess Lieven and Earl Grey, 1824-1834, ed. and trans. by G. Le Strange, 3 vol. (1890); J. R. M. Butler, The Passing of the Great Reform Bill (1914); G. M. Trevelyan, Lord Grey of the Reform Bill, 2nd ed. (1929).
(M. G. B.)

GREY, SIR EDWARD: see GREY OF FALLODON, EDWARD GREY, 1st Viscount.

GREY, SIR GEORGE (1812-1898), British colonial administrator, notable for his service as governor of the Cape Colony and New Zealand, and as prime minister of New Zealand. The only son of Lieut. Col. George Grey of the 30th foot regiment, he was born in Lisbon, Port., on April 14, 1812. He passed through Sandhurst with credit, received his commission in 1829, and left the army ten years later. He undertook two lengthy explorations in Western Australia between 1837 and 1839, in the course of which he showed striking courage and endurance. In 1839 he married Eliza, daughter of Adm. Richard Spencer. On his return to England in 1840, he was appointed governor of South Australia, which was at that time suffering acutely from depression, bad administration and land speculation. Here his career, though stormy, was successful; by the time he left in 1845, the public finances were in good order, agriculture was expanding, and copper mining had begun. In this period, he formed definite ideas on native policy which he attempted to implement in New Zealand and South Africa, for the whole of his official career. He held that a rapid assimilation of native races to European civilization was both possible and desirable; he contended that its promotion should be the aim of official policy in settlement colonies.

Grey's transfer in Nov. 1845 to New Zealand, where he succeeded Robert FitzRoy as governor, brought him into contact with an acute and prolonged situation of racial disharmony. Here many Maori tribes had become so disturbed at the progress of settlement that they were either restless or in a state of active resistance. Grey, better equipped with troops and money than his predecessors, took vigorous and successful military action in the trouble centres. He then tried to implement policies to hasten the assimilation of the Maori, especially in regard to education, health and agriculture. He purchased vast areas of land, including the whole of the South Island, from the Maori for settlement, thereby accelerating the process which ended in renewed warfare in 1860. He was widely respected among the Maori, became well versed in their traditions, and may be considered an early exponent of indirect rule: nevertheless, his efforts were on such a small scale that they affected only a small part of the Maori population.

During his governorship Grey fell out with the leading settlers, who were engaged upon a crusade for self-government. He persuaded the colonial office to withhold a new constitution pending his successful solution of the native and land problems. Temperamentally Grey was autocratic; intellectually he was a radical. He sought, through land sales policy, to ensure a future in which small landowners, not owners of large estates, would characterize New Zealand society. The 1852 Imperial act, of which Grey had been a chief author, was put into partial operation, since he was by then certain that his policies had been successful. He then returned to Great Britain pursued by the animosity of the settlers' leaders.

Grey was appointed governor of Cape Colony in 1854, where disturbed conditions again gave him ample scope. He subdued the Kaffirs, encouraged settlement and again attempted to promote assimilation, earning the respect of the native races. During the Indian mutiny (1857) he sent supplies, men and money to the British authorities. His major effort in South Africa was to promote the federation of the Boer and British settlements; the Orange Free State favoured this, but the process was halted by the colonial office. Grey's reluctance to accept this decision and his attempt to reverse the direction of policy (a recurrent feature of his official career) led to his recall. Grey was reinstated by Lord Palmerston (who superseded Lord Derby as prime minister in 1859), but he was not permitted to take federation any further.

Meanwhile war had broken out in New Zealand between settlers and the Maori, largely over the land issue and sweeping government policies. Grey was sent to New Zealand again in 1861 but his second governorship showed no spectacular successes. The colony was now self-governing, except for native policy, which was quarreled over by New Zealand ministries bent upon land confiscation, British colonial secretaries suspicious of settler cupidity, army officers in the field hostile to the governor, and Grey himself, caught among all three and seeking to implement his own policy. By the time of his recall in April 1867 Maori resistance had largely collapsed; Grey was irretrievably in disgrace with the colonial office but at least popular with the settlers, with whose views he was in substantial sympathy.

His later life is noted by an unsuccessful attempt to enter British politics as a Liberal, a period of seclusion at Kawau, on his return to New Zealand, devoted largely to book collection, and a career in New Zealand politics beginning in 1874. He proved immensely effective as an orator, even as a radical demagogue, but his single premiership (1877-79) was marked by administrative disorder, debt and inaction. He remained for years a member of parliament, on occasion able to destroy ministries. From 1894 till his death on Sept. 19, 1898, he lived in London.

See J. Rutherford, *Sir George Grey, K.C.B. 1812-1898* (1961).
(W. H. Ol.)

GREY, HENRY GEORGE GREY, 3RD EARL (1802-1894), English statesman, born Dec. 28, 1802, at Howick, Northumberland, was the eldest son of the 2nd Earl Grey (*q.v.*). As Viscount Howick, he sat in the house of commons for Winchelsea, 1826-30, for Higham Ferrers, 1830-31, for Northumberland, 1831-41, and for Sunderland, 1841-45, when he succeeded his father. He became undersecretary for the colonies in his father's ministry in 1830. He belonged to the more advanced party of colonial reformers, sharing the views of Edward Gibbon Wakefield on questions of land and emigration, and he resigned in 1833 from dissatisfaction that slave emancipation was made gradual instead of immediate. In 1835 he entered Lord Melbourne's cabinet as secretary at war, but in 1839 he again resigned, disapproving of the more liberal views of some of his colleagues. He became secretary for war and the colonies in 1846, and the six years of his administration effected a revolution in the relations between England and its colonies. Grey was the first minister to proclaim that the colonies were to be governed for their own benefit as well as for that of England; the first systematically to accord them self-government so far as then seemed possible; and the first to introduce free trade into their relations with Great Britain and Ireland. The concession by which colonies were allowed to tax imports from the mother country ad libitum was not his; he protested against it, but was overruled. His greatest success was in Canada, where his appointment of Lord Elgin as governor general and wise support of Elgin's policy led to the recognition of responsible government (1847). He also drafted constitutions for the Australian colonies and for New Zealand, but the latter proved unworkable and had to be suspended, leaving the conduct of affairs in the masterful hands of Sir George Grey (*q.v.*). His policy in the West Indies and Ceylon was criticized as repressive, and he aggravated the difficult situation in the Cape Colony by an ill-judged attempt to settle convicts there. He resigned with his colleagues in 1852 and never again held office. In retirement he wrote a history and defense of his colonial policy in the form of letters to Lord John Russell, a dry but instructive book (*Colonial Policy of Lord John Russell's Administration*, 1853).

During the remainder of his long life, he exercised a vigilant criticism of public affairs. His principal parliamentary appearances were when he moved for a committee on Irish affairs in 1866, and when in 1878 he passionately opposed the policy of the Beaconsfield cabinet in India. He died at Howick on Oct. 9, 1894.

GREY, LADY JANE (1537-1554), for nine days queen of England, was the great-granddaughter of Henry VII. She was the daughter of Henry Grey, marquess of Dorset, by his wife, Lady Frances Brandon, daughter of Princess Mary of England by her second marriage, with Charles Brandon, duke of Suffolk.

Lady Jane was born at Bradgate, Leicestershire, in Sept. 1537. Her parents bestowed more than ordinary care upon her education, and she became the marvel of the age for her acquirements. She spoke and wrote Greek and Latin with an accuracy that satisfied even such critics as Roger Ascham and her tutor John Aylmer, afterward bishop of London. She is also said to have acquired some knowledge of at least three oriental tongues, Hebrew, Chaldee and Arabic. In his *Schoolmaster* Ascham records her devotion to her studies and the harshness she experienced from her parents. Learning was her solace; in reading Demosthenes and Plato she found a refuge from domestic unhappiness. When she was nine years old Thomas, Lord Seymour, obtained her wardship, and induced her parents to let her stay with him, even after the death of his wife, Queen Catherine, by promising to marry her to his nephew, King Edward VI. Lord Seymour, however, was attainted of high treason and beheaded in 1549. Jane returned to her studies at Bradgate.

The duke of Somerset was beheaded three years after his brother, and, the dukedom of Suffolk having become extinct by the deaths of Charles Brandon and his two sons, this title (Suf-

folk) was conferred upon the marquess of Dorset, Jane's father. Jane was now constantly at court. The duke of Northumberland, who was all-powerful, endeavoured to secure his position by family alliances. His fourth son, Lord Guildford Dudley, was accordingly wedded to Lady Jane Grey on May 21, 1553. The bride went to live with her husband's parents, whom she disliked, and the misery of her marriage brought on a severe illness. The match had the full approval of Edward VI, who was now persuaded by Northumberland to break through his father's will and make a new settlement of the succession to the crown in favour of Lady Jane and her male heirs. The document was witnessed (June 21) by the signatures of all the council and of all but one of the judges; but those of the judges were obtained only with difficulty by threats and intimidation.

Edward VI died on July 6, 1553, and it was announced to Lady Jane that she was queen. She was 16 years of age. The news was a most unwelcome surprise; she fainted and for some time resisted all persuasion to accept the fatal dignity, but eventually she yielded. The better to mature their plans the cabal had kept the king's death secret for two days; Queen Jane's proclamation was issued on July 10. Mary, however, had received early news of her brother's death, and, retiring from Hunsdon into Suffolk, gathered around her the nobility and commons of those parts. The army with which Northumberland went to oppose her began to melt away. In London many of the councilors met at Baynard's castle, revoked their former acts as done under coercion and caused the lord mayor to proclaim Queen Mary, which he did (July 19) amid the shouts of the citizens. The duke of Suffolk told his daughter that she must lay aside her royal dignity; she replied that she relinquished most willingly a crown that she had only accepted out of obedience to him and her mother, and her nine days' reign was over.

Lady Jane and her father were committed to the Tower of London; but Suffolk procured a pardon. Lady Jane, her husband Dudley and others were arraigned for high treason at the Guildhall (Nov. 14). She pleaded guilty and was sentenced to death. The execution of the sentence was suspended, but the participation of her father in the Wyat rebellion sealed her fate. She and her husband were beheaded on Feb. 12, 1554, her husband on Tower Hill, and herself within the Tower an hour afterward, amid universal sympathy and compassion. *See also* ENGLISH HISTORY.

See Sir N. H. Nicolas, *Literary Remains of Lady Jane Grey* (1825); R. Davey, *The Nine Days' Queen* (1909).
(R. B. WM.)

GREY, ZANE (1875-1939), U.S. writer of western fiction, was born in Zanesville, O., on Jan. 31, 1875, and was trained as a dentist, practising in New York from 1898 to 1904. In the latter year he published privately a story of pioneer life, *Betty Zane*, based on a journal by a maternal ancestor, Ebenezer Zane (*see* ZANESVILLE), and abandoned dentistry for full-time writing. *The Spirit of the Border* (1905), also based on Zane's notes, became a best seller. Grey wrote 54 novels, of which over 15,000,000 copies were sold; *Riders of the Purple Sage* (1912) was the most popular. He died at Altadena, Calif., on Oct. 23, 1939.
(F. L. Mt.)

GREYHOUND RACING: *see* DOG RACING.

GREY OF FALLODON, EDWARD GREY, 1ST VISCOUNT (1862-1933), British statesman, who was foreign secretary during the critical period which preceded and included the outbreak of World War I, was born in London on April 25, 1862, the eldest son of Col. George Grey and Harriet Pearson and grandson of Sir George Grey, the 2nd baronet. The Greys were collaterally related to Earl Grey, the prime minister who carried the Reform bill of 1832, and Edward Grey was brought up in a strong Whig Liberal tradition. His early years were largely spent at the family seat, Fallodon, in the wilder part of Northumberland. There he acquired that deep love for fishing and bird watching which remained his hobby and solace for most of his life. He became a leading expert upon both subjects. In 1874 his father died suddenly. Two years later Grey went to Winchester and then in 1880 to Balliol college, Oxford. That college, under its great master Benjamin Jowett, often had a significant formative influence upon future statesmen. Not so in the case of Grey. He was sent down in 1884 for incorrigible idleness, and he himself later described his life at Oxford as "one of pure pleasure."

He had succeeded to his grandfather's title and estate in 1882. Greatly influenced by Mandell Creighton, the vicar of Embleton (in which Falloden stood) and author of the famous *History of the Papacy*, Grey was never idle again. He was elected as Liberal member of parliament for Berwick-upon-Tweed in 1885 and he kept his seat even in the worst periods of Liberal depression. In Oct. 1885 he married Dorothy, daughter of Fitzherbert Widdrington, a neighbouring squire. It was an ideally happy marriage.

Grey was in office from 1892 to 1895 as parliamentary under-secretary for the foreign office. His successive chiefs, Lord Rosebery and Lord Kimberley, were both in the house of lords and Grey's post was all the more important for that reason. For the next ten years the Liberals were in opposition and sharply divided. In the party's internal feuds at the time of the South African War Grey was firmly on the side of the so-called Liberal Imperialists, led by H. H. Asquith and R. B. Haldane. He mistrusted the leader, Sir Henry Campbell-Bannerman, and was only reluctantly persuaded by Asquith and Haldane to accept the foreign office in Dec. 1905.

On assuming office he at once had to make a major decision. Was he to continue Lord Lansdowne's policy of support for France against Germany over the Morocco crisis? There was much doubt in Europe, most diplomats expecting a reversal of the previous policy. Grey, however, with Campbell-Bannerman's full agreement, allowed it to be known that he believed, though he could not guarantee, that in the event of German attack Britain would come to the aid of France. He also permitted military conversations to take place between the British and French general staffs. This latter decision was deliberately—and with the prime minister's consent—withheld from the cabinet in order to avoid the difficulties which its more radical members might have created. There was much retrospective criticism of this suppression.

These two decisions shaped the whole of Grey's foreign policy until the outbreak of World War I. Profoundly pacific, determined not to commit Britain irrevocably, he nonetheless warned Germany of the consequences of aggression. It was not his fault that the warning went unheeded. Thereafter Grey pursued the policy of the balance of power consistently and farsightedly. He came to an agreement with Russia in 1907 which, though highly unpopular with the radicals, went far to consolidate the anti-German forces in Europe. Meanwhile tragedy darkened his private life; in Feb. 1906 Lady Grey was killed in a carriage accident. It may be doubted whether Grey would have remained in office so long had it not been for this disaster which made him seek distraction in constant and unremitting work. In home affairs his views inclined to the right of centre and he did not approve of David Lloyd George's more ebullient declarations but he took little active part. During the cabinet crisis of 1909 he strongly supported increased naval estimates. Grey received unexpected support from Lloyd George in 1911 over the Agadir crisis, another instance of German sabre-rattling. When the assassination of the Archduke Francis Ferdinand at Sarajevo in 1914 set in train the events that led to war, Grey with moderation and skill managed to bring a cabinet profoundly divided at the outset into almost unanimous acceptance of military intervention on the side of France.

Grey hated war and was not the ideal foreign minister in wartime, but on one matter, the question of the blockade, he displayed great skill. But for his care for American public opinion the U.S. might not have entered the war on the side of the Allies. Grey was also responsible for the secret treaty of London (April 1915) which brought Italy into the war. Its provisions have been criticized but it was truly a case of necessity knowing no law. In the summer of 1916 Grey began to have trouble with his eyes. To diminish his work he entered the house of lords as Viscount Grey of Falloden. At the end of the year Asquith was replaced by Lloyd George and Grey gladly quitted the office which he had held for 11 years—the longest consecutive period in history. He was never in office again, and no longer took a leading part in public affairs. His later life was clouded by tragedy. He married again, in 1922, Genevieve Wyndham, the widow of the first Lord Glenconner, but she died six years later. His youngest brother, Charles, was killed in an accident. Falloden was burned down. Increasing and eventually complete blindness descended upon Grey. It was some consolation that in 1928 Oxford university conferred the highest honour in its gift by electing him chancellor. He remained serene and uncomplaining to the end, dying at Falloden on Sept. 7, 1933. He had no children and his peerage became extinct. He wrote a number of books, of which his political memoirs, *Twenty-five Years* (1925), is perhaps the best known. In 1912 he was made a knight of the Garter.

See G. M. Trevelyan, *Grey of Falloden* (1937). (R. N. W. B.)

GREY OF WILTON and GREY OF RUTHYN. The first Lord Grey of Wilton was Sir Reynold de Grey (d. 1308) of Wilton, Herefordshire, and of Shirland, Derbyshire, who was summoned to parliament as a baron in or before 1290. From him descended successive generations of Lords Grey of Wilton, none of whom achieved distinction until William (d. 1562), 13th lord, came of age in 1529. He held commands in France under Henry VIII, was a leader of the English army which defeated the Scots at the battle of Pinkie (1547) and helped to suppress the west country rebellion (1549). Imprisoned (1551) as a friend of the fallen Protector Somerset and afterward implicated in the attempt (1553) to put Lady Jane Grey on the throne, he was pardoned by Queen Mary and was entrusted with the defense of Guînes. In Jan. 1558 he was forced to surrender the town to the French. He later served in Scotland and besieged Leith in May 1560. His son Arthur (d. 1593), 14th lord, fought in France and Scotland with his father. As lord deputy in Ireland (1580–82) he reduced the Irish rebels to submission, but was afterward charged with having ordered the massacre of about 500 Italians and Spaniards at Smerwick (Nov. 1580). While in Ireland Grey was served as secretary by Edmund Spenser, and it is perhaps the he who figures as Artegall in the *Faerie Queene*. He was a commissioner for the trial of Mary, queen of Scots (1586). His son Thomas (d. 1614), 15th and last lord, became involved in the Bye plot and in Nov. 1603 forfeited his honours and was imprisoned in the Tower until his death. With him the male line of the family came to an end, but the title was revived (1784), in the archaic form Grey de Wilton, for a descendant of his sister Bridget (d. 1648), Sir Thomas Egerton (d. 1814), who was created Viscount Grey de Wilton and earl of Wilton (1801). The barony expired at his death.

In 1282 Edward I rewarded Reynold, Lord Grey of Wilton, for his services in the Welsh wars with a grant of the lordship of Ruthyn, Denbighshire. John (d. 1323), 2nd lord of Ruthyn, settled Ruthyn on his younger son, Roger (d. 1353), who in 1325 was summoned to parliament as Lord Grey of Ruthyn. Roger's grandson Reynold Grey (d. 1440), 3rd lord, was appointed lieutenant (1402) in north Wales to deal with the Welsh rebels, but was himself captured by Owen Glendower and was afterward ransomed. He was succeeded by his grandson Edmund Grey (d. 1490), who deserted to the Yorkist cause while in command of the royal vanguard at the battle of Northampton (1460). He soon found favour with Edward IV, who appointed him treasurer of England (1463) and created him earl of Kent (1465). The title descended with the earldom of Kent until 1639 (see Kent, Earls and Dukes of) and the barony passed to the families of Longueville (1639), Yelverton (1676), Rawdon-Hastings (1858), Clifton (1887) and Butler-Bowdon (1939). Sir John Grey, Lord Ferrers of Groby, grandson of the 3rd Lord Grey of Ruthyn, married Elizabeth Woodville, afterward queen of Edward IV.

See Arthur Grey, *A Commentary of the Services and Charges of William, Lord Grey of Wilton, K.G.*, ed. by P. de M. Grey Egerton (1847). (C. D. R.)

GREYTOWN: see San Juan del Norte.

GRIBOEDOV, ALEKSANDR SERGEEVICH (1795–1829), Russian playwright whose comedy *Gore ot uma* is one of the finest in Russian literature, was born on Jan. 15 (new style; 4, old style), 1795, in Moscow, where he graduated from the university in literature, law, physics and mathematics. A man of wide culture, he led an active and eventful life, joined the hussars during the war of 1812 against Napoleon and served in White Russia. After resigning his commission in 1816 he lived in St. Petersburg (Leningrad), joining the diplomatic service two years later and becoming a member of the Russian mission to Persia during that year. A friend of Aleksandr Pushkin (*q.v.*) and a sympathizer with the Decembrist revolt of 1825 against Nicholas I, he was arrested in the following year, but soon released. In 1828 he was appointed Russian minister in Teheran, and he died on Feb. 11 (N.S.; Jan. 30, O.S.), 1829, at the hands of a Persian mob, which attacked the Russian embassy.

Although Griboedov has left an interesting correspondence and several plays, which include *Molodye suprugi* (1815; "Young Married People") and *Student* (1817; "The Student"), his reputation rests on a single work—*Gore ot uma* (1822–24; Eng. trans., *Wit Works Woe*, 1933), a satirical play in rhymed iambic lines of varying length. After being published in fragments in 1825 and circulating in thousands of manuscript copies, it was first published in full in 1833. To Russians it is their most important play, with the possible exception of Nikolai Gogol's *Revizor* (Eng. trans., *The Government Inspector*), but its virtues are likely to elude those foreigners who do not possess a thorough knowledge of Russian. The style is a masterpiece of conciseness, colloquialism and wit, so that many of Griboedov's lines have found a permanent place in the language. The same is true of many of the characters, especially those through which Griboedov satirizes the old-fashioned Russia of bribery, place-seeking and pomposity. Such are the fatuous high official Famusov, the cringing careerist Molchalin and the empty phrase-monger Repetilov. Set against these caricatures is the eloquent hero of the play, Chatski, who is portrayed as having just returned to Russia from three years' stay abroad. Part of the plot is devoted to his unsuccessful wooing of Famusov's daughter, but the real meat of the play lies in his splendidly witty and rhetorical denunciations. Together with Pushkin's hero Evgeni Onegin, Chatski is the first example in Russian literature of the "superfluous man," a type later much discussed by critics.

GRID, in an electron tube such as is used in electrical communication, is an electrode having openings through which the electron stream, between cathode and anode, may pass. The relative electrical potential of the grid controls the current flowing between the anode and the cathode. *See also* ELECTRON TUBE.

GRIEG, EDVARD (HAGERUP) (1843–1907), Norwegian composer who contributed to the romantic movement and founded the Norwegian national school. He was born on June 15, 1843, in Bergen, where his father, Alexander Grieg, was British consul. The Grieg (formerly Greig) family was of Scottish origin, the composer's great-grandfather having emigrated after the battle of Culloden. His mother, Gesine Hagerup, who belonged to a well-established Norwegian family, studied music at Hamburg. From the age of six, Grieg received piano lessons from her and in 1858, at the recommendation of Ole Bull, he entered the Leipzig conservatory, where he studied with I. Moscheles and Karl Reinecke and came under the influence of Mendelssohn and Schumann. During this period he suffered a severe attack of pleurisy from which he never really recovered. In 1863 he went to Copenhagen, where he studied with Niels Gade and Emil Hartmann, both illustrating a sentimental rather than a radical aspect of the Scandinavian temperament. Grieg developed through his association in 1864 with the young Norwegian nationalist composer Rikard Nordraak. "Through him," said Grieg, "I first learned to know the northern folk tunes and my own nature." In the winter of 1864–65 Grieg became one of the founders of the Copenhagen concert society, Euterpe, for the production of works by young Scandinavian composers. In 1867 he married his cousin, Nina Hagerup, who became an authoritative interpreter of his songs. He spent the winters of 1865–66 and 1869–70 in Rome, where he first met Ibsen and also Liszt, who was roused to enthusiasm by his piano concerto. In 1866 he settled in Christiania (Oslo), remaining there until 1874, when he was granted an annual stipend of 1,600 kroner by the Norwegian government. In 1885 he built his home "Troldhaugen," near Bergen. In spite of poor health, Grieg made several tours in Scandinavia, on the continent and in

England, playing his piano concerto in London in 1888. He died at Bergen on Sept. 4, 1907.

Rooted in the national folk tradition of Norway, Grieg's music displays a refined lyrical sense. Between 1867 and 1901 he wrote ten collections of "Lyric Pieces" (*Lyriske Stykker*) for piano. His spirited rhythms often have a folk music association. His harmonies are novel, developed from the late romantic style, and anticipate the impressionists. In his relatively few works in the larger forms, the Piano Concerto (op. 16), the String Quartet in G minor (op. 27) and the three violin and piano sonatas, he makes use of a free sonata form. His original "Ballade" for piano (op. 24) is a set of variations on a folk theme. Among his most popular works are his incidental music to *Peer Gynt* (op. 23) and the suite *Fra Holbergs tid* (op. 40). His arrangements of Norwegian dances and songs (op. 17 and 66) and especially his *Slaatter*, Norwegian peasant dances (op. 72), show his characteristic sense of rhythm and harmony. His vocal works include the songs on texts of A. O. Vinje (op. 33) and the *Haugtussa* cycle (op. 67). Intuitively, he identified himself with the poet's imagery in these songs and discovered its musical equivalent.

BIBLIOGRAPHY.—O. Gaukstad, *Bibliography of Grieg's Works and Writings on Him* (1942); David Monrad-Johansen, *E. Grieg* (1934; Eng. trans. by M. Robertson (1938); F. Törnblom, *E. Grieg* (1943); A. E. Cherbuliez, *E. Grieg: Leben und Werk* (1947); G. Abraham (ed.), *Grieg, a Symposium* (1948); J. Horton, *Grieg* (1950); D. Schjelderup-Ebbe, *E. Grieg 1858–1867* (1964). (Sk. H. B.)

GRIEG, (JOHAN) NORDAHL BRUN (1902–1943), Norwegian writer, who combined strong patriotic feelings with a wide cosmopolitan outlook, was born at Bergen on Nov. 1, 1902. After studying literature and languages in Oslo and later in Oxford he combined extensive traveling with journalism, and a strong social conscience was already evident in his first books, the sea poems *Rundt Kap det gode Haab* ("Round the Cape of Good Hope"; 1922) influenced by Kipling, and the novel *Skibet gaar videre* (1924; Eng. trans., *The Ship Sails On*, 1927).

Grieg's love for Norway, especially northern Norway, was expressed without reserve in the poems *Norge i våre hjerter* ("Norway in Our Hearts"; 1929). After publishing six highly personal essays on Keats, Shelley, Byron, Rupert Brooke, C. H. Sorley and Wilfred Owen, *De unge døde* ("The Young, Dead Ones"; 1932), he spent two years in Moscow (1932–34). There his Russian theatre and social consciousness turned communist. The cinema inspired his most powerful social play, *Vår ære og vår makt* ("Our Honour and Our Power"; 1935). When Germany occupied Norway in 1940, Grieg escaped to Britain and in his war poems became the leading voice of free Norway. He was killed while on a bombing raid over Berlin on Dec. 2, 1943.

Collected works: *Samlede Verker*, 7 vol. (1947); *Samlede dikt* (1948). *See also* Harald Engberg, *Nordahl Grieg og Tidens Drama* (1946); Kjølv Egeland, *Nordahl Grieg* (1953). (To. S.)

GRIEN, HANS: *see* BALDUNG, HANS.
GRIERSON, SIR GEORGE ABRAHAM (1851–1941), Anglo-Irish linguist, notable for his researches into the languages of India, was born Jan. 7, 1851, at Glanageary, County Dublin, of an Anglo-Irish family of publishers and printers. He acquired his first taste for Indian languages at Trinity college, Dublin, where he took prizes in Sanskrit and Hindi. He qualified for the Indian civil service in 1871 and arrived in Bengal in Oct. 1873.

Grierson spent the next 26 years mostly in Bihar and western Bengal, where he held various posts as magistrate and collector of revenue.

Grierson's first book, *Bihar Peasant Life* (1885), contains vast information on the language, techniques, usages and superstitions of the peasantry among whom he had lived. This book was followed by numerous monographs published in *The Indian Antiquary* and in *The Journal of the Asiatic Society of Bengal*, as Grierson's researches spread to Hindi, to the northwestern Dardic languages, which he termed Pisaca, and to Kashmiri. In 1898 he was appointed superintendent of the *Linguistic Survey* of India, a work which engaged his attention from 1898 to 1928, and in which he had the assistance of the Norwegian linguist Sten Konow. The *Survey*, in 19 folio volumes, furnishes vocabularies for 364 lan-

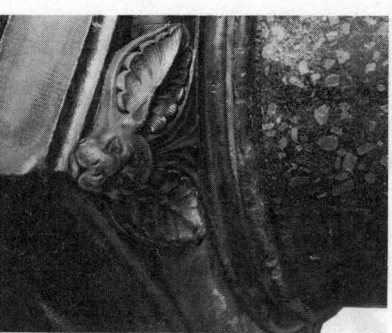

guages and dialects of India. For most of these a skeleton grammar and brief texts are given as well.

Grierson had also a deep interest in Indian popular literature and Indian religion.

Grierson was knighted in 1912, and received the honour of Order of Merit in 1928. A bibliography of his numerous works appears in the *Bulletin of the London School of Oriental and African Studies* for 1936. A brief memoir of his life has been printed in the *Proceedings of the British Academy*, vol. xxviii.

(D. H. H. I.)

GRIFFE, in architecture, a small ornament, generally triangular, which fills the space between the round torus of a column base and the square corner of the plinth below; sometimes known as a spur.

The use of the griffe is particularly characteristic of the later Romanesque period; it usually takes the form of a group of leaves or a single curling leaf. Grotesque animals are occasionally found.

GRIFFENFELD, PEDER SCHUMACHER, COUNT (1635–1699), the greatest Danish statesman of his time, was born at Copenhagen on Aug. 24, 1635, the son of a wealthy wine merchant. He was a precocious child and received an excellent education. From 1654 to 1662 he traveled abroad, visiting Germany, studying at the universities of Leiden and Utrecht in the Netherlands and staying (1657–60) at Queen's college, Oxford. Arriving in Paris in autumn 1660, he was much impressed by the superiority of the administration of a strong centralized monarchy and came to admire and to adopt French manners. In 1661 he went to Spain, where he perfected his knowledge of Spanish language and literature; and he also spent some time in Italy.

On his return to Copenhagen in 1662, Schumacher found the absolute monarchy established and the aristocracy's monopoly of state offices abolished by King Frederick III. Schumacher hastened to find protectors among prominent men and was appointed royal librarian in 1663. Gifted, charming and well mannered, he soon made a complete conquest of the king as well as the king's old and trusted adviser and confidant Christoffer Gabel, who had now become very influential and held several offices of state. Schumacher's career as statesman dates from April 1665, when he was appointed secretary of the king's chamber. From 1666 he moreover acted as a secretary of the Danish chancellery. This promotion was probably due to his admirable drafting of the *Kongelov*, the "royal charter," which is dated Nov. 1665. Before Frederick III's death in 1670 Schumacher had become a member of the supreme court and of the state council; and on his deathbed Frederick recommended him to his son and successor, Christian V. The new king took his father's advice. As Schumacher also allied himself with Frederick III's bastard son, Ulrik Frederik Gyldenlove, statholder in Norway, and with Frederik Ahlefeldt, statholder of Schleswig-Holstein, he soon became the leading Danish statesman. Measures now taken to reform the central administration (already begun in the early 1660s) were undoubtedly due to Schumacher's initiative. He was made the principal secretary of the newly created a count, ennobled under the name of Griffenfeld (1670), and finally appointed high chancellor of the kingdom (1674).

Griffenfeld thus obtained complete control of both chancelleries, including to a large extent the conduct of Danish foreign policy. This was to prove fatal to his career. His chief concern was to maintain Danish neutrality, fortified by a share of the subsidies which France so lavishly disbursed and of which Sweden obtained the greater part. Christian V, on the other hand, was clamouring with increasing urgency for a war of revenge against Sweden.

When war was declared in Aug. 1675 Griffenfeld had to acquiesce, but still entertained some hope that it would be possible to maintain friendly relations with France. To this end he took great risks; and most foolhardily he did not take the king in his confidence. Moreover, his ambition, vanity and frailness of character had made him very unpopular, and his enemies now won the king over.

On March 11, 1676, Griffenfeld was arrested in the king's name as a prisoner of state. On May 3 he was tried by an extraordinary tribunal of ten dignitaries, and conducted his own defense on a variety of charges. For 46 days before his trial he had been closely confined in a dungeon without lights, books or writing materials. Though legal assistance was illegally denied him, he yet proved more than a match for his accusers. Even so he was condemned to degradation and decapitation. His primary offense was the taking of bribes, which no twisting of the law could convert into a capital offense, while the charge of treason had not been substantiated. Griffenfeld was pardoned on the scaffold, his sentence being commuted to life imprisonment. After years in a lonely state prison, first in the fortress of Copenhagen, finally at Munkholm on Trondheim fjord, he died at Trondheim on March 12, 1699.

See A. D. Jorgensen, *Peter Schumacher-Griffenfeld* (1893–94); K. Fabricius, *Griffenfeld* (1910) and *Kongeloven* (1920). (As. F.)

GRIFFES, CHARLES TOMLINSON (1884–1920), first native U.S. composer to write impressionistic music, was born in Elmira, N.Y., Sept. 17, 1884. In 1903 he went to Berlin where he took lessons with E. Humperdinck, returning to the U.S. in 1907. Fascinated by the new French music, he studied assiduously the scores of Debussy and Ravel and his own music reflects this preoccupation. His symphonic poems *The White Peacock* (1917) and *The Pleasure Dome of Kubla Khan* (1919), and the piano suites *Three Tone Pictures, Fantasy Pieces* and *Four Roman Sketches* successfully capture the exotic colours of an impressionist palette. He died in New York city on April 8, 1920.

See E. M. Maisel, *Charles Tomlinson Griffes* (1943). (N. Sy.)

GRIFFIN (GRIFFON or GRYPHON), a composite creature with lion body, winged or wingless, and bird (usually eagle) head. The name is from the Greek *gryps* via the Latin *gryphus*. Like the sphinx (*q.v.*), the griffin is a favourite motif in decorative arts in the ancient near east and classical lands. Probably originating in the Levant in the 2nd millennium B.C., it occurred on seals and ivories all over western Asia by about 1500 B.C.; it was common in Crete around the same time and by the 14th century B.C. was known in Greece also. The Asiatic griffin has a crested head, while the Minoan and Greek griffin usually has a mane of spiral curls. It may be recumbent or seated on its haunches, often paired with a sphinx; occasionally it acts as a beast of prey, leaping on another animal, but it may itself be the victim of a predator. The large griffins painted on the throne room wall of the palace of Minos in Crete suggest a protective function for the beast.

In the Iron Age the griffin again appeared in both Asia and Greece. At Carchemish on the upper Euphrates it is carved on a palace wall of the 10th century, and Assyrian reliefs of the next three centuries show griffin-demons. It occurred in the 8th century among the cast bronzes of Urartu in the Armenian mountains and apparently traveled westward through Anatolia to Greece. From the 8th to the 6th centuries (orientalizing and archaic periods) the griffin is common on Greek metalwork and occurs also on painted vases. Greek metalworkers evolved a handsome, stylized rendering, with the beak open to show the curling tongue and the head provided with horses' ears and a large knob on top. Often griffin heads ornamented the rims of huge bronze caldrons, and similar caldrons are known from Armenia to the Etruscan tombs of Italy. Apparently the griffin was in some sense sacred, appearing frequently in sanctuary and tomb furnishings, but its precise meaning is unknown. The few references in the ancient authors give no clear idea of the nature of the creature or its role in cult and legend. (A. Ps.)

GRIFFITH, ARTHUR (1872–1922), Irish revolutionary leader, was born in Dublin on March 31, 1872, and began his working life as a printer. Like many other young men of the generation after Parnell, Griffith despaired of winning Irish freedom by constitutional means. He joined the Gaelic league, was an active member of the Celtic Literary society and became a member of the Irish Republican brotherhood (I.R.B.). After a brief spell in South Africa (1896-98), he began to write for the *United Irishman*, a weekly paper founded in 1899, of which he became editor in 1901. The paper was savagely political, but Griffith cared passionately also for the things of the mind. He welcomed voluntary contributions from the principal writers in Ireland, including W. B. Yeats and "A.E." No contributor expected to be paid, for all knew that Griffith himself lived on a pittance.

Griffith's aim was both destructive and constructive. He sought first to divert his countrymen from the attempt to win self-government through parliamentary action at Westminster and second to persuade them to work for it in their own country. Although all his intimate associates were Fenians, he recognized that the majority of Irish nationalists did not think separation from Britain possible. He therefore resigned membership of the I.R.B. in 1906 and aimed at winning over the separatists to work for a parliament in Ireland united to that of England only by the link of the crown. As a means to this end, he proposed passive resistance and an appeal to moral force. Payment of taxes was to be refused. Members elected to parliament were to absent themselves from Westminster and to sit in Ireland as a council and govern only by the assent of the nation. Tribunals were to be set up to which cases should be brought.

This policy was first publicly announced at a meeting in Dublin in Oct. 1902. The body which met called itself Cumann na nGaedheal (Society of the Gaels); the name chosen to represent their policy was Sinn Fein ("ourselves"—Irish words which in their proverbial use mean roughly "stand together"). The name was soon transferred from the policy to its adherents. The new policy at first did not make much headway; resistance to taxation proved difficult because all taxation except income tax was indirect and a large proportion of income-tax payers were unionists. The only effective forces were the personality and the pen of Arthur Griffith. His paper changed its name in 1906, when damages for libel were awarded against the *United Irishman*, to *Sinn Fein*. In 1907 *Sinn Fein* appeared as a daily paper, but this experiment soon had to be abandoned and after another bankruptcy its name became *Eire*. Griffith wrote no books, but he published in 1905 a pamphlet called *The Resurrection of Hungary*, putting forward the Magyars as an example for the Irish. Griffith condemned the third Home Rule bill (1912) in the strongest terms, his most furious opposition being directed against any suggestion of such partition of Ireland as he was later constrained to accept. When the formation of the Ulster Volunteers in 1912 revived the hopes of the physical force party, he supported the counterorganization of the Irish Volunteers by word and deed. He was one of those who received the rifles landed at Howth in July 1914.

Griffith took no part in the Easter rising of 1916 and thereby lost influence with the extremists. The British authorities remedied this by putting him into Frongoch, the detention camp in Wales, which became a crowded academy of Sinn Fein. Yet when the prisoners were released in 1917, Eamon de Valera was chosen as their leader. Griffith proposed this election at the convention of Sinn Fein, while he himself returned to his desk, reissuing his paper as *Nationality*; this also was suppressed and he was again put in jail in 1918. After the Sinn Fein election triumph in Dec. 1918, the elected members assembled as *dáil éireann* (the assembly of Ireland), but, going beyond Griffith's plan, they declared for an Irish republic, electing De Valera as president and Griffith as vice-president.

During De Valera's absence in America, from June 1919 to the close of 1920, Griffith acted as head of the "Irish Republic." His policy now was carried out in its entirety. The elected bodies, county councils and municipalities refused to take orders from the British authorities in Dublin castle; Sinn Fein courts were set up and functioned with notable success; income tax was withheld. But these forms of passive resistance were effective only because active resistance was in progress. In the conduct of military operations, power rested with Michael Collins and other young men. Griffith, however, was chosen to lead the Irish delegation to the treaty negotiations in London in the autumn of 1921, and he was the first member of that delegation to indicate his acceptance of the British terms, later embodied in the Anglo-Irish treaty, 1921. In the bitter controversy that followed, Griffith stood by the treaty, not as the best thing but as giving Ireland the opportunity to advance peacefully toward the full freedom for which the Irish had fought. When the treaty was approved by the narrow majority of seven in the *dáil*, De Valera resigned and Griffith was elected president. He continued to occupy this office until his death, but under the terms of the treaty there was to set up a provisional government of which Collins was chairman side-by-side with the *dáil* ministry. This resulted in an illogical division of authority and Griffith's public utterances as president were sometimes contradicted by the action or inaction of the provisional government. Griffith died suddenly on the morning of Aug. 12, 1922, on the way to his office in Dublin. Essentially he ranks as a publicist, an educator and an inspirer of action, but when called upon late in life to deal with difficult and dangerous questions he showed that he also possessed qualities of statesmanship. *See also* IRELAND, REPUBLIC OF: *History*.

See Padraic Colum, *Life of Arthur Griffith* (1960).
(S. G.; P. N. S. M.)

GRIFFITH, DAVID (LEWELYN) WARK (1875-1948), U.S. motion-picture director and producer, under whose direction the camera developed into a superb instrument for the expression of emotions and ideas, was born in Oldham county, Ky., on Jan. 22, 1875. After various jobs in Louisville, he played small parts with the Mefert stock company (1897-99) and later toured with other stock companies. In 1907 he sold his first play, *A Fool and a Girl*, for $1,000. The production was a failure, and he then turned to the new medium of motion pictures. He was hired for a leading role in *Rescued From the Eagle's Nest* (1907) and sold several stories to Biograph studios.

In 1908 Griffith went to work as a director for Biograph, continuing until 1913 when he became associated with Mutual Films. In 1914 he began work on a film based on *The Clansman*, a Civil War novel by Thomas Dixon. It was an epochal picture. Opening in New York city in March 1915 with the title *The Birth of a Nation*, it established motion pictures both as popular entertainment and as an art. The racial aspects of the picture aroused much controversy. In 1916 Griffith released *Intolerance*, an epic sermon against injustice and despotism. With Charlie Chaplin, Douglas Fairbanks and Mary Pickford, he formed United Artists Corp. in 1919.

Among Griffith's other famous pictures were *Broken Blossoms* (1919), *Way Down East* (1920) and *Orphans of the Storm* (1922). His two talking pictures were less notable. He retired from directing in 1932.

Griffith was a genius in the art of the film. He originated or improved upon the long shot, the close-up, the pan shot, high- and low-angle shots, the moving shot, the dissolve, soft focus, crosscutting, the flashback, night photography and back lighting. His contributions to editing and his use of tempo, scenery and crowds were equally remarkable. He died in Hollywood, Calif., on July 23, 1948.
(M. S. By.)

GRIFFITHS, JOHN WILLIS (1809-1882), U.S. naval architect, creator of the first notable clipper sailing ship, was born in New York city on Oct. 6, 1809. He was apprenticed to his father's trade of shipwright, and at the age of 19 laid the lines of the frigate "Macedonia." In 1835 he suggested the ram for the bow of warships; in 1836 he published a series of articles embodying his ideas on shipbuilding in the *Advocate* at Portsmouth, Va.; in 1842 he gave a series of lectures on naval architecture in New York city and elsewhere, the first notable discourses on the subject to be given in the United States. In the same year he opened a free school for instruction in shipbuilding.

In 1841 he proposed departures from the accepted standards in ship construction and began the construction of a ship embodying his proposals in 1843 for William H. Aspinwall, a New York merchant engaged in the China trade. This ship, christened the "Rainbow" and launched in 1845, was the first renowned clipper and introduced a new era in shipbuilding. Expressing an important tenet of modern aesthetics, Griffiths argued that form produced in accordance with functional needs not only sails fastest and carries large cargoes, but is beautiful. Continuing his experiments, Griffiths invented, in 1848, iron keelsons for wooden ships, and exhibited a steamboat model at the 1851 London exhibition.

He became co-editor and associate proprietor of the *Nautical Magazine and Naval Journal* in 1856, but upon his appointment by the U.S. government as special naval constructor in 1858 the magazine ceased publication. He then built the U.S. gunboat "Pawnee," incorporating several new features including twin screws and a drop bilge, which was one of the widest and lightest draft vessels of similar displacement ever built. Then followed a series of inventions: bilge keels to prevent rolling (1863), a timber-bending machine which he used with success in the "New Era," Boston, 1870, and triple screws for great speed (1866). He was engaged by the U.S. government in 1871–72 to erect timber-bending machinery, and in 1872 built the "Enterprise" for the government at Portsmouth, N.H. In 1879–82 he was engaged in editorial work on the *American Ship*, a New York city weekly journal. He died in Brooklyn, N.Y., on April 29, 1882.

His *Treatise on Marine and Naval Architecture*, 2 vol. (1850), was republished in England, and brought him recognition from many maritime nations. He also published *The Progressive Shipbuilder*, 2 vol. (1853); *The Shipbuilder's Manual*, 2 vol. (A. B.-B.)

GRIGNARD, VICTOR (1871–1935), French chemist, who shared the 1912 Nobel prize in chemistry with Paul Sabatier (*q.v.*), for his discovery of the so-called Grignard reaction, was born at Cherbourg, May 6, 1871. He studied at Lyons under Louis Bouveault and Philippe Barbier. It was Barbier who in 1898 had Grignard repeat some experiments on the preparation of a tertiary alcohol from a mixture of methyl heptyl ketone, magnesium and methyl iodide. Grignard hit upon the idea of treating the iodide with the magnesium first, and, following older experiments of Sir Edward Frankland on the preparation of zinc alkyls, carried out the reaction in ether.

This first of the Grignard reagents (*q.v.*) was a complete success, and by 1901 Grignard was able to obtain a doctor's degree on the synthesis of acids, alcohols and hydrocarbons. Other syntheses followed, including the discovery by Grignard's pupil, Émile Blaise that organometallic compounds of other metals are most conveniently prepared from Grignard reagents. Grignard became professor of organic chemistry at Nancy in 1910 and at Lyons in 1919. He died at Lyons Dec. 13, 1935.

For biographical details *see* H. Gilman, *J. Amer. Chem. Soc.*, Proc. 59, 17 (1937); H. Rheinboldt, *J. Chem. Educ.*, 27:476–488 (1950).

GRIGNARD REAGENTS are organic derivatives of magnesium, commonly prepared by the reaction of an organic halide (RX, where R represents an organic radical and X represents chlorine, bromine, or iodine) in a solvent which is usually diethyl ether. They are usefully represented by the general formula RMgX, though they have somewhat complex constitutions (*see* below). Their very high chemical reactivity makes them one of the most valuable classes of synthetic reagents, a typical and simple reaction being the formation of ethyl phenyl carbinol from benzaldehyde and ethylmagnesium bromide:

$$C_2H_5MgBr + C_6H_5CHO \rightarrow C_6H_5CH(OMgBr)C_2H_5$$
$$\xrightarrow{H_2O} C_6H_5CH(OH)C_2H_5 + MgBrOH$$

They are named after Victor Grignard (1871–1935), who developed their chemistry in 1900 and the following years. Organomagnesium compounds (R₂Mg) had first been prepared, with some difficulty, by Auguste André Thomas Cahours in 1860. Grignard's contribution, for which he was awarded the Nobel Prize for Chemistry in 1912, was the discovery that organomagnesium halides could be prepared, and used for a great variety of synthetic purposes, from an organic halide and metallic magnesium provided that a suitable solvent is used. The solvent is normally diethyl ether, but other solvents which share the common characteristic of donor character can also be used.

The preparation, composition in solution, typical reactions, and synthetic applications of Grignard reagents are briefly reviewed below.

Preparation Using Diethyl Ether as the Solvent.—Grignard reagents are normally prepared by the slow addition of a solution of the appropriate organic halide in diethyl ether to a stirred suspension of magnesium in the same solvent. It is desirable to distill both the organic halide and the solvent in a nitrogen atmosphere prior to reaction. Diethyl ether is suitably purified by distillation from LiAlH₄. The reaction should be performed under a nitrogen atmosphere since the Grignard reagent is very reactive toward oxygen and moisture in air.

$$RMgX + O_2 \rightarrow ROOMgX \xrightarrow{RMgX} 2ROMgX$$
$$RMgX + H_2O \rightarrow RH + MgXOH$$

Since metallic magnesium, once exposed to air, is always coated with a thin film of oxide, the reaction cannot start until this film has been broken down. The formation of a Grignard reagent is therefore slow at the beginning, but the reaction usually accelerates very markedly once an appreciable amount of reagent has been formed. One method for starting the reaction is to crush some of the metal (turnings are generally used) with a glass rod after a little halide has been added. Addition of a small crystal of iodine, or the use of magnesium which has previously been heated to about 200° C in the presence of some iodine, are more favoured methods for starting the reaction; these methods owe their efficacy to the attack of iodine on the magnesium, affording ether-soluble magnesium iodide and exposing an active metal surface. Magnesium bromide and iodide also form ether-insoluble hydrates which have a most advantageous effect in further drying the ether present. A similar effect may be achieved by the use of a little ethylene dibromide, which attacks magnesium rapidly, forming ethylene and magnesium bromide. More recently triply sublimed magnesium has become available which has very little oxide coating. Using this type of magnesium, induction periods are much shorter (usually of the order of one to two minutes) and clear, colourless solutions containing the Grignard reagent are produced.

Organic halides vary greatly in their rates of reaction with magnesium. For example, alkyl iodides generally react very rapidly whereas most aryl chlorides react very slowly, if at all. The most reactive halides are liable to undergo side reactions such as the Wurtz reaction, or the formation of olefins by dehydrohalogenation. If a choice between a chloride, bromide, and an iodide is possible, it is best to use the least reactive halide which reacts sufficiently rapidly.

The formation of Grignard reagents is a strongly exothermic reaction, so care is necessary to avoid the addition of too much halide before the reaction is well started. Once reaction has begun, the halide is usually added at a rate sufficient to maintain steady boiling of the ether.

Di-Grignard reagents (XMgRMgX) have considerable synthetic value, but are obtainable as a rule only with difficulty. *Meta* and *para* aromatic dihalides have not been converted satisfactorily to di-Grignard reagents by any direct route, though, for example, paradibromobenzene affords paradilithiobenzene by reaction with *n*-butyl-lithium. *Ortho* dihalides such as *o*-bromoiodobenzene have afforded di-Grignard reagents which have found application in the synthesis of *o*-phenylene tertiary diphosphines (F. G. Mann). A peculiar complication in the case of *o*-dihalides is the side reaction resulting in elimination of magnesium halide and formation of the very reactive "benzyne" intermediate which immediately undergoes addition reactions (F. G. Mann, G. Wittig), with furan for example:

Indirect methods for the preparation of Grignard reagents are not so widely used as the indirect methods for organolithium compounds. However, the metal-hydrogen exchange reaction is particularly useful for obtaining Grignard reagents derived from relatively acidic hydrocarbons. These hydrocarbons derive their acidity from the enhanced electronegativity of acetylenic carbon,

$$C_6H_5C{\equiv}CH + C_2H_5MgBr \rightarrow C_6H_5C{\equiv}CMgBr + C_2H_6$$

or from the formation of an aromatic from a nonaromatic system,

$$\text{(cyclopentadiene)} + C_2H_5MgBr \rightarrow \text{(cyclopentadienyl)} MgBr^+ + C_2H_6$$

It is probable that both these types of Grignard reagent, the acetylenic and the cyclopentadienyl (both most useful synthetic reagents), have essentially ionic constitutions. Carbanions of these types are much less reactive than those derived from alkyl or simple aryl groups and do not attack ether. Acetylene itself affords a di-Grignard reagent,

$$C_2H_2 + 2C_2H_5MgBr \rightarrow BrMgC{\equiv}CMgBr + 2C_2H_6$$

but the mono-Grignard reagent has been prepared by the slow addition of ethyl magnesium bromide to tetrahydrofuran which is kept saturated with acetylene (E. R. H. Jones, L. Skattebøl and M. C. Whiting),

$$C_2H_2(\text{excess}) + C_2H_5MgBr \xrightarrow{\text{THF}} HC{\equiv}CMgBr + C_2H_6$$

The formation of a Grignard reagent is believed to be a free radical reaction. The most direct evidence for this comes from the fact that partial racemization is observed when optically active 1-methyl-2, 2-diphenylcyclopropyl bromide is allowed to react with magnesium whereas the Grignard prepared by an indirect route maintains its stereochemical integrity (ϕ = phenyl, C_6H_5-).

$$\phi \begin{array}{c} CH_3 \\ Br \end{array} \xrightarrow{Mg} \phi \begin{array}{c} CH_3 \\ MgBr \end{array} \xrightarrow{CO_2} \phi \begin{array}{c} CH_3 \\ CO_2H \end{array}$$

(12% retention of configuration)

$$\phi \begin{array}{c} CH_3 \\ Li \end{array} \xrightarrow{\downarrow BuLi} \phi \begin{array}{c} CH_3 \\ MgBr_2 \end{array} \xrightarrow{CO_2} \phi \begin{array}{c} CH_3 \\ CO_2H \end{array}$$

(100% retention of configuration)

Preparation Using Solvents Other Than Ether.—Grignard reagents are prepared and used in diethyl ether far more than in any other solvent. However, other solvents are preferred (1) when high reaction temperatures are necessary; (2) when the reaction products have a volatility comparable with that of diethyl ether; and (3) when the use of ethers of more strongly donor character than diethyl ether is necessary to promote the formation of Grignard reagents from relatively unreactive halides.

The first case is the simplest; the Grignard reagent may be prepared in the usual way, the chosen reactant added, followed by a higher boiling solvent such as benzene, xylene, or di-n-butyl ether. The reaction mixture may then be heated well above the boiling point (b.p.) of ether, when much ether (but not all) will distill away. In carrying out such reactions subsequent working up is often facilitated if the ether distillate is returned to the cooled reaction mixture before the hydrolysis step.

The second case requires the absence of diethyl ether. The preparation of trimethylarsine (b.p. 50.4° C),

$$AsCl_3 + 3CH_3MgI \rightarrow (CH_3)_3As + 3MgCII$$

is an example in which a difficult separation of the product from diethyl ether can be rendered quite easy by the use of di-n-butyl ether (b.p. 142° C) as solvent.

The third case is perhaps the most interesting. It has been shown (H. Normant) that vinyl halides (preferably chlorides or bromides) form Grignard reagents if the reaction is carried out in tetrahydrofuran. This cyclic ether (I) has a stronger donor char-

$$\begin{array}{c} CH_2-CH_2 \\ CH_2 \quad CH_2 \\ \diagdown O \diagup \end{array}$$
I

$$CH_3OCH_2-CH_2OCH_3$$
II

acter than diethyl ether because it possesses less steric requirement resulting in less F-strain in the solvated Grignard species. The chelating di-ether (II), ethylene glycol dimethyl ether, also promotes the formation of Grignard reagents in difficult cases. The preferred reaction temperature is 40°–50° C and a final concentration of just under 2-molar is suitable. The use of tetrahydrofuran may be further illustrated by the formation of phenylmagnesium chloride from chlorobenzene and magnesium in that solvent; chlorobenzene does not react with magnesium in diethyl ether.

Benzene and other hydrocarbons have been used as a diluent in Grignard reagent preparations. Although the product is not soluble in such nonpolar solvents, this method has the advantages of a low cost, nonperoxide forming diluent and the resulting product undergoes the usual reactions of Grignard reagents.

Tertiary amines have been used as solvents with no apparent advantage over ether solvents due to the low solubility of Grignard reagents in typical tertiary amines, such as triethylamine.

Until 1965 Grignard reagents of α-halo and α-alkoxyalkylhalides could not be prepared without considerable decomposition. Recent techniques of preparation involving the use of tetrahydrofuran or hexamethylphosphoramide at −80° to −110° C have resulted in the preparation of stable solutions of these Grignard reagents. This discovery has resulted in the widespread use of α-halo and α-alkoxy Grignard reagents in organic synthesis.

$$CH_2Br_2 + Mg \xrightarrow[-80°C]{\text{THF}} BrCH_2MgBr \xrightarrow{SiCl_4} Si(CH_2Br)_4$$

Grignard reagents, such as benzylmagnesium bromide, prepared in hexamethylphosphoramide produce highly coloured solutions indicating dissociation in solution.

$$C_6H_5CH_2MgBr \underset{\text{HMPA}}{\rightleftharpoons} C_6H_5CH_2^- + MgBr^+$$

Estimation of Grignard Reagents.—The simplest method is the hydrolysis of an aliquot, the addition of a known amount of acid, followed by back-titration with alkali:

$$2RMgX + 2H_2O \rightarrow 2RH + MgX_2 + Mg(OH)_2$$

A very useful method has been developed (H. Gilman and F. Schulze) for the detection of Grignard reagents or other reactive organometallic compounds. A small sample of the test solution is added to about an equal volume of a 1% solution of Michler's ketone in dry benzene; after hydrolysis, the reaction product is oxidized by the addition of a little 0.2% solution of iodine in glacial acetic acid. Development of a blue to green colour indicates the presence in the test solution of a Grignard reagent (or organometallic compound sufficiently reactive to add to a ketone). The test involves the formation of a di- or tri-phenylmethane-type dye. Thus phenylmagnesium bromide gives malachite green:

$$(p\text{-}Me_2NC_6H_4)_2CO + PhMgBr \rightarrow (p\text{-}Me_2NC_6H_4)_2PhCOMgBr$$
$$\downarrow H_2O$$
$$[(p\text{-}Me_2NC_6H_4)_2PhC]^+I^- \xleftarrow{I_2} (p\text{-}Me_2NC_6H_4)_2PhCOH$$
malachite green iodide

Composition of Grignard Reagents.—For a number of years it was thought that the composition of Grignard reagents in diethyl ether solvent was best represented by an equilibrium not involving RMgX species.

$$R_2Mg + MgX_2 \rightleftharpoons R_2Mg{\cdot}MgX_2$$

This belief originated from isotopic labeling experiments in which admixture of diethyl ether solutions of $(C_2H_5)_2Mg$ and $Mg^{28}Br_2$ did not result in redistribution. Thus the possibility of a Schlenk equilibrium and the existence of C_2H_5MgBr in solution was eliminated.

$$R_2Mg + MgX_2 \rightleftharpoons 2RMgX$$

GRIGNARD REAGENTS

More recently (1963–67) evidence has accumulated to indicate that redistribution does occur in the R_2Mg—MgX_2 system and thus $RMgX$ species do exist in solutions of Grignard reagents. A reinvestigation of the isotopic labeling experiments reported earlier also substantiates the existence of a Schlenk equilibrium. Molecular association, infrared and selective crystallization studies indicate that the composition of Grignard reagents in tetrahydrofuran is best represented by a Schlenk equilibrium.

Molecular association studies in diethyl ether indicated a similar description in this solvent except that the Schlenk equilibrium must be expanded to include dimeric and trimeric species.

$$\text{trimer} \rightleftharpoons \text{dimer} \rightleftharpoons R_2Mg + MgX_2 \rightleftharpoons 2RMgX \rightleftharpoons \text{dimer} \rightleftharpoons \text{trimer}$$

The bonding involved in the dimer and trimer molecules appears to be best represented by a single halogen bridge bond in some cases.

$$\left[\begin{array}{c} R \\ \downarrow \\ \cdots Mg \cdots \\ OEt_2 \end{array} \quad \begin{array}{c} R \\ \downarrow \\ Mg \cdots \\ OEt_2 \end{array} X \right]$$

Double halogen bridge bonding proposed earlier does not appear to be consistent with molecular association studies reported for methyl- and phenylmagnesium bromide.

$$R_2Mg + MgX_2 \rightleftharpoons \quad \begin{array}{c} R-Mg \\ \diagdown \\ X \; Mg-R \\ \diagup \end{array} \quad \rightleftharpoons 2RMgX$$

Although a mixed halogen-alkyl bridged intermediate does not appear to be present in substantial concentration, nevertheless this type of intermediate has been proposed to explain the mechanism whereby redistribution in the system R_2Mg–MgX_2 takes place.

In triethylamine solvent Grignard reagents are also represented by a Schlenk equilibrium. However in this case the equilibrium constant is very large indicating that the equilibrium lies predominantly, if not entirely, to the right, whereas the equilibrium constant for the Schlenk equilibrium of representative Grignard reagents in diethyl ether is ~400 and in THF ~4.

Reactions of Grignard Reagents.—With the exception of ethers and tert-amines there are very few organic functional groups which fail to react with Grignard reagents, though by no means all these reactions have achieved any notable importance.

Active Hydrogen.—Since such weakly acidic substances as acetylene and cyclopentadiene (see above) react with Grignard reagents, it is not surprising to find that all substances containing —OH, —SH or —NH groups also behave as acids. For example, piperidine reacts as follows:

$$C_5H_{10}NH + CH_3MgI \rightarrow C_5H_{10}NMgI + CH_4$$

Volumetric measurement of the methane formed in such reactions is the basis of an analytical method for the determination of "active hydrogen."

Carbon Dioxide.—The formation of carboxylic acids takes place by addition of carbon dioxide followed by acid hydrolysis:

$$RMgX + CO_2 \rightarrow RCO_2MgX \xrightarrow[H_2O]{HX} RCO_2H + MgX_2$$

Inorganic Halides.—The halides of the alkali or alkaline earth metals do not react except for halogen exchange, with the further exception of the beryllium halides which afford organoberyllium compounds:

$$2CH_3MgI + BeCl_2 \rightarrow (CH_3)_2Be + MgCl_2 + MgI_2$$

This is an example of one of the most generally useful methods for the preparation of organometallic compounds. The reactions often proceed in stages, for example,

$$C_2H_5MgBr + HgBr_2 \rightarrow MgBr_2 + C_2H_5HgBr$$
$$C_2H_5HgBr + C_2H_5MgBr \rightarrow MgBr_2 + (C_2H_5)_2Hg$$

Most nonmetallic halides form organic derivatives on treatment with Grignard reagents. Thus phosphorus trichloride and phenylmagnesium bromide affords triphenylphosphine in good yield:

$$PCl_3 + 3C_6H_5MgBr \rightarrow (C_6H_5)_3P + 3MgClBr$$

The halides of metals which do not easily form organic derivatives also react with Grignard reagents, and the ultimate products of such reactions are usually consistent with the formation of unstable organometallic compounds and their subsequent decomposition.

Most transition metal halides give hydrocarbons as the main organic product of reaction with Grignard reagents, the halides being in effect reduced to the metal:

$$CuI + C_2H_5MgI \rightarrow Cu + MgI_2 + C_2H_4 + C_2H_6$$

The hydrocarbon products are usually those to be expected on the basis of the unstable organometallic intermediate decomposing to form organic free radicals, which generally disproportionate or react with the solvent by hydrogen abstraction. Grignard reagents derived from cyclopentadiene and indene form a variety of organometallic compounds on reaction with certain transition metal halides.

$$2C_5H_5MgBr + FeCl_2 \rightarrow (C_5H_5)_2Fe + MgCl_2 + MgBr_2$$

Ferrocene (dicyclopentadienyliron) is the most stable member of this large class of compounds, in most of which the metal atom is bound to the cyclopentadienyl ring by π rather than by σ bonds.

Organic Halides.—Aryl and vinyl halides are not usually reactive to Grignard reagents. Alkyl halides can react in several ways and the course of reaction is not always easy to predict; several products are formed in many instances.

Only in special cases is reaction between a Grignard reagent and an organic halide a good preparative method.

Carbonyl Halides.—These usually react very rapidly to give, after hydrolysis and working up, tertiary alcohols:

$$RCOX + 2R'MgX \rightarrow RR'_2COH$$

By "reverse addition," i.e., addition of the Grignard reagent to the solution of carbonyl halide, it is possible to obtain moderate yields of ketones:

$$RCOX + R'MgX \rightarrow RCOR'$$

The transference of a Grignard reagent from the vessel in which it is prepared to a dropping funnel must be carried out in an inert atmosphere and sometimes presents experimental difficulties. A much better method for ketone synthesis involves the addition of dry cadmium chloride to the Grignard reagent, whereby it is converted to an organocadmium compound:

$$2RMgX + CdCl_2 \rightarrow R_2Cd + MgX_2 + MgCl_2$$

Organocadmium compounds, being considerably less reactive than Grignard reagents, react only with the halogen of a carbonyl halide. The acid chloride may thus be added to the solution of cadmium compound:

$$R_2Cd + 2R'COX \rightarrow 2RCOR' + CdX_2$$

Aldehydes.—The normal product, after hydrolysis, is a secondary alcohol:

$$RMgX + R'CHO \rightarrow RR'CHOMgX \rightarrow RR'CHOH$$

Poor yields can result from condensation reactions, and by the Grignard compound acting as a reducing agent leading to primary alcohol formation.

Formaldehyde, of course, affords primary alcohols, often in rather poor yield:

$H_2CO + C_2H_5MgBr \rightarrow nC_3H_7OH \text{ (low yield)} + CH_2(OC_2H_5)_2$

$H_2CO + C_6H_5MgBr \rightarrow C_6H_5CH_2OH \text{ (about 70\%)}$

The formaldehyde is commonly generated by thermal depolymerization of paraformaldehyde, or the polymer may be added to the Grignard reagent and the suspension boiled with reflux.

Ketones.—The normal reaction product is a tertiary alcohol:

$RMgX + R'COR'' \rightarrow RR'R''COMgX \rightarrow RR'R''COH$

The main complications of this synthesis are reduction to secondary alcohols and enolization.

Carboxylic Esters.—The reaction between esters and Grignard reagents is a common method for preparing tertiary alcohols:

$RCO_2R' + 2R''MgX \rightarrow RR''_2COH + R'OH$

The reactions of certain esters are of particular importance. Formic esters afford secondary alcohols, or aldehydes:

$HCO_2C_2H_5 + 2C_2H_5MgBr \rightarrow (C_2H_5)_2CHOH$

$HCO_2C_2H_5 + C_6H_5MgBr \rightarrow C_6H_5CHO$

Orthoformic esters (generally ethyl orthoformate) are used for the preparation of acetals or the corresponding aldehydes:

$HC(OC_2H_5)_3 + 2C_2H_5MgBr \rightarrow C_2H_5OMgBr \rightarrow C_2H_5CH(OC_2H_5)_2$

Cyanides.—Though rather less reactive to Grignard reagents than most substances already mentioned, cyanides are attacked in the usual way, the organic component of the Grignard reagent becoming bound to the carbon atom.

$RMgX + R'CN \rightarrow RR'C = NMgX \xrightarrow{H_2O} RR'C = NH \xrightarrow{H_2O} RR'CO$

BIBLIOGRAPHY.—M. S. Kharasch and O. Reimruth, *Grignard Reactions of Nonmetallic Substances* (1954); G. E. Coates, *Organometallic Compounds* (1968); E. C. Ashby, *Quarterly Reviews*, 21, 259 (1967).
(G. E. Cs.; E. C. A.)

GRIGNION DE MONTFORT, SAINT LOUIS MARIE DE: see MONTFORT, SAINT LOUIS MARIE GRIGNION DE.

GRILLPARZER, FRANZ

(1791–1872), recognized, belatedly, as the greatest Austrian dramatist, was born in Vienna on Jan. 15, 1791. His father, a reticent, patriotic lawyer, died in debt in 1809; his markedly neurotic mother belonged to the talented musical family of Sonnenleithner. In 1807 Grillparzer entered the University of Vienna to study law but, as the eldest son, was obliged to turn to private tutoring to help his family. Later he became a clerk in the department of revenue and, in 1818, poet to the *Hofburgtheater* and clerk in the exchequer. By 1832, when he was appointed director of the exchequer archives, it was clear that he would not be promoted to high office. In 1856 he retired from government service.

In 1817 the first performance of his tragedy *Die Ahnfrau* evoked public interest. Previously he had written many dramatic fragments, mainly on historical themes, and a play in blank verse, *Blanka von Castilien*, obviously modeled on Schiller's *Don Carlos* but already embodying the principal idea of several later works—the contrast between a quiet, idyllic existence and a life of action. *Die Ahnfrau*, written in the trochaic Spanish verse form, has many of the outward features of the then popular "fate tragedy" (*Schicksalsdrama*), but the characters are themselves ultimately responsible for their own destruction. A striking advance was the swiftly written tragedy *Sappho* (1818), which is worthy of comparison with Goethe's *Tasso*. Here Sappho's tragic fate is attributed to her unhappy love for an ordinary man and to her inability to reconcile life and art, clearly an enduring problem for Grillparzer. Work on the trilogy *Das Goldene Vlies* (1821) was interrupted by the suicide of Grillparzer's mother and by illness. This drama, with Medea's assertion that life is not worth living, is the most pessimistic of his works and offers mankind little hope. Once more the conflict between a life of meditation and one of action seems to lead inevitably to renunciation or despair. More satisfying, both aesthetically and emotionally, is the historical tragedy *König Ottokars Glück und Ende* (written 1823, but because of censorship difficulties not performed or published until 1825). Here the action is drawn from Austrian history, and the rise of Rudolph of Habsburg (the first of Grillparzer's characters to avoid guilt and tragedy) is contrasted with the fall of the tyrant Ottokar of Bohemia, so that Ottokar's fate is not presented as representative of all humanity. In another historical tragedy, *Ein treuer Diener seines Herrn* (1826, performed 1828), the self-effacement of the hero Bancban in the name of duty is not suited to theatrical representation. Grillparzer was disappointed at the reception given to both these plays and became discouraged by the objections of the censor. Although he loved Katharina Fröhlich (1800–79), whom he had met in the winter of 1820–21, he felt unable to marry, possibly because of a conviction that as an artist he had no right to personal happiness. His misery during these years is reflected not only in his diaries but also in the impressive cycle of poems significantly entitled *Tristia ex Ponto* (1835).

Des Meeres und der Liebe Wellen (1831), often judged to be Grillparzer's greatest tragedy because of the degree of harmony achieved between content and form, marks a return to the classical theme in treating the story of Hero and Leander, which is, however, interpreted with a psychological insight anticipating the plays of Friedrich Hebbel and Ibsen. Hero, the priestess, who lacks a true sense of vocation, forgets her vows in her blind passion for Leander and, when her lover is ensnared to his death, she dies of a broken heart. The following of vital instincts is shown to rob the individual of inner harmony and self-possession. *Der Traum ein Leben* (1834) owes most, particularly in form, to Grillparzer's intensive and prolonged studies of Spanish drama, especially the plays of Lope de Vega and Calderón. This Austrian *Faust* ends happily, for the ambitious young peasant Rustan only dreams the adventures which involve him in crime and awakes to a realization of the vanity of earthly aspirations. Grillparzer's only comedy, *Weh dem, der lügt!* (1838), was a failure, despite the humour of its situations and the brilliance of its dialogue, chiefly because the theme—the hero succeeds because he tells the truth when everyone thinks he is lying—was too subtle and too serious for comic treatment.

Grillparzer wrote no more for the stage and very little at all after the 1840s. The honours which were heaped on him in old age came too late. In 1861 he was elected to the *Herrenhaus*, his 80th birthday was the occasion for a national celebration and his death in Vienna on Jan. 21, 1872, was widely mourned. Three tragedies, apparently complete, were found among his papers. *Die Jüdin von Toledo*, based on a Spanish theme, portrays the tragic infatuation of a king for a young Jewess. He is only brought back to a sense of his responsibilities after she has been killed at the queen's command. *Ein Bruderzwist in Habsburg*, a profound and moving historical tragedy, lacks the theatrical action which would make it successful in performance and is chiefly remarkable for the portrayal of the emperor Rudolph II. Grillparzer's sympathetic attitude to Rudolph is sometimes regarded as a justification of Metternich's conservatism. Much of Grillparzer's most mature thought forms the basis of the third play, *Libussa*, in which he foresees human development beyond the rationalist stage of civilization. Its advent is foretold by Libussa who desires a natural community guided by intuition and ruled by love. She submits, however, to the views of her practical consort Primislaus who, although devoted to the task of building the state, understands that justice based on reason is necessary in government.

Apart from the critical studies on Spanish drama and the posthumous autobiography, Grillparzer's finest prose work is *Der arme Spielmann* (1848), the story of a poor musician who cheerfully accepts life's failures and dies through his efforts to help others, an attitude to life which is encountered elsewhere in *Biedermeier* literature, e.g., in *Kalkstein* by Adalbert Stifter (1805–68).

Features of the *Biedermeier* outlook are clearly traceable in Grillparzer's work: the looking back to the great classical and romantic achievements and the painful evolution from the disillusionment of idealism to a compromise with reality. Grillparzer is unusually gifted not only as a dramatic poet but also as a playwright capable of creating dramas suitable for performance. The influence of Shakespeare, Lope de Vega and Calderón and of the productions of the popular Viennese theatre is to be seen in the details of many of his dramas. Unlike his great predecessors, Goethe and Schiller, he distinguishes between the speech of the cultured person and that of the uneducated. Also he introduces colloquialisms, humour and elements from the popular farce. Although the central dramatic conflict is often rooted in his personal problems, it is presented objectively. Grillparzer's solution is renunciation rather than acceptance. He suffered undoubtedly from the restrictions imposed by the Metternich regime, but it is probable that his unhappiness originated principally in an inability to resolve his own difficulties of character. For a portrait of Grillparzer see article GERMAN LITERATURE.

BIBLIOGRAPHY.—*Editions:* The critical edition of Grillparzer's works, letters and diaries by August Sauer, Reinhold Backmann *et al.* began to appear in 1909 (42 vol. up to 1944). Other reliable editions include those by Stefan Hock, 4 vol. (1911) and Reinhold Backmann, 5 vol. (1952). English editions include those of *Des Meeres und der Liebe Wellen* by D. Yates (1947); of *König Ottokars Glück und Ende* by H. C. Thomas (1953); and of *Der Traum ein Leben* by W. E. Yuill (1955). English translations of many works have been made by H. Stevens or A. Burkhard.

Life: Descriptions of Grillparzer and conversations with him by his contemporaries appeared in *Grillparzers Gespräche und die Charakteristiken seiner Persönlichkeit*, ed. by August Sauer, 7 vol. (1904–41). Biographies include: H. Laube, *Die Tragik in Drama und Persönlichkeit Franz Grillparzers Lebensgeschichte* (1884); Marie von Ebner-Eschenbach, *Meine Erinnerungen an Grillparzer* (1916); E. Alker, *Franz Grillparzer* (1930); Douglas Yates, *Franz Grillparzer* (1946; in English, only first vol. published); J. Nadler, *Franz Grillparzer* (1948).

Criticism: E. Reich, *Franz Grillparzers Dramen* (1894; 4th ed. 1938); Friedrich Gundolf, in *Jahrbuch des Freien Deutschen Hochstifts* (1931); Ilse Münch, *Die Tragik in Drama und Persönlichkeit Franz Grillparzers* (1931); Gerhart Baumann, *Franz Grillparzer. Sein Werk und das österreichische Wesen* (1954); Walter Naumann, *Grillparzer-Studien* (1924); K. Glossy (ed.), *Jahrbuch der Grillparzer-Gesellschaft* (1891–); and for bibliographies of the numerous publications on Grillparzer, Karl Goedeke's *Grundriss zur Geschichte der deutschen Dichtung*, vol. viii (1905) and vol. xi (1953). (F. G.)

GRIMALD (GRIMOALD), **NICHOLAS** (1519–c. 1559), English poet, whose best-known work was contributed to the first edition of *Tottel's Miscellany*, was born in Huntingdonshire in 1519. He studied at Oxford and at Cambridge and became chaplain to Bishop Ridley. To the original edition (June 1557) of *Songes and Sonettes* (known as *Tottel's Miscellany*), which he may have edited, he contributed 40 poems and translations, only 10 of which were retained in the second edition (July 1557). Some of his pieces were in blank verse, in which he followed the style of the earl of Surrey, yet not without originality. He handles the metre competently and produces an occasional fine-sounding line. His other works include two Latin tragedies—*Christus redivivus* (1543) and *Archipropheta* (1548)—and a translation of Cicero's *De Officiis* (1556). Grimald died about 1559. (L. H. C. T.)

GRIMALDI FOSSILS are a group of human remains from the caves carved out of a high cliff, the Baoussé-Roussé (the Red rocks), which borders the Riviera in Italian territory, 2 km. (1¼ mi.) E. of Menton. These remains, totaling 16 individuals, were found in four caves called the Grotte des Enfants, the Grotte du Cavillon, the Barma Grande and the Baousso de Torre. They were found in excavations by E. Rivière, L. Julien, F. Abbo and, to a greater extent, by L. de Villeneuve during his systematic excavations organized by the prince of Monaco in 1901. All were found in implementiferous Upper Paleolitic deposits (Aurignacian and Grimaldian) but at quite different levels, some being only about 6 ft. below the surface, others nearly 30 ft. and almost in contact with the adjoining Mousterian layers. They all date from the second half of the last glacial period, from about 30,-000 to 40,000 years ago.

The major part of the remains are of the skeletons of very tall men of the Cro-Magnon race, of which many other specimens from the same epoch are known in Europe, and which is the ancestor of certain present-day Europeans. The skulls are elongated, with low vaults, short faces and orbits, and the bones are particularly robust. Quite different from these, the two skeletons from the lowest level of the Grotte des Enfants belong to a type of shorter stature and with facial prognathism—the "race" of Grimaldi which R. Verneau considered Negroid and which he thought preceded the Cro-Magnon people in this region. In the 1960s the idea of such a race was moot; other Negroid fossils had not been found in Europe, and it seems that the prognatism of the so-called Negroids was essentially the result of a posthumous deformation; possibly they may be interpreted as primitive Cro-Magnons.

See also CRO-MAGNON MAN.

See L. de Villeneuve, M. Boule, R. Verneau and E. Cartailhac, *Les Grottes de Grimaldi* (1906–12); M. Boule and H. V. Vallois, *Fossil Men* (1957). (H. V. V.)

GRIMKÉ, SARAH MOORE (1792–1873) and **ANGELINA EMILY** (1805–1879), U.S. antislavery crusaders and advocates of women's rights, were born in Charleston, S.C., Sarah on Nov. 26, 1792, and Angelina on Feb. 20, 1805. Both developed an early dislike of slavery. After several visits to Philadelphia, Sarah joined the Society of Friends in 1821; Angelina did the same in 1829. The sisters then moved to the north and became interested in the antislavery movement, with Angelina as the leader. After publication in the *Liberator* of her letter of approval to William Lloyd Garrison, the abolitionist leader, the sisters joined the American Anti-Slavery society. In 1836 Angelina published "An Appeal to the Christian Women of the South," in which she urged southern women to speak and act against slavery. Later in the year Sarah made a similar plea in "An Epistle to the Clergy of the Southern States."

The career of the Grimkés as antislavery speakers began when Angelina appeared before small groups of Philadelphia women in private homes. In 1836 the sisters moved to New York where both spoke to larger gatherings in churches and public halls. Their talks in New England before mixed audiences prompted a pastoral letter from the General Association of Congregational Ministers of Massachusetts against women preachers and reformers. As a result of such opposition the sisters became pioneers in the women's rights movement and were largely responsible for linking it to the antislavery crusade.

Following Angelina's marriage to the noted abolitionist Theodore Dwight Weld in 1838, both she and Sarah were expelled from the Society of Friends for breach of the "discipline." Ill-health forced Angelina shortly afterward to give up public speaking and Sarah followed her into retirement. The sisters helped Weld in the schools he started in New Jersey. The Welds and Sarah later moved to Hyde Park, Mass., where Sarah died on Dec. 23, 1873, and Angelina on Oct. 26, 1879.

BIBLIOGRAPHY.—Catherine H. Birney, *The Grimké Sisters* (1885); G. H. Barnes and D. L. Dumond (eds.), *Letters of Theodore Dwight Weld, Angelina Grimké Weld, and Sarah Grimké* (1934); Benjamin P. Thomas, *Theodore Dwight Weld* (1950). (M. H. Rı.)

GRIMM, FRIEDRICH MELCHIOR, BARON DE (1723–1807), Franco-German critic and diplomat, whose *Correspondance littéraire* played a considerable part in the dissemination of French culture in Europe, was born on Sept. 26, 1723, in Ratisbon (Regensburg). He was educated (1743–45) at Leipzig university where he came under the influence of the professor of poetry, Johann Christoph Gottsched (q.v.), who was then trying to create a German drama on the French classical model. Grimm's one and only tragedy, *Banise*, was published in Gottsched's *Deutsche Schaubühne* (1743). Grimm had to make his own way in the world and he accordingly attached himself to the powerful Schoenberg family. With a sound knowledge of the French language and already strongly attracted by French civilization, he eagerly seized, in 1748, the opportunity of escorting the second son to Paris, where he was appointed in turn reader to the prince of Saxe-Gotha, secretary to the count of Friesen and, in 1755, *secrétaire des commandements* of the duc d'Orléans.

At the same time he succeeded in gaining an entry into fashionable, progressive literary and philosophical circles through his acquaintance with J. J. Rousseau (q.v.) who introduced him to D'Holbach, Helvétius, Denis Diderot (q.v.) and, in 1750, to Mme d'Épinay (q.v.), whose lover he became three years later. When Mme d'Épinay went to Geneva in 1757 on account of her health, difficulties arose as to who should accompany her; this was the immediate cause of Grimm's quarrel with Rousseau, who unjustly blackened his former friend's character in his *Con-*

fessions. Yet Grimm retained the esteem and affection of Diderot, with whom he formed a lifelong, devoted friendship. It is difficult to estimate precisely what each man owed to the other, but it would seem that whereas Diderot had by far the richer mind, Grimm often stimulated him to activity, particularly in the dramatic field, and sometimes tempered his exuberance with methodical sobriety. He certainly shared most of Diderot's ideas and wrote one article, *Du Poème lyrique*, for the *Encyclopédie*, which he helped to edit and advertised abroad through his many correspondents and friends.

The number and importance of Grimm's connections indeed grew rapidly, for he promoted his career with great astuteness. He quickly became a person of note in the Parisian literary world. Two letters to the *Mercure de France* (1750 and 1751) on German literature made little impression; but in 1753, during the famous controversy over the merits of French and Italian music (*guerre des bouffons*), he achieved a certain notoriety with his *Petit Prophète de Boehmischbroda* in which, like Rousseau and Diderot, he extolled Italian to the detriment of French composers.

In this same year Grimm decided to establish a private news service for foreign princes anxious to keep in touch with life in Paris. Every fortnight after May 15, 1753, usually through diplomatic channels, subscribers received a manuscript newsletter, normally composed by Grimm who was, however, frequently helped by Mme d'Épinay and Diderot who contributed, for instance, his famous *Salons* (1759–81). The venture was successful, attracting subscriptions from many minor European rulers as well as from Catherine the Great of Russia. But in March 1773, increasingly absorbed by diplomatic work, Grimm handed over his task to Jakob Heinrich Meister.

Frank because confidential, Grimm's letters constitute a social and literary document of outstanding importance. They chronicle events of all kinds, transmit social and literary gossip, record songs, epigrams and parodies and divertingly analyze and evaluate new publications in all spheres. The impartiality and sureness with which Grimm appraised contemporary French writers, even Rousseau and Voltaire, is increasingly appreciated. The *Correspondance littéraire*, first published in 1812, has been described as the first great work of modern criticism.

Grimm's correspondence and his acknowledged tact served him well in the furtherance of his ambitions. He was appointed to a number of minor diplomatic posts and created successively a baron of the Holy Roman empire (1772) and Russian councilor of state (1777). He acted as Paris agent for some of his patrons, particularly for Catherine II, for whom he bought works of art and the libraries of Diderot and Voltaire. His activities brought him opportunities to travel extensively in Germany, England (1771), Italy (1776) and Russia (1773–74, 1776–77).

The position Grimm had thus built up was wrecked by the French Revolution. Horrified, faithful to the *ancien régime* and therefore suspect to the republic, which confiscated his property and ruined him financially, Grimm left France in 1792. In 1793, he settled in Gotha where he died, impoverished and embittered, on Dec. 19, 1807.

BIBLIOGRAPHY.—*Correspondance littéraire, philosophique et critique, par Grimm, Diderot, Raynal, Meister, etc.*, ed. by M. Tourneux, 16 vol. (1877–82); E. Scherer *Melchior Grimm* (1887); A. Cazes, *Grimm et les Encyclopédistes* (1933); J. R. Smiley, *Diderot's Relations With Grimm* (1950). (O. R. T.)

GRIMM, JACOB (LUDWIG CARL) (1785–1863) and **WILHELM (CARL)** (1786–1859), together were the collectors and editors of Grimms' *Fairy Tales* and were generally known as "the brothers Grimm"; Jacob Grimm, the grammarian, was the formulator of "Grimm's law" (*see below*), and Wilhelm Grimm was the literary scholar. They were born little more than a year apart and spent their entire lives together in a happy community of interests. As children they were inseparable, at the university they studied and lived together, as mature scholars they worked together in the same room, and they were buried side by side in Berlin.

Lives.—Jacob was born on Jan. 4, 1785, Wilhelm on Feb. 24, 1786. They attended the public school at Kassel and later studied at Marburg, where the lectures of Friedrich von Savigny awakened in both the love for antiquarian investigation which formed the real basis of all their later work. While still university students they laid plans for collaboration on medieval German literature, and in 1805 Jacob wrote from Paris to Wilhelm that he hoped they would never again be separated. By a happy combination of good fortune and early recognition of their great talents they remained together and became the most distinguished brother-scholars of the German romantic period.

Following long periods of service in the Kassel library, the brothers moved in 1830 to Göttingen, where Jacob received the appointment of professor and librarian, Wilhelm that of under-librarian. Jacob lectured on legal antiquities, historical grammar, literary history, interpreted ancient Germanic literature and commented on the *Germania* of Tacitus. The years at Göttingen were fruitful ones, despite the severe illness of Wilhelm; in 1835 Wilhelm was named to a professorship and Jacob was given the title of *Hofrat* in recognition of their accomplishments. In 1837, however, the brothers being two of the seven professors who had signed a protest against the new king of Hanover's abrogation of the constitution, they were dismissed from their professorships and banished from the kingdom of Hanover. They returned to Kassel but in 1841 went to Berlin, where they both received professorships and were elected members of the Academy of Sciences. They seldom lectured; but they worked assiduously together at the great dictionary of the German language, a task so large, even when first projected, as to make it impossible for the brothers to finish it themselves. The first volume was published in 1854; after the work had been apportioned among many other hands, the last volume was completed in 1960 by the combined efforts of scholars from eastern and western Germany.

Wilhelm, never in robust health, died in Berlin on Dec. 16, 1859; Jacob, never ill, continued working until he died quite suddenly on Sept. 20, 1863.

Of the two, Jacob was the stronger, the more vigorous and the more strictly scientific; Wilhelm was the weaker physically, the more sensitive and the more literary; Jacob became the great grammarian; Wilhelm gave literary form to the fairy tales.

Works.—The purely scientific side of Jacob's character developed slowly. Led by his careful study of Middle High German poetry to take up grammatical investigation, he apparently soon felt the need of a regular method of work in etymology, but he long grasped for scientific principles without finding them. He set himself against the use of logical concepts in the analysis of a language, and he called observation the soul of grammar; but his own almost exclusive interest in history, the variety of the evidence which he and his contemporaries collected and examined, and the necessarily slow evolution of a methodical procedure for dealing with very complex linguistic phenomena so controlled his talents as to make of him rather a careful collector and arranger of data than a great intuitive expositor or inventive theoretician. Even the ordering of the correspondences among consonants in the Germanic and other Indo-European languages which bears his name had to wait 50 years for its final clear and simple treatment.

Jacob Grimm's *Deutsche Grammatik* (4 vol, 1819–37) was, moreover, the linguistic outcome of both brothers' previous philological work. In 1811 Jacob published a work of purely literary character, *Über den altdeutschen Meistergesang*, and Wilhelm brought out his volume of translations *Altdänische Heldenlieder, Balladen und Märchen übersetzt*. In 1812 the brothers jointly edited the two ancient fragments of the *Hildebrandslied* and the *Weissenbrunner Gebet*, and in 1812–15 they jointly brought out the first edition of the *Kinder-und Hausmärchen* (the *Fairy Tales*, of which one of many English translations was edited by Joseph Campbell in 1944) which have carried their name into every household of the civilized world. In 1816–18 an analysis of the oldest Germanic epic traditions appeared under the title *Deutsche Sagen*, and in 1815 one volume of an edition of the Poetic Eddas was published over both their names. This edition, however, was never completed; and Jacob, who had little taste for text editing, about this time began to turn his mind to other things. Although he did occasionally bring out a new edition of an old text (*e.g., Reinhart*

Fuchs, 1834), and although medieval literature and comparative mythology continued to interest him, more and more his activity became focused on grammar, lexicography and the history of the German language.

Grimm's Law.—Jacob had not at first intended to include languages other than German in his *Deutsche Grammatik*; but he soon found that Old High German postulated Gothic, that the later stages of German could not be understood without the help of the Low German dialects, including English, and that the evidence from the Scandinavian languages could likewise not be ignored. The first volume of the *Grammar* appeared in 1819, its revised edition in 1822. While the first edition gives only the inflections, in the second, phonology takes up no fewer than 600 pages, more than half of the whole work. The striking difference is evidence of the increasing interest in linguistic method which marked the early years of the 19th century. This advance must be credited mainly to the influence of Rasmus Rask (*q.v.*). To Rask belongs the credit for having first demonstrated the regularity of correspondence among sounds in genetically related languages, but the first full demonstration of the validity of this principle of regularity was made by Jacob Grimm in the long lists of correspondences of consonants in the Germanic and other Indo-European languages which he published in the second edition (1822) of his *Deutsche Grammatik*. It is the regularity in these correspondences which has come to be known as Grimm's law (*see* GERMANIC LANGUAGES). Thus, the initial sound of the inherited Indo-European word for "father" is represented in Latin writing by *þ* and in English writing by *f* (Latin *pater*; English "father"). This correspondence is regular under conditions which can be clearly and certainly stated. Such regular correspondences for all consonants in all the Indo-European languages can now be given with similar certainty, only marginal problems remaining.

The question of who discovered what is known as Grimm's law is answerable only after much qualification. The correspondence of single consonants had been more or less clearly recognized by several of Jacob Grimm's predecessors; but the one who came nearest to the discovery of the complete law was the Swedish scholar J. Ihre, who established a considerable number of *litterarum permutationes*, "changes of letters." Rask, in his essay on the origin of the Icelandic language, gives the same comparisons, with a few additions. As Grimm in the preface to his first edition expressly mentions this essay of Rask, there is every probability that it gave the first impulse to his own investigations. There is, however, a wide difference between the isolated permutations of his predecessors and Grimm's comprehensive generalizations and massive assembling of evidence. The extension of the law to High German is also entirely Grimm's own.

The importance of Grimm's generalization in the history of linguistics can hardly be overestimated, but much of the merit belongs to his predecessors, and some to his immediate successors; the completion of the solution, the demonstration of symmetry existent in complexity and the simple formulation which could finally be given to the discovery are, all taken together, a unique triumph and one large enough to be shared by many. Grimm's law proved that a simple, coherent and complete demonstration of order in the process of language was possible. Jacob Grimm and his contemporaries in the mid-19th century thus made the study of linguistic phenomena scientific.

The Fairy Tales.—The criticism and interpretation of the two brothers' fairy tales began early. Wilhelm himself in 1856 stated the brothers' theory that the Germanic folk tales were versions of Indo-European myths. Theodor Benfey, the Sanskritist, sought their origins in India. Joseph Bédier and others supported the view of polygenesis, the possibility of which had also been admitted by the Grimms. The Finnish school of folklorists attempted a strict historical and geographically limited approach—a procedure which may be said to have culminated in the unhistorical typological arrangement of Stith Thompson's *Motif-Index of Folklore Classification*.

A similarly unhistorical but otherwise totally different point of view is that of the psychoanalytic school of criticism which, following Freud's hypotheses, sees in fairy tales the dreams of the human race and thus interprets them as externalizings of unfulfilled wishes, of feelings of guilt and of profound anxieties deeply buried in the unconscious. Many essays expressing this view can be found in the pages of the periodical *Imago*. Still another judgment has been expressed by Albert Wesselski in his *Versuch einer Theorie des Märchens*; according to him the "people" never create; only storytellers, authors, create, and all collections of "folk stories," including the Grimms' fairy tales, come directly or indirectly from books.

Collaboration.—So harmonious was the collaboration of the brothers Grimm and so happy their lifelong association that it is unjust to both to discriminate between them except only to show how perfectly their slight differences complemented each other. Wilhelm remained to the end of his life a literary scholar, historian and critic and, according to his brother, always loved the collections of fairy tales the most; while Jacob was occupied with grammatical problems and the history of the German language, Wilhelm continued his work on Germanic heroic legends and wrote beautifully, delightfully and learnedly about such matters as elves and children's games and customs. But these tasks for the last decade of Wilhelm's life were secondary or ancillary ones; the great work was the dictionary on which both brothers worked always harmoniously together.

The Grimm brothers' patriotism and love of historical investigation received full satisfaction in the study of the language, traditions, mythology, laws and literature of their countrymen and their nearest kindred. Both acted together for the sake of principle without bitterness and almost without complaint. Their work together was so harmonious that their genuine human kindness, which shows in their letters, made them both gently, modestly serene.

Jacob never married; Wilhelm was both a husband and a father. In a memorial address delivered in the Academy of Sciences in Berlin six months after his brother's death, Jacob said of himself that he in early youth had found an iron devotion to work which Wilhelm's weaker health denied him, but that Wilhelm's work was shot through with flashes of silver, as his own was not. Wilhelm, he also said, was fond of happy company, music and laughter; but of himself Jacob remarked that his joy arose from work itself.

See the series of critical essays (entitled *Anmerkungen*) on the Grimms' fairy tales which were published by Johannes Bolte and Georg Polívka between 1913–31. A bibliography of the principal writings of both brothers and the principal critical works about them is given in Herman Gerstner's *Die Brüder Grimm* (1952). (Mr. F.)

GRIMMELSHAUSEN, HANS JAKOB CHRISTOPHER (JOHANN JAKOB CHRISTOPHER) **VON** (1621/22–1676), German novelist, author of *Simplicissimus*, the greatest German novel of the 17th century and one of the great works of German literature. The troubled times in which he lived and which found expression in his work are reflected in uncertainties about his birth, parentage, and early life. Born at Gelnhausen, near Hanau, Hesse-Kassel, in 1621 or 1622, he lost his parents early, probably in the sack of Gelnhausen (1634). His father was apparently an innkeeper, a member of a noble family that had been assimilated back into the *Bürgertum* (or middle classes). Grimmelshausen lived in Gelnhausen until kidnapped as a child by Hessian and Croat troops; his experiences with them are mirrored in *Simplicissimus*. He joined the Imperial Army, probably in 1636, and in 1639 became secretary to Reinhard von Schauenburg, the commandant at Offenburg, on whose staff he served until May 1647. In 1648 he was with the commandant on the Inn. Soon after the war ended he became steward of the Schauenburg estates. His marriage in 1649 may have been the occasion of his becoming Catholic; his parents and education were certainly Lutheran. His stewardship was no sinecure in a period of claims and counterclaims in a divided family and a despoiled countryside, but he found time for writing, which he had begun in the army, and opened an inn at Gaisbach, near Oberkirch.

In 1660 Grimmelshausen was discharged, and became until 1665 administrator of the Ullenburg estate. In 1667 he was appointed magistrate and tax collector at Renchen, a town belonging to the bishopric of Strasbourg. After 1674 his life was again disturbed by invading armies. The district was occupied by the Lorrainers, the inhabitants fled, and Grimmelshausen's household was broken up. He died at Renchen, perhaps after service on the imperial staff, on Aug. 17, 1676.

His first published works, *Traumgesicht von dir und mir* ("A Vision of You and Me," 1658) and *Reisebeschreibung nach der oberen Mondswelt* ("A Journey to the Other Side of the Moon," 1660), are mainly derivative: satiric in intent, yet lacking the single-mindedness of pure satire and showing the tendencies developed in his later work—keen, humorous observation, ridicule of convention, and power of episodic invention. In 1669 he published *Der abenteuerliche Simplicissimus, Teutsch, das hist: Die Beschreibung dess Lebens eines seltzamen Vaganten, genannt Melchior Sternfels von Fuchshaim* . . . (Eng. trans. by A. T. S. Goodrick, *Simplicissimus, the Vagabond; that is, The Life of a Strange Adventurer Named Melchior Sternfels von Fuchshaim* . . ., 1912, and by H. Weissenborn and L. MacDonald, 1964), in five volumes. This is the story of an innocent child brought into contact with life through his experiences of the Thirty Years' War. Modeled on the Spanish picaresque romance (see PICARESQUE NOVEL), but with a metaphysical purpose in which the development of a human soul is measured against the depraving background of a Germany riven by warfare, it gives full rein to Grimmelshausen's power of narration, eye for realistic detail, creation of convincing minor characters, coarse humour, and criticism of society.

Simplicissimus is a masterpiece in its own right and valuable as a historical document for its vivid picture of 17th-century Germany. Its success led Grimmelshausen to write continuations, the so-called *Simplicianische Schriften*, the first being the "sixth" book of *Simplicissimus*, in which the hero retires to a desert island and there lives a sort of Robinson Crusoe life. Other continuations were *Die Landstörtzerin Courasche* (1669; Eng. trans. by H. Speier, *Courage, the Adventuress*, 1964; used by Bertolt Brecht for his play *Mutter Courage*), *Der seltsame Springinsfeld* ("The Remarkable Scamp," 1670), and *Das wunderbarliche Vogelnest* ("The Magical Bird's Nest," 1672; Eng. trans. of nine chapters by H. Speier as *The False Messiah*, 1964). Grimmelshausen also wrote satires, and courtly "gallant" novels (*Der keusche Joseph*, "The Chaste Joseph," 1666; *Dietwald und Amelinde*, 1670; and *Proximus und Lympida*, 1672) but it is on *Simplicissimus* that his fame remains secure.

BIBLIOGRAPHY.—The best modern edition of *Simplicissimus* is by J. H. Scholte (1938–39; 3rd ed. by K. Henniger, 1955); Scholte also edited the *Simplicianische Schriften* (1923–43). Selected works, ed. by A. von Keller, 4 vol. (1852–62); H. Kurz, 4 vol. (1863–64); and H. H. Borcherdt, 3 vol. (1921); and S. Streller, 4 vol. (1960). See also A. Bechtold, *Grimmelshausen und seine Zeit*, 2nd ed. (1919); G. Könnecke and J. H. Scholte, *Quellen und Forschungen zur Lebensgeschichte Grimmelshausens*, 2 vol. (1926–28); K. C. Hayens, *Grimmelshausen* (in English, 1932); J. H. Scholte, *Der Simplicissimus und sein Dichter* (1950); G. Herbst, *Die Entwicklung des Grimmelshausenbildes in der wissenschaftlichen Literatur* (1957). (D. G. D.)

GRIMSBY, formerly called GREAT GRIMSBY, a municipal, county and parliamentary borough of Lincolnshire, Eng., on the south bank of the Humber estuary, 35½ mi. N.E. of Lincoln by road. Pop. (1971 prelim.) 95,685.

Grimsby was a Danish settlement and is mentioned in the Icelandic sagas. The name derives from Grim the fisherman, foster father of Havelok the Dane in the legend of that name. King John granted the first royal charter to the town in 1201, and Henry III granted a further charter in 1227. These grants were confirmed and extended by later sovereigns, the last charter being given by James II in 1688. An annual fair and weekly market are held under charter rights. The parish church of St. James contains Norman, Early English and transitional work; it was extensively restored after suffering severe war damage in 1943. Grimsby has a bishop suffragan in the diocese of Lincoln.

Up to the end of the middle ages, Grimsby was an important seaport, but it declined as the old haven silted up. In 1796 a statutory company was formed by a private act of parliament to improve the harbour, and the first dock was built in 1800. The modern development of the town is due largely to its favourable situation as regards the North sea and other fishing grounds. The docks were rebuilt and modernized after 1846, and fishing smacks began trawling in 1856. The use of the steam trawler from the 1880s extended the area covered by the fishing fleet as far as Greenland and the White sea. At the same time the increase in the population of England, the construction of railways and the use of ice for preserving fish made possible for the first time a supply of fresh fish in bulk to all parts of the country. Approximately one-third of the fish landed in Great Britain passes through Grimsby docks. The trade greatly developed with the introduction of modern methods of curing and quick freezing, and there is a considerable export trade in frozen fish. A second fish dock was built in 1900 and a third (35 ac.) with slipways and coaling facilities was opened in 1934. The total dock area is 139 ac., 64 ac. of which are fish docks. Immingham (q.v.) dock, 6 mi. N., is the deepwater port for Grimsby.

Grimsby was a mine sweeper base in World War II. After the war, Grimsby became a centre of the heavy chemical industry, and several large modern plants were erected. The town is one of the greatest single manufacturing centres of titanium oxide in the world. The commercial docks handle imports of timber, food, wood pulp and raw materials for the chemical industry. Coal and general merchandise are exported. There are regular commercial services to the Scandinavian countries.

GRIMTHORPE, EDMUND BECKETT, 1ST BARON (1816–1905), English lawyer, horologist, Gothic revivalist and public controversialist, was born near Newark on May 12, 1816, the eldest son of Edmund Beckett Denison, later 4th baronet. Educated at Eton and Trinity college, Cambridge, he was called to the bar in 1841 and became queen's counsel in 1854. Between 1877 and 1900 he was chancellor and vicar-general of York, receiving a peerage in 1886. He rapidly acquired a large practice, achieving the leadership of the parliamentary bar by 1860—a position he owed more to vigorous self-assertiveness than to legal erudition. After 1880 he withdrew from legal work. An expert, inventive horologist, Beckett designed, despite bitter opposition, the clock for the houses of parliament (Big Ben), installed in 1859. Clocks at Leeds town hall and at Worcester, Lincoln and St. Paul's cathedrals were also designed by him on new principles.

He was passionately interested in the revival of Gothic architecture, publishing *Lectures on Gothic Architecture* (1855), designing churches and secular buildings at Doncaster and elsewhere. His magnum opus was the "restoration" of St. Albans cathedral, where, having virtually bought the faculty in 1880, he raised the roof pitch, recast the west front in a new style, redesigned the transept windows and vestries. His ruthlessness aroused a storm of protest and did much, as a negative exemplar, to provoke those better, sensitive conceptions of restoration since prevalent. Nevertheless, his Gothic designs there and elsewhere have a coarse vitality typical of the man. Throughout his life, in parliament, in the *Times*, pamphlets and libel cases, he was a famous controversialist. Among subjects of his virulent, dogmatic outbursts were architects, doctors, trade unions and ecclesiastical affairs. Though clever, versatile and dynamic, he was brutal, insensitive and wrongheaded. Leaving more than £2,000,000, he died at St. Albans on April 29, 1905. (R. J. LA.)

GRINDAL, EDMUND (1519?–1583), archbishop of Canterbury, whose Puritan sympathies brought him into serious conflict with Elizabeth I, was born at St. Bees, Cumberland, and educated at Magdalene and Christ's colleges, Cambridge. He became fellow and president (i.e., vice-master) of Pembroke college during the mastership of Nicholas Ridley, and during the visit of Edward VI's commissioners to the university he took part in a disputation against transubstantiation. When Ridley became bishop of London, he appointed Grindal his domestic chaplain in 1550 and precentor of St. Paul's cathedral. In 1551 Grindal became a royal chaplain and prebendary of Westminster, and in 1552 Ridley pressed his name for a bishopric. During the reign of Mary I, Grindal went to Strasbourg, being sent thence to Frankfurt as member of a deputation to mediate between the contending factions of "Coxians" (see Cox, RICHARD), who desired to keep "the face of an English church" by using the 1552 prayer book with omissions, and the "Knoxians" who desired a liturgy after the pattern of John Knox's later Genevan liturgy. He also assisted John Foxe, the martyrologist, in his work. On the accession of Elizabeth I he returned home, became one of the disputants against the Marian bishops in 1559, preached in St. Paul's cathedral on May 15, 1559, the day on which the Elizabethan prayer book came into use, was appointed one of the royal commissioners for the visitation of the northern province, and was elected master of Pembroke college, Cambridge. In the same year, 1559, he was nominated bishop of London, but hesitated to accept because of his scruples about the "ornaments" rubric in that prayer book, the outdoor habit of the clergy and the use of wafer bread for Holy Communion. He consulted Peter Martyr, who advised acceptance so that they might work from within for the removal of the remaining relics of popery. As bishop of London Grindal was a thorn in the side of Archbishop Matthew Parker, who wished to enforce the wearing of the surplice but enjoyed little support from Grindal.

In 1570 Grindal was made archbishop of York, where the chief difficulties arose from papists rather than from Puritans. But though sympathetic with the latter so long as the dispute turned upon the surplice, he became a determined opponent of Thomas Cartwright and the Presbyterianizing party, which desired the abolition of the prayer book and of episcopacy. Accordingly he was nominated to the archbishopric of Canterbury in 1576 in the hope that he might drive a wedge between the moderate Puritans and the new party of revolution. He introduced a series of moderate reforms of abuses, which might have been effective ten years earlier. Unfortunately he fell foul of Elizabeth in regard to "prophesyings," or meetings of clergy for mutual edification and study, since he wished to regulate and continue them, she to prevent their meeting. Grindal thereupon addressed to the queen a remonstrance, in which he pointed out to her the limits of her authority in ecclesiastical matters and exhorted her to respect that of the bishops, in terms as unaccustomed as unwelcome to Elizabeth. She retorted by suspending him from the exercise of his metropolitan functions, and the dispute dragged on until his death at Croydon on July 6, 1583. Because of this conflict it is impossible to say whether Grindal might have succeeded in winning over a majority of moderate Puritans and isolating the minority of extremists. It has been held that it was a mistake to make a Marian exile archbishop of Canterbury; probably it was too late for a policy of appeasement with the Puritans to be effective.

See J. Strype, *Life of Grindal* (1707); *Cambridge Modern History*, vol. iii (1934).

(N. S.)

GRINDELWALD, a valley in the Bernese Oberland and one of the chief summer and winter tourist resorts in Switzerland. It is shut in on the south by the Wetterhorn, Mettenberg and Eiger, between which are two famous ice streams known as the Upper and Lower Grindelwald glaciers. On the north it is sheltered by the Faulhorn range, while on the east the Great Scheidegg pass leads over to Meiringen; and on the southwest the Little Scheidegg and Wengernalp (railway across) divide it from Lauterbrunnen. The main village is connected with Interlaken by a rack railway (13 mi.) while the Jungfrau railway ascends from there to the highest Alpine railway station in Europe—Jungfraujoch (11,342 ft.). The First, the longest chair lift in Europe, also starts from Grindelwald.

The valley possesses excellent pastures, as well as fruit trees, though little corn is grown. It is watered by the Black Lütschine, a tributary of the Aar. The parish church is 3,468 ft. above sea level. The population is practically all Protestant and German speaking.

The valley was originally inhabited during the summer for pasturage by serfs of various great lords. A chapel in a cave was superseded about 1146 by a wooden church, replaced about 1180 by a stone church, which was pulled down in 1793 to make way for the present building. Gradually the Austin canons of Interlaken bought out all the other owners of the valley, but when that house was suppressed in 1528 by the town of Bern the inhabitants gained their freedom.

(S. Ri.)

GRINDING MACHINE, a device using an abrasive wheel to produce a desired size, shape or surface finish on parts made of metal or other hard materials. The first cylindrical grinder was made in the 1860s in the United States by replacing the single-point tool of an engine lathe with a rotating abrasive wheel. At first the grinding wheel was made of natural sandstone, but later, for faster production and better control of quality, manufactured abrasives were formed into wheels by the ceramic process. By 1876 the universal cylindrical grinder had been developed to about its present state.

Many types of grinding machines have been developed for modern industry. They comprise a wide range of sizes and varieties, each designed to perform a particular type of work to best advantage. Polishing, buffing, lapping, honing and superfinishing are additional abrasive processes, each requiring a machine of special type. Some grinders use abrasive-faced belts instead of wheels.

Common Types of Grinders.—In cylindrical grinding of external surfaces, the work, with conically countersunk ends, is held rigidly on centres and rotated slowly, and the rapidly rotating wheel is fed against the work (for internal grinding, some form of chuck or clamp holds the work). When the surface to be ground is longer than the width of the wheel, the work is mounted on a cross slide and traversed slowly past the grinding wheel by hydraulic, mechanical or manual means. When the wheel face is as wide as the length of the surface being ground, the wheel may be fed in with no traversing movement; this is called plunge grinding. The wheel speed (usually about 6,000 ft. per minute), the work feed (about 0.001 in. per traverse), the work speed (50–100 ft. per minute), the table-traverse speed and the length of traverse are all independently adjustable to suit the machine and the type of work. The universal cylindrical grinder has a table mounted on a graduated base so that it may be swiveled for grinding tapered shapes.

The plain cylindrical grinder has been modified to perform roll grinding on piston rods, turbine shafts and rolling-mill parts requiring great accuracy and superior finish. Other machines have been adapted for grinding the crank and main bearings of crankshafts; in these, the shaft is chucked so that its main journal bearings revolve in an orbit, while the crank pins being ground run concentrically. Camshaft-grinding machines are provided with master cams which cause a movement between the wheel and the cam being ground that evolves the desired contour of the cams. Other modifications are constructed for tool and cutter sharpening, drill pointing, saw and milling-cutter sharpening, etc.

The centreless grinding machine for external cylindrical or circular-section work consists of two abrasive wheels, each mounted on a horizontal axis with the wheel surfaces opposed to each other. An adjustable work-supporting blade is mounted between the two wheels. The smaller of the wheels, known as the regulating wheel, rotates slowly and acts as a brake to prevent the work from spinning as it is forced against the grinding wheel. For cylindrical

BY COURTESY OF GRINDING MACHINE DIV., CINCINNATI MILLING MACHINE CO.

WATER-PUMP SHAFTS BEING GROUND BY THE "THROUGH-FEED" METHOD ON A CENTRELESS GRINDING MACHINE

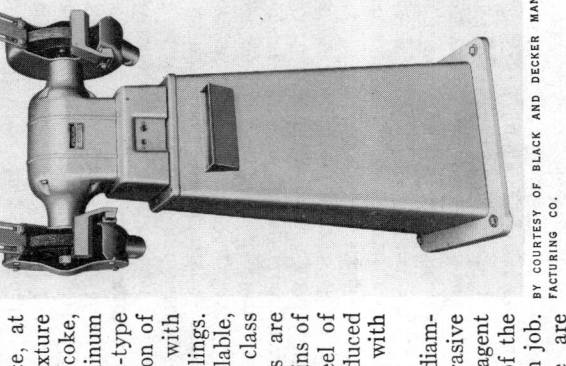

shapes, the work is fed axially between the wheels. For formed work it is placed on the rest between the two wheels while the regulating wheel is fed forward.

Internal grinding machines have been developed for finishing holes to required sizes and surface conditions. These machines employ a small-diameter grinding wheel, rotating at high speed, which is traversed in and out of the hole as it is fed radially, to produce the correct diameter. Many grinding machines used for mass production have automatic measuring devices so that the grinding continues until the specified size is reached.

Several types of surface-grinding machines are available for grinding flat surfaces. One, with a reciprocating table carrying the work, moves under a straight wheel (which grinds on its periphery) mounted on a horizontal spindle or under a face-grinding wheel on a vertical or horizontal spindle. Other types have rotary tables employing a cup wheel on a vertical spindle or a straight wheel on a horizontal spindle. The rotary table supports the work in mechanical fixtures or on a magnetic chuck. There are also single- and double-opposed disk grinders in which the work is forced against the face of a single disk or fed between opposed disks to be ground to a desired thickness.

Special Grinding Machines.—Gear grinders finish gear teeth to an involute form. This is usually done after the gear teeth have been machined and hardened. One type of grinder uses a straight wheel formed to the desired tooth space. The wheel is traversed through the previously roughed-out tooth space as it is fed, at each stroke, to the depth that gives the desired tooth thickness. Another type of grinder uses a straight wheel with the faces dressed to straight bevel sides; the wheel simulates a tooth of a gear having a very large number of teeth. As the wheel traverses the rough tooth space it is fed gradually to a depth that gives the desired tooth thickness; and at the same time the wheel and gear are rolled back and forth together, just as one finished gear engages another.

Another gear grinder, using the generating process, employs a single large-diameter flat-face wheel with a thin edge tilted at an angle. The whole wheel is traversed across the meshing gear teeth.

The thread grinder for finishing screw threads employs a wheel the face of which has the form of the thread space. The wheel is fed inward as it traverses back and forth along the axis of the screw, while the screw slowly rotates.

Finishing Operations.—The lapping or final finish of the teeth of spur, bevel or hypoid gears is done by running two gears together at crossed axes to provide a sliding action. An oil containing a fine abrasive is poured on the meshing gear teeth.

Polishing is done with an abrasive glued to the face of a flexible wheel, usually made of cotton or felt. Coarse or medium-size abrasive grain is used for fast metal removal with a resulting coarse finish, and fine grain for a good surface finish. Buffing follows finish polishing and involves a soft, pliable wheel with a very fine abrasive, such as tripoli powder mixed with grease, pressed against the wheel at intervals. This process produces a high lustre.

Honing involves the use of small honing stones supported in an adjustable head which is rotated slowly as it is reciprocated in, for example, the bore of a cylinder. The stones are forced radially against the cylinder wall so that a small amount of metal is removed. The bore is thus given a fine finish and accurate size. Superfinishing, quite similar to honing, uses fine honing stones supported flexibly and forced gently against slowly moving work, such as cylindrical bearings. This is done after grinding to give a smooth, accurate surface.

Grinding-Wheel Abrasives.—Abrasives for metal removal may be natural or manufactured. Natural abrasives such as sandstone (quartz), emery and corundum were used for centuries but have been largely replaced by manufactured abrasives, which are more uniform in composition and performance. Diamonds are used for making up solid wheels and honing stones and as a powder for lapping very hard material.

The manufactured abrasives are of two principal compositions: silicon carbide is manufactured in an electric furnace, at about 4,000° F., from a mixture of a silica sand, petroleum coke, salt and sawdust; aluminum oxide is produced in an arc-type electric furnace by the fusion of the mineral bauxite mixed with ground coke and iron filings. Several hardnesses are available, each adapted to a specific class of work. These abrasives are crushed and sorted into grains of various mesh size. A wheel of desired shape and size is produced by baking the grains, mixed with a bonding agent.

The size, shape and bore diameter of the wheel, the abrasive type, grain size, bonding agent and structure are all part of the wheel specifications for each job. Wheels of silicon carbide are used generally to grind materials of low tensile strength (cast iron, brass, aluminum); aluminum oxide wheels are used for high strength materials, such as steel of all types. Grinding wheels must rotate at high speeds, and it is therefore important that they run true and are dynamically balanced and free of cracks. Adequate guards should be provided to minimize damage in the event of wheel breakage, and the operator should wear safety glasses.

See also references under "Grinding Machine" in the Index volume.

(O. W. B.)

GRINGORE (GRINGOIRE), **PIERRE** (c. 1475–c. 1538), French poet, dramatist and satirist, was born in Normandy, perhaps at Thury-Harcourt (Calvados). His name, Gringore, found in acrostics in his poems, is the Norman equivalent of central French Gringoire, the latter form being already found in records of payments made to him at the court of Lorraine (see below). Fairly well educated by medieval standards, he enjoyed great popularity, particularly as an actor-manager and playwright between 1506 and 1512, in Paris, where he helped to produce a play for the entry of Archduke Philip of Austria in 1501 and had other similar commissions, including the mimed *Sotie des Chroniqueurs* for the entry of Mary Tudor (1514). His first extant work, *Le Chasteau de Labour* (1499; Eng. trans. by Alexander Barclay, 1506; ed. by A. W. Pollard, 1905), is an allegorical poem in which a despondent young husband learns how to overcome adversity by diligence. But Gringore is best known as a writer of satirical plays for the *Confrérie des Enfants Sans Souci* or *Sots*, with their Prince and *Mère Sotte* the most famous guild of comic actors in France at the time. As *Mère Sotte* (a title which he kept until his death) he wielded great authority and enjoyed the favour of Louis XII, who "loved truth, even against himself" and employed Gringore and his fellow *Sots* as the mouthpiece of his antipapal policy. Gringore served Louis well, satirizing the Venetians and Swiss as well as condemning the temporal pretensions of Pope Julius II. He first attacked Julius II in his poem *La Chasse du cerf des cerfs* (1510), parodying the papal title of *Servus servorum Dei* (*le serf des serfs de Dieu*); then on Shrove Tuesday, 1511 (old style; 1512, new style), when the pope was at its bitterest, he staged a trilogy (*sotie, moralité* and *farce*), *Le Jeu du Prince des Sots et Mère Sotte*, the pope being *L'Homme obstiné* of the morality, but Holy Church, scathingly exposed in the *sotie*, being after all only *notre Mère Sotte*.

Gringore's strikingly different *Vie Monseigneur Sainct Loys par personnaiges* (1514?), a piously conceived mystery play about Louis IX, sometimes considered his masterpiece, was written for the Paris guild of masons and carpenters. With Francis I's accession (1515), restrictions were imposed on playwriting, and royal favour passed to the Italian players, so Gringore moved to Lorraine in 1518, to be herald to the duke with the title of Vaudémont, but also to continue and revise plays and to organize court festivities. In 1518, too, he married Catherine Roger (his poem *La Complaincte de Trop Tard Marié* may be earlier in date). His *Blazon des hérétiques* (1524), a tedious enumeration of heretics down to Luther, whom he attacks, was dedicated to the duke. The exact date, place and manner of his death are unknown.

Gringore is best as a polemist and imitator; he is often labelled but he can be vigorous and witty, and his sound dramatic sense made him much sought after as a reviser of plays. His motto, *Tout par Raison, Raison par Tout, Par tout Raison*, framing *Mère Sotte* on the title page of several works, characterizes the love of order and good sense, rather than any corrective purpose, in his writing; and he was a good Catholic despite his difficulties with the Sorbonne over translations in his *Heures de Notre-Dame* (1525). His other works include satirical poems and other satires such as *Les Folles Entreprises* (1505), *L'Entreprise de Venise* (1509), *Les Abus du Monde* (1509), *L'Espoir de Paix* (1509?), *La Coqueluche* (1510), *L'Obstination des Suysses* (1512-13?); religious verse such as *La Quenouille spirituelle* (1524?) and *Chants Royaux* (1527); and collections of tales, *Les Fantasies de Mère Sotte* (1516) and *Les Menus Propos et le Testament de Lucifer* (1521).

BIBLIOGRAPHY.—The *Oeuvres complètes*, vol. 1 edited by C. d'Héricault and A. de Montaiglon (1858), vol. 2 by Montaiglon and J. de Rothschild (1877), is now inadequate. *See* also E. Picot, *Gringore et les comédiens italiens* (1878); C. Oulmont, *Pierre Gringore* (1911); N. Hamper, *Die Stellung des Dichters Pierre Gringore zur französischen Kirchenpolitik unter Ludwig XII*, in *Jahrbuch der Gesellschaft für lothring. Geschichte*, vol. xxiv, pp. 167-217 (1912); W. Dittmann, *Pierre Gringore als Dramatiker* (1923); C. R. Baskervill, *Pierre Gringore's Pageants for the Entry of Mary Tudor into Paris* (1934).
(F. J. We.)

GRINIUS, KAZYS (1866-1950), Lithuanian statesman, prime minister and president of the republic during the period of liberal democracy, a key figure of the Lithuanian Peasant party, was born on Dec. 17, 1866, near Marijampole. He studied medicine in Moscow and then, from 1893, practised as a doctor in several Lithuanian towns. Before World War I his house at Marijampole was a gathering place of Lithuanian democrats. For his patriotic activity he was persecuted by the tsarist Russian government. A member of the Lithuanian constituent assembly, he formed a cabinet on June 19, 1920, which on July 12, 1920, signed a peace treaty with the U.S.S.R. He resigned on Feb. 1, 1922. On June 7, 1926, Grinius was elected president of Lithuania and served until the military *coup d'état* in favour of a Nationalist government on Dec. 17, 1926. He then resumed his medical and social work. He escaped the second Soviet occupation by fleeing to Germany in 1944 and went to the United States in 1947. He died in Chicago on June 4, 1950.
(MA. G.)

GRINNELL, a city of east central Iowa, U.S., 50 mi. E. of Des Moines, the seat of Grinnell college. A coeducational school, Grinnell was founded in 1846 by pioneer settlers in Iowa who were Congregationalists and graduates of Andover (Mass.) Theological seminary, who went west in 1843 as educational missionaries. The college was opened at Davenport in 1848 as Iowa college and in 1859 moved to Grinnell, where it absorbed Grinnell university (founded 1855). Known popularly as Grinnell college, the school did not officially change its name until 1909. The city was settled in 1854 and was named after one of its founders, Josiah Bushnell Grinnell (1821-91), a Congregational clergyman, abolitionist, congressman and railway promoter. Grinnell was incorporated as a town in 1865 and as a city in 1882. It adopted the council-manager form of government in 1955. Manufactures include sporting goods, gloves, chemical fertilizers and shoes. For comparative population figures *see* table in IOWA: *Population*.

GRIPENBERG, BERTEL JOHAN SEBASTIAN, BARON (1878-1947), one of the most outstanding of the Finnish poets who wrote in Swedish, was born on Sept. 10, 1878, in St. Petersburg, the son of a senator. He studied law at Helsinki university, became a free-lance writer and spent the last years of his life on his estate at Sääksmäki in southwest Finland. Gripenberg's first collection, *Dikter* (1903), attracted attention for its richness of colour and sensualism. This and other early collections, of which the most important are *Gallergrinden* (1905) and *Svarta sonetter* (1908), show his proud individualism, love of beauty and skilful handling of the sonnet form in particular. He gradually found in the landscape of central Finland a solace for the feelings of loneliness and anger so apparent in *Svarta sonetter*. The collections *Drivsnö* (1909), *Aftnar i Tavastland* (1911), *Skuggspel* (1912) and *Spillror* (1917) include more tranquil contemplative poetry, often dwelling on the idea of death. Later collections contain some fine patriotic poems, *e.g.*, on the events of the 1918 war of independence, but in some Gripenberg degenerates into theatrical attitudes and empty pathos. In his last collections, *Vid grönsen* (1930), *Livets eko* (1932) and *Sista ronden* (1941), the tone is again calmer and more sombre.

He also published some prose works, including his memoirs, *Det var de tiderna* (1943), and translated into Swedish the "Ballad of Reading Gaol" by Oscar Wilde, whose influence is apparent in his own works. He died in Sweden at the Sävsjö sanatorium on May 6, 1947.

See M. Björkenheim, *B. Gripenbergs ungdomsdiktning* (1950); J. Louhija, *Symbolit ja kielikuvat B. Gripenbergin tuotannossa* (1959).
(K. L. K. L.)

GRIQUALAND EAST AND GRIQUALAND WEST are historical divisions of the Cape of Good Hope province in the Republic of South Africa. Geographically they are widely separate; historically they are linked by the fact that in 1861 Adam Kok III (1835-76) of Griqualand West sold his land rights in what is now the Orange Free State. He trekked thence with about 3,000 Griquas across the Drakensberg and settled south of Natal and east of Basutoland in the no man's land, now called Griqualand East, between the Cape, Natal and Pondoland.

Griqualand West lies north of the Orange river and stretches from the Cape plateau eastward across the junction of the Vaal and the Hartz rivers, with Kimberley almost on its eastern frontier. Its foundation dates from 1803, when wandering groups of Hottentots and Bastaards (offspring of mixed marriages) under Barend Barends were induced by the missionaries William Anderson and Cornelius Adrian Kramer to settle at Klaarwater (modern Griquatown). They were joined by Korana and Bechuana groups, and by 1823 the settlement numbered about 4,000 who called themselves collectively the Griqua people.

By the 1830s there were three Griqua communities with some claim to rank as states. The oldest, at Griquatown, had elected as captain Andries Waterboer, of part Bushman, part Hottentot extraction. He rescued the Kuruman mission station from attack by the Mantatees in 1823 and the following year gave shelter to Moshesh of Basutoland. North and east of Waterboer's lands lay Campbell, another mission station, where the Griquas were ruled by Cornelis Kok. About 150 mi. S.E. of both, Adam Kok's group had settled round the London Missionary society centre at Philippolis.

In Dec. 1834 Sir Benjamin D'Urban, then governor of Cape colony, signed a treaty with Waterboer recognizing his territorial rights as far east as Ramah, and sent a British resident to Griquatown. By 1835, when the great trek was launched by the Afrikaners, it was Adam Kok, farther to the east, who found himself in the path of the trekkers. In 1843 he concluded a treaty with Sir George Napier, D'Urban's successor. In 1838 Adam Kok had concluded a treaty fixing the frontier as between himself and Cornelis Kok on the west, and he now thought that the Napier treaty would cover his eastern line facing the Boers. An attempt to exercise the duties imposed by Britain in terms of the Cape of Good Hope Punishment act led to a clash with the Boers at Zwartkopjes (May 1845). In 1845 Napier's treaty was revised by his successor, Adam Kok's lands were divided into an inalienable tribal area south of the Riet river and a leasable area north of it. In 1848 the governor, Sir Henry Smith, converted those Boer farms in the leasable area into freeholds in return for cash compensation to Adam Kok, and stipulated that the Griquas pay compensation for improvement when leases terminated in the inalienable land. Notoriously improvident, the Griquas rarely had the money to pay this, and the Boers either usurped or bought freehold even in the inalienable area. In 1854, when Britain recognized the independence of the

Free State, no security for Griqua lands was predicated; so the quasi-legal expropriation continued, and, in terms of the convention of Bloemfontein (1854), Free State, not Griqua, jurisdiction extended to European farmers in Griqua lands. In 1857 Cornelis Kok bequeathed the Campbell lands to Adam Kok, who four years later sold his lands to the Free State and, in an epic trek, moved eastward to settle in Griqualand East, where the British hoped the Griquas would be a buffer between the Basuto and the Pondo. Adam Kok died in 1876; and between 1878 and 1879 the control of European magistrates increased until, in 1879, Griqualand East was annexed to the Cape. In 1903, the district of East Griqualand, now called Emboland, was established as a native council and was admitted into the Transkeian Territories (see TRANSKEI).

Unfortunately, when Adam Kok's lands were sold to the Free State, his agent, without authorization, included the very dubious claim to the ill-defined Campbell lands, which the Griquas said should have reverted to Waterboer. Thus the Free State and Waterboer were rival claimants of territory that had strategic importance because it lay across the missionary road to the north. The road was vital to traders and, after the discovery of the Tati gold fields, sectors of the road were claimed by the Transvaal. Because of this the road was the focus of dispute between Britain, which protected the missionaries; Waterboer and the Free State, which claimed the Campbell lands; and Marthinius Pretorius of the Transvaal, whose westward claim to territory swung right across the road. (See PRETORIUS.) The Keate arbitration (1871) determined against the Transvaal frontier claim and defined the north and west limits of Griqualand West.

Meanwhile, confusion was increased by the discovery of diamonds, first in the Klipdrift area between the Vaal and the Hartz rivers, and then in dry diggings on the fringe of the eastern boundary of Campbell territory claimed by Waterboer. At Klipdrift the diggers had established a republic under the presidency of a former sailor, Stafford Parker. There, and in the dry diggings of what is now Kimberley, each of the interested powers—Britain, the Orange Free State and the Transvaal—claimed control they dared not exert without the risk of war, while the diggers appealed to eacn in turn as seemed opportune. When in 1870 Waterboer and Pretorius and J. H. Brand failed to make an agreement, Waterboer offered his land, about which there was no dispute, together with his disputed Campbell claims, to Britain. In 1871, following the Keate arbitration (see SOUTH AFRICA, REPUBLIC OF), Sir Henry Barkly annexed the full Waterboer claim as Griqualand West. Legally the decision was premature, as was revealed when a land court was set up to settle matters of title. The judge ruled that Waterboer's sovereignty had not extended to the Campbell lands, though he did not establish the converse, namely that Free State sovereignty had so extended. Two political factors ranked as extenuating circumstances. First, control was urgently needed to stop the acceleration of the gun traffic, and the Langalibalele crisis (see NATAL) demonstrated this. Second, had a plan for federation proposed by the earl of Carnarvon matured, Griqualand would have been one unit in a new state. In 1876 Britain paid £90,000 compensation as a final settlement of Free State claims. Even so, the annexation crisis of 1871 exercised a profound and adverse effect on Afrikaner sentiment.

Although formally annexed in 1871, Griqualand West was not taken over by the Cape until 1880. Order was restored and maintained first by Sir Richard Southey and then by Sir William Owen Lanyon, both scrupulous and able lieutenant governors. Land was surveyed and the Griquas were settled, some on farms, some in rural villages. But unrestricted freehold and improvidence led to systematic expropriation. By the early 1900s, the Griquas were almost extinct as landowners. (W. A. Ml.)

GRIS, JUAN (real name JOSÉ VICTORIANO GONZÁLEZ) (1887–1927), major Spanish Cubist painter closely associated with Georges Braque and Pablo Picasso, was born in Madrid on March 23, 1887, and was given a scientific education before being allowed to follow his inclination and study art. In 1906 Gris moved to Paris, where he made drawings (in an art nouveau style) for papers such as Le Charivari and Le Témoin. He settled in Montmartre in the Bateau-Lavoir, an artists' dwelling where his compatriot Picasso also lived. During his vital prentice years, Gris was thus closely in touch with the gradual evolution of Cubism. His first paintings in an analytical manner (including a "Portrait of Picasso") were exhibited at the Salon des Indépendants and Section d'Or in 1912. In 1913–14 he arrived at a personal and mature version of synthetic Cubism in which the use of papier collé was all-important. Gris envisaged the basis of every painting as "a sort of flat coloured architecture." He was, however, equally aware that "the essence of painting is the expression of certain relationships between the painter and the outside world"; pictures "with no representational purpose" were for him "incomplete technical exercises." He created synthetically an image of reality out of purely pictorial elements, and his greatness results from his having been able to temper intellectual and mathematical calculation with intuition and sensibility. Gris's version of Cubism was more severe and classical, less spontaneous and instinctive, than that of Braque and Picasso; at the same time he was not the victim of a system or theory. Between 1921 and 1927, Gris transformed his synthetic Cubist idiom so that his style became increasingly free, bold and lyrical; formal rhymes abound, curves prevail over angles, the colours are lighter and softer and objects assume more volume. In 1925, his health began to fail and Gris died at Boulogne-sur-Seine on May 11, 1927.

BIBLIOGRAPHY.—D. Cooper (ed.), *Letters of Juan Gris* (1956), *Juan Gris ou Le Goût du Solonnel* (1949); D. H. Kahnweiler, *Juan Gris: His Life and Work* (Eng. trans., 1947). (Ds. Cr.)

GRISAILLE is a kind of decorative painting done in a monochrome of grays, usually handled in severe or bold modeling in the manner of bas-reliefs. In French it is used as a general term to describe any painting technique that employs a completely developed monotone underpainting, in shades of gray or sometimes in brown, over which transparent or translucent oil colours are laid. It distinguishes between such a twofold method of colouring and the direct or alla prima method of putting down the final colours directly, but it does not include the type of painting in which transparent colours or glazes are applied over a multicoloured underpainting. Monochrome or single-toned paintings, or those in which two or three tones are used without regard for actual or realistic colour, intended as finished works in themselves are called camaïeu. Among glass painters the term grisaille has still another meaning: it is the name of a gray vitreous colour or pigment used in the art of colouring glass for stained glass (q.v.). Neither the term grisaille nor the two technical procedures which it denotes are very widely used. Nevertheless monochrome decorations and monochrome underpainting methods are significant in the development of western art, and they have been practised to some extent in every period from Greek times to the present. See also OIL PAINTING, TECHNIQUE OF. (RH. M.)

GRISI, CARLOTTA (1819–1899), was the Italian ballerina who created the title role in Giselle in 1841. Born in Visinada, Italy, June 28, 1819, she studied at the ballet school of La Scala, in Milan. Dancing with Jules Perrot in Naples in 1834, she became his pupil and later his wife.

Following brilliant successes in Vienna and London, she was engaged at the Paris Opéra in 1841. She inspired the profound devotion of Théophile Gautier (q.v.), author of Giselle, who also wrote La Péri for her. She danced in Perrot's Pas de Quatre in London (1845), appeared in Russia, and at the age of 35 retired to Geneva, Switz., where she died, May 20, 1899. (LN. ME.)

GRISI, GIULIA (1811–1869), Italian opera singer, daughter of one of Napoleon's Italian officers, was born in Milan on July 28, 1811. She came from a musical family and made her stage debut in 1828 in Rossini's Zelmira. Later at Milan she was the first Adalgisa in Bellini's Norma, in which Giuditta Pasta took the title part. Grisi first appeared in Paris in 1832 as Semiramide in Rossini's opera, and continued to be successful there until 1849, while in the summers from 1834 onward she appeared in London. Her voice was a brilliant dramatic soprano, and her established position as a prima donna continued for 30 years. In 1830 Bellini wrote for her the part of Giuletta in I Capuleti ed i Montecchi, her sister Giuditta Grisi taking the part of Romeo, and five years later Bellini wrote I Puritani for the great quartet of Grisi, Luigi Lablache,

Giovanni Battista Rubini and Antonio Tamburini. Later, Giovanni Mario took the place of Rubini in this quartet, and for them Donizetti wrote *Don Pasquale*. Grisi married Count Gérard de Melcy in 1836 and, in 1844, Mario (G. M. de Candia), touring the U.S. with him in 1854. She died on Nov. 29, 1869.

GRISON, a weasellike mammal (*Grison* or *Galictis vittata*) found in Central and South America. It is about two feet long with an eight-inch tail. The small ears are broad, Grisons, skilled burrowers, climbers and swimmers, prefer to feed on flesh but will eat berries, nuts, etc. The lower parts are blackish, the back bluish-gray.

A smaller species (*G. furax*) lives in southern Brazil. The so-called least grison (*Lyncodon patagonicus*) occurs in Argentina; it is brown with a whitish crown, blackish nape and gray back. The tayra (*Eira* or *Galera barbara*), an otter, with a long tail and ears, has been confused with the grison.
(J. E. HL.)

ROBERT C. HERMES

GRISON (*GRISON VITTATA*), NATIVE IN CENTRAL AND SOUTH AMERICA

GRISONS: see GRAUBÜNDEN.

GRISWOLD, RUFUS WILMOT (1815–1857), U.S. editor who as literary executor edited the writings of Edgar Allan Poe (1850), was born in Benson, Vt., on Feb. 15, 1815. He was a Baptist clergyman for a time, then became a journalist in New York city, and succeeded Poe as literary editor of *Graham's Magazine* (Philadelphia.). He died in New York city on Aug. 27, 1857.
See Honor McCusker, "The Correspondence of R. W. Griswold" *More Books*, vol. xvi, xviii (1941, 1943), continued by Zoltan Haraszti, *Boston Public Library Quarterly*, vol. ii (1949, 1950); Killis Campbell, "The Poe-Griswold Controversy," *Modern Language Association Publications*, vol. xxxiv, pp. 436–464 (1919); Joy Bayless, *Rufus Wilmot Griswold, Poe's Literary Executor* (1943).

GRIZZLY BEAR (*Ursus horribilis*) and its close relatives include some of the largest bears. The coat colour is brownish to buff; the hairs are usually pale-tipped, producing a frosted, grizzled effect. A large animal may be nine feet long and weigh over 1,000 lb. and can easily kill and carry a cow. The height of these bears at the shoulders produces a humped appearance. Because of their great bulk and long, straight claws, they seldom climb, even as cubs.

Formerly they occurred over western North America from northern Alaska to central Mexico, especially in open country. Because of their aversion to man, the disappearance of suitable food and relentless hunting they are almost extinct in the United States and Mexico and much reduced in numbers elsewhere. They are omnivorous, feeding on big game, rodents, fish, berries and occasionally even grass. Food is often cached in shallow holes and covered with brush or grass. The grizzly digs readily in search of rodents, often leaving a hillside thoroughly plowed. The home range of a grizzly may comprise several hundred square miles. A methodical animal, it prefers well-developed trails, each passing animal treading in the footsteps of its predecessor until the trail is deeply rutted. Despite their great bulk, grizzlies are surprisingly agile and when pressed run with a light gallop as fast as 30 m.p.h. When fleeing or charging, they can crash through brushy thickets or deep, matted grass with seeming ease. They are unpredictable, often sullen and ill-tempered and exceedingly dangerous when they feel themselves threatened. *See also* BEAR; CARNIVORE.

GROCK (stage name of CHARLES ADRIEN WETTACH) (1880–1959), the clown whose blunders with piano and violin became proverbial, was born at Moulin de Loveresse, near Reconvilier, Switz., on Jan. 10, 1880. His father, a watchmaker, was an amateur acrobat, and his son grew up with such a love of the sawdust ring that he was allowed to spend each summer with a circus, where he performed first as a tumbler and then as a violinist, pianist and xylophonist. When he was 19 he clowned in a café, but the draw of the circus proved irresistible, though it brought him a wandering life of hardship from Hamburg to Bucharest. He then became the partner of a clown named Brick, and changed his name to Grock on Oct. 7, 1903. Together they appeared in France, North Africa and South America. When Brick married, Grock joined the celebrated Antonet. At Berlin, appearing on a stage instead of in an arena, they failed at first; but by mastering the stage technique they obtained, through C. B. Cochran, an engagement at the Palace theatre, London, in 1911. Two years later Grock, with an anonymous partner, perfected those adventures of a simpleton among musical instruments that to where the strings had gone when he held his fiddle the wrong side up, and at his labours to sit nearer the piano by pushing it toward the stool. In 1924 he left England and remained on the continent until his farewell at Hamburg in 1954. He died at Imperia, Italy, on July 14, 1959.

Grock wrote several books, among which is his autobiography, *Die Memoiren des Königs der Clowns* (1956), translated by Basil Creighton as *Grock, King of Clowns* (1957).
(M. W. D.)

GROCYN, WILLIAM (c. 1446–1519), humanist scholar and reputedly the first Englishman to teach Greek, was born at Colerne in Wiltshire. He entered Winchester college in 1463 and New college, Oxford, in 1465, becoming a fellow two years later. If he learned Greek before visiting Italy, as Erasmus claims, his teacher was probably a Greek scribe working at Oxford, John Serbopoulos, or Emanuel of Constantinople. He was divinity reader at Magdalen college (1483–88) and disputed before Richard III. He then visited Italy (1488–90) where he attended the lectures of Politian and Demetrius Chalcondyles at Florence. In 1491 he returned to Oxford, to Exeter college, and five years later accepted a living in London. There he taught Thomas More and met Erasmus in 1499. He lectured (1501) on the *Ecclesiastical Hierarchy* of Dionysius the Areopagite and correctly questioned the identification of the author with the Dionysius of Acts xvii, 34. In 1506 he became warden of All Hallows college, Maidstone, where he died in 1519. His only published work is a letter printed in Aldo Manuzio's *Astronomici veteres* (1499). The manuscripts copied for him by Serbopoulos show him interested in Greek primarily as an aid to theological studies. But as a friend of John Colet and Thomas Linacre, who sympathized with the new learning, he certainly helped to prepare the ground for the rise of English humanism.
See M. Burrows' memoir of Grocyn, *Collectanea*, 2nd series, part 5 (1890); R. Weiss, *Humanism in England during the Fifteenth Century* (1957).
(R. R. Bo.)

GRODNO, an *oblast* and town in the Belorussian Soviet Socialist Republic of the U.S.S.R. The *oblast* covers 9,652 sq.mi. (25,000 sq.km.) in the northwest of the republic. Pop. (1970 prelim.) 1,121,000. It was formed in 1944 from former Polish territory and in 1960 the southwestern part of the former Molodechno Oblast was added to it. Most of the *oblast* consists of the level, often swampy plain of the Neman River. Around the western, southern, and eastern margins rises a series of morainic uplands, the Grodnenskiye, Volkovyskiye, Slonim, and Novogrudskiye, the last reaching 1,060 ft. in Zamkova Gora. The Neman Lowlands (Nemanskaya Nizina) have sandy or alluvial soils, often acidic, with considerable mixed forest cover in which pine is dominant. Along the rivers are broad meadows. The uplands have been cleared for agriculture and much gully erosion has occurred.

Of the population in 1970 only 33% (369,000) was urban. Most are Belorussians, although there are also Russians, Lithuanians, and Poles. Most Poles were removed to Poland after World War II. Agriculture forms the most important sector of the economy, with the emphasis on cattle and dairy produce, based on abundant natural pasture, and in the upland areas on industrial crops, especially sugar beet, flax, and tobacco. Rye and oats are the dominant grains. Industry is chiefly concerned with processing agricultural products and timber working. There is a large cardboard mill at Albertin.

Grodno, the administrative centre of the *oblast*, lies on the Neman River. Pop. (1970 prelim.) 132,000. It is one of the oldest Russian towns and is first mentioned in 1126, when it was already the seat of a princedom with a stormy history. It was sacked by the Tatars in 1241 and by the Teutonic knights in 1284 and 1391. In the 13th century Grodno was taken by the Lithuanians who made it their capital, Gardinas. It later came under Poland. There Stephen (István) Báthory, king of Poland, died in 1586. The second partition of Poland was signed there in 1793 and Grodno passed to Russia by the third partition of 1795. From 1919 to 1939, the city was once more under Polish rule. Many architectural relics of its varied history remain: the 12th-century princes' chapel and Borisogleb Church, the late 16th- to early 17th-century *fara* (parish) church, and two castles, that of Báthory, built about 1580, and that of Augustus III, of the 18th century. Modern Grodno is a growing chemical centre, making nitrogenous fertilizer and man-made fibre, with the use of natural gas piped from Dashava in the Ukraine. It also makes electrical equipment, vehicle parts, glass, furniture, tobacco and food products, textiles, leather goods, and shoes.

(R. A. F.)

GROENER, WILHELM (1867–1939), German general of World War I and Democratic statesman under the Weimar republic, was born on Nov. 22, 1867, at Ludwigsburg, Württemberg. He became a Württemberg officer in 1884 and head of the railway section of the German general staff in 1914. When war broke out he was responsible for the rail arrangements for the concentration of the armies and their subsequent reinforcement and supply by rail in both west and east. From May 1916 until Aug. 1917 he was head of the personnel and supply departments of the war office, but his solicitude for the munitions workers and his fight against war profiteers brought him into conflict with the supreme command, and he was sent to the eastern front.

On Oct. 26, 1918, Groener succeeded Ludendorff as quartermaster general. Together with Hindenburg, he brought about the emperor William II's abdication. After the armistice he showed considerable ability and political finesse in bringing the troops home and co-operating with Friedrich Ebert against the threat of a Communist dictatorship. Perhaps more than any other man he was responsible for maintaining the discipline of the army in the immediate postwar period.

Having retired from the army in 1919, Groener entered politics and joined the Democratic party. He was minister of communications from June 1920 to Aug. 1923, minister of defense from 1928 to 1932 and, from 1931, minister of the interior as well. His rigorous measures against the National Socialist storm troopers caused his dismissal by Hindenburg. He died at Bornstedt, near Potsdam, on May 3, 1939. His studies of generals Alfred von Schlieffen (*Das Testament des Grafen Schlieffen*, 1927) and the younger Moltke (*Der Feldherr wider Willen*, 1930) are military classics.

(C. N. B.)

GROEN VAN PRINSTERER, GUILLAUME (1801–1876), Dutch Protestant political leader, religious thinker and historian to whom can be traced the Antirevolutionary and Christian-Historical trend in the Netherlands party system, was born at Voorburg near The Hague, on Aug. 21, 1801. He studied at Leiden university and from 1827 to 1833 acted as secretary to King William I of the Netherlands. A liberal in his early years, Groen was converted in about 1830 to a strictly orthodox dogmatism, becoming one of the pillars of the Reveil, a religious revival and anti-Liberal movement. He became critical of the "enlightened," vaguely Christian and undogmatic character of a church open to state interference. He defended for a time the denominational state schools in the belief that the state had to provide an orthodox Protestant education for all Protestant children. In politics Groen was influenced by conservative thinkers such as Edmund Burke, Karl Ludwig von Haller (1768–1854) and, afterward, Friedrich Julius Stahl (1802–1861), and he prepared the way for the subsequent foundation of the Antirevolutionary party formed in 1878 in opposition to the principles of the French Revolution. As a theoretical scholar and an aristocrat, lacking organizational capacities, he was not capable of rallying the orthodox lower middle classes. Nevertheless, he must be considered to be a founder of the typically Dutch denominational party system. Although Groen was a member of the second chamber (1849–57 and 1862–65) his significance rests on his published works. His handbook of Dutch history (1st ed. 1846) gives his views on the

providential genesis of the Dutch republic and makes the same Protestant claims for the kingdom as well. In *Ongeloof en Revolutie* (1847) he identified unbelief with the spirit of the French Revolution. He was the main opponent of the Liberal leader and minister J. R. Thorbecke. That he promulgated a manifesto of principles rather than a political program is demonstrated by his words about himself: "A statesman—no, a follower of the Gospel." As a historian he edited many documents about the rise of the Dutch republic. He died at The Hague on May 19, 1876.

BIBLIOGRAPHY.—T. de Vries, *Mr. Guillaume Groen van Prinsterer, een bibliografie* (1908); P. A. Diepenhorst, *Groen van Prinsterer* (1932); H. Smitskamp, *Groen van Prinsterer als historicus* (1940); *see* also chapters in P. Geyl, *Reacties* (1952). (H. A. Bo.)

GROIN, in architecture, the edges formed at the intersections of two vaults at an angle to each other. If the vaults intersect at right angles and are of the same height and radius, these intersections will all lie on a vertical plane at 45° to the planes of the two vaults. If, however, one vault is lower than the other, or the curvatures are different, winding and distorted curves will result. Both the Roman and Renaissance constructors of vaults frequently regularized the rib shapes and slightly warped the surfaces of the vaults until they met at this regularized groin line. Thus in the coved, penetrated ceilings of the 16th century, where an elliptical vault was intersected by smaller vaults, the

EDWIN SMITH

GROIN VAULTING AS SEEN AT THE CHURCH AT LASTINGHAM PRIORY, YORKSHIRE

groins would often be given simple segmental curves, meeting at a point in the centre of each penetration, and the smaller vaults forming the penetrations given a surface almost conical in order to meet this line. The term Welsh groin is often applied to the groin resulting from such an intersection of a smaller cross vault with a higher main vault. In the medieval period, when ribbed vaulting became common, the groin ribs under the groins (groin ribs or diagonal ribs), being built first, were usually on curves lying in a simple plane. The web, or filling in of small stones between the ribs, could be warped or twisted at will, so as to start correctly from the wall or cross ribs of different sizes and yet meet over the groin rib. *See* ARCH AND VAULT.

GROLIER, JEAN, VICOMTE D'AGUISY (1479–1565), French bibliophile, well known as a patron of writers and printers, was born at Lyons, the son of Étienne Grolier. Between 1509 and 1521 he was treasurer to the French army in Italy and subsequently became one of the four treasurers of France. He was the friend of the scholar and humanist Guillaume Budé and patron of the Aldi, the famous family of printers (*see* MANUTIUS). Of his great library of 3,000 volumes, dispersed in 1676, about 550 are known to be in existence. They are richly bound in morocco or calf decorated with intricate designs in gold and colours, bearing the *ex libris* of their owner *Jo. Grolierii et amicorum*. Many also bear his motto, the prayer *Portio mea, Domine, sit in terra viventium* ("O Lord, may my portion be in the land of the living:" *cf.* Ps. cxlii, 5). There is an early series of 25 decorated in Milan with plaquettes, but the majority were bound by the best Parisian binders of the day. Grolier was also famous for his large collection of coins and medals. He died in Paris on Oct. 22, 1565.

See A. Le Roux de Lincy, *Researches Concerning Jean Grolier*, rev. and trans. by C. Shipman (1907); G. D. Hobson, *Notes on Grolier* (1929). (H. M. N.)

GROMATICI (AGRIMENSORES), in the ancient Roman world, were land surveyors and later writers about land surveying. The word is derived from *groma* or *gruma*, the special pole used by the surveyors who were called at first *finitores*, then usually *mensores* or (like the writers) *agrimensores*, "field measurers." Land surveying for civil ownership, camps and communities, cultivation and for census, probably begun by the augurs, was developed through the republican era into a trained and paid profession, with schools, mathematical and legal knowledge and a didactic literature, which flourished from the 1st to the 6th century A.D. The surviving writings deal with rules of land tenure, mensuration, marking of boundaries and making of maps.

The first recorded professional surveyor is L. Decidius Saxa (d. 40 B.C.), and the first recorded writing is one attributed to Sextus Julius Frontinus (q.v.) of which extracts survive in a commentary on it. Next there is a handbook on geometry for land surveyors, based perhaps on a work by Hero of Alexandria (q.v.), ascribed to one Balbus who served under the emperor Trajan in Dacia in A.D. 101-104. About the same time one (or possibly two persons) known as Hyginus Gromaticus wrote four treatises, surviving in part, on boundaries, land disputes and land tenure. Somewhat later M. Junius Nipsus wrote about mensuration, boundary stones and surveying of rivers; fragments survive. The *De controversiis agrorum* by Siculus Flaccus is complete, as is Innocentius' strange so-called *De casis litterarum* (portions of land named from letters of the alphabet) written in obscure and barbarous Latin, perhaps for practice in map reading in schools in the 4th or the 5th century. Some treatises attributed to the 6th-century philosopher Boethius (q.v.) can hardly belong to him. There are also a few other records and extracts, probably of the 5th century, from official registers connected with colonial and other surveys, passages from the law code of the emperor Theodosius II and lists and descriptions of boundary stones. Some boundary stones also survive.

BIBLIOGRAPHY.—Writings: F Blume, K Lachmann *et al.*, *Gromatici Veteres* (*Schriften der römischen Feldmesser*), 2 vol. (1848-52); C. Thulin, *Corpus Agrimensorum Romanorum* (1913-) in the Teubner series. See also E. Fabricius in Pauly-Wissowa, *Real-Encyclopädie der classischen Altertumswissenschaft*, vol. xiii, 672-701 (1926); A. Déléage in *Études de Papyrologie*, vol. ii, pp. 147 ff. (1934); Sir H. Lyons, "Ancient Surveying Instruments," in *Geographical Journal*, vol. lxix, pp. 137 ff. (1927).

(E. H. W.)

GRONINGEN, a province and town of the Netherlands. Groningen province is the most northerly in the country and is bounded south by Drenthe, west by Friesland and the Lauwers Zee, north and northeast by the Wadden Zee and the Ems estuary (with the Dollart) and southeast by Germany. It includes the island Rottumeroog, belonging to the Frisian Islands (q.v.). Pop. (1971 est.) 522,400. The sandy tongue of the Hondsrug extends from the Drenthe plateau into Groningen, the capital. The northern part of the province is flat and consists of marine clay or sandy clay, the latter especially in the reclaimed estuaries that in the early middle ages intersected this region, and in the reclaimed polders of later times along the northern coast. The reclaimed inundation of the Dollart (15th century) consists of a heavy marine clay. The southwest of the province (southern Westerkwartier) has mainly sandy soil. Except for the sandy islands of the Westerwolds region, the southeast of the province until the end of the 16th century formed an extensive peat bog. Its reclamation was started with a vast network of canals through which the excavated peat was exported. Subsequently the sandy subsoil, transformed into arable land by manuring and fertilizing, became an agricultural region (*Groninger Veenkoloniën*). The morass on the German border had been long considered a natural frontier and so its impassable condition was retained and it was not until the second half of the 19th century that the work of reclamation was begun.

The rivers of Groningen descending from the Drenthe plateau meet at the capital, whence they are continued by the Reitdiep to the Lauwers Zee (closed by dikes in 1969); the Ems canal (1876) connects with the Ems at Delfzijl. The southeastern corner of the province is traversed by the Westerwolde Aa, which discharges into the Dollart Zee. The railways afford communication with the rest of the Netherlands and with Germany (Bremen).

On the clay regions agriculture is the main industry with wheat, barley, oats, potatoes, sugar beet and oil seeds as the most important crops. The holdings are in general large by Dutch standards, often more than 250 ac., and there is a high proportion of landowners. Cattle rearing is concentrated in a low-lying clay region round the capital exclusively devoted to grass. In the *Veenkoloniën* agriculture has specialized in rye, oats and potatoes, and this type of agriculture has been adopted by the adjoining regions of Westerwolde and the Woldstreek. By heavy manuring a high yield of straw is acquired, to be worked in the strawboard factories. The southern Westerkwartier has mixed farming with much cattle rearing. Horse breeding and equestrian sports form a favourite activity in most agricultural regions of the province.

Groningen, the only large town (*see below*), has various industries. The *Veenkoloniën* is the most industrialized district of the province, with potato flour mills, chemical industries, strawboard, paper and cardboard factories and engineering (Hoogezand, Veendam); shipbuilding yards (Hoogezand); electrotechnical industries (Stadskanaal); and textile and hosiery (Wildervank, Ter Apel). Groningen by the Ems ship canal, is an important port (imports: coal, wood, artificial fertilizers; exports: strawboard, potato flour, salt); moreover it has large chemical industries and aluminum manufacturing. Winschoten is a marketing and shopping centre.

The history of the province is chiefly of the almost continuous quarrels between the town of Groningen and the surrounding districts. During the middle ages these districts consisted of a number of independent farmers' republics (Hunsingo, Fivelgo, etc.), forming together the Ommelanden, whereas the town kept their own government, finance and sometimes even their own army. Although Groningen at length succeeded in acquiring a dominant position in the region (*e.g.*, in getting the supremacy in the Oldambt in 1401, in buying the seigniory of Westerwolde in 1619 and taking an important part in the reclaiming of the peat bog region), the disputes persisted. Thus the Ommelanden joined the revolt against the Spaniards, whereas the town of Groningen remained loyal to the Spanish king. After 1594 the two parties were merged into one republic, but until the French occupation the Ommelanden kept their own government. Only in 1795 were the town and the Ommelanden united into one province.

GRONINGEN TOWN, the capital of the province, lies at the confluence of the two canalized rivers the Drentsche Aa and the Hunse (which are continued to the Lauwers Zee as the Reitdiep), 16 mi. N. of Assen and 33 mi. E. of Leeuwarden by rail. Pop. (1971 est., 171,334 [mun.]). The ancient part of the town is still surrounded by the former moat and in the centre lies a group of market places. The chief church is the Martinikerk, founded in the 13th century but in its present form dating from 1452; the Akerk was founded in 1253. The provincial museum of antiquities contains an interesting Germanic collection, as well as medieval and modern porcelain, and pictures. The old Ommelanderhuis, the former extraterritorial site of the representatives of the Ommelanden, is the remaining part of the *refugium* of an abbey; there were many of these *refugia* in the town belonging to a number of powerful abbeys in the Ommelanden. There are many ancient and picturesque foundations for old people and 16th- and 17th-century brick houses. The University of Groningen, founded in 1614, has among its auxiliary establishments a large modern hospital and a library which contains a copy of Erasmus' New Testament with marginal annotations by Martin Luther.

Groningen is the centre from which several important canals radiate. It is the junction of railways and motor bus services. The importance of Groningen is both administrative and commercial. It maintains a considerable trade, chiefly in cereals, oilseed, wood and cattle. It is also a shopping centre for the whole province and for large parts of the adjoining provinces of Drenthe and Friesland. The chief industries are men's clothing, sugar refining, book printing, tobacco, coffee and tea, chemicals for agriculture, machinery and bicycles.

The town of Groningen, mentioned first in 1006, originally belonged to the tribe Triantha (Drenthe), the countship of which was bestowed in 1024 on the bishop of Utrecht. In 1040 the emperor Henry III gave the church of Utrecht the royal domain of Groningen, where down to the 15th century the bishops were represented by a prefect or burgrave, whose authority also extended over the neighbouring districts known as the Gorecht; in 1460 the bishop of Utrecht finally sold to the city his rights over the Gorecht. Originally an agricultural settlement, trade and commerce gradually developed because of its situation on the navigable river Aa. Already in the 13th century Groningen merchants were trading in the Baltic. About the same time the town, sometimes aided by the neighbouring Frisians, succeeded in freeing itself from the episcopal yoke. The city was walled in 1255; before 1284 it had become a member of the Hanseatic League; and by the end of the 14th century it was practically an independent republic, which to a high degree also controlled the (Frisian) Ommelanden between the Ems and the Lauwers Zee.

The medieval constitution of Groningen, unlike that of Utrecht, was aristocratic. There were no merchant guilds and the craft guilds were without direct influence on the city government that held them in subjection. Membership of the governing council was confined to men of approved "wisdom," and "wisdom" was measured in terms of money. This *raad* of wealthy burghers gradually monopolized all power. The council was supreme and in 1439 it decreed that no one might trade in the district between the Ems and the Lauwers Zee except burghers and those who had purchased the right of residence in the city and the freedom of the guilds. In 1536 the city passed into the hands of the emperor Charles V, and in the great wars of the 16th century suffered all the miseries of siege and military occupation. From 1581 onward, Groningen, still held by the Spaniards, was constantly at war with the Ommelanden which had declared against the king of Spain. In 1672 the town was besieged by the bishop of Münster, but it was successfully defended and in 1698 its fortifications were improved under Menno van Coehoorn's direction. The French Republicans were in control from 1795 until 1814. The fortifications of the city were pulled down in 1874. German troops occupied Groningen during the invasion of May 1940 and destroyed the centre of the city on their retreat in April 1945. It has since been rebuilt.

(H. J. Ke.)

GROOTE, GERHARD (GEERT GROOT or GROETE; Lat. GERARDUS MAGNUS) (1340–1384), founder of the Brethren of the Common Life (*q.v.*) and also (through his disciple Florentius Radewyns) of the Windesheim Congregation of Canons Regular, was the father of the *devotio moderna*, the influential spiritual movement of the 15th century. Born of a wealthy family at Deventer, Neth., he was well educated (arts, canon and civil law, medicine, theology) at Aachen, Cologne, Paris and Prague. Influenced by a Carthusian friend, he abandoned the worldly life he was leading, renounced his two benefices (Utrecht and Aachen) and many possessions, gave over most of his home to devout women (first beginning of the Sisters of Common Life) and on the advice of Jan van Ruysbroeck (*q.v.*) went to a Carthusian monastery (*c.* 1375). Desiring apostolic activity, he left after two years, was ordained deacon (never a priest) and began zealously preaching the gospel in the diocese of Utrecht. His preaching was immensely fruitful, but he made enemies by rebuking lax priests and religious. They persuaded the bishop to retract his permission to preach. Groote obeyed but appealed to the pope. Before the response came, he died on Aug. 20, 1384. By preaching Groote gathered many disciples who became the nucleus of the Brethren of the Common Life, and from them was formed, at Groote's direction but after his death, the Windesheim congregation. Through these two groups he had his greatest influence, especially in spirituality. His spirituality was affective, practical, moderate and methodical. Groote has been claimed to be the author of *The Imitation of Christ* (*q.v.*).

See A. Hyma, *Brethren of the Common Life* (1950), with a biography of Groote, a history of the Brethren of the Common Life and the Windesheim congregation and a fine bibliography.   (T. G. O'C.)

GROPIUS, WALTER (1883–1969). German-U.S. architect. internationally famous for his leadership in modern architecture. was born May 18, 1883, in Berlin. After a brilliant early start. continued struggles against the German ruling taste made his life and career difficult. From 1903 to 1907 he studied at the institutes of technology in Berlin and Munich. He was Peter Behrens' chief assistant in Berlin from 1907 to 1910, and in 1910 he set up his own architectural practice.

With his design of the Fagus works at Alfeld (1911). Gropius became, as Ludwig Mies van der Rohe put it, "with one stroke one of the leading architects of Europe." By employing an interior

ARTHUR HERZOG FROM BLACK STAR

GROPIUS

framework of steel, Gropius eliminated the need for supportive walls. His walls, light and transparent—later known as curtain walls—functioned only to admit light and as protection from the elements. The Fagus factory is preserved as a national monument.

At the Werkbund Exhibition at Cologne (1914), great architectural excitement was aroused by Gropius' model factory connected to an administration building, with its transparent staircase and glass-walled offices and roof terrace. Among his other exhibits were: the Paris Exhibition's "Salon des Artistes Decorateurs" (1930) and the Pennsylvania Pavilion for the New York World's Fair (1939). His famous Bauhaus at Dessau (1925–26) revealed the potentialities of new forms and spaces in a large building complex composed of two schools and a students' dormitory. The glass curtain wall, drawn around the corners of the main building, dominated the scene. The Impington Village College, Cambridge, Eng. (1936), was designed to provide for the education of both children and adults. His most important work in the United States is the Harvard graduate centre (1949–50).

Gropius' faith in teamwork is rooted in his qualities as a teacher. That the Bauhaus at Weimar and Dessau (1919–28) could stand up against its adversaries is a tribute to his talent for inspiring associates to cooperate in the service of an ideal. This emphasis on teamwork was largely responsible for his great influence as chairman of the graduate school of design at Harvard (1937–52). In all his activities he sought to bridge the gulf between artistic form and industrial production. At the Bauhaus students were required to learn at firsthand the problems of the craftsman in production. From 1934 to 1937 Gropius was a voluntary exile in London until he was summoned to Harvard. Beginning in 1946, as founder and member of the Architects' Collaborative, he associated himself successfully with young American architects engaged in extensive building activity, including the U.S. embassy in Athens (1957). Gropius' plans for Iraq's University of Baghdad were being executed in the early 1970s, as were various other projects of the Architects' Collaborative, including a satellite city (Gropiusstadt) outside Berlin, a medical complex in Boston, and the IBM World Trade Centre in Teheran. Gropius died on July 5, 1969, in Boston, Mass. *See further* BAUHAUS; MODERN ARCHITECTURE; and references under "Gropius, Walter" in the Index.

BIBLIOGRAPHY.—H. Bayer, W. Gropius, and I. Gropius (eds.), *Bauhaus, 1919–1928* (1952); S. Giedion, *Walter Gropius: Work and Teamwork* (1954); James Marston Fitch, *Walter Gropius*, Masters of World Architecture Series (1960); Hans Wingler, *The Bauhaus* (1969)

(S. GN.: X.)

GROS, ANTOINE JEAN, BARON (1771–1835), French (history) painter especially known for his pictures of Napoleon's campaigns, was born in Paris on March 16, 1771, the son of a painter of miniatures, who gave him his first lessons in painting and drawing. Toward the end of 1785 he entered the studio of J. L. David; while revering him as a teacher, he was equally impressed by the works of Rubens, whose influence can be seen in his brilliant colouring and crowded compositions. In 1793, with David's help, Gros went to Italy, made his way to Genoa, and there met Joséphine de Beauharnais and through her his hero Napoleon. In 1796 he followed the French army to Arcole and was present when Napoleon planted the flag on the bridge, an incident commemorated in his first major work, "Napoleon sur le Pont d'Arcole" (Louvre, Paris). Napoleon gave him the formal rank of *inspecteur aux revues*, which enabled him to accompany the army on its campaigns, and he also served on the commission to select works of art from Italy for the Louvre.

The Salon of 1804 saw the second of Gros's masterpieces, "Les Pestiférés de Jaffa" (Louvre), which shows Napoleon not only visiting the leper hospital but touching the sores in the way that former kings of France touched for the plague. This was followed two years later by "La Bataille d'Aboukir" (Versailles), of which the hero is Murat, and in 1808 by "La Bataille d'Eylau" (Versailles), in which Napoleon on the battlefield almost has the attributes of sanctity. Although he continued to paint large compositions containing passages of fine painting ("Départ de Louis XVIII," 1815, Versailles.), Gros never repeated the great climaxes of Jaffa or Eylau. The decoration of the dome of Ste. Geneviève (1811) is a cold and disconnected work. After the fall of Napoleon, Gros's finest pictures were portraits, many of which are masterpieces; e.g., "Jeune Fille au Collier de Jais" (Musée Magnin, Dijon), "Mme Récamier âgée" (Zagreb).

Constantly worried by David's criticism of his work, Gros made an effort to paint in a more academic, classical manner, in the ceiling of the Egyptian room of the Louvre in 1824. But it was too late; his brilliant, crowded compositions of some 20 years earlier had already sown the seeds of the Romantic reaction to classicism. Eugène Delacroix and Théodore Géricault would not have been possible without Gros. A sense of failure exacerbated his already strong tendency toward melancholia and on June 26, 1835, he was found drowned in the Seine.

BIBLIOGRAPHY.—E. J. Delécluze, *Louis David, son école et son temps* (1855); J. B. Delestre (pupil of Gros), *Gros, sa vie et ses ouvrages* (1867); G. Dargenty, *Le Baron Gros* (1887).

(AA. B.)

GROSE, FRANCIS (c. 1731-1791), English antiquary and artist, was born at Greenford, Middlesex. He studied art and for some years after 1769 exhibited at the Royal Academy, but his main interests were in antiquities, heraldry and military affairs. He was Richmond herald from 1755 until 1763 when he resigned to become adjutant and paymaster of the Hampshire militia. Grose was also captain and adjutant of the Surrey militia from 1778 until his death. He produced several serious books on military history, among them *Military Antiquities*, two volumes (1786-88), and a satire, *Advice to the Officers of the British Army* (1782).

Grose was elected fellow of the Society of Antiquaries in 1757 and his most important works arose from a fusion of antiquarianism and the picturesque, so much in vogue in the late 18th century. He had run through the money left him by his father and producing these historical and topographical works became one of his main sources of livelihood. The series began in 1773 with *The Antiquities of England and Wales*, six volumes (1773-87); then followed a tour through Scotland in 1789, when he met Robert Burns, which led to the publication of *The Antiquities of Scotland*, two volumes (1789-91). It was while Grose was touring to gather material for a similar work on Ireland that he died in Dublin on June 12, 1791. *The Antiquities of Ireland*, two volumes (1791-95), was completed by Edward Ledwich.

GROSSETESTE, ROBERT (c. 1168-1253), bishop of Lincoln, *magister scholarum* (or chancellor) of the University of Oxford and one of the greatest of medieval statesmen and philosophical scholars, was born in Suffolk, Eng., according to most authorities of humble parents. He was educated possibly first at Lincoln, then at Oxford, and was in the household of William de Vere, bishop of Hereford, by 1198. He then almost certainly taught at Oxford (before 1209), and he must have taken his mastership in theology, probably at Paris, at some time before his appointment to the office of chancellor of the university. He held this office, though with the title of master of the schools, probably c. 1215-21. He was given a number of ecclesiastical preferments and sinecures, including the archdeaconry of Leicester (1229), but in 1232 he resigned them all except for a prebend at Lincoln, writing to his sister, a nun; "If I am poorer by my own choice, I am made richer in virtues." From 1229 or 1230 to 1235 Grosseteste was first *lector* (lecturer) in theology to the Franciscans, who had come to Oxford in 1224. His influence there was profound, and continued after he left Oxford in 1235 on becoming bishop of Lincoln, in whose diocese Oxford lay and under whose jurisdiction its schools came. He contributed largely to directing the interests of the English Franciscans toward the study of the Bible, of languages and of mathematics and natural science. During his episcopate he attended the Council of Lyons in 1245 and argued before the papal curia at Lyons again in 1250. He died on Oct. 9, 1253, at Buckden, Buckinghamshire, and was buried in Lincoln cathedral.

Grosseteste's career thus falls into two main parts, the first that of a university scholar and teacher and the second that of a bishop and ecclesiastical statesman. His writings fall roughly into the same periods, to the former belonging his commentaries on Aristotle and on the Bible and the bulk of a number of independent treatises, and to the latter his translations from the Greek. Living at a time when western intellectual horizons were being greatly extended by the Latin translations of Greek and Arabic philosophical and scientific writings, Grosseteste took a leading part in introducing this new learning into the world of Latin Christendom. His commentary on Aristotle's *Posterior Analytics* was one of the first and most influential of the medieval commentaries on this fundamental work. Other important writings belonging to the first period are his commentary on Aristotle's *Physics*, independent treatises on astronomy and cosmology, the calendar (with intelligent proposals for the reform of the inaccurate calendar then in use), sound, comets, heat, optics (including lenses and the rainbow) and other scientific subjects, and his scriptural commentaries, especially the *Moralitates in evangelica*, *De cessacione legalium*, *Hexaemeron* and commentaries on the Pauline Epistles and the Psalms. Having begun to study Greek in 1230-31, he used his learning fruitfully during the period of his episcopate by making Latin translations of Aristotle's *Nicomachean Ethics* and *De caelo* (with Simplicius' commentary), of the *De fide orthodoxa* of John of Damascus, of pseudo-Dionysius and of other theological writings. For this work he brought to Lincoln assistants who knew Greek; he also arranged for a translation of the Psalms to be made from the Hebrew and seems himself to have learned something of the language.

Though in content a somewhat eclectic blend of Aristotelian and Neoplatonic ideas, Grosseteste's philosophical thinking shows a strong intellect curious about natural things and searching for a consistently rational scheme of things both natural and divine. His search for rational explanations was conducted within the framework of the Aristotelian distinction between "the fact" (*quia*) and "the reason for the fact" (*propter quid*). In natural philosophy he thought the latter to be provided only by mathematical explanations which he based specifically on his theory that the fundamental corporeal substance was light. He held that light was the first form to be created in prime matter, propagating itself from an original point into a sphere and thus giving rise to spatial dimensions and all else according to immanent laws. Hence his conception of optics as the basis of science. Grosseteste's rational scheme included revelation as well as reason, and he was one of the first medieval thinkers to attempt to deal with the conflict between the Scriptures and the new Aristotle. Especially interesting are his discussions of the problems of the eternity or creation of the world, of the relation of will to intellect, of angelology, of divine knowledge of particulars and of the use of allegorical interpretations of Scripture.

Grosseteste's public life as bishop of Lincoln was informed by both his outlook on the universe as a scholar and his conception of his duties as a prelate dedicated to the salvation of souls. In particular, he was governed by three principles: a belief in the supreme importance of the cure of souls; a highly centralized and hierarchical conception of the church, in which the papacy, under God, is the centre and source of spiritual life and energy; and a belief in the superiority of the church over the state, because its function, the salvation of souls, is more vital. Such views were widely accepted, but Grosseteste was unique in the ruthlessness and thoroughness with which he applied them. He was thus led to challenge the widespread practice whereby ecclesiastical benefices, intended for the cure of souls, were used to endow officials in the service of the crown and the papacy. This led him, among other things, to criticize papal provisions, not as a general principle, for he believed that the pope had the right to dispose of all benefices, but where he thought the practice led to unsuitable appointments. He expounded his views on this in a memorandum presented to the pope at Lyons in 1250, and in 1253, in a famous letter to a papal notary, he refused to admit the pope's nephew to a canonry at Lincoln. Similarly he was prepared to oppose any ecclesiastical corporation which seemed to him to be obstructing the disciplinary work of the church, and this brought him into conflict with his own cathedral chapter of Lincoln. On the other hand as well as actively encouraging the Franciscans in the pursuit of learning, he welcomed the friars for pastoral reasons and was glad to use them as missioners.

His views also brought him into conflict with the crown, particularly where he thought royal writs of prohibition were impeding the jurisdiction or discipline of the church, or where the secular law clashed with church law, as over the question of bastardy (see ENGLISH HISTORY: *The Personal Rule of Henry III*), or where churchmen were employed as judges or in other secular offices; there was strong opposition from the king when he tried to make laymen give evidence on oath at diocesan visitations.

Grosseteste was a close friend of the Franciscan Adam Marsh and of Simon de Montfort. He was to some extent De Montfort's spiritual director and took charge of the education of his sons; but the degree to which Grosseteste shared in or influenced De Montfort's political ideals has probably been exaggerated. As Sir Maurice Powicke has put it, he was not an Englishman with a grievance; he was a bishop with an ideal. After Stephen Langton Grosseteste is probably the greatest example in 13th-century England of the new type of bishop trained in the universities.

BIBLIOGRAPHY.—H. Luard (ed.), *Roberti Grosseteste epistolae* (1861); F. N. Davis (ed.), *Rotuli Roberti Grosseteste episcopi Lincolniensis* (1913). *See also* L. Baur, *Die philosophischen Werke des Robert Grosseteste* (1912) and *Die Philosophie des Robert Grosseteste* (1917); E. Franceschini, "Roberto Grossatesta .. e le sue traduzioni latine," *Atti del reale instituto Veneto di scienze lettere ed arti*, vol. xciii (1933); D. E. Sharp, *Franciscan Philosophy at Oxford in the Thirteenth Century* (1930); S. H. Thomson, *The Writings of Robert Grosseteste* (1940) and "Grosseteste's *Questio de calore, de cometis and de operacionibus solis*," *Medievalia et humanistica*, vol. xi (1957); A. C. Crombie, *Robert Grosseteste and the Origins of Experimental Science, 1100–1700* (1953); R. C. Dales, "Robert Grosseteste's *Commentarius in octo libros physicorum Aristotelis*," *Medievalia et humanistica*, vol. xi (1957). For biographical accounts *see* F. S. Stevenson, *Robert Grosseteste* (1899); D. A. Callus, "The Oxford Career of Robert Grosseteste," *Oxoniensia*, vol. x (1945) and (ed.) *Robert Grosseteste* (1955). (A. C. CE.)

GROSSETO, an episcopal see and the chief town of the province of the same name in Tuscany, Italy, lies 70 km. (43 mi.) southwest of Siena and 12 km. (7½ mi.) inland from the Tyrrhenian sea. Pop. (1961) 51,842 (commune). It is in a low-lying plain (until the 18th century a malarial swamp) through which flows the Ombrone river. (The river flooded the town and its country disastrously in 1966.) The old town is enclosed by a hexagonal wall (mainly 16th century); a projecting corner of a bastion bears the arms of the Medici (15th century). The new town was much developed after 1930. The Duomo (1190, restored 1294 and later) has a Romanesque façade of red and white striped marble; the interior is in the form of a Latin cross. The churches of S. Pietro and S. Francesco are of the 14th century. The archaeological museum contains Etruscan and Roman antiquities, among them a black bowl on which is scratched an Etruscan alphabet. Grosseto is an important commercial and agricultural centre and is on the railway from Rome to Pisa. About 5 mi. N.E. of Grosseto, near the mineral springs of Roselle Terme, may be traced remains of the Etruscan settlement which became the Roman Rusellae. This town was an episcopal see in the 5th century, but in 935 it was destroyed by the Saracens. (M. T. A. N.)

GROSSMITH, GEORGE (1847–1912), English comedian, noted for his roles in Gilbert and Sullivan productions, and for his authorship, with his brother, WALTER WEEDON GROSSMITH (1852–1919), of *The Diary of a Nobody* (1894), was born in London on Dec. 9, 1847. After several years of journalistic work he started about 1870 as a public entertainer, with songs and recitations. In 1877 he began a long connection with the Gilbert and Sullivan operas at the Opera Comique, London, in *The Sorcerer*. He appeared regularly thereafter at that theatre and from 1881 at the new Savoy theatre, London. His capacity for "patter songs," and his humorous acting, dancing and singing marked his creations of the chief characters in the Gilbert and Sullivan operas as the expression of a highly original individuality. In 1889 he left the Savoy and again set up as an entertainer, visiting all the major cities of Great Britain and the United States. He died at Folkestone, Eng., March 1, 1912. His two sons, GEORGE (1874–1935) and LAURENCE GROSSMITH (1877–1944), were both actors.

See S. Naylor, *Gaiety and George Grossmith* (1913).

GROSS NATIONAL PRODUCT, a term used in economics to indicate the total market value of the goods and services produced by a nation's economy during a specific period of time (usually a year), computed before allowance is made for depreciation and other forms of capital consumption. It is distinguished from net national product, which is computed after such an allowance is made. Gross national product, or GNP as it is often abbreviated, is a convenient indicator of the level of a nation's economic activity. *See* NATIONAL INCOME ACCOUNTING; UNITED STATES (OF AMERICA): *The Economy*.

GROSVENOR, GILBERT HOVEY (1875–1966), U.S. geographer, writer and longtime editor of the *National Geographic Magazine*, was born in Constantinople, Turkey, Oct. 28, 1875. He was graduated from Amherst college, Amherst, Mass., and in 1899 became director and president of the National Geographic society, and, in 1900, editor of the *National Geographic*. Under his directorship the society membership grew from 900 to over 1,900,000. He resigned as editor in 1954 and became board chairman.

During Grosvenor's administration the society sent out numerous expeditions to the north and south poles, into the stratosphere, to the ocean depths, and conducted a myriad of other investigations. In addition to his articles in the *National Geographic Magazine* he wrote a history of the society, chapters on exploration for the Smithsonian institution report and Adm. R. E. Peary's *The North Pole*. He was long a leader in the conservation and protection of wildlife. Grosvenor died Feb. 4, 1966, at his home in Nova Scotia.

GROS VENTRES, a name (Fr. "big bellies") applied to two distinct North American Indian groups:

1. The Hidatsa or Minitari, also known as the Gros Ventres of the Missouri. A Siouan-speaking tribe, linguistically related to the Crow and closely connected historically with the Mandan, they have been settled since the mid-19th century on Fort Berthold reservation, N.D. (*see* HIDATSA; MANDAN).

2. The Atsina, sometimes called the Gros Ventres of the Prairie (or Plains). An offshoot of the Algonkian-speaking Arapaho tribe, from which they may have separated as early as 1700, they were living in what is now northern Montana and adjacent regions of Canada in late historic times, and were culturally similar to other Plains tribes. Together with the Assiniboin, they were settled on Fort Belknap reservation, Montana, where the combined population totaled about 2,000 in the 1960s. (*See also* ARAPAHO; PLAINS INDIANS.)

The term Gros Ventres has been interpreted as a French-Canadian misunderstanding of Indian gestures designating the two tribes—possibly indicating hunger or greediness in the case of the Atsina and a pattern of body tattooing in the case of the Hidatsa.

See F. W. Hodge (ed.), *Handbook of American Indians North of Mexico*, part 1 (reprinted, 1959); A. L. Kroeber, *Ethnology of the Gros Ventre*, Anthropological Papers of the American Museum of Natural History, vol. i, part 4 (1908).

GROTE, GEORGE (1794–1871), English historian of Greece, was born at Clay Hill near Beckenham in Kent on Nov. 17, 1794, the son of George Grote and Selina Mary Peckwell. His grandfather Andreas Grote had come from Bremen and had founded a banking house in Threadneedle street, London, with George Prescott in 1766. Grote was educated at Charterhouse. At the age of 16 he joined his father's bank and worked in it until 1843. In 1820 he married Harriet Lewin, who shared his intellectual interests, supported him in his public life and became his biographer. For many years Grote worked in his spare time to perfect his command of Greek and to learn German, economics and philosophy. He inherited freethinking from his father and soon entered the circle of Jeremy Bentham and James Mill. Later

G. C. Lewis was a considerable influence on him, and by repeated visits to France he came to know well the leading French liberals.

His first published work was, characteristically, a *Statement on the Question of Parliamentary Reform* (1821), in which he advocated voting by ballot and frequent elections: in 1831 he restated his argument in *Essentials of Parliamentary Reform*. In 1822 he edited and practically rewrote some papers by Bentham under the title *Analysis of the Influence of Natural Religion on the Temporal Happiness of Mankind*, using the pseudonym "Philip Beauchamp." About that time he was already working on his Greek history. With J. S. Mill and H. P. (later Lord) Brougham he exerted himself to set up the new London university in Gower street (later University college, London). He was a member of its council between 1826 and 1830, but resigned after disagreement with J. S. Mill. From 1832 to 1841 he was an M.P. for the City of London. A Radical, he found himself in increasing isolation in the house of commons. He retired to devote himself to the *History of Greece* which was published in 12 volumes between 1846 and 1856: it ended with the events of 301 B.C.

Grote's *History* was quickly recognized (in the original or in translation) as the best Greek history in any language, and its authority remained unchallenged for almost half a century. Grote applied to Greek history the critical methods of B. G. Niebuhr, but distrusted Niebuhr's excessive subjectivism and tried to correct it by his epoch-making distinction between two periods of Greek history (legendary Greece and historical Greece), the dividing line of which he put about 776 B.C. In Greece Grote found the origins of all that he most admired: of democratic government, the principles of freedom of thought and of rational inquiry. Athens—not Sparta—was the centre of his Greece, and in Athens he revalued the sophists as the champions of intellectual progress, perhaps his greatest contribution to the understanding of Greece. In his love for Greece there was no romantic element.

Grote never visited Greece, but in 1847 went to Switzerland because he thought that the political system of modern Switzerland was analogous to that of ancient Greece: his articles on the subject in the *Spectator* were reprinted as *Seven Letters on the Recent Politics of Switzerland* (1847). Later he turned to the analysis of *Plato and the Other Companions of Socrates* (3 vol., 1865) and of *Aristotle* (unfinished and published posthumously, 1872). In these works the limitations of his utilitarian point of view and of his Greek scholarship are more evident.

In 1849 he reassumed his active interest in University college, London. He became its treasurer in 1860 and its president in 1868. From 1862 until his death he was also vice-chancellor of the University of London. He became a trustee of the British museum in 1859 but refused a peerage which Gladstone offered him in 1869.

Grote died on June 18, 1871, and was buried in Westminster abbey.

The fifth edition (1888) of his *History of Greece* was reprinted in 12 volumes in the Everyman Library (1907). His minor works were edited by A. Bain after his death as *The Minor Works of George Grote* (1873) and *Fragments on Ethical Subjects* (1876).

BIBLIOGRAPHY.—Harriet Grote, *The Personal Life of George Grote* (1873); G. Croom Robertson in *Dictionary of National Biography* corrects and adds details. *See also* H. Hale Bellot, *University College, London, 1826–1926* (1929); A. Momigliano, *George Grote and the Study of Greek History* (1952) with bibl.; A. Toynbee, *A Study of History*, vol. x, Annex (1954); M. L. Clarke, *George Grote: a Biography* (1962).
(A. D. Mo.)

GROTEFEND, GEORG FRIEDRICH (1775–1853), German epigraphist, who was instrumental in the decipherment of ancient Persian cuneiform script, was born at Münden in Hanover on June 9, 1775. He studied at Göttingen, became corrector of the Frankfurt *Gymnasium* and then director of the *Gymnasium* at Hanover. He published some important works on the Umbrian and Oscan dialects, on the coins of Bactria and other subjects. But it was in the east rather than in the west that Grotefend did his greatest work. The cuneiform inscriptions of Persia had for some time been attracting attention in Europe; exact copies of them had been published by the elder Niebuhr, who lost his eyesight over the work; and Grotefend's friend, O. G. Tychsen of Rostock, believed that he had ascertained the characters in the column, now known to be Persian, to be alphabetic.

At this point Grotefend took the matter up. His first discovery was communicated to the Royal Society of Göttingen in 1800 and an account of it in Arnold Heeren's great work on ancient history, and in 1837 published his *Neue Beiträge zur Erläuterung der persepolitanischen Keilschrift*. Three years later appeared his *Neue Beiträge zur Erläuterung der babylonischen Keilschrift*. His discovery may be summed up as follows: (1) that the Persian inscriptions contain three different forms of cuneiform writing, so that the decipherment of the one would give the key to the decipherment of the others; (2) that the characters of the Persian column are alphabetic and not syllabic; (3) that they must be read from left to right; (4) that the alphabet consists of 40 letters, including signs for long and short vowels; and (5) that the Persepolitan inscriptions are written in Zend (which, however, is not the case), and must be ascribed to the age of the Achaemenid princes. The process whereby Grotefend arrived at these conclusions illustrated his persevering genius (*see* CUNEIFORM: *Decipherment*).

Grotefend died on Dec. 15, 1853, at Hanover.

GROTH, KLAUS (1819–1899), German poet, whose book *Quickborn* (1852) first showed the poetic possibilities of *Plattdeutsch*, or Low German, was born in Heide, Holstein, on April 24, 1819. He became a school teacher but tireless energy in self-education and learning finally won him a chair at Kiel university (1866). He died in Kiel, June 1, 1899. Groth was inspired to explore the possibilities of his native Dithmarschen dialect by Burns and J. P. Hebel, and *Quickborn* first revealed (to a public already politically interested in Schleswig-Holstein) that *Plattdeutsch* was capable not only of humour but of deep feeling. A second part to *Quickborn* (1871) was less successful except for *De Heisterkrog*, one of Groth's most moving stories. He also published *Vertelln*, successful stories (1855–59) and essays on the use of dialect. His work influenced Fritz Reuter and John Brinckman and Brahms is among the composers who set his poems to music.

BIBLIOGRAPHY.—*Werke*, ed. by F. Pauly *et al.* (1952 *et seq.*); *Briefe*, ed. by W. Schröder (1931); V. Pauls, *Um den "Quickborn" Briefwechsel* (1938); biographies by H. Siercks (1899); T. Kröger (1905); G. Seelig (1924); D. Cölln (1926); A. Bartels, 2nd ed. (1943). Criticism includes P. Jørgensen, *Die dithmarschische Mundart in Groth's "Quickborn"* (1934). *See also* articles in *Niederdeutsches Jahrbuch* (1915 *et seq.*).
(K. Sc.)

GROTIUS, HUGO (HUIGH DE GROOT) (1583–1645), Dutch jurist and statesman, philologist, poet, theologian and historian, a "man of all-embracing learning" (R. Fruin) whose writings were of fundamental importance in the formulation of international law, was born at Delft on April 10, 1583. His father, a friend of men such as Simon Stevin and Justus Lipsius (*qq.v.*), had been burgomaster of Delft and curator of Leiden university and took a keen interest in his son's career. Grotius was a precocious but normal boy and became a student at Leiden in the faculty of letters at the age of 11. There his professor Junius imbued him with an undogmatic but profound religious outlook; and the great Joseph Scaliger was his preferred scientific mentor. At the age of 15 Grotius edited Martianus Capella's encyclopaedia and accompanied the leading statesman J. van Oldenbarnevelt (*q.v.*) on his embassy to Henry IV of France. Grotius was welcomed by the king of France as the "miracle of Holland." In a remarkable poem Grotius depicted the complicated international situation of the period and on his way back to Holland took the degree of doctor of law at Orleans. He became distinguished as an advocate in The Hague, moved in government circles and in 1601 was appointed historiographer of the States of Holland. His literary work at this time included the writing of two dramas in Latin and the editing of the literary remains of Aratus of Soli.

In 1604 the Dutch East India company, in order to justify the action of one of its admirals in seizing a Portuguese vessel, asked Grotius to write on the lawfulness of the capture of merchant ships. In his treatise *De jure praedae* ("On the Law of Prize and Booty"; published only in 1868) Grotius began by describing the law of mankind in general. The law of nature deriving from God's will contains four primary precepts: neither state nor individual may attack another state or individual; neither state nor individual may appropriate what belongs to another state or individual; neither state nor individual may disregard treaties or contracts; precepts must be upheld by judges and, if there are no judges, by private litigation. It follows from these precepts that because Portugal deprived the Dutch of the right to sail to the East Indies for commercial purposes, and as there was no judge, the East India company was entitled to capture Portuguese merchantmen in order to compensate itself for its losses. This is, in a nutshell, the content of Grotius' concise treatise, characterized by Jules Basdevant, a judge of the International Court of Justice, as "a triumph of juridical argument." Grotius thus maintains that the ocean is free to all nations, and one chapter of the *De jure praedae* was published in 1609 as the *Mare liberum*.

In his famous work *De jure belli ac pacis* ("On the Law of War and Peace", 1625) Grotius describes (in the second book) the whole law of mankind, private, penal and constitutional as well as international, exactly based on the four precepts of the *De jure praedae*. In the case of nonobservance, any rule of that law may be upheld, if there is no judge, by war or by individual action. The third book explains the rules of warfare. In the *De jure praedae* Grotius had already pointed out that the harsh rules of the law of warfare ought to be mitigated by equity. This statement is developed in the famous *temperamenta* ("moderations") of the third book, as well as in an analogous way at the end of the second book. The introductory first book contains general observations on law and wars and private litigation. The *De jure belli ac pacis* in fact constitutes the second edition of the general part of the *De jure praedae*, as C. van Vollenhoven pointed out in the preface of its 1919 edition. In later years the *De jure belli ac pacis* was erroneously considered to be a book on international law and on a great number of things that have, in fact, nothing to do with international law. Van Vollenhoven showed that the book describes the whole law of mankind, of which international law is only a part. Giambattista Vico in 1719 rightly styled Grotius *generis humani jurisconsultus* ("the jurist of the human race"). Indeed, in the 20th century, international law has largely developed on the lines judged by Grotius to be positive law.

In 1607 Grotius became *advocaat fiscaal* (attorney general) of the province of Holland and in the following year he married Maria van Reigersberch, the daughter of the burgomaster of Veere; she remained his courageous helpmeet until the end of his life. In 1612 he began his practical attempts to bring about the reunion of the Christian churches. He hoped that King James I would take the lead and to that end started a correspondence with Isaac Casaubon, the king's adviser in theological matters. In 1613 there was a great demand for Grotius' services from the town of Rotterdam, the high court of justice, the states-general and the pensionary of Rotterdam, Grotius now began his political career. He was one of the representatives of that town in the States of Holland and in that capacity he represented these states, together with Oldenbarnevelt, in the states-general, the government of the Republic of the United Provinces. When Oldenbarnevelt's health began to fail it was generally understood that Grotius would become his successor.

After the conclusion of a 12 years' truce with Spain (1609) the republic had been torn by a religious dispute. In its origin a theological difference about predestination between two Leiden professors, Jacobus Arminius and Franciscus Gomarus, it evolved into a quarrel between church and state and ended as a conflict between the provinces of Holland and Utrecht on the one hand and the orthodox Calvinist majority in the states-general supported by the head of the army, Prince Maurice, on the other (*see*

ARMINIANISM; DORT, SYNOD OF). While upholding the authority of the state over the church, the States of Holland tried to restore ecclesiastical peace. At last the schism in the republic ended in a show of force by Prince Maurice. Grotius had been the spokesman of the States of Holland, had drafted their peace resolutions and defended the policy of the states in his *Ordinum pietas*, although he did not always agree with Oldenbarnevelt. A short time before the final episode he proposed a skillfully drafted compromise solution of the problem at issue, but without success. Oldenbarnevelt and Grotius were arrested on Aug. 29, 1618. The latter was sentenced to life imprisonment (May 18, 1619) and taken to the castle of Loevestein. Through the resourcefulness of his wife Maria, however, he managed to escape from prison hidden in a chest. Grotius then made his way to Paris, where he was well received as a statesman in exile by old friends and by the king, Louis XIII, who granted him a pension. Its irregular payment was attributed by Grotius to the fact that he was not prepared to become a Roman Catholic and accept a high position. Nor would he accept a position in commerce, which would probably do harm to Dutch interests and about which rumours reached Amsterdam.

Grotius continued to produce an extraordinary quantity of scientific and literary work in prison and exile. This included the *De veritate religionis Christianae* ("On the Truth of the Christian Religion"), *Annotations on the New and the Old Testament*, an *Introduction to the Jurisprudence of Holland*, an *Apology* on behalf of the States of Holland, the *De jure belli ac pacis* and a translation of Euripides' *Phoenissae* with an introduction on the subject of classical tragedy.

In 1631 Grotius made an attempt to return to his native country, but, after hot debates in the States of Holland and notwithstanding the intervention of his old friend Prince Frederick Henry of Orange, he was obliged to become an exile once more and went to Hamburg. An attempt was made to use his abilities outside his country by appointing him governor general in the East Indies, but he refused. Until that time Grotius had also rejected overtures from foreign countries, which he considered incompatible with his Dutch nationality. However, when the Swedish chancellor, Oxenstierna, approached him in 1634 he accepted service under Sweden as ambassador to France, Sweden being at that time ally of the republic. The example of Joseph in the Old Testament who, as minister of Egypt, nevertheless served his Jewish people taught him that he was right to accept. In his drama *Sophompaneas* Grotius showed his gratitude to his mentor.

His hope that he would be in a position to promote the restoration of a general peace was not fulfilled; his task consisted mainly in insisting that France should give sufficient assistance to Sweden during the Thirty Years' War. It must be borne in mind that the great diplomatic centre of the two allies was neither Stockholm nor Paris but Hamburg, where permanent embassies were installed. Grotius' letters to Oxenstierna are of great historic interest. When France's statesman Cardinal Richelieu met Grotius for the first time in 1625 in order to be informed about the political situation in the republic after the death of Prince Maurice, he pointed out that in matters of state the weakest must always be in the wrong. Grotius answered that God and time would show the truth, whereby Richelieu at once understood that he could not handle the Swedish ambassador as he used to do. It was a disappointment to Grotius when in 1643 he was not invited to become a member of the Swedish peace embassy. He equally deplored the fact that his persistent efforts to promote the reunion of the Christian churches were misinterpreted in Holland. In his testament of March 27, 1645, he prayed God "to unite the Christians in one church under a holy reformation." When France recalled its ambassador at Stockholm, Sweden recalled Grotius. He was then received in Sweden with great honour, but he refused to settle there as Queen Christina suggested. On his way back to Holland he died at Rostock on Aug. 28, 1645.

Grotius' varied interests included philology, poetry, theology and history. His Latin is splendid but often difficult, especially in his poetry, and his Latin translations of Greek poets are notable. His first drama, *Adamus Exul* (1601), has been called the greatest dramatic representation of the subject. *See* also references under "Grotius, Hugo," in the Index.

BIBLIOGRAPHY.—For a bibliography of the works of Grotius see J. ter Meulen and P. J. J. Diermanse, *Bibliographie des écrits imprimés de Hugo Grotius* (1950). Biographical works include: C. Brandt, *Historie van het leven des Heeren Huig de Groot,...*, *The Life and Works of Hugo Grotius* ...; W. S. M. Knight, *Hugo Grotius. Eine biographische Skizze* (1952); W. J. M. van Eysinga, collected by H. and J. de Groot in *H. Grotii ... epistolae quotquot reperiri potuerunt* (1687). Those addressed to Oxenstierna were published in 2 vol. as *Hugonis Grotii epistolae ad Axelium Oxenstierna* (1889; 1890). A more recent collection of Grotius' correspondence: P. C. Molhuijsen (ed.), *Briefwisseling van Hugo Grotius*, 2 vol. (1936). Editions of Grotius' works on jurisprudence include: R. Fruin (ed.), *De iure praedae commentarius* (1868). This appeared in an English translation as: *De jure praedae commentarius. Commentary on the Law of Prize and Booty*, 2 vol. (1950). An essay by Fruin in the Bibliotheca Visseriana, vol. 5 (Leiden, 1925). For the *De iure* see P. C. Molhuijsen (ed.), *Hugonis Grotii de Jure Belli ac Pacis libri tres* (1919). This was translated into English and appeared in "The Classics of International Law," with an introduction by J. B. Scott (1925). *See* also: C. van Vollenhoven, *Verspreide geschriften*, pp. 349–602 (1934) and *The Framework of Grotius' Book De Jure Belli ac Pacis, 1625* (1931); G. N. Clark and W. J. M. van Eysinga (eds.), *The Colonial Conferences between England and the Netherlands in 1613 and 1615*, 2 vol. (1940; 1951); Sir Hersch Lauterpacht, "The Grotian Tradition in International Law," *British Year Book of International Law*, vol. 23 (1946); W. J. M. van Eysinga, "Grotius resurgens," *Netherlands International Law Review*, vol. 7 (1953).

(W. J. M. van E.)

GROUND BASS, *basso ostinato* in Italian, a term used to describe a bass pattern several times repeated, upon which a musical composition is constructed. The immediate ancestry of the ground bass is found in the 15th-century *cantus firmus* dances of Italy and France. In the 16th century the practice of composing a counterpoint upon a repeated bass pattern became popular in Italy and Spain, and such well-known "grounds" as the *passemezzo antico*, *Romanesca*, *folia* (all closely related), *Ruggiero* and *passemezzo moderno* spread throughout Europe. The early grounds implied an invariable harmonic structure that provided an ideal framework for improvisation.

Many 16th- and 17th-century dances were written on pre-existing or newly composed grounds. Closely allied to the "harmonic" ground is the "melodic" ground that first appeared in the 17th century. In this the harmony may be varied at each repetition, the phrase lengths of the upper parts may overlap those of the ground and the ground itself may be transposed during the course of the piece.

Ex. 1

Ex. 2

The use of the ground bass has a more or less continuous history from the 16th to the 20th century. Among the composers who have employed it with outstanding success are Monteverdi, Purcell, Bach, Beethoven, Brahms, Britten and Berg. *See* VARIATIONS.

GROUND BEETLE: *see* BEETLE.

GROUND-EFFECT MACHINE (GEM), sometimes called air-cushion vehicle, ducted-fan vehicle or Hovercraft, a craft that has the ability to hover and move about close to the surface of the earth, either land or water, obtaining the major portion of its support from a cushion of air trapped between the vehicle and the surface. These machines are severely limited in altitude since the lifting force depends on the close proximity of the ground.

History of Ground Effect.—It has been well known for some years that an airplane flying very close to the ground exhibits a decrease in drag and an increase in lift. The major effect of proximity to the ground is an increase in one measure of an airplane's efficiency called the lift/drag ratio. Although not necessarily a logical development from other aircraft, early efforts to take advantage of ground effect began in the 1930s when T. J. Kaario in Finland and D. K. Warner in the U.S. constructed GEMs usually known as "ram" type.

Devices now called GEMs include first the plenum (fig. 1) which is the more elementary type. This general configuration dates back to 1859, when a French patent was issued for a steam-supported machine of plenum design. The other category, the peripheral jet (fig. 2), is somewhat more sophisticated. The peripheral jet concept is much more recent than the plenum. Several individuals and groups began working with peripheral jet devices early in the 1950s. Among these pioneers were C. S. Cockerell in England, Carl Weiland in Switzerland, J. C. M. Frost in Canada and M. W. Beardsley and U. H. von Glahn in the U.S. Cockerell and Weiland approached the GEM concept through trying to eliminate water friction on the hulls of the boats. The first Hovercraft, the SRN-1, crossed the English channel in 1959.

Fundamental Principles.—The plenum is essentially an open-bottom box into which air is pumped under pressure and allowed to leak out along the ground. The fundamental characteristic of a fan, or any air-moving system, is to produce a mass flow of air and a corresponding rise in pressure. Thus, the air horsepower (a.h.p.) delivered by the fan is a function of both of these parameters; and a.h.p. = $f(\Delta P, m)$ where ΔP is pressure rise per unit area and m is mass flow.

A given air-moving system may be designed so that these two parameters vary with the back pressure against which the fan operates, and keep air horsepower constant. Another more easily understood characteristic of a rotating fan is the production of thrust. In the case of a plenum GEM this thrust is in the direction of lift. The total lift L of such a device is the sum of the thrust T of the rotating fan and the unit pressure rise ΔP multiplied by the platform area S, or $L = T + \Delta P(S)$. Planform area refers to the area covered by the fan when at rest (excluding inlet area).

If the above equation is divided by thrust T, the following expression results: $L/T = 1 + \Delta P(S)/T = A$, where A is the augmentation ratio. This ratio of lift to thrust, L/T, expresses the magnification of the thrust lift of the rotating fan by the proximity of the ground to the planform area of the machine. This is the most distinctive characteristic of a GEM and has been the reason for the general interest in these vehicles. The equation for A also points out the effect of unit pressure rise ΔP on the lift-augmentation ratio. The other air horsepower parameter, mass flow m, in combination with ΔP determines the height at which the machine will fly.

It should be emphasized that this is a greatly simplified treatment of the factors affecting the hovering performance of a plenum GEM. Such influences on the over-all performance as the effects of flow contraction at the periphery and of trapped vortices within the chamber must be considered in actual design.

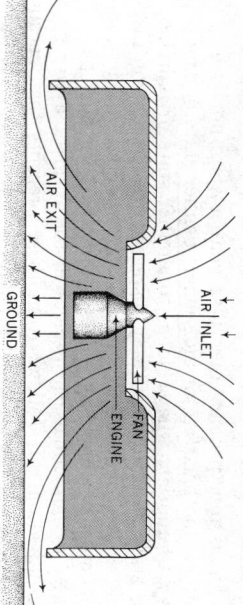

BY COURTESY OF T. E. SWEENEY

FIG. 1.—SCHEMATIC DIAGRAM SHOWING SIDE VIEW OF PLENUM GROUND-EFFECT MACHINE

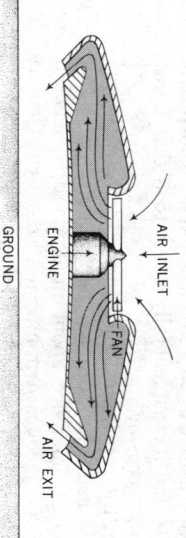

BY COURTESY OF T. E. SWEENEY

FIG. 2.—SCHEMATIC DIAGRAM SHOWING SIDE VIEW OF PERIPHERAL JET GROUND-EFFECT MACHINE

FIG. 5.—VICKERS VA-3 HOVERCRAFT, THE FIRST BRITISH GROUND-EFFECT MACHINE IN COMMERCIAL SERVICE

VICKERS-ARMSTRONGS

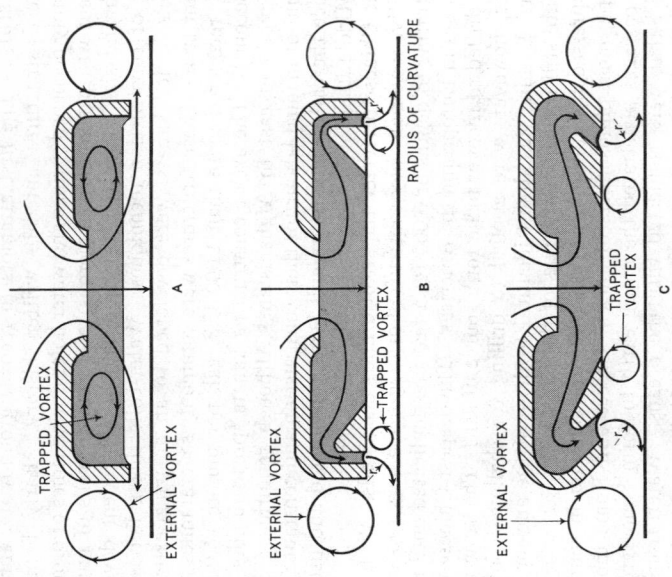

FIG. 3.—TYPICAL INTERNAL AND BASE FLOW PATTERNS

Engines and fans are omitted. (A) plenum; (B) peripheral jet (vertical blowing); (C) peripheral jet (blowing inward 45°)

BY COURTESY OF T. E. SWEENEY

The peripheral jet GEM up to a certain point is similar to the plenum in principle. All equations given apply to the peripheral jet machine with the modification that T represents the thrust lift of the air ejecting downward through the nozzle. This nozzle-flow condition is contrasted with the flow in a plenum in fig. 3.

In order to turn the downward peripheral flow of air outward, a certain force is necessary. This force is generated as the jet impinges on the ground, raising the base pressure exactly enough to turn the flow outward. The smaller the radius of curvature of this turning air stream and the greater the number of degrees of rotation of the stream, the higher will be the base pressures needed to apply the necessary force to the stream. Thus, the closer the machine is to the ground (smaller radius of curvature) and the greater the angle of inward blowing (more degrees of rotation), the higher the lift augmentation should be. From the power standpoint, it is best to fly quite close to the ground, and from the standpoint of lift it is best to angle the peripheral nozzle inward.

In this simplified discussion of the peripheral jet such effects as the mixing of the jet with relatively quiescent outside air, the effects of the trapped toroidal vortex within the jet curtain on performance and stability, and the method for providing the most favourable initial jet angle have been ignored.

The fundamentals governing the hovering performance of these two types of ground-effect machine indicate that the peripheral jet is inherently capable of substantially higher altitudes than the plenum for equal planform areas, weights and mass flow of air. This is demonstrated in fig. 4, where typical experimental lift-augmentation curves for both types are shown.

Static Stability and Control.—Static stability may be simply defined as the tendency of the GEM to right itself to a level attitude after being tilted by some external force. The plenum demonstrated static stability through a range of heights that are generally quite close to the ground. The peripheral jet, on the other hand, demonstrated inherent static stability up to heights about 5% of a base diameter for the circular planform configuration, above which it becomes increasingly unstable with height. Several devices can give inherent static stability to the peripheral jet machine at hovering heights in excess of 5% of a base diameter. These involve segmenting the base of the craft with additional nozzle slots for ejecting air downward. The stability of noncircular planforms is a function of the aspect ratio (ratio of width to length). As this ratio decreases, the longitudinal stability increases while the lateral static stability drops.

Even though the hovering heights of GEMs are greatly limited these machines must be considered aircraft in terms of control and propulsion. These craft must be capable of being trimmed about each of their three axes to compensate for pitching, rolling and yawing moments generated by asymmetric loading and by aerodynamic moments generated in forward flight. In addition, they must be able to produce sufficient horizontal force to provide for propulsion and braking, and side force to compensate for cross winds and to resist skidding in turns. The trim requirement can be accomplished by throttling a portion of the peripheral nozzle. Thus, if the forward portion of the periphery is partially throttled, the nose of the machine will tend to drop. A nose-up attitude is produced by throttling a portion of the aft slot or nozzle, and right and left roll can be produced in a similar manner.

An effective method of producing horizontal force uses external propellers oriented and controlled to allow the pilot to create a resultant force in any direction and to create a moment for yaw or directional control. Horizontal forces can also be produced by tilting the machine to generate lift components in the direction of tilt by installing vertical vanes in the peripheral nozzle to partially turn the discharging air away from the desired direction of motion, and by venting some of the air through

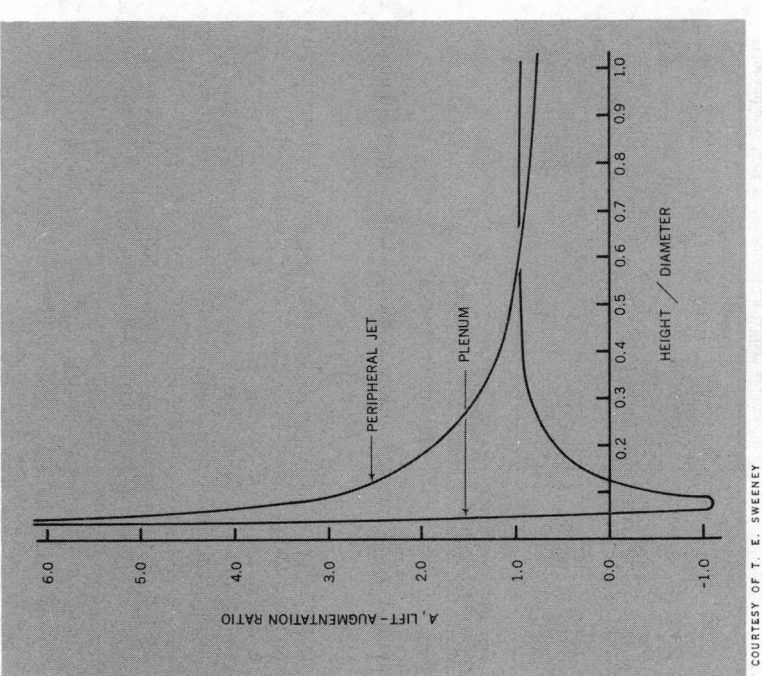

FIG. 4.—TYPICAL LIFT-AUGMENTATION CURVES

BY COURTESY OF T. E. SWEENEY

nozzles in the sides of the machine to produce a jet-propulsion effect.

The GEM is seen as filling the gap between ship and rail vehicles that offer low speed and large payload capacity, and conventional aircraft with their high speed but relatively low payload capacity.

BIBLIOGRAPHY—Harvey R. Chaplin, *Theory of the Annular Nozzle in Proximity to the Ground*, David Taylor Model Basin Aero Report no. 923 (1957); *Effect of Jet Mixing on the Annular Jet*, David Taylor Model Basin Aero Report no. 953 (1959); W. B. Nixon and T. E. Sweeney, *Some Qualitative Characteristics of a Two Dimensional Peripheral Jet*, Princeton University Aero Report no. 484 (1959); W. B. Nixon, *Maneuvering Capability of an Annular Jet Ground Effect Machine*, Princeton University Aero Report no. 515 (1960); D. E. Wright, *The Effect of Configuration on the Lift Augmentation Ratio of a Two Dimensional Open Plenum Ground Effect Machine*, Princeton University Aero Report no. 516 (1960); T. E. Sweeney and W. B. Nixon, *The Effect of Planform on the Static Characteristics of Peripheral Jet Wings*, Princeton University Aero Report no. 524 (1961). (T. E. S.)

GROUND HOG, a North American burrowing rodent. *See* WOODCHUCK.

GROUNDHOG DAY (Feb. 2). According to popular tradition in the United States, the ground hog or woodchuck comes out of his hole on this day after a long winter sleep to look for his shadow. If he sees it, he regards it as an omen of six more weeks of bad weather, and returns to his hole for that period. If the day is cloudy, and hence shadowless, the animal takes it as a sign of coming spring, and is content to stay above ground. The tradition, sometimes including the bear or badger, stems from similar beliefs associated with Candlemas (*q.v.*; also Feb. 2) in England, according to an old English song: "If Candlemas be fair and bright, Come, Winter, have another flight; If Candlemas bring clouds and rain, Go, Winter, and come not again."

(A. McQ.)

GROUND ICE, ice formed at the bottom of streams while the temperature of the water is above the freezing point. It is also known as anchor ice and bottom ice. Radiation of heat from the stream bottom probably is the prime cause of the formation of ground ice. It is formed only under a clear sky, never in cloudy weather; it is most readily formed on dark rocks, never under any covering such as a bridge, and rarely under surface ice. On a cold clear night the rocks on the bottom may radiate heat rapidly, cooling below the freezing point and resulting in the formation of loosely grown spongy masses of anchor or ground ice. On the next bright sunny day heat from the sun may detach them and they will rise to the surface with considerable force. Probably a thin film of stationary water rests upon the boulders and sand over which a stream flows, and this, becoming frozen, forms the foundation for the anchor ice and produces a surface upon which descending frazil ice (a Canadian term for surface ice formed in rapids) can lodge.

GROUNDSEL: *see* SENECIO.

GROUND SLOTH, a common term applied to the diverse group of extinct terrestrial relatives of the living tree sloths. *See* EDENTATA.

GROUNDWATER. Water beneath the land surface that feeds wells and springs is called groundwater. It maintains the dry-weather flow of streams and helps maintain the levels of lakes and ponds after overland runoff from rain and melting snow has ceased. Most groundwater originates from excess surface water seeping downward until it reaches a zone in which all the natural pore space is fully saturated. Under natural conditions, it moves slowly from the areas of origin to areas of discharge. These may be springs, swamps, or zones of diffuse upward seepage along shorelines and the margins of river valleys.

Wells intercept the naturally migrating groundwater and provide an important source of municipal, agricultural, and industrial water in almost all parts of the world. Even in regions of abundant surface water, the general absence of pathogenic organisms, an almost constant temperature, and the lack of turbidity in groundwater make it favoured for most uses. In the U.S., about 25% of all water, exclusive of water used for navigation and power generation, is supplied from wells.

History.—The first attempts to recover groundwater through artificial structures antedate written history. Early hominids probably deepened springs and water holes during times of drought. Ancient writings contain numerous references to wells of unusual depth and size, suggesting a long period of antecedent development of construction techniques. Water-collecting galleries and tunnels, called kanats, were developed to an amazing extent in ancient Iran. These structures were commonly several miles long; many recovered more than 1,000 U.S. gal. per minute (63 litres per second). The art of constructing kanats spread rapidly west to Egypt and east to Afghanistan. Although requiring a large amount of manual labour for their construction and constant maintenance thereafter, kanats are still being constructed and used in the Middle East.

The Chinese perfected the art of drilling deep wells. With only primitive materials they constructed drilling machinery capable of penetrating to depths of 5,000 ft., a feat not duplicated until modern times in Europe and the Americas. The deepest Chinese wells were drilled to recover brine for a source of salt. The same techniques, however, were applied to drilling for shallower potable water. Drilling rigs almost identical to those of the ancient Chinese are still used in rural areas of the Far East.

Impressed by limestone caverns that are common in southern Europe, most philosophers of ancient Greece and Rome thought such passages penetrated the entire earth to form "underground rivers" that were connected with the oceans. Water from the ocean was thought to be forced into the rocks by wind and waves, eventually to emerge as springs in the high mountains. The salt was thought to be removed by an evaporation and condensation cycle in the hot interior of the earth; a later version of this theory considered that the salt water was freshened by a process of earth metabolism. Although caverns can be important local conduits for groundwater movement, the concept of a widespread network of underground rivers is not correct. Furthermore, solar evaporation in the ocean is the only significant natural process by which potable water is separated from ocean salts. The chemistry of ocean water is changed slightly when it moves beneath the land, but it is still salty and can cause damage to groundwater supplies in coastal regions.

The relatively low precipitation in the region suggested to the Greeks and Romans that rainfall and snow was insufficient to account for large springs and rivers. Neither Plato nor Vitruvius fully shared this viewpoint; nevertheless natural process by which educated people did not generally accept the atmospheric origin of river and groundwater until early in the 18th century. This final acceptance was due to the careful work of two Frenchmen: Pierre Perrault (1608–80), who showed that the discharge of the Seine River from 1668 to 1670 was only one-sixth of the total volume of rainfall, and Edme Mariotte (1620–84), who measured infiltration of rainwater into the subsurface and also measured the discharge of the Seine, thus verifying Perrault's work. (*See also* GEOLOGY: *Geomorphology*.)

The mathematical law governing flow of groundwater was first stated clearly by Henri Darcy (1803–58), a noted French engineer. The modern form of his equation states

$$q = kA \frac{\rho}{\mu}\left(-\frac{\delta h}{\delta l}\right)$$

in which q is the volume of water flowing per unit of time through

Water of the World

Location	Surface area (sq.mi.)	Water volume (cu.mi.)*	Percentage of total water
Surface water			
Freshwater lakes	330,000	30,000	.009
Saline lakes and inland seas	270,000	25,000	.008
Average in stream channels	—	300	.0001
Subsurface water			
Vadose water (includes soil moisture)		16,000	.005
Groundwater within depth of half a mile	50,000,000	1,000,000	.31
Groundwater—deep lying		1,000,000	.31
Other water locations			
Icecaps and glaciers	6,900,000	7,000,000	2.15
Atmosphere (at sea level)	197,000,000	3,100	.001
World ocean	139,500,000	317,000,000	97.2
Totals (rounded)	—	326,000,000	100

*One cubic mile of water equals 1.1 trillion gallons.
Source: U.S. Geological Survey.

the cross-sectional area, A; k is a proportionality factor called permeability; ρ is the density of the fluid; μ is the viscosity; g is gravitational acceleration; and $\frac{\delta h}{\delta l}$ is the hydraulic gradient (see PERMEABILITY, FLUID). In a simple linear groundwater system, the hydraulic gradient is the slope of the surface that is defined by water levels in wells, i.e., the change in elevation, Δh, between water levels in adjacent wells divided by the distance, Δl, between the wells, provided the wells are aligned with the direction of groundwater flow.

Forces Causing Water Movement.—Most groundwater movement can be related to differences in elevation and pressure. Water completely saturating horizontal conduits, whether in small artificial pipes or in natural rocks and sediments, will move in response to pressure differences. Freely falling water, on the other hand, will move almost entirely because of the gravitational force acting on the water through the distance of fall. Groundwater velocities are very small, so inertial forces normally present in surface water can be ignored in all flow regimens except those near large-capacity wells and springs and in unusually permeable gravel, limestone, and volcanic rocks.

In the general case, where the water is neither falling freely nor flowing in a perfectly horizontal direction, the potential for movement, Φ, as defined by M. K. Hubbert, represents the combined effect of pressure and vertical position in the gravitational field,

$$\Phi = gz + \frac{p}{\rho}$$

in which z is the vertical distance of an element of water above a given datum, for example, sea level, and p is the gauge pressure (see PRESSURE GAUGE: *Bourdon Tube*) imposed on the same element. But inasmuch as

$$\Phi = gh$$

then

$$h = z + \frac{p}{\rho g}$$

For practical purposes, the exceedingly small changes in the field of gravity are ignored, and the potential for movement of a given particle of water is considered to be directly proportional to the hydraulic head, h, measured at the position of the particle (see fig. 2). This means, in turn, that water levels in wells that measure the hydraulic heads in a given water-bearing zone will also measure indirectly the potential field.

Chemical, electrical, and thermal forces as well as surface tension will also cause movement of water below the land surface. These forces normally will be negligible within shallow zones containing potable groundwater. Unusual pressures encountered in some oil wells have been explained by some researchers in terms of chemical and electrical forces. Surface tension becomes important where two fluids are in contact in restricted openings, such as oil in contact with water within a sandstone. Surface tension is of utmost importance in controlling the movement of water in soils and other unsaturated materials above the fully saturated zone containing groundwater (see also SURFACE TENSION).

Migration of Groundwater.—Water moving downward from the surface will usually traverse a zone that is only partly saturated before entering the fully saturated zone of groundwater flow. Water that is held by surface tension above the saturated zone will not enter wells; only water that enters the fully saturated zone below the influence of capillary forces can be intercepted by wells.

Natural zones that have permeabilities high enough to allow the easy entrance of water into wells are called aquifers. The size and shape of aquifers can range from restricted fracture zones in otherwise dense granite to tabular bodies of sedimentary rock underlying thousands of square miles. Some of the most extensive aquifers known are sandstones in northeastern Africa and east-central to north-central Australia. Some of the deepest fresh-water wells in the world have been drilled to tap Australian sandstone aquifers.

Rates of groundwater movement depend on the permeability, the amount of effective pore space available for water migration, and the hydraulic gradient. Water in materials having low permeabilities, such as clay and shale, may move with a velocity of less than one foot per century. Water in cavernous limestone, in contrast, may move more than one mile in a single hour. Velocities in normal aquifers under natural conditions range more commonly from a few feet per day to a few feet per month. Some aquifers of great extent have recharge areas along distant borders. Computed water velocities as well as radioactive dating of the water from these aquifers demonstrate that the water must be at least several thousand years old.

The exact paths of water migration are difficult to predict in all but the most simple natural situations. Permeability changes and locations of groundwater recharge and discharge are the most important variables determining the directions of water movement. Despite the complexities, graphical, analog, and digital methods have enabled modern researchers to solve many complex problems of groundwater flow.

Chemical Quality of Groundwater.—All groundwater contains dissolved mineral matter which may range in concentration from only slightly more than that found in rainwater to brine which is completely saturated with respect to common salt. The brine may have more than 30%, or 30 parts per hundred, by weight of dissolved solids. Potable water will generally contain less than 0.1%, or more conveniently 1,000 parts per million (ppm), of

WELL

SHALE

SANDSTONE AQUIFER

SHALE

FLOW

GROUNDWATER

SEA LEVEL

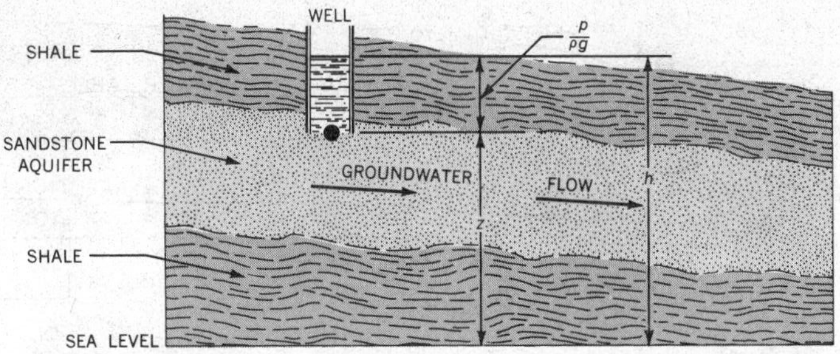

FIG. 2.—HYDRAULIC HEAD IN SANDSTONE AQUIFER CONFINED BETWEEN TWO LAYERS OF SHALE (see TEXT)

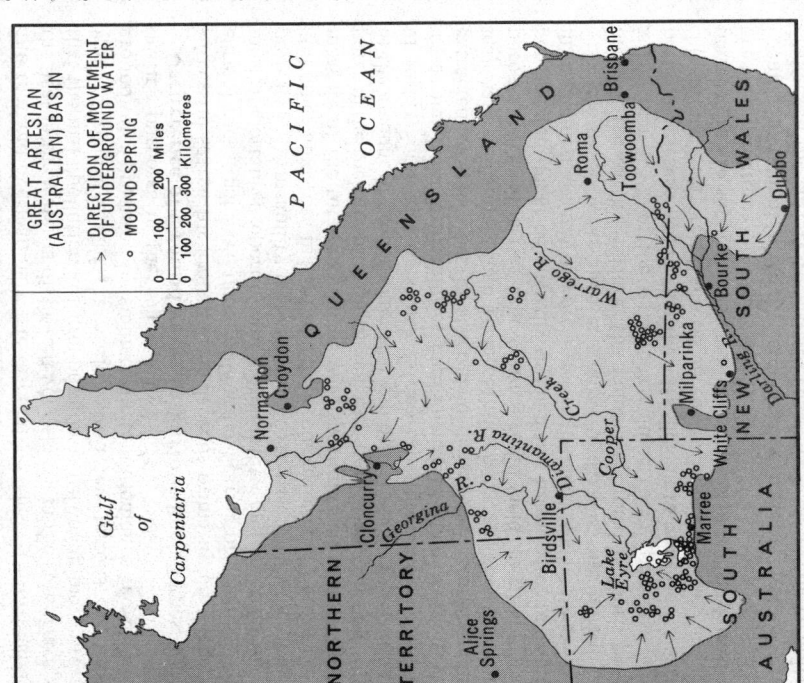

GREAT ARTESIAN (AUSTRALIAN) BASIN

→ DIRECTION OF MOVEMENT OF UNDERGROUND WATER

○ MOUND SPRING

0 100 200 Miles
0 100 200 300 Kilometres

FROM L. KEITH WARD, GEOLOGICAL SURVEY OF SOUTH AUSTRALIA, 1946

FIG. 1.—GREAT ARTESIAN (AUSTRALIAN) BASIN

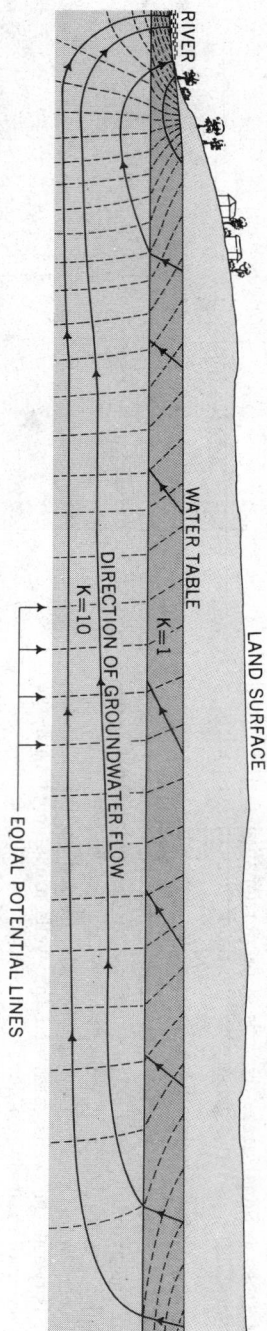

FIG. 3.—GROUNDWATER CIRCULATION IN TWO UNCONFINED AQUIFERS. THE UPPER AQUIFER HAS A PERMEABILITY (K) EQUAL TO 1/10 OF THE PERMEABILITY OF THE LOWER AQUIFER

ADAPTED FROM FREEZE AND WITHERSPOON, "WATER RESOURCES RESEARCH," 1967

dissolved solids. Rainwater will most commonly contain between 3 and 30 ppm dissolved solids.

Calcium, sodium, magnesium, bicarbonate, sulfate, chloride, and silica are the most abundant dissolved constituents in groundwater and, in potable water, generally range in concentrations from 5 to 500 ppm. Potassium, strontium, iron, fluoride, boron, carbonate, and nitrate are secondary constituents most commonly found in concentrations that range from 0.05 to 5 ppm in potable water.

A host of minor and trace elements have been found in groundwater. Some of the most interesting are radioactive constituents. Two general types of natural radioactive constituents are present. The first type is related to very ancient radioactive material that was probably present when the earth formed. Thorium, uranium, radioactive potassium, and their products of disintegration such as radon and radium are examples of the first type. Concentrations of uranium and radium in natural waters rarely exceed 1 ppm in natural waters. Owing to the slow disintegration rates of thorium, potassium, and uranium, they do not produce radiation hazards in natural waters. Radium, however, has a relatively rapid disintegration rate. Furthermore, it tends to accumulate permanently in the bones of vertebrates. Radium, as a consequence, is the most hazardous inorganic material known to be transported in water. As little as 3×10^{-6} ppm radium can be a matter of concern. Fortunately, even such minute concentrations are rarely found in normal groundwater.

The second type of natural radioactive materials found in groundwater has its origin in cosmic radiation of the atmosphere and the earth's surface. Radioactive hydrogen (H3 or tritium) and carbon (C^{14}) are the two most important products from the standpoint of groundwater studies. Tritium disintegrates rapidly and is used to obtain approximate dates in terms of a few decades. Carbon-14 disintegrates more slowly and is useful for dates of several thousand years. Neither tritium nor carbon-14 gives rise to health hazards when in natural concentrations.

Groundwater has long had the reputation of being free of chemical and biological contamination. Rapid expansion of urban, suburban, and manufacturing areas throughout the world has created problems not only in pollution of air and surface water but of groundwater as well. Aquifers in contact with polluted rivers may be contaminated. Pits and ponds at the surface built for the disposal of wastes will commonly leak and pollute nearby aquifers. Overproduction of groundwater will lower water levels and allow underlying saline groundwater and sea water near coastlines to enter aquifers. The slow movement of groundwater makes the correction of groundwater pollution both time-consuming and expensive.

Groundwater Temperature.—Most people are impressed by a cool drink of water from wells or springs during hot summer months and are surprised to learn that groundwater is actually warmer than the mean annual temperature of the region. Groundwater generally flows so slowly that its temperature is controlled by conduction of heat in the earth. The normal increase in temperature, caused by heat being conducted outward from the interior of the earth, will range from 1° F for every 20 ft. of depth, down to 1° F for every 200 ft. of depth. The terminal temperature at the earth's surface is controlled by the mean annual temperature of the surface soil. In Australia water in 6,000-ft.-deep wells drilled where the mean annual temperature is nearly 70° F boiled at surface pressures, indicating a rise over the surface temperature of 150° F or 1° for every 40 ft. of depth. Water from most wells having depths greater than 3,000 ft. must be cooled before it is used for domestic or stock purposes.

Warm springs with temperatures 10° to 30° F higher than the mean annual temperatures of the regions in which they are found owe their origin to the deep circulation of groundwater followed by a rapid rise of the water to the surface along faults and other natural conduits. Hot springs which have temperatures near the boiling point of water are almost everywhere associated with volcanic activity of the last one or two million years. Steam and other gases will carry heat from slowly cooling igneous rocks into aquifers near the surface. Although part of the hot-spring water may be condensed volcanic steam, most of the water originates from surface rain and snow which is heated by the steam and hot rocks.

Warm water is commonly produced by various heat-exchange processes in air conditioning and manufacturing. The warm water may be injected into the subsurface in order to conserve water and to avoid overloading waste-disposal systems. Unfortunately, the heat in the water is dissipated very slowly in the subsurface so that thermal "pollution" of groundwater is becoming more prevalent in urban areas of the world. In a few regions the warm groundwater produced by summer air conditioning is recycled for heating purposes in the winter.

Occurrence of Groundwater in Various Rock Types.—The successful search for groundwater depends primarily on the presence of rocks that have favourable water-bearing properties. The most important properties are permeability and interconnected porosity. Permeability is a measure of the ease with which water and other fluids can move through porous material. Porosity is a measure of the total amount of void space present in a rock. If pores in the rock are interconnected, then porosity is also a measure of the amount of groundwater that can be stored in a given volume of rock. Some materials such as clay can store vast amounts of water but lack permeabilities high enough to allow water to be extracted by wells. On the other hand, dense but fractured granite may have moderately high permeabilities but may lack significant porosity. A well in this type of rock could yield initially 40 gal. per min. but might be virtually dry in a few hours, after the water in the limited amount of pore space is drained.

Where dense rocks such as granite and gneiss are buried far beneath the earth's surface, the volume occupied by open pores is less than 0.5% of the total rock volume (0.5% porosity), and permeabilities are so low that they are difficult to measure. Nearer the surface, scattered fractures in the rock may produce enough permeability to supply small amounts of water to wells. Porosity, even with fractures, however, is still generally less than 1%. The chemical action of rainwater and organic material will produce changes in the surface rock that eventually leads to the complete breakdown of the rock into loose soil. The porosity of the soil ranges from 35 to 50% and the permeability is high enough to sustain water wells having modest yields.

Water-bearing properties of volcanic rocks depend largely on the geologic history of the rocks. For example, basalt that does not reach the land surface but cools in a tabular body below the surface is about as dense and nonpermeable as deeply buried granite. Basalt of the same composition but having been cooled and solidified at the surface in a lava flow may form some of the most permeable aquifers known. Lava flowing down a mountain slope will tend to produce a crust at the surface due to cooling. Continued movement of the underlying lava buckles and fractures the crust which forms an extremely permeable zone when the lava is solidified. Holes in the lava formed by gas bubbles and burned vegetation together with shrinkage cracks formed during cooling adds further porosity and permeability to the volcanic rock. Thick, viscous lava flows, however, form layers that are dense and almost nonpermeable except along upper and lower surfaces. If the viscosity becomes too great, volcanic eruptions tend to produce explosions rather than lava flows. The fragmental material that is ejected is coarse and blocky near the volcano and commonly is both porous and permeable. At some distance, most of the ejecta is mixed with fine-grained volcanic ash. The resulting deposits are porous but the size of the pores is so small that the permeability is very low.

Volcanic rocks slowly lose their porosity and permeability as they are compacted and as circulating groundwater deposits minerals in the pore spaces. Most volcanic rocks more than 100,000,-000 years old are permeable only where secondary fractures have formed.

Sedimentary rocks such as shale, sandstone, and limestone will have highly variable hydraulic properties that depend on antecedent compaction, cementation, fracturing, and solution of the rocks. Shale has a porosity that ranges from about 15% in deeply buried rocks to 50% in rocks near the surface. With the exception of shale within 200 ft. of the surface, permeability is so low that significant amounts of water will not flow from the shale into wells. Near the surface, shale can be fractured to form secondary aquifers. The porosity of sandstone varies with the amount of cementing material that has been deposited between sand grains. Minimum porosities are about 1% and maximum porosities about 30%. Most sandstone has enough permeability to sustain wells having small to moderate yields.

Yields of some wells in limestone in Florida and Texas rival the high yields of wells in volcanic aquifers. Geologically young limestones formed from coarse shell fragments and reef-building organisms have porosities of from 15 to 30% and permeabilities so high that they are difficult to measure. Limestones formed from calcareous muds and older compacted limestone will have porosities between 2 and 20% and significant permeabilities only where the rock is fractured and partly dissolved by circulating groundwater. Water levels in older compacted limestones are variable in their yields, being for the most part quite poor but occasionally encountering fractures and solution openings that produce more than 500 gal. per minute.

Some of the world's most spectacular springs come from limestone aquifers. The largest is probably near the town of Ras-el-Ain in Syria where a spring gives rise to a river with a discharge of 886,000,000 gal. per day (38.7 cu.m. per second). The Fontaine de Vaucluse in France and Silver Springs of Florida each have an average discharge of about 500,000,000 gal. per day. Many other large limestone springs in Lebanon, Yugoslavia, Spain, the U.S., and Greece have discharges of more than 10,000,000 gal. per day.

Material that is not solidified into firm rock mantles much of the earth's surface. Sand dunes, river alluvium, lake clays, glacial till, and beach deposits are but a few of the more common examples of nonsolidified material. Porosities of most of this material are between 35 and 50%. Permeabilities, however, may be very high as in the case of coarse alluvial gravel or very low as in the case of lake clays.

River alluvium is one of the most favoured places to search for water. Test drilling is inexpensive; permeable sands and gravels are common; large amounts of groundwater are stored in the pore space; and nearby rivers provide an active source of water to recharge aquifers.

Groundwater Development.—Overproduction of groundwater in urban and agricultural areas has caused serious lowering of water levels in wells in many parts of the world. (*See also* Irrigation.) Besides the simple depletion of water supplies, overproduction increases pumping costs, induces the inflow of saline water into aquifers, and produces, in some areas, land subsidence. Water pressure in aquifers helps support the weight of overlying materials. When the pressure is reduced, the weight rests more directly on the aquifer, causing it and adjacent materials to compact, which in turn lowers the land surface. Subsidence due to groundwater pumping has been a serious problem in Mexico City, Tokyo, Houston, and other metropolitan regions. Subsidence has also adversely affected agricultural areas in Arizona and California.

Despite local overproduction and contamination, groundwater supplies as a whole are underproduced. In the United States, far more fresh water is stored in aquifers than in all the nation's rivers, reservoirs, and lakes, including the Great Lakes. With proper legislation and planning, this vast storehouse of fresh water can be managed as effectively as surface reservoirs. The quality of water can be protected, local overproduction prevented, and excess surface water used to recharge the groundwater supply. (*See also* International Hydrological Decade.)

In most groundwater planning, an attempt is made to balance the rate of extraction with the rate of natural recharge in an aquifer. Some lowering of water levels in wells is necessary to induce water to flow to well fields and to make subsurface storage space available for occasional recharge with surplus surface water. The concept of an extraction system balanced with nature, however, is not practical in arid and semiarid regions because natural recharge is too low. Wells, pits, and spreading basins are constructed in arid regions to recharge surplus stream water. Unfortunately, physical conditions are not favourable for artificial recharge in many regions. Within these regions where aquifers are present, a philosophy of groundwater mining has been proposed. The water can be treated as a nonrenewable resource, the same as oil, coal, or iron ore. Water can be mined for many decades, then wells can be abandoned when the supply is exhausted. Communities, farms, and industries need not be abandoned, because with proper planning a vigorous economy can be established that could support eventual importation of surface water even though this would be impossible economically prior to the groundwater mining program.

See also Natural Resources: Water; Well; Spring; Water Supply and Purification; Hydrology.

Bibliography.—C. L. McGuinness, "The Role of Ground Water in the National Water Situation," *U.S. Geological Survey Water-Supply Paper 1800* (1963); H. E. Thomas, *Conservation of Ground Water* (1951); S. N. Davis and R. J. M. DeWiest, *Hydrogeology* (1966); R. C. Heath and F. W. Trainer, *Introduction to Ground-Water Hydrology* (1968); M. K. Hubbert, "Entrapment of Petroleum Under Hydrodynamic Conditions," *Bull. Am. Ass. Petrol. Geol.* 37:1954–2026 (1955). (S. N. Da.)

GROUP INSURANCE is a 20th-century development of insurance business in the United States, Great Britain and other countries. In a sense, all insurance is based on the group concept, for the underlying element of insurance is the pooling of an enormous number of risks. The vast majority of insurance policies are issued to individuals, but the group technique can be and is applied in different classes of business, notably life insurance, annuities and health insurance.

Group insurance is characterized by one master contract, issued by an insurance company, the insurer, to a policyholder, usually an employer, providing insurance for insureds, usually employees, and often for the benefit of fourth parties, the beneficiaries named by the insured employees. The employer normally receives a master policy from the insurance company, and each employee receives a certificate of insurance outlining the benefits of the plan. Depending on state regulatory rules, group insurance in the United States may be available to employee groups as small as ten. Even smaller groups are sometimes underwritten. In Great Britain, where such detailed control as state regulations obviously does not exist, group policies may be issued by a company for such numbers, large or small, as its own practice and competitive conditions determine.

Another basic characteristic of group insurance is that, with few exceptions, it is issued without medical examination or other evidence of individual insurability, thus permitting all active employees to receive coverage under the group policy regardless of the state of their health.

Group insurance is essentially low-cost, wholesale protection. Mass distribution and mass administrative methods afford economies of operation not available in individual insurance. Further, most group life and health insurance is temporary or current-cost insurance, with the consequent elimination of the necessary reserve element found in level premium insurance. Since active employees typically make up the group, there is a constant flow into the group of younger persons and a flow out of the group of the older and infirm persons. A trend in the second half of the 20th century is to retain retired employees under the plan, thus necessitating the building of some reserve element.

Although the majority of all group insurance is provided through contracts issued to individual employer groups (in the United States, at any rate) it may also be issued to multiple employer groups, labour union groups, creditor-debtor groups and such miscellaneous groups as associations of public employees, fraternal society members, state police, savings account plan depositors, professional associations and the like.

Group life insurance is the most popular form of group insurance, representing about one-third of all life insurance. A benefit schedule, normally related to earnings, determines the amount of death benefit for each employee. The employee may or may not contribute to the cost of the coverage. Often a disability provision provides for continuance of coverage in the event of total disability. Group permanent or group paid-up life insurance has a reserve element accumulated during the life of the contract.

Group annuities typically are issued to employers for the purpose of financing retirement benefits of employees. Group methods of marketing and administration afford cost advantages over the individual annuity plan.

Group health insurance represents the application of group principles and practices to a variety of health insurance coverages. Group disability income insurance provides cash benefits to replace lost earnings in the event of disability. Benefits may be paid for total or partial disability, and for temporary or permanent disability. Benefits may be provided for a stated number of weeks, until a certain age or for life. Coverage may be limited to disability from accident only, or from accident and sickness. Group medical expense insurance provides cash benefits or service benefits to meet hospital charges, surgical bills, doctor's bills, drug and X-ray charges and similar costs.

A great variety of coverages is available in the United States from insurance companies and from privately financed health insurance organizations such as Blue Cross and Blue Shield. Broad blanket coverage of medical expenses is provided under "comprehensive medical expense" and "major medical" policies. Group travel accident contracts typically provide death, dismemberment and disability income benefits for accidents experienced while traveling. Group accidental death and dismemberment insurance providing additional benefits for accidental death and dismemberment normally is used as a supplemental coverage to group life insurance.

BIBLIOGRAPHY.—Davis W. Gregg, Group Life Insurance, 3rd ed. (1962); Kenneth Black, Jr., Group Annuities (1955); Jesse F. Pickrell, Group Disability Insurance, rev. ed. (1961).
(D. W. G.)

GROUP MARRIAGE, the marriage of several men with several women. It has been found among various peoples who practise polyandry (q.v.)—in Tibet, India and Ceylon. In many of these cases it is said that if one of the brothers who have a wife in common brings a new wife, he shares, or has to share, her with his brothers. In the other cases, also, the group marriage seems to have arisen as a combination of polygyny (q.v.) with polyandry, which may be inferred from the facts that both in Tibet and India polyandry is much more prevalent than group marriage; that the latter occurs nowhere except side by side with polyandry; and that the occasional combination of polygyny with polyandry, when the circumstances permit it, is easy to explain, whereas no satisfactory reason has been given for the opinion held by some sociologists that polyandry has developed out of an earlier stage of group marriage.

It is possible that Caesar's statement about the marriages of the ancient Britons, if correct, likewise refers to a combination of polygyny with polyandry. He says: "In their domestic life they practise a form of community of wives, ten or twelve combining in a group, especially brothers with brothers and fathers with sons."

While genuine group marriage has been found only side by side with polyandry, there are peoples—such as the Chukchi, the Herero in southwest Africa, the Masai and Kamba in east Africa, certain communities in New Guinea, and some Australian tribes—who have a kind of sex communism, in which several men have the right of access to several women, although none of the women is properly married to more than one of the men. Thus the pirrauru relation among the central Australian Dieri and the piraungaru relation among their neighbours, the Urabunna, almost exclusively imply sexual licence. Yet these relations have been considered to give support to the hypothesis of ancient group marriage in Australia, according to which the men of one division or class had as wives the women of another division or class. Marriages of this sort no longer exist anywhere in Australia. No person becomes a pirrauru or piraungaru as a matter of course because of his or her status. An agreement must be made with the husband, the pirrauru may have to pay for it, and the relation may even be of short duration (in the case of a visitor); while the licence allowed at the performance of certain ceremonies when the ordinary rules of morality are more or less suspended, the levirate (q.v.), and the use of classificatory terms of relationship which group together under single designations many distinct degrees and kinds of relationship.

See also MARRIAGE, PRIMITIVE.

BIBLIOGRAPHY.—E. Westermarck, The History of Human Marriage, vol. iii (1921); B. Malinowski, The Family Among the Australian Aborigines (1913; rev. ed. 1963); R. Briffault, The Mothers (1927; rev. ed. 1963).
(E. W. X.)

GROUPS, in mathematics, are sets of elements with a composition law that satisfies certain conditions (see below). Group-theoretical methods can be traced back to the geometric construction of beautiful ornamental figures in ancient Egypt as well as to the theory of regular polygons and polyhedra in classical Greece. However it was only toward the end of the 18th century that various mathematicians gradually recognized the real importance of groups. In studying the solution of algebraic equations of higher degrees, they encountered groups of permutations (see below) on the set of roots of algebraic equations; and the study of such groups culminated in the outstanding results of E. Galois (1811–32) known in the 1960s as Galois theory. The theory of groups then developed with its various applications and finally established itself as a new branch of mathematics at about the start of the 20th century.

The notion of a group is now one of the most fundamental concepts in the whole structure of mathematics; for instance, F. Klein (1872) defined geometry as the study of those properties of a space that are invariant under a certain specific group of transformations on the space. The theory of groups, its results and methods, is now indispensable in almost all main branches of mathematics; for examples see TOPOLOGY, ALGEBRAIC: The Homology Groups; ANALYSIS, ABSTRACT; ALGEBRA: Some Central Topics and Results; GEOMETRIES, FINITE; ALGEBRA: Modern Algebra; ALGEBRAIC GEOMETRY: Algebraic Surfaces.

Concepts from the theory of groups also have important applications outside of mathematics in such fields as quantum mechanics and crystallography. Crystals, for example, are classified by treating them as sets of points (lattices) in n-dimensional

Euclidean space in terms of the theory of groups (see CRYSTALLOGRAPHY: *Rotational Order in Crystals: The 32 Crystal Classes*).

In modern mathematics, a new concept is usually introduced by abstracting certain essential properties from a number of important mathematical objects that have these properties in common; these individual objects then provide concrete examples of the theory developed upon the new abstract concept thus defined. The definition of a group presents a typical example of this procedure. In what follows, a group will be defined first; some examples to illustrate the abstract definition will be given later. The discussion assumes the reader to have some familiarity with such topics as those covered in LOGIC: *Type Theory and Set Theory*; FIELDS; SET THEORY (THEORY OF AGGREGATES).

Definition of Group.—Let G be a nonempty set. Suppose that G is given a rule that assigns to each (ordered) pair of elements x,y in G a third element z in G called the composite of x and y; it is customary to denote the composite z of x and y: that is, $z = xy$. The set G is then called a group if the rule of composition satisfies the following three conditions:

1. Associative law: $a(bc) = (ab)c$, for any a, b and c in G.
2. There is an element e in G such that $ea = a$ for every a in G.
3. For each a in G, there is an element x in G such that $xa = e$.

Let G be a group. It can be proved that the element e in (2) satisfies $ae = ea = a$ for every a in G and is the unique element in G with this property; e is called the identity (unit or neutral element) of the group G. Also, the element x in (3) satisfies $ax = xa = e$ and is uniquely determined by this property; it is called the inverse of a and is denoted by a^{-1}; that is, $aa^{-1} = a^{-1}a = e$.

A group G is called an abelian (or commutative) group if $xy = yx$ for every x,y in G. In an abelian group, the composite of x and y is often denoted by $x + y$ instead of xy and is called the sum of x and y accordingly; the identity is then denoted by 0 and the inverse of a by $-a$. An abelian group with such additive notation is also called a module.

The number of elements contained in a group is called the order of the group. The group is called a finite or infinite group according as the order is finite or infinite.

Subgroups.—Let a be an element of a group G and A a subset of G. By aA, Aa and aAa^{-1} the sets of all elements of the form ax, xa and axa^{-1} are respectively denoted, with arbitrary x in A. Similarly, if B is also a subset of G, AB denotes the set of all products of the form xy with x in A and y in B.

A subgroup of a group G is a subset of G that itself is a group with respect to the rule of composition defined in G. A subgroup always contains the identity e of G, and the intersection of any number of subgroups of G is again a subgroup of G.

Let H be a subgroup of G. A right (or left) coset of H in G is any set of the form aH (Ha) with a in G; it is a subset of G containing $a = ae$ ($a = ea$). Two right (or left) cosets of H either completely coincide or have no element in common. Hence G is divided into a number of mutually disjoint right (or left) cosets of H. The number of distinct right cosets of H in G is then equal to the number of distinct left cosets of H in G, and it is called the index of H in G. When G is a finite group, the order of G is the product of the order of H and the index of H in G.

If H is a subgroup of G, the set aHa^{-1} is also a subgroup of G for any a in G. Such a subgroup is called a conjugate subgroup of H in G.

A subgroup N of G is called a normal (or invariant) subgroup of G if N coincides with all its conjugate subgroups in G, or, equivalently, if $aN = Na$ holds for every a in G. For a normal subgroup N, there is no distinction between the right and the left cosets of N; and the product AB of any two such cosets A and B is again a coset of N in G. The set of all cosets of N in G then forms a group with respect to this multiplication; it is called the factor group (quotient group) of G with respect to N and is denoted by G/N.

The set $\{e\}$ consisting of the identity e alone is a normal subgroup of G, and G itself is also a normal subgroup of G. If there is no other normal subgroup in G, then G is called a simple group. Let Z_G denote the set of all elements a in a group G such that $ax = xa$ for every x in G. Then Z_G is also a normal subgroup of G, and it is called the centre of G.

Permutation Groups.—A mapping f of a set M into a set M' is a rule that assigns to each element s in M a certain element s' in M'; s' is called the image of s under the mapping f and is denoted by $f(s)$; that is, $s' = f(s)$. The mapping f is called injective if different elements in M' are assigned to different elements in M under f (i.e., $f(s) \neq f(t)$ for $s \neq t$ in M), and it is called surjective if every element in M' is the image of some element in M under f.

A permutation of a set M is a mapping of M into itself that is both injective and surjective. Let both f and g be permutations of M. Then there is a unique permutation h of M such that $h(s) = f(g(s))$ for every s in M. Such a permutation h is called the product of f and g, and is denoted by fg; that is, $h = fg$. The set, P_M, of all permutations of M then satisfies (1), (2) and (3), and hence forms a group with respect to the rule of composition defined above. Any subgroup of the group P_M is called a permutation (or transformation) group on the set M. When the set M consists of letters $1, 2, \ldots, n$, the group P_M is denoted by S_n and is called the symmetric group of degree n; it is a finite group of order $n!$. For example, the symmetric group S_3 consists of the following six permutations on 1, 2, 3:

$$\begin{pmatrix} 1\,2\,3 \\ 1\,2\,3 \end{pmatrix} \quad \begin{pmatrix} 1\,2\,3 \\ 2\,3\,1 \end{pmatrix} \quad \begin{pmatrix} 1\,2\,3 \\ 3\,1\,2 \end{pmatrix} \quad \begin{pmatrix} 1\,2\,3 \\ 1\,3\,2 \end{pmatrix} \quad \begin{pmatrix} 1\,2\,3 \\ 3\,2\,1 \end{pmatrix} \quad \begin{pmatrix} 1\,2\,3 \\ 2\,1\,3 \end{pmatrix}$$

Here $\begin{pmatrix} 1\,2\,3 \\ 3\,1\,2 \end{pmatrix}$, for instance, denotes the permutation f such that

$$f(1) = 3, \quad f(2) = 1, \quad f(3) = 2.$$

Further Examples.—(1) Let C and R respectively denote the set of all complex numbers and the set of all real numbers. Then C is an abelian group with respect to ordinary addition as the rule of composition, and R is a subgroup of C. The set Z of all integers $0, \pm 1, \pm 2, \ldots$, is a subgroup of both C and R.

(2) The set C^* of all nonzero complex numbers forms an abelian group with respect to ordinary multiplication as the rule of composition. The set of all nonzero real numbers is a subgroup of C^*.

(3) For any integer $n \geq 1$, let $GL(n; C)$ ($GL(n; R)$) denote the set of all $n \times n$ nonsingular matrices with entries in C (in R). Then $GL(n; C)$ is a group with respect to matrix multiplication and $GL(n; R)$ is a subgroup of $GL(n; C)$ (see MATRIX). The set $SL(n; C)$ ($SL(n; R)$) of all matrices in $GL(n; C)$ ($GL(n; R)$) with determinants 1 is a normal subgroup of $GL(n; C)$ ($GL(n; R)$). The set $U(n)$ of all $n \times n$ unitary matrices and the set $O(n)$ of all $n \times n$ orthogonal matrices are also subgroups of $GL(n; C)$; $O(n)$ is the intersection of $U(n)$ and $GL(n; R)$. These groups belong to an important class of groups called classical groups.

(4) A mapping f of n-dimensional Euclidean space E_n ($n \geq 1$) into itself is called a motion in E_n if it does not change the distance of any two points in E_n (i.e., if $d(s,t) = d(f(s), f(t))$ for any s,t in E_n, d being the distance). The set of all such motions forms a subgroup of the group of all permutations on the set E_n; it is called the group of motions in E_n. Similarly, the group of motions in a non-Euclidean space (Riemannian space) is defined by the set of all mappings of the space into itself that leave invariant the non-Euclidean (Riemannian) distance of any two points in the space (see RIEMANNIAN GEOMETRY). More generally, the set of all permutations on a geometric space that leave invariant certain geometric properties of the space forms a subgroup of the group of all permutations on that space.

Isomorphisms.—A homomorphism of a group G into a group G' is a mapping f of G into G' such that $f(a)f(b) = f(ab)$ for any a,b in G. If furthermore f is both injective and surjective, then it is called an isomorphism of G onto G'; in other words, an isomorphism is a one-one correspondence between G and G' that preserves the rule of composition in these groups. When there exists such an isomorphism, it is said that G is isomorphic to G' (written $G \cong G'$). It then follows that $G \cong G$; $G \cong G'$ implies $G' \cong G$; while $G \cong G'$ and $G' \cong G''$ imply $G \cong G''$.

Let N be a normal subgroup of a group G and let ϕ be a mapping of G into the factor group G/N defined by $\phi(a) = aN$ for any a in G. Then ϕ is a surjective homomorphism of G into G/N and is called the canonical homomorphism of G into the factor group

G/N. Let f be a homomorphism of G into a group G' and let K denote the set of all elements x in G such that $f(x) = e'$, where e' is the identity of G'. Then K is a normal subgroup of G and is called the kernel of the homomorphism f. On the other hand, the set of all images $f(a)$ of elements a in G under f forms a subgroup of G'. It is called the image of G in G' under f and is denoted by $f(G)$. One of the fundamental theorems in the theory of groups says that given such a homomorphism f of G into G', there is an isomorphism g of G/K onto $f(G)$ such that $g(\phi(x)) = f(x)$ for any x in G, where ϕ is the canonical homomorphism of G into G/K; in particular, $G/K \cong f(G)$. For example, let f be a mapping of R into C^* (see [1] and [2] above) defined by $f(x) = e^{2\pi i x}$ for any x in R. Then f is a homomorphism of R into C^*; the kernel of f is the group Z of all integers, and the image $f(R)$ is the group C_1 of all complex numbers z with $|z| = 1$. Hence $R/Z \cong C_1$.

An isomorphism of a group G onto itself is called an automorphism of G. The set of all automorphisms of G then forms a subgroup of the group of all permutations on the set G.

When two groups are isomorphic to each other, it is said that they have the same abstract group structure or they are of the same type; these groups may then be considered to represent the same abstract group in two different ways. In developing the theory of groups, interest focuses on the abstract structure of groups and efforts are made to find out what possible types of (abstract) groups there are.

Normal Chains.—A normal chain of a group G is a sequence of groups, $G = G_0, G_1, \ldots, G_n = \{e\}$, such that each G_i is a normal subgroup of G_{i-1}. Such a normal chain is called a composition series of G if furthermore each G_{i-1}/G_i is a simple group different from the identity. A group G does not always have a composition series. But the theorem of Jordan-Hölder says that if for G there exist two composition series: $G = G_0, G_1, \ldots, G_n = \{e\}$ and $G = G_0', G_1', \ldots, G_m' = \{e\}$, then $n = m$ and the factor groups G_{i-1}/G_i are isomorphic to the factor groups G_{j-1}'/G_j' in some order.

A normal chain, $G = G_0, G_1, \ldots, G_n = \{e\}$, is called a central chain of G if each G_i is a normal subgroup of G, and G_{i-1}/G_i is contained in the centre of G/G_i. A group that has such a central chain is called a nilpotent group.

A group G is called a solvable (soluble) group if there is a normal chain, $G = G_0, G_1, \ldots, G_n = \{e\}$, such that each G_{i-1}/G_i is an abelian group. Solvable groups are so named because they are associated in Galois theory with algebraic equations that can be solved by algebraic means.

An abelian group is nilpotent, and a nilpotent group is solvable.

Construction of Groups.—Given two groups G_1 and G_2, let $G_1 \times G_2$ denote the set of all pairs (x_1, x_2) with x_1 in G_1 and x_2 in G_2. If the product of two such pairs (x_1, x_2) and (y_1, y_2) is defined to be $(x_1 y_1, x_2 y_2)$, then the set $G_1 \times G_2$ becomes a group; it is called the direct product of G_1 and G_2. If e_1 and e_2 denote the identities of G_1 and G_2 respectively, then (e_1, e_2) gives the identity of $G_1 \times G_2$. Let G_1' be the set of all pairs of the form (x_1, e_2) with arbitrary x_1 in G_1, and let G_2' be defined similarly interchanging G_1 and G_2. Then both G_1' and G_2' are normal subgroups of G and have the following properties: $G_1' G_2' = G_1 \times G_2$; $G_1' \cap G_2' = \{e\}$; $G_1' \cong G_1$; $G_2' \cong G_2$. If a group G has two normal subgroups G_1 and G_2 such that $G_1 G_2 = G$, and $G_1 \cap G_2 = \{e\}$, then G is isomorphic to the direct product $G_1 \times G_2$. The direct product of more than two groups can be defined similarly; for example, $G_1 \times G_2 \times G_3$ is the group consisting of all triples (x_1, x_2, x_3) with x_i in G_i ($i = 1, 2, 3$).

Again, let G_1 and G_2 be any given groups. A group G is called an extension of G_2 by G_1 if G had a normal subgroup N such that $G/N \cong G_1$, and $N \cong G_2$. O. Schreier (1926) studied the structure of such an extension. To study the structure of extensions of G_2 by G_1 and explicitly described how all extensions can be obtained from any given groups G_1 and G_2.

Representations.—A homomorphism of a group G into a group G' is also called a representation of G in G'. To study the structure of a given (finite) group G, consideration is often given to representations of G in the groups S_n and $GL(n; C), n \geq 1$ (see *Permutation Groups; Further Examples:* [3], above). Let f be a representation of G in $GL(n; C)$, and let $\chi(x)$ denote the trace (sum of the diagonal entries) of the matrix $f(x)$ for any x in G. The function χ on G thus defined is called the character of f; it is also called a character of G without referring to f. If χ_1 and χ_2 are characters of G, then the sum $\chi_1 + \chi_2$ is also a character of G. A character χ is called irreducible if it is not the sum of two other characters of G. Every character of G is then the sum of a finite number of irreducible characters. Two representations f_1 and f_2 of G in $GL(n; C)$ are called equivalent if there is an element u in $GL(n; C)$ such that $f_2(x) = u f_1(x) u^{-1}$ for every x in G. Equivalent representations define the same character.

In general, a group G can be divided into a number of disjoint subsets called conjugate classes of G such that any two elements x and y in G belong to the same conjugate class if and only if $y = a x a^{-1}$ with some a in G; those x and y are then called conjugate elements and they satisfy $\chi(x) = \chi(y)$ for every character χ of G. Suppose that G is a finite group; then two representations of G are equivalent if they define the same character; two elements x and y in G are conjugate if $\chi(x) = \chi(y)$ for every character χ; the number of irreducible characters of G is equal to the number of different conjugate classes in G, and those irreducible characters satisfy the so-called orthogonality relations that are important in various applications.

For any "field" K, let $GL(n; K)$ denote the multiplicative group of all $n \times n$ nonsingular matrices with entries in K. Representations of finite groups in such $GL(n; K)$ are also studied; when K has prime characteristic, they are called modular representations.

Abelian Groups.—A set of elements in a group G is called a set of generators of G if every element of G can be expressed as a product of elements in that set and of their inverses. If there is a finite set of generators, the group is called finitely generated.

A cyclic group C is a group generated by a single element; it consists of powers of an element a as follows: $e = a^0, a^{\pm 1}, a^{\pm 2}, \ldots$, with $a^n = e$. Here $a^{\pm 2}$, for instance, denotes the elements aa, and $a^{-1} a^{-1} = (aa)^{-1}$. A cyclic group is abelian. For each $n = 1, 2, \ldots, \infty$, there is a unique type of cyclic group C with order n. If $n = \infty$, it is isomorphic to the group Z of all integers. If $n < \infty$, then C consists of the n elements, $e = a^0, a, a^2, \ldots, a^{n-1}$, with $a^n = e$.

A fundamental theorem on abelian groups says that a finitely generated abelian group G is (isomorphic to) the direct product of a finite number of cyclic groups each of which has order either ∞ or a power of a prime number, and that the orders of these cyclic groups are uniquely determined by G. Using this theorem, all possible types of finite abelian groups of order n can be found for any given integer $n \geq 1$. For example, there exist four different types of abelian groups of order 100.

Finite Groups.—Let p be any prime number. Let p^e be the exact power of p dividing the order of a finite group G. L. Sylow (1873) proved that G contains subgroups of order p^e, called Sylow p-subgroups of G, and that these subgroups are conjugate to each other in G. In general, a finite group with order a power of p is called a p-group. A p-group is nilpotent; a finite group is nilpotent if and only if it is the direct product of its Sylow subgroups. Hence the study of nilpotent finite groups is reduced to that of p-groups.

A finite group G always has a composition series: $G = G_0, G_1, \ldots, G_n = \{e\}$. Each G_{i-1}/G_i ($1 \leq i \leq n$) is a simple group, and G is constructed from these simple groups G_{i-1}/G_i ($1 \leq i \leq n$) by means of successive group extensions (see *Construction of Groups*, above). The group G is then solvable if and only if every G_{i-1}/G_i is abelian. But an abelian simple group is a cyclic group with order a prime number, and its structure is completely known. On the other hand, the structure of nonabelian simple groups is very complex; the study of solvable finite groups is much easier than that of nonsolvable finite groups. To determine the structure of nonabelian simple finite groups is one of the most important problems in the theory of groups. See INVARIANTS; GROUPS, CONTINUOUS; GROUPS, TRANSFORMATION; GROUPS AND ALGEBRAS, REPRESENTATIONS OF; see also references under "Groups" in the Index.

BIBLIOGRAPHY.—C. Jordan, *Traité des substitutions et des équations algébriques* (1870); W. Burnside, *Theory of Groups of Finite Order*, 2nd ed. (1955); B. L. v. d. Waerden, *Gruppen von linearen Transformationen* (1935); I. Kaplansky, *Infinite Abelian Groups* (1954); A. G. Kurosh, *The Theory of Groups* I, II (trans. from Russian) (1955); A. Speiser, *Die Theorie der Gruppen von endlicher Ordnung*, 4th ed. (1956); H. Zassenhaus, *The Theory of Groups*, 2nd ed. (1958); M. Hall, Jr., *The Theory of Groups* (1959); V. Heine, *Group Theory in Quantum Mechanics* (1960); G. Lyubarskii, *Application of Group Theory in Physics* (1960); G. d. B. Robinson, *Representation Theory of a Symmetric Group* (1961). Textbooks on modern algebra, such as G. Birkhoff and S. MacLane, *A Survey of Modern Algebra* (1953), also give an introduction to the theory of groups.
(K. Iw.)

GROUPS, CONTINUOUS. This subject comprises a fundamental branch of modern mathematics with applications to theoretical physics. The expression "continuous groups" has been employed since the 19th century for a variety of mathematical structures, some of which are not even groups (q.v.). Roughly speaking, the study arose from situations in which there is an infinite number of symmetries present. The set of symmetries is called "the group of transformations admitted by" the situation. In the early days of the theory, which was fathered largely by M. Sophus Lie, much of the research was devoted to applications to the theory of differential equations. As one might expect, the presence of symmetries serves to reduce many difficulties by drastically limiting possibilities. Toward the end of the 19th century, the work of E. Cartan shifted the course of investigation toward a deeper analysis, both algebraic and topological, of the continuous group itself. So fruitful were some of Cartan's ideas that they molded some of the basic notions of algebra and topology. The threefold structure of continuous groups—algebraic, topological and analytic—has attracted a variety of methods of attack, some of them marked by brilliant developments. The work of Lie and of Cartan had revealed many of the fundamental properties of continuous groups before the end of the 19th century. Rather than retrace their steps, this article will begin by introducing some 20th-century terms necessary for an adequate description of the basic ideas. The early developments in the relations between groups and differential equations will be presented later in the article.

Topological Groups.—A topological group G is a group G whose elements are the points of a topological space (*see* TOPOLOGY, GENERAL) for which the group operations are continuous. In greater detail, the elements of G satisfy the postulates for a group:

(G1) There is a binary operation assigning to any two elements x and y in G an element in G denoted by xy and called the group product of x and y.

(G2) There is an element e in G such that $ex = xe = x$ for all x in G; e is called the identity.

(G3) For each element x in G, there is an element denoted by x^{-1} such that $x^{-1}x = e$; the element x^{-1} is called the inverse of x.

The condition that G is a topological space for which the group operations are continuous means that there is a notion of "nearness" among the various elements of G so that if x' is near x then x'^{-1} is near x^{-1} and if y' is near y then $x'y'$ is near xy.

The following are familiar examples of topological groups:

Example 1. G is the set of all real numbers with addition as the group product.

Example 2. G is the set of all complex numbers z with $|z| = 1$ and with multiplication as the group product.

Example 3. G is the set of all rigid motions in Euclidean space which keep some point O fixed. Here the group product is taken as composition of motions; that is, if T_2 and T_1 are in G, $T_2 \cdot T_1$ is the motion which takes any point p into $T_2(T_1(p))$.

Example 4. G is the group of all $n \cdot n$ matrices with complex coefficients and nonzero determinant, the group product being the usual matrix multiplication.

The groups in examples 1 and 2 above are abelian; that is, $xy = yx$ for any two elements x and y. The groups in examples 2 and 3 above are compact; that is, any infinite sequence of elements $x_1, x_2, \ldots, x_m, \ldots$ contains a subsequence converging to an element of the group. The group in example 4 above is neither abelian nor compact, but it is locally compact; that is, each element has a compact neighbourhood. Each of the groups in the examples is locally Euclidean; that is, each point has a neighbourhood resembling topologically a solid ball in Euclidean space of dimensions 1, 1, 3 and n^2 respectively.

The theory of topological groups has developed in three principal directions: the theory of the algebraic structure, of the topological structure and of representations by transformation groups.

The algebraic structure of a topological group is especially accessible to investigation in case the group operations are analytic. In greater detail, in a topological space, one can define a continuous function as any real-valued function f with the property that $f(x')$ is close to $f(x)$ if x' is close to x. But one cannot speak of differentiable or analytic functions on a locally Euclidean topological space in a self-consistent fashion unless one is given a rule by which to pick out from the totality of continuous functions the differentiable and analytic functions. A locally Euclidean space with such a rule is called a differentiable or analytic manifold, as the case may be. For simplicity, this article deals with analytic manifolds.

An analytic co-ordinate system around a point p in an analytic manifold is a set of functions $(x_1, \ldots, x_k)$ defined near p with the property: a function f is analytic around p if and only if it is expressible as a convergent power series in $x_1, \ldots, x_k$ in some neighbourhood of the point p. In an analytic manifold M there is of course an analytic co-ordinate system around each point, but in general the co-ordinate system is not defined throughout the manifold.

If $(x_1, \ldots, x_k)$ is an analytic co-ordinate system, the map Φ : $p \to (x_1(p), \ldots, x_k(p))$ is a map of a neighbourhood of p onto a neighbourhood in Euclidean k-space E^k and the map Φ is a topological equivalence or homeomorphism of some neighbourhood of p onto a solid ball in E^k.

A map ϕ (taking possibly many points into a single point) of a manifold M into a manifold N is called an analytic map if for any analytic function f defined in a region of N, the composite function $f \circ \phi$ is analytic in M (recall $f \circ \phi(m) = f(\phi(m))$).

A Lie group G is a topological group of a special kind: the underlying space is an analytic manifold for which the group operations are analytic. That is, the map $(x,y) \to xy$ of the analytic manifold of ordered pairs $G \cdot G$ into G is an analytic map, and the map $x \to x^{-1}$ of G into G also is analytic.

Infinitesimal Transformations.—One of the basic notions in the theory of Lie groups is that of infinitesimal transformation. Let M be an analytic manifold and let m be a point of M. We wish first to speak of a tangent vector to M at m. In case M is a surface in Euclidean space, one regards, extrinsically, a tangent vector to a surface as a vector in the containing Euclidean space.

However, it is possible to make a mathematically satisfactory intrinsic definition of a tangent vector to a manifold (*i.e.*, without reference to a containing Euclidean space) by means of the following consideration: a tangent vector X is completely determined once one knows how functions vary along it, that is, the directional derivative of functions along X. Hence for all purposes we can equate the notion of tangent vector X with the operation of taking the directional derivative along X. In this pragmatic spirit one adopts the definition: a tangent vector X to a manifold M at a point m is an operator that assigns to each real-valued function f analytic around m a real number Xf, called the directional derivative of f along X, such that

$$X(f + g) = Xf + Xg$$
$$X(fg) = (Xf)g(m) + f(m)X(g)$$
$$X(af) = aXf$$

where f and g are analytic functions around p, and a is a constant. It is easily proved that the set of all tangent vectors at a point m of a k-dimensional manifold constitutes a linear or vector space whose dimension is k (over the field of real numbers). This linear space is called the tangent space to M at m and is denoted by $\dot{M}_m$. A vector field on a manifold M is a rule which assigns to each point m of M an element of $\dot{M}_m$. To illustrate, let $(x_1, \ldots, x_k)$ be an analytic co-ordinate system on a neighbourhood V of manifold M. We denote by $\frac{\delta}{\delta x_i}(m)$ the operator which assigns to the analytic function $f(x_1,\ldots,x_k)$ the value of $\frac{\delta f}{\delta x_i}$ at the point m. Then $\frac{\delta}{\delta x_i}(m),\ldots,\frac{\delta}{\delta x_k}(m)$ form a base for the vector space $\dot{M}_m$.

We denote by $\frac{\delta}{\delta x_i}$ the vector field $p \to \frac{\delta}{\delta x_i}(p)$ on the neighbourhood V. The most general vector field on V has the form $\Sigma_i A_i \frac{\delta}{\delta x_i}$, where $A_1,\ldots,A_k$ are functions on V. An infinitesimal transformation on an (analytic) manifold is a vector field X such that for any analytic function f on M, the function $Xf: p \to X(p)f$ is analytic. An infinitesimal transformation on the neighbourhood V above is any vector field $X = \Sigma A_i \frac{\delta}{\delta x_i}$ such that the functions $A_1,\ldots,A_k$ are analytic. If $(y_1,\ldots,y_k)$ is a second co-ordinate system, then $\frac{\delta}{\delta x_i} = \Sigma_i \frac{\delta f}{\delta y_i}\frac{\delta y_i}{\delta x_i}$, so that

$$\frac{\delta}{\delta x_i} = \frac{\delta y_1}{\delta x_i}\frac{\delta}{\delta y_1} + \frac{\delta y_2}{\delta x_i}\frac{\delta}{\delta y_2} + \cdots + \frac{\delta y_k}{\delta x_i}\frac{\delta}{\delta y_k}$$

An infinitesimal transformation X can also be equated with the operation $f \to Xf$ taking any analytic function f into the analytic function Xf. Indeed, any operation X assigning to any analytic function f an analytic function Xf such that

$$X(f+g) = Xf + Xg \tag{1}$$
$$X(fg) = Xf\cdot g + fXg \tag{2}$$
$$X(af) = aXf \tag{3}$$

for any analytic functions f and g, a being any constant, determines a unique infinitesimal transformation.

A map ϕ of an analytic manifold M into an analytic manifold N induces a map of the tangent space $\dot{M}_m$ into the tangent space $\dot{N}_{\phi(m)}$ called the differential of ϕ at M and denoted by $d\phi_m$, as follows: $d\phi_m(X) = X(\phi)$ for any function f analytic in M around the point m.

For example, if ϕ is an analytic curve in N, that is an analytic map of the manifold of real numbers (t) into N, then $d\phi_t(\frac{d}{dt})$ is the tangent vector at the point $\phi(t)$ which assigns to any function f on N the value $\frac{d}{dt}f(\phi(t))$; in case ϕ is a real-valued function on M, then for any tangent vector X in $\dot{M}_m$,

$d\phi(X)$ is a numerical factor of the tangent vector $\frac{d}{dt_{\phi(m)}}$; the numerical factor is also denoted by $d\phi(X)$. By this convention, $d\phi$ becomes a real-valued function of tangent vectors in case ϕ is an analytic (or differentiable) real-valued function on M; this $d\phi$ coincides with the classical definition of differential.

Suppose now that X is an infinitesimal transformation on an analytic manifold M. Then, by the fundamental existence and uniqueness theorem of ordinary differential equations, there passes through each point p of M a unique trajectory to X with initial point p; that is, an analytic curve $\phi(p,t)$ in M with $\phi(p,0) = p$ and the tangent to the curve at any point q coinciding with the tangent vector $X(q)$; more explicitly, $\frac{d}{dt'}\phi(\phi(p,t)) = Xf(\phi(p,t))$ for any t and for any function f analytic in M. We denote by "exp tX" the map $p \to \phi(p,t)$; for any point p, exp tX is defined for suitably small values of t (but not necessarily all). We can think thus of an infinitesimal transformation as the velocity field of a steady flow on a manifold, and exp tX is the displacement of points after t units of time.

In the special case that M is the set of real numbers and $X = \frac{\delta}{\delta x} = \frac{d}{dx}$, $x(\exp tX(\phi)) = \frac{dx}{dx} = 1$ and $\exp tX(\phi) = p + t$. If $X = x^2\frac{d}{dx}$, then $\exp tX(p)$ is the trajectory to $\frac{dx}{dt} = x^2$, and $\exp tX(\phi) = \frac{p}{1-pt}$, which is not defined for $t = 1/p$. The term "infinitesimal transformation" owes its origin to the fact that for small values of the parameter t, the transformation $\exp tX$ consists of the displacement

$$(x_1,\ldots,x_k) \to (x_1+tA_1,\ldots,x_k+tA_k)$$

up to infinitesimals of order t^2 if $X = \Sigma_i A_i \frac{\delta}{\delta x_i}$. If X is an infinitesimal transformation on a manifold then $f(\exp tX(p)) = $

$$\sum_{n=0}^{\infty}(n!)^{-1}t^n X^n(f)$$

whenever both sides are defined. This identity can be stated in a more familiar form when we adopt the following notational convention: if ϕ is a map of a space M into a space N, we denote by $\phi(f)$ the composite function $f\circ\phi$ where f is a function on N. Thus by definition, $f(\phi(m)) = (\phi(f))(m)$. By this convention we regard ϕ not only as a map of points of M into points of N but also as the equivalent indicated map of functions on N into functions on M. Adhering to this convention, the identity above states

$$\exp tX = \sum_{n=0}^{\infty}(n!)^{-1}t^n X^n \tag{4}$$

as operators on analytic functions on M, whenever both sides can be applied.

It is clear from (4) that a point m is fixed under the transformations $\exp tX$ for all t if and only if the point m is a zero of X; i.e., $X(m) = 0$ or $X_f(m) = 0$ for any analytic function f.

Local (Pseudo-) Groups of Transformations.—Let G be a topological group and M a topological space. Let $P(M)$ denote the set of all permutations of M; i.e., all transformations of M which have inverses. An operation of G on M is a rule T which assigns to each g in G an element $T(g)$ in $P(M)$ such that

(T1) $T(g_1 g_2) = T(g_1)\circ T(g_2)$
(T2) The element $T(g)(m)$ depends continuously on g and m.

If G is a Lie group and M is an analytic manifold, an operation is called analytic if the point $T(g)(m)$ depends analytically on g and m. An important variation on this idea is that of a local pseudo-group (sometimes called simply local group) operating on a manifold. Briefly, a local Lie group is a structure which resembles a neighbourhood of the identity in a Lie group; products are not always defined but, when they are, the group postulates are fulfilled. The celebrated first and second fundamental theorems of Lie describe the relation between local Lie groups on a manifold and infinitesimal transformations.

Let N and M be analytic manifolds and let T be a one-to-one map of N into $P(M)$ such that $T(n)(m)$ depends analytically on n and m. Assume that for some n_0 in N, $T(n_0)$ is the identity transformation of M. One considers the map T_n which assigns to each tangent vector $X\epsilon N_n$ an infinitesimal transformation $T_n(X)$ by the following rule:

$$\tilde{T}_n(X)(m) = d\phi_m(X) \tag{5}$$

where $\phi: p \to (T(p)\cdot T(n)^{-1})(m)$ maps N into M and n into m. T is an analytic operation of N on M. If this is the case, the infinitesimal transformation $T_n(X)$ is called the infinitesimal transformation of M along a path whose tangent vector at n is X.

Lie's first fundamental theorem states that $T_n(N_n)$ is independent of the point n if and only if N is a local Lie group and T is an analytic operation of N on M. If this is the case, the infinitesimal transformations $T_n(X)$ form a local Lie group of transformations on M, the operator $XY - YX$ satisfies conditions (1),

(2) and (3), and is thus an infinitesimal transformation. $XY - YX$ is denoted by $[X,Y]$ and is called the Poisson bracket of X and Y. If $(x_1, \ldots, x_k)$ is an analytic co-ordinate system on a neighbourhood v, then $X = \Sigma_i A_i \frac{\delta}{\delta x_i}$, $Y = \Sigma_i B_i \frac{\delta}{\delta x_i}$ and $[X,Y] =$

$$\Sigma_{ij}\left(A_j \frac{\delta B_i}{\delta x_j} - B_j \frac{\delta A_i}{\delta x_j}\right) \frac{\delta}{\delta x_i}.$$

Directly from definitions, it may be seen that

$$[X,Y] = -[Y,X] \text{ and } [[X,Y],Z] + [[Y,Z],X] + [[Z,X],Y] = 0$$

the latter being the Jacobi identity.

Suppose now that $\mathcal{J}$ is a set of infinitesimal transformations. $\mathcal{J}$ is called a Lie algebra of infinitesimal transformations if (1) $\mathcal{J}$ is a linear family, that is, $\mathcal{J}$ contains any linear combination of its elements with constant coefficients; and (2) $\mathcal{J}$ contains the Poisson brackets of any of its elements.

Lie's second fundamental theorem states that a family of infinitesimal transformations $\mathcal{J}$ is the infinitesimal generator of a finite dimensional local Lie group of transformations if and only if $\mathcal{J}$ is a finite dimensional (over the field of constants) Lie algebra of infinitesimal transformations. The corresponding local Lie group of transformations is the set of all transformations of the form

$$\exp t_1 X_1 \cdot \exp t_2 X_2 \cdot \ldots \cdot \exp t_r X_r \quad (6)$$

where $X_1, \ldots, X_r$ is a base for $\mathcal{J}$ and $t_1, \ldots, t_r$ is any set of real numbers which are suitably small. The elements of the corresponding local group can also be described as the set of all transformations

$$\exp X = X \epsilon \mathcal{J} \quad (7)$$

It may happen that the corresponding local group G is indeed a genuine group. In that case neither the elements of the form (6) nor (7) necessarily exhaust G; they merely cover a neighbourhood of the identity in G in general.

In case the family $\mathcal{J}$ of Lie's second fundamental theorem is infinite dimensional, there arises a so-called infinite Lie pseudo-group. These pseudo-groups were studied extensively by Cartan, but basic questions about the nature of such structures were left unanswered. In the 1950s several independent investigations into some of these questions were initiated. In this article, however, the term Lie group is reserved for the finite dimensional case alone.

With the help of his second fundamental theorem, Lie was able to determine all the local groups of transformations depending on a finite number of parameters which operate on the line, plane and, in certain cases, on higher dimensional spaces. For example, it is relatively easy to show that the only finite dimensional Lie algebras of infinitesimal transformations on the line which have no common zeros have in suitable co-ordinates one of the following three bases $(a) \frac{d}{dx}$; $(b) \frac{d}{dx}, x\frac{d}{dx}$; or $(c) \frac{d}{dx}, x\frac{d}{dx}, x^2 \frac{d}{dx}$.

These are the generators of the
(a) one-parameter translation group: $x \to x + t$;
(b) two-parameter affine group: $x \to ax + b$;
(c) three-parameter projective group: $x \to \frac{ax + b}{cx + d}$,

$$\det \begin{vmatrix} a & b \\ c & d \end{vmatrix} \neq 0.$$

These three are thus up to equivalence the only finite dimensional local Lie groups operating transitively on the line.

The last example shows clearly that a local group of transformations of the line need not be a piece of a global group of transformations of the line. However, it is true that any local Lie group has a neighbourhood of its identity which is *in abstracto* isomorphic to a neighbourhood of the identity in some genuine (global) Lie group.

The Lie Algebra of a Lie Group.—Consider now a Lie group G. For each g in G, let $T(g)$ denote the left translation map $x \to gx$ of G onto G. Then T is an analytic operation of G on G.

By Lie's first fundamental theorem, the group $T(G)$ has an infinitesimal generator, and by Lie's second fundamental theorem, the infinitesimal generator is a Lie algebra of infinitesimal transformations; this infinitesimal generator is denoted by $\dot{G}$ and is called the Lie algebra of G. It is readily proved that $\dot{G}$ consists of precisely those infinitesimal transformations on G which are left unchanged by the right translations $x \to xg$ of G into G. It follows at once that each infinitesimal translation in G is uniquely determined by its value at the origin. Thus as a linear space, $\dot{G}$ is equivalent to $\dot{G}_e$, the tangent space of G at the identity element e. If X is an element of $\dot{G}_e$, and $\bar{X}$ is the element of G determined by X, then one defines $\exp X = \bar{X}(e)$. Also, one defines $[X,Y]$ to be the value at e of $[\bar{X},\bar{Y}]$, where $\bar{X}$ and $\bar{Y}$ are the elements of G with $\bar{X}(e) = X$ and $\bar{Y}(e) = Y$. In the special case that G is the group $GL(n)$ of all invertible linear transformations of an n-dimensional linear space V_n over the real numbers, the tangent space to G at the identity element can be identified with the set of all linear transformations of V_n. Then for any $X \epsilon \dot{G}_e$, $\exp X$ coincides with the classical exponential of the transformation X; *i.e.*, $\exp X = \Sigma_i \frac{X^i}{i!}$. Moreover, for any X and Y in $\dot{G}$, $[X,Y] = XY - YX$, where the multiplication on the right is the usual multiplication of linear transformations.

If we abstract from $\dot{G}$ its algebraic structure alone, we see that it is an algebra with Poisson brackets as multiplication. This multiplication is nonassociative, but the structure of such algebras is capable of a virtually exhaustive description. On the other hand, there is a very close connection between the algebraic structure of a Lie group and the algebraic structure of its Lie algebra. Indeed, there is a one-to-one correspondence between the subalgebras of the Lie algebra $\dot{G}$ and the connected Lie subgroups of G, the correspondence being: a connected Lie subgroup H corresponds to the subalgebra of $\dot{G}$ that is determined by the tangent subspace H_e to H at the identity. A connected Lie subgroup H is normal in G if and only if the corresponding subalgebra $\dot{H}$ is an ideal in $\dot{G}$; that is, $[\dot{G},\dot{H}]$ is contained in $\dot{H}$. To the commutator subgroup of G generated by the elements of the form $xyz^{-1}y^{-1}$, there corresponds the "derived" subalgebra which is generated by the elements $[X,Y]$ with X and Y in $\dot{G}$. In particular, a connected Lie group G is abelian if and only if $[X,Y] = 0$ for all X and Y in $\dot{G}$.

The most elementary type of Lie algebra is one wherein the multiplication is trivial; *i.e.*, $[G,\dot{G}] = 0$. Such a Lie algebra is called abelian. Next in complexity is a Lie algebra wherein the product of some finite number of any elements is zero; *i.e.*, if setting $\dot{G}^{(1)} = \dot{G}$, $\dot{G}^{(n+1)} = [\dot{G}^{(n)}, \dot{G}^{(1)}]$, then $\dot{G}^{(n)} = 0$ for some n. Such a $\dot{G}$ is called nilpotent. One step more complex are Lie algebras $\dot{G}$ which have a decreasing sequence of ideals, $\dot{G} \supset \dot{G}_1 \supset \ldots \supset \dot{G}_n \ldots$ with the quotient algebra $\dot{G}_i/\dot{G}_{i+1}$ abelian and $\dot{G}_n = 0$ for some n; such a Lie algebra is called solvable. The maximum solvable ideal of a Lie algebra is called its radical. If $\dot{G}$ is a Lie algebra and $\mathcal{R}$ denotes its radical, then $\dot{G}/\mathcal{R}$ has no nonzero radical; such a Lie algebra is called semisimple. If a Lie algebra has no nonzero properly smaller ideal, it is called simple. The basic theorems describing the structure of Lie algebras over any field of characteristic zero areas follows:

1. Any Lie algebra is a semidirect sum of its radical and a semisimple subalgebra.
2. Any semisimple Lie algebra is a direct sum of simple Lie algebras.
3. Any simple Lie algebra over the field of complex numbers is one of the following type:

A_n: the Lie algebra of the group of all complex-valued matrices of determinant 1;

B_n: the Lie subalgebra of A_{2n+1} which annihilates the quadratic form
$$X_1^2 + X_2^2 + \ldots + X_{2n+1}^2;$$

C_n: the Lie subalgebra of A_{2n} which annihilates the alternating bilinear form
$$x_1 y_{n+1} - y_1 x_{n+1} + x_2 y_{n+2} - y_2 x_{n+2} + \ldots + x_n y_{2n} - y_n x_{2n};$$

D_n: the Lie subalgebra of A_{2n} which annihilates the quadratic form
$$x_1^2 + \ldots + x_{2n}^2.$$

The five "exceptional" simple Lie algebras G_2, F_4, E_6, E_7, E_8 discovered by W. Killing are of dimensions 14, 52, 78, 133, 248 respectively.

This remarkable classification is achieved by a study of the so-called root diagram of the Lie algebra.

Although each Lie group has a unique Lie algebra, a Lie algebra in the abstract (i.e., divorced from its presentation as the infinitesimal generator of a Lie group) may arise from inequivalent or nonisomorphic groups. For example, the one-dimension abelian Lie algebra over the field of real numbers is the Lie algebra of both example G1 and example G2 above. The problem of determining the relation between the various connected Lie groups having abstractly isomorphic Lie algebras was solved by Otto Schreier. The situation is: to each abstract Lie algebra $\mathfrak{g}$ (over the field of real numbers) there corresponds a unique (up to isomorphism) simply connected Lie group G; that is, a connected Lie group in which every closed curve can be deformed continuously to a point; any other Lie group G_1 whose Lie algebra is isomorphic to $\mathfrak{g}$ is obtained from G by a homomorphism with a discrete kernel. Thus G_1 is evenly covered by G, and all connected Lie groups whose Lie algebras are isomorphic to G have the same simply connected covering group.

The spin representation of physics provides another example of this phenomenon.

It should be emphasized, however, that in a neighbourhood of the identity, any two Lie groups having isomorphic Lie algebras are isomorphic. This can be seen from the Baker-Campbell-Hausdorff formula.

$$\exp X \exp Y = \exp (X + Y - \tfrac{1}{2}[X,Y] + \cdots)\qquad(8)$$

the dots denoting an infinite sum of terms built from X and Y with Poisson brackets. By a process known as "complexification" it can be proved that the classification of complex simple Lie algebras also applies to compact Lie algebras.

The Topological Structure of Lie Groups.—We have seen that to a given abstract Lie algebra there may correspond Lie groups which are not topologically equivalent. Therefore, one cannot expect that the abstract Lie algebra $\hat{G}$ of a Lie group G determines the topological structure of G completely. However, one of the greatest contributions of E. Cartan to mathematics was his demonstration that the Lie algebra $\hat{G}$ determines the important topological invariants called Betti numbers of the group G in the very important case that the Lie group G is compact and connected. Cartan's researches on this problem led him to invent his theory of exterior differential forms and to conjecture the celebrated De Rham theorems, which were proved by his student, G. de Rham.

Exterior Differential Calculus.—If V is a vector space, then, by the exterior algebra over V we mean an associative algebra $E(V)$ generated by the elements of V together with a unit element 1 such that the product of p elements of V is not zero in $E(V)$ if and only if $x_1, \ldots, x_p$ are linearly independent in V. Since $x^2 = 0$ for any x in V, it follows that $x\cdot y = -y\cdot x$ for any x and y in V, then $E(V^*)$ can be identified in a natural way with the set of skew-symmetric multilinear functions on V, the multiplication being

$$\varphi_p\cdot\psi_q(X_1,\ldots,X_{p+q}) =$$
$$(p+q)!^{-1}\Sigma(-1)^{\epsilon(\sigma)}\varphi_p(X_{\sigma(1)},\ldots,X_{\sigma(p)})\psi_q(X_{\sigma(p+1)},\ldots,X_{\sigma(p+q)})\qquad(9)$$

where φ_p and ψ_q are respectively p- and q-linear, $X_1,\ldots,X_{p+q}$ are any $p+q$ elements of V, $\epsilon(\sigma)$ denotes the parity of the permutation σ, and σ ranges over all the permutations of $1,\ldots,p+q$. The algebra $E(V^*)$ is called the Grassmann algebra of V. An exterior differential p-form on an analytic manifold M is a rule which assigns to each point m of M an element of degree p of the Grassmann algebra $E(M_m^*)$, M_m being the tangent space to M at m. In the language of tensors, an exterior differential p-form is a covariant skew-symmetric tensor field of degree p. The novel operation introduced by Cartan is "exterior differentiation" of exterior differential forms. This operation assigns to any exterior differential p-form w a $p+1$-form dw such that

(D1) d is linear.
(D2) d applied to a function or zero form is the usual differential.
(D3) $d(w_1\cdot w_2) = dw_1\cdot w_2 + (-1)^p w_1\cdot dw_2$ where p is the degree of w_1.
(D4) $ddw = 0$ for any form w.

The geometric significance of exterior differentiations is seen in the generalized Green-Stokes theorem: If S is a p-dimensional hypersurface bounding the $p+1$ dimensional solid region R, then

$$\int_S w = \int_R dw\qquad(10)$$

For example, if $w = Pdx + Qdy + Rdz$, $dw = \left(\frac{\partial Q}{\partial x} - \frac{\partial P}{\partial y}\right)dxdy + \left(\frac{\partial P}{\partial z} - \frac{\partial R}{\partial x}\right)dzdx$; if $w = Rdxdy + Qdydx + Pdzdx$, then $dw = \left(\frac{\partial P}{\partial x} + \frac{\partial Q}{\partial y} + \frac{\partial R}{\partial z}\right)dxdydz$.

Exterior differentiation has the fundamental property that it commutes with maps. That is, suppose ϕ is a map of a manifold M into a manifold N, and ω is an exterior differential p-form on N. Extending the notational convention adopted above, one denotes by $\phi(\omega)$ the p-form on M which is given by

$$\phi(\omega)(X_1,\ldots,X_p) = \omega(d\phi(X_1),\ldots,d\phi(X_p))$$

It follows from the properties D1 through D4 that for any analytic map ϕ,

$$\phi(d\omega) = d(\phi(\omega))\qquad(11)$$

In addition, since ϕ preserves the addition and multiplication of exterior forms, one can say that ϕ yields a differential algebra homomorphism.

An exterior differential form ω is called closed if $d\omega = 0$; it is called exact if $\omega = du$. Since $d^2 = 0$, every exact form is closed. Conversely, if ω is exact, then in any suitably small neighbourhood V there is a form u such that $du = \omega$ in V. But nevertheless a closed form need not be exact. The set of closed forms constitutes a vector space and the set of exact forms is a subspace. The quotient space of closed exterior p-forms by the exact p-forms is the p-dimensional Betti group, and the dimension of this space is the pth Betti number of M, denoted $B_p(M)$. Since locally, every closed form is exact, the number $B_p(M)$ must clearly depend on the global structure of M. Cartan showed that for a compact connected Lie group G, $B_p(G)$ is determined by the Lie algebra $\hat{G}$. This success of Cartan encouraged a closer study of the topological structure of Lie groups in an attempt to determine for them the various finer topological invariants that were being introduced in topology.

The central position occupied by compact groups in topological questions concerning Lie groups was clearly established when it was discovered that any Lie group with a finite number of connected components is topologically a product of any of its maximal compact subgroups and a Euclidean space. Thereby the question of topological structure of Lie groups was reduced to the case of compact Lie groups, which are more amenable to topological treatment. The principal results on topological structure of compact groups are that the cohomology ring with real coefficients of a compact Lie group is isomorphic to the cohomology ring of a direct product of spheres; but a compact Lie group is not in general (even in the simply connected case) topologically equivalent to a direct product of spheres. This last result follows from a computation of the Steenrod reduced power operations in compact Lie groups that was carried out by A. Borel and J. P. Serre.

The torsion groups of nearly all compact Lie groups have also been determined. The compact Lie groups Su(n) and Sp(n) (the unitary unimodular group and symplectic group respectively) have no torsion; Spin (n), the two-sheeted covering group of the orthogonal group, has no torsion for $n \leq 6$. Su(n) ($n \geq 3$) and Spin (n) ($n \geq 7$) have 2-torsion and all their torsion coefficients are equal to 2.

Representation as Transformation Groups.—It is natural to compare general topological groups with special ones, and in particular much attention has been devoted to the study of homomorphisms of topological groups into groups of linear transformations or matrix groups. This study has achieved far-reaching results which throw fresh light on the classical Fourier transform and the theory of special functions. Only two results will be mentioned here.

1. The theorem of F. Peter and H. Weyl states that any compact Lie group is isomorphic to a subgroup of the unitary group.

2. The theorem of I. Ado states that any real Lie algebra is isomorphic to a Lie algebra of matrices. Thus any Lie group has a neighbourhood of its identity in which multiplication is isomorphic to multiplication in some matrix group.

Turning now to more general types of representations, there have been several investigations of the global relations between topological groups and the types of spaces in which they can operate as groups of continuous transformations, as well as special properties of the operations themselves. To indicate the scope of such investigations, we mention several results:

1. The only two-dimensional surfaces on which a Lie group can operate transitively (i.e., carrying any point into any other point) are the plane, sphere, torus, projective plane, cylinder, Möbius band and Klein bottle.

2. A compact connected Lie group operating transitively and effectively (i.e., so that each element other than the identity moves some point) on an even-dimensional sphere is simple; more generally if M is a manifold whose Euler-Poincaré characteristic $(=\Sigma(-1)^p \beta_p(M))$ is a prime number, then any compact connected Lie group operating on M is simple.

3. If a Lie group G operates transitively on a compact simply connected space M, then some compact subgroup of G operates transitively on M.

4. If a Lie group operates transitively on a space M having no "holes" (that is, all the homotopy groups are zero), then M is topologically Euclidean space.

5. If a compact Lie group G operates on a manifold M, then the operation is topologically equivalent to the operation of a group of rotations of some (higher dimensional) Euclidean space on a subspace that is topologically equivalent to M.

6. If a compact connected abelian Lie group operates on the Euclidean space, then it must leave some point fixed, and the set of fixed points resemble a hyperplane topologically.

Hilbert's Fifth Problem.—Among the celebrated 23 problems for research that were proposed by David Hilbert in his address to the International Congress of Mathematicians of 1900 was the conjecture that any locally Euclidean topological group can be given the structure of an analytic manifold so as to become a Lie group. The first great inroad on this problem came with the discovery by A. Haar in 1932 that in any locally compact topological group one can introduce a measure and an integral which is invariant under all group translations $x \rightarrow yx$; that is, for any function f defined on a locally compact group G, the integral $\int_G f(x)dx$ satisfies, in addition to the usual rule of linearity, the condition

$$\int_G f(yx)dx = \int_G f(x)dx$$

In 1933 J. von Neumann was able to exploit Haar's integral by adapting the theory of integral equations on a Lie group that had been developed in 1927 by Peter and Weyl and thereafter succeeded in solving the Hilbert problem for compact groups. In 1934 L. Pontryagin was able to prove Hilbert's conjecture for abelian groups as a by-product of his theory of characters on locally compact abelian groups.

The final complete solution of Hilbert's fifth problem came in 1952 as a result of the work of A. Gleason, D. Montgomery and L. Zippin. Indeed, it was found that any locally compact topological group is a limit of Lie groups. This profound result affirmed the central position of Lie groups in the theory of continuous groups.

Algebraic Linear Groups.—An algebraic linear group is a subgroup of the group of all nonsingular $n \cdot n$ matrices $L(n)$ which is defined by the vanishing of polynomials in the matrix coefficients, that is a subgroup of $L(n)$ which is the intersection of $L(n)$ with an algebraic variety. If the underlying field is the field of real or complex numbers, then any algebraic linear group is a Lie group, but not conversely. On the other hand, most of the questions involving linear groups that arise in mathematics reduce to problems concerning groups which are algebraic. It is natural therefore to seek the special properties which characterize algebraic linear groups and their Lie algebras. This study was initiated by L. Maurer in the 19th century and resumed in mid-20th century by C. Chevalley and others.

The theory of algebraic linear groups has thrown fresh light on the relation between an arbitrary Lie group and the set of all its finite dimensional linear representations; this development was initiated by T. Tannaka in an effort to generalize Pontryagin's duality theory of characters, and was carried further by G. Hochschild and G. D. Mostow.

Chevalley's theory of algebraic groups was carried out for arbitrary ground field, even fields of prime characteristic p. This theory in characteristic p rested on very different considerations from the classical theory in characteristic zero but arrived at identical conclusions about the classification of simple groups. Moreover, Chevalley's work established a significant connection between finite simple groups and simple Lie groups.

Invariants of an Exterior Differential System.—The principal application of continuous groups to the solution of differential equations consists in forming first integrals of a system of differential equations from the infinitesimal generators of a group admitted by the system. The number of unknowns involved in the system is thereby reduced.

For simplicity of illustration, we consider only systems of the type

$$w_1 = \ldots = w_n = 0 \quad (12)$$

where $w_1, \ldots, w_n$ are independent differential 1-forms (i.e., linear differential forms) on an $n+1$ dimensional manifold. The solutions of (12) are called integral curves, functions that are constant on solutions are called first integrals, and differential forms expressible in terms of first integrals and their differentials are called invariant forms. A first integral is thus an invariant 0-form. The system (12) is said to admit a transformation ϕ if ϕ carries solutions of (12) into solutions and to admit the infinitesimal transformation X if it admits the transformations $\exp tX$ for all small t.

The passage from groups of transformations admitted by (12) to first integrals of (12) is via invariant forms of (12). There are three simple principles for the formation of invariant forms out of given ones:

(A) If w is an invariant form, then dw is also invariant.

(B) If the system (12) admits the infinitesimal transformation X, and if w is an invariant form, then Xw is an invariant form.

(C) Under the hypotheses of (B), the form $\partial_X w$ is an invariant form, where, for any p-form w, $\partial_X w$ is the $p-1$ form defined by $\partial_X w(X_1, \ldots, X_{p-1}) = w(X, X_1, \ldots, X_p)$.

Suppose the system (12) admits an n-dimensional Lie group of transformations G whose Lie algebra G has a base $X_1, \ldots, X_n$ such that the determinant $w_i(X_j)$ is not zero.

We replace the forms $w_1, \ldots, w_n$ by linear combinations $w_1', \ldots, w_n'$ such that $w_i'(X_j) = \delta_{ij}$ — for $i,j = 1, \ldots, n$. The linear forms $w_1', \ldots, w_n'$ are invariant forms of (12) and are called the forms dual to $X_1, \ldots, X_n$. If $(X_i, X_j) = \Sigma_s c_{ijs} X_s$, then $dw_s' = - \Sigma_{ij} c_{ijs} w_i' w_j'$. It follows that if G is solvable, then the equation (12) can be solved by n successive quadratures. This is an analogue of E. Galois's celebrated theorem on the solution of algebraic equations by radicals. For example, the equation

$$\frac{d^2y}{dx^2} = F\left(\frac{dy}{dx}\right) \quad (13)$$

is invariant under the group G generated by translations along the x-axis and by uniform stretchings. The system (13) is put in form (12) by introducing the new variable y' and (13) then becomes

$$\begin{aligned} dy - y'dx &= 0 \\ ydy' - F(y')dx &= 0 \end{aligned} \quad (14)$$

The group G operates in (x,y,y')-space and its infinitesimal generators are $X_1 = \frac{\partial}{\partial x}$, $X_2 = x\frac{\partial}{\partial x} + y\frac{\partial}{\partial y}$. The dual forms are

$$w_1 = dx - \frac{y - xy'}{F(y')}dy - \frac{y - xy'}{F(y')}dy' \quad \text{and} \quad w_2' = \frac{dy}{y} - \frac{y'}{F(y')}dy. \quad \text{Since}$$

$[X_1, X_2] = X_1$, we have

$$dw_2' = 0$$
$$dw_1' = w_1'w_2'$$

Thus w_2' is exact and gives by integration the first integral u_2 with $dw_2 = w_2'$. On the surface $u_2 = C_1$, we have $w_1' = 0$ and thus $w_1' = 0$ can be integrated. The result of the two successive integrations are

$$x = C_1 \exp\left(\int \frac{1}{F(y')}\left(\exp \int \frac{y'dy'}{F(y')}\right)dy'\right) + C_2 \qquad (16)$$

The Poincaré Invariant Integral and Cartan's Associated Form.—H. Poincaré has shown that for any Hamiltonian system

$$\frac{dp_i}{dt} = -\frac{\partial H}{\partial q_i}; \qquad \frac{dq_i}{dt} = \frac{\partial H}{\partial p_i} \quad i = 1, \dots, n \qquad (17)$$

the form $w = \Sigma_i dp_i dq_i$ has the property that $\int_D w$ over any region in $(p_1, \dots, p_n, q_1, \dots, q_n)$-space taken at a simultaneous time t is independent of t. A differential form with such a property is called a Poincaré integral invariant. If $F(x_1, \dots, x_k, t, dx_1, \dots, dx_k)$ is a Poincaré integral invariant of a system

then $F(x_1, \dots, x_k, t, dx_1, \dots, dx_k)$, and by integration one gets first integrals. In this way one can derive the known first integrals of the n-body problem.

Poisson Parentheses and Contact Transformations.—A nondegenerate bilinear form B on a finite dimensional vector space V determines a one-to-one linear map B_1 of V onto its dual space of linear functions V^* by the rule $B_1(v)(w) = B(v, w)$. This map produces out of functions on V functions on V^*. In particular the function B produces the bilinear function B^* in V^*

$$B^*(x, y) = B(B_1^{-1}(x), B_1^{-1}(y)) \qquad (21)$$

for any elements x and y in V^*.

Now let M be a manifold (necessarily of even dimension) on which there is defined an exterior differential closed 2-form β which is nondegenerate at all points. If f and g are functions on M, set

$$(f, g) = \beta^*(df \, dg) \qquad (22)$$

The function (f, g) is called the Poisson parentheses of f and g with respect to β. In the neighbourhood of any point one can find co-ordinates $(p_1, \dots, p_n, q_1, \dots, q_n)$ such that $\beta = \Sigma_i dp_i dq_i$. A simple computation gives

$$(f, g) = \Sigma_i \frac{\partial f}{\partial p_i} \frac{\partial g}{\partial q_i} - \frac{\partial f}{\partial q_i} \frac{\partial g}{\partial p_i} \qquad (23)$$
$$df \cdot dg \cdot \beta^{n-1} = (f, g)\beta^n$$

where the dot is exterior multiplication and $\beta^n = \Sigma_i dp_i dq_i$. Transformations of a manifold of dimension $2n$ or $2n + 1$ pre-

but actually determines the system (20), namely, (20) is the first Pfaffian (or associated characteristic) system of w'. Any infinitesimal transformation admitted by the equations of motion leads to an invariant 1-form via the principle in (C) applied to w'. Quite frequently, such 1-forms are exact and by integration one gets first integrals. In this way one can derive the known first integrals of the n-body problem.

and it is called the associated Cartan form. The associated Cartan form of $\Sigma_i dp_i dq_i$ is thus $w' = \Sigma_i (dp_i + \frac{\partial H}{\partial q_i}dt)(dq_i - \frac{\partial H}{\partial p_i}dt) = \Sigma_i dp_i dq_i - dH dt$. This Cartan form is not only an invariant of the system

$$\frac{dp_1}{-\frac{\partial H}{\partial q_1}} = \dots = \frac{dp_n}{-\frac{\partial H}{\partial q_n}}$$
$$= \frac{dq_1}{\frac{\partial H}{\partial p_1}} = \dots = \frac{dq_n}{\frac{\partial H}{\partial p_n}} \qquad (20)$$

$$\frac{dx_i}{dt} = A_i(x_1, \dots, x_k, t) \quad i = 1, \dots, k$$

$$\frac{dx_1}{A_1} = \frac{dx_2}{A_2} = \dots = \frac{dx_k}{A_k} \qquad (18)$$

then $F(x_1, \dots, x_k, t, dx_1 - A_1 dt, \dots, dx_k - A_k dt)$ is an invariant form of this system

$$dx_1 - A_1 dt, \dots, dx - A_k dt \qquad (19)$$

serving an exterior 2-form β of maximum possible rank were called by Lie restricted nonhomogeneous contact transformations with respect to β. Lie studied more general nonhomogeneous contact transformations which preserve the equation $w = 0$ where w is a differential 1-form on $2n + 1$ dimensional manifold such that $w dw^n \neq 0$; also, homogeneous contact transformations of a $2n$-dimensional manifold preserving a 1-form w such that $dw^n = 0$. The best example of a one parameter group of restricted nonhomogeneous contact transformations is given by the movement of a wave front according to Huygens' principle.

Another example is the motion of a conservative dynamical system in Hamiltonian form—the mathematical foreshadowing of quantum mechanics. If H is the Hamiltonian of a conservative dynamical system, then the infinitesimal transformation defined by equations (17) is the operator X_H, where X_θ denotes the infinitesimal transformation defined by the operator

$$f \to (g, f)$$

parentheses being with respect to the Poincaré integral invariant $\beta = \Sigma_i dp_i dq_i$. The most general (analytic) infinitesimal transformation of $(p_1, \dots, p_n, q_1, \dots, q_n)$-space which preserves β is of the form X_θ with θ an arbitrary analytic function. The Hamiltonian form (20) of the equations of motion is preserved by any contact transformation with respect to β, and the equations (20) admit the infinitesimal contact transformation X_θ only if θ is a first integral or if X_θ preserves the associated Cartan form of β. Thus if g_1 and g_2 are first integrals of (20), then their Poisson parentheses is a first integral by the principle (B). Poisson parentheses are related to Poisson brackets by the

$$[X_i, X_\theta] = X_{(i,\theta)} \qquad (25)$$

identity

$$[X_i, X_\theta] = X_{(i,\theta)} \qquad (26)$$

See also INVARIANTS; GROUPS; TRANSFORMATION; GROUPS AND ALGEBRAS, REPRESENTATIONS OF.

BIBLIOGRAPHY.—L. Pontryagin, *Topological Groups* (1939); D. Montgomery and L. Zippin, *Topological Transformation Groups* (1955); C. Chevalley, *Theory of Lie Groups, I* (1946), *Theorie des groupes de Lie II, III* (1951, 1955); H. Weyl, *Classical Groups, Semi-naire "Sophus Lie"* (1955); Ecole Normale Supérieure, *Theory of Groups and Quantum Mechanics* (1931); L. H. Loomis, *An Introduction to Abstract Harmonic Analysis* (1953); A. Weil, *L'Intégration dans les groupes topologiques et ses applications* (1940); E. Wigner, *Gruppentheorie und ihre Anwendungen auf die Quantenmechanik der Atomspektren* (1931); L. P. Eisenhart, *Continuous Groups of Transformations* (1933); E. T. Whittaker, *Treatise on the Analytical Dynamics of Particles and Rigid Bodies* (1937); E. Cartan, *Oeuvres complètes* (1952), *Leçons sur les invariant intégraux* (1922), *Les Systèmes différentiels extérieurs* (1945); S. Lie and F. Engel, *Theorie der Transformationsgruppen*, 3 vol. (1930); J. Auslander and C. C. Moore, *Unitary Representations of Solvable Lie Groups* (1966). (G. D. M.)

GROUPS, TRANSFORMATION. Transformation groups in geometry comprise a branch of theoretical mathematics that has received increasing attention in the 20th century and has close relations with important aspects of physics and with other phases of higher geometry.

Preliminary Definitions.—An abstract group (see GROUPS) is a system of elements in which a multiplication is defined satisfying certain simple rules (see below). A transformation group is always associated with a space of points and is an abstract group whose elements are one-one correspondences between the points; furthermore, the space has some kind of structure which is preserved by the correspondences. For example, the transformation group of principal interest in Euclidean geometry is the collection of congruences; these preserve distances between points and are called isometries. The correspondences, also called transformations, have this character: (1) to each point of space regarded as preimage they associate an image point; (2) each point is image of one and only one preimage. If T denotes a correspondence one writes $T(A) = A'$ to say that A' is image of A.

The set of all such transformations (and also certain subsets called subgroups) forms an abstract group; i.e., an associative multiplication can be defined, there is an identity and each element has an inverse. Thus the product $S \cdot T$ of transformations S and T associates to A the image $A'' = S(T(A)) = S(S(A))$, where $S(A)$ is image of A under S; S denotes $S(T(A)) = S(A)$. The inverse of T denoted by T^{-1} interchanges image and preimage; denoted by I, is defined by $I(A) = A$ for all A. If for two elements S and T, $S(A) = T(A)$ for all A, this means that $S = T$; in this sense $TT^{-1} = I = T^{-1}T$, and for three elements $R \cdot ST = RS \cdot T$ (associativity), as is easily verified.

S and T are said to commute, if $ST = TS$; if every pair commute, the group is called commutative.

Historical Survey.—High points in the development of this subject in the century (1830–1930) after the invention of group theory were as follows. (1) Discovery of Bolyai-Lobachevski plane geometry. This has distance-preserving transformations which give rise to "rigid motions" different from Euclidean motions. (2) Papers by B. Riemann and by H. L. F. von Helmholtz on the foundations of geometry; their investigations clarified the mathematical nature of space and motion and led to new geometries in all dimensions. (3) Studies by Arthur Cayley and by Felix Klein on the relation of metric geometries to subgroups of the projective group; the latter preserves collinearity (if A, B, C are on a line so are the images A', B', C') but distorts distance. (4) M. S. Lie's work on continuous transformation groups (now called Lie groups); here the group regarded as a spacelike structure (group manifold) plays a dominant role. (5) David Hilbert's axiomatization based on transformation groups of the two metric geometries on the plane. (6) Relativity theory with its emphasis on the principle of invariance—physical entities such as space-time intervals, forces, displacements, expressible in appropriate co-ordinate systems by some mathematical formalism, must keep their form after transformations of co-ordinates. In consequence the group of allowable transformations of co-ordinates reflects the nature of the physical world. This is the Lorentz group in relativity theory and the Newton-Galileo group in the older physics. (7) Studies by E. Cartan and H. Weyl on group manifolds whose structure is describable in local co-ordinate systems (Lie groups). (8) Studies by A. Haar, J. von Neumann and L. Pontryagin on the construction of co-ordinate systems in more general group manifolds.

General Concepts.—Let G denote a group acting on a space. The set of images of a point A under all elements of G is called the orbit of A, denoted by $G(A)$. Those elements S for which A is a fixed point, i.e., $S(A) = A$, form a subgroup (possibly trivial; i.e., consisting of the identity) called the stability group (also isotropy group) of A, denoted by G_A. G carries each point of $G(A)$ to every other point and is called transitive on the orbit. If G_A is the identity, G is simply transitive on $G(A)$; then each point can be associated to a unique element of G. In this case G and $G(A)$ have similar structure as spaces.

For example: (1) a line L can be reflected into itself across each point. The collection of these transformations and all their products forms a transitive group; each stability group has two elements, the identity and one reflection. G has a subgroup called the line-translation group, which is simply transitive on L. (2) the group of rotations of a circle is simply transitive on the circle, and is called a circle group.

Space is partitioned into distinct orbits each of which is a point in an abstract space called the orbit space. For example, if G is the group of rotations of the plane about a fixed origin, then all orbits (with one exception) are circles, and the orbit space is a half line whose end point corresponds to the one point left fixed by all elements of the group.

As this example shows, the stability groups associated with points on different orbits need not be similar. However, if A and B are on the same orbit, then G_A and G_B are actually conjugate groups; i.e., there is an element T in G such that, for every element S in G_A, TST^{-1} is in G_B. It should be remarked for those familiar with group theory that the orbit $G(A)$ is directly related to the coset space (either left or right) of G by G_A.

Euclidean Plane Geometry.—One of the simplest substantial illustrations of the foregoing is the Euclidean plane group. This can be defined on the basis of the first dozen or so propositions of Euclid's book i, as follows. Let ABC and $A'B'C'$ be a pair of congruent triangles and let D be an arbitrary point in the plane. There is a unique point D' such that the distances AD, BD, CD equal AD', BD', CD' respectively. Thus the natural correspondence $T(A) = A'$, $T(B) = B'$, $T(C) = C'$ can be extended to a transformation of the entire plane: to each point D one simply associates the appropriate D'. The totality of all these transformations for all choices of a pair of congruent triangles constitutes the Euclidean group of isometries (distance-preserving transformations); let us call this G.

In the light of Euclid's fourth postulate (see L. W. Young, *Fundamental Concepts of Algebra and Geometry*, 1911, for a discussion of Euclid's geometry) that all right angles are equal, one sees that an ordered pair of perpendicular lines L_1, L_2 can be carried by an isometry into any other such pair. This corresponds to choosing reference axes in the plane, and is the first step in introducing rectangular co-ordinates.

It is instructive to see how other postulates of Euclid are related to properties of G and its subgroups. The third postulate, that to each pair of points A,B there is a circle with centre A passing through B, expresses the fact that stability groups G_A have circle orbits $G_A(B)$. The first and second postulates, covering the existence and uniqueness and extendibility of a line segment AB, express the fact that for each A,B there is in G a unique subgroup which is a line-translation group and for which A and B are on the same orbit.

The fifth and last, the "parallel" postulate, expresses the fact that for each of these line groups in G, the family of orbits is a system of parallel lines. The set of all elements on all of these line groups forms a commutative subgroup of G, called the translation group. It is the existence of this commutative, simply transitive subgroup which distinguishes Euclidean geometry from all other metric geometries and lends it a much simpler structure. This is also the group that, in applications to physics, gives rise to the "parallelogram law" of the addition of vectors.

Examples of Transformation Groups.—1. The affine group in the plane carries parallel lines to parallels but may distort shape (of triangles, for example) and size. To describe it, let x,y denote co-ordinates in the plane. Each transformation T is identified by six parameters (a,b,c,d,e,f) subject only to the condition $(ad - bc)$ not zero, to ensure that T^{-1} exists. T can be represented by

$$T : \begin{aligned} \bar{x} &= ax + by + e \\ \bar{y} &= cx + dy + f \end{aligned}$$

Here x,y are co-ordinates of A; $\bar{x},\bar{y}$ are co-ordinates of A'; and $T(A) = A'$.

2. There is a corresponding affine group in n-dimensions whose elements depend on $n^2 + n$ parameters (also called co-ordinates).

3. The equiaffine plane group, with $ad - bc = 1$, preserves area of triangles but alters shape.

4. If one regards T, above, as a substitution (transformation of co-ordinates) then one can find the Euclidean group as a subgroup of the affine by the requirement that the distance formula be left "invariant"; i.e., $\sqrt{(\bar{x}_1 - \bar{x}_2)^2 + (\bar{y}_1 - \bar{y}_2)^2}$ goes over to $\sqrt{(x_1 - x_2)^2 + (y_1 - y_2)^2}$.

5. The group of homeomorphisms of a metric space M is defined as follows. An infinite sequence of points $A_0, A_1, A_2, A_3, \ldots$, is called fundamental if the distances $A_0A_1, A_0A_2, A_0A_3, \ldots$, grow smaller approaching zero. A transformation T is called topological if T and T^{-1} preserve fundamental sequences; T is also called a homeomorphism. The totality of these T constitutes the group.

6. In every metric space one can define the group of isometries, but in general this group will be trivial; i.e., reducing to the identity.

7. Two metrics on a space M are said to be topologically equivalent if every sequence which is fundamental in one metric is also fundamental in the other. Thus the Bolyai-Lobachevski and the Euclidean metrics on the plane are topologically equivalent. However, the two groups of isometries are very different.

A Theorem of Hilbert.—A topological transformation of the plane distorts linearity; nonetheless the images of all lines and circles under a fixed transformation of this kind form a system of point sets (called open curves and closed curves, respectively) which can be interpreted as the new lines and circles of an abstract geometry in the plane. This system satisfies all the postulates of Euclid's geometry.

In 1903 Hilbert proved a theorem equivalent to the following. Hypotheses: (1) we are given the plane and a metric which is only topologically equivalent to the Euclidean metric; (2) in this new metric the group of isometries G is transitive; (3) the orbits $G_A(B)$ are infinite sets (i.e., not finite). Conclusions: (1) it is possible to define straight lines, circles, angles, etc., in terms of the geometry of G; and (2) one obtains either the Euclidean or the Bolyai-Lobachevski geometry and nothing else.

Modern Developments.—In the early 1950s, as the culmination of work by A. M. Gleason, K. Iwasawa, D. Montgomery, H. Yamabe and others on topological grounds and that of H. Busemann, H. Freudenthal, J. Tits, H. C. Wang and others on the geometry of transformation groups, the theorem of Hilbert was extended and generalized in many ways. The following theorem is most quotable, and in its way definitive.

Hypotheses: M is an abstractly given metric space which is locally compact and connected and the group G of isometries has this property: if the distances between points A,B,C equal corresponding distances between A',B',C' then the two triples are congruent under some element of G.

Conclusions: M is a manifold on which one can define lines, angles and circles, giving rise to one of the four types of metric geometries, and G is the group appropriate to that geometry.

A remarkable feature of this theorem is the following: each type of geometry has a representative in each dimension n, from $n = 2$ upward, so that the theorem is about a fourfold infinity of geometries. To distinguish a particular one from among the others, it is merely necessary to choose the desired dimension and type.

See also GEOMETRY, NON-EUCLIDEAN; GROUPS; GROUPS, CONTINUOUS; GROUPS AND ALGEBRAS, REPRESENTATIONS OF.

BIBLIOGRAPHY.—H. Weyl, *Symmetry* (1952); L. W. Young, *Fundamental Concepts of Algebra and Geometry* (1911); L. Pontryagin, *Topological Groups* (1939); D. Montgomery and L. Zippin, *Topological Transformation Groups* (1955); P. M. Cohn, *Lie Groups* (1957); A. Borel, *Seminar on Transformation Groups* (1960). (L. ZN.)

GROUPS AND ALGEBRAS, REPRESENTATIONS OF.

Since their formal introduction in the early 19th century, groups have been one of the principal objects of mathematical attention. Their widespread and profound applications to such physical subjects as crystallography, quantum mechanics and hydrodynamics and to such other mathematical regimes as number theory, harmonic analysis and geometry have demonstrated their importance.

The main general technique for studying groups is the method of "group representation." Technically, a representation of a group is a homomorphism of it into another group, most commonly, into the group of invertible linear transformations (or matrices) on some linear space. Less technically, this method amounts to comparing the given group with better known examples of groups. Representation theory plays a significant part in all branches of mathematics in various ways; it also is important in theoretical physics, particularly in quantum theory.

To sketch briefly, a group is a set on which a multiplication satisfying certain specific properties is defined. Corresponding to each pair of elements a, b (in a given order) is another element (written ab) and this law of combination has the properties: (1) $a(bc) = (ab)c$; (2) there is an element e, called the group identity element, such that $ae = ea = a$; and (3) for each a there is an element a^{-1} called the inverse of a such that $aa^{-1} = a^{-1}a = e$. If in addition $ab = ba$ for each a and b, the group is said to be abelian (also commutative). A homomorphism is a mapping (function, correspondence) f of one group G into another group H such that $f(ab) = f(a)f(b)$ for each a and b in G; i.e., f "preserves" multiplication. The positive and negative integers with their usual addition provide an example of an infinite abelian group (here, addition plays the role of group multiplication, 0 is the group identity and, for example, -5 is the group inverse to 5). The two integers 0 and 1 with the usual addition as group multiplication (except that 1 is to combine with 1 to give 0) provide an example of a finite abelian group, as does the set of two integers $+1$ and -1 with the usual multiplication. The mapping of an integer into 0 if it is even and into 1 if it is odd provides an homomorphism of the group of integers onto the first two-element group. The function which assigns 0 to $+1$ and 1 to -1 is an example of an isomorphism (i.e., one-to-one homomorphism) of the second two-element group onto the first. Structurally (as far as group theoretical properties are concerned), the existence of this isomorphism indicates that both two-element groups are the same—they are different (isomorphic) representations of the same abstract group, so to speak.

The process of group representation may be likened to measuring some physical object with a ruler. By comparing the object to be studied with the known object (the ruler), special information is obtained. Spreading the object out completely along the ruler might be thought of as an isomorphic representation, but such a procedure may not be possible. For example, a polyhedron would have to be studied by applying a series of partial measurements and combining them (corresponding to combining information from homomorphic representations). It would be hoped that sufficiently many measurements could be made to give detailed information—corresponding to the case of sufficiently many (a separating family of) representations so that each pair of distinct elements is carried into a pair of distinct elements by at least one of the representations. An instance of "combining" information is afforded by the simple fact that a group which has a separating family of representations in abelian groups is itself abelian (ab and ba are identified by all such representations). It would help little to make measurements with an unmarked straightedge; in the same way, the representations would be expected to take place in groups with some discernible structure. On the other hand, if the ruler is too specialized, for example, circular, it is available for only a limited type of measurement; by analogy, the class of groups in which the representations take place should remain broad enough to have general application. The so-called linear groups, groups of invertible linear transformations on a linear vector space, are well suited to this task. Representations in such groups often are referred to as "linear" representations, or simply as representations if confusion is unlikely. In particular, representations by unitary operators on Hilbert spaces, called unitary representations, and representations by operators on finite-dimensional linear spaces, called finite-dimensional representations, have proved very useful.

In applying the technique of representations to the study of groups, the allied method of associating an algebra, the so-called group algebra, with the group has a key function. (An algebra is a linear space, with a multiplication satisfying certain specific conditions; *see* ALGEBRAS [LINEAR].) For finite groups and the complex group algebra, this amounts to associating with the group sums of formal complex multiples of the group elements and multiplying two such sums by distributing products in the usual way, "commuting" numbers past group elements and multiplying group elements by means of the group multiplication.

A linear representation of the group can be extended to the group algebra by assigning to each sum of multiples of group elements the same sum of multiples of the operators (matrices) corresponding to those group elements under the given representation. This extension is a representation of the group algebra (a mapping into the algebra of operators on the "representation space" which preserves both products and sums). The analysis of the algebra representation is somewhat simpler than that of the group representation and yields much information about the group representation. The process of extension can be reversed, for the group elements are found in a natural way among those of the group algebra; i.e., a representation of the group algebra gives rise to a representation of the group.

There are several ways of constructing new representations from one or more given representations. The first, restriction of a representation, starts with a representation f of a group G (or algebra) and a subspace V of the representation space which is mapped into itself by each of the representing operators (a so-called reducing or invariant subspace). The restricted representation assigns to each g in G the operator $f_V(g)$ on V which is $f(g)$ restricted (in its action) to V. If V is not 0 or the full space, the representation f is said to be reducible. If no such "proper" invariant subspace exists, the representation is said to be irreducible. (In the case of representations on Hilbert spaces, "subspace" is understood to mean "closed subspace.") Representations of finite groups enjoy the important property of complete reducibility. If V is a reducing subspace, there is a complementary space V' which is also invariant (V and V' have only 0 in common and each vector in the representation space is the sum of one from V and one from V').

The representation f is said to be the direct sum of f_V and $f_{V'}$. This description of direct sum from an internal viewpoint has an external counterpart. If f and f' are representations of G on spaces V and V', respectively, a representation $f \oplus f'$, called the direct sum of f and f', on the direct sum $V \oplus V'$ of V and V' (i.e., the linear space of pairs of elements, one from V and one from V') is defined by assigning to each group element g the operator on $V \oplus V'$ which transforms a pair (v, v') into the pair $([f(g)](v), [f'(g)](v'))$. In the case of reducing complementary spaces V and V' for a representation f, it is an easy matter to see that $f_V \oplus f_{V'}$ is f when the full space is viewed as $V \oplus V'$. In a similar manner, direct sums of more than two representations can be defined. For finite groups, the process of decomposition of a representation may be continued on each of the restricted representations until a full reduction into irreducible representations is effected (the representation is a direct sum of irreducible representations and such a decomposition is unique).

A more complicated procedure for constructing representations from families of representations, the tensor product, stems from the tensor product of linear spaces (the space of sums of multiples of formal products of basis elements one from each space in a given order—the dimension is the product of the dimensions of the individual spaces as contrasted with that of the direct sum which is the sum of the dimensions). If f and f' are representations of G on spaces V and V', respectively, then $f \otimes f'$, their tensor product, assigns to each g in G the operator $f(g) \otimes f'(g)$ which transforms one of the generating elements $v \otimes v'$ of the tensor product $V \otimes V'$ of V and V' into $[f(g)](v) \otimes [f'(g)](v')$. In particular, the square of a representation consists of tensoring it with itself (similarly for higher powers).

A problem of some importance and difficulty is that of describing the irreducible representations which appear in the decomposition of the higher powers of irreducible representations of specific groups (these higher powers are not themselves irreducible, in general). Of course, the basic problem of the theory is the description of the irreducible representations of specific groups, for these are the basic representations not only of the general theory but of the fundamental physical situation to which the theory applies. Speaking of the possible occurrence of a representation which is reducible in the description of a general scheme for quantum mechanics, H. Weyl, one of the founders of modern representation theory, wrote, "Nature could hardly be expected to indulge in such a superfluous luxury."

In dealing with representations of a given group, there is clearly no additional information to be obtained by passing from one representation to a second whose space can be identified with that of the first in such a way that the operators corresponding to each group element under both representations act in the same way on the spaces (relative to the identification). In this case, the representations are said to be equivalent. (Technically, if f and f' are the equivalent representations of G on spaces V and V', there is a linear isomorphism P of V onto V' such that $Pf(g)P^{-1} = f'(g)$ for each g in G.) When a representation f of a group is expressed as the direct sum of irreducible representations and precisely n of these are equivalent to a given irreducible representation f', then f' is said to occur in f with multiplicity n. If the group G has m elements the set of complex-valued functions on G is a linear space of dimension m (addition and scalar multiplication performed pointwise). A natural representation of G on this space is available—to the function a assign the function a_g whose value at g' is $a(g^{-1}g')$, and let $f(g)$ be the transformation of the function space so defined. Then f is a representation of G (called the "left regular" representation of G). In a similar manner, there is the "reflected" situation of the right regular representation of

G. The crucial property of the regular representation is that each contains every irreducible representation of G in its direct sum decomposition (with multiplicity equal to the dimension of the representation space—as a consequence of the reflection situation of the right and left regular representations). The regular representation is an isomorphic one, from which one concludes that the group G has a separating family of irreducible representations. If f is a representation of the finite group G as operators on a Hilbert space, then the function which assigns to a pair of vectors x,y in the space the number $\sum_g (f(g)x, f(g)y)$ is again an inner product equivalent to the original one and relative to which each $f(g)$ is a unitary operator (orthogonal transformation, in the real case), so that each such representation of G is equivalent to a unitary representation of G. If f and f' are a pair of inequivalent (irreducible) unitary representations of G, then

$$\sum_g (f(g)x, y)(f'(g^{-1})x', y') = 0$$

where x,y and x',y' are orthonormal pairs of vectors in their respective spaces (the same holds when $f' = f$ and x',y',x,y is an orthonormal set such that not both $x = x'$ and $y = y'$); while $\sum_g |(f(g)x, y)|^2$ is the number of elements in G (called the order of G) divided by the dimension of the representation. These are the so-called orthogonality relations. The sum of the diagonal entries of the matrix corresponding to an operator on and a basis for some finite-dimensional space is called the trace of the operator. It is independent of the basis chosen. If f is a representation of the finite group G on a finite-dimensional space, the function which assigns to each element of G the trace of its representing operator is called the character of f. A critical result of the theory states that two such representations are equivalent if and only if their characters are identical—the study of such representations is reduced to the study of the characters of G. The character of a direct sum of representations is the sum of their characters and that of a tensor product is their product. The character of the n-dimensional "identity" representation (which assigns the identity operator on n-dimensional space to each group element) has the constant function n as its character, and that of the regular representation is 0 at each group element except the identity where it takes the value equal to the order of the group (this is easily checked on the basis consisting of functions which are 1 at some group element and 0 at all others). The characters of the irreducible representations are precisely those characters k such that $\sum_g |k(g)|^2$ is the order of G.

Schur's lemma, which states that the only operators that commute with a unitary irreducible representation are the scalar multiples of the identity operator, is a key result in the development of representation theory. (Since each representation of a finite group is equivalent to a unitary representation, Schur's lemma covers all such representations.) Applying this fact to abelian groups, it follows that each irreducible unitary representation of such a group is 1-dimensional—each group element is mapped into a complex multiple (having absolute value 1) of the identity operator. The function on the group which assigns to each element its corresponding complex number is the character of the representation. There is, of course, no need to distinguish between the representation and its character, in this situation. The complex conjugate of such a character is again a character as is the product of two such characters. With this multiplication, the characters form a group—the character or dual group (to the original group). If G is an abelian group and G' its dual, then each g in G gives rise to a character of G' which assigns to an element of G' its value at g. The duality theorem for abelian groups states that the mapping of G just described is an isomorphism of G onto the character group of G' (roughly speaking, G is the dual group of its dual group). A function a on G may be viewed as the element $\sum_g a(g)g$ in the group algebra of G, and each character g' of G has the extension to this group algebra which assigns to $\sum_g a(g)g$ the number $\sum_g a(g)g'(g)$. Denoting this number by $a'(g')$, the transformation which maps a onto a' is an isomorphism of the group algebra of G onto the function algebra of G' (the linear space of functions on G' with pointwise multiplication). For finite abelian groups, this function mapping is the counterpart of the Fourier transform, so important in mathematical analysis (see FOURIER SERIES).

The "symmetric group on n letters," S_n, is the set of all one-one transformations of n objects (letters) onto itself (i.e., the set of all permutations or arrangements of the n objects) as the group multiplication. Thus S_2 can be viewed as the permutations of the numbers 1, 2: one permutation (the identity) leaving 1 and 2 fixed and the other interchanging 1 and 2 (the square of this last is the identity). It follows that S_2 has 2 elements; S_3 has $1 \cdot 2 \cdot 3 \, (= 6)$ elements, and quite generally, S_n has $1 \cdot 2 \cdots n \, (= n!)$ elements. The natural combinatorial character of the symmetric groups results in their dominance of representation theory for finite groups—wherever physical quantities exhibit combinatorial symmetries (e.g., in the quantum mechanics of a system of several identical electrons) the symmetric groups make their appearance. Group-theoretically, their importance is obvious from the fact that each finite group is isomorphic with a subgroup of some symmetric group. In fact, if G has n elements, the mapping that assigns to each element g of G the permutation of the n elements of G effected by (left) multiplying each by g is an isomorphism of G with a subgroup of S_n. From the general theory, one sees that the study of the representations of S_n can be carried out by a detailed analysis of its group algebra and, in particular, of the regular representation. For arbitrary finite groups, the number of inequivalent irreducible representation is the linear dimension of the centre of the group algebra (those elements of the group algebra which commute with all others); and this is seen to be the number of distinct conjugate classes of group elements. (Two group elements a and b are "conjugate" if there is some group element g such that $a = gbg^{-1}$. A conjugate class in a group is the set of conjugates of some fixed element.) For symmetric groups each conjugate class can be associated with a certain symmetry pattern. Each permutation on n letters permutes various disjoint subsets of the letters cyclically among themselves (i.e., placing the letters of one subset along the rim of a wheel at equal intervals and in the proper order, the permutation affects these letters as would a rotation of the wheel carrying one into the next). Two permutations are conjugate precisely when the subsets of one can be matched with those of the other so that matching subsets have the same number of elements. Thus there are as many inequivalent irreducible representations of S_n as there are ways of expressing n as a sum of nonnegative integers (independent of order). The subsets corresponding to a partition of n constitute a particular symmetry pattern. Relative to these, a generalized process of symmetrization and alternation is defined which gives rise to special elements of the group algebra, the so-called Young symmetrizers, in terms of which the irreducible representation corresponding to the pattern can be described. If a particular pattern has $m_1, m_2, \ldots, m_k$ elements in the respective subsets (listed in decreasing order of size), the dimension of the corresponding irreducible representation is the quotient of $s(n!)$ by $(n_1!)(n_2!) \cdots (n_k!)$, where s is the product of all the differences $n_j - n_h$ with j less than i and $n_j = m_j + k - j$. Applied to S_5, for example, these results assert the existence of seven inequivalent irreducible representations corresponding to the partitions $5, 4+1, 3+2, 3+1+1, 2+2+1, 2+1+1+1$ and $1+1+1+1+1$, with dimensions $5, 4, 5, 6, 5, 4$ and 1, respectively. It is no accident that the sums of the squares of these dimensions (120) is the order of S_5—it is a consequence of the fact that the regular representation takes place on 120-dimensional space and each irreducible representation occurs in it with multiplicity equal to its dimension.

The applications of the theory of group representations to mathematical analysis and to physics entail, for the most part, the description of the representations of infinite groups which have a topological structure related to their group structure—the so-called topological groups. (The topological structure is a mathematical formulation of the concepts of "nearness." The topological groups are those in which nearness is so defined that the product of an element and the inverse of another element are themselves is near to the group identity provided both elements are themselves

near the identity.) The most important and the most intensively studied of these groups are the Lie groups. These are the topological groups in which the topology near each point is like that of n-dimensional Euclidean space for some fixed n. A more general class of topological groups, the locally compact groups, have received some attention. These include the discrete groups (those in which no group element is "infinitely near" the others—every group can be given such a topology), the Lie groups, and those which can be constructed from these two classes by certain group-theoretic processes. The various Euclidean spaces with vector addition as group multiplication and the complex numbers of modulus 1 (the circle group) with the usual multiplication of complex numbers each with its usual notion of nearness are examples of abelian Lie groups. The invertible operators on n-dimensional Euclidean space, with nearness described in terms of nearness of the images of a specific vector and group multiplication the multiplication of operators, is an example of a nonabelian Lie group (the general linear group of dimension n).

The crucial property of locally compact groups is the existence of a measure on them, Haar measure (a notion of "volume" for subsets), which assigns the same number (measure) to a subset of the group and to the subset obtained from it by left multiplying each element of the subset by a fixed group element (each "left translate" of the set). Those groups with finite total measure constitute an especially important subclass, the compact groups. The circle group and the subgroup of the general linear group consisting of those operators which preserve the lengths of vectors, the orthogonal group (unitary group in the complex case), are examples of compact Lie groups. The finite groups are compact (discrete) groups.

Several different possibilities for group algebras and regular representations present themselves in the case of locally compact groups, each shedding some light on the representation theory of these groups. The set of finite sums of complex multiples of group elements is a direct generalization of the group algebra for a finite group, but it takes no account of the group topology. The integrable functions on the group with multiplication like that in the finite case (each function thought of as the sum of the products of each group element by the function value at that group element), except that integration replaces ordinary summation, is an effective generalization which respects the group topology. (This group algebra is the L_1 group algebra and its multiplication is convolution.) The space of square integrable functions on G (i.e., $L_2(G)$) is a Hilbert space which is available for the various regular representations. Assign to each group element the operator which left translates an L_2 function by g^{-1} (as in the finite group case). This operator is unitary, and the algebra of finite sums of multiples of these operators is the (left) regular representation of the "finite" group algebra. The integrable functions on the group generalize too—the (left) $L_2(G)$ with the given L_2 function. This association is a bounded operator on $L_2(G)$ with the given L_1 function. "Convolving" operators so obtained is not closed in the various relevant topologies on the set of bounded operators, and the various closures of this algebra are reasonable candidates for a group algebra (in particular, the uniform and the weak closures are of special interest). It is not to be expected that a general unitary representation of G can be "extended" to the L_1 group algebra (an essentially topological construct) without some further topological restriction. The unitary representations which appear in practice are the "strongly continuous" representations—those which represent elements near the group identity by unitary operators (strongly) near the identity operator (equivalently: "weakly continuous" and "measurable" unitary representations), and these representations are so extendible to the L_1 group algebra. They are often but not always extendible to the uniform closure of this group algebra (in its regular representation on $L_2(G)$); and the question of just when they can be so extended is related to some of the most delicate problems of mathematical analysis. They are rarely extendible to the weakly closed group algebra (i.e., to the weak closure of the regular representation of the L_1 group algebra).

The most satisfactory aspects of this general theory are to be found in its application to the classes of compact groups and of abelian (locally compact) groups. The theory of representations developed for finite groups is valid for continuous representations of compact groups on Hilbert spaces, once summation over the finite group (divided by the group order) is replaced by integration with respect to Haar measure (normalized so that the group has measure 1). The equivalence of such representations with unitary ones, the character theory, direct sum decomposition into irreducible representations, the orthogonality relations and the existence of a separating family of (finite-dimensional) irreducible unitary representations are valid for compact groups. The critical new fact which must be established in the general case is the finite dimensionality of each irreducible representation. The duality theory for finite abelian groups carries over intact to the general case. The dual (character) group of a compact abelian group is discrete (and that of a discrete group is compact). In particular, the character group of the circle is the additive group of integers—the correspondence between (L_2) functions on the circle and those on the integers (described for finite abelian groups) is the Fourier series expansion of periodic functions. The additive group of real numbers (i.e., 1-dimensional Euclidean space) is its own dual and the function mapping, in this case, is the important Fourier transform.

A foreshadowing of the complexities of the theory of representations for more general locally compact groups is afforded by the decomposition problem for reducible representations of abelian groups which are locally compact but not compact. Here a direct sum decomposition into irreducible representations (i.e., characters) is not always possible as such. Rather, a direct integral decomposition, which bears the same relation to a direct sum decomposition as integration does to summation (ordinary addition), replaces the direct sum decomposition.

The representations of the 3-dimensional rotation group, R_3, supply an excellent and physically significant illustration of the theory for compact groups. The group R_3 consists of linear transformations of (real) 3-dimensional space which preserve the lengths of vectors and have determinant 1. The rotations preserve area on the unit sphere about the origin (best described in terms of 3-dimensional polar co-ordinates), so that each such rotation induces a unitary transformation on the Hilbert space of square integrable functions over the sphere. The resulting unitary representation decomposes into a direct sum of irreducible, finite-dimensional unitary representations. From a direct analytical study this representation can be shown to decompose into a direct sum of spaces of odd dimension, one for each odd number. This decomposition is effected by means of the spherical harmonic functions on 3-space and their associated surface harmonics on the sphere. The orthogonality relations for the surface harmonics establish the fact that this decomposition yields all the irreducible representations of R_3.

For general locally compact groups it is still possible to establish the existence of a separating family of strongly continuous irreducible unitary representations, and it is still possible to decompose reducible representations into a direct integral of irreducible representations; but much of the value of this fact is lost in the observation that the decomposition can often be performed in many totally distinct ways (i.e., so that no irreducible component of one decomposition is equivalent to any component of the others). These developments have given rise to the opinion that the appropriate process is not decomposition into irreducible representations but rather into factor representations. (A unitary representation is said to be a factor representation when the weak closure of the sums of multiples of the representing unitary operators has only multiples of the identity operator in its centre. The factors have been broadly classified into types depending on the nature of a dimension function on the projections in the factor (its discreteness or nondiscreteness, its finiteness or infiniteness). The so-called factors of type I are the most manageable type, from the point of view of group representations. These are the factors isomorphic with the algebra of all bounded operators on some Hilbert space. The (direct integral) decomposition of a group

representation into factor representations is essentially unique. When the resulting factors are of type I the decomposition of the representation into irreducible components is also essentially unique. The problem of the types of factor representations a specific group has (the so-called type problem) is central to the general theory. In particular, establishing that specific classes of groups have only type I representations is of vital importance to the general theory.

The detailed investigation of a Lie group and its representations proceeds via the study of its associated Lie algebra. If the Lie group with its associated topology is thought of as a surface in 3-dimensional space (or, more generally, a manifold in n-dimensional space) each vector in the tangent plane (space) at the group identity determines a unique vector at each group element by means of (left) translation by that group element. Relative to (i.e., in the direction of) the invariant vector field so obtained, (differentiable) functions can be differentiated to give another function on the group. If two such vector fields are involved, differentiation is performed with respect to each successively in both orders, and the result of one is subtracted from that of the other, the mapping on functions obtained by this process is the same as that due to differentiation with respect to some third invariant vector field. This third vector field is said to be the Lie product or bracket of the other two. These vector fields, or—what amounts to the same thing since each is determined by a tangent vector at the group identity e—the tangent space at e, with the Lie product is the Lie algebra of the group (it is a nonassociative algebra). Since differentiation is a local process, depending only on the points near a point at which it takes place, the Lie algebra of a group is in reality a construct associated only with that portion of the group near the identity—the so-called local Lie group. Several Lie groups which are distinct "globally" may have the same local structure and hence the same Lie algebra (e.g., the circle group and the group of real numbers both have the real line with the Lie product of each pair of elements 0 as their Lie algebra). The distinction between Lie groups which have the same Lie algebra is a (global) topological one. Loosely speaking they differ in the number and relation of the "holes" in them. A particular one of them "covers" the other; i.e., maps homomorphically onto the other by a mapping which is an isomorphism near the identity. For example, the circle has a hole, the real line does not, and the real line may be "wrapped" homomorphically around the circle. In the family of Lie groups with a given Lie algebra there is one which covers all the others—the so-called universal covering group of the others (also called simply connected covering group—the one which has no holes). The group of reals is the universal covering group of the circle. The rotation groups in dimensions 3 and higher are not themselves simply connected, but have a twofold universal covering group (i.e., each point in the rotation group is the image of precisely two points in this covering group). These are the "spinor groups" (Spin(n) for the n-dimensional rotation group R_n).

The Lie algebra of a Lie group may be thought of as a linear approximation to the local Lie group in the same sense that a tangent plane to a surface is the best planar approximation in the neighbourhood of the point of tangency. The multiplicative nature of the local group is made linear (additive) by the transition to the Lie algebra in much the same way that the logarithm converts multiplicative numerical problems into additive ones. In fact, there is a generalized logarithmic mapping (which preserves differentiability) carrying the local Lie group onto a neighbourhood of the origin in the Lie algebra—or, technically more manageable, an exponential mapping of the entire Lie algebra into the group. By means of this mapping (local) questions about the group can be transferred to questions about the Lie algebra (which are more easily handled because of the added linearity). A (differentiable) homomorphism f of a Lie group G into another H induces a mapping of the functions on H into those on G and consequently of the differentiations with respect to invariant vector fields on G into those on H; i.e., f gives rise to a mapping df of the Lie algebra h of H into the Lie algebra g of G. The mapping df is a homomorphism of g into h; i.e., a linear mapping which preserves the Lie product. Conversely, a Lie algebra homomorphism stems from a homomorphism of the local Lie group which may or may not be extendible to the full group. It is always extendible if the first group is simply connected. Applied to finite-dimensional representations of G (i.e., a homomorphism of G into the n-dimensional general linear group) this process yields a representation of $\mathfrak{g}$; for the Lie algebra of the general linear group can be viewed as the set of all n-dimensional operators with the Lie product of two operators A and B as $AB - BA$. The n-dimensional rotation group of 2-dimensional unitary operators with determinant 1 and also as the group of unit quaternions; the representation theory, in this case, is related to the physical phenomena associated with electron spin.

The deeper analysis of the representation theory of Lie groups whose finite-dimensional representations are completely reducible (the semisimple Lie groups) involves a profound analysis of the semisimple Lie algebras and the so-called theory of weights associated with their representations. It has been established for such groups that their unitary representations on Hilbert spaces are of type I.

Historical Development.—The general representation theory for finite groups was developed by G. Frobenius, I. Schur and W. Burnside at the end of the 19th and the beginning of the 20th century. Nothing of the deeper theory of finite groups developed by such later workers as E. Artin and R. Brauer has been discussed here. The extension of the finite group theory to compact groups is due in part to Schur, who developed the representation theory of the rotation group in those terms. The general extension to compact groups of the completeness and orthogonality of the finite-dimensional irreducible unitary representations is known as the Peter-Weyl theorem (published in 1927). Lie groups are named after M. Sophus Lie, who discovered their fundamental properties in the last decades of the 19th century. A deeper analysis of their properties and, in particular, the classification of the semisimple groups was carried out by E. Cartan in the early part of the 20th century. The general finite-dimensional representation theory for semisimple Lie groups was developed principally by Weyl in the mid-1920s as were the connections between group theory and quantum mechanics. The general representation theory for topological groups started with the discovery by A. Haar in the early 1930s of an invariant measure on locally compact groups. The existence of a separating family of irreducible unitary representations for locally compact groups was established by I. Gelfand and D. Raikov in the early 1940s. The decomposition of unitary representations of locally compact groups into irreducible and factor unitary representations was carried out by F. Mautner at the end of the 1940s. This decomposition was based on the powerful theory of operator algebras developed by J. von Neumann in collaboration with F. Murray in the 1930s and early 1940s. In particular, the theory of factors is their creation. A general duality operator algebras was developed by I. Segal in the early 1950s. G. Mackey created a forceful technique for the analysis of representations of groups with type I representations by generalizing the Frobenius theory of induced representations. The detailed analysis of the infinite-dimensional representations of the semisimple Lie groups is the work of Gelfand, M. Neumark and Harish Chandra. The fact that these groups have type I representations is a consequence of Harish Chandra's results. J. Dixmier established this same fact for the so-called nilpotent Lie groups. Examples of Lie groups with representations not of type I are known. *See also* FIELDS; GROUPS; GROUPS, CONTINUOUS; GROUPS, TRANSFORMATION; INTEGRATION AND MEASURE; MATRIX; OPERATORS, THEORY OF; TOPOLOGY, ALGEBRAIC.—C. Chevalley.

BIBLIOGRAPHY.—C. Chevalley, *Theory of Lie Groups* (1946); L. H. Loomis, *An Introduction to Abstract Harmonic Analysis* (1953); F. Murnaghan, *The Theory of Group Representations* (1938); L. Pontryagin, *Topological Groups* (1939); A. Weil, *L'Intégration dans les groupes topologiques et ses applications* (1940); H. Weyl, *Theory of Groups and Quantum Mechanics* (1949); *Classical Groups* (1946); R. V. Kadison, *Representation Theory for Commutative Topological Algebra* (1951); G. B. Robinson, *Representation Theory of the Symmetric Group* (1961). (R. V. K.)

GROUP THEATRE, New York, was founded in 1931 for the purpose of establishing a permanent company of stage craftsmen under a unified policy in the choice of plays and in production. The group preferred plays it considered relevant to the American social scene. The technique of acting employed emphasized personal as well as artistic truth—a technique derived from the so-called Stanislavski method. (*See* STANISLAVSKI, KONSTANTIN SERGEEVICH ALEKSEEV.)

The three director-founders of the organization were Harold Clurman (sole director after 1937), previously an actor, stage manager and playreader for the Theatre Guild; Cheryl Crawford, who had been the Theatre Guild's casting director; and Lee Strasberg, an actor and occasional director of amateur productions at a New York city settlement house. The Group Theatre's first two productions, Paul Green's *The House of Connelly* and *1931*—by Claire and Paul Sifton, were produced under the auspices of the Theatre Guild. Subsequent productions, 25 in all, were presented independently and financed piecemeal, the latter condition being the cause for the final breakdown of the enterprise.

Though the first plays were critically acclaimed for the quality of their performances, financial success was not achieved until 1933 with the presentation of Sidney Kingsley's *Men in White*. Other outstanding plays produced by the Group Theatre were by Clifford Odets, a member of the acting company from its inception—notably *Awake and Sing, Waiting for Lefty* and *Golden Boy*; *Johnny Johnson* by Paul Green, music by Kurt Weill, and *My Heart's in the Highlands* by William Saroyan were also presented.

The Group Theatre exercised a considerable influence on the American stage in three ways: (1) its acting and production methods became virtually standard after 1945; (2) its emphasis on social themes was characteristic of the period and helped foster new writing talent; and (3) its personnel came to occupy prominent places in the years following the Group's demise (1941). Harold Clurman, Elia Kazan and Robert Lewis came to rank among the leading directors of the American theatre. Stella Adler (Studio), Sanford Meisner (Neighborhood Playhouse school) and Lee Strasberg (Actors' Studio) were outstanding teachers of acting.

See H. Clurman, *Fervent Years; the Story of the Group Theatre and the Thirties* (1945). (Hd. E. C.)

GROUSE, many well-known game birds belonging to the family Tetraonidae, plump-bodied, fowllike birds, with strong, feathered legs and mottled plumage, lacking the brilliant colours of the pheasants but well adapted for concealment. They are of medium to moderately large size; fly swiftly for short distances; feed on or near the ground on seeds, berries and young plant shoots; and nest on the ground, usually laying six to ten or more eggs. They are confined to the northern hemisphere, six genera being found only in North America, four only in the old world, and one—the

MALE SHARP-TAILED GROUSE (PEDIOECETES PHASIANELLUS) COMPETING ON DISPLAY GROUNDS

ptarmigans (*Lagopus*)—circumpolar in distribution. The white-tailed ptarmigan (*L. leucurus*) is found in the mountains of western North America, while the willow ptarmigan (*L. lagopus*) and rock ptarmigan (*L. mutus*) are circumpolar in range. The willow and the rock ptarmigan are remarkable for their seasonal changes in plumage. The rock ptarmigan is pure white in winter blending with the snow, close-barred, grayish-brown in summer to blend with tundra vegetation and mixed brown and white in autumn to match the dying grasses and first light snows—a three-molt sequence that is nearly unique.

A very popular woodland game bird of North America is the ruffed grouse (*Bonasa umbellus*), so named because it has a ruff of large feathers on the sides and back of the neck which are elevated somewhat in display. The cock's performance consists of posing rather stiffly erect and rapidly beating his wings to and fro to make a loud drumming sound. The bird has a favourite log from which it drums repeatedly in the spring and early summer. In the winter the scales on the toes grow out laterally forming a fringe which has been described as "snowshoes" and which may assist the birds in walking about in the snow.

The grouse of the British Isles is the red grouse (*L. scoticus*), one of the four species of ptarmigan. It does not turn white.

Two species of capercaillies (*Tetrao*), two species of black grouse (*Lyrurus*) and two species of hazel hens (*Tetrastes*) occur in Europe and Asia. In North America there are two species of prairie chickens or pinnated grouse (*Tympanuchus*), the sharp-tailed grouse (*Pedioecetes phasianellus*) and the large sage hen (*Centrocercus urophasianus*). The Canada spruce grouse (*Canachites canadensis*) is a less wary bird, as is its smaller relative, Franklin's grouse (*Canachites franklini*), also known as the fool hen. The sharp-winged grouse (*Falcipennis falcipennis*) of northeastern Asia is rather like the Canada spruce grouse. The blue grouse (*Dendragapus obscurus*) has two forms, sooty and dusky.

See BLACKCOCK; CAPERCAILLIE; HEATH HEN; PTARMIGAN; PRAIRIE CHICKEN. (G. F. Ss.; HT. FN.)

GROUSE LOCUST (PYGMY GRASSHOPPER), an insect of the orthopterous family Tetrigidae, related to the true grasshoppers or

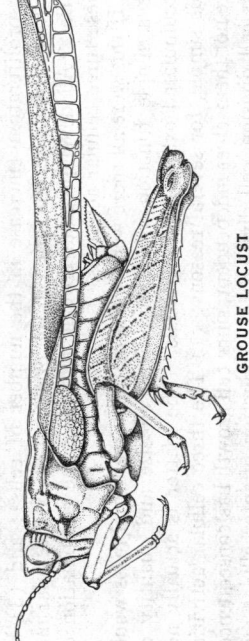

GROUSE LOCUST

Acrididae (*see* GRASSHOPPER). Grouse locusts are small (seldom over an inch long), commonly brown, gray or moss green and often blotched or lined with whitish. They are usually abundant on moist soil or among dead leaves along the edges of ponds, but are also found in dry places. Unlike the true grasshoppers their fore-wings are reduced to small pads or are absent, the folded membranous hind wings being protectively covered by a pointed prolongation of the thoracic shield. Many species are dimorphic —one form short, with reduced hind wings, the other long, with functional hind wings. Sound-producing and hearing organs are absent.

The family is world-wide, but is best represented in the tropics, where are found bizarre forms with humped backs, spines or high crests. The inheritance of form and coloration in species of the genus *Paratettix* has been much studied by geneticists. Although grouse locusts are vegetarians, they are not economically important pests.

BIBLIOGRAPHY.—W. S. Blatchley, *Orthoptera of Northeastern America* (1920); L. Chopard, *Biologie des Orthopteres* (1938); R. K. Nabours, "The Genetics of the Tettigidae," *Bibliogr. Genet.*, vol. 5 (1929). (T. H. HL.)

GROVE, FREDERICK PHILIP (1871?-1948), outstanding Canadian novelist, was one of the first to write realistically about the pioneers of the Canadian west. Born in northeastern Europe of a Swedish father and Scottish mother, he spent much of his youth traveling in Europe with his mother. He was stranded in Toronto in 1892, while on a pleasure tour, by the sudden death and bankruptcy of his father. For the next 20 years he led the life of a hobo in the American and Canadian west. In 1912 he became a schoolteacher in Manitoba, where he lived until 1929. In that year he moved to Ontario, first to Ottawa and then to Simcoe, where he owned a farm and wrote his later novels. He died at Simcoe on Aug. 19, 1948. Soon after his arrival in Canada, Grove began to write his realistic novels of prairie life, but they remained in manuscript for a generation. It was not until 1922 that he found a publisher for his first book, *Over Prairie Trails*, a series of descriptive and narrative sketches. A similar book, *The Turn of the Year*, appeared in 1923. His first novel, *Settlers of the Marsh*, when it finally was published in 1925, caused a sensation by its frankness and realism. He subsequently published seven more novels, of which the best known are *A Search for America* (1927), *Our Daily Bread* (1928), and *The Yoke of Life* (1930); a book of essays, *It Needs to Be Said* (1929); and his autobiography, *In Search of Myself* (1946).

Grove's novels are somewhat stiff in style and clumsy in construction, but they live by virtue of the honesty of his vision. His pictures of prairie life (often bleak and sombre) bring out the rugged perseverance of the pioneers and have great documentary value.

See D. Pacey, *Frederick Philip Grove* (1945), *Creative Writing in Canada* (1961). (D. P.)

GROVE, SIR GEORGE (1820-1900), English writer on music, was born at Clapham, London, on Aug. 13, 1820. He began his career as a civil engineer and then became secretary to the Society of Arts in 1850 and to the Crystal Palace in 1852. He collaborated with William Smith in the *Dictionary of the Bible* and was largely responsible for organizing the Palestine Exploration fund in 1865. Besides having a beneficial influence on the choice of music at the Crystal Palace, for more than 40 seasons Grove wrote analytical notes for the concerts; these notes were marked by enthusiasm, insight and thoroughness and established a standard that was long admired. In 1867 he visited Vienna with Arthur Sullivan and there discovered the part books of the whole of Schubert's music to *Rosamunde*, which had been left unregarded for 44 years. Grove was editor of *Macmillan's Magazine* from 1868 to 1883. During the years 1879-89 his famous *Dictionary of Music and Musicians* was published. Subsequent editions were: second edition edited by J. A. Fuller-Maitland (1904-10); third edition (1927) and fourth edition with supplement (1940), both edited by H. C. Colles; fifth edition edited by Eric Blom (1955), with supplement edited by Blom and Denis Stevens (1961). When the Royal College of Music was founded in 1882 Grove was appointed its first director and was knighted. His book, *Beethoven and His Nine Symphonies*, was published in 1896. He died at Sydenham, London, on May 28, 1900.

See C. L. Graves, *Life and Letters of Sir George Grove* (1903). (H. Ru.)

GROWTH, in its simplest definition, designates increase—whether measured as area, volume, mass, number or intensity. In this descriptive sense the term is applied very generally to very different phenomena: persons, animals, plants, cities, libraries, crystals and knowledge are said to grow. The common attribute displayed by all of these entities when they grow is increasing magnitude, denoted purely descriptively with no assumption that there is commonness in what is increasing or in how the increase occurs.

As soon as one concerns oneself with what is growing and how, growth becomes more difficult to define. What grows in persons, libraries and knowledge clearly is not the same, and similarly how these grow is unlikely to be the same. So different is growth in these several connotations that it requires very different competences even to discuss them. The growth of animals and plants is a problem for the biologist; the growth of human beings, for the biologist and physician; the growth of crystals, for the physical chemist and crystallographer; and the growth of cities, for the sociologist and city planner. Emphasis on major differences in the things that grow does not exclude the possibility that there may be important, perhaps fundamental, similarities in the nature of growth of such things as cities, anthills and ants. It makes evident, however, that what is designated generally as growth is an aspect of diverse phenomena rather than a unitary phenomenon in and of itself. Growth can be abstracted for analysis, but it cannot be safely assumed that statements made about growth in one context are equally applicable to others.

BIOLOGICAL GROWTH

Growth probably is analyzed most frequently in its biological connotation, in reference to orderly increase in number or size of cells, organisms or populations. It is in this sense that growth is a characteristic of living things, the result of numerous metabolic processes at work continuously during life (see NUTRITION; BIOCHEMISTRY). Lower animals, such as corals and sea anemones, and many plants, especially trees, are capable of unlimited growth (said to be indeterminate); their proliferative tissues remain active throughout life (see PLANTS AND PLANT SCIENCE; see also LIFE SPAN). Many higher animals, including man, on the other hand, usually attain a maximum size and a characteristically limited adult form (there is some evidence, however, to indicate that certain higher animals, e.g., fish and turtles, may grow indefinitely).

Descriptively, biological growth, like growth in general, can be defined simply as has already been done. Analytically, however, complications soon emerge. Growth of populations involves replication of individuals; growth of individuals involves replication of cells; growth of cells involves replication of molecules; and replication of molecules involves mobilization of precursors. What grows, and how it grows, is different at each level, and yet all are involved in the over-all phenomenon. For this reason a full statement about human population growth, for example, must take into account factors ranging from, on the one hand, the psychological, social and economic influences on human reproduction to, on the other hand, the pathways of electron transport in respiration.

Rate of Growth.—Organisms grow characteristically and, within reasonable limits, predictably. When size is plotted against time, curves of rate of growth (growth curves) are obtained that are as characteristic for the members of a species as is their morphology or behaviour. Thus the rate and duration of growth is as much a part of the hereditary endowment of the organism as is any other property. But the regularity and relative simplicity of the over-all growth curve gives way to an astonishing complexity when growth of parts of the organism is examined. Each part has its own growth curve, and no two seem to behave in exactly the same way. In extreme instances certain parts may even be decreasing in size, "degrowing," while over-all growth continues. Clearly the regularity of over-all growth is the resultant of many individual part-growths proceeding at different rates.

Factors Regulating Growth.—Such regularity of the whole despite diversity of the parts may be statistical and fortuitous, but it strongly suggests mutual interaction and control. This impression is heightened by the finding that the growth of parts, while dissimilar, is not at all anarchic. Frequently part-growth can be expressed as a relatively simple mathematical function of the growth of the whole or of other parts. Such mathematical relationships among the differential growth rates of parts clearly have consequences for shape and form of the whole and have attracted the interest of many students of growth. Interest is fed by some spectacular correspondences between the results of purely mathematical transformation of growth rates and form and the actual changes undergone by organisms during individual development and evolutionary history. The mathematical approach to growth, however, has so far failed to yield an encompassing function that captures the full subtlety and variety of organismal growth. What it has accomplished is to call attention to the dearth of physiological information on interactive mechanisms that must smooth the apparent disorder of diverse growth rates of parts into a unitary organismal growth curve.

Growth curves vary in detail from species to species but they resemble each other in their approach to a sigmoid or S-shaped curve. This kind of curve indicates that growth of individuals tends to begin slowly, to accelerate to a sustained maximum and then to decline. The level of the sustained growth rate, and the period over which it is sustained, are the chief variables correlating with the great differences in size among living organisms. But the changes in rate at the beginning and end of the curve seem to indicate that the size attained is itself a regulator of growth, that is, that growth is in some measure self-regulating. The organism behaves as though it were at first too small for maximum growth: it slowly achieves optimum size, but then the very consequences of rapid growth act to limit it. The implication that fairly potent growth regulators must exist within the organism is borne out by the demonstration of auxins (growth-promoting hormones) in plants and of the growth-influencing effects of certain hormones in animals (see PLANTS AND PLANT SCIENCE: Plant Physiology: Growth; HORMONES). Despite supporting physiological information of this type for the existence of regulatory mechanisms, a fully satisfactory explanation of the self-limiting characteristic of over-all growth, and particularly of the hereditary influence on final size, has yet to be given.

Disruption of the regulating mechanisms of growth may result in various abnormalities. Under certain conditions animal cells reproduce rapidly and haphazardly, resulting in neoplasms (see TUMOUR; CANCER), or respond to developmental cues unlike the normal ones for the species, resulting in physical defectives (see MONSTER; DWARFISM AND GIGANTISM). Plant cells can be triggered by various agents into unregulated growth as galls, excrescences and fusions of parts normally separate (see PLANT DISEASES; GALL, PLANT).

Manner of Growth.—With advancing knowledge the true complexity of the disarmingly simple over-all growth curve has gradually become apparent. Growth is one of the striking components of the development of a multicellular organism from a single-celled zygote to an adult. As a first approximation there are three ways in which this developmental increase may occur: (1) by cell growth or synthesis (increased size of individual cells); (2) by cell division or proliferation (increase in the number of cells); and (3) by production and accumulation in the organism of extracellular material. All developmental growth involves some combination of these three cellular activities.

If this were all there were to the matter, organismal mass would be a simple function of cell number, cell size and quantity of accumulated extracellular materials. The matter is actually not this simple, for several reasons: (1) The three cellular activities are not themselves independent, since cell growth has consequences for cell division, cell division for production of intercellular material, etc. (2) Although not independent, the three activities are not so invariably coupled as to fit a simple calculus—the relations among them differ in different circumstances and so far have defied generalization. (3) Over-all growth frequently is a net effect of several cellular processes, some of which reinforce and some of which cancel each other. (4) No sharp distinction can be drawn between cellular processes that merely maintain organismal size and those that increase it; growth is more a shift of equilibrium than the addition of a new and unique process.

The growth of human skin will serve to illustrate some of the changes that take place during growth. In the early stages of development the skin is represented by a single surface layer of cells. As the embryo increases in size the surface layer must increase as well, otherwise it would be spread thinner and thinner. No cells are added to the surface layer from below, the entire increase in the surface being due to division of component cells, with the divided products subsequently growing to the size of the original cells. In this type of growth essentially nothing changes but cell number. This growth can be expressed by plotting the number of cells against time, the number of cells being found to approximately double during one division cycle of all cells. Soon, however, the surface layer increases not only in area but in thickness as well. Microscopic examination shows that the increased thickness is not due to increased height of individual cells but to increased number of layers. In the change from a single to a multiple layer, cells move out of the original layer to form new ones above. Only the cells in the original layer continue to divide; the ones in the new layers do not. As a result the cell population now has two components: a basal germinal layer, which continues to divide and from which cells continue to move outward; and outer non-dividing layers, which remain quiescent so far as division. In simple consequence, as the number of nondividing cells increases, the number of cells produced by one division cycle of the germinal cells becomes a smaller proportion of the total number of skin cells. Without altering the intrinsic growth activity of the germinal cells, a reduction in the rate of growth of the whole skin has occurred.

The cells that move out of the basal layer do not divide, but they do undergo differentiation or specialization. It is a general observation that as cells specialize in their activities the probability of their undergoing division is reduced. With advancing development, therefore, the proportion of dividing cells is steadily reduced. In the case of skin, specialization takes the form of synthesis of keratin, a major component of the horny outer protective layer of the adult. In the process of keratinization the cell dies. The bulk of adult skin epithelium is made up of non-proliferating cells that are in the process of becoming, or have become, horny. The various stages in the process can be seen progressing outward in regular order, from the unspecialized, proliferative germinal layer to the dead, completely horny layer on the outer surface.

Clearly, if the accumulation of horny cells continued indefinitely, the skin would become progressively thicker. This does not occur—not because germinal proliferation ceases but because horny material is constantly rubbed off and shed from the surface. The skin ceases to increase in mass when the rate of proliferation in the germinal layer just balances the rate of loss at the surface. Growth in the sense of net increase has then stopped—not because the proliferative process has ceased but because it is balanced by loss. At any time, factors that affect the balance of proliferation and shedding may change the mass of the skin locally or generally.

From this course of events it is clear that cessation of growth does not always mean cessation of all growth activity. Rather it implies a balance—first, between proliferating and differentiating cells, and second, between production and loss.

Growth as Equilibrium.—Such "steady state" growth systems are not uncommon. Bone marrow operates this way in the production of blood cells, and the ovary and testis in forming gametes. Even the tiny, fingerlike villi of the wall of the small intestine are covered by a population of cells subject to steady loss and replacement. These instances, which could be greatly multiplied, emphasize the fact that growth of the organism and of its parts is not the result of a peculiar and unitary growth process that turns off and on. Rather it is a dynamic resultant, slowing and accelerating with changes in the steady state of the manifold cellular activities of the organism (see also CELL).

Complexity is not eliminated and no unitary growth process emerges even when attention is shifted from the organism as a whole and is focused on the growth of cells themselves. For many years microbiologists have been studying the growth of populations of bacterial cells under relatively simple and well-defined conditions. More recently cells of higher organisms, both plant and animal, have been studied in similar ways under the controlled conditions of cell and tissue culture (see TISSUE CULTURE). The general growth of cell populations is very much the same in all cases. A suitable number of cells introduced into an appropriate nutrient medium provides a characteristic growth curve of sigmoid shape. A short preliminary "lag" period of little or no

growth—usually interpreted as involving adjustment of the cells to their new environment—is followed by increase at maximum rate. This rate is exponential, numbers of cells doubling in equal intervals of time, and the period frequently is referred to as the "log" phase because cell number plotted on logarithmic co-ordinates behaves as a straight line.

Subsequent to the log phase growth rate declines. Depending upon circumstances it may approach zero (tend toward the maximum stationary phase), reach zero ("plateau") or become negative ("decline"), in which case the size of the population becomes smaller.

The striking similarity of the shape of the growth curve of a free cell population and of an intact multicellular organism could not help attracting the attention of biologists. It raised the question, in particular, whether the declining growth rate (senescence) of multicellular organisms might be due to some intrinsic limitation in their cells. It is now known that this is not the case. Certain cells, at least, cease growth and die because the organism dies, and not vice versa (see also DEATH [BIOLOGICAL]; GERONTOLOGY AND GERIATRICS). By providing a suitable and frequently renewed culture environment microbial cells and some cells extracted from living organisms can be held in the log phase indefinitely. The growth of microbial cells evidently follows a sigmoid curve because factors in their environment limit their growth. In the case of the cells taken from higher organisms cellular growth activity within the organism is regulated by relations with the entire organism. Removed from these relationships, and provided with a favourable artificial growth environment, constituent cells may grow indefinitely and are potentially immortal.

Growth of Individual Cells.—Microorganisms and cells in culture afford opportunity to study growth as it occurs in an individual cell. This requires very special circumstances, but it has been accomplished by ingenious techniques applied to the free-living, single-celled ameba. Individual amebae can actually be weighed, to the order of 1 millimicrogram (one thousandth of one thousandth of a milligram). When an ameba divides, its daughter cells are of approximately equal weight, and each is half the weight of the mother cell. Daughter cell weight begins immediately to increase at maximum rate, with no lag period as in population growth. Growth continues for about 20 hours, or until the weight has doubled; i.e., becomes equal to that of the original mother cell. There then occurs a four-hour period of growth stasis, which is again terminated by division into two new daughter cells. When division is completed, renewed growth ensues at a maximum rate.

It is possible to interfere with the normal growth cycle of the ameba in several illuminating ways. Division of a mother cell can be caused to be unequal, yielding an unusually small and an unusually large daughter cell. These two cells subsequently grow at unequal rates but, despite their initial size difference, reach the same final size before themselves dividing. Moreover if portions of the cytoplasm of a growing cell are surgically removed, requiring it to take longer to reach its "dividing weight," then division is postponed. In fact if cytoplasm is removed repeatedly, the cell will remain in continuous growth without ever dividing. It appears that some level of cytoplasmic mass must be achieved before the division process can be initiated. Cell growth and cell division are thus very closely interrelated in single-celled organisms. As has been noted earlier, less direct observations than are possible on ameba imply that a similar relation may underlie some of the complexity of multicellular growth.

Chemical Study of Growth.—Single cells pose technical difficulties for more detailed analysis, particularly for chemical studies during the growth cycle. Cell populations, on the other hand, provide more material for chemical analysis, but interpretation is complicated unless the population is "in phase", that is, all cells are at a given stage of the growth cycle at the same time. Such "phased" populations are observed in a limited number of natural situations and in some cases can be produced artificially. Analysis of artificially phased ameba cultures shows that complexity and heterogeneity, as in over-all organismal growth, underly the seeming simplicity of the growth curve of a single cell. Cell mass, cell volume and content of protein increase synchronously, but

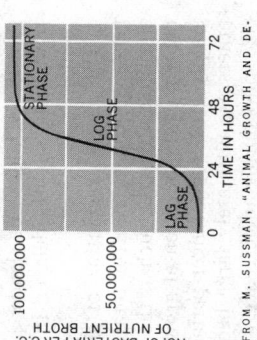

NO. OF BACTERIA PER C.C. OF NUTRIENT BROTH

100,000,000

50,000,000

LAG PHASE   LOG PHASE   STATIONARY PHASE

0   24   48   72
TIME IN HOURS

FROM M. SUSSMAN, "ANIMAL GROWTH AND DEVELOPMENT," 1960, PRENTICE-HALL

GROWTH CURVE OF POPULATION OF BACTERIA; THE SHAPE OF THIS CURVE IS TYPICAL OF NATURAL GROWTH OF CELLS, ORGANISMS AND POPULATIONS IN GENERAL

nuclear volume lags behind these and increases rapidly only when over-all growth has reached its plateau. Similarly the amount of deoxyribonucleic acid—an important nuclear constituent implicated in heredity and the control of general synthetic activity—remains constant through most of the growth cycle but doubles shortly before the division process begins. Over-all cell growth, like over-all organismal growth, is a result of part-processes preceding at different rates. Interaction and integration among cell parts and cell processes is implied, and these are only barely beginning to be discerned in detail.

Moreover, it is clear that, at the subcellular level, growth is intimately related to metabolism—the turnover of chemical materials within living systems (see BIOCHEMISTRY). Synthesis of larger and more complex molecules—indispensable for growth—is closely coupled with energy-yielding reactions frequently involving degradation of larger molecules to smaller ones. When synthesis of retained material exceeds degradation and loss, growth occurs.

Since cells may synthesize many kinds of materials, growth may vary quantitatively (in total net synthesis) or qualitatively (in the kind of material chiefly produced). The increase of total net synthesis is spoken of as growth; change in the kind of synthesis is spoken of as transformation. When the transformation results from hereditary change it is called mutation (q.v.); when it occurs in the normal course of development in higher organisms, it is called differentiation (see EMBRYOLOGY AND DEVELOPMENT, ANIMAL). In the study of metabolism at the cellular level, students of heredity, growth and development meet on common ground.

Summary.—What emerges as the essential quality of biological growth? Certainly no single process controlled by a master reaction and expressible in an all-encompassing equation. Growth as increase from within is one of the most characteristic features of living things. In its elementary and perhaps earliest form growth is replication, one thing making another fundamentally like it. Replication, at all levels, continues to play a part in all growth processes—making more like molecules, more like cells and more like organisms in growing populations. But at each successive level the mechanisms of control of replication become more complex and the nonreplicative by-products tend to increase. In a sense regulation is added to regulation as the increasing price of more abundant replication. Growth involves all of this; it is the quantitative extension of living systems at whatever level and by whatever mechanism. In its widest and perhaps most profound sense biological growth is the thrust of the living against the nonliving, the indomitable impulse of life.

(Cr. G.)

HUMAN GROWTH

Although growth in human beings resembles that in other mammals, in both over-all course and specific determinants, there are many features in which human growth is either unique or exaggerates tendencies found in other mammals. Moreover, human beings grow under a wide variety of nutritional extremes, and are highly variable in genetic makeup. Human beings now attempt to regulate the growth of their young for optimum health, and are increasingly aware of the important relationships between growth rate and length of life.

The newborn human being is neither so advanced developmentally as the colt, nor so unformed as the fetal opossum. The size of an infant is a compromise between the advantages of developmental advancement and the problems that the larger human brain and head pose to the birth process. Furthermore, the newborn human being is, among mammals, uncommonly fat and uncommonly scant in hair; it is uncommonly dependent on the care of its parents and uncommonly equipped with the vocal mechanisms to demand it.

In most children, growth can be divided into a series of phases. The first six or nine months after birth constitute a phase of rapid growth and fat gain, followed by an apparent slowing-up as fat is lost while muscle is gained. A second shift appears in the pre-school to early school years. The onset of the steroid-mediated phase of growth, in turn, is heralded by an increase in food intake, metabolic activity and tissue mass.

COURSE OF GROWTH—Size and Growth at Birth.—The size of the infant at birth is the result of many factors, chief among them being the size of his parents and the length of gestation. Generally, the larger the parents (taller or greater in muscle mass), the larger the infant, even for equal length of gestation, and the longer the term of intra-uterine life, the larger the body size at birth.

There are wide variations in size and proportions at all fetal stages and at birth. Girls are generally smaller than boys, yet further along in development. Racial differences in body proportions are evident as early as the third month of gestation. Japanese babies at birth are relatively short legged while American Negro babies tend to be longer legged, when compared with American white babies. During the first few years after birth the influence of parental body size is clearly evident. Big parents have big babies, who are advanced over smaller babies in sitting up, crawling and walking. Yet girls, though smaller, are consistently advanced in nearly every motor skill, and especially in talking.

Despite congenital differences, size in human infants is highly amenable to nutritional control. Malnourished, sick or debilitated infants show major delays in growth and behaviour. In the Western world improved nutrition and improved medical care have resulted in faster growth during infancy.

Nutritional Effects During Childhood.—During childhood, the effects of nutrition and medical care on growth are clearly apparent. A 6-year-old child in Central America or in Africa may be smaller than a 4-year-old in North America or in northwestern Europe. Poverty and plenty may each produce growth problems. Caloric and protein deprivation limit childhood growth in two-thirds of the world's population. At the same time, children in economically advanced areas suffer from overnutrition and underexercise, which have now created a new class of medical problems.

The state of nutrition clearly determines the rate of growth, all other things being equal. Under "nutrition" are included the limiting nutrients; even though the diet has an adequate caloric content, it may be deficient in other essential nutrients such as vitamins, deficiencies that can limit growth. In many parts of the world today, protein deficiency is growth-limiting. In Central and South America, and in Africa, Asia and Indonesia, children fail to grow optimally because of a lack of quality protein such as is provided by meat, milk or cheese. Low-cost protein supplements, including fish meal, milk powder or a mixture of cereal proteins are being developed for distribution to areas where the populace is chronically undernourished and limited in growth attainment.

Genetic Mediation.—Genetically determined differences in growth rate and skeletal development are marked. Genes are the basic determinants of size and growth. In well-nourished populations, genes are the major determinants, accounting for perhaps 90% of size variance. Tall parents have tall children, and short parents have short children. Tall × short parental combinations produce children who are quite variable in size during growth. It does not seem to be important whether the mother is tall and the father short, or vice versa, though there are slightly greater father-daughter similarities in size during growth. Children of slender parents tend to be slender and also tend to be slightly delayed in their skeletal and dental development.

The genetic regulation of size and growth is complex. Some genes appear to control total size. Others control the size of specific body parts, such as the legs or the spinal column. Genetic control of the duration of growth is also involved. Some children simply grow for a longer period of time (i.e., they mature late); others are ultimately large because they have a disproportionate size spurt during adolescence.

This complex combination of genes, nutrition and state of health makes competent medical supervision a necessity. No system of charts and tables can replace the need for regular medical care, nor can the doctor effectively appraise the growth of a child without thorough knowledge of his parentage.

Hormonal Mediation.—By the 10th year in the female, and about the 11th in the male, hormones of gonadal origin begin to appear in appreciable amounts. As these steroid hormones increase in potency and amount, many physical changes take place, and the course of growth is greatly altered. The period of steroid-mediated growth is long in man, lasting from at least the 10th year until well after statural growth has apparently ceased. Puberty (time of appearance of pubic hair) and menarche (time of the first menstruation) are two significant events in this long period that mark approaching sexual maturity.

Under the influence of steroid hormones there is a tremendous increase in the rate of growth, an adolescent sometimes gaining a maximum of 7 in. in a single year. Caloric requirements for growth are then very great, as are calcium requirements for the increase in the skeletal mass. Fat accumulations increase in the female, especially over the breasts, hips, thighs and upper arms. The hairline recedes in both sexes, coarse body hair appears, and sebaceous gland activity heightens, the latter is often associated with acne.

As the epiphyses (end plates) of the long bones unite with the shafts, linear growth comes to an end. But the individual rate and duration of bone growth varies considerably, resulting in a wide range of body types.

In man, as in other primates, fertility is attained rather early in the steroid growth phase. The girl may be able to conceive at 14 (usually one year after menarche), she may be married at 20, but she will not attain maximal skeletal or muscular development until she is 25, or thereabouts.

Cessation of Growth.—By the time growth has ceased, aging sets in, the onset varying with different tissues and organs of the body. The muscle mass continues to increase through the mid-20s, thereafter gradually decreasing. The skeletal mass increases until age 30 or so, and then begins to decrease, first in the central skeleton (the pelvis and spine) and last in the peripheral skeleton (the fingers and toes). Along with aging in general, there is deposition of cholesterol in the arteries, more extensive and heavier in the overnourished. Changes in the central nervous system take place as strength and endurance wane. In some animals, aging appears to be delayed by slowing growth—thereby postponing maturity—and by maximizing activity. It is not certain whether this phenomenon occurs in man.

Predicting Adult Size.—At birth, a full-term baby boy is about 27% as long as he will be when he is 18 years old. A new-born baby girl is nearly 30% of her final stature. A 6-year-old American boy already stands two-thirds his probable height at age 18, and this is true for the 5-year-old American girl. On the average, a full 90% of final length is attained by contemporary American boys in their 14th year, and this percentage of final size is already true for girls between ages 11 and 12. Within rather broad limits, then, it is possible to predict adult size from the size at any age, using the simple multipliers given in the accompanying table, which has been especially calculated for this article.

The values given in this table do have certain limitations, however. They apply specifically to children of contemporary U.S. parents whose heights when added equal 134 in. (or average 67 in.). If the parental stature is much higher or markedly lower than these values, the true multipliers will be somewhat different. Stature prediction of children is necessarily more unreliable in cases where either parent is of extreme size, or where the size disparity between the parents is great. Stature prediction is most reliable when the parents are near the middle of their appropriate size distributions, and where there is little relative disparity in absolute dimensions.

A further complication to size prediction is the rate of skeletal development. Skeletal age, or bone age, as measured from X-rays of the hand, may be retarded or advanced over the child's actual age. A healthy child who is retarded in skeletal age has a longer time to grow; he will be bigger than predictions based on age and size would suggest. On the other hand, a child who is advanced in skeletal development will ordinarily stop growing sooner, and his final stature will probably be less than the prediction tables alone suggest.

If skeletal age is known, it should be substituted for chronological age in using the prediction table. For a 7-year-old boy with a skeletal age of 6 years, the multiplier listed for 6 years of age should be used (1.54). Conversely, if a 10-year-old girl has a skeletal age of 11 years, then the multiplier for age 11 should be used (1.12) instead of that for age 10 (1.17). In this way it is possible to make use of biological, or physiological, age as a reference standard, greatly improving stature prediction. Growth experts, medical experts concerned with the very short or the very tall child, and orthopedists, who may have to perform "pinning" operations to balance out leg length, use a combination of stature tables and bone-age corrections to come to their final decisions. When working with older children—12 years or so in girls and 14 years or more in boys—with careful attention to skeletal status, predictions of final stature can be made with an effective accuracy of one inch or better.

Except for very late-maturing children, or children who have been delayed in growth for various reasons, values for size at age 18 are used as the standard; stature prediction is generally based on such values, even though some adolescents may continue to add height after age 18.

Trends in Growth

Size and Maturity.—For the last 170 years, people have been growing bigger and maturing earlier. In most countries the average size of the adult has been increasing at the rate of one inch every 30 to 50 years. The age of the first menstruation has decreased from about 15 years in 1800 to slightly under 13 years in 1960.

These changes are based on improved nutrition, reduced energy expenditure and better medical care. In all countries, better nourished children grow taller and mature earlier. The level of nutrition has been raised considerably in most parts of the world by the elimination of vitamin deficiencies, the provision of more and higher quality protein, and the supplementation of caloric intake. Energy expenditure is reduced in childhood because of warmer homes, better clothing, elimination of child labour and simply less activity. Energy not expended to keep warm, or for work, or in transportation is energy spared for growth. The elimination and control of childhood diseases, particularly the dysenteries, has corresponded with increase in growth among children.

Growth Research.—It is clearly possible to regulate the rate of growth, the timing of maturation and final adult size within genetically set limits by controlling caloric intake and energy expenditure. By increasing energy intake or decreasing energy expenditure during growth, energy is stored as fat, growth is promoted, maturation is earlier and adult size will be larger.

Restricting growth, either by nutritional deprivation or increased energy expenditure, is of course deleterious. Malnourished children are more susceptible to infectious diseases and have lower life expectancy than properly nourished children. Complications

Stature-Prediction Tables for Children of Parents With a Combined Height of 134 in.*

Boys				Girls			
Age	Standard height (in.)	Percent of age 18	Multiplier	Age	Standard height (in.)	Percent of age 18	Multiplier
1	29	41	2.46	1	28¾	44	2.30
2	34½	49	2.06	2	32¼	50	2.01
3	38¼	54	1.86	3	36¼	57	1.76
4	41¼	58	1.73	4	40	62	1.62
5	44	62	1.62	5	42¼	66	1.51
6	46¼	65	1.54	6	45¼	70	1.43
7	48¼	68	1.47	7	47¼	74	1.35
8	50¾	71	1.40	8	50¼	78	1.29
9	52¾	74	1.35	9	52¾	81	1.23
10	55	78	1.29	10	55¼	85	1.17
11	57¼	81	1.24	11	58	90	1.12
12	59¼	84	1.19	12	60¼	93	1.07
13	62¼	88	1.14	13	62¾	97	1.03
14	65¼	92	1.09	14	64¼	99	1.01
15	67¾	96	1.04	15	64½	100	1.002
16	69¾	98	1.02	16	64½	100	1.002
17	70½	99	1.01	17	64¾	100	1.001
18	71	100	1.00	18	64¾	100	1.000

*Average for both parents = 67 in.

of childbearing are more severe in mothers who have undergone growth restriction in childhood.

Overnutrition also is dangerous. Size is greater and sexual maturation earlier in overnourished children, features that set them aside from their age mates and frequently engender psychological problems. From the strictly physical viewpoint, fat children generally become fat adults, with decreased life expectancy and all the ills the obese are prone to contract.

Growth research is aimed at determining the optimum rate of growth, defined by the fewest childhood diseases and the greatest life expectancy. A great deal is known about the growth of people in North America, western Europe and Japan. Growth knowledge is spotty for other areas. Information on the growth of African pygmy children or that of Australian aborigines is essential to understanding the entire range of normal human growth. The study of growth following recovery from disease or malnutrition is a subject that needs investigation. Very often there is heightened growth during recovery termed "catch-up growth," a little-understood compensatory period.

The goal of growth research is not merely to determine optimal individual growth or to achieve optimum health and growth of populations but to acquire a fundamental knowledge of the growth processes and mechanisms from the time of conception through the period of senility.

Specific articles relating to growth processes include ADOLESCENCE; DIET AND DIETETICS; GERONTOLOGY AND GERIATRICS; INFANTS, CARE OF; MALNUTRITION; NUTRITION.

See also references under "Growth" in the Index.

(S. M. G.)

BIBLIOGRAPHY.—L. B. Arey, Developmental Anatomy, 6th ed. (1954); Leona Bayer and Nancy Bayley, Growth Diagnosis (1959); N.J. Berrill, Growth, Development, and Pattern (1961); Agatha H. Bowley, Natural Development of the Child, 4th ed. (1957).; Edith Boyd, Growth of the Surface Area of the Human Body (1935) and Outline of Physical Growth and Development (1941); W. E. LeGros Clark and P. B. Medawar, Essays on Growth and Form (1945); G. W. Gray, "Human Growth," Scientific American, 189, 4:65–76 (Oct. 1953); J.S. Huxley, Problems in Relative Growth (1932); R. Pearl, The Natural History of Populations (1939); Dorothy Price (ed.), Dynamics of Proliferating Tissues (1958); W. J. Robbins et al., Growth (1928); Dorothea Rudnick (ed.), Aspects of Synthesis and Order in Growth (1955), Cellular Mechanisms in Differentiation and Growth (1956), Rhythmic and Synthetic Processes in Growth (1957) and Cell, Organism and Milieu (1959); J. M. Tanner, Growth at Adolescence, 2nd ed. (1955); J.S. Huxley (ed.), Third Symposium on Human Growth (1959); D'Arcy W. Thompson, On Growth and Form (1942); E. H. Watson and G. H. Lowrey, Growth and Development of Children, 2nd ed. (1954); V. B. Wigglesworth, Control of Growth and Form (1954); E. B. Wilson, The Cell in Development and Heredity, 3rd ed. (1928); M. X. Zarrow et al. (eds.), Growth in Living Systems (1961).

GROYNE (GROIN), a structure erected out from a shoreline to limit erosion and control water flow. On the coasts of the Netherlands and Belgium low groynes constructed of fascine mattress work and rubble stone are commonly employed. Groynes similar in form to those used on seashores are employed for training the flow of rivers, protecting their banks from erosion, and deepening their channels. Groynes built out over river banks and which are perpendicular to the flow of the current are sometimes termed spur groynes (see RIVER ENGINEERING). In architecture, the word groin (q.v.) refers to the edges formed at the intersections of vaults. See also JETTY.

(N. G. G.)

GROZNY, a town and the administrative centre of the Chechen-Ingush Autonomous Soviet Socialist Republic of the Russian Soviet Federated Socialist Republic in the U.S.S.R., stands on the Sunzha River, at the foot of the Sunzha Range (Sunzhenski Khrebet) of the north Caucasian foothills, 300 mi. NW of Baku. Pop. (1970 prelim.) 341,000. The town was founded in 1818 as a fortress against the warlike Chechens and both L. N. Tolstoi and M. Y. Lermontov (qq.v.) served there. From 1944 to 1957 the autonomous republic was known as Grozny Oblast. The presence of petroleum at Grozny was known from 1833 but large-scale commercial production began only with the first bore in 1893, and the year when the railway reached the town. Thereafter Grozny grew rapidly as one of the major oil centres of Russia, being by the time of the Revolution second only to Baku. The growth of new Soviet oil fields reduced the relative importance of the area, but with new oil finds in the 1950s Grozny remained a significant producer. Pipelines run to Makhachkala on the Caspian, Tuapse on the Black Sea, and the Donbass industrial area. There is large-scale refining, processing, and the manufacture of petro-chemicals and machinery for the petroleum industry. Grozny has also sawmilling, timber-working, and food-processing industries. It is joined by railway to Makhachkala and, via Ordzhonikidze and Armavir, to Tuapse.

(R. A. F.)

GRUDZIADZ (Ger. GRAUDENZ), a town in the Bydgoszcz wojewodztwo (province) of northern Poland, is situated on the lower Vistula, 95 km. (59 mi.) S of Danzig (Gdansk). Pop. (1968 est.) 75,100. Located on the Torun–Gdansk railway and a road junction, it is an industrial centre with foundries and breweries and factories producing agricultural implements, rubber, ceramics, and footwear. From the 13th century it was heavily fortified under the Teutonic Knights, and in 1291 received municipal rights. It was acquired by Poland in 1466. After the first partition in 1772 the town became a powerful fortress under Prussia. The Versailles Treaty of 1919 returned it to Poland. A large forced-labour camp was established there during the German occupation in 1939–42.

(K. M. WI.)

GRUIFORMES, an order of birds, the best-known members of which are the cranes and rails. See BIRD; BUSTARD; COOT; CRANE; FINFOOT; GALLINULE; LIMPKIN; NOTORNIS; PHORORHACOS; SERIEMA; SUN BITTERN; TRUMPETER.

GRUMBACH, WILHELM VON (1503–1567), German adventurer, chiefly known through his connection with the so-called "Grumbach feuds," the last attempt of the German knights to destroy the power of the territorial princes, was born near Würzburg on June 1, 1503. In about 1540 Grumbach became associated with Albert Alcibiades, margrave of Brandenburg, whom he served both in peace and war. After the conclusion of the peace of Passau in 1552, Grumbach assisted Albert in his career of plunder in Franconia and was thus able to take some revenge upon his enemy, Melchior von Zobel, bishop of Würzburg. Grumbach held his lands in fief from the bishops of Würzburg, and had held office at the court of Conrad of Bibra, who was bishop from 1540 to 1544. Albert's career, however, was checked by his defeat at Sievershausen in July 1553 and his subsequent flight into France, and the bishop seized Grumbach's lands. The knight obtained an order of restitution from the imperial court of justice, but he was unable to execute it; and in April 1558 some of his partisans killed the bishop.

Grumbach fled to France. Returning to Germany, he pleaded his cause, unsuccessfully, before the diet at Augsburg in 1559. He had found a new patron in John Frederick II (q.v.), duke of Saxony, whose father, John Frederick, had been obliged to surrender the electoral dignity to the Albertine branch of his family. Grumbach suggested to the duke a general rising of the German knights as a means to the recovery of the electorate. Magical charms were employed against the duke's enemies, and communications from angels were invented which helped to stir up the people. In 1563 Grumbach attacked Würzburg, plundered the city and compelled the bishop to restore his lands. He was consequently placed under the imperial ban, but John Frederick refused to withdraw his protection. Meanwhile Grumbach planned the assassination of the Saxon elector, Augustus; proclamations were issued calling for assistance; and alliances both without and within Germany were concluded. In Nov. 1566 John Frederick was placed under the ban, which had been renewed against Grumbach earlier in the year, and Augustus marched against Gotha. A mutiny led to the capitulation of the town. Grumbach was tortured, and executed at Gotha on April 18, 1567.

GRUMENTUM, an ancient town of Italy, in Lucania (modern Basilicata), 33 mi. S of Potentia (Potenza). It seems to have been native Lucanian, not a Greek settlement. In 215 B.C. the Carthaginian general Hanno was defeated under its walls, and in 207 B.C. Hannibal made it his headquarters. In the Social War it seems to have been held by both sides at different times. Its site is a ridge on the right bank of the Aciris (Agri) about 1,960 ft. above sea level, ½ mi. below the modern Saponara. Its ruins include scanty traces of a large amphitheatre, the only one in Lucania, except that at Paestum (Pesto).

GRÜN, HANS: see BALDUNG, HANS.

GRUNDTVIG, NIKOLAI FREDERIK SEVERIN (1783–1872), Danish bishop and poet, founder of a theological movement (Grundtvigianism) which revitalized the Danish church, and also outstanding as hymn writer, historian, pioneer of studies on early Scandinavian literature, and educationalist, was born at Udby parsonage, Zealand, Sept. 8, 1783. After taking a degree in theology (1803), he studied the *Eddas* and Icelandic sagas. His *Nordens mytologi* (1808) marks a turning point in this research: like his early poems, it was inspired by the romantic movement. As a poet he rivaled Adam Oehlenschläger (*q.v.*) in his *Optrin af Nordens Kaempeliv*, 2 vol. ("Scenes From Heroic Life in the North," 1809–11).

In 1811, after a spiritual and emotional conflict which ended in a "Christian awakening," he became his father's curate. His first attempt to write history from a Christian standpoint, *Kort Begreb af Verdens Kronike i Sammenhaeng* (1812), attracted much attention. From his father's death in 1813, however, until 1821, his criticism of rationalist tendencies in the Danish church made it impossible for him to find a pastorate, but in poems such as those in *Roskilde-Riim* (1814) and other collections, and in *Bibelske Praedikener* ("Biblical Sermons," 1816), he called for a renewal of the spirit of Luther, and in his opposition to the romantic philosophers, especially Schelling, he foreshadowed Kierkegaard. During these years he also translated Saxo Grammaticus and Snorri Sturluson into vigorous, racy Danish and opened the way for research into Anglo-Saxon literature by his version of *Beowulf* (1820). On three later visits to England (1829–31) he continued this work by drawing attention to the early manuscripts.

In 1825, he became the central figure in the "Church controversy," when in his *Kirkens Gienmaele* ("The Church's Reply") he accused the theologian H. N. Clausen of treating Christianity as a philosophical idea. Grundtvig maintained that it was a historical revelation, handed down by the unbroken chain of a living sacramental tradition at baptism and Holy Communion. His writings were placed under censorship, and in 1826 he resigned his living, but he continued to develop his view of the church in theological writings and in *Christelige Praedikener* (3 vol., 1827–30). His visits to England had helped to clarify his view of the need for freedom in church and state and of what he called "the great natural law of the spiritual life," *i.e.* "the necessity of the spoken word for the awakening of life and the transmission of the spirit." He expounded his philosophy in a new and inspired *Nordens Mytologi* (1832) and in his *Haandbog in Verdenshistorien* (3 vol., 1833–43). As an educationalist—*e.g.*, in *Skolen for Livet og Academiet i Soer* (1838)—he stressed the need for a thorough knowledge of the mother tongue, national and biblical history, through narrative and song, in opposition to the Latinists, and put forward the idea that the years after 18 are those of awakening to life. This inspired the founding, after 1844, of voluntary residential folk high schools, in which young people of every class were encouraged to educate themselves and one another.

In 1839, Grundtvig was allowed to receive the living of Vartov, Copenhagen, and in 1861 he was given the rank of bishop. His liberal outlook found political expression in his active part in the movement leading to the introduction of parliamentary government in 1849. He died at Copenhagen, Sept. 2, 1872.

As "father of the folk high school," which spread through Scandinavia and inspired adult education in many other countries, notably Switzerland, England and the United States, as the founder of Grundtvigianism, the strongest trend in the Danish church after 1848 and also influential in Norway, Grundtvig's position is assured. His work made it possible for the 19th-century religious revivals in Denmark to remain within the national church. Perhaps even more lasting is his position as the greatest Scandinavian hymn writer. His *Sang-Vaerk til den Danske Kirke*, 5 vol. (1837–81), contains new versions of the hymns of the whole Christian church, as well as a wealth of original hymns, many of them well known in Norwegian, Swedish, German and English

translations, and is a Christian counterpart of J. G. Herder's *Stimmen der Völker.*

BIBLIOGRAPHY.—N. Davies, *Education for Life* (1931) and *Grundtvig of Denmark* (1944); E. Sontag, *N. F. S. Grundtvig, Erzieher seines Volkes* (1946); E. L. Allen, *Bishop Grundtvig: a Prophet of the North* (1947); H. Begtrup, H. Lund and P. Manniche, *The Folk High Schools of Denmark,* 4th ed. (1949); P. G. Lindhardt, *Grundtvig: an Introduction* (1951); Hal Koch, *Grundtvig* (Eng. trans. 1952); J. Knudsen, *Danish Rebel: a Study of N. F. S. Grundtvig* (1955); E. Simon, *Réveil national et culture populaire en Scandinavie* (1960); S. Johansen, *Bibliografi over N. F. S. Grundtvigs Skrifter,* 4 vol. (1948–54). *Grundtvig-Studier* (1948–   ), with English summaries, gives information about new literature. (HE. N. H.)

GRUNDY, MRS., an imaginary English character who typifies the control of the conventional "proprieties" of society over conduct, the tyrannical pressure of the opinion of neighbours on the acts of others. The name first appears in a play by Thomas Morton, *Speed the Plough* (produced in 1798), in which one of the characters, Dame Ashfield, continually refers to what her neighbour Mrs. Grundy will say as the criterion of respectability. Mrs. Grundy does not appear in the play, but is a mythical character similar to Mrs. Harris, Mrs. Gamp's friend, in Dickens' *Martin Chuzzlewit* (1844).

GRUNDY, SYDNEY (1848–1914), English dramatist, was born at Manchester on March 23, 1848. He was educated at Owens College, Manchester, and was called to the bar in 1869. He became well known as an adapter of plays, his early successes being *The Snowball* (1879) from *Oscar, ou le mari qui trompe sa femme* by A. E. Scribe and Duvergne; and *In Honour Bound* (1880) from Scribe's *Une Chaine.* Among his most successful adaptations was *Pair of Spectacles* (1890) from *Les Petits Oiseaux* of Labiche and Delacour. Grundy died on July 4, 1914.

GRÜNEWALD, MATHIAS (*c.* 1460–1528), the painter so named by J. von Sandrart in his *Teutschen Academie* (1675), the creator of the pictures on the leaves of the great Isenheim altarpiece, one of the greatest artists of his time, was in fact called Mathis Gothardt Neithardt and was born in Würzburg about 1460. He was probably a pupil in a studio on the middle Rhine. In 1485 he was resident in Aschaffenburg; all the work belonging to this period has been lost. In 1490, he moved away and disappeared from sight for a decade. In 1501 he settled in Seligenstadt and lived in this specially privileged little town on the Main river until 1520. In 1503 he painted the "Mocking of Christ" (Pinakothek, Munich) for the cathedral at Aschaffenburg, and about the same time a small "Crucifixion" (art museum, Basel). Both pictures already show his bold composition, expressive drawing and dramatic colouring. In 1509 he became court painter to the archbishop of Mainz, Ulrich von Gemmingen, who lived in Aschaffenburg. As artistic and technical adviser, Grünewald had to supervise the rebuilding of the castle; at the same time, he reached great heights as a painter. In 1510 the Frankfurt patrician Jakob Heller commissioned him to paint a two-leaved standing screen for the altar in the Dominican church. Two of the panels, painted gray on gray, depicting St. Lawrence and St. Cyriacus, have been preserved in Frankfurt (Städel); two others, with St. Elizabeth and St. Lucy, are in the museum at Donaueschingen.

Grünewald created his masterpiece in Isenheim, Upper Alsace, for the monastery church of St. Anthony upon commission by Abbot Guido Guersi. In 1505, the Strasbourg sculptor Niklaus Hagnower had delivered a carved screen for the high altar in the church, which had been expanded; now, Grünewald was commissioned to paint the pictures for four movable and two fixed wings. His subjects were taken from the mystical world of Antonine thought: Christ's early years; the Passion; and St. Anthony (the saint's temptation and his conversation with Paul the Hermit). The altar, preserved in the museum in Colmar, was finished about 1515–16. Later, but before 1519, Grünewald painted an altarpiece for the Maria Schnee chapel in the church of SS. Peter and Alexander in Aschaffenburg; its central picture (the Mother of God as guardian of the church) is now in Stuppach, Württemberg, and its right wing (the miraculous foundation of Sta. Maria Maggiore) is in the museum in Freiburg im Breisgau. In 1520, Grünewald delivered various altar pictures for the cathedral in Mainz, all of which were destroyed in the Thirty Years' War.

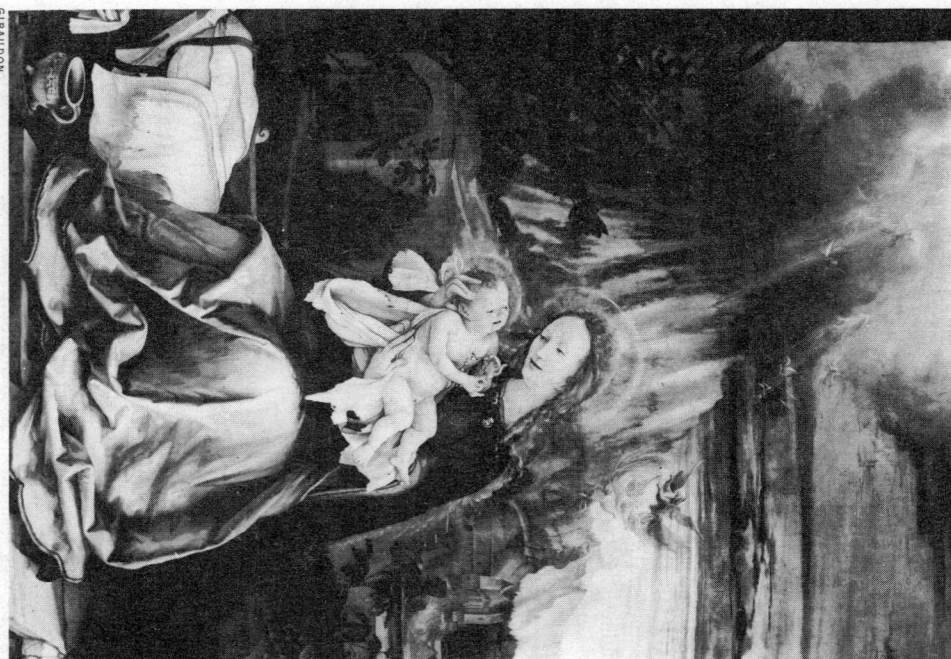

GIRAUDON

"VIRGIN AND CHILD" BY MATHIAS GRÜNEWALD: 1516. IN THE MUSEE D'UNTERLINDEN, COLMAR, FRANCE

In the years following, commissioned by the young archbishop of Mainz, Albrecht Cardinal von Brandenburg, he painted the great panel with the meeting of St. Erasmus and St. Mauritius (Munich); for an unknown patron he painted an altarpiece for the city church in Tauberbischofsheim ("Carrying of the Cross" and "Crucifixion" in Karlsruhe; predella with the "Lamentation of Christ" in Aschaffenburg cathedral). Apparently Grünewald soon had differences with Albrecht von Brandenburg, and in 1526 there was an open breach between them over the painter's support of the Reformation. He was dismissed from court service and went to Halle, dying there in 1528.

Grünewald depicted the suffering Christ with cruel naturalism, yet was the master of a transfiguring colour and a transcendental light. His drawings (only about 40 survive, most of them in Berlin, others in Dresden, Erlangen, Karlsruhe, Oxford, Paris and Stockholm) also grow out of light. Grünewald always approached form as if he felt the necessity to translate it into light. Above all, however, his pictures are all the result of an introspective gaze which expressed itself in the objectivity of its religious content. Thus he became a visionary interpreter, which was in his time accounted to be the highest artistic achievement.

BIBLIOGRAPHY.—H. A. Schmid, Gemälde und Zeichnungen von M. Grünewald (1907–11); M. J. Friedländer, Grünewald's Isenheimer Altar (1908), Die Zeichnungen von M. Grünewald (1927); A. Burkhard, Mathias Grünewald, Personality and Accomplishment (1936); W. C. Züch, Der historische Grünewald (1938); M. Hürlimann and W. R. Deusch, Grünewald (1939); Guido Schoenberger, The Drawings of Mathis Gothart Nithart called Gruenewald (1948); Anthony Bertram, Grünewald (1950); Stengel, "Der neue Grünewald—Fund," Zeitschrift für Kunstwissenschaft, 6, s. 65 (1952); L. Behling, Die Handzeichnungen des Mathis Gothart Nithart, genannt Grünewald (1955). (A. Se.)

GRUNION (Leuresthes tenuis), a small edible fish (five to seven inches long) of the silverside family (Atherinidae), found along the shores of California and Lower California. Its spawning habits are correlated with the tides. During spring and summer grunion spawn on the beach during the highest tide, which occurs every two weeks. Adults swim onto the beach with the waves and are temporarily stranded; the female wriggles two to three inches into the sand and lays 1,000 to 3,000 eggs, which are at the same time fertilized by the male. Two weeks later the next high tides wash out the eggs, which will hatch only after they have been disturbed. During their spawning period grunion can be readily caught by fishermen, even with the bare hands.
(C. Hu.)

GRUNT, the name for several species of perchlike marine fishes of the family Pomadasyidae, a group abundant in warm waters. The name refers to the curious grunting sound that these fishes produce by grating the upper throat teeth (pharyngeal) against the lower, the swim bladder acting as a resonator. Members of the genus Haemulon, which have large mouths lined with brilliant red, are found in the Atlantic ocean.

Grunts are important food fish. Some are brightly coloured; most are small, of pan fish size. The porkfish (Anisotremus virginicus), margate (Haemulon album) and pigfish (Orthopristis chrysopterus) belong to the same family. The drum (q.v.), a perchlike fish of the family Sciaenidae, is sometimes called grunt, or grunter. See also FISH.
(J. T. N.; X.)

GRUNWALD, BATTLE OF, the name given by the Poles to their victorious battle against the Teutonic Order, which marked the end of German colonization in the lands on the southeastern coast of the Baltic. The engagement is also known as the battle of Tannenberg. The military decision had been politically prepared since 1385 by the union of Poland and Lithuania under King Wladyslaw II Jagiello. The battle itself took place on July 15, 1410, between the villages Stebark (Tannenberg) and Grunwald (Grünfelde), about 60 mi. E. of Grudziadz and 25 mi. S.W. of Olsztyn. In order to obtain the shortest line of attack against Malbork (Marienburg), the order's headquarters, Wladyslaw had assembled his forces much farther to the east than his enemies had expected. An attack by the armoured horsemen of the order under their high master, Ulrich von Jungingen, defeated the Lithuanian army group under Vytautas (Witold); but the ranks of the Polish gentry, which were directed by Wladyslaw from outside the battle, remained unbroken. At the end of a long day the forces of the order were outflanked. Jungingen, who had led the charges in the medieval style of chivalrous fighting, was killed with most of his commanders and 205 of his knights. The survivors of his army were dispersed. Immediately after the battle the order's morale broke down; a great number of castles surrendered without a fight. But during August and September the defense of Malbork by Heinrich Reuss von Plauen reduced this effect for the time being. The loss of prestige, however, was permanent; and in 1466 the order's power in the Baltic lands collapsed completely. See also POLAND: History. For the German victory over the Russians in World War I see WORLD WARS: World War I: The Eastern Front, 1915.
(H. Lz.)

GRUSON, HERMANN AUGUST JACQUES (1821–1895), German engineer, inventor and industrialist, was born on March 13, 1821, in Magdeburg. From 1840 to 1847 he worked as an unpaid assistant at the Borsig locomotive works in Berlin, attending university lectures on natural science in his spare time. He spent the years 1845–55 gaining engineering and managerial experience. In 1855 he opened, in Magdeburg-Buckau, a small shipyard together with a factory and an iron foundry and, in 1857, as a result of successful production of a high-grade chill casting by the process of mixing together various types of German pig iron, his iron foundry prospered while the shipyard and factory lay idle. Following English and U.S. examples, he used this new process for the production of railway equipment and later for the production of cast-iron shell cases and armour plate. In 1882 he bought a construction patent for armoured gun turrets. Besides defense armaments, Gruson manufactured grinding machines and ore-concentration machines, as well as machines for oil, rubber and other factories. In 1893 his business was amalgamated into the firm of Friedrich Krupp.

Gruson died at Magdeburg on Jan. 30, 1895.

See *Beiträge zur Geschichte der Technik und Industrie*, vol. 16, pp. 65–93 (1926).

GRUYÈRE (Ger. GREYERZ), the southernmost district of the Swiss canton of Fribourg (*q.v.*), is situated between the cities of Montreux and Fribourg, and its green pasture land scattered with chalets spreads along the middle reach of the Sarine (Saane) river on the edge of the Vaudois uplands and of the Bernese Oberland (Vanil Noir, 7,838 ft.). The capital is Bulle (pop. [1960] 5,983, the majority French-speaking and Roman Catholic) with sawmills, furniture factories and cellars where the famous Gruyère cheeses are stored. Gruyère lace is also sold and there are large cattle fairs. Its castle was built about 1230–39 by Boniface, bishop of Lausanne, and the chapel of Notre-Dame de la Compassion dates from the 13th century. The village of Broc has a chocolate industry with an international market.

Gruyères (pop. [1960] 1,349), the historical capital of the district, is a walled town with a 15th-century castle (keep of much earlier date), now the property of the canton of Fribourg, and a church of St. Théodule (1254). Its name is derived either from *gruyer*, a forestry officer, or from the crane (*grue*), which appears on its coat of arms and its standard.

Gruyère is served by railways and motor coaches that pass through Bulle. The national road from Bern to Vevey was under construction in the 1960s. The road of the Col du Bruch (Juan pass) 4,948 ft. high, joins Suisse Romande to the Spiez-Interlaken region by way of Gruyère and Simmental. (G. Cu.)

GRYPHIUS, ANDREAS (1616–1664), German lyric poet and dramatist, the leading German writer of the 17th century, was born on Oct. 11, 1616, at Glogau in Silesia, the son of a Lutheran parson who died by poison when the poet was still a child. The family name was Greif, latinized, according to the prevailing fashion, as Gryphius. The horrors of the Thirty Years' War soon cast a shadow over Gryphius' unsettled childhood. A refugee from his native town, he was educated in various places, revealing himself in the process as a brilliant scholar. Crowned *poeta laureatus* by Count Georg von Schönborn, whose sons he tutored, Gryphius went to Leiden and stayed there six years, both as student and teacher. After extensive travels in Holland, France and Italy, he finally returned in 1650 to take up the important administrative post of syndic in Glogau, a post he filled until his death there on July 16, 1664.

Gryphius' reputation has increased enormously during the 20th century. His work is distinguished by a deep sense of melancholy and pessimism and is threaded through with a fervent religious strain which, faced with the transitoriness of earthly things and the fight for survival in the ravaged Germany of the time, borders on despair. He wrote five tragedies, which owe less than has been supposed to the influence of Seneca, the Dutch dramatists P. C. Hooft and J. van den Vondel, and the Jesuit dramatists. They are *Leo Armenius* (1646); *Catharina von Georgien, Carolus Stuardus* and *Cardenio und Celinde* (all printed 1657), and *Papinianus* (1659). They deal with the themes of stoicism and constancy unto martyrdom, of the Christian ruler and the Machiavellian tyrant, and of illusion and reality, a theme used with telling effect against the middle-class background of *Cardenio und Celinde*. The theme of illusion and reality is a fundamental one in his three comedies, the best of which is *Die geliebte Dornrose* (1660). *Herr Peter Squentz* (1657) handles the theme of the Bottom scenes in *A Midsummer Night's Dream*. His lyric poetry covers a wide range of verse forms and is characterized by a technical mastery and assurance and a portrayal of human emotions in adversity, the sincerity and compulsive power of which stamp him, particularly in his sonnets, as a great poet.

BIBLIOGRAPHY.—Gryphius' complete works, *Lustspiele, Trauerspiele, Lyrische Gedichte*, ed. by H. Palm, *Stuttgarter Literarischer Verein*, 3 vol. (1878–84), augmented by the *Lateinische und deutsche Jugenddichtungen*, ed. by F. W. Wentzlaff-Eggebert (1938). *See also* V. Mannheimer, *Die Lyrik des Andreas Gryphius* (1904); W. Harring, *Gryphius und das Drama der Jesuiten* (1907); W. Flemming, *Gryphius und die Bühne* (1921); G. Fricke, *Die Bildlichkeit in der Dichtung des Gryphius* (1933); E. Lunding, *Das schlesische Kunstdrama* (1940). (D. G. D.)

GUADALAJARA, a province and city of Spain in the region of New Castile. The town, capital of the province, lies on the Henares river 56 km. (35 mi.) N.E. of Madrid by road. Pop. (1960) 21,230 (mun.). It has been the administrative and commercial centre of the region since the middle ages. In the past it had important fairs and a thriving woolen industry. Modern industries are based on agriculture. The city is Iberian in origin but its name is Arabic (Wad al Hadjarah, "river of stones"). Its chief artistic monument is the Palace of the Duques del Infantado dating from the end of the 15th century and belonging to the Mendoza family. It was burned down during the civil war (1936–39) and only the façade remains. The church of Santa María, dating from the 13th century, and that of San Ginés, once part of a Dominican monastery, were also badly damaged in the civil war. The baroque church of San Nicolás (1691) belonged to the Jesuits.

GUADALAJARA PROVINCE (pop. [1960] 183,545; area 4,707 sq.mi.) forms part of the uplifted northeastern edge of the Meseta (*see* SPAIN: *Physiography*) and consequently the high ground is in the north while in the south the land slopes into the plateau basin of New Castile. The extreme southeast rises again to form the Sierra de Albarracín. The northern highlands reach their greatest heights in Ocejón (6,744 ft.), Cerro de San Felipe (7,214 ft.), Sierra Alta and other peaks in the Guadarrama mountains. The main pass is over the Sierra Ministra which carries the railway from Madrid to Saragossa. The remainder of the province has a mean altitude of 3,300 ft. and is crossed by several rivers most of which are tributaries of the Tagus. The chief of these are the Henares, Jarama and Tajuña which have been utilized for hydroelectric power and irrigation through the dams of Entrepeñas, Buendía and Bolarque.

The province has more than 400 municipalities and is divided into nine judicial areas. The plains have a greater population density than the mountains. The 1950 census showed that the drop in the population figure was considerable. This was caused by emigration to Madrid because of the poor economic resources of the area. The Madrid-Saragossa railway and the main road from Madrid to France pass through the provincial capital. The railway also passes through the ancient cathedral town and episcopal see of Sigüenza (pop. 4,620 [mun.]), which stands 3,245 ft. above sea level. Molina de Aragón (pop. 3,181 [mun.]), on the Gallo river, is a fortified town dominated by a 12th- to 13th-century castle.

The natural regions are Serranía, Campiña, Parameras de Molina and La Alcarria. About half the country is unproductive but sheep rearing on the pastures provides the biggest contribution to the economy. Cereals are the most widely grown crops; olives and vines are cultivated. Alcarria in the southwest is noted for its honey.

BIBLIOGRAPHY.—A. Pareja, *La Alcarria* (1918); Manuel Teran, *Sigüenza*, no. 26 (1946); Layna Serrano, *Guadalajara y sus Mendozas* (1942). (M. B. F.)

GUADALAJARA, the second largest city of Mexico and the capital of the state of Jalisco, is 275 mi. W.N.W. of Mexico City. It is in the Antemarac valley, near the Río Grande de Santiago, at an elevation of 5,092 ft. Except for the rainy season, which extends from about July 1 to Sept. 15, its climate is dry and mild. The city is connected by rail with Nogales on the Arizona border and Mexico City. All-weather highways connect it with those two cities as well as with cities on the central and Pan-American highways. An excellent highway leads to Lake Chapala, a popular resort 23 mi. from the city. Guadalajara is served by major national airlines which provide connections with all major cities of the republic and with the United States.

The city was founded in 1531 by Nuño de Guzmán. During the first decade of its existence its site was changed several times under pressure from the Indians. From its beginning the city was the centre for Indian slave hunting and remained so throughout much of the 16th century. Father Hidalgo y Costilla, who initiated the independence movement in Mexico, occupied the city late in 1810, and it was there that he decreed the abolition of slavery in Mexico. On Jan. 17, 1811, he suffered a disastrous defeat at Calderón bridge near the city. During the French intervention of the 1860s,

Guadalajara was occupied by the invading forces. The city suffered from severe earthquakes on May 31, 1818, and March 11, 1875.

Guadalajara has experienced a significant population growth in the 20th century; the population increased from 179,600 in 1930 to 736,800 in 1960. After 1940 Guadalajara added to its traditional roles of political capital and commercial entrepôt for an extensive agricultural region (devoted primarily to corn growing and live-stock raising) that of a major industrial producer. In the second half of the 20th century it ranked as one of the republic's important industrial centres; manufactures included textiles, shoes, chemicals, building materials, tobacco products and soft drinks. Handicraft industries, carried on in Guadalajara and the suburbs of San Pedro (commonly known as Tlaquepaque) and Tonolá, include glass blowing, leather tooling, pottery making, silver- and coppersmithing and weaving.

Industrial and commercial establishments are often quartered in ultramodern buildings, and modern residential suburbs have attracted members of the upper classes and the rapidly expanding middle classes from the older parts of the city. The city was made the seat of a bishopric in 1549, and the cathedral, built between 1571 and 1618, is richly decorated. Many of the city's more than 50 churches also date from the colonial period.

During the summer months religious processions bear the image of the Virgin of Zapopan, the patroness of the city, to each of the churches; afterward there are secular festivals with elaborate moving fireworks displays (castillos). The governor's palace, begun in 1743, is generally considered to be one of the finest examples of Spanish architecture in Mexico. Guadalajara has two universities—the University of Guadalajara dating from 1792 and the Autonomous University of Guadalajara founded in 1935. The Teatro Degollado is one of the largest and most ornate theatres in Latin America.

Guadalajara was the home of the painter José Clemente Orozco (1883–1949), and among his numerous murals in the governor's palace, the Autonomous university and the Hospicio (orphanage) are to be found some of his finest works. The family home is a museum.

Mariachis (strolling orchestras) specializing in Mexican folk music, and found throughout most of the republic, originated in Guadalajara.

(J. J. J.)

GUADALQUIVIR (Lat. BAETIS, Moorish WADI AL KEBIR, "the great river"), the chief river of southern Spain, rises at about 4,593 ft. between the Sierra de Cazorla and Sierra del Pozo in Jaen province. It descends rapidly between precipitous banks to Baeza (932 ft.) but it does not become a large river until joined by the right-bank tributary, the Guadalmena. The Guadalquivir is the only Spanish river with a large coastal plain, which it enters at Córdoba (328 ft.), and Seville is the only big river port in the country. Below Coria the Guadalquivir traverses the largest swamps in Spain, Las Marismas; navigation to Seville has been facilitated by a cut, the Corte de Tablada, for vessels up to 1,200-1,500 tons. Below Sanlúcar de Barrameda the river enters the Atlantic after a course of 348 mi. The Guadalquivir receives more than 800 affluents, of which several exceed 100 mi. in length, the chief of which is the Genil (222 mi.) fed by the ice field of the Corral del Veleta. Apart from the Guadalquivir dam at El Tranco de Beas and two on the Genil, the other ten dams are constructed on the swiftly flowing tributaries coming from the Sierra Morena (q.v.). The Guadalquivir valley is irrigated in four main sections: Andújar, Córdoba, Lora del Río and above Seville.

(J. M. Ho.)

GUADALUPE, a river, mountain range, monastery (formerly Franciscan) and puebla (village) in the northeast of the Cáceres province of the Extremadura region in Spain. The river rises in the Sierra de Guadalupe, or Sierra de las Villuercas, and flows into the Guadiana. The mountains rise 1,736 m. (5,695 ft.) and form the watershed between the Tagus to the north and the Guadiana to the southeast. Oil, chestnuts and cork are products of the region. The puebla (pop. [1960] 4,079 [mun.]) has 14th- to 17th-century houses surrounding the monastery which was built where a shepherd found an image of the Virgin that had been hidden during the Moorish domination. Alfonso XI of Castile visited the shrine in 1337 and it became a centre of pilgrimage. In 1389 the Hieronymites (hermits of St. Jerome) took over the sanctuary; their first prior, Yañez (d. 1412), built the church, the mudéjar (Moorish) style cloister with a fountain, and hospices. The flamboyant St. Anne's chapel with a tomb by the Brussels sculptor Egas was added later, as were the Gothic cloister, chapter hall and library. The main retable by Juan Gomez de Mora was completed by Vincenzo Carducci and Eugenio Caxesi; the sculptures are by Merlo. There are tombs of Henry IV of Castile and his mother Maria of Aragon. In 1638–39 Francisco de Zurbaran painted eight large canvasses for the sacristy, two for the adjoining chapel, and for its altar the "Glory of St. Jerome" and little figures of Hieronymite saints on the predella. From the vault hangs a Turkish lantern seized at the battle of Lepanto. The Camarin has nine paintings by Luca Giordano. The monks of Guadalupe were skilful embroiderers, miniaturists, ironworkers and silversmiths, and their surviving works are on display together with illuminated books, portraits by Juan Carreño de Miranda and other art treasures.

(M. L. Ca.)

GUADALUPE HIDALGO: see GUSTAVO A. MADERO.

GUADELOUPE (LA GUADELOUPE), the largest territory of the French Antilles, consists of twin islands of the Leeward group, in the eastern Caribbean at 16° 15' N. and 61° 35' W. Basse-Terre to the west and Grande-Terre to the east are separated by swamps and a narrow channel, the Rivière Salée. A few miles east and south lie the smaller islands of Marie-Galante and La Désirade and the islets called the Îles des Saintes and the Îles de la Petite Terre. These, together with St. Barthélemy and the northern part of St. Martin, situated respectively about 130 mi. and 140 mi. to the northwest, are dependencies of Guadeloupe. The total area is 687 sq.mi.

Relief and Geology.—Physically the western and eastern parts of Guadeloupe are strongly contrasted. Basse-Terre is high and rugged with a central chain of volcanic peaks and ridges which increases in height southward and culminates in Soufrière (4,869 ft.), the highest mountain in the Lesser Antilles. This volcano is dormant but it erupted in 1797 and again in 1836, causing considerable destruction. Thermal springs and solfataras are its only present signs of activity. From the mountainous spine of Basse-Terre the ground slopes steeply to the west coast, but eastward a gently sloping plain descends toward the Rivière Salée. Grande-Terre is by contrast flat and low-lying. It nowhere rises above 450 ft. and consists mainly of limestone, as do the adjacent islands of Marie-Galante, La Désirade and La Petite Terre. Les Saintes, off the south coast of Basse-Terre, are volcanic. Thus the western half of Guadeloupe forms part of the inner, volcanic arc of the Lesser Antilles and the eastern half part of the outer, sedimentary arc.

The volcanic rocks of Basse-Terre are mainly andesite, agglomerate and ash built up during Miocene, Pliocene and Pleistocene times, whereas the rocks of Grande-Terre are older. There horizontal limestones lie conformably upon fine tuffs and ashes, the whole series being of Eocene and Oligocene age. Some younger, Pliocene limestones rest unconformably upon these older beds and near the coast there are recently exposed coral reefs. Numerous streams drain the mountain slopes of Basse-Terre, but Grande-Terre has few permanent watercourses and depends largely on reservoirs, ponds and cisterns for its water supply.

Climate.—Climatic conditions vary greatly despite the small area of Guadeloupe. The seasonal range of temperature varies only from a minimum monthly mean of 28° C. (82° F.) in June to a minimum of 24° (75°) in January, but the mountains are always distinctly cooler than the lowlands. Variation of rainfall is much more pronounced. Only 40 in. annually are received by parts of Grande-Terre and serious droughts occur in the dry season from January to May, whereas the mountains of Basse-Terre, lying across the path of the prevailing northeast trade winds, receive well over 100 in. a year and their summits are usually blanketed in cloud. Hurricanes are liable to occur in the rainy season from July to November; in Sept. 1928 Guadeloupe, with much of the West Indies, was devastated by a hurricane and by the succeeding

GUADELOUPE

tidal wave. Guadeloupe was also hit hard by a hurricane in Sept. 1960.

Vegetation and Animal Life.—There is a marked contrast in the vegetation of western and eastern Guadaloupe. The mountains of Basse-Terre are clad in dense tropical rain forest which remains the finest virgin forest in the Lesser Antilles. Grande-Terre, on the other hand, has been cleared of its original forest cover and only scattered patches of dry scrub woodland remain. Near the Rivière Salée there are extensive mangrove swamps.

The fauna of Guadeloupe has been much altered since European settlement began. Numerous animals have been introduced and a large number of native species exterminated. The Indian mongoose was brought to the island about 1880 to control the spread of rats, but it has also caused the extermination of several species of birds, lizards and snakes as well as threatening the existence of native mammals such as the agouti. Forest clearance and hunting have also contributed to the extermination of native species, notably parrots, macaws, the diablotin or blackcapped petrel (*Pterodoma hasitata*) and the crapaud or mountain chicken, a large edible frog (*Leptodactylus fallax*).

History.—Prior to its discovery in 1493 by Christopher Columbus on his second voyage, Guadeloupe was occupied by Caribs, themselves relative newcomers who had migrated from South America and supplanted a pre-existing population of Arawaks. Columbus named the island after the monastery of Santa Maria de la Guadeloupe in Extremadura, Spain, but the Spaniards, prevented with the larger islands to the west and discouraged by Carib hostility, made no attempt at settlement. In 1635 Guadeloupe was occupied by Liénart de l'Olive and his companion Du

Plessis for the French Compagnie des îles de l'Amérique, and the Caribs were gradually exterminated. Four chartered companies were ruined in successive attempts to colonize Guadeloupe and in 1674 it passed to the French crown, becoming a dependency of Martinique, which it remained until 1775.

During the 17th and 18th centuries the British attacked Guadeloupe several times but were successful in occupying it only from 1759 to 1763 and again briefly in 1794. In 1810 they took it again and retained it until 1816 when it was returned to the French government.

Between 1816 and 1825 Guadeloupe's legal code was introduced. In 1837 municipal institutions were established and in 1848 slavery was abolished, 93,000 slaves being freed. During World War II Guadeloupe adhered to the resistance movement of Gen. Charles de Gaulle in 1943 and in 1946 became an integral part of the French Union.

Population.—In the 17th and 18th centuries growth of the population depended largely on the immigration of French settlers and the importation of Negro slaves. Following the abolition of slavery, labourers, artisans and traders from India, Syria and elsewhere increased the size and racial diversity of the population. By the mid-1960s the total, with the dependencies, was more than 300,000. Negroes and mulattoes predominate, except in Les Saintes whose inhabitants are mainly white. The principal town, Pointe-à-Pitre (*q.v.*), in the mid-1960s had a population of about 50,000. The administrative capital is Basse-Terre (pop. about 15,000).

Administration.—In 1946 Guadeloupe, with its dependencies, became an oversea *département* of France. It is divided into two *arrondissements* comprising 34 communes, each administered by an elected municipal council. Executive government is conducted by a prefect and other appointed officials, and legislative authority is vested in a general council of 36 members elected by popular vote. The territory is represented in the National Assembly by three deputies and in the Senate by two senators. There were 3 secondary and about 190 primary schools in the early 1960s, most of which were public and provided free education.

Economy.—Economically Guadeloupe remains, as it was before World War II, dependent on the export of agricultural produce to France. Sugarcane occupies a larger area than any other crop, and sugar and rum are the most valuable exports. There are sugar factories at Pointe-à-Pitre, Le Moule and St. Anne on Grande-Terre, where most of the sugar is grown, and also at Basse-Terre and at Grande Anse on Marie-Galante.

Bananas are the other main export crop, about 90,000 metric tons being produced annually. Minor exports are coffee, cocoa, vanilla, pineapples, citrus fruit and cotton, the latter grown in the drier areas. Subsistence farming, the raising of livestock, and fishing occupy most of the population not engaged in the production of cash crops for export. The forests of Basse-Terre proved too difficult of access to be ex-

SCHOONERS DOCKED AT THE QUAY, AT POINTE-À-PITRE. SCHOONERS ARE WIDELY USED FOR INTERISLAND TRADE IN THE CARIBBEAN

ploited for timber, which is imported. Mineral production is limited to small amounts of salt and sulfur.

Ships of French and North American lines regularly visit the harbour of Pointe-à-Pitre and scheduled flights of French, U.S., British and Dutch airlines call at Le Raizet airport north of the town. Local steamers serve the dependencies, and the main island has a network of about 450 mi. of roads.

St. Martin and St. Barthélemy.—These islands lie near the northwest end of the outer arc of the Lesser Antilles and though small are rugged, with hills rising to 1,332 ft. and 991 ft. respectively. St. Martin was amicably divided between the French and the Dutch in 1648 and has remained so. About two-thirds of the island is French with a mainly Negro population of 4,502 (1961) and one town, Marigot, which is a free port. Both parts of the island are served by an airport near Philipsburg in the Dutch sector.

St. Barthélemy was occupied by the French in 1648, ceded to Sweden in 1784 and returned to France in 1877. There is one town, Gustavia, and the population of 2,176 (1961) is almost exclusively of European origin.

See also references under "Guadeloupe" in the Index.

BIBLIOGRAPHY.—L. Blanche, *Histoire de la Guadeloupe* (1938); J. Gottmann, "The Isles of Guadeloupe," *Geogr. Rev.* vol. xxxv (1945); E. Revert, *La Guadeloupe*, 2 vol. (1961); G. de Chamberrand, *La Guadeloupe et Dépendances* (1965); *Annuaire de la Guadeloupe* (1957); Maurice Nicolas, *La France d'Amérique* (1949); *Les Antilles* (1954); G. Lasserre, *La Guadeloupe et Dépendances* (1965); Current history and statistics are summarized annually in *Britannica Book of the Year*.
(D. R. H.)

GUADET, MARGUERITE ELIE (1758–1794), French Revolutionary politician, was born at St. Emilion near Bordeaux on July 20, 1758, and became a lawyer. When the French Revolution broke out he had already gained a reputation as a leading advocate at Bordeaux. In 1790 he was made administrator of the Gironde and in 1791 president of the criminal tribunal. In that year also he was elected to the legislative assembly as one of the group of deputies who were subsequently known as Girondins or Girondists.

As a supporter of the constitution of 1791, Guadet joined the Jacobin club, and there and in the assembly became an eloquent advocate of all the measures directed against real or supposed traitors to the constitution. He bitterly attacked the ministers of Louis XVI and was largely instrumental in forcing the king to accept the Girondin ministry of March 15, 1792. Although an advocate of the policy of forcing the king into harmony with the Revolution, Guadet remained a royalist and, with others, even addressed a letter to the king soliciting a private interview. Whatever negotiations might have resulted from such an interview, however, were cut short by the uprising of Aug. 10 when insurrectionists occupied the Tuileries and imprisoned the royal family. Guadet, who presided over the assembly during part of that fateful day, unsuccessfully opposed the insurrectionist group.

As a convention deputy in September, he voted for an appeal to the people at the trial of Louis XVI and for the death sentence, but with a respite pending appeal. In March 1793 during the war in La Vendée Guadet refused to co-operate with Danton whom he held responsible for the September massacres. He was involved in the fall of the Girondins and his arrest was ordered in June 1793. He fled to Caen, however, and afterward hid in his father's house at St. Emilion. Discovered, he was taken to Bordeaux where, after he had been positively identified, he was guillotined on June 17, 1794.

GUADIANA (Lat. ANAS, Moorish WADI ANA), a river of the southwestern Iberian Peninsula. Despite its drainage area of 23,455 sq.mi. (60,748 sq.km.), a length of 359 mi. (578 km.) and about 30 major tributaries, the flow is relatively meagre, only about half that of the Tagus or Douro. This is because its basin drains the Montes de Toledo and the Sierra Morena, and the plains of La Mancha, with their low rainfall. The Zancara (the true source of the upper Guadiana) and the Gigüela rise in the more pluviose mountains of Cuenca. They then form temporary lakes to the west of Daimel. These marshes are known as *los Ojos del Guadiana* ("the eyes of the Guadiana"), a noted sanctuary of wildfowl. In contrast, the porous limestones of the southern basin form a shallow water table and the karstic flow of the Guadiana Alto, Azuer, Cárcoles, and Guadiana en los Ojos produces intermittent streams that disappear underground, though eventually feeding the Zancara.

To the west, the Guadiana cuts a series of defiles through the quarzitic ridges of the Montes de Toledo, now utilized by ten dams with a reservoir capacity of 3,786,000,000 cu.m. There are four major dams, the Cíjara being the largest single dam in Spain (completed 1956); and the last to be completed is the Zújar (1963). These dams are the basis of electrification and irrigation for the Badajoz Plan, boldly launched in 1952 to develop an area the size of Belgium and one of the poorest in Spain. It was expected to be completed in 1970, with about 292,600 ac. (118,402 ha.) under irrigation between Mérida and Badajoz, the establishment of some 10,000 families in new colonies, and some 90 new industrial enterprises. By 1962, all the towns and villages of Badajoz province were electrified.

Between Badajoz and Monsaraz and again downstream from Pomarão, the river forms the frontier between Spain and Portugal. But the rocky defiles and the sandbars at its mouth make the river suited to the navigation of small boats only for 42 mi. (67.6 km.) upstream to Mértola. Larger vessels ply only between Pomarão and the coastal ports of Ayamonte (Spain) and Vila Real de Santo António (Portugal).
(J. M. Ho.)

GUADIX, a town of southern Spain in the province of Granada, is situated between two mountain ranges on the Verde or Guadix river, 58 km. (36 mi.) E. of Granada by road. Pop. (1960) 24,704 (mun.). It has a cathedral in Renaissance and baroque styles. The town is surrounded by caves excavated in the mountainside, which are inhabited and very picturesque. Guadix is on the railway from Madrid to Almería and on the main Granada-Murcia highway. Agriculture is the chief occupation; chief crops are wheat, olives, flax and hemp. Guadix is the ancient Acci of the Romans but its present name is of Arabic origin.
(M. B. F.)

GUAHIBO, a small family of South American Indian languages, including the languages spoken by the Guahibo and Chiricoa as well as those of several other little-known tribes. The Guahibo and Chiricoa were closely related culturally as well as linguistically, and inhabited adjoining areas in the savannas west of the Orinoco river in eastern Colombia. Both were nomadic peoples who derived their subsistence from hunting a variety of animals and gathering wild roots and palm fruits. The political unit was a fairly large band with a hereditary leader, but the food-gathering group was composed of only a few families. These tribes had a rather complex technology for a nomadic people and made painted pottery as well as hammocks and many kinds of baskets. Throughout the historic period there had been a fairly extensive trade between the nomads of the savanna and the sedentary farming tribes in the forests to the south, and some of the nomads have adopted agriculture and permanent dwellings as a result of this contact.

Although census data were unavailable in the early 1970s, Guahibo were estimated to number about 20,000.

See Paul Kirchhoff, "The Guahibo and Chiricoa," in *Handbook of South American Indians*, ed. by Julian H. Steward, Bureau of American Ethnology Bulletin 143, vol. 4, pp. 446–455 (1948).
(Se. L.)

GUAIACUM (GUAJACUM), a genus of trees, important for their exceptionally hard, resinous wood, belonging to the family Zygophyllaceae. The common guaiacum or lignum vitae tree (G. officinale) is a native of the West Indies and the north coast of South America, where it attains a height of 20 to 30 ft. G. sanctum grows in the Bahamas and Cuba, and at Key West in Florida. G. arboreum, the guaiacum tree of Colombia, is found in the valley of the Magdalena up to altitudes of 2,600 ft., and reaches considerable dimensions. Guaiacum wood is of a yellow colour merging into green, and has an almost powdery fracture. This resinous wood (viz, the resin itself) was once thought to have great remedial qualities against many illnesses; hence the term lignum vitae ("wood of life").

The wood is exported in large logs or blocks, generally divested of bark, and presents in transverse section very slightly marked

UMATAC BAY AT THE FOOT OF MT. BOLANOS, BELIEVED TO BE THE LANDING SITE OF MAGELLAN IN 1521

concentric rings of growth, and scarcely any traces of pith; with the aid of a magnifying glass the medullary rays are seen to be equidistant and very numerous. The outer wood is pale yellow and devoid of resin; the inner, which is by far the larger proportion, is dark greenish-brown, contains in its pores 26% of resin and has a specific gravity of 1.333, and therefore sinks in water. Owing to the diagonal and oblique arrangement of the successive layers of its fibres, the wood, unlike that of most trees, cannot be split lengthwise; because of its hardness, density and durability it is much valued for the manufacture of rulers, mallets, etc.

Guaiac resin, procured chiefly from *G. officinale*, is obtained from the wood as a natural exudate from the living trees; by heating logs about three feet in length, bored to permit the outflow of the resin; or by boiling chips and raspings in salt water. It occurs in rounded or oval tears, or in large brownish or greenish-brown masses, translucent at the edges; fuses at 85° C. (185° F.); is brittle, has a vitreous fracture and a slightly balsamic odour; and is at first tasteless when chewed but subsequently produces a sense of heat in the throat. The resin is readily soluble in alcohol, ether, chloroform, creosote, oil of cloves and solutions of caustic alkalies; with glycerine it gives a clear solution and with nitrous ether a bluish-green gelatinous mass. The chief constituents are: guaiaconic acid (70%), guaiacic acid, which is closely allied to benzoic acid, and guaiaretic acid.

Guaiacum wood was first introduced into Europe by the Spaniards in 1508 but the first edition of the *London Pharmacopoeia* in which the resin is mentioned is that of 1677. Although now little used in medicine (in the form of derivatives), the resin gives rise to a sensitive chemical indicator of oxygen and has also been used as an antioxidant, especially in commercial lard. The active principle apparently is guaiaretic acid.

GUAIRÁ, a department of central eastern Paraguay, contains fertile lowlands and hill slopes which are well peopled and produce large crops of tobacco, cotton, maté and sugar. Pop. (1962) 114,297; area 1,236 sq.mi. A German agricultural colony at Independencia is famous for its wineries. Villarrica, one of Paraguay's most important cities, is the capital, and Borja is a market centre and railway junction, serving also the department of Caazapá to the south. The principal railway of Paraguay (from Asunción to Encarnación) bisects the department, and a major road links it to Coronel Oviedo to the north. (G. J. B.)

GUAM, the largest, most populous and southernmost island of the Marianas and an unincorporated territory of the United States, lies in the Pacific ocean at latitude 13° 26′ N. and longitude 144° 39′ E., about 6,000 mi. W. of San Francisco, 3,340 mi. W. of Honolulu and 1,500 mi. E. of Manila. Area 209 sq.mi. Pop. (1964) 44,892, excluding military personnel. Agana, the capital, had a population of 1,827 in 1964. The larger populated villages include Sinajana, Barrigada, Tamuning and Agana Heights.

Physical Geography.—The island is sharply divided into a northern limestone plateau with a general elevation of about 500 ft. and an area of high, volcanic hills to the south. The plateau is covered with a thick growth of jungle; the volcanic hills support mainly sword grass. They rise more than 1,000 ft. above sea level and their lower slopes to the east (and also in part to the west) are covered with younger limestones, generally similar to those of the northern limestone plateau. The higher hills are found in the west-central and southern parts of the island: Mt. Lamlam rises to an elevation of 1,334 ft., Mt. Jumullong Manglo to 1,086 ft., Mt. Bolanos to 1,220 ft. and Mt. Sasalaguan to 1,109 ft.

Guam has a pleasant tropical climate. Temperatures range from 20° to 32° C. (70° to 90° F.) and are fairly even throughout the year. Average annual rainfall is about 95 in., three-fourths of which falls during the wet season, generally starting in May or June and lasting through November. The climate is punctuated by destructive typhoons that occur at irregular intervals.

The People.—The native Guamanians, ethnically called Chamorros, are basically of Indonesian stock with a considerable admixture of Spanish, Filipino (Tagalog) and other strains. Their vernacular, called the Chamorro language, is not a Micronesian dialect but a distinct language with its own vocabulary and grammar. The word Chamorro is derived from *Chamorri,* or *Chamoli,*

the ancient name for chief. Pure-blooded Chamorros are no longer found in Guam, but the Chamorro language is still used in many native homes, though English is the official language of the island. The predominant religion is Roman Catholic.

At the end of World War II, the Guamanians were faced with tremendous tasks. They had to reconstruct the parts of their island that had suffered war damage, to discover and develop profitable home industries and to fulfill Guam's potential position as an important new hub of Pacific activity. Agana, the seat of Guam's government and formerly a city of 12,000 inhabitants, was completely destroyed by bombardment during the war.

Before World War II the villages were the main social and economic units, preserving customs and traditions similar to those of 19th-century Europe. A family would work for a year, for example, in preparation for a costly wedding. The fiesta held in memory of a patron saint was the great social and religious event of the year in the village, for it was one of the few occasions when people traveled from one village to another. Fiesta customs similar to those of earlier days are still observed in modern Guam. Changes in the social life and institutions of Guamanians, however, have come about with the economic improvement of the people and their closer contacts with western civilization.

History.—It is believed, but has not been definitely proved, that Guam was discovered by Ferdinand Magellan in 1521. There was no attempt to conquer the island until the latter part of the 17th century, when the Spaniards subdued it after considerable bloodshed. War and disease, particularly smallpox and influenza, played an important role in the decimation of the population. While the reduction of the population was due primarily to the intermittent warfare with the Spaniards that continued for a period of 25 years, typhoons in 1671 and 1693 and influenza epidemics, especially that of 1688, contributed to the tragic loss of life. Guam remained a Spanish possession until 1898, when, in the course of the Spanish-American War, the U.S. warship "Charleston" steamed into the harbour of Apra and shelled the old fort. Guam was ceded to the United States and the other islands of the Marianas were sold by Spain to Germany in 1899. From that time until 1950 (excepting World War II) the governor of the island was always a naval officer appointed by the president of the United States.

During World War I Japan occupied Germany's island possessions north of the equator and after the war Japan received the Marianas (except Guam) and the Caroline and Marshall groups, as a mandate under the League of Nations. Japan retained possession of the islands even after it withdrew from the league in 1933. In World War II the Japanese landed on Guam just after the attack on Pearl Harbor and occupied the island by Dec. 12, 1941. U.S. marine and army forces retook Guam by Aug. 10, 1944. It was a major air and naval base for the squadrons of bombers that attacked Japan near the end of the war. (See WORLD WARS: *World War II: The Allied Offensive in the Pacific, 1944.*)

The U.S. department of the interior took over the administration of the island on Aug. 1, 1950. Although Guam no longer serves as headquarters of the Trust Territory of the Pacific Islands, the headquarters having been relocated at Saipan, it is the site of major naval and air force bases. The navy's facilities include a nuclear submarine base and a large ship-repair facility. Andersen Air Force base, at the opposite end of the island, has a nuclear capability, and its B-52s carried out bombing raids over Vietnam in the 1960s.

Government.—Guam is an unincorporated territory of the United States, governed under the Organic Act of Guam, passed by the U.S. congress and approved by the president on Aug. 1, 1950. Before that date the Guamanians had been "nationals" of the United States but the Organic act made them citizens of the U.S., although they were not given the right to vote in national elections. Under that act, the governor was appointed by the president of the United States.

The Organic Act was amended in 1968 to provide for the popular election, beginning in 1970, of a governor and lieutenant governor for four-year terms.

The legislature is a unicameral body with 21 members elected at large for a term of two years. All persons 18 years of age or over, both men and women, are permitted to vote. The legislature has the power to override the governor's veto by a two-thirds vote, but until 1971 the governor could transmit the repassed bill to the president of the United States, who made the final decision on legislation referred to him. The U.S. congress may still annul any law passed by the legislature.

The judiciary consists of the district court of Guam, whose judge is appointed by the U.S. president for a term of eight years. There are also two interior courts—the island court, with two judges appointed by the governor for a four-year term with the consent of the legislature, and the police court in which an island court judge presides. The municipal commissioners are authorized to try a few minor offenses but rarely do so.

Each of the island's 19 "municipalities" is headed by a popularly elected native commissioner who serves for a four-year term. The municipalities are the districts into which the entire territory is divided. A chief commissioner, appointed by the governor, acts as liaison between the governor and the municipalities.

The law codes of the island were revised in 1933 and incorporated many provisions of a bill of rights drawn up in 1930.

Finance and Trade.—All federal income taxes collected from U.S. government employees in Guam are remitted to the Guamanian government. Other persons in Guam are subject to the territorial income tax, which consists of the income tax laws of the U.S. re-enacted by congress by reference as a separate local tax, and enforced by the government of Guam. Most of Guam's imports come from the United States. Except for scrap and military surplus materials, exports are imported items that are resold, primarily to the Trust Territory of the Pacific Islands. (See TRUSTEESHIP SYSTEM.)

Transportation.—Guam is served by Pan American World Airways, which makes regular stops on its route between Honolulu and Manila. Pan American also has direct flights between Guam and Tokyo. Guam is the hub of air transportation serving the Trust Territory of the Pacific Islands.

Guam is also the port of call for two major shipping lines. Ships call on an average of twice a month bringing cargo from both the east and west coasts of the U.S. Both lines carry a limited number of passengers; however, P&O Orient lines cruise ships call twice yearly.

Agriculture.—The development of Guam into an important military base brought about profound changes in the island's agricultural pattern after World War II. The availability of work on military establishments drew off many workers who had formerly engaged in subsistence farming. In the late 1960s the government of Guam was making strenuous efforts to increase agricultural production. There were about 2,000 ac. under cultivation, worked by 520 full-time and 600 part-time farmers. Principal crops were bananas, beans, cucumbers, cabbages, melons, eggplants, okra, papayas, peppers, squash, onions, sweet potatoes, taro and yams. Annual production in the mid-1960s totaled almost 2,000,000 lb. of fresh fruits and vegetables valued at $366,000. This included produce moved only through major market outlets. Egg production, the most stable agricultural enterprise, averaged about 2,000 doz. daily. A pilot poultry processing plant went into operation in 1966. During the 1960s about 1,800,000 lb. of broilers were imported annually, and it was expected that within a short time locally grown broilers would cut imports by half. The livestock population included about 7,000 hogs, 6,500 cattle, 655 carabaos, the traditional beast of burden, and 88 horses. It was hoped that private enterprise would establish a feed mill and a slaughterhouse, in addition to possible off-shore commercial fishing. There is licensed hunting on the island for deer, pigs, doves and fruit bats.

Industry.—Considerable emphasis was being given, in the late 1960s, to the development of industrial and commercial enterprises compatible with Guam's access to materials from the far east. Increased air transport was a significant factor. The Guam Economic Development authority was organized with the basic purpose of encouraging new industries. It was actively engaged in promoting and assisting new business ventures.

The successful organization of watch-assembly operations on Guam proved the feasibility of assembly-type operations. The first year of active operations started with one company and expanded to seven, with a total output of 600,000 watches.

Tourism was seen as the greatest potential for the island. A large tourist hotel was being planned, and secondary tourist accommodations were expanding rapidly.

Education.—The Organic Act of Guam provided that all children between the ages of 6 and 16 must attend school. In the late 1960s there were 21 public elementary schools, 5 junior high schools, 2 senior high schools, a school for the physically and mentally handicapped and a trade and technical school. Enrollment in the public schools totaled more than 21,000 with more than 16,000 pupils in elementary grades from kindergarten through the eighth grade, and approximately 5,000 pupils in secondary grades from 9 through 12. More than 5,000 students were enrolled in parochial schools. There were nearly 700 public school teachers and more than 160 parochial school teachers.

The University of Guam, opened in June 1952, had an enrollment of more than 2,000 in the late 1960s, and the faculty numbered more than 130.

See also references under "Guam" in the Index.

BIBLIOGRAPHY.—Rupert Emerson *et al.*, *Guam and Its People*, *America's Pacific Dependencies* (1949); Annual Reports of the Governor of Guam to the U.S. Secretary of the Interior and to the United Nations; John Wesley Coulter, *The Pacific Dependencies of the United States* (1957); Charles Beardsley, *Guam, Past and Present* (1964); P. Carano and P. C. Sanchez, *A Complete History of Guam* (1964); Current history and statistics are summarized annually in the *Britannica Book of the Year.* (J. W. CR.)

GUAN, a tropical American chickenlike bird related to the chachalacas and curassows (*q.v.*) and with them constituting the family Cracidae of the order Galliformes. The dozen species include the crested guan (*Penelope purpurascens*), the wattled guan (*Aburria aburri*) and the sickle-winged guan (*Chamaepetes goudotii*). Nearly all have a bare throat, from which, in some forms, hangs a wattle. The horned guan (*Oreophasis derbianus*) has a long, bare spike between its eyes. Like their allies, the fruit-loving guans are most often seen hopping and flying about in the treetops. Attempts to domesticate these birds for their tasty flesh have been unsuccessful. Except for the few that extend to Central America, Mexico and the Antilles, the guans are confined to the South American continent.

Chachalacas, named for their ringing chatter, are the smallest and most terrestrial members of the family. The dozen species, mainly Central American, include the plain chachalaca, *Ortalis vetula*, a long-tailed brown bird that ranges northward to the Texas border.

GUANABACOA, a former city of Havana Province, Cuba, and now part of Greater Havana, is situated in a hilly section. It was essentially a residential suburb of the capital, although a number of industries had been established. In 1953 its population was 32,490. Guanabacoa (meaning "site of waters") was originally an old Indian town. Established by the Spanish in 1617, it became a summer place for fashionable families during the colonial period because of its medicinal springs. Interesting old structures include churches, monasteries, and administrative buildings.

(D. R. D.; X.)

GUANABARA, a state of Brazil bounded north by Rio de Janeiro state, east by Guanabara bay, south by the Atlantic and west by Sepetiba bay. Area 524 sq.mi.; pop. (1960) 3,307,163, of which nearly all live in Rio de Janeiro (q.v.), now the state capital. Three massifs dominate the topography, occupying a third of the area and reaching a height of 3,360 ft. Guanabara was created from the former federal district in 1960, when Brasília (q.v.) succeeded Rio de Janeiro as the national capital. The state's first governor and legislature were elected on Oct. 3, 1960.

(R. M. M.)

GUANACASTE, a province of Costa Rica located on the Pacific coast and bordering Nicaragua. Area 4,015 sq.mi., pop. (1970 est.) 188,972. Shortly after independence from Spain this area separated itself from Nicaragua and in 1825 officially became a province of Costa Rica. As a result, Guanacaste was the source of ill-feeling between the two nations during the 19th century. It was also the centre of much of the warfare between the Central Americans and William Walker (q.v.) in the 1850s. Guanacaste, bisected by the Inter-American highway, has impressive agricultural prospects. Occupying 20% of Costa Rica it is a frontier of flat grassland with dry forests in the north. The chief income is from cattle, which are driven to market in Alajuela. About one-half of the beef, corn and rice consumed by Costa Ricans comes from Guanacaste province. The largest towns are Nicoya and Liberia, the provincial capital.

(T. L. K.)

GUANACO (Lama guanicoe), one of the four lamoids (Lama species) of the camel family (Camelidae), range from the snow lines of the highest grasslands to sea level throughout the Andes from the equator to Cape Horn. The guanaco is scarce in the range of the llama, alpaca and vicuña, and is most abundant at the southern tip of South America, including Tierra del Fuego and other islands. Although usually found in herds of 10 to 30,

about 500 were seen together on Santa Cruz by Charles Darwin. The guanaco and vicuña (q.v.) are wild and shy, and, unlike the llama and alpaca (qq.v.), they cannot be domesticated. The Andean people hunt guanacos for food and manufacture robes from the hides of the very young animals. The adult guanaco stands about four feet high at the shoulder, and has the typical long, gracefully curved neck of lamoids and camels. It is fawn coloured above and white below; the head is grayish. Extremely alert and curious, guanacos are adept at climbing and swimming. Their droppings are left in selected spots, located close to grounds used as dust baths. Salty water is taken as readily as fresh water. Some authorities believe that the llama and alpaca were derived evolutionarily from the guanaco. See also TYLOPOD. (H. K. B.)

GUANAJUATO, an inland state of Mexico, lies wholly within the limits of the great central plateau of Mexico, and has an average elevation of about 6,000 ft. Area 11,810 sq.mi.; pop. (1970) 2,270,000. The northern half of Guanajuato is mountainous, but its southern half is covered by fertile plains, called the Bajío, largely devoted to agriculture. It is drained by the Río Lerma and its tributaries, the Río Turbio and the Río de la Laja. The climate is semitropical and healthful, and the summer rainfall, 20 to 30 in., is sufficient to ensure good results in agriculture and stock raising. Indian corn, beans, barley and wheat are grown.

The principal industry of the state is mining, the mineral wealth being enormous. Among its mineral products are silver, gold, tin, lead, mercury, copper and opals. Silver has been extracted since the early days of the Spanish conquest. Some of the more productive mining sites are the Veta Madre (mother lode), the San Bernabé lode and the Rayas mines of Guanajuato, and the La Valenciana mine, the output of which is said to have been $226,-000,000 between 1766 and 1826. Industries include flour mills, tanneries and leather factories, cotton and woolen mills, distilleries, foundries and potteries.

The first Spanish settlement in the state was San Miguel de Allende, 1542, a picturesque colonial town now an art and study centre. The capital, the city of Guanajuato (q.v.), also has great colonial charm. As the silver mines poured forth their wealth Mexican baroque architecture flowered in this area. Miguel Hidalgo y Costilla (q.v.) began the Mexican War for independence in the village of Dolores Hidalgo in 1810. That same year his forces took the capital and looted it. Later, the Spaniards executed Hidalgo and his three lieutenants and displayed their heads on the Alhóndiga de Granaditas in Guanajuato for a period of ten years. Other important cities of the state are León (q.v.) and Celaya. Alvaro Obregón decisively defeated Pancho Villa at Celaya in 1915. Until 1824 Guanajuato with Querétaro was administered as a Spanish intendancy.

(J. A. Cw.)

GUANAJUATO, capital of Guanajuato state, Mexico, is 175 mi. N.W. of Mexico City. Pop. (1970) 65,258 (munic.). It is served by a branch of the Mexican National railway, which joins the main line at Silao, and a paved road branching 13 mi. N.E. from that city. Guanajuato's dry climate is considered healthful.

Guanajuato is situated at an elevation of 6,835 ft. in the Cañada de Marfil at the junction of three ravines. The city stands essentially as a foremost example of a Spanish colonial centre, whose location and mineral riches determined its plan and historical role. It gives the appearance of being crowded. The narrow tortuous streets (some are built as steps) rise steeply up the hillsides. Balconies which overhang the narrow streets are a distinctive feature of the city. There are a few modern buildings.

During the late 1520s and early 1530s Spaniards overran the area which remained little more than a military frontier until silver was discovered. Guanajuato was founded in 1554 and became a city in 1741. The town, along with Zacatecas to the north and Potosí in Bolivia, became one of the three greatest silver mining centres of the 16th century. Its celebrated Veta Madre (mother lode) was described as the richest in the world. The mineral wealth of Guanajuato—over 1,800 mines were in operation at one time—was largely responsible for making Mexico City the most splendid jewel in Spain's new world empire. In Guanajuato itself fabulous wealth was most manifest in the elaborate and richly endowed churches, notably La Valenciana and La Parroquia. The

GUANACO (LAMA GUANICOE)

only post-Spanish building of significance is the Teatro Juárez, built during the Díaz regime, and an excellent example of both the romanticism and the ostentation which characterized the era.

Guanajuato was the first major city to fall to the independence leader Hidalgo y Costilla in 1810. The plundering and destruction which accompanied the overrunning of the Alhóndiga de Granaditas (granary used as a fortress) were followed by subsequent struggles for control of the mines, through flooding, and the greatly reduced output of the city which by 1822 had resulted in a decline, which continued until the 1930s, when as a result of the exodus of many wealthy families. Guanajuato entered a period of increased tourist trade and federal support of mining and agriculture in the state, the city began a slow recovery which appeared to be continuing in the 1960s. It is the site of a national college. The Panteón, or public cemetery, has catacombs which contain mummies.

(J. J. J.)

GUANCHES were the inhabitants of the Canary Islands met by the Spaniards when they undertook the conquest of those islands at the beginning of the 15th century. The name is more precisely applied to the primitive inhabitants of the western group of islands; those of the eastern group, notwithstanding their affinity to the Guanches, form a separate type called Canarios. Both populations are thought to be of Cro-Magnon origin (see CRO-MAGNON MAN). They perhaps came to northern Africa with other populations from central and southern Europe. Ultimately they settled in the Canary Islands where they lived for centuries in complete isolation. They were vigorous, brawny and well-shaped, the Guanches rather taller than the Canarios. Of brown complexion, they had blue or gray eyes and light-coloured hair. These are still distinctive characteristics of a large number of the present inhabitants of the islands. They were sturdy and bellicose, frugal, industrious and proud of their independence. They covered their bodies with leather tunics or vests made of plaited rushes. Their food consisted mainly of milk, butter, goat flesh and pork and the fruits of some shrubs. Their industry was mainly Paleolithic, but pottery was rather advanced in the Neolithic. They had hand mills to make *gofio* (meal). Alphabetiform engravings and characters have been discovered as curious vestiges of their culture. They were monotheists and held courts in the open air. Corpses were interred in graves, sometimes deposited in tombs or even embalmed.

See also CANARY ISLANDS: *Population and Administration.*

(S. J. Sz.)

GUANIDINE is an organic compound of formula $HN:C(NH_2)_2$. It was first prepared by Adolph Strecker in 1861 from guanine, which had been obtained from guano, and this is the origin of the name. The compound has been detected in small amounts in a variety of plant and animal products, but some of its derivatives are widely distributed and are of considerable importance, especially in the action of muscular tissue. It is closely related to urea, into which it is converted by hydrolysis. Guanidine is readily prepared from calcium cyanamide. This, when heated with water, gives dicyandiamide, which gives a good yield of guanidine when fused with an ammonium salt.

$$2H_2N.CN \rightarrow HN:C\Big\langle{}^{NH.CN}_{NH_2} \xrightarrow{NH_3} 2HN=C\Big\langle{}^{NH_2}_{NH_2}$$

A variety of other syntheses are known, some of which (*e.g.,* the reduction of tetranitromethane and the action of ammonia on carbonyl chloride) give a simple indication of the constitution of the compound. Guanidine itself is a colourless crystalline solid that absorbs water and carbon dioxide from the air and is thus not easy to prepare pure, but the salts crystallize well, notably the carbonate and the nitrate. Guanidine as a base is much stronger than the majority of organic bases; its aqueous solutions have a conductivity approaching that of the alkali hydroxides and it forms stable salts even with acids as weak as boric and silicic acids. It behaves as a monacidic base only, and forms a cation—a positively charged ion—that can be written as

$$H_2N=\overset{+}{C}\Big\langle{}^{NH_2}_{NH_2}$$

An X-ray crystal analysis of the iodide (W. Theilacker, 1935) shows, however, that, as might be expected, all three nitrogen atoms are identically linked in the ion and are symmetrically arranged in a plane around the carbon atom. This is caused by resonance between the three structures which can be written by allotting the positive charge to each of the three nitrogen atoms in turn. The resonance energy is the cause of the stability of the ion and hence of the strong basic character of the compound.

Of the derivatives, nitroguanidine, obtained by the action of sulfuric acid on the nitrate, has been used to some extent as a constituent of explosives; its peculiarity is the low temperature produced in the explosion. Aminoguanidine and substituted aminoguanidine are intermediates in the synthesis of a variety of dyes and other heterocyclic compounds.

Two amino acid derivatives are of great physiological interest. Arginine, or 1-amino-4-guanidovaleric acid, $HN:C(NH_2).NH.(CH_2)_3.CHNH_2.COOH$, is a constituent of proteins and particularly of protamines, but also plays an important part in nitrogen excretion in animals. With mammals this is largely excreted as urea, which is synthesized in the liver from ammonia and carbon dioxide by a series of reactions in which arginine is an intermediate. Creatine (methylguanidinoacetic acid, $HN:C(NH_2).NMe.CH_2.COOH$) is present in large amounts in mammalian muscle, and its internal amide, creatinine, is excreted by mammals especially during growth. The contraction of muscle is known to derive its energy from the enzymatic hydrolysis of adenosine triphosphate and it is also known that one of the mechanisms whereby this substance is reformed in the muscle is by the action of creatine phosphate. The importance of the guanidine group in muscle is further shown by the fact that certain types of tetanus are associated with the occurrence of guanidine itself or of methylguanidine in the body. Other guanidine derivatives have proved to be of value as therapeutic agents. Decamethylenediguanidine (Synthalin) and related compounds have a specific effect in destroying trypanosomes; and sulfaguanidine, one of the least soluble of the sulfanilamide derivatives, is of great value in bacillary dysentery. Chlorguanide hydrochloride, the synthetic antimalarial, is a substituted biguanide (N_1-p-chlorophenyl-N_5-isopropylbiguanide):

$$Cl-\!\!\bigcirc\!\!-NH-C-NH-C-NH-CH\Big\langle{}^{CH_3}_{CH_3}$$
$$\quad\quad\quad\;\;\;\| NH \quad\;\; \| NH$$

(T. W. J. T.)

GUANO, the accumulated excrement and dead bodies of birds, bats or seals. Bird guano is mainly from fish-eating cormorants, pelicans and gannets which populate some islands off the west coast of Peru, Lower California and Africa, up to 5,600,000 per square mile, and consume 1,000 tons of fish daily. Exports from the Peruvian deposits began about 1810 and reached 50,000 tons in 1856. The government protects the seafowls and processes the guano which contains about 11% to 16% nitrogen, 8% to 12% phosphoric acid and 2% to 3% potash, in fertilizer terminology. Bat guano is found in caves throughout the world with significant deposits in Missouri (16,000 tons) and in a cave of the Grand Canyon (100,000 tons). Seal guano has accumulated to 230 ft. on the Lobos Islands off South America and to a lesser extent on Tortuga Island. Bat and seal guano are lower in fertilizing value than Peruvian guano. See also FERTILIZERS AND MANURES; PERU; *The Economy.*

(S. R. A.)

GUANTÁNAMO, a city in Oriente province, Cuba, about 40 mi. E. of Santiago de Cuba and about 60 mi. from the eastern end of the southern coast. Pop. (1964 est.) 122,400. It is 10 mi.

N. of Guantánamo bay, one of the largest and best-sheltered bays in the world, having a narrow entrance into a harbour about 4 mi. wide and 12 mi. long, capable of accommodating large vessels. The bay is served by the ports of Caimanera and Boquerón which are linked by rail to Guantánamo.

The strategic importance of the bay close to the Windward passage, which is between Cuba and Haiti and links the Atlantic to the Caribbean and Panama, was recognized by the United States during the Spanish-American War, when U.S. marines landed at the bay. A large U.S. naval base, which now includes fortifications and airfields, was established by treaty in 1903. The difficulty of land communications in the mountainous eastern region of Cuba.

Guantánamo bay was named Cumberland bay in 1741 when an English force landed and attacked Santiago. The town was founded in 1819 and was called Santa Catalina del Saltadero del Guaso until 1843. French refugees from Haiti aided in the colonization of the area and many cultural characteristics, such as architecture, stem from their influence, as well as from a number of Catalan settlers. (D. R. D.)

GUAPORÉ (Spanish IRÉNEZ), a river of northeast Bolivia, which, with the Paraguay river, rises in the mountains of the state of Mato Grosso, Brazil. It flows to the northwest marking the frontier with Brazil until its confluence with the Mamoré river (q.v.) several miles above the town of Guayaremerín. Proceeding north, the Amazon (q.v.) may then be reached by way of the Madeira river (q.v.), formed by the juncture of the Mamoré and Beni (q.v.) near the river port of Villa Bella, and the Madeira-Mamoré railroad via Pôrto Velho. The Guaporé is the largest affluent of the Mamoré and is navigable along its course of 1,087 mi. at any season of the year. The town of Mato Grosso, lying less than 100 mi. from the source of the Guaporé, may be reached by river craft. The Guaporé constitutes the border between the Brazilian state of Mato Grosso and the federal territory of Rondônia to the east, and the Bolivian departments of Santa Cruz and Beni to the west. It flows through a forested region having a hot and humid climate which is almost uninhabited except for occasional settlements of Indians and mestizos along the banks. The Guaporé, in contrast with the brown silt-laden Mamoré, is a beautiful river with unusually clear water. For several miles below their juncture, the identity of the two streams can still be readily perceived.

The upper tributaries of the Guaporé, flowing largely from the slopes of the Serra dos Parecis, include the Branco, the Corumbiari, the Colorado, the São Miguel and the Cautario. Its affluents flowing from the south and southwest comprise the Paraguá, the Baures and the Itonamas. Ports of the Guaporé are Príncipe da Beira, which may be reached by air, Versalles, Pedras Negras and Santa Isabel. Historically, the region was witness to numerous frontier conflicts between the Spanish and Portuguese and the struggles of both with hostile Indians. Forte Príncipe de Beira, constructed near the confluence of the Guaporé and Mamoré in the late 18th century, is a reminder of this era. (J. L. TR.)

GUARANA (Paullinia cupana or sorbilis), a woody climbing plant, of the soapberry family (Sapindaceae), native to the Amazon valley. Its seeds are used to prepare a stimulant beverage popular in parts of South America. The plant has a smooth, erect stem; large leaves with five oblong-oval leaflets; narrow panicles of short-stalked flowers; and ovoid fruit about as large as a grape and usually containing one seed shaped like a minute horse chestnut.

Guarana beverage is prepared from the seeds as follows. In October and November, when ripe, the seeds are sun-dried and then ground in a stone mortar or deep dish of hard sandstone. The resulting powder, moistened with water, is made into a paste with a certain proportion of whole or broken seeds and worked up, usually into rolls 5–8 in. in length and 12–16 oz. in weight. After drying by heat, the product is packed between broad leaves in sacks or baskets. Thus prepared, it is of extreme hardness, has a brown hue, a bitter, astringent taste and an odour faintly resembling that of roasted coffee. An inferior kind is manufactured by admixture of cocoa or cassava. For use, a portion of the roll (about one-half teaspoon for each cup) is rasped or grated into hot or cold water. The beverage owes its stimulant properties to its caffeine content (about three times that of a similar amount of strong coffee) and its astringent action to tannin. In addition, guarana yields the glucoside saponin, with starch, gum, several volatile oils and an acrid, green fixed oil.

GUARANÍ, a group of South American Indian tribes once centred mostly in eastern Paraguay but also extending into adjacent parts of Argentina and Brazil. They were members of the Tupian (q.v.) language stock which was widespread in South America, and in most respects resembled the other Indian tribes of the tropical forests, living from the gardening of maize, manioc and sweet potatoes by the women and hunting and fishing by the men. Like the others, the Guaraní were warlike and lived in large thatched houses with the whole village surrounded by a defensive palisade of upright logs. Their history after the Spanish conquest, however, was unusual, and the name Guaraní is now better known than that of the other forest Indians.

Early in the 17th century Jesuit missionaries established settlements (Reducciones) of Guaraní Indians along the Paraná river and eventually about 30 large and successful mission towns constituted the famous "Jesuit Utopia," the Doctrinas de Guaranies. The Jesuit order was expelled from the new world in 1767, and the mission Indians were scattered or taken into slavery. The ruins of the missions can still be seen in eastern Paraguay.

Much earlier (1537), in the region of Asunción, the present capital of Paraguay, the first Spanish colonists, unsuccessful in their search for gold, settled down peacefully among the Guaraní and established their notorious "harems" of Guaraní women. Their racially mixed descendants gradually grew into the rural population of modern Paraguay, which still speaks the Guaraní language and still considers itself to be Guaraní in custom and habits of mind. Actually, a Spanish colonial way of life had been established among the people very early in their history, and no truly aboriginal customs have survived except for the use of the now much-altered language.

A few scattered communities of true Guaraní Indians still survive marginally in the forests of northeastern Paraguay, but they were rapidly dwindling in the 1960s. The best known of these were the Apapocuva.

See J. H. Steward and L. C. Faron, Native Peoples of South America, ch. 12 (1959); E. R. Service and H. S. Service, Tobati: Paraguayan Town (1954). (E. R. SE.)

GUARANTEE, in law, a contract to answer for the payment of some debt, or the performance of some duty, in the event of the failure of another person who is primarily liable. The agreement is expressly conditioned upon a breach by the principal debtor. The debtor is not a party to the guarantee, and the guarantor is not a party to the principal obligation. A contract of guarantee must be distinguished from a contract of indemnity, in which the indemnitor is primarily liable if the conditions of the agreement are fulfilled. The distinction is important, for a contract of guarantee, unlike one of indemnity, is not enforceable unless it is evidenced by some note or memorandum in writing. (E. G. S.)

See FIDELITY AND SURETY BONDS.

GUARAUNAN: see WARRAU.

GUARDA, the name of a district and of its capital city, in Portugal. Guarda is a largely rural district located in Beira Alta province in north-central Portugal. Area 2,122 sq.mi. Pop. (1960) 276,470. The chief occupation of the district is sheep-raising; vines are cultivated in the valleys of the Douro and Mondego rivers. The town of Guarda, 137 mi. S.E. of Oporto on the northeast side of the Serra de Estrela, is Portugal's highest town, altitude 3,443 ft. Pop. (1960) 9,345. Its manufactures include leatherwork and distilling, and it is known as a health resort. The town's first royal charter was given it, as a "guard" against the Moors, by Sancho I in 1199. The Gothic cathedral was built between 1390 and 1540. Other old structures include the Blacksmith's tower and the two gates, all of the 12th-13th centuries; the chapel of Mileu, 11th-12th centuries; and the castle, 12th-13th centuries.

(J. P. Go.)

GUARDI, FRANCESCO (1712–1793), Venetian landscape and figure painter, and his brother Giovanni Nicolò (1715–86), were trained under their elder brother, Giovanni Antonio Guardi (q.v.).

By 1731 the brothers are recorded as collaborating in a studio which specialized in supplying paintings together with copies of others' works. About 1738 an uncle presented a group of religious and decorative paintings produced in this studio to the church at Vigo d'Anaunia (Trentino) of which he was the parish priest. Works of like character are also known, notably altarpieces at Belvedere di Aquileia (c. 1746) and Cerete Basso (c. 1755), the celebrated "Story of Tobias" panels in the church of the Angelo Raffaele in Venice (before 1750), two large allegorical figures in the Ringling museum, Sarasota, and two secular paintings, the "Ridotto" and the "Parlatorio" in the Museo Correr (Cà Rezzonico). Very few works of this type are signed, but a number of figure paintings, still lifes, etc., have been attributed to the Guardi studio; though the individual contributions of Francesco and Gianantonio are hotly disputed, it would seem there was fairly extensive collaboration between them. Nicolò's part remains completely obscure.

Francesco does not appear to have adopted the practice of view painting, on which his fame rests, before the mid-1750s or later. Perhaps he was impelled by the approaching death of Gianantonio and the relative absence of competition in this profitable field except from the aging and then unproductive Canaletto. It is possible, but not certain, that he actually worked with Canaletto at this period. His earliest views are almost always signed or initialed as though to draw attention to his new artistic aims and seem inspired by Canaletto's own works of 30 years before. Francesco certainly copied Canaletto's compositions, notably in the "Feste Dogali" painted from engravings after Canaletto drawings; he often based capricious landscape compositions (like his earlier subject paintings) on the works of other artists.

In 1782 he depicted the official celebrations in honour of the grand duke Paul's visit to Venice, basing at least one of the compositions on commonplace contemporary engravings. Later in the year he was commissioned by the republic to make similar records of Pius VI's visit, the contract specifically forbidding such copying. He enjoyed considerable favour with the English and other foreigners and his late election to the Academy (1784) was doubtless, like Canaletto's, due only to the low esteem which landscape painting then enjoyed. His works are not easily datable, though the costumes occasionally provide a clue; his later landscapes are generally more sparkling and lighter than his first view

"SANTA MARIA DELLA SALUTE" BY FRANCESCO GUARDI. IN THE WALLACE COLLECTION, LONDON

paintings. He was an exceedingly prolific artist whose scintillating and romantic impressions of the declining city are in marked contrast to Canaletto's limpid photographic records of its architecture.

BIBLIOGRAPHY.—G. Fiocco, Francesco Guardi (1923); J. Byam Shaw, The Drawings of Francesco Guardi (1951); A. Morassi, Conclusioni su Antonio e Francesco Guardi (1951); V. Moschini, Francesco Guardi (English trans. with full bibliography, 1957).

(F. J. B. W.)

GUARDI, GIOVANNI ANTONIO (GIANANTONIO) (1699–1760), Venetian painter of religious and figure subjects, was born in Vienna in May 1699, the son of a modest painter, Domenico Guardi, in whose studio at Venice he was trained. After his father's death in 1716 Gianantonio worked for a time under Pittoni before opening his own studio. Here, he and his brothers Francesco (q.v.) and Nicolò, specialized in paintings of religious and genre subjects as well as copies of earlier masters, frequently of minimal significance. Only one painting signed by Gianantonio, a "Death of St. Joseph" (Berlin), survives, though a few signed drawings are known. With his brothers he probably worked on the decoration of the sacristy of the parish church at Vigo d'Anaunia in the Trentino (1735–38).

There is still much dispute about the precise part played by each of the three brothers in these and other works, such as the now famous paintings on the organ loft in the church of the Angelo Raffaele at Venice with the story of Tobias (before 1750) and the altarpieces in the parish churches at Belvedere di Aquileia and Cerete Basso (c. 1755). Gianantonio Guardi died in 1760 at SS. Apostoli.

See F. de Maffei, Gian Antonio Guardi, pittore di figure (1951); C. Donzelli, I Pittori Veneti del Settecento (1957), with up-to-date bibliography.

(F. J. B. W.)

GUARDIANSHIP, in law, refers to the care and management of the person or property of a minor, of one mentally ill, or of anyone else incapable of administering his own affairs. The father and mother of a ward are called natural guardians, those appointed and supervised by a court, general guardians and those designated by will, testamentary guardians. It is not uncommon for a trust company to be appointed guardian of property. See CHILDREN, LAWS CONCERNING; INSANITY: Insanity in the Civil Law; TRUST COMPANY.

GUARDS AND HOUSEHOLD TROOPS. From antiquity heads of state have maintained special troops who served as personal bodyguards. Such was the function of the praetorian guard, founded in 27 B.C. by Augustus Caesar, and of the housecarls of the Anglo-Saxon kings. Steady expansion in numbers of such picked troops led to their employment as a corps d'élite in battle. This occurred with the "Immortals" of Xerxes and Philip II of Macedon's "Companions," and later the Mamelukes of Egypt and the Turkish Janizaries. (See JANIZARIES; MAMELUKE; STRELTSY.)

Early Bodyguards.—In the Hundred Years' War a contingent of Scottish archers was recruited in 1418 as an elementary garde du corps for the French monarch. When Charles VII formed his maison du roi in 1449, this company took senior rank. The second company of the garde du corps was enrolled by Louis XI in 1479, the third by Louis XII in 1514 and the fourth by Francis I in 1545. Sir Walter Scott's Quentin Durward gives a picture of life in the corps as it was under Louis XI. Only marshals of France could be captains of the garde du corps. As minister of state to Louis XIII, Cardinal Richelieu recruited a personal bodyguard of musketeers. In 1671 came the establishment of the maison militaire du roi, of which the senior corps was the gendarmes de sa majestie. Then came the chevaux légers (given the standing of household troops by Henry III), the première and seconde compagnie de mousquetaires à cheval, who provided their own equipment and were trained as dragoons. Lastly, companies of gendarmes were titularly commanded by the queen, the dauphin and the royal dukes. The duties of the gardes de la porte and the cent Suisses were more those of a personal bodyguard.

In England, the king's bodyguard or the yeomen of the guard (q.v.), raised by Henry VII in 1485, was not called upon to take the field. But the present-day honourable corps of gentlemen-at-

...arms, instituted as "the nearest guard" or "king's speres" by Henry VIII in 1509, accompanied the king to France and was actively engaged at Guinegate (the battle of the Spurs) in 1513 and in the siege of Boulogne in 1544. The corps was sometimes known as the gentlemen-pensioners. It last appeared under arms at the time of the Chartist disturbances in 1848. Reconstituted on a purely military basis in 1862, only officers entitled to a war decoration were eligible for appointment. The establishment consists of a captain, lieutenant, standard-bearer, clerk of the cheque and adjutant, suboffcer and 39 gentlemen-at-arms. The office of captain is a political appointment, the holder (always a peer) relinquishing his post on a change of government.

The English gentlemen-at-arms and the pope's Swiss guard, founded in 1505 and still garbed in the uniform designed by Michelangelo, are the two oldest bodyguards surviving; the pontiff's noble guard was not founded until 1801. In 1527, when the Austrians invaded Rome, the Swiss guard perished to a man in covering the flight of Clement VII from the Vatican.

Mounted Guards.—During England's Civil War, Charles I's life guard consisted of four companies of Cavalier gentlemen. Parliament also established a body of life guards, which was reviewed by Oliver Cromwell in Tuttle fields in April 1656.

During Charles II's exile about 80 expatriate Cavaliers, under Lord Gerrard, served as the king's life guard. With the Restoration in 1660 these faithful followers formed the "1st or his majesty's own troop of guards." The 2nd troop was mostly made up of men who had soldiered as the "duke of York's guards" in the Spanish service. On the death of Gen. George Monk in 1670 his "duke of Albemarle's troop" became the 2nd or queen's troop, the duke of York's troop becoming the 3rd. In 1685 the 1st and 2nd troops were styled Life Guards of Horse. Two years later the blue-coated Royal Regiment of Horse, a parliamentary "New Model" regiment disembodied in 1660 and immediately re-enrolled, was elevated to the status of a household cavalry corps. In 1690, while on station in Ireland with some of William III's Dutch "Blue guards," the name of the "Oxford Blues" was bestowed on the 1st British formation, after the earl of Oxford, its colonel. The 1st troop (1693–1788) and Scots troop (1702–88) of Horse Grenadier guards were absorbed when the household cavalry was reorganized to form the 1st and 2nd regiments of Life guards and the Royal Horseguards Blue, the latter title being officially changed to that of the Royal Horse guards (the "Blues") in 1819. In 1922 the 1st and 2nd Life guards were amalgamated.

The "Tins" (Life guards) and the "Blues" wear a scarlet and a deep blue tunic respectively, white metal helmets with white or (for the "Blues") red horsehair plumes, steel cuirasses, buckskin breeches and jack boots with spurs. Their bands are arrayed in richly laced coats and wear blue velvet "jockey" caps. Their senior noncommissioned officers are known as corporal majors and corporals of horse. Since the battle of Dettingen in 1743 they have participated in all major wars, particularly distinguishing themselves at Waterloo.

Foot Guards.—In 1656, during his exile in Holland, Charles II of England recruited a small bodyguard of foot, which was merged in the regiment of guards enrolled at the Restoration in 1660. On St. Valentine's day, 1661, on Tower hill, what had been the Lord General's Regiment of Foot guards, formed by Oliver Cromwell in 1650, took up its arms as an "extraordinary guard" for the sovereign. Having marched from Coldstream, near Berwick-upon-Tweed, it acquired the title of the Coldstream guards; and its motto of *nulli secundus* sufficiently denotes its denial of precedence to the 1st guards. The latter acquired their title of Grenadier guards and their bearskin headdress—subsequently adopted by the rest of the guards' brigade—by virtue of their defeat of Napoleon's grenadier guards at Waterloo. The Scots guards, at one time known as the Scots Fusilier guards, were raised in 1662, being a re-creation of Charles I's Scottish Foot guards of 1643. They were put on the same footing as the other two guards regiments with the Act of Union of 1707.

No further addition was made to the brigade until 1900, when Queen Victoria was pleased to command that the Irish guards be formed, in tribute to the fighting quality of the Irish regiments in the South African War. In 1915 the representational nature of the brigade was rounded off by the formation of the Welsh guards.

The guards brigade serves as a *corps d'élite* in the field. There has been no major conflict in which it has not taken full part; and it can expand into machine-gun companies, armoured formations and other specialized units as occasion may demand. The battalions regularly take their turn of garrison duty overseas.

The governor general's bodyguard in Canada is furnished by a guards formation organized, equipped and uniformed on similar lines to the British guards brigade. In India, up to 1947, the viceroy's bodyguard consisted of scarlet-coated native lancers with British and Indian officers.

The Royal Company of Archers, the British sovereign's bodyguard for Scotland, derives from the ancient archer guard of the kings of Scotland. It was constituted in its present form in 1676.

Bodies of Guards Containing Both Cavalry and Foot.—Frederick William of Brandenburg (1620–88) scoured Europe for giants to lure into his regiment of household guards. But Frederick the Great substituted an effective fighting force for what hitherto had been largely an ornamental bodyguard. The tradition was preserved by imperial Germany, whose white-clad, silver-helmeted *Kürassier* headed the heavy cavalry in 1870 and, in field gray, were again in action in 1914, as were the Prussian foot-guard regiments. The national guard of revolutionary France, composed of citizen-soldiery, was neither a bodyguard nor a *corps d'élite*, but a kind of militia. Napoleon created a small corps of "guides," to act as a personal escort throughout his Italian and Egyptian campaigns. A consular guard was instituted in 1799, and out of this grew the formidable body of troops, representative of all arms of the service and including the veteran "old guard," the "middle guard" and the "young guard," that made up the emperor's imperial guard. In 1813 this totaled 81,000 officers and men. Napoleon III sought to revive the glories of the imperial guard, adding the decorative *cent gardes* to his household troops. The *garde républicaine* was made responsible for ceremonial duties about the French president. (R. C. H.)

GUÁRICO, a state in central Venezuela, bordered on the north by outliers of the central highlands and on the south by the Orinoco River and two of its tributaries, the Apure and the Portuguesa rivers. Pop. (1961) 244,966. Area 25,091 sq.mi. (64,986 sq.km.). Typical of the llanos, Guárico in the 1960s ranked second among Venezuelan states in number of cattle. This was declining, however, due to the increasing need for farmland.

In the 1950s the government constructed the Guárico River Reclamation Project near Calabozo; it built a 9-mi.-long dam across the river, which formed a lake of 90 sq.mi. and irrigates (1963) over 50,000 ac. of llanos. In the area are large farms; rice is a major crop and Guárico ranks first among the states in its cultivation. In the eastern part of the state cotton is of importance, and corn, coffee (in the north), tobacco, and feed crops are grown. Petroleum has been discovered, a number of fields have been developed, and the state ranks fifth in annual output. The state capital is San Juán de los Morros (pop. [1961] 28,556). Calabozo (q.v.) and Valle de la Pascua are important trading and agricultural centres. (L. WE.)

GUARIENTO (d. between 1368 and 1370), Italian painter who was, under the influence of Giotto, the first Paduan artist to detach himself from the Byzantine tradition. He is mentioned in Paduan records as early as 1338. In 1365 he was invited by the Venetian authorities to paint a "Paradise," and some incidents of the war of Spoleto, in the great council hall of Venice. These works were greatly admired at the time, but disappeared under overpaintings of later periods. In 1903 the fresco of "Paradise" was uncovered, transferred onto canvas and exhibited at the Doge's palace. Guariento's works in Padua have suffered much. In the church of the Eremitani are allegories of the Planets, and, in its choir, some small sacred histories in dead colour, such as an "Ecce Homo"; also, on the upper walls, the life of St. Augustine, with some other subjects. A few fragments of other paintings by Guariento are still extant in Padua. In the gallery of Bassano is a "Crucifixion" by him.

GUARINI, GIOVANNI BATTISTA (1538–1612), Italian poet, author of *Il Pastor fido*, a pastoral dramatic poem which became very popular throughout Europe, and reflected and influenced the manners of the age. He was born at Ferrara, Dec. 10, 1538, six years before Tasso whose friend he became, and whose poetic achievement he rivaled, at least in contemporary esteem. He studied at Pisa and Padua, and, before he was 20, became professor of moral philosophy in his native city. In 1567 he entered the service of Alfonso II, duke of Ferrara. Guarini aimed at state employment as the serious business of his life, and was sent on various embassies and missions by the duke. But he spent his time and money to little purpose, suffered from the spite and ill will of two successive secretaries to the duke, quarreled with his old friend Tasso and at the end of 14 years of service found himself half ruined, with a large family and no prospects. When Tasso was condemned to Sant' Anna, the duke promoted Guarini to the vacant post of court poet. He found the position uncongenial, and retired in 1582 to his ancestral farm, the Villa Guarina, where he wrote *Il Pastor fido*. In 1585 he was at Turin whence Alfonso recalled him to Ferrara, and gave him the office of secretary of state. This reconciliation did not last long. Guarini moved to Florence, then to Rome, and back again to Florence, to the court of Ferdinand de' Medici, and finally took refuge in Ferrara. His last years were passed in study, lawsuits and polemical disputes with his critics, until his death at Venice, Oct. 7, 1612.

Il Pastor fido, published in 1590 and first performed at the carnival at Crema in 1595, is a pastoral tragicomedy, set in an Arcadia of idyllic urbanity. It is occasionally reminiscent of *Aminta*, Tasso's earlier work in the same *genre*, but lacks his lyrical simplicity. The brilliant polish of its diction is sometimes flawed by the contemporary faults of frigid conceits and forced antitheses, and by sententious maxims revealing the moralist rather than the poet. Yet it lives as an expression of late 16th-century Italian society, and of an attitude toward social life at once pagan, sensual and refined, proper to an age of social decadence. Its fame was widespread and its influence great, and for nearly two centuries it was regarded as a code of gallantry and shared with *Aminta* a prominent position in European literature, becoming a guide to manners as well as their mirror. It was several times translated into English, most notably by Sir Richard Fanshawe (1647). Contemporaries criticized its departure from Aristotelian rules of dramatic structure, against which Guarini wrote an able defense, in *Compendio della poesia tragicomica*. He also wrote a comedy in prose, *L'Idropica*, miscellaneous *Rime*, and polemics.

BIBLIOGRAPHY.—Guarini's works were published in 4 vol. (1737–38). The best contemporary edition of *Il Pastor fido* is the 20th (1602); there is a modern critical edition, *Il Pastor Fido e Il Compendio della poesia tragicomica*, by G. Brognoligo (1914). *See also* V. Rossi, *G. B. Guarini ed il Pastor Fido* (1886); G. Grillo, *Poets at the Court of Ferrara* (1943).

GUARINI, GUARINO (properly CAMILLO) (1624–1683), Italian architect, priest, mathematician, and theologian, whose designs and books on architecture made him a major source for later Baroque architects in Central Europe and North Italy, was born in Modena on Jan. 17, 1624. He was in Rome during 1639–47 when Borromini (q.v.) was most active. Later he taught in Modena, Messina, and Paris, and finally, in 1666, went to Turin where he stayed for the greater part of the remainder of his life. He died in Milan on March 6, 1683.

While in Turin in the service of the dukes of Savoy Guarini built (or furnished designs for) at least six churches and chapels, five palaces, and a city gate; published six books, two on architecture and four on mathematics and astronomy; and sent palace designs to the duke of Bavaria and the margrave of Baden. In S. Lorenzo (1668–87) and SS. Sindone (1667–90) in Turin, Guarini, working on a centralized plan, converted domes to an open lacework of interwoven masonry arches. His longitudinal churches—of which the most spectacular was S. Maria della Divina Providenza, in Lisbon, built from his design but destroyed by earthquake in 1755—with their veiled light sources and interwoven spaces served as models for much of the church development in Central Europe. The Palazzo Carignano, Turin (1679), is Guarini's masterpiece of palace design. With its billowing façade,

its magnificent curved double stair, and its astonishing double dome in the main salon, it well deserves to be acclaimed the finest urban palace of the second half of the 17th century in Italy. Guarini's principal architectural treatise, *Architettura Civile*, was published posthumously in Turin in 1737.

See P. Portoghesi, *Guarino Guarini* (1956); R. Wittkower, *Art and Architecture in Italy, 1600–1750* (1958), both with further bibliography.

(H. Mn.; X.)

GUARNERI (GUARNERIUS), a celebrated family of violin-makers of Cremona. The first was ANDREAS (c. 1626–98), who worked with Antonio Stradivari in the workshop of Nicolò Amati (son of Girolamo). Violins of a model original to him are dated from the "sign of St. Theresa" in Cremona. His son GIUSEPPE (1666–c. 1739) made instruments at first like his father's but later in a style of his own with a narrow waist; his son PIETRO "of Venice" (1695–1762) was also a fine maker. Another son of Andreas, PIETRO GIOVANNI (1655–1728), moved from Cremona and settled at Mantua, where he too worked "sub signo Sanctae Teresae." Pietro's violins showed considerable variations from those of the other Guarneris. G. Hart, in his work on the violin, says, "There is increased breadth between the sound holes; the sound hole is rounder and more perpendicular; the middle bouts are more contracted, and the model is more raised."

The greatest of all the Guarneris, however, was a nephew of Andreas, GIUSEPPE, known as "Giuseppe del Gesù" (1687–1744), whose title originates in the I.H.S. inscribed on his labels. He was much influenced by the earlier works of the Brescian school, particularly those of G. P. Maggini, whom he followed in the boldness of outline and the massive construction that aim at the production of tone rather than visual perfection of form. The great variety of his work in size, model and related features represents his various experiments in the direction of discovering this tone. A stain or sap mark running parallel with the finger board on both sides appears on the bellies of many of his instruments. Since the middle of the 18th century spurious instruments ascribed to the master have been abundant. It was not until Paganini played on a "Joseph" that the taste of amateurs turned from the sweetness of the Amati and the Stradivari violins in favour of the more robust tone of the Giuseppe Guarneri. Paganini's instrument is preserved in the Municipal palace of Genoa. *See* VIOLIN FAMILY.

GUASTALLA, a small town in Italy, on the right bank of the Po, in the region of Emilia-Romagna, province of Reggio nell' Emilia. Pop. (1961) 13,525 (commune). It is an episcopal see, an agricultural centre, and has some manufactures. Guastalla was probably founded in the 7th century by the Lombards and was later under the families of Torello and Gonzaga. In 1859 the town proclaimed its allegiance to the kingdom of Italy. Principal historical monuments are a bronze statue of Ferrante I Gonzaga, a 16th-century work by Leone Leoni; the Gonzaga palace; the Romanesque churches of Pieve and S. Giorgio; and the Maldotti library, containing 50,000 volumes and precious incunabula.

(Er. C.)

GUATEMALA (REPÚBLICA DE GUATEMALA), the northernmost of the Central American republics, extending between the Caribbean sea on the northeast and the Pacific ocean in the south. Pop. (1964) 4,284,473. Area 42,042 sq.mi. The country has a coastline of about 55 mi. on the Caribbean (Gulf of Honduras) and 160 mi. on the Pacific.

Its boundaries on the north and west, which touch Mexico, were fixed by treaty, on May 8, 1899. This set the Suchiate river, from the Pacific inland, as the start of an irregular line that runs generally northwestward, in part following the Chixoy or Upper Usumacinta and the Usumacinta rivers, until it strikes the parallel of 17° 49′ N., which it follows to the border of Belice (Belize) or British Honduras (q.v.), to which Guatemala lays claim. The eastern border, with Belice, follows the meridian of 89° 20′ W. southward to the Gulf of Honduras on the Caribbean sea; this boundary was set by the treaty of July 9, 1893. The boundary follows eastward to the Sarstún (Sarstoon) river, which it follows eastward to the Gulf of Honduras on the Caribbean sea; the eastern section was long in dispute but, by treaty in 1930, was submitted to the arbitration of the U.S.; Chile and

GUATEMALA

Costa Rica, and a final decision was rendered in 1933. The award was "essentially on the basis of *status quo* of operation," and made the Motagua river the frontier in most of the disputed area. The southeastern part of the boundary with Honduras and El Salvador was never in serious dispute.

Further aspects of Guatemala can be found in the article CENTRAL AMERICA and the short articles on the departments and more important cities.

PHYSICAL GEOGRAPHY

Geology and Surface Features.—Guatemala is located within the Central American-Antillean region. This is a region of folded and faulted geologic structures running more or less from west to east from Central America through the Greater Antilles to and beyond Puerto Rico. On the southwest, facing the Pacific coast of Central America from the Gulf of Fonseca to about latitude 20° N. in Mexico, there is much volcanic activity and the underlying west-east structures are buried under a deep accumulation of lava and ash.

The national territory of Guatemala includes four major surface divisions. These are: (1) the Pacific coastal lowland; (2) the highlands; (3) the valleys and ridges of central Guatemala; and (4) the plains of Petén, a part of the Yucatán peninsula.

The Pacific Coastal Lowland.—This is a southeastward continuation of the coastal lowland of Chiapas in Mexico. At the Mexico-Guatemala border it is about 25 mi. wide, and it continues for about 150 mi. across Guatemala into El Salvador. The coast is bordered by long sand bars and has few indentations. In back of the lagoons the land rises gradually toward the base of the mountains.

The Highlands.—These rise steeply from the inner edge of the coastal lowlands to elevations between 3,500 and 8,000 ft. Numerous cone-shaped volcanoes rise above this general level. The highest is Tajumulco (13,845 ft.), but there are at least six others nearby that are over 11,500 ft. Among the volcanic peaks there is a series of more or less isolated basins, deeply filled with volcanic ash. In one such basin is the well-known and spectacularly beautiful Lake Atitlán.

The Valleys and Ridges of Central Guatemala.—These emerge from under the cover of volcanic material proceeding away from the Pacific coast. The buried structures of the Central American-Antillean region have been etched by the rivers draining toward the Caribbean into a series of more or less west-to-east deep valleys separated by steep, sharply crested ridges. Within the territory of Guatemala there are two major structural depressions. The northern one is occupied by the headwaters of the Chixoy river. The Usumacinta river, which forms the border between Mexico and northern Guatemala, has cut headward to capture the upper Chixoy and carry its waters northward. The lower part of the structural valley in Guatemala is occupied by Lake Izabal and drains out through the Dulce river to the Gulf of Honduras.

The southern of the two structural valleys is occupied throughout its length by the Motagua river. The ridges that separate these deep structural depressions extend all the way to the Caribbean. Another, but smaller, depression, parallel to the larger ones, is occupied by the Sarstún river, on the border between Guatemala and British Honduras.

The Plains of Petén.—These are a part of the peninsula of Yucatán and consist of a limestone tableland, honeycombed with sinks and underground channels with much of the water draining off through solution caverns.

Climate.—The pattern of climatic conditions, as in all mountainous lands, is quite complex. Along the Pacific coast and on the volcanic highlands there is a distinctive "monsoon" climate, with very heavy rainfall in summer (May to October) when the winds are onshore from the south, and a very dry season in winter (November to April) when the prevailing wind is offshore from the north. On the Caribbean side, however, rainfall is heavy throughout the year on east-facing slopes. There are dry pockets in the rain shadow of the mountains, such as, for example, the middle part of the Motagua valley. Temperature varies with altitude but is never cold. At sea level the average annual tempera-

GEORGE HOLTON FROM PHOTO RESEARCHERS
INDIAN FISHERMEN IN DUGOUT CANOES ON LAKE ATITLÁN; IN THE BACK-GROUND IS SAN PEDRO VOLCANO

ture is about 77° F. (25° C.), with very little difference between summer and winter. The old concept of steaming jungles refers to the high humidity rather than high air temperature. At Guatemala City (4,872 ft. above sea level) the average annual temperature is about 64.4° (18°), ranging from an average of about 60.8° (16°) in December to about 69.8° (21°) in May just before the beginning of the rainy season. In the higher basins of western Guatemala, between 5,000 and 10,000 ft. above sea level, average temperatures are between 64.4° (18°) and 55.4° (13°). There is seldom much variety in the day-to-day weather, although occasionally hurricanes reach the Caribbean coast of Guatemala in September or October.

Vegetation.—The vegetation cover of Guatemala exhibits two basic characteristics of mountain geography: a general zoning by altitude and an intricacy of detail that makes the vertical zoning in places difficult to identify. Along the wet coastal lowlands on the Caribbean and on the lower east-facing mountain slopes there is a heavy tropical rain forest which comes as close to exhibiting the popular idea of a jungle as any place in the tropics. Along the Pacific lowland and the lower slopes of the south-facing volcanic highlands there is very little rain and the vegetation cover is a tropical semideciduous forest with patches of tall-grass savanna. Some of the species of trees in the forest, like all the species in the rain forest on the Caribbean side, are evergreen. During the dry season some of the trees in the semideciduous forest shed their leaves, which reappear when the rains come again. The colour of the forest changes from dark green in the rainy season to grayish in the dry season and that of the savannas from green to brown.

As one ascends the mountains, contrasts in vegetation appear in what Alexander von Humboldt described as "vertical zones." The lowland species of trees give way to evergreen forests of oak and cypress. Above 5,000 ft. the oak is mixed with North American species of pine. However, the vegetation reflects the lack of rain wherever there are dry pockets in the mountain valleys. In the dry middle part of the Motagua valley the vegetation is xerophytic, with many species of cactus and other drought-resistant plants.

Above 10,000 ft. the pines become thinner and grow only in patches in sheltered places. The trees are then replaced by a cover of mountain tall grass, similar to the paramos of the northern Andes. In no part of Guatemala are the mountains high enough to rise above the mountain grasslands. At these latitudes (between 14° and 16° N. of the equator) the zone of permanent snow is between 14,000 and 15,000 ft., and none of the Guatemalan volcanoes reaches such an altitude.

Animal Life.—Apart from domesticated cattle, sheep, pigs and mules, deer, monkeys and peccaries are common, especially in the less settled areas. Jaguars, tapirs and pumas are rarer. Crocodiles are found in the Polochic river and manatees in Lake Izabal and elsewhere. The bird life of the country is remarkably rich—wild turkeys and ducks, doves and pheasants abound; one almost extinct bird of magnificent plumage, the quetzal, has been chosen as the national emblem.

GEOGRAPHIC REGIONS

There are two major geographic divisions of Guatemala: the highlands and the lowlands. But because of human action each of these two divisions is subdivided—the highlands into two parts, the lowlands into three.

The Highlands.—Including the volcanic region and the ridges and valleys of central Guatemala, these are the most densely populated sections of the country. The highlands are sharply marked off into two distinctive regions—one region occupied by Indians, the other by people of Spanish and Spanish-Indian ancestry.

The Indian region is that part of the highlands that stands more than 5,000 ft. above sea level. It begins a short distance west of Guatemala City and includes the whole western part of the country. The Indians are descendants of the Mayas. Although there are a few large commercial towns, such as Quezaltenango and Huehuetenango, there are also many smaller village communities with fewer than 500 inhabitants. In some areas the people live in towns and villages and go out daily to work their farms—a pattern of living well developed around Lake Atitlán. In other areas the individual farmer lives on the land he is cultivating. The land is sometimes held in common and cannot be sold, although it can be used by the farmer as long as he continues to live on it. The chief Indian crop is corn (maize), which can be grown up to elevations of about 9,500 ft. It yields well and makes up the greater part of the Indian diet, along with beans, chili and other vegetables. The one crop above the upper limit of corn is the potato, which can be cultivated up to 10,500 ft. Still higher, there are a few Indian communities that are supported only by the pasture of sheep on the high grasslands. But even in the more productive wheat and corn-growing parts of the highlands, the Indian farms

are too small to provide adequate support for farm families.

The other part of the highlands was divided up long ago among the Spanish conquerors. Most of the properties are large, and in many cases only partly utilized. The largest area is used for the pasture of cattle. But the chief commercial crop, which ordinarily provides over 70% of Guatemala's exports, is coffee. This crop grows well at altitudes of between 1,000 and 5,000 ft. The chief coffee-growing section of the country is westward from Guatemala City to Lake Atitlán and down to the coast below Quezaltenango. To the east of the gap where the Chixoy river turns northward to form the Usumacinta river, there is another coffee-growing district centring on the town of Cobán. This area was developed by German planters, most of whom lost their properties by expropriation during World War II.

The two highland regions are crossed by the Inter-American highway, which now connects Guatemala with both Mexico and El Salvador.

The Lowlands.—These were never utilized by people of Spanish ancestry until after the development of the banana plantations by the United Fruit company. The first banana plantations were created in clearings carved out of the rain forest in the lower Motagua valley, and Puerto Barrios was built as a banana-shipping port. When disease hit the banana plantations on the Caribbean side in the 1920s and '30s, the company moved its operations to the Pacific lowland. The company also built a railroad to connect Guatemala City with Puerto Barrios and later from the capital to the Pacific port of San José. The line was extended along the Pacific base of the highlands to connect with the Mexican railroads.

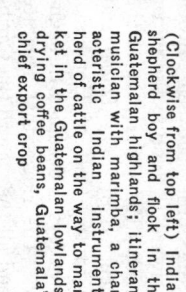

(Clockwise from top left) Indian shepherd boy and flock in the Guatemalan highlands; itinerant musician with marimba, a characteristic Indian instrument; herd of cattle on the way to market in the Guatemalan lowlands; drying coffee beans, Guatemala's chief export crop

Another line reaches El Salvador. The banana plantations of the United Fruit company were in part expropriated by the government during the early 1950s; but when the government again became more friendly, the company began to rebuild its plantations in the late 1950s. (See *The Economy*, below.)

The third part of the lowlands—more than a third of the total area of Guatemala—is in the plains of Petén. This is a very thinly populated area. There are few permanent settlements. Most of the inhabitants are engaged in the work of gathering and shipping chicle, the major ingredient in chewing gum. A maze of foot trails winds through the forest over which porters carry the chicle to collecting stations. Some is brought out by mules or canoes, some by small airplanes. Petén is isolated from the rest of the country by vast stretches of empty, forest-covered areas.

(P. E. J.)

THE PEOPLE

More than half of the population of Guatemala is Indian (see *Population*, below), and most of the remainder is composed of Ladinos, who are europeanized in culture and usually of mixed Spanish-Indian ancestry. The two groups are not always physically distinguishable, but are demarcated by speech—whether an Indian language or Spanish—by dress—whether native or western—and by community membership.

The Indian cultures of Guatemala are remarkable for the high degree of native custom retained. The modern Indians of Guatemala come, in general, from the Maya or the kindred Quiché (*q.v.*) strain. The Indian settlements are predominantly in the highlands (see *Geographic Regions*, above). It is estimated that about 18 different Indian languages are spoken in Guatemala. Costume and dialect vary from one village to another, although Quiché serves as a trade language to some extent, and Spanish is a second language learned by some of the Indians. Traditional arts and crafts pursued in the villages include pottery, basketry, hand-tooled leather articles and colourful textiles. The social life of the Indians is centred in markets and *fiestas*.

The Indians differ but slightly among themselves, being of dark copper skin, stocky build, with coarse, straight black hair, high cheekbones and low foreheads. Formerly the Indians, who are the chief labour supply for the large coffee plantations at harvest time, were treated in almost feudal fashion by the coffee planters. With the constitutions of 1945 and 1956, which guaranteed many basic liberties, and the enactment of the labour code of 1947, which abolished the so-called vagrancy laws, the situation of the Indians was considerably ameliorated, although some abuses undoubtedly were continued.

The cultural isolation of the Indians results in their underrepresentation in the national life; Ladino leadership in public affairs is predominant. However, since the two groups, Indian and Ladino, are distinguished mainly by speech, dress and community membership, Spanish-speaking Indians can and sometimes do become "ladinoized," particularly in the cities. (*See also* INDIAN, LATIN-AMERICAN; CENTRAL AMERICA: *Population: Composition*; MAYA INDIANS.)

The prevailing form of religion in Guatemala is Roman Catholic, the church claiming virtually 90% of the population as communicants. The archbishop of Guatemala is the primate of Central America, and church influence is considerable. There are some Protestant missionaries and mission schools. The Indians are nominally Roman Catholic but retain elements of native religions, such as deities and ceremonies associated with soil fertility. Much of the white population is notably religious, and while there is sometimes a division on political lines, and the church has at times been accused of opposing the prevailing liberal government with serious consequences, the religious attitude of the people of the higher classes has not been greatly affected.

(X.)

HISTORY

Since the European conquest of the new world, Guatemala has been a colony of Spain (1524–1821), a part of the Mexican empire set up by Agustín de Iturbide (1822–23), a state in the Central American Federation (1823–47) and an independent republic (since 1847). Its history has been coloured by the fact that

SEMINARY STUDENTS VISITING THE RUINS OF SAN FRANCISCO, ONE OF MANY LARGE RELIGIOUS RUINS IN ANTIGUA. ONCE THE CAPITAL OF THE SPANISH COLONIAL CAPTAINCY GENERAL. ANTIGUA WAS LARGELY DESTROYED BY AN EARTHQUAKE IN 1773

Europeans settled among Indians whom they dominated but whose culture has kept them a people apart.

The territory which is now Guatemala was inhabited at the time of the European conquest by a sedentary, agricultural, highland people of Mayan stock organized in tribal societies headed by "kings," who frequently warred on each other. For reasons not definitely established, the brilliant Mayan culture, which once flourished in the tropical forests that bordered the central plateau on the north, had declined, and the magnificent cities, possibly as a result of drought and soil erosion, were deserted. (*See* MAYA INDIANS.) Trade and conquests from the west had already brought the area under strong Mexican influences.

Guatemala was conquered (1524) by Pedro de Alvarado (*q.v.*), one of the principal officers of Hernán Cortés, who was sent from Mexico in command of a force of Spaniards and Indian allies to punish and subdue the rebellious natives of the south. The invaders defeated in sequence the warriors sent out by the chiefs of the disunited local tribes, reduced many Indians to vassalage and appropriated the more accessible lands. The conquest completed, Alvarado was appointed the first captain general of an area which included modern Central America and the adjacent portions of contemporary Mexico.

The origin of the name Guatemala is certainly Indian, but its derivation and meaning are undetermined. Some hold that the original form was Quauhtemallan (which indicates an Aztec rather than a Mayan origin), meaning "land of trees," and others hold its origin was Guhatezmalha, meaning "mountain of vomiting water," referring no doubt to the so-called volcano of water which destroyed Ciudad Vieja (Santiago), the first permanent Spanish capital of the captaincy general.

Colonial Period.—The colony was organized in the typical Spanish pattern. The conquerors were assigned lands and Indians to support them, the capital was eventually established at Antigua (q.v.) and Spanish officials, subject in some matters to the viceroy of Mexico but in local affairs independent, were appointed to administer the area. Public buildings, churches and monasteries were constructed, and a university was established under clerical control. The capital achieved a certain magnificence and the major towns acquired some aspects of Spanish culture, but the outlying areas were only lightly affected. When Antigua was razed by an earthquake in 1773, the capital was moved by royal order to the site of modern Guatemala City (q.v.).

The colony developed no great degree of economic prosperity. The cultivation for export of agricultural staples, principally cacao and indigo, by Indian or Negro labour was the major economic activity, exclusive of production for subsistence. Commerce, however, was never extensive; a satisfactory port was never developed, internal transportation was difficult and pirates harassed the coasts and preyed on shipping.

Independence.—Successful termination of the war for independence in Mexico led to a declaration in Guatemala City of Central American independence from Spain on Sept. 15, 1821. Shortly thereafter, the former captaincy general, which included the modern republics of Guatemala, El Salvador, Honduras, Costa Rica, Nicaragua and Chiapas state (Mexico), joined the empire which Agustín de Iturbide, the successful general of the Mexican independence movement, proclaimed in that country. When Iturbide fell from power in 1823, Central America determined upon separate nationhood, and the Republic of the United Provinces of Central America (Central American Federation) was formed with its capital in Guatemala City.

The federation had a brief and stormy life. Manuel José Arce, the first president, came into conflict with the Liberal state authorities in Guatemala and El Salvador, and was overthrown (1829) by a military force under Francisco Morazán (q.v.), who was shortly elected to the presidency. Morazán's government, with the cooperation of friendly authorities in some of the states, attempted to carry through the Liberal program of reform, one feature of which was subordination of the church to the civil authorities. The rapid and drastic changes produced a reaction which, coupled with other divisive factors, threw the union into civil war, and by 1838 the federation had, for practical purposes, ceased to exist. The Guatemalan government functioned independently after 1839.

Morazán was defeated decisively and exiled in 1840, and his attempt to regain power in 1842 ended in his execution.

The principal factor in the overthrow of Morazán was the back-country uprising in Guatemala of which Rafael Carrera assumed leadership. This astute but illiterate rustic established himself as the military arbiter of the state (1838) and, from the executive's chair or from behind it, controlled policy until his death in 1865. The formality of elections was dispensed with in 1854 when the presidency was conferred upon him for life.

Carrera, with Conservative support, returned Guatemala to a regime similar to that of the colonial period. He restored the church to its position of privilege and power and catered to its aristocracy. He followed a nationalistic policy and in March 1847 formally declared Guatemala an independent and sovereign nation. In 1859 he made a treaty with Great Britain defining the status and boundaries of British Honduras (Belice), the interpretation of which is still an issue between the two governments.

In 1871 a revolution headed by Miguel García Granados and Justo Rufino Barrios (q.v.) overthrew Gen. Vicente Cerna, Carrera's Conservative successor in office, and inaugurated a period of "Liberal" ascendancy that extended almost unbroken to 1944. After a brief period in the presidency, García Granados ceded to Barrios (1873), who became known as the "Reformer" because of the sweeping changes he introduced.

With the approval of the assembly Barrios broke the power of the local aristocracy; brought the church under civil control and confiscated its properties; instituted lay education; promulgated a new constitution (1876); fostered the construction of roads, railways and telegraph lines; encouraged development by private initiative of the resources of the country; and opened the country to foreign capital. He stimulated the cultivation of coffee to replace the declining trade in cochineal and enacted legis-lation designed to assure producers of a ready supply of labour. He was an ardent exponent of the idea of Central American union, and, when persuasion failed to produce the ends he desired, he invaded El Salvador and lost his life at the battle of Chalchuapa (1885) in an attempt to accomplish them by force.

After the death of Barrios, Manuel Lisandro Barillas occupied the presidency and was succeeded by José María Reina Barrios, nephew of the "Reformer," who was elected in 1892 and assassinated in 1898. Manuel Estrada Cabrera became provisional president, regularized his status by an election and by repeated re-elections (1904, 1910, 1916) maintained himself in power until leaders of the opposition Unionist party, with the co-operation of some former adherents of the dictator, forced him from office by the novel expedient of having the assembly declare him insane (1920).

During his long tenure in power, Estrada Cabrera fostered economic development and progress along the lines established by Barrios. He encouraged improvements in agriculture, made the first concessions to the United Fruit company (1906), continued to build roads, supported railroad construction and had the satisfaction of seeing the railroad to the Atlantic completed. Health conditions were improved and education stimulated, especially in practical fields. His political policies were less admirable. He persecuted political opponents, disregarded individual rights and liberties, muzzled the press and summarily disposed of his enemies.

After the fall of Estrada Cabrera, the presidency was held by Carlos Herrera, Gen. José M. Orellana, Lázaro Chacón, Baudilio Palma, Gen. Manuel Orellana and José María Reina Andrade, for periods ranging from a few days to nearly a full six-year term. In 1931 Jorge Ubico was elected president and began the fourth of the extended dictatorships that covered a century of Guatemalan history.

Contemporary Period.—Ubico stressed economic development and, in particular, improvement and diversification of agriculture and the construction of roads. He balanced the national budget and transformed a deficit into a surplus. In part his financial achievement was due to economies, in part to the efficiency and honesty of his administration. Although his vagrancy law (1934) made workers, especially Indians, liable to periods of forced labour at critical seasons, Ubico's paternalistic policies toward the natives established him as their patron. During his motorcycle tours of the country, or in his office, he listened to their complaints and dispensed immediate "justice." This relationship deluded Ubico (called Tata, "father") into stating that Guatemala no longer had an Indian problem.

Education, which had received considerable emphasis under preceding Liberal regimes, was of but slight interest to Ubico. He closed several of the few institutions of secondary level outside the capital, allowed teachers' salaries to remain at levels incompatible with decency and, as a final disparagement, militarized the schools and required teachers and students to march in his parades and festivals.

Ubico's administration dramatized the degree to which Liberal thought had lost its idealism and was concerned principally with material progress. The new socioeconomic groups that had been brought into existence by such innovations as lay education, mechanized transportation and industrial development found no stimulation and no hope in the dreary materialism and military repression which had come to characterize Liberal regimes.

These latent sources of opposition were solidified and focused by the increasing disregard which the dictator showed for individual rights and liberties. The familiar trappings of military dictatorship became increasingly evident, and the reorganized national police came to be regarded as an espionage force. Protests were answered by sterner restrictions and even by violence. The discontent was increased by the economic dislocation incident to World War II, and by the unfavourable contrast between the idealistic pronouncements of Allied war leaders and conditions in Guatemala. Ubico was thought to admire the totalitarian dictators, but in Dec. 1941 his government declared war on Japan, Germany and Italy.

In June 1944 a general strike forced Ubico to resign. Labour was allowed to organize, political parties were formed and a presidential electoral campaign was begun in which Juan José Arévalo soon emerged as the most popular candidate. Gen. Federico Ponce Vaides, head of the interim government, was ousted on Oct. 20, 1944, by an uprising headed by students and teachers, workers and younger elements of the military. A revolutionary junta presided over the drafting of a new constitution, the electoral campaign and, in March 1945, the inauguration of Arévalo.

The Arévalo administration attempted to consolidate the social revolution implicit in the October uprising. A favourable labour code was enacted and a social security system that promised progressive extension of benefits was inaugurated. Urban labour increased in strength, and organization of agricultural workers began. Public-school education was expanded and improved, teachers' salaries were increased and the university was granted autonomy. Arévalo also pressed the Belice issue with Great Britain. He subjected foreign enterprises to regulation that he conceived to be in the national interest and attempted to guarantee to Guatemalan labourers a larger share of the benefits produced by their toil and improved status in comparison with foreign employees of foreign corporations operating in the country. Thus the revolution and the Arévalo regime accomplished the transfer of political power in Guatemala from the military to a popular group of which organized labour was the most important single element.

This development Guatemalan Communists turned to their peculiar advantage. Lack of leadership from the rank and file allowed Communists to organize the labour movement and use it for their own ends. Arévalo was not friendly to their activities, but his nationalistic bent gave them opportunity to establish themselves as his most enthusiastic and reliable backers on issues for which he badly needed support. In this fashion they won for themselves a degree of toleration which permitted them to operate.

The most likely candidates to succeed Arévalo were Francisco Arana and Jacobo Arbenz Guzmán (q.v.), but Arana was assassinated. Arbenz Guzmán became the official candidate, was elected, with Communist support, over Gen. Miguel Ydígoras Fuentes, and assumed office on March 1951. Arbenz Guzmán made agrarian reform the central project of his administration. With strong Communist support, the assembly passed a measure providing for the expropriation of unused portions of landholdings in excess of a specified acreage, and the distribution of the land, title to which remained with the government, among landless peasants.

The growth of Communist influence in Guatemala became the most controversial issue of the Arbenz Guzmán regime. The president's toleration allowed the party to operate openly, and individual Communists to hold key posts in government, official agencies and organized labour. Internal opposition to the trend was eventually stifled by increasingly terroristic means, but exiles and foreign recruits headed by Col. Carlos Castillo Armas planned outside the country to overthrow the government. When the blow fell, military officers informed Arbenz Guzmán that the army would not fight in his defense and forced him to resign (June 1954).

Castillo Armas emerged from a military junta as provisional president, and a plebiscite subsequently regularized his status. He attempted to extirpate Communist influence, moderate the social reforms inaugurated by his predecessors and restore the confidence of foreign investment capital, but he was assassinated in July 1957. After two temporary governments and an election nullified by the congress, Gen. Miguel Ydígoras Fuentes (National Democratic Reconciliation party) was declared elected to the presidency and took office March 2, 1958. In March 1963 a coup led by the defense minister, Enrique Peralta Azurdia, ousted Ydígoras, on grounds that his failure to prevent the return of former President Arévalo heightened the possibility of an "extremist" victory in the coming election. The provisional president, Peralta Azurdia, canceled the election, promising to hold one later.

On March 6, 1966, Guatemalans elected a new president and a new congress. Violence was feared, but orderly balloting gave a law professor, Julio César Méndez Montenegro, candidate of the moderately left-wing Revolutionary party, an unexpectedly large plurality over Col. Juan de Dios Aguilar de León, candidate of the military regime, and Col. Miguel Angel Ponciano Samayoa. Méndez Montenegro did not obtain the majority of votes required for election, but the new congress, in which the Revolutionary party had gained a majority, declared him elected. The government was thus returned to a civilian head, but its hopes of reform were largely frustrated, and its attention was absorbed by increasing acts of violence and terrorism, including the assassination of the U.S. ambassador and two members of the U.S. military mission in 1968.

The presidential election of March 1, 1970, also was orderly, although violence and the kidnapping of the Guatemalan foreign minister, Alberto Fuentes Mohr, marked the pre-election period. None of the three candidates—Col. Carlos Arana Osorio, backed by the right-wing, anti-Communist coalition; Mario Fuentes Pieruccini of the Revolutionary party; Jorge Lucas Caballeros of the Christian Democratic party—received a majority of the vote. On March 21, the congress named Colonel Arana president. Later that month the West German ambassador to Guatemala was kidnapped and subsequently murdered when the Guatemalan government refused to release a number of political prisoners and to pay $700,000 as ransom. A mounting wave of terrorism caused Arana to declare a state of siege in November, which was lifted a year later when the situation seemed to have calmed down. On the economic front, Arana announced a five-year plan (1971–75), with particular emphasis on agriculture.

POPULATION

The population of Guatemala has increased, according to census figures, from 2,004,900 in 1921 to 2,790,868 in 1950 and 4,284,473 in 1964. The estimated population in 1971 was 5,347,787. Guatemala's rate of population increase at more than 3% per year is

Population of Guatemala by Department Census of 1964*

Department	Area (sq.mi.)	Population	Capital city	Population
Alta Verapaz	3,354	259,873	Cobán	38,426
Baja Verapaz	1,206	95,663	Salamá	18,632
Chimaltenango	764	163,753	Chimaltenango	15,372
Chiquimula	917	151,241	Chiquimula	35,848
El Progreso	742	66,734	El Progreso	9,534
Escuintla	1,693	269,813	Escuintla	54,191
Guatemala	821	813,696	Guatemala City	572,937
Huehuetenango	2,857	286,965	Huehuetenango	25,279
Izabal	3,489	114,404	Puerto Barrios	32,071
Jalapa	796	97,996	Jalapa	36,157
Jutiapa	1,243	199,053	Jutiapa	43,775
Petén	13,843	26,720	Flores	3,690
Quezaltenango	753	268,962	Quezaltenango	56,921
Quiché	3,235	247,775	Santa Cruz del Quiché	30,079
Retalhuleu	717	122,829	Retalhuleu	36,919
Sacatepéquez	179	80,479	Antigua	21,984
San Marcos	1,464	332,303	San Marcos	10,557
Santa Rosa	1,141	155,488	Cuilapa	12,621
Sololá	410	108,815	Sololá	21,382
Suchitepéquez	969	186,299	Mazatenango	32,416
Totonicapán	410	139,636	Totonicapán	42,335
Zacapa	1,039	95,976	Zacapa	30,187
Total	42,042	4,284,473		

*Preliminary.

one of the highest in the world. Population is concentrated in the highlands paralleling the Pacific, but clusters occur in the lowlands on either side and particularly on the Pacific slope. One-third of the population is classified as urban.

On the basis of cultural traits (not ancestry), inhabitants are classified as Indian (54%) and Ladino. Less than 5% of the population is white, and about 5% is Negro or mixed Negro and Indian (such as the "Black Caribs" of the Caribbean coast). Indigenous highland communities, particularly in isolated locations, maintain their traditional tribal customs and language and their distinctive village dress and mode of life. These characteristics keep Indian groups apart from European (Ladino) culture, as well as separate from each other. This division into two distinct culture groups is a basic national problem.   (W. J. G.)

ADMINISTRATION AND SOCIAL CONDITIONS

Constitution and Government.—The constitution of Guatemala, which became effective on March 1, 1956, was preceded by those of 1851, 1876, 1879 and 1945. The government is divided into three equal branches, executive, legislative and judicial.

Executive power is vested in the president, who is elected for a term of 6 years by popular vote and is ineligible for re-election

GUATEMALA

for 12 years after leaving office. The president must be a native Guatemalan over 35 years of age. He appoints and presides over the council of ministers or cabinet whose members are responsible to him, although congress may under certain conditions bring about the dismissal of one or more of them. They have the right to participate in congressional debates and are obliged to appear and answer questions put to them by members of congress.

Legislative power is delegated to the congress, which is unicameral and composed of one deputy for each 50,000 inhabitants or fraction thereof in excess of 25,000, each deputy having the right to elect at least one deputy. Deputies are elected by popular direct suffrage for a term of four years, with half the congress being elected every two years. A nine-member permanent committee composed of eight members elected by congress and the president of congress acts during recesses. Deputies must be native Guatemalans over 21 years of age and may be re-elected.

The judicial power is exercised by the judges of the tribunals of the republic. The judges of the supreme court of justice and of the court of appeals, which may be composed of one or more chambers, are elected by congress for terms of four years and may be re-elected. Judges of first instance and lower judges are appointed and removed by the supreme court.

Guatemala is divided for administrative purposes into 22 departments (see *Population*, above), each headed by a governor appointed by the president. The departments consist of municipalities controlled by popularly elected municipal corporations.

The constitution contains broad guarantees of rights to citizens, including life, liberty, equality and security of person, honour and property, freedom of movement in or out of the country, freedom of religion, the right of association and peaceful assembly and freedom of speech, but outlaws the Communist party. Detailed social guarantees are established for labour, public employees, the family and culture. Certain guarantees may be suspended by the president in agreement with the council of ministers, subject to ratification by congress.

All males over 18 years of age may vote but only those women over 18 who can read and write Spanish may vote. Male illiterates may hold municipal but not national office. Voting is compulsory for literate males and optional for women and illiterates.

Living Conditions.—The Guatemalan cost-of-living index showed a steady rise after mid-20th century although living standards were low. During the revolutionary period from 1944 to 1954, the Guatemalan government placed heavy emphasis on labour reforms. A labour code adopted in 1947, designed to stimulate the growth of trade unions, provided for collective bargaining, settlement of labour disputes in labour courts and compulsory arbitration of disputes involving public services. Amendments

in 1948 required severance pay and permitted farm workers to join unions. Despite these measures, relatively few Guatemalan workers became members of internationally affiliated unions.

Welfare Services.—Guatemala's social security coverage was also expanded during the period 1944-54. Laws passed in 1946 provided cash and medical benefits for both occupational and nonoccupational injuries, insurance being compulsory for employers of five or more persons. Benefits are financed by employer, employee and government contributions. Severe problems characterize health and sanitation conditions in Guatemala. In the mid-1960s, the infant mortality rate averaged about 90 per 1,000 births; there were about 3,700 persons per physician, and 25,000 people per dentist; and fewer than three hospital beds existed for every 1,000 Guatemalans. As a result of its strained relations with the United States, particularly during the administration of Arbenz Guzmán, Guatemala curtailed its participation in bilateral technical assistance programs designed to cope with these problems, although the country continued its contracts for the multilateral programs of the United Nations. After the revolution of 1954, Guatemala resumed interest in the bilateral programs.

Education.—Education is in theory free, secular and compulsory. According to an official estimate in 1965 36.7% of persons seven years old and over were illiterate. Some progress has been made in combating illiteracy by extending the school system, but there are handicaps, such as the language barrier (with non-Spanish-speaking Indians). The University of San Carlos de Guatemala (originally founded in Antigua, Jan. 31, 1676, as the University of San Carlos de Borromeo) was reestablished May 2, 1918, with seven faculties and schools. The 1956 constitution provided that the university receive no less than 2% of the annual national budget. The National library and government archives contain more than 100,000 volumes.

Defense.—Military service is legally compulsory between the ages of 18 and 50 but not observed. The size of the armed forces is limited by agreement with the other Central American nations. There is a small air force. The president is chief of the armed forces.

(G. I. B.)

THE ECONOMY

Production.—From 1946 to the mid-1960s total annual production in Guatemala rose from $250,000,000 to about $700,000,-000, an increase in annual production per capita from about $100 to $175. Much of this increase represented genuine improvement in living levels, for Guatemala had experienced only modest price inflation during the period. However, the growth rate slowed during the 1960s.

More than 90% of the country's production originates in private enterprise. Less than 10% comes from general government and state enterprises. In the private sector agriculture and forestry account for approximately one-third of the output, while mining, cottage industry, light manufacturing, utilities, commerce, communications and finance contribute the other two-thirds.

Agriculture.—Guatemala is well suited to diversified agriculture. Corn (maize) and beans, the chief subsistence crops, are grown everywhere. Other crops, mainly for home consumption, are rice, wheat, sugarcane, tobacco, potatoes, plantains, and miscellaneous fruits and vegetables. The 1960 agricultural census numbered more than 1,000,000 cattle; about 750,000 sheep; more than 400,000 pigs; 250,000 horses, mules and asses; and 80,000 goats.

Leading commercial crops are coffee, cotton and bananas. Coffee, mainly the Arabica and Bourbon types, is grown between 1,000 and 5,000 ft. above sea level. There are about 12,000 growers, but the largest 1,500 produce 80% of the crop. State-owned *fincas nacionales* ("national farms" expropriated from German settlers during World War II) are the largest producers. Annual production of coffee in the mid-1960s was about 100,000 metric tons.

Principal cotton cultivations are located in the Pacific coastal area where cotton first was introduced during the early 1950s. By the 1960s production for export had surpassed 33,070 short tons (30,000 metric tons), and cotton had displaced bananas in

NATIONAL PALACE IN GUATEMALA CITY, GUATEMALA'S CAPITAL AND LARGEST CITY

ACE WILLIAMS FROM BLACK STAR
WOODSELLERS ON THE STEPS OF THE CHURCH OF SANTO TOMÁS, IN CHICHICASTENANGO

value as Guatemala's second commercial product.

Bananas are grown throughout the moist lowlands, but commercial production centres around United Fruit's Bananera division in the Motagua river basin near the Caribbean. A larger development, the Tiquisate division in the Pacific lowlands, was gradually shut down during the early 1960s because of labour disputes, hurricanes, volcanic damage and plant diseases. Tiquisate closed altogether in 1964 after 35 years of production, and United Fruit sold most of the land to ranchers and cotton farmers. Smaller private plantations near Mazatenango and Retalhuleu sell fruit on contract for export by United Fruit or Standard Fruit.

An extensive agrarian reform program was initiated by law in 1952. It gave the government power to expropriate uncultivated land on farms larger than 664 ac. Owners were compensated only for tax valuation with unsecured 25-year bonds bearing 3% simple interest. Redistribution provided for leaseholds of 45 ac. or less. Implementation was vested in local agrarian committees, which often went beyond provisions of the law. Expropriations were halted in 1954 after a change of government, and the 1952 legislation was replaced in 1956 and 1962 by new acts that provided improved expropriation compensation, grants of title to redistributed lands and minimum family-farm allocations of 45 ac.

Forestry.—Nearly two-thirds of Guatemala is forested, including about 15,000,000 ac. of hardwoods and 3,000,000 ac. of softwoods, but forest resources remain little exploited because of their inaccessibility. Petén is especially significant for mahogany and dyewoods. Production of chicle dropped sharply after World War II because of destructive harvesting practices and competition from synthetic substitutes and natural latex. Nevertheless, chicle exports showed some recovery by the 1960s.

Mining.—Major known mineral resources include gold, silver, lead, zinc, copper, chromium and sulfur. The leading mining area is near Cobán, where lead and zinc are produced. Lead also is produced near San Miguel Acatán, in the department of Huehuetenango. In the 1960s approximately 11,000 tons of lead concentrate and 16,000 tons of zinc concentrate were produced annually. Petroleum deposits may exist in northeastern Guatemala. A new petroleum code in 1955 was followed by applications by 29 international and local companies for exploration permits, chiefly in Petén.

Industries.—Manufacturing occupies a growing place in the national economy. Production is chiefly for domestic purposes, and enterprises tend to be small. Output includes electricity, textiles, alcoholic beverages, soft drinks, food products, cement, shoes and leather goods, soap, candles, cigarettes, matches, furniture and Indian handicrafts. Production of brown sugar (*panela*) and molasses is significant on the southern coast. The first rubber tire factory in Central America was opened, with U.S. participation, in 1958.

Industrial expansion is hampered by lack of power, which is relatively expensive because coal and oil must be imported. However, there is a large potential for hydroelectric power development on rivers running to the two coasts.

Trade and Finance.—The U.S. is Guatemala's chief trading partner, both for imports and exports. However, significant trade also exists with West Germany, Japan and the United Kingdom. Major imports include machinery, motor vehicles, petroleum, textiles, flour, chemicals, and iron and steel manufactures. Major exports are coffee, cotton and bananas, with lesser amounts of chicle, essential oils (mainly citronella and lemon grass), abaca, cacao, sugar, meat, zinc, lead and timber.

Although coffee exports have increased, diversified exports have grown more rapidly. Consequently, coffee supplied about 50% of export value in the mid-1960s, while cotton ranked second with 15% to 20% and bananas were third with less than 10%. Before 1960 coffee normally supplied 75% of exports, and cotton was a minor item. Bananas, which ranked second to coffee before 1960, have declined since the 1930s, when they represented about 30% of exports.

Despite rising exports, the trade balance on merchandise has been consistently unfavourable. In 1960 the International Monetary fund authorized credit up to $15,000,000 to support the quetzal when it was threatened further by declining coffee prices. The quetzal, the monetary unit of Guatemala, is officially at par with the U.S. dollar.

Communications.—Guatemala has 720 mi. (1,159 km.) of railway, mostly operated by International Railways of Central America, a majority share of which is owned by the Transportation Corporation of America. The main line extends from Puerto Barrios, on the Caribbean, through Guatemala City to Ayutla, a point for connection with the National Railways of Mexico. Branch lines run to El Salvador and to San José, on the Pacific.

About 8,051 mi. (12,957 km.) of roads exist, although most are unpaved. Exceptions are the highway from Guatemala City to San José and sections of the Pan-American, Pacific Coast and Atlantic (Guatemala City-Puerto Barrios) highways. Puerto Barrios is the most important port. Three ports of lesser significance are Santo Tomás, on the Caribbean, and San José and Champerico, on the Pacific.

Air transportation is supplied by international lines and by the government-owned Aviateca, which provides the principal domestic service.

Most domestic telecommunications facilities, including telephone, telegraph and radio, are government owned. They provide contact between principal points in the country, but equipment and service are inadequate. Good local telephone networks are almost nonexistent except in the capital. International cable services connect with the government telegraph lines.

See also references under "Guatemala" in the Index.
(R. A. LaB.)

BIBLIOGRAPHY.—Chester L. Jones, *Guatemala, Past and Present* (1940); David Vela, *Literatura Guatemalteca*, 2 vol. (1943); F. W. McBryde, *Cultural and Historical Geography of Southwest Guatemala* (1947); L. Aguirre, *The Land of Eternal Spring* (1949); Mary P. Holleran, *Church and State in Guatemala* (1949); International Bank for Reconstruction and Development, *The Economic Development of Guatemala* (1951); Sol Tax et al., *Heritage of Conquest: the Ethnology of Middle America* (1952); J. H. Adler et al., *Public Finance and Economic Development in Guatemala* (1952); P. J. E. Male, *Economic and Commercial Conditions in Guatemala* (H.M.S.O. 1956); Sol Tax, *Penny Capitalism, a Guatemalan Indian Economy*, rev. ed. (1963); Luis Cardoza y Aragón, *Guatemala, las líneas de su mano* (1955); Amy E. Jensen, *Guatemala, a Historical Survey* (1955); W. J. Griffith, *Empires in the Wilderness* (1965); Seymour Menton, *Historia crítica de la novela guatemalteca* (1960); V. Kelsey and L. de J. Osborne, *Four Keys to Guatemala*, rev. ed. (1961); Nathan L. Whetten, *Guatemala, the Land and the People* (1961); Richard A. La Barge, *Impact of the United Fruit Company on the Economic Development of Guatemala, 1946–1954* (1960). Current history and statistics are summarized annually in *Britannica Book of the Year.*
(L. W. Be.; M. L. M.; L. L. LL.)

GUATEMALA, a department in central Guatemala. Area 821 sq.mi. Pop. (1964) 813,696. A volcanic highland region, it extends northward to the Motagua River. In the southern part, in the midst of volcanoes, is Lake Amatitlán, a popular resort area with Indian villages on its shores and also the chief coffee-growing region of Guatemala. Other crops include maize, beans, and sugarcane. There is much pasture land for beef cattle.

Guatemala City (q.v.) is both the departmental and the national capital and is connected by paved highway and railroad to the lake district. Roads and railroads provide communications with Mexico to the west and El Salvador to the east, and also with the Pacific port of San José and the Caribbean ports of Puerto Barrios and Santo Tomás.
(P. E. J.)

GUATEMALA CITY is the largest city in Central America (pop. [1964] 572,937 [mun.]), the political and social capital, the cultural centre and the economic heart of Guatemala. It is also the capital of Guatemala department. The city is 150 mi. (241 km.) SW of Puerto Barrios in an intermontane valley of the central highlands at an elevation of slightly less than 5,000 ft. (1,500 m.), and enjoys the temperate climate and invigorating fresh atmosphere characteristic of high altitudes in the tropics.

Guatemala City was founded (1776) to replace Antigua (q.v.), ruined by an earthquake in 1773, as the capital of the captaincy general of Guatemala. After independence from Spain was declared (1821), it served successively as the capital of the province of Central America under the Mexican Empire of Agustín de Iturbide (1822–23), the Central American Federation (1823–33), the state, and, finally, the independent republic of Guatemala. The tradition of government from Guatemala caused distrust of the city in other areas of Central America that was a factor in the demise of the federation and the failure of subsequent attempts to revive it.

The modern city was largely rebuilt after the disastrous earthquakes of 1917–18. The characteristic appearance created by low, massive structures has been somewhat modified by the erection of steel and concrete multistoried hotels and office and apartment buildings of modern design. Elegant residential districts have grown up on the borders of the old city, particularly toward the south in the direction of La Aurora Airport, and low-cost housing units have been constructed in various parts of the urban area. Most streets are well paved and well lighted.

In addition to the government offices and services concentrated there, Guatemala City employs nearly half of the capital invested in the country, accommodates more than half of the industrial establishments, and accounts for a like proportion of the industrial production of the republic. It is the focus of transport, both local and international, by highway, railroad, and air, and is the commercial and banking metropolis of the country.

The cultural role of the city is equally dominating. It is the seat of the principal faculties of the University of San Carlos; the major institutions for artistic, commercial, vocational, and military education; the Society of Geography and History; and several of the important museums and related institutions of the country. Most performances by the national orchestra and the national ballet company and those of foreign artists on tour are given in the capital.

Public buildings of note include the National Palace, the post office, police headquarters, the National Archives, the National Library, and the modern cluster about the new city hall. Among the major religious structures are the Cathedral and the churches of San Francisco, Santo Domingo, and La Merced. Other points of interest include the remarkable relief map of the country in Minerva Park (constructed in 1905 by Francisco Vela), the archaeological and historical museums, the colonial aqueduct, the central market, and the Olympic City built for the 1950 Central American Olympic games.

In the environs of Guatemala City are the villages of Chinautla, famous for hand-formed pottery, and Mixco, which supplies the capital with fruits and vegetables. Nearby are the Indian towns of San Pedro and San Juan Sacatepéquez.
(W. J. G.)

GUAVA, in Spanish *guayaba,* is the name applied to numerous tropical American trees and shrubs of the genus *Psidium,* of the myrtle family (Myrtaceae), and to their fruit, which is eaten in many ways where it is grown. Horticulturally the two important species are the so-called common guava, *P. guajava,* and the cattley or strawberry guava, *P. cattleianum,* which occurs in two forms, one with maroon-red fruits and the other with bright yellow ones. The latter is sometimes listed botanically as *P. lucidum.*

The common guava is a large shrub or small tree with quadrangular branchlets, oval to oblong leaves about three inches in length and white four-petaled flowers an inch broad. The fruits are round to pear shaped, sometimes as much as three inches in diameter, though usually less; the flesh, which is white to salmon red, contains numerous small, hard seeds—more abundant in primitive forms of the fruit than in the modern improved varieties. The musky, at times pungent, odour of the sweet flesh is characteristic and not always appreciated. The Brazilian guava (*P. guineense*) has smaller but similar fruit.

Guavas are pre-eminently suited for the preparation of jellies, jams and preserves, highly popular in many tropical countries and exported from a few, notably Cuba. Fresh guavas are rich in vitamin C; they are eaten out of hand or may be sliced and served with sugar and cream as a dessert.

J. HORACE MCFARLAND CO.

COMMON GUAVA (PSIDIUM GUAJAVA)

The common guava resists little frost, hence is not cultivated in many parts of California but is successfully grown throughout southern Florida; in several tropical regions it grows so abundantly in a half-wild state as to become a pest.

Propagation of the plant is usually by seeds, but the fine varieties that have been developed in Florida, California and a few other parts of the world must be perpetuated by some vegetative means. Because of its hard, dry wood and thin bark, propagation by cuttings and by conventional methods of grafting are not practical, but veneer grafting, using as rootstocks young plants in vigorous growth, and covering the grafts with strips of polyethylene plastic, gives excellent results. A method known as modified Forkert budding has been recommended in Hawaii.

The cattley or strawberry guava is considerably more frost resistant and is popular in many subtropical regions. It is a large shrub, attractive for its thick, glossy-green oval leaves and its white flowers. The fruits are round, occasionally as much as two inches in diameter, and contain numerous hard seeds like those of the common guava. The flavour of the soft whitish flesh has been likened to that of the strawberry, hence one of the common names. This species is frequently planted in gardens throughout southern California and several other subtropical regions; nowhere has it attained commercial importance.

Other guavas used to a limited extent in parts of tropical America include the cás of Costa Rica (*P. friedrichsthalianum*) and the guisaro (*P. molle*), both of which yield highly acid, not very pungent, fruits. The so-called pineapple guava is the feijoa (q.v.), a related fruit tree.
(W. Po.)

GUAYAQUIL, chief port and largest city of Ecuador, capital of the province of Guayas (q.v.) located on the west bank of the Guayas river (q.v.) about 45 mi. upstream from the Gulf of Guayaquil. Pop. (1962) 515,489. The main part of the city is on high ground at the foot of a hill which has two humps called Cerro Santa Ana and Cerro Santa Carmen, about 30 ft. above sea level, and stands above the highest floods of the river although the lower town is at times inundated.

The climate of Guayaquil is equatorial but temperatures are never extreme: the average of the warmest month (April) is 27° C. (80° F.), and for the coldest month (July), 24° C. (75° F.). Rainfall is heavy from January to May, but there is little rain during the rest of the year. Violent storms and heavy winds are unknown, but the humidity is high, especially in the rainy season. The average annual rainfall is 38.8 in.

A settlement was established near modern Guayaquil in 1535 by Sebastián de Belalcázar. This site, at the mouth of the Babahoyo river, was subject to flooding and disease. The location was moved, and finally in 1538 Francisco de Orellana established the town in its present location, naming it Santiago de Guayaquil to honour both the saint on whose day it was founded and the Indian chief Quaya and his wife Quila. The city has survived attacks by buccaneers, fires, earthquakes and pestilence. For many years Guayaquil, which is slightly more than 2° south of the equator, was regarded as a plague spot. In the 20th century notable engineering and hygienic achievements were accomplished by the government in co-operation with the Rockefeller foundation, and after 1920 health hazards were reduced to a minimum. In 1822 Guayaquil was the scene of the conference that took place between Simón Bolívar and José de San Martín, after which Bolívar emerged as sole leader of the South American liberation movement.

Traditionally the products of the Guayas lowland are brought to Guayaquil by river boat. Even in the dry season, shallow-draft steamboats are able to ascend the Guayas river for about 80 mi. to Babahoyo and to navigate the Daule river for about 40 mi. A branch of the Inter-American highway descends from the highlands to Durán on the left bank of the Guayas river opposite Guayaquil. This is also the western terminal of the Guayaquil to Quevedo railway (288 mi.). Passengers and goods cross the river in ferries. An all-weather highway runs from Guayaquil to Quevedo and thence up into the highlands at Latacunga, connecting there with the Inter-American highway; another highway connects Guayaquil with Salinas to the west. In the early 1960s a new highway was being built from Quevedo more directly to Quito by way of Santo Domingo de los Colorados. Guayaquil is served by both international and domestic airlines.

The port of Guayaquil can accommodate ships of up to 22-ft. draft. Larger ships, however, anchor about 40 mi. below Guayaquil at Puná Island and are met there by lighters and ferries. A new port on the Salado estuary, about 10 mi. S.W. of Guayaquil, was completed. Most of the exports and imports of Ecuador pass through the port. The decline in the importance of cacao, however, means that no longer is Guayaquil filled with the odour of the drying cacao kernels, which once were spread on the streets in the dry season and gave the city a distinctive aroma.

Guayaquil has numerous industrial plants, producing leather goods, alcohol, soap, candles, textiles, beer and cement. There are sugar refineries, iron foundries, machine shops, tanneries and sawmills. It has one of Ecuador's two leading universities, founded 1867, and among its older buildings are some notable examples of colonial architecture. Since the earthquake of 1942 much of the city has been rebuilt. (P. E. J.)

GUAYAS, a coastal province of Ecuador, bounded west by the Pacific ocean, north by Manabí, Pichincha and Los Ríos, east by Los Ríos, Cañar and Azuay and south by El Oro. Area 7,368 sq.mi. Pop. (1962) 979,223. The provincial capital is Guayaquil (q.v.). The greater part of the province is a lowland surrounding the Gulf of Guayaquil. It is rainy and covered with tropical forest in the north, and becomes drier toward the south.

The flood plains of the Guayas river (q.v.) system and along the Guayas itself below Guayaquil, including the swampy Puná Island at the mouth of the river, are inundated each year during the rainy season from December to May. Above the flood plains, plantations produce cacao, bananas, rice, cotton, coffee and fruit. Much of the land, including the flood plains, is used for the pasture of beef cattle.

At the end of the Santa Elena peninsula, 75 mi. W. of Guayaquil, is Ecuador's only oil field. At the town of Salinas, in the midst of the oil field, there are salt-extracting works and a rapidly growing seaside resort. Salinas enjoys an arid climate, with blue skies and comfortable ocean winds, and sandy beaches.

The Galápagos Islands (q.v.), which form a separate territory of Ecuador, are administered from Guayas province. (P. E. J.)

GUAYAS RIVER, a river in the coastal region of Ecuador. Its tributaries rise on the western slopes of the Western Cordillera and descend to drain the wet lowland, upstream from Guayaquil. Chief among these are the Daule, the Vinces, the Chimbo (Yaguachi in its lower course) and the Babahoyo. These tributaries join to form the Guayas which carries all this water about 40 mi. to the Gulf of Guayaquil.

The whole length to the end of the longest tributary is about 200 mi. Steamers drawing 22 ft. can ascend even in the dry season to Guayaquil (q.v.), where the river is 1 mi. wide, and smaller river steamers can reach Babahoyo. In the rainy season small steamers can navigate to Zapotal, 90 mi. S.W. of Quito. The river enters the Gulf of Guayaquil through an estuary on either side of Puná Island. (P. E. J.)

GUAYCURUAN (GUAICURUAN, WAICURUAN), a South American Indian linguistic family comprising a number of tribes formerly inhabiting much of the Gran Chaco. The best known tribes generally assigned to this family include the Abipón (Callagá), Mbayá (including the Caduveo), Mocoví (Mocobí), Payaguá, Pilagá, and Toba. Many Guaycuruan-speaking groups acquired the horse from the Spaniards and became famous in the 17th and 18th centuries for their highly stratified, warlike societies. The Mbayá tribe, for example, developed definite classes of nobles, serfs and slaves. Such Guaycuruan tribes campaigned eastward across the Paraná river and northward into the southern Mato Grosso. Constant warfare and epidemics eventually reduced their numbers, and in the 1960s these tribes were either extinct or were being assimilated.

See also INDIAN, LATIN-AMERICAN.

BIBLIOGRAPHY.—Martin Dobrizhoffer (Dobrizhofer), *An Account of the Abipones, an Equestrian People of Paraguay,* 3 vol. (1822); Alfred Métraux, "Ethnography of the Chaco," in *Handbook of South American Indians,* Bureau of American Ethnoloy Bulletin 143, vol. 1, pp. 197–370 (1946); José Sánchez Labrador, *El Paraguay Católico,* 3 vol. (1910–17). (M. J. H.)

GUAYMÍ: see CHIBCHAN; MIDDLE AMERICA: *Lower Central America.*

GUAYULE (*Parthenium argentatum*), a rubber-bearing desert shrub of the family Compositae (q.v.), native to the north central plateau of Mexico and the Texas Big Bend area. Prehistoric Indians are believed to have obtained the rubber by chewing the bark. The modern method is to macerate the shrub mechanically. Rubber was extracted in Mexico from wild plants during the early part of the 20th century, and vigorous efforts were made to cultivate guayule in southwestern United States during World War II. Commercial production of guayule rubber ceased soon after the end of the war, but research plantings have been continued in Spain, Turkey and the United States.

See Alton I. Moyle, *Bibliography and Collected Abstracts on Rubber Producing Plants (Other Than Species of Hevea),* Texas Agricultural Experiment Station *Circular 99* (Nov. 1942); K. W. Taylor, "Guayule—An American Source of Rubber," *Econ. Bot.* 5:255 (1951). (L. G. P.)

GUBBIO (ancient IGUVIUM), a town of central Italy, province of Perugia, 19 mi. N.E. of the city of Perugia. Pop. (1961) 30,146 (commune). The town, situated at the foot of Mt. Ingino, dominates a large plateau; its climate is temperate and healthful. The commune produces cereals, wine and olive oil. Tobacco products, cement and brick are manufactured. The craft of ceramics is highly developed (Gubbio was noted for majolica in the 16th century), as are those of wrought iron, embroidery and lace. Gubbio retains much of the middle ages in its appearance. Principal monuments include the 14th-century Palazzo dei Consoli, now the town hall, where the Iguvine tables are preserved (see IGUVINE TABLES); the Palazzo Pretorio; the cathedral (12th–13th centuries) and other churches. The Roman theatre, probably dating from the republican period and restored under Augustus, is the chief Roman relic. Gubbio has two traditional regional festivals.

Iguvium was a flourishing town of ancient Umbria; subsequently it was an ally of Rome and later a Roman *municipio.* A bishop of Iguvium is mentioned in A.D. 413. In the middle ages Gubbio was a free commune, rich and powerful, alternately Guelph and Ghibelline; in 1400 it passed to the duchy of Urbino, under which it remained till 1624 when it was ceded to the church. In 1860 it was united with the kingdom of Italy.

GUCHKOV, ALEKSANDR IVANOVICH (1862–1936), Russian political leader, a spokesman for constitutionalism in the last years of the tsarist regime, was born in 1862 into a wealthy Moscow commercial family. A man of active and energetic disposition, he volunteered for service with the Boers in the South African War (1899–1900) and was made prisoner by the British. Politically, he was a moderate liberal. In 1905 he helped to found the Octobrist party, which sought to consolidate the constitutional regime granted by Nicholas II in his October manifesto. In the third duma (1907–12) his investigations into irregularities of the military administration earned him the hostility of the prime minister, P. A. Stolypin, who had looked to the Octobrists for support. Guchkov was elected president of the duma in March 1910, but resigned a year later in protest against Stolypin's unconstitutional measures. During World War I, as chairman of the War Industries committee, he struggled desperately to keep the front supplied. From the autumn of 1916 he worked clandestinely to bring about a palace coup d'état as a means of staving off revolution, but his plans were overtaken by events. As minister for war and for the navy in the provisional government after Nicholas II's abdication, he was obliged, under pressure from the Petrograd soviet, to sanction far-reaching military reforms. This undermined his standing with many senior officers; and he resigned on May 5, 1917. After the Bolshevik revolution he emigrated to Paris, where he died on Feb. 14, 1936. Extracts from his memoirs were published in Paris in *Posledniya Novosti* (Aug. 26–30, 1936).

(J. L. H. K.)

GUDGEON (*Gobio gobio*, sometimes called *G. fluviatilis*), an edible fish of the carp family (Cyprinidae), found in fresh waters of Europe and northern Asia, especially in sandy or gravelly

shallows. It rarely exceeds a length of eight inches; it has a barbel at each corner of the mouth and a row of blackish spots along the side of the body. Other species of *Gobio* inhabit China and Japan.

(C. Hu.)

GUELDER-ROSE, so called from Gelderland (a province of the Netherlands), its assumed source, is commonly called snowball or snowball bush in the United States. It is *Viburnum opulus sterile* (or *V. o. roseum*), a sterile-flowered variety of the European true cranberry; *q.v.*), a member of the honeysuckle family (Caprifoliaceae) and native throughout temperate Eurasia. The guelder-rose is much cultivated for its showy, spring-flowering, ball-like clusters of white, sterile flowers; but, lacking fruit, it does not have the showy autumnal colour of the red drupes of *V. opulus*. In England the term guelder-rose is more often applied to *V. opulus* itself, which there also is called rose elder. *See also* VIBURNUM.

(N. Tr.; X.)

GUELPH, a city and the seat of Wellington county, southeastern Ontario, Canada, is 28 mi. N.W. of Hamilton and 45 mi. W. of Toronto. On the Canadian National and Canadian Pacific railways, it is in one of the more densely populated areas of Canada—within 13 mi. of the cities of Kitchener and Galt and the towns of Fergus, Elora, Acton, Hespeler and Preston. Founded by the Scottish writer John Galt in 1827 at a power site on the Speed river, a tributary of the Grand, the settlement was named after the British royal family. Guelph was incorporated as a village in 1851, a town in 1856 and a city in 1879. The Ontario Agricultural college (1874) and the Ontario Veterinary college (1862) helped make Guelph an important centre for research and training in scientific agriculture. Among products manufactured are electrical apparatus, hardware, stoves, flour, biscuits, pharmaceutical supplies, leather goods and textiles. Pop. (1966) 50,714.

(G. Fn.)

GUELPHS AND GHIBELLINES, the names of two parties in medieval Italian politics, respectively derived from the family name of the German house of Welf (*q.v.*) and from the local name of Waiblingen, a seat of the Hohenstaufen in Swabia. The names appear in Florence in the early years of the 13th century, at first as parties of the Guelph and of the Ghibelline, to indicate the adherents of the Welf Otto IV and those of the Hohenstaufen Frederick II, rivals for the German kingship and the Holy Roman empire. During the subsequent struggles between Frederick II and the papacy, the *parte Guelfa* in Florence came to mean the papal party, the *parte Ghibellina* the imperial. Generally in use in Tuscany by the middle of the 13th century, the names spread from there to the rest of Italy.

The division into papalists and imperialists, or Guelphs and Ghibellines, was preceded, in many communes of Italy, by a division into two rival local factions, which often assumed the names of their leading families. These, by adhering to pope or to emperor, were drawn into the wider struggles—without, however, losing their local character. The adoption of the names of Guelphs or Ghibellines, while making little difference to their allegiances, helped to accentuate the common interests that existed between parties in different towns. Such links were particularly important after expulsions following on the victory of one of the parties and acted as regional or even national elements in Italian politics by binding citizens of different towns together. At the same time, exiles might intensify interstate conflicts, just as they could determine a town's adhesion to one or the other party.

The Florentine Guelphs and Ghibellines were organized under captains and councils on the model of the commune (*see* COMMUNE (MEDIEVAL)); during periods of exile, this internal organization would foster cohesion and thus increase a party's chances of return. After their return from exile to Florence in 1266, the Guelphs used their party organization to control the government. After 1280 they lost this control, but the *parte Guelfa* remained a pillar of the Guelph commune; having acquired Ghibelline property, it enjoyed vast wealth, and its captains were among the highest Florentine officials. Only between 1346 and 1378 did the *parte* once more succeed in gaining political power. Though the struggles between the papacy and the Hohenstaufen,

GUDBRANDSDAL, a district of south central Norway, comprises the valley of the Lågen river from Lake Mjösa to its source in the famed Dovrefjell (Lake Lesjaskogen), together with tributary valleys and the vast stretches of the encircling fjells. Though the fjells are barren and rugged, the narrow valley and its slopes, where arable, are richly fertile. Transhumance of cows, goats and sheep in summer to mountain pastures is important. The crude forest economy of the 17th and 18th centuries has disappeared, but the region still produces much timber. Lillehammer, at the southern end, is a thriving town; other communities are small. The district offers excellent fishing and hunting, especially for fowl. A railway and a road through the valley connect Oslo with Trondheim, and from Dombås both rail and road lead to Åndalsnes.

Like the other valleys of the country, Gudbrandsdal has developed its own culture and dialect but long has possessed a deeply national sentiment. A historic trade route and the site of ancient graves, it is associated with several sagas and legends including *Peer Gynt*.

(L. H. Hg.)

GUDERIAN, HEINZ (1888–1954), German army officer, an outstanding tank expert in World War II, was born at Kulm (Polish Chelmno) on June 17, 1888, the son of an army officer. After serving as a staff officer in World War I, he vigorously advocated development of armoured forces. In 1935 he attracted Hitler's attention and was promoted rapidly. Designated chief of mobile troops in Nov. 1938, he proved the soundness of his tank warfare theories in the Polish campaign (1939) and in the conquest of France (1940). Following his unsuccessful drive on Moscow in Oct. 1941, he became inspector general of Panzer troops with authority to establish priorities in the production of armoured vehicles as well as to direct their employment. After the attempted assassination of Hitler on July 20, 1944, Guderian became acting chief of staff, a position he held until March 28, 1945.

Guderian was a highly competent officer of the Prussian school who accepted Hitler's leadership as a matter of duty. Of special interest among his several books are *Achtung! Panzer!* ("Attention, Tanks," 1937) and *Erinnerungen eines Soldaten* (1951), published in English as *Panzer Leader* (1952). Guderian died in West Germany on May 14, 1954.

(P. N. T.)

which had given rise to the party names, came to an end after the death of Conradin in 1268, the Guelph and Ghibelline parties survived as something more than merely local factions. The Guelph city like Florence did not hesitate to go to war against the pope (1375–78); while cities like Siena and Pisa, with a long Ghibelline tradition, were still regarded in the 15th century as potential allies of the emperors. The Italian expeditions of Henry VII (1310–13) and of Louis IV the Bavarian (1327–30) led to a temporary revival of Ghibellinism in Lombardy and Tuscany; several despots, such as Matteo Visconti and Castruccio Castracani, strengthened their local position by taking the emperor's side.

The decline of imperial influence in Italy is reflected in the occasional use of the names Guelphs and Ghibellines by local parties in the 15th century without any reference to either pope or emperor; thus toward the middle of the century, the pro-Venetian faction at Cremona was called Ghibelline, the pro-Venetian faction Guelph. In the 16th century, the revival of imperial power in Italy affected in its turn the use of the party names: during the Italian wars between the French kings and the emperor Charles V, the adherents of the former in the Romagna were called Guelphs, those of the latter Ghibellines.

The meaning and origins of the names early attracted the attention of Italian writers. The 14th-century jurist Bartolus of Sassoferrato, in his treatise *De Guelphis et Ghibellinis*, lists a number of contemporary explanations and provides valuable evidence for the parties' political and social significance in his time.

BIBLIOGRAPHY.—R. Davidsohn, *Forschungen zur Geschichte von Florenz*, vol. iv (1908); E. Jordan, *Les Origines de la domination angevine en Italie* (1909); G. A. Brucker, *Florentine Politics and Society, 1343–1378* (1962); E. Emerton, *Humanism and Tyranny* (1925), for an Eng. trans. of Bartolus' treatise. (N. R.)

GUENON, a group of the commonest African monkeys, frequently brightly coloured, constituting the large genus *Cercopithecus*, of which the diana, mona, green, grivet and vervet monkeys are representatives. Some species have been introduced into the new world tropics. Most guenons have a small, slender body (about the size of a house cat), long legs, a long nonprehensile tail and a short face. Many species are tamable and are among the finest zoo monkeys because of their hardiness, activity, good nature and fondness for grimacing at observers. *See* MONKEY; PRIMATES.

GUÉRANDE, TREATY OF (1365), the agreement that ended the War of the Breton Succession (*see* BRITTANY). After the defeat and death of Charles (*q.v.*) of Blois at Auray on Sept. 29, 1364, and the flight of his widow, Joan of Penthièvre, to Anjou, the victorious John of Montfort reduced the Breton towns that had been withstanding him. Thereupon Charles V of France resolved to negotiate a peace that would compensate Joan without driving John of Montfort back into the arms of Edward III of England—who had recognized French suzerainty over Brittany in the treaty of Brétigny (1360).

Negotiations began in Dec. 1364 between the representatives of Joan of Penthièvre and those of the king of France, and peace was signed at Guérande on April 12, 1365. John of Montfort was to have the duchy of Brittany, but Joan was to keep the countship of Penthièvre without having to pay homage for it to the duke of Brittany (though after her death her heirs would pay homage). Further, John was to renounce his claim to the viscountcy of Limoges in Joan's favour; Joan and her heirs were to receive in perpetuity an annuity of 10,000 livres from the duke; and Joan's son John was to marry John of Montfort's sister. Finally, the order of succession to the duchy was regulated to exclude women so long as any male descendant of the house of Brittany survived, so that if the male line of Montfort should die out, the duchy would revert to the branch of Penthièvre. Charles V ratified the treaty on May 31, 1366, and John did homage to him on Dec. 13.

See P. H. Morice, *Mémoires pour servir de preuves à l'histoire ecclésiastique et civile de Bretagne* (1742–46); R. Delachenal, *Histoire de Charles V*, vol. iii (1916). (Mr. M.)

GUÉRANGER, PROSPER LOUIS PASCAL (1805–1875), French Benedictine monk, restorer of Benedictine monachism in France and pioneer in the modern liturgical revival, was born on April 4, 1805. Reacting while still a theological student against the lingering Gallicanism (*q.v.*) of his day, he was ordained priest in 1827. Although strongly sympathizing with the views of Hugues Félicité Robert de Lamennais (*q.v.*), he never identified himself intimately with the views of that erratic genius. His studies in Christian antiquity and the history of Christian institutions led to a strong feeling for the Roman liturgy and to the beginning of a campaign for the abolition of the various local liturgies then flourishing in France. It was not long before the idea of restoring Benedictine monachism, extinct in France as a result of the Revolution and the legislation of the Napoleonic era, took hold of him. In Dec. 1832 he acquired the monastic buildings and lands of Solesmes (in Sarthe *département*), an 11th-century foundation. In spite of numerous difficulties, within five years Solesmes was confirmed as an abbey by the Holy See with Guéranger as first abbot and head of the Benedictine Congregation of France. A great advance had been made, and in spite of recurring administrative problems, studies long interrupted could now be resumed.

In 1840 appeared the first volume of Guéranger's *Institutions liturgiques*, an ambitious project never carried to completion, but the second volume is still important for the history of the liturgy in France in the 17th century and in the two centuries following. When the three volumes were re-edited after the author's death, a fourth was added (1885) containing several controversial letters, written in reply to criticisms which the work had evoked. Of quite a different character—that is, strictly devotional—is another work which began to appear in the same year as the *Institutions*, the *Année liturgique*, of which nine volumes—from Advent through Paschaltide—were published in the author's lifetime. Six volumes, the work of Dom Lucien Fromage, who dealt with the period after Pentecost, completed the series (1878–1901), which was frequently reprinted, not only in the original but also in more than one of the languages into which it had been translated. A complete list of Guéranger's works is to be found in the *Bibliographie des bénédictines de la Congrégation de France*, 2nd ed., 55–71 and 167–168 (1906). Guéranger died on Jan. 30, 1875.

BIBLIOGRAPHY.—Paul Delatte, *Dom Guéranger, abbé de Solesmes*, 2 vol. (1909–10); Ernest Sevrin, *Dom Guéranger et la Mennais* (1933); Fernand Cabrol, article in *Dictionnaire d'archéologie chrétienne et de liturgie*, vol. vi, pp. 1875–79; B. Heurtebize in *Dictionnaire de théologie catholique*, vol. vi, pp. 1894–98; A. Genestout in *Enciclopedia Cattolica*, vol. vi, p. 1226 ff.; Olivier Rousseau, *L'Histoire du mouvement liturgique* 1945; Eng. trans., *The Progress of the Liturgy*, 1951; John Higgens, "Dom Guéranger and the Founding of Solesmes," *American Benedictine Review*, 6:53–75 (1955); Louis Bouyer, *Liturgical Piety* (1955), noteworthy criticisms; and the rejoinder by Damasus Winzen, "Guéranger and the Liturgical Movement," *American Benedictine Review*, 6:419–426 (1955). (AM. S.)

GUERCINO, the name given to GIOVANNI FRANCESCO BARBERI (1591–1666), Italian baroque painter, because of his squint. He was born on Feb. 8, 1591, at Cento, near Ferrara, and received his earliest training locally. But the formative influence on his style came from Bologna, especially from the work of Lodovico Carracci. His first pictures (*e.g.*, the "Madonna in Glory With Saints and a Donor," at the Brussels museum) have large, rather uncouth forms, strong colour, unbalanced compositions and broad, vigorous brushwork. The lights are scattered over the surface in patches, leaving much of the picture in shadow (*cf.* Carracci's Cento "Madonna" of 1591). This method of using light and shadow was unrelated to the discoveries of Caravaggio and was derived from Bologna and Venice, which Guercino visited in 1618; the tendencies toward realism in his style were general in 17th-century Italy.

In 1621 Guercino went to Rome, and there, among many other commissions, decorated the Casino Ludovisi. The main fresco,

"Aurora," on the *gran' salone* ceiling, is a spirited, romantic work; yet it already reveals something of the crucial experience of his stay in Rome, which was his contact with Pope Gregory XV's private secretary, Monsignor Agucchi, a propagandist for the classicism of Annibale Carracci's Roman style. Guercino seems to have tried to make his own style conform with Carraccesque principles, an effort reflected in his "Sta. Petronilla" (Vatican gallery).

On the death of Gregory in 1623, Guercino returned to northern Italy, continuing to smooth out the unclassical features of his style. The result was not entirely happy and Guido Reni's unassailable position in Bologna as heir to Annibale Carracci increased his difficulties. But Guercino was continually employed by ecclesiastical and private patrons. Some of the later works—e.g., the "Death of Dido" (Spada gallery, Rome) and the "Hercules and Antaeus" (Palazzo Zampieri, Bologna), both of 1631—are considerable achievements; others are weak and empty. In 1642 Guido died and Guercino settled in Bologna, where he died on Dec. 22, 1666.

See D. Mahon, *Studies in Seicento Art and Theory* (1947).

(M. W. L. K.)

GUÉRET, a market town of central France, *préfecture* of the *département* of Creuse, lies 73 km. (45 mi.) by road N.E. of Limoges and on the Limoges-Montluçon railway. Pop. (1968) 12,801. The feudal capital of La Marche, Guéret grew up around a 7th-century abbey sited on granite slopes at 1,440 ft. It was only a small foothill market town at the beginning of the 19th century, but grew slowly with the coming of the railway, and later became the centre of agricultural co-operatives. Industries include sawmilling, tanning and leather working, and basketwork. The Hôtel des Monneyroux, a 15th-century mansion used as the *préfecture*, is the most notable building.

(M. W. L. K.)

GUEREZA, a long-tailed black and white Ethiopian monkey, *Colobus abyssinicus*, often called bishop monkey from the attractive robelike mantle of fine, silky white hair; the name is sometimes extended to embrace all the darker thumbless monkeys of the genus *Colobus*. They resemble the langurs (q.v.) with which they agree in their slender build. These gentle herbivores seldom leave the tops of tall trees.

See also PRIMATES.

GUERICKE, OTTO VON (1602–1686), German natural philosopher, notable for his studies of air pressure, was born at Magdeburg, in Prussian Saxony, on Nov. 20, 1602. Having studied law and mathematics in Germany and at Leyden, he visited France and England, and in 1636 became engineer-in-chief at Erfurt. In 1627 he was elected alderman of Magdeburg, and in 1646 mayor of that city and a magistrate of Brandenburg. His leisure was devoted to scientific pursuits, especially in pneumatics. Incited by the discoveries of Galileo, Pascal and Torricelli, he attempted the creation of a vacuum.

After a number of partially successful experiments he invented the air pump (1650). Besides investigating other phenomena connected with a vacuum, he constructed an electrical machine which depended on the electrification of a rotating ball of sulfur; he also made successful researches in astronomy, predicting the periodicity of the return of comets. In 1681 he gave up office, and retired to Hamburg, where he resided until his death on May 11, 1686.

His principal observations are given in his work, *Experimenta nova, ut vocant, Magdeburgica de vacuo spatio* (1672). He is also the author of a *Geschichte der Belagerung und Eroberung von Magdeburg*. See F. W. Hoffmann, *Otto von Guericke* (1874); A. L. Mann and C. Vivian, *Famous Physicists* (1963).

GUÉRILLA: see GUERRILLA WARFARE.

GUÉRIN, (GEORGES) MAURICE DE (1810–1839), French writer, a skilful exponent of the prose poem, was born at Le Cayla, Tarn, Aug. 5, 1810. He was brought up by his possessive sister Eugénie and was educated at the Collège Stanislas in Paris. There he met Jules Barbey d'Aurevilly (q.v.), who became a close friend. Guérin joined the community of the Abbé Félicité de Lamennais (q.v.) at La Chênaie, Brittany, and there studied and took part in discussions, some of which he recorded in his journal, published as *Le Cahier vert* (1861). In 1832 Lamennais was condemned and the community was dissolved. Guérin, having lost his faith, went to Paris where he had a romantic association with a married woman, Mme. Henriette Marie de Maistre. In 1837 he fell ill and returned to Le Cayla where he recovered and married a rich young Creole, Caroline Gervain. This proved unhappy but short-lived, for on July 19, 1839, he died at Le Cayla, of tuberculosis.

Although Guérin wrote several poems his chief works are his two prose poems "La Bacchante" and "Le Centaure," both remarkable for their rich, pantheistic natural descriptions. Also in prose is the "Méditation sur la mort de Marie." Recognition came when his works were published after his death through the efforts of his sister and his friends Barbey d'Aurevilly and Guillaume Trébutien. In 1840 *La Revue des deux mondes* printed "Le Centaure" with a memoir by George Sand, and in 1861 Trébutien published the works in two volumes entitled *Reliquiae*. A "Guérin cult" arose, causing the publication of every scrap of writing by Maurice and Eugénie, including their most intimate correspondence.

The *Journal* (1862) and *Lettres* (1865) of Eugénie de Guérin (1805–1848) show that she possessed gifts as rare as her brother's, but her mysticism assumed a more strictly religious form. She died on May 31, 1848, at Le Cayla.

BIBLIOGRAPHY.—*Oeuvres*, ed. by B. d'Harcourt, 2 vol. (1947); E. Decahors, *Maurice de Guérin, Essai de biographie psychologique* (1932); E. Barthès, *Eugénie de Guérin*, 2 vol. (1929). *See also* the periodical review *L'Amitié guérinienne* (1933–).

GUÉRIN, PIERRE NARCISSE, BARON (1774–1833), French painter, the teacher of both E. Delacroix and J. Géricault, was born at Paris on May 13, 1774. He had an early success with his topical "Marcus Sextus" (1799, Louvre). "Phèdre et Hippolyte" (1802, Louvre) and "Andromaque" (1810, Louvre) are melodramatic and highly calculated pieces. His best painting, the only one to show feeling for colour and atmosphere, is "Enée racontant à Didon les malheurs de Troie" (1817, Louvre). He died in Rome on July 16, 1833.

(AA. B.)

GUERNIERI (properly WERNER, duke of Urslingen) (d. 1354?), one of the mercenary captains who plagued and plundered Italy during the middle decades of the 14th century. After serving Pisa against Florence in 1342, he formed his own marauding band, called by him the Grand Company. Secretly encouraged by the Pisans and others, he moved with this force of about 3,000 horse into Romagna, where he levied large sums of money from the Malatesta of Rimini and the Pepoli of Bologna. He came to Italy again in 1347 with Louis I of Hungary's expedition against Naples and then resumed his career of pillage for four more years before returning to Germany for good in 1351. The story went that he wore a breastplate inscribed "Enemy of God, of pity and of mercy."

See E. Ricotti, *Storia delle compagnie di ventura in Italia*, 4 vol. (1844–45); K. H. Schäfer, *Deutsche Ritter und Edelknechte in Italien während des 14. Jahrhunderts* (1911).

(P. J. J.)

GUERNSEY, the second largest of the Channel Islands (q.v.) and the westernmost of their important members, lies 30 mi. W. of Normandy, France. Pop. (1971 prelim.) 51,351. Area 24.5 sq. mi. The island is roughly triangular, about 9 mi. in length from northeast to southwest and about 5 mi. broad in the south. With Alderney and Sark (qq.v.), Herm, Jethou and associated islets, it forms the bailiwick of Guernsey. Pop. (1971 prelim.) 53,734. Its capital is St. Peter Port on the east coast.

Physiography.—In the south Guernsey rises in a plateau to about 300 ft., with ragged cliffs along the south coast. The plateau, having been notched by the sea at various levels, descends in steps and is drained mainly by streams flowing northward in deep valleys; its soils are developed on loess. Except in the south, rocky beach platforms are extensive, especially around Perelle bay and the off-lying Lihou island (38 ac.); this western coast, exposed to the Atlantic, has a long history of wrecks. Northern Guernsey is low lying, although small outcrops of resistant rock form hills locally called *hougues*. The Braye du Valle, an arm of the sea that at high tide formerly isolated the north of the island, has been reclaimed but its eastern end forms St. Sampson harbour. The soil on the lower ground is of blown sand, raised beach deposits and the fills of old lagoons. Vraic (Fr. *varec*, wrack or seaweed) is the traditional manure, its harvesting being regulated by strict custom.

The climate is markedly maritime, snow and severe frost are rare, the annual range of temperature is only about 17° F. (−8° C.) and sunshine averages 1,905 hr. annually. Mean annual rainfall declines from 35 in. in the south to below 30 in. along the northwestern fringes. The somewhat scanty water supplies were in 1960 supplemented by a sea-water distillation plant. (For vegetation and animal life see CHANNEL ISLANDS.)

(G. H. D.)

History.—Although Guernsey was probably inhabited continuously from Neolithic times, evidence suggests that it was colonized from Normandy early in the 11th century, no doubt during the reconstruction of western Normandy after the ravages of the Northmen. The earliest surviving documents, which date from that time, show that the chief landowners were the lords of Saint Sauveur (hereditary *vicomtes* of the Cotentin), the *vicomtes* of the Bessin, the abbey of Le Mont Saint Michel and the duke of Normandy himself. They also show the ten parish churches, brought effectively under the bishop of Coutances by Geoffrey de Montbrai (1049–93; *see* MOWBRAY). By the end of the 12th century about a dozen Norman and French abbeys held property in Guernsey, many more lay tenants are known and there are indications of the form of the king-duke's government there. Guernsey formed a unit for the collection of his revenue, his justices visited the island and a local *curia regis* (king's court) was held by a *vicomte*.

After separation from continental Normandy in the reign of King John, Guernsey preserved its Norman law and local customs. The Channel Islands as a group were put in charge of a warden (*custos, gardien*) and sometimes—regularly in the 15th century— granted to a lord (*dominus, seigneur*). From the end of the 15th century, however, Guernsey (with Alderney and Sark) was put under a "captain," who gradually changed his title to governor, an office abolished in 1835. The duties devolved upon a lieutenant governor, who had in fact performed them for more than a century and still performs them. Since the warden could not conduct the frequent sessions of the king's courts regularly in four islands, his judicial responsibilities in Guernsey fell to a bailiff: at first his deputy, but soon the "king's bailiff" and frequently a Guernseyman. He presided over the Royal court, as it has come to be called, in which judgment was given and the law declared by 12 jurats.

The executive officer, the *prévot*, was elective; a clerk kept the records and the ancestors of the law officers of the crown appeared in the 14th century. The court has survived substantially in this form to the present day, administering the law of Guernsey founded on the custom of Normandy and local usage.

From 1299 until 1331 the island was visited by itinerant justices from England. Thereafter the highest judicial powers were given to the warden—in effect to the bailiff and jurats. From their practice of referring difficult points of law to those occasions when tenants of the king attended the court, the deliberative and legislative assembly, the "States of Deliberation," ultimately grew. Although separate records do not begin until 1605, the States remained an enlarged session of the court until 1948, added elements being the rectors and constables of the parishes probably in the 16th century, 15 deputies of the *douzaines* (representatives of the parishes) in 1845 and 18 additional deputies in 1899. In the 19th century the States emerged as a mature legislative assembly administering the island through executive committees.

It has been Guernsey's good fortune never to be dominated by one great family; there have been divisions within the community, but never a rending feud. The peasantry has always been free; the early growth of commerce in St. Peter Port (*q.v.*), with the smuggling and privateering of later times and the industrial development of the 19th century, weakened the hold of the feudal landlord. Part of the population was evacuated to England in 1940 prior to the German occupation during World War II. (*See* also CHANNEL ISLANDS: *History*.)

(Le P.)

Population and Administration.—The population, mainly of Norman descent with an admixture of Breton blood, numbered 20,302 in 1821, 29,757 in 1851, 40,446 in 1901 and 38,283 in 1921. The increase in the late 19th century, stimulated by quarrying and the spread of market gardening, was later more than offset by emigration. St. Peter Port had a population of 16,303 in 1971, and St. Sampson had a population of 6,534; settlement in the country parts is largely dispersed.

The two bailiwicks of the Channel Islands are not part of the United Kingdom but are attached directly to the crown; they are not affected by acts of the Westminster parliament unless specified therein. Guernsey is governed by the States of Deliberation, presided over by the bailiff and consisting of 12 counselors, 33 elected peoples' deputies and 10 *douzaine* representatives, with two deputies from Alderney. The Royal court consists of the bailiff as president and 12 elected jurats. The proceedings are conducted in English. The lieutenant governor is personal representative of the sovereign.

The Economy.—Dairy farming with the famous Guernsey breed of dairy cattle is largely confined to the high land in the south. It requires far fewer workers than market gardening, which is concentrated chiefly in the north where extensive greenhouses produce tomatoes, flowers and grapes, mostly exported to England.

Market gardening and tourism sustain the island's economy. Both rely increasingly on airline services. Little fishing is practised, although lobsters and ormers (*Haliotis tuberculata*) are taken as delicacies. The principal imports are foodstuffs, solid fuel and building materials; the chief exports are tomatoes, flowers and stone.

Passenger and cargo vessels connect Guernsey with Jersey, Alderney and Sark; Weymouth, Eng.; and St. Malo, France. Seaborne cargo services include those with London and there are extensive air links. Internal passenger transport relies on bus services.

(G. H. D.)

GUERRAZZI, FRANCESCO DOMENICO (1804–1873), Italian patriot and writer of historical novels through which he expressed his political opinions. Born at Leghorn on Aug. 12, 1804, he was educated for a legal career at Pisa, where in 1821 he met Byron. In 1829, with Guiseppi Mazzini and Carlo Bini, he founded at Leghorn a political journal, the *Indicatore livornese*, which was soon suppressed. Several times imprisoned for his activity in the cause of Young Italy, he wrote his most famous novel, *Assedio di Firenze* (1836), in prison. He became a liberal leader at Leghorn, and in 1848 was made a minister. In 1849, on the proclamation of the republic of Tuscany and the flight of the grand duke, he was one of the triumvirate, with Mazzini and Guiseppi Montanelli, and then became dictator, but after the restoration he was arrested and imprisoned, and exiled to Corsica. He was later allowed to live at Genoa and, after 1862, became a deputy at Turin.

Guerrazzi died near Cecina, Sept. 23, 1873. His many romantic novels, in which artistic and historical truth is sacrificed to political enthusiasm, reveal the fieriness of temperament which made him an effective political speaker.

See R. Guastalla, *La vita e le opere di F. D. Guerrazzi* (1903); P. Miniati, *F. D. Guerrazzi* (1927).

GUERRERO, FRANCISCO (1527–1599), one of the most outstanding composers of the Spanish polyphonic school of the 16th century. He was born in May 1527 in Seville, where he spent nearly all his working life. Guerrero received his early musical training from his brother Pedro and in 1545, at the unusually early age of 18, he was appointed *maestro de capilla* at Jaén cathedral. In 1548 he was appointed cantor at Seville cathedral under Pedro Fernández de Castilleja. In 1551 he assumed the effective directorship of the cathedral and became *maestro de capilla* in 1574. He died in Seville on Nov. 8, 1599. A most accomplished contrapuntist, Guerrero wrote music that is eminently vocal, strongly Spanish in character and evocative of a vivid and serene spirituality. His compositions include 18 Masses, two Requiems, setting of two Passions (St. Matthew and St. John), motets, and a volume of *Canciones y Villanescas espirituales* (1589), which has been reprinted as vol. 1 of the *Opera Omnia* (1955 *et seq.*) prepared by the Instituto Español Musicología.

See G. Reese, *Music in the Renaissance* (1954). (J. T. A. H.)

GUERRERO, VICENTE (1783-1831), Mexican independence hero born at Tixtla, began his military career in 1810. José María Morelos commissioned him to promote the revolutionary movement in the south. By 1817 the movement was virtually suppressed, but Guerrero continued guerrilla warfare until he accepted (1821) Agustín de Iturbide's invitation to consummate Mexican independence.

When Iturbide had himself crowned emperor (1822), Guerrero participated in the military and political struggles which followed. In March 1829 he was chosen president but proved to be less adept at political administration. The troops of Antonio López de Santa Ana rebelled and Guerrero was betrayed, tried and executed in Chilapa on Feb. 14, 1831. (S. R. R.)

GUERRERO, a Pacific coast state of México, bounded north-west by Michoacán, north by México (state) and Morelos, north-east and east by Puebla and Oaxaca, and south and west by the Pacific. Area 24,631 sq.mi. Pop. (1960) 1,186,716, largely composed of Indians and mestizos. The state is roughly broken by the Sierra Madre del Sur and its spurs, which cover its entire surface with the exception of the Pacific coastal plain. The valleys are usually narrow, fertile, and heavily forested, but difficult of access. Guerrero is divided into two distinct zones—the *tierras calientes* of the coast and lower river courses where tropical conditions prevail, and the *tierras templadas* of the mountain region, celebrated for its climate. The principal river is the Balsas. Its baroque church of Santa Prisca is one of the most famous in Mexico.

Agricultural products include cotton, coffee, tobacco, and cereals, and the forests produce rubber, vanilla, and various textile fibres. Mineral resources include silver, gold, mercury, lead, iron, coal, sulfur, and precious stones.

Guerrero became a state in 1849, and was named after Vicente Guerrero, a leader of Mexico's war for independence. Chilpancingo (pop. 18,022), the capital, is an agricultural centre. Two well-known cities are Taxco (pop. 14,773) and Acapulco (q.v.), a famous colonial port now has a fashionable resort. Taxco, because of its colonial character, has been declared a national monument, and is a great tourist and art centre. (J. A. Cw.)

GUERRILLA WARFARE is a type of warfare characterized by irregular forces fighting small-scale, limited actions, generally in conjunction with a larger political-military strategy, against orthodox military forces. The guerrillas are usually non-descript in dress, unconventional in weapons and equipment, lack formal supply lines, and employ highly unorthodox tactics which in addition to extremely mobile, aggressive operations embrace all aspects of psychological warfare including the use of sabotage and terrorism. Although this type of warfare occurs throughout history, the word "guerrilla" (the diminutive of Spanish *guerra*, the word for "war," which traces to French *guerre*, O.H.G. *werra*), literally meaning "little war," stems from the duke of Wellington's Iberian campaigns (1809-13) when Spanish-Portuguese irregulars or *guerrilleros* (also referred to at the time as partisans and insurgents) helped drive the French from the peninsula. In World War II the word partisan became synonymous with guerrilla; more recently the word insurgent has come into vogue, the result of a specific political dimension having been added to guerrilla warfare.

Function.—Guerrilla warfare by tradition is a weapon of protest employed to rectify real or imagined wrongs levied on a people either by a foreign invader or by the ruling government. As such, it may be employed independently, or it may be used to complement orthodox military operations in which case it can be employed either inside enemy territory or in those areas which have been seized and occupied by an enemy.

In either capacity the importance of its role has varied considerably through history. Currently, it is a highly prized weapon playing an integral role in what has been termed revolutionary or insurgency warfare (one student, the French officer Roger Trinquier, insists on the term modern, as is apparent in his *Modern Warfare*)—and what international Communism calls "people's wars" and "wars of national liberation."

Since World War II guerrilla warfare has been independently employed by non-Communist insurgencies in such countries as Indonesia, Cyprus, and Algeria (qq.v.), where it was successful, and by Communist insurgencies in Malaya and the Philippines, where it ultimately failed. In a complementary role, in which the guerrilla force first fights independently and later evolves into an orthodox insurgent army, it has been successfully employed by Communist insurgencies in China and Indochina.

History.—Ancient and medieval chronicles offer countless examples of guerrilla actions, usually of an independent type undertaken by peasant bands and normally resulting in little more than temporary embarrassment to the incumbent ruler or temporary harassment to the invader. These chronicles also describe numerous campaigns undertaken by marauding tribes which practised an offensive style of warfare often marked with definite guerrilla overtones. The genesis of modern guerrilla warfare, however, is found in the American Revolution when the colonists, many of them veterans of Indian fighting, formed loosely knitted bands of riflemen which practised highly unorthodox tactics against the formally trained British redcoats. Despite George Washington's tendency remained. In 1780 one of the former Indian fighters, Francis ("the Swamp Fox") Marion, organized a rag-tag group of guerillas which complemented orthodox warfare in South Carolina by continual, devastating raids in the rear of Cornwallis' lines.

A far more important role, however, was played by Spanish-Portuguese guerrillas in Wellington's campaigns in Portugal and Spain. Throughout this long war, effectively commanded guerrilla bands made life miserable for the French armies by completely disrupting their lines of communication—"by blocking the roads, or intercepting couriers and convoys" and even "waging regular war" (Charles Oman, *A History of the Peninsular War*, 6 vol., Oxford University Press, 1902). Numbering no more in the field than 20,000 and "despite their weakness in the open field, their intestine quarrels, their frequent oppression of the countryside, and their ferocity, they rendered good service.... by pinning down ... twice their own numbers of good French troops. Any one who has read the dispatches of the commandants of Napoleon's 'military governments,' or the diaries of the officers who served in Reille's or Dorsenne's or Caffarelli's flying columns, will recognize a remarkable likeness between the situation of affairs in Northern Spain during 1810 and 1811 and that in South Africa during 1900 and 1901." In 1812 Napoleon himself was to suffer heavily from guerrilla strikes during his long retreat from Moscow. In Tolstoi's words, bands of Russian peasants, working with mounted Cossacks, "belabored the French until the whole invading army had been driven out."

Guerrilla warfare in both its independent and complementary roles was employed extensively from Napoleon's day to the present. A striking example of the protest role is the T'ai P'ing Rebellion (1851-64) in China. Begun by impoverished peasants "and

THE BETTMANN ARCHIVE

FRANCIS MARION (1732-95), THE "SWAMP FOX" OF THE AMERICAN REVOLUTION, ESCAPING BRITISH TROOPS BY CROSSING THE PEE DEE RIVER IN NORTH CAROLINA: FROM A PAINTING BY J. A. O'NEILL

GUERRILLA WARFARE

by jobless coolie porters, opium smugglers, and pirates," the unsuccessful rebellion against the Manchu dynasty cost an estimated 20,000,000 lives and, in the opinion of some sinologists, constituted one of "the great social upheavals of modern times" (Ssu-yu Teng and J. K. Fairbank, *China's Response to the West*, Atheneum Publishers, New York, 1963).

Lesser but nonetheless significant independent guerrilla actions were fought against the British in India and Africa, the French and Spanish in Morocco, the Turks and Austro-Hungarians in the Balkans, and the Americans in the opening of the West. In 1900 the Boxer Rebellion in China constituted a protest action against a foreign invader (in the form of the Western powers whose influence ironically had grown as the result of the T'ai P'ing Rebellion) as did both the Philippine insurrection, in which Aguinaldo's guerrillas ultimately lost to American regulars, and the South African War in which the Afrikaners quickly abandoned orthodox tactics in favour of highly mobile, irregular operations undertaken by mounted groups called "commandos," which the British regulars defeated only with the greatest difficulty.

Equally impressive is the concurrent record of complementary guerrilla operations. The most successful guerrilla leader in the American Civil War was a Confederate cavalry officer, John Mosby. Leading a small band of mounted volunteers, Mosby so disrupted Union operations by his constant, dashing raids in northern Virginia that Sheridan finally was forced to devastate the region in order to deprive the guerrilla force of its base.

The static nature of World War I prevented guerrilla warfare on the Western Front, but subsidiary theatres offered two splendid actions. In the Middle East a British officer, T. E. Lawrence (*q.v.*), led a revolt of Arab tribesmen in a prolonged guerrilla action which claimed the lives of some 35,000 Turkish soldiers and another 35,000 captured and wounded; the guerrillas finished the war in control of about 100,000 sq.mi.—without question, a significant contribution to Allenby's victory in Palestine. In German East Africa (today's Tanganyika), a German officer, Lieutenant Colonel Lettow-Vorbeck, led a small force of German regulars supplemented by a few hundred tribesmen in a holding operation against vastly larger British forces which could have been used on the Western Front. Although bereft of supply and nearly physically exhausted, this officer with a handful of followers had still not surrendered when the war ended.

Meanwhile guerrilla fighting of a different nature had broken out in southern Ireland which was in rebellion against British rule. Beginning in Dublin on Easter Monday, 1916, the original insurrection had not proved popular and was instantly put down by the British army garrison. But then the military authorities made a major political-psychological error by court-martialing and condemning to death the 15 principals. The easygoing Irish public was horrified—"horror turned to anger against the government and admiration for the insurgents. The British authorities were, as Bernard Shaw warned them at the time, 'canonizing their prisoners'" (J. C. Beckett, *The Making of Modern Ireland, 1603–1923*, Faber and Faber Ltd., London, Alfred A. Knopf Inc., New York, 1966). The result was a guerrilla war characterized by the most brutal terroristic killings and ambushes and lasting until settlement in 1921.

A still different type of guerrilla action meanwhile was being fought in Russia where in 1918 Lenin's Bolsheviks had stolen control of the revolution and were fighting White Russian counter-revolutionary forces supported by various of the great powers including the United States. This support was probably unwise since, as was the case in Ireland, the new government had not proved particularly popular. The intervention of foreign powers, however, brought a great wave of patriotism to the Russian masses, with many peasants joining partisan movements. Not all guerrillas, however, fought for the Bolshevik cause: "...in the Ukraine the peasant anarchist Nestor Makhno led partisans against, successively, Denikin's Whites, Trotsky's Reds, Wrangel's Whites, and finally everybody, until he fled to Rumania in 1921" (F. L. Schuman, *Russia Since 1917*, Alfred A. Knopf Inc., New York, 1957). This anarchic tendency was repeated in the Ukraine in 1940–45.

The victory of the Russian Reds loosed an international Communist movement which would affect profoundly the history of guerrilla warfare. An almost immediate offshoot of this victory was the establishment of a Communist Party in China. After many vicissitudes and under the later leadership of Mao Tse-tung this movement survived to fight the Japanese invader and, after World War II, to wrest control of the country from Chiang Kai-shek's Nationalist government. The new political factor in warfare became obvious in the Spanish Civil War. In July 1936 a regular army officer, Francisco Franco Bahamonde, led an army mutiny which quickly spread from Spanish Morocco to the mainland. To defeat this force of mutinous Nationalists, the Popular Front left-wing government had to rely primarily on guerrilla forces holding the Nationalist armies while the government built regular armies, a tragic, confused period splendidly presented in Ernest Hemingway's novel *For Whom the Bell Tolls* (1940). The war quickly assumed a political character, the Nationalists being supplied with arms and air power primarily by the Fascist governments of Germany and Italy, the Loyalists being supplied by Communist Russia. It was also characterized by the most brutal cruelties practised by both sides; it lasted three years and claimed an estimated 1,000,000 lives before ending in a Nationalist victory.

Guerrilla warfare in World War II was also marked with strong political overtones. Since Communist parties had been operating, usually clandestinely, in most of the invaded countries, their members were ideally suited for underground warfare, the more so since capture by the German or Japanese enemy meant execution, torture, or banishment to a slave labour camp. In the West, primarily in France and Italy, the Communists either formed their own bands or joined other bands such as the French and Belgian *maquis*, covert organizations engaged in espionage, sabotage, and terrorist activities while performing special missions such as aiding downed Allied pilots to escape back to England. Communist cadres in the Balkans and the Orient formed guerrilla bands which usually operated independently, sometimes in competition with guerrillas representing the legal governments, as Tito did in Yugoslavia. Although some of these groups spent as much time eliminating indigenous opposition while consolidating their own hold on the country as in fighting the enemy, they nonetheless contributed sufficiently to the war effort to continue receiving impressive shipments of arms and equipment from the Western powers—the result of a still controversial Allied decision in which the political goal was subordinated to the demands of military strategy. Rightly or wrongly, the decision resulted in supplying Communist bands in Yugoslavia, Greece, Burma, Thailand, Indochina, the Philippines, and Indonesia; indirectly, the West also equipped Mao Tse-tung's Communist army in that many of Chiang Kai-shek's Nationalist divisions, which were given large amounts of American weapons and equipment, defected in wholesale lots to the Communists.

A slightly different political factor is found in one of the most important guerrilla actions fought in World War II. This resulted from the political error made by the Germans when their armies invaded the U.S.S.R. in 1941. The Russian peasantry in the vast area of the Ukraine were fully prepared to accept the invading Germans as "liberators"; by acting as conquerors and exterminators, the Germans quickly forfeited this immense advantage, a grievous mistake which caused the formation of numerous partisan bands in their rear. Once these semi-independent bands were organized by the Soviet high command (which never entirely trusted them), they caused widespread and at times vital damage to German communications. In the autumn of 1943, in addition to large police and security forces, the German command in the U.S.S.R. was expending 10% of its strength—25 field divisions—in fighting the partisans. Although estimates vary, these guerrillas probably killed more than 250,000 German soldiers while blowing up thousands of trains and trucks and inflicting an inestimable psychological pressure.

The Communist guerrilla forces formed in World War II provided natural political instruments for postwar ambitions. In some cases, such as Yugoslavia, take-over of government was simple and direct, in other cases such as Czechoslovakia and China, it was complicated and delayed. In Vietnam it was only partially accomplished; in Malaya and the Philippines it was foiled. Meanwhile, however, non-Communist insurgencies began using guerrilla warfare with considerable success in such countries as Indonesia, Cyprus, Kenya, and Algeria. In the late 1960s guerrilla warfare was being employed in a complementary role in Vietnam, in a lesser role in Hong Kong, and in a preliminary role in Colombia and other South American countries, as well as in central Africa and Thailand.

Strategy and Tactics.—The broad strategy underlying successful guerrilla warfare is that of protracted harassment accomplished by extremely subtle, flexible tactics designed to wear down the enemy while gaining time either to develop sufficient military strength to defeat him in orthodox battle, or to subject him to internal and external political and military pressures sufficient to cause him to seek peace. This strategy embodies political, social, economic, and psychological factors to which the military element is often subordinated. Essentially a strategy for the morally strong and materially weak, it apparently was practised in antiquity as may be inferred from the warning of the wily Chinese general Sun Tzu (q.v.; c. 350 B.C.): "There has never been a protracted war from which a country has benefited" (Sun Tzu, *The Art of War*, trans. by S. B. Griffith, Oxford University Press, 1963).

Presumably to avoid such, Sun Tzu instructed his generals in words familiar to the successful, latter-day guerrilla leaders: "And therefore I say: Know the enemy, know yourself; your victory will never be endangered. Know the ground, know the weather; your victory will then be total." A successful general "avoids strength and strikes weakness"; the use of tactics based on deception and surprise is the hallmark of a victorious commander.

Sun Tzu's indirect approach was largely ignored in the written commentary covering the wars of centuries. Such an approach does appear now and again—Xenophon wrote in the 4th century B.C. of the importance of the psychological factor in warfare while in the 18th century the French commander Marshal Saxe suggested that it is possible to win a war without fighting battles. Saxe was writing in a time of limited, formal wars which soon gave way to the "total" warfare introduced in the Napoleonic era and which was subsequently treated by the famed Prussian officer-scholar Karl von Clausewitz (q.v.).

Since wars should be fought only for political aims, Clausewitz argued that they must differ in scope and duration. A weaker adversary does not have to destroy the stronger's army in order to gain victory, but rather he must destroy the other's will to wage war. With extensive guerrilla fighting in Spain and Russia still fresh in mind, Clausewitz agreed that partisan warfare could aid the wearing process, provided the theatre of operations was large

enough, the terrain sufficiently rugged, and the partisans themselves temperamentally suited to this type of fighting. A contemporary, the Cossack general Denis Vasilievich Davidov, who led a partisan force during Napoleon's retreat from Moscow, later wrote that this type of warfare "is concerned with the entire area which separates the enemy from his operational base." Its objectives are "to cut the communication lines, destroy all units and wagons wanting to join up with him, inflict surprise blows on the enemy left without food and cartridges and at the same time block his retreat. This is the real meaning of partisan war" (Otto Heilbrunn, *Warfare in the Enemy's Rear*, George Allen & Unwin Ltd., London, 1963, Frederick A. Praeger, Publishers, New York, 1964).

Nearly a century later a young British archaeologist-turned-soldier, Lawrence, offered the world a dramatic demonstration of Davidov's definition. Sent to lead dissident Arab tribes in revolt against the Turks, Lawrence followed a Clausewitzian precept by isolating the Arab political aim which "was unmistakably geographical, to occupy all Arabic-speaking lands in Asia."

To accomplish this aim, Lawrence formed a strategy based on three elements: "one algebraical, one biological, a third psychological," the sum of which defined the war: "The Turkish army was an accident, not a target. Our true strategic aim was to seek its weakest link, and bear only on that till time made the mass of it fall. The Arab army must impose the longest possible passive defense on the Turks (this being the most materially expensive form of war) by extending its own front to the maximum. Tactically, it must develop a highly mobile, highly equipped type of force, of the smallest size, and use it successively at distributed points of the Turkish line." By making the Arabs "an influence, a thing invulnerable, intangible, without front or back, drifting about like a gas," Lawrence would gain "five times the mobility of the Turks [thus] the Arabs could be on terms with them with one-fifth their number."

About the time that Lawrence was incorporating these thoughts for an article for the *Encyclopædia Britannica*, a Communist school-teacher–turned–politician-soldier was developing a doctrine of peasant warfare in China: Mao Tse-tung (q.v.), a young, devoted student of revolution as preached by Marx, practised by Lenin, and qualified by Mao's own considerable experience. Since 1927 he and a band of comrades had been on the run from the Nationalist generalissimo Chiang Kai-shek. In the Fukien-Kiangsi borderlands Mao had helped turn peasants and bandit bands into the first crude Chinese Communist army, one that spent the next eight years fighting for its life against Chiang's forces. Mao's experience had led him to defy his Russian teachers by concluding that the Communist revolution in China could come only from the country peasants, not from the urban proletariat as Russian doctrine demanded. His theory was tested when pressure from Chiang's armies forced him and his followers to undertake a 6,000-mi. march to the north, to Yenan, a mountain hideout in Shensi Province.

The 43-year-old rebel leader now began to codify a doctrine of revolutionary warfare which ultimately would influence his world. Mao looked out from the Yenan mountains and saw two enemies: the Japanese invader and the regularly constituted Kuomintang armies headed by Chiang Kai-shek. He looked on a country "half colonial and half feudal; it is a country that is politically, militarily, and economically backward . . . a vast country with great resources and tremendous population, a country in which the terrain is complicated and the facilities for communication are poor. All these factors favor a protracted war; they all favor the application of mobile [that is, orthodox] warfare and guerrilla operations" (Mao Tse-tung, *On Guerrilla Warfare*, trans. by S. B. Griffith, Frederick A. Praeger, Publishers, New York, 1961, Cassell & Co. Ltd., London, 1962).

Echoing Clausewitz, whom he had studied, Mao insisted on subordinating his war to an overall political strategy. He was too weak to fight both the Japanese and the Kuomintang. He would use one war as a means of growth to fight another more important war. As he put it, "to drive out Japanese imperialism and build an independent, free and happy new China." To accomplish this meant first a truce with Chiang's armies which Mao needed. In

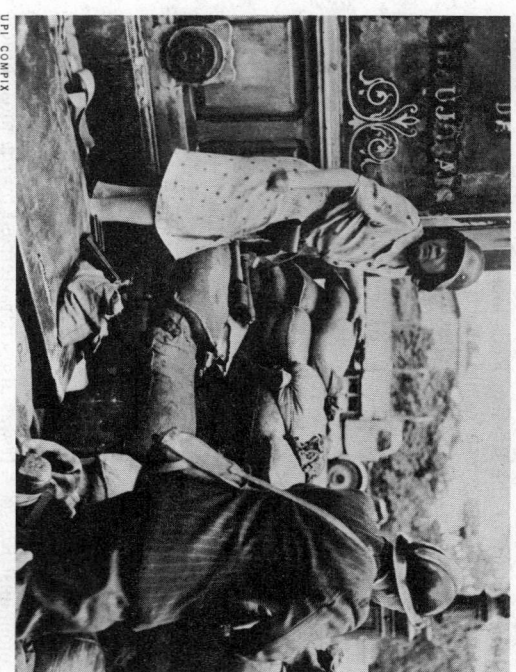

BARRICADED BEHIND SANDBAGS, FRENCH GUERRILLAS, ARMED WITH CAPTURED GERMAN WEAPONS, FIGHT NAZIS DURING THE WEEK BEFORE PARIS WAS LIBERATED IN AUGUST 1944

his famous work, *Yu Chi Chan (On Guerrilla Warfare)*, Mao wrote: "The concept that guerrilla warfare is an end in itself and that guerrilla activities can be divorced from those of the regular forces is incorrect . . . in sum, while we must promote guerrilla warfare as a necessary strategical auxiliary to orthodox operations, we must neither assign it the primary position in our war strategy nor substitute it for mobile and positional warfare as conducted by orthodox forces." With regard to the whole war, "mobile warfare is primary and guerrilla warfare supplementary; with regard to each part, guerrilla warfare is primary and mobile warfare supplementary." Since Mao's force, the Eighth Route Army, was fighting "a part," he called for a basic strategy of "guerrilla warfare"—"but lose no chance for mobile warfare [that is, operations of regular armies] under favorable conditions."

Mao borrowed freely from Sun Tzu's thesis of the indirect approach: "Guerrilla strategy must be based primarily on alertness, mobility, and attack. It must be adjusted to the enemy situation, the terrain, and the existing lines of communication, the relative strengths, the weather, and the situation of the people." It should be used "to exterminate small forces of the enemy; to harass and weaken large forces; to attack enemy lines of communication; to establish bases capable of supporting independent operations in the enemy's rear; to force the enemy to disperse his strength; and to coordinate all these activities with those of the regular armies on distant battle fronts."

To accomplish these goals, Mao demanded tactics based on surprise and deception: "In guerrilla warfare, select the tactic of seeming to come from the east and attacking from the west; avoid the solid, attack the hollow; attack, withdraw; deliver a lightning blow, seek a lightning decision." As opposed to orthodox warfare, which is frequently static, Mao wanted "constant activity and movement. There is in guerrilla warfare no such thing as a decisive battle; there is nothing comparable to the fixed, passive defense that characterizes orthodox war. In guerrilla warfare, the transformation of a moving situation into a positional defensive situation never arises. The general features of reconnaissance, partial deployment, general deployment, and development of the attack that are usual in mobile warfare are not common in guerrilla war." Instead of fixed defense, Mao calls for "alert shifting . . . when the enemy feels the danger of guerrillas, he will generally send troops out to attack them. The guerrillas must consider the situation and decide at what time and at what place they wish to fight. If they find that they cannot fight, they must immediately shift." Although the guerrilla will defend his own operational bases, these must be abandoned when necessary. "We must observe the principle, 'To gain territory is no cause for joy, and to lose territory is no cause for sorrow.'"

Such tactics demand "careful planning . . . those who fight without method do not understand the nature of guerrilla action. A plan is necessary regardless of the size of the unit involved; a prudent plan is as necessary in the case of the squad as in the case of the regiment." As Lawrence put it, "Guerrilla war is far more intellectual than a bayonet charge."

Good planning depends on superior intelligence, of course, and this can only be gained from the people who, in turn, must withhold such from the enemy: "Many people think it impossible for guerrillas to exist for long in the enemy's rear. Such a belief reveals lack of comprehension of the relationship that should exist between the people and the troops. The former may be likened to water and the latter to the fish who inhabit it. How may it be said that these two cannot exist together? It is only undisciplined troops who make the people their enemies and who, like the fish out of its native element, cannot live."

Mao's basic strength came from the people—from the water which produced then supported the fish. From the Yenan haven his agents went forth to select suitable base areas for organization and consolidation, a process in which volunteers were trained and indoctrinated as agitators and propagandists, who in turn went forth to the countryside to enlist peasant support, a process "conspiratorial, clandestine, methodical, and progressive."

In Mao's scheme of things, this phase merges into one of limited direct action, mainly sabotage and terrorism designed to eliminate members of the opposition including the police and other loyal government officials, and to gain arms and supplies for the embryo guerrilla force. This expansion phase may last for years, but if it succeeds it merges into a decisive phase: the destruction of the enemy with the main effort undertaken by orthodox military forces which, however, grew out of the people who were once peasant guerrillas.

Mao's teachings, though perhaps only partially utilized, nonetheless underlie most of the revolutionary wars fought since World War II. In fact his doctrine has become a blueprint for the "national wars of liberation" which Russia, China, and Cuba have promised to foment and support in Asia, Africa, and Central and South America.

Basic Characteristics.—*Motivation.*—Fundamental to the revolutionary process is a cause, which unfortunately is not difficult to find in the underdeveloped countries of the world. The cause may assume several guises: to the world it may be presented as liberating a country from the colonial yoke; to the peasant being converted to Communism, it may be freedom from serfdom, from oppressive taxation, or from payment of oppressive rents to absentee landlords—propaganda which purposely downplays the Communist Party line.

Whether natural or synthetic, whether inspired by international Communism or by virulent nationalism, the political goal is fundamental in motivating people to action. Mao leaves no doubt as to its importance: "Without a political goal, guerrilla warfare must fail, as it must if its political objectives do not coincide with the aspirations of the people and their sympathy, cooperation, and assistance cannot be gained."

Popular Support.—The guerrillas' affiliation with the people is constantly stressed in revolutionary writings. Guerrillas spring from the people who in turn support their spawn, not only by furnishing their sons to the cause, but, when called upon, by furnishing money, food, shelter, refuge, transport, medical aid, intelligence—support which they must attempt to deny the enemy. Although Lawrence called for no more than "a friendly population, not actively friendly, but sympathetic to the point of not betraying rebel movements to the enemy," he also wrote that his rebels "had won a province when the civilians in it had been taught to die for the ideal of freedom: the presence or absence of the enemy was a secondary matter." Gen. George Grivas, the non-Communist, professional soldier who led the Cypriot rebellion wrote that a guerrilla war, no matter who its leader may be, stands no chance of success unless having "the complete and unreserved support of the majority of the country's inhabitants" (G. Grivas, *General Grivas on Guerrilla Warfare,* trans. by A. A. Pallis, Longmans, Green & Co. Ltd., Harlow, Eng., 1964, Frederick A. Praeger, Publishers, New York, 1965).

Organization.—Protracted revolutionary warfare as defined by Mao demands a complicated organization both on the political and military levels. Mao recommends a clandestine system of parallel hierarchy beginning with the cadre or cellular party structure at the hamlet-village level and proceeding to the top via district, province, and regional command structures. This organization comprises regular military forces supplemented by territorial forces, both on a regional and local basis. The latter, which Ho Chi Minh's government in North Vietnam calls "popular forces," comprises guerrilla units, militia or "home guard" units, and auxiliary service units.

The tactical organization of guerrilla units varies according to operational demands. Mao called for a guerrilla squad of 9 to 11; Grivas employed sabotage groups of 4 or 5. In the Vietnam fighting the Vietminh and later the Viet Cong ranged from small squads up to battalion and even regimental strengths.

Arms.—The guerrilla by necessity employs a wide variety of weapons, some self-manufactured, some captured, and some supplied from outside sources. In the earlier stages of the war, the weapons are usually primitive—in Mao's words, "a kitchen knife, a wooden cudgel, an axe, a hoe, a wooden stool, or a stone" (Mao Tse-tung, *Basic Tactics,* trans. by Stuart R. Schram, Frederick A. Praeger, Publishers, New York, 1966, Pall Mall Press, Ltd., London, 1967). Americans in Vietnam have frequently encountered homemade rifles, hand grenades, and Claymore mines; trails booby-trapped with punji stakes soaked in urine; and shallow pits lined with nail boards. Nearly every guerrilla war has produced ingenious improvisation, both because of necessity and to avoid a cumbersome logistic "tail." Nothing can be simpler to construct and use than a Molotov cocktail or a *plastique* bomb, yet under certain conditions nothing can be more effective. Castro's guerrillas employed an effective antitank weapon "rigged up from a shotgun; it was made of a cartridge with a long wooden rod substituted for the projectile, and the [Molotov] cocktail fastened on the forward end of the rod" (Ernesto Guevara, *Che Guevara on Guerrilla Warfare*, ed. by Harries-Clichy Peterson, Frederick A. Praeger, Publishers, New York, 1961, Cassell & Co. Ltd., London, 1962). When tarred roads prevented Cypriot guerrillas from planting mines they constructed "a small cannon—a tube of any size, closed at one end and filled with explosive or gunpowder mixed with fragments of iron which acted as projectiles. This contraption was made fast to a tree or wall by the side of the road at a suitable height and angle, so that when it was electrically detonated the projectile should strike the target . . . it yielded excellent results" (Grivas, *op. cit.*).

Terrain.—It is axiomatic with Mao and his followers that revolution begins in the country. Once sufficient "base" and "guerrilla" areas are established, "operations may be extended to include cities and lines of communication not strongly held." This rural strategy is influenced by such factors as the political goal, geography, the insurgent strength, and the government's strength.

Such was the combination of these in Russia that the 1917 revolution was decided in the cities, and only later successfully defended in the country by orthodox Communist armies employing guerrilla forces in a complementary role. The Irish Rebellion was also fought largely in the cities. Taking a page from that book, General Grivas opened the semisuccessful Cypriot rebellion with a few combat groups especially trained in terrorist-sabotage tactics. As his strength grew, he resorted to guerrilla warfare with which he transformed "the whole island into one general field of combat." On the basis of this and other examples, Grivas later argued that, contrary to Mao's teachings, guerrilla warfare need not be rural-based, and further that it sometimes is possible for guerrilla warfare alone to accomplish the political objective.

Terror.—As Goya makes clear in his famous etchings, "Los Desastres de la Guerra," there is nothing attractive about guerrilla warfare. One of its most hideous characteristics is the use of terror: assassination, a hand grenade thrown into a crowd, an indiscriminate bombing—actions familiar to any insurgency. Although the Communists usually practise selective terrorism in the early stages of an insurgency, they quickly employ mass terrorist tactics, usually kidnapping and assassination, when the war begins to go against them. In Vietnam they killed thousands of loyal government officials who were trying to implement social and economic reforms; to bolster their own strength they "increasingly

resorted to coercing, kidnapping and pressing young peasants into the Viet Cong organization" (George K. Tanham, *War Without Guns*, Frederick A. Praeger, Publishers, New York, 1966).

Terror is used for several reasons: to focus world attention on the rebel cause, to eliminate opposition leaders, to paralyze normal government activity, to intimidate the general populace, to keep one's own guerrillas from defecting. It is difficult to assess the psychological impact of terrorist tactics on the general population. Apparently, within limits most people accept it as a necessary part of revolutionary warfare. Should the method be unduly exaggerated, however, public opinion is apt to turn sharply against the guerrillas as it did against the Mau Maus in Kenya and the Huks in the Philippines, and, in some cases, the Viet Cong in Vietnam.

Sanctuary.—Guerrilla forces cannot fight all the time. They must control safe areas to which they can retire, voluntarily or involuntarily, for rest, recuperation, repair of arms, clothing, and equipment, and where recruits can be indoctrinated, trained, and equipped. Such areas traditionally are located in remote, rugged terrain, usually mountains, forests, and jungles; but "guerrilla areas" may be developed in which whole villages and hamlets serve a sanctuary role. The sea can also provide sanctuary, as in the Peninsular War when the British navy succored Wellington's cooperating Portuguese-Spanish guerrillas.

Sanctuary may also be provided by sympathetic neighbouring countries; during the Greek Civil War the Communist guerrillas frequently retreated into Yugoslavia, which not only offered physical sanctuary but also arms and supplies; and it was only after Tito closed the border that these guerrillas were finally defeated.

Similarly, Ho Chi Minh's guerrillas, in the later stages of the war against France, relied on China for refuge, training, and supply of arms and equipment. It is doubtful if Ho's army commander, Vo Nguyen Giap, could have won the Battle of Dien Bien Phu without artillery supplied by China; it is also doubtful if he could have maintained orthodox military operations against South Vietnam and the United States without continuing aid from China and Russia.

Successful prosecution of a revolutionary war does not always demand a foreign sanctuary. The Huks in the Philippines and the Chinese in Malaya fought long and hard without this advantage; the vast expense of China offered Mao ample room for guerrilla tactics against the Japanese and later against Chiang's demoralized divisions that resulted in the capture of generous quantities of arms, ammunition, and equipment. Despite the sanctuary of North Vietnam, the Viet Cong used Mao's guerrilla tactics in South Vietnam, that is the development of regional base areas supplemented by "guerrilla areas," which Mao defined as smaller bases controlled by guerrillas only when in physical occupation.

The people offer a final form of sanctuary. At one time during the Cypriot revolt, Grivas was surrounded by a British force for nearly two months, "but though the enemy had spotted me . . . I was able again and again to escape capture or death." An Algerian rebel leader was able to install himself within two hundred yards of the army commandant's headquarters in Algiers "and remain there without being found for several months before his arrest." (Trinquier, *op. cit.*) In South Vietnam in 1964 American officials discovered that several thousand supposedly government-controlled "fortified" hamlets were in fact controlled by Viet Cong guerrillas "who often used them for supply and rest havens" (Staff of the Senate Republican Policy Committee, *The War in Vietnam*, Public Affairs Press, Washington, D.C., 1967).

Guerrilla Forces.—*The Leaders.*—The unusual requirements of guerrilla warfare call for outstanding leadership at all levels if a guerrilla force is to survive and prosper. The vicissitudes of these wars demand a leader not only endowed with extraordinary intelligence and courage, but one buttressed by an almost fanatic belief in himself and his cause. Lenin, Trotski, Lawrence, Lettow-Vorbeck, Michael Collins, Eamon de Valera, Mao, Tito, the Filipino Louis Taruc, the Kenyan Jomo Kenyatta, Ho Chi Minh, Vo Nguyen Giap, the Algerian Ahmed ben Bella, Castro, Ernesto ("Che") Guevara—these and dozens of their lieutenants at lower levels: unusual, unorthodox personalities generally with civilian

FILIPINO GUERRILLAS DURING WORLD WAR II SEARCH FOR JAPANESE SNIPERS ON LEYTE

backgrounds and holding political philosophies virtually incomprehensible to the average professional officer. Yet each proved able to attract a handful of followers, to organize them and instill a disciplined zeal matched only in the most elite military organizations, to lead them often against great odds, to suffer hunger, humiliation, misery, wounds, prison, sometimes torture and death—and, for some of them, finally to win.

The Recruit.—Selectivity is the key in nearly all "hard-core" cases. Mao preferred "volunteers," but went to great administrative lengths to attract them. Lawrence wanted fighters offering "special initiative, endurance and enthusiasm." Grivas demanded "to the highest degree the qualities of boldness, resourcefulness, cunning initiative, optimism, a strong constitution, sobriety, and resistance to hardships." Che Guevara, who in 1967 was killed while leading a guerrilla force in Bolivia, wanted young men at once "audacious and optimistic . . . adaptable, imaginative, and inventive."

It is easier to attract suitable recruits early in an insurgency or during the course of a particularly successful one than later or when success seems doubtful. Protracted war, however, works both for and against the guerrilla leader. In the war against the French in Indochina, the Vietminh "put great effort into sporadic recruiting campaigns, which combined pressure with propaganda and enticement. It is known that some young men were forcibly dragged into the armed forces, and that in other cases indirect pressure was brought to bear on families or village leaders to supply recruits. Usually, a strong-arm and other pressure methods were accompanied by propaganda appeals to the prospective recruits to serve their country against the European imperialists and for the betterment of society" (George K. Tanham, *Communist Revolutionary Warfare*, Frederick A. Praeger, Publishers, New York, 1961).

Communist recruiting normally begins at the village level, generally by inducing peasant-candidates to join one or more front groups and participate, if only indirectly, in the war effort. After exposure to suitable propaganda as well as political indoctrination, the candidate will join the village guerrilla cell after which he can be promoted to the regional and regular forces.

Training.—As might be expected, formal military training of the guerrilla soldier is variable, but generally rudimentary. In such instances as Mao's Long March or Tito's and Ho's World War II resistance movements in Yugoslavia and Indochina, both leaders and followers were self-taught. In Arabia, where tribal organization existed, training was confined to weapons which Lawrence judged necessary for the mission: elementary demolition techniques and light machine guns "for use not as machine guns, but as automatic rifles, snipers' tools." Grivas, on the other hand, started with men "of no war experience or even trained in

the use of arms." He organized 4 or 5 man combat groups which he trained "under the noses of the British," then allowed on-the-job training in skirmishes against the police and finally against British army forces. Castro's original band was largely self-taught; only later did he establish special schools to teach recruits "commando" tactics which included stress on "rifle marksmanship and ammunition discipline" (Guevara, *op. cit.*).

During Ho's war against the French, the Communists relied largely on a self-training program which included "some instruction in the use of personal weapons, as well as lessons in sabotage." More advanced guerrilla units received "close-order drill and even instruction on automatic weapons" (Tanham, *op. cit.*). In view of the supply of modern Chinese and Russian weapons, the Viet Cong guerrilla undoubtedly received more advanced training.

The Communist camp has always emphasized political training. Guerrilla leaders in Vietnam continually stress political education in order "to produce politically reliable and enthusiastic soldiers and to provide effective propaganda agents" (Tanham, *op. cit.*). Mao insisted that his guerrillas be taught "a precise conception of the political goal of the struggle and the political organization to be used in attaining that goal" in order to "carry out the political activities that are the life of both the guerrilla armies and of revolutionary warfare."

Discipline.—Although Communist leaders preach a rejection of the normal concept of military or group discipline in favour of that stemming from the individual conscience, they go to enormous trouble to keep their disciples in an unquestioning frame of mind. At a very early stage the Communist recruit is taught that failure to carry out orders unquestioningly will result in harsh punishment. The omniscience of the party hierarchy is pounded home through an incessant barrage of lectures, propaganda broadcasts, and entertainments while individual behaviour is constantly examined and judged in self-criticism group sessions, which continue throughout a guerrilla's connection with the party.

Since it is essential for the guerrilla to win and retain popular support, he is also taught to practise circumspect behaviour when among the people. Communist leaders in China, Cuba, and Vietnam have drawn up lengthy codes of individual behaviour: the Chinese guerrilla, for example, was required to pay a peasant for food, to respect his property, and not to offend propriety by undressing in front of a peasant woman. In discussing this code, Guevara added a typically Latin touch: if the guerrilla had no money, he was to offer an IOU.

It is questionable to what depth party-imposed discipline descends in the average Communist guerrilla, no matter the nationality. Unquestionably the hard-core guerrilla practises an almost ascetic association with the people while approaching his military tasks with dogged determination. But, judging from interrogations of Viet Cong guerrilla prisoners and from the number of Viet Cong defectors, the guerrilla's discipline varies as ideological beliefs ebb and flow in the physical and moral tides of war.

Counterguerrilla Warfare.—In waging this type of warfare, which calls for location, isolation, and elimination of the entire guerrilla apparatus (political as well as military), orthodox military commanders have employed and continue to employ a wide range of weapons and tactics which, judged by results, are more appropriate to a conventional warfare situation. Wholesale bombings and mass artillery interdictions of suspected sanctuary areas, division and corps strength "sweeping" operations in which a few guerrillas are captured or killed but whole villages are destroyed, the establishment of defended but isolated chains of military outposts, mass arrests and interrogations—each has failed to achieve notable triumphs. In a preface to Colonel Trinquier's book on revolutionary warfare, Bernard Fall aptly wrote: "American readers—particularly those who are concerned with today's operations in South Vietnam—will find to their surprise that their various seemingly 'new' counter-insurgency gambits, from strategic hamlets to large-scale pacification, are mere rehashes of old tactics to which helicopters, weed killers, and rapid-firing rifles merely add a new dimension of speed and bloodiness without basically changing the character of the struggle—nor its outcome, if the same *political* errors that the French have made are repeated."

UPI COMPIX
MARSHAL TITO (RIGHT), LEADER OF YUGOSLAV PARTISANS DURING WORLD WAR II, AND AN ASSISTANT AT WORK IN A CAVE THAT SERVED AS THE PARTISAN COMMAND POST

Although Fall's conclusion stems from a realistic appraisal of Mao Tse-tung's codification of revolutionary warfare, even as modified by other insurgent leaders, it was scarcely a revolutionary pronouncement. Throughout history, nations have impelled insurgencies because of political errors and military commanders have failed to quell insurgencies because of political ignorance.

The political consideration is always important; in Communist revolutionary warfare it is paramount. If the Communist guerrilla is not supported by the people—if he is not a fish in the sea of humanity—he cannot effectively operate for any length of time. Consequently the government must win the people's support, both to deprive the guerrilla of this support and to obtain information on which to base tactics of destruction. It is not enough to break up guerrilla bands and kill individual guerrillas. A government can claim victory only when the subversive organization behind each level of an insurgency has been destroyed and when viable government has been achieved—a process conveniently described by a French officer, General Allard, as "destruction" and "construction" (Peter Paret, *French Revolutionary Warfare from Indochina to Algeria*, Frederick A. Praeger, Publishers, New York, 1964).

Such counterinsurgency campaigns as those conducted in the Philippines and in Malaya prove that the Communist guerrilla ultimately can be defeated (but not necessarily eliminated). The means of defeat, however, lie only in a patient and judicious application of a host of civil and military measures—a blend of social-economic-police-military factors. Although in the course of a counterinsurgency campaign one or another of these factors may assume a temporary supremacy, in the end each must remain integral to an overall political consideration.

Indeed, political realism is the first essential in conducting a counterinsurgency: the recognition of weakness as well as strength, of failure as well as success. An insurgency indicates a breakdown of government in that a minority is able to defy law and order while coercing others to offer either active or passive support to the cause. The opening phase of a Communist insurgency, what can be called "subversion supported by selective terrorism" (Robert Thompson, *Defeating Communist Insurgency*, Frederick A. Praeger, Publishers, New York, Chatto and Windus Ltd., London, 1966), must be recognized for what it is, and must be met by specific governmental measures, both covert and overt. Because this phase is generally covert, the government, usually the police, must practise considerable subtlety in a difficult environment at best; where internal weakness, ineptness, or corruption are at work, or where an outside force, usually war, has disrupted the normal functioning of government, then the task becomes almost insuperable. In such cases the insurgency usually flares into the second "armed struggle" phase, which brings guerrilla warfare into the open.

In the opening phase or phases of an insurgency, a government is usually on the defensive. In Malaya this was the period in which the government "prevented the enemy from taking over and kept the insurgency from escalating." The general theme was security both by maintaining police functions and, militarily, by splitting up (but not attempting to destroy) the larger guerrilla units. These "holding" operations gave the government time to marshal its forces (not just police and military) in order to fight the second or offensive phase "in which the enemy's power to beat us was broken," and, finally, the third or victory phase which destroyed the last remnants of guerrilla forces while establishing a stable, independent government (R. L. Clutterbuck, *The Long, Long War*, Frederick A. Praeger, Publishers, New York, 1966).

One veteran of the Malayan campaign ascribes the government's success to certain basic principles, which he holds essential for the conduct of any counterinsurgency: (1) the government must have a clear political aim, ideally "to establish and maintain a free, independent and united country which is politically and economically stable and viable"; (2) in ferreting out, neutralizing, and destroying guerrillas, the government, no matter how tempted, must function in accordance with law and with a carefully developed counterinsurgency plan, which grants priority to defeating the political subversion, not the guerrillas per se; (3) finally, in fighting the guerrillas, the government must first develop base areas before commencing aggressive tactics (Thompson, *op. cit.*).

These principles need not unduly restrict the counterguerrilla efforts. Most authorities agree that emergency regulations, often harsh, must be legally invoked. In Malaya these included compulsory census, an enforceable identity-card system, suspension of habeas corpus (but with carefully publicized safeguards) permission to search private property without a warrant, the death sentence for persons caught with unauthorized weapons, harsh sentences for those aiding the Communists, flexible power of curfew; later extraordinary measures included the right to shoot on sight in prohibited areas, the right to resettle whole villages, the right to control food distribution with harsh penalties, including death, for those found guilty of aiding the enemy.

Such regulations, of course, are not attractive. If indiscriminately applied, as unfortunately is sometimes the case, they will lead to an increasing alienation of the civil population from the government. Where properly applied, however, they will aid greatly the police and military forces in their essential mission of providing security to the civil populace, which, in turn, will then feel more free to provide essential information on which to base further counterguerrilla operations.

The exact nature of such operations must vary in accordance with the enemy's strength and the area concerned. The first priority of government is to reestablish law and order, which, in a rural area, means revitalizing the rural police function. The military effort, the strength of which is dictated by necessity, concentrates on "clearing" operations designed to break up and disperse large guerrilla formations, then to keep them deprived of the initiative by small-unit tactics, mainly patrols and ambushes based on valid intelligence. The "clearing" operation is followed by the "holding" operation, which is designed to "restore government authority . . . and to establish a firm security framework" (Thompson, *op. cit.*). The "holding operation" is the period of "winning the hearts and minds" of the people, first by providing security, which will be maintained by strategic hamlets defended by organized hamlet militias working in conjunction with government forces where necessary, second by providing social reforms (land reform, schools, hospitals, community projects) which will identify the government with the people's best interests. Once won over, the people will deprive the guerrillas of vital support besides furnishing information necessary for police and military forces to penetrate and destroy the local Communist organization. At the same time the government must make every effort to capture guerrillas (who will then be "turned" against their own) as well as to establish defector programs based along the lines of Ramón Magsaysay's classic program in the Philippines in the 1950s (N. D. Valeriano and C. T. R. Bohannan, *Counter-Guerrilla Operations*, Frederick A. Praeger, Publishers, New York, 1962).

The "clearing" and "holding" operations provide the key to successful counterguerrilla warfare. Where they have been applied qualitatively, as in Malaya, they have proven successful; where applied quantitatively, as in Vietnam, they have in large part failed. Even under the most favourable circumstances, most governments lack the necessary civil, police, and military resources to carry out "clear and hold" operations simultaneously in all areas. For this reason, the military effort may have to extend to secondary operations in lower priority areas. These are designed to keep the guerrilla off-balance until the civil effort can be enlarged. Such operations may include large-scale "sweep and clear" actions in which units are parachuted into guerrilla sanctuaries and supplied by air drop while establishing and maintaining permanent ambushes, sometimes with the aid of friendly tribes.

Such may be the strength of the insurgency and the weakness of the legal government that outside aid is called for, as happened in Vietnam. Unless limited to supply, technical training, and professional advice, outside aid may well prove a two-edged sword. If the donor government underestimates the dimensions of the conflict, as happened with the United States in the case of Vietnam, it is persuaded with a military intervention which, by escalating the war from the extent needed for victory, tends to "take-over" the host government, thus widening the gulf between the people and the host government

and their government and providing the Communist enemy with propaganda for the familiar charge of imperialist aggression.

Legal Status.—For understandable reasons, the orthodox military commander has always placed the guerrilla in an extralegal status. After the British were stung several times by Francis Marion in the **Revolutionary War**, they complained that he fought neither "like a gentleman" or "a Christian." Napoleon's marshals on the Spanish peninsula were driven to violent reprisals against Spanish-Portuguese guerrillas with one result that for every guerrilla shot a French prisoner paid with his life, a "barbarous system" finally concluded by mutual agreement. The problem arose again in the American Civil War; when Gen. Eleazar A. Paine, the Union commander in western Kentucky, was unduly harassed by guerrillas he published this proclamation: "I shall shoot every guerrilla taken in my district, and if your Southern brethren retaliate by shooting a Federal soldier, I will walk out five of your rich bankers, and cotton men, and make you kneel down and shoot them. I will do it, so help me God" (Richard Bennett, *The Black and Tans*, Hulton, David Higham Associates, London, 1959).

The Brussels international conference of 1874 provided that in order to be recognized as lawful belligerents guerrillas must answer to a specific commander, must wear a distinctive badge, carry arms openly, and must conform in operations to the laws and customs of war. The Hague conferences on the rules of land warfare in 1899 and 1907 adopted this definition with a few modifications.

The Hague ruling has not prospered mainly because conformance would nullify the advantages of guerrilla warfare, but also because sabotage and terrorist tactics often breed brutal reprisals far removed from the rules of warfare. From the Philippine insurrection (1899–1902) to the present, the guerrilla has been held fair game for torture or for execution without trial. A French veteran of guerrilla warfare, Colonel Trinquier, wrote concerning the Algerian war: "No lawyer is present for such an interrogation [of the terrorist]. If the prisoner gives the information requested, the examination is quickly terminated; if not, specialists must force his secret from him. Then, as a soldier, he must face the suffering, and perhaps the death, he has heretofore managed to avoid. The terrorist must accept this as a condition inherent in his trade and in the method of warfare that, with full knowledge, his superiors and he himself have chosen" (Roger Trinquier, *Modern Warfare*, Frederick A. Praeger, Publishers, New York, Pall Mall Press, Ltd, London, 1964). As in the Peninsular War of the early 19th century, the guerrilla, unable to expect just treatment, has continued to render unjust treatment, a cycle of horror reaching its zenith in the Spanish Civil War and in the partisan actions of World War II.

The advent of revolutionary warfare has further complicated the legal aspects of guerrilla warfare. What statute of international law can deal with the legality of a neighbouring country providing sympathetic sanctuary for a guerrilla force? What is the legal status of the counterguerrilla who disguises himself as a guerrilla? Is it morally correct for a government to grant amnesty to and even reward guerrillas who are known to have murdered loyal citizens? Is it morally correct that the fate of a captured guerrilla should be subject to the whim of the individual military commander? Can torture, no matter the information at stake, ever be condoned by a civilized government? What is the legal status of an outside belligerent such as the American soldier fighting an undeclared war in Vietnam?

Perhaps because of the complexity of such questions, a trend is under way to tame the guerrilla with the aid of various defector programs or, in the case of captives, rehabilitation by political education and psychological persuasion.

Despite this new approach the guerrilla will probably remain the bandit of the battlefield.

BIBLIOGRAPHY.—Sir John Fortescue, *Wellington* (1925); Deneys Reitz, *Commando* (1929); Karl von Clausewitz, *On War*, trans. by J. J. Graham, 3 vol. (1940); Stuart Schram, *Mao Tse-tung* (1966); Richard Goodwin, *Triumph or Tragedy: Reflections on Vietnam* (1966); V. D. Sokolovskii, *Soviet Military Strategy*, trans. by H. S. Dinerstein et al. (1963); Charles Oman, *A History of the Peninsular War*, 6 vol. (1902); Gabriel Jackson, *The Spanish Republic and the Civil War, 1931–1939* (1965); James Cameron, *The African Revolution* (1961); Ian Henderson and Philip C. Goodhart, *Man Hunt in Kenya* (1958); Sun Tzu, *The Art of War*, trans. by S. B. Griffith (1963); George K. Tanham, *Communist Revolutionary Warfare* (1961); *War Without Guns* (1966); Mao Tse-tung, *On Guerrilla Warfare*, trans. by S. B. Griffith (1961); Peter Paret, *French Revolutionary Warfare from Indochina to Algeria* (1964); David Galula, *Counterinsurgency Warfare* (1964); T. E. Lawrence, *Seven Pillars of Wisdom* (1935); J. C. Beckett, *The Making of Modern Ireland, 1603–1923* (1966); Richard Bennett, *The Black and Tans* (1959); Edgar Holt, *Protest in Arms* (1960); Otto Heilbrunn, *Warfare in the Enemy's Rear* (1963); N. D. Valeriano and C. T. R. Bohannan, *Counter-Guerrilla Operations* (1962); G. Grivas, *General Grivas on Guerrilla Warfare* (1965); Abdul H. Nasution, *Fundamentals of Guerrilla Warfare* (1965); Roger Trinquier, *Modern Warfare* (1964); Richard L. Clutterbuck, *The Long, Long War* (1966); Bernard B. Fall, *Hell in a Very Small Place* (1966); L. Huberman and P. M. Sweezy, *Cuba: Anatomy of a Revolution* (1960); Charles Thayer, *Guerrilla* (1963). (R. B. As.)

GUESDE, JULES (legal name, MATHIEU BASLE) (1845–1922), organizer and early leader of the Marxist wing of the French labour movement, was born in Paris, Nov. 11, 1845. Guesde began his career as a radical journalist, and in 1877 founded one of the first modern socialist weeklies, *Égalité*. Guesde consulted with Karl Marx and Paul Lafargue (a son-in-law of Marx) in 1880 on a socialist program of French labour action. Adopted by a national labour congress in 1880, the program called on workers to elect representatives sworn to "conduct the class struggle in the halls of parliament"; *i.e.*, to stand uncompromisingly for the establishment of the socialist state. Guesde was opposed by labour opportunists—in French usage, the "possibilists"—who sought labour's gains by tactics of economic and political pressure-group action—aggressive collective bargaining, strikes and the promise of workingmen's votes to favourable political candidates regardless of their party affiliations. The split between "Guesdists" and "possibilists" is an early French manifestation of a fundamental line along which the labour movements of the western world continue to be divided. Guesde served in the chamber of deputies beginning in 1893 and as minister without portfolio in 1914 and 1915. A fertile author and powerful orator, he died July 28, 1922, at St. Mandé, Seine.

See Alexandre Zévaès, *Jules Guesde, 1845–1922* (1929), which contains a complete list of his writings; Suzanne Lacore, *Jules Guesde* (1945). (G. W. Z.)

GUEST, EDGAR ALBERT (1881–1959), U.S. writer of verse which was widely syndicated in newspapers, was born in Birmingham, Eng., on Aug. 20, 1881, and was brought to the United States in 1891. Four years later he went to work for the *Detroit Free Press*, first as a police reporter and then as a writer of daily rhymes which became so popular that they were eventually distributed to newspapers throughout the country and made his name a household word. His first commercially published book, *A Heap o' Livin'* (1916), became a best seller and was followed by similar collections of his optimistic rhymes on such subjects as home, mother and the virtue of hard work. Guest, who became a U.S. citizen in 1902, also appeared on radio and television. He died Aug. 5, 1959, in Detroit, Mich.

GUEUX (GEUZEN; that is, BEGGARS), the nickname of the Netherlands insurgents against Philip II of Spain, particularly the Calvinists. On April 5, 1566, when the members of the nobility who had signed the "Compromise" (*see* NETHERLANDS, THE: *History*), led by Hendrik of Brederode (*q.v.*), presented their "Request" to the regent, Margaret of Austria, duchess of Parma, at Brussels, Charles, comte de Berlaymont, is said to have contemptuously referred to these petitioners as *gueux*, possibly an allusion to the impoverished state of many of them. They at once adopted this name and gloried in it. At a banquet Brederode, wearing a beggar's wallet and holding a beggar's bowl, proposed a toast to the "Beggars," which was answered by cries of "*Vivent les Gueux!*" Afterward, the name was applied to rebels of all ranks. (A. G. J.)

GUEVARA, ANTONIO DE (1481?–1545), Spanish moralist, court preacher and chronicler, born near Santillana, is best known for his didactic novel *Reloj de príncipes* (1529), one of the most influential and widely translated books of the 16th century despite contemporaries' annoyance at his mischievous attribution of parts of it to Marcus Aurelius, whose *Meditations* only came to light in 1558. The *Epistolas familiares* (1539–42), better known abroad as the *Epîtres dorées*, achieved almost equal success. Guevara aimed at creating an aureate diction for prose as antithetical character of his style was much exaggerated by his English translators (Lord Berners, *Golden Boke of M. Aurelius*, 1535; Sir Thomas North, *Diall of Princes*, 1557), and John Lyly (*q.v.*) is indebted to him for matter rather than manner. His other chief work, dealing as usual with a commonplace (here the antithesis of town and country), is the *Menosprecio de Corte* (1539).

BIBLIOGRAPHY.—M. de Riquer, *Prosa escogida de Fray Antonio de Guevara* (1943); L. Karl, "La Fortune des oeuvres d'A. de Guevara à l'étranger," in *Bulletin Hispanique* (1938); M. R. Lida, articles in *Revista de filología hispánica* (1945) and *Archivo Ibero-Americano* (1946). (F. S. R.)

GUEVARA, LUIS VÉLEZ DE: see VÉLEZ DE GUEVARA, LUIS.

GUGGENHEIM, the name of a family of U.S. industrialists founded by Meyer Guggenheim (1828–1905) who, together with his seven sons, developed world-wide mining interests. Meyer Guggenheim, born in Lengnau, Switz., Feb. 1, 1828, emigrated to the U.S. when he was 19, settling in Philadelphia, Pa. In 1872 he established the firm of Guggenheim and Pulaski, importers of Swiss embroideries, later reorganized as Guggenheim and Sons, with the four oldest sons as partners. In 1888 the company sold its lace business and entered copper mining and smelting, forming the Philadelphia Smelting and Refining Co. in 1888. Smelters were built at Philadelphia and in Colorado and Mexico, and ore deposits were acquired throughout the world. Alliances with mine owners were established in an attempt to integrate and control both mining and processing operations. The Guggenheims defeated the American Smelting and Refining Co. in a struggle for control of the industry, and took control of that company in 1901. Meyer Guggenheim died March 15, 1905; his sons continued the management.

DANIEL GUGGENHEIM (1856–1930) was largely responsible for the smelting operations of the firm, and his operations were international in scope. He developed tin mines in Bolivia, gold mines in Alaska, diamond fields in Africa, copper mines in Utah, nitrate fields in Chile and rubber plantations in the Congo. The firm established smelting and refining plants all over the world. Simon GUGGENHEIM (1867–1941) was United States senator from Colorado (1907–13). In 1925 he and his wife established, as a memorial to their son, the John Simon Guggenheim Memorial foundation "to further the development of scholars and artists by assisting them to engage in research ... under the freest possible conditions." HARRY F. GUGGENHEIM (1890–1971), industrialist and foundation executive, was born Aug. 23, 1890, son of Daniel Guggenheim. He graduated at the University of Cambridge. He was associated with the company properties and headed the Daniel and Florence Guggenheim foundation for research in aeronautics and the Solomon Guggenheim foundation. In 1929–33 he was United States ambassador to Cuba. (J. R. LT.)

GUIANA, FRENCH. French Guiana (Guyane Française), an overseas *département* of France, lies on the north coast of South America. It is bounded on the south and the east by Brazil, on the west by Surinam, and on the north by the Atlantic Ocean. Among the numerous islands offshore are the Îles du Salut, of which Devil's Island (*q.v.*), the French penal settlement, became the most famous. The frontiers, long in dispute, were fixed along the Maroni River with Surinam by the arbitration of the tsar of Russia in 1891, and along the Oyapock River with Brazil by Swiss arbitration in 1900.

GEOGRAPHY

Geology and Structure.—Geologically, the country falls into three distinct zones. In the extreme south lies part of the great range of the Guiana Highlands, formed from ancient granites and characterized by low tabular mountains, some of volcanic origin, reaching a height of 600–700 m. (1,950–2,300 ft.). This area is bounded to the north and west by a region of foothills, never rising higher than 350 m. (1,148 ft.) with steep sides and flattish tops, running parallel with the coast. The coastal strip, about 15 to 40 km. (10–25 mi.) wide, itself comprises low plains formed from Quaternary marine deposits, from which spring occasional small isolated hills, dignified by the inhabitants with the appellation "mountain" or "mount."

Climate.—Guiana as a whole lies in an equatorial zone, mainly on the thermal equator, but its climate is profoundly influenced by its proximity to the sea. It is continually affected by the trade winds, especially those from the northeast. Rainfall is heavy on the east coast (4 m. [157 in.] per year) but is less excessive inland. The seasons are determined by the regular periods of rainfall. A short rainy season between mid-December and February is followed by a short dry season (described locally as the "little March summer") lasting from the end of February until mid-April. The main dry season from August to December. The main rainy season extends from April to July and the humidity is always very great, as much as 90%. The temperature is almost constant throughout the year, the average for January being 25° C (77° F) and that for October 27° C (81° F). Temperatures rise during the daytime, and the nights can be cold.

Drainage.—The high rainfall and the unabsorbent nature of the ground have combined to produce in French Guiana a large number of rivers. Depressions at the feet of the mountain regions tend to hold surplus water accumulated during the rainy seasons, with the result that the level of the rivers is normally uniform throughout the year. These rivers, running in general northeastward, have numerous rapids, some of which are about 500 m. (546 yd.) long. The main rivers, enumerated from east to west, are the Oyapock (with its tributaries the Yaroupi and the Camopi flowing in to it from the west); the Approuague; the Kaw River, which is joined, from the west, by the Comté; the Sinnamary, joined by the Courcibo; the Iracoubo; the Mana; and the Maroni, into which the Tampoc, Ouaqui, the Inini, and the Abounamy flow, all from French Guianian territory.

Soils.—French Guiana has three types of soil, roughly corresponding to the three distinct geological zones. The earth in the interior highland region, made up of decomposed granite, newly formed shale, and dolerites, is usually of poor quality except in the patches of volcanic deposits. Along the rivers and across a fairly wide strip of land running parallel to the coast between

DEVIL'S ISLAND, A FORMER FRENCH PENAL COLONY, OFF THE COAST OF FRENCH GUIANA

GUIANA

Cayenne and Iracoubo the soil is alluvial. On the coastal plains, comprising mainly 200,000 ha. (494,200 ac.) of swamp, forest land, and bush to the east of Cayenne, the soil is exceptionally rich because of the nature of the underlying clay and the absence of erosion. If adequate drainage were installed, the 100,000 ha. (247,100 ac.) of land between the Mahury and Approuague rivers would become first-class agricultural land.

Vegetation.—Almost 90% of the whole territory of French Guiana (8,000,000 ha. [19,769,000 ac.]) is covered by tropical forest (*selva*). It contains about 25–50 cu.m. of commercial timber per hectare. Among the species represented are the Angelica, the crabwood, the grignon franc, the grignon fu, the sapotac, and the yayamadou. All these trees are resistant to tree borers, termites, insects, and fungoid growths; because they are naturally hard and resistant they provide particularly suitable wood for cabinetmaking.

Animal Life.—The fauna of French Guiana is exactly the same as that of Surinam and Guyana. Although only the insects and birds are ordinarily visible, mammal, reptile, fish, and insect life is immensely varied and teeming. The fiercer mammals include the ocelot, the haka tiger or yaguarundi, and the jaguar. The largest land animal is the tapir, which is fairly rare. The manatee is a herbivorous aquatic mammal. Other exotic creatures are the sloth, the great anteater, the capybara or bush pig, and the armadillo. Monkeys and deer are among the commonest of the wild mammals.

The birds of the coast include vultures, some species of which are useful scavengers, the chicken hawk, finfoot (*Heliornis*), the muscovy duck, snipe, teal, plover, pigeon, and heron. The kiskadee is the "sparrow of Guiana." The blue sacki and the hummingbird are very common. The kingfisher and the beautiful scarlet ibis are seen on rivers. In the forests bird life is indescribably rich in variety and plumage. It includes the tinamou, the gorgeous cock of the rock (*Rupicola rupicola*), the marudi or bush turkey, the vividly coloured macaw, and the bellbird with a note like a silver gong. Flocks of parrots are common in the savannas.

Caymans, related to alligators and the commonest of the larger water creatures, infest the fresh waters of the coastlands, particularly the great rivers. Of the many varieties of snake, the giant anaconda or water boa is the biggest and the bushmaster the most vicious. Lizards are extremely numerous; the larger types include the iguanas of the lower rivers; smaller ground and arboreal forms are found also. Fish life abounds in the sea and rivers. Sharks and stingrays are found offshore. Snappers and groupers are the most esteemed of the sea fish commonly landed. River fish include the voracious predatory piranha (*Serrasalmus*)

and the lukanani (*Cichla*). Invertebrate life is the most abundant of all. Especially obvious are mosquitoes, sand flies, grasshoppers, termites, ants, and spiders.

Minerals.—Gold, tantalic columbite, and bauxite comprise the three great mineral resources of French Guiana. Gold-mining was discontinued in 1964 for various reasons (production in 1960 had been 589 kg.; 1963, 217 kg.), but in 1966 a new working was begun in the Paul Island alluvial minefields in the Decou-Decou massif. Beginning in 1963 tantalic columbite found in small mineral outcrops was mined by individual prospectors or small groups.

HISTORY

For early history, *see* GUYANA.

French Guiana, occupied by Anglo-Portuguese forces in 1809, was restored to France in 1817. Thereafter for some years the country enjoyed a certain degree of prosperity, shown, for example, in the work between 1827 and 1846 of Mother Anne Marie Javouhey, superior of the community of Saint-Joseph of Cluny, who organized a flourishing colony for freed slaves at Mana. During the same period the interior of the country was explored. The sudden abolition of slavery in 1848 caused a severe financial crisis. Several different groups were introduced in order to ease the labour shortage, but only the Asian Indians were at all effective. The situation was made worse when in 1855 gold was discovered and labour was lured away from agriculture to the mines. In 1852 a convict settlement was started at Saint-Laurent-du-Maroni, but Europeans were quite unable to work in the tropical climate and died quickly, and the settlement contributed nothing to the development of the country. The decision to abolish it was taken in 1936 but did not become effective until 1945. The convict settlements there and on the Îles du Salut near Cayenne gave French Guiana a sinister reputation which to some extent endures. (*See also* DEVIL'S ISLAND.)

The inhabitants of French Guiana have had full French citizenship and the right to vote since 1848, and the colony has been represented in the French Parliament since 1877. French Guiana became an overseas *département* of France in 1946. French Pres. Charles de Gaulle visited the territory in 1964.

POPULATION AND PEOPLE

The 1967 census showed a total population of 44,392 (1961, 33,505), of whom 36,270 lived in the *arrondissement* (district) of Cayenne and 8,122 in the *arrondissement* of Saint-Laurent-du-Maroni. The capital, Cayenne (*q.v.*), had 19,668 inhabitants and Saint-Laurent-du-Maroni 3,486.

The Amerindians, numbering about 1,000, are divided into five principal tribes: the Galibi, permanently settled on the coast; and the Palicur, Oyampi, Rucuyen, and Emerillon, who are residual riverine tribes of the forest and are somewhat pampered by the administration, particularly since the formation in 1956 of a government service for the protection of primitive peoples.

The Negroes are groups (Bosh, Boni, Youca, Saramaka) descended from freed slaves. The first three groups dwell only along the Maroni and in the north; the Bosh are adopting the French way of life. The Saramaka make only brief sojourns in the territory. In addition there are about 5,000 foreigners, including a number from the British West Indies (chiefly from St. Lucia) and Hong Kong, and some Surinam Chinese. An attempt in the 1950s to form a settlement of European "displaced persons" at Saint-Jean on the Maroni suc-

PHOTOGRAPHS, E. AUBERT DE LA RÜE

(LEFT) INDIAN CANOES BEACHED ON THE MARONI RIVER. (RIGHT) EQUATORIAL RAIN FOREST ALONG THE OYAPOCK RIVER

ceeded only partially and 150-200 people of Czech, Polish, and Hungarian origin remain there.

The Creoles are those who, whatever the colour of their skin, have adopted a European way of life. They make up 80% of the population and speak an Antillean Creole dialect of French, rich in folklore. The population is predominantly Roman Catholic, with Cayenne as the episcopal see, but there is a Protestant minority of about 500 persons who originally came from British territories or were Salvation Army converts when in the convict prison.

GOVERNMENT AND ADMINISTRATION

The *département* is administered by a prefect, assisted by an elected general council, and is represented in the French Parliament by a deputy and a senator. The Cayenne coastal *arrondissement* is divided into 14 communes, administered by municipal councils. Justice is administered through tribunals of first instance, a High Court and a Court of Appeal.

French social legislation, social security measures, and family grants are applicable. There are primary schools in all the centres of French Guiana and secondary education is given at a *lycée*. There is also a technical college for girls. Furthermore, there are courses in law which provide the student with the equivalent of the first year's study for a license to practise and to some extent equip him as a teacher. The Institut Français d'Amérique Tropicale is a scientific authority recognized throughout South America, particularly in geology and the study of soils, oceanography, and ichthyology.

Health.—There is a hospital at Cayenne (400 beds), one at Saint-Laurent (280 beds), and physicians' offices in each commune. Besides this service, there is a private hospital run by the sisters of the Order of Saint-Paul of Chartres and a sanatorium operated by the Sisters of Saint-Joseph of Cluny. This latter is a continuation of the order's original work for lepers. Guiana is thus medically one of the best equipped of the French dependencies. The Pasteur Institute in Cayenne has been successful in combating yellow fever, malaria, and leprosy, and its chemical laboratory has discovered important sources of vitamins A and C in the Guiana flora.

ECONOMY

Agriculture takes up little more than 3,000 ha. (11½ sq.mi.) and French Guiana has to import foodstuffs. The chief crops are yams, cassava, bananas, and sugarcane. The government agricultural and forestry services have undertaken a twofold project: to utilize the lowlands and to develop the experimental breeding station at Kourou.

Guiana, which exported meat regularly during the 19th century, has seen its livestock decrease from more than 9,000 cattle and buffalo to about 3,300 in the mid-1960s. On the other hand, over the same period there was an increase in the number of pigs (5,900 against 1,800) and of sheep (1,200 against 900). The decline in the number of cattle was the result of various bacterial diseases, of viruses, and of parasites and the various deficiency diseases they produce.

The forests are a vast source of wealth, despite the fact that limited communications make it practicable to work only those portions which lie below the rapids of the rivers. The volume of felled and stripped timber exceeded 14,800 cu.m. in 1964, and rose to 30,000 cu.m. in 1965. In the same period the output of sawed logs rose from 18,000 to 19,000 cu.m. Exports to Europe, to the Antilles, and to Surinam are very important.

In addition to gold and bauxite, tantalic columbite exists, though the deposits are generally insufficient for exploitation unless by hydraulic methods. Reserves of bauxite represent 42,000,000 tons of ore with an aluminum content of 41.5%. Lithium minerals may exist in the Maroni River region.

The main exports are gold, wood, essence of rosewood, and balata rubber. Their value is greatly exceeded by that of imports which (except petroleum products) come almost wholly from France. The unit of currency is the metropolitan French franc.

Communications.—Rivers and coastal navigation have for long afforded the chief means of communication between the settlements, but the road from Cayenne to Iracoubo, extended to Organabo and Saint-Laurent, has assisted the economic development of the regions traversed. By the mid-1960s there were about 170 mi. (273 km.) of main roads, of which 100 mi. (160 km.) were tarred, and 120 mi. (193 km.) of secondary roads, of which 30 mi. (48 km.) were tarred.

Regular shipping services link Cayenne with France (Bordeaux and Le Havre). Minor ports are Larivot near Cayenne and Saint-Laurent. Rochambeau airport near Cayenne is served by French and U.S. airlines and there are domestic air services to a number of centres in the *département*.

BIBLIOGRAPHY.—E. Revert, *La France d'Amérique* (1949); B. Choubert, *Géologie et pétrologie de la Guyane française* (1949); E. Aubert de la Rue, *Reconnaissance géologique de la Guyane française méridionale, 1948-50* (1955); R. Abonnenc, J. Hurault and R. Saban, *Bibliographie de la Guyane française* (1957); "La Guyane française: Histoire-Géographie-Ethnographie" (*Notes et études documentaires*, no. 1721 (March 30, 1953); Alix Resse, *Guyane française, terre de l'espace* (1964). Current history and statistics are summarized annually in *Britannica Book of the Year*.
(Ro. C.)

GUIANA HIGHLANDS

are located mainly in the Guiana region of South America, north of the Amazon and south of the Orinoco river. Consisting of a heavily forested plateau, they cover the southern half of Venezuela, all of the Guianas except for the low coastal plain, the northern part of Brazil and a part of southeastern Colombia. These highlands are similar in geology and surface form to the Brazilian highlands, from which they are separated by the narrow eastern part of the Amazon lowland. The rocks are geologically ancient granites and gneisses, covered in places by more recent sandstones and lava flows. The terrain is made up of a mixture of three elements: a basement of rolling hilly upland, standing mostly less than 1,000 ft. above sea level; surmounted in places near the stream divides by low mountains that stand above the hilly upland between 2,000 and 3,000 ft. above sea level; and surmounted by tabular plateaus where the sandstones and lava flows cover the crystalline rocks. The highest elevations are formed by these tabular uplands, such as Mt. Roraima (9,094 ft.) where the boundaries of Brazil, Venezuela and Guyana come together. The highlands extend westward across the upper Orinoco (and across the Casiquiare canal, a torrential stream that connects the Orinoco with the Amazon via the Negro river) and in southeastern Colombia reach the eastern front of the Andes, thus separating the Orinoco lowland from the Amazon lowland.

The whole region receives an abundance of rainfall and no season is really dry. The vegetation is mostly tropical rain forest, but there are certain parts of the area with savanna. Much of southern Venezuela is a mixture of semideciduous forest and woodland savanna. From the forests come valuable cabinet woods, balata, chicle, vanilla, divi-divi, insecticides and medicinal plants. The crystalline rocks carry a wealth of minerals, but exploration is difficult due to the plant cover. Gold and diamonds are mined, and the Sierra Imataca of Venezuela is a major source of iron ore.

See also GUYANA: *Physical Geography and Natural Resources*; VENEZUELA: *Brazil*; COLOMBIA; SOUTH AMERICA. (P. E. J.)

GUIART (GUIARD), GUILLAUME

(d. c. 1316), French chronicler and poet, was probably born at Orléans, and served in the French army in Flanders in 1304. He lived at Arras and then in Paris, afterward appearing as a *ménestrel de bouche*. Guiart's poem *Branche des royaulx lignages* was written and then rewritten between 1304 and 1307, in honour of the French king Philip IV, and in answer to the aspersions of a Flemish poet. Its 21,000 verses deal with the history of the French kings from the time of Louis VIII, but it is only really important for the period after 1296 and for the war in Flanders from 1301 to 1304, for which it is a high authority. Unfortunately the style of the poem is very slipshod. It was first published by A. Buchon (1828), and again in vol. xxii of the *Recueil des historiens des Gaules et de la France* (1865).

See A. Molinier, *Les Sources de l'histoire de France*, vol. iii (1903).
(M. PAC.)

GUIBERT OF RAVENNA, antipope under the title of Clement III. See CLEMENT.

GUICCIARDINI, FRANCESCO (1483–1540), Italian historian and statesman whose *Storia d'Italia* has remained one of the monuments of Italian historiography, was born at Florence on March 6, 1483, of an aristocratic family which played a prominent role under Lorenzo de' Medici (*see* MEDICI). From 1498 to 1505 he studied civil law at Florence, Ferrara and Padua, and subsequently set up legal practice at Florence. In 1508 he married Maria, daughter of Alamanno Salviati. Francesco was elected in 1511 ambassador to King Ferdinand of Aragon. He was at the Spanish court when the Florentines restored the Medici under the pressure of Spanish troops. On his return to Florence in 1514 he resumed his legal practice; in 1514 he was member of the Eight and in 1515 of the Signoria. In 1513 Cardinal Giovanni de' Medici became Pope Leo X; in 1516 he appointed Guicciardini governor of Modena, and in 1517 of Reggio. Until 1534 Guicciardini served the papacy almost continuously.

As governor of an exposed and recently acquired part of the papal states, in which he had to face internal disorders as well as external dangers, Guicciardini showed outstanding administrative gifts. His severe and sometimes ruthless measures were effective in restoring order, but also caused him unpopularity. The renewed outbreak of the war between Spain and France made Reggio into a military outpost of the papal states, and in July 1521 Guicciardini was appointed commissioner-general of the papal army. In this capacity, he prevented, by his courage and determination, Parma from falling into French hands in Dec. 1521. But the death of Leo X in the same month jeopardized his career temporarily; after the election of Adrian VI, he was at first deprived of the governorships of Modena and Reggio, but recovered them at the end of 1522. In 1523, after Adrian's death, he had to defend both cities against their original ruler, the duke of Ferrara. Reggio capitulated, but Modena was held by Guicciardini against superior odds. After the election of Cardinal Giulio de' Medici as Clement VII, he earned his reward by being appointed, in 1524, president of the Romagna. In the critical situation after the battle of Pavia, when the imperial army was preparing to advance south, he conveyed to the pope much advice, and in Jan. 1526 he was summoned to Rome. There he played a prominent role in the papal counsels, advocating an alliance with France against Charles V. The League of Cognac, concluded in May 1526, was to no small extent his work, and in June he was appointed papal lieutenant general with the army of the league. The failure of the league to prevent the army of German *Landsknechte* under the duke of Bourbon from advancing on Florence and Rome involved him once more in the fate of his native city.

The danger in which Florence found herself as a result of Clement's policy had increased the opposition to the Medici regime. When, on the arrival of the duke of Urbino with his army near Florence, the Medici left the city to welcome him (April 26, 1527), a revolt broke out. Guicciardini, who had arrived shortly before to help protect the city, succeeded in preventing the duke from assaulting the palace of the Signoria by negotiating a free pardon in return for surrender. A few days later, Bourbon's army captured Rome; and this led to a second, and this time successful, rising in Florence against Medicean rule.

The collapse of the pope's authority rendered Guicciardini's position untenable, while his long association with the Medici made him suspect in republican Florence. There he supported the attempts of the gonfalonier Niccolò Capponi to come to terms with the pope. The victory of the intransigent faction and the fall of Capponi (April 1529), followed by the advance of the imperial army on the city, endangered Guicciardini's position and, in September, he left Florentine territory for the papal court. From now onward he fully supported Clement's bid for Florence, although trying to obtain favourable conditions for the Florentines. In March 1530 he was condemned as a rebel at Florence. After the city's surrender, he returned as papal representative, and took a leading part in the persecution of the republicans. In 1531 Clement appointed him governor of Bologna, but he lost this post after the accession of Paul III in 1534. Back in Florence, he acted as legal adviser to Duke Alessandro de' Medici. After the murder of Alessandro in 1537, he helped secure the succession for

Cosimo, probably hoping to limit the ducal powers which he considered excessive. Disappointed in his hopes and personal ambitions, although still holding high office under the new ruler, he devoted the last years of his life, in his villa at S. Margherita a Montici, to the composition of his *Storia d'Italia*. He died on May 22, 1540.

This *History of Italy* was the crowning achievement of Guicciardini's literary production which began, in 1508–09, with the composition of his family memoirs and of his *History of Florence* from 1378 to 1509. The latter constitutes one of the major sources for the history of the republican regime after 1494; it reveals Guicciardini's gifts for historical analysis and narrative. He did not return to historical writing until 1528, when he began to draft a second and more ambitious history of Florence from 1375 to his own time, which he never completed. After his return to Florence from Bologna, he began work on a history of Italy during his lieutenantship which, redrafted during the following years, became the nucleus of his far more ambitious *History of Italy* from 1492 to 1534. He began the work probably in 1536; the final revision was not completed when he died. Written by a statesman closely associated with many of the events he described, and by a historian who in his critical use of evidence followed and surpassed his humanist predecessors, the work is the most important contemporary history of Italy during the Italian wars.

Guicciardini was also a prolific political writer, composing numerous memoranda and treatises, mostly in the form of discourses on political problems of the day, often in connection with his official duties. A number of them deal with the government of Florence, on which he also wrote, between 1521 and 1525, the *Dialogo del reggimento di Firenze*. In this he advocates an aristocratic regime on the Venetian model as the ideal constitution for his city. The most concise and varied expression of his views on politics and society is, however, found in his collection of maxims and observations, the *Ricordi*, compiled in 1528 and 1530. His political thought is frequently akin to, and sometimes more radical than, that of his friend Niccolò Machiavelli (*q.v.*), with whom he shares, despite his long service with the papacy, a criticism of the contemporary church. He disagreed, however, in his *Considerations on the Discourses of Machiavelli* (c. 1530), with Machiavelli's interpretation of Roman history as evidence for a political science. Of his works, only the *History of Italy* and the *Ricordi* were published before the 19th century (*editiones principes* 1561 and 1576 respectively). Most of his other works were published between 1857 and 1867 by G. Canestrini in the *Opere inedite*. The second history of Florence was edited for the first time by R. Ridolfi in 1945 under the title *Le cose fiorentine*. For a portrait of Guicciardini *see* ITALIAN LITERATURE.

BIBLIOGRAPHY.—*Storia d'Italia*, ed. by A. Gherardi (1919), and by C. Panigada (in *Scrittori d'Italia*, 1929); *Storie fiorentine, Dialogo del reggimento di Firenze, Ricordi*, the political discourses, the family memoirs and the personal diaries, ed. by R. Palmarocchi (in *Scrittori d'Italia*, 1931–36). The fundamental critical edition of the *Ricordi* is by R. Spongano (1951). The new edition of Guicciardini's letters (*Carteggi*), ed. by R. Palmarocchi, vol. 5–9 (1522–26) ed. by P. G. Ricci. *See also* A. Otetea, *François Guichardin* (1926); and especially R. Ridolfi, *Vita di Francesco Guicciardini* (1960); with bibliography; specialized studies include A. Rossi, *Francesco Guicciardini e il governo fiorentino dal 1527 al 1540* (1896–99) ; V. Luciani, *Francesco Guicciardini e la fortuna dell' opera sua*, ed. by P. Guicciardini (1949).

GUIDANCE. Guidance, educational, vocational and psychological, exists to enable an individual to discover and to develop his potentialities and thereby to achieve an optimal level of personal happiness and social usefulness. The concept of guidance is essentially democratic in that the assumptions underlying its theory and practice are, first, that each individual has the right to shape his own destiny and, second, that the relatively mature and experienced members of the community are responsible for ensuring that each person's choice shall serve both his own interests and those of the society to which he belongs. It is implicit in the philosophy of guidance that these objectives are complementary rather than conflicting. The function of those who guide children and young people is not to effect a compromise between the requirements of individuals on the one hand and the demands of the community on the other. It is rather to orient the individual toward those opportunities afforded by his environment which can best guarantee the fulfillment of his personal needs and aspirations.

Guidance, in this sense, is a pervasive activity in which many persons and organizations take part. It is afforded to individuals by their parents, relatives and friends and by the community at large through various social, religious and political agencies and, particularly, through the press and broadcasting services. The term is usually confined, however, to the more systematic attempts made by schools and educational authorities to help their pupils to satisfy their personal needs and to develop their potentialities to the full.

DEVELOPMENT OF GUIDANCE IN THE SCHOOLS

School guidance programs traditionally have been described as serving the educational, vocational and psychological, or personal-social, needs of the child. Often programs have been set up to serve primarily one or another of these needs, dealing with the others only secondarily or incidentally. Even though the trend has been to view a child's educational, vocational and personal-social aspirations and achievements—or problems—as interrelated concerns of an over-all guidance program, it may be well first to discuss them separately.

Educational Guidance.—Educational guidance has always been an integral part of a teacher's function. Since formal education began there can have been few teachers who perceived their role solely in terms of purveying instruction. It has long been recognized that effective teaching involves the regular assessment of each pupil's progress and attainments. It is necessary to determine the extent to which he is absorbing and benefiting from his instruction, to assess his strengths and weaknesses and then to encourage the development of the former and, as far as possible, to remedy the latter. These are the essential rudiments of educational guidance. The techniques traditionally employed by teachers to serve these purposes have been: (1) regular observation of their pupils' reactions to instruction; and (2) the periodic use of more formal methods of assessment, such as oral or written examinations.

During the 20th century, and particularly since about 1930, educational guidance has become a complex operation involving, in some countries, the employment of specially trained people to assist teachers in carrying out this part of their function. These developments have involved a widening of the scope of the guidance that is offered and a considerable refinement of the methods employed; but the essential features of the traditional approach still remain, in that guidance continues to be based on close observation of each pupil's progress and on his results in tests and examinations. The observation becomes increasingly objective and systematized. It is a common practice, for example, to keep cumulative record cards or files for each pupil so that various aspects of his progress can be charted and to submit him to more multifarious and efficient tests and examinations. Considerable advances have been made in the analysis of human abilities and in devising instruments for their effective measurement. It is no longer necessary to base the assessment of a child's potential solely on the subjective judgment of his teachers or on his attainments in scholastic subjects. Tests have been developed and are widely used which serve to measure a number of basic intellectual abilities and which enable reliable predictions to be made concerning the likelihood of a pupil's success in a specific educational course.

A striking feature of the development of educational guidance is the extent to which its methods have been evaluated by research. It has become characteristic of modern educators to seek empirical justification for their practices rather than to content themselves with a priori assumptions. A number of rigorously controlled follow-up studies have been carried out, particularly in the United States, and these have supplied convincing evidence that professionally directed, contemporary programs of guidance, based on objective measurements of abilities and aptitudes, on cumulative records and on the results of counseling interviews, yield results significantly superior to those obtained by the less systematic traditional methods.

Current trends in educational guidance are clearly moving toward broadening the scope of the service and making it available to every child. In the past the major emphasis was on the evaluation of children's intellectual achievements or disabilities. A child was advised to pursue or to avoid a particular educational course mainly according to his possession or lack of the necessary intellectual attributes. It has become increasingly recognized, however, that the totality of an individual's attributes and characteristics must be taken into account. It is not enough to ensure only that a child has the intellectual equipment necessary for a particular course of study. It is equally important to ascertain that he has sufficient nervous stamina and balance, to assess his interests, his degree of motivation and the likelihood of his finding the course emotionally satisfying. A past tendency was to regard educational guidance as a process appropriate only for the child who experienced some specific difficulty in his school career; but research has amply demonstrated that the progress and orientation of all pupils can be improved by an effective system of guidance.

A further trend deserving of comment is for guidance to become increasingly "child-centred." There is a risk, clearly recognized by those responsible for this service, that guidance might become something akin to direction. A teacher or counselor who has systematically analyzed a child's abilities and aptitudes and has reached the conclusion that a particular course is ideally suited to his capacities may be tempted to press the case for this course too strongly. Admittedly, it would be irresponsible to allow a child to make for himself a wholly unrealistic choice involving a strong likelihood of subsequent failure and frustration; on the other hand, if he has a preference contrary to the counselor's and is not allowed to follow it he may, for that reason, be inadequately motivated to succeed in whatever alternative he has been persuaded to accept.

Clearly, educational guidance calls for tact and nice judgment as well as a skilful assessment of a child's needs and capabilities. Its ultimate aim, moreover, is recognized as being to develop in each child the insight that will enable him eventually to undertake the sensible direction of his own affairs.

Vocational Guidance.—Vocational guidance may be regarded as an aspect or a branch of educational guidance and it employs basically the same techniques. It aims, by assessing a candidate's abilities and aptitudes, to enable him to choose a career that will exercise his talents and from which he can derive adequate personal satisfaction. Cumulative records, the results of standardized objective tests of ability, attainment and aptitude, questionnaires, attitude scales, inventories and interviews designed to assess the candidate's interests and preferences provide the evidence on which guidance is based.

The methods of vocational guidance, too, have been evaluated by research, which shows that scientifically based guidance increases the probability that an individual will give and receive satisfaction in the career he enters, and that guidance serves to reduce maladjustment and delinquency. Those responsible for vocational guidance need to be just as knowledgeable concerning the rapidly developing field of mental measurement as do those in charge of educational guidance. They also need to be well-informed about the changing pattern of vocational opportunities in modern society. Industrial and vocational psychologists, by means of job analysis and similar techniques, have provided a considerable amount of information concerning the requirements of a wide range of occupations in terms of specific skills and abilities. The vocational counselor or careers master needs to be familiar with these findings if he is to perform his function satisfactorily.

Perhaps the most notable modern trend in vocational guidance is the tendency to counter the somewhat facile optimism fostered in the 1930s by the spectacular advances in aptitude-testing techniques of that period. It then seemed that it would become possible to guide each individual toward a specific career with a reasonable degree of precision. Later, increasing emphasis was placed on the need to take into consideration factors other than skill and intellectual prowess, such as motivation, temperament, etc.; to make due allowance for human powers of adaptation; and, largely because of the changing pattern of society's requirements in a scientific and technological age, to encourage most young people to defer a definite choice of career for as long as possible.

Psychological Guidance.—Psychological guidance assists young people to adjust themselves to their environment, to solve their personal problems and to achieve a well-balanced and integrated personality relative to their educational and vocational goals. The role of the school in this respect used to be perceived as secondary and supportive. Guidance of this kind was regarded as appropriate only for children who developed emotional disorders or other forms of maladjustment and its administration was considered to be the prerogative of professionally qualified persons. The normal procedure was for a child who exhibited symptoms of maladjustment to be referred to a clinic where his disorder would be diagnosed and treated by a team of specialists including psychiatrists, psychologists and, usually, psychiatric social workers, who provided the necessary link with his home.

The activities of the school in this regard tended to be confined to co-operating with the specialists and to carrying out such supportive measures as the latter advised.

This procedure, indeed, is still generally followed; but a more positive attitude is now adopted toward the problems of mental health. Just as educational guidance is no longer regarded as the prerogative of the minority of children with specific educational difficulties but is extended to all children, so psychological guidance for all children is regarded as the proper concern of the schools. Increasing attention is paid to the relationship between a school's organization and educational practices and the mental health of its pupils. Indeed, the concept is developing of a comprehensive program of educational guidance that includes adequate psychological guidance as one of its major services.

TRENDS

As indicated above, there has been a trend toward integrated guidance programs to serve the over-all educational, vocational and other personal-social or psychological needs of schoolchildren. As these programs met with more and more widespread acceptance a further trend developed toward accentuating developmental and preventive functions in preference to the more traditional diagnostic and remedial approaches, and toward extending such services both downward into lower and elementary schools and upward into higher educational and young adult and adult vocational situations.

The Expansion of Guidance Services.—Since World War II the number of organized guidance programs has increased rapidly, particularly in secondary schools. In the United States this growth resulted from the activities of state governments and local communities, augmented by the adoption of the National Defense Education act (1958) which, among other things, helped states and local school systems to train counselors, establish guidance programs and identify and guide talented youth. In urban areas nearly every high school had a guidance program by the 1960s. Such programs were less evident in rural high schools but were increasing; in some instances one counselor was employed to serve several schools.

In the United States, counseling, that is, the use of modern psychological principles and methods in helping the individual to achieve a better understanding of his problems and potentialities, is regarded as the primary service of the guidance program. Personal interviewing is the principal method used. Guidance services are performed by trained counselors who work co-operatively with teachers, principals and other specialists and include testing and other measurements of interests and aptitudes, vocational and educational information and placement, follow-up contacts and research.

At the college and university level guidance is usually identified with student personnel work. Most institutions of higher education in the United States have more elaborate and more formal student personnel programs than are found at similar institutions in other countries. A typical U.S. program would include a counseling centre, non-academic student activities, educational and vocational placement services, academic advisement, health services, residence-hall supervision and administration of admissions and financial aid. Each service has its own specialized personnel, and services are usually co-ordinated by a dean of students. Student personnel programs in colleges have gradually increased in size and number, but growth has not kept pace with enrollment.

Elementary schools have a long history of interest and concern for the guidance of pupils by classroom teachers. Relatively few such schools, however, employ special guidance counselors, school psychologists or social workers, although their numbers are increasing. Many educators believe that guidance specialists would be more effective in elementary schools than in high schools because personality seems to be less firmly fixed at earlier ages and there is more time to help the child.

Guidance programs for persons out of school lag far behind those for students. Nevertheless, thousands of adults are benefiting from agencies that offer various types of guidance, such as employment offices, vocational training, retraining and counseling bureaus, family welfare and mental health clinics, rehabilitation institutes and industrial personnel offices.

Changing Concepts.—The 20th century has witnessed the growth of new guidance professions, including those of counselor, school psychologist and school social worker. In the United States these and related professions are represented by the American Personnel and Guidance association, the American Psychological association, and the National Association of Social Workers, each having state and local branches. Graduate-level university preparation is derived largely from the social sciences. Counselors and other professional guidance workers offer assistance to youth and adults that is intended to supplement the help of traditional guidance authorities: parents; teachers; clergymen and doctors of medicine. This trend toward guidance by specialists trained in relatively new professions seems to be firmly established, as a result of increased public sensitivity to personal and social problems, and the accumulation of more useful knowledge about human behaviour.

A view of guidance prevailed from about 1910 until after 1930 in which counselors were supposed to guide persons only with regard to one of several problem areas: vocational, educational, or personal-social guidance. Many high school counselors still are assigned to guide students on single areas, one growing specialty being college admissions counseling. However, the main trend of thinking about school programs is toward the guidance of a person's total mental and social development, with an emphasis on helping him to prevent unusually severe maladjustments. Vocational, educational and personal-social development are viewed as part of the larger whole of growth toward greater maturity. The counselor's intent is to help the individual learn to solve his own problems and become a self-guiding person. Under this concept of guidance, a counselor would be responsible for the general school welfare of a number of students, and he would not be restricted to providing guidance on only one type of problem or in one area of interest.

Professional guidance originally was provided mainly for special categories of people, for example, high-school dropouts or leavers looking for jobs, emotionally disturbed children, college-bound youth, slow-learning pupils or juvenile delinquents. Many private and public guidance agencies still serve special groups such as these. Since World War II, however, guidance has come to be viewed as valuable for all students. Similarly, there has been revealed an increasingly popular conception of guidance as a practical support for national welfare by identifying and encouraging the development of human talents in order to inventory, develop and conserve manpower more efficiently.

See also CHILD PSYCHOLOGY; EXAMINATIONS; PSYCHOLOGICAL TESTS AND MEASUREMENTS; PSYCHOLOGY, APPLIED; EDUCATIONAL PSYCHOLOGY.

(R. W. ST.)

BIBLIOGRAPHY.—C. A. Oakley and A. Macrae, *Handbook of Vocational Guidance* (1937); C. R. Rogers, *Counseling and Psychotherapy*

(1942); G. Forrester, *Methods of Vocational Guidance* (1944); J. W. M. Rothney and B. A. Roens, *Guidance of American Youth* (1944); A. J. Jones, *Principles of Guidance*, rev. ed. (1957); A. H. Brayfield (ed.), *Readings in Modern Methods of Counseling* (1950); C. P. Froehlich, *The Evaluation of Counseling* (1951); L. E. Tyler, *The Work of the Counselor*, 2nd ed. (1961); *The National Defense Counseling and Guidance Training Institutes Program: a Report of the First 50 Institutes* (1960); National Society for the Study of Education, *Mental Health in Modern Education* (1955); Year Book of Education, vol. 3, R. K. Hall and J. A. Lauwerys (eds.), *Guidance and Counseling* (1955); D. E. Super, *The Psychology of Careers* (1957).

Commission on Guidance in American Schools, C. Gilbert Wrenn, Director, *The Counselor in a Changing World* (1962), Educational Policies Commission, *Manpower and Education* (1956); P. W. Hutson, *The Guidance Function in Education* (1958); R. A. Martinson and H. Smallenburg, *Guidance in Elementary Schools* (1958); C. H. Miller, *Foundations of Guidance* (1961); National Society for the Study of Education, *Personnel Services in Education* (1959); J. Warters, *Techniques of Counseling* (1954); C. G. Wrenn, *Student Personnel Work in College* (1951).

GUIDED MISSILES: see ROCKETS AND GUIDED MISSILES.

GUIDI, an Italian feudal family that originated in the Romagna in the 10th century and succeeded in extending its feudal dominions from the *contado* of Pistoia over large parts of Tuscany, the Romagna and Emilia. By the middle of the 12th century they were the most powerful feudal house of the Florentine *contado*. Their possessions were situated in its eastern region; and they had extensive lands in the Tuscan Romagna, in the *contadi* of Bologna, Faenza, Forlì and Ravenna and in the Casentino (the hill country of the upper Arno). In the 13th century they had to yield, from the 12th century onward, to the expansion of the communes and were drawn into the conflicts between cities and between Guelphs and Ghibellines. They were further weakened by their division into several branches which sometimes took opposite sides. In the Casentino, the branch of the counts of Poppi succeeded in preserving feudal independence until 1440, when the Florentines annexed the lands of Count Francesco da Battifolle who had allied himself with Milan against them.

BIBLIOGRAPHY.—L. Passerini, "Guidi di Romagna," in *Famiglie celebri italiane*, vol. xxv (1866-67); R. Davidsohn, *Geschichte von Florenz*, vol. i, ii (1896, 1908); P. Santini, "Studi sull'antica costituzione del comune di Firenze," *Archivio Storico Italiano*, 5th series, vol. xxv, xxvi (1900). (N. R.)

GUIDO OF AREZZO (c. 990–1050), Italian musical theorist who developed the system of modern musical notation. Of Italian descent, Guido was originally a monk at the Benedictine abbey of Pomposa. Driven from the monastery as a result of jealousies aroused by his musical innovations, he probably settled at Arezzo. At the invitation of Pope John XIX he went to Rome not later than the summer of 1032, accompanied by the Bishop Theobald of Arezzo, to whom he had dedicated his treatise on notation, *Micrologus*, and by two Arezzo priests. The pope greatly admired his system of notation, but illness compelled Guido to return to northern Italy, where the abbot of Pomposa vainly sought his return to the monastery. After travels that may have taken him to France, he appears to have ended his life at the Camaldolite monastery of S. Croce di Fonte Avellana, in Umbria. The chronicles of this order show that he was at the monastery in 1030, becoming a prior in 1047, and that he died in 1050. Theories attempting to refute this evidence on the ground that Guido was a hermit and a recluse are unfounded since the Camaldolites were themselves hermits, meeting only to sing at offices. Other theories suggesting that Guido was French or that, as an Italian, he had early settled at St. Maur near Paris derive from a confusion of names and monasteries. Guido certainly traveled, but knowledge of his journey to France is scanty. It is known only that staff notation, obviously derived from Guido's research into this field, early appeared in the north of France (though not at St. Maur), as it did in central Italy.

Guido established the staff of four lines as well as the names of the degrees of the hexachord (q.v.). At the same time he developed the alphabetic notation now common to the Germanic countries. It is not possible, however, to ascribe to him the invention, widely used in the middle ages, of the "Guidonian hand," in which notes are represented by the joints of the five fingers; though the theory of notation based on this invention bears his name it is not mentioned in his works.

The staff was certainly the most far-reaching of his achievements. Before Guido's time melodies were learned by heart, since neumes were unable to express intervals precisely. Guido declared that with his system the ten years normally required to become an ecclesiastical singer could be reduced to five months. Earlier, certain manuscripts from Aquitania and Lorraine had used a single line for notation. This was originally intended for the inscription of the verbal text but, by custom, it became used for musical notation. Moreover, Pseudo Hucbald (*see* HUCBALD) had previously used a system of several lines, and it is believed that there were other such experiments. These manuscripts must surely have been known to Guido. The idea of a single line led logically to a staff of several lines to which he gave different colours so that the position of the semitones was clearly defined.

The disadvantage of Guido's system was that melodies tended to become desiccated. Many of the ornaments that appear in early manuscripts on neumes are not to be found in those on staves. It is not known if all western musicians were able to seize the subtle intervals represented by the neume signs—they still form part of the oriental Christian chants—nor to what extent this tradition was established in the west. As in modern times, not everyone was able to grasp them. However this may be, the west was ready to establish the diatonic system, and this movement was followed by Guido, who may not himself have been entirely appreciative of the earlier significance of neumes. In any case the values of neumes could not be represented on the staff, which, though precise in notation, was not designed to record intervals smaller than the semitone. On the other hand, Guido's discovery allowed the diffusion of musical theory, a precise notation of polyphony and the development of the musical language leading to the modern system.

Guido is credited with the composition of the Latin hymn to St. John the Baptist, *Ut queant laxis*; the first syllable of each line, *ut, re, mi, fa, sol, la*, is used in Latin countries as the name of the first six ascending notes of the C major scale. Probably he modified the hymn so that the first notes of the lines formed this succession. Before Guido an alphabetical system of musical notation is found in France at the time of the monastic reforms of Guillaume de Volpiano, as early as 996, probably introduced from the region of Vercelli in Italy. This system used the letters of the alphabet from *a* to *þ*. Guido used other forms consisting of a series of capital letters, small letters and double small letters, using the letters *a* to *g*.

BIBLIOGRAPHY.—Smits van Waesberghe, *Guidonis Aretini Micrologus* (1955), *Expositiones in Micrologum Guidonis Aretini* (1957), *De musico-paedagogico et theoretico Guidone Aretino eiusque vita et morbus* (1953); "Les origines de la notation alphabétique" in *Annuario Musical*, vol. ii (1957); Hans Oesch, *Guido von Arezzo, Biographisches und Theoretisches unter besonderer Berücksichtigung der sogenannten odonischen Traktate* (1954); S. Corbin, "Sens et valeur de la notation alphabétique à Jumièges et en Normandie," in *Jumièges, Congrès scientifique* (1956). On the hymn *Ut queant laxis*, see C. A. Moberg, "Die Musik in Guido von Arezzos Solmisationshymne," in *Archiv für Musikwissenschaft*, vol. xvi (1959). (S. Co.)

GUIDO DA SIENA (active c. 1250–1275), Italian painter, who, if certain assumptions regarding him may be accepted as true, is the earliest representative of a new school of neo-Byzantine art that flourished in Siena in the 13th century. A large painting of the "Virgin and Child Enthroned," once in the church of S. Domenico at Siena and later moved to the Palazzo Pubblico, bears a rhymed Latin inscription, giving the painter's name as "Gu . . . o de Senis," with the date 1221. Milanesi alleged that the inscription had been tampered with and should read 1281, while Wickhoff maintained that the date 1221 was genuine. Later art criticism inclined toward the latter view. Milanesi thought that the work in S. Domenico was due to Guido Graziani, of whom no other record remains earlier than 1278, when he is mentioned as the painter of a banner.

GUIDO RENI: see RENI, GUIDO.

GUIENNE (GUYENNE), the old name for a region of southwestern France, merged with Gascony (q.v.) for the last centuries of the *ancien régime* in the *gouvernement* of Guyenne-et-Gascogne.

In this *gouvernement* the areas regarded as Guienne were Bordeaux (*q.v.*), the capital, with its vicinity, Bordelais; Médoc; Blaye and Blayais; Bazas and Bazadais; Agen and Agenais; Périgord; Quercy; and Rouergue. Guienne in this sense therefore corresponded to the modern *départements* of Gironde, most of Lot-et-Garonne, most of Tarn-et-Garonne, Dordogne, Lot and Aveyron.

The name Guienne had various meanings in the middle ages. In the language of the troubadours Guiana appears to correspond to Aquitania (*see* AQUITAINE). Historically, however, the name Guienne first became important through the treaty of Paris (1259), between Louis IX of France and Henry III of England. Aquitaine and Gascony had passed together to the English through Henry Plantagenet's marriage to Eleanor of Aquitaine in 1152, but in the ensuing century of warfare the French had reconquered nearly all Aquitaine proper. By the treaty of Paris, however, Louis IX accepted Henry III as his vassal for the duchy of "Guienne," which was then specified as including not only lands in the Aquitanian dioceses of Limoges, Périgueux and Cahors—that is to say, parts of Limousin, Périgord and Quercy (*qq.v.*), to which, as the rump of Aquitaine, the name Guienne was perfectly appropriate—but also Gascony, hitherto held by the English as an allodial possession, not as a fief. Moreover, he granted to the English the conditional reversion of Agenais (an ancient fief of Gascony), lower Saintonge and the rest of Quercy, all at that time held by the counts of Toulouse. Agenais in fact passed to the English in 1279 and lower Saintonge and Toulousain Quercy in 1286, but juridical arguments on extraterritorial areas were brought up to delay the actual delivery of the lands in the dioceses into English hands.

Philip IV of France in his quarrel with Edward III of England declared Guienne confiscated in 1294, and French armies occupied the whole country except Bayonne and its vicinity, but peace was made in 1303, restoring the *status quo ante*. Charles IV repeated the sentence of confiscation in 1324 and kept Agenais and Bazadais under the peace of 1327, leaving the English little more than the coastal areas, Saintonge, Bordeaux and Gascony. This remnant likewise was declared forfeit by Philip VI in 1337 at the beginning of the Hundred Years' War (*q.v.*), but the treaty of Brétigny (*q.v.*) in 1360 ceded not only the Guienne of 1259 but the whole of the old Aquitaine, with Rouergue also attached, to the English as a sovereign principality.

The later phases of the war, however, saw the gradual French reconquest of the country; the battle of Castillon (*q.v.*), in 1453, was decisive.

Louis XI gave the duchy of Guienne as an apanage to his brother Charles in 1469. On the latter's death (1472) it was reunited to the French crown. During the wars between Catholics and Huguenots in the 16th century (*see* FRANCE: *History*) and during the Fronde (*q.v.*) in the 17th, Guienne was the scene of bitter fighting. In the 18th century it was highly prosperous.

GUILBERT, YVETTE (1867?–1944), French *diseuse*, born in Paris, won an immense vogue by her rendering of songs drawn from Parisian lower-class life and from the humours of the Latin Quarter. Her adoption of a habitual yellow dress and long black gloves, her studied simplicity of diction and her ingenuous delivery of songs charged with risqué meaning made her famous. She owed something to Xanrof (Léon Fourneau), who for a long time composed songs especially for her, and perhaps still more to Aristide Bruant, who wrote many of her argot songs. She is also remembered as the subject of a famous poster by H. Toulouse-Lautrec.

Her publications include *La Vedette* and *Les Demi-vieilles*, both novels (1902), and *Song of My Life: My Memories* (1927; Eng. trans., 1929).

GUILD may be defined as a confraternity, brotherhood, or society formed for the mutual aid and protection of its members or for the prosecution of some common cause. The term is now primarily applied either to the associations of this type which flourished in Western Europe between the 11th and 16th centuries or to societies of other periods and places which reveal features characteristic of the medieval guild in general and the medieval craft guild in particular.

The word is common to most modern North European languages and is derived from the Old Germanic root—*gelt*, *geld*, or *gild*, with an early meaning of "payment" or "offering." (*Guild* remains the common English spelling despite several attempts to revive the original *gild*.) The etymological argument suggests that the earliest guilds would be associations of men grouped together to pay money for a common object. The mysterious *gegildan* or "geld-comrades," found in Anglo-Saxon England as early as the late 7th century, were in fact required by the law codes of Ine and Alfred of Wessex to help one another pay the *wergild* (homicide price). However, it would be dangerous to assume that all the early medieval guilds were merely associations of geld payers, if only because the linguistic evidence is itself indecisive. Other meanings of *gild* or *geld* include "sacrifice," "worship," "idol," "feast," and "banquet." Thus the theory that at least some medieval guilds derived from early Germanic or Scandinavian combinations for sacrificial banquets must be regarded as nonproven rather than inherently impossible.

It would in any case clearly be unwise to look for a single origin for so complex and heterogeneous a series of societies as the medieval guilds. By the 12th century, when evidence first survives in quantity, the Western European guilds were already bodies of widely differing degrees of organization, directed at a multiplicity of aims. Although any attempt to classify these associations is bound to distort the complicated realities of the medieval situation, most of them can be said to fall within one of the following four classes: (1) frith (peace) guilds; (2) religious guilds; (3) merchant guilds; and (4) craft guilds. All four categories contained a strong religious element; only in the case of the last two was the aim predominantly or primarily that of economic regulation and control. The craft guild has come to be considered as especially typical of the Middle Ages although there is no doubt that many of its characteristics had been anticipated during the classical period.

Guilds in Antiquity and Medieval Byzantium.—There is no direct documentary evidence for the existence of permanent associations of traders or craftsmen in ancient Mesopotamia and pharaonic Egypt. Nor is much known about such societies in pre-Hellenistic Greece, despite references to corporations of *emporoi* and *naukleroi* (shipowners) at Athens and Piraeus by the end of the 5th century B.C. These associations appear to have played relatively little part in public affairs during the classical Greek period, and it is generally agreed that at this stage their aims were primarily social and religious rather than political or commercial: the majority were probably informal and voluntary clubs. Despite Plutarch's comment that of all the establishments of Numa (Numa Pompilius; the semilegendary second king of Rome) "the most commended was his distribution of the people by their trades into companies or guilds," the Roman *collegia opificum* seem to have emerged only very gradually and hesitantly during the later years of the republic. The colleges, of which there were over 30 in Rome itself at the beginning of the 3rd century A.D., were normally based on statutory authority (the *lex collegii*) and their members subjected to the authority of *magistri*. From the reign of Diocletian onward the imperial government deliberately exploited the guilds in the interests of public authority and social order. The *collegia* or *corpora* of Rome and Constantinople were placed under the direct supervision of the city prefect and the children of *corporati* were compelled to enter the profession or trade to which their parents belonged. Although this imperial attempt to confine membership of the guilds to a hereditary caste of skilled artisans was not unsuccessful, the increasing financial demands imposed by the state reduced most colleges to a very precarious position by the mid-4th century A.D.

The fate of the Roman *collegia* and *corpora* after the fall of the Western Empire in 476 remains extremely mysterious and the question whether there was any link between them and the medieval guilds has been long debated. In Northern Europe not one of the several attempts made to demonstrate survival has proved at all convincing; but early medieval Italy does furnish a few examples of trading and artisan societies which may have descended from late imperial *collegia*. In the admittedly exceptional case of the exclusive and powerful society of moneyers, R. S. Lopez has been able to show that there was chronological continuity, except for a period of Lombard disruption at the end of the 6th century. However, in most Italian towns, including Rome itself, all the *collegia* seem to have disappeared and it would be unwise to over-emphasize the significance of survivals. Only in the Byzantine Empire, and perhaps only in the city of Byzantium (Constantinople) itself, did the traditions of the Roman *collegia* continue to survive more or less intact until the fall of Constantinople in 1453. The famous *Book of the Prefect* (a series of instructions probably drawn up by the emperor Leo VI about the year 900) provides a comprehensive picture of an elaborate guild organization whose primary function was the imposition of a rigid control, especially for financial purposes, on every craft and trade in the city.

Frith (Peace) Guilds.—As social groups intermediate between the family and the larger political units of city, territorial lordship, or state, the earliest guilds of northern Europe not unnaturally emerged at a period when many individuals could no longer rely for their own security on either kindred or public authority. The first indisputable reference to guilds as societies with some degree of continuity and coherence occurs in one of Charlemagne's Capitularies of 779 where members of the *ghildonia* are forbidden to bind themselves by oaths. In 852, Archbishop Hincmar of Reims passed statutes to which such associations (*geldoniae* or *confratriae*) gave rise. Common to these and other early references to north European guilds are the assumptions that such fraternities were not yet associations of merchants or craftsmen, that they were formed by means of a mutual oath or *conjuratio*, and that they were spontaneous growths from below which often faced the hostility of the Carolingians because of their danger to established authority. These early guilds may therefore be most plausibly interpreted as substitute or ersatz kindred groups designed to provide mutual self-protection at a time when the wider kin, or *maegth*, to the seven degrees of kindred, showed obvious signs of dissolution. Although it is no longer possible to accept Max Pappenheim's oversimplified theory that all medieval guilds originated from sworn "foster-brotherhoods," this hypothesis had the virtue of stressing that several of the early fraternities were clearly directed at the preservation of life and property in the absence of an alternative protector. Many lords, moreover, were quick to see the possibilities of harnessing a general social movement toward voluntary association in the interests of public order. The *Judicia civitatis Londoniae* of Aethelstan's reign (924–939) reveals the existence of a highly regulated London frith guild whose primary purpose was the pursuit of thieves.

The aim of mutual self-protection is still very much in evidence among the ordinances of the late Anglo-Saxon guilds at Exeter, Bedwyn, Abbotsbury, Woodbury, and Cambridge, which are of particular interest as the earliest medieval guild statutes in existence. Regulations concerning the payment of the *wergild* and the pursuit of the blood feud were now, however, combined with several features characteristic of all later medieval guilds. These surviving Anglo-Saxon guild ordinances assume a continuous corporate organization, expressing itself by means of a solemn entrance oath, a central treasury based on contributions from members, and periodical meetings in a guildhall. By the middle of the 11th century it would seem that both in England and on the Continent, the religious and social functions of the guilds were replacing the protection of life and property as the central preoccupations of their members.

Religious Guilds.—Christian confraternities are as old as Christianity itself and it is impossible to exaggerate the influence of the doctrine and practice of the Church on the evolution of the medieval guild. When missionaries first appeared in Northern Europe they found themselves confronted with a medley of pagan fraternities, many of which they successfully converted into Christian brotherhoods. SS. Boniface (d. 754), Lull (d. 786), and Benedict of Aniane (d. 821) deliberately propagated fraternities uniting faithful Christians to their local abbey, and by the 10th century most of Western Europe was honeycombed with monastic colonies of suppliants. From this time onward all mediæval guilds were inescapably religious organizations, although it seems legitimate to reserve the phrase "religious guild" for those associations whose aims remained more or less exclusively spiritual. The popularity of the latter remained immense throughout the Middle Ages and beyond; and no sharp line can be said to separate the parish fraternities of medieval Europe from their equivalents in present-day Italy or Spain. As most religious guilds were small and private associations with a very limited sphere of operations, they rarely found their way into the sparse public and governmental records of the early Middle Ages. They were already numerous by 1300, and there are good grounds for believing that their multiplication in the late 14th and 15th centuries was one of the most remarkable social phenomena of that period. At least 180 distinct guilds have been detected in later medieval York and many more in London and Norwich. The returns made in 1389 to a governmental inquiry into the origins, usages, and property of the English guilds reveal numerous fraternities of widely differing types in almost every town; all had originated as voluntary associations and relatively few had sought authorization by royal charter. Nor were such religious guilds necessarily confined to the towns. By the 15th century the extremely popular Guilds of Corpus Christi were to be found in virtually all substantial English villages. In southern and south-eastern France a similar role was played by the *Confrérie du Saint-Esprit*, which often enrolled the total population of an Alpine village within its ranks. Characteristic of all such guilds was an oath of admission and a generally small contribution by members to the common fund, customarily expended on the giving of alms, the sayings of masses for the dead, and the holding of feasts and processions. Attachment to a local church, or to a particular altar within a church, was almost universal.

Although the great majority of medieval religious guilds functioned as small religious and social clubs, several pursued more expensive and specialized objectives like the Guilds of the Virgin Mary and of Corpus Christi at Cambridge, which undertook the foundation of an academic college (Corpus Christi) in 1352. At Genoa a century later a new guild was formed to provide a sumptuous chapel in the cathedral of S. Lorenzo as a fitting repository for the newly acquired relics of St. John the Baptist. Some fraternities were semi-international in character (like the *Feste du Puii*, whose ordinances reveal the convivial and musical activities of the late 13th-century London patriciate) and a few, like the Trinity Guild at Coventry, founded in 1364, were partly aristocratic in character. Several religious fraternities, *e.g.*, the Guilds of Corpus Christi and Our Lord's Prayer in 15th-century York, made the promotion of ceremonial processions, pageants, and plays their main *raison d'être*, though only at the risk of arousing the hostility of the craft guilds. The latter, acting in cooperation and under municipal sanction, tended to dominate the formal rituals of city life. Few religious guilds were wealthy or powerful enough to compete with the crafts and almost all were affected, more or less adversely, by the religious upheavals of the 16th century. In England, the Chantries Act of 1547 with its explicit denunciation of the "vain opinions of Purgatory and Masses" and its outright secularization of revenues devoted to spiritual purposes dealt an immediate death-blow to the religious guilds.

Merchant Guilds.—No problem in the history of medieval guild organization has proved more intractable or elusive than the exact economic and political role played by the merchant guilds (the *gilda mercatoria* of most Latin charters, usually synonymous with the Italian *mercanzia* and the German *hanse* or *kopgilde*). However, it is now generally accepted that the merchant guild was never of quite such fundamental significance to the European economy as was once believed. Thus Henri Pirenne's belief that the merchant guild was the initiator of urban autonomy in the West seems highly suspect, especially as it reflects his questionable thesis that the vast majority of European towns originated as settlements of long-distance peddlers and merchants. This is not to deny that the first recorded merchant guilds were associations of traders interested in international commerce. The privileged fraternity formed by the merchants of Tiel in Guelders about 1020 is the first undoubted precursor of the merchant guilds, and the statutes of a similar body at St. Omer actually use the term *gilda mercatoria* before the end of the 11th century. Al- though associations of merchants from different towns continued to flourish in the later Middle Ages (the so-called Hanse of London is the best known 12th-century example; *see also* HANSEATIC LEAGUE), most merchant guilds naturally confined their member- ship to the inhabitants of one city. In most European towns the imposition of a high entrance fee gave the merchant guild an ex- clusive character, although it is clear that the merchant patriciate normally exercised authority through its control of the urban constitution rather than through the merchant guild as such. It followed that such guilds were unlikely to survive the urban social upheavals of the late 13th and 14th centuries, the so-called *Zunftrevolution* ("guild revolution"), which transferred all or part of the political and economic powers of the patriciate to the crafts and mysteries (see *Craft Guilds*, below). By the early years of the 15th century most continental merchant guilds had disappeared into oblivion or survived as attenuated bodies, deprived of any genuine economic function.

An instructive parallel is provided by the history of the merchant guilds in Scottish cities; here, because of the general backwardness of the Scottish economy, the violent collisions between the guildry and the crafts seem to have been postponed to the 16th and 17th centuries. Although merchants successfully retained much of their influence in the town councils (a dean of guild, although deprived of nearly all his ancient functions, still survives in many Scottish burghs), the result of the struggle was generally favourable—as in continental Europe 200 years earlier—to the craftsmen.

The history of the English guild merchant has aroused particular interest because of its distinctive features. First emerging soon after the Norman Conquest, it is recorded in about 40 English towns (but not London, Exeter, or Norwich) before the death of King John. Like its Anglo-Saxon predecessors, the guild merchant had its charitable, social, and convivial activities, usually centred on the *Morwenspeches* or "morning-speeches" where new members were elected, ordinances were revised, and erring guildsmen fined in ale. But its essential characteristic, one highly prized by English burgesses and conveyed to them by a royal grant of *gilda merca- toria*, was the unrestricted and monopolistic right to regulate all trading within the borough. There now seems little doubt that the English guild merchant originated primarily as a fiscal device, a mechanism through which all burgesses with an interest in urban trade could "geld together" and by contributing toward a common fund secure their individual exemption from royal tolls. In essence the guild merchant was not a fraternity of merchants (*mercator* was in any case a much wider term than the modern "merchant") but a market guild, popular rather than exclusive in character: there were no less than 200 members of the guild merchant at Totnes in 1260. The obvious advantages of a common fund and an independent body of officials headed by an alderman made the guild merchant an eminently suitable instrument for the transac- tion of general urban affairs. This was, however, a temporary phenomenon and by the 13th century the powers of the guild merchant were already being undermined by the growth of the craft guilds. At the time of the Reformation, the organization of the guild merchant had collapsed almost everywhere, the name occasionally surviving as a vague term applied to a periodical feast (that at Preston [*q.v.*] is the best-known and longest-lived ex- ample) or the municipal corporation as a whole.

Craft Guilds.—A medieval craft guild was an occupational as- sociation, usually comprising all the artisans—and often the sup- pliers, retailers, and wholesale merchants—concerned with a spe- cific branch of industry or commerce. Such associations were commonly called mysteries (misteries) in late medieval England, a word which rightly stresses, like the French *métier*, the Italian *arte*, the German *Zunft* or *Handwerk*, and the Latin *ministerium* (from which it was derived) or *officium*, the professional nature of the fraternity. As an essentially urban phenomenon, finding its most favourable conditions within towns large enough to en- courage extensive division of labour and yet not given over too exclusively (like Venice) to the needs of large-scale international trade, it was inevitable that the craft guild should emerge in

the wake of the commercial revolution of early medieval Europe. A weavers' guild is recorded at Mainz as early as 1099 and in London, Lincoln, Winchester, Oxford, and Huntingdon during the reign of Henry I; but the greatest period of guild expansion occurred after rather than before 1250. Most craft organizations naturally modeled themselves on existing religious guilds and it was extremely common for mysteries to originate as social and religious fraternities which only developed economic functions at a later date. By a natural process of extension, the principles of the craft guild were applied to the "arts" of masonry, carpen- try, painting, and music. A very early example is the corporation of architects and sculptors at Siena in 1212. Guild records are among the few sources to provide biographical information about medieval and Renaissance artists, since membership of their local fraternity was generally compulsory for all painters not in the personal service of a ruling prince. Because of the widespread tendency for existing crafts to amalgamate, many artists found themselves linked with practitioners of very different trades: Florentine painters belonged to the guild of surgeon apothecaries in the 14th century (*see* ART, SOCIETIES OF). Several associations of painters and musicians did, however, preserve their separate identity (*see also* MINSTREL; MEISTERSINGER).

The general characteristics of the medieval craft guild are well known and were in general remarkably alike throughout Eu- rope. Assemblies of all members enjoyed some legislative powers but the control of guild policy lay in the hands of a few officials (from two to four wardens in the case of most English crafts) and a council of advisers or assistants. From an early stage in its development, the typical mystery tended to be an extremely hier- archical body, divided into the three categories of masters, jour- neymen, and apprentices. In the largest and wealthiest trades the master craftsmen formed a select inner circle, open only to those apprentices and journeymen who could provide proof not only of their technical competence (the "masterpiece") but also of their wealth and social eligibility. Antagonism between the master employer and journeyman labourer within the same craft was increasingly common from the 14th century onward and found expression in the formation of separate yeomen or journeymen's guilds. The political and economic significance of the latter has been much exaggerated in the past, and except in 15th-century Germany, where masters occasionally formed interurban defensive leagues against the *knechten* (journeymen) of their respective crafts, they rarely offered a seriously sustained challenge to the authority of the existing mysteries. Apprenticeship, although not always compulsory, remains perhaps the most fundamental element in the constitution of the craft guild, as it secured the continuity of practice, tradition, and personnel on which the welfare of all such bodies depended (*see* APPRENTICESHIP).

Because the primary economic objective of most craft guilds was the establishment of a complete monopoly over all who were associated together in the pursuit of a common profession, it has often been argued that they "embodied a whole social system into which the individual was completely absorbed by the pressure of moral and social conventions" (E. Lipson). A closer investigation of the complex economic and social problems affecting the medieval town suggests that the ability of the craft guilds to exercise their authority was subject to serious practical limitations. Many of the innumerable extant craft guild regulations can never have been applied continuously and guild monopoly power was usually too weak to take the blame (as it once did) for the economic difficul- ties of late medieval Europe. Despite frequent attempts at price- fixing, it seems unlikely that many guilds were able to exert permanent influence on local selling prices and wage rates. The aims of urban producers as expressed in their craft ordinances were normally held in check by the needs of the local consumer and the long-distance merchant. The very multiplicity of crafts within a given city tended to prevent any one mystery from pursuing its monopolistic ambitions to extremes, as the perennial conflicts throughout Europe between weavers and fullers or between the victualing and nonvictualing guilds fully demonstrate. Even when, as was usual in the 14th century, a group of particularly power- ful crafts succeeded in securing direct or indirect control of the town government, they normally found it essential to subordinate their own economic interests to those of the city as a whole. Municipal supervision and interference in matters of craft policy is common at all stages of guild history and from the 15th century onward was being increasingly supplemented by the intervention of national governments: an Elizabethan statute of 1563 made the length of apprenticeship customary in London (seven years) compulsory for craft guilds throughout England. During the later Middle Ages, prominent mysteries were finding it advisable to secure royal charters of incorporation, charters which were to launch the London Livery Companies in particular into a long and flourishing career before attaining their present position as the most celebrated survivors of the medieval craft guilds (see LIVERY COMPANIES).

The decline of the medieval craft guilds was a slow and tortuous process. New fraternities were still being founded throughout Europe in the 17th century and the London companies were attempting to enforce the registration of apprentices as late as 1800. Nevertheless the 16th century can be said to have marked a decisive turn in the fortunes of most mysteries. Apart from the disruptive effects of the Reformation and the growth of governmental power, the craft guilds were seriously weakened by the appearance of new markets and greater capital resources. An entrepreneurial class had emerged with little to gain from the preservation of urban craft restrictions. Contemporaries believed with justice that Antwerp's economic primacy in early 16th-century Europe was the direct result of the unrestricted freedom offered to merchants and bankers who resided there. The drift of industrial activity away from the towns into the countryside, very evident in the case of English and Flemish cloth production, left the guilds increasingly isolated from the main currents of economic power, as did the emergence of regulated companies and other associations of wealthy merchant-capitalists. It is perhaps a sign of the general insignificance of the surviving guilds that they evoked surprisingly little serious criticism until the 18th-century Enlightenment. By the time of the decrees abolishing craft associations in France (1791), Rome (1807), Spain (1840), Austria and Germany (1859–60), and Italy (1864), the bases of their authority had been long eroded. In England the Municipal Corporations Act of 1835 which formally removed all guild restrictions on trade and industry was generally regarded as the recognition of a *fait accompli*.

Occupational guilds continued to flourish in India, China, Japan, and the Muslim countries until quite recent times, but they too have been unable to withstand the impact of modern Western industrial organization.

See also references under "Guild" in the Index.

BIBLIOGRAPHY.—W. E. Wilda, *Das Gildenwesen im Mittelalter* (1831); J. Toulmin Smith, ed., *English Gilds*, with introductory essay by L. Brentano, "On the History and Development of Gilds" (1870; reprinted 1924); C. Gross, *The Gild Merchant*, 2 vol. (1890; reprinted 1927 and 1965); *Bibliography of British Municipal History*, *Including Gilds and Parliamentary Representation*, 2nd ed. (1966); S. Kramer, *The English Craft Gilds and the Government* (1905); *The English Craft Gilds: Studies in Their Progress and Decline* (1927); G. Unwin, *The Gilds and Companies of London* (1908; 4th ed. 1963); G. von Below, "Die Motive der Zunftbildung im deutschen Mittelalter," *Historische Zeitschrift*, cix, pp. 23–48 (1912); H. F. Westlake, *The Parish Gilds of Medieval England* (1919); F. Valsecchi, *Le corporazioni nell'organismo politico del medioevo* (1931); G. Mickwitz, *Die Kartellfunktionen der Zünfte und ihre Bedeutung bei der Entstehung des Zunftwesens* (1936); H. Pirenne, *Les Villes et les institutions urbaines* (1939); R. S. Smith, *The Spanish Guild Merchant: a History of the Consulado, 1250–1700* (1940); E. Coornaert, *Les Corporations en France avant 1789* (1941); G. Espinas, *Les Origines de l'association*, 2 vol. (1941–42); S. L. Thrupp, "Medieval Gilds Reconsidered," *The Journal of Economic History*, ii, pp. 164–173 (1942); son, *The Merchant Class of Medieval London, 1300–1500* (1948); E. Lipson, *Economic History of England*, 9th ed., vol. i (1947); M. M. Postan *et al.* (eds.), *The Cambridge Economic History of Europe*, vol. ii and iii (1952–63); excellent bibliographies; R. S. Lopez, "An Aristocracy of Money in the Early Middle Ages," *Speculum*, xxviii, pp. 1–43 (1953); W. F. Kahl, *The Development of London Livery Companies* (1960; with biblíog.); J. Bromley, *Armorial Bearings of the Guilds of London* (1961); G. A. Williams, *Medieval London* (1963); M. Wischnitzer, *History of Jewish Crafts and Guilds* (1965); G. Baer, *Egyptian Guilds in Modern Times* (1967); S. W. Wells, *Chinese Commercial Guild*, 5th ed. (1966). (R. B. Do.)

GUILDFORD, a municipal borough, cathedral and market town, and the county town of Surrey, Eng., is situated on the River Wey where it breaks through the North Downs, 28 mi. (45 km.) SW of London. Pop. (1971 prelim.) 56,887. First mentioned in the will of Alfred the Great, Guildford was a royal manor in Saxon times. Vestiges of a shell-keep and the Saxon church tower of St. Mary's Church are of pre-Conquest date. The town's earliest known charter dates from 1257. The Norman castle was part of the medieval perimeter defense of London and was much visited by Plantagenet kings. In the steep High Street are many historical buildings including the Tudor Royal Grammar School (founded 1507), now the town's art gallery and library; Guildford House (founded 1660), a magnificent almshouse founded by Archbishop George Abbot, a native of Guildford; the Church of Holy Trinity (1760), opposite, which is one of two Georgian churches in Surrey; and the Guildhall, a Tudor building with a 17th-century facade.

On Stag Hill stands the Cathedral of the Holy Spirit, designed by Sir Edward Maufe (started in 1936 and completed in 1968), the second Anglican cathedral to be built on a new site in England since the Reformation. On the western slopes of Stag Hill rise the buildings of the University of Surrey (incorporated 1966). Charles Lutwidge Dodgson (Lewis Carroll) died in Guildford in 1898 and is buried in the Mount Cemetery.

Guildford lies in the Greater London green belt, and its river, the Wey, is the first river in England to belong to the National Trust. Public parks, sports and swimming facilities and conserved open spaces abound. The town has a professional municipal symphony orchestra, a College of Art and Design, many further education institutions and a College of Law. The Yvonne Arnaud Theatre was opened in 1965 and a modern Sports Centre and new Law Courts heralded a Municipal Town Centre development. Light industries in knitwear, plastics, and engineering developed after World War II alongside the older Dennis automobile works.

BIBLIOGRAPHY.—G. C. Williamson, *Guildford in the Olden Time* (1904); *Victoria County History of Surrey*, vol. iii (1911); J. W. Penycate, *History of Guildford* (1968); *Guide to Guildford Cathedral* (1960). (M. D. L.)

GUILD SOCIALISM, the name of a school of socialist thought which became prominent in Great Britain in the early 20th century (see SOCIALISM). Its governing idea was that of self-government in industry—the application of democratic principles to industrial as well as to political affairs—and the organization of the economic life of the community on a "functional" basis. As the name implies, guild socialism had, in the minds of its founders, a relation to the forms of industrial organization that existed throughout the medieval world, and was based on an attempt, in some measure, to apply medieval ideas to the solution of modern problems. This does not mean that guild socialists wished to restore the medieval guild system or to revive handicraft in place of machine production. This element was indeed present in the early stages but had dropped away before it acquired any wide influence.

Origin.—The origin of the movement is to be found in the work of an architect, Arthur J. Penty, who published *The Restoration of the Guild System* in 1906, and of A. R. Orage, for many years editor of the *New Age*, in which journal the new doctrine gradually developed in the next few years. The fruit of this development was the book *National Guilds*, written by S. G. Hobson and edited by A. R. Orage, first published in the *New Age* in 1912. In this work, guild socialism first assumed its distinctive form as an attempt to convert the trade unions to the idea of "workers' control" in industry, and to create, with their aid, self-governing functional organizations for the government of industry in conjunction with the state.

So far the guild movement had not spread beyond a small circle of theoretical adherents. But in the years before 1914 a great wave of labour unrest spread over Great Britain. There were many strikes, and a new spirit of economic revolt entered into the trade-union movement. At the same time the doctrines of industrial unionism were imported from America (see INDUSTRIAL

WORKERS OF THE WORLD), and those of syndicalism (*q.v.*) from France; both these doctrines found numerous adherents among the younger trade unionists and excited vigorous controversy. Guild socialism was influenced by these movements and was more and more presented as a reconciliation of syndicalist and socialist doctrines. Like the syndicalists it denounced bureaucracy and state control. Unlike them, it repudiated anarchism, and recognized the necessity of the state as an instrument of political organization and control. It was not, however, until a group of the younger men began, in 1913, regularly to advocate guild socialism in the newly founded *Daily Herald* that the movement attained any widespread influence. And it was not until 1915 that it assumed, with the foundation of the National Guilds league by G. D. H. Cole, W. Mellor, M. B. Reckitt and others, an organized form.

World War I and After.—The industrial situation during World War I undoubtedly helped the growth of the new movement. For the war, by making necessary large and frequent changes in industrial organization, profoundly stirred the trade unions, and created in the minds of trade unionists a keen desire for control and self-government in industry. During the war the influence of guild socialism was widely felt in the shop stewards' movement and in the redrafting of many trade-union programs so as to include the demand for "workers' control." Thus, the Miners' federation, which before the war had demanded nationalization and state administration of the mines, changed its program in 1918 to a demand for national ownership and democratic control by the workers, and put forward its new guild socialist claim before the famous Sankey commission of 1919. The socialist bodies, such as the Independent Labour party and the Labour party itself, also altered their programs so as to include the demand for some measure of workers' control in industry.

Immediately after the war guild socialism spread still more rapidly, and entered on a new phase with the formation of actual working guilds, under trade-union auspices, in the building and other industries. The National Building guild and its local centres executed, between 1920 and 1922, a number of important housing contracts and were generally agreed to have done excellent work. But the guild had no capital, and the abandonment of the Addison housing scheme in 1921 was fatal to it. Driven to depend on bank and commercial credits, it overtraded and got into financial difficulties which in 1922 led to its collapse. Certain of its local centres survived and were still active for several years longer, as were the tailoring guilds in Glasgow and Leeds, the piano workers' guild in London and certain others.

Guild Socialism and Collectivism.—These practical ventures, however, were, from the standpoint of the main body of guild socialists, only of minor importance. For the guild was for them essentially a part of the mechanism of a socialist community, and "guilds" formed in a capitalist society could be guilds only in a quite incomplete sense. Guild socialism involves the ownership of industries by the whole community, as well as their administration by the "workers by hand and brain" (a phrase originally coined by the guild socialists) engaged in them. It is essentially a socialist doctrine, accepting the socialist idea of public ownership, and differing from the collectivist or state socialist school of thought only in its insistence on the idea of industrial self-government and its hostility to bureaucracy and political control of industrial affairs. Guild socialists differed, indeed, in their views about the form and structure of the state in a guild society. Some believed in the continued supremacy of the state as the political organ of government, while others held that the state in its present form is destined to disappear and to be replaced by a sort of federal authority representing the community in its various functional aspects. This latter view has been associated with the philosophical ideas of political pluralism. It must not be confused with proposals for "industrial self-government" under capitalist control.

Industrial self-government was, for the guild socialists, the application to economics of a general principle that is of far wider significance. They believed that democracy can be real only if it is "functional"—that is, if it is specifically related to each of the main activities of society. It is absurd, they held, to speak of

political democracy where industry is organized on autocratic lines, for the conditions of a man's daily work will inevitably affect his attitude and status as a citizen. Moreover, the existing economic system fails because it does not call out what is best in men. Instead of a co-operative fellowship of service we have contending groups of masters and men, alike wasted by "the sickness of an acquisitive society" (R. H. Tawney). It is necessary so to organize the economic and social system as to make each service a responsible fellowship, whose members are "on their honour" to do their best in the interest of all. (G. D. H. C.)

Appraisal.—Guild socialism as such lost appeal in Great Britain, and elsewhere had no theoretical or practical impact. The reasons became manifest as critical thought was brought to bear on the ideas of guild socialism in the decade after 1919.

It became clear that the division of economic power, political power and representation in sovereign legislatures is not as distinct as guild socialists had implied. Legislatures that represent territorial divisions in which each voter has one vote tend, indeed, to be overly general in their representation, but the consultation, formal and informal, by both legislatures and administrative bodies with various interest groups steadily remedied this weakness; thus the suggestions of guild socialists had nothing to do with the remedy. In Germany, France and Italy native and traditional needs and ideas produced special formal "corporative" advisory bodies. (*See* CORPORATE STATE.) If political representation of the voters was not everywhere as incessantly active as guild socialists thought it ought to be in a guild organization, political parties, the mediums of democratic representation, improved themselves in the techniques of continuous operative linkage between people, groups, legislatures and the executive. Workers' control of industry was contrived in part through trade unions which brought direct pressure on employers, or through the establishment of some form of workers' elected councils in the workshops with some rights of joint determination of business policy. It became apparent that the vesting of sovereign power in numerous guilds must lead to insoluble disputes over the weight of representation to be accorded to each guild. Also, the number of guilds (each a segment of the national economy) must be so large as virtually to substitute a multiplicity of parties, each based on an economic interest, for a usually much smaller number of conventional political parties (in some nations, only two), with a consequent grave divisive effect on society. The belief that workers would more actively share in guild operation than in the activities of political parties could not be proved; but their demonstrated passivity in their own trade unions and consumers' co-operative societies engendered skepticism of the faith of guild socialists.

The essence of guild socialist doctrine, that political representation in great societies is a gross wholesale process that needs remedies, however, remained valuable. French syndicalism, German *Ständestaat* ("estate") or "corporative" theories and Latin state "corporativism" and institutions contained this germ and were variant answers to the anxieties which guild socialism expressed. (H. Fi.)

BIBLIOGRAPHY.—S. G. Hobson and A. R. Orage, *National Guilds* (1914); G. D. H. Cole, *Self-Government in Industry* (1917), *Guild Socialism Re-stated* (1920), *Social Theory* (1920) *The Next Ten Years* (1929); M. B. Reckitt and C. E. Bechhofer, *The Meaning of National Guilds* (1918). For guild socialist political theory, see G. R. de Maeztu, *Authority, Liberty and Function* (1916); Bertrand Russell, *Roads to Freedom* (1919); R. H. Tawney, *The Acquisitive Society* (1921). For criticisms, see G. C. Field, *Guild Socialism* (1920); N. Carpenter, *Guild Socialism* (1922); R. Bowen, *German Theories of the Corporative State* (1947); M. H. Elbow, *French Corporative Theory, 1789–1948* (1953); H. Finer, *Mussolini's Italy* (1935). (G. D. H. C.; H. Fi.)

GUILFORD, BARONS AND EARLS OF. The English barony of Guilford was first created in 1683 for FRANCIS NORTH (1637–1685), second or third son of the 4th Baron North (*see* NORTH, BARONS), after he had become lord keeper in succession to Lord Nottingham. He had been an eminent lawyer, solicitor general (1671), attorney general (1673) and chief justice of the common pleas (1675), and in 1679 was made a member of the council of 30 and, on its dissolution, of the cabinet. North was a man of wide culture and a stanch royalist. He married in 1672 Lady Frances Pope, daughter and co-heiress of the earl of Downe, who inherited the Wroxton estate. He was succeeded by his son FRANCIS (1673-1729), 2nd baron, whose eldest son, FRANCIS (1704-90), 3rd baron, inherited the barony of North in 1734 from his kinsman the 6th Baron North. This 3rd Baron Guilford was in 1752 created earl of Halifax, and his son and successor FREDERICK (1732-92), 2nd earl, is best known as Lord North (q.v.), the English prime minister. The titles passed in 1949 to EDWARD FRANCIS (1933-), 9th earl.

GUILLAUME DE CHAMPEAUX (Lat. GUGLIELMUS DE CAMPELLIS; Eng. WILLIAM OF CHAMPEAUX) (c. 1070-1121), French philosopher and theologian prominent in the scholastic controversy on the nature of universals. Having studied under Manegold of Lautenbach in Paris, under Anselm of Laon and under Roscelin at Compiègne, he taught in the cathedral school of Notre Dame in Paris and had Abelard among his pupils. In 1108, however, perhaps because of the polemics between him and Abelard, he withdrew to the abbey of St. Victor, where he taught rhetoric, logic and theology and may have inspired the mystical trend characteristic of that abbey. From 1113 he was bishop of Châlons-sur-Marne.

On the question of universals, Guillaume before his disputes with Abelard was an extreme realist, holding that the universal had real being as the common essence simultaneously present in its entirety in every individual member of a genus or species. Subsequently he maintained a theory of "indifference" (i.e., non-difference), maintaining that the universal really consisted in the features of similarity or identity whereby individuals, though essentially distinct, are recognized as members of genus or species. Guillaume's surviving works are all theological. The *De sacramento altaris*, the *De origine animae* (perhaps apocryphal) and the *Altercatio cujusdam Christiani et Judaei* are printed by J. P. Migne in *Patrologia latina*, vol. clxiii (1854). He also wrote *De essentia Dei* and *Sententiae seu Quaestiones*.

BIBLIOGRAPHY.—V. Cousin, *Fragments philosophiques*, 5th ed., vol. ii, *Philosophie du moyen âge* (1865); E. Michaud, *Guillaume de Champeaux et les écoles de Paris au XIIe siècle*, 2nd ed. (1868); G. Lefèvre, *Les Variations de Guillaume de Champeaux et la question des universaux* (1899); M. Grabmann, *Geschichte der scholastischen Methode*, vol. ii (1911); H. Weisweiler, *Das Schrifttum der Schule Anselms von Laon und Wilhelms von Champeaux in deutschen Bibliotheken* (1936).

GUILLAUME D'ORANGE, the central hero of about 24 medieval French epic poems of the 12th and 13th centuries. Of the secular life of the historical Wilhelmus, a Frankish nobleman and cousin of Charlemagne, who died in 812, the chroniclers record but little. Appointed count of Toulouse in 789, he was in frequent conflict with Moorish invaders; in 793, although halting their advance, he suffered defeat at the battle of the Orbiel, and about ten years later participated as *primus signifer* in the siege of Barcelona by Louis I. In 804 he withdrew to the Benedictine abbey of Aniane and soon after founded the *cella* of Gellone (St. Guilhem-du-Désert, Hérault), where he died. There is no doubt that he is the same person as the Guillaume d'Orange, or Guillaume Fière-brace, or Guillaume *au court* (also, and perhaps originally, *courb*) *nez*, of the epic poems.

The *Couronnement Louis* portrays him as a young knight zealously upholding his weakling sovereign Louis the Pious, son of Charlemagne, forcing him to overcome his reluctance to accept the crown, and killing an overambitious rival. While on a pilgrimage to Rome he delivers the city from the Saracens, and in order to return to the service of Louis, abandons at the altar the princess whose hand had been his reward. He subdues a revolt of the barons who on Charlemagne's death had imprisoned Louis and then returns to Italy to overcome a German invader. In the *Charroi de Nîmes* Guillaume sets out to gain Nîmes, Orange and "Spain" (i.e., Moorish-held lands), with which the king had invested him if he was able to conquer them. The *Prise d'Orange* tells how Guillaume, lured by reports of the beauty of Orable, wife of the Saracen king Tiébaut, captures the city of Orange where she is guarded by his son. He marries Orable who is baptized and takes the name Guibourc (one of the wives of the historical Wilhelmus was called Vitiburgis). In the *Chevalerie Vivien* Guillaume is no longer a youth and shares the principal role with his nephew Vivien—a character apparently owing much to Roland, another chief hero of the epics of this period. When he is knighted, Vivien vows never to give ground to the Saracens. Having provoked the Saracen king, Déramé (Abd-er-Rahman), Vivien is attacked by him with overwhelmingly superior forces, and, despite the arrival of Guillaume with an army, is defeated at the battle of Archant (or *les Archanz*, or *Larchamp*), a name of doubtful origin but which the poets equated with Les Aliscans d'Arles). The narrative continues in *Aliscans*; Vivien, despite his heroism, is finally overcome, and, in one of the most moving scenes in French epic poetry, dies in the arms of Guillaume, who, his army wiped out and his nephews captured, flees in disguise to Orange, where Guibourc persuades him to seek help from Louis. The king, despite Guillaume's past services, at first refuses but is finally driven, to grant him an army. With this, accompanied by his brothers, Guillaume returns and puts Déramé to flight, principally with the aid of a giant kitchen boy, Rainoart, (later to be revealed as Guibourc's brother) who wields a *tinel*, or club, in lieu of lance and sword and whose absence introduces something of a burlesque note. At last, heavy with years, Guillaume retires to Aniane and Gellone, but even now his travails are not ended; again, in the *Moniage Guillaume*, he must take up arms for Louis, this time against the Saxons, who are besieging the king in Paris itself. He retrieves his arms and charger, defeats Isoré under the walls of the capital and returns to Gellone, there to die.

These poems are bound together not only by the characters but also by a unity underlying the imaginary events they relate, for pervading them all is the theme of the devotion of Guillaume and his family—to each other, to their self-assumed championship of Christendom against the infidel in Spain and the south, and above all to a consistently pusillanimous, ungrateful and unco-operative king.

These themes are developed in the additions to the cycle by later poets: the deeds of Guillaume's father are recounted in *Aimeri de Narbonne* and the *Mort Aimeri*, and those of his six brothers in the *Narbonnais*. These, with others, constitute a cycle within a cycle, the *cycle d'Aimeri*; Guillaume is provided with a prothalamion in the *Enfances Guillaume*, and the wars against the Saracens are further continued by nephews and nephews of nephews in *Foulque de Candie*, *Le Siège de Barbastre*, *La Bataille Loquifer*, etc., until finally the canvas covers some seven or eight generations.

The principal poems are mostly anonymous and their relationship to each other is obscure. They are with few exceptions incorporated in cyclic manuscripts—library or collectors' pieces at least a century younger than the earlier poems, which appear to date from the middle and second half of the 12th century—and in some cases these manuscripts show evidence of material accretions; in addition, there are many internal inconsistencies which do not always seem to be explained by the fact that the texts in their conserved forms appear to be recensions of earlier versions. For some critics, the starting point of the cycle lies in the events surrounding the death of Vivien, although there are good grounds for regarding the death as a relative newcomer to the poems, while other scholars look rather in the direction of the capture of Orange. It is difficult, however, in view of the underlying theme, to fragment the narratives in this way. The whole problem is further complicated by the *Chanson de Guillaume*, a 13th-century Anglo-Norman text discovered in 1903 and at first generally assumed to represent, despite its obvious corruptions, the earliest form of the Vivien episodes. But the early dating of this poem is not unchallenged, and the enigma of the *Chanson de Guillaume*, part of which is clearly a derivative of *Aliscans*, remains to be solved.

The researches of Joseph Bédier (q.v.; see also *Bibliography*) established the link between these poems and their propagation through the sanctuaries of the pilgrim routes of France and Spain, especially that of Santiago de Compostela; his theory that their genesis is to be explained in these terms, however, is less certain. The cult of St. Guillaume appears to have been originally a local one, and there is irrefutable evidence of collaboration between jongleurs and the monks of Aniane and Gellone as early as 1139,

But scholars remain sharply divided between the traditionalist and the individualist interpretation (*see* CHANSONS DE GESTE) of the many problems surrounding these poems and allied texts, including the *Fragment de la Haye*, an apparently early 11th-century fragment in Latin prose, probably rewritten from hexameters, but of unknown origin, in which figure a group of protagonists bearing names identical to those of certain characters appearing in the Guillaume poems (although not that of Guillaume himself). Some modern toponymic and onomastic research, especially by E. von Richthofen, suggests that part of the legend may have been originally localized in the Spanish March—where sons and nephews of the historical Wilhelmus played a part in the political events of the 9th century.

The popularity of these poems was not confined to France. They were adapted into German by Wolfram von Eschenbach (*q.v.*) in his *Willehalm*, the compiler of the Old Norse *Karlamagnussaga* incorporated them in his Branch ix, and in the 15th century Andrea da Barberino rewrote them as *I Nerbonesi*.

BIBLIOGRAPHY.—P. Tuffrau, *La Légende de Guillaume d'Orange* (1923); J. Bédier, *Les Légendes épiques*, vol. i, *Le Cycle de Guillaume d'Orange* (1st ed., 1908; 3rd ed., 1926); P. A. Becker, *Das Werden der Wilhelm-und der Aimerigeste* (1939); J. Frappier, *Les Chansons de geste du cycle Guillaume d'Orange*, vol. i, *La Chanson de Guillaume, Aliscans, La Chevalerie Vivien* (1955); M. de Riquer, *Les Chansons de geste françaises*, 2nd ed., trans. by I. Cluzel (1957). *See also* R. Bossuat, *Manuel bibliographique de la littérature française du moyen âge* (1951; supplements 1955, 1961); and the annual *Bulletin bibliographique de la Société Rencesvals* (1958–). (D. McMi.)

GUILLAUMIN, JEAN BAPTISTE ARMAND (1841–1927), French landscape painter and engraver, an important member of the Impressionist movement, was born in Paris, Feb. 16, 1841. He spent his boyhood at Moulins-sur-Allier and at the age of 17 went to Paris. He studied drawing under the sculptor Caillouette, and he painted views in the neighbourhood of Montmartre and Meudon and on the banks of the Seine. He also worked on portraiture and still life. In 1874 Guillaumin took part in an exhibition of Impressionist paintings with C. Pissarro, C. Monet and Sisley. By 1892 he was in a position to give up his post and to concentrate entirely on his art. After that date, he painted many seascapes on both the Atlantic and Mediterranean coasts. His execution is direct, bold and sometimes vehement, his colour harmonious.

GUILLEMOT (*Uria aalge*), or, as it is usually called in North America, common murre, a sea bird, the size of a small duck, breeds on the rocky coasts of the North Atlantic in vast numbers. It is a member of the auk family (Alcidae). The head, slender bill, back and wings are dark, the under parts being white. A second species, Brünnich's guillemot, or thick-billed murre (*U. lomvia*), is very similar to and ranges the same area as *U. aalge*. Each has varieties in the cold North Pacific and the west coast of North America and elsewhere.

The black guillemot, *Cepphus* (or *Uria*) *grylle*, known to sailors as the "dovekie," is almost entirely black in summer plumage. It is also found along cold northern coasts. Unlike the common form, which lays a single egg, the black guillemot produces two or three in a clutch. The pigeon guillemot (not definitely distinct from the black guillemot) is more southerly in range, sometimes occurring along the coast of southern California. *See also* AUK.

GUILLERAGUES, GABRIEL JOSEPH DE LAVERGNE, VICOMTE DE (1628–1685), French author and diplomat, who wrote the *Letters of a Portuguese Nun*, was born at Bordeaux on Nov. 18, 1628, and educated at the Collège de Navarre in Paris. After studying law in Paris, he returned to his native city to become a barrister in the *parlement* of Bordeaux. In 1651 he met the prince de Conti and five years later became his steward, a post which he occupied until Conti's death in 1666. He then left Bordeaux for Paris, where he frequented Mme de Sablé's salon and was on friendly terms with Molière, Boileau and La Rochefoucauld. In 1669 he published what appears to have been his entire literary work: some rhymed *Valentins*, and the famous *Lettres portugaises*, an alleged translation of five love letters written by a Portuguese nun, who in 1810 was identified as one Mariana Alcoforado (*q.v.*). Guilleragues entered Louis XIV's service in 1669 as his private secretary, and ten years later was appointed French ambassador at Constantinople, where he died on March 4, 1685.

For over two centuries his fame depended on personal tributes by Boileau, who called him "the most agreeable man in France," and Antoine Galland (*q.v.*), his secretary at Constantinople. In 1926, however, with F. C. Green's discovery that he was the author of the *Lettres portugaises*, he won a small but secure place in literary history. (R. BA.)

GUILLOTINE, the instrument for inflicting capital punishment by decapitation, introduced into France at the period of the Revolution. It consists of two upright posts surmounted by a crossbeam, and grooved so as to guide an oblique-edged knife, the back of which is heavily weighted to make it fall forcefully when the cord by which it is held aloft is released. Previous to the period when it obtained notoriety under its present name, it had been in use in Scotland, England and various parts of the continent. There is still preserved in the antiquarian museum of Edinburgh the rude guillotine called the "maiden," by which the regent Morton was decapitated in 1581. No similar machine seems to have ever been in general use in England; but until 1650 there existed in the forest of Hardwick a mode of trial and execution called the gibbet law, by which a felon convicted of theft within the liberty was sentenced to be decapitated by a machine called the Halifax gibbet.

In Germany the machine was in general use during the middle ages, under the name of the *Diele*, the *Hobel* or the *Dolabra*. From the 13th century it was used in Italy under the name of *Mannaia* for the execution of criminals of noble birth. It had fallen into general disuse on the continent until Joseph Ignace Guillotin, a French physician, suggested its use in modern times.

Guillotin, who was born at Saintes, May 28, 1738, and elected to the constituent assembly in 1789, was instrumental in having a law passed requiring all sentences of death to be carried out by "means of a machine." This was done so that the privilege of execution by decapitation would no longer be confined to the nobles and the process of execution would be as painless as possible. After the machine had been used in several satisfactory experiments on dead bodies in the hospital of Bicêtre, it was erected on the Place de Grève for the execution of the highwayman Nicolas Jacques Pelletier on April 25, 1792. At first the machine was called *Louisette* or *La Petite Louison*, but was later referred to as *la guillotine*, the name by which it since has been known both popularly and officially.

BIBLIOGRAPHY.—H. Herschmann, *La Guillotine en 1793, d'après dés documents inédits des archives nationales* (1908); A. Kershaw, *History of the Guillotine* (1959). (R. G. CL.; X.)

GUINEA is a loosely used term for the coastal region of west Africa between Cape Verde (latitude 15° N.) and Moçâmedes, Angola (15° S.). There is a distinction between Upper and Lower Guinea, westward and southward respectively of the line of volcanic peaks that runs northeast from Annobón through São Tomé to Mt. Cameroon. The Gulf of Guinea is a part of the Atlantic ocean adjacent to this coastal area. The name Guinea appears on maps from about 1350, though it came into common usage in Europe only during the 15th century. It may derive from the 8th-century kingdom of the upper Niger known variously as Ghinea,

ERIC HOSKING
COMMON MURRES OR GUILLEMOTS (URIA AALGE); (LEFT) BRIDLED AND (RIGHT) COMMON VARIETIES

Genii, Jenné or Djenné; or from Ghana, "the land of gold," the oldest known state of the western Sudan (from which modern Ghana, formerly the Gold Coast, takes its name).

Convincing evidence is lacking for the French claim that ships from Dieppe reached the Guinea coast in 1364–65 and that their merchants established trading posts as far east as São Jorge da Mina (modern Elmina, Ghana). Cape Bojador (latitude 26° N.) was rounded by the Portuguese seaman Gilianes or Gil Eannes in 1434, and some years later the first cargoes of slaves and gold were brought back to Lisbon. A papal bull gave Portugal exclusive rights over the west coast of Africa, and in 1469 Fernão Gomes was granted a trade monopoly provided 300 mi. of new coast were explored annually. The equator was reached in 1471 and the Congo discovered by Diogo Cam (q.v.) in 1482. After 1530 other Europeans, including English, Dutch, French, Danish and Branden-burgers, established trading posts or forts. Sections of the coast were known by their chief products, such as the Grain coast (from Sierra Leone to Cape Palmas), the source of the grains of paradise (Guinea pepper, *Aframomum meleguetta*); the Ivory coast (beyond Cape Palmas); the Gold coast (east of Cape Three Points); and the Slave coast (between the Volta river and the Niger delta, the latter known as the Oil rivers).

European penetration of Guinea was hindered by the hot, humid and unhealthy climate, the density of the rain forest, the scarcity of harbours along the generally surf-bound coast and the difficulties of river navigation. *See also* Angola; Dahomey, Republic of; Equatorial Guinea; Gabon Republic; Gambia, Ghana; Guinea, Republic of; Ivory Coast, Republic of; Liberia; Nigeria; Portuguese Guinea; Sierra Leone.
(R. W. Sl.)

GUINEA, GULF OF, that part of the South Atlantic ocean east of longitude 7° W. (Cape Palmas) and north of the equator, bordered by the countries between the Ivory Coast and Gabon republics. Between Ghana and the Niger delta a broad indentation forms the Bight of Benin. From the delta the coast trends east and then south; the corner of the gulf includes a line of volcanic islands running northeast from Annobón to Fernando Pó, which faces Cameroon mountain on the mainland. Between these islands and the coast eastward lies the Bight of Biafra. The warm Guinea current, flowing eastward near the coast, swings round in this bight to join the westward-moving south equatorial current, composed mainly of cooler water from the Benguela current moving up from the south. Thus a marked contrast (both in direction and temperature) exists between surface currents along the northern and southern margins of the gulf, although a local upwelling of cold water near the Volta delta has important effects on the coastal climate.
(J. C. Ph.)

GUINEA, REPUBLIC OF (République du Guinée), since 1958 an independent republic and formerly a territory of French West Africa, is situated in the northern wet tropical zone. It is bounded west by the Atlantic Ocean and Portuguese Guinea, north by the republics of Senegal and Mali, and east and south by Ivory Coast, Liberia, and Sierra Leone. Pop. (1967 est.) 3,702,-000. Area 94,925 sq.mi. (245,855 sq.km.). The capital is Conakry (q.v.).

Physical Geography.—The coast is low and fringed with mangroves, much broken by estuaries and with off-lying swampy islands. Four regions can be distinguished inland.

Lower Guinea comprises a coastal plain 30–55 mi. broad crossed by winding rivers (Mellacorée, Konkouré, Rio Kapatchez, Rio Nuñez, and the Cogon or Rio Componi) that form deltas and are tidal for about 25 mi. The crystalline rocks of the plain are generally covered by alluvial formations and laterites. From a line of high sandstone cliffs about 30 mi. inland the Kakoulima massif rises to 3,688 ft., composed of volcanic rock, as are the Kaloum Peninsula, the island of Tombo on which Conakry stands, and the nearby Los Islands (q.v.).

Middle Guinea is formed by the Fouta Djallon (Futa Jallon) massif of about 30,000 sq.mi. and of average elevation 3,000 ft. It consists of stepped plateaus, some detached, of thick sandstone layers interstratified with basalt. Faulting in a northwesterly direction has caused the massif to rise in the southeast. In the Fouta Djallon can be distinguished: (1) the high central plateau

around Labé and Pita, crossed by deep valleys; (2) the more level eastern plateau, the Bafing, a headstream of the Senegal River, offering a route into Sudanese (Mali) territory; (3) the northern borderlands, sloping down toward Youkounkoun and dominated by Mt. Loura (4,970 ft.), near which rises the Gambia River; and (4) the lower western plateau around Gaoual and Télimélé, dissected by the Cogon, Tominé, and Fatala rivers.

Upper Guinea, in the northeast of the republic, is a land of grassy plains and savanna of stunted trees traversed by the Tinkisso River, which joins the Niger near Siguiri.

Southern Guinea is a distinct region lying inland of Sierra Leone and northern Liberia. Its uplands of granitic gneisses and quartzite rise in sharp relief, reaching 6,069 ft. in Mt. Nimba. Variegated forest, often deteriorated, covers the moist slopes.

Climate.—The humid, tropical climate exhibits two seasons: one dry and the other wet (June–December), accompanied by frequent tornadoes. In the dry season the harmattan (q.v.) blows from the northeast. Rainfall is heavy near the coast and on exposed slopes, reaching 169 in. annually at Conakry, where the temperature is fairly constant (average 80° F [26.7° C]). At Mamou, about 125 mi. inland, the rainfall decreases to 79 in. and the Fouta Djallon is generally well watered. In Upper Guinea the temperature range is greater (64°–104° F [17.7°–40° C]) and the annual rainfall less (Siguiri, 50 in.).

Vegetation.—Oil palms grow on the coastal plain, but the Fouta Djallon is mainly grassland. The Guinea plum (*Parinarium excelsum*) and the Guinea peach or country fig (*Sarcocephalus esculentus*) grow on the higher ground; oranges, lemons, and bananas are cultivated; and the coffee plant is indigenous. The baobab and shea tree (karite) are common in Upper Guinea.
(J. D.)

Animal Life.—The coastal forest strip has a fauna like that of Sierra Leone (q.v.). The better quality savanna woodlands merge into the dry semidesert with mammalian fauna typical of inland West Africa. Larger animals include roan antelope, waterbuck, kob, reedbuck, western and Senegal hartebeeste, gazelle, wart hog, elephant, and lion. The giant (Derbian) eland exists in one area. The hippopotamus and manatee may survive in some of the larger rivers but the great demand for meat in West Africa encourages

PAUL CONKLIN—PIX FROM PUBLIX
FISHERMEN MENDING THEIR NETS IN CONAKRY, THE CAPITAL AND PRINCIPAL PORT OF GUINEA

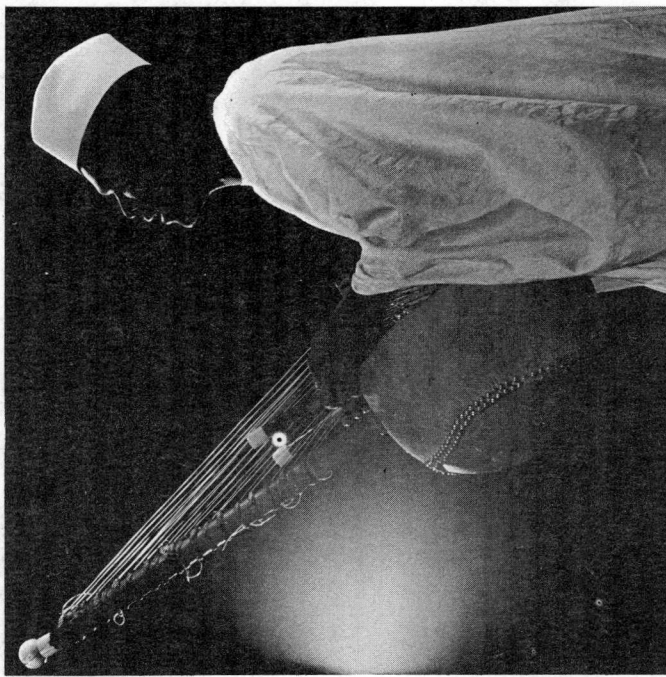

GUINEA

a profitable international traffic in dried meat that endangers the existence of all the larger animals. There are also crocodiles and venomous snakes.

The People.—The main groups are: (1) along the coast, the Baga (*q.v.*) farmers of the swamps; (2) in the Conakry-Kindia region, the Susu (*q.v.*); (3) on the Fouta Djallon plateau, agricultural peoples dominated by the pastoral Peul or Fulani (*q.v.*); the Dialonké, related to the Malinké, dwell on the eastern slopes; (4) north of the plateau, the Bassari, Koniagi, and Tenda, paleo-negritic farmers; (5) on the eastern plains and in Upper Guinea, the Malinké (*q.v.*); (6) in the forest along the Sierra Leone border, the Kissi (*q.v.*); (7) in the forest along the Liberian border, more primitive tribes such as the Manon, Guerzé, and Toma. Groups (1), (4), and (7) are pagan and have no large states; the others have been largely converted to Islam and wear the ample wide-sleeved robe common among the peoples of Senegal and Mali. Groups (2), (3), (4), and (7) speak various Mande languages; Fula is spoken on the Fouta Djallon. The Fulani, Malinké, and Susu are numerically and culturally the most important groups and are gradually spreading their way of life and the influence of Islam. The family is patrilineal; among the pagans secret societies, ritual dances, and religious feasts are features of the social system. Following independence the non-African population decreased considerably to about 2,000–3,000 (1959 est.), mostly Lebanese traders.

The population density is approximately 13 inhabitants to the square kilometre and the average annual increase is about 2.2%.

History.—The Susu, a group related to the Malinké (Mandingo), seem to have driven the Baga to the coast. The Fulani established domination over the Fouta Djallon by the 16th century. The upper Niger was the domain of the Malinké, forming the ancient kingdom of Mali. The coast was made known by Portuguese voyagers of the 15th century and was for long a resort of slave traders. In 1827 the French explorer René Caillié (*q.v.*) traversed the country on his journey from the Rio Nuñez to Tombouctou. From 1838 L. E. Bouët-Willaumez and other French naval officers surveyed the coast and established a settlement on the Rio Nuñez which was annexed in 1849. In 1880 Tomba Island was occupied and in 1881 the *almamy* (amir) of Fouta Djallon placed his country under French protection. The protectorate was called Rivières du Sud until 1890, when it was detached from Senegal and became a separate colony, later renamed French Guinea, which in 1895 became part of the federation of French West Africa.

The colony was enlarged by addition of territories on the right bank of the Niger and in the hinterland of Sierra Leone and Liberia, and by the cession in 1904 of the Los Islands from Great Britain. Pacification of the Fouta Djallon and of southern Guinea was achieved with difficulty.

Under the constitution of 1946 Guinea became an overseas territory of France and its people French citizens. In 1958 it was the only territory to vote against the constitution of the French Community and thus achieved complete independence. Guinea became a kind of popular democracy under Pres. Sékou Touré, strong supporter of the policy of African unity extolled by Kwame Nkrumah of Ghana. Deprived of French assistance, Guinea contracted loans and economic and trade agreements with the U.S.S.R. and China. In 1960 Guinea left the franc area but later in the year concluded an agreement providing for technical and economic aid from the United States. Guinean relations were resumed with the neighbouring republics and on May 22, 1963, with France, but the economic situation of the country scarcely improved and the power of Sékou Touré remained somewhat uncertain. (Hu. De.)

Administration and Social Conditions.—Guinea is a republic of presidential type, in which the president is the head of state and of the armed forces and is elected by the assembly for seven years. A single chamber national assembly of 75 members is elected for five years by universal suffrage; the president controls the administration through a council of ministers. The Republic of Guinea is divided into 29 administrative regions controlled by governors with the assistance of regional secretaries-general. Local budgets are discussed by elected regional councils at Beyla,

F. B. GRUNZWEIG—PHOTO RESEARCHERS, INC.

A MUSICIAN OF GUINEA PLAYING THE CORA, A STRINGED INSTRUMENT WITH A BASE MADE FROM A LARGE LEATHER-COVERED CALABASH. IN GUINEA, ONLY THE HEREDITARY CASTE OF MUSICIANS, GRIOTS, IS ALLOWED TO PLAY THE CORA; THEY SING SATIRICAL SONGS WHILE PLAYING

Boffa, Boké, Conakry, Dabola, Dalaba, Dinguiraye, Dubréka, Faranah, Forécariah, Fria, Gaoual, Guéckédou, Kankan, Kérouané, Kindia, Kissidougou, Kouroussa, Labé, Macenta, Mali, Mamou, Nzérékoré, Pita, Siguiri, Télimélé, Tougué, Yomou, and Youkounkoun. Five supraregional inspection units are established at Conakry, Kankan, Kindia, Labé, and Nzérékoré. The villages, based on a system of collective farming, are administered by village chiefs with the advice of village councils.

In 1966 more than half the children of school age in Guinea attended schools: 188,717 went to primary schools (where they were taught by 4,050 teachers of Guinean nationality), 6,678 went to secondary schools, and 3,465 attended technical colleges.

Economy.—The agricultural and pastoral economy of Guinea is reinforced by rich mineral resources. The chief food crops are rice, fonio (millet), sorghum, and cassava. Mountain rice, grown on forest plots cleared by burning, is supplemented by plains rice grown in the flooded valleys of the Niger and its affluents and on the coastal plain. Millet is grown in upper Guinea. Bananas, from the coastal plain and the Fouta Djallon around Mamou, were the chief export crop (87,000 metric tons in 1965) with coffee (13,500 metric tons in 1965), grown in southern Guinea, where tobacco, quinine, tea, and rubber were also introduced. Other export crops are palm kernels, pineapples, oranges, and groundnuts (peanuts). Cattle are raised on the Fouta Djallon and in upper Guinea and exported on the hoof to neighbouring countries, with considerable exports of hides and leather. A trawler fleet supplies fish for a cannery at Conakry.

Alluvial gold deposits near Siguiri have long been worked by Africans and more recently diamonds have been mined in southern Guinea; these industries were nationalized in 1961. Important deposits of iron ore in lower Guinea were first worked in 1953 at the Kaloum Peninsula near Conakry and yielded 700,000 metric tons in 1965 for export. The bauxite deposits are rich; those in the Los Islands were first exploited in 1949, followed by mining near Boké on the Rio Nuñez and smelting for aluminum with hydroelectric power at Fria on the Konkouré River. Further bauxite deposits were located at Dabola (about 200 mi. up the railway from Conakry), around Kindia, and near the Mali border.

The chief imports by value are textiles, petroleum products, cement, and manufactured goods; the chief exports are coffee, bananas, iron ore, palm kernels, and bauxite. After leaving the franc area in 1960 Guinea created its own currency at par with the "old" overseas French franc, or CFA franc, so that 1 Guinga franc (GFr.) equaled 2 "new" (1960) French centimes.

Guinea is traversed from northwest to southwest by the highway from Dakar in Senegal to Abidjan on the Ivory Coast; this is joined at Mamou by the road from Conakry and at Kankan by the road to Bamako in the Sudanese Republic (Mali). A metre-gauge railway, completed in 1913, links the port of Conakry by an iron bridge with the mainland and thence through Kouroussa on the Niger with Kankan, 411 mi. E of Conakry.

See also references under "Guinea" in the Index.   (J. D.)

BIBLIOGRAPHY.—J. R. Molard, *La Guinée française* (1952); B. Ameillon, *La Guinée française* (1953); F. Gigon, *Guinée, état-pilote* (1959); B. Ameillon, *La Guinée, bilan d'une indépendance* (1964); current history and statistics are summarized annually in *Britannica Book of the Year.*

GUINEA FOWL, a name based on the western African origin of the first known of these birds and now used for the seven species of gallinaceous (fowllike) birds comprising the family Numididae and closely related to poultry. Guinea fowl are native to Africa and southern Arabia. They are from 17 to 30 in. long. The drooping tail, heavily overlaid with upper tail coverts, and the more or less bare head give these birds a distinctive appearance. Some have a casque and wattles, or a crest (as in *Guttera* species). The usual plumage of the guinea fowl is blue-black, spotted with white or gray; however, among some forest species the feathers are black (e.g., *Phasidus niger*) or boldly marked with black and white. An Ethiopian species, the vulturine guinea fowl (*Acrylium vulturinum*), has elongated, lance-shaped, white-shafted feathers originating on the neck and draping over the breast and back.

Best-known is the helmet guinea fowl (*Numida meleagris*), with many local varieties widespread in the savannas and brushlands of Africa and introduced into the West Indies and elsewhere. It lives in flocks and walks about on the ground, feeding on seeds, tubers and some insects. When alarmed the birds run, but when pressed they fly with a flapping motion for a short distance. At night they sleep in trees. They are noisy birds, giving harsh, often repeated calls. The nest, a hollow in the ground, scantily lined with vegetation, contains about 12 finely spotted tan eggs, which require about 30 days' incubation. The downy young are active immediately after hatching and accompany the parents.

Birds selected by man from the helmet guinea fowl have changed little under domestication except for the occurrence of some albinistic varieties. Although they are not so important as poultry and easily revert to a half-wild state, guineas are raised for market in some countries. In North America these alert, noisy birds are kept around farms as "watchdogs."   (A. L. Rd.)

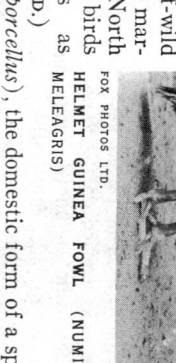

FOX PHOTOS LTD.

HELMET GUINEA FOWL (NUMIDA MELEAGRIS)

GUINEA PIG (*Cavia porcellus*), the domestic form of a species of cavy (*q.v.*; *C. cutleri*). This rodent was domesticated by the Indians of Peru, Ecuador and Colombia long before the arrival of the Spaniards. Guinea pigs were kept for their meat, which was prized as a delicacy, and were first introduced into Europe for the same purpose soon after the discovery of America. Now these animals are rarely eaten but are kept as pets or used as valuable experimental subjects in medical and biological research.

The two sexes are similar in general features, being about ten inches long and weighing about two pounds. There is no external tail, although internally there are seven caudal vertebrae. The ears are naked and relatively small. The forefeet have four toes, the hind feet only three; all toes are armed with broad claws, although guinea pigs are not burrowing in habit. They walk on the entire sole and palm. The legs are short, the body stout and the head large.

The several varieties differ greatly in colour: black, tan, cream, chocolate, reddish and white animals are common, as well as combinations of these in various patterns described as tortoise shell, Dutch belted, Himalayan, etc. Some are "agouti," that is, they have banded hairs, black and ochraceous or buff, like the wild cavies. Size also varies somewhat in the different breeds. Long-haired cavies with silky pelage are called Peruvians. The so-called Abyssinian cavies have coarse hair forming odd whorls or rosettes. Short-haired varieties are usually called English or Bolivian cavies.

Guinea pigs feed largely on grass and other green vegetation. If plenty of this is supplied, they can get along without water. In captivity they may be kept on rabbit or rat food, but then they need water. Wild cavies breed only once a year and only one or two young are born at a time, but guinea pigs have litters of two to eight or more, twice or three times a year. The young are born after 63 to 75 days' gestation and are highly developed even at birth, being furry, open-eyed and able to eat solid food. In a few hours they can run with the mother; they are weaned at about two weeks. Females may reproduce at the age of two or three months, but it is better, when breeding them, to wait until they are fully grown, at about nine months. The average life span is two years, but some individuals may live longer than six years.

GUINEA-WORM INFECTION (DRACONTIASIS, DRACUNCULOSIS) involves the viscera, with subsequent manifestations in the subcutaneous tissues and the skin. The causative agent is *Dracunculus medinensis,* a distant relative of the filarial worms (*see* FILARIASIS). The disease is endemic in India, the middle east and tropical Africa. The adult worms, minute males and cordlike females, which attain the length of a metre, mature in the viscera and deeper tissues. The pregnant female then migrates through the subcutaneous tissues to the skin, usually of an extremity, where a small blister is produced. On contact with fresh water the blister bursts, discharging a swarm of larvae into the water. If these are ingested by the water flea (*Cyclops*), they migrate into the body cavity of the *Cyclops* and become infective for man when the water flea is accidentally swallowed in raw drinking water. The disease may become epidemic following annual holy pilgrimages of Hindus and Muslims who wade into sacred streams and rinse out their mouths with the polluted water; accidentally swallowing some of the infected *Cyclops* and simultaneously contributing a new supply of larvae for the *Cyclops.*

Clinical manifestations, including hypersensitization, which develop as the females migrate from the deeper tissues to the skin, are readily controlled by the administration of adrenaline. The long, patent sinuous tunnel in which the worm resides becomes readily infected with bacteria. The worm resists attempts to pull it out intact, and if too much traction is produced it breaks off. Since the days of Moses natives have contented themselves with winding a small length of the worm each day on a stick at the site of the open blister, until finally the entire worm has been withdrawn. Introduction of phenothiazine ointment into the tissues immediately around the tunnel stupefies the worm and allows it to be removed intact.

Plankton-feeding fish, when stocked in infested waters, will eat the *Cyclops* and thus break the vicious cycle.   (J. E. Hl.; X.)

W. SUSCHITZKY

CAVIA CUTLERI, PARENTAL STOCK OF THE GUINEA PIG

See also ROUNDWORM.

BIBLIOGRAPHY.—M. Elliott, "A New Treatment for Dracontiasis," *Trans. R. Soc. Trop. Med. and Hyg.*, 35:291–301 (1942); V. N. Moorthy, "A Redescription of *Dracunculus medinensis*," *J. Parasitol.*, 23: 220–224 (1937).
(E. C. F.)

GUINEVERE, in Arthurian romance, the wife of King Arthur (*q.v.*). The name appears as Gwenhwyfar, "the first lady of this island," in *Culhwch and Olwen*, and in the Welsh *Triads* there are no fewer than three Gwenhwyfars, perhaps to be explained by a tendency toward reduplication.

Geoffrey of Monmouth (*q.v.*) in his *Historia regum Britanniae*, calls her Guanhamara and makes her a Roman lady. Wace (*q.v.*), in his *Roman de Brut*, gives her Roman parentage on the mother's side, but says that she was cousin to Cador of Cornwall by whom she was brought up. According to the Vulgate cycle; *see* ARTHURIAN LEGEND) her father was King Leodegan of Carmelide and he gave the Round Table to King Arthur as her dowry. An impostor, the false Guinevere, comes to Arthur's court, claiming to have been kidnaped on the wedding night, but the true Guinevere is vindicated by Lancelot in a judicial combat. According to the account by Giraldus Cambrensis of the discovery of the royal tombs in Glastonbury (*q.v.*), the body with Arthur was that of his second wife, and in the prose *Lancelot* there is a reference to Arthur's son Lohout whom he had by "la bele Lisanor" before he married Guinevere.

There seems to have been an early tradition of abduction and infidelity involving Guinevere. The *Vita Gildae* of Caradoc of Llancarfan (probably late 11th or early 12th century) relates how she was carried off by Melwas, king of Aestiva Regio, to Glastonbury and how Arthur and his army went to the rescue. A similar abduction and rescue seems to be taking place on the 12th-century archivolt of Modena, which depicts Winlogee being rescued by Artus. In the *Chevalier de la Charrette* (*Lancelot*) by Chrétien de Troyes (*q.v.*) she is abducted by Meleagant to the land of Gorre and is rescued by Lancelot, and this story is incorporated in the Vulgate cycle. In the *Lanzelet* of Ulrich von Zatzikhoven the would-be abductor is Valerin, a magician. Some scholars see in all these accounts traces of the theme of an abductor from the other world. In the chronicles and the prose romances another abduction of Guinevere, this time by Mordred, the king's nephew or, in some texts, his incestuous son, is closely connected with the death of Arthur and the end of the Round Table. In Geoffrey of Monmouth and Wace the queen is not unwilling; in the Vulgate cycle and the *Morte Darthur* of Sir Thomas Malory (*q.v.*) she is an unhappy victim as far as Mordred is concerned but must nevertheless bear some responsibility for the final disaster, as her love for Lancelot caused bitter dissension.

It is indeed through Lancelot's love for her that she is best known in Arthurian romance. Chrétien presents her as the typical lady of the Provençal lyric, receiving or refusing love, but she plays a more active role in pursuit of Lancelot in parts of the Vulgate cycle. Through Lancelot's adoration of her, courtly love is exalted in *Le Chevalier de la Charrette* and the first part of the prose *Lancelot*, and condemned in the Vulgate cycle *Queste del Saint Graal*; and it was through reading the description of Lancelot and Guinevere's first kiss that Dante's Paolo and Francesca succumbed to temptation and were damned.

See also LANCELOT.

BIBLIOGRAPHY.—J. Frappier, *Chrétien de Troyes* (1957); F. Lot, *Étude sur le Lancelot en prose* (1918; 1954). For further bibliography *see* J. D. Bruce, *Evolution of Arthurian Romance*, 2 vol., 2nd ed., (1959); *Arthurian Literature in the Middle Ages*, ed. by R. S. Loomis (1959).
(E. M. K.)

GUINGAMP, a town of northwestern France in the *département* of Côtes-du-Nord, lies on the right bank of the Trieux 71 mi. (114 km.) E.N.E. of Brest by road. Pop. (1962) 8,829. It dates from the 11th century and parts of its ancient fortifications still remain. It became the capital of the countship (subsequently the duchy) of Penthièvre and was a centre of resistance against Charles of Blois (*q.v.*). The ramparts of the castle built in 1437 by Count Peter I of Guingamp and dismantled under Louis XIV stand above the town. There too is the 11th-century church of Notre Dame, rebuilt in the 14th century; one of its two towers and the great west door were restored in the 16th century and are magnificent examples of Renaissance architecture. The most celebrated chapel dates from the 13th century and is outside the church proper; it is dedicated to the Black Virgin under the name of Notre-Dame de Bon-Secours. The statue is the object of one of Brittany's most interesting "pardons" or religious pilgrimages. This dates from the 17th century and takes place on the night preceding the first Sunday in July when the statue is carried in torchlight procession through the town to the central square where the bishop lights three huge bonfires. In the square is a graceful Renaissance fountain (1588, restored 1745). During the week of the pardon a big fair is held in the public park. In 1944 the whole town was consecrated to Our Lady.

Guingamp has a market for dairy cattle and is a tourist centre. Its industries include flour milling and the manufacture of wool, agricultural machinery and central heating equipment.

GUINNESS, the name of a family of Irish brewers. ARTHUR GUINNESS (d. 1855) owned a small brewing plant at Leixlip on the river Liffey and also purchased a small porter brewery at St. James's Gate, Dublin. The business prospered under his direction but his porter and stout were confined to the Irish market. Under Arthur's third son, SIR BENJAMIN LEE GUINNESS (1798–1868), who took sole control of the firm (Arthur Guinness & Sons) in about 1855, agencies were established in the United Kingdom, on the continent, in the British colonies and in the United States. The export trade soon rose in volume and the business became one of the largest of its kind in the world. Sir Benjamin was elected first lord mayor of Dublin in 1851 and represented Dublin in parliament from 1865 until his death. St. Patrick's cathedral in Dublin was restored at his expense and in 1867 he was created a baronet. He died in London on May 19, 1868. He was succeeded in control of the business by his eldest son, SIR ARTHUR EDWARD GUINNESS (1840–1915), and his third son, EDWARD CECIL GUINNESS (1847–1927). When Arthur Edward became Lord Ardilaun in 1880 he disposed of his share in the family business to Edward Cecil. In 1886 the business became a limited liability company in which Edward Cecil was the largest shareholder. He amassed a large fortune, was created a baronet in 1885 and became earl of Iveagh in 1919. He made large contributions to charity and scientific research. After his death in 1927 his business interests were taken over by his son, Rupert, Viscount Elvedon.
(H. J. SG.)

GUIPÚZCOA, a Basque province of northern Spain, is situated between Vizcaya (Biscay) province and the French frontier. Pop. (1960) 478,337; area 771 sq.mi.; density of population, 620 per sq.mi. The name was used as a geographical entity from the end of the 10th century and, as a county, it was unified with Castile in 1200. Its chief towns were founded or resettled during the 13th and 14th centuries. Its central position in the Basque provinces (Vascongadas) has enabled it to preserve its dialects and ancient traditions more conservatively than either Vizcaya or Alava.

To the east and west the valleys of the Bidasoa and Deva are clearly defined provincial boundaries. Guipúzcoa is backed to the south by the mountainous ramparts of Aralar (3,682 ft.) and Aritz (3,494 ft.), forming the main watershed of the short Atlantic streams. The Bidasoa, Urumea, Oria, Urola and Deva are rapid and unnavigable rivers that carve out transverse corridors across the W.S.W.–E.N.E. folded mountain ranges. This trellis pattern permits relatively easy if indirect lines of communication within the province. The southern and western ranges tend to form a rugged relief of limestone scarps, but the younger marls and sandstones of the coastal ranges break down into deeper soils with thick forests. Humid air streams, aided by the configuration of the coast at the head of the Bay of Biscay, bring heavy rainfall rising from 50 in. annually on the coast to more than 90 in. in some of the mountains. Temperatures are mild and on the high mountain slopes an Atlantic silva of deciduous oaks and chestnuts prevail. Everywhere there is a careful and intensive cropping of the lower valley slopes and much of the land is under pasture. Only about 17% of the total area is cropped, however, chiefly under maize (corn), beans and numerous small apple orchards. A stock-rearing economy dominates the province, especially of Swiss stall-fed dairy cattle.

Scattered sources of iron ore in the Deva valley originally fostered the light metallurgical industries. Apart from the older manufactures of Mondragón (pop. [1960] 14,148 [mun.]), Vergara (13,162) and Eibar a wide range of metallurgical goods are also made at Tolosa (16,281), Beasain (7,610) and Rentería (18,642). Paper mills in the Oria valley, textile factories more widely scattered, and a miscellaneous group at San Sebastian (*q.v.*; 135,149) the provincial capital and seaside resort, all contribute to the relative prosperity of the province. Irún (29,814) is the nation's chief customs town, and Pasajes (11,700) a busy port.

(J. M. Ho.)

GÜIRALDES, RICARDO (1886-1927), Argentine novelist and poet, was famous for his poetic interpretation of the Argentinian gaucho. He was born in Buenos Aires on Feb. 13, 1886, son of a wealthy landowner. He died in Paris on Oct. 8, 1927. His masterpiece, *Don Segundo Sombra* (1926; English trans. by Harriet de Onís, 1935; 1966), is a poematic novel recreating the mythical gaucho that all Argentinians worship as a national symbol. This book combines the objectivity of country life and the subtlety of a poetic vision; it shows Güiraldes' twofold personality —the cosmopolitan spirit of an insatiable traveler well acquainted with French literary circles and the devoted admirer of his native land. A double view of the gaucho is presented, one through Don Segundo, the mature centaur, who is a model of manliness, and the other through the emerging personality of a young man, who follows undauntedly in the footsteps of his friend and mentor.

Güiraldes was also a forerunner of post-World War I literary innovations in Argentina. Imbued with an audacious spirit, he found little receptiveness for his first volume of verses, *El cencerro de cristal* (1915). Two early novels, *Raucho* (1917; 1968) and *Xaimaca* (1923), are important as records of his literary convictions. *Rosaura* (1922; 1967), a poignant love story, shows the author's dramatic power and insight into human motives. *Croquis, dibujos y poema de Ricardo Güiraldes* was published in 1967.

(E. N-S.)

GUISE, HOUSE OF, a junior branch of the ducal house of Lorraine, conspicuous in French politics in the 16th century.

The countship of Guise, in the Île-de-France, became a possession of the house of Lorraine in 1333, when it was included in the dowry of Mary of Blois on her marriage with Rudolph (Raoul) duke of Lorraine. When René II, duke of Lorraine, died in 1508, his lands were divided between his eldest sons by his marriage with Philippa, daughter of Adolf, duke of Gelre: the first, Antony (d. 1544), received the duchy of Lorraine, while the second, Claude, received Guise and other French fiefs, namely the countships of Aumale and Harcourt, the marquisate of Elbeuf and the lordships of Joinville, Lillebonne, Brionne and Mayenne. This partition was confirmed by an agreement of Oct. 27, 1530. Of René II's other sons, Jean (*see below*) became the 1st cardinal de Lorraine, and Ferry, Louis and François died fighting on the French side at Marignano (1515), at Naples (1528) and at Pavia (1525) respectively.

CLAUDE DE LORRAINE (1496-1550), comte and later 1st duc de Guise, was born at Condé-sur-Moselle on Oct. 20, 1496. He was brought up at the French court and on April 18, 1513, married Antoinette de Bourbon (1493-1583), daughter of François, comte de Vendôme. In 1514 he defeated Charles Brandon, duke of Suffolk, in a tournament held in celebration of Louis XII's marriage with Mary Tudor; in 1515 he fought at Marignano and was seriously wounded; in 1521 he distinguished himself at the siege of Fuenterrabia. With the rewards that he received from the crown he built up the wealth and prestige of his family. He avoided further service in Italy and concentrated his military activities in northern France. His successes against the English suffered by the French in Italy and won him the admiration and gratitude of the people of Paris. In 1523 he was appointed governor of Champagne and Burgundy and became responsible for the defense of France's eastern border. At Neufchâteau, he routed the Holy Roman emperor's army. In 1525, after Francis I of France had been defeated and captured at Pavia, Guise assumed a prominent place in Louis of Savoy's council of regency. Although he was criticized for using troops needed for the defense of the realm to crush a peasant revolt in Lorraine, he gained the reputation of being a champion of religious and social orthodoxy, and in 1527 Francis I acknowledged his services by enlarging his estates and creating him duke and peer, a dignity hitherto reserved to princes of the blood. Guise claimed precedence over all other French nobles and eventually aroused the king's distrust; as provincial governor he acted so independently of the crown as to incur the displeasure of the *parlement* of Paris. In 1536 and 1537 he fought the imperial troops in northern France, relieving Péronne; and in 1542 took part in the short-lived conquest of Luxembourg. Toward the end of his life, he tended to efface himself before the growing fortunes of his sons. He died at his château of Joinville on April 12, 1550. It was believed at the time that he had been poisoned in revenge for his suspected complicity in the death of François de Bourbon, lord of Enghien (1546), his wife's nephew, whose victory at Ceresole had revived the prestige of the rival house of Bourbon.

The 1st duc de Guise was supported in his activities by his younger brother JEAN (1498-1550), cardinal de Lorraine, who was born at Bar on April 9, 1498, and became coadjutor of the bishop of Metz at the age of 3 and cardinal at 20. In the course of his life, the cardinal held many archbishoprics, bishoprics and abbeys, some of which he subsequently conferred on his nephews. He was dissolute and extravagant, lavishing vast sums of money on entertainments at the hôtel de Cluny, his Paris residence; as a patron of scholars, writers and artists, including Erasmus, Clément Marot and Benvenuto Cellini, and as an almsgiver he had few equals. By his munificence he helped to build up a clientele for the Guises at court. The cardinal served Francis I as councilor and diplomat, but toward the end of Francis' reign fell from favour and retired to Rome. His hopes of becoming pope were never fulfilled. He died at Nogent-sur-Yonne on May 18, 1550, as he was returning from Italy.

Claude de Lorraine had an illegitimate son, CLAUDE, who became abbot of Cluny (d. 1612), and 12 legitimate children, including FRANÇOIS, 2nd duc de Guise (*see below*); CHARLES (1524-1574), 2nd cardinal de Lorraine; CLAUDE (1526-1573), marquis de Mayenne and later duc d'Aumale, who married Louise de Brézé, daughter of Diane de Poitiers; LOUIS (1527-1578), bishop of Troyes, archbishop of Sens and 1st cardinal de Guise; another FRANÇOIS (1534-1563), grand prior of the Order of the Knights of Malta in France and general of the galleys; RENÉ (1536-1566), marquis d'Elbeuf, from whom descended the lines of Harcourt, Armagnac, Marsan and Lillebonne; and MARY (*q.v.*), who married James V of Scotland and was the mother of Mary, queen of Scots.

FRANÇOIS DE LORRAINE (1519-1563), 2nd duc de Guise, was born at Bar on Feb. 17, 1519. As comte d'Aumale he fought in Francis I's army and was wounded almost fatally at the siege of Boulogne (1545). His life was saved by the skill of Ambroise Paré, the king's surgeon, and the scar that remained on his face won him the nickname of "le Balafré" ("the Scarred"). In 1546 he was appointed governor of Dauphiné, and in 1547 his countship of Aumale was turned into a duchy. On the accession of Henry II (1547) he was made master of the king's hunt and great chamberlain. He had to share the king's favour, however, with the constable Anne de Montmorency. The humanity with which he quelled a revolt over the *gabelle* (*q.v.*) in Saintonge in 1548 was favourably contrasted with Montmorency's severe repression of a similar rising in Guienne. After failing to win the hand of Jeanne d'Albret, niece of Francis I and heiress of Navarre, Aumale married, on Dec. 4, 1549, Anne d'Este, the beautiful and cultivated daughter of Ercole II, duke of Ferrara. This marriage buttressed the ambitions of his family, for Anne was of royal blood, being the granddaughter of Louis XII of France, and her father could be a useful ally if the house of Lorraine should decide to press the claim (which it had inherited from its Angevin ancestry) to the kingdom of Naples. François succeeded to the duchy of Guise in April 1550, and soon after became prince de Joinville (1552) and hereditary seneschal of Champagne. In 1551 he had helped to prepare Henry II's German campaign, and in Aug. 1552 he was placed in charge of the defense of Metz against the emperor Charles V. Having repaired the fortifications within a remarkably short time, he repelled every assault on the city and obliged the emperor to withdraw, but Henry II failed to take advantage of this success. In Aug. 1554 Guise again distinguished himself by routing an imperial army at Renty.

In Jan. 1557 Guise was sent at the head of a military expedition to Italy, after Pope Paul IV had sought French help against the Spaniards in the kingdom of Naples. The expedition had the backing of the duc's brother Charles, cardinal de Lorraine, who saw in it an opportunity of securing the crown of Naples for his family. Guise had doubts which proved justified: Ercole II of Ferrara and Paul IV allowed their selfish and conflicting interests to impede rather than assist his march, while the duque de Alba, who commanded the Spanish army, consistently avoided battle. Guise cannot be blamed for the failure of the Italian expedition: he remained tactically supreme throughout and showed great qualities of leadership. In August he was hurriedly recalled to repel a Spanish army, which had invaded northern France; it was no mean achievement that he was able to bring back his army virtually intact. On being appointed lieutenant general of the kingdom, he realized the need for some brilliant coup to revive the morale of the French nation. He chose to attack the English in Calais, and within six days forced them to surrender (Jan. 6, 1558); he then completed their expulsion from France by capturing Guines and Ham. Such victories served to strengthen the prestige of his family, and in April 1558 Guise had the satisfaction of seeing his niece, Mary Stuart, married to the dauphin, Francis. By seizing Thionville and Arlon from the imperial army in May, Guise hastened the signing of the treaty of Cateau-Cambrésis (April 3, 1559), but its terms were such as to reduce his family's hopes of ever gaining the crown of Naples.

The accession of Francis II (1559) produced a change of ministers: Montmorency was replaced as grand master of the royal household by Guise, who shared the chief power in the state with his brother, the cardinal de Lorraine. The Bourbons, as first princes of the blood, had a stronger claim to being the king's advisers, but were deficient in political sense. Their leader, Antoine de Bourbon, was principally interested in recovering his wife's kingdom of Navarre from Spain and would not ally himself with Montmorency, whom he accused of having overlooked his interests at the recent peace talks. Antoine's brother Louis, prince de Condé, however, was more inclined to take advantage of the discontent caused among the nobles and Huguenots by the government's economic and religious reforms. With Condé's approval a conspiracy was formed to overthrow the Guises; but they got wind of the plot. The duc de Guise was again appointed lieutenant general of the kingdom with full powers to deal with the conspirators (March 17, 1560). His firm handling of the situation proved their undoing. Their attack on the court at Amboise, the so-called *tumulte*, was a failure and many were either hanged, beheaded or drowned in the Loire. The slaughter, which lasted for several days, intensified hatred of the Guises in certain quarters. For his part in the conspiracy, Condé was tried by a special commission and condemned to death (Nov. 1560), but the king's death (Dec. 1560) prevented his execution.

On the accession of the young Charles IX to the French crown, the queen mother, Catherine de Médicis, emerged as the dominant figure in the state. By assuming the regency herself, appointing Antoine de Bourbon as her chief councilor and restoring Montmorency to favour, she indicated clearly that Guise domination would no longer be tolerated. The duc de Guise, however, was allowed to remain grand master. The Bourbons gained ground: Condé was cleared of the charges against him, and Antoine de Bourbon was made lieutenant general of the kingdom, but Catherine refused their demand that the Guises be excluded from court. The rise of the Bourbons, who were leaders of the Huguenot movement, and the policy of religious toleration pursued by the government brought about the dramatic reconciliation of Guise and Montmorency (March, 1561); together with the

marshal de Saint-André (Jacques d'Albon) they formed a "triumvirate" in defense of the Catholic faith. To signify their disapproval of Catherine's policy they retired from the court to their estates after the attempt to reconcile Catholics and Huguenots at the colloquy of Poissy. The Huguenots were left almost in control of the government and in Jan. 1562 a royal edict gave them freedom of worship outside towns. In February, Guise held talks with Christopher, duke of Württemberg, at Saverne, possibly with a view to reconciling the Lutherans and the Catholics. On March 1, he and his suite were traveling to Nanteuil when they came across a Huguenot congregation at Vassy; a clash ensued in the course of which several Huguenots were killed and wounded. On learning of the "massacre" Condé summoned his coreligionists to arms, and Theodore Beza urged the queen mother to bring Guise to justice. She summoned him to court, but he disobeyed by marching on Paris with Montmorency and Saint-André; after being enthusiastically received by the citizens (March 16), they prevailed on Catherine and her children to join them, while Condé gathered his forces at Orléans.

The first of the wars of religion again showed Guise to be an outstanding soldier. His timely intervention in the battle of Dreux (Dec. 19) ensured the defeat of the Huguenots. Montmorency and Condé were both captured, so that Guise became the sole commander of the royal army while the admiral Gaspard de Coligny took over the direction of the Huguenot troops. As lieutenant general of the kingdom, Guise moved to besiege Orléans; but on Feb. 18, 1563, he was shot by Jean Poltrot de Méré, and on Feb. 24 he died of his wounds. Coligny's complicity in the assassination has never been proved: while admitting that he had given Poltrot money and acclaiming the duke's death as "the greatest good to this realm and to the church of God," he denied all foreknowledge of the act.

Guise was less of a political intriguer than his brother, the cardinal de Lorraine. He was ambitious, like other members of his house, but was generally loyal to the crown and served it well. He was primarily a man of action endowed with a handsome physique, charm, clear-sightedness, courage and energy. As a soldier he was loved by his men and feared by his enemies. He was survived by five of his children: HENRY, 3rd duc de Guise (*see below*); CHARLES (1554–1611), duc de Mayenne (*q.v.*), who consolidated the League; CATHERINE (1552–1596), who married Louis de Bourbon, duc de Montpensier; LOUIS (1555–1588), 2nd cardinal de Guise, afterward cardinal de Lorraine; and FRANÇOIS (1558–1573).

HENRY DE LORRAINE (1550–1588), 3rd duc de Guise, was born on Dec. 31, 1550. His career was largely determined by the desire to avenge his father's death, for which he held Coligny responsible. Though he was only a child in 1563, Catherine de Médicis allowed him to succeed his father as grand master and as governor of Champagne. In 1566 he went to Vienna in the hope of gaining military experience by fighting the Turks, but the war ended before he could go into action. He returned home in time to take part in the second religious war and soon showed that his judgment was not equal to his courage. He was tricked by Coligny into defending Sens, thereby allowing the Huguenot leader to link up with German reinforcements. After the peace of Longjumeau (March 1568), Catherine de Médicis adopted a policy favourable to the Catholic party: Michel de L'Hospital, the chief advocate of toleration, was dismissed from the chancellorship and the Guises regained their former influence at court. When civil war broke out anew in Aug. 1568, Guise served under the king's brother, Henry, duc d'Anjou; at Jazeneuil (Nov. 1568), at Jarnac (March 1569) and at St. Yrieix (June 1569) he performed deeds as daring as they were useless. His successful defense of Poitiers (Sept. 1569), however, earned him admission to the king's council. At the battle on Montcontour (Oct. 1569) he received a leg wound, which kept him in bed for three months. After the peace of St. Germain (Aug. 1570) Guise returned to court, the idol of the younger nobility; his bold wooing of Margaret of Valois provoked the anger of her brother, Charles IX, which could only be appeased by Guise's hurriedly marrying Catherine de Clèves, daughter of François, duc de Nevers, and of Marguerite de Bourbon (Oct. 4, 1570). While the king succumbed to Coligny's influence, Guise took care to ingratiate himself with the people of Paris.

In 1572 Catherine de Médicis turned to the Guises for help in getting rid of Coligny, who was pressing the king to adopt policies at variance with her aims. After an attempt on the admiral's life had failed, Guise attended the secret meeting (Aug. 23) which planned the massacre of St. Bartholomew's day (see SAINT BARTHOLOMEW'S DAY, MASSACRE OF). On Aug. 24 he personally supervised Coligny's murder, thereby avenging his father's death, but otherwise took no part in the massacre and even sheltered about 100 Huguenots in his house. In Feb. 1573 he narrowly escaped death at the siege of La Rochelle. The election of Henry, duc d'Anjou, as king of Poland (June 1573) left him without a serious rival as head of the Catholic party; Catherine de Médicis came to depend on him to protect her from the intrigues of her son François, duc d'Alençon and later duc d'Anjou, and Henry of Navarre.

At Henry III's accession (May 1574) the duc de Guise occupied a unique position at court as well as in the affections of the people of Paris. The king's marriage to Guise's cousin Louise de Vaudémont (Feb. 1575) further strengthened his influence. In Oct. 1575 he calmed the anxieties of the Parisians by defeating a German army at Dormans; during the action a bullet carried off part of his left cheek and ear, leaving a scar that won him his father's nickname of "le Balafré." Fearing Guise's growing popularity, Henry III made peace with the Huguenots (May 1576). Guise, angered by what he regarded as a betrayal, formed a league of nobles in defense of the Catholic cause (see LEAGUE, HOLY); it professed loyalty to the king but implicitly challenged his authority. Henry III countered the move by placing himself at the head of the movement. His relations with Guise deteriorated further after the peace of Poitiers (Sept. 1577) and the official dissolution of the League. While the king fell under the spell of new favourites, Guise strengthened the ties which existed for some time between his family and the Spanish monarchy. He became the friend of Don John (q.v.) of Austria, with whom he proposed to invade England in Mary Stuart's interest (1583); and from 1578 onward he had a pension from Philip II of Spain. His need of money was acute, his heavy debts even obliging him to sell his property of Nanteuille-Haudoin.

When François d'Anjou died (June 1584), the Huguenot leader, Henry of Navarre, became heir presumptive to the crown, and the League was revived in order to exclude him from the succession. By settling the succession on Charles, cardinal de Bourbon, it concealed Guise's own designs on the throne. In March 1585 Guise and his supporters issued the manifesto of Péronne, which attacked Henry III for his lukewarm policy. As half the kingdom rallied to the League, the king yielded to its demands at Nemours (July 1585) and halfheartedly assumed the direction of the war against the Huguenots. While the royal army under Anne, duc de Joyeuse, was routed at Coutras, Guise defeated German allies of the Huguenots at Vimory (Oct. 1587) and Auneau (Nov. 1587).

In May 1588 Guise returned to Paris, where his sister Catherine, duchesse de Montpensier, had been agitating on his behalf. On May 12—the Day of the Barricades—the people rose against the king, but instead of seizing the throne, Guise helped to appease the mob, and Henry III was able to escape to Chartres. By the Edict of Union (July) the king surrendered to the League's demands, and on Aug. 4 Guise was appointed lieutenant general of the kingdom. When the estates-general met at Blois in October, Henry III tried to reassert his authority, but the deputies, unmoved by his eloquence, obliged him to adhere to the Edict of Union. It was then that he decided to destroy Guise. On Dec. 23 Guise fell into a carefully laid trap. As he left a council meeting in answer to a royal summons, he was set upon by the king's bodyguard. Even after he had been repeatedly stabbed, he put up a fierce resistance before collapsing at the foot of the king's bed. His body and that of his brother Louis, cardinal de Lorraine, who was murdered next day, were burned and the ashes thrown in the Loire.

Posterity has treated Henry de Lorraine harshly; he has been condemned for his foolhardiness and treasonable activities. However, his contempt for Henry II appears to have concealed a fundamental respect for the dynasty of Valois, which explains the indecision that characterized his political behaviour. His popularity was largely based on his handsome appearance, charm of manner, humanity and courage.

Henry de Guise was outlived by 7 of his 14 children, notably CHARLES, 4th duc de Guise; CLAUDE (1578–1657), duc de Chevreuse; and LOUIS (1585–1621), 3rd cardinal de Guise.

CHARLES (1571–1640), 4th duc de Guise, was imprisoned for three years after his father's death. In 1611 he married Henriette Catherine de Joyeuse, heiress to the duchy of Joyeuse and widow of Henry de Bourbon, duc de Montpensier. Of his ten children, HENRY (1614–1664) was archbishop of Reims before he became the 5th duc de Guise. In 1647 and 1654 he tried unsuccessfully to secure the crown of Naples, spending part of the intervening period as a prisoner in Spain. The 6th duke was his nephew LOUIS JOSEPH (1650–1671), who married Elizabeth, daughter of Louis XIII's brother Gaston, duc d'Orléans. The 7th and last duc de Guise of the house of Lorraine was Louis Joseph's son FRANÇOIS JOSEPH (1670–1675); and the senior line of the Guises died out with MARIE DE LORRAINE (1615–1688), called Mademoiselle de Guise, a daughter of the 4th duke. Though the male line of Elbeuf survived, the duchy-peerage of Guise became extinct. Revived in 1704 for the Bourbon princes de Condé, it passed with their inheritance to the house of Bourbon-Orléans in the 19th century (see BOURBON).

BIBLIOGRAPHY.—The best guide to sources relevant to the Guises is H. Hauser, Les Sources de l'histoire de France au XVIe siècle 1494–1610, 4 vol. (1906–16). Among original authorities see Mémoires pour servir à l'histoire de France, ed. by J. F. Michaud and J. J. Poujoulat, vol. vi (1839). Apart from general histories of France in the 16th century, see R. de Bouillé, Histoire des ducs de Guise, 4 vol. (1849); L. H. Forneron, Les Ducs de Guise et leur époque, 2 vol. (1893); L. Romier, Les Origines politiques des guerres de religion, 2 vol. (1913–14), Le Royaume de Catherine de Médicis, 2 vol. (1922), La Conjuration d'Amboise (1923) and Catholiques et Huguenots à la cour de Charles IX, 4 vol. (1922–24); A. Bailly, Henri le Balafré (1953).
(R. J. K.)

GUITAR, a plucked stringed instrument with a wide, flat shallow body of waisted outline. Although deriving ultimately from the common stock of medieval necked stringed instruments played with plectrum, fingers or bow, the guitar probably originated in Spain in the early 16th century and was probably a development of the gittern. With seven gut strings arranged in three pairs, or "courses," and a single top string, the tuning (two fourths with a third in the middle) of the early guitar was by means of pegs in a violllike pegbox fitted to a long neck on which gut frets were tied. The neck was mortised into an end block and the finger board was flush with the table (belly). In the table was a circular sound hole, often elaborately decorated. The bridge was glued to the table, thus sustaining the direct pull of the strings. This instrument was closely related to the vihuela de mano, which in Spain took the place of the lute. Books of vihuela music from the middle years of the 16th century often include music for the four-course guitar.

Before the end of the 16th century a fifth course was added, tuned a fourth below the fourth course. This instrument, small bodied and narrow in outline, with a flat, slightly reflexed head in place of the earlier pegbox, remained popular mainly with amateurs during the 17th and 18th centuries, although some music of interest was written by virtuoso professional players.

In the late 18th century a sixth course was added, the stringing subsequently being reduced to six single strings tuned E-A-d-g-b-e', which has since remained standard. At this period the finger board remained flush with the table, the frets were of metal or ivory, the 12th or octave fret was at the junction of the neck with the body and five higher frets were mounted on the table itself.

Thereafter, most European makers sought to produce greater sonority. In Spain the tradition of guitar playing remained unbroken and it was there, in the early 19th century, that further developments were introduced. The body became broader and shallower with a very thin table, an important internal feature of which was the spreading of radial bars from just below the sound hole in place of the earlier transverse bars. The base of the neck was formed into a "shoe" which projected a short distance inside the body and was glued to the back; this gave extra stability against the pull of the strings. A raised hardwood finger board with metal frets extended down the neck and upper part of the table as far as the sound hole.

Elsewhere in Europe, makers, on the whole, favoured a narrow-waisted body and a rather heavier construction. Radial bars were adopted, however, together with the raised finger board and the "shoe." Most northern instruments were fitted with machine heads instead of pegs for tuning.

The guitar in its modern form was introduced by the Spanish maker Antonio Torres in the mid-19th century; this large instrument with a fuller, deeper tone is suitable for use in the concert hall. The strings of the classical guitar were of gut and metal-covered silk, but plastics later largely replaced gut for the upper strings. Other modern developments include the dance band guitar, metal strung and played with a plectrum; the "cello guitar," with a violin-type bridge and tailpiece; the Hawaiian guitar, in which the strings are stopped with a metal bar which is used to produce a portamento effect; and the electric guitar, where the tone depends not on body resonance but on amplification.

From the 16th to the 18th century guitar music was written either in tablature (see LUTE) or in a system of chord symbols known as *abecedario Italiano*. Sometimes the two were combined. Since the 18th century the method normally used is a single stave upon which the music is notated an octave higher than it sounds.

In many parts of Europe the guitar has played an important part in folk and popular music and in the hands of Spanish flamenco players a very high technical standard has been achieved. Modern classical guitar technique owes much to the Spaniard Francisco Tarrega, whose transcriptions of works by Bach, Mozart and other classical composers formed the basis of the concert repertoire. The position of the guitar in the concert world is mainly due to the Andrés Segovia. Many first-rate executants appeared in modern Europe and America, serving as a fresh impulse to composers to produce serious works for the instrument. (E. HA.)

GUITRY, the name of two French actors, father and son, the latter being also a producer and playwright.

LUCIEN GERMAIN GUITRY (1860–1925) was born in Paris on Dec. 13, 1860. Immediately after leaving the Conservatoire he first appeared at the Gymnase in *La Dame aux Camélias* (1878). His style of acting, sparing in gesture and theatrical effects, at first surprised rather than pleased the public and the critics. Sarah Bernhardt asked him to play at the Théâtre de la Renaissance, and it was there that he achieved his first successes.

He appeared in plays of the most varied character, from Charles Maurice Donnay's *Amants* (1895) to Anatole France's *Crainquebille*. He succeeded in representing the utmost frenzy of passion with the greatest economy of method. From 1918 onward he frequently acted in the plays of his son Sacha Guitry; he was remarkably successful in creating the principal parts in *Pasteur* and *Mon Père avait raison*. He died in Paris, June 1, 1925.

SACHA GUITRY (1885–1957), dramatist, actor and producer, was born at St. Petersburg, Russia, on Feb. 21, 1885, the son of the foregoing. He was only 21 when he achieved success with his first play, *Nono*. This was followed by *Chez les Zoaques* (1906), *Petite Hollande* (1908), *Le Scandale de Monte Carlo* (1908), *Le Veilleur de nuit* (1911)—one of his best plays—and *Un Beau mariage* (1911).

Sacha Guitry generally acted in his own plays; it is difficult to draw an absolute distinction between his work as an actor and as a playwright, for his art was always to some extent in the nature of brilliant improvisation. His output was enormous; he had over 90 plays produced out of 130 that he wrote. Special mention is given to those more serious pieces which he wrote for his father to act in: *Debureau* (1918), *Pasteur* (1919) and *Béranger* (1920). He wrote, directed and acted in many motion pictures of which the best known was perhaps *Roman d'un tricheur* ("The Cheat"). His autobiography, *Mémoires d'un tricheur* (translated into English as *If I Remember Right*), appeared in 1935. He was promoted commander of the Legion of Honour in 1936 and elected to the Académie Goncourt in 1939.

Married five times, he taught all his wives, of whom Yvonne Printemps was the most celebrated, to act. He died in Paris on July 24, 1957.

See S. Guitry, *Lucien Guitry, sa carrière et sa vie* (1930); A. Madis, *Sacha* (1950). (W. A. DN.)

GUITTONE D'AREZZO (c. 1235–1294), Italian poet, a founder of the school of Tuscan courtly poetry before the *Stil Nuovo* (see ITALIAN LITERATURE). He belonged (after 1265) to both the military and religious orders of the Milites Beatae Virginis Mariae and from these two periods of his life arise the love poems and, in contrast, the sonnets and difficult moral lyrics. His 41 letters are among the oldest documents of epistolary prose in Italian and he can be considered the inventor of the sacred ballad (*Lauda*). He was severely judged by Dante, and Francesco de Sanctis defined him as "not . . . a poet, but a subtle reasoner in verse."

See *Le Rime di Guittone d'Arezzo*, ed. by F. Egidi (1940); *Le Lettere di Frate Guittone*, ed. by F. Meriano (1923). (FR. M.)

GUIZOT, FRANÇOIS PIERRE GUILLAUME (1787–1874), French statesman and historian, a Protestant who, as a champion of conservative monarchy, opposed Napoleon, supported the Restoration and for nearly eight years was the master spirit of the last government of Louis Philippe, was born at Nîmes, the son of a lawyer, on Oct. 4, 1787, a few weeks before the promulgation in Languedoc of the royal edict restoring civil rights to the Protestants. His father was one of the leaders of the "Patriot" party in the town in the first days of the Revolution but was executed on April 8, 1794, as a member of the federalist insurrection against the Convention. His mother took refuge with her two sons in Geneva, where François learned Latin, Greek, Italian, German and English. His years of exile and study in a pious Calvinist environment, together with the influence of his mother, a woman of strong will but very sensible and devoted, seem to have had a profound effect on Guizot, whose later life bore witness to his moral fortitude and to his puritan probity. After six years in Geneva, however, the family returned to Nîmes.

In Oct. 1805 François went as a law student to Paris, where he also served as a tutor in the house of Philipp Albert Stapfer, the Swiss Protestant minister in France. At the same time he began frequenting literary circles, generally those in opposition to Napoleon I's government (his letters to his mother never mention the military parades of these years of the triumphant empire; and during a stay in Geneva he visited the exiled Mme de Staël). The 34-year-old authoress Pauline de Meulan, whom he met in 1807, introduced him to other writers and journalists, and for nearly four years he worked with her as the principal reporter for *Le Publiciste* till it disappeared under the imperial restrictions on the Parisian press. He finally married Pauline in 1812. Guizot also did much work as a translator, as a commentator for a critical edition of Edward Gibbon's *Decline and Fall of the Roman Empire* in French (1812) and as a contributor to the *Biographie universelle* (for which he wrote chiefly on German subjects) and to the *Annales de l'éducation* (founded by Pauline de Meulan and himself in 1811).

He published his first original work, *De l'état des beaux-arts en France et du Salon de 1810*, in 1811. In 1812 he was appointed assistant to J. C. D. de Lacretelle, professor of history at the University of Paris; and a few months later a new chair of modern history was created for him. His teaching of history followed the Christian lines advocated by Louis de Fontanes (q.v.).

After the fall of Napoleon in 1814, Guizot became secretary-general of the ministry of the interior and a leading exponent of the moderate policy of the first Restoration. During the Hundred

ANTHONY BAINES

MODERN SIX-STRINGED GUITAR

Days, he emigrated to Ghent, where he advised Louis XVIII to follow a liberal trend in the probable event of a second Restoration. This advice caused the reactionary Ultras to regard him as one of the most dangerous enemies of the monarchy, while his flight from France had on the other hand alienated the Bonapartists. Louis XVIII, however, on the second Restoration, let judging probably that the presence of a well-known Protestant Guizot be appointed secretary-general of the ministry of justice, would give some satisfaction to the allied powers worried by the excesses of the "white terror." The minister of justice, François de Barbé-Marbois, and Guizot resigned simultaneously in May 1816.

Guizot's *Du Gouvernement représentatif et de l'état actuel de la France* (1816) was the best statement of the program of the Doctrinaires (*q.v.*), for a constitutional monarchy, and in 1819 he was called to administrative office as director of the local government section in the ministry of the interior. After the fall of Élie Decazes in Feb. 1820, Guizot went back to the university and resumed work as a historian and as a journalist. Though he wrote many pamphlets expressing the liberal and constitutional views and served the opposition to the reactionary government through his writings *Des Moyens de gouvernement et d'opposition dans l'état actuel de la France* (1821) and *Histoire des origines du gouvernement représentatif*, 2 vol. (1821-22; Eng. trans. 1852), he did not join any of the secret societies that organized conspiracies in the years 1820-23. In 1823, Guizot began the publication of the *Collection des mémoires relatifs à l'histoire de France*, 31 vol., and of the *Collection des mémoires relatifs à l'histoire de la révolution d'Angleterre*, 25 vol. The theme of the struggle against Charles I in England, which Guizot moreover treated in his *Histoire de la révolution d'Angleterre*, part i, 2 vol., (1826-27; Eng. trans. 1838) was later to provide the ideological groundwork on which the Orleanists based their program. He also wrote an *Histoire de la civilisation en Europe*, 3 vol. (1828; Eng. trans. 1837), and an *Histoire de la civilisation en France*, 4 vol. (1830).

Despite all this literary work Guizot devoted considerable energy in the 1820s to acting as secretary-general to the liberal league "Aide-toi, le ciel t'aidera," which played a great role in the general elections of 1827 and 1830. Supported by this league, Guizot was on Jan. 23, 1830, elected deputy for Lisieux (Calvados) and so began an 18-year political career. He spoke against Prince Jules de Polignac's ministry and voted the address of the 221 which made King Charles X decide to dissolve the chamber and to run the risk of new elections. Re-elected on June 23, 1830, Guizot lost his faith in Charles X's liberal intentions when Charles published the "Three ordinances"; and the declaration of the 63 deputies against the ordinances was written by Guizot (July 27). After three days of rioting the July revolution triumphed (*see* CHARLES X, king of France).

Under Louis Philippe (*q.v.*), Guizot first became minister of the interior (Aug. 1-Nov. 2, 1830) and quickly reorganized the administration. He refused, however, to take part in Jacques Laffitte's ministry because he thought the tendency of the new government too revolutionary. From this time he was considered as one of the leaders of the "quasi-Legitimists" among the supporters of constitutional monarchy. As minister of education from Oct. 1832 to March 1839, with an interruption of six months in 1836, he prepared and put into action the first law on primary education (June 28, 1833); created the Commission des Travaux Historiques et Scientifiques; revived the Académie des Sciences Morales et Politiques (suppressed during the Restoration) and founded the Société d'Histoire de France. Politically, Guizot supported the Conservative party against the Republicans; and the period in which he, Adolphe Thiers and Victor, duc de Broglie, were ministers together was perhaps the best in the history of the July monarchy. From 1836, however, the Conservatives were split by dissensions, and in Feb. 1840 Guizot accepted the post of ambassador to London at the time when troubles in Syria between Ottoman Turks and Egyptians were giving Thiers an opportunity for an adventurous foreign policy (*see* EASTERN QUESTION).

Guizot helped Louis Philippe's efforts to maintain peace with Great Britain; and on Oct. 29, 1840, he was appointed minister for foreign affairs in Marshal Soult's ministry. This ministry proved to be the longest in Louis Philippe's reign, and from the beginning Guizot rather than the aged Soult was the real head of it. First he had to calm public opinion, which the bragging of Thiers had excited, and to restore friendly relations with powers alarmed by France's recent attitude on the Eastern question. He had to fight not only the Republican and Legitimist opposition but also Thiers' friends and some liberal deputies—chiefly those elected by the great maritime constituencies. Guizot surmounted every difficulty with courage, and the great eloquence with which he upheld the principle of a *juste milieu* between reaction and republicanism was an important element in the continuous strengthening of the Conservative party. In foreign affairs he exercised a real influence, his major achievement being the understanding with Great Britain reached through his personal good relations with the earl of Aberdeen, foreign secretary in Sir Robert Peel's government. In domestic affairs, however, Guizot was confronted with problems arising from dispositions taken by previous governments: for instance, the building of the Paris fortifications provoked resentment because land had to be expropriated; the census of 1841, with its inquiry into private wealth, caused dissatisfaction and even widespread riots; and the return to France of Napoleon's remains in Dec. 1840 (a move inaugurated by Thiers) served Bonapartist propaganda. Guizot refused any modification of the electoral law restricting the vote to men who paid more than 200 francs in taxes. During one of the numerous debates he answered the demand for reform by pointing out that anyone could attain the franchise if he paid enough tax, and added *Enrichissez vous par le travail et par l'épargne* ("Get rich by work and savings")—a sentence usually misrepresented by quoting only the first two words. The opposition, therefore, principally of the left, could stress the distinction between the "real" and the "legal" country, the *pays réel* which was largely unrepresented and the *pays légal* of the electorate, but in the chamber of deputies Guizot's majority seemed rather to be strengthened by the elections of 1842 and 1846. Prosperity, indeed, was his best support. Then came the economic crisis of 1846-47, coinciding with political and financial scandals in which some conservatives were involved. This gave a new impulse to the left opposition, and a new campaign for electoral reform found support even in moderate circles, while some Legitimists used the schools question to detach a number of Catholics from their adherence to a monarchy which had nevertheless done much for the church. When a reformist "banquet" was forbidden in Paris, secret republican societies started troubles which grew into the revolution of Feb. 1848. Guizot, who in Nov. 1847 had at last taken Soult's place as prime minister, resigned to let the king try a new ministry, but he could not save the monarchy.

Guizot took refuge in Belgium and then in England, where he spent a year going back to his historical works and collecting material for his future books. He returned to France in 1849 and spent his last years either in Paris or on his estate of Val Richer, near Lisieux, where he had acquired a former monastery, and where his two daughters and sons-in-law, both from the old Dutch family of De Witt, lived with him. The publications of his later years include *Histoire de la république d'Angleterre et de Cromwell*, 2 vol. (1854); *Histoire du protectorat de Richard Cromwell et du rétablissement des Stuart*, 2 vol. (1856); *Mémoires pour servir à l'histoire de mon temps*, 8 vol. (1858-67); and *Histoire parlementaire de la France*, 5 vol. (1863). After the failure of the attempt to reconcile Orleanists and Legitimists in 1849, Guizot consistently refused to take part in any political plots and the last 25 years of his life were spent in a retirement characterized by a great dignity and gave further proof of that rigid honesty which his most determined opponents could never call in question. A member of three of the five academies of the Institut de France, he had a great influence on their deliberations and so played a part in selecting new members, without any concern for flattery toward Napoleon III's government. He was also an important member of the French Protestant Church and encouraged it to behave sympathetically toward other churches; *e.g.*, in defending the Roman

Catholic position about the papal states in 1861. He tried, too, to use his personal contacts to obtain British mediation during informal discussions for the Franco-German peace treaty of 1871. Guizot died at Val Richer on Oct. 12, 1874. One of his daughters, Henriette de Witt, edited his letters to his family and friends (1884).

BIBLIOGRAPHY.—C. H. Pouthas, *Guizot pendant la Restauration* (1923) and *La Jeunesse de Guizot* (1936); Elizabeth P. Brush, *Guizot in the Early Years of the Orleanist Monarchy* (1927). *See also* Henriette de Witt, *Monsieur Guizot dans sa famille* (1880); Jules Simon, *Thiers, Guizot, Rémusat* (1885); Maurice Guizot, *Les Années de retraite de M. Guizot* (1902); Douglas Johnson, *Guizot: Aspects of French History* (1963); *Lettres de François Guizot et de la princesse de Lieven* (1963).
(J. E. V.)

GUJARAT (also GUJRAT or GUJERAT), a state of the Republic of India which came into existence under the Bombay Reorganization act on May 1, 1960. Before that, the term Gujarat was loosely applied to a region lying north of Bombay city where Gujarati is spoken. When India became independent in 1947 there came the Bombay state (*q.v.*). In the years which followed there was a successive reorganization of former princely states, notably the rich state of Baroda and the numerous small units which made up the peninsulas of Kathiawar and Cutch (Kutch). From 1948 to 1956 the greater part of the Kathiawar peninsula formed the separate Rajpramukh's state of Saurashtra with capital at Rajkot. When the states of peninsular India were reorganized on a linguistic basis in 1956 there was difficulty in separating the Gujarati-speaking and the Marathi-speaking parts of Bombay state and the separation was deferred till 1960. In broad terms Gujarat is that part of India where Gujarati is the dominant language, comprising Cutch, Kathiawar and the parts of the former Bombay state north of Daman (Damão). Its area is 72,236 sq.mi, bounded by Pakistan and Rajasthan on the north, Madhya Pradesh, Maharashtra and Daman on the east and south.

Physical Features.—The state of Gujarat is one of great contrasts; it stretches from the wet fertile rice-growing plains of the west coast north of Bombay city to the almost rainless salt deserts of Cutch. The state is best considered on a basis of its natural divisions. In the northwest, Cutch (*q.v.*) comprises a single district so arid as to be almost desert; it is bounded on the south by the Gulf of Cutch and on the north and east is separated from Pakistan and the mainland of India by the Great Rann of Cutch best described as a vast salt marsh covering about 8,000 sq.mi. The Rann floods during the rainy season, slight though the rains may be, and Cutch is converted into an island; in the dry season it is a sandy salty plain plagued by duststorms. To the south of Cutch is the large peninsula of Kathiawar lying between the Gulf of Cutch and the Gulf of Cambay. It also is arid and rises from the coasts to a low rolling area of hill land in the centre, covered with scrub or sparse woodland. The chief towns are found in the more fertile spots and were formerly the capitals of small states; now six of them are headquarters of districts. Soils are mostly poor being derived from a variety of the old crystalline rocks but among the products of value are the fine building stones of Porbunder. Rivers, except for seasonal streams, are absent. On the southern shores of the peninsula is the former Portuguese territory of Diu (*q.v.*). Northern Gujarat, using the old regional name, occupies the northeastern part of the new state and is mainly a country of small plains and low hills, through which runs the main line of the Western railway (formerly the Bombay, Baroda and Central Indian) from Bombay to Delhi. Rainfall is low; January temperatures may drop almost to freezing point while 48° C. (118° F.) has been recorded in the hot season. Dry zone crops of millet with some cotton are grown; Ahmedabad is an important cotton town.

Southward in central Gujarat the rainfall increases, temperature ranges are less, soils are more fertile being derived partly from the Deccan basalts. The focus of this area is the city of Baroda, formerly the capital of a rich and powerful state. South of what is now the Baroda district, the Narmada (formerly Narbada) river empties into the Gulf of Cambay and it is the silt borne by this river as well as the Tapti river which is responsible for the shallowing of the Gulf of Cambay and the decline of its former ports.

Southern Gujarat, the districts of Broach and Surat, are famed for their rich soils and fine crops of cotton. The great river Tapti, flowing in a deep trench from the east, cuts through Surat and in the eastern parts of south Gujarat the country is mountainous. This is indeed the northern extension of the Sahyadri mountains or Western Ghats, so important in Maharashtra state and which attract a heavy rainfall from the summer monsoon. Farther south, the mountains are forested and the small district of the Dangs (*q.v.*) lies here. Along the coastal plains conditions begin to approach the equable climate, with rainfall nearing 80 in., characteristic of Bombay city. Almost the only unifying factor in the varied state of Gujarat is the Gujarati language.
(L. D. S.)

History.—Rich in Paleolithic and microlithic finds, the area included in Gujarat state has been inhabited from prehistoric times. It is believed that there was contact with the Indus Valley civilization, for a cult of the Mother Goddess has been traced along with more characteristic Hindu faiths. Between the 4th and the 8th centuries A.D., Gujarat was ruled successively by the Mauryas, the Sakas, the Guptas and the Valabhis. It was during the 8th century that the Parsees entered the country from Iran. The Chalukya (*q.v.*) dynasty reigned from the 10th to the 13th century. Their power was then usurped by the Vaghelas who ruled until the Muslim conquest (*c.* 1298). The imperial rule of the sultans of Delhi ended with the usurpation of the first sultan of Gujarat, whose capital was at Anhilvada (Patan). Sultan Ahmed I founded Ahmedabad in 1411. From 1515 to 1572–73, when Akbar conquered Gujarat, the sultans were constantly embroiled with their Hindu, Rajput neighbours. About that time Affonso de Albuquerque and other Portuguese leaders made strenuous efforts to establish trading posts and forts in the coastal areas. Diu was obtained in 1535 and Daman in 1558, but relations with the Muslim rulers were seldom easy. Bassein (Vasai) was founded in 1534–35, and became an important centre of Portuguese and missionary activity, but it was taken by the Marathas in 1739. Between 1719 and 1758 the Marathas infiltrated through Gujarat. After the collapse of Maratha power, the former princely states entered into treaty relations with the British. They included Cambay, Chota Udaipur, Bariya, Balasinor and numerous petty states. The Gaekwar of Baroda was left as the principal representative of Maratha dominance, and his state was famed for enlightened administration. In 1937 the political agencies Rewa Kantha, Surat, Kaira, Nasik and Thana combined with Baroda to form the Gujarat States Agency with headquarters at Baroda city. In July 1947, on the eve of Indian independence, all the component states joined the union of India and were subsequently incorporated into the state of Bombay. The latter was reorganized in 1960 to form the states of Gujarat and Maharashtra.

Apart from the areas that were formerly under direct British control, much of the modern Gujarat state still awaits development and socially and (except for the textile industry) economically also it retains archaic features. Its architecture is exceptionally rich, particularly in elaborate tracery and highly ornate temples and sculpture. Jainism there reached a high pitch of intellectual development, being patronized lavishly by the wealthy, numerous and abstemious Hindu mercantile classes.

(*See also* INDIA, INDIA-PAKISTAN, SUBCONTINENT OF: *History*.)
(J. D. M. D.)

Population, Administration and Social Conditions.—At the 1971 census the population figure for Gujarat was 26,687,186, giving a density of 369 persons per square mile. This was an increase of 6,053,836, or 30%, over the 1961 census. Ahmedabad is the provisional capital; the projected new capital, 15 mi. N. of Ahmedabad, is to be called Gandhinagar. There are about 220 towns and more than 19,000 villages in the state; the chief towns are Ahmedabad (pop., 1971, 1,588,378), Baroda (467,422), Surat (471,815), Rajkot (300,152), Bhavnagar (226,072), Jamnagar (214,853), Nadiad (108,268); all the others have fewer than 100,-000 persons.

Gujarat comprises 19 districts. They are Cutch; six which make up most of the Kathiawar peninsula, Jamnagar, Junagadh, Rajkot, Amreli, Bhavnagar (Gohilwad) and Surendranagar (Zalawad); and twelve in the old Gujarat region, Surat, Dangs, Kaira, Mehsana, Sabarkantha, Baroda, Bulsar (Valsad), Gandhinagar, Banaskantha, Broach, Baroda, Panch Mahals and Ahmedabad.

By the early 1970s Gujarat, with more than 35% of the population literate, ranked fourth among the Indian states in literacy. There were more than 25,000 schools and educational institutions, including seven universities. Primary education for children aged 7 to 11 is free and compulsory in all districts of Baroda division. The Gujarati language (*q.v.*) is spoken by most people.

About 1,270 hospitals and dispensaries provide nominally free medical treatment. There are a number of labour welfare centres that have free recreational facilities and cultural activities for industrial workers. The state government spends about Rs. 56,-000,000 annually on educational, housing, medical and cultural facilities.

(S. Ch.; S. B. L. N.)

Economy.—The main products of the state are cotton, rice, wheat, jowar, bajri and pulses. Forests produce teak, bamboos and sandalwood. The Gir forests contain the only lions' sanctuary in India. Minerals include calcite and limestone in Jamnagar and manganese in Baroda. Kaira has bauxite and limestone and Saurashtra has gypsum. There are cement works at Porbunder, Dwarka and Sikka, and factories for drugs and medicines near Bulsar and in Baroda. Silk goods are produced and there is a smaller output of gold and silver thread, carved sandalwood, and leather goods. When completed the Ukai project will irrigate 400,000 ac. of land and help the industrial development of southern Gujarat.

The industrialization characteristic of the city of Bombay (*q.v.*), and especially the textile industry, extends northward into Gujarat with such centres as Surat, Broach, Baroda and Ahmedabad well served by rail and road. To relieve the pressure on this main railway and the port of Bombay, the policy of the central government of India is to develop railways and modern deepwater ports in Cutch and Kathiawar (the Gulf of Cambay is too shallow). Okha at the western tip of the Kathiawar peninsula has proved too distant and involves a long rail haul; Port Kandla on the Gulf of Cutch has accordingly been developed. Gujarat has 3,515 mi. of railway, and road construction in the drier parts is relatively easy; but Gujarat has less than half of the number of factories and of factory workers found in Maharashtra.

(L. D. S.)

BIBLIOGRAPHY.—A. K. Forbes, *Ras Mala*, ed. by H. G. Rawlinson, 2 vol. (1924); H. Wilberforce-Bell, *The History of Kathiawad* (1916); M. S. Commissariat, *History of Gujarat*, 2 vol. (1938–57); K. M. Munshi, *Glory That Was Gurjaradeśa*, vol. i (1943); A. K. Majumdar, *Chaulukyas of Gujarat* (1956); M. R. Majumdar (ed.), *Historical and Cultural Chronology of Gujarat* (1960).

(J. D. M. D.)

GUJARATI LANGUAGE, spoken by about 20,000,000 persons in the Indian states of Gujarat and Maharashtra and adjoining districts, is one of the Indo-Aryan languages (*q.v.*). Its neighbour east and northeast is the Rajasthani language (*q.v.*), into which it merges so gradually that it is difficult to assign border dialects to either language. Gujarati, one of the 14 regional languages specified in the Indian constitution, has a number of dialects and class variations; *e.g.*, Parsis make distinctions between cerebrals and dentals that are disregarded by Muslims. Both communities have borrowed Persian and Arabic words more freely than standard Gujarati, which, because of its maritime connections, has borrowed occasional words from other parts of Asia and from Europe, especially in the dialect of the Kathiawar sailors. There are differences in pronunciation among the Hindus, too, *e.g.*, variation between *ē* and *ĕ* and *c*, *kh* and *ch*, *s* and *ch*, as well as loss of *h*, confusion of cerebrals and dentals and alternation of *ḍ*, *r*, *l* and *l*. (For standard Gujarati grammar, *see* G. P. Taylor, *The Student's Gujarati Grammar*, 3rd ed., 1944).

Gujarati has a long literary tradition with an almost unbroken evolution from Gaurjara Apabhraṃśa to Old Gujarati (or Old Western Rajasthani), the latter generally considered to begin with the Bhakta or devotional poems of Narasimha Mehta (15th century) and, in the same period, the writings of the great poetess Mira Bai. Premanand, the 17th-century master of narrative poetry, adapted themes from the Sanskrit epics "Mahābhārata" and "Rāmāyana." The last great poet of Old Gujarati was Dayaram (1767–1852). Jain *bhandārs* or libraries are veritable storehouses of Old Gujarati manuscripts.

On the impact of European civilization Narmadashankar (1833–1886), in his prose and verse innovations, gave direction to a literary revival; he is justly termed the founder of modern Gujarati literature. Govardhanram Tripathi's (1855–1907) novel *Sarasvaticandra* depicts Gujarati life; it marks a renaissance and gives a literary inspiration to the period. K. M. Munshi (1887–1971) captured a wide public with his historical novels. The Gujarati writings and speeches of Mohandas K. Gandhi (1869–1948) had a strong literary influence. Panalal Patel wrote novels about village life.

BIBLIOGRAPHY.—Sir George Grierson, *Linguistic Survey of India*, vol. ix, pt. ii, pp. 340–343 (1903–28); B. N. Mehta & B. K. Mehta, *Modern Gujarati Dictionary* (1925); M. B. Belsare, *An Etymological Gujarati-English Dictionary* (1940); *Bhagvad Gomandal*, Gujarati dictionary, 7 vol.; N. B. Divatia, *Gujarati Language and Literature*, 2 vol. (1920–21); T. N. Dave, *A Study of the Gujarati Language in the 16th Century* (1935); K. M. Munshi, *Gujarat and Its Literature*, 2nd ed. (1954); J. H. Dave, "Gujarati," *The Indian Literatures of Today* (1947); K. Chavada, "Gujarati," *Writers in Free India* (1950); E. Bender (trans.), *Nalarayadavadanticarita* ("Adventures of King Nala and Davadanti") (1951); M. Jhaveri, "Gujarati," *Contemporary Indian Literature*, 2nd ed. (1959); K. M. Munshi, "Gujarati Literature" and M. Joshi, "Gujarati Literature," *Literatures in Modern Indian Languages* (1957); J. R. Firth, "Phonetic Observations on Gujarati," *Bulletin of the School of Oriental and African Studies* (1957); P. B. Pandit, "Duration, Syllable and Juncture in Gujarati," *Indian Linguistics* (1958), and *Phonemic and Morphemic Frequencies of the Gujarati Language* (1961), and *Phonemic and Morphemic Frequencies of the Gujarati Language* (1965); G. Cardona, *A Gujarati Reference Grammar* (1965); R. L. Turner, *A Comparative Dictionary of the Indo-Aryan Languages* (1966).

(Er. B.)

GUJRANWALA, a municipal town, a district and a *tehsil* in Lahore division, Pakistan. The town, headquarters of the district, lies 41 mi. N of Lahore. Pop. (1969 est.), including refugee camp, 289,300. Originally a village founded by Gujars, it was renamed Khanpur by some settlers, Sansi Jats of Amritsar, but its old name survived. Little is known of its history until the Sikh period. Places of interest include the grave of Mahan Singh, Mahan Singh's garden and a lofty cupola covering part of the ashes of the great maharaja. There are two degree colleges, for men and women, both affiliated to the Punjab university.

Gujranwala lies on the railway line to Peshawar, and on the Grand Trunk road, and is the chief market of the district and an important industrial centre. Manufacturing of iron safes and aluminum, brass and copper utensils are the old industries for which it occupies an important position in Pakistan. New industries have grown since independence, including manufactures of textiles, hosiery, sanitary fittings and electric fans, and tanneries.

GUJRANWALA TEHSIL, area 936 sq.mi, had a population in 1961 of 745,393.

GUJRANWALA DISTRICT comprises an area of 2,312 sq.mi. Pop. (1961) 1,291,886. In 1847 the district came under British influence in connection with the regency at Lahore. In 1849 it was included in the territory annexed after the second Sikh War, and became a part of Pakistan in 1947. Located in the Rechna doab it consists of a featureless plain that naturally falls into two divisions: the low-lying lands fringing the Chenab and the Degh, and the upland between them. Wheat, rice and cotton are the chief crops.

(K. S. Ad.)

GUJRAT, a municipal town, *tehsil* and district in Rawalpindi division, Pakistan. The town, headquarters of the district, stands about 5 mi. from the right bank of the Chenab river, 70 mi. N of Lahore by rail. Pop. (1961) 59,608; (1969 est.) 73,000. It is built upon an ancient site formerly occupied, according to tradition, by two successive cities, the second supposedly destroyed in 1303, the year of a Mongol invasion. The existing town probably grew up round the fort made by Akbar in 1580. The town has factories for furniture, brassware, boots, cotton goods, shawls and electric fans, and is known for its potteries. There are two colleges, Zamindar college and the Government college for women, affiliated to the Punjab university.

(K. S. Ad.)

GUJRAT DISTRICT (area 2,264 sq.mi.; pop. [1961] 1,326,012);

GUJRAT TEHSIL covers an area of 565 sq.mi. Pop. (1961) 433,-340.

comprises a narrow strip of sub-Himalayan plain country. A range of low barren hills, known as the Pabbi, traverses the northern angle. Wheat and millets are the principal crops. The rainfall is good and large areas are irrigated. Lower Jhelum canal takes off from the Jhelum (q.v.) at Rasul, where the fall between the upper and lower canals has also been used to generate electricity. Numerous relics of antiquity stud the surface of the district. A mound occupied by the village of Moga (Mong) has been identified as the site of Nicaea, the city built by Alexander the Great on the field of his victory over Porus (see HYDASPES, BATTLE OF THE). Construction of a great cantonment began at Kharian in 1960.

(K. S. Ab.)

GULA, a name written with the prefix for deity, occurs for the first time on Sumerian tablets of the 3rd dynasty of Ur (late 3rd and early 2nd millennium B.C.), found at Lagash, Drehem, Umma, Ur and Nippur. *Gu-la,* "great," "mighty," may be merely an epithet which served as a substitute name for goddesses of the "great mother" class. Post-Sumerian catalogues of the Sumero-Akkadian pantheon show that Gula was identified with such goddesses—e.g., Bau, much honoured in cult at Lagash, and Nininsina. "Lady of Isin." The earliest Lagash texts, however, mention Bau often but Gula hardly at all; whereas contemporary texts of Umma and Drehem refer rarely to Bau by name and frequently to Gula; and texts of Ur mention Gula only in relation to cult. Tablets of this period mention too a "Gula of Umma" and a "Nininsina of Umma"; and a tablet from Lagash refers to Nininsina(k) gu-la.

On Kassite *kudurru* (boundary stones) Gula is represented seated, sometimes with a dog, and named in association with Ninurta, god of war and the hunt. In Assyrian ritual prayers she is addressed as "the lady who dwells in the pure heavens, merciful, restorer of life, whose command heals." There were temples to Gula at Babylon and Borsippa and at Isin. The Assyrian Ashurnasirpal II (884–859 B.C.) built a temple for her at Ashur.

See A. Deimel, *Pantheon Babylonicum,* no. 547 (1914); E. Dhorme, *Les Religions de Babylonie et d'Assyrie* (1949). (T. FH.)

GULBARGA, a city and district in Mysore, India. The city, headquarters of the district, lies about 100 mi. W. of Hyderabad. Pop. (1961) 97,069. Originally included in the territory of the Kakatiyas of Warangal, it was annexed to the kingdom of Delhi in the early 14th century by Ulugh Khan, afterward Mohammed Tughluq; after his death it fell to the Bahmani kingdom and, upon the breakup of that power, to Bijapur. With the conquest of the Deccan by Aurangzeb it was again included in the empire of Delhi, but was separated from it by the establishment of Hyderabad state in the early 18th century.

There are many ancient monuments. In the eastern quarter of the city are the tombs of the Bahmani kings; the most notable building is a mosque said to be modeled upon that of Córdoba in Spain. Gulbarga is also a centre of the cotton trade with ginning and pressing factories and spinning and weaving mills, and also flour and oil mills and paint factories. It is situated on the main line from Bombay to Madras.

GULBARGA DISTRICT (pop. [1961] 1,399,457; area 6,332 sq. mi.) lies on the north bank of the river Krishna and mainly in the valley of its tributary, the Bhima. The rainfall is low, seldom exceeding 30 in. The chief crops are millets, pulses, cotton and linseed. Limestone is quarried in places, but the majority of the population is engaged in agriculture. Formerly in Hyderabad state, the district became part of Mysore in 1956. (S. AH.)

GULDBERG, OVE HÖEGH- (1731–1808), Danish statesman, one of the principal ministers of Christian VII's reign, was born at Horsens on Sept. 1, 1731, the son of a shopkeeper. He grew up in straitened circumstances and worked for a time as a tutor before taking a degree in theology in 1753. He then occupied himself with historical studies, but became professor of rhetoric at Sorö academy in 1761. In 1764, however, he was appointed tutor to Prince Frederick, half brother of the future King Christian VII (q.v.). He became Frederick's private secretary in 1771 and shared his indignation at the usurpation of power by J. F. Struensee (q.v.). After contributing to Struensee's fall in 1772, he began, in collaboration with Prince Frederick and the dowager queen Juliana Maria, to exert considerable influence over internal affairs; and in 1774 he was appointed confidential cabinet secretary. Mild in manner but ambitious, Guldberg gradually increased his power. From his office issued increasing numbers of cabinet orders which bypassed his colleagues and the council but were signed by the unbalanced Christian VII. By this means the important law concerning citizenship, which reserved the holding of public office to Danish citizens, was passed. Guldberg concerned himself with educational and religious affairs, but was conservative in the matter of land reform and wished to preserve the landowners' authority over the peasants. When the foreign minister Andreas Peter Bernstorff (q.v.) opposed the influence of the cabinet and conducted a foreign policy of his own, Guldberg had him dismissed (1780) and tried to pursue a policy based exclusively on cooperation with Russia. A director of several companies, he also controlled Denmark's financial policy from 1782 and so could secure government support for his companies during the economic difficulties after the close of the American Revolution in 1783. In April 1784, just as he was about to be admitted to the privy council, Guldberg was overthrown by the crown prince Frederick's *coup d'état.* (See FREDERICK VI, king of Denmark.) For the next 18 years Guldberg was a loyal and active provincial civil servant. At his death on Feb. 7, 1808, in Hald, he was a landowner.

See Aage Friis, *Andreas Peter Bernstorff og Ove Höegh Guldberg* (1899); E. Holm, *Danmark-Norges Historie 1720–1814,* vol. v–vi (1906–09). (F. SK.)

GULF INTRACOASTAL WATERWAY, an improved navigable waterway along the Gulf of Mexico coast of the United States, extends from Apalachee bay, Fla., westward to the Mexican border at Brownsville, Tex., a distance of more than 1,100 mi. In part artificial, the waterway consists of a channel paralleling the coast behind barrier beaches, linked by a series of canals and maintained at a minimum depth of 12 ft. by the U.S. army corps of engineers.

The Gulf Intracoastal waterway is an important route for barges, and several sections of it furnish access to major gulf ports for

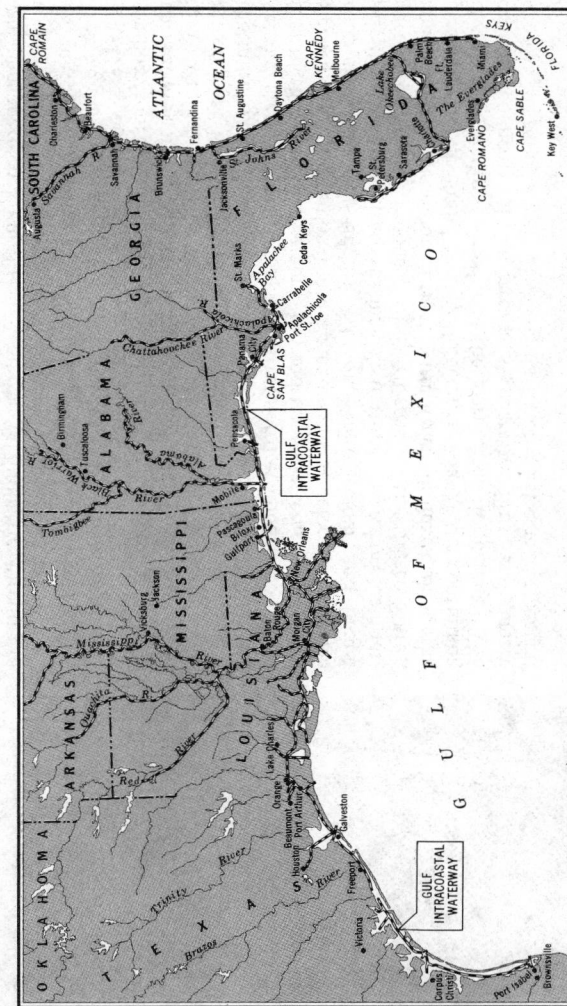

THE GULF INTRACOASTAL WATERWAY SYSTEM OF SOUTHEASTERN UNITED STATES

ocean-going vessels. Among the major ports along the waterway are Panama City, and Pensacola, Fla.; Mobile, Ala.; Gulfport, Miss.; New Orleans and Lake Charles, La.; and Port Arthur, Freeport, Beaumont, Galveston, Corpus Christi and Brownsville, Tex.

Although much of the traffic is short haul, averaging about 170 mi., the waterway is connected with the Mississippi valley system of inland waterways; through barge traffic is handled between such ports as Chicago, Pittsburgh, St. Louis and Memphis and points on the Gulf Intracoastal waterway and its branches. Among the principal items moved on the waterway are petroleum and its products, industrial chemicals, pipe and other supplies for the oil fields and sulfur.

At its eastern end, the waterway is not directly connected with the Atlantic Intracoastal waterway, except via the open waters of the Gulf of Mexico and the Okeechobee Waterway. Traffic is concentrated in that section of the waterway connecting the Warrior-Tombigbee system on the east at Mobile bay, Ala., with the Mississippi river system at New Orleans, La., and between the Mississippi river and the major Texas ports. A cut-off route, the Plaquemine waterway, provides direct connection west of New Orleans between the Gulf Intracoastal waterway and the Mississippi river. The waterway is at sea level. The Harvey lock at New Orleans provides entrance from the Mississippi river. Part of the route of the waterway at New Orleans consists of the Inner Harbor Navigation canal, an artificial waterway which is the axis of a major industrial district.

See also WATER TRANSPORT, INLAND.

(H. M. M.)

GULFPORT, a city and seat of Harrison county in southeastern Mississippi, U.S., on the Gulf of Mexico, is midway between Mobile, Ala., and New Orleans, La., on the Old Spanish trail. Gulfport was founded in 1887 by Capt. William H. Hardy, Confederate soldier and engineer, who selected the site for the southern terminus of his Gulf and Ship Island railroad. Its development, however, was made possible by Capt. Joseph T. Jones of the Bradford (Pennsylvania) Construction company, who completed the railroad, secured controlling interest and moved to the city in 1902. Jones and his family were leaders in the building of the city, including its excellent harbour, transferred to the U.S. government in 1907.

Gulfport is in the centre of what has been called the world's longest man-made sand beach (28 mi. long and 300 ft. wide) which helped make the city a year-around resort.

Gulfport was incorporated as a city in 1904. (For comparative population figures see table in MISSISSIPPI: Population.)

There is a frontage of 6 mi. on the Gulf which includes a modern deepwater port, consisting of two moles, separated by a harbour one-half mile long. The commerce of the port is chiefly in wood products, creosoted piling, cottonseed products, salt of potash, phosphate rock and fish. A number of industries produce a variety of goods, including textile products, concrete and building materials, fertilizers, small craft and drugs. There is also a U.S. Veterans hospital there.

(J. T. D.)

GULF STREAM, the western and northern quadrants, extending from Florida to the Grand Banks of Newfoundland, of the current system which sets clockwise around the North Atlantic in mid-latitudes. Fed by water from the Gulf of Mexico and reinforced off Florida by some water from the trade-wind current, the initial Gulf stream is relatively narrow and deep. Maximum velocities exceed four knots, with a rate of flow about 1,000 times that of the Mississippi river. Beyond Cape Hatteras it broadens, slackens and breaks down into a meandering streaky pattern with countercurrents and eddies. Its deep blue colour and higher salinity and temperature distinguish it from the inshore countercurrent (Cold Wall) along the eastern coast of the United States, and from the Labrador current with which it mixes along the periphery of the Grand Banks. East of the Banks the continuing current is normally referred to as the North Atlantic current. The offshore boundary of the stream is generally diffuse and poorly defined, the result in part of the similarity of the stream and central Atlantic waters.

See also ATLANTIC OCEAN: Surface Currents; OCEAN AND OCEANOGRAPHY: Movement of Sea Water.

(C. A. Bs.)

GULFWEED, a popular name given to a species of the brown seaweeds (Phaeophyta) belonging to the genus Sargassum, more particularly the species (Sargassum natans) that grows in free-floating masses in the Gulf stream and the Sargasso sea (q.v.). It is remarkable among seaweeds for its form, which resembles branches bearing leaves and berries; the latter are hollow floats answering the same purpose as the bladders in another brown seaweed, Fucus vesiculosus, common around the British Isles between high and low water. See also ALGAE.

GULL, the common name for a group of more than 40 species of web-footed, usually white, gray or black sea birds of the subfamily Larinae, family Laridae. One of the most attractive is the pinkish white Ross's gull (Rhodostethia rosea) which breeds in northern Siberia and wanders widely over the Arctic ocean. The black-legged kittiwake (Rissa tridactyla), a gull that inhabits the seas of the northern hemisphere, breeds as far south as the coast of France and the Gulf of St. Lawrence and winters south to the Mediterranean and Japan; this species, which has a wingspread of 36 in., is the only truly pelagic gull, and the only one that dives from the surface and swims under water (see also KITTI-WAKE).

Of the 35 species of the genus Larus, the largest is the great black-backed gull (L. marinus), with a wingspread of 65 in.; it is nearly circumpolar but does not occur between western Labrador and Japan. The large species of Larus are more or less raptorial; they prey on the eggs and young of many species of sea birds and rob smaller gulls of their food. The little gull (L. minutus) of Europe and, occasionally, of North America, a black-headed species, is the smallest gull, with a wingspread of 24 in. The black-headed gull (L. ridibundus), a dark-headed bird with crimson legs, breeds in Eurasia and Iceland and winters south to India, the Philippines and, infrequently, to the Atlantic coast of North America. This gull gets on well with man, feeding commonly in Europe in crop fields where its chief food is insects. In America its counterpart is the Franklin's gull (L. pipixcan) or "prairie dove," a trusting species that hawks for flying insects and that breeds in large colonies on inland marshes. Sabine's gull (Xema sabini), a ternlike species that abounds in the Arctic, has a forked tail and a curious habit of running and picking up food like a plover. The herring gull (L. argentatus) is by far the commonest of the Atlantic gulls; adults are gray-mantled with flesh-coloured legs and feet and black and white spotted wing tips. Many races breed over the northern part of the northern hemisphere, and the species is generally increasing as a result of expanding food supplies, chiefly garbage and sewage in and near coastal waters, for this gull is primarily a scavenger. The laughing gull (L. atricilla), which often gives vent to a strident laughing call, is a medium-sized species with, in summer, a black head, red bill and

ERIC HOSKING FROM NATIONAL AUDUBON SOCIETY

BLACK-HEADED GULL (LARUS RIDIBUNDUS)

red feet. It breeds from Maine to northern South America and winters south to Brazil, often on fresh waters quite far inland, although it is a coastal species; it is the only gull that breeds in the Caribbean area and South Atlantic ocean. The ring-billed gull (*L. delawarensis*), a well-named species, much resembles the herring gull, but is smaller; it is widespread on inland lakes and often gathers in large flocks to feed in plowed fields in North America. The California gull (*L. californicus*), smaller but much like the herring gull, breeds inland and often moves about in large flocks, which serve as powerful checks to insects and rodents. This is the species that is credited with saving the crops of the early Mormon settlers in the Salt Lake City region from destruction by the Mormon cricket, a long-horned grasshopper—an event commemorated by the erection of a monument. The kelp gull (*L. dominicanus*) is a very wide-ranging, black-headed species of the southern hemisphere, including Antarctica.

The only gull with a strikingly forked tail is the swallow-tailed gull (*Creagus furcatus*) of the Galápagos Islands. The large gray-ish Pacific gull (*Gabianus pacificus*) breeds in the region of Tasmania and southern Australia. Curiously, no gulls are found between South America and Australasia. (E. T. GI.)

GULLAH is the dialect of former slaves and their descendants (also called Gullahs and Geechees, West African tribal names) on the Sea Islands of South Carolina and Georgia and on the mainland nearby. It reveals characteristics of the speech of British settlers in that region during the 17th and 18th centuries and of several West African languages—including Vai, Mende, Twi, Ewe, Hausa, Yoruba, Ibo, Kikongo and others. The influence of these languages upon Gullah is evident in its vocabulary, sounds, syntax, morphology, intonation and word formations.

RALPH E. LAWRENCE

RING-BILLED GULL (LARUS DELAWARENSIS)

Nearly 6,000 African words have been identified in Gullah, most of which are now used as personal names, such as *Abiona*, "born by the wayside" (Yoruba); *Adanse*, a place name in Ghana; *Anyika*, "she is beautiful" (Vai); *Pitipa*, a Mende name given children born during a rain; etc. Many African words in Gullah are fairly common in American English, such as *cooter*, "tortoise"; *goober*, "peanut"; *gumbo*, "okra"; *juke* as in "jukebox"; *voodoo*, "witchcraft"; etc. Gullah speakers simplify English words and constructions, speak rapidly with no southern drawl, and use an intonation unlike that of English. The following sentences reveal features of Gullah: *Dey fa go shum*, "They went to see her," literally, "They take go see her"; *Shishuh tall pass una*, "Sister is taller than you"; *'E yedi wulisankpankpan, but cyan' shum*, "He hears the woodpecker, but can't see it"; *'Twix' me na una 'e duh badmout 'em fuh trut, enti?*, "Between me and you he surely put a curse on them, didn't he?"; *Uma-chil' nyamnyam fufu an' t'ree roll-roun', but 'e ain' been satify*, "The girl ate mush and three biscuits, but she wasn't satisfied."

For an analysis of Gullah with illustrative texts, *see* Lorenzo D. Turner, "Notes on the Sounds and Vocabulary of Gullah," *Am. Dialect Soc.* (May 1945), "Problems Confronting the Investigator of Gullah," *Am. Dialect Soc.* (April 1948) and *Africanisms in the Gullah Dialect* (1949). For Gullah stories, *see* Ambrose E. Gonzales, *The Black Border* (1922); S. G. Stoney and G. Shelby, *Black Genesis* (1930); R. I. McDavid and V. G. McDavid, "The Relationship of the Speech of American Negroes to the Speech of Whites," *American Speech*, vol. 26 (1951); J. Mason, "Etymology of Buckaroo (Gullah Word Buckra)," *American Speech*, vol. 35 (1960). (L. D. T.)

GULLANE, a village in the parish of Dirleton, East Lothian, Scot., on the southern shore of the Firth of Forth, lies 17 mi. E. of Edinburgh. Pop. (1951) 1,482. The 12th-century kirk of St. Andrew (now disused) has a Norman chancel arch and a 15th-century north transept. Gullane's associations with Knights Templar are indicated in such names as Templar lane. The 16th century Saltcoats castle, ½ mi. S.W., belonged to the Livingston family, whose ancestor obtained a grant of land for killing a wild boar, the last in Scotland, which terrorized the neighbourhood. Gullane possesses three excellent golf courses. (W. BE.)

GULLSTRAND, ALLVAR (1862–1930), Swedish physician, winner of the 1911 Nobel prize for medicine for his work on the dioptrics of the eye, was born on June 5, 1862, at Landskrona. He became professor of diseases of the eye at Uppsala in 1894 and in 1913 was appointed professor of physiological and physical optics there. His investigations concerned the general laws of dioptrics, a new conception of the theory of optical images; the extrication of the optical images in the eye; and the eye's relation to the diffusion of light. Among Gullstrand's works are *Allgemeine Theorie der monochromatischen Aberrationen* (1900), *Die optische Abbildung in heterogenen Medien und die Dioptrik der Kristallinse des Menschen* (1908) and *Einführung in die Methoden der Dioptrik des Auges des Menschen* (1911). He died in Stockholm on July 28, 1930.

GULLY, JOHN (1783–1863), British prize fighter, racing man and politician, a light of the 19th-century English sporting world, was born Aug. 21, 1783, at Wick near Bristol, the son of an innkeeper. In 1805, having failed as a butcher, he was in the king's bench prison when he was visited by his Bristol pugilist friend Henry Pearce, the "Game Chicken." As the result of an informal bout between them Gully's debts were paid and he was matched against Pearce. They met at Hailsham, before the duke of Clarence (afterward William IV), when Gully lost after 59 rounds. In 1807 he twice beat the huge Bob Gregson. He then retired from the ring, was landlord of "The Plough" in Carey street in London and took to horse racing. He executed betting commissions for important patrons during the prince regent. In 1827 he lost £40,000 in backing Mameluke (which he had bought for 4,000 guineas) in the St. Leger. With Robert Ridsdale as his confederate in 1832 he won the Derby and St. Leger with St. Giles and Margrave respectively. In alliance with John Day he won the Two Thousand Guineas with The Ugly Buck in 1844 and two years later the Derby with Pyrrhus the First and the Oaks with Mendicant. In 1854 he won the Two Thousand Guineas with The Hermit and, in partnership with Henry Padwick, the Derby with Andover. For many years his horses were trained at Danebury in Hampshire, where he and his betting associates were called the Danebury confederacy. He bought Ackworth park, Yorkshire, and was member of parliament for the pocket borough of Pontefract from Dec. 1832 to July 1837. In 1862 he bought the Wingate estate and collieries in Durham. Gully married twice and had 24 children, 12 by each wife. He died on March 9, 1863, in Durham. He was a fine figure, six feet tall and immensely strong. He was a man of resolute character who lived in an age of dubious sporting ethics and scandal has not wholly spared him; he probably kept to his own reasonably high standard of honesty and was always ready to fly to arms if defamed. (B. DN.)

GUMAL (GOMAL) **PASS**, the route that leads along the valley of the Gumal river, through South Waziristan agency, connecting Ghazni in eastern Afghanistan with Tank and Dera Ismail Khan in Pakistan, via Domandi, Gulkach (Gul Katch) post, Nilikach and Kot Murtaza near the entrance of the pass. The name is sometimes applied to the whole course of the Gumal river. The actual Gumal pass is a four-mile defile, and the most important pass between the Khyber and Bolan passes (*qq.v.*), providing the oldest of the trade routes in that area. It has been traditionally used by traders called Powindahs, who carry all their goods on the backs of camels or donkeys. They spend the summer in Afghanistan and on the approach of winter cross over to Pakistan in caravans. The Powindahs are mostly of the Ghilzai clan (mainly Nasir and Sulaiman Khel tribes) who live on the Afghan side of the frontier. They trail their camels along the borders of the territory of the Mahsud Waziris, bringing fruits, skins and cloth for disposal in the frontier markets or in the plains of Dera Ismail Khan. The entry of Powindahs into Pakistan is no longer free.

GUMAL RIVER rises near Sarwandi on the Koh Nak range in Afghanistan. Between Waziristan and the highland plateau of Afghanistan there is a belt of hills, in more or less parallel lines, which forms the barrier through which the Gumal breaks before it enters Pakistan near Domandi, where it is joined by the Kundar. It is joined by the Wana Toi (from the north) at Toi Khula and by the Zhob (from the south) at Khajuri Kach, and falls into the Indus a few miles south of Dera Ismail Khan cantonment. Al- most all its water is used for irrigation.

In the early 1960s plans were in hand to construct a multipur- pose dam at Khajuri Kach, below the junction of the Zhob and the Gumal, to form a reservoir with a storage capacity of 2,500,000 ac.ft. It was designed to provide irrigation to about 115,000 ac., to produce 73,000 kw. of hydroelectric power and also to control floods in the area.

(K. S. Ad.)

GUM ARABIC (Gum Acacia), an exudation from various varieties of acacia, much used in the arts. See Gums, Plant.

GUMBO, the name for the young mucilaginous pods of okra (gumbo is derived from an African word meaning "okra") and for the dishes and soups prepared from the pods. See Okra.

GUMMA, Japanese prefecture located in the western Kantō plain. Pop. (1970) 1,659,000, area 2,445 sq.mi. Gumma is mostly mountainous, with two-thirds of its territory over 1,640 ft. eleva- tion with volcanic peaks towering over 6,560 ft. The capital Mae- bashi (q.v.) and most of the population are on a small segment of the Kantō plain in the southeastern corner. Sericulture and wheat growing are the most important activities in its pre- dominantly agricultural economy. Mountain forests and mineral deposits (sulfur, manganese, limestone) are exploited. The silk- reeling industry, conducted on a small workshop scale, is centred in Maebashi, Tomioka, Kiryū (q.v.) and Isezaki.

(J. D. Ee.)

GUMS, PLANT, are adhesive substances of plant origin that are carbohydrate in nature and are usually produced as exudates from the bark of trees or shrubs. The term plant gums does not normally include the so-called varnish gums which, although they are of natural origin, are in fact resins and quite different chemi- cally (see Resins: Natural Resins). Some plant gums, such as gum arabic, are soluble in water, dissolving to give clear solutions. Others including gum tragacanth give mucilages by the absorption of large amounts of water. When the water evaporates after the application of gum solutions, a film with considerable adhesive properties is formed.

Plant gums are produced by trees either after mechanical dam- age to the bark or after a bacterial, insect or fungal attack upon it. It may therefore be possible that the formation of gums (a proc- ess often referred to as gummosis) is associated with some protec- tive mechanism. However, all reasons for gummosis are not completely understood. Concerning this, it may be mentioned that the yield of gum acacia from the Acacia senegal tree is greatest when the trees are in an unhealthy condition, but methods of good culture reduce the yield of plant gum.

The production of plant gums for commercial use involves mak- ing an incision in the bark of the tree and after a month or so col- lecting the exudate. The collection is repeated throughout the season and the gums so obtained consist of small lumps, each about the size of a walnut, which are usually transparent and light yellow in colour.

A number of plant gums are used on a considerable scale com- mercially. They come from many parts of the world: some origi- nate in Africa and include Sudan gum and Kordofan gum from Sudan and Senegal gum from Senegal. These are varieties of gum arabic which is also collected in northern Nigeria, Tripoli, Tunisia and Tanganyika. Gum ghatti is collected in India, gum tragacanth comes from Asia Minor and Iran and wattle gum from Australia.

Gum arabic is the most widely used of the truly water-soluble gums. True gum arabic (gum acacia) is produced by species of Acacia only, but the term is sometimes used to include gum arabic substitutes obtained from other sources. Gum sudan and gum kordofan are names which refer to their geographical origin, but they are also a type of gum arabic in that they are produced from various Acacia trees.

Gum tragacanth is the second most important commercial gum and is produced by several shrubs which belong to the Astragalus genus. Astragalus gummifer is the source of most of the gum tragacanth, and is endemic in the arid regions of Iran, Asia Minor and Greece. The exudate is produced spontaneously on the bark of the shrub, but the yield is often increased by making an incision and driving wooden wedges into it. Gum tragacanth is not totally soluble in water, but forms a mucilage on treatment with water. It is one of the oldest drugs known and its use has dated from pre- Christian times. It is still used pharmaceutically as a demulcent and as an adhesive agent in pill manufacture. It is also used in food manufacture as an emulsifying agent and as a thickener in sauces.

Other plant gums include gum ghatti which has been used as a gum arabic substitute. Gum karaya and carob gum have been used as substitutes for gum tragacanth, but their use is limited. Many cultivated trees yield plant gums including cherry (Prunus cerasus) and plum (P. domestica), while other miscellaneous sources yield cholla gum (Opuntia fulgida) and mesquite gum (Prosopis species). Some of these gums are used in cosmetics, pharmaceuti- cals and food; an examination of their chemical nature (see below) has shown that they have a close relationship to other plant gums, which are not true gums (see below). Rubber, chicle and other latex products, which are not true gums, are discussed in the articles Rubber; Chicle; Latex.

Chemical Investigations and Structure of Plant Gums.— The plant gums are complex carbohydrate derivatives which are polysaccharide in nature (see Carbohydrates). Their chemical study is complementary to the detailed study of the other polysac- charides that has been made. The polysaccharides are an impor- tant group of natural products and the chemistry of the plant gums has contributed to knowledge regarding their structure and func- tion.

Plant gums are the neutral potassium, magnesium or calcium salts of acidic polysaccharides, whose acidity is due to the presence of uronic acid functions in their structure. Hydrolysis of plant gums gives a mixture of monosaccharides, including D-galactose (I) and L-arabinose (II) in all cases and D-xylose (III) fairly fre- quently. With the exception of gum tragacanth, which yields D-galacturonic acid (V), all plant gums yield D-glucuronic acid (IV) on acid hydrolysis. Thus the acidity of gum tragacanth is due to D-galacturonic acid residues, whereas the acidity of the other plant gums is due to D-glucuronic acid residues. Sugars such as L-rhamnose (VI) and L-fucose occur rather rarely as plant gum hydrolysis products.

CH_2OH — D-galactose (I)

HO_2C / H, OH — L-arabinose (II)

D-xylose (III)

CO_2H — D-glucuronic acid (IV)

CO_2H — D-galacturonic acid (V)

Me — L-rhamnose (VI)

The problem of determining the complete structure of a plant gum is really the determination of the order of the various mono- saccharide residues in the parent polysaccharide molecule. The researches of E. L. Hirst, J. K. N. Jones and F. Smith have en- abled substantial progress to be made with this problem and the determination of the structure of gum arabic is illustrative of the methods which have been used.

The sugar units of which the gum arabic molecule is composed are indicated by the acid hydrolysis products which are D-galactose (I), L-arabinose (II), L-rhamnose (VI), and D-glucuronic acid (IV), and the problem of structure determination is really (a) the identification of the repeating unit in the macromolecular polysac- charide structure and (b) the determination of the arrangement of the monosaccharide components within this repeating unit.

A possible repeating unit in the gum arabic molecule

Several formulas are possible for the gum arabic molecules and one of them is indicated. Comparison of this structure with the structures of the monosaccharide units (I, II, IV and VI) show the way in which they are linked together.

It can be seen therefore that gum arabic has a highly branched structure which is no doubt responsible for its special physical properties. Similar studies have been made of several different plant gums and a similarity between their structures is detectable.

BIBLIOGRAPHY.—C. L. Mantell, "The Water-Soluble Gums—Their Botany, Sources and Utilization," *Economic Botany*, 3:3 (1949); J. K. N. Jones and F. Smith, "Plant Gums and Mucilages," *Advanc. in Carbohyd. Chem.*, 4:243 (1949); W. W. Pigman and R. M. Goepp, *Carbohydrate Chemistry* (1948). (W. D. Os.)

GUMTI, a river of northern India now called GOMATI. It rises in Pilibhit district, Uttar Pradesh, and after a sinuous southeasterly course of 500 mi. past Lucknow and Jaunpur joins the Ganges (Ganga) in Ghazipur district. At Jaunpur it is spanned by a 16th-century bridge and is navigable. Another Gumti river rises in Tripura state, India, and enters the Meghna in Tippera district. Bangladesh (formerly East Pakistan), after a 143-mi. course.

GUM TREE (STRINGYBARK TREE), a name commonly given in Australia to eucalyptus trees. See EUCALYPTUS.

GUMUSANE (GUMUSHANE, "silver workshop"), chief town of an *il* (province) of the same name in northeast Turkey, is situated on the Harsit river, 40 mi. S.S.W. of Trabzon. Pop. (1960) 5,373. Though an ancient town, its origin and development are obscure; a few remains of castles lie nearby. The silver mines from which the town takes its name were known in ancient times and were mentioned by Marco Polo. Since their exhaustion the old town has experienced some development, which mainly depends on its position on the main road from Trabzon to Iran. It has a simple economy and the standard of living is low. The main income is supplied by the orchards along the Harsit valley, the principal fruits being apples and pears.

GUMUSANE PROVINCE is bordered north by Trabzon province, east by Erzurum, south by Erzincan and west by Giresun. Area 3,897 sq.mi.; pop. (1960) 243,232. It is drained by the Harsit, Kelkit and Coruh rivers. The country is mountainous and rugged and settlements are clustered in the river valleys. Agriculture is of subsistence character and some cereals are grown. Bayburt, a district centre (pop. [1960] 11,968), is the other main town of the province. (N. Tu.; E. Tu.; S. Er.)

GUN: see AIR GUNS; ARTILLERY; CARBINE; MACHINE GUN; RIFLE; SMALL ARMS, MILITARY.

GUN, MACHINE: see MACHINE GUN.

GUNCOTTON, a high-grade type of nitrocellulose (cellulose nitrate) resembling cotton in appearance. It contains more than 13% nitrogen and is prepared by the nitration of cotton fibres with a strong mixture of nitric and sulfuric acids.

Commonly a batch process of nitration in iron or earthenware pots is used. After nitration care must be taken to hydrolyze unstable chemicals by boiling the final product in slightly acidified water (stabilization) and washing it free of all acid. Unless this is done the inherent instability associated with nitric esters of this type is enhanced even at ordinary temperatures.

Guncotton, like other forms of nitrocellulose, will decompose with time forming nitrogen dioxide in air which promotes further decomposition.

Guncotton is insoluble in water, alcohol and ether but will dissolve in acetone, nitrobenzene and ethyl acetate. The essential constituent of cotton is cellulose which is a long chain polymer of anhydroglucose units having the empirical formula of $C_6H_{10}O_5$. Cotton linters may have as many as 1,000 to 1,500 of these units in a single molecular chain. In the nitration process the three hydroxyl (OH) groups of each unit can be replaced by a nitrate (ONO_2) ion. If this replacement is complete the resulting guncotton would contain 14.14% nitrogen.

Actually complete nitration is not accomplished and the attached nitrate groups are believed to be distributed randomly along the chain among the three possible positions for each unit. For military purposes in the United States a minimum nitrogen content of 13.35% is used. This represents a somewhat more complete nitration of the cellulose than the *coton-poudre* no. 1 (CP₁) used in World War I.

A characteristic property of this highly nitrated cellulose is its low solubility in an ether-ethanol solution. This property distinguishes guncotton from the less nitrated celluloses which are referred to as collodion cotton or soluble nitrocellulose because of the fact that they dissolve in the ether-alcohol solvent. Guncotton has superior explosive properties to those of collodion and has been extensively employed in conjunction with nitroglycerin for the production of cordite, the British service propellant. The blending of the two ingredients is brought about by acetone, but by the use of collodion with a large proportion of nitroglycerin a cordite is obtainable without the employment of acetone.

During the mid-19th century numerous attempts were made, particularly in Austria, to employ guncotton alone and unmodified as a military propellant, the necessity for tempering its explosive violence by colloiding processes being as yet unrecognized. All ended in failure.

Moist guncotton has been used as a high explosive, but is quite unsatisfactory because of the hazards in handling. Dry guncotton is even more hazardous, being sensitive to all forms of initiation—friction, impact, heat, sparks, etc. Its sensitivity is comparable with other primary explosives such as mercury fulminate or lead azide. It propagates detonation and has a brisance (shattering effect) comparable with TNT.

See NITROCELLULOSE.

See T. E. Thorpe, *Dictionary of Applied Chemistry*, vol. iii (1922); Tenney L. Davis, *The Chemistry of Powder and Explosives* (1943). (P. M. FE.)

GUNGL, JOSEPH (1810-1889), Austro-Hungarian composer of popular marches and dances in the light Viennese style, was born at Zsámbék, Hung., on Dec. 1, 1810. He was an oboist and later a bandmaster in the Austrian army. In 1843 he formed a celebrated light orchestra in Berlin. In 1848 he toured the U.S. and the following year became director of music of the king of Prussia. In 1864 he founded a second orchestra in Munich with which he traveled extensively. His *Hungarian March* for orchestra, Opus 1, was transcribed for the piano by Liszt. He wrote more than 400 dance pieces for orchestra, many of which long remained popular. He died at Weimar, Ger., on Feb. 1, 1889.

GUNKEL, HERMANN (1862-1932), German Old Testament scholar and one of the first to develop the method of form criticism, was born on May 23, 1862, at Springe near Hanover. He became *Privatdozent* in Old Testament theology at Göttingen university in 1888 and at Halle in 1889, university reader in Berlin (1894-1907) and professor at Giessen (1907-20) and at Halle (1920-27). He died in Halle on March 11, 1932.

A leading member of the *Religionsgeschichtliche Schule* ("History of Religion school"), Gunkel was one of the first to stress the literary values of the Old Testament by the comparative study of the legends on which it draws, particularly in Genesis, Psalms and the prophets, on which he published works in 1901, 1903 and 1917, respectively. Extending his researches beyond current dogmatic interpretations of the Old Testament, he promoted the study on literary-historical lines of the religious history of Israel, publishing in 1906 *Die israelitische Literatur* and in 1911 *Die Urgeschichte und die Patriarchen*. He contributed to the *Göttinger Handkommentar zum Alten Testament* (1910), assisted in the first edition of the religious dictionary *Die Religion in Geschichte und Gegenwart* (1903-13) and was co-editor of the second edition of the series *Forschungen zur Religion und Literatur des Alten Testaments und des Neuen Testaments* (1903-). Gunkel's work stimulated much further Old Testament research, especially in Germany.

BIBLIOGRAPHY.—H. Schmidt, *In memoriam Hermann Gunkels* (1932); H. J. Kraus, *Geschichte der historisch-kritischen Forschung des Alten Testaments* (1956); W. Baumgartner, *In memoriam Hermann Gunkel*, Fifth International Congress for Old Testament Study (1962).
(E. AU.)

GUN METAL, a variety of bronze (*q.v.*), formerly used for ordnance. Gun or "G" metals are copper-base casting alloys of the general type: 88% copper, 10% tin and 2% zinc or 86% copper, 10% tin and 4% zinc. Usually up to 1% nickel is present in the modern alloys to add strength, promote grain refinement and reduce segregation. The addition of 0.5% lead improves machinability without harming the cold mechanical properties. A small quantity (0.05% max.) of phosphorus may be used as a deoxidizer to promote metal fluidity and soundness of the casting.

The 88-10-2 alloys are used frequently for gears and bearings subjected to heavy loads and low speeds. They also withstand atmospheric, steam and sea-water corrosion, and thus are suitable for valves, pump parts and steam fittings. The mechanical properties of the "as cast" alloy are: tensile strength, 36,000-46,000 lb. per square inch (p.s.i.), yield point 18,000-26,000 (p.s.i.); elongation 15%-25% (in 2 in.), reduction of area 12%-26% and Brinell hardness 65-80.

GUNNERY, AERIAL. Aerial gunnery is the term applied to the art or practice of aiming and firing guns mounted on aircraft in flight at targets in the air or on the surface of the earth. There are two basic types of aerial gunnery, fixed and flexible, each requiring techniques of gun handling different from the other. Fixed aerial gunnery pertains to the use of guns that are stationary relative to the aircraft on which they are mounted, while flexible aerial gunnery pertains to aircraft guns on mounts that allow them to be elevated and traversed.

Origins.—Aerial gunnery evolved during World War I. At the beginning of the war in 1914 aircraft were employed primarily for purposes of observation and reconnaissance; no country had planes that were equipped or intended for employment in a primary role involving the use of guns. As the military value of aerial observation became apparent, however, both sides began arming their aircraft crews. Pistols, shotguns and rifles were used at first, but by the end of 1915 aircraft were equipped with machine guns to drive enemy aircraft away from the front lines and to prevent themselves driven away by the enemy.

This led to the development of the armed fighter plane whose primary function was to employ its guns against enemy aircraft of all types and provide protection for friendly observation craft. Pilots of fighter aircraft became popular heroes, particularly such aces (those who had shot down five or more enemy aircraft) as Max Immelmann and Manfred von Richthofen of Germany, William A. Bishop of Canada and Edward V. Rickenbacker of the U.S. Fighter aircraft also employed their guns against ground targets, observation balloons and, in the case of Allied aircraft, against the great German Zeppelins.

By the end of the war the fundamental principles and theories underlying aerial gunnery had been established and, with minor refinements and improvements, the types of aerial guns, gun sights and gun mounts that had been developed were continued in use until shortly before the start of World War II.

Gun Requirements.—Since military aircraft operate at extremes of altitude and temperature aircraft guns must be able to function under all conditions. At low temperatures, *e.g.*, —55° C. at 40,000 ft., heat usually is applied to the guns' actions to keep them warm and ready to operate. Air-cooling of guns to compensate for the heat generated by firing has been the most common practice although water-cooled guns were often used in World War I. Aircraft guns must also be designed to operate under either positive or negative gravity or "g" forces induced by maneuvering of the aircraft. Thus when an aircraft makes a 4g turn in flight, the guns must be capable of operating under a force four times that of gravity. Since added weight and bulk detract from the performance of an aircraft, the guns must also be as light and compact as possible.

High rates of fire with guns of large calibre are necessary to inflict maximum damage, since the aircraft often is in position to fire for only a few seconds or, in the case of jets, for only a fraction of a second. Aerial gun calibres have ranged from the .30 cal. Lewis machine gun of World War I to the .50 cal. aerial machine gun and 20 mm. aerial cannon which saw much use in World War II. Larger guns have also been used on occasion. During World War II one type of U.S. bomber-attack plane had a fixed 75 mm. cannon in its nose, primarily for use against ground targets. Rates of fire were greatly increased by the development of multi-barreled Gatling gun-type aerial cannon and machine guns. These guns were used extensively and with devastating effect in both limited war and counterinsurgency applications, as in Vietnam.

Fixed Aerial Gunnery.—Fixed gun installations have been used most extensively in fighter and attack aircraft, employed primarily in an offensive role to destroy other aircraft or ground targets. It has been the practice to mount these forward-firing guns in available spaces such as the wings, nose and on the top and sides of the fuselage. As many guns as could be mounted without impairing the plane's handling qualities have been used in order to get a maximum volume of fire on target in the least time. Fixed guns may be mounted to fire directly through the arc of an aircraft propeller. When this was first done, during World War I, pilots often shot away their own propellers. Metal deflection plates were then installed on the propellers to protect them, but this led to a danger from ricochets. Later, the firing mechanisms of the guns were interconnected with the aircraft engine in such a manner that the bullets passed between the blades as the propeller rotated. Guns governed by this arrangement are called synchronized guns, and their rate of fire is governed by the rotational speed of the propeller. On aircraft without propellers, such as jet fighters, or on aircraft whose guns are so placed that their fire is not masked by the propeller, the rate of fire is not restricted and the guns fire as rapidly as their design permits.

When fixed guns are installed they must be aligned with the gun sight and with the fore and aft axis of the aircraft. To do this, the aircraft is placed in a flying attitude (when jacked up on the ground) and the pilot's gun sight is adjusted to aim directly ahead at a target that has been aligned with the aircraft's fore and aft axis. Then by boresighting the guns (*i.e.*, sighting through each barrel) they are adjusted to aim at the same target that is seen through the gun sight. This complete process is called harmonization.

In harmonizing sights and guns it is important that the target be sufficiently far away to avoid or compensate for errors which might be induced by parallax. If the guns are set fairly close together, as in the nose of a jet, and it is desired that their lines of fire should be parallel, they would be sighted on a target at infinity or far enough away to be considered infinity for all practical purposes. If, however, the guns are far apart, e.g., in the wings, they might be positioned so that their fire would converge at a specific range. In this case the target selected for the harmonization would be set up at this range. Corrections for the effect of gravity might also have to be made in harmonization so that the line of sight from the gun sight and the fire from the guns intersect at the proper time.

Cameras designed to take moving pictures of a target as it is being fired upon, commonly referred to as aerial gun cameras, may be mounted on fighter aircraft and harmonized in the same manner as the guns. These cameras are also used in place of guns for simulated combat during training exercises.

Gun sights in a fighter aircraft may vary in complexity from two fixed iron posts, over which the pilot will sight as in aiming an ordinary rifle, to electronic sights which measure range to the target and automatically compute the proper lead. An aircraft equipped with fixed guns is, in effect, a flying gun platform, and the guns are aimed by aiming the whole aircraft. The pilot has essentially the same problem of range and lead estimation in shooting at a moving target in the air as the hunter on the ground who shoots at ducks flying past his blind. The difference is that the pilot, whose guns are fixed in a forward-firing position, is always moving toward his target when tracking and firing. The pilot must turn his aircraft to keep his guns aimed ahead of a moving target, flying a curved course called the curve of pursuit as he approaches and fires. One of the defensive measures which can be taken by a moving target is to fly in a curve of equal or smaller radius than the curve of pursuit. If this is done properly and at the right time the pursuer cannot lead the target sufficiently to score any hits. Indeed, if the target can fly a tight enough curve it may turn the tables and shoot down the pursuer. Such maneuvers were the basis for the famous "dogfights" of World War I.

Flexible Aerial Gunnery.—Flexible guns, attached to mounts that can be swivelled both vertically and horizontally, customarily have been employed by bombers and other less maneuverable aircraft to provide defensive firepower against attack by enemy fighters. This type of gun installation has been used on the top, bottom and both sides of the fuselage, and in the nose and tail, so that the fields of fire can cover every point of possible attack and, in some places, reinforce each other. Although flexible gun installations may consist of either a single gun or multiple guns, the use of twin guns at each of the positions has been customary practice where space permits. These may be aimed and fired manually or by using power-driven devices. In manual aiming the gun mounts usually incorporate mechanisms designed to counterbalance the weight of the guns and the blast of the rushing air if the gun position is not enclosed. In order to prevent the gunner from inadvertently shooting into his own aircraft, flexible gun mounts limit the travel of the guns or stop the firing mechanism when the guns are pointed at any part of the plane.

The problem of accurately aiming and firing flexible guns from a moving aircraft at another moving aircraft is a complex one in which the speed, relative flight paths and maneuvering of both aircraft have to be considered. To assist the gunner in manual aiming, a movable wind vane type of gun sight, calibrated and designed to compensate for the forward motion of the gunner's own aircraft, is often placed on the forward end of the gun barrel. As the barrel of the gun is swung about in the air stream the wind vane sight also swings a compensating amount, reaching maximum deflection when the gun barrel is at right angles to the flight path. Another aid is the use of tracer bullets whose path can be followed with the eye and a correction made to bring the fire onto the target.

Flexible guns may be mounted inside a power-driven device called a gun turret which encloses the gunner and the actions of his guns, giving both of them protection against the rushing air and low temperatures. Turrets generally revolve from side to side, while the guns are mounted in such a manner that they swing up and down, with only the barrels protruding. Most turrets can be operated manually in an emergency, but such operation is usually slow and fire from a manually-operated turret is generally ineffective. Systems of remote control have been used which connect several gun turrets to one central control position, from which the guns may be aimed and fired by one gunner using an electronic sight which automatically computes the proper target lead for each turret.

With the advent of jet aircraft, the functions of aerial guns were largely taken over by heat-seeking and radar-guided missiles by the early 1960s. Experience gained in the war in Vietnam later reaffirmed a need for guns as well as missiles on tactical aircraft, both for strafing and aerial combat. Also, research and development in aerial guns and weapons of all types was intensified when the helicopter "gunship" was battle-tested and proven in Vietnam. Armed with rockets and machine guns, these helicopters were used to suppress enemy ground fire, while escorting helicopter-lifted troops in combat operations.

See also AIR POWER; MACHINE GUN.

BIBLIOGRAPHY.—L. Bruchiss, *Aircraft Armament* (1945); J. C. Boyce, *New Weapons for Air Warfare* (1947); H. Woodhouse, *Textbook of Military Aeronautics* (1918).
(B. S. P.)

GUNNERY, NAVAL. Naval gunnery is the art and science of using naval guns and rocket and missile launchers. It is distinguished from land-based military gunnery in that the naval gun fires from an unsteady and moving platform. The task of the military gunner is to fire at one fixed point from another fixed point. The naval gunner has a task comparable to firing at a fast automobile moving along a bumpy and twisting road from another fast automobile also moving along a bumpy and twisting road. In this respect it has points of similarity with aerial gunnery. (*See also* ARTILLERY: *Technique*.)

The principal developments in naval gunnery of modern times have been in fire control, automatic fire, antiaircraft guns and missiles. Fire control improvements included use of radar, greatly improved directors and more accurate ballistic computing devices. Automatic fire was improved by the introduction of more reliable ammunition as well as new and improved loading mechanisms. Antiaircraft gunnery was improved by the introduction of larger guns with a higher rate of fire. Missile development greatly increased range and the probability of hits on high-speed air targets.

Types of Guns.—It is convenient to classify naval guns by the type of breech-operating mechanisms employed.

Automatic.—An automatic gun is one that uses part of the energy of explosion (recoil energy) to eject the empty cartridge case and to load another cartridge; it continues to fire as long as the firing circuit is closed and the ammunition supply is maintained. Examples are the 40-mm. and 3-in. antiaircraft guns.

Semiautomatic.—A semiautomatic gun is one in which part of the energy of explosion is first stored and later used to open the breech, eject the empty cartridge case and close the breech after another round is loaded, either by hand or by auxiliary power. Most naval guns are of this type.

Nonautomatic.—A nonautomatic gun is one in which none of the energy of the explosion is used to operate any part of the operating mechanism except a device that prevents the unintentional opening of the breech of a loaded gun. The main battery guns of battleships and most heavy cruisers are of this type.

Gun Mounts.—The naval gun mount is the entire system of gun-supporting parts, elevating and training mechanisms, recoil and counterrecoil (run-out) equipment. The two classes of mounts are deck mounts and turret mounts. Deck mounts may be worked either manually or by power; turret mounts are invariably worked by power, either electric, hydraulic or a combination of both.

The principal parts of the deck mount are the slide (cradle), carriage and stand. The slide is a hollow cylindrical support in which the rear part of the gun barrel is housed. During recoil and counterrecoil, the gun rides back and forth in this support. Two horizontal projections on the slide, called trunnions, provide the axis about which the gun is free to move in the vertical plane. The carriage supports the slide and rests on roller bearings. It is free to rotate in a horizontal plane and provides means for training the gun. The stand is the stationary part of the mount, bolted to the deck of the ship and containing the lower roller path on which the carriage rests. It supports the combined gun, slide and carriage. Movement of the gun in the horizontal and vertical planes is by a system of handwheels, shafting and gearing. Movement may also be accomplished by a power source through suitable shafting and gearing. Deck mounts may be partially or completely shielded by armour.

The turret mount consists of the barbette, the turret revolving structure, the gunhouse and the turret foundation. The barbette is a heavy fixed cylinder of armour extending from the gunhouse to the lowest armoured deck. Its sole function is to protect the turret revolving structure and the turret foundation. The gun-house is a heavily armoured rotatable structure containing the guns. The turret revolving structure, which corresponds to the carriage of the deck mount, extends from the gunhouse down to the magazine handling rooms (located outside the barbette) and is composed of steel girders and bulkheads that form the various compartments for the turret machinery and personnel. The turret foundation is composed of steel girders built into the hull of the ship to support the turret revolving structure and the gunhouse. Training of the turret is accomplished by a system of power-driven gears and a toothed rack fitted inside, but not attached to, the barbette. Elevation may be accomplished by means of a long, power-driven shaft and pinion.

Recoil and Counterrecoil.—In naval gun mounts the recoil mechanism is generally a hydraulic brake consisting of one or more cylinders secured to the slide of the mount; in the slide, pistons fixed to the gun operate so that they move to the rear during recoil and forward during counterrecoil. The cylinders are filled with hydraulic fluid that must pass through orifices in the pistons which are so designed that the resistance to flow is approximately constant (or increases) throughout the length of the piston's travel. The work done by the recoil in forcing the piston through the liquid absorbs the momentum of the gun in recoil.

The counterrecoil mechanism may be either mechanical, pneumatic, hydraulic or a combination of all three. The counterrecoil system must not only return the gun to firing position (battery), but must be able to hold it there at all angles of elevation.

Fire Control.—The practical application of exterior ballistics and the methods and devices used to control guns and other weapons are known as fire control. In the early days of naval gunnery and until well past Nelson's time, fire control was a simple matter. Each gunner peered along the barrel of his muzzle-loader and trained his gun by means of a lever; he also estimated the range and elevated his gun by means of a wedge under the breech or by a threaded shaft.

As guns became more powerful and ranges increased from a few hundred to several thousand yards, this hit-or-miss system was no longer effective. Range finders were introduced to determine the exact distance to the target, and guns were elevated according to the number of degrees required to shoot a given distance.

By World War I, battle ranges exceeded 10,000 yd. and additional problems arose: (1) It was no longer possible to fire at the target directly; allowance had to be made for movement of the target while the projectile was in flight. (2) Allowances were necessary for the wear of gun barrels (called bore erosion), temperature of the powder, effects of air density and upper air wind velocity. (3) Allowance had to be made for the ship's roll and pitch. Failure to allow for any one of these might change the range of the projectile by several thousand yards. To meet these problems, director firing was instituted. Director firing is essentially the firing of all guns in one battery by use of a director, a range-determining device and a computer.

The director itself is a master gun sight for all the guns in its battery. The director is trained continuously on the target, giving the line-of-sight bearing and elevation. These, and the distance to the target as given by the range-determining equipment, are fed directly to the computer. Other information sent to the computer includes: firing ship's motion with respect to the horizontal plane, from a stable element; firing ship's course and speed; surface wind velocity, projectile muzzle velocity loss through gun erosion and powder temperature; time; and certain other nonstandard variables such as air density and unavoidable errors in calculations. These data are combined by the computer and result in a continuous output of the following: present target range and bearing; advance range, used in setting gun sights; train and elevation orders to position the guns; and fuze orders or time of flight. (*See* Sights, Gun.)

In earlier director systems, train and elevation orders were sent by electrical connections to pointers at the guns. The gunners kept the gun trained and elevated by keeping pointers connected to the guns in coincidence with the director pointers. Firing took place at a predetermined point of the ship's roll. In later director systems, the guns were trained and elevated automatically, and stabilizing devices discounted the roll and pitch of the firing ship. Antiaircraft fire presents a quite different problem. The antiaircraft battery must cope with high-speed targets that may attack from several directions simultaneously. To achieve the necessary flexibility, the battery is divided into four groups, each capable of independent operation in its own sector, or of combining with an adjacent group to defend a sector common to both. Each group has its own director system, and in cases where two groups fire together, one director handles the fire control problem for both groups.

The introduction of radar changed naval gunnery drastically. It permitted the automatic tracking of targets and accurate firing under adverse conditions. The effective range of large guns formerly had been limited to the visible range; haze, fog, smoke or darkness sometimes reduced this range to a few hundred yards. Radar not only permitted finding the range of targets under conditions of poor or limited visibility, but allowed effective firing at them. Battle ranges often exceeded 25,000 yd.

The introduction of high-speed aircraft and bombs with a large destructive radius also introduced new problems. It became necessary to destroy the most dangerous, not necessarily the nearest, target first. This destruction had to be accomplished quickly before the target could arrive at a position, such as the bomb release point, where it could damage the ship. This involved early detection of the target, rapid determination of the firing data and fast, accurate firing.

Before the end of World War II, it had become apparent that self-propelled, guided missiles were necessary to cope with the increased speed of aircraft. By the early 1950s, all major naval powers had operational antiaircraft missiles available for use in their fleets. These missiles were capable of rapid launching, of receiving post-launching guidance during the intermediate part of their flight and of automatically seeking the target at long range. Some of these antiaircraft or antimissile missiles were capable of destruction of the target at ranges up to 65 mi. from the launching ship. The use of such missiles combined with nuclear warheads seemed to be the answer to the problem of improving the range, accuracy and destructive effect of naval weapons. *See* Rockets and Guided Missiles.

Bibliography.—France, Ministère de la Marine, *Manuel du Canonnier* (1946); Harold Kimble Hines, *Ordnance and Gunnery* (1910); James Inman, *An Introduction to Naval Gunnery* (1928); Bureau of Naval Personnel, U.S. Navy Department, *Evolution of Naval Weapons* (1949); U.S. Navy Department, *Naval Weapons and Their Uses* (1943).
(R. L. Ne.; H. J. Sт.)

GUNPOWDER (Black Powder), generic names applied originally to a mechanical mixture of saltpetre (potassium nitrate), charcoal (carbon) and sulfur. Gunpowder is the older and more commonly used term but black powder is preferred in military circles in the United States. Prepared in approximately the correct proportions (74.6% saltpetre, 13.5% charcoal, 11.9% sulfur) it will, when ignited, burn rapidly and evolve a large volume of whitish gas. In a confined space this pent-up gas can be used for blasting or for propelling missiles. Black powder is a low explosive rather than a high explosive like TNT. It is easily ignited and is widely used for primers, fuzes and blank fire charges in military

PLATE I

GUNNERY, NAVAL

Forward turrets of H.M.S. "Duke of York," with 14-in. guns

A salvo from the 15-in. guns of the British battle cruiser "Repulse," sunk Dec. 10, 1941, off Malaya

Firing incendiary tracer shells from 20-mm. antiaircraft guns on the flight deck of a U.S. aircraft carrier

Manning 5-in. gun mount on the U.S.S. "Tarawa"

A 40-mm. gun of the U.S.S. "Rochester"

Firing 16-in. guns of the number one turret of the U.S.S. "North Carolina"

NAVAL ORDNANCE

BY COURTESY OF (ALL EXCEPT TOP ROW) U.S. NAVY; OFFICIAL PHOTOS; PHOTOGRAPHS, (TOP ROW) BRITISH COMBINE FROM PUBLIX

PLATE II

GUNNERY, NAVAL

Sea Slug, surface-to-air missile of the British Royal navy

Polaris, shown in a firing from a surface ship, but designed chiefly for use firing underwater from a submarine (surface-to-surface); U.S. navy

Regulus I, the first operational attack missile of the U.S. navy; surface-to-air type

Terrier, surface-to-air missile, U.S. navy

Talos installation aboard a guided missile cruiser; surface-to-air, U.S. navy

NAVAL MISSILES

ammunition. *See* AMMUNITION, ARTILLERY.

History.—Discovery of black powder and its adaptation to firearms marks one of the most important events in the history of civilization. The blasting power of black powder enabled men to do work that had formerly required brute force, and its use to propel missiles gave civilized men ascendancy over barbarians. On the other hand the introduction of siege artillery toward the end of the middle ages diminished the defensive value of feudal castles and other fortifications. Black powder was the sole explosive material available for about 600 years, from the time of its discovery to mid-19th century when nitroglycerin and nitrocellulose were discovered.

There is no certainty as to the actual date of the invention of black powder, but early experiments with such materials as oil, pitch, sulfur and other ingredients were all steps on the road to its discovery. These predecessors were of a sticky nature; they not only adhered to objects they hit, but their fire was difficult to extinguish, especially with water. Best known of these mixtures was Greek fire (*q.v.*), long a terror to the enemies of the ancient Byzantine empire.

There is some evidence that the Chinese possessed black powder in ancient times, but the evidence is not conclusive. It may be significant that saltpetre (or nitre), an essential ingredient of black powder, was mentioned for the first time in the writings of the Arabian Abd Allah, about A.D. 1200. Nevertheless, it may have been used in rockets or in "Roman candles" in the 10th century or even earlier.

Among the many claimants of the honour of discovering black powder are Chinese, Hindus, Greeks, Arabs, English (Roger Bacon) and Germans (Berthold Schwarz). The subject attained greater prominence when the first guns were invented to utilize black powder as a propellant, early in the 14th century. The actual loading of the powder into cannon required considerable artistry to get uniform and maximum results, and therefore good gunners were in great demand. There had to be just the right density of loading for optimum propagation of the flame, since burning occurs mostly on exposed powder surfaces. (*See* ARTILLERY.) Other applications followed slowly. For example, no record is found of the use of black powder for blasting for nearly 300 years.

Early Manufacture.—The preparation of black powder from solid ingredients requires fine particle sizes for uniform mixing and blending of the saltpetre, carbon and sulfur. In the earliest processes these were combined by simple mortar-and-pestle methods, often with improvised equipment—even to the point of using hollowed-out logs as mortars.

A little later methods were devised to raise the pestle mechanically, using horse or water power, and to drop it by the automatic tripping of a trigger. These rather violent blows increased the danger of spontaneous fires and explosions, so these "stamp mills" were banned in some quarters (notably England, in 1772).

One of the main problems at first was to secure sufficiently pure ingredients, especially important being the purity of the saltpetre. This material is found in many parts of India and in Spain and southern Andalusia. Various means of developing it from other sources, such as the decomposition of organic matter, were devised by governments of most European countries. Near the end of the 19th century the discovery in Chile of huge deposits of sodium nitrate (Chilean saltpetre), which could readily be converted to potassium nitrate by treatment with potassium chloride, improved the world supply situation.

As the powdered form of black powder burned too rapidly, 15th-century powder makers introduced a process for corning or graining the powder. The mixture of ingredients was moistened while being pounded in the pestle, using various fluids such as alcohol and urine. The paste so formed was beaten into a more or less coherent cake under the action of the pestle, then removed and broken into chunks. These chunks were broken down into smaller particles by agitation with metal balls in the mass; the resulting particles were "classified" by passing through various meshes of sieve. The final "grains" were irregular in shape and left ample space for the passage of flame throughout the charge. Particles of different sizes were readily adapted to varying sizes of cannon

to furnish burning rates that were effective ballistically but did not create excessive pressures.

As elongated projectiles replaced round balls and rifling of gun tubes was adopted to rotate and stabilize the projectile, ordnance specialists searched for slower burning propellants. Capt. (later Brig. Gen.) Thomas J. Rodman, of the U.S. army, conducted many experiments in the 1850s and finally came up with grains of controlled shape and size. The shape was hexagonal with a number of perforations parallel to the edges. These perforations provided expanding burning surfaces, thus promoting progressive burning rates as the projectile traveled down the bore of the gun. These grains could be made in various sizes, by pressing the ordinary black powder particles into specially designed dies.

For even slower burning in heavy ordnance, brown or "cocoa" powder was introduced in the late 19th century. Here the carbonaceous material was prepared from rye straw and was undercharred. For dependable burning the saltpetre content was increased from 75% to 80% and the sulfur reduced to 3%. This powder, made in the prism form devised by Rodman, proved to be the best evolved. With it the U.S. navy fought the Spanish-American War (1898) but that was the last great conflict in which black powder played an important role as a propellant.

Properties and Variations.—The early composition of black powder saw little change in the proportions of ingredients for 400 years or more. Since then, however, the properties, and especially the burning rate, have been altered for various uses by changing the percentage of saltpetre, using different types of wood to make the charcoal, substituting powdered coal for the charcoal and substituting sodium nitrate for the saltpetre. The original material is no longer used as a propellant but still finds valuable application as an igniting medium. In an artillery shell, for example, it apparently projects almost an optimum mixture of hot gases and incandescent solid particles onto the surface of the propellant grains. In the absence of moisture, black powder is quite stable chemically, its ingredients being essentially nonreactive with each other even at 120° C. Presence of moisture causes black powder to react with some metals such as steel, brass and copper. The high degree of accidental explosion hazard is attributable to its great sensitivity to ignition by flame, incandescent particles or electric spark.

In addition to use as an igniting material, black powder (with variations in compositions as described above) finds useful application in time fuzes, saluting charges, squibs, smoke-puff charges, "spotting" charges for practice bombs and, of course, many commercial applications such as fireworks and signals. For blasting purposes it is still employed in large quantities and is especially effective where a relatively slow "push" is required to avoid excessive break-up of the material being excavated. This property would be ideal for coal mining except for the fact that the resultant flames cannot be tolerated because of flammable gases present in many mines.

One may wonder at the sudden demise of black powder as a propellant, for centuries its most dramatic use. The question is partly answered by the terminology of its replacement, "smokeless" powder. Nitrocellulose propellants burn more completely and thus produce less smoke, because both the fuel (carbon and hydrogen) and the oxygen exist together in the same molecule. Furthermore, modern propellants deliver much more mechanical work per unit of weight, and from many weapons the undesirable muzzle flash can be prevented by addition of certain alkali metal salts (as K_2SO_4) or cooling agents (as dibutylphthalate) in the colloid. Curiously, the term "powder" still is applied in some quarters to modern propellants, even though a single grain for rockets may have a diametre of many inches and a length measured in feet. Fortunately, the single word propellant is rapidly replacing the inaccurate terms gunpowder and smokeless powder.

Following World War II the production rate of most types of black powder dropped off considerably as military requirements were reduced and substitute materials were utilized for special purpose application. For example, such metals as magnesium and aluminum, with an oxidizer, give higher burning rates, much more heat energy and cleaner burning. Nevertheless, black powder has served mankind well for many centuries. It has acted as a most important tool and steppingstone in the rapid march toward the modern concept of civilization.

See also references under "Gunpowder" in the Index volume.

Bibliography.—H. W. L. Hime, *Gunpowder and Ammunition* (1904); Anon., *The Rise and Progress of the British Explosives Industry* (1909); A. P. Van Gelder and H. Schlatter, *History of the Explosives Industry in America* (1927); C. J. Ffoulkes, *The Gun-Founders of England* (1937); Tenney L. Davis, *The Chemistry of Powder and Explosives*, 2 vol. (1941); Jules Bebie, *Manual of Explosives, Military Pyrotechnics, and Chemical Warfare Agents* (1943); W. Y. Carman, *A History of Firearms from Earliest Times to 1914* (1955); U.S. Dept. of the Army, Technical Manual TM9-1910, *Military Explosives* (1955).
(B. E. An.)

GUNPOWDER PLOT,

the name given to a conspiracy in England for blowing up King James I and the parliament on Nov. 5, 1605. The chief instigator of the plot was Robert Catesby, a zealous Roman Catholic who was angered by James's failure to keep his promise, made before he ascended the throne, to grant more toleration to the English Catholics. Catesby's objectives are not entirely clear, but he apparently hoped that by achieving the murder of the king, the queen and their eldest son, Prince Henry, as well as the privy councilors and the members of parliament, the English Catholics could take over the country. Catesby thought of the plot as early as May 1603, but he did not make definite plans until 1604, after the government had issued a proclamation banishing priests. The original group of conspirators consisted of five men: Catesby; his cousin, Thomas Winter; two friends, Thomas Percy and John Wright; and Guy Fawkes (*q.v.*), a soldier brought over from the Netherlands. The conspirators rented a house about-ting upon the parliament building in May 1604, and in the following December they began to dig a subterranean passage to a point directly under the chamber of the house of lords.

Progress was slow and the plan changed when in March 1605 the conspirators were able to rent the cellar next door, directly beneath the palace of Westminster. They opened a passageway between the two cellars, and Fawkes was given the task of preparing the explosive. He brought into the cellar at least 20 barrels of gunpowder, placed several iron bars upon them to increase the impact of the explosion and concealed the barrels and iron bars with a covering of faggots and coals. Then the conspirators separated until the meeting of parliament, which was expected in October but did not take place until Nov. 5. Catesby and his colleagues realized, of course, that during the ceremonies of the first day of the new session most of the royal family, as well as the great ministers of state, would be present. On that day the explosion was to take place. What the conspirators intended to do after the explosion is

not wholly clear. Catesby made plans during the summer of 1605 to hold a large hunting party in Warwickshire at the time parliament met. Several of the Catholic gentry were to be invited to this party and presumably would act as leaders of the hoped-for insurrection. Plans were also made to capture Prince Charles, if he were not present at parliament, and Princess Elizabeth, who was living at Combe abbey, and enthrone one or other of them.

The need for more money, as well as for arms and horses, persuaded Catesby to bring other people into the plot. By November numbers had risen to 13, among them Francis Tresham, a gentleman of some means whose brother-in-law, Lord Monteagle, was a member of the house of lords and hence would perish in the explosion. When Tresham learned that Catesby opposed sending warnings to Catholics who would be present at the opening of parliament, he decided to take matters in his own hands and warn his brother-in-law. On Oct. 26 Monteagle received an anonymous letter that told him not to attend the opening meeting of parliament. "Retire yourself into your country . . .," the letter stated, "for though there be no appearance of any stir, yet I say they shall receive a terrible blow this Parliament, and yet they shall not see who hurts them." Monteagle glanced at the letter and handed it to his servant to read aloud, most likely with the intent that the servant should warn the plotters that the secret was out. Monteagle then took the letter to the earl of Salisbury, the king's chief minister, who was dining with several members of the privy council. The ministers studied the letter, guessed that it might refer to an explosion by gunpowder, but decided to postpone a search until the day before the opening of parliament. On Nov. 4, after two search parties had been sent to the cellar, the gunpowder was discovered and Guy Fawkes, who was the only conspirator present, was arrested. The other conspirators quickly fled from London, but all were soon apprehended. Catesby, Percy and two others were killed while resisting arrest, Tresham died in prison and the remaining eight were tried and executed (Feb. 1, 1606).

In Jan. 1606 the parliament which was to have been destroyed by the Gunpowder plot passed an act establishing Nov. 5 as a day of public thanksgiving. The day, now known as Guy Fawkes day, is still celebrated by bonfires, fireworks and the carrying of "guys" through the streets.
(R. C. Jo.)

GUNS, SPORTING AND TARGET,

are the firearms used in hunting game and in target shooting competitions. This article deals with modern sporting, or hunting, firearms—rifles, shotguns, and handguns—used for different types of game; and with modern target firearms employed in competitive shooting. For uses of guns for hunting in general *see* Hunting; for shooting techniques and competitive target shooting with rifles (including muzzle-loading rifles), shotguns, and handguns *see* Shooting and Trapshooting and Skeet Shooting. The history and development of firearms are covered in Small Arms, Military, and Pistol and Revolver. Additional technical information may be found in Ballistics; Propellants; and Sights, Gun.

MODERN SPORTING FIREARMS

Rifles

Game.—Hunting rifles vary according to the type of game for which they are intended. In general, the larger the game the larger and more powerful the weapon. A rifle for game usually shot at close range and in areas with dense underbrush must be quick handling and able to kill quickly. For game usually shot at long range, accuracy and flat trajectory are more important. Conceivably, many different rifles could each be best for a particular type of game, but practical considerations limit rifle classes to big, medium, and small. Similarly, there are two range requirements, short and long. Under this system, sporting rifles can be divided into six different classes. It must be understood, however, that one weapon can often fit into more than one category. Furthermore, a hunter's skill in using a gun is more important than the gun itself.

Rifles for dangerous big game, such as is hunted in Africa and southern Asia, must be of the most powerful class and capable of being handled quickly where ranges are short. Hunters will oc-

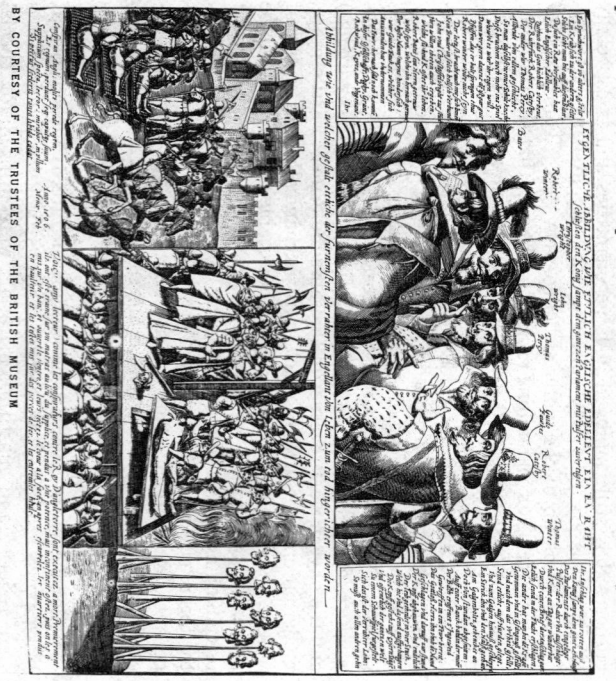

casionally have shots at game of this type at medium and even long range, but in weapons used for this work long-range accuracy is of secondary value. The ability to deliver a quick second shot is essential. Nondangerous big game can safely be hunted with an accurate rifle of less knockdown power.

Dangerous medium game, the cat family particularly, requires a rifle that can be used to best advantage at close range; a fairly quick second shot is necessary. Medium nondangerous game is often taken at long range where fast handling can be sacrificed for flat trajectory and accuracy.

Small game rifles for close range are mainly the calibre-22 rimfire types common throughout the world. At long range small game is generally shot with small-calibre, high-velocity centre-fire rifles which are noted for their accuracy and ultraflat trajectories.

Actions.—Bolt-action rifles similar to military weapons are most common for hunting. This form of action is efficient, reliable, and easy to produce with several forms of magazines, or as a single shot. Properly assembled, it has great accuracy. The disadvantage of bolt-action weapons is that the total overall length for any given barrel length is greater than for other actions. Also, the delivery of a second shot is slower and not so certain.

The top-break, double-barreled shotgun-type of rifle action is expensive and very few are produced, but it produces a shorter, handier hunting weapon. Such a double-barreled rifle, almost always side-by-side, has a quick second shot available, if needed. Chambered for powerful cartridges, these are best for close range against dangerous game. Moderate power weapons of this type are made with two, three, or even more barrels that combine rifle and shotgun capability.

Semiautomatic hunting rifles are rare, save in calibre-22 rimfire; they can be more subject to stoppages. Lever-action sporting rifles have been popular in North America for almost a century; slide- or pump-action types are much less common.

Cartridges.—The performance of a rifle depends on the bullet; power and trajectory determine its suitability for type of game and for range. The same rifle can give different capacities, if ammunition is varied. Bullet energy varies directly in accordance with the weight of the bullet, and also according to the square of its velocity (kinetic energy = $\frac{1}{2}$ mass × velocity^2). Weight remains constant throughout a bullet's flight, of course, but velocity decreases rather rapidly. It would appear probable that in the case of large and dangerous game the actual stopping power of a heavy bullet is greater than that of a lighter one with the same energy.

Dangerous game is normally considered to require at least 2,500 ft-lb. of bullet energy. This can be achieved by a 200-gr. bullet traveling at 2,400 feet per second (fps), by a 300-gr. bullet traveling at 1,950 fps, or by a 500-gr. bullet traveling at 1,700 fps. These velocities and bullet weights can be found in a calibre-.30-06 rifle out to about 100 yd., a calibre .375 out to about 175 yd., and a calibre .458 out to about 300 yd. High-intensity magnum cartridges like those in the Weatherby series extend power for any given calibre at least one class; the .300 Weatherby Magnum loaded with a 180-gr. bullet is almost as powerful as a standard .458. The .460 Weatherby Magnum and the .577 and .600 British nitro-express cartridges for double-barreled rifles give enormous power, 5,000 ft-lb. or more over all ranges at which these guns are normally employed. The reason for using guns with this extra power is, of course, that they provide greater safety for the hunter against charging animals.

More bullet power means more recoil which must be absorbed by the firer. Not everyone has the experience and physical makeup to take heavy recoil. Too much rifle power can lead to fear of recoil which will cause flinching, particularly where game is not dangerous. A hunter should not choose a weapon that has more recoil than he can handle comfortably. It is better to shoot a lower powered rifle well than a more powerful arm poorly.

Sights and Stocks.—Sporting rifles have either iron or telescope sights. The iron sights can be either open or of the peep variety. Open iron sights are preferred for short-range dangerous game shooting. A rear peep sight has some optical advantages and affords greater accuracy. Most serious and experienced hunters use telescope sights for medium and long range. When properly adjusted, the crosshairs of the sight indicate the exact point at which the bullet will strike. This feature is particularly valuable to those who do not have a great deal of time to practice. A good telescope sight also extends hunting time in the morning and evening because it gathers light better than the naked eye and makes precise shooting possible under poorer light conditions.

Rifle stocks should be chosen for the type of sights to be used. Iron sights are normally lower, closer to the axis of the bore than telescope sights. The stock of a telescope-sighted rifle should therefore be higher so that the eye readily finds the telescope when the rifle is brought to firing position.

SHOTGUNS

Game.—Sporting shotguns are used primarily to kill birds in flight. There is some variation in the size of the game taken and the range at which it is shot, but these are not so important as in hunting with rifles. Small animals, such as rabbits and hares, are also taken with shotguns. Although in some countries hunting deer with anything other than rifled weapons is regarded as cruel and unsportsmanlike, shotguns are used for deer in many U.S. states. A solid projectile, or "rifled slug," usually is preferred over buckshot or smaller pellets.

Actions and Barrels.—Throughout the world except in the U.S. the top-break type of shotgun is the type most widely accepted; most of these are double barreled, either side-by-side or over-and-under. As mentioned above, three or more barrels (rifle and shotgun) can be combined into a single weapon of this type.

To be effective, double-barreled shotguns must be made so that both barrels shoot to the same point of aim at normal ranges for the gun. The skilled labour required in manufacture and the fine finish generally found in first-class weapons of this type, such as the world famous Browning over-and-under as made at Fabrique Nationale in Belgium, account for their high price, although some moderately priced models are available. A double-barreled shotgun can deliver a second shot more reliably and speedily than any other type of action; it also produces a weapon with minimum length for any given barrel.

The high cost of quality doubles and the lack of a fairly rapid third shot have led to the development of other types of shotguns. Semiautomatic weapons, made in many countries, are popular with hunters except where sporting custom frowns on their use. These weapons are cheaper than doubles of the same class of workmanship and can usually deliver more shots. But all autoloaders are subject to inherent functional difficulties and are not quite as reliable as other types of actions. The long-

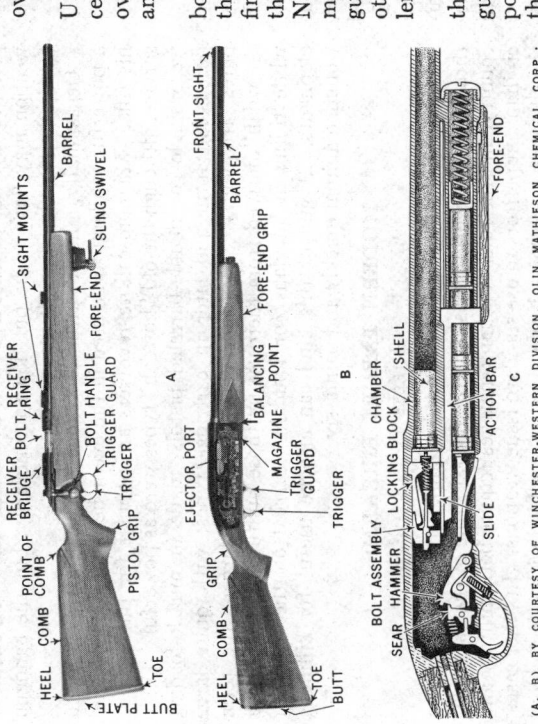

FIG. 1.—(A) COMPETITION TARGET RIFLE; (B) MODERN SHOTGUN; (C) SHOTGUN MECHANISM IN POSITION FOR FIRING

(A, B) BY COURTESY OF WINCHESTER-WESTERN DIVISION, OLIN MATHIESON CHEMICAL CORP.; (C) FROM J. O'CONNOR, "COMPLETE BOOK OF RIFLES AND SHOTGUNS," COPYRIGHT 1961 BY OUTDOOR LIFE

recoil type Brownings have been popular, however, for more than 50 years, and the newer gas-operated weapons are giving reliable service.

Slide- or pump-action shotguns have been popular in the United States for many years and have gained in favour in other countries. When the wooden fore-end is pulled smartly to the rear as far as it will go after each shot and then pushed forward again, the empty shell is ejected and a new round is chambered. A hunter experienced with a pump gun is hardly conscious of operating it and is able to give his entire attention to his shooting. In general, shotguns of this type are the cheapest and most reliable practical repeaters. Bolt-action shotguns are still cheaper, but they are not really satisfactory because they are excessively long for a given barrel length and cannot be fired faster than some top-break single-barreled weapons—usually the cheapest model of all.

Gauges, Chokes, and Shot Patterns.—Shotguns are made in several standard barrel sizes or bores. The usual designation is a bore or gauge number which was originally the number of bore-diameter spherical lead balls which would make a pound. A 12-bore, or 12-gauge, had a bore of such diameter that 12 lead balls to fit it weighed one pound. Thus, the smaller the designation, the larger the bore diameter. There are five standard bores in wide use: 10-, 12-, 16-, 20-, and 28-gauge. A few 24-gauge and 32-gauge guns are sold in Europe. There is another common size, the "four-ten." This gun is calibre .41, but is frequently, although incorrectly, designated .410-gauge. A shot charge from a shotgun is most popular in the U.S. and Great Britain, but elsewhere the preference is sometimes for the 16-gauge. A 12-gauge is most

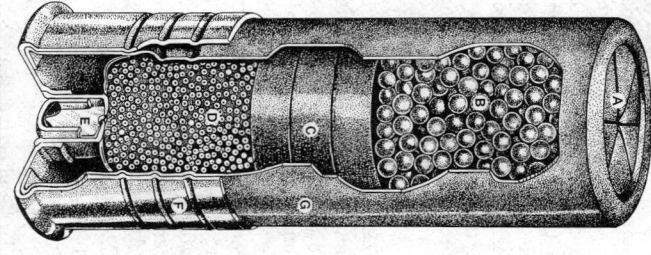

FIG. 2.—CUTAWAY DIAGRAM SHOWING PARTS OF A SHOTGUN SHELL: (A) SEAL: (B) SHOT: (C) WADS: (D) POWDER: (E) PRIMER: (F) BRASS BASE: (G) CARTRIDGE

popular in the U.S. and Great Britain, but elsewhere the preference is sometimes for the 16-gauge. A shot charge from a shotgun with a uniform, or straight-cylinder, bore would distribute itself more or less evenly in a circular "pattern" on a surface placed perpendicular to the line of flight. The density of the pattern would depend upon the number of pellets in the cartridge and the distance from the muzzle to the target. For quick shooting at close range, the broad circle or pattern thrown by a cylinder bore is desirable; for longer shots, a tighter pattern is better to overcome dispersion caused by increases in range.

If the muzzle end of the barrel is smaller inside than the rest of the bore the shotgun is "choked." A charge of shot fired through this restriction will be to some extent concentrated, that is, the pattern at any given range will be tighter than from a cylinder bore. Chokes are of several degrees; in general, the greater the reduction in bore diameter at the muzzle, the tighter the pattern. But there are limits to the efficiency of this constricting of the muzzle. Maximum, or full, chokes have a reduction in diameter of about .045 in. and cause an increase in effective range of about 15 yd. compared to cylinder bores, at the distances where full-choked guns are needed. Great skill is required to hit fast flying birds at long range regardless of gun choke; any reduction in pattern size handicaps a shooter at close range. Improvements in ammunition have slightly tightened and evened shot patterns and somewhat reduced the need for full chokes, except for long-range wild fowling.

Shotgun barrels normally have a choke built into them, but choking devices can also be attached to the end of any single-barreled gun. These allow a hunter the choice of several chokes, either by attaching a new tube or by rotating a single variable-

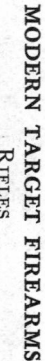

diameter sleeve arrangement. These can also be used in conjunction with recoil-reducing compensators.

Sights and Stocks.—Rifle-type rear sights and even telescope sights have been installed on shotguns, but infrequently. Normally, there is only a front sight, and sometimes a middle sight; the idea in wing shooting is to point the entire gun, rather than to sight at a bird rifle-style. But sight picture—the front sight, the target, and part of the top of the gun—is still important. Good shotgun shots usually require a gun that fits them, that is, a gun that will throw the charge of shot evenly into the area which they see around the front sight when they place the gun in normal firing position. If this does not happen, the weapon will handicap the shooter unless he realizes the discrepancy and allows for it.

The three important points of fit are the length of the stock, the distance from the line of sight to the top of the stock where a shooter habitually puts his cheek, and the angle made between the plane of the buttplate and the line of sight. There is no way of measuring a shooter and then making a perfect shotgun for him. In general, the length of the shooter's arm and neck is important, but so is the position that he assumes when he fires a gun. Stock-makers have special techniques and devices for determining individual fit, but the final form will probably be dependent on a shooter's own experiments after he has done enough firing to acquire automatic reactions and a definite firing position.

HANDGUNS

Game.—Small game is frequently taken with calibre .22 rimfire handguns carried by sportsmen for this purpose while hunting other game with a rifle or shotgun. Game birds on the ground can be taken with such guns but the practice is considered not sporting; smoothbore shot-throwing handguns, however, are used to some extent throughout the world to take flying birds, although such shooting is very difficult. Besides, these guns are often illegal or controlled in countries where a shotgun is not.

On the other hand, single-shot, rifled handguns are used regularly by a few hunters for medium game. For the most part, originally designed either for military or police use, handguns used in shooting of this type often are equipped with telescope sights, extra long barrels, and other gadgets. Occasionally, the guns resemble restocked hunting rifles more than they do pistols or revolvers.

Personal Defense.—Hunters, trappers, explorers, and others who have gone into primitive or unsettled regions sometimes have carried with them not only a shoulder weapon but also a holstered handgun for personal defense. Many hunting rifles have a very limited magazine capacity, whereas a revolver or semiautomatic pistol always has at least five shots available. Also, the shoulder weapon may have to be put down temporarily, but the handgun can be kept at hand at all times.

Occasionally, a hunter after dangerous game will carry with him a powerful handgun to be used in the event he is unable to reload his rifle. Magnum-calibre revolvers are popular for this type of service, although the old "howdah" types were as powerful. These were single- or double-barreled pistols, made in muzzle-loading percussion form and later in cartridge types, with quite large bores, frequently .577 calibre but sometimes larger; the term "howdah" derived from their use by those hunting tigers in India while riding in howdahs (or houdahs) carried on the backs of elephants. A gun of this kind can also be useful for killing a wounded animal quickly and painlessly.

MODERN TARGET FIREARMS

RIFLES

Military and Similar Types.—Competitive rifle shooting throughout the world is based on the military rifle of the particular country, and the rules for many matches require both military and civilian competitors to use standard issue weapons. In other cases, the rifle may be reworked, and even reassembled with selected and special components including sights.

Fine accuracy can be obtained from a selected bolt-action military rifle such as the U.S. M1903 and the British Rifle No. 4, but these usually must have better sights installed and be worked over in critical areas, with special attention given to the uniformity of internal barrel dimensions and the fit of the stocks to the actions. The newer U.S. M1 Garand and U.S. M14 rifles as well as the British SLR and the Canadian C1—the last two are essentially the Fabrique Nationale (Belgium) post-World War II military rifle firing the 7.62 mm. NATO round—can all be made into accurate target rifles. In unlimited or nonservice competition in the United States, Canada, and Britain, however, competitors frequently use weapons similar to old military bolt-action types, but not necessarily identical with them.

Free or Unrestricted Firearms.—For international competition and for other matches in which a completely nonmilitary rifle is allowed, an extremely specialized target weapon has been developed. This type of rifle is heavy—some run to 18 or more pounds—and is ordinarily a single shot. With stock adjustments it can deliver the most accurate fire possible from the three international positions: standing, kneeling, and prone. The stock is usually of the thumbhole type, with a hook buttplate, interchangeable with a rubber palm plate for the prone position, and adjustable palm rest, and a front-end hand stop (see illustration). A wide

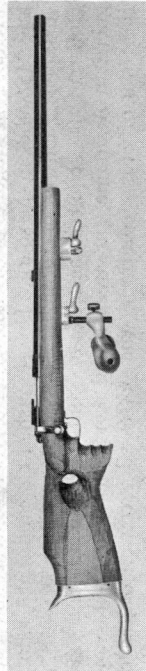

BY COURTESY OF REMINGTON ARMS CO., INC.
AN INTERNATIONAL MATCH FREE RIFLE. THUMBHOLE STOCK IS UN-FINISHED, READY FOR FITTING TO INDIVIDUAL SHOOTER

arm-cuff is allowed on slings, and almost any form of metallic sights may be used; the weapon is generally bolt action and the barrel usually free floating—it does not touch the wooden stock at all. Triggers are adjustable down to let-off pressures of less than one ounce. This sensitive trigger causes the weapon to be dangerous for any other use. But, in free-rifle competition, a shot accidentally fired while loading does not count against the competitor.

Since international free-rifle shooting with centre-fire calibres is normally at 300 m. (328 yd.), a relatively fast, heavy bullet is required so that changes in wind velocity and direction will affect it as little as possible. Most of these weapons are between calibre .25 and .30 and use bullets longer and heavier than standard. A similar rifle in calibre .22 rimfire is used in free-rifle competitions at 100 yd. (91.4 m.). An intermediate class of de-calibre .22 rimfire target rifle has also been developed for more restricted shorter range competition; these rifles are larger than sporting weapons and nonmilitary in general outline, but not as specialized as the free rifles.

Benchrest Weapons.—In benchrest competition, the rifles are aimed and fired while resting in various types of supports, or "benchrests," to ensure maximum steadiness. In general, the idea is to compete not only in shooting ability, but in equipment and ammunition as well. Almost all competitors load their own cartridges. There are several classifications by weight of weapon, calibre, and sight magnification, but all rifles are relatively heavy, long barreled, and of no more than moderate power. Many weapons used in these competitions will place an entire string of 10 bullets in less than one minute of angle, or about 1 in. (2.54 cm.) at 100 yd. Group size (the distance between the centre points of the two bullet holes that are the farthest apart) determines the winners. In good weather, various .22 centre-fire cartridges seem to have the advantage. At 200 yd. and under poor weather conditions, however, scores are better with longer, heavier bullets, which are less affected by wind.

SHOTGUNS

Live Bird Shotguns.—The most realistic shotgun competition is afforded by shooting at live birds, normally pigeons, released from small cages or "box traps." The sport is prohibited by law in some countries. Where it is still practised various rules determine the weapons that are used. Range can be varied but it is

normally about 20 to 25 yd. (18 to 23 m.) from the point where the competitor stands to the line of traps. The birds can, of course, fly in any direction, either increasing or decreasing the initial range.

Since a second shot can be taken at each bird, without penalty, double-barreled guns are favoured by most competitors, with semi-automatics and pumps far behind. Maximum bore size is limited to 12-gauge; few competitors handicap themselves by using smaller weapons. The choke of the barrel that is fired first is tight and that of the second barrel even tighter. Barrels are normally long, at least 30 in. (76.2 cm.). Good shots have relatively little trouble with incoming birds, but want every advantage possible in taking those that fly directly away. Since the competitors usually are experienced shooters who have their guns in position before they call for a bird, the weapons are relatively heavy and have straighter stocks than those normally used in the field.

Trapshooting Shotguns.—Since international clay-bird trap rules allow two shots at each target thrown and relatively heavy charges of shot, the guns used are similar to those used for live-bird shooting. Other rules govern other types of clay-bird trap-shooting, particularly in the United States. Where (as in most U.S. matches) a single shot only is fired at each bird, and the clays are thrown one at a time, two barrels are not required and a simpler, less expensive shotgun can be used. But even in these events, years of competition have evolved a specialized shotgun—fine top-break, single-barreled trap guns with straight stocks. Many other types, including pumps, doubles of both varieties, and semiauto-matics, are also used to fire at single targets; and another popular form of trapshooting, in which two birds are thrown at the same time and fired at successively, requires repeaters of these types. Triggers are sometimes altered so that the gun fires when the trigger is released, rather than when pulled. Since guns are not loaded until all competitors are ready and facing their targets, normal safety devices frequently are omitted.

Skeet Shotguns.—Weapons used in the specialized clay-bird competition known as skeet are normally like upland game guns, but in the U.S. they can have straighter stocks since the competitors can bring the gun to shoulder position before calling for a clay pigeon. This is not allowed under international skeet rules. But all skeet guns are shorter barreled and quicker handling than trap guns, and looser bored since all targets are shot at relatively close range. Skeet chokes seldom concentrate the shot pattern, but they do tend to make it more even. Since each skeet round includes four "doubles"—two birds thrown at the same time, with one shot at each—all skeet guns must be capable of delivering two shots. Pumps, semiautomatics, and doubles of both types are popular, often with recoil reducing devices mounted on the muzzle end of the barrels. (See also TRAPSHOOTING AND SKEET SHOOTING.)

HANDGUNS

Police and Military Types.—Most handgun competitions throughout the world are conducted with the standard weapons of the local police and national armed forces. Servicemen and police officers use their issue weapons; civilians in such matches use the same type of arms. As in the case of service rifles used for competition, issue handguns are often less accurate than they could be. To the extent permitted by the rules governing a particular competition, competent reassembling with special component parts can improve accuracy. Special target ammunition also can raise the scores. Adjustable sights are required for top performance.

The most accurate service pistol in the world today is probably the calibre-.45 Colt U.S. Army M1911 A1 semiautomatic (popularly, the "Colt .45 Automatic"). It must be emphasized, however, that maximum accuracy with this weapon is obtained only when special components and sights are used in a selective assembly by experts. A police revolver, the Colt Official Police Special calibre .38, is used in many matches. Maximum accuracy is possible with this weapon also only after reassembly and the installing of special sights which may prevent the weapon from being put into a normal holster. (For detailed views of these weapons see PISTOL AND REVOLVER.)

Calibre-.22 Target Weapons.—Soon after metallic cartridges were introduced, the smallest standard variety, the .22 rimfire, became popular for pistol shooting because of its low cost and the low cost of .22 ammunition, and its small amount of noise and combined. Fine accuracy can be achieved in revolvers, in semi-automatic pistols, and in single shot weapons of this type. Where a number of shots have to be fired within a limited time, semi-automatics or revolvers are preferred; in the Olympic rapid-fire matches, which require the fastest kind of shooting, semiautomatics are almost universal. The popular Smith & Wesson Model 41 calibre-.22 Long Rifle is an autoloader with a recoil-reducing device at the muzzle; it also is available in a model that uses extra low-power .22 short ammunition.

Free or Unrestricted Types.—For international slow-fire pistol competition and other similar matches, a special free pistol has been developed. These weapons resemble to some extent the free rifles already discussed and, like the international free rifle, calibre-.22 rimfire single-shot weapons, useful for no other purpose. Their trigger pulls are extremely light and the stocks usually are shaped to fit the individual hand of each competitor. They are heavy, long barreled, and have as long a sight radius (distance between front and rear sights) as the rules will allow.

BIBLIOGRAPHY.—Sir Gerald Burrard, *The Modern Shotgun*, 3 vol. (1950); *Notes on Sporting Rifles*, 4th ed. (1953); Walter H. B. Smith, *N.R.A. Book of Small Arms*, vol. i, *Pistols and Revolvers* (1946), vol. ii, *Rifles* (1948); Henry M. Stebbins, *Rifles: a Modern Encyclopedia* (1958); Jack O'Connor, *Complete Book of Rifles and Shotguns* (1961); Phillip Burdette Sharpe, *The Rifle in America* (1938). (J. We.)

GUNTER, EDMUND (1581-1626), English mathematician, inventor of several useful measuring devices, was born, of Welsh extraction, in Hertfordshire in 1581. He was educated at Westminster school, and in 1599 was elected a student of Christ Church, Oxford. He was professor of astronomy at Gresham college from 1619 until his death. Descriptions of some of his inventions were given in his treatises on the sector, cross-staff, bow, quadrant and other instruments. In 1620 he published his *Canon triangulorum*. There is reason to believe that Gunter was the first to discover (in 1622 or 1625) that the magnetic declination at one place varies (*see* GEOMAGNETISM). He introduced the words cosine and cotangent (*see* TRIGONOMETRY), and he suggested to Henry Briggs, his friend and colleague, the use of the arithmetical complement (*see* Briggs's *Arithmetica logarithmica*, ch. xv; *see also* LOGARITHMS).

His practical inventions included Gunter's chain, the chain in common use for surveying, 22 yd. long and divided into 100 links; Gunter's line, a logarithmic line, the forerunner of the slide rule; Gunter's quadrant, used to find the hour of the day, the sun's azimuth, etc., and also to take the altitude of an object in degrees; and Gunter's scale, generally called by seamen the gunter, a large plane scale engraved with various lines of numbers and used to solve problems in navigation, trigonometry, etc., with the aid of a pair of compasses. He died on Dec. 10, 1626. (O. OE.)

GÜNTHER OF SCHWARZBURG (1304-1349), German king in 1349 in opposition to Charles IV, was a descendant of the counts of Schwarzburg in Thuringia and the younger son of Henry VII, count of Blankenburg. Charles IV had been chosen by a majority of the electors to supplant Louis IV the Bavarian as German king in 1346. After Louis IV's death (1347), however, four of the electors offered the crown to Edward III of England, who declined it (1348). The four finally elected Günther at Frankfurt on Jan. 30, 1349, but on May 26 Charles forced him to accept the treaties of Eltville, which ended the conflict. Günther recognized Charles as German king and was given 20,000 marks. He died at Frankfurt on June 12, 1349, and was buried in the cathedral.

See K. Janson, *Das Königtum Günthers von Schwarzburg* (1880).

GÜNTHER, JOHANN CHRISTIAN (1695-1723), German poet, outstanding for his lyrical poetry, was born on April 8, 1695, at Striegau, Silesia, the son of a physician. He studied medicine at Wittenberg but after two years of dissolute life went in 1717 to Leipzig, where the efforts of J. B. Mencke (1674-1732) to procure him the post of stipendiary poet at the Saxon-Polish court at Dresden ended in a fiasco, for which Günther was partly to blame. In 1719 his father, who for long had opposed his son's poetical ambitions, disinherited him, despite Günther's pathetic attempts at reconciliation. He died at Jena on March 15, 1723.

Apart from Paul Fleming and Andreas Gryphius, Günther is the most important German lyric poet of the period between the middle ages and the early Goethe. In his Leipzig *Lieder* he breaks away from baroque mannerism and the learned traditions of humanism into classical lyricism. His true poetic quality, however, emerges when he writes of his personal sufferings in such poems as the *Leonorenlieder* and in the confessional poem in which he pleads to his father for mercy.

BIBLIOGRAPHY.—*Sämtliche Werke*, ed. by W. Krämer, 6 vol. (1930-37). *See also* W. Krämer, *Das Leben des schlesischen Dichters J. Chr. Günther* (1950); F. Delbono, *Umanità e Poesia di Christian Günther* (1959); H. Dahlke, *J. Chr. Günther* (1960). (K. Sc.)

GUNTRAM (d. A.D. 592), Merovingian Frankish king of Burgundy and Orléans, was one of the four sons of Clotaire I, on whose death in 561 he inherited a vast territory, comprising the ancient kingdom of Burgundy (extended northward as far as Melun); the kingdom of Orléans, with Berry, in the west; and Arles and Marseilles in the south. He established his capital at Chalon-sur-Saône. On the death of his eldest brother, Charibert (567), Guntram also acquired the cities of Saintes, Angoulême and Périgueux in Aquitaine, the areas round Avranches and Nantes and the town of Sées. Guntram, who possessed a certain degree of political ability, tried to maintain a balance of power between his warring brothers Sigebert I (d. 575) and Chilperic I. He formally adopted Sigebert's son Childebert II at a meeting at Pompierre (577). But the cordiality was short-lived, as Childebert's adherents seized Guntram's city of Marseilles, while Chilperic, having taken Périgord and Agenais, moved on to attack the town of Sées. After the assassination of Chilperic (584) and the revolt of the pretender Gundobald, Guntram sought a fresh alliance with Childebert, by which he gained control of other territory, including Paris (584). The treaty of Andelot (Nov. 28, 587) between Guntram, Childebert and the latter's mother, Brunhilda, settled the disputes that had arisen out of the succession to Charibert, established the irrevocable nature of royal grants to churches and to nobles and so brought a few years' internal peace.

Guntram sent two unsuccessful expeditions into Septimania against the Visigoths and a fleet to Galicia (586) in a vain attempt to help the Suebi against them. He was more successful against the Lombards, decisively repelling their two attempted invasions of Provence and occupying Aosta and Susa to prevent their crossing the Alps. Guntram died on March 28, 592, and was buried in the church of St. Marcellus, which he had built at Chalon. Described as a good king by Gregory of Tours (his contemporary), he was subsequently venerated as a saint at Chalon. (JE. H.)

GUNTUR, a town and district of Andhra Pradesh, India. The town, headquarters of the district, is situated about 250 mi. S.E. of Hyderabad on the Vijayavada-Guntakal metre-gauge section of the Southern railway, and on the main road from Vishakhapatnam to Madras. Pop. (1951) 125,255; (1961) 187,122. It has six colleges: three arts and science, one medical, one women's training and one oriental, all affiliated to the Andhra university; also an engineering institute and the Andhra Christian college. There are a jute mill, oil and rice mills, tobacco establishments and engineering works. Guntur appears to have been founded by the French in the second half of the 18th century. In 1788 it came into British possession, the cession being confirmed in 1823. It became a municipality in 1866.

GUNTUR DISTRICT, constituted in 1904 from territory till then divided between Kistna and Nellore, has an area of 5,802 sq.mi. Pop. (1961) 3,009,900. It is bounded east and north by the Kistna river, from which an extensive area is irrigated by canals. Rice is the main crop, and other crops are millets, chilies, peanuts and tobacco. The district has vegetable-oil mills, textile mills, a cement factory and many tobacco establishments. There are famous ancient Buddhist monuments at Amaravati (1st-3rd centuries A.D.) and at Nagarjunakonda, which would be submerged

GUNZBURG, the name of a leading Jewish family of financiers, philanthropists, communal workers and bibliophiles in Russia in the 19th century.

JOSEPH (YOZEL) GUNZBURG (1812–1878) made a fortune and settled in St. Petersburg. An influential financier, he often appealed to the government on behalf of the persecuted Jews. In 1863 he founded the Society for the Diffusion of Enlightenment among the Jews, to "disseminate among the Jews the knowledge of the Russian language and other useful subjects," in the hope that thereby "the Jews will become full-fledged citizens of the country." His son, Horace, and grandson, David, continued to work for the society.

HORACE GUNZBURG (1833–1909), even more than his father, was recognized as the spokesman of Russian Jewry, on whose behalf he was incessantly appealing to the government. In 1908 he organized the Russian Jewish Ethnographic society.

DAVID GUNZBURG (1857–1910), son of Horace Gunzburg, a trained orientalist, edited medieval Hebrew and Arabic texts and published a major work on Jewish art, *L'Ornement Hébreu* (1903). Like his predecessors he, too, was active in communal affairs.

An outstanding achievement of the Gunzburg family was their accumulation of rare books, manuscripts and incunabula of Jewish lore. During the Russian Revolution many books were destroyed, even burned as fuel. In 1956 Abraham Katsh of New York university examined what was left of the collection and microfilmed some of it. Remains of the collection (about 6,000 rare items) were housed in the Lenin library in Moscow. (I. M. F.)

GUPPY (*Lebistes reticulatus*), one of the live-bearing fishes of the family Poeciliidae, order Cyprinodontiformes. They were discovered in 1866 on Trinidad by R. J. L. Guppy, whose name was later given them. Because they are hardy and reproduce prolifically, guppies are often the first fishes kept by the beginner collector, and the diverse and brilliant colours appeal to the breeding skills of the experienced aquarist.

Guppies occur in brackish and fresh waters of northern South America and the Lesser Antilles. They are most common at the surface of ponds and quiet streams. They eat a variety of foods but are primarily insect feeders. Guppies often eat large numbers of mosquito larvae and are sometimes used as a mosquito control agent. They will also eat their own young when hungry.

The females grow continuously but seldom exceed two inches in length; the males seldom exceed one inch and do not grow appreciably after sexual maturity. In nature females seldom have bright colours but some aquarium strains have coloured females. On the other hand, males are almost always marked with brilliant colours; the fins, which are often long, may be marked with red and blue hues. The anal fin is used to transfer sperm to the female. The eggs are fertilized internally and the young are born alive. The gestation period is about four weeks, and each female produces broods at this interval throughout the year. Maturity is attained about three months after birth. The number of young per brood varies considerably with the size of the female. Since sperm can be retained for months within a female, she may produce several broods after she has been isolated from males, and a brood may contain the young of several fathers.

Most guppy colours are controlled by the male hormones, and males play a more active role in courtship and are more important in selecting mates than are the females. *See also* AQUARIUM; FISH: *Survey of the Bony Fishes.* (C. HU.)

GUPTA, the dynastic title of emperors who ruled in India in the 4th–5th centuries A.D. (and later, with lessened authority). The name was also borne by Chandragupta Maurya, founder of the Maurya dynasty. *See* INDIA-PAKISTAN, SUBCONTINENT OF: *History*; CHANDRAGUPTA; CHANDRA GUPTA I; CHANDRA GUPTA II; SAMUDRA GUPTA.

GURAGE, in southern Ethiopia, a region on the northwest of Lake Zeway inhabited by people of Sidama (*q.v.*) stock heavily overlaid by a military colonization from Tigré and by an influx of later refugees from Harar. Though the population is not large (estimates range from 40,000 to 350,000), there is much diversity, especially in religion, for which the proportion is about five-twelfths pagan, one-third Muslim, and one-fourth Christian. The dominant language, Gurage, is the southernmost Semitic Ethiopic language (*see* SEMITIC LANGUAGES: *Ethiopic*). The people are largely agricultural; their staple food is ensete (Abyssinian banana).

Until conquered by Ethiopia in 1875, the country was divided into independent tribal groups each under a "king," though formerly they paid tribute to Ethiopia. In the 17th century this took the form of gold figures of animals, hides and cattle; at this time the kings of Ethiopia appointed governors, but their rule was only nominal. The chief tribal divisions are Aymallal (north); Silte, Ulbarag (Werbarag), Walane (eastern); and Chaha, Ennamor, Endageny, Muher, Masqan, Gogot (western). For a long time Gurage was a stronghold of slavery and slave trading. *See* also ETHIOPIA: *The People; History*; CUSHITIC PEOPLES.

BIBLIOGRAPHY.—A. Cecchi, *Da Zeila alle frontiere del Caffa*, vol. i, ch. 30 (1886); C. F. Beckingham and G. W. B. Huntingford (eds.), *Some Records of Ethiopia: 1593–1646* (1954); W. Leslau, *Ethiopic Documents: Gurage* (1950); G. A. Lipsky et al., *Ethiopia* (1962).
(G. W. B. H.)

GURJARA-PRATIHARA, the name generally given to two dynasties of medieval Hindu India. The line of Harichandra ruled in Mandor (Jodhpur, Rajasthan) during the 6th–9th centuries A.D., generally with feudatory status. The line of Nagabhata ruled first at Ujjain and later at Kannauj (*qq.v.*) during the 8th–11th centuries. Other Gurjara lines existed, but these did not take the surname Pratihara.

The origin of the Gurjaras is uncertain. A view once widely held was that they entered India in the wake of the Hunas (*see* HEPHTHALITES) and were connected with the Khazars. There is some evidence in favour of this theory, but it is nowadays contested by most Indian historians, who believe that they had an indigenous origin. The name Gurjara is not to be found before the end of the 6th century A.D.

Of the two Gurjara-Pratihara lines the earlier was that descended from Harichandra. The relations of this line with the later and more important line of Nagabhata are uncertain, but there may have been some connection. Its founder, Nagabhata I, appears to have ruled in Malwa (*q.v.*), and his great-nephew Vatsaraja is attested as king of Ujjain in A.D. 783. Vatsaraja and his son Nagabhata II came in the way of the Rashtrakutas of the Deccan in their frequent attacks on the north, and seem to have accepted Rashtrakuta suzerainty for a time. In the complicated and badly documented wars of the early 9th century, involving Pratiharas, Rashtrakutas and Palas, Nagabhata played a very important part, and ultimately wrested Kannauj from the local king Chakrayudha, who had the protection of the Pala ruler Dharmapala. At this time the power of the Rashtrakutas weakened, and Nagabhata II estab-

GUPPIES (LEBISTES RETICULATUS): FEMALE DISTENDED WITH YOUNG; MALE WITH EXTENDED ANAL RAYS AND RAGGED-EDGED TAIL

lished himself in his new capital of Kannauj as the most powerful ruler of northern India.

Nagabhata was succeeded by his son Ramabhadra c. 833. This king had a very brief reign and was in turn succeeded by his son and successor Mihira Bhoja in 836 or a little earlier. Under Bhoja and his successor Mahendrapala (c. 890–910) the Pratihara empire reached its apogee of prosperity and power. In extent the territory of the Pratiharas rivaled that of the Guptas and of Harsha, reaching in the time of Mahendrapala from Gujarat and Kathiawar to northern Bengal, though much of it was loosely held under vassal kings. The prosperity and grandeur of Kannauj at about this time are attested by the Arab travelers Suleiman the Merchant and al-Mas'udi, and by the poet Rajasekhara, who was the *guru* (religious preceptor) of Mahendrapala.

After the death of Mahendrapala the succession is obscure, and the power of the Pratiharas was apparently weakened by dynastic strife. It was further diminished as a result of a great raid from the Deccan, led by the Rashtrakuta king Indra III, who in c. 916 sacked Kannauj. Under a succession of rather obscure kings the Pratiharas never regained their former influence. Their feudatories became more and more powerful, one by one throwing off their allegiance until by the end of the 10th century the Pratiharas controlled little more than the Gangetic *doab*. Their last important king, Rajyapala, was driven from Kannauj by Mahmud of Ghazni in 1018, and was later killed by the forces of the Chandella king Vidyadhara. For about a generation longer a small Pratihara principality apparently survived in the Allahabad district.

The Pratiharas were the most important Hindu dynasty of medieval northern India, and their disappearance marked a stage in the political decline which resulted in the Muslim conquest.

See also INDIA-PAKISTAN, SUBCONTINENT OF: *History.*

See R. S. Tripathi, *History of Kanauj to the Moslem Conquest* (1937); B. N. Puri, *The History of the Gurjara-Pratiharas* (1957).
(A. L. BA.)

GURKHA (GORKHA), a small straggling town in Nepal, is the ancestral home of the ruling house of that country. In 1559 Drabya Sah, the younger son of the king of Lamjung, seized the town and established his own little kingdom. His descendant Prithwi Narayan Shah conquered the Malla kingdoms of Nepal and consolidated the numerous petty principalities into the state of Nepal. Since this event (1768), generally described as the Gurkha conquest, the term Gurkha has often been used synonymously with Nepal, and the ruling dynasty is known as the house of Gurkha. Similarly, the Aryan Nepali language is often referred to as Gurkhali. Nepalese serving in the British Indian army were described as Gurkhas, and there were still Gurkha regiments in the armies of both England and India in the 1960s. In this loose sense the term is applied to all soldiers of Nepalese descent, whether or not they differ in caste, language or race from the martial people of Nepal. In fact, most Nepalese who enlist in foreign armies come from other castes; British Gurkha regiments are largely recruited from the Gurung, Magar, Tamang, Rai and Limbu tribes. The Magars are regarded as Hindus and the Tamangs as Buddhists, while the Gurungs, Rais and Limbus in the main have their own tribal religions. The modern town of Gurkha is famous for the shrine of Gorakhnath, the patron saint of the house of Gurkha, a small sanctuary hidden in a cave. There is also a fine durbar and a temple to the Hindu goddess Bhavani (Devi). The town is of little importance for trade but it is the administrative centre of the district of the same name. See also NEPAL.

See F. Tuker, *Gorkha: the Story of the Gurkhas of Nepal* (1957); T. Hagen, *Nepal* (1961).

GURKO, IOSIF VLADIMIROVICH (1828–1901), Russian army officer who distinguished himself during the Russo-Turkish War of 1877–78, was born in the Mogilev province on Nov. 27 (new style; 15, old style), 1828. Gurko took part in the Crimean War and in the suppression of the Polish insurrection of 1863. After the outbreak of the Russo-Turkish War he led an initially successful attack against Turnovo and Shipka, but in July 1877 his advance was checked by the Russian attack and the fall of Pleven in December, Gurko crossed the Balkan mountains, defeated the Turkish armies and occupied Sofia, Plovdiv and Edirne. The war ended in Jan. 1878 and in March the Ottoman empire signed the treaty of San Stefano. In 1879, Gurko was appointed governor-general of St. Petersburg, but he was replaced in 1880 when he failed to stop an attempt on the life of the emperor Alexander II. In 1882–83 he served as governor-general and military commander in Odessa. From 1883 to 1894 he served as governor-general and military commander in Warsaw, where he carried out the repression of all Polish nationalist agitation. In the field of education Gurko's policy of russification led to the reduction of the use of Polish in favour of Russian in instruction. While serving in Poland he strengthened the defenses of the area, and developed strategic highways. In 1884 he was made a member of the imperial council. He left the service as field marshal in 1894 and died at Zakharovo, Moscow region, on Feb. 10 (N.S.; Jan. 28, O.S.), 1901.
(B. J.)

GURKO, VASILI IOSIFOVICH (1864–1937), Russian army officer, last chief of the general staff of tsarist Russia and Russian commander in chief from March to June 1917, was the son of Field Marshal I. V. Gurko (*q.v.*). Educated in the corps of pages, he joined the Grodno hussar regiment in 1885. He took part in the Russo-Japanese War and later edited the official work on the war. In Aug. 1914, as commander of a cavalry division, he participated in the advance into and retreat from East Prussia. From Nov. 1914 he was in command of the VI corps and in 1916 he was commander on the Rumanian front. From Nov. 23, 1916, to March 1917 he acted as chief of staff when Gen. M. V. Alekseev became ill. Because he did not believe that an offensive should be undertaken by the weakened Russian forces, he came into conflict with A. F. Kerenski, minister of war, who dismissed him. On Aug. 4 Gurko was arrested and imprisoned. On Sept. 8 he was allowed to leave the country. Gurko's memoirs are entitled *Memories and Impressions of War and Revolution in Russia, 1914–17* (1918). His interpretation of the causes of the fall of the Romanov dynasty is contained in his book *Tsar i Tsaritsa* (1927). He died in Paris in 1937.
(B. J.)

GURNARD (*Trigla*), a genus of fishes of the sea robin family (Triglidae), recognized by the three first fin rays of the pectoral fin being detached to form movable fingerlike appendages, serving as organs of touch and of locomotion along the bottom, and by the large, angular, bony head. Gurnards are generally distributed over the tropical and temperate areas. Although never found far from the coast, gurnards descend to several hundred fathoms; they are caught chiefly by the trawl. In young gurnards the pectorals are comparatively longer than in the adult, extending to the end of the body. These fins are beautifully coloured, especially in the young. When taken out of the water, gurnards emit a grunting noise produced by the vibrations of a perforated diaphragm across the cavity of the air bladder. Their flesh is white, firm and wholesome. The so-called flying gurnard is *Dactylopterus volitans* (family Dactylopteridae), which is said to be able to propel itself out of the water. See also FLYING FISH.

GURNEY, the name of a distinguished English Quaker family of bankers and philanthropists. In 1770 the brothers JOHN (d. 1809) and HENRY GURNEY founded a banking house at Norwich, the business passing in 1809 to SAMUEL GURNEY (1786–1856), second son of John. At approximately the same time Samuel Gurney took control of the firm of Richardson, Overend and Co., which dealt in bills of exchange. For 40 years Overend, Gurney and Co. was the greatest discount house in the world, competing effectively with the Bank of England as a "banker's banker." JOSEPH JOHN GURNEY (1788–1847), third son of John Gurney, was an active philanthropist, sharing the prison reform views and interest of his older sister, Elizabeth Fry (*q.v.*) and his brother-in-law, Sir Thomas Fowell Buxton (*q.v.*). He was also active in the cause of emancipation of the slaves. He toured the United States many times in the service of the Society of Friends and to promote abolition of slavery and of capital punishment. DANIEL GURNEY (1791–1880), youngest son of John, was for more than 60 years a partner in the family firm.

See, for the family, P. Lubbock, *Earlham* (1922; reissued 1963);

D. E. Swift, *Joseph John Gurney: Banker, Reformer and Quaker* (1962).

GURU, in Indian religion, a spiritual teacher. From at least the time of the Upanishads India has stressed the importance of the tutorial method in matters of spiritual pursuit. The learner presents himself to a guru to be instructed in that wisdom which leads to an awareness of the identity of the deep self, Atman, with ultimate reality, Brahman. In the tradition of Bhakti Marga, the pathway of devotional faith in a personalized deity, a pathway that became important after the period of the Upanishads, increasing stress was placed upon the role of the guru, who in effect assumed the role of the personal deity. In at least one sect, the Vallabhacharis, the devotee offered his body, soul and substance to the guru who was identified with the deity. In all sects, including the well-known Vedanta, the devotee is expected to give perfect obedience to the guru. Through this identification with a concrete exemplar of the ideal of devotion, the devotee is led to discover the same immanent ideal within himself. The guru prescribes whatever disciplines are called for and gives to the student an initiatory formula known as a mantra (*q.v.*) to assist in meditation. (F. H. R.)

GURYEV (GURYEV), an *oblast* and town at the northeastern end of the Caspian Sea in the Kazakh Soviet Socialist Republic of the U.S.S.R. The *oblast* (formed 1938) adjoins Astrakhan Oblast on the west, the Karakalpak A.S.S.R. on the east, and the Turkmen S.S.R. on the south. It is generally flat except in the Mangyshlak Peninsula in the southeast, where there are hills rising to 1,821 ft. (555 m.). The mainly sandy terrain is interspersed with salt marshes. The climate is continental and subject to severe droughts. The Ural River runs through the *oblast*.

Oil extraction and fishing are the chief industries. The long-established Emba oil field was eclipsed by the discovery of major oil and natural-gas deposits in the waterless and largely uninhabited Mangyshlak Peninsula in 1961. An oil pipeline from the latter field is linked to the Guryev-Orsk pipeline and was being extended at the beginning of the 1970s to Kuibyshev. The Caspian and Ural fisheries and fish-canning industry are important. Agriculture is mainly concerned with stockbreeding though wheat is grown.

The population was 499,000 (1970 prelim.); 330,000 were urban. There are three towns—Guryev, Fort Shevchenko, and the new oil town of Shevchenko. Railways are Kandagach-Guryev, Makat-Shevchenko-Novy Uzen (1965), and Guryev-Astrakhan (1967). In the early 1970s Beyneu on the Makat-Shevchenko line was being linked to the Kungrad-Chardzhou line to the south. There is navigation on the Caspian and the Ural.

GURYEV, the *oblast* centre, is a port on the Ural River near its mouth on the Caspian Sea. Pop. (1970 prelim.) 113,000. It was founded as a fishing settlement in 1645 and is an important centre of the fishing and oil industries with an oil refinery, a fish cannery, and associated technical colleges. Other industries include construction materials, a meat-packing plant, and ship repair yards. There is a pedagogic institute and a theatre. (G. E. WR.; A. SH.)

GUSTAVO A. MADERO, a town in Mexico's federal district named in honour of the brother of Francisco I. Madero, revolutionary hero and former president of Mexico. Pop. (1960) 102,602. It is situated about 3 mi. N.E. of the central plaza of Mexico City. Prior to 1931 the town was known as Guadalupe Hidalgo and is the site of the famous basilica of the Virgin of Guadalupe, patron saint of Mexico. The basilica was erected near the spot where an apparition of the Virgin is said to have appeared to an Indian convert in 1531 and commanded that a church be built. A painting of the Virgin, which is said to have miraculously appeared on the inside of the Indian's cloak, hangs in the church. The apparition did much to hasten the conversion of the Indians. In 1754 a papal bull made the Virgin of Guadalupe patroness and protector of New Spain, and in 1810 she became the symbol of the Mexican independence movement when the patriot-priest Miguel Hidalgo y Costilla raised her picture to his banner. Each year, hundreds of thousands of pilgrims from all parts of the world are attracted to the shrine, holiest in Mexico, which was given the status of basilica by Pope Pius X in 1904. Also in this town, on Feb. 2, 1848, the United States and Mexican governments signed the treaty of Guadalupe Hidalgo, which provided that Mexico cede its territories of New Mexico and Upper California along with a cash payment of $15,000,000 to the U.S. in return for cancellation of numerous claims. (H. R. HY.)

GUSTAVUS I VASA (Swed. GUSTAV ERIKSSON) (1496?-1560), king of Sweden from 1523, came of a noble family whose members had played a prominent part in the factious aristocratic politics of 15th-century Scandinavia, and was connected by marriage with the family of Sture, which had supplied Sweden with three regents. Gustavus fought in the army of Sten Sture the Younger against Christian II of Denmark in 1517-18 and was one of the hostages sent by Sten to Christian in 1518 as part of the terms of an armistice. Christian violated the agreement and carried Gustavus off to Denmark. In 1519 Gustavus fled from his captivity to Lübeck, where he made friends who were to be of great importance later, and on May 31, 1520, he returned to Sweden. Sten Sture had meanwhile died of wounds, and Christian was master of almost all Sweden save Stockholm. In November, by the "Stockholm

BY COURTESY OF THE SVENSKA PORTRÄTT-ARKIVET, STOCKHOLM

GUSTAVUS I, AFTER A PORTRAIT BY J. BINCK, 1542. IN THE UNIVERSITY OF UPPSALA

blood-bath," Christian removed the most dangerous of his opponents, including Gustavus' father and two of his uncles.

Gustavus, faced with the alternative of rebellion or flight, chose the former. He succeeded in rousing Dalarna to resist; purchased by judicious concessions the support of lay and ecclesiastical magnates to whom a union of the three Scandinavian kingdoms under Christian had become unwelcome; and was able (since Sten Sture's son Nils was a mere boy) to pass as leader of the surviving Sture party. A considerable body of folk legend deals with his real and supposed adventures at this period. For the eviction of the Danes, as he soon found, outside help was necessary; and he obtained it from Lübeck, whose merchants felt themselves threatened by Christian's aggressive economic policies. This aid enabled Gustavus to establish Sweden's independence and may have been responsible for his election as king (June 6, 1523). In return for it, Lübeck extorted far-reaching commercial privileges; and it was to be one of Gustavus' main concerns to emancipate his country from its dependence on his former backers.

Meanwhile Gustavus' crown continued for some years to be precarious. Christian II had indeed been driven out of Denmark by his uncle, who succeeded him as Frederick I, and a common fear of Christian's restoration soon drew Frederick and Gustavus together, so that despite recurrent periods of tension the threat from Christian, and afterward from his heirs, enforced a measure of harmony between Sweden and Denmark. But Gustavus had to face serious internal dangers: from aggrieved members of the old Sture party who resented his favour to some of their former enemies; from the men of Dalarna, who added to this grievance complaints on economic and religious grounds; and from great nobles, who found Gustavus a more formidable ruler than they had expected.

The need to pay his debts to Lübeck, and the need to strengthen the royal authority, forced Gustavus to impose heavy taxes; and it was essentially with a view to tapping the church's wealth that he embarked on the measures which led to the Reformation in Sweden. The diet at Västerås in 1527 put the church's property at his mercy. Gustavus had few theological interests or preferences; but he resented the presence in Sweden of any authority which challenged his own, and he had some sympathy with the idea of services in Swedish, for he was an indifferent Latinist himself. The move toward Lutheranism, however, was accelerated or retarded by purely political considerations. Sweden did not become irrevocably a Lutheran country till 1544 at the earliest, and it was a long time before Protestantism was popular outside Stockholm.

The last great revolt of the reign, that of Nils Dacke in 1542-43, had a strong anti-Protestant strain. Gustavus' vain attempts to become a member of the League of Schmalkalden, formed by the German Protestants, were dictated by a desire to provide himself, indeed, he inclined always to caution and a husbanding of resources. If he intervened in the so-called Count's War between pretenders to the Danish crown (1534-36), it was because he saw at last a chance of liberating Sweden from Lübeck's tutelage; and the later war with Muscovy (1555-57) was probably inevitable.

Gustavus' greatest achievement was the creation of a strong monarchy. He based his power on a massive agglomeration of crown and family lands, acquired for the most part by confiscation from the church, which put him beyond the rivalry of any other noble house. The supervision and exploitation of these lands was his personal concern, and with it went an infinite solicitude for the smallest details of fiscal policy. He treated Sweden as though it were a gigantic manor of which he was the all-seeing lord; and though in the early 1540s a shortage of competent Swedish administrators led him to experiment with Burgundian administrative techniques applied by imported Germans, this was a brief episode: at the close of his reign the government remained almost as personal and intimate as at the beginning. As the political heir of a faction, he found it expedient to bribe his nobility with church lands, and he was successful in many policies which the Stures had attempted. In 1544, for instance, he induced the diet to declare the monarchy hereditary rather than elective. He summoned the estates frequently in the uncertain years at the beginning of his reign, though less often thereafter; and his use of them to endorse his policies undoubtedly aided their development as an effective parliamentary body. On the other hand, he reduced to a position of relative insignificance the aristocratic council of state, which had played the leading part in the constitutional struggles of the preceding century.

Gustavus was a harsh master and an exigent lord: his suspiciousness, irritability and violence drove a succession of faithful servants into embittered exile; his ruthless ferocity put an end to the political pretensions of Dalarna. He was mendacious and cruel, vengeful and capricious, and to his enemies he seemed to have most of the attributes of a tyrant. He cared little for learning or the arts, though he was fond of music and a skilful performer on the lute. Yet he handled the Swedish language with superb vigour and effect: his speeches to the commonalty—at the diet, or at fairs and markets—were brilliant examples of calculated demagogic art, and his letters are those of a great letter writer. He was indeed one of the great rulers of his age, wise, shrewd, tireless in his care for his country. He made Sweden an independent state; he gave his country, for the first time for a century, nearly 40 years of stable and intelligent government; he ensured the triumph of the Reformation; he established the first truly national standing army of modern times; and he founded the Swedish navy. By his first wife, Catherine of Saxe-Lauenburg (1513-35; married 1531), he had one son, who succeeded him as Eric XIV (q.v.); by his second, Margareta Leijonhufvud (1516-51; married 1536), he had a numerous family; his third was Katarina Stenbock (1535-1621; married 1552). He died in Stockholm on Sept. 29, 1560. A selection of his letters has been edited by N. Edén (1917).

BIBLIOGRAPHY.—S. Wikberg, *Gustav Vasa*, 2 vol. (1944-45); I. Svalenius, *Gustav Vasa* (1950). See further G. Landberg, *De nordiska rikena under Brömsebroförbundet* (1925); H. Holmquist, *Svenska kyrkans historia*, vol. iii (1933); I. Svalenius, *Georg Norman* (1937); G. Olsson, *Stat och kyrka i Sverige vid medeltidens slut* (1947); E. Lönnroth, *En annan uppfattning* (1949); N. Ahnlund, *Den svenska utrikespolitikens historia*, vol. i (1956). (Mr. R.)

GUSTAVUS II ADOLPHUS (1594-1632), king of Sweden from 1611, was born in Stockholm on Dec. 9, 1594, the eldest son of Charles IX and his second wife Christina of Holstein. He succeeded his father on Oct. 30, 1611, shortly before his 17th birthday, at an extremely critical moment for his country (*see* SWEDEN: *History*). He had been carefully educated for kingship by his tutor, Johan Skytte, and had acquired at second hand some insight into the new Dutch school of tactics which he was later so successfully to develop. His accession was not to be taken for granted, for his cousin John of Östergötland had a better title, and by the succession pact of Norrköping (1604) it had been laid down that a regency was to continue until Gustavus had completed his 23rd year. His father's government had been hateful to the high nobility, and his cousin Sigismund III of Poland, who had been deposed from the Swedish throne in 1600 and was now at war with Sweden, long continued to intrigue for his restoration.

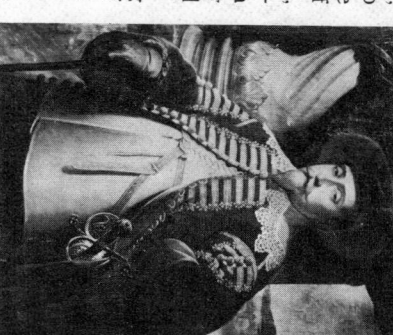

BY COURTESY OF THE SVENSKA ARKIVET, STOCKHOLM

GUSTAVUS ADOLPHUS, PORTRAIT BY M. MERIAN THE ELDER, 1632. AT SKOKLOSTER, UPPLAND

Gustavus was forced to purchase the consent of his council to his immediate accession by the grant of a charter (1612) which seemed to imply a curtailment of the royal prerogative, and his appointment of Axel Oxenstierna (q.v.) as his chancellor appeared to ensure the predominance of the high nobility in the central government. Gustavus, however, was more favourably inclined to the nobility than his father had been, and more tactful in his handling of men, and between him and Oxenstierna developed a lifelong intimacy and friendship which provided him with invaluable support. He was also more orthodox in his Lutheranism than Charles IX. He was able, therefore, to reconcile both nobility and church to the crown; and, since he followed his father's example of using the *riksdag* (diet) to support and endorse his policies, he was able to evade the restrictions of the charter. By the close of his reign he had become more popular and more powerful than any king before him. Gustavus tackled with success the internal problems of the country, reforming the abuses of the administration, remodeling local government, providing better judicature; his reform of *riksdag* procedure (1617) decided that there should be no more than four estates represented in the diet.

Gustavus was one of the great reforming monarchs of Swedish history, and his reign laid the bases upon which the state was to develop for the next two centuries. A brilliant stylist, a keen musician, he had an insatiable intellectual curiosity which developed a remarkable *expertise* in the most varied matters, from the details of a ship's rig to the cabalistic implications of runology. He had a lively interest in education, as to which his views, under Skytte's influence, were Ramist (*see* RAMUS, PETRUS), and his reign was of decisive importance for the future of Swedish education: he was the real father of the Swedish grammar schools (*gymnasia*), and it was to his exertions (and to his magnificent donation of 1624) that the University of Upsala owed its recovery and its advancement to equality of status with other continental universities. He had strong views and clear, if narrow, insight into economic matters; he desired to convert the royal income from payments in kind to payments in cash, and consequently deliberately sold or pawned crown lands and revenues to the nobility—a policy which was later to have unfortunate constitutional and social consequences. In an attempt to control the nation's commerce he founded many towns which experience showed not to be economically viable, though to this generalization Gothenburg was a notable exception. He perceived, however, that one of Sweden's most urgent needs was capital investment to develop her mineral resources; and it was to his initiative in attracting foreign capitalists that the spectacular development of Sweden's metallurgical industries (first copper, later iron) was very largely due.

For the first ten years of the reign the foreign policy of Gustavus was necessarily mainly defensive. The disastrous war with Denmark was ended by the onerous peace of Knäred (1613), and Sweden's intervention in the "troubles" in Russia (*see* RUSSIAN HISTORY) was brought to a successful conclusion by the treaty of Stolbova (1617). Gustavus feared the latent expansive force of Muscovy and sought to erect barriers against it while the tsardom was weak: at Stolbova he succeeded in acquiring territory in Ingria (Ingermanland) and Karelia which linked the Swedish possessions in Estonia with Finland and completely excluded Russia from the Baltic. The irreconcilable dynastic quarrel with Sigismund III of Poland proved less easy of solution, and by 1620 no decision was in sight here. Meanwhile Gustavus sought to cultivate the good will of Protestant Europe, partly as an insurance against renewed Danish attack, partly in the hope that Protestants might be brought to recognize his struggle against Poland as an aspect of the wider struggle of Protestantism against the Counter-Reformation: it was with this end in view that he married, in 1620, Maria Eleonora (1599–1655), daughter of the elector John Sigismund of Brandenburg.

The outbreak of the Bohemian War in 1618 (see THIRTY YEARS' WAR) had aroused the close attention of Gustavus, and he seems from the beginning to have been convinced of the need for Protestant solidarity in the crisis. He was, however, preoccupied with his war with Poland, which he began again in 1621, seizing a favourable opportunity when Sigismund was heavily committed against the Turks; and until this complication could be disposed of it was difficult for him to intervene in Germany. He felt, moreover, that his campaigns in Poland should be recognized as a valuable diversion, particularly in view of the active aid which the Holy Roman emperor Ferdinand II sent to Sigismund and of the plans for Spanish-Austrian naval collaboration in the Baltic. The capture of Riga in 1621 was his first major military success; and in Jan. 1626 he rounded off five years' campaigning in the Düna valley by the brilliant victory of Wallhof. Wallhof ensured his conquest of Livonia and made it possible for him to transfer the main theatre of activity to the Vistula valley: he hoped by throttling Poland's corn exports to constrain Sigismund to a speedy peace. Despite victories at Mewe (Pol. Gniew), Dirschau (Tczew) and Gorzno, however, it was not until 1629 that he was able to conclude the six years' truce of Altmark, which left the Prussian ports with their valuable revenues in his hands and freed him for the expedition to Germany which he had for some years seen to be inevitable.

The progress of the emperor's forces in northern Germany was by 1627 threatening the security of the Baltic; in 1628 Gustavus, sinking his differences with Christian IV of Denmark, had collaborated to save Stralsund from capture by Wallenstein. But all attempts to create a Protestant league had broken down; Denmark made peace in 1629; and when Gustavus crossed into Germany he did so without an ally. The interests of Sweden and the cause of Protestantism were in his view almost identical, and he regarded his expedition as essentially an attempt to obtain security: he probably had no long-distance plans beyond the permanent eviction of the imperial armies from the coast lands. The Protestant princes of Germany viewed him with jealousy, and it was several months before he was able to secure allies; but the Protestant masses saw him as a destined saviour, the "Lion of the North" of whom Paracelsus had prophesied. His failure to relieve Magdeburg, which had committed itself to support of his cause in reliance on his promises, was probably justified by military considerations and did little permanent damage to his reputation; his extraordinary victory at Breitenfeld on Sept. 17 (new style; 7, old style) was at once a landmark in the art of war and in the history of Europe. It ensured the survival of German Protestantism, and it made Gustavus for a time the arbiter of Germany. His advance thereafter on Mainz has been criticized; but there is little doubt that he was right to reject Oxenstierna's advice to thrust for Vienna. It was now the Swedish king's object to ensure that his German allies should be bound together in a league effective enough to win the war and solid enough to afford real security when peace should be made. This led him to impose terms upon them which were stringent, and has given rise to the mistaken belief that he aspired to a permanent feudal superiority over them. It was widely suggested that he might make himself emperor. On this last point his own views are unknown; it is very unlikely, however, that he would have accepted such a solution save in the last resort. Nor does it seem that he desired any permanent authority over his allies. His object was security, for Sweden and for Protestantism, but he fell too easily into the assumption that security could only

be won by total victory; hence in the interests of military efficiency he treated his allies with a roughness which alienated many of them from his cause.

In 1632 Gustavus invaded Bavaria, forced the line of the Lech in a brilliant operation and captured Munich. Wallenstein's threat to Saxony, however, forced him to turn northward, and he sustained a sharp reverse in an extraordinarily daring attack on his enemy's entrenched camp near Nürnberg (Aug. 1632). After a period of maneuvering, in which each threatened the bases of the other, the adversaries met again at Lützen, on Nov. 16 (N.S.; 6, O.S.), 1632. In a most bloody battle, fought in dense mist, the Swedes were victorious, but Gustavus was killed leading a cavalry attack.

The victories of Gustavus had been made possible by his thorough reform of the recruiting, training, discipline, armament and administration of the Swedish army and by the revolution in tactics which he effected. Conscript subjects rather than mercenaries formed the nucleus of his forces, and their performance confounded the military experts. His linear tactics, an improvement of those of Maurice of Orange, combined mobility and striking power; pike and musket, cavalry and artillery as no other commander of the age could combine them, and inaugurated a revolution in the art of war; his new mobile artillery soon set a standard for other armies. He was a commander of the very first rank. But he was also, independently of his military achievements, one of the greatest of kings. He combined in his character a fervent piety with an irresistible charm; his magnanimity and tolerance were matched by his integrity and his devotion to duty; and his naturally hot and suspicious temper was offset by a bubbling fount of high spirits and an ability to get on terms with the common man.

He was succeeded on the throne by his only legitimate child, his daughter Christina (q.v.).

BIBLIOGRAPHY.—G. Wittrock, *Gustav II Adolf* (1927); J. Paul, *Gustav Adolf*, 3 vol. (1927–32); N. Ahnlund, *Gustav Adolf den store* (1932; Eng. trans., *Gustav Adolf the Great*, 1940); N. Ahnlund, *Axel Oxenstierna inkl Gustav Adolfs död* (1940); M. Roberts, *Gustavus Adolphus: a History of Sweden 1611–1632*, 2 vol. (1953–58). Older works include J. Hallenberg, *Svea Rikes Historia under konung Gustaf Adolf den stores regering*, 5 vol. (1790–96); A. Cronholm, *Sveriges Historia under Gustav II Adolphs regering*, 6 vol. (1857–72). *See also Sveriges Krig, 1611–32*, ed. by the Swedish general staff, 8 vol. (1936–39). See also references under "Gustavus II" in the Index volume.

(Mr. R.)

GUSTAVUS III (1746–1792), king of Sweden from 1771, was born in Stockholm on Jan. 24, 1746, the eldest son of the future king Adolphus Frederick and Louisa Ulrica, sister of Frederick the Great of Prussia. Educated under the care of the statesmen Carl Gustaf Tessin and Carl Scheffer, he had the poet and historian Olof von Dalin as one of his tutors. Brilliantly talented and enthusiastic for the Enlightenment, he early began to exercise that charm of manner which later made him so fascinating and so dangerous; also he showed a strong instinct for drama, which was to win him an honourable place in literature. His marriage (Oct. 1, 1766) to Sophia Magdalena, daughter of Frederick V of Denmark, proved unhappy.

Gustavus first intervened in politics in 1768, when his father temporarily resigned the crown to compel the dominant Cap faction (*see* SWEDEN: *History*) to summon the four estates to an extraordinary *riksdag*, from which he hoped for the reform of the constitution in a monarchical direction. The Hat faction, however, dominant in the new *riksdag*, failed to redeem the pledges which it had given before the elections. When Adolphus Frederick died, on Feb. 12, 1771, Gustavus was

GUSTAVUS III. PORTRAIT BY LORENS PASCH

absent from Sweden on a political mission in Paris (Feb. 4–March 25). The new king secured the French government's undertaking to pay the outstanding subsidies to Sweden, in return for which he was to bring about a revision of the Swedish constitution by strengthening the monarchy against the warring factions of the nobility. On his way home he visited his uncle, Frederick the Great, in Potsdam. Frederick bluntly informed him that, in concert with Russia and Denmark, he had guaranteed the existing Swedish constitution and advised him to abstain from violence.

Back in Sweden Gustavus made a last attempt to mediate between the Hats and Caps, who were ruining the country between them. On June 25, 1771, he opened his first *riksdag* with a moving speech in which he proposed a reconciliation between contending factions. A composition committee was actually formed, but it proved illusory from the first. The subsequent attempts of the Caps—now dominant again and bent on making Sweden a Russian satellite—to limit still further the royal prerogative induced Gustavus to carry out his revolution. Two of his confidants, Johan Kristoffer Toll and Jacob Magnus Sprengtporten, secured for him the key fortresses of Kristianstad in Skåne (Aug. 12, 1772) and Sveaborg in Finland (Aug. 16). Apprised of this success, the king on Aug. 19 won over the officers of the Stockholm garrison and dictated a new oath of allegiance, absolving them from their allegiance to the estates and binding them to obey only their king. Meanwhile the senate and the governor general, Ture Rudbeck, had been arrested and the fleet secured. On the evening of Aug. 20 heralds proclaimed that the estates were to meet on the following day. On Aug. 21 the king appeared in full regalia and reproached the estates for their unpatriotic venality in the past. A new constitution was laid before the estates and accepted by them unanimously. The *riksdag* was then dissolved.

Gustavus was inspired by enthusiasm for the greatness and welfare of Sweden and worked in the same reformatory direction as contemporary sovereigns of the Enlightenment. He took an active part in every department of business and relied far more on counselors of his own choosing than on the senate. Measures were taken to reform the administration and the judicial procedure (torture as an instrument of legal investigation was abolished); an ordinance of 1774 provided for the liberty of the press; religious toleration was accorded; the finances were set in good order by the "currency realization ordinance" of 1777; and the national defenses, especially the navy, were strengthened, though the king's foreign policy was at first both wise and wary. Thus, when he convened the *riksdag* at Stockholm, on Sept. 9, 1778, he could give a brilliant account of the first six years of the new regime. Yet, short as the session was, it was long enough to open the eyes of the deputies to the fact that their political supremacy had departed.

The *riksdag* of 1778 had been obsequious; that of 1786 was mutinous. The consequence was that nearly all the royal propositions were either rejected outright or so modified that Gustavus himself withdrew them. Thenceforth Gustavus was determined to rule with even less dependence on the *riksdag*. His opportunity came when the political complications arising out of the war against Russia, that he had begun in the summer of 1788, enabled him by the Act of Unity and Security (on Feb. 21, 1789) to override the opposition of the gentry and, with the approbation of the three lower estates, to establish a new constitution, in which, though the estates still held the power of the purse, the royal authority largely predominated. Throughout 1789 and 1790 Gustavus gallantly conducted the unequal struggle with Russia, finally winning in the Svensksund (July 9–10) the most glorious naval victory ever gained by the Swedish arms. A month later, on Aug. 14, 1790, peace was signed between Russia and Sweden at Väräla. It saved Sweden from humiliating concessions, and in Oct. 1791 Gustavus took the bold step of concluding an eight years' defensive alliance with the Russian empress Catherine the Great, who thereby bound herself to pay her new ally annual subsidies amounting to 300,000 rubles.

Free to concentrate his attention on the European problems arising from the French Revolution, Gustavus now aimed at forming a counterrevolutionary league of princes, but was hampered by poverty and by the jealousy of the other powers. Then, shortly after the meeting of the *riksdag* at Gefle (Jan. 23–Feb. 24, 1792), he fell a victim to a widespread aristocratic conspiracy. Shot in the back by Capt. Jacob Johan Anckarström at a midnight masquerade at the Stockholm opera house on March 16, 1792, he died on March 29.

Though he had many foibles and extravagances, Gustavus III was indisputably one of the greatest Swedish sovereigns, and his death was a national misfortune for his country. He was, moreover, a distinguished author and a munificent patron of all the arts. He founded the Swedish academy (1786) and gave such encouragement to the theatre in Sweden as to inaugurate a new era in its history. His own plays combine the influence of Voltaire with patriotic feeling (notably *Gustaf Adolphs ädelmod*, 1783), and it was he who drafted the plot of the opera *Gustaf Vasa* (1786), for which Johan Kellgren wrote the libretto. For his cultural activity no less than for his political achievement, his reign is rightly remembered as the Gustavian age.

BIBLIOGRAPHY.—C. T. Odhner, *Sveriges politiska historia under Konung Gustaf III:s regering* (1885–96); O. Levertin, *Gustaf III som dramatisk författare* (1894) and *Från Gustaf III:s dagar* (1909); H. Schück, *Gustaf III. En karaktärsstudie* (1904); R. N. Bain, *Gustavus III and His Contemporaries*, 2 vol. (1904); L. Stavenow, *Konung Gustaf III*, 3rd ed. (1925); A. Söderhjelm, *Sverige och den franska revolutionen* (1920); B. Hennings, *Gustaf III, en biografi* (1957); Olof Jägerskiöld, *Den svenska utrikespolitikens historia*, vol. ii, part 2, 1721–1792 (1957).
(R. N. B.; E. O. H. J.)

GUSTAVUS IV (GUSTAF ADOLF) (1778–1837), king of Sweden from 1792 to 1809, was born in Stockholm on Nov. 1, 1778, the son of Gustavus III and Sophia Magdalena. Carefully educated, he grew up serious and conscientious. On the assassination of his father (March 1792), he became king under the regency of his uncle, Charles, duke of Södermanland. Negotiations for his marriage to the grand duchess Alexandra, a granddaughter of the Russian empress Catherine the Great, were broken off when, at the end of the regency, he refused to concede her freedom to practice the Orthodox religion (1796). Instead, in 1797, he married Frederica Dorothea, daughter of Charles Louis of Baden. This might have led to a war with Russia but for the hatred of Revolutionary France shared by Catherine's successor Paul and Gustavus IV, whose morbid horror of Jacobinism drove him to adopt all sorts of reactionary measures and to postpone his coronation so as to avoid calling together a diet; but the disorder of the finances, caused partly by the continental war and partly by the failure of the crops in 1798 and 1799, compelled him to summon the estates to Norrköping in March 1800, and on April 3 he was crowned.

For the change which now took place in Sweden's foreign policy and its consequences *see* SWEDEN: *History*. By the end of 1808 the situation was desperate. The king's violence had alienated his most faithful supporters, while his obstinacy was paralyzing the national efforts. To remove Gustavus by force was the one remaining expedient; this was accomplished by a conspiracy of officers of the western army. On March 13, 1809, seven of the conspirators broke into the royal apartments, seized the king and conducted him to Drottningholm (whence he was soon moved to Gripsholm); his uncle Charles accepted the leadership of a provisional government; and a diet, hastily summoned, approved the revolution. On March 29, Gustavus IV, in order to save the crown for his son Gustavus (1799–1877; styled the prince of Vasa from 1829), voluntarily abdicated; however, on May 10 the estates, dominated by the army, declared that his whole issue had forfeited the throne. On June 6 the duke regent was proclaimed king under the title of Charles XIII after accepting the new liberal constitution which the diet ratified. In December Gustavus and his family were transported to Germany.

Gustavus now assumed the title of count of Gottorp, but subsequently called himself Colonel Gustafsson, under which pseudonym he published some books, notably the *Mémorial* (1829) and *La Journée du treize mars* (1835). Separated from his family, he led an erratic life for several years; was divorced in 1812; and finally settled at St. Gall in Switzerland in loneliness and indigence. He died there on Feb. 7, 1837. At the suggestion of King Oscar II his body was brought to Sweden and interred in the Riddarholm-skyrka in 1884, after the marriage of the future Gustavus V (q.v.) in 1881 to a granddaughter of Gustavus IV's daughter Sophia.

BIBLIOGRAPHY.—K. V. Key-Aberg, *De diplomatiska förbindelserna mellan Sverige och Storbrittannien under Gustaf IV...*, 2 vol. (1890-91); K. Ullrich, *Die deutsche Politik Gustavus IV... 1799-1806* (1914); R. Petiet, *Gustave IV Adolphe et la Révolution Française* (1914); Sten Carlsson, *Gustaf IV Adolf* (1946).

GUSTAVUS V (1858-1950), king of Sweden from 1907, was born at Drottningholm Castle, near Stockholm, on June 16, 1858, the eldest son of the future king Oscar II of Sweden and Norway and Sophia of Nassau. Duke of Värmland and, from 1872, crown prince, he entered the army and also traveled widely. His marriage (Sept. 20, 1881), to Victoria (1862-1930), daughter of the grand duke Frederick I of Baden, reunited the Bernadotte dynasty with the royal house of Vasa, since his bride's paternal grandmother was Sophia, daughter of Gustavus IV of Sweden.

Having frequently acted as regent, Gustavus became king of Sweden at his father's death on Dec. 8, 1907. He took as his motto "With the people for the Fatherland." During World Wars I and II he was a firm believer in Swedish neutrality; in World War II his country was soon left as the one neutral state in northern Europe. Until his severe illness in 1942, he was an enthusiastic tennis player and continued to travel. He was also skilful at needlework. Gustavus V died in Stockholm on Oct. 29, 1950.

GUSTAVUS VI (GUSTAF ADOLF) (1882-), king of Sweden from 1950, was born in Stockholm on Nov. 11, 1882, the eldest son of the future king Gustavus V. By his first marriage (1905), to Princess Margaret of Connaught (1882-1920), he had five children: Gustaf Adolf, duke of Västerbotten (1906-47); Sigvard, duke of Uppland (1907-); Ingrid (1910-), queen consort of Denmark (1947-72); Bertil, duke of Halland (1912-); and Carl Johan, duke of Dalarna (1916-). His second marriage (1923) was to Lady Louise Mountbatten (1889-1965), daughter of the first marquess of Milford Haven. During his father's long reign the crown prince showed himself to be a keen archaeologist: he excavated ancient Swedish monuments and sponsored expeditions overseas. Considered as an authority on Chinese ceramics, he formed one of the largest private collections of Asian pottery in the world. He became king in 1950. His grandson Charles Gustavus (1946- ; son of the duke of Västerbotten) then became crown prince. In 1965, though the king was then over 82 and his heir only 19, the *riksdag* raised the age at which a king might start to rule from 21 to 25. In 1967 the question of replacing the monarchy by a republic was shelved for five years, by which time the crown prince would be 25.

GUSTAVUS ADOLPHUS UNION (since Jan. 31, 1946, known as the Gustav-Adolf-Werk der Evangelischen Kirche Deutschlands; formerly the Evangelischer Verein der Gustav Adolf Stiftung) was founded by Gottlob Grossmann at Leipzig in 1834 after the bicentennial celebration of the battle of Lützen, Nov. 16 (N.S.; 6 O.S.), 1632, as a memorial to the Swedish king Gustavus II Adolphus, who was killed at Lützen. Based on the biblical idea of the Diaspora, it was to aid Protestant minority churches in Germany and abroad, and in 1842 it received an additional impulse from amalgamation with Karl Zimmermann's similar society in Darmstadt. Membership was open to all denominations of Protestants and even included a few Catholics. Aid, chiefly from voluntary contributions, was given in the form of buildings for churches and schools, provision of pastors and teachers and, after 1945, the support of refugee communities. World War II greatly increased the work, which developed into a worldwide organization for the spreading of the Christian faith.

See O. Lerche, "Hundert Jahre Arbeit an der Diaspora," in *Nachweisungen aus den Veröffentlichungen des Centralvorstandes des Evangelischen Vereins der Gustav Adolf Stiftung* (1932); P. W. Gennrich, "Das Gustav Adolf Werk der Evangelischen Kirche Deutschlands," *Kirchliches Jahrbuch*, vol. 82 (1955).

GÜSTROW, a town of Germany which after partition of the nation following World War II became a regional capital in the German Democratic Republic. *Bezirk* (district) of Schwerin in the German Democratic Republic. Pop. (1970 est.) 37,213. The town is about 25 mi. S. of Rostock on the Berlin-Rostock railway line and is a rail and traffic junction. The little Nebel river flows through Güstrow. Wood and engineering enterprises are of primary importance. The town, which is in a fertile agricultural district, had already achieved significance as a market and commercial centre in the 13th century. In 1219 it was granted special privileges by Schwerin. From 1316 to 1436 the princes of the Wends resided there, and from 1555 to 1695 it was the seat of the dukes of Mecklenburg-Güstrow. The town has a number of historic structures, including the 16th-century castle and town hall and a 13th-century church. An institute of animal husbandry and a pedagogical institute are located there.

GUTENBERG, JOHANN (c. 1398-1468), inventor of printing in Europe, was born between 1394 and 1399, the third child of Friele Gensfleisch, patrician of Mainz, Ger., alternatively named (zum) Gutenberg from a family estate, and his second wife, Else Wirich. Johann became a goldsmith, acquiring skill in metalwork which served and perhaps inspired his invention. He was exiled, probably in Sept. 1428, through discord between the patricians of Mainz and the city council and guilds. Between 1430 and 1444 he is found at Strassburg (mod. Strasbourg, France), arresting the city clerk of Mainz for an alleged debt of 310 guilders (March 28, 1430); sued for breach of promise by a Strassburg patrician lady, Ennelin zu der Iserin Thüre (1436-37); paying tax on a well-stocked wine cellar (July 9, 1439); and borrowing 80 Strassburg pounds (Nov. 17, 1442). Meanwhile he was already working on the invention of printing. About early 1438 he entered into partnership with the Strassburg citizens Andreas Dritzehen (whom he had trained some years before in gem cutting) and Andreas Heilmann, undertaking for a fee of 160 guilders to instruct them in a new method of manufacturing mirrors to be sold at the Aachen pilgrimage fair the next year. Finding that the pilgrimage would not occur until 1440, Gutenberg promised, for a further 250 guilders under a five-year contract, to teach them yet another new process. Andreas Dritzehen died at Christmas 1438, and his brothers Georg and Claus sued Gutenberg for admission to the partnership or alternatively for the money advanced by Andreas. On Dec. 12, 1439, judgment was given in Gutenberg's favour. The witnesses' evidence shows conclusively that Gutenberg had constructed a printing press complete with type, for it mentions a press, type (*Formen*), a stock of lead and other metals and a mysterious instrument in four pieces secured by two handscrews (probably a type-casting mold). Hans Dünne, a goldsmith, testified that he sold to Gutenberg 100 guilders' worth of "material pertaining to printing," as early as 1436, and Heilmann owned a paper mill. Presumably Gutenberg printed something at Strassburg, since all necessary equipment was available, but no known specimen survives. Gutenberg last appears as a Strassburg taxpayer on March 12, 1444, and after four blank years is found at Mainz, borrowing 150 guilders on Oct. 17, 1448. It is remotely possible that he was connected during the interval with the abortive printing venture of Procopius Waldvogel at Avignon (1444-46).

In 1450 Gutenberg borrowed 800 guilders from the Mainz burgher Johann Fust (q.v.), on the security of his printing equipment, and about two years later received a further 800 guilders on condition of taking Fust into partnership. Gutenberg's allegation that Fust agreed to pay 300 guilders annually for board, keep, wages, rent, paper, parchment and ink, and to forego interest, is open to doubt. In 1455 Fust foreclosed on loans and interest, demanding 2,026 guilders in all and calling Peter Schoeffer, Gutenberg's most skilled employee, to testify on his behalf. Judgment was passed against Gutenberg on Nov. 6, 1455. Fust thus obtained possession of Gutenberg's materials, or at least of the 42-line Bible and Psalter types, and continued to print in association with Schoeffer.

No surviving printed matter bears Gutenberg's name as printer; however the monumental 42-line Bible, printed on six presses simultaneously, in one copy of which the hand rubrication was finished on Aug. 24, 1456, and the Psalter, completed by Fust and Schoeffer on Aug. 14, 1457, must both have been well in hand before his break with Fust. It is a moot point how the credit for the superb type design and setting of these books should be divided between Gutenberg and Schoeffer.

On June 21, 1457, Gutenberg was still in Mainz. In 1458 and thereafter he defaulted on interest payments for the Strassburg loan of 1442. On Jan. 17, 1465, he was appointed courtier to Archbishop Adolf of Mainz with the rank of nobleman, clothing, keep and other perquisites. He died on Feb. 3, 1468, and was buried in the Franciscan church at Mainz. At the time of his death he had possession of "forms, letters, instruments, tools, and other things pertaining to the work of printing," the property of Dr. Conrad Homery, who acknowledged receipt thereof from the archbishop on Feb. 26, 1468, promising not to use it outside Mainz and in case of sale to give preference to a resident citizen.

Two groups of books exist which it is natural and attractive, but far from proved correct, to assign to Gutenberg (whether or not acting as his own master), because they conveniently fill the period between his break with Fust and the 1460s. The first is printed in type resembling, but apparently preceding in design, that of the 42-line Bible and presumably begins with the 31-line Indulgence of 1454. Next, in a sequence marked by slight progressive modifications of the type, come other small works, including a German poem on the Last Judgment, an indeterminate number (maximum 24) of editions of Donatus' Latin Grammar, and four calendars, one of which, the so-called Astronomical Calendar, was once wrongly assigned to c. 1447 but belongs typographically to c. 1457. In the latest state of the type is the 36-line Bible, reprinted from the 42-line Bible c. 1458–59. In 1460 this type was in the hands of Albrecht Pfister at Bamberg. Immediately after, the Catholicon, a large encyclopaedic dictionary, appeared in a small gothic type, including in 1459–62, which boasts, possibly in Gutenberg's own words, that the book was printed at Mainz in 1460 "with the protection of the All-Highest, Who often reveals to the humble what He conceals from the wise." A Missale speciale, printed in an earlier state of the smaller of the two 1457 Psalter types, was legitimately dated c. 1454 until evidence from paper, liturgiology, etc., showed that it was printed c. 1473–74, probably at Basel, Switz., perhaps with type acquired from Homery after Gutenberg's death.

Gutenberg's priority as inventor of western printing from movable type cannot be seriously contested. The essential and unique elements of his invention consisted of a hand mold, with punch-stamped matrices, for precision casting of type in large quantities; a type-metal alloy (probably lead with tin and antimony) with low melting point and quick, undistorted solidification; a press adapted from those used, e.g., by papermakers and bookbinders; and an oil-based printing ink. None of these features existed in Chinese or Korean printing (of which it is unlikely that Gutenberg had ever heard) or in the European techniques of stamping letters on bookbindings, textiles, etc., or in woodcut printing. Woodcut block-books date only from the 1460s onward. The type-set works formerly attributed to the semimythical Laurens Coster of Haarlem, c. 1440, are now assigned to the early 1470s at Utrecht. No authentic portrait, autograph or press material of Gutenberg is known.

BIBLIOGRAPHY.—Checklist of literature: D. C. McMurtrie, The Invention of Printing, (1942). Original documents: K. Schorbach, "Die urkundlichen Nachrichten über Gutenberg," in Festschrift zum 500-jährigen Geburtstag Gutenbergs (1900); trans. in D. C. McMurtrie, The Gutenberg Documents (1941). General studies with bibliographies: A. Ruppel, Johannes Gutenberg (1947). See also O. W. Fuhrmann, Die Technik Gutenbergs und ihre Vorstufe (1961); V. Scholderer, "The Invention of Printing," in The Dolphin, no. 3 (1938); V. Fuhrmann; C. Wehmer, "The Invention of Printing," in The Library, ser. 4, vol. 21 (1940); C. Wehmer, Mainzer Probedrucke (1948), reviewed by V. Scholderer in The Library, ser. 5, vol. 5 (1951); Sir I. Masson, The Mainz Psalters and the Missale Speciale," (1954); A. H. Stevenson, "Paper Evidence and the Missale Speciale," Gutenberg-Jahrbuch (1962).

(G. D. P.)

GÜTERSLOH, a town of Germany which after partition of the nation following World War II was located in the Land (state) of North Rhine-Westphalia in the Federal Republic of Germany. Pop. (1961) 52,346. Gütersloh is well served by railway and the Cologne-Berlin Autobahn, which, together with the railway route from Gütersloh to the Teutoburg forest, connect the town with all the main industrial and trade centres of the Federal Republic. It has a wide variety of industries, particularly machinery, metal goods, furniture, silk and cotton, printing and meat products. Well-tended parks and gardens give the town and its surrounding districts an attractive appearance. There are modern primary, secondary, vocational and commercial schools. (H. Dr.)

GUTHRUM (GODRUM or GUTHORM) (d. 890). Danish invader of England who fought against King Alfred and later became king of East Anglia, is first mentioned in the Anglo-Saxon Chronicle under the year 875 as one of three Danish "kings" (i.e., warriors of royal blood) who advanced to Cambridge to attack Wessex when the original "Great Army" of 865 split into two parts and the followers of Healfdene settled in the north. Guthrum's part in the southern fighting of 876–878 is not specified, but he clearly emerged as the leader of the Danes, on whose behalf he made peace with Alfred in 878 at Aller in Somerset, accepting baptism under the name Aethelstan. Alfred himself stood godfather. Guthrum withdrew to Cirencester and subsequently to East Anglia, where he founded in 880 a partially Christian state and issued a coinage under his baptismal name. He made peace with Alfred about 886 in a treaty still extant. Guthrum's death is noticed by the Chronicle in 890, and he appears to have been vaguely remembered in Danish and Norman traditions preserved by Saxo Grammaticus and Dudo of St. Quentin. (AL. C.)

GUTIERREZ NAJERA, MANUEL (1859–1895), Mexican poet, who in 1894 founded the Revista azul, Mexico's first modernist journal. Born in Mexico City on Dec. 22, 1859, he received his early education from his mother, and later studied French and Latin. His first article appeared in the newspaper La Iberia when he was 13; and until his death he published several a week. He used many pseudonyms, "El Duque Job" being his favourite.

His prose and verse show the influence of Alfred de Musset, Théophile Gautier, Paul Verlaine and other French writers, and represent the transition between romanticism and modernism. His poems are musical, elegant, melancholy and often witty. The best known are "La Duquesa Job," "La Serenata de Schubert," and "De blanco." Modernist writers were influenced by his graceful and light prose style, in which he wrote *crónicas* or sketches (a genre he created) and excellent short stories, as *Rip-Rip—* reminiscent of Washington Irving—and the *Historia de un peso falso*. He died in Mexico City on Feb. 3, 1895.

BIBLIOGRAPHY.—*Obras completas*, 4 vol. (1898-1910); Nell Walker, *The Life and Works of Manuel Gutiérrez Nájera* (1927); Boyd G. Carter, *Manuel Gutiérrez Nájera* (1956).
(L. Ll.)

GUTIÉRREZ SOLANA, JOSÉ (1886-1945), Spanish painter of the Castilian school, was born on Feb. 28, 1886, in Madrid and died there on June 24, 1945. He lived in Madrid throughout his life, except for a few trips in Spain and abroad.

He is remarkable for his devotion to his chosen subject matter and for his treatment of it in a tragic and restrained style in which the influence of academic training is modified by the romantic-expressionist tradition of Goya and James Ensor. His technique is austere and tortured; his colours are dull and earthy, with yellowish ochres, blacks and grays. He depicts the most desolate aspects of human existence, with solitary figures dominated by a lifeless environment. The usual characters of Spanish painting, in gloomy landscapes and taverns full of masked faces, skulls and old carvings are essential themes of his work.

But Gutiérrez Solana's whole view of life in all its sourness, with its brothel scenes, dreary suburban bars and corteges, is transfigured by the powerful internal consistency of his design and by the subtlety of his colour scheme. His vigorous nudes are particularly notable, being quite unlike those of most other painters; so also are his conversation pieces showing family reunions, assemblies of professional men or parties of friends, such as "La Botica" in the Barcelona museum.

BIBLIOGRAPHY.—M. Sánchez Camargo, *Solana* (1945); Emilio M. Aguilera, *Solana* (1947); also special number devoted to Gutiérrez Solana of *Papeles de Son Armadans*, year iii, vol. xi, no. 33 (1958).
(J. GL.)

GUTTA-PERCHA, the name applied to the evaporated milky fluid or latex furnished by several trees chiefly found in the islands of the Malay archipelago, also in Brazil. The hard, non-brittle characteristics of gutta-percha find use in such varied articles as golf ball covers, electrical insulation, cable coverings and chewing gum. Because of its high cost, gutta-percha is gradually being replaced by newer synthetic materials such as polyethylene, vinyl resins and nylon.

Botanical Origin and Distribution.—The best gutta-percha of Malaya was chiefly derived from two trees belonging to the family Sapotaceae—*Palaquium gutta* (no longer cultivated) and *P. oblongifolia*. Allied trees of the same genus and of the same family yield similar but usually inferior products. Among them may be mentioned species of *Payena*.

Gutta-percha trees often attain a height of 70 to 100 ft. and the trunk may have a diameter of from 2 to 3 ft. They are mature when about 30 years old. The leaves of *Palaquium*, which are obovate-lanceolate with a distinct pointed apex, occur in clusters at the end of the branches and are bright green and smooth on the upper surface but on the lower surface are yellowish-brown and covered with silky hairs. The leaves are usually about 6 in. long and about 2 in. wide at the centre. The flowers are white, and the seeds are contained in an ovoid berry about 1 in. long.

The gutta-percha tree is almost entirely confined to the Malay peninsula and its immediate neighbourhood. It includes a region within 6° north and south of the equator and 93°-119° longitude, where the temperature ranges from 66° to 90° F. and the atmosphere is exceedingly moist. The trees may be grown from seeds or from cuttings.

Preparation of Gutta-Percha.—The gutta is furnished by the grayish milky fluid, the latex, chiefly secreted in cylindrical vessels or cells in the cortex. Latex also occurs in the leaves of the tree and may be removed from the powdered leaves by the use of

appropriate solvents, but the process is not practicable commercially. The latex flows slowly where an incision is made through the bark, but not nearly so freely as the India rubber latex. On this account the Malays usually fell the tree to collect the latex, which is done by chopping off the branches and removing circles of the bark, forming cylindrical channels about an inch wide at various points about a foot apart down the trunk. The latex exudes and fills these channels, from which it is removed and converted into gutta by boiling in open vessels over wood fires.

The work is usually carried on in the wet season when the latex is more fluid and more abundant. Sometimes, when the latex is thick, water is added before boiling. The best results are obtained from mature trees, which furnish about two to three pounds of gutta.

The Chinese and Malays were acquainted with the characteristic property of gutta-percha of softening in warm water and of regaining its hardness when cold, but this plastic property seems to have been utilized only for ornamental purposes, the construction of walking sticks, knife handles, whips, etc. John Tradescant brought samples of the curious material to Europe about the middle of the 17th century. (X.)

Character and Properties.—Gutta-percha appears in commerce as gray blocks, often with a reddish tinge. It is a hard, inelastic solid, just soft enough to be indented by the nail and is tough at ordinary temperature. Gutta-percha from the tree is in a crystalline form (called alpha), which melts at about 65° C. Above this temperature it becomes soft and plastic but is still inelastic. On slow cooling again gutta-percha returns to the alpha crystalline form, but with rapid cooling a different crystalline form (called beta) is obtained, which melts at 56° C. These two forms differ in the pattern in which the molecules are arranged and can be distinguished by X-ray methods. The beta form is unstable and can be converted to the alpha form by slight warming. About 60% of gutta-percha is normally crystalline at ordinary temperature, the remainder being amorphous.

Composition and Structure.—The principal constituent of gutta-percha is a hydrocarbon *gutta* of the empirical formula C_5H_8, having a molecular weight of about 30,000. Each molecule is composed of isoprene units, joined in regular fashion into a long chain. There are two possible geometric configurations of isoprene units within a molecule: the *trans* form, exemplified by gutta-percha, and the *cis* form, typical of India rubber or caoutchouc. The *trans* and *cis* forms are identical chemically. The difference in physical character lies in the geometry of the molecules.

The hydrocarbon of gutta-percha is unsaturated, having one double bond for each *gutta* unit. It will react with chlorine. The reaction with sulfur is utilized to vulcanize gutta-percha, rendering it nonplastic and insoluble. Gutta-percha is dissolved by carbon disulfide, chloroform and benzene. Alkaline solutions or dilute acids do not affect it. Strong sulfuric acid chars it when warm and nitric acid effects complete oxidation. When exposed to air and light, gutta-percha rapidly deteriorates, absorbing oxygen and producing a brittle resin. Ozone attacks gutta-percha extremely rapidly with similar results. The attack by air or ozone is slowed greatly by adding antioxidants, generally aromatic amines or phenols. When heated in the absence of air at a high temperature, gutta-percha decomposes into a mixture of isoprene and higher hydrocarbons. Crude gutta-percha contains resinous materials, which are usually deleterious. These resinous components can be removed by solvents.

Gutta-percha is identical in nature to balata, which is obtained from *Bumelia retusa*. Chicle (*q.v.*) is a similar material, having about half the molecular weight of gutta-percha.
(A. W. MR.; J. A. DN.)

GUTTER, in architecture, a horizontal channel or trough contrived to carry away the water from a flat or sloping roof to its discharge down a vertical pipe or through a spout or gargoyle; more specifically, but loosely, the similar channel at the side of a street. In Greek and Roman temples the cymatium of the cornice was the gutter, and the water was discharged through the mouths of carved lions' heads. In medieval work the gutter rested on the top of the wall or on a corbel table, and the water was discharged through gargoyles. Sometimes, however, a parapet or pierced balustrade was carried outside the gutter. In many buildings the parapet is only a continuation of the wall below, and the gutter is set back and carried in a trough resting on the lower end of the roof timbers. The most practical form is an eaves gutter which projects more or less in front of the wall and is secured to and carried by the rafters of the roof. In French Renaissance work the gutter is frequently concealed behind a rich cresting in stone, lead or copper at the edge of the main cornice.

GUY, THOMAS (c. 1644-1724), founder of Guy's hospital, London, was the son of a lighterman and coal dealer at Southwark. After an apprenticeship of eight years with a bookseller, he began business on his own account in 1668. He dealt largely in Bibles, which were poorly and incorrectly printed in England. These he at first imported from the Netherlands but subsequently he obtained from the University of Oxford the privilege of printing. He died on Dec. 27, 1724. Having accumulated a substantial fortune through printing and from various investments, Guy acquired a reputation for his philanthropies. He established an almshouse at Tamworth, and in 1707 built three wards of St. Thomas's hospital, as well as assisting many distressed persons individually and supporting a number of poor relations. He erected Guy's hospital, leaving for its endowment more than £200,000, and endowed other charities. He was member of parliament for Tamworth from 1695 to 1707. He was chosen sheriff of London, but declined to serve.

See S. Wilkes and G. T. Bettany, *A Biographical History of Guy's Hospital* (1892); H. C. Cameron, *Mr. Guy's Hospital, 1726-1948* (1954).

GÜTZLAFF, KARL FRIEDRICH AUGUST (1803-1851), German Lutheran pastor, pioneer of mission work in China, was born at Pyritz, Pomerania (now Pyrzyce, Pol.) July 8, 1803, and attended J. Jänicke's missionary school in Berlin. In 1826 he was sent to Java by the Dutch Missionary society, but soon became a *Freimissionar* (independent missionary). As interpreter to the British East India company he obtained entrance to a China otherwise closed to foreigners, proselytized successfully, despite hostility aroused by the Opium War (1839-42), trained Chinese as preachers, and in 1847 formed 300 of them into a society that evangelized in 12 out of 18 provinces. Returning to Germany once (1849-50), he gained enthusiastic support and new assistants, though criticized for the superficiality of his work. He was aided first by the Berliner Hilfsverein, then (1873) by the Rheinische and (1882) the Berliner Missionsgesellschaft. He translated the Bible into Chinese, published a *Journal of Three Voyages Along the Coast of China in 1831, 1832 and 1833* (1834), *Bericht einer Reise von China nach England* ... (1851) and a *Sketch of Chinese History, Ancient and Modern* (1834). He died in Hong Kong, Aug. 9, 1851. Many of his plans were realized by his admirer, Hudson Taylor, founder of the interdenominational China Inland mission.

See H. Schlyter, *Karl Gützlaff als Missionar in China* (1946).
(C. L. A. R. H.)

GUTZKOW, KARL FERDINAND (1811-1878), German novelist and dramatist, who opened a way to the German social novel of the 20th century, was born March 17, 1811, at Berlin. In 1832 he published anonymously his *Briefe eines Narren an eine Närrin*, and in 1833 appeared *Maha-Guru, Geschichte eines Gottes*, a fantastic and satirical romance. In 1835 he published *Wally, die Zweiflerin*, an attack on marriage which marks the beginning of the revolt of "Young Germany" against romanticism. He was violently attacked by Wolfgang Menzel, and the federal diet condemned Gutzkow to three months' imprisonment and ordered the suppression of all he had written or might yet write. During his imprisonment at Mannheim, Gutzkow wrote his treatise *Zur Philosophie der Geschichte* (1836). On his release he produced *Richard Savage* (1839), a play which immediately made the round of all the German theatres. Of his numerous other plays a few keep a place in the German repertory. In 1847, Gutzkow went to Dresden, where he succeeded J. L. Tieck as literary adviser to the court theatre. Meanwhile he had written the novels *Seraphine* (1838) and *Blasedow und seine Söhne* (3 vol.; 1838), a satire on the educational theories of the time. In 1850 appeared the first of the nine volumes of *Die Ritter vom Geiste*, which may be regarded as the starting point for the modern German social novel. *Der Zauberer von Rom* (9 vol.; 1858-61) is a powerful study of Roman Catholic life in southern Germany. Gutzkow died at Sachsenhausen on Dec. 16, 1878.

BIBLIOGRAPHY.—Gutzkow's dramatic works were published in 20 vol. (1873-75) and his collected works in 12 vol. (1872-76). For Gutzkow's life *see* his various autobiographical writings: *Aus der Knabenzeit* (1852), *Rückblicke auf mein Leben* (1875) and the biography in the selected works (1908). *See* also H. H. Houben, *Studien über die Dramen Gutzkows* (1898), *Gutzkow-Funde* (1901); J. E. Dresch, *Gutzkow et la jeune Allemagne* (1904); E. Metis, *Karl Gutzkow als Dramatiker* (1915); P. Westra, *Gutzkows religiöse Ansichten* (1948).

GUYANA (formerly BRITISH GUIANA), a republic and an independent member of the Commonwealth of Nations, lies in the northeastern part of South America. Its area is 83,000 sq.mi. (215,000 sq.km.); its seaboard extends about 230 mi. (370 km.). The geographical term "Guiana" (probably "land of waters") applies to the entire region between the Amazon, Orinoco, and Negro rivers.

PHYSICAL GEOGRAPHY

Geology and Structure.—The main structural features are similar to those of eastern Brazil (*see* Brazil: *Physical Geography: Geology and Surface Features*; *see* also Guiana Highlands). Most of the country consists of an ancient crystalline plateau of Precambrian (Archean) age, generally less than 500 ft. (152 m.) above sea level. The crystalline platform was depressed below the sea in late Tertiary and early Quaternary times. Granite islands crumbled to form the white sands which overlie the platform inland of the coast alluvium.

The platform was raised and given a slight seaward tilt in geologically recent times. Important features of the platform are veins of gold and diamonds, and bauxite deposits derived from

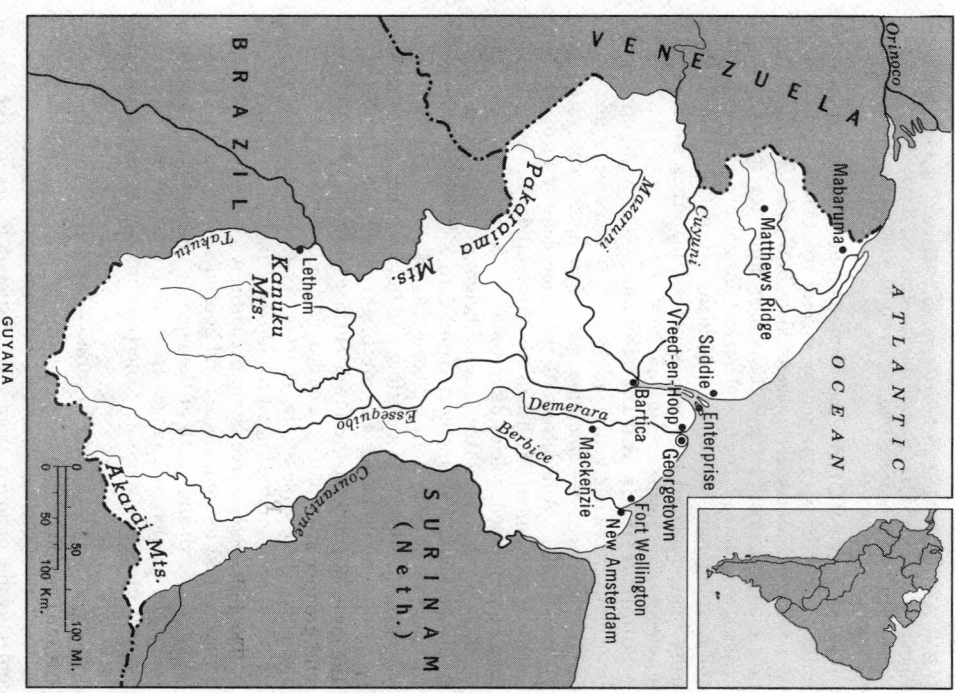

GUYANA

lateritic earths under conditions of intense weathering.

Relief and Drainage.—The massive sandstones of the interior form steep, almost vertical faces, down which streams plunge in immense falls, cutting deep canyons. The more prominent heights include the Akarai Mountains, or Serra Acarai, on the southern frontier at about 2,000 ft. (610 m.) and the Pakaraima Mountains on the western frontier, which culminate in the great massif of Roraima at 9,219 ft. (2,810 m.). On either side of the western Kanuku Mountains is a savanna area.

The drainage in Guyana is poor, and the headstreams of Amazon and Essequibo tributaries are often confused. The ill-defined Lake Amuku may be the site of Manoa, the city of Eldorado (q.v.). The rivers draining the crystalline platform have few tributaries and are separated from their neighbours only by low divides. The average gradient is only one foot to one mile. (*See* BERBICE; COURANTYNE; DEMERARA; ESSEQUIBO.)

Climate.—Guyana has the climatic characteristics of an equatorial lowland, namely rather high temperatures, heavy rainfall with relatively small seasonal differences, high humidity, and high average cloud cover. Temperatures are remarkably uniform. At Georgetown, the average monthly temperature varies from 26° to 28° C (79° to 82° F) with a daily range of about 8.3° C (15° F). The effects of constant heat and high humidity are mitigated near the coast by the northeast trade winds.

Rainfall derives mainly from the movement of the intertropical front, or doldrums. It is heavy everywhere in the forested zone and on the coast. The annual average at Georgetown is about 90 in. (2,286 mm.). On the interior savannas it is about 70 in. (1,780 mm.). On the coast, a long wet season from April to August, and a short wet season from December to early February are sufficiently well marked on the average, but in the southern savannas the short wet season is not experienced. Total annual rainfall is variable and years of drought occur.

Vegetation.—Many plants of the coast grow in shallow brackish water and help to protect or extend the land. The mangrove and many salt-water grasses are among these. The wet savanna behind the coast has coarse tufted grasses and a wide scattering of palms, notably the coconut, truli, and manicole. The high forest or selva covers most of the country and is of extraordinary variety and magnificence. Prominent trees include the greenheart and the wallaba on the sandy soils of the northern edge; the giant mora and crabwood on swampy sites; the balata and other latex producers; and many trees yielding handsome cabinet woods. The interior savanna is mostly open grassland, with much bare rock, many termite hills, and clumps of ita palm.

Animal Life.—All forms are immensely varied and abundant, though few, apart from birds and insects, are normally visible. The tapir is the largest land mammal, the ocelot the fiercest, and monkeys and deer the commonest. Among the more exotic are the sloth, the great anteater, the capybara or bush pig, and the armadillo. Bird life includes the vulture, kiskadee, blue sacki, hummingbird, kingfisher, and scarlet ibis of the coast and lower rivers; and the macaw, tinamou, bellbird, and cock-of-the-rock in the forest and savanna. The cayman is the commonest of the larger freshwater creatures. The giant anaconda, or water boa, is the largest of many kinds of snake, and the bushmaster the most vicious. Lizards are numerous, and include the iguana of the lower rivers. Shark and sting rays are found offshore. Snapper and grouper are the most esteemed of the fish commonly landed.

PEOPLE AND POPULATION

The indigenous peoples are collectively known as Amerindians. Their numbers in Guyana in the mid-1960s were estimated at approximately 29,500, a threefold increase since 1930 and a reversal of centuries of decline. They include the Warraus, Arawaks, Caribs, Wapisianas (Wapishanas) Arecunas, the mixed "Spanish Arawaks" of the Moruka River, and many more in the forest areas. The Makusi (Macussi or Macushi) are the most prominent of the savanna peoples.

Until the 19th century the forest peoples had in common the manufacture of polished stone implements and coil pottery, weav-

ing (including bead decoration and the manufacture of hammocks), cassava cultivation, the use of the blowgun, vegetable poisons for hunting and fishing, and fish traps.

The Amerindians are rarely seen in the populated coastal areas. Since 1953 they have had important rights in reservations totaling more than 6,000 sq.mi. (15,540 sq.km.) but are not confined to them. They are useful workers in the cattle and logging industries.

The other major elements in the population of Guyana are all predominantly coastal dwellers. Descendants of African slaves form the oldest group of nonindigenous peoples in Guyana. They abandoned the plantations after emancipation to become independent peasantry or town dwellers. The "East Indians" of Guyana came predominantly as indentured labour from India to replace the Africans in plantation work. They form the largest racial group in the country and have been increasing more rapidly than any of the others. They are the mainstay of plantation agriculture, and many are independent farmers and landowners, have done well in trade, and are well represented among the professions.

The Chinese and Portuguese also entered originally as agricultural labourers but are now rarely found outside the towns. They are active in business and the professions, and their influence is disproportionate to their numbers, but they have not been increasing. Europeans other than Portuguese are few and most are short-term inhabitants. While every kind of racial mixture may be found, mulattoes are by far the commonest. Most of them live in towns, and a high proportion are in clerical and professional work.

At the census of 1960 the total population was 560,330; in mid-1965 it was estimated at 647,000. All but a small proportion live on the coastal plain east of the Pomeroon River. Georgetown (q.v.), the capital, had, with its environs, a population of approximately 162,000; New Amsterdam, for long the second town, had about 15,000 inhabitants but has been exceeded by the bauxite centre, Mackenzie, with about 20,000.

Medical and sanitary improvements resulted in a rapid increase in the population after the 1930s. Between 1946 and 1960 population increased by nearly 50%. The estimated proportions of the racial groups were (December 1964): East Indian 50% (1931, 42%); of African descent 31%; of mixed descent 9%; Amerindians 4.6%; Portuguese 1%; other Europeans and Chinese less than 1% each.

HISTORY

The coast of Guiana was sighted by Columbus in 1498, but the area, long known as the Wild Coast, proved unattractive to the Spanish and Portuguese because of the lack of gold and the difficulties of movement. Although Spain resisted for awhile, the Guiana coast was left to the Dutch, French, and English. Their attempts at colonization and exploration were almost wholly abortive until early in the 17th century. During the 17th and 18th centuries the Dutch were the leading colonists; most British activity was an offshoot of developments in the West Indies.

The early settlements were typically a few miles up the larger rivers. Dutch settlements existed on the Courantyne, Essequibo, and Cayenne rivers by 1616. The Dutch West India Company (q.v.) was founded (1621), the slave trade was established, and official appointments in command of settlements were made. The Essequibo settlements centred on Fort Kyk-over-all, on an island at the junction of the Mazaruni and the Essequibo. The colony of Berbice was established in 1627 at Fort Nassau, about 50 mi. (80 km.) from the sea, and was virtually run by the van Peere family for more than a century. A successful British colony was planted on the Suriname River by Lord Willoughby of Parham in 1651, the colonists coming mainly from Barbados. Cayenne was finally established as French only in 1674.

Early in the 18th century, colonists were attracted to the sea coasts by the fertility of the soil. The Berbice estuary was settled in 1732, and a fort was established on Fort Island in the Essequibo estuary. The greatest figure in 18th-century history was Laurens Storm van's Gravesande, who was in Essequibo from 1738 to 1772. He began the orderly development of Demerara; kept the slave population in order by firm but humane action; established free immigration for all nationalities and remitted taxation for the immigrants' first ten years; and encouraged exploration, notably in the case of Nicholas Horstman, who penetrated the Rupununi savanna and descended the Rio Negro in 1739-41.

Settlements changed hands with bewildering frequency during the wars of the period 1780-1815. During a brief French occupation, Longchamps, later called Georgetown, was established at the mouth of the Demerara; the Dutch renamed it Stabroek and continued to develop it. The British took over in 1796 and remained in possession except for short intervals until 1814, when they purchased Demerara, Berbice, and Essequibo in the settlement that ended the Napoleonic Wars. Surinam went to the Dutch and Cayenne to the French. The 19th-century pattern was finally established when Berbice, Demerara, and Essequibo were united in 1831 as the colony of British Guiana.

During 1835-44 Sir Robert H. Schomburgk (q.v.) surveyed the main geographical features of British Guiana with a view to fixing boundaries. However, a large proportion of the forested area is still virtually unknown in any detail.

The slave trade was abolished in 1807, when there were about 100,000 slaves in the three British colonies. After emancipation in 1834 African labour left the plantations, and large areas of land went out of cultivation. Of the many attempts to organize immigration of suitable labour, only that for Asian Indians was at all successful.

During the rest of the 19th century the colony was almost overwhelmed with difficulties, and was not helped by the indifference of Britain. Reliance on a single crop, sugarcane, was the main fault, and this was not corrected until well into the 20th century.

Settlement began on the Rupununi savanna in 1860 but proceeded very slowly. Gold was discovered in 1879, and a boom in the 1890s helped the colony over a difficult spell. The North Western District was organized in 1889 and was the cause of a sharp international flurry in 1895 when the U.S. supported Venezuela's claims to the territory. In the early 1960s Venezuela revived its territorial claims on British Guiana.

The Report of the Moyne Commission, not published in full until 1945 although the Commission had been appointed in 1938, led to substantial welfare and development grants from Britain. The British inherited from the Dutch a singularly complicated constitutional structure. Except for a major change in 1891 (which simplified it) this remained until 1928 when a typical crown colony system was introduced. In 1953 a new constitution, with universal adult suffrage, a bicameral elected legislature, and a ministerial system was introduced, and, subject to several revisions, has remained in force.

From 1953 to 1966, the political history of the colony was very stormy. The first elected government, formed by the People's Progressive Party (PPP) led by Cheddi Jagan, seemed so pro-Communist that the British government suspended the constitution in October 1953 and sent in troops. The constitution was not restored until 1957. The PPP split along racial lines, Jagan leading a predominantly East Indian party and Forbes Burnham leading a party of African descendants, the People's National Congress (PNC). At the elections of 1957 and 1961, the PPP was returned with working majorities and formed governments which pursued moderate policies. From 1961 to 1964 severe rioting and a long general strike led to the return of British troops to keep order, and the country was in grave economic difficulties.

To answer the PNC allegation that the existing electoral system unduly favoured the PPP, the British government introduced for the elections of December 1964 a new system of proportional representation. The result reflected racial divisions with considerable accuracy. The PNC formed a coalition government thereafter with the United Force Party, a group broadly representative of European and mixed racial interests. This government, led by Forbes Burnham, took the colony into independence under its new name, Guyana, in May 1966. The PNC was returned to power by the general elections of December 1968 and on Feb. 23, 1970. Guyana became a republic within the Commonwealth. Raymond A. Chung, a high court trial judge and the son of a Chinese farmer, was elected by Parliament as the first president of the Republic of Guyana.

ADMINISTRATION AND SOCIAL CONDITIONS

The Government.—The constitution for independent Guyana provided for a governor general and a government consisting of a prime minister and a cabinet collectively responsible to a National Assembly of 53 members elected by proportional representation. With the establishment of the republic in 1970, the president, appointed by the Assembly, is the head of state.

Apart from Georgetown and New Amsterdam, which are municipalities, the country is divided for local government purposes into six coastal and three interior divisions. The coastal divisions are subdivided into villages and country districts, with councils responsible to a local government board. The interior divisions comprise seven-eighths of the area of the country but have a population of less than 40,000. They are directly administered by the central government. A number of "Amerindian districts" have been demarcated for the sole occupation of Amerindians, and local councils have been formed in some of them.

Employment.—Trade unionism was officially encouraged in the mid-1960s and the unions became fairly powerful. In the sugar industry piece-rate wage systems prevailed, and incentive schemes were particularly directed at improving regularity of work. The sugar industry was by far the largest employer, but its labour force of 18,000 was being steadily diminished by mechanization. The bauxite industry was a relatively small employer. Rice cultivation was mainly a peasant industry. Rice milling was on a small-scale except where connected with government irrigation schemes. The timber industry was the only other considerable employer.

Sugar and rice growing are seasonal occupations, so there has always been unemployment, underemployment, and casual labour. The rapid rise of population has aggravated the problem. It was being countered by efforts to make more drained land available and to introduce new local industries.

Health.—The standard of health was generally good. Control of malaria and other formerly endemic diseases was very effective in populous areas. Low dietary standards were being gradually raised by education and propaganda.

Education.—Education was free and compulsory from 6 to 14 years in the mid-1960s, though attendance was far from complete, especially in rural areas. There was a teachers' training college in Georgetown. Well-organized educational broadcasting helped the schools. The Queen's College, founded in 1844, was government-maintained. A technical institute has made progress since 1945, and the Carnegie School of Home Economics has had a long and distinguished history. In 1963 the University of Guyana was established in Georgetown, initially for part-time students.

NATURAL RESOURCES AND THE ECONOMY

Land Use. *The Coast.*—Beginning in the early 18th century a narrow strip of coastland, three to six miles deep, was turned into plantation land by damming back the swamp waters inland and erecting a dike against the sea. The superfluous water drained toward the sea through sluices in the sea dam, which could be opened only as the tide receded. Parts of this elaborate system became ruined during periods of decline of plantation agriculture, and the agricultural wealth of Guyana depended on the efficient exploitation of the relatively few miles of drained land remaining. The soil won from the swamp and the sea is fertile though hard, and a great variety of crops has been produced on it. Sugarcane reigned supreme for more than a century and continued to do so in the mid-1960s. Readiness to use new strains of sugarcane and mechanization produced more sugar than ever before.

Rice growing was the second industry of the coast. It was mainly in peasant hands and had been the object of much official encouragement through provision of drainage facilities, marketing schemes, and modern rice mills. Much of the coastland was devoted to small-scale farming for sugarcane, cassava, corn (maize), vegetables, fruit, cattle, and poultry. The sandier areas are suited to coconuts, which were the third most important commercial crop. The coastal belt, though incompletely drained, offered the most obvious scope for settlement. Though only 10% of the area of the country, it directly supported about 90% of the population.

The Forest.—High forest (selva) covered 85% of the country in the mid-1960s, and was magnificent in its size and luxuriance. The timbers were difficult to cut and transport, however, and in spite of great effort the forest remained a mainly latent resource.

The Interior Savanna.—In the southwest is grassland, interspersed with bare rock and termite hills. Cattle are reared on the open-range system, and tobacco is grown for local consumption.

Minerals.—Gold production virtually ceased after 1958. Diamonds were produced steadily on a small scale. Of a number of known minerals, only bauxite, near Mackenzie on the Demerara River, and manganese in the North West District were actually mined. Bauxite was the second main resource of the country and the deposits were of world importance. Synthetic mullite, a high-grade refractory mineral, was being produced at a plant in Mackenzie as a by-product.

Trade.—Domestic trade was mainly in foodstuffs, and local industry was mainly devoted to processing them. Coconuts occupied about 40,000 ac. (16,187 ha.), but did not fully meet the local demand for cooking oil.

The principal exports were: sugar, bauxite, rum, diamonds, timber and lumber, toilet preparations, and manganese. The principal imports were machinery, food, fuels, and lubricants. About 30% of Guyana's foreign trade was with Great Britain, 18% with Canada, 15% with other Commonwealth countries (mainly in the West Indies), and 22% with the U.S. Great Britain took almost 40% of exports and Canada 25%.

Finance.—The money of account was long the British Indian dollar ($4.80 = £ sterling) until in 1955 U.K. coinage was replaced. Guyana note currency was introduced in 1965. The Guyana dollar (U.S. $.59) was devalued in Nov. 1967 (U.S. $.50) following the devaluation of the British pound. Heavy investment and welfare-scheme investments produced unfavourable annual balances.

Communications.—There were about 1,100 mi. (1,770 km.) of road in the mid-1960s, of which about 300 mi. (482 km.) were bitumen- or concrete-surfaced. The remainder were of burnt clay. A development scheme for the late 1960s envisaged the improvement of 400 mi. (644 km.) of existing road and the building of 300 mi. (482 km.) of new road; and the Demerara was being bridged at Mackenzie. There were also 400 mi. (644 km.) of "vehicular trails" in the Rupununi savanna. The interior had few roads.

Coastal railways ran from Georgetown to the Berbice and Essequibo rivers. A 30-mi. (48-km.) line connected the manganese mines at Matthews Ridge with Port Kaituma on the Barima River. Internal airways services used landing strips and the quieter stretches of rivers. Passengers and equipment were the chief freight. Atkinson Field is an international airport.

Water transport constituted by far the greatest mileage. It was used along the coast, on the canals of the sugar estates, by the ferry and steamer services of the lower rivers, and by the light craft of the interior.

Bauxite was loaded into oceangoing ships at Mackenzie, and manganese ore at Port Kaituma, but otherwise the whole of the country's external trade passed through Georgetown, which maintained direct connections with the West Indies, Surinam, French Guiana, the United Kingdom, Canada, and the United States.

BIBLIOGRAPHY—C. A. Harris and J. A. de Villiers, *Storm van's Gravesande, the Rise of British Guiana* (1911); S. Bracewell, "Geology and Mineral Resources of British Guiana," *Bull. Imp. Inst., Lond.,* vol. 45-i (1947); G. Lighton, "British Guiana" parts i and ii in *Geography* (1950); Dwarka Nath, *History of Indians in British Guiana* (1950); D. B. Fanshawe, *The Vegetation of British Guiana* (1952); International Bank for Reconstruction and Development, *Economic Development of British Guiana* (1954); Michael Swan, *British Guiana* (1957); R. T. Smith, *British Guiana* (1962); J. H. Parry and P. M. Sherlock, *A Short History of the West Indies,* 2nd ed. (1963); Sir Alan Burns, *History of the British West Indies,* 2nd ed. (1965). See also *Colonial Reports British Guiana* (annually); British Guiana Department of Agriculture, *Agric. J. Br. Guiana* (quarterly), 1906 et seq.), and counterparts of the above renamed for "Guyana" from 1966. Current history and statistics are summarized annually in *Britannica Book of the Year.* (G. Ln.)

GUYNEMER, GEORGES MARIE (1894–1917), the most famous French fighter pilot of World War I, was born in Paris on Dec. 24, 1894. He was educated at the Lycée Stanislas and took an early interest in aeronautics. Nevertheless, on the outbreak of World War I he tried unsuccessfully to join the infantry and the cavalry and turned only as a last resort to the air service. He enlisted as a student mechanic, but was later accepted as a pupil pilot and made his first flight on Feb. 17, 1915. He received his pilot's certificate a month later and, on June 8, joined M.S.3 Squadron (*Les Cigognes,* "the Storks") as a corporal pilot. He remained with this squadron for the rest of his life, flying successively Morane-Saulnier two-seaters, Nieuport single-seaters, and Spad fighters. He had phenomenal success as a fighter pilot, shooting down 53 enemy aircraft. Guynemer took off from Saint-Pol Airport on Sept. 11, 1917, on a flight from which he never returned. It was later established that he had been shot down near Poelcapelle, Belg., on that day.

See H. Bordeaux, *Le Chevalier de l'air, Guynemer* (1919). (D. Cr.)

GUY OF WARWICK, a romance popular in France and England from the 13th to the 17th century, and found in English broadside ballads as late as the 19th century. Four versions, translated from French or Anglo-Norman, survive in English: the two earliest, probably dating from c. 1300, are preserved in a manuscript of c. 1330–40. One, in two parts, is followed by a continuation about Guy's son Reinbrun. The earliest French version probably dates from the 12th century, and there are 13th-century versions in French and Anglo-Norman manuscripts. (*See also* FRENCH LITERATURE; ANGLO-NORMAN LITERATURE.)

The earliest English versions, with the Reinbrun continuation, contain most of the incidents on which later verse and prose romances, ballads, a play, and other works are based. The version in two parts has already been recast: it combines the popular romance themes of the hero who wins his lady by deeds of bravery in foreign lands and of the knight who, repenting of his worldly life, becomes a pilgrim. The first part, like the other three English versions, is in short couplets; the second and the sequel are in a 12-line tail-rhyme stanza.

In the first part Guy, son of Sigurd, Saxon steward of the Norman earl of Warwick, wins the earl's daughter Felice by heroic deeds abroad and by killing a dragon in Northumbria. In the second he abandons wife and unborn child, goes on pilgrimage, and kills the Saracen giant Amorant. Returning home an old man, he defeats in a duel near Winchester the African giant Colbrand, the representative of the Danish invaders under Anlaf (Olaf, q.v.), and after living as a hermit dies in his wife's arms.

The romance (first printed in 1500 in England), like the works derived from it, has little literary merit. It lacks structural unity or distinction of style, and probably owes its popularity to its combination of secular with religious interest, and in England to the patriotic appeal of the duel with Colbrand. (This may have a historical origin, not identified.) Otherwise the story is a blend of English traditional with French romance material, in which the French courtly style, with its emphasis on description and analysis, prevails. *See also* ROMANCE.

BIBLIOGRAPHY.—J. E. Wells, *A Manual of the Writings in Middle English 1050–1400* (1916), with bibliography; L. A. Hibbard, *Medieval Romance in England . . . the Sources and Analogues of the Non-Cyclic Metrical Romances* (1924); R. S. Crane, "The Vogue of Guy of Warwick from the Close of the Middle Ages to the Romantic Revival," in *PMLA,* vol. xxx (1915).

GUYON, JEANNE MARIE BOUVIER DE LA MOTTE (1648–1717), French mystic, is best known for her advocacy of Quietism (q.v.). Born at Montargis, April 13, 1648, she was married in 1664 to Jacques Guyon. After his death in 1676 she devoted herself to religion and went, in 1681, to Savoy to work for a foundation of New Catholics, where she was inspired by the teaching of a Barnabite friar, François Lacombe (1643–1715). As her spiritual director he encouraged her particular convictions about the nature of prayer; an emphasis on passivity and an indifference even to eternal salvation. The dissemination of these doctrines aroused the suspicions of the bishop of Geneva and, with Lacombe in attendance, Mme Guyon set out on a period of wandering which took her to Turin and Grenoble. In 1685 she published the most influential of her writings: *Moyen court et très facile de faire oraison.* In 1687 Lacombe was recalled to Paris, imprisoned and remained so until his death. Mme Guyon herself was arrested in 1688, but was released after a few months at the intervention of Mme de Maintenon, who introduced her into the royal circle and allowed her to teach in the girls' school at St. Cyr. She began to correspond with Fénelon (q.v.), who was attracted by a teaching which solved some of his own problems as a spiritual director. The enthusiasm with which Fénelon propagated doctrines coloured by Quietism disturbed J. B. Bossuet (q.v.), who by 1694 became thoroughly alarmed. Mme Guyon asked to be cleared of the accusations against her and in 1695 a conference convened at Issy, where Fénelon undertook her defense. The result was a condemnation of the Quietist teaching. Mme Guyon was arrested; the controversy between Bossuet and Fénelon continued in a pamphlet war. Quietism received papal condemnation in 1699; but it was not until 1703 that her imprisonment ended. Her last years were spent at Blois, where she died on June 9, 1717.

BIBLIOGRAPHY.—Mme Guyon's writings (45 vol.) were published from 1712 to 1720 (reprinted 1767-90). There is no modern critical biography; the best, though out of date, is L. Guerrier, *Mme. Guyon, sa vie, sa doctrine et son influence* (1881). See also A. Largent in *Dictionnaire Théologie Catholique*, vol. 6, col. 1997-2006; R. A. Knox, *Enthusiasm* (1950), pp. 319-352; L. Cognet, *Crépuscule des Mystiques* (1958). (L. Co.)

GUYOT, ARNOLD HENRY (1807-1884), Swiss-U.S. geologist and geographer whose name is perpetuated in the term "guyot," used to describe submerged flat-topped peaks rising from the floor of the ocean, was born at Boudevilliers, near Neuchâtel, Switz., on Sept. 28, 1807. He studied at the College of Neuchâtel and in Germany. In 1838, under the influence of Louis Agassiz, he took up the study of glaciology, making important observations on glacial motion, the structure of glaciers and the movement of moraines. In 1835-40 he was teaching in Paris, and in 1839 he was appointed to the chair of history and physical geography at the Academy of Neuchâtel. In 1848 he settled in the United States at Cambridge, Mass., and was employed until 1854 by the Massachusetts board of education to lecture on geography and teaching methods. The ideas he formulated were incorporated later in his series of school textbooks which served as models in American education for many years. He taught his pupils to observe their own environment, and to consult the topographical map as an introduction to regional studies.

In 1854 Guyot became professor of geology and physical geography at Princeton university, where he remained until his death, on Feb. 8, 1884. He made extensive meteorological observations which led to the establishment of the U.S. weather bureau. For his topographical maps of the Appalachian mountains, and the Catskill region he plotted altitude by means of readings of barometric pressure. His standard works were *Tables, Meteorological and Physical* . . . (4th ed., by W. Libbey, 1887) and *The Earth and Man* . . . (Eng. trans. by C. C. Felton, 1850). From his early years a devout Protestant, he published in 1884 *Creation, or the Biblical Cosmogony in the Light of Modern Science*. (H. M. Ws.)

GUYTON DE MORVEAU, LOUIS BERNARD, BARON (1737-1816), French chemist and co-author of proposals for a revised chemical nomenclature which helped establish the distinction between elements and compounds, was born on Jan. 4, 1737, at Dijon. He studied law at Dijon, and became advocate-general in the *parlement*, until 1782. He devoted his leisure to the study of chemistry, and in 1772 published *Digressions académiques*, containing his views on phlogiston and crystallization. An essay on chemical nomenclature in the *Journal de physique* (May 1782) was developed, with the aid of Antoine L. Lavoisier, Claude L. Berthollet and Antoine F. Fourcroy, into the *Méthode d'une nomenclature chimique* (1787), the principles of which were adopted by chemists throughout Europe. He adopted Lavoisier's views on combustion and published his reasons in the first volume of the section "Chymie, Pharmacie et Metallurgie" of the *Encyclopédie méthodique* (1786), the chemical articles in which were written by him. In 1791 he was elected as member of the legislative assembly, and in 1792 of the convention, becoming a member of the committee of public safety. From 1795 to 1805 he taught at the École Polytechnique, Paris, of which he was the director. He was master of the mint from 1800 to 1814.

In 1811 he was made baron of the French empire. He died in Paris on Jan. 2, 1816.

In addition to many scientific papers, Guyton wrote *Mémoire sur l'éducation publique* (1762); a satirical poem "Le Rat iconoclaste, ou le Jésuite croqué" (1763); *Discours publics et éloges* (1775-82); *Plaidoyers sur plusieurs questions de droit* (1785).

GUZMÁN, NUÑO DE (d. 1542), Spanish conquistador and colonial administrator noted for his cruelty and rapacity. Guzmán was appointed governor of Pánuco (northeastern Mexico) in 1525 and president of the *Audiencia* of New Spain in 1527. As president, he ruled in a highhanded manner. Between 1529 and 1531 he undertook the conquest of New Galicia (northwestern Mexico), and abused the native population so badly that serious revolts subsequently developed in the area. He was deprived of his offices for his misdeeds and, upon his return to Mexico City in 1536, was imprisoned and sent back to Spain, where he died in obscurity in 1542.

(L. N. McA.)

GUZMÁN BLANCO, ANTONIO (1829-1899), Venezuelan dictator, was born in Caracas, Venez., on Feb. 29, 1829, the son of Antonio Leocardio Guzmán, who was prominent in the governments of Simón Bolívar and José Antonio Páez. After exile and travel in the United States, where he represented his country in several capacities, Guzmán Blanco returned to Venezuela in 1859 to take part in a revolution staged by Gen. Juan Crisóstomo Falcón, which was successful in 1863. The Falcón government fell in 1868 while Guzmán Blanco was in Europe as a special finance commissioner. In Feb. 1870 he headed a counterrevolt, set up a dictatorship (April 1870) and had himself elected constitutional president in 1873. He was re-elected in 1880, 1882 and 1886 and, until 1888, was absolute ruler of Venezuela, although he spent much of his time in Europe.

Guzmán Blanco brought order but with it servility and insufferable arrogance. From personal resentment rather than ideological conflicts, he waged an unmerciful attack upon the Roman Catholic Church. The press was gagged. Like many Latin-American tyrants of his day he believed that order was a small price to pay for progress and his rule was signalized by solid economic achievements. He sponsored public education, restored the public credit, subsidized agriculture, promoted international trade, and laid the groundwork for an era of significant technological advance, particularly in railroad construction. In the process the dictator grew rich representing the nation before foreign bankers and contractors but the life of the Venezuelan masses changed little as they continued to live like serfs on the edge of starvation.

In 1888, during one of his numerous trips to Europe, a revolt broke out in Caracas. The man Guzmán Blanco had placed in the presidency repudiated his authority, and the army deserted him. He remained in Paris, where he died on July 20, 1899.

See George S. Wise, *Caudillo* (1951). (J. J.)

GWADAR (GWADUR; ancient BARNA), a seaport of Pakistan, is situated on the Makran (Baluchistan) coast of the Arabian sea, 287 mi. W. of Karachi. Pop. (1961) 8,146. The town (with small fortress) lies below a rocky cliff on the east side of Gwadar bay on the narrow neck of the Ras Nuh peninsula, which shelters the roadstead of the port. Gwadar exports fish, dates and wool. It is on the telegraph routes from India and Pakistan to the Persian gulf and Europe.

Sultan Ibu Ahmad of Muscat added Gwadar and other Makran coastal townships to his dominions in 1797. During the subsequent rise of the khanate of Kalat and the consolidation of Persian control to the west of it, Muscadine possessions on the north coast of the Gulf of Oman were reduced to Gwadar, and this last remnant disappeared with its transfer to Pakistan in 1958. (L. D. S.)

GWALIOR, a city and district located in Madhya Pradesh, India, and a former princely state. The city of Gwalior is the headquarters of the district. Pop. (1971 prelim.) 406,755. It is a centre of industry, the chief products being textiles, pottery, footwear, silks, carpets, biscuits, confectionery, plastics, glass and matches. The Agra-Bombay road, a national highway, passes through the town, which is also connected to Bhind, Sheopur and Shivpuri by narrow-gauge railways. There are nine colleges (including engineering, medical and agricultural colleges) connected

WIDE WORLD PHOTOS

FORTRESS WALLS AT GWALIOR; THE FORT IS BUILT ON A FLATTOPPED SANDSTONE HILL ABOVE THE TOWN

with Vikram university at Ujjain (q.v.), a central technical institute, an industrial research laboratory, a school of arts and a college of music. Near the town is the tomb of Tansen, one of India's best-known musicians, and Gwalior is still a centre of music with its own distinctive style and tradition.

The city centres around a fortress built on a rocky escarpment and guarding the main road which leads from the fertile plains of the north to central India. The fort is first mentioned in a temple inscription of about A.D. 525. It was in the hands of Hindu rulers till 1232 when it was taken by the Muslim ruler Altamsh. In 1398 it was captured by the Rajputs. Raja Man Singh built two of the palaces within the fort; in one the coloured tiles are still brilliant. Recovered by Akbar in 1559, the fort was used by the Moguls as a prison till 1751 when it was conquered by the Marathas. In 1777 it became the headquarters of the Sindhia (q.v.) family. It was taken by the British in 1780, recaptured by the Marathas in 1783, retaken in 1804 and restored to the Sindhia in 1805. In 1844 the fort was garrisoned by British troops. In 1853 it was handed over to the Sindhia, who held it until 1857, when it was seized by rebel sepoys who in 1858 surrendered to the British. In 1886 the fort, one of the most famous in India, was restored to the Sindhia in exchange for Jhansi. It contains eight tanks, six palaces, six temples, a mosque and other buildings. The Telika Mandir (11th century), the Man Mandir, the Gujari Mahal and the surviving atrium of the Great Sas Bahu temple (dedicated 1093) are fine examples of early Hindu architecture. The rock face of the fort is covered with Brahmanical and Jain scriptures.

The Former Gwalior State.—Prominent among those Maratha military leaders who were gaining their independence of the peshwas (the hereditary Maratha rulers) in the second quarter of the 18th century was Ranoji Sindhia (d. 1745), who laid the foundations of the state of Gwalior. The defeat of the peshwa at Panipat in 1761 accentuated the tendency to independence among the generals. Power now passed from the peshwas of Poona to their generals, the most important of whom was Mahadaji Sindhia of Gwalior, a son of Ranoji. In 1785 Mahadaji re-established Shah Alam on the imperial throne at Delhi. Though nominally a deputy of the peshwa, Mahadaji was the ruler of a vast territory, including parts of central India and Hindustan proper, while his officers exacted tribute from the chiefs of Rajputana. Mahadaji was succeeded in 1794 by his grandnephew Daulat Rao, who lost considerable territory to the British in 1803 and 1818. In the 1857 mutiny the maharaja of Gwalior, under the influence of the resident, Major Macpherson, remained loyal to the British even after his troops had joined the mutineers.

The princely state of Gwalior was divided as follows: (1) a large northern tract southeast of the Chambal river extending southward to the Bhopal border; (2) a large tract about the headwaters of the Kali Sindh river north of the Vindhya mountains; (3) three smaller areas west of this, the southernmost containing Ujjain, the original Sindhia capital; (4) a further division to the southeast, north of the Narmada river. The administrative headquarters of the state were at Lashkar, founded c. 1800, 4 mi. S. of old Gwalior. Lashkar contains many palaces and the cenotaph of the rani of Jhansi (see INDIAN MUTINY). At Antri, near Gwalior town, stands the tomb of Abu'l-Fazl 'Allami (q.v.). The famous fort of Narwar, where ruled Raja Nala whose story has been immortalized in the Mahabharata, is in the Shirpur district. Near the tomb of Tansen is that of Mohammed Ghaus; it is a fine example of Mogul architecture.

GWALIOR DISTRICT has an area of 2,002 sq.mi. and a population (1961) of 657,876. One-fifth of the district is under forests and the rest is of fine alluvium, growing wheat, rice (irrigated), maize (corn) and sugarcane. An outcrop of Vindyar sandstone is quarried for building and Gwalior city is largely built from it. The people speak Hindi.

The district, previously the core of the former princely state of Gwalior, was absorbed in Madhya Bharat on May 28, 1948, and subsequently (Nov. 1, 1956) in Madhya Pradesh. In the early 1960s it was progressing with the rapid growth of Gwalior city.

GWALIOR DIVISION comprises the districts of Bhind, Morena, Shivpuri, Goona, Datia and Gwalior. Area 17,216 sq.mi. Pop. (1961) 3,436,639. (D. G. NA.; S. M. A.)

GWINNETT, BUTTON (c. 1735-1777), American merchant, patriot, and signer of the Declaration of Independence, known chiefly because his autographs are of extreme rarity and collectors of the signers have forced their value to a high figure. He was born in Gloucester, Eng., probably in 1735, and moved to Georgia some time before 1765. On Feb. 2, 1776, he was elected a delegate from that colony to the Continental Congress, and as such signed the Declaration. Returning to Georgia, he was a member of the convention to frame a new state constitution. He was wounded in a duel and died at his home on St. Catherine's Island on May 19, 1777.

GWYN, NELL (ELEANOR GWYN, GWYNNE OR GWYNN) (1650-1687), English actress and mistress of Charles II, whose frank recklessness, generosity, invariable good temper, ready wit, infectious high spirits and amazing indiscretions appealed irresistibly to a generation that welcomed in her the living antithesis of Puritanism, was born on Feb. 2, 1650, probably in an alley near Covent Garden, London. Her father's name is unknown; according to tradition he died in a debtors' prison in Oxford during Nell's infancy. Her mother, Helena Gwyn, kept a bawdyhouse in the Covent Garden district, where Nell was brought up "to fill strong waters [brandy] to the guests" (Pepys, Diary, Oct. 26, 1667). In 1664, through the influence of her older sister, Rose, Nell became an orange-girl in the King's theatre. Quickly attracting the attention of the leading actor, Charles Hart (whose mistress she became), Nell mounted to the stage, making her first appearance as Paulina, a courtesan, in Thomas Killigrew's Thomaso, probably in Dec. 1664.

From 1666 to 1669 Nell was the leading comedienne of the King's company, playing continuously save for a brief absence in the summer of 1667 when she lived at Epsom as the mistress of Lord Buckhurst, afterward 6th earl of Dorset (q.v.). She created such popular roles as Florimel in Dryden's Secret Love, Mirida in James Howard's All Mistaken and Jacinta in Dryden's An Evening's Love. An excellent singer and dancer, and much in demand as a speaker of impudent prologues and epilogues, "pretty, witty Nell" was ill-suited to serious parts, yet she was often cast for roles in romantic dramas.

BY COURTESY OF THE NATIONAL PORTRAIT GALLERY, LONDON

NELL GWYN, PROBABLE PORTRAIT ATTRIBUTED TO SIR PETER LELY, c. 1675

Her last appearance was as Almahide to the Almanzor of Hart in Dryden's two-part heroic play *The Conquest of Granada* (Dec. 1670–Jan. 1671), the production of which had been postponed several months for her return to the stage after the birth of her first son by the king (May 14, 1670).

Established in a fine house in Pall Mall and admitted to the inner circles of the court, Nell spent the rest of her life entertaining the king and his friends, living extravagantly and intriguing against her rivals. She persuaded the king to create her son Charles Beauclerk, Baron Heddington and earl of Burford, and, subsequently, duke of St. Albans. Her second son, James, Lord Beauclerk (b. Dec. 25, 1671), died in 1680. Nell settled her mother in a house in Chelsea, where, in July 1679, overcome by brandy, Madam Gwyn fell into a nearby brook and was drowned.

Of all the mistresses of Charles II, Nell was the only one beloved by the public. Her popularity was due partly, no doubt, to the disgust inspired by her rival, Louise de Kéroualle, duchess of Portsmouth, and to the fact that, while the Frenchwoman was a Catholic, Nell was a Protestant. But very largely it was the result of exactly those personal qualities that appealed to the monarch himself. She was small, slender and shapely, with a heart-shaped face, hazel eyes and chestnut-brown hair. She was, nor to interfere in matters outside the special sphere assigned to her; she made no ministers, she appointed to no bishoprics, and for the high issues of international politics she had no concern. She never forgot her old friends and, as far as is known, remained faithful to her royal lover from the beginning of their intimacy until his death and, after his death, to his memory.

When Charles II died in Feb. 1685, Nell was so deeply in debt that she was outlawed by her creditors. However, the king's deathbed request to his brother, "Let not poor Nelly starve," was faithfully carried out by James II, who paid off enough of her debts to re-establish her credit, gave her sizable amounts in cash and settled on her a pension of £1,500 a year. In March 1687 Nell was stricken by apoplexy and partial paralysis. She died Nov. 14, 1687, and on Nov. 17 was buried, according to her request, in the church of St. Martin's-in-the-Fields. Her funeral sermon was preached by the vicar, Thomas Tennison (afterward archbishop of Canterbury), who took as his text, "Joy shall be in Heaven over one sinner that repenteth, more than over ninety and nine just persons who need no repentance."

BIBLIOGRAPHY.—Peter Cunningham, *The Story of Nell Gwyn* (1852); J. H. Wilson, *Nell Gwyn: Royal Mistress* (1952).
(J. H. W.)

GYANGTSE (GYANTSE; ROYAL-RTSE in Tibetan), the third largest town in Tibet, is located 40 mi. upstream from Zhikatse (q.v.) in Gtsang Province. A massive fort on a ridge dominating Gyangtse, which serves as the seat of the local government, was the scene of heavy fighting and prolonged siege during the civil war (1727–28). Gyangtse, on the main route from India to Lhasa via the Chumbi Valley (q.v.), is a commercial town and a manufacturing centre for woolen cloth and carpets. A British, and later Indian, trade agency was established there in 1904 and remained in operation until 1962, when it was closed following the expiration of the 1954 Sino-Indian trade agreement.

Before the Communist Chinese occupation of Tibet, traders from western and upper Tibet brought wool, furs, musk, borax salt, and butter to Gyangtse to exchange for a variety of products, including barley flour from central Tibet; tea from China; tobacco, sugar, cotton goods, dried fruits, and hardware from India and Nepal; and wooden bowls and rice from Bhutan. Much of the town was rebuilt after a disastrous flood in July 1954 swept away most of the residential buildings and drowned more than 1,500 people. The population was estimated in 1953 at 10,000. Gyangtse was linked by motor road with Lhasa, Zhikatse, and Yatung, near the Sikkimese border, after the Communist Chinese occupation.

On the northwest side of Gyangtse stands the famous Dpal-'khor chos-sde (pronounced *Bä-ko chö-de*) monastery, founded in 1418 by Rab-brtan kun-bzang phags-pa.
(T. V. W.)

GYGES, king of Lydia c. 680–c. 648 B.C. (his dates are uncertain) and founder of the Mermnad dynasty, was according to all ancient sources a usurper who slew his predecessor and married the queen. Greek literature was much interested in him, as it was contemporary the poet Archilochus. He is mentioned as a type of royal power by his contemporary the poet Archilochus. Herodotus tells how, as an officer under King Candaules, Gyges was forced by the queen to kill the king or perish himself when Candaules, inordinately proud of his wife's beauty, had compelled Gyges to see her naked (the queen, discovering this, pleaded that she had been dishonoured). A papyrus fragment survives of a tragedy on the same story, either late and based on Herodotus, or early and actually Herodotus' source. R. D. Barnett suggests that the tale is an irreverent Greek parody of Gyges' propaganda line that he was the chosen spouse of the naked goddess Kybebe; since "lover of the goddess" was a common Oriental royal title. Plato in *The Republic* tells how an ancestor of Gyges (according to the manuscripts, though most scholars emend to make the statement refer to Gyges) was a shepherd who found a ring that made him invisible, and by this means seduced the queen and murdered the king. Nicholas of Damascus, writing in the 1st century B.C., who used the 5th-century Lydian historian Xanthus, makes him an officer of a northern family already intermittently suspect to the royal house, who was sent to bring home the king's bride and tried to seduce her on the way. She complained to her husband, whom Gyges then killed.

Under Gyges Lydia emerged as a military power. The Cimmerians had overrun Phrygia and Asia Minor was in turmoil. Gyges concerted operations with King Ashurbanipal of Assyria against the Cimmerians and defeated them. He is perhaps the "Gog" known vaguely to the prophet Ezekiel among northern barbarians. He invaded Ionia, overthrowing Colophon and attacking Miletus. He also made offerings at Delphi. Having, however, rejected Assyrian suzerainty and dispatched troops to aid the revolt of Psamtik I in Egypt, he was left to face another Cimmerian invasion and was defeated and killed c. 648 (some authorities prefer an earlier date).

See also LYDIA.

See R. D. Barnett in *Journal of Hellenic Studies*, vol. lxviii, p. 22 (1948); D. L. Page, *A New Chapter in the History of Greek Tragedy* (1951); A. E. Raubitscheck in *Classical Weekly*, vol. 48, no. 4, pp. 48 ff. (January 1955) with full bibliography.
(A. R. Bu.)

GYLLENBORG, GUSTAF FREDRIK, COUNT (1731–1808), Swedish poet, a friend of G. Ph. Creutz and Hedvig Charlotta Nordenflycht (qq.v.), known for his satirical and reflective poetry, was born on Nov. 25, 1731, in Svinstad (Bankekind), Östergötland. Although his family were prominent in political life, he refused to engage in party battles, and attacked the weaknesses of modern society in the spirit of Rousseau in such poems as "Verldsföraktaren" ("The Misanthrope," 1762). A pessimism typical of the late 18th century is expressed in his most famous poem, "Menniskjans Elände" ("Misery of Man," 1762). After parting with Creutz and Fru Nordenflycht in 1763, Gyllenborg wrote little of importance, but devoted himself to a career in the civil service.

Gyllenborg's poems were published in *Vitterhetsarbeten af Creutz och Gyllenborg* (1795); his memoirs, *Mitt lefverne 1731–1775*, appeared in 1885.

He died in Stockholm, March 30, 1808.

See M. Lamm, *Upplysningstidens romantik*, vol. 1, pp. 263–308 (1918); G. Sahlberg, *G. F. Gyllenborg* (1943).
(L. G. Bz.)

GYLLENSTIERNA (GYLLENSTJERNA), **JOHAN, COUNT** (1636–1680), Swedish statesman and chief adviser of King Charles XI, was born at Bränkyrka on Feb. 18, 1636, a scion of the high aristocracy but closely connected with the anti-aristocratic and royalist civil service through his maternal grandfather Johan Skytte, the tutor of Gustavus II Adolphus. From the beginning of his career (at the *riksdag* of 1660), he advocated a strong royal authority, opposition to the nobles of the council of state or *riksråd*, and an effective pursuit of national interests. During Charles XI's minority, an opposition group in the regency and in the council had Gyllenstierna elected president of the *riksdag* of 1668 and later appointed councilor of state. He strongly opposed the chancellor Magnus Gabriel De la Gardie's policy both in foreign and in economic affairs (*see* DE LA GARDIE, MAGNUS GABRIEL); he tried in vain to prevent the French alliance of 1672 and wanted the "reduction" decreed in 1655 for the restoration of royal control over the lands of the kingdom to be implemented.

After Charles had attained his majority in 1672 the government was at first still dominated by De la Gardie, who was married to a cousin of the young king; but when the outbreak of war with Denmark in 1675 revealed the complete failure of the chancellor's foreign and financial policies, Gyllenstierna, with the aid of lesser officials, built up at the royal headquarters in Skåne a position of power which almost amounted to a military dictatorship. Though the great nobles of the Stockholm bureaucracy sought by various means, including impeachment, to bring about his fall, he enjoyed the king's full confidence. He concluded an advantageous peace and an alliance with Denmark at Lund in 1679. Appointed governor general of Skåne, Gyllenstierna died suddenly at Landskrona on June 10, 1680, before all his far-reaching plans could be realized. The confirmation of royal autocracy by the *riksdag* in Dec. 1680, when the council's powers were entirely set aside, was the fulfillment of his idea.

See G. Landberg, *Johan Gyllenstiernas nordiska förbundspolitik* (1935); G. Rystad, *Johan Gyllenstierna, rådet och kungamakten* (1955); *Johan Gyllenstierna* (1957). (N. G. R.)

GYMEL, a medieval musical style of two-part polyphonic composition, possibly of popular origin, in which the voices move mainly in consecutive thirds or sixths. Crossing of parts is frequently found. Although compositions in gymel form have been preserved in manuscripts dating from the beginning of the 13th century, the name itself (derived from *cantus gemellus,* "twin song") is first found in the 15th century when a detailed description of gymel is given by the music theoretician Guilielmus Monachus. Gymel seems to have been favoured in England during the 13th century and this style of composition had a marked influence on the development of English polyphony in the following century. In late 15th- and early 16th-century English choral music the word gymel denotes a duo, also the splitting of a part into two parts. (S. Co.)

GYMNASIUM. The history of the gymnasium dates back to ancient Greece where the literal meaning of the word was "school for naked exercise." The gymnasiums were of great significance to the ancient Greeks and every important city had at least one. These were usually built by the state and from a humble beginning of merely a gathering place where exercises were performed grew to imposing structures with dressing rooms, baths, training quarters and special areas for contests.

Originally these gymnasiums were public institutions where only male athletes over the age of 18 received training for competition in the public games of that time as opposed to the palestrae which were private schools where boys were trained in physical exercises. The supervision of the gymnasiums was entrusted to "gymnasiarchs," who were public officials responsible for the conduct of sports and games at public festivals and who directed the schools and supervised the competitors. The "gymnastae" were the teachers, coaches and trainers of the athletes.

Gradually, the gymnasiums developed into institutions of learning and schools of intellectual culture. In the German-speaking countries, the term *Gymnasium* is still applied to the higher grades in secondary schools and has no association with athletics or sports; the name *Turnverein* is used to designate a site for physical exercise. However, in the English-speaking countries the gymnasium's connection with philosophy and mental culture has been dropped and it ordinarily designates a room or building for the practice of physical culture. Although the Greeks attempted to establish their gymnasiums in the Roman empire, the Romans had little regard for the institution as they felt it was too effete and contributed little to the military training which was paramount for their youth.

One of the first gymnasiums of modern times was the Berlin *Turnverein* established by Friedrich Ludwig Jahn (*q.v.*) in

1811. A military gymnasium was established at the United States Military academy at West Point in 1817, and in 1822 Capt. P. H. Clias, a Swiss army officer, was appointed gymnastics instructor in the English army and instructed at the gymnasium established at Aldershot, Eng. The first school gymnasium in England was opened in 1859 at Uppingham school.

Round Hill school at Northampton, Mass., first offered systematic instruction in a gymnasium in 1823 and the first German *Turnverein* in the United States was built in 1848 in Cincinnati, O. In the same year the British government erected apparatus for an open-air gymnasium at Primrose Hill, London. Princeton erected the first college gymnasium building in the U.S. in 1856 and in 1879 Harvard university built the Hemenway gymnasium which was considered the finest of its time.

Gymnastic instruction at a college for women was first offered in 1862 by Mount Holyoke college, South Hadley, Mass., in a storeroom over the wood and coal shed; a gymnasium was erected in 1865.

The famous Czech (Bohemian) gymnastic society, the *Sokol*, established its first gymnasium in Prague in 1862, and its first gymnasium in the United States at St. Louis, Mo., in 1865. The first Y.M.C.A. gymnasium was opened in 1869, in San Francisco, Calif.

The main purpose of these early institutions was to provide a suitable place for physical exercise and the practice of the sport of gymnastics on the various apparatus (*see* GYMNASTICS). Gradually, however, the scope of the activities carried on in gymnasiums broadened so that 20th-century gymnasiums have facilities for a great many other sports and games such as basketball, volleyball, tennis, handball, etc.

(For special equipment, dimensions of playing areas, etc., *see* separate articles on the various sports.)

In addition, most gymnasiums are equipped with dressing and locker rooms, shower rooms and swimming pools, special exercise rooms for remedial gymnastics, boxing, wrestling, weight-lifting and fencing rooms, running tracks, etc.

A typical list of standard gymnasium equipment includes the following:

1. Apparatus specified by the Fédération Internationale de Gymnastique (F.I.G.) for international gymnastic competitions, *i.e.,* pommeled or side horses, long (vaulting) horses; parallel bars, horizontal bars, stationary rings, balance beams (for detailed description *see* GYMNASTICS: *Men's Events and Apparatus; Women's Events and Apparatus.*

2. Climbing ropes, $1\frac{1}{2}$ to 2 in. in diameter (competitive climbing for time is for a distance of 20 ft. under U.S. collegiate and Amateur Athletic union rules).

3. Swinging (flying) rings, similar to the stationary rings, except that they are suspended from a height of 23 to 24 ft. and the rings may be made of wood, metal or metal covered with seamless rubber or leather, weighing not less than 4 and not more than 6 lb. per ring. Exercises are performed on the swinging rings while they are in motion, maintaining an angle of at least 40° on each side of vertical (making a total swing of 80°).

4. Elementary apparatus such as low horizontal and parallel bars, vaulting bucks, wall bars and horizontal and oblique ladders.

5. High-jump and pole vaulting standards, together with the necessary sticks and poles for indoor practice of these activities.

6. Mats, provided for safety when exercising on the apparatus and also large sized, single-piece mats for wrestling and tumbling.

7. Necessary equipment for games such as volleyball and tennis nets, basketball goals and backstops. Cabinets provide for the neat and protective storing of equipment such as basketballs, medicine balls, volleyballs and the portable hand apparatus such as Indian clubs, wands, dumbbells, etc.

8. Special exercise rooms contain such equipment as pulleys, chest weights and weightlifting equipment. Boxing and fencing rooms are equipped with the accessories for these sports.

9. Handball and squash courts, requiring specially constructed walls, are often included in a modern gymnasium.

In design, the recommended dimensions of a gymnasium are a minimum width of 60 ft., with a ratio of width to length of 3 to 5. Height should be a minimum of 23 ft., and running tracks or galleries should be not less than 10 ft. above the floor. The space required for each person exercising is 40 to 50 sq.ft. The floor, usually of maple, should have a hard, clear finish and may be permanently marked to designate boundary lines for basketball, volleyball, tennis courts, etc.

Accommodations for spectators at sporting events may be provided by bleachers—a series of tiered benches—which may be permanent in nature or portable, in that they may be folded up against the walls when not in use.

School gymnasiums often provide the facilities for holding social functions such as dances, receptions, bazaars, fairs, etc., as well as facilities for physical education and intramural and interscholastic athletics. (*See* PHYSICAL EDUCATION.) Many gymnasiums include meeting rooms, lounges, auditoriums, theatres, cafeterias, workshops and other facilities to provide recreational and leisure-time activities for an entire community.

In Great Britain public gymnasiums are not common. Most gymnasiums form part of a school, college or university. The recommended dimensions of a school gymnasium are 40 by 70 ft. and the building is equipped for education gymnastics. The apparatus shows strong Scandinavian influence although much experimental apparatus also has been installed.

(J. F. HY.)

See also STADIUM.

GYMNASIUM (GERMANY), a secondary school traditionally offering an academic classical education (*q.v.*) and leading to university matriculation. In the Federal Republic of Germany the *Gymnasium* is differentiated into three main types: classical, including Latin, Greek and one modern language; modern, with Latin and two modern languages; and mathematics and science, with two modern languages, optional Latin, and greater emphasis on mathematics and science. Senior departments of elementary schools, middle schools (*Mittelschulen*), and teachers training, commercial and senior girls' colleges provide general secondary or postprimary education and training for technical, commercial and civil service occupations.

See SECONDARY EDUCATION; EDUCATION, HISTORY OF.

(X.)

GYMNASTICS, a system of physical exercises practised either to promote physical development or as a sport. The history of gymnastics dates back to the public games of ancient Greece, where the general term included activities which have since developed as separate sports, for example, track and field athletics, fencing, wrestling, boxing, etc. A primitive form of modern gymnastics was practised as training for the more strenuous combative sports and later developed into a competitive sport of its own to the extent of forming part of the ancient Olympic games (*q.v.*). With the termination of the ancient Olympic games all sports fell into a decline. In the middle ages jousts and various field sports were popular, but the systematic training of the body which the Greeks had associated with gymnastics fell into neglect.

The modern development of gymnastics started in the 19th century when there was a revival of interest in all sports, and gymnastics early came to be recognized as a systematized form of physical exercise having not only recreational but therapeutic value, and offering a means of developing a high degree of discipline of both mind and body.

Gymnastic societies were founded first in Germany (*Turnvereine*) and in the Bohemia of the Austro-Hungarian empire (*Sokols*), followed by France and Switzerland (where a system of gymnastics performed in unison by groups was developed) then gradually spread throughout western Europe. Gymnastics was one of the first sports to recognize that its recreational and therapeutic advantages were as valuable to women as to men. The European gymnastic societies also provided children's classes starting youngsters as early as the age of five.

While interest in gymnastics in England and Canada has been mainly in its remedial and physical training qualities, particularly in connection with the military, its recreational and competitive aspects have slowly gained recognition.

The original impetus to gymnastics in the United States came in the 1880s with the advent of the great tide of immigrants from the European countries, who brought with them the ideas of their gymnastic societies and founded these wherever they settled.

In Sweden a system of free exercises on the ground was developed in mid-19th century with the objective of developing perfect rhythm of movement. This system was introduced in England in 1879 and in the United States in about 1889 and for the next 20 years the relative merits of Swedish (rhythmic) gymnastics and the German gymnastic system (apparatus work of a formal nature, stressing muscular development) were debated intensively by both the educational authorities and adherents of the sport. A solution was found by the Fédération Internationale de Gymnastique (F.I.G.) in the 1920s which blends the rhythmic, fluent movements of the Swedish system with the precision and developmental emphasis of the German system.

Although the Swedish system is still popular in the country of its origin, the combined version has been adopted by sport authorities. For additional historical details *see* GYMNASIUM.

COMPETITIVE GYMNASTICS

As a competitive sport gymnastics is akin to diving and figure skating in that it is a "demonstration" sport and the effectiveness of the competitor is assessed solely by the judgment of officials who have a knowledge of the technical rules and regulations governing the competition.

In international competition these rules and regulations are promulgated by the F.I.G., which prescribes international standards for the apparatus to be used, the types of exercises to be performed and the conduct of the competition. It is charged with the conduct of the gymnastic competition at the Olympic games and holds world championships in gymnastics every four years (two years after each Olympic games).

Governing bodies in the different countries (such as the amateur athletic unions of England, the United States, Canada, etc.) hold membership in the F.I.G. and conduct gymnastic competitions under the F.I.G. rules.

The men's competition in the international program of competitive gymnastics consists of seven events: the horizontal bar, parallel bars, side or pommeled horse, long or vaulting horse, stationary rings, floor exercises or calisthenics and the all-around event consisting of the combined scores in the first six events (international rules require that a gymnast perform in all events, similar to the decathlon event in track and field).

The women's competition consists of the balancing beam, uneven parallel bars, vaulting horse, floor exercises or calisthenics and the all-around event.

On the apparatus and in calisthenics each competitor performs two exercises, one a prescribed exercise which all competitors must perform. This prescribed exercise is composed by the governing administrative body of the sport (the amateur athletic unions of the different countries, and the F.I.G. for international competitions). The performance of this exercise is judged solely on its execution, that is, the form of the gymnast, the fluency of his performance, the correctness of the execution and the beauty of combining the component parts of the exercise.

In addition, an optional exercise, composed by the gymnast himself, must also be performed. The element of difficulty of the component movements of the exercise enters into the evaluation of the optional exercise. Beside difficulty, other elements of the optional exercise are originality, beauty of combining of the various movements and the fluency and perfection of its execution.

Four judges, supervised by a "superior judge" evaluate and score each exercise on a one-tenth basis, *i.e.* 8.8, 9.3, etc., with 10 for a perfect exercise. For the prescribed exercise the entire 10 points are confined to the execution of the exercise inasmuch as all competitors perform the same exercise. In the evaluation of the optional exercise, 2.4 points are allotted for the difficulty of the exercise, 1.6 points for the element of combination of the various movements and 5 points for the execution of the exercise as a whole. All four judges evaluate and score each exercise independently. Then, in order to eliminate gross errors of judgment, the scorers delete the highest and the lowest marks of the four judges, and the two middle marks are averaged for the score of the exercise. For example, if the four judges' marks are 9.6, 9.2, 9.1, 8.7, the 9.6 and 8.7 are deleted and the 9.2 and 9.1 are averaged, giving the final score of 9.15. The average score of the prescribed exercise is added to that of the optional exercise to determine the final score of the competitor in the event and his standing as compared with the other competitors. To obtain the all-around score, the final scores of the six events (four in the case of women) are added and the total comprises the score of the gymnast in the all-around competition.

Since the dimensions and specifications of the apparatus used in the Olympic games and other international gymnastic competitions, as well as the type of exercises performed thereon, are standardized by the F.I.G., when gymnasts from all parts of the world gather for an international competition they have all trained on the same type of apparatus and have a common knowledge of the conditions and requirements of the competition. The F.I.G. delegates the task of prescribing these rules and regulations to two technical committees, one for the men's and one for the women's program, composed of experts who have made a study of the technical aspects of the sport and are alert to changes in the trend of gymnastics and change the programs accordingly.

It should be noted that there was a gradual change in the trend of competitive gymnastics from its earlier concept of emphasizing strength and the holding of classical poses to a more liberal interpretation, and the phrase "artistic gymnastics" came to describe perfection of execution and fluency of movement. Ballet movements, particularly in calisthenics, gained approval and on the apparatus fluent movements and swinging exercises requiring changes of grasps and position were encouraged to the extent of limiting movements requiring strength and pressing.

Any changes in the rules by its technical committees are published by the F.I.G. and are disseminated to the governing bodies of the sport in the various countries holding membership so that they in turn may keep gymnasts currently informed.

The following is a description of the apparatus as specified by the F.I.G. and the types of ex-

ercises to be performed thereon. Inasmuch as most of the countries use the metric system of measurement, the dimensions are so stated rather than in English linear measurements.

MEN'S EVENTS AND APPARATUS

Horizontal Bar.—This is a polished steel bar, 28 mm. in diameter, 2.35 to 2.50 m. long and 2.40 to 2.50 m. high from the floor, supported at the ends by steel poles which are held upright by guy wires. Only movements of swinging and vaulting, without pause, are permitted. Such exercises as upstarts, back and front (by which the gymnast swings himself from a hang to a support above the bar); giant circles forward and backward (rotating around the bar from a handstand position with the arms fully extended) and with inverted or dislocated grips and changes from one to another; vaulting over the bar, releasing the grip and regrasping the bar; movements requiring turns and changes of the position of the body and the releasing and regrasping of the bar; and finishes with straddles over the bar or forward and backward somersaults from the bar are performed on this apparatus.

Parallel Bars.—The two bars, made of wood, are oval in form, 42 to 48 cm. apart, 3.50 m. long and 1.60 to 1.70 m. high. The requirements for this apparatus are movements combining swings, vaults, strength and balances, although the elements of swings, and vaults must predominate. There may not be more than three balances (such as handstands) in an exercise (a sequence of at least ten different movements or tricks) and there must be at least one movement of strength (as a handstand which is pressed into by strength from a support, rather than swung up into). Movements below the bars and the release and regrasping of the bars are also required.

Side or Pommeled Horse.—This apparatus is a leather-covered form, 1.60 m. long, 35 to 37 cm. wide and raised 1.08 m. from the floor (measured to its top) by a support in its centre. Curved wooden pommels, 12 cm. high, are inserted in the top of the horse 40 to 45 cm. apart in the centre, or "saddle," of the horse. The gymnast supports himself on the pommels over the horse and performs movements of the trunk and legs, without stops, such as single or double leg circles, crosses of the legs (scissors); with turns and changes of the grasp to the forward (neck) part of the horse, the centre (saddle) and the rear (croup). It is necessary to vary the movements and also to perform them both to the left (clockwise) and to the right.

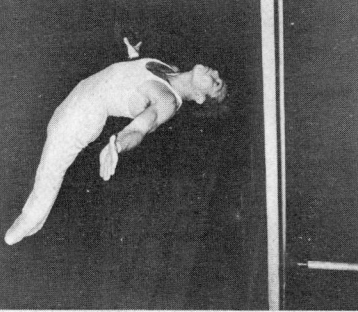
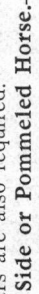

JOHN NICOLAS

PARALLEL BARS: BACK SOMERSAULT

JOHN NICOLAS

TWO EVENTS IN MEN'S GYMNASTICS COMPETITION: (LEFT) GIANT CARTWHEEL VAULT ON THE LONG OR VAULTING HORSE; (RIGHT) "MOORE" TURN ON SIDE OR POMMELED HORSE

JOHN NICOLAS

FULL TURN (PIROUETTE) AT END OF BACKWARD SWING ON THE HORIZONTAL BAR (RELEASING GRASP)

Long or Vaulting Horse.—The same apparatus is used as for the side horse, except that the pommels are withdrawn and the horse is placed lengthwise so that when the gymnast faces it the part nearest to his stand is the croup, and the neck is farthest away from him, with the saddle in between. The height of the horse is raised to 1.35 m. The Reuther-type elastic board, placed in front of the croup end of the horse, is 1.20 m. long, 60 cm. wide and raised 12 cm. on the end nearest to the horse, tapering back to the floor. The gymnast takes a run; gathers momentum as he nears the horse, rebounds off the elastic board and, supporting his hands on the horse, vaults over it. A variety of vaults is performed such as vaulting over with straddled legs, with the legs together and bent into a squatting position or the legs straight with the hips bent into a "stooping" position; a handspring over the horse, a cartwheel, etc. The hands may be placed on either the croup or the neck end of the horse, but the space for the support of the hands is limited and encroaching beyond this space inflicts a penalty on the scoring of the vault. Each vault is evaluated by a table as to its difficulty.

Stationary Rings.—The rings are made of wood, 28 mm. in thickness and 18 cm. in diameter (inside). They are suspended by straps at a height of 5.50 m. from the floor to the point of suspension, with the rings themselves hanging 2.40 to 2.50 m. above the floor. The exercise must be performed with the rings in a stationary position (without a swinging or pendulum movement of the rings) and must combine swinging movements of the body, strength and holding of positions. There must be at least two handstands in an exercise, one of which must be pressed into by strength from a support above the rings, and the other swung up into from a hanging position below the rings, and at least one other part of strength such as a cross (holding the body vertical with the arms fully stretched sideways); or a lever (hanging with straight arms, with the body stretched out horizontally, either in front of the arms or in a dislocated hang (i.e. hanging in an inverted position, with the head

JOHN NICOLAS
STATIONARY RINGS: "CROSS" HANG WITH LEGS IN "L" POSITION

nearest the floor, and then lowering the body backward, stretching it in a horizontal position with the body stretched backward in back of the arms). Combined with such required movements may be movements of upstarts, either forward or backward, forward or backward uprises, straight or inverted hangs, and dislocate circles of the body, either forward or backward.

Floor Exercises or Calisthenics.—No apparatus is used in the floor exercises or calisthenic event. The exercise is done on the floor, which may be covered by canvas or felt, in an area 12 by 12 m. and must be at least 50 seconds and not more than 70 seconds in duration. The type of exercise required is a series of combined movements of the elements of flexibility (tumbling movements such as handsprings, cartwheels, somersaults in the air, etc.), jumps, strength, holding of poses, balances and other tricks. The exercise must be performed with rhythm and harmony and the gymnast must move in different directions and utilize a major portion of the allotted area. The exercise usually starts and finishes with a series of tumbling movements such as a cartwheel with half a turn ("round-off") continuing with handsprings and somersaults backward or forward in the air. In between the start and finish balances are held on one leg in the air.

JOHN NICOLAS
HANDSTAND: MEN'S EXERCISE

WOMEN'S EVENTS AND APPARATUS

Balance Beam.—This is a wooden beam 5 m. long, 10 cm. wide and raised 120 cm. from the floor. The performer begins the exercise by mounting the beam either by a vault or a jump and executes movements which must include steps, running, jumps, turns, sitting and lying positions and some held or posed positions (scales), handstands are pressed into by strength, movements resembling ballet and tumbling movements and jumps are interposed. The duration of the exercise is from 1 min. 20 sec. to 1 min. 45 sec.

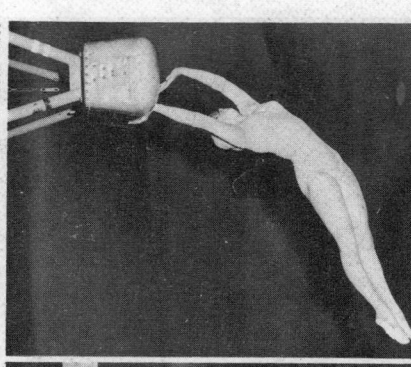

JOHN NICOLAS
TWO EVENTS IN WOMEN'S GYMNASTICS COMPETITION: (LEFT) PIVOT CARTWHEEL ON WOMEN'S SIDE HORSE VAULT; (RIGHT) FRONT OR HORIZONTAL SCALE ON WOMEN'S BALANCE BEAM

Uneven Parallel Bars.—These are of the same dimensions and construction as the men's parallel bars, except that the top bar is 2.30 m. above the floor while the lower bar is only 1.50 m. high. This apparatus is the latest to be developed, being first used in the 1936 Olympic games, and permits of a great variety of movements, although hanging and swinging exercises predominate (such as hanging from the higher bar and transferring to a support on the lower bar), interspersed with support and balance movements. The performer uses either of the bars, or combines movements using both bars.

JOHN NICOLAS
CROSS HANDSTAND: WOMEN'S UNEVEN PARALLEL BARS

Vaulting Horse.—This is the same as men's long horse, except that it is only 1.10 m. high and is placed sideways instead of lengthwise. Women also use the Reuther-type elastic board and perform similar vaults to those done by men except that the vault is much shorter, inasmuch as it is performed over the width of the horse, rather than its length.

Floor Exercises or Calisthenics.—This event is similar to the men's except it is performed to music and lasts from 1 to 1½ min.

Other Apparatus

Mats.—Mats to protect the gymnasts against injury in the event of a fall off the apparatus or when dismounting are placed around the apparatus at all times for both men and women.

Elementary Apparatus.—In addition to the apparatus used in competitive gymnastics, an elementary form of apparatus is usually employed by children's classes or beginners in gymnastics to learn the rudiments and elementary movements of the sport and for body development. Examples of such elementary apparatus are the low parallel bars (3 ft. 4 in. high), the low horizontal bar (about chest height), the vaulting buck, climbing ropes and poles, wall bars and horizontal and oblique ladders.

Rebound Tumbling Apparatus.—To the traditional gymnastic apparatus may be added an apparatus developed in the late 1930s—for rebound tumbling—a table-height metal frame to which is attached a canvas or a webbing bed, the elasticity of which permits the performer to continue springing upward by rebound and perform acrobatics in his flight.

JOHN NICOLAS

BALLET MOVEMENT (GRANDE JETÉ) IN WOMEN'S FLOOR EXERCISES

School and College Gymnastics

Although gymnastics had been practised as a competitive sport in the schools and colleges for many years in the United States it wasn't until shortly after World War II that it came into prominence and gained recognition as a major sport with dual meets and sectional and national championships being regularly scheduled. The school and college program does not comply with the F.I.G. rules inasmuch as it does not require the performance of prescribed exercises and lays more stress on the difficulty of the optional exercise rather than on its execution. The schools and colleges also have competition in events not recognized by the F.I.G. such as tumbling on the mats, rebound tumbling, a 20-ft. rope climb for speed and the flying or swinging rings (the same apparatus as the stationary rings except that the rings are suspended from a point 24 ft. from the floor and the gymnast performs on them while they are swinging). While women participate in physical training, competition in gymnastics in the schools and colleges is confined to men only.

Amateur Athletic Union

The Amateur Athletic union (A.A.U.) is responsible for the administration of amateur gymnastics in the United States. It conducts local, district and national championships under F.I.G. rules and sponsors visiting groups of foreign gymnasts and trips of U.S. gymnasts abroad for international competition. It publishes the rules and regulations governing competitions in its *Gymnastic Yearbook*, basing them on F.I.G. rules and amending them whenever the F.I.G. promulgates changes.

To provide for competition in events which, although not on the international program, still hold a wide interest in the United States, the A.A.U. also includes in its program events such as tumbling, rebound tumbling, rope climb and swinging rings for men and tumbling and rebound tumbling for women. No prescribed exercises are required in these events. Also, the A.A.U. does not require a gymnast to compete in every event (although it encourages all-around gymnasts) but permits competition in individual events.

The various gymnastic clubs holding membership in the A.A.U., such as the German and Swiss *Turnvereins*, *Sokols* and Y.M.C.A.'s, as well as the colleges, participate in the A.A.U. program and are the nucleus of developing gymnasts to represent the United States in the Olympic games (*q.v.*) and other international competitions.

OTHER TYPES OF GYMNASTICS

Festivals and Demonstrations.—Although gymnastics as a sport also has its recreational qualities, this form is popular mainly in the European countries where it is practised by groups ranging from a few gymnasts to mass demonstrations of many thousands. The *Sokols*, gymnastic societies, in Czechoslovakia have promoted gymnastic festivals in which as many as 10,000 gymnasts participated simultaneously in a mass calisthenic drill. The *Turnvereine* of Germany and the gymnastic societies of the Scandinavian countries also participate in mass demonstrations not only in calisthenic drills but also on apparatus.

Physical Education.—The value of physical education had long been recognized in military circles as a means of promoting general health and self-discipline and had become an essential part of the training of the army recruit, particularly in England and the United States during World Wars I and II, when untrained civilians were inducted into the armed forces. In the elementary schools the term physical education appeared in England and the United States in 1880 and took the imagination of the educational authorities at the beginning of the 20th century. The principal object was the introduction of a balanced and graduated system of exercises to children in the early grades, progressing to more advanced exercise in the secondary schools and colleges. *See also* Physical Education.

Remedial Gymnastics.—Much study and research has been made of the value of remedial gymnastics in connection with the rehabilitation of men badly wounded in wartime and persons with injuries caused by industrial accidents and those handicapped by such diseases as cerebral palsy, poliomyelitis, etc. It was found that with specially graduated exercises constructed for individual needs it was possible to enable a crippled or handicapped individual to enjoy greater mobility by flexing and moving atrophied muscles. Incorporating many of the theories and movements used in gymnastics is a regular feature of practice in orthopedic hospitals. Great progress has been made in the development of remedial gymnastics and the application of its therapeutic qualities. *See* Physical Therapy.

(J. F. Hy.)

GYMNOSOPHISTS, the English form of the name *gymnosophistai*, by which the ancient Greeks sometimes designated the ascetic philosophers of India (*gymnos* "naked" and *sophistes* "teacher of wisdom"). Diogenes Laërtius quotes Aristotle as mentioning Indian gymnosophists in a catalogue of the names for wise men and wonder-workers current among non-Greek peoples. Strabo, however, who writes at some length, though rather superficially, about Indian philosophers and wise men (*Geographica*, sections 703 and 711–715), does not speak of "gymnosophists" but cites Megasthenes as having drawn a distinction between Brachmanes (Brahmans) and the ascetic "dwellers in the forests," who fed on leaves and wild fruits and made what covering they wore from bark.

GYMNOSPERMS. Most of the trees commonly referred to as evergreens belong to the group of seed plants called gymnosperms. They are abundant in nature in many parts of the world and are to be seen everywhere in cultivation. In addition to these common representatives of the group, however, the interesting and often bizarre cycads and Gnetales also belong here. As a group the gymnosperms are particularly interesting to the biologist because of their antiquity, their excellent fossil record and their great diversity of form and life cycle.

All living seed plants customarily are divided into two main groups, the gymnosperms and the angiosperms (*q.v.*). By definition the gymnosperms have naked ovules, exposed to the pollen at the time of pollination, and naked seeds. The angiosperms have ovules enclosed within the ovary of a pistil (gynoecium), with the pollen falling on the stigma at its tip, so that the pollen tube must grow through considerable tissue before reaching the ovules. The seeds of the angiosperms throughout their development are enclosed within the ovary, which later becomes a fruit that may be single seeded or many seeded.

The ovules of some gymnosperms are buried rather deeply between the scales of the cone in which they are produced, but the pollen is able to sift down through to them. In a few angiosperms the carpels are open and the ovules exposed, but the pollen only develops on the stigma. The basic difference between the two groups thus lies in the behaviour of the pollen, which produces a long tube growing down the style in the angiosperms, but which usually enters the ovule directly in the gymnosperms.

All the seed plants have an alternation of generations and the prominent plant seen is the sporophytic or asexual generation. Spores, or pollen of these plants, give rise to the alternating generation, the gametophytes. In the lower plants the gametophyte is the dominant generation, and even in the ferns it is relatively conspicuous. On the other hand, in the gymnosperms and angiosperms the gametophytes are usually quite small, the pollen grain being transported through the air to the ovule, from which the female gametophyte never escapes and where the male gametophyte develops from the pollen grain.

Another basic difference between the two groups lies in the gametophytic generations. The male gametophyte of the gymnosperms always produces more sterile cells than the male gametophyte of the angiosperms. The female gametophyte of most gymnosperms is comparatively large and, like that of the ferns, produces large cells in cellular structures called archegonia. No archegonia are formed in the angiosperms in which the gametophyte is small and produces but one egg.

As a consequence of there being several eggs, the gymnosperms are nearly always polyembryonic—that is, they have several embryos beginning their development, depending upon how many eggs are fertilized. Actually only one embryo usually survives the intense competition to maturity. Angiosperms, having usually a single egg and embryo in an ovule, are rarely polyembryonic.

There are anatomical differences between the gymnosperms and the angiosperms, as well. The phloem of gymnosperms lacks companion cells associated with the sieve cells (which are not sufficiently specialized to be called sieve tubes, as in the angiosperms). Vessels and vessel elements are characteristic of the angiosperms and they are lacking in all the gymnosperms except the Gnetales. In the latter group, as will be seen below, it can be shown that the vessels arose independently of those in the angiosperms.

In addition to the living gymnosperms there are several entire groups that have become completely extinct. The fossil seed ferns (Pteridospermae) are related to the cycads and the Cordaitales (Cycadoidales) are of uncertain affinities.

The only other plants that might be considered to have descendants are fossil. These belong to the group of club mosses (Lycopsida) and there are differences of opinion as to whether the structures produced by them can properly be regarded as seeds. They are so similar to seeds, however, as to suggest that even this characteristic probably has arisen more than once in the evolution of the vascular plants and that perhaps the true gymnosperms are not the homogeneous group they are often thought to be.

Present day gymnosperms include only woody perennial plants, which are usually evergreen trees, seldom shrubs or lianas. There are several more or less distinct growth forms: the palm or tree fern type of the cycads; the profusely branched evergreen tree type of nearly all conifers, conical in their youth and often becoming irregular with age; and the shrubby types represented by dwarf conifers and most of the Gnetales. Nearly all of the latter are either shrubs or woody vines. These growth forms are associated with pronounced differences in size. Whereas the cycads may remain small palmlike trees, with a trunk about a foot in diameter and less than 10 to 20 ft. high, surmounted by a crown of compound palm- or fernlike leaves, the conifers include the largest trees known.

The giant sequoia or big tree (Sequoia gigantea) is the world's most massive organism, but it has not been proved to be, as was once thought, the oldest. The latter distinction belongs to another conifer, the bristlecone pine (Pinus aristata). The redwood (Sequoia sempervirens) is probably the tallest tree known. The cycads, though small in comparison, grow relatively slowly and may become very old. Even the small Welwitschia mirabilis of the coastal desert region of western South Africa may live for a century.

Gymnosperms are sometimes referred to as "living fossils." In many features they remain essentially unchanged from their fossil ancestors and their history extends back in an uninterrupted series to the Paleozoic era. There are apparently at least eight phyletic branches of gymnosperms, of which three are entirely extinct and one is represented by a single living representative, the ginkgo, or maidenhair tree (Ginkgo). Two other divisions of the gymnosperms include relatively rare plants; only one group, the Coniferales (including pines, cedars, firs, spruces, redwoods, cypresses, etc.), constitutes a really large, conspicuous and important part of our existing vegetation.

If the view is accepted that all gymnosperms had a common origin, it seems likely that they evolved from the same stock that included the Filicales or true ferns. There are other possible interpretations, however, and there is not even general agreement that the group is a natural one with a single common ancestor. The earliest fossil types date from the Devonian and they are relatively advanced. An important part of the divergence they show in their fundamental structures was attained during the close of the Paleozoic era. They were dominant land plants during the greater part of the Mesozoic era. Angiosperms did not become abundant until the latter part of the Mesozoic era. Gymnosperms were contemporaneous with the dinosaurs but, unlike these reptiles a fairly representative group of them, including some of the most massive organisms that ever existed, remain as a part of our living vegetation.

One of several proposed taxonomic schemes includes eight major divisions (or orders) of gymnosperms as follows:

1. Pteridospermae or Cycadofilicales. These so-called seed ferns, which combine a fernlike habit with seed production, are wholly extinct.

2. Cycadales. The cycads, comprising about nine living tropical or subtropical genera, were more abundant in the Mesozoic than today.

3. Cycadeoidales or Bennettitales. A group of wholly extinct cycadlike plants whose relations are uncertain.

4. Cordaitales. The cordaites are now completely extinct, but apparently gave rise to the Ginkgoales, Cordaitales, and possibly the Ephedraceae in the Gnetales.

5. Ginkgoales. Mostly extinct but with a single surviving species.

6. Coniferales. The largest and most important order of living gymnosperms; 45 genera with many Mesozoic fossil representatives (see CONIFERS).

7. Taxales. A small group of gymnosperms (the yews) formerly (and by some, still) included in the Coniferales.

8. Gnetales. An order including three peculiar genera of uncertain affinities, mostly tropical and subtropical, with few, if any fossil representatives.

For more information on the major extinct groups of gymnosperms, see PALEOBOTANY.

The general relationships of the gymnosperms is diagramed in fig. 1, which also shows the major divisions of the geological time scale. Representations of this sort are very general and tentative but may be useful in visualizing one hypothesis of the evolutionary history. Each of the larger divisions represented by living forms has had a continuous history down to the present. Only the Gnetales have no history of which one can be certain. They must have been derived in relatively recent times in areas where fossils rarely, if ever, were formed.

Gymnosperms are classified primarily on the basis of their reproductive structures. Although these structures are often described as flowers, especially in the original descriptions, it is better to avoid that term and speak of cones or strobili. All of the living gymnosperms have cones of two kinds: the pollen or staminate cones; and the seed or ovulate cones. The latter are greatly reduced in some species so that the cone structure is scarcely or

The tuberous forms have stems that are subterranean or remain very short and are often branched, but are otherwise similar. The stems of the columnar forms may have an armour of persistent leaf bases covering the younger portion only or occurring throughout their entire length, whereas in the tuberous forms the leaf bases may scale off. In some of the tuberous forms only the tip of the stem, the cones and the crown of leaves appear above the ground.

Though cycads are regarded as woody plants, they really have only a scant zone of wood, surrounding a very large pith and enclosed by a very large cortex. Thus the stem is relatively weak in comparison with other gymnosperms. The softer tissues are often permeated with mucilage canals. All cycads grow very slowly. Cycads of the columnar type attain their maximum height only after many centuries of growth. A new crown of leaves is produced annually in some species, biennially in others and the leaves of each successive crown usually persist for several years. Whenever cones are produced, a new crown of leaves is not formed until the following year or the plant may remain dormant for several years before growth is resumed.

The leaves of cycads are pinnately compound and remarkably like those of the palms in appearance. Usually the cuticle is relatively thick and hard and the leaves have a tough texture. In some species the tips of the leaflets are spiny and the entire plant with the spines pointing outward from all of the leaflets makes a formidable barrier.

The following genera of cycads are known:

Cycas, with about 16 species extending from southern Japan and Asia, through Indonesia to Australia, includes only columnar forms, which differ from the remaining genera in having the seed cones produced terminally. Upon resumption of vegetative growth, the crown of new leaves appears at the tip of the seed cone axis and individual cone scales are cast off rather than the entire cone. In all other genera the seed cone is crowded aside and may become detached as a unit if it has not previously disintegrated. The meristem forming the new crown of leaves then appears laterally to the base of the old cone. This condition holds for the pollen cones of all species. *Cycas revoluta* is frequently found in cultivation, in conservatories or as decorative ornamental tub plants or growing in the open in subtropical or warm temperate regions. The leaflets of *Cycas* have a single median vein. The seed-bearing members of the cone have in several species a dissected terminal blade with several ovules or seeds attached laterally to the rachis (*see* fig. 2). The pollen-bearing scales are narrower and have a broad pointed tip.

Macrozamia, with about 14 species, is confined to Australia. This genus includes columnar as well as tuberous species. The leaflets are parallel veined without a midrib and some species have a gland at the base of the leaflet. In many of them both kinds of cone scales are terminated by very long flat spines and in these, as well as in all remaining genera of cycads, only two ovules are produced on the ovulate scales. The seed cones of *Macrozamia denisonii* may become a yard long and weigh up to 85 lb.

Bowenia is also found in Australia. It has two species. These are both low tuberous forms, with the subterranean stem resembling a gigantic carrot. They differ from all other cycads in having leaves that are twice pinnate.

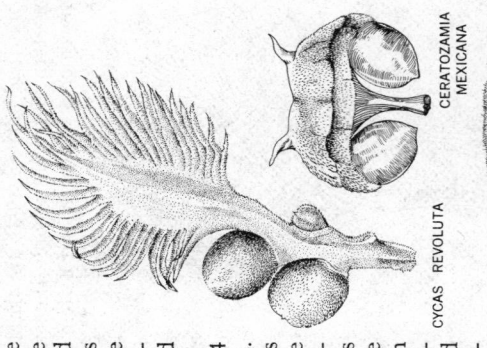

CYCAS REVOLUTA
CERATOZAMIA MEXICANA
DIOON EDULE

FROM ADRIANCE S. FOSTER AND ERNEST M. GIFFORD, JR., "COMPARATIVE MORPHOLOGY OF VASCULAR PLANTS," SAN FRANCISCO; W. H. FREEMAN AND COMPANY, 1959

FIG. 2.—SEED CONE SCALES OF CERTAIN CYCADS

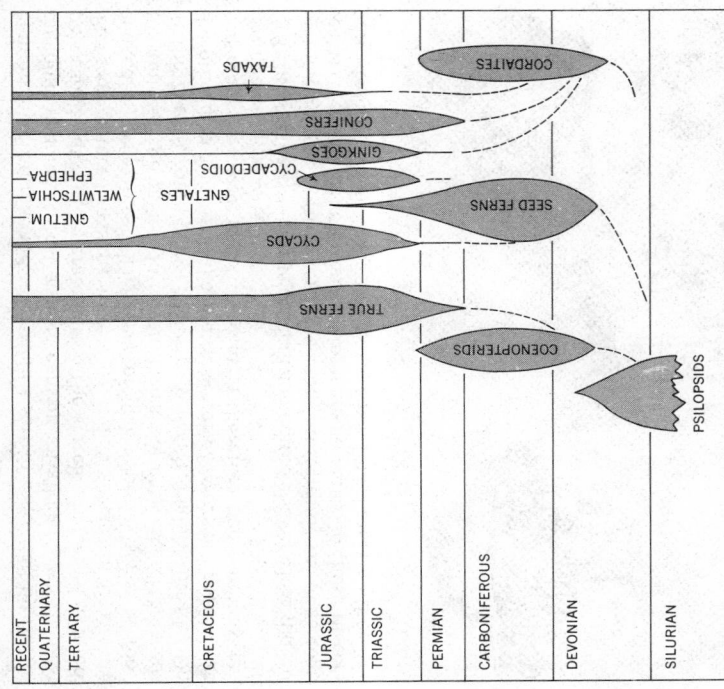

FIG. 1.—DIAGRAM SHOWING EVOLUTION AND RELATIONSHIPS OF GYMNOSPERMS

not at all obvious; some orders, such as the Ginkgoales and Taxales, probably never had ovulate cones. In those conifers that are monoecious both kinds of cones are borne on the same plant. In other conifers and in all other living gymnosperms, the species are dioecious with pollen cones and seed cones formed on different plants.

The pollen producing plant is often referred to as the male plant and the seed bearing plant as the female. This terminology is not strictly accurate, for the gymnosperms, like the mosses, ferns and angiosperms, have an alternation of an asexual sporophytic generation with the sexual or gametophytic generation. Although the gametophytic plants in gymnosperms and angiosperms are quite small (sometimes comprising only three cells), they are nonetheless individual plants of a separate generation and are properly called male or female. Since there is not general agreement as to whether the gymnosperms are truly heterosporous, rather than merely heterothallic, it appears preferable to avoid using the terms microspore and megaspore for the spores that give rise to the male and female gametophytes respectively.

The classification in all groups involves many histological details including the succession of events that go on within the ovules of the cones that bear them. Much of the following discussion necessarily has to do with these internal microscopic details. It is possible to distinguish the gymnosperms on the basis of vegetative characteristics, such as the morphology of the leaves, stems, buds, and on the externally obvious characteristics of the cones. But their classification and phylogenetic position is determined by their reproductive mechanism. *See also* PALEOBOTANY.

CYCADALES

This division includes about 85 species situated in the tropics and subtropics and includes also a large group of Mesozoic fossil cycads not placed with the Cycadeoidales. The living species belong to nine genera; all are dioecious, bearing only one kind of a cone on a particular plant, either seed cone or pollen cone. Four genera are found in the new world, five in the old world. There are two slightly different growth forms, those with columnar stems and those with stems usually referred to as tuberous. The columnar types consist of erect cylindrical stems, seldom branched, that may become 10 to 30 ft. high, surmounted by a crown of large compound leaves at the top giving the appearance of a palm.

GYMNOSPERMS

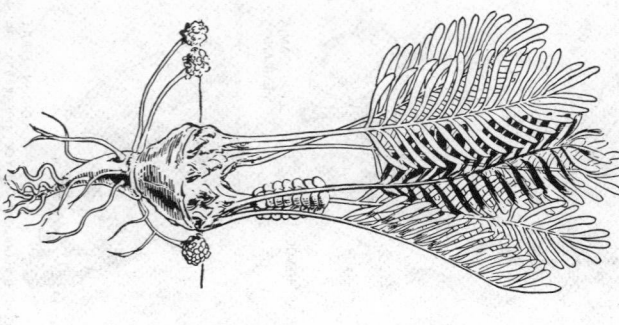

FIG. 3.—MATURE SPOROPHYTE OF ZAMIA BEARING A SEED CONE

The cones are relatively small and have peltate scales bearing two ovules each.

Encephalartos is a genus with 12 species, all South African cycads. Some are tuberous but most of them are of columnar habit. The margins of the leaves or the tips of the leaflets of many of these species are very jagged or spinous. The "bread palm," or kaffir bread, *Encephalartos caffer*, produces the largest known cone, sometimes fully a yard in length and weighing up to 100 lb. The other species have much smaller cones, but in several species these are borne in great numbers.

Stangeria, the other South African cycad, a genus with one (or possibly two) species, is a tuberous plant the leaflets of which have dichotomous veins branching off from a central midvein. Its leaves are so similar to those of some ferns that this plant was originally named and classified as a species of the fern *Lomaria*; not until many years later, when seed cones were found, was its status as a cycad recognized. The cones are terminal, their scales having a distinct lamina terminating the stalk.

The four remaining genera are all new world plants. *Dioon*, with four species, occurs in central Mexico. The leaflets, without a midrib, are parallel veined and have a broad insertion on the rachis. The dioons are all columnar in habit and have terminal cones. The ovulate cone scales are especially broad with the two ovules borne laterally on the stalks as shown in fig. 2. The pollen-bearing scales are also very broad at the apex, which is broad, triangular and turned upward.

Ceratozamia is another Mexican and Central American genus, with three to four species. The leaflets are pointed and narrowed below at their insertion on the rachis. They are short, columnar in habit and bear terminal cones. The cone scales are tipped by two firm laterally divergent spines (*see* fig. 2).

Microcycas is a monotypic genus of western Cuba, columnar in habit and up to 20 ft. high, with stems that sometimes branch. The leaflets are parallel veined and strongly reflexed on the rachis. The cones are large, the scales bearing two ovules each terminated by a rounded pyramidal extension. The single species, *Microcycas calocoma*, has not been successfully grown in cultivation.

Zamia is a genus of about 13 species, ranging from Florida through the Caribbean islands, Mexico, Central and South America to Brazil and Peru. Zamias are all tuberous in habit and frequently branched. The leaflets are parallel veined. *Zamia pygmaea*, of western Cuba, is probably the smallest cycad, with leaves only a few inches in length and a stem less than a half inch thick. It bears a correspondingly small seed cone with seeds less than 8 mm. long. Most species of *Zamia* are much larger and may produce more than a single cone, especially the pollen cones. The cone scales of *Zamia* are always shield shaped and though actually in a spiral arrangement, they are so regularly spaced that they appear to be attached in vertical rows. (*See* fig. 3.)

Uses of Cycads.

The cycads are valued as decorative, ornamental and conservatory plants. They are not hardy and only a few species may be used as tub plants in temperate regions. In subtropical regions, *Cycas revoluta* and a few species of *Dioon*, *Encephalartos* and *Macrozamia*, are sometimes grown outdoors. Their firm leathery leaves find floricultural use, both while fresh (as ceremonial "palm" leaves) or dried (sometimes dyed green and used in permanent decorations). The stems of *Cycas*, *Zamia*, *Encephalartos* and other genera contain much starch, and some yield a sort of sago used by the indigenous peoples. Most species contain an alkaloid, which must be washed out and separated from the starch when used as food. The very young leaves of some *Cycas* are cooked as vegetables. The seeds of many species serve as food for animals and man. In South Africa the natives use the seeds of the "bread palm," *Encephalartos caffer*, in making bread. On the other hand, in Australia the leaves of *Macrozamia moorei* are poisonous to cattle, and this plant is therefore being rapidly exterminated.

Relationships.

Of the genera enumerated above, when judged by morphology, *Cycas* is regarded as the most primitive. The cone scales of some of these show a closer resemblance to those of certain Mesozoic fossils than to the extremes found among other living species of *Cycas*.

In the old world the Australian *Macrozamia* includes several species that would stand close to *Cycas*, and some of the species of *Encephalartos* would stand only slightly higher in the scale of evolution.

The Australian *Bowenia* is in some respects the most highly specialized genus, but has twice compound leaves, which may be among the most primitive, and likewise, *Stangeria* is primitive with respect to its fernlike leaves and cone scales, but more specialized in other directions. Among the American genera *Dioon* is the most primitive genus. In some respects it is not far removed from *Cycas*. *Zamia* is the most advanced. *Ceratozamia* and *Microcycas* lie between these extremes, and each of them is somewhat specialized.

Reproductive Morphology.

The development of the reproductive structures in the cycads is so little variable that a general description of the phases of the life cycle for any one of them will serve as a general outline for most of the other genera.

The spores, or pollen, from which the male gametophytes develop, are produced on the scales of the pollen cone in sporangia that are arranged in groups (sori) on the lower surface of the scale and are similar in appearance to those of the Eusporangiate ferns. Fig. 4 shows the sporangia and sori of several species. The sporogenous tissue that will eventually give rise to the spores arises below the epidermis, and the sporangium has a jacket several cell layers thick. Within this is the tapetum, a layer of nutritive cells that produce materials needed by the developing spores.

The spore mother cells undergo a specialized type of cell division, called meiosis, which reduces the chromosome number by one-half and produces four cells, each of which is a spore. This reduction of chromosome number from the sporophytic (symbolized by $2n$) to the gametophytic number (n) is necessary, of course, since fertilization subsequently will double the gametic number. The division of the spore (pollen grain) nucleus results in the formation of a gametophytic plant—even though very small—equivalent to the prothallus of a fern or to a leafy moss plant. In the development of

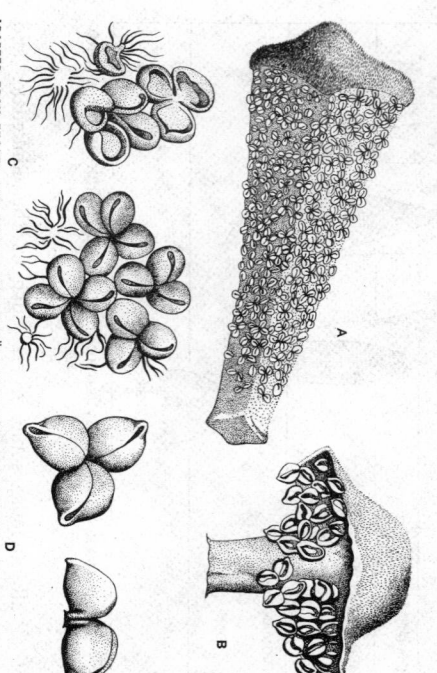

FIG. 4.—SCALES OF THE POLLEN CONES OF CYCADS: (A) CYCAS CIRCINALIS: (B) ZAMIA INTEGRIFOLIA; (C) PARTS OF A; (D) PARTS OF B SHOWING SPORANGIA GROUPED INTO SORI

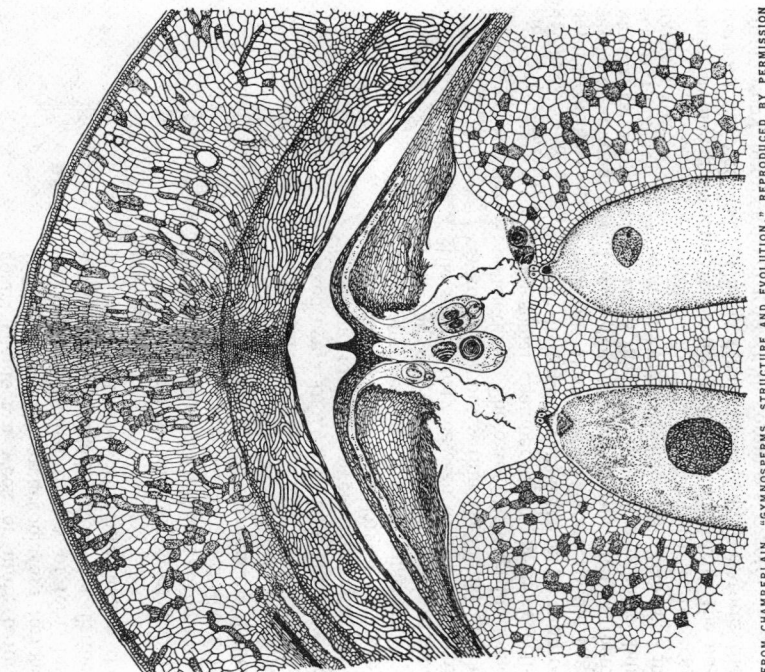

pollen in cycads, a single vegetative cell is formed, the prothallial cell, and it persists. The remaining nucleus divides again, giving rise to the tube nucleus and a generative cell. By this time the pollen grain has developed a specialized coat consisting of an outer layer, the exine, and an inner layer, the intine. Only the intine is capable of extension as the pollen tube in later stages of development. The pollen grains are in this three-celled condition at the time of shedding and all subsequent development must be observed in the nucellus of the ovules where some of the pollen eventually becomes lodged in the process of pollination. Fig. 5(A) and (B) shows the stages before the pollen grain is shed and (C) and (D) after it germinates on the nucellus.

Pollination is accomplished by the wind in all of the genera; reports of possible insect pollination in one of the African species may indicate the evolution of another type of pollination. In the cycads that have been observed closely a pollination droplet appears at this time at the micropyle, a small opening through the integument of the ovule. This droplet originates from the tissues at the tip of the nucellus, which is the tissue of the ovule in which the spore producing the female gametophyte arises. The formation of the pollination droplet produces the pollen chamber in the nucellus at its tip below the micropyle. The pollen grains falling upon the droplet are held within it by surface tension. As the liquid is resorbed into the nucellus, the entrapped pollen grains are brought into intimate contact with the cells lining the pollen chamber and here they germinate.

The pollen tubes are formed by an extension of the intine, which emerges at the side where the exine is thinnest. The tubes grow out into the nucellus and penetrate this tissue laterally. Usually there are several radiating outward and downward in all directions. The exine is spread open and adheres to the exposed end, where it may be seen throughout the period of pollen tube growth. When the growing end has penetrated deeply into the nucellus, this opposite exposed end, tipped by the exine, elongates and bends downward toward the female gametophyte. Meanwhile the generative cell within the pollen tube has divided to form two cells, the stalk cell and the body cell. The stalk cell clasps or partially surrounds the prothallial cell and maintains contact with the body cell, which enlarges greatly as the exposed end of the pollen tube expands and elongates. Fig. 5(C) and (D) shows stages in germination of the pollen grains and the formation of the pollen tube, of which only the lower end is shown. The body cell divides later to form two cells within each of which a sperm is organized. Fig. 6 shows later stages of several pollen tubes in position above the eggs of the female gametophyte.

As the time of division of the body cell approaches, two conspicuous structures, the blepharoplasts, appear in the cytoplasm of the body cell on opposite sides of the nucleus. Similar blepharoplasts are found in sperm-producing cells of ferns. During division of the nucleus these play a role similar to that of the centrosome of animal cells in marking the poles of the spindle. After mitosis they organize the cilia of the sperm.

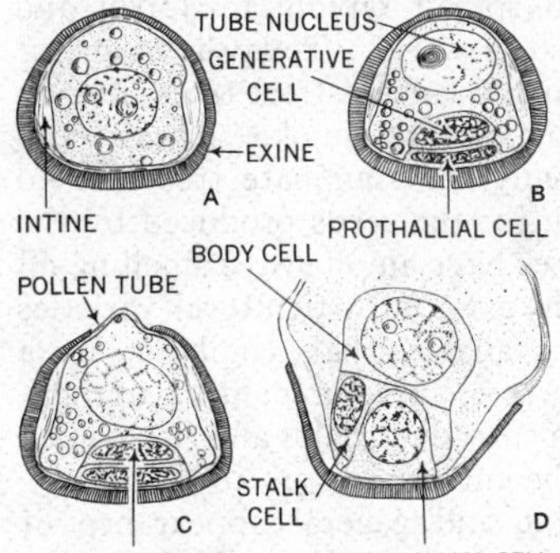

The sperms of cycads, nearly .3 mm. in diameter, are large enough to be observed with a hand lens. They are top-shaped cells, the greater part of which is occupied by nucleus. From the pointed end is a spiral row of thousands of cilia that emerge from the cytoplasm in a single spiral band that encircles the sperm several times between the apex and the outer margin.

As the female gametophyte enlarges, the nucellar tissue between the exposed ends of the pollen tubes and the female gametophyte breaks down completely. Meanwhile, the opening above the pollen

FIG. 5.—DEVELOPMENT OF MALE GAMETOPHYTE IN DIOON EDULE

FROM CHAMBERLAIN, "GYMNOSPERMS, STRUCTURE AND EVOLUTION," REPRODUCED BY PERMISSION OF THE UNIVERSITY OF CHICAGO PRESS

(A) microspore; (B) germinating microspore, or pollen grain; (C) later stage in which generative cell has given rise to stalk cell and body cell

FIG. 6.—DIOON EDULE

FROM CHAMBERLAIN, "GYMNOSPERMS, STRUCTURE AND EVOLUTION," REPRODUCED BY PERMISSION OF THE UNIVERSITY OF CHICAGO PRESS

Part of a longitudinal section of an ovule at the time of fertilization. Pollen tube on the left shows the body cell undivided; middle tube shows two sperms and the remains of the prothallial and stalk cells; right pollen tube shows two sperm mother cells and the spiral ciliated band beginning to develop. Two pollen tubes have discharged their sperms. A sperm has entered the egg on the left. Two sperms, in the liquid discharged from the pollen tube, are ready to enter the egg on the right

chamber at the top of the nucellar tip extending into the lower end of the micropyle is closed. The nucellus becomes a very thin and membranous cap, tipped by a brown point, as shown in fig. 6.

Ovule and Seed.—As previously stated, the ovulate cones of cycads vary considerably in appearance depending upon the size and shape of the scales of a particular species. Fig. 2 shows how the ovules are attached in three different genera. Ovules are borne at the lateral margins of species with peltate scales, as well as those having spatulate cone scales. They are only partially developed at the time of pollination, but become full grown before fertilization takes place.

Young ovules consist of a central ovoidal mass of tissue, the nucellus, surrounded by a thick integument that leaves only a narrow passageway, the micropyle, leading to the tip of the nucellus. The ovules are always attached at the end opposite the micropyle and are thus regarded as atropous or erect.

Deep within the tissue of the nucellus an enlarged cell, the spore mother cell, appears. This cell undergoes meiosis during which the chromosome number is reduced from $2n$ to n in forming spores. Only one of the row of four spores persists; the three on the side toward the micropyle are usually aborted. This haploid (n) cell gives rise to the female gametophyte. The latter begins to develop by free-nuclear division, that is, no cell walls are formed between the nuclei at first. Soon it becomes an oval cellular structure situated in the centre of the nucellus. At the upper end of the gametophyte several cells enlarge greatly and form the archegonia, or egg-containing structures. These may usually be recognized long before they are fully developed.

The early formation of the archegonia checks the growth and enlargement of the gametophyte in this region so that these egg-bearing structures come to lie in a cylindrical depression, the archegonial chamber (fig. 6). The wall of the spore becomes thick and remains to envelop the entire gametophyte as a distinct tough spore coat. It is ruptured only in the region above the archegonial chamber a week or more before fertilization. The archegonia are formed in a manner similar to that of ferns but are deeply embedded and have a distinct jacket of nutritive cells surrounding the eggs.

Fig. 6 shows the disposition of the female gametophyte with the archegonia and its relation to the pollen tubes above in the nucellus and to the surrounding tissues of the ovule. The eggs of cycads are so large that they are easily visible to the naked eye. In *Dioon edule* they are up to 4 mm. long and over 1 mm. in diameter, unquestionably the largest eggs produced anywhere in the plant kingdom.

At the time of fertilization a pair of motile sperms may be seen with a hand lens swimming about within the liquid of the pollen tube. These are discharged into the archegonial chamber upon the neck cells of the archegonia causing them to rupture and thus afford direct access to the egg. The motility of the sperms enables them to enter the neck of the archegonia, but soon afterward the cilia are left behind in the upper part of the cytoplasm of the egg.

Only the naked nucleus penetrates the nucleus of the egg cell. This is fertilization, and it restores the chromosome number from n to $2n$ in forming a zygote.

Sometimes additional sperms enter the upper part of the egg. However, these remain lodged near the neck of the archegonium, where they may still be found and recognized by their spiral bands of cilia in the embryos dissected out weeks or months later.

Microcycas calocoma, of Cuba, differs from other cycads in having a large number of smaller archegonia situated over the surface of the gametophyte. Its pollen tubes differ also in giving rise to many sperms each, instead of the usual two.

The embryo of all cycads is formed from the repeated division of the zygotic nucleus. These early free-nuclear divisions and all stages before cell elongation has begun are included in what is called the proembryo stage. Nuclear divisions take place until there are from 500 to 1,000 free nuclei. Walls appear between the nuclei situated in the lower part of the archegonium and in some genera the entire egg may be blocked off into cell areas, but the growing meristem of the embryo is always confined to the lowest group of cells. The cells immediately above this meristem elongate to form a suspensor, which, by elongating tremendously, thrusts the embryonic tip into the tissue of the gametophyte as the latter becomes the nutritive endosperm of the seed. This process is both mechanical and digestive. The embryonic structures secrete an enzyme that hollows out a cavity within the gametophyte while the suspensor, which becomes long and coiled, keeps the embryo pushed as far forward as possible.

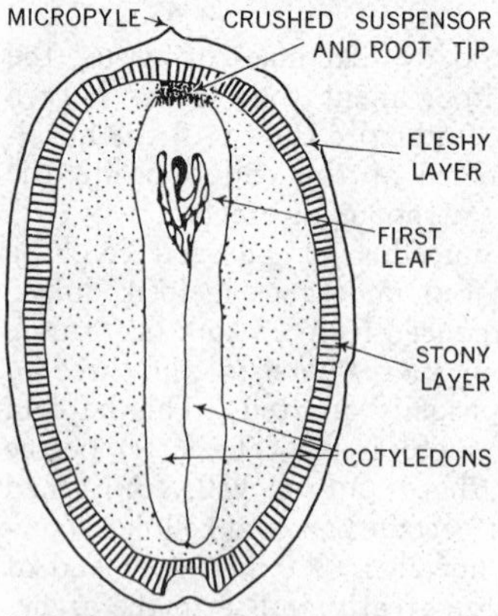

Since there are several eggs that may be fertilized, an embryo may begin to develop from more than one of them, a condition referred to as simple polyembryony. However the plural embryos are in intimate competition with each other. All save one are usually eliminated long before this embryo begins to form cotyledons and only a single embryo develops fully as the embryo of the seed.

Fig. 7 shows a tangle of suspensors originating from five fertilized eggs shown at the top, as they appear when dissected out about a month after fertilization. The largest embryo that has survived competition is shown at the tip; this embryo is still very small.

Fig. 8 shows a similar seed at maturity. A single dicotyledonous embryo occupying a central position is surrounded by the endosperm (female gametophyte) and with the ovule wall, which now has a stony layer, forming the testa.

Fig. 9 shows a seed of *Dioon edule* in germination. Fig. 10 is a seedling with its first leaf expanded. The stem bearing this leaf and the scale leaves is still so small that it remains hidden, while the primary root bearing secondary branches has become fleshy.

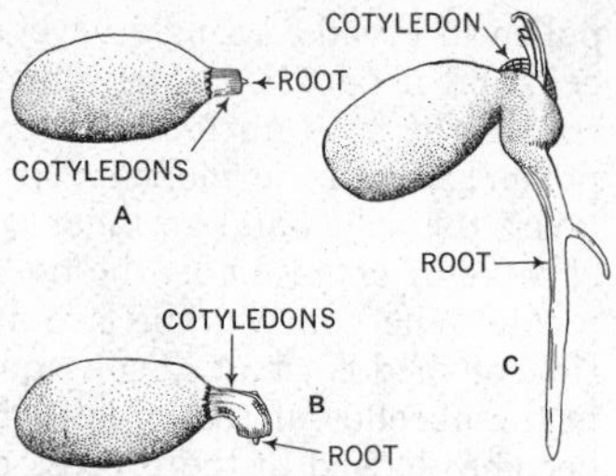

GINKGOALES

This order of gymnosperms has only a single living representative: *Ginkgo biloba*, the ginkgo, or maidenhair tree. It is native to China, although it has not been found forming native forests in any part of Asia. The tree is frequently cultivated in temperate regions, and in China it is usually found at temples and shrines, or under circumstances that could account for it as escaped from such cultivation.

Apparently, the maidenhair tree was unknown to the ancient Chinese and occurs in the literature for the first time in the 11th century. Not only was it brought into cultivation, but it was introduced into poetry and painting, where it remains an important object of representation. This early interest in the plant stems from its literary name of the seed, the fleshy outer layer of which has a waxy bloom, is Silver Apricot. From these beginnings the ginkgo spread rapidly to Japan and to the western world. Today it is one of the most highly valued street trees because of its resistance to smoke, disease and insects. Only the staminate trees should be planted, for the seeds produced by the ovulate trees have an offensive smelling oil in the fleshy coat. Horticultural varieties are now available that combine, in a staminate tree, predominantly upright, rather than spreading, habit and rich golden leaves in the autumn.

The habit and general appearance of ginkgo is that of a conifer. The wood is similar to that of conifers; its wedge-shaped leaves, which are not evergreen, have dichotomous veins that remind one of the leaflets of the maidenhair fern, though they are much larger and thicker and show considerable variability in size, shape and lobing. In winter the tree is not conspicuously different from the trees of many deciduous angiosperms. However, a closer examination of the twigs shows that these are long shoots bearing many dwarf

FROM CHAMBERLAIN, "GYMNOSPERMS, STRUCTURE AND EVOLUTION," REPRODUCED BY PERMISSION OF THE UNIVERSITY OF CHICAGO PRESS

FIG. 7.—CERATOZAMIA MEXICANA: YOUNG EMBRYOS WITH SUSPENSORS, SHOWING THE TOUGH EGG MEMBRANES AT THE TOP; SLIGHTLY LARGER THAN NATURAL SIZE

MICROPYLE

CRUSHED SUSPENSOR AND ROOT TIP

COTYLEDONS

FIRST LEAF

FLESHY LAYER

STONY LAYER

FROM CHAMBERLAIN, "GYMNOSPERMS, STRUCTURE AND EVOLUTION," REPRODUCED BY PERMISSION OF THE UNIVERSITY OF CHICAGO PRESS

FIG. 8.—MATURE SEED OF DIOON EDULE

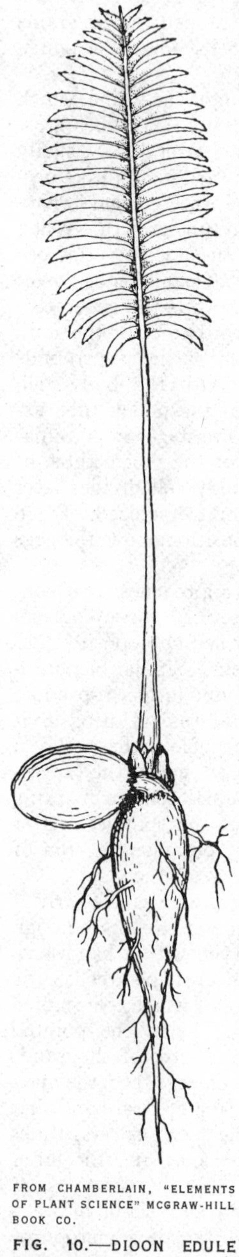

FROM CHAMBERLAIN, "ELEMENTS OF PLANT SCIENCE," McGRAW-HILL BOOK CO.

FIG. 10.—DIOON EDULE SEEDLING

COTYLEDONS

ROOT

COTYLEDON

ROOT

FROM CHAMBERLAIN, "THE LIVING CYCADS," REPRODUCED BY PERMISSION OF THE UNIVERSITY OF CHICAGO PRESS

FIG. 9.—DIOON EDULE SEEDLING: (A, B) ROOT TIP AND COTYLEDONS EMERGING AND TURNING DOWN (ABOUT TWO-THIRDS OF THE PROTRUDING PART IS THE COTYLEDON, WITH THE ROOT VISIBLE AT THE END); (C) LATER STAGE WITH THREE LEAVES BETWEEN THE COTYLEDONS. ABOUT HALF NATURAL SIZE

branches. The long shoots continue the growth on the end of long shoots of the previous year, bearing leaves that alternate in a spiral arrangement. Along these twigs two or more years old are the dwarf branches, which originated from buds in the axils of the leaves of the first year's shoots. These spurs vary in length with their age, and bear groups of leaves that arise from the bud at the tip in annual succession for many years. Occasionally, the dwarf branches give rise to long shoots growing out from their tips. Dwarf branches have a relatively thick cortex and large pith with the wood zone correspondingly narrowed; taken as individual units they are comparable to a miniature cycad trunk with its terminal crown of leaves. It is on these dwarf branches that the reproductive structures are borne, and like all living cycads, the trees are strictly dioecious. Fig. 11 shows these branches with ovule-bearing stalks and pollen cones near the time of pollination, when the new leaves appearing in the spring are half grown. The ovules are always paired, though it is not usual that both ovules are developed; more frequently only one of the pair enlarges to develop fully (fig. 11[C]). The aborted ovule remains as a scar at the base of the enlarged seed.

The reproductive morphology differs only in minor details from that of cycads. The pollen is borne in sporangial appendages of which there are many that make up the pollen cone. Each appendage bears a pair of deflexed sporangia on the end of a short stalk as shown in fig. 11(E). The pollen grains, formed from spore mother cells as in cycads, also have double spore coats with several cells formed internally at the time of pollination. Likewise, the pollen is wind borne, with the pollen falling into pollination droplets that appear at the micropyles of the ovules. The ovules enlarge and are soon full grown as represented by fig. 12, which shows a longitudinal section through a fully enlarged ovule near the time of fertilization (A) and a matured seed (B).

After fertilization, which is accomplished, as in cycads, by motile sperms, the proembryo initiates its development in the same manner. However, after about 250 free nuclei have been formed, cell walls appear between all of the nuclei so that the entire egg cavity is filled with cellular tissue. The cells of the lower part of the proembryo divide rapidly, while those near the upper part begin to elongate and push the embryo downward into the gametophyte (which becomes the endosperm of the seed), but usually not farther than one-third the length of this tissue before the seed is shed. The seeds usually fall from the tree in au-

tumn before they are fully matured, and the soft, outer, fleshy seed coat soon develops a very putrid odour. If planted, the seed will not germinate for many months, but this delay is due only to the immaturity of the embryo. A small percentage of the seeds may contain two embryos matured to the stage with cotyledons, which may develop internally in the ginkgo seed with somewhat less close competition in their earliest stages than in cycads. This is due to the fact that the smaller archegonia are slightly separated and long coiled suspensors are not formed. Still, in several species embryos from simple polyembryony are usually eliminated; less than 2% of the ripe seeds contain more than a single embryo.

Although the reproductive morphology of ginkgo has much in common with that of the cycads, they differ in other respects. The stem anatomy, aside from that of the spur shoots, is much closer to that of the conifers; the long stems have relatively little pith, a narrow cortex and a very large volume of wood that grows rapidly from a cambium and forms distinct annual growth rings. In the spur branches the pith, wood zone and cortex are proportioned more nearly as in a cycad trunk.

Ginkgo is regarded as a descendant of the Cordaitales, to which it is linked by a series of many Mesozoic fossil forms—*Baiera, Ginkgoites,* etc.—found in widely scattered regions of North America, Europe and Asia.

TAXALES

The Taxales are a small order of gymnosperms usually included in the Coniferales. They are separated here since, according to the work of Rudolph Florin and others, the taxads proper have never had ovulate cones. That is, the ovules are borne terminally and singly on axes of the plant and are not aggregated into cone-like structures. Their evolutionary history can be traced back separately, well into the Mesozoic. There are four or five genera recognized: *Taxus* (yew), *Torreya* (California nutmeg or stinking cedar), *Austrotaxus, Amentotaxus,* and *Nothotaxus.* All of them are shrubs or trees (rarely reaching a maximum height of 90 ft.).

The usually spirally arranged leaves are needlelike, but flat, fairly wide, and sharp pointed. The Upper Triassic genus *Paleo-taxus* is similar to modern forms, and *Taxus* and *Torreya* extend back to the Jurassic.

Taxus with about seven species is widely distributed in Europe, North America, eastern Asia and Asia Minor. It is the only member of economic significance, having wood used for cabinetmaking, bows, etc., and having poisonous properties. *Torreya* has five or six species found in

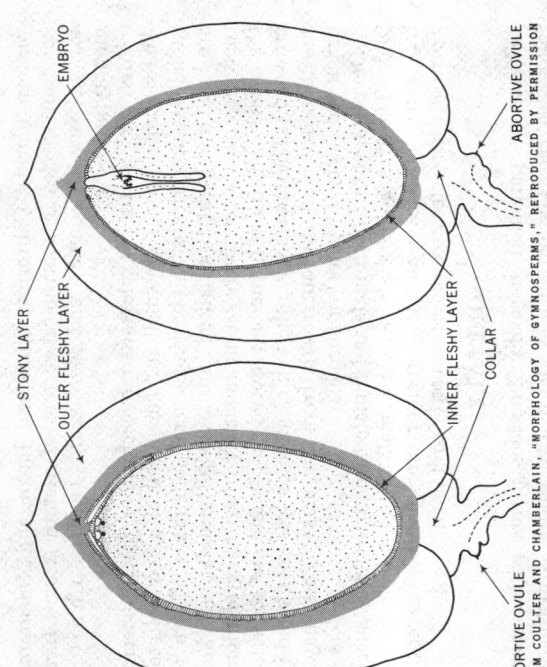

EMBRYO
STONY LAYER
OUTER FLESHY LAYER
ABORTIVE OVULE
INNER FLESHY LAYER
COLLAR
ABORTIVE OVULE

FROM COULTER AND CHAMBERLAIN, "MORPHOLOGY OF GYMNOSPERMS." REPRODUCED BY PERMISSION OF THE UNIVERSITY OF CHICAGO PRESS

FIG. 12.—GINKGO BILOBA: (A) LONGITUDINAL SECTION OF AN OVULE WHEN FULLY ENLARGED, SOME TIME AFTER POLLINATION: (B) SIMILAR SECTION WITH THE STONY LAYER HARD, THE INNER FLESHY LAYER DRY AND PAPERY. MAGNIFICATION ABOUT X 2

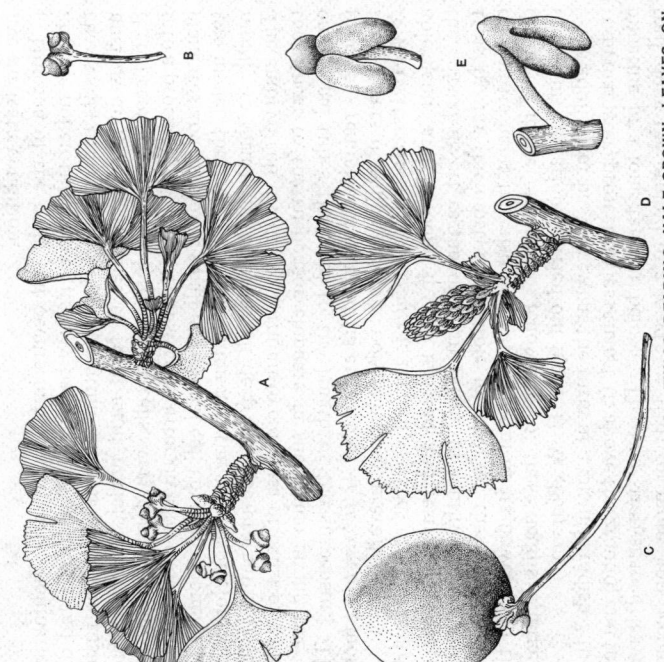

FIG. 11.—GINKGO BILOBA: (A) TWIGS BEARING HALF-GROWN LEAVES ON DWARF BRANCHES WITH OVULATE STALKS: (B) OVULATE STALKS AS THEY APPEAR AT TIME OF POLLINATION: (C) AN OVULE AFTER ENLARGEMENT: (D) TWIG BEARING A POLLEN CONE; (E) SPORANGIA OF CONE ENLARGED

western Florida, California, China and Japan, and *Amentotaxus* has four species in subtropical regions of eastern Asia. *Austrotaxus* (New Caledonia) and *Nothotaxus* (eastern China) are monotypic.

Members of the Taxales are monoecious or often dioecious. The staminate cones are small and composed of a few peltate or radially symmetrical scales bearing several pollen sacs. The ovules are large and highly specialized and basically terminal. In *Taxus* there has been a relatively recent tendency toward aggregation of the ovules, which are borne on reduced shoots and are sometimes crowded. The taxads have the ovules more or less enveloped in a so-called aril, a fleshy outgrowth from the axis. This may be bright red (as in the yews) or purple.

Development of both male and female gametophytes is special-ized. The archegonia are often very small and may lack the ven-tral canal nucleus. Simple polyembryony prevails except in *Torreya* where cleavage polyembryony is retained.

GNETALES

These are perennial, normally dioecious plants with opposite simple leaves. The perianth of one or two whorls is distinctive, and sharply contrasts this division with other gymnosperms. The cones are more complex than in other forms, consisting of an axis bearing crossed pairs of bracts or a number of superposed whorls of bracts, each whorl connate in a cuplike form. In either case the ovulate or staminate structures, which for convenience may be called "flowers," are axillary to these bracts. The flower always consists of one or two pairs of free or connate bracts, enclosing either a single ovule with a long projecting perianth, or from one to six stamens.

It is evident that it is the flowers of Gnetales, especially the ovulate flowers, which are equivalent to the cones of conifers (*e.g.*, compare the female cone of *Torreya*) and not the whole "cone." This group of flowers, which might well be called a compound cone, is also comparable to the catkinlike inflorescence of certain flower-ing plants.

The Gnetales are superficially similar to the angiosperms in their anatomy, for though the phloem remains typical of the gymno-sperms in general, true vessels are associated with the typical gymnospermous tracheids and there are no resin canals. The tracheids have very large circular bordered pits; the vessels of Gnetales have evolved from them by the dissolution of the closing membrane of these pits. The cells, placed end to end, function as long tubes for the conduction of water. Vessels in the angio-sperms have evolved from tracheids with an entirely different type of pitting and are a completely independent acquisition.

The order Gnetales includes only three genera, which are so entirely different as to suggest that each should be regarded as the type of a different order. Perhaps such a taxonomic treatment would be preferable to that usually followed; an intermediate course, recognizing each as the type of a family, will be followed here. The Gnetales, in the broad sense, have had only a very recent fossil history and the relationships of the plants are still imperfectly understood. It seems clear that none of the three can be regarded as ancestral to the flowering plants despite some interesting examples of convergent evolution. From the work of A. J. Eames there is considerable evidence that the Ephedraceae are related to the extinct Cordaitales; and there is some evidence that the other two families are not. Until the latter have been thoroughly studied they are better placed with the Ephedraceae in what is probably an unnatural order. The three families are characterized as follows:

The Ephedraceae includes only the genus *Ephedra*, consisting of much branched, small-leaved xerophytic shrubs. The ovule has two integuments containing a female gametophyte with arche-gonia, similar to that of the Coniferales.

Welwitschia is the only genus of the Welwitschiaceae; it contains a single species. The plants are large, tuberous and mostly under-ground. After the formation of the cotyledons (seed leaves) they develop only two enormously long and straggling parallel-veined leaves. The ovule has one integument and no archegonia are formed.

The Gnetaceae are all put into the genus *Gnetum*, and are either trees or large woody climbers with numerous net-veined leaves superficially indistinguishable from those of a dicotyledonous angiosperm. The ovule has two integuments and there are no archegonia in the female gametophyte.

Ephedra.—This largest genus of Gnetales has about 35 species, represented in America, Asia and Europe. It is confined to more or less arid warm-temperature and tropical regions; one species is common on sand dunes along parts of the Mediterranean coast. The finer branches are green; the surface of the long internodes is marked by fine longitudinal ribs; and at the nodes are borne pairs of small, partially connate scale leaves, the general appear-ance being similar to that of a stem of a horsetail (*Equisetum*) or a twig of *Casuarina*. Some of the branches bear pairs of small cones in the axis of the scale leaves. The cone scales are broad and imbricate. Each staminate flower (fig. 13) consists of an inconspicuous peri-anth, composed of two more or less con-crescent bracts, enclosing an axis project-ing beyond the perianth and terminating in two (sometimes more, up to six or eight) sporangia. The resemblance of this struc-ture to a stamen is obvious, but it is no less clearly homologous with the cone scale of conifers.

The ovulate flower is enveloped in a closely fitting perianth of two more or less connate bracts, as in the staminate flower. This perianth encloses a single ovule with two integuments; the inner, which is not

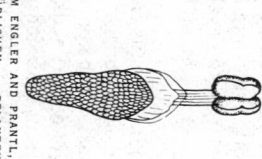

FIG. 13.—A STAMINATE FLOWER OF EPHEDRA FRAGILIS

more than two cells thick, prolonged upward as a beaklike micro-pyle; the outer, which is thicker and later becomes woody, only reaching about halfway up the micropylar beak. The micro-pyle secretes a pollination drop, as in conifers.

A prothallus is organized exactly as in conifers, the two to five archegonia being developed from separate superficial cells at the apex, and having long, multicellular necks. About the time when they first appear, the tip of the nucellus begins to break down, this disorganization proceeding downward until there is (when the archegonia are mature) a broad circular pollen chamber open to the top of the prothallus, thus permitting the pollen grains to rest on the necks of the archegonia. The development of the pollen grain is closely similar to that of *Larix* and it is shed in the five-nucleate condition.

Division of the body cell occurs immediately after pollination, and the pollen tube forces its way between the neck cells and dis-charges its contents into the egg within a few hours. The fusion nucleus divides three times to form eight nuclei, some of which then become organized into walled cells, very loosely connected into a proembryo. Each of these cells, after division of its nucleus, elongates and cuts off a small embryonal cell containing one of the two nuclei; the larger cell remaining and the suspensor elongating rapidly to thrust the embryo cell deep into the prothallus tissue. The embryo cell divides to form an ovoid mass of cells, of which those next to the suspensor elongate in succession giving rise to embryonal tubes that add to the length of the suspensor. The process is reminiscent of what takes place in *Actinostrobus* among the conifers in which cleavage polyembryony prevails.

Welwitschia.—*W. mirabilis* is the only species of this remark-able genus and is found in two isolated and restricted areas of the coastal desert region of Damaraland in southwestern Africa. It is by far the most remarkable member of the Gnetales not only in its habit but also both in the form of its flowers and the details of its development. Knowledge of these details is largely due to investigations carried out by H. H. W. Pearson.

An adult plant has somewhat the form of a gigantic radish 2 to 4 ft. in diameter, projecting less than 1 ft. above the ground, and ter-minating in a long taproot below. The two strap-shaped leaves trail along the ground to a length of 10 ft. or more, and become split into a number of narrow thonglike strips. They retain the power of growth at the base throughout the life of the plant, which probably exceeds 100 years. The characteristics of the plant accord well with the interesting suggestion that it may represent an "adult seedling." Numerous circular pits occur on the concentric ridges of the depressed and wrinkled crown, marking the positions of former inflorescences, new ridges subsequently appearing outside the old ones. The inflorescences have the form of two-branched stalks bearing the cones, from 1 to 20 in the ovulate plant and up to 50 in the staminate. The ovulate cone is about 1 in. long and scarlet in colour, the staminate smaller and more slender. Each consists of an axis that bears a large number of alternating pairs of overlapping bracts, in the axils of which are the flowers. The staminate flower (fig. 14[A]) is enclosed by a perianth of two opposite pairs of bracts, surrounding a ring of six stamens, united below but free above, each terminating in a three-chambered anther. In the centre of the flower is an abortive ovule, the integument of which projects upward as a spirally twisted tube with a stigmalike expansion at its apex. In the development of the pollen grain a single prothallial nucleus is cut off, disappearing about the time of pollination. There are only two further divisions, resulting in a tube nucleus and two male nuclei; the formation of a stalk cell, which occurs without exception in all conifers, as well as in *Ephedra*, is omitted. There is evidence that pollination is effected by insect agency. The ovulate flower consists of an erect ovule with two investments: the outer is winged and represents the perianth, formed of a pair of completely connate bracts; and the inner is the integument, which has the usual long tubular micropyle (fig. 14[B]). No pollen chamber is formed, but numerous pollen tubes grow downward in the nucellar cap. The spore begins to develop as usual, becoming filled with protoplasm containing over 1,000 nuclei before walls appear; the latter divide the whole sac into multinucleate compartments, those in the micropylar end and containing fewer and larger nuclei, any of which may function as eggs. The remainder contain about a dozen nuclei each, all of which fuse together in the compartment, thus forming a tissue of uninucleate cells, which then grows considerably and may be termed the endosperm.

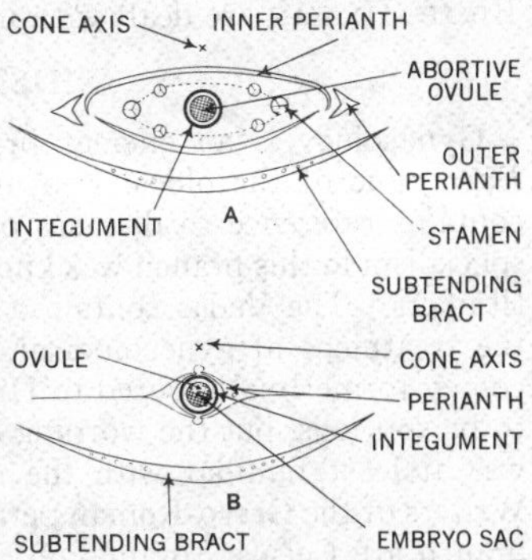

The micropylar multinucleate cells put out long tubes that grow upward into the nucellar cap, and into which the egg nuclei pass. These ascending prothallial tubes meet and fuse with the descending pollen tubes; at the point of fusion, fertilization occurs.

The fertilized egg forms a wall and elongates into a tube from which an embryo tip cell is cut off, the remainder of the tube being the suspensor, which carries the embryo deep into the endosperm. Thus it appears that only a single embryo is produced from each zygote, in contrast with cleavage polyembryony in *Ephedra*. The further development is similar to that in *Ephedra*, including the formation of embryonal tubes from the young embryo.

Gnetum.—This is represented by about 30 species, mostly climbers, found both in tropical Amer-

ica and in tropical regions of the old world. The oval leaves are 2 or 3 in. long and are borne in pairs, at the swollen nodes. The cones are long and cylindrical and bear whorls of flowers at each node, accompanied by numerous sterile hairs, in the axil of cup-like concrescent bracts. In a staminate inflorescence very numerous flowers may be found, up to about 3,000 in one species. whereas in an ovulate spike the number of flowers probably does not reach 100. The staminate flower consists of a perianth of two concrescent bracts enclosing a slender axis projecting above the perianth and terminating in two sporangia. The pollen appears to be formed in precisely the same manner as that of *Welwitschia*. Incomplete ovulate flowers are often found in the staminate inflorescence containing ovules with one integument instead of two, but these rarely set seed.

A perfect ovulate flower (fig. 15) consists of an ovule with three investments of which the outer is generally regarded as a perianth of two concrescent bracts. Of the other two the inner arises first and develops the long slender micropylar tube characteristic of all Gnetales and is followed by a much shorter outer covering, the outer integument.

Several spores may begin to develop in a young ovule, but only one attains full size. In all species the embryo sac, as in *Welwitschia*, becomes filled with numerous free nuclei, and in some species (probably in the large majority) fertilization occurs at this stage, the contents of pollen tubes being discharged into the embryo sac, any of the nuclei near the micropylar end apparently functioning as eggs. The lower half of the sac then becomes partitioned, as in *Welwitschia*, into multinucleate compartments, the nuclei of each subsequently fusing so that an endosperm of uninucleate cells results, into which the developing embryos penetrate.

Each zygote of *Gnetum gnemon* is stated to elongate and form a long tortuous multinucleate suspensor, from the lower end of which a small, also multinucleate, embryo cell is cut off. Walls are said to appear in this "cell" and so reduce it to a tissue of uninucleate cells. Although this account may not apply to all species of *Gnetum*, it is surprising to find certain resemblances to the embryogeny of some Cupressaceae, notably *Juniperus*, in which suspensor-embryo initial cells give rise to embryos in a specialized type of cleavage polyembryony.

The later development of the embryo is similar to that of *Welwitschia*, and in both genera a rodlike outgrowth is formed from the hypocotyl at its junction with the radicle, which serves as a feeder and draws nourishment from the endosperm during the germination of the seed. The climbing species of *Gnetum* are characterized by the production of several concentric cylinders of wood and bast from as many successively formed cambium cylinders; they are produced in the pericycle, as in *Cycas*.

(J. T. Bz.; W. T. Sa.; R. W. H.; X.)

BIBLIOGRAPHY.—E. Strasburger, *Die Coniferen und Gnetaceen* (1872), *Die Angiospermen und die Gymnospermen* (1879); A. B. Rendle, *The Classification of the Flowering Plants*, vol. 1 (1904); J. M. Coulter and C. J. Chamberlain, *Morphology of Gymnosperms* (1917), *Gymnosperms: Structure and Evolution* (1935); *The Living Cycads* (1919); R. Pilger, in Engler and Prantl, *Die natürlichen Pflanzenfamilien*, vol. 13, 2nd ed. (1926); K. Schnarf, "Embryologie der Gymnospermen," in Linsbauer, *Handbuch der Pflanzenanatomie*, vol. 10, part 2 (1933); J. Schuster, "Cycadaceae," in Engler, *Das Pflanzenreich*, iv, 1 (1932); H. H. W. Pearson, *Gnetales* (1929); T. M. Harris, "The Relationship of the Caytoniales," *Phytomorphology*, 1:29–39 (1951); A. C. Seward, "The Story of the Maidenhair Tree," *Sci. Prog.*, 32:420–440 (1938); A. S. Foster and E. M. Gifford, Jr., *Comparative Morphology of Vascular Plants* (1959); K. Esau, *Anatomy of Seed Plants* (1960).

(J. T. Bz.; W. T. Sa.; R. W. H.; X.)

GYMPIE, a city of March county, Queensland, Austr., lies on the Mary river 107 mi. N. of Brisbane by rail. Pop. (1966) 11,279. Gold was discovered by James Nash in 1867 and mining continued to 1930, the total yield of gold being 4,500,000 oz. Gympie became a municipality in 1880 and a city in 1905. The district is one of the state's best dairying, agricultural and fruitgrowing areas. Powdered milk and baby foods are manufactured.

GYNANDROMORPH (GYNANDER), a zoological term denoting an organism in which the body is of fundamentally different constitution in different regions, male in some, female in others, the areas being quite clearly demarked.

INNER PERIANTH
CONE AXIS
ABORTIVE OVULE
OUTER PERIANTH
STAMEN
SUBTENDING BRACT
CONE AXIS
INTEGUMENT
A
PERIANTH
OVULE
INTEGUMENT
B
EMBRYO SAC
SUBTENDING BRACT
FROM H. H. W. PEARSON, "PROCEEDINGS OF THE ROYAL SOCIETY"

FIG. 14.—WELWITSCHIA: CROSS SECTION OF FLORAL STRUCTURE: (A) STAMINATE FLOWER; (B) OVULATE FLOWER

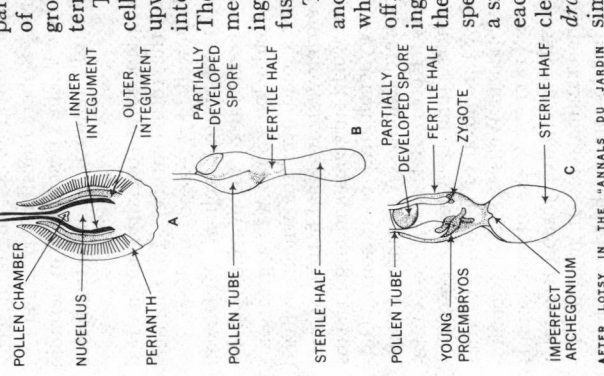

POLLEN CHAMBER
INNER INTEGUMENT
OUTER INTEGUMENT
NUCELLUS
PERIANTH
POLLEN TUBE
PARTIALLY DEVELOPED SPORE
FERTILE HALF
STERILE HALF
A
B
POLLEN TUBE
PARTIALLY DEVELOPED SPORE
FERTILE HALF
YOUNG PROEMBRYOS
ZYGOTE
STERILE HALF
IMPERFECT ARCHEGONIUM
C

AFTER LOTSY IN THE "ANNALS DU JARDIN BOTANIQUE DE BINTENZORG," E. J. BRILL

FIG. 15.—GNETUM GNEMON: (A) LONGITUDINAL SECTION OF OVULATE FLOWER; (B) PROTHALLUS AT TIME OF FERTILIZATION; (C) PROTHALLUS AFTER FERTILIZATION

A hermaphrodite (q.v.) or an intersex may likewise show male characteristics in some parts of its body, female characteristics in others, but its mosaicism is only apparent. Fundamentally all parts are of the same sex.

Gynanders are reported in many invertebrates, especially in insects. In certain butterflies in which there is extreme sex difference in colour and wing form, they are very striking in appearance. In the fruit fly *Drosophila*, the genetic conditions of the formation of gynanders have been analyzed by use of mutant traits. In this fly most gynanders begin development as females with two sex chromosomes. One of these chromosomes is lost from a cell giving rise to part of the body, thus resulting in a patch of male tissue, which may be large or small according to whether the loss occurred early or late in development. In other cases certain mutant genes cause elimination of a sex chromosome in many minute regions of the body surface, resulting in a gynander that is mostly female with many small male spots. Recessive mutant traits carried by the sex chromosomes supplement secondary sex characters in making the gynanders very conspicuous by their asymmetry in colour or form.

Many gynanders are reported in ants, bees and wasps, but some of these are undoubtedly intersexes. The genetic method of use of mutant traits has been employed in investigations with the parasitic wasp *Habrobracon*. Here the female parts are biparental, derived from a fertilized nucleus, whereas the male parts develop parthenogenetically (without fertilization) from a second egg nucleus or, much more rarely, from a second sperm nucleus.

Male regions of gynanders may be completely separated from female, as left v. right or anterior v. posterior. There may be one or more male islands in the female region or the reverse, or there may be considerable intermixture. These differences depend primarily upon chance distribution of the two types of nuclei in the insect egg preceding the formation of cells in the early embryo.

Reproductive reactions, mating, egg laying, etc., in the wasp *Habrobracon* have been shown to depend upon the sex type of certain regions of the head.

Tendency toward formation of gynanders is hereditary. Extensive breeding work with certain species of moths (*e.g.*, gypsy moth) has failed to reveal more than one or two gynandric individuals, but in other species (beeswax moth, silkworm moth) gynanders are frequent, especially in certain stocks. In moths both nuclei of the binucleate eggs must be fertilized in order that a gynander may develop.

In vertebrates there have been many reports of gynanders, but the cases are doubtful. In certain species of birds (pheasants and finches) in which the males differ strikingly from the females in form and colour of feathers, a few apparent sex mosaics have been found, with male plumage on one side, female on the other. It has been suggested that a critical difference in rate of growth between the two sides of the body resulting in a threshold effect may account for this condition.

Such birds would then be intersexes or hermaphrodites rather than gynanders. It is, nevertheless, possible that gynandrism may occur in vertebrates with its influence masked by sex hormones circulating in the blood. This would produce apparent asymmetry of development despite a fundamental asymmetry of sex mosaicism. *See* Sex.

Bibliography.—F. A. E. Crew, *Sex Determination*, 3rd ed. (1954); F. W. Rogers Brambell, *Development of Sex in Vertebrates*, pp. 206-219 (1930); J. T. Patterson and Wilson Stone, "Gynandromorphs in *Drosophila melanogaster*," University of Texas Pub. No.3825 (1938).
(P. W. Wg.)

GYNANDER OF PARASITIC WASP HAB-ROBRACON

Ventral view (X9); note the shorter antenna, the heavier structure of the abdomen and the elongate sting or ovipositor on the female side (right), the mother of this specimen had the mutant trait white eyes, shown on the mutant trait white head side. The dominant paternal black eye colour is visible on the female side

GYNECOLOGY is that branch of medicine which deals primarily with disorders of the female reproductive tract. The practice of gynecology requires skill in surgery, especially pelvic surgery; in obstetrics; in female urologic conditions, because the symptoms of diseases of the urinary tract and the genital tract are often similar; in endocrinology as it applies to gynecology; in gynecological pathology; and in dealing with minor psychiatric problems which commonly arise among gynecologic patients.

The anatomy and physiology of the female genital tract are discussed in the article Reproductive System. Pregnancy and Birth, Human are dealt with in those articles.

HISTORY

Gynecology is an ancient branch of medicine. The *Papyrus Ebers*, one of the oldest known works on medicine (1550 B.C.), contains reference to diseases of women, and it is recorded that specialism in this branch was known among Egyptian medical practitioners. The Vedas contain a list of therapeutic agents used in the treatment of gynecological diseases. The treatises on gynecology formerly attributed to Hippocrates (460 B.C.) are now said to be spurious, but the wording of the famous oath shows that he was at least familiar with the use of gynecological instruments. Writers of the Greco-Roman period of medicine who treated of this branch are Celsus, Soranus of Ephesus and Galen. It is evident that during this period much gynecological work was in the hands of female healers. Martial (Marcus Valerius Martialis) refers to these *feminae medicae* in his epigram on Leda. These women must not be confused with the midwives, who are always described as *obstetrices*. Throughout the Byzantine and medieval periods of medicine, which comprise a period of more than 1,000 years, gynecology shared in the general sterility and even decadence which accompanied medical and all other branches of scientific learning; such writers on gynecology as Oribasius (A.D. c. 325-c. 400) were mere compilers of the work of their predecessors, and practice was bound by ancient authority and tradition. The growth of interest in diseases of women during the Renaissance is shown in the huge "Gynecia" or encyclopaedia of gynecology issued by Caspar Wolf of Zürich in 1566. In the 17th century what has been described as the first work on operative gynecology in the modern sense was written by Hendrik van Roonhuze; it contains case reports on extrauterine pregnancy and rupture of the uterus and the description of a scientific operation for vesicovaginal fistula.

Among contributions to gynecology in the 18th century are William Hunter's proposal for excision of ovarian cyst and his description of retroversion of the uterus; Robert Houston's treatment of ovarian cysts by tapping; Matthew Baillie's description of dermoid cysts of the ovary; and John Bard's removal of an extrauterine pregnancy.

Operative gynecology, as an independent specialty, had no real existence until the first half of the 19th century. Its founders may be said to be Ephraim McDowell (1771-1830) of Kentucky and James Marion Sims (1813-83) of South Carolina. McDowell performed the first ovariotomy (removal of an ovarian cyst by abdominal section) in 1809 in Kentucky. Sims was a great surgical genius whose fame quickly spread over the whole civilized world because of his success in curing vesicovaginal fistula. Gradually the medical centres of the world surgeons and obstetricians undertook a limited variety of gynecological operations. Outstanding among these pioneers were Thomas A. Emmet (1828-1919), plastic gynecologic surgery; Robert Battey (1828-95), removal of both ovaries; the brothers, John L. Atlee (1799-1885) and Washington L. Atlee (1808-78), removal of fibroids; Charles Clay (1801-93) and Sir Thomas Spencer Wells (1818-97), oophorectomy; Sir James Y. Simpson (1811-70), the uterine sound; Robert Lawson Tait (1845-99), salpingectomy; Joseph Récamier (1774-1852), revival of speculum examination. It must be remembered that all these pioneers had to combat the violent prejudice of the public against any exposure or examination of the female organs. This prejudice, fostered at first by midwives, was supported by the clergy and by many members of the medical profession.

The two great advances which finally and in spite of vigorous opposition made all surgery generally available were anesthesia and antisepsis.

DISORDERS OF THE FEMALE REPRODUCTIVE TRACT

CONGENITAL ABNORMALITIES

Congenital abnormalities of the female reproductive tract are relatively rare. Among these abnormalities is absence of the vagina which may be complete or partial. In either case, the uterus may or may not also be absent. In most instances the uterus is absent, but the ovaries are present and the patient is completely feminine, with all the secondary sexual characteristics. When the uterus is present and the vagina partially or completely absent, there is no egress for the menstrual blood, which is retained within the uterus or an upper compartment of the vagina and often regresses through the tubes and into the peritoneal cavity. Complete absence of the vagina may be corrected by forming surgically, lining it with a skin graft from the thigh; such vaginas usually function well.

Septate vagina, with a tissue partition, is commoner than absent vagina. Such a double vagina may give no trouble, and the patient may be unaware of its presence. If it bothers the patient at intercourse, the septum may be excised easily.

Underdevelopment of the uterus may exist in all degrees, to the point of complete absence. Small uteri, two-thirds to one-half normal size, are not uncommon. Underdevelopment of the uterus is sometimes associated with infantile external genitalia and breasts, but in many cases the other genital organs are normal.

Double uterus is the result of failure of complete fusion of the bilateral Müllerian ducts which are present in the embryo. These are cordlike masses of tissue from which the tubes, uterus and vagina are formed. In the normal fetus the lower portions of these ducts unite to form the vagina and uterus; the upper ends, which do not fuse, form the two Fallopian tubes. When union fails completely, there results a double vagina and double uterus. All degrees of failure are encountered; thus the uterus may be completely double (didelphic) or partially united (bicornuate). Women with these abnormalities usually have great difficulty in carrying a fetus to term. Unification of the double uterus may be carried out by surgery, after which successful pregnancy may occur.

See also HERMAPHRODITE; URINARY SYSTEM.

COMMON DISORDERS OF MENSTRUATION

Amenorrhea.—Amenorrhea, or absent menstruation, occurs physiologically prior to puberty, with pregnancy, during lactation and at the menopause. Amenorrhea also occurs with absent uterus. When the uterus is present and the vagina completely or partially absent, there is no visible evidence of menstruation but hidden menstruation actually occurs (cryptomenstruation). Hidden menstruation also occurs when the hymen is imperforate. At the start of menstrual life there may be long periods of amenorrhea before the regular monthly tempo is established. Likewise, in the late 40s, before menstruation ceases, there are often lapses of menstruation for variable periods of time (*see* MENOPAUSE). Constitutional causes of amenorrhea are undernutrition and severe illnesses such as tuberculosis and typhoid fever. Mental depressions are also frequently associated with a cessation of menstruation. Periods sometimes cease for months and even years when there is no demonstrable cause; in such cases, the cause must be ascribed to an endocrine disorder. In some such cases the endocrine disorder can be recognized (thyroid or adrenal disease), but in others the primary cause is thought to be malfunction of the pituitary.

Hypermenorrhea.—Hypermenorrhea, or menorrhagia, is excessive bleeding at the time of the menstrual period. The flow of blood may be extremely profuse, prolonged or both. Menorrhagia may be a symptom of organic disease or may be simply functional, without any demonstrable cause. The commonest organic condition causing excessive bleeding is uterine fibromyoma (see *Tumours*, below). When fibromyomas grow into the uterine cavity, they also may cause intermenstrual bleeding. Cancer of the cervix or the body of the uterus rarely manifests itself by excessive bleed-ing at the periods. Functional uterine bleeding, in which there is no demonstrable organic disease, often manifests itself by menorrhagia, although it can also cause intermenstrual bleeding.

Metrorrhagia.—Bleeding between the periods may be an indication of organic or functional disease. Cancer of the cervix or body of the uterus in a premenopausal woman usually manifests itself by intermenstrual bleeding, which is thus more diagnostic of malignancy than is excessive bleeding at the time of the period. Intermenstrual bleeding, though not prima facie evidence of malignancy—often benign disease (as cervical polyp) manifests itself thus—always demands thorough investigation of the cause.

Dysmenorrhea.—Painful menstruation is present to some degree in a high percentage of menstruating women. The exact percentage is impossible to state, for it is difficult to determine just how much discomfort is required to be considered dysmenorrhea. Some women are truly incapacitated with real physical pain; others may complain bitterly when there probably is only slight discomfort. A small percentage of women have no discomfort whatever at menstruation, and an even smaller number state that they feel better at the time of menstruation than at any other time of the month. Causes of real menstrual pain are varied; among them are endometriosis (*see below*), salpingitis, myomata, cervical canal obstruction and, in some instances, retrodisplacement of the uterus. In the majority of cases of dysmenorrhea, however, the pelvic organs are anatomically normal, and the real cause of the pain is not known. There is undoubtedly often a great psychic factor. Cervical dilatation relieves the pain in cases of congenital or acquired obstruction in the cervical canal. Childbearing, which dilates the cervical canal better than all other procedures combined, cures more cases of dysmenorrhea than all other procedures combined. In severe cases, the sensory nerves of the uterus may be cut surgically. Very rarely, hysterectomy is performed for severe dysmenorrhea in women past the age when childbearing is desired or feasible. When organic disease is present, surgery is indicated if the symptoms are sufficiently severe. In most cases, nonhabit-forming pain-relieving drugs are sufficient to give relief.

See also MENSTRUATION.

TUBAL (ECTOPIC, EXTRAUTERINE) PREGNANCY

Union of sperm and ovum normally takes place in the tube. If, for some reason, the migration of the fertilized ovum down the tube to the uterus is interfered with, the embryo develops within the tube. Previous inflammation within the tube (salpingitis), causing adhesions and partial blockage of the passage way; is the commonest cause, but many cases of tubal pregnancy occur in tubes in which there has been no previous infection; congenital abnormality of development may be responsible. The conditions under which the embryo develops within the tube are not so favourable to normal growth as those within the uterus, and for that reason the embryo is often cast from its site into the tube; or, as the embryo grows, the thin-walled tube is stretched and ruptures. Either of these eventualities results in hemorrhage from the tube into the abdominal cavity, with sudden severe pain and often with fainting from pain or loss of blood. The treatment is immediate surgery, the operation usually consisting of simple removal of the tube. Very rarely tubal pregnancies go to term, but the chances of this are so slight that the gynecologist is not justified in gambling on the possibility.

ENDOMETRIOSIS

Endometriosis is a condition in which the uterine mucosa (endometrium) grows in places other than its normal habitat within the uterine cavity; no other benign tissue possesses this ability to invade other tissues. The mechanism whereby endometrium is transported to these abnormal sites is not completely understood.

Endometriosis is of two types, internal and external. In internal endometriosis the endometrial tissue grows within the musculature of the uterus itself. Minor degrees of internal endometriosis occur frequently without symptoms, but when the condition is more extensive it may be responsible for excessive and painful menstruation. If the symptoms are sufficiently severe it can be cured by hysterectomy.

Of much greater clinical importance is external endometriosis, in which the endometrium grows outside the uterus, on and in various pelvic structures. Endometrium growing between the rectum and vagina was first described in 1897, and it was first discovered in an ovary in 1899. Since then it has been found on all the organs in the lower abdomen, and more rarely, at the umbilicus and in the vagina and vulva. As the uterine endometrium goes through a monthly cycle under the influence of the ovary, so do these bits of endometrium growing outside the uterus, and at menstrual periods they bleed, causing severe pain in some women. The sudden occurrence of menstrual pain or aggravation of menstrual pain in a woman in her 20s or 30s should always arouse a suspicion of endometriosis (although, of course, there are several other possible causes). The sterility rate is high in women with this condition.

J. A. Sampson in 1921 began a series of publications which made physicians aware of this disease. He also brought forth his theory of retrograde menstruation as its cause, suggesting that the particles of endometrium cast off at the time of menstruation, instead of going down through the cervical canal and into the vagina, might go out through the Fallopian tubes in a retrograde manner, then grow within the abdomen and be further disseminated. Sampson's ideas were objected to by some who believed that endometriosis was the result of morphological changes in the pelvic peritoneum; they contended that the particles of endometrium cast off with the menstrual blood were dead and incapable of growth. In 1950 R. W. TeLinde and R. B. Scott produced endometriosis in monkeys by surgical rearrangement of the uterus so that the monkeys menstruated directly into the peritoneal cavity. By this method they established the fact that the particles of endometrium as cast off at menstruation are capable of growth, thus greatly strengthening Sampson's theory.

Endometriosis that produces no symptoms requires no treatment, since the growth is benign. When treatment is required for the relief of pain or sterility, surgery may be conservative or radical, depending upon the age of the patient, her desire for further children, and the extent of the disease process. Many women have been relieved of their symptoms by conservative surgery and thereafter have borne children. In some instances, however, hysterectomy and removal of both ovaries is necessary. Endometriosis in these abnormal positions, as in the uterus, requires the ovarian hormones (estrogens) for its growth, and removal of ovarian function by menopause, surgery or irradiation stops the progress of the growth.

INFECTION

Infections of the reproductive organs may be divided into two groups: those affecting the upper tract (the body of the uterus, the tubes and ovaries) and those affecting the lower tract (cervix, vagina and vulva). Upper tract infections are principally of three types: gonorrheal, puerperal and tuberculous. The incidence is in the order named.

Gonorrhea.—Gonorrheal infections result from sexual intercourse with an infected male. The lower tract is infected first, and the infection may remain there. In a certain percentage of cases, the infection spreads upward, involving first the uterine cavity and then the tubes. Gonococcal inflammation of the tubes (salpingitis) may be of varying degree: sometimes it is slight, leaving the tubes with very little damage; in other instances, the entire tube may become distended with pus (pyosalpinx). Such tubes usually become sealed off, and the patient is permanently sterilized. Gonococcal salpingitis is not the serious condition it once was. If recognized and treated early, the progress of the inflammation may be stopped and healing take place. The sulfonamide drugs were the first to prove effective against the gonococcus, and penicillin is even more so, penicillin therapy greatly reducing the percentage of cases in which surgical removal of the tubes is necessary. The ovaries, lying in close proximity to the tubes, are often involved in the inflammatory process. (See also VENEREAL DISEASES.)

Puerperal Infections.—These occur at childbirth or as a result of abortion. Use of antibiotics has greatly reduced their incidence. The usual infecting agent is the streptococcus, although other organisms may be involved. Puerperal infections are less likely than gonococcal infections to close the tubes and thus sterilize the woman; also surgery is less often necessary.

Tuberculosis.—Tuberculous infection of the pelvic organs almost always takes place through the blood stream rather than by way of the vagina, as in gonococcal and streptococcal infections. The blood stream is infected from a distant part of the body, usually the chest. The Fallopian tubes are generally the first organs involved in the pelvis, but in many cases the uterus and ovaries are also affected. Formerly, surgical removal of the involved organs was the only treatment, but in modern times the antituberculosis drugs are used in conjunction with surgery and in some instances are able to conquer the disease alone. (See also TUBERCULOSIS.)

Lower Tract Infections.—In the lower generative tract, the cervix, Bartholin glands and urethra may be infected by the gonococcus. Vigorous penicillin therapy helps prevent the spread of the disease into the uterus and tubes, where such infection is of more serious consequence. Gonococcal infection of the vaginal wall does not occur in adults, but it may be found in prepubertal girls. Nongonorrheal infection of the cervix is one of the commonest gynecological conditions. Many of these infections gain entrance to the cervix at the time of delivery, when the cervix is torn and the open wound is exposed to the bacteria which are ever present in the vagina. The cervix also may be infected in women who have never had children and even in virginal women. The infection has a tendency to irritate the mucus glands of the cervix and cause them to secrete an excess of mucus mixed with pus. This vaginal secretion, leukorrhea, is one of the commonest complaints of women. Often douching is sufficient to keep the woman comfortable; in severe cases eradication of the infected glands by cautery usually results in cure.

The vagina and vulva of adult women are frequently infected by Trichomonas vaginalis and by yeast, which may give rise to an irritating discharge that is often quite resistant to treatment. These infections are not venereal in origin, and they are of little consequence except for the annoying discharge.

TUMOURS

Vulva.—Benign growths of the vulva are rare. Fatty tumours and fibrous tumours occasionally attain such size as to inconvenience the patient and require removal. The only growth of importance in this region is cancer, which may arise in the skin or mucosa of the vulva; this is rare, however, representing only about 3% of the malignancies of the pelvic organs. It makes its appearance as a small lump or ulcer, usually in elderly women. The treatment is radical excision of the entire vulva, together with the lymph nodes in the groin.

Vagina.—Primary tumours of the vagina, either benign or malignant, are exceedingly rare. Benign fibromyomas and polyps are so unusual as to be almost curiosities. Primary cancer of the vagina, much less common than that of the cervix, usually becomes manifest by the appearance of a bloody discharge. Because of the proximity to the bladder and rectum, treatment by surgery or irradiation is difficult. For the most part irradiation treatment is used; there is a small rate of cure.

Cervix.—The cervix is commonly the site of small benign polyps. These small tumours appear as reddish, tonguelike growths projecting from the cervical canal. They commonly cause bleeding between the periods or, in older women, after the menopause. These small growths can usually be safely removed in the physician's office. They should be examined pathologically, but malignant change in them is exceedingly rare.

Cancer of the cervix is the second commonest malignancy in women, being exceeded in frequency only by breast cancer. It is most often a disease of middle life, the age of maximum occurrence being 48 years, but it is not uncommon in the 30s and not at all rare after the menopause. For unknown reasons it is extremely rare in Jewish women; it has been suggested that this is due to ritual circumcision of the males, but other peoples who practise circumcision regularly do not share this immunity. It is also rare in nuns, suggesting that infections in the cervix due to sexual contact may be a factor in the subsequent development of cancer.

The symptom of cervical cancer which should cause the woman to consult a gynecologist is bleeding, which in the premenopausal woman usually takes the form of spotting between periods. During the menopausal years any abnormal bleeding should arouse suspicion. It is true that bleeding at this time of life is more likely to be of benign origin but it is also true that the menopausal years are the years of the greatest incidence of cervical cancer. In a woman who has not menstruated for a year or more, the sight of even a small amount of blood from the vagina should arouse a suspicion of cervical cancer. Though the initial symptom of cervical cancer is usually slight bleeding, as the disease advances the bleeding may become profuse and the patient very anemic. Most, but not all, cases of cervical cancer are curable when the bleeding first appears. Late in the course of the disease, the signs and symptoms of advanced malignancy—anemia, loss of weight, weakness and pain—appear.

Cervical cancer has been classified into four stages, according to the extent of the growth. This was first done by the League of Nations, and later the classification was modified by an international committee of gynecologists, which to the original four stages added a stage zero, indicating preinvasive cancer. In this stage the individual cells which are involved have the typical appearance of the cells of invasive cancer, but they are found on the surface of the cervix and have not invaded the underlying tissue. It now appears quite certain that many invasive cervical cancers begin as the preinvasive condition, remaining on the surface for many years before invading the tissues. In the preinvasive stage, cervical cancer is almost 100% curable. If it could be detected in this stage in all women, invasive cancer could practically be eliminated, and there would be few if any deaths from cervical cancer.

Early detection of cervical cancer depends in great measure on the detection of cancer cells in the vaginal secretions. After the work of G. N. Papanicolaou and H. F. Traut, published in 1943, on the diagnosis of uterine cancer by the study of individual cells, there was an ever-increasing interest in this subject. Cytological examination of the vaginal secretions is a remarkably accurate diagnostic measure for early cervical cancer, the percentage of error in good laboratories being less than 1%. It is less accurate in diagnosing cancer of the body of the uterus, but many cases of cancer of this type are first suspected by this procedure. Diagnosis of cervical cancer is confirmed by curettage or cervical biopsy, or both. Not until the exact origin, location and extent of the malignant tissue are ascertained should definitive treatment be carried out.

Treatment of cervical cancer is not standardized. In early days the lesions were cauterized, with little success. E. Wertheim made popular a radical type of hysterectomy, but even after this over three-fourths of the women with cervical cancer died of the disease; also the Wertheim operation had a mortality rate, even in good hands, of about 10%. Soon after the discovery of radium cervical cancer was treated by it. Many early cases and a few advanced cases were cured; in most cases, there was at least temporary alleviation. With the addition of deep X-ray therapy the number of five-year cures has increased until about 50% of properly treated cervical cancer patients remain well for at least five years. There is general agreement that advanced cervical cancer is best treated with irradiation, but there is no such uniformity of opinion regarding the treatment of the disease in stage I (limited to the cervix). Notable among the surgeons who have revived and modified the radical surgical approach is J. Meigs of Boston, Mass., whose five-year cure rate in selected cases equals that of the better clinics where irradiation is used as the primary treatment. In cancer limited entirely to the cervix, the five-year salvage by surgery or irradiation in the better clinics ranges from 70% to 80%. Most gynecologists are agreed that in stage O (preinvasive) the treatment of choice is hysterectomy; cures in this stage approach 100%.

Corpus Uteri.—There are only two tumours of the body of the uterus sufficiently common to warrant mention.

Fibromyoma.—Fibromyomas, commonly called myomas or fibroids, of the uterus are the commonest tumours in the female genital tract; in fact, they are the commonest tumours in women. Fibromyomas vary in size from pinhead to enormous tumours of 50 lb. or more. They are usually multiple but may occur singly. They are benign, but very rarely malignant change takes place in them. The incidence of malignant change in a large series removed at the Mayo clinic, Rochester, Minn., was 0.7%, and the incidence based on all existing tumours is much smaller than that. Fibroids grow under the influence of the ovarian secretions, the estrogens. After the menopause, when the ovaries no longer secrete estrogen, fibroids fail to grow and usually shrink, sometimes to the point of disappearing completely. When they do grow after the menopause, it is almost a sure sign of malignant change.

Since fibroids are benign growths, they do not require removal unless they give rise to symptoms. A large proportion of them never do this, and the woman would be unconscious of their existence if she were not told of their presence by a physician. The symptoms for which removal is indicated are: (1) excessive bleeding, usually at the time of menstruation; (2) pain from pressure of large tumours; (3) symptoms of pressure on other organs (such as the bladder, causing frequency of urination); (4) distortion of the abdomen due to the large size of the tumour; (5) history of miscarriages for which, after proper endocrinological studies, it seems likely that the fibroids are responsible; (6) rapid growth or any growth after the menopause, which may indicate malignant change.

Treatment consists of removal of the tumour (or tumours) or hysterectomy. In young women who wish to have more children it is desirable and sometimes possible to remove the tumours and save the uterus (myomectomy). Since childbearing is usually past or has been found impossible in the late 30s or 40s when these tumours commonly occur, the usual treatment is hysterectomy. Total hysterectomy is preferable, for removal of the cervix is prophylaxis against cervical cancer. In selected cases in women approaching the menopause, successful treatment of small tumours can be carried out by radium implanted within the uterine cavity for a short time, or by X-ray therapy.

Carcinoma.—The malignant tumour occurring in the body of the uterus is carcinoma, which arises in the endometrium. It is less common than cancer of the cervix, the average ratio of uterine carcinoma to cervical cancer being 1 to 5 or 6. Carcinoma of the corpus uteri is essentially a disease of the postmenopausal years. The average age of occurrence is 58 years, approximately a decade later than that of cervical cancer; it may occur before the menopause, but its appearance in the 30s is rare. The commonest symptom is vaginal bleeding after the menopause. Often this is not profuse and is described by the patient as "spotting." Sometimes there occurs a watery discharge which contains too little blood to be recognized by the patient. When the disease occurs before the menopause, bleeding takes place between periods. The appearance of vaginal blood a year or more after the menopause is an indication for curettage without delay.

Treatment in most clinics is the administration of radium within the uterine cavity, followed by total hysterectomy and removal of both tubes and ovaries five to six weeks later. In a few clinics, the value of preoperative irradiation is questioned, and hysterectomy is done without the application of radium. Reports of five-year "cures" vary widely, salvage rates ranging from 50% to 90% being reported; the rate of cure exceeds that of cervical cancer by a fairly wide margin. In a few patients of very advanced age the risk of operation is greater than seems justifiable, and irradiation alone is used; salvage in these cases is about half that obtained by irradiation combined with surgery.

Ovaries.—Ovarian tumours, benign and malignant, are common in occurrence. They vary greatly in size; in former days tumours up to 100 lb. were reported, and though they seldom attain that size today, because surgical help is called for earlier, tumours of 15 to 20 lb. still are occasionally seen. Benign ovarian tumours are fortunately commoner than malignant ones. Ovarian tumours may be benign for years and secondarily become malignant, but it is probable that most ovarian cancers start as malignant growths.

Unfortunately, ovarian tumours are generally silent growers until they get so large that they cause distortion of the abdomen or pressure symptoms. If the tumour is malignant this usually means that the condition is incurable. Both benign and malignant ovarian tumours may occur at any age, but in general the chances of malignancy are greater in advanced age. Of special interest are ovarian tumours which secrete hormones. Certain tumours secrete an excess of feminizing estrogenic hormone and when these occur in young children they cause precocious sexual development; in post-menopausal women they may cause uterine bleeding resembling a recurrence of menstruation. Ovarian tumours which secrete the male hormone, androgen, cause masculinizing changes, such as deepening of the voice and excessive growth of hair.

Treatment of ovarian tumours varies with the type of tumour and the age of the patient. Malignant tumours require removal of both ovaries, the tubes and the uterus, regardless of age. In some instances, such surgery is followed by deep X-ray therapy. When dealing with benign unilateral tumours in young women, it is usually sufficient to remove only the ovary involved, usually with the tube. In women past the menopause, the opposite ovary and uterus are also removed, whether the ovarian growth is unilateral or bilateral. In women in midmenstrual life, the question of conservative or radical surgery depends upon the judgment of the operator as to the probability of later tumour formation in the opposite ovary. Some tumours have a great tendency to bilaterality, while others have much less tendency to involve both ovaries.

See also CANCER; TUMOUR.

SURGERY OF THE FEMALE REPRODUCTIVE TRACT

Surgery is performed in the female pelvis chiefly for determining or ruling out the presence of malignancy; for removal of tumours, benign and malignant; for correcting malpositions of the uterus; and for reconstructing the vagina after damage resulting from childbirth or other trauma.

DILATATION AND CURETTAGE

Dilatation and curettage is the operative procedure most frequently performed in gynecology. Dilatation of the cervical canal may be done alone to permit easier egress of menstrual blood when the patient suffers from menstrual pain, but much more often dilatation and curettage are done concurrently. The cervical canal is dilated to permit the introduction of the curette, an instrument that might be described as a miniature hoe, with which the endometrium is scraped off. Curettage of the uterine cavity may be done for either diagnostic or therapeutic purposes; in some instances both are accomplished by the same operation. The uterus is most often curetted to establish the cause of abnormal uterine bleeding. The tissue obtained by curettage is prepared for examination in the pathological laboratory and examined microscopically. It is only by this study that the condition of the tissue can be determined and the cause of the bleeding established. When the bleeding is not due to malignancy, curettage frequently temporarily, and sometimes permanently, relieves the bleeding. Curettage is never a cure for malignancy. It simply permits the gynecologist to make an accurate diagnosis and plan definitive treatment. On some occasions, dilatation and curettage are done with therapeutic intent, as after incomplete abortion, when some of the products of conception remain in the uterus and cause bleeding; removal of these remnants stops the bleeding.

In most clinics biopsy of the cervix, to detect early cervical cancer, is done routinely at the time of curettage.

HYSTERECTOMY

Hysterectomy, removal of the uterus, is the most commonly performed major gynecological operation. The uterus is most commonly removed through an abdominal incision (abdominal hysterectomy), and must be so removed when tumours have caused the organ to be greatly enlarged. When the uterus is normal in size or only slightly enlarged, it can be removed through the vagina (vaginal hysterectomy). Although vaginal hysterectomy is often more difficult to perform than abdominal hysterectomy, there is

great advantage to the patient in having the operation done by this route, since recuperation is usually faster and there is no visible scar.

The uterus may be removed *in toto*, the body and the cervix, and this is known as total or complete hysterectomy. When only the body of the uterus is removed, leaving the cervix attached to the vagina, the operation is called subtotal hysterectomy. The obvious advantage of total hysterectomy is that the patient cannot subsequently develop cervical cancer. Most gynecologists do it almost routinely, but occasionally, for reasons of technical difficulty, subtotal hysterectomy, which is simpler and more quickly done, is performed. It is commonly believed that "complete hysterectomy" means removal of the entire uterus together with the tubes and ovaries; this is incorrect. Such an operation is properly called total hysterectomy and double salpingo-oophorectomy. Removal of the uterus naturally stops menstruation, but it does not precipitate early menopause, since the ovaries continue to function.

OOPHORECTOMY

Oophorectomy, the surgical removal of the ovaries, is done most often for ovarian tumours or pelvic inflammatory disease. Bilateral oophorectomy in young women is a regrettable procedure, but in case of ovarian malignancy it is unavoidable and with bilateral benign ovarian tumours is usually necessary. When hysterectomy is done after the menopause for any reason it is customary to remove the tubes and ovaries also. It is almost certain that the ovaries are functionless after the menopause, and their removal is prophylaxis against ovarian malignancy. The younger the woman, the more conservative the surgeon should be in dealing with the ovaries.

RESTORATION OF UTERINE POSITION

Operations for the restoration of the uterus from retrodisplacement to its normal position were formerly done very frequently. Today the operation is performed occasionally when the symptoms are sufficiently severe and further childbearing is desired. When the uterus has fallen to a much lower level than normal (prolapse) it commonly causes bearing-down discomfort in the pelvis and may even annoy the patient by protruding from the vagina. Such a prolapse of the uterus is commonly associated with faulty support of the vagina. When the anterior vaginal wall lacks support, herniation of the bladder may occur (cystocele). When the posterior wall is defective, the rectum may bulge into the vagina (rectocele). There are many different operations for correction of uterine prolapse and restoration of the vaginal supports. Removal of the entire uterus or part of the uterus through the vagina is commonly done. When there are defects in the vaginal walls, simple removal of the uterus in whole or in part does not correct the condition. Under those circumstances, the supporting structures (fascias) of the vagina should also be repaired. Often the muscles forming the floor of the pelvis (levator ani) are separated or torn as a result of childbirth. Under these conditions they are restored to their normal position as part of the vaginal plastic operation.

See OBSTETRICS.

BIBLIOGRAPHY.—Emil Novak, *Textbook of Gynecology* (1944); G. N. Papanicolaou and H. F. Traut, *Diagnosis of Uterine Cancer by the Vaginal Smear* (1943); Joe V. Meigs, "Cancer of the Cervix—the Wertheim Operation," *Surg. Gynec. & Obst.*, 78:195 (1944), *Am. J. Obst. & Gynec.*, 49:542 (1945); J. A. Sampson, "Peritoneal Endometriosis, Due to Menstrual Dissemination of Endometrial Tissue Into Peritoneal Cavity," *Am. J. Obst. & Gynec.*, 14:422 (1927); R. B. Scott and R. W. TeLinde, "External Endometriosis—the Scourge of the Private Patient," *Ann. Surg.*, 131:697 (1950), and "Experimental Endometriosis," *Am. J. Obst. & Gynec.*, 60:1147 (1950); R. W. TeLinde, *Operative Gynecology* (1946); J. M. M. Kerr et al., *Combined Textbook of Obstetrics and Gynaecology for Students and Practitioners*, 6th ed. by D. Baird (1957); A. W. Bourne and L. H. M. Williams, *Recent Advances in Obstetrics and Gynaecology*, 9th ed. (1958); J. H. Peel, *Textbook of Gynaecology*, 5th ed. (1960). (R. W. TEL.)

GYŐR (Ger. RAAB), an ancient town of northwest Hungary and chief town of Győr-Sopron *megye* (county). Pop. (1960) 70,812 (mun.). Its site is remarkable for its relation to three rivers. The course of the Danube branches freely in northwest Hungary; the middle and main channel forms the frontier with

GYPSUM

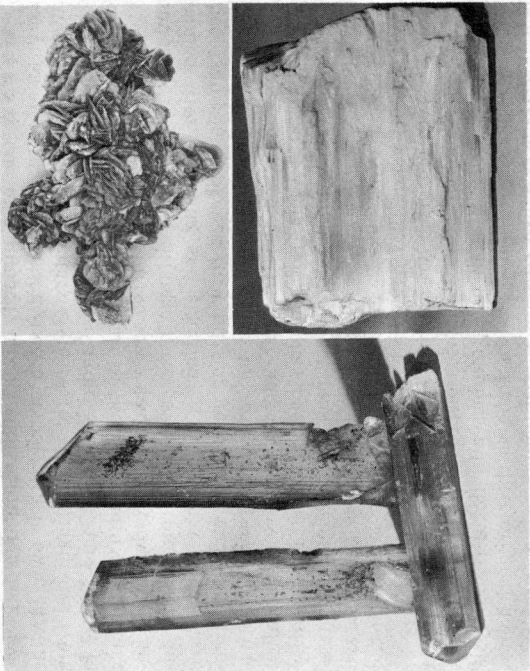

(LEFT) SELENITE, LARGE TWINNED CRYSTALS, NAICA, MEX.; (TOP RIGHT) SELENITE PRISMATIC CRYSTALS, MEXICO; (BOTTOM RIGHT) SATIN SPAR, EAST BRIDGEFORD, ENG.

Czechoslovakia; the northern channel is in Slovakia; the southern, with extreme meandering, is in Hungary. Győr lies on the outer curve of a sharp bend in this southern channel 66 mi. W.N.W. of Budapest. Two south bank tributaries converge on the bend, the Rábca and the much larger Rába. The town and its neighbourhood are therefore interlaced with meandering river channels. The site was that of the Roman Arabona, and Győr has been for centuries a prosperous market for a fertile farming neighbourhood with special interests in horse breeding and grain and wine production. The town's trade is supplemented by some industry: flour milling and distilling and continued production of linen, wool and textiles. It is linked by road and rail to Budapest and Vienna and is a centre of secondary roads.

In the 17th century Győr was fortified by Raimund Montecuccoli (q.v.) and became a strong point against the Turks. In the 19th century some manufacture developed, largely as small enterprises subsidiary to industrial concerns in Budapest. On a northern spur of the Bakony hills 11 mi. S.E. are the immense buildings of the Benedictine abbey of Pannonhalma, founded by Géza, the father of Stephen I, and receiving its title deed from Stephen in 1001. This was for a long time one of the wealthiest landowning communities in Hungary, and its authorities had many privileges.
(H. G. S.)

GYPSUM, a common mineral consisting of calcium sulfate dihydrate, $CaSO_4,2H_2O$, named from the Greek *gypsos*, "chalk," a word used by Theophrastus to denote both the naturally occurring mineral and also the product of its calcination, plaster of paris (the hemihydrate, $2CaSO_4.H_2O$), which was used in ancient times, as it still is, as a plaster. In well developed crystals the mineral commonly has been called selenite, from *selene*, "the moon," probably in reference to the pale moonlike lustre of its faces, or, after legend, because it was found nocturnally when the moon was on the increase. The mineral also occurs as anhedral granular aggregates (alabaster), as cross-fibre veinlets (commonly referred to as satin spar because of the silky lustre); and as impure earthy pulverulent masses (gypsite). The mineral may be scratched by means of the fingernail, having a hardness of only 2. Most gypsum is colourless to white, but because of impurities may be gray, yellowish, pink or brownish. The specific gravity is 2.317. The streak is white, the lustre subvitreous; cleavage pieces show a pearly lustre. Gypsum is used in the crude form as a fluxing agent, fertilizer, filler in paper and textiles, and retarder in portland cement. About three-fourths produced is calcined for use as plaster of paris in molding, casting and pottery plasters and dental plasters; and as building materials in plaster, Keene's cement, board products and tiles and blocks.

The granular form called alabaster (the alabaster of the ancients actually was a marble) is used for statuary and carved ornamental objects.

Most gypsum occurs in sedimentary strata associated with other evaporite minerals, such as rock anhydrite and rock salt, and also limestone and shale. Other minerals commonly present include anhydrite, calcite, dolomite, halite, sulfur, barite, quartz and clay, and many strata are relatively impure, fine- to coarse-grained, equigranular to heterogranular. The gypsum appears as fine grains, as large prismatic crystals, as large plates, as parallel fibrous aggregates and as spherulites. Very commonly it may replace anhydrite, but the converse relation also has been noted. Individual strata of rock gypsum range from a few feet to hundreds of feet in thickness. In addition, gypsum also is an important constituent of cap rock, an anhydrite-gypsum rock forming a covering on salt domes (q.v.), especially in the Texas and Louisiana Gulf coast area, where it may be an important source of native sulfur. Gypsum also may be deposited directly from sea water by evaporation, at 30° C. and at a salinity of 3.35 times that of normal sea water. In sedimentary strata where gypsum has been formed by the replacement of anhydrite, the process gives rise to a 30% to 50% volume increase, resulting in intense, tight folding of the remaining anhydrite layers. This replacement is the result of hydration by surface and ground waters; thus in many cases gypsiferous strata grade downward into anhydrite rocks. In addition, gypsum also occurs as a disseminated mineral in limestones and dolomitic limestones, especially with anhydrite, barite, celestite and fluorite, as well as in similar fashion in some shales. Unusual crystals of gypsum are known from solution caves in limestone regions; some of these are highly twisted, others are of extraordinary size. It is a gangue mineral of some relatively low-temperature hydrothermal mineral deposits, and is found in deposits of native sulfur, as in Sicily, and results from the reaction of sulfureous gases and waters on calcium-bearing minerals around fumaroles and solfataras in volcanic regions. In the United States commercial sedimentary gypsum deposits occur in rocks of Silurian age in New York, in rocks of Mississippian age in Michigan. Other significant economic deposits occur in Virginia, Ohio, Iowa, Kansas, Texas, Nevada and southern California. In Canada gypsum is produced for export in Nova Scotia and New Brunswick. Deposits occur in many countries but the United States, Canada, France, Germany, the U.S.S.R. and the United Kingdom are leading producers. In France gypsum is common in Tertiary marls and clays of the Paris basin (hence the name plaster of paris), especially in Montmartre; in England near Chellaston in Derbyshire, Newark in Nottinghamshire and Fauld in Staffordshire. Crystals up to 5 ft. long have been found in caves in Naica, Chihuahua, Mex. Northern Italy is the leading source of alabaster, also found in England, Colorado and other localities.

Upon calcination gypsum loses three-fourths of its water between 120° C. and about 165° C., yielding the hemihydrate (plaster of paris). When this is mixed with water it rehydrates and sets to a white solid mass of interlocking fibrous crystals of gypsum. Heating of gypsum for three hours at about 240° C. ("dead-burnt") expels all water to produce anhydrite (q.v.).

Crystallography.—Gypsum crystallizes in the monoclinic system, forming thin to thickly tabular crystals which commonly show coarse striations parallel with the c-axis. Crystals may also be lenticular, resulting from rounding of terminal faces. Other crystals are warped, with extreme examples bent into irregular or helical forms twisted about the c-axis. Twinning on (100) is very common as swallow-tailed or cruciform penetration twins or as multiple lamellar twins. The side pinacoid cleavage (010) is well developed and the front pinacoid cleavage (100) is distinct. Many crystals contain inclusions of sand or clay particles which may show crystallographically oriented concentrations, parallel with edges or certain faces.

See also references under "Gypsum" in the Index volume.
BIBLIOGRAPHY.—American Inst. Min. and Metal. Eng., *Industrial Minerals and Rocks*, 2nd ed. (1949); E. H. Kraus, W. F. Hunt and L. S. Ramsdell, *Mineralogy*, 4th ed. (1951); C. Palache, H. Berman and C. Frondel, *The System of Mineralogy of James Dwight Dana and Edward Salisbury Dana*, vol. ii, 7th ed. (1951); E. W. Heinrich, *Microscopic Petrography* (1956).
(E. W. Hh.)

GYPSY

GYPSY, one of a minority group with distinctive folkways, traditional occupations, and a speech uniquely their own. In the Western world, the sedentary Gypsies are also distinguished from the migratory Gypsies by culture and dialect. At Sacro Monte in Granada, Spain, in the second half of the 20th century, sedentary Gypsies constituted one of the few remaining cave-dwelling communities in the world although their caves were comfortably installed with carpeting and electricity. Although Gypsies have been sometimes likened to wandering Jews, they lack the directional symbol of a promised land and, as a group, own to no nationality other than that of their adopted country. The alien conservatism of their traditions has been a target for majority groups, resulting in repeated persecutions and systematic deportations of the Gypsies. For the Gypsies themselves it has served as an armour preserving their cultural identity in largely hostile environments where they have made a selective adaptation.

In the 19th century, Gypsiology (Gypsy studies) had become a branch of ethnology. Early theories disputed the Gypsy's origin but later evidence from blood groupings and linguistic analysis strongly suggest the Indus Basin in India as their original homeland. Certain castelike patterns of behaviour such as preferred endogamy, rules of commensality and impurity, and preferred occupations add substance to this theory. Later theories tracing their puzzling migrations showed that they must have been well established, especially in Greek-speaking regions of southeastern Europe, prior to their dispersion throughout Europe after the year 1417. Since then, when the original 200 "Secani" arrived in Lüneburg, Ger., thousands have spread as far abroad as Hawaii, the Americas, and Australia. Modern writings emphasize the exotic character of their life styles or mark their differential adaptation to modern technological society. Many studies—past and current—either repeat or compound the doubtful scholarship of their predecessors and show evidence of a concern, perhaps emotional rather than scholarly, for a people who were gradually losing their unique character in the second half of the 20th century.

True Gypsies refer to themselves by one generic name (*Rom*—*lom* or *dom* in Armenia, Persia, and Syria—meaning "man" or "husband") and to all non-Gypsies by another term, *gadje* (or variants in different countries, *e.g.*, *gorgios* in England and *payos* in Spain); this exclusive term has the pejorative connotation of "bumpkin," "yokel," or "barbarian." Other popular names for Gypsies are: in France *bohémiens, manouches, romanichels, boumianes*; in Germany *zigeuner*; in Portugal *ciganos*; and among Arabs *zutt*. The English word *Gypsy* (and, in the past, *Egyptian*), the Greek *Gyphtoi*, the Spanish *Gitano*, the Turkish *Faraoni*, and the Magyar *Pharao nepe* ("Pharaoh's folk") reflect a misguided belief in their Egyptian origin, a belief common in southeast Europe even before the western migration. F. H. Groome notes the presence in 1322 of large numbers of captives in Egypt from the Danubian territories and speculatively suggests this fact as a cause for stereotyping the Gypsies thus. He adds that these captives were later converted to Islam, an event that accounts for the story told by western immigrant Gypsies (1417–34) of their falling away from the Christian faith.

Well-established myths and legends romanticized their origin in the East or in the world of the Bible. All myths are refashioned by their subjects and garnished by others who profess a belief in them. However fantastic some of the legends may be, the Gypsies themselves are, in part, responsible for perpetuating them. Whether it is the myth of Black Sara, the Egyptian handmaiden to the Virgin Mary's sisters; the familiar legend of the Gypsy blacksmith forging (or stealing) the fourth nail for the crucifixion of Christ; or that which has them as the cursed descendants of Cain, most Gypsies accept and even relate a guilt-form of legend that condemns them to a life of wandering. A rootless people, perhaps greatly desirous of establishing roots, their chiefs called themselves "Dukes of Little Egypt" when first their bands spread across Europe.

If the legends about Gypsies were at best fanciful, then various hypotheses as to their origin were no less so. Bonaventura in 1697 claimed Nubia as their homeland; A. Baudrimont saw them as destitute Babylonians; J. A. Vaillant gave them a Pelasgian nationality; and Voltaire saw them as degenerate descendants of the priests of Isis. The best-known, though not necessarily the most tenable, theories are those of P. Bataillard, Lord Avebury, and Forbin, who independently concluded in the 1860s that modern Western man owes his first knowledge of metallurgy to prehistoric Gypsies in Europe who were probably nomad smiths like the Komodromoi of the 7th century A.D. and the Ishmaelites of the 12th century A.D. Counter-theories place their origin in India. The Bahram Gor theory, adopted by A. F. Pott, T. J. Newbold, Sir Richard Burton, and others, holds that in A.D. 420, Bahram Gor of Persia imported 12,000 Jat minstrels from India, and that their descendants entered Europe in 1025 or as late as the 14th century (there is however a marked dissimilarity between the Jat and Gypsy languages).

H. M. G. Grellmann's Tamerlane theory claims that Gypsies were expelled by Tamerlane from India and first reached Europe in 1417. Other theories identified Gypsies with various Indian migrants: D. L. Richardson (1803) with the Nats; R. Mitra (1870) with the Bediyas; and C. G. Leland and Sir G. A. Grierson (1873–88) with the Doms. F. H. Groome (1899) shows them to be carriers of Oriental folktales. S. Roberts (1842), who gave them a pre-Christian Egyptian origin, also thought they were great travelers even then and actually credited them with the building of pre-Columbian pyramids in Mexico.

Speculation, often based on a slender linguistic, occupational, or physical similarity, became fashionable. Thus, the Gypsy Atsingkanoi of 11th-century Constantinople were thought to be one and the same with the heretical Athinganoi, a branch of the Manichaean sect of the Paulicians. Much confusion has therefore arisen because of conjecture linking the Gypsies with marginal or minority groups, for example, the camp followers of Charlemagne's armies, or the goliards (European students or clerks who became wandering minstrels), so that the terms "bohemian" and "goliard" came to mean the same. They have also been linked with many varieties of nomadic smiths in Europe and other such client groups, or unclassified tribes and low-caste groups such as the Luri and Dom in India, the myriad groups of vagabonds, tinkers, professional entertainers and charlatans, beggars and thieves that take to the road, and even with Jews. It is not surprising, therefore, that Gypsies have earned the opprobrium accorded by sedentary folk to most migratory peoples; nor is it to be wondered at, though it can be deployed, that their own tongue *Romani* (anglicized as *Romany*) has been confused with thieves' slang.

The migratory nature of the Gypsies, their absence in official census returns, and their popular classification with other nomadic groups makes the estimating of the total numbers of Gypsies a formidable task. Just before World War II, M. Block gave a figure of between one to one and a half million for Europe and not more than two million in the world. C. Winick (1956), in the *Dictionary of Anthropology*, gives an approximate world figure of 2,000,000; J. P. Clébert (1963) claims that the total number can certainly be estimated at approximately 5,000,000. A significant statistical picture cannot be gained from the sporadic reporting by Gypsiologists in different countries; at the time of these studies, however, figures given for each country may be more reliable than any global estimate. The majority of Gypsies were still in Europe in the 1960s, especially in the central and southern regions.

The exotic stereotype of the nomadic Gypsy has often disguised the fact that fewer and fewer have remained truly migratory. Writers on Gypsies disagree on this point. C. G. Leland, in 1874, was afraid that Gypsies in England were passing away as rapidly as Indians in North America. In 1899 F. H. Groome claimed that only "a small portion" of Gypsies were still "intensely nomadic." Just over 60 years later, Clébert stated that the great majority of authentic Gypsies were still uncompromising nomads. Block, too, in 1939, referred to their "unquenchable wanderlust... fundamental in their character." He noted that the southeast was now their European home and that the great migration from India in the 10th century, and that from the Near East in the 14th and 15th centuries were followed by one from southeastern Europe (especially west from Macedonia) in the 19th and 20th centuries. Since then no large groups had come from Greece and the movement from the Near East to Europe had ceased entirely (few, if any, Arabic words are found in Romany).

Nomadism by the Gypsies in Britain was largely insular; yet many of them, like many of their continental brethren, overcame their aversion to sea travel sufficiently to emigrate to the New World. All nomadic Gypsies migrate at least seasonally, along patterned routes that ignore national boundaries. They also follow along a chain, as it were, of kin or tribal links so that, e.g., in the São Paulo area of Brazil, one tends to find Gypsies of Rumanian origin only; those of Greek and of Yugoslav origin are to be found in the Rio Grande do Sul area, where apparently they formed rival political factions—progressive versus conservative. Of the four "tribes" reported as based in Philadelphia in 1942, only one traveled consistently; another moved regularly with carnivals in the summer only.

Their own supposed disposition to wander has been forcibly furthered by exile or deportation. Only 80 years after their first appearance in western Europe, they fell under the penalty of banishment: Germany (1497); Spain (1499); France (1504); England (1541); and Poland (1557). Some of their migratory patterns can be elicited from official policies of deportation; from England to France and Norway (1544); from Scotland to Barbados, Jamaica, and the American plantations in Virginia (1665, 1699, 1715); from Portugal to Africa and also to Brazil (1574); from Spain to Louisiana some time before 1800; and from the Basque country en masse to Africa (1802). By 1864, the first Gypsies, deported from Britain, had appeared in penal settlements in Australia. Despite this systematic exile, or transportation abroad, Gypsies continued to reappear in one guise or another back in the countries they had left.

All unsettled tribes who live among settled peoples seem to become convenient scapegoats. So it is with the Gypsies who have regularly been accused by the local populace of all the evils common to the so-called antisocial or dangerous classes as a prelude to later official and legal persecution.

Their relations with the authorities in the host country have been marked by consistent contradiction. Official decrees were often aimed at settling or assimilating them, yet local authorities systematically refuse them the bare hospitality of a campsite to this day. Philip II of Spain is credited with making an early attempt (1560) at settling the nomadic Gypsies. Laws were modified to allow them permanent residence so that Gypsies began to establish themselves in reserved neighbourhoods of large cities such as the Triana barrio in Seville, or in marginal areas such as the Sacro Monte caves near Granada. Yet by 1633, Philip IV, in a further attempt to integrate them forcibly by breaking down their solidarity as a group, had prohibited their residence in distinctive quarters, their costume and dialect, marriage among themselves, and even the name Gitano. Forced settlement is simply another form of persecution that has had the counter-productive effect of fortifying rather than weakening Gypsy cultural solidarity. By 1783 Charles III of Spain, in a more liberal decree, enjoined Spaniards to treat Gypsies not as strange members of an impure race, but as subjects of equal stature—"neo-Castilians" (compare the Hungarian queen Maria Theresa's term "neo-Hungarian" in 1761); yet the ban on their own language and on their mobility remained. The philosophy of the Nazis favouring those of Aryan stock during World War II did not prevent them from a methodical extermination of an estimated 400,000 Gypsies. French laws in modern times forbade them campsites and subjected them to police supervision, yet the Gypsies were taxed and drafted for military service like ordinary citizens. Spain and Wales are two countries often cited as examples where the Gypsies have become settled, if not wholly assimilated. In modern times, the Socialist republics of Eastern Europe have attempted a program of enforced settlement to end Gypsy migration.

Despite their seeming contempt for the non-Gypsy world it would appear that Gypsies have consistently sought protection and patronage. As early as 1387 archives in Bucharest show that

Mircea I, a voivode (local chief) of Walachia, renewed a "grant" made by his uncle 17 years earlier, of 40 families to the monastery of St. Anthony at Voditza. It is difficult to understand this self-imposed serfdom (for such it seems), which continued for Gypsies in general in much of Rumania till 1856, especially when history indicates the brutal treatment as slaves that they received during this long period. But in Rumania, as in Russia, where they were settled as serfs in the crown lands of Catherine II, there has been a marked assimilation of the Gypsies. Nevertheless, isolated instances suggest that they were befriended, even championed, by distinguished personalities or patrons: the Gypsies in Barcelona in 1447 bore papal letters with them on their travels; Sigismund, king of Hungary, supplied some bands with letters of protection in 1433; and James V of Scotland in 1540 afforded "Johnie Faur, lord and erle of Litill Egypt," juridical rights over his own Gypsy bands. Even when Gypsies became the object of official persecution they were often given refuge or protection by many of the gentry, a fact which several edicts in Spain and France (e.g., that of Louis XIV in 1682) recognize. Some Gypsiologists state that common Gypsy surnames in Britain such as Boswell, Buckland, Cooper, Gray, Herne, and Lee indicate that Gypsies there readily assumed the names of their patrons.

During the late 18th and 19th centuries the Gypsies were at times positively cultivated, in some cases by royalty, and, of course, by Gypsiologists. Block refers to this period as the missionary era and cites individual attempts, in Poland and Prussia by princes of the realm, to found settled colonies of Gypsies, none generally in the long term successful. The then prince of Wales visited a well-known Gypsy "queen" at Norwood in England in 1750; Prince Viktor of Hohenlohe visited Lazarus Petulengro at the Liverpool Exhibition of 1886. Since 1936 in England, when commoners' rights of camping on racecourses such as the Epsom Downs were abolished, various members of Parliament have championed their cause for permanent sites.

The type of Gypsy occupations always had something to do with the nature of their nomadic or semisettled existence, e.g., hawkers and tinkers. Their work has been therefore either part-time, sporadic, or seasonal such as hop-picking in Kent, Eng., or in circuses and at fairs. Furthermore, since they were a marginal, perhaps pariah, group, they filled those marginal and fractionalized gaps in the economy by which they supplied services or goods unavailable or undesirable to the general native population (e.g., entertaining, leatherwork, and tinkering in India; latrine cleaning in Hungary; serving as undertakers, dogcatchers, and knackers in Rumania; as hangmen in Bulgaria; and as slave traffickers in Brazil). Gypsy men exercised their talents as smiths, musicians, and horse dealers without parallel. Gypsy women ensured themselves an income as tricksters, beggars, fortune-tellers, and entertainers in environments that failed to make adequate use of their men's craft skills. Mircea Eliade has noted, as a sign of great antiquity, the close bond between the art of the smith, the occult sciences, and the arts of song, dance, and poetry. Tradition and heredity sometimes determined the means of livelihood; there have always been some Gypsy jockeys in England; the Balkan Ursari (bear leaders) seem to have been quite a separate guild or group; combmakers and brickmakers pursue the same trade as did their slave forefathers in settled villages in Rumania.

Gypsies did not become peasants, however long they had settled on the land, but simply settled artisans. Where horse transportation gave way to the automobile Gypsy men quite easily and logically became dealers in secondhand autos or their parts. Nor did they become fisher folk or sailors except in one reported case of some 40 families at Ciboure and Saint-Jean-de-Luz in the French Basque country about the year 1860. Other Gypsies in that Basque area were grooms and basket makers. These latter, included in the generic term Barengres (non-Gypsy nomads), occupy the lowest status in what seems to be an ill-defined hierarchy.

Gypsies recognize tribal divisions among themselves with some sense of territoriality emphasized by certain cultural and dialectal differences. Mateo Maximoff, the Gypsy writer, himself a Kalderash Tchoukouresti, has classified the three main groups who each assert their authentic "Gypsy blood" as (1) the Kalderash (smiths,

GYPSY

especially coppersmiths as their name indicates, who came from the Balkans and then from central Europe)—the most numerous; (2) the Gitanos (French *Gitans*, mostly in the Iberian Peninsula, North Africa, and south France), strong in the arts of entertainment); (3) the Manush (French *Manouches*—the "Bohemians"—also known as *Siniti*, mostly in France, Alsace, and Germany, often traveling showmen and circus people). Each of these main divisions was further divided into two or more subgroups distinguished by occupational specialization (e.g., the Kalderash Boyhas—animal exhibitors) or territorial origin (e.g., the Manush Piedmontesi, from Italy), or both. Each "tribe," or "subtribe," tended to marry among themselves and their bands followed the dictates of their respective tribunals.

Of the approximate 50,000 in Britain, collectively referred to as Gypsies legally and also by the populace, only about 10,000 considered themselves true Romanies (*Rom*); the others were divided into *Poshrats*, *Didikais*, or "travelers" according to the degree of mixed heritage. Sedentary Gypsies include in their numbers groups or families who for one reason or another, such as the violation of the Gypsy code (exogamy, murder, or theft among themselves), were exiled from the band or suspended as "unclean" (*marimé*).

There has never been on record any one authority, either congress or "king," accepted by all Gypsies. "International" congresses of Gypsies have been held in Munich, Moscow, Bucharest, Sofia (1906), and at Rowne in Poland (1936; presided over by eight Gypsy "kings"). Much was made in 1930 of the crowning of Michael II, king of the European Gypsies, a ceremony at which a representative of the president of the Polish Republic was present. This ceremony has been called misleading and unjustifiable by Gypsiologists since it could, at best, apply only to a small number of Gypsies who would recognize such a king (witness a second "election" in Poland a year later that declared the first election null and void). It was nevertheless good publicity for the Gypsies as a whole. Even so, a so-called International Gypsy Committee has been created with headquarters in Paris. In 1966 it sent a representative to the newly formed Gypsy Council in Britain, an organization that later displayed unusual (for the Gypsies) political militancy.

If Gypsy kings are a romantic popular fiction, the existence of political authorities among the Gypsies is an established fact. The use of the word "tribe" by writers on Gypsies has been ambiguous. Those who affected noble titles such as "duke" or "count" in their early historical dealings with local nationals were probably no more than chieftains of bands, who moved in groups of anything from ten to a few hundred households. These chieftains (*voivodes*) are elected for life from among outstanding families of the group, and the office is not heritable. Their power and authority vary according to the size of the band, its traditions, and its relationships with other bands within a tribe.

It was the *voivode* who acted as treasurer for the whole band, decided the pattern of its migration, and became its spokesman to local municipal authorities. He governed through a council of elders that also consulted with the *phuri dai*, a senior woman in the band. The *phuri dai*'s influence was strong, particularly in regard to the fate of the women and children, and seemed to rest much on the evident earning power and organization of the women as a group within the band.

Strongest among the Gypsy institutions of social control was the Romany *kris*, connoting both the body of customary law and values of justice as well as the ritual and formation of the tribunal. Basic to the Gypsy code were the all-embracing concepts of fidelity, cohesiveness, and reciprocity within the recognized political unit. The ultimate negative sanction of the *kris* tribunal, which dealt with all disputes and breaches of the Gypsy code, was excommunication from the band—e.g., for a breach of endogamy. Where this punishment took the form of permanent exile, it was often sanctioned also by other tribal groups. However, a sentence of ostracism might exclude the individual from participation in certain band activities and punish him with menial tasks. In some cases, rehabilitation was granted by the elders and followed by a feast of reconciliation. Writers have not failed to draw comparisons with caste councils, taboos, and outcasting in India; the Gypsies believe in a concept of defilement (*marimé*) by the wrongdoer that may pollute their whole community. The more sedentary the Gypsies, as in Andalusia in Spain, the more they accept systems of local justice.

Such was the power of the *kris* that acceptance of its authority as supreme was sufficient to legalize client groups of questionable Gypsy pedigree to proper Romhood in the eyes of the adopting band or tribe. The new Russ and Meksikaia tribes became proper *Rom* by these means in the course of a dynastic and tribal political struggle between the Kalderasa and the Mačvaya in New York during the years 1931 and 1963 (reported by R. C. Gropper). There is a similarity here to the process of sanskritization in India. A band that was chiefless—however temporarily—could "sue" for client status with another, stronger band and, where necessary, upgrade its status to *Rom*, with the support of its patron group. This acceptance of a not necessarily permanent suzerainty of another group accounted for much intermarriage and the emergence of new combinations of bands and tribes, often the basis for temporary economic alliances (*Kumpania*).

Bands are made up of *vitsas*, which are name groups of extended families with common descent either patrilineal or matrilineal, as many as 200 strong. A large *vitsa* may have its own chief and council. *Vitsa* membership can be claimed if offspring result through marrying into the *vitsa*. Within each *vitsa* there is at the very least a recognition that one member's pollution (*marimé*) affects the remainder, and among *vitsas* there is some stratification. Gropper states that just as a man belongs to the tribe of his father, so he inherits his father's *vitsa* and *familia* affiliations. Loyalty and economic cooperation are expected at the household (rather than the *vitsa*) level though the *familia* may exist in single or multiple household form. For cooperation, a man probably relies on an action-set composed of a circle of meaningful kinsmen with whom he is physically close and not, at the time, in dispute. Ritual kinship, created through the institution of co-godparenthood, expands this circle. Nevertheless, according to G. Coker's report on Gypsies in Philadelphia, a structural principle functions in all types of households, stabilizing them around a core of women who constitute essentially a team. Each woman's earnings go into a common fund controlled by the senior woman.

It has been suggested (by A. H. Bonos) that Gypsies would become more assimilated if the men were forced to assume financial responsibilities for their families. Although their role is apparently subservient within the Gypsy household, women have always been the steadier providers of income from the outside world.

Brideprice among Gypsies everywhere is an important institution, as is cousin marriage; in Philadelphia, brideprice in 1942 was valued at $1,000, rising to $8,000 in the late 1960s. A consequent co-parent-in-law relationship (*xanamik*) was formerly of great social importance. Women are both the personification and guardians of the Gypsy moral code, as is witnessed by their supposed powers of cursing (especially their own men folk) and the purity taboos surrounding them. Little juvenile delinquency is reported among the Gypsies. Despite popular views of their shamelessness, prostitution is most rare among Gypsy women. Much of the cult of the Gypsy among the well-to-do in the past may have sprung from a desire to be temporarily released from those standards of behaviour which the Gypsies were mistakenly thought not to obey.

Accusations of sorcery, witchcraft, even cannibalism, and consequent persecutions against marginal groups like Gypsies who appear to have no religion of their own are not uncommon, given especially the Gypsy women's predilection for divination and fortune-telling (and their use of Tarot cards). Gypsies judiciously adopted the most convenient religion of their host country, especially where a church provides them with practical services of a welfare or educational nature such as in 20th-century Spain (the Apostolado de los Nómadas, 1967). Thousands of Gypsies participate in an annual international pilgrimage on May 25 to Les Saintes-Maries-de-la-Mer in Provence, France, and in another to Zaragoza, Spain. Many writers have attributed to them a vague set of magical beliefs rather than a religious system: the evil eye, serpent worship, medical magic, even moon worship (though others cite their fear of the night), not uncommon to many folk peoples throughout the world.

Gypsies have been one of the vehicles through which folk beliefs and practices have been disseminated; and in areas where they are settled (e.g., Rumania) have been positive guardians of "national" customs, dances, and the like, which were disappearing among the peasantry in the second half of the 20th century.

Gypsy social life is shaped both by the calendrical rhythm of the seasons and by their celebration of critical events. Spring feasts and autumn feasts (the Feast of the Kettles) mark the parting and the reunion of family groups divided by a summer's travel. Every life crisis—baptism, brideprice transaction and wedding, and especially death—is an occasion for bringing together kindred often from long distances away in an expression of solidarity. Of these the funeral feast (*pomana*)—actually a series of feasts—is especially lavish and well attended, particularly for a chieftain. *Slava* is a feast given for an individual to bring him good luck or avert bad luck at a critical period.

Although Gypsies have been the carriers of customs and ideas, have enriched the arts of music and the dance, and have been innovators in certain basic crafts, they have not contributed to the world of literature. Romany is not a written language any more than flamenco is a written music. Illiteracy, no longer an accepted norm, was not the only reason; reluctance to reveal the inner world of an exclusive culture was certainly another reason. Mateo Maximoff, whose first novel appeared in the 1940s, is one of very few full blood Gypsy writers. A Gypsy academic, Svetslav Simitch, published a Gypsy newspaper, *Diario Cigano*, in Belgrade during the 1930s. Modern scholars such as W. Cohn (1969) testify to the remarkable linguistic homogeneity of Romany. Leland noted in 1874 that in more than 300 years not one English word had been incorporated into Romany; on the contrary, he cited English borrowings from Romany such as *pal, row* (in the sense of "ruckus"), *trash*, and *niggling*, though linguists would agree only on *pal*. Moreover, nomadic Gypsies use a most complex set of conventional signs (*patrin*) at vantage points for visual communication as they travel.

Gypsies, once called a self-constituted caste (by A. Kroeber), and transplanted folk at midpoint between tribal and urban peoples (by R. Redfield), receive scant mention from anthropologists. Increasingly in the second half of the 20th century Gypsies struggled with contradictions in their culture. No longer did they defend themselves so much against persecution from a hostile society but rather against erosion to their life styles from urban influences in industrialized societies (as B. B. Quintana has shown). Themes of familial and ethnic loyalty typified in the Andalusian *canto hondo* ("deep song") helped to preserve the conservatism of Gypsy ways, yet some of the younger and more talented exponents of this music, drawn away by the material rewards in the outside world, were thereby threatening the integrity and economic security of the culture whose virtues they sang. Integrated housing, economic independence, and intermarriage with non-Gypsies undermined Gypsy law. If it is true that, unlike the peasant, the Gypsy wants to remain a Gypsy, then his classical ability to select and adapt to his own cultural advantage features from the outside world was undergoing perhaps its severest test.

BIBLIOGRAPHY.—H. M. G. Grellmann, *Dissertation on the Gypseys* (1807); J. Hoyland, *A Historical Survey of the Customs, Habits, and Present State of the Gypsies* (1816); G. Borrow, *The Zincali*, 2 vol. (1841), *The Bible in Spain*, 3 vol. (1843), *Lavengro*, 3 vol. (1851), *The Romany Rye*, 2 vol. (1857); C. G. Leland, *Gypsy Sorcery and Fortune Telling* (1890), *The Gypsies* (1882), *The English Gypsies and Their Language* (1873); F. A. Coelho, *Os Ciganos em Portugal* (1892); R. Salillas, *El Delincuente Español* (1896); Sir Richard Burton, *The Jew, the Gypsy, and El Islam* (1897); F. H. Groome, *Gypsy Folk Tales* (1899); G. F. Black, *A Gypsy Bibliography*, new ed. (1914); F. M. Pabano, *Historia y Costumbres de los Gitanos* (1915); E. Pittard, *Les Peuples des Balkans* (1920); I. Brown, *Deep Song* (1929); *Gypsy Fires in America* (1930); K. Bercovici, *Story of the Gypsies* (1928); C. J. Popp Serboianu, *Les Tsiganes* (1930); J. O. China, *Os Ciganos do Brasil* (1936); M. Block, *Gypsies, Their Life and Their Customs* (1939); W. F. Starkie, *Don Gypsy* (1937), *Raggle-Taggle* (1935), *In Sara's Tents* (1953); A. H. Bonos, "Roumany Rye in Philadelphia," *Am. Anthrop.*, 44:257-274 (1942); C. Cimorra, *Los Gitanos* (1944); B. Vesey-Fitzgerald, *Gypsies of Britain* (1944); M. Maximoff, *Les Ursitory* (1946), *Savina* (1956), "The Gypsies of Montreuil-sous-Bois: Some Observations On His Own Tribe," *J. Gypsy Lore Soc.*, 26:37-42 (1947); S. Murin, "Hawaii's Gypsies," *Social Process in Hawaii*, 14:14-38 (1950); D. Yates, *My Gypsy Days* (1953); R. M. Cotten, "An Anthropologist Looks at Gypsiology," *J. Gypsy Lore Soc.*, 33:107-120, 34:20-37 (1954-55); B. B. Quintana, *The Deep Song of the Andalusian Gypsies*, Ph.D. thesis, New York Univ. (1960), "Stress and Individuation in Andalusian Gypsy Culture," MS (1967); G. E. C. Webb, *Gypsies: the Secret People* (1960); Jean-Paul Clebert, *The Gypsies* (1963); G. Çoker, "Romany Rye in Philadelphia: a Sequel," *SWest. J. Anthrop.*, 22:85-100 (1966); R. C. Gropper, "Urban Nomads: the Gypsies of New York City," *Trans. N.Y. Acad. Sci.*, ser. 2, vol. 29 (1966-67); J. Yoors, *The Gypsies* (1967); W. Cohn, "Some Comparisons Between Gypsy (North American *rom*) and American English Kinship Terms," *Am. Anthrop.*, 71:3:476-482 (1969); *Journal of the Gypsy Lore Society*, three series (1888-92; 1907 *et seq.*; 1922-). (Mt. K.)

GYPSY MOTH, a European moth (*Porthetria dispar*) brought to the United States for experiment in 1869 but, on escaping from confinement, multiplied slowly and eventually became a serious pest of shade, fruit and woodland trees in the New England states.

The adult female moth is a heavy-bodied, light-coloured insect, with zigzag blackish marks on the wings. The body is so heavy that it makes it impossible for the female to fly. It has a wingspread of $2\frac{1}{2}$-in. The male, however, is much smaller and flies readily. It is dark in colour. The winter is passed in the egg stage. The eggs are laid during July in clusters of 400 or more, on the bark of trees, fence rails, fallen logs, under loose bark, in cavities in tree trunks or branches, and are sometimes placed on stones where they may be concealed from view. Each cluster is covered with buff-coloured hair.

With the appearance of the leaves in the following spring the eggs hatch and the young larvae feed rapidly, becoming full-grown early in July. When these ravenous eaters are numerous they may completely strip the trees before the end of June. At this time they are 2-in.-long, flattened, pale-brown caterpillars with long tufts of stiff brown and yellow hairs standing out from the sides of the body; a further distinguishing feature are the tubercles found in two rows down the back: five pairs of blue nodules followed by six pairs of red ones. The pupae or chrysalids, into which the larvae are changed, give out the adult moths after about ten days. There is one generation each year.

The gypsy moth spreads commercially on nursery stock, young trees, lumber, stone or other products likely to be sent away. They also spread as newly hatched caterpillars, in which condition they are blown to considerable distances by the wind on warm sunny days. In New England thousands of trees have been killed. Apple and oak have suffered more than other species, but pine and other coniferous trees have been killed when mixed with deciduous growth.

BY COURTESY OF U.S. DEPARTMENT OF AGRICULTURE

GYPSY MOTH (PORTHETRIA DISPAR)

Left: Leaf-eating caterpillars. Right: Moths; male (upper), and female laying eggs

With the expansion of the infested area in the early 1900s the federal government took active part in the work and since then has co-operated with states in an effort to control and prevent its spread. These activities include the enforcement of a quarantine regulating the movement of articles which might carry the insect into new areas.

The insect spread by natural means into new areas in the New England states, however, and in 1923 it was felt that natural spread to the west could best be prevented by eliminating all infestations which developed in an area along the eastern border of New York and adjoining states to the east. This barrier zone was maintained by the federal government and the state of New York.

The insect by the 1950s was found throughout most of New England, in several counties in eastern New York and in an isolated area in Pennsylvania. Infestation varied greatly from year to year. Developments in the application of DDT sprays with aircraft greatly reduced the cost of artificial control operations. The remedial measures adopted after long investigation consisted of spraying with a suspension of lead arsenate, banding the trees to prevent the climbing of the caterpillars and treatment of the egg masses with creosote. Many species of parasites have been introduced from Europe and certain of these, especially the Braconids and the Tachina flies, have proved reasonably effective. A predatory beetle known as *Calosoma sycophanta* has also been introduced as a means of aiding very considerably in the control of the insect.

See ENTOMOLOGY: *Agricultural and Forest Entomology.*

BIBLIOGRAPHY.—C. L. Metcalf, W. P. Flint and R. L. Metcalf, *Destructive and Useful Insects* (1951); U.S. Department of Agriculture, *Yearbook, Insects* (1952); U.S. Department of Agriculture, *Farmers' Bulletin 1335, Circular 464* and *Technical Bulletin 86*; Massachusetts Forest and Park Association, *Bulletin 157.*
(L. O. H.; X)

GYROCOMPASS or **GYROSCOPIC COMPASS** is a navigational instrument which makes use of a continuously driven gyroscope (*q.v.*) to accurately seek the direction of true (geographic) north. It operates by seeking an equilibrium direction under the combined effects of the force of gravity and the daily rotation of the earth. As such, it is immune to magnetic interferences such as those caused by ore deposits, steel structures or electric circuits. These properties make the gyrocompass a prime navigational device in ships and submarines. It has found extensive use on ore ships on the Great Lakes, as the azimuth reference for gun and torpedo control on warships and as a reliable compass for navigation of any ship. It is not suitable as an aircraft compass because the speed of several hundred knots associated with such vehicles seriously affects the north-seeking properties of the instrument. (*See also* COMPASS.)

Although the apparent effect of the earth's rotation on gyroscopes was first shown by Léon Foucault in 1852, the ability to construct sufficiently accurate units did not exist until the first decade of the 20th century. The first seaworthy gyrocompass was produced in 1908 by the firm of Hermann Anschütz in Germany, largely through the efforts of Max Schuler who developed the principles on which a practical ship borne gyrocompass depends. This compass was a marvel of mechanical ingenuity. In 1911 Elmer A. Sperry in the United States produced a gyrocompass that was easier to manufacture. In England, S. G. Brown, working with John Perry along somewhat the same lines as Sperry, produced a gyrocompass in 1916. Later the Arma corporation in the U.S. produced a unit that was a modification of the Anschütz.

Operating Principles.—One form of gyroscope is a spinning wheel mounted so that the direction of its spin axis has universal rotational freedom. The spin allows the mass, or inertial, properties of the material in the wheel to be used continuously and thereby gives rise to a relatively large gyroscopic momentum or inertia in a moderate sized wheel. The important property of a practical gyroscope is its angular momentum—the product of its spin and its inertia about the spin axis. This quantity is a vector.

All gyrocompasses operate on the same basic principle. They differ in their methods of supporting the gyroscopic element (the spinning wheel), of applying the pendulosity which is required for the north-seeking property and in the means used to damp out oscillations and thus cause the unit to settle on north.

since it has both direction and magnitude. The angular momentum vector may be conveniently represented by curling the fingers of the right hand in the rotational sense of the spin, the extended thumb of the right hand then pointing in the direction of the angular momentum vector. The angular momentum is nearly parallel to the spin axis in a practical gyrocompass.

In the same manner the moment of a force (torque, or turning effect) is directed along the extended thumb of the right hand when the fingers of the hand curl in the sense of the rotation that the force is trying to produce. The following is the basic law of gyroscopics: when a torque is applied to a gyroscope, it will rotate (or precess) so as to attempt to align its angular momentum with the torque. The precession is with respect to inertial space, *i.e.*, a reference space that is nonrotating relative to the "fixed stars." Note that the earth is not part of inertial space because of its daily rotation. The magnitude of the precession is directly proportional to the magnitude of the torque and inversely proportional to the magnitude of the angular momentum. When no torque is applied, the spin axis remains motionless relative to inertial space; if aimed at a star it remains aimed at the star, and consequently one end of the axis appears to an earth observer, in the course of a day, to rise in the east and set in the west. This is shown in fig. 1 as the path encircling the pole. When an applied torque attempts to rotate a gyroscope about the vertical axis, the spin axis will rise or dip, *i.e.*, precess about a horizontal axis, as it attempts to align its angular momentum with the torque. Similarly, an applied torque about a horizontal axis will cause the spin axis to precess about the vertical axis.

A gyrocompass is a gyroscope having a frame with a mass unbalance giving it a pendulosity at right angles to the spin axis. In normal operation the spin axis will be nearly horizontal and pointed north, while the pendulosity is downward. Consider a gyrocompass started with its spin axis horizontal and pointing a few degrees east of north. The earth's rotation then causes the spin axis to rise above the horizon as seen by an earth observer (more accurately, the horizon dips below the spin axis, which initially remains motionless in inertial space). The earth's rotation as seen by the spin axis causes a horizontal torque directed westward due to the effect of gravity on the pendulosity. The spin axis, obeying the basic law of gyroscopics, precesses about the vertical toward the meridian, continuing to rise because of the earth's rotation until the meridian is reached. At this point the pendulous torque is maximum and the spin axis continues to precess through the meridian. When the spin axis is west of the meridian the earth's rotation causes the spin axis to set, thus reducing the pendulous torque. At the same dis-

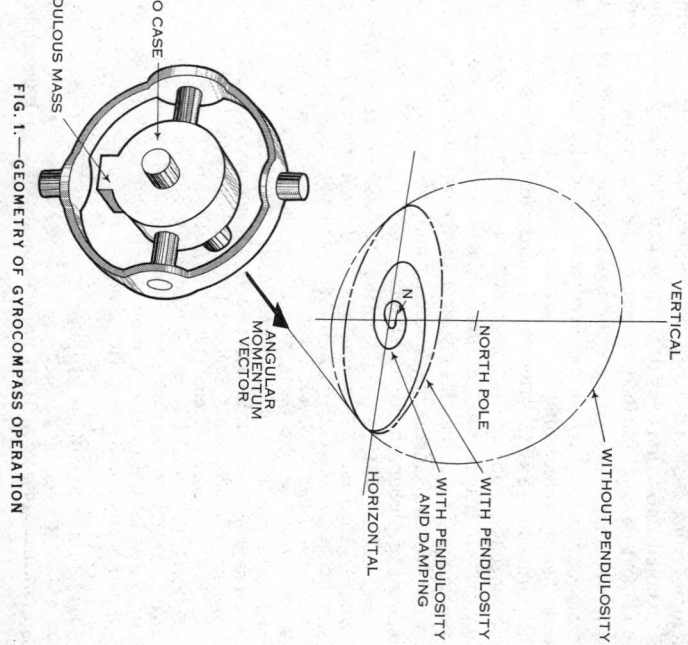

PENDULOUS MASS — GYRO CASE — ANGULAR MOMENTUM VECTOR

VERTICAL — NORTH POLE — HORIZONTAL — WITHOUT PENDULOSITY — WITH PENDULOSITY — WITH PENDULOSITY AND DAMPING — N

FIG. 1.—GEOMETRY OF GYROCOMPASS OPERATION

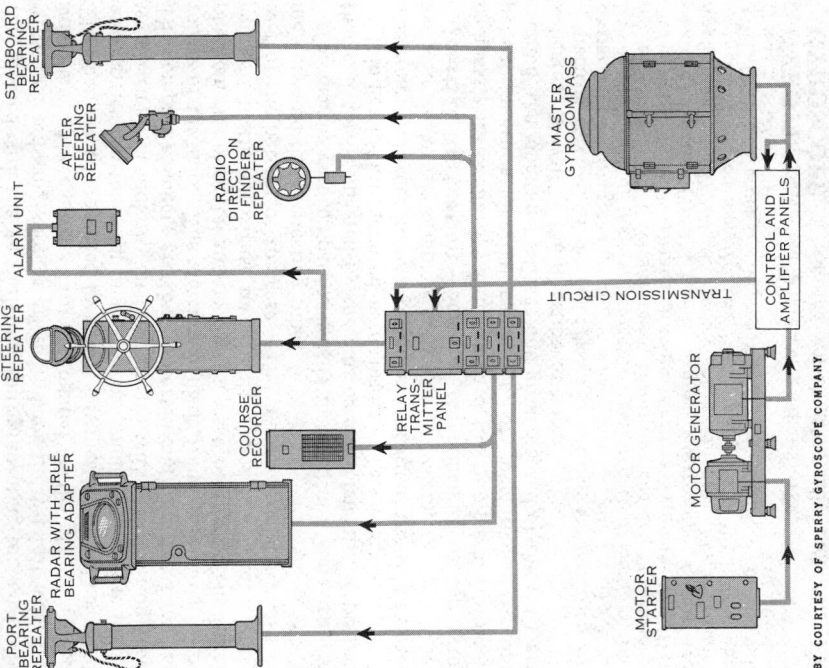

BY COURTESY OF SPERRY GYROSCOPE COMPANY

FIG. 2.—COMPLETE GYROCOMPASS SYSTEM

tance west of north as the starting direction was east of north, the spin axis is horizontal again, but because of earth rotation continues to set. This causes the spin axis to dip below the horizon and produces an eastward pendulous torque, which causes the spin axis to precess toward the meridian again and eventually precess past the meridian and back to its starting direction, where this whole process is repeated. The spin axis thus traces out an ellipse about the meridian and horizontal, as shown in fig. 1. The flatness of the ellipse and the period of the oscillation depend on the strength of the pendulosity.

For a gyrocompass to point north, it is necessary that the oscillation be damped out so that the unit can settle on the meridian and not keep passing through it. Damping an oscillator involves changing its energy state by opposing the velocity of the body. Two methods for damping have been used. The first, used in all gyrocompasses except the Sperry, is due to Schuler. It consists in applying an antipendulous torque caused by the restricted flow of a viscous fluid responding to the tilt of the gyroscopic element. Viscosity and direction of flow through the constriction are combined so that the torque is applied in the proper phase for damping. The torque is horizontal and ideally is directed so as to precess the gyro toward the meridian at all times, i.e., it points west when the spin axis is east of the meridian and east when the spin axis is west of the meridian. The combined action of pendulous and damping torques changes the previously mentioned elliptical motion of the undamped regime to a spiraling-in motion toward the meridian, as is shown in fig. 1. Viscous friction absorbs the energy withdrawn to effect the damping. The second method of damping is used in the Sperry gyrocompass. The Sperry compass is supported by a wire suspension with a power-driven follow-up, known as a phantom ring, which is a type of servomechanism. Damping involves applying the pendulous torque in such a manner that its interaction with the phantom ring and follow-up motor produces a torque along the vertical axis. This attempts to reduce the tilt of the gyroscopic element. Since tilt and motion in the horizontal plane are coupled together in a gyrocompass, this method also serves to damp the spin axis toward the meridian. The energy for damping is furnished by the motor that operates the phantom ring. This system has antipendulous action and damping is obtained by adding energy to the system.

In its steady state a gyrocompass has a slight upward tilt on the north side of its spin axis in the northern hemisphere and a downward tilt in the southern hemisphere. This produces the torque required to precess the gyrocompass relative to inertial space about the vertical axis at the same rate that the meridian is rotating about that axis due to the earth rotation. This rate is zero at the equator and increases to full earth rate at the poles. Because of this equilibrium tilt the damping method used in the Sperry gyrocompass causes the spin axis to settle slightly east of the meridian in the northern hemisphere and west in the southern. This is a small known angle that is readily compensated for in the heading indication.

The Anschütz and Arma compasses are supported by flotation. The pendulous torque is obtained by simply mounting the unit with the centre of gravity below the pivot. Damping is obtained by restricted flow of a viscous fluid in a tube. The Brown compass is supported by a pulsing oil column. The pendulous torque is obtained by the flow of oil between two tanks. Air pressure generated by the spin of the gyro wheel forces the oil uphill to give it pendulosity, since it is naturally antipendulous or top-heavy. It is damped by restricted flow of a viscous fluid in a tube. The Sperry compass is supported by a wire suspension with a power-driven follow-up motor, which receives a signal proportional to the displacement of the phantom ring from the wheel-supporting gimbal.

Dynamic Requirements (Schuler Tuning).—The period of oscillation of a gyrocompass is determined by the requirement that the compass operate usefully in an accelerated vehicle. The pendulosity that produces the north-seeking property responds to vehicle accelerations as well as to gravity. The torques associated with north-south accelerations (east-west accelerations are not important because of the system configuration) would cause a corresponding wander of the gyrocompass about north and would render the instrument useless for navigation. Furthermore, when a vehicle travels north or south it acquires in its motion over the spherical earth an angular velocity relative to inertial space that is perpendicular to the earth's daily rotation. This means that the apparent meridian, relative to which stars would appear from a moving vehicle to rise and set, is rotated about a vertical axis from the true meridian, westward for northerly velocity and eastward for southerly motion. The tangent of this angle of rotation is the vehicle's north-south speed divided by the product of earth rate (speed of a point on the equator: nine-hundred knots) and the cosine of the latitude. At ship speeds this angle is generally less than 4°. A major contribution by Schuler was the discovery that, when the period of oscillation is $2\pi\sqrt{\text{earth radius/gravity}}$, the heading precession of the gyroscope spin-axis due to acceleration is exactly the rate of change of the angle between the apparent and true meridians seen on a moving vehicle. The gyrocompass will then read true north at all times if its indicating reference is offset by the angle between these two meridians. The angle, at ship speeds, is a direct function of the north-south speed and is easily set into the system. The need for accurate speed measurement for this offset is the main reason why a gyrocompass is not usable in aircraft.

Description of Parts.—Only one type of gyrocompass is described because of space limitations; the Sperry unit is chosen as one that is representative and in extensive use at sea. The gyro wheel is electrically driven and mounted on spin-axis ball bearings within the rotor case. This case in turn is mounted to tilt on ball bearings about a horizontal, and nearly east-west, axis in the vertical ring. The vertical ring is pivoted about a vertical axis within the phantom ring, but its weight is borne by strands of steel wire from the phantom head. A follow-up system keeps the phantom ring aligned with the vertical ring, thus preventing torsion in the wires and reducing support friction about the vertical axis to a minimum. The phantom is supported by thrust bearings in the spider which also carries the follow-up motor. This whole device is mounted with a small pendulosity in the binnacle within a covering case. The compass elements are thus protected and also free from the rolling of the ship. The mercury ballistic frame is pivoted to the phantom on horizontal and nearly east-west bearings. The frame connects to the rotor case by a link that makes contact slightly east of the bottom of the case. The frame carries the tanks of mercury and the connecting tubes.

The master gyrocompass is usually installed in a compartment that will not be affected by the outside environment. Repeaters of its indication are mounted on the bridge and elsewhere as needed. The course recorder keeps a permanent record of the ship's heading. Fig. 2 shows a complete gyrocompass system.

Inertial Navigation.—Some of the principles of the gyrocompass were extended, starting in 1950, to a new method of navigation, known as inertial navigation, of submarines. In this method, the longitude, latitude and ground speed of the craft are indicated, as well as the direction of north.

BIBLIOGRAPHY.—E. S. Ferry, *Applied Gyrodynamics for Students, Engineers, and Users of the Gyroscopic Apparatus*, rev. ed. (1933); A. L. Rawlings, *Theory of the Gyroscopic Compass and Its Deviations*, 2nd rev. ed. (1944); M. Davidson (ed.), *Gyroscope and Its Applications*, rev. ed. (1946); R. F. Deimel, *Mechanics of the Gyroscope; the Dynamics of Rotation* (1952); J. B. Scarborough, *Gyroscope: Theory and Applications* (1958); W. R. Markey and J. Hovorka, *The Mechanics of Inertial Position and Heading Indication* (1961); W. Burger and A. G. Corbet, *Marine Gyro-compasses and Automatic Pilots*, 3 vol. (1964). (W. Wy.)

GYROPLANE: *see* AIRPLANE; HELICOPTER.

GYROSCOPE, a rotating wheel universally mounted; *i.e.,* mounted in such a manner that it is free to turn about any axis. In 1852 the French physicist Léon Foucault used such a device to demonstrate the rotation of earth and coined the word "gyroscope." This comes from two Greek words, *gyros* meaning "turn or revolution," and *skopein* meaning "to view." Thus a literal meaning of the word *gyroscope* is "to view the turning."

One of the first of these rotating devices was constructed about 1810 by G. C. Bohnenberger and is described in Gilbert's *Annalen* for 1818. It consisted of a heavy spheroid which could rotate on an axis passing through its diameter, which axis was mounted along the diameter of an outer circular ring. This ring with its contained spheroid was similarly made movable, inside a second ring, about an axis at right angles to the axis of the spheroid. In the same way the second ring with its contents could rotate, inside a third ring, about an axis at right angles to each of the others. From this it will be seen that the spheroid had all degrees of free rotation, one point only within it being fixed: namely, the intersection of the three axes.

In 1836, in a paper read before the Royal Scottish Society of Arts, Edward Sang suggested an experiment, with a universally mounted rotating wheel, by which the rotation of the earth on its axis could be directly proved. He said: "While using Troughton's top an idea occurred to me that a similar principle might be applied to the exhibition of the rotation of the earth. Conceive a large flat wheel, poised on several axes all passing directly through its center of gravity, and whose axis of motion is coincident with its principal axis of permanent rotation, to be put in very rapid motion. The direction of its axis would then remain unchanged. But the directions of all surrounding objects varying, on account of the motion of the earth, it would result that the axis of the rotating wheel would appear to move slowly." This suggested experiment was actually carried out in 1852 by Foucault, probably without any knowledge of Sang's suggestion. Foucault's experiment for demonstrating the rotation of the earth by means of a gyroscope became widely known and stimulated much thought and research on the uses of the gyroscope.

In order to conduct these early experiments successfully it was necessary to construct the instruments with the utmost exactness. Further difficulty hindered the development of the gyroscope, in that rotation could not be kept up for any length of time without

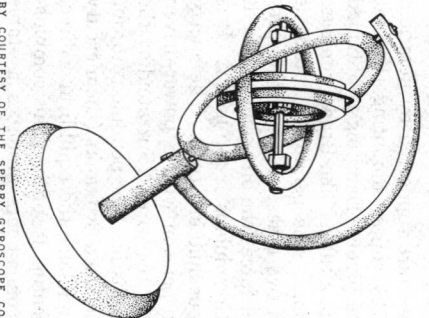

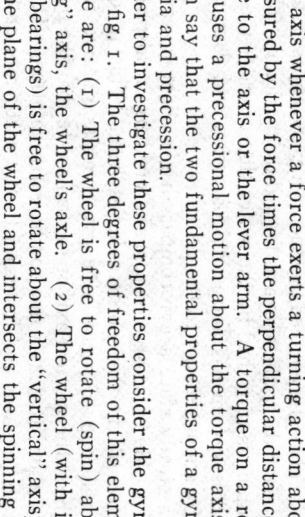

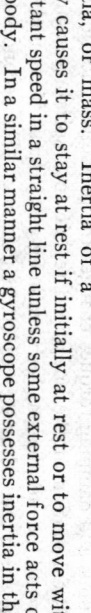

BY COURTESY OF THE SPERRY GYROSCOPE CO.

FIG. 2.—TILTED GYROSCOPE SHOWING THAT THE ORIGINAL PLANE OF ROTATION IS MAINTAINED WHEN THE BASE IS MOVED

functional interference causing the rotor to be inaccurate. Consequently, the gyroscope remained largely an instrument used only for demonstration purposes. It was not until the latter part of the 19th century, when G. M. Hopkins introduced the first electrically driven rotor, that the utility of the gyroscope could be fully realized. It was about the turn of the century that Elmer A. Sperry visited France and became interested in the historic Foucault gyroscope. From this interest was built up the Sperry Gyroscope company, which supplies ships and planes with gyroscopic devices for indicating direction, for steering and for stabilization.

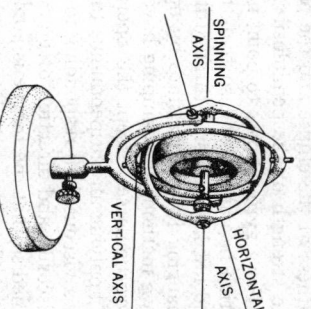

BY COURTESY OF THE SPERRY GYROSCOPE CO.

FIG. 1.—AN ELEMENTARY FORM OF GYROSCOPE THAT CAN SPIN WITH ITS AXES IN ANY DIRECTION

SPINNING AXIS

VERTICAL AXIS

HORIZONTAL AXIS

Fundamental Principles of the Gyroscope.—The explanation of the phenomena displayed by a gyroscope can be given in terms of Newton's laws of motion.

These laws are adapted to spinning objects without the introduction of any new physical laws, though new concepts are introduced. Newton's first law has to do with the fundamental property of all bodies that they have inertia, or mass. Inertia of a body causes it to stay at rest if initially at rest or to move with constant speed in a straight line unless some external force acts on the body. In a similar manner a gyroscope possesses inertia in that a freely rotating body will maintain a fixed direction in space.

In order to change either the amount or the direction, or both, of the speed of a body, Newton's second law states that an external force is necessary. This force depends both on the inertia or mass of the body and the amount of the change of speed; *i.e.,* its acceleration. For a rotating body a torque is necessary to change the direction of the axis of spin of a gyroscope. A torque exists about an axis whenever a force exerts a turning action about the axis measured by the force times the perpendicular distance from the force to the axis or the lever arm. A torque on a rotating wheel causes a precessional motion about the torque axis. We may then say that the two fundamental properties of a gyroscope are inertia and precession.

In order to investigate these properties consider the gyroscope shown in fig. 1. The three degrees of freedom of this elementary gyroscope are: (1) The wheel is free to rotate (spin) about its "spinning" axis, the wheel's axle. (2) The wheel (with its axle and axle bearings) is free to rotate about the "vertical" axis, which axis is the plane of the wheel and intersects the spinning axis at right angles. (3) The wheel (with its axle, axle bearings, vertical axis and vertical axis bearings) is free to rotate about the "horizontal" axis, which axis intersects the vertical axis at right angles at the intersection with the spinning axis.

vertical axes are always at right angles to each other, as are also the horizontal and vertical axes, but the spinning axis may make any angle with the horizontal axis. The spinning axis may also be in any direction horizontally, and therefore in any direction relative to space.

The spinning wheel is made so that most of its mass, or weight, is near its periphery, or rim. This gives the wheel a large rotational inertia or moment of inertia. Rotational inertia is measured by the sum of the products of the masses of the body and the square of their distance from the axis of rotation. Thus as the rim of the wheel is made larger and heavier its moment of inertia is increased. Suppose the wheel of this gyroscope is set into rapid rotation and the system is tilted about the horizontal axis. If the wheel is perfectly balanced then, instead of its tilting with the base, it would maintain its original plane of rotation. As shown in fig. 2, no matter how the base is moved the original plane of rotation of the wheel is maintained in space so long as friction at the bearings does not become sufficiently great so as to reduce the spin velocity. This experiment demonstrates the phenomenon of gyroscopic inertia that so long as no torques act on the wheel of the gyroscope it will maintain its orientation in space.

The second important property of a gyroscope is that of precession which occurs when a torque is applied to it. In order to demonstrate this, let us imagine a wheel, such as a bicycle wheel, hung up by a cord attached to the end of the axle, or preferably to an extension attached to the axle, as shown in fig. 3. If the wheel is held in a vertical plane and is not rotating, then immediately after release it will fall. The weight of the wheel, acting at its centre of gravity; i.e., at its geometrical centre, exerts a torque, or moment of force, about the point where the cord is attached. The moment of this torque is the weight of the wheel multiplied by its lever arm, Wl (the distance between the centre of gravity and point of support when the axle is horizontal). This torque Wl, if the wheel were not spinning, would cause a clockwise rotation about O, or about an axis perpendicular to the plane of the page, if W and l are in the plane of the page. The direction of this torque is given by the direction in which a right-handed screw would progress if turned in the direction of the torque. This clockwise rotation of W about O, whose torque or moment is Wl, would be represented by a line perpendicular to and into the page.

Suppose that the wheel now is set into rotation with a large spin velocity s, in the direction shown in fig. 3. If a right-handed screw is turned in the direction of s, the screw would progress to the right so that the spin velocity s is represented by a line through the centre of the wheel to the right. The rotating wheel then has an angular momentum to the right which depends on the moment of inertia of the wheel and the spin velocity s. Placing a heavy lead strip on the outer rim of the wheel increases the moment of inertia and angular momentum of the wheel. Suppose the suspended spinning wheel is now released, then the wheel does not fall but starts to turn around the cord, or to precess, with a precessional spin velocity s'. This precessional motion may be considered in the following manner: By Newton's laws of motion the torque Wl about O tends to cause motion or produce angular momentum in the direction indicated by the arrow Wl. Thus the wheel tends to turn its spin velocity; i.e., to precess into this direction. Specifically the arrow representing the spin velocity s of the wheel turns into the direction of the torque arrow. Now the precessional spin velocity s' depends on the moment of inertia I, the spin velocity s of the wheel and the value of the torque Wl. If the moment of inertia of the wheel is increased then the precessional spin velocity s' is correspondingly increased. In this case the precessional spin velocity s' is given by Wl/Is where Is is the angular momentum of the spinning wheel.

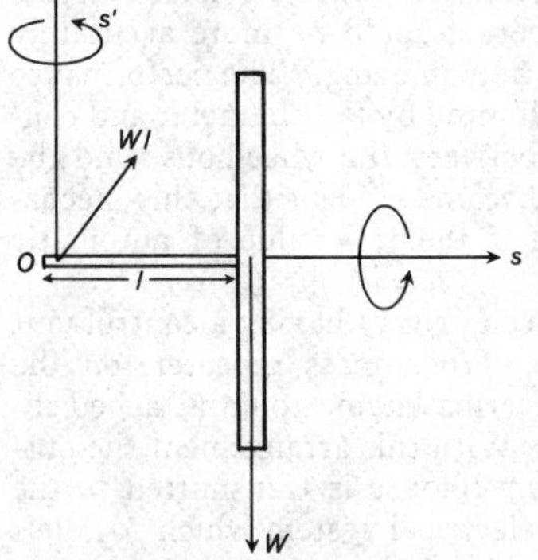

Actually, the above analysis is only approximate for the case in which the angular momentum Is of the spinning wheel is considerably larger than that of the precessional spin angular momentum. If this is not the case, the axis of the wheel does not precess in a horizontal circle but wobbles about this circle with a motion called nutation, or nodding. This nutational motion is seen when the wheel slows down; i.e., its angular momentum decreases. It

FIG. 3.—DIAGRAM SHOWING THE PRECESSIONAL PROPERTY OF A GYRO-SCOPE AS ADAPTED IN A SPINNING WHEEL SUSPENDED BY A CORD (see TEXT)

may also be seen with a spinning top or a toy gyroscope having one point on the table.

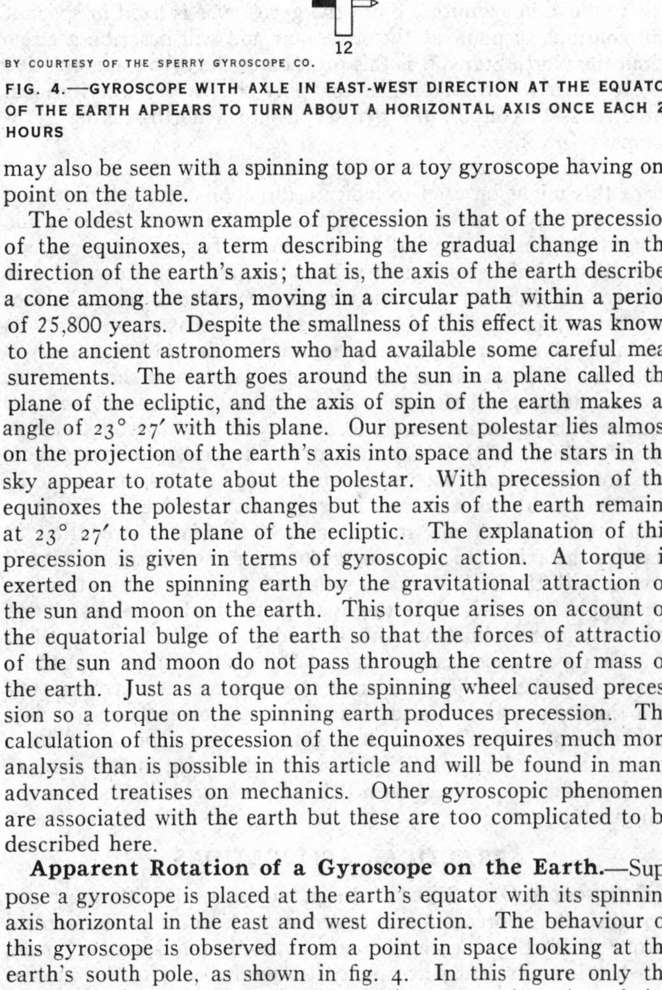

The oldest known example of precession is that of the precession of the equinoxes, a term describing the gradual change in the direction of the earth's axis; that is, the axis of the earth describes a cone among the stars, moving in a circular path within a period of 25,800 years. Despite the smallness of this effect it was known to the ancient astronomers who had available some careful measurements. The earth goes around the sun in a plane called the plane of the ecliptic, and the axis of spin of the earth makes an angle of 23° 27' with this plane. Our present polestar lies almost on the projection of the earth's axis into space and the stars in the sky appear to rotate about the polestar. With precession of the equinoxes the polestar changes but the axis of the earth remains at 23° 27' to the plane of the ecliptic. The explanation of this precession is given in terms of gyroscopic action. A torque is exerted on the spinning earth by the gravitational attraction of the sun and moon on the earth. This torque arises on account of the equatorial bulge of the earth so that the forces of attraction of the sun and moon do not pass through the centre of mass of the earth. Just as a torque on the spinning wheel caused precession so a torque on the spinning earth produces precession. The calculation of this precession of the equinoxes requires much more analysis than is possible in this article and will be found in many advanced treatises on mechanics. Other gyroscopic phenomena are associated with the earth but these are too complicated to be described here.

Apparent Rotation of a Gyroscope on the Earth.—Suppose a gyroscope is placed at the earth's equator with its spinning axis horizontal in the east and west direction. The behaviour of this gyroscope is observed from a point in space looking at the earth's south pole, as shown in fig. 4. In this figure only the wheel of the gyroscope is shown, the supporting rings being omitted for the sake of clarity. During the course of a day the gyroscope appears to rotate about a horizontal axis at right angles to the spinning axis. As seen from the earth at zero time the axis is along the horizontal while after three hours it is at 45° to the horizontal and after six hours it is along the vertical, making one rotation about the horizontal axis in a day. Actually, however, the gyro-spinning axis has remained parallel to its original direction in space, though the gyroscope has been carried along with the earth, including the revolution of the latter about its

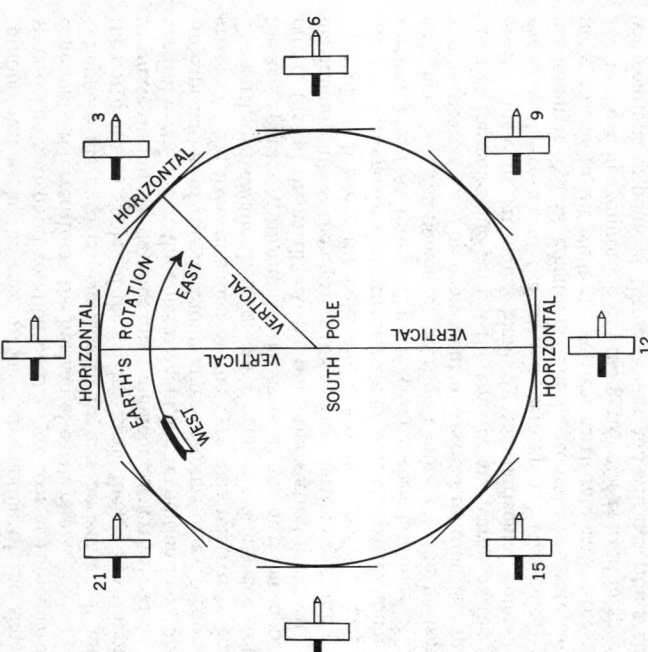

BY COURTESY OF THE SPERRY GYROSCOPE CO.

FIG. 4.—GYROSCOPE WITH AXLE IN EAST-WEST DIRECTION AT THE EQUATOR OF THE EARTH APPEARS TO TURN ABOUT A HORIZONTAL AXIS ONCE EACH 24 HOURS

polar axis. Thus the rotation of the gyro axis is an apparent rotation just as in the case of the daily motion of the sun and stars. The horizontal rotation of the gyro axis at the equator is commonly referred to as the horizontal earth rate.

Suppose the gyro is placed, with its axis horizontal, at either the north or south poles of the earth. Again the gyro axis appears to rotate during the day but this time about a vertical axis. The vertical earth rate at the poles is again one revolution in 24 hours. An explanation of this is readily given in terms of gyroscopic inertia; i.e., the fixed direction of the gyro axis relative to space. The earth turns while the gyro axis remains fixed in space so that the axis appears to turn under the earth at an equal and opposite rate to that of the earth. At the poles the vertical earth rate is a maximum, while at the equator the vertical earth rate is zero.

At places between the poles and the equator the gyro axis appears to turn partly about the horizontal axis and partly about the vertical axis. At intermediate places between latitudes 0° and 90° there is a component of rotation about both the horizontal and vertical axes. The component of vertical rotation is a maximum at the poles and zero at the equator and varies as the sine of the angle of latitude. Similarly the horizontal component varies as the cosine of the latitude, zero at 90° (the poles) and maximum at 0° (the equator). The horizontal earth rate causes the gyro axis to tilt while the vertical earth rate causes the gyro axis to move in azimuth. Since the gyro's axis is fixed in space it will continue to point at the same star and will describe a circle about the North Star. It is this rotation of the gyro's axis relative to the earth which enables us to apply the earth's gravitational force so as to convert the gyroscope into a north-seeking gyrocompass (q.v.).

It might be thought that since the gyro axis remains fixed in space this might be used to indicate direction. Unfortunately in practice the gyro axis does not remain fixed in space. Even while using the highest quality ball bearings and balancing the gyroscope carefully in gimbals so that there is no torque due to gravity, it has not been possible to reduce the rate of precession to zero. In fact in practice a precession of less than 2° per hour is very difficult to attain. For a short laboratory experiment this may seem negligible, but for practical use, for instance in steering a ship, it is not good enough. If the gyro wandered only 2° per hour and in the same direction for a whole day it would change by 48°, which, of course, would render it useless for navigation. It is for this reason that a gyrocompass (q.v.) must make use of both the earth's rotation and its gravitational force.

In other applications, it must always be remembered that in practice the axis of the spinning gyro is not fixed in space but will deviate with time. It has been proposed at various times to use a gyroscope as a clock by setting it to point at some fixed star and then using its inclination with a fixed pointer to indicate time. If such a gyroscope really remained fixed with respect to space it could be used to indicate sidereal or star time. An error of 1% in a timekeeper amounts to about a quarter of an hour per day, and to keep time even as well as this the gyroscope would have to maintain its direction in space with a deviation of less than 4° per day, whereas we have seen that 2° per hour is better than we can guarantee.

PRACTICAL APPLICATIONS

Gyroscopic Gun Sights.—In an earlier section it was shown that the rate of precession of a gyroscope is equal to the applied torque divided by the angular momentum of the spinning wheel, or what is equivalent, the applied torque is equal to the rate of precession multiplied by the angular momentum. This principle is applied in the design of a naval gun sight which has been successfully used to defend ships against dive bombers. Suppose a gyroscope is mounted on the barrel of a gun with the spin axle constrained to be horizontal and at right angles to the barrel. Then when the gun is slued from one direction to another the gyroscope is slued with it, and if the wheel is spinning this motion is, in fact, precession. The axle will only slue with the gun because a torque is being applied to the gyro about an axis parallel to the gun barrel. If the mounting is all solid and unyielding there is no means of knowing how great the torque is, but if the gyro is put in gimbals and the axle constrained to keep horizontal by a spring, then the pull of the spring will be proportional to the tilt of the gun. This pull on the spring will be a measure of the rate of precession of the gyro and therefore of the rate of sluing of the gyroscope. The pull of the spring will be proportional to the tilt of the gyroscope round the gun axis. From a measurement of the tilt the rate of slue can be obtained. In this case the precession initiates the torque, and the torque makes the precession go on. The information obtained from the gyro can be used either by reading the tilt and making calculations based on it, or better by making the gyro sight offset the gun sight by just the right amount required to make the shell hit the moving target instead of lagging behind it.

The first major tryout of gyroscopic gun sights produced during World War II occurred when the U.S.S. "South Dakota" virtually annihilated a force of attacking planes on Oct. 26, 1942. Since that time gyros have been used to compute the correct lead for guns, bombs or rockets fired from jet fighter planes. These were used in Korea. Gyros are also used to stabilize all types of fire control systems and as a controlling mechanism for guided missiles.

(R. J. SN.)

Gyrocompass.—In the case of the marine gyrocompass (q.v.), both the gyroscopic inertia and the precession characteristics of the gyroscope are utilized, but the sensitive or rotating element is harnessed by the force of gravity so that the spinning axis of the gyro is brought into line with the north-south axis of the earth and is caused to remain there. The gyrocompass is a necessity in naval work where the great masses of iron and steel seriously impair the accuracy of the magnetic compass and where a high degree of accuracy is required for gun fire control. The gyrocompass is also in use in practically every large merchant fleet in the world because of the safety and added economy of navigation it affords. Vessels ranging from small power yachts to ocean liners use the gyrocompass.

Gyropilot for Ships.—The gyropilot was originally developed (1921) to serve the single purpose of automatic steering. Its introduction was the logical step which followed as soon as the gyrocompass had established a fixed reference by which a ship could be steered. With such a reference available it was obvious that the purely mechanical function of steering could be more accurately performed by a machine than by a human being. The performance of the early models, however, was limited by the character and condition of the connecting medium between the wheelhouse and the steering engine room, and it soon became evident that this mechanism would have to be improved if the full value of automatic steering was to be realized.

A gyropilot was therefore produced (1925) having a control unit or steering stand, containing the gyrocompass repeater, on the bridge, and a power unit in the steering engine room attached directly to the steering gear control. With this arrangement the output of the steering stand in the wheelhouse is transmitted to the power unit aft by an independent electrical system which parallels the existing ship's telemotor. Through this system course changes may be effected while steering automatically, and the ship may also be steered manually through the electrical system by means of a wheel on the steering stand.

Facilities are provided in the equipment to take care of variable factors which influence the steering of the vessel. Under certain conditions, for instance, it is desirable to let the vessel have a small amount of "weather yaw." An adjustment is provided on the bridge unit for this purpose. Another adjustment varies the amount of rudder applied for a given amount of departure from the set course. It will be seen, therefore, that the gyropilot can steer a loaded ship as well as it can a light one and that it is effective in heavy weather as well as in a smooth sea.

Course Recorder.—The course recorder, operated electrically from the gyrocompass, automatically provides on a moving chart a chronological, graphic record of all movements of the ship's head in azimuth. From this record the quality of the steering, the mean course steered and the times and amounts of alterations of course may be ascertained, either at the time of recording or at any sub-

sequent time. These course records have frequently proved invaluable in cases of litigation following accidents and collisions.

Gyrostabilizer for Ships.—In order to add materially to the pleasure and comfort of ocean travel, as well as to reduce the stresses and strains imposed on a ship's framework when rolling in a heavy sea, many different forms of apparatus have been devised, one of which is shown in fig. 5. The only kind which met with any great degree of success was the gyroscopic stabilizer developed by Sperry. This stabilizer is a compact unit generally located below decks on the centre line of the ship. It consists of a rotor of special steel and a supporting casing resting in horizontal "thwartships" gudgeon bearings, so that the rotor axle, when central, is vertical, with the ship on an even keel. The only apparent movement of the stabilizer other than the spinning of its rotor is a tilting or precessing fore and aft in the thwartships bearings. In so doing, however, the gyro exerts a righting force against the action of the wave as it tends to roll the vessel over. By dealing with each wave increment individually and by exerting a small counteracting force against it at just the right moment, the gyrostabilizer quenches the force of each wave and never allows the vessel to build up a roll averaging more than 3° or 4°. With the increase in ship size in the 20th century, the use of the gyroscopic stabilizer began to give way to retractable fins near the bottom of the hull on each side amidships. Gyroscopes were still used with the fins to control the angle of tilt needed to offset the roll of the ship.

Roll and Pitch Recorder.—This is an instrument employing a gyroscopic pendulum to determine the amplitude of a vessel's roll and pitch and the period of these motions. It consists of a small gyroscope with controlling mechanism for two pens, one of which makes a record of the roll, the other of the pitch of the vessel. A sheet of recording paper is automatically drawn under the two pens, and a third operated by clockwork makes marks on the paper at fixed intervals of time.

Gyroscopic Track Recorder.—A Sperry gyroscopic pendulum has also been used with success in a mechanism employed to record the condition of a railroad rail bed. It has been used to record differences of elevation of the two rails on both curves and straightaway track, magnitude and location of rail spreads, depressions, depth of low rail joints and other inequalities in the roadbed at the time the track is subjected to the actual impact of the car passing over the rails at normal speed.

Aircraft Instruments.—The most widespread applications of the gyroscope are to be found in aircraft, since the airplane travels in a medium which makes possible not only changes in direction but changes in attitude as well. The gyroscope has become indispensable in the control of aircraft. Two instruments in particular have long been standard for flying blind or without reference to the earth. These instruments are the directional gyro and the artificial horizon.

The directional gyro is an excellent example of practical use being made of the property of a free gyroscope to maintain a fixed plane in space without reference to the earth. It is a small instrument which goes on the instrument panel in front of the human pilot. It consists of a small gyro spun by an air jet. This gyro is so mounted in gimbals as to have three degrees of freedom. The normal positions of this gyro are with its axes horizontal or parallel to the earth's surface. Around the vertical gimbal ring of this gyroscope is mounted an azimuth card. By means of a manual setting knob, this gyroscope, together with its azimuth card, may be moved so that the indication of the card at the plane's head will correspond with that of the magnetic compass. The gyro then maintains this specific directional line in space with a possible error caused by drift of possibly two or three degrees in each half hour that the gyro is left free. The utility of this instrument may appear to be very limited but it happens to complement the magnetic compass in a remarkable degree. By itself, neither is satisfactory as a directional reference, but a combination of the directional gyro with a magnetic compass gives the pilot complete and stable directional information. The magnetic compass is useful in an airplane only so long as the airplane continues on a straight course and in smooth air. While the airplane is making banked turns, the magnetic compass may have errors of 90° or more. Therefore, if the pilot desires to change his course by a definite number of degrees, the magnetic compass will be of little use to him. On the other hand, the directional gyro is not affected by banked turns or rough air. It therefore gives a positive and gyrostabilized indication of the exact number of degrees of turn that the airplane may make at any time. Since its indication is not affected by rough air, it is possible for the human pilot to steer a straighter and more accurate course to his destination. The relatively slow drift of the directional gyro from its heading may be corrected manually from time to time by comparing its heading with that of the magnetic compass when the airplane is in straight and level flight.

Another important aircraft instrument is the artificial horizon, which is used to give accurate indications to the human pilot of the bank and pitch attitude of his airplane. This instrument is also a small gyroscope mounted in such a manner as to have three degrees of freedom but with its axle maintained in a vertical position with reference to the earth by means of a gravity-actuated pendulum-type erecting system. Therefore, throughout any maneuvers of the airplane, the axle of the vertical gyro in the artificial horizon is always vertical and the indicating mechanisms attached to this gyroscope give the human pilot the exact bank, dive or climb angle at which his airplane is flying. This information to the human pilot is essential when flying blind, since human senses are not able to determine accurately the true direction of gravity without reference to the earth's surface by visual means.

The artificial horizon is a good example of the averaging ability of the gyro. The vertical position of the gyro axle in the artificial horizon is the average of all the positions assumed by the small pendulum-actuated erecting system which controls this gyroscope. Because of small changes of course or attitude caused, for instance, by rough air or turns, the pendulum is constantly swinging about the mean position which, in itself, is a true vertical. The artificial horizon gyroscope endeavours to follow these swings of the pendulum mechanism but does it so slowly that, for all practical purposes, the gyroscope remains with its axle fixed about the mean of all positions assumed by the erecting pendulum.

These two fundamental gyroscopes used in all aircraft are a basis of many control, calculating and indicating devices used on airplanes. The gyroscopes may be driven by air jets or by electric motors. By means of relays and pickup mechanisms of various types angular indications may be secured from the basic gyro reference and used to actuate servo mechanisms by which complete

BY COURTESY OF THE SPERRY GYROSCOPE COMPANY

FIG. 5.—SHIP GYROSTABILIZER. THE STABILIZER OPERATES UNDER THE DIRECTION OF A SMALL, SENSITIVE CONTROL GYROSCOPE MOUNTED ON ITS BASE. BOTH INSTRUMENTS HAVE ROTORS OR SPINNING FLY WHEELS. THE CONTROL GYROSCOPE RESPONDS INSTANTLY TO THE SLIGHTEST ROLL OF THE SHIP, TRANSMITTING PRECESSION OR COUNTERACTING MOTION TO THE GYROSTABILIZER WHICH SERVES TO BALANCE THE SHIP'S HULL

automatic control of the airplane may be secured as in the automatic gyropilot. The information from these basic gyroscopes may be fed into calculating devices which will compute true ground speed, as in the ground speed meter, or may be used as a basis for taking celestial fixes, as in the gyro sextant, or they may be used to provide the basic directional information for the air position indicator which indicates constantly the latitude and longitude at which the airplane is located. Other gyroscopes of the same basic type are used for the control of many types of computing sights, stabilized gun turrets and other fire-control mechanisms used on military aircraft. In the final analysis, the vertical and the horizontal gyroscope form the basis by which the modern airplane is controlled and navigated from its starting point to its destination.

(R. E. G.; A. L. R.; R. J. Sn.)

BIBLIOGRAPHY.—Ervin Sidney Ferry, *Applied Gyrodynamics, for Students, Engineers, and Users of Gyroscopic Apparatus*, rev. ed. (1933); Petr Petrovich Shilovskii, *Gyroscope: Its Practical Construction and Application* (1938); Richard F. Deimel, *Mechanics of the Gyroscope: the Dynamics of Rotation* (1952); Kenneth Ian Trevor Richardson, *Gyroscope Applied* (1954).

GYTHIUM (GYTHEION, YITHION), a town of Laconia, south Peloponnese, Greece, lies at the northwest extremity of the Laconian Gulf (Lakonikos Kolpos), in a small fertile plain at the mouth of the Gythius. In antiquity it served as the harbour and arsenal of Sparta, which is 48 km. (30 mi.) NNW. Pop. (1961) 4,992. The modern town is a busy port with a good harbour protected by Cranae Island (Marathonisi), now connected by a mole with the mainland.

Its reputed founders were Heracles and Apollo, who frequently appeared on its coins. In classical times a community of perioeci (*q.v.*), it later formed the most important of the Eleutherolaconian towns (*see* LACONIA). Pausanias (iii, 21 ff) describes the Roman town, the agora, the Acropolis, the island of Cranae where Paris celebrated his nuptials with Helen, the Migonium or precinct of Aphrodite Migonitis (occupied by the modern town), and the hill Larysium (Koumaro) rising above it. Extant remains are all of Roman date; the theatre, a temple of Augustus and Tiberius, and the buildings partially submerged by the sea are noteworthy.

(W. G. F.)

17 68

THIS letter corresponds to Semitic ☐ (cheth, consonantal) and Greek ☐ H (eta). It may derive from an early symbol for fence. In the early Greek alphabets both the form ☐ with three horizontal bars and the simpler form H were widely distributed. In Etruscan the prevailing form was ☐, and the same or a similar form occurs in very early Latin inscriptions, but the form H came into general use in Latin, either from the Chalcidic Greek alphabet of Cumae or from some other source. The modern majuscule H is derived directly from the Latin. The cursive Latin form ʰ resembled the modern minuscule, and the uncial form was h. Both these forms result from writing the letter without taking the pen from the paper, the right-hand vertical bar being thus foreshortened and the horizontal stroke rounded. From these came the Carolingian h and the modern minuscule h. (See ALPHABET.)

from the western Greek alphabets into the Etruscan alphabets and then into the Latin and other alphabets of ancient Italy. In the Romance languages the sound has largely disappeared, but the letter is still extensively used, partly with only etymological value, (e.g., French *homme*), partly with fancied etymological value (e.g., French *haut* from Latin *altus*, with *h* through the influence of *hoh*, the Old High German word of the same meaning), partly with special orthographical functions; for example, in Italian in combination with *c*, *g* to indicate the hard sound before a front vowel (e.g., *chi*, *ghetto*).

In English, the initial *h* is pronounced in words of Germanic origin (e.g., "hunt," "hook"); in some words of Romance origin, the *h* remains unpronounced (e.g., "heir," "honour"), but in others it has been restored (e.g., "humble," "humour"). The initial *h* often disappears in unaccented syllables (e.g., "What did he say?"). In chemistry, H is the symbol for the element hydrogen.

(B. F. C. A.; J. W. P.)

In music in the German nomenclature, H stands for B natural, while the letter B is used for B flat. This confusing arrangement dates back to earlier centuries when, to get the semitone in the right place (between the 3rd and 4th notes) in the hexachord beginning on F, a new B, a half tone lower than the normal B, was introduced. This lowered B was called B *molle* (soft) and indicated by a rounded B (B *rotundum*) to distinguish it from the square sign of the natural B (B *quadratum*). B rotundum was later adopted as a general sign in the form of a flat (♭) to indicate the lowering of a note by a semitone, while B quadratum became the sign, in the form of a natural (♮), for a note not so lowered; and in this way, from the resemblance of the latter sign to an H, this letter came to be adopted in Germany for the natural or unlowered B. In other words, H is here really an erroneous and misleading form of what was originally a square-shaped B.

HAAKON (Old Norse Hákon), the name of a number of kings and rulers of Norway.

Haakon I the Good (10th century A.D.) was the youngest son of Harald Haarfager and one of the most eminent rulers of his period. When he was one year old, his father sent him to England, where he was brought up at the court of King Aethelstan (d. 939). When he heard of the death of his father, Haakon, then 15 years old, sped to Norway supported by English arms. His elder half brother, Eric Bloodaxe, was by this time supreme ruler, but his ruthless tyranny had made him so unpopular that Haakon quickly gained support and Eric was forced to flee to England. Eric was killed soon afterward, but his sons took refuge in Denmark and harried Norway with the help of Danish forces. Haakon resisted successfully for a time, but was finally killed in battle against Eric's sons on the island of Fitjar in the southwest of Norway.

Haakon had grown up in England as a Christian. He brought English missionaries to Norway and established some churches, but the heathen chiefs were unshakable in their resistance and in the end compelled him to adopt their own religious practices. He was remembered as an able and humane ruler. His regnal dates are obscure. Medieval historians supposed that he ruled c. 933–960, but his reign was probably shorter and might be dated c. 946–961.

Haakon the Great (d. 995) ruled the greater part of Norway for many years after the death of Harald Greycloak. He never assumed the title of king, but was *jarl* (earl) as his ancestors had been before him. He held his dominions nominally as a fief of

NAME OF FORM	APPROXIMATE DATE	FORM OF LETTER
PHOENICIAN	1200 B.C.	☒
CRETAN	600	☐ H
THERAEAN	700-600	☐
ARCHAIC LATIN	700-500	(H)
ATTIC	600	☐
CORINTHIAN	600	☐
CHALCIDIAN	600	☐
IONIC	403	H
ROMAN COLONIAL	PRECLASSICAL AND CLASSICAL TIMES	H
URBAN ROMAN		☐
FALISCAN		☐
OSCAN		⊘
UMBRIAN		H
CLASSICAL LATIN AND ONWARD		

THE DEVELOPMENT OF THE LETTER "H" FROM THE PHOENICIAN THROUGH CLASSICAL LATIN TO THE PRESENT FORM

In the alphabets used to write the East Ionic dialect of Greek the letter became superfluous as a result of the disappearance of the aspirate which it represented in that dialect. It was accordingly put to a new use to indicate the open long *e* which had arisen through alteration of the primitive Greek long *a*. In a few inscriptions from Thera, Naxos and several other localities the letter was used with syllabic value; that is, it included *he*, thus showing its old consonantal and its new vocalic value at the same time. But eventually, as a result of the spread of the Ionic alphabet, its use for the long vowel *e* or *η* became general throughout Greece, while its consonantal value as the aspirate *h* passed

Denmark and, in 974, fought at the side of Harald Gormsson, king of Denmark, against the Holy Roman emperor Otto II. Haakon was afterward forced by the king to submit to baptism, but after leaving Denmark he publicly renounced Christianity and declined henceforth to pay tribute to the king. Haakon successfully resisted Danish attacks and won immense popularity as the foremost upholder of the ancient Norse religion. Toward the end of his life his morals declined and many of his subjects turned against him. When Olaf I Tryggvason invaded Norway in 995, asserting his claims to the crown, Haakon found few supporters and was finally murdered by his own thrall in a pigsty.

HAAKON II THE BROAD-SHOULDERED (c. 1147-1162) was an illegitimate son of Sigurd Munn (d. 1155). On the death of his uncle King Eystein in 1157, the ten-year-old Haakon received the support of Eystein's partisans against the rival king, Ingi I, whom they finally defeated and killed in 1161. In 1162, however, the supporters of another pretender, Magnus Erlingsson, defeated the forces of the boy king Haakon and killed him.

HAAKON III (d. 1204) was the illegitimate son of King Sverre Sigurdsson. During his short reign (from 1202), he tried to heal the breach between the crown and the church, so that exiled bishops returned to their sees. It was said that the sickness which caused his sudden death was the result of poison put into his drink at the instigation of his Swedish stepmother, Margaret.

HAAKON IV HAAKONSSON (1204-1263) was acknowledged as the illegitimate, posthumous son of Haakon III and thus grandson of Sverre Sigurdsson. He was brought up at the court of King Ingi II and on Ingi's death (1217) was proclaimed the king by the Birchlegs, the adherents of Sverre. The archbishop and other ecclesiastical leaders were at first suspicious of Haakon, doubting his paternity, but after his mother had come through the ordeal by hot irons (1218) his rights were widely acknowledged.

The early years of Haakon's reign were disturbed by revolts on behalf of other pretenders, which were supported by some sections of the church. Government, in the first years, was conducted chiefly by Jarl Skuli, an elder kinsman of Haakon, but Skuli's ambition led to a rift between him and the king. Attempts were made to reconcile them: Haakon married Skuli's daughter Margaret and conferred the first Norwegian dukedom on Skuli (1237). In the end, however, Skuli revolted openly and proclaimed himself king, but was quickly defeated and killed by Haakon's forces (1240).

After reigning many years, Haakon appealed to the pope to authorize his coronation, a ceremony then rare in Norway. He was crowned in 1247 by a papal legate, Cardinal William of Sabena. Haakon showed strong colonial ambitions and secured the submission of Greenland in 1261 and that of Iceland in 1262. In 1263 he sailed with a large fleet to the Hebrides, intending to assert Norway's traditional rights there, but after some skirmishes with the Scots, he retired to Orkney, where he died in Dec. 1263.

Haakon is remembered as a patron of letters as well as a statesman. At his instigation a Norse version of the story of Tristram was made in 1226 and many other French romances appeared in Norse versions during his reign. A detailed biography of Haakon was written some years after his death by the Icelander Sturla Thordarson (d. 1284).

HAAKON V MAGNUSSON (1270-1319), a younger son of Magnus Lagabøter (d. 1280), succeeded his elder brother Eric in 1299. Throughout his reign he engaged in intermittent wars with the Danes and Swedes. He checked the growing power of the nobility and introduced many social reforms. He left no son, but revised the law of succession so that he was succeeded in 1319 by Magnus VII, the son of his daughter Ingeborg, who had married the Swedish prince Eric. Since Magnus was also acknowledged king of Sweden (Magnus II), the two crowns were united.

HAAKON VI (1340-1380) was the younger son of Magnus VII and II of Norway and Sweden. In 1343 it was agreed that he should eventually succeed to Norway but that his elder brother Eric should succeed to Sweden. When Sweden was torn by pestilence and grave political strife, he intervened on his father's side. His marriage to Margaret, daughter of Valdemar IV of Denmark, paved the way for the union of the three kingdoms, Norway, Sweden and Denmark, after his death (1380).

(G. T.-P.)

HAAKON VII (1872-1957), first king of Norway after its restoration to independence, was born at Charlottenlund, in Denmark, on Aug. 3, 1872, the second son of the Danish crown prince Frederick, later king of Denmark as Frederick VIII. Known at first as Prince Charles of Denmark, he was trained as a naval officer. On July 22, 1896, he married the English princess Maud, youngest daughter of Edward VII. After the dissolution of the union of Norway with Sweden in 1905, the Norwegian government offered the vacant crown to Prince Charles, who accepted it with the proviso that the Norwegian people's approval must first be demonstrated by a plebiscite. This condition was opposed by the Norwegian government, which feared an unfavourable verdict; but when the plebiscite was held (Nov. 12), the overwhelming favourable result (259,563 votes against 69,264) strikingly vindicated the prince's political insight. On Nov. 18 he was unanimously elected by the *storting*, assuming the old Norse name of Haakon.

Haakon's long reign covered a critical period including two world wars and the sudden rise to power of the Labour party or *Arbeiderparti*. The Labour ministers, new to governmental responsibility, owed much to the king's tactful guidance, which he always associated with the strictest loyalty to democratic principle. When the Germans invaded Norway in 1940, during World War II, Haakon's value was conspicuously illustrated. Faced by a German ultimatum, the ministers who accompanied his escape from Oslo to England were at first divided and hesitant, but the king, though he insisted that the decision must be theirs, declared that he himself would abdicate rather than accept terms which violated the constitution. Thus he rallied the doubters and saved a most dangerous situation. Two months later, when the presidential board of the *storting*, under German pressure, requested him to abdicate, his firm and clearly reasoned refusal heartened the country's will to resistance. It moreover reflected unmistakably the true wishes of the nation: thenceforward Norwegians, without distinction of class or party, regarded him as the rallying point and inspiration of their struggles. His return to Oslo in 1945 was warmly acclaimed, and to the day of his death, which took place in Oslo, on Sept. 21, 1957, he commanded his people's devotion.

(G. M. G.-H.)

HAARLEM, a city of the Netherlands, capital of the province of North Holland, lies on the Spaarne river, 4½ mi. from the North sea, 13 mi. (21 km.) W. of Amsterdam by rail. Pop. (1960) 167,673. It is connected by bus lines with Zandvoort, Leiden, Amsterdam and Alkmaar and with its residential suburbs Bloemendaal, Aerdenhout, Bentveld, Heemstede, Overveen and Santpoort. Haarlem is the seat of a Roman Catholic and a Jansenist bishopric and of a court. It is rapidly expanding on modern town-planning lines; a satellite town, Schalkwijk, for 40,000 inhabitants, is under construction. The centre is formed by the old town, with numerous canals and gabled houses.

Weaving of wool and brewing, the town's early industries, declined in the course of the 17th century when silk, lace and damask weaving were introduced by French refugees and became very important in the economy. About the close of the 18th century the town's prosperity came to an end, and it was not until the second half of the 19th century that it was regained when Haarlem developed the industries in which it is now chiefly engaged. Among the most important of these are printing, type founding, ship and construction yards, machine building, hosiery and clothing manufacture, cocoa and chocolate processing, pharmaceutical chemistry and plastic packings. After World War II foreign industries, mostly from the United States, were located in Haarlem. Though retail distribution and civil administration are important, most of the town's inhabitants work in industry. Horticulture, especially market gardening, is extensively practised in the vicinity, and Haarlem has a large trade in bulbs, which it exports to all parts of the world.

With its beach and dunes (including the Kennemerduinen national park) on the west side, sailing centre on the east side and bulb fields to the south, Haarlem has a remarkably good recreation area for a town situated in one of the most densely populated districts of the world. It is also an important regional shopping centre.

Of the fortifications, the ancient Spaarnwouder gate, the moats and some earthworks remain. In the great market square are the town hall (about 1350, with 17th-century additions), the Vleeshal, or meat market (1603), and the Grote Kerk (390 ft. long, 180 ft. wide, with a tower 250 ft. high). The choir of the Grote Kerk was built in 1397–1400, transept and nave 1472–96; a crossing tower (wood, covered with lead) was added in 1519–20. The church possesses, among other interesting objects, carved choir stalls (1512) with armorial decoration, a monumental brass lectern in the shape of a pelican (1499), a brass choir screen (1509–17) and two organs, of which the greater was built in 1738 by Christian Müller. Frans Hals is buried in the choir.

Of the other churches mention may be made of the former chapel of the Béguinage (the oldest of the city); the Bakenesserkerk (Our Lady), with a delicate tower of 1530; the Dutch baroque Nieuwe Kerk (New or St. Anne's church), 1645–49; and the Roman Catholic cathedral, 1895–1930.

The provincial government is housed in a charming building (1785–88), originally the country seat of an Amsterdam banker, later the residence of King Louis Napoleon. It is located in the Hout (Wood), a municipal park of medieval origin, remodeled in landscape style in 1835.

The city possesses the Frans Hals museum containing historical objects and an important picture gallery (works of the Haarlem school, group portraits by Hals); and the Roman Catholic Episcopal museum of ecclesiastical art and history. The Teyler museum has Italian 16th-century and Dutch 17th-century drawings, the former collection of Christina of Sweden; physical instruments, including a 31-tone organ tuned according to the theory of Christiaan Huygens; paleontological, geological and mineralogical collections, etc. The city library (founded 1596) contains several old manuscripts, incunabula and a collection of early Dutch literature. The Dutch Society of Sciences (founded 1752) and the Teyler foundation (1778) are located in Haarlem.

Haarlem was a prosperous place in the 12th century and received its town charter in 1245. It played a considerable part in the wars with the Frisians. In 1492 it was captured by insurgent peasants of North Holland, and after being retaken by the regular troops was deprived of its privileges. In 1572 Haarlem joined the revolt of the Netherlands against Spain, but in July 1573 after a seven months' siege was forced by starvation to surrender to the duque de Alba's son Frederick, who exacted terrible vengeance. In 1577 the town was recaptured by William of Orange and permanently incorporated in the united Netherlands. Since the 15th century Haarlem has been a centre of artistic activity. The sculptor Claus Sluter was born there; the Haarlem school of painting had many illustrious names, including the Ruisdaels, Philips Wouwerman and the Ostades and Frans Hals. (C. F. JA.; J. F. ME.; P. MK.)

HAARLEM LAKE (Dutch HAARLEMMERMEER) is a polder, coextensive with the commune of Haarlemmermeer, in the province of North Holland, Neth. It has an area of 45,700 ac. (71 sq.mi.). The region was formerly a number of lakes which gradually increased in extent. In 1531 the Haarlemmermeer, the Leydermeer and some smaller sheets of water in their vicinity had a united area of about 14,000 ac. These lakes were formed into one by successive inundations and by 1647 the new Haarlem lake had an area of about 37,000 ac., which a century later had increased to more than 42,000 ac. As early as 1643 Jan Adriaanszoon Leeghwater proposed to endike and drain the lake with pumping power provided by 160 windmills; and similar schemes were brought forward from time to time. A hurricane in Nov. 1836 drove the waters as far as the gates of Amsterdam, and another on Christmas day sent them in the opposite direction to submerge the streets of Leiden. In Aug. 1837 the king appointed a royal commission of inquiry; the scheme proposed by the commission received the sanction of the second chamber in March 1839, and in May 1840 the work was begun. A canal was first dug around the lake for the reception of the water and the accommodation of the traffic which the lake had previously carried. Since the water from the lake had no natural outfall, pumping by steam engines began in 1848, and the lake was dry by July 1852. The whole area of 42,096 ac. recovered from the waters brought in about £780,000, exactly covering the cost of the enterprise; so that the actual cost to the nation was only the amount of the interest on the capital. The soil is of various kinds, mainly clay and loam, and most of it is fertile. About 80% of the reclaimed lake is arable land, 15% is meadow and about 2.3% is used for horticulture. A road fork, a detour from the *autosnelweg* from Leiden to Amsterdam, crosses the Haarlemmermeer. (H. J. KE.)

HAARLEMMERMEER, a commune and polder near Amsterdam in the province of North Holland, Neth. Pop. (1962 est.) 46,531. The lake (*see* HAARLEM LAKE) was drained 1840–52. Within the enclosing canal and dike is a network of roads and ditches at right angles. The population (1961 est.) lives in the central villages of Hoofddorp (6,000) and Nieuw-Vennep (3,500), the northern garden villages of Badhoevedorp (10,000) and Zwanenburg (7,500), along the dike (10,000) and in the polder (9,000). There is a polder museum (Cruquius). In the northeast is Amsterdam's large airport, Schiphol. Bus services run to Amsterdam, Haarlem, Utrecht and Leiden. The main occupations of the population are agriculture (wheat, beets, potatoes), dairy farming, horticulture (flowers, bulbs, vegetables), industry (aircraft, steel furniture, agricultural implements, draining machines, lifeboats) and services connected with the airport. (J. Ac.)

HAAST, SIR JOHN FRANCIS JULIUS VON (JOHANN FRANZ JULIUS VON HAAST) (1824–1887), German-born British geologist and explorer, was born at Bonn on May 1, 1824. In 1858 he journeyed to New Zealand and there he assisted Austrian geologist Ferdinand von Hochstetter in his preliminary geological survey. The governments of Nelson and Canterbury then employed Haast to investigate the geology of those districts. He discovered gold and coal in Nelson, and carried on important researches with reference to the extinct wingless birds, the moas. His *Geology of the Provinces of Canterbury and Westland, N.Z.,* was published in 1879. He was the founder and director of the Canterbury museum at Christchurch, surveyor general of Canterbury from 1861 to 1871 and professor of geology at Canterbury University college (affiliate of the University of New Zealand). He was elected a fellow in the Royal society in 1867; and he was knighted in 1887. He died at Wellington, N.Z., on Aug. 15, 1887.

HABAKKUK, BOOK OF, the eighth in order of the collection of 12 prophetic books in the Old Testament known as the 12 Prophets or the Minor Prophets. Its author, Habakkuk (Ambacum in the Septuagint and the Vulgate), was probably a professional Hebrew prophet (i, 1) living at the end of the 7th century B.C., who spoke by inspiration (i, 11) and saw visions (i, 1; ii, 1, 2) which he wrote down (ii, 2) in a style borrowed from sacred poetry and from prophecy. He was thus probably a professional seer employed in the worship of the Temple (*cf.* also ii, 20).

Contents and Themes.—Literary analysis reveals the following: two lamentations, each followed by an oracle, and then five imprecations, or woes, and a final *tefilla* ("prayer" or "psalm") in the third chapter after a liturgical silence (ii, 20) required before the appearance of God outside the sanctuary. This combination of lamentation and oracle, which occurs elsewhere in the Old Testament (*e.g.,* Jos. vii, 7 ff.), is consonant with Hebrew liturgical usage.

In the lamentations, Habakkuk, as a representative of Israel, bewails the national misfortunes, and in the oracles he pronounces the response of God's consolation. The imprecations then curse an enemy who is somewhat enigmatically described. The appearance (theophany) of the Lord in the third chapter celebrates God's victory over his enemies.

The detailed outline of the book is as follows:

i, 1:	title
i, 2–4:	first lamentation
i, 5–11:	oracle on the "bitter and hasty nation"
i, 12–17:	second lamentation
ii, 1–5:	oracle from the tower
ii, 6–19;	five imprecations
ii, 6–8:	on oppression

Literary History.—There are three main problems: the literary unity of the book, the identity of the enemy and the date of composition.

Literary Unity.—Too artificial an analysis has sometimes exaggerated the internal contradictions of the book and hence split it up among different authors. But careful attention to composition, thought, style and vocabulary shows that it is by one man. The symmetrical texture of the book, its organic architecture and the logical progression of its thought—from lamentations echoed by oracles, to imprecations damning the enemy to disaster, and culminating in a theophany of God the avenger—all indicate a planned composition typical of an author who was at once singer and prophet and who was familiar with the Temple worship and with prophetic liturgy. The Book of Habakkuk is thus, according to this view, organically and deliberately put together and not merely a juxtaposition of various passages. Its vocabulary is closely related to that of sacred poetry and of prophecy at the end of the 7th century B.C.

The third chapter shares the double character of the rest of the book, to which it forms the climax. Many scholars have jettisoned it as inauthentic, and this view finds support in the chapter's absence from the Habakkuk manuscript found at 'Ain Feshkha, near the Dead sea, in 1947-48. This manuscript, variously estimated to date from the 1st century B.C. or A.D., contains the text of ch. i-ii, with a commentary. However, ch. iii was part of the text of Habakkuk much earlier, in the (Greek) Septuagint version, probably of the 2nd century B.C., and it is clearly an original part of the text.

Identity of the Enemy and Date of the Book.—The enemy ("the wicked," i, 4) of Habakkuk's vision has been variously identified. Some suggest the Assyrians, against whom God will send the Chaldeans (*i.e.*, Babylonians) as liberators (i, 6). Holders of this theory must either reject Hab. i, 5-11 as spurious, for there the Chaldeans (Babylonians) are represented as instruments of divine vengeance, or place these verses before i, 2-4 as a prelude to the coming of the Babylonians who later became a threat. In either case the symmetrical composition analyzed above would be spoiled. In addition, it would be paradoxical to treat as an agent of God (i, 5, 6) those very Babylonians who, according to this hypothesis, are the oppressors of Judah.

Yet a third answer is to identify the enemy with Jehoiakim (*q.v.*), king of Judah. The struggle between "the righteous" and "the wicked" (i, 4) would then be within Israel itself, and the Babylonians would only appear at the end of the 7th century as the imminent agent of Judah's salvation. The objection to this theory is that it would be an exaggeration to describe Jehoiakim as an oppressive tyrant.

Finally, some would identify the enemy with Alexander the Great (d. 323 B.C.) or even with the eschatological adversary, but these theories collapse before the express mention of the contemporary Babylonians (i, 6).

Though no one of these theories can be definitely accepted, some conclusions can be taken as certain: i, 5-11 envisages the coming of the Babylonians as imminent (*i.e.*, before the destruction of Jerusalem in 586 B.C.). Difficulties are raised if the whole passage ii, 6-19 refers to foreign domination; and i, 6 expressly

Others claim that the enemy is to be identified with the Babylonian oppressors of Judah and that Habakkuk was writing just before or even during the Exile (which began in 596 B.C.). Holders of this theory must either reject Hab. i, 5-11 as spurious, for places the scene between 626, when the Babylonian Nabopolassar came to power, and 612, when the Assyrian city of Nineveh was captured by the Babylonians and the Medes. The objection to this dating is that by the last decades of the 7th century Assyria was no longer an imperial power.

calls the Babylonians an agent of God. The identity of the enemy thus remains a problem, but it may be concluded that Habakkuk was a cult prophet of the end of the 7th century, as indeed his vocabulary confirms. His liturgy, no doubt composed for solemn ceremonial in the Temple, is on any interpretation a fierce criticism of a contemporary despotism and the triumphant assertion of God's sovereignty, which will annihilate the enemy: "the just," which is Judah, can then rest assured in faithfulness (ii, 4).

Habakkuk in Later Literature.—The exegesis of the 'Ain Feshkha commentary on Habakkuk is allegorical, not historical, the Chaldeans being interpreted as Kittim (*i.e.*, Romans, the enemy in that later period) and the prophecies being applied to the contemporary Jewish reaction to Roman domination. The commentary's running quotations from Habakkuk are of interest for the textual criticism of the biblical book, since they show some variation from the standard Hebrew text.

In the New Testament Paul twice makes Habakkuk's allusion to faithfulness (ii, 4) apply on a universal and purely spiritual level, identifying it with "faith" and thus assuring it a place at the centre of the Christian gospel: "the just shall live by faith" (Rom. i, 17; Gal. iii, 11). *See also* BIBLE.

BIBLIOGRAPHY.—English commentaries by A. B. Davidson in *Cambridge Bible*, pp. 45-94 (1896); G. W. Wade, *Westminster Commentaries*, pp. 141-215 (1929); and Charles L. Taylor, Jr., in *The Interpreter's Bible*, vol. vi, pp. 973-1003 (1956). German trans. with commentary by E. Sellin, *Das Zwölfprophetenbuch* (1930) and by F. Horst in *Handbuch zum Alten Testament*, 2nd ed. (1954). *See also* J. Lachmann, *Das Buch Habakkuk* (1932); P. Humbert, *Problèmes du livre d'Habacuc* (1944); K. Elliger, *Studien zum Habakuk-Kommentar vom Toten Meer* (1953); Millar Burrows, *The Dead Sea Scrolls* (1956).
(P. Hr.)

HABBANIYAH, LAKE (HAWR AL HABBANIYAH), lying about 50 mi. W. of Baghdad in Ramadi *liwa* (province) between Ar Ramadi and Al Fallujah, is a sheet of slightly saline water about 19 mi. long, separated from the Euphrates by the Asibi and Zaban (Dhiban) ridges. Since ancient times it has been used to take floodwater from the Euphrates; two "cuts,"—Aziziyah and the Habbaniyah escape—link it on the northwest with a further channel, Majora (Majarrah) escape, leading off to a second basin, the Jira depression. In 1956 the long-discussed project of a cut allowing return of water to the Euphrates in the dry season was begun. The town of Habbaniyah lies on the northeastern bank, where the lake comes closest to the river, and consists mostly of air force installations (formerly British).
(W. B. Fr.)

HABDALAH, in Judaism, the concluding ceremony of sabbaths and festivals. *See* KIDDUSH AND HABDALAH.

HABEAS CORPUS, an ancient common-law writ, issued by a court or judge directing one who holds another in his custody to produce the body of the person before the court for some specified purpose. Many varieties of the writ were recognized at common law. Thus, habeas corpus *ad respondendum* was employed to remove a prisoner from the process of an inferior court to answer a cause of action in a higher court. A prisoner against whom a judgment had been obtained in an inferior court could be removed to a higher court on habeas corpus *ad satisfaciendum* in order that he might there be subjected to process of execution. The form of the writ *ad prosequendum, testificandum, deliberandum* authorized the removal of the prisoner from confinement so that he might prosecute, testify or be tried in the proper jurisdiction. Habeas corpus *ad faciendum et recipiendum* was employed by one sued in some inferior jurisdiction to remove the cause to any of the courts at Westminster. But the form of greatest importance, referred to by Blackstone as "the great and efficacious writ," is habeas corpus *ad subjiciendum*, which is employed to correct violations of personal liberty by directing judicial inquiry into the legality of the detention. The habeas corpus remedy is recognized in the countries of the Anglo-American legal system, and comparable procedures have been adopted in some nations whose institutions are the product of other legal traditions.

England.—The origins of the writ cannot be stated with certainty. Prior to Magna Carta (1215) a variety of writs performed some of the functions of habeas corpus, such as the writ *de odio et atia* which was used to prevent imprisonment on vexatious appeals of felony. In the later middle ages habeas corpus was frequently employed to bring cases from inferior tribunals into the king's courts and thus served primarily as an instrument of royal prerogative rather than of individual right. By the closing decades of the 15th century the common-law courts used the writ to assert their jurisdiction against the competing claims of the court of chancery. The modern history of the writ as a device for protection of personal liberty against official authority may be said to date from the reign of Henry VII (1485–1509) when efforts were made to employ habeas corpus *ad subjiciendum* in behalf of persons imprisoned by the privy council. By the reign of Charles I, in the 17th century, the writ was fully established as the appropriate process for checking illegal imprisonment by inferior courts or public officials. But legislation was ultimately required to establish the writ in its present significance.

The modern law of habeas corpus is closely associated with the constitutional struggles of 17th-century England. In Darnel's case (1627) it was decided that a writ of habeas corpus *ad subjiciendum* is sufficiently answered by a showing that the prisoner was detained by command of the king. Parliament sought to remedy this situation in the Petition of Right (1628) which recited that the king's subjects had "of late been imprisoned without any cause shewed" but were detained by the king's "special command" and prayed that "no freeman, in any such manner as is before mentioned, be imprisoned or detained." The Act of 1641 (16 Car. I, c. 10), which abolished the court of star chamber, provided that anyone imprisoned by a court of like jurisdiction, the king or the privy council should have the right of habeas corpus to test the legality of the commitment. But by far the most important legislation is the celebrated Habeas Corpus act of 1679 (31 Car. II, c. 2) which, although it created no new rights of personal freedom, provided procedures which made significant contributions to the effective assertion of such rights. The act authorized the judges to issue the writ when the courts were in vacation and provided severe penalties for any judge who without good cause refused to entertain a writ and for any officer who refused to comply with it. The act of 1679 applied only to persons imprisoned on criminal charges. Legislation enacted in 1816 (56 Geo. III, c. 100) made the writ available to persons confined under private authority.

The Administration of Justice act, 1960, made some important changes in the law and practice relating to habeas corpus proceedings in England. Section 14 deals with procedure and provides: (1) that in a criminal application an order for the release of the person detained shall be refused only by a divisional court of the queen's bench division, whether the application be made in the first instance to such a court or to a single judge; (2) that where an application has been made to a court or judge, no further application shall be made to another court without fresh evidence; and that no application shall be made to the lord chancellor; (3) that applications on behalf of certain defined classes of mental patients shall be deemed to constitute a criminal cause or matter. Section 15 of this act altered the law as to appeals in habeas corpus proceedings, so that appeal now lies in any such proceedings, whether an order is granted or refused, except when (granting the application). In criminal cases appeal lies from the divisional court to the house of lords by leave of the court or the house (unlike other criminal appeals), without the need for either to certify that a point of law of general public importance is involved; in civil cases appeal lies from the divisional court to the court of appeal without leave and thence to the house of lords by leave either of the court of appeal or the house.

United States.—Although the use of habeas corpus has never been adequately traced in the colonial history of the United States, it is clear that the writ was adopted by many colonial courts as part of the common-law heritage. As early as 1692 South Carolina and Massachusetts enacted legislation similar to the English act of 1679, and cases in which the writ was granted may be found in other colonies. By the outbreak of the American Revolution the rights to habeas corpus were popularly regarded as among the basic protections of individual liberty. Thus in the Address to the People of Quebec, issued by the continental congress in

1774 in an effort to gain the assistance of the French Canadians in its struggle with the English crown, reference is made to the "liberty of the person" protected in the American law by "a writ, termed a Habeas Corpus." The U.S. constitution provides that the privilege of the writ of habeas corpus "shall not be suspended, unless when in cases of rebellion or invasion the public safety may require it" (art. i, sec. 9, par. 2). The first congress enacted legislation empowering justices of the supreme court and judges of the district court to grant the writ.

In England the writ of habeas corpus was suspended by annual acts of parliament from 1794 to 1801 and in 1817. In the United States, President Lincoln suspended the writ by executive proclamation at the outbreak of the Civil War in 1861. The presidential act was challenged by Chief Justice Taney who, in the well-known case of *Ex Parte Merryman* (Fed. Cases no. 9487), vigorously contended that the power of suspension resides only in the national legislature. Lincoln ignored the order of the court in the *Merryman* case, but the weight of modern opinion appears to support the view that suspension of the writ requires the consent of congress. In 1863 congress, with considerable reluctance, delegated to the president power to suspend the writ "during the present rebellion . . . whenever, in his judgment, the public safety may require it." Again in 1871, congress authorized the president to suspend the writ in connection with certain difficulties of the postwar Reconstruction. President Grant's executive order, which suspended the writ in nine counties of South Carolina, referred to the congressional act as the source of legal authority. Following the attack on Pearl Harbor in 1941, the governor of Hawaii suspended the writ of habeas corpus and declared martial law. The governor's proclamation was promptly approved by the president of the United States, as required by law. Later, in the case of *Duncan* v. *Kahanamoku*, 327 U.S. 304 (1946), convictions of civilian offenders tried before a military commission were set aside by the supreme court on the ground that military necessity did not justify the supplanting of the civil courts at the time of the trials. The state constitutions contain provisions for the writ of habeas corpus and its suspension during periods of public emergency. The privilege of the writ was suspended in Massachusetts during Shay's rebellion (1786–87).

The writ of habeas corpus mentioned in state constitutional provisions has ordinarily been held to possess the attributes of the common-law writ. Procedures relating to the issuance of the writ are regulated by legislation in most jurisdictions. Relief by way of habeas corpus is conceived as an extraordinary remedy and generally is not granted if other procedures are available. Thus it is frequently said that habeas corpus cannot be used as a substitute for an appeal or writ of error in criminal cases. Since the enactment of the legislation of 1789, the habeas corpus jurisdiction of the federal courts has been expanded by a series of congressional acts. The Force act of 1833 (4 Stat. 634) authorized the granting of writs in cases of prisoners committed pursuant to any law of the United States or by an order of a federal judge or court. Of primary significance, however, is the act of 1867 (14 Stat. 385), which enlarged the existing habeas corpus jurisdiction to include cases of any person who may be restrained "in violation of the constitution, or of any treaty or law of the United States." These provisions, codified in 1874, survived without important change until 1948.

The U.S. supreme court's increasingly liberal interpretations of the constitutional rights of those accused of crime led in mid-20th century to the filing of many habeas corpus petitions by prisoners in state and federal custody. In the leading case of *Johnson* v. *Zerbst*, 304 U.S. 458 (1938), the supreme court held that the failure of the trial judge in a federal criminal prosecution to appoint counsel for an indigent defendant constituted a "jurisdictional" error and hence one appropriate for habeas corpus relief. The marked increase in the number of habeas corpus petitions filed by federal prisoners following the *Johnson* case and similar decisions of the supreme court led congress in 1948 to enact a substitute procedure (28 U.S.C., sec. 2255). This provision authorizes a federal prisoner to attack his conviction in the sentencing court on a variety of grounds, including lack of jurisdiction in the trial court and denial of defendant's constitutional rights. The motion for relief may be made at any time, but the court need not entertain successive motions for similar relief by the same prisoner. An application for habeas corpus must be denied when the prisoner has failed to utilize the statutory motion or when the motion has been denied, unless the statutory remedy appears inadequate to test the legality of the prisoner's detention. The validity of the statutory procedure has been upheld by the supreme court.

The habeas corpus jurisdiction of the federal courts as it relates to prisoners convicted in the state courts gives rise to even more difficult and delicate problems. Since 1867 the federal district courts have had jurisdiction over both federal and state prisoners who claim that their confinement is in violation of the federal constitution or federal law. A considerable number of cases involving state prisoners were decided in the 19th century, but the modern problems date from the 1930s when the rights of accused persons in the state courts were first significantly enlarged by the supreme court's interpretations of the due process clause of the 14th amendment. It has long been understood that federal habeas corpus relief is not available to the state prisoner until his state remedies have been exhausted, and this principle was given statutory expression in a provision enacted by congress in 1948. The precise definition of the exhaustion requirement has been the source of judicial controversy, however; and other problems relating to the scope and availability of federal habeas corpus relief have proved difficult. In the 1950s various legislative proposals were made for eliminating or drastically reducing federal habeas corpus jurisdiction over persons held under state process. These proposals often failed to take into account the substantial contributions to the quality of state criminal justice that have resulted from the supervision of state procedures by the federal courts. The proposals were defended primarily by reference to the administrative burden on the federal district courts caused by the proliferation of habeas corpus petitions by state prisoners and by the supposed impropriety of subjecting a state judgment to the scrutiny of the lower federal courts. Although these proposals gained considerable support, none had been enacted into law by the beginning of the 1960s.

The writ of habeas corpus is recognized by the law of the states, as well as the federal government. It has been held, however, that a state court may not issue the writ to effect the release of one held by an officer of the United States who claims authority for the detention under federal law. There is considerable diversity in the law of the states as to the scope and function of the habeas corpus remedy and the procedures required to invoke it. A convicted criminal is ordinarily not permitted to raise issues that were or could have been raised in an appeal of his criminal conviction. Even apart from this restriction, however, the writ may be strictly limited to attacks on the jurisdiction of the court in which the petitioner was convicted. Thus errors at the trial, even those denying the accused's constitutional rights, may not provide a basis for habeas corpus relief. In such states, other postconviction remedies may be available for the assertion of constitutional rights, such as the writ of error *coram nobis*. Since World War II many states have created statutory postconviction procedures to provide expeditious means for testing alleged deprivations of constitutional rights. In some states, however, the writ of habeas corpus has been adapted to this end and has become the customary mode of challenging the constitutional validity of a conviction when the criminal appeal is unavailable for this purpose. The law of postconviction remedies in many of the states at the beginning of the 1960s was ill-defined and poorly adapted to deal with the problems created by the more liberal judicial definitions of the constitutional rights of accused persons.

The use of habeas corpus, however, is by no means confined to challenges to the validity of criminal convictions on constitutional or other grounds. Frequently a writ may be requested in behalf of one in police custody for the purpose of requiring the police either to charge the arrested person with an offense or to release him. Habeas corpus proceedings may be employed to obtain release of the accused prior to trial on the ground that the bail set by the magistrate is excessive. On occasion habeas corpus relief has been granted a prisoner who is unlawfully detained after expiration of his sentence. In cases of one arrested on a warrant of extradition or of interstate rendition, a proceeding in habeas corpus may be instituted to challenge the validity of the warrant. The writ may also be employed in a wide variety of situations not involving criminal proceedings. Thus competing claims to the custody of a minor may be adjudicated in habeas corpus. One confined in a mental hospital may in some states bring about his release by showing at the habeas corpus hearing that he has recovered his sanity. The writ has also been employed to challenge the right of the military forces to retain the petitioner in their custody. Many other occasions for use of the writ occur in the modern law.

(F. A. A.)

HABENARIA, a genus of plants of the orchid family (Orchidaceae), comprising in its most inclusive sense some 500 temperate and tropical species. In North America several handsome kinds occur, usually in boglike acid soil. Among them are the small purple-fringed orchis (*H. psycodes*), the white-fringed orchis (*H. blephariglottis*), the ragged orchis (*H. lacera*), the prairie fringed orchis (*H. leucophaea*), the yellow-fringed orchis (*H. ciliaris*), the white bog orchis (*H. dilatata*), the round-leaved orchis (*H. orbiculata*), the slender white orchis (*H. elegans*) and the western green orchis (*H. unalaschensis*). The frog orchis (*H. viridis*), scented orchis (*H. conopsea*) and butterfly orchis (*H. bifolia*) are native to the British Isles. See ORCHID.

HABER, FRITZ (1868–1934), German physical chemist, winner of the Nobel prize for chemistry in 1918 for his direct synthesis of ammonia from nitrogen and hydrogen, was born at Breslau, Dec. 9, 1868, and took his doctorate in organic chemistry at the Technische Hochschule, Berlin. He was essentially self-taught in his chosen field—physical chemistry with emphasis on technical application. His remarkable output of research began at Karlsruhe in 1894, beginning with a study of the thermal decomposition of hydrocarbons and combustion of gases in contact with cooled surfaces. This was a real contribution to the understanding of the cracking processes that have since become tremendously important.

Haber's work in electrochemistry was outstanding. He unraveled the complicated course of the electrolytic reduction of nitrobenzene. He was the first to demonstrate the significance of the electrode potential in oxidations and reductions, and developed the first general theory of electrochemical reduction. He destroyed the hopes that had been placed in fuel cells as a means for the direct electrochemical transformation of the energy of coal into electrical power. He showed that Faraday's law is valid for solid electrolytes. He worked out the theory of the glass electrode and developed its practical application. He provided standard methods for investigating and remedying the corrosion of underground gas and water mains due to stray currents from tramway systems. He studied beryllium compounds, the production of aluminum, the passivity of iron, the gas-water equilibrium in the Bunsen flame, the speed of reaction in heterogeneous systems, the separation of gases by centrifugal force and the escape of electrons from metals. His studies of the optical analysis of gases led to the gas interferometer that bears his name. He devised a vibrating quartz manometer to measure low gas pressures, and constructed a firedamp whistle for use in mines. Among his later studies were: the chemical applications of Planck's quantum theory; the conditions determining the structure of precipitates; adsorption, chemiluminescence; chain reactions in gases; free radicals; the mechanism of combustion.

Haber's greatest achievement, which brought him the Nobel prize in 1918, was his successful synthesis of ammonia (*q.v.*). This was an outcome of his studies of the thermodynamics of gas reactions. He developed a small apparatus, but at first was quite skeptical about the feasibility of carrying out, on a technical scale, a reaction at red heat and under several hundred atmospheres of pressure. Eventually, he perfected his equipment so that the translation to the industrial scale, though still presenting gigantic problems, was far from hopeless. The credit for the large-scale development of the Haber process belongs mostly to Karl Bosch.

In 1911, Haber was called to direct the Kaiser Wilhelm Institut für Physikalische Chemie und Elektrochemie at Dahlem, Berlin. This research institute, which he headed until 1933, became the finest laboratory of its kind in the world, and mature chemists from all nations came there to work. In 1914, he placed his services at the disposal of the German imperial government, though he hated war and its horrors. He sensed at once that the issue could be decided by a lack of nitric acid, the essential raw material for high explosives. Haber's first efforts were to increase the supply of ammonia, which could then be oxidized to nitric acid. He also headed the organization of the gas warfare, and directed the chlorine gas attack at Ypres on April 22, 1915. He was made chief of the chemical warfare service in 1916.

Svante A. Arrhenius (q.v.) estimated that the oceans contain 8,000,000,000 tons of gold. When Germany was asked to pay in reparations the equivalent of 50,000 tons, Haber conceived the dramatic idea of securing the fabulous amount from the sea. He devised processes for the extraction of the metal from the water, whose gold content was believed to be at least five milligrams per ton. However, actual trials gave disappointing results, as it was discovered that the analyses had been erroneously high because of the gold content of the reagents and vessels. The actual content is about one-thousandth of a milligram per ton. The project was abandoned in 1928.

On a journey around the world, Haber spent two months in Japan, a nation with which he had great sympathy. In 1930 he established the Japan institute, with headquarters in Berlin and Tokyo, to promote mutual understanding and cultural interests. The anti-Jewish policy of the Nazi regime brought his resignation in 1933, and he accepted an invitation to work at the University of Cambridge. En route to Italy, to escape the dangers of the English winter, he suffered a heart attack at Basel and died there on Jan. 29, 1934.

Besides his numerous scientific papers and published academic lectures, he was the author of: Grundriss der technischen Elektrochemie auf theoretischer Grundlage (1898); Thermodynamik technischer Gasreaktionen (1905; English translation by Lamb, 1908); Die elektrolytischen Prozesse der organischen Chemie, with Moser (1910); Beitrag zur Kenntnis der Metalle (1919); Aus Luft durch Kohle zum Stickstoffdünger, zu Brot und reichlicher Nahrung, with Ramm and Caro (1920); Über die Synthese des Ammoniaks (1922); Die Chemie im Kriege (1922); Fünf Vorträge aus den Jahren 1920–1923 (1924); Über die Herstellung des Ammoniaks aus Stickstoff und Wasserstoff (1924); Aus Leben und Beruf, Aufsätze, Reden, Vorträge (1927).
See H. Kallmann, Das Andenken von Fritz Haber (1946). (R. E. O.)

HABERL, FRANZ XAVER (1840–1910), German musical scholar and editor of ecclesiastical music. Born at Oberellenbach, Bavaria, April 12, 1840, he was ordained at Passau and in 1862 was appointed choirmaster of the cathedral. In 1867 he became organist at Sta. Maria dell'Anima in Rome, and in 1874 founded a school of ecclesiastical music at Regensburg which became an international centre of learning. He was appointed canon of the cathedral of Palestrina in 1879 and in the same year founded the Palestrina society. The publication of Palestrina's works had been begun in 1862, but Haberl discovered much new music and by 1894 had brought out 33 volumes of his works, followed by a supplement in 1907. He then began a similar publication of the works of Orlando di Lasso, in which he was assisted by Adolf Sandberger, who completed it (21 vol.; 1894–1927). Haberl wrote many works on the theory and practice of early ecclesiastical music, notably Magister Choralis (1864), and compiled a thematic catalogue of the archives of the Sistine choir. Toward the end of his life he was disappointed at seeing his studies of plain chant, on which he had spent 30 years, replaced by the official Vatican edition. His original research, particularly his editions of Palestrina and Di Lasso, remained the foundation of the work of later scholars. He died at Regensburg, Sept. 5, 1910.
See Musica Sacra ed. by F. Commer no. 10 and 12 (1910).

HABERLANDT, GOTTLIEB (1854–1945), Austrian plant physiologist best known for his studies in functional plant anatomy, was born at Ungarisch-Altenburg on Nov. 28, 1854. He received a doctorate from Vienna in 1876 and then studied under Simon Schwendener at Tübingen. He became a Privatdozent of botany at Vienna in 1878, and in 1880 became professor of botany at Graz, where he remained until 1909. He visited the botanical gardens at Buitenzorg, Java, in 1891–92. His account of the journey appeared as Eine botanische Tropenreise (1893; 3rd ed., 1926). He accepted the chair of plant physiology at Berlin in 1909 and was founder-director of the plant physiology institute there until his retirement in 1923. He continued research as professor emeritus. He died at Berlin-Wilmersdorf on Jan. 30, 1945.

One of the foremost plant physiologists of his time, Haberlandt was the first to formulate the idea of plant-tissue culture (1902). However, his attempts at such culture were unsuccessful. He was also the first to present experimental evidence (1913, 1921) for the existence of "wound hormones" in plant tissues. He proposed several theories, e.g., the "statolith theory," to explain geo- and phototropic movements of plants. Physiologische Pflanzenanatomie (1884; 6th ed., 1926), his best-known work, presents a classification of tissues based upon function, i.e., dermal, photosynthetic, mechanical, absorptive, etc. Haberlandt's relating of physiology to anatomy had a profound influence on subsequent research and teaching.
See Phyton (article and bibliography), 6:1–14 (1955). Haberlandt's memoirs were published as Erinnerungen: Bekenntnisse und Betrachtungen (1933). (J. W. Tr.)

HABIBULLAH KHAN (1872–1919), amir of Afghanistan from 1901 to 1919, was born at Tashkent, the eldest son of Amir Abdurrahman Khan. He succeeded peacefully to his father's throne in Oct. 1901. Thanks to his father's strict measures Habibullah had little trouble with his own people during his reign, but he was beset with foreign troubles from an early date. The British and Russian authorities, expecting that the death of Abdurrahman would be the occasion for trouble in central Asia, took prompt measures to avail themselves of any opportunity that might arise. Gen. Aleksei Kuropatkin, Russian minister of war, left immediately for central Asia, and the British were active along the frontier. Fortunately, however, no untoward incident occurred. During Lord Curzon's viceroyalty relations between Afghanistan and the government of India were strained, although as a result of a mission to Kabul headed by Sir Louis Dane a treaty of friendship was signed in March 1905. During Lord Minto's viceroyalty Habibullah paid a state visit to India (1907) which resulted in much-improved relations between the two countries. The outbreak of World War I and particularly Turkey's participation placed Habibullah in a difficult position. The sultan of Turkey was regarded as the spiritual head of the Muslim world. Yet, despite the efforts of the Central Powers to embroil Afghanistan, Habibullah maintained strict neutrality.

Habibullah was an enlightened monarch. He founded the Habibia school in 1904 and established a military academy. He started the weekly paper (in Persian) Siraj-ul-Akhbar advocating external independence and internal reforms, and he abolished the espionage system and severe punishments introduced by his father. Other projects he favoured were the extension of western medical and surgical methods, widespread road improvements, piped water supplies and the introduction of automobiles and electricity.
Habibullah was assassinated in his shooting camp at Kalagosh in the Laghman valley on Feb. 20, 1919. See also AFGHANISTAN: History. (MD. A.)

HABIMA THEATRE, a Jewish theatrical group which was originally founded in Bialystok, Pol., in 1909 by Nahum L. Zemach, who wished to prepare a Hebrew acting group for eventual establishment in Palestine. This earlier venture was suppressed by tsarist police but revived by Zemach in 1916 in Moscow, where the group's first efforts gained the support of Maksim Gorki, and Konstantin Stanislavski of the Moscow Art theatre. Evgheny Vakhtangov, assistant to Stanislavski but critical of his extreme naturalism, became Habima's director. He found Jewish lore, especially Chassidic mysticism, congenial to his purpose and developed a new method, which he called fantastic realism, a dynamic theatricalism applying music, dance and intense stylization to an essentially realistic intent. Characteristic Habima plays are Salomon Rappoport Anski's *The Dybbuk*, Halper Leivick's *Der Golem*, David Pinski's *Wandering Jew* and Richard Beer-Hofmann's *Jacob's Dream*. Habima has also applied its method to non-Jewish plays.

In Russia, Habima laboured under constant tension, even after the revolution. In 1926, two years after the death of Vakhtangov, the group obtained permission to leave the country and tour Europe and America. It never returned. In 1928 it made a triumphant tour of Palestine and settled permanently in Tel Aviv in 1931. Further tours abroad were made in 1937 and 1948. In 1945 a theatre building, including a dramatic school and library, was opened in Tel Aviv. (M. Rs.)

HABIT, in psychology, a customary or automatic way of acting, usually as a result of frequent usage rather than of inborn origin. In a different sense "habit" is used to indicate the natural appearance, place and manner of growth of plants and animals. It is also a term for a coat or a form of clothing, especially one that is common to a species or is worn for a particular purpose. In botany and zoology "habit" may refer to innate tendencies and actions of plants or animals. Psychologists use "habit" to designate either a specific learned unit of behaviour or generically to refer to the several classes of acquired modes of acting or perceiving. Thus, a conditioned response is a habit, acquired and again modifiable. It shows variations in strength among individuals and in the same individual from one occasion to the next. Persons and animals exhibit changing tendencies to select and reorganize incoming stimulation from the environment. They acquire habitual rhythms of action that are independent of the immediate environment.

The acquisition and alteration of habits constitute topics of central concern in the study of behaviour. Psychologists and physiologists have concerned themselves with both the environmental and the organismic conditions and consequences of habit formation. They have shown that organisms differ in their susceptibility to the stimulus patterns which contribute to a change in behaviour. The social consequences of the use of habit-forming drugs have produced a highly specialized research area in applied psychophysiology.

The nature and optimum scheduling of reinforcement have been studied extensively in relation to the control of habitual activities of animals and people. Some investigators have stated that a full understanding of mechanisms of reinforcement promises to give a full understanding of how habits are changed. They assert that complexities of human behaviour arise out of the compounding of many habits based on many sources of reinforcement, some obvious and some extremely subtle. Other students of the subject have adopted an associationistic principle without recourse to a "law of effect," the action of rewards or punishment being subsumed under a concept of motivation and acting only secondarily in habit formation.

William James discussed in his *Principles of Psychology* both the biological utility of habits as the means for conserving higher mental processes for more demanding tasks, and their more unfortunate consequences in behavioural inflexibility. He also theorized concerning their physiological basis in the nervous system. During the first half of the 20th century improved neurosurgical techniques and electrophysiological methods brought forth a body of evidence on the structures necessary for habit formation, but answers to the fundamental biochemical questions remained elusive. R. W. Sperry, R. E. Myers and their co-workers isolated visual and tactual discrimination habits to either half of the brain by cutting only certain essential nerve bundles that interconnect the right and left halves through the *corpus callosum*. Animals so prepared learned antagonistic habits depending upon which eye was uncovered or which paw was used in feeling the object. Careful experiments during 1955 to 1957 showed that cats so prepared developed independent sets of habits in the right and left hemispheres of the brain, where such habits were learned *following* the operation. Otherwise they behaved normally, as have human patients following similar brain surgery. H. F. Harlow, D. O. Hebb and others showed that animals or children learn new habits with greater ease or difficulty depending upon previous experience in habit formation. The insightful solving of problems, once regarded by experts in the field of perception as being independent of previous learning, was shown to occur only after appropriate tool-using habits had been established, or, in the case of spatial detour problems, only after skills for discriminating relative positions in space had been developed. Spatial intelligence in man and animal depends in part upon early learning. Work in language and other symbol-using habits increased in response to the evidence that conceptual thinking requires prior acquisition of basic perceptual skills. One series of experiments showed that both early experience and frontal lobes of the brain are essential to the performance by dogs of spatial delayed-response problems.

The durability of emotional conditioning and the permanence of certain imprinted social discrimination habits in birds impressed scientists at mid-century with the need for continuing research on the effects of habits learned in infancy. *See also* ANIMAL BEHAVIOUR; BEHAVIOUR; CONDITIONING; LEARNING.

BIBLIOGRAPHY.—William James, *The Principles of Psychology* (1890); N. Kleitman, *Sleep and Wakefulness* (1939); J. P. Zubek and P. A. Solberg, *Human Development* (1954); W. H. Thorpe, *Learning and Instinct in Animals* (1956); C. B. Ferster and B. F. Skinner, *Schedules of Reinforcement* (1957); R. S. Woodworth, *Dynamics of Behavior* (1958).
(A. H. R.)

HABITUAL OFFENDERS. A habitual criminal is one who has frequently been apprehended and convicted, who has manifested a settled practice in crime, and who presents a danger to the society in which he lives. Penal systems of the United States, Great Britain and the Commonwealth, and most European countries provide for more protracted imprisonment of such criminals than would normally be imposed in respect to their last crimes. The primary purpose of such provisions is the greater protection of the community. (N. R. M)

United States.—Every state, as well as the national government, makes special provision for additional punishment of recidivists. The laws differ markedly, however, in their definitions of a habitual offender and on the punishment to be meted out to convicted defendants who have records of previous convictions. Although one can trace the statutory concept of extra punishment for recidivists back to American colonial days, detailed legislation providing for specialized treatment of habitual offenders became common in the more populous states only in the latter part of the 19th century and more prevalent in the 20th century. In general, the statutes provide that a habitual offender—he may be called by other names—may or shall be sentenced to an additional number of years of imprisonment—or even to death—on proof of his earlier conviction or convictions. In some jurisdictions the prior offense must have been a felony to warrant the increased sanctions. Some states, such as New York, have a sliding scale of increased punishment dependent on the number of prior offenses. An Oklahoma statute providing for sterilization of some habitual offenders was held unconstitutional by the United States Supreme Court in *Skinner v. Oklahoma*, 316 U.S. 535 (1942), on the ground that it violated the equal protection clause of the 14th Amendment.

There are essential differences among the laws in the methods of proof of prior criminal record. Some provide for the judge to make the determination, others for a jury. Some require the same jury that is passing on guilt or innocence to make the finding, the jury sometimes being informed of the prior convictions before verdict and sometimes not until after verdict. The power of the states to choose among the varying methods of proof of prior conviction was sustained by the Supreme Court in *Spencer v. Texas*, 385 U.S. 554 (1967).

Despite the popularity of the concept, it was not possible in the early 1970s to say that the statutes had accomplished any desirable goal, if that goal is described either as the removal of dangerous criminals from society or the affording to penologists of additional time within which to effect rehabilitation of the convict. The statutes do seem to satisfy society's unconscious demands for retribution. It is doubtful, however, that all of the rational objectives of habitual-offender laws could not be accomplished under procedures for invoking greater expertise in

fixing criminal sanctions than is generally available to judges.
(P. B. K.)

English and European Law.—By the Prevention of Crime Act, 1908, power was given to English courts to sentence habitual criminals to a period of preventive detention in addition to one of penal servitude in respect of their last conviction. Owing to several complexities in this act and to the reluctance of the courts to impose what seemed to be a double punishment, these provisions of the 1908 act fell into disuse. This situation led to the appointment in 1930 of a departmental committee on persistent offenders. The report of this committee (1932) made recommendations that were embodied in the Criminal Justice Act, 1948. This act attempted to distinguish between offenders who though not yet hardened showed every sign of becoming so and those whose persistent criminality was evident. For the former a sentence of corrective training was introduced and, for the latter, preventive detention. In practice the training offered to corrective trainees was not significantly different from that given to ordinary prisoners. The failure of this system, too, was partly attributable to the inability, in practice, appreciably to differentiate preventive detention and corrective training from common imprisonment. Another source of difficulty was the selection of persons suitable for these treatments. At all events, this act was superseded by the Criminal Justice Act of 1967, which abolished both preventive detention and corrective training. In their place this act provides that the habitual offender may be detained, for the protection of the public, for a period in excess of the maximum punishment for his last crime, but not as long as was previously available under the 1948 act. The extended sentence may be for five years if the last crime was punishable with a period of less than five years, or for up to ten years if the last crime could attract a penalty of five years or more. Qualification as a habitual criminal depends on the frequency of previous offenses, on their proximity to the present offense, on the total length of previous imprisonment, or on a prior sentence for preventive detention or corrective training.

From 1854 France had transported certain criminals to its penal colonies. In 1885 this punishment was made applicable to habitual criminals and, called *relégation*, from then to the abolition of deportation (*q.v.*) in 1938 it was extensively applied.

The Swiss Draft Penal Code of 1893, prepared by Carl Stoos, provided for the indeterminate detention of habitual criminals in institutions specially adapted to that purpose, such detention to take the place of punishment for their last offenses. He coined the phrase *mesure de sûreté* to describe this type of sentence. In 1937 this plan was accepted in Switzerland, though it had by then, with various modifications, been applied widely throughout Western Europe—Norway, in 1902, had been the first country to test it. The main differences between continental and English penal practice are the wider discretion that tends to be given to courts on the continent in determining which offenders may be punished as habitual offenders and the wider discretion there held by the penal administrators or special administrative tribunals to determine the date of conditional or final release of the habitual criminal.

Germany's current draft code (1962) contains revisions similar to the English act, including the reduction of the extremely protracted detention period previously provided for habitual criminals. It also incorporates preventive detention for young offenders while maintaining a form of protective custody over them. The court retains its ability to extend sentences for repeated offenses, although in Germany, as in many other countries, this power to impose additional terms of preventive detention is seldom used.

The purpose of sentences of this type being primarily to segregate and only secondarily to deter and reform, those administering European and English penal systems have endeavoured to ameliorate the penal conditions of such prisoners, particularly toward the end of their terms. Much of the struggle and controversy in the current movements for modification in the treatment of the habitual criminal has been concerned with achieving more positive reform. The process has necessitated a more effective means of classification of offenders and ultimately a reexamination of the necessity for satisfaction of the public's desires for vengeance by this type of legislation.

See also PAROLE; PRISON; RECIDIVISM; REFORMATORY.

BIBLIOGRAPHY.—N. Morris, *The Habitual Criminal* (1951); W. H. Hammond and Edna Chayen, *Persistent Criminals* (1963); A. Dunham and F. M. Merrifield, *University of Chicago Law School Law Revision Studies*, no. 1 (1955); *McGill Law Journal*, "The Habitual Criminal," vol. 13, no. 4 (1967); J. B. Waite, *The Prevention of Repeated Crime* (1943); P. W. Tappan, "Habitual Offender Laws and Sentencing Practices in Relation to Organized Crime and Law Enforcement" in American Bar Association, Commission on Organized Crime, *Organized Crime and Law Enforcement* (1952). (N. R. M.)

HABSBURG (HABSPURG or HAPSBURG), also known as the HOUSE OF AUSTRIA, one of the greatest of the formerly sovereign dynasties of Europe.

Origins.—The name Habsburg is derived from the castle of Habsburg or Habichtsburg ("Hawk's castle"), built in 1020 by Werner, bishop of Strasbourg, and his brother-in-law, Count Radbot, in the Swiss Aargau overlooking the Aar river. Radbot's grandfather, Guntram the Rich, the earliest traceable ancestor of the house, may perhaps be identified with a Count Guntram who rebelled against the German king Otto I in 950. Radbot's son Werner I (d. 1096) bore the title count of Habsburg and was the great-grandfather of Albert III (d. c. 1200), who was count of Zürich and landgrave of Upper Alsace. Rudolf II of Habsburg (d. 1232) acquired Laufenburg and the "Waldstätte" (Schwyz, Uri, Unterwalden and Lucerne), but on his death his sons Albert IV and Rudolf III partitioned the inheritance. Rudolf III's descendants, however, forming the house of Habsburg-Laufenburg, sold Laufenburg and other districts to Albert IV's descendants before dying out in 1408.

Austria and the Rise of the Habsburgs in Germany.—Albert IV's son Rudolf IV of Habsburg became German king as Rudolf I in 1273 (see GERMANY: *History*). It was he who, in 1282, bestowed Austria and Styria on his two sons Albert (the future German king Albert I) and Rudolf (reckoned as Rudolf II of Austria). From this date the age-long identification of the Habsburgs with Austria begins (see AUSTRIA, EMPIRE OF). The family's custom, however, was to vest the government of its hereditary domains not in individuals but in all male members of the family in common, and though Rudolf II renounced his share in 1283, difficulties arose again when King Albert I died (1308). After a system of condominium had been tried, Rudolf IV of Austria in 1364 made a compact with his younger brothers which acknowledged the principle of equal rights but secured *de facto* supremacy for the head of the house. Even so, after his death the brothers Albert III and Leopold III of Austria agreed on a partition (treaty of Neuburg, 1379): Albert took Austria, Leopold took Styria, Carinthia and Tirol.

Albert I's son Rudolf I had been king of Bohemia from 1306 to 1307, and his brother Frederick I of Austria had been German king as Frederick III (in rivalry or conjointly with Louis IV the Bavarian) from 1314 to 1330. Albert V of Austria was in 1438 elected king of Hungary, German king (as Albert II) and king of Bohemia; his only surviving son, Ladislas Posthumus, was also king of Hungary from 1440 and of Bohemia from 1453. With Ladislas the male descendants of Albert III of Austria died out in 1457. Meanwhile the Styrian line descended from Leopold III had been subdivided into Inner Austrian and Tirolean branches. Frederick V, senior representative of this line, was elected German king in 1440 and crowned Holy Roman emperor, as Frederick III (*q.v.*), in 1452. While the elective crowns of Hungary and Bohemia were lost to the dynasty on the death of Ladislas Posthumus, the death without issue of Sigismund of Tirol in 1496 meant that all the hereditary possessions of the Habsburgs—except the Swiss territories lost from 1315 onward and finally renounced in 1474 (see SWITZERLAND: *History*)—were reunited in the hands of Frederick's son Maximilian I (*q.v.*). For a title peculiar to the dynasty from the middle ages onward see ARCHDUKE.

The Empire, Burgundy and Spain.—The policy of dynastic aggrandizement by marriage to heiresses, already practised with success by his ancestors, was carried on with unprecedented brilliance by Maximilian I. His father had adopted the motto

TABLE I.—*The Habsburgs to 1493*

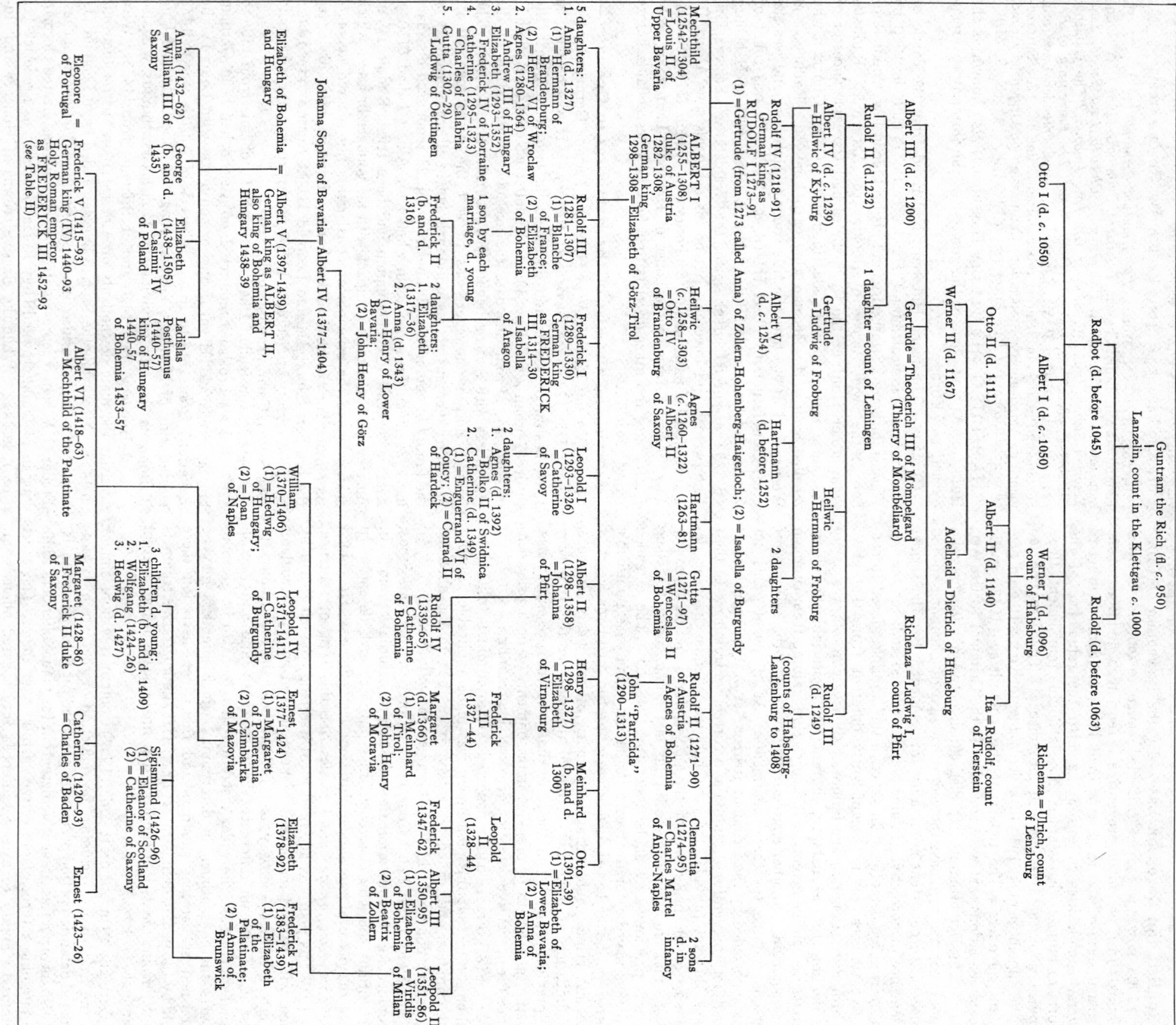

A.E.I.O.U., interpreted in Latin as *Austriae est imperare orbi universo* or in German as *Alles Erdreich ist Oesterreich unterthan*, this aspiration to universal empire for the house of Austria was vastly strengthened by Maximilian's matrimonial achievements. These were the occasion of the famous hexameter *Bella gerant alii, tu felix Austria nube* (Let others make wars, you, fortunate Austria, marry). Maximilian himself married Mary, heiress of Charles the Bold, thus securing the greater part of the inheritance of Burgundy for his son by her, namely the Netherlands, Artois and Franche-Comté; by marrying this son, Philip, to Joan the Mad, heiress of Castile and Aragon, he ensured that Spain, with that kingdom's immense dominions in America as well as Naples-Sicily and Sardinia, would pass likewise into the house of Habsburg. Philip's son Charles was thus already sovereign of the Burgundian territories and king of Spain as Charles I when in 1519 he succeeded his grandfather in the Austrian territories proper and was elected emperor as Charles V (*q.v.*).

By the treaty of Brussels (1522) Charles V assigned the old Habsburg-Austrian possessions to his brother, the future emperor Ferdinand I, who in 1521 had married Anna, sister of Louis II,

HABSBURG

TABLE II.—*The Imperial Succession of the Habsburgs, 1493-1740*

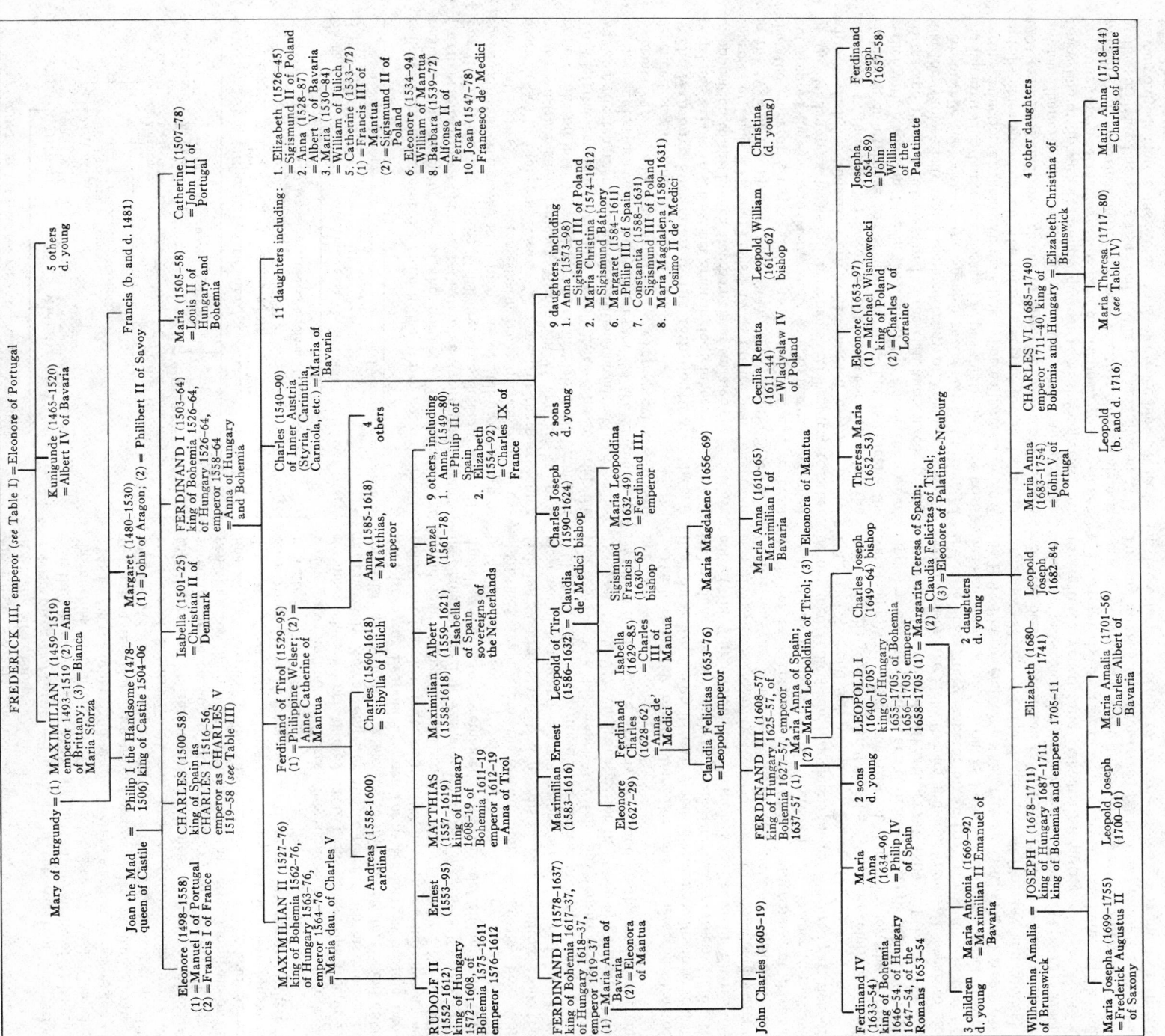

his son, Philip II of Spain, whose male descendants were to be kings of Spain till they died out with Charles II in 1700. The early failure of the Spanish line may be attributed very largely to the intermarriage of the Spanish and the imperial Habsburgs: six of Charles II's great-grandparents were Habsburg, two of them being also his grandparents. (*See* Table III; SPAIN: *History;* and biographical articles on the Habsburg kings of Spain.)

The great heritage of Charles V was thus partitioned between the imperial and the Spanish lines of the Habsburgs. The ensuing 140 years saw some decline in the dynasty's divided fortunes,

king of Hungary and Bohemia. Louis II's untimely death in 1526 led ultimately to Ferdinand's becoming king in his place. Apart from intervals of rebellion and invasion, Hungary (together with the kingdom of Croatia) and Bohemia, as well as the Austrian lands, were to remain with Ferdinand's male descendants, holders also of the imperial title, till 1740. For the Holy Roman emperors from Frederick III to Charles VI *see* Table II; *see* also the separate biographical articles on the emperors indicated.

By the series of abdications at the end of his life Charles V transmitted his Burgundian, Spanish and Italian possessions to

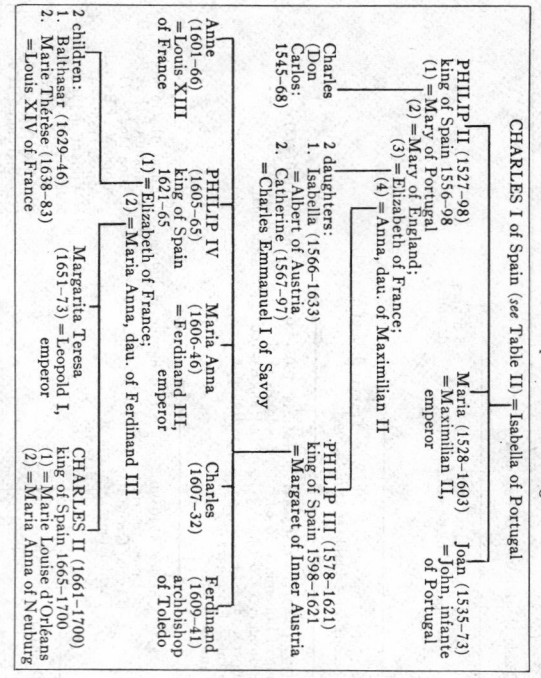

TABLE III.—*The Spanish Habsburgs*

CHARLES I of Spain (*see* Table II) = Isabella of Portugal

- PHILIP II (1527-98) king of Spain 1556-98
  - (1) = Mary of Portugal
  - (2) = Mary of England
  - (3) = Elizabeth of France
  - (4) = Anna, dau. of Maximilian II
- Maria (1528-1603) = Maximilian II, emperor
- Joan (1535-73) = John, infante of Portugal

Charles (Don Carlos; 1545-68)

2 daughters:
1. Isabella (1566-1633) = Albert of Austria
2. Catherine (1567-97) = Charles Emmanuel I of Savoy

PHILIP III (1578-1621) king of Spain 1598-1621 = Margaret of Inner Austria

- Anne (1601-66) = Louis XIII of France
- PHILIP IV (1605-1665) king of Spain 1621-65
  - (1) = Elizabeth of France
  - (2) = Maria Anna, dau. of Ferdinand III
- Maria Anna (1606-46) = Ferdinand III, emperor
- Charles (1607-32)
- Ferdinand (1609-41) archbishop of Toledo

2 children:
1. Balthasar (1629-46)
2. Marie Thérèse (1638-83) = Louis XIV of France

Margarita Teresa (1651-73) = Leopold I, emperor

CHARLES II (1661-1700) king of Spain 1665-1700
(1) = Marie Louise d'Orléans
(2) = Maria Anna of Neuburg

---

mainly at the expense of the Spanish line, which not only had to recognize the independence of the northern Netherlands (*see* NETHERLANDS, THE) but also lost extensive territories to France. For the imperial line of the Habsburgs, the diminution of its specifically imperial power in Germany as a result of the peace of Westphalia (1648) was of more lasting consequence than its dynastic losses to France in Alsace. The effect of the partitioning of the Austrian lands between Maximilian II and his brothers came to an end in 1665, when the death of Sigismund Francis of Tirol left the emperor Leopold I as sole heir. The imperial line was able to strengthen its dynastic position considerably by securing recognition of its hereditary succession to the kingdoms of Bohemia (1627) and Hungary (1687), where previously it had depended on election.

The Habsburg Succession in the 18th Century.—The imperial line's claim to the extinct Spanish line's inheritance in 1700, in opposition to the French Bourbon claim through the Habsburg consorts of Louis XIII and Louis XIV of France, was fought out in the War of the Spanish Succession. The result (1714) was that the emperor Charles VI had to forgo Spain and America but secured the southern Netherlands (*see* BELGIUM) and most of the Italian possessions of the Spanish Habsburgs, together with the duchy of Mantua, which he had annexed in 1708. Sicily, conceded to the house of Savoy in 1714, was recovered for the Habsburgs in exchange for Sardinia in 1717 but lost again, together with Naples, in 1735 in the War of the Polish Succession. Parma and Piacenza were assured to the Habsburgs in compensation for Naples-Sicily under the final treaty of Vienna (1738).

Meanwhile the crisis of the Spanish succession had prompted the imperial Habsburgs to envisage the possibility of a like crisis on the extinction of their own male line. The emperor Leopold I and his elder son and heir, the future emperor Joseph I, had in 1703 renounced their own claims to Spain in favour of Joseph's brother Charles so that he, as Charles III of Spain, might found a new line of Spanish Habsburgs distinct from the imperial. At the same time a secret *Pactum mutuae successionis* was concluded whereby, on the extinction of male heirs of either line, a male heir of the surviving line was to succeed. When Joseph died in 1711 leaving only daughters, his brother thus succeeded him as Charles VI. Though the plans for the Spanish succession came to nothing (*see* above), Charles now had to consider the Austrian, since he himself had at this time no children. Thus the famous Pragmatic sanction of April 19, 1713, came to be formulated, in order to assure the undivided succession, if Charles should have no male heir, as follows: (1) to any heiress, under primogeniture, that might be born to him; next (2) to Joseph I's daughters, under primogeniture, if Charles left no children; and finally (3) if Joseph's line should have failed, to the heirs of Leopold I's daughters, by primogeniture. The attempt to secure general recognition of the Pragmatic sanction was Charles VI's main concern from

the death of his son Leopold (1716). His death in 1740, leaving his daughter Maria Theresa as his heiress, led to the War of the Austrian Succession.

Habsburg-Lorraine.—The War of the Austrian Succession cost the Habsburgs most of Silesia, part of the duchy of Milan and the duchies of Parma and Piacenza (treaty of Aix-la-Chapelle, 1748). On the other hand Maria Theresa was left in possession of the rest of the Habsburg inheritance, and her husband, Francis Stephen of Lorraine, was recognized as Holy Roman emperor, with the style of Francis I. Moreover, as a further consequence of the War of the Polish Succession, Francis Stephen had been assured of the succession to the grand duchy of Tuscany (in compensation for the loss of Lorraine) on the extinction of the male line of the Medici, which died out in 1737. His and Maria Theresa's descendants form the house of Habsburg-Lorraine. (*See* Table IV and biographical articles on the emperors therein indicated.)

The Austrian and the Tuscan inheritances, however, were kept distinct: when Francis I died (1765), his eldest son Joseph II became Holy Roman emperor and co-regent with his mother of the Austrian dominions, while the second son became grand duke of Tuscany as Leopold I; when the latter in turn became Leopold II as Joseph's successor in 1790, his own second son became grand duke of Tuscany as Ferdinand III. Thereafter Ferdinand's descendants ruled in Tuscany till 1859 (*see* Table V), while the Austrian inheritance remained with the descendants of Leopold II's eldest son.

Distinct again from these two branches of the house of Habsburg-Lorraine was that of Austria-Este, resulting from the marriage of Ferdinand, a younger brother of Joseph II and Leopold II, to Maria Beatrice d'Este, heiress of Modena (*see* ESTE, HOUSE OF). For this branch, sovereign in Modena from 1814 to 1859, *see* Table VI. On its extinction in 1875 its rights passed by legacy to the archduke Francis Ferdinand, of the senior Austrian line.

The imperial line of Habsburg-Lorraine in the second half of the 18th century, with its own dynastic arrangements firm at last and nothing but the southern Netherlands and northern Italy left out of the Burgundian and Spanish inheritance of Charles V, turned its attention away from the west to central and eastern Europe and the Balkans. Joseph II's plans to consolidate his dominions by exchanging the Austrian Netherlands for Bavaria resulted only in his getting the Innviertel, but farther to the east he obtained Galicia and Lodomeria under the first partition of Poland (1772) and Bukovina from Turkey (1775).

During the period covered by the French Revolutionary and Napoleonic Wars (*qq.v.*) the Austrian Habsburgs lost the Netherlands forever and acquired and then lost "Western Galicia" (1795-1809) and Venetia and Dalmatia (1797-1809). Leopold II's son and successor, the Holy Roman emperor Francis II, began to use the style "hereditary emperor of Austria" from 1804, so that he was still emperor of Austria, as Francis I, after his dissolution of the Holy Roman empire in 1806 (*see also* AUSTRIA, EMPIRE OF; GERMANY: *History*). The Habsburgs of Tuscany and Modena, who had been dispossessed by the French, were restored to their hereditary possessions by the congress of Vienna (1814-15), which also restored Venetia and Dalmatia to Austria.

The formerly ecclesiastical territory of Salzburg, which had been secularized and given to the dispossessed Ferdinand III of Tuscany in 1803 and transferred by him to Francis I of Austria in 1805 but then ceded to Bavaria in 1809, was finally restored to Austria in 1816. The Austrian Habsburgs also annexed Cracow in 1846. Parma and Piacenza were assigned by the congress of Vienna to Napoleon's Habsburg consort Marie Louise, but on her death they reverted to the Bourbons (1847). In the Wars of Italian Independence the Habsburgs lost Lombardy, Tuscany and Modena (1859) and then Venetia (1866). The Mexican empire of Maximilian, brother of the Austrian emperor Francis Joseph I, lasted only from 1864 to 1867 (*see* MEXICO: *Independent Mexico*).

After the Prussian victory in the Seven Weeks' War (1866) had put an end to all hopes of restoring Austrian hegemony in Ger-

HABSBURG

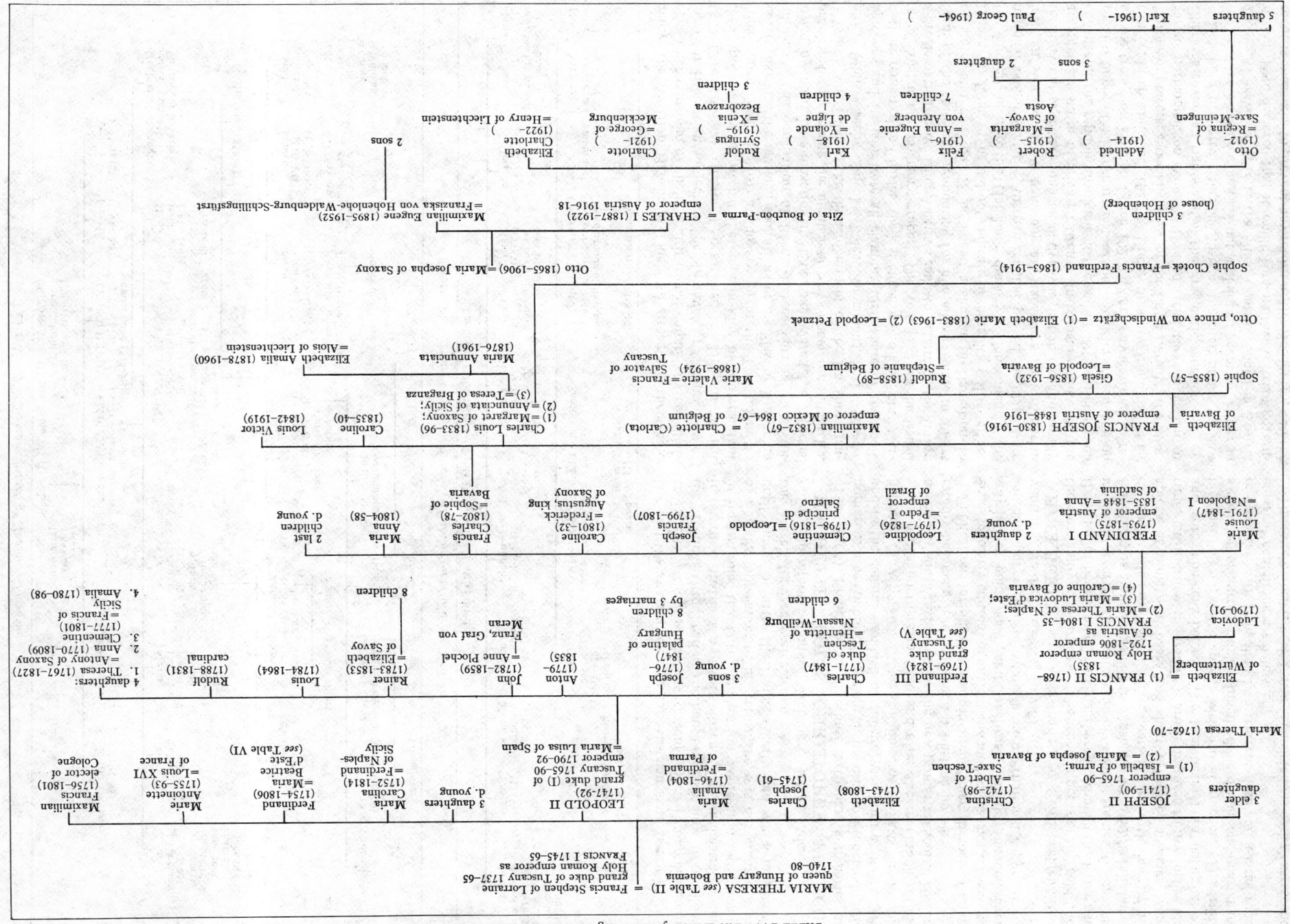

TABLE IV.—*The House of Habsburg-Lorraine in Austria*

many, the Austrian Habsburgs sought to strengthen their hold over what remained of their "multinational empire" by conciliating their Hungarian subjects. The *Ausgleich* or Compromise of 1867 (*see* HUNGARY: *History*) so satisfied the Hungarians that they opposed any steps that the emperor-king of the resultant "dual monarchy" of Austria-Hungary might think of taking to satisfy likewise the national aspirations of his Slav or Rumanian subjects. The occupation of Bosnia-Hercegovina in 1878, followed by outright annexation in 1908, aggravated the national problem by increasing the number of Slavs under the monarchy. World War I led to the dismemberment of the Habsburg empire. While Czechs, Slovaks, Poles, Rumanians, Serbs, Croats, Slovenes and Italians were all claiming their share of the spoil, nothing remained to Charles, the last emperor and king, but "German" Austria and Hungary proper. On Nov. 11, 1918, he issued a proclamation recognizing Austria's right to determine the future form of the state and renouncing for himself any share in affairs of state, and on Nov. 13 he issued a similar proclamation to Hungary. Even so, he did not abdicate his hereditary titles either for himself or for the Habsburg dynasty. Consequently the national assembly of the Austrian republic passed the "Habsburg law" of April 3, 1919, banishing all Habsburgs from Austrian territory unless they renounced all dynastic pretensions and loyally accepted the status of private citizens. In Hungary, however, the collapse of the republican regime at the end of 1919 raised strong royalist hopes of a Habsburg restoration, and after the conclusion of the treaty of Trianon (June 1920) Charles twice tried to return (March and Oct. 1921). Under pressure from the other European powers, especially those of the Little Entente, the Hungarian parliament on Nov. 3, 1921, decreed the abrogation of Charles's sovereign rights and of the Pragmatic sanction. Habsburg property rights in Austria, forfeited under the law of 1919, were restored in 1935 but withdrawn again by Hitler in 1938. After World War II the Allied Control council in Austria in 1946 declared that it would support the Austrian government in measures to prevent any return of the Habsburgs, and the

law of 1919 was written into the Austrian state treaty of 1955. In June 1961 the Austrian government rejected an application by the archduke Otto, head of the house of Habsburg, to be allowed to return to Austria as a private citizen. The administrative court of Austria ruled that Otto's application was legal in 1963; because of Socialist opposition to his return, he was not granted a visa until June 1966 after the People's Party had won a majority in the March 1966 general election.

See also references under "Habsburg" in the Index.

HACHETTE, LOUIS CHRISTOPHE FRANÇOIS (1800–1864), French publisher whose textbooks, dictionaries, and numerous other publications gave an impetus to French education and to the general standard of culture, was born at Rethel (Ardennes), May 5, 1800. After studying law in Paris, he bought a small bookshop there in 1826 and after the revolution of 1830 began to publish textbooks for the new primary schools. His firm rapidly became a leading French publishing house.

Publications included manuals in almost every branch of knowledge, scholarly editions of ancient and modern classics, a cheap railway library, guide books, and directories. He also founded several journals and worked to establish an international copyright convention. He died in Paris, July 31, 1864.

HACKBERRY, a popular shade tree, *Celtis occidentalis*, of the elm family (Ulmaceae). The wood is occasionally sold under the name of beaver wood and sugarberry, although the latter name is usually reserved for another closely related species, *C. laevigata*. Hackberry is a medium-sized tree, usually 40 to 60 ft. tall, but occasionally attaining 130 ft. The ovate leaves, with long tapering apices, asymmetrical bases and sharply toothed margins (sometimes entire below the middle), are from three to five inches long, and soft-pubescent below. The tree bears both unisexual and bisexual flowers, which appear with leaf emergence. The fruit is a dark red or purple, thick-skinned edible drupe, one-quarter inch in diameter, with thin, slightly astringent flesh and a large rough-ened pit containing a single seed.

The tough, fibrous bark features conspicuous corky excrescences

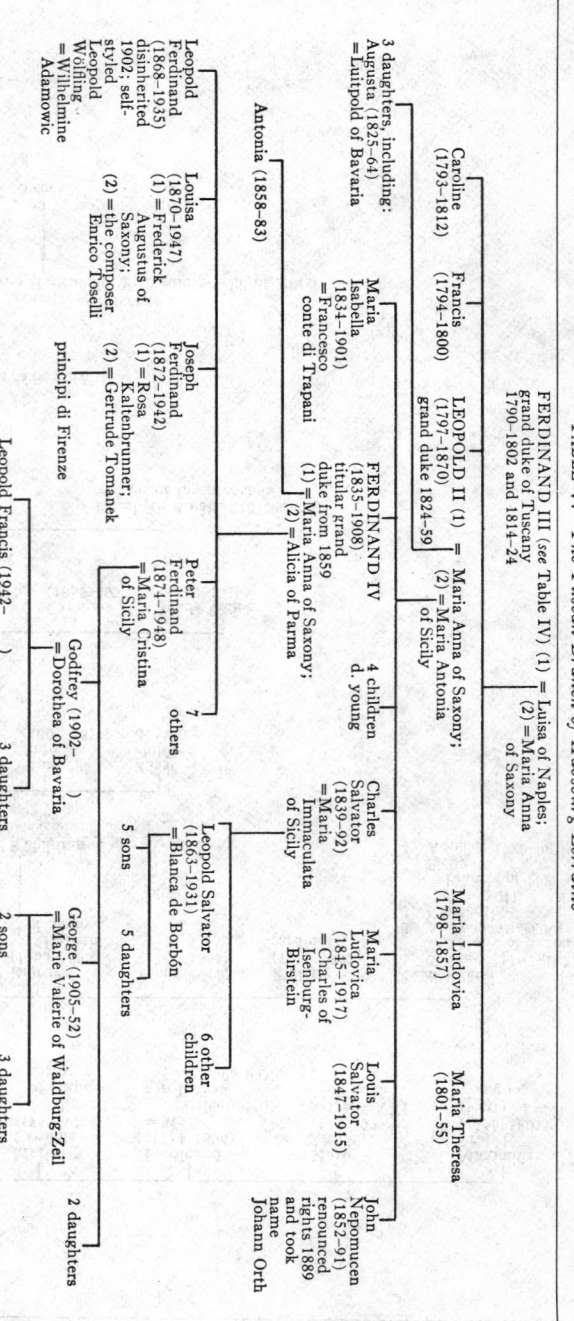

TABLE V.—*The Tuscan Branch of Habsburg-Lorraine*

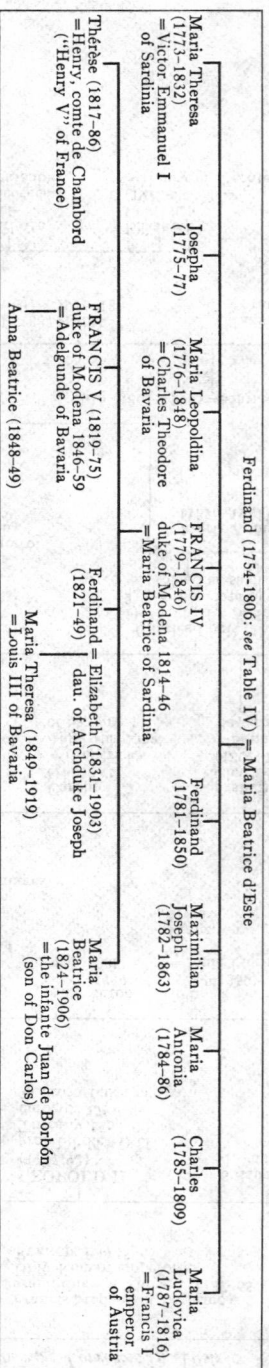

TABLE VI.—*Austria-Este: the House of Habsburg-Lorraine in Modena*

and ridges. The wood is grayish white to yellow, coarse-grained and sometimes fragile. It is used for boxes, baskets, planing mill products, furniture and wooden novelties. The root contains a dye principle suitable for dyeing linen. Hackberry ranges over eastern U.S. and occurs sparingly in southern Canada in the vicinity of the Great Lakes. It is also grown in Europe. It attains its best development on rich, moist, alluvial soils.   (E. S. HR.)

HACKENSACK, a city of northeastern New Jersey, U.S., on the Hackensack River, 13 mi. N of Jersey City; the seat of Bergen County.

The site was settled first by the Dutch, who called it New Barbadoes, and later by the British. Its name is supposedly of Indian origin, variously spelled Achkinchesacky, Hockumdachque, and in other ways. A popular theory is that the town was named after the Hock and Sack, an old tavern. Many streets still bear pioneer Dutch family names. The Green, opposite the county courthouse, was the camping ground of both British and American troops during the American Revolution. The community was not chartered as a city with the official name of Hackensack until 1921 although it had been called Hackensack for many years.

Located in the geographical centre of the county, Hackensack serves a densely populated area of more than 1,000,000 people within the Paterson-Clifton-Passaic standard metropolitan statistical area. Its business establishments consist of a wide variety of small industries, insurance companies, and banks. Pop. (1970) 35,911. For comparative population figures *see* table in NEW JERSEY: *Population.*

HACKETT, JAMES HENRY (1800–1871), U.S. actor, whose importance lies chiefly in his encouragement of the native American drama, was born in New York city, March 15, 1800. Upon leaving Columbia university because of ill health, he tried various businesses. In 1825, after Hackett lost his money in speculation, his wife, a former actress, returned to the stage, and the following year Hackett, who had achieved a social reputation for impersonations, began playing character parts. In 1828 his Falstaff, in *Henry IV,* part i, was successful, remaining one of his most popular roles. His *Rip Van Winkle* (1830) was the best prior to Joseph Jefferson's.

In answer to a prize competition established by Hackett, James Kirke Paulding submitted in 1831 his *Lion of the West,* a comic satirization of Davy Crockett, and as Nimrod Wildfire in this play, Hackett was successful in the U.S. and in England. He was manager of the Astor Place opera house at the time of the Macready riot (*see* FORREST, EDWIN).

In 1863 he published his *Notes and Comments on Shakespeare,* which included a correspondence between himself and John Quincy Adams. He died Dec. 28, 1871.   (S. W. H.)

HACKNEY, one of the 32 London boroughs constituting Greater London, Eng., is bounded north by Haringey, northeast by Waltham Forest and Newham (and separated from them by the ancient commercial navigation of the River Lea or Lee), southeast by Tower Hamlets and the City of London, and west by Islington. This inner London Borough was established on April 1, 1965, under the London Government Act 1963 (*see* LONDON) by the amalgamation of the former metropolitan boroughs of Hackney, Shoreditch, and Stoke Newington. Area 7.5 sq.mi. (19 sq.km.); pop. (1971 prelim.) 216,659. The parliamentary constituencies are Stoke Newington and Hackney North, Hackney Central, Shoreditch and Finsbury (in part), and Bethnal Green (in part). The districts of Dalston, Kingsland, Homerton, Clapton, Hackney Wick, Stamford Hill, Haggerston, and Hoxton are within the borough.

Shoreditch, near the City, is industrial and commercial. The rest of Hackney is predominantly residential with small areas of industry. The development of the area has been conditioned by its nearness to the City and because it lies on a main route from London to the north (Shoreditch High Street–Kingsland Road) which follows the course of the Roman Ermine Street. Hackney is served by the Eastern and Midland Regions of British Rail and, in the southwest, by the Northern Line of the London Underground. Principal shopping centres are at Dalston and in Mare Street. The traditional associations of the borough with furniture,

cabinetmaking, and garment trades are reflected by the London College of Furniture, the Shoreditch College for the Clothing Industry, and the Geffrye Museum (mainly period furniture and household utensils; formerly erected as almshouses in 1712 from a bequest of Sir Robert Geffrye, lord mayor of London in 1685). The Cordwainers Technical College testifies to a past link with the leather industry. There has been substantial rehousing and redevelopment since World War II. By the late 1960s more than 30% of all the dwellings were municipally owned, some by the Greater London Council. Education is administered by the Inner London Education Authority. Several comprehensive schools have been built since the war and the former Grocers' Company's School flourishes as the Hackney Downs Grammar School.

Parks and open spaces include part of Victoria Park (218 ac. [88 ha.]), Hackney Downs, Clissold Park, Springfield Park, London Fields, and Millfields. Hackney Marshes (used mainly as playing fields) are expected to become part of the Lee Valley Regional Park. There are stadiums at Hackney Wick and Clapton (mainly for greyhound racing). The New River empties into reservoirs north of Clissold Park, and the Grand Union Canal runs through the borough.

The parish church of St. John at Hackney (1790–97) is the successor to that of St. Augustine (probably 13th century) of which the ancient tower remains. St. Leonard's at Shoreditch (opened 1740) was designed by George Dance, the elder. St. Mary's at Stoke Newington (consecrated 1858) was the work of Sir George Gilbert Scott; Old St. Mary's parish church, largely restored but still bearing the stamp of antiquity, stands opposite.

The Knights Templars and the Knights Hospitallers held substantial land in Hackney. From the Tudor period onward many notables had mansions there and subsequently Stoke Newington and Hackney became fashionable residential areas. Daniel Defoe was educated at Newington Green (where Edgar Allan Poe also attended school [1817–20]); later Defoe built a large house (in Defoe Road) where he wrote *Robinson Crusoe.* Most of the mansions have been demolished, but Brooke House, one of the oldest (and possibly the manor house of Kings-Hold), survived until it sustained heavy air raid damage during World War II. Sutton House in Homerton, built by Thomas Sutton (d. 1611), the founder of the Charterhouse, remains and is owned by the National Trust. The first Elizabethan playhouse, the Theatre, was built (1576) in Holywell Lane, Shoreditch, for Sir James Burbage, to circumvent the ban on play acting in the City; the Curtain was built nearby in Curtain Road a little later. Two large theatres, the Hackney Empire in Mare Street and the Britannia at Hoxton, reached their heyday during the music hall period.   (L. G. HU.)

HACKNEY: *see* CARRIAGE; HORSE: *Breeds of Horses.*

HADAMARD, JACQUES SALOMON (1865–1963), French mathematician, distinguished for his work in various branches of pure mathematics, was born at Versailles on Dec. 8, 1865. He studied at the École Normale and the École Polytechnique, and became a professor at the Collège de France, the École Polytechnique and the École Centrales des Arts et Manufactures. In 1912, he became a member of l'Institut de France (Académie des Sciences).

Hadamard's early work contained many important contributions to the theory of functions of a complex variable, in particular to the general theory of integral functions and to the theory of the singularities of functions represented by Taylor's series. In 1896, Hadamard proved the prime number theorem at the same time as de la Vallée Poussin but independently of him. He also obtained important results in connection with the partial differential equations of mathematical physics.

Hadamard's work on the calculus of variations helped to lay the foundations of the modern theory of functional analysis, and in particular he introduced the name functional. A result of Hadamard's on determinants is important in the theory of integral equations. He died in Paris on Oct. 17, 1963. His books include *La Série de Taylor* (1902); *Leçons sur la propagation des ondes et les équations de l'hydrodynamique* (1903); *Leçons sur le calcul des variations* (1910); *An Essay on the Psychology of Invention in the Mathematical Field* (1945).   (M. L. C.)

HADASSAH, the Women's Zionist Organization of America, was founded in 1912 by Henrietta Szold (q.v.). It numbers about 350,000 U.S. Jewish women, organized in more than 1,400 chapters. Initiated for the purposes of sponsoring health work in Palestine and fostering Jewish ideals in the U.S. Jewish community, Hadassah later vastly broadened its objectives. In the United States it conducts intensive Jewish youth education and civic affairs programs for hundreds of groups. In Israel its activity has deeply influenced the life of the country. Its youth rescue and training program (Youth Aliyah) has resettled and rehabilitated 140,000 children from 72 lands. In cooperation with the Hebrew University of Jerusalem, it sponsors the only medical school in Israel and a new dental research centre. Its medical program in Israel includes several hospitals and clinics, district health services, etc. In 1970 it established Israel's first community college, in Jerusalem. (A. L. Sa.)

HADDINGTON, EARLS OF. In 1627 THOMAS HAMILTON (1563–1637), earl of Melrose, was created earl of Haddington, in the Scots peerage. He was a lawyer who had become a lord of session as Lord Drumcairn in 1592. He was one of the "Octavians" appointed to manage the finances of Scotland in 1596 and was on very friendly terms with James VI who called him "Tam o' the Cowgate," after the name of the street in which he lived. Hamilton was secretary (1612–26) and was raised to the peerage as Lord Binning in 1613. He was lord president of the court of session (1616–26) and in 1619 was created earl of Melrose, a title exchanged in Aug. 1627 for that of earl of Haddington. He had by then ceased to be lord president, but in Oct. 1627 he was appointed lord privy seal.

The 1st earl's eldest son, THOMAS (1600–1640), 2nd earl, was a covenanter and a soldier who was blown up at Dunglass castle (Aug. 30, 1640). His sons, THOMAS (c. 1625–1645) and JOHN (1626–1669), became respectively the 3rd and 4th earls of Haddington, and John's grandson THOMAS (1680–1735) succeeded his father, CHARLES (1650–1685), as 6th earl in 1685, although he was his second son. Charles had married Margaret (d. 1700), the heiress of the earldom of Rothes. It was agreed that the two earldoms should be left separate; thus the elder son, John, became earl of Rothes, while Thomas became earl of Haddington. Thomas is chiefly remembered as a tree planter and agrarian improver.

THOMAS (1780–1858), 9th earl, was lord lieutenant of Ireland (1834–35) under Sir Robert Peel, and in Peel's second administration (1841–46) he was first lord of the admiralty and then lord privy seal. At his death the earldom passed to his cousin GEORGE BAILLIE (1802–1870), a descendant of the 6th earl. He took the name of Baillie-Hamilton, and his son GEORGE (1827–1917) became 11th earl of Haddington in 1870. In 1917 he was succeeded by his grandson GEORGE (1894–), 12th earl. (G. S. P.)

HADDINGTON, a royal and small burgh and the county town of East Lothian (formerly Haddingtonshire), Scot. Pop. (1971 prelim.) 6,505. It is on the left bank of the Tyne, 16½ mi. E. of Edinburgh. The town, originally built round a triangular space, consists mainly of Georgian gray stone buildings; the townhouse (1748–1831), with its 170-ft. steeple, stands where Court street branches into Market and High streets. In the early 15th century Haddington was Scotland's largest town. On the right bank of the river lies the old industrial suburb of the Nungate, which contains the Giffordgate, where John Knox is believed to have been born, and the 12th-century church of St. Martin. St. Mary's abbey church is a 14th-century building in red and gray

THOMAS HAMILTON, FIRST EARL OF HADDINGTON, BY AN UNKNOWN ARTIST

sandstone; the nave, restored in 1892, is used as the parish church, but the choir and transepts are roofless, though otherwise kept in repair. In the ancient vestry is a fine monument in alabaster of John, Lord Maitland of Thirlestane (1545–95), chancellor of Scotland, and his wife, with a laudatory sonnet by James VI. John, duke of Lauderdale (1616–82), is also buried there. In the choir is the tombstone which Thomas Carlyle erected over the grave of his wife, Jane Welsh, a native of the town. Samuel Smiles (q.v.) was born in the burgh. The corn exchange (1854), next to that of Edinburgh, is the largest in Scotland. The Knox memorial institute was founded in 1879 to replace the old and famous grammar school, where John Knox, William Dunbar, John Major and possibly George Buchanan and Sir David Lyndsay were educated. The chief industries are fellmongery, flour milling, malting and the manufacture of agricultural machinery, textiles and woolens; its grain markets (Fridays), once the largest in Scotland, are still of considerable importance.

Haddington was created a royal burgh about 1130 by David I. It also received charters from Robert the Bruce, Robert II and James VI. In 1139 it was given as a dowry to Ada, daughter of William de Warenne, earl of Surrey, on her marriage to Prince Henry, only son of David I. Alexander II was born there in 1198. Lying in the direct road of the English invaders, the town was burned by King John in 1216 and by Henry III in 1244. Fortified in 1548 by Lord Grey of Wilton, it was besieged the next year by the Scots and French, who forced the garrison to withdraw.

HADDOCK (*Melanogrammus aeglefinus*), an edible fish of the North Atlantic belonging to the cod family (Gadidae), distinguished by the presence of three dorsal and two anal fins, a small barbel projecting from the chin, a black lateral line and a black spot on the side over the pectoral fin. The upper jaw does

ST. MARY'S ABBEY CHURCH, 14TH CENTURY

HADDOCK (MELANOGRAMMUS AEGLEFINUS)

not extend back as far as the eye. Haddock occur on continental shelf areas off Newfoundland, Iceland, the Faeroe Islands, Norway and the Barents sea and extend as far south as New Jersey (occasionally to Cape Hatteras) on the American side and the Bay of Biscay on the European. Although its distribution overlaps that of the cod, the haddock prefers somewhat warmer waters.

The haddock lives close to the bottom, mostly in depths of about 150–450 ft. It eats a large variety of bottom-living invertebrates as well as squids and small fishes. The spawning season varies with local conditions but in general extends from February to early June. The eggs, about 1¼ mm. in diameter, drift in the plankton and hatch in 12–20 days. The young fish drift for about three months, living on invertebrates of the plankton until large enough to descend to bottom. The largest haddock on record, caught in Iceland, was 44 in. and weighed 37 lb.; the average length at age eight is about 2 ft. Haddock is one of the most valuable bottom fishes; over 900,000 metric tons are caught annually by North American and European fishermen, mostly with otter trawls. Smoked haddock is popularly known as finnan haddie. *See also* FISH: *Survey of the Bony Fishes.* (L. A. WD.)

HADDON, ALFRED CORT (1855–1940), one of the founders of modern British anthropology, was born in London on May 24, 1855, and educated at various schools and at Christ's college, Cambridge. He distinguished himself in comparative anatomy and zoology and in 1880 was appointed professor of zoology at the Royal College of Science, Dublin. His first book, *Introduction to the Study of Embryology*, appeared in 1887, followed by a succession of papers on marine biology.

In 1888 he went to Torres straits to study marine biology but instead found himself irresistibly drawn to the indigenous people; thereafter, his interests lay in the study of man. Having moved his home to Cambridge in 1893 (though he did not relinquish his Dublin professorship until 1901), he gave lectures in physical anthropology. In 1898 he organized and led the Cambridge anthropological expedition to Torres straits, New Guinea and Sarawak, in which were worked out some of the basic techniques of modern anthropological field work; *e.g.*, the use of genealogies. On his return, Cambridge recognized his services by a lectureship, and his college by a fellowship (1901). The Board of Anthropological studies in Cambridge was instituted in 1904, and from 1909 to 1926 Haddon was reader in ethnology. Virtually the sole exponent of anthropology at Cambridge for 30 years, it was largely through his work and especially his teaching that the subject assumed its rightful place among the observational sciences. Widely traveled, he received recognition from learned societies throughout the world.

Haddon's publications, over 600 in number, include *Evolution in Art* (1895); *Head-Hunters, Black, White and Brown* (1901); (with Sir J. S. Huxley) *We Europeans* (1935); and *Reports of the Cambridge Anthropological Expedition to Torres Straits* (1901, etc.). He died at Cambridge on April 20, 1940. (D. F. R.)

HADEN, SIR FRANCIS SEYMOUR (1818–1910), English etcher whose unaffected use of the lessons learned from the great masters place some of his works among the undeniable masterpieces of printmaking. He was born on Sept. 16, 1818, in London, the son of Charles Haden, a surgeon. After pursuing a medical education in England and France, Haden became in 1842 a member of the Royal College of Surgeons.

In 1843–44 he traveled in Italy and made his first sketches from nature. He studied the works of the great original engravers, Dürer, Lucas van Leyden and Rembrandt, and these studies influenced his own efforts, leading to his important monograph (1897) on the etchings of Rembrandt. In 1847 he married the sister of James McNeill Whistler. He received the Grand prix in Paris in 1889 and 1900 and was made a member of the Institut de France, Académie des Beaux-Arts and Société des Artistes Français. He was knighted in 1894. He retired in 1887 from his London medical practice and went to live in the neighbourhood of Alresford, Hampshire, where he died, on June 1, 1910.

Of Haden's original etched plates, more than 250 in number, one of the most notable is the large "Breaking Up of the Agamem-

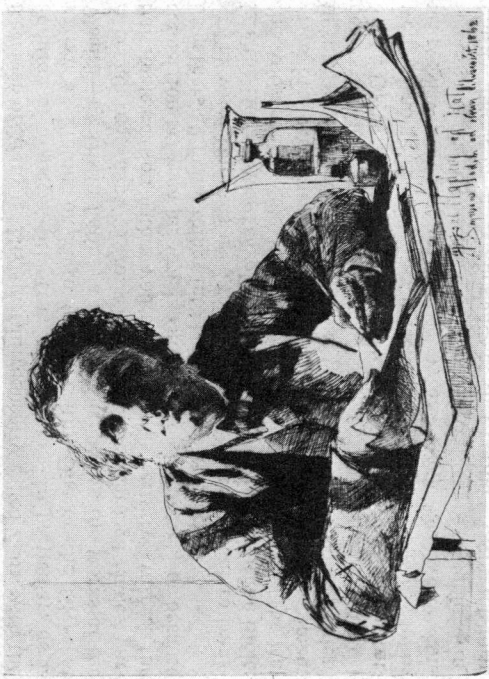
SELF PORTRAIT BY SIR FRANCIS SEYMOUR HADEN. ETCHING AND DRYPOINT. 1802

non." Some of his early and most beautiful etchings are "Thames Fishermen," "Sub Tegmine," and "Early Morning—Richmond." Other notable works, long popular with collectors, are "A By-Road in Tipperary," "Combe Bottom," "Shere Mill Pond" (both the small study and the larger plate), "Sunset in Ireland" and "Evening Fishing, Longparish." Toward the end of his life Haden began to practise mezzotint, and he also produced some charcoal drawings of landscape subjects. He wrote several well-known monographs, including *About Etching* (1878–79) and *The Art of the Painter-Etchers* (1890).

See H. Nazeby Harrington, *The Engraved Work of Sir Francis Seymour Haden* (1910). (H. Es.)

HADENDOA: see BEJA.

HADERSLEV, a town of Denmark in the *amt* (county) of Sønderjylland, is 48 km. (29 mi.) N of the German frontier by road. Pop. (1970 est.) 29,620 (municipality). It lies in a valley on the fjord, which is about 7½ mi. long and communicates with the Little Belt (Lille Bælt).

The magnificent Cathedral of Our Lady at Haderslev dates from the 13th century. Industries include the production of textiles, plastic boats, screws, compressors, malt and beer, and cheese. Haderslev is a railway junction and the harbour is accessible to small vessels. The town was first mentioned in 1228 and received municipal rights from Duke Waldemar II in 1292. It suffered in the 15th-century wars between Slesvig and Holstein. In November 1864 it passed with Slesvig to Prussia and was called Hadersleben. It was returned to Denmark with North Slesvig by plebiscite in 1920.

The nearby town of Christiansfeld, which was laid out in 1773 by the Moravians, has a famous honey-cake bakery, and its museum and cemetery (Gudsageren, "God's field") are of interest. (Ro. H. T.)

HADES (possibly Greek AIDES, "the Unseen"), son of the Titans Cronus and Rhea, brother of Zeus and Poseidon. After deposing Cronus the three brothers cast lots for the kingdoms of the heaven, the sea and the infernal regions. To Hades fell the underworld, where he ruled with his queen, Persephone (*q.v.*), over the infernal powers and over the dead, in what was often called "the House of Hades." Though he supervised the trial and punishment of the wicked after death, he was not normally one of the judges in the underworld; nor does he personally torture the guilty, a task assigned to the Furies (Erinyes; *q.v.*). He is depicted as stern and pitiless; unmoved (like death itself) by prayer or sacrifice; forbidding, aloof, never quite emerging as a personality from the shadowy darkness of his realm. The city of Elis was unique in worshiping Hades under his own name. Elsewhere direct mention of so ill-omened a deity was avoided and euphemistic epithets were substituted: Clymenus (the Illustrious), Eubuleus (the Giver of Good Counsel) and Polydectes (the

Receiver of Many). He is not infrequently called Zeus, with the addition of a special title (e.g. *chthonios*). In particular, he is known as Pluton, or Pluto (the Wealthy One or the Giver of Wealth—*cf.* Dis in Latin), a name first found in the works of the Athenian tragedians. It may have originated through Hades' partial amalgamation with a god of the earth's fertility (witness the connection between his worship and that of Demeter); or because he gathers all living things into his treasury at death.

The word Hades is used in the Greek Old Testament to translate the Hebrew word *sheol*. Among English versions of the Bible, the Authorized (King James) does not use Hades at all; the Revised Standard uses it at several places in the New Testament in substitution for "hell" at points where the Greek word "Hades" occurs in the text. *See* HELL.

(D. E. W. W.)

HADEWYCH, a 13th-century mystic, probably born in Antwerp of noble descent, was influential among the *béguines* living near Nijvel. Her lyrical poetry, in which she wrote consciously as the troubadour of divine love, attains a sublime intensity unique in the Netherlands at that period. Using the form and terminology of the Provençal troubadours (*q.v.*), she releases powers of a timeless validity from a language dulled by the urbanities of the romances, and by dedicating her intellect and literary gifts with the singleness of purpose evident throughout her writings, she became a highly skilled craftsman in both prose and poetry. Her letters and 14 *Visioenen*, in prose, are too esoteric, and her *Strofische Gedichten* are too personal, ever to attain a wide appeal. Yet an understanding of her use of symbol and parodox discloses a person with simple desires heroically surrendering a complex personality to the demands of the religious life. Her mystical approach is derived from the Augustinian modification of the neoplatonic ideal current among certain French religious of the 12th century. The rhapsodic fervour constantly restrained by awe and humility reveals, in tensely disciplined stanzas, the greatness of a poet who saw her own creative genius as the only barrier to a selfless approach to God. Her expression of the soul's relationship to Christ as that of a lover to the Beloved led to the systematic mysticism of *Die Chierheit der geesteliker Brulocht* by Jan van Ruysbroeck (*q.v.*), so different from the introspective approach of the German Johannes Eckhart (*q.v.*), although Hadewych herself later became well known in southern Germany by the name of Adelwip.

BIBLIOGRAPHY.—*Strofische gedichten*, ed. by E. Rombauts and N. de Paepe (1961); *Hadewijch. Een Bloemlezing uit hare Werken* (1950), *De Visioenen van Hadewijch* (1924), *Brieven* (1947), all ed. by J. van Mierlo; Th. Weevers, *Poetry of the Netherlands in Its European Context, 1170–1930,* pp. 27–39 (1960).

(P. K. K.)

HADFIELD, SIR ROBERT ABBOTT (1858–1940), British metallurgist, was born in Sheffield, Eng., on Nov. 29, 1858, and was educated at Sheffield Collegiate school. He interested himself at an early age in metallurgy and in 1883 patented his process for the production of manganese steel (*see* MANGANESE). He became famous as the inventor and improver of various metallurgical processes, including low hysteresis steel and many other special ferrous alloys.

In 1908 he was knighted, the following year became a fellow of the Royal Society, and was created a baronet in 1917. Hadfield published more than 220 scientific and technical papers and his book *Metallurgy and Its Influence on Modern Progress; With a Survey of Education and Research* (1925) became a standard work of reference. In 1914, soon after the beginning of World War I, Hadfield and his wife founded a hospital at Wimereux, France. Hadfield died in London on Sept. 30, 1940.

HADHRAMAUT (HADRAMAWT), a region forming the eastern part of the People's Democratic Republic of Yemen, in the southern part of the Arabian Peninsula, bounded west by the 'Aulaqi country, east by the Mahrah country, north by the Rub' al Khali, and south by the Indian Ocean.

The region includes: the former Qu'aiti sultanate Shihr and Mukalla and the former Kathiri sultanate, known as the Hadhramaut states; the former Wahidi sultanates of Balhaf and Bir 'Ali; and the two tiny coastal former sheikhdoms of Haura and 'Irqa. All of them were in treaty relations with the United Kingdom, and with the former Mahra sultanate of Qishn and Socotra (*q.v.*), have since 1967 been included in the People's Republic of Southern Yemen (after Nov. 30, 1970, the People's Democratic Republic of Yemen). The population in 1961 was about 300,000. Al Mukalla (20,000) is the principal seaport. The other chief towns are Ash Shihr, also a seaport; Shibam in the Wadi Hadhramaut; Al Khuraybah in the Wadi Daw'an; and Ghayl ba Wazir.

The Hadhramaut is a poor country, and about one in four Hadhramis live and work abroad, mostly in Java, Singapore, East Africa, Egypt, and Saudi Arabia, sending money home. Little agricultural development is possible, but the use of diesel pumps has considerably increased in the Wadi Hadhramaut, and a little grain has been exported westward. Principal exports by sea are tobacco, honey, lime, and fish products; principal food crops are dates and millet. *See further* ARABIA; SOUTHERN YEMEN.

(W. H. Is.)

HADITH, the Arabic term for "news," "story," and thence the technical term for the narratives or traditions that relate a saying or an action of Mohammed, of one of his companions or of a later authority. These traditions embody the Sunna ("right custom") of the community of Muslims. Every complete Hadith consists of two parts, the text proper and the *isnad* ("chain of transmitters") which precedes it; *e.g.*, "It has been related to me by Yahya on the authority of Malik on the authority of Nafi' on the authority of Abdallah ibn Omar that the Prophet said: 'If someone sells a palm-tree which has been fertilized, its fruit belongs to the seller, unless the buyer stipulate it for himself.'"

This literary form came into being early in the 2nd century of the hegira (soon after A.D. 720), and was at once put into writing. The emergence of traditions was mainly due to the activity of the *ahl al-hadith* ("traditionists"), who tried to base the Islamic way of life not on custom as it had developed in the centres of the Muslim world but on individual precedents going back to the Prophet. This led to a wholesale creation of traditions with ever more elaborate *isnads*. As a result, most of the early opinions held on the religious law and dogma of Islam as well as on its early history (which provided legal and political precedents), not to mention prophecies expressing political and other expectations, were cast in the form of traditions, which often attempted to conceal their underlying tendencies. The Muslim scholars were aware of this, but being bound, on principle, to accept any formally reliable statement of what the Prophet had said or done, had to restrict themselves to the scrutiny of *isnads*, the truthfulness and orthodoxy of transmitters, etc., although their unavowed criterion was the acceptability to the majority of the traditions in question. The result of that scrutiny is represented by six collections of traditions recognized as authoritative in orthodox Islam, the works of al-Bukhari, Muslim ibn al-Hajjaj, Abu Dawud, al-Tirmidhi, Ibn Maja and al-Nasa'i (all of the 9th or early 10th centuries). By that time, Islamic law had already taken its final shape, so that the study of traditions became of antiquarian and edifying interest, but they have deeply influenced Muslim thought. For critical scholarship, traditions are the main source for the study of doctrinal development during the first few centuries of Islam. *See* ISLAM: *Development of the Shari'a.*

BIBLIOGRAPHY.—I. Goldziher, *Muhammedanische Studien,* vol. ii (1890), partially translated as *Études sur la tradition islamique* (1952); J. Robson in B. Lewis *et al.* (eds.), *Encyclopaedia of Islam,* new ed., vol. iii, pp. 23–28 (1965); J. Schacht, "A Revaluation of Islamic Traditions," *Journal of the Royal Asiatic Society,* pp. 143–154 (1949), *The Origins of Muhammadan Jurisprudence,* 4th ed. (1967); M. Z. Siddiqi, *Hadith Literature, Its Origins, Development, Special Features and Criticism* (1961).

(J. Sc.)

HADLEIGH, a market town and urban district in the Sudbury and Woodbridge parliamentary division of Suffolk, Eng. 10 mi. W. of Ipswich on the Brett, a tributary of the Stour. Pop. (1971 prelim.) 5,101. Hadleigh, the capital city of the East Angles, was called by the Saxons Heapde-leag and appears in Domesday Book as Hetlega. About 886 Aethelflaed, with the consent of Aethelred, her husband, gave Hadleigh to Christ Church, Canterbury. The dean and chapter of Canterbury have held it since the Dissolution. Flemings arrived in medieval times to make cloth and in the 17th century Hadleigh was famous for woolen manufacture. The town was incorporated in 1618, and in 1635, in a list of the corporate towns of Suffolk to be assessed for ship money, Hadleigh was named as third in importance. It declined after the plague in 1636 and in 1687 was deprived of its charter; an unsuccessful attempt to recover it was made in 1701.

James I granted fairs on Monday and Tuesday in Whitsun week and confirmed an ancient fair at Michaelmas and a market on Monday. The church of St. Mary the Virgin is Perpendicular, with an Early English tower and Decorated spire. The Deanery tower, a turreted gatehouse of brick, dates from 1495 and has associations with the Oxford movement. The Guild hall nearby is a Tudor building and the High street contains many half-timbered houses. Coir matting, sacks, malting, milling, egg packing and agriculture are the main trades.

There is a Hadleigh in Essex near Southend-on-Sea.

HADLEY, ARTHUR TWINING (1856–1930), U.S. economist, specialist in railroads and educator, was president of Yale university from 1899 to 1921. He was born in New Haven, Conn., on April 23, 1856, the son of a Yale professor, and graduated from Yale in 1876. After two years of further study in Germany and the U.S. he became a member of the Yale faculty. His early reputation as an economist was based on his *Railroad Transportation* (1885) in which he pointed out the importance of the high proportion of fixed to variable costs in the railroad industry as a source of cutthroat competition and instability. Hadley expanded his emphasis on fixed costs to include the manufacturing industries and argued that an increase in mergers and combinations was inevitable if instability was to be avoided. In his most influential work, *Economics: an Account of the Relations between Private Property and Public Welfare*, Hadley argued that even though greater power had been placed in the hands of private business, government control of industry was not the answer. He contended that the development of an enlightened, responsible community of the highest moral character would prove to be the ultimate solution of the economic problem. This line of reasoning led him to an increasing concern with moral problems. Hadley attempted to resolve the conflict between responsibility and individualism. He dealt directly with this issue in his *The Relations between Freedom and Responsibility in the Evolution of Democratic Government* (1903) and returned to the problem in his last important work, *The Conflict between Liberty and Equality* (1925). On the whole Hadley is identified with the conservative tradition, but his moral emphasis, like that of the later Victorian economists, was on the co-operative rather than the individualistic aspects of society. After retirement from Yale he was active as director of several railroad companies and lectured extensively. He died in Kobe, Japan, on March 6, 1930.

(L. N.)

HADLEY, HENRY KIMBALL (1871–1937), U.S. conductor and composer of operatic and symphonic music in a neoromantic manner, was born in Somerville, Mass., Dec. 20, 1871. He studied composition with G. W. Chadwick in Boston. He went to Germany in 1904 and on April 4, 1909, conducted in Mainz his one-act opera *Safié*. His later operas, *Azora, Daughter of Montezuma* (1917), *Bianca* (1918) and *Cleopatra's Night* (1920), were given in Chicago and New York.

His orchestral works include five symphonies (1897–1934); the symphonic poems *Salomé, Lucifer* and *The Ocean*; and the symphonic suites *San Francisco* and *Streets of Pekin*. He also wrote choral works, chamber music and about 150 songs. His music is cast in a Wagnerian mold, with occasional impressionistic touches.

Hadley conducted the Seattle Symphony orchestra (1909–11), the San Francisco Symphony orchestra (1911–15) and the Manhattan Symphony orchestra (1929–32). From 1920 to 1927 he was associate conductor of the New York Philharmonic orchestra and in 1930 he conducted concerts in Tokyo. He died in New York city on Sept. 6, 1937.

See H. R. Boardman, *Henry Hadley, Ambassador of Harmony* (1932). (N. Sv.)

HADOW, SIR (WILLIAM) HENRY (1859–1937), English educationist and musician, was born at Ebrington, Gloucestershire, on Dec. 27, 1859. Educated at Malvern and Oxford, where he lectured on music from 1890 to 1899, Hadow was principal of

Armstrong college, Newcastle (1909–19), and vice-chancellor of Sheffield university (1919–30). He was knighted in 1918 and in 1927 presided over the committee that produced the Hadow report on education. His *Studies in Modern Music* (2 vol. 1892–95) revealed critical perception and wide knowledge. He was editor of *The Oxford History of Music* (1901–05) and author of the fifth volume, *The Viennese Period* (1904). He died in London on April 8, 1937. (H. Ru.)

HADRIAN (PUBLIUS AELIUS HADRIANUS) (A.D. 76–138), Roman emperor A.D. 117–138, was born on Jan. 24, 76, at Italica (near modern Seville) in Spain, of a Roman family long domiciled there. He was the emperor Trajan's nearest blood relation (grandson of Trajan's aunt), and from the moment of Trajan's accession was given a career of rapid promotion, marking him out as the likely successor. He had the support of Trajan's closest friend and adviser, L. Licinius Sura. Nevertheless, the transition of power when Trajan died was not smooth. Trajan failed to make his wishes clear and consequently the adoption of Hadrian by the dying emperor was believed by some to be an invention put about by Hadrian and the empress Plotina, who was devoted to him. Moreover, since the death of Sura, Trajan's main support in his policy of military expansion had come from certain eminent military commanders, who had good reason to suspect Hadrian's intentions. When, therefore, Hadrian learned on Aug. 11, 117, in Syria, of Trajan's death at Selinus in Cilicia and assumed the government, he was faced with internal dissatisfaction as well as a large number of pressing external problems.

ANDERSON—MANSELL

HADRIAN. PORTRAIT BUST IN THE MUSEO NAZIONALE, NAPLES, ITALY

He at once abandoned the lands beyond the Euphrates river overrun by Trajan's armies. There is evidence that he wanted to give up also Trajan's other conquest, Dacia. The tribes bordering that province were certainly causing trouble in the absence of Danube.legions; Dacia, however, was retained. The Jewish rebellion in Cyrene and Egypt had left a trail of desolation, and north Britain was in turmoil. Before Hadrian reached Rome four senior marshals of Trajan had been executed on a charge of conspiracy.

The nature of the plot, if indeed there was one, and the responsibility for these summary executions are never likely to be accurately determined, but Roman opinion certainly saddled Hadrian with the deed, and his principate began under a cloud. His first measures were therefore a massive attempt to recover popularity and included the cancellation of 900,000,000 sesterces of debts by Roman citizens to the treasury and the extension and reorganization of the *alimenta* (institutions for bringing up children of the poor in Italy).

Probably in 121 Hadrian left Rome on the first of those travels about the Roman world which are the most notable feature of his principate. Between 121 and 125 he toured first the west and then the east; in 128 he spent a summer in north Africa and after a short return to Rome departed in the same year again for the east, where he journeyed up and down continuously until 134. For 12 of his 20 years as emperor Hadrian was absent from Rome, and the effect of these absences was inevitably to concentrate government and policy round the person of the emperor, wherever he might be, and to reduce the importance of Rome and Italy, hitherto the nucleus and leading element in the empire.

Hadrian's journeys exemplify at every turn his eagerness to appreciate the diverse circumstances and problems of the empire, to redress and improve, to build and create. In Britain he ordered the building of the great frontier wall that bears his name (*see* HADRIAN'S WALL). In north Africa he repopulated the lands devastated in the Jewish rebellion. He engaged in personal negotiations with the Parthian king on the far eastern frontier. In Africa, and wherever there were troops, he held vigorous maneuvers, taking part himself; and *disciplina militum* is one of the most characteristic legends on his coinage. Athens was the city he most loved; he visited it three times, revised its constitution, was archon and initiate of Eleusis, established a united Greek league, the Panhellenion, with Athens as its centre, and built, in the midst of a whole new portion of the city, the vast temple of Olympian Zeus (see ATHENS).

One of Hadrian's creative efforts proved a disastrous mistake. He ordered the building of a new city on the desolate site of Jerusalem, to be called Aelia Capitolina and peopled with gentile Roman citizens. He failed to calculate the effect of this upon the Jews, and in 132 Palestine blazed with the last and most desperate of its rebellions, led by a messiah, "son of the star," proclaimed by Rabbi Akiba (see BAR-COCHBA). Guerrilla warfare, waged with utter savagery and bitterness on both sides, ended only in 135 with Palestine ruined and largely depopulated.

In Egypt Hadrian lost the object of his homosexual devotion, the Bithynian Antinous (q.v.), drowned in the Nile in 130. To honour him Hadrian built another new city, Antinoopolis, in Egypt, and lavished privileges upon it; and over much of the Roman world official cult was offered to Hadrian's favourite, now counted among the gods. From 134 to the end of his life the emperor was in or near Rome, nostalgically making ever larger and more reminiscent of the past his fantastic villa at Tivoli. He was sad, lonely and increasingly ill, and the problem of the succession now beset him. His attempts to solve it made him at the end, as he had been at the beginning, *invisus omnibus* ("hated by all"). There was no heir; his nearest relative was his brother-in-law L. Julius Ursus Servianus, honoured outstandingly in 134 with a third consulship. Servianus was over 80, but may have expected to succeed as a stopgap for his grandson. However, in 136 Hadrian adopted, with every sign of intending him as successor, L. Ceionius Commodus (thereafter called L. Aelius Caesar), a senator of good family but no particular distinction compared with many others. It has been conjectured that this man was Hadrian's illegitimate son, but on suspect evidence; in any case, Servianus and his grandson were put to death. Aelius Caesar died in Jan. 138, and Hadrian had to think again. His second solution appears sensible and solid, though it too met with opposition; he adopted T. Aurelius Antoninus, the future emperor Antoninus Pius, who in his turn adopted M. Annius Verus and L. Ceionius Commodus (the son of Hadrian's former choice); who in due course became the emperors Marcus Aurelius and Lucius Verus. Hadrian died at Baiae on July 10, 138. The senate is said to have wanted to annul his acts and refuse him the title *Divus*, but to have been dissuaded by his successor.

Later antiquity saw Hadrian's principate as a milestone on the road to the centralized bureaucracy of the late empire, and modern historians have tended to endorse this judgment; but the development of the empire was in most aspects a continuous, longterm process and it is not clear that the innovations of Hadrian were particularly fundamental. An important and undoubtedly bureaucratic step was taken in the codification of the praetor's edict, source of *ius honorarium* and hitherto a means by which law could be made independently of the emperor (see ROMAN LAW). This innovation may be connected with the fact that Hadrian in some way made greater use of the jurists in taking advice on the law (though the "permanent legislative *consilium principis*" is a figment of the imagination of historians) and that by the mid-2nd century at least the emperor's role as supreme legislating and also judicial authority was clearly enough recognized, and the praetorian prefect had a court of law as the emperor's delegate. Hadrian's is said to have made fundamental changes in military affairs; he was certainly interested in the regulation of military discipline and law, but more cannot be shown. The main change that was taking place in the army, the tendency of the legions to be recruited from the population of their localities, spread over a long period and was not begun by Hadrian. The continued expansion of the equestrian civil service and the eventual abandonment of the "farming" system of tax collection in favour of direct collec-

tion by civil servants were also general developments over a long period. Much is sometimes made of what on present evidence seems to have been a Hadrianic innovation—the growth of an equestrian career that bypassed military service, hitherto a necessary preliminary—but there are few such careers in Hadrian's principate and they are almost all of men going into specialized literary or legal posts. The unique position of Italy was gradually being undermined; one symptom of this process was Hadrian's appointment of four special assize officers for Italy (an institution that already existed in the provinces).

The character of Hadrian is an epitome of his age—an age of culture, sensitivity and growing religiosity. He was a competent amateur in literature, painting and mathematics; he had a prodigious memory and wit and loved the company of scholars; he shared the contemporary taste for the archaic in literature; he was an initiate of the mysteries and dabbled in astrology and magic; his travels were at least partly motivated by geographical and antiquarian curiosity.

There survive as monuments to him three notable works of architecture: his mausoleum, now the Castel Sant'Angelo, beside the Tiber, the present form of the Pantheon and the remains of his villa at Tivoli.

See also references under "Hadrian" in the Index volume.

BIBLIOGRAPHY.—Scriptores Historiae Augustae, *De vita Hadriani*; Cassius Dio, lxix; P. von Rohden in Pauly-Wissowa, *Real-Encyclopädie*, vol. i, pp. 493–520 (1894); G. Mancini and D. Vaglieri in E. Ruggiero, *Dizionario epigrafico*, vol. iii, pp. 600–640 (1922); E. Groag and A. Stein, *Prosopographia Imperii Romani*, 2nd ed., A 184 (1933); F. Gregorovius, *The Emperor Hadrian*, trans. by Mary E. Robinson (1898); W. Weber, *Untersuchungen zur Geschichte des Kaisers Hadrianus* (1907); R. H. Lacey, *Equestrian Officials of Trajan and Hadrian* (1917); B. W. Henderson, *Life and Principate of the Emperor Hadrian* (1923); P. Strack, *Untersuchungen zur römischen Reichsprägung des 2. Jahrhunderts*, ii (1933); F. Pringsheim, "The Legal Policy and Reforms of Hadrian," in *Journal of Roman Studies*, xxiv, pp. 141 ff. (1934); P. Graindor, *Athènes sous Hadrien* (1934); J. M. C. Toynbee, *The Hadrianic School* (1934); P. J. Alexander, "Letters and Speeches of Hadrian," in *Harvard Studies in Classical Philology*, xlix, pp. 141 ff. (1938); J. Carcopino, "L'Hérédité dynastique chez les Antonins," in *Revue des études anciennes*, li, pp. 262 ff. (1949); B. d'Orgeval, *L'Empereur Hadrien, l'oeuvre législative* (1950); J. A. Crook, *Consilium Principis*, ch. 5 and append. 3 (1955); J. Beaujeu, *La religion romaine à l'apogée de l'empire*, i, esp. ch. 3 (1955); M. Hammond, *The Antonine Monarchy* (1959); Marguerite Yourcenar, *Memoirs of Hadrian* (Eng. trans. 1955; fiction).   (J. A. CR.)

HADRIAN'S WALL, the continuous barrier that defended the northern frontier of the Roman province of Britain. The wall extends from Wallsend (Segedunum) on the river Tyne to Bowness on the river Solway, 80 Roman and about 73½ English miles, and was erected by order of the emperor Hadrian under A. Platorius Nepos, governor of Britain from A.D. 122 to c. 126. The work was not built to a single plan, but had reached its final form by about A.D. 136 in four stages. First, a continuous barrier

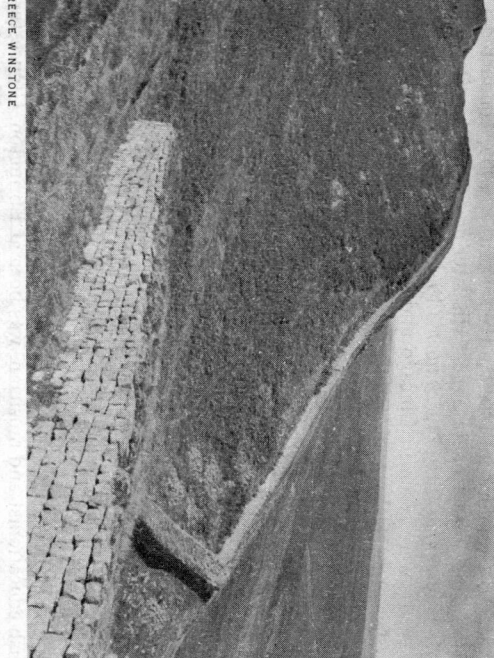

REECE WINSTONE

HADRIAN'S WALL, WHICH MARKED THE FRONTIER OF THE ROMAN EMPIRE IN BRITAIN

comprising 45 Roman miles of stone wall, from Newcastle upon Tyne (Pons Aelius) to the river Irthing, and 31 Roman miles of turf wall from the Irthing to Bowness on Solway, both equipped with regularly spaced milecastles and turrets (two per mile) for a patrolling garrison, while forts for fighting men lay behind. Coastal milecastles and towers were built along the Cumberland shore to the west; also outpost forts to the northwest where the view from the wall is not good. Second, the forts were moved forward on to the wall itself, where about ten were built before A.D. 126; the stone wall was extended to Wallsend and gradually substituted for the turf wall. Forts were built to accompany the coastal defense. Third, the *vallum*, a flat-bottomed ditch running along a wide cleared strip delimited by mounds, was added as a rearward barrier to the military zone of the wall and its new forts. Fourth, forts blocking less obvious lines of approach were added to the new series on the wall, bringing the number up to 16.

The wall was twice destroyed by northern tribes, in 197 and 296, when its garrison was withdrawn for civil war, and again in 367–369 by concerted attack from land and sea. It appears to have been evacuated after 383.

See J. C. Bruce, *Handbook to the Roman Wall*, 11th ed., by I. A. Richmond (1957), wherein a detailed bibliography is contained.
(I. A. Rd.)

HADRUMETUM, the ancient name of Susah (*q.v.*) on the east coast of Tunisia. It was said to be a Phoenician colony, though the settlement may have been made from Carthage. A sanctuary and graves of Phoenician type from the 6th century B.C. have been discovered. The city grew fast and was probably one of the most important communities within the Carthaginian territory in north Africa. It was attacked by the Sicilian leader Agathocles in 310 B.C. during his invasion of Africa, and through it Hannibal escaped after the battle of Zama in 202 B.C. In the Third Punic War (149–146 B.C.) Hadrumetum sided with Rome and was rewarded with the status of a *civitas libera*. Roman and Italian merchants and settlers began to come to the coast from the time of Gaius Gracchus (122 B.C.), as it was a good trading centre, and a *conventus civium Romanorum* ("assemblage of Roman citizens") was formed alongside the Punic community. Both were heavily fined in 46 by Julius Caesar for having supported his enemies in the civil war, at which time Hadrumetum probably ranked with Utica as the most important African city. It is possible that it received colonial rank from Augustus but more probable that this occurred under Trajan (A.D. 98–117); the full name of the city was later *Colonia Concordia Ulpia Traiana Augusta Frugifera Hadrumetina*. The racially predominant Punic element became more or less romanized in the 2nd century A.D. Inland from Hadrumetum was a fertile territory of farms and large estates with a number of native Libyan villages but few Roman settlements; surplus products from this territory, particularly olive oil, were probably exported through Hadrumetum. The city was a centre for the administration of imperial estates in the eastern part of Tunisia, and became capital of the province of Byzacena formed by Diocletian about A.D. 300. Hadrumetum was still flourishing during the Vandal supremacy in north Africa in the 5th century A.D. but in danger of attack from nomadic tribes as the walls had been dismantled by the Vandals. It was again important after the Byzantine reconquest of Africa by Justinian I in 533, receiving the name Justinianopolis and substantial new defenses.

Since the site was occupied throughout the Arab period, few remains of any consequence survive from the Roman period, though the foundations of a number have been discovered; a substantial cemetery of the Christian period has been found, and bishops of Hadrumetum are recorded at church councils from the 3rd to the 7th centuries.
(B. H. WA.)

HAECKEL, ERNST HEINRICH (1834–1919), German zoologist, well known for his early adoption of the doctrine of evolution and for his confident construction of genealogical trees of living organisms, was born at Potsdam on Feb. 16, 1834. He studied medicine and science at Würzburg, Berlin and Vienna under such men as Johannes Müller, R. Virchow and R. A. Kölliker. In 1862 he became professor of comparative anatomy and director

of the zoological institute at Jena, where a chair of zoology was created for him in 1865. He spent his life at Jena, with the exception of the time devoted to various tours. As a field naturalist (he coined the term ecology in 1866), Haeckel had extraordinary power and industry, displayed in his publications on *Radiolaria* (1862), *Siphonophora* (1869), *Monera* (1870) and *Calcareous Sponges* (1872), as well as several *Challenger* reports, viz., *Deep-Sea Medusae* (1881), *Siphonophora* (1888), *Deep-Sea Keratosa* (1889) and *Radiolaria* (1887).

Darwin believed that Haeckel's enthusiastic propagation of the doctrine of organic evolution was the chief factor in the success of the doctrine in Germany. His *General Morphology* (1866) was a suggestive attempt to work out the practical application of evolution to its final results. *Natürliche Schöpfungsgeschichte* (1867; 10th ed., 1902; Eng. trans., *History of Creation*, 1892) laid particular stress on the "fundamental biogenetic law," that ontogeny recapitulates phylogeny, that the organism in its development is to a great extent an epitome of the form modifications undergone by the successive ancestors of the species in the course of their historic evolution. Haeckel's well-known "gastraea" theory is an outcome of this generalization. He divided animal creation into the Protozoa or unicellular animals, and the Metazoa or multicellular animals. In the Metazoa the single primitive egg cell is transformed by cleavage into a globular mass of cells (morula), which first becomes a hollow vesicle and then changes into the gastrula. The simplest multicellular animal resembles this gastrula with its two primary layers, ectoderm and endoderm, and the earliest hypothetical form of this kind, from which the higher animals are probably descended, may be called the gastraea.

Haeckel's genealogical constructions culminated in the paper he read before the fourth international zoological congress, held at Cambridge in 1898, when he traced the descent of the human race in 26 stages from organisms like the still existing Monera, simple structureless masses of protoplasm, and the unicellular Protista through the chimpanzees and the *Pithecanthropus erectus*, which he regarded as the link between primitive man and the anthropoid apes.

Haeckel's attempt to apply the doctrine of evolution to the problems of philosophy and religion appeared in *Die Welträtsel* (1899; Eng. trans., *The Riddle of the Universe*, 1900). Adopting an uncompromising monistic attitude, he asserted the essential unity of organic and inorganic nature. For him the chemicophysical properties of carbon in its complex albuminoid compounds are the sole and the mechanical cause of the specific phenomena of movement which distinguish organic from inorganic substances, and the first development of living protoplasm, as seen in the Monera, arises from such nitrogenous carbon compounds by spontaneous generation. Psychology he regarded as merely a branch of physiology. Every living cell has psychic properties, and the psychic life of multicellular organisms is the sum total of the psychic functions of the cells of which they are composed. Moreover, just as the highest animals have evolved from the simplest forms of life, so the highest human faculties have evolved from the soul of animals. Consequently Haeckel denied the immortality of the soul, the freedom of the will and the existence of a personal God.

Haeckel occupies no serious position in the history of philosophy, and it can be held that in the formulation of his ideas he was somewhat unscrupulous in his treatment of scientific facts. He is thus exposed to criticism, but he was very widely read in his own day and was very typical of the school of extreme evolutionist thought. He died at Jena on Aug. 8, 1919.

Haeckel's other works include: *Die systematische Phylogenie* (1894), which has been pronounced his best book; *Anthropogenie* (1874; 5th ed., 1903; Eng. trans., 1879), dealing with the evolution of man; *Über unsere gegenwärtige Kenntnis vom Ursprung des Menschen* (1898; Eng. trans., *On Our Present Knowledge Regarding the Origin of Man*, 1898); *Der Kampf um den Entwicklungsgedanken* (1905; Eng. trans., *The Struggle Over Ideas Concerning Evolution*, 1906); books of travel such as *Indische Reisebriefe* (1882; 6th ed., 1922) and *Aus Insulinde* (1901). *Kunstformen* der Natur (1904), in 11 parts, consists of exceptionally fine paintings of protozoan organisms. Haeckel was an excellent artist but tended to be led by his imagination.

See W. Bölsche, E. Haeckel. Ein Lebensbild (1900; Eng. trans. 1906); H. Schmidt (ed.) Was wir Ernst Haeckel verdanken, 2 vol. (1914).

HAEMATOPODIDAE, a family of stout-bodied black-and-white shore birds, with bright red bills, breeding mainly along sea coasts. See OYSTER CATCHER.

HAEMOSPORIDIA, an order of parasitic single-celled animals (Protozoa; q.v.) which live in and gradually destroy the red blood corpuscles of vertebrates. Prominent among the Haemosporidia are certain species of Plasmodium, organisms that cause the various kinds of malaria (q.v.).

HAFIZ (SHAMSUDDIN MOHAMMED) (c. 1325-1389 or 1390), the most famous lyric poet of Persia, was born at Shiraz, where he lived all his life. Never a man of substance, he lectured on Koranic and other theological subjects (his surname of Hafiz designates one who has learned the Koran by heart) and wrote commentaries on a number of religious classics. As a court poet, he enjoyed the patronage of several rulers of Shiraz and of other distinguished men, all of whom are mentioned in his poems.

Hafiz lived in troubled times; sovereigns were overthrown, Shiraz was taken by force more than once, and over the last years of his life loomed the menacing shadow of the world-conqueror Timur (Tamerlane). There are many echoes of these events in his poems; but they tell more of the "café" life of Shiraz, of the vagaries of his princely patrons and of his disputes with his orthodox and sectarian contemporaries. For the guiding influence in Hafiz's own life was Sufism, the mystical movement that demanded of its adherents complete self-abandonment to the pursuit of union with the Ultimate Reality, and the rejection of the restraints of conventional religion and morality.

Hafiz' principal medium of expression, and one that he brought to a perfection never achieved before or since, was the ghazal, a lyric poem of 6 to 15 couplets linked by unity of thought and symbolism rather than by a logical sequence of ideas. Traditionally the ghazal dealt with love and wine, motifs that, in their association with ecstasy and freedom from restraint, lent themselves naturally to the expression of Sufi ideas. Hafiz' achievement was to give these conventions a freshness and subtlety that completely relieves his poetry of tedious formalism. The western reader can appreciate this, even if he misses the hidden associations that make the imagery so potent to the sophisticated Persian audience.

It has been well pointed out that almost any poem of Hafiz can be read on at least three levels of significance—at its face value as an expression of the gay and civilized life of medieval Shiraz, as a tribute to his princely patron and, lastly and above all, in terms of Sufi mystical theology.

The extraordinary popularity of his poetry in all Persian-speaking lands, however, is to be sought rather in his simple and often colloquial language, free from artificial virtuosity, and his unaffected use of homely images and proverbial expressions. Above all, his poetry is characterized by love of humanity, sympathy for the problems of ordinary men, contempt for hypocrisy and mediocrity and an ability to universalize everyday experience and to relate it to the mystic's unending search for the reality of God. It is for these qualities that Hafiz' poems are sung even by the Persian villager. His wide appeal in the west is indicated by the fact that apart from several complete translations of his works, numerous translators (including 30 in English and German and English) published translations of selections of his poems.

The best edition of the Persian text of the poems is by Mohammed Qazvini and Qasem Ghani (1941); there are English translations by H. Wilberforce Clarke, Hafiz Shirazi. The Divan . . . (1891), and by John Payne, The Poems of Shemseddin Mohammed Hafiz of Shiraz (1901). English translations of selected poems include those by Sir William Jones, with introductory notes, in Grammar of the Persian Language (1771); by Gertrude L. Bell, Poems from the Divan of Hafiz, 2nd ed. (1928); by A. J. Arberry, Fifty Poems of Hafiz (1947), which includes many samples of earlier translations; and by Peter Avery and John Heath-Stubbs, Hafiz of Shiraz, Thirty Poems (1952).

BIBLIOGRAPHY.—E. G. Browne, A Literary History of Persia, vol. iii, pp. 271-319 (1928); K. Süssheim in Encyclopaedia of Islam, vol. ii, pp. 210-212 (1927); M. Farzaad, Haafez and his Poems (1949); H. R. Roemer, Probleme der Hafizforschung (1951).
(L. P. E.-S.)

HAFIZ IBRAHIM, MOHAMMED (1872-1932), Egyptian poet known as the "poet of the Nile," was born at Dayrut, the son of an irrigation engineer. After serving first as a court pleader and later as a lieutenant in the Egyptian army Hafiz Ibrahim retired on a small pension in 1901. The next ten years formed his most creative period, during which he wrote his well-known odes denouncing imperialism and his nationalistic poems. His superb skill as a reciter of poetry won him a prominent place in the society and in 1911 he became director of literature in the national library at Cairo. He held this post until 1931, but these years were unaccountably unproductive of literary work. He died in Cairo on July 21, 1932.

The political poems have nothing profound to recommend them. Hafiz' real talent may well have been in prose as can be seen from his unfinished works Al Bu'asa and Layali Satih. His collected poems were edited by Ahmad Amin et al., two volumes, 2nd ed. (1939).
(A. EL-T.)

HAFNIUM, a metallic element that was a laboratory curiosity for many years, became an important material of construction for certain nuclear power reactors in the early 1950s. Here its particular virtues of moderate strength, excellent corrosion resistance and high neutron absorption capacity make it an excellent regulator to control the rate of burn-up of atomic fuel (see Use and Production, below).

Hafnium is a metal having the symbol Hf. It is a higher homologue of zirconium, its atomic number being 72 and its atomic weight 178.49. Hafnium has six stable isotopes with the mass numbers 174, 176, 177, 178, 179 and 180, the last-named isotope being the most abundant (abundance 35%). The arrangement of electrons in the outer levels (O and P) and sublevels is: $5s^2, 5p^6, 5d^2, 6s^2$.

DISCOVERY AND OCCURRENCE

The element was discovered by D. Coster and G. C. de Hevesy in 1923 and was named hafnium, the Latin name of Copenhagen, where the discovery was made (earlier G. Urbain and A. Dauvillier had given the name celtium to the element of atomic number 72, for which Urbain obtained some evidence from X-ray spectra in 1911). The missing element 72 had been considered to be a member of the rare-earth group, but Niels Bohr, in putting forward his views on the electronic arrangement in the atom (q.v.), reached the conclusion that the number of rare-earth elements, including cerium, could not exceed 14. Cerium having the atomic number 58, the last rare-earth element must have the atomic number 71 and, correspondingly, element 72 must belong to the titanium group, IVa in the periodic system, which includes zirconium, and should have properties resembling the latter rather than the rare earths.

This conclusion induced Coster and De Hevesy to search for the missing element in zirconium minerals. The investigation of the X-ray spectra emitted by samples of Norwegian and Greenland zircons revealed the presence of element 72.

Later investigations showed the presence of hafnium in each zirconium mineral and in every commercial zirconium preparation; in no other case is the "camouflage" phenomenon more pronounced. The lowest hafnium content is shown by the zircons of Brazil. Zirconium/hafnium ratios up to 700:1 are found there. In the products of siliceous residual crystallization, on the other hand, there is sometimes a very appreciable decrease in the above ratio.

Altered zircons like some alvites and cyrtolites, products of residual crystallization, show an atomic ratio even as low as 6:1 (the $ZrO_2 + HfO_2$ content of such minerals amounting to about 50%). The highest hafnium content (17% HfO_2) was found in cyrtolite from Rockport, Mass. Hafnium-bearing zirconium minerals are found in beach sands and river gravels along with monazite, rutile, etc. Commercial sources exist in the United

HAFNIUM

States (principally Florida), Australia, Brazil, western Africa and India. The share of hafnium in building up the earth's crust is about $\frac{1}{180,000}$. The presence of hafnium vapour in the solar atmosphere has been ascertained.

USE AND PRODUCTION

Nuclear Energy Regulator.—An atomic bomb is simply an uncontrolled reactor while a power producing reactor, in its simplest sense, is a slow burning atomic bomb. In the construction of nuclear reactors it is important that a material of low neutron absorption capacity be used as a protective material for the atomic fuels because neutrons are the "bullets" that make possible splitting of the atom. Zirconium, with a specific absorption of 0.18 barns, is almost an ideal cladding material for reactors using thermal neutrons (it must be emphasized in this application that the absorption figures are for thermal neutrons, i.e. the lowest speed neutrons used in nuclear energy work). Conversely, a material of high neutron absorption capacity is needed to regulate the rate of burn-up of atomic fuel.

Hafnium with a specific absorption of 105 barns makes an excellent throttle or regulator; by raising or lowering the control rods of hafnium metal properly inserted in a nuclear pile, the neutron density which controls the atomic reaction can be exactly controlled. For such special purposes, the cost of $75 a pound for sponge hafnium can be tolerated.

Separation From Zirconium.—As noted at the Geneva conference on peaceful uses of atomic energy in 1955, the separation of hafnium from zirconium can be accomplished in five different ways: (1) fractional crystallization; (2) selective extraction; (3) ion exchange; (4) fractional precipitation; and (5) disproportionation or fractional distillation.

The first hafnium salts in the late 1920s and early 1930s were prepared by fractional crystallization. In this method the difference in solubility of, say, the phosphate or fluoride salts is used to precipitate a less soluble from a more soluble salt. The method is laborious and in general does not lend itself to modern continuous production procedures. Selective extraction, which involves the preferential solubility of hafnium or zirconium in an organic liquid, has been the preferred commercial separation method. The two best known processes are the thiocyanate-isobutyl ketone and the tributyl phosphate-nitric acid separation systems. In either case a hafnium hydroxide is obtained which is calcined to produce pure hafnium oxide.

Production.—The commercial production of hafnium metal is accomplished by the use of both the Kroll and De Boer-Van Arkel processes. The Kroll process, developed by William J. Kroll for the production of ductile titanium, consists essentially of the reduction of titanium tetrachloride by molten magnesium under an inert atmosphere of helium or argon to produce titanium metal and magnesium chloride; the resultant magnesium chloride can be melted and distilled to leave behind the pure metal. The process can be used with hafnium tetrachloride: the conversion of hafnium oxide obtained by separation, as explained above, to hafnium tetrachloride can be accomplished in two ways: (1) by heating with carbon at a temperature above 800° C. the hafnium oxide can be made into hafnium carbide which is then chlorinated in a simple vertical shaft furnace to produce hafnium tetrachloride and carbon monoxide; or (2) the hafnium oxide can be briquetted with a sugar solution and lamp black and chlorinated directly at temperatures above 700° C. to produce hafnium tetrachloride. The latter method is preferred commercially. Hafnium chloride is a white solid that sublimes at 320°–330°. Before reduction, hafnyl chloride (HfOCl$_2$) must be removed from the chloride since it contains oxygen. This is performed by heating under helium and partial vacuum at temperatures up to 200° C. After the chloride purification, the material is transferred to another furnace in the bottom of which is a container holding the calculated amount of magnesium required to accomplish the reduction $HfCl_4 + 2Mg \rightarrow Hf + 2MgCl_2$ plus 40% excess. After evacuating the reduction furnace and backfilling with helium, the magnesium is melted and the chloride of hafnium is heated to a temperature above 350° C. to force it to sublime. As it passes over the molten

magnesium surface it is reduced to hafnium metal which settles to the bottom of the pot and the resultant magnesium chloride remains as an intermediate layer in the pot. At the end of the reduction stage, the material is allowed to cool and is then removed to a second furnace where the pot is placed upside down in the top of a vertical furnace and heated under vacuum to a temperature of about 900° C. The magnesium chloride melts and is collected in a suitable container in the lower portion of the furnace. Residual magnesium and magnesium chloride in the final stages are removed by so-called vacuum distillation. The resulting sponge metal is cleaned of surface contamination or residues and then further purified by the iodide purification process.

Due to its higher atomic weight hafnium does not have the same tolerance for a given amount of oxygen as does titanium and zirconium. Consequently, the Kroll process sponge hafnium, which contains 1,000 to 1,500 p.p.m. (0.01% = 100 p.p.m.) oxygen must be purified by the iodide (De Boer—Van Arkel) process to reduce this level to 200 to 500 p.p.m. to obtain ductile hafnium metal.

The purified bars of hafnium must be melted under special conditions to avoid contamination. The molten metal reacts with virtually every refractory container known to man as well as with oxygen and nitrogen of the atmosphere. The only satisfactory method is that of consumable electrode arc melting in a water-cooled copper crucible under an inert gas cover. If necessary, alloying elements can be added during the course of melting. The resulting ingot freezes at the copper wall without sticking or contamination.

Once melted, the dense metal offers less surface for oxidation and can be heated for forming purposes to temperatures of the order of 1,000° C. It is then shaped by standard metallurgical methods of forging, rolling and welding to produce control rod material for nuclear reactors. Several tons of hafnium are used each year for this purpose. (E. T. H.)

PHYSICAL AND CHEMICAL PROPERTIES

In the laboratory the reduction of K$_2$HfF$_6$ with potassium, that of hafnium tetrachloride with sodium or of zirconium oxide with calcium and sodium leads to the formation of hafnium powder. Hafnium metal, even ductile single crystals, may be prepared by reducing hafnium tetraiodide, prepared from hafnium powder and iodine, on glowing tungsten wire. Physical constants of hafnium and zirconium metals are seen in Table I.

TABLE I.—*Some Physical Constants of Hafnium and Zirconium Metals*

Properties	Hafnium	Zirconium
Density (g./ml.)	13.31	6.52
Atomic volume (ml.)	13.42	13.97
Electrical resistance at 0° C., $\rho \times 10^4$ (in ohm cm.)	0.30	0.41
Temperature coefficient of the resistance $\rho \times 10^2$	0.44	0.44
Temperature of the maximum resistance (° K.)*	1,775	1,150
Temperature of the minimum resistance (° K.)*	1,900	1,430
Maximum resistance, $\rho \times 10^4$ (in ohm cm.)	1.75	1.44
Minimum resistance, $\rho \times 10^4$ (in ohm cm.)	1.62	1.26
Melting point (° K.)*	2,500	2,130
Work necessary to release the electrons: above the transition point (in ev)	3.53	4.13
below the transition point (in ev)	3.20	....

*Kelvin, or absolute temperature ($qx.$), scale.

The structure of hafnium, like that of zirconium, is hexagonal, the value of a being 3.223, and $c = 5.123$, the log of vapour pressure is determined by

$$\log \rho = \frac{-30\,200}{T} + 9.46$$

Hafnium is not superconductive at 1.35° K. on the absolute temperature scale; between 4.12° K. and 1.35° K. the resistance does not change and is 0.0947 of the resistance at 0° C. Hafnium attains its maximum resistance (1.75×10^{-4} ohm) at 1,775° K., and its minimum (1.62×10^{-4} ohm) at 1,900° K. The resistance (maximum and minimum) of hafnium indicates the existence of allotropic modifications which unfits this metal for use in lamps and valves.

Hafnium was first isolated by fractional crystallization of the hexafluoride, the hafnium concentrating in the mother liquor. Commercial hafnium compounds, available previous to World War II, were prepared by this method. Another method is based on the fractional precipitation of complex phosphates or fractional precipitation of the phosphates from concentrated sulfuric acid. A further method of isolation is the crystallization of the oxychloride from about 10 N hydrochloric acid. Separation of zirconium and hafnium as negative fluo-ions has been obtained by using anion exchange resins, or as perchlorate applying a cation exchanger. Hafnium in zirconium may be reduced to less than 0.1% by passing a solution of the chlorides in methanol through a silica gel column.

The ions of hafnium are tetravalent; in many compounds the hafnyl (HfO^{2+}) ion is present. Prolonged ignition of sulfate and oxychloride leads to the formation of a monoclinic modification of the oxide, while by heating the hydroxide to about 400° C. a tetragonal modification (mol. vol. = 20.10, density = 6.13, melting point = 2,812° C.) is obtained. When ignited above 1,000° C., a third modification of the oxide can be obtained, this time in the cubic system. The molecular volumes of zirconium oxide and hafnium oxide of tetragonal type are identical within 0.5% and the molecular volumes of the monoclinic modifications of the two oxides differ by less than 0.8%. These data illustrate the very close resemblance between the hafnium and the zirconium.

Atoms of different nuclear charges show practically the same behaviour provided the quantum numbers of the valency electrons differ sufficiently to compensate exactly the effect of the difference in the nuclear charge. Hafnium and zirconium are examples of such atoms, the compensation of the effect of the difference in the nuclear charge being due to the appearance of the 14 rare-earth elements. Without the existence of these elements, the hafnium ion would show the properties of the ceric ion, which is the pseudo homologue of the zirconium ion.

The diamagnetic susceptibility of the oxide is 0.110×10^{-6}. Hafnium peroxide, which has the formula $Hf(OOH)(OH)_3$, is scarcely soluble in ice-cold alkaline hydrogen peroxide. The ratio of oxide: active oxygen: water is 1:1:2. The melting point of hafnium carbide (HfC) is 4,160° K.; the specific resistance of HfC ($W_{18}. \times 10^{-4}$) is 1.09. The mixture of four molecules of hafnium carbide and one molecule of hafnium carbide was found to melt at 4,215° K. No higher melting point is known for any substance. The melting point of hafnium boride was found to be 3.335° K. Hafnium nitride has been prepared from a mixture of hafnium tetrachloride, nitrogen and hydrogen. When a glowing filament was introduced into this mixture hafnium nitride formed in the vicinity of the filament and was deposited thereon. The bromide was prepared in a similar manner, substituting boron tribromide for the mixture of nitrogen and hydrogen. The crystal structure of

TABLE II.—*Solubility of Hafnium and Zirconium Fluorides at 20° C.*

Compound	Solvent	Solubility (mol. per litre)
$(NH_4)_2ZrF_6$	Water	1.050
$(NH_4)_2HfF_6$	Water	1.425
$(NH_4)_3ZrF_7$	Water	0.551
$(NH_4)_3HfF_7$	Water	0.558

hexafluoride is similar to that of K_2PtCl_6; that of the heptasalts, such as $(NH_4)_3HfF_7$, is regular; its molecular volume is 125.7. The solubility of the hafnium and zirconium fluorides is seen in Table II.

The refractive indexes of the corresponding zirconium and hafnium salts show only slight differences, as may be seen from Table III.

Hafnium tetrachloride is prepared through the action of chlorine on a mixture of hafnium oxide and charcoal. Above 200° C. the tetrachloride sublimes. The tetrachloride hydrolyses immedi-

TABLE III.—*Refractive Indexes of Hafnium and Zirconium Fluorides*

		n	Δn
(1)	K_2ZrF_6, monoclinic twins n (max.)—1.466; n (min.)—1.455		
	K_2HfF_6, monoclinic twins n (max.)—1.461; n (min.)—1.449		
(2)	K_3ZrF_7, regular octahedron	1.408	0.005
	K_3HfF_7, regular octahedron	1.403	
(3)	$(NH_4)_2ZrF_7$, regular octahedron	1.433	0.007
	$(NH_4)_3HfF_7$, regular octahedron	1.426	

ately when coming in contact with water, leading to the formation of the fairly stable $HfO(4H_2O)^{2+}$. Hafnium oxychloride crystallizes in tetragonal needlelike crystals. The refractive index of the needlelike crystals of $HfOCl_2,8H_2O$ is $n(\omega) = 1.557$; $n(\epsilon) = 1.543$. With increasing hydrochloric acid concentration the solubility of the oxychloride first decreases and then increases after a concentration of eight mols per litre is reached. Hafnium tetrachloride prepared through the action of bromine vapour on a mixture of hafnium oxide and sugar charcoal was used in the determination of the atomic weight of hafnium. The solubility of hafnium oxybromide decreases with increasing hydrobromic acid concentration. The heat of decomposition of hafnium sulfate is 110 cal. per mol. Hafnium phosphate $HfO(H_2PO_4)_2$ is the phosphate of lowest solubility known. Solubility figures are given in Table IV.

TABLE IV.—*Solubilities of Zirconium and Hafnium Phosphates*

Concentration of HCl (N)	Weight of residue ignited per 100 cu.cm. of solution (gram)	$M^{IV}O(H_2PO_4)_2$ per litre of solution (mol)
	Zirconium phosphate	
10.00	.0033	0.00023
6.01	.0061	.00012
	Hafnium phosphate	
10.48	.0046	0.00013
10.21	.0043	.00012
5.94	.0031	.0009

Hafnium acetylacetonate $[Hf(C_6H_7O_2)_4,10H_2O]$ crystallizes in strongly birefringent monoclinic crystals. The density of the compound is 1.679; its melting point, 194° C. In a vacuum of 0.001 mm. a slight sublimation is observed at 82° C. One litre of ethylene bromide dissolves at 25° C. 0.620 mol of the salt. Hafnium can best be estimated and determined by X-ray spectroscopy. Optical spectroscopy is also applied in the estimation of hafnium in the arc spectrum; the strongest persistent Hf I line has the wave length of 4093.17 Å (Å = angstrom = 10^{-8} cm.); and the strongest Hf II line, 3399.80 Å (4093.17 Å, for ionized atoms). The determination of the density of the zirconium oxide-hafnium oxide mixture is a suitable method to determine the hafnium content of zirconium. Denoting the density of the mixed crystal by d, the atomic ratio is

$$\frac{HfO_2}{ZrO_2} = \frac{d - 5.73}{9.74 - d}$$

A pure or very concentrated hafnium preparation shows a slightly different behaviour toward rufigallic acid, the colouring being more quickly obtained in the presence of hafnium. The absence of the formation of $Hf_2O_6SO_4,8H_2O$ when hydrogen peroxide is added to an acid hafnium solution, in contrast with the formation of a corresponding zirconium compound, can also be used to distinguish between a pure or concentrated hafnium and a zirconium preparation.

BIBLIOGRAPHY.—G. C. de Hevesy, *Recherches sur les propriétés du hafnium* (1925); D. R. Martin and P. J. Pizzolato, "Hafnium," *Chemical Analysis by X-rays and Its Applications Handbook*, ed. by C. A. Hampel, 2nd ed. (1961); U.S. Bureau of Mines, *Minerals Yearbook*, "Zirconium and Hafnium" chapter (annual).

(G. C. DE H.)

HAFSIDS, an eastern Berber dynasty (13th-16th century A.D.) founded by Abu Zakariyya, the Almohad governor of Afrikiya (Tunisia), who declared himself independent c. 1229. Al-Mustansir (caliph from 1253) raised the prestige of the kingdom to its highest point. Further, he came to terms with the Christian kingdoms and emerged unscathed from St. Louis's crusade. A period of internal dissension followed (1277–1318), during which time Constantine rose in rebellion (1284–85). On the death of Abu 'Asida (reigned 1295–1309) the amir of Bejaïa, Abu'l Baqa, restored the unity of Hafsid rule, but he was deposed (1311) by the usurper Ibn al-Lihyani. Abu Yahya Abu Bakr, amir of Bejaïa, again restored Hafsid unity in 1318; he quelled many rebellions, entrusted the government of the provinces to his sons, defeated the Arabs and reduced their factiousness thanks partly to the all-powerful chamberlain Ibn Tafragin. The Marinid Abu'l Hasan conquered Tunisia (1347) but was later defeated by the Arabs and the Hafsid dynasty was restored.

In the reign of Abu Ishaq Abu Inan Faris achieved a second lustre of al-Mustansir's era. He pacified the country and repulsed a Franco-Genoese expedition against Mahdia (1390), thus increasing the insolence of the Hafsid corsairs. Abu Faris (1394–1434) completed his father's work. He conquered Tlemçen and repulsed a Christian force at Djerba. Under Othman (1435–88), worthy successor of Abu Faris, Hafsid power retained its vigour despite Abu'l Hasan's rebellion (1435–52) and other troubles, but after Othman's reign dynastic struggles heralded the decline of Hafsid power. The country fell again into Arab hands and was split up. Later the Spaniards established themselves on the coast. Khair ud-din (Barbarossa), founder of the regency of Algiers, seized Tunis in 1534 but it was immediately returned to the Hafsids by the emperor Charles V. Finally a struggle for control between Spanish and Turkish forces ended with the conquest of Tunisia by the Turks. Tunisia was granted the status of a pashalik in 1574.

The features of the Hafsid period were: progress of arabization and of the Malikite school of Islamic law and mysticism; considerable intellectual and architectural activity (under Andalusian influence); successful piracy and the maintenance of relations with Christian Europe.

BIBLIOGRAPHY.—R. Brunschvig, *La Berbérie orientale sous les Hafsides . . .*, 2 vol. (1940–47); *Encyclopaedia of Islam*, "Hafsids," vol. iii, 2nd ed. (1965); C. A. Julien, *Histoire de l'Afrique du nord*, vol. ii, 2nd ed. (1952).

HAFSTEIN, HANNES THORDUR (1861–1922), Icelandic statesman and poet, was born at Mödhruvellir, on Dec. 4, 1861, the son of a provincial governor. After secondary studies in Reykjavik, he took his degree in law at Copenhagen university in 1886. A civil servant for 15 years, he was elected in 1901 to the Icelandic *althing* and soon became the leader of the Home Rule party. It was chiefly because of his influence that Denmark consented in 1903 to the transfer of the residency of the minister for Icelandic affairs from Copenhagen to Reykjavik. Appointed to this office on Jan. 31, 1904, Hafstein inaugurated a new era of practical reforms: Iceland's cable connections with abroad, internal telephone system and first reafforestation and land-reclamation acts, as well as much educational progress, were due to him. Dissatisfaction over the union with Denmark led to his defeat at the general election of 1908, whereupon he resigned; but after the victory of the Home Rule party in 1911, he again became minister in 1912. He had to resign again, however, in 1914, after new and fruitless efforts to achieve national unity over the union problem. Two years later, having lost his health, he retired from public service. He died in Reykjavik on Dec. 13, 1922.

Hafstein was also a skilful and fluent lyrical poet. Influenced by realism, he was a cofounder in 1882 of the periodical *Verdandi* ("The Future"). A collection of his poems appeared in 1893; an enlarged edition (1916) was reprinted in 1925 and 1951. (T. J.)

HAFTARAH (pl. Haftaroth), in synagogue services, selected readings from the Prophets, following the readings from the Pentateuch. The word means literally "conclusion," signifying the end of the scriptural lesson. The custom of adding a chapter from the Prophets to the pentateuchal reading long antedated the destruction of the Temple. It derived additional significance from the fact that it implied the sanctity of the prophetic books of the Old Testament, in opposition to the Samaritans who accepted only the five books of Moses. In the New Testament, the custom of preaching on the Haftarah is mentioned. (Acts xiii, 15. Luke iv, 17.)

In the modern synagogue, boys are usually trained to chant the Haftarah on the Sabbath of their Bar Mitzvah. In Conservative synagogues, in addition to the boys' rites, a similar rite for girls known as Bat Mitzvah has become widely accepted. (J. B. A.)

HAGEDORN, FRIEDRICH VON (1708–1754), German poet whose fables, love songs and anacreontics introduced a new lightness and grace into his country's poetry, was born on April 23, 1708, at Hamburg, where his father was Danish ambassador. In 1729 he became unpaid private secretary to the Danish ambassador in London. He returned to Hamburg in 1731, and in 1733 was appointed secretary to the *Englischer Hof*, an English trading company established there in the 13th century. He died at Hamburg, Oct. 28, 1754.

His first collection of verse appeared in 1729: most of the best of it—fables and tales in verse which stand comparison with those of his master La Fontaine both in neatness of form and lightness of touch, and love lyrics echoing Horace—appeared in *Versuch in poetischen Fabeln und Erzählungen* (1738) and *Oden und Lieder*, 3 vol. (1742–52). Hagedorn's works were edited by J. J. Eschenburg, 5 vol. (1800).

See H. Stierlung, *Leben und Bildnis Friedrichs von Hagedorn* (1911); K. Epting, *Der Stil in den lyrischen und didaktischen Gedichten Hagedorns* (1929).

HAGEN, JOHANNES GEORG (1847–1930), Austrian Jesuit priest and astronomer known especially for his work on variable stars, was born at Bregenz, on March 6, 1847. Educated at Feldkirch in Austria and at Münster and Bonn in Germany, he did some of his theological studies in England. He became director of Georgetown observatory, Washington. D.C., in 1888. In 1906 Pope Pius X appointed him director of the Vatican observatory. Hagen died in Rome on Sept. 6, 1930, while still engaged in research. His many publications include: *Atlas Stellarum Variabilium*, Ser. i–vii (1890–1908); *Astrographic Catalogue of the Vatican Zone*, 10 vol. (1914–28). (D. J. K. O.)

HAGEN, a town of Germany which after partition of the nation following World War II was in the *Land* (state) of North Rhine-Westphalia in the Federal Republic of Germany, on the eastern edge of the Ruhr district. Pop. (1969 est.) 200,266. To the south it is bordered by the Sauerland, a mountainous district of forests and lakes. Four rivers flow through the town, which is also situated at the junction of many railway routes and served by highways. The principal industry is light engineering. Others are engaged in manufacture of batteries, chains and accessories for bicycles, paper and confectionery, in die-casting, heavy engineering and brewing. Of the many historical buildings that were formerly to be seen, many were destroyed in World War II when Hagen, as one of the Ruhr manufacturing cities, was heavily bombed. The town has always been renowned for its schools. It has a large number of open spaces and parks and numerous children's playgrounds, as well as two indoor and two outdoor swimming pools. It also has a municipal theatre, an orchestra, an art museum and a local history museum.

The first mention of Hagen in historical documents occurs in the 8th century. Until the end of the middle ages its economy was based on agriculture, but then the population turned to iron ore mining and iron founding. Numerous and varied crafts also were established. In 1661 the Great Elector, Frederick William, settled cutlers and armourers from Solingen there, and about 30 years later a paper mill was erected, followed in 1712 by another. At the beginning of the 18th century cloth manufacturers, bleachers and dyers from Berg and Jülich established themselves in Hagen, and until the beginning of the 19th century they represented the principal industry. Hagen was granted civic rights in 1746.

During the Seven Years' War the town suffered severe damage, but by the end of the 18th century it was once more flourishing. After the Napoleonic Wars it was assigned to the newly formed province of Westphalia and an era of continuous industrial development and population expansion began. The reassignment of town boundaries before World War II in the Ruhr district led to the merger of Hagen, Haspe, Boele and Vorhalle. About half of Hagen was destroyed in World War II; the town centre in particular was completely demolished. Reconstruction began on a large scale after 1945.

(K. BA.)

HAGERSTOWN, a city of Maryland, U.S., and seat of Washington county, 70 mi. W.N.W. of Baltimore, is a commercial centre for the rich Cumberland valley between the Blue Ridge and Allegheny mountains.

Wide diversification of manufacturing includes pipe organs, aircraft, blast-cleaning and dust-collecting equipment, refrigerator doors, furniture, shoes and textiles.

Scotch-Irish and Germans moved into the valley from Pennsylvania in the 1730s. In 1762 Jonathan Hager, a German, laid out the town around his stone farmhouse, which is still standing near the centre of the city. He named it Elizabeth Town after his wife, but neighbours soon called the place Hagerstown, under which name it was incorporated in 1814. Ft. Frederick (1756) in the state park of the same name is nearby, and is said to be the only fort of the French and Indian War remaining with its original walls. In the 1820s the town became a major stopping point on the Cumberland road to the west, and subsequently it became a railroad centre. It changed hands several times during the American Civil War, and within 30 mi. are a number of battlefields including Harpers Ferry, Antietam and Gettysburg. About 5,000 Confederate soldiers are buried in the city.

Artisan labour, neat farmland and distinctive architecture give the area a typically German mellowness. Symbol for the city is "Little Heiskell," a tin soldier weathervane which has stood on successive town halls since 1769. The city has a fine library and an outstanding art museum. For comparative population figures see table in MARYLAND: *Population.*

(K. BA.)

HAGFISH, a blind, eel-shaped, parasitic marine fish, less than two feet long, that feeds on other living fishes by boring into the flesh and devouring everything but skin and bones. Also known as slime eels, the hagfishes constitute one suborder (Hyperotreti or Myxiniformes) of the primitive vertebrate group Cyclostomata. Best known genera are *Myxine* and *Eptatretus.* About 20 species inhabit the coastal regions, from shallow water to depths exceeding 1,000 fathoms. Hagfishes inflict considerable damage by feeding on fishes caught in nets, setlines or traps. When held in a container they excrete a surprisingly large quantity of mucus. *See* CYCLOSTOME.

(G. H. CR.)

HAGGADAH (pl. HAGGADOTH; Aramaic AGGADA; "narrative," "saying" or "legend"), a variety of rabbinical literature that is not legal (as *halaka*) but rather consists of legends, proverbs, allegorical exegetical writings, etc., all with didactic intent. In a restricted sense the word means also the history of the Exodus recited by the family at the Seder, the festal meal of the first night of Passover. *See* JEWISH HOLIDAYS: *Pesach;* MIDRASH; TALMUD: *The Talmud's: Character of the Talmud.*

(C. L. HS.)

HAGGAI, BOOK OF (in the Douai version of the Bible, PROPHECY OF AGGEUS), the tenth of the 12 prophetic books of the Old Testament known to Christians as the Minor Prophets. Its two chapters contain four oracles, delivered in Jerusalem between September and December in the second year of the reign of the Persian king Darius I (522–486 B.C.).

Historical Background.—In 537/536 B.C. the Jewish exiles in Babylon had been allowed to return home to Palestine and had begun to resume their religious life in the promised land. The rebuilding of the Temple, which was the centre of the Jewish faith, should have been the first call on their energies, as it had been the chief reason for their return. But the work did not progress until in 520 B.C., against the background of the rebellion and political upheaval at the beginning of Darius' reign (cf. Hag. ii, 7; "shake all nations" being interpreted as referring to this upheaval), the prophets Haggai and Zechariah got the people to make a new start.

It is uncertain whether the rebuilding of the Temple was carried out by the returned exiles from Babylon (cf. Ezra iii, 8) or by the remnant of the Jews left behind in Palestine during the Exile (cf. Hag. i, 12, 14; ii, 2, 4). The Babylonian connection of the name Zerubbabel (probably "shoot of Babylon," cf. Zech. vi, 12) suggests that the returned exiles gave the lead. It is also uncertain when the rebuilding actually began. Ezra i, 1 indicates that a start was made in 537/536 B.C. (that is, "the first year of Cyrus" as ruler of Babylon), whereas Hag. i, 2 in 520 B.C. implies that nothing has yet been done. Perhaps Ezra v, 16 is an attempt to harmonize the two traditions by introducing a 16-year delay after the beginning of the work.

Contents.—The first oracle (i, 1–11), delivered by Haggai on the first day of the sixth month (*i.e.,* Aug. 29, 520 B.C.), calls on a descendant of David (cf. I Chron. iii, 19), Zerubbabel, the governor of Judaea, and Joshua, the high priest, to rebuild the Temple. Economic distress, inflation, bad harvests and drought are God's judgments upon the people, who live in paneled (i, 4) dwellings themselves but do not rebuild the house of God. The guarantee of God's presence (i, 13) reinforces the people's wholehearted and immediate response to the prophet's appeal (i, 12–15). The second oracle (ii, 1–9), addressed to Zerubbabel, Joshua and "the remnant of the people" on the 21st day of the seventh month (*i.e.,* Oct. 18), reassures those disappointed at the contrast between the new Temple and the old. God promises that through an imminent cosmic upheaval "the treasures of all nations shall come in" (ii, 7) and "the latter splendor of this house shall be greater than the former" (ii, 9). The presence of God's glory will be a sign of the prosperity he will grant.

The third oracle (ii, 10–19), on the 24th of the ninth month (*i.e.,* Dec. 18/19), invokes a priestly ruling to prove that, whereas ritual uncleanness is contagious, holiness is not. This ruling is used to accuse "this people" of uncleanness. Economic distress, caused by bad harvests, is due to the failure to rebuild the Temple, but blessing is certain from the moment of its foundation.

The fourth oracle (ii, 20–23), addressed to Zerubbabel on the same day, reaffirms the impending upheaval, but guarantees Zerubbabel's unshakable position as God's "servant" and "signet."

Author.—Haggai is named in this book, always in the third person, as the mouthpiece of God's word. He is mentioned twice in Ezra (v, 1; vi, 14) along with his contemporary the prophet Zechariah. His name (Heb. Chaggai; Gr. Haggaios; Lat. Aggeus) means "festal," perhaps indicating that he was born on a festival. The question of ii, 3 would perhaps gain in point and pathos if the prophet had himself seen the Temple of Solomon before its destruction in 586 B.C. This, however, would make him very old at the time of rebuilding, and there is a patristic tradition that describes him as being young at that time. In view of the repetition in i, 1 and 3, the historical comment in i, 12–14, the misplaced date in i, 15, the lack of connection between ii, 10–14 and ii, 15–19, and the interpolated phrases or glosses in ii, 5, 17 and 18, as well as further additions in the Greek translation, it is unlikely that the prophet was himself responsible for the book.

Interpretation.—*Temple Rebuilding.*—The whole duty of Jewish man is to rebuild the Temple. Haggai's material and local preoccupation may seem an anticlimax after the spiritual universalism of Deutero-Isaiah, but how can the idea of the holy be realized on earth except through some particular embodiment of the holy? True sacramentalism is the only safeguard against materialism and pseudo-spirituality.

Economic Theory.—There is a direct connection between neglect of the Temple and economic distress. Haggai's objectively demonstrable interpretation of the connection may seem naive, but it makes clear that God is as much concerned with money and meteorology as with morals and religion.

Messianic Hope.—Universal convulsions will precede the peace of God. It is this teaching of Haggai (ii, 6, 21) that alone is quoted in the New Testament (Heb. xii, 26). Haggai's imminent apocalyptic expectations may seem crude, but at least they affirm God's triumph on this earth. Confidence in God, not optimism about man, is the only safeguard against ultimate defeatism. In the patristic period Hag. ii, 7 was taken as a prophecy of the coming of Christ, but by "treasures" (Vulgate *desideratus*) Haggai means Temple offerings. His messianic hopes were concentrated on the

Davidic Zerubbabel and were not fulfilled, but the dynastic messianism he preached—a safeguard against hopeless cynicism and sentimental utopianism—was not abolished but reinterpreted by David's "greater son," Jesus Christ. *See also* BIBLE.

BIBLIOGRAPHY.—Eng. trans. with commentary by George Adam Smith, *The Book of the Twelve Prophets*, new ed., vol. ii (1928); and by D. Winton Thomas and W. L. Sperry in G. A. Buttrick (ed.), *Interpreter's Bible*, vol. vi, pp. 1037–49 (1956); commentary by P. R. Ackroyd in *Peake's Commentary on the Bible* (1962). German trans. with commentary by K. Elliger, *Das alte Testament deutsch*, series 1, vol. xiv, 2nd ed. (1954). *See also* P. R. Ackroyd in *Journal of Jewish Studies*, vol. ii–iii (1951–52); vol. vii (1956), *Journal of Near Eastern Studies*, vol. xvii (1958); L. E. Browne, *Early Judaism* (1920); D. R. Jones, *Haggai, Zechariah and Malachi* (1962). (Jo. E. F.)

HAGGARD, SIR HENRY RIDER (1856–1925), English novelist and agriculturalist, best known for his imaginative adventure stories about Africa, was born at Bradenham, Norfolk, on June 22, 1856. He served on Sir Theophilus Shepstone's staff in South Africa and himself hoisted the flag at the annexation of the Transvaal in 1877. He then became master of the high court there. After the retrocession (1881) he returned to England, wrote a history of recent events in South Africa, *Cetywayo and His White Neighbours* (1882), and read for the bar. He published two novels, both unsuccessful, but captured the public—young and old—with his African adventure story, *King Solomon's Mines* (1885). He followed this with *She* (1887), and further stories of Africa, notably *Allan Quatermain* (1887), *Nada the Lily* (1892), *Queen Sheba's Ring* (1910), *Marie* (1912) and *The Ivory Child* (1916). He wrote memorably of ancient Egypt in *Cleopatra* (1889), *The World's Desire* (1890), *Morning Star* (1910) and *Queen of the Dawn* (1925); while *Lysbeth* (1901), *The Brethren* (1904) and *Red Eve* (1911) are outstanding historical romances. Haggard was also a practical farmer; he served on several government commissions concerning agriculture, and was knighted in 1912 (*Knight of the British Empire*, 1919) for these services. *A Farmer's Year* (1899) and *Rural England*, two volumes (1902), are works of permanent importance. He died in London on May 14, 1925.

BIBLIOGRAPHY.—Modern editions of his best-known stories in Dent's Library; Nelson's Classics, etc. *See* Haggard's autobiography, *The Days of My Life*, 2 vol. (1926); Lilias Rider Haggard, *The Cloak That I Left: a Biography* (1951); M. N. Cohen, *Rider Haggard: His Life and Work* (1960). *See also* J. E. Scott, *A Bibliography of the Works of Sir H. Rider Haggard* (1947). (R. L. GR.)

HAGGIS, a pudding made from the heart, lungs and liver of a sheep or other animal, finely minced with suet and oatmeal, seasoned with salt, pepper, onion, etc., and boiled in the animal's everted stomach. Though regarded since the mid-18th century as a distinctively Scottish dish, it was long popular in England, as English references to *hagges*, *haggus* and *hagas* in the early 15th century precede the earliest Scottish mention in the *Flyting of Dunbar and Kennedy* (1508). Its origin is, however, more ancient, for Marcus Apicius, Aristophanes and even Homer allude to dishes of similar composition. The derivation of the term is unknown.

Haggis is cheap, savoury and nourishing. In Scotland it was formerly considered a rustic dish and was so celebrated in Burns's lines *To a Haggis* (1786), but today it is popular with all classes, being served with some ceremony on national anniversaries. Instructions for making it are given by Hannah Glasse in *The Art of Cookery* (1796), Margaret Dods, *The Cook and Housewife's Manual* (1826), and Marian McNeill, *The Scots Kitchen* (1929). (JA. F.)

HAGIOLOGY (HAGIOGRAPHY), derived from the Greek *hagios* ("holy," "saint"), is the branch of historical studies dealing with the lives of the saints and the devotion paid to them throughout the centuries (*see* SAINT). The need for this specialized study was created by the special nature of the documents concerned: acts of the martyrs, lives of saintly monks, bishops, princes or virgins, and accounts of miracles taking place at their tombs or in connection with their relics, icons or statues. These form a type of literature in a class of its own, inspired as it is by keen admiration, by a desire to instruct the reader and often also by the intention of attracting pilgrims to the shrine of a miracle worker. These pious writings, although presenting great variety, yet share so many

common characteristics that they form a special branch of literature and should be studied as a group.

The importance of hagiology derives in the first place from the vital role which the veneration of the saints played throughout medieval civilization in both the east and the west. Second, this type of literature preserves an amazing amount of valuable information not only about religious beliefs and customs but also about daily life, institutions and happenings in periods for which other evidence is either imprecise or nonexistent.

The sources of hagiology fall into two groups, literary and liturgical. Beside documents concerned only with a single saint or with a number martyred on the same occasion, there are works devoted to a class of saints, such as Eusebius of Caesarea's account of the martyrs of Palestine (4th century), Theodoret's of the monks of Syria (5th century) and Gregory the Great's of the monks of Italy (6th century). Most lives of saints are anonymous, but some are attributed, rightly or wrongly, to the greatest names in Christian literature. When it became customary to read at divine office and in the refectory the lives of the principal saints on their feast days, these readings were arranged in calendrical order and collected in books called menologies in the east and passionals or legendaries in the west. As some lives were too long for reading aloud in this way they were abridged, as for example the lives in the imperial Byzantine menology (11th century) and in the Golden Legend of Jacobus de Voragine (13th century).

The liturgical sources of hagiology are those documents, chiefly calendars, which give information about devotion paid to the saints. Originally the festival of a saint was celebrated at his tomb on the anniversary of his death. Both these points, the place and the day, if attested in early documents, are generally sufficient to establish the legitimacy of the cult of a saint. In addition to local calendars, universal calendars, which have no strictly liturgical importance, soon began to appear.

Among these martyrologies, as they are called in the west, the chief are the Hieronymian (5th century), those of Bede (8th century), of Adon and of Usuard (9th century) and finally the Roman martyrology (end of the 16th century). The Eastern Church uses synaxaries rather than martyrologies; these contain a brief biography of each saint. (*See also* MARTYR.)

Modern critical hagiography began with Heribert Rosweyde and Jean Bolland. In addition to the Bollandists (*q.v.*), there are distinguished scholars of all nationalities in this field, from J. Mabillon (*q.v.*) and S. de Tillemont to Charles Plummer, P. Franchi de' Cavalieri, Wilhelm Levison, A. Papadopoulos-Kerameus and V. V. Latysev.

Hagiography has a threefold task: to collect all the material relevant to each particular saint, to edit the documents according to the best methods of textual criticism and to interpret the evidence by using literary, historical and any other pertinent criteria. For instance, some acts of the martyrs are contemporary factual accounts of their trials and deaths, some are in epic style, while some saints' lives are mainly fictional. The scholar must seek to discover the author's intentions and the sources at his disposal, and also to criticize his statements in the light of information gained from other disciplines such as archaeology and epigraphy and from secular and religious history.

BIBLIOGRAPHY.—For editions of martyrologies, etc., and collections of hagiographic material *see* the publications referred to in BOLLANDISTS. *See also* R. Aigrain, *L'Hagiographie: Ses sources, ses méthodes, son histoire* (1953); H. Quentin, *Les Martyrologes historiques* (1908); A. Ehrhard, *Überlieferung und Bestand der hagiographischen Literatur der griechischen Kirche* (1937–52). *See especially* the standard works by the Bollandist H. Delehaye, *Les Légendes hagiographiques*, 4th ed. (1955), *Les Passions des martyrs et les genres littéraires*, 2nd ed. (1966), *Les Origines du culte des martyrs*, 2nd ed. (1933), *Sanctus: Essai sur le culte des saints dans l'antiquité*, 2nd ed. (1954), *Cinq Leçons sur la méthode hagiographique* (1934). (F. HA.)

HAGIOSCOPE, in architecture, any opening, usually oblique, through the side or front walls of a church chancel to enable the congregation in transepts, chapels or other portions of the church, from which the altar would not otherwise be visible, to witness the elevation of the host during mass. Similar openings are sometimes furnished to allow an attendant to ring the sanctus bell at the proper time, or to permit someone in a vestry vision of the service so that he can notify the bell ringer. Hagioscopes or squints are more common in England than on the continent of Europe.

HAGUE, THE (Dutch, 's Gravenhage or Den Haag; Fr., La Haye), the seat of the government of the Netherlands and capital of the province of South Holland, lies on a plain about 3 km. (2 mi.) from the North sea. Pop. (1962 est.) 605,213, including Scheveningen, Loosduinen and Kijkduin.

The city's name recalls the hunting lodge of the counts of Holland which was located in a small woodland community called Haghe or "hedge" whence 's Gravenhage, meaning counts' hedge or wood. A town grew up around the castle, built by Count William II in 1248, which comprised the first of a group of buildings called the Binnenhof ("inner court"). Of the great halls around this courtyard, the Ridderzaal or Knight's hall (c. 1280) is now the throne room, and the northwestern and southeastern sides of the square are occupied by the estates-general and contain the Armistice or Truce hall, designed by Daniel Marot in 1697. The estates-general sat in The Hague from the establishment of the republic until the revolution in 1795, and again from 1815 until 1830, during which time they sat alternately in Brussels and The Hague. The Binnenhof is surrounded by 15th- to 18th-century buildings, and remnants of post 14th-century architecture are still to be found in the spacious layout of the Buitenhof ("outer court"), Plaats, Lange Vijverberg, Kneuterdijk and Lange Voorhout. In the 13th and 14th centuries a commercial district grew up around the central buildings, still to be seen in the shopping streets, such as Veenestraat, Spuistraat, Gravenstraat and Hoogstraat. At the beginning of the 17th century wide avenues and canals, lined by imposing aristocratic mansions, were constructed on the eastern side of this district (Tournooiveld, Korte Vijverberg, Korte Voorhout, Herengracht and Plein); to the southeast there grew up the Spui (craftsmen's district) and small inner harbours; and to the west the Prinsegracht (wealthy middle class) which was connected to the Westland by the Loosduinse canal. Under Prince Maurits a belt of canals was constructed from 1613 to 1619 as a fortification for the town. Within this belt there was ample space for the town development until long after the period of French domination.

In the first half of the 20th century a town grew up, characterized by broad avenues, parks and public gardens, in the surroundings of Nieuwe Parklaan, Laan van Meerdervoort, Weinarstraat, Bezuidenhoutseweg and Laan van N. O. Indië. In the north the Benoordenhout quarter was built, and near Wassenaar the fine residential park district of Marlot. In the southwest the Zuiderpark districts were laid out, containing many blocks of flats. Along the dunes in the west and near the Laan van Meerdervoort and Loosduinseweg small villas were built, and the Bomen and Bloemen district and the Fruit quarter (for middle-class people) were laid out. Between 1930 and 1940 radical improvements took place in Scheveningen. Old slums disappeared and were replaced by the new fishermen's district of Duindorp.

Surrounded as The Hague is by the North sea, the water works in the dunes, the adjoining municipalities and the nurseries of the horticultural area, called the Westland, the city had extended almost to its limits after World War II. The only possibility of expansion was toward the southeast, in the polders. Three feet below sea level, there arose a new town quarter for more than 100,000 inhabitants.

The Buitenhof is one of the centres of the town's activities, and contains several hotels and restaurants. The original entrance to it was the Gevangenpoort ("prisoners' gate"), which was built about 1400 and consists of a tower and a gate, now a museum. Just north of the Binnenhof lies the Hofvijver, a big rectangular sheet of water, with a small island in the centre. Close by is the Church of the Old Catholics (1722) with a beautiful baroque interior. The royal palace in the Noordeinde (now occupied by the International Institute for Social Studies) was first built in the 16th century. The other royal palace, Huis ten Bosch, dates from 1640 and was designed by Pieter Post and Jacob van Campen. It has a beautiful hall with a domed roof. Northeast of the Binnenhof is the Mauritshuis (1633–44), originally built for Prince Johan Maurits van Nassau, governor of Brazil, and now

the great Royal Museum of Painting of The Hague. Other artistic collections are contained in the Municipal museum, housing modern paintings, musical instruments, etc.; the Mesdag museum, with European paintings of the 19th century; the Bredius museum (1645), with old pictures of the Dutch school; and many others. The Royal library, designed by Marot in 1798, contains a collection of more than 1,000,000 volumes and manuscripts. The old Renaissance town hall of 1564 stands southwest of the Buitenhof. It was enlarged in 1733 and again during the 19th century, but as it eventually proved too small, a new one was completed in 1953.

Near the old town hall stands the Great Church (Grote Kerk) of St. James or Jacob (15th and 16th centuries), which has a hexagonal tower and a richly decorated late Gothic choir; the new spire, designed as a copy of an old one and completed in 1957, has the largest carillon in the Netherlands (51 bells). The Royal theatre, in the Korte Voorhout, with its elegant façade by Peter de Swart, was originally the Nassau-Weilburg palace. The Nieuwe Kerk (New church), built between 1649 and 1656, contains the tombs of the De Witt brothers, who were murdered in the city in 1672, and of the philosopher Spinoza. The Peace palace (1907–13) is the seat of the International Court of Justice and of the Permanent Court of Arbitration. The more striking modern buildings include the Shell building (1941), the KLM (Royal Dutch Airlines) building (1949) and the United States embassy (1959).

A considerable part of The Hague is composed of woods, public gardens, parks and recreation grounds, chief among which are Westdun park (617 ac.), Zuiderpark (210 ac.); Scheveningen woods (210 ac.) and Westbroek park (25 ac.) with an exhibition garden.

There is a variety of educational institutions including the International school, the American school, the Royal Conservatory of Music, the Academy of International Law and the Institute of Social Studies.

The city has rail connections with Amsterdam, Utrecht, Rotterdam and Paris, and there are also waterway communications with various parts of the Netherlands. The airfield is at Schiphol near Amsterdam. The main industries are metallurgy (electrical appliances, hardware, stoves, coachwork), building, and the manufacture of foodstuffs, clothing, luxury articles, chemicals, pottery and glass, and printing. The Hague is the headquarters of a large number of international firms, including more than 30 oil companies, and is a centre for international conferences (see HAGUE CONFERENCES).

Madurodam, Holland's miniature city, is a noted tourist attraction. Scheveningen, which is the Netherlands' principal herring

EIGHTEENTH-CENTURY PATRICIANS' HOUSES ALONG THE PRINCESS CANAL, THE HAGUE

harbour, is also an important seaside resort. At Loosduinen there are extensive horticultural grounds from which early fruit and vegetables are exported by air.

See Municipal Publications, *Enige grondslagen van de Stedebouwkundige ontwikkling van 's-Gravenhage* (1948); *The Hague, City in Expansion* (1957). (D. P. M.)

HAGUE CONFERENCES, the two international conferences held at The Hague in the Netherlands in 1899 and 1907, known also as the Hague Peace conferences. The first was called at the instance of Tsar Nicholas II of Russia, by a note of the Russian minister of foreign affairs, Count Mikhail N. Muraviev, under date of Jan. 11, 1899, addressed to the diplomatic representatives at St. Petersburg, in which the purpose of the conference was stated to be that of "a real and lasting peace and, above all, of limiting the progressive development of existing armaments," followed by details with respect to the regulation of specific instruments of warfare. Twenty-six states were represented at the conference, which sat from May 18 to July 29, 1899. Only two American states, the United States and Mexico, took part.

The conference failed to attain its chief objective of the limitation of armaments; the larger powers, particularly Germany, opposing any specific measures. Instead, two conventions dealing with the regulation of war were adopted, one concerning the laws and customs of war on land and a second adapting the principles of the Geneva convention of 1864 to maritime war (see GENEVA CONVENTIONS). Three declarations were adopted, one prohibiting the discharge of projectiles from balloons, a second prohibiting the use of asphyxiating gases and a third prohibiting the use of expanding bullets. More important, however, was the Convention for the Pacific Settlement of International Disputes creating the Hague Permanent Court of Arbitration, a list of judges from which the parties in controversy might select the members of an arbitral tribunal for their particular case. (*See* ARBITRATION, INTERNATIONAL.)

The conference of 1907, likewise called by the tsar after Pres. Theodore Roosevelt had first taken the initiative, was attended by representatives of 44 states and sat from June 15 to Oct. 18. Again the proposal of a limitation of armaments failed of acceptance. But two constructive steps were taken—the revision of the Convention for the Pacific Settlement of International Disputes and a new Convention Respecting the Limitation of the Employment of Force for the Recovery of Contract Debts. Eleven additional conventions were signed, two of them revising and renewing the conventions on the laws of war on land and the version of merchant ships into warships, the laying of automatic submarine contact mines, bombardment by naval forces in time of war, restrictions on the exercise of the right of capture in maritime war, the establishment of an international prize court and the rights and duties of neutral powers in maritime war. (*See* also CONTRABAND.) The conference renewed the declaration of 1899 prohibiting the discharge of projectiles and explosives from balloons; but the declarations of 1899 with respect to asphyxiating gases and expanding bullets were not renewed, the United States having opposed both declarations and Great Britain having signed them only on the eve of the conference.

The final act of the conference proclaimed the unanimity of the delegates in admitting the principle of compulsory arbitration and expressed a number of *voeux* (resolutions), the first of which declared the advisability of adopting the draft Convention for the Creation of a Judicial Arbitration Court and the last recommending the assembly of a third peace conference within another period corresponding to that between the first and second conferences. The other *voeux* dealt with topics that had not been included in the conventions, namely, relations between the inhabitants of the belligerent states and neutral countries, the position of foreigners in respect to military service and the future codification of the laws and customs of naval war.

The conference planned for 1915 failed to meet because of the outbreak of war in 1914, no provision having been made to meet emergencies. At the close of the war the League of Nations replaced the Hague conference system. In the light of history the Hague conferences failed because they accepted war as inevitable and merely sought to regulate it as a legal procedure. *See* WAR; AGGRESSION; INTERNATIONAL LAW, PUBLIC; *see* also references under "Hague Conferences" in the Index. (C. G. Fk.)

HAHN, OTTO (1879–1968), German chemist, who received the Nobel Prize in 1944 for splitting the uranium atom, was born March 8, 1879, in Frankfurt am Main, and studied at the universities of Marburg and Munich, receiving his doctorate at the former in 1901. For many years Hahn was the outstanding radiochemist in Germany. His early interest in this field brought him to Sir William Ramsay's laboratory in London in 1904–05, and in the following year to Lord Ernest Rutherford's institute in Montreal, Que. Upon his return to Germany he worked first at the chemistry laboratory of the University of Berlin, headed at that time by Emil Fischer, and from 1912 on as member and later (1928–44) as director of the Kaiser Wilhelm Institute for Chemistry in Berlin-Dahlem. Hahn's cooperation with Lise Meitner, the physics partner of this group, started in 1907 in Fischer's institute and lasted until 1938 when the Hitler regime forced her to leave the country. The highlights of Hahn's scientific career were the detection of radiothorium, mesothorium, and protactinium with Lise Meitner (1917) and finally uranium and thorium fission with Fritz Strassmann (1938). The latter discovery (*see* ATOMIC ENERGY) is the basis for all methods to tap atomic energy, including the development of the atomic bomb. Hahn had a foreboding that his discovery could be used for military purposes but, as his publications indicate, fervently hoped this would prove impossible. After World War II he became president of the Max Planck Gesellschaft in Göttingen, which took over the functions of the Kaiser Wilhelm Institute in West Germany.

In April 1957 he joined with 17 other West German nuclear physicists in stating that they would refuse to cooperate in any way in the development of atomic weapons, and in the same month supported Albert Schweitzer in urging that world opinion demand the ending of atomic bomb tests. In 1966 he was co-winner of the Enrico Fermi Award with Lise Meitner and Fritz Strassman. Hahn died in Göttingen on July 28, 1968.

Hahn's writings include: *Applied Radiochemistry* (1936); *Künstliche Atomumwandlungen und die Spaltung schwerer Kerne* (1944); *Die Kettenreaktion des Urans und ihre Bedeutung* (1948); *Die Nutzbarmachung der Energie der Atomkerne* (1950); *New Atoms* (1950); *Cobalt 60* (1955); *A Scientific Autobiography* (trans. 1967). (Js. F.; X.)

HAHN, REYNALDO (1875–1947), French composer of light operas and songs in the tradition of Offenbach and Messager. Born at Caracas, Venez. Aug. 9, 1875, he went to Paris when a child and studied at the Conservatoire under Massenet. In 1898 his *L'île du rêve* was given at the Opéra Comique, and from then until 1939 he produced many light operas, the best of which is *Ciboulette* (1923), ballets (notably *La Fête chez Thérèse*, 1910) and *Le Dieu bleu* (1912), and incidental music for plays by Edmond Rostand, Sacha Guitry and others. His songs include the *Chansons grises* and the *Chansons latines* and the well-known "Si mes vers avaient des ailes." He was also known as a conductor of the operas of Mozart and gave *Don Giovanni* at Salzburg. His piano suite, *Portraits de peintres*, was inspired by early poems of Marcel Proust who portrayed Hahn in his novel *Jean Santeuil*. He was music critic of *Le Figaro* from 1934 and was appointed director of the Paris Opéra in 1945. His work is melodious, usually slender, but gracefully written. With André Messager he was responsible during his day for the main developments in the French operetta which had been established by Offenbach. His memoirs are valuable sources for the musical and literary life of his time. He died in Paris, Jan. 28, 1947. (E. Lr.)

HAHNEMANN, (CHRISTIAN FRIEDRICH) SAMUEL (1755–1843), German physician, founder of homeopathy, was born at Meissen, Saxony, on April 10, 1755. He studied medicine at Leipzig and Vienna and settled in Leipzig in 1789. In the following year, while translating W. Cullen's *Materia medica* into German, he was struck by the fact that the symptoms produced by quinine on the healthy body were similar to those of the disordered states it was used to cure. This observation led him to assert the truth of the "law of similars," *similia similibus curantur*; i.e., diseases are cured (or should be treated) by those drugs which produce symptoms similar to them in the healthy. He promulgated his principle in a paper published in 1796, and four years later, convinced that drugs in much smaller doses than were generally employed effectually exerted their curative powers, he advanced his doctrine of their potentization of dynamization. His chief work, *Organon der rationellen Heilkunst* (1810), contains an exposition of his system, which he called homeopathy. His *Reine Arzneimittellehre* (6 vol., 1811) detailed the symptoms produced by "proving" a large number of drugs; i.e., by systematically administering them to healthy subjects. In 1821 the hostility of established interests, and especially of the apothecaries, forced him to leave Leipzig, and at the invitation of the grand duke of Anhalt-Köthen he went to live at Köthen. Fourteen years later he moved to Paris, where he practised until his death, on July 2, 1843. Statues were erected to his memory at Leipzig and at Köthen.

See T. Bradford, *Life and Letters of Dr. Samuel Hahnemann* (1912).

See also HOMEOPATHY.

HAHN-HAHN, IDA, COUNTESS VON (1805–1880), German writer of poetry, travel books and a large number of novels which incorporate many of her own experiences in sentimental plots written in an artificial, aristocratic style. She was born at Tressow, Mecklenburg-Schwerin, on June 22, 1805, daughter of the theatrical producer Count Karl Friedrich von Hahn (1782–1857). An unhappy marriage to her cousin F. von Hahn-Basedow ended in divorce, and she also had several unsuccessful friendships. She was converted to Roman Catholicism in 1850 and thereafter produced pious stories and poems. *Aus der Gesellschaft* (8 volumes, 1835–46) was the title given to a collection of her novels. Her style was parodied by her rival for public acclaim, Fanny Lewald (q.v.), in *Diogena* (1847). She published a justification of her conversion in *Von Babylon nach Jerusalem* (1851). Her collected works appeared in two series, *Gesamtausgabe der protestantischen Zeit* (21 vol., 1851) and *Gesammelte Werke der katholischen Zeit* (45 vol., 1902–05). Her best novels are *Gräfin Faustine* (1841) and *Sibylle* (1846). She died at Mainz on Jan. 12, 1880.

See R. M. Meyer in *Allgemeine Deutsche Biographie*, vol. 49 (1904). (W. D. Wi.)

HAI BEN SHERIRA (939–1038), last of the outstanding Babylonian *geonim* (see GAON), under whose presidency the Pumbeditha academy reached its greatest heights. Though the office of *gaon* was not necessarily hereditary, Hai was the fourth in a direct line, in a family which traced its origin to the Davidic dynasty, to occupy the gaonate of Pumbeditha, situated in Baghdad since the late 9th century. Hai first assisted his father, Sherira ben Hanina, in teaching and later as chief of court of the academy. A false accusation caused the imprisonment of father and son (997), but when they were proved innocent and freed, Hai was appointed *gaon* (998) during the lifetime of his father.

Close to 1,000 *responsa* (advice or decisions on points in the Talmud) written by Hai, equaling the number of extant *responsa* written by all other *geonim*, have come down to modern times. He steered a middle course between the rationalistic and fundamentalist philosophical schools, explaining all anthropomorphisms as metaphors and upholding free will against predetermination. He couched his *responsa* in the same languages (Hebrew, Aramaic or Arabic) in which the questions were written. Hai died at the age of 99 on the eve of the last day of Passover 1038, and was eulogized by the famous Judaeo-Spanish poets Solomon ibn Gabirol and Samuel ha-Nagid as one who left no children but countless disciples in all countries of the world.
(S. K. M.)

HAIDA, the Indians of Queen Charlotte Islands, B.C., and the southern half of Prince of Wales Island, Alaska. The Alaskan branch, called Kaigani, occupy former Tlingit territory, having moved north from Langara Island in the 18th century. Following the earliest visits by European and American trading ships in the 1770s and '80s, the number of Haida decreased sharply. A Hudson's Bay company census about 1841 listed 6,600 Haida in 13 Queen Charlotte villages and 1,700 in 6 Kaigani villages. By 1880 they had declined to 900 and 800 respectively, leaving most villages abandoned. The modern Haida occupy three villages—Skidegate Mission, Masset and Hydaburg (Kaigani); in the 1960s about 210 were reported from Alaska and about 650 from Canada.

Notwithstanding popular speculations of a supposed Polynesian or other exotic origin, the Haida are typical North Pacific Coast Indians in physical type, speech and culture. Of medium height compared with other American Indians, they and their neighbours also tend to have lighter skins, more luxuriant hair, heavier trunks, larger and wider faces and heads. Their language is distantly related to Tlingit, spoken on the coast to the north, and to the Athapaskan family, spoken over a large part of North America (see CENTRAL AND NORTH AMERICAN LANGUAGES). With their mainland neighbours the Tlingit, Tsimshian and northern Kwakiutl, the Haida shared the highest attainments of the Northwest Coast culture area. Founded on a rich, sea-oriented fishing and hunting economy and a skilful woodworking technology, their culture produced uniqueness in social organization, ceremonialism and art.

Territories, houses and the crests displayed on totem poles were owned by maternal lineages. There were two major divisions, Ravens and Eagles, within which intermarriage was prohibited. Their arts and crafts have brought the Haida their widest acclaim. Even in precontact times their decorated wooden boxes and seagoing dugout canoes were sought in trade by other tribes, and their masks and ceremonial equipment, costumes, household furnishings and other products are still prized by museums. The totem poles in their old villages were more elaborate and numerous than those of any other tribe. Shortly after 1800 they began to carve a local argillite or "black slate" into pipes, dishes, figures and model totem poles. This new art form found a ready market, and is still being produced. See also INDIANS, NORTHWEST COAST.

BIBLIOGRAPHY.—J. R. Swanton, *Contributions to the Ethnology of the Haida*, American Museum of Natural History Memoirs, vol. 8 (1910); G. P. Murdock, *Rank and Potlatch Among the Haida*, Yale University Publications in Anthropology, vol. 13 (1936); P. Drucker, *Indians of the Northwest Coast* (1955). (W. Du.)

HAIDAR (HYDER) ALI (c. 1722–1782), Indian ruler and military commander who played a redoubtable part in the wars in southern India in the 18th century. A Muslim soldier-adventurer, he was the great-grandson of a fakir who came from the Punjab to Gulbarga in the Deccan, and the second son of a naik (chief constable) at Budikota, near Kolar in Mysore. His elder brother rose to command a brigade in the Mysore army while Haidar acquired a useful familiarity with the tactics of the French under Joseph Dupleix. He is said to have induced his brother to employ a Parsee to purchase artillery and small arms from the Bombay government and to enroll about 30 European sailors as gunners and is thus credited with having been "the first Indian who formed a corps of sepoys armed with firelocks and bayonets, and who had a train of artillery served by Europeans."

After the siege of Devanhalli (1749), Haidar received an independent command in Mysore; within the next 12 years his energy and ability had made him master of minister and raja alike. In everything but in name he was ruler of the kingdom. In 1763 the conquest of Kanara gave him the most splendid capital in India, under his own name, thenceforth changed from Haidar Naik to Haidar Ali Khan Bahadur; and in 1765 he retrieved previous defeat by the Marathas by destroying the Nairs or military caste of the Malabar coast and by conquering Calicut (Kozhikode).

Haidar Ali now occupied the serious attention of the Madras government, which in 1766 agreed to furnish the nizam of the Deccan with troops to be used against the common foe. But a secret arrangement was agreed upon between the two Indian powers, the result of which was that Col. Joseph Smith's small force was met with a united army of 80,000 men and 100 guns. British dash and sepoy fidelity, however, prevailed, first in the battle of Chengam (Sept. 2, 1767) and again still more remarkably in that of Tiruvannamalai (Trinomalai).

On the loss of his recently made fleet and forts on the western coast, Haidar Ali offered peace overtures; on their rejection, bringing all his resources and strategy into play, he forced Smith to raise the siege of Bangalore and brought his army within five miles of Madras. The result was the treaty of April 1769, providing for the mutual restitution of all conquests and for mutual aid and alliance in defensive war; it was followed by a commercial treaty in 1770 with the authorities of Bombay. Under these arrangements Haidar Ali, when defeated by the Marathas in 1772, claimed British assistance, but in vain; this breach of faith aroused in him a desire for vengeance.

His time came when in 1778 the British, on the declaration of war with France, resolved to drive the French out of India. The capture of Mahé on the Malabar coast in 1779, followed by the annexation of lands belonging to a dependent of his own, gave him a pretext. Again master of all that the Marathas had taken from him, and with empire extended to the Krishna river, he descended through the passes of the Ghats amid burning villages, reaching Kancheepuram (Conjeeveram), only 45 mi. from Madras, unopposed. Not till the smoke was seen from St. Thomas' Mount, where Sir Hector Munro commanded 5,200 troops, was any movement made; then, however, the British general sought to join a smaller body under Col. William Baillie recalled from Guntur. The incapacity of the officers resulted in the destruction of Baillie's force of 2,800 (Sept. 10, 1780). Warren Hastings sent from Bengal Sir Eyre Coote, who, though repulsed at Chidambaram, defeated Haidar thrice successively in the battles of Porto Novo, Pollilur and Sholingarh, while his son Tipu (*see* Tipu Sultan) was forced to raise the siege of Wandiwash, and Vellore was provisioned. On the arrival of Lord Macartney as governor of Madras, the British fleet captured Negapatinam and forced Haidar Ali to confess that he could never ruin a power which had command of the sea. He had sent Tipu to the west coast, to seek the assistance of the French fleet, when his death took place at Chittoor on Dec. 7, 1782.

Bibliography.—L. B. Bowring, *Haidar Ali and Tipu Sultan* (1893). For the personal character and administration of Haidar Ali *see* the *History of Hydur Naik*, written by Mir Hussein Ali Khan Kirmani, trans. from the Persian by W. Miles and published by the Oriental Translation Fund (1842), and the curious work written by Maistre de la Tour, commandant of his artillery, *Histoire d'Ayder-Ali Khan* (1783). For the whole life and times *see* Mark Wilks, *Historical Sketches of the South of India,* 2 vol., 2nd ed. (1869); H. N. Pearson, *Memoirs of Schwartz* (1839); N. K. Sinha, *Haidar Ali* (1949).

HAIFA, the chief port of Israel and administrative headquarters of Haifa district, lies at the southern foot of Mt. Carmel at the southern end of the Bay of Acre and 55 mi. N.N.E. of Tel Aviv. Pop. (1961) 183,021. The Sycaminum of Byzantine times, during the crusades it was an important stronghold (Caiphas or Caiffa) assailed and destroyed by Saladin in 1191. It was captured by Napoleon in 1799 and by Ibrahim Pasha in 1839.

Modern Haifa has three main sections. The business and commercial quarters are by the harbour, the main street being Independence avenue (formerly Kingsway), on reclaimed land. The main shopping, administrative and residential quarter, Hadar Hacarmel ("the Grace of Carmel"), is on the lower slopes of Carmel and contains government and municipal offices, law courts, the museum of archaeology, and the original buildings of the Technion (Israel's Institute of Technology, founded 1924) with a secondary school. New buildings of the institute are northeast of the city, on a wooded ridge. New residential quarters are on the higher parts of Carmel, while on the slopes are a gilded and domed shrine and a building in classical Greek style, approached by a Persian garden, which are memorials to the founders of the Baha'i religious creed. Below them is the main avenue of the former German colony, occupied till World War II by a Württemberg religious sect who migrated to Palestine in the 1880s and were pioneers of scientific agriculture. The principal access to the top of Carmel is the United Nations avenue. On Carmel are Mother's park (Gan Haem), a nature reserve, and Panorama road commanding fine views of town and bay.

Haifa has good sea communications with Mediterranean countries. An underground funicular railway (1959) connects the port

with suburbs on Carmel. Haifa is the terminus of three railways: one, laid by the British along the coast in World War I, formerly connected with the Egyptian system; the second is a branch of the Hejaz railway, which formerly ran from Haifa to Damascus but is now used only for freight to Semakh station on the Sea of Galilee; the third is an extension of the coastal railway to the northern frontier at Nakura, which formerly connected with Beirut. An airfield is linked with Cyprus.

The principal industries are to the north of the town and include a steel mill, a superphosphate and chemical plant, a textile industry, the original cement factory of Palestine, the principal electric power station, and the oil refinery formerly worked by the Iraq Petroleum company. Israel's small navy is based on Haifa, and there is a fishing industry. The majority of the country's imports and exports pass through Haifa. A supplementary port for oil tankers is at the mouth of the Kishon river. Haifa has a university college attached academically to the Hebrew university of Jerusalem.   (No. B.)

HAIG, DOUGLAS HAIG, 1st Earl (1861–1928), British field marshal, commander in chief of the British forces in France during most of World War I, was born in Edinburgh on June 19, 1861. He was educated at Clifton college, Brasenose college, Oxford, and at the Royal Military academy, Sandhurst. Haig joined the 7th hussars in 1885 and served in the Nile campaign (1898) and in the South African War (1899–1902). After commanding the 17th lancers, he was made inspector general of cavalry in India (1903–06), becoming a major general in 1905. He served in the war office as director of military training (1906–09) and published *Cavalry Studies* in 1907. He was chief of the general staff in India (1909–12), became a lieutenant general in 1910 and took over the Aldershot command in 1912.

Haig led the I corps to France in 1914 and became commander of the 1st army early in 1915. During that year he fought the battles of Neuve Chapelle, Festubert and Loos. He succeeded Sir John French in command of the British expeditionary force in France in Dec. 1915. This command by then largely consisted of new armies which had to be trained and integrated with the territorial army and what remained of the regular army to form a coherent force. As Haig was constantly being pressed by the French to take over a larger sector of the Allied front, it was not easy to meet his requirements for training. The heavy battles of the Somme, fought in 1916 at the insistence of the French commander Gen. Joseph Joffre against Haig's better judgment, with insufficient artillery and ammunition, led, however, to great exhaustion of the German forces and contributed much to the relief of the French. But the heavy casualties alarmed both governments; controversy arose over the correctness of the strategy followed, which appeared to result in little territorial gain for disproportionate expenditure of lives. This strategy can now be seen in its proper perspective as having led to the weakening of the German army and to its eventual defeat in 1918. Reserved by nature, Haig was not the man to make optimistic promises for the future but rather to base his arguments on solid military grounds. The casualties of the battles in 1916 were therefore a factor in the political arrangements made between the British and French governments under which Gen. Robert Nivelle, the French army commander who had superseded Joffre, directed the operations of the British army in 1917.

Impetuous and overoptimistic, Nivelle issued instructions to Haig which did not inspire confidence. Subsequent events, in which the British army did better than the French, led to Nivelle's downfall and to the temporary enhancement of Haig's prestige. Gen. Henri Philippe Pétain succeeded to the French command and appealed to Haig to bear the brunt of the fighting while the French army was reorganized. The bitter fighting of Passchendaele in 1917. was the result. The French army was reorganized by October, but Passchendaele still went on. The French soon renewed their demands upon the British to take over more of their front.

Meanwhile Haig had been fortified by a letter from King George V at the close of 1916 announcing his promotion to field marshal. The former war minister, Lord Haldane, took the opportunity to tell him that he was almost the only British military leader with the power of thinking. A new supreme war council had been set up and met in Jan. 1918, and Haig eventually agreed to extend the British front southward. He had asked for reinforcements in expectation of an enemy attack, but these were denied him and in March the expected German offensive opened against the 5th army in the sector recently taken over from the French. As a result of Haig's representations, Ferdinand Foch was appointed generalissimo to direct the Allied armies. This arrangement, in which the British and French armies were separately under their own commanders, was quite different from the disastrous course imposed on Haig in 1917, when the British army was placed directly under French command. After fierce fighting, during which Haig issued his famous "backs to the wall" message, the German attack was held and then the two commanders, working in close harmony, began the series of assaults which led to the defeat of the Germans in 1918, in which the brunt of the fighting was borne by the British army.

Haig was a simple and humble man of great character: unshakable in purpose, farseeing and determined. He had under his command what was at that time the largest British army that had ever taken the field, with complicated problems of supply, organization and training. He had to deal with politicians, such as Lloyd George, who did not always support him, when they were not actually intriguing against him, nor did they try to understand his problems or his strategy. But even when they sought means to destroy him, he never threatened to resign: he viewed his duty as being to continue with his task until he was replaced. He had difficulties with the French, to whom he was always loyal in his pursuit of the ultimate aim of victory. He always had the trust of his men and the moral support of the king.

After the war, Haig devoted himself to the welfare of ex-servicemen and united various organizations into the British legion. He organized the collection of money for the benefit of ex-servicemen, and traveled throughout the British empire in his efforts to alleviate and improve their circumstances. He was given an earldom in 1919. He died in London on Jan. 29, 1928, and was buried in Dryburgh abbey. See also WORLD WARS: World War I.

BIBLIOGRAPHY.—Duff Cooper, Haig, 2 vol. (1935-36); Robert Blake (ed.), The Private Papers of Douglas Haig, 1914-1919 (1952). See also Sir F. Maurice, History of the War in South Africa, 1899-1902 (1906-10); J. H. Boraston (ed.), Sir Douglas Haig's Despatches, Dec. 1915-April 1919, 2 vol. (1919); G. A. B. Dewar and J. H. Boraston, Sir Douglas Haig's Command (1922); J. E. Edmonds, Military Operations, France and Belgium, 1914-15, 2nd ed. (1925). (R. G. TH.)

HA'IL (HAYIL), the capital town of Jabal Shammar in the northern Najd, Saudi Arabia, lies near the southern edge of Jabal Aja' on one of the main pilgrim routes from Iraq to Mecca, 3,170 ft. above sea level. It superseded the former capital, Fayd (50 mi. S.E.), about the mid-19th century, after the establishment of the dynasty of Ibn Rashid, who ruled the desert from the great clay castle of Barzán. The castle dominated the market place and beside it was the Great Mosque. Under the first and fourth amirs, Abdullah and Mohammad, Ha'il rivaled Riyadh (q.v.), the Saudi capital, in influence and importance, being in direct contact with the Turkish government and controlling the principal pilgrim route from the east.

For a decade (1891-1902) it was the undisputed capital of all desert Arabia, but the notorious family feuds of the Ibn Rashid dynasty, and its constant wars with its neighbours, led in 1921 to its collapse under attack by Ibn Saud (q.v.). The population (about 30,000 in 1961) is ruled by a Saudi governor. The town has shared to some extent in the general prosperity of the kingdom, with a number of modern palatial buildings, including schools and hospitals, as well as a serviceable airport for local traffic. Ha'il is not endowed with any natural resources; the days of its greatness ended with the Rashid dynasty. (H. ST. J. B. P.)

HAILE SELASSIE (SELASSIE) (1892–), "Lion of Judah, Elect of God, King of Kings of Ethiopia," was crowned as emperor of Ethiopia on Nov. 2, 1930. A great-grandson of King Sahela Selassie of Shoa, with whom Queen Victoria concluded a treaty of friendship and commerce in 1841, and a son of Ras Makonnen, who was the emperor Menelik II's right-hand man, he was born (as Lij Tafari) on July 23, 1892, near Harar and was

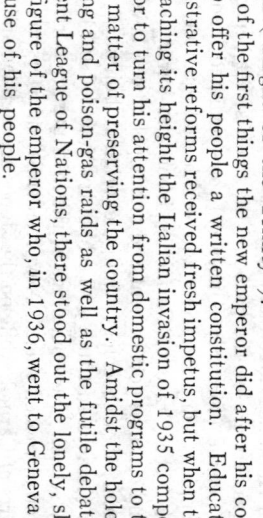
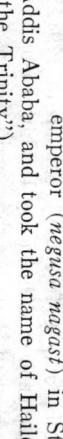

MARC AND EVELYNE BERNHEIM FROM RAPHO GUILLUMETTE

THE EMPEROR HAILE SELASSIE

educated at home by teachers employed by the French mission at Harar. At the age of 14 he was created dejazmatch ("Commander of the Door," a title of senior dignitaries, district chiefs, etc.), and in 1908 he was appointed governor of the large southern province of Sidamo. Two years later, upon the death of his father and of his elder brother, he became governor of his native province of Harar. In 1911 he married Wayzaro Menen, later empress, by whom he had three sons and three daughters.

Dejazmatch Tafari was born without any reasonable prospect of ascending the throne. His education was that traditionally given to young Ethiopian noblemen, but his attainments, intellectual powers and great personal dignity soon became apparent and had, indeed, already been recognized by the emperor Menelik. Upon the latter's death in 1913 Lij Yasu (Lidj Iyasu), his grandson, succeeded to the throne, but his weakness and unreliability as well as his flirtation with Islam made him obnoxious to the Christian majority of his people. Dejazmatch Tafari became the rallying point of the forces of resistance which finally brought about the deposition of Lij Yasu in 1916 and the crowning of Zauditu (Zawditu), Menelik's daughter, as empress, with Ras Tafari (as he now became) as regent and heir to the throne.

The dyarchy of the empress Zauditu and the young regent was a delicate arrangement, but it brought peace and prosperity to Ethiopia. Zauditu was conservative in outlook, while Ras Tafari was progressive and became the focus of the aspirations of the modernist younger generation. Yet as regent and emperor he showed a remarkable feeling for the pace of reform and progress at which his country could move without disturbance or upheaval. He always insisted that Ethiopia must evolve its own concepts and forms suitable to conditions prevailing in that ancient realm.

Ras Tafari concentrated at first on foreign affairs. In 1923 he had a conspicuous success in the admission of Ethiopia to the League of Nations. In the following year he visited Rome, Paris and London, and was thus the first Ethiopian ruler ever to go abroad. In 1928 he assumed the title of negus ("king"), and two years later, when the empress Zauditu died, he was crowned emperor (negusa nagast) in St. George's cathedral, Addis Ababa, and took the name of Haile Selassie ("Might of the Trinity").

One of the first things the new emperor did after his coronation was to offer his people a written constitution. Education and administrative reforms received fresh impetus, but when this work was reaching its height the Italian invasion of 1935 compelled the emperor to turn his attention from domestic programs to the more urgent matter of preserving the country. Amidst the holocaust of bombing and poison-gas raids as well as the futile debates of an impotent League of Nations, there stood out the lonely, slight and noble figure of the emperor who, in 1936, went to Geneva to plead the cause of his people.

After four years of exile in Britain, Haile Selassie went to Khartoum in 1940, shortly after Italy's entry into World War II, and helped to organize the Ethiopian campaign which culminated in the emperor's re-entry into his capital in May 1941. The transformation of the country from chaos, destruction and political fragmentation into a viable and stable structure was the abiding achievement of the emperor. On the 25th anniversary of his coronation, in 1955, he promulgated a revised constitution under which several elections have since been held.

By the time Haile Selassie had been ruler for 50 years (1966), he had made Ethiopia the centre of the Organization of African Unity and of the United Nations Economic Commission for Africa. A short-lived revolt in 1960 somewhat loosened the texture of Ethiopian society without materially impairing the emperor's authority. He remains the very embodiment of Ethiopia.

BIBLIOGRAPHY.—Christine Sandford, *The Lion of Judah Hath Prevailed* (1955); Edward Ullendorff, *The Ethiopians*, 2nd ed. (1965); L. Mosley, *Haile Selassie* (1964).   (E.U.)

HAINAN ISLAND (HAI-NAN TAO), China's second largest offshore island, is that country's most extensive tropical possession. Long known but little explored, it is rich in iron ore, tin, bauxite, possibly in copper, and in tropical hardwoods, and has a great potential for tropical commercial crops. That it has been so sparsely settled by the Chinese despite ample opportunity and convenience to the coast and to southeast Asia trade routes is a puzzle of historic interest.

The island lies south of the Luichow (Leichow) peninsula, between 19° 9′ and 20° 15′ N., extending 160 mi. east-west, and 90 mi. north-south. Hai-k'ou (Hoihow), the main port on the north coast, is 250 mi. E. of Haiphong in North Vietnam and 300 mi. W. of Hong Kong. In total area Hainan covers 13,124 sq.mi., slightly less than Formosa, which totals 13,807 sq.mi. The 1953 population of Hainan was reported at 2,800,000, one-third being tribal peoples.

Structurally, Hainan is the southern flank of a graben (depression), Hainan strait occupying the bottom, and is also the southern end of an older structural massif which extends northeastward into Manchuria. Basaltic lavas are found in the northern part of the island, and in the southern half granites and porphyries form the Five Finger mountains (Wu-chi shan), which reach over 6,000 ft. elevation. The mountains show a radial drainage pattern flowing in all directions into the South China sea, and form a refuge for aboriginal tribes and for flora and fauna not widely distributed in other parts of the island.

The tropical climate provides a 12-month growing season, with temperature averages for lowland areas of 18° C. (65° F.) for January and 29° C. (85° F.) for June. Rainfall on the southern half of the island exceeds 70 in., being about 60 in. in the north, with a strong monsoonal seasonality (dry winter) in the south but a less emphatic one in the north. Strong autumnal typhoons often affect the island.

Natural vegetation is tropical in nature, including many palms, bamboos, rattans, fruit trees, tropical hardwoods and fragrant woods, though tribal shifting cultivation reduced the original cover in many parts of the island. The native fauna also is rich and varied, being notably more tropical than that of the mainland. Both streams and offshore waters abound in fish. Agriculturally, Hainan is capable of producing practically all of the crops grown in southeast Asia.

With such favourable conditions, Hainan's lack of development historically and in modern times is striking. Following Chinese subjugation of Kuangtung in the Early Han dynasty (206 B.C.–A.D. 8), Li tribes moved south to the island. Later Chinese settlements on the coastal plain compressed them toward the forested mountain interior, repeating the mainland pattern of economic control and suppressing their frequent uprisings. Thereafter they were interspersed with smaller and later Miao tribes from southwest China, living by hunting, gathering, shifting cultivation, and settled wet-rice cultivation.

During the past 19 centuries various Chinese groups have migrated to Hainan in small numbers: the Hoklo from south Fukien, clustered around Wen-ch'ang in the northeast, providing the main source of Hainanese emigrants to Thailand and Singapore and the standard "Hainan dialect"; Hakka from Kuangtung, mostly at Na-ta in the northwest; a Mandarin-speaking enclave at Tan-hsien, probably descendants of Hunanese troops landed in 1885; about 2,000 Chinese-Li Muslims at San-ya in the south believed to be descended from shipwrecked Arabs; and merchant families from Canton, Swatow and Hong Kong. From the T'ang dynasty (A.D. 618–906) to the Republic (1911) Hainan was a place of political exile from court, the most famous exile (A.D. 1098–1101) being the Sung poet Su Tung-p'o (1036–1101). Distance from the mainland culture, coastal piracy, malignant malaria and frequent tribal rebellions all discouraged sizable Chinese immigration and settlement. The tropical environment, so different from that of mainland China beyond the south coast, was not congenial to traditional Chinese economy, and this may be a good part of the reason the Chinese did not early develop the island.

Western contact began under the Portuguese Jesuits in 1630, but the lack of a developed economy restricted western interest. Repeated missionary contacts were made, Hai-k'ou was opened to foreign trade in 1858, and foreign commercial residence began in 1876, but it never expanded productively. Hainan was held by a foreign power only once—by the Japanese, 1939–45.

Repeated small Chinese efforts at development mark the modern period. In 1910 two Chinese companies from Singapore started rubber plantations, but they ceased operations after 1920 because of low prices and insufficient capital. Other small attempts were made to produce such tropical products as coffee, cacao, pepper, sisal, ramie and coconut. The first real developments resulted from Japanese occupation, when rubber production was resumed, and a start was made with other tropical products. The Japanese built a paved road around the island shore, and built narrow-gauge rail lines in the southwest to exploit iron and copper ores. They improved several harbours, transforming Yü-lin on the southwest coast into a naval base, and extracted nearly 3,000,000 tons of iron ore from deposits in the southwest at Shih-lu and Tien-tu, took out considerable bauxite from Yai-hsien on the south coast, and mined alluvial tin at Na-ta on the north coast.

In April 1950 Hainan came under the Chinese Communists. On July 1, 1952, the tribal areas in the mountainous south were designated the Li-Miao Autonomous District for the 360,000 non-Chinese tribesmen there. Rubber plantings were expanded, and processing plants built. Irrigation dams were built to increase wet-rice production. Mineral surveys and mining were extended, and both air bases and the Yü-lin naval base were reported to have been expanded.

Hainan was long a neglected frontier region. Tribal shifting cultivation, with extraction of forest products, continued in the interior, and limited Chinese settlement on the coastal fringes occurred. In the second half of the 20th century Hainan still constituted a frontier region, but was beginning to undergo development of mineral resources, transport facilities and large-scale experimentation with tropical agriculture.
                                    (TE. H.; J. E. SR.)

HAINAUT (HAINAULT; Flemish HENEGOUWEN), a province of Belgium, occupies much of the southwest of the country, extending along the French frontier for nearly 150 mi. It consists of 6 administrative *arrondissements* (Ath, Charleroi, Mons, Soignies, Thuin and Tournai), 34 judicial cantons and 443 communes. The population estimate, which is mostly French-speaking, was 1,248,854 in 1961. Area 1,466 sq.mi. The mean density of population is 852 per square mile, appreciably above the average for Belgium, but it varies from the sparsely populated Ardennes to the dense agglomerations on the coal field. The provincial capital is Mons (q.v.).

Physical Characteristics.—Topographically one of the most varied parts of Belgium, its relief ranges from the Flanders plain to the Ardennes. The first division is the broad valley of the upper Scheldt in the west, overlain by alluvium; the river is joined by the Haine, a westward-flowing tributary in central Hainaut. The second division is the interfluve between the Scheldt and the upper Dender (Dendre) and part of interior Flanders. Most of this area is covered with Flanders Clay (Eocene), with residual patches of Pliocene sands which form the gently undulating Ronse hills with several rounded summits: Pottelberg (515 ft.) east of Ronse, Mt. St. Aubert (489 ft.) north of Tournai, and the Kluisberg (463 ft.). The third division, in the east, lies between the upper Dender, Senne and Sennette. This is part of the central plateaus of Belgium, consisting of underlying Paleozoic rocks, covered with Flanders Clay and *limon*, but exposed in the valleys. A porphyritic diorite is worked at Lessines, and in the upper Senne and Sennette valleys Carboniferous limestone is quarried. A bluish limestone, known in the district as *petit granit*, is worked at Les Ecaussines and Soignies. The plateau rises gently southward to about 620 ft., whence it drops markedly to the Haine and Sambre valleys. The fourth division comprises the Sambre valley extending eastward from the French frontier and occupying part of a synclinal furrow flanking the northern edge of the Ardennes. The Meuse follows the line of the Sambre, its main tributary. The fifth division includes the most westerly portion of the Ardennes in the neighbourhood of Chimay, the highest point rising to 1,123 ft. The rocks are mainly Devonian sandstones, shales and limestones, with some Cambrian slates along the French frontier extending into the Rocroi massif.

(F. J. M.)

History.—The county of Hainaut (Ger. Hennegau, Lat. Hannonia) had a considerably larger area than the modern Belgian province. It was bounded north by Flanders; east by Brabant and by part of the bishopric of Liège; southeast by the French Rethelois and Thiérache; southwest by the bishopric of Cambrai and by the county of Artois; and west by the district of Tournai. This territory, inhabited in ancient times by the Celto-German tribe of the Nervii, was included in the kingdom of Austrasia under the Merovingian Franks and in those of Lotharingia and then of East Francia (Germany) under the Carolingians. Formed from a number of *pagi* (*pays*), the countship emerges as a unit at the end of the 9th century under Rainier (Ragnerus, Regnar, etc.) I. This Rainier, who in his latter years was in control of Lower Lorraine, had two sons: the elder, Giselbert, eventually became duke of Lorraine; the younger, Rainier II, succeeded his father in Hainaut in 916. Rainier III was dispossessed of his countship c. 957, but his son Rainier IV recovered it in 998. Rainier V, count from 1013 to 1029 or perhaps later, left only a daughter, Richildis (d. 1086), whose second marriage, to the future Baldwin VI of Flanders (Baldwin I of Hainaut), led to a temporary union of Hainaut and Flanders; but this was dissolved on Baldwin's death (1070). Hainaut being reserved for Baldwin II, second son of Richildis. His great-grandson Baldwin V, however, became Baldwin VIII of Flanders in 1191 (*see* FLANDERS, COUNTY OF). Baldwin VI and IX became Latin emperor of Constantinople as Baldwin I. His second daughter, Margaret, agreed however in 1246 to leave Hainaut to the son of her first marriage, Flanders to the son of her second; so that on her death (1280) John of Avesnes, her elder son's heir from 1257, became count of Hainaut. John became count of distant Holland in 1299 (*see* HOLLAND, COUNTY AND PROVINCE OF). Thenceforward Hainaut was linked with Holland under the house of Avesnes, the Wittelsbachs, the Burgundians and finally the Habsburgs (*see* NETHERLANDS, THE: *History*).

The Spanish Habsburgs had to cede Le Quesnoy, Landrecies and Avesnes to France under the treaty of the Pyrenees (1659) and Valenciennes, Condé, Bavay and Maubeuge to France under that of Nijmegen (1678): Valenciennes then became the capital of French Hainaut (now part of Nord *département*). The rest of Hainaut was annexed to France during the French Revolutionary and Napoleonic Wars and formed into the *département* of Jemappes, but given to the kingdom of the Netherlands in 1814, whence it passed to Belgium in 1831.

Economy.—Except for the small portion of the Ardennes where heath, moorland and coniferous plantations dominate, Hainaut is a well-farmed province. The soils developed on the Flanders Clay are found on the valley alluvium are damp and heavy, but better soils are found on the *limon*. More than half of the farmland is under permanent pasture, and fodder crops are widely grown. Pigs, beef and dairy cattle are raised while large numbers of heavy draft horses are bred for farm use. In some parts, particularly where loamy soils have developed on the *limon* covering, wheat and sugar beet are grown.

The activity of the industrial region known as the Borinage consists mainly of coal mining, steel manufacture and use, and textile manufacture. Three of the main districts of the southern Belgian coal field lie within the province: Mons in the west, around La Louvière in the centre, and Charleroi in the east. The nature and quality of output is varied: long-flame, high-volatile coals are found in the west of the Mons field, and some good coking coals near La Louvière and Charleroi. Because of high production costs many mines have been closed, although a few new shafts have been sunk near Mons. Gas is piped to a large chemical plant at Tertre, near Mons. Mons, besides collieries, has coke ovens, plants for making briquettes and chemical by-products, and light industries (pottery, refractory ware, soap, tobacco and cement). La Louvière (1961 pop. 23,107) has steelworks and manufactures machinery, wire, locomotives and rolling stock, chemicals and cement. The main industrial centre is Charleroi, the heart of an urban agglomeration; the population of the commune in 1961 was 26,175, but with the satellite towns of Jumet, Gilly, Montignies, Marcinelle and Marchienne-au-Pont the total was about 150,000. This area has steelworks and many factories making machinery, electrical apparatus, machine tools, nuts and bolts, chemicals and glass. Textile manufacturing in western Hainaut is part of the long-established industry of the Flanders plain. The chief centre is Tournai where production is varied, carpets being a speciality.

Main-line railways of the province include the Paris-Mons-Brussels line, which passes through Tournai, and farther south the Paris-Liège line via Charleroi. The Mons-Condé canal is a straight waterway 16 mi. long, from the French Scheldt at Condé across the frontier to Mons. A second link joins the Scheldt near Antoing with the Mons-Condé canal at Pommeroeul; the Blaton-Ath canal uses 21 locks to cross from Ath in the Dender valley to the Antoing-Pommeroeul canal, and the Centre canal continues the Mons-Condé canal eastward through the coal field to join the Brussels-Charleroi canal at Houdeng-Goegnies. The Centre canal has the steepest rise of any Belgian waterway, a gradient of 1 in 230. Ath and Chimay are two interesting places in the province, Ath being well known for its antiquity, interesting architecture, including a 12th-century tower, and its ancient society of archers. Chimay, near the French frontier, has been the scene of many sieges including the one in 1640 under Turenne when the town was reduced to ruins. It is also famous for its ruined castle and has a Tudor-style château built in the 18th century.

(F. J. M.)

(X.)

HAIPHONG, a city-province and port of North Vietnam, lies on the northeastern edge of the Red River delta beside a distributary of the Song Thai Binh, the Cua Cam. Pop. (1960) 369,248 (municipality). The name means "where the sun sinks into the sea." Haiphong is the outport of Hanoi (*q.v.*) and is the chief national harbour and a major industrial centre. Power depends on coal from mines across the bay at Quang Yen. A new (1964) 24,000-kw.-hr. Soviet-built power plant at Uong-Bi was destroyed by U.S. bombers in December 1965. The area had a cement plant, cotton and rice mills, as well as glass, chemical, and fish-canning factories and a small shipyard. Silting and winter mists hinder the sea approaches and the coast is a jigsaw of lagoons and sandbars, confused northward by dangerous rocks of the Cac Ba (Catba) and Ke Bao islands. Haiphong became a seaport in 1874. It was occupied by the Japanese from September 1940 to August 1945. During 1965-66 more than 200 Western ships called on the port, the largest group being of British registry from Hong Kong. Oil and gasoline storage facilities of Haiphong were destroyed by U.S. bombing raids during 1967 and 1968.

In May 1972 the U.S. mined the harbour, virtually sealing it off from ships bringing in supplies, and once again subjected the city to intensive air raids.

(F. J. M.)

HAIR, in mammals, the characteristic threadlike outgrowths of the outer layer of skin (epidermis) forming the coat or pelage. By analogy the filamentous bristles on nonmammalian forms and on plants are often called hairs.

See also SKIN; FIBRE and allied articles; BALDNESS; FUR; LEATHER.

Anthropology.—One of the traditional bases for racial classifications of man has been the characteristics of hair—its growth, form and microscopic appearance. Although the general structure of all human hairs is similar, some variation occurs among ethnic groups. In fact, differences occur even among hairs of the same region of any person.

The hair of the scalp (capillus) has been studied more exhaustively than that of other regions of the body, perhaps because of its greater abundance and accessibility. Its length, colour and type are gross characteristics seen with the naked eye, which are useful to the anthropologist in distinguishing ethnological groups. Microscopic studies have disclosed differences that are correlated with the gross characteristics. Certain of the microscopic differences, if found in the large majority of hairs of an adequate sample, are sufficiently specific to determine racial origin. Further, a single hair can be shown to have come from only one of a number of individuals of the same ethnological group. Thus, a single hair provides evidence for individual as well as racial identification.

Peter A. Browne of Philadelphia in 1853 was the first to demonstrate a relationship between the form and behaviour of hair and to correlate different forms with specific races. Ten years later M. Pruner-Bey published similar observations in Paris and to him the credit was almost invariably given until C. H. Danforth in 1926 pointed out the discrepancy. The form of the hair was said to be crisped or frizzled and the shape of a cross section of the hair was said to be circular or oval. In the latter part of the 19th century anthropologists classified hair as leiotrichous (including straight and wavy) and as ulotrichous (crisp, woolly or tufted). Early in the 20th century a third term was introduced, cymotrichous, to stand between the other two and to include the wavy and curly hair.

As the 20th century has progressed there has been a slow and gradual change in the point of view of students of hair and with it the nomenclature of hair types has been expanded. The tendency has been away from the two or three large groupings and toward smaller and more clearly defined categories. Thus, in Hrdlička's *Practical Anthropometry* the following classification was recommended: (1) straight, (2) wavy (slightly or markedly), (3) curly (slightly or markedly), (4) frizzly, (5) woolly, (6) peppercorn, i.e., in more or less widely separated close spirals, *en rouleux* ("in little rolls").

Likewise, the study of race differentiation has produced evidence of many overlapping characteristics which have resulted in a less rigid classification. In 1944 W. Howells wrote that no two persons would classify races in the same way. He pointed out that the three familiar great racial stocks (yellow, black and white) obviously represent an ancient separation and that the fourth, the Australian aborigines, is the most primitive of all races. The hair of the yellow race is straight, lank, long and coarse, round or nearly so in section, with a medulla usually present, and dark brown or black in colour (Chinese, American Indians). Frizzly, woolly and peppercorn hair of dark brown or black is found in the black race (African Negroes). It is short, coarse and crisp, elliptical or kidney-shaped in section, with a medulla which is masked by dense pigment granules.

Wavy and curly hair is smooth and silky, oval in section, with a medulla present more often than not. This is the hair of the white race (Europeans) and varies in colour from ash blond (Scandinavians) through the different tones of brown to black (Greeks, southern Italians) and is occasionally red. In length, wavy and curly hair holds an intermediate position. The hair of the Australian aborigines, although wavy or curly and oval in section like that of the white race, is consistently dark brown or black in colour and coarse like that of the black and yellow races. (*See* fig. 2.)

The index of the hair (the figure determined by multiplying the smallest transverse diameter of the hair's shaft by 100 and dividing by the largest diameter) is used to indicate the form of the hair or the degree of flattening. The index of straight and wavy hair varies generally between 80 and 100; of curly and frizzly hair between 75 and 80; and of the woolly and peppercorn form between 50 and 75. Hairs that grow side by side on the same head may vary in their index by 30 points or more. Although there is much variation in form among hairs of the same head, there does exist an undeniable connection between cross section and form. Also, the degree of curliness of the shaft is believed to be determined by the degree of obliquity of the hair follicle. The follicles are straight in races with straight and wavy hair and their direction is more or less parallel; the hairs leave them at the surface of the skin at an acute angle. In the curly haired the direction is not uniform and there is convergency toward many little centres at the surface. The follicle of Negro hair is strongly curved or sabre-shaped.

Since this suggested relationship between the direction of the follicle and the form of its hair is borne out only in a general way, Danforth called attention to other factors that, if not the fundamental cause of the form of the hair, undoubtedly contribute to it, viz., a slight inequality between the two sides of the more or less flattened shaft and a twisting of the shaft on its long axis.

To the former is due the primary curl seen in wavy hair and to the latter the change in direction of the primary curl from one side to the other seen in curly, frizzly, woolly and peppercorn hair. The degree of kinkiness increases as the number of twists along the shaft increases.

Other morphologic and genetic features that are used in classifying races may be found in ANTHROPOLOGY and RACES OF MANKIND.
(M. Tr.)

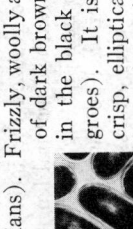
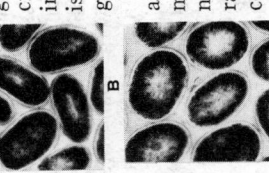

Diagrammatic sketches: (A) straight, (B) wavy, (C) curly, (D) woolly and (E) peppercorn hair; single hairs: (F) wavy, (G) curly and (H) woolly

(A, B, C, D, E) MODIFIED FROM RUDOLPH MARTIN, "LEHRBUCH DER ANTHROPOLOGIE" (VOL. I); (F, G, H) BY COURTESY OF C. H. DANFORTH

FIG. 1.—TYPES OF HAIR

HAIR IN MAMMALS

The most important function of hair in most mammals is that of insulation against cold. A second function is that of a sensory organ—snout hairs or whiskers sensitive to touch (vibrissae) are very helpful to many night-prowling animals. Man's eyelashes consist of sensory vibrissae which cause the reflex shutting of the eyelid when a speck of dust hits them. Important from the standpoint of survival is the coloration and pattern of coats, which serve both as a camouflage to enemies and as an allurement to mates.

Mammalian hairs are developed in relatively deep pits in the skin, the hair follicles, which extend downward into the thickness of the dermis, or even into the subcutaneous tissue. In man the hair rudiments begin to appear about the third or fourth month of fetal life as small solid down growths from the Malpighian layer of the epidermis, their growth being completed about the fifth or sixth month, when they constitute the very delicate hairy covering, the lanugo, which is entirely shed either before birth or soon after. The hairs constituting the downy lanugo are fine, slender, faintly or not pigmented, with large cortical scales and no medulla, and possess some of the characteristics of wool.

At birth the hairs of the eyelashes, eyebrows and scalp, though still soft and more or less retaining the characteristics of lanugo, already show a much more vigorous growth and may be pigmented. During the first few months of infancy this growth is shed, being replaced by the typical coarser hair of the eyebrows and head, while over the rest of the body grows the fine, short, generally unpigmented down hair or vellus. Finally, at and following puberty, coarse, longer and more heavily pigmented hair (terminal hair) is developed in armpits (axilla), pubes, certain areas of the trunk and limbs, and in males on the upper lip and chin.

The amount of terminal hair varies according to race, sex and even individual, though it is generally more abundant in males, the

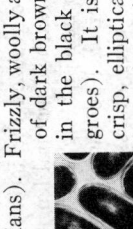
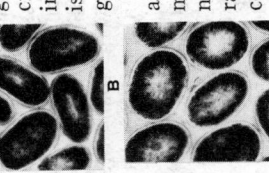
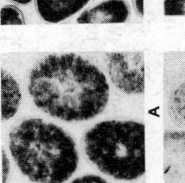
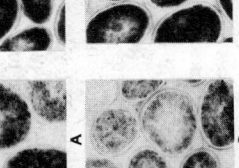

FIG. 2.—CROSS SECTIONS OF HAIRS

Exemplifying four types: (A) Mongoloid, from a Thai, Bangkok; (B) Negroid, from a Comorian, Madagascar; (C) Caucasoid, from a French Canadian, Quebec; and (D) Australoid, from an Australian aborigine, Cairns, Qsld. (enlarged approx. 50X)

greater part of the body in adult females still being covered by vellus. While there are little or no sexual differences distinguishing the auxiliary hairs, slight differences are observed in the pubic hairs, which appear rather longer and more abundant in men and relatively coarser in women. One characteristic human trait is that most of the body hairs never develop beyond more or less rudimentary vellus, whereas in other mammals the coarser forms predominate, and, in addition, tactile hairs (sensory vibrissae) are present. The total area of really hairless skin in man is relatively small, being confined to the palms of the hands, soles of the feet, undersurface of the fingers and toes, the margin of the lips, areolae of the nipples, umbilicus and immediate vicinity of the urogenital and anal openings.

The Hair Follicle.—This structure, which is essentially a recess of the skin, is composed of two tissue elements—one, of epithelial origin, closely invests the hair root, while the second is connective tissue. A cross section of a hair follicle shows that the epithelial layer consists of an outer layer of polyhedral cells forming the outer root sheath, and an inner, horny stratum, the inner root sheath, composed of three layers, known respectively as Henle's layer (the outermost) of horny, fibrous, oblong cells; Huxley's layer, consisting of polyhedral, nucleated cells containing pigment granules; and the cuticle of the root sheath, composed of a layer of downwardly imbricated scales (overlapping as roof tiles) that fit over the upwardly imbricate scales of the hair proper.

The connective tissue element consists internally of a vascular layer separated from the root sheath by a basement membrane, the hyaline layer of the follicle, and externally has a more open texture corresponding to the deeper part of the cutis containing the larger branches of the arteries and veins.

Process of Growth.—The hair grows upward from the bottom of the follicle by multiplication of the soft cells that cover the papilla, and these become elongated and pigmented to form the fibrous substance of the hair shaft, and are otherwise modified to produce the central medulla and cuticle of the hair.

The hair shaft is chiefly composed of a pigmented, horny, fibrous material, which consists of long, tapering, fibrillated cells that have coalesced. Externally this fibrous substance is covered by a delicate later of imbricated scales forming the cuticle. In many hairs the centre of the shaft is occupied by an axial substance, the medulla, formed of angular cells containing granules of eleidin (a substance allied to keratin) and frequently, in addition, minute air bubbles that give the cells a dark appearance.

The medullary cells tend to be grouped along the central axis of the hair as a core; continuous or interrupted in single, double or multiple columns. The variations in the medulla may be summarized as: (a) the continuous type, which may be homogeneous, as in the chimpanzee, or nodose (having a knotty appearance) as in the gelada baboon; (b) discontinuous medullas, which in simple forms may be ovate, elongated, or flattened (in the gibbon it is discontinuous and elongated); (c) a fragmental type, as in the langur, a common oriental monkey.

Cuticular Scales.—The delicate cuticular scales are most varied in shape and size and constitute the most important microscopical structure of the mammalian hair, for they possess definite and constant specific characters. The dominant form is an imbricate scale, like a tile of irregular shape, having its edges rounded, minutely notched or flattened. There are many varieties of the imbricate scale, each typical of its species; thus in man, chimpanzee, gorilla and orangutan, the hairs have imbricate scales which are, however, quite distinctive in size, shape and structure of the edge—slightly oval in chimpanzee, slightly ovate and shallowly notched in man and gorilla, with more deeply notched edges in orangutan. The second type of cuticular scale is the coronal, in which each individual cuticular cell completely encircles the hair shaft and may have a smooth or saw-toothed edge. While the imbricate scale is typical of the higher Primates, the coronal scale in its simpler form is present in the Lemuridae and Tarsius, becoming in the Insectivora more specialized, with saw-tooth edges.

In some Indian bats the cuticular scales are developed as leaflet-like processes arranged in whorls at regular intervals along the hair shaft. In many deer (Cervus), the cortical substance is nearly indistinguishable, almost the entire hair appearing to be composed of thin-walled polygonal cells. In the peccary the cortical envelope sends inward radial prolongations, the interspaces being occupied by medullary substance; and this, on a larger scale, is the structure of the porcupine's "quills." One of the most remarkable mammalian hairs is that of the Australian duckbill or platypus (Ornithorhynchus), in which the lower portion of the shaft is slender and woollike, while the free end terminates as a flattened, spear-shaped, pigmented hair with broad imbricated scales.

In the three-toed sloth (Bradypus tridactylus), a microscopic alga grows between the cuticular scales of the hairs and would appear to be symbiotic, inasmuch that its presence, giving a curious greenish-gray hue to the coat of the sloth, helps to disguise the animal among the trees, giving it when viewed from the ground almost the appearance of a mass of moss.

Tactile Hairs.—These occur in all mammals except man, and are large, stiff hairs of pre-eminently sensory character, having highly specialized follicles, the root being embedded in a mass of true erectile tissue (corpus cavernosum, corpus spongiosum pili), and having a rich sensory nerve supply, presumably controlled by the sympathetic nervous system. These specialized hairs are few in number, their distribution being chiefly confined to the lips, cheeks and supraorbital regions, occasionally occurring elsewhere.

See also references under "Hair" in the Index volume.

(F. M. Du.)

BIBLIOGRAPHY.—M. Pruner-Bey, "De la Chevelure comme caractéristique des races humaines d'après des recherches microscopiques," Mém. Soc. d'anthropol. de Paris, vol. ii, pp. 1–36 (1863); C. H. Danforth, "The Hair," Nat. History, vol. xxvi, no. 1, pp. 75–79 (1926); W. Howells, Mankind So Far (1944); T. D. Stewart (ed.), Hrdlička's Practical Anthropometry, 3rd ed. (1947); W. Montagna and R. A. Ellis, Biology of Hair Growth (1958); M. Trotter, "The Form, Size and Color of Head Hair in American Whites," Am. J. Phys. Anthrop., vol. xiv, pp. 433–445 (1930); "A Review of the Classifications of Hair," Am. J. Phys. Anthrop., vol. xxiv, pp. 105–126 (1938); "Classifications of Hair Color," Am. J. Phys. Anthrop., vol. xxv, pp. 237–260 (1939) and with O. H. Duggins and F. M. Setzler, "Hair of Australian Aborigines," Am. J. Phys. Anthrop., n.s. vol. xiv, pp. 639–659 (1956).

HAIRDRESSING.

Both men and women, even in primitive times, seem to have realized the inconvenience of allowing the hair of the head to reach its natural length of growth. From the custom of cutting or manipulating it, a short step led to hairdressing as a means of personal adornment. Early records show that the ancient Assyrians wore a mass of curls falling over the shoulders. Kings and other great men wore on top of this a kind of helmet, women a simple headband. Hebrew women wore their hair in a net or caul ornamented with "round tires like the moon" (presumably metal fillets). Men wore their hair loose over the shoulders. By contrast, the ancient Egyptians shaved the head, but on ceremonial occasions wore wigs.

Classical Times.—Ancient Greek customs were simpler, at least until the period of the decadence. The Spartan women, in particular, kept for nearly 600 years their manner of wearing a simple ribbon to keep the hair in place over the temples, allowing it to flow loose at the back. In other parts of Greece a kind of bandeau was worn, sometimes replaced by a wreath of laurel leaves or fresh flowers. The back hair was frequently twisted into a chignon. Statues of goddesses often show a diadem or tiara, ornaments presumably worn by the wealthy. As early as 400 B.C. some women dyed their hair. False hair also was known, but, unlike the

Egyptian wig, was made to look as natural as possible. It was the custom for Greek boys when they attained to manhood to cut their hair and dedicate it to a god.

Etruscan women, even after having adopted much from Greece, continued to wear the *tutulus*, a kind of cloth cap entirely concealing the hair. Roman manners were, at first, even more austere, women's heads being almost completely veiled. Men wore short hair. As luxury increased, Roman women dressed their hair more elaborately, replacing the simple bandeaux copied from Greece by broad gold-embroidered bands of stuff adorned with pearls and cameos. The hair itself was intricately twisted and curled; many Roman headdresses must have required the curling iron. Roman portrait busts record the quick changes of hairdressing styles; for some Roman *grandes dames* the sculptured hair was made separately from the rest of the bust and could be changed when desired. Hairpins and combs appear, some of them of gold or ivory. Indeed, most later styles are found already in the coiffures worn by patrician Roman ladies. Dyeing and bleaching of hair were very common. Much false hair obtained from the Gaulish and Germanic tribes had the advantage of being naturally fair.

From the Early Middle Ages Onward.—Among the barbarians who overthrew the Roman empire, short hair, even among men, was the mark of the slave. Many women wore their hair in long plaits emerging from the veils with which they covered their heads. Such veils were universally worn and continued throughout the middle ages. Saxon men wore their hair long, but the Normans were close-cropped.

Not until the mid-14th century did women's hair become visible again. It first appeared in small knobs, like earphones held in a decorated mesh. By the end of the 15th century the veil, especially in the form of the "butterfly" headdress, had become so transparent that the hair, confined in its net, could be plainly seen through it. Men's hair was worn long in the 14th century, but with the development of armour early in the 15th men cut off their hair and beards. Short hair continued to be usual with men until the reign of Charles I.

At the beginning of the 16th century women's hair was almost entirely hidden by the "Tudor arch" headdress. This gradually changed, slipping back until it became the charming "French hood" affected by Mary, queen of Scots. Elizabethan women, freed at last from any kind of veil, tried various fantastic styles. The back hair was generally hidden, but the front was parted in the middle and turned back over a pad; or the hair was raised without parting over a wire support known as a "palisadoe." There was a brief freak fashion for wiring the hair up into two horns. Much false hair was used. John Stow, the historian, says that the periwig (a corruption of the French *perruque*) was first brought into England about the time of the massacre of St. Bartholomew's day and that the fashion had become so general toward the end of the century that children were frequently lured away to be robbed of their hair. Queen Elizabeth I undoubtedly wore a wig. In her youth she had had sufficient of her own reddish-gold hair, but her later portraits clearly show a *perruque*. The queen of James I wore her hair even higher than Elizabeth, but this mode vanished entirely under Charles I, giving place to a fringe low over the forehead and side curls. Many men, however, began to wear their hair long in "cavalier" fashion, as a mark of royalist sympathies; short hair was the sign of the parliament man, called a "roundhead."

At the Restoration Charles II, like his courtiers, was wearing his own long hair, but shortly afterward followed the lead of Louis XIV of France, who had taken to wearing false hair. All civilized men in western Europe felt compelled to do the same. By 1673 the fashion was so entrenched in France that Louis created no fewer than 200 posts of *perruquiers* at court.

By the end of the century the full-bottomed wig was firmly established. Women's hairdressing styles also became more formal. The *fontange*, called after a French court lady, was a towering lace cap, made with several frills and wired up to a considerable height. It was fashionable in the 1690s but by 1710 most women were wearing their hair close to the head. It was frequently powdered white or gray.

The full-bottomed wig for men was hot, and somewhat unstable. Soon something less cumbrous, the "campaign" or "traveling" wig, became popular. There were also black riding wigs, bagwigs and nightcap wigs; and the duke of Marlborough's victory at Ramillies brought in the so-called "Ramillie wig," which sat fairly close to the head and had a long, plaited tail tied with a bow at the top and a smaller bow at the bottom. By the 1740s bob wigs were replacing the long, curled kind for ordinary use. Until 1800 wigs became steadily smaller. Soon after the accession of George III the wig ceased to be indispensable, many gentlemen preferring to wear their own hair dressed and powdered like a wig.

In the late 1760s women's hair began to rise from the head, and headdresses soon assumed fantastic proportions. Women, in general, did not wear wigs; they wore their own hair (no doubt with additions) elaborately dressed and powdered, draped over a foundation of wire or basketwork and crowned with anything that took the fancy: clusters of feathers, bunches of flowers, baskets of fruit and even a miniature ship in full sail. The coiffure of the 1780s was broad rather than high but still very large. By the end of the century, powder had gone out of fashion for both sexes. Men had abandoned wigs and, the pigtail having been cut off (except by naval and military men, who retained it into the next century), the hair was worn fairly short.

Women's hair also became short in the 1790s. Side-curls began to reappear only in 1815. These curls, smoothed out at the end of the 1830s, became the typical early Victorian coiffure with flat pads over the ears, a style that remained almost unchanged until the 1870s. Thereafter hair began to be worn rather high on the head with an immense bunch of curls behind, later confined in a chignon, often with some false hair. From 1882 the fringe was much in vogue, frizzed, crimped or sometimes quite straight and low on the forehead. Toward the end of the decade the hair began to be turned back over a pad, foreshadowing the more elaborate styles of the 1890s and the Edwardian period.

Modern Times.—The most significant developments in women's hairdressing in the western countries in the 20th century were the permanent wave and short hair styles. Curled or waved hair had long been regarded as desirable and, if not naturally present, was obtained by various means: temporarily by rolling the hair on various types of curlers, for a longer time by the use of curling irons and similar devices. The modern permanent wave, which changes the shape of the hair affected and therefore remains until the hair grows out, dates from 1905, when Charles Nessler, a German living in London at the time, gave the first demonstration of the permanent wave. It had long been known that alkaline solutions could soften hair sufficiently to permit changing its shape; the problem was to soften the hair relatively quickly and then heat it high enough to dry it in the new form before it could be damaged by the alkali. Nessler's invention involved softening by borax and heating, first by irons and later by electricity.

Permanent waving was introduced in the United States in 1908 and was well received from the beginning. Early permanent waves were expensive, lengthy and complicated operations. Subsequently many improvements were made in the process.

Nessler recommended cutting the hair to a length of three feet for his method and he waved only the hair around the hairline. Bobbed hair, introduced about 1915 and popularized by Irene Castle, the dancer, was a great stimulus to permanent waving, and beauty salons in their present form began to be common in the 1920s. Another important development was the invention about 1930 of the cold wave (steaming by chemical action), which prepared the way for the modern home permanent.

Hair colouring, which has been practised by many peoples from the earliest times, also underwent significant modern developments. In the period prior to World War II most hair colouring was done for women who objected to gray hair; after World War II the practice became more widespread. Contributing to this were improvements in the kinds of colouring agents: bleaches, permanent tints (which last until new hair grows out) and temporary tints (most of which wash out in the next shampoo).

Basic to hair beauty are good general health and cleanliness, and in styles for short hair the cut is important. A vast array of products for the care of the hair is available; much of their efficacy depends upon the proper selection of the product for the result desired, and skill in using it.

Men's hair (except with some groups of youths) remained short, sometimes very short and *en brosse* in imitation of the U.S. soldier and college boy, until the mid-1960s when long hair became popular among young men of high school and college age, and developed into a symbol of social and political change. Razor-shaped haircuts and long sideburns also became popular. Wigs were increasingly common in both men's and women's fashions in the late 1960s. Women's hairpieces ranged in size from the small chignon to full, high-fashion wigs. The use of men's toupees was supplemented by the introduction of false moustaches, sideburns, and beards. (*See also* WIG.)

The East and Africa.—The hairdressing of non-European nations falls into a different category, for fluctuating fashion hardly enters into it at all. A significant exception is to be found in the elaborate coiffures of the women of the Japanese Yoshiwara, that is, of women whose function it was to please and whose hair styles changed sufficiently quickly (between, say, 1780 and 1810) for it to be possible to date Japanese prints by this means alone. Some African tribes have elaborate hairdressing, the hair of Zulu women, for example, being built up into a solid cone, stiffened with dung. What hairdressing there is in the middle east is, in general, invisible, the women wearing veils and the men turbans. In India and the far east hairdressing had a ritualistic significance, being, in fact, a form of tonsure, originally practised by Hindu Brahmins and Buddhist monks to signify rebirth. Hence it became associated with every rite of initiation. In India and Indochina alike, when a child completes his first month of age and again when he reaches puberty, his head is shaved, a single tuft being left which is then braided or wound up into a knot. Among the Mongols, Tatars and Manchus this became transformed into a pendant pigtail; and during the Manchu dynasty in China (1644-1911) the pigtail was imposed by the conquerors on the Chinese. Indian and Chinese women have continued to dress the hair very simply.

BIBLIOGRAPHY.—J. B. Thiers, *Histoire des Perruques* (1690); J. Comtesse M. Hennequin de Villermont, *Histoire de la coiffure féminine* (1891); R. Steininger, *Die weiblichen Haartrachten im ersten Jahrhundert* (1891); H. Hofmann, *Untersuchungen über die Darstellung des Haares in der archaischen griechischen Kunst* (1900); Stéphane, *L'Art de la coiffure féminine* (1932); G. E. Gerini, *Chulakantamangala, or the Tonsure Ceremony as Performed in Siam* (1893).
Hair Care: Miriam Cordwell and Marion Rudoy, *Hair Design and Fashion,* rev. ed. (1962); S. C. Thorpe, *Practice and Science of Standard Barbering* (1951).   (J. LR.)

HAITI (RÉPUBLIQUE D'HAÏTI), a republic occupying the western third (10,714 sq.mi.) of the Caribbean island Hispaniola, which it shares with the Dominican Republic. This article deals with Haitian history, people, administration, social conditions, and economy. The geography of Haiti is treated with that of the Dominican Republic in the article HISPANIOLA. *See also* DOMINICAN REPUBLIC.

HISTORY

The aboriginal Arawak Indians called the entire island Quisqueya, or Haiti, but when Columbus landed on the north coast in December 1492 he named it Española, later anglicized to Hispaniola. After his flagship, the "Santa Maria," was wrecked near the present site of Cap-Haïtien, Columbus left 38 of his men in a fort on the shore. All were killed by the Indians before he returned on his second voyage, but a new settlement which he established in 1493 on the coast farther east and which was later moved to the south coast became the Spanish city of Santo Domingo. It was from there that further exploration and conquest of the new world were carried on during the next 25 years.

By the end of the 16th century most of the Indians had died from disease or mistreatment, and many of the Spanish settlers had moved to the richer colonies on the mainland. French buccaneers from Tortuga took advantage of the virtual abandonment of the western end of the island to establish settlements there, and in 1664 the French West India Company took possession of these. Spain ceded the area to France by the Treaty of Rijswijk

(1697). In the 18th century exports of sugar, coffee, and other tropical products made French St. Domingue one of the richest colonial possessions in the world, and great numbers of Negro slaves were brought from Africa. On the eve of the French Revolution (1789) 450,000 of the total population of about 520,000 were slaves, while 27,500 were freedmen of mixed ancestry, some of whom themselves owned plantations and slaves. The mulattoes were restive under the humiliating restrictions imposed on them by the whites, and the whites themselves were divided into several bitterly hostile groups.

When the French government's control was weakened by the Revolution in France, these enmities led to disorders which culminated in a general slave revolt in 1791. There were some years of confused fighting between whites and mulattoes and blacks until one of the black leaders, Pierre-Dominique Toussaint L'Ouverture (*q.v.*), obtained control. In 1801 Toussaint conquered the former Spanish colony also and proclaimed himself governor-general for life. He put the peasants back to work on the plantations under military rule and encouraged many of the French proprietors to return.

Though Toussaint professed allegiance to France, he was virtually independent, and in December 1801 Napoleon sent an army under his brother-in-law, Gen. Charles Leclerc, to reestablish French authority. Alexandre Sabès Pétion and several other mulatto exiles accompanied the expedition. After some months of fierce resistance, Toussaint accepted terms of peace, only to be treacherously arrested and sent to France, where he died in prison on April 7, 1803. Some of his lieutenants, who had retained their commands in the army, resumed the war and were soon joined by Pétion and other mulatto leaders, who were infuriated by the restoration of the restrictions on their caste. Reports that France had reestablished slavery in Guadeloupe and Martinique made the natives more desperate and the struggle was carried on with the greatest savagery on both sides. The French were weakened by an epidemic of yellow fever, and their position became hopeless with the renewal of hostilities between France

BYRON CORONEOS—PIX FROM PUBLIX

CITADELLE LAFERRIÈRE, SOUTH OF CAP-HAÏTIEN

and Britain in May 1803. In November 1803 Gen. Jean Baptiste Rochambeau, who had assumed command after Leclerc died of yellow fever, surrendered to a British admiral. On Jan. 1, 1804, Jean Jacques Dessalines (q.v.), the principal leader in the revolt, declared the independence of Haiti, with himself as governor-general. French forces retained the former Spanish colony in the eastern end of the island until Spain regained possession in 1809.

Dessalines massacred most of the whites who had not already fled from the island and treated all native opponents with brutal severity. In September 1804 he proclaimed himself Emperor Jacques I. He was killed Oct. 17, 1806, while attempting to put down a mulatto revolt at Port-au-Prince. His lieutenant, Henry Christophe (q.v.), took control of the northern part of the country with his capital at Cap-Haïtien, where he proclaimed himself king in 1811; but he failed during several years of civil war to defeat the mulatto leaders who set up a separate republic in the South with Alexandre Pétion as president. It was King Henry who built the famous Citadelle Laferrière, a fortress south of Cap-Haïtien. Pétion ruled the South as president until his death in 1818. His successor, Jean Pierre Boyer, took control of the North also when Christophe killed himself, after suffering a stroke, in 1820. In 1822 Boyer conquered the eastern end of the island, which had just declared its independence from Spain.

Dessalines and Christophe had forced the peasants to work on the plantations and some sugar was produced, despite the destruction of many mills during the slave revolt and the deterioration of the irrigation systems. In the South, on the other hand, Pétion did not enforce the law which forbade the peasants to abandon the plantations where they worked, and under Boyer sugar production virtually ceased throughout the island. During the rest of the 19th century the country's chief export was coffee picked from the half-wild bushes on the old French plantations.

Boyer ruled Haiti for 25 years. France recognized his government in 1825, after exacting the promise of an indemnity of 150,000,000 francs, only a part of which was actually paid. Britain recognized Haiti in 1833, but opposition in the slave-holding states delayed U.S. recognition until 1862. There was little active opposition to the regime in Haiti until 1843, when a group of young liberals revolted and overthrew it. Boyer's former supporters regained control in 1844, but in the meantime the Spanish-speaking inhabitants of the eastern end of the island, who had been unhappy under Haitian rule, revolted and regained their independence, establishing the Dominican Republic.

Since Christophe's death the government had been controlled by the mulatto elite at Port-au-Prince, who were a small minority as compared with the black masses and who faced opposition particularly in the North, where black leaders had much influence. After the disorders of 1843–45 the situation of the elite became more precarious. Its leaders tried to strengthen their position by giving the presidency to a series of black military leaders whom they expected to control, but Faustin Soulouque, chosen in 1847, turned against them and killed great numbers of mulattoes when they opposed him. In 1849 Soulouque proclaimed himself Emperor Faustin I, and created a large nobility. He attempted to reconquer the Dominican Republic, but was restrained by the diplomatic intervention of the U.S., Great Britain, and France.

Soulouque was ousted in 1859 by his own chief of staff, Nicholas Fabre Geffrard. The new ruler, a dark mulatto, sought the support of both of the country's racial groups but cruelly repressed all opposition. A concordat with the papacy in 1860 improved the hitherto deplorable condition of the Haitian church and made possible the establishment of several schools by foreign religious orders. Until then there had been few schools of any sort. Geffrard was overthrown in 1867 by a revolt in which young liberals of the Port-au-Prince elite played an important part, and after two years of unusually destructive civil war the liberals came into power in 1870 with Nissage Saget as president. The liberals controlled the government during much of the next nine years, but there were frequent revolts and their effort to establish constitutional republican government collapsed when a black leader named Lysius Salomon seized power in 1879.

Salomon, who had been Soulouque's chief adviser, was a ruthless dictator, but he established a national bank and tried to promote public education and agriculture. High coffee prices gave the country a relative prosperity, which continued during the administration of Florvil Hyppolite, who took the presidency in 1889 after some months of civil war. There was much excitement in 1891 when the United States tried unsuccessfully to obtain a lease of the port Môle Saint-Nicolas, which several other foreign powers also coveted as a strategic position of great importance. Tiresius Simon Sam took office peacefully when Hyppolite died in 1896, but there was a civil war at the end of his term in 1902 which brought to power Nord Alexis, an uneducated but able soldier who ruled as a dictator until he was defeated in a revolution in 1908. Cincinnatus Leconte, the next president, was ousted by a revolution in 1911.

In the four years that followed there were increasingly frequent revolutions and an almost complete breakdown of organized government. The situation caused concern to several foreign governments and particularly to the U.S. Since the administration of Pres. Theodore Roosevelt, the U.S. had been endeavouring to promote political stability and better financial administration in the more disorderly of the Caribbean states because disorder and failure to pay debts was an invitation to European intervention. U.S. Pres. Woodrow Wilson, like his predecessors, thought that foreign political influence in a country close to the Panama Canal would imperil U.S. security, and he considered it the duty of the United States as a neighbour to help the Caribbean countries to achieve orderly democratic government. The U.S. Department of State had been especially apprehensive of possible European intervention in Haiti because both France and Germany had special interests there. French investors held the country's foreign debt and half of the stock in the National Bank, and the priests and the teachers in many schools were French citizens. Germans had taken over much of the retail trade and owned important public utilities, and German merchants were financing revolutions, simply as a profitable business. Neither the number of resident foreigners nor the value of their investments was very great, but the U.S. government suspected Germany, especially, of a desire to build up its influence in Haiti, possibly with a view to acquiring Môle Saint-Nicolas.

U.S. financial interests had also made small investments in Haiti, in railroad building and in the stock of the National Bank. The U.S. State Department's efforts to protect these from despoliation or extortion by irresponsible revolutionary authorities had involved it in several annoying controversies, which had increased the feeling that something should be done. Between 1913 and 1915 the U.S. government repeatedly attempted to persuade the Haitian authorities to permit the establishment of a U.S. customs collectorship which might prevent the impending default on the foreign debt, but the increasingly frequent and always successful revolutions made it difficult to negotiate.

In July 1915, after a mob infuriated by the massacre of 167 political prisoners dragged Pres. Guillaume Sam from his refuge in the French legation and killed him, United States Marines intervened to restore order. Under their protection the Haitian Congress elected Sudre Dartiguenave president. The Haitian government was compelled to accept a treaty which gave officials nominated by the president of the United States control of the finances and the public works and public health administrations, and provided that U.S. officers should train a constabulary to maintain order. A brigade of U.S. Marines remained in Haiti to support the new constabulary. The treaty, as amended in 1917, was to remain in force until 1936.

In the first years of the intervention the U.S. effort was poorly organized, and there were frequent quarrels between U.S. and Haitian officials. A revolt in the interior, which began in 1918, was suppressed by the U.S. Marines after more than a year of fighting in which 1,500 Haitians were said to have been killed. Conditions improved rapidly after 1922, when Brig. Gen. John H. Russell of the U.S. Marines was appointed U.S. high commissioner with full authority over the Marine brigade and the treaty services. Russell established a cordial working relationship with Pres. Louis Borno, who succeeded Dartiguenave in 1922 and was reelected in 1926. A $16,000,000 loan was contracted in New York City to refund the foreign debt and finance public works, and another $5,000,000 internal loan made possible the payment of foreign claims and the internal floating debt. The Public Works Service, directed by engineers of the U.S. Navy, built roads and irrigation systems and port works, and U.S. Navy doctors improved the deplorable sanitary conditions in the towns. In 1923 another treaty service was established to promote agriculture and establish vocational and agricultural schools.

Many Haitians resented the U.S. military occupation, and many of the elite objected both to the U.S. officials' efforts to improve the condition of other social groups and to the emphasis on vocational education at the expense of the traditional academic curriculum. There was much opposition to Borno, who had taken advantage of a transitory provision of the constitution of 1918 to put off the election of a Congress and to rule with the aid of a Council of State which he himself appointed. The Council of State had reelected Borno in 1926, and the other political leaders feared that it would choose his successor in 1930. Demands for a congressional election led to minor strikes and disorders late in 1929, and early in 1930 U.S. Pres. Herbert Hoover appointed a commission headed by W. Cameron Forbes to look into the situation and to consider "when and how we are to withdraw from Haiti" and "what we shall do in the meantime." Through the mediation of the commission and General Russell, Borno and his opponents agreed that Eugene Roy should be installed as temporary president to arrange for the popular election of a Congress. In November 1930 the new Congress elected Sténio Vincent, one of the nationalist leaders, as president.

The commission did not advise an immediate withdrawal of the U.S. occupation forces, but it recommended that the high commissioner be replaced by a civilian minister who would negotiate agreements for the reduction of U.S. control. President Hoover approved this course, and in 1931 the Public Works Administration and Public Health Service work outside of Port-au-Prince and Cap-Haïtien were turned over to Haitians who had been trained in the services. At the same time, U.S. personnel were withdrawn from agricultural and educational work, and the technical state of martial law, proclaimed by the Marines in 1915, was ended. A treaty signed in September 1932, which would have abrogated most of the provisions of the 1915 treaty and fixed times for the completion of the training of the constabulary and the withdrawal of the Marines, was rejected by the Haitian Congress, but an executive agreement signed in August 1933 provided that the constabulary should be turned over to Haitian command and that the U.S. Marines withdrawn in August 1934. U.S. financial control continued because of promises made by both governments to purchasers of the bonds issued in 1922, but it was made less rigorous. It was further reduced in 1941 and abolished in 1947, when the 1922 bonds were paid off by an internal loan.

A plebiscite in 1935 extended President Vincent's term to 1941 and amended the constitution to provide that future presidents be chosen by popular vote instead of by Congress. In 1937 the Dominican Army massacred several thousand Haitians who had been working in the Dominican Republic, but war was averted by the good offices of other American nations and the payment by the Dominican Republic of a large indemnity to Haiti. Under Élie Lescot, who became president in 1941, Haiti cooperated in the allied war effort by increasing the production of sisal and joining with the U.S. in an ambitious but costly and unsuccessful attempt to produce rubber from cryptostegia. In 1946, after Lescot had the Congress extend his term to 1951, the army ousted him. Dumarsais Estimé took his place, but he in turn was forced out by the army in 1950.

Col. Paul Magloire, who was elected president, was forced to resign in December 1956, when his opponents stirred up popular opposition to his alleged plan to continue in office for another term. There was a period of disorder during which short-lived governments, backed by rival factions in the army, rose and fell. In September 1957, after a popular election in which rival candidates campaigned actively and an unusually large number of voters participated, François Duvalier became president.

The new president, a black physician who had studied at one time in the United States, soon made it clear that he proposed to rule as a dictator. He sought the support of the black masses and excluded most of the mulatto leaders from the government. Persons who were suspected of plotting against him were exiled or killed and there were ugly reports of the torture of political prisoners in the president's palace. The Tontons Macoutes, a group of armed thugs, terrorized political opponents and at the same time preyed on businessmen and property owners. Mulattoes were persecuted and humiliated, partly to intimidate them and partly, apparently, in an effort to destroy the prestige of the elite class. The president's policies seemed to meet with little opposition among the masses of the people. His enemies organized small revolutionary expeditions from nearby countries in 1959, 1964, and 1968, but all of these failed.

The army, which had dominated politics for some years before 1957, was brought under control by the elimination of leaders whom the president distrusted. To increase its efficiency, the Haitian government in 1958 obtained a military mission from the U.S. Marine Corps. This was withdrawn in 1963 after relations with the United States deteriorated and after the mission had opposed Duvalier's plan to create a militia of peasants and workers to offset the army's power. The president still distrusted the army leaders, and in 1967, 19 officers were executed after the discovery of an alleged plot to murder him. Duvalier's own son-in-law and daughter were exiled. Several civilians were shot, and others, including trusted advisers, simply disappeared.

Duvalier's policies, and particularly the mistreatment of foreigners by the Tontons Macoutes, led to controversies with other governments. Some foreign diplomatic representatives left Haiti after receiving offensive treatment, and in 1963 the Organization of American States (OAS) had to use its good offices to prevent war when Haitian soldiers invaded the Dominican embassy at Port-au-Prince. There were also controversies with the Roman Catholic Church, which led to the expulsion of the archbishop and several other priests and to Duvalier's excommunication. The Haitian government resumed normal diplomatic relations with the Dominican Republic and with the Vatican in 1966.

The U.S. from time to time indicated its disapproval of Duvalier's actions. Before 1957 the U.S. government had an extensive aid program in Haiti and was financing the irrigation of the Artibonite Valley. Disputes about the conduct of the work and the diversion of the aid funds for improper purposes made continuance of the program difficult, and most U.S. aid was suspended in 1962. Diplomatic relations continued despite the Haitian government's offensive treatment of U.S. representatives.

In 1964 Duvalier had had a special provision written for the new constitution making him president for life. In January 1971, apparently because of his failing health, he had the constitution amended to lower the legal age of the president from 40 to 18 and to provide that his successor also be made president for life. He took this step so that his 19-year-old son, Jean-Claude, could succeed him. When Duvalier died on April 21, 1971, Jean-Claude Duvalier was immediately sworn in as president.

THE PEOPLE

Haiti is one of the most densely populated countries in the Americas. According to the first official census, taken in 1950 with the aid of the U.S. Census Bureau, there were 3,097,220 inhabitants, or 291 persons per square mile. A 1968 estimate showed a total of 4,671,000, or 436 per square mile. The population is predominantly rural. Port-au-Prince, the capital, with 340,175 inhabitants, and Cap-Haïtien (35,000) are the only towns with more than 20,000 people. Most of the country is mountainous, and a large proportion of the people are crowded into the relatively small areas of arable land.

Practically all of the natives are of Negro or mixed Negro and white descent. Perhaps 5%, most of them mulattoes, form the upper class, the so-called elite, who live in the principal towns. The great bulk of the people, most of them of pure or almost pure African descent, are peasant farmers, or workmen or servants in the towns. There are a few resident foreigners, including a number of merchants of Syrian descent.

The elite speak French, which is the official language, and take pride in their French culture. Some are professional or businessmen, and some have distinguished themselves as scholars and artists, but the majority have traditionally looked to government employment or government favours as their chief means of support. As the only people who could read and write and who had any understanding of governmental problems, they have usually held many positions in the administration even when black leaders were in power. The mulatto elite, a rather exclusive group based mainly on family, has traditionally been indifferent to the condition of the peasants and has discriminated socially against the growing number of educated darker-skinned people, many of whom, especially in recent years, have studied abroad and achieved prominence in intellectual or professional work.

Most of the elite, nominally at least, are Roman Catholics. There were no bishops and few priests in Haiti until the signature of the concordat with the papacy (1860) regularized the position of the church and provided for its support by the Haitian government. As late as the 1930s nearly all of the priests were recruited in France, but in later years the majority were of other nationalities and nearly 25% were Haitians.

The peasants cultivate small plots of land, usually as owners or squatters, or as renters from the government or other land owners. They live in wooden-framed huts with mud-daubed walls and thatched roofs, sleeping on mats on the floor and possessing only the scantiest furniture. Water must often be carried from considerable distances. Most of the farmers produce a bare subsistence, for a hoe and a machete are usually the peasant's only implements and agricultural methods are extremely primitive. Even coffee, the chief money crop, grows half-wild. When outside work is available, wages are 20-40 cents per day, and the per capita annual income probably does not exceed $63.

The country people are almost universally illiterate and speak a Creole patois with a small vocabulary of archaic French and a few Spanish and African words. Their religion is voodoo, a mixture of African superstitions with some elements derived from Catholicism. Voodoo priests and priestesses, and sorcerers of various types, have much influence. Despite the work done by traveling clinics during the U.S. occupation and the more recent health program sponsored by the United Nations, tuberculosis, malaria, yaws, and diseases of malnutrition are still prevalent in Haiti.

While there is no real middle class, there are some groups which are beginning to occupy a position between the elite and the peasants: artisans and other skilled labourers in the towns, minor government employees, and some of the more intelligent and successful peasant farmers. The building of roads and the establishment of cheap bus services has tended to break down the isolation in which most of the rural communities formerly existed. In the cities there are small and weak labour unions, which have been allowed little freedom in recent years.

ADMINISTRATION

In 1961 President Duvalier dissolved the Senate and the Chamber of Deputies and appointed a unicameral National Assembly of 58 members. In 1964 this body approved the submission to the voters of a new constitution which made Duvalier president for life and gave him power to dissolve the National Assembly and rule by decree in case of emergency. The voters gave their approval, "almost unanimously," in a plebiscite in June 1964. The president is assisted by a Cabinet and an appointed Council of Government. Judicial power is vested in a Court of Cassation, courts of appeal, and lower courts, all appointed by the executive. Haiti's legal system is based on the Napoleonic code.

The capital of Haiti is Port-au-Prince (q.v.), which is also the chief port and commercial centre. The second city of the republic is historic Cap-Haïtien. (q.v.).

EDUCATION

Primary education is legally free and compulsory, but there has never been a school system which could provide even elementary instruction for more than a very small fraction of the children of school age. Before the U.S. occupation there was no effort to educate the peasants and the small sums which the government appropriated for public schools in the towns were generally stolen or misused. Most of the children of the elite attended schools maintained by foreign religious orders. Between 1923 and 1930 one of the U.S. treaty services began to set up great numbers of farm schools, where peasants could learn to read and write and be given practical instruction in agriculture. It also built schools for vocational training in some of the larger towns, in the hope of eventually building up a Haitian middle class. These programs were unpopular with the elite and collapsed even before the U.S. withdrawal. Recent governments took somewhat more interest in education, and it was reported that in the mid-1960s about one-fifth of the children were in school.

Secondary and higher education are also theoretically free to all, but the number of secondary schools is inadequate and a very small proportion of children reach them. There is a university at Port-au-Prince. According to the 1950 census, 89.3% of those ten years of age and over were illiterate.

ECONOMY

Haiti's economy is basically agricultural, with coffee, sisal, cotton, castor beans, sugar, logwood, and essential oils as the chief products. As a French colony, it was one of the most productive regions of the Caribbean, but the large colonial estates and the irrigation systems were mostly destroyed during the wars for independence. (See History, above.) Those members of the new ruling class who still owned land were often prevented from cultivating it by the hostility of the peasants, and Haiti became a country of small farms, which grew still smaller as the population grew. Primitive agricultural methods and erosion, especially on the mountain slopes, depleted the soil and made it increasingly difficult for the farmers to obtain even a bare subsistence. The country continued, however, to produce a considerable amount of coffee, which commanded a good market abroad despite careless cultivation and poor preparation. Logwood, a dyewood, was also cut and exported. U.S. experts, during the occupation, demonstrated the cultivation of sisal, and large quantities of this have been produced for export, chiefly by means of U.S. capital.

U.S. engineers serving under the treaty of 1915 began to restore the irrigation systems on which much of the wealth of Haiti had depended, but lack of funds made progress slow. The irrigation of the valley of the Artibonite, Haiti's largest river, would greatly increase the amount of productive land, and after World War II the United States government provided large sums of aid for this project. The Peligre Dam was completed in 1956, but much work remained to be done and the conduct of the Duvalier regime, which brought about the suspension of U.S. aid in 1962, delayed the completion of the project.

In the 1950s Haiti began to attract many foreign tourists. Several hotels were built, especially in Port-au-Prince, and many cruise ships stopped at Haitian ports. After 1956, however, the disorders that preceded Duvalier's election and the unpleasant reports published abroad about the Duvalier regime discouraged the tourist trade, which had once promised to become a major source of national income. Tourism began to revive in 1969.

In 1967 and 1968 Haitian agriculture was disastrously affected by a severe drought, and low prices for the country's agricultural products made matters worse. The production of copper and bauxite was increasing and a few new industries were being established by foreign capital to take advantage of the very low cost of Haitian labour, but the general picture was one of growing poverty and economic deterioration. The per capita annual income, already one of the lowest in the Western Hemisphere, decreased to an estimated $63.

Trade and Finance.—Coffee accounts for approximately half of Haiti's exports, followed in importance, in recent years, by bauxite and copper. It was reported in 1967 that the exportation of sisal, formerly an important source of income, had virtually ceased. Some sugar, cacao, and logwood are exported. The total value of exports fluctuates considerably from year to year: $38,-

000,000 in 1950, $55,000,000 in 1954, $32,000,000 in 1960, and $36,000,000 in 1965. The total value of imports also fluctuates: $36,000,000 in 1950, $47,000,000 in 1954, $35,000,000 in 1960, and $36,000,000 in 1965. Food and textiles account for about 70% of the imports. The government's revenues, of which about 70% are derived from customs duties, averaged about $25,000,000 per year in the early 1960s. By the late 1960s they had decreased considerably, leaving the administration with a rapidly mounting deficit.

The monetary unit is the gourde. The rate of exchange is five gourdes for one U.S. dollar.

Transport and Communication.—The Compagnie Nationale des Chemins de Fer, the government-owned passenger railway from Port-au-Prince to Saint-Marc and Verrettes, was reported to have discontinued operations in the late 1960s except for the carriage of some local freight. Other railways are privately owned and serve mainly to carry freight. Roads, some of them asphalted but most of them now in bad condition, connect the various towns and give the peasants a means of transporting their produce. Air services link Port-au-Prince with other Caribbean islands and New York City, and a domestic airline, Corps d'Aviation de la Garde d'Haiti, serves the interior. Haiti's seaports are served by U.S., British, Dutch, West German, and Panamanian shipping lines. Worldwide cable and telegraph services are maintained, but local telephone service has deteriorated. *See also* references under "Haiti" in the Index.

BIBLIOGRAPHY.—H. P. Davis, *Black Democracy* (1936); Ludwell Lee Montague, *Haiti and the United States 1714–1938* (1940); James G. Leyburn, *The Haitian People* (1941); United Nations, *Mission to Haiti* (1949); R. W. Logan, "The United States Mission to Haiti, 1915–1952," *Inter-American Economic Affairs*, 6:18–28 (1953) and *Haiti and the Dominican Republic* (1968); S. Rodman, *Haiti* (1954); A. C. Millspaugh, *Haiti Under American Control, 1915–1930* (1931); M. J. Herskovits, *Life in a Haitian Valley* (1937). For a fictional (hostile) account of the Duvalier regime, *see* G. Greene, *The Comedians* (1966). Current history and statistics are summarized annually in *Britannica Book of the Year*.
(R. W. LN.; D. G. MO.)

HAJDUBÖSZÖRMÉNY, a town of northeastern Hungary in Hajdu-Bihar *megye* (county), lies about 13 mi. N.N.W. of Debrecen. Pop. (1960) 32,199 (mun.). Several smaller towns in this region have the same prefix (Hajduszoboszló, Hajdunánás, Hajdudorog, Hajduhadház). The prefix possibly originates from the Turkish *haiduk* and originally meant "robber" or "brigand," but in Hungary it applied to mercenary foot soldiers of Magyar origin, who in the early 17th century were given grants of land east of the Tisza as a reward for faithful service to Calvinist Hungary. The area became Hajdu county in 1876. These settlements are by tradition the nucleated village-towns of the Great Alföld and in particular of the Hortobágy *puszta*, or steppe, but the countryside has changed fast with the success of irrigation from the upper Tisza. The discovery of natural gas south of Debrecen made the growth of several secondary roads and is linked with Debrecen by rail. The early 16th-century Protestant church survives, with an unfinished tower.
(H. G. S.)

HAJJ (HADJ), the pilgrimage to Mecca, which every adult Muslim (with certain exceptions) must perform at least once in his lifetime. *See* MECCA: *The Pilgrimage*; PILGRIMAGE.

HAKE, EDWARD (fl. 1579), English Puritan satirist, who resided in Gray's Inn and Barnard's Inn, London, and held civic office at New Windsor, is known for *Newes Out of Powles Churchyard* (1567?; 2nd ed. 1579), a dialogue between Bertulph and Paul, who meet in the aisles of the cathedral. It is in rhymed 14-syllable metre and divided into eight "satyrs," dealing with the corruption of the higher clergy and of judges, the greed of attorneys, the tricks of physicians and apothecaries, the sumptuary laws, extravagant living, Sunday sports and the abuse of St. Paul's cathedral as a meeting place for business and conversation, usury, etc. Hake's other works include a translation of Thomas à Kempis, *The Imitation, or Following of Christ* (1567, 1568); another satire, *A Touchestone for This Time Present* (1574); and *Of Golds Kingdome* (1604), a collection of pieces in prose and verse, inveighing against the power of gold.

HAKE, a common name for various fishes of the cod family (Gadidae), especially the genera *Merluccius* and *Urophycis*. The European hake (*M. merluccius*), an important food fish of the Mediterranean and the Atlantic coast of Europe, is most abundant south of the British Isles. It differs from other fishes of the Gadidae in skeletal characters, and is perhaps best placed in a separate family. It is a slender fish, with long, acute snout, large terminal mouth and sharp teeth, and reaches a length of four feet; it is a voracious fish, living in rather deep water; the flesh is soft. Other species of *Merluccius* are known from both coasts of North America, and from Chile and Patagonia, South Africa and New Zealand. *Urophycis* includes the squirrel, gulf, Carolina, southern, spotted and white hakes, all of which are found along the Atlantic coast of North America.

HAKIM, AL- (ABU 'ALI MANSUR AL-HAKIM) (985–1021), sixth Fatimid caliph (996–1021), son of the caliph al-Aziz, ascended the throne in Cairo at the age of 11. The first years of his reign were filled by the intrigues of various generals striving for power. His personal rule is marked by the intermittent persecution of the non-Muslim population of Egypt and by a number of capricious edicts, as well as by building and the promotion of cultural and religious activities. In his last years he was proclaimed by some of the extreme followers of Isma'ilism (the state religion of the Fatimid dynasty) as the last incarnation of the divinity. Out of this movement, led by Hamza al-Zuzani, grew the sect of the Druzes (*see* DRUZE). During the night of Feb. 23, 1021, al-Hakim mysteriously disappeared from his palace never to be seen again. *See also* FATIMIDS.
(S. M. SN.)

HAKKA ("guest family"), a people of south China living mainly in Fukien and Kwangtung. They are most numerous in the Ka-ying district of Kwangtung but also live in Kwangsi, Taiwan (Formosa), Hainan Island and Hong Kong, in Malaya, Singapore, Thailand, North Borneo and Sarawak and as far away as Jamaica. Their language has affinities with both Mandarin and Cantonese; it has six tones and many of its initial sounds are a bridge between these dialects (*see* CHINESE LANGUAGE: *History and Dialects*). There are conflicting traditions about Hakka origins, many genealogy books indicating a northern centre in Shantung in the 3rd century B.C.; poorer clans without such books trace their wanderings no farther than Fukien. It is certain however that the Hakka have migrated in successive stages from somewhere in central or northern China, pushed by population pressure from the north. In the middle of the 19th century many Hakka in Kwangtung were active in the T'ai P'ing rebellion (*see* CHINA: *History*) and after it in skirmishes with the local population, as a result of which many emigrated to neighbouring countries. Except where they are the dominant group they tend to live on the less fertile uplands and intermarry little with other Chinese. The women have never bound their feet, and both sexes are extremely industrious. They are basically farmers, but when they go overseas tend to follow specialized occupations; *e.g.*, most of the building workers in Hong Kong and the shoemakers in Singapore are Hakka.
(J. A. PR.)

HAKLUYT, RICHARD (*c.* 1552–1616), British geographer and publicist, was born in or near London about 1552. The Hakluyts were of some standing in the Welsh Marches and held property at Eaton, near Leominster in Herefordshire. A Richard Hakluyt of a cadet branch was apprenticed to a member of the Skinners' company in 1510, and was himself later admitted to the company. He died in 1557, leaving his family, Richard Hakluyt the geographer being his third son, to the care of a cousin, another Richard Hakluyt. This Richard, a lawyer of the Middle Temple, had numerous friends among prominent city merchants, geographers and explorers of the day and was expert in overseas trade and economics. He was well placed to assist the future geographer in his life work.

Young Richard, with the help of various exhibitions, was educated at Westminster school, and Christ Church, Oxford, entering in 1570 and taking his M.A. degree in 1577. His interest in geography and travel had been aroused some years earlier on a visit to the Middle Temple when his cousin, supported by "certain books of cosmographie, an universall mappe, and the Bible," had discoursed on the recent discoveries and the new opportunities for trade. The schoolboy had thereupon resolved to "prosecute that knowledge and kind of literature" at the university. Some time before 1580 he took holy orders. "My exercises of duty first performed, I fell to my intended course and by degrees read over whatsoever printed or written discoveries and voyages I found extant" in several languages.

Hakluyt also gave public lectures—he is regarded as the first professor of modern geography at Oxford—and was the first to display "both the old imperfectly composed and the new, lately reformed maps, globes, spheres and other instruments of this Art for demonstration in the common schools." He made a point also of getting to know "the chiefest Captains at sea, the greatest merchants, and the best Mariners of our nation." This was the time when English attention was fixed on the northeast and northwest passages, and on Francis Drake's circumnavigation. Hakluyt was concerned with the activities of Sir Humphrey Gilbert and Martin Frobisher, was consulting Abraham Ortelius and Gerardus Mercator on cosmographical problems and was gaining the approval of Lord Burghley, Sir Francis Walsingham and Sir Robert Cecil (later earl of Salisbury). He thus embarked upon his career as a "publicist and a counselor for present and future national enterprises across the ocean." His policy, constantly expounded, was the exploration of temperate North America in conjunction with the northwest passage, the establishment of England's claim to possession based on the discoveries of the Cabots and the foundation of a "plantation" to foster national trade and national well-being. These views are first set out in the preface to a translation of Jacques Cartier's voyage to Canada, which he induced John Florio to make from G. B. Ramusio's *Viaggi* in 1580, and are further developed in his first work of importance, *Divers Voyages touching the Discouerie of America* (1582). In this he pleaded also for the establishment of a lectureship in navigation. In 1583 Walsingham sent him to Paris as chaplain to Sir Edward Stafford. There he served also as a kind of intelligence officer, collecting information on the fur trade of Canada and on overseas enterprises from French and exiled Portuguese pilots. In support of Walter Raleigh's colonizing project in Virginia, he prepared a report, known briefly as *The Discourse on the Western Planting* (1584), which set out very forcefully the political and economic benefits from such a colony, and the necessity for state backing. This was presented to Queen Elizabeth I, who rewarded Hakluyt with a prebend at Bristol but took no steps to help Raleigh. *The Principall Navigations, Voiages and Discoveries of the English nation . . .*, and the first edition, in one volume, appeared in 1589. In 1590 he married Duglasse Cavendish, a relation of Thomas Cavendish, the circumnavigator, and was presented to the living of Wetheringsett in Suffolk. Until after the death of his wife in 1597, little is heard of any geographical work, but he then completed the greatly enlarged second edition of *The Principall Navigations*, which appeared in three volumes between 1598 and 1600. Shortly before its completion, he was granted by the queen the next vacant prebend at Westminster, that he might be at hand to advise on colonial affairs. He gave information to the newly formed East India company, and continued his interest in the North American colonizing project, being a patentee of the Virginia company in 1606 and contemplating a voyage to the colony. Nor did his belief in the possibility of arctic passages to the east fade, for he was also a charter member of the North-west Passage company of 1612. In 1613 appeared the *Pilgrimage* of Samuel Purchas (*q.v.*), in spirit a continuation of his own work, and the two editors probably became acquainted. Purchas procured some of Hakluyt's manuscripts after his death and was able to use them in *Purchas His Pilgrimes* of 1625. Hakluyt died on Nov. 23, 1616, and was buried in Westminster abbey.

Works by Hakluyt in addition to those mentioned above include

translations of Antonio Galvão's *The Discoveries of the World* . . . (1601), and of Hernando de Soto's account of Florida, under the title *Virginia Richly Valued by the Description of . . Florida* (1609). But it is the *Voyages* which remain his memorial. This, "the prose epic of the English nation," is more than a documentary history of exploration and adventure; with tales of daring it mingles historical, diplomatic and economic papers to establish British right to sovereignty at sea and to a place in overseas settlement. Its overriding purpose was to stimulate, guide and encourage an undertaking of incalculable national import. At the same time he was not blind to the profits arising from foreign trade. Sir Thomas Smith asserted that the income of the East India company was increased by twenty thousand pounds through a careful study of Hakluyt's *Voyages*.

BIBLIOGRAPHY.—*The Principall Navigations* were reprinted with additional matter as *Hakluyt's Collection of the Early Voyages, Travels, and Discoveries of the English Nation*, 4 vol. (1809–12), and for the Hakluyt Society with a preface by Walter Raleigh, 12 vol. (1903–05). The *Divers Voyages* was edited by the Hakluyt Society (1850). The best text of *The Discourse on the Western Planting* is in E. G. R. Taylor (*see below*). Many narratives from Hakluyt's collection have been republished by the Hakluyt Society (founded 1846). For his life, the dedications to the two early editions of *The Principall Navigations* should be consulted (*see above*). *See also* G. B. Parks, *Richard Hakluyt and the English Voyages* (1928); E. G. R. Taylor, *The Original Writings and Correspondence of the Two Richard Hakluyts*, Hakluyt Society, 2nd ser., vol. 76, 77 (1935); J. A. Williamson, "Richard Hakluyt," in *Richard Hakluyt and His Successors*, Hakluyt Society, 2nd ser., vol. 93 (1946). (G. R. CE.)

HAKODATE, a city and one of the early open ports of Japan, is on the south coast of the island of Hokkaido. For many years Hakodate was regarded as the capital of the island until Sapporo was officially raised to that rank. Pop. (1965) 243,418. The city is built along the northwestern base of a rocky promontory (1,157 ft.), which forms the eastern boundary of a bay. The bay is easy of access and spacious. Hakodate was opened to U.S. commerce in 1854 and to general foreign trade in 1857. It has declined in importance, though it remains an important point of transit between Hokkaido and Honshu. The principal industry is fishing.

HAKO-NIWA: *see* MINIATURE LANDSCAPE.

HAKUIN (1685–1768), Japanese Zen priest, artist, and writer, who saved Japanese Zen from extinction. E-kaku Hakuin (title Zenji; "Zen Teacher"; posthumous titles Shinki-Dokumyō, "Divine-Opportunity-Independent-Wonder," and Shōshū Kokushi, "True-Religion-National-Teacher") was born in Hara-machi (near Mt. Fuji) on Dec. 25, 1685. Educated at the local temple of Shōinji, he studied under priests of various sects and finally (1708) settled for Zen, owing to a mystic experience when a "wonderful thought suddenly came into his mind and filled him with assurance and joy." He belonged to the Rinzai (not the Sōtō) branch of Zen. (*See* BUDDHISM: *Regional Variations in Buddhism: Japan.*) From then on he gave his life to helping others to the same state of bliss. In 1716 he settled at the temple of Shōinji where he died in December 1768. In contrast to the haughty Zen priests who served the shogunate, he lived in great poverty among his peasant parishioners, who called him "our dear priest." His spirituality, humility, and contentment to live in poverty attracted large numbers of earnest young men, who would have gone to other forms of Buddhism. They became a new foundation of Zen in Japan.

Hakuin's teaching may be summed up thus: direct knowledge of the truth is available to all, even to peasants. A moral life must accompany religious practice. The body must not be treated too harshly in the effort toward Enlightenment. The Zen motto of his life was: "Having heard the Way in the evening, let me die in the morning." He is also well known as an artist and calligraphist of the Zen tradition. His chief writings are *Keisō Dokozui* ("Poisonous Stamens and Pistils of Thorns"), written in Chinese and intended for advanced Zen students; *Orate-gama* ("The Embossed Tea Kettle"), practical advice for ordinary people; *Hogo-Roku* ("Records of Talks on the Law," including his parochial sermons for the peasants), in which he "accommodates" Zen doctrines to the condition of each; and *Yasen Kanna* ("A Chat on a Boat in the Evening"), a warning not to treat the body too harshly in meditation.

BIBLIOGRAPHY.—Eng. trans. of the three Japanese works, with introduction, by R. D. M. Shaw, *The Embossed Tea Kettle* (1963); *See* also H. Dumoulin, *A History of Zen Buddhism*, ch. 14 (1963); Sir Charles Eliot, *Japanese Buddhism* (1959); K. Brasch, *Hakuin and die Zen-Malerei* (1957).
(R. D. M. S.)

HALAKA (pl. HALAKOT; literally "the proper way"), a word that in its widest meaning denotes the Jewish postbiblical laws concerning religion and society, in contrast to the nonlegal writings (*haggadah*) and the biblical law as embodied in the Torah. *See* MIDRASH; TALMUD.

HALBERSTADT, a town of Germany which following partition of the nation after World War II became part of the German Democratic Republic, is a regional capital in the *Bezirk* (district) of Magdeburg and lies 47 km. (29 mi.) S.W. of Magdeburg in the fertile northern approaches to the Harz mountains. Pop. (1964) 45,903. Despite bombing in World War II Halberstadt is still rich in old timber-framed buildings. The Marienkirche built between the 11th and 13th centuries in Romanesque style with a basilica and four towers, the Gothic cathedral built in the 13th and 14th centuries and the old town hall (*Rathaus*) dating from the 14th century are among the most interesting buildings. There is an extensive bird museum.

Halberstadt is on the railway from Magdeburg to Goslar and is a junction. It has various industrial enterprises: machinery, agricultural implements, rubber and woven goods, railway repair shops, a punch and die works, and a large meat and food conserving plant in which Halberstadt's speciality, the Halberstadt sausage, is produced.

The history of Halberstadt goes back to the 9th century. It became a diocese in 820 and had received its municipal charter by 998, thus being one of the oldest German towns. After the Thirty Years' War the peace of Westphalia of 1648 granted it to the electors of Brandenburg. By the treaty of Tilsit in 1807 it became part of the kingdom of Westphalia set up by Napoleon, but after his downfall it reverted to Prussia. The town was heavily damaged by air attacks in World War II.

HALBERT, HALBERD or HALBARD, a weapon consisting of an axe blade balanced by a pick and having an elongated pike head at the end of the staff, which was usually about 5 or 6 ft. in length. The utility of such a weapon in the wars of the later middle ages was that it gave the foot soldier the means of dealing with an armoured man on horseback. The pike could do no more than keep the horseman at a distance. This ensured security for the foot soldier but did not enable him to strike a mortal blow, for which a long-handled, powerful weapon capable of striking a heavy cleaving blow, was required. Several different forms of weapon responding to these requirements are described and illustrated below; it will be noticed that the thrusting pike is almost always combined with the cutting-bill hook or axehead, so that the individual billman or halberdier should not be at a disadvantage if caught alone by a mounted opponent, or if his first descending blow missed its object. It will be noticed further that, concurrently with the disuse of complete armour and the development of firearms, the pike or thrusting element gradually displaced the axe or cleaving element in these weapons, until there evolved the court halberts and partisans of the late 16th and early 17th centuries and the so-called "halbert" of the infantry officer and sergeant in the 18th, which can scarcely be classed even as partisans.

Figs. 1–6 represent types of these long cutting, cut and thrust weapons of the middle ages, details being omitted for the sake of clearness. The most primitive is the vouge (fig. 1), which is simply a heavy cleaver on a pole, with a point added. The next form, the gisarme (fig. 2), appears in infinite variety but is always distinguished from vouges, etc., by the hook, which was used to pull down mounted men, and generally resembles the modern agricultural bill hook. The glaive (fig. 3) is a broad, heavy, slightly curved sword blade on a stave; it is often combined with the hooked gisarme as a glaive-gisarme (fig. 4). A gisarme-vouge is shown in fig. 5.

The weapon best known to Englishmen is the bill, which was originally a sort of scythe blade, sharp on the concave side (whereas the glaive has the cutting edge on the convex side), but in its best-known form it should be called a bill-gisarme

(fig. 6). The partisans, *ranseurs* and halberts proper developed naturally from the earlier types. The feature common to all is the combination of spear and axe. In the halberts the axe predominates (*see* figs. 10, 11, 12). In the partisan the pike is the more important, the axeheads being reduced to little more than an ornamental feature. A south German specimen (fig. 9) shows how this was compensated by the broadening of the spearhead, the edges of which in such weapons were sharpened. Fig. 8, a service weapon of simple form, merely has projections on either side, and from this developed the *ranseur* (fig. 7), a partisan with a very long and narrow point, like the blade of a rapier, and with forklike projections intended to act as "sword breakers," instead of the atrophied axeheads of the partisan proper.

The halbert played almost as conspicuous a part in the military history of middle Europe during the 15th and early 16th centuries as the pike. But, even in a form distinguishable from the vouge and the glaive, it dates from the early part of the 13th century, and for many generations thereafter it was the special weapon of the Swiss. It was also in the 15th and 16th centuries that the halberts became larger; the blades were formed in many varieties of shape, often engraved, inlaid or pierced in open work and exquisitely finished as works of art.

This weapon was in use in England from the reign of Henry VII to the reign of George III, when it was still carried (though in shape it had certainly lost its original characteristics and had become half partisan, half pike) by sergeants in the guards and other infantry regiments. It is still retained as the symbol of authority borne before the magistrates on public occasions in some of the burghs of Scotland.

The Lochaber axe may be called a species of halbert furnished with a hook on the end of the staff at the back of the blade. The godendag (Fr. *godendart*) is the Flemish name of the halbert in its original form.

HALDANE, the name of a Scottish family distinguished for several members who, in addition to excelling in their professions, were notable in public life and as writers.

RICHARD BURDON HALDANE, Viscount Haldane of Cloan (1856–1928), British statesman, a great military reformer, was born in Edinburgh, on July 30, 1856, second son of Robert Haldane, writer to the signet, and Mary Burdon-Sanderson. His family background was a blend of evangelical piety and high intellectualism. He was educated at Edinburgh Academy and at the universities of Göttingen and Edinburgh. He was called to the bar by Lincoln's Inn in 1879 and soon acquired a large practice, eventually becoming a queen's counsel in 1890. He was elected to Parliament in 1885 as Liberal member for East Lothian, a seat he held for 26 years. His principal interest during these years, apart from law and politics, was philosophy—a sort of neo-Hegelianism which he expounded with much energy and little clarity.

Together with H. H. Asquith and Sir Edward Grey, Haldane belonged to the imperialist wing of the Liberal Party, and like them

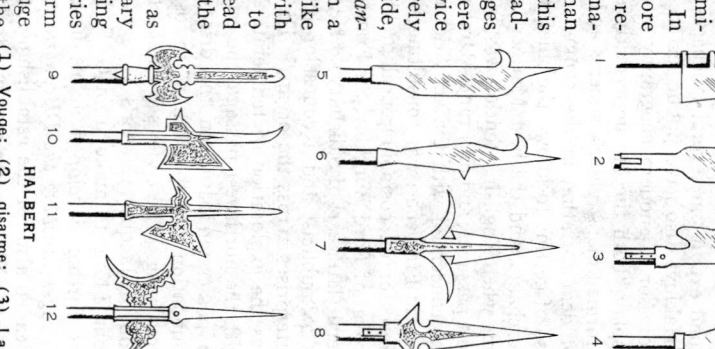

HALBERT

(1) Vouge; (2) gisarme; (3) glaive; (4) Burgundian glaive-gisarme, c. 1480; (5) Swiss gisarme-vouge, 14th century; (6) bill-gisarme; (7) ranseur; (8) service halbert; (9) German partisan, 1615; (10) Swiss halbert, early 15th century; (11) Swiss halbert, mid-16th century; (12) German court halbert, mid-16th century

he distrusted the leader, Sir Henry Campbell-Bannerman; but their attempt failed in 1905 to force Campbell-Bannerman into taking a peerage and leading the government from the House of Lords (see CAMPBELL-BANNERMAN, SIR HENRY). It was in something of a spirit of mild revenge that Campbell-Bannerman then offered Haldane the War Office, that grave of political reputations. However, it turned out to be a brilliant appointment. Haldane was an administrator of genius, and reform was in the air. He was also a man of infinite patience, great persuasiveness, and much personal charm; the hospitality of his table was famous. Knowing that it would be fatal to quarrel with the military hierarchy, he instead secured their confidence. Acting largely through Douglas Haig, the director of military training, he achieved three major reforms: the creation of a continental expeditionary force capable of speedy mobilization, the establishment of the territorial army as an efficient reserve for the regular forces, and the setting up of a general staff. Without these changes, Great Britain might well have succumbed in the early stages of World War I.

Haldane accepted a viscountcy in 1911 and became lord chancellor in 1912. In 1915 Asquith was forced to form a coalition government and under great pressure from the Conservatives consented to drop Haldane, whom they disliked and who was the victim of a discreditable and wholly unjustified charge of being "pro-German." Apart from assisting in the judicial work of the House of Lords, Haldane could do little in public life for the remainder of the war. It became clear, however, when the war ended that his sympathies had moved to the left. He believed that on education, a subject that greatly interested him, the Liberals were insufficiently progressive. Haldane accepted James Ramsay MacDonald's invitation in 1924 to become lord chancellor in the first Labour government, where his wisdom and experience were of great value.

Haldane never married, and after his death at his Scottish home, Cloan, on Aug. 19, 1928, his peerage became extinct. His *Autobiography* was published posthumously in 1929. *See also* his *Pathway to Reality* (1903), *The Reign of Relativity* (1921), and *The Philosophy of Humanism* (1922).

See Sir F. Maurice, *Lord Haldane*, 2 vol. (1937-39); Dudley Sommer, *Haldane of Cloan* (1960).
(R. N. W. B.)

JOHN SCOTT HALDANE (1860-1936), physiologist noted for his researches on respiration, many of which were outcomes of problems connected with coal mining, was born in Edinburgh, May 3, 1860, the son of Robert Haldane and brother of Richard Burdon Haldane and Elizabeth Sanderson Haldane. He studied at Edinburgh University, where he was graduated in medicine in 1884, and the University of Jena. He was a demonstrator in physiology at University College, Dundee, and in 1887 became a demonstrator in physiology at Oxford University where he was a reader in physiology from 1907 until he resigned in 1913. He also lectured at Yale University (1916), Glasgow University (1927-28), and Dublin University (1930). He had been elected to the Royal Society in 1897.

Haldane's principal contribution to science was the elucidation of gas exchanges during respiration. He also developed apparatus for the investigation of respiration and for blood-gas analysis. In 1905 he reported his fundamental discovery that the regulation of breathing is usually determined by the effect of the tension of carbon dioxide in the blood on the respiratory centre in the brain. In 1911 he led an expedition to Pikes Peak, Colo., where he studied the effect of low barometric pressure. He investigated the action of gases that caused suffocation in coal mines and the pathological effects of the carbon monoxide present after a mine explosion. His report to the home secretary on the causes of death in mine explosions and fires (1896) was an important contribution to mine safety, and from that time he was a member of several government advisory committees and commissions. In 1912 he became director of a mining research laboratory founded near Doncaster by the mine owners; when it was transferred to Birmingham in 1921, he became an honorary professor of mining at Birmingham University. He was also president of the Institution of Mining Engineers, 1924-28, and contributed to the solution of such mining problems as rescue equipment and pulmonary disease. In 1907 he

developed a method of stage decompression which made it possible for a deep-sea diver to ascend to the surface safely. Haldane was also a notable thinker, who throughout his life tried to clarify the philosophical basis of biology, its relation to physics and chemistry, and the problems of mechanism and personality.

His publications include *Organism and Environment* (1917), *Methods of Air Analysis* (1920); *Respiration* (1922, 2nd ed. with J. G. Priestley, 1935), *The Sciences and Philosophy* (1929), and *The Philosophy of a Biologist*, 2nd ed. (1936). He died at Oxford at midnight, March 14-15, 1936.

ELIZABETH SANDERSON HALDANE (1862-1937), associated with many projects of social welfare, was born in Edinburgh, May 27, 1862, the only daughter of Robert Haldane. After a rather retiring early life, she became actively involved in many public works. She was closely associated with nursing services in Britain and served in a number of appointed posts relating to welfare programs. Miss Haldane was the first woman to be made a Justice of the Peace in Scotland (1920). She has several biographical books to her credit and translations of philosophical works from German, French, and Latin. She died at Auchterarder, Perthshire, Scot., Dec. 24, 1937.

Her books include *The British Nurse in Peace and War* (1923), *George Eliot and Her Times* (1927), *Mrs. Gaskell and Her Friends* (1930), and *From One Century to Another* (1937).

JOHN BURDON SANDERSON HALDANE (1892-1964), geneticist, biometrician, physiologist, noted popularizer of science and philosopher of biology, who opened new paths of research in population genetics and evolution. He was born at Oxford, Eng., Nov. 5, 1892, the son of John Scott Haldane. His formal education, in the classics, was taken at Eton and New College, Oxford. His scientific training, as assistant to his father, began at about age 8. His own researches were interrupted by World War I, in which he saw action with the Black Watch Regiment. After the war, Haldane served as a Fellow of New College and, from 1922 to 1932 (when he was elected a fellow of the Royal Society), as a reader in biochemistry at Cambridge. After a year as visiting professor at the University of California, in 1932, he became a professor of genetics at London University (1933-57), and later professor of biometry at University College (1937-57).

He announced himself a Marxist in the 1930s and was for several years editor of the Communist *Daily Worker*. He later became disillusioned with the official party line and the rise to power of the controversial biologist T. D. Lysenko. In 1957 Haldane left for India, in protest over several aspects of British policy. At the time of his death, of cancer, Dec. 1, 1964, at Bhubaneswar, India, Haldane was an Indian citizen and head of the Genetics and Biometry Laboratory of the Government of Orissa, India. He was decorated and honoured widely in academic circles. His unusual combination of analytical thought, range of knowledge, literary prowess, and force of personality produced not only a considerable number of discoveries in many fields but also had a notable general effect on a whole generation of research workers.

His many works include: *Animal Biology* (with J. S. Huxley, 1927), *Science and Ethics* (1928), *The Inequality of Man* (1932), *The Causes of Evolution* (1933), *The Marxist Philosophy and the Sciences* (1939), *Heredity and Politics* (1938), *New Paths on Genetics* (1941), *Science Advances* (1947), and *The Biochemistry of Genetics* (1954).

BIBLIOGRAPHY.—For more complete biographical and bibliographical data on certain members of the Haldane family, *see* the *Dictionary of National Biography*.
(X; H. K.)

HALDEN (formerly FREDRIKSHALD), a town in the *fylke* (county) of Ostfold in southern Norway, is situated at the mouth of the Tista river near the border of Sweden, 118 km. (73 mi.) S.S.E. of Oslo by road. Pop. (1960) 10,006. Features of interest include the Fredriksten fort, begun in the 17th century, the medieval Berg church and the Norwegian national war memorial at Rodsberg. Svinesund bridge, linking Norway and Sweden, is 9 km. (5.6 mi.) west. Main industries include sawing, pulp and paper mills, and the manufacture of boots, shoes and textiles; granite is exported. The town has good boat and rail communications.

Halden has an atomic reactor. In early times there existed a settlement called Halden on the same site. The town was founded in 1661, and from 1665 was called Fredrikshald; in 1928 the name reverted to Halden. The Fredrikssten fort repeatedly had to take the brunt of the conflicts between Sweden and Denmark-Norway. In the siege of 1718 Charles XII of Sweden was killed there. In 1906, after the separation of Norway and Sweden, the fort was demilitarized.

HALDIMAND, SIR FREDERICK (1718–1791), British general and governor of Quebec, was born in the canton of Neuchâtel, Switz., on Aug. 11, 1718. He entered the British service in 1756 with rank of lieutenant colonel in the Royal American regiment. He was with Lord Jeffrey Amherst's expedition against Montreal in 1760 and after the capitulation remained there as second-in-command. He became military governor of Trois-Rivières in 1762, commander at Pensacola, Fla., in 1767, and commander in chief of the British army in North America while Thomas Gage was on leave in 1773–74. He succeeded Sir Guy Carleton as governor in chief of the province of Quebec in 1778. Although he did not conduct any major operations during the American Revolutionary War, he directed border raids and defended the St. Lawrence against privateers. He returned to England in 1784, was knighted in 1785, and died at Yverdon, Switz., on June 5, 1791.

See J. N. McIlwraith, *Sir Frederick Haldimand*, 2nd ed. (1926); A. L. Burt, *The Old Province of Quebec* (1933). (J.E.E.M.)

HALE, EDWARD EVERETT (1822–1909), U.S. clergyman and author, is best remembered for his short story *The Man Without a Country* (1863), "a document of the Civil War." Hale was born in Boston, April 3, 1822, a grandnephew of Edward Everett, the orator. Trained on his father's newspaper, the *Boston Daily Advertiser*, Hale turned early to letters. For 70 years newspaper articles, historical essays, short stories, pamphlets, sermons, and novels poured from his pen. He was intimately associated with the *North American Review*, *Atlantic Monthly* and *Christian Examiner*. From 1870 to 1875 he published and edited the Unitarian journal *Old and New*. "My Double and How He Undid Me" (1859) established the vein of realistic fantasy which was Hale's forte and introduced a group of loosely related characters figuring in *If, Yes, and Perhaps* (1868), *The Ingham Papers* (1869), *Sybaris and Other Homes* (1869), *His Level Best* (1872), and other collections. *East and West* (1892) and *In His Name* (1873) were his most popular novels.

Hale became pastor of the Church of the Unity at Worcester, Mass., in 1846. He married into the crusading Beecher family and took an active interest in western emigration and the Kansas-Nebraska controversy. In 1856 he became pastor of the South Congregational (Unitarian) Church of Boston. His forceful personality, organizing genius and liberal theology placed him in the vanguard of the "social gospel" movement. Many of his 150 books and pamphlets were tracts for such causes as emigrant aid, Negro education, workman's housing and world peace. A moralistic novel, *Ten Times One Is Ten* (1871), inspired the organization of several young people's groups. The reminiscent writings of his later years are rich and colourful: *A New England Boyhood* (1893), *James Russell Lowell and His Friends* (1899), and *Memories of a Hundred Years* (1902). His *Works*, in ten volumes, appeared in 1898–1900. In 1903 he was named chaplain of the United States senate. He died at Roxbury, Mass., June 10, 1909.

See E. E. Hale, Jr., *The Life and Letters of Edward Everett Hale* (1917); Jean Holloway, "Checklist," *Bulletin of Bibliography* (1954), and *Edward Everett Hale: a Biography* (1956).

HALE, GEORGE ELLERY (1868–1938), U.S. astronomer, was known for his development of great astronomical instruments, including the 200-in. Palomar telescope, and for his pioneering researches in solar physics, particularly his discovery of magnetic fields in sun spots. He was born at Chicago, Ill., on June 29, 1868. He graduated from Massachusetts Institute of Technology in 1890 and carried out research work at the Harvard College observatory (1889–90) and the University of Berlin (winter 1893–94). In 1888–91 he organized the Kenwood observatory in Chicago, where he invented and developed the spectroheliograph (*q.v.*), an instrument for photographing the sun in monochromatic light. In 1892, when he became associate professor of astrophysics (later professor) at The University of Chicago, he began the organization of the Yerkes observatory, of which he was director until 1904. Here he built the 40-in. refracting telescope which remains the largest of its type in the world. He established the *Astrophysical Journal*, an international review of spectroscopy and astronomical physics, in 1895. In 1904 he organized the Mt. Wilson observatory of the Carnegie Institution of Washington and was its director until 1923. Here he built solar apparatus of great power as well as the huge 60-in. and 100-in. stellar telescopes, both of the reflecting type. He helped organize the National Research council (1916). His plans and efforts led to the construction by the California Institute of Technology (with funds supplied by the Rockefeller foundation) of the 200-in. reflecting telescope on Palomar mountain. His work was recognized by the awarding of many honours and by his election as a foreign member of most of the world's leading academies of science. He assisted in the organization of the Henry E. Huntington Library and Art gallery (San Marino, Calif.), and in the improvement of the city of Pasadena as a member of the city planning commission.

Hale took a leading part in the expansion and strengthening of the California Institute of Technology. He died at Pasadena on Feb. 21, 1938. His books include *The Study of Stellar Evolution* (1908), *Ten Years' Work of a Mountain Observatory*, *The New Heavens* (1922), *The Depths of the Universe* (1924), *Beyond the Milky Way* (1926), and *Signals From the Stars* (1931). (P.W.M.)

HALE, JOHN PARKER (1806–1873), U.S. senator and candidate for the presidency in 1852, was born at Rochester, N.H., on March 31, 1806. He graduated from Bowdoin college, Brunswick, Me., in 1827 and was admitted to the New Hampshire bar in 1830. He was a state representative in 1832 and a U.S. district attorney, 1834–41. He served one term in the U.S. house of representatives, 1843–45. In June 1846 he was elected to the U.S. senate by a coalition of Whigs and antislavery Democrats. During his first term, 1847–53, he was conspicuous as the first of several outspoken critics of slavery who came into the senate during this period. Hale was nominated for president in 1847 by the Liberty party but withdrew in favour of Martin Van Buren, candidate of the Free Soil party. In 1852 he was presidential candidate for the Free Soil party but received only about 155,000 votes. From 1855 to 1865 he was again U.S. senator. He was one of the founders of the Republican party in New Hampshire and during the Civil War was an eloquent supporter of the Union and chairman of the senate naval committee. From 1865 to 1869 he was U.S. minister to Spain. He died at Dover, N.H., Nov. 19, 1873. (H.S.S.)

HALE, SIR MATTHEW (1609–1676), lord chief justice of England under Charles II and one of the most learned and capable lawyers in English legal history, was born on Nov. 1, 1609, at Alderley, Gloucestershire. He entered Lincoln's Inn, probably in 1628, and immediately devoted himself to legal studies. He was called to the bar in 1637 and within a very few years was at the head of his profession. He entered public life shortly before the onset of the Puritan revolution and in the confused and critical period that followed he conscientiously sought to steer a middle course. He played a prominent role in the trials of political offenders that characterized the times. Some believe he was engaged as counsel for the earl of Strafford; it is certain that he acted for Archbishop Laud, Lord Maguire, Christopher Love, the duke of Hamilton and others. The assertion that Hale signed the Solemn League and Covenant, regarding the constitution of the Anglican church (*see* COVENANTERS), is not supported by satisfactory evidence. He did, however, take the engagement of loyalty to the Commonwealth required of all lawyers, and in 1653, already serjeant, he became a judge in the court of common pleas. Two years later he sat in Cromwell's parliament as one of the members for Gloucestershire. After the death of the protector he declined to act as a judge under Richard Cromwell, although he represented Oxford in Richard's parliament. At the Restoration in 1660 he was graciously received by Charles II, and in the same year he was appointed chief baron of the exchequer, and accepted, apparently with reluctance, the honor of knighthood. After holding the office of chief baron for 11 years he became chief justice of the king's bench in 1671. He resigned his office in 1676 and retired to his native Alderley, where he died on Dec. 25 of the same year.

As a judge Hale made a remarkable impression on his contemporaries for his probity, fairness, piety and moderation, traits that too often did not characterize those who then exercised judicial functions. It was these qualities that secured his position in the violent and shifting political life of the 17th century. The principal blot on his record involves the conviction of two women for witchcraft in 1661 or 1662.

Hale was a prolific writer, his works including discussions of theological and scientific matters as well as legal studies; most of them were left in manuscript and published posthumously. Perhaps his most important work is the *Historia placitorium coronae*, or *History of the Pleas of the Crown* (1685; 2 vol. 1736), one of the most influential treatises on the criminal law of England ever produced. Hale's other legal work of continuing importance is the *History of the Common Law of England* (1713). Among his religious writings the *Contemplations, Moral and Divine* (1676-77) occupies first place.

BIBLIOGRAPHY.—Hale's life has been written by G. Burnet (1682); by J. B. Williams (1835); by H. Roscoe, in *Lives of Eminent Lawyers* (1838); by Lord Campbell, in *Lives of the Chief Justices* (1849); and by E. Foss in *Lives of the Judges* (1848-70). (F. A. A.)

HALE, NATHAN (1755-1776), American Revolutionary officer and hero, was born at Coventry, Conn., on June 6, 1755. After he graduated from Yale in 1773, he became a school teacher. He joined a Connecticut regiment after war broke out, served in the siege of Boston and was commissioned a captain at the opening of 1776. When William Heath's brigade departed for New York he went with them, and the tradition is that he was one of a small and daring band who captured a provision sloop from under the very guns of a man-of-war. On Sept. 21, having volunteered to enter the British lines to obtain information concerning the enemy, he was captured in his disguise of a Dutch school teacher and was hanged the next day. The penalty was in accordance with military law, but young Hale's act was a brave one, and he has always been glorified as a martyr. Tradition attributes to him the saying (similar to a remark in Joseph Addison's play *Cato*) that he only regretted that he had but one life to lose for his country; and it is said that his request for a Bible and the services of a minister was refused by his captors.

BIBLIOGRAPHY.—W. O. Partridge, *Nathan Hale, the Ideal Patriot* (1902); H. P. Johnston, *Nathan Hale, 1776* (1914); J. C. Root, *Nathan Hale* (1915); G. D. Seymour, *Documentary Life of Nathan Hale* (1941).

HALES, JOHN (1584-1656), English scholar, author of sermons and religious tracts whose learning earned him the title "the ever memorable," was born at Bath on April 19, 1584. He was educated at Bath grammar school and at Corpus Christi and Merton colleges, Oxford. He became public lecturer in Greek at Oxford in 1612, and in 1613 he was elected a fellow at Eton college. His tract *Schism and Schismaticks* (1636), containing thoughts on ways of achieving ecclesiastical concord, earned him the disapproval of Archbishop Laud, but his impressive defense of his ideas led the archbishop to make Hales one of his chaplains and canon of Windsor in 1639. His knowledge earned him the admiration of Lord Falkland, Sir John Suckling (who mentions him in his "A Session of the Poets"), Sir William Davenant and Ben Jonson. Because of his royalist views he was deprived of his canonry in 1642 and he was formally dispossessed of his fellowship in 1649. He died at Eton on May 19, 1656.

Much of Hales's work was printed without his consent, including *Schism and Schismaticks* in 1642. His famous funeral oration on Sir Thomas Bodley (1613) and his sermon *Concerning the Abuses of the Obscure Places of Holy Scripture* (1617) were also printed, and in 1659 appeared *The Golden Remains*, sermons and letters collected by the bookseller Timothy Garthwait. This contains letters written while Hales was in Holland from 1616 to 1619 as chaplain to Sir Dudley Carleton, the English ambassador, and among them are several reporting the synod at Dort in 1618, at which the five points of Calvinism were formulated. Hales's work combines clarity of thought with lightness of touch, fully justifying Andrew Marvell's contemporary description of him as "One of the clearest heads and best prepared breasts in Christendom."

See *Works*, ed. by D. Dalrymple, 3. vol. (1765); J. H. Elson, *John Hales of Eton* (1948).

HALES, STEPHEN (1677-1761), English clergyman, physiologist, chemist and inventor, famous for his pioneering studies in animal and plant physiology, was born at Bekesbourne, Kent, on Sept. 7, 1677. Educated at Corpus Christi college, Cambridge, he took holy orders at Cambridge and in 1709 was presented to the perpetual curacy of Teddington, Middlesex, where Alexander Pope was his neighbour and friend; there he spent his life. In 1718 he was elected fellow of the Royal society, which awarded him the Copley medal in 1739, and in 1753 he became foreign associate of the French Académie des Sciences. He died at Teddington on Jan. 4, 1761.

Hales is best known for his *Statical Essays*. The first volume, *Vegetable Staticks* (1727), describes experiments in plant physiology: transpiration, the rate of growth of shoots and leaves, variations in root force at different times of the day and the nourishment taken in by plants from the air. In his experiments he was able to collect gases over water in vessels separate from those in which they were generated, and thus used what was to all intents the pneumatic trough, later perfected by Joseph Priestley. The second volume, *Haemastaticks* (1733), was the most important contribution to the physiology of blood circulation after William Harvey. Hales made the first quantitative estimate of blood pressure, and his work led to the development of the instruments now in general use for that purpose.

Like Robert Whytt, Hales showed the necessity of the spinal cord for reflex movements. He also devised a ventilator (a modified organ bellows) by which fresh air could be conveyed into jails, hospitals and ships' holds, and invented a sea gauge for sounding and processes for distilling fresh from sea water, for protecting corn from weevils by fumigation with brimstone and for salting animals whole by passing brine into their arteries. His *A Friendly Admonition to the Drinkers of Brandy and Other Distilled Spirit* was published anonymously in 1734 and had six editions, and *A Description of Ventilators*, a pioneer work of great practical importance, appeared in 1743.

See A. E. Clark-Kennedy, *Stephen Hales: an Eighteenth Century Biography* (1929); C. J. Singer et al. (eds.), *A History of Technology*, vol. iv (1958). (W. J. BP.; X.)

HALESOWEN, a municipal borough (1936) in the Oldbury and Halesowen parliamentary division of Worcestershire, Eng., 7 mi. WSW of Birmingham. Pop. (1971 prelim.) 53,933. Mentioned as Halas in Domesday, Halesowen had a Premonstratensian monastery (1214-1539), ruins of which exist. William Caslon (1692-1766), inventor of the Caslon type face, was born at Cradley, and the Leasowes Estate was the birthplace and residence of William Shenstone, the poet. Halesowen has a grammar school (1652) and a county technical school (1939).

HALEVI, JUDAH BEN SAMUEL (c. 1085-1141), Jewish poet and philosopher, born in Tudela, c. 1085, is considered the greatest of the Hebrew poets of Spain, both in courtly and liturgical poetry, in which he followed the conventions of the Spanish school. His *Songs of Zion*, devoted to his plan to emigrate to Palestine, are, however, entirely personal. Similarly, in his philosophy (expounded in Arabic in his *al-Khazari* or *Kuzari*, an imaginary dialogue between a Jewish scholar and the king of the Khazars, converted to Judaism), he follows a line of his own, inasmuch as he rejects the main tenets of contemporary philosophy and emphasizes the irrational and national elements of Jewish religion. (His book was mainly read in the Hebrew translation by Judah ibn Tibbon.) Having decided to leave Spain and make a pilgrimage to Jerusalem, he died on his way in 1141.

BIBLIOGRAPHY.—*Poems*: ed. by H. Brody, 4 vol. (1894-1930); *Selected Poems*, trans. by N. Salaman (1924); *Sechzig Hymnen und Gedichte*, trans. by F. Rosenzweig (1924); *Kuzari*, Arabic and Hebrew ed. by H. Hirschfeld (1887), Eng. trans. (1905); *Selections*, trans. by I. Heinemann (1948). *See also* J. M. Millás Vallicrosa, *Yehuda Ha-Levi como poeta y apologista* (1947); S. D. Goitein, "The Biography of Rabbi Judah ha-Levi...," *Proceedings of the American Academy for Jewish Research*, pp. 41-56 (1959).
(S. M. SN.)

HALÉVY, ÉLIE (1870-1937), French historian, the author of an important history of 19th-century England, was born at Étretat (Seine-Inférieure), Sept. 6, 1870, a son of the playwright Ludovic Halévy. He became professor at the École Libre des Sciences Politiques in 1898. His *History of the English People in the Nineteenth Century*, which is better known in English translation, was begun shortly before World War I. After three volumes dealing with the years 1815-41, Halévy turned to the end of the century in his two-volume *Épilogue* covering 1895-1914 (Paris, 1926-32). He projected a further three volumes for the period 1841-95, but died, at Sucy-en-Brie (Seine-et-Oise), Aug. 21, 1937, before the work could be completed. A volume dealing with the years 1841-52 was later prepared from his notes (Paris, 1946). A translation was published as follows: *England in 1815* (1949); *The Liberal Awakening, 1815-1830* (1949); *The Triumph of Reform, 1830-1841* (1950); *Victorian Years, 1841-1895* (1951); *Imperialism and the Rise of Labour, 1895-1905* (1951); *The Rule of Democracy, 1905-1914* (1952). Halévy's work remains the best detailed general account of English history in the 19th century and his introductory survey of England in 1815 is particularly brilliant. As an informed foreign observer he was at an advantage when passing judgment on English history, especially where non-conformity, in which he was very interested, was concerned. He was the first to suggest that the absence of any revolt in England during the French revolutionary period might be due to the influence of Wesleyanism. Another service rendered by Halévy to English history was the revival of interest in Bentham, both in England and France, through his *La Formation du radicalisme philosophique*, 3 vol. (1901-04).

HALÉVY, JACQUES FRANÇOIS FROMENTAL ÉLIE (1799-1862), French composer known for his romantic opera *La Juive*. Born May 27, 1799, in Paris of a Jewish family originally named Lévy, he studied under Henri Berton and Cherubini. In 1819 he won the Prix de Rome with his cantata *Herminie*. He wrote more than 30 operas, from *L'Artisan* (1827) to *La Magicienne* (1858). Among the earlier operas *La Dilettante d'Avignon* (1829) was a satire on the poverty of contemporary Italian librettos. In 1835 he wrote the five-act grand opera *La Juive* on a libretto by Eugène Scribe, based on episodes from *The Merchant of Venice* and *Ivanhoe*. Remarkable for its choral writing, psychological characterization and imaginative orchestration, *La Juive* was, with Meyerbeer's *Les Huguenots*, the prototype of early French romantic opera. Equally successful was *L'Éclair* (1835) in which Halévy revived the 18th-century traditions of *opéra comique*. *La Tempesta*, based on *The Tempest*, was written in Italian for production in London (1850) and introduced the air completed by his pupil Bizet who married Halévy's daughter, Geneviève, later portrayed as the Duchesse de Guermantes in Proust's *À la recherche du temps perdu*. Halévy was greatly influenced by Meyerbeer, and in his day overshadowed by him, though some of Meyerbeer's more delicate orchestral effects were borrowed from *La Juive*. He published *Souvenirs et portraits* (1861) and *Derniers Souvenirs* (1863). He died at Nice, March 17, 1862.

BIBLIOGRAPHY.—L. Halévy, *François Halévy, sa vie et ses oeuvres*, 2nd ed. (1863); A. Pougin, *François Halévy écrivain* (1865); M. Curtiss, *Bizet and His World* (1958).
(E. LR.)

HALÉVY, LUDOVIC (1834-1908), French playwright and novelist, who in collaboration with Henri Meilhac wrote the librettos for the operettas of Offenbach and satirical comedies about contemporary Parisian life. He was born in Paris, Jan. 1, 1834, the son of Léon Halévy, a versatile writer, and the nephew of the composer Fromental Halévy. While still a member of the civil service he began writing for the stage and collaborated anonymously in *Orphée aux enfers* (1858, music by Offenbach). In 1861 he entered into a partnership with Meilhac which was to last more than 20 years. While Halévy concentrated on the subject and its development and also directed the productions, the script was left to his partner. *La belle Hélène* (1864), a burlesque on the Homeric theme, opened a brilliant series of operettas with music by Offenbach. Among the best known of their plays are *Fanny* (1868) and the sentimental *Froufrou* (1869). They also wrote the libretto for *Carmen* (1875, music by Bizet).

Halévy's own nondramatic works, which are of a high quality, include *L'Invasion* (1872)—impressions of the Franco-German War and the Commune; *Monsieur et Madame Cardinal* (1873)—amusing studies of the theatrical world; and short stories and novels, in particular *L'Abbé Constantin* (1882). After his election to the Académie Française in 1884, he almost ceased to write. He died in Paris, May 8, 1908.
(D. KS.)

HALFBEAK, fishes belonging to the family Hemiramphidae, distinguished from the gars and needlefish, which they closely resemble by the shortness of the upper jaw, whence they take their name. Many are small attractively coloured fish native to the coasts of tropical countries. The largest grow to about 18 in., the smaller to 6 in. or less. The North American halfbeak, *Hyporhamphus unifasciatus*, is found along the Atlantic coast,

HALFPENNY, WILLIAM (fl. 1752), English 18th-century architectural designer, was also known as Michael Hoare. He published about 20 books dealing almost entirely with domestic architecture and especially with country houses in the Gothic and Chinese fashions of his period. His most influential works were *New Designs for Chinese Temples* (1750-52); *Rural Architecture in the Gothic Taste* (1752); *Chinese and Gothic Architecture Properly Ornamented* (1752); and *Rural Architecture in the Chinese Taste* (1750-52). The first of these books disproves the statement that Thomas Chippendale and Sir William Chambers introduced the Chinese taste into England. John Halfpenny, said to have been his son, was associated with William.

HALF-TIMBER WORK, in building, a method which exposes to view the heavy wood framing of the walls. Spaces between the structural members are filled with contrasting materials such as brick, plaster or wattle and daub. The strong, cagelike skeleton is often stiffened with corner braces. Traditionally it is made of squared oak timbers joined by mortises, tenons and wooden pegs. The nature of the structure is expressed in rectangular buildings, the rhythmic spacing of posts and beams facilitating division into boxlike rooms. In the country, units of various sizes can be combined domino fashion to produce rambling plans and picturesque silhouettes, while in crowded towns narrow buildings with steep gables may rise six or seven stories. Although occasional structures are still built to take advantage of the strength and slow-burning properties of heavy timbers, the universal method today is to use light sills, studs, and joists only 2 in. thick, nailed together to make "balloon frames" in place of the old pegged girts, beams and braces. Where the decorative effect of half-timber work is desired, boards are applied to the wall surface in a sham version of the old structural pattern. A more genuine, if unintentional, reflection is seen when the framing of concrete and steel buildings is made visible as part of the exterior effect.

Half-timber work is used where the climate is moderate, suitable wood is available, and there are craftsmen skilled in working with hand tools. It was common in China, and, in a refined form, in Japan, and was used for domestic architecture throughout northern Europe until the 17th century. At Pompeii there are remains of many houses whose upper floors were constructed in half-timber technique.

Extant medieval examples, from the 12th century, have projecting upper stories. The overhang, which probably originated in military construction, gains a small amount of space on the upper levels and gives some weather protection for walls and openings below. However, the main advantage is structural, since the cantilevers at the ends of the beams partially counterbalance the load carried by their spanning portions. The system permitted a

A. F. KERSTING.   LITTLE MORETON HALL, CHESHIRE. ENG.: 1550–59.

series of open panels to serve as windows. Originally provided with shutters, louvres, or bars, in the 13th century these began to be fitted with leaded glass. The use of many studs set close together gives a pronounced vertical rhythm to the exteriors of this era. Along both coasts of the English channel this effect was retained even after the squarer panel forms of the Renaissance had been adopted elsewhere. The wooden frames of 13th- and 14th-century structures were elaborately ornamented, the moldings and carvings displaying the same forms used in Gothic artifacts and buildings of stone. Exposed ground floor posts, hewn from tree trunks and placed upside down, were often carved with the images of craftsman inhabitants or patron saints, while other framing elements were enriched with delicate running patterns. In France the latter emphasized the vertical elements, while in England the tendency was to stress the horizontals and the raking bargeboards which follow the edge of the roof. In the 15th and 16th centuries the decorative contrast between timber and filling was fully exploited. Panels were made of brick in herringbone patterns, of plaster molded or incised with floral forms or with inlays of slate, tile or marl. Carved ornament was lavish and fanciful, and showed classical motives. Many wooden members were added without structural necessity. These were often crisscrossed under windows, and, in England where more timberwork was exposed, they were assembled in cusped shapes or chevrons to create the striking patterns of the "black and white" manor houses of Cheshire and Lancashire. In Germany a bolder and cruder effect was obtained by using fewer elements and emphasizing angle bracing. In the American colonies the English found it expedient to use an insulating layer of wood siding (clapboards or weatherboarding), and half-timbering was not visible from outside. In the French and German settlements, however, the buildings were faithful copies of the European models, an occasional one appearing as late as mid-19th century. *See also* CARPENTRY.

BIBLIOGRAPHY.—F. H. Crossley, *Timber Building in England* (1951); Nathaniel Lloyd, *A History of the English House*, 2nd ed. (1949); H. S. Morrison, *Early American Architecture* (1952).   (S. W. J.)

HALFTONE: *see* PHOTOENGRAVING.

HALIBURTON, THOMAS CHANDLER (1796–1865), Canadian humourist and satirist, is best known as the creator of Sam Slick, the Yankee clock peddler and cracker-barrel philosopher. Born in Windsor, Nova Scotia on Dec. 17, 1796, he was educated at King's college, Windsor. In 1820 he was admitted to the

bar and became in turn a justice of the court of common pleas (1829) and a judge of the supreme court (1841). But the formative development of his career was his election in 1826 to the provincial house of assembly and his subsequent involvement in the assembly's struggle against the misuse of powers by the ruling clique. For a time Haliburton led the popular movement for reform; but when, as it seemed to him, agitation for responsible government began to threaten the colony's ties with Great Britain and the crown, his Tory convictions reasserted themselves. He resigned his seat in the assembly and turned to writing as an outlet for his opinions. Of the 16 books he wrote, nearly all were rooted in his strongly conservative views on political and social questions.

Sam Slick made his first appearance in the *Novascotian* newspaper in 1835; and in the three series of *The Clockmaker* (1836, 1838, 1840), in *The Attaché; or, Sam Slick in England* (1843–44) and in *Sam Slick's Wise Saws and Modern Instances* (1853) Haliburton pressed home his attack against the political shiftlessness of the Nova Scotians, against the shortcomings of American "mobocracy," and indeed against the whole broad front (Britain not excepted) of the levelling tendencies of the age. In sum it is a remarkable body of writing—sometimes too blunt in its preachment or merely bad-tempered, but constantly quickened by the tremendous vitality of Sam Slick's colloquial speech and by his fund of anecdotes and tall tales. Artemus Ward is said to have called Haliburton "the father of the American school of humor." Important volumes in similar vein, though without Mr. Slick, are *The Old Judge* (1849) and *The Season Ticket* (1860).

In 1856 Haliburton moved to England, where he represented Launceston in the house of commons for six years prior to his death in Middlesex, on Aug. 27, 1865. A son, Robert Grant Haliburton (1831–1901), was a prominent figure in literary circles at the time of Canadian confederation.

See V. L. O. Chittick, *Thomas Chandler Haliburton* (1924).   (R. L. McD.)

HALIBUT (*Hippoglossus hippoglossus*), the largest of the flatfishes (order Pleuronectiformes), is a member of the family Pleuronectidae and is highly valued as a food fish. Its eyes are on the right side of the head; only the eyed side has colour (dark brown, often with pale blotches), the other side is white. The halibut is a fish of boreal and subarctic waters, living on the continental shelf and offshore banks of both sides of the North Atlantic and of the North Pacific. On the basis of slight anatomical differences from its Atlantic counterpart, the Pacific halibut is considered by some authorities as belonging to a separate species (*H. stenolepis*).

Evidently halibut spawn near the bottom, generally at depths of 900–1,350 ft., in spring but sometimes as early as December. The eggs are about 3½ mm. in diameter, are buoyant and drift suspended in the water; the larvae continue to drift an undetermined period after hatching. The growth rate varies widely from one region to another: a 20-year-old specimen may attain more than five feet in length and several hundred pounds in weight; however, occasional individuals are much larger. Halibut feed on a variety of fishes, crustaceans and mollusks. The reported annual commercial catch is more than 1,800,000 metric tons, about 60% of which comes from the Atlantic. Formerly in danger of depletion, halibut have responded well to scientific management of fishing rates, as demonstrated in the northeastern Pacific.

The California halibut (*Paralichthys californicus*), with eyes on the left side, belongs to the family Bothidae. *See* FLATFISH.   (L. A. WD.)

PRINTED IN THE U.S.A. BY R. R. DONNELLEY & SONS CO.

1768